New York 1960

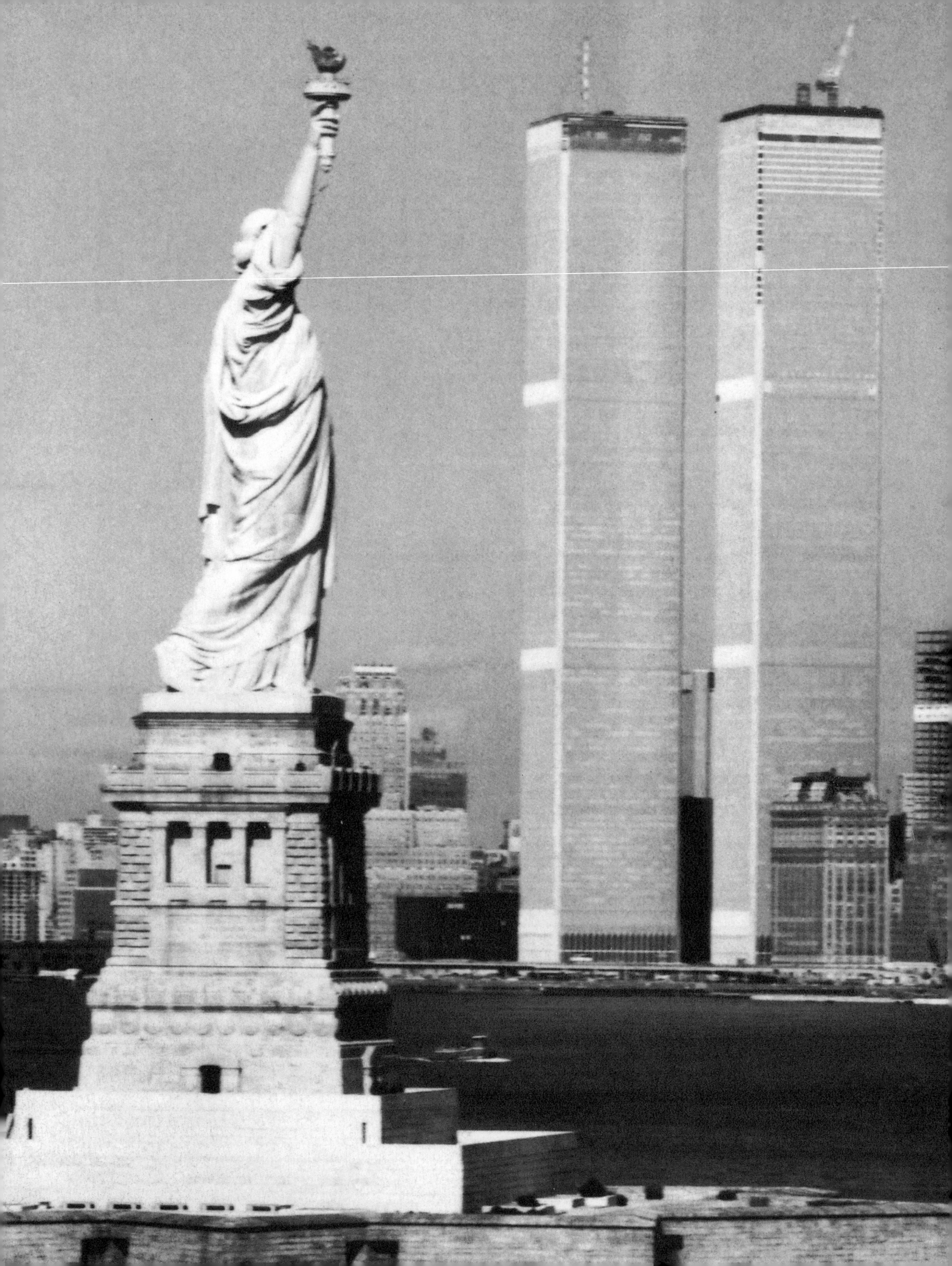

New York 1960

Architecture and
Urbanism Between the
Second World War and
the Bicentennial

Robert A. M. Stern

Thomas Mellins

David Fishman

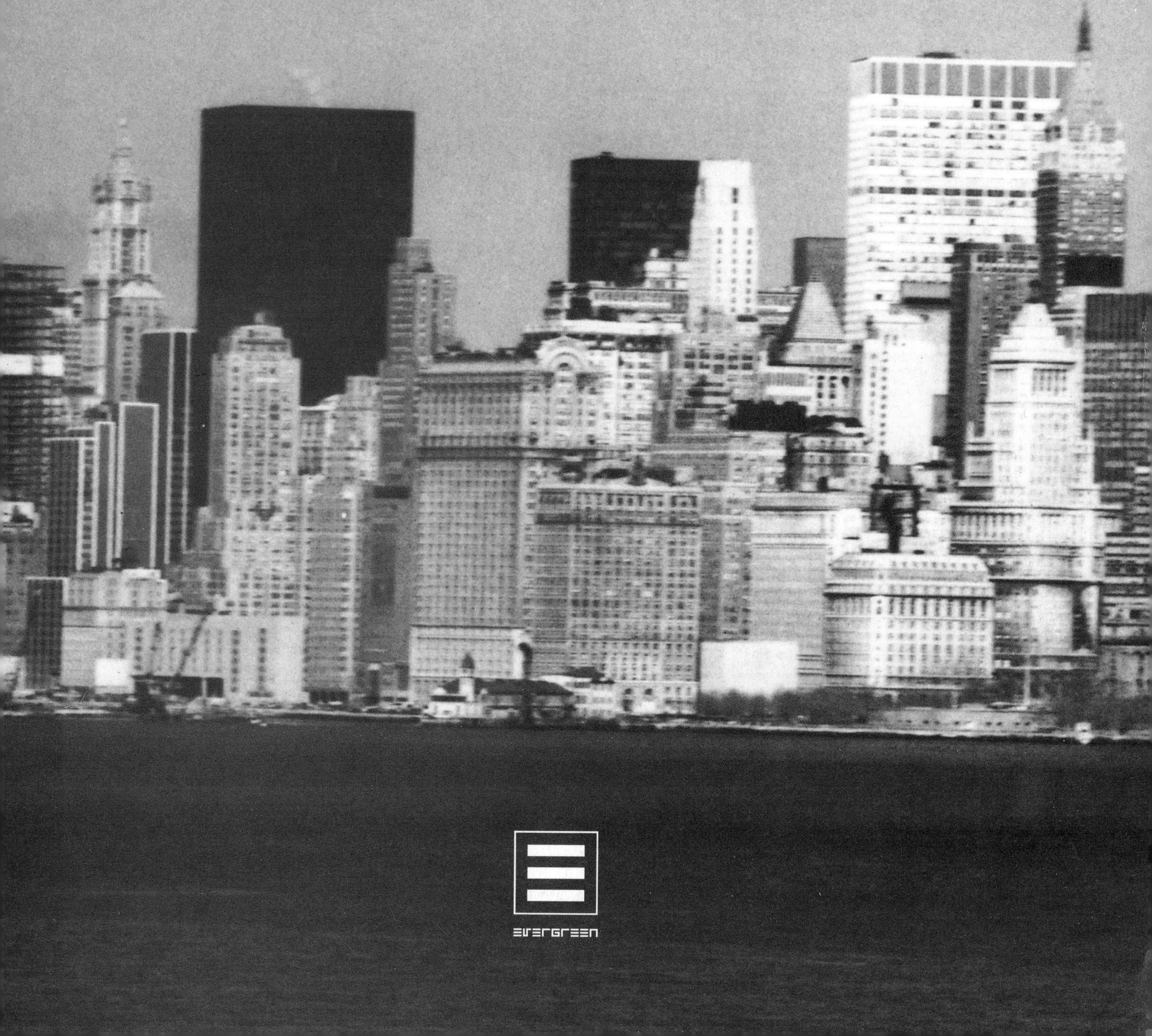

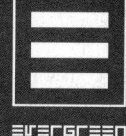

EVERGREEN

Frontispiece: View to the northeast of Upper New York Harbor
with the Statue of Liberty (Frédéric Auguste Bartholdi, sculptor,
Alexandre Gustave Eiffel, engineer, and Richard Morris Hunt,
architect of the base, 1886) on the left and, behind, One and Two
World Trade Center (Minoru Yamasaki and Emery Roth & Sons,
1973). ERS

New edition published throughout the world
(except on the North American continent) in 1997 by
Benedikt Taschen Verlag GmbH
Hohenzollernring 53, D–50672 Köln
Germany

First published in 1995 by
The Monacelli Press, Inc.
10 East 92nd St, New York, New York 10128

Copyright © 1995 The Monacelli Press, Inc., and Robert A. M. Stern

Designed by Abigail Sturges
Set in type by MEM Totally Graphics, Inc.

ISBN: 3–8228–7741–7
Printed in Italy

Acknowledgments

An undertaking as large and complex as *New York 1960* would not have been possible without the help of many people. Limitations of space prevent us from acknowledging everyone individually, but we would like to give particular thanks to Christopher Gray and Suzanne Braley at the Office for Metropolitan History, who generously shared with us their knowledge of New York architecture. We would also like to thank our indefatigable research assistants: Michael Adams, Lindsay Bierman, Max Hillaire, Elizabeth Kraft, Juong Yoon Lym and Goteh Nzidee. Don Shillingburg provided invaluable assistance during the final stages of production. The staff of the Landmarks Preservation Commission of the City of New York was always helpful. Throughout the entire process, Angela Giral, Avery Libarian, Janet Parks, Curator of Drawings, as well as Katherine Chibnik, Kathe Chipman, Paula Gabbard, Edward Goodman, Daniel R. Kany, Katherine Keller, Deborah Kempe, Herbert Mitchell, William O'Malley, Christine Sala, Barbara Sykes-Austin and the entire staff of Columbia University's Avery Architecture and Fine Arts Library, made every effort to assist us; without their help, this book truly could not have been written. Additionally, Dwight Primiano spent long hours in the library photographing material from Columbia's collections.

We are greatly indebted to the individuals and institutions who helped us find photographs and gave us permission to use them. Regretfully, we cannot individually acknowledge the architects and the members of their staffs who assisted us, but we give our heartfelt thanks to them all. We would also like to thank the numerous photographers whose work is represented here; they are each credited in captions throughout the book. Thanks are also due to Terry Ariano, Museum of the City of New York; Jacqueline Cancro, Port Authority of New York and New Jersey; Kenneth R. Cobb, Municipal Archives; Laura Harris, *New York Post*; Judith Johnson, Archive of Lincoln Center for the Performing Arts, Inc.; Jonathan Kuhn, New York City Department of Parks and Recreation; Oscar Muñoz, Frank Lloyd Wright Archives; Ford Peatross and Marilyn Ibach, Library of Congress; Laura Rosen, Triborough Bridge and Tunnel Authority; Erica Stoller, Esto; and Robert Tuggle and John Pennino, Metropolitan Opera Archives.

Our special thanks go to those who helped in the book's production. Beverly Johnson-Godette heroically typed first drafts. Abigail Sturges designed and oversaw production of the book and Michael Bertrand and Michael Molfetto helped put her elegant and evocative scheme on paper. Kathleen Cromwell and Alice Smith Duncan served as the book's proofreaders. Steve Sears guided the book through the phases of production. We are particularly grateful for the clear head and fine hand of our editor, Kate Norment; Lois Nesbitt was also a valuable member of the editorial team. Finally, the support and vision of our publisher, Gianfranco Monacelli, was indispensable in bringing *New York 1960* to fruition.

Contents

This book documents New York's architectural and urbanistic evolution from the outbreak of World War II in 1941 to the nation's bicentennial celebration in 1976. As in *New York 1900* and *New York 1930*, the two previous volumes in the series, we have sought to let the city tell its own complex story rather than to impose a contemporary perspective on it. To this end, we have emphasized primary over secondary sources, drawing extensively on the commentaries of the major architecture critics of the day, as well as the architects, urban planners and city officials who directly participated in New York's building and rebuilding. To present as clear and direct a picture of the city as possible, we have maintained the model established by the previous books and illustrated the text exclusively with period photographs.

New York 1900 and *New York 1930* described the flowering of Metropolitanism, and *New York 1960* continues that discussion by analyzing the concept's virtual demise and its replacement with a new reality: the city as but a component of a superconurbation called Megalopolis. Prior to World War II, New York embodied the metropolitan ideal, in which the city sought to provide to its own citizens the resources and opportunities offered by the nation as a whole; in fact, it set out to establish the prototypes, the standards, by which the federal government would meet its responsibilities. For example, it had great museums of art and natural history before the national institutions in Washington, it had great parks before the federal government had a park service, and it had public housing before Washington embarked on a program to address this urgent problem.

Reflecting the country's pluralist, democratic society, metropolitan New York was both a miniature and a distillation of America, encompassing within its boundaries the most disparate urban forms, from the man-made canyons of the financial district to the leafy green idyll of suburban enclaves within the outer boroughs, all linked by a network of roads and railroads that was an internationally recognized model of efficiency, comparable to and in many ways a model for that of the nation as a whole. Even more than constituting a paradigm of efficiently organized diversity, the metropolitan city was de facto a world capital, the highest representation of cultured life in

America. Urban density, rather than being seen as the evil it would come to be regarded as later, was celebrated in a so-called cult of congestion inextricably linked to the advantages and aspirations of a progressive civilization. All this would change rapidly following World War II, when the city would become the primary but not sole focus of a sprawling suburbanism, the boundaries of which far exceeded not only those of the consolidated city established in 1898 but also those of any traditional region. This almost unimaginably large conurbation, stretching from northern Virginia to southern New Hampshire, came to be known in 1961 as Megalopolis, a name given it by the French urban geographer Jean Gottmann.[1]

Radical change occurred not just at the city's periphery but at its core. At the same time that the city's role within the surrounding region, and its relationship to the nation as a whole, underwent redefinition, entire precincts of the city itself were virtually rebuilt. Because of the massive scope of redevelopment, *New York 1960* is organized on a geographic basis—a departure from the emphasis on building type that characterized the previous volumes in the series—with chapters dedicated to each of Manhattan's principal areas, as well as the outer boroughs and, to a lesser extent, the suburbs.

Large-scale construction was, of necessity, accompanied by large-scale destruction—often of architecturally significant buildings. In another departure from the previous volumes in this series, *New York 1960* includes an extensive discussion of historic preservation efforts, not only examining successful campaigns to protect the city's architectural heritage but cataloguing the numerous buildings that fell victim to the wrecker's ball, many of which were first discussed as new examples of the architect's art in *New York 1900* and *New York 1930*. It was during the post–World War II period, and particularly after the tragic destruction of Pennsylvania Station in 1963, that many New Yorkers began to fully recognize the architectural richness of their own city as well as the need to preserve it. At the same time, what had previously been the domain primarily of well-heeled ladies with a taste for colonial houses first became a "movement" supported by members of both the architectural community and the public at large, and later evolved into an integral part of municipal government, wielding immense, legally

Preface

mandated power. Not only did the Landmarks Preservation Commission, established in 1965, go a long way toward saving important buildings, it pursued what some observers would argue was New York's most proactive form of planning in light of the City Planning Commission's repeated failure to establish effective comprehensive planning strategies.

Why 1960? In a survey of the years from World War II to the bicentennial, the year 1960, falling nearly at the period's midpoint, marks a watershed for the city's physical growth. From 1960 on, the baseline of urban development would no longer be the metropolitan ideal of city-state, but the concept of the city as the largest but not necessarily the most prosperous place within Megalopolis. In terms of architecture and urbanism, 1960 marks a decisive moment when the waning Classicism of the nineteenth century gave way almost completely to the Modernism that had been making significant inroads in America since the early 1930s. This shift, typical of American architecture and urbanism as a whole, was nowhere more vividly realized than in New York, where the complete revision of the zoning ordinance virtually legislated not only Modernist urbanism but also Modernist aesthetics.

On December 15, 1960, the city's pioneering zoning ordinance of 1916 was completely overhauled and one year later the new code took effect. The old ordinance, with its solid roots in the traditional spacemaking of streets and avenues bounded by walls of buildings that filled up city blocks to near solidity, was abandoned. The new regulations encouraged unmodulated, independently spaced skyscraper tower slabs rising from generously scaled plazas—an "open" city, a city that was space positive rather than mass positive, a city that, were it to be rebuilt completely along the lines of the new code, would become one with the continuous open space of the essential ruralism of Megalopolis. After 1960 the physical fabric of the city would never be the same again; not only would the character of the streets and blocks change, but also the very idea of community. And, of course, so too would the city's architecture be completely different. Whereas the zoning ordinance of 1916 adapted traditional urbanism to the giant scale of American building practice, that of 1960–61 broke with the past completely. The new urbanism legislated the disintegration of the traditional city;

its authors probably did not see clearly enough that with the collapse of traditional street architecture would come the collapse of traditional street life and perhaps of the very idea of neighborhood. After 1960, as the city began to become in reality what Le Corbusier, thirty-five years before, had conceived and designated as a vertical garden city, one in which generously scaled open areas would "in fact, make the city itself one vast garden,"[2] the camaraderie of street and neighborhood life, so long the glue that kept the city's social fabric together, began to harden and dry, tearing apart the fabric of daily life.

Other key changes coming around 1960 tended to reinforce the sense that the city had turned a not necessarily welcome corner. Robert Moses, the master builder and public servant, so long a metropolitan hero, began to reveal himself as petty and not a little deceitful. As the result of widely publicized scandals in the administration of large-scale federally funded urban renewal projects, in which Moses appeared both venal and callous, he began to be stripped of his vast powers. At the same time, increasing demands made by local communities for self-determination rendered politically insupportable Moses's Haussmann-like approach to redevelopment.

The year 1960 was an important watershed in another, highly ironic way: just as the new zoning was taking effect, many of the planning notions that had led to its adoption were devastatingly criticized. The new thinking was given shape by Jane Jacobs in her polemical book, *The Death and Life of Great American Cities*, published in 1961.[3] So it could be argued that the collapse of the old order came just at the time when many of its characteristics were being favorably reassessed, although it would take another fifteen years or so, until the era that has come to be called Post-Modernist, for the lessons of Jacobs to become absorbed into the patterns of the city's architecture and urbanism. That story belongs to *New York 2000*.

It was also in 1960 that the city's postwar building boom got under way in earnest. On the one hand, the boom was prompted by a speculators' rush to construct as much as possible under the more permissive 1916 code. But so great was the city's capacity to absorb new office and dwelling space that the new zoning soon enough made its mark—far more quickly than the changes that followed the ratification of the 1916 zoning,

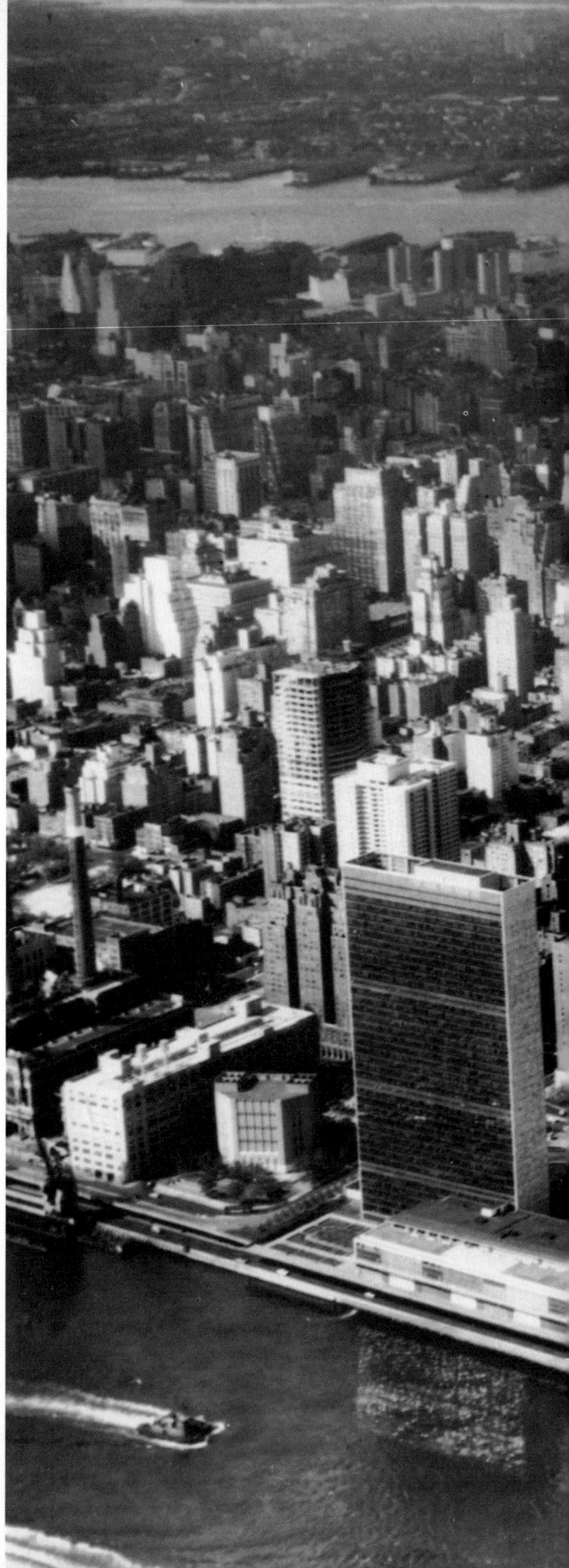

View to the southwest of midtown Manhattan, showing the United Nations Headquarters (Board of Design, Wallace K. Harrison, Director of Planning, 1947–52) on the lower left and the Empire State Building (Shreve, Lamb & Harmon, 1931) on the upper left. Wurts. MCNY

which, because of World War I and the depression of 1920–21, did not significantly affect the shape of the city for six or seven years after its adoption.

The boom of 1960–69 also made it possible for long-anticipated urban schemes to be realized. In 1960 lower Manhattan, on a steady decline as the city's business center since the war, was given a new lease on life with the completion of Skidmore, Owings & Merrill's catalytic Chase Manhattan Bank Building. Now New York would have two equally viable business centers, downtown and midtown, fulfilling a fifty-year-old dream. Just a year earlier, completion of Harrison, Abramovitz & Harris's Time & Life Building marked the first key step in the reconstruction of Sixth Avenue, renamed the Avenue of the Americas in 1945.

Perhaps most important of all, 1960 was a time when many residents and observers of New York began to critically reevaluate the city's potential. Writers, urbanists and to a considerable extent ordinary people began to discuss what came to be called the "urban crisis"—a notion, as James Lardner wrote in 1993, "that reflected a sense of opportunity as well as alarm. The city, with its neighborhoods, its parks, its landmarks, and its cohesiveness, was a great resource, which could be saved; there might even be some fun to be had in saving it."[4]

While *New York 1900* and *New York 1930* were each confined to a relatively small canvas, *New York 1960* explodes to a broad mosaic of events and geography. But at its core lies Manhattan, which the developer William Zeckendorf, in a phrase picked up by the editors of *Fortune* in 1960, labeled "Headquarters Town."[5] Despite our opening up of the discussion to cover not only the outer boroughs but also the suburbs, our concentration on Manhattan seems justified. As the city planner Charles Abrams noted in 1961: "What saves New York is Manhattan—the city's 'downtown.' It is a kind of national downtown, a crossroads of America."[6] To a greater extent than ever before, Manhattan was the representative city of America. With the election of John F. Kennedy as president in 1960, the American century was at a climactic moment, and New York, in many ways even more visibly than Washington, D.C., occupied center position on the world's stage.

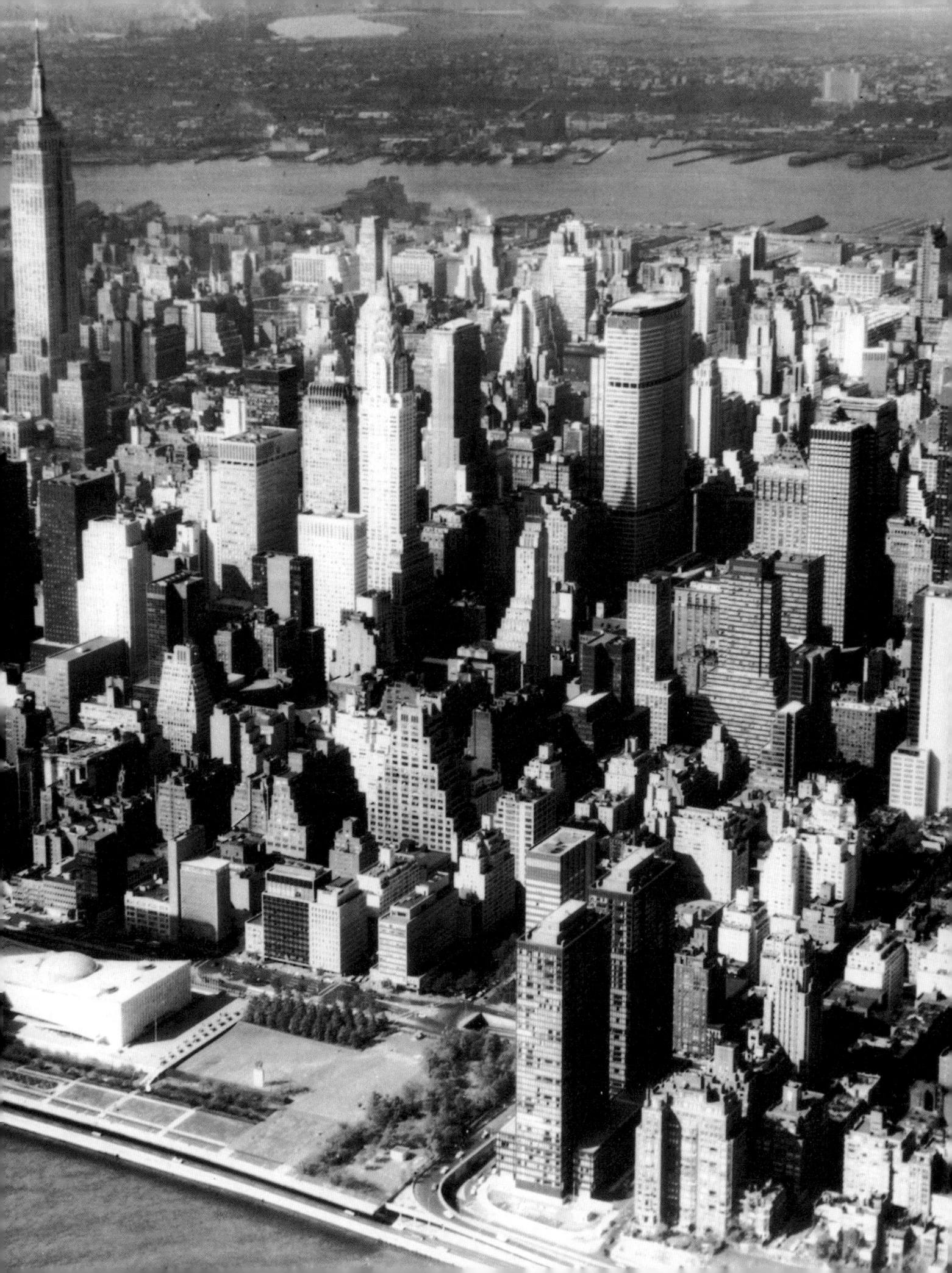

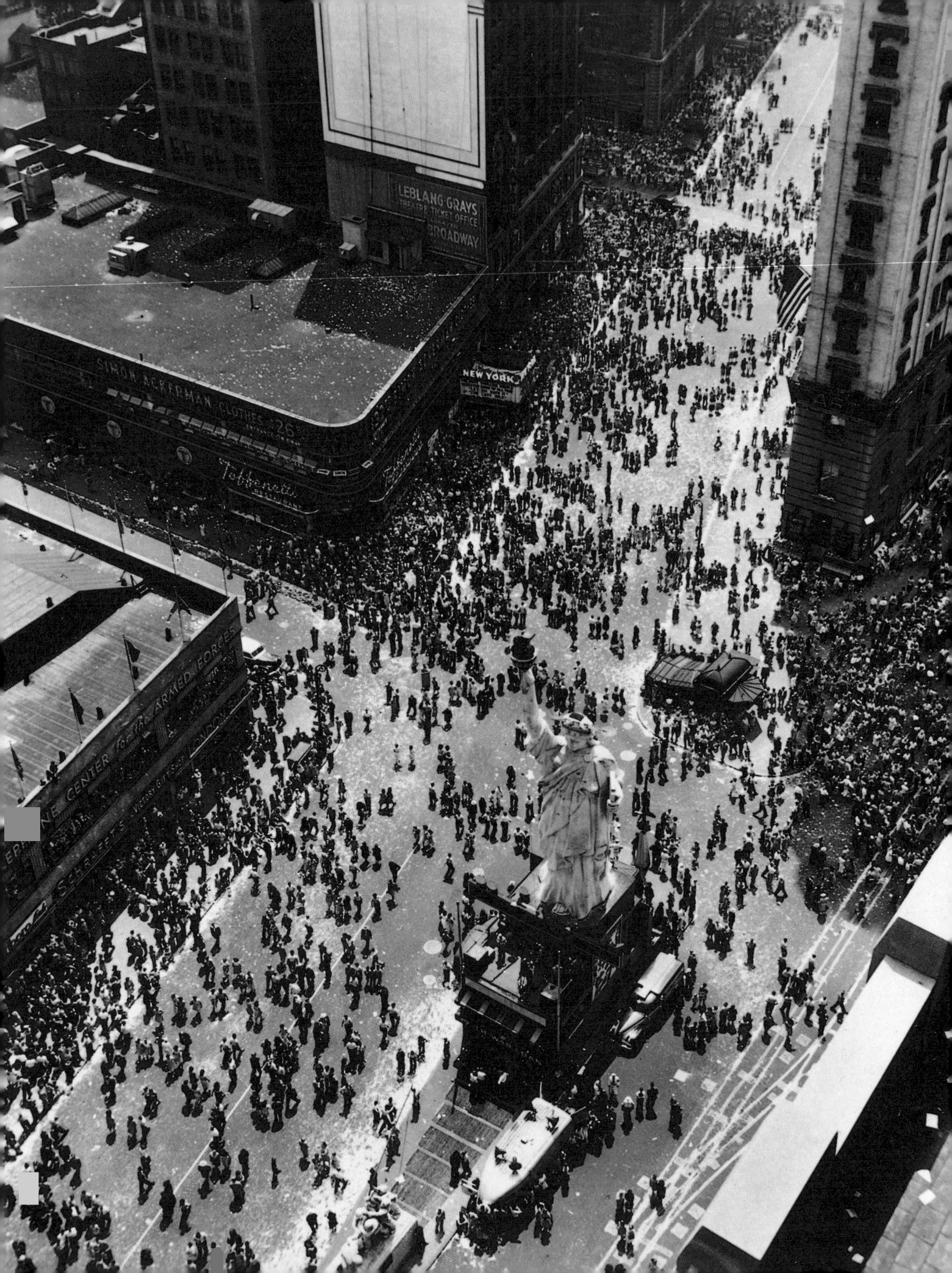

Introduction

I don't think New York City is like other cities. It does not have character like Los Angeles or New Orleans. It is all characters— in fact, it is everything. It can destroy a man, but if his eyes are open it cannot bore him.
New York is an ugly city, a dirty city. Its climate is a scandal, its politics are used to frighten children, its traffic is madness, its competition is murderous. But there is one thing about it— once you have lived in New York and it has become your home, no place else is good enough.
—John Steinbeck, 1953[1]

From World Capital to Near Collapse

This is the story of New York's architecture and urbanism in the age of Megalopolis. It is the story of a city fighting for survival amidst naysayers who in the name of humanism argued for its transformation into a smaller, lesser, more suburban place. It is the story of a city that in order to survive and prosper too often set aside its quirks and ideals yet somehow managed to retain a healthy measure of its identity and vitality. It is the story of a city that became the world's capital in 1945 yet found itself thirty years later at the brink of economic collapse.

New York in 1940 was a relatively quiet place, at least as compared to the way it had been in the booming 1920s. For ten years in the 1920s New York had exulted in and been celebrated for its size and, more important, its congestion. Now, after a decade of economic depression, with many of its office towers and luxury apartment houses empty, the pace of city life was comparatively slow. Moreover, many New Yorkers seemed to like it that way, deeming the boom times of the 1920s an age of excess well left behind. Even the city's vaunted skyline seemed too much, at least to such observers as the editors of the *New York Times*, who in 1940 applauded Manhattan's "gradually sinking

skyline. Hard on Times Square there are now three street corners on which tall buildings of the pre-skyscraper age—say ten or twelve stories—have been lately replaced by two-story 'taxpayers.' Esthetically the change is enormously for the better. The new buildings are much handsomer than their predecessors, and above the new low buildings one catches a glimpse of the sky."[2]

The Depression had virtually put a stop to private development; but the government-supported projects of Robert Moses in many ways made up for this loss of commercial activity by providing jobs as well as useful public works on a scale of civic grandeur the city had not seen since the construction of Frederick Law Olmsted and Calvert Vaux's Central Park. Not only was the city still feeling the effects of the malingering Depression, it also appeared that it was losing jobs and population to the suburbs, a factor that seriously concerned Manhattan real estate interests but not most city planners, who welcomed low densities and decentralization.[3] Even with the exodus to the suburbs, the city's overall population continued to grow, replenishing itself in its traditional way, through immigration—from war-threatened and war-ravaged Europe, which contributed an exceptional number of artists and intellectuals as well as ordinary citizens, and from the rural areas of the South and Puerto Rico.

Although the city's population was growing, it was doing so at a much slower rate than in the past. In 1941 the Regional Plan Association analyzed the 1940 census data and predicted that by 1970 there would be 8,405,000 New Yorkers, a million more than in 1940. By comparison, between 1920 and 1930 the city's population had grown from 5,620,048 to 6,930,446. Manhattan, the city's focus, which had been experiencing a steady decline in population since its peak of 2.3 million in 1910, was on something of an upswing. In 1940 it was home to 1.9 million, representing a modest growth in the 1930s.[4] Despite the slower rate of population growth, New York was still a very big place: it was the second largest city in the world, its 7,454,995 people and 322.83 square miles exceeded only by those of London.

The World's Fair of 1939–40, though it promised the future, proved in effect to be the embodiment of the recent past. In terms of the city's preparations, the fair stimulated the realization of many of the transportation projects that were proposed in the *Regional Plan of New York and Its Environs* (1928–31).[5] The

V-J Day celebration, Times Square, August 14, 1945. View to the southeast, of intersection of Seventh Avenue, Broadway and West Forty-third Street, showing temporary replica of the Statue of Liberty in the center, Toffenetti's (Skidmore, Owings & Merrill, in association with Walker & Gillette, 1940) on the upper left, and the base of the Times Tower (Cyrus L. W. Eidlitz, 1904) on the upper right. LOC road-building and land-use policies of Robert Moses, who never acknowledged his debt to the 1929–31 plan, opened up the countryside to the inner-city dweller as never before and set in motion the process of deurbanization that in the postwar years would unalterably change the composition of the city's social and economic mosaic. Though the fair's exhibits celebrated ways of living that were fundamentally anti-urban, taken as a whole the fair offered strong affirmation of New York's status as the nation's cultural and economic capital.

So much had been built in the 1920s and so traumatic was the effect of the Depression on its population that the city was almost unrecognizable to those who had not been there since World War I. Clair Price, an expatriate writer returning to the city in 1941 after having lived in Europe since 1920, found a town that looked "a bit more mature, a bit more like a city whose children have been falling in love with it. It looked new and full of light." Price went on to write:

> The New York of 1920 has rearranged and expanded itself into the New York of 1941. Its heaving uptown surge has crashed through the old Fifth Avenue mansions and left towering shops and offices in their stead, spilling over whole streetfulls of smart shops into Fifty-Seventh Street and Madison Avenue. It has torn out miles of the old residences in Park Avenue and West End Avenue, replacing them with fifteen-story apartment houses. It has raised the thirty-story factories of the new midtown garment center and flung up climactic midtown peaks.

Price also saw other, "less spectacular but more pervasive changes," like the new highways sweeping "beneath its bold escarpments, new housing and new playgrounds," as well as a greater sense of open sky that had resulted from the 1916 zoning.[6]

"For perhaps the first time in its ruthless, headlong history," he reflected, "some new impulse, something apart from commerce, industry and finance, had been acting on the town. Some sense of community design and purpose has tempered the obsession with buying and selling. . . . Out of the old demonic energy has come a new ambition to build a city more fit for human use and aspiration." In the calamity of the Depression, Price concluded, New York had discovered a new sense of itself: "There is a new maturity, a new tranquility, on the faces of the seven-million. The old fury-for-fury's-sake has gone. . . . But what is more heartening in the gathering darkness of this time is that democracy in New York, which seemed to be curdling and turning sour in 1920, has today been sweetened, invigorated and made strong."[7]

Following two years of "preparedness," America went to war in December 1941. New York took the war in stride. After the initial shocks of blackouts and air-raid drills, buildings were dimmed not out of any real fear of air attack but because the glow of city lights silhouetted shipping for enemy U-boats lurking offshore. Quickly settling down to the business of manufacturing goods and moving them, as well as a large portion of the American troops fighting in Europe, onto ships to be sent abroad, New York played a key role in the war effort. Yet, except for the sight of servicemen on leave and of cargo vessels and tankers being loaded with goods or repaired in dry dock, New Yorkers who were without close friends or relatives in the armed services or living overseas were largely insulated from the war.[8]

War returned something of pre-Crash prosperity, rekindling the city's nightlife to levels of activity not seen since the 1920s. To the casual observer, like Tania Loring, returning to the city in 1943 after two years in London, New York seemed "brilliant,

dazzling, filled with good things to wear and to eat."[9] But to war refugees this surface glitter could be very off-putting. Before the Philippine journalist and statesman Carlos Romulo understood the city's commitment to the war effort, he found it nothing short of a carnival.[10]

At the war's conclusion in 1945, New York was the world's most powerful city: London was severely damaged, while Berlin and Tokyo lay in near ruin; Paris, though not physically injured, was demoralized by years of occupation. New York was not only physically intact, it was prosperous and optimistic, symbolizing the best American values to Europeans and to the returning GI's. "Of all the big cities," Sergeant Milton Lehman, a reporter for the *Stars and Stripes* newspaper, assured readers of the *New York Times* in 1945, "New York is still the promised land."[11] As the military men and women from New York returned home, a holiday spirit spread out into the neighborhoods, with so many block parties being held that the *New York Times* could report "dancing in the streets" all over the city.[12]

The mobilization for war and then war itself temporarily solved many of New York's systemic problems. Wartime rations on gasoline made suburban living much less convenient, and many families who could, closed up their suburban houses and rented apartments in Manhattan. The war returned New York to prosperity, causing a boom in its principal heavy industry, shipbuilding. And with factories everywhere else in the United States working at full capacity, New York's plants, outmoded though they might be, were humming as well, except for those of the garment trades, which were hampered by government restrictions and competition from the South.[13] Nonetheless, more people worked in the garment trades than in Detroit's automobile industry. From the point of view of industrial activity, New York seemed prepared for the future as no other American city was; its industries did not need to be retooled for peacetime, because they made in wartime what they'd always made, small-scale items easily adaptable to the consumer market.

New Yorkers were not only busy making things: 440,000 of them helped keep shop, and of the 500,000 workers estimated to enter and leave Manhattan's central business districts each working day many went to Wall Street to help manage the nation's and increasingly the world's finances. Wall Street had been nearly moribund during the 1930s, but wartime brought new life to its precincts as capitalists and brokers devised a vast panoply of techniques to democratize business ownership and create a financial industry of unprecedented size and value to the city's economy. By war's end the city was the world's financial capital, and after December 1946, when the United Nations agreed to locate its permanent headquarters in Manhattan, it became the world's political capital as well.[14]

True, there were obvious problems: the city housing stock was bursting at the seams, with 165,400 families living doubled up, mostly young couples unwillingly camped with their in-laws, waiting to move into new apartments and houses as soon as they could be built. New York was the densest of American cities, with 21,000 persons living on each of its 323 square miles. Its next nearest rival, Chicago, had only 16,000 per square mile, while in the United States as a whole the density level was only forty-one per square mile. With population density came even more diversity than before: it was a city more representative of the world than the United Nations itself, with some sixty nationalities living within its borders: two million of its residents were foreign-born; 2.75 million were natives of foreign or mixed parentage; and almost half a million were black, making New York the world's largest black metropolis.

Oddly enough, New York was in many ways also like a small town—more so than it had been in the 1920s. Though 3.5 million meals were consumed each day at New York's 22,000 restaurants, soda fountains, snack bars, sandwich shops and clubs, the vast majority of meals served in the city were served at home. But in one respect, at least, New York was different from any other American city—it was obsessed with entertaining itself. The Consolidated Edison Company estimated that New Yorkers used only a little more than half the kilowatts of electricity used by Americans elsewhere in a year, sure confirmation that Gothamites were much more likely to be out at night than their fellow Americans, probably visiting the city's 700 movie theaters, 1,315 dance halls, cabarets or nightclubs, 6,679 bars, 8 concert halls and 64 "legitimate" theaters.[15] To move its citizens about, New York ran a twenty-four-hour transit system, carrying 2.5 billion passengers in 1945 on 2,453 buses, 585 trolleys and along 554 route miles of subways using 1,233 miles of track, enough to connect New York and Chicago, with track left over for a jaunt to Omaha. The city's trolleys, long the object of planners' derision, were outnumbered more than four to one by buses, but even in the process of being scrapped as outdated, they nonetheless carried twice as many passengers as did the buses. And they moved them faster.

New York's immediate postwar situation was dichotomous—expanded influence amidst internal decline; after the jubilation of V-E and V-J days, when the people of the city gathered in celebration (see chapter 5), New York's grip on itself began to loosen. On February 12, 1946, Lincoln's Birthday, in an effort to preserve fuel during a strike by the tugboat workers who towed oil and coal barges that brought heating supplies the city depended on, newly elected Mayor William F. O'Dwyer closed the city's services down.[16] It was a dramatic gesture that was respected by the public, and the strike ended within a day. Observing the shutdown from a vantage point in Central Park, the editors of the New Yorker found it "the equivalent not of Martial Law, but of the Mardi Gras."[17] Yet to Marya Mannes, the postwar era, recalled fifteen years later, seemed to signal a decline in the city's ability to "cope with its people, when—through overcrowding, inefficiency, corruption and greed—" it seemed to sacrifice "those amenities which spell civilized living."[18]

During the 1940s and 1950s, 1.2 million whites moved out of the city, mostly to nearby suburban counties in New York and New Jersey.[19] At the same time, the city benefited from an influx of southern blacks and Puerto Ricans. By November 1957 New York would become the first city in the world to have a black population of more than one million. Still, New York remained a largely white city, with a white population estimated at about 6.7 million, including 600,000 Puerto Ricans. In the same period, the population of Nassau County on Long Island grew from 407,000 to 1,300,000, while comparatively remote Suffolk swelled from 197,000 to 667,000. The shift of middle-class population away from the center, where it found employment, was paralleled by a shift of manufacturing jobs to the periphery, where the working class found few opportunities for housing, thereby setting in motion a pattern that would put an endless burden of commutation by automobile on all classes and would hamper the ability of the poor to seek employment. The establishment of suburban branch department stores to suit the convenience of, in particular, affluent clientele had begun in 1929 when Best & Company opened a store in Garden City. By 1949, according to the Regional Plan Association, there were forty-eight suburban branches of New York stores.[20]

But the move of industry to the suburbs, more or less by-

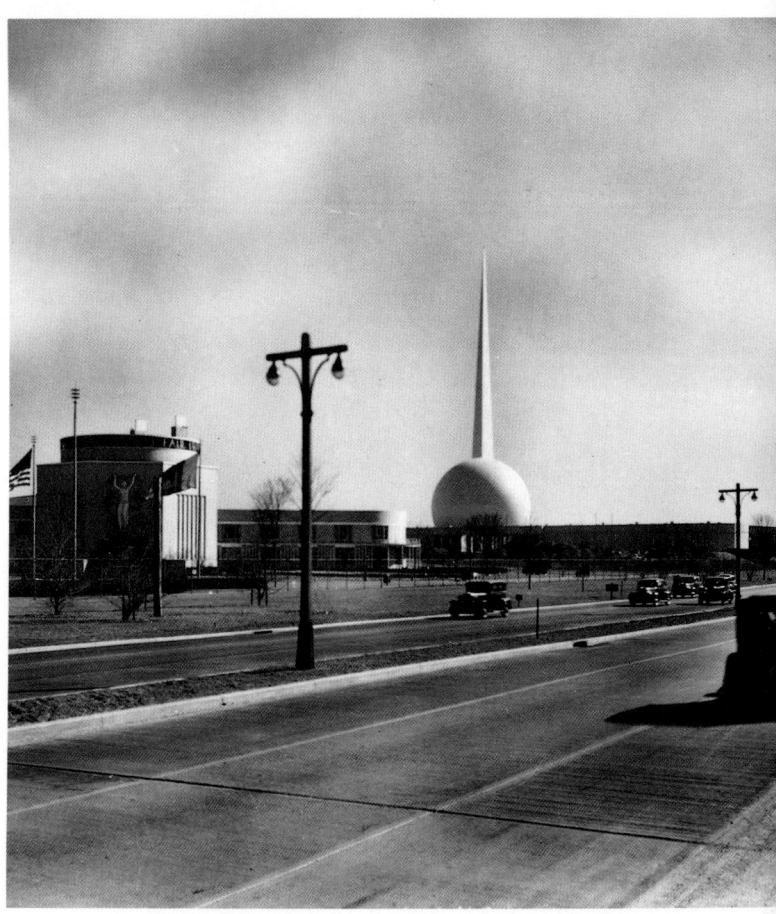

Trylon and Perisphere, New York World's Fair, Flushing, Queens. Harrison & Foulhoux, 1939. View to the southeast from Grand Central Parkway. Underhill. LOC

Overleaf: V-E Day celebration, East Forty-second Street and Lexington Avenue, May 8, 1945. View to the southeast. LOC

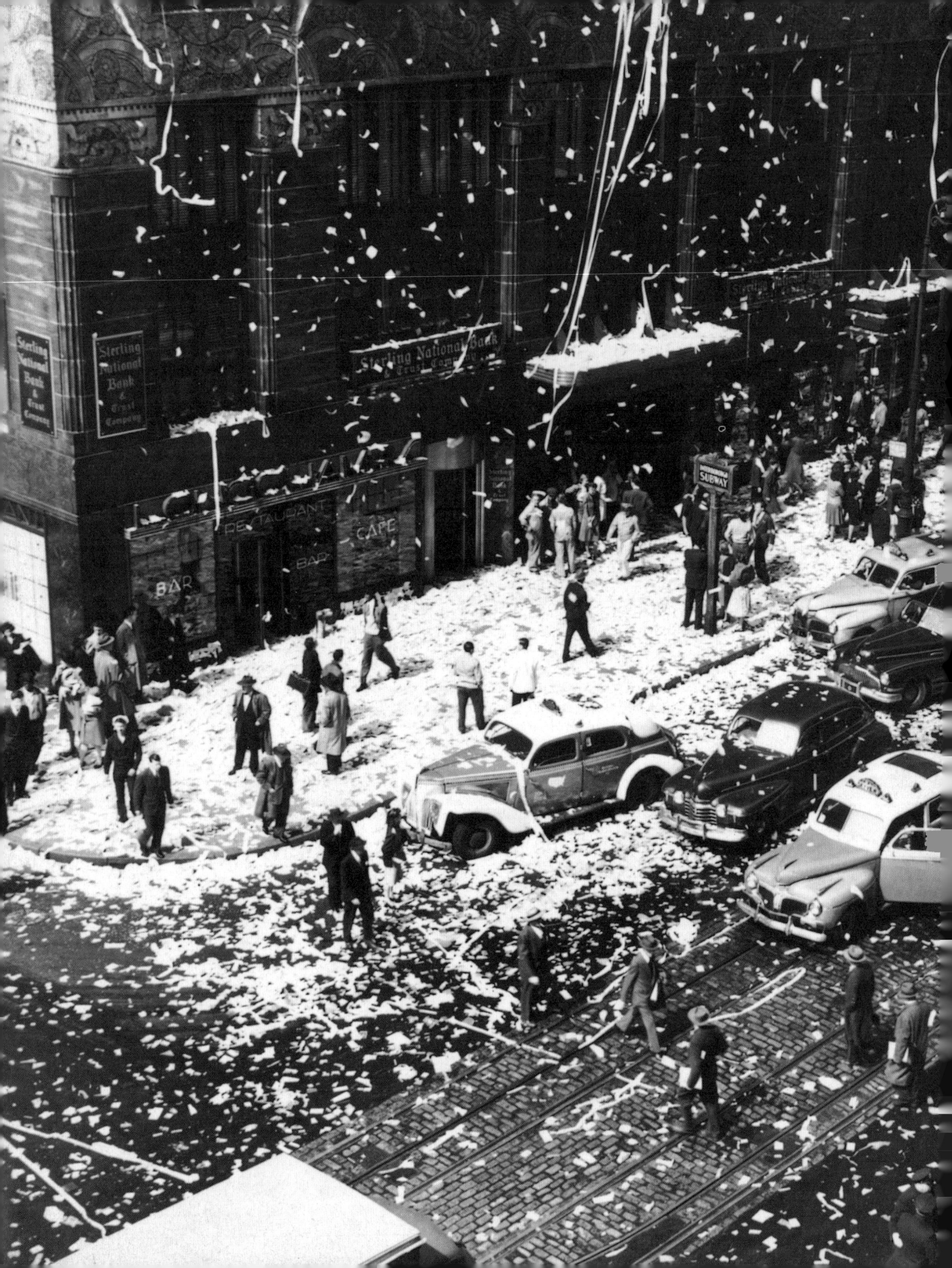

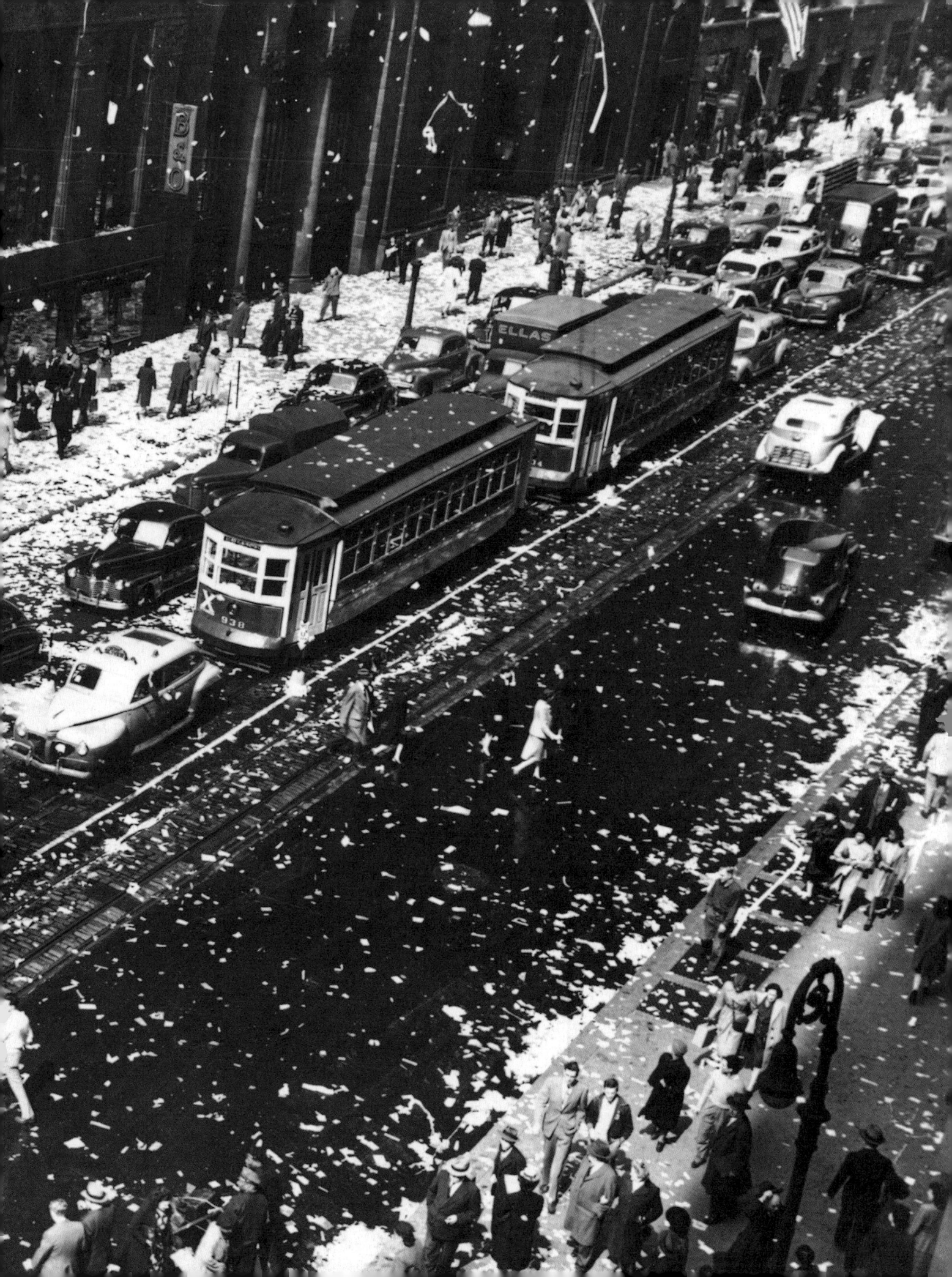

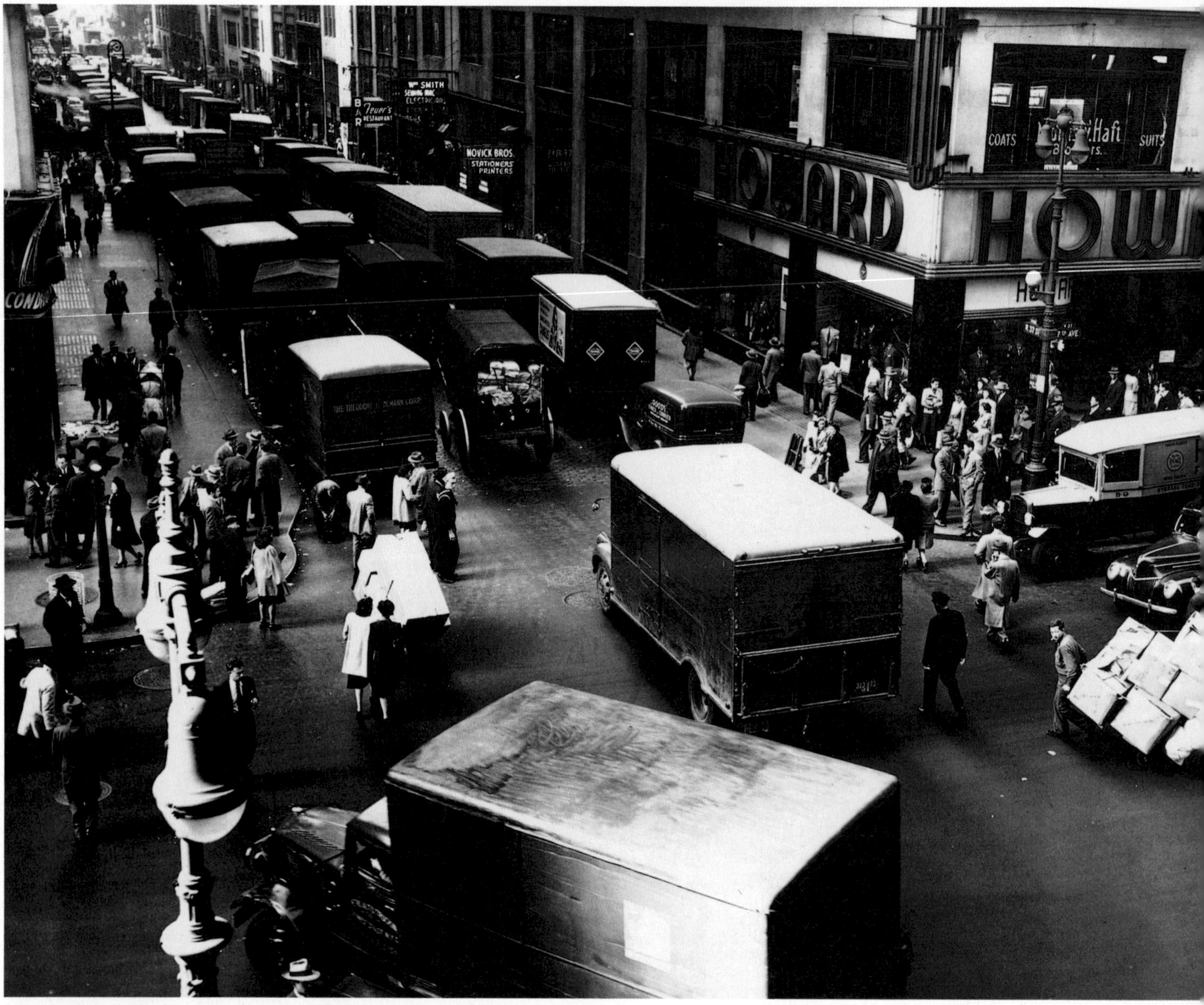

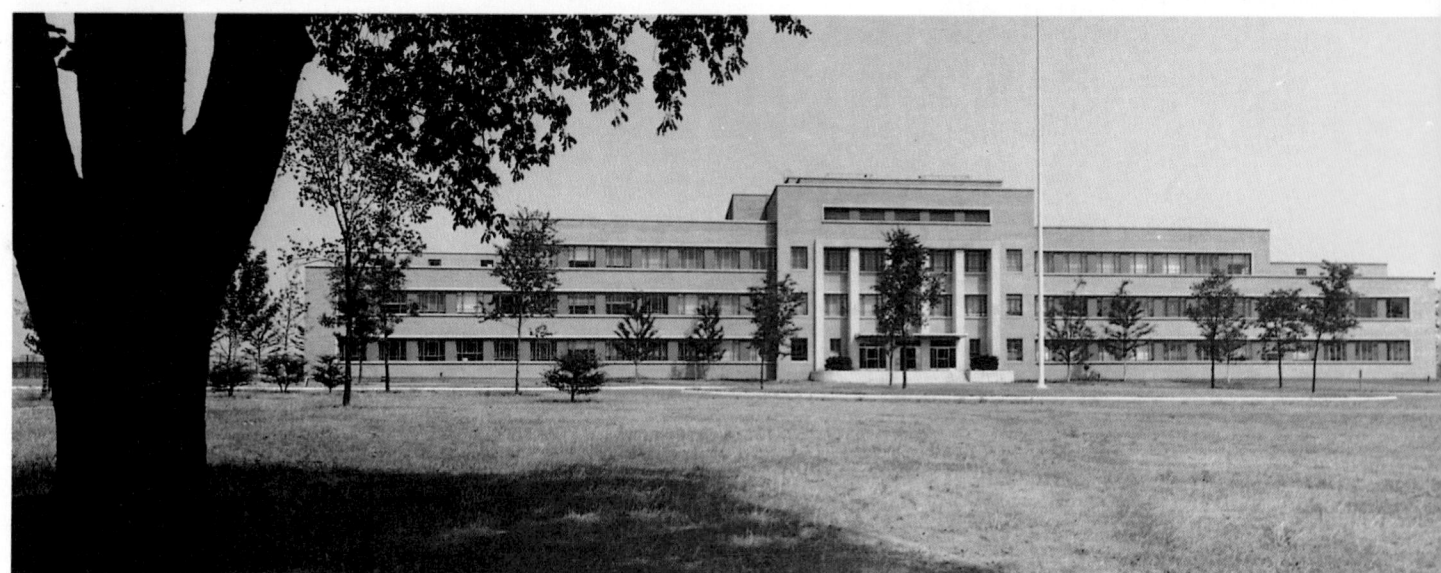

Garment district, West Thirty-seventh Street and Seventh Avenue, 1945. View to the west. LOC

Johns-Manville Research Center, Manville, New Jersey. Shreve, Lamb & Harmon, 1949. Gottscho-Schleisner. LOC passing the outlying sections of the outer boroughs, which were already filling up with houses, was more troubling. In 1946 New York was the nation's largest manufacturing town. But in 1952 the Regional Plan Association, after surveying 2,658 plants built between 1946 and 1951, reported "a postwar trend to decentralize manufacturing throughout the metropolitan area," noting that five-sixths of the new factories "were built beyond the limits of the major industrial districts existing at the close of World War II."[21] While the efficiency of horizontal organization of the manufacturing process was no doubt an important factor in determining plant locations, it was also likely that placement convenient to the increasingly suburbanized managerial work force was also a significant factor; little attention seemed to have been paid to the hardships placed on the ordinary factory worker by locating plants in relatively remote suburban areas.

The changing demographics, combined with the suburbanization of industry and the middle class, quickly transformed postwar optimism into pessimism; in fact, as the French geographer Jean Gottmann put it, in those years

there was practically common agreement that New York would decline in importance in the future. It was not advantageously located for the new era of airplanes then opening up. The time seemed over when transportation by sea made it essential to have the main economic center in a seaport. . . . It was also agreed that Manhattan was far too crowded, that the rest of New York was too blighted, and that it would cost too much to improve the situation. Every major corporation which did not have particularly local roots—and even some that did—were planning new headquarters somewhere else in America.[22]

Concern for the future had first been fielded in April 1943, when the so-called Hanes Committee, appointed by Governor Thomas E. Dewey to study business and employment opportunities in the city, came up with some shocking findings that portended a sagging postwar economy.[23] The report pointed to current less-than-full employment, attributed to the city's manufacturing companies' concentration on consumer goods and the comparatively high cost of doing business in the city. But light manufacturing and port activities, traditionally the source of the city's economic strength, were doing well. A third factor—financial management and especially business management—was also very strong and, according to some observers, would grow and prosper. The *Herald Tribune* saw the future more clearly than most when it editorialized: "New York's position as business-management headquarters far outweighs its importance as the financial center."[24] In 1944, in the pages of *American Mercury*, Richard H. Rovere contended that "the truth of the matter" was that though "New York may still be the financial and cultural center of the nation," this might not be "the case twenty years from now. For more than a century New York was the golden city, draining riches and talent away from the rest of the country. Recently, talent and riches have been leaving New York. If it were otherwise, the proud metropolis would not be trying, like Zenith or Eureka, to lure new enterprise its way."[25]

But not everyone was negative about the city's future. "It's going to be quite a town," Robert Moses proclaimed in a 1947 *New York Times Magazine* article. Citing recently released figures gathered by the Consolidated Edison Company that projected a 1960 population of 8.4 million, Moses revealed plans for rebuilding the East River waterfront from Beekman Place in the north to City Hall in the south, including the complete reconstruction of Second Avenue in the vicinity of the

Queensboro Bridge, where an elaborate cloverleaf interchange would be constructed. In the same article, Moses extolled the creation of a new Civic Center in Brooklyn, which would remove "the old cancerous weakness" of that borough's traditional downtown. He also touched on other projects and raised the issue of the Narrows crossing, stating that while the city could not afford to build a tunnel for at least twenty years, if the United States Army Corps of Engineers were to give their approval to the request before then, a bridge could be financed immediately after the Brooklyn-Battery Tunnel was opened.[26]

Looking forward to 1960, Moses predicted that New York would be the most important air center in this country and probably in the world, as well as "the undisputed headquarters of business management" and "a major financial center." But he feared for its future as a manufacturing center "unless the diseases and troubles which afflict our local industries are honestly diagnosed by capital, labor and officialdom, and are frankly combatted." Moses did not picture "the New York of 1960 as completely rebuilt, and so changed as to be unrecognizable by a modern Rip Van Winkle." But he did see a new Metropolitan Opera, a new Carnegie Hall, a new Madison Square Garden, "more apartment houses towering over Central Park, Columbia Heights, Flushing Bay, the Narrows and the Hudson at Riverdale."[27]

Postwar malaise began to give way in 1948, when the fiftieth anniversary of the city's consolidation was celebrated with a large exhibition, designed by A. Gordon Lorimer and held at the Grand Central Palace, as well as a torchlight parade up Lexington Avenue and an air show.[28] For its Golden Jubilee year, the city seemed on top of the world. As *Travel* magazine reported: "For a city that puts out no glittering travel folders and stages no publicity ceremonies, New York has established itself as America's leading all-year-round tourist resort."[29] The best measure of the city's renewed state of health was the return of construction, particularly the construction of office buildings in midtown and, some time after, in lower Manhattan. Another sign of the city's increased activity was the Post Office's 1953 decision to abandon the underground pneumatic mail-delivery system that had served most of Manhattan since 1877, now deemed inadequate to handle the dramatically rising volume of mail.[30]

By the mid-1950s New York's pace and self-confidence began to pick up so notably that some became frightened lest it spin out of control. In *Seize the Day* (1956), the novelist Saul Bellow's protagonist, Tommy Wilhelm, who lives on the increasingly seedy Upper West Side, complains: "I'm not used to New York anymore. For a native, that's very peculiar, isn't it? It was never so noisy at night as now, and every little thing's a strain, like the alternate parking."[31] Alternate-side-of-the-street parking was a perfect metaphor for the situation: it represented to average citizens the price they would have to pay for maintaining essential services and traditional civilities in the face of a postwar "autopia" that was inherently anti-urban but, by virtue of the growth of suburbs, was inextricably linked with the city's destiny, perhaps even in charge of it. The system was introduced in 1950 to facilitate street cleaning, which had become nearly impossible given the shortage and the high cost of garage space. Most New Yorkers, who now owned cars in record numbers but tended to use them only on weekends, had no choice but to park them on the city's streets for long periods of time.[32] Alternate parking was but one aspect of the postwar explosion of traffic in the region, and especially in Manhattan, which at times became virtually impassable. In a special issue devoted to New York's traffic, the editors of the *Reporter* stated in 1955:

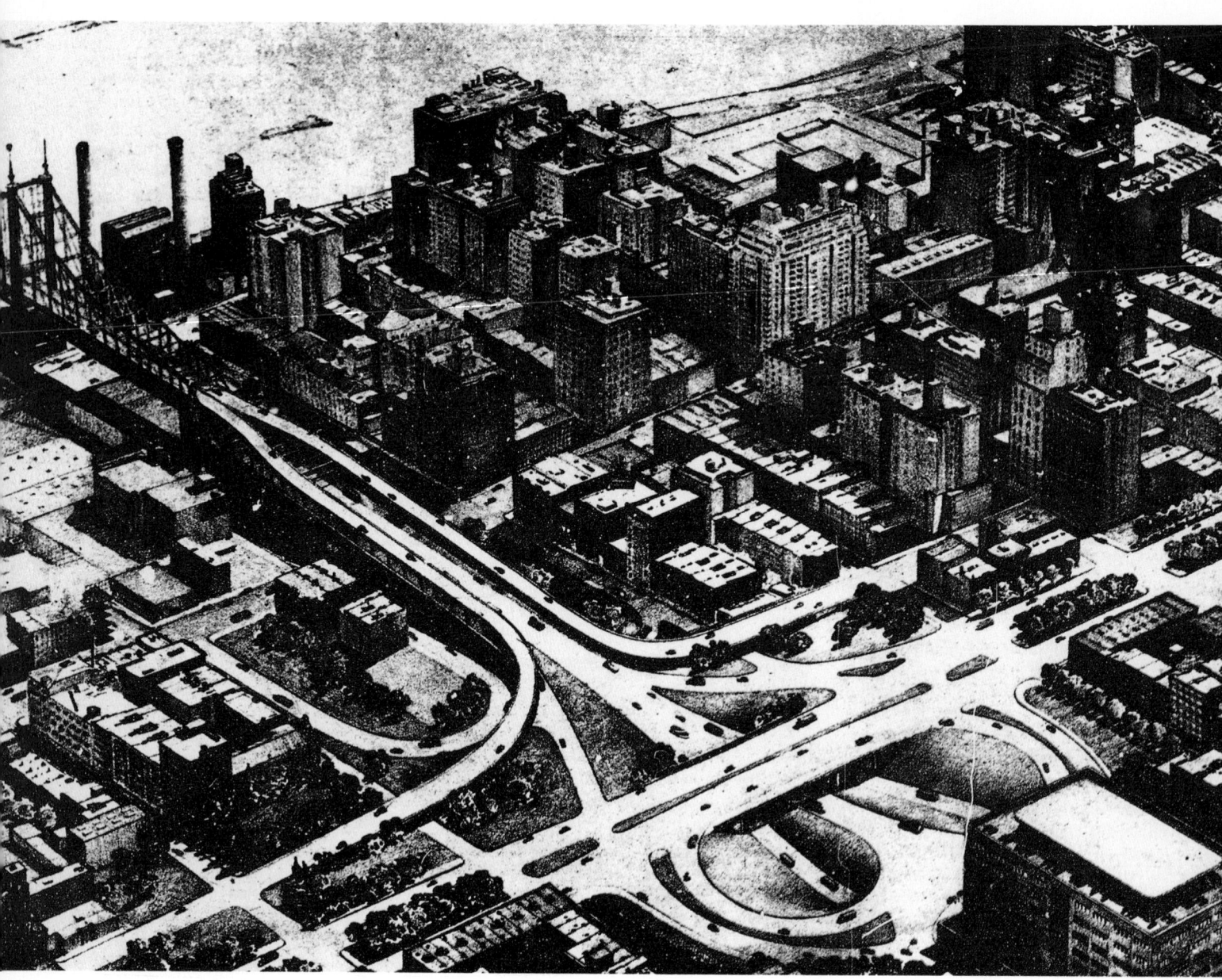

Manhattan approach to the Queensboro Bridge. Proposal by Robert
Moses, 1947. View to the southeast. NYT

Every great city has a contemporary problem of movement and access, but none can match in madness what has happened in downtown New York, in what is called the "Manhattan Cordon." The Manhattan Cordon is an engineering definition of the lower half of Manhattan from Fifty-ninth Street to the Battery. . . . Into this area each day some four million people come to work and in the evening they leave. . . . What has been happening in the Manhattan Cordon since the war is that two great developments arising from sources far beyond the city's ability to control them have interlocked. One is the fantastic growth of the suburban belt . . . , the second is the development of superhighways to deliver the suburbanite to the city by car. Only seven years ago New Yorkers cried out that traffic conditions were impossible when 320,000 automobiles were counted entering and leaving New York's confines daily. Since then the daily total has grown to 550,000 and the inelastic city streets are choked. . . . Each new trunk line or expressway thrown up on the approaches to New York City further congests life within it. . . . A suburban county on the fringe—for a notable example, Nassau County on Long Island, which has grown by 360,000 people in the past five years—creates further congestion in the pivot city.[33]

The postwar effort to "manage" New York's, and in particular Manhattan's, traffic along scientific lines had a profound effect on the city, reaching far beyond the efficient movement of vehicles, or even the safety of pedestrians and motorists, to influence the very rhythm and character of city life. After the comparative inactivity of wartime, when gas rationing had kept streets free of cars, the postwar years quickly brought with them nearly intolerable levels of congestion.[34] In 1949 T. T. Wiley was appointed executive director of the New York City Traffic Commission.[35] Working with Lloyd B. Reid, an engineer who would soon become the first commissioner of a newly constituted Department of Traffic Engineering, Wiley, who would become its deputy commissioner and after 1952 its commissioner, set out to reorganize the parking and movement patterns of the city's streets. They introduced parking meters, one-way traffic on major avenues with "progressively" timed lights to ensure an even flow, and the shortening of intervals between red and green signals from sixty seconds of green and thirty seconds of red on the avenues (and the reverse on the side streets) to thirty seconds of each in each direction.[36] Wiley's system was first put into effect in 1949 on Ninth and Tenth avenues, bringing with it not only the sudden quickening of the pace of traffic but also a noticeable reduction in the civility of street life, with increased noise and a growing sense that for the first time in its history the motor car and not the pedestrian now had pride of place on the city's streets. Nonetheless, Wiley's vision prevailed and First and Second avenues were turned into one-way pairs on June 4, 1951;[37] three years later Seventh and Eighth avenues were made one-way.[38] One-way travel for Fifth Avenue was originally proposed in 1959 but was not implemented until 1966—by Mayor John V. Lindsay during the transit strike that rocked his first days in office; Madison Avenue was also made one-way at that time.[39]

In 1946 enabling legislation was put through the State Legislature permitting the city to finance and build parking garages. On-street parking had been a problem in New York's various business and shopping districts since the First World War. By 1941, even with the Depression just barely over, there were one million vehicles registered in New York City, clogging the streets with traffic and filling almost all curbsides with parked cars.[40] A number of garages had been built by private interests in the late 1920s and early 1930s, including the skyscraping Kent

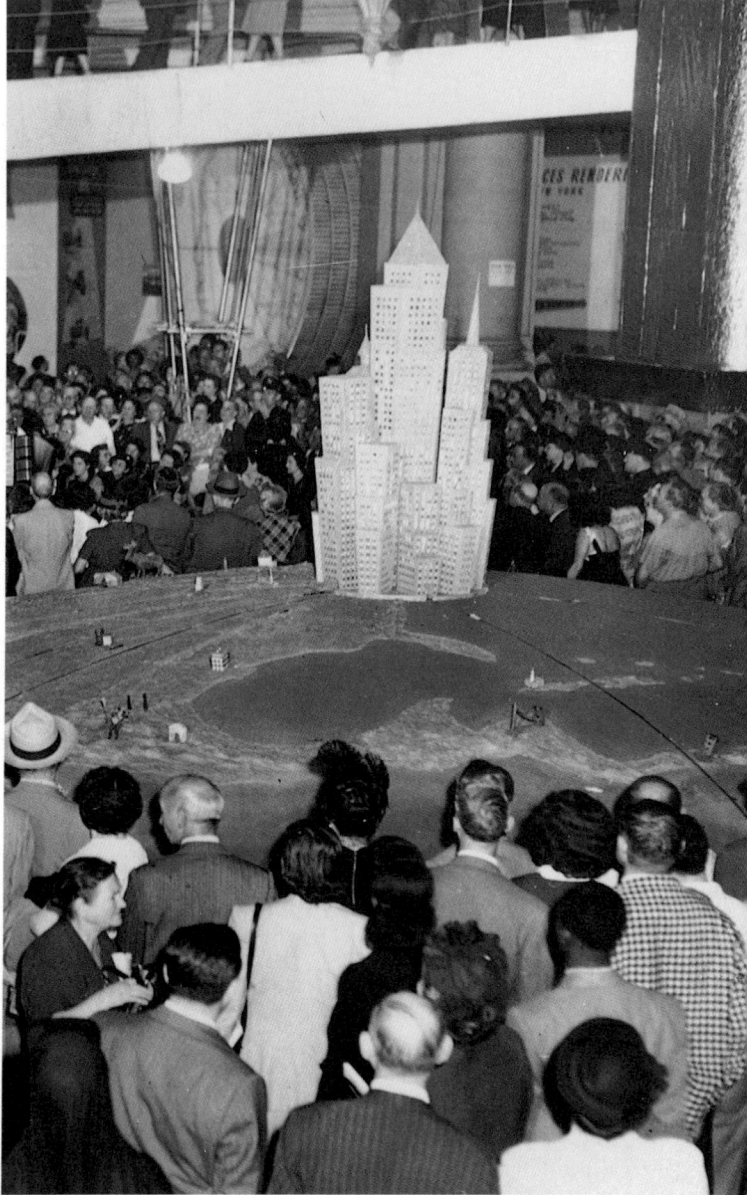

Greater New York Anniversary Exhibition, Grand Central Palace. Installation by A. Gordon Lorimer, 1948. MA

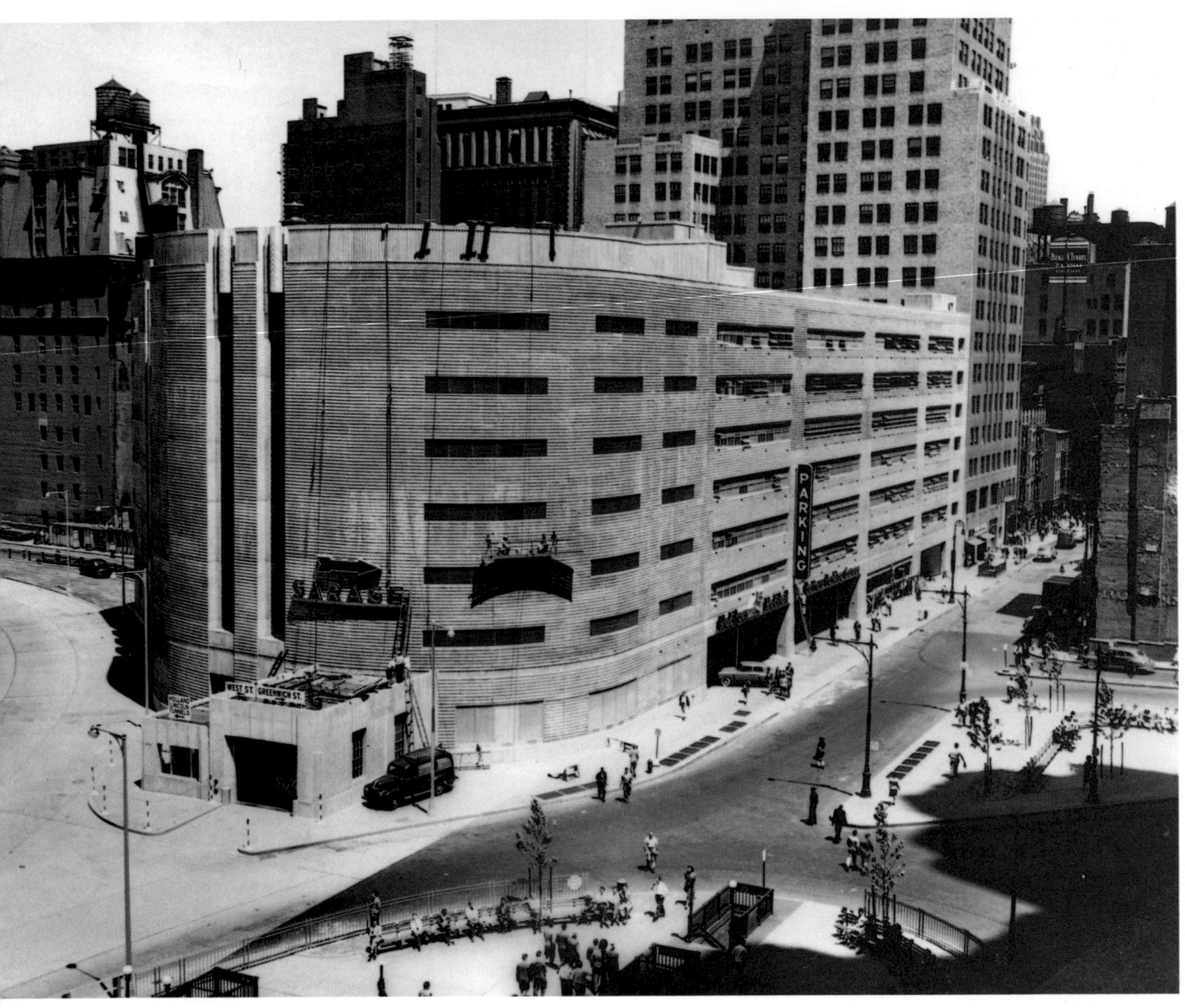

Battery Park Garage, 56 Greenwich Street. Ole Singstad, 1950. View to
the northwest. TBTA

Automatic Parking Garages and the subterranean garage at Rockefeller Center,[41] but these efforts were costly and unable to satisfy the needs of the average citizen. The relief of the parking problem through the construction of large-scale, publicly financed, inner-city garages became a postwar priority.[42]

In August 1946, with the new legislation in hand, the Board of Estimate asked a firm of consulting engineers to prepare a report for the City Planning Commission dealing with the traffic problem, particularly in mid-Manhattan.[43] The report dealt with off-street parking, parking meters, a midtown elevated expressway along Thirtieth Street, street underpasses, a lower Manhattan elevated crosstown expressway, subsurface pedestrian ways, off-street loading, bus terminals and channelization of public franchised buses. But the cost of the programs necessary to achieve the commission's goals was enormous, well beyond the city's capacity to fund them.

On-street loading, with double and even triple parking, was a principal cause of Manhattan's congestion. To provide off-street parking, Wiley and others proposed that garages be built under public parks, as at Union Square in San Francisco. But many independent citizens as well as Robert Moses were opposed to this idea. In 1947 Moses argued against a plan of Manhattan Borough President Hugo E. Rogers to dig up Bryant and Madison Square parks and build parking garages under them.[44] Moses objected to the garages on the issues of location, cost and, most important, park encroachment. He objected to the borough president's statement that the facilities for 4,000 cars had more value than anything the parks could provide. Moses, however, appears to have supported the agreement entered into in 1948 by the city and the New York Life Insurance Company to build a 1,400-car garage topped by a new public park on land immediately south of the insurance company's Manhattan House project. The project was not realized, though preliminary designs were prepared.

In 1951 the City Planning Commission recommended that all new residential construction include off-street parking, a plan endorsed by leading city apartment builders.[45] In addition, the prospect of a tax on overnight street parking encouraged developers to voluntarily include parking as part of their plans.[46] In 1953 the City Planning Commission proposed to amend the zoning laws to require parking in commercial buildings as well. Again, developers favored the change. As Robert H. Arnow, of Swig-Weiler-Arnow, put it, "since we cannot keep vehicles out of the city, it is only good business that we provide enough space for them to stay in while they are here."[47]

Meanwhile, T. T. Wiley, having found that progressive timing failed to quicken New York's traffic flow to the extent he once believed it would, was busy installing parking meters, first in outer-borough and uptown Manhattan business locations and then, after 1954, in all business districts except mid-Manhattan: "We've no intention of encouraging short-term parkers to bring their cars into the very heart of town."[48] By April 1954, 26,000 parking meters were in operation. To further discourage suburbanites from driving into town, the city began to develop large parking lots at or near the ends of the subway lines. The first one, opened on April 27, 1954, was at Flushing, Queens, where it could also serve shoppers.[49] A similar facility exclusively for commuters was already in operation at the Willets Point subway station, where it took advantage of existing parking fields left over from the 1939–40 World's Fair.

Without any strong policy to discourage motorists from driving into Manhattan, the solution to the problems caused by too many cars remained not only the construction of garage

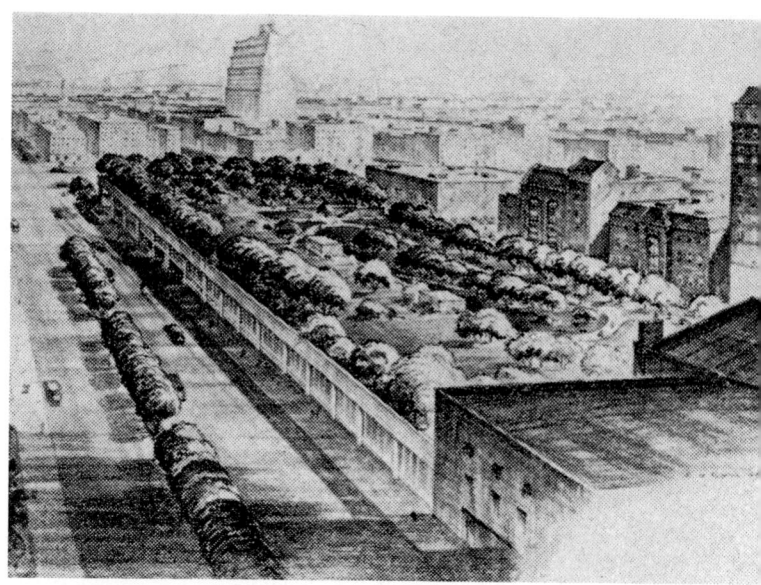

Top: Parking garage, between East Sixty-fourth and East Sixty-fifth streets, between Second and Third avenues. Proposal by the New York Life Insurance Company, 1948. View to the southeast. IN. CU

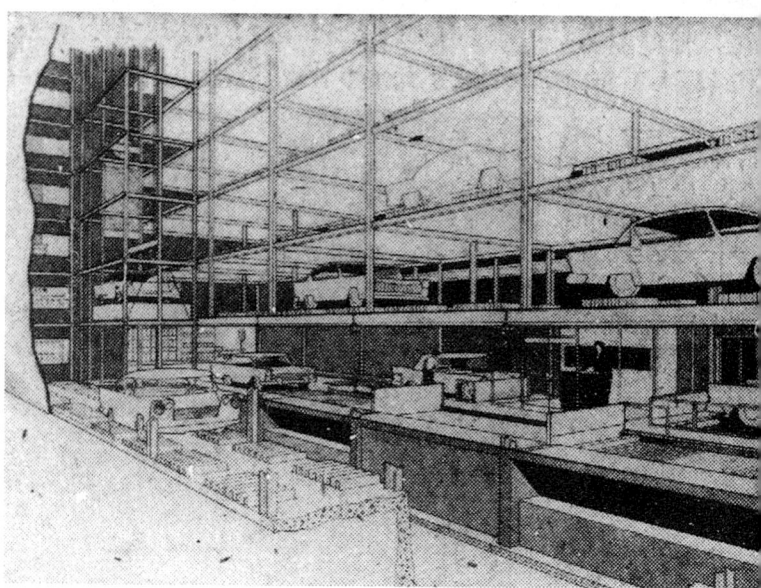

Bottom: Speed-Park Garage, West Forty-second to West Forty-third Street, west of Eighth Avenue. Mihai Alimanestianu, engineer; Francisco & Jacobus, architects, 1961. Cutaway axonometric. NYT

space in new buildings but the construction of additional, independent garage buildings to take up the overflow. The Triborough Bridge and Tunnel Authority's Battery Garage (Ole Singstad, 1950), at once stylishly streamlined and tectonically heavy-handed, was near ideal in its location as possible, taking the cars of drivers bound for the financial district directly out of the tunnel and off major approach roads.[50]

A number of private investors built parking garages on the fringes of midtown, especially near the Times Square theater district. Because the self-park garage took up a lot of space, many engineers and inventors explored systems employing elevators and rotating platforms to pack as many cars in as small a site as possible. Albert F. Burnalli's Rotogarage was ingenious, combining a continuous spiral with a central elevator.[51] Huntington Hartford, the food-chain heir, was also interested in the problem, and his Speed-Park, Inc. proposed to build the first completely automatic parking structure on a vacant site extending from Forty-second to Forty-third Street, west of Eighth Avenue. Hartford stated that his structurally direct facility, based on a system invented by Mihai Alimanestianu, an engineer, would be "a most worthwhile civic endeavor. We feel that the attractive exterior of the structure will make a substantial contribution to the facelifting of 42nd Street and the entire Times Square area."[52] In 1961 the awkwardly proportioned and detailed open steel framework was built with the assistance of Francisco & Jacobus, architects.

In 1960 Commissioner Wiley advanced a plan calling for the construction of 10,000 car spaces in fifteen municipal garages to be located in mid-Manhattan.[53] Wiley's program was based on a belief that midtown retailers were losing sales because suburbanites who might prefer to shop downtown rather than closer to home were unable to find a place to park. The new garages would provide the required convenient short-term parking. Victor Gruen, the architect-planner, opposed Wiley's proposal to locate garages in the central city and applauded the City Planning Commission's opposition, which contributed to Wiley's downfall. In a debate with Gruen, Wiley argued that traffic congestion was highly desirable: "No city has ever died from too much traffic, but many have deteriorated because of too little."[54] In a thoughtful response, Gruen pointed out that many factors contributed to the center's decline, including its distance from the expanding periphery, the traffic encountered along the way and the cost of the trip, including that of the in-city parking itself.

Moreover, Gruen argued, the principal attraction of regular trips to midtown was not shopping or entertainment but employment. Workers, he continued, "were shoppers and drivers and consumers of entertainment. Those who do not come to Manhattan to work, frequently do so for a number of purposes at once including health care, culture, entertainment and shopping." Claiming that Wiley's proposal called for too few spaces given the capacity of the roads that had been built to get the traffic on and off the island, he called for a "rim garage program" of multidecked facilities built near principal peripheral cross-points, with no private cars permitted within the core area and truck traffic confined to nighttime and early morning hours.[55] Taxis, buses and repair and emergency vehicles would of course be given free access to the core at all times. The key issue for Gruen was not traffic per se but congestion, which he believed had reached intolerable levels, to the point that when in the early 1960s the Daily News arranged a race across midtown involving an automobile, a bus, a taxi and a pedestrian, the pedestrian won hands down.[56]

Flying in the face of Wiley's program and prevailing planning policy, Gruen raised perhaps for the first time the propriety of accommodating the automobile in the city's central business district at all: "Instead of contributing to the solution of Manhattan's traffic problems and of New York's general problems," Wiley's plan "would increase them significantly. It is in essence nothing but a continuation of the mistaken policy of one-sided investments for a single type of transportation, which is the inefficient one. It is another step on the road to 'suicide by automobile.'"[57] Wiley's garage program did go ahead, but only one garage was built in Manhattan, the extremely banal 455-car facility on the east side of Eighth Avenue between Fifty-third and Fifty-fourth streets (Alton Craft and Seelye, Stevenson, Value & Knecht, 1960).[58]

Just as the Eighth Avenue garage was being completed, the City Planning Commission, "flexing muscles it had trained during the passage of the new zoning resolution," as Housing and Planning News put it, announced its intention to oppose the plan for construction of daytime garages in midtown.[59] The day of this announcement, March 16, 1961, was for Edward T. Chase, a writer specializing in urban transportation issues, "the greatest day in the modern history of New York."[60] The commission argued that the garages would produce congestion and have "serious long term effects on the integrity and function of the most valuable midtown core area."[61] Nonetheless, Wiley continued to battle for garages, even reviving the long-dormant plan to park cars under Madison Square Park, which was opposed by the Park Association, the Council for Parks and Playgrounds and the Municipal Art Society.[62]

But Wiley's days as the city's traffic czar were numbered: it was not the revival of the unpopular proposal to park cars under city parks that cost him his job but the disastrous Christmastime crush that ensued when throngs of kids and teenagers packed midtown, resulting in an hours-long near halt of traffic on December 27, 1961.[63] Meanwhile, as Chase pointed out, the usual discussion of the city's transportation bogged down in minutiae of traffic flow, while the "real issue is reducible to the question: do we take positive steps to discourage automobile travel in New York City; or do we accede to it as an 'uncontrollable' fact of life; or do we encourage it?"[64]

For Percival and Paul Goodman there were to be no halfway measures. In 1961 they called for a total ban on cars in Manhattan except for buses, small taxis, vehicles for essential services and the trucking used in light industry. They also argued in favor of a pattern of superblocking at unprecedented scale, calling for the elimination of four out of five crosstown streets, a move justified by the Goodmans' claim that 35 percent of Manhattan's land surface was taken up by roads. Such a plan, its proponents argued, would provide "a great fund of land" for neighborhood redevelopment; their superblocks, though superficially similar to those created by the Housing Authority as part of its urban renewal projects, were significantly different in key ways—they would accommodate mixed uses and house families of mixed income.[65] To park the cars of commuters and unreconstructed islanders who would want them for trips, the Goodmans proposed to build pierlike garages on the river.

The proposed garage under Madison Square Park was taken up again in 1964 when the new traffic commissioner, Henry Barnes, fresh from triumphs in Baltimore, resurrected a three-year-old feasibility study prepared by Skidmore, Owings & Merrill that had been paid for by the Chase Manhattan Bank and the New York Bank for Savings.[66] The idea was again opposed by the community and by the park commissioner, who were joined by William F. R. Ballard, the new chairman of the City

Planning Commission.[67] The issue of the Madison Square garage continued to raise community ire, which escalated to high indignation in March 1965 when a so-called secret agreement to build the garage was leaked to the press.[68] Learning of this, the Committee to Save Madison Square Park immediately fired off protest telegrams to the mayor and city officials. The parking garage under Madison Square Park was never built.

Traffic, like many of the city's ills, was not something that could be solved locally. As the Regional Plan Association had been stressing since the 1920s, by the late 1950s it was clear that New York City was part of a large collection of independent small cities, towns, villages and open spaces that affected each other. Just as New Yorkers were beginning to understand or at least accept the fact that their city was part of a larger region, a new term and a new definition burst on the public consciousness, identifying the geographic scope of that region as nothing short of alarming. In 1961 the French geographer Jean Gottmann published a book, *Megalopolis: The Urbanized Northeastern Seaboard of the United States*, in which he observed that between Washington, D.C., and Boston there had grown up an almost continuous, extensively urbanized region of thirty-eight million people.[69] The term Megalopolis, frightening as it sounded to many, was not a neologism. When the Ancient Greeks planned a new city-state in the Peloponnesus they called it "Megalopolis," or "very large city," a name the Jewish philosopher Philo of Alexandria adopted for his concept of a city of ideas that would govern the secular world. Postwar Megalopolis was a fancy term for urban sprawl, or what the Regional Plan Association took to calling "spread city."[70] Quintessentially suburban in character, Megalopolis incorporated traditional cities and villages as well as open countryside within its vast borders.

According to Gottmann, America's Megalopolis was no new phenomenon either, having its origin in the late nineteenth century, when "suburban sprawl and coalescence between neighboring centers were already becoming obvious." Because Gottmann's focus was the region and not one component city in particular, he was, naturally enough, not alarmed by New York's comparative decline in relation to the whole, which he saw in glowing, almost transcendent terms: "No other section has a comparable role within the nation or a comparable importance in the world. Here has been developed a kind of supremacy in politics, in economics, and possibly even in cultural activities, seldom before attained by an area of this size."[71]

The idea of Megalopolis frightened and irritated urbanists almost as much as it did the public at large. It hit a raw nerve, pointing to the symptoms of a gradual but perhaps very long decline that lay in the city's future. Even those who were not troubled with the term, or the idea of so large and diverse a form of urbanism, found Megalopolis a disturbing reminder of a dramatically changed world. "Megalopolis," according to the urban historian Andrew Sinclair, "is interested in *control* rather than manufacture, in *services* rather than raw materials. And here it resembles many of the great cities of the past, where labor became specialized in the arts of government and luxury trades. Megalopolis contains one-fifth of the population of the United States, but two-fifths of the nation's bank deposits. Thus, through the control of capital, it organizes the work of others and reaps its profits."[72]

In 1959 the first volume of the much-anticipated nine-volume "second" regional plan was published by the Regional Plan Association. When *Anatomy of the Metropolis: The Changing Distribution of People and Jobs Within the New York Metropolitan Region*, written by Edgar M. Hoover and Raymond

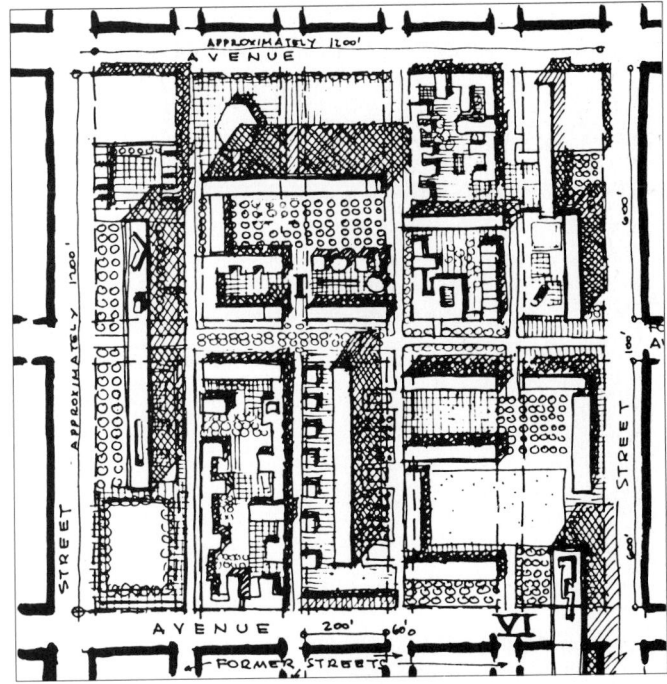

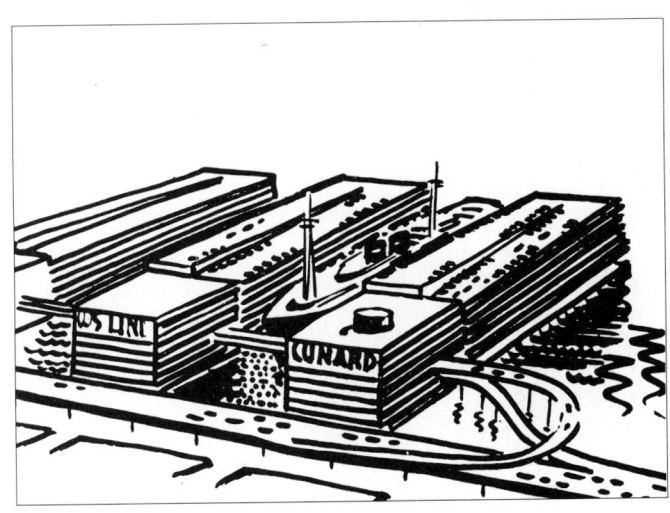

Proposal to ban cars from Manhattan streets. Paul and Percival Goodman, 1961. Top: Proposed remapping of Manhattan into superblocks. Bottom: Proposed parking garages on piers along the Hudson River. NG

25

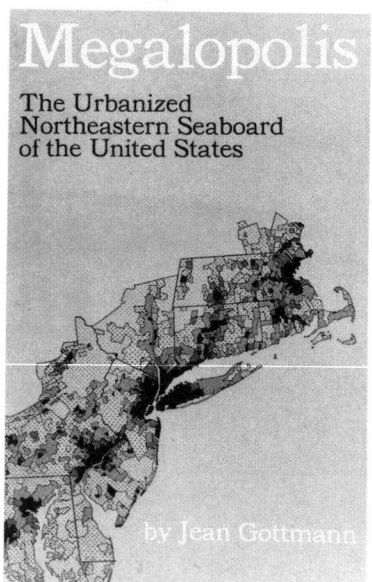

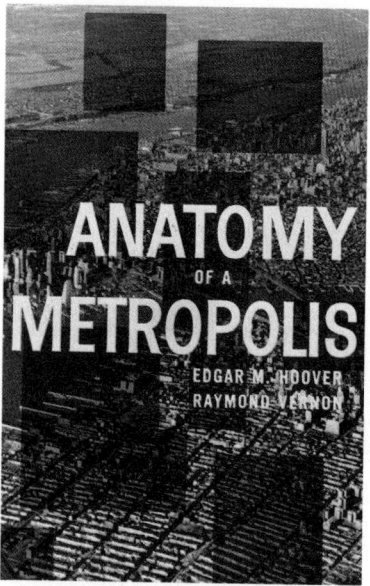

Top: *Megalopolis: The Urbanized Northeastern Seaboard of the United States.* Census map of population density, 1960. TCF

Bottom: *Anatomy of a Metropolis: The Changing Distribution of People and Jobs within the New York Metropolitan Region.* Cover design by Marcia R. Lambrecht, 1959. RPA

Top right: *Made in New York: Case Studies in Metropolitan Manufacturing.* Cover design by Marcia R. Lambrecht, 1959. RPA

Center right: *The Newcomers: Negroes and Puerto Ricans in a Changing Metropolis.* Cover design by Marcia R. Lambrecht, 1959. RPA

Bottom right: *Money Metropolis: A Locational Study of Financial Activities in the New York Region.* Cover design by Marcia R. Lambrecht, 1960. RPA

Vernon, was released in June, their prediction of "continuing growth and prosperity" in the region as a whole was tempered by a dire warning for New York and the other established cities in the region, pointing to population loss and declining employment, particularly for blue-collar workers.[73] The report, which drew attention to outworn areas at the periphery such as Newark, Jersey City and Yonkers, warned of comparable problems in traditional middle-city neighborhoods, anticipating the growth of a gray belt of blight between the city center and its healthy peripheral residential edges. It baldly stated that, lacking any middle-class areas, Manhattan as a whole would be recast as a place of extremes, increasingly a managerial center, home only to "the very rich and the very poor."[74]

Not only did the *New York Times* broadcast these distressing facts, but so did the national media, including *Newsweek*, which followed the publication of the Hoover and Vernon book with a special report, "Metropolis in a Mess."[75] So negative was the article that it provoked a five-point rebuttal by Mayor Robert F. Wagner, published several weeks later as "The Big Town— The Big Mess."[76] While *Newsweek*'s essay had been exaggerated in tone and in its claims of impending disaster, as the mayor's response effectively demonstrated, it nonetheless pointed to quite serious, systemic problems, ranging from those of race relations to fiscal irresponsibility. It included an indictment of the hitherto virtually sacrosanct public housing projects, criticizing them as "million-dollar barracks." *Newsweek*'s swipes were followed in October 1959 by an entire issue of the *Nation*, "The Shame of New York," edited by Fred J. Cook and Gene Gleason, who pointedly took their title from Lincoln Steffens's fifty-five-year-old muckraking text, *The Shame of the Cities*.[77] Cook and Gleason's orientation was political, but their revelations concerning the administration of the Title I slum-clearance program led to a massive shake-up that would have profound effects on the city's physical redevelopment.

The Regional Plan Association followed Hoover and Vernon's book with *Made in New York*, which dealt with the region's three major industries (the garment trades, electronics, and printing and publishing), and continued with books on race, a variety of specific economic issues, transportation, and the 1,400 governments in the region. The series concluded with Raymond Vernon's *Metropolis 1985: An Interpretation of the Findings of the New York Metropolitan Region Study*.[78] Reviewing the entire series, *Business Week* confidently headlined, "New York 1985: Still the Leader."[79] In *Metropolis 1985* Vernon, the study's leader, made some key predictions: that Manhattan would prosper as an office center although there would be some dispersion to the suburbs; that manufacturing would move to the outer boroughs and suburban counties; that population would follow jobs, resulting in a growth of upper-income housing in Manhattan and an exodus of the middle class from the outer boroughs to the suburbs, their place being taken by low-income, largely nonwhite workers, who would move into better apartments abandoned by middle-class whites. According to Vernon, however, the supply of old housing coming onto the market in the so-called outer borough gray areas was likely to exceed demand, spreading blight as the population thinned out.

In some ways *Metropolis 1985* was an elixir of hope. By measuring New York's health in a different way than might be used to assess that of other cities, Vernon seemed to see strength where others saw weakness. Key was his emphasis on the city's ability to initiate new specialized economic activities. As Vernon saw it, New York was continually able to replace one innovation with another, seeming to lose activities it had begun to other parts of the country where manufacturing was cheaper, but in fact moving on to new things all the time, a process Vernon believed would continue in the future. For example, even though the high cost of labor would mean that clothing would not be manufactured in the city, dresses would be designed and fashions set there. Similarly, though telecommunications would make it possible to have back-office business operations take place virtually anywhere, top-level management would continue to find New York a useful and stimulating environment. On balance, Vernon thought that business would concentrate in New York, which would grow as a white-collar employment center until 1985.

The revelations of *Megalopolis* and the findings of the Regional Plan Association were quickly absorbed—or ignored—amidst the enormous prosperity that the region, and the city in particular, were enjoying. Most especially, given a building boom the likes of which New York had not seen since the 1920s and which no other American city was then undergoing, it was understandably hard to face the long-term implications of the two reports. In 1960 alone, in addition to a host of more or less typical office buildings in midtown designed by firms like Emery Roth & Sons, high-profile headquarter buildings for Time & Life, Union Carbide, Pepsi-Cola and, most significant, Chase Manhattan were completed, the latter opening up a second wave of development in the financial district, which in turn triggered a downtown building boom that would last a decade.

While office-building construction, concentrated in Manhattan, was the most visible manifestation of the city's construction boom, it was by no means the only one: Robert Moses's express-highway building program was at its zenith, spurred on by recently released funds as part of the federal government's defense highway program. According to the Citizens Budget Commission, in 1960 $6 billion in city, state and federal funds were committed for roads and bridges, including the Verrazano-Narrows crossing. Billions were also committed to private and public residential construction, schools and other educational facilities, leading the budget commission's president, the realtor Robert W. Dowling, to state: "Should all the projects be achieved tomorrow, New York, great as it is today, would be a vastly different place. The pending construction plans are of such colossal magnitude that they might remake the city—or at least greatly change its way of life."[80]

Despite the exodus of a large segment of the middle class to the suburbs, New York managed to hold a balance between the classes. Remarkably, unlike most other American cities, many of the very rich remained, adopting a two-residence pattern that combined apartments in town with houses in exurbia or rural or shore properties even farther away to be visited on weekends or vacations. And many members of the middle class chose to remain as well; more important still, by the late 1950s the first wave of post–Depression era suburbanites began to return to the city. With their children now grown, these affluent middle-aged couples returned, usually to Manhattan, attracted by its convenience and its cultural life. Clearly, New York, and especially Manhattan, was about to enter a new phase of prosperity that was unique in American cities at the time: it would flourish as an office center, its retailing would continue to prosper and it would grow as an upmarket residential center as well.

Fueling the Manhattan boom was the expansion of offices. Cushman & Wakefield, an office-building management firm, conducted a survey in August 1960 to find out how much office space would be needed in New York. It revealed that not only

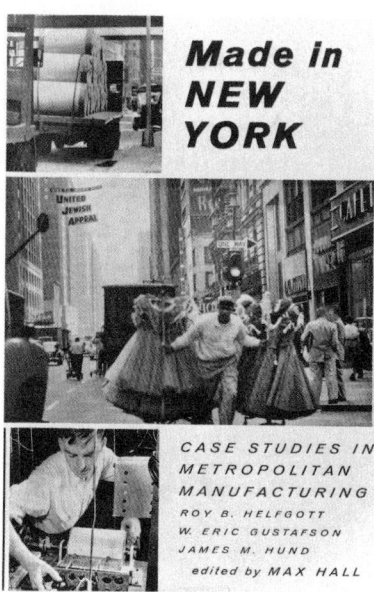

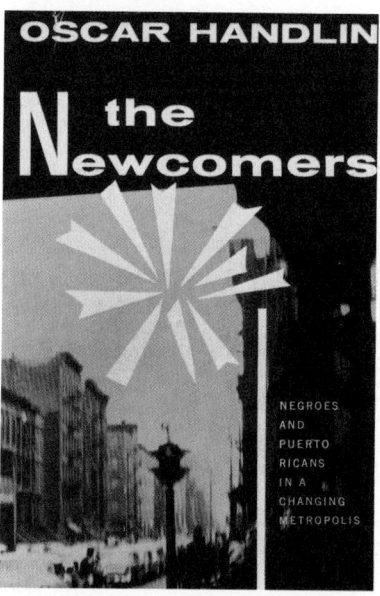

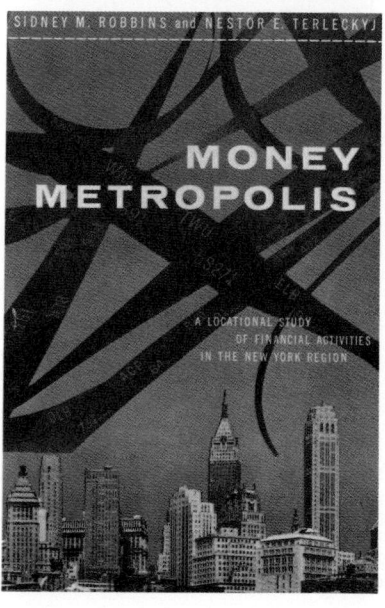

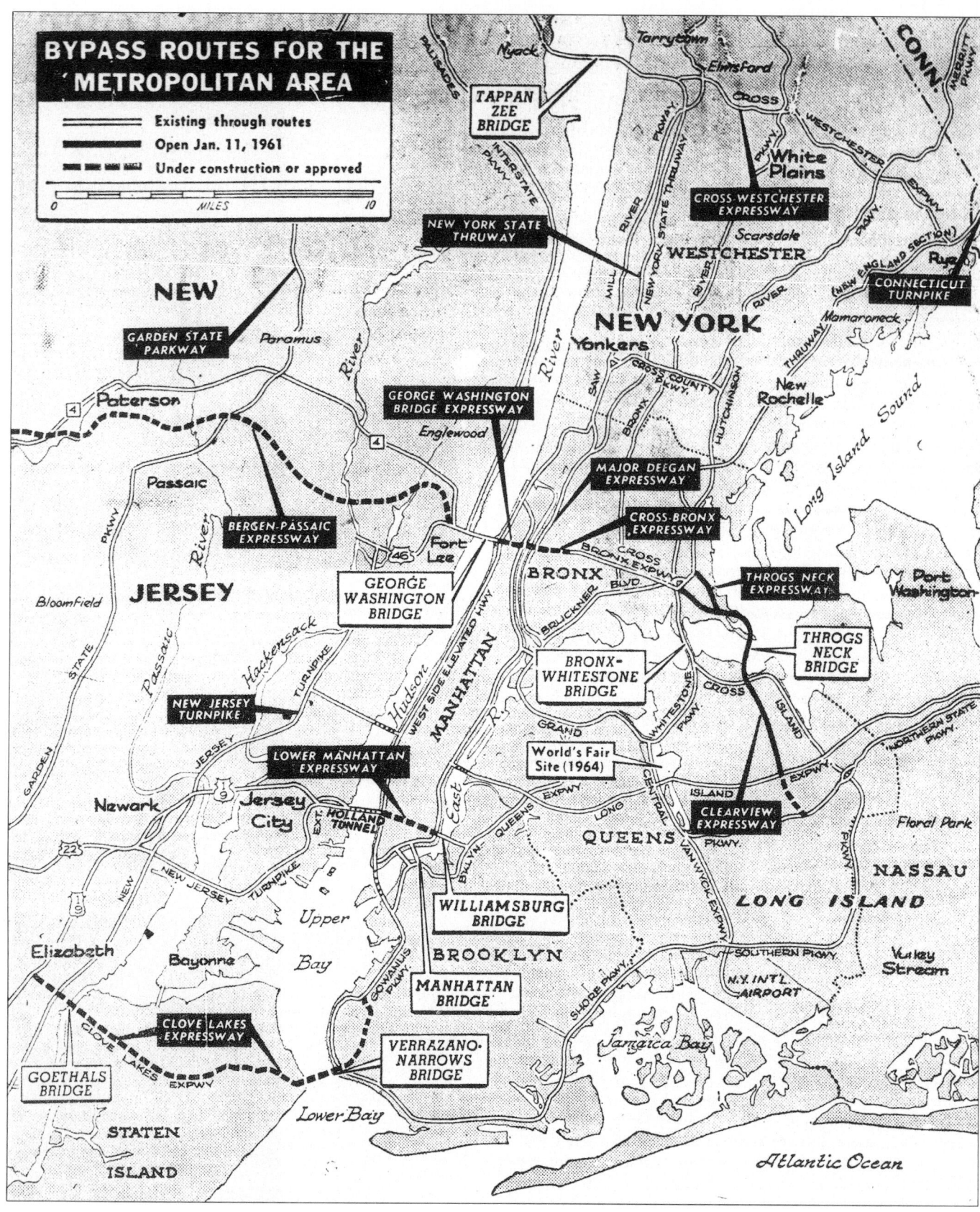

Map of express highway bypass routes in the New York City
metropolitan region, 1961. NYT

were 25 percent of the nation's five hundred largest corporations headquartered in the city, but of those that were not, more than 69 percent had sales offices there.[81] No one understood this trend better than William Zeckendorf, who, in *Fortune's* 1960 feature on New York as "Headquarters Town," exulted: "Precisely because New York is a national headquarters, it is also a middle income as well as a high-income town."[82] In this belief Zeckendorf was supported by Charles E. Silberman, who, writing in the same issue of *Fortune*, noted that the "facts about New York's economy upset some long-standing notions—most notably the cliché that it is the residence of only the very rich and the very poor. . . . To be sure, the population of New York City has been growing very slowly and that of Manhattan not at all. But what distinguishes New York from U.S. cities in general is the fact that its low-income group is smaller and its middle and upper-income groups larger."[83]

Though the region's margin of economic superiority over the U.S. as a whole was less than it was in 1929, when per capita income was 75 percent higher, the difference did not spell a decline in wealth but a shift from an independently wealthy, property-owning class at the top to "civic leaders . . . now drawn largely from the ranks of corporate top management. . . . In headquarters town," Silberman noted, "even the wealthy belong to the working class."[84] With so many of the country's top corporations headquartered in the city, New York was developing a new kind of economy—one based on managerial skills, information processing and services. Again Zeckendorf had seen this coming and sensed its virtues when in 1956 he shocked economists and politicians by describing the city's loss of manufacturing jobs as "magnificent" and went on to chart the city's destiny in the service field. "And as we have lost industrial workers from the population," he said, "we have gained higher paid, higher educated administrative personnel that make New York an unparalleled consumer's market."[85]

Along with the new prosperity came a renewed sense of pride, much of it directed to the city as a unique, if evolving, artifact worth visiting and studying. The urban historian Andrew Sinclair believed mid-century New York to be "in its golden age," based on the five major roles it played:

> As the home of the United Nations and as the richest seaport in the world, it is the center of the globe. As the hub of the great American Megalopolis of some 40 million people . . . it is the laboratory of the gigantic cities of tomorrow. With its heart in Manhattan Island, the city shows others how to create infinite riches in a little room. With its districts and its ghettoes, it explains how the immigrants of the world may live together in opportunity if not always in amity. And with its varied streets, New York City produces the most complex and diverse culture that has been known to man.[86]

Even normally blasé New Yorkers began to take pride in their city and exhibit an interest in its history, especially its physical history. Citizens began to take walking tours of traditional New York neighborhoods such as the financial district, Greenwich Village and upper Fifth Avenue organized by Henry Hope Reed for the Museum of the City of New York.[87] In addition, books about the city began to proliferate, beginning with the photographer Andreas Feininger's *The Face of New York* (1954), with a text by Susan E. Lyman.[88] Gilbert Millstein's *New York: True North* (1964), with photographs by Sam Falk, comprised a series of interviews with local citizens, some famous, many not, commenting on the city and daily life in it.[89] The writer and photographer Louis B. Schlivek's *Man in Metropolis*

(1965) also profiled ordinary city residents but enlarged its scope to include suburban commuters as well.[90] The eighty-five-year-old architect and planner Arthur C. Holden's *Sonnets for My City: An Essay on the Kinship of Art and Finance* (1965) was an unusual plea for a better urban environment, consisting of a collection of two hundred sonnets, short essays and pen-and-ink sketches devoted to specific neighborhoods and issues of aesthetics, planning and land use.[91] Holden bemoaned the lack of coordination between architects and the businessmen who financed construction, arguing that more enlightened credit policies, better zoning laws and increased cooperation between the two groups could greatly improve New York's physical and fiscal condition. Marya Mannes's *The New York I Know* (1961), with photographs by Herb Snitzer, made up of a collection of essays previously published in the *Reporter*, included a notable argument in behalf of preservation. But hers was not a misty-eyed paean to a lost world: "It is painful to watch the wrecking of the old and good: when the great iron ball crashes into a fine old cornice it is like a savage blow in a defenseless aging groin. But when it buckles the walls of a filthy tenement with a roaring cascade of bricks and a cloud of dust, the heart leaps up. Smash it, smash it and clear the ground of evil."[92]

The city's new sense of itself, and its growing sophistication, could be measured in countless ways, none more visible than the proliferation of sidewalk cafés, expressive of the enthusiasm of ordinary citizens for participatory urbanism, and a willingness to forsake the private pleasures of suburban backyards for the public pleasures of the street. Cafés sprang up despite innumerable bureaucratic obstacles that were fought by the Park Association.[93] In 1964 there were only twenty-four sidewalk cafés in the city, all in Manhattan; a change in city licensing policy resulted in a doubling of that number the next summer.[94] Rules were further simplified in 1967, and again in 1968, permitting cafés to be covered with canopies and enclosed in winter, a departure from previous rules that had the support of William S. Paley, chairman of the Urban Design Council.[95] So many new cafés opened that they began to be regarded as a nuisance, with many operators building enclosures so dense as to constitute near buildings, leading the city to consider new, stricter rules.[96] By 1976 there were 105 authorized sidewalk cafés in the city, but only twenty-five of them were open air, in the Paris manner. Many neighborhood groups objected to requests for any more.[97]

Another sign of the public's newfound enthusiasm for the city was their rediscovery of the bicycle. By the late 1960s the city's streets were filled with bicyclists, young dedicated city dwellers who took to traveling around on two wheels as New Yorkers had never done before. (The bike craze of the 1890s was recreational; this one, though recreational on weekends, satisfied the transportation needs of many during the week.) As a result, safety on the city's streets became an even more serious issue than before: New York drivers didn't seem to take cyclists seriously, and often didn't seem to see them either.[98] Pedestrians were also careless and frequently at risk. On Wednesday morning, September 16, 1970, a thousand bicyclists, including Mayor Lindsay and Environmental Protection Administrator Jerome Kretchmer, pedaled from Central Park to City Hall via Fifth Avenue to demonstrate that New York would be better if more people biked to work.[99]

The city in the 1960s was as full of life as it had been during the wartime forties. "New York was a glorious place to live in 1965," Stephen Zoll recalled in 1973. "Anything seemed possible, even the purification of the air and the reconstruction of vast deterioration. There was a willingness among most New

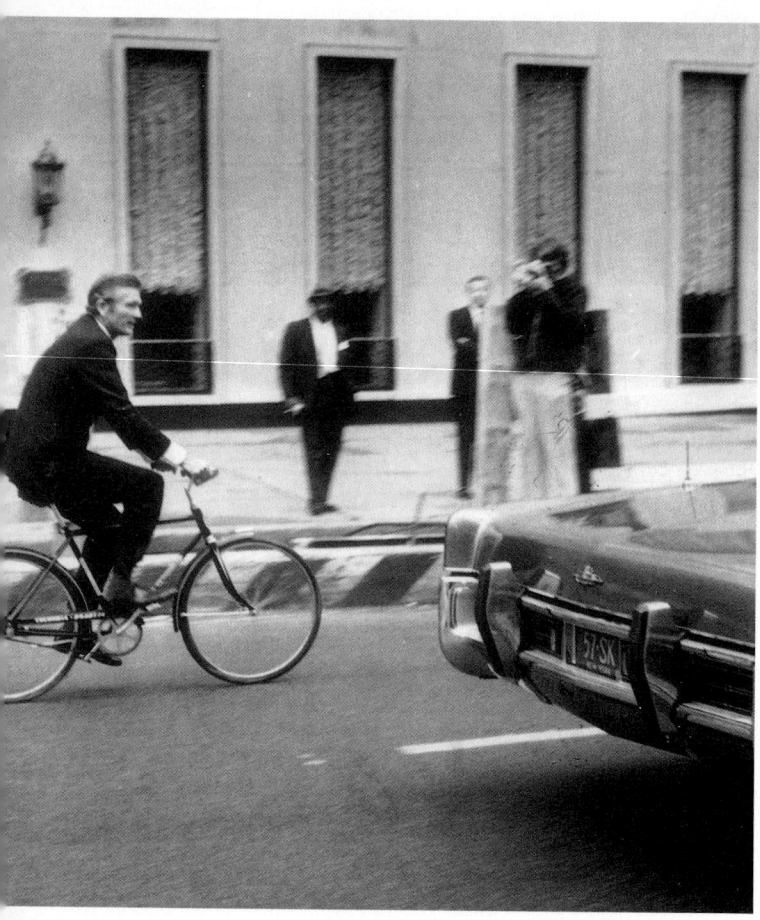

Mayor John V. Lindsay participating in demonstration asserting the viability of bicycling to work, September 16, 1970. Jones. NYT

Yorkers to see things from a determinedly liberal point of view." Although "the process of neighborhood collapse due to ethnic turnover" had not been stabilized and 1.8 million white families had left the city since 1950,

> the city was still functioning as New York historically always functioned: the median real income indicated an increase in purchasing power of 40% during the decade of the 1950s. The feeling of crowding was acute on the streets, but inside one's home space standards had expanded by the addition of 1.4 million rooms in 1965 over 1950. When John Lindsay stood for mayor of New York in 1965, it wasn't completely ludicrous to refer to New York as Fun City. He was elected because of a widespread optimism about the city's future as a place to live.[100]

In November 1965 John V. Lindsay, a liberal Republican who represented Manhattan's 17th (Silk Stocking) District in Congress, running as a "fusion" candidate, was elected mayor, succeeding Robert F. Wagner, who had served for three terms (1954–66). Wagner had been an able politician, a reasonably skilled administrator and in many instances a forceful advocate of sound planning. He had a strong social conscience and was committed to slum clearance and urban renewal. But he was not glamorous or even inspiring, two things Lindsay was. Later in Lindsay's tenure in Gracie Mansion, when his style and wit began to be seen as a detriment, one of his waggish critics put it like this: "If a letter carrier in Brooklyn awakened with sore feet, Bob Wagner's arches hurt, and Lindsay wondered where Brooklyn was."[101] Yet for all the criticism of Lindsay as a mayor who, like James Walker a generation before him, was seen as too often putting style over substance, it is not to be overlooked that Wagner's social commitment and his consensus approach to governance was in no small way responsible for the city's ultimate downfall. Wagner was on one occasion said to have stated: "I do not propose to permit our fiscal problems to set the limits of our commitments to meet the essential needs of the city."[102]

Lindsay's first mayoral campaign coincided with a dramatic shift in the national mood: unlike the postwar middle class, people now regarded big cities not only as places to work in and occasionally visit but also as highly desirable places to live in. This new sensibility was reflected in the pages of the August 1965 issue of the normally suburban *House Beautiful*, which was devoted to "The Lure of the City,"[103] featuring desirable urban enclaves such as Amster Yard and offering encomiums on urban living such as August Heckscher's "I Happen to Be a City Man," political writer Andy Logan's gently antisuburban "We Never Left" and Mary Scott Welch's "We Moved Back to the City."[104]

Like Fiorello H. La Guardia before him, Lindsay was the man for the moment: his campaign proclaimed to the straphanging electorate that this young, clean-cut, white-shirted urban Galahad touring ghetto streets with his suit jacket slung over his shoulder was fresh, while all the rest of the politicians were tired. Lindsay surrounded himself with bright idealists, many of them politically naive, but all of them imbued with a sense that New York was a great city that had lost its way, but not irretrievably so.[105] Spurred on by such close advisers as the art curator Thomas P. F. Hoving, Lindsay recognized that physical planning was a key issue that could unite a wide section of an electorate that was seriously divided over issues of race, ethnicity and class. In the early days of his campaign in July 1965 Lindsay took a widely publicized helicopter tour over the city accompanied by Philip Johnson and Robert L. Zion, following it up with a press conference at which he articulated ideas based on groundwork laid by Hoving, Eli S. Jacobs, a young banker interested in architecture and planning, Robert A. M. Stern, Jaquelin Robertson and other advisers that would become policy once he was elected. The primary issues he discussed were the need to recapture the waterfront, the need to curb development on Staten Island, the need to protect available parkland and to expand it where possible and the need to discourage cars from entering Manhattan's central business districts.[106] Lindsay also reiterated his opposition to the construction of the Lower Manhattan Expressway and criticized the proposed construction of the Columbia gymnasium in Morningside Park.

When Lindsay beat Abraham D. Beame, the former comptroller, he tackled a city that many argued was ungovernable, with a business climate that showed signs of ill health as industry moved out and automation threatened to reduce the white-collar work force. Some observers, Lindsay among them, knew the city was perilously near bankruptcy.[107] At his gala inaugural ball most of the guests knew they were closer to disaster than they cared to admit, with total urban paralysis less than a day away because of the sure certainty that the Transport Workers Union would strike for the first time ever—a result of a breakdown in negotiations with the former city administration.[108] Lindsay took to the microphones to ask New Yorkers and suburbanites to either walk to or stay home from work in an effort to manage traffic on the city's streets during the strike.

According to Roger Starr, the phrase "Fun City" was used by the mayor in his first days in office, "setting a peculiarly inappropriate context for the request that working people give up their livelihood."[109] As the city grappled with the transit strike, Lindsay, after leading a contingent of thirty reporters in a brisk, rain-soaked, early morning, forty-five-minute walk to City Hall from his temporary residence at the Roosevelt Hotel on Madison Avenue and Forty-sixth Street, assumed the role of cheerleader: "It's fun being Mayor of New York City. New York is a fun city."[110] The strike by the 34,000-member union brought the city to its knees. It lasted twelve days, giving New Yorkers an opportunity to rally together and cope with disaster. While negotiating with the union, Lindsay and Traffic Commissioner Henry Barnes, held over from Mayor Wagner's administration, took advantage of the emergency to implement long-opposed plans for one-way travel on Fifth and Madison avenues, initiating a change that would increasingly compromise their function as pedestrian-oriented shopping streets. In the settlement, Lindsay granted significant wage hikes to transit workers and a twenty-year retirement plan that quickly robbed the system of almost all of its experienced maintenance and operations personnel.

Unlike most of New York's mayors, who left the city's physical shape to others, Lindsay was deeply concerned with issues of urban planning and civic design. Within six months in office he blocked Huntington Hartford's plan for a restaurant in Central Park; vetoed projected garages and other intrusions that park conservationists had protested under Wagner's administration; barred cars from Central Park from 6 A.M. to noon on Sundays; killed Robert Moses's plan for the Thirtieth Street elevated expressway across Manhattan; temporarily blocked construction of the World Trade Center; and attempted to introduce logical land planning on Staten Island.[111] His first summer in office was marked by notable calm in the city's black and Hispanic ghettos—a significant difference from other American cities that were experiencing considerable unrest.

Lindsay understood, as Wagner before him had not quite, the increasing importance of community action groups. Despite

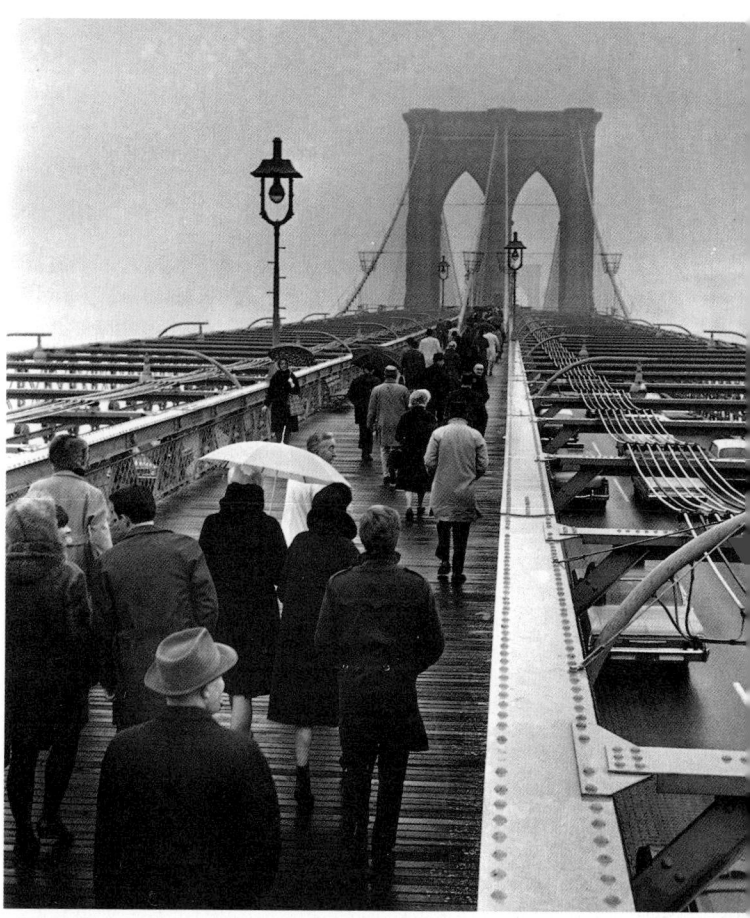

Commuters walking to work over the Brooklyn Bridge during the Transit Workers Union strike, January 3, 1966. NYT

an outburst in the East New York section of Brooklyn, New Yorkers seemed enchanted with Lindsay's persona and impressed with his efforts to deal directly with local groups through negotiation. Lindsay seemed to understand the city's changing demographics and the feeling of empowerment that minorities were beginning to enjoy. He understood and he acted. Suddenly, New York seemed a model city.[112] Just as he worked tirelessly to keep the neighborhoods cool during the long hot summer, Lindsay struggled to prevent the lid on the city's Pandora's box of finance and labor problems from bursting open, pleading for aid from legislators in Albany and helping to turn national attention to the plight of cities and the need for federal aid.[113]

While Lindsay's first term was hardly the Camelot-like paradise many had hoped for, in the area of planning and architecture the mayor had effectively wrested control of the city's future away from old-style politicians and traditional City Hall hangers-on. In a city that had, under Wagner, rarely turned to architects or community groups for advice about issues of planning, Lindsay, as Peter Blake put it, "consistently made excellence in architecture, planning, urban design and in all the associated arts and disciplines a top-priority public policy."[114] Meanwhile, the phrase "Fun City" became something of a sick joke, commercialized in the form of Fun City Discotheque, on the southeast corner of Forty-seventh Street and Broadway, where go-go dancers could be seen by passersby gazing up through second-story windows, stopping traffic.[115]

In 1975 the political scientist Andrew Hacker summed up Lindsay's impact:

> John Lindsay's presence in Gracie Mansion awakened the consciousness of people who might otherwise have stayed with the mood and mentality of earlier eras. During this eight-year period whole classes of individuals became more assertive than they had ever been in the past. . . . In New York from 1965 to 1973 countless citizens apparently believed that the time was ripe to vent grievances and assert ambitions. . . . New Yorkers were ready for John Lindsay. Sentiments he would arouse lay near the surface. The demography of the city was beginning to fashion the contours of a new civic personality.[116]

The years of Mayor Lindsay's second term were marked by an increasing malaise, a sense that the city was in decline, despite relative prosperity in the construction, service and entertainment industries. That growing sense of inadequacy, the city's seeming inability to cope with its problems, became international news when a February 1969 snowstorm crippled Kennedy Airport, stranding six thousand people and highlighting the city's failure to respond quickly. As Saul Bellow's Mr. Sammler observed in 1970: "New York makes one think about the collapse of civilization, about Sodom and Gomorrah, the end of the world. The end wouldn't come as a surprise here. Many people already bank on it."[117]

But all was not gloomy. In 1969–70 the statistically improbable fantasy of three of the city's professional basketball, football and baseball teams—the Knicks, the Jets and the Mets—winning world championships proved a significant morale booster, if not a last gasp of the heyday of Fun City. Besides the dramatic coincidence of the victories, the teams found themselves inextricably intertwined with the image, mood and pace of city life as the top stars in each sport became New York's most visible national ambassadors. The Knicks were the team of Walter (Clyde) Frazier, who sported long sideburns, wore a fur coat and drove a Rolls-Royce, and Dollar Bill Bradley, the

Princeton-trained Rhodes scholar with the unerring jump shot.[118] The brashest and most prominent of the city's sports stars was Jets quarterback Broadway Joe Namath, the Beaver Falls, Pennsylvania, native who loved Manhattan's nightlife and occupied a penthouse apartment on First Avenue and Seventy-sixth Street that was flamboyantly decorated with Siberian snow-leopard throw pillows, a cheetah-skin bench, a black leather bar, an oval bed topped by green satin sheets and the pièce de résistance, a wall-to-wall, six-inch-thick, white llama rug.[119] Namath's decision to live in the city was itself notable, bucking a decade-long trend of athletes who had decamped to suburbs in New Jersey or Long Island and recalling the tradition of celebrated pros who lived the glamorous life in Manhattan that was inaugurated in the 1920s when Babe Ruth took up residence in the Ansonia Apartment Hotel.[120] The turnaround of the perennial last-place Mets also energized the reelection efforts of Lindsay, who was forced to run on the Liberal and Independent lines after his narrow, first-ever loss in the Republican primary to State Senator John Marchi.[121] His appearance in the Mets' locker room after the win, being doused with champagne like he was one of the players, seemed to confer upon Lindsay a measure of that team's popularity as underdogs who came back against all odds to defy the pundits, contributing to his victory in the general election less than three weeks later against Marchi and the Democratic challenger, city comptroller Mario Procaccino.

New Yorkers were becoming aware not only of the dramatic schism growing in the city between the "haves," who were largely white, and the "have nots," who were largely but by no means exclusively black and Hispanic, but also of the extent of the city's poverty, with 1964 figures revealing one in every five New Yorkers living on below-standard incomes. To supplement the incomes of the poor and provide them with essential social services the city embarked on extensive welfare programs, the costs of which were staggering but largely supported with state and federal funds in this period. When those funds were cut off by Albany and Washington in the early 1970s, the burden of the services fell to the city's own inadequate resources, contributing to the near collapse of its finances in 1975. New York's failure was in this sense a failure of metropolitanism, because as a city-state it had developed not only institutions comparable to those of the federal government but also social programs, programs now abandoned by the nation as a whole but still very much a part of the city's own self-image, its sense of social mission.

Still, despite its social problems and a host of other maladies, New York remained a mecca for the bright, young and ambitious from the hinterlands and for foreigners, who continued to pour in. The change in the national immigration law in 1965, which came into effect in 1968, brought a new wave of immigrants to the city: by the late 1960s the Caribbean, Latin America and Asia were the dominant sources of newcomers, with some 954,000 persons settling in the city between 1965 and 1978. Thus, despite an outmigration in the economically slumped early and mid-1970s of over 1,162,000 people, New York's population declined only 11 percent. As Nathan Glazer put it: "The immigrant flow into New York seemed unaffected, or scarcely affected by changing economic circumstances, by the phenomenal decline in manufacturing jobs, by the massive destruction of low-cost housing in the great waves of abandonment of the 1970s. Whatever the changes that were affecting New York for the worse in the 1970s, to the immigrant it was still apparently the city of opportunity."[122]

New York's problems really began after 1970, when the collapse of the stock market cut deeply into Wall Street payrolls and undermined commercial real estate. The situation was not helped by the growing animosity between Lindsay and Governor Nelson A. Rockefeller, whose support was needed in the annual battle for funds from the State Legislature.[123] Tensions between city and state were not new. As long ago as 1861 the notoriously corrupt Mayor Fernando Wood argued for a break between city and state, complaining that "The political connection between the people of the city and the state has been used by the latter to our injury. Our burdens have been increased, our substance eaten out and our municipal liberty destroyed. Why may not New York disrupt the bonds that bind her to a corrupt and venal master?"[124] The idea was raised again by William Randolph Hearst, the publisher and would-be mayor, by mayors Walker and La Guardia and in 1953 by the editors of *Look* magazine, who proposed that the city "should rise in its majesty, secede from the state, set up on its own and proceed to tax hell out of non-residents employed in Manhattan. This would leave the city rolling in the wealth to which it is entitled, and would reduce the state to a position in society consonant with petty farming and a few clusters of heavy industry."[125] Jane Jacobs, a brilliant journalist concentrating on urban planning issues, on the other hand, had suggested breaking up the consolidated city into a collection of federated units but with some authority left to a larger metropolitan government. When the idea of statehood was taken up again, and much more seriously, things had changed. Not only were the city's finances in a mess, but the balance of economic and social power had shifted, with many members of the middle class living and voting in suburban towns and resenting the city where they worked and to which, since 1966, they had paid a commuter's tax.[126]

In 1959 the New York City Council approved the creation of a committee to study secession, and a bill for a referendum on the establishment of city statehood was introduced in the State Legislature.[127] The idea died for lack of interest, not to be revived until 1969, when the novelist Norman Mailer, running for the Democratic nomination for mayor, made it the key issue of his campaign. Mailer chose as his running mate the journalist Jimmy Breslin, who sought the slot of City Council president. In an essay, "Why Are We in New York?" published in the *New York Times Magazine*, Mailer, after reciting a litany of the city's ills, including air pollution, traffic, housing and public finances, and musing on the city's fading greatness, got to the heart of the issue: "The style of New York has shifted since the Second World War (along with the rest of the American cities) from a scene of local neighborhoods and personalities to a large dull impersonal style of life which deadens us with its architecture, its highways, its abstract welfare, and its bureaucratic reflex to look for government solutions which come into the city from without (and do not work)."[128]

Pushing on with his point, Mailer rhetorically asked how we can save the city: "New York will not begin to be saved until its men and women begin to believe that it must become the greatest city in the world, the most magnificent, most creative, most extraordinary, most just, dazzling, bewildering and balanced of cities." "By the most brutal view," he continued, the city "is today a legislative pail of dismembered organs strewn from Washington to Albany. We are without a comprehensive function which will become our skin. We cannot begin until we become a state of the United States separate from New York State: the Fifty-first, in fact, of the United States. New York City State or The State of New York City. It is strange on the tongue, but not so strange."[129] Once a state, the city could write a new charter, "built upon one concept so fundamental that all others would depend upon it. This concept might state that power would return to the neighborhoods."[130]

Mayor Lindsay took the idea of statehood up again in 1971, appointing a commission to study the problem, only to discover that he lacked the support of various borough officials, especially Staten Island Borough President Robert T. Connor, who recalled that borough officials had recently studied "how to get the hell out of New York City."[131] Lindsay saw New York as a federally chartered "national city," which, once independent, could deal directly with the federal government on such key issues as welfare, health and trade. Pete Hamill, the columnist, also gave the idea some play in 1972 and again in 1975 when he suggested that the city become a state and then secede from the union.[132]

Bella Abzug, the outspoken feminist congresswoman, also advocated the city's breaking away from the state.[133] But others, such as Michael Harrington, the author of the landmark book on poverty, *The Other America* (1962), took a less extreme position. Commenting on a *New York* magazine poll in which 90.2 percent of the 5,713 people sampled favored New York City's withdrawing from the state,[134] Harrington made it clear that though the "relationship between New York City and New York State is indeed an intolerable anachronism," the city "is not economically or socially independent. It is part of a gigantic megalopolitan system which reaches into New Jersey, Connecticut, Pennsylvania and other parts of New York State, most notably Long Island. It is this area, and not the five boroughs or New York State, which constitutes a labor market, a transportation system, a unified—and deteriorating—environment and the other crucial determinants of modern life." Harrington advocated instead "the development of functional regional government on the one hand and organs of neighborhood, or small community, rule on the other."[135]

On the opposite side of the argument, yet at the same time complementary to it, was the suggestion of B. Bruce-Briggs, an historian, that the consolidated city be abolished not by breaking it up into the boroughs that were largely created along the lines of the region's nineteenth-century development but by creating a host of villages and small towns—Flushing, Flatbush, Jamaica and so on, each becoming towns within their respective counties.[136]

Just as the city's situation began to worsen and talk about a fifty-first state became commonplace, Charles Gillett, president of the New York Convention and Visitors Bureau, mounted a promotional campaign for the city, which took as its symbol a red apple, based on the increasingly frequent use of the phrase "The Big Apple," a term of endearment for New York.[137] According to Gerald Leonard Cohen, New York, or at least Broadway, was first called the Big Apple in the 1920s; the term was also used in the 1920s to refer to New York's racetracks.[138] During the 1930s black jazz musicians began to use the term to refer to the city as a whole and to Harlem in particular, where a nightclub of the same name was located. The Big Apple was also a dance step that became a national craze in the 1930s. The term was well suited to the city. As William Safire wrote in 1975: "an apple is shaped like the world, and by synecdoche, the Big Apple has come to stand for the place where opportunities—and problems—converge. If you can make it in New York, you can make it anywhere."[139]

By 1973 the predictions about New York's future growth made in 1960 by Raymond Vernon (see above) were beginning to reveal themselves as overoptimistic. Employment, though

33

high, was not so high as he had implied it would be, and telecommunications had made a central-city location less than indispensable for corporate management as well as for the innovative entrepreneur, who could locate himself near his suburban home on Long Island or Westchester, or in new specialized areas, like Route 128 outside Boston or the Silicon Valley outside San Jose, California.

Nevertheless, in 1973, during Lindsay's last year in office, despite the collapse of financial markets in 1969–70 and the ensuing halt of the office-building boom, the city seemed in better health than it had been for quite a while.[140] At the same time, Eli Ginzberg, head of Columbia University's Conservation of Human Resources Staff, published his study of metropolitan labor and economics, *New York Is Very Much Alive*.[141] There he authoritatively reflected the popular wisdom that the city's increasingly nonwhite population was finding it hard to compete with whites in the marketplace and that public welfare represented the preferred alternative to employment within a large segment of the population, but he refuted claims that the suburbs had drained the city of its vitality or that the city's economy was faltering.

The summer of 1974 was a watershed for the country at large, which witnessed the fall of Richard M. Nixon's presidency amidst the Watergate scandal, accompanied by the disintegration of the economy, which had a particularly strong impact on New York. As stock prices collapsed, throwing many brokerages into chaos and leaving many New Yorkers out of work, the emergence of double-digit inflation began to affect the bond market, while the banks, which had to cope with corporate loans that had turned sour, were further squeezed when the real estate investments they had sponsored began to fail. The situation was disastrous for the Urban Development Corporation (UDC), a state agency that was created in 1968 under the administration of Governor Rockefeller as a public developer of moderate-cost housing and was critical to the city's redevelopment plans in places like Roosevelt Island and Coney Island. With state revenues off, the "moral-commitment obligation" bonds the state issued to finance UDC projects, backed by no specific revenues, began to lose their appeal with investors, making it difficult for the corporation to raise capital for new projects or meet its commitments on projects already under way.

When Abraham D. Beame took office as mayor in January 1974, he inherited municipal debts that had begun to pile up under Mayor Wagner and had grown alarmingly under Mayor Lindsay. On June 30, 1974, the city's short-term debt was $3.4 billion, three times what it had been four years before. Like the UDC's debt, the city's was largely incurred in finance charges for mortgages needed for its publicly assisted housing programs. By late 1974 the city, which in a desperate effort to stay afloat had been selling municipal securities on an unparalleled scale and at very favorable rates to bondholders, was at the end of its line of credit, requiring almost $1.5 billion each year just to finance its debts. On top of this, the city had resorted to what Felix Rohatyn, who was to head the Municipal Assistance Corporation, created in 1975 to help the city restore its financial health, described as "accounting gimmicks," including a trend to pay expenses out of the capital budget, hastening the physical deterioration of infrastructure and buildings while halting the construction of new facilities.[142]

In the spring of 1975 the UDC found itself unable to sell its new series of one-year notes and therefore unable to pay off its notes from the previous year.[143] In other words, an agency of the State of New York was broke, thereby suggesting to financiers that the state itself might not be so healthy either. But the state had a "moral obligation" to the UDC's bondholders and, to avoid the agency's default, Governor Hugh Carey's administration cobbled together an arrangement using federal housing subsidies to create the Project Finance Agency, which was able to sell bonds to refinance the UDC's maturing debt and save it from liquidation.

The UDC's problems and the city's recklessness combined to produce the fiscal crisis of 1975. The city was able to hang on until spring 1975, but the UDC's dilemma convinced New York City's bankers that they could not invest in the city anymore unless severe measures were taken to cut back on expenses. By April 7 *Time* could tell its readers that the Big Apple was "on the brink" of bankruptcy.[144] A month later Martin Mayer told the readers of the *New York Times*: "The city is in fact bankrupt, and the time has come to go to the bankruptcy court, recognize what has happened, and pick up the pieces under court supervision and protection."[145] When Governor Carey, who succeeded Nelson Rockefeller in 1975, became alarmed that the city's fiscal collapse would engulf the state as a whole, he won legislative approval for the establishment of the Municipal Assistance Corporation, which quickly became known as "Big Mac."[146] Empowered to borrow up to $3 billion on behalf of the city backed by its sales and stock-transfer taxes, Big Mac was a variant on the moral-obligation type of financing that had created the UDC. When squabbles between the city, the state and the unions rendered Big Mac nearly helpless, the city sent emissaries to Washington, where both houses of congress and the president turned a cold shoulder.[147]

On October 30, 1975, the *New York Times'* banner headline read: "Ford, Castigating City, Asserts He'd Veto Fund Guarantee; Offers Bankruptcy Bill."[148] But the *Daily News* was more succinct, headlining: "Ford to City: Drop Dead."[149] In his speech dealing with the city's crisis, President Gerald R. Ford pinpointed the cause of the city's ills: bad fiscal management that awarded excessive salaries and benefits to municipal employees, that sloppily administered welfare and that let the city's budget grow at a far faster rate than its income would allow. Ford presented New York as a metaphor for the nation as a whole (only he neglected to note that the federal government could, to put it simply, print more money as it ran short):

> None of us can point a completely guiltless finger at New York City. None of us should now derive comfort or pleasure from New York's anguish. But neither can we let that contagion spread. As we work with the wonderful people of New York to overcome their difficulties—and they will—we must never forget what brought us to the brink. If we go on spending more than we have, providing more benefits and more services than we can pay for, then a day of reckoning will come to Washington and the whole country just as it has to New York City. . . . When that day of reckoning comes, who will bail out the United States of America?[150]

The city prepared for bankruptcy in the waning months of 1975.[151] A near-siege mentality took over as budgets were slashed and the public was warned about municipal services to be cut back or eliminated.[152] The threat was so real that it finally forced the city, the state and even the federal government to face the situation; with the cooperation of the municipal labor unions, the major city banks and the Municipal Assistance Corporation, a deal was worked out and default was averted. With the offer of federal loans, the city was saved, although President Ford insisted that it had "bailed itself out."[153]

Though the city was in dire financial straits and its self-esteem was at an all-time low, President Ford's callous attitude seemed to tap a deep reserve of natural goodwill. As *Newsweek* put it: "for all its immediate problems, the city still possesses remarkable resilience, and there is a widespread feeling that writing off New York is premature, if not foolhardy."[154] But what did the financial crisis really mean for the city's future? To Richard Wade, the urban historian, the crisis marked the end of "the era of the self-sufficient metropolis." But, Wade advised, as cities needed to turn to states and to the federal government for help, there would be "a new sense of sacrifice in the city." He explained:

> The city must be borne equitably; not just by the children, the young and the poorly paid. The rich and middle class can run away to the suburbs or chase the sun in the Southwest. But their relief will be short-lived. The acid of urban decay will not stop at the municipal boundaries or the Mason-Dixon line. It must be handled somewhere and sometime. And where better than here in New York where the modern urban age began more than a century ago and where the future of American cities will either be lost or won.[155]

As Roger Starr, commissioner of the Housing and Redevelopment Administration, put it, "Imprudent borrowing to finance moderate rental housing in New York City produced the fiscal crisis, only coincidentally with the U.D.C.'s problems in 1975. It would ultimately have produced a crisis all by itself."[156] While the money needed to build housing was the principal source of indebtedness, it was by no means the full measure of the problem. The city had become "a social democracy," as Lou Winnick, deputy vice president of the Ford Foundation, put it: "It was taxing the rich to help the poor. It began to act like a country, like Denmark."[157]

Thomas Bender, in his book *New York Intellect*, which he began writing in 1975, has speculated that the meaning of the crisis extended "far wider than the political and economic commentary on it suggested. It was . . . just as much a cultural and intellectual crisis," marked by "the inability of New York's intellectuals to generate compelling general ideas about New York as a democratic city. No one seemed to know how to initiate—within the context of a local, urban culture—a serious and general discourse about the most important city in the world. The city, it seemed, was a mere incident in various discourses of organized, professionalized interest groups, some local, some not, but all sectorial in orientation."[158]

If on the whole the collapse of the city's markets and its finances brought forth a real camaraderie and spirit, it also elicited its share of I-told-you-so's, none more irritating and self-serving than those retailed by the developer Samuel J. Lefrak. Early in 1974 he sought to lay blame on the city's planners, calling them slaves of fashion, who first advocated greenery and vest pocket parks, which proved dangerous and less valuable as social condensers than the mom-and-pop grocery shops and candy stores they frequently replaced; then became enamored with Jane Jacobs's ideas; and finally placed all their emphasis on Manhattan Island. According to Lefrak, the planners deemed the outer boroughs inconsequential—"Isn't that where people go to sleep and where people are buried?"—as they pushed for high-density office development in Manhattan, sneering at the type of "six-story apartment houses in Brooklyn and Queens" that were Lefrak's stock-in-trade. "They were basic," Lefrak wrote. "The windows opened and closed. You opened them in the summer and closed them in the winter. Middle-class New Yorkers could

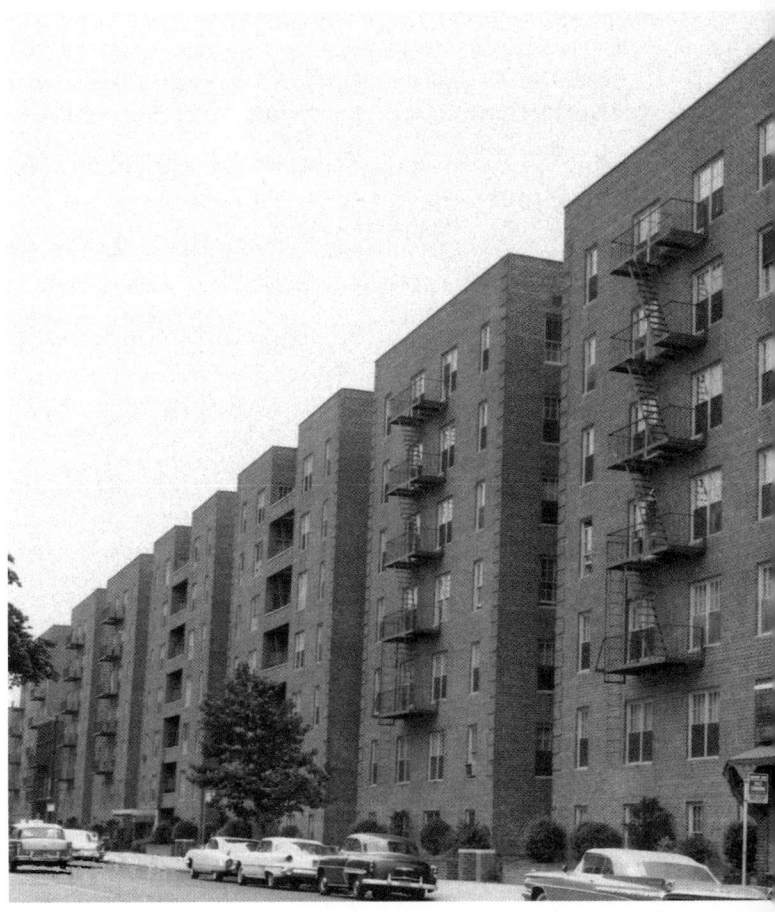

The Dakota, 2425 Nostrand Avenue, Flatbush, Brooklyn. Jack Brown, 1955. Developed by Samuel J. Lefrak. LO

afford to live in them and raise families. The planners didn't like them so I can't build them anymore. But the planners like nice 50-story luxury apartment houses in Manhattan." Lefrak concluded with a note of cautionary optimism: "The era of nonsense is over. Let's get back to reality."[159]

Still, despite all of the city's vicissitudes, amidst New York's collapse, 54 percent of the citizens interviewed in a survey conducted for the *New York Times* in 1974 said that they stayed there because they wanted to, not because economic necessity forced them to. In response, Andrew Hacker observed that "New York . . . can claim the loyalty of about half of its inhabitants, no small proportion, considering the national opinion of urban life."[160] Instead of breaking New York's spirit, the crisis seemed to make those who loved the city all the more passionate in their ardor and all the more vocal in their praise. But the praise was not naive boosterism. Rather it was a sense that New York was improbable but utterly special. As the writer Kurt Vonnegut, Jr., put it in the lead article in a collection of paeans to the city published by *Harper's* magazine in August 1975:

> The city is permanently cruel. It has always been what it is today—a sort of polluted lake on which splendid vessels bob. Many people can't even afford water wings, so an awful lot of drowning in untreated sewage goes on. Too bad. It is time for a revolution here, with so much incompetence at the top and in the middle and at the bottom, with the wealth so capriciously distributed, with so many people unemployed. . . . The trouble with the city as a birthplace for revolution is that Manhattan Island, at its center, inspires utterly baseless optimism—even in me, even in drunks sleeping in doorways and in little old ladies whose houses are shopping bags. . . . Crazy.[161]

Amidst the general mood of self-flagellation, Roger Starr argued for a continuation of the city's spirit:

> The extravagances with which New Yorkers now reproach themselves were imprudent; no doubt they were mistaken, and yet the mistakes were essentially allied to the character of New York City itself. They were the mistakes of size, the mistakes of too great a faith in the future, too high a confidence in the ability of the future to catch up with and perhaps even to surpass the patent extravagances of the present. But if the mistakes of largeness are imprudent, mistakes of smallness are mean. The task facing New York's leadership today is not simply to develop prudence, but to shrink extravagance without shrinking the spirit that produced it and above all, perhaps, to resist the pressures to impose rural or small-town values on what must be cosmopolitan to be worth having. Unless the city can find the basic economic justification for a continuing largeness of spirit, this task will be impossible.[162]

In 1974 Lee Levitt, a public relations executive who served as president of New York Upbeat, a volunteer task force created by the New York Chapter of the Public Relations Society of America to study the city's public relations problems, argued that New York had been the victim of biased reporting by the media, which had consistently focused on and frequently distorted its problems while ignoring those of other cities. As the nation's principal city and home to most of its print and broadcast media, it also garnered the most attention: "In an era when much of the news from cities is bad, the largest city inevitably makes more bad news than any other." Levitt observed: "Many leaders of the effort to 'save' America's cities during the 1960s were based in New York, and they naturally used New York for their examples of problems to be remedied. In their zeal, they frequently exaggerated. For this reason, the media never noticed that New York actually escaped many of the ills afflicting other U.S. cities—desertion of the central business district, a net loss of jobs, a net drop in population." Most of all, Levitt continued, there were "two special factors" that prejudiced the editors of out-of-town local media against New York: "resentment and envy on the part of older economic and social leaders in their American cities," caused by the fact that the preponderant "flow" of business and culture in the twentieth century had been from the country and the older towns to New York.[163]

Years later, Marshall Berman was to echo this assessement: "Our own media mythicized us into America's Other, which could be blamed for everything that the country didn't want to see in itself. The demonization of New York reached orgiastic heights in the mid-1970s, during our fiscal crisis, when many politicians and media pundits spoke as if social peace would return to all America if only New York could somehow be wiped off the map."[164] Lewis Lapham, in his column in *Harper's*, presented a similar view in 1976 when he pointedly observed that though many reasons had been voiced for New York's catastrophe, little had been said about "the principal reason for it . . . the national hatred for the freedom of a great city. . . . To say, as so many people do, that New York is a dark and terrible inferno, is to say that they hate and fear the multiplicity of both the human face and the human imagination."[165]

In 1975 Andrew Hacker published *The New Yorkers*, which he subtitled *A Profile of an American Metropolis*. Acknowledging from the book's outset that the city "has problems" and that "by virtually every accepted measure, it is deteriorating," Hacker, to a considerable extent, ascribed its current state to the changing character of its population: "new people with a new spirit of self-importance." This renewal of population and purpose, having made the city "an unpalatable place for some people," was a sure sign for others that the city remained a desirable "center of excitement and innovation." Quite obviously the city had lost much of its appeal for Americans in the hinterlands and for its own citizens who decamped to the suburbs and the Sunbelt. This, Hacker conceded, "is bad for pride. People who once made New York their goal now go elsewhere. . . . Nevertheless, persons of all races and classes continue to move to New York. On the whole they come voluntarily: the city is what they want."[166]

By the indices usually cited, Hacker said,

> New York is in a bad way. More of its citizens display selfish and destructive behavior, inflicting injuries on both themselves and one another. . . . Even so, the statistics provide a one-dimensional picture. Despite the crime, vandalism, and its contracting economy, New York contains a more interesting collection of people than at any time in its history. There is more going on in terms of variety and self-enjoyment than in any urban center on this continent or most others. It is an adventuresome place to live for those who want that kind of life. And enough apparently do.[167]

Perhaps Felix Rohatyn summed up the situation best: "The evil that has been done to this city has been done through philosophic desire and through illusion, not by intent."[168]

Two Power Brokers:
Robert Moses and Jane Jacobs

Two figures personify the struggle between New York as the grandest metropolis in the world on the one hand and as the world's biggest village on the other, between the power of the purse, whether public or private, and the power of the public will: Robert Moses, the master builder, and Jane Jacobs, the urban theorist and activist.

For Robert Moses city life was the daily grind, a fundamental fact of modern existence but basically unsympathetic to the good life. City life meant sacrifice, with the individual bending his will to the collective, exemplified by Moses's oft-repeated phrase about large-scale projects: "You can't make an omelet without breaking eggs." For Jane Jacobs the city was a great liberation, the ultimate freedom, an intricate web of individuals, buildings and streets, a mosaic or tapestry that somehow amounted to more than any singular vision and was absolute anathema to the idea of a grand plan. In Jacobs's view, New York, or at least the parts of it she admired, had the ingredients of a post-industrial-age utopia; it was definitely not an ordeal to be endured.

At one time Robert Moses was as powerful as any person in New York City—perhaps the most powerful of all; and his influence was not only vast but also enduring, extending from the 1920s to the 1960s. He came to power in the city in 1934 and went on to hold key positions at various quasi-public agencies with large building funds, including the Triborough Bridge and Tunnel Authority. He also served as Park Commissioner and City Construction Coordinator as well as being a member of the City Planning Commission, a seat he was appointed to by Mayor La Guardia in 1942 and held through the administration of Mayor Wagner. By virtue of these positions, as Eugene Lewis has recently written, he "achieved a magic circle. . . . Moses . . . proposed *and* disposed."[169]

Robert Moses's first job in government was at the state level: he served as chief of staff of the New York State Reconstruction Commission from 1919 to 1921. In 1924 he was named by Governor Alfred E. Smith as the first chairman of the State Council of Parks and the first president of the Long Island State Park Commission. Moses was then appointed New York's Secretary of State (1927–28). By the late 1920s he had embarked on what would be his principal project of the 1930s and unquestionably the great work of his lifetime, the construction of a network of parkways leading to a system of parks on Long Island.[170] In this he exhibited an unprecedented breadth of vision as a planner who, working with teams of engineers, architects and landscape architects, was able to realize one of history's incomparable public works.

Moses's organization of parks and parkways was more than a sophisticated roadway system, more even than the fulfillment of the Regional Plan's proposals of 1929–31. For Moses, an arterial system of highways was the backbone of an overall urban vision about how cities would be rebuilt and how they would expand. Yet Moses was not a proponent of sweeping reform; he believed in the inherited structure of the city. In the roads he built to accommodate the automobile he saw a way to break through traditional social and physical barriers, whether in the country estates of the wealthy on Long Island's North Shore or the lower-middle-class tenement and apartment house neighborhoods of the Central Bronx, in an effort to spread the city out, to disperse populations and homogenize ethnicity.

The Second World War interrupted Moses's park and highway program, and when he resumed his work in the postwar era, he seemed to have lost his way. His postwar highways and parks lacked the quality of those built in his glory days in the 1930s. Gone were the beautiful details and the bold vistas; gone, most of all, was a sense that the parks and highways together represented an overall vision. Moses's postwar work seemed in every way composed of expedient solutions to slum clearance and traffic alleviation rather than broad strategies. Any impression he or his programs had managed to convey of an enlightened social vision fell by the wayside as road building overwhelmed park building in his plans and as hosts of citizens were forced to give up their homes to make way for his projects. By the late 1950s Moses, who was just turning seventy, seemed drained not only of ideals but also of ideas. Ten years later, when his public career was virtually over, Moses seemed actively hostile to the city he had so long served.

In the introduction to their book, *Beyond the Melting Pot* (1963), Nathan Glazer and Daniel Patrick Moynihan offered what may well have been the first serious criticism of the postwar Moses: everyone was so overwhelmed by Moses's capacity to get things done, they wrote, "that for a long time it hardly mattered that what he was getting done on a scale appropriate to the city's size was brutal and ugly, and only exacerbated its problems."[171] Glazer and Moynihan's indictment would become a litany for intellectuals in the 1960s and 1970s, culminating in Robert Caro's discrediting biography, *The Power Broker: Robert Moses and the Fall of New York* (1974).[172] In 1982 Marshall Berman, a professor of political science at the City University of New York, tried to explain why the master builder's postwar projects were so inferior to those from before:

> Moses' projects of the 1950s and 60s had virtually none of the beauty of design and human sensitivity that had distinguished his early works. Drive twenty miles or so on the Northern State Parkway (1920s), then turn around and cover those same twenty miles on the parallel Long Island Expressway (1950s/60s), and wonder and weep. . . . Now Moses seemed scornfully indifferent to the human quality of what he did: sheer quantity—of moving vehicles, tons of cement, dollars received and spent—seemed to be all that drove him now.[173]

Berman attributed the public's rejection of Moses's postwar work not only to its declining quality but also to the "advent of the New Left and 'counter culture,'" which led Americans to ask some serious questions about the progressive visions of the 1930s:

> Mobility for what? These middle-class children of the dream forced our whole culture to ask: Where are we running, and for what human end, and at what human cost? . . . It is striking that two of the most stirring actions of the Sixties involved sitting down on construction sites and stopping the works: a gymnasium in a park at Columbia [see chapter 9], a parking lot on "free space" at People's Park [Berkeley, California]. . . . Suddenly, for the first time anyone could remember, America's master builders were on the defensive, publicly despised for their "public works"; there was a vast wave of free-floating popular sympathy for "the people" in the way and this sympathy could often be utilized to block the way. All through the Sixties, all over America, by force or by vote, great machines and great works were stopped. In the New York version of the drama, Robert Moses played a crucial role: he was sitting on top of the world we were trying to stop, lashing his men and machines to move faster as resistance grew.[174]

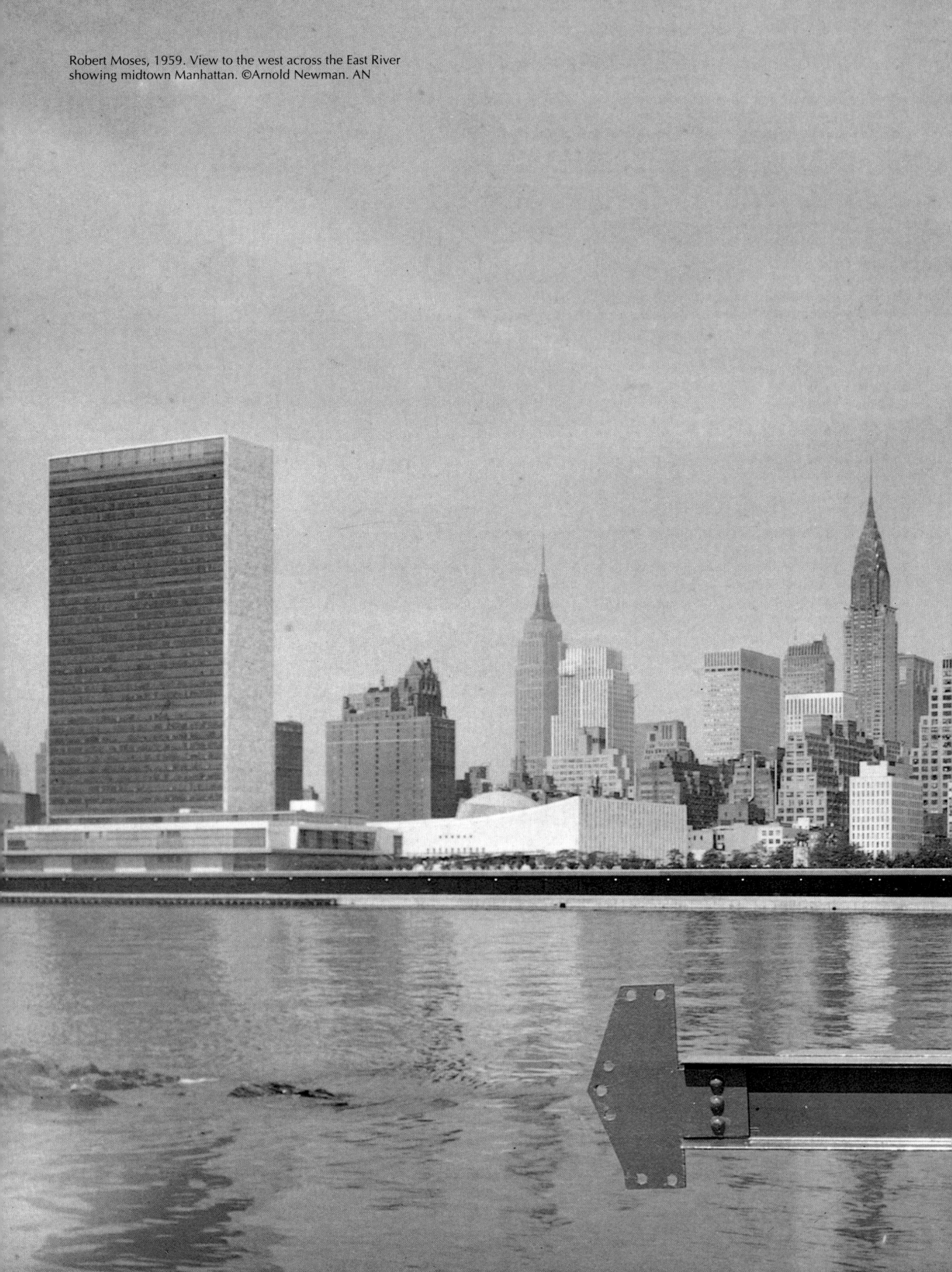

Robert Moses, 1959. View to the west across the East River showing midtown Manhattan. ©Arnold Newman. AN

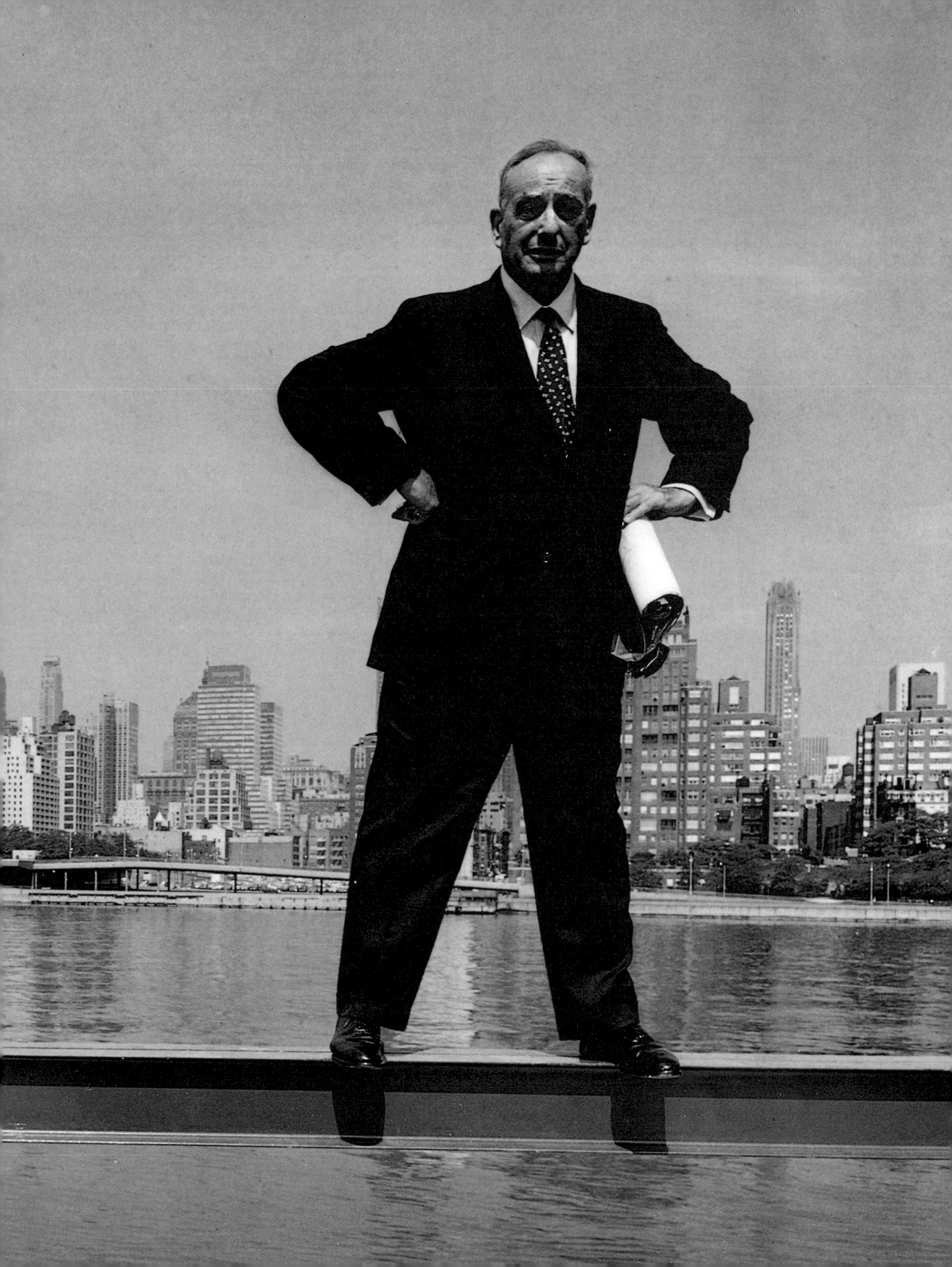

The collapse of Moses's influence cannot simply be attributed to a change in attitude on the part of intellectuals or the public at large. Moses contributed mightily to his own downfall, attacking intellectuals and public-spirited citizens who disagreed with him, whom he dismissed as do-gooders and, more familiarly, "goo-goos." He courted further contempt by exhibiting a swaggering superiority to any average citizen who might oppose him and in particular to nonwhite minorities. By the 1960s Moses's natural arrogance had gotten in the way of his better judgment. As the city's Construction Coordinator, he became the principal planner and developer of the large-scale housing projects that replaced park and highway construction in the postwar era as the most characteristic public project type. While thwarting the City Planning Commission's efforts to produce a master plan that would develop an overall strategy for urban redevelopment, Moses combined his official powers with the financial clout of federal funds to rebuild whole areas of the city, usurping the commission's role and planning the city with what was in effect no plan at all. Ironically, Moses also became the principal exponent of Modernist towers-in-the-park urbanism because it proved to be a relatively expedient way to rehouse large populations on cleared sites. Ignoring those who advised him to be more sensitive to the changing nature of the politics of redevelopment, Moses refused to recognize that his housing projects and expressways were cutting not only through the fabric of old neighborhoods but through the tissue of human lives and relationships, creating racial and social schisms that could not be easily mended. In his book *New York Plans for the Future* (1943), Cleveland Rodgers described Moses's planning methods as similar to those of a "military leader who concentrates on limited objectives and makes definite gains in given sectors without disclosing larger purposes or strategy."[175] But perhaps Frances Perkins, America's first Secretary of Labor (in Franklin Roosevelt's administration) and a long-time observer of Moses, put it best: "He loved the public, but not as people."[176]

Moses's first big downfall came in 1956 in the so-called Battle of the Tavern on the Green (see chapter 10). That was but a minor skirmish compared with the scandal that broke three years later surrounding his casual, callous and perhaps dishonest handling of the Title I program of federal redevelopment funds.[177] It was logical for the city's Title I program, initiated by the federal government's Housing Act of 1949, to be handled by Moses. As Eugene Lewis has written: "By the time the federal presence came to be felt strongly in New York City, through its bureaucratic agencies dominated by engineers, managers and other technocrats, Robert Moses was among the more qualified and experienced hands in government familiar with construction projects of all kinds. He was in many ways the model entrepreneur of mythical capitalism evolved into a more powerful, better-adapted creature."[178]

But Moses chose to administer the program in his own way. In an article in a special issue devoted to New York in the journal *Dissent*, Fred J. Cook explained Moses's system:

> Throughout most of the nation, municipalities condemned the land, moved off the people and razed the buildings before turning the sites over to private developers who then had no choice except to build as quickly as possible. But Moses insisted that the system that had worked elsewhere wouldn't work in New York. Instead, he turned entire tenement areas over to private developers at knock-down prices, with buildings still standing, fully populated, producing hundreds of thousands of dollars in rents. The result was inevitable: the temptation to milk the slum dwellers as long as possible before tearing down the tenements and rebuilding, proved irresistible.[179]

The scandals that swirled around the Title I program revealed an approach that was costing the taxpayers too much money and, worse still, was playing fast and loose with human lives, forcing mostly immigrant families to live in derelict housing and moving them from neighborhood to neighborhood. In April 1959, culminating years of controversy over Title I's administration that had first surfaced in 1954, a major scandal involving shady financial deals and preferential treatment began to break; it continued to gobble up headlines throughout the hot summer. Although Moses was never directly implicated, the public was appalled by the fact that banker Thomas Shanahan, his close associate, and George E. Spargo, his top assistant, were. While it was possible to exonerate Moses in the Title I scandal—his worst sin may have been sloppy management—his callousness to the human dimension of city building was becoming increasingly hard to justify. Yet even the Title I scandal failed to topple Moses, who seemed to remain virtually unassailable, a phenomenon that baffled even his severest critics. Fred Cook called his survival a "genuine, crowning achievement": "He has created and successfully defended within the fabric of American democracy an island of unbreachable, untouchable despotism. At the same time he remains the paragon without rival, an exemplar of vision and efficiency within the framework of democracy; a colossus untarnished, unsullied, inimitable in his indispensability and perfection. It is no mean achievement."[180]

Soon enough, however, Moses's career began to slide and the public esteem he enjoyed began to seriously wane, so that by 1964 his power was largely stripped from him, except for his chairmanship of the Triborough Bridge and Tunnel Authority, which he maintained until 1968, when he retired and began to serve it as a consultant.[181] By the time Moses retired, the Triborough had lost its hegemony as well, becoming a component of the newly constituted Metropolitan Transportation Authority (MTA). The 1964–65 World's Fair, Moses's last great public project, was, as Richard Wade put it, a "kind of gold watch for public service."[182] His staunch advocacy of the Lower Manhattan Expressway brought him up against determined and articulate opponents. Moreover, his refusal to support the concept of an integrated metropolitan transportation policy by surrendering a portion of the profits from tolls on the bridges and tunnels under his jurisdiction to help support the subways and commuter railroads brought him head to head with Mayor Lindsay, who in his first term was as popular a mayor as any the city had seen since La Guardia. Moses's contempt for Lindsay was unqualified. In his autobiography of 1970 he wrote:

> It has yet to be shown that essentially honest, youthful municipal administration based on impulse rather than experience—with Haroun al-Raschid tours of the slums, extravagant promises and announcements, invitations to disorder and lawlessness in the name of satisfying youth, contrived, extraordinary, uncontrollable events and happenings as distinguished from steady progress—can maintain New York's supremacy and livability. We must soon decide whether we want a fun town rather than one guaranteeing outward order and decency.[183]

Moses's reputation hit its nadir in 1974, when Robert Caro published his monumental biography, *The Power Broker: Robert Moses and the Fall of New York*. One of the book's underlying themes was the then prevailing antiplanning philosophy associated with Moses's antithesis and, as it turned out, nemesis as well, Jane Jacobs. Caro's book perfectly mirrored the city's and the nation's post-Vietnam mood: it was an era when, to paraphrase E. F. Schumacher's title, small was beautiful.[184] On this point, Moses saw the bias and weakness of Caro's book clearly. In his written response to it, he offered a thinly veiled attack on Jacobs and the idea of community participation:

> The current fiction is that any overnight ersatz bagel and lox boardwalk merchant, any down to earth commentator or barfly, any busy housewife who gets her expertise from newspaper, television, radio and telephone is ipso facto endowed to plan in detail a huge metropolitan arterial complex good for a century. In the absence of prompt decisions by experts, no work, no payrolls, no arts, parks, no nothing will move. Honest public officials will be denounced as wheelers and dealers, oppressors of the poor, dictators, fixers and power brokers intolerable in a true democracy. . . . I raise my stein to the builder who can remove ghettos without moving people as I hail the chef who can make omelets without breaking eggs.[185]

Other thoughtful observers tended to support Moses's point. In his review for the New York Times, Richard Wade argued that Caro's book, remarkable though it was as a document of the recent past, was also a document of its own time and in ways limited by this:

> For Caro is not only against Robert Moses of New York; he is against all the Robert Moses of the country. He rejects the kind of planning—or perhaps better said, of building—that has governed American urban policy for the past two generations. . . . Caro's view stems from a new perspective popularly associated with Jane Jacobs. . . . This view emphasizes decentralization of power and planning, neighborhood participation, smaller construction everywhere. . . . Caro's adherence to this school underlies his entire work and informs every episode, often overtly, but always subliminally. Hence, what seems on the surface to be a narrative biography is also a partisan discussion of one of the central questions of our time.[186]

To this, Dick Netzer, an urban economist, added that Caro's belief that Moses's policies were the source of all that was wrong in New York was nothing more than "the familiar and conventional liberal theology."[187]

Caro's book not only focused new attention on Moses but also provided an opportunity for a host of intellectuals, many quite young, to assess, usually unfavorably, the master builder's programs and persona and, more important, to comment on the book's not-so-hidden agendas: the advocacy of participatory democracy and the lamentation over "the Fall of New York." Marshall Berman, writing in the March 1975 issue of Ramparts, a leftist journal, called Caro's work "the most exciting American book on the city since the works of Paul and Percival Goodman, Lewis Mumford and Jane Jacobs, in the glorious sunrise of the early Sixties." But, unlike other intellectuals who expressed their enthusiasm for Caro's faultfinding biography by excoriating Moses, Berman had a more measured view of him as a complex figure: while Moses was guilty of overreaching arrogance and a contempt for the individual, Berman said, he was also "one of the greatest heroes of modern construction. . . . In the first 20 years of his work he did more than any man in American history to nourish the romance of construction and bring it to a climax: in his next 20 years of building, he would do more than any man to poison that romance and tear it down."[188] Berman's admiration for Moses, and especially his call to leftist liberals to draw out of the Moses experience a new synthesis, a revived romance of construction that would combine grandeur with humanity,

failed to unleash a reaction. The times were not right; this was not the age of Robert Moses but of Jane Jacobs, who, more than any postwar figure in planning, altered how Americans, and New Yorkers in particular, viewed cities.

In 1961 Jane Jacobs's book The Death and Life of Great American Cities burst on the scene with a force unlike that of any other previous book on architecture and urbanism.[189] Jacobs had pursued a career in journalism after her high school graduation, first in Scranton and then in New York, where she took some classes at Columbia University. In 1944 she married an architect, Robert Hyde Jacobs. Working for the Office of War Information, Jacobs began writing articles about diverse subjects for their overseas publications. For ten years beginning in 1952 Jacobs was an editor at Architectural Forum, where, according to Suzanne Stephens, "her blunt prose, hard-hitting comments, and liberal use of slang and hyperbole gave the articles she wrote . . . a distinct punch mixed with common sense."[190] Jacobs's prose was not only breezy and pithy, it was also joyously iconoclastic. In an article titled "New York's Office Boom," published in March 1957, Jacobs castigated New York office-building design:

> Three main faults are evident. First, simple industrial materials with regular industrial rhythms can, when used with great care and subtlety, give us Lever Houses and U.N. Secretariats; but seized upon by simple minds, these ingredients produce plain lack of character and retreat from design responsibility. The second trouble is New York's 1917 [sic] ziggurat or cake-mold zoning formula; combined with simple-minded modern this yields a cityscape that appears to have been wallpapered over bumps. The third evil is the way these products . . . are slapped along a seventeenth-century street pattern with which they are out of scale, in the usual pre-Rockefeller Center fashion, but minus even the small deferences to scale which past fashions permitted.

Observing several buildings under construction that featured plazas, such as the Seagram Building and the Time & Life Building, Jacobs anticipated some of the weaknesses of the zoning ordinance adopted four years later, in 1961: "No one . . . building can stand as an isolated gem with setting. If owner and architect follow habit in regarding it thus, instead of as a problem also in town planning, coincidental plazas can total up to happenstance, blobbed-together meanders. This kind of problem cannot be solved very well by municipal regulation; deft application of governmental design rules is no American characteristic."[191]

Jacobs combined her interests in architecture and urbanism with a developing concern for the role of government in the life of cities and for the economies of cities as a whole. In 1957, reviving what would become an ongoing discussion about statehood for New York City, she suggested changing city government to a series of federated units within a large metropolitan area "with some sovereignty surrendered to a metropolitan government."[192] The next year she tackled the problems of urban redevelopment in an article published in Fortune, "Downtown Is for People," which was reprinted in the widely read book The Exploding Metropolis.[193]

Jacobs took a two-year leave from Architectural Forum between 1959 and 1961 to write The Death and Life of Great American Cities. She opened her book, which, given the complacent suburbanism of the period, achieved remarkable sales for a debunking discussion of planning and a celebration of the grittier forms of city life, with an attention-grabbing assertion:

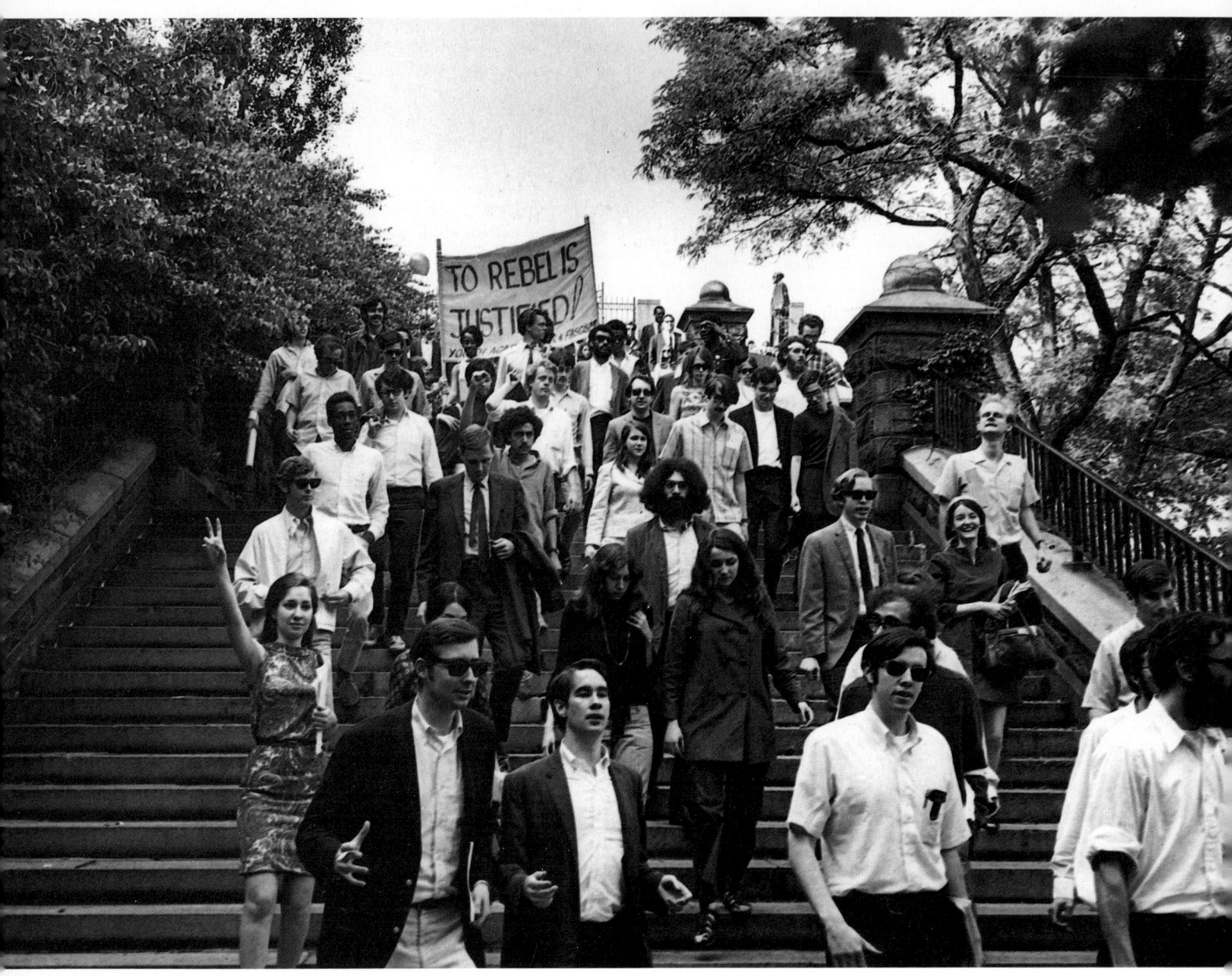

Columbia University student demonstration, Morningside Park, 1968.
Rogers. CCT

This book is an attack on current city planning and rebuilding. It is also, and mostly, an attempt to introduce new principles of city planning and rebuilding, different and even opposite from those now taught in everything from schools of architecture and planning to the Sunday supplements and women's magazines. My attack is not based on quibbles about rebuilding methods or hair-splitting about fashions in design. It is an attack, rather, on the principles and aims that have shaped modern, orthodox city planning and rebuilding.

In a few daring pages, Jacobs went on to overturn the holistic urbanism that had dominated architects and urbanists since the publication of Le Corbusier's key tract on planning and city design, *Urbanisme* (1925), in which the author elaborately articulated his idea of the Radiant City, a geometry-obsessed, high-rise version of the Garden City. Jacobs stated:

To approach a city or even a city neighborhood as if it were capable of being given order by converting it into a disciplined work of art is to make the mistake of substituting art for life. The results of such profound confusion between art and life are neither life nor art. They are taxidermy. In its place, taxidermy can be a useful and decent craft. However, it goes too far when the specimens . . . are exhibitions of dead, stuffed cities.[194]

Just as Modernist planning seemed to have reached its ultimate goal, becoming the legislated model for New York, Jacobs took it on not only by attacking its principles but also by criticizing the city planning profession as an entrenched establishment, thereby cutting to the heart of a point of view that prided itself on being the exact opposite: "It is understandable that men who were young in the 1920s were captivated by the vision of the freeway Radiant City, with the specious promise that it would be appropriate to an automobile age. At least it was then a new idea." But, Jacobs trenchantly argued, "It is disturbing to think that men who are young today, men who are being trained now for their careers, should accept on the grounds that they must be 'modern' in their thinking, conceptions about cities and traffic which are not only unworkable, but also to which nothing new of any significance has been added since their fathers were children."[195]

While Jacobs's book addressed city planning issues that affected the nation as a whole, it focused on New York City and in particular Manhattan, where she lived with her family in an unprepossessing house at 555 Hudson Street in the West Village.[196] Jacobs celebrated life on Hudson Street, and the buildings and other physical phenomena that housed and supported that life, as representative of what a city should be. She praised the "seeming disorder of the old city" and its streets as "a complex order . . . all composed of movement and change, and although it is life, not art, we may fancifully call it the art form of the city and liken it to the dance. . . . The ballet of the good city sidewalk never repeats itself from place to place, and in any one place is always replete with new improvisations." Most important, she observed that on Hudson Street, with its myriad shops and its mixed sociology, safety and civility prospered in contrast to the "bland-eyed city" of the Modernists' functionally stratified ideal, exemplified in large-scale single-class housing projects.[197]

Jacobs's attack on city planning cut right to the core of that discipline's fundamental anti-urbanism. She mocked urban renewal, which sought to turn each targeted slum area into an in-town suburbia, no matter how high the buildings. She exposed the obsessive tidiness of the planning method as inappropriate

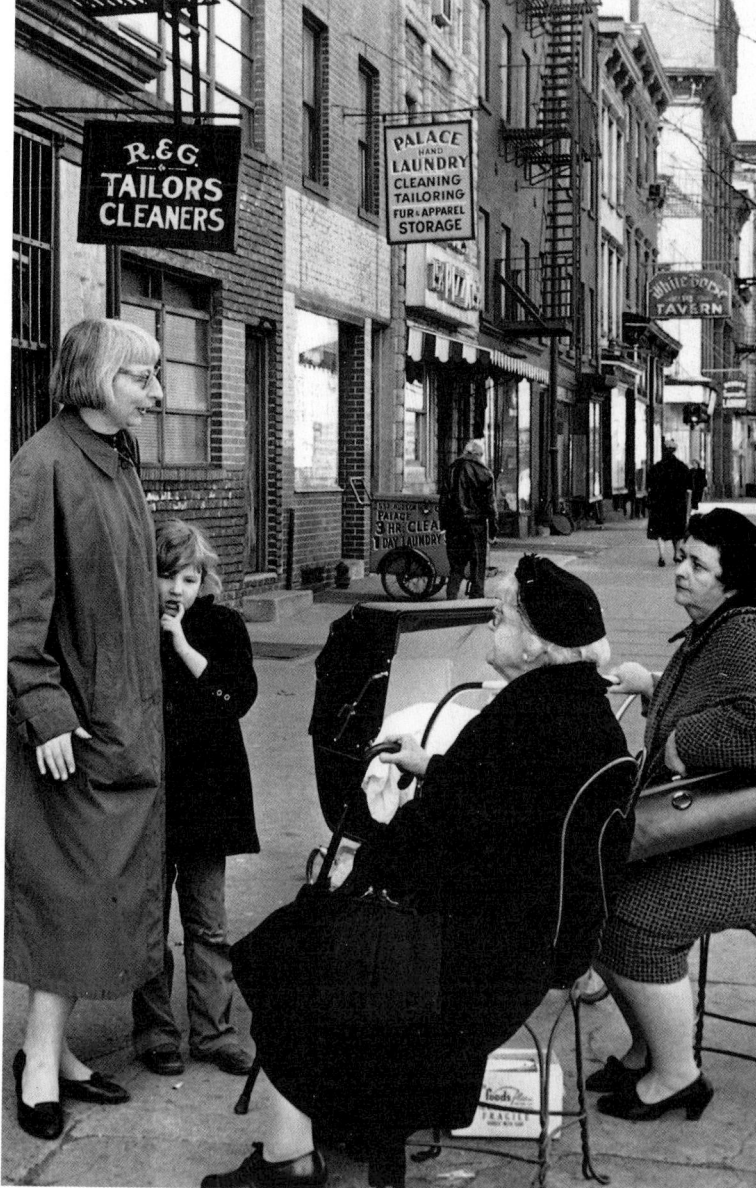

Jane Jacobs (standing) on Hudson Street, 1961. NYT

43

to New York: "There is a quality even meaner than outright ugliness or disorder, and this meaner quality is the dishonest mask of pretended order."[198] But Jacobs's contribution wasn't confined merely to an attack on prevailing planning theory; it was a celebration of cities—and not of the grand representative places in cities but of the typical neighborhoods that constituted the overall warp and woof of urbanism. As Jerome Charyn has written, "She was a woman who cared about great cities, particularly her own. . . . She revealed New York the way no one had ever revealed it before."[199]

Jacobs's critique of high-rise housing was a bold, startling and controversial attack on all large-scale urban redevelopment schemes, whether along the lines of the Radiant City, the Radiant Garden City or the Radiant Garden City Beautiful, to use her terms. "Wherever the rebuilt city rises the barbaric concept of Turf must follow," she stated, because each new enclave or city-within-a-city is stratified by class and economics and "because the rebuilt city has junked a basic function of the city street and with it, necessarily, the freedom of the city."[200] Flying in the face of accepted planning theory, Jacobs argued for concentration of activity and population. In contrast to Greenwich Village, where "relatively little is left open and unbuilt upon," the housing projects, "with their expanses of open land are . . . hard to control . . . and produce so much vacuity and trouble." With the open land typical of housing projects, "it is impossible to reconcile high densities with variety. Elevator apartments, and often very high ones, are unavoidable." Jacobs pointed out that though Stuyvesant Town, with 125 dwellings per net acre, was lower in density than Greenwich Village, its low ground coverage, with only 25 percent of the site covered by buildings, was forced into a rigid format. Perhaps "more imaginative architects and site planners" than those employed to design Stuyvesant Town could have come up with a more creative scheme, but such superficial changes would have made "no possible difference. . . . Mathematical impossibility would defy genius itself to introduce substantial variety at these low ground coverages with these densities."[201]

Jacobs was aware of—and indeed deliberately called attention to—the unorthodoxy of her plea for urban density and diversity: "To say that cities need high dwelling densities and high net ground coverages, as I am saying they do, is conventionally regarded as lower than taking sides with the man-eating shark."[202] But Jacobs, for all her praise of the wonders of Hudson Street, was no Pollyanna. Recognizing the reality of slums, she refused to acknowledge that wholesale clearance was the way to solve the problem:

> The method fails. At best, it merely shifts slums from here to there, adding its own tincture of extra hardship and disruption. At worst, it destroys neighborhoods where constructive and improving communities exist and where the situation calls for encouragement rather than destruction. Like Fight Blight and Conservation campaigns in neighborhoods declining into slums, slum shifting fails because it tries to overcome causes of trouble by diddling with symptoms.[203]

Jacobs argued that the way to stem the slide of a neighborhood into slumdom was to retain a considerable part of its population.

But as much as she believed in the redemption of old-time slum areas, Jacobs believed in the elimination of existing large-scale projects: "To think of salvaging or improving projects, *as projects*, is to repeat this root mistake. The aim should be to get that project, that patch upon the city, rewoven back into the fabric—and in the process of doing so, strengthening the surrounding fabric too." Large-scale public housing projects, Jacobs argued, "like any slums, need to be unslummed." To do this, Jacobs advocated reurbanizing the blank ground planes of the projects with "real streets which are to receive buildings and new uses along them; not 'promenades' through vacuous 'parks.'"[204] The new streets had to tie into the existing surrounding city grid and link all the buildings within the project's boundaries. "The apartment buildings," Jacobs noted, "which we have been thinking of as floating above the site, attached only by elevators and stairs, can become street buildings, with their ground floors redesigned and incorporated into streetside uses. . . . The general aim should be to bring in uses different from residence, because lack of enough mixed uses is precisely one of the causes of deadness, danger and plain inconvenience."[205]

Jacobs also recognized the problems that plagued the interiors of high-rise housing projects: the traplike corridors and the malfunctioning elevators. "The only solution I can see to [the elevator] problem, and to the related corridor problem, is to provide elevator attendants," a seemingly expensive solution yet one whose cost she said was minuscule compared to the capital investment already made to build such projects.[206] Finally, she argued, "To unslum, public housing projects must be capable of holding people by choice when they develop choice." To achieve this, both physical and administrative changes must occur, "which means that maximum income limits must be abandoned. It is not enough to raise limits; the tie of residency to income price tags must be abandoned altogether. So long as it remains, not only will all the most successful or lucky inexorably be drained away, but all the others must pyschologically identify themselves with their homes either as transients or as 'failures.'"[207]

Jacobs did not confine her argument to housing projects, nor even to issues raised by large-scale development. She tackled the traffic planners and spoke out for pedestrians, she argued for decentralized city government and she took a strong stand in favor of historic preservation. In her concluding chapter, Jacobs attempted to define "the kind of problem a city is," closing with a pessimistic view of postwar progress:

> City planning, as a field, has stagnated. It bustles but it does not advance. Today's plans show little if any perceptible progress in comparison with plans devised a generation ago. In transportation, either regional or local, nothing is offered which was not already offered and popularized in 1939 in the General Motors diorama at the New York World's Fair, and before that by Le Corbusier. None of today's pallid imitations of Rockefeller Center is as good as the original. . . . Even in conventional planning's *own given terms*, today's housing projects are no improvement, and usually a retrogression, in comparison with those of the 1930's.[208]

The essayist Marya Mannes was one of the first to write in praise of Jacobs's book, offering the readers of *Architectural Forum* a succinct summary of its arguments and predicting that they would "undoubtedly raise a howl from the planners. But to a city-dwelling layman [the book] is not only a fresh and fascinating look at our life but a revolutionary and revelatory volume of common sense."[209] In his rather skeptical review of the book, Herbert Gans, the sociologist whose own research Jacobs drew on, revealed himself somewhat out of touch with evolving behavior patterns among the urban middle class:

In proposing that cities be planned to stimulate an abundant street life, Mrs. Jacobs not only overestimates the power of planning in shaping behavior, but she in effect demands that middle-class people adopt working-class styles of family life, child rearing, and sociability. The truth is that the new forms of residential building—in suburb as well as city—are not products of orthodox planning theory, but expressions of the middle-class culture which guides the housing market, and which planners serve. Often the planners serve it too loyally, and they ignore the needs of a working-class population. Thus, Jane Jacobs' criticism is most relevant to the planning of public housing projects, for its middle-class designers have made no provision for the street life that these particular tenants probably want. But middle-class people, especially those raising children, do not want working class—or even bohemian—neighborhoods.[210]

Gans also quarreled with Jacobs's claim that people left when neighborhoods became dull, leading to the development of slums. Gans found "this analysis . . . too simple. People leave such areas not to seek diversity but to practice new life styles, and additional diversity would not persuade them to stay." While he applauded her distinction between low-rent areas, which may look dilapidated to the casual observer but were viable communities, and "perpetual slums," the term she used for areas in which physical decay was deep, he pointed out that such low-rent neighborhoods as the west part of Greenwich Village were numerically unimportant in most cities and that their population was mostly lily-white besides. "Their improvement cannot solve the problem of the real slums," which Gans laid at the door of deteriorating and overcrowded buildings.[211] Recognizing that the solution for these slums was the construction of new housing, Gans supported Jacobs's proposal for building housing on scattered sites and for developing a system of government subsidies that would foster economic, social and racial integration.

Even though he thought she overstated her case against the planners, Gans was a Jacobs enthusiast:

> No one, it is true, has stated these ideas as forcefully as she, or integrated them into an over-all approach before. The neighborhoods with which she is most concerned cannot serve as models for future planning, but the way in which she has observed them, the insights she has derived, and the principles she has inferred from her observations, can—and ought to be— adapted for use in planning cities and suburbs in the future. Her book is a pathbreaking achievement, and because she is so often right, I am all the more disappointed by the fact that it is also so often wrong.[212]

On February 8, 1962, as the third event of a five-part series titled "The Building Boom: Architecture in Decline," cosponsored by the Museum of Modern Art and the Architectural League, three speakers were invited to talk about cities from the platform of the museum's auditorium.[213] The evening, called "The Laws of the Asphalt Jungle," was well cast, with the architect-journalist Peter Blake serving as moderator. Two of the debaters were the architect-planner Edmund Bacon, Executive Director of Philadelphia's City Planning Commission, and the lawyer Edward Logue, Development Administrator of the Boston Redevelopment Authority. Logue, who was to become active and influential in New York's planning in the 1970s, was described by Walter McQuade, writing in the Nation, as "rather strongly a non-architect" and was said to have labeled architecture "a silly profession." Jane Jacobs was the "third star of the evening," as McQuade put it, describing

her not only as the author of a controversial book but as "a political heroine [who] when her own neighborhood in West Greenwich Village was marked for demolition by the City Planning Commission," together with her neighbors, "rose up and clawed back, forcing Mayor Wagner to call off the renewers."[214] Jacobs declined to deliver a speech from the rostrum but chose instead to comment from the speaker's table, waiting for her turn to "quickly, but not really unkindly, butcher both professional planners," who talked a Jacobs-derived line of humanistic antirenewalism but were in fact engaged in large-scale development projects.[215]

In addition to the discussion at the museum, the editors of Architectural Forum asked Logue and Edward Chase to debate the merits of Jacobs's book in the pages of their March 1962 issue. Logue attacked Jacobs as provincial: "Jane Jacobs' window on the world of cities is Hudson Street." For Logue, Jacobs's argument in behalf of what existed was a "plea for the status quo."[216] But according to Chase, a writer and advertising executive, Jacobs was on the right track: "In each generation there are relatively few books that set a whole body of specialists on their ear as Mrs. Jacobs' has. How have the planners reacted to the toppling of their dogmas? Rather badly, I would say. There is resort to ridicule; there is patronizing dismissal of Mrs. Jacobs as a crackpot anti-intellectual, antiplanner." As to the accusation that the book was fundamentally flawed because New York was its focus, Chase, while calling attention to Jacobs's wide range of references in it, argued that the claim was "essentially irrelevant. New York is America's preeminent urban confine. It is a splendid 'for instance.'" Chase also responded to the claim, made by Logue among others, that her stand against projects made Jacobs a fall guy for rightists who opposed any federal spending in cities. He argued that to say Jacobs should remain silent "because she discloses the malign effects of current urban renewal and public housing programs, and because these programs are unpopular with illiterate reactionaries and well-heeled, irresponsible suburbanites," was to invoke "the guilt-by-association McCarthy era."[217]

Chase argued on: "No writer has demonstrated a more intense devotion to and comprehension of city values than Mrs. Jacobs. None has shown more perception in unmasking the essentially antiurban bias of urban specialists, especially the old-hat sentimentalists who have failed to think through their 'Garden City' fabrication." Finally, Chase understood Jacobs's point of view more clearly than most: "The important thing is that Mrs. Jacobs would give city planning an entirely new orientation conceived in terms of ecology. . . . The approach is not unlike that of the naturalist. . . . Mrs. Jacobs has reaffirmed better than anyone else that perceptive social planning is the indispensable city planning."[218]

But it was the response of Lewis Mumford that was the most thoughtful, widely discussed and puzzling. Mumford's assessment in the New Yorker began on a surprising note, with a denunciation of the housing that had been built since the passage of the National Urban Renewal Act in 1948: "These large-scale operations have brought only small-scale benefits. The people who gain by the government's handout are not the displaced slum dwellers but the new investors and occupants." Unable to wholly dismiss the housing projects he had so long defended, Mumford claimed to have called attention to their limitations as early as 1942. He then went on to discuss Jacobs's book, which "has been an exciting theme for dinner-table conversation all over the country this past year." Mumford first encountered Jacobs at a Harvard conference where her direct style "blew like a fresh, off-shore breeze to present a picture, dramatic but not distorted, of the results of displacing large neighborhood populations to facilitate large-scale building. . . . Mrs. Jacobs gave firm shape to a misgiving that many people had begun to express. But she saw more deeply into the plight of both those who were evicted and those who came back to living in homogenized and sterilized barracks."[219]

Despite Mumford's praise of Jacobs, he went on to write that whereas "'Sense and Sensibility' could have been the title of her Harvard discourse," her new book "comes close to deserving the secondary title of 'Pride and Prejudice.'" He found her outlook to be overly concerned with the prevention of criminal violence and lacking in a "total view of the great metropolis. . . . She beholds it just in fragments." Replying to Jacobs's argument from the Olympian height of his generation's view, Mumford claimed to have lived "in every kind of neighborhood and in every type of housing . . . [but] like a majority of my fellow citizens, I am still unregenerate enough to prefer the quiet flat with a back garden . . . the kind of well-planned neighborhood Mrs. Jacobs despises."[220]

Mumford found Jacobs's argument not merely anti-architectural but anti-aesthetic:

Mrs. Jacobs has jumped from the quite defensible position that good physical structures and handsome design are not everything in city planning to the callow notion that they do not matter at all. That beauty, order, spaciousness, clarity of purpose may be worth having for their direct effect on the human spirit even if they do not promote dynamism, increase the turnover of goods, or reduce criminal violence seems not to occur to Mrs. Jacobs. This is aesthetic philistinism with a vengeance.[221]

Not surprisingly, it was Jacobs's espousal of high-density urbanism that was most offensive to Mumford, the anti-urban city planning theorist who twenty-five years before had left New York for an upstate farm. Although Mumford was forced to acknowledge that Jacobs's emphasis on neighborhood life and her support of local government was sound, he could not accept her fundamental pragmatism, and he concluded his review with the assertion:

One cannot control destructive automatisms at the top unless one begins with the smallest units and restores life and initiative to them—to the person as a responsible human being, to the neighborhood as the primary organ not merely of social life but of moral behavior, and finally to the city, as an organic embodiment of the common life, in ecological balance with other cities, big and little, within the larger region in which they lie. A quick, purely local answer to these problems is no better than applying a homemade poultice for the cure of a cancer. And that, I am afraid, is what the more "original" Jacobean proposals in The Death and Life of Great American Cities comes to.[222]

Mumford's was the most august voice raised against Jacobs, but he was by no means alone among serious commentators in criticizing her. Though essentially sympathetic to Jacobs's point of view, Wolf Von Eckardt, the architecture critic and historian, felt obliged to point out that "rats, slumlords, stench, and frustration [were] the other side of the romantic coin" of what he called Jane Jacobism, a phenomenon "which, in a strange alliance of liberals and reactionaries, has mounted a crusade against the federal urban renewal bulldozers. At its best, this crusade keeps charging the drab old windmills of public housing projects. . . . At its worst, it represents the same profit-greedy interests that turned the romantic old neighborhoods into slums

in the first place."[223] Sibyl Moholy-Nagy, the critic and historian, laced into Jacobs for her presumed anti-architectural stance. In a confused but impassioned letter to the Architectural Forum's editors, Moholy-Nagy, echoing Ayn Rand's The Fountainhead, grew irate over Jacobs's claim that "a city cannot be a work of art."[224]

Roger Starr, the conservative and contrary-minded urbanist, also had very little tolerance for Jacobs's point of view. In response to her concept of mixed primary uses, where industrial and residential uses were intermingled, Starr argued:

The connection between the mixed uses and the charms of the West Village was . . . not that the intrusion of industry into a residence section was attractive; but rather that the mixed uses were literally repulsive. In other old but unmixed sections of the city, the market value of older buildings had long since soared; if the land itself had become very valuable, the old house had long since given way to apartment house development. To confuse the characteristic that led to the survival of the buildings with the qualities that made them beautiful is to succumb to a curious kind of logical fallacy, much as though Mrs. Jacobs had visited Pompeii and concluded that nothing makes a city so beautiful as covering it with ashes.[225]

The liberal establishment outside those specifically concerned with architecture and urbanism also rejected her arguments, seeing them as a justification for conservative antipathy to welfare, urban renewal and other social entitlements. But in contrast to these voices of negativism, there was the public who embraced Jacobs and her book. To New Yorkers, Jacobs was a breath of fresh air; she was "one of us." And she rescued the city and planning as a whole from the Mumfordian gloom that had hung over it since the 1930s. Mumford's urbanism was anti-city. He believed in villages and towns, not metropolises. But Jane Jacobs was the opposite; since the publication of her book, as Jerome Charyn put it, "our sense of the city has never been the same."[226]

In 1969 Jacobs published a second book, The Economy of Cities, in which, in attempting to understand why "some cities grow and others stagnate and decay," she argued that "rural economies, including agricultural work, are directly built upon city economies and city work," a reversal of the generally held view.[227] This book was not as specifically focused on New York as her first had been; and, published at a time when Americans were concerned with the war in Vietnam and the struggle to keep cities from blowing themselves apart in race and antiwar riots, it did not enjoy anything like the impact of its predecessor. Nonetheless, The Economy of Cities contained some pithy observations about New York, most notably that the $300 million spent building housing in Harlem would have been better spent investing in local minority enterprise.

Styles and Stylists

To the new generation that would come to political and cultural power after World War II, the stripped-down International Style Modernism that originated in Europe in the 1920s and slowly began to influence American architecture a decade later perfectly expressed the corporate giantism that dominated American business practice. As nearly as any structure, Raymond Hood's McGraw-Hill Building (1931) had pioneered this trend in New York, but coming at the end of the 1920s building boom it understandably had no impact, as virtually no corporate buildings were built in the city for the next fifteen years.[228] But by the late 1940s, as the swaggering individual entrepreneur of the past was transformed into the team-playing corporate man in the gray flannel suit, so the instantly identifiable cathedrals of commerce that exemplified the city's architecture from 1900 to 1929 gave way to an architecture that celebrated repetition to the point of anonymity. The nearly identical glass-and-steel office buildings that dominated New York's architecture from 1950 to 1970 confirmed the generally held belief that cities were little more than machines for working in. Thus the high social, urban and technological ideals of European Modernism's leading architects—Walter Gropius, Le Corbusier and Ludwig Mies van der Rohe—were subverted to serve the purposes of expedient commercialism, its aesthetics reduced to a singular, obsessive minimalism.

In 1940 the field of battle between traditionalism and Modernism was still quite open. When the Architectural League's "Versus" exhibition devoted one floor to traditional work and another to Modernist work, each contained accomplished examples. But the Modernists, represented by houses designed by Walter Gropius, Marcel Breuer, George Howe, Edward Durell Stone, Frank Lloyd Wright and William Wurster, clearly had the edge, with fresh images that seemed to render the traditional styles weak and sentimental by comparison and their practitioners lacking in conviction.[229] By war's end, Modernism seemed clearly victorious, causing even traditionalists to modify their approach and attempt a synthesis. This synthetic trend was initiated in the 1930s, when architects began to strip the forms of Classicism while retaining its basic compositional grammar to create work that was at once traditional and spare. Two commercial buildings, both completed in 1950 and both the work of firms that had produced some of the most significant and memorable buildings of the interwar period, illustrated this attempt to hybridize what many believed to be incompatible styles: Shreve, Lamb & Harmon Associates' headquarters for the Mutual of New York Insurance Company (see chapter 5) and Walker & Poor's Parke-Bernet Galleries (see chapter 11).

Despite the continued construction of buildings that to varying degrees explicitly maintained formal links to the past, it was International Style Modernism, first directly experienced by a broad American audience at the New York World's Fair of 1939–40, that would come to dominate postwar architecture in New York. Whereas Modern Classicism sought to marry traditional architecture and urbanistic conventions with a minimalistic and machine-inspired aesthetic that seemed an appropriate expression of contemporary conditions, International Style Modernism sought to fully supersede old aesthetic systems and criteria, most often dispensing with symmetrical composition, planning hierarchies and applied ornament. Replacing fundamental aspects of traditional architecture, including the representation of natural forms and building typology, International Style Modernism attempted to transform all aesthetic and functional requirements into pure geometry. Denying architecture its validity as a narrative art, International Style Modernists asserted that their approach was not a style but simply a way of building. In some sense they were right; a technology-driven architecture inevitably became highly self-referential. At the same time, as disseminated in postwar America, International Style Modernism was less of an ideology and certainly far less of a utopian blueprint for a brave new world than it had been in prewar Europe, and more of a style. And, like all styles, it would undergo a period of ascendancy and a period of decline. So it was that in America, and preeminently in New York, International

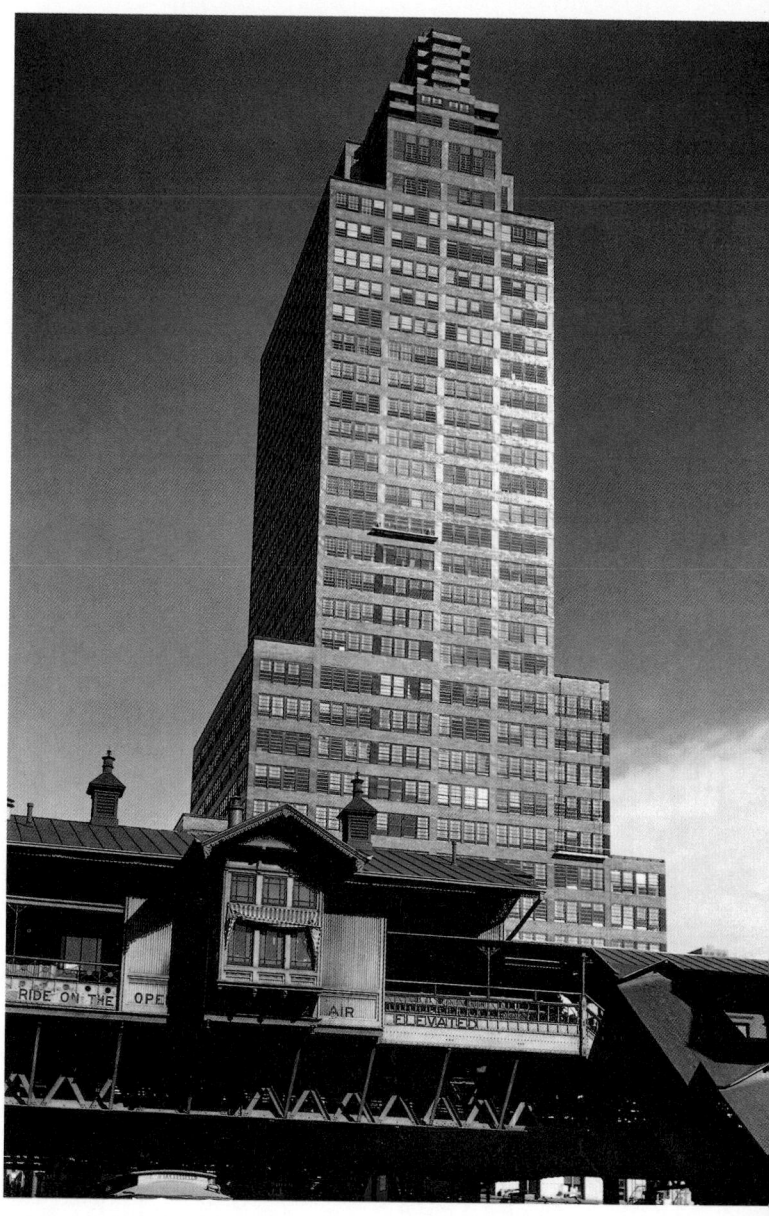

McGraw-Hill Building, 330 West Forty-second Street. Raymond Hood, Godley & Fouilhoux, 1931. View to the southeast from Ninth Avenue. Abbott. MCNY

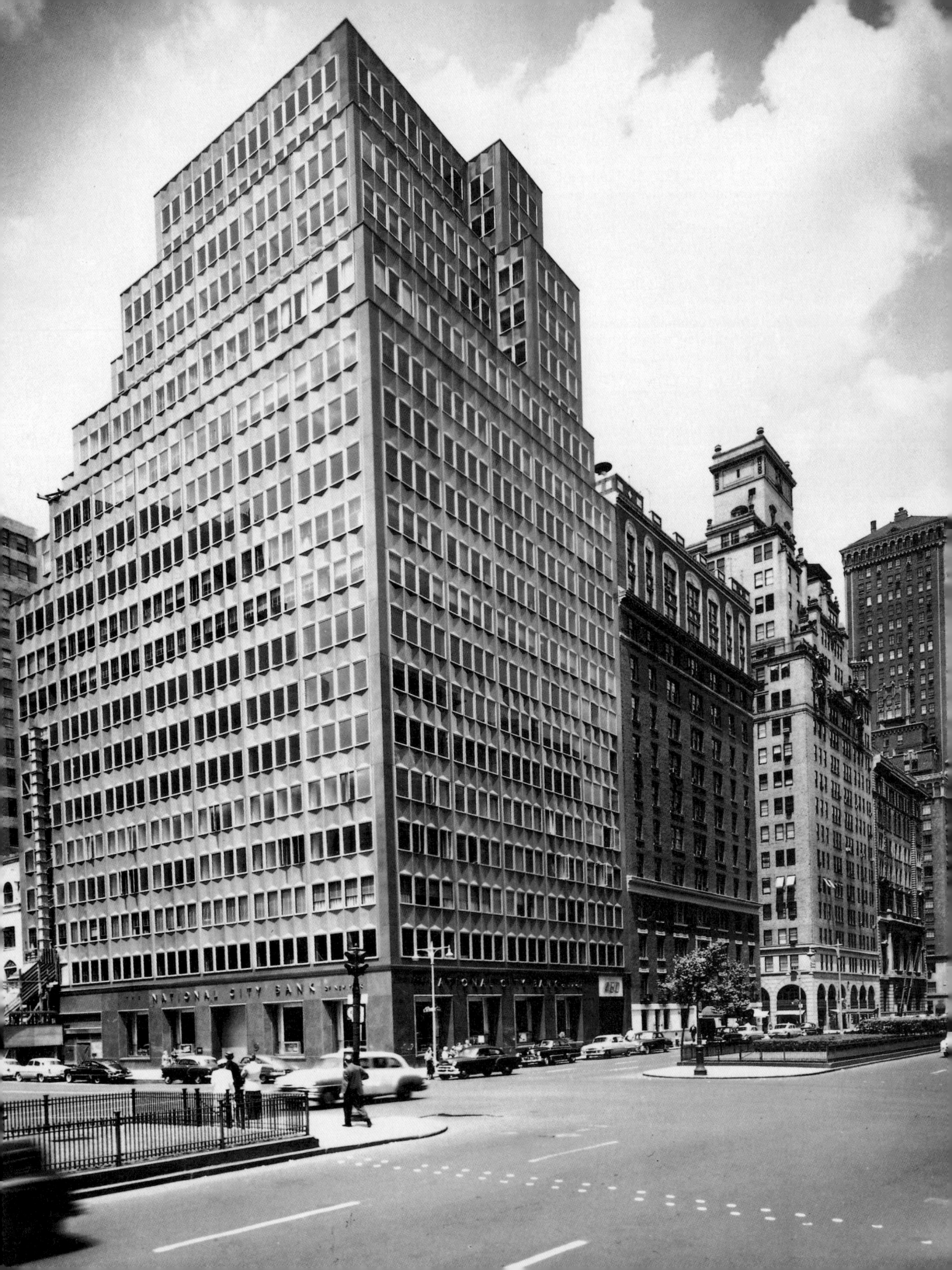

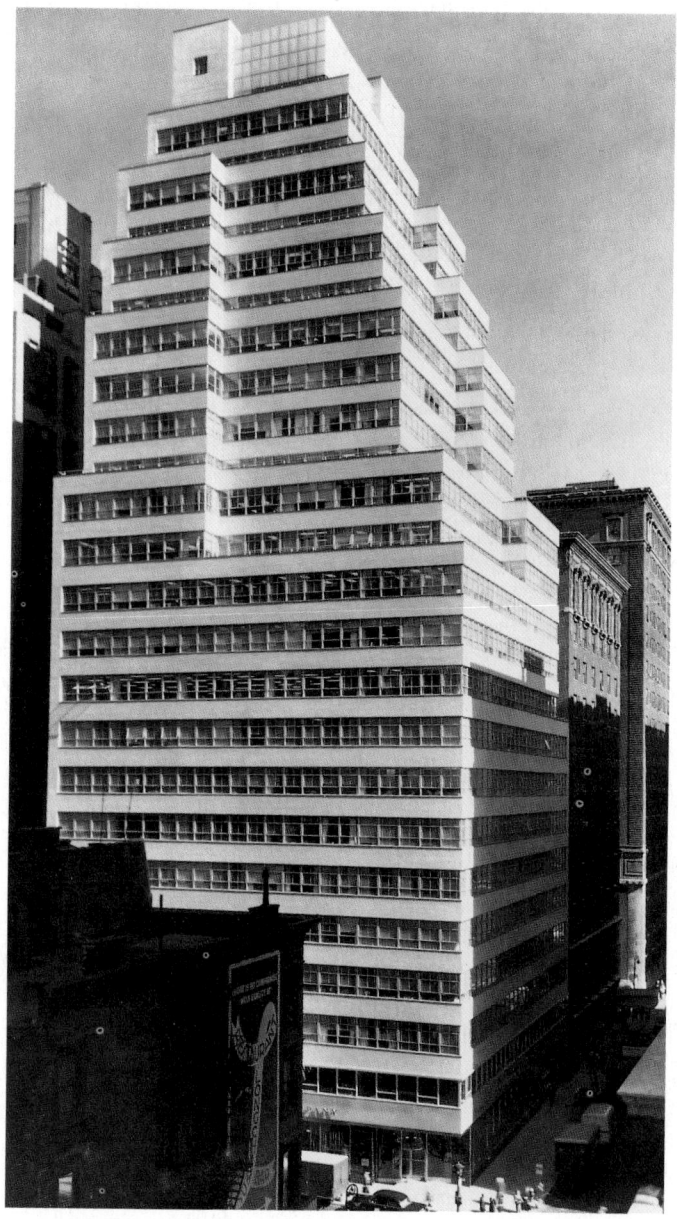

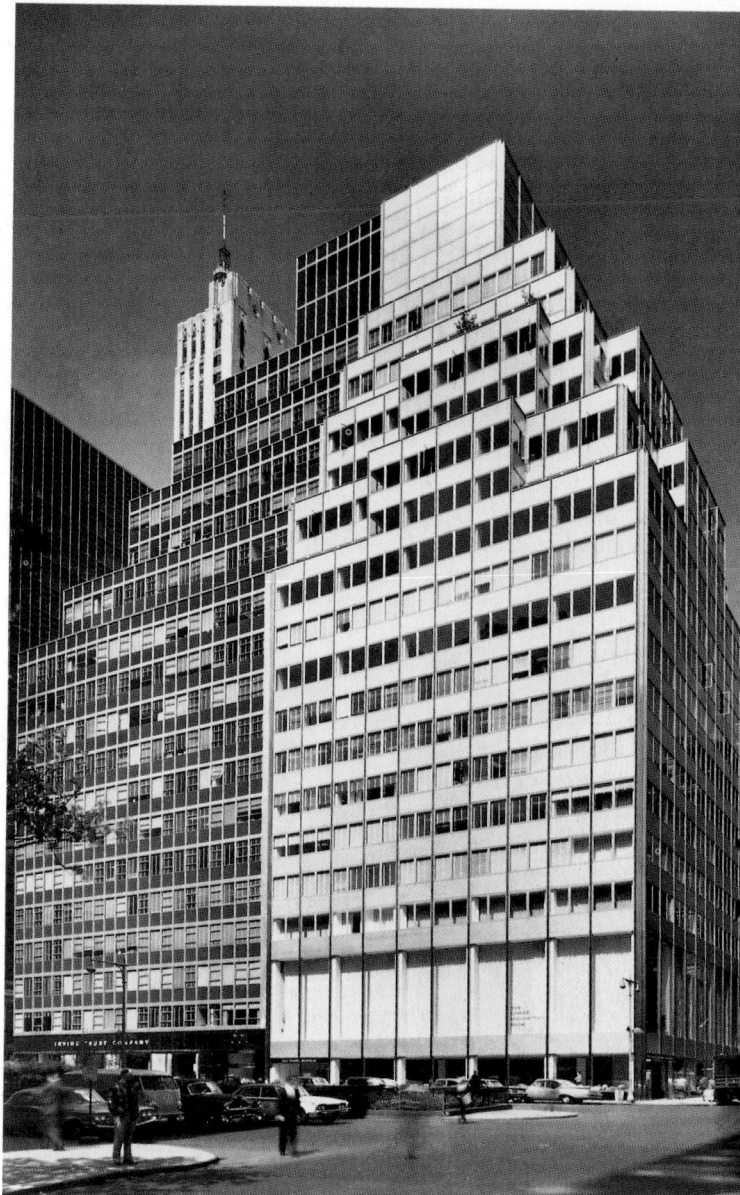

Left: 460 Park Avenue, northwest corner of East Fifty-seventh Street. Emery Roth & Sons, 1955. View to the northwest. Langley. ERS

Top left: 415 Madison Avenue, northeast corner of East Forty-eighth Street. Emery Roth & Sons, 1956. View to the east. ERS

Top right: 400 Park Avenue (1958), on the left, and 410 Park Avenue (1959), on the right, East Fifty-fourth to East Fifty-fifth Street. Emery Roth & Sons. View to the southwest. Studly. ERS

Style Modernism, adapted to the problems of the high-rise office building—the quintessential building type of the twentieth century—reached its zenith of achievement and influence in the 1950s and 1960s and began to colapse in the 1970s.

In the 1930s the International Style's rightness for America was argued largely on sociological grounds, particularly in the realm of housing, where it was presumed that its adoption would be accompanied by, and indeed would stimulate, a more equitable distribution of wealth and a greater realization of social justice. But after World War II the argument was refocused, perhaps more logically, on the corporate arena; it was argued that only International Style Modernism could directly and honestly express the genius of twentieth-century capitalism. At the same time, the wholesale adoption of International Style Modernism by corporate America would have a practical, and some would feel insidious, motivation: the increased cost of the labor required in a traditionally designed building and the comparatively decreased cost of mass-produced materials used in a Modernist building gave Modernism a competitive financial edge. By the early 1960s the dictum attributed to Ludwig Mies van der Rohe, "Less is more," had crudely, perhaps shrewdly, been translated into "Less costs less."

No sector of the American economy embraced architectural Modernism more wholeheartedly than big business. In 1957 the Museum of Modern Art reflected the triumph of its by-then historical mission to legitimize the new aesthetic with an exhibition, "Buildings for Business and Government," featuring six Modernist buildings, including the Seagram Building and the Chase Manhattan Bank headquarters.[230] Two firms—Skidmore, Owings & Merrill and Emery Roth & Sons—would quickly come to be New York's principal exponents of what would soon be labeled Corporate Modernism, in effect defining the style as the sheer number of their projects transformed entire precincts of the city.

While the obsessively minimalist aesthetic of Skidmore, Owings & Merrill, widely known as SOM and derided by many as "three blind Mies," was giving architectural definition to corporate America, the firm was also bringing an unprecedented degree of corporate management and size to architectural practice.[231] Given the economic climate of the 1930s and the building slowdown of the early 1940s, the firm's growth had been nothing short of explosive: founded in 1936, by 1974 SOM employed a professional staff of approximately one thousand people in seven principal offices in the United States as well as in Paris. SOM began when Louis Skidmore formed a Chicago-based architectural firm with his brother-in-law, Nathaniel Owings; the two already had a proven track record of effective collaboration, having worked together in 1933 on Chicago's Century of Progress Exposition. Seeking large-scale projects, the partners soon adopted an interdisciplinary approach, teaming up with the engineer John Merrill in 1939.

Though the founding partners were often self-effacing concerning their design talents, they did tout their ability in one essential aspect of corporate organization—personnel management—asserting that they could "produce the people who produce the architecture."[232] The most telling proof of their ability to discern and foster talent and turn it into profit was the presence of Gordon Bunshaft, who in 1937, at the age of twenty-eight, was hired as the chief designer of Skidmore and Owings's newly established New York office, formed in response to a commission from the American Radiator Company but soon sustained by commissions for the New York World's Fair of 1939–40.[233] Bunshaft had completed both his undergraduate

and graduate studies in architecture at the Massachusetts Institute of Technology and had endured brief, unsatisfying stints with several architects, including Edward Durell Stone, before landing the job with SOM. Once there, he was quick to reach artistic maturity. He was principally responsible for the design of many of the firm's most important works, including Lever House (1952) and the Manufacturers Trust branch on Fifth Avenue (1954), both of which were immediately acknowledged as undisputed landmarks of Corporate Modernism (see chapter 5). As Bunshaft's biographer, Carol Herselle Krinsky, has observed:

> Throughout the Bunshaft years, there is recognizable in the vast production of SOM a sufficient coherence that one might identify a corporate agenda: a commitment to the inventions and abstract formal constructs of modernism; a will to serve, unstintingly, the large corporate institutions through rationalized and often innovative planning; and an unswerving pursuit of available technology. . . . SOM set the standard for postwar office buildings in the United States, which in effect meant the world.[234]

The sheer volume and consistency of SOM's carefully modulated interpretation of International Style Modernism distinguished the firm's output; the firm's work also strongly embodied Modernism's urbanistic agenda. As the critic and historian Henry-Russell Hitchcock stated in 1963, the significance of the firm's work lay

> not in the creation of individual structures of intense personal expression . . . conceived in isolation from an urban context and serving rather specialized cultural functions, but in the rebuilding of our cities. . . . Although their most conspicuous works have perforce been fitted into the inherited urban scene with only some slight amelioration of the immediate neighborhood by the introduction of open plazas at the base and crisper outlines at the top, they have provided many of the most important and useful architectural ingredients of the later 20th-century city.[235]

Though SOM was doubtless *the* corporate architecture firm catering to high-profile clients, Emery Roth & Sons provided the bread-and-butter vernacular buildings that would even more noticeably transform whole sections of Manhattan from stone to glass. At the outset of his career the firm's founder, Hungarian-born Emery Roth, had designed the Saxony apartment house (1901)[236] and the Hotel Belleclaire (1903).[237] His Ritz Tower (1925) with Thomas Hastings, the Oliver Cromwell (1927), the San Remo (1930) and, in collaboration with Margon & Holder, the Eldorado (1931) were each landmarks of the interwar skyline.[238] Because Roth was able to keep busy in the 1930s, his firm was one of the few large, well-organized, highly efficient organizations available to postwar developers. In the early 1920s Roth brought his son Julian into the firm, and in 1928, his younger son Richard, who had just graduated from the Massachusetts Institute of Technology, also joined the firm. By the late 1930s both sons had become partners, though the firm's name did not change to Emery Roth & Sons until 1947. Upon their father's death the following year, Julian and Richard took over.

The Look Building (1949), 488 Madison Avenue, was the firm's first architecturally significant building completed after its founder's death. Its asymmetrically arranged setbacks and curve-cornered masonry spandrels rendered it a distinctive addition to midtown, and to some extent a stylistic trendsetter. The Roths followed up with other buildings echoing Look's design, but it was their adoption of the glass-and-metal curtain wall to low-budget speculative office buildings that would become their signature. The Roth-designed glass-and-metal box would soon be a ubiquitous feature of the city, particularly in east mid-town, where real estate activity during the 1950s and 1960s was intense. Between 1950 and 1970 the Roths completed seventy New York office buildings, collectively containing in excess of thirty million square feet of space, or half of the total amount of office space created during that period. In 1967 Ada Louise Huxtable could rightly state that the Roths were "as responsible for the face of modern New York as Sixtus V was for baroque Rome."[239]

While Dennis Duggan was arguably correct when, writing in the *New York Herald Tribune* in 1963, he stated that "The Roths, man and boys, have had more to do with the way New York has looked over the last half-century than any other archi-tectural office that ever wielded a T-square," it was, from the real estate developer's or client's point of view, not so much the wrapping of a Roth building as its "belly" that made it desirable. Roth buildings were distinguished first and foremost by their faultless provision of the maximum amount of rentable space; furthermore, they were characterized by a flexibility of plan and imaginative use of state-of-the-art technology, including high-speed elevators and year-round climate control. Indeed, so su-perior was the Roths' ability to design a skyscraper's "belly" that, beginning in the mid-1960s, the firm was hired to do "produc-tion work," that is, to serve as associate architects who produced the working drawings for high-profile buildings designed by well-known architects. The Roths were associate architects for Walter Gropius and Pietro Belluschi's Pan Am Building (1963), Edward Durell Stone's General Motors Building (1968), Minoru Yamasaki's World Trade Center (1972–77) and Hugh Stubbins's Citicorp Center (1977).

In 1963 Richard Roth flatly stated that "What separates the men from the boys in skyscraper architecture is how these inte-rior components fit together. In one building, everything will dovetail; in another you'll have the air-conditioning tripping over the plumbing."[240] Richard Roth would later somewhat de-fensively charge, "we are sometimes criticized unfairly, because of the way in which we are judged: ours is not a field of archi-tecture in which we create or try to create masterpieces. The en-tire endeavor in our office is to create the best that can be pro-duced within the restrictions that are placed upon us; and these restrictions are seldom those of our client, but rather of lending institutions, economics and municipal authorities' laws."[241] the exterior banality of many of the Roths' buildings was further jus-tified not only on practical and logistical grounds but on the rather curious notion that to make aesthetic considerations para-mount was equivalent to denying architecture its basic human dimension. Richard Roth stated that "A facade is what it says—a face. All of us are taught not to judge a person by appearance. Well, the same is true of a building. A building is not a picture. It is almost flesh and blood, like its occupants." Perhaps hinting at his own frustration that architectural imagination had not more powerfully surpassed the limits of circumstance in his firm's work, Roth candidly stated that "Architecture reflects society, and this is not a great age."[242]

Roth was wrong: the 1950s and 1960s were a great age—the great age of the American corporation—and the glass-and-metal Modernist high rise became one of its principal representations, just as the gray flannel suit became its sartorial signature. In the interwar period, in contrast, the skyscraper type had been bril-liantly exploited as a kind of inhabited billboard, an instantly identifiable symbol of a corporation's pride in its product, which

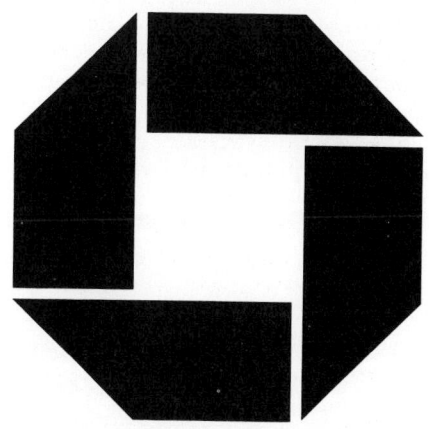

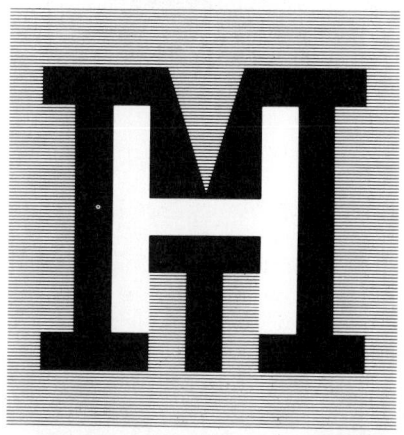

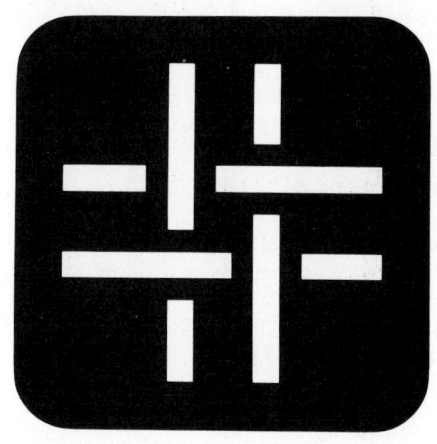

Corporate logos. Thomas Geismar. From top to bottom: Chase Manhattan Bank (1960), Manufacturers Hanover Trust Co. (1961), Burlington Industries (1966). CG

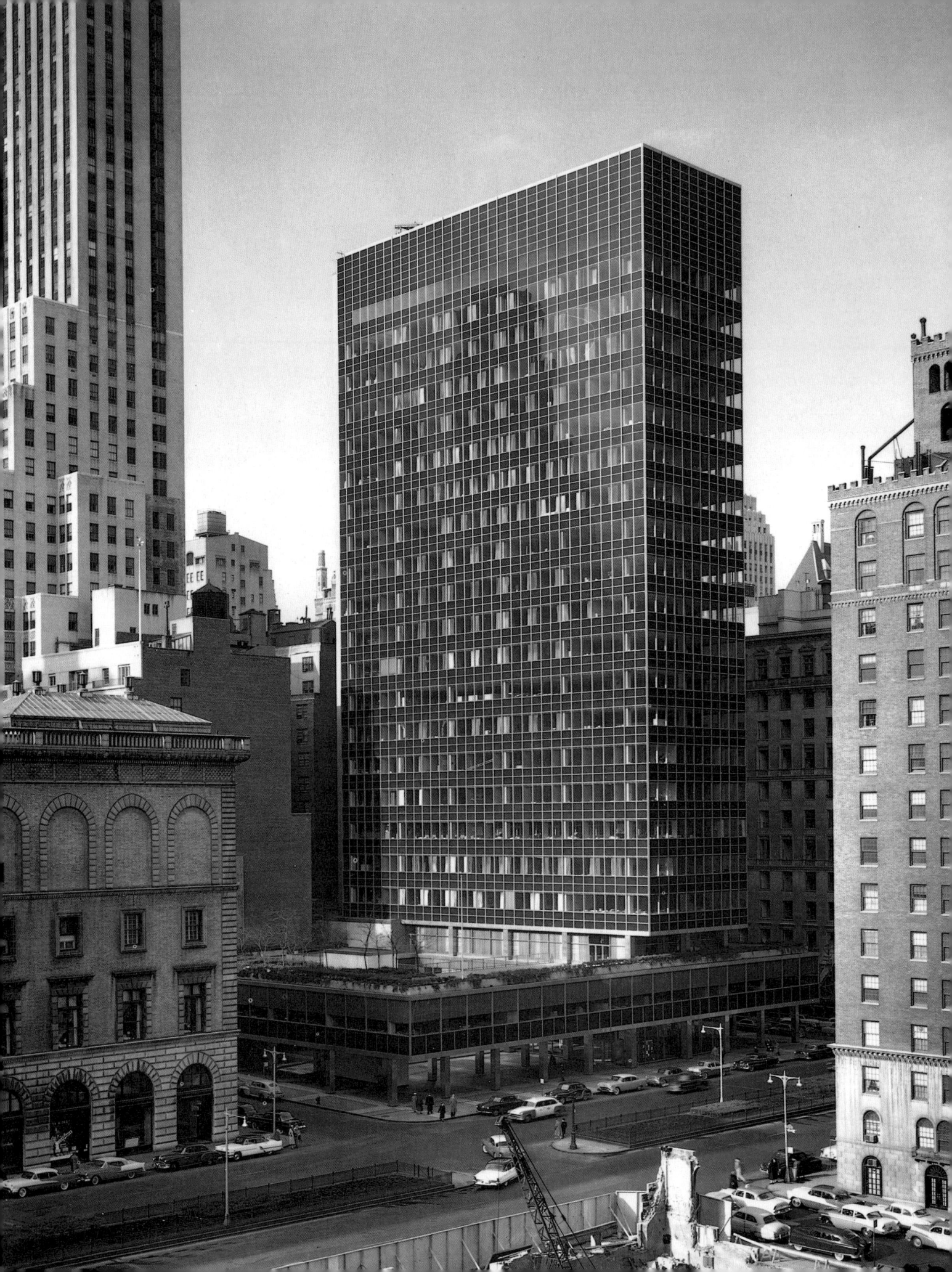

was sometimes celebrated in the building's elaborate ornamental embellishments, as for example in the case of William Van Alen's Chrysler Building (1930).[243] The 1920s and early 1930s corporate building was monumental and nearly religious in its aspirational power. But in the postwar period the proud, spire-topped tower was generally denigrated. What was valued was almost oxymoronic: anonymously detailed, blandly profiled, bulky buildings, amounting to little more than real estate ventures, were touted as proud corporate symbols. Because these were so much alike, a new design industry called "corporate identity" evolved, in which graphic designers such as Ivan Chermayeff and Thomas Geismar collaborated with marketing specialists to create easily identifiable and memorable symbols—corporate logos—with which to embellish office buildings and letterheads and advertisement. The era's conspicuously anonymous Corporate Modernist buildings seemed to visually make way for the graphic designer's contribution, as if the building were a bland piece of stationery awaiting the addition of a letterhead.

Despite the essential homogeneity of so much postwar corporate architecture, there were two distinct phases in its development. In the first phase, Corporate Modernism took up the streamlined, horizontally banded, strip-windowed aesthetic of the work initially conceptualized in Europe during the 1920s and early 1930s by such German architects as Erich Mendelsohn, whose Schocken department store (1928–29) in Chemnitz and Columbus Haus office building (1931) in Berlin were particularly influential.[244] William Lescaze favored this approach in his unrealized project for CBS in New York (1935), in his executed CBS Building (1936–38) in Hollywood, California, in his Longfellow Building (1941) in Washington, D.C., and in his 711 Third Avenue (1954–56) office building.[245] This style was also used by Emery Roth & Sons in their Look Building. In its second, longer, and more prolific phase, Corporate Modernism was epitomized by a single construction feature: the almost neutral, gridded glass-and-metal curtain wall. The innovation was derived from Le Corbusier's *pan verre*, first realized at the Salvation Army Building in Paris (1929–33).[246] The feature also referred back to Mies van der Rohe's unrealized 1919 and 1921 skyscraper projects, as well as Willis Polk's Hallidie Building (1917), San Francisco, which was rediscovered as a progenitor of the type.[247]

Gordon Bunshaft's Lever House pioneered the glass curtain wall in New York, but existing fire laws necessitated that brick walls be built behind the glass to the height of parapets, thus reducing the expanse of view glass, seen from within the building, to an amount not significantly greater than that in a standard masonry-clad building with punched windows. Ironically, by the time municipal building codes permitted a closer approximation of the crystalline towers that European architects had first envisioned following World War I, the need for a visual structure had modified that ideal. Thus Mies van der Rohe's Seagram Building of 1958, in which exterior walls were glazed nearly floor to ceiling, incorporated a meticulously detailed curtain wall, fabricated not of comparatively cheap steel or aluminum but of bronze, visible on the building's facades. This established a visual antiphony between solidity and transparency as it elevated the I-beam of ordinary engineering to the level of a Classical order within a rigorously defined and articulated Modernism. In this sense, Mies's design was much more in the Classically inspired tradition of Louis Sullivan's office buildings of the 1890s, such as his Bayard Building (1897) in New York.[248]

By the late 1950s International Style Modernism, having been adopted by a wide segment of the building community

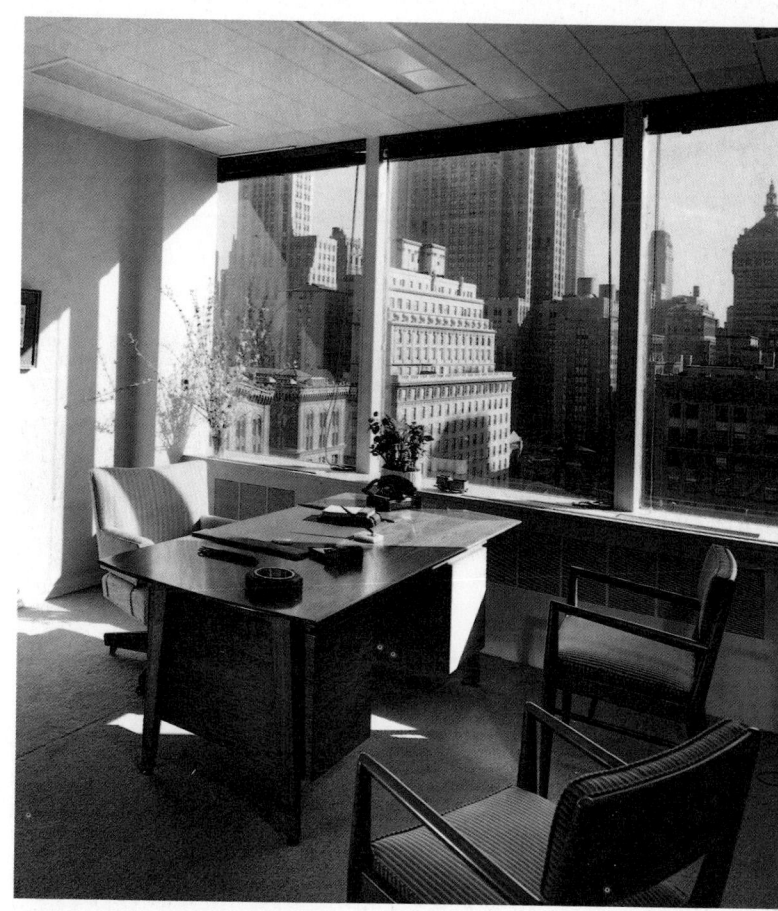

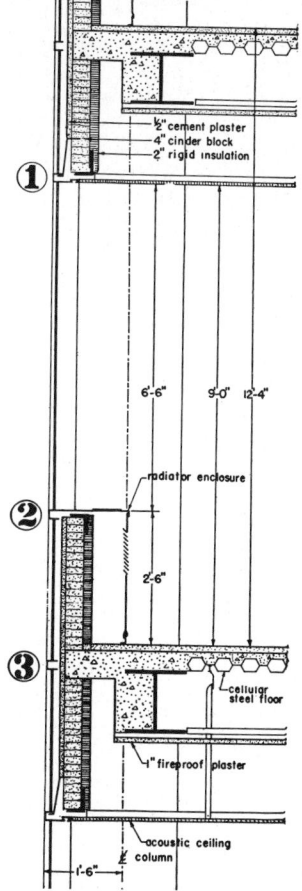

Far left: Lever House, 390 Park Avenue, East Fifty-third to East Fifty-fourth Street. Skidmore, Owings & Merrill, 1952. View to the northwest. Stoller. ©ESTO

Above: Lever House. Office interior. View to the southeast. SOM

Left: Lever House. Cross-section of curtain wall. SOM

53

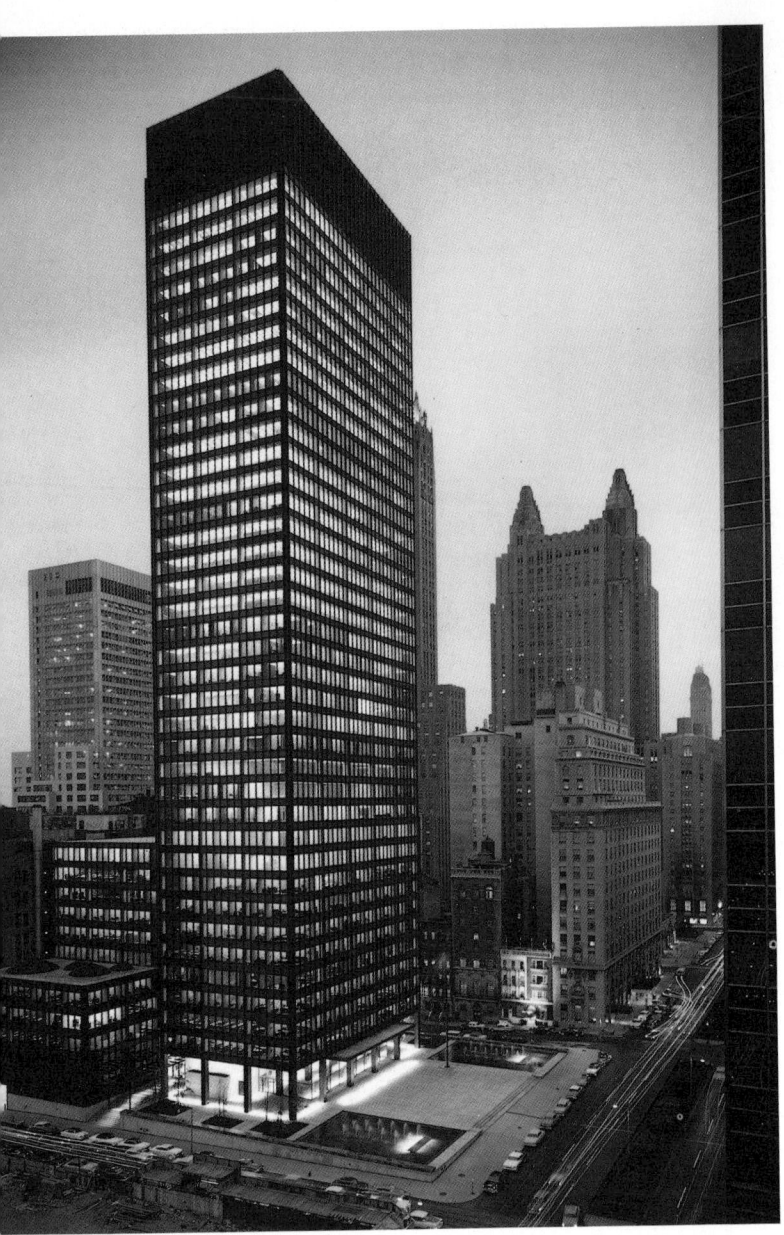

Seagram Building, 375 Park Avenue, East Fifty-second to East Fifty-third Street. Ludwig Mies van der Rohe, Philip Johnson and Kahn & Jacobs, 1958. View to the southeast. Stoller. ©ESTO

with breathtaking speed, began to lose its force as polemic. Moreover, its popularity with the public, even at its peak never very great, was now ebbing. As an alternative to the ahistoricism of the International Style, a new approach, Historicist Modernism, began to emerge, which, by emphasizing planning and stylistic continuities with the modern tradition as a whole, argued for the enduring validity of Classicism. Perhaps not surprisingly, this new trend was enthusiastically taken up by institutional clients such as Lincoln Center, for whom a tradition-based architecture communicated a sense of stability and permanence, in contrast to Corporate Modernism's obsession with structural lightness, transparency and impermanence.

As Historicist Modernism began to emerge, Philip Johnson, whose polemicizing on behalf of the International Style had been so effective in its early days, became both an ardent polemicist for and practitioner of the new approach. While not directly repudiating the tenets of the International Style, Johnson's exhortation that one "cannot *not* know history" was clearly reflected in his work at Lincoln Center. There he led his fellow architects, including Wallace K. Harrison and Max Abramovitz, in the direction of more Classically designed buildings and a more Classical form of urbanism, exemplified by his proposal to construct an enclosing colonnade to connect and unify the center's constituent buildings. Johnson would later state that while he expected his proposal to be defeated, "that wasn't the point."[249] The point, it seemed, was to relearn Classical lessons concerning not only compositional and planning principles but also architecture's role as a narrative art that surpassed considerations of function and building technology. Johnson's design for the New York State Theater (1964) was the most historically referential of the center's buildings. In 1960, while the theater's design was under way, Johnson stated that the building "will look very much like the Altes Museum in Berlin. . . . They will probably tell me I am a fascist."[250] Though the critical response to the completed building was mixed, Johnson had decisively established a direction, or at least contributed mightily to restoring architecture's participation in a dialogue across time. Designed more or less concurrently with Johnson's theater, Edward Durell Stone's Gallery of Modern Art (1964), built nearby at Two Columbus Circle for the grocery store heir and art patron Huntington Hartford, similarly mined the architectural past for inspiration. Stone's museum was more unabashedly decorative, constituting a Venetian-derived vertical palazzo. Having tired of the International Style's ascetic formalism, the critic Olga Gueft found the design to be one that "only a Bauhaus ogre with hardened arteries could fail to smile at."[251]

Nine years later Minoru Yamasaki's 110-story twin towers at the World Trade Center took Historicist Modernism into the corporate realm. The style was a shotgun marriage between the austerity of the by-then iconic Seagram Building and the delicately decorative, Gothic-inspired motifs that Yamasaki had been exploring for a decade or more on a much smaller scale, perhaps best represented by his work at Wayne State University (1958) in Detroit.[252] Thin columns at the base of each building formed pointed-arch arcades that were surmounted by grilles of thinner piers rising to the building's full height. Visually, the transition from base to shaft, though finely articulated, seemed awkward at best; indeed the idea of lifting a 110-story building on narrow stilts seemed inherently ungainly and a bit precarious. Metaphorically, the composition was more disturbing still. The towers' historicism failed to provide a sturdy foundation for the Modernist superstructure; instead, the past appeared like an obligatory but unwanted guest. Far from imbuing the modern

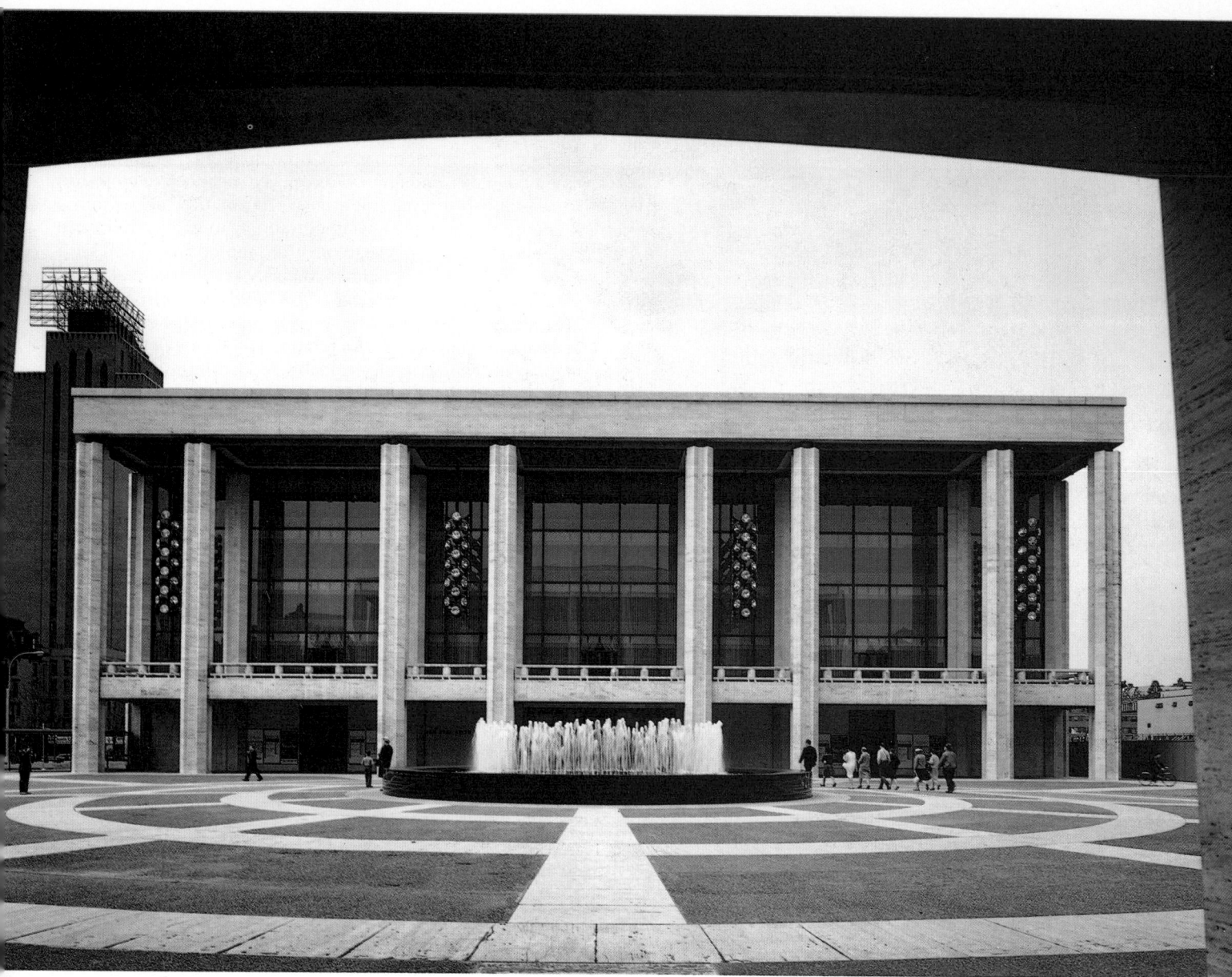

New York State Theater, Lincoln Center, southwest corner of Columbus Avenue and West Sixty-third Street. Philip Johnson, 1964. View to the south from Philharmonic Hall (Max Abramovitz, 1961). Stoller. ©ESTO

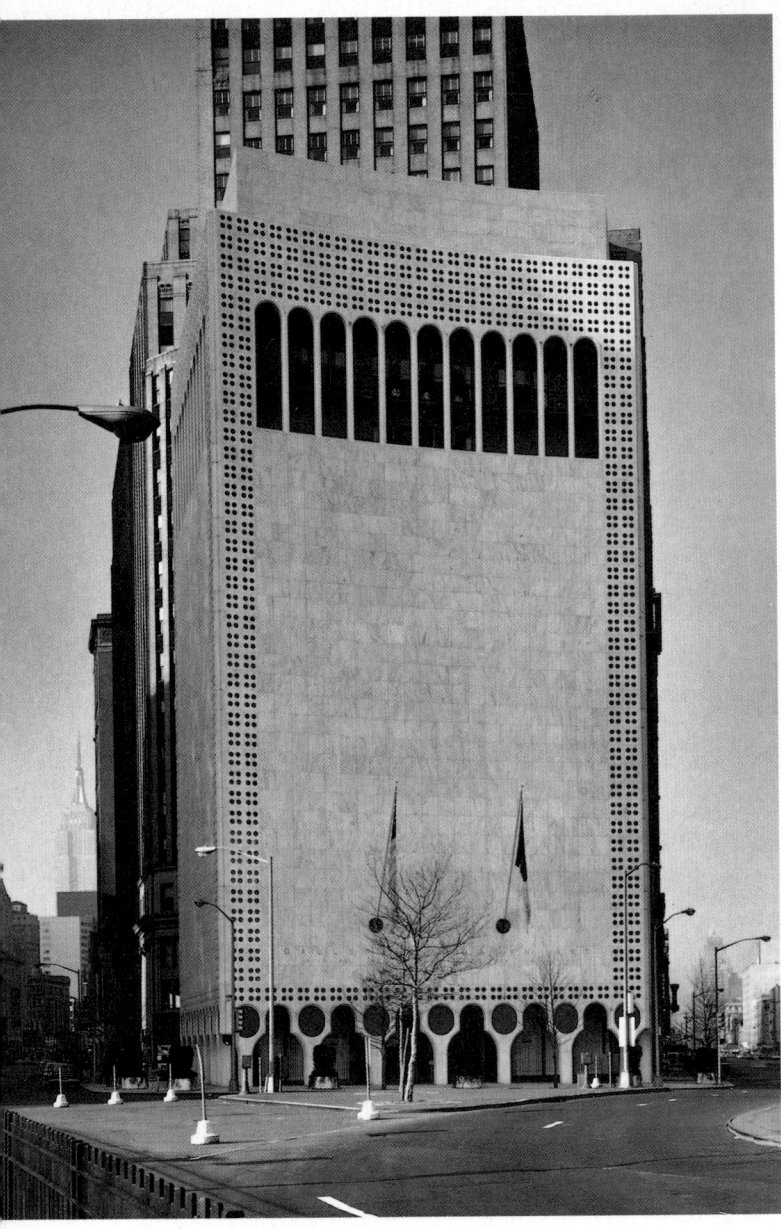

Above: Gallery of Modern Art, Two Columbus Circle. Edward Durell Stone, 1964. View to the south. Stoller. ©ESTO

Right: One (left) and Two (right) World Trade Center, Church to West Street, Liberty to Vesey Street. Minoru Yamasaki and Emery Roth & Sons, 1973. View to the east across the Hudson River from Jersey City, New Jersey. Molitor. JWM

present with a spiritual quality, the Gothic past appeared at best quaint, at worst ersatz.

While Historicist Modernism was the most prevalent antidote to Corporate Modernism in New York, another trend, more visible elsewhere but not without important representation in the city, was also emerging—that of an expressive or thematic Modernism. This approach was compellingly advocated in many buildings (and few words) by Eero Saarinen, who sought to reestablish the narrative power of architecture within a Modernist point of view without resorting to explicit historicist references. Saarinen's search for an appropriate, expressive Modernism sometimes led him to highly keyed structural strategies, as in his TWA terminal (1962) at Idlewild Airport, but it also led him in his CBS Building (1965) to challenge Mies's Seagram Building with a structurally "honest" solution to the exterior wall. Though unquestionably Modernist in its insistently abstract form, CBS nonetheless evoked Gothic architecture's lithic celebration of verticality to communicate a complex, albeit somewhat ambiguous critique of the clichéd glass-and-metal curtain wall.

By the mid-1960s architects such as Johnson, Stone, Yamasaki and Saarinen, a second and distinctly American generation of Modernists, were joined by a younger generation of theorists and practitioners who, though they sometimes claimed status as Modernists, were so against the work of the recent past as to constitute a new and distinct position. By the mid-1970s this approach had come to be widely known as Post-Modernism. While the major impact of Post-Modernism does not come until after 1976, its presence from the late 1960s on can be found not only in the work of a number of young firms, most notably Hardy Holzman Pfeiffer, but also in the writings of Jane Jacobs and the novelist and essayist Norman Mailer, who in 1963 became Modernism's most articulate nemesis. Mailer's attack on Modernist architecture, first published in *Esquire*, sent shock waves through the profession as it confirmed increasingly common beliefs among the public.[253] In the *Esquire* article Mailer offered a devastating critique of the city's public housing efforts (see chapter 2). Less than a year later Mailer resumed his invective:

> People who admire the new architecture find it of value because it obliterates the past. They are sufficiently totalitarian to wish to avoid the consequences of the past. Which of course is not to say that they see themselves as totalitarian. The totalitarian passion is an unconscious one. Which liberal, fighting for bigger housing and additional cubic feet of air space in elementary schools, does not see himself as a benefactor? . . . Yes, the people who admire the new architecture are unconsciously totalitarian. . . . The landscape of America will be stolen for half a century if a Resistance does not form. Indeed it may be stolen forever if we are not sufficiently courageous to enter the depression of contemplating what we have already lost and what we have yet to lose.[254]

In 1965 Mailer extended his critique into the realm of actual design, with a surprising, even contradictory, proposal for a 3,000-foot-tall, 15,000-unit apartment building, represented in a large model made with children's Lego blocks that he proudly displayed in the living room of his Brooklyn Heights home.[255]

In spite of, or perhaps to some degree because of, Mailer's flair for antic showmanship, his diatribe turned even potential supporters into antagonists. At the request of Peter Blake, the editor of *Architectural Forum*, Mailer and the historian and critic Vincent Scully exchanged views in the journal's pages. Scully argued:

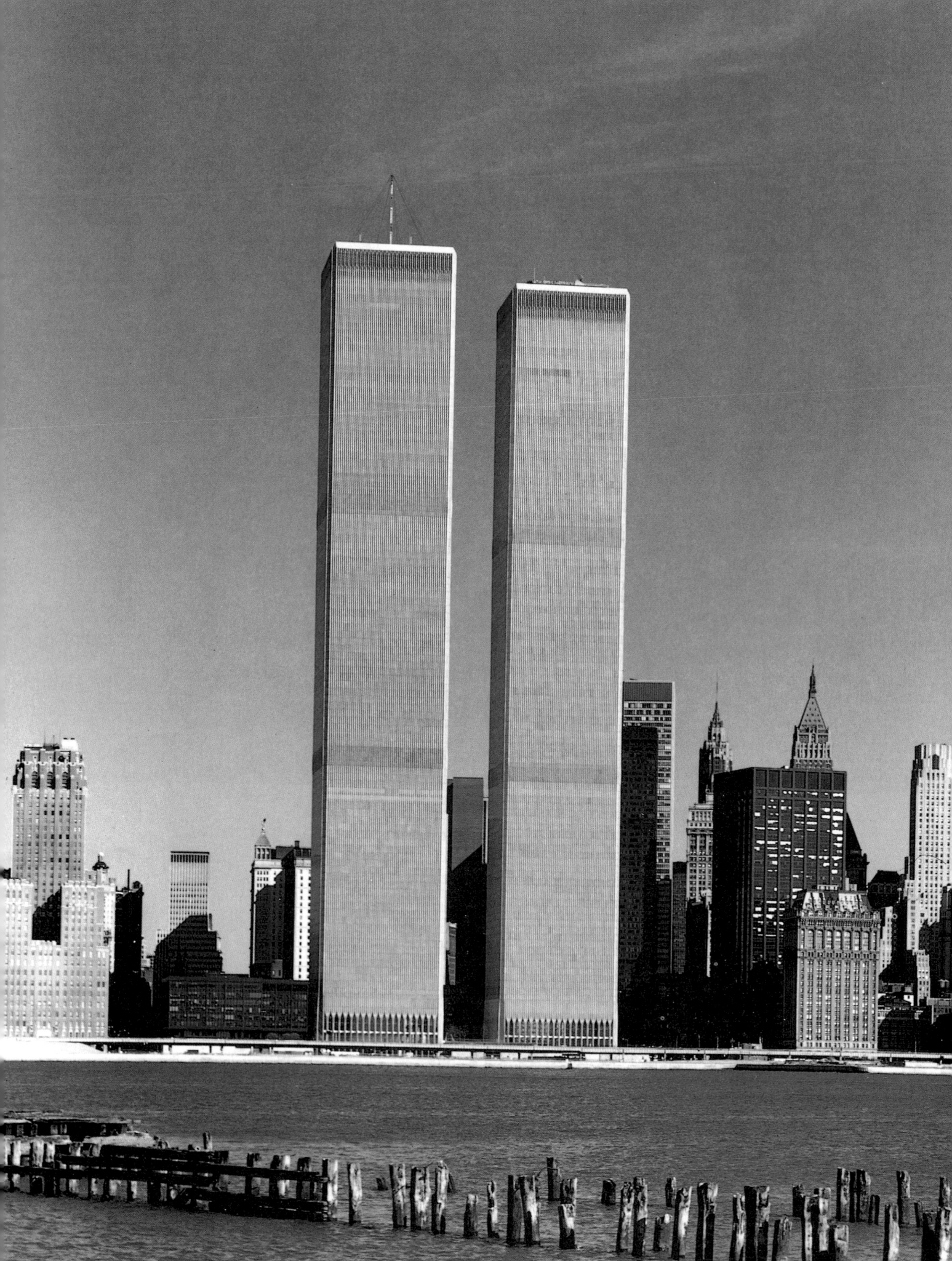

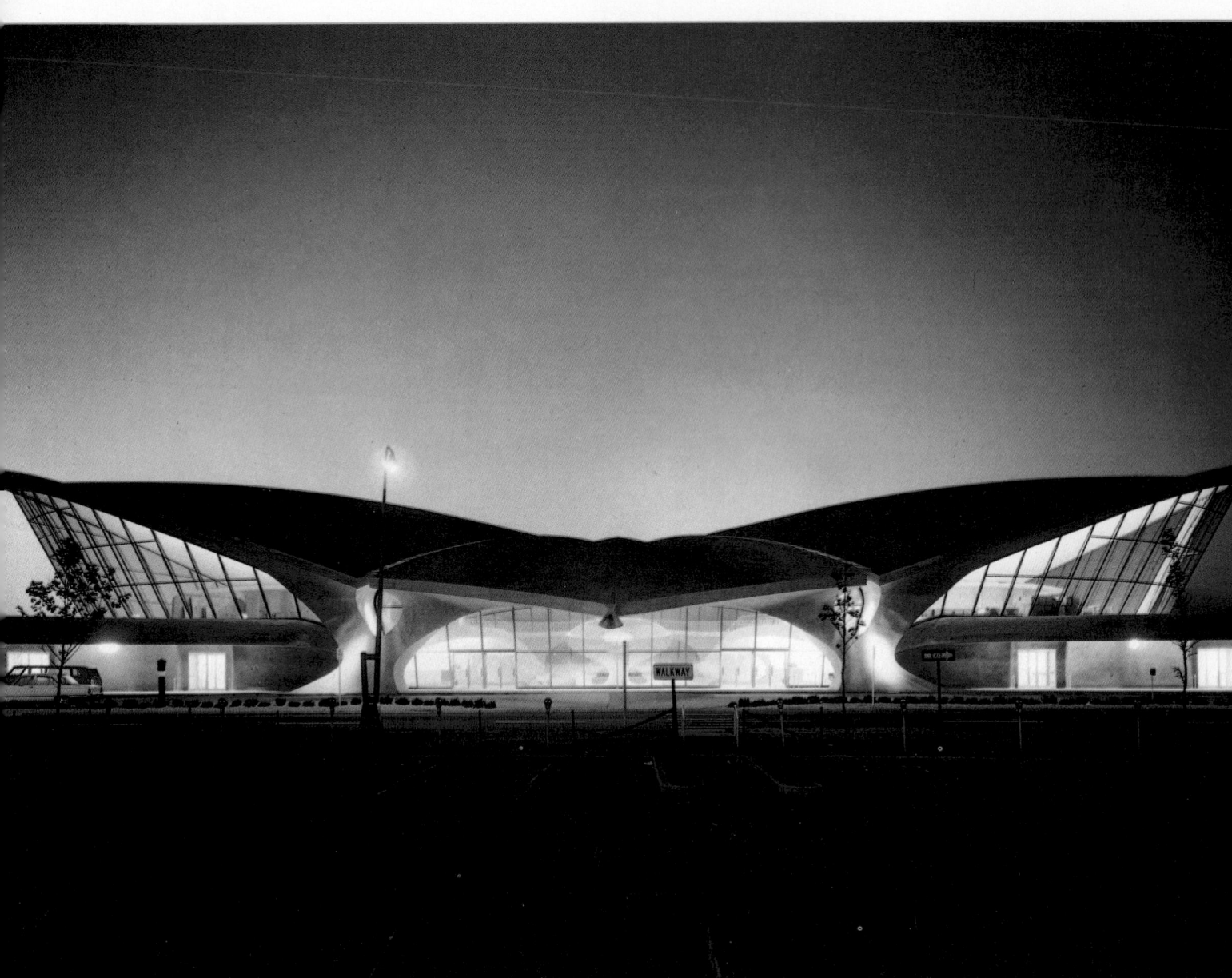

TWA terminal, Idlewild Airport, Queens. Eero Saarinen & Associates,
1962. Stoller. ©ESTO

To equate modern architecture, which was banned by all the most totalitarian of the totalitarian countries, *with* totalitarianism, is historically speaking, the Big Lie at its most majestic. I should prefer to believe that Mr. Mailer is simply uninformed, and his articles do have that lovely loose quality which only pure indifference can provide. For example, the work of Wright, Le Corbusier, and Aalto—not, surely, to mention that of Lou Kahn—flatly contradicts everything, absolutely everything, Mr. Mailer has to say. Just read it in reverse and you've got it, especially that bit about destroying the past.

Despite the vehemence of his rebuttal, Scully did admit that "Mr. Mailer, with his fierce, restless, innocent artist's eye—flecked though it is by some neo-Romantic sunspots and pretentious motes—is more right than wrong in terms of what is generally to be seen around us. Indeed, I think that the architectural situation relative to humanity and the earth is a good deal more serious even than he seems to find it."[256]

The most eloquent and influential practitioner-spokesman for the emerging generation of architects pursuing historically referential vocabularies was the Philadelphia-based architect Robert Venturi. His seminal book, *Complexity and Contradiction in Architecture* (1966), proposed a serious reappraisal of Modernism, calling into question its rigidity, its abstractness and its willful disregard for context and history in favor of an entirely new order. Ironically, *Complexity and Contradiction in Architecture* was published by the Museum of Modern Art, which staunchly supported the very Modernism that the book argued against and undermined. Equally ironic was the fact that while Venturi's observations reflected an invigorated regard for long-honored traditions, they struck a contemporary audience as radical. On a simple level, Venturi turned prevailing Modernist canon upside down, celebrating much that its leading polemicists looked upon as base, vulgar. In reference to Times Square, for instance, Venturi argued that "The seemingly chaotic juxtapositions of honky-tonk elements express an intriguing kind of vitality and validity, and they produce an unexpected approach to unity as well."[257]

Venturi's ideas were picked up by younger New York architects, many of whom were involved with Mayor John V. Lindsay's administration (see chapter 2). Though the new stylistic approach took many different stances, its advocates shared a belief in the importance and relevance of the architectural past and the vernacular context of cities; in most cases this meant the pre-Modernist past, but in some cases, principally those of Charles Gwathmey and Richard Meier, the past was defined as the high-style Modernism of the 1920s. Venturi, Denise Scott Brown and Steven Izenour's 1970 proposal for a neon-sign-wrapped mixed-use complex on the west side of Broadway between Forty-fifth and Forty-sixth streets, recalling Times Square's interwar glory, promised to be New York's first major expression of Post-Modernism, but the innovative project went unrealized. Throughout the mid-1970s New Yorkers eager to see examples of the new architectural trend had to content themselves with relatively small-scale projects, mostly interiors.

Nonetheless, by 1970 it was clear that a radical reevaluation of the International Style had entered mainstream architectural discourse and that the so-called battle of the styles, having been seen less than a decade earlier as inexorably concluded in favor of an anonymous Modernism, was raging once again, this time between Modernism, which had become a sytlistic battleground in its own right, and Post-Modernism, a hybrid point of view that welcomed stylistic diversity and, most maddening to purists, even welcomed the various styles of Modernism itself.

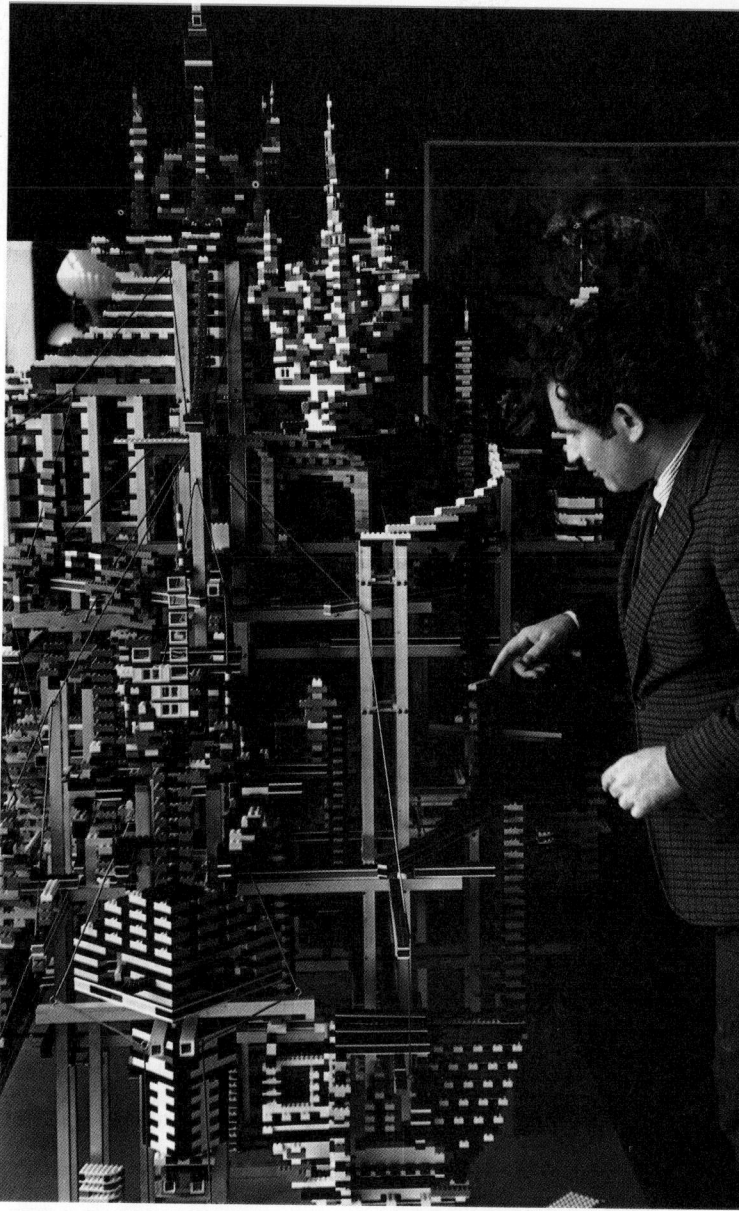

Norman Mailer presenting his proposed 15,000-unit apartment building, 1965. Model made of Lego blocks. Fred W. McDarrah. FWM

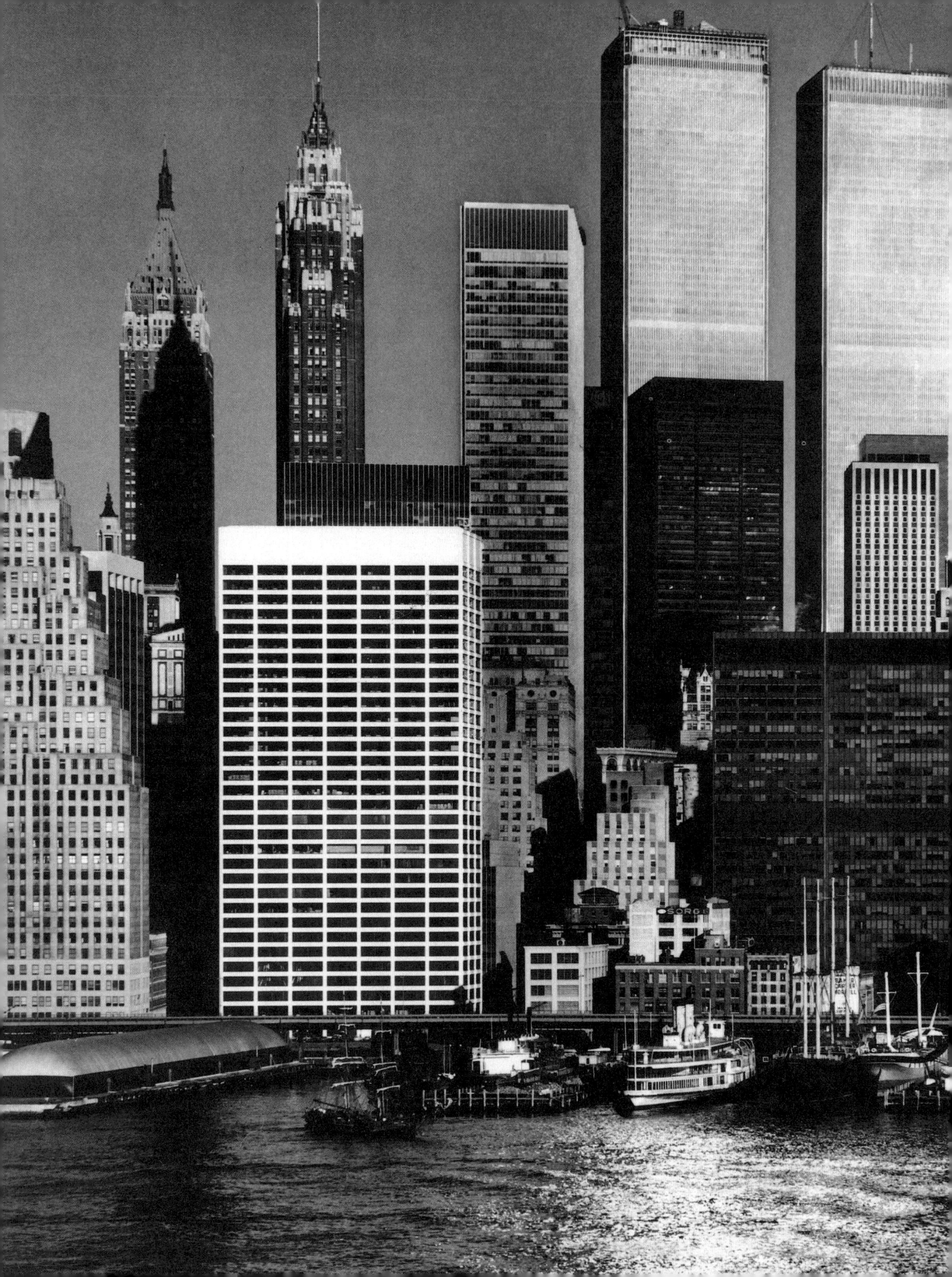

Chapter 2

Death by Development

The pneumatic noisemaker is becoming
the emblematic Sound of New York,
the way the bells of Big Ben are The Sound of London.
—Horace Sutton, 1961[1]

More as Less: The Office-Building Boom

Although there was some new commercial building in the late 1940s, such as Kahn & Jacobs's Universal Building, it was not until the United Nations and Lever House were completed in 1952 that the office-building boom and the subsequent growth of the city's two principal business districts seemed to really take off. The development was triggered by a phenomenon that the editors of the *Herald Tribune,* but few other observers, had anticipated as early as 1943: the near-exponential growth of white-collar front- and back-office operations in the central city.[2] By the 1950s the conclusions reached by the *Herald Tribune* were being echoed in many quarters. In 1953 the editors of *Time* recognized the impact of corporate activities on the city by celebrating "The Great Manhattan Boom" in a photographic essay.[3] The following year William Zeckendorf, the imaginative real estate entrepreneur, re-envisioned postwar New York's prosperity as an office center, predicting that the city "would experience a 'rebirth' and certainly not a 'demise.'"[4] By 1956 the city's Department of Commerce was positively crowing over a postwar boom that was "utopia come true."[5]

Despite all its faults—traffic, high living costs, crowded living conditions (or long commutes to the suburbs), high taxes and so on—New York grew dramatically as a corporate headquarters in the postwar era. The presence of banking and financial institutions on Wall Street, the city's closeness to Washington for

dealing with the increasingly important role of the federal government in private enterprise, its accessibility to other important American cities and to Europe, and its varied, vigorous, and sophisticated cultural life unquestionably helped to offset New York's disadvantages in the minds of many enthusiasts. But the greatest reason for New York's attractiveness, it would seem, was its proximity to the media. As the architect turned business executive Charles Luckman put it, just after he made the decision to relocate the far-flung enterprises of Lever Brothers, the soap manufacturers, to the city: "New York is the inevitable answer to our major problem—selling. . . . All advertising centers in New York, all show business except the movies. The platform from which to sell goods to America is New York." In choosing New York, Lever, which had been scattered in several New York buildings as well as locations in Cambridge, Massachusetts, and Chicago, rejected a suburban setting, like *Reader's Digest*'s in Pleasantville: "A nice spot to relax in," Luckman observed. "A good place to edit a magazine and to do many other jobs no doubt, but no place to sell soap. . . . Lever's selling philosophy thrives on congestion. Congestion is people. . . . Where the most people are is where we should be."[6]

Social considerations also played a part in attracting business to New York. As Wesley W. Stout put it in 1950, "Success attracts success. New York is the great success among cities. Here the success-minded have a feeling of being in the show-window, in the big time."[7] The sociologist Daniel Bell expressed a similar line of thought in his key essay about New York published in 1961:

> The convergence of corporations on New York can . . . be seen as the final stage in the breakup of family capitalism. Where an enterprise has family roots, the prestige and power of the head of the firm are displayed in the town or city where the enterprise has begun, and where the family has its social power. . . . When the "deracinated" manager "makes it" in the impersonal world of corporate capitalism, he wants other people to know about it, these other people being the tribe of corporate managers; hence the lure of New York.[8]

The stream of corporations migrating to New York swelled to a flood in the late 1950s.[9] In October 1956 the editors of *Business Week* labeled New York "the executive city," the

---

View to the west of lower Manhattan from the Promenade, Brooklyn Heights, Brooklyn, showing in foreground: 120 Wall Street (Buchman & Kahn, 1931), on the left, and 88 Pine Street (I. M. Pei & Partners, 1973), on the right; in background, from left to right: Bank of the Manhattan Company (H. Craig Severance and Yasuo Matsui, 1930), Cities Service Building (Clinton & Russell with Holton & George, 1932), Chase Manhattan Bank (Skidmore, Owings & Merrill, 1960) and Two and One World Trade Center (Minoru Yamasaki and Emery Roth & Sons, 1973). Lieberman. PCF

home base for the "business executive on the run." It was not only the concentration of business activity but also its variety that helped make New York unique; unlike Detroit or Houston, New York was built not around a single industry but "a complex of businesses," each with its own geographical area, like the financial or insurance districts downtown, the garment center in west midtown, or Madison Avenue, where advertising was centered. As *Business Week* put it: "It is more than just big. It's the quality of its bigness that makes New York the capital of this modern business age."[10] New York had 136 of the 500 top industrial companies headquartered in the city, as well as eleven of the fifty largest commercial banks, nineteen of the fifty biggest merchandising firms, ten of the fifty largest transportation companies, thirteen of the fifty biggest utilities and seven of the major life insurance companies. But most of all, as *Business Week* reported in another article published in October 1956, New York was a vast supermarket for goods, services and, especially, ideas: "New York is a gigantic communication center. Here . . . the man with an idea meets the man with money. . . . It is a magnet for big men, big deals, big money, and big ideas." Despite its declining population growth rate and its lagging trade and manufacturing growth, *Business Week* said, the "city is explosively alive, and its national and world importance are growing steadily. . . . Its health can't be assessed by the disease symptoms of other cities, for its metabolism is not the same."[11]

By 1960 New York was not only the nation's corporate headquarters but also the world's finance center. Although the jolts of the 1929 Crash, the Depression and the increasing role of the federal government in setting monetary policy had seriously threatened that position, the Second World War and its aftermath did much to enhance it. The appetite of corporations stimulated the office-building boom, which between 1947 and 1960 resulted in the construction of a third as much office space as then existed in all of Chicago, and the needs of the financial services industry extended that boom for another decade.[12]

Although the postwar office-building boom could be explained in part by the influx of corporations to New York, it could also be linked to three other factors: the expansion of the office labor force required by big business; the increase of space assigned to each office worker; and the need to replace old space with new, air-conditioned facilities geared to the requirements of the increasingly automated office. While the increase of white-collar workers was estimated as 18 percent between 1947 and 1960, the growth in the space allotted to each worker grew as much as 25 percent. This was attributed to the increase in managerial-level workers, office machines, service operations such as libraries and cafeterias, and reception areas where image was crucial, as well as to simple relief from overcrowding. According to *Fortune*, a 10 percent rise in space per worker over the thirteen years between 1947 and 1960 would alone have required about fifteen million square feet, or about a third of the new construction built in Manhattan.[13]

Replacement of old facilities was also a considerable factor: between 1947 and 1960 five million gross square feet were torn down to be replaced by forty million square feet on the same sites. Chase Manhattan replaced 400,000 square feet of space in seven buildings ranging from nine to seventeen stories to create its new, 1.7 million-square-foot building; the Commercial Cable Building at 20 Broad Street and the Blair Building were torn down to create expansion space for the New York Stock Exchange; and the twenty-five-story St. Paul Building was torn down as part of the assemblage that made possible the Western Electric Building at 222 Broadway.

Dramatically different from the typical office building of the prewar era, which was carried forward into the early boom of the 1950s, the large-floor offices that began to be typical after 1960 were planned not to provide maximum light to office workers but to provide as much unencumbered floor space as possible which might be taken up by machines or by workers arranged in flexible "open plan" groupings. The rising demand for this kind of superscaled office building, notable not so much for its height, which was hardly a novelty, as for its enormous bulk, perfectly coincided with the adoption of the new zoning code, which encouraged large lots developed with towers and slabs unbroken by setbacks.

In addition to the need to provide more space, the desire to enhance corporate identity and prestige fueled the building boom, reviving a phenomenon well known before the Crash, when many buildings had been built for similar reasons. Most notable among these was F. W. Woolworth's sixty-story building (Cass Gilbert, 1910–13), which was justified by its owner in terms of its advertising potential.[14] It was not just that the building bore the name of a corporation, or a single entrepreneur, but that its design in some way embodied the sponsor's institutional or individual persona: the Chrysler Building (William Van Alen, 1930) was a significant interwar example of this trend.[15] The office buildings of the immediate postwar era, however, were largely anonymous, frequently identifying principal tenants with little more than a raised metal sign above the principal entrance. Lever House (1952) was a departure from this tendency, but its small size rendered it less than influential.

It was not until the Seagram Building opened in 1958 that the second great age of the corporate monument began in earnest. Louis Sill, a prominent realtor, observed in 1961 that corporate leaders were coming to value new office buildings not just as efficient business instruments but as symbols of corporate stature and reflections of a corporation's progressive outlook: "In an age of lightning change, American industry is looking for symbols that reflect its progress. They want office buildings that reflect the dynamic qualities of the people who 'live' in them."[16] Daniel Bell made a similar point about New York's lure: "What draws the rationalized, bureaucratized corporate behemoths to New York is now a new bazaar, the sleek symbols glorifying 'Seagram' or 'Pan Am' or 'Lever Brothers' or 'Pepsi-Cola'—the new doges of Park Avenue."[17]

While the postwar boom in office buildings was to be expected, given the lack of virtually any new construction since the beginning of the Depression and a vacancy rate in 1947 of 0.2 percent, builders, still smarting from the beating the real estate industry took after the Crash, moved cautiously at first. Only two new office buildings were completed in 1947, three in 1948 and two more in 1949, for a total of 1.2 million square feet of new space. But by 1950 developers and planners alike began to realize that the city was not merely engaging in a catch-up process but experiencing a tremendous expansion of its business economy, comparable to that of the 1920s.[18] In 1950 twelve new office buildings were completed, supplying four million square feet of space; aside from a slight slowdown resulting from material shortages caused by the Korean War, the boom continued throughout the decade.[19]

By 1956 *Newsweek*, reporting on the "New New York," stated that since World War II, construction had begun on more than eighty new office buildings with 22,418,000 square feet of rentable office space, more than enough room for the entire working population of Pittsburgh.[20] The pace of this construction far outstripped that of any other American city at the time and ensured New York's status as the nation's office capital. This claim was confirmed in a 1956 New York City Department of

Commerce study which found that twenty-nine of the seventy national corporations with assets of $1 billion or more were headquartered in New York and that most of the rest had branch offices in the city. New York also contained the headquarters of 1,205 corporations having assets of $1 million or more; 713 more corporations in this category had city branches. According to the survey, midtown Manhattan was "beyond any doubt the gravitational pinpoint of American management." In addition, the study revealed "very definite indicators" of a renaissance in the downtown business district.[21] It also reported that even though it was neither a national nor a local government capital, New York was host to one of the largest concentrations of government services in the world, as well as the headquarters of many nonprofit agencies like the Girl Scouts.

The office boom slowed in the late 1950s as a result of a recession in the national economy.[22] Even so, many observers felt that in the long run the demand for new space was as strong as ever. Norman Tishman, a leading developer, was optimistic and prophetic when he stated in 1958 that "Despite the high level of office construction since the end of World War II, new buildings have not kept pace with the growing needs of business. With our economy still being accelerated because of the wider use of automation, increasing population, and the rise of new technologies and business services, the demand for new office space should continue as strong as ever." Tishman attributed the growth in the economy as a whole to the demands of an expanding population of consumers, but he believed that automation was an important factor in changing the character of the economy and, as a by-product, in spurring office-building development:

> The advent of automation has shifted the emphasis in our society from a people primarily employed in production fields to an economy of specialists employed in an ever increasing number of service occupations. . . . Inasmuch as expanding businesses need more space to house their larger service staffs, which at present account for more than half of the nation's total labor force, the expansion of existing businesses and the development of new products and businesses means a continuing demand for more and more office space.[23]

Eleven new office buildings were built in Manhattan in 1960, so vast in every way that they represented a new scale of development. With the Chase bank, Union Carbide and 320, 350 and 399 Park Avenue among the eleven, they supplied only 35,750 square feet less than the 6,838,250 square feet contained in the twenty-one structures completed in the previous year. As the 1960s continued, the boom went on and on; despite 129 major office buildings completed in Manhattan since 1947, there still seemed no end to it. New buildings proliferated and, amazingly, they were fully rented up: the occupancy rate remained remarkably high, with 97.2 percent of all office buildings in Manhattan leased in 1960 and 97.1 percent in 1961.[24] The continuing boom was fueled not only by the growth of corporations that had moved into new quarters ten or so years before but also by builders rushing to complete as much new construction under the old zoning, generally believed to be less space-restrictive than the new zoning, which would take effect on January 1, 1962.[25] A crest in the boom came in 1963, when 7,286,083 square feet of space were completed in thirteen buildings, among them the vast Pan Am Building, which had 2.4 million square feet of space, making it the world's largest commercial office building in terms of floor space. When the market paused in the mid-1960s the boom merely slowed down to what *Architectural Forum* described as a "boomlet."[26]

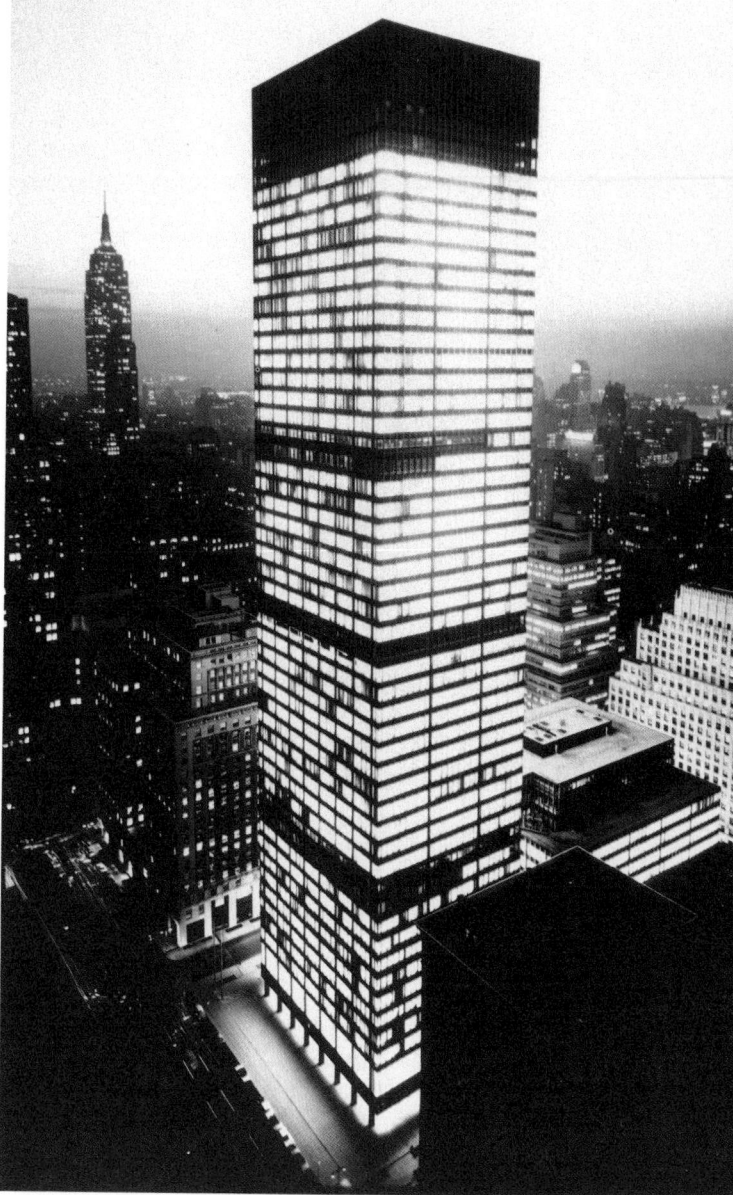

Union Carbide Building, 270 Park Avenue, East Forty-seventh to East Forty-eighth Street. Skidmore, Owings & Merrill, 1955–60. View to the southwest. MA

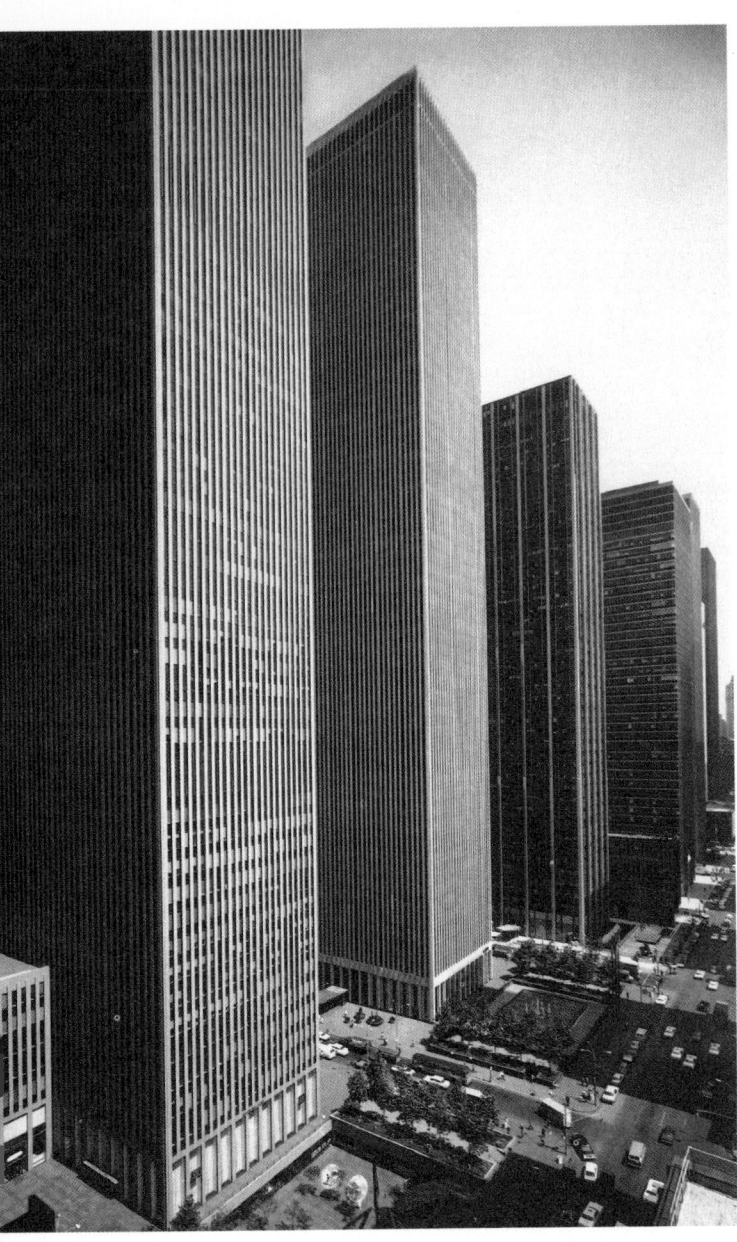

View to the northwest along Sixth Avenue from West Forty-eighth Street showing, from left to right: McGraw-Hill Building (Harrison, Abramovitz & Harris, 1972), Exxon Building (Harrison, Abramovitz & Harris, 1971), Time & Life Building (Harrison, Abramovitz & Harris, 1959) and Equitable Building (Skidmore, Owings & Merrill, 1959–61). Stoller. ©ESTO

With comparatively few buildings slated for completion in the mid-1960s, one experienced observer, George Studley, began as early as 1963 to forecast a second boom for the decade's end, which he based on the 2-4 percent annual growth in the number of white-collar workers in Manhattan. Studley, arguing for a speedup in office-building construction starts, pointed to United States Department of Labor statistics which predicted that in contrast to a 10 percent rise in blue-collar workers there would be 21 percent more nongovernment office workers in Manhattan by the end of the decade, a rise from 1,360,000 workers in 1963 to 1,633,000. White-collar workers would represent 65 percent of the work force in Manhattan, already home to one in every twelve of the nation's service-industry jobs. Significantly, Studley pointed out that the Labor Department did not believe that automation would curtail the increase of clerical employees, who would be needed more than ever to help with record keeping and communication within corporations and to handle the increasing demand put on corporations to prepare tax and other reports.[27]

By mid-summer 1965 Studley's call for a speedup had been heeded and, after a fourteen-month lull, *Business Week* was able to report that a "fuse is lit for another office building boom."[28] This came not a moment too soon, as an "acute shortage of new Manhattan offices" was reported in 1966.[29] The second boom of the postwar era was the city's greatest ever: more office space was under construction in Manhattan during the first six months of 1967 than in any other comparable period in the city's history.[30] Though fewer new buildings were under construction, they were taller and bulkier than ever before: 48 percent (thirteen out of twenty-seven) of the buildings under construction were forty stories or higher, as compared with only 9 percent (seventeen out of 187) of those built between 1947 and 1966. On the average, each of the new buildings contained 800,000 square feet of space, while the 187 completed between 1947 and 1966 averaged only 362,000 square feet each. Ten of the new buildings contained a million square feet, compared with only thirteen structures of a million square feet in the entire duration of the first boom. The second boom was fueled largely by the tremendous expansion in the financial markets. Trading on the New York Stock Exchange climbed from a daily average of three million shares in 1960 to more than ten million shares in 1967; related banking and brokerage business expanded apace. The Chase bank, for example, having completed its 1.7 million-square-foot headquarters in 1960, negotiated a lease in 1967 for an additional 1.1 million square feet in the fifty-story One New York Plaza.[31]

Although the 7,806,000 square feet of new space in 1967 set a postwar record, the boom continued to pick up speed, with 8,820,000 square feet built in 1968, 10,187,000 square feet in 1969 and 14,280,000 square feet in 1970, which included the three million square feet of the World Trade Center.[32] All in all, the amount built in this three-year period not only represented half the total production of all the postwar years combined but also was greater than that erected during the entire period of the city's post–World War I office-building boom.[33] On top of this, confidence in the market's potential for expansion continued. In January 1969 S. Dudley Nostrand, a prominent realtor, predicted that the "office boom will accelerate," fueled by growth in the financial industry as well as the expansion needs of cosmetics companies, advertising agencies, electronics firms, publishers and airlines.[34] With the exception of the World Trade Center, which was slated for completion in 1975, most of the new buildings were planned to be completed by 1971. But soaring construction costs and interest rates began to slow the rate of speculative construction, making developers increasingly reluctant to initiate a project until a major tenant was guaranteed. Even if such a tenant were available, the developer had to take a considerable risk in hoping that the remainder of the building, usually about 50 percent of its space, could be quickly leased.

At last, despite construction sites everywhere in the financial district and in midtown, by October 1969 *Fortune* reported that "cracks" were beginning to show in New York's "endless" office-building boom.[35] Late in 1969 Julian J. Studley began to see a glut of office space coming on the market at a time when New York City's fortunes were beginning to decline as a result of the bear market on Wall Street.[36] Along with the bear market, the increasing number of mergers, particularly among financially troubled brokerages, caused a decrease in the demand for space. By the end of 1970 the situation had worsened, with the excess space of retracting businesses in all fields being added to the pool of new office space. The resulting glut was so serious that the term "slump" began to be widely used and the dread word "depression" was even whispered. With seven million square feet of space unrented, the real estate industry was further alarmed at the prospect of an additional eleven million square feet of new space being completed in 1971.

In addition to business being slow in the city, the fact that many corporations were relocating elsewhere increased the growing fear for the city's business future: eighteen companies, including American Can, Pepsico, Shell Oil and U.S. Tobacco, had decamped between 1968 and 1970, and fourteen more had announced their intentions to follow, including Uniroyal, Borden, Stauffer Chemical and General Telephone & Electronics. Only two major companies had moved to New York during the same two years, Atlantic Richfield and Norton Simon, while a third, UMC Industries, Inc., had just announced its intention to move to New York from St. Louis. Whether it was the stagnating economy or the changing perception of New York as a desirable place to do business in, it was clear, as H. D. Harvey, Sr., chairman of the Uris Brothers finance committee, put it at the end of 1970, that "there won't be any new major buildings started here for quite a while."[37]

In February 1971 *Fortune* took a second look at the New York office-building scene, following up its prediction of trouble in October 1969 with an analysis of the current state.[38] "The situation is really bad," Charles Urstadt, State Housing Commissioner, was quoted as saying. "Without our backbone, which is offices, what is going to happen to the city?"[39] While the bulk of the discussion concerned the changing economics of office-building construction and leasing, the article also identified more systemic problems: though the decline in the market was largely attributable to the nationwide economic slowdown, there were increasing signs that when business picked up again, New York might no longer be the nation's corporate capital. According to George Sternlieb, a prominent urban economist, New York also might not maintain its status as the nation's financial center, given the emerging communications technology. Sternlieb stated that "New York City is—with the possible exception of Washington, D.C.—the only city in the United States which . . . does have the market capacity to reshape itself. It still has that vital critical mass. But I am afraid that its capacity is rapidly being dissipated."[40] Concern over the corporate exodus was widespread, with close to seventy-five corporations reported to be considering a move out of the city. In addition, whole divisions of corporations choosing to remain were being moved out, frequently to cheaper back-office locations. The repercussions of the exodus extended beyond the direct contributions corporations made to the city's economy; there was a fear that the exodus would diminish the growth of the city's business-service industries—lawyers, accountants and consultants.

"At a time when emphasis on quality of life is greater than ever," *Fortune*'s reporter noted, "New York no longer seems worth the trouble to a lot of people."[41] The negative state of the city was attributed to the local government's inability to handle issues like crime, housing and education, but was also blamed on the development community's greed. An unnamed member of the "real-estate fraternity" said: "[Developers] just haven't cared. Most of them are greedy beyond anyone's conception. The builders are selling New York, but they haven't added to it. Park Avenue is a canyon, Sixth Avenue is almost there, and now Fifth. They are part of the reason people don't want to be here. We are losing the people who can make the contribution."[42]

In 1971, as the building boom was fizzling, the Regional Plan Association released a study that predicted a surge in office jobs and growth in and around New York over the next thirty years. The study, which was prepared by Regina Belz Armstrong and later published as a book, raised questions about the shape the city and its suburban ring would take as a result of this growth, arguing that unless urban problems such as declining mass transit, poor schools and inadequate housing were addressed by the city, the growth would be felt primarily in the suburbs and not downtown.[43] The Regional Plan Association defended its optimistic growth projections by pointing out that nationally, white-collar jobs, which had moved ahead of blue-collar jobs in the mid-1950s, would exceed all other types of employment by 1980, requiring a virtual doubling of office space in the New York region alone.

Despite the current overbuilding, this meant that new jobs combined with the replacement of obsolete buildings by the year 2000 would require 200 million square feet of new office buildings on Manhattan Island alone, with another 400 million square feet needed in the rest of the region. But the Regional Plan Association cautioned that the quality of suburban life would not necessarily benefit from this growth. As William Shore, its vice-president, put it, "The suburbs are at their peak as attractions for offices. They can only go down."[44] Taking this long view, the association remained confident that the urban center would retain its attractiveness to many companies.

The postwar office-building boom transformed the city as perhaps no other physical phenomenon had, but in key ways it was not a positive transformation. Though a myriad of tall buildings were built, they did little to enhance the city's skyline, compromising its "naturalistic" pinnacles with abstract, boxy shapes. Worse, they did serious damage to the city's streets. As Marya Mannes put it: "They altered the *feeling* of New York . . . profoundly, street by street. For the excitement of Manhattan, the optical spur is diversity." But the vast size and essential repetitiveness of the new building type weakened that diversity:

> You have only to look at Park Avenue between Forty-eighth and Fifty-ninth street to know what this is: a shining gauntlet of glass, without expression or response. Clean and high and bright and sometimes handsome, like the Lever and Union Carbide Buildings, they are like the surrealist facades of a dream in which oneself, a single figure, runs down infinite vistas crying to be heard. But no one answers. No one can, because these new glass skins are tightly sealed. No window opens, no air flows in, no sound comes out. The people inside are flies in amber: between them and the outer world there is no communication or contact. In all this sterilization and insu-

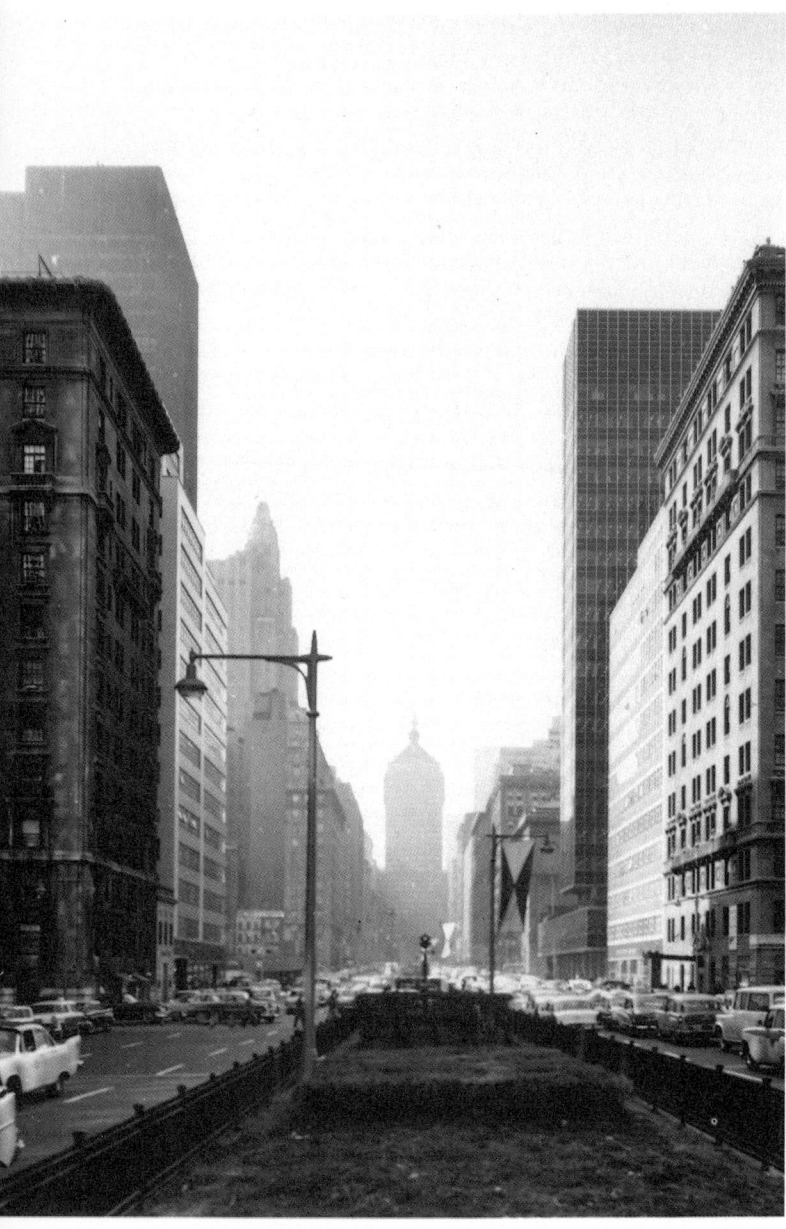

View to the south along Park Avenue from East Fifty-sixth Street, 1957. Gottscho-Schleisner. LOC

lation there is, I think, an emotional deadness that not even the bright clean colors and sharp forms of the modern interior can circumvent.

These buildings, Mannes felt, did away with the old city order of brownstones and tenements, the "little old crummy rows, the occasional mansion, the fancy facades," that once provided office workers with "the gentle prods of pleasure" they needed, the "roughage" in their daily architectural diet.[45]

Dull Utopias: Public Housing

Between 1935, when First Houses (Frederick L. Ackerman) was completed by the New York City Housing Authority, and 1975, when public funds for housing had virtually dried up, New York City was the nation's principal housing laboratory, leading in the number of units of public and publicly assisted housing built.[46] The late 1940s and early 1950s were the boom years for public housing. While the city's leadership in this area was undisputed, it was not accompanied by equal success in thinking through the problems that go with such large-scale residential development. There was no consistent attitude to rehousing New York, for as Cleveland Rodgers and Rebecca Ranken observed in 1948, "Most theories and generalizations concerning housing in New York are subject to modification on short notice."[47] Nonetheless, the city's efforts, if only by virtue of sheer size, established the basis for evaluating every major housing program and trend that would emerge across the nation as cities struggled for their survival in the face of suburbia.

By 1940, with eight projects totaling over 10,000 apartments in operation, the New York City Housing Authority was a significant factor in New York's complex housing market. According to the *Real Estate Record and Guide*, the Housing Authority had received 174,000 applications for apartments, but only 13.6 percent of those applying were eligible—that is, were American citizens who had lived in the city for two years and in a substandard dwelling for at least one and who met the Housing Authority's income requirements.[48] By 1941 the number of public housing projects had been increased by three, and three more were under way.[49] Even as the entry of the United States into the war brought new construction to a halt, plans were being made for additional public housing after the cessation of hostilities.[50]

Unquestionably, the public housing movement was guided by high ideals, compellingly articulated amidst wartime doubts by Edmond Borgia Butler, chairman of the Housing Authority, in a speech delivered before a meeting of housing officials:

> To justify further public housing, it is necessary to base it on something more secure than the improvement of the physical condition of a city by substituting new bricks, steel and mortar for old. . . . Poverty is not the sin of the poor. It is the sin of Society. Neither God nor the poor created slums. Society is their parent. Then let Society clean its own house. With this as our justification we can plan future public housing without fear and with the consciousness of doing what is our duty to our fellow men.

Butler warned, however, against the dangers of paternalism: "We owe an obligation to those who are our tenants. We must not forget that they are the masters of their homes. . . . Public housing must not be used to regiment the tenants." He also warned those in charge against believing that their way was better than any other: "We have to integrate our program into

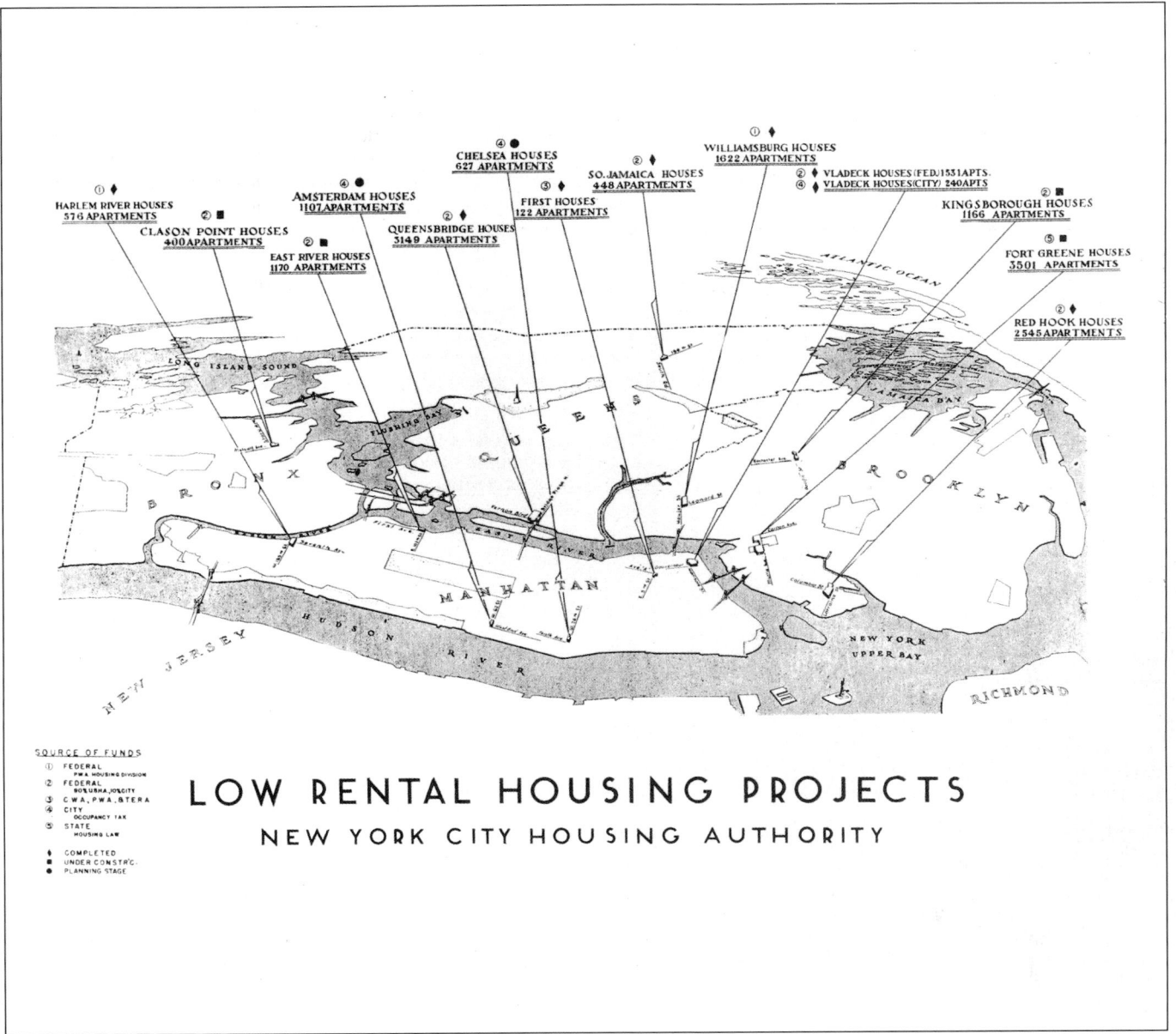

HARLEM RIVER HOUSES
576 APARTMENTS
①♦

CLASON POINT HOUSES
400 APARTMENTS
②■

EAST RIVER HOUSES
1170 APARTMENTS
②♦

AMSTERDAM HOUSES
1107 APARTMENTS
④●

QUEENSBRIDGE HOUSES
3149 APARTMENTS
②♦

CHELSEA HOUSES
627 APARTMENTS
④●

FIRST HOUSES
122 APARTMENTS
③♦

SO. JAMAICA HOUSES
448 APARTMENTS
②●

WILLIAMSBURG HOUSES
1622 APARTMENTS
①♦

VLADECK HOUSES (FED.) 1531 APTS.
VLADECK HOUSES (CITY) 240 APTS
②♦
④♦

KINGSBOROUGH HOUSES
1166 APARTMENTS
②■

FORT GREENE HOUSES
3501 APARTMENTS
⑤■

RED HOOK HOUSES
2545 APARTMENTS
②♦

SOURCE OF FUNDS
① FEDERAL
  PWA HOUSING DIVISION
② FEDERAL
  BOSURHA IOSCITY
③ C.W.A., P.W.A., & T.E.R.A.
④ CITY
  OCCUPANCY TAX
⑤ STATE
  HOUSING LAW

♦ COMPLETED
■ UNDER CONSTR'C.
● PLANNING STAGE

LOW RENTAL HOUSING PROJECTS
NEW YORK CITY HOUSING AUTHORITY

Map of New York City Housing Authority projects, 1941. RERG. CU

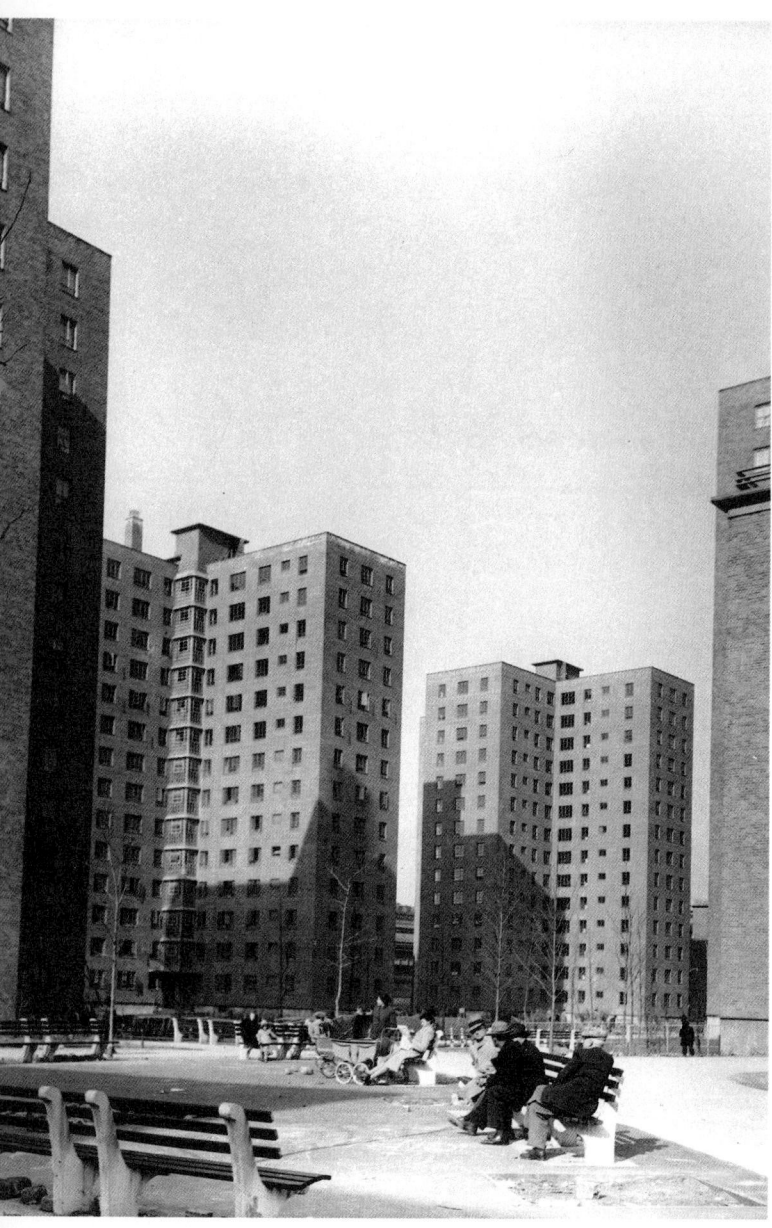

Above: James Weldon Johnson Houses, Park to Third Avenue, East 112th to East 115th Street. Julian Whittlesey, Harry M. Prince and Robert J. Reiley, 1947. NYCHA

Overleaf: View to the northwest of the Lower East Side from the Williamsburg Bridge showing, from left to right: Baruch Houses (Emery Roth & Sons, 1954–59), Lillian Wald Houses (Frederick L. Ackerman and Lafayette A. Goldstone, 1949) and Jacob Riis Houses (James Mackenzie, Sidney Strauss and Walker & Gillette, 1949). East River Park is in the foreground. NYCHA

the community. Public housing is not Utopia nor is it a city within a city."[51]

Public awareness of and enthusiasm for the public housing program reached a peak in May 1944, when the Citizens' Housing Council organized "Housing Week," which included department store window displays, citizen meetings, "farewell-to-slums" block parties at public housing projects, a film shown at all Loew's theaters and a panel discussion at the Museum of Modern Art.[52] Although the city's Housing Authority had already demolished 50,000 slum units, according to the prevailing wisdom another half million units still required substantial upgrading or demolition. At the present rate of renewal, it was estimated that this process of rehousing would take until the year 2110. A principal feature of Housing Week was an exhibition of the Housing Authority's projected postwar projects, which were not welcomed with unqualified enthusiasm. City Councilman Stanley M. Isaacs assessed the proposed projects as "a huge number of costly individual structures with no attempt to combine buildings, no effort at neighborhood planning."[53] The issue of planning was also raised by the Committee on Civic Design and Development of the New York Chapter of the American Institute of Architects. Under its chairman, Grosvenor Atterbury, the committee pointed out in a 1943 report that projects housing 25,000 people and covering more than fifty acres were large towns in themselves and should be developed as integrated, self-contained neighborhoods, including places to work as well as live.[54]

Other voices were also being raised in criticism of the prevailing planning approach, which was typical not only of the Housing Authority's work but also of the large-scale developments sponsored by insurance companies. Eugene Henry Klaber, a veteran houser, viewed superscale projects such as the Lillian Wald Houses, the Alfred E. Smith Houses and Stuyvesant Town as "walled towns destroying existing social values in the neighborhoods and precluding the development of new and healthy neighborhood characteristics. Even a competent master plan of development would not do the trick, since what we term 'the walled city' is, in large measure, the result of the architectural arrangements of buildings and open spaces." Accepting the value of large-scale projects, and especially of superblocking, which it was believed turned excess streets into valuable land, Klaber argued that any new project should include a site set aside for a public school, as well as a public park "so located and planned that it will be a binding element (not a separation) between private development and a proposed adjacent housing project." He also recommended that the "recreation areas of the development be around its perimeter (not walled in by buildings) and that they be maintained and operated by the city but access granted to everyone, not merely to the tenants of the new buildings."[55]

With the war barely over, the Housing Authority pushed forward with major projects for the first time since 1942: late in 1945 clearance began on the sites of the Brownsville Houses in Brooklyn, and the Jacob Riis, James Weldon Johnson and Abraham Lincoln houses in Manhattan. In January 1946 the site of the Amsterdam Houses in Manhattan, most of which had been cleared in 1942, was completely demolished.[56] But these projects, which when completed would total over 6,700 units, were hardly enough to alleviate the housing crisis. As Architectural Forum editorialized in June 1946: "Biggest, richest US city, New York had after four fumbling months, found house room for about 45 veterans," or so claimed various groups who demonstrated as part of Housing Day in May 1946.[57]

Clearly, the situation was complicated by political shenanigans and planning anomalies. Emergency housing units assigned the city by the federal government were not delivered because sites could not be found for them; only forty-five units had been set up, in Canarsie, and the federal government threatened to withdraw its offer of two thousand more unless the city took swift action. One thousand families were rehoused in state-converted barracks at Manhattan Beach, Brooklyn. Meanwhile, Robert Moses, responding to criticism that he was busily demolishing housing to make way for new highways, claimed that "You cannot make an omelet without cracking eggs."[58] Moses was also under fire for advocating tax abatements to tenement landlords who undertook renovations, a state-supported program he devised to quiet opposition to the superscale slum clearance required for Stuyvesant Town.

Virtually every civic group was convinced that "slum clearance" was the best solution to inner-city problems, but the Housing Authority's policy of total clearance of entire areas was becoming suspect. In 1948 the architect Charles C. Platt, president of the Municipal Art Society, proposed studying the preservation and "beautifying" of slum areas, confining demolition only to those buildings beyond repair.[59] This was a radical view that Thomas Creighton, editor of *Progressive Architecture* and a member of the society, did not support. He felt the proposal was dangerous, and explained: "The objections are obvious—this is, in a sense, putting sugar candy on what remains a bitter pill. Palliative measures can never take the place of replanning. The buildings should be torn down and the land should be redeveloped. And yet—will these things be done—would they, for many generations, even under the most favorable conditions?"[60] Despite his objections, Creighton had to admit that the proposal, derived from an aesthetic as opposed to a statistical approach to the problem, might be a way out of the housing impasse.

While public housing seemed sufficiently established to ensure some relief to the housing plight of the very poor, except for the controversial superprojects of the life insurance companies, very little hope was held out for the middle class. Experienced apartment house developer-builders like Sam Minskoff called for tax abatements similar to those that had spurred construction after World War I.[61] This was echoed by architects such as George F. Pelham II, who pointed to inflated construction costs and to the fact that the threat of rent control over new construction also repressed activity in the field.[62]

In 1945 the Housing Authority celebrated its tenth anniversary with a report that, while it congratulated itself on its fiscal acuity, left many unanswered questions about the product itself—at least as far as the Citizens' Housing Council was concerned. Particularly troubling to that group of civic watchdogs were the issues of tenant relocation and the high density typical of Manhattan projects—a result of high land costs and the lack of an established mechanism for "writing down" these costs. As they observed: "The optimum density usually advanced for urban redevelopment by competent planners is 200 persons per acre. On the James Weldon Johnson site, practically the same number of families will be accommodated as lived on the slum site; its density will be 463 persons per acre."[63]

Postwar inflation dealt the Housing Authority's programs a crippling blow: the John Lovejoy Elliott Houses had been budgeted at a 30 percent increase over 1940 building costs, but the lowest bids opened in late 1945 came in at about 68 percent over 1940 costs. The Housing Authority turned the bids down, deciding to construct only the foundations of this and other projects while waiting for prices to decline.[64] In June 1946 Mayor O'Dwyer offered a new plan, prepared by Robert Moses, which accelerated the Housing Authority's timetable as well as proposing projects funded by other programs such as the Urban Redevelopment Law to provide new housing for 1,268,400 people by the end of 1949.[65] The Citizens' Housing Council quickly castigated the city for delays and criticized Moses's plan as overly optimistic. While the council's proposals to remedy the situation were not particularly imaginative, its report had the benefit of calling public attention to what was quickly developing into a political issue: "There can be no adequate housing program for New York City until the Mayor recognizes—and recognizes not merely in words—that this is New York's No.1 problem; that it must be met with the same energy that war emergencies were dealt with."[66] The *New York Times* went on to editorialize that the city's housing project had "bogged down," with only 1,700 temporary units for returning service personnel constructed instead of the 43,300 projected in December 1945.[67]

The situation was alarming: no new apartments were built during the first ten months of 1946, and only 1,603 one-family and twenty-two two-family units were completed.[68] The conditions began to ease in 1947 both in the private and public sectors, where three new Housing Authority projects accommodating 3,680 families were completed and many more were under construction.[69] In March 1948 the Housing Authority's plan for 17,000 more apartments was approved by the Board of Estimate.[70] By 1948–49 public housing construction was steaming ahead, with the Housing Authority in the throes of its greatest sustained construction schedule ever: fourteen projects providing 15,000 units of housing were under way, with three more, housing another 5,550 families, in the construction-documents stage and four more, providing 2,500 units, being forwarded to the City Planning Commission and the Board of Estimate for approval.[71] So vast had the Housing Authority's role grown to be that, as Robert Moses observed in 1949, "In less than ten years, one person out of every ten in New York will look to the City Housing Authority as his landlord—a sobering thought."[72]

Just how sobering a thought it was could be measured by the May 1949 report prepared by the Committee on Housing of the New York Chapter of the American Institute of Architects.[73] Under the leadership of its chairman, Arthur C. Holden, the committee not only assessed various housing projects in detail, ranking them for livability, but also extended its reach into the more controversial issues of public policy. In particular, it criticized the Housing Authority for eliminating such "seeming luxuries" as closet doors, toilet-seat covers, adequate electrical outlets and soundproofing in order to make tenants "slightly uncomfortable" so that they would be spurred on to improve their lot and seek market-rate housing.

In what was perhaps the first such serious attack, the committee criticized the standardized architecture of the projects as well as their lack of community facilities: "The danger now is that the public has been educated to the acceptance of large-scale projects of a grim, barracks-like character because that is the type . . . which public opinion has expected the public authorities to construct for low-income families—and unfortunately . . . has set a standard which private industry seems to follow in estimating the needs and desires of families capable of paying an economic rent." The report also criticized the City Planning Commission, which "has not yet reached its full level of effectiveness" and has not exercised leadership in locating new housing or relating "these new concentrations of housing to

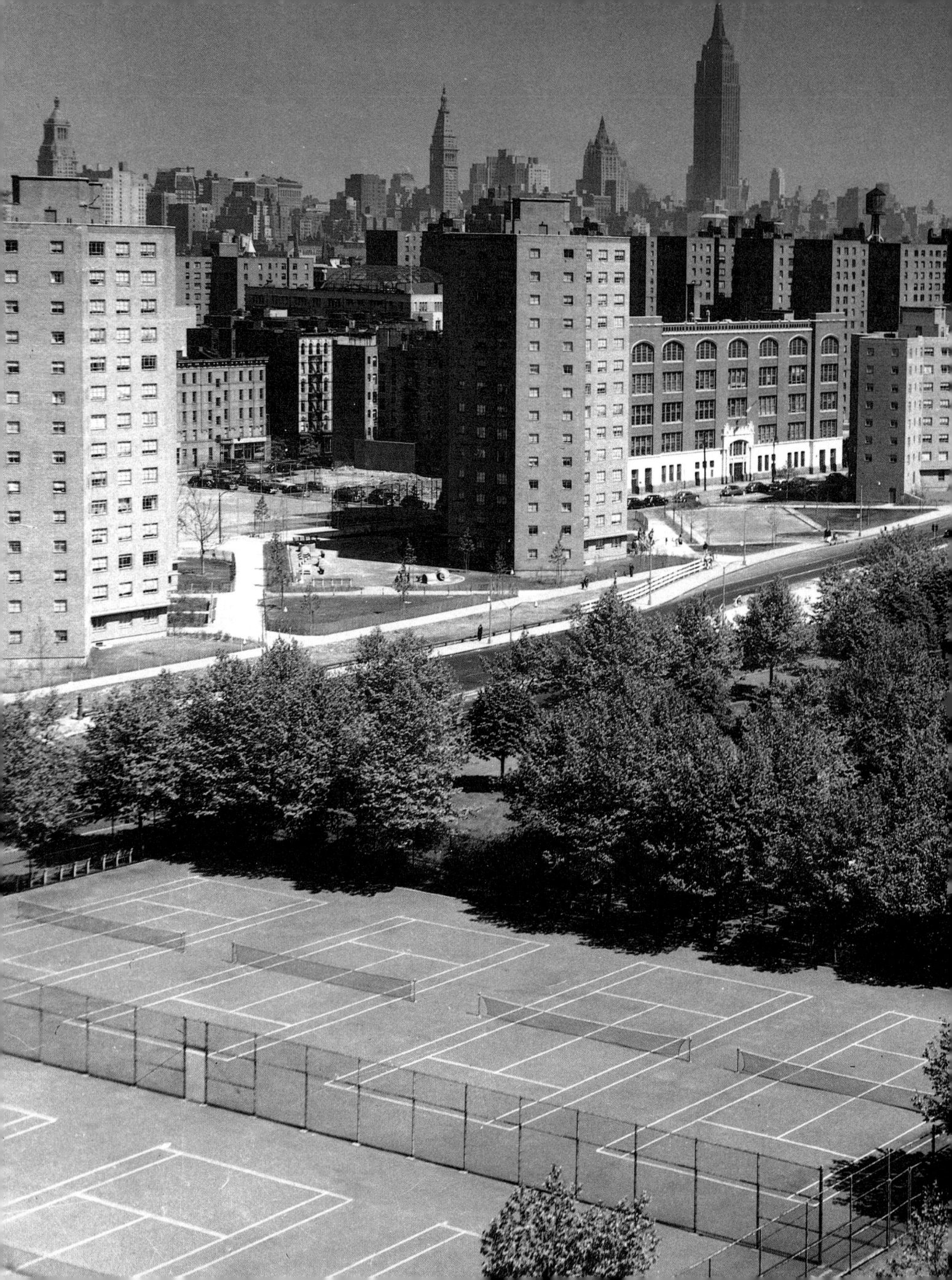

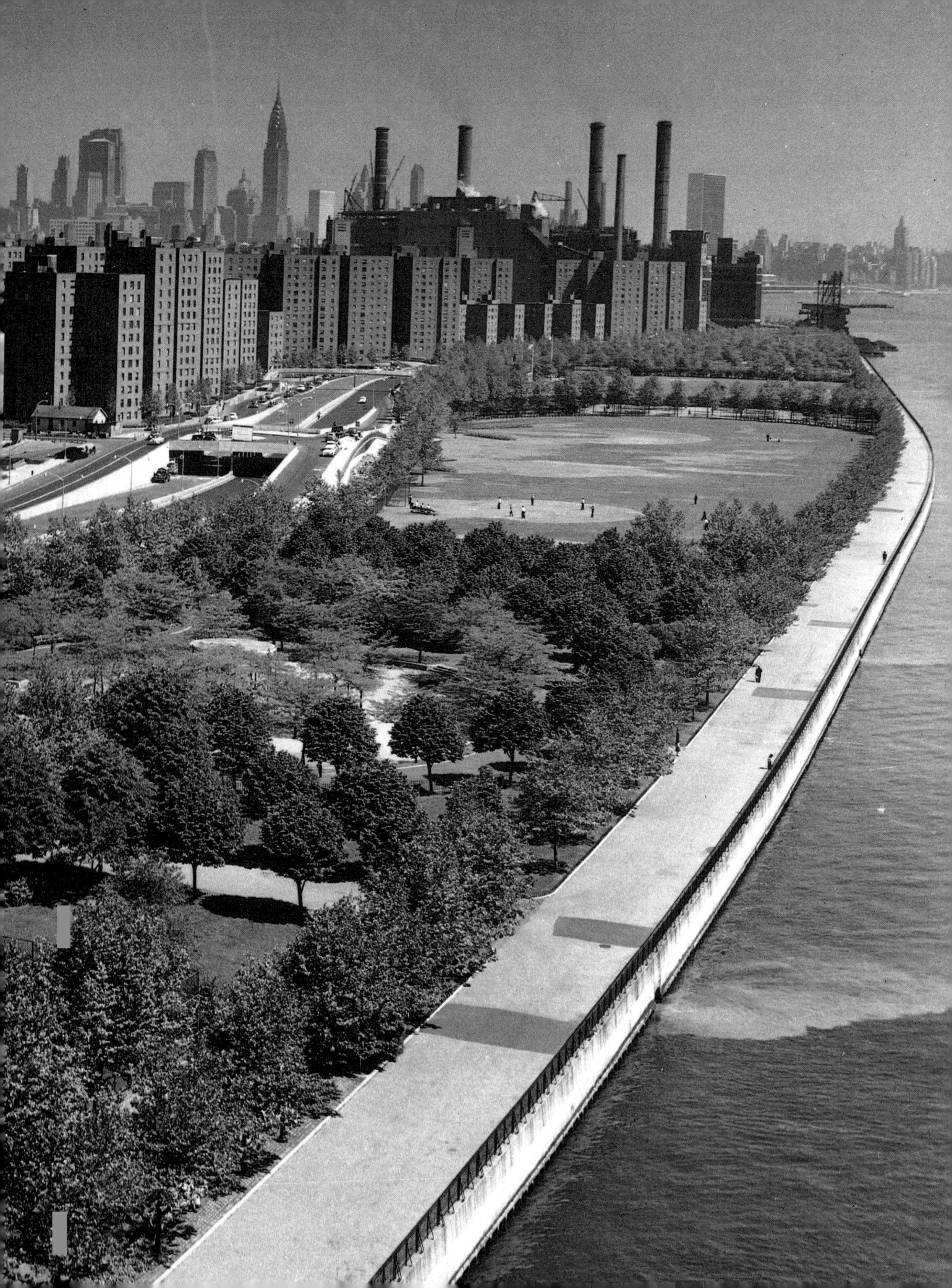

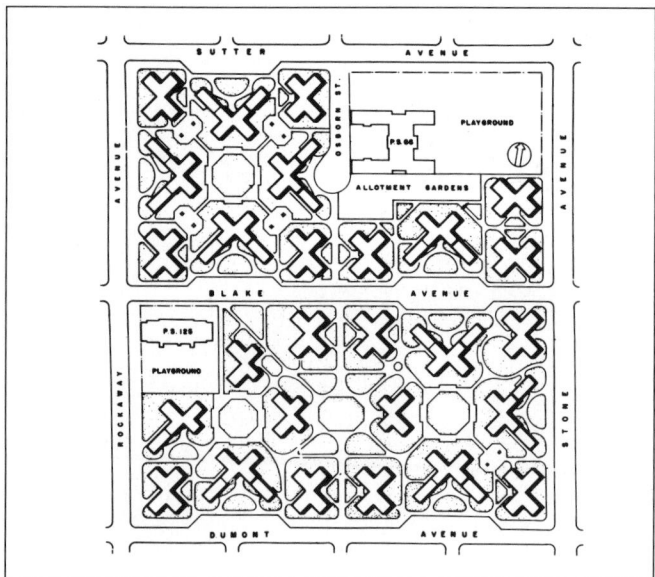

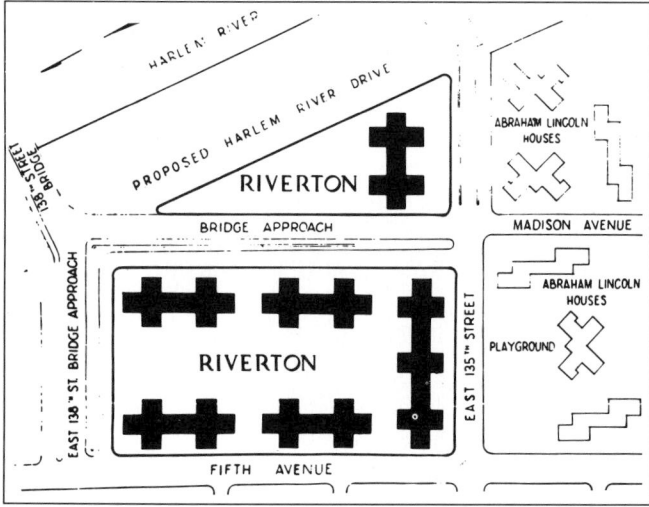

Top: Brownsville Houses, Sutter to Dumont Avenue, Rockaway to Stone Avenue, Brownsville, Brooklyn. Frederick G. Frost and John Ambrose Thompson, 1947. Site plan. NYCHA

Bottom: Riverton Houses, Fifth Avenue to the Harlem River Drive, East 135th to East 138th Street. Irwin Clavan, 1945. Site plan. CHCHN. CU

the organism of the city as a whole." Moreover, the committee felt that the Planning Commission was derelict in its duties in permitting public housing "to preempt the most immediately available land," land that was sometimes remarkably valuable as potential open space or high-yield private development.[74]

In 1950 Lewis Mumford assessed the city's large-scale housing projects, which he characterized as "red-brick bee-hives." A trip along Manhattan's East River waterfront from the Brooklyn Bridge to the Harlem River revealed, he said, "occasional groupings of brand-new oblong prisms of red brick, ten to fourteen stories high, set at brief intervals and looking like enormous building blocks arranged by a tidy but not too methodical child." He continued his observations:

> From the outside, these new buildings look as if they had all been designed by one mind, carried out by one organization, intended for one class of people, bred like bees to fit into these honeycombs. But though the differences are trivial, some of these projects are the work of the New York City Housing Authority, some belong to the big life-insurance companies; some are for the lowest-income groups, whose old slum dwellings have been razed, and some for middle-class and, as in the case of Peter Cooper Village, even upper-middle-class occupants; some are subsidized by the federal government or the state, some are the investments, and profitable ones, of corporations. Strange to say, dozens of architectural firms in free rivalry produced these masterpieces of regimentation.[75]

Mumford was, however, willing to admit that the brick bee-hives were superior in "such essentials as air, light, open space, and quiet" not only to the tenements they replaced but also to the so-called model tenements of prewar housing reform. Although he failed to question the large-scale, towers-in-the-park planning strategies they embodied, he complained about the high density of the new developments:

> The urgent need of housing is doubtless the chief justification for the bad precedent the Housing Authority has set in overcrowding the land. Most of the buildings are freestanding units, from six to fourteen stories high; by far the largest number of apartments are in buildings over ten stories. The ground plans of these structures differ considerably, forming crosses, double crosses, "H"s and "T"s and "Y"s and even pinwheels, but whatever the device, the result of crowding as many apartments as possible around each elevator shaft is to deprive a great number of rooms of either cross or through ventilation, and to deprive many so-called dining foyers not only of ventilation but of light.

He went on to lament the introduction of high-density, high-rise units, particularly in the outer boroughs, where they frequently replaced worn-out housing stock that was only two or three stories tall. "What reasoning has persuaded our city officials, to say nothing of our life-insurance-company administrators, that this congestion of population is desirable? Is this new housing so good that we should endeavor to make over the rest of the city on this plan? How livable will the city be if the standards the municipal and life-insurance projects have set up become universal?"[76]

In a second critique, "The Gentle Art of Overcrowding," Mumford argued that the Housing Authority and the City Planning Commission had taken a "shortsighted" view of the situation: "They have treated the shortage of lower-income housing as a disease that can be cured by segregating the sufferers in an isolation ward, and they have overlooked the fact that their favorite type of high-density building has by now created a new pattern of municipal congestion more widespread than the original slum pattern." In a devastating but succinct summation, Mumford characterized the Housing Authority's work to date: "To correct a pathological condition, it employed a pathological remedy."[77]

Mumford's critique extended beyond the building practices of the Housing Authority to analyze the inherently segregational character of the legislation that governed its activities:

> Though the Housing Authority, with admirable zeal, has abolished racial segregation, the law under which it operates has established segregation by income, a class distinction concept all too plainly embodied in the Authority's great building units. Again, under the terms of the law, this housing has been separated from every other normal manifestation of neighborhood life, so although these estates are physically neighborhoods, or even small cities, they lack most of the organs and attributes of a full-fledged domestic community. The fourteen thousand people who live on the thirty-four acres occupied by the adjoining Jacob Riis and Lillian Wald Houses . . . haven't a single church or synagogue or motion-picture house or public market within their whole area.

Yet Mumford was caught in a dilemma: on the one hand he was critical of the architectural type that the Housing Authority built while on the other he seemed unable to see that, in its way, it was the direct expression of the Functionalist-Modernist argument he had long since adopted as his own. So he continued: "The provision of these facilities, in low, freestanding buildings, would do more to compensate for the bleak uniformity of the huge brick prisms the tenants occupy than any amount of fancy ornament. There is no substitute for the variety and stir and color of a real neighborhood."[78]

His reservations notwithstanding, Mumford basically went along with the Housing Authority's approach. Pointing to the mildly critical 1949 report of the New York Chapter of the American Institute of Architects, to growing federal concern over the quality of life in these projects and to "a certain amount of stocktaking and heart searching . . . going on in the Housing Authority itself," Mumford visited more than a dozen projects to derive some generalizations. He admired their size, "big enough to form a neighborhood, or at least to make a decisive mark on the surrounding area." He admired, in addition, the fact that the superblocks were traffic-free: "This is the most important contribution these projects have made to the concept of a new city. The super-block not only is economical, because it does away with the need of maintaining long stretches of street and with unnecessary duplications of water, sewer, and gas mains, but it provides pools of quiet in residential areas. The people who live in these housing projects probably sleep better than the inhabitants of most other parts of the city."[79]

Less satisfactory for Mumford were the uniform brick walls that surrounded the towers: "In small buildings, such as those in Sunnyside Gardens, unadorned brick walls are pleasant, but in larger ones, completely devoid of detail or embellishment, the effect is depressing." The buildings, he said, had an "inhuman scale" and a "barrackslike air," justifying, despite all measure of landscaping, "Herman Melville's epithet for New York: a Babylonish brick kiln." Mumford recognized that some of the austerity came from a fear that decoration and planting "might be regarded as coddling the underprivileged citizens. . . . The laudable purpose was economy, but the unlaudable outcome is poor design and living quarters not as comfortable as they could be."[80]

Mumford went on to say that while most critics of New York's public housing used terms like "standardization" and "monotony" to castigate the architecture, he preferred the term

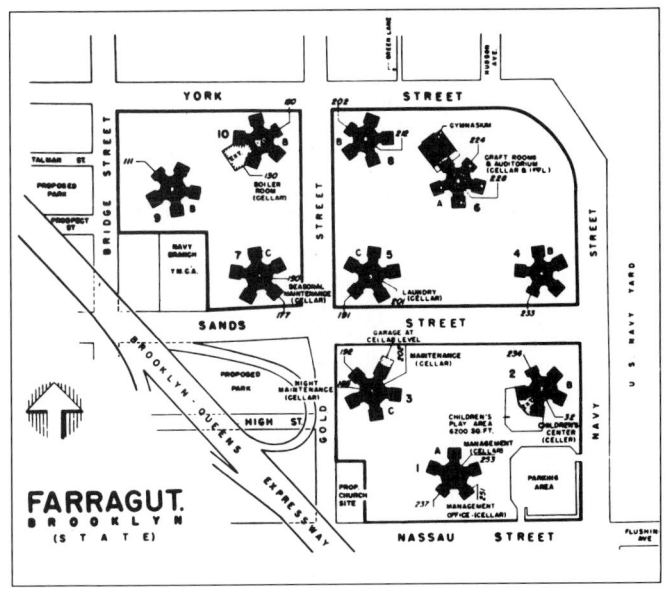

Farragut Houses, bounded by Brooklyn-Queens Expressway, York, Concord and Navy streets. Fort Greene, Brooklyn. Alfred Fellheimer, Stewart Wagner and Carl A. Vollmer, 1952. Site plan. *A History of Housing.* RP

"formalism," which he described as "the inflexible carrying out of a system that has no regard for the site or the needs of its inhabitants." He explained: "It is formalism to provide better housing accommodation for the poorest families in fourteen-story elevator apartments without considering whether such tall buildings increase the difficulties of a busy mother faced with the problem of looking after young children and doing her household chores." Mumford also took exception to the Housing Authority's decision to provide mostly small, two- and three-room apartments in the face of increasingly large family units (a trend that ran counter to the projections of the wartime years), and its skimping on landscape features. Most of all, he criticized the practice of high-density urban development, calling it "formalism of the most opaque bureaucratic variety":

> The core of this concept of housing is not a family, a neighborhood, and a livable city, but an elevator shaft. If this new pattern of building becomes more widely imitated, it will create urban disabilities that will be more difficult to remove than the old slums. At the end of a dozen years of zealous construction, the New York City Housing Authority is farther away from a good civic standard for the rebuilding of the greater city than it was when, in 1937, it completed Harlem River Houses. If that is progress, then what is lost motion?[81]

The new housing, Mumford felt, was draining the city of its inherent vitality and endangering its future, making the suburbs and the city equally bland, but with the rich people enjoying the presumed benefits of lower densities:

> Each year, thousands of taxpayers are driven to the suburbs because a pattern of life does not exist within the heart of the city. That is poor planning and poor business. We must abandon the old habit of giving housing the isolation-ward treatment. We must set sane limits of density in both business and residential parts of the city, we must decentralize many commercial and manufacturing activities that are now overconcentrated, to no one's real benefit, in Manhattan. . . . As for the Housing Authority, it is time that it . . . urged the city to use the new Federal Housing Act's beneficencies to establish lower densities. . . . Should we go on rebuilding New York on the obsolete patterns of . . . the municipal housing projects, we should merely be exchanging slums for super-slums.[82]

Mumford and the architects were quickly joined in their critique by the principal source of housing funds, the federal government itself. Through the enactment of the Housing Act of 1949, the government subsidized the purchase of sites, presumably encouraging local housing authorities to redevelop them at lower densities than they had previously been able to. But even the comparatively enlightened federal legislation seemed incapable of deflecting professional housers from their self-proclaimed mission to standardize the product, to pile as many people on a site as possible in order to alleviate perceived slumlike conditions, and to physically break with the city's traditional urban patterns, a mission Mumford traced to a mistaken interpretation of Le Corbusier's "meretricous" City of the Future.

The Housing Authority's response to the growing criticism of superscale development was to initiate, in 1956, a "scatter-site" or "vest-pocket" program (see below). Instead of the earlier program of six or eight superblocks, federal funds would be used for a program of small-scale interventions ranging from a simple building to no more than one superblock, thereby helping to stabilize existing neighborhoods rather than replacing them.[83] Meanwhile, the Housing Authority itself came under political attack when, between February 18 and March 7, 1957, the *Daily*

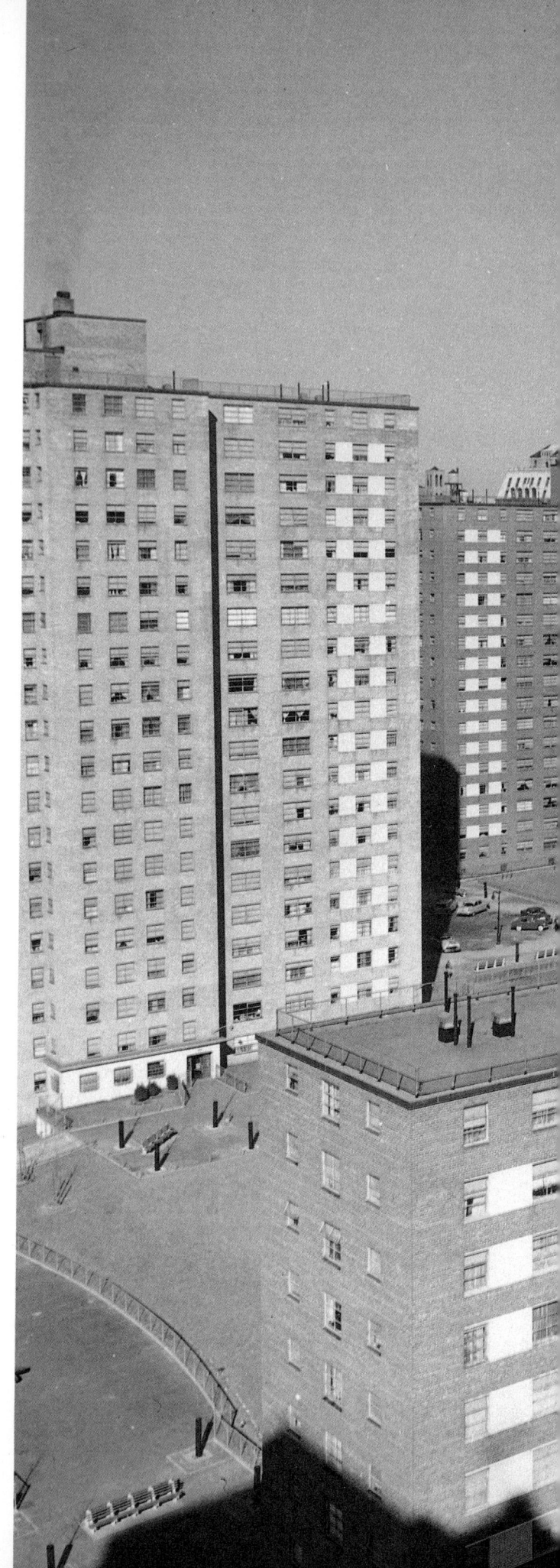

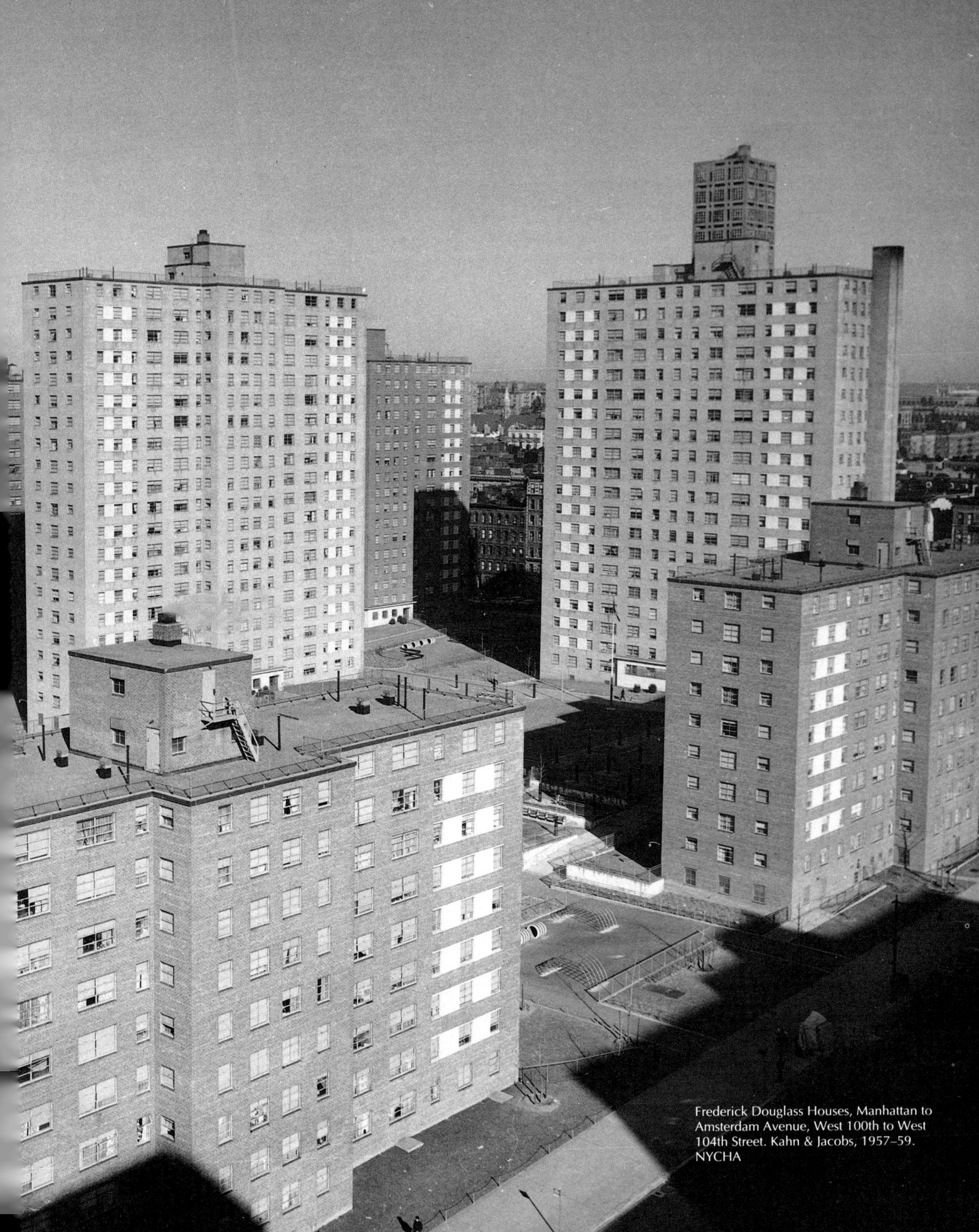

Frederick Douglass Houses, Manhattan to Amsterdam Avenue, West 100th to West 104th Street. Kahn & Jacobs, 1957–59. NYCHA

News ran a series of fifteen articles critical of the agency. The stories charged that the Housing Authority had not only mismanaged its mandate but had been virtually taken over "by a communist clique; that their principal strategy, to undermine the project by fostering deterioration, had begun to succeed; and that public housing had become a center of racial tension, vandalism and juvenile crime."[84] The headline of the series' first article, "Reds Peril N.Y. City Housing," set the rabid tone.[85] While many of the charges could be shrugged off as by-products of the era's McCarthyism, the articles nonetheless pointed up a hitherto unrecognized situation, one that Mumford had anticipated: the "projects" were becoming a new kind of slum.

In 1957 veteran houser Catherine Bauer, in a widely read article published in *Architectural Forum*, argued that public housing in general had become "ossified" and that, although its ideals were as valid as they were in the 1930s, over twenty years' experience had revealed two fundamental fallacies. First was "the notion that slum rehousing should be established permanently as an independent program. . . . This insured the segregation of the low-income slum dweller and fortified his isolation as a special charity case." The second fallacy was that this "'extreme form of paternalistic class-segregation' had been dramatized architecturally in the name of 'modern community planning,'" institutionalizing what had been an idealistic questioning of prevailing urban patterns into a new, equally rigid set of patterns. As Bauer saw it, the ossification of the program distanced it not only from the public it was intended to serve but also from the public whose support it needed to survive: "Life in the usual public housing project just is not the way most American families want to live. Nor does it reflect our accepted values as to the way people should live."[86]

At a symposium organized by *Architectural Forum*, a number of New York housing and planning experts—including Ellen Lurie, a community worker with the Union Settlement; Charles Abrams, an economist and planner; Elizabeth Wood, a veteran houser; and Stanley Tankel, a planner—discussed Bauer's ideas. Abrams charged that "Public housing is the product of finance and legislation more than of the drawing board," while Tankel, daring to speak the unspeakable, asked, "Why is it just occurring to us to see if the slums, themselves, have some of the ingredients of good housing policy?" Tankel went on to completely undermine the assumptions, however well intentioned, of a generation of public housing experts: "We are discovering suddenly that slums are human in scale; that slum families don't necessarily move when their incomes grow up; that independence in slums is not stifled by paternalistic management policy; and finally that slum people, like other people, don't like being booted out of their neighborhoods. We are coming to realize that it is not people and social institutions which are properly the subject of attack, but their housing conditions." Tankel went further still to shake the very foundations of the urban renewal process itself, at least insofar as it affected the design of residential communities: "We will have to admit that it is beyond the scope of *anyone's* imagination to *create* a community. We must learn to cherish the communities we have; they are hard to come by. 'Fix the buildings but leave the people!' 'No relocation outside the neighborhood.'—These must be the slogans if public housing is to be popular."[87]

In March 1958 Harrison E. Salisbury, in a series of seven searing articles on juvenile delinquency entitled "The Shook-Up Generation," first published in the *New York Times* and later as a book, brought to public attention the shocking facts of life in New York's public housing projects.[88] One out of twenty of the city's families lived in projects, and when the city's current projects were completed in the early 1960s, one out of fourteen families would be housed there. Salisbury opened the third article in the series with the following revelations:

> Most visitors to the Fort Greene Houses in Brooklyn prefer to walk up three or four flights instead of taking the elevator. They choose the steep, cold staircases rather than face the stench of stale urine that pervades the elevators. Nowhere this side of Moscow are you likely to find public housing so closely duplicating the squalor it was designed to supplant. . . . Many New Yorkers have the comfortable feeling that slums are a thing of the past. . . . What they do not know until their nostrils ferret out Fort Greene's fetid story or until they see the inside of some apartments at Marcy Houses or St. Nicholas Houses is that . . . the slums have merely been institutionalized. The slums have been shut up within new brick and steel. The horror and deprivation have been immured behind those cold new walls.

Salisbury blamed the situation largely on the rigid income controls that created a single-class ghetto and on the social disruption of the slum-clearance process: "Housing projects are rammed into one neighborhood after another. The primary concentration is on providing new walls, floors and ceilings at the cheapest possible cost. But the social consequences are bypassed."[89]

In a symposium organized by *Architectural Record* and subsequently reported on in the *New York Times*, architects from around the country joined in criticizing not only New York's program but national efforts as well. New York architect Percival Goodman was the most direct in his critique. "Housing architects regard the works as shelter engineering, not architecture," he said. "A hard-boiled program is given to them to be translated into concrete and brick. The result can hardly be other than thoughtless, mechanical—a design by robots for robots. An architect cannot function effectively unless he is part of the program making. He is citizen prior to artist, artist prior to technician."[90]

William H. Whyte, a journalist and *Fortune* editor who had begun to turn his attention away from the sociology of the "organization man" and toward the problem of cities, carried the argument further, emphasizing that large-scale public housing projects were the worst example of a wider urban illness that came to be called "projectitis." Speaking before a packed meeting of the Washington Square Joint Emergency Committee in June 1958, Whyte said:

> Rebuilding doesn't have to be repulsive to be economic. The trouble with urban redevelopment is that with pitifully few exceptions, the projects are being planned by people who don't like cities, and in far too many cases, they are not designing for people at all. If you've seen one redevelopment project, you've seen almost them all. No hint of tradition, nothing native to the architecture is allowed to interrupt their vast redundancy . . . the same basic design is repeated over and over.

Criticizing the projects' lack of "intimacy or of things being on a human scale," Whyte quoted the architect and urbanist Henry Churchill's observation that "'Most of the architects wouldn't be caught dead inside their dull utopias.'"[91]

The "housing establishment" itself was bitterly divided over the criticisms being leveled against public housing with increased frequency during the late 1950s. A 1959 editorial, "Public and/or Housing," in *Housing and Planning News* argued that an impatience with government ownership was the basic reason for public disappointment in public housing, and that specific criticisms were superficial:

America is in a period of relatively full employment, when most Americans, at least those not handicapped by minority group status, believe that their own efforts should produce comfortable living, and that failure to achieve this is more a reflection on themselves than on the "system." More than architectural dullness, anti-urban street fronts, and excessive densities, it may be the "shame" at requiring some sort of public assistance that keeps many eligible residents from accepting public housing under today's conditions. Reliable forecasts indicated that in a rebuilt City, public housing will eventually provide homes for 1,200,000 New Yorkers. Are these all to be members of minority groups? Shall people be forced to live in public housing against their will? There are two alternatives. One is to try to reconstruct in our citizens a feeling of pride in the achievement of their government, as the expression of their own desires and abilities. The other is to find a different mode—assisted by co-operatives, private management—in which to produce fully-subsidized living units without direct public ownership.[92]

By the early 1960s the problems of public housing had to be understood in terms of new urban demographics. Although the racial balance in many other cities had shifted more dramatically than in New York, where in 1960 only 12 percent of the population was nonwhite, the influx of approximately 10,000 blacks per year from the rural South and between 20,000 and 30,000 Puerto Ricans per year pointed to a new urban character and to new problems of urban acculturation.[93] This assimilation process was certainly not well served by the superscale, high-density public housing projects. Thus, as David Carlson wrote in Architectural Forum in 1960, "despite 26 years of effort and a total of 110,000 units built, New York's public housing, though it has greatly augmented the supply and quality of housing for the least privileged, has hardly made a dent in the cruel pattern of segregated, congested slums."[94]

Worse still, as S. Anthony Panuch revealed in a report he prepared for the Citizens' Housing and Planning Council, the city, despite 380,000 new housing units built by the combined public and private sectors since 1950, had made virtually no progress in closing the gap between supply and demand, still lacking 430,000 needed units.[95] Part of the seeming lack of progress could be attributed to the very process of urban renewal itself, which was firmly rooted in the idea of slum clearance rather than building new housing on vacant sites and rehabilitating existing housing.

Despite the bold optimism of the Kennedy era with regard to issues of housing and urbanism, New Yorkers were becoming increasingly suspicious of the value of slum clearance and public housing as strategies for redeveloping the city. John Crosby, the critic, devoted one of his columns in the Herald Tribune to the question, "Who says what is a slum?" referring to President Kennedy's March 9, 1961, message on housing, which called for extending the funding and scope of existing policies. Crosby asked why any neighborhood should "look forward to the prospect of public housing when the concrete pillboxes being erected in the name of public housing have created the most dangerous and depressing slums yet. . . . The psychology of cities and of people is being absolutely ignored in those brick monstrosities of appalling conformity and ugliness called 'urban renewal.'"[96] Mary Perot Nichols was an equally outspoken critic of prevailing public housing models: "There is something about

the puritanical viciousness of the people in the richest city in the richest country in the world who house their poor in great barren blocks of buildings—like prisons and insane asylums."[97]

While it was becoming increasingly clear that to enjoy community acceptability any new publicly assisted housing would have to break with the rigid superblock mold of the 1940s and 1950s, the issue of how to ameliorate the problems in existing housing superprojects began to receive some attention as well. In 1961 Elizabeth Wood, a professor of English at Vassar College and a former director of the Chicago Housing Authority, working under the aegis of the Phelps-Stokes Fund and the Citizens' Housing and Planning Council, published a thirty-two-page pamphlet called Housing Design: A Social Theory.[98] Among Wood's proposals were the installation of "concierges" whose apartments would open off enlarged, glassy lobbies with no "raping corners," and a "corner candy story" to help supply opportunities for healthy socialization in the public spaces of the projects. Wood even advocated pubs, arguing that "drinking beer in company is recreation," a bold point that flew in the face of the prevailing wisdom of "most administrators, and, perhaps . . . the critical public that likes its poor to be pure, or at least to be protected from temptation." Similarly, Wood's belief in the value of the candy store was realistic rather than idealistic: "To design for teenage loitering is not to say that it is a good form of recreation, merely that it seems to be a fact of teenage life, and design should make the best of it. Forbidding is not a solution." Wood's criticism was unsentimental, the observations of a serious, committed professional who understood the situation from the inside. In her desire to reform public housing, she cautioned against abandoning "the large-scale planning that lies behind projects" as the failures of the existing large-scale projects came to be better understood.[99]

The publication in 1961 of Jane Jacobs's book The Death and Life of Great American Cities, which became a national best-seller, hit the architectural and planning community with the force of a bomb (see chapter 1). While the book was intended, as Jacobs's opening sentence makes perfectly clear, as "an attack on city planning and rebuilding," to a considerable extent the book was an attack on public housing. For Jacobs crystallized the feelings of many observers when she said that "low-income projects . . . become worse centers of delinquency, vandalism and general social hopelessness than the slums they were supposed to replace." But, she went on to note, new middle-income housing projects, "truly marvels of dullness and regimentation, sealed against any buoyancy or vitality of city life," were essentially no better. Luxury housing projects were about the same, but they "mitigate their inanity, or try to, with a vapid vulgarity."[100]

Charles Abrams was an early champion of Jacobs's ideas, and he took on in more specific terms the problems of large-scale urban renewal efforts. In an article in Architectural Record in May 1962, Abrams wrote: "The urban renewal process is relatively young, the disciplines are in the process of formation, the experts few, all of them groping for solutions. . . . It is less than a quarter century since the U.S. advanced from the general orientation of building on 20-to-200-ft urban lots to acquiring land for large-scale projects by compulsory purchase." Abrams cautioned against tearing down too much: "When we destroy and rebuild . . . it is better to graft onto what is valid. First Houses, the first public housing project in America, was not the work of an architectural genius, but it is far better than Fort Greene. It was set within the neighborhood, not superimposed upon it." He criticized the quality of the new housing, finding "many old

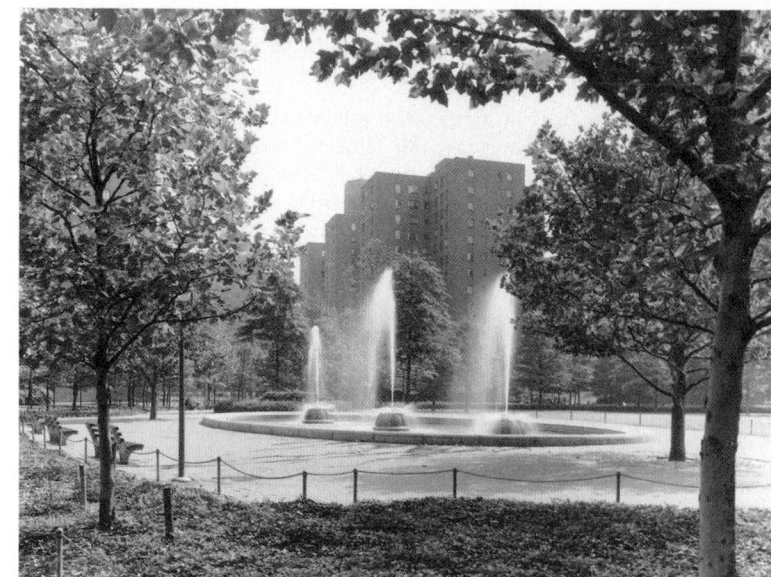

Top: Stuyvesant Town, First Avenue to Avenue C and the East River Drive, East Fourteenth to East Twentieth Street. Irwin Clavan, 1947. Gottscho-Schleisner. LOC

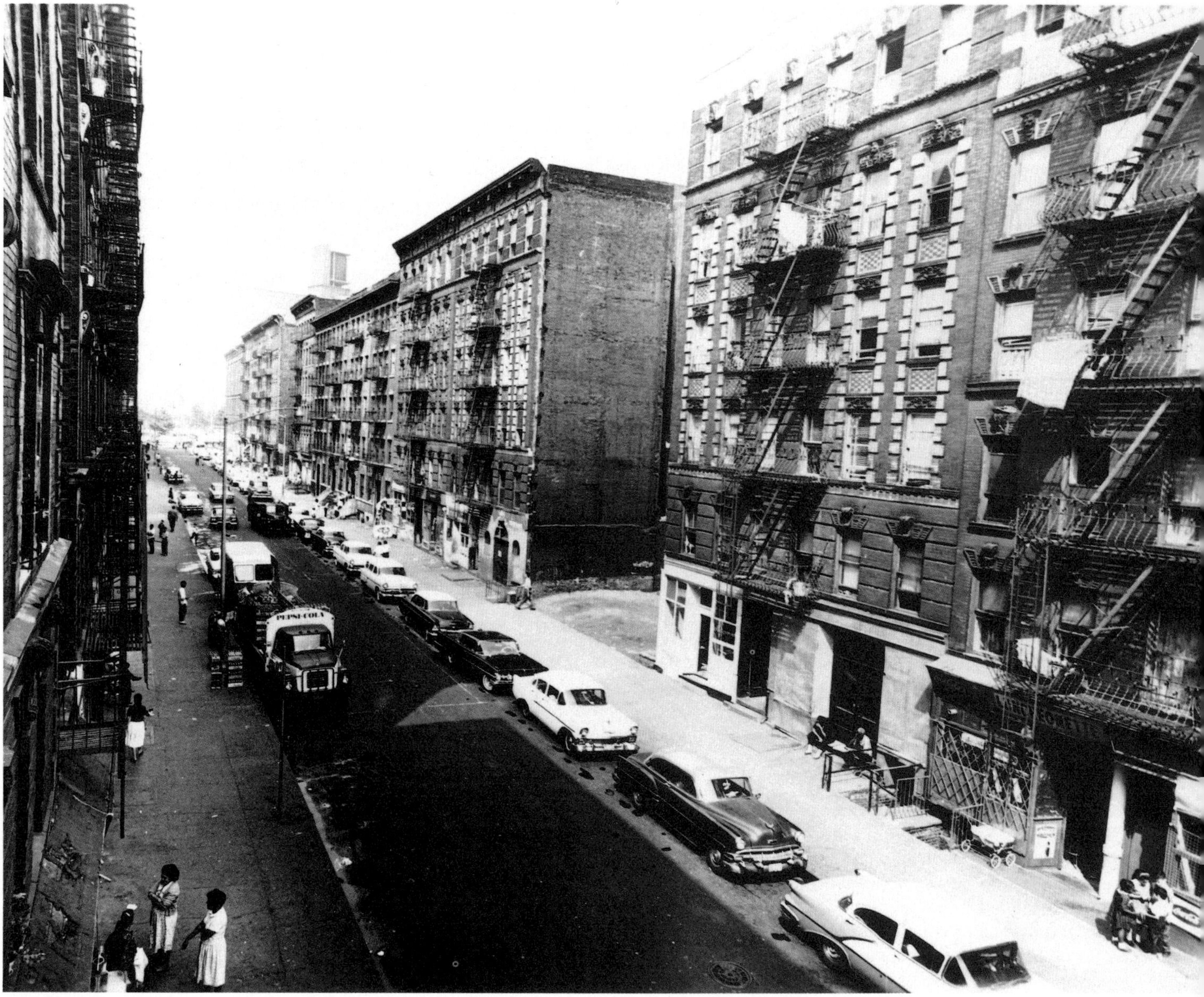

Bottom: East 100th Street, 1962. View to the northwest from First Avenue. DeMarsico. LOC

houses in New York . . . better in standard than the new multiple dwellings that are being built. This is as true of most of the private projects as of those built under the new urban renewal law, and even of some public housing projects." Abrams also criticized the "straightjacket" that publicly assisted housing subjected most tenants to, arguing that people should be given a chance to "improve their neighborhoods and create something that reflects their own contributions, efforts and personalities." Moreover, he felt that projects must contribute to a city's diversity, which was not the case in New York, where he observed a "superimposition of multiple dwellings of the same type; as the projects grow larger the patterns are repeated, while existing foci of interest are destroyed." He described the relationship a project should have with its surroundings:

> A new building must give a feeling of belonging: i.e., its belonging to them or them belonging to it . . . [it] must harmonize with the voice of the city. This means it must look and feel as if it were part of the city, and not be so overpowering in its dimensions that we avoid it. . . . It must leave room for something to grow around it. . . . This has not been the case in public housing projects nor even in places like Stuyvesant Town, which are insulated from the neighborhood by wide streets and have done very little to spark adjoining improvements.[101]

In his book *The City Is the Frontier* (1965), Abrams expanded on his ideas while providing an extensive analysis of American postwar urban renewal policy.[102]

By 1962 even Lewis Mumford, challenged perhaps as much by Jacobs's critique as by the grim realities of the public housing landscape, came to the realization that the projects were not really desirable:

> On sound hygienic terms, the one way of meeting this demand [for low-cost housing] within the limited areas provided is the erection of tall buildings, whose grim walls are overshadowing ever-larger sections of Manhattan. There is nothing wrong with these buildings except that, humanly speaking, they stink . . . though the hygiene of these new structures was incomparably superior to anything the market had offered in the past—and in sunlight, air, and view, definitely superior to the congested super-slums of the rich on Park Avenue—most of the other desirable facilities and opportunities had descended to a lower level.[103]

In 1963 the novelist and essayist Norman Mailer summed up the failure of the public housing movement, which he saw as a metaphor for the dismal state of modern architecture as a whole, and offered a few ideas of his own about how to get beyond the seeming dead end that urban redevelopment had reached: "Now in the cities, an architectural plague is near upon us. For we have tried to settle the problem of slums by housing, and the void in education by new schools. So we have housing projects which look like prisons which look like hospitals which in turn look like schools which look like luxury hotels. . . . One can no longer tell the purpose of a building by looking at its face." Mailer homed in on the housing projects, claiming, as almost no other observer dared to do, that the design of the buildings themselves actually contributed to the decline and behavioral problems so typical of life in them. Mailer advocated a self-help sweat-equity program in which individual tenants would be given money to improve their slum apartments, which would require "a fraction of the money it cost to dispossess and relocate slum tenants, demolish buildings, erect twenty stories of massed barracks." If such a program were instituted, he speculated,

slum apartments in the city would be different. Some would be worse, some would be improved, a few would be beautified. But each man would know at least whether he wished to improve his home, or truly didn't care. And that might be better than moving into scientifically allotted living space halfway between a hospital and a prison. For the housing projects radiate depression in two directions. The people who live in them are deadened by receiving a gift which has no beauty. The people who go past the housing projects in their automobiles are gloomy for an instant, because the future, or that part of the future we sense in our architecture, is telling us that the powers who erected these buildings expect us to become more like one another as the years go by.[104]

Despite the fact that by 1965, 135,000 units of public housing had been built in New York, 100,000 names of people requesting apartments remained on the Housing Authority's lists. Nor had slum conditions improved: although by 1965 East 100th Street between First and Second avenues in Manhattan was, in the words of the journalist Woody Klein, "a slum showplace" visited by "every important politician, social worker, clergyman and newspaperman in and out of New York . . . it is still the slum it always was."[105] In 1964 Klein published a book documenting what Congressman John V. Lindsay described as "the life and death" of the tenement building at 311 East 100th Street (see chapter 12).[106]

By the mid-1960s, as the last great infusions of federal funds were being injected into the city's housing pipeline, the criticism of the late 1950s had begun to reap benefits. For one thing, the appointment in April 1961 of Marie C. McGuire as commissioner of the Federal Public Housing Administration led to a loosening of the rules imposed by Washington. McGuire's comparatively sympathetic view of the role aesthetics could play in urban redevelopment was in turn supplemented by a change in the composition of the city's Housing Authority, which was reorganized by Mayor Wagner in 1958 and which instituted an advisory council on the arts in 1960. Suddenly the poor, who previously had not been deemed worthy of community centers—or of closets with doors, bathrooms with showers, or toilet bowls with seat covers—were now being treated to some of the "amenities" that most average citizens outside the projects took for granted.[107] But amenities were only one part of the reform; the very concept of the large-scale project began to be replaced with the idea of smaller units of development, frequently described as "vest-pocket" projects. This shift in emphasis was not made solely on the basis of theory or even common sense. It was also made as a result of the changing political climate: as citizen groups became increasingly vocal in their opposition to slum clearance and urban renewal, the Housing Authority was prevented from pursuing large-scale projects. Thus, the average size of housing projects dropped from 1,500 units in the 1950s to 500 in the early 1960s, when seven two-building projects, housing 270 to 400 families, and fourteen single-building projects, housing 70 to 175 families, were built. The vest-pocket projects, however, were fraught with a new set of problems stemming from the objections of citizens in established neighborhoods to the construction of such facilities in their midst. The community battles at Riverdale and most notably Forest Hills (see chapter 13) were fiercely fought.

In December 1965, during the waning days of Mayor Wagner's administration, a report prepared by private consultants, *New York's Renewal Strategy 1965,* was described by planning and housing officials as "the most important document ever produced about renewal in New York City." The report was critical of the city's emphasis on middle-income housing under its Title I urban renewal projects, and emphasized rehabilitation of slum areas now estimated to house 1.75 million people in order to nurture a "new middle class" and "restore a solid environment."[108] It was the first report ever to present a comprehensive overview of the city's housing in relationship to its urban renewal activities, urging the abandonment of the project-by-project, community-by-community, agency-by-agency, socially stratified and bureaucratically compartmentalized approach that had been standard up to that time.

Still, the complexities and the vastness of the city's housing problem, despite a generation of consistent effort, remained staggering. Housing professionals and the general public alike were beginning to feel the problem could not be solved. To begin with, there was the never-ending shortage of units. According to the Wagner administration's report, 450,000 to 550,000 families, seven out of ten of them black or Puerto Rican, could not find housing of appropriate size and cost. And what had been built or was under way was proving to be a social and environmental failure. In 1965 Frank S. Kristof, chief of the Bureau of Planning and Program Research of the City's Housing and Redevelopment Board, offered an extremely thoughtful, dispassionate assessment of the situation. He pointed out that, contrary to the pessimistic statistics of the so-called Panuch report, which had declared a shortfall of 430,000 units, the city had made progress during the 1950s—the decade in which it had first begun to recognize the magnitude of the housing problem. Yet, he admitted, the quality of the city's housing remained deplorable. According to Kristof: "Even with the limited count of substandard housing units obtainable from Census classifications, the City had enough substandard housing units in 1960 to unsatisfactorily house the entire population of Cleveland, Ohio, the eighth largest city in the nation!"[109]

Housing was also a priority consideration for Mayor John Lindsay, who hoped to lure to New York Edward J. Logue, chief administrator of the Boston Renewal Authority (BRA) and, after Robert Moses, the most effective city builder of the postwar era. Logue, like Moses, recognized that housing programs had to be closely coordinated with other planning activities. As a condition of his coming to New York, he required that the City Planning Commission be absorbed into a new development agency which he would head, as proposed in a report prepared with private and foundation funds.[110] The title of Logue's report, *Let There Be Commitment*, was a phrase used by President Johnson in his proposal for a Demonstration Cities program, which in 1967 became the Model Cities program of the federal government.

Logue's report, prepared with the assistance of David A. Crane, Anthony C. Adinolfi and M. Justin Herman, among others, offered a program that was citywide in nature but concentrated on an all-out effort to rehabilitate the city's major slum ghettos: Harlem–East Harlem, the South Bronx and Central Brooklyn. It isolated bad housing as the city's number one problem and called for the creation of 45,000 units a year for the following ten years. It criticized the City Planning Commission for failing to take an active role in shaping the city's future and proposed the establishment of a Housing Planning Development Agency, comparable in scope and organization to the new federal Department of Housing and Urban Development, with "area administrations" established in ten city districts: "We think New York City too large to be governed from the City Hall area. We are both impressed and depressed with the lack of identification between the people and their government and the peo-

ple's sense of helplessness in obtaining satisfaction on even the most routine requests."

Logue's plan would require $1.5 billion in federal renewal and Demonstration Cities funds over the next six years as well as substantial increases in public housing and mortgage insurance authorization. But he believed the time was "propitious . . . to ask for Federal assistance for New York City" even though the war in Vietnam, the space race and inflation also made it "inconvenient."[111] Though the Logue report concentrated on technical issues of redevelopment and community organization, and proposed a superagency that would wield great power, it also emphasized the role of design in the redevelopment process. This turned the city's attention to the quality of the physical environment in ways that had not been focused on at the highest governmental levels for a generation or more.

As a supplement to *Let There Be Commitment*, David Crane, an architect specializing in urban design, prepared a "background report," *Planning and Design in New York*. In Crane's view the city, outside its core, was a monotonous physical environment punctuated by isolated large-scale housing developments, "project-islands of helter-skelter hi-rise apartments; little bits of ground space and large areas of chain-link fencing; cheerless architecture; and sharp boundaries," places that "look all the same, despite the fact that each is a product of a different and ingenious piece of legislation and financing. . . . The stereotypes of apartment architecture and site planning are nowhere so strongly aligned with the forces of social stratification as in New York."[112]

Liberal pundits were skeptical of Logue's approach, fearing a renaissance of Moses-like development and especially of Moses-like high-handedness.[113] And Logue himself did little to comfort the skeptics, claiming that "Planners can either rest comfortably in the reviewing stands watching the marchers go by, or they can lead the parade. In this town, they have sat on their behinds." Although Logue did not join the Lindsay administration, he did the city a service when, perhaps for the first time, he made the scope of the problem crystal clear by announcing that it would take $1.5 billion of public money to rebuild the city's slums—a staggering amount given that federal urban renewal grants for all cities combined was then $725 million per year. "I didn't dream up Harlem," Logue said, "and I'm not going to foster the illusion you can solve it with a small-scale program. We're not recommending anything more than what Lyndon Johnson proposed in his demonstration-cities message. All we're doing is saying, 'Hello, Lyndon, here we are.'"[114] Significantly, as Allan Tallot, an urban consultant who had helped Logue formulate his plan, pointed out in *Harper's* magazine, the $1.5 billion needed over six years was little more than the amount estimated to cover twelve months of aircraft replacement in the Vietnam War.[115]

Essential aspects of Logue's report were adopted as policy by Lindsay. A number of agencies were consolidated as the Housing and Development Administration, but the City Planning Commission remained independent; planning and renewal activities were concentrated in three "Model Cities" areas: Central Harlem, the South Bronx and Bedford-Stuyvesant. Existing renewal programs that had already obtained federal planning money were expedited, but others were withdrawn. In addition, housing rehabilitation programs were stepped up in keeping with the growing recognition of the social value of existing neighborhoods.[116]

In an effort to stem the tide of building decay, concentrated code-enforcement programs were established for marginally stable neighborhoods. But the new programs quickly faltered, not

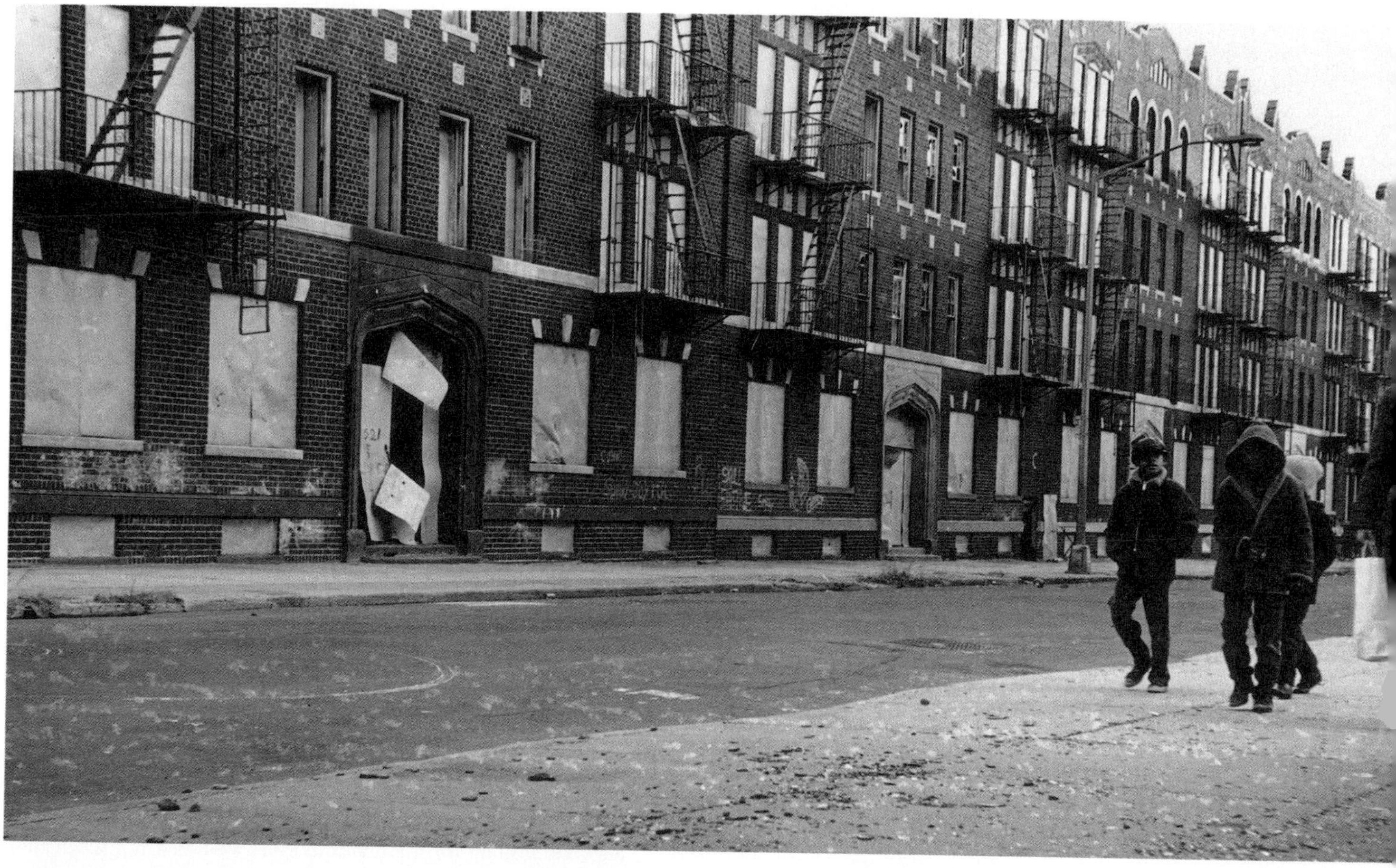

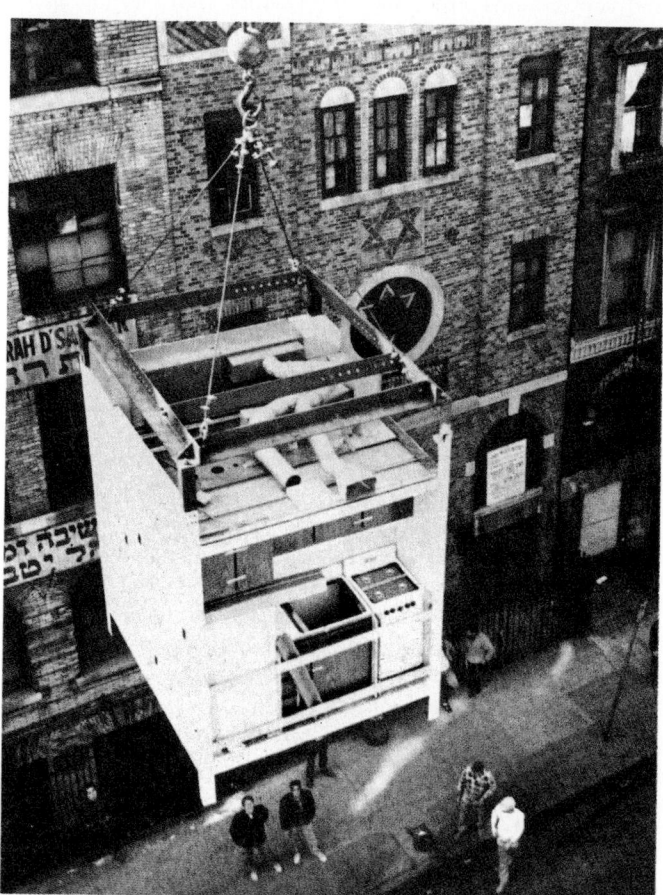

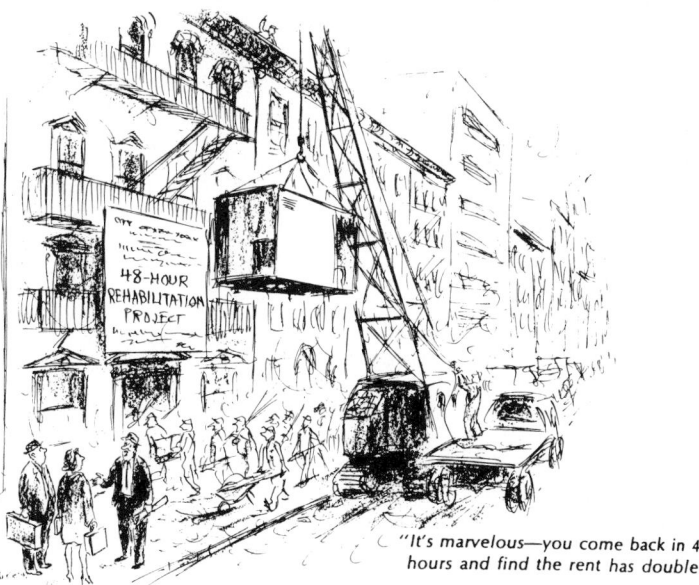

"It's marvelous—you come back in 48 hours and find the rent has doubled!"

Top: Abandoned buildings, Brooklyn, 1970. Fred W. McDarrah. FWM

Bottom left: Mechanical core including finished bathroom and kitchen being installed as part of "instant rehabilitation" of 635 East Fifth Street, between Avenue B and Avenue C. Edward K. Rice of Conrad Engineers with Tishman Research Corporation, 1967. AR. CU

Bottom right: Cartoon. Alan Dunn, 1967. PDE

only because of the magnitude of the problems but also because the necessary federal funding began to dry up as the nation plunged deeper and deeper into the Vietnam War. By 1969 the *New York Times* could report a "housing paralysis": with 130,801 names on the waiting list for public housing, it would take fifty-one years for everyone on the list to get an apartment. According to the *Times*, New York needed 780,000 new subsidized apartments—only 20,000 short of the total number produced by the federal housing program in its thirty-four-year history. The *Times* was quick to point out that though the Lindsay administration, "which inherited these problems, has not been able to run fast enough even to stand still," it had nonetheless taken strides toward allowing the poor to plan the renewal of their own neighborhoods, "in paying careful attention to the quality of design, in attempting to eliminate past cruelties of relocation."[117] But the bottom line—quantity—was not significantly improved. While 13,257 new units were begun in 1968, experts claimed that their impact would be dissipated by the vast number of existing units that decayed each year.

Rent control, initiated as a wartime measure in 1943 but not terminated after the war as it had been in most other cities, combined with the sheer old age of a lot of housing, was fostering a growing and alarming trend: housing abandonment. Abandonment resulted from the frustration of property owners who could not realize a reasonable return on their investment and were therefore unable to finance necessary repairs. The abandonment of the worst housing affected the poorest class; although they may have been able to pay more than what they were being charged for housing, they could not make the necessary leap to a substantially higher class of accommodation. In 1961, 1,000 abandoned buildings were on record. By 1968 some 13,000 buildings, previously housing some 275,000 people, had been abandoned by their owners and ordered by the city to be either bricked up or demolished.

The city was unable to stay ahead of the abandonment process. As a result, the *New York Times* noted:

> More and more vacant structures are left standing with a depressing and demoralizing impact on surrounding property and residents. Their infection spreads quickly through whole blocks, until some sections of the city now resemble bombed-out areas of wartime Europe. . . . A vacant apartment falls prey to drug addicts, who rip out plumbing and sell it to support their habits. The old boiler, in need of repair, stops providing heat. Water freezes, bursts the pipes and drips into electrical wiring, putting out the lights and perhaps starting a fire. The tenants leave, one by one, and the building is gone.[118]

This trend could be seen as beneficial, cleansing the city's housing stock of its least valuable buildings, if the citizenry were experiencing a rising income level and were therefore able to afford better accommodation, but this was not the case.

Clearly, the extent and apparent intractability of this crisis were extraordinary. The city had built so much housing that the continuing shortage could not be explained away as the by-product of bureaucratic inefficiency or callous municipal indifference. The situation was more complex. For one thing, the standards for an adequately housed family had increased, so that much of the housing once deemed adequate was no longer acceptable. Secondly, the number of independent households in the city's population at large had grown: families were smaller, and many more people lived alone rather than with relatives or as boarders, creating an increased demand for dwelling units despite the population decline of the postwar era.[119]

Given the near failure of traditional methods of slum clearance and project development, the late 1960s abounded in new strategies for providing housing for low-income families. Of all the methods advanced, none better suited the frenetic, technologically obsessed mood of the period than "instant rehabilitation," a strategy owing more to the processes of assembly-line factory production than to hands-on field-based building construction. As described in *Scientific American*, the instant rehabilitation technique called for cutting a shaft through each vertical stack of apartments in a tenement, stripping most of the insides of the building, removing the old materials through the shaft by means of a crane and lowering materials for reconstruction through the shaft.[120] The object of this exercise was to transform a worn-out tenement within forty-eight hours. Costly and disruptive tenant relocation would be eliminated, since families living in the building would simply stay in a hotel for the two days and nights that the work was taking place; and the cost of providing upgraded housing would be reduced by as much as $2,000 per apartment over conventional rehabilitation methods and $15,000 to $17,000 over the cost of new units.

The instant rehabilitation system was the brainchild of a California engineer, Edward K. Rice of Conrad Engineers, who collaborated with the Tishman Research Corporation. It was first demonstrated in three neighboring buildings in Manhattan—633, 635 and 637 East Fifth Street (owned by the Carol W. Haussamen Foundation)—where, under a grant from the U.S. Department of Housing and Urban Development, various techniques and materials were being field-tested to refine the system. Key to the system was a mechanical core built off-site containing a finished bathroom and kitchen, the heating and air conditioning for the apartment, as well as a hot water tank and vent systems. Once the core was lowered into the apartment, all that remained was to hook it up with the existing systems that workers had installed in the various rooms. Specially designed telescoping windows that could fit all likely sizes of openings were installed, and a coat of special plaster requiring no paint was troweled on. *Voila!*—a rehabilitated apartment. But, as *Architectural Record* put it, "instant rehab [was] not so instant. Few ideas for rehabilitation have been more highly touted, or caused as much talk, as New York's drop-in kitchen-bathroom core concept. But the realities of old, sagging buildings and high costs of construction labor raise practical questions about both cost and speed for the new system."[121]

In April 1967, after a winter of testing on two of the East Fifth Street buildings, the demonstration of the perfected system commenced at the third, 633 East Fifth Street, a seventy-two-year-old tenement.[122] On Tuesday, April 11, the twelve resident families were moved out and demolition crews of the Wrecking Corporation of America, temporarily abandoning their work on the old Metropolitan Opera building, cleaned the tenement out. By 3:00 A.M., Wednesday morning, the cores were being dropped into the eight-foot-square hole cut through the building. Forty-seven hours, fifty-two minutes and twenty-four seconds from the start, the building's families returned from their two nights at the Broadway Central Hotel to find their apartments transformed, their spirits lifted and their rents raised by almost 100 percent (although no tenants were obliged to pay more than 25 percent of their income on rent).[123]

While instant rehabilitation was spectacular, it was never employed on a large scale, primarily because the field conditions of old, neglected tenements were too idiosyncratic to easily accommodate the prefabricated cores. In addition, unions refused to permit the cores to be factory produced but insisted on construction workers assembling them on nearby sites, thereby driving up costs. Despite the seeming success of the demonstration, Robert Weaver, the secretary of the Department of Housing and Urban Development, was guarded in his assessment at the ceremony marking the conclusion of the forty-eight-hour marathon. It was "not the whole answer by any means," he said. "But it is one . . . way to get moving toward saving buildings and therefore saving neighborhoods for the people who live in them."[124] Perhaps the real benefit of the experiment was the focus it put on the inherent values, both physical and social, of tenement structures. The experiment itself had a direct influence on its immediate environs, where it triggered a spate of conventional renovations in the neighboring buildings.

Quality Lost?

Nothing was more ubiquitous in the postwar era than the new apartment houses that catered to an affluent tenantry but barely exceeded the minimum standards of public housing. As Jason Epstein put it in 1965, when the boom in "luxury" housing and hotels was at its peak, "Hardly anything in history [is] less solidly built than the new buildings that already crumble and tilt, creaking and groaning along Park Avenue, or the new hotels that are really tents made of glass."[125] Typically, the new "luxury" apartments, most of which were built on the Upper East Side and in and around Greenwich Village between 1955 and 1965, had plasterboard walls instead of the prewar plaster; low ceilings (8'6" was usual, but 8'0" was not unheard of); wood tile rather than parquet flooring; no dedicated service elevators and therefore no separate service halls or service entrances to kitchens; and long public corridors serving eight, ten or even twelve apartments. Outside, except for fancy entrances and whatever balconies and, on pre-1961 buildings, setbacks were provided, there was nothing to ornament the white glazed brick that was the cladding of choice.

Efforts to explain the collapse of standards were less than satisfactory. In 1960 Edward L. Friedman, architect in charge of I. M. Pei's research efforts into concrete technology, offered what was as logical an explanation as any:

> Shortly after World War II, the steel shortage, coupled with the appearance of the flat slab, gave impetus to reinforced-concrete construction. Cities where zoning regulations limited building heights, gratefully received the shallower floor-to-floor height of flat-slab construction. An entire floor could be gained. . . . The advantage of flat-slab design was further augmented by "scatter columns" which could be shaped and placed at will according to plan dictates. Taller and more powerful cranes and improved ready-mix concrete service were additional encouragements. There were drawbacks, but of an architectural character. The freedom allowed to column layout condoned development of floor plans devoid of structural coherence. This did not damage rental attraction. The buildings were cloaked in brick skins which were penetrated by window openings determined by plan only, oblivious to any refinement of facade design.[126]

For Marya Mannes, a resident of an old Central Park West apartment building, the new buildings, though justified by the technology, economics and aesthetics of the time, failed to measure up:

> When I visit one of the gleaming white apartment houses recently finished, my appreciation of the new techniques of liv-

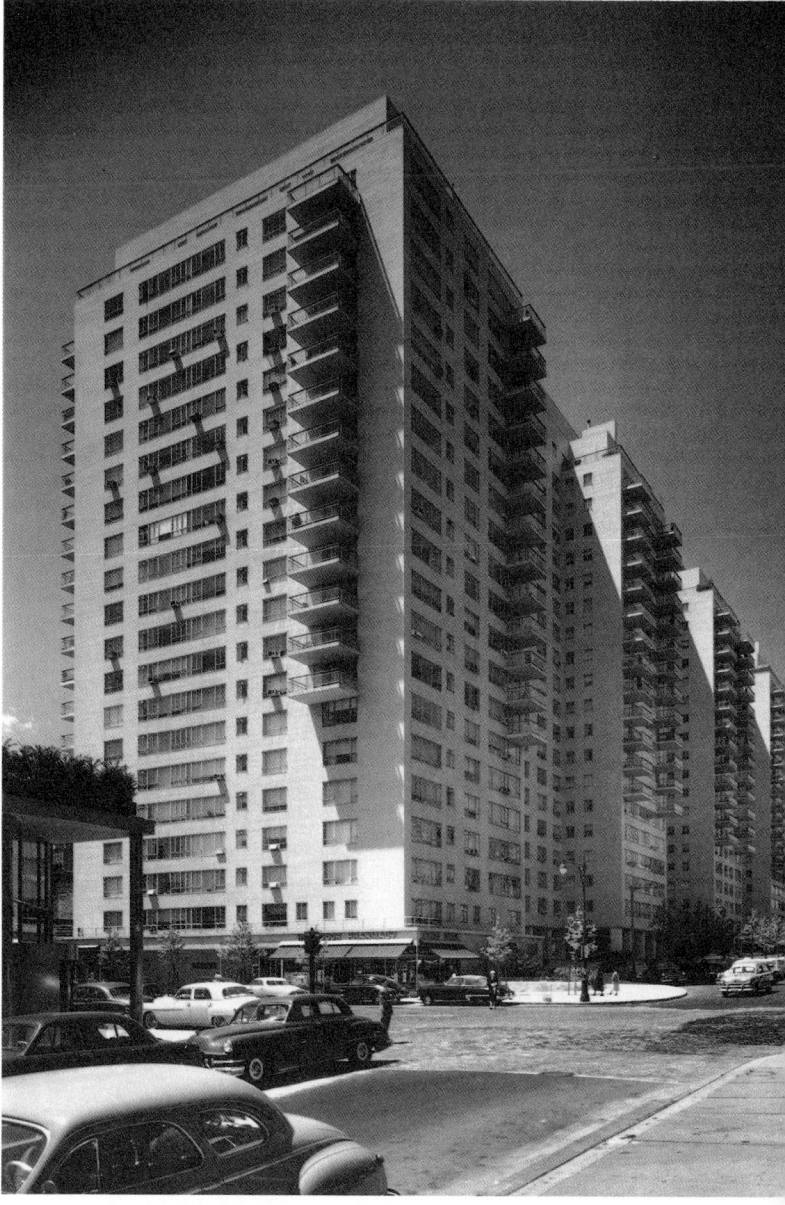

Manhattan House, Second to Third Avenue, East Sixty-fifth to East Sixty-sixth Street. Skidmore, Owings & Merrill and Mayer & Whittlesey, 1950. View to the southwest from Second Avenue. Stoller. ©ESTO

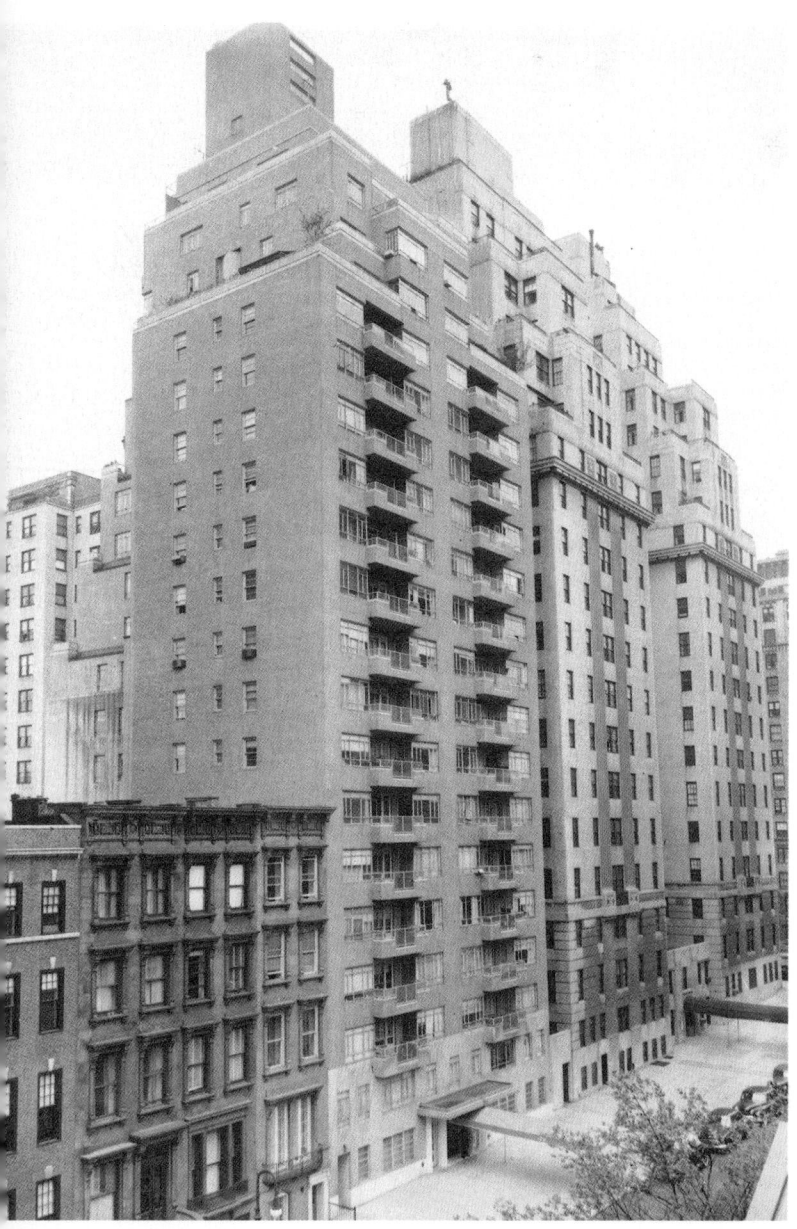

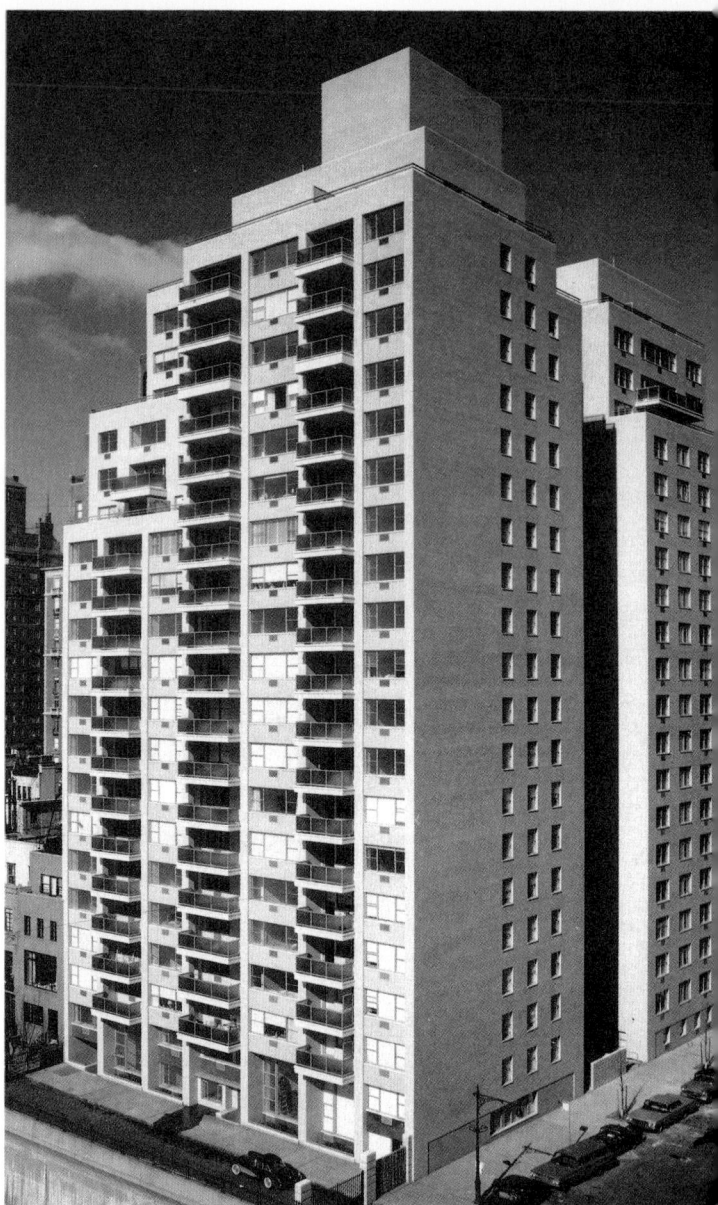

120 East Seventy-ninth Street. Sylvan Bien, 1947. View to the southwest showing 895 Park Avenue (Sloan & Robertson, 1929), on the right. EG

35 Sutton Place. Robert L. Bien, 1961. View to the southwest. EG

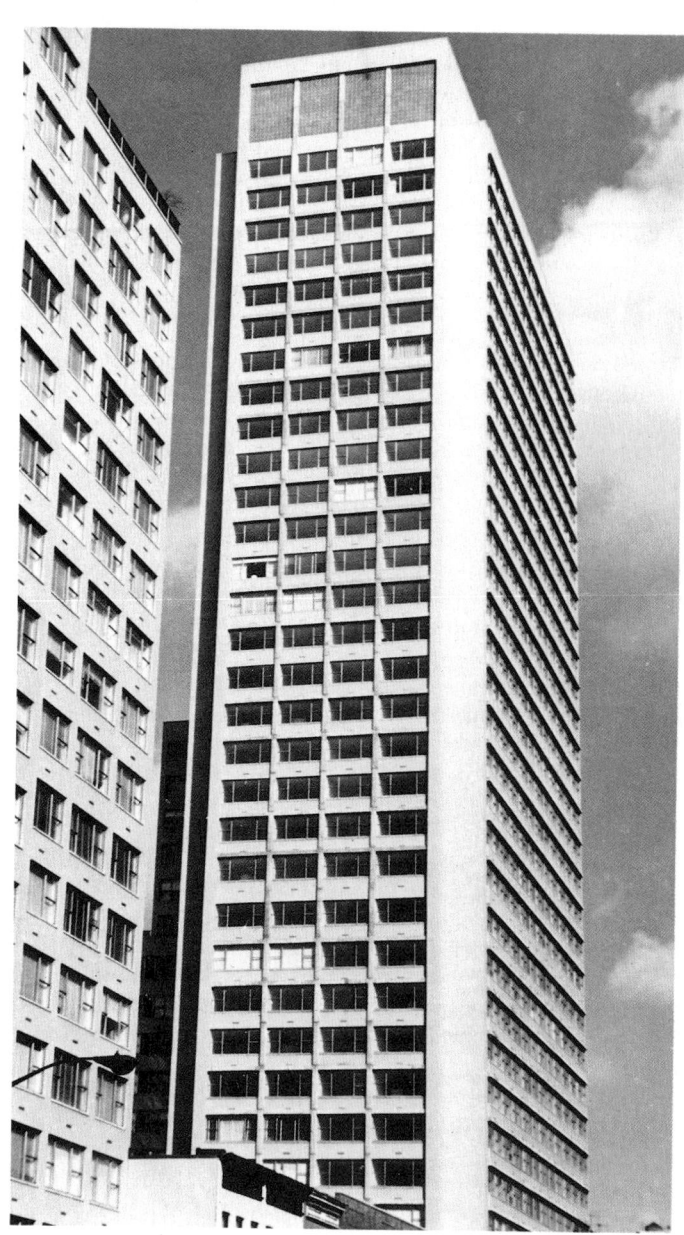

444 East Eighty-second Street. Robert L. Bien, 1964. View to the northwest. EG

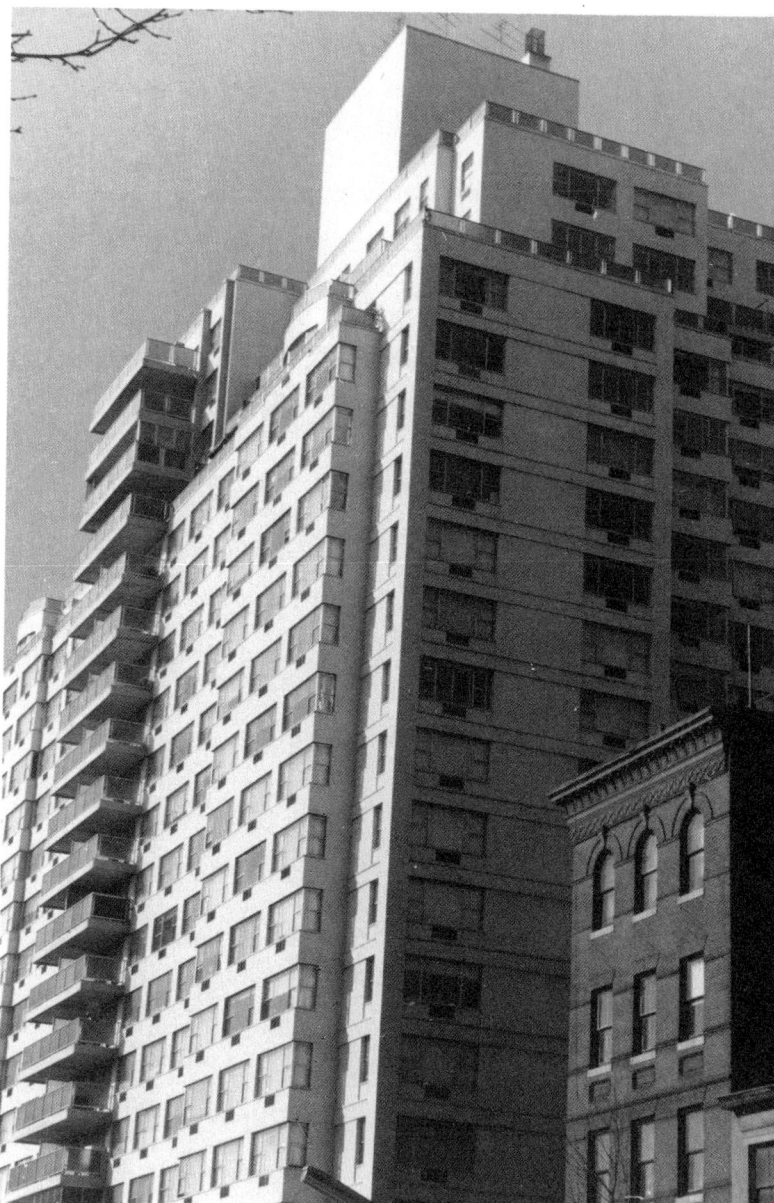

115 East Ninth Street. Robert L. Bien, 1964. View to the southwest. EG

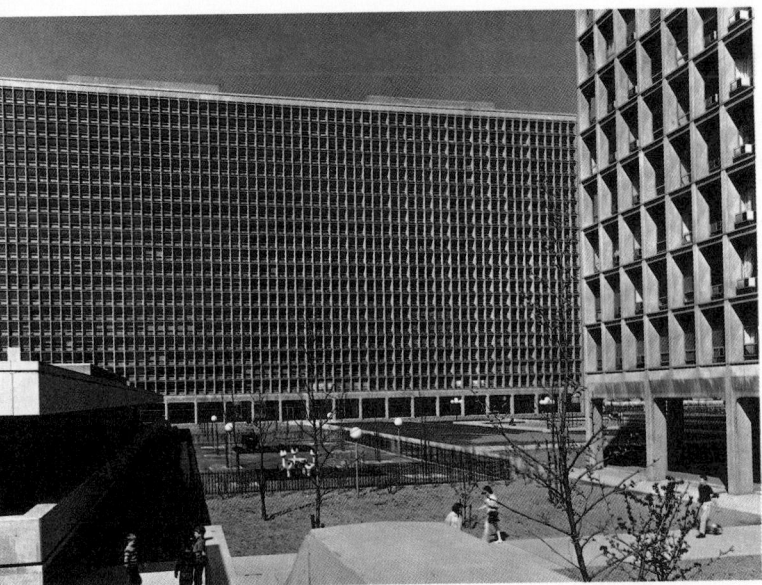

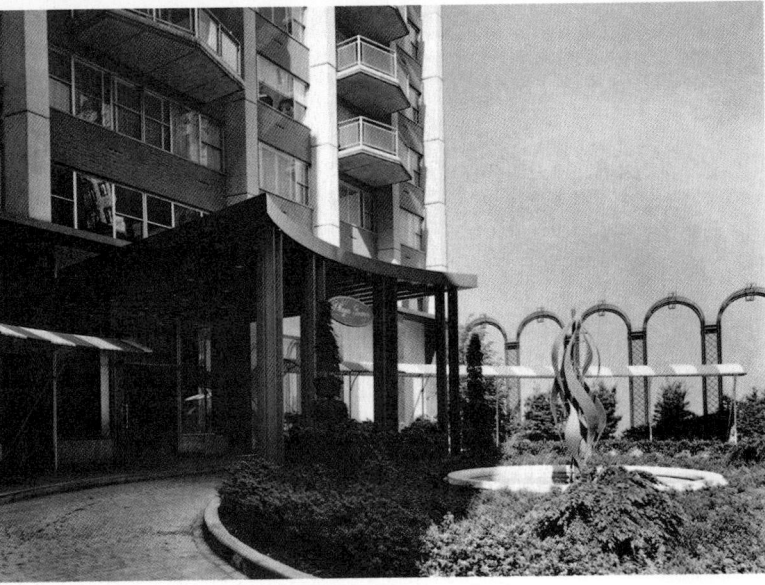

Top: Kips Bay Plaza, First to Second Avenue, East Thirtieth to East Thirty-third Street. I. M. Pei, 1958-66. View to the northeast. Cserna. PCF

Bottom: Plaza Tower, 118 East Sixtieth Street. Samuel Paul and Seymour Jarmul, 1965. View to the southwest. SPDP

ing, the functional gain, is matched by a sense of poverty. The rooms may be large but they are entirely predictable; there is a distinct limit to what you can do to them. . . . In the old apartment houses, as in brownstones, capricious corners and unexpected hallways allow imagination to range: you can do a number of different things in the same space. But the newest apartments strike me like filing cabinets for the human species, one to a drawer, equipped with everything needed for living except that mysterious marriage of man and environment called mood. Space has become mechanical rather than mystical.

Surprisingly, Mannes admired the exteriors of the new apartment houses; she was particularly fond of Manhattan House, describing it as "an exciting block . . . with the particular quality of glamour you find in a huge ocean liner." She even praised "the less imaginative developments" whose "simple whiteness is good for the New York air and light and sky," imposing "cheer and cleanliness on the neighborhood." But the price for this modernity was steep: "Here too, the gain is matched by a definite loss. The shops on the ground floors of most of these buildings are as bright and predictable as their predecessors were cluttered and enticing."[127]

Roger Starr was perhaps the first to publicly articulate how much the minimums of public housing had been carried over into the private sector: "The status of the modern apartment house is expressed in the color of its brick. Since the public housing developments have concentrated on red brick . . . the luxury development is likely to be a house of another color. Any other color. Yellow, white, or water-color. It is difficult for the builder now to brag about the height of his ceilings, because all have become so low that they are dwarfed beside floor heights of even the old tenement house."[128]

By 1962 public criticism of new multifamily housing at all economic levels had grown so vocal that Pease and Elliman, Inc., a prominent firm of rental and management agents, was moved to organize a symposium on the subject, held in March at the Overseas Press Club. The architects on the panel were actively involved in apartment house design: Bernard Guenther of Brown & Guenther; Harold C. Bernhart of Shreve, Lamb & Harmon Associates; Allen Kramer of Kramer & Kramer; H. I. Feldman; Robert L. Bien; Zareh Sourian; and Burton Nowell. The architects discussed the overall lack of design quality in apartment buildings. One architect, quoted anonymously, observed: "We are forced to put our architectural concepts in the background when we design new buildings. Today's architect is really just a room bookkeeper." Allen Kramer noted that "most of today's apartments lack individuality" and that "people are not deceived by superficial differences such as lobbies that look like Chinese restaurants." These themes of uniformity and banality were picked up as well by Zarek Sourian, who pointed out succinctly: "We lack pride and we go in for vulgar flashiness." Bernard Guenther offered a positive suggestion, proposing that apartment buildings be built like office buildings: "When a tenant moves into an apartment, he is committed to the spaces we have partitioned within the apartment. Perhaps we should just build a 'shell,' put the essential facilities in it, give the tenant 2,000 square feet of space and tell him: 'Go ahead and subdivide the space to your heart's content.'"[129]

One solution to the housing-quality problem, for those who could afford it, was to move into older, "prewar" buildings, many of which were being converted into cooperatives. As the *New York Times* put it: "The older, more substantial buildings with high ceilings, soundproof walls and proper entrance halls and dining rooms are coming back into their own, with the result that most of them are being converted into co-ops by tenants who want to ensure their footholds."[130] Brownstones and townhouses were also increasingly attractive alternatives to living in new apartment houses. According to *Time* magazine, one "refugee" from a new twenty-eighth-floor apartment "overhanging the river" said: "Sure, we had a great view but it was like living in a cruise ship. Now we have a parlor floor in a sweet old brownstone in the Village and they'll have to blast to get us out. The only trouble is, I'm afraid they will."[131]

John Berendt, in a provocative essay in *Esquire*, "Patterns of Decay," argued that "new slums are just around the corner for six major cities," New York among them. He characterized the city's "great glassy building spree . . . as profitable (for the builders), expensive (for the tenants) and monolithic for all to look at." The quality of this "gigantic feat of rebuilding," he said, was symbolized by the collapse of the garden of Imperial House (Emery Roth & Sons, 1960), "one of the plushest new apartment houses," into an underground garage. "It is no secret," Berendt continued, "that the construction has been done mostly by speculators in quest of the quick buck: get it up fast, cheap, and then sell it. Walls are thin, details shoddy, and these buildings may achieve the dubious distinction of needing rehabilitation only a short time after being built. One builder, when asked why the best materials were not used, said, 'We expect this thing to be torn down in twenty years.'"[132]

Balconies were one of the most controversial elements of the new apartment houses. While they provided for some kind of outdoor living—which particularly appealed to returning suburbanites—they were hard to keep clean and typically offered less than alluring views of traffic-clogged Upper East Side avenues, as was made clear in Neil Simon's tragicomedy, *The Prisoner of Second Avenue*.[133] But it was pure economics, not tenant preference, that gave the balcony terrace its wide popularity: the cost of building a balcony was only about one-quarter the cost of building a fully enclosed room, yet it could be rented at the equivalent of half a room's rent. More important, the balcony counted as half a room when the builder applied for his FHA mortgage, so he could borrow twice as much as the feature cost him.

In 1941, 240 Central Park South was the first Manhattan apartment house to make extensive use of balconies, and by the mid-1950s they had become a relatively standard feature.[134] But with the nearly universal adoption of air conditioning by the mid-1960s, balconies began to be criticized by architects who, in accordance with the prevailing taste for sleek forms, preferred not to have them. Also, as middle-income projects, such as the ILGWU's Penn Station South project, began to adopt balconies, their earlier status as an exclusive feature of "luxury housing" was challenged. Moreover, with increasing affluence, not only the rich but even the middle class began to get weekend houses and the balcony's usefulness diminished. "In the good old days," Richard Roth observed in 1964, "before people had a lot of money, we used to build balconies. They added a feature to the building. But today, too many people are rich. If they can pay $1,200 a room per year, they can afford a country club in the summer."[135]

With regard to the question of building balconies, logic only sometimes prevailed over taste: at Tower East, Roth based his argument against balconies on the lackluster view over Third Avenue, while Peter Tishman, the developer, thought the view was dandy and wanted panoramic large windows unblocked by balconies. Further downtown, I. M. Pei argued to have the area

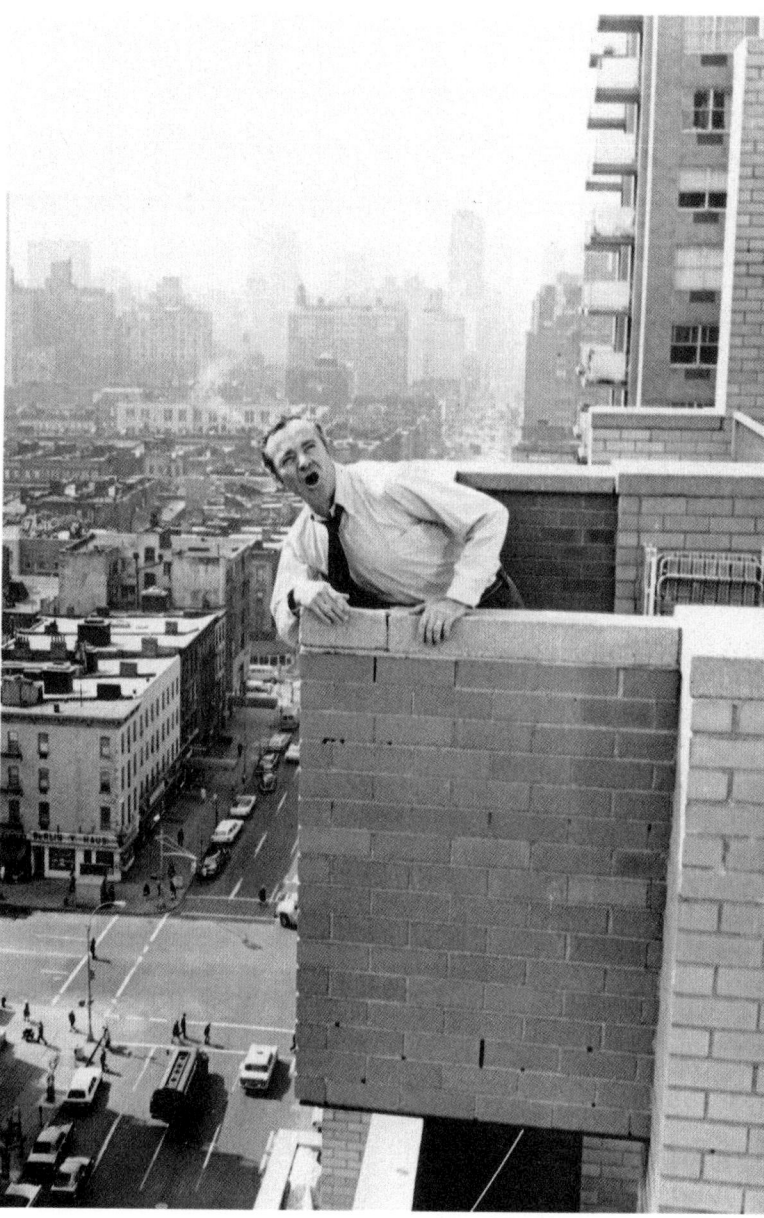

The Prisoner of Second Avenue, 1975. Film still. Art director, Preston Ames; director, Melvin Frank. MOMA

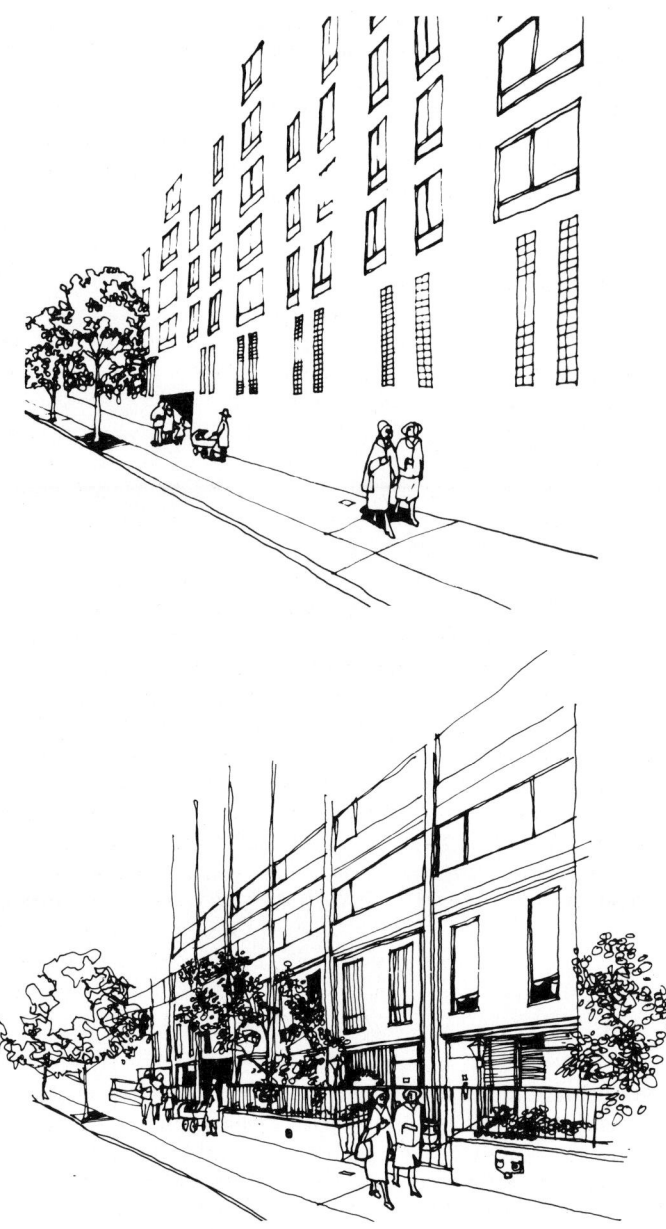

Housing Quality: A Program for Zoning Reform. Urban Design Council, 1973. Top: Drawing of typical postwar apartment building facade. Bottom: Drawing of streetscape enlivened by ground-level maisonettes. NYC

values assigned by the FHA to balconies applied to interior space at his Kips Bay Plaza, not for aesthetic reasons, it would seem, but to provide the tenants with larger rooms that could be used all year. As a result of Pei's arguments about the wastefulness of open-air balconies, the FHA revised its standards in 1961 and allowed only a one-quarter-room allowance. But the 1961 zoning laws revived balconies. While eliminating the setbacks that had functioned as integral terraces, the new code permitted balconies appended to the building mass outside the maximum plot coverage allowed for the building enclosure, in effect increasing the buildable area (and leasable square footage) of apartment houses.

By the mid-1960s the glut of new housing that had been rushed to completion to take advantage of the old zoning was fully absorbed by the marketplace, and new apartment houses began to be built. Where the pre-1961 designs honored the street wall, housed shops that enlivened building wall and street alike, and achieved some interest at the top as the floors stepped back, the new buildings were towers or slabs that rose in unbroken mass to greater height than housing typically had before, with endless stacks of balconies. At the street level the plaza was frequently no more than an automobile drop-off and turn-around—as at the Plaza Tower, 118 East Sixtieth Street. Where that was not feasible, the plazas were deliberately designed to discourage malingering. The plaza of 200 East Sixty-second Street, on the southeast corner of Third Avenue, was notorious: its surface was relieved at three points by ventilators for the building's below-level parking, the top surfaces of which were deliberately rendered useless as seating by the addition of serrated metal strips.

The proliferation of ill-conceived plazas combined with the inherent burdens the new zoning put on the residential development process, particularly in the low-density neighborhoods of the outer boroughs, led Mayor Lindsay to request that the Urban Design Council study the issue. In July 1973, after fifteen months' work spearheaded by Alexander Cooper, the council's executive director, and council members Michael Kwartler and Charles Reiss, a proposal, *Housing Quality: A Program for Zoning Reform,* was offered by Lindsay as a major overhaul of the city's residential zoning law.[136] The changes proposed were dramatic to the point of being revolutionary, reflecting a near-complete repudiation of the fundamental biases of the 1961 ordinance toward the "open city" of isolated towers-in-the-park. The revision drew on arguments advanced by Jane Jacobs and the architect and urban planner Oscar Newman, whose book *Defensible Space* (1972) claimed that the design of buildings and the spaces around them could inhibit crime.[137]

The purpose of the new rules would be to discourage high-rise housing in low-rise neighborhoods and to encourage designs that opened up lobby interiors to easy view from the street and provided useful social and recreational amenities such as day-care facilities. The method for achieving extra bulk, hitherto awarded only for additional open space at ground level or below twenty-three feet, would now be based on various explicit "quality" factors related to a point system. These factors were arranged in four broad categories: neighborhood impact, recreational space, security and safety, and the individual apartment units themselves. Specific items to be rewarded were sunny open spaces, street trees, new buildings that matched the setbacks of adjacent buildings, daylight in hallways and covered parking.

The new housing-quality plan was generally admired by architects, especially the more adventurous ones like William Conklin, who had been railing against the tower model though he recognized that it was popular with developers because it was a cheap way to build. Some older practitioners, however, saw it as a throwback. Philip Birnbaum, the veteran apartment house architect, found "the basic idea . . . sound if the plot is large enough," but he feared that narrow sites might lead to a revival of "the old narrow 'hello neighbor' deep courts of the nineteen-twenties." Simon Breines was even less sympathetic. He compared the report and its motivation to the policies of the Luddites, who "made a kind of convulsive but understandable reaction to the Industrial Revolution."[138]

Despite the fact that the proposal was put forward in the waning days of Mayor Lindsay's second and final term of office, it was taken up by his successor, Abraham D. Beame, and adopted as an option in 1976.[139] A new section was added to the city's charter allowing the establishment of a special permit for housing developments that met the criteria of the program.

The decline of aesthetic and tectonic quality in postwar building was by no means confined to market-rate high-rise housing. For the first time, many observers felt unconvinced that new projects, either in the private or public realm, were beneficial to the city's architecture and urbanism. Publicly sponsored projects seemed increasingly to amount to little more than attempts at problem solving, not the self-confident essays in civicism they had once been. On May 13, 1963, the City Club of New York announced that a jury of three architects and one layman had failed to find a single work of civic architecture created in the city since 1958 worthy of winning the newly established Albert S. Bard award for excellence in civic architecture, named in honor of a recently deceased former club trustee and civic leader who was devoted, according to the club, to "electoral reform and making American cities beautiful."[140] The architects on the jury were Gordon Bunshaft of Skidmore, Owings & Merrill, Charles R. Colbert, former dean of Columbia's architecture school, and Jan C. Rowan, editor of *Progressive Architecture.* Richard W. Childs, chairman of the executive committee of the National Municipal League, was the nonprofessional member. Not content with just announcing its jury's report, the City Club published a brochure, subtitled "a fruitless search for excellence," which achieved wide circulation. The publication included recommendations for architect selection, fee enhancement, and streamlining of review processes, as well as a plea for cultural leadership from city hall.

Ada Louise Huxtable greeted the news—which she labeled a "well-placed stick of dynamite"—with a kind of inverse optimism: "The announcement . . . may mark New York's official awakening to the state of its municipal design. . . . It may well be the initial wave of increased general interest in municipal architecture. The chief significance of this 'no-award fiasco,' as the club's report terms it, is that it brings the questions and criticisms into the open."[141] Two days later, the *New York Times* editorialized, "Government architecture, which should lead, doesn't even follow."[142]

Even though the frequently balky Roger Starr saw some merit in the jury's decision, when asked by the club to comment on the lack of a prize, he pointed out some fundamental dilemmas in municipal architecture:

> [The club's] members should have awarded themselves a special prize for doing so much to make outstanding public buildings impossible. Throughout its life, the club had insisted on equitable specifications, democratic review of proposals, objective criteria, and promotions in accordance with a merit system. A lobby for good municipal architecture might well support the official who flouts these very accomplishments. . . . Good political architecture is a political demand, a demand that money be spent on this instead of other worthy causes.[143]

The jury's report came as a shock to the city's architects. The New York Chapter of the American Institute of Architects denounced the City Club's competition as "misleading and irresponsible," resulting in a "hoax."[144] In a speech at the Architectural League, Simon Breines, speaking for the New York Chapter's executive committee, described the Bard jury's report as exaggerated. He pointed out that only twenty-four buildings completed since 1958 had been reviewed, and that these were submitted by "architects who had decided for themselves to go to the expense and effort to prepare the special brochure of plans and photos required and to pay an entry fee as well."[145] But forty-two members of the chapter, calling themselves the Ad Hoc Committee of Architects for Better City Architecture in New York and including Philip Johnson, Edgar Tafel, John Johansen, William J. Conklin and Norval White, rebuked the official stand as not representing "the views of the Chapter at large." The dissenting group of architects, mostly younger, referred to Breines's speech as "intemperate and selfish—a defensive whitewash with which we do not agree."[146]

Buildings were not the only part of the postwar municipal realm that seemed far less aesthetically satisfying than before. The adoption of new nighttime illumination standards for city streets and the design of new lamp standards was a visible representation of how utilitarian functionalism had almost totally usurped aesthetics in civic design. While the city had never chosen a universal street lamppost, the majority of those in place in 1940 were based on the so-called bishop's crook design prepared in 1892 by the Edison Electric Illuminating Company under the direction of Richard Rodgers Bowker.[147] After the Second World War the development of various high-intensity bulbs led to their adoption for street lighting, increasing visibility for pedestrians and drivers. Rather than adapting the traditional light standard to meet the requirements of the new technology, the city set out to create new designs, beginning in 1948 with the introduction of a stripped-down version of the old type executed in aluminum.[148] Lewis Mumford was not pleased with the improvement:

> Our old-fashioned lamp standards, with the heavy base, the indentations, the melancholy laurel and acanthus leaves, the scrolly horizontal supports, might have been adequate and appropriate in 1900, but they no longer are, and the new ones on Park Avenue, with their uncouth and fussy changes of outline, are even worse. Just because they are less conventional in conception than the old ones, their every departure from strict simplicity is that much more irritating and unlovely.[149]

Other models followed, each progressively more "modern," that is to say more stripped of detail and more aggressively profiled, until an absolutely bare stainless steel post carrying a fluorescent luminaire set at about a 120-degree angle was chosen in 1956. Henry Hope Reed, Jr., contrasted this new fixture with Bowker's elegantly curved bishop's crook in his book *The Golden City* (1959), and not to the new design's advantage.[150] The city's bureaucrats continued to tinker with designs so that by 1959 sixty-four types of light poles could be found on the city's streets. In an effort to establish a uniform type that could be used throughout the city, the industrial designer Donald Deskey was commissioned in 1958 to come up with a new design, which was finally accepted two years later.[151] An early proposal by Deskey to integrate in one post many of the items of street furniture typical of New York's streets—litter bins, fire hydrants, mailboxes, fire-alarm boxes and public telephones—proved unfeasible, but that quirkily awkward design was surely more interesting than his cobralike standards that were adopted.

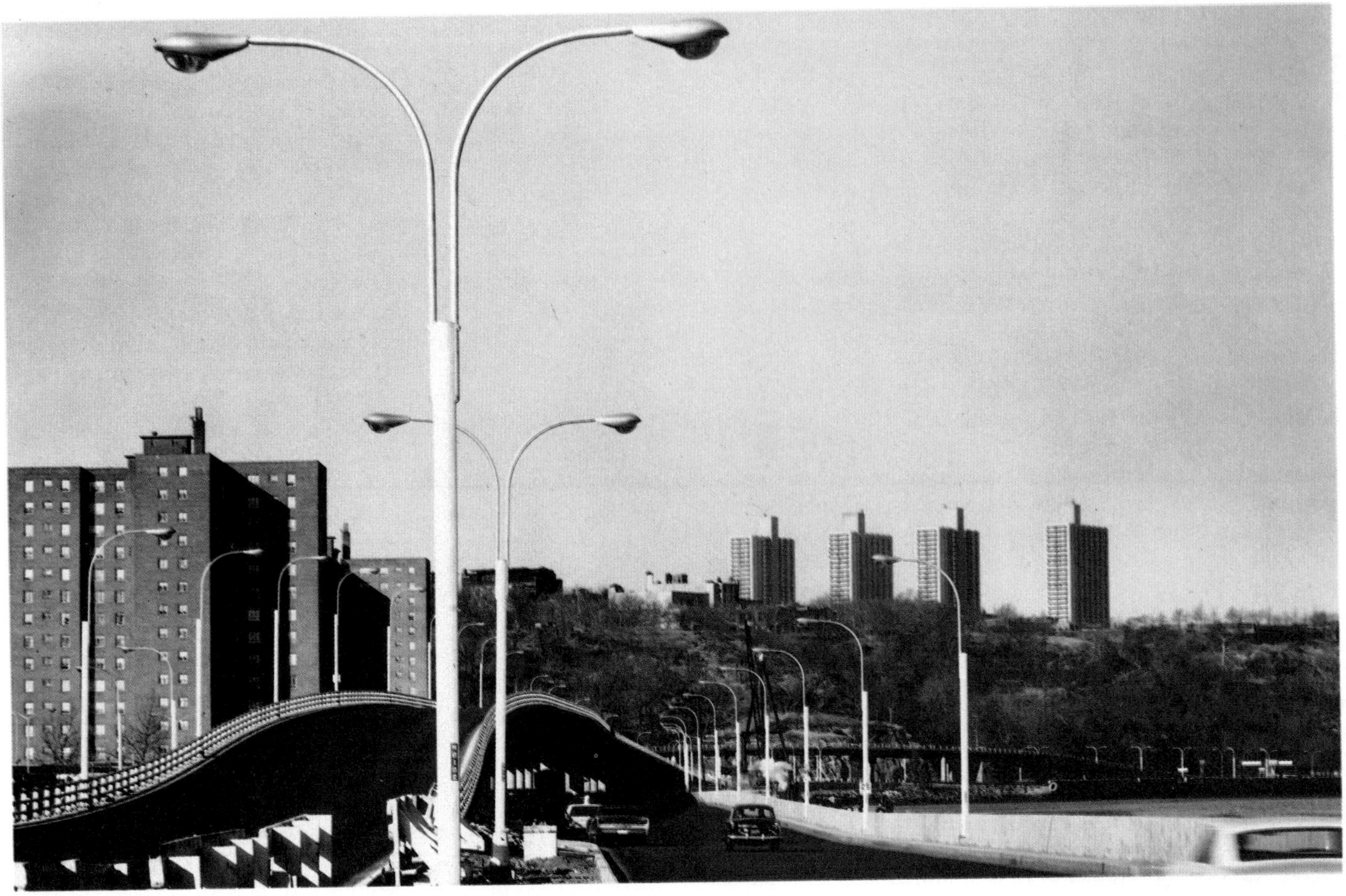

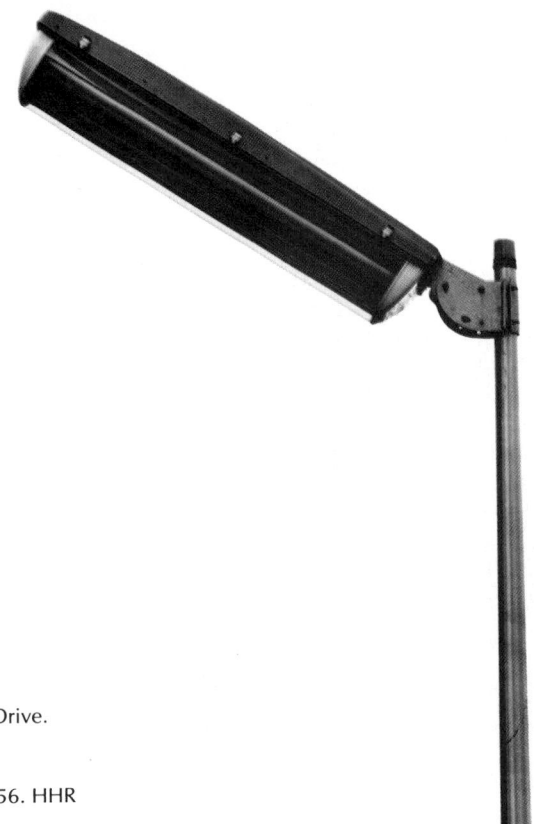

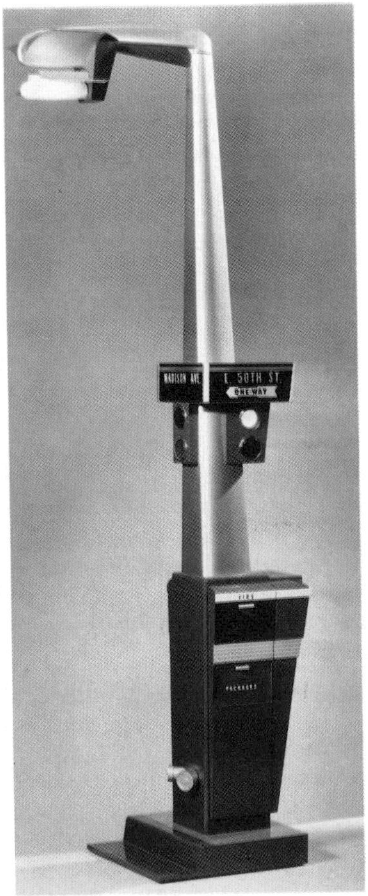

Top: Lamp standards along the Harlem River Drive.
Donald Deskey, 1960. View to the north. CH

Bottom left: New York City lamp standard, 1956. HHR

Bottom right: Proposed lamp standard incorporating street
signs, traffic lights, litter bin, fire hydrant, mailbox, fire-
alarm box and public telephone. Donald Deskey, 1958. CH

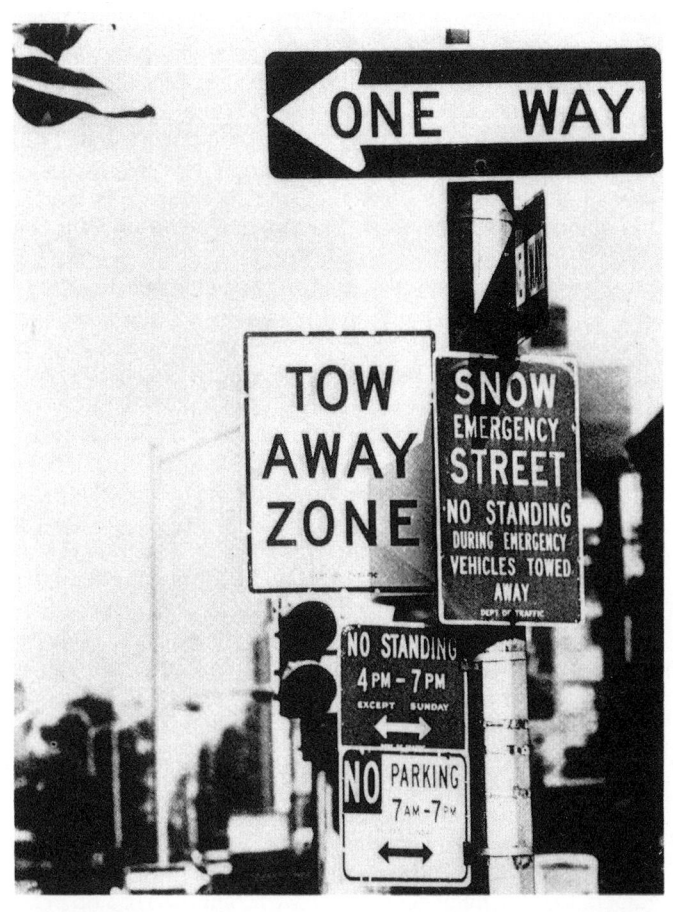

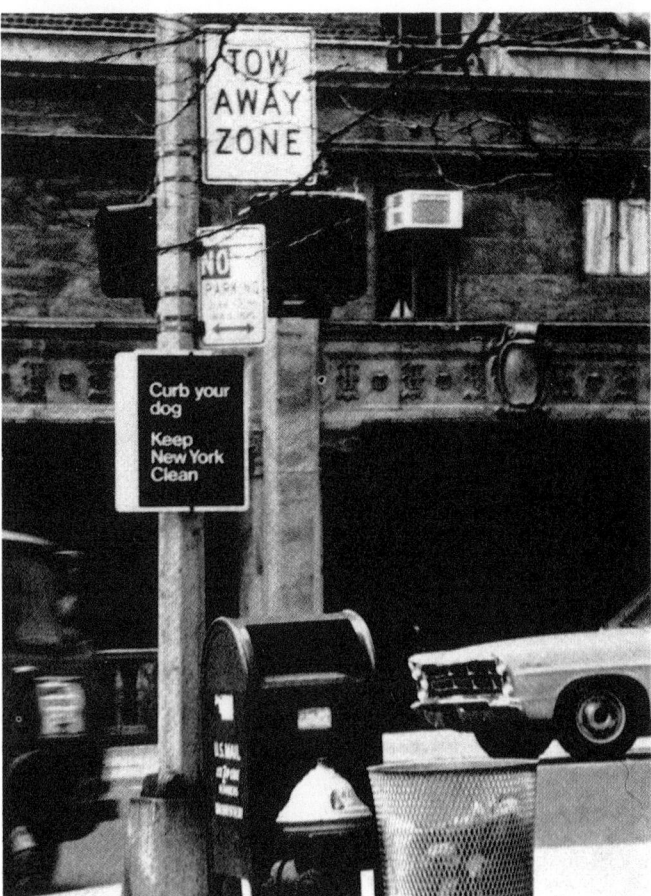

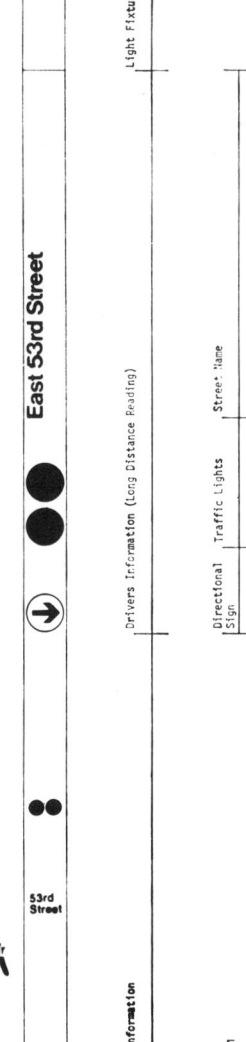

Existing signage contrasted with signage
proposed by Massimo Vignelli and
Seymour Evans for East Fifty-third Street,
1969. CA. CU

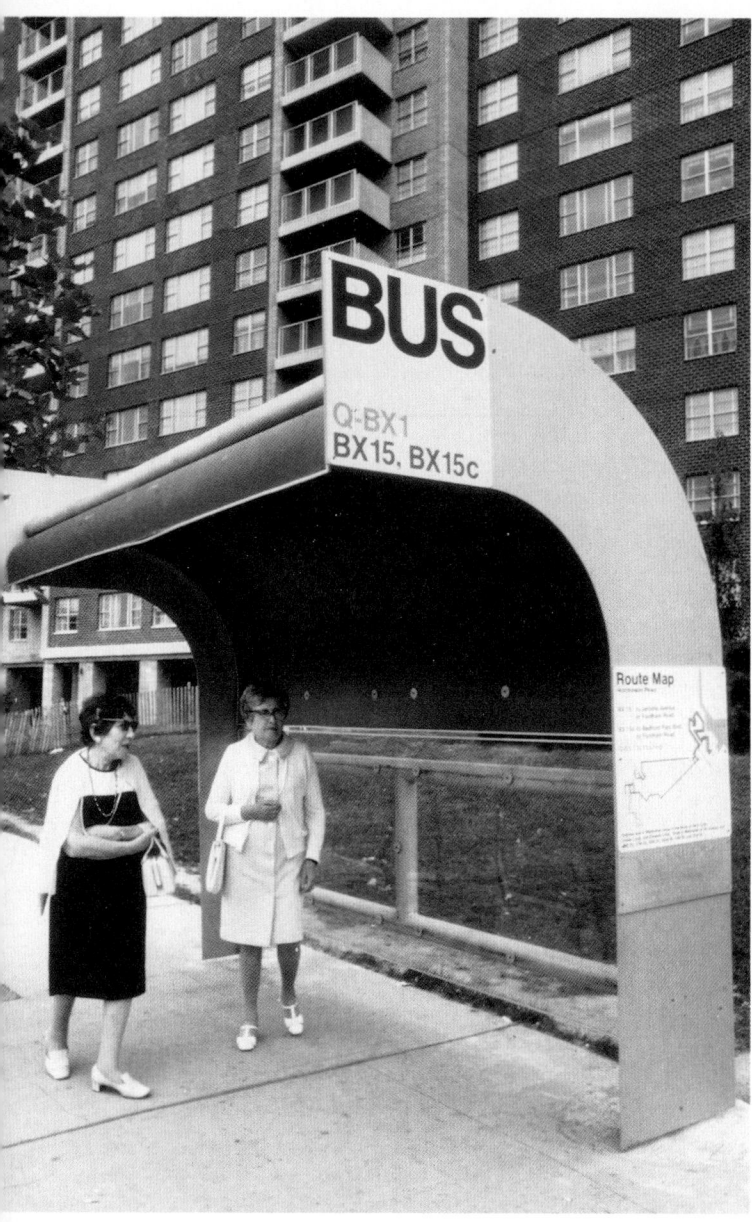

Bus shelter. James Stewart Polshek, 1971. JSP

Still, the streetscape remained a cacophony of directional and instructional signs, traffic lights and the like, a fact that had been criticized by the tidy-minded Museum of Modern Art in its 1954 exhibition "Signs in the Street."[152] In 1969 the designer Massimo Vignelli and the lighting consultant Seymour Evans were commissioned by the city to study the problem of street signage along Fifty-third Street, eventually resulting in the special standards (Designetics, 1978) installed on the Citicorp block.[153]

Not only was the city inept in achieving distinction; it seemed intent on thwarting the development of even the most commonplace amenities. In 1969, after years of resistance, the city undertook a pilot program to develop a bus-shelter prototype.[154] Two companies came forward with proposals, but neither was adopted. Some fifty shelters were built, however, and the Columbia Equipment Corporation's blandly straightforward prefabricated anodized-aluminum design, featuring transparent shatterproof walls made of plexiglass, was well received by the public. Two years later, a more stylish shelter was developed by James Stewart Polshek, and about a hundred structures based on his design were built.[155] When Polshek set to work on the design, he staged an informal intra-office competition, which resulted in a simple, arc-shaped structure that featured fluorescent lighting and large, clear signage. Without funds to properly maintain the shelters, however, they became covered with graffiti.

In 1975 a new shelter design was proposed by William E. Bouchara, a French businessman who formed Bustop Shelters, Inc.[156] What made Bouchara's scheme different was that it included paid advertising on the shelters, with a percentage of the advertising revenue to be remitted to the city. The aluminum-framed, De Stijl–influenced design was composed of a fiberglass roof and clear glass panels for wind protection, with a lighted glass-enclosed showcase with room for two posters. The eight-foot-high, 1,000-pound structures also featured photocells that automatically switched on the lighting at nightfall. In less than a year 250 of Bouchara's shelters were installed in Manhattan and the Bronx, and plans for 600 more were approved by the city.

Quality Regained?

In his campaign for office, John Lindsay set a high value on city design.[157] Once he became mayor, he manifested his commitment to architecture and urbanism in a number of ways, first by commissioning a report, prepared by Edward J. Logue, which included a detailed assessment of the city's design approach to planning, redevelopment and even neighborhood conservation (see "Dull Utopias: Public Housing," above). He then established a blue-ribbon commission, the Mayor's Task Force on Urban Design, and its successor, the Urban Design Council, to help him evolve policy, and formed the Urban Design Group within the City Planning Commission, a body that had been notably devoid of an architectural component since its inception in 1938.

In April 1966 Lindsay announced the appointment of William S. Paley, chairman of the Columbia Broadcasting System, as chairman of the urban design task force.[158] Also appointed to the task force were bankers Eli S. Jacobs and James M. Clark, Jr.; Stephen Currier, president of the Taconic Foundation, who died in an airplane accident before the committee began its deliberations; Joan Davidson, trustee of the J. M. Kaplan Fund; George Lindsay, the mayor's brother; Walter Thayer, president of the New York Herald Tribune; and four architects: Philip

Johnson, I. M. Pei, Jaquelin Robertson and Robert A. M. Stern. On February 7, 1967, the task force issued its report, *The Threatened City*, which was divided into four sections: "The Trouble," "Opportunities," "Toward a Method" and "Proposals."[159] The report was largely drafted by the architectural critic Walter McQuade and was prefaced by a letter to Mayor Lindsay that emphasized the essential problem: "The subject is quality, the quality of living in the sometimes overpowering environment of the world's greatest city." The letter called attention to the importance of design to the city's environment as a whole: "Design is not a small enterprise in New York City today, nor should it be considered narrowly as merely a matter of aesthetics, a frail word. In our increasingly crowded man-shaped urban world, aesthetics must now include not only the marble statue in the garden but the house, the street, the neighborhood, and the city as a cumulative expression of its residents."[160]

The report pulled no punches, bemoaning the decline of civic architecture, contrasting the 1907 ferry terminal at Whitehall (Walker & Morris)[161] with that completed for the Department of Marine and Aviation in 1956 (Roberts & Schaefer), and categorizing the subway system as "probably . . . the most squalid public environment of the United States: dark, dingily lit, fetid, raucous with screeching clatter; one of the world's meanest transit facilities."[162] It lamented the overall lack of attention to design in the postwar reconstruction of Third Avenue and the city's failure to land-bank the 12,000 acres of vacant land on Staten Island that sold for $9,000 an acre in 1957 and now commanded $40,000. And it focused on the Bedford-Stuyvesant area of Brooklyn, an "overpopulated wilderness" consisting of 500 blocks of low-rise, walk-up housing that accommodated 200,000 people in 1900 but now was home to twice that number: "Here one sees the city's central agony, the racial stockade, the solution to which is far beyond the redesign of physical surroundings or any other single remedy."[163] The report also reminded people of the good places that existed within the city and cautioned the citizenry to struggle for their preservation.

The Threatened City went on to analyze the government's failure to build imaginatively and to influence the private sector to improve its contribution, placing the responsibility directly in the hands of the mayor. If he used "the full strength of his position," the report said, the mayor could transform the way the city as a whole viewed its environment. It proposed the appointment of five citizens, serving without pay, to advise the mayor as a council on urban design. More important, it called for "a full-time staff of technical design specialists" to work within the Department of City Planning, "an urban design force of trained professionals of the highest competence, to be headed by an architect-planner of proven ability and personal force. This group should be charged with the developing—or commissioning—of concept-designs for rebuilding special-use sections of New York."

The report suggested that the group (which a few months later was implemented as the Urban Design Group) be supported by a force of not less than sixty people, with approximately fifteen design specialists plus supporting personnel, forming a cadre of dedicated urban design activists that would make municipal service for young architects and urban designers "as compelling as that of the gifted young lawyers who sign up for service as assistant district attorneys in New York to saturate themselves in the practice of their profession before moving on to private practice." The report also called for the creation within the group of sixty of a "unit of development-instigators . . . to work full-time on the correlation of private and public con-

struction into plans for special-use areas."[164] These would eventually be realized as various special development offices for lower and midtown Manhattan, downtown Brooklyn and so on. The report further recommended the abolition of the notorious Board of Standards and Appeals—a recommendation not acted upon—to concentrate all matters of zoning administration and interpretation in the city planning department, and urged the use of the zoning resolution to foster good design through special district legislation and through the use of floor-area bonuses to achieve desired goals. It also recommended that all mapping, now done in the various borough president offices, be concentrated in the planning department, and that the Site Selection Board be discontinued and its advisory functions turned over to the planning department.

The *New York Times* was not impressed with *The Threatened City*, finding it "overly preoccupied with traditional views and vistas" and dependent on a "conventional brand of nineteenth-century urban esthetics [that] has limited value for the dynamic disorders of the twentieth-century city."[165] Taking umbrage at this criticism of the report, the four architect-members of the commission responded in a letter to the newspaper, observing:

> If by "nineteenth-century urban esthetics" you mean access to the water's edge for all, imaginative design for our major avenues, an over-all plan for plazas and parks, then we are for it. . . . Design, we say, should not be considered narrowly as merely a matter of esthetics. . . . It must include the house, the street, the neighborhood and the city as a cumulative expression of its residents. By far the greater part of the report was concerned with these things. Still the main burden of our report was more political than architectural. We tried to suggest to Mayor Lindsay that if he can succeed in establishing the machinery and the procedures which will permit New York to take advantage of its incomparable design opportunities, he will have forged a tool which will be of incalculable help in restoring and strengthening those intangibles known as pride, tone and *esprit* upon which the good health of all human institutions, such as cities, must ultimately rest.[166]

Stephen Zoll, reviewing the work of the Paley task force in 1973, found it to be based on "naive optimism," but he believed it made two important points: "that the city's endless process of redevelopment was conceived piecemeal," and "that pretty much under existing law the city could exert enormous municipal control over both public and private design."[167] This latter point was made powerfully in the report, which stated: "No one can build in this city without exposing himself to a bargaining position with the [municipal] government."[168] But, according to Zoll, the report "made basic errors" in assuming "that the way to save the city from being destroyed by social polarity was to design into the fabric of the city the kinds of amenities that would hold or lure back the middle class." He continued:

> To a great extent, this insistence on reform by architectural design was . . . based on the faulty premise of visual improvement. The effort was bound to fail because the only available subsidy to provide amenity . . . was higher density; but greater bulk in the CBD [Central Business District] sterilizes development in the rest of the city. . . . The only possible effect higher commercial density can have on the middle class is to disperse them further yet beyond the municipal tax jurisdiction.[169]

In 1967 Lindsay followed up on the report of the task force, forming the Urban Design Council of New York, some of whose members—Paley, Pei and Johnson—had served on the earlier commission.[170] In 1970 the council, at Lindsay's request, undertook "to review the ways in which public works projects are initiated, architects selected and design review carried out, with an end toward recommending major changes in this process to insure a higher quality of design in schools, libraries, firehouses and other civic buildings."[171] Their findings, *A Report on the Working Relationships of Architects and the City of New York*, published in November 1971, outlined procedures and advocated higher rates of compensation to attract topflight professional talent. But by the time its recommendations were broadcast, the economic recession and the city's fiscal crisis rendered the report relatively moot. The council undertook a second report, *Housing Quality: A Program for Zoning Reform*, which would have long-term effects (see "Quality Lost?" above).

Lindsay also established the Urban Design Group, announcing his decision in a speech given before the annual convention of the American Institute of Architects, which was held at the New York Hilton in May 1967.[172] Jonathan Barnett, Jaquelin Robertson, Richard Weinstein and Myles Weintraub, who had already served as consultants to the city for one of the vest-pocket park programs, and one of whom, Robertson, had served on the Paley committee, were the Urban Design Group's founding members.[173] Suddenly the city became a laboratory for urban design experimentation and a mecca for students and recent graduates, particularly from Yale's architecture school—not a surprising connection given that three of the Urban Design Group's four leaders had graduated from Yale (Weinstein went to the University of Pennsylvania). Other Yale graduates who quickly joined them were Alexander Cooper and Michael Dobbins. The members of the Urban Design Group, the glamorous corps d'elite of Lindsay's revitalized planning department and commission, which was headed by a young lawyer, Donald Elliott, considered themselves "true" advocacy planners, arguing that the more radical groups were adversary planners.[174] The group worked quickly, and within two years it was so well established and—in the eyes of many observers—so accomplished that the Architectural League asked Jonathan Barnett to organize an exhibition of its work in May 1969.[175]

The Urban Design Group seized as its principal bargaining chip the granting or withholding of bonus floor area in return for which the developer would provide a plaza. By expanding the concept of the plaza bonus through the establishment of special-use districts calling for other types of design amenities, the Urban Design Group recharted the course of the 1961 zoning resolution and the very concept of zoning as a whole. As Stephen Zoll put it: "Instead of being asked to work negatively—by excluding incompatible uses and restraining intensity of use and forbidding encroaching placement of buildings on their sites—zoning was, from 1967, to be used positively as a planning instrument." In so doing, the Urban Design Group introduced coordinated design for entire areas of the city, as the Paley report had recommended. But, as Zoll observed, the use of zoning as the instrument of coordinated planning was problematic, given that it had only "higher bulk" to offer as an incentive. "It was a formal heresy," he wrote, but one that could be defended because it not only achieved a presumed social benefit—better planning and design—but also increased the city's tax base. Zoll saw this type of incentive zoning as nothing short of "an essay to create a new order" out of the existing city. "The question of what bulk would be right for the city became subtly changed to: how do we get the greatest bulk level and tax return in order to support the *stricken* city? Before our mystified eyes, zoning has been turned from a hope of restraint to a strategy of expansion."[176]

By the early 1970s the original members of the Urban Design Group had scattered: Richard Weinstein had become director of the city's Office of Lower Manhattan Development in 1968, a position he held until 1974, when he opened a private practice; Jaquelin Robertson headed the city's Office of Midtown Development between 1969 and 1972 before leaving for private practice and becoming, in 1973, a member of the City Planning Commission, only to quit soon afterward and take on a major redevelopment project for Tehran, Iran;[177] Jonathan Barnett left the group to head up an urban design program at the City College of New York in 1971; and, in December 1973, Alexander Cooper was appointed to succeed Robertson on the City Planning Commission. This move, according to *Architecture Plus*, was "Lindsay's last major appointment before stepping down as mayor and one of his best."[178]

All in all, Lindsay's intentions notwithstanding, the city seemed unable to turn the tide against its own venality. The problem lay in the very strategy the Mayor's Task Force on Urban Design had urged Lindsay to exploit: incentive zoning. So it was that Norman Mailer, in assessing Lindsay's tenure in office, blamed him for what he was only partially responsible for fostering, a course of action he had pursued in the name of amelioration if not reform:

> If Lindsay had in part carried through a program of increasing self-government and opportunity in the ghettoes, he had also worked with the most powerful real estate interests in the city. No question that in his eight years, the ugliest architecture in the history of New York had also gone up. The new flat tops of the skyline now left New York as undistinguished in much of its appearance as Cleveland or Dallas. It is possible that Lindsay had bought social relief at the price of aesthetic stultification, call it desecration—the view of New York's offices and high rise apartments proving sacrilegious to the mood of any living eye—Wasp balance had done it again.[179]

Disaster City

In 1949, as part of his bittersweet tribute to New York life, E. B. White called attention to New York's toughness in the face of disaster: "By rights New York should have destroyed itself long ago, from panic or fire or rioting or failure of some vital supply line in its circulatory system or from some deep labyrinthine short circuit. . . . Mass hysteria is a terrible force, yet New Yorkers seem always to escape it by some tiny margin: they sit stalled in subways without claustrophobia . . . they meet confusion and congestion with patience and grit—a sort of perpetual muddling through."[180]

While White's assessment concentrated on the everyday disasters with which most New Yorkers routinely coped, there were some that were exceptional and, in their specialness, closely related to the city's physical character. The 1940s began for the city not only with a world's fair carried over from the previous decade but with preparations for a war, the seeds of which were sown ten or more years before. Though the United States did not enter World War II until December 7, 1941, news of German air raids on London in 1940 had led New Yorkers to contemplate the possibility of air attacks on the city, so that eight days after the Japanese invasion of Pearl Harbor, the city was prepared to undertake for the benefit of newsreel cameramen two practice air-raid drills in Times Square.[181] New Yorkers were slow to react to the first alarm, but the second time around they cleared the busy streets in less than ninety seconds.

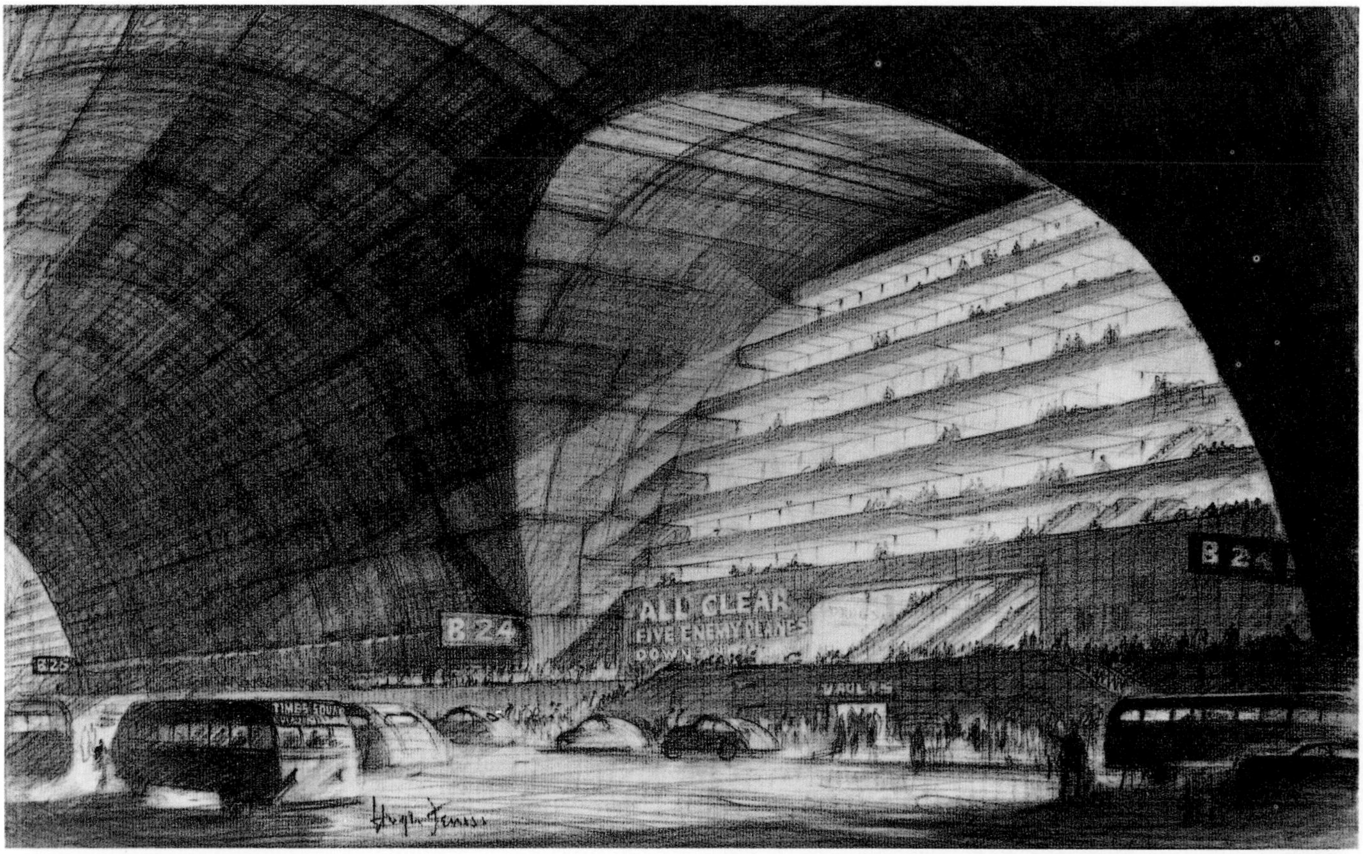

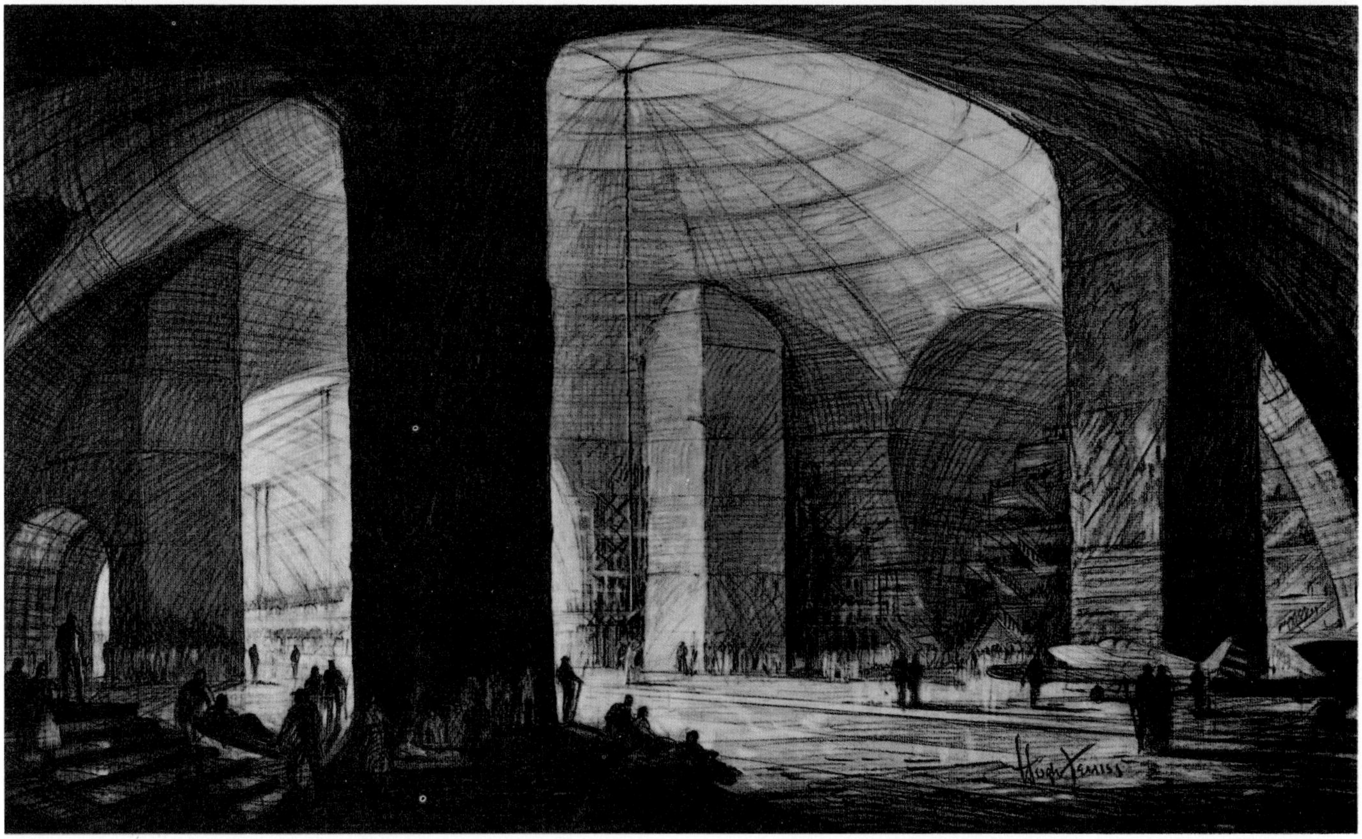

Top: Proposed bomb shelter in the Palisades, New Jersey. George J.
Atwell, John Evans and Hugh Ferriss, 1943. Rendering by Hugh Ferriss.
CU

Bottom: Proposed bomb shelter in the Palisades, New Jersey.
Rendering by Hugh Ferriss. CU

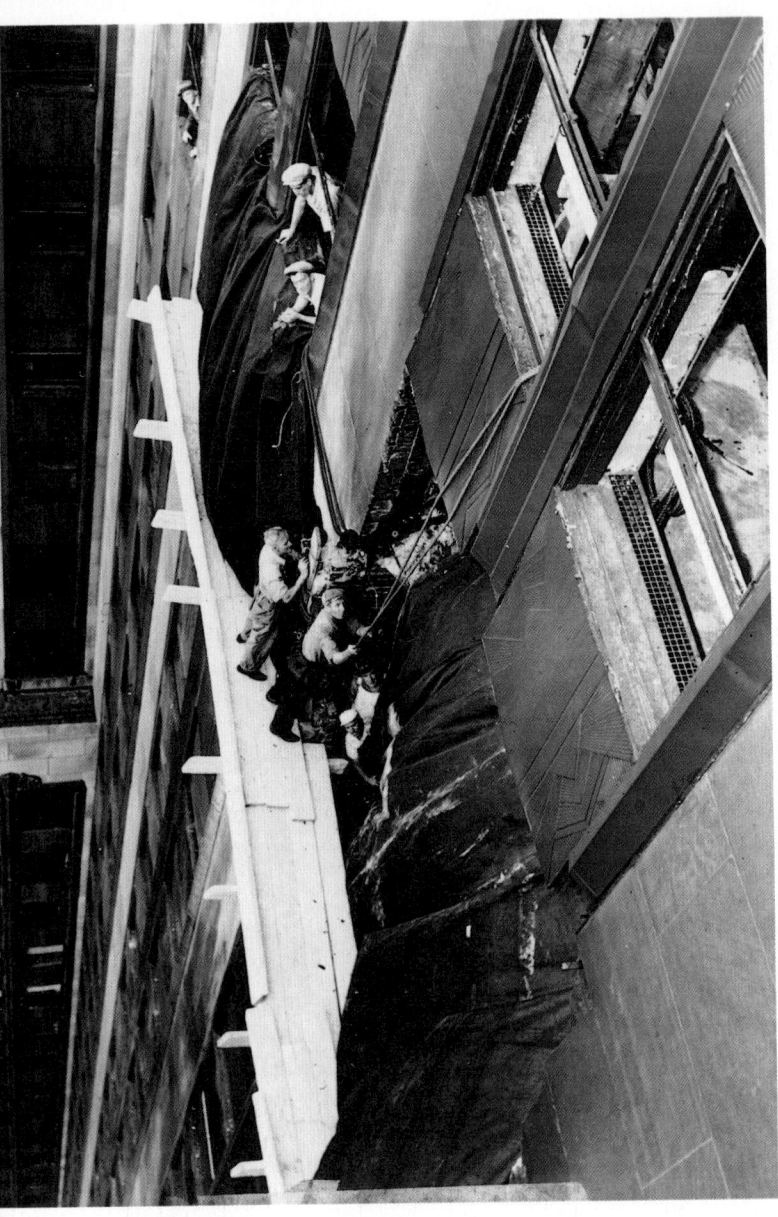

Army bomber plane crashes into the Empire State Building, July 28, 1945. LOC

Although most citizens were appalled by the prospect of air attacks on the city, the threat was grist for the mill of decentralists like Lewis Mumford[182] and Frank Lloyd Wright, who hyped his Broadacre City proposal as "bomb proof."[183]

With war a fact, New York, like other coastal cities, responded to the threatened attacks with nighttime dimouts and blackouts, including the darkening of Times Square.[184] The city had been darkened during World War I, but with the object of saving electricity; now the threat of invasion was the more urgent motivation. Blackout requirements resulted in the tarring over of most of the city's skylights—many of which would not see daylight again for a generation or more.[185] It also caused a rush on fabric needed for blackout curtains, depleting supplies in department stores and inspiring the publicity-obsessed decorator Dorothy Draper to suggest an alternative. According to the New York Times, she made the recommendation that instead of draping windows with heavy fabric to blacken them at night as a precaution against air raids, New Yorkers should adopt a cheaper and more decorative strategy by stenciling or painting designs on opaque roller shades and inserting them between the venetian blinds and the windows.[186]

The prospect of attack raised questions for New York. In particular, there was great concern for the safety of people working in skyscrapers and for those who might be walking or driving in the skyscraper districts during an enemy air attack. In a report to the American Institute of Architects, William Orr Ludlow, the architect of a number of pre-Crash skyscrapers, attempted to quell fears over large-scale disasters that might befall very tall buildings.[187] According to Ludlow, skyscraper construction was more rigid than most other types of building; in addition, he believed that their slender proportions presented difficult targets for bombers. Nonetheless, he cautioned that the high concentration of people in the skyscrapers and their access to the sight and sound of the enemy's planes in the event of attack presented increased risk of panic.

Despite fears about the security of tall buildings, preparations were made to use skyscrapers as bomb shelters. But George J. Atwell, head of the country's largest foundation-construction company, working with John Evans, chief engineer of the Port of New York Authority, and Hugh Ferriss, also developed designs to blast enormous shelters in the Palisades, across the Hudson from Manhattan. His plans called for the construction of a rock-hewn tunnel 100 feet high, 200 feet wide and a mile and a half long that would shelter 200,000 people in Piranesian splendor with room left over for munitions plants and fleets of fighter planes.[188]

Surprisingly, it was not enemy forces that caused one wartime crash in New York City. On a foggy Saturday morning at 9:49, July 28, 1945, Lt. Col. William F. Smith, Jr., a highly decorated and experienced flyer, crashed his Army B-25 Mitchell bomber into the seventy-eighth and seventy-ninth floors of the Empire State Building, killing fourteen people, including himself, and injuring some thirty others.[189] Although the air traffic controllers at La Guardia Airport had ominously warned the pilot that they were "unable to see the top of the Empire State Building,"[190] Smith decided to continue his flight from New Bedford, Massachusetts, to Newark Airport, declining to land at La Guardia. Less than a minute after passing La Guardia, the pilot was lost and apparently mistook the East River for the Hudson and began his descent. Eyewitnesses report seeing the plane buzz Rockefeller Center and pass the New York Central Building at around the level of the twenty-second floor before hitting the Empire State. But less than forty-eight hours after the catastrophe, after inspections by architects and engineers, the building was deemed safe and, except for the eighty-sixth-floor observatory, was back open for business.

With the war's end, New Yorkers momentarily relaxed, only to grow more apprehensive than ever as they began to appreciate their increased vulnerability in an age of jet propulsion and nuclear fission. As E. B. White wrote in 1949:

> The subtlest change in New York is something people don't speak much about but that is in everyone's mind. The city, for the first time in its long history, is destructible. A single flight of planes no bigger than a wedge of geese can quickly end this island fantasy, burn the towers, crumble the bridges, turn the underground passages into lethal chambers, cremate the millions. The intimation of mortality is part of New York now: in the sound of jets overhead, in the black headlines of the latest edition.[191]

As the last rivet was being driven in the new Sinclair Oil Building, workmen on the job as well as nearby office workers shared their concerns for the future in a post-nuclear age with *Life* magazine's editors.[192] Meanwhile, Jerry Finkelstein, the newly appointed chairman of the City Planning Commission, sought to reassure the population that "there are ways in which substantial protection against the atomic bomb can be provided for many of those in greatest danger."[193] Deemed a "prime target area" in the event of war, New York grimly set out to protect itself against attack as the United States and the USSR locked horns in the so-called Cold War.

In discussions of civil defense, New York was most frequently used as the case in point. For example, in vivid detail *Time* magazine outlined a scenario of doom should the Russians attack New York with an atom bomb on an overcast autumn morning, targeting its weapon to explode a half mile in the air over Union Square.[194] Assessing the situation after Civil Defense Week, 1951, *Business Week* reported that New York was remarkably prepared for such a disaster: "One reason is the cooperation of some of the bigger buildings on Manhattan Island—at the bulls eye of the target area."[195] Civil defense plans were drafted for major buildings and public places.[196] Rockefeller Center was a model of preparedness, with a thousand civil defense workers organized to help protect the complex's 35,000 residents and 100,000 transients. Plans were made to evacuate the top five floors of each building in the event of attack. Shelter areas were carefully labeled; the designated areas were located in the center of buildings, away from windows and open areas where tenants were most likely to be exposed to heat, radiation and flying glass. The center's nearly mile-long underground concourse, possibly big enough to house all the people working in its offices at one time, was designated a shelter area as well.

On November 28, 1951, for seven minutes beginning at 10:33 A.M., the city ground to a halt as a thousand sirens screamed, calling into action what *Life* described as "the biggest air-raid drill of the atomic age."[197] Fear of nuclear attack continued unabated throughout the decade, with nationwide tests in 1954 and 1956 that chilled the populace.[198] The *New York Times* warned that though the 1954 test was a success, had there been real bombs, 2,175,000 New Yorkers would have died.[199] On December 29, 1959, Sidney H. Bingham, chairman of the city's Board of Transportation, announced a plan that would provide emergency sleeping accommodations for 100,000 people and temporary shelter for one million others that would be built as future subway stations or tunnels (most of the existing subways were not deep enough to provide adequate protection).[200]

Plans for shelters continued to be developed throughout the 1950s, achieving what *Progressive Architecture* called an

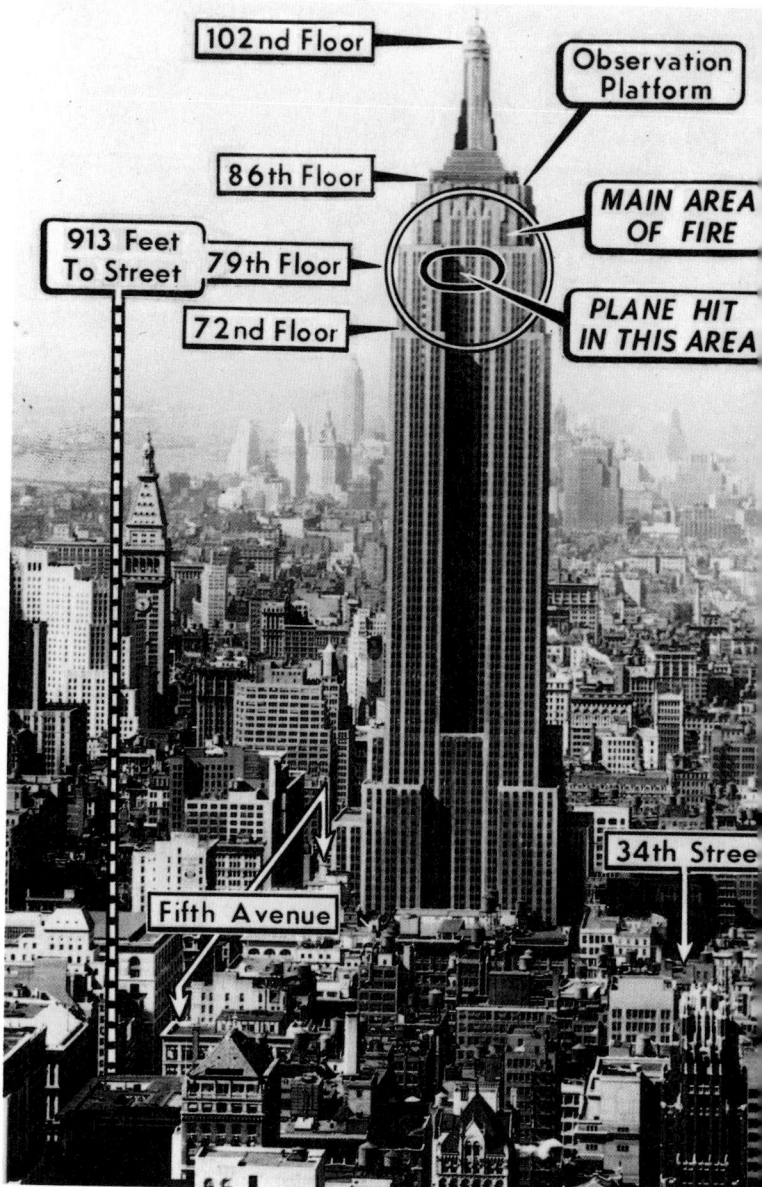

Army bomber plane crashes into the Empire State Building. LOC

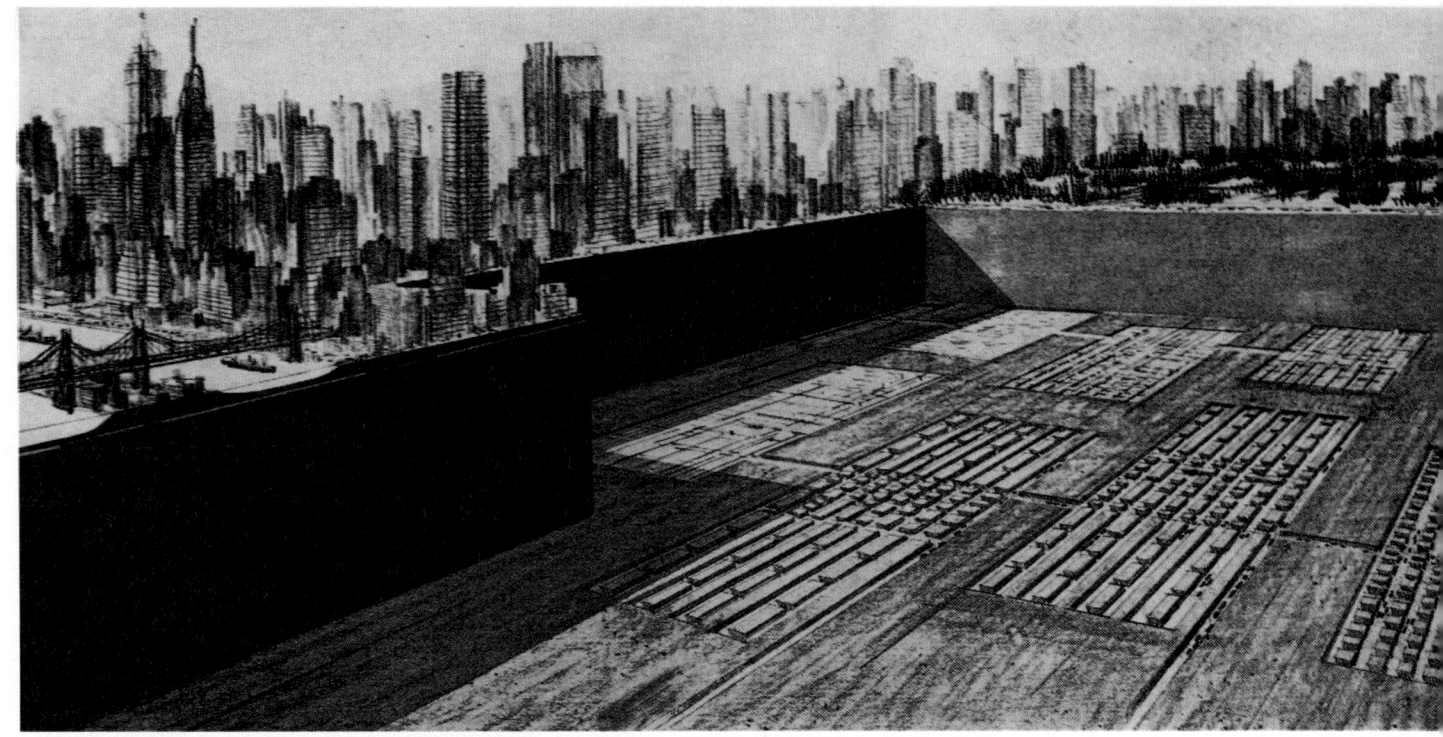

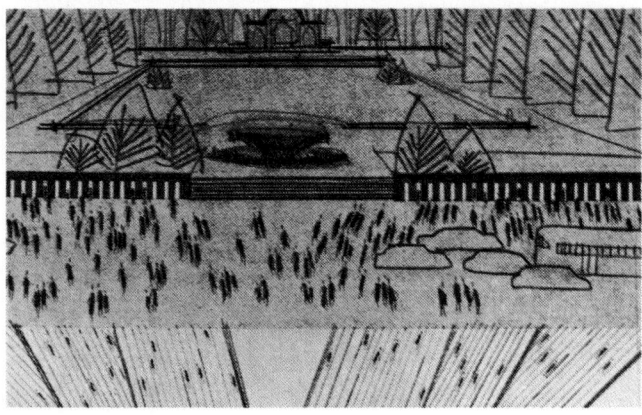

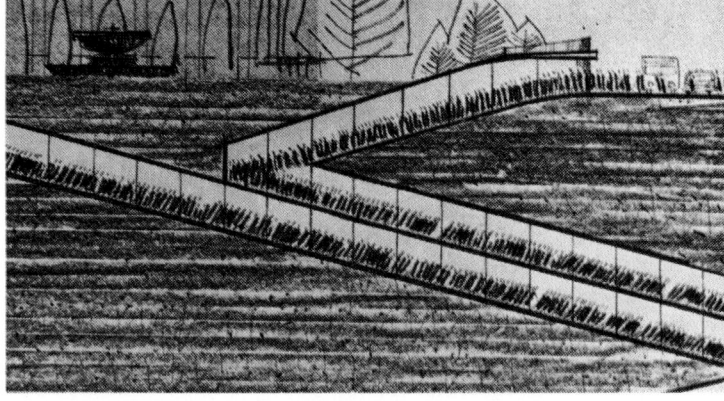

Top: Proposed bomb and fallout shelter beneath the east side of Manhattan and the East River. Guy B. Panero Engineers in association with Paul Weidlinger and Hood & Manice, 1959. Cutaway rendering by Cristof showing view to the southwest. PA. CU

Bottom left: Proposed chutes leading to bomb and fallout shelter beneath Bryant Park. Guy B. Panero Engineers in association with Paul Weidlinger and Hood & Manice, 1959. Cutaway rendering by Cristof showing view to the east. PA. CU

Bottom right: Proposed ramps leading to bomb and fallout shelter beneath Bryant Park. Cutaway rendering by Cristof showing view to the south. PA. CU

"Orwellian" character in 1959 when Guy B. Panero Engineers in association with Paul Weidlinger and Hood & Manice prepared designs for sheltering the four million people who lived in, worked in or visited Manhattan on any given day.[201] The scheme provided for ninety-day occupancy of twenty-five shelter groups, or "base modules," that would each accommodate 160,000 people. Each module was to be sunk 800 feet beneath Manhattan and reached by steep ramps and chutes as well as by elevators or rock conveyors reserved for the elderly and handicapped. The base modules would be broken up into five submodules, plus a 5,000-member headquarters area where the "secure area cadre" were to be housed. But New Yorkers would have none of it; their fatalism and optimism combined to cause the shelter program to be abandoned as citizens resigned themselves to take their chances.[202]

Not only did New York face serious threats from outside forces; a certain self-destructive tendency increasingly became a hallmark of the postwar era. Although the problem of air pollution was first recognized in the 1930s, until the 1950s little attention was paid to the quality of the city's air as compared, for example, to the purity of its water. A city agency for air-pollution control was not established until 1952.[203] While the Pollution Control Board, working with Consolidated Edison, succeeded in holding to prevailing amounts of air pollution despite the enormous postwar growth in energy production—a principal source of pollutants—the situation was serious. The public began to focus on the problem in earnest in the mid-1960s after the *New Yorker* published a lengthy discussion of it in 1964.[204] Air quality quickly became a major issue. A report released by the City Council in June 1965 claimed that for a non-cigarette-smoking New Yorker, walking down the street each day was equivalent to inhaling as much cancer-causing benzopyrene as would be inhaled by smoking two packs of cigarettes a day.[205] New York's dust was among the nation's worst, with 640 tons falling on the city each day from furnaces, incinerators and sewer plants. In 1966, after reports about the lethal effects of a "lid" that rendered the air at street level dangerous, the city began to take positive steps to lower pollution levels, inaugurating rules about the sulphur content of coal and fuel oil used and banning the use of soft coal after 1968. But the city alone was not able to control its air quality; much of the pollution came from factories and power plants in New Jersey.[206] When a mass of heavily polluted air settled over the New York region in November 1966, President Johnson was persuaded that air quality was a federal issue.[207] In February 1967 Johnson submitted a special message to Congress calling for regional air-quality commissions.[208]

Senator Robert Kennedy actively lobbied for better air and for federal controls. Kennedy was particularly affected by the ghastly condition that prevailed at the Bridge Apartments (see chapter 12), four middle-income slabs straddling the Manhattan approach to the George Washington Bridge that he visited in June 1967. The air rising from the highway was so bad that, according to one tenant, Roger Minkoff, "below the twentieth floor, it's impossible to open your windows. . . . No one can sit on their balconies."[209] Tenants of the buildings had organized to try to get some respite, but the city deemed the pollution level "tolerable."

By 1970 New York was said to have the worst air of any major American city, with the rate of death due to emphysema having increased 500 percent since 1960.[210] But 1970 was a key year for air-pollution control: not only did the city's Environmental Protection Administration begin to reduce ac-

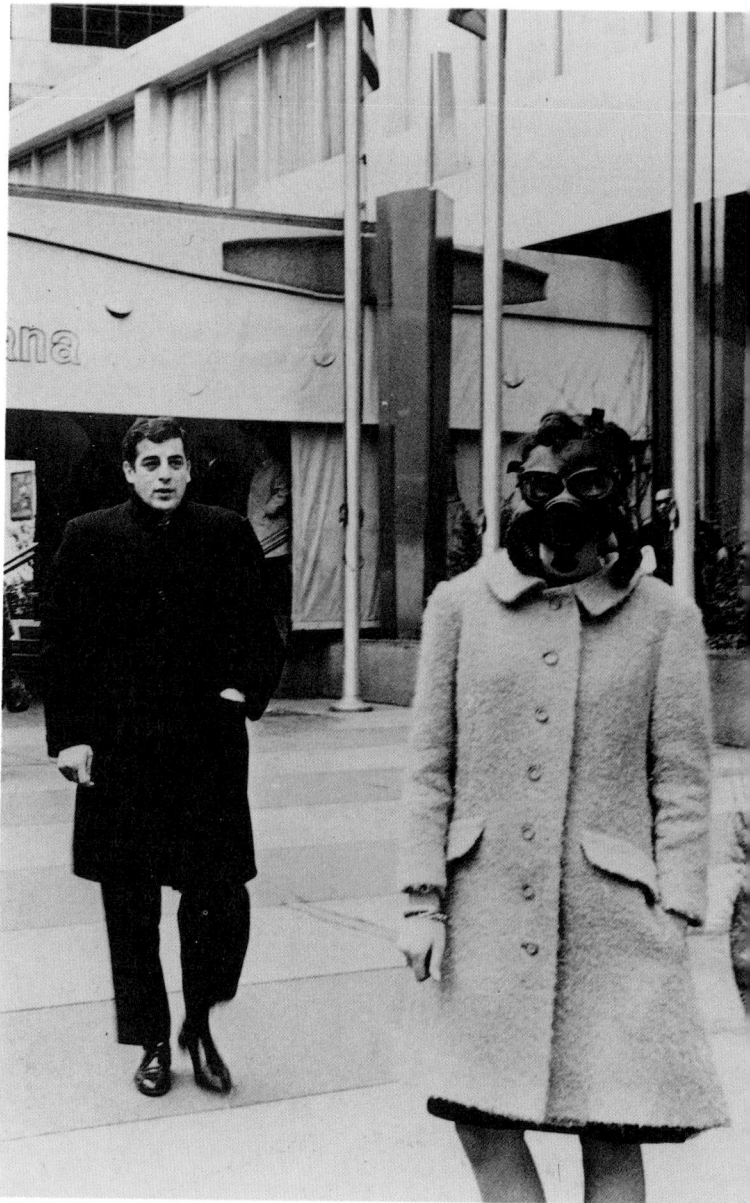

Woman wearing gas mask, 1967. View to the northeast showing the Americana Hotel (Morris Lapidus, Kornblath, Harle & Liebman, 1962), 811 Seventh Avenue, between West Fifty-second and West Fifty-third streets. LOC

ceptable levels of sulphur and other fuel-related pollutants, but it also established the nation's first regulations for the control of airborne asbestos, a fire-protection material commonly used in steel-framed construction that had come to be regarded as a source of cancer.[211] In April 1970 Robert W. Rickles became head of the city's Department of Air Resources,[212] just a few months before the city experienced its worst pollution ever amidst an August heat wave, the effects of which were compounded by a power shortage owing to the breakdown of "Big Allis," a million-kilowatt generator in Queens.[213]

As a symbolic gesture of concern, Mayor Lindsay ordered the stretch of Fifth Avenue between Forty-second and Fifty-seventh streets closed to vehicles for four successive Saturdays beginning July 11, 1970.[214] Citizens for Clean Air, a 4,000-member civic group, effectively lobbied against the expansion of Consolidated Edison's Astoria plant and urged that cars be banned below Fifty-ninth Street during the day.[215] Rickles advocated traffic limitations and went so far as to question the wisdom of having cars in the city at all. He successfully fought for strong auto-emission standards as part of the federal Clean Air Act of 1970. In 1971 he opposed the transportation bond proposition, which he felt would help bring more auto traffic into the city. For his efforts against the bond issue he was forced to resign.[216] The 1970 statute set national goals for healthy air quality, but Congress left to the states and cities the responsibility of achieving them. New York State took the lead and designed a Transportation Control Plan in 1973, which called for restrictions on traffic, including a ban on traffic in Manhattan below Sixtieth Street.[217] The plan was approved as a model for the nation, which it essentially was, being the only federally approved plan of its kind in the country.

Less dramatic but nonetheless a sign of the city's vulnerability as well as of its increasing age was the growing deterioration of its infrastructure: the pipes, conduits and subways beneath the streets, as well as the streets themselves, and even the limited-access highways that seemed brand new to many observers yet were in some cases fifty or more years old. Concern for the city's infrastructure began to become widespread only in the late 1960s, when the term "disaster area" became an increasingly common epithet for New York.[218] But serious problems had begun to surface a decade earlier. On August 17, 1959, uptown Manhattan, from Fifty-ninth street to Harlem, was without electricity for up to twelve hours, bringing with the inconvenience a genial camaraderie among those affected.[219]

It was the blackout of November 9, 1965, that awakened the population to the fragility of New York's physical structure as no previous event had.[220] Affecting the entire city and virtually the entire northeast section of the United States from New York to Canada and from Lake Huron to Boston, this blackout was also not without its camaraderie. But as it heightened everyone's sense of the vulnerability of modern technology, it reminded New Yorkers of just how inextricably linked their city was to the entire region, bringing into focus the realities of Megalopolis as never before. Although the city was the most dramatically affected area in the afflicted region, and although most New Yorkers initially believed that the power failure was a local phenomenon, the source of the problem that led to the blackout was the malfunctioning of a relay station near Canada. The power failure, which began at 5:28 P.M., at the peak of the evening rush hour, stranded between 600,000 and 800,000 commuters in packed subway trains and jammed rail-

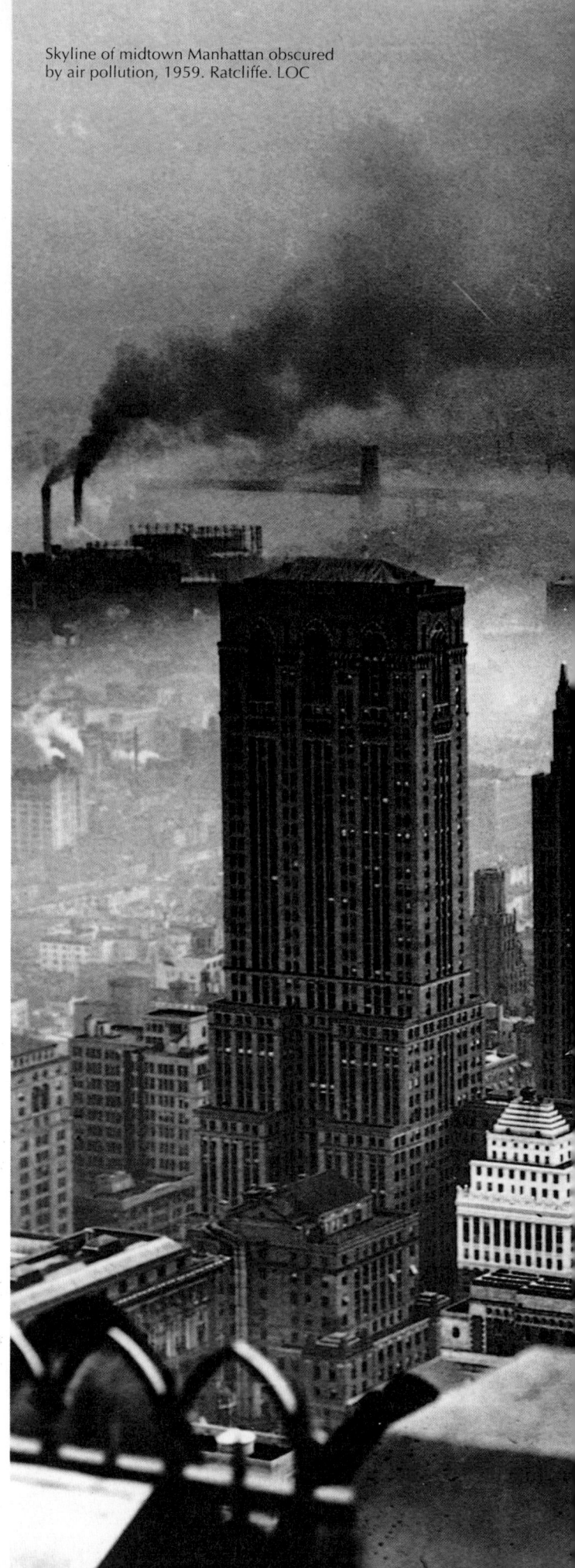

Skyline of midtown Manhattan obscured by air pollution, 1959. Ratcliffe. LOC

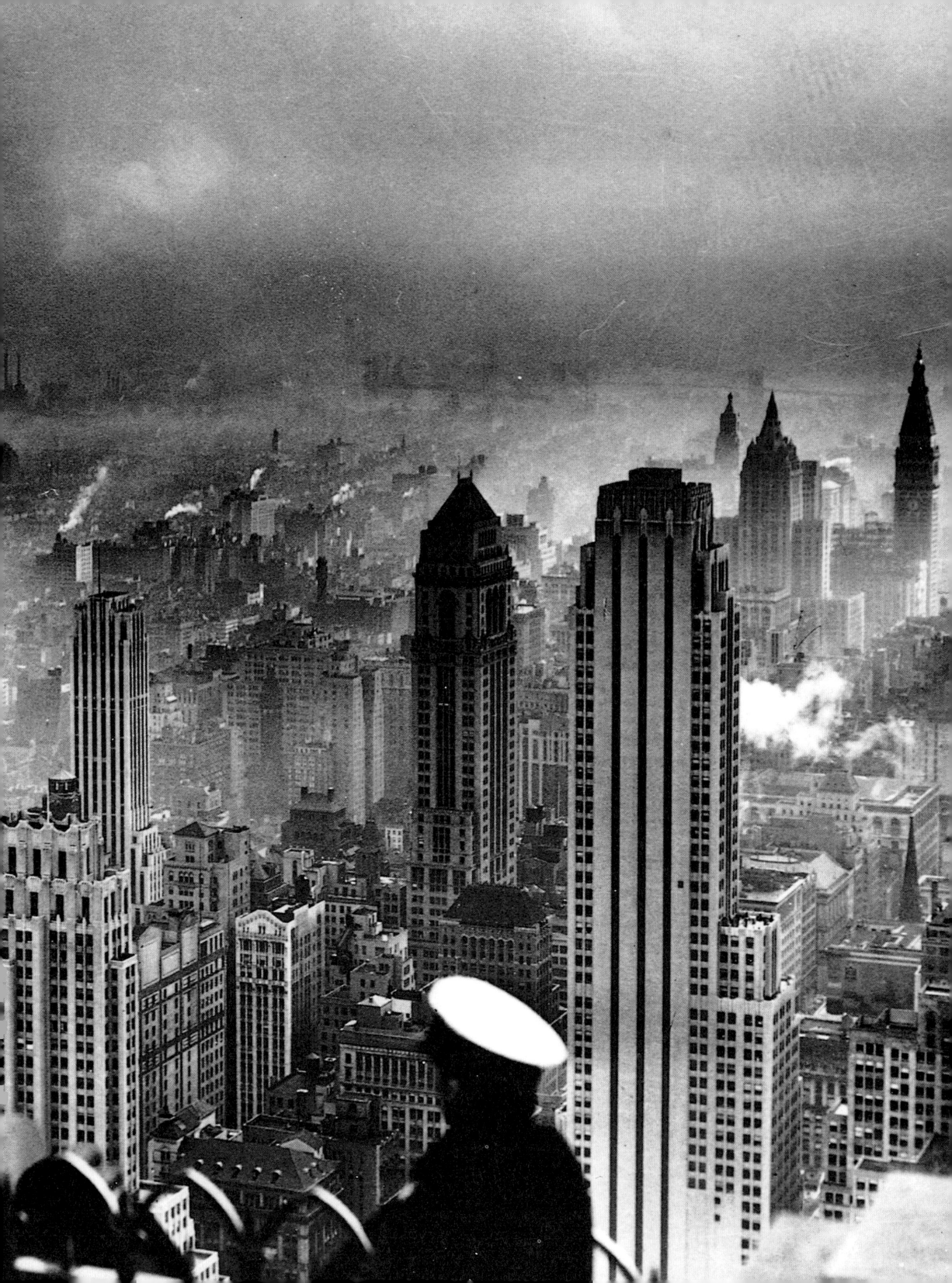

road stations, not to mention hundreds in office-building elevators. Lights began to return in the early hours of the next morning.

Air-raid drills, power blackouts and even high-pollution days constituted dramatic breaks with daily routine; but day after day New Yorkers put up with little disasters, many of them associated with the aggravating assault on the senses that comprised the daily trip between home and place of work. In many ways the subways, which were the most critical component of the city's arterial system, were also in the worst shape. Not only overtaxed during rush hours, they were also frayed and in some places pretty well worn out. In 1940 the city's subway system was at last unified when title to the Interborough Rapid Transit Company, which had been in receivership for eight years, and the uncondemned elevated lines of the Manhattan Railway Company passed to the city, bringing to a conclusion the campaign for a coordinated transit system that had been pursued since 1921.[221] The unified system consisted of 790 track miles of subway and elevated lines, 437 track miles of street railway and 80 miles of bus routes, all to be operated as the New York City Transit System and managed by the Board of Transportation. As part of the ceremony marking the transfer, Mayor La Guardia paid his respects to Contract 3, the agreement between the city and Interborough guaranteeing the five-cent fare that had been signed in 1913.

As 1940 drew to a close, there was occasion for yet more transit-oriented celebration. At a midnight fete on the night of December 15, Mayor La Guardia and 2,000 guests, including Mr. and Mrs. John D. Rockefeller, Jr., jammed the first two trains to operate on the Sixth Avenue subway. They rode from the Thirty-fourth Street station, where they boarded after a supper given at Gimbel Brothers department store, to the Rockefeller Center station, where they moved through the underground passageways to the Center Theater. There they were treated to a tribute to the new line featuring players from the Center Theater and Radio City Music Hall as well as other entertainers. Ben Grauer, the radio announcer and the evening's master of ceremonies, praised the mayor, who "For last Christmas . . . gave us 'No El, No El,' and for this Christmas . . . gives us the splendid new subway."[222] Asked if this was his first subway ride, John D. Rockefeller, Jr., replied: "I rode in the first city subway many years ago, and I have been using the subways ever since."[223]

Wartime restrictions on gasoline combined with the city's prosperity to pack the subways with people. But at war's end, the crowds began to thin as the more prosperous took cabs or drove their own cars, leaving the composition of subway riders an increasingly unrepresentative cross section of the democracy. Declining ridership created significant financial problems, and maintenance was neglected. Fares were at last raised to ten cents on July 1, 1948, but few capital improvements were undertaken.[224] By 1950 the state of the subway system had become serious: although the city-built IND line (1930–40) was still relatively new, the IRT system, built mostly between 1900 and 1917, was definitely in need of modernization. A few steps were taken to improve the situation: in 1947 the platforms on the west side IRT line were lengthened between the 103rd and Dyckman Street stations.[225]

In 1949 the IND Fulton Street line was extended in Brooklyn. Although Lewis Mumford said the four new stations on the Fulton Street line were "at least more radiant" than their predecessors, which "in the course of fifteen years . . . have become grimy and prematurely dilapidated," he was not overly impressed with their quality. "For all our boasting about American ingenuity," he wrote, "we still haven't produced a subway station in New York that compares with any of those done in London by Adams, Holden & Pearson during the last twenty years."[226] At the same time, a new design was adopted for the cars added to the IND system to handle increased traffic.[227] In the postwar era observers seemed to expect more in the way of design than they had during the Depression. In an effort to improve performance and enhance its image, the Board of Transportation commissioned some new prototypes, including the experimental stainless-steel-clad R-11 car, which cost $43,000 more than the $80,000 R-10, the fluorescent-lighted standard of the postwar era.[228] The R-11 was intended to lure passengers with an improved ride, a loudspeaker system, ultraviolet-ray lamps to sterilize recirculated air, and gray, cream and blue interiors. It was not adopted.

In September 1951 a $500 million program for expanding and improving the city's rapid transit service was approved by the Board of Estimate.[229] The program would be funded by the sale of bonds, and because of the vast amount of money involved, it required the approval of the voters of New York State, which was granted the following November. The purpose of the allocation was the construction of a new subway under Second Avenue, needed to relieve the Lexington Avenue line, already overburdened because of the destruction of the Second Avenue elevated line in 1941–42 and soon, with the removal of the Third Avenue Elevated, to become the only rapid-transit service on the east side of Manhattan. The Second Avenue subway was to be a six-track trunk line running from Grand Street in Manhattan to 149th Street and Third Avenue in the Bronx. The program also called for the reorganization of the DeKalb Avenue station in Brooklyn, long a bottleneck, permitting an additional eighteen trains per hour to get through; the construction of a long-projected express line under Sixth Avenue running between the West Fourth and West Thirty-fourth Street stations; the construction of a crosstown subway under Fifty-seventh Street to connect the Sixth Avenue line with the new one under Second Avenue; and a branch line, extending from Seventy-sixth Street and Second Avenue to Rego Park, Queens, where it would tap into the Rockaway line of the Long Island Railroad, the purchase price of which was also covered in the bond package. This new Queens line was intended to provide subway service to the Rockaways. With the completion of the Rockaway extension, it would be possible to make a thirty-mile journey from the far corners of the Bronx to the city's most expansive seashore playground.

The ambitious 1951 plan for the system's expansion also included a branch line along Utica Avenue, Brooklyn, connecting the IRT to Flatlands; an extension of the IRT's Nostrand Avenue line to Sheepshead Bay; and the alteration of the Pelham Bay line to carry the larger IND and BMT cars that would operate on the Second Avenue route. Not cited among the improvements proposed in 1951 was the reconstruction of the Forty-second Street shuttle, an anomalous but heavily traveled service that was put into operation in 1918 when the original IRT subway system was expanded into two parallel east- and west-side lines.[230] One of the system's worst bottlenecks, the Forty-second Street shuttle consisted of two- or three-car trains that ferried back and forth between Times Square and Grand Central, using the tracks of the old subway, which had run along Park Avenue south of Forty-second Street and along Broadway north of Forty-second Street. The shuttle was no great timesaver, requiring passengers to do just about as much walking and waiting as riding.

In 1951 the Goodyear Tire & Rubber Co. and Stevens-Adamson Manufacturing Co. advanced a plan to replace the existing shuttle with individual six-passenger cars riding on an endless belt.[231] The system resembled the one developed to move visitors through General Motors' Futurama exhibition at the New York World's Fair of 1939–40.[232] Carrying more than 500 people a minute along the line, the new shuttle, like the General Motors ride, would be boarded from a platform moving at the same speed as the train. In 1952 the Board of Transportation studied the shuttle and in its capital budget for 1953 requested $3.6 million to rebuild it. The board also expressed interest in the Goodyear system. In 1953 a full-size working mock-up of the conveyor belt system was tested in Aurora, Illinois, and proved satisfactory for all, including the physically disabled. Later in 1953 the company established a "speedwalk" to carry New Jersey commuters 227 feet from the Hudson & Manhattan Railroad's Jersey City terminal up an incline to the Erie Railroad station. So confident was Goodyear of its adaptability to New York's needs that it established a separate company, Passenger Belt Conveyor, Inc., to develop the system.

On June 15, 1953, the Board of Transportation gave way to the New York City Transit Authority.[233] Created by the New York State Legislature, the Transit Authority was responsible for all day-to-day operations. Originally headed by an unsalaried five-member board (two each chosen by the mayor and the governor, the final one chosen by the other four members), two years later its makeup was changed to a three-member paid panel. The Transit Authority was mandated by law to avoid deficits. Funds for capital improvements were to be raised primarily through municipal bonds, although in 1962 it was granted limited power to issue its own bonds to pay for new rolling stock. After only one month in operation, the Transit Authority raised the subway fare to fifteen cents in a major effort to eliminate operating deficits said to run as high as $50 million per year. With this in mind, planning was halted for the Second Avenue subway, a principal feature of the upgraded system that the voters had endorsed and that was initially to have begun construction in 1952. Civic-minded observers saw the delay as a benefit, providing more time to plan the facility along ideal lines. One provocative scheme was volunteered in 1954 by Pomerance & Breines.[234] In a plan that was reminiscent in many ways of the original Regional Plan, the architects called for adding two tracks for freight traffic to the six tracks already planned for passenger service.

By the early 1960s steps toward the implementation of the master plan for transit were being taken. In 1962 the Transit Authority once again announced its intention to extend the Sixth Avenue line north to West Fifty-seventh Street as part of the $100 million DeKalb Avenue–Chrystie Street–Sixth Avenue improvement. Portions of this project, such as the improvements to the DeKalb Avenue station and two additional tracks under Sixth Avenue, were already under construction. The entire project was intended to feed BMT trains coming over the Manhattan and Williamsburg bridges into the Sixth Avenue line, increasing by forty-five per hour the number of rush-hour trains that could pass between Manhattan and Brooklyn.[235]

Subway service and ridership declined steadily beginning in the 1950s. By the late 1960s many people thought the system was near collapse, caught in a squeeze between declining ridership and escalating labor costs. This became all too obvious in January 1966, when newly elected Mayor Lindsay, upon taking office, was faced with a crippling transit strike that lasted twelve days. The strike ended only when the city agreed to substantial

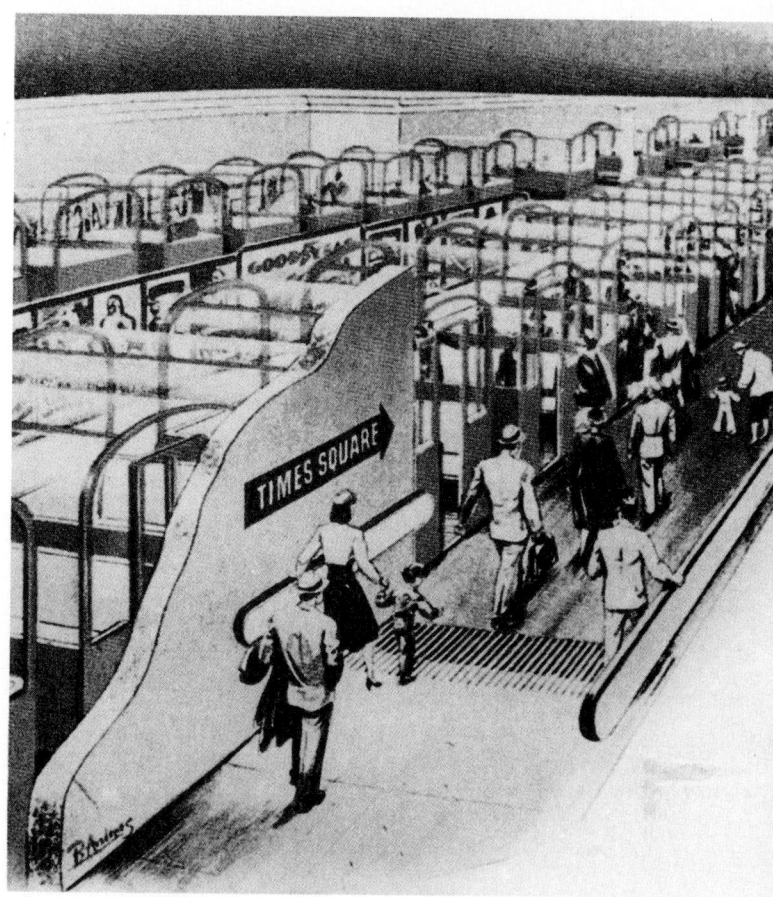

Above: Forty-second Street shuttle replacement proposed by the Goodyear Tire and Rubber Company, 1951. PS. TMM

Overleaf: Blackout, August 17, 1959. View to the west of lower Manhattan from the Promenade, Brooklyn Heights, Brooklyn. LOC

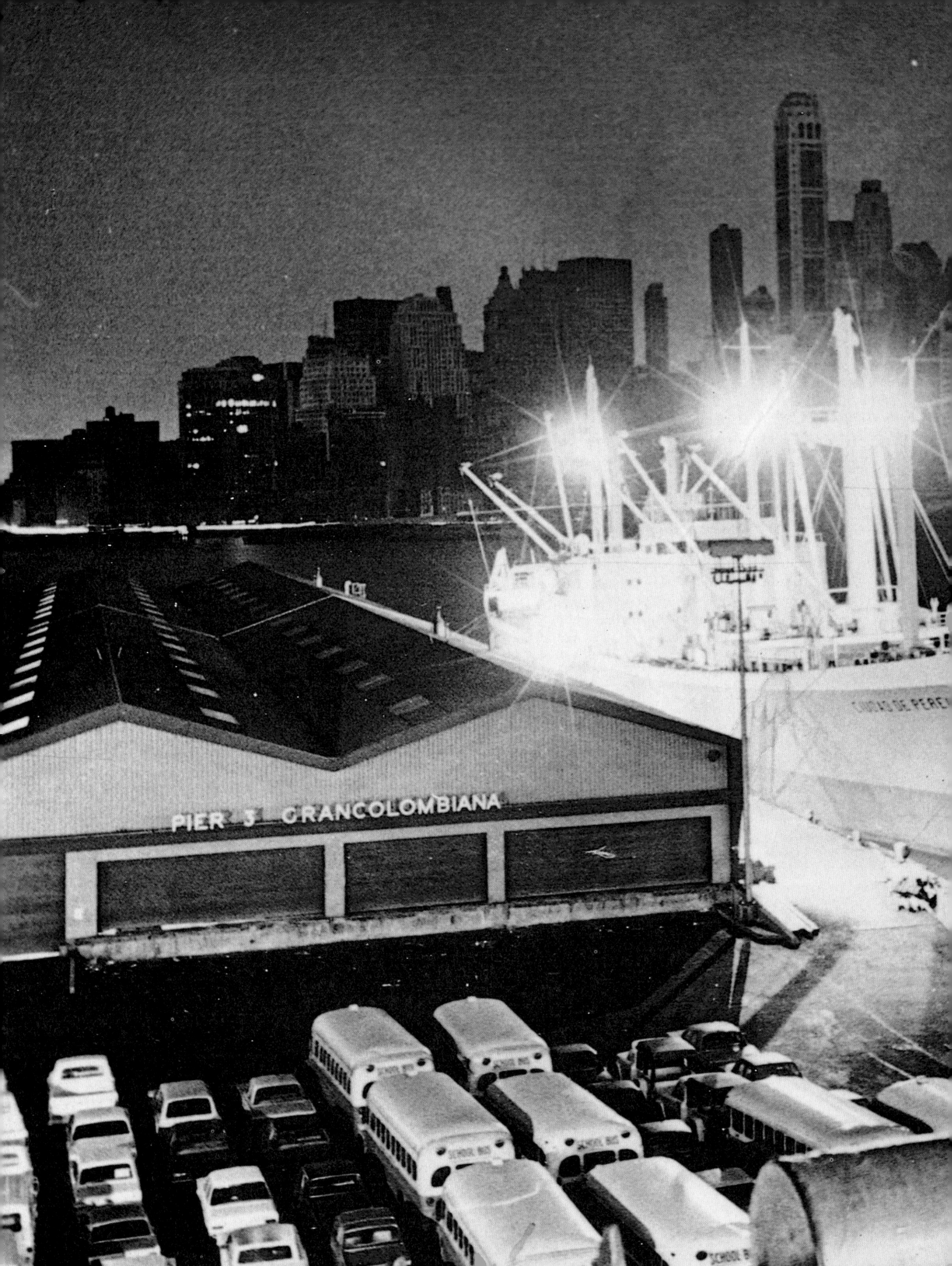

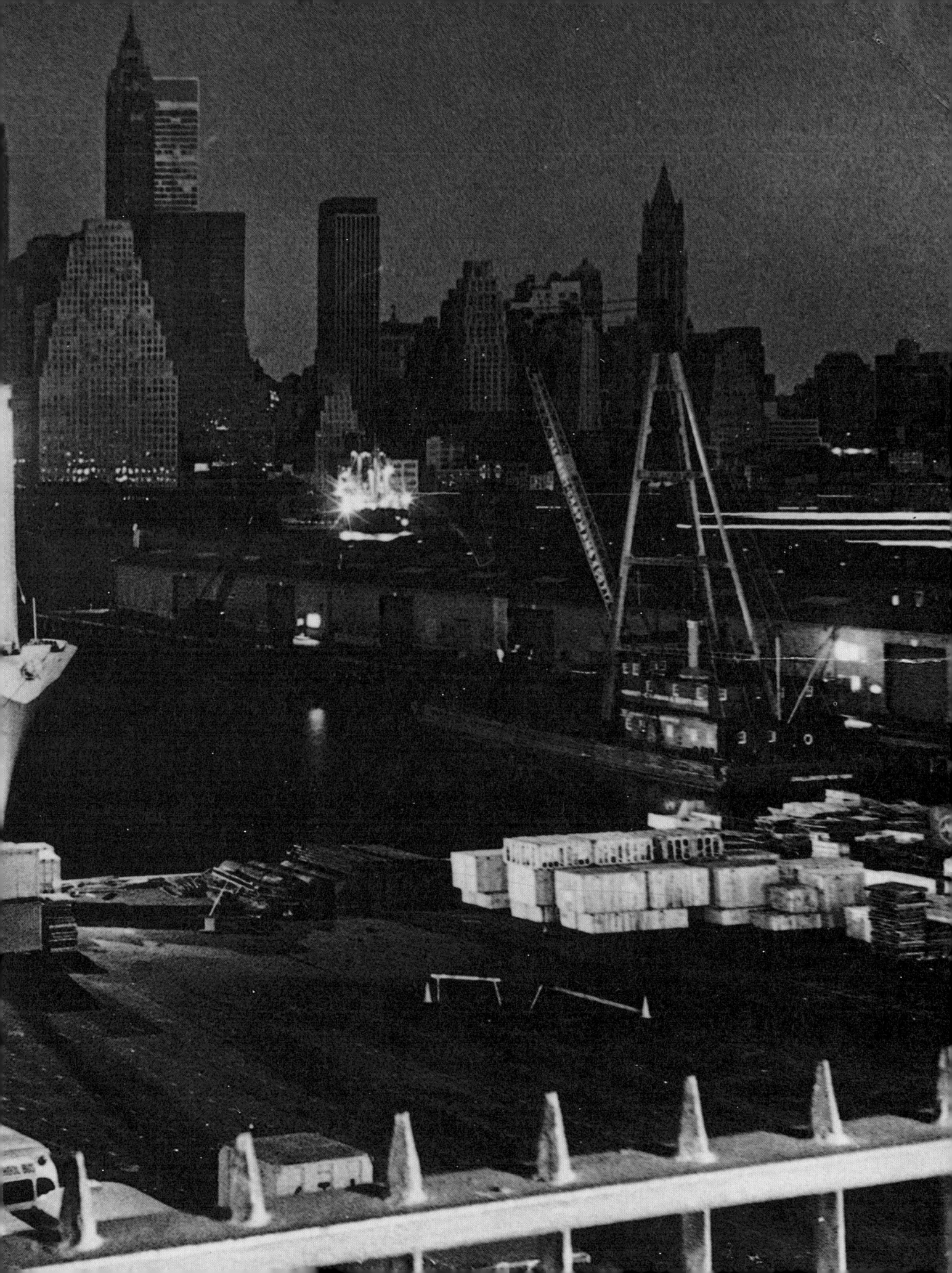

pay increases for striking workers and to their retirement at a high pension after twenty years' service, thereby robbing management of its most skilled maintenance personnel.

The situation grew even more desperate two years later when express buses from outer-borough locations were permitted to enter the downtown and midtown areas. By 1979 there were fifty-six express routes—run either by the Metropolitan Transit Authority or by private concerns—serving Queens, Staten Island, the Bronx and Brooklyn as well as two starting in Manhattan neighborhoods and going to midtown and downtown, adding about 550 buses to Manhattan traffic each morning and seriously exacerbating congestion as they marshaled near origin points at the evening rush hours. While the express buses were originally advocated as a way of luring people out of their automobiles, they principally drained the subways of commuters, despite the buses' higher fares. As Sigurd Grava, a transportation planner, noted, the success of the express bus experiment chiefly indicated the depth of the "dissatisfaction (also fear, contempt, unease, and scorn) that most New York subway riders have with that service."[236]

Lindsay's main goal for the subways was not new lines but the development of air-conditioned subway cars—a difficult task given the cramped headroom of existing tunnels, particularly on the IRT lines. Lindsay achieved his goal in the summer of 1969 when the first of 400 air-conditioned cars were put in service and a new prototype was released for a car that was insulated against noise as well as extreme temperatures.[237] The new cars, designed by Sundberg-Ferar, were fifteen feet longer than the traditional sixty-foot model and had brighter fluorescent lighting. More important, they could achieve speeds of seventy miles per hour (the previous top speed was fifty miles per hour). But the new cars were only as good as the roadbed they traveled on and the electrical systems that regulated the safe flow of traffic.

Between May 20 and August 3, 1970, the subway, customarily regarded as the world's safest railroad, experienced four accidents that killed three people and injured 164 others.[238] As Newsweek reported: "The causes of this mayhem seemed plain enough. A frightening amount of the equipment on the New York subways is both dangerously old and badly maintained. On a brief tour of the system recently, a New York Post reporter found railroad spikes that could be pulled out by hand and empty fire extinguishers in darkened tunnels." In addition, Newsweek continued, the qualified employees were retiring and the new help was inexperienced: "One motorman, who piled a train carrying some 1,800 people into the rear of another train last month, admitted that he was 'a very poor judge of distance.'"[239]

Aside from the danger of subway accidents, most riders were dismayed by the inability of the subway's management to keep the stations clean. In 1970 the subway stations and the rolling stock became an almost inexhaustible canvas for an age-old urban phenomenon, graffiti, which came to be celebrated by some supporters as a vital art form.[240] The transformation of graffiti to the level of public art was begun by a man named Demetrius, a resident of 183rd Street in Washington Heights who identified himself as Taki 183 (Taki is the Greek diminutive of Demetrius) when he set out to work his felt-pen magic. By 1973 Taki had spawned hundreds of imitators and graffiti had burgeoned into an uncontrollable visual onslaught; almost none of the city's 6,802 subway cars remained untransformed by the boldly scaled, wildly colored designs executed in spray paints and multisize markers. Virtually all the graffiti was signed; in fact, the signature was the art. According to psychology professor Gary Winkel of the City University, the signature graffiti re-

vealed "the importance one feels when one sees one's name so big."[241] But Dr. Fredric Wertham, an expert in violent behavior, saw graffiti as "part of the widespread vandalism, the mood to destroy, the brutalism that is everywhere."[242]

Many established artists rose up in praise of the graffiti. Saul Steinberg saw it as "a necessity for entering the art scene," noting that the graffitists avoided advertisement billboards because they were regularly replaced, concentrating instead on walls and subway cars, which could be cleaned of their art only at great expense.[243] Artist Claes Oldenburg was ecstatic about the new art: "You're standing there in the station, everything is gray and gloomy, and all of a sudden one of those graffiti trains slides in and brightens the place like a big bouquet from Latin America. At first it seems anarchical—makes you wonder if the subways are working properly. Then you get used to it. The city is like a newspaper anyway, so it's natural to see writing all over the place."[244] The dancer and choreographer Twyla Tharp employed graffitists to spray away on stage at the City Center in 1973 as part of her dance "Deuce Coupe," which was performed by her company in collaboration with the Joffrey Ballet to the rhythms of a Beach Boys recording. In 1973 New York magazine inaugurated its TAKI awards (which it said would henceforth be known as the T.A.s), citing the 103rd Street and Broadway station as the city's most graffiti-saturated, and a car with dots, drops, vibes, arrows and crown motifs by a graffitist named Spin as the grandest design of the season.[245] For a while, only Mayor Lindsay seemed less than smitten with subway graffiti.[246]

Norman Mailer's 1974 celebration of graffiti, rich in hyperbole, was a landmark of the so-called new journalism. Mailer managed to irritate both officials and average Joes who wanted to tidy up the system, and he gave the movement some stature as self-proclamation, as social art: "Graffiti is the expression of a ghetto which is near to the plague, for civilization is now inimical to the ghetto. Too huge are the obstacles to any natural development of a civilized man. In the ghetto it is almost impossible to find some quiet location for your identity. No, in the environment of the slum, the courage to display yourself is your only capital, and crime is the productive process which converts such capital to the modern powers of the world, ego and money."[247]

While the explosion of subway graffiti captured the public's imagination, perhaps the most significant development in the city's subway system during the 1970s was the proposed construction of the Second Avenue line, an idea that had been tossed about for decades, taking on an almost mythic quality in the process. First conceived in 1927, the subway was discussed seriously three years later when public hearings were held. With a 1940 completion date in mind, its construction was to be tied to the removal of the Second Avenue Elevated, Manhattan's fourth and last constructed line, opened in 1880. Efforts to begin the new subway were stalled by the Depression. But in 1941 the stretch of the Second Avenue Elevated between Fifty-ninth and 129th streets was demolished, as was the section from Fifty-ninth Street south to Chatham Square one year later.[248] While the wartime freeze on new construction negated the supposed economic benefits of removing the Elevated, the light and fresh air that now poured into the tight Lower East Side streets it had snaked through for more than fifty years were seen as benefit enough, improving living conditions and stimulating retail sales in the "cloak and suit" district along Division Street.

In 1955–56, after some improvement in the financial condition of the recently created Transit Authority, and with everyone now confident of the Second Avenue line's imminent construction, the Third Avenue El was demolished. But things did not work out as planned. With postwar inflation, the bond money bought much less than had been anticipated, and what was available was dissipated in many relatively small projects and in subsidizing the system as a whole, which was believed essential as subway ridership declined. Nonetheless, the Second Avenue line remained a priority, and in 1963 the City Planning Commission reaffirmed its value in a report, although no funds for its construction were available.

In his 1965 campaign white paper on transportation, John Lindsay supported the Second Avenue line, for which some planning money had been found to prepare route maps and engineering studies. At this point the idea for a Sixty-fourth Street (later Sixty-third Street) tunnel that would also run under Central Park (see chapter 10) emerged as a key element in the political future of the Second Avenue line because it appealed to transit-starved Queens voters who represented the system's only postwar growth area. The 1967 bond issue, and the establishment of the Metropolitan Transit Authority (MTA) one year later, gave the project a new lease on life. In 1970, when the federal government began to allocate increasing amounts of financial assistance, the construction of the Second Avenue subway seemed at last likely, despite the fact that the project was so costly that there still seemed to be not quite enough money.

When construction on the Second Avenue subway began in 1972, it was scheduled for operation in 1980.[249] The new line was to extend from Broad and Water streets to 125th Street and Second Avenue in Manhattan, extending to East 180th Street in the Bronx, where it would join the existing Pelham Bay Park and Dyre Avenue lines. A controversial, so-called East Side Loop, to serve the working-class population of the East Village, was added to the plans by the Board of Estimate at the last minute in March 1970. At the same time, pressured by the Downtown–Lower Manhattan Association, the board agreed to build the southern— below Thirty-fourth Street—portion of the line, which had originally been slated for construction in the 1980s.[250] Suddenly the line began to be seen as one earmarked for white-collar workers commuting between the financial district and the high-income Upper East Side, and critics began to call it the "Second Avenue snobway," choosing to ignore the fact that the line would continue north for 5.7 miles into the Bronx.

At the request of the Board of Estimate, an initial plan calling for four tracks was trimmed to a scheme providing only two. But in recognition of the need to accommodate Bronx and East Harlem residents traveling to midtown and downtown, a decision was made to provide just three stations above Sixty-third Street in Manhattan: at Eighty-sixth, 106th and 125th streets. Stops in midtown and farther south would be more closely spaced. From the moment the plan was inadvertently and prematurely released to the press in August 1971, Upper East Side groups began to demand more stations, arguing for locations close to intensively used facilities such as New York and Metropolitan hospitals. After many public hearings, most of them angry, the MTA in 1971 proposed new stations at Ninety-sixth and Seventy-second streets. The strength of the community's protests caught the authority off guard. Times had surely changed, one official nostalgically mused, from the days "when La Guardia built the Eighth Avenue subway [and] there was no nonsense about consulting the communities on where the stations were to be located. There was no discussion. It was all under wraps. One day the jackhammers appeared and that's when you knew where the stations would be."[251] Despite the fact that the Bronx portion represented one-third of the line, most of the public attention, and that of the city

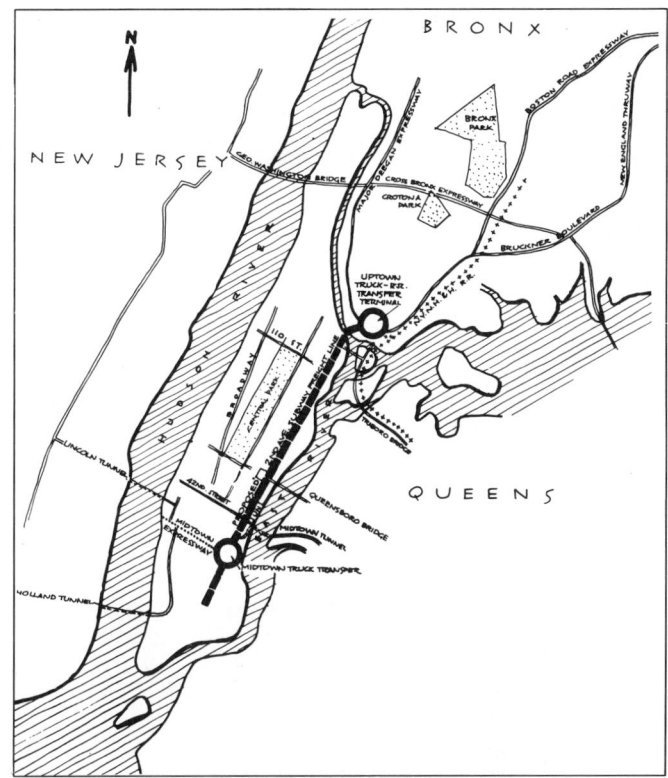

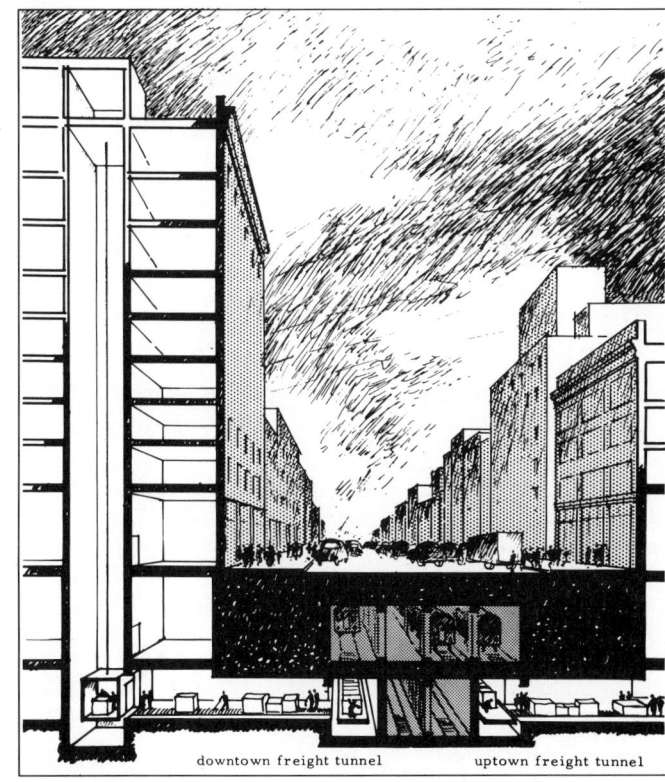

Top: Map of proposed Second Avenue subway freight line. Pomerance & Breines, 1950. PB

Bottom: Proposed Second Avenue subway passenger and freight lines. Pomerance & Breines, 1950. Section perspective looking north. PB

107

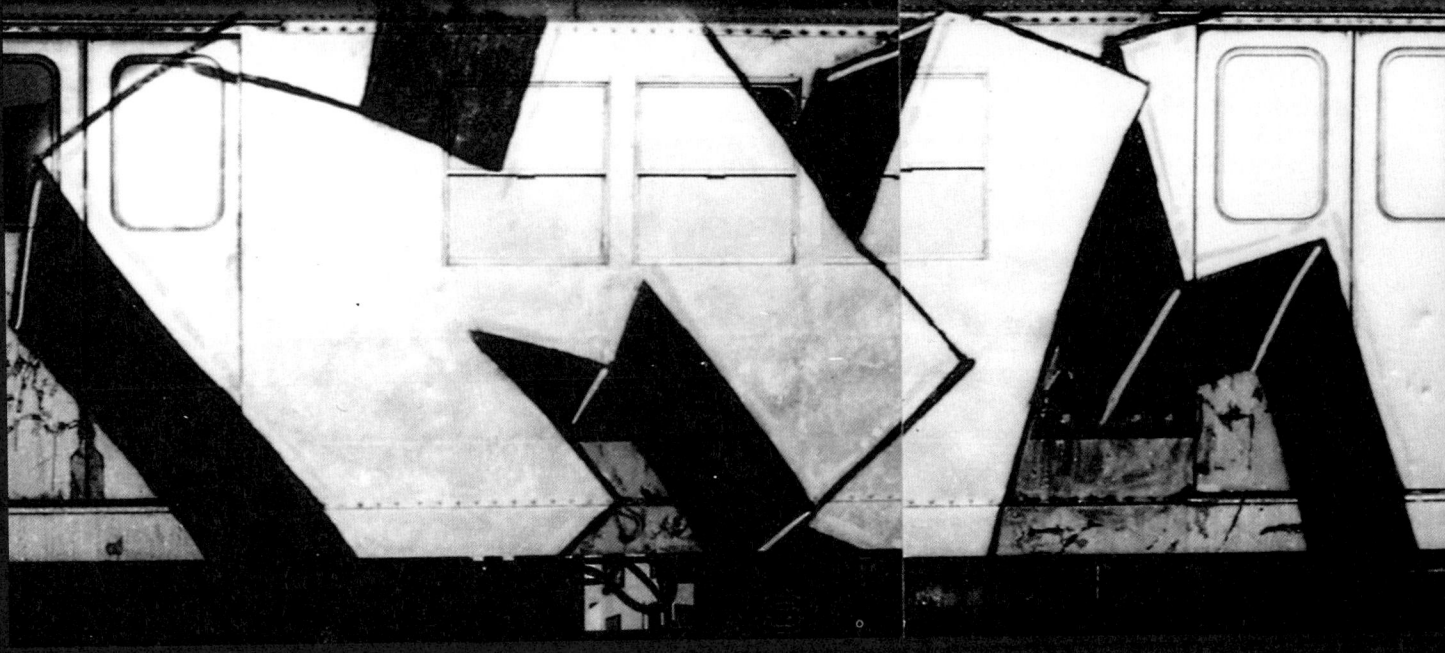

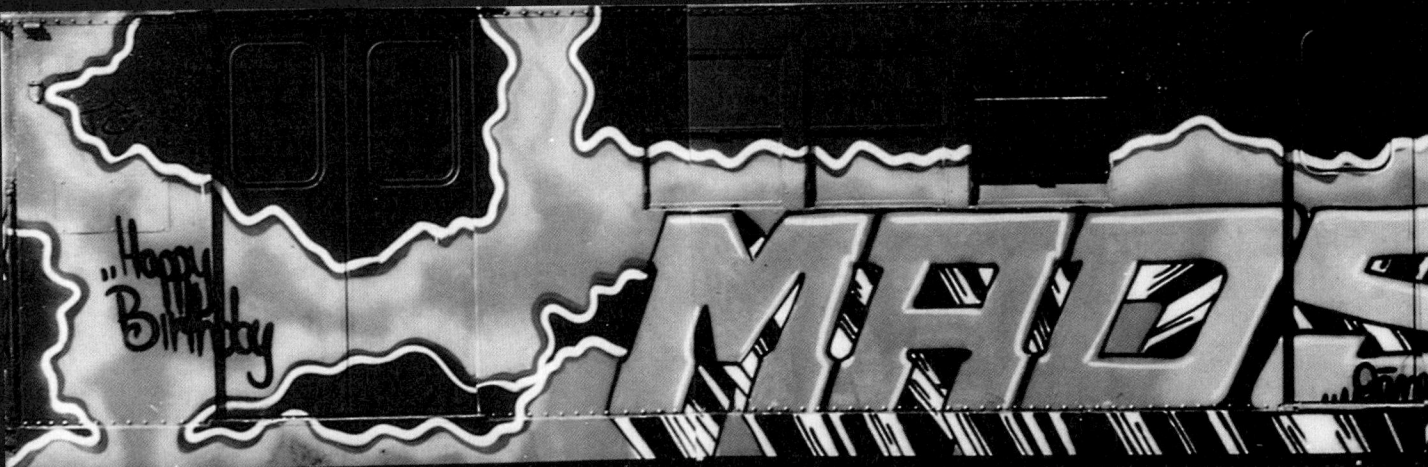

Top: "Mitch," subway graffiti, 1980. Chalfant. HC

Middle: "Madseen," subway graffiti, 1980. Chalfant. HC

Bottom left: Graffiti-covered subway station. Fred W. McDarrah. FWM

Bottom right: "Deuce Coupe," dance by Twyla Tharp, performed by Twyla Tharp and the Joffrey Ballet, 1973. Backdrops by United Graffiti Artists. Migdoll. JOF

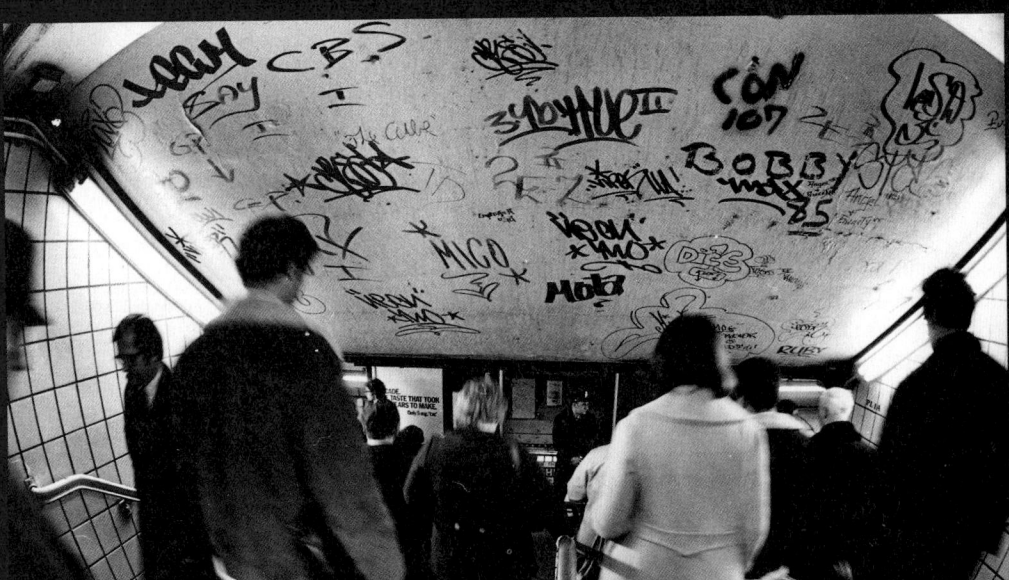

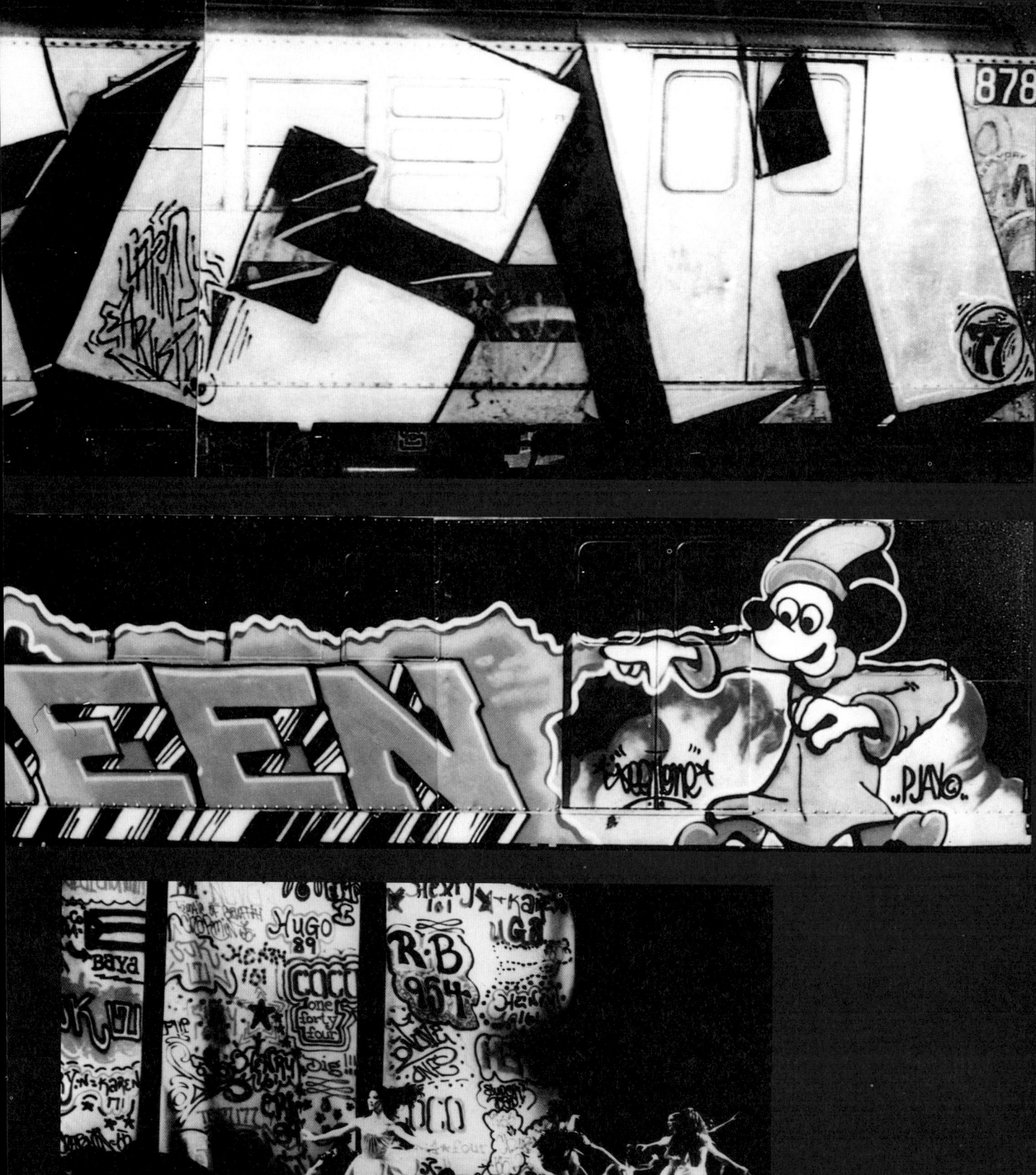

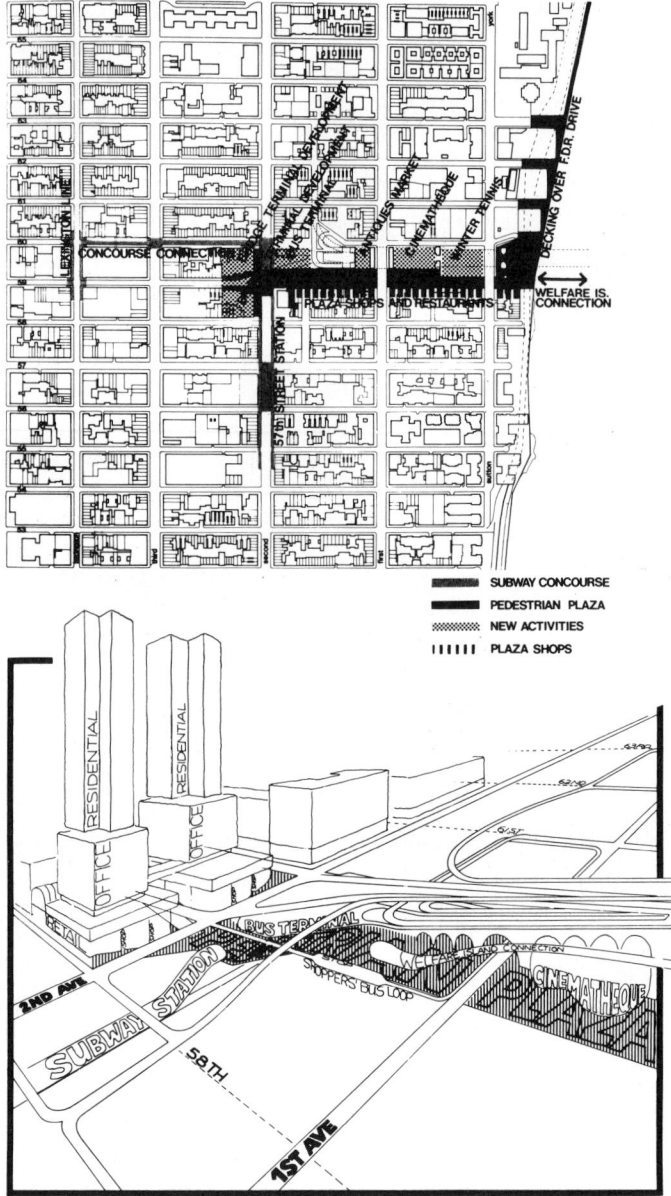

Plan for coordinating development near Second Avenue subway station at East Fifty-seventh Street. Urban Design Group, 1972. Map and perspective. JB and NYC

SUBWAY CONCOURSE
PEDESTRIAN PLAZA
NEW ACTIVITIES
PLAZA SHOPS

planners, was focused on Manhattan. True bored tunnel construction was rejected on the grounds of cost; except in a few areas, the new subway would be built by the time-honored, traffic-disrupting cut-and-cover method.

As groundbreaking approached, the Urban Design Group developed special zoning regulations for areas around the stations to control land use, help integrate new and existing buildings with the stations and develop more environmentally desirable circulation patterns for passengers as they moved between the street and the trains.[252] In 1974 the Board of Estimate adopted legislation extending the city's zoning power to cover below-grade conditions by requiring that new development along the Second Avenue subway route take underground access into consideration. Establishing a "special land use district" for the duration of the construction, it required off-street subway entrances through plazas, underground concourses or lobbies of buildings. The legislation, evolving out of a six-month-long study sponsored jointly by the City Planning Commission and the Municipal Art Society, was prepared under a grant from the National Endowment for the Arts. It was directed by Raquel Ramati, an architect on the commission's staff and from 1974 to 1980 director of the Urban Design Group, who collaborated with Ada Karmi-Melamede, the chief designer, on three prototypical subway stations along the route meant to serve as "guidelines for architects."[253]

Construction got under way in October 1972, four months after the federal government, through the Urban Mass Transportation Administration (UMTA), announced its approval of and intended participation in the project, granting $25 million toward the construction but suggesting that as much as two-thirds of the total cost might be forthcoming. The first contract covered work between Ninety-eighth and 105th streets. In March 1973 a second contract was let covering work between 110th and 120th streets, and in October 1973 work on the southern section was begun at Canal Street. In July 1974 construction was begun at Ninth Street, although the city's financial situation was so bad that this section of the work never progressed as far as the actual building of a tunnel.

The first commission to design a station went to Damaz & Weigel, whose project designer was James Hadley. Tackling the Ninety-sixth Street station, they produced a scheme that was, as Architecture Plus observed, "ordinary" compared to stations in other major cities but "glorious" compared to those in New York.[254] The station's constrained dimensions, with only ten-foot ceilings in the mezzanine, had been determined by DeLeuw, Cather & Company, engineers for the entire line. The materials—brick walls and brick pavers in combination with stainless steel—were chosen for durability. At this point other firms were at work: Johnson & Hanchard for the station at 106th Street; Gruzen & Partners for Eighty-sixth Street; Carson, Lundin & Thorsen for Seventy-second Street; I. M. Pei & Partners for Fifty-seventh Street; Harrison & Abramovitz for Forty-eighth Street; Poor & Swanke & Partners for Twenty-third Street; Haines, Lundberg & Waehler for Grand Street; and Morris Ketchum, Jr. & Associates for Chatham Square.

In 1971 the general euphoria over the line's likely construction was somewhat jolted by the voters' rejection of that year's transportation bond issue, which forced the financially strapped city to come up with the $150 million estimated for the line's southern portion. It became increasingly clear in 1972–74 that city officials were initiating a grand project with hopes of raising the funds later. Meanwhile, an increasingly vocal segment of the population began to suggest that, given

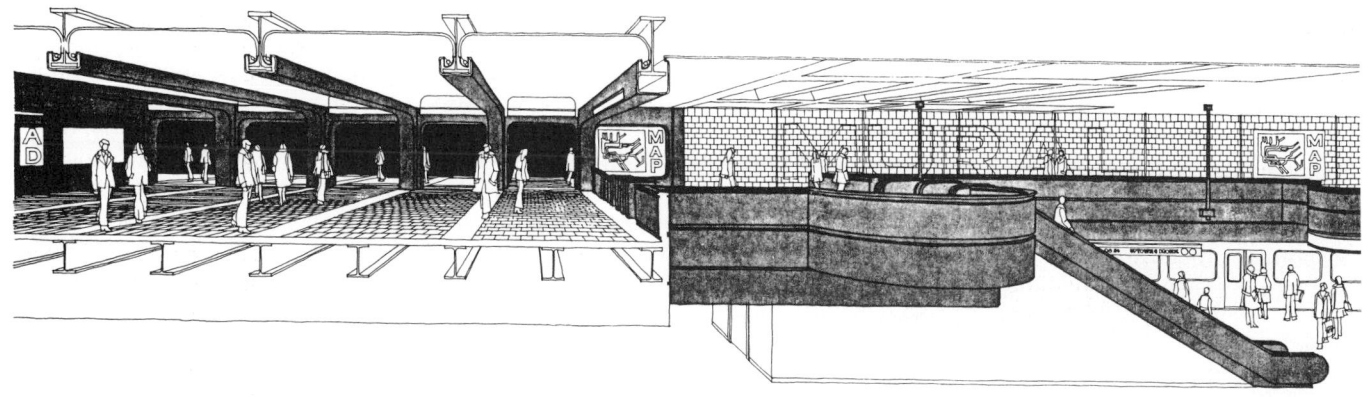

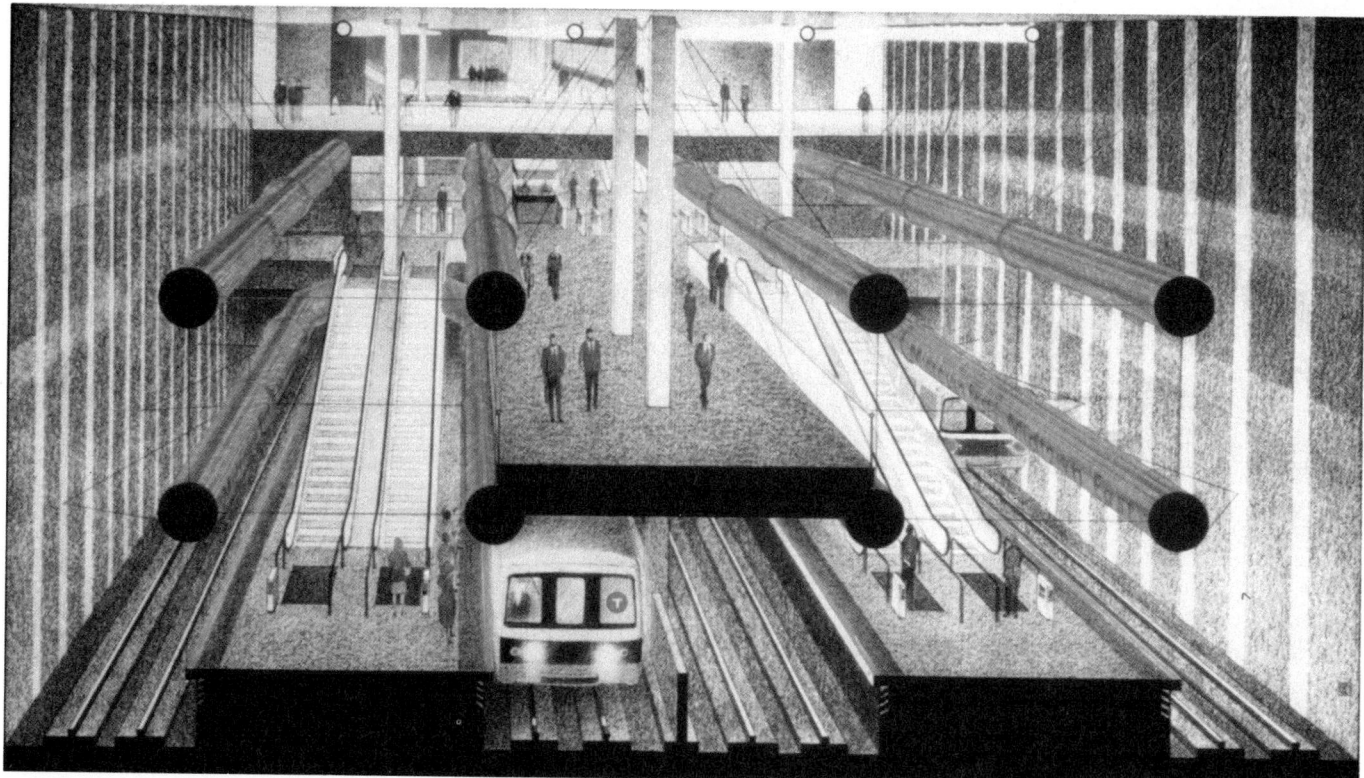

Top: Proposed Second Avenue subway station at East Ninety-sixth
Street. Damaz & Weigel, 1974. Section perspective by James Hadley.
JH

Bottom: Proposed Second Avenue subway station at East Fifty-seventh
Street. I. M. Pei & Partners, 1977. Section perspective. PCF

the declining ridership on the entire system, including the Lexington Avenue line, and the collapse of the city's postwar building boom, the emphasis should not be on new construction but on maintenance and rehabilitation of the aging and critically neglected system. Maintenance, performance and safety, not new construction, were emphasized in a five-part series about the subway system published in the *New York Times* a month before the November 1973 referendum on the transportation bond issue.[255] When the voters went to the polls, they defeated the bond proposal; officials, citing mysterious "alternate" forms of financing, continued to paint an optimistic picture.

In November 1974, as the city was struggling with its financial crisis, construction of the Second Avenue subway was discontinued, with 1986 given as the earliest likely date for its resumption. A month after construction stopped, Mayor Beame announced new transportation policies: fare stabilization, system modernization and completion of the new Queens lines. In his *Transportation Policy and Programs* report for 1975, the mayor stated: "Astronomical construction costs confront us with the choice of either concentrating our resources or spreading them so thinly that no new service could become operational until the last decade of the century. . . . We are not abandoning the Second Avenue subway. However, we must defer it."[256]

Once again delay was not without its value, for as Sigurd Grava observed in his 1980 assessment, despite the previous delays, "the basic premises of the Second Avenue Subway were never re-examined." It was, in its way, a textbook case of a facility that was assumed to be needed with no real studies ever having been made to support these presumptions. Grava wrote: "Any such project today and in the future would have to be certain about the expected patronage, would have to examine all social-economic-community-environmental impacts, would have to know where the funds are coming from, and would have to select the most appropriate mode—not necessarily heavy rail." The physical record of the Second Avenue subway project is one of the more notable oddities of New York's history, leaving behind, as Grava described them, "three elongated and unconnected holes under the pavement more or less lined up . . . neatly finished but never actually used . . . tangible monuments to an exuberant era of city management that came to an abrupt turning point in the 1970s."[257]

Even older than the city's subways were its principal bridges, the oldest of which, the Brooklyn Bridge (John A. Roebling and Washington Roebling, 1883), was completely overhauled beginning in 1950 (see chapter 13). In April 1953, while the Brooklyn Bridge was still under reconstruction, the city's Department of Public Works revealed that the forty-four-year old Manhattan Bridge (Carrère & Hastings and Leon Morsieff, 1909) had broken a truss.[258] The Madison Avenue Bridge (A. P. Boller, 1910) over the Harlem River was closed for repairs for over a year beginning in February 1959.[259] The city's prized water-supply system, in place since 1890, was also showing signs of wear. In July 1957 water-main breaks on Sixth Avenue, attributed to ground settlement beneath the city's surface as well as old age, flooded subways and disrupted traffic in midtown, wreaking havoc for almost a month, only to recur a few blocks away near Times Square in November.[260] Even the surface conditions of the city's streets, once a model for the nation, were becoming a problem. In 1963 the city filled 950,000 potholes, yet the problem would not go away.[261] By April 1964,

at the conclusion of the city's spring "Fill 'Em Up" campaign, another 264,124 potholes were plugged.[262]

The city's highway system, the newest component of its arterial system, was also in bad shape. Not surprisingly, no part was worse off than the earliest segment of the network of expressways and parkways that hugged the city's shores: Manhattan's elevated West Side Highway, officially known as the Miller Highway, portions of which were forty years old in 1970. With narrow and twisting roadways and left-hand exit and entrance ramps, the West Side Highway, one of the city's busiest, was inadequate to handle modern traffic loads. Part of the highway was structurally unsound. In 1973 a $1 million repair program began to arrest the highway's serious decline and stabilize it until a permanent solution was found.[263] Repairs had barely gotten under way when a truck and a car fell to the ground as a portion of the highway collapsed near Gansevoort and Little West Twelfth streets, leading to an indefinite closing of the entire highway south of Twenty-third Street.[264] Subsequently, the stretch of the Henry Hudson Parkway between Seventy-second and Seventy-ninth streets was also closed for repairs, clogging Riverside Drive with traffic and inflaming tempers.[265] By June 1974 the entire West Side Highway south of Forty-sixth Street was indefinitely closed as well.[266] Two years later, in September 1976, workers began to demolish the road, which had been serving many residents as a bikeway and promenade; demolition south of Forty-sixth Street was completed in 1983.[267]

In 1971, just as the serious condition of the West Side Highway was beginning to be understood, New York State's Urban Development Corporation (UDC) released its Wateredge Development Study, a proposal to expand Manhattan by 700 acres of virgin territory, principally along the lower west side, simply by moving the land mass into the river to the limits of the pierhead line established by the federal government.[268] The study had precedents in proposals by the Regional Plan Association (1966) and by a group of fifty architects and student architects designating themselves the Hudson Riverfront Committee who, sponsored by Manhattan Borough President Percy Sutton, had produced a visionary plan for its development in 1968.[269]

The UDC's study was directed by Samuel Ratensky, who had been instrumental in seeing Waterside built on an East River platform (see chapter 5) and who had worked with the developer Carol W. Haussamen to find similar potential sites between the pierhead and bulkhead lines for the Moshe Safdie–designed housing she hoped to build (see chapters 3 and 11). Wateredge called for the complete reconstruction of the West Side Highway, which would be rebuilt along the shore at a cost of $25 to $50 million a mile. But the proposal, which was developed in detail by a young Yale-trained architect-urbanist, Craig Whitaker, met resistance from the first, initially from city and state officials. They feared that the project would disrupt plans for Battery Park City (see chapter 3), delay construction of the city's proposed convention center (see chapter 5) and undermine the fragile agreements that still kept some shipping operations in Manhattan, including those of passenger cruise ships, for which a new superliner terminal was being planned (see chapter 5). Only later did they realize that the objections of Village and Upper West Side residents would pose the greatest threat to the project.

The state's Department of Transportation was authorized to study various alternate alignments in its effort to obtain federal funds that would cover 90 percent of the cost of construction. In order to get these funds, the new highway would have to link

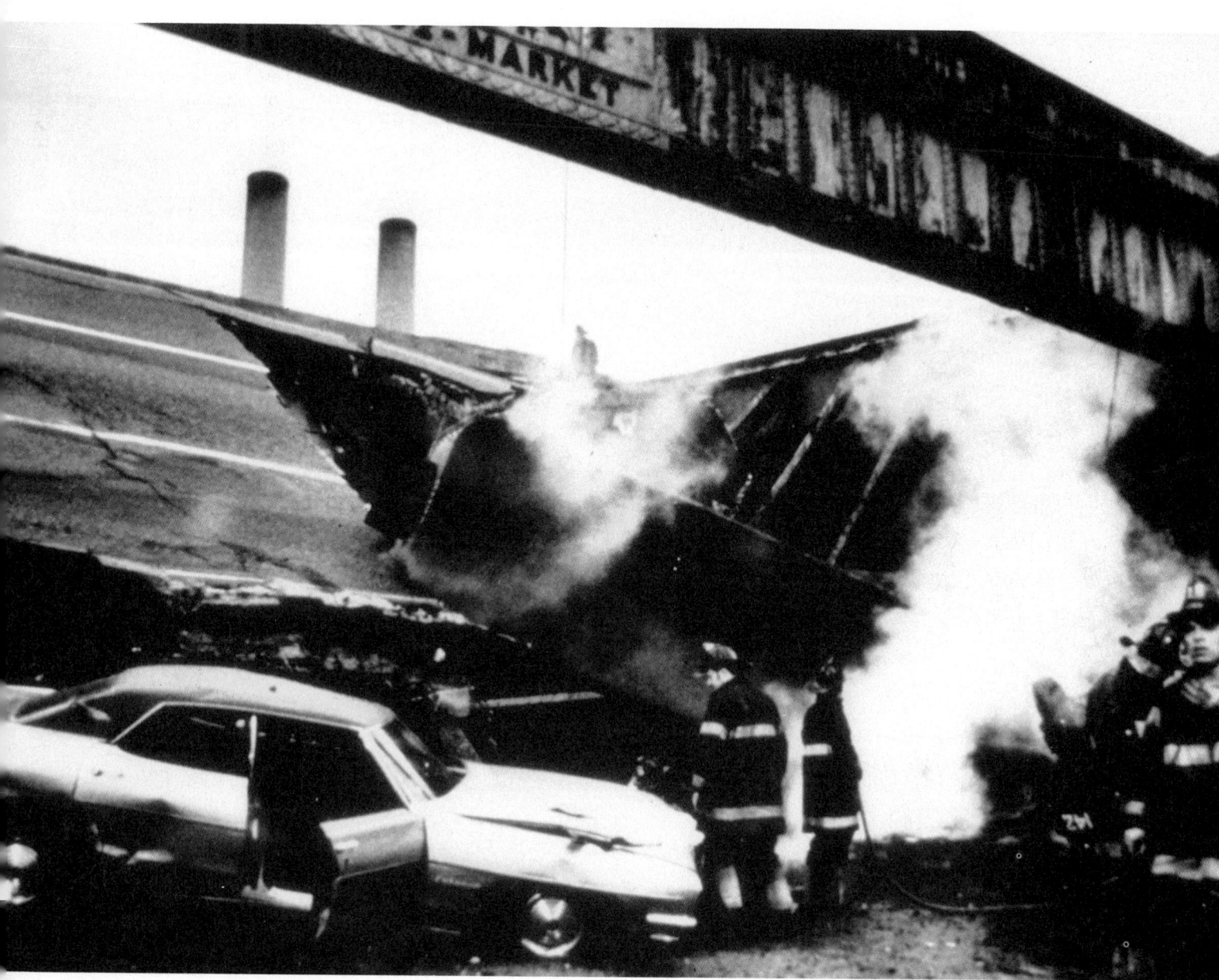

Collapse of the West Side Highway, between Little West Twelfth and
Gansevoort streets, December 15, 1973. CW

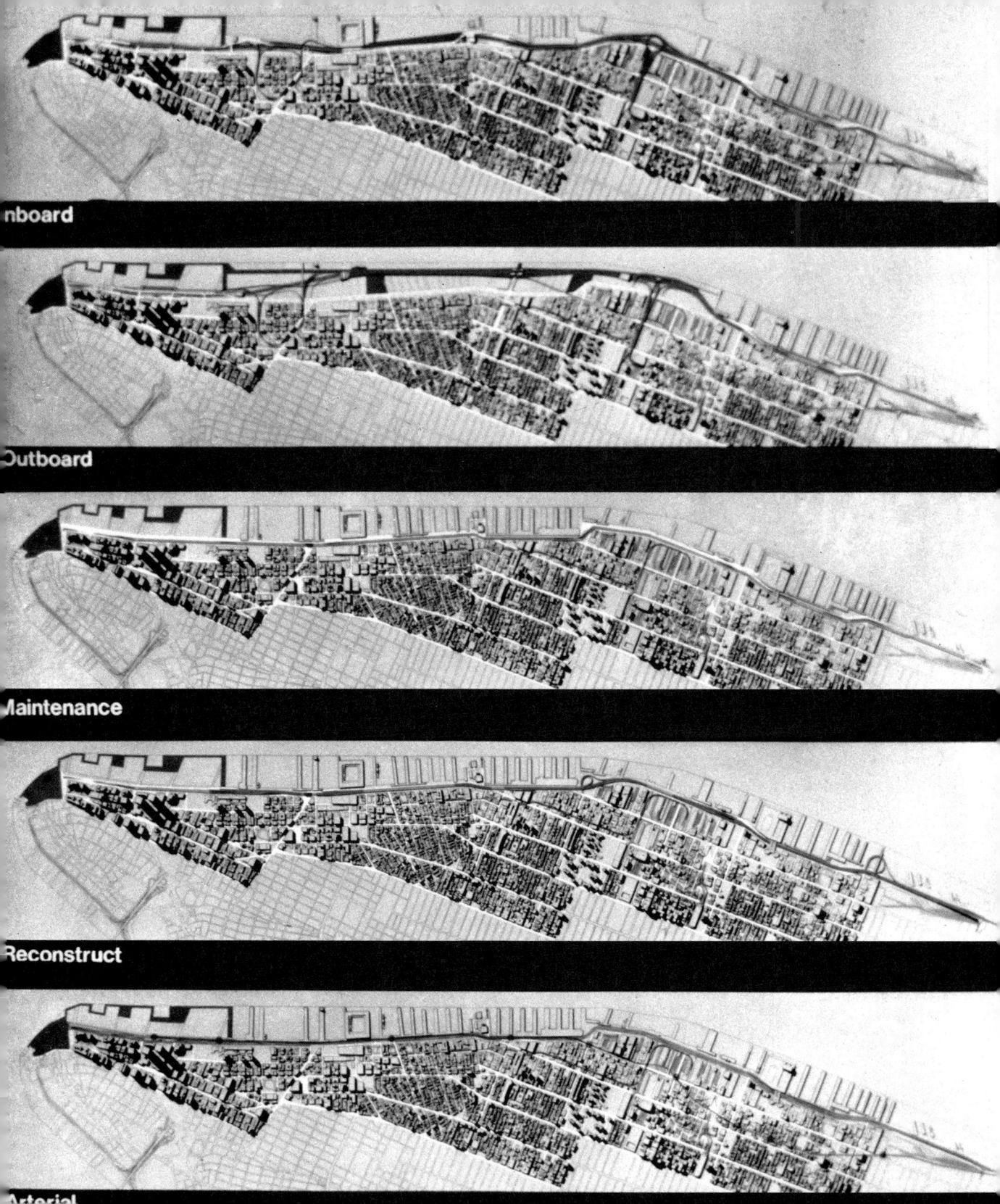

Inboard

Outboard

Maintenance

Reconstruct

Arterial

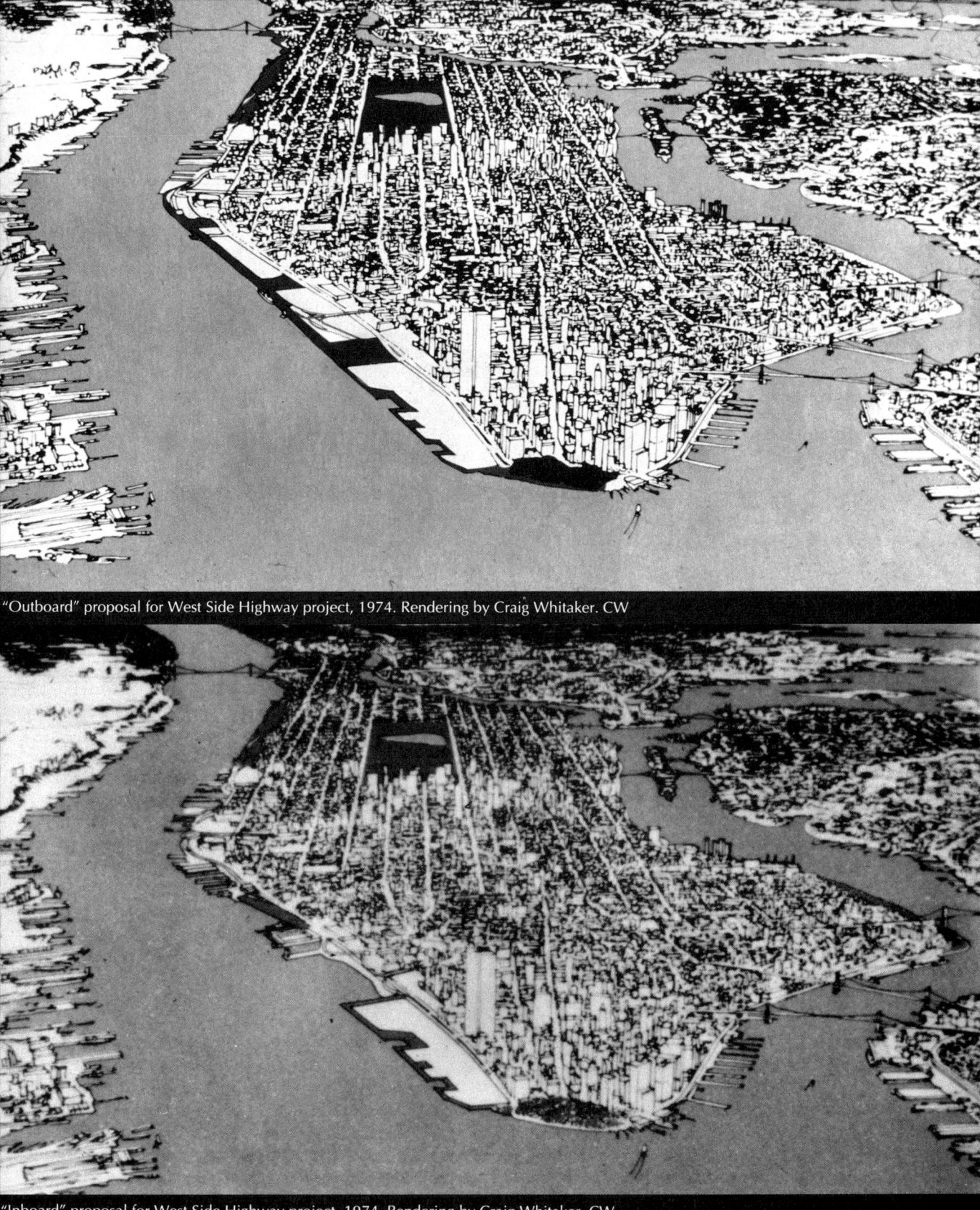

"Outboard" proposal for West Side Highway project, 1974. Rendering by Craig Whitaker. CW

"Inboard" proposal for West Side Highway project, 1974. Rendering by Craig Whitaker. CW

two states, thereby making connection with New Jersey via the Henry Hudson Parkway almost essential—the two Hudson River tunnels could not qualify because they were not part of the interstate system—and creating the threat of a massive reconstruction of one of Moses's most beautiful urban parkways.

As Ratensky and Whitaker conceived it, the project was more than a conventional plan for a highway: its landfill would create a development area of between 650 and 700 acres capable of housing 75,000 to 85,000 families. The plan called for the construction of an eight- or ten-lane highway set 100 feet back from the pierhead line, the line established by the United States Army Corps of Engineers beyond which no construction was permitted in the Hudson River's channel. This routing meant that in some areas the highway would be located 1,000 feet or more from the present shoreline, in which area the new development could take place. As initially proposed, the highway was to be built at or near grade level but would be covered, so that shipping could continue at quays, and parking and other services could be tucked beneath a landscaped deck that would become a waterfront park, similar to Finley Walk and Carl Schurz Park over the East River Drive. Inboard of the highway, city streets would be extended to form building blocks for future development. The new top deck would slope gently back to connect with the city's edge at grade level.

In 1971, as a result of intense community lobbying, Governor Rockefeller and Mayor Lindsay agreed to an amendment to the state's highway law that would protect Riverside Park from encroachment by the expressway. The law, championed by Al Blumenthal, deputy minority leader of the New York State Assembly, carried his name. By the end of the year community groups, especially in the West Village and Chelsea, were beginning to become concerned. By January 1972 the city and state had entered into a "memorandum of understanding," drafted mostly by Alexander Cooper of the Urban Design Group, and signed by Mayor Lindsay and Governor Rockefeller, creating a twenty-member steering committee to coordinate the highway's redesign and to determine future land uses along the water. The committee consisted of eight city, six state and two independent officials as well as the chairmen of the four affected community planning boards. Key to the memorandum was the provision that should the groups not be able to come up with a plan, the mayor and the governor could negotiate an agreement of their own.

In 1972 Samuel Ratensky became ill and was replaced by Lowell K. Bridwell, a former Federal Highway Administrator, who was named executive director of the project, and Whitaker continued on. On April 1, 1972, Wateredge was reconstituted as an independent West Side Highway project with a working committee overseeing its progress that included Edward Logue, president of the Urban Development Corporation, and Donald Elliott, chairman of the City Planning Commission. While Bridwell was sympathetic to a mixed-use approach, he asserted that "there's no doubt we're trying to do a highway here." And he assured the community planning boards of the West Side that he was not willing to build "at all social, economic, and other costs." In fact, "no build" was one of nine alternate strategies that were studied in 1972–73.[270]

On March 30, 1973, seven possible strategies were reported under consideration, but by the time the first public hearings were scheduled in May 1973, only four alternatives were being considered—and the no-build scheme was not among them. While objections to the new road focused on environmental issues, it was clear that the creation of so much

new land posed a genuine threat to the established upland neighborhoods. As the New York Times noted, the new highway had not only to "meet the needs of the shipping and railroad industries, which have fallen into deep decline," but also to "handle the reborn concept that the needs of neighborhoods cannot be ground down by City Hall. Words like ecology, air pollution and traffic patterns did not bother the original builders of the highway, but now these words are essential in plans for a new roadway."[271]

By late 1974 it was clear that the West Side Highway project was in trouble with the community, although nothing like a consensus could be drawn about what if anything was to be done. In October and November 1974 all groups were induced by the Regional Plan Association to meet together at the American Arbitration Association, where Donald Strauss, its research director, made what New York Affairs described as a "quixotic effort to help all sides reach a compromise."[272]

Not surprisingly, many groups and individuals had their own proposals, including Robert Moses, causing the editors of New York Affairs to speculate that "perhaps the threat of a Moses comeback will finally jar the West Side Highway disputants out of their ... stalemate."[273] Moses, eighty-five years old and a consultant to the Triborough Bridge and Tunnel Authority, recommended that the section from the Battery to Canal Street be replaced by a street-level highway, that the portion between Canal and Fifty-ninth streets be rebuilt to eliminate its sharp curves and that the section between Fifty-ninth and Seventy-second streets be relocated to the east, permitting a southern extension of Riverside Park on land soon to be abandoned by the Penn-Central Railroad. Donald Trump and his architects, Gruzen & Partners, adopted Moses's realignment when Trump became the redeveloper of the Penn-Central yards, proposing in 1976 that three residential communities housing 14,500 families be built on the 100-acre site (forty-five acres of which were still under water).

Early in 1974 five alternate plans were released in preparation for a public hearing to be scheduled in late April or May pursuant to the Environmental Impact Statement prepared by the project team. To the shock of many observers, the various alternatives were accompanied by a proposal to tunnel under Riverside Park as far north as the George Washington Bridge—a seeming threat to the integrity of the Blumenthal amendment. Bowing to community groups who argued that more time was needed to respond to the detailed proposals, city officials delayed the hearings and broke them into two sessions, on June 20 and 27 and on September 5 and 12. By then the community understood the choices: rebuild the present highway; reconstruct it, straightening out the worst curves; create an "arterial" route by removing the highway altogether and making West Street into a six-lane surface boulevard; build a new highway "inboard" that would hug the present west side edges and be served by major interchanges at key intersections; or build a covered highway "outboard," along the pierhead line, that would also be served by interchanges. The last alternative would create 243 acres of new land.

While hearings were taking place, the Citizens' Housing and Planning Council editorialized on the irony that "during the great debate" on the project, Robert Caro's book on Robert Moses was being published, reminding them "of the contrasts between Moses who spoke and acted abruptly, often arbitrarily, and occasionally ruthlessly for what he regarded as the public interest and the West Side Highway Project which so far has no spokesman who presumes or even dares to speak for the public interest." The editorial continued: "Our point is not to mourn the

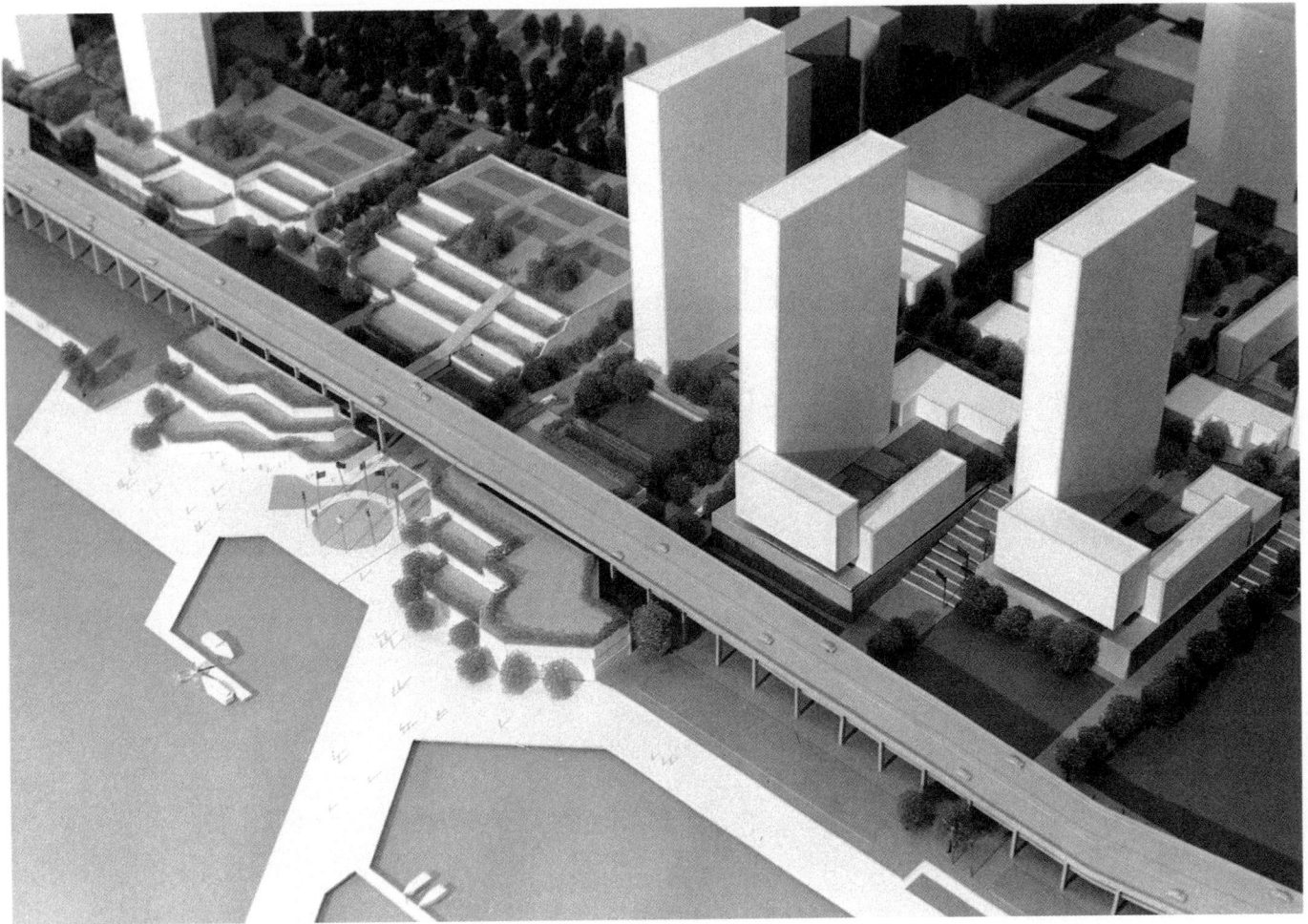

Residential community along the Hudson River, West Fifty-ninth to West Seventy-second Street, proposed by Donald Trump. Gruzen & Partners, 1976. GS

departure of Moses, but to wonder whether there is a public interest left to be spoken for."[274] According to the Citizens' Housing and Planning Council, the project, like so many others of a period dominated by community review, was "in danger of being chipped, chopped, and delayed until death by a combination of conflicting spokesmen for very divergent and really rather special points of view: limousine riders who want comfort; residents fearing traffic and change; developers who want a piece of the action; environmentalists who prefer that developers, as well as road builders, have no action at all."[275] The council supported the outboard plan because it promised to bring in federal funds and to create new land.

Faced with a stalemate, on November 26, 1974, John E. Zuccotti, City Planning Commissioner, and Michael J. Lazar, City Transportation Administrator—both members of the West Side Highway Project's steering committee—unveiled the Beame administration's compromise plan. The plan, called Westway, consisted of a six-lane interstate highway burrowing through landfill but without the great network of service roads and elaborate interchanges called for in Bridwell's outboard scheme. In March 1975 Westway became the official proposal of the city and state. But a coalition of more than thirty environmental groups had already brought suit in Federal District Court

to block any kind of interstate project. Also in March the Regional Plan Association called for an even more limited facility, with a four-lane surface boulevard below Twenty-third Street and six lanes, also at grade, above, gradually rising to join the Henry Hudson Parkway north of Forty-second Street.

By October 1976 federal endorsement of Westway seemed assured, thereby guaranteeing 90 percent of the highway's construction cost, but the plan was still being challenged in the courts. In addition, many level-headed citizens' groups were lobbying for an even more reduced highway, trading in the majority of the federal funds for mass transit in accord with a policy initiated by the Ford administration to give local communities more control over their transportation systems.

In January 1977 Paul Goldberger began an assessment of the Westway project by quoting an anonymous spokesman of the West Side Highway Project: "Not since the building of Central Park or the covering of the railroad tracks on Park Avenue has there been a decision that will change the physical shape of the city as much as Westway."[276] But in an era of incremental planning it was the very enormity of such projects that frightened citizens' groups, so much so that Congressman Edward I. Koch, campaigning for mayor in October 1977, called for a transit-fund trade-in and labeled Westway a "disaster" that would "never be

117

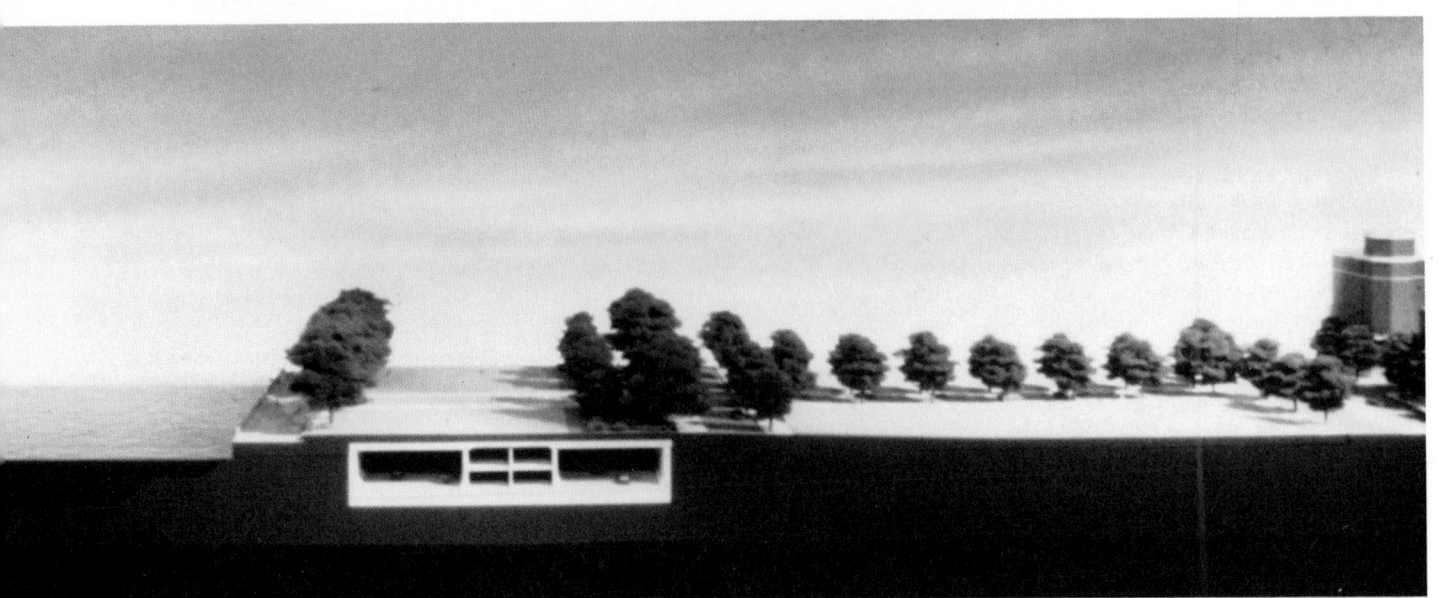

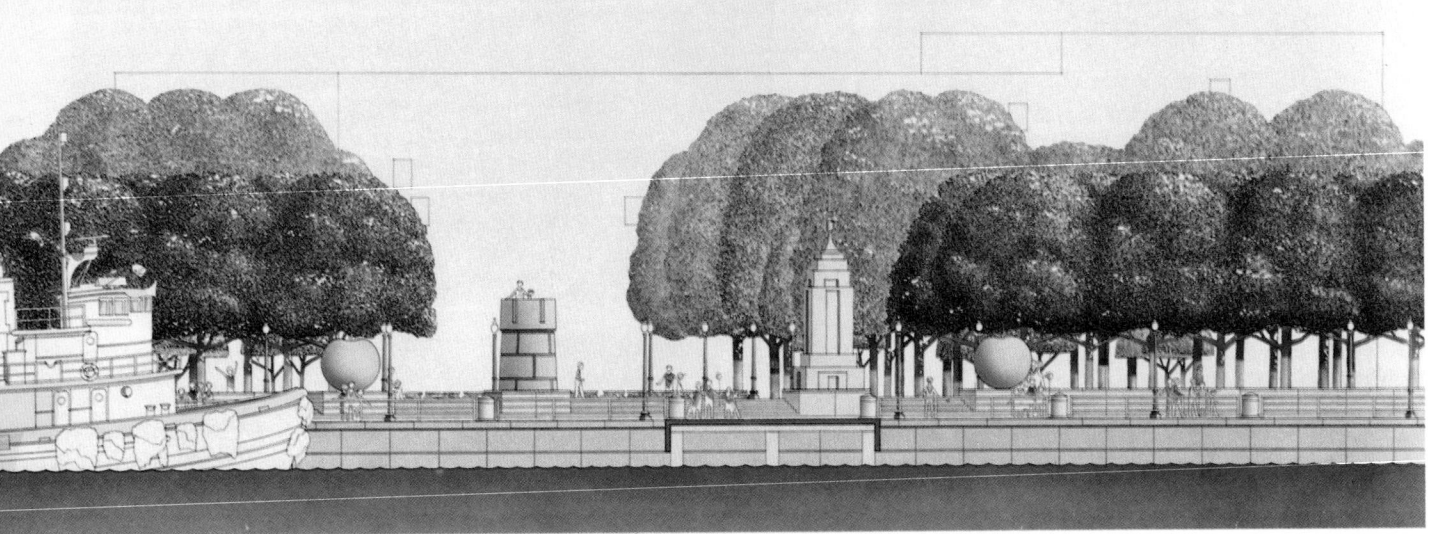

Top: Model of Westway, 1980. Lowell K. Bridwell, executive director
of the project. CW

Bottom: Proposed Westway State Park, along the Hudson River from
Chambers to West Thirty-sixth Street. Venturi, Rauch & Scott Brown,
Clarke & Rapuano and Craig Whitaker, 1980–84. Elevation. VSBA

built."[277] A few months later State Environmental Commissioner Peter A. A. Berle denied the project an air-quality permit vital to the highway's realization, claiming that the designers had underestimated the traffic and pollution the facility would produce. The Westway project drifted on through the courts until its death in 1985, and the old West Side Highway was replaced by a surface boulevard.[278] Dying along with Westway was Venturi, Rauch & Scott Brown, Clarke & Rapuano and Craig Whitaker's elegant terraced waterfront park (1980–84), with its imaginative playgrounds using miniature skyscrapers as climbing tops and its "big apple" sculptures.[279]

From No Plan to Non-Plan

The pseudoscience of planning seems almost neurotic in its determination to imitate empiric failure and ignore empiric success.
—Jane Jacobs, 1961[280]

With the revision of the city's charter in 1936, the first planning commission was called into existence, replacing the farcical 500-member New York City Committee on Plan and Survey, set up in 1926 by Mayor Walker, and the ad hoc Mayor's Committee on City Planning, formed by Mayor La Guardia in 1934. The new commission, which had as one of its principal responsibilities the drafting of a master plan for the city's future, consisted of five members who were appointed by the mayor: Adolf A. Berle, Jr., was chairman, taking the position after Robert Moses declined it; the other members were Cleveland Rodgers, Lawrence Orton, Edwin A. Salmon and Arthur V. Sheridan.[281] The commission met for the first time in January 1938. When Berle resigned his post in April 1938 to become Assistant Secretary of State in the federal government, he was replaced by another prominent New Dealer, Rexford Guy Tugwell, who closed down the Master Plan Division after it had been at work for only two months. Tugwell's approach relied on "continuing economic and social research" rather than definitive physical planning.[282] His vision, supported by the *New York Times*, was of a planning commission that would act as a "clearing-house."[283]

In April 1939 the commission issued its first annual report, rather schizophrenically advocating the location of housing near the main centers of work while proposing the dispersion of new business and industrial districts away from the heart of the city.[284] The report went on to comment on New York's status as a part of New York State, "without political power commensurate with its population, to say nothing of its wealth and responsibilities." It speculated on the benefits that would accrue to the metropolitan area if it were an independent state or "a single geographical and political unit, as closely integrated otherwise as it is economically." The report focused on the city as a marketplace for commodities, goods and ideas but ignored its potential as a creative center in its own right: "New York is not inhabited by a superior class of individuals who surpass the rest of the country in ideas or in other ways. The metropolis is merely the place where idea exchanges are operated. . . . The ideas come from everywhere and are brought to New York because this is the place where ideas are evaluated, exploited and exchanged."[285]

On November 20, 1940, the commission unveiled the proposed first and second stages of its Master Plan of Land Use. A few weeks later, on December 5, Tugwell reviewed his ideas with 500 civic and business leaders gathered in the auditorium of Hunter College.[286] The presentation consisted of five written pages and three maps, showing where New Yorkers now lived and worked, where the next generation could be expected to live and work after slum-clearance programs had been undertaken, and what the city of the future, perhaps three generations hence, might be like. The plan focused on the middle-income wage earner, seen as the "forgotten man" who had been squeezed out of Manhattan. According to Charles Bennett, the real estate reporter for the *New York Times*, "As it emerges into its new character the city will become more and more a cluster of well-knit residential communities complete with small parks and playgrounds" and other facilities, "all factors essential to a satisfactory neighborhood environment."[287] The proposed land-use plan, which included a district plan showing health centers and other public facilities, a plan outlining areas suited to low-rent housing, and an extensive map of highways, was based on a belief that the city would experience slower population growth in the future and that decentralization was a logical and desirable goal. By far the most controversial aspect of Tugwell's plan was the notion that by 1990 the city would transform one-third of its land surface into public open space.

Though the plan was endorsed by architects and planners such as Eliel Saarinen, who hailed it as a brilliant vision, it was attacked from the start by Park Commissioner Robert Moses, who launched a stream of objections to its "visionary," "irresponsible" and "fantastic" ideas. Recommending that the plan be "filed away and forgotten," he denounced it as the work of ivory-tower theorists who dressed up revolutionary ideas in obscure and newly invented words like "greenbelts" and "decentralization."[288] Moses's vitriol was at its peak when he came to discuss the plan's call for vastly expanded parklands. Citing the achievements of park planners in the 1920s and 1930s, "people who labored day and night for limited objectives in the face of great difficulties," he characterized the commission's proposals as those of "itinerant carpet-bag experts splashing at a ten-league canvas with brushes of comet's hair." Moses believed that the plan was too long-range in its implications and that too little thought had been given to "the status of the airplane and motor car half a century hence."[289] Therefore, he urged that the city proceed with more limited objectives in mind.

Moses mustered wide support for his opposition to the plan: the Citizen's Budget Commission opposed it, as did savings-bank groups and industrial, commercial and real estate interests, who condemned the plan as too grandiose in the scope of its public improvements and too dependent on decentralization. The *Real Estate Record and Guide* contended that decentralization contradicted the "fundamental purpose of a city": "The need is not flight from devalued areas but rather restoration of values by modernizing neighborhoods."[290] Moses succeeded in killing the plan.

On November 27, 1941, after Tugwell's resignation the previous July,[291] Moses was appointed to the City Planning Commission by Mayor La Guardia, who also elevated Edwin A. Salmon to the position of chairman.[292] At the same time, Public Works Commissioner Irving V. A. Huie replaced Arthur Sheridan.[293] "Now we will have one happy family," crowed La Guardia, who had effectively located control over the commission within his own administration.[294] Some saw the appointment of Moses and Huie as letting the foxes into the chicken coop. The move was opposed by the Citizens Union, whose president, Robert S. Childs, brought suit on July 7, 1942, seeking to restrain payment to the two commissioners because in their principal city jobs they held office at the mayor's pleasure while as City Planning Commissioners they were appointed to fixed terms. "If the suit is successful," the Citizens Union said in its statement, "these two capable commissioners can resign from the City Planning Commission and be reappointed as heads of their respective departments, and the Mayor will be required to appoint a real City Planning Commission whose viewpoint can be independent and based on full-time attention as the City Charter intended."[295] The issue, of course, was not that the joint appointments compromised the commission's independence. What was troubling was the overwhelming power of Moses, who was also commissioner of the city's Park Department; chairman of the New York State Department of Parks; president of the Long Island State Park Commission, the Bethpage Park Authority and Jones Beach State Parkway Authority; chairman of the Triborough Bridge Authority; and sole member of the New York City Parkway Authority. The Appellate Division dismissed the suit almost a year later, in May 1943.[296]

Despite the decisive role his highway system played in dispersing the city's middle class into the suburbs, Moses opposed decentralization, arguing in 1940 that those "who would drastically decentralize the metropolis, break it up into satellite forms, rebuild it in its entirety, make sheer logic prevail in the relocation of trade, residence, art and recreation, may continue to live in Ivory Towers. . . . This town is too tough for them and they had better keep out of the rough and tumble of the market place."[297] For Moses, large-scale planning seemed inextricably bound up with decentralization, an approach that did not fit with his vision of how to rejuvenate the city. In 1943, meditating on postwar planning, he stated:

> We do not believe in revolution. The city is not going to be torn up and rebuilt as a decentralized satellite or other academic theory. Therefore, we do not have to wait for the painting of the new, big, over-all picture constantly referred to by revolutionary planners. We believe that the older, run-down sections of the city will be rebuilt. We believe that there will be a much slower development of outlying open lands within the city and its suburbs, that subway extensions will be limited, and that efforts will be directed to making what we have inherited more livable and attractive—as against abandoning it, letting trade and population drift away, and continuing a trend toward suburban dormitory living and commuting.[298]

In June 1944 Moses went after the planner-idealists again in a highly public way. In an article in the New York Times Magazine, "Mr. Moses Dissects the 'Long-Haired Planners,'" he revealed himself to be shamelessly intolerant of their point of view. Portraying planning idealists as little more than political subversives, Moses said: "In municipal planning we must decide between revolution and common sense—between the subsidized llamas in their remote mountain temples and those who must work in the market place." In particular, Moses attacked the Finnish-born Eliel Saarinen, who supported the first master plan's emphasis on decentralization, claiming that Saarinen's city planning led "straight into communal land ownership." Carried away with his cause, Moses descended to a xenophobic attack not only on Saarinen but also on the German-born architects Walter Gropius and Erich Mendelsohn. Moses's tone would be regarded as odious under any circumstances, but in the middle of a war against a virulently nationalistic political system from which these last two figures had fled it was insupportable. As if to make amends, Moses also went after the American-born Frank Lloyd Wright, telling readers that the author of The Disappearing City was "regarded in Russia as our greatest builder."[299] After taking on Lewis Mumford, Moses reserved for the finale of his diatribe an attack on the former chair-

man of the City Planning Commission, Adolf A. Berle, Jr., and his successor, Rexford Guy Tugwell, who specialized in "the kind of watercolor planning which consists of splashing green paint at a map and labeling the resulting blobs as 'open areas,' 'green belts,' breathing spaces, etc." He concluded with as clear a statement of the political mores of his planning philosophy as he was ever able to articulate: "The patriotic conservative will find plenty of faults at home. He should be eager to remedy them, but he must be loyal to the institutions and to the local scene in which his lot is cast."[300]

Moses's tirade quickly became a cause célèbre and was widely commented on. Time magazine ran an article called "Moses—Or the Bull Rushes," and a number of individuals took the time to comment as well.[301] Among these none was more thoughtful than the architect Joseph Hudnut, dean of Harvard's School of Design, where Gropius was the leading professor. In an article published in the New York Times Magazine, Hudnut reminded Moses of the European sources of America's city plans and its architecture.[302] Moses replied to Hudnut twice, heating up the argument in his second letter, where he wrote: "I never said great principles of art did not originate abroad. Of course they do. I am a traditionalist not a revolutionary. Progress is not made by wholesale destruction, but slowly and by concentration on limited objectives." Defending his parkways and parks, he concluded with a final dig at decentralization, claiming that given "the theory that big cities will be abandoned entirely, these little accomplishments are futile."[303]

In May 1944 the city put its "postwar program" of public works on display in an exhibition held on the ground floor of 500 Park Avenue (Napoleon Le Brun, 1893), the former headquarters of the Board of Education. The exhibition presented not only projects intended for immediate postwar realization but also those in preparation, forming, as Mayor La Guardia put it, "a shelf or backlog of worthwhile projects which could be put under contract immediately after the war to help relieve a possible unemployment situation."[304] The central feature of the stylish exhibition, designed by Skidmore, Owings & Merrill, was a large, fifty-by-twenty-foot floor model of New York City indicating the locations of the postwar projects. Viewed from a curving ramp, the model showed the future New York bright with green parks and playgrounds, red crosses marking new hospitals and small slates indicating new schools. The remainder of the exhibition, divided into sections by boroughs, presented individual projects in somewhat more detail. The projects were designed for the most part in a manner that sought to bridge the gap between traditional modes of expression and those of Modernism. Anxious to avoid the four-year-old controversy over the master plan, the program was presented not as a "city plan but a building replacement scheme."[305]

"At first glance," a writer in Architectural Forum reported after a visit to the exhibition, "the program is staggering in scope. Map after map and model after model leave New Yorkers slightly dizzy. They discover that future plans include 60 new elementary schools, 10 health centers, 94 playgrounds, 14 hospital buildings, 16 fire houses, 12 police stations, 8 new parkways and expressways, 13 housing projects, 7 sewage treatment works and well over 500 extensions and additions to existing facilities." All of this would cost over a billion dollars, with less than 50 percent funded out of federal and state aid and the greater portion to be borne by New York itself. In short, Forum observed, "all these facts and figures add up to the most gigantic postwar program as yet undertaken by any city." But despite the size of the program, given the city's vast needs, it was a fragmentary effort at best: "New York's present planning could be compared to a small town's decision to build one new school, one new hospital, one fire station, one police station, a park and a couple of streets."[306] The program was quintessential Moses: immediate and practical rather than long-range and idealistic.

Talbot Hamlin was stinging in his critique. Outlining New York's present deficiencies, which rendered the city "less rewarding to live in than it was fifty years ago," a theme that would become almost a litany as the decades passed, he chastised the City Planning Commission for answering the "question of what the new city is to be" with promises of "more of the same—a billion dollars more." Hamlin went on to observe that "One thing new alone is evident: that the planners are obsessed with the problem of automobile traffic." He decried as well the almost "complete failure of human imagination" demonstrated in the program:

> The history of blight in our cities is certainly a fact. The downward population trend is a fact. Growing decentralization in our cities, with consequent waste of time and energy, is a fact. Behind flight lies everywhere the attempt to use land more intensively than human beings can tolerate. But every effort of this post-war program seems directed toward increasing in the city of the future every single element that is evil and, in the long run, economically destructive.[307]

Though Hamlin saw good things in some of the schools proposed, he deplored many of them, like Eric Kebbon's Junior High School 117, which seemed "designed not to be the happy gathering places of children, but to look like the 'architected' factories of twenty years ago." Nor was he impressed with SOM's Concessions Building, "which shows a violation of the simplest rules of harmonious design." Hamlin damned both the program, which he said was "no plan," and the architects charged with fleshing it out, who "in most cases have lamentably failed to rise to the superb opportunity." In summary, he said, "There is little evidence of love or enthusiasm in these designs; much of boredom, disintegration, a sort of aesthetic defeatism, and despair."[308]

The vast display of postwar projects only served to increase the pressure from various civic groups on the City Planning Commission to formulate some sort of plan for postwar development.[309] To make up for the commission's failure to do so, Clarence Stein offered his own proposals for the city's future, not surprisingly calling for "a place predominately of green and open spaces."[310] The National Association of Housing Officials also offered its opinion, emphasizing the need for emergency war housing. Alfred Rheinstein, a builder and former chairman of the New York City Housing Authority, called for architectural competitions to determine the best designs for large areas that would then be parceled out to developers by the city. The Committee on Civic Design and Development of the New York Chapter of the American Institute of Architects took a more provocative position in October 1943, questioning large-scale projects like Stuyvesant Town in a public report, prepared under the direction of Grosvenor Atterbury, that proposed a more integrative approach combining new construction with existing neighborhoods.[311]

Without a strong overall vision from Moses, the City Planning Commission or the leading professional organization, the brothers Paul and Percival Goodman took matters into their own hands. Paul, a writer, therapist and social critic, and Percival, a Modernist architect, presented to the readers of the *New Republic* (in November 1944) and of the *Journal of the American Institute of Architects* (in February 1945) a radical

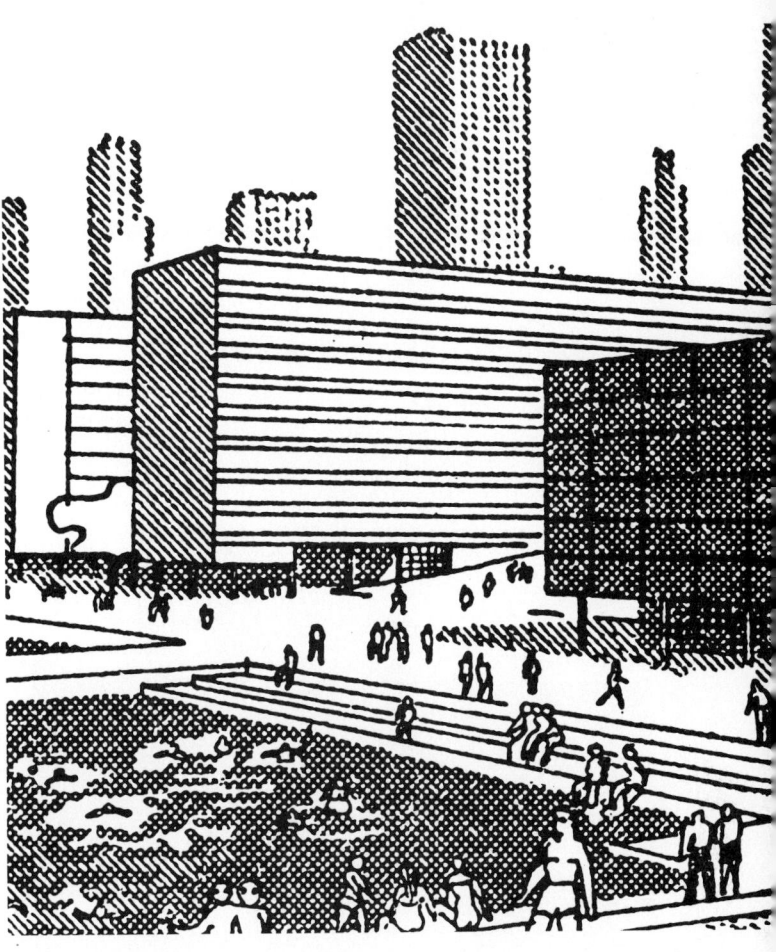

Proposed redevelopment of Manhattan with north-south spine of commercial buildings and riverfront recreational facilities. Paul and Percival Goodman, 1944. View to the southwest along the East River. NG

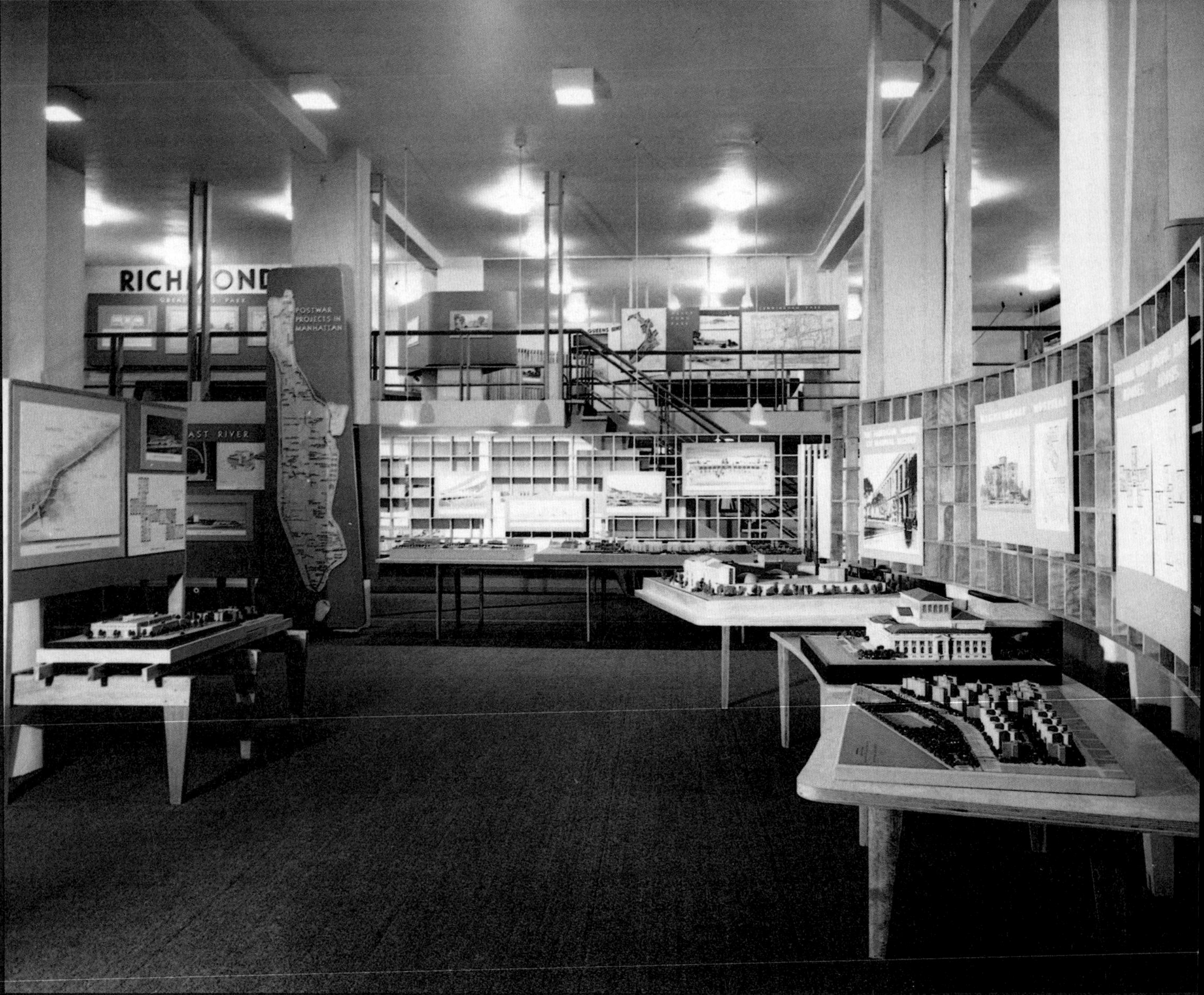

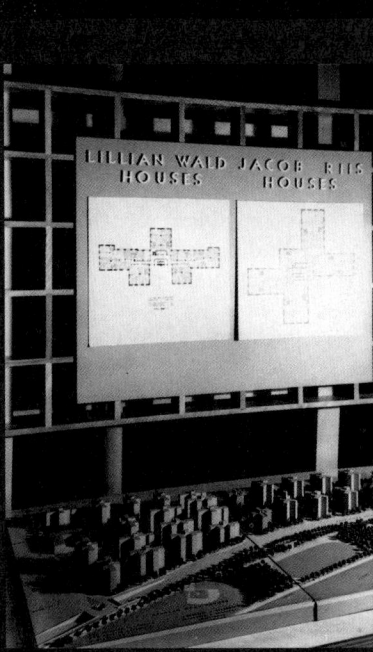

Above: New York City Postwar Planning Exhibition, 500 Park Avenue. Installation by Skidmore, Owings & Merrill, 1944. General view. Gottscho-Schleisner. LOC

Right: New York City Postwar Planning Exhibition. Rendering of proposed Oceanarium (Harrison, Fouilhoux & Abramovitz and Aymar Embury II), Coney Island, Brooklyn. Gottscho-Schleisner. LOC

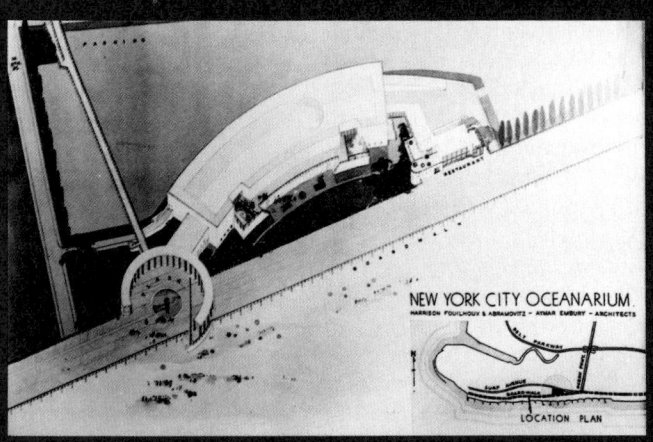

Far right: New York City Postwar Planning Exhibition. Model showing Lillian Wald Houses (Frederick L. Ackerman and Lafayette A. Goldstone), East Houston to East Sixth Street, Avenue D to East River Drive, on the left, and Jacob Riis Houses (James Mackenzie, Sidney Strauss and Walker & Gillette), East Sixth to East Fourteenth Street, Avenue D to East River Drive, on the right. Gottscho-Schleisner. LOC

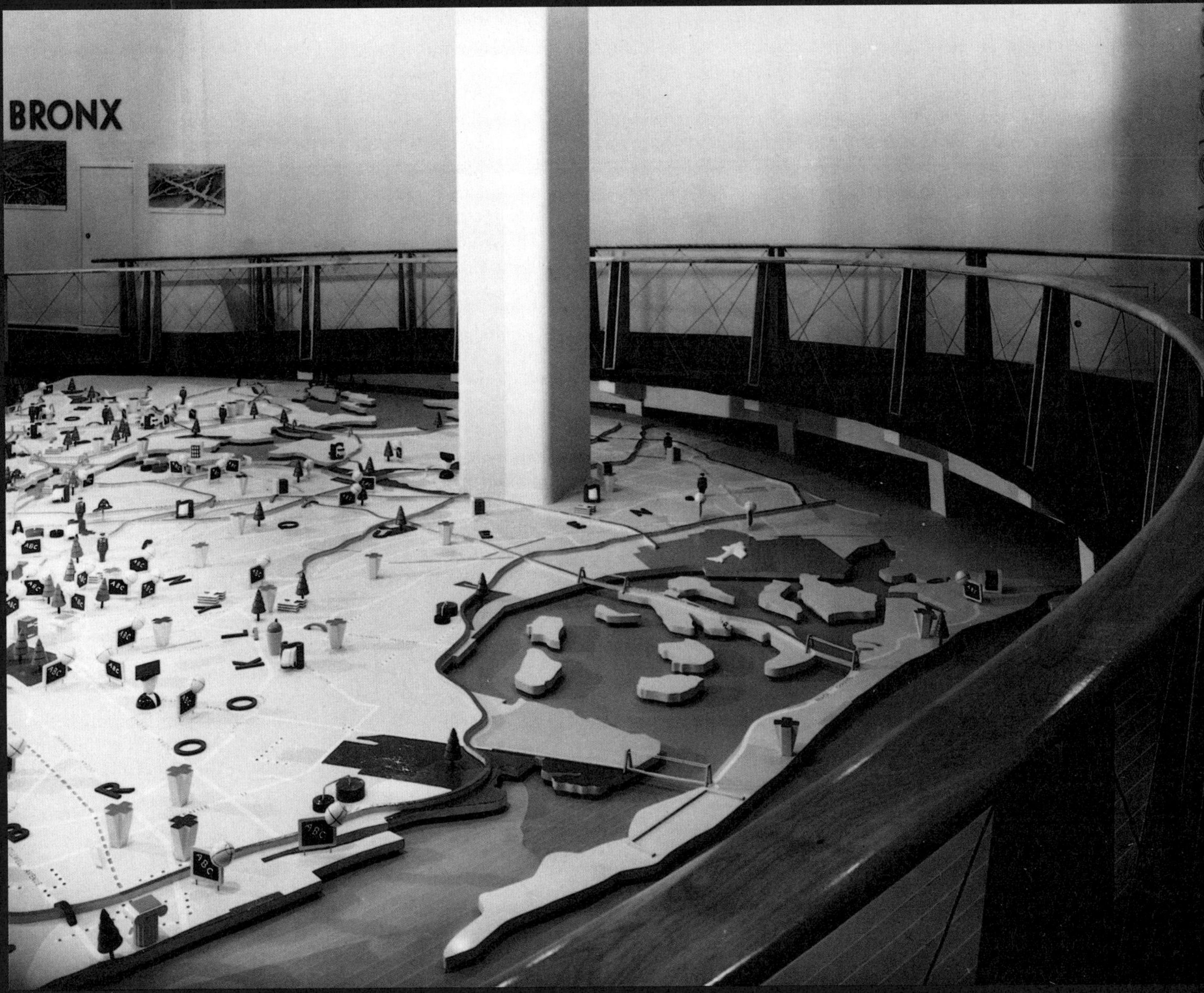

BRONX

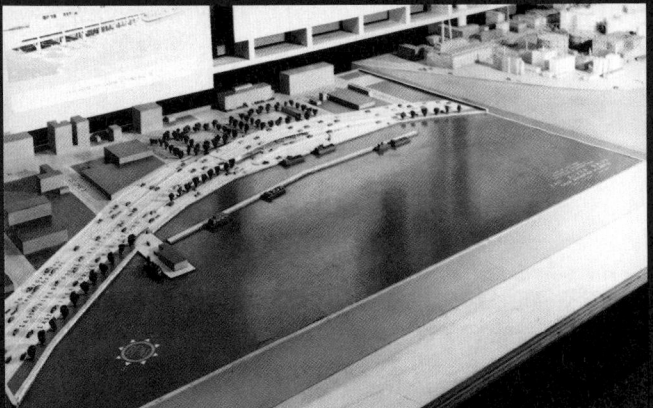

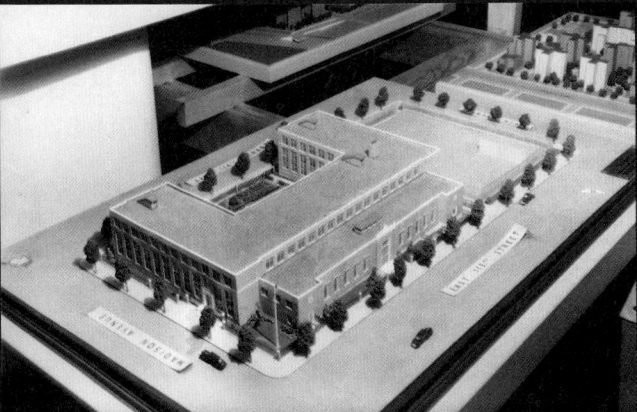

Top: New York City Postwar Planning Exhibition. Diorama of southern Brooklyn and Queens. Gottscho-Schleisner. LOC

Bottom left: New York City Postwar Planning Exhibition. Model of grade separation at East River Drive and East Ninety-sixth Street. Gottscho-Schleisner. LOC

Bottom right: New York City Postwar Planning Exhibition. Model of Junior High School 117 (Eric Kebbon), between Fifth and Madison avenues, East 114th to East 115th Street. Gottscho-Schleisner. LOC master plan for Manhattan that would confine all business and light industry to a north-south spine in the center of the island.[312] The Goodmans' plan, which would be expanded upon as the key element of their influential book of 1947, *Communitas: Means of Livelihood and Ways of Life*,[313] carried the Corbusier-inspired superblocks favored by the Housing Authority to an even bolder scale: it proposed the elimination of every other cross street to redevelop the island as parklike residential neighborhoods opening up to two rivers, the shores of which would be redeveloped above Twenty-third Street as bathing beaches and boating areas. Tackling one of the city's thorniest new problems, that of airports, the Goodmans offered a "tentative proposal" to construct along the Hudson River shore between Twenty-third and Forty-second streets an enormous warehouse, the roof of which would provide a landing strip, an idea that William Zeckendorf would soon adopt as his own (see chapter 9). To achieve this sweeping plan, the Goodmans, like Ernest Flagg before them,[314] called for demapping Central Park in order to create a massive land reservoir so as to be able to rearrange the functional components of the city.

In presenting their plan, the Goodmans made what was perhaps the first strong argument in defense of Manhattan as a special and distinct case, different from that of New York as a whole and from typical American cities. Initiating a vision that would not be taken up again by architects so forcefully until 1978, when the Dutch architect Rem Koolhaas would publish *Delirious New York: A Retroactive Manifesto for Manhattan*,[315] the Goodmans proclaimed "The Idea of Manhattan." Manhattan, they said, played a "peculiar role not only in the New York region but in the world (which is the true region of our cosmopolis). . . . There is no need to defend Manhattan Island; she has her own rule; there is no need to praise her, though we who are her sons are often betrayed into doing so. She has long been the capital not of a region but of a nation."[316]

In February 1949 Moses was one of five architects and planners whose predictions for New York in 1999 were published in the *New York Times Magazine*.[317] For the *Times*' readers, Harvey Wiley Corbett reinvoked his ideas from the 1920s, proposing a multilevel city to handle the traffic. He also envisioned superblock-scaled buildings, designed like terraced domes, in which balconied apartments, "like frosting on a great cake," would wrap the edges of a structure holding "stores, businesses, theaters, athletic club facilities and many other things not needing outside light." Such an arrangement would counteract population dispersion by keeping "the people living on the outer crust in closer contact with their work as it goes on inside this great structure," simultaneously solving the problem of traffic by letting people live nearer to their work.[318]

Moses saw the New York of 1999 as "not so different in its broader aspects or vistas, not so changed in its life and spirit." Countering many planners' contention that cities would decline and disperse, Moses believed that the population would grow and that housing would improve, with "the worst of the old slums . . . gone, and new forms of obsolescence, neither as extensive or as troublesome," to worry about. "There will be other new and as yet unimagined problems, but who wants to live in an age without challenges?"[319]

Eliel Saarinen, an unrepentant decentralist despite the rough treatment meted out to him by Moses five years before, saw Manhattan divided into three principal areas—downtown, midtown and uptown—separated by large areas of greenery. The waterfront would largely be devoted to recreation, with shipping activity relocated to more remote shores. Fewer sky-scrapers would crowd the skyline. Outside Manhattan, "scattered along the extended waterfront will be small integrated shipping communities, each with its own particular function, handling the world trade now concentrated around the shores of Manhattan. Separated by protective zones of green land, these communities will be enclosed in a spacious green-belt system."[320] All in all, the city would be dispersed, and downtown and midtown would be but slightly more important foci than other communities scattered throughout the region.

Wallace K. Harrison, who joined Corbett and Moses in eschewing "neighborhood utopias," reminded readers that the postwar city was so vulnerable to wartime attack that its future could be ensured only by peace. Harrison, too, was an unrepentant advocate of the urban concentration last heralded in the 1920s, arguing that the city would continue to enlarge and concentrate. "I would rather preserve the neighborliness of a quiet little restaurant in New York, with its sawdust on the floor and smell of good food, than have fifty neighborhood dining rooms run by sanitary and efficient food experts." Harrison confessed himself an island citizen, a man who was "very happy to let the people of the Bronx, Brooklyn and Queens, and the outer regions of Kings and Richmond, live and develop their borough [*sic*] as they will." But Harrison's call for more north-south arteries, a new north-south subway, elevated expressways across midtown and across lower Manhattan, and massive housing projects eating "into the cancer of the Lower East Side" was hardly calculated to foster the small-scale charms he espoused.[321]

Hugh Ferriss, the fifth of the contributors, chose to submit a drawing, a dramatically rendered vision of a large-scale landscaped enclave of low monumental buildings and tall slabs set atop sunken highways, like an expanded version of the United Nations, which he was working on at the time. Ferriss included a caption with his drawing: "Fifty years from now New York will be a capital city in a united world. A city of several levels, of glass and light, with building masses set wide apart and separated by tree-lined malls. It will, I hope, be run by atomic power, working for peace, not war."[322]

As efforts to create a master plan were stymied, the City Planning Commission's attention turned to zoning, the principal tool at its disposal to shape the city. On June 2, 1941, New York marked the twenty-fifth anniversary of the day when the Commission on Building Districts and Restrictions submitted the report that would give the city the nation's first comprehensive system of zoning.[323] Outside the tenement laws, New York had few use, height or bulk restrictions of any kind until the first Building Zone Resolution was adopted in 1916. This resolution divided the city into three classes of districts—business, residential and unrestricted—each with defined limitations on permitted uses, as well as height and bulk of buildings. It was site-specific, relating building heights to street widths, although buildings or parts of buildings that occupied less than 25 percent of a site could rise to unrestricted heights.

Although the 1916 resolution survived significant court tests, its administration by the Board of Estimate and Apportionment during the 1920s was sloppy and even corrupt. The Seabury inquiry in 1931–32 inspired the authors of the new city charter to place zoning under a new entity, the City Planning Commission.[324] At the time the new charter was being debated, the obsolescence of the existing zoning ordinance was clear enough that, according to Lawrence Orton, a draft of an "entirely new type of zoning based upon direct resolution of density" was included in the final report of the Mayor's Committee on City Planning (1936). The draft came before the newly established

City Planning Commission in 1938 and it was debated for a year before the conclusion was drawn that the new commission "was not in a position to tackle the comprehensive revision implied . . . but that it should undertake the most complete revision of the existing zoning within its capability."[325] This revision was adopted in 1941, modernizing provisions affecting automobiles and parking, and including some direct density controls.

In May 1944, in a report prepared by John Taylor Boyd, Jr., and Jacob Moscowitz, the Committee on Civic Design and Development of the New York Chapter of the American Institute of Architects questioned the belief that the "New York Zoning Ordinance satisfactorily controls the physical development of the City and the distribution of its population," and called for an "effective master plan and a comprehensive re-zoning of the City's land uses."[326] In June 1944 Robert Moses, now ensconced on the City Planning Commission, in a surprising move, proposed sweeping changes to the ordinance, dramatically reducing area coverage in all categories and proportionately reducing building heights in relationship to street width.[327] Moses also proposed to further restrict the amount of ground area that could be covered in retail zones.

Hearings on the zoning plan were held in September. Moses's proposals received the qualified support of architects, but real estate interests angrily battled the new rules, which constituted the first substantial change in the controls since 1916. After deliberation, the City Planning Commission released its report to the Board of Estimate, which approved it in December 1944, despite the objections of four borough presidents and more than fifty business, real estate and civic organizations.[328] According to the plan, the height and area of new buildings in retail business districts would be more restricted than ever before, with buildings allowed to occupy only 65 percent of their lots, except in special situations where parking was included, in which case a low base with shops could fill the site to permit garage entrances in the rear. This feature promised to drastically alter and even suburbanize the physical character of midtown streets, with buildings for the first time set behind the building line for most of their lower floors as well as those in the setback areas above. According to Lawrence Orton, the "sound and fury" generated by the new rules vastly "exceeded their importance," but because there was not unanimous approval in the Board of Estimate, the revised ordinance was taken to the courts by embattled owners of property in the highest-density district. The opposition was led by Robert Dowling, who in July 1946 succeeded in having the entire amendment defeated in the State Court of Appeals after retailers had already gotten the provisions curtailing ground-floor space overturned.[329]

But the clamor for a new zoning ordinance only seemed to grow, so that in 1948 the Board of Estimate was moved to appropriate funds to hire the housing and planning firm of Harrison, Ballard & Allen to undertake a comprehensive survey of the city's zoning.[330] To knowledgeable observers, most of whom were decentralists—either of the low-rise "garden city" persuasion epitomized by Lewis Mumford or of the high-rise, open-city, towers-in-the-park philosophy espoused by Le Corbusier—the existing ordinance, amended 1,440 times between 1916 and 1949, needed more than tinkering, or even overhaul: it needed to be reformed.[331] Robert Moses, who had supported zoning reform only four years before, objected, fearing that the outside consultants were too much in the pocket of the City Planning Commission's professional planners, who favored decentralization. In a speech at Dartmouth College, he seemed to reverse himself and take the side of real estate inter-

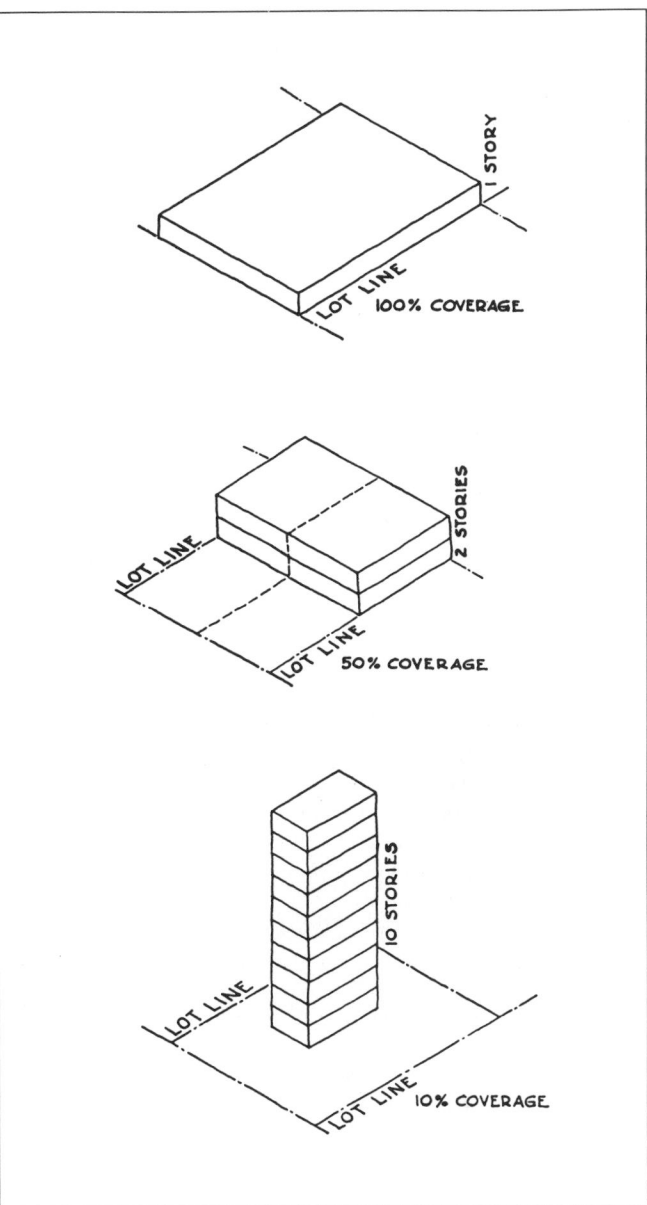

Diagrams illustrating the concept of floor area ratio (FAR). Harrison, Ballard & Allen, 1950. Each of the three building masses has the same FAR. NYC

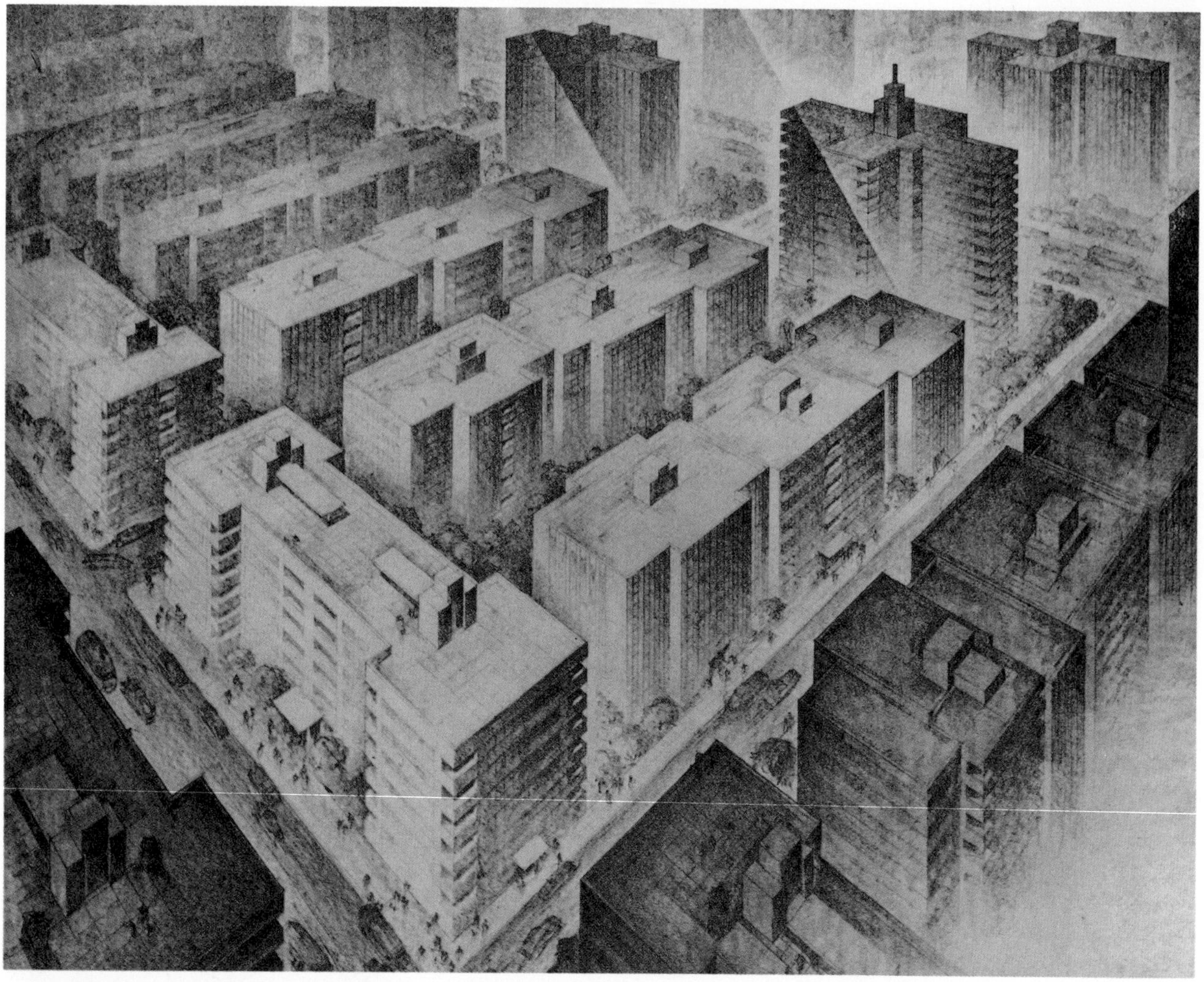

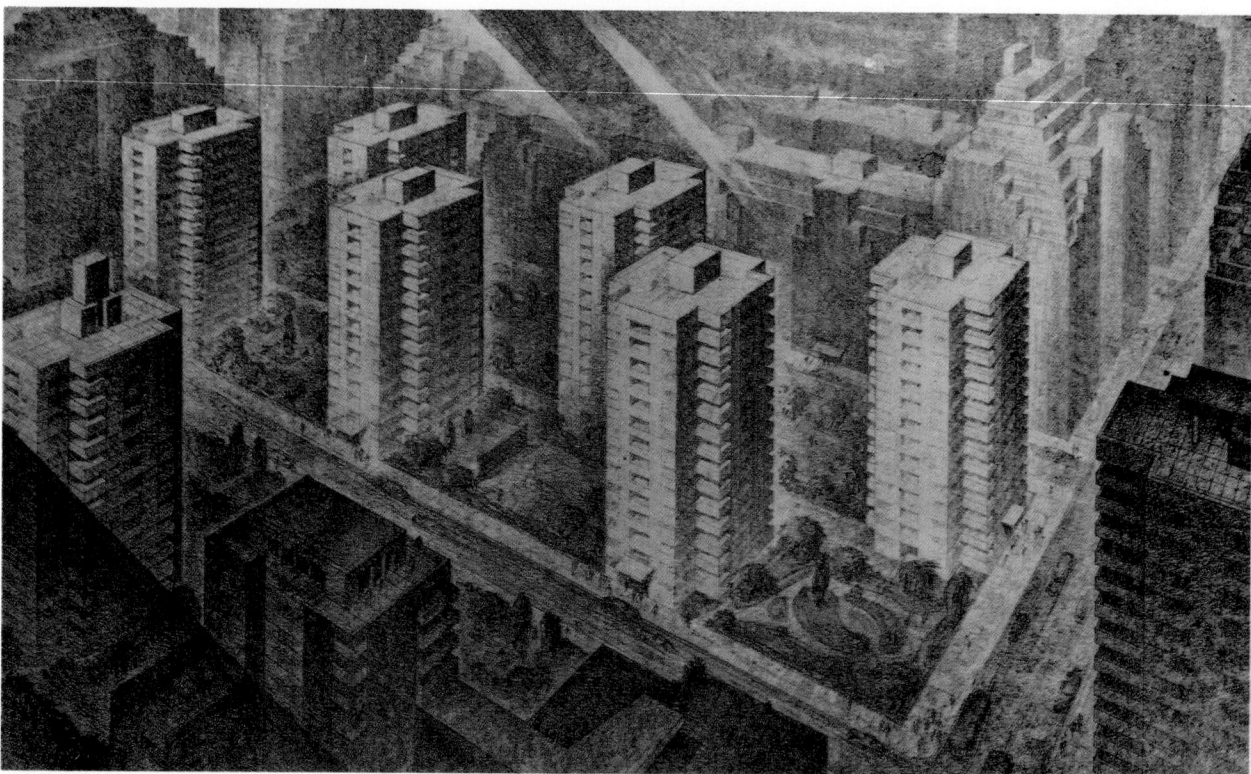

ests, arguing in behalf of "the merchants and property owners who must pay most of the bills—what is to become of them and of the City's credit while irresponsible greenbelters are declaring half the City's real estate worthless for complete rezoning on new bulk and angle-of-light theories."[332]

Harrison, Ballard & Allen's *Plan for Rezoning the City of New York* was released in the fall of 1950.[333] It proposed to limit New York's population to 12.6 million, as opposed to the 66 million it estimated could be squeezed in under the prevailing law. Given the decreasing birthrate, the planners estimated that from 1940 to 1970 there could be a 35 percent rise in the number of families in the city, but only a 15 percent population increase. The plan called for a modest reduction of population from fifty-one people per usable acre in 1940 to forty-five by 1970, still a much denser arrangement than in any other American city. It also foresaw a labor force of four million New Yorkers by 1970, 400,000 more than in 1948. For Manhattan, the new plan would bring a drastic reduction of manufacturing districts, particularly on the East Side, with much of the area reverting to residential use, although manufacturing districts in east midtown, around the United Nations, would be rezoned for commercial uses.

If adopted, the plan would also have environmental effects that would profoundly alter the city's architecture and urbanism. The plan proposed to determine building bulk not by street width and use district, as had been done in the past, but by the new principle of floor area ratio, defined as the horizontal area of the floors of a building divided by the area of the lot on which it is placed. The idea of the floor area ratio, though presented almost as a technical correction to limitations in the old system, was a revolutionary mechanism devised by architects and planners to transform the traditional city of attached or close-packed buildings forming continuous blocks bounding streets and interior courtyards. The 1916 zoning had established a fixed physical relationship between street width and building cornice height, resulting in a street wall of constant height along every street. The principle of floor area ratio, however, would set an overall limit on bulk but give the designer more or less free choice on how to distribute that bulk and shape the building. The new zoning would result in an "open city" of continuous greenery populated by isolated buildings, like the scheme Le Corbusier had most compellingly articulated in his redevelopment plans for Paris, which he first proposed in the 1920s.[334] That the promulgators of the plan had a specific vision of the future city in mind was never in doubt, as the report's renderings of typical build-outs—prepared by Nicholas B. Vassilieve in an evocative, Hugh Ferriss–inspired style—made all too clear.

In an effort to encourage architectural variety, a complicated formula for determining bulk was devised so that building heights controlled by the angle of light obstruction could be averaged, permitting a building to rise to a greater height at one point of the site if it fell below the setback line at another. This provision would permit freestanding slablike towers to sit on low, site-covering bases in a manner similar to that of Lever House, then being realized on Park Avenue by Skidmore, Owings & Merrill. Richard A. Miller described the evolution of the new formula, arguing for it as the logical third stage in the development of urban controls: from the oldest technique, height controls; to the "recession plane," the principle behind New York's 1916 law; to the combination of floor area ratio and the recession plane, which structured the new plan.[335] In contrast to the 1916 regulations, which categorized the city's buildings by use, height and bulk, with each category delineated on a separate

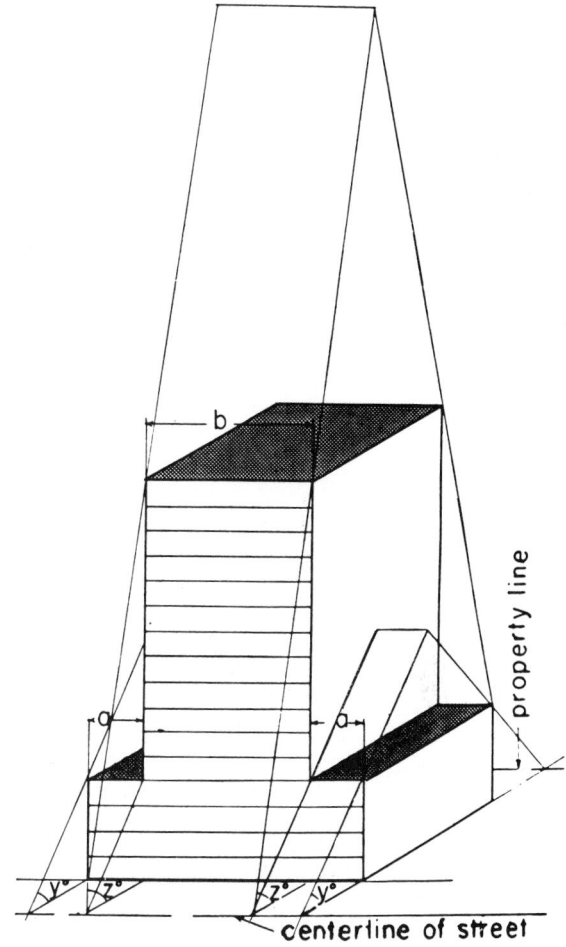

Top left: Maximum bulk permitted under proposed residential district zoning regulations. Harrison, Ballard & Allen, 1950. Rendering by Nicholas B. Vassilieve. NYC

Bottom left: Alternative massing permissible under proposed residential district zoning regulations. Harrison, Ballard & Allen, 1950. Rendering by Nicholas B. Vassilieve. NYC

Above: Illustration of the concept of averaging a building's angles of light obstruction. Harrison, Ballard & Allen, 1950. NYC

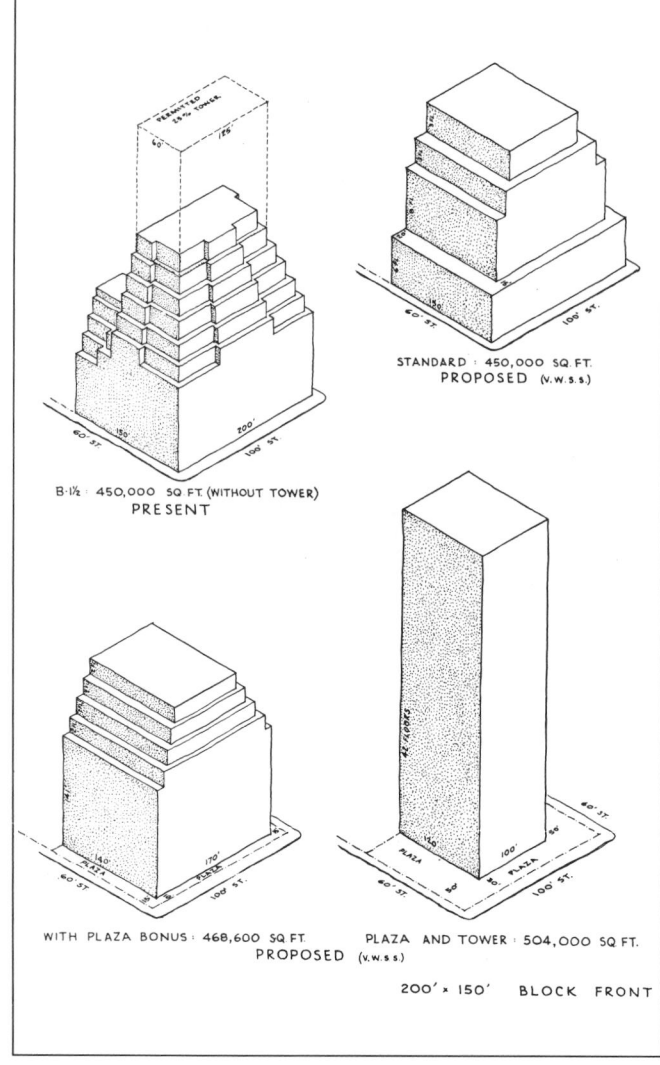

B·1½ · 450,000 SQ FT (WITHOUT TOWER)
PRESENT

STANDARD · 450,000 SQ.FT.
PROPOSED (V.W.S.S.)

WITH PLAZA BONUS · 468,600 SQ FT
PROPOSED (V.W.S.S.)

PLAZA AND TOWER · 504,000 SQ FT.
PROPOSED (V.W.S.S.)

200' × 150'   BLOCK FRONT

Contrasting effects of existing zoning regulations and those proposed by the New York Chapter of the American Institute of Architects, 1959. *Final Report.* CU

map, the new proposal divided the city into districts, each with its own set of use and bulk restrictions. The information would be presented on a single map.

Aline B. Louchheim, art critic for the *New York Times*, saw the proposed law as a way to counter the aesthetic limitations of earlier zoning: "Our town is becoming a hideous mountain range of layer cakes, questionably proportioned, insensitively detailed, selfishly dominating their entire sites, content to repeat clichés of construction and unimaginative use of materials, and above all, indifferent to eloquent architectural expression."[336] For Henry Churchill, the key benefit of the new ordinance was that it would allow for design choices rather than dictating a single "style," as the fixed rules of 1916 had done: "It was the requirements for setbacks . . . that produced the 'style' of architecture which has been characteristic of New York for the past thirty-five years. This is a real style, as inevitable under the conditions of the culture which imposed it as any of the great styles of the past. Regardless of whether the architect chose to dress his structure vertically, horizontally, paste pilasters on it, or just to poke holes in it, underneath it is all the same." The proposed law, "instead of confining" architects "in a mathematical strait jacket," would encourage them to pursue "a choice of forms."[337]

Despite such positive critical reception, and despite close to a thousand public meetings that thrashed out issues and garnered widespread support, Harrison, Ballard & Allen's zoning plan failed to be adopted for one simple reason: Robert Moses was against it. Given the weakness of the mayor, Vincent Impellitteri, and of the chairman of the City Planning Commission, John Bennett, who was also a Moses supporter, the plan didn't have a chance. But with the election of Robert F. Wagner as mayor in 1954, zoning reform got a new lease on life, although it was still an uphill fight. In 1956, when Mayor Wagner asked James Felt, a respected realtor, to assume the chairmanship of the City Planning Commission, public confidence in that body was so low that its very survival was in question. Felt saw zoning reform as the issue with which he could most effectively rally support for the commission; after all, in previous zoning battles in 1944 and 1951, the commission had stood its ground only to be defeated in the political arena largely because of Robert Moses's controversial persona. Given Felt's credentials as a realtor and his close ties to Mayor Wagner, his decision to take on rezoning as "a must" for the city was critical.[338]

Instead of fiddling with the Harrison, Ballard & Allen report, Felt decided to start fresh. On August 30, 1956, the architecture firm of Voorhees, Walker, Smith & Smith was hired to help formulate a new plan, which was released in draft form in August 1958 and in its final form on February 16, 1959, as *Rezoning New York City.*[339] In addition to Chairman Felt, the commission then had as its members Francis Blaustein, a lawyer; Robert Moses; Lawrence Orton; Charles J. Sturla, a Queens real estate broker and active Democratic politician; Goodhue Livingston, Jr.; and Robert G. McCullogh, ex officio member, who was chief engineer of the Board of Estimate. The new proposal incorporated many of the features of Harrison, Ballard & Allen's aborted effort, especially the principle of the floor area ratio, the maximum number of square feet of floor space that could be built for each 100 square feet of lot area, a figure that would vary from district to district. In addition to the floor area ratio method, it introduced a bonus system, devised to encourage plaza and mall space inside mapped building lines by rewarding builders with three additional square feet of leasable space for every square foot of open space provided at grade. The plan also reduced the city's commercial acreage by about 50 percent, and "ribbon" developments that lined block after block of important arteries in residential neighborhoods were targeted for elimination.

The zoning proposal divided the city's land into forty-seven types of residence, commercial and manufacturing districts, balancing current use and desirable future use patterns. It also recognized "the fact and economics of large-scale projects," and provided for their accommodation. The plan foresaw a resident population of only 10,940,000—55,000,000 less than the population theoretically obtainable under the 1916 ordinance, and 1,660,000 less than was projected by the Harrison, Ballard & Allen plan. It accepted "the existence of the automobile," requiring off-street parking in residential districts and in all commercial and manufacturing districts, "except for the most congested downtown areas where mandatory off-street parking would be uneconomic and impractical."[340] According to the *New York Times*, the planners explained this "seeming paradox" by arguing that the exception was made "to avoid attracting more automobiles and compounding the present intolerable traffic congestion" in the worst areas.[341]

The New York Chapter of the American Institute of Architects quickly endorsed the new plan.[342] But opposition soon began to build among real estate developers, who believed that by restricting the bulk of new buildings the plan would make construction uneconomical and discourage new projects, thereby undermining land values and ultimately adversely affecting the city's tax base.[343] Robert Dowling, who had opposed both the Moses and the Harrison, Ballard & Allen plans, stepped up to support the new proposal, forming the Committee for Modern Zoning, similar to the group established in 1913–14 to support the original ordinance.[344] A key issue blocking support was the absence of a grace period between the code's enactment and its implementation, which the Committee for Modern Zoning persuaded the City Planning Commission to adopt. The commission conducted a public hearing to discuss the proposed code on April 13, 1959. While most objections came from real estate interests concerned with potential loss of value, one observer, Victor Gruen, faulted the code for its accommodation of the automobile, arguing that "what is not recognized in the new zoning resolution is the fact that a new land use of most destructive qualities has developed: the automobile as a means of transport."[345] In the section on "Off-Street Parking Regulations," the draft code observed: "Since 1947 the tidal wave of half a million more automobiles owned by residents of the City has swept New York into the unenviable position of having traffic problems comparable with Detroit and other 'automobile cities.'"[346] It also pointed out that almost one million people drove to work. Gruen observed that if New York's projected eleven million people were to have one car per family unit, space to store three million cars would be needed, requiring about 4.8 billion square feet of area, or 120,000 acres, more than half of the city's total acreage. To stem the tide of the automobile, Gruen opposed the proposed requirement that every new building provide off-street parking.

By December 1959 the adoption of the new code seemed fairly certain, with enactment scheduled for the summer of 1960, yet revisions were continually being made.[347] In their final report, the New York Chapter of the American Institute of Architects, combining an urge to institutionalize the Modernist open city with a street-savvy feeling for real estate pragmatics, suggested sweeter bonuses than the ones originally proposed for creating street-level plazas, as well as a bonus for street-level arcades, concourses, rear yards and interior courts that were connected to the street, and for side yards that were more than thirty feet wide.

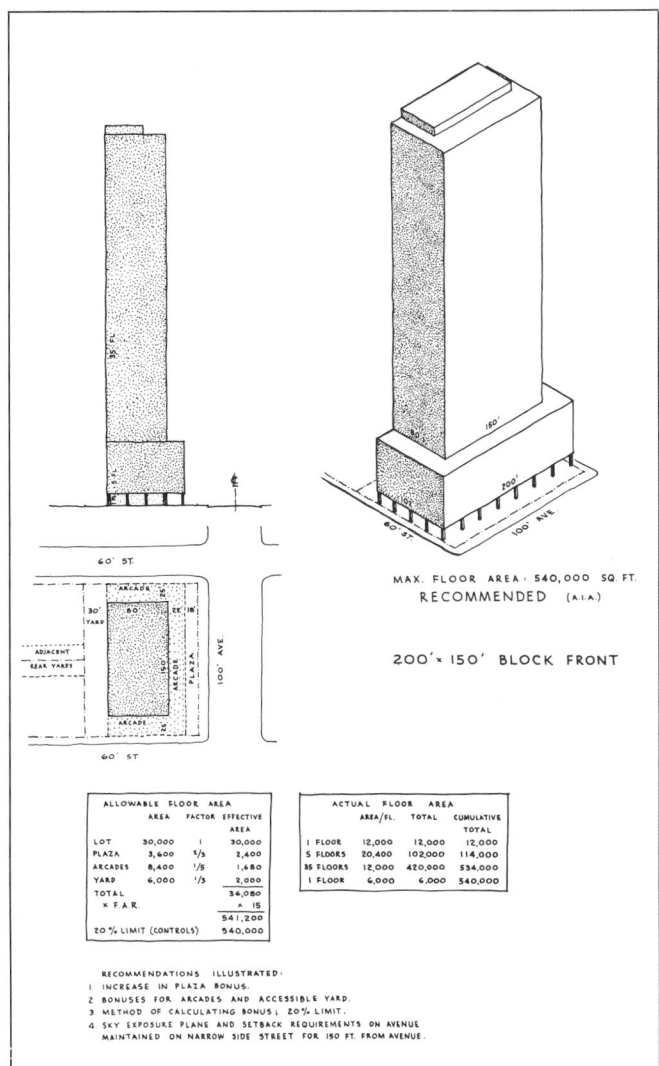

Zoning recommendations proposed by the New York Chapter of the American Institute of Architects, 1959. *Final Report.* CU

All of these moves were deliberately intended to replace New York's traditional street-oriented urbanism with continuous open space punctuated by freestanding, objectlike buildings. The architects also called for increased lot coverage for towers, claiming that the buildings allowed by the proposed 40 percent coverage would be too slender to be feasible, and proposed that no off-street parking be built in crowded areas. As a sop to the growing popular sentiment that development was destroying New York's traditional character—which, by the evidence of their report, they otherwise clearly applauded—the architects proposed that the mapping be revised to protect historic areas and the character of certain neighborhoods such as Greenwich Village, Gramercy Park, Hanover Square and the remaining early-nineteenth-century portions of Washington Square.[348]

The commission scheduled seven public hearings to review the document and Chairman Felt announced his determination to see the document adopted: "This is the fight of my life," he said.[349] But the Real Estate Board of New York remained unconvinced, claiming that the new zoning would result in higher rents because the size of buildings would be more strictly regulated.[350] With so much opposition, the City Planning Commission decided not to submit the new ordinance to the Board of Estimate in June but to delay. Between June 1959 and March 1960, when hearings on the new law began, the commission, under Felt's direction, relaxed some of the provisions and provided key interest groups such as the Fifth Avenue Association with special language describing use districts that conformed to prevailing patterns. Moses raised his voice in protest, attacking the overall plan as an "alphabet soup" and a "panacea." He focused in particular on the floor area ratio formula, which he had opposed when it was first advanced by Harrison, Ballard & Allen because it was an abstract concept and not specifically tied to the physical requirements of individual sites, a key point that was never adequately debated.[351] But eventually Felt and Mayor Wagner persuaded him to back off.

Final hearings were held on September 12–14, 1960, and the proposal was passed on October 18 and forwarded to the Board of Estimate, which, with only modest opposition at the public hearing, approved it on December 15, 1960.[352] In order "to insure maximum stability in the building and real estate industries during the important transition period," the City Planning Commission directed that the new zoning would not become effective until one year after its approval by the Board of Estimate.[353] As finally approved, the plan incorporated 850 revisions to the original proposal, over 500 more than in the previous document of December 1959. Among these were dropping the requirement that nonconforming industries in residential districts move out within twenty-five years; adding greater incentives for plazas and greater bulk for commercial buildings in the central business district; and allowing for greater population density, targeting the city's ultimate growth at 12,273,000, which was essentially what Harrison, Ballard & Allen had initially proposed.

The passage of the new zoning was postwar New York's pivotal architectural event, irrevocably changing the relationship between buildings and streets that had prevailed for over three hundred years. As with the 1916 zoning ordinance, it would have a profound effect on the design of cities across the United States and, in keeping with New York's new, international prominence and prestige, on the design of cities worldwide. From the point of view of architecture and urban design, the most notable provision of the new zoning was the plaza bonus, a feature pressed for by architects who pointed to the Seagram and Time & Life buildings as models.[354] Felt was com-

pletely sold on the plaza provision: "We are now saying for the first time in New York City that open space is not to be considered as a gouge here and a notch there, depriving builders of valuable floor space but as a usable commodity worth more than the office it replaces."[355]

In his 1973 essay, "Superville: New York—Aspects of Very High Bulk," Stephen Zoll argued that by introducing the bonus system the 1961 zoning reversed the original purpose of zoning—"to control its logical bulk"—and encouraged larger projects by rewarding developers for providing public amenities. While the need to use a reward system was probably inevitable given that the city had no master plan spelling out desirable public benefits in any given area, Zoll saw the introduction of incentive zoning as a reflection of the city's sense of helplessness in the face of competition from other cities. He called such zoning an "applied cure" that "only intensifies the malady": "Incentive zoning is a reconciliation of the incompatible idea of buildings so large as to destroy public amenities and the idea that such buildings can also be made to provide public amenities. . . . Incentive zoning regards tall buildings with a mixture of a planner's horror and a comptroller's glorification."[356]

No sooner was the new zoning adopted than developers rushed to file plans under the old rules, which remained in effect until December 31, 1961. As a result, 1961 proved to be New York's biggest year ever for building.[357] Given that the new code reduced the allowable density on many sites, real estate prices at first began to drop. But developers were quick to see possibilities for profit. While the city's ultimate theoretical population was lowered from 66 million to 12.3 million, the business cores were not nearly so severely affected. Large-scale developers of commercial office space and apartment houses had no trouble adjusting to the code's provisions because they realized that the bonus system combined with the elimination of setbacks made it possible for them to build bigger and more efficiently engineered buildings than ever before.[358] Though the new code would not have permitted 666 Fifth Avenue, 300 Park Avenue, 1407 Broadway and 20 Broad Street, all with a floor area ratio (FAR) of 20, it encouraged new structures that somewhat resembled Seagram's and its large plaza but were almost twice its size. For example, the Seagram Building, in many ways the yardstick for the new ordinance, had an FAR of 11.1; but the new code allowed an FAR of 15 for its neighborhood, a figure that could, with the provision of open plazas, arcades or terraces, rise to as high as 18.

The new rules had a less positive effect on small-scale enterprises, resulting in a significant reduction in the amount of medium-size, medium-height housing that had traditionally met the needs of the middle-class market in the outer boroughs and even in the "soft" areas of Manhattan.[359] The zoning's impact on apartment house design was a result not only of the emphasis on large site assemblages but of the tight density requirements imposed by the desire to limit the city's population to 12.3 million: a 15,000-square-foot, 100-by-150-foot plot on East Sixty-third Street, which would have supported 154 apartments under the old rules, could contain only 115 units under the new; to achieve the old number an additional 5,000 square feet of land would be needed. Even more dramatically, a similar plot in upper Manhattan in the new R7-2 zone would result in only forty-two apartments, whereas fifty-six units would have been permitted before.[360] Midblock sites, traditionally the most desirable for apartment houses because of the quiet they afforded, were virtually ruled out for development because, in order to achieve a reasonable density, they had to be set so far back on the plot as to provide virtually no buildable area.

Despite initial skepticism about the aesthetic impact of the new code,[361] and the glut that occurred when developers rushed projects through to take advantage of the old code, the city's real estate appetite was so great that by 1970, less than ten years after the new code went into effect, it had completely transformed the fabric of Manhattan's two principal business districts as well as whole areas of the Upper East Side. But many observers were not happy about the changes. While many of New York's best architects had remained enthralled with the 1916 zoning ten years after its passage, and the architecture it mandated had become an example to the world at large, in an equal time the 1961 ordinance was in severe disrepute at home, though its principles were widely adopted by other cities. Architects and members of the city's development community were quick to see it not only as urbanistically destructive but also as the cause of an increased density of development in the commercial core, rather than the reduction so many had hoped for.

The new zoning also had the result of creating an overabundance of one particular building type. As the New York Times reported in 1969: "The new code, while limiting building bulk, provided incentives for including open space at street level. This had the practical effect of making most profitable from the owner's standpoint a sheer tower set well back from the curb to create a plaza." Edward Sulzberger, a prominent realtor, pointed out that the zoning change did little more than to substitute one design cliché for another. As the Times put it: "In the annals of Manhattan's skyscraper architecture, the 1950s might best be described as the era of the wedding cake, and the 1960s as the age of the plaza."[362] Between 1961 and 1973 some 1.1 million square feet of new open space was created in the city because of the plaza bonus provision. According to a subsequent cost-benefit analysis computed by Jerold S. Kayden, the construction costs of these plazas to the developers came to $3,820,278, in return for which they were able to build 7,640,556 square feet of additional commercial space, yielding by conservative estimates a bonus value of $186,199,350 to them; succinctly put, each dollar spent for a plaza yielded forty-eight dollars worth of extra space.[363]

But the plazas were not all equally useful and almost none were comparable to that of Seagram's; some were in fact designed to discourage actual use. As a result of the analysis of William H. Whyte, who organized the Street Life Project, the zoning was amended in May 1975 to set standards for bonus plaza design.[364] Drafted by the City Planning Commission's Urban Design Group, under its director, Raquel Ramati, the new legislation specified types of amenities to be provided on the plazas, such as kiosks and cafés, and prescribed conditions for seating, including the number of chairs per square foot of open space. In addition, to ensure that mandatory tree planting, bench installations and maintenance would be performed, it required the developer to post a performance bond before receiving a certificate of occupancy.

As a result of the new zoning, post-1961 buildings were not only bulkier, they were taller. The typical Manhattan office building built in the 1950s was between thirty and forty stories high; in the 1960s the average rose to between forty and fifty stories, making the streets seem more crowded than ever and even darker in some cases. The buildings were also more expensive: the lower costs of uninterrupted vertical structures and the towers' smaller foundations were more than offset by the costs of increased elevators, which enlarged the percentage of space occupied by the building's core on a typical floor. As a result, cheaper finishes and more diagrammatic designs and detailing became a commonplace.

The situation had become so bad that even some realtors were concerned; as Edward Sulzberger told the New York Times, perhaps it was time for a change. Sulzberger suggested that new incentives be written into the zoning code to encourage more variety in skyscraper design: "This could get away from the single-note theme song of the sixties in Manhattan architecture."[365] In April 1965 the City Planning Commission voted a revision to the zoning law that would "take the shackles off architects" who had once believed that the 1916 ordinance restricted their creativity, only to find themselves bound in a new architectural serfdom, cranking out "cheesebox" designs.[366] The 1965 revision was intended to encourage artistic freedom—that is, to add circular, hexagonal and other nonrectilinear shapes to the prevailing repertoire of rectangular towers. It further advocated a departure from the constraints of street-hugging architecture by encouraging designs that were not parallel to the building line and permitting buildings to occupy a limited area within fifty feet of the street line on streets less than seventy-five feet wide or within forty feet of the line on wider streets. The first building to take advantage of this change was one built in 1967 by the New York Telephone Company at 233 East Thirty-seventh Street (see chapter 5). A twenty-four-story hexagonal structure designed by Kahn & Jacobs, who had initiated the revision, this prowlike building occupied a midblock site that extended through to Thirty-eighth Street and featured plazas facing both streets. But the design of the building was otherwise banal, and it offered no real direction for a renewal of architectural aesthetics or an improved urbanism.

On October 15, 1963, William F. R. Ballard became chairman of the City Planning Commission, replacing James Felt, who resigned late in 1962, in part to avoid suggestions of conflict of interest because of his brother Irving's role in developing a new Madison Square Garden on the site of the old Pennsylvania Station.[367] Ballard, the first architect ever to hold the job, was a member of the team that had developed the abortive zoning reform of 1950. As president of the Citizens' Housing and Planning Council, he was a highly respected member of New York's planning world.[368] With a new zoning amendment in place and a new chairman at the helm, the commission once again turned to the production of a master plan. This was done for two reasons: because federal agencies were beginning to threaten to cut off funds to the city until it had a plan, and because the prevailing redevelopment strategies were beginning to be widely questioned by the public. In particular, the tide of public opinion was beginning to turn against the city's dependence on the federal government's urban renewal program, which was waggishly derided as "urban removal" or—because of the program's unenlightened attitude toward race—as "Negro removal," a phrase coined by the novelist James Baldwin.[369] The Federal Bulldozer, a book written by Martin Anderson, a Columbia University finance professor, offered a devastating critique of urban renewal as it fanned the flames of community discontent.[370]

While the generation of New York architects who dominated the scene in the 1950s—whether high-style artists such as Philip Johnson or Gordon Bunshaft, or yeomen such as the Roths—eschewed debates about city planning, a younger generation was now emerging who eagerly took up issues of urbanism. They began to attack the urban renewal process and the city's lackluster planning, for which they held their fellow architects in large measure responsible, dismissing the city's professional planners as lacking in vision and hopelessly bureaucratic. In July 1964 some of the younger architects, including Richard B. Snow, Lathrop Douglass, Sheldon Licht, Jeanne M. Davern,

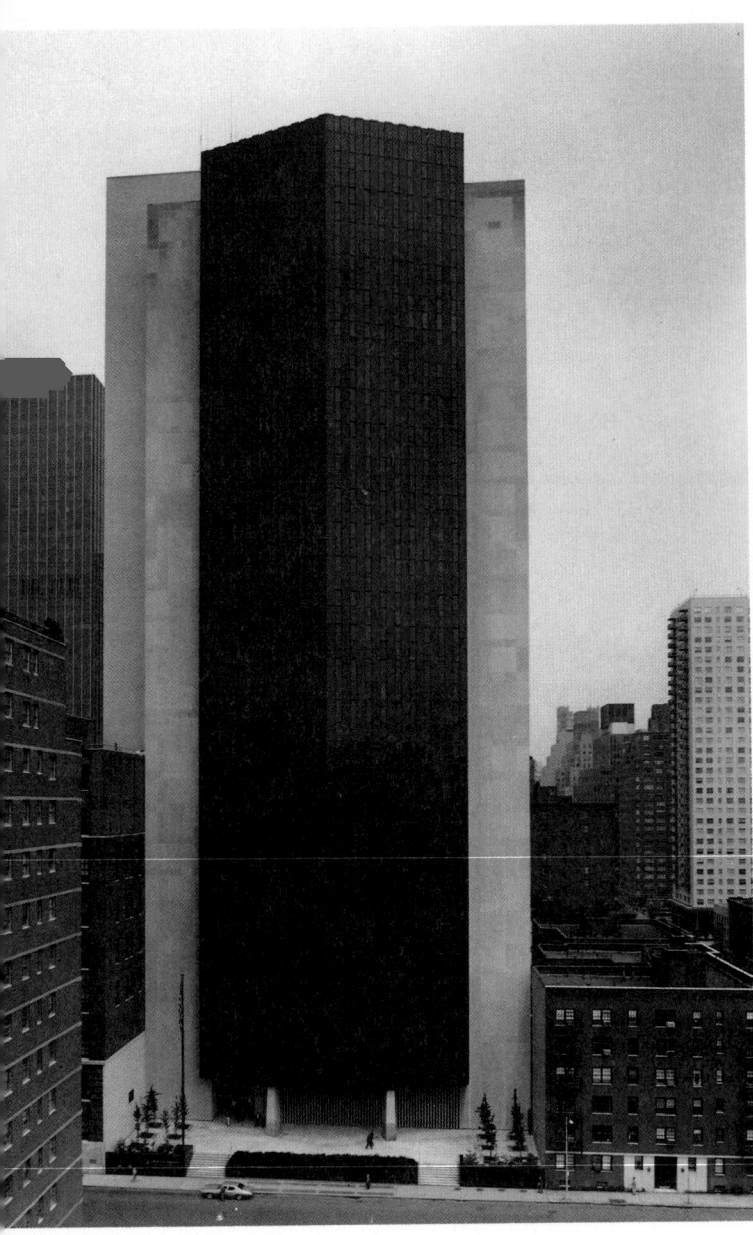

New York Telephone Company Building, 233 East Thirty-seventh Street. Kahn & Jacobs, 1967. View to the north. OMH

A. Corwin Frost, Jan Pokorny and Arvin Shaw III, combined forces to issue a twelve-page report, *The State of the City*, that was a politely worded yet nonetheless harsh assessment of the current situation. Not surprisingly, it called for a master plan, by now a time-honored cry, but it went further to castigate the profession for participating in a process of "churning destruction and frantic rebuilding." The report advocated an aggressive urbanism: "city residential neighborhoods must be made more competitive with Suburbs," the report said, and "better arrangement of neighborhoods, parks, and housing . . . [must] be planned to create environments which offer more than spartan utility, which have character and private pleasure for those who live there."[371] The architects also made a strong call for landmarks preservation, praising Mayor Wagner's formation of a commission charged with planning legislation for a landmarks law (see chapter 16). The architects' report, together with Ballard's appointment, helped create a new climate for planning, and work was begun in earnest on the master plan, although it quickly became bogged down by the statistical approach that the city planning staff had inherited from Tugwell and seemed unable or unwilling to shed.[372]

On October 14–16, 1964, the City Planning Commission sponsored a symposium on planning in New York, "The Future by Design." Though it led to no specific program of action, the symposium was, as Ada Louise Huxtable wrote, useful as "a catalyst for an awakening community concern. It was education and catharsis."[373] Among twenty-five notable speakers, Huxtable singled out Henry Fagin, professor of planning at the University of Wisconsin, who stated that the "number one priority in New York is a city planning process that can plan. You just don't have it."[374] Dr. Martin Cherkasky, director of Montefiore Hospital, came close to predicting the course of planning in the next ten or so years: "This society moves only when it's in trouble. Then every emergency program in the wrong place becomes a vested interest with which future city planning must deal."[375] Another speaker, Allan Temko, an architecture critic and a displaced New Yorker living in San Francisco, said that "the Harlem riots [of the] summer were no surprise to those outside the city that watched the administration direct a billion dollars into a world's fair." A billion dollars, he wryly observed, "could have done quite a bit to improve Harlem."[376]

The City Planning Commission's effectiveness was never more caustically characterized than in Richard J. Whalen's book of 1965, *A City Destroying Itself*:

> The City's Planning Commission has described Manhattan as "the most preferred real-estate location in the world"—so choice, apparently, that planning officials are not allowed to trespass on it. The real power lies in hands holding private purse strings. Through their collective decisions, the speculative builders and, even more important, the mortgage lenders in the banks and insurance companies have reshaped the contours of New York, determining how the city functions and how inhabitants live.[377]

Two years later, commenting on the fact that no plan had yet been drafted, Barry Gottehrer wrote: "It is not difficult to understand why much of the city's physical development has been disorderly and unsound, based less on social goals and indications of any relevance than in politics and pressure of the moment."[378]

Walter McQuade, a planning commissioner, later offered his own explanations for the City Planning Commission's tardiness in developing a master plan. He pointed out that the commission had also been charged by Mayor La Guardia in 1938 with the administration of the zoning ordinance and the preparation of its capital budget, which approached a billion dollars annually. But the real reason no master plan had appeared, he said, "may have been the presence on the political and planning scene of that great city-shaper Robert Moses, who prevailed completely in the 1930s, 1940s, 1950s and the early half of the 1960s. The mighty Moses is said to have preferred to wear his private master plan for New York in the lining of his hat, where it could be adjusted to the exigencies of political reality."[379]

But in 1969 and 1970 the City Planning Commission did at last manage to release a master plan.[380] The first volume, *Critical Issues*, consisted of four sections. The first, "National Center," was devoted to Manhattan and called for a westward expansion of midtown, an expansion of the landmass in lower Manhattan to support new offices and housing, incentive zoning to encourage construction in the public interest, and greater use of eminent domain to help acquire land areas for large-scale development. Significantly, the plan did not call for the decentralization of Manhattan's core; in fact, it argued for density: "Concentration is the genius of the City, a reason for being, the source of its stability and its excitement. We believe the center should be strengthened, not weakened, and we are not afraid of the bogey of high density." The plan contended that "concentration does not have to mean congestion" if pedestrian malls, wide plazas, and vest-pocket parks were created to help ventilate the urban fabric.[381] It came out strongly in favor of mass transit for access to Manhattan, proposing high tariffs in garages and tolls on East River bridges to discourage automobile commutation.

Section two of the first volume, "Opportunity," addressed the need for job-training programs to help workers make the transition from a blue-collar economy to an almost exclusively white-collar economy. The third section, "Environment," emphasized neighborhood preservation and rehabilitation, calling for stricter air-pollution controls and for experimentation with innovative solid-waste disposal techniques. Volume one concluded with a fourth section, "Government," in effect a plea for governmental reform that advocated greater "house rule" for the city and substantial amounts of federal and state financial aid. The next five volumes of the plan were devoted to separate examinations of the city's boroughs, concluding with a discussion of Staten Island that was released on December 7, 1970, slightly more than a year after the first volume's release.[382]

The master plan unleashed a torrent of criticism.[383] For example, at a midweek discussion of the plan attended by 2,000 people and sponsored by the Regional Plan Association, sixty militant blacks and Puerto Ricans chanted that it was "the master's plan" and complained about lack of community participation in its formulation. Ada Louise Huxtable said that despite the plan's "folksy, plain-spoken" style, it "has been generating about as much heat as *Portnoy's Complaint*," Philip Roth's novel published around the same time. Huxtable saw the plan as very different from what she (perhaps wrongly) believed was intended in 1938, when the City Planning Commission was first charged with the task of preparing a master plan: "Its renewal strategies are not the familiar redevelopment schemes in which the city is divided into neatly wrapped areas with before and after pictures of blight and beauty and a vision for the year 2000." She described the new plan as essentially strategic, concerned "with the renewal of people," a contradiction "of all the tenets dear to the doctrinaire planners' heart." She believed that such an approach was necessary in New York City: "New York's chaos, its very problems, are a result of dynamic vitality—the pressures of the ongoing process of growth, building, demand and development."[384]

Much of the plan was written by William H. Whyte, whose "almost chatty tone," according to Huxtable, "with heavy emphasis on what 'we are doing' may seem like political proselytizing to many, since it stresses programs begun by the Lindsay administration."[385] Beverly Moss Spatt, a "midnight" appointee of Mayor Wagner's and a notable Lindsay-era dissenter, attacked it as a "wordy non-plan."[386] Spatt's principal objection was the plan's overriding emphasis on density, especially at the core, a point that represented "much of its thrust and guiding spirit."[387] Spatt also objected to the plan's lack of regional scope—"This non-plan is particularly short sighted in dealing with the region of which New York City is a part"—as well as its approach to housing, calling its goals for new construction inadequate and criticizing its emphasis on rehabilitation. In sum, she characterized the plan as "at best, comprehensively equivocal," saying that it avoided specific solutions to specific problems.[388] Spatt was not alone in believing that the plan was not really a plan at all. Even City Planning Commission Chairman Donald Elliott called it only a proposal. And even those who were not so negative were disappointed by its breezy catalogue of urban problems peppered with barbed knocks at the failure of state and federal governments to support needed programs.

The intention was for the plan to be debated for a year and then voted on, so that, if adopted, it could be submitted to the federal government's Department of Housing and Urban Development, which in turn had to pass on it before certifying that the city was eligible to receive funds for some programs. But the plan did not fare well with the sixty-two local community planning boards that were established by charter in 1969, almost at the precise time the plan was released.[389] Most of these boards, typically infused with the era's "people power" polemics, resented the plan's Manhattancentric bias. This opposition had a powerful effect, forcing the new chairman of the commission, John Zuccotti, a former supporter of the plan, to declare in 1973 that the plan was "invaluable and heroic" but also "outdated."[390] To cope with the new reality of community participation, the master plan was turned into little more than a reference tool, and a new set of neighborhood "miniplans" was developed. As Zuccotti said: "This, we think, is planning for the seventies."[391]

As Paul Goldberger explained in the *New York Times*, the miniplan approach was intended to be tailored to the needs of different neighborhoods and incremental in its realization. While acknowledging that the new strategy was no panacea for New York's problems, Goldberger felt that it effectively responded to the city's diversity and the now firmly entrenched power structure of local communities. Zuccotti saw this strategy as a vindication of Jane Jacobs, whose work he admired. In a 1973 speech at Columbia's architecture school, Zuccotti characterized himself as "neo-Jacobean" and explained: "We have adjusted our sensibilities to the pulse and scale of the neighborhoods. We have changed our focus to work on the detailed fabric of the city, rather than seek to improve the pattern by cutting it new from whole cloth."[392]

As Zuccotti and others acknowledged, the 1969 master plan contained several proposals that were not that different from the new miniplan principles. But, as Goldberger noted, "while the master plan was sympathetic to neighborhood concerns and community participation in the planning process, its very existence as an overview of the city has made it less than an asset in today's political climate. The little plans Daniel Burnham decried, seem to be the only schemes likely to win acceptance today."[393]

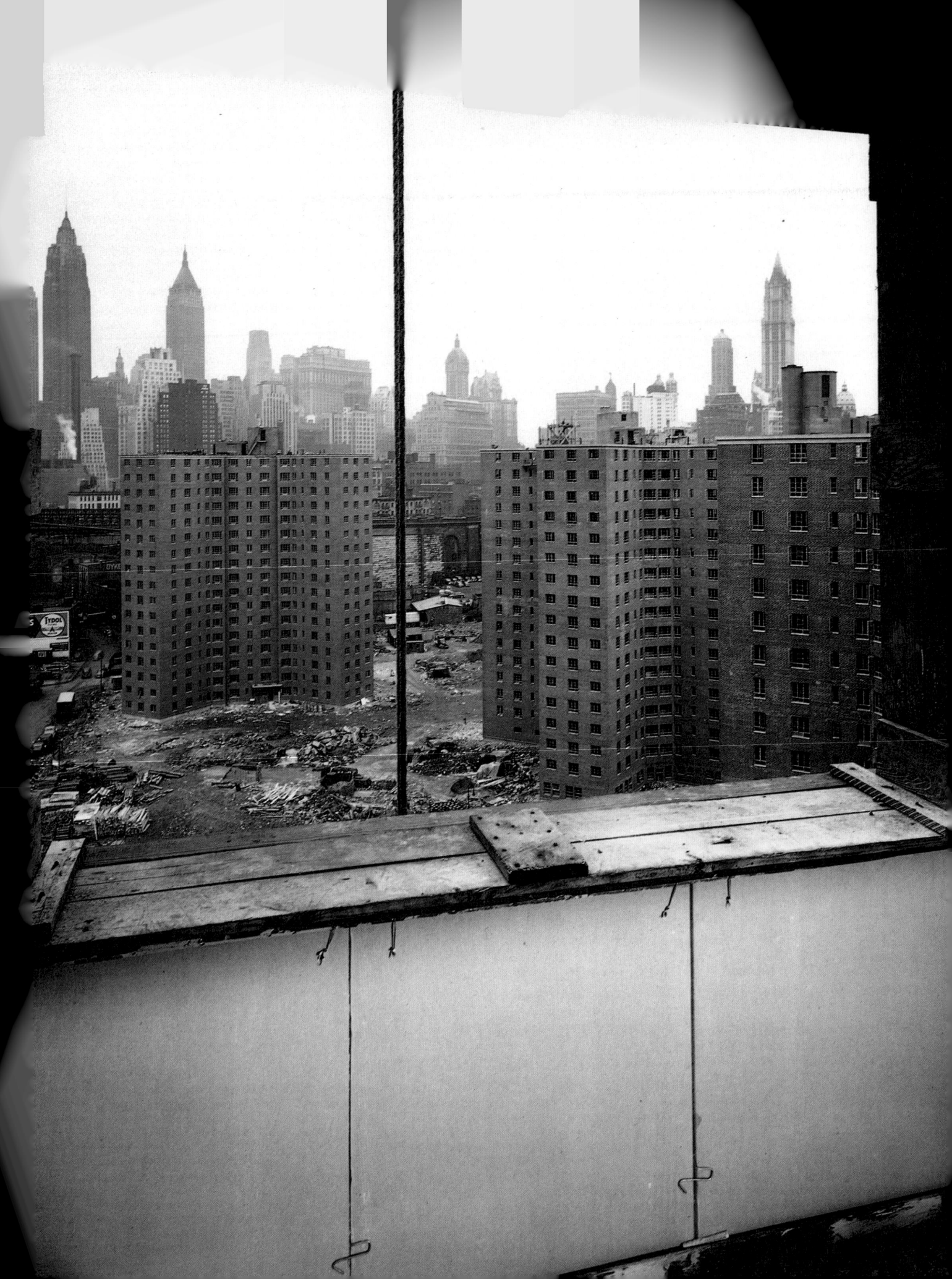

Chapter 3

Lower Manhattan

Here, past and present come together, not in the gentle partnership of the ideal city, but in the dramatic clash of the city desperate to make itself new at the expense of the old.
—*Paul Goldberger, 1979*[1]

LOWER EAST SIDE

Slum though it was, the Lower East Side was a real community. As the authors of the *WPA Guide to New York City* noted in 1939, "Crowded, noisy, squalid in many of its aspects, no other section of the city is more typical of New York." The area's character was in large measure defined by its legacy of poverty; originally a "melting pot" of ethnicity, by the advent of World War I it constituted the world's largest Jewish community, although many Italians also lived there. Remarkably, despite the overcrowding, or perhaps because of it, the area was on the whole one of the safest neighborhoods in the city. Moreover, it was full of life, with packed streets lined by shops and pushcart vendors, cafés, cafeterias and movie theaters as well as live theaters featuring Yiddish-language plays that attracted the notice of uptown critics. The cultural life of the Lower East Side was equal to that of any neighborhood in the city.

To the nation as a whole, the Lower East Side represented not merely poverty but also possibility. "The district is best known as a slum, as a community of immigrants, and as a ghetto," the WPA writers observed, "yet not all of the district is blighted, not all of its people are of foreign stock, and not all are Jewish. From its dark tenements, generations of American workers of many different national origins and an amazing number of public figures have emerged; politicians, artists, gangsters, composers, prize fighters, labor leaders."[1] The complexity of the area's character and composition resulted in the paradoxical situation that it was at once revered and loathed, a place to be proud of and a place to escape from, a place where dream journeys from rags to riches did come true despite enormous obstacles.

Alfred E. Smith Houses, bounded by Pearl, Madison and Catherine streets, Franklin Delano Roosevelt Drive and the approach to the Brooklyn Bridge. Eggers & Higgins, 1952. View to the southwest showing buildings under construction. Stoller. ©ESTO

At the outbreak of World War II the Lower East Side for the most part remained what it had been since the 1890s: a teeming slum of five- and six-story tenements, some built before the Civil War, many more before the "old law" type was outlawed by the Tenement House Act of 1901.[2] The physical wretchedness of the setting was appalling. In 1933, 78 percent of the apartment buildings in the area lacked steam heating.[3] As late as 1940, 37.5 percent of the area's apartments lacked plumbing facilities, 33 percent lacked toilets and 1.6 percent lacked running water.

By the war's end the goal of eradicating the slums was paramount. For one thing, the population that tolerated the tenements was rapidly aging, and suburban-minded young people were no longer willing to take their place. In addition, the immigrant Jews and their children were increasingly prosperous. Clearly the tenements had to go, and the area's future began to be redefined in terms of large-scale urban reconstruction. Unfortunately, reconstruction imposed a radically different pattern on the place. As proven by the continued vitality of what was allowed to remain in Chinatown, Little Italy and the vicinity of Tompkins Square Park, the destruction of Lower East Side buildings would also eliminate the patterns of daily life that the structures had so successfully reinforced. Still, even the most banal of the new super-scale housing projects were, in strictly material terms, a significant improvement over the tenements they replaced, whatever the projects' shortcomings or the magnitude of the unanticipated social problems that would emerge from reconstruction.

In 1947, surveying several large-scale public housing projects then on the boards, *New York Times* staff writer Murray Schumach could write with confidence, "The city's shame, its historic lower East Side slums, will become its pride in ten years."[4] Profound sociological changes accompanied the massive architectural transformation; with many of the area's Jewish and Italian residents gone to the outer boroughs or the suburbs, a new, even more complex mixture of ethnicity evolved, consisting of Chinese and blacks and, later, dominated by Puerto Ricans. Except in small pockets, everything on the Lower East Side changed, even its boundaries. Traditionally the area had been considered to be bounded on the north by Fourteenth Street, on the east by the East River, on the south by the approach to the Brooklyn Bridge and on the west by Pearl Street

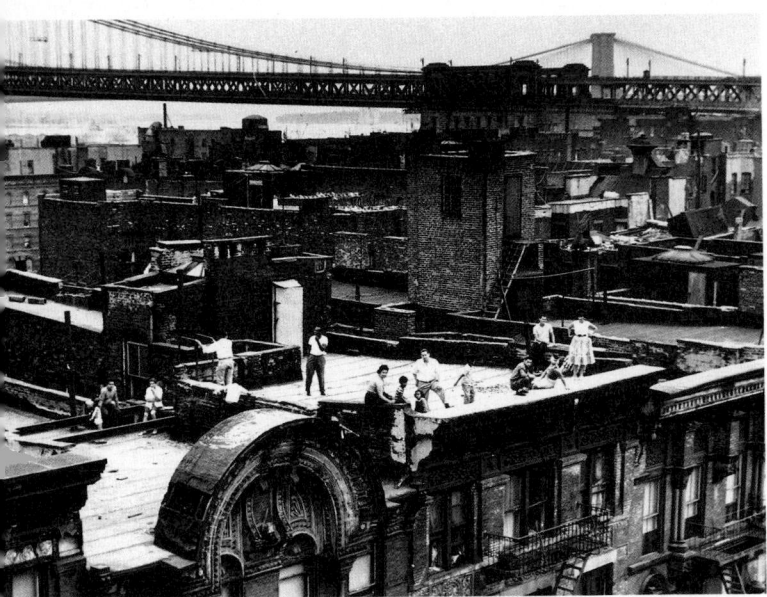

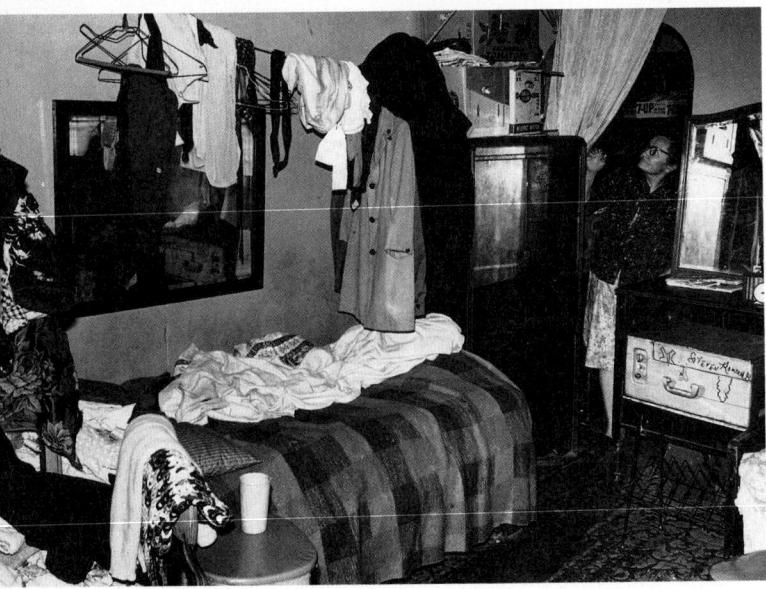

Top: View of area to the south of Henry Street, 1959. Fred W. McDarrah. FWM

Bottom: Tenement interior, Lower East Side, 1968. Fred W. McDarrah. FWM

Right: Lillian Wald Houses, East Houston to East Sixth Street, Avenue D to Franklin Delano Roosevelt Drive. Frederick L. Ackerman and Lafayette A. Goldstone, 1949. NYCHA

and Broadway. In the 1960s developmental pressures pushed some of Greenwich Village's younger and less well-heeled residents east of Third Avenue, causing part of the Lower East Side to be recast and redubbed the East Village (see chapter 4). This area, however, along with the area below Fourteenth Street and east of First Avenue, where the lettered avenues gave rise to the term "Alphabet City," remained physically the least transformed section of the historical slum neighborhood.

While the housing stock was almost completely replaced, institutional buildings, in particular those devoted to religion, remained isolated, alienated reminders of earlier street patterns and of bygone social conditions. Many of the area's most beautiful religous buildings were synagogues, some of which had originally been built as churches. As demographics changed, the synagogues increasingly fell victim to neglect.[5] Although the synagogues suffered, a few icons of Jewish ethnicity managed to survive. The culinary mecca Yonah Shimmel's Knishes Bakery, at 137 East Houston Street, proved indispensable to the city as a whole if not necessarily to the rebuilt neighborhood in which it was located. As the graphic artists and gourmets Milton Glaser and Jerome Snyder proclaimed in 1967, "The *raison d'etre* of this landmark has always been and is today the potato knish. The knish has played an active role in many New York political campaigns. In fact, no New York politician in the last 50 years has been elected to public office without at least one photograph showing him on the Lower East Side with a knish in his face."[6] Orchard Street, where the original tenement buildings largely remained, also continued to thrive as an area for discount shopping.[7]

Notwithstanding the remnants of the old Lower East Side, what had been was not just transformed; it was obliterated. Nowhere was the area's rebuilding more apparent than along the East River, where new parkland had been created as part of the construction of the East River Drive in 1941.[8] By the 1960s a near-continuous line of public housing defined the riverfront and vast stretches of the upland area, providing some residents with ample light, air and river views while effectively cutting off the rest of the neighborhood from the river. In a matter of a few years, the mean if lively streets of a vital slum gave way to an impersonal parkified nowhere realm punctuated by repetitious, banal housing blocks.

In 1941 the city signed contracts for the Lillian Wald Houses, to shelter 1,816 families on a seventeen-acre superblock site bounded by Sixth and East Houston streets, Avenue D and the East River Drive; by 1943 Frederick L. Ackerman and Lafayette A. Goldstone had been appointed the architects for the project.[9] Opened in 1949, the Wald Houses, named in honor of the founder of the Henry Street Settlement,[10] consisted of sixteen five-winged red-brick buildings, ranging in height from ten to thirteen stories and serviced by pairs of elevators stopping on alternate floors. The buildings collectively occupied less than 20 percent of the site's total acreage. From the first, the Housing Authority had recognized that the tenants of the large-scale projects would encounter economic and social problems as they relocated from the tenements to the superblocks. At the Wald Houses, these issues were rather naively addressed when the authority commissioned students at the Pratt Institute School of Home Economics to design a model apartment, which included a fabric-covered dressing table made of orange crates, as well as other street finds.

Occupying a superblock site bounded by Sixth and Fourteenth streets, Avenue D and the Franklin Delano Roosevelt Drive (formerly the East River Drive), the Housing Authority

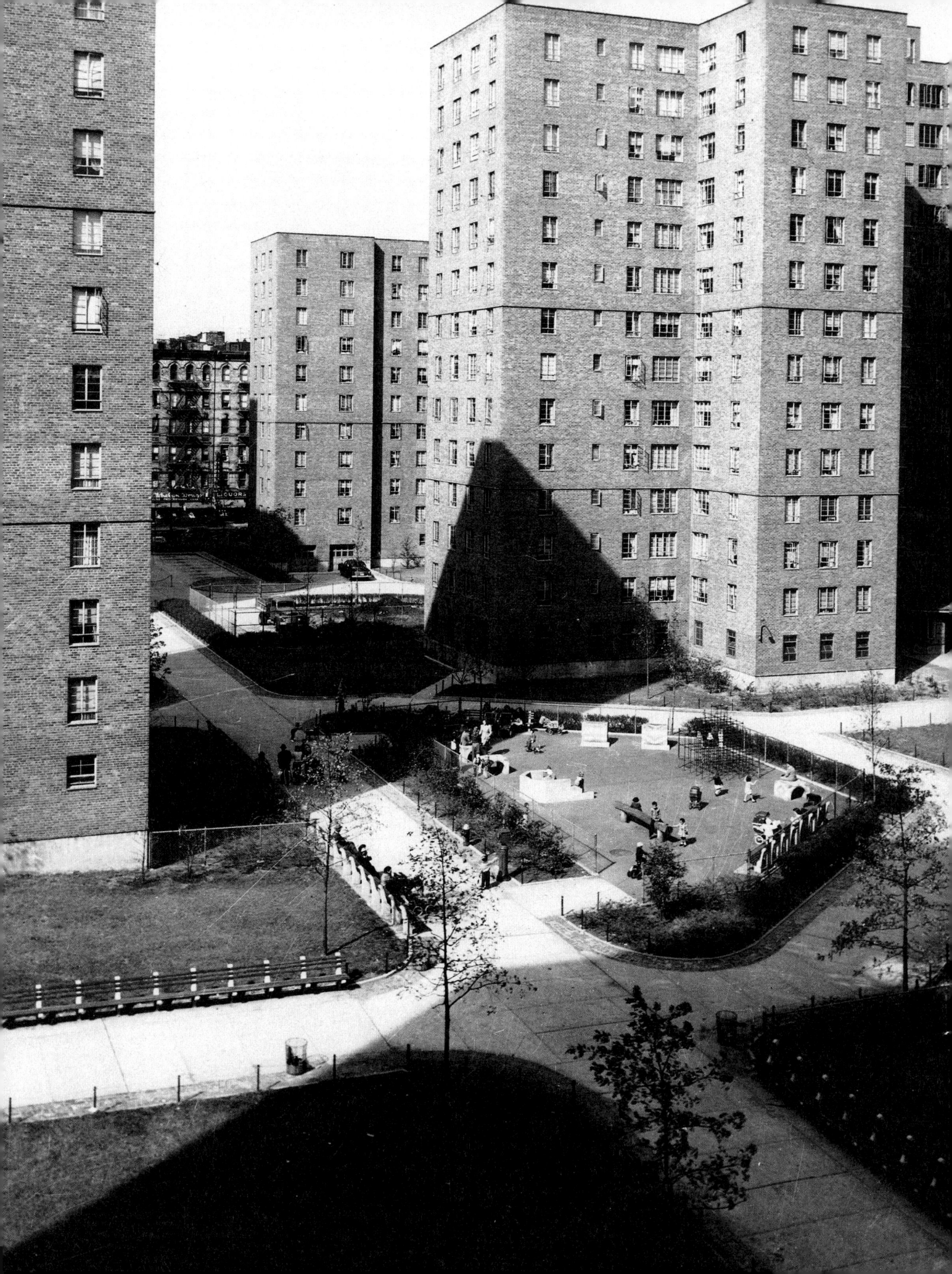

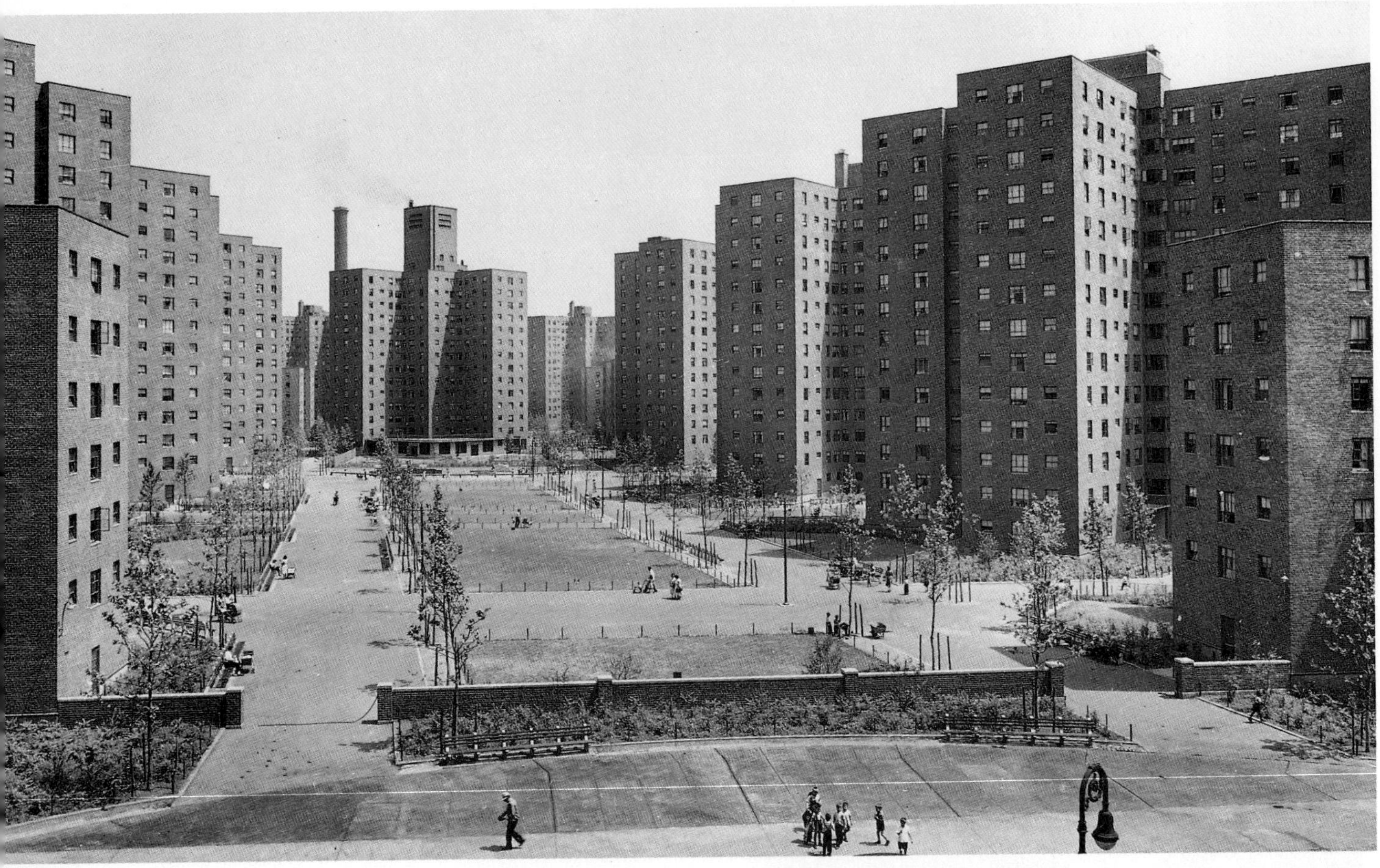

Above: Jacob Riis Houses, East Sixth to East Fourteenth Street, Avenue D to Franklin Delano Roosevelt Drive. James MacKenzie, Sidney Strauss and Walker & Gillette, 1949. NYCHA

Right: Riis Plaza, Jacob Riis Houses. M. Paul Friedberg, 1966. NYCHA

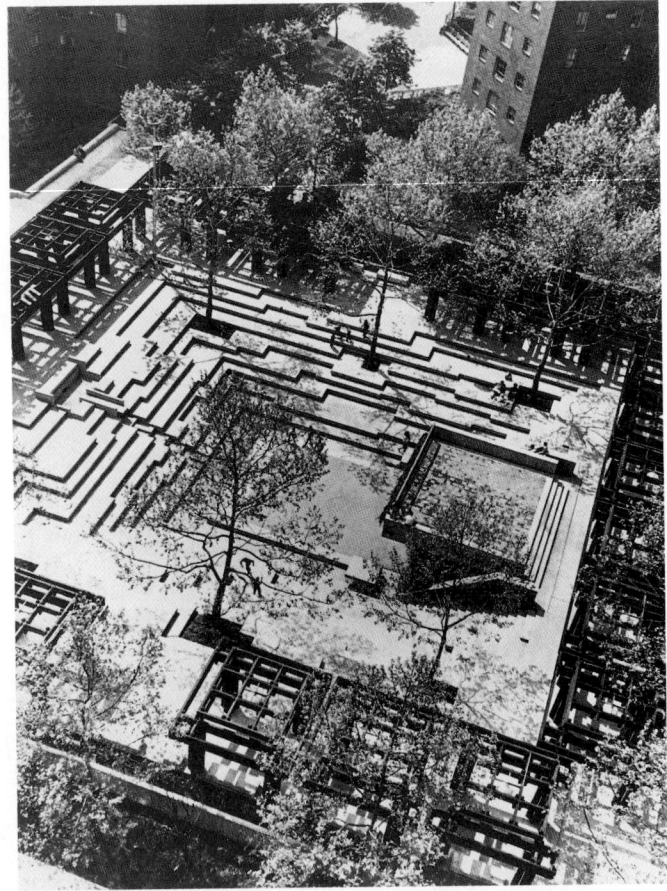

worked its way north from the Wald Houses with the Jacob Riis Houses (1949), providing an additional 1,700 apartments.[11] These buildings offered no more in the way of architectural interest or urbanistic vitality than the earlier project had. The Riis Houses, named for the Danish-born social reformer and writer,[12] were designed by the architects James Mackenzie and Sidney Strauss and the architectural firm of Walker & Gillette, and sponsored both by the city and the federal government. The development consisted of nineteen buildings, ranging in height from six to fourteen stories, placed on the site at a forty-five-degree angle to Manhattan's street grid. A long mall-like rectangle of tree-bordered turf was intended to serve as a central park.

In a "Sky Line" essay in the New Yorker titled "The Red-Brick Beehives," Lewis Mumford dismissed both the Wald and Riis houses as jointly creating "a broken palisade of red brick."[13] Finding fault with the design of the Riis Houses, Mumford linked its aesthetic shortcomings to broader problems with the city's efforts to clear and rebuild slum neighborhoods. Though he found the generous south-facing fenestration "praiseworthy," he asked, "what possessed the site planner to 'balance' the facades that face south with facades whose more numerous windows face north?" Mumford answered his own question: "Sheer formalism . . . formalism that looks good on a drawing board but disregards the desirability, both for summer and for winter, of a southern exposure." Mumford went on to criticize the density of the Riis Houses:

> It is formalism of the most opaque bureaucratic variety to go on with urban housing developments whose density of population averages over three hundred and fifty to the acre, ignoring the effect of such congestion on the traffic, the park and playground space, and the neighborhood schools. The core of this concept of housing is not a family, a neighborhood, and a livable city but an elevator shaft. If this new pattern of building becomes more widely imitated, it will create urban disabilities that will be more difficult to remove than the old slums.[14]

Though he failed to question other underlying premises of the wholesale urban renewal and "scientific" site and unit planning favored by housing officials, Mumford was one of a very few observers in the 1940s and 1950s who raised any questions at all about the program. As far as most New Yorkers were concerned, projects such as the Wald and Riis houses constituted very real progress. This view had radically changed by the mid-1960s, when the Wald and Riis houses, and other projects like them, were seen to be a source of an urban illness that brought with it vandalism, senseless crime and a host of other problems. While it was difficult to fight such a disease without tearing the projects down, certain palliatives were attempted. In 1965 the landscape architect M. Paul Friedberg and the architectural firm of Pomerance & Breines, working with funds from the Astor Foundation, transformed the central open area of the Riis Houses into one of the few attractive and engaging outdoor gathering spaces in a public housing project.[15] Private funding was the key ingredient in the new plaza's fruition. As Thomas P. F. Hoving, the city's newly appointed Park Commissioner, pointed out, with characteristic hyperbole: "[The plaza] cost the Vincent Astor Foundation nine hundred thousand dollars and it was constructed in nine months. If it had been built with city funds, it would have cost more than two million dollars, and it would have taken at least three years."[16]

As with most postwar public housing projects, the Riis Houses originally contained a flat lawn lined by pathways, concrete and wood park benches and rows of London plane trees.

Over the years the space had acquired "Keep Off" signs, chain-link fences and, eventually, paving instead of grass, degenerating into what the editors of Progressive Architecture described as "a barren concrete pit."[17] Following Jacob Riis's putative wishes, as well as those of the many project tenants interviewed by the designers, Paul Friedberg, the project's principal designer, sought to eradicate the existing "cages for incarceration" by "taking away the rigid, coercive path structure imposed on old projects and looking on the entire space as one big path." To transform the project's open space into "almost a happening"[18]—a concept Friedberg borrowed from Thomas Hoving—the designers divided the two-block-long space, renamed Jacob Riis Plaza, into four connected but distinct areas: an innovative children's playground featuring sand-covered areas, a stone "igloo" and balancing beams; a series of brick-paved enclaves incorporating trellises and visually centered around a monumental abstract sculpture by William Tarr; a thousand-person, pergola-enclosed, sunken amphitheater, for which the theatrical impresario Joseph Papp served as a design consultant; and a sitting area distinguished by a fountain and intended particularly for use by the elderly. Lampposts supporting large white globes provided nocturnal illumination but were also visually festive by day. The newly designed space was built on numerous levels; existing trees were saved and welled where the ground plane had been elevated. Because grass was considered too difficult to maintain, rough-surfaced paving was used throughout. Elevated flower beds containing geraniums and begonias were cleverly designed to accommodate pedestrian traffic. Architect Simon Breines, one of the designers of the plaza, said that it was meant to respond directly to its users' needs and desires: "The most important lesson is that you can't make people do what they don't want to do. You've got to find out what they like to do and design for it. It's like rediscovering the wheel."[19]

After the plaza's official opening on May 23, 1966, an event deemed important enough for President Johnson's wife, Lady Bird, to attend, the redesigned space attracted wide attention and universal praise. The editors of the New Yorker described it as a work of "remarkable beauty," noting in particular the plane trees growing inside the amphitheater, "more or less as permanent members of the audience."[20] The urban planner and author William H. Whyte called the place "very attractive," adding that it was "in fact, downright chic"; if the Riis Houses were luxury apartments, he said, "the residents would consider themselves lucky to have such a commons."[21] The editors of the Village Voice, labeling Riis Plaza "New York's most spectacular playground," also addressed the class issue, bluntly stating: "For once, the poor of the city have the best of it."[22] Mildred F. Schmertz, an editor at Architectural Record, contended that Friedberg's "genuinely distinguished solution" succeeded in eschewing not only the prototypical asphalt jungle but the supposedly cheerful look of concrete tables and multicolored metal umbrellas—"a grim proletarian parody of the country-club terrace."[23] The editors of Progressive Architecture noted the plaza's aesthetic effect on the existing buildings, saying that it "has transformed the public housing surrounding it the way a maiden's kiss transforms frogs into princes."[24]

Following the completion of Riis Plaza, Friedberg and Pomerance & Breines, who had prepared for Riis Plaza with a similar effort at Carver Houses in Harlem (see chapter 12), proposed that its scope be expanded into the upland unredeveloped community in an effort to reunite the riverfront and upland areas that the housing projects had split apart. Friedberg proposed additional landscaped pedestrian malls to link Riis Plaza

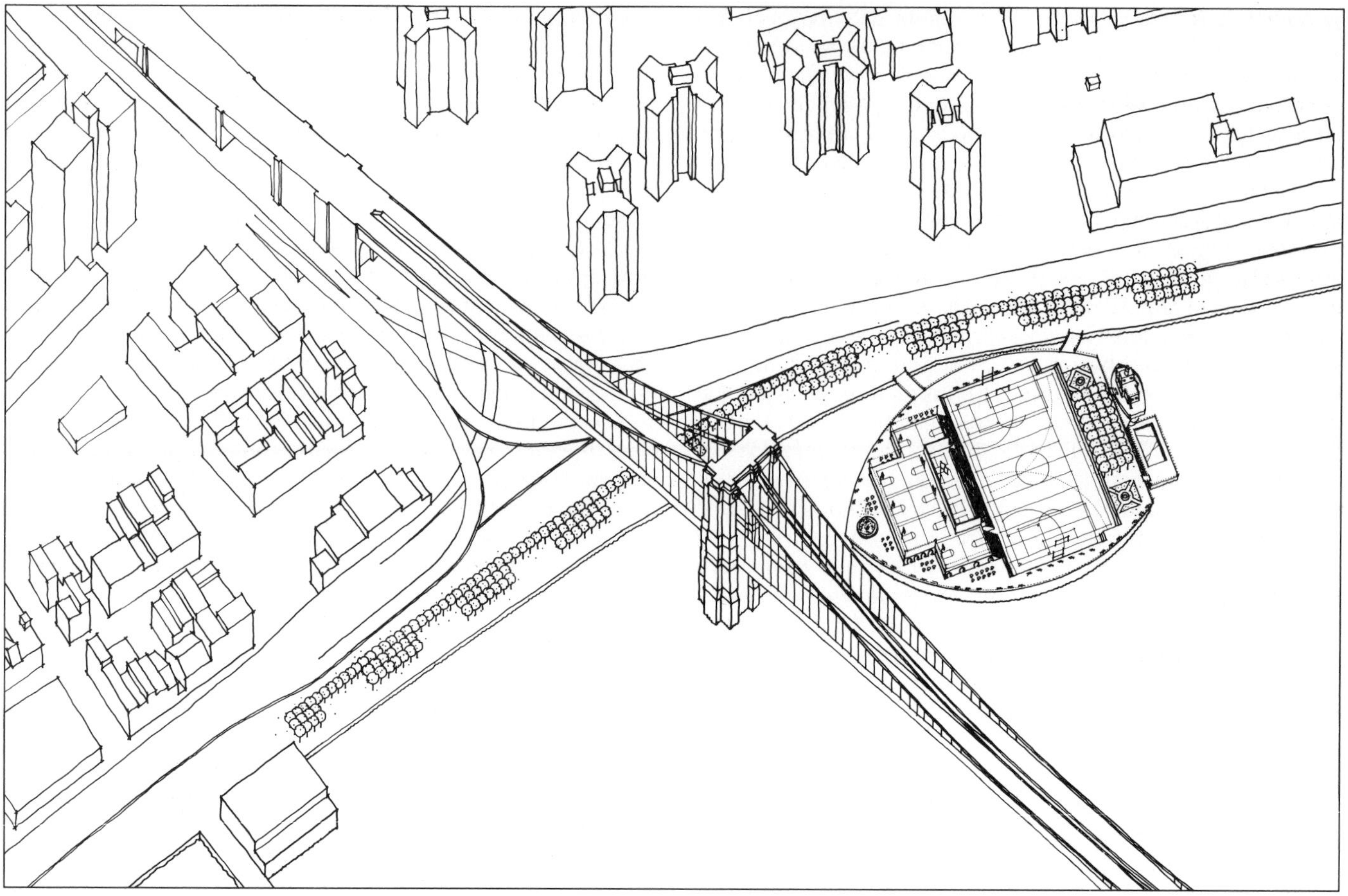

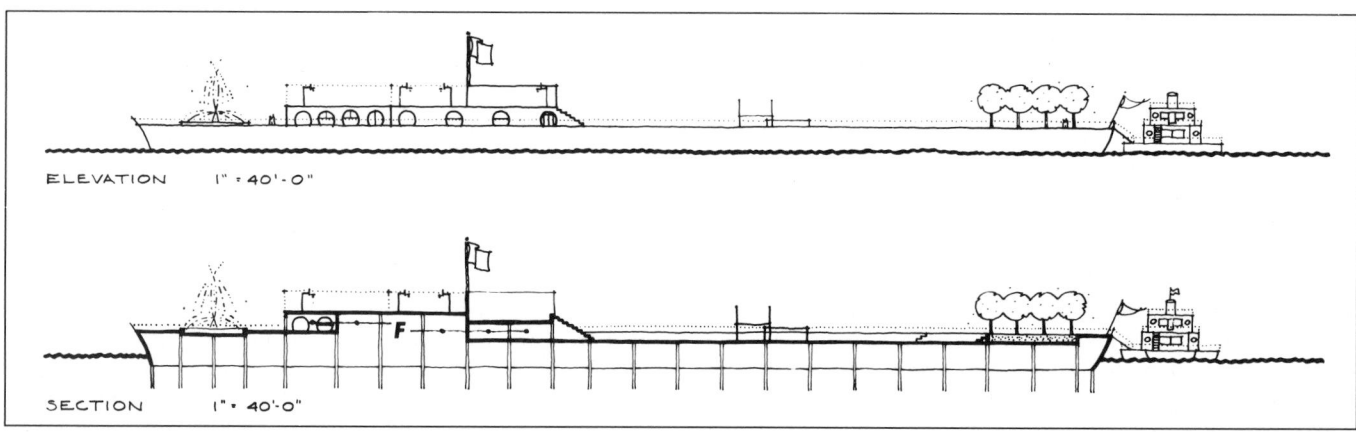

ELEVATION   1" = 40'-0"

SECTION   1" = 40'-0"

Proposed East River Park, East River opposite the Alfred E. Smith
Houses. Venturi & Rauch, 1973. Top: Axonometric. Center: Elevation.
Bottom: Section. VSBA

with Tompkins Square Park two blocks to the west, suggesting that Eighth and Ninth streets between Avenue B and Avenue D be permanently closed to all but service vehicles and serve as the extension's principal east-west element. The plan also called for four midblock plazas to be built above one-story parking garages to the north and south of the extension. The proposal, however, failed to receive funding, which Friedberg took as a sign that, without the support of an extra-governmental sponsor like the Astor Foundation, the business of housing and urban renewal would continue to be practiced according to the conventional wisdom of the 1940s and 1950s. "I wish," Friedberg lamented, "I could honestly say that the nationwide attention Riis Plaza has received has somehow altered public-housing policy, but I can't. They're a little more generous with funds for landscaping, but they still haven't bought the idea of plazas like Riis becoming community centers that could spark the renewal of whole slum communities."[25]

Riis Plaza was perhaps the inspiration for another, albeit much smaller, outdoor space built on the Lower East Side by the architect Charles Platt. Also supported by private funds, Platt's scheme transformed the backyards of four adjacent tenements at 130–136 Suffolk Street into what the New York Times described as a "back-pocket park."[26] The prototype for this design was the transformation of slum yards to form Sullivan-MacDougal Gardens and Turtle Bay Gardens nearly half a century earlier.[27] But on Suffolk Street the buildings were not transformed or gentrified; it was only the outdoor space that was reclaimed. Neighborhood participation in this project was even greater than at Riis Plaza: the residents built the 16-by-100-foot park themselves. Funding came from the J. M. Kaplan Fund, while Consolidated Edison donated the cable spools that were used as outdoor furniture and the Long Island Rail Road provided the wood ties used as play equipment.

In 1973 the architectural firm of Venturi & Rauch proposed what would have been, if realized, arguably the most innovative addition to the Lower East Side's recreational facilities.[28] A four-acre, wedge-shaped platform, evoking a boat sailing downstream, was to be located in the East River just north of the Brooklyn Bridge and opposite the Alfred E. Smith Houses. Connected to the mainland by means of two gangplanks, the facility was to include five basketball courts, a playing field that could serve as either two softball fields or a single football field, a garden, playgrounds and cafés. In addition, on the park's north side, a swimming pool was to be attached to a tugboat, as if it was being towed. While intended to serve the needs of the Lower East Side, the floating facility could be moved anywhere along the city's waterfront. Budgeted at $5.5 million, the project fell victim to the city's impending fiscal crisis.

To whatever degree park projects ameliorated the environmental brutality of the renewed Lower East Side, in the end they could not significantly compensate for the overall impact of the housing projects themselves. The Alfred E. Smith Houses, named for the recently deceased, charismatic former governor and presidential candidate who had been born nearby in a tenement at 174 South Street, were designed by Eggers & Higgins and opened in stages between 1949 and 1952.[29] The project was yet another superscaled element in the wall of public housing being built along the East River. In June 1943, anticipating the cessation of World War II and the resultant postwar housing shortage, Mayor La Guardia announced that the city would utilize state funds to build a public housing project to be located on a 21.4-acre superblock site bounded by Pearl, Madison and Catherine streets, the Franklin Delano Roosevelt (FDR) Drive

and the approach to the Brooklyn Bridge. Acting Housing Authority commissioner Ira S. Robbins was angered by La Guardia's preemptive public announcement, claiming that leaking information about the agency's acquisition of the proposed site would stimulate landowners to raise their prices.

Whereas 1,718 families had been housed previously on the site, the Smith Houses accommodated 1,935 families in twelve sixteen-story, red-brick buildings, each containing a central slab from which four wings emanated at forty-five-degree angles. Enjoying the dubious distinction of being the largest public housing project in Manhattan built to date as well as the tallest such project completed or planned in the city as a whole, its architectural mass was brutal and its exterior banal. In 1950 a privately funded memorial to the former governor was erected in Alfred E. Smith Memorial Park, located at the superblock's border along Catherine Street. The memorial incorporated a pedestal designed by Eggers & Higgins and a sculpture by Charles Keck. Next to a low granite wall, the back of which supported a bas-relief sculpture of nostalgic street scenes titled The Sidewalks of New York, stood a likeness of Smith; a sculpted version of Smith's sartorial signature—a derby hat—rested on a ledge nearby. Directly north of the sculpture, a flagpole surmounted a base, sculpted by Paul Manship, depicting animals native to the New York City region, a sophisticated and whimsical design that helped relieve the overall anonymity.

Nearly three decades after the completion of the Smith Houses, at a time when such towers had become not only a design cliché but to a large degree a universal symbol of the failure of government-sponsored urban renewal, Paul Goldberger offered a thoughtful assessment of Eggers & Higgins's project, putting as positive a spin as possible on the stylistic and urbanistic context that set the urban renewal agenda of the postwar era:

[The project] is worth seeing, mainly because it is not so terribly bad—yes, Jane Jacobs, there is light and air made available to people who never had it before—but also because of the juxtaposition its site offers with other, more conventional parts of the cityscape. . . . The towers have the Brooklyn Bridge to one side, the buildings of the civic center to the west, and the skyline of the financial district to the south. They play off not against a grid but against a complex urban landscape, and as a result, their own absolute order becomes all the more insistent by contrast.[30]

Located within the project's confines, but more aesthetically satisfying than the housing towers, were Public School 126, known as the Jacob Riis School, at 80 Catherine Street, and, directly behind it, the Alfred E. Smith Recreation Center.[31] Designed by Percival Goodman and completed in 1966, the four-story school and the two-story recreation center were skillfully executed Modernist compositions incorporating exposed-concrete structures filled in with red brick and industrial sash. The recreation center was further distinguished by its pitched roof. The stylistically consistent buildings brought not only some degree of visual interest but a welcome dose of human scale to the development as a whole.

The Baruch Houses, completed in three sections between 1954 and 1959, were designed by Emery Roth & Sons and constructed with federal funds.[32] The 2,194-unit complex, named for Simon Baruch, a physician and father of the financier Bernard Baruch, consisted of seventeen multiwinged buildings ranging in height from seven to fourteen stories.[33] Apartment plans incorporating diagonal axes were externally expressed by

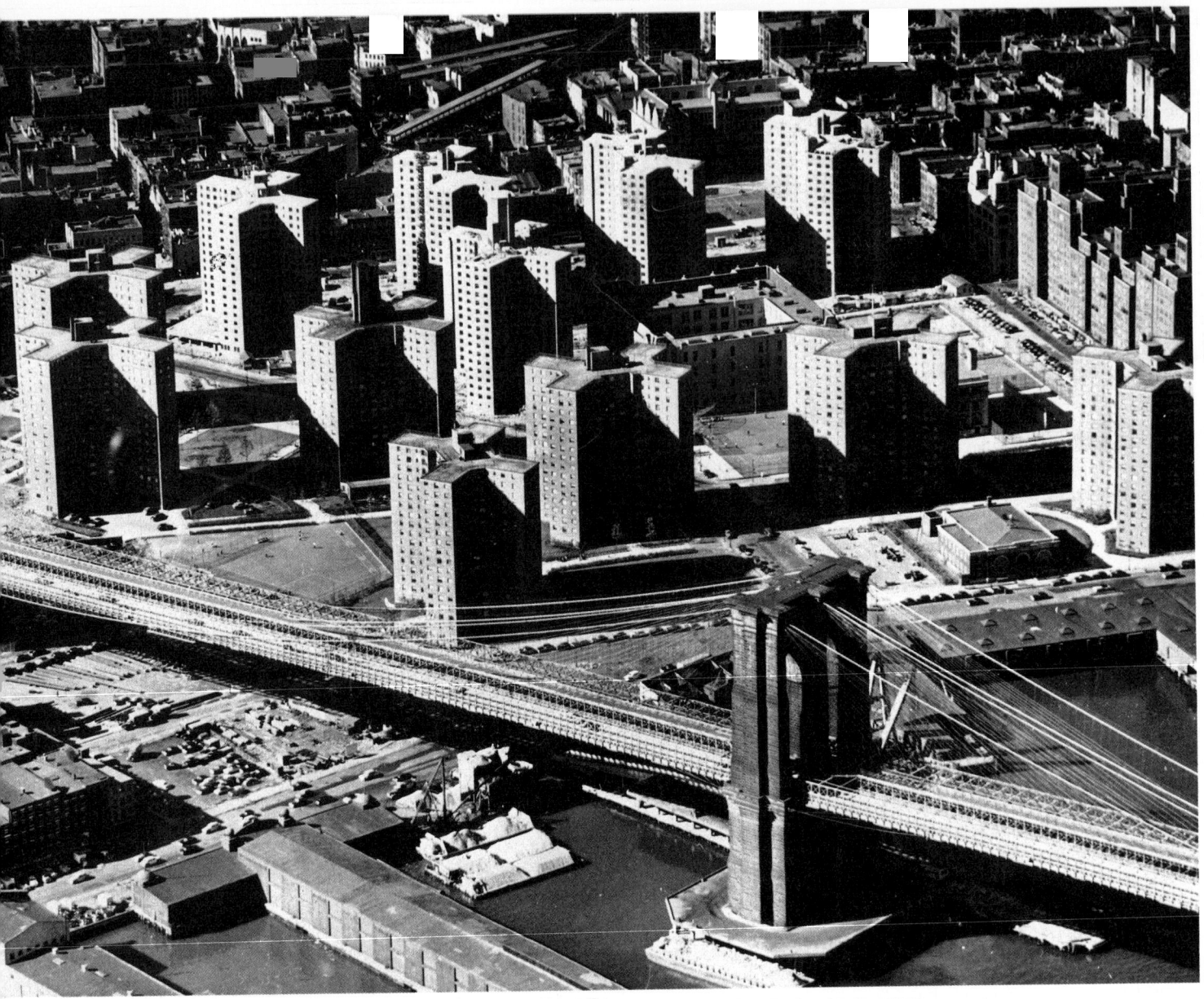

Above: Alfred E. Smith Houses, bounded by Pearl, Madison and
Catherine streets, Franklin Delano Roosevelt Drive and the approach to
the Brooklyn Bridge. Eggers & Higgins, 1952. View to the northwest.
NYCHA

Top right: Baruch Houses, East Houston to Delancey Street, Franklin
Delano Roosevelt Drive to Columbia Street. Emery Roth & Sons, 1959.
View to the west. NYCHA

Bottom right: Baruch Houses. Site plan. NYCHA

saw-toothed facades that, while adding a measure of visual complexity, also gave the development a decidedly aggressive and even forbidding appearance. The buildings covered 13.4 percent of a 27.5-acre superblock that was bounded by Delancey, Columbia and East Houston streets and the FDR Drive but interrupted by a surviving portion of Rivington Street, which terminated east of Columbia Street in a cul-de-sac, and by Baruch Drive, a new north-south street that meandered in a serpentine path.

Though the site was enormous, the development was a model of placelessness, not only breaking connections with upland neighborhoods but also failing to define itself as an urban enclave: there was neither a strong boundary nor a dominant central space. Furthermore, the usefulness of the Baruch Houses' generously scaled if randomly configured open spaces was severely compromised by the presence of parking lots. The architect and historian Richard Plunz later claimed that the Baruch Houses were the culmination of "the spatial pathology of public housing in New York City during the 1950s. . . . Because there were no discernible criteria for site organization, the orientation of the buildings was quite random." As Plunz pointed out, however, the individual buildings "were an interesting hybrid form that combined the characteristics of the slab and the asterisk," a configuration that succeeded in providing 70 percent of the apartments with river views.[34] The site of the Baruch Houses, along with those of the Wald and Riis projects, was undeniably spectacular. Helen Hall, the longtime director of the Henry Street Settlement, wondered why real estate interests had not developed land in "such a beautiful location" for high-rent apartments. "But they didn't," she said, "and our neighbors who had borne the heat of the day in the old tenements have the lovely view on the East River."[35]

A staggering 12,600 tenement apartments fell victim to the wrecker's ball in order to make way for the Baruch Houses. The destruction of such a long-established and socially cohesive section of the city was poignantly described by the *New York Times* journalist Meyer Berger:

> A group of the displaced who had lived in the easternmost rookeries on the Baruch city housing site by the East River shivered in the raw wind at Rivington Street and Baruch Place last night, proof of the saying that misery loves company. They stared at the vacated flats, at windowglass shards and rubble on the sidewalks about them. They watched prowling cats and sad-looking mongrels, left behind by neighbors who were told they could not bring their pets to the new homes found for them by the city. Barely a soul moved in what had once been a teeming neighborhood. Hardly a light showed in the blackened, empty tenements. The river wind hit the banshee note. The whole quarter, huddled in dark melancholy in anticipation of demolition crews . . . was a weird deserted village. It will pass forever as Baruch City goes up.[36]

In 1953, prior to the project's completion, the builders of the Baruch Houses reported a large number of broken windows due to vandalism, attributed to neighborhood youths. Though attacks on buildings under construction were common, the scope of the damage was unprecedented. Considered in light of the publicized social tensions stemming from the rebuilding and relocating processes that were rapidly transforming the Lower East Side, such vandalism was a harbinger of the disaffection and violence that the new urbanism would encourage.

In 1957 the DeWitt Reformed Church, designed by Edgar Tafel, was completed within the Baruch project superblock on the northeast corner of Columbia and Rivington streets.[37] The

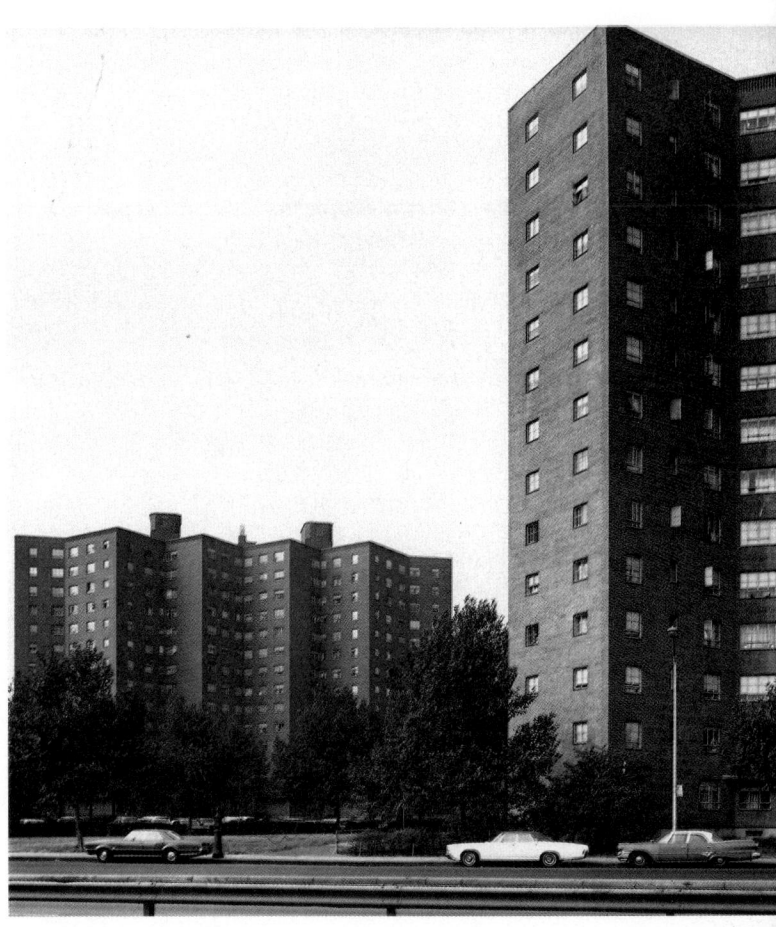

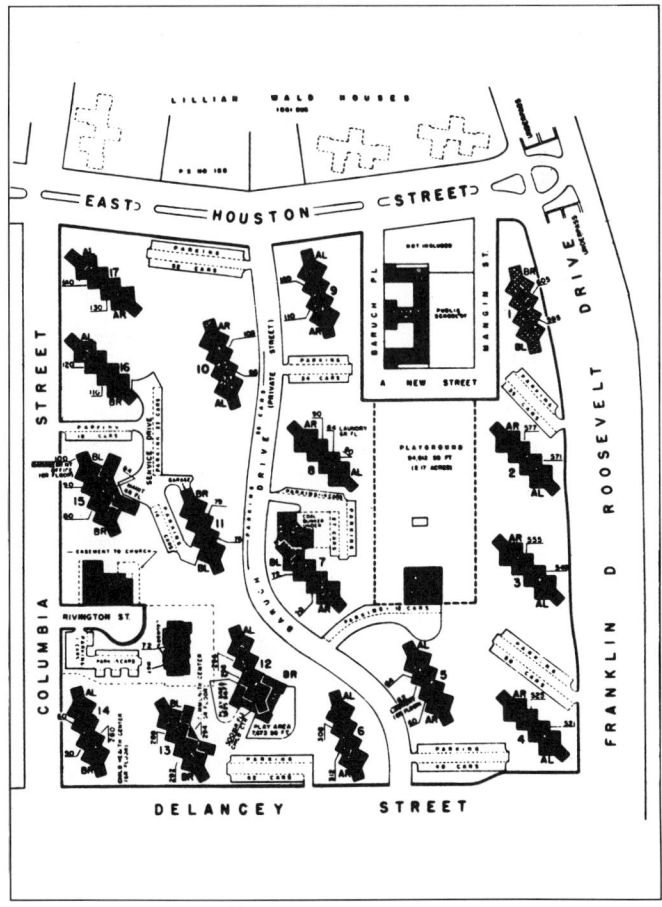

only religious building to be built on the Lower East Side during the postwar period, the church eschewed the imposing Moorish and Gothic vocabularies that dominated the area's traditional religious architecture in favor of a distinctly understated Modernism inspired by the work of Frank Lloyd Wright, the architect's mentor. Incorporating a pitched roof over the sanctuary, the church lacked a steeple because, Tafel argued, "it would be impossible to compete for a feeling of height with the 14-story buildings in the vicinity," although the principal facade featured a large crucifix made of two tree trunks that clearly identified the building's function.[38] The Reverend Norman Vincent Peale, who attended the church's dedication on January 5, 1958, asserted that "the new, completely modern, entirely up-to-date plant of the DeWitt Church is the answer of a dynamic and creative Protestantism to the problems of New York City."[39] Norval White and Elliot Willensky saw even broader implications in the design; they praised the church for imbuing the surrounding housing project with a "very human element."[40]

Completed in 1956, the Corlears Hook Houses, also known as the International Ladies Garment Workers Union Cooperative Village, were middle-income cooperative apartments sponsored by the labor union under Title I of the Federal Housing Act of 1949.[41] Designed by the architect Herman Jessor, who would later design the gargantuan Co-op City complex in the Bronx (see chapter 13), the Corlears Hook Houses filled in the brick-clad riverside housing palisade so that it was now virtually unbroken from the Brooklyn Bridge to Twenty-third Street. But the Hook Houses were a departure from the area's typical housing projects. Built by a union, the project was not financed through conventional methods: the ILGWU invested its own money in a federally insured mortgage loan.

The Corlears Hook Houses consisted of four eight-winged, red-brick apartment buildings, as well as landscaped open areas and parking lots, occupying a twelve-acre site straddling Grand Street and bounded on the west by Jackson, Lewis and Madison streets and on the east by the FDR Drive. A one- and two-story shopping center occupying a triangular site bounded by Grand, Jackson and Madison streets completed the development, virtually the only new commercial space provided in the neighborhood, since government-financed public housing was enjoined from providing commercial space. The apartment buildings, two with twenty stories and two with twenty-one stories, contained a total of 1,668 apartments and covered one-fourth of the site. Until clearance commenced in 1953, the area had had a site coverage exceeding 90 percent, consisting predominantly of five- and six-story nineteenth-century tenements. At the time of demolition the tenements housed only 718 families, fewer than half the number that could be accommodated in the new development.

To the journalist Charles Grutzner, writing in the New York Times in January 1957, the Corlears Hook Houses, which he applauded as housing that was "within the means of average factory and white-collar workers," constituted a paradigm of postwar urban renewal. The project, Grutzner contended, "is one of the best examples of the urban renewal program under which the Federal Government may spend $1,000,000,000 to help cities and built-up areas in the sprawling suburbs fight decay. This decay is more than just a side effect of the spread of urbanization; it is as much a part of it as the rise of the Levittowns."[42]

Efforts to counteract not only the spread of slums but also the lure of suburbia could be discerned in Jessor's design, which, in contrast to typical public housing projects such as the adjacent Vladeck Houses (Shreve, Lamb & Harmon, 1940),[43] featured 945 recessed corner balconies. Though they could hardly compete with leafy backyards as slices of arcadian pie, the balconies nonetheless opened typical Manhattan cliff dwellers up to the possibilities of "indoor-outdoor" living as never before. The buildings' massing gained some interest at the top, where setbacks accommodated thirty-six penthouses that seemed to approach the level of amenities offered by more fashionable apartment buildings uptown.

A year after the completion of the Corlears Hook Houses, the widening of Grand Street between Columbia Street and the FDR Drive, as well as the creation of a new street known as Delancey Street South connecting Lewis Street to the highway—which were touted as traffic "improvements"—dealt yet another blow to the area's vitality. As Morris Kaplan reported in the New York Times in 1957, "No traces remain of the area's colorful past—sailing ships, saloons and shanghaied sailors. Grand Street is indeed no longer a grand shopping district."[44]

As was often the case with public housing projects, the city-built Mary K. Simkhovitch Houses (F. P. Wiedersum Associates, 1963), named after the social reformer and settlement-house founder, was more interesting for its economic underpinnings and its reflection of evolving public policy than for its architecture.[45] The project was an attempt to address the needs of lower-middle-class families who were customarily left out of public housing programs. Consisting of six twenty-one-story slabs, the Simkhovitch Houses occupied a riverfront superblock site bounded by the FDR Drive and Gouverneur, Water and Jackson streets, as well as two other superblock sites to the west and north. The design incorporated terraces—an innovation for the Housing Authority—and covered less than 13 percent of the three-part, seven-acre site. Reflecting a growing sense that individual ownership and private management provided a far more effective and efficient means of financing and maintaining such housing, in the late 1960s the city began to convert the Simkhovitch Houses and seven other similar projects to privately owned cooperatives. Shedding its stigma-laden origins as a "project," the development's name was changed to the tonier Gouverneur Gardens.

In 1962 the firm of Mayer, Whittlesey & Conklin presented a design for the Two Bridges Urban Renewal Project, an extensive development proposed in two parts: the upland portion would run from Market Slip to Montgomery Street between Cherry Street and the FDR Drive; and, on the east side of the highway, a landfill portion would be built into the river itself and connected to the rest of the development by means of two pedestrian bridges.[46] The upland site, largely industrial in character, though no longer central to the city's economy, did not present the massive residential relocation problems typical of renewal projects. In addition to containing housing for 10,000 residents, stores, an elementary school, indoor parking and outdoor recreational areas, Two Bridges, which was to mix five- and twenty-two-story buildings, was to include shipping facilities for the Belgian Line. According to the city's Housing and Redevelopment Board, the proposal was the first urban renewal project in which residential units were to be combined with nonretail commercial facilities. The five-story residential buildings were to contain interlocking split-level units and the high-rise buildings would be distinguished by balcony-covered, "ski-jump" sloping facades. Together the high- and low-rise buildings were to define open pedestrian plazas. Despite Conklin's confident assertion that the project's "public spaces . . . are designed to capture something of the color and life of the old lower east side," including street-level stores, the firm's sketches suggested that its plazas would be more typical of the overly

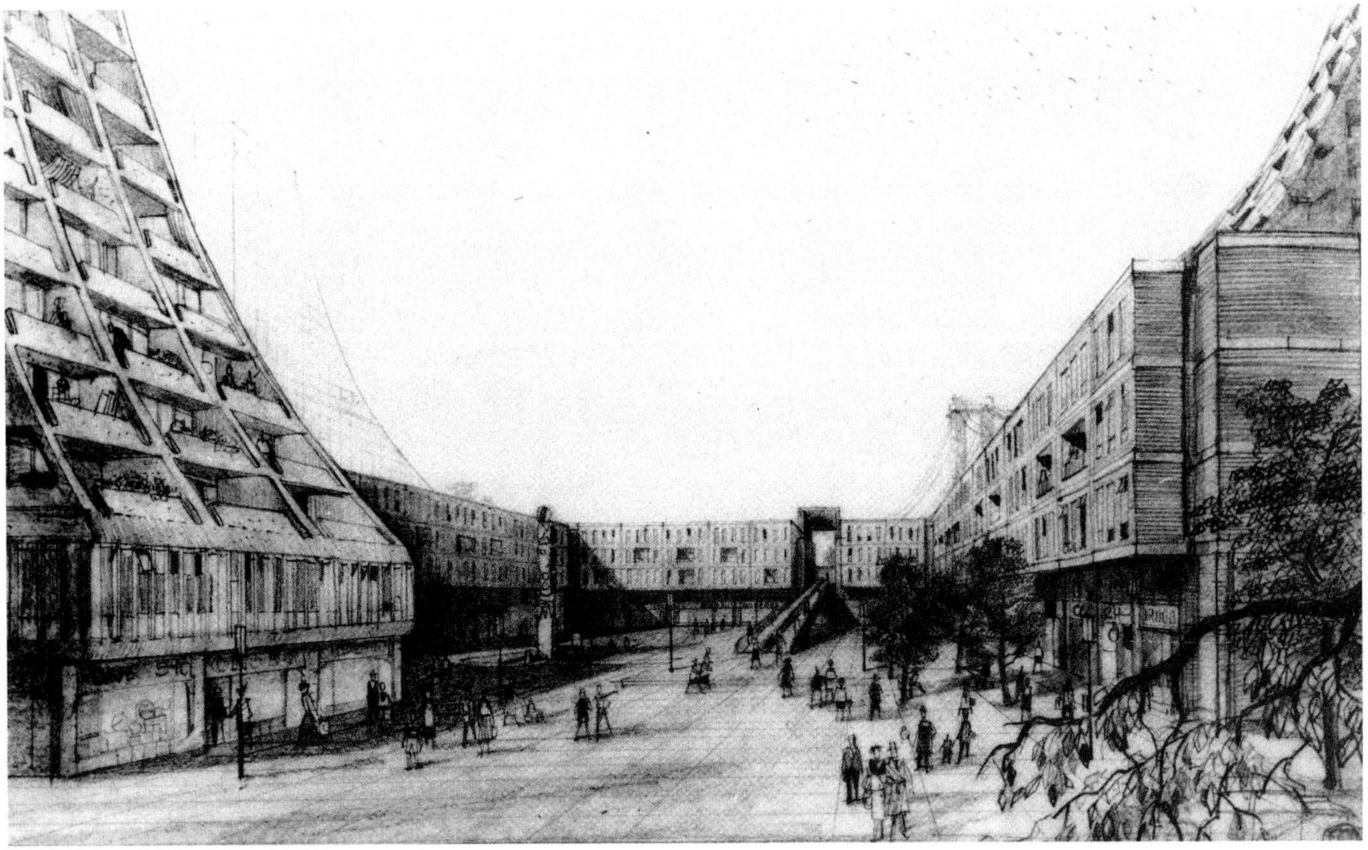

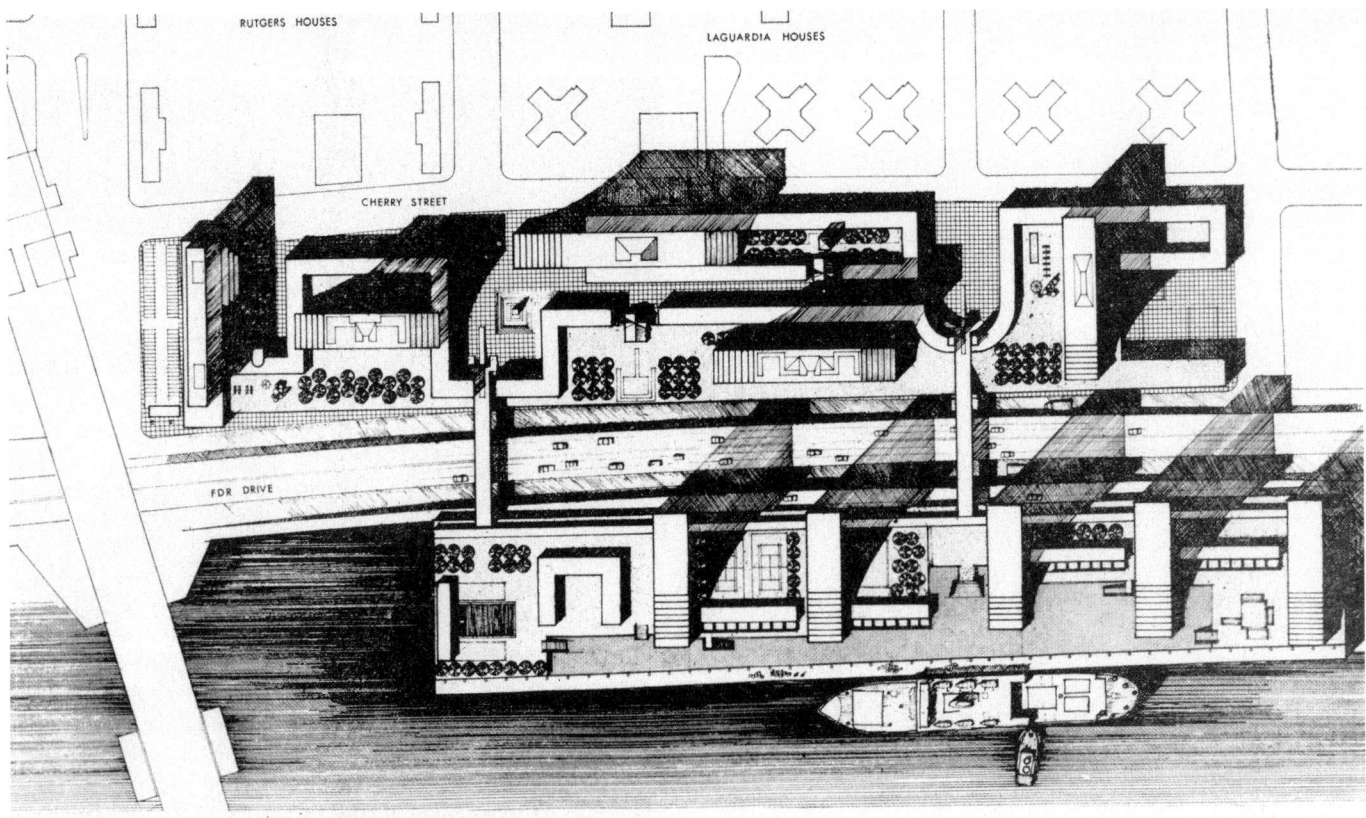

Top: Proposed Two Bridges Urban Renewal Project, Market Slip to Montgomery Street, Cherry Street to Franklin Delano Roosevelt Drive, landfill in the East River from Rutgers Slip to Montgomery Street. Mayer, Whittlesey & Conklin, 1962. Perspective by James Rossant. CR

Bottom: Proposed Two Bridges Urban Renewal Project. Site plan. CR

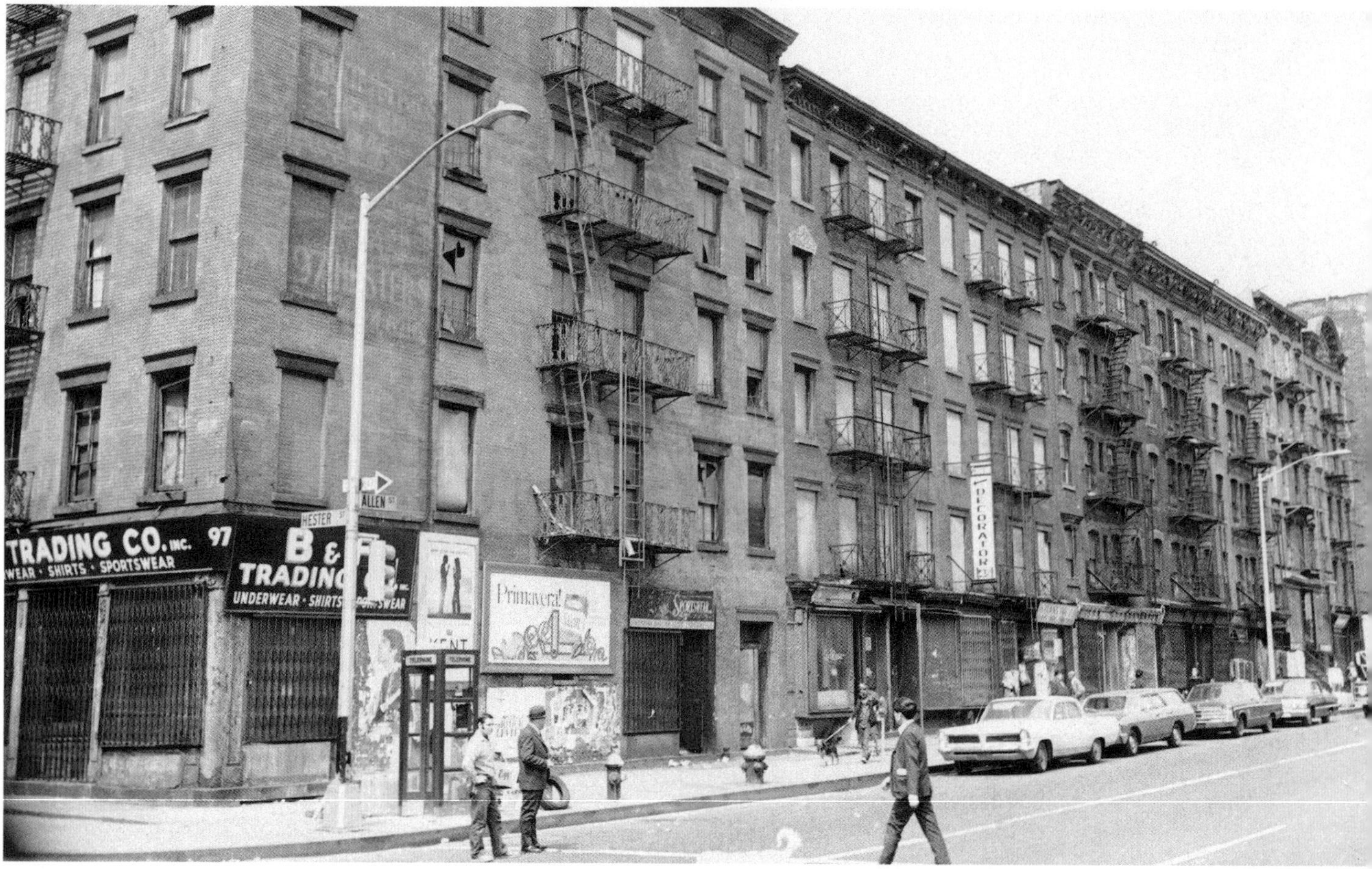

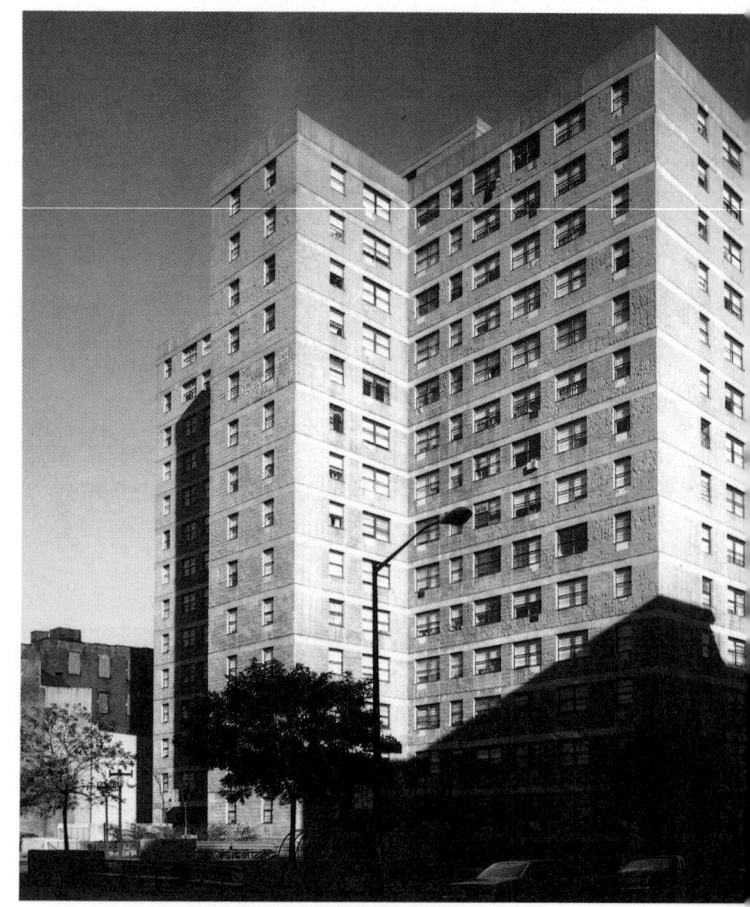

Above: Site of proposed Hester-Allen Turnkey Housing, northwest corner of Hester and Allen streets, 1971. NYCHA

Right: Hester-Allen Turnkey Housing, 45 Hester Street, northwest corner of Allen Street. Edelman & Salzman, 1973. NYCHA

generous but ill-defined spaces that formed the neighborhood's new anti-urban urbanism.[47]

Two Bridges languished amid complex negotiations and numerous plan revisions. Meanwhile, plans were being hatched for the further renewal of the still-considerable area that remained of the old Lower East Side. In 1971, following three years of study, the planning firm of Abeles, Schwartz and Associates completed a comprehensive report, *Forging a Future for the Lower East Side*, prepared for the City Planning Commission and the City Housing and Development Administration.[48] The report declared that 35,000 neighborhood apartments were "not fit to live in" and advocated that they be demolished incrementally and replaced, in part, by new housing to be built on landfill in the East River, extending from the Brooklyn Bridge to north of the Manhattan Bridge, overlapping the area previously slated for the Two Bridges project.[49] Additionally, the report recommended that underutilized streets be closed to make way for new housing, and that Sara Roosevelt Park (1934), bounded by East Houston, Forsyth, Canal and Chrystie streets, also be used for housing, as had been proposed by Howe & Lescaze in their attempt to realize a revolutionary urbanism along Chrystie and Forsyth streets in 1932.[50] In addition to forwarding building proposals, the report focused on a broad range of issues including education, health care, poverty and job training. Implicit in its recommendations was the recognition, gained after decades of experience, that the beneficial results of public housing were at best finite in scope and were most lasting when combined with economic change.

While Two Bridges offered an alternate model for redevelopment, involving almost no slum clearance, the city continued to pursue its traditional renewal programs for the Lower East Side with little new thinking. The federally funded, low-income La Guardia Houses (H. I. Feldman, 1957), named for the Lower East Side–born mayor who in 1935 had established the New York City Housing Authority, occupied two adjacent superblock sites collectively bounded by Cherry, Rutgers, Madison and Montgomery streets, and separated by Clinton Street.[51] The 607 apartments of the La Guardia Houses were accommodated in nine brick buildings, ranging in height from twelve to sixteen stories. Three years after their completion, Ira S. Robbins, vice chairman of the City Housing Authority, in an effort to relieve what he described as the "plainness and depressing monotony" that had come to characterize so much low-income public housing, announced that an authority-appointed panel had selected Elmer Polony, a Hungarian refugee artist, to install a mural in the project's community center.[52] The five-by-twenty-nine-foot mural, funded privately because the authority was legally prohibited from financing art projects, depicted the arrival and assimilation of immigrants into the neighborhood.

The state-sponsored, five-building, 718-unit Rutgers Houses (Hart, Jerman & Associates, 1965) were yet another architecturally undistinguished public housing project, occupying a superblock site bounded by Cherry, Pike, Madison and Rutgers streets.[53] Equally banal were the federally funded Gompers Houses (Lama, Proskauer & Prober, 1965), named for the labor leader, where 475 apartments were packaged in two twenty-story buildings that occupied only 15 percent of a 7.5-acre, L-shaped superblock site on the northwest corner of Delancey and Pitt streets.[54] Intended for large poor families, Gompers Houses featured apartments ranging in size from two and a half to five and a half rooms. Located directly to its east, a municipally sponsored, middle-income project called Columbia Houses, also designed by Lama, Proskauer & Prober, consisted of four twenty-one-story buildings containing a total of 1,108 apartments.[55] Federal and city housing officials coordinated the development of the adjacent projects in an effort to avoid, as New York City Housing Authority chairman William Reid put it, the "economic segregation" that increasingly was becoming a hallmark of urban renewal projects.[56]

The New York City Housing Authority's Hester-Allen Turnkey Housing (1973) marked an aesthetic departure from the red and brown brick slabs and towers that were the agency's norm.[57] But more significant than the design by the firm of Edelman & Salzman, which included horizontal bands in smooth and ribbed concrete block, was the method of financing used to realize the project. In 1968 new legislation was passed that set the groundwork for the so-called turnkey financing method, in which private-sector landowners could build housing and sell it to a local public housing authority. This was a contrast to the conventional process, in which the housing authority bought the land or acquired it through eminent domain and subsequently used the services of its own architects and contractors—an approach that was coming under increasing attack because of its slowness and inefficiency.

Masaryk Towers (Lama, Proskauer & Prober, 1966) were distinguished by an on-site gymnasium containing an Olympic-size indoor swimming pool, if not by the architecture of the four twenty-one-story, buff-brick slabs. The project, named for the first president of Czechoslovakia, Tomás Masaryk (whose wife was American), occupied the southeast portion of a superblock site bounded by East Houston, Columbia, Delancey and Pitt streets.[58] The 1,109-unit middle-income cooperative shared the block with Gompers Houses and Hamilton Fish Park, as well as with Kelly & Gruzen's stylish combined building for the Hamilton Fish Park branch library and Junior High School 22 (1956), at the southwest corner of East Houston and Columbia streets.[59] Gruzen's Le Corbusier–inspired, three-story, reinforced-concrete building was partially raised on stilts, leaving street-level space available to serve, at least in theory, as a protected recreational area. A generously proportioned interior court contained a ramp leading directly to the building's second floor.

Spurred on by the success of the Corlears Hook project, the ILGWU built Seward Park Houses (Herman Jessor, 1960), a Title I housing project occupying most of a triangular site bounded by East Broadway, Grand Street and Essex Street and traversed by Clinton Street. The development had some distinction because of its wide range of public amenities, which included a recreation center, a branch of the public library and, perhaps most significant, a first-run movie theater, the first such facility built in the area in twenty-five years. Designed by William Kahn as a freestanding, one-story, white-glazed-brick box, the theater was located at the southeast corner of Grand and Norfolk streets.[60]

In 1962 the city's Housing and Redevelopment Board proposed a renewal plan, which came to be known as the Seward Park Extension, for the area bounded by Grand, Essex and Willett streets and Delancey Street South.[61] The innovative plan called for the creation of several adjacent superblock sites, some of them interlocking L shapes, separated by narrow, newly created streets but crisscrossed by midblock pedestrian walkways. As was typical of all superblocks, surrounding streets were to be widened. Mixed low- and high-rise buildings were to contain low- and middle-income housing as well as commercial and institutional space. The plan reflected an increased sensitivity toward the existing urban fabric; several important neighborhood institutions would be retained, including Synagogue Beth

Hamedrash Hagodol (originally Norfolk Street Baptist Church, 1859), at 60–64 Norfolk Street;[62] St. Mary's Roman Catholic Church (1833; P. C. Keely, 1871), at 438 Grand Street;[63] and the Bialystoker Synagogue (originally Willett Street Methodist Church, 1826), at 7–13 Willett Street.[64]

Eventually William F. Pedersen proposed a plan for an extension to the Seward Park Houses that, in a bold departure from typical postwar practice, featured a vast courtyard.[65] Although this plan was not implemented, Pedersen did complete a two-part extension that brought to the area an unusually high level of design and urbanistic sensitivity.[66] Located at 64–66 Essex Street and occupying the full square block bounded by Essex, Broome, Norfolk and Grand streets, the western component of the project (1973) consisted of a twenty-two-story, buff-brick slab built out to the lot line at the site's northern end. The slab's unornamented street-facing elevations, simple to the point of banality, were offset by one richly faceted facade with corner windows and terraces that faced south toward a landscaped courtyard. At the site's southern end, a one-story building containing community facilities shielded the outdoor room from the traffic along Grand Street. The courtyard, not extensive enough to provide a real sense of *rus in urbe*, more closely resembled the open spaces of privately funded interwar projects in the outer boroughs than the typical postwar public housing project. The editors of *Architectural Record* nonetheless praised the Seward Park Extension as constituting "an enclave away from urban din."[67] The extension's eastern component, a similarly designed apartment tower, was completed in the same year at 154–156 Broome Street, between Clinton and Ridge streets. Here the slab's modeled facade faced east toward a landscaped open space, but the lack of an adjacent low-rise development, as well as the development's proximity to the approach of the Williamsburg Bridge, made the space considerably less tranquil and inviting.

Located immediately east of the Seward Park Extension's eastern component, Pedersen's combined facility for the Seventh Precinct of the New York City Police Department and Engine Company Seventeen and Ladder Company Eighteen, at 19½–25 Pitt Street, on the northwest corner of Broome Street, added a measure of architectural distinction to the area.[68] Completed in 1975, the two- and three-story building eschewed a traditional vocabulary while successfully achieving a vivid sense of civic authority. The design was a sculptural essay rendered in textured red brick, with deeply recessed windows, some of them vertical slits, and a recessed corner entrance marked by a column extended into a rounded corner above. Visually separating the fire and police facilities, a centrally located tower gave the building a notable skyline silhouette.

Although of less architectural interest than Pedersen's projects, three twenty-six-story low- and middle-income apartment towers surrounding St. Mary's Church helped to realize some of the practical if not aesthetic goals of the original Seward Park Extension proposal.[69] As designed by Frost Associates for the Grand Street Guild of St. Mary's Parish, the three red-brick towers were set back from the surrounding streets on generously scaled plazas. While the church was left intact and served as a much-needed grace note, it appeared dwarfed and stranded by its towering neighbors.

In 1973 the architects Roger A. Cumming and Waltrude Schleicher-Woods proposed a redevelopment plan—ultimately not realized—for the two blocks between the Bowery and Chrystie Street, directly north and south of East Houston Street.[70] The scheme proposed for the southern side a plan of buildings,

with chamfered corners, ranging in height from eight to fourteen stories. A small building housing a day-care center was to punctuate the landscaped space; ground-level stores, underground parking and rooftop recreational areas were to complete the plan. A similar scheme was proposed for the northern block, the most significant difference being that the northern perimeter wall, as well as portions of the eastern one, were to incorporate previously existing buildings. While the proposal reflected the designers' association with the architect and urban planner Shadrach Woods, who began his career in the office of Le Corbusier, and the work Woods did with his partners Georges Candilis and Alexis Josic, it was more notable as a return to traditional New York housing types. Perhaps the most important local influence was Andrew J. Thomas's extensive courtyard apartment house developments, built in Jackson Heights during the interwar period.[71]

Though the eradication of substandard housing on the Lower East Side was without question the primary goal of both public- and private-sector interests, one of the architectural high points of the area's postwar transformation was not a residential project but a community center. The Arts for Living Center (1975), at the northwest corner of Grand and Willett streets, was the only truly significant antidote to the dreary uniformity imposed by so many of the surrounding public housing projects.[72] The art center's sophisticated design, by Lo-Yi Chan of Prentice & Chan, Ohlhausen, also offered a trenchant reflection of evolving Modernist aesthetics and popular attitudes toward urbanistic contextualism. It was built by the venerable Henry Street Settlement, which the social reformer Lillian Wald had founded in 1893 to serve the practical and cultural needs of the area's poor. The new building housed extensive facilities for dance, music and art, an underground eighty-seat recital hall and an experimental performance space. It also contained backstage facilities for, and was internally linked to, the settlement's well-known Federal-style Henry Street Playhouse (F. Burrall Hoffman and Harry Creighton Ingalls, 1915), at the northeast corner of Grand and Pitt streets, the auditorium of which was renovated as part of the new building program.

Chan arranged his building in an arc surrounding a generously proportioned entrance courtyard opening out to Grand Street. The courtyard, which could be utilized as an outdoor performance space, contained four distinct levels separated by short, curved flights of stairs that served double duty as bleacher seats. To the plaza's west, a narrow wing was built out to the lot line. Rising to the height of the adjacent playhouse, it helped maintain the existing street wall and, with its red-brick cladding and dark mortar, visually enhanced and honored the surrounding historic buildings. The connection between the playhouse and the art center was further emphasized by the continuation of the white coping that decorated the parapet and roofline of the older building; changes in the art center's brick patterns coordinated with the playhouse's stringcourses.

Directly north of the new arts center stood the Bialystoker Synagogue. Between the arts center and the synagogue, an enclosed plaza terminated in a curved wall facing the street. The regular window pattern of the art center's southern facade achieved at least some visual harmony with the synagogue's severe symmetries and stood in sharp contrast to the syncopated fenestration of both the straight and curved facades defining the Grand Street courtyard.

For all this, Chan's design was modest. As Suzanne Stephens wrote: "This building may not necessarily elicit exalted rhetoric to evoke its architectonic forms or spaces. Nor may it swiftly stir

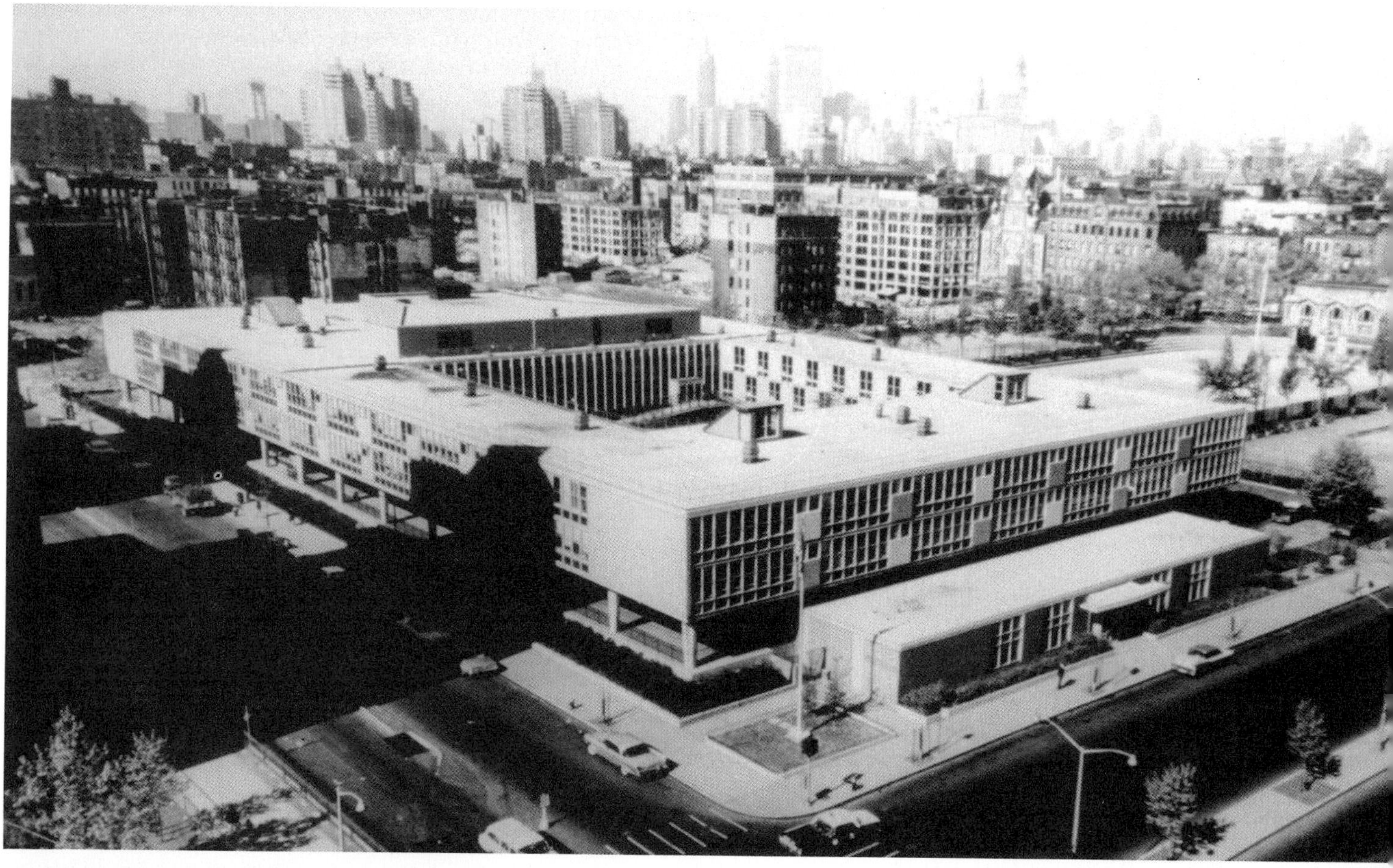

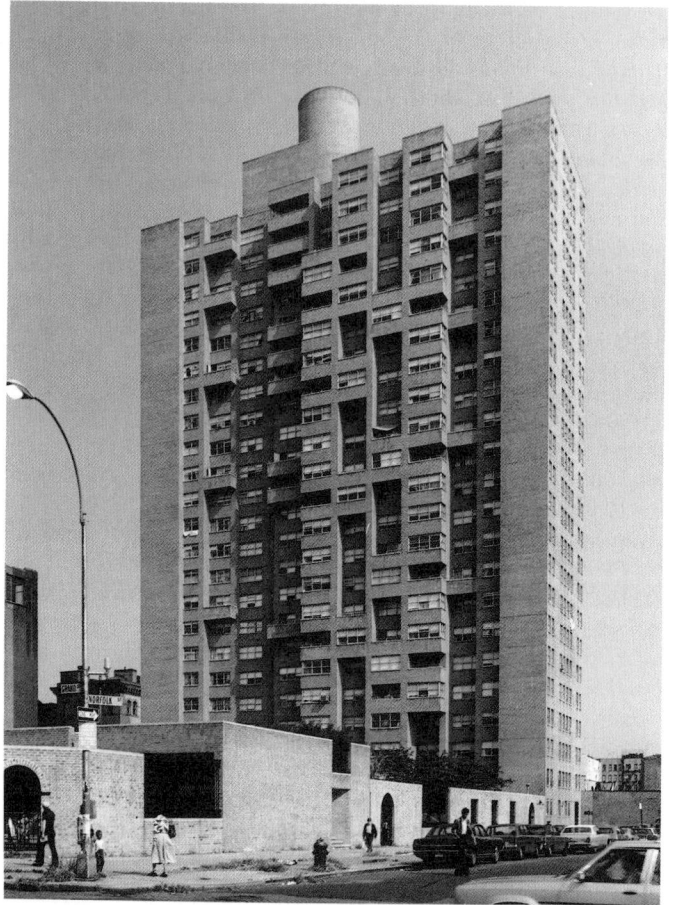

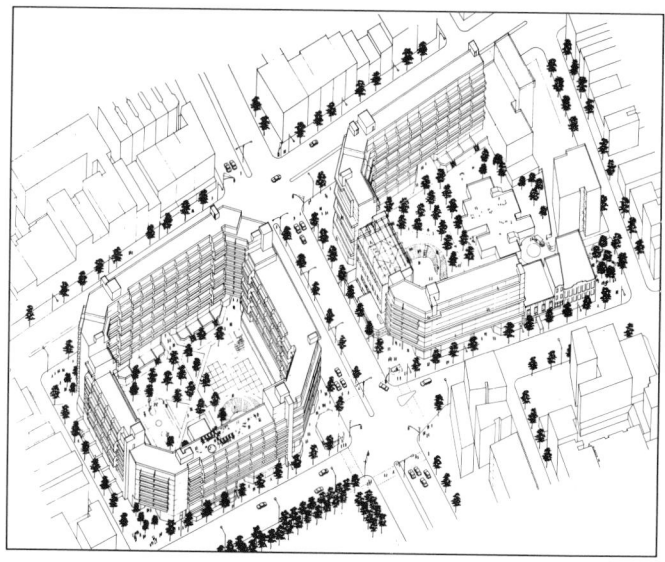

Top: Hamilton Fish Park branch of the New York Public Library and Junior High School 22, southwest corner of East Houston and Columbia streets. Kelly & Gruzen, 1956. View to the southwest. GS

Bottom left: Extension to the Seward Park Houses, Grand to Broome Street, Essex to Norfolk Street. William F. Pedersen, 1973. View to the northwest. NYCHA

Bottom right: Proposal for redevelopment of two blocks, one bounded by the Bowery, Stanton, Christie and East Houston streets and the other by the Bowery, East Second Street, Second Avenue and East Houston Street. Roger A. Cumming and Waltrude Schleicher-Woods, 1973. RAC architects to controversy and diatribe." Yet, Stephens noted, the building's contextualism was significant: "Architecturally, the center could best be described as a 'background' building [that] with its dark red brick takes on the 'dumb and ordinary' character of its surroundings. . . . Not too long ago . . . a building, if it were a well-designed thing unto itself, would de facto harmonize with the surrounding environment. Several hundred travertine blockbusters later, a new attitude pervades."[73] Ada Louise Huxtable was even more lavish in her praise:

> The Arts for Living Center . . . is a building meant to serve and expand the life of a community, and no better definition of architecture exists than that. The fact that it is a good building, not only in the fulfillment of the basic objective but also in terms of the more esthetic qualitative criteria in which architecture deals, makes it doubly satisfying. . . . [The] public area carved out of the building site and flowing in from the street, yet part of the building itself, demonstrates architecture as a social and urban art in the very best sense.

Huxtable also acknowledged a hidden agenda within the building program: the provision for security in a high-crime, multiethnic and multiracial neighborhood. "Nothing in a building like this can be closed or hidden," she wrote. "Part of its function is to turn energies commonly directed to vandalism to other interests and pursuits. . . . Design becomes a kind of behavioral or architectural fencing to the end of making the building something more than an adversary environment."[74] Norval White and Elliot Willensky also praised the arts complex for its contribution to the neighborhood, saying that it was "a civic space in this wasteland of amorphous streets" and represented "a high moment of architecture."[75]

Chinatown

As many of Manhattan's most distinctive, ethnically defined neighborhoods began to lose some measure of their colorful and often rather gritty identities due to massive rebuilding programs, Chinatown seemed to hold on.[76] Even though Chinatown, like the rest of the Lower East Side, would become home to major publicly assisted housing projects, the special nature of the community, the fervent desire of residents to remain there despite cramped conditions, and the seemingly endless in-migration of Chinese, especially after the Communist takeover of their homeland in 1949, created special challenges to housing reformers. From the first, it was clear that any Pollyannaish notion of the "melting pot" would not apply. A tiny area bounded by the Bowery and Canal, Baxter and Worth streets, Chinatown's eleven blocks were estimated to contain 25,000 residents, nearly 80 percent of whom were of Chinese origin or descent. Most of the area's buildings were old- and new-law tenements that ranged in height from four to seven stories; the editors of the New York Times contended that "few, if any," contained elevators.[77] Sixty percent of Chinatown's buildings had been built before 1900 and nearly all were residential, with most containing commercial enterprises—often restaurants, groceries or funeral parlors—at street level. Though the desire to retain the area's distinct character was strong, it did not diminish the widely perceived need for some kind of renewal. Even more than in other parts of the Lower East Side, Chinatown's living conditions were deplorable, with small apartments commonly housing as many as ten people in rooms that lacked adequate light and ventilation. More than 70 percent of the area's apartments did not have private bathrooms.

In 1950, shortly after mainland China's fall to Communism, Herman T. Stichman, New York State Housing Commissioner, announced plans for massive slum clearance in Chinatown, to be sponsored in part by the American Legion.[78] According to the New York Times, Stichman "had asked the help of President Truman for his favorite project of clearing the slums of Chinatown and setting up a 'China Village' neighborhood community there."[79] Stichman's plan called for the construction of three housing projects that would, as the Times described it, help transform "a quaint city landmark of 25,000 cramped residents into a sun-lit, park-filled area retaining aspects of Chinese life such as 'pagoda touched' architecture."[80] While cautioning local residents that new antidiscrimination laws required housing projects to be open to all, Stichman also promised them that existing businesses would be accommodated and that the rebuilt district would retain its distinctly Chinese identity. He explained, for instance, that new housing projects would contain floors reserved exclusively for the large number of Chinese bachelors—as a result of the mass migration of Chinese men in the mid-nineteenth century and the subsequent Chinese Exclusion Act of 1882, four-fifths of Chinatown's residents were male.

Employing his characteristically caustic tone, Robert Moses, in his role as New York City Construction Coordinator, ridiculed Stichman's proposal as a "celestial promise" that would inevitably take the community for "a lovely rickshaw ride." Moses charged that the State Housing Commissioner had passed off "as an accomplished fact something that is only a figment of [Stichman's] busy imagination" and that the plan's public announcement amounted to little more than "what might be called a slip of the Tong." Arguing that the plan was economically unfeasible, Moses sniped, "Perhaps you have Chinese money available for this purpose."[81] Stichman responded to Moses's comments in a seven-page letter, labeling Moses the "City Construction Obstructor" and dismissing his humor as sophomoric and derogatory. Defending the proposal's intention to at least in part incorporate a traditional Chinese architectural vocabulary, Stichman asked, "Must all New York housing have vertical lines, no adornment, no imagination, and much red brick and dullness?" Seemingly offered as a warning to Moses, if not a prediction, Stichman quoted a Chinese saying: "Those who would control the world eventually embrace only emptiness."[82]

Stichman proceeded with his plans, consulting with the China Institute on the possibility of establishing a cultural center in Chinatown, as well as other ways to integrate aspects of Chinese culture into the area's development. The institute's director suggested the construction of tea gardens and pagodas. In 1954 Stichman released drawings that showed two anonymously designed perpendicular slabs rising from a parking lot on a two-acre triangular site bounded by Park Row, Worth and Baxter streets and incorporating the southernmost block of Mulberry Street, which was to be closed.[83] In an essentially misguided attempt at contexuality, the building's elevator penthouses were to be treated as pagodas, and a two-story commercial building, to be located at the corner of Worth and Baxter streets, was to feature a Chinese roof and pagoda. Despite Stichman's perseverance, Moses's original charges of insufficient funds seemed to have been true, and the project was never realized.

With the demolition of the Third Avenue Elevated in 1955, the eastern edge of Chinatown was particularly ripe for redevelopment. In 1956 plans were announced for a large-scale housing development just east of Chinatown's traditional bound-

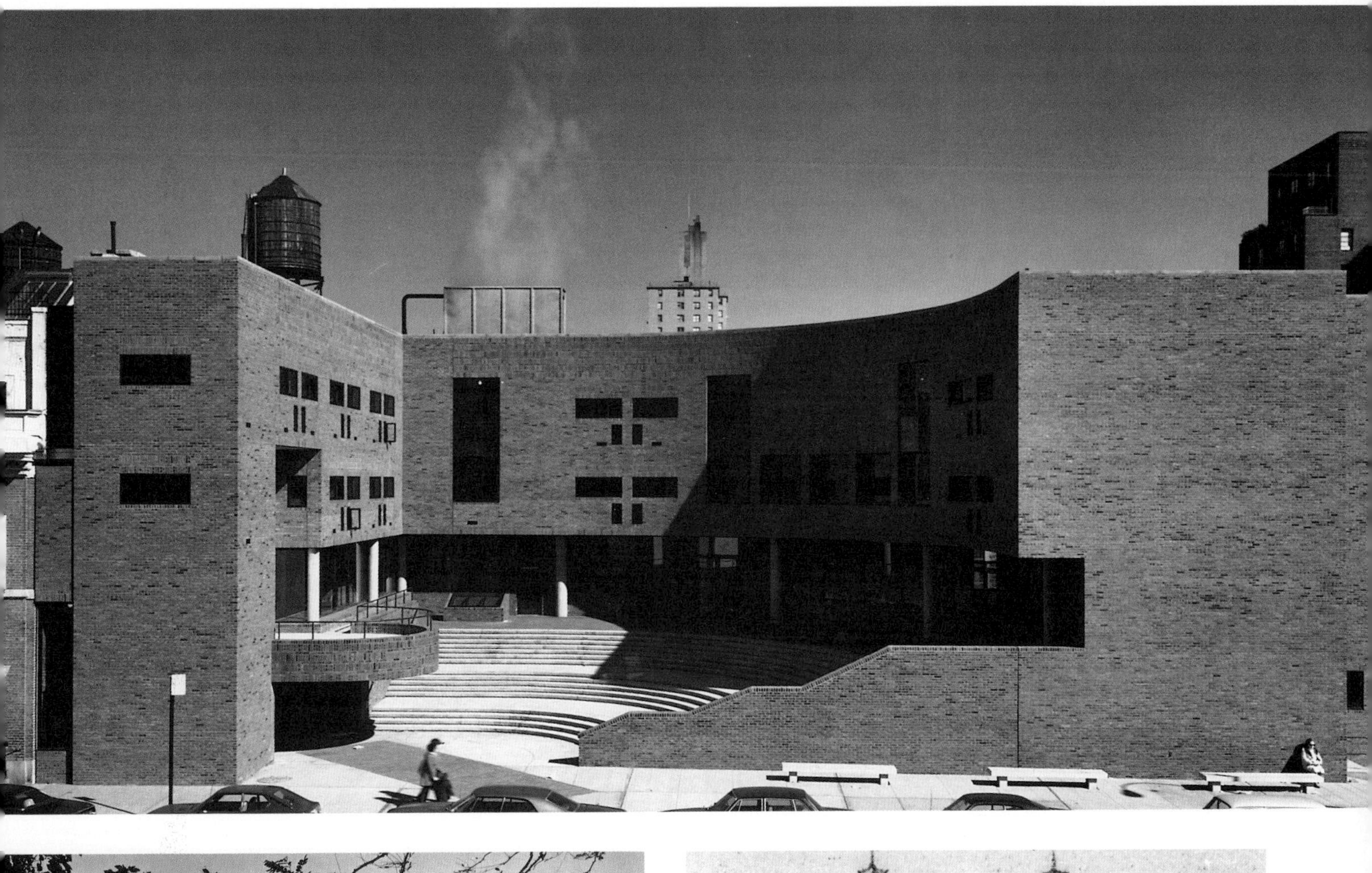

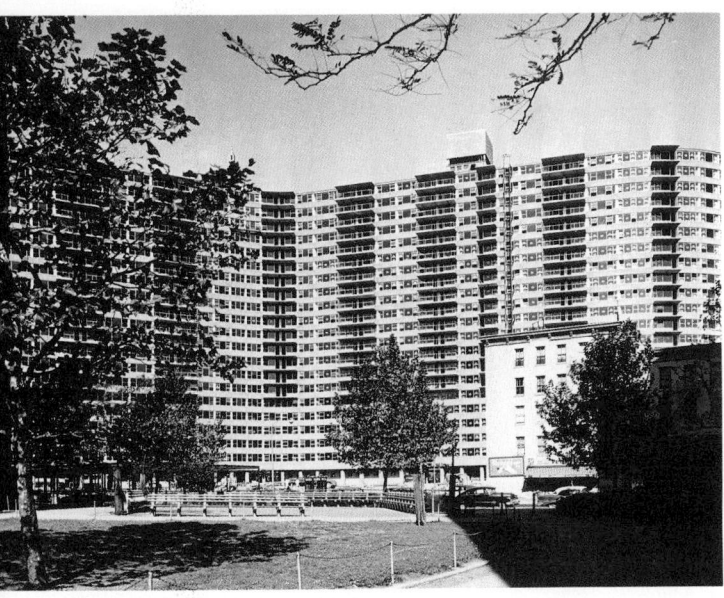

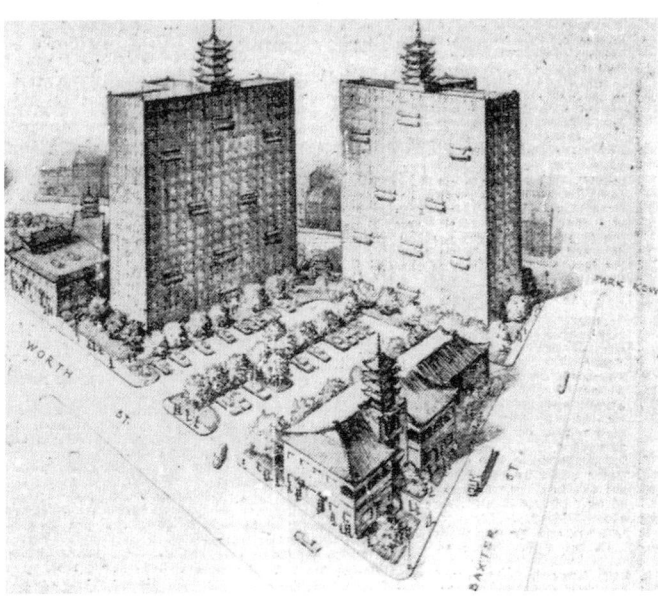

Top: Arts for Living Center, northwest corner of Grand and Willett streets. Prentice & Chan, Ohlhausen, 1975. View to the north showing the Henry Street Playhouse (F. Burrall Hoffman and Harry Creighton Ingalls, 1915) on the left. PCO

Bottom left: Chatham Green, Pearl Street to St. James Place, Park Row to Madison Street. Kelly & Gruzen, 1961. View to the northwest. GS

Bottom right: Proposed China Village, block bounded by Park Row, Worth and Baxter streets, 1954. Rendering of view to the southeast. NYT

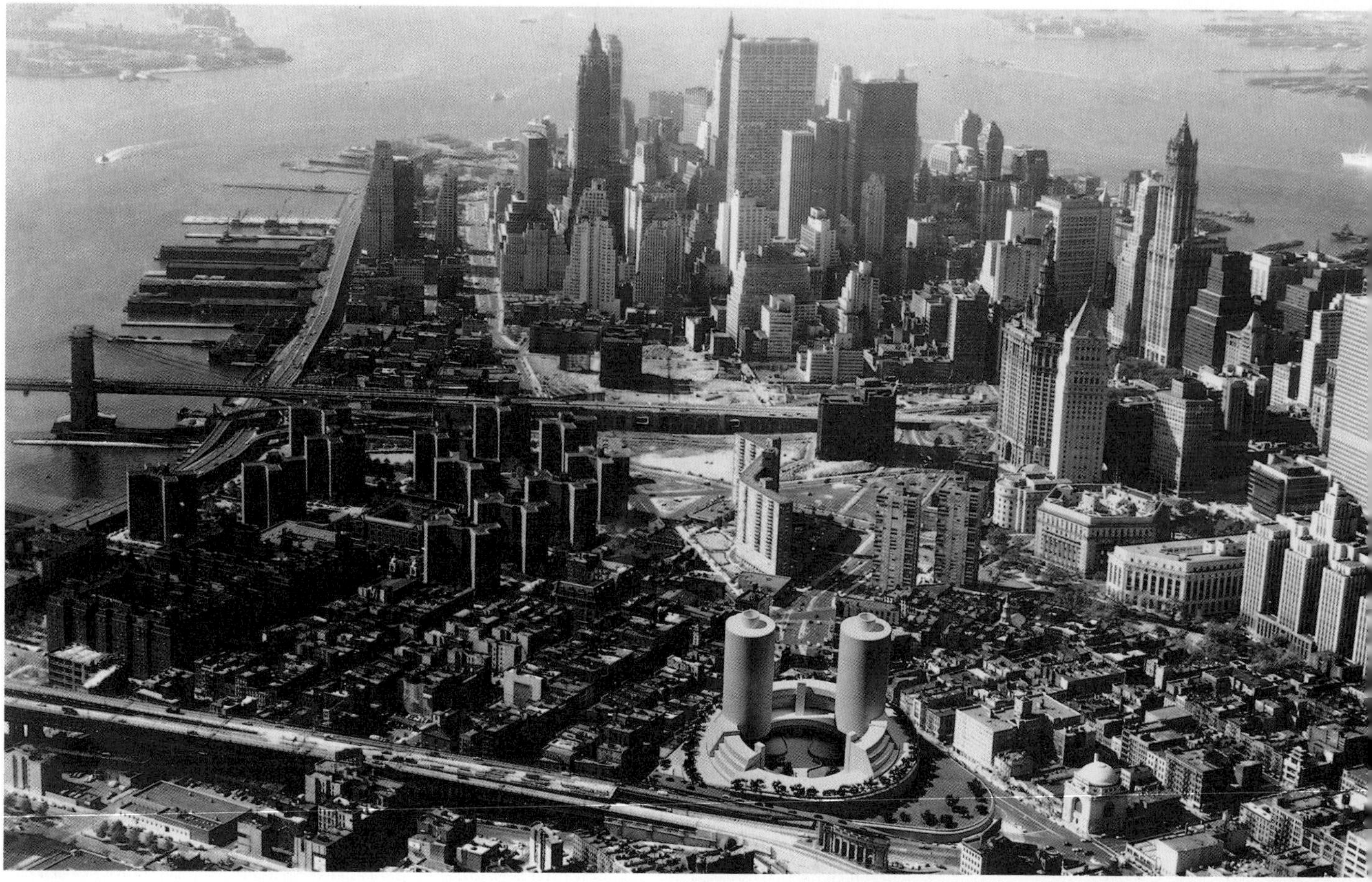

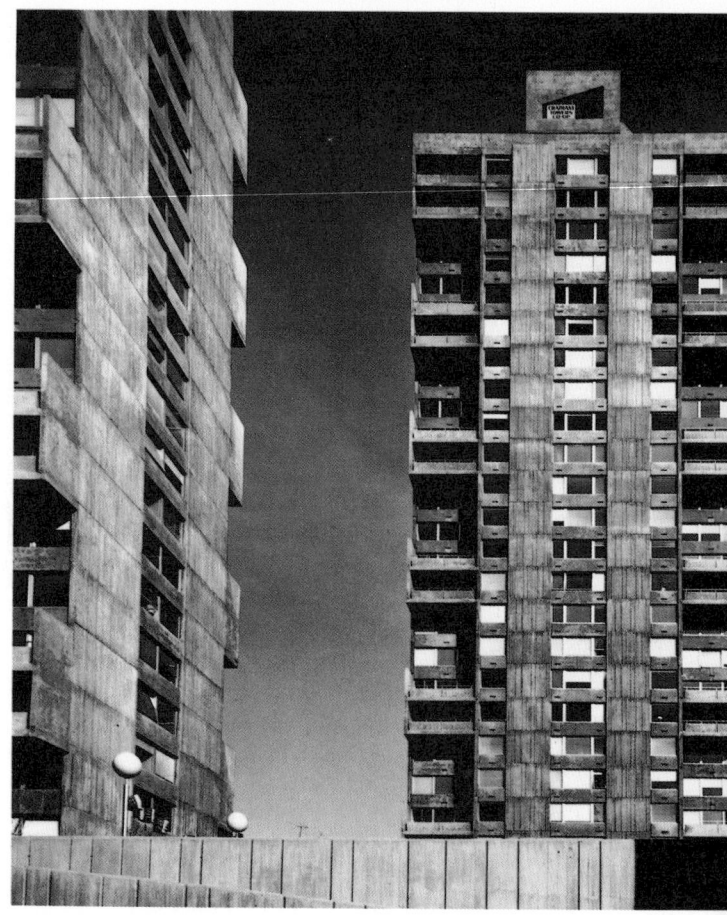

Above: Proposed Confucius Plaza, block bounded by the Bowery, Canal Street and the approach to the Manhattan Bridge. Horowitz & Chun, 1969. Photographic montage showing view to the south. WFC

Right: Chatham Towers, between Park Row, Worth and Baxter streets. Kelly & Gruzen, 1965. View to the east. GS

aries, north of the Brooklyn Bridge along Park Row. The project, Chatham Green, completed in 1961, was a twenty-one-story, middle-income cooperative housing 450 families.[84] Sponsored by the Municipal Credit Union and the New York State Credit Union League under Title I provisions, the project occupied a 4.5-acre site bounded by Park Row, Pearl Street, Madison Street and St. James Place, located directly east of Stichman's unrealized project. Given its proximity to the civic center area and to the financial district, Chatham Green was, as Manhattan Borough President Hulan Jack put it, a "central factor" in the city's plans to revitalize lower Manhattan as a "walk-to-work" community.[85] Designed by the firm of Kelly & Gruzen, Chatham Green was a colossally long brick-clad serpentine structure that reflected the form of Le Corbusier's Obus Plan of 1931 for the rebuilding of Algiers as interpreted by Affonso Eduardo Reidy, whose Pedregulho housing project, begun in 1947 outside Rio de Janeiro, Brazil, had recently been visited by Barney Gruzen.[86] Abandoning traditional interior corridors, Chatham Green incorporated open-access galleries that provided through-ventilation and a minimum of two exposures for each apartment. By 1979 Paul Goldberger found that the serpentine housing project, though "a well-meaning attempt at innovation," seemed "dated" and "too earnest, too eager to be 'designed' to be convincing."[87]

In 1960 a new project, Chatham Towers, was announced for the crowded two-acre site previously slated for Stichman's development.[88] The site was covered by thirty-one buildings, the last remaining fragment of Five Points, the notorious nineteenth-century slum. Among the run-down, architecturally undistinguished buildings, however, was one beloved local landmark, O'Rourke's Saloon, at 446 Pearl Street, which the New York Times described as "a high-toned 'hangout' for a weird assortment of millionaire playboys, boxers, promoters, showgirls, politicians and bums" and "one of the last links with the gay life on the Bowery in the old days."[89] Chatham Towers, a cooperative development catering to a somewhat more affluent group than Chatham Green, was built by the Committee for Middle Income Housing under Title I. The complex consisted of two twenty-five-story towers, each containing 120 units. Kelly & Gruzen were also the architects for Chatham Towers, but this time Gruzen gave the project to a team of young designers, including his son Jordan, as well as Richard D. Kaplan and Mario Romanach.

Despite a tight budget, the design of Chatham Towers conveyed a sense of luxury and decisively broke with the prevailing institutional look of subsidized housing. The towers occupied only 15 percent of the site; parking for 125 cars was tucked underground and the resulting open space was imaginatively designed by the landscape architect M. Paul Friedberg with play areas as well as a formal plaza. The slender tower *parti* made it possible to have only five apartments to a floor, with all but one having corner exposures. Half of the towers' apartments had terraces. The use of exposed, board-formed concrete succeeded, to some extent, in visually linking the buildings to the limestone and granite buildings of the nearby civic center and at the same time set them apart not only from the typical tenements of Chinatown but also from the more mundane red brick of Chatham Green and the Alfred E. Smith Houses, both of which were just to the east. The towers featured a number of technological innovations: they were the first to incorporate the exclusive use of drywall as opposed to more labor-intensive plaster, and the first high-rise apartments in the city to use urethane insulation behind their exterior walls. They also introduced a

Swedish-designed window that sandwiched a venetian blind between two layers of glass and pivoted open for ventilation and cleaning.

For Norval White and Elliot Willensky, the complex immediately joined the ranks of "distinguished housing architecture," along with the Dakota, Butterfield House (see chapter 4), 131–135 East 66th Street and Williamsburg Houses, "its peers from all eras."[90] Paul Goldberger, writing in 1979, said that Chatham Towers, in contrast to its neighbor, Chatham Green, "has aged well, and even though it could be called heavy-handed Corbusier (which it clearly is), it is well-scaled, comfortable, and visually attractive—qualities which help any building survive the passage of time."[91] Also writing in 1979, John Tauranac described the towers as "remarkable" and noted that at the time of their completion, "nothing like them had ever been seen in New York, a pair of towers that seem carved out of gritty cliffs of concrete."[92]

Successful as the composition of Chatham Towers was, with its bold sculptural presence, the design lacked the crucial linkages to the overall neighborhood fabric that might have rescued it from the status of a "project." While the building's outdoor spaces were formally successful, their designer, M. Paul Friedberg, astutely pointed out that "what is wrong with the whole thing, and it's a major point, is that it is an insular development, focussing in on itself. This plaza should open out and link up with others."[93] Writing in Progressive Architecture, the critic Ellen Perry turned her attention more toward the project's handling of broad housing and urban renewal issues than to its design aspects. Reflecting the increased populism of the late 1960s, Perry questioned the Corbusier-inspired aesthetics of the design: "We know very little about what people respond to, and want, and need in their environment. It may be that form is irrelevant. . . . Many buildings, today, are being built with chinoiserie and its esthetic (or ethnic) equivalents. Are such buildings necessarily, and by that fact alone, worse to live in than Chatham Towers?"[94]

By 1969 the explosive growth of Chinatown's population led to Confucius Plaza, a massive development on a triangular, 6.5-acre site bounded by the Manhattan Bridge, the Bowery, Division and Canal streets. As originally planned by the firm of Horowitz & Chun, the project was to be jointly financed by the city's Educational Construction Fund and its Housing and Development Administration.[95] The scheme was to incorporate an access road for the proposed Lower Manhattan Expressway (see chapter 4), wrapping around a nine-story base that would contain a three-story-school—Public School 124—and a playground in an "open air core," as well as six stories of duplex apartments. The base would support a pair of twenty-five-story cylindrical apartment towers providing a total of 550 units on a site that before demolition had contained only sixty-four residential and twenty-four commercial tenants.

By the time of its opening in 1976, Confucius Plaza, which was initially projected for a 1972 completion, had been completely redesigned by W. F. Chun, and its site had become one of the most intensively developed in the city.[96] It contained 762 apartments, as well as a 1,200-student school, 55,000 square feet of shops and community space, a 7,500-square-foot day-care center and a 230-car subterranean garage. The previous tower-on-base scheme had been abandoned, along with the idea of wrapping it with the access ramp (the Lower Manhattan Expressway had by this time been defeated). Chun adopted a bent-slab *parti*, gathering the apartments into a stepped semicircle that at its extremities was nineteen stories tall and reached a forty-four-story height at the center. The enormous building sheltered a south-facing plaza, along the edges of which the lower three stories projected forward to create a more intimate scale and to help buffer the apartments above from the lower-floor public realm. Norval White and Elliot Willensky found the curving slab of the unusually shaped building "arbitrary, but a pleasant skyline form."[97] Inside, the curving configuration resulted in apartments that, according to Suzanne Stephens, were "unusual (if not quirky)."[98] The double-loaded corridor condemned many units to an exclusively northern orientation, but the absence of direct sunlight in these units was more than compensated for by spectacular views toward midtown. While the curving slab did provide amenities, such as the partially enclosed, 24,000-square-foot public plaza, which the initial tower-on-podium scheme would not have included, the height and length of the wall it created along the low-scale boundary streets was overpowering.

CIVIC CENTER

The struggle to conceive of and articulate a suitable and comprehensive architectural expression of New York's civic identity—a struggle that had plagued the city since the 1890s—continued almost unabated throughout the postwar period.[1] Once again the struggle seemed, at least in part, to be a reflection of New York's obsession with its own relentlessly commercial character and its peculiar status as one of a few internationally important cities in the world that was not also a national capital. As in the past, New York's postwar efforts to build a coherent civic center in lower Manhattan were hampered by aesthetic confusion, bureaucratic inefficiency and public ambivalence.

On June 24, 1948, the City Planning Commission released a plan for the redevelopment of the City Hall area.[2] Titled *Manhattan Civic Center and Related Improvements*, the commission's report asserted that City Hall (John McComb, Jr., and Joseph F. Mangin, 1803–12) was one of the nation's most architecturally distinguished civic buildings and accordingly should serve as the focus of a district that "deserves special consideration and offers unusual opportunities for appropriate planning to provide for various activities of the City government."[3] To this end, the commission proposed that the former New York County Courthouse (Thomas Little, John Kellum and Leopold Eidlitz, 1861–81), popularly known as the Tweed Courthouse after the notoriously crooked politician William Marcy ("Boss") Tweed, under whose administration it was built, be demolished to make way for parkland. It also recommended that a new municipal courts building, as well as municipal office buildings, be erected on the west side of Foley Square; that warehouses and office buildings clustered near the Manhattan approach to the Brooklyn Bridge be torn down to provide a suitably monumental landscaped setting for the bridge; and that major traffic improvements be implemented, including the widening of Chambers Street, the extension of Lafayette Street south from Worth to Chambers Street, and the construction of a road tunneled under City Hall Park to run from the Brooklyn Bridge to Chambers Street. Prior to the plan's first public hearing, the editors of the *New York Times*, pinpointing problems that had long plagued previous efforts to realize a coherent civic center, stated that the plan "proposes the rehabilitation of an area in the city that has existed without plan and with few alterations in almost a century." The editors also noted that, as Alexander Chapin, executive manager of the Borough of Manhattan, had

charged, "public apathy to the project could be as dangerous as organized opposition."[4]

Approval of the plan, which did not grant the authority to realize specific projects but was intended to serve merely as a guideline for future development, proceeded, as the editors of *Interiors* put it, "at a snail's pace."[5] Final commission approval was granted on May 24, 1949. On August 10, 1950, the commission approved map changes that permitted the widening of Frankfort Street, an improvement that required the demolition of the Pulitzer Building, also known as the New York World-Telegram Building (George B. Post, 1890), and the Brooklyn Bridge Freezing and Cold Storage Company plant; they were demolished in 1955.

The same year saw the completion of Lorimer Rich Associates' New York State Insurance Fund Building.[6] Located at 199 Church Street, between Thomas and Duane streets, the fifteen-story building was a competent if not particularly distinguished essay in Le Corbusier–inspired Modernism. Above a base clad in polished red granite, white-glazed-brick spandrels alternated with strip windows framed by metal eyebrows. The principal entrance was marked by a stainless-steel canopy. In 1979 Paul Goldberger would write that "there is nothing remarkable about the building except for the fact that it is visually pleasing, which few fifteen-story white-brick structures with horizontal strip windows in New York are."[7]

The Civil Courthouse and Municipal Courts Building, designed by William Lescaze and Matthew Del Gaudio, became the first municipally sponsored postwar addition to the civic center area when it was completed in 1960 on the former site of the Criminal Courts Building (Thom, Wilson & Schaarschmidt, 1894), bounded by Center, Elm, Franklin and White streets.[8] The old building, which at the time of its completion had been lambasted by the editors of *Architectural Record* as "the most discreditable edifice the city has ever erected," had previously been connected, by a "bridge of sighs" over Franklin Street, to the castellated municipal prison, widely known as the Tombs (Withers & Dick, 1897), at 53–67 Lafayette Street.[9] With the completion of the new courts building, the block of Franklin Street between Lafayette and Centre streets was closed and the site of the former prison unified with the new building's site.

Twenty years earlier Park Commissioner Robert Moses had advocated the replacement of the Tombs with a park.[10] Though Moses criticized the prison as the area's "only blot on the landscape" and an "ugly and obsolete building," his efforts to tear it down were thwarted, at least for a while.[11] In February 1942, three months after the correctional facility was closed, its function having been taken over by a new Criminal Courts Building and Prison (Harvey Wiley Corbett and Charles B. Meyers, 1939),[12] the city Fire Department announced that it would remodel the building to serve as a "college" for training firemen.[13] As part of the city's participation in the war, the iron bars of the prison cells were to be removed and donated to the federal government as scrap metal. Alternate plans to convert the former prison into an office building were also considered. In 1948, however, the building was torn down and replaced by nothing more than a city-owned parking lot.[14] Though the elimination of the Franklin Street block in 1960 helped the site to serve visually as a forecourt to the new building, the area was still maintained as a parking lot.

Lescaze and Del Gaudio's near-cubic, twelve-story courthouse was clad in limestone, with the exception of a one-story base of glass and dark polished granite. A large expanse of aluminum-framed windows alternating with dark polished span-

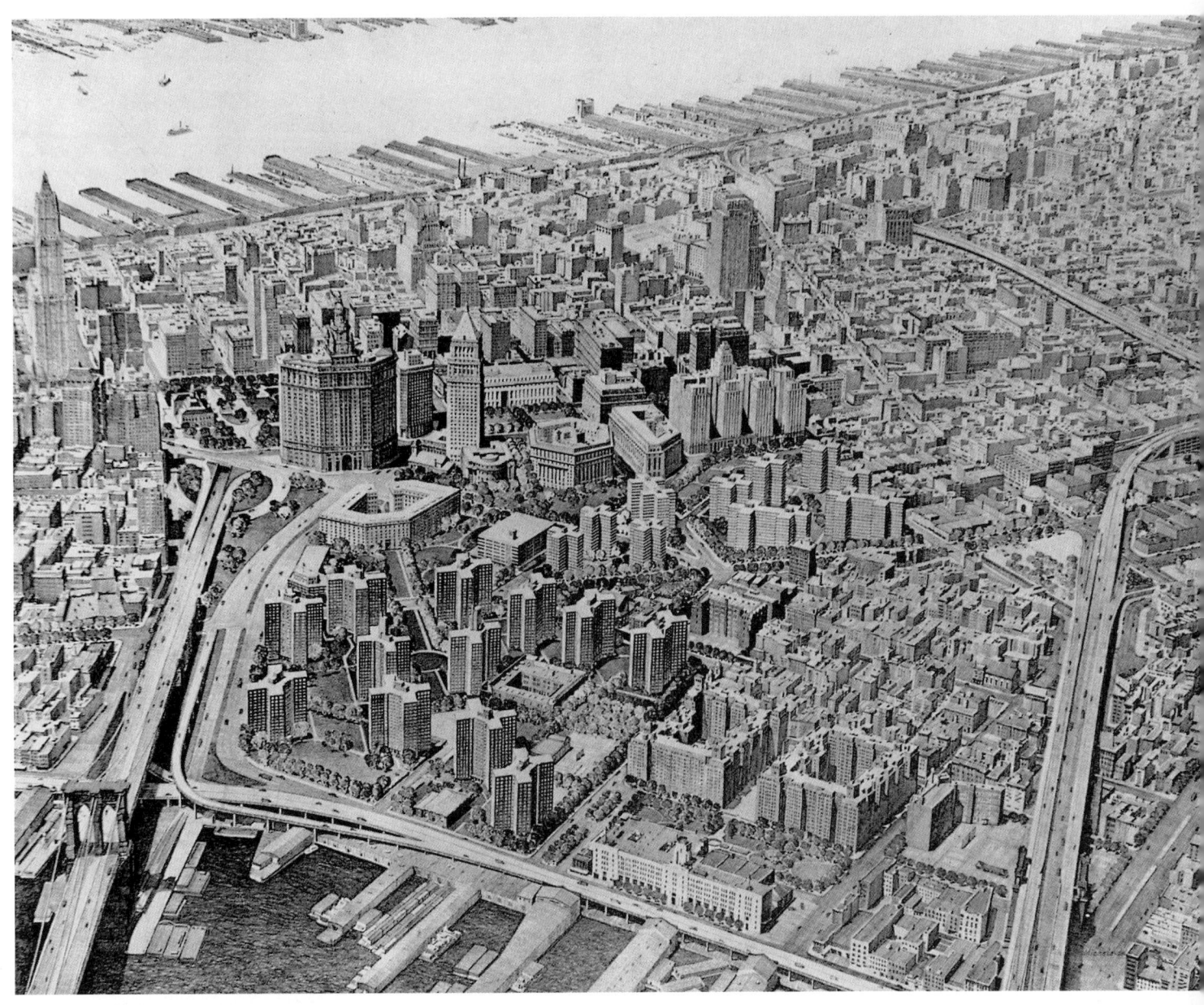

Proposed redevelopment of the Civic Center area by the New York City
Planning Commission, 1948. Rendering of view to the west with
proposed Lower Manhattan Expressway on the right. NYC

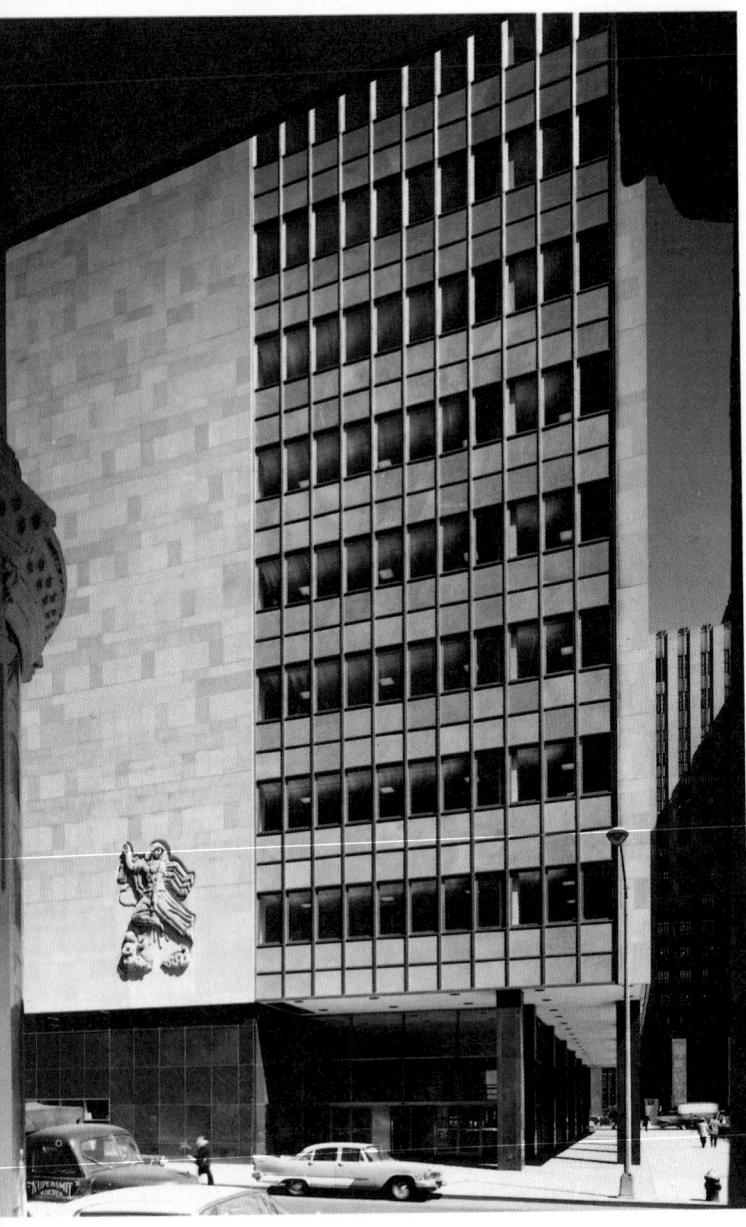

Civil Courthouse and Municipal Courts Building, Franklin to White Street, Lafayette to Centre Street. William Lescaze and Matthew Del Gaudio, 1960. View to the east. Molitor. JWM

drels faced the park. Narrow, similarly articulated glass areas punctuated the facades fronting Centre and Lafayette streets. Inside, the building incorporated windowless courtrooms and two distinct circulation systems: one intended for jurors and judges, another for lawyers and the general public. The court building was characterized by Norval White and Elliot Willensky as "a sleek but dull cube."[15] A similar assessment was made by Paul Goldberger, writing in 1979, nineteen years after the building's completion: "[This] is what happens when the modernists make it clear that they know better than all that old fancy stuff and try to strip it down. . . . [The] building is just a bland box, period."[16]

The severity of the building's predominantly limestone facades was relieved to some degree by two bas-relief sculptures. Facing Lafayette Street, Joseph Kiselewski's *Justice* (1960) depicted the allegorical figure of Justice protecting a baby from a snake.[17] Facing Centre Street, *Law* (1960), a work by William Zorach, one of the country's leading practitioners of direct carving, presented a family surrounding a judge in the process of taking an oath, as well as a young woman reading a book (a symbolic representation of wisdom), all set against an abstract evocation of New York City.[18]

The two sculptures, as well as an interior mural by the painter Umberto Romano, were commissioned by the Department of Public Works after the building's design had been completed. Though Lescaze publicly stated at the building's dedication on April 30, 1961, that he did not object to the artists' work, he vehemently protested the fact that he was excluded from the selection process. Lescaze later said that he was "fed up" with traditional artistic treatments such as those adorning the courthouse,[19] but a spokesman for the Department of Public Works cavalierly dismissed Lescaze's criticism, responding: "The courthouse is a public building. It is not a work of art or a work of culture. It is a place to work."[20] Several notable members of the artistic and architectural communities quickly rallied behind Lescaze. Harold Weston, who served as the president of the National Council on Arts and Government, stated, "We're 100 percent behind [Lescaze]. They should have worked together from the start instead of being brought in as an afterthought—an embellishment."[21] The architect Wallace K. Harrison said, "Certainly the architect should be in charge, otherwise, there will be no unified design."[22] The editors of the *New York Times* also defended Lescaze, stating: "For the architect to select the team is a reasonable and even imperative arrangement if our public buildings are not to run the risk of esthetic scrambling." The editors went on to raise broader and more profound issues: "A master plan for the relationship of the elements composing such projects as city centers is as necessary esthetically as it is practically. Architecture, traditionally the mother of sculpture and painting, has social responsibilities today on a scale not even approached in the past. A very large part of that responsibility is the creation of a harmonious environment from the hodge-podge of our cities."[23]

On June 11, 1959, the Board of Estimate approved preliminary plans for a major group of buildings, including a new eighteen- to twenty-one-story municipal building, to augment McKim, Mead & White's monumental Municipal Building of 1907–14.[24] Separate records and archives buildings were also planned, as well as a 640-car public garage. To accommodate the new buildings, two adjacent superblocks northeast of City Hall were to be created, collectively bounded by Park Row, Pearl Street, St. James Place and the extension of Robert F. Wagner, Sr. Place, and divided by Madison Street. The city commissioned Eggers & Higgins to design the new municipal building, the engineering and architectural firm of Praeger-Kavanagh-Waterbury to design the archives building, and the engineering and architectural firm of Rouse, Dubin & Ventura to design the garage; the designer of the records building was not announced.

In 1960, dismissing the city's proposal as "horse and buggy thinking" that would merely create "islands in a sea of traffic," the architect Nathan R. Ginsburg offered an alternate scheme wherein the city would acquire land to the east and south of City Hall Park and create a roughly circular plaza more than twice the size of the park.[25] Motor traffic would wind around the plaza in a semicircular loop connecting Foley Square to Broadway at Ann Street. The Brooklyn Bridge would be directly linked to the new loop road, as well as to Chambers Street via a tunnel beneath the plaza. New civic buildings, including a vast arc-shaped municipal building, would be built at the plaza's periphery. A public parking garage and a concourse connecting the area's subway lines would be built beneath the plaza. Though the editors of *Architectural Forum* asserted that "to advocate a course of action in New York City as an individual, or without diverse, widespread support is usually about as effective as a voice crying in the wilderness,"[26] by 1961 Ginsburg had succeeded in garnering the support of the New York Chapter of the American Institute of Architects and the Municipal Art Society, along with the 600-member Architects Council of New York, of which he served as president.

In February 1962, responding to Ginsburg's challenge, the city hired Max Abramovitz, Simon Breines and Robert W. Cutler of Skidmore, Owings & Merrill, assisted by the traffic planning specialists Day & Zimmerman, to survey the area and present yet another proposal.[27] Overseeing the coordination of the plan was Mayor Wagner's Civic Center Committee, consisting of James Felt, the chairman of the City Planning Commission; Peter Reidy, the commissioner of the Department of Public Works; William F. Shea, municipal budget director; Edward Dudley, Manhattan borough president; and Henry A. Barnes, the director of the Department of Traffic. The proposal, known as the ABC plan after the architects who devised it, defined the civic center as a roughly triangular, sixty-acre area bounded on the north by Canal Street, on the west by Broadway and on the east by Baxter Street and Park Row, with the eastern and western sides coming together at the triangle's apex south of City Hall. According to the ABC plan, all through streets below Worth Street were to be either totally or partially eliminated. The so-called Tweed Courthouse was to be demolished and a municipal office building erected on the northeast corner of Broadway and Chambers Street, with the latter artery reduced to a cul-de-sac.

The new office building would replace the New York Sun Building (originally the A. T. Stewart department store, John B. Snook, 1845–46; additions by Trench & Snook, 1850–51, and Edward D. Harris, 1884)[28] and, together with City Hall and the Hall of Records (John R. Thomas and Horgan & Slattery, 1899–1911),[29] form a triangle of prominent civic buildings set in a parklike setting. Bisecting the triangle, a grandly scaled, three-level landscaped mall would extend north of City Hall, incorporating subterranean parking for 1,100 cars, as well as a public concourse lined with shops and restaurants. The mall, which would span the remaining portion of Reade Street and necessitate the demolition of the robustly detailed, Modern French–style Emigrant Savings Bank Building (Raymond F. Almirall, 1909–10), at 51 Chambers Street,[30] would terminate in a towering new municipal building approximately forty stories tall. As indicated by a preliminary massing model, the new mu-

nicipal building would be a narrow slab, placed parallel to the remaining portion of Duane Street directly to the north, and would serve visually as a monumental backdrop to the gemlike City Hall.

Under the ABC plan, the site east of Park Row, where in 1948 the City Planning Commission had proposed a major concentration of civic buildings, would be utilized for middle-income housing. In addition, the ABC plan called for the widening of Worth Street to four lanes and the creation of an expressway connecting the Brooklyn Bridge to Canal Street. A family court building would also be located within the district, possibly on the west side of Lafayette Street, along with a police headquarters, perhaps at the district's northeast corner, on the full block bounded by Canal, Baxter, White and Centre streets. The Mayor's Civic Center Committee, overseeing the implementation of the plan, also petitioned the federal government's General Services Administration to move a projected federal office building and courthouse, which had been announced in 1960 but was not yet under construction, from its proposed site on the west side of Foley Square between Worth and Duane streets further west to abut Broadway. This would allow Broadway's street wall to be maintained and a more gracious distribution of buildings within the proposed parklike setting to be achieved.

Because the ABC plan had to incorporate many previously proposed buildings, it was a less than cohesive overall vision. So much was already committed to, if not necessarily designed, that the plan's realization required the allocation of only 10 percent more funding than had been earmarked for construction in the civic center area to date. Noting this advantageous financial situation, as well as the fact that the completion of the proposed buildings would save the city $2.5 million annually in office rentals, the Civic Center Committee urged that the ABC plan be adopted swiftly, and they outlined a schedule under which the center would be completed by 1967. As committee member James Felt somewhat dramatically stated: "To be sure we need more schools, hospitals, libraries and other improvements. But despite [New York City's] austerity program, we must move ahead with our Civic Center program at this time because we will never again have the opportunity that lies within our grasp."[31]

From the start the ABC plan proved highly controversial, especially with architects. Though City Planning Commission approval was granted in April 1963 and the city signed contracts with the architects Edward Durell Stone and the firm of Eggers & Higgins in the fall of 1963 to realize at least the general parameters of the plan, there was widespread, heated debate. Not surprisingly, Nathan Ginsburg criticized it, charging that the city was "working at breakneck speed to freeze things in the plan so that no changes can be made."[32] Elliot Willensky, head of the Action Group for Better Architecture in New York (AGBANY), which had spearheaded efforts to save Pennsylvania Station (see chapter 16), sought to promote public discussion of the plan, noting that a citywide newspaper strike immediately following its initial announcement had stymied proper discourse. The architect Norval White, who served as the acting chairman of the newly created advocacy group New Yorkers for a Civic Center of Excellence (NYCCE), claimed that the architects of the ABC plan had been presented "a very timid directive" by the city, gingerly adding that NYCCE was "criticizing those who gave the directive, not the architects."[33] Other architects were, however, not so diplomatic; a divisive debate raged within the New York Chapter of the American Institute of Architects, where some

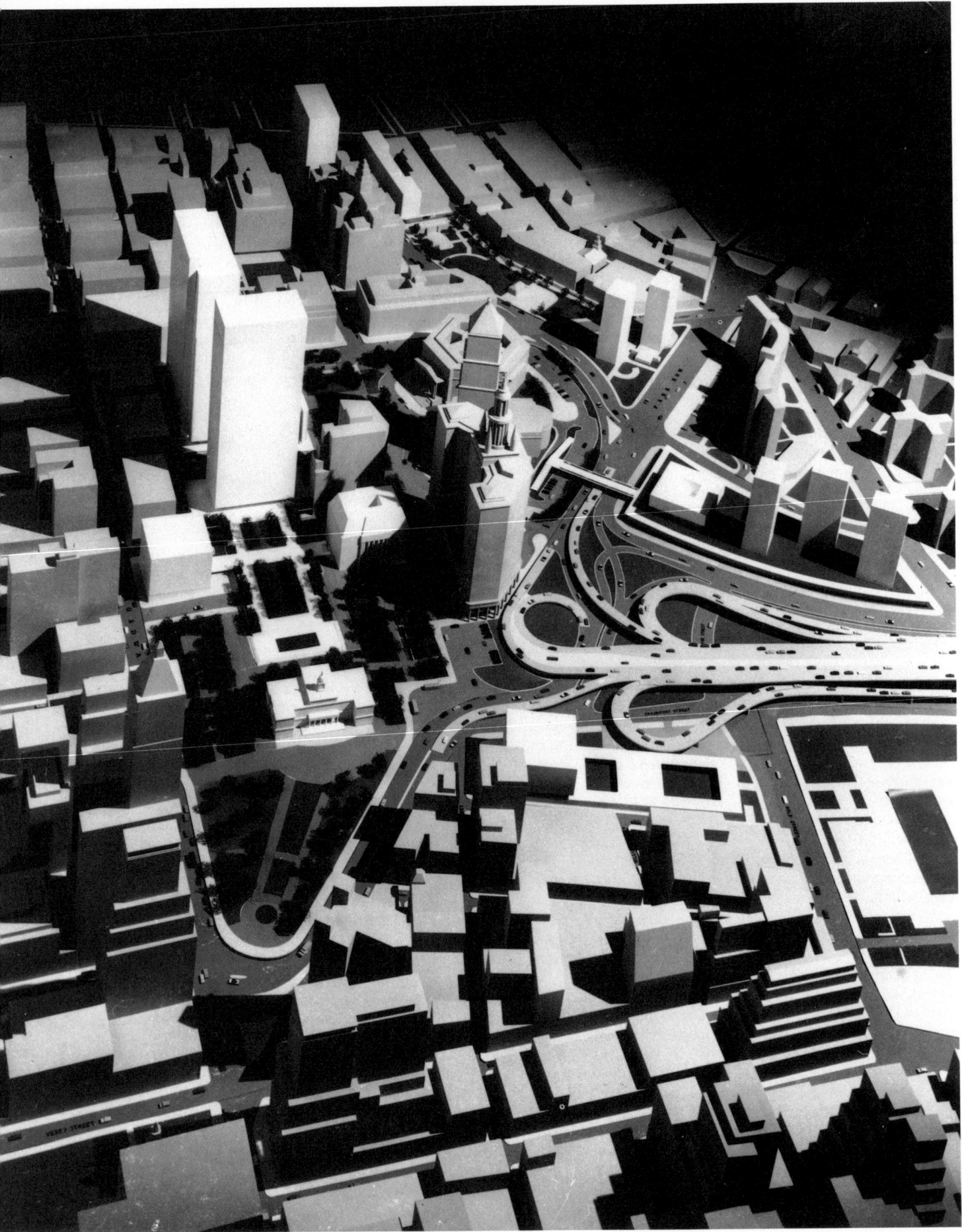

members pressed for an open design competition while others argued that because contracts had already been signed, such a competition was tantamount to a public assault on the commissioned architects' competence.

In August 1963, prior to the hiring of Stone and Eggers & Higgins, the businessman and philanthropist J. M. Kaplan had directly approached Mayor Wagner, offering in excess of $50,000 to sponsor a design competition. Wagner definitively rejected the suggestion, saying, according to Kaplan, "We have a good plan now."[34] Not everyone agreed. The esteemed British architect and urban planner Sir William Holford, who was responsible for the postwar reconstruction of the precincts around London's St. Paul's Cathedral, stated: "From a look at the proposed plan and model, the open space is merely an absence of building or what is left over between traffic lanes: it does not seem to have any amenity value in its own right."[35] The critic Lewis Mumford was even harsher: "Even at a glance," Mumford argued, "the plan shows that the major decision has already been made, not by architects or planners, but by highway engineers, whose Brooklyn Bridge interchange will sufficiently mangle the site to make its redemption all but impossible. In deference to the engineers' wishes, it would be wise to put all the buildings underground and turn the surface, now preempt, into even more complicated traffic spirals for achieving the ultimate triumph of the motor age: maximum speed and zero destination."[36] Even Le Corbusier offered his opinion, succinctly characterizing the plan as one of "frightful confusion."[37]

Kaplan continued to press the case for redesign, enlisting the participation of several members of the architectural community, who subsequently organized themselves into a group known as the Architectural 13; the group consisted of the architects Edward Larrabee Barnes, Marcel Breuer, Walter Gropius, Philip Johnson, I. M. Pei, Paul Rudolph and José Luis Sert; the scholar Burnham Kelly; the planner G. Holmes Perkins; the landscape architect Hideo Sasaki; Peter Blake and Douglas Haskell, critics and editors of *Architectural Forum*; and the critic and managing editor of *Progressive Architecture*, Jan Rowan. The group faulted the plan for failing to anticipate future governmental needs, provide for expansion, coordinate with surrounding areas and with other large-scale projects planned for lower Manhattan, and adequately handle traffic. The group's spokesman, Jan Rowan, claimed that as it had been presented, the ABC plan was "doomed to failure."[38]

Roger Starr, the director of the Citizens' Housing and Planning Council and a member of the Downtown–Lower Manhattan Association, forcefully countered Rowan's prediction; arguing that further delays in the design and approval processes might prevent any civic center plan from being realized, Starr said that the Architectural 13 "reduce themselves ultimately to the proposition that you cannot plan a civic center until you plan the area around it, that you cannot plan the area around it until you plan an even larger area around that, and carried to its ultimate conclusion, that you cannot plan a New York City Civic Center until successive landings have been made on the moon to discover the relevance of conditions there."[39] Despite Starr's strong stance, however, the mayor agreed to meet with the Architectural 13. Following several planning sessions, Stone and Eggers & Higgins modified their scheme, in part reflecting the group's suggestions.

The revised plan was presented in April 1964.[40] In place of the forty-story municipal office building to be erected directly behind City Hall, the modified and now fully articulated plan called for a fifty-four-story tower. Explaining his design, Stone

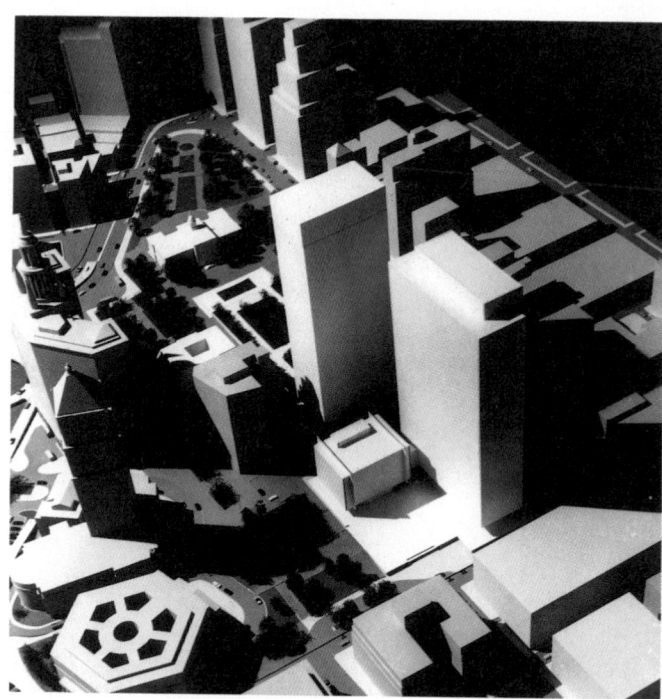

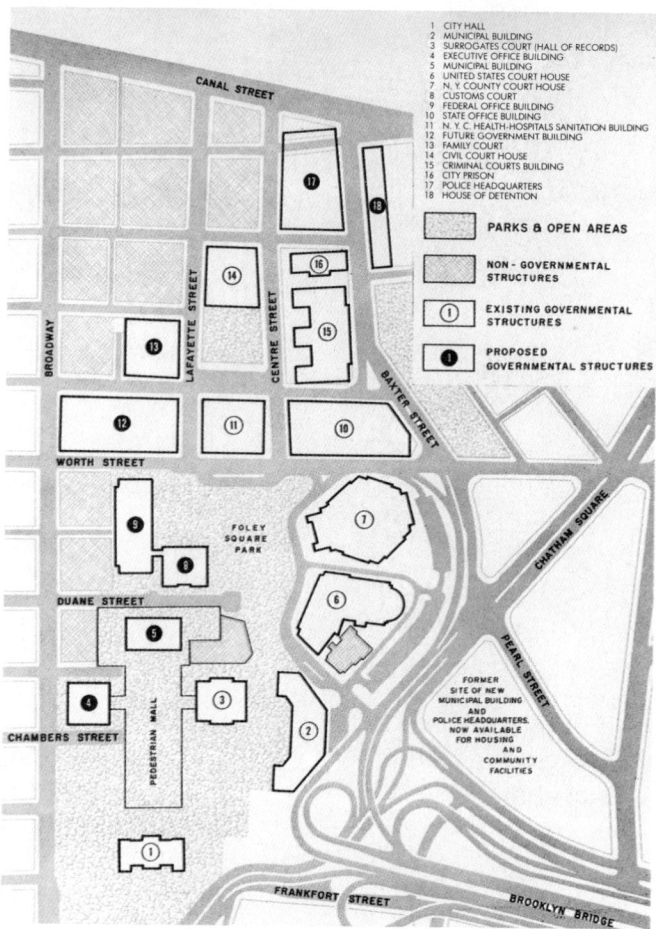

Left: ABC plan. Max Abramovitz, Simon Breines and Robert W. Cutler, 1962. Model. View to the northeast. AKS

Top: ABC plan. Model. View to the southwest. AKS

Bottom: ABC plan. Site plan. PB

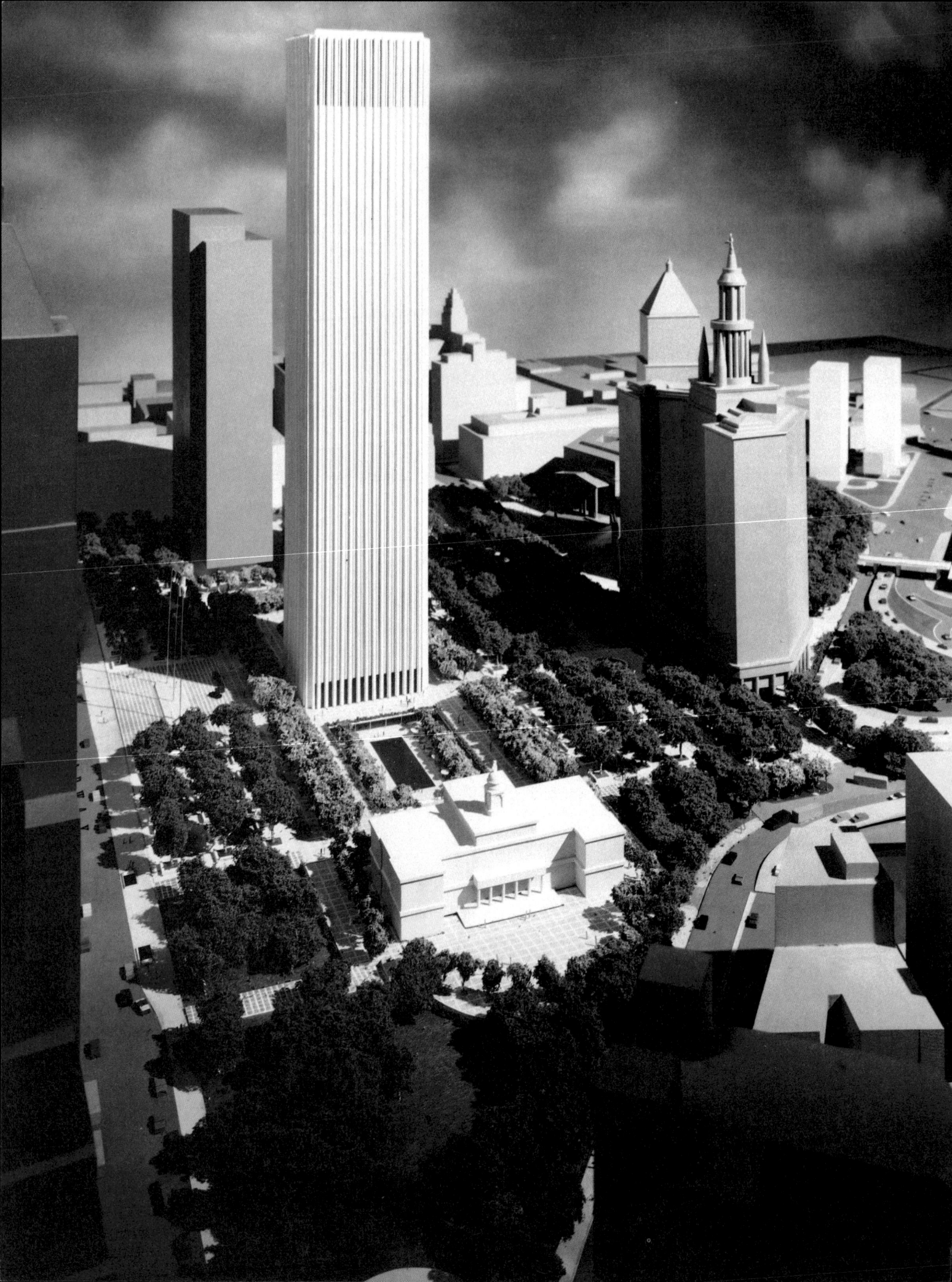

said, "It would be fitting that New York City, with its skyscraper skyline, use a tower for its Civic Center."[41] The new building would house a top-floor mayoral suite and incorporate offices that, under the earlier scheme, would have been housed in the building to be built on the northeast corner of Broadway and Chambers Street. Stone's building would serve the daily utilitarian needs of city government, while City Hall would take on a ceremonial function. A sunken, 220-by-140-foot landscaped plaza lined with shops and restaurants, evocative of the one at Rockefeller Center, would link the skyscraper and City Hall. The steel-framed tower, rising without a single setback, was to be clad with narrow, slightly curved, pierlike white marble aggregate panels separating vertical strips of gray glass windows. According to Ada Louise Huxtable, "The delicacy of scale of this surface treatment is meant to lessen the impact of its size in relationship to the diminutive 19th-century City Hall."[42] Altogether, Stone's design was similar to the one he was concurrently working on uptown—his General Motors Building of 1964–68 (see chapter 5). The new plan also called for the simplification of the Brooklyn Bridge approach.

The Architectural 13, which by the time of the revised plan's release numbered twelve (Philip Johnson had left for unspecified reasons), praised the redesign as a "considerable advance" reflecting an enhanced "awareness of a larger whole." Though the group lauded the bridge approach and the sunken mall, it was critical of the skyscraper, which "intrudes into and dominates the main space"; the group suggested that it be redesigned as a collection of lower buildings "handled less as a tower and more as a 'wall,' to define the Civic Center space."[43] In January 1965, while acknowledging that "plans for major civic improvements in New York have a way of taking approximately the same time it took to build Notre Dame," the editors of *Progressive Architecture* were confident that the redesign would produce "a really significant Civic Center." The editors optimistically stated, "It should not escape the notice of architects in other cities that the 'go fight City Hall' attitude of architects who thought a better job could be done was a major factor in getting this new Civic Center plan."[44] *Progressive Architecture*'s optimism proved unwarranted. While Mayor Lindsay approved the plan on June 9, 1966, and the buildings north of Chambers Street were acquired by the city, funds for their demolition and for new construction were not forthcoming and the grand proposal languished, ultimately joining earlier unsuccessful attempts to build a monumental civic center. Writing in 1973, Huxtable would rather matter-of-factly conclude that Stone and Eggers & Higgins's "saccharine scheme . . . died a natural death."[45]

As the saga of the ill-fated civic center unfolded, the intertwined story of the United States Federal Building and Customs Courthouse (Alfred Easton Poor; Kahn & Jacobs; and Eggers & Higgins, 1967) became an unintended object lesson not only in the creation of architectural mediocrity but, to use Huxtable's phrase, in "how not to build a city."[46] The city's request in 1962 that the federal government move its building complex was flatly rejected; the government argued that the proposed change would cost between $9 million and $15 million and cause a delay of two years. In Huxtable's view, however, the inability to alter plans was "apparently based on the fact that while the wheels of government grind slowly they cannot reverse or change direction."[47] In an exquisite if unfortunate irony, excavation of the federal government building undermined the foundations of the neighboring buildings on Broadway, forcing the government to demolish them and leaving empty the site pre-

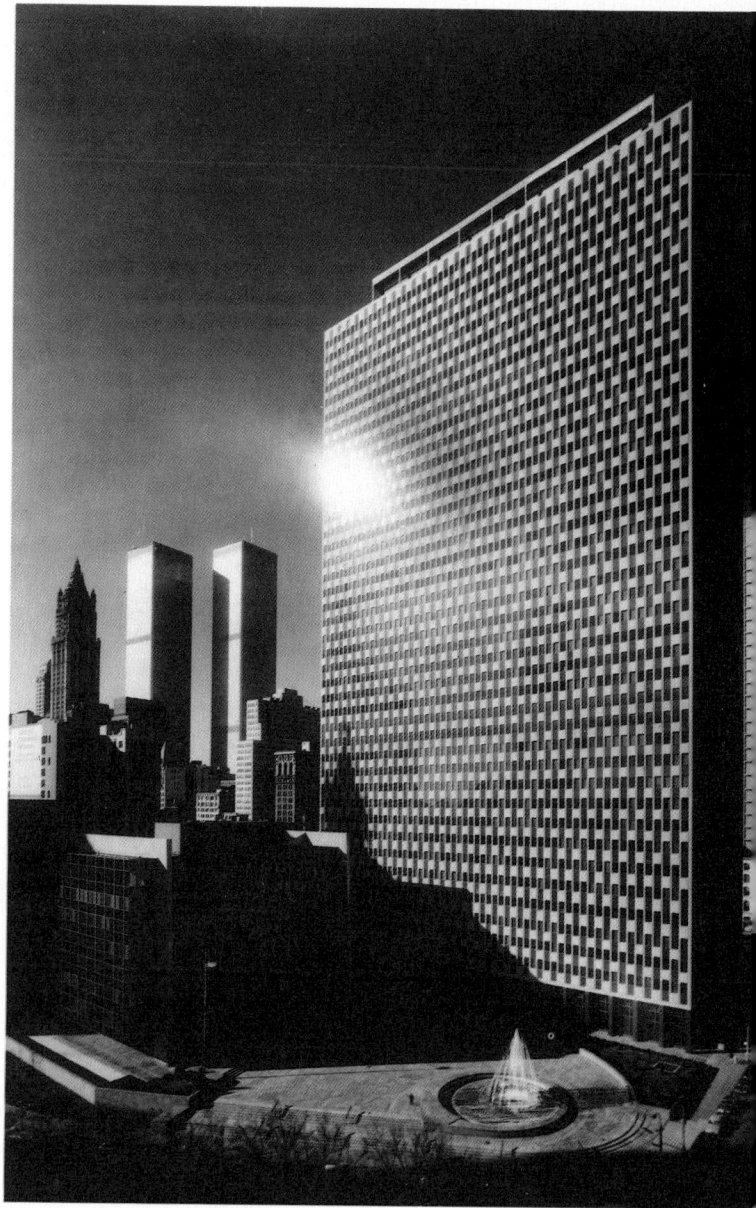

Left: Revised ABC plan. Edward Durell Stone and Eggers & Higgins, 1964. Model. View to the northeast of Stone's proposed municipal office building, in the center, and City Hall (Mangin & McComb, 1803–11), in the foreground. Stoller. ©ESTO

Above: United States Federal Building (right) and Customs Courthouse (left), Foley Square, Duane to Worth Street. Alfred Easton Poor, Kahn & Jacobs and Eggers & Higgins, 1967. View to the southwest. ©Gil Amiaga. EG

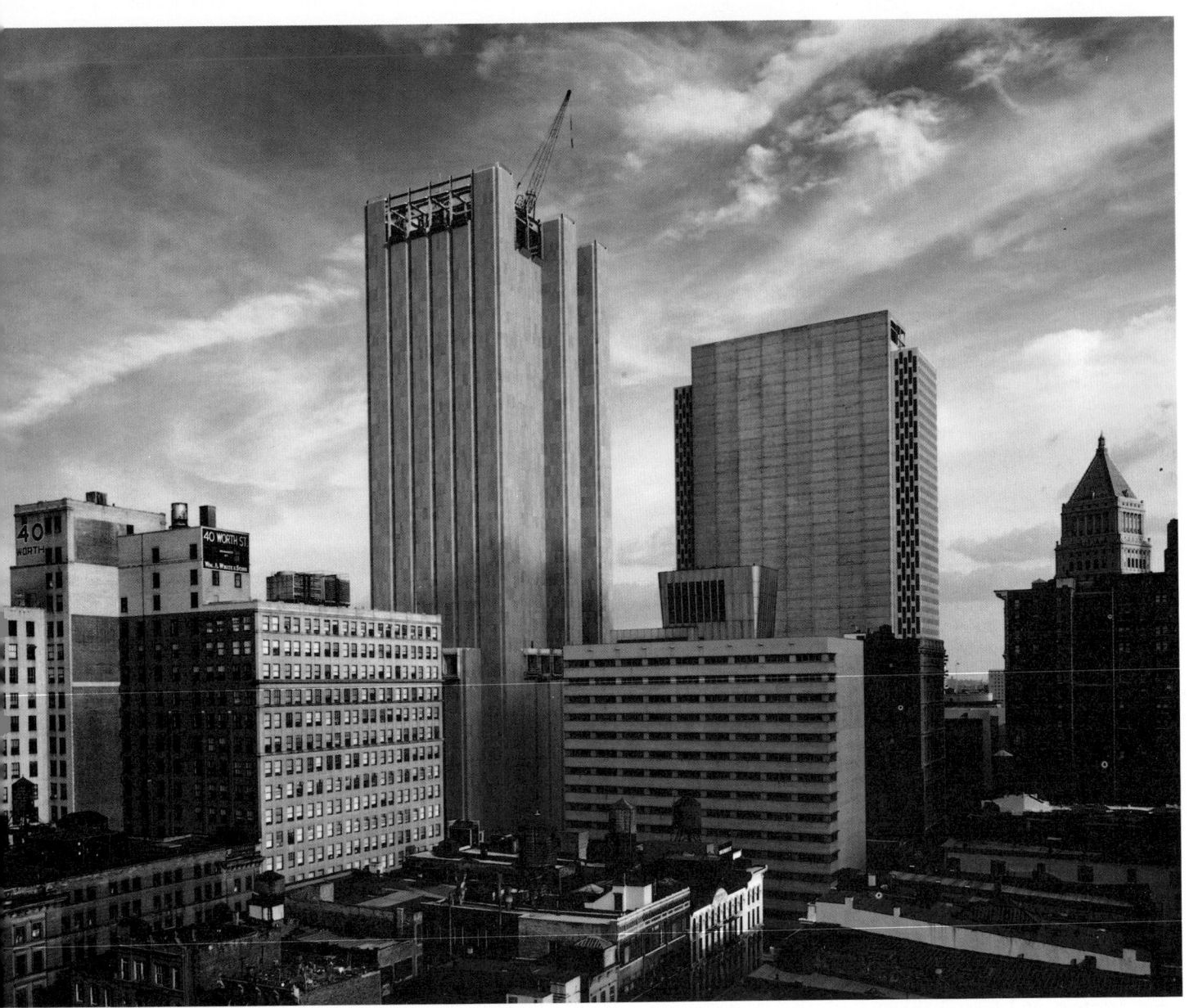

American Telephone & Telegraph Long Lines Building, Broadway to
Church Street, Worth to Thomas Street, under construction. John Carl
Warnecke, 1974. Also shown are the United States Federal Building
(Alfred Easton Poor, Kahn & Jacobs and Eggers & Higgins, 1967), on
the right, and New York State Insurance Fund Building (Lorimer Rich
Associates, 1955), in the center foreground. View to the east.
Lieberman. TL

ferred by the city for the federal building. The city reiterated its request that the federal government move to the new site, but to no avail. One of the building's architects, David L. Eggers, suggested that the Broadway site be utilized as a park covering a subterranean garage. He also proposed that an expansive entrance lobby be built to link the skyscraper to Broadway and that the blank party wall facing Broadway be developed "with vertical accents and texturing."[48]

Despite these proposals, the tower was erected as originally designed, with a mammoth undecorated wall oriented toward Broadway. In 1965, two years before the building was completed, the federal government announced its intention to extend the tower to cover the adjacent vacant site. Anticipating the building's expansion, Huxtable stated, "Considering its size now, and what can only be called its belligerent banality, this might be called Washington's gift of double disaster to New York."[49] As built, the United States Federal Building consisted of a forty-one-story slab housing an array of federal government agencies, and an eight-story structure housing the United States Customs Court and four district facilities. The federal building was oriented parallel to Broadway; the court building was located at the site's southeast corner, where it overlooked Foley Square. A large, triangular plaza occupied the site's northeast corner, eroding the building wall that defined the oddly shaped space of Foley Square. The tower, clad in glass and metal panels arranged in a syncopated domino pattern, loomed over the visually quieter courthouse, which was clad in dark glass.

Huxtable lambasted the complex as "one of the most monumentally mediocre Federal buildings in history." Dismissing the tower as "the biggest checkerboard in the world," she focused on the courthouse: "The office tower is attached to a smaller building with structural paranoia; hung by trusses, supported by columns and cantilevered at the edges behind a standard glass skin. Is it a suspended structure or isn't it? Only its architects know for sure." Huxtable recapped the long process leading to the building's completion: "While New York backed and filled and restudied plans for the environs of City Hall, the Federal Government went ahead and built a forty-one-story office building and courthouse in City Hall's backyard that dominate and destroy the entire Civic Center area."[50]

Though Huxtable's assessment was perhaps an overstatement, she effectively homed in on the key issue when she described the federal building as "so horribly visible from anywhere at all that its placement is academic."[51] Writing in 1978, two years after the building had been expanded west to Broadway, Norval White and Elliot Willensky characterized it as "an ungainly checkerboard . . . now extended . . . with a continuing heavy hand."[52] In 1979 Paul Goldberger made his contribution to the existing body of overwhelmingly negative criticism: "Surely the architects are full of all sorts of clever theories about how well the low, separate, more formal courthouse and the bigger, blander office area behind it are appropriate expressions of their different roles. Claptrap. Both are designed with the subtlety of an airport concourse—each, in its own way, strikes a deep blow at the compositional order of Foley Square as a whole, which is hardly given coherence by a pair of clashing boxes."[53]

The civic center area's increasingly disjointed ensemble of buildings received yet another brutal blow in 1974 with the completion of John Carl Warnecke's American Telephone & Telegraph Long Lines Building, occupying the block bounded by Broadway and Worth, Church and Thomas streets.[54] The construction of Warnecke's building necessitated the demoli-

tion of cast-iron loft buildings at 58–60 Worth Street and 31–37 Thomas Street, though their principal facades were dismantled and preserved. The building's design was determined in large measure by the requirements of housing sensitive electronic equipment in a windowless mass. Like the telephone company's building at 811 Eleventh Avenue (Kahn & Jacobs, 1964) (see chapter 5), Warnecke's building was specifically designed to resist nuclear fallout and was to be provided with enough energy and food storage to keep it self-sufficient for two weeks' operation. In order to accommodate the telephone equipment, which generated enough heat to warm the building, each floor had a height of eighteen feet, giving the twenty-nine-story building a total height of 550 feet, equivalent to that of a typical fifty-story building. The building was clad in red granite placed over precast-concrete slabs, and its chief feature was the grid of superscaled exterior columns that ran its full height, housing elevators, stairs, and ducts required for air-conditioning and other mechanical systems. In almost parodic emulation of Louis I. Kahn's lyric cluster of laboratories and service towers at his Richards Medical Research Building (1957-61) at the University of Pennsylvania, Philadelphia,[55] the columns were punctuated by visually prominent air intakes and exhaust louvers on the tenth and twenty-ninth floors.

The editors of *Architectural Record* wrote that though the building was designed principally with machines in mind, it had a "definite concern for its impact on people and on the city itself."[56] White and Willensky disagreed, castigating the building as a "giant electronic complex in the guise of a building" and a "stylish leviathan that looms over the city with architectural eyebrows."[57] Goldberger was more generous in his assessment, stating that it was "the only one of the several windowless equipment buildings around town that makes sense architecturally. . . . Warnecke has made the building itself an enormous piece of equipment. . . . One might say, in fact, that the form attempts to express the building's role as part of the cityscape—a successful and visually pleasing way of pulling off a double-barreled challenge."[58]

The postwar development of the civic center area ended on a more distinguished note than might have been expected with a succession of imaginative if heavy-handed buildings designed by Gruzen & Partners. These began in 1973 with the firm's Police Headquarters and adjacent public plaza, designed in association with the landscape architect M. Paul Friedberg.[59] The Police Headquarters replaced the previous facility (Hoppin & Koen, 1909), at 240 Centre Street, between Grand and Broome streets.[60] Located directly east of McKim, Mead & White's Municipal Building, the new headquarters was a corporate version of the Brutalist Boston City Hall (Kallmann, McKinnell & Knowles, 1963–68), itself an awkward amalgam of ideas from Le Corbusier's La Tourette monastery and the postwar work of Alvar Aalto.[61]

Rather than build the fifteen-foot-high overpass bridging Park Row that would have been necessary to make the new building easily accessible from the west, the architects succeeded in having the street depressed below the grade of Chambers Street, which was closed to vehicular traffic east of Centre Street. This permitted pedestrians to reach the Police Headquarters by walking under the Municipal Building's grand arch and across a seventy-five-foot-wide brick-paved plaza. Part of Duane Street was also closed to motor traffic and repaved in brick to serve as a pedestrian passageway leading from the Police Headquarters to Foley Square. Approach roads to the Brooklyn Bridge were simplified to accommodate the new

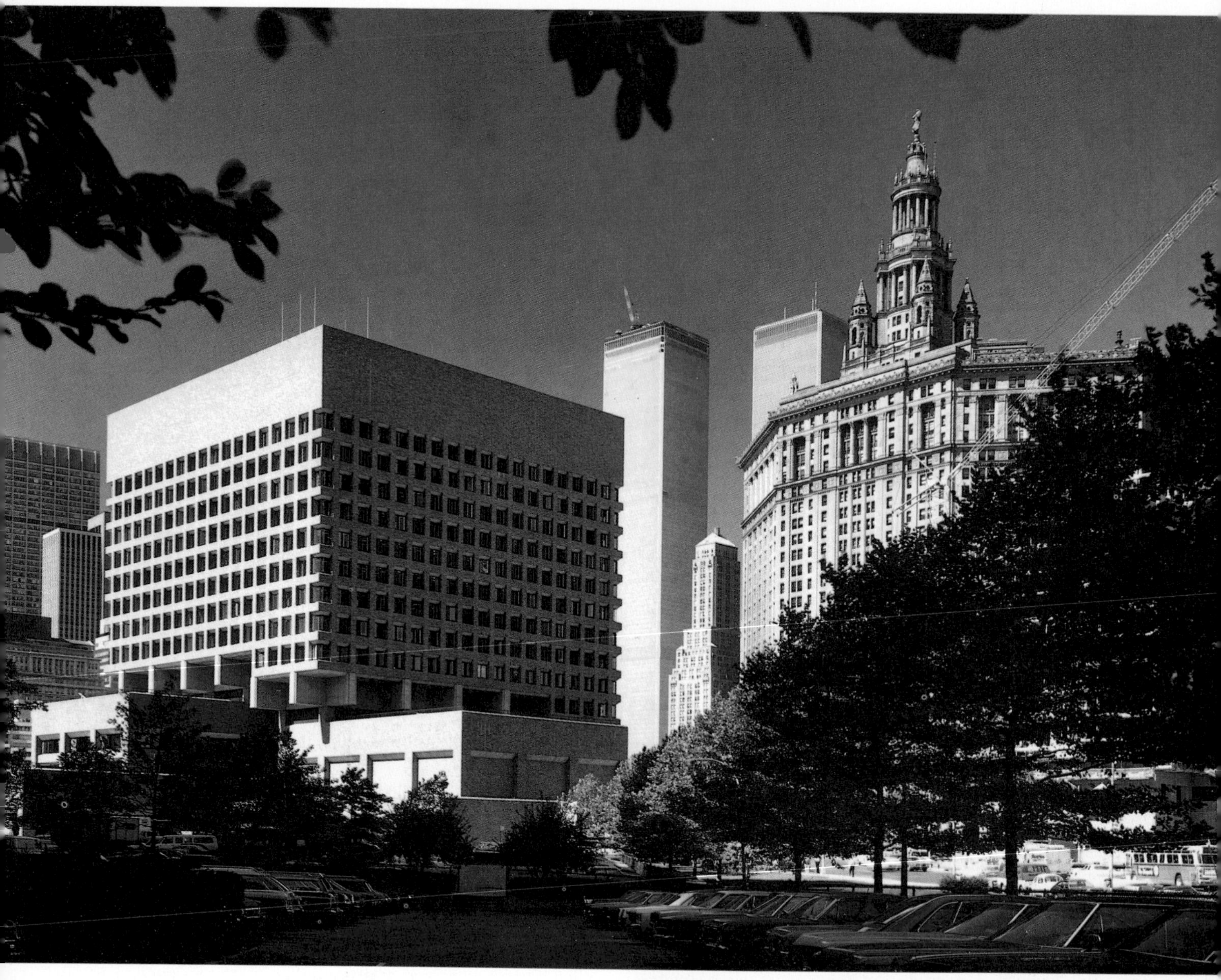

Above: Police Headquarters, One Police Plaza, bounded by Avenue of the Finest, Pearl and Madison streets. Gruzen & Partners, 1973. View to the west showing the Police Headquarters, on the left, and the Municipal Building (McKim, Mead & White, 1914), on the right. Hirsch. GS

Right: Police Headquarters. Lobby. Hirsch. GS

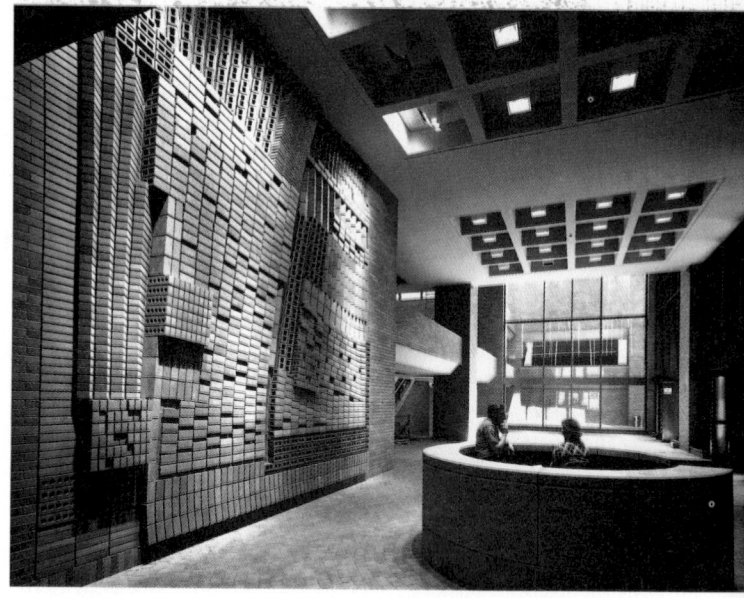

plaza. Noting the complex bureaucratic aspect of the building's design process, Barclay F. Gordon, writing in *Architectural Record*, said that the depression of Park Row and the creation of Police Plaza "meant the cooperation of a spate of city agencies . . . as well as all the patience and persuasive powers the architects (and designer Peter Samton in particular) could muster."[62]

The police building consisted of a ten-story, near-cubic volume supported on cantilevered trusses above a rather sprawling complex of one- to five-story structures. All four facades of the building's upper portion incorporated grids of deep-punched windows, including corner windows, and contrasted with the virtually windowless base. Both the tower, housing offices, and the base, housing a public parking garage, detention cells, a pistol range and an array of other specialized facilities, were clad in dark brown brick; the intervening exposed-concrete trusses were continued inside as walls. Inside, a spacious, glassed-in lobby, entered from a plaza-level entrance aligned with the Municipal Building's arch, incorporated dramatically modeled brick walls.

Though the building's formal merits were considerable, the Police Headquarters was most noteworthy as urban planning, and as a triumph of optimism, perseverance and stamina in the face of sometimes daunting obstacles. Ada Louise Huxtable wrote rather extensively about the building throughout the long course of its development. In a 1969 *New York Times* article titled "Beating the System," she stated: "There are several important things about this particular project. It is huge; in design quality it is light years beyond the New York City norm; it is part of an over-all Civic Center plan . . . that attempts to pull together what may be the world's worst municipal planning mess; and it is being built." Noting the changing cast of characters associated with the project over the years, Huxtable said: "It took a decade and seven Public Works Commissioners, of whom three died—there seems to be an inordinately high mortality rate among Public Works Commissioners—to get the building out of the ground."[63] Upon the building's completion in 1973, Huxtable further observed: "You've got to be around New York about ten years and watch the progress of a major project or two to develop a proper sense of the ludicrous, or the miraculous, or both. That the two are not mutually exclusive gives this city its special flavor. . . . The Police Headquarters comes in the miracle class."[64] Barclay Gordon asserted that the architects' patience and determination resulted not only in a splendid building but, perhaps even more important, in "a sound and coherent piece of civic planning in a portion of the city where this virtue has been absent too long."[65] The critic James D. Morgan, writing in *Architecture Plus*, similarly noted that the building's "relationship to existing conditions is especially masterful."[66]

It was the generously scaled and well-designed plaza, containing rows of honey locust trees, a fountain, benches and a monumental abstract sculpture by Bernard (Tony) Rosenthal, that charmed the public and received critical praise even more than the building itself. In addition to providing an appropriately monumental entrance to the Police Headquarters and effectively blocking out the sights and sounds of the heavy traffic that plagued the area, the plaza invited, as Gordon put it, "strollers to pause, lovers to dally, city brownbaggers to linger over sandwiches and apples."[67] In keeping with the lively spirit of the place, Rosenthal intended his sculpture, an evocation of the city's five boroughs titled *5 in One*, to be "a participation piece . . . it can be walked through."[68] The plaza was undeniably a success. In contrast to the "empty and monumental plazas now found in other cities around public buildings," Morgan said, the Police Headquarters plaza helped to establish "a dense, rich urban fabric."[69] Huxtable was

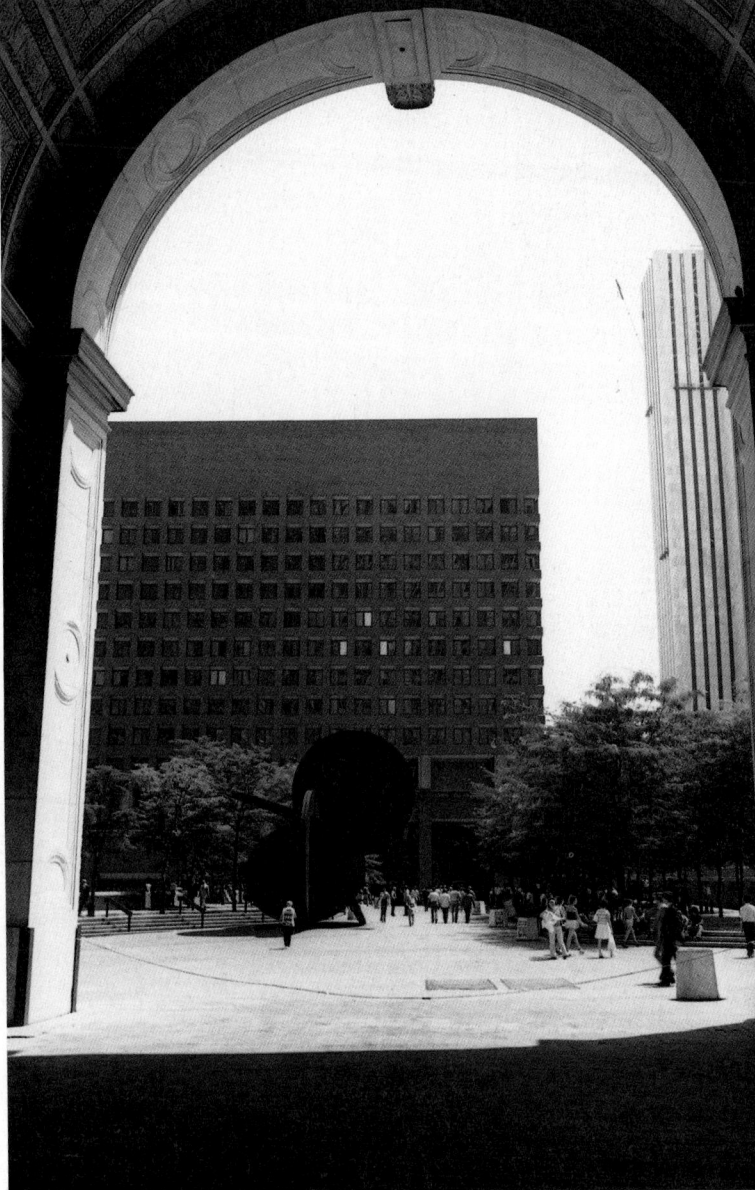

Police Plaza, elevated structure spanning Park Row, from Pearl Street to Avenue of the Finest. M. Paul Friedberg, 1973. View to the east from the Municipal Building showing sculpture *5 in One* (1974) by Bernard (Tony) Rosenthal. MPF

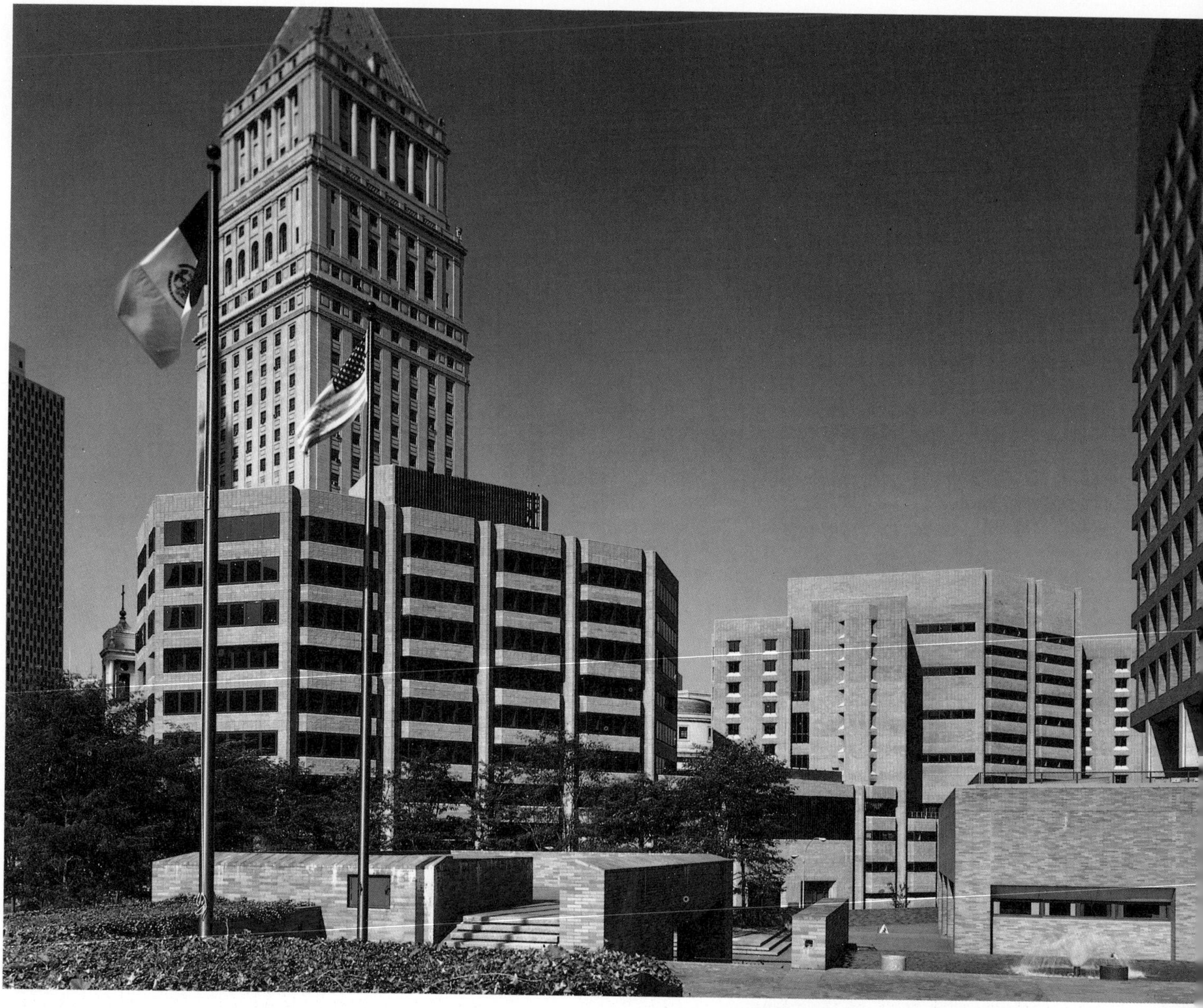

Above: Annex to the United States Courthouse, housing offices of the
United States Attorney (left) and the Metropolitan Correction Center
(right), bounded by Park Row, Pearl Street and Police Plaza. Gruzen &
Partners, 1975. View to the north showing the United States
Courthouse (Cass Gilbert, 1936), in the background. GS

Right: Murray Bergtraum High School, southeast corner of Madison
Street and Avenue of the Finest. Gruzen & Partners, 1976. View to the
east showing the New York Telephone Company Switching Station
(Rose, Beaton & Rose, 1976), in the background. Hirsch. GS

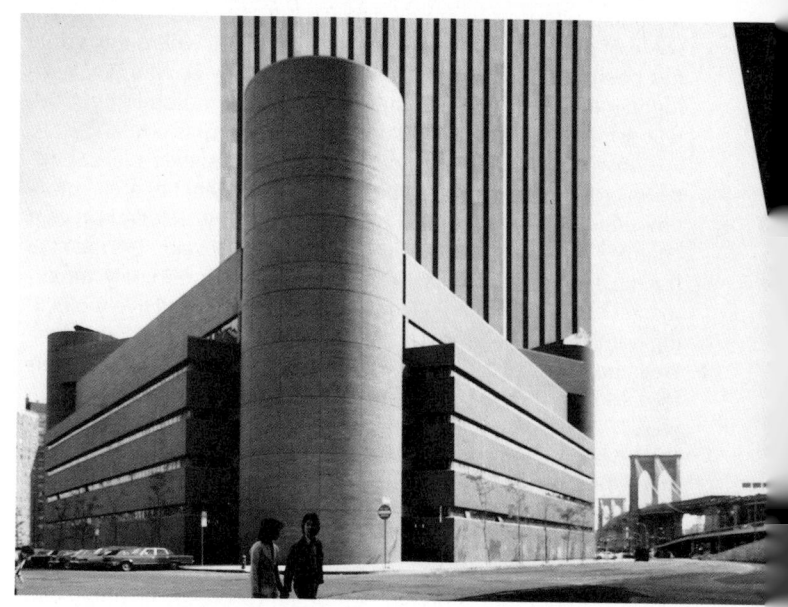

once again lavish in her praise, calling the new outdoor space "the city's finest public plaza" and explaining: "The plaza is connector and catalyst for everything around it, all the spaces and structures it touches take on totally new meanings and relationships, where before there were no relationships at all."[70]

Gruzen & Partners' next project in the area, the annex to the United States Courthouse (Cass Gilbert, 1936), was completed in 1975.[71] It consisted of two connected buildings, one housing the offices of the United States Attorney, the other housing the Metropolitan Correction Center; the annex backed onto Park Row and was accessible from Police Plaza to the south. To blend with Gilbert's limestone-clad facades, the ten-story building complex featured ribbed precast-concrete facades punctuated by horizontal strip windows placed in long bays. The rather stridently horizontal character of Gruzen's buildings, however, also provided strong contrast to the verticality of Gilbert's courthouse. Paul Goldberger praised the project as "a significant improvement in the level of Federal architecture in New York" and went further to comment on its success as prison architecture, which, he said, "once sounded like a contradiction in terms [but] has become a major and creative field within the architectural profession." Goldberger lauded the building as "a superb example of an intelligently conceived, fully secure environment that nonetheless manages to be comfortable and even, to the extent that any prison can, feel welcoming." Goldberger described the cells as "spartan, but comfortable. . . . The over-all sense is as much that of a new college dormitory room as that of a prison cell."[72] Goldberger later added that the two buildings forming the annex were "discreet and helpful in providing a sense of overall continuity in the area, and good reminders of how additions can be presences in themselves and yet not detract from the main event."[73]

Another design by Gruzen & Partners, the Murray Bergtraum High School, was built by the New York City Board of Education and Educational Construction Fund.[74] It occupied a triangular site, the apex of which was formed by the intersection of Madison Street and the Avenue of the Finest. Completed in 1976, the school was the last of the firm's projects in the civic center area. Though Gruzen and his firm had been associated with the civic center since the 1920s, when B. Sumner (Barney) Gruzen had worked on the drawings of Guy Lowell's New York County Courthouse,[75] the firm had in no way succeeded in stamping the place with a singular identity or any continuous body of ideas. Rather, Gruzen's work in the civic center itself and in the housing projects at its edges had merely reflected changing design ideas widely held in the profession as a whole. The six-story Bergtraum building was clad in dark brown brick, punctuated by thin horizontal strip windows. Three cylindrical towers, located at the building's corners and housing stairways and mechanical equipment, accentuated the building's imposing mass while imbuing it with an almost fortresslike appearance that seemed at once a powerful expression of civic authority and an appropriate reflection of the declining state of the public school system. With Bergtraum, the civic center returned to the medievalism of the Tombs and its additions; a style that only a few decades before had been deemed offensive for penitentiaries was now being praised for high schools.

In some ways the school's financial underpinnings were more interesting than its architecture. The school traded its air rights to the New York Telephone Company for a zoning credit that made possible the construction of a thirty-two-story switching center on an adjacent site to the east. The telephone company, in turn, paid off the municipal bonds that had been issued

to finance the school. The two buildings shared more than economics. As designed by the firm of Rose, Beaton & Rose, the switching center, located at 375 Pearl Street, was equally brutal, though more ordinary in its appearance.[76] White and Willensky characterized the tower as a "humorless . . . high-rise monster,"[77] and Goldberger dismissed it as "a massive and utterly banal intrusion" that performed "what can only be called an act of cruelty, as it cuts off much of the view of the Brooklyn Bridge."[78]

The Family Court Building reverted to the heavy-handed mediocrity that characterized the 1950s and early 1960s.[79] Completed in 1976 and designed by Haines, Lundberg & Waehler, the building housed offices and courtrooms and was located at 60 Lafayette Street, on the west blockfront between Leonard and Franklin streets. Although the design may have achieved a monumentality suited to its civic function, it lacked any sensitivity to its delicate mission. The eleven-story, polished black granite building was an aggressively active composition, with numerous recessions piercing the building's mass at forty-five-degree angles and an asymmetrical arrangement of windows varying widely in size and shape. A soaring colonnade formed of narrow slablike columns placed at forty-five-degree angles framed the main entrance.

Paul Goldberger found the design disappointing: "While the materials used are dignified and handsome, the facade as a composition has little real grace to it. Its abstract quality is an obvious attempt to break free of the classical vocabulary while holding onto the symbolic value of a formal masonry structure, but the attempt comes off as merely overbearing."[80] Goldberger later stated that the design was "so contorted, so needlessly agonized, as to be more a piece of narcissism than of architecture."[81] Inside the building, Goldberger found little more to enjoy: "The interiors are a bizarre mix of trendy materials—polished stainless steel, tile, molded plastic chairs—and tired Government-standard design, as if a jail had been remodeled by Bloomingdale's."[82]

DOWNTOWN

Although the anticipated conclusion of World War II brought with it announcements of new office buildings for the city's historic downtown—the financial center along Wall Street and the insurance center along John Street—almost nothing was actually built until the mid-1950s.[1] With its greater access to fashionable Manhattan residential neighborhoods, to suburban railroads, to restaurants, shops, theaters and other cultural activities, midtown seemed to be the exclusive focus of postwar commercial development. By 1950 its role as the choice location for corporate management centers was unchallenged.[2]

Meanwhile, the financial and insurance districts slumbered. Only a handful of new buildings in the immediate postwar era stood in contrast to the burst of construction being experienced farther uptown. Downtown's first postwar office building of consequence was 99 Church Street (Reinhard, Hofmeister & Walquist, 1951), an eleven-story, 330,000-square-foot facility occupying the east blockfront between Barclay Street and Park Place.[3] The new home office for Dun & Bradstreet, the mercantile agency, and the largest office building built in lower Manhattan in twenty years, it was more notable for the sophisticated technology of its vertical transportation system—its basement and lower five floors were connected by twelve escalators—than for its stolid massing or its conservative,

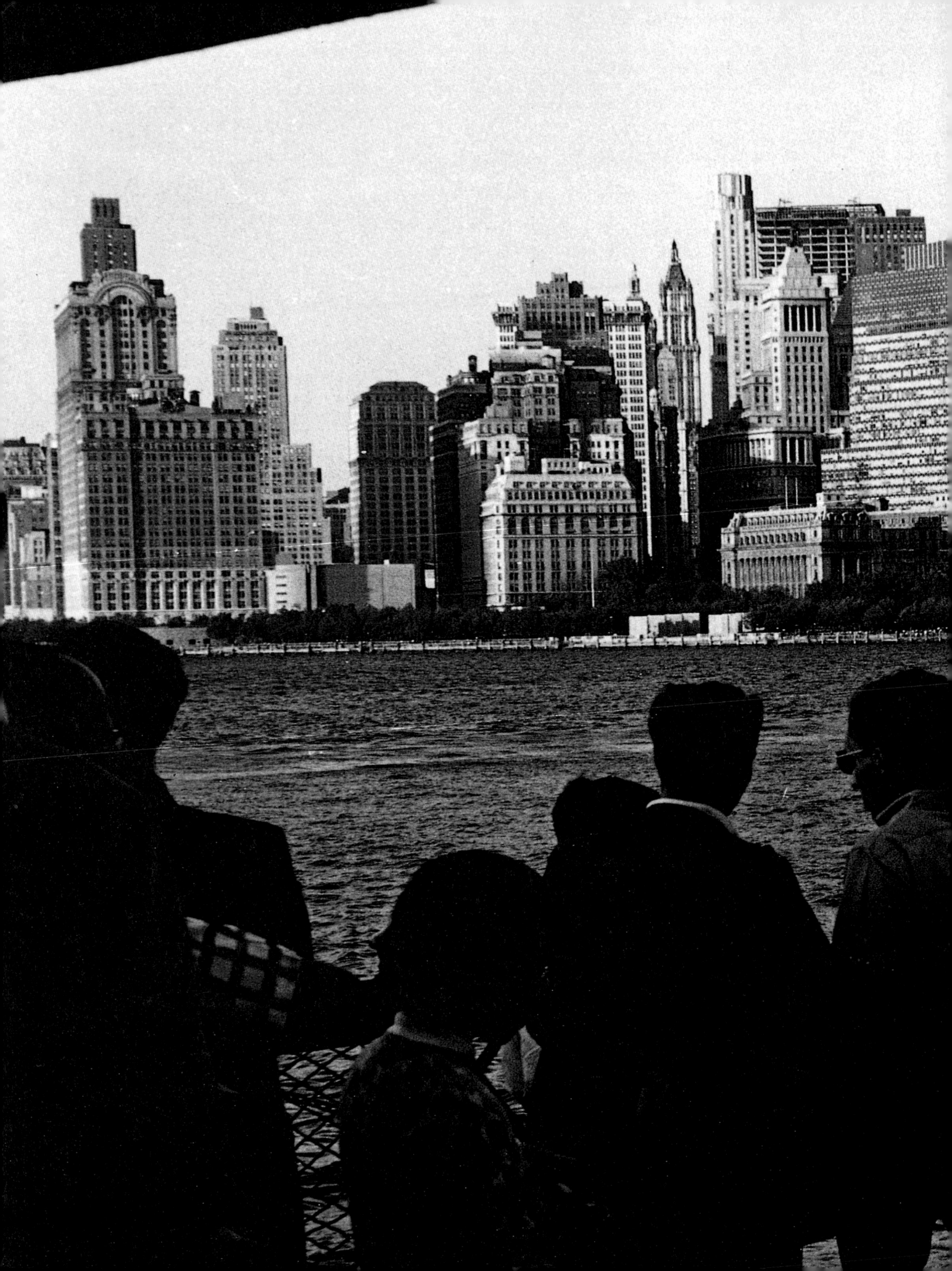

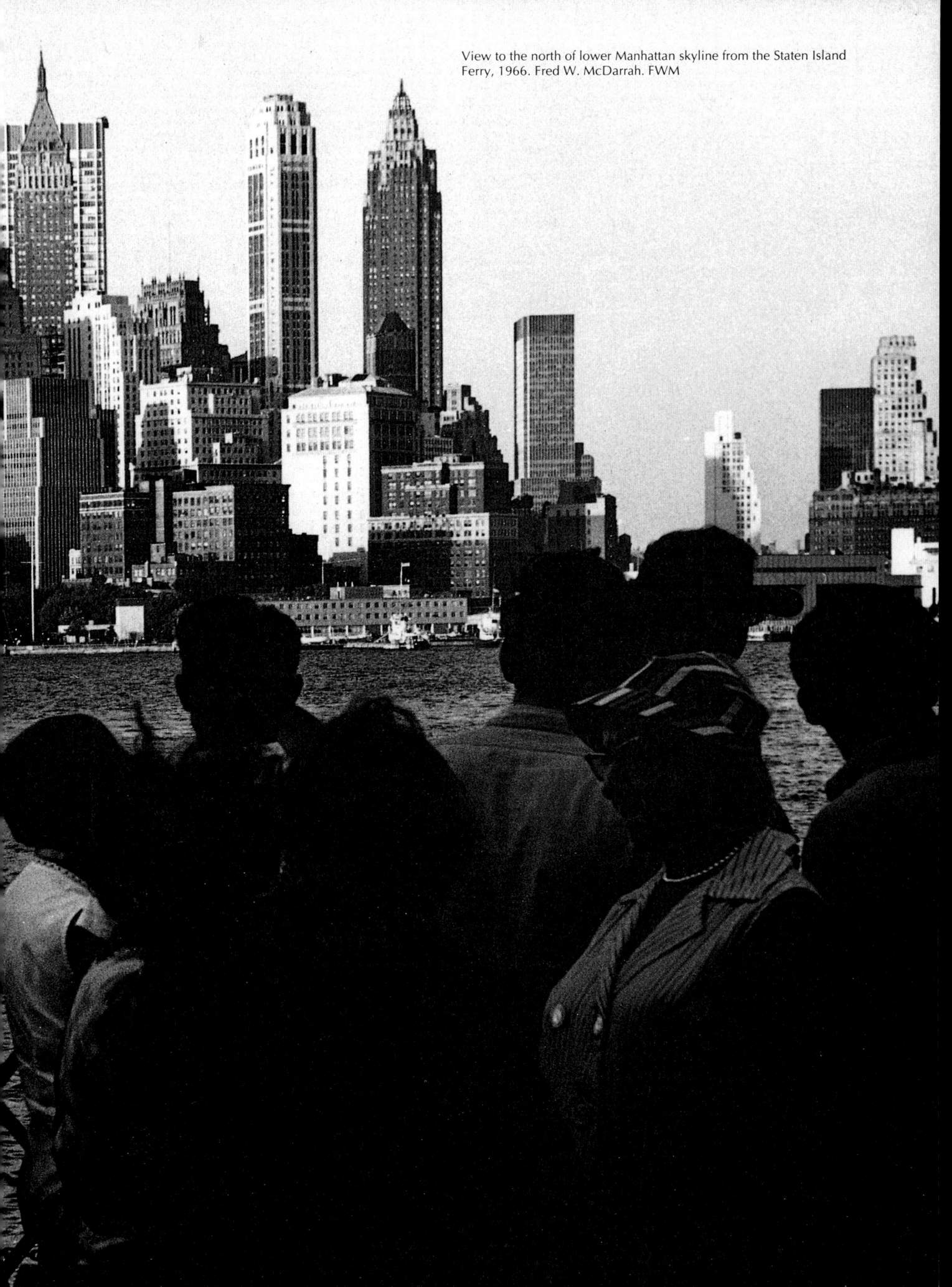

View to the north of lower Manhattan skyline from the Staten Island
Ferry, 1966. Fred W. McDarrah. FWM

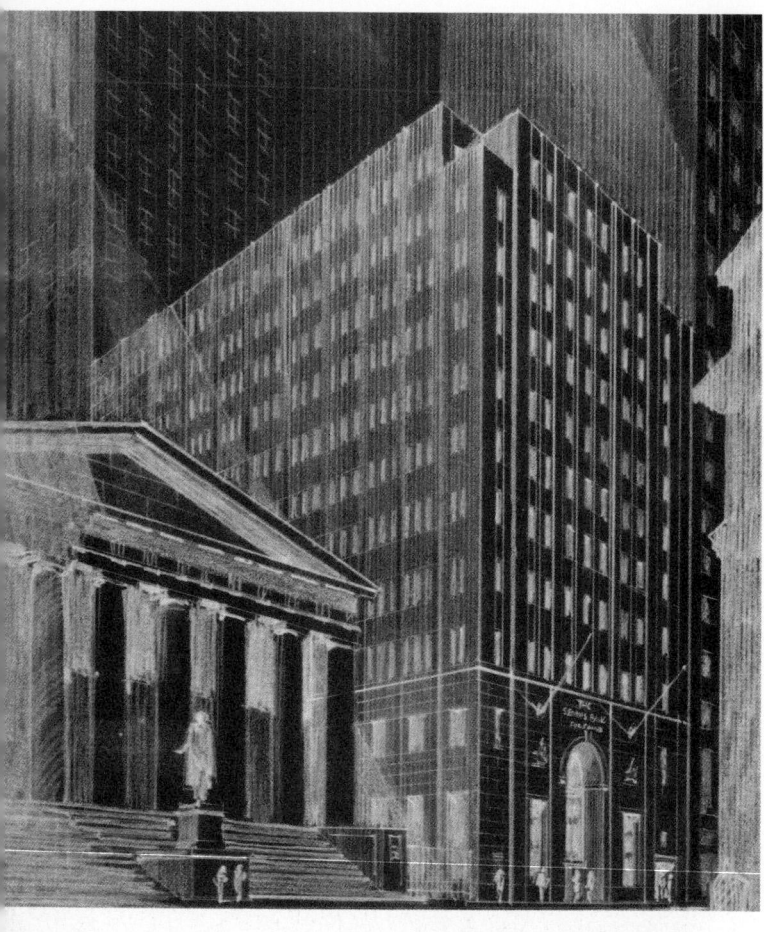

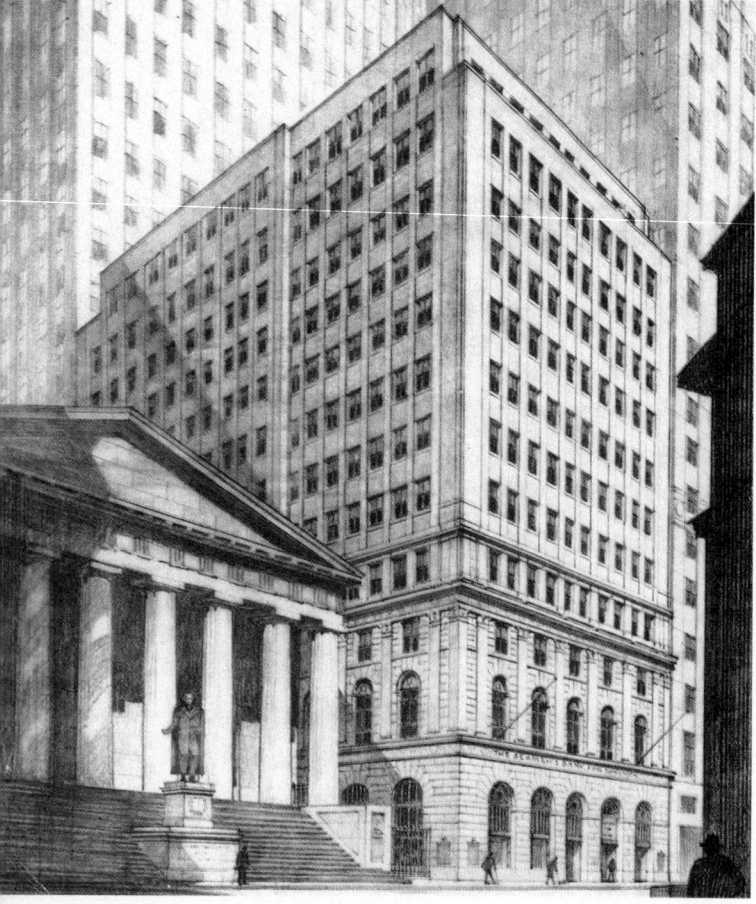

stripped-down, limestone-clad facades. A year later, 99 Church Street was followed by lower Manhattan's first postwar speculative office building, 161 William Street, a banal, twenty-one-story, 153,000-square-foot essay in the International Style designed by Sylvan Bien.[4]

But two buildings do not constitute a boom, and to many observers lower Manhattan seemed not so much asleep as dead. In 1952 the *Journal of Commerce* ran a series of articles assessing the area's future in which it implied that before long banks and corporations would decamp to midtown locations and Wall Street would become a residential backwater.[5] While more new office space had been added to midtown's supply between 1947 and 1956 than existed in all of Chicago's central business district, Wall Street languished. One hopeful note came in 1953 when John D. Butt, president of the Seaman's Bank for Savings, announced that the bank had bought the Assay Office (York & Sawyer, 1925), at 30 Wall Street, next to the Subtreasury (Town & Davis, with John Frazee and Samuel Thompson, 1842), and planned to build a new building on the site.[6] As originally designed by Halsey, McCormick & Helmer, the office tower was to incorporate a two-story base with a traditionally articulated, arched entranceway. This scheme did not go forward. Instead, the Assay Office was preserved and remodeled to function as the base of Halsey, McCormick & Helmer's otherwise banal twelve-story building, completed in 1955.

In 1955 confidence in downtown's future began to pick up with the announcement that 20 Broad Street was to be developed by the New York Stock Exchange on a site immediately to the south of its headquarters.[7] Two buildings on the site were demolished: Harding & Gooch's Commercial Cable Building (1897) and Carrère & Hastings's Blair Building (1902–03), both of which the exchange had purchased in the late 1920s. The twenty-seven-story, 421,000-square-foot 20 Broad Street, designed by Kahn & Jacobs with Sidney Goldstone, was a bulky version of the lead architects' 100 Park Avenue (see chapter 5), completed six years before. Similarly, 156 William Street (1956), a twelve-story, horizontally banded, 87,000-square-foot building designed by Emery Roth & Sons, was a warmed-over version of uptown work, in this case the firm's Look Building of 1950 (see chapter 5).[8] In 1957 the Roths added a six-story addition to the building next door at 158 William Street. Another in the first wave of postwar speculative office buildings was the Roths' 123 William Street, a twenty-six-story, 415,000-square-foot infill building with an aluminum-and-glass curtain wall, located in the insurance district.[9]

By virtue of its size, location and the historic preservation issues it raised, the Roth firm's Two Broadway (1959), a thirty-two-story, 1,390,000-square-foot office building on the site of George B. Post's Produce Exchange Building (1881–84) opposite Bowling Green, was the most significant postwar building in lower Manhattan up to that time.[10] The project was first announced in 1953 when, after twenty years of virtually no construction downtown, the prospect of an important new building was greeted with elation, even though it meant the loss of a fine old one. Two Broadway was initially designed by William Lescaze in association with Kahn & Jacobs, who proposed a thirty-story, million-square-foot building consisting of an eleven-story base that virtually filled the 50,000-square-foot site, surmounted by a slightly hexagonal tower slab that ran east-west. The second floor of Lescaze's design was to project from the mass as a kind of inhabited sidewalk marquee. Lescaze called for a gridded facade for the lower floors facing Bowling Green, but for the south elevations of both base and tower he

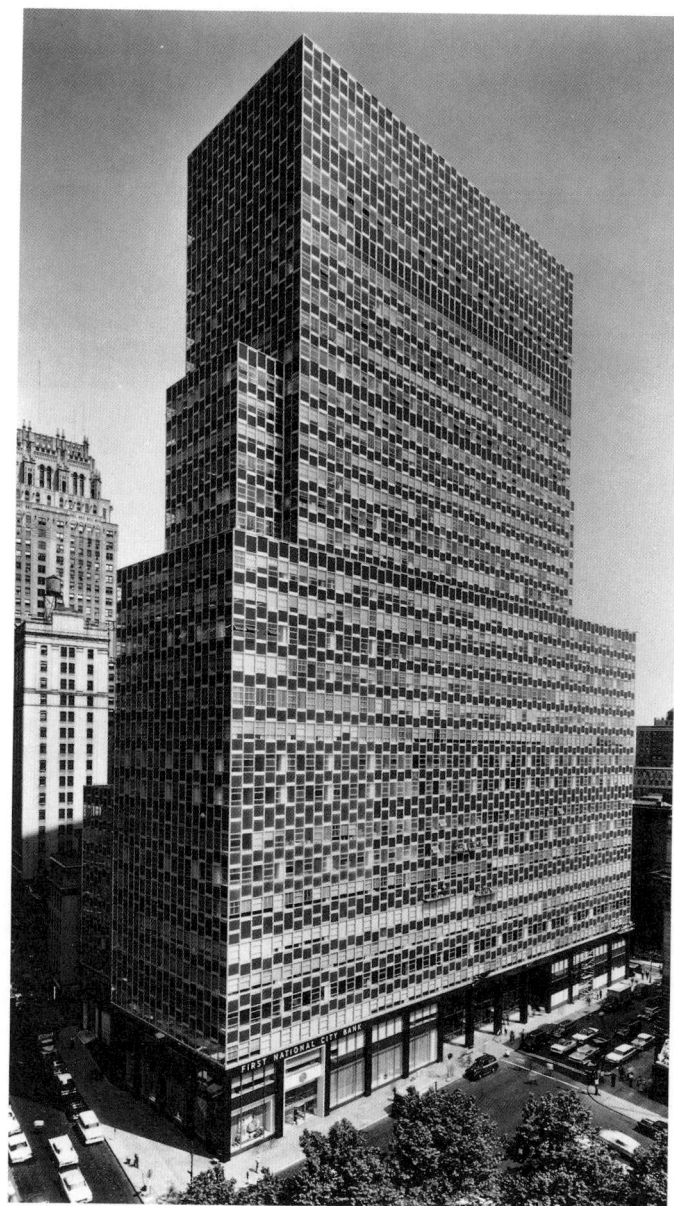

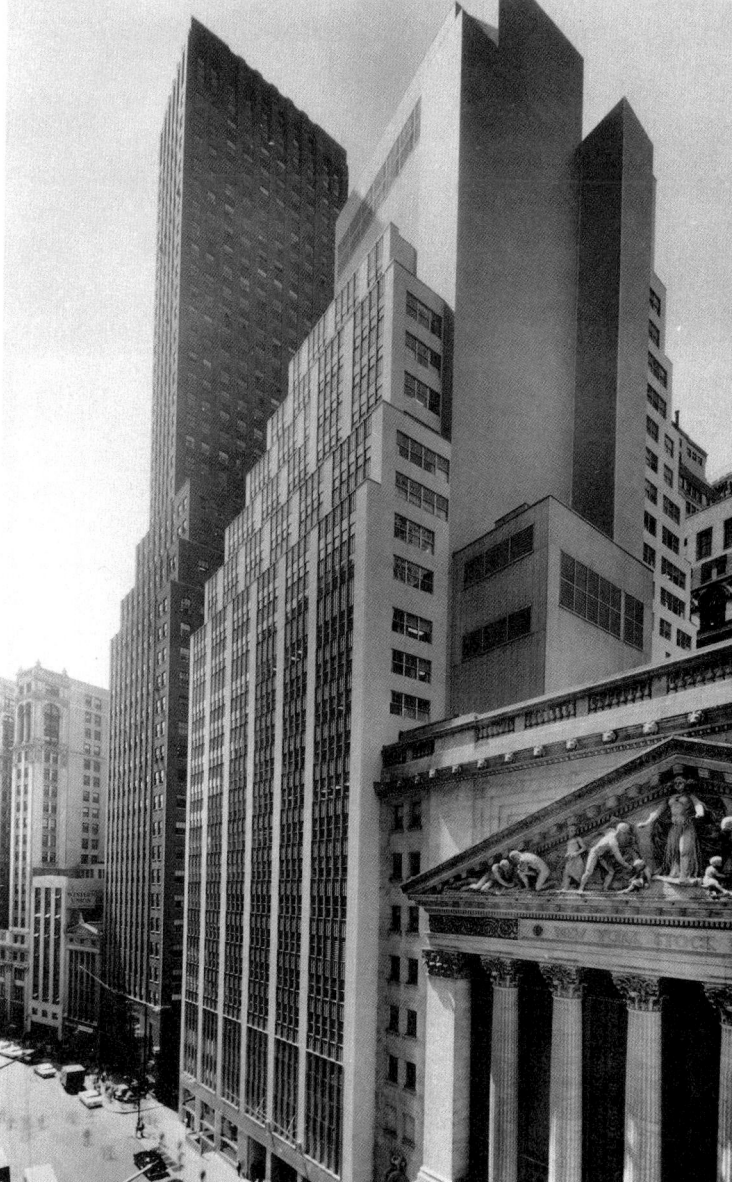

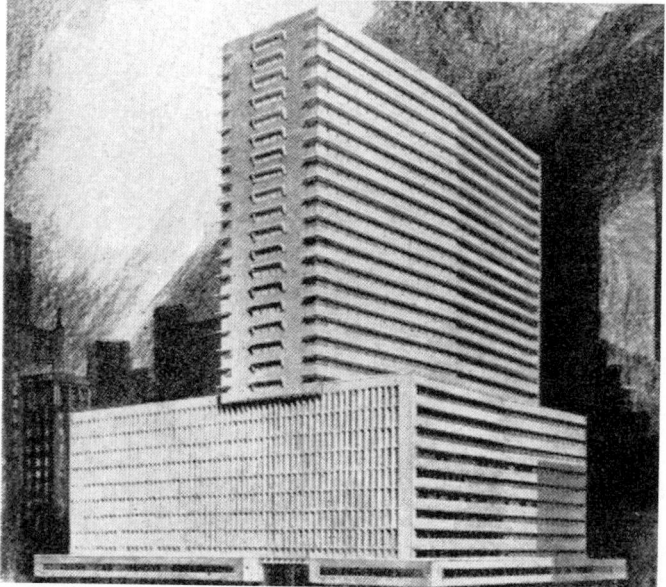

Top far left: Proposal for 30 Wall Street. Halsey, McCormick & Helmer, 1953. Rendering by L. Rutis of view to the northeast showing Subtreasury (Town & Davis, with John Frazee and Samuel Thompson. 1842), on the left. MD

Bottom far left: Proposal for 30 Wall Street, incorporating the existing Assay Office (York & Sawyer, 1925) at the base of the new building. Rendering by L. Rutis of view to the northeast. MD

Top left: Two Broadway, Stone to Beaver Street. Emery Roth & Sons, 1959. View to the southeast. Wurts. MCNY

Bottom left: Proposal for Two Broadway. William Lescaze in association with Kahn & Jacobs, 1954. Rendering of view to the northeast. AR. CU

Top right: 20 Broadway, between Exchange Place and Wall Street. Kahn & Jacobs with Sidney Goldstone, 1956. View to the southwest showing the New York Stock Exchange (George B. Post, 1903), in the foreground. Wurts. MCNY

171

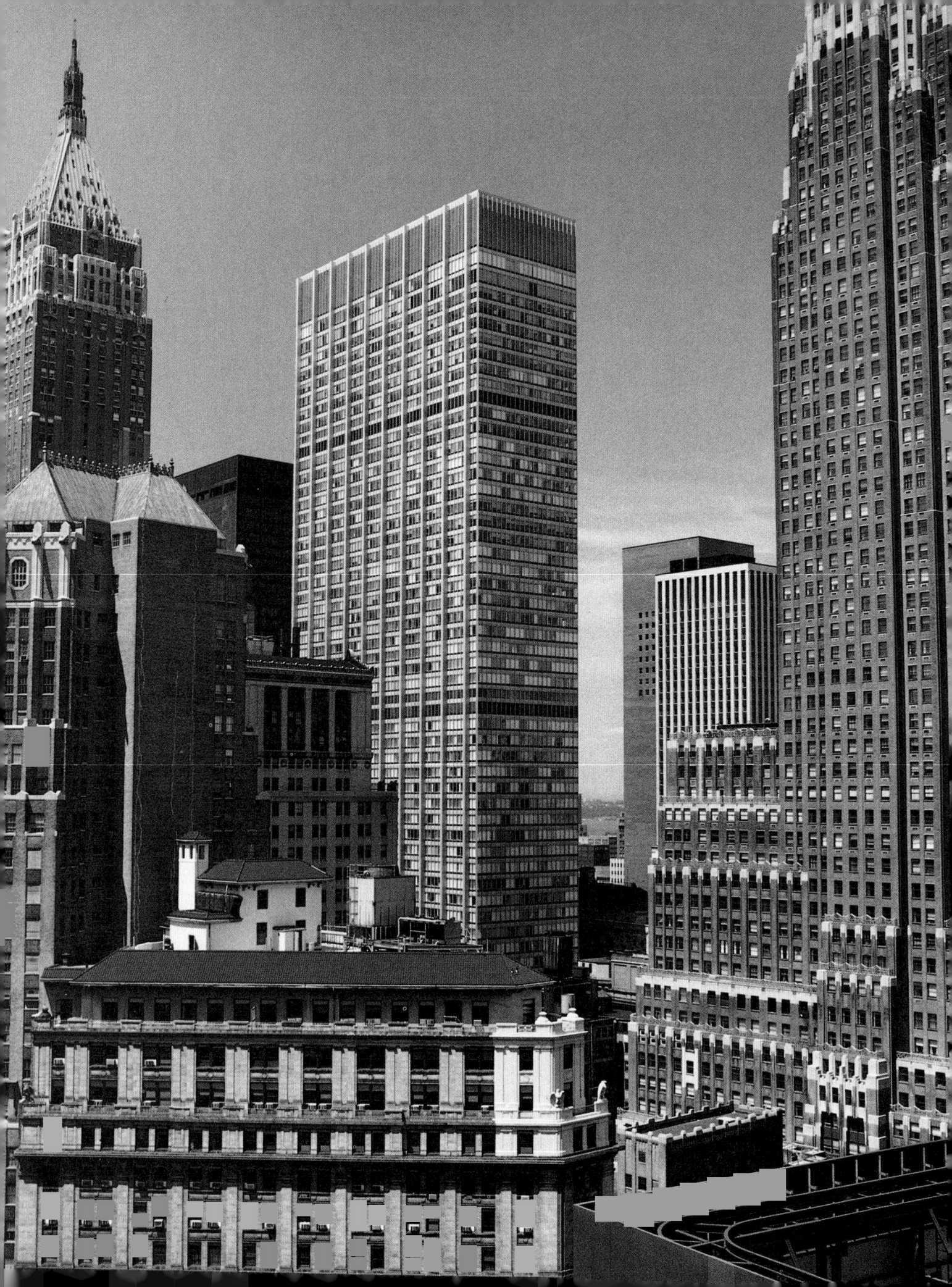

proposed horizontal strip windows shaded by projecting over-hangs similar to ones he had employed in his Longfellow Building, Washington, D.C., of 1939–41.[11] Lescaze's scheme had been developed for the partnership of Jack D. Weiler and Benjamin H. Swig, but they were unable to go forward with the project.

In January 1957, when demand for downtown space intensified, the project was revived by new developers, the Uris Brothers, who brought in their favorite architects, Emery Roth & Sons, to completely redesign it. The Roth scheme would also rise thirty stories, but it would fill the zoning envelope to the maximum allowed, yielding an additional 200,000 square feet of net rentable area. The building's typical floors of about 59,000 square feet, the largest in the financial district, were very well suited to banks' growing needs for back-office space. The final design for Two Broadway was an overwhelming, thirty-two-story gridded mass sheathed in a curtain wall of blue-gray spandrel panels and silvery windows, constituting the first break with the dense masonry wall that had been the hallmark of Broadway's business canyon since the 1870s. Though a bold break with the past, the design of Two Broadway did not seem the optimistic symbol of a new urban order that the Lever Brothers headquarters had been for Park Avenue, nor was it a rival to the Chase bank's new headquarters (see below), plans for which were released as Two Broadway neared completion. Instead, the Roth design seemed to many a brutal affront to accepted canons of beauty, a fact exemplified by the decision of the Uris Brothers, spearheaded in these matters by B. H. Friedman, a Uris executive who was intensely interested in abstract art, to commission two mosaic panels from the painter Lee Krasner, working in collaboration with her nephew, Ronald Stein. One of the works, approximately fifteen feet square and placed over the Broad Street entrance, was composed of floral and organic forms executed in various shades of green, ultramarine, crimson and black, accented with yellow. The second panel, rendered in the same color scheme and compressed into a narrow, eighty-six-foot-long horizontal frieze that ran above the main entrance, featured oval shapes that were twisted and turned to create a dynamic, rhythmic pattern.

Douglas Haskell, the editor of *Architectural Forum*, found Two Broadway seriously wanting. His assessment, aptly entitled "Off-Tune on Broadway," criticized the Roths' building as no more than an ordinary speculative building placed in an extraordinarily prominent place. He particularly disliked the handling of the window wall, finding its "over-all pattern . . . a jazzy staggered one" that failed to attain "its ambitions to be interesting and different" because it was too crude for the size of the surface it was meant to enliven: "In this instance the internal proportions of the design itself would not be called distinguished, and its directional emphasis on the building is neither vertical nor horizontal but neutral: from a distance the wall looks not unlike a great piece of magnified and glass-filled chain mail." Haskell saw some value in the curtain-wall design as it applied to the building's rear elevations, where the need to maximize space within the restrictions of the setback ordinance led to a "cubistic method of composition":

> When the building lot ramifies in all directions, as this property does, the result is setback prisms of all manner of shapes; and when the building is all glass and all covered with the same filigree pattern of aluminum, like this building, and the edges of the prisms are the thinnest aluminum bars, exact definition becomes all but impossible to the eye of a stationary observer. Under the bewildering play of light and shade and reflection and cross-reflection, the whole cubistic pileup takes on a fasci-

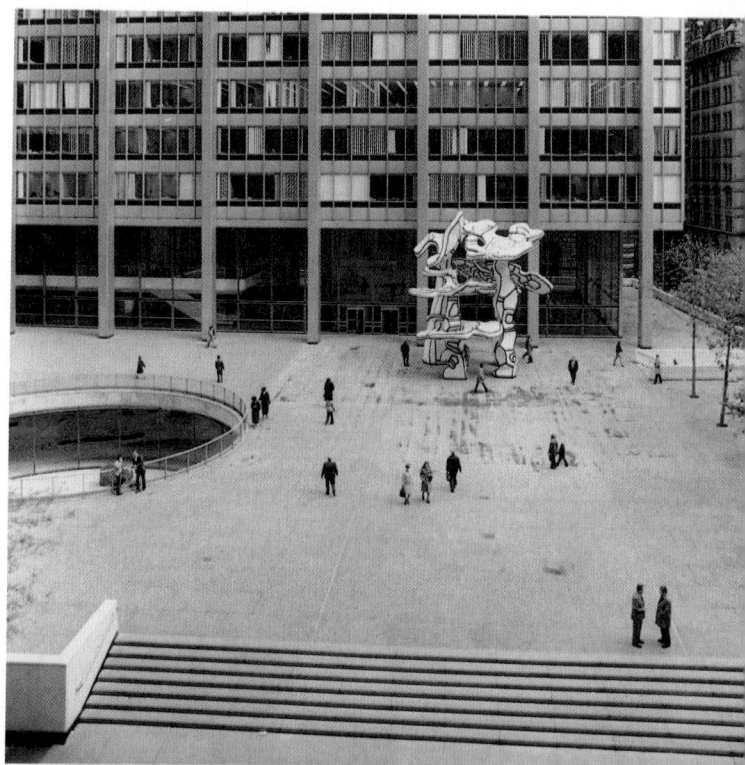

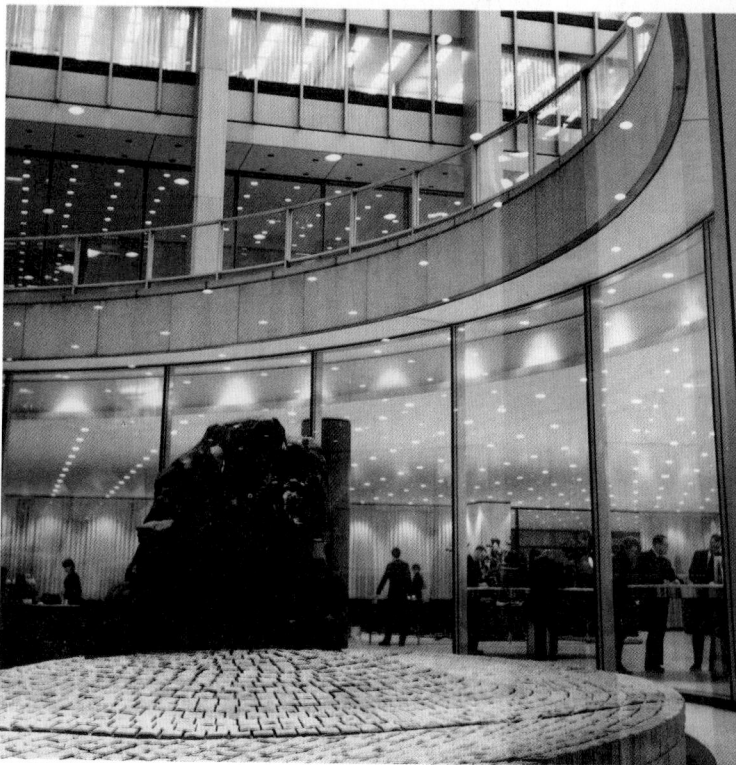

Left: Chase Manhattan Bank, One Chase Manhattan Plaza, between Pine, Nassau, Liberty and William streets. Skidmore, Owings & Merrill, 1960. View to the northwest. Lavine. CMA

Top: Chase Manhattan Bank. View to the north showing sunken garden by Isamu Noguchi (1960), plaza and sculpture *Group of Four Trees* (1972) by Jean Dubuffet. CMA

Bottom: Chase Manhattan Bank. View to the north from sunken garden. Lavine. CMA

nating aerial quality. Moreover, as in modern jazz, and in some kinds of modern painting, the process seems simply to go on and on, being "made up as it goes along," and there is no such thing as a definite, strongly willed final shape, but simply an endless play with a set of themes.[12]

In November 1955 the Chase Manhattan Bank electrified the city's development community with the announcement that it intended to consolidate 8,700 employees working in nine different locations in a skyscraper headquarters building in the financial district, to be designed by Skidmore, Owings & Merrill (SOM).[13] The significance of the Chase bank's decision went beyond the building's contribution as architecture. The announcement of the project, more than any other single factor, triggered the economic revitalization of lower Manhattan, which had been so threatened by decline that the board of directors of the New York Stock Exchange had become alarmed for the entire financial community's physical stability. When the Chase National Bank absorbed the Bank of the Manhattan Company in 1955, the time seemed appropriate to make a decisive move and the bank acquired from the Guaranty Trust Company a 64,000-square-foot parcel fronting on Liberty Street.

According to *Fortune*, when SOM partner Edward James Matthews got wind of the potential project, he put the firm's principal partner, Nathaniel Owings, on the case.[14] Owings assembled a team of partners who succeeded in meeting informally with top Chase executives on June 10, 1955, and the firm was retained on a "time card" basis to begin preparing schematic designs. By July 15 SOM had prepared a full-scale analysis of the downtown site and its context; from the first the new headquarters building was seen not as an isolated project but as the anchor of the financial district's process of self-renewal. At this time Owings proposed the bold strategy the bank was to adopt: the creation of a superblock that would combine its holdings with the recently acquired property. From July 16 to August 30, when Gordon Bunshaft, the New York office's design partner, was in Europe, his chief assistant, Roy Allen, Jr., and Jacques Guiton, a senior designer with the firm, began developing alternate plans for the use of the site while other SOM executives began to explore the superblock concept with city officials. As a "control," the design team developed a scheme for two buildings, a fifty-two-story tower and an adjunct fifteen-story building. But at the first full-dress presentation to the Chase board of directors on September 26, an alternate scheme calling for a single slab was also presented. Though the board favored this scheme, it asked that the "control" be developed as well. Bunshaft did not return from Europe until October 15, only then taking over the design. By December 6 Chase was persuaded that the single slab on a plaza was the way to go and the other scheme was dropped. Construction began on January 28, 1957, and the building was completed in the summer of 1960; the plaza followed two years later.

With the announcement of the Chase building's imminent construction, the editors of *Fortune* magazine, believing that a period of dramatic change for the financial district lay ahead, commissioned the photographer Walker Evans to take "a last look backward," documenting an area that had changed very little since the 1920s: "Its cacographic towers; its peeling lunch joints; its meek little Morgan Bank looking like a fairly respectable Indianapolis branch office; its ubiquitous hardware shops glutted with sleazy pliers—all this familiar furniture looks almost exactly the way it looked thirty years ago down to the lapel cut of the suits worn by passing brokers."[15]

The proposed Chase Manhattan Bank was by far the biggest new building downtown; in fact, among postwar buildings throughout the city it was rivaled in size only by the Socony-Mobil Building (see chapter 5). To achieve the 2.5-acre site needed for such a large building, a superblock bounded by Liberty Street on the north, William Street on the east, Pine Street on the south and Nassau Street on the west was created, incorporating one block of Cedar Street that would be demapped. The Chase project was nicknamed "little Rockefeller Center," although the midtown colossus was a large-scale development, not a superblock. In fact, Rockefeller Center created additional streets, although their ownership was kept private, while Chase reduced the number of streets. In return for the closed street, the perimeter streets were widened so that the city lost no public real estate. The city was also given $100,000, and Chase paid the costs for relocating utilities. The new superblock would be cleared of all buildings, including the massive Mutual Life Insurance Building (Charles W. Clinton, 1884).[16] The only exception was the current Chase headquarters, a thirty-eight-story building at 18 Pine Street, designed in 1928 by the Chicago firm of Graham, Anderson, Probst & White; it was to remain standing, though it would be renovated to provide a sidewalk arcade along Pine Street.[17]

Superblocking was advantageous in many ways. Had there been no street closing, Chase could have built about 1,250,000 square feet of usable space on the site north of Cedar Street and another 150,000 square feet in buildings it intended to modernize on the eastern half of the block south of Cedar Street. But the SOM proposal creating the superblock offered the possibility of a single, sheer, 813-foot-tall slab rising to sixty stories and occupying only 30 percent of the site, only 5 percent more coverage than the zoning permitted for towers of unlimited height. In return for the generous open space, the tower slab would yield 1.7 million square feet of usable space, 300,000 square feet more than the conventional approach would have generated. The slab provided 30,000-square-foot floors with twenty columns of approximately three by five feet along the outside perimeter, in the manner pioneered by Howe & Lescaze in their Philadelphia Saving Fund Society Building of 1929–31.[18] This allowed for office floors that were encumbered only by the mechanical and service core.

SOM's elegantly detailed Chase tower was sheathed in 28-by-107-foot panels of anodized aluminum. Stainless steel was rejected for cost reasons, while granite was rejected because Frederick Ecker, the senior building committee member, considered that time-honored material too traditional. The decision to use aluminum was a bold stroke: the building's silvery metallic sheen, enhanced by its glassiness, created an instantly identifiable and virtually unforgettable contrast with the traditional masonry mass of the lower Manhattan skyline. While not the tallest building in lower Manhattan, Chase dominated and drastically altered the area's by now historic skyline by virtue of its singular shape and its bright finish. As *Architectural Forum* put it in the unprecedented thirty-page section it devoted to the building in 1961, "The big, broad-shouldered Chase stated crisply the mood and abilities of a newer age. It was not so much a cathedral of money as a powerful and superbly equipped machine for handling it."[19]

Because of the site's slope, many of the functions of the massive building were housed below grade. A 94,000-square-foot lower lobby level was used primarily as a banking floor, and there were four more full-site basement floors and a fifth level, occupying about half the site, that contained a vault. The building had major entries at the plaza level (which was more or less level with Pine Street) and at the lower lobby level, entered directly from Liberty Street. Although the plaza was large, it was somewhat flawed by its limited access. Even at its south end, along Pine Street, pedestrians needed to climb shallow steps to reach it, while at the northeast corner of the site, where the land sloped away, it was twenty feet above sidewalk level, in part to provide pedestrian access to the building's lower ground floor and headroom for a truck entrance to the below-grade service docks. A circular cut was made in the 98,000-square-foot plaza floor to form a sunken garden, designed by the sculptor Isamu Noguchi. Visually connecting the two levels and providing light to the lower level, Noguchi's garden consisted of a sixty-foot-diameter pool paved with granite cubes and punctuated by seven basalt blocks selected from the bed of the Uji River in Japan. In 1972 a ten-year search for an appropriately scaled monumental work for the building's plaza finally culminated in the installation of a forty-two-foot-high construction designed by the French artist Jean Dubuffet as part of his *L'Hourloupe* series, a word he coined to connote physical grotesquerie and tragedy. The Chase piece, called *Group of Four Trees*, a gift to the city from David Rockefeller, was a twenty-five-ton black-and-white abstraction fabricated in concrete, steel and fiberglass-sheathed aluminum.

The building's interiors were also distinctive, and the thirty-foot-tall main lobby at plaza level was particularly impressive. Like the Seagram's lobby, it was a glass-enclosed room whose principal ornaments were the exterior boundary features—the landscaped plaza and the traditional, lavishly detailed masonry buildings that framed the site, most notably York & Sawyer's Florentine-style Federal Reserve Bank of 1924.[20] The column-free office floors were ingeniously organized. For one thing, the elevator core was placed off-center, creating deeper space on the choicer southern side of the building and gaining some variety and flexibility in space planning as well. Most of the departments were housed in open-plan configurations, so that despite 7,500 Chase employees working in 1.2 million square feet of the building (about 500,000 square feet of space was rented to outside tenants), there were only 150 private offices. Top-level executives were housed on the seventeenth floor, which was accessible from the street by a special express elevator that could also whisk them to the executive dining room on the sixtieth floor. This dining room was the most impressive place in the building. Ada Louise Huxtable noted that the effect of the glass-walled aerie, where one is "greeted by the incomparable vista of New York harbor and the view of a luminous, mist-shrouded Manhattan Island," was that of an "overwhelming assault . . . on the imagination and the senses."[21] The original plan for the sixtieth floor had called for placing a spectacular piece of sculpture just off the elevator landing, intended as a principal element in the spatial sequence guiding visitors to the dining room. But, according to Bunshaft, once the sixtieth floor was framed in, it became clear that the sculpture had been provided free of charge, so to speak, by H. Craig Severance and Yasuo Matsui when they designed the spectacular pyramidal roof and spire of their Bank of the Manhattan Company Building at 40 Wall Street.[22]

The interior fittings were in keeping with the machinelike precision of the curtain wall. As much as any other large-scale office building of the period, even more than Seagram's and perhaps CBS, Chase was a work of total design. Its extraordinary interior design program was handled by Davis Allen of SOM, assisted by interior designer Ward Bennett, who designed some of the furniture and tabletop items and selected many of the

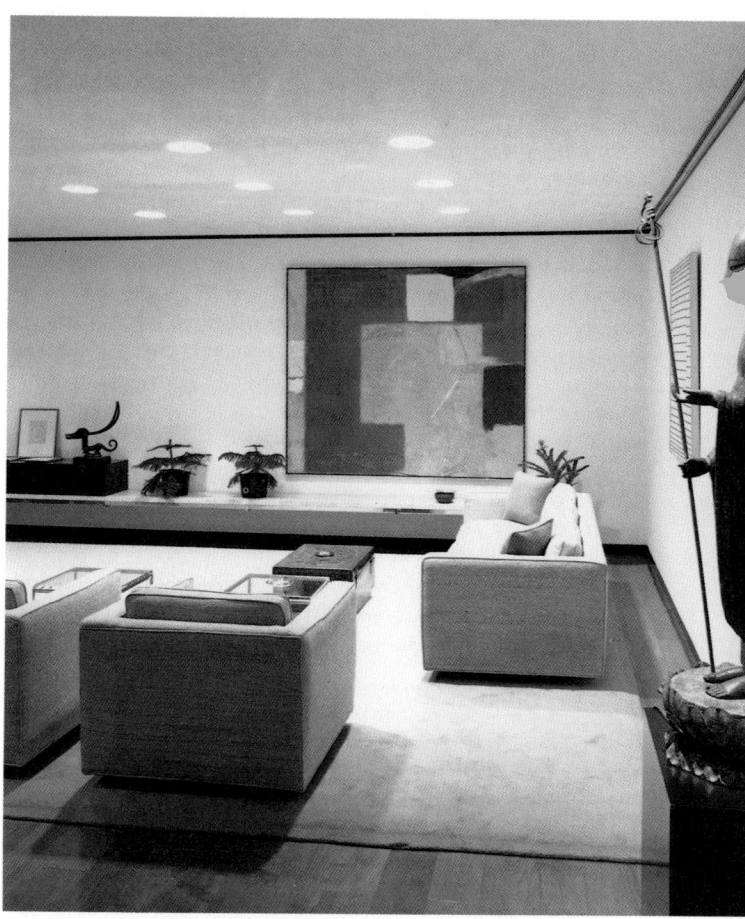

Chase Manhattan Bank, One Chase Manhattan Plaza, between Pine, Nassau, Liberty and William streets. Skidmore, Owings & Merrill, 1960. Executive office designed by Ward Bennett. Stoller. ©ESTO

175

accent pieces used in the executive offices and employee facilities. Although Bennett's furniture and accessories (including twenty different types of ashtrays, manufactured by top craftsmen like Hermès and Gucci) were remarkable, it was the lavish use of art in public areas and executive offices that established an important trend in corporate culture. The art was drawn from a large collection assembled by the company with the help of a selection board that included museum curators Alfred H. Barr, Jr., and James J. Sweeney, as well as David Rockefeller and Gordon Bunshaft, who continued to serve the bank in this capacity for eighteen years; Bennett was also involved in the art program. Rockefeller, the bank's president, assigned a $500,000 budget for the purchase and commissioning of artwork. In addition to a remarkable art collection and specially designed furnishings, not to mention custom-designed faucets and taps in the bathrooms, the building's decor also included a sophisticated program of graphics developed by the firm of Chermayeff & Geismar, most notable for the corporate logo they created for Chase (see chapter 1).

In the appraisal that concluded its exhaustive presentation of the Chase building, *Architectural Forum* described the building as more a culmination than an innovation :

> Chase is a milestone, perhaps even an end point, in the best development of the American skyscraper, which for decades has been the summit meeting place of business, engineering and art. In many big office buildings, the result speaks of a clear victory for one of these, or at best an uneasy truce. Chase reconciles and balances the three, and each in its most advanced form; it works, and looks, like a big, handsomely designed business machine, its complex anatomy of systems multiplies the efforts of its users . . . ; art has not been spooned on for appearances, but carefully integrated into every detail down to the paperweights on the desks. Architecture is already moving restlessly on, as architecture will. But it can look back on Chase as a remarkably complete statement of a set of long-held, long-developed ideas. It is not just a superbly efficient instrument for work, but a totally considered environment as well.[23]

But despite its innumerable merits, the Chase building also raised serious questions. The *Forum* article brought up some important issues about the wisdom of retaining the bank's former headquarters building, which had prevented the creation of a truly generous plaza; about the new building's sheer size and its population density; and, finally, about its very configuration: "Is a lone, flat-topped slab of this size really a graceful and fitting addition to a romantically pinnacled sky line?"[24] This last point was to be developed by a young Austrian architect, Hans Hollein. After traveling across America Hollein returned to Vienna and prepared a drawing that showed his version of the bland box of the Chase: a superwide slab, wittily decorated with a Classical pediment, overshadowing its surroundings and blocking out the pinnacles of Wall Street buildings.[25] His version of the building, not so different from the radiator grille of a Rolls-Royce, served as not only a warning about the consequences of unlimited size but also a call for architects to recapture the symbolic possibilities of great height and romantic profiles. Other negative responses emerged in the months following the building's initial publication. Adolf De Roy Mark, a Philadelphia architect, in a letter to *Forum*, characterized Chase as a "stacked subway concourse,"[26] while the conservative gadfly Walter C. Kidney, in his letter, derided the building's art program as "a warning to everyone who contemplates becoming a businessman in this day and age. It seems to me that Mr. Ward Bennett has built into the new Chase the datedness of the future."[27]

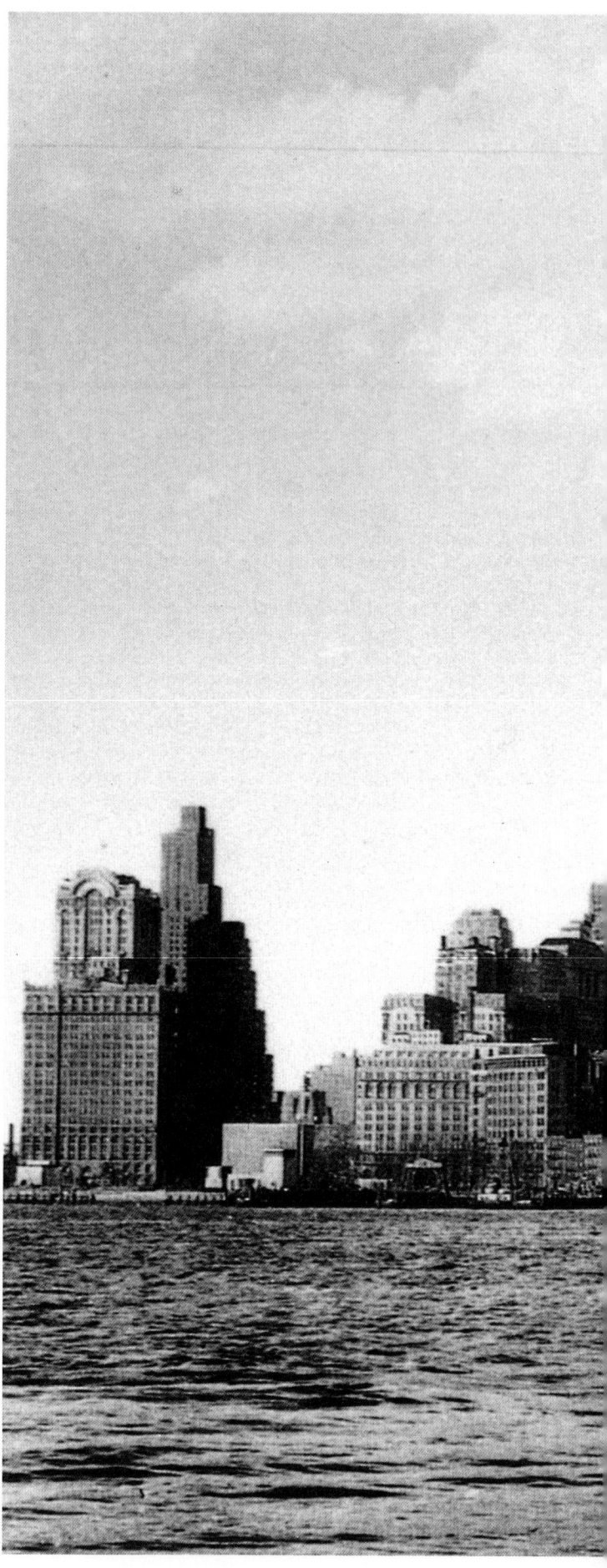

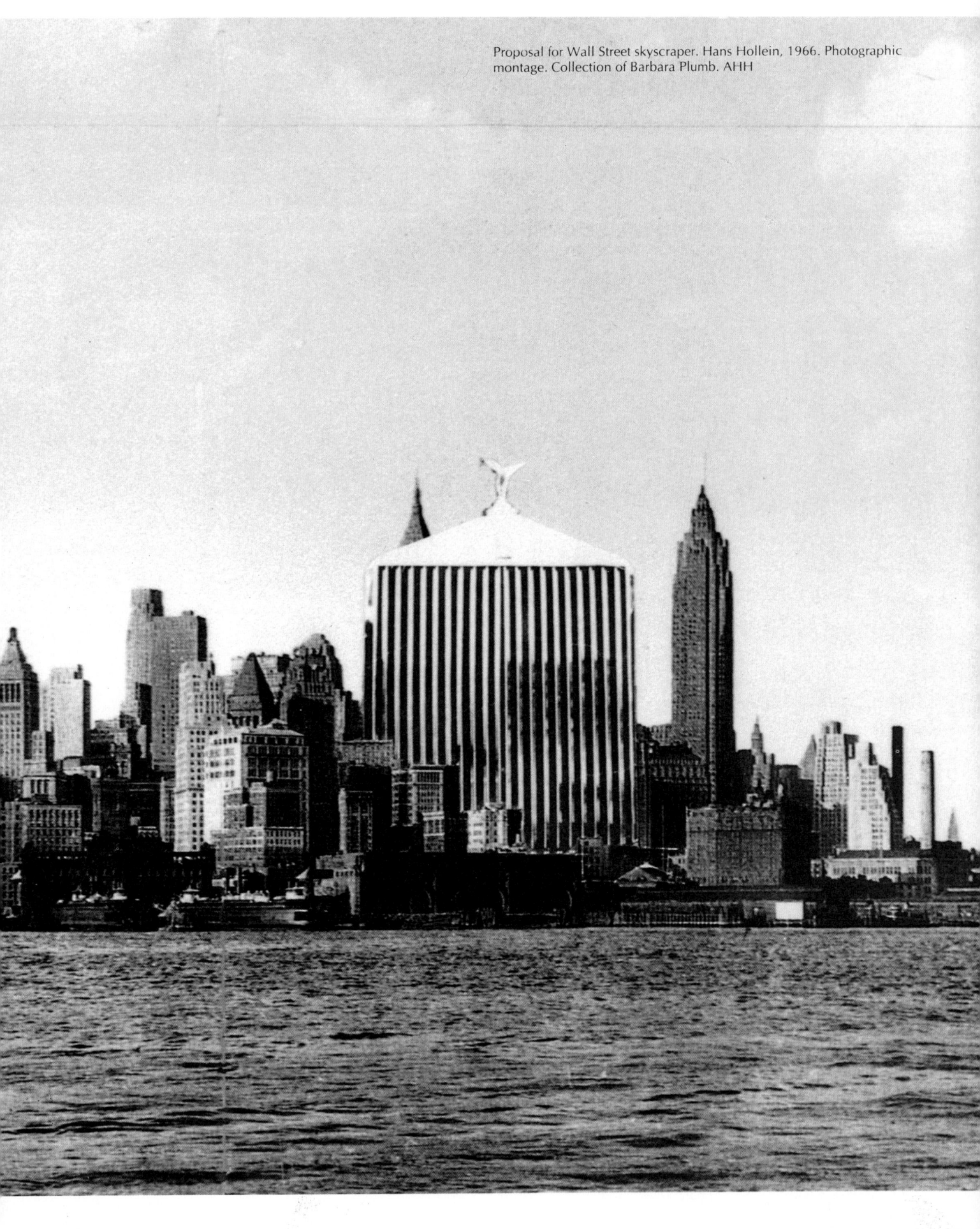

Proposal for Wall Street skyscraper. Hans Hollein, 1966. Photographic montage. Collection of Barbara Plumb. AHH

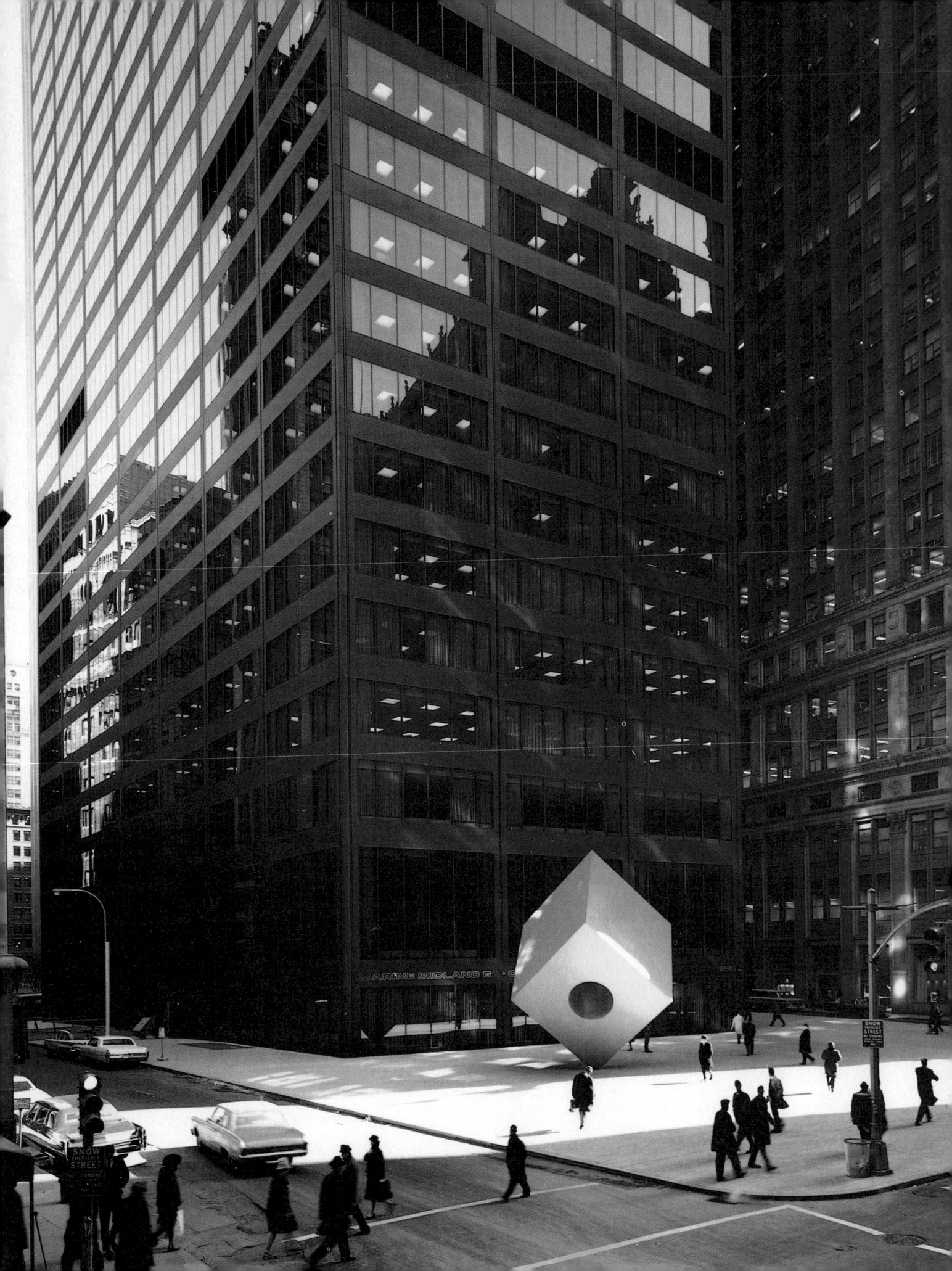

Though Chase's commitment to build stimulated a boom in downtown office construction, it did not do much, at least at first, to stimulate quality design. Many of the new buildings were banal: 110 William Street, Sylvan and Robert Bien's thirty-two-story, 696,000-square-foot building of 1956–58, which utilized the frame of a 1918 office building (Frank H. Quimby);[28] 80 Pine Street, a forty-story, 983,000-square-foot building designed by Emery Roth & Sons in 1957–60;[29] and 100 Church Street, a twenty-story, 860,000-square-foot building of 1957–58, also by the Roth firm.[30] Almost as bland was 30 West Broadway (1959), designed by William Lescaze, a fourteen-story bare-bones back-office interpretation of the designer's high-style Modernism of the 1930s and a crude version of his more successful uptown building at 711 Third Avenue (see chapter 5).[31] AT&T's subsidiary, Western Electric, built a home office building at 222 Broadway (1959–61), at the northeast corner of Fulton Street, which was designed by Shreve, Lamb & Harmon.[32] Replacing a number of buildings, including George B. Post's St. Paul Building of 1897–99 and Donn Barber's National Park Bank of 1904, the new thirty-one-story building was a dowdy, clumsily massed, beige-brick banality, a sad comedown from the glories of William Welles Bosworth's AT&T headquarters building of 1914–17, diagonally across the street at 195 Broadway.[33]

In 1961 plans were announced for 140 Broadway, a new building that would rival Chase in the quality of its architectural and urban design.[34] Also known as the Marine Midland Building, 140 Broadway (1967) was designed by Gordon Bunshaft of Skidmore, Owings & Merrill. The first scheme, initially developed by Erwin Wolfson shortly before his death, called for a thirty-two-story tower similar to the Chase bank in design, with two plazas to break up and "aerate" the lower Broadway canyon. This scheme was to have masonry sunshades projecting beyond the floor slab. When the project was taken over by Harry Helmsley at the invitation of Carl Morse, the builder, it was redesigned. As it evolved, the fifty-two-story tower slab became an essay in curtain-wall minimalism, rising without setbacks from its slightly trapezoidal site, bounded by Broadway, Liberty, Nassau and Cedar streets. One of the first tall buildings built under the 1961 zoning ordinance, it replaced York & Sawyer's Guaranty Trust Company Building of 1913.

Though the revised building, with its virtually flat facades, seemed the embodiment of an aesthetic minimalism driven by economics, it was in fact costlier to build than the typical commercial product. As Bunshaft was to recall: "This building, due to the wisdom of Wolfson initially, Helmsley waking up, and Carl Morse urging that it not be the cheapest building in the world but the most economical one, set higher standards somewhat—not up to what Chase would do, but more than an Emery Roth building would have."[35] The building occupied 40 percent of the site and rose 677 feet, leaving wide areas of travertine-paved sidewalk on all sides. Not exactly a plaza, and certainly not an outdoor room, the open space of the second scheme was nonetheless a very welcome relief to the area. By virtue of its connections to the Chase plaza, the wide sidewalks created an element that planners and architects began to seize upon as the beginning of a network of linked pedestrian open spaces crossing the island. The first two floors of the building contained a branch office of the Marine Midland Bank. Its sleekly Modernist interiors were an appropriate extension of the building's exterior minimalism.

One of the most memorable aspects of 140 Broadway was its dialogue with the red cube designed by Isamu Noguchi for the Broadway plaza. At first, Bunshaft, fresh from a trip to

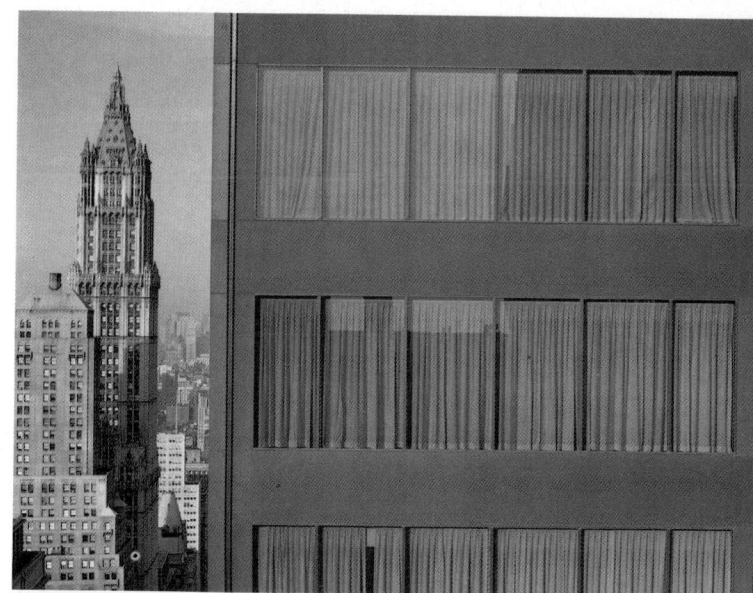

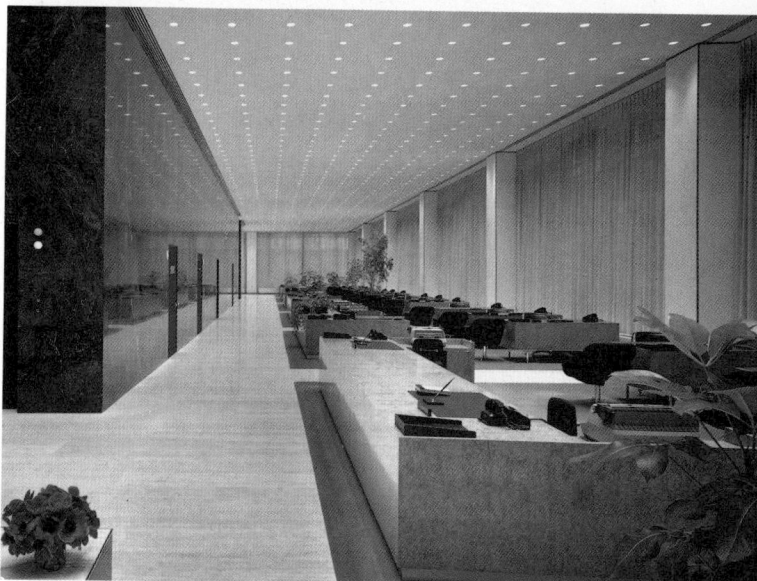

Left: 140 Broadway, Broadway to Nassau Street, Cedar to Liberty Street. Skidmore, Owings & Merrill, 1967. View to the southeast showing Broadway plaza with sculpture *The Red Cube* (1967) by Isamu Noguchi. Stoller. ©ESTO

Top: 140 Broadway. View to the north showing facade detail. Robinson. CERO

Bottom: 140 Broadway. Interior of Marine Midland Bank branch. Stoller. ©ESTO

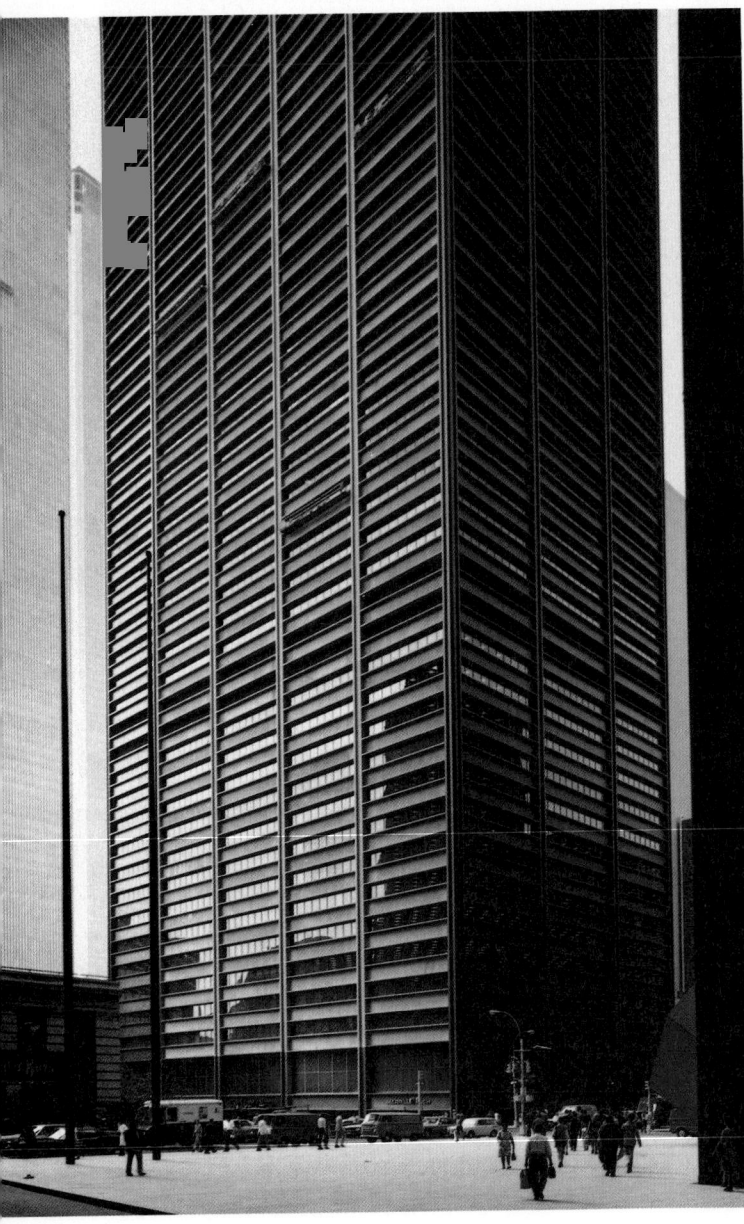

Above: United States Steel Building, One Liberty Plaza, Church Street to Broadway, Liberty to Cortlandt Street. Roy Allen, 1972. View to the northwest. Stoller. ©ESTO

Top right: 88 Pine Street, bounded by Maiden Lane, Water and Front streets. I. M. Pei & Partners, 1973. View to the southwest. Lieberman. PCF

Bottom right: 88 Pine Street. Entrance detail. Cserna. PCF

Stonehenge, proposed that Noguchi create a megalith, but Helmsley felt the estimate for such a piece was too high. The architect then proposed a cube to Noguchi, who took the idea further, producing a rhombohedron pierced by a cylindrical hole, the verticality of which complemented the slender verticality of the building behind it. As Bunshaft's biographer Carol Krinsky was to later write: "This is probably Noguchi's most popular work of art done in conjunction with architecture, partly because it requires no interpretation. It is a teasingly precarious-looking object for a sober building."[36] *Fortune* was more ambivalent: surveying lower Manhattan's new office buildings in 1969, it observed that "the few attempts at decoration, like Isamu Noguchi's punctured cube . . . show how far U.S. culture has moved from romantic humanism since *Prometheus* was installed at Rockefeller Center in 1934."[37]

Ada Louise Huxtable praised Bunshaft's "skin" building, although she said it was "the kind of flat, sheer, curtain wall that it has become chic to reject." She went on to explain that "younger architects, off on a wild, Arthurian search for the nouveau picturesque, and an uninformed public that have never understood or accepted what was happening have turned their backs on one of the miracles of modern building: the skyscraper wall reduced to gossamer minimums of shining, thin material hung on a frame of extraordinary strength through superb contemporary technology." She described 140 Broadway as "a commercial building, not a monument," one that avoids "'artful' plasticity" to take its place "as a foil for the ornate masonry around it."[38] Six years later, in 1974, Huxtable was to go even further in her praise, saying that it was "not only one of [the] buildings I admire most in New York, but that I admire most anywhere."[39]

Perhaps Arthur Drexler, director of the Museum of Modern Art's Department of Architecture and Design, delivered the most understanding assessment of 140 Broadway:

> The notion of minimal form as skin rather than bones . . . reaches its apogee in New York with Gordon Bunshaft's Marine Midland Building. . . . The "function" of the building is recognized as analogous to that of a package; what is offered is a commodity: portions of space. Marine Midland is thus a commodity in a glass and metal wrapping so flat that it appears to have been printed rather than built. . . . The building is surrounded by a field of travertine paving and this, together with a bright red metal cube designed by Isamu Noguchi, completes a tripartite composition. . . . Together the three elements—building, paving, cube—are somehow more than they seem to be, as if the composition had been created by a sculptor of the minimal school intent on transposing the empiricism of architecture into the metaphysics of abstract form.[40]

Just as the finishing touches were being put on 140 Broadway, diagonally to its west demolition was already under way on Ernest Flagg's inventive and elegantly slender Singer Tower, which at the time of its completion in 1908 had been the world's tallest building (see chapter 16). Taking the place of the Singer Tower and the earlier Singer Building, also by Flagg, as well as a number of other buildings, including Francis H. Kimball's City Investing Building (1906–08), was the United States Steel Building (1972), designed by SOM partner Roy Allen.[41] The building filled the block bounded by Broadway, Liberty, Church and Cortlandt streets, while the block immediately to its south, bounded by Broadway, Cedar, Church and Liberty streets, was also cleared to create a public open space dubbed Liberty Plaza. This lay immediately to the west of 140 Broadway and formed a third link in the chain of pedestrian-only open spaces that was being forged from the Chase plaza on the east to the World Trade Center. The unused development rights from the Liberty Plaza site were combined with those of the block to the north to permit the construction of 1.8 million square feet of net office space, piled in an exceptionally bulky 250-by-150-foot slab rising fifty-four stories or 772 feet high. The plaza, however, was not fully realized until 1980, because the Chock full o'Nuts restaurant, a ground-floor tenant of one of the buildings on the site, refused to give up its very valuable lease. This forced the developers, U.S. Steel in joint venture with the Galbreath-Ruffin Corporation, to demolish all the other buildings on the site as well as eleven stories above the Chock full o'Nuts restaurant and develop the plaza in stages.

The huge mass of One Liberty Plaza was made to seem even more hulking by the unusual structural system devised by the architects working in close collaboration with U.S. Steel, who viewed the headquarters building as a showcase for their principal product. The building consisted of exceptionally wide (fifty feet) structural bays spanned by six-foot-deep plate girders. This solution was influenced by the design for the Civic Center in Chicago, which SOM worked on with two other architectural firms, C. F. Murphy Associates and Loebl, Schlossman & Bennett.[42] The superscale structural frame was exposed on the outside of the building. To prevent the possibility of fire-induced structural failure, flame canopies were developed to conceal the fireproofing between the top and bottom beam flanges as well as between the spandrels and girders. This fireproofing was in turn cased in more steel so that, in effect, what appears to be the structure is not. The enormous size of the spandrels, combined with the extra depth of their flanges due to the flame canopies, resulted in a highly sculptured window wall that heightened the sense of mass.

In his introduction to a survey of SOM's work, Arthur Drexler found little to praise in the design for U.S. Steel:

> Here the intent is to use steel as visibly and assertively as possible: it is what the client sells. . . . The immediate visual impression is that if the U.S. Steel building is structurally sound, then everything around it must be unsafe; if the others are safe, then the U.S. Steel building must be something of an exaggeration. The sheer quantity of metal displayed to the eye is perhaps no more than would be consumed by dividing the structural bays with closely spaced vertical mullions, or using some other cladding system; it is, of course, the reversal of proportions between solid and void that makes the difference. This is not a glass building with a skeleton frame; it is a steel wall with glazed slots, hypnotically compelling, especially as the eye climbs the rungs of the facade and the glass disappears altogether.[43]

One other building in the financial district exemplifed the structurally determined minimalism typical of SOM's work, but with considerably more finesse in the handling of the details: I. M. Pei & Partners' 88 Pine Street (1973).[44] The superblock site, bounded by Maiden Lane, Water, Front and Pine streets, was created by demapping De Peyster Street between Water and Front streets. In addition, Pine Street was closed to traffic between Water and Front streets to create a plaza that would link up with the plaza on the Pine Street side of 100 Wall Street (1969), the massively inarticulate, twenty-nine-story, 420,000-square-foot building designed by Emery Roth & Sons.[45]

The Pei firm's first New York City office building, 88 Pine Street was designed by associate partner James Ingo Freed. In some ways it synthesized aspects of Chase, 140 Broadway and U.S. Steel: set in a plaza, the skin-and-bones building was little

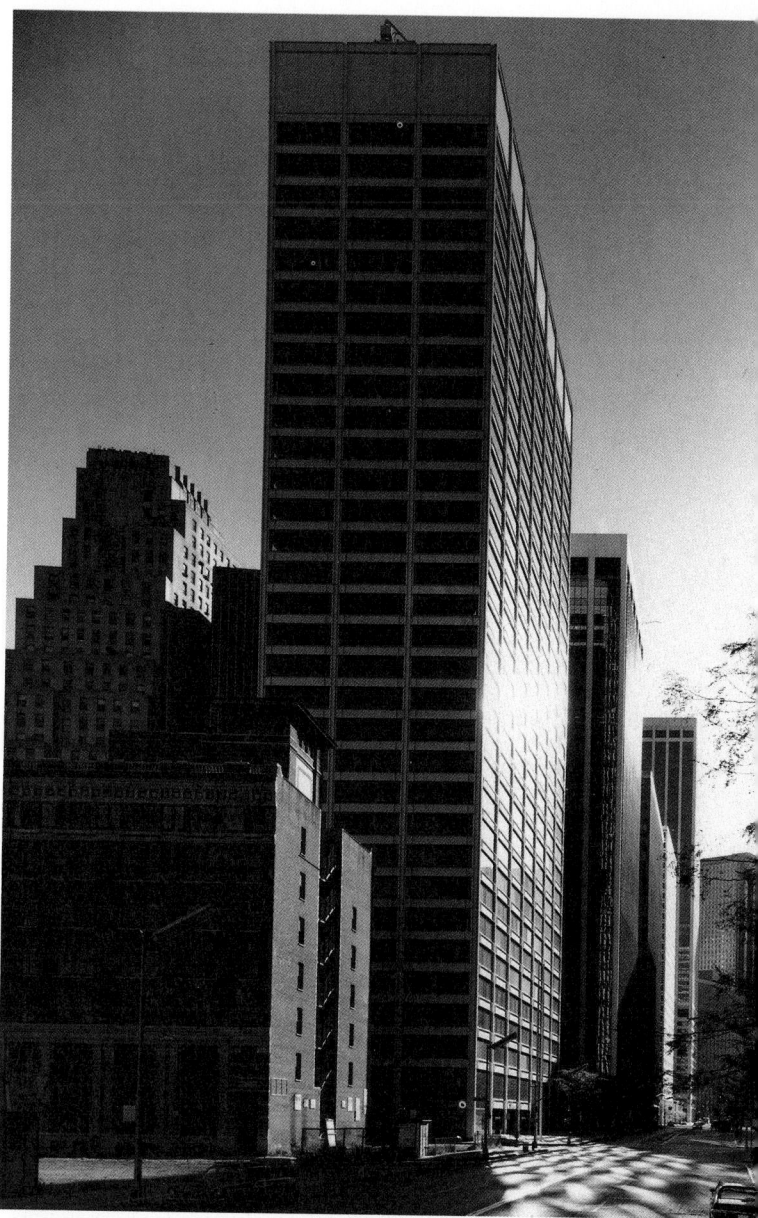

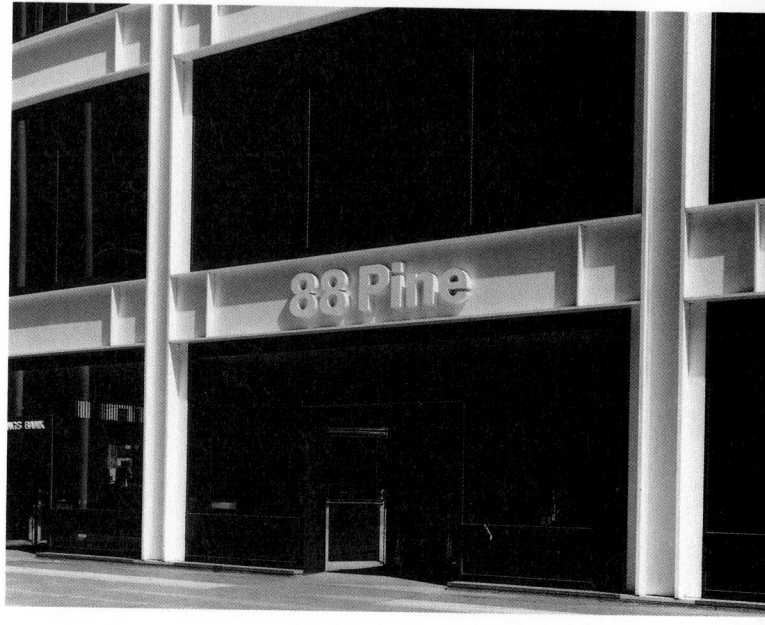

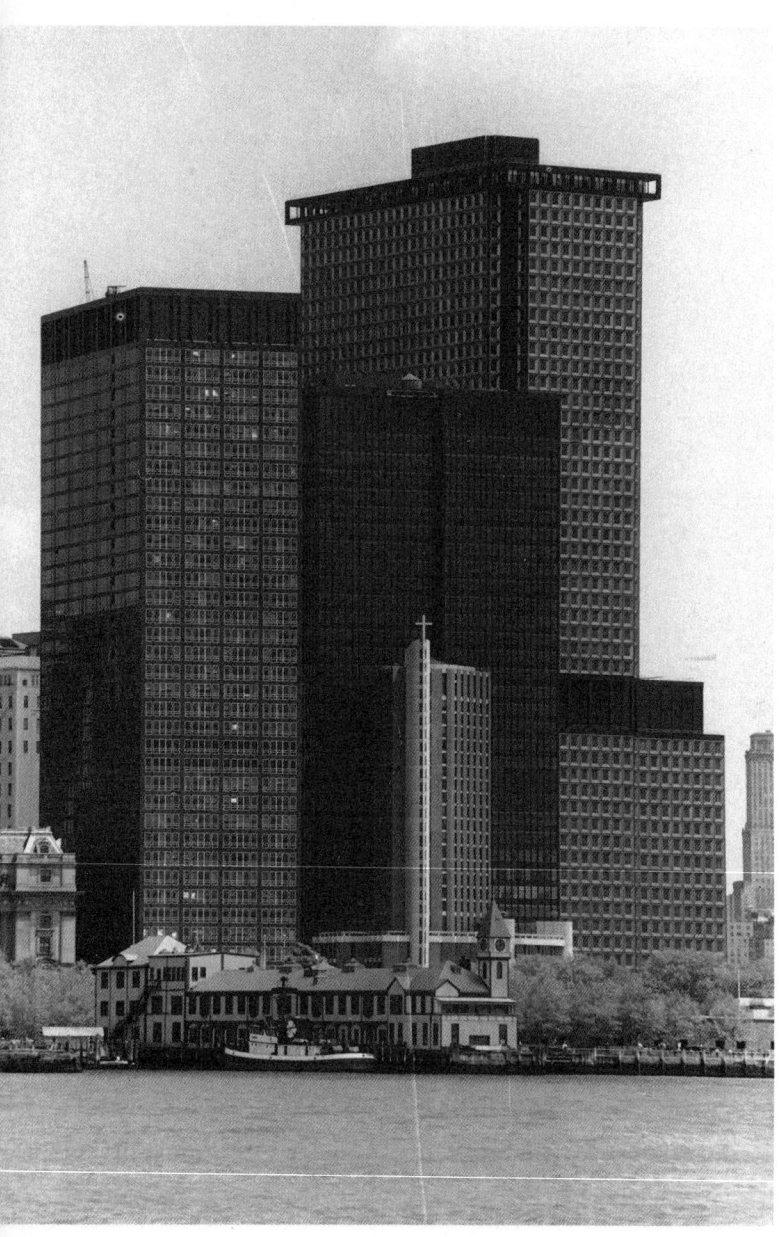

View to the northwest showing, from left to right: One Battery Park Plaza (Emery Roth & Sons, 1971), One State Street Plaza (Emery Roth & Sons, 1969), Seamen's Church Institute (Eggers & Higgins, 1969) and One New York Plaza (William Lescaze and Kahn & Jacobs, 1969). Fred W. McDarrah. FWM

more than a white-painted aluminum frame infilled with recessed, butt-jointed twenty-six-foot-wide glass panels to maximize the contrast between the "solid" of structure and the "void" of enclosure. To the editors of *Architecture Plus*, it was "the prototypical, late-20th century American office tower—straightforward, economical, and clean." No ordinary problem solver, it was a building with "a sophistication of detail and of proportion that gives it considerable distinction on a street lined with curtain-wall catalogues."[46] But the building was, in fact, not comparable with a purely speculative undertaking: it cost three dollars more per square foot to build. The high-ceiling lobby and adjoining bank were impeccably detailed, with glinting curved surfaces of polished stainless steel and Chinese-red elevator cabs. The thirty-two-story tower slab rose uninterrupted from its site, creating a twenty-five-foot-wide, tree-lined sidewalk plaza along Water Street. The sidewalk plaza was punctuated by abstract constructions in stainless steel by Yu Yu Yang, commemorating the fire that destroyed the ocean liner *Queen Elizabeth I* while it was docked in Hong Kong (the building's owner, Morley Cho, head of Associated Maritime Industries, Inc., was also the ship's last owner).

Despite *Architecture Plus*'s encomium, Pei and Freed's building seemed rather conservative at the time of its completion, when commercial architecture was moving toward more glittery effects using reflecting glass or more sculptural effects employing masonry. Unfortunately, New York had no distinguished commercial examples of either of these trends in the early 1970s. Among those that sought the effects of sculpted masonry, there were a number of aesthetic failures, none more prominent or less happy than One New York Plaza, the 2.3 million-square-foot, fifty-story behemoth.[47] Designed by William Lescaze & Associates (with Kahn & Jacobs), it was the first of a four-building group that Huxtable described as "a private development of singularly aggressive lack of distinction or urban coordination, built without city design supervision."[48] But not without city involvement: the seven-block site that would eventually include One, Two and Four New York Plaza and 55 Water Street was first proposed by Robert Moses as an urban renewal area in 1959. Much of the southern portion of the site was owned by Atlas-McGrath, an investment firm that acquired the land, intending to build a new headquarters for the stock exchange. This did not go forward, nor did the renewal project, which the city was unable to fund.[49] Huxtable saw Atlas-McGrath's operation as a typical New York plot by real estate interests to thwart planning:

> The investment firm of Atlas-McGrath assembled enough prime lower Manhattan land not only to frustrate the city's urban renewal designation for the area, but to make it possible to create, with ease and art and single ownership, a small-scale Rockefeller Center on one of the city's most superb waterfront sites. This would have been compensation for historic destruction. It is not being done. Instead of coordinated planning and design, the *modus operandi* has been simply to milk the most out of each separate, negotiable parcel independently.[50]

Designed under the direction of Nevio Maggiora, the facade of One New York Plaza consisted of an absolutely regular grid of ten-by-twelve-foot prefabricated aluminum-and-glass panels. The building was popularly known, according to Ada Louise Huxtable, "as the waffle iron or barber shop building for its insistent pattern of prefabricated, shaped aluminum window framing that reminds one of stamped in barber shop ceilings at a massively blown up scale."[51] To Paul Goldberger, the facade looked like "fifty stories of Otis elevator buttons (or blank TV screens),"[52] and to Norval White and Elliot Willensky, the panels were just so many "interior decorators' picture frames."[53] At the corners, the air-conditioning risers were designed to create a visual frame, which was concluded at the top by a "cornice" housing an exclusive dining club. The building's bulk and uniformity made it the most prominent if not the most distinguished new building to rise along the hitherto low-scale East River landscape. A fire in the building on August 5, 1970, which killed two people and injured thirty-five, raised serious questions about whether prevailing building and fire codes provided sufficient protection in sealed buildings, particularly those with large office floors.

Two New York Plaza, a forty-story tower designed by Kahn & Jacobs, also with Nevio Maggiora in charge, was equally banal and equally single-minded.[54] Huxtable observed that "it makes the flashy commercial formula of vertical aluminum strips inescapable by land or sea." She found it, like One New York Plaza, a "drop dead" building "in bulk and visual aspect."[55] Paul Goldberger described its plaza as "a windswept wasteland," and its exterior as "sheathed with a dreary skin of vertical stripes which indent in an exaggerated expression of exhaust equipment on mechanical floors."[56] Two New York Plaza was also an economic disaster. As the market for office space dried up in 1969–70, it became, according to *Fortune*, "the undisputed white elephant of the office building boom."[57] When it was completed in 1971, it did not have a single tenant for its 1.1 million square feet of space, and Atlas-McGrath, its developers, were in serious financial trouble.

Development along the East River waterfront had begun to have disturbing effects, not only compromising the mountain-range effect of the lower Manhattan skyline and bringing the loss of the historic, small-scale buildings that had traditionally formed its foothills, but also, because of superblocking, cutting off vistas to the water from the upland streets. Alarmed by the urbanistic implications of such trends and spurred on by strong criticism from Ada Louise Huxtable,[58] the city's Office of Lower Manhattan Development, an offshoot of the City Planning Commission, developed a set of design guidelines for development along the East River waterfront.

The first building to be built under the new plan was 55 Water Street (1972).[59] Located on a superblock created by joining together four small-scale blocks, 55 Water Street occupied a 165,000-square-foot site bounded by Water and South streets, Old Slip and Jeannette Park, which the Uris Brothers, the developers, agreed to rebuild as part of their project. Sacrificed to the site were Coenties Slip and Cuyler's Alley, as well as part of Front Street. In clearing the site the thirteen-story Seamen's Church Institute (Warren & Wetmore, 1907; additions 1913 and 1929, also by Warren & Wetmore) was demolished. The institute moved to a new twenty-three-story, red-brick headquarters at 15 State Street, on the southeast corner of Pearl Street, designed by Eggers & Higgins in 1969.[60] To Huxtable, the new Seamen's Church Institute, which had a "projecting stair tower topped by a lighted cross, and walls of textured brick and exposed concrete," exemplified "institutional skyscraper style."[61] Though it attempted to complement the delicate Watson house (attributed to John McComb, Jr., 1793–1806), which it abutted, it had the opposite effect of overwhelming it.

Designed by Emery Roth & Sons, 55 Water Street was extraordinarily bulky; it was, in fact, the second largest office building in the world (only the Pentagon in Washington was larger) and the largest commercial office building, with over three million square feet of rentable space. The project consisted

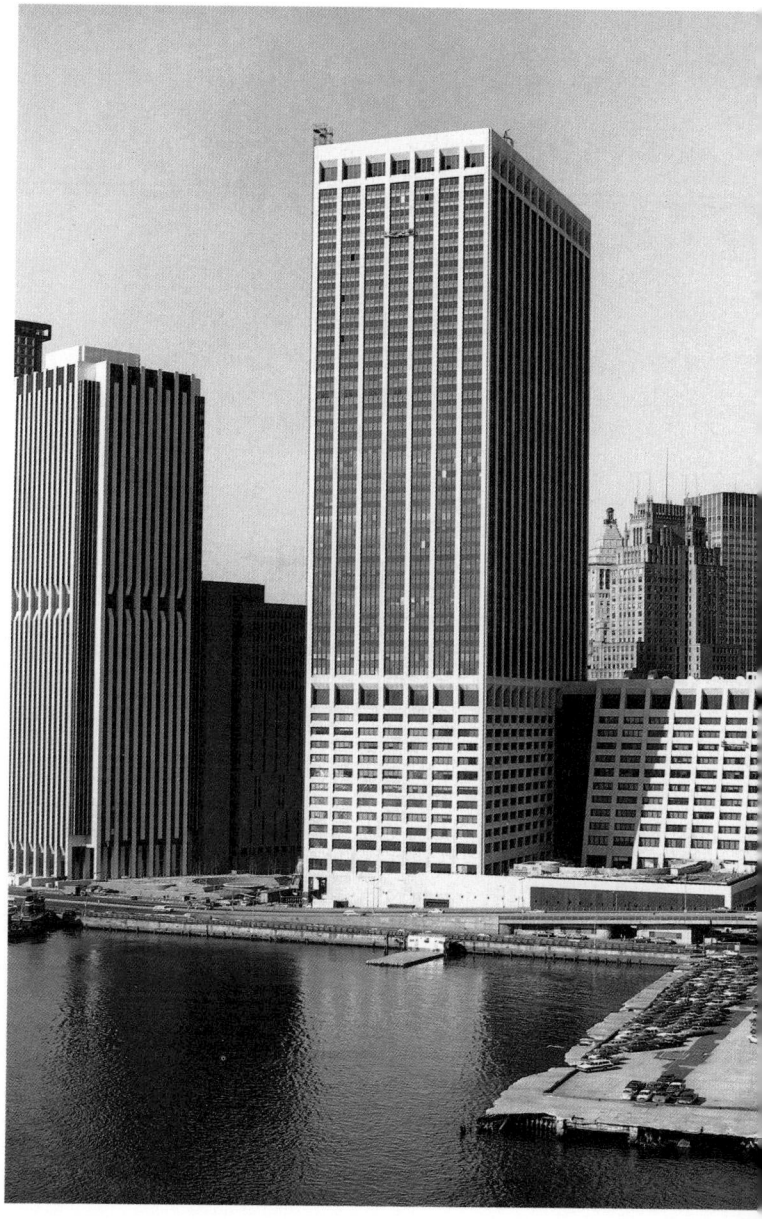

55 Water Street, Water to South Street, Jeanette Park to Old Slip. Emery Roth & Sons, 1972. View to the west showing Two New York Plaza (Kahn & Jacobs, 1971), on the left. ©Gil Amiaga. ERS

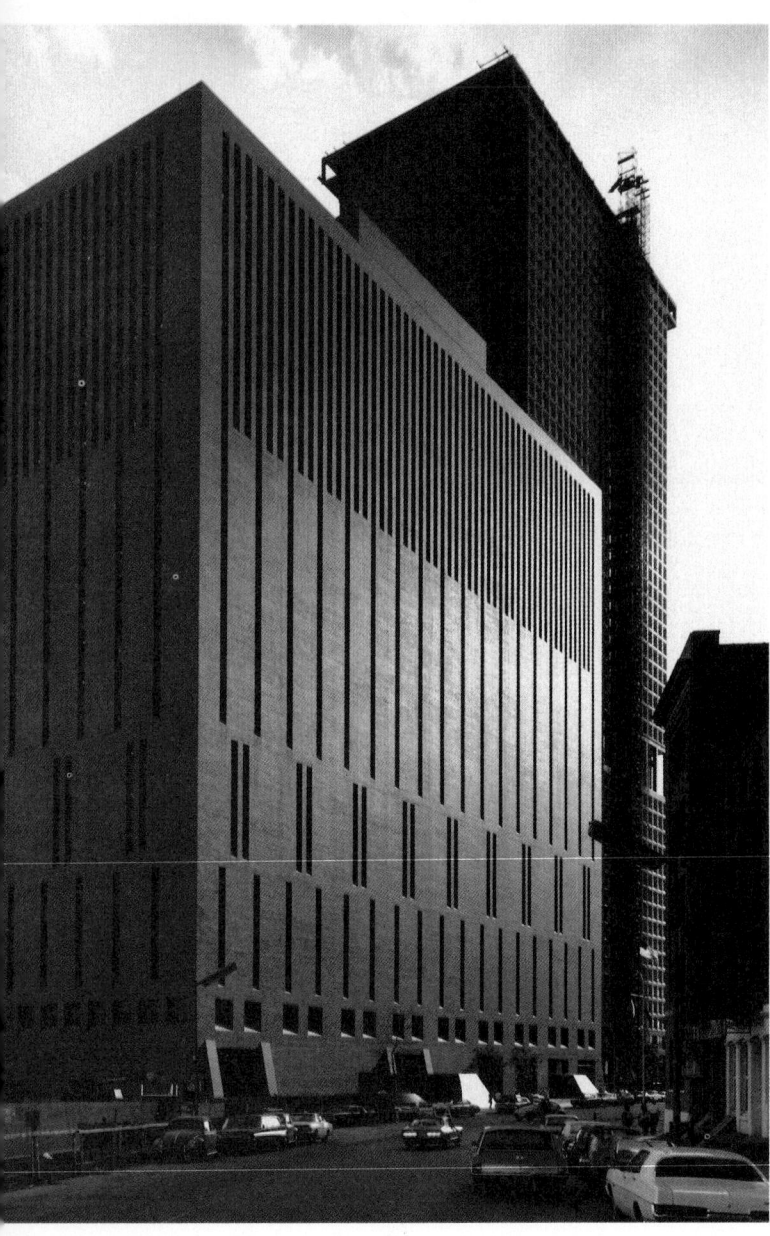

Four New York Plaza, southeast corner of Water and Broad streets. Carson, Lundin & Shaw, 1969. View to the south. Stoller. ©ESTO

of a massive fifty-six-story slab set perpendicular to Water Street and a fifteen-story slope-walled wing at right angles to it. The typical tower floors contained over 55,000 square feet of space, and the lower fifteen floors almost double that amount. The crudely detailed, Brutalist exterior, with its insistently gridded base and dark glass tower, was surely no worse than its neighbors at One and Two New York Plaza, but, as Huxtable noted when the project was announced in 1969, at "this scale the question of aesthetics ceases to be the main consideration. Architectural design of the individual structure almost becomes irrelevant in the face of what it does to the city. . . . What really matters is the planning that will make one building relate to another and to the area and its supporting facilities."[62]

Ironically, the very existence of the building was due to the intervention of the city government. Through the Office of Lower Manhattan Development, under the direction of Richard Buford (who was also the executive director of the City Planning Department), the city negotiated a deal with the Uris Brothers permitting the street closings in return for a number of planning concessions and civic amenities, including a new park as well as a plaza elevated twelve feet above grade (to permit parking of 521 cars below). To achieve this particular public benefit, a special zoning amendment was passed so that the raised plaza could be considered as open space. Future connections to a proposed east side subway were also promised by the developer. The building was, in fact, the first structure to conform to the general principles of the Lower Manhattan Plan, which had been submitted to the city in 1966 (see "On the Waterfront," below). While the plan called for new development on landfill to the east of Water Street, 55 Water Street occupied land filled in long ago, but its site formed a key link between the upland and the new waterfront.

Lawrence Halprin & Associates, landscape architects headquartered in San Francisco, were initially hired to design the new Jeannette Park and the elevated plaza. Halprin's early sketch models suggested a design similar to one he had recently executed to much acclaim in Portland, Oregon, with extensive use of abstract, rocklike reinforced-concrete outcroppings, water and grass.[63] The plaza was intended eventually to span the elevated highway along South Street and to connect with Manhattan Landing, a development for a riverside site to be created on pilings (see "On the Waterfront," below). Halprin's design was not carried out, however, and by 1970 the commission was in the hands of M. Paul Friedberg & Associates, who created a plaza paved in brick and embellished with pools. But, as Huxtable lamented in 1973, shortly after the complex was completed, "Although the park is handsome, it is oppressively hard-surfaced. . . . A bit of greenery can go a long way, but even landscape architects seem to be allergic to it."[64]

To further enhance the building's image as a contribution to the city, a branch of the Whitney Museum of American Art, the first undertaken by the museum, was established on the third-floor plaza level.[65] In 1969 David Hupert, the museum's education director, had begun to look for downtown space, and the museum considered locations in the United States Customs House, the Staten Island Ferry Terminal and the World Trade Center, still under construction. Following the suggestion of the Office of Lower Manhattan Development, the Whitney's director, John I. H. Baur, approached the Urises about renting space in 55 Water Street. They quickly agreed to lease the museum space for $1 per year; the new museum's operating costs were to be covered by twenty-nine Wall Street area corporations. Percy Uris, who was a Whitney Museum benefactor, would later recall, "We thought it was a good idea to have something of the cultural nature of the Whitney down there. We also felt it would contribute nicely to the feel of the building and the amenities it offers to people who work there."[66] A long, narrow space that could be reached directly from the street by means of an exterior escalator, as well as from within 55 Water Street, the 4,800-square-foot museum contained architecturally straightforward, minimally detailed galleries.

While no building along the new Water Street approached the elegance of 88 Pine, three others achieved some distinction: Four New York Plaza (Manufacturers Hanover Operations Center), at the northeast corner of Water and Broad streets (1969); 77 Water Street, occupying a site between Old Slip, Gouverneur Lane and Front Street (1970); and 127 John Street, occupying most of the block bounded by Water and Pearl, John and Fulton streets (1971). In designing Four New York Plaza, the architects, Carson, Lundin & Shaw, attempted to ingratiate their building to the area's remaining early-nineteenth-century buildings by cladding its bulky twenty-two-story frame in brick.[67] The Manufacturers Hanover Trust Operations Center presented a new functional program for office buildings: back-office space for the banking and securities industries in which clerical workers and computers functioned round-the-clock to process buy and sell orders and to keep pace with worldwide markets. Though the building's orange-toned brick was intended to blend in with the neighborhood, the use of supersize (twelve-inch-long) Norman brick and the punch-card-like arrangement of the narrow vertical window bands made its mass seem unnecessarily aggressive. Huxtable, however, considered it "an above-average building" that "displays some of the best brickwork in New York."[68]

Huxtable also had praise for 77 Water Street, which she called "a small gem . . . [with] a sleek glass and aluminum 'skin' structure of considerable finesse."[69] Designed by Emery Roth & Sons, it was a straightforward, slickly detailed, twenty-six-story, 507,000-square-foot office building of only slightly more than normal interest. What was unusual was the attempt to make the plazas—which were virtually mandated by zoning—"useful" and entertaining. Witty special effects at the street and roof level were designed by graphic designers Corchia–de Harak Associates and landscape architect A. E. Bye. William Tarr, the artist, reconstructed a Sopwith Camel (a World War I aircraft) on the building's roof solely for the delight of denizens of neighboring skyscrapers. At street level, in addition to water pools traversed by bridges, the designers provided a replica of an old-fashioned candy store that would provide a functioning symbol of an earlier, more personable urbanism. The Corchia–de Harak firm also designed "heat trees," illuminated metal umbrellas that would render the open space under the building more usable in winter. According to the developer, Melvyn Kaufman, who worked in a similar vein in midtown buildings along Third Avenue (see chapter 5), this policy of fun and games made serious economic sense. Imbued with the era's enthusiasm for Pop Art, he saw in supergraphics and painted finishes a way to be contemporary and penny-pinching at the same time. Most of all, he saw it as a way to deliver "something to the people," that something being lively if gimmicky street furniture rather than great architecture. For Kaufman, the building itself was little more than a container, "a good building, mostly because it's a nonbuilding. . . . You can pull it right out of a catalog."[70]

The Kaufman organization was also responsible for 127 John Street (1971), a thirty-two-story, 511,000-square-foot building on the northwest corner of Water Street.[71] This building

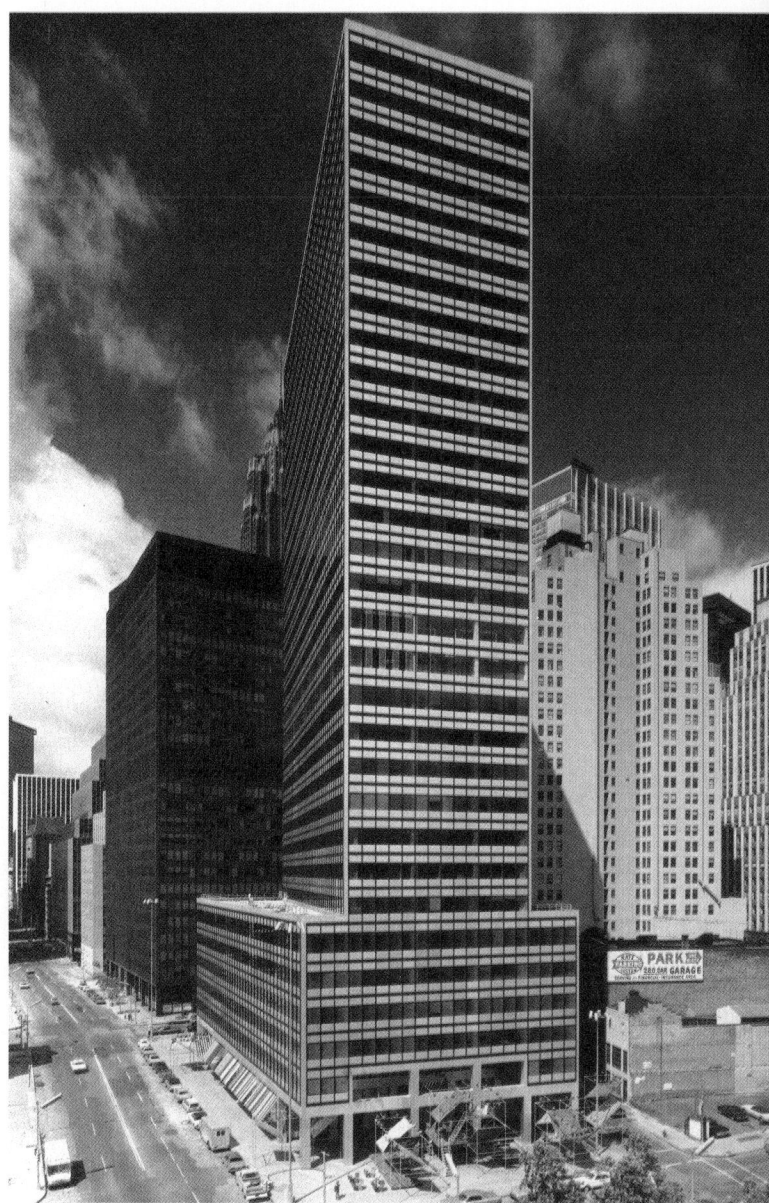

127 John Street, northwest corner of Water Street. Emery Roth & Sons, 1971. View to the south. Lieberman. TL

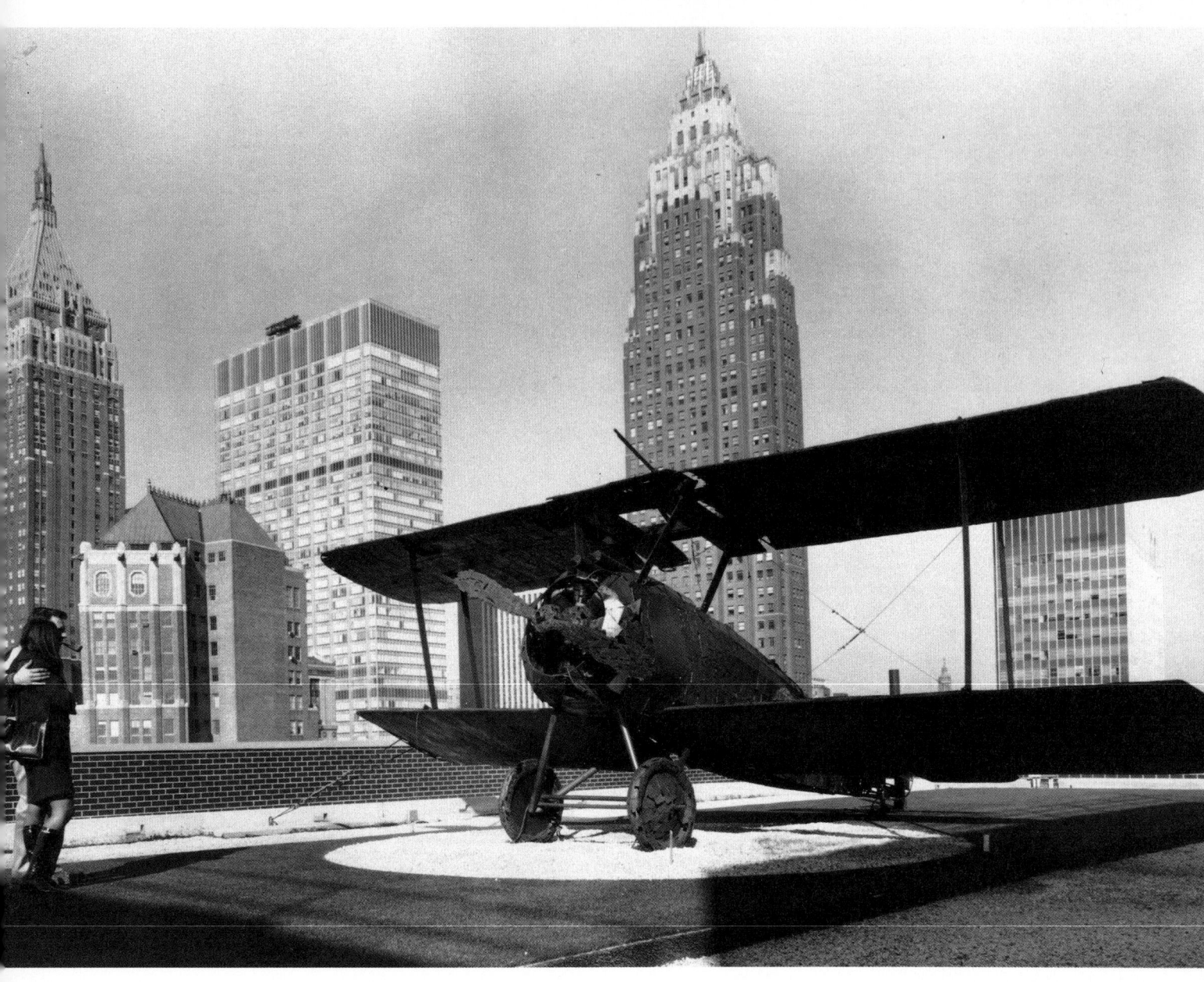

Reconstruction of a Sopwith Camel aircraft (William Tarr, 1970) on the roof of 77 Water Street (Emery Roth & Sons, 1970), Water to Front Street, Old Slip to Gouverneur Lane. View to the northwest. Oakley. ERS

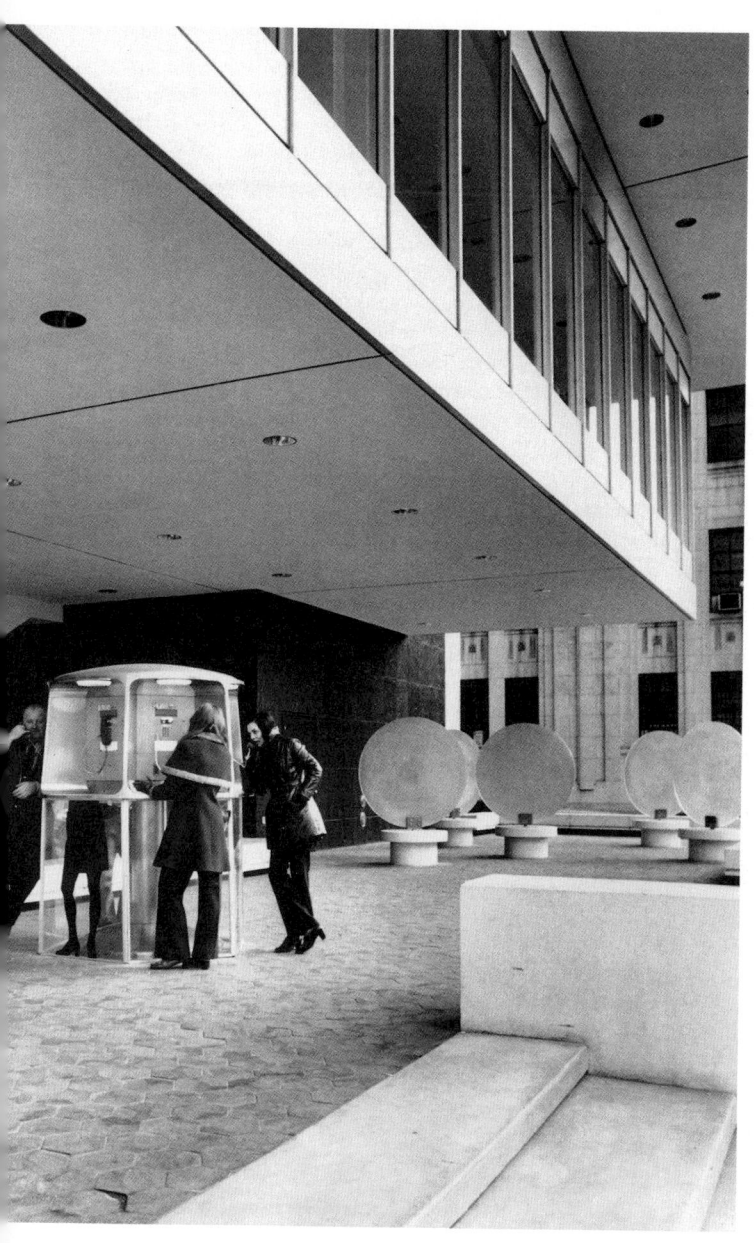

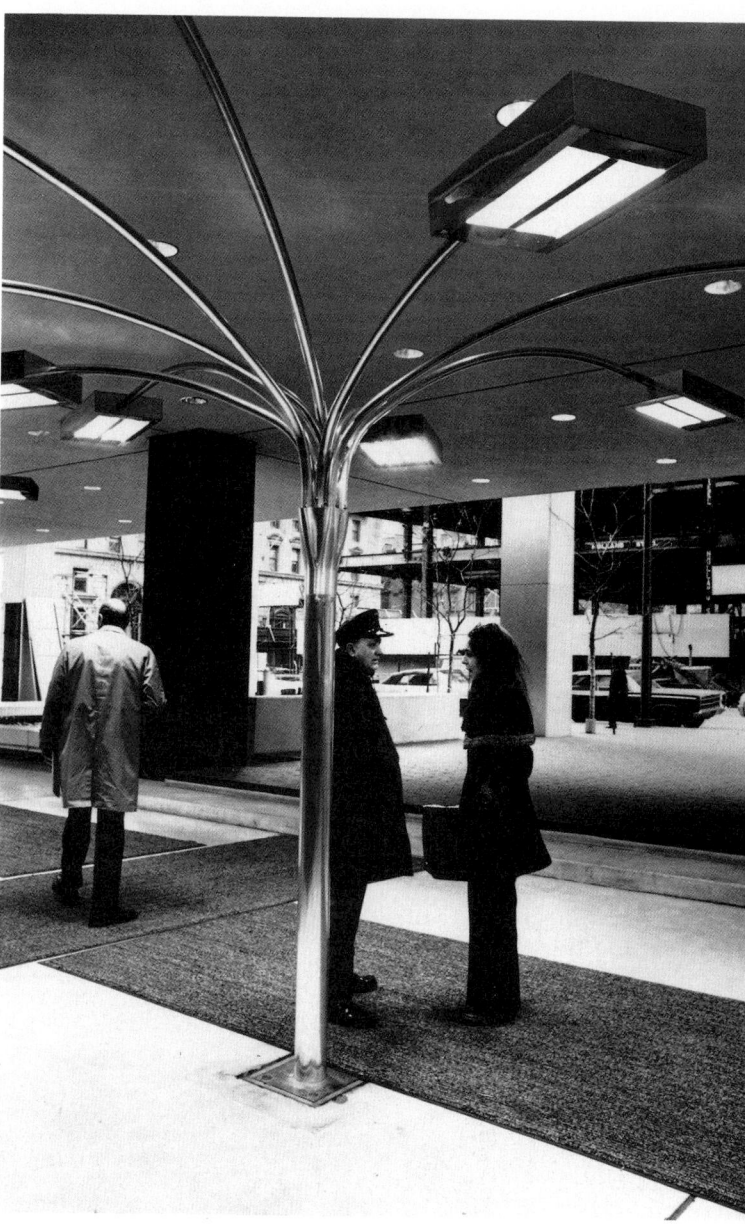

77 Water Street. Ground-level plaza designed by Corchia–de Harak Associates and A. E. Bye. Graham. ERS

77 Water Street. "Heat trees" designed by Corchia–de Harak. Graham. ERS

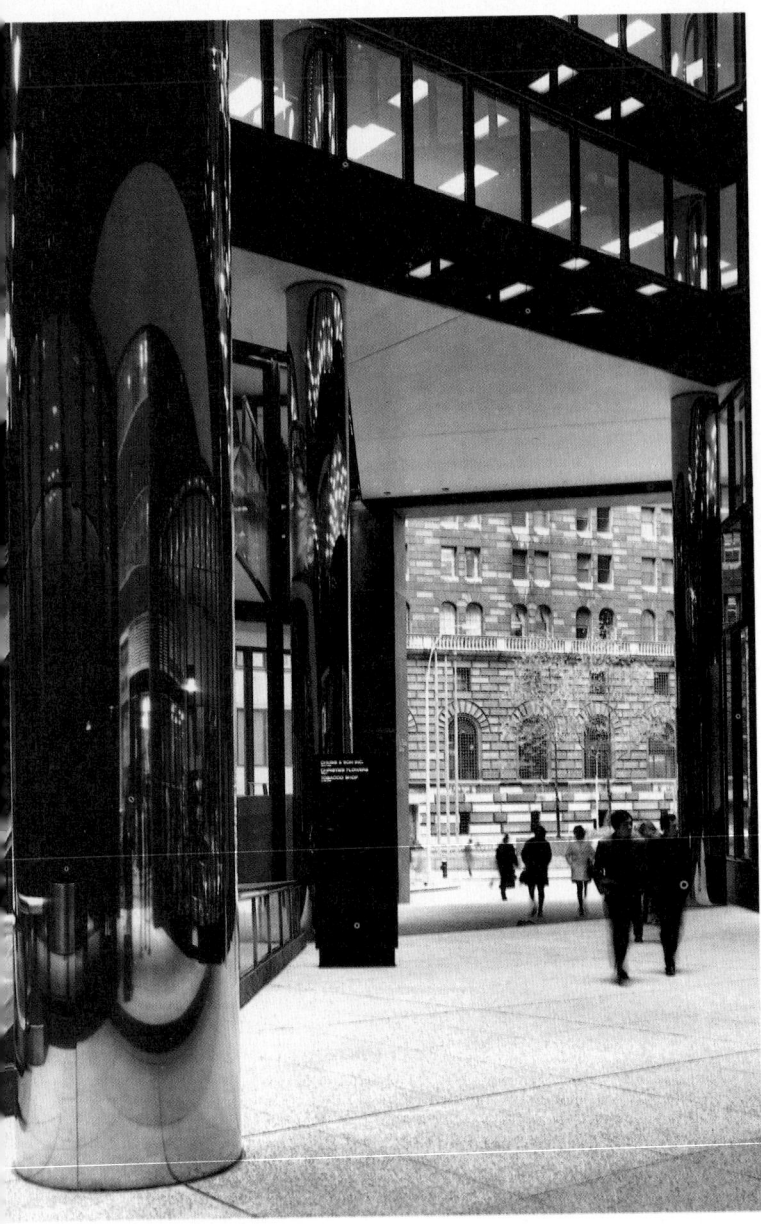

Above: 100 William Street, Platt to John Street. Davis, Brody & Associates in association with Emery Roth & Sons, 1974. View to the southwest showing galleria connecting John Street and the northeast corner of William and Platt streets. DBA

Right: View to the south along William Street showing 100 William Street on the left, the Federal Reserve Bank (York & Sawyer, 1924) on the lower right, and the Chase Manhattan Bank (Skidmore, Owings & Merrill, 1960) in the background. DBA

was also designed by the Roth office and was equally dedicated to the ideal that commercial architecture could "create an atmosphere of pleasure, humor and excitement for people."[72] The building itself was a somewhat better than usual version of a typical glass-curtain-walled slab set atop a colonnaded base, notched on one corner to accommodate two preexisting structures whose owners had held out for excessive purchase prices. Kaufman embellished the building with a funhouselike sequence of spatial effects that entertained visitors as they traveled from the front entrance to the elevators, which were located at the back of the site. Even before entering the building the visitor was greeted with a supersized digital clock covering the exposed flank of one of the old buildings. Once on Kaufman's turf, the visitor was sheltered by a metal frame from which brightly colored canvas panels were stretched. Visitors then wandered through a short neon-lit tunnel that led to the lobby, designed by Corchia–de Harak, who included Oriental rugs and warm lighting to calm potentially jangled nerves. On the seventh-floor roof setback a mural depicting a cat following bird tracks was executed in gravel by the artist Pamela Waters to entertain upper-floor workers. Waters also helped with the thirteenth- and fourteenth-floor mechanical rooms, which were visible through clear windows; when illuminated at night with blinking lights, these floors seemed to express the building's pulse. In many of these effects the lighting designer, Howard Brandston, played an important role. While critics frequently derided Kaufman's efforts as a patron of architecture, most admitted that as a showman he was quite successful.

Although less user-friendly than Kaufman's typical product, the more dignified, even somber, twenty-one-story, slate-banded office building at 100 William Street (1974) offered much in the way of street-level amenities.[73] Designed by Alexander Purves of Davis, Brody & Associates in association with Emery Roth & Sons, the building filled the site, except at the corner, where a diagonal chamfer inflected the mass toward the Chase bank plaza across the street to the southwest. Its principal feature was an eighty-foot-tall galleria carved out of the building's 300,000-square-foot mass to create a diagonal passageway through the site from John Street to the corner of William and Platt streets. Three levels of office space looked over the passage. The galleria, which was completely open to the street at each end, combined the functions of the building's lobby with a shopping arcade (at street level and one level below) and access to an improved subway station.

This was the first building to take advantage of the revised zoning that provided additional leasable space in return for a public amenity—in this case the galleria. The new zoning was developed by the City Planning Commission, which worked with the Office of Lower Manhattan Development and the architects as the building was being designed. The revised zoning offered a bonus of eleven square feet of building space for each square foot of covered pedestrian space; at 100 William Street this resulted in 55,308 square feet for the developer. The new zoning provision also established controls guaranteeing the public value of the covered spaces: to qualify they had to be at least twenty-five feet wide and 150 feet long; if longer than 150 feet, the arcade had to be thirty feet wide. In addition, to stimulate a lively pedestrian scene, the shops along the arcade could not be leased to banks or travel agents, and 50 percent of the retail space had to be filled with shops of no more than twenty-five-foot frontage (the rest could be as wide as forty feet). At first the law made no distinction between open-air and enclosed gallerias, but the developer of 100 William Street, Sylvan

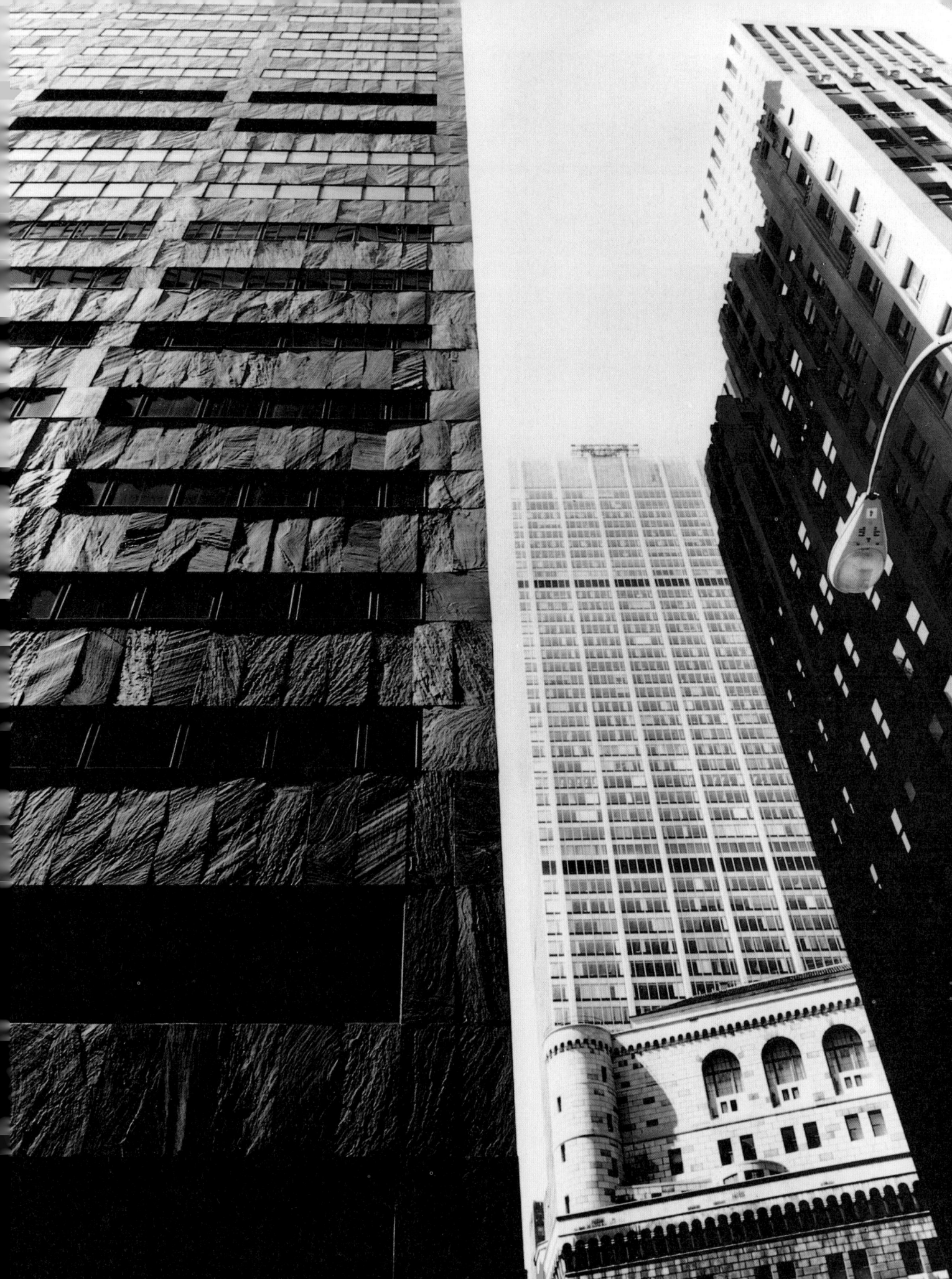

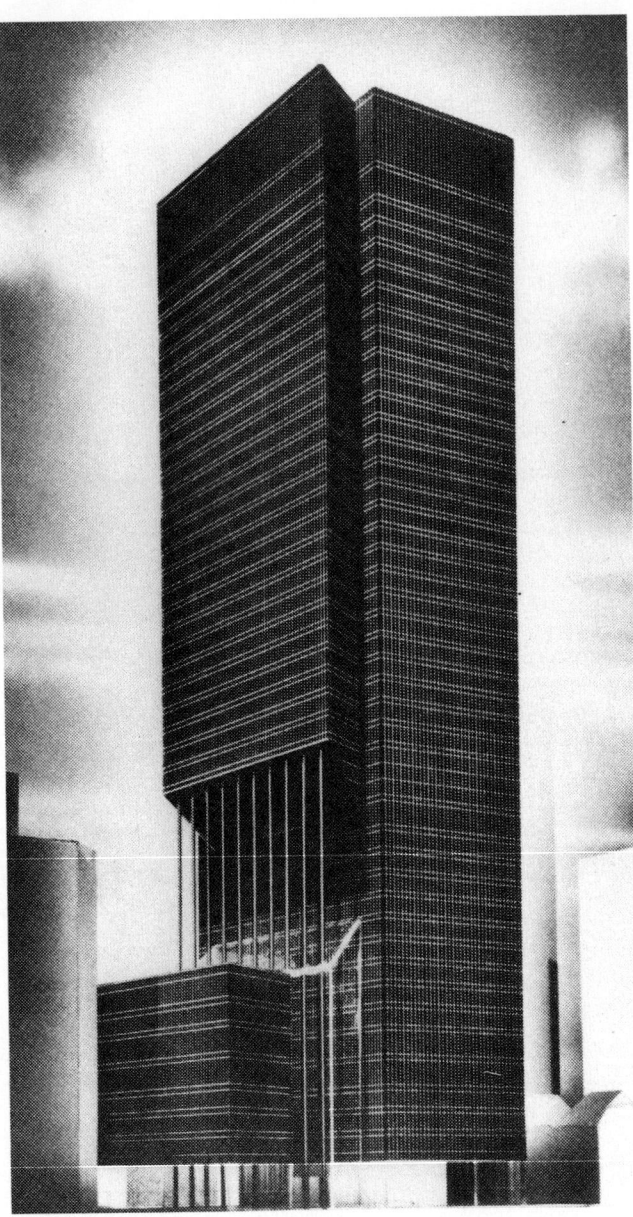

Proposed Lehman Brothers headquarters, Pearl Street, east of Broad Street. Philip Johnson and John Burgee, 1967. PJA

Lawrence, and his architects advocated the open type, citing its obviously public nature, and they were so persuasive that the law was amended to prohibit enclosed gallerias.

Most of the new construction of the 1960s boom occurred along lower Manhattan's edges, dramatically and, in the opinion of many observers, disastrously altering the character of its historic skyline. Once a mountain range crowned by pinnacled peaks at its center, it was now a field of cubic megaliths, which outside of a few notable exceptions—such as the Chase bank, 140 Broadway and 88 Pine—were architecturally undistinguished. One anomaly was the area's core of prewar banking institutions, mid-rise office blocks and towerlike skyscrapers that had been left largely undisturbed. In 1967 Lehman Brothers, the venerable investment bankers, did undertake to build something significant in the hitherto ignored, near no-man's-land that lay between Water Street and the financial district's heart, proposing to build on the site of several old buildings on Pearl Street near Broad Street, across from Fraunces Tavern.[74] Working in conjunction with two real estate concerns, Arlen Properties and Cushman & Wakefield, Lehman retained the newly formed partnership of Philip Johnson and John Burgee, who prepared plans for a 1.2 million-square-foot tower slashed through with diagonal cuts to articulate the corners and create an eight-story-high galleria running through the base. The building was to be sheathed in black glass held in place by silvery aluminum mullions. The galleria and the ten exposed columns that held a portion of the upper tower aloft projected a sculptural monumentality that promised a reinvigorated direction in corporate Modernism. The design, however, proved to be too expensive for the clients, who then asked Skidmore, Owings & Merrill to prepare plans for a much cheaper building. But even though the SOM scheme cost "a little less," as an anonymous spokesman for Lehman Brothers put it, it was "still too rich for our blood."[75]

While most of the new buildings ignored the architecture and urbanism of the interwar years, Kevin Roche and John Dinkeloo's proposal for a forty-two-story office tower that would provide expansion space for the Federal Reserve Bank of New York did come to terms with one of its most notable monuments, York & Sawyer's headquarters building for the Federal Reserve (1924).[76] The building Roche proposed for the irregular, 21,300-square-foot site bounded by Nassau and John streets and Maiden Lane was to have been a tower lifted 160 feet off the ground on four colossal columns, creating a covered, open-air plaza whose ceiling height would be just above the cornice of York & Sawyer's bank. Roche believed that a conventional plaza would be too small to provide real relief to the area's density, and that any tall building on the site would destroy the scale of the remaining small buildings around it. His solution, to raise the offices above the surrounding area, was a bold scheme, to say the least. Roche commented: "I never like to miss an opportunity for a little spectacle."[77] The project, which was to be completed in 1976, was approved by the city in 1973, but construction was delayed because of market conditions. The project was completely abandoned in November 1976, when Paul A. Volcker, president of the Federal Reserve Bank of New York, citing rising construction and other costs, decided not to proceed. With all but one of the six buildings on the site demolished, the city was left with a vacant lot that much too clearly expressed the dramatic devaluation of its real estate.

Although the commercial office building, with its near-tyrannical singularity of mass and style, was almost the only building type to be realized in postwar lower Manhattan, examples of a few other building types helped enliven the scene. Two religious buildings—a church and a synagogue—powerfully reflected the difficulty Americans had in coping with traditional building types in the face of the increasingly dominant Modernism. Eggers & Higgins's Church of Our Lady of Victory (1945), on the southwest corner of Pine and William streets, represented one kind of reaction: the complete rejection of Modernism.[78] A large Palladian window dominated the principal facade of the Georgian-style red brick and stone building, while a series of five arched windows punctuated the secondary facade. Above a 478-seat basement-level chapel and a 416-seat ground-level sanctuary, the building incorporated a two-story rectory. Despite its size, the church managed to exert a strong presence amid its taller office-building neighbors.

Almost twenty years later, William Breger's Shaare Zedek Synagogue (1967), at 47 White Street, between Broadway and Church Street, took quite the opposite approach.[79] Also known as the Civic Center Synagogue, Shaare Zedek served an orthodox congregation established in 1938 to serve the weekday needs of civil servants working in lower Manhattan; by the beginning of the 1960s the congregation occupied an industrial loft building located at 80 Duane Street. In 1965, when that building was torn down to make way for construction of the United States Federal Building and Customs Courthouse, the congregation purchased a stylistically unusual, Classically detailed brownstone-fronted loft building at 47 White Street, which they demolished to make way for their first purpose-built synagogue. The demolition of the loft building left the block, which had enjoyed a regularity of scale and a remarkable degree of urban cohesiveness despite stylistic diversity, with a gaping hole. Breger's design for the synagogue's new home did little to ameliorate the situation: making no attempt to fill the fifty-foot-wide interstice with the equivalent of cosmetic bridgework, Breger drew the building back behind the street wall, inserting a seven-inch-thick undulating concrete shell, externally faced with narrow strips of marble, between the party walls of the two adjoining structures. This shell, in effect both wall and floor of the synagogue's sanctuary, bowed out toward the street and seemed to float a story above a landscaped entrance court, where two reflecting pools and a sculpture by Alexander Liberman flanked the building's principal entrance.

Inside, the concrete-shell facade was covered with horizontal birch slats. Two other curved concrete shells formed the space's roof and rear wall. A gap between the roof and the front wall was filled with a space frame surmounted by a skylight. The editors of *Architectural Forum* praised the sanctuary as "impressive" and "beautifully lit by day and night": "It has been suggested that the form of the sanctuary was inspired by that of the flame in an eternal light. However that may be, it is an unmistakably religious space: Breger says that he wanted to give fluidity to contrast with what he considers to be the 'directional quality' of a Christian church. It is certainly unlike the latter."[80]

In addition to the church and the synagogue, several buildings for education enriched the area during the postwar period. The New York University Graduate School of Business Administration's Nichols Hall (Skidmore, Owings & Merrill, 1959), at 100 Trinity Place between Thames and Cedar streets, struck an up-to-date if severe Modernist note, particulary in contrast to Richard Upjohn's adjacent school building (1872–74), built for the Trinity Church. The rather squat ten-story building, windowless from the second to the seventh floor, incorporated a dark-color cast-stone grid filled in with enamelized brick. Sixteen years later, SOM replaced Upjohn's building with another building for NYU's business school, Charles E. Merrill

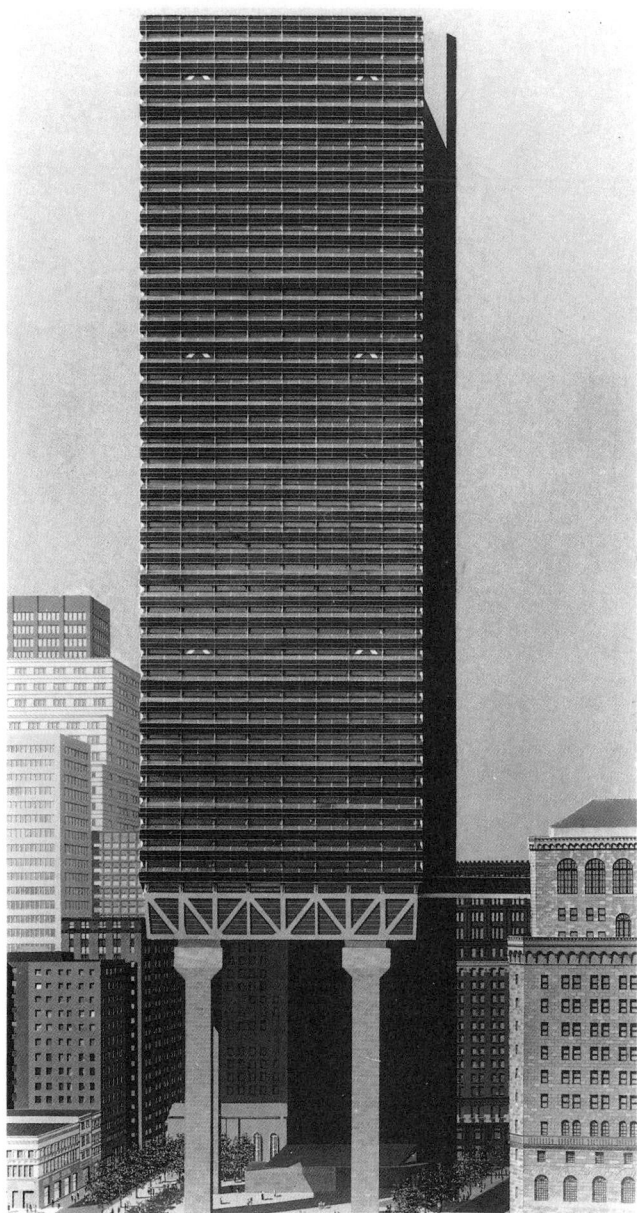

Proposed office building for the Federal Reserve Bank of New York, east blockfront of Nassau Street, Maiden Lane to John Street. Kevin Roche and John Dinkeloo, 1973. Perspective. KRJDA

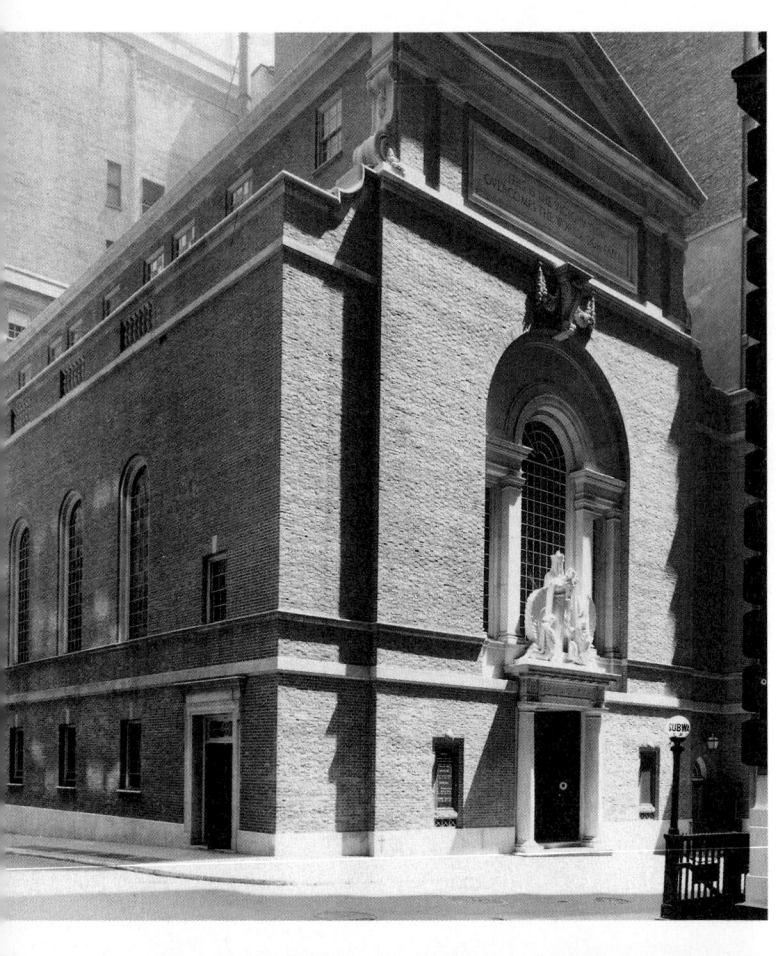
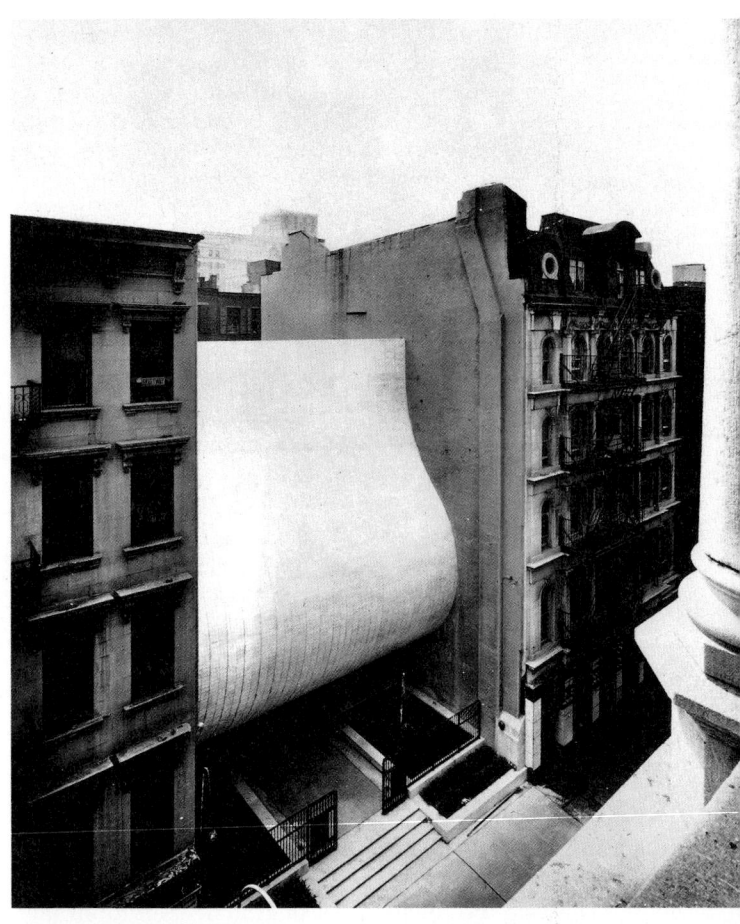
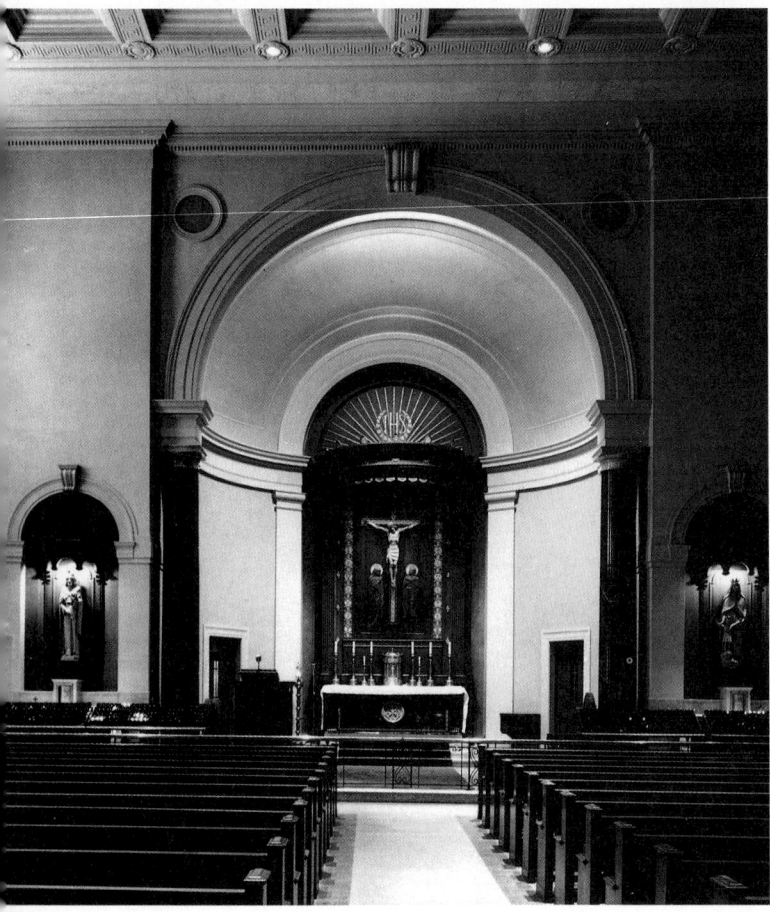
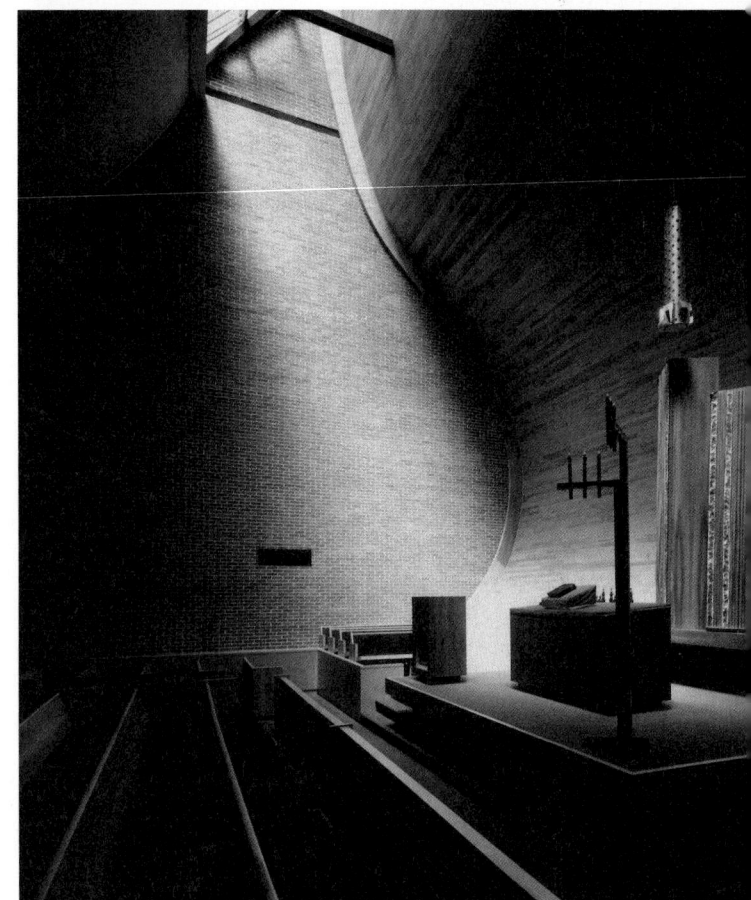

Hall, at 90 Trinity Place, on the southwest corner of Thames Street.[81] The dark-stone-clad building with deeply recessed windows seemed to Norval White and Elliot Willensky to be a "classic background modern monument" that, in spite of its self-effacing minimalism, reduced its once-stylish neighbor to the status of "a dull white-speckled brick ancestor."[82]

Pace College's Civic Center Campus (1970) added little in the way of architectural grace to the area.[83] Planned as part of the fifteen-acre Brooklyn Bridge Southwest Urban Renewal Area,[84] the campus, serving 10,000 students, occupied two full blocks bounded by Nassau, Spruce, Gold and Frankfort streets, directly east of City Hall Park and south of an approach road to the Brooklyn Bridge. In essence the campus replaced the printers' row that in the late nineteenth century had contained not only some of the city's leading newspapers but also some of its most notable tall buildings, including Richard Morris Hunt's New York Tribune Building (1876), which was demolished to make way for the new construction. George B. Post's Pulitzer Building, which had also stood on the site, had already been victimized by the wrecker's ball in 1955 to help make way for a new Brooklyn Bridge approach.

As designed by the Eggers Partnership, with C. Gates Beckwith serving as partner-in-charge and Peter B. Halfon overseeing the interiors, the university was housed in a sprawling complex of connected five-story buildings that formed a podium for a thirteen-story dormitory. The low buildings surrounded an internal courtyard. The new Pace campus was clad in limestone punctuated by narrow vertical strips of bronze-anodized, aluminum-framed windows. Writing in 1978, White and Willensky dismissed the building group, which powerfully exemplified the era's enchantment with "megastructures," as "an ungainly form . . . unhappily squeezed between its neighbors."[85] More satisfying was the school's acquisition and reuse of the robustly rusticated former New York Times Building (George B. Post, 1889; Robert Maynicke, 1905).[86] In 1973, however, when the twenty-five-year-old college was granted university status by the New York State Board of Regents, its president, Edward J. Mertola, announced plans to replace the Times Building with a thirty-story graduate-study building designed by the firm of I. M. Pei & Partners.[87] At the base of the tower, which was to rise without setbacks, retail space would link the campus to the lively commercial environment of Nassau Street. The building, for which only preliminary designs were drawn, was never realized.

In 1970, as part of the Washington Market Urban Renewal Area plan, Caudill Rowlett Scott, an architectural and urban-planning firm specializing in school buildings, presented a master plan for the Borough of Manhattan Community College.[88] Conceived of as a sprawling megastructure, the single-building campus was intended to serve 5,000 daytime students and 10,000 evening students of the six-year-old college, which had been housed in what was described as a "patchwork of run-down rooms" in five undistinguished midtown office buildings between Forty-seventh and Sixty-eighth streets.[89] The ramshackle quarters were a factor in the 1978 decision of the Middle States Association of Colleges and Schools to withhold the school's accreditation; the board charged that the facilities were "so inadequate as to defy description."[90] Completion of the new complex had originally been scheduled for 1977, but the city's fiscal crisis brought construction to a halt in 1976, and it was not resumed until 1980.

Finally, in 1981, the building was opened, providing the college with not only a comparatively grand physical plant but

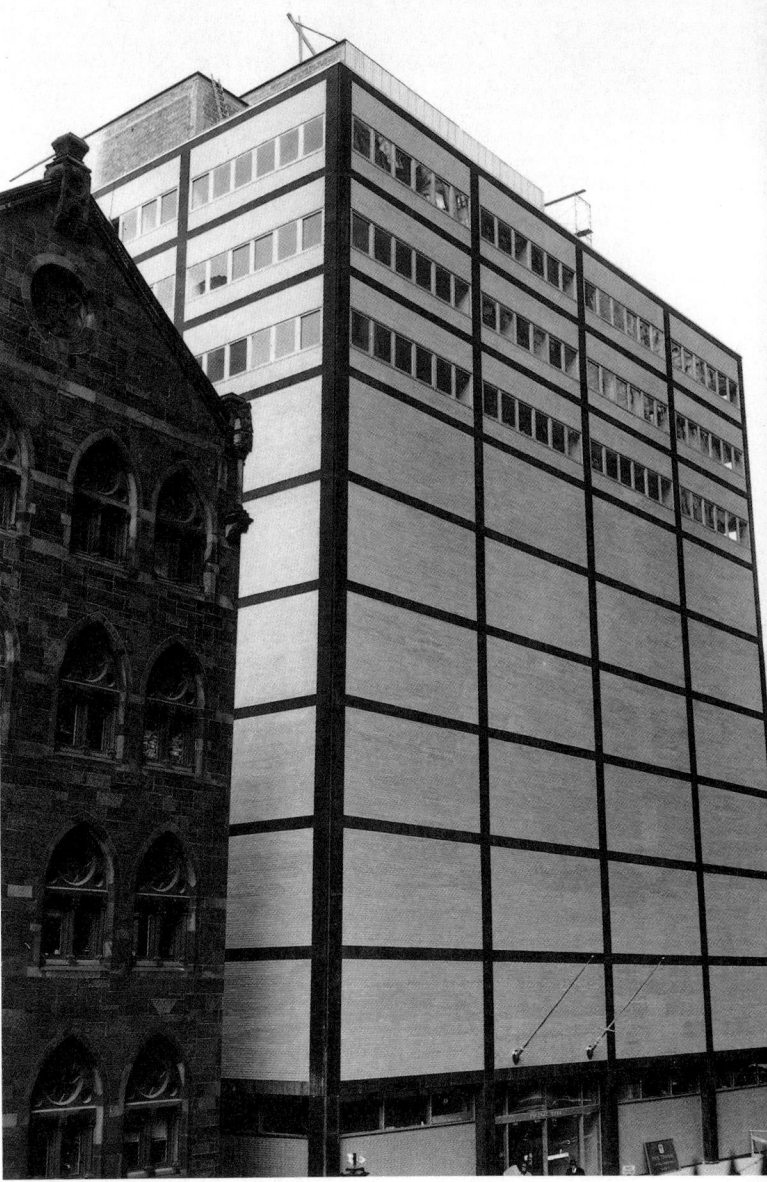

Top far left: Church of Our Lady of Victory, northeast corner of Pine and William streets. Eggers & Higgins, 1945. View to the northeast. Gottscho-Schleisner. LOC

Bottom far left: Church of Our Lady of Victory. View of the altar. Gottscho-Schleisner. LOC

Top right: Shaare Zedek Synagogue, 47 White Street, between Broadway and Church Street. William Breger, 1967. View to the southwest. BTA

Bottom right: Shaare Zedek Synagogue. View of the sanctuary. BTA

Above: Nichols Hall, New York University Graduate School of Business Administration, 100 Trinity Place, Thames to Cedar Street. Skidmore, Owings & Merrill, 1959. View to the northwest. NYU

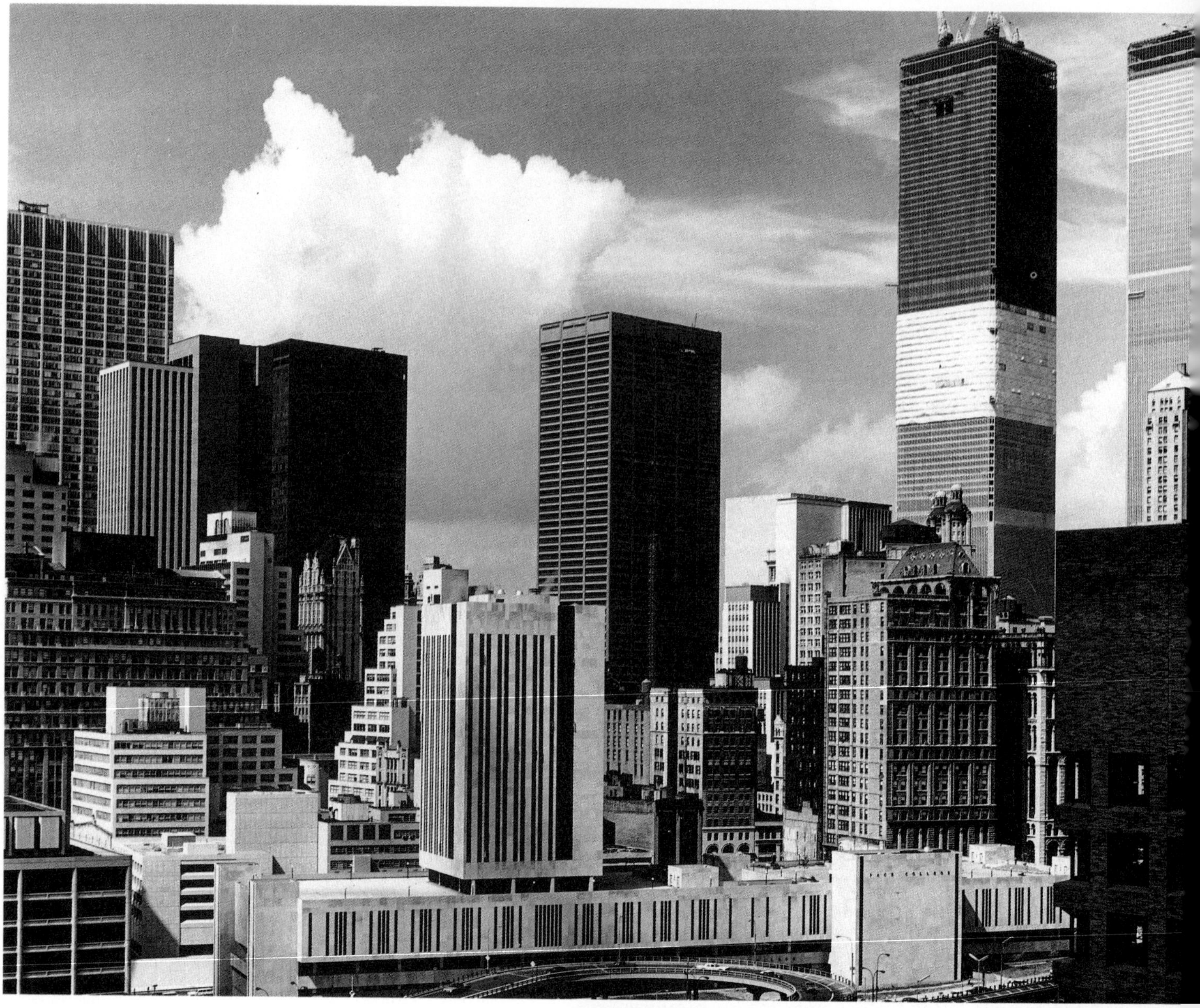

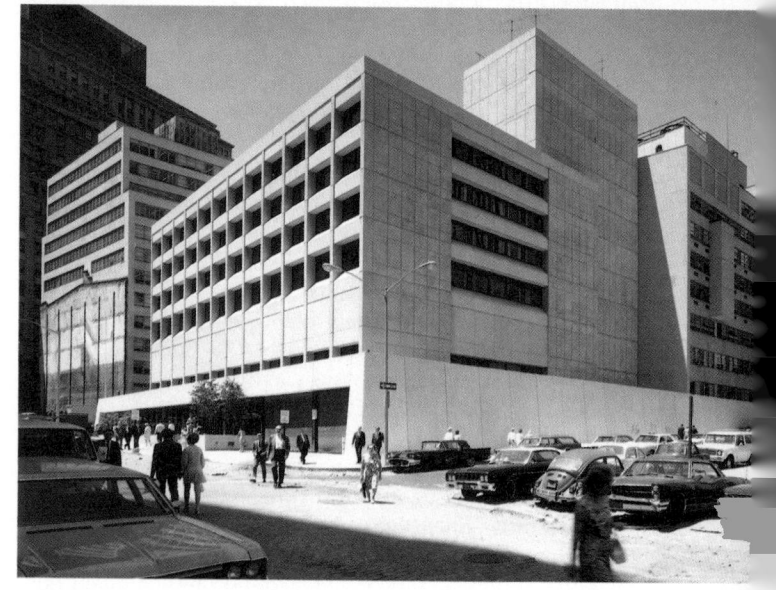

Above: Pace College Civic Center Campus, Nassau to Gold Street, Spruce to Frankfort Street. Eggers Partnership, 1970. View to the southwest with campus in the center foreground. ©Gil Amiaga. EG

Right: Beekman Downtown Hospital addition, southwest corner of Spruce and Gold streets. Skidmore, Owings & Merrill, 1971. The original hospital building (Lorimer & Rose, 1953) wraps the addition on the south and west. Stoller. ©ESTO

also a sought-after location in lower Manhattan. Filling much of a 4.3-acre superblock site east of West Street and the West Side Highway and extending north the equivalent of five blocks from Chambers to North Moore Street, the monumentally scaled but relatively low-lying seven-story building was, as a reporter in *Architectural Record* put it, "designed with passing highway and river traffic in mind, as well as the view from the New Jersey shore, giving a strong unified impression at high speeds or at a distance."[91] The complexly massed design, incorporating numerous cantilevered sections and angular projections, was clad in masonry over a steel frame and incorporated aluminum-framed windows. Internally, the mammoth complex was tied together by concourses that led to multiple entrances and elevator banks. A large gymnasium and swimming pool, open to the community, were visible from the concourses. In recognition of the projected student body's particular needs, the school contained a day-care center.

One major health-care facility was completed in lower Manhattan during the postwar period: the Beekman Downtown Hospital (Lorimer & Rose, 1953), occupying the full east blockfront of William Street between Spruce and Beekman streets.[92] Taking the shape of a modified U, the stylishly Modernist, eight-story hospital, clad in light gray brick, incorporated a midblock courtyard, accessible from both Spruce and Beekman streets and used by ambulances and delivery vehicles, as well as staff parking. The dedication of the 170-bed hospital on April 7, 1953, was festively marked by Governor Thomas E. Dewey cutting a gauze ribbon with gold surgical scissors. In 1971 Skidmore, Owings & Merrill completed a new wing facing Gold Street, which closed in the courtyard.[93] Though this was a competent if uninspired Modernist essay, its bulky mass robbed the earlier building of much of its grace.

One of the reasons lower Manhattan failed to attract postwar development was its lack of cultural amenities, a problem addressed by plans for the Lower Manhattan Cultural Center, which, had it been built, would have brought a futuristic, world's fair type of fun to the area.[94] Proposed in 1971 for an unspecified waterfront site by Thomas Pelham Miller, a thirty-one-year-old entrepreneur, the museum, as designed by Der Scutt of Kahn & Jacobs, was to be housed in a soaring cone-shaped structure made of exposed concrete and steel covered with heat-resistant reflective glass. The boldly shaped building, which would jut into the river, was to be surrounded by sweeping, curvilinear decks. Inside, the vast undivided space was to house highly flexible exhibition space as well as three restaurants. Olga Gueft characterized the building as "strange but idyllic . . . a translucent chambered nautilus more gigantic than the United States' bubble pavilion at Expo 67." It would provide, she said, a "sun-filled shelter within which trees can bloom and an aquarium remain unfrozen no matter how wintry the weather outside."[95] Specially designed fiberglass-enclosed barges would augment the museum's programs, serving as "mini-museums" as they traveled upriver to outer-borough and suburban locations.

The area's principal outdoor public space, Battery Park, had been slated for redevelopment as part of Robert Moses's ambitious Battery-Brooklyn Bridge project of 1939.[96] Following the demise of Moses's controversial proposal, the park languished until 1952, when it was redesigned by the Park Department.[97] The rather banal scheme failed to establish a convincing sense of either intimacy or monumentality, although an axial mall linking Castle Clinton to Bowling Green did pro-

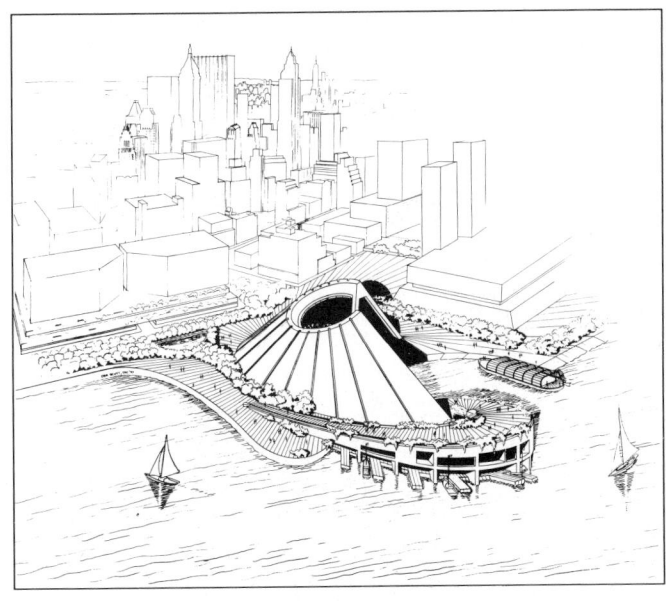

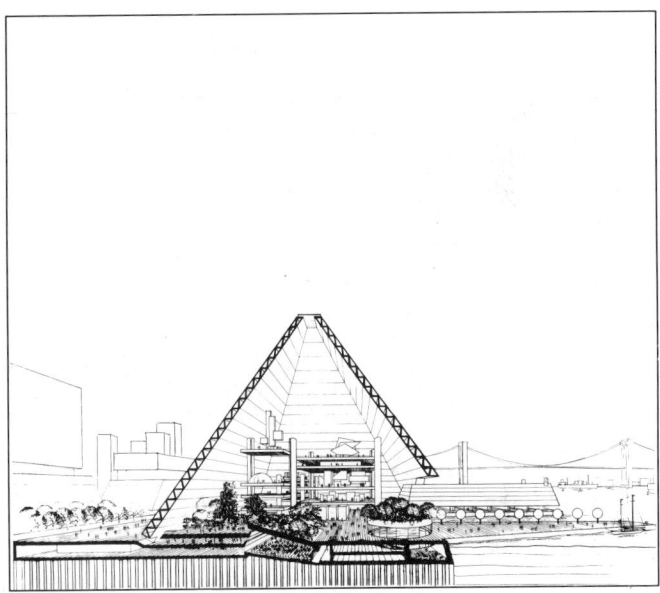

Top: Proposed Lower Manhattan Cultural Center, landfill in the East River. Kahn & Jacobs, 1971. Rendering of view to the northwest. DSA

Bottom: Lower Manhattan Cultural Center. Section perspective showing view to the north. DSA

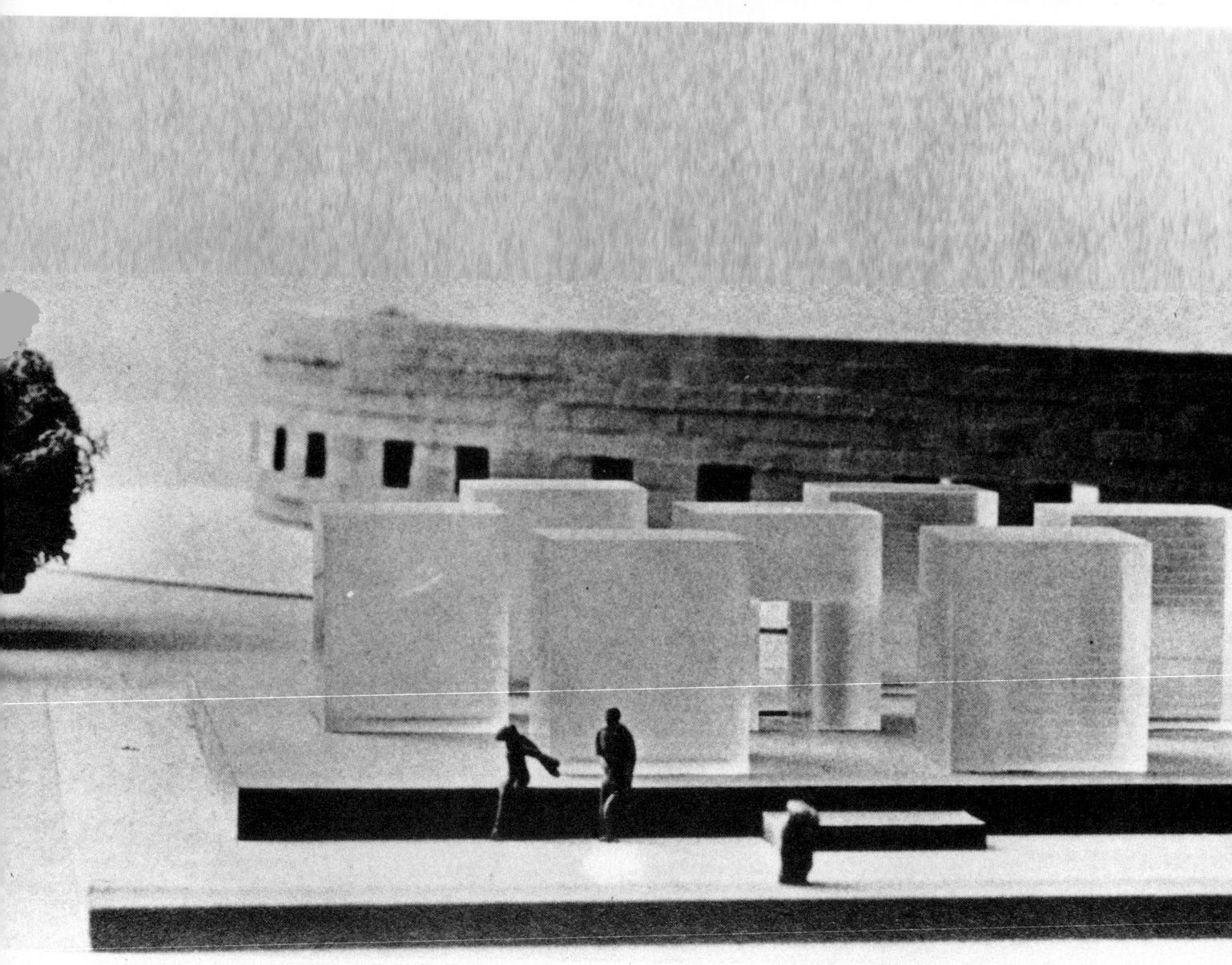

Proposed Memorial to the Six Million Jewish Martyrs, Battery Park.
Louis I. Kahn, 1968. Model. View to the northeast. LIK

vide a small measure of grandeur. While the graceful structure of the Brooklyn-Battery Bridge proposed by Moses would have in a curious way reinforced the Battery's functional and symbolic role as the city's most memorable gateway, the completion of the new Staten Island Ferry Terminal in 1956 delivered a serious aesthetic blow to the park.[98]

Designed by the engineering firm of Roberts & Schaefer, the terminal building was erected in part over the steel frame of half of Walker & Morris's exuberant Modern French–style Whitehall Ferry Terminal of 1907.[99] The new terminal, opened one year after the beloved, nickel-fare municipal ferry line celebrated its fiftieth year of operation, featured a semicircular principal facade facing north. A sweeping ramp provided pedestrian access to the building's second level, where it was extended as a cantilevered, curvilinear terrace. On the ground level, a roadway penetrated the building, allowing motor vehicles to board the ferry without interfering with pedestrian traffic. Inside, escalators led to the terrazzo-floored, second-story main waiting room, enclosed by 3,000 square feet of windows looking out onto the terrace as well as the city and harbor beyond. An early rendering for the project also included a bulky ten-story building flanking the terminal that was instead realized as a three-story facility for the U.S. Coast Guard. If the terminal succeeded as an efficient traffic-conveying machine, it did not fare as well as an expression of civic pride. Whereas Walker & Morris's terminal, influenced by the design of the Grand Palais at the Paris Exposition of 1900, was distinguished by a delicate latticework of steel, copper and bronze, the new building struck the editors of the *New York Times* as resembling "a taxpayer store building, something dreamed up for a world's fair or a modern factory."[100] Norval White and Elliot Willensky would later be far less kind in their assessment, lambasting the building as "the world's most banal portal to joy (a public men's room en route to Mecca). Kafka would have had the shivers: a disservice to the celebration of arrival and departure in New York."[101]

The possibility of Battery Park regaining some sense of place was raised in 1966, when the city offered the park to a newly formed alliance of Jewish organizations, the Committee to Commemorate the Six Million Jewish Martyrs, as a site for a memorial to victims of the Holocaust.[102] Several different Jewish organizations had been attempting to erect a large-scale memorial in Riverside Park since 1947, including proposals by the architect Erich Mendelsohn (see chapter 9). When those efforts proved unsuccessful, the new alliance approached Louis Kahn to design a memorial for a site between Castle Clinton and Battery Park's Hudson River promenade. As publicly revealed in a six-foot-high model exhibited at the Museum of Modern Art in October 1968, Kahn's abstract design called for a sixty-six-foot-square, gray granite podium, low enough to accommodate seating, on which seven glass piers would stand. Each pier was to be ten feet square and eleven feet high, and the central pier would be hollow and open to the sky; this pier would serve as an *ohel*, or chapel, and its walls would carry English and Hebrew inscriptions. Technical limitations in manufacturing the glass piers necessitated that each one be composed of layers of glass blocks six inches thick and six feet long. The piers would be constructed, as Kahn said, "without the use of mortar, reminiscent of how the Greeks laid solid marble blocks in their temples."[103]

At first Kahn had envisioned a concrete structure studded with glass, but he soon decided on glass as the principal material. Initial configurations for the glass piers included sixteen piers placed at eight-foot intervals and twelve piers placed at ten-foot intervals; Kahn also considered a scheme employing four piers as well as one focused on a single pier. Kahn's first presentation to the sponsoring committee indicated nine piers; committee members rejected the proposal, citing the fact that according to Jewish numerological symbolism, the number nine stood for the period of gestation and was thus inappropriate for the purpose of this memorial. He then considered six identical piers, which the committee found a fitting symbol of the six million victims, and finally settled on seven, with one harboring a chapel.

Kahn described the memorial in characteristically eloquent and mystical terms: "The glass makes the monument sensitive to everything around it and gives it a sense of life and hope rather than of death. One is conscious of light. Light is what we come from: we are born out of light. Light is maker of all things, of all presences."[104] Ada Louise Huxtable reacted favorably to the design, describing it almost as poetically as Kahn himself:

> In an age of violence that has made a flat mockery of conventional memorial values and platitudes, Mr. Kahn's solution is a cool, abstract, poetic, powerful and absolute statement of unspeakable tragedy. It could rank with the great works of commemorative art in which man has attempted to capture spirit, in symbol, for the ages. . . . The design is beautiful and chilling. There is about it a silent, almost frozen formality, a crystalline sense of the eternal emptiness of death. . . . This is architecture and, at the same time, sculpture, and it is symbolism of the highest order, timeless and contemporary. Mr. Kahn weds poetry and philosophy to form.[105]

Despite her lavish praise for Kahn's design, Huxtable questioned the appropriateness of the proposed Battery Park site, arguing that "the quality of the design and tragic importance of the cause do not cancel out the basic question that still must be faced: whether monuments belong in parks at all." She advocated that a different site be found, one that could be physically defined to function within the larger urban context. Kahn's design, she said, "deserves nothing less and will be compromised by anything less, because there is, potentially, overwhelming art and symbolism here. It is a suitable memorial if a suitable site can be found."[106]

Whatever the validity of Huxtable's suggestion, the monument's sponsoring committee found fault with the design, putting forward a variety of suggestions, including the addition of a roof to the chapel. Kahn reluctantly complied, spanning the outer piers with a flat roof and the chapel with a conical one. After the committee charged that the monument's cost was too great, Kahn instituted cost-cutting design changes. When the committee argued that the money would be better spent in support of Soviet Jewry and Israel, it became clear that the group no longer intended to raise the funds necessary to build the monument. The inability to realize Kahn's compelling design became one more failed attempt to erect a Holocaust memorial in New York, one more unrealized scheme for a monument in Battery Park,[107] and, saddest of all, a failure to realize one of the most provocative visions of late-twentieth-century Modernism.

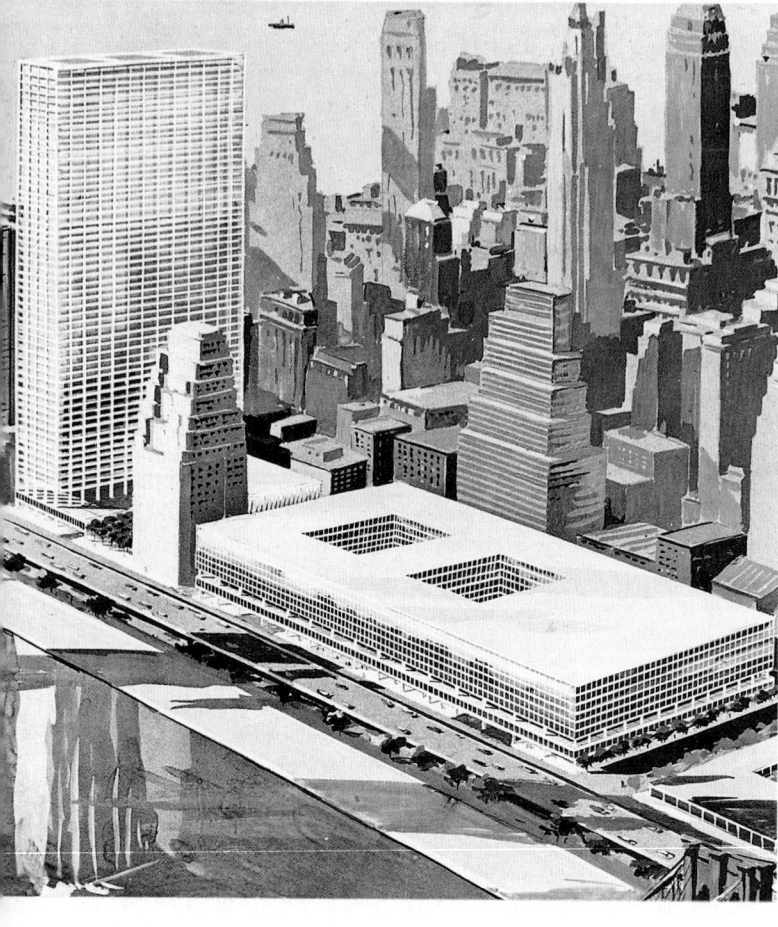

ON THE WATERFRONT

World Trade Center

Lower Manhattan's most dramatic development during this period took place along its waterfront edges, on both existing land and newly created landfill. Though the Chase Manhattan Bank headquarters and the series of office buildings that followed in its wake signaled the revitalization of lower Manhattan as a 9-to-5 office and brokerage center, they failed to contribute to the broad physical reconfiguration and business diversification that David Rockefeller had hoped to stimulate in the area. What was needed, he believed, was a new kind of center for global commerce that would function as a natural complement to the activities of an increasingly international-minded stock exchange and would help New York reposition itself in the area of international trade, which was being dramatically changed by a variety of forces from air cargo to global telecommunications.

The idea of the World Trade Center began to take form in January 1960, when the Rockefeller-supported Downtown–Lower Manhattan Association issued a plan calling for a combination office and hotel structure of fifty to seventy stories, a six-story international trade mart and exhibition hall and a central securities exchange building in which it hoped the New York Stock Exchange would relocate. All of these facilities would sit on a three-story podium that would virtually fill a 13.5-acre site along the East River bounded by Old Slip, Fulton, Water and South streets.[1] The platform's roof would provide a promenade with views over the river; inside, the podium would include a five-block-long arcade lined with shops, restaurants and a theater. The office components were depicted as uniformly gridded slablike structures; only the securities exchange and the sparsely planted 600-by-400-foot enclosed five-level concourse provided some suggestion of human scale. The report said that it believed planning assistance from the Port Authority of New York and New Jersey would be forthcoming. Preliminary concepts for the development were prepared by Skidmore, Owings & Merrill under Edward James Matthews's direction. To the north of the site lay the Brooklyn Bridge Southwest project. Initially announced in conjunction with the start of the Chase bank building, this project was to supply 21,000 units of housing in the expectation that the entire east side of lower Manhattan, with its hundred-year-old houses and warehouses, having served recently as marginal office and storage space but now largely unoccupied and considered derelict by planners, would be replaced by a new twenty-four-hour community.

In 1961 the Port Authority prepared its own report and by November 1962 announced its intentions to proceed in earnest with the World Trade Center, the story of which had actually begun earlier, when in 1946 the New York State Legislature created a World Trade Center Corporation to examine the feasibility of creating such a facility for New York City.[2] After some study the idea was dropped, not to be picked up again until 1958, when it became a pet project of David Rockefeller, who described it to a *New Yorker* reporter in 1960 as "the hottest thing I'm involved in at the moment." Rockefeller saw the East River waterfront as a commercial slum, "right next to the greatest concentration of real-estate values in the city. In a way, the existence of these slums presents a great opportunity, because they propose a minimum problem of relocation." The World Trade Center was, as Rockefeller and his colleagues in the Downtown–Lower Manhattan Association saw it, a way to create new downtown office space without competing with exist-

Above: Downtown–Lower Manhattan Association's proposed World Trade Center, Fulton Street to Old Slip, Water to South Street. Skidmore, Owings & Merrill, 1960. Perspective of view to the southwest. *World Trade Center.* CU

Top right: Proposed World Trade Center, Fulton Street to Old Slip, Pearl and Water streets to South Street. Richard M. Adler, 1961. Model. View to the west. Stoller. ©ESTO

Bottom right: Proposed World Trade Center. Section perspective of view to the south. PANY

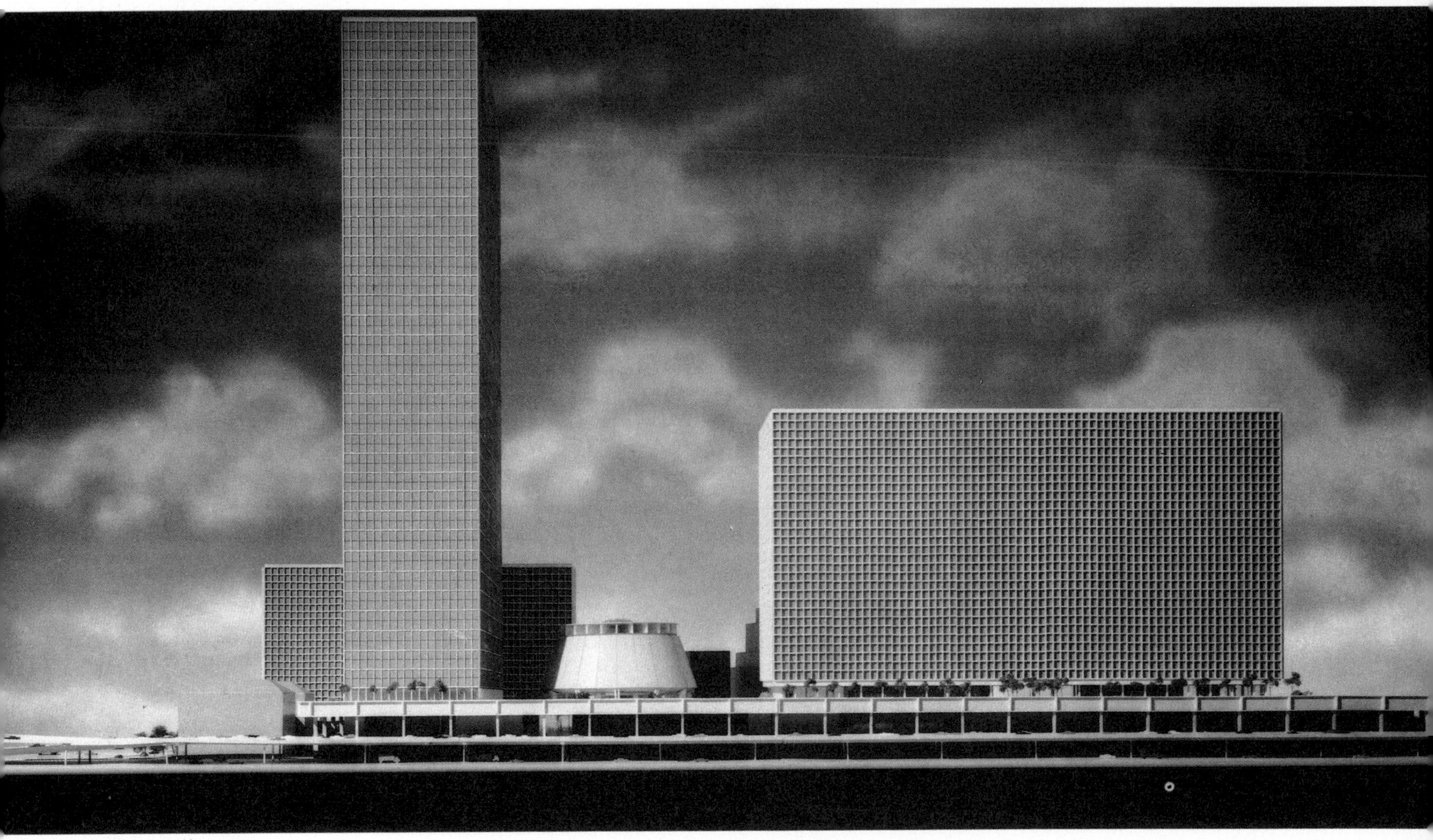

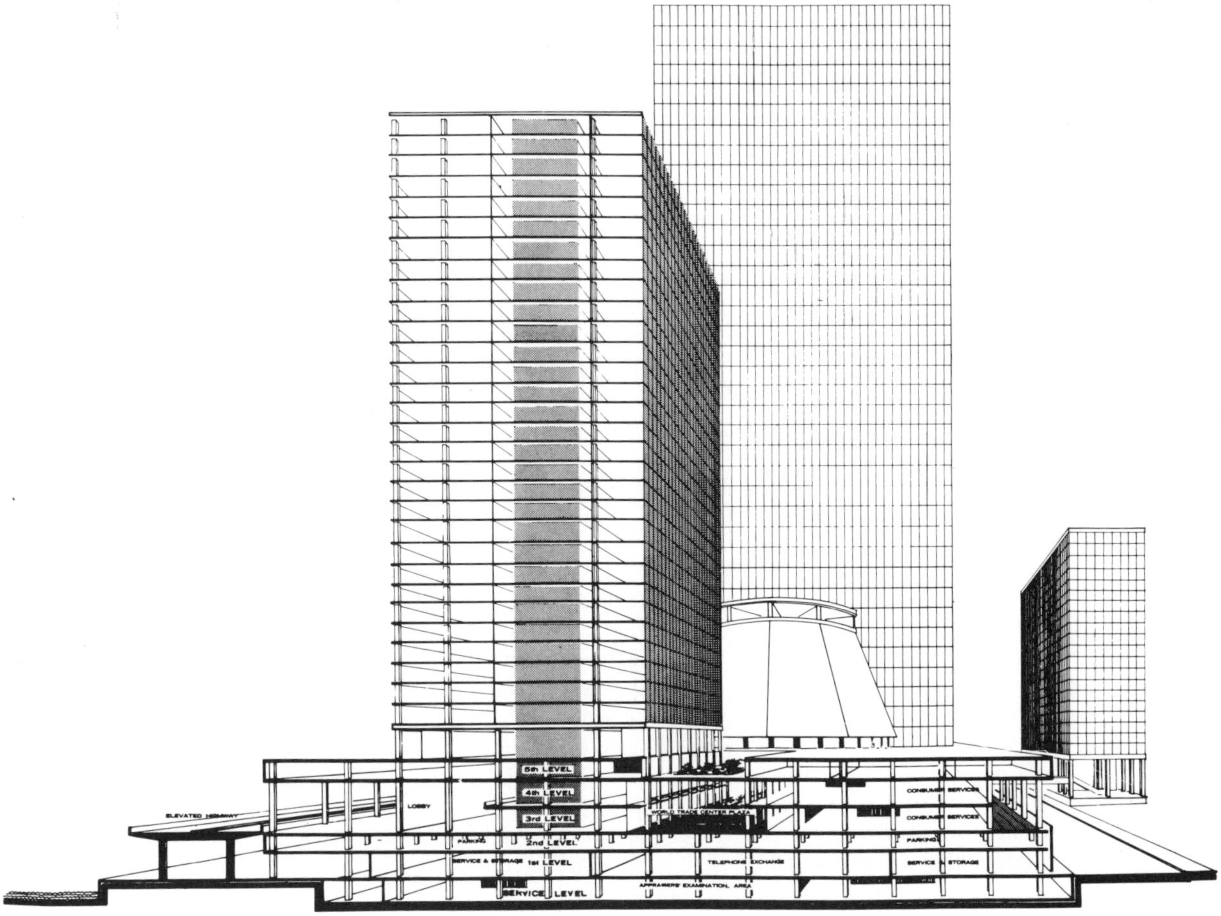

ELEVATED HIGHWAY   5th LEVEL   LOBBY   4th LEVEL   3rd LEVEL   CONSUMER SERVICE   CONSUMER SERVICE   PARKING   2nd LEVEL   WORLD TRADE CENTER PLAZA   SERVICE & STORAGE 1st LEVEL   TELEPHONE EXCHANGE   SERVICE & STORAGE   SERVICE LEVEL   APPRAISERS EXAMINATION AREA

ing office space: "We want to provide some new use. A World Trade Center seems logical, and it seems logical to have it near the banks that service the bulk of United States foreign trade."[3]

The Port Authority's 1961 report included a comprehensive design devised by the architect Richard M. Adler, a principal in the firm of Brodsky, Hopf & Adler, working with a board of architects consisting of Gordon Bunshaft, Wallace K. Harrison and Edward Durell Stone. The design called for a five-story concourse surmounted by four buildings, including the seventy-two-story World Commerce Exchange, housing a 350-room hotel as well as extensive office and exhibition space, the thirty-story World Trade Mart, and the twenty-story Trade Center Building, which was to be raised on fifty-foot-high columns defining an entrance colonnade. All three buildings were to be, at least according to the preliminary model, rather typically articulated Modernist slabs. The fourth building was to be an eight-story truncated cone housing the New York Stock Exchange.

By March 1962, when the center had officially become a project of the Port Authority, its site was shifted to the west side, where its construction would be coordinated with improvements to the nearly bankrupt Hudson & Manhattan Railroad, which the authority had agreed to take over in return for New Jersey's support of the project and its willingness to go along with a location in New York. While a good deal of the rehabilitation work was to take place along the railroad's right-of-way, the plan also called for the demolition of the terminal and its office buildings, landmarks of the lower Manhattan skyline since their completion in 1908.[4] By October 1962 the Port Authority had put together its architectural team, consisting of the Michigan-based design architect Minoru Yamasaki, who would collaborate with the New York office building specialists Emery Roth & Sons. At the outset Yamasaki stated: "The basic problem . . . is to find a beautiful solution of form and silhouette which fits well into lower Manhattan and gives the World Trade Center the importance it deserves."[5] The project, he said, just as design was beginning, will be "tremendous . . . a great complex of structures . . . separate and apart from the rest of New York, with an identity of its own."[6] Yamasaki explored over a hundred schemes for the project, including one with a series of lower towers that he rejected because "it looked too much like a housing project," and one that called for a single, 150-story shaft, which was judged to be too big.[7]

The choice of Yamasaki was bold and controversial. At the peak of his career, fresh from the popular and critical triumph of his Federal Service Pavilion at the Seattle World's Fair (1962), Yamasaki was well known for what Ada Louise Huxtable described as an "experimental architecture [that] goes beyond conventional standards to explore a more adventurous and evocative world (Xanadu and Shalimar) for a broader, richer and more ornamental contemporary architecture." Huxtable had high hopes that the World Trade Center would be "one of the loveliest buildings of our time," and she concluded: "One thing is certain: this large and important group of structures will be unlike anything that New York has ever seen before."[8]

Progress on the Trade Center was slow, bogged down through most of 1963 by court actions taken by businessmen threatened with eviction from the fifteen-block, sixteen-acre site, bounded by West, Vesey, Church and Liberty streets. Two additional blocks between Washington Street and West Broadway extended the site as far north as Barclay Street. The design was at last presented to the public in January 1964. No longer was the project the asymmetrical grouping of various-size buildings set on a podium that had been proposed for the East River site. Yamasaki's bold and instantly identifiable plan was simple in the extreme: two identical 1,350-foot-tall, 110-story towers (quickly dubbed Nelson and David, after the Rockefeller brothers who were ardent proponents of the project) rising from a five-acre plaza bounded by seventy-foot-tall, five-story exhibition and hotel buildings that were intended to modify the towers' superscale and shield the plaza from Hudson River winds. From the first, the plaza was seen as a kind of twin-campanied San Marco. Perhaps the goal was to restate the *parti* for Rockefeller Center in postwar terms, but the open spaces, the low buildings and the towers were all too diagrammatic and bland. Along Church Street, low, eight-story, black anodized-aluminum office blocks served not only to help define the monumental plaza but to continue the traditional scale of the street wall. The plaza's key eastern edge, however, was left unresolved, since Walker & Gillette's 1935 branch for the East River Savings Bank, located on a site bounded by Church, Cortlandt and Dey streets, was not large enough to form the kind of closure that Saks Fifth Avenue did at Rockefeller Center.[9]

The aluminum-clad towers seemed far less fragile and flimsy than the typical office buildings of the period, largely because of the window wall that placed 18¾-inch-wide structural ribs at 22-inch intervals and reduced the amount of glass to 30 percent of the building's surface. *Time* likened the resultant windows—high and narrow (19¼ inches)—to bowman's slots in a medieval fortification.[10] At the base, the module was doubled and the metal "tracery" was gathered together to form Gothic-inspired "lancet windows," a motif that reappeared at the buildings' tops, but without breaking the overall module. In order to create an efficient plan despite the sheer unbroken rise of each building—the Trade Center towers were 75 percent efficient, as opposed to the 52 percent typical of most tall office buildings—Yamasaki divided his towers into three zones and established "sky lobbies" at the forty-first and seventy-second floors. Yamasaki's elevator system could be likened to the express and local service of New York's subway system, with the sky lobbies connected to the street level via special express elevators. Stacked "locals" made it possible for the elevator core to be fairly uniform throughout.

The buildings would be not only the world's tallest but the world's biggest: their gross space was nearly triple that of the Pentagon in Washington, D.C. The space of two Pan Am buildings could fit inside each of the Trade Center's twin towers. In all, the plan called for ten million square feet of rentable space, four million of this to be used by private firms engaged in international trade. But the chief tenant was to be the State of New York itself, occupying two million square feet for the New York City offices of its various agencies.

As designed by the architects and their structural engineer, John Skilling, the Trade Center was structurally innovative. Rather than a typical frame building curtained in stone or glass, it was in essence a giant steel lattice, acting almost like a bearing-wall structure: that is, it was held up mostly by the closely spaced exterior columns, which, together with their cross members, formed a right-square or Vierendeel-type truss. The four walls of the tower, locked into place on completion of the building's framing, constituted, in effect, a hollow tube punched through with windows. The narrow, deep-set windows were seen as a positive feature that would help to counteract acrophobia. As a result of the structural system, the acre-large office floors were column-free, interrupted only by the elevator and service core. The Port Authority adopted an open-plan arrangement for 80 percent of its own space, designed by the Detroit-based firm of Ford & Earl Design Associates. Although the sea of desks and conference tables, separated only by flexible low partitions, was at once visually monotonous and spatially confusing, the scheme did succeed, as Olga Gueft observed, in providing "most of the interiors [with] exceptional light and view—an exhilarating effect of floating free over more than a city—over a whole region."[11]

The Trade Center was a statistician's dream: it was expected to provide office space for 50,000 people; to attract about 80,000 visitors per day; to require 60,000 kilowatt-hours of electricity (enough to light an entire city of 400,000); and to have 40,000 tons of air conditioning (enough to cool refrigerators in a city of one million). As the modest, five-foot-one-inch-tall Yamasaki stated when the plans were first shown, "It was a terrifying program from the standpoint of size. . . . You just run scared before you get adjusted."[12]

Despite these impressive figures, the Trade Center's size and technological daring did not seem to thrill the public as the great height and structural feats of the pre-Depression skyscrapers had. Just after the scheme was unveiled, the *Daily News* editorialized: "Must these structures be the ugly, boxlike things now planned?"[13] Moreover, the Trade Center was criticized not merely for its aesthetics but for its very size and for the large-scale temporary and permanent disruptions it would cause in the city's physical and human fabric. Many saw the project less as the "public benefit" it had been represented to be in the numerous court battles connected with the site's condemnation and more as a real estate deal that would give the Port Authority a surefire money-maker at the expense of private enterprise. Others felt that the $3 million the Port Authority was to pay the city in lieu of the real estate taxes the project was technically exempt from was far less than the $15 million that would come to it from equivalent private development. Most of all, there was concern for the scale of the buildings themselves, not because they were so tall, but because their height would disrupt the coherence of the traditional, low-scaled buildings along the river's edge. As the eighteen students of Architectural Design 112X at City College put it in a letter to the editors of *Architectural Forum*, the towers would throw "the whole of Manhattan . . . into a different scale and ruin what is now one of the most exciting spatial arrangements in the world. If the Chase Manhattan building can be challenged for the destruction of Wall Street's consistency, then the twin towers will add the final touches to this fatal feat."[14]

After persistent court battles and relocation delays, the project went forward with Yamasaki's original concept largely intact. The most significant change was the decision to abandon the raised podium of the original plaza in favor of one at sidewalk level. Also gone was the idea of hotel and exhibition buildings forming a continuous wall around the plaza. This was replaced with a plan for four separate ten-story buildings that would open the site to the west, where further development was already being contemplated. One of the four dark gray concrete buildings (a change from previous designs that called for the low buildings to be clad with the same materials as the towers) was to house the United States Custom Court, which would be relocated from Cass Gilbert's Custom House facing Bowling Green.[15] Also, the stainless steel originally proposed to sheath the towers had been downgraded to aluminum.

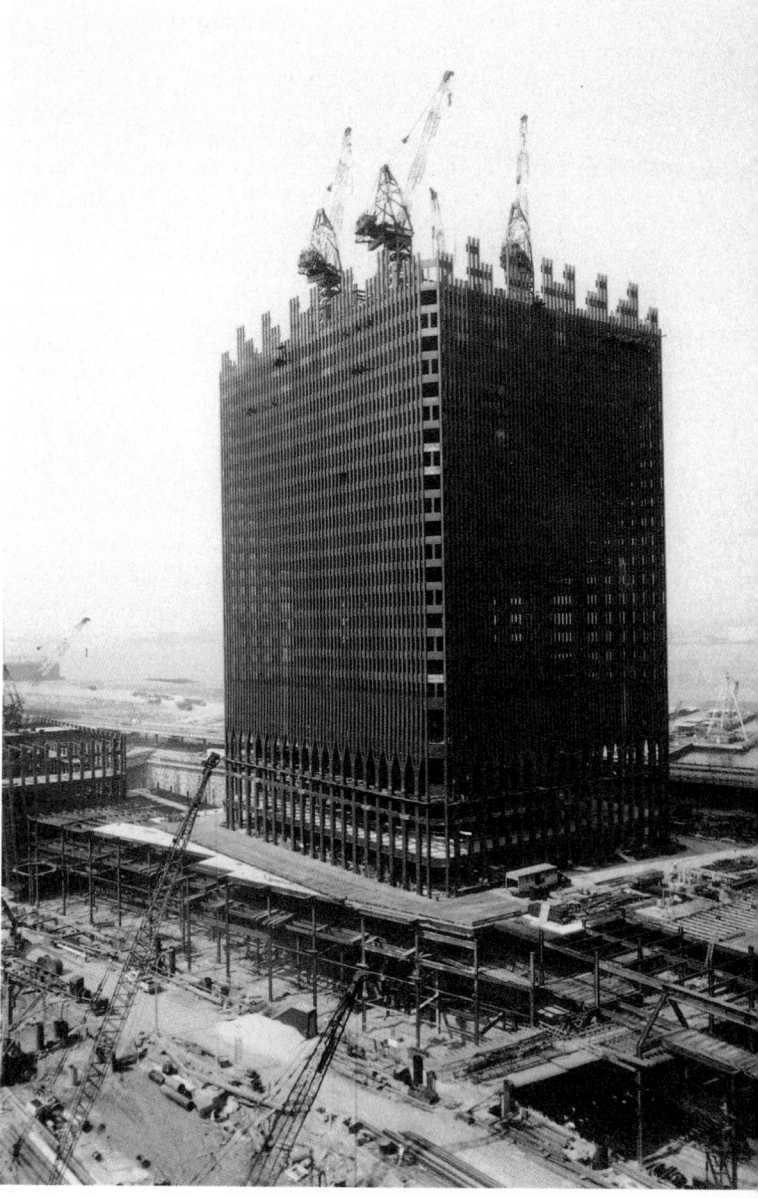

Two World Trade Center, Liberty to Vesey Street, West to Church Street. Minoru Yamasaki and Emery Roth & Sons, 1973. View to the southwest during construction. OMH

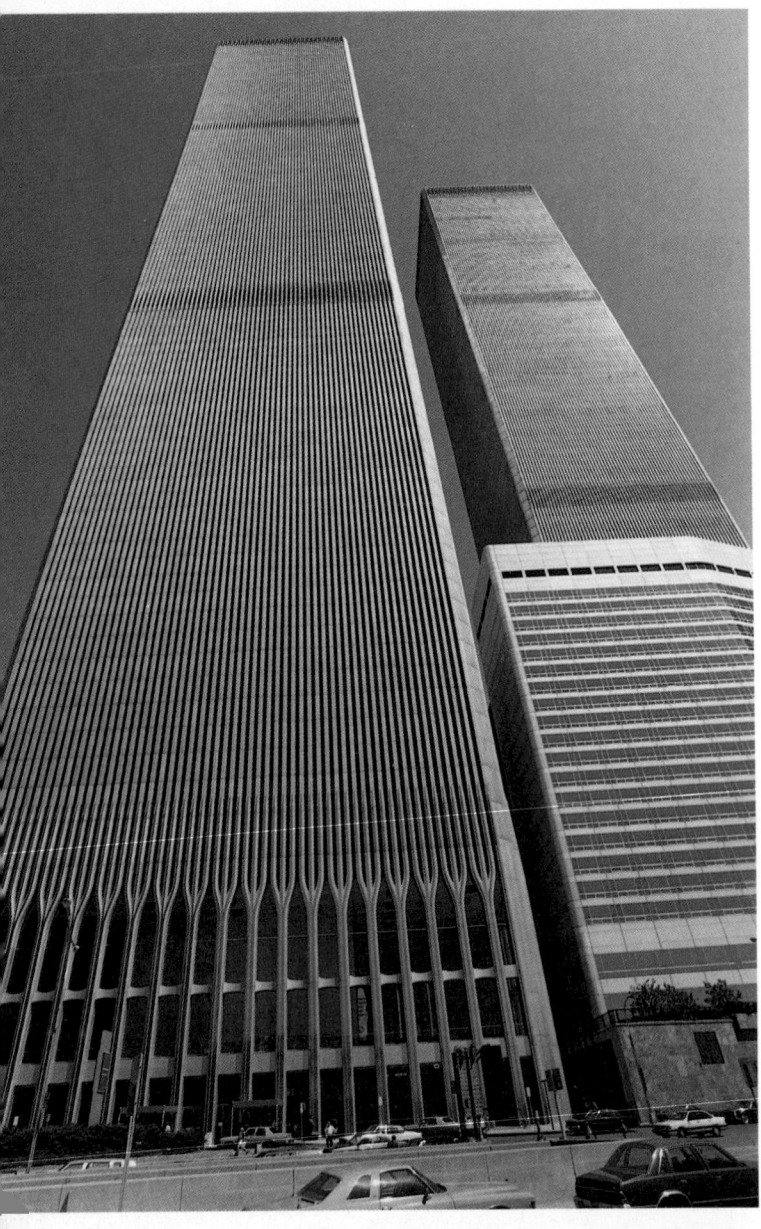

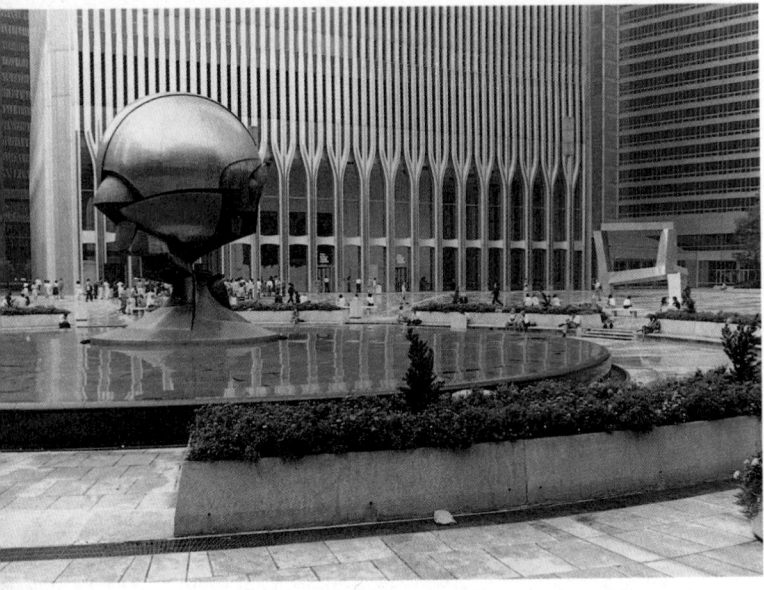

By now Huxtable had begun to have reservations about the design. Yamasaki, she said, "has developed a curiously unsettling style, which involves decorative traceries of exotic extraction applied over structure or worked into it. His choice of delicate detail on massive construction as a means of reconciling modern structural scale to the human scale of the viewer is often more disturbing than reassuring. . . . Here we have the world's daintiest architecture for the world's biggest buildings."[16] But the architect saw it differently: "I was trained in the twenties and early thirties, when classic design was the theme of the day. Though the traditional historic architectures I was taught then are not appropriate to our present-day techniques of building, their graceful proportions are still vital to any structure."[17]

The public remained cool to the design, and though only halfhearted efforts to block its construction were organized, the project stimulated widespread debate about the extra-legislative decision-making process that the Port Authority enjoyed. The protests were not without some success, and a new agreement between the city and the Port Authority, hammered out in August 1966, resulted in greater revenues to the city. In addition, the Port Authority agreed to finance $146 million in off-site public improvements and to use the excess fill from the Trade Center excavations to create twenty-three acres of new land along the waterfront as part of the proposal for Battery Park City.

Construction began on August 5, 1966, although protests continued. As late as April 12, 1967, the *New York Times* editorialized: "It is almost but not quite too late to stop the juggernaut."[18] More public hearings were held in May 1967 before the City Planning Commission and the Board of Estimate, but these two bodies decided to support the project. The towers began to rise on their foundations in March 1969; by January 1970, with steel on the north tower up to the forty-third-floor level, the Trade Center was beginning to make its presence felt on the skyline amidst a declining market for office space and an increasing perception that the facility was well beyond the needs of the international trade community. As the first tower was nearing occupancy, an army of workers were being trained to maintain and clean the behemoth in a program sponsored by the Port Authority to meet its increasing sense of social responsibility.

On April 4, 1973, the Trade Center was officially dedicated, two years before its projected completion. Though it was no larger than when it was originally planned, economic inflation and vast overruns had combined to push its price tag from $350 million to $800 million. Ten thousand people were already at work in it and 80 percent of its office space was spoken for. But the Trade Center was not much loved; it was seen as little more than an engineering marvel. Huxtable had lost all the enchantment she once had for Yamasaki's approach and had few kind words to say about the finished product:

> The towers are pure technology, the lobbies are pure schmaltz, and the impact on New York . . . is pure speculation. . . . In spite of their size, the towers emphasize an almost miniature module. . . . The module is so small, and the 22-inch-wide windows so narrow, that one of the miraculous benefits of the tall building, the panoramic view out, is destroyed. . . . These are big buildings but they are not great architecture. The grill-like metal facade stripes are curiously without scale. They taper into the more widely-spaced columns of "Gothic trees" at the lower stories, a detail that does not express structure so much as tart it up. The Port Authority has built the ultimate Disneyland fairytale blockbuster. It is General Motors Gothic.[19]

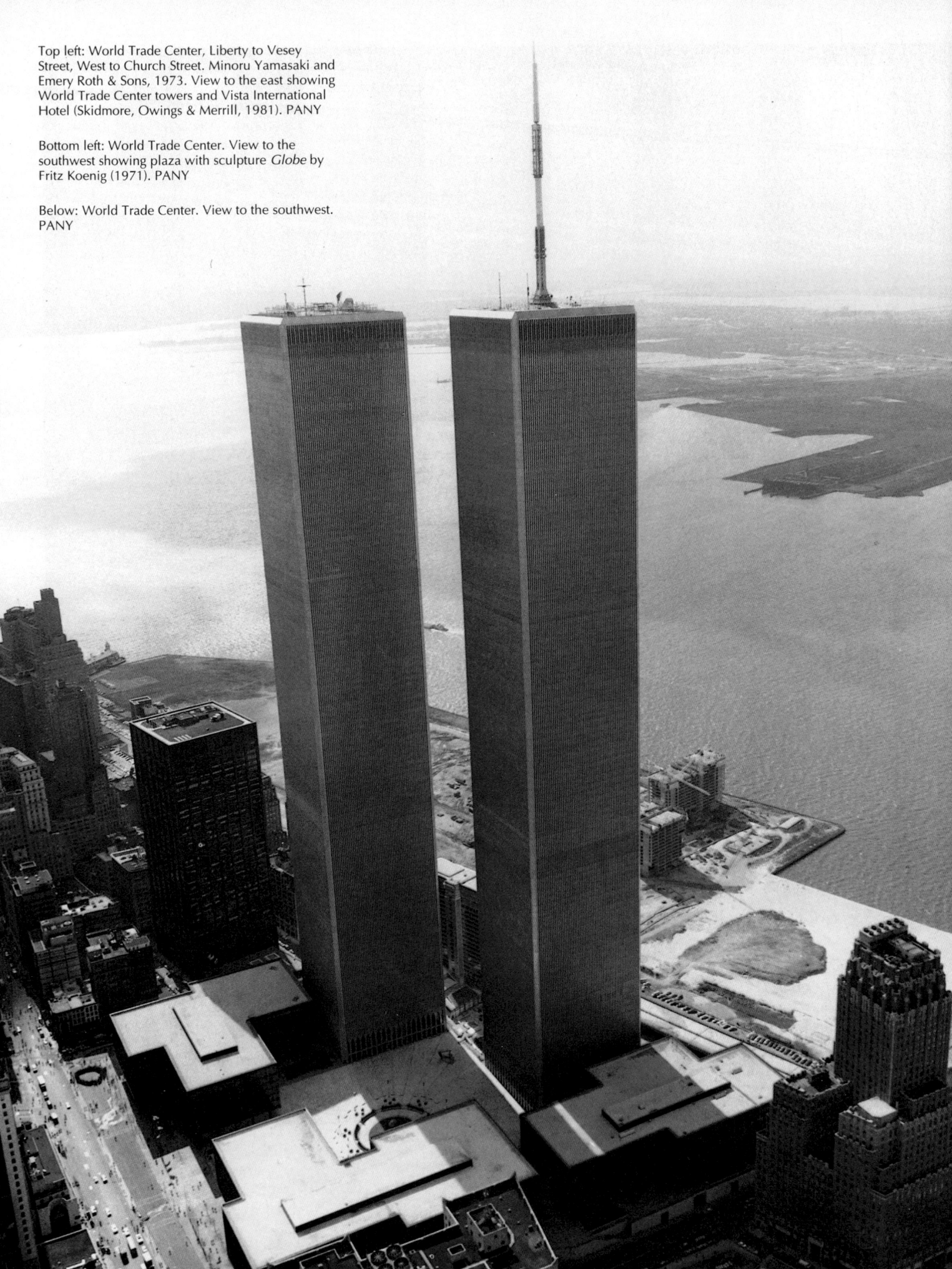

Top left: World Trade Center, Liberty to Vesey Street, West to Church Street. Minoru Yamasaki and Emery Roth & Sons, 1973. View to the east showing World Trade Center towers and Vista International Hotel (Skidmore, Owings & Merrill, 1981). PANY

Bottom left: World Trade Center. View to the southwest showing plaza with sculpture *Globe* by Fritz Koenig (1971). PANY

Below: World Trade Center. View to the southwest. PANY

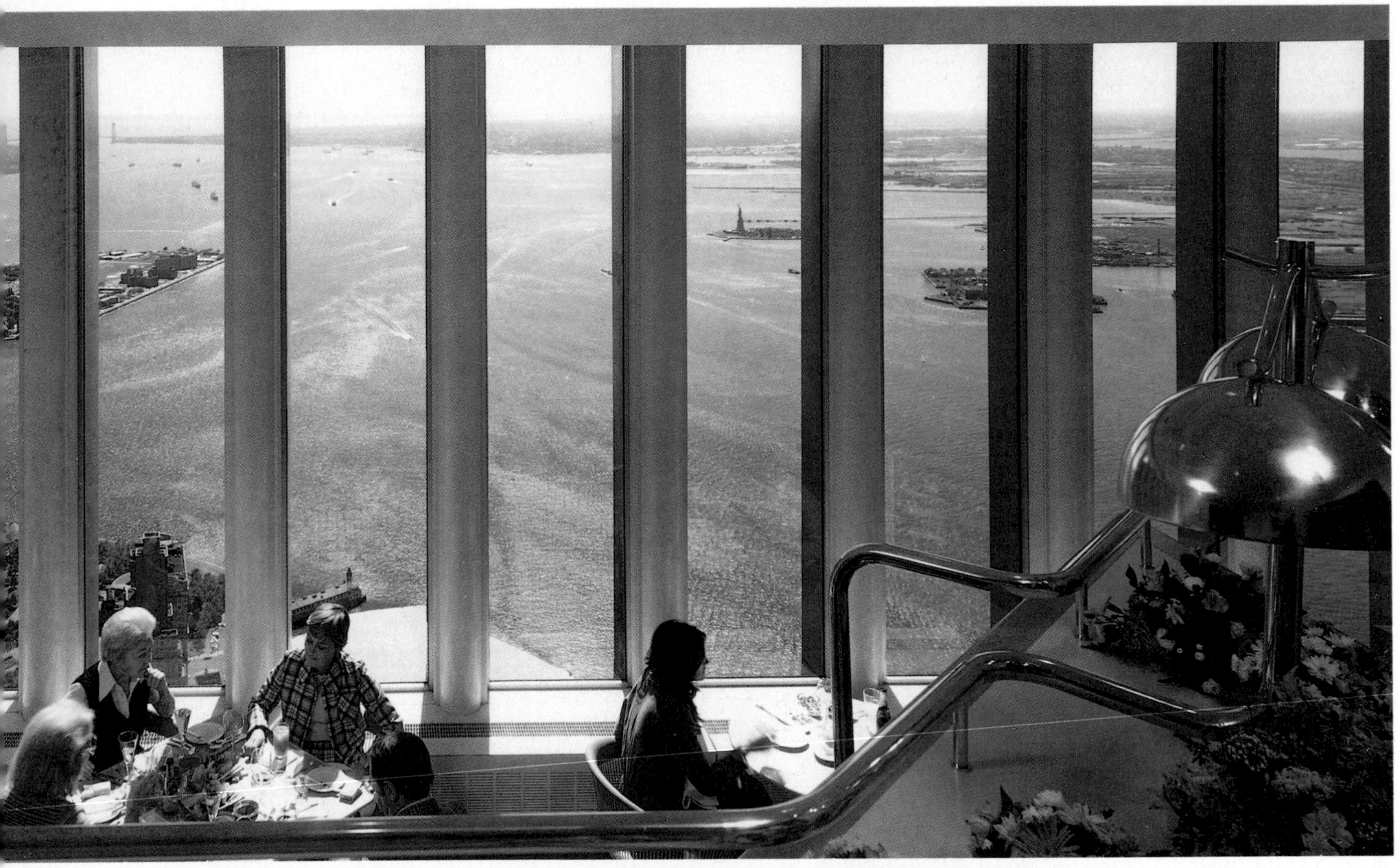

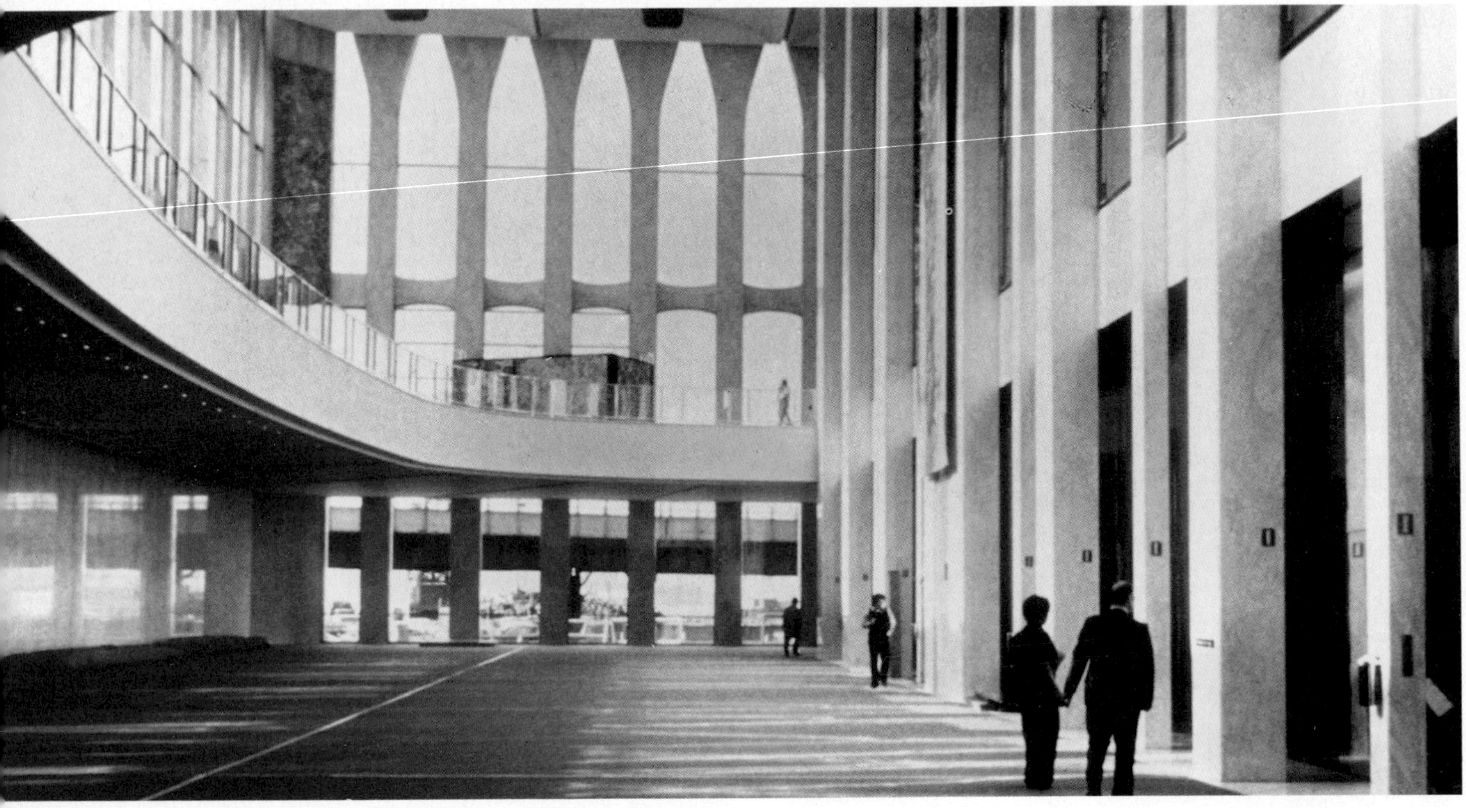

Top: Windows on the World, 107th floor of One World Trade Center. Warren Platner Associates, architects and designers, 1976. View to the southwest. Stoller. ©ESTO

Bottom: Two World Trade Center, Liberty to Vesey Street, West to Church Street. Minoru Yamasaki and Emery Roth & Sons, 1973. Lobby. ERS

An extraordinary event brought some much-needed positive attention to the World Trade Center the year after its dedication. At 7:30 A.M. on Wednesday, August 7, 1974, a twenty-five-year-old Frenchman, Philippe Petit, set out on a forty-five-minute, 131-foot-long walk—a walk along a tightrope that he had secretly stretched between the roofs of the two towers during the night—astounding thousands of office-bound workers in the plaza below as he entertained them with knee bends and other stunts. Asked why he did it, Petit, a professional stuntman who was to develop architectural high-wire walking into a speciality, replied: "If I see three oranges I have to juggle. And if I see two towers, I have to walk."[20] Reflecting on the stunt, the editors of the *New Yorker* said that Petit "did for the Trade Center what King Kong did for the Empire State Building."[21] Petit's feat was ephemeral; but in 1976, the Trade Center made a bid for lasting fame when, in Dino De Laurentiis's remake of King Kong, it usurped the role the Empire State Building had played in the original version (see chapter 17).

In 1975 the general public was for the first time permitted to experience the thrilling views from the top floors when the 110th-floor rooftop observation deck was opened above the south tower along with an enclosed observatory three floors below. Designed by the interior architect Warren Platner and the graphic designer Milton Glaser, the observatory not only offered extraordinary views of the city, the harbor and the suburban areas beyond, but also treated visitors to an informative exhibition about marketing around the world.

The towers even gained a measure of glamour in 1976 with the opening of Windows on the World, an elegant restaurant on the north tower's 107th floor, designed by Warren Platner and masterminded by the restaurateur Joe Baum. As food critic Gael Greene pointed out, Windows on the World opened at just the right time. Not only did it deflect negative public opinion about the Trade Center, but it also demonstrated that New York could build the world's largest office complex and then create at its top a restaurant that would take the best possible advantage of its location and serve delicious food in a glamorous setting. As the bottom was falling out of New York's economy, and its self-esteem seemed lower than it had ever been, here was something to put the city back on top—literally: "Suddenly I knew," Greene wrote, "absolutely *knew*—New York would survive. . . . If money and power and ego and a passion for perfection could create this extraordinary pleasure . . . this instant landmark . . . money and power and ego could rescue the city from its ashes." For Greene, Windows on the World was a "post-industrial enchantment": "In the Statue of Liberty Lounge the harbor's heroic blue sweep makes you feel like the ruler of some extraordinary universe. All the bridges of Brooklyn and Queens and Staten Island stretch across the restaurant's promenade. Even New Jersey looks good from here." Greene described Platner's design as "an extraordinary luxury liner sailing through blue skies 107 stories above the sea. You get the message in the sleek dress uniforms, the epaulets, the gold braid, the brass railings."[22]

To achieve this skyward paradise, Platner and Baum had to go over Yamasaki's head to Guy Tozzoli, the Trade Center's director, to widen the windows by six inches (which was also done at the top of the south tower to help the view from the 107th-floor observation area). Although Platner challenged Yamasaki on this one point, in the overall design he seemed to have captured the very romantic Modernism that Yamasaki was known for but which seemed to have otherwise eluded him in the design of the Trade Center as a whole. Platner, a former colleague of Eero Saarinen's, organized the restaurant as a series of

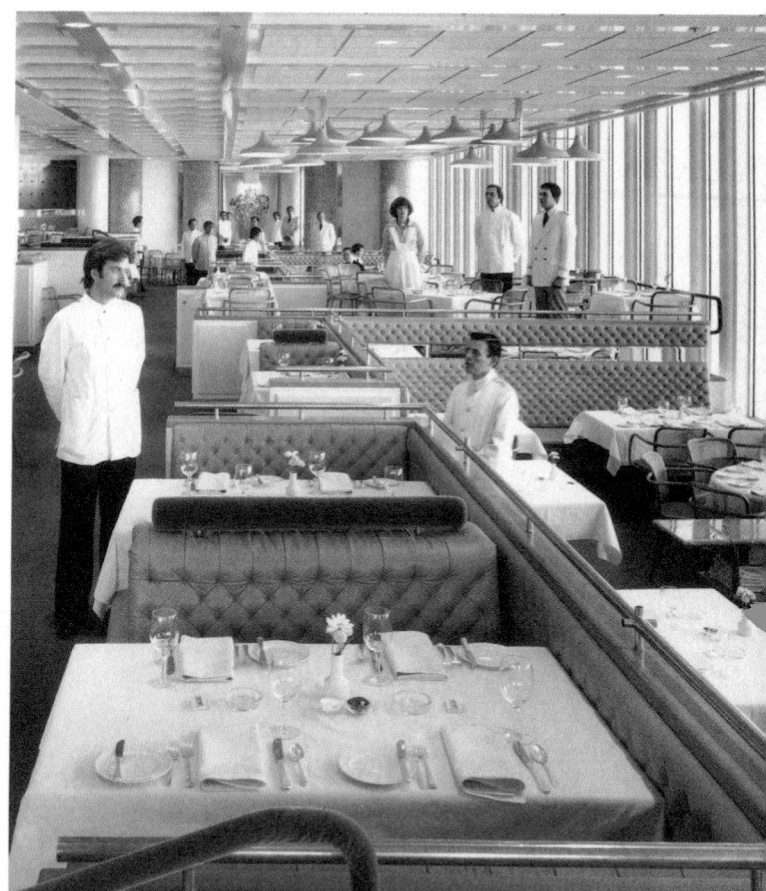

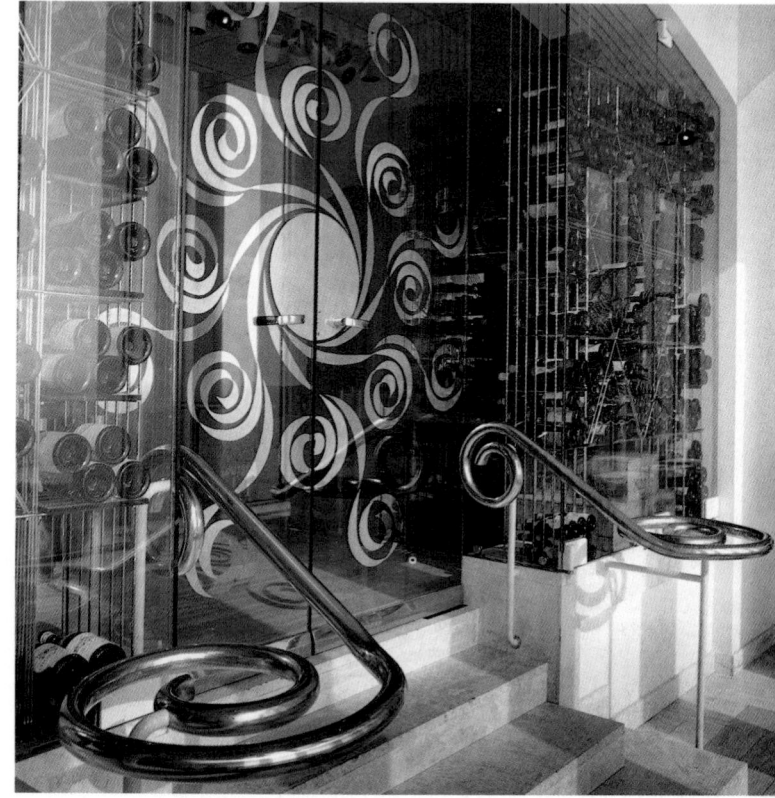

Top: Windows on the World. Georges. WPA

Bottom: Windows on the World. Wine cellar. Georges. WPA

205

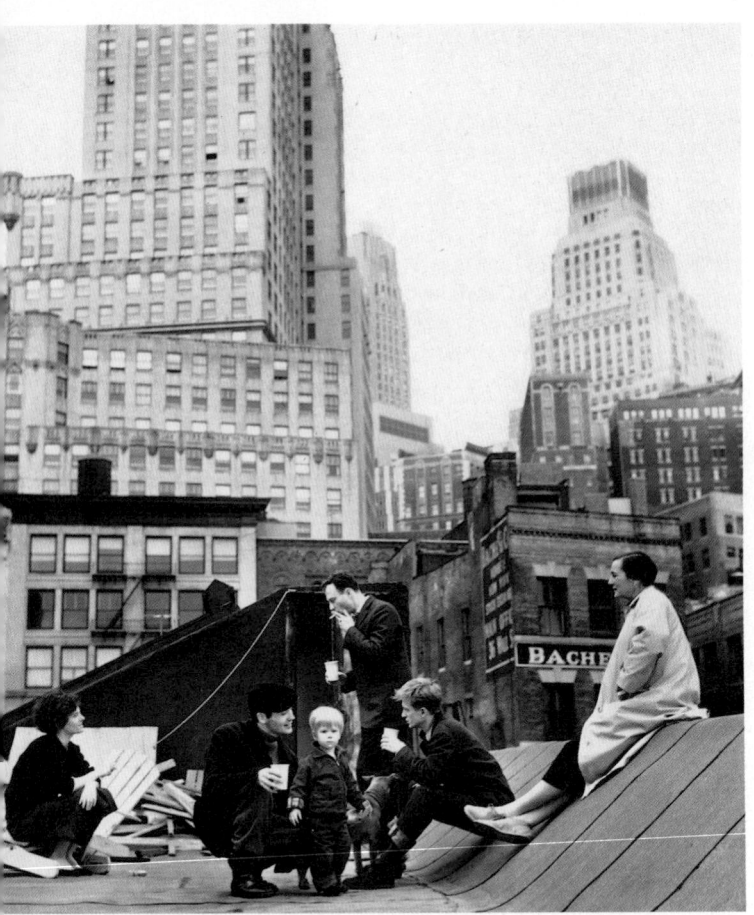

View to the west from a rooftop on Coenties Slip, 1958. Showing, from left to right: Delphine Seyrig, Robert Indiana, Ellsworth Kelly (standing), Jack Youngerman and Agnes Martin. The child is the son of Seyrig and Youngerman. Hans Namuth. CCP

levels terraced up from the windows to best take advantage of the views, creating a sensuous if fussy environment combining brass, marble, light-colored woods and soft beige fabrics.

After the dazzle of Windows on the World and the observation deck wore off, a less heady assessment was made and the twin towers were seen as a "standing monument to architectural boredom,"[23] their facades characterized as "the largest aluminum siding job in the history of the world."[24]

Battery Park City

While no one could dispute lower Manhattan's rebirth following the construction of the Chase bank, midtown, with its variety of commercial and cultural activities, still remained the city's most desirable corporate center. Not only did lower Manhattan offer no mix of activities; it also provided no room to grow. While midtown could easily expand west from the Grand Central–Central Park corridor, downtown growth necessarily had to follow a time-honored but very expensive process—landfill.[25] But given the postwar slump, the potential rewards did not seem to justify the cost of landfill. It was not until the Port Authority was persuaded to use the fill excavated in building the World Trade Center to create twenty-three acres of new land that lower Manhattan began to expand. In so doing, the authority would provide for housing and other amenities that would mark the area's rebirth as a round-the-clock, functionally diversified neighborhood. Just as public pressure against the commercial expansion of midtown was beginning to grow, largely exerted by preservationists concerned with Grand Central (see chapter 16) and by residents of Clinton (see chapter 5), lower Manhattan's new land resource came to seem very valuable indeed: here was the city's best opportunity to develop an asset without sacrificing an existing neighborhood. In lower Manhattan there could be development without redevelopment.

As early as 1941, in a letter to the *New York Times*, Harold A. Caparn articulated a vision for a residential neighborhood in lower Manhattan that would take advantage of the largely underutilized real estate east of Pearl Street.[26] But the war and the slow postwar recovery of lower Manhattan forestalled any further thought about the area's evolution. The situation remained stagnant until 1956, when, as part of his decision to keep the Chase Manhattan Bank headquartered downtown, David Rockefeller organized a group of downtown businessmen, including the leading executives of major banks and the president of the New York Stock Exchange, to consider the future.[27] This high-powered group soon merged with the old Downtown Manhattan Association to form the new Downtown–Lower Manhattan Association, which in 1958 released a set of proposals for the area prepared with the assistance of Skidmore, Owings & Merrill.[28] A broadly sketched master plan, the report focused on three areas: traffic, zoning and redevelopment. Citing the area's unique accessibility by rapid transit and automobile, the plan endorsed proposed street widenings along Water and Fulton streets and suggested further improvements along the west side, as well as arguing for the construction of the Lower Manhattan Expressway (see chapter 4). The plan also recommended rezoning to restrict key areas to commercial use, and to prevent them from being used for manufacturing, which existing zoning permitted. The plan proposed restricting manufacturing to the triangular area on the west side of Church Street below Canal and above Cortlandt, which would come to be known as TriBeCa (short for triangle below Canal Street). Most important, it called for the removal of the Fulton Fish Market to create a major new landmass that, in combination with the expansion of the island out onto the pierhead line of the East River, would permit the financial and insurance districts to expand to the east. This new land would also allow for the development of significant new residential enclaves north of Fulton Street and near the Battery between Pearl and Water streets, the area Harold Caparn had recommended over fifteen years before.

When the plan was submitted to Mayor Wagner for consideration by the Board of Estimate, it ran into heavy opposition from area merchants. Though the Board of Estimate failed to take any action on the plan, the ideas it contained, and the positive demonstration the Chase bank building made in behalf of a new urban order, continued to inspire the community. Even some real estate developers, such as Wylie F. L. Tuttle, argued for the plan, especially its call for housing, which would help transform the area into a twenty-four-hour neighborhood. "With housing in the area," Tuttle said, "the district will no longer become a ghost town after 5 every night."[29]

The area had, in fact, already been discovered by artists, who in the mid-1950s had begun to colonize it as a place in which to both live and work. Coenties Slip attracted a number of artists who rejected the clannish atmosphere of Tenth Street, then the primary locus of activity for the New York Abstract Expressionist school, in favor of the isolated and in large measure defunct waterfront.[30] In 1954 the watercolorist Fred Mitchell set up a studio at 31 Coenties Slip and romantically dubbed the area New Rome. Two years later Mitchell was joined by Ellsworth Kelly and Robert Indiana; Kelly encouraged Agnes Martin as well as Jack Youngerman and his wife, the French film actress Delphine Seyrig, to move. Youngerman established a life-drawing studio there in 1957 that was frequented by James Rosenquist, who subsequently moved to Coenties Slip in 1960. By then the emergent artists' community along the waterfront included Charles Hinman, Jasper Johns, Malcolm Morley, Robert Rauschenberg, Leonore Tawney, Ann Wilson and the composer John Cage. The painter Cy Twombly, unable to afford a loft there himself, used Indiana's space during the day while Indiana was at work in an art-supply store on Fifty-seventh Street.

The artists were attracted not only by the spacious and relatively inexpensive studios but by the area's nonresidential ambience and its isolation from people in general and from other, often more established artists in particular. Youngerman would later recollect, "Consciously or not, everyone who lived [on Coenties Slip] was trying to live apart from the Tenth Street group. My time there was, on the whole, a kind of solitary struggle with my own work and not competition with other people's."[31] So valued was the sense of privacy that many of the resident artists endured the inconvenience of having to go to the Seamen's Church Institute to pick up something to eat or take a shower. But along with the difficulties of living in the area, artists found pleasures, as John Cage would fondly recall: "It was comfortable there. Even though we were poor, we lived with such a view—from Brooklyn and Queens across to the Statue of Liberty—that life was enjoyable and not oppressive."[32] By the mid-1960s the area's aesthetic qualities had attracted the attention of Ada Louise Huxtable, who documented its architectural significance in her 1964 guidebook, *Classic New York: Georgian Gentility to Greek Elegance*.[33] Huxtable was also an early advocate of the area's preservation, but by the decade's close nearly all of the loft buildings on Coenties Slip had been demolished to make way for monolithic office towers.

In 1958 plans were announced for three major housing developments in lower Manhattan: the 3,000-unit Brooklyn Bridge South, along the East River; the 1,224-unit Battery Park Houses; and the 300-unit Battery Park North project.[34] William Zeckendorf had hoped to become the developer of the Battery Park project. In September 1956 full-page national advertisements for Universal Atlas Cement featured three high, circular "Helix" apartment buildings in a parklike setting against the backdrop of the lower Manhattan skyline, presumably presented as part of the proposed redevelopment of the Battery Park City area.[35] A scheme for the site, developed by I. M. Pei & Associates, was similar to the proposal Zeckendorf and Pei had made for the earlier Helix apartments over the East River Drive (see chapter 11). But by March 1957 the head of Metropolitan Structures, Inc., Herbert S. Greenwald, a Chicago-based developer who had worked with Mies van der Rohe, was rumored to be the favored developer.[36]

On January 19, 1959, Robert Moses submitted a designation plan for the Battery Park Urban Renewal Area to Mayor Wagner and the Board of Estimate.[37] The seven-block area of the proposed site, bounded by South, Whitehall, Water and Broad streets, Coenties Slip and Jeannette Park, was to be cleared of its late-eighteenth- and early-nineteenth-century buildings to make way for three twenty-four-story apartment buildings containing 1,224 apartments in all, to be developed by Greenwald. Planned as a Title I Urban Renewal and Slum Clearance project, Battery Park was seen as the first phase in the billion-dollar redevelopment announced three months previously by the Downtown–Lower Manhattan Association. In 1962 plans were announced for the development of the Battery Park project with three forty-four-story slabs oriented east-west in a gently radiating arrangement that in its way respected the area's historic plan.[38] Designed by Mies van der Rohe for Metropolitan Structures, Inc., these did not go forward.

In 1963, as part of a comprehensive plan prepared for the entire Hudson River waterfront from the Battery to West Seventy-second Street by the engineering-management firm Ebasco Services, Inc., in consultation with architects Eggers & Higgins, among others, the city proposed extensive landfill between the Battery and Chambers Street. This would be occupied primarily by a continuous pattern of high-rise housing towers set amid greenery.[39] Opposite Battery Park itself there was to be no landfill but instead a futuristic cylindrical office tower rising on its own island-pier and connected back to the mainland by a bridge.

The Battery Park project languished until May 1966, when Governor Rockefeller announced plans for Battery Park City, a $600 million "coordinated community" to be built on ninety-eight acres of landfill west of West Street, extending north for fifteen blocks from Battery Park to Chambers Street.[40] The project's complex financing called for $138 million from the state to pay for 7,500 units of middle- and low-income housing and $42 million from the city for schools and other public facilities. Private enterprise would supply the rest of the capital to build the complex, which would include eight million square feet of office space. The highly diagrammatic plan, said to have been prepared over eighteen months, though signed by Wallace Harrison was in fact designed by the governor, who did much of the drafting himself.[41] The plan called for a double row of sixteen widely spaced apartment slabs oriented east-west along a central north-south avenue, which would be concluded at each end by identical pairs of flanking sixty-seven-story office towers. Herein lay the birth of the World Trade Center's twin towers.

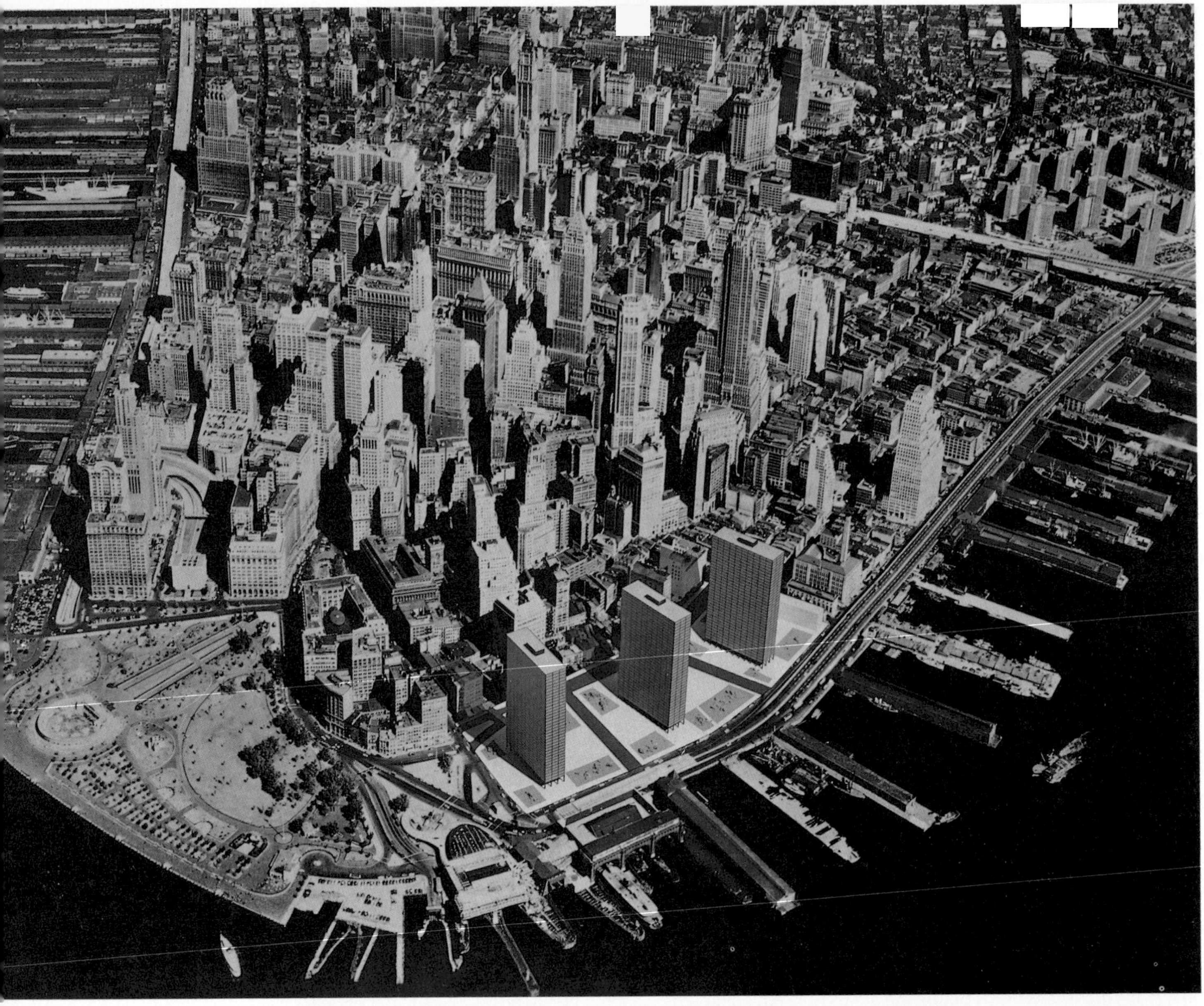

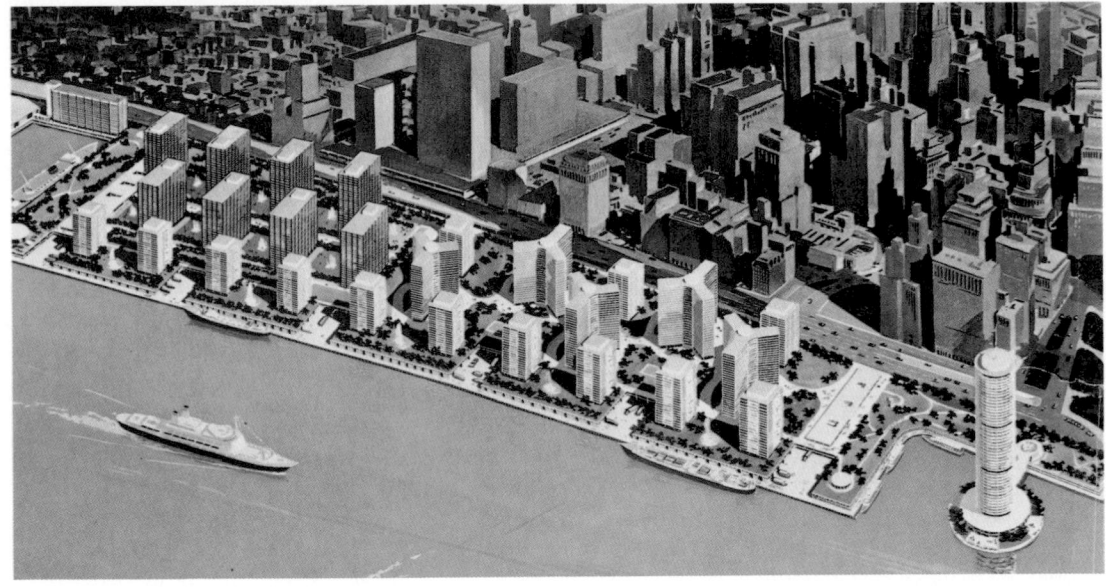

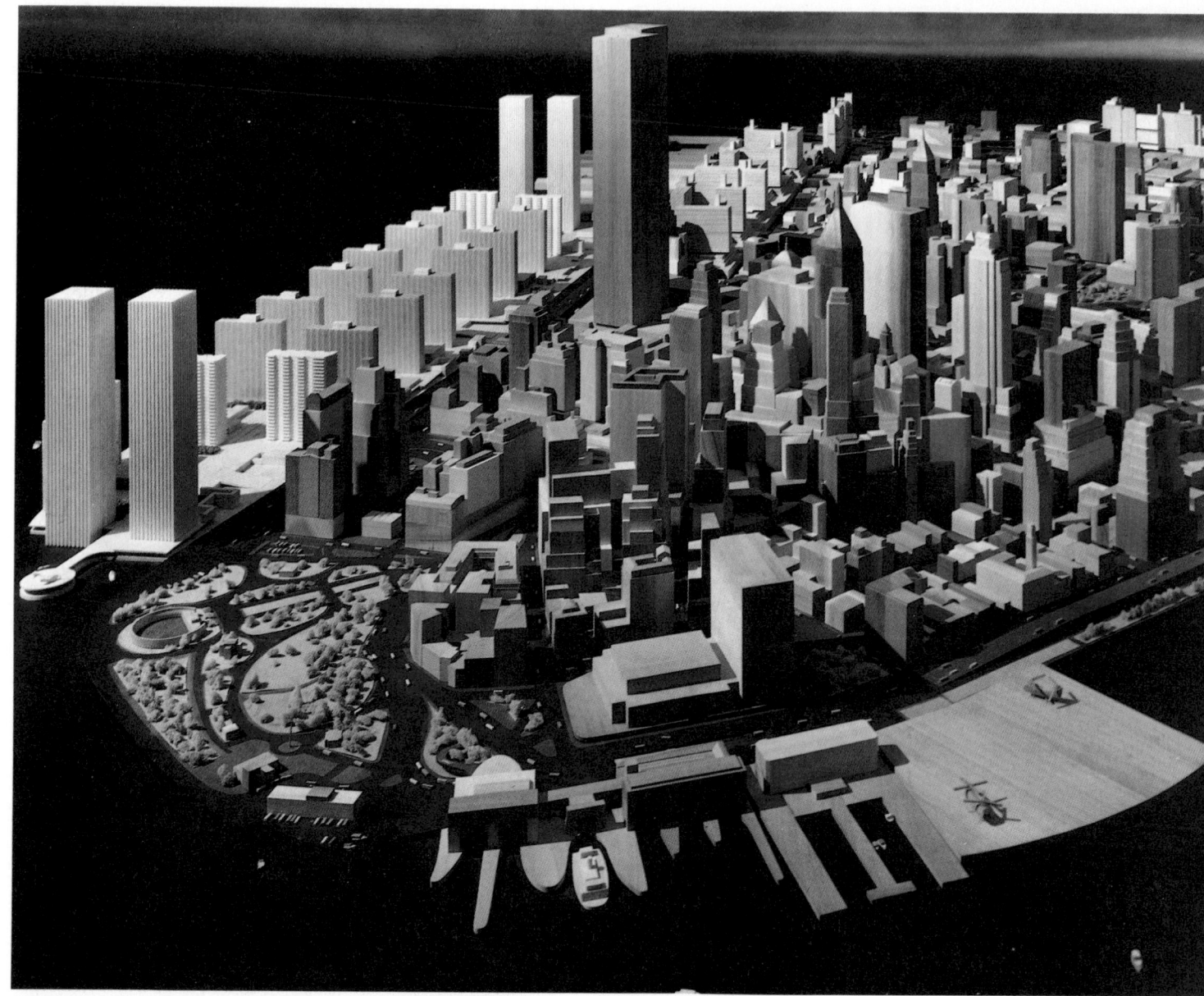

Top left: Proposal for the Battery Park Urban Renewal Area, Whitehall Street to Coenties Slip and Jeannette Park, Water to South Street. Ludwig Mies van der Rohe, 1962. Photographic montage showing view to the north. Hedrich-Blessing. CHS

Bottom left: Proposal for Hudson River landfill project, Battery Park to Chambers Street. Ebasco Services, Inc. in consultation with Moran, Proctor, Mueser & Ruttledge and Eggers & Higgins, 1962. Rendering of view to the northeast. *The Port of New York.* CU

Above: Battery Park City, landfill in the Hudson River, Battery Park to Chambers Street. Nelson A. Rockefeller and Wallace K. Harrison, 1966. Model. View to the northwest. Checkman. LC

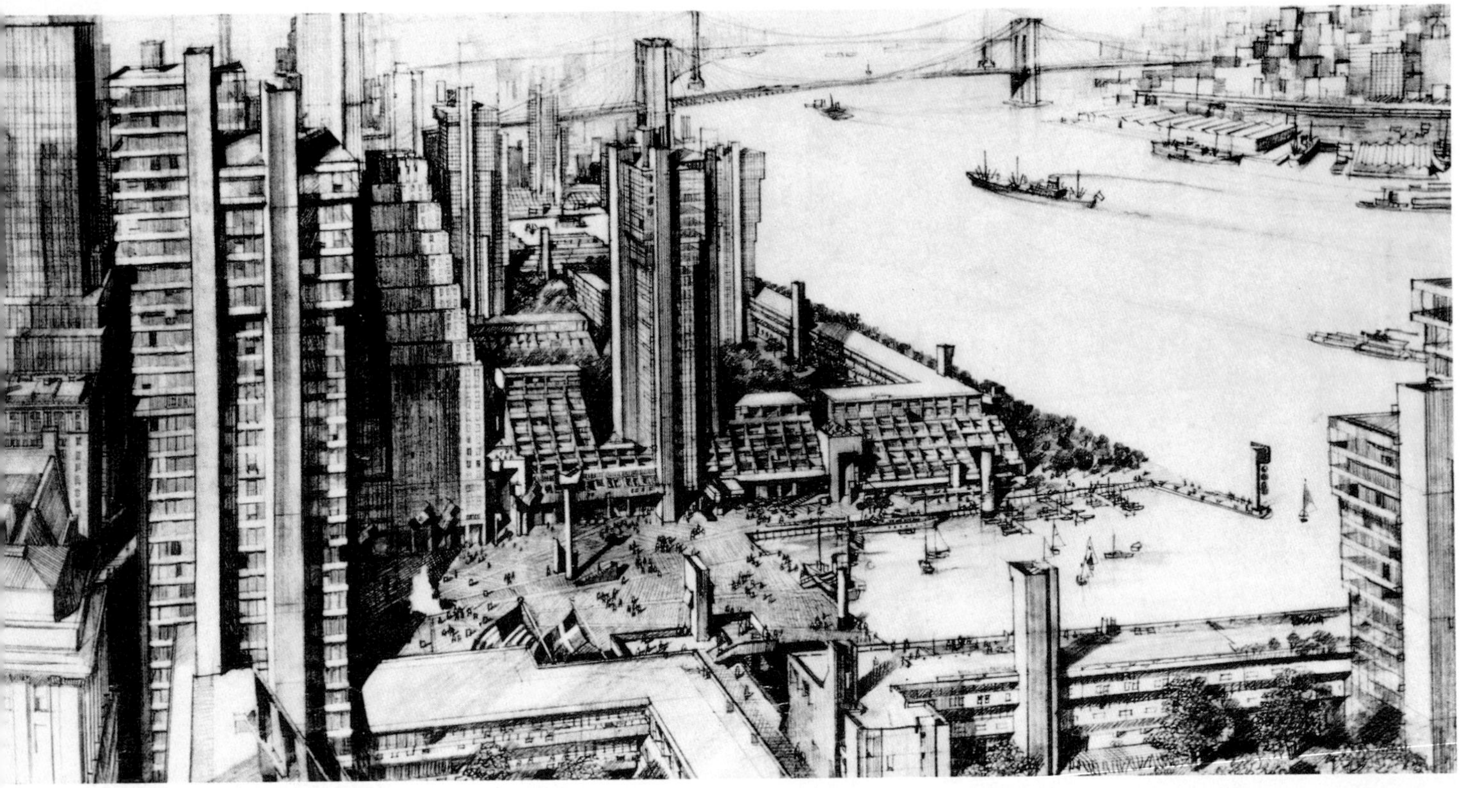

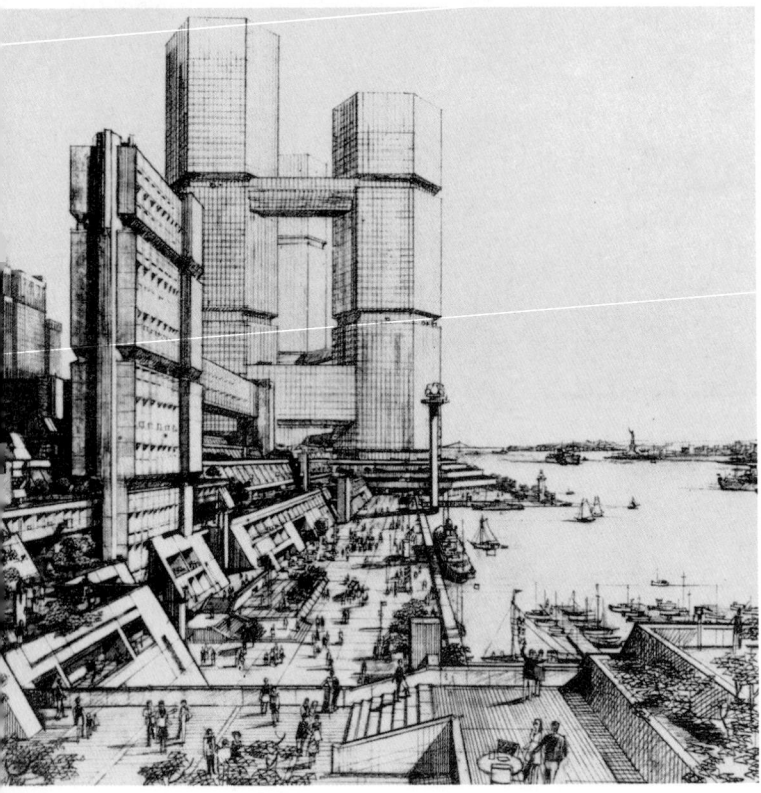

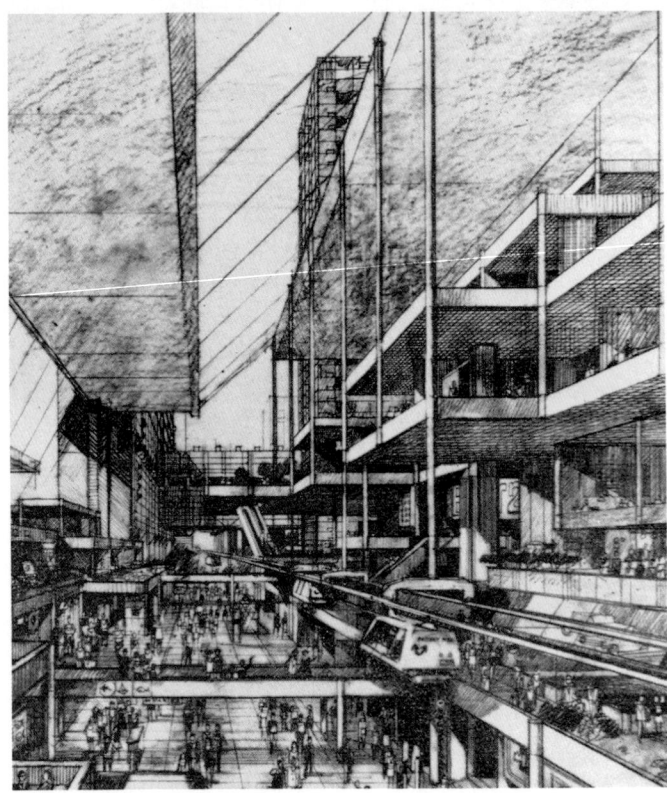

Top: Lower Manhattan Plan, landfill in the East River south of the Brooklyn Bridge. Wallace, McHarg, Roberts, and Todd; Whittlesey, Conklin & Rossant; and Alan M. Voorhees & Associates, 1966. Rendering of view to the northeast. NYC

Bottom left: Battery Park City, landfill in the Hudson River, Battery Park to Chambers Street. Wallace K. Harrison, William Conklin, Philip Johnson and Alan M. Voorhees & Associates, 1969. Rendering of view to the south. AD. CU

Bottom right: Battery Park City, 1969. Rendering of view to the north showing enclosed circulation-shopping spine and "people mover," on the right. AD. CU

Schools, religious buildings, a library-museum, a waterfront hotel and stores would be interspersed among the housing, but the overall feeling was that of a continuous plaza built above garages to create a city not so much within as apart from the city. Ada Louise Huxtable characterized the plan as "'box-top architecture'—something that can be torn off at the dotted line, because it has no relation to anything around it."[42]

The governor's plan was revealed at a press conference held in the Astor Hotel and attended by many officials, including Mayor Lindsay, who called the proposal "an excellent one . . . a balanced, progressive, and proper use of this part of New York City . . . entirely consistent, even identical, with the plans drafted by the City Planning Commission."[43] In fact, the governor, whose relations with the mayor were at best tense, had jumped the gun in an attempt to steal the thunder from the city, whose long-awaited plan was about to be released. But in so doing, and in announcing the creation of the Battery Park City Authority, to be headed by the experienced developer-builder John W. Galbreath, he provided the state's commitment to the area's future, which would prove essential to realizing any coordinated development on the site.

Less than a month later, on June 21, 1966, the City Planning Commission came forward with its proposal.[44] The Lower Manhattan Plan, which was prepared by a staff coordinated by Jack C. Smith and consultants including the landscape architects Wallace, McHarg, Roberts, and Todd of Philadelphia, and the architects, urban planners and urban designers Whittlesey, Conklin & Rossant of New York, was initiated in February 1965. Portions of the findings were previewed in December 1965, when the job of William F. R. Ballard, chairman of the City Planning Commission, was threatened by the mayor because of the commission's traditional inaction in the area of master planning.[45] While much of the plan was concerned with short-range and urbanistically questionable palliatives such as street widenings to deal with the massive new construction in the area—including office buildings, expanded facilities in the civic center and housing—the study was boldly innovative in the breadth of its vision. It looked forward to the year 2000 with two major development strategies: it called for wrapping virtually the entire area with landfill, in part created from the excavations for the Trade Center; and it offered a precise urban design strategy, extending the existing streets out to waterfront parks and plazas in an effort to countermand standard superblocking by renewing the traditional pattern of streets that presented "windows on the water." This concept was illustrated with evocative sketches showing sculpturally modeled apartment towers rising from low townhouselike apartment buildings that wrapped around lively riverfront yacht harbors. Here was a decisive break with the "domino" planning of New York's typical postwar housing, a real contrast to the Rockefeller-Harrison proposal for Battery Park City. Writing in 1967, the architect Wallace Berger observed that the plan "adroitly combines historical continuity with conceptual boldness and proposes an environment in which the district can grow, prosper, and continue to develop its own unique forms. The plan is comprehensive, long-range, and exciting. . . . For a city which in the past has been notoriously inept at just such planning foresight, there is hope that a far-reaching precedent has been established."[46]

Work toward the realization of Battery Park City continued, and in April 1968 Governor Rockefeller and Mayor Lindsay announced an agreement that would permit the Battery Park City Authority, a nonprofit corporation, to hold a ninety-nine-year lease on what had become a 104-acre site and a $1.1 billion residential and commercial complex.[47] The additional acreage was to be created by platforming over a submerged West Side Highway. Now there would be 21,000 apartments, two-thirds of them financed at market rate, the remaining one-third divided among lower- and middle-income families. The amount of office space in the 1966 proposal had been drastically curtailed, from eight to five million square feet.

As a result of this agreement, a new plan would be undertaken by a team of architects and traffic consultant Alan M. Voorhees & Associates. The principal participants on the team were Wallace Harrison and William Conklin, who had so successfully contributed to the mayor's Lower Manhattan Plan. Philip Johnson, who was respected by both the governor and the mayor, was brought in as a kind of referee. Here, as Ada Louise Huxtable was later to put it, was "a team of designers that could only have been put together by a clubhouse deal or a marriage broker, or both."[48] But when the Harrison, Conklin and Johnson plan was released in April 1969, it failed to please several contingents. The longshoremen regretted losing their hegemony over the Manhattan waterfront, even though it was in fact virtually dormant in terms of shipping. And low-cost housing advocates were angered that only 1,266 of the 21,000 housing units were earmarked for the poor; civil rights leader Bayard Rustin and Manhattan Borough President Percy Sutton denounced the project as "the Riviera of the Hudson."[49]

The architecture called for in the new plan was radically different from that of the Rockefeller-Harrison scheme, but the plan incorporated some of the features of its predecessor, in particular the north-south avenue. In keeping with current megastructural tendencies in urban design, the avenue was treated as a multilevel enclosed circulation-shopping spine complete with a "people mover" system. But instead of the simpleminded scheme of parallel superslabs, a more complex network of courtyards and plazas was devised. Two major harbors, acting as windows on the water, were established, one opposite the Trade Center, the other at the foot of Morris Street, where it buffered the residential quarter from the office buildings, now designed as three glass-skinned hexagonal towers of varying heights linked by skybridges.

Despite some misgivings, Huxtable greeted the plan with enthusiasm: "Battery Park City . . . is an outstanding effort to establish comprehensive guidelines for desperately needed housing and commercial development within the framework of a totally planned community set into the larger city. . . . [It] is a progressive, sophisticated and promising development. . . . Is this any way to plan a city? You bet it is."[50] Looking back four years later in 1973, Huxtable saw the design as "a brilliant, schematic compromise."[51]

Despite an improved plan and government support, the softening market for office space hampered financing and the decision was made to go ahead with the housing only.[52] As the project's fiscal prospects declined, relations between the Battery Park City Authority and the city declined. The three-firm architectural coalition was abandoned, in part because the City Planning Commission's urban designers began to have strong reservations about the plan's superscale urbanism. Increasingly, the virtues of the time-honored, incremental, building-by-building, block-by-block approach to development and redevelopment were coming to be appreciated. As Huxtable put it: "The city's urban designers at the Office of Lower Manhattan Development grew increasingly disturbed at the plan's lack of relationship to existing configurations of Lower Manhattan. . . .

They feared a 'Chinese wall' effect offshore and wanted connections and continuity with the new development."[53]

By 1973, when the Battery Park City Authority finally abandoned the hope of building offices to subsidize the project and settled on a starting project of 5,800 housing units using $4.5 million of state-supplied Mitchell-Lama funds, it set out to redesign the project.[54] At this point the authority brought in Samuel Lefrak and the Fisher Brothers as potential housing developers, and Wallace Harrison's partner, Max Abramovitz, took on the role of architectural consultant to the authority, which hired William Halsey as its director of architecture. The new developers first hired the Israeli-born Canadian architect Moshe Safdie, who, fresh from his triumph at Habitat, built for the Expo '67 World's Fair in Montreal, proposed five concrete ziggurats. Safdie lasted but a short time before Lefrak brought his favorite in-house architect, Jack Brown, on board. Quickly Battery Park City began to look like Lefrak City (see chapter 13), or, as Huxtable put it, "outer borough limbo."[55] With the buildings becoming increasingly banal and the spaces between them widening, the landscape architect Lawrence Halprin was called in for help.[56] But all the talent in the world couldn't help the project, which foundered on the shaky sands of a declining financial market.

It was not until September 1974 that any actual construction began, with a whimper and not much of a bang, as 1,642 units of dreary, brownish red brick subsidized middle-income housing were designed by Max Abramovitz, Jack Brown and Irving Gershon for Lefrak and the Fisher Brothers.[57] Even as construction was under way, it was not clear whether Lefrak-Fisher would invest in the project or merely act as construction managers; the design of the buildings and the spaces between them was also as yet undetermined. Paul Goldberger observed that "The evolution of Battery Park City's still-uncertain physical appearance has been a classic study in the politics of design. The stakes are high: the buildings that are to be constructed on the prominent site will be seen by visitors from all over the world and will permanently alter the skyline of lower Manhattan. And the project is viewed as a test case for the city's desire to turn lower Manhattan into a mixed-use '24-hour' community."[58] In 1976, as foundations for the project were at last being dug on the 5,000-person complex, Huxtable found a few things to admire, including Abramovitz's redesign of Brown and Gershon's buildings, which included towers and lower elements "clustered . . . in 'pods,' or neighborhood groups." She also praised Halprin's "integrated design of the open space": "It is the way this open space is handled that has brought about the miraculous transformation of Battery Park City from a wasteland to a place any lucky New Yorker would want to live. . . . What has finally been clearly understood and dealt with is the quality of urban life and how it can be created through urban design."[59] Nonetheless, failure to achieve required federal loan guarantees halted the project again, so that after ten years all that had been realized was the site itself, slightly over ninety flat acres of dirt.

Habitat New York

Without question, one of the most technologically daring postwar building proposals for the lower Manhattan waterfront—or indeed for anywhere in New York—was Moshe Safdie's Habitat II, to be built on platforms in the East River, east of South Street, extending roughly from Fulton to Wall Street.[60] After the success of his widely publicized Habitat modular housing project for the Expo '67 World's Fair in Montreal, the architect released designs for Habitat II, also known as Habitat New York, in 1968. Among the many visitors to Habitat in Montreal was Carol W. Haussamen, a sponsor of both for-profit and not-for-profit building projects in New York. Subsequent to discussions between Haussamen and Mayor Lindsay, who had also visited Habitat and been favorably impressed, Safdie met with members of the New York City Housing Authority and the City Planning Commission, as well as with Haussamen, to examine the possiblity of creating a municipally organized urban renewal site along the East River to house a Habitat-type project.

Two sites were chosen: one near Ninety-first Street and the other between Fulton and Wall streets. Haussamen, who sought to develop the project as upmarket housing, thought the Upper East Side location more economically viable. Safdie had designed a scheme for the uptown site (see chapter 11) and initiated the cost-estimating process when Haussamen decided to move the project to the lower Manhattan location. An increase in the cost of acquiring the property necessitated an increase in the height and density of the proposed building complex; whereas the earlier plan had called for a twenty-two-story building planned on the basis of a density of 200 units per acre, the revised plan called for a building fifty stories high and a density of 300 units per acre, as permitted by zoning. These new programmatic requirements in turn necessitated technological innovation: Safdie's previous design, if amplified in height, would not be able to withstand high winds or earthquakes.

Safdie's design for Habitat New York reflected his interest in intricate geometries and his commitment to finding a technological, almost futuristic solution to the complex problems the project posed. A triangular compression tower was to stand in the center of the complex; between the tower and three similarly designed towers arranged in a surrounding triangle were to be three enormous catenaries from which stacks of modular apartments were to be suspended. Each of the three towers were to support two more spokes of housing. Safdie described this arrangement both as "somewhat like a suspension bridge going in three directions" and as "masts off which in three directions are suspended enormous sails of housing." Amazingly, the supporting cables, wrapped in fireproof material, were less than three inches in diameter. As Safdie enthusiastically put it, the resulting "efficiency in terms of the materials and useable interior space was almost incredible."[61]

The complex was to be composed of thin-shell precast-concrete units manufactured in Queens. Because they would be shipped by barge to the site, circumventing highway transport, the units could be wider than the standard mobile home. Unlike the prefabricated units of the Montreal Habitat, which were slipped into a comprehensive superstructure, here the units merely hung from a cable. Despite the lack of a rigid overall structure, however, the physics of suspension required that each module need only be strong enough to support itself. Pairs of modules could be connected or installed separately, providing residents with a choice of simplex or split-level units. Many apartments were to be provided with generously scaled terraces, described by the architect as "gardens."

Beneath the looming, tentacular apartment towers, eleven-story stepped-profile buildings were to house one million square feet of office space, a hotel, a shopping center and a 3,000-car garage, located partially underwater; the project was also to contain a marina. Though structurally independent, the ground-level buildings were attached to the towers above, anchoring the suspended structure and controlling sway. Landscaped open spaces located between these facilities would provide greenery

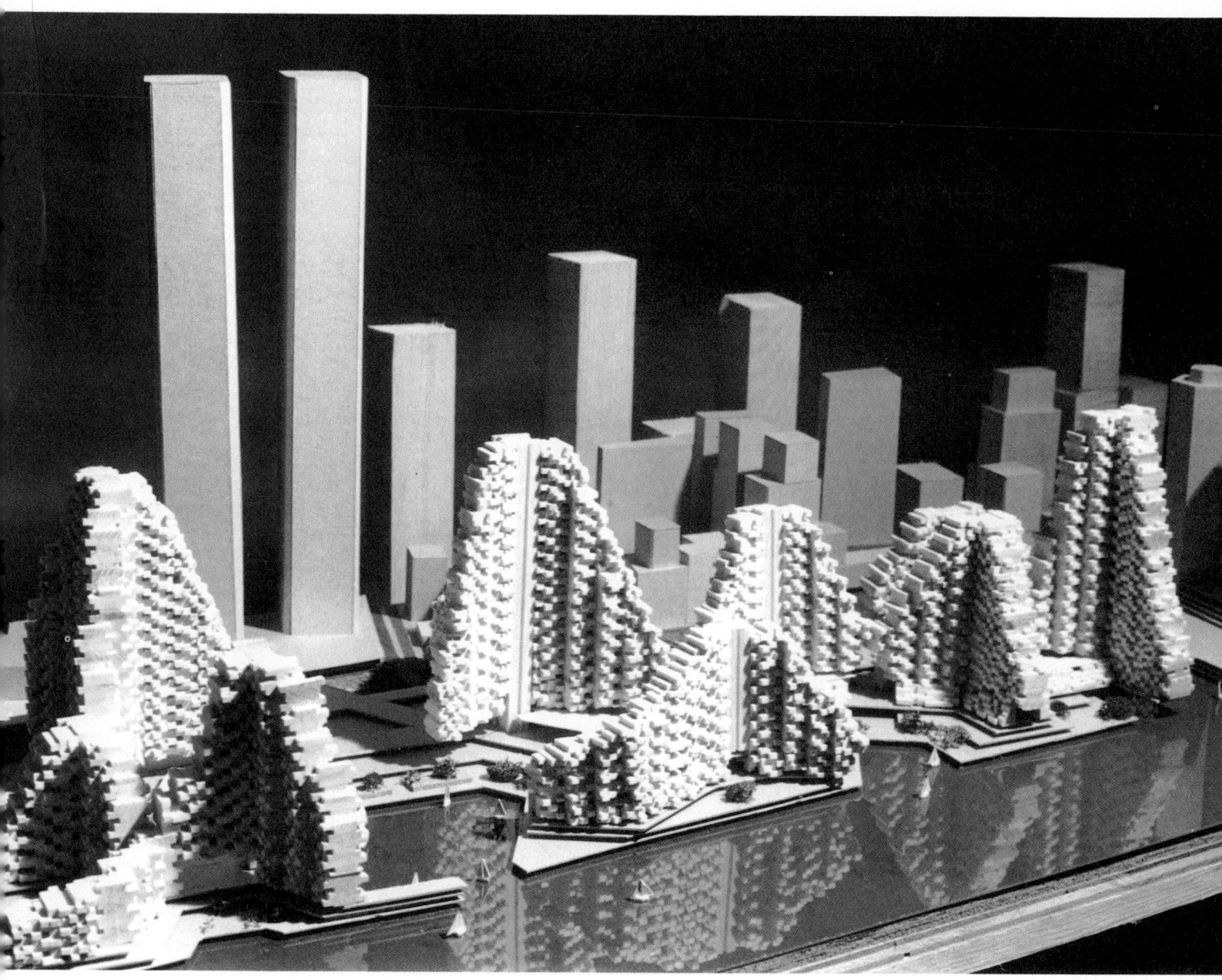

Habitat New York, platforms in the East River, Wall to Fulton Street.
Moshe Safdie, 1968. Model. View to the northwest. MSA

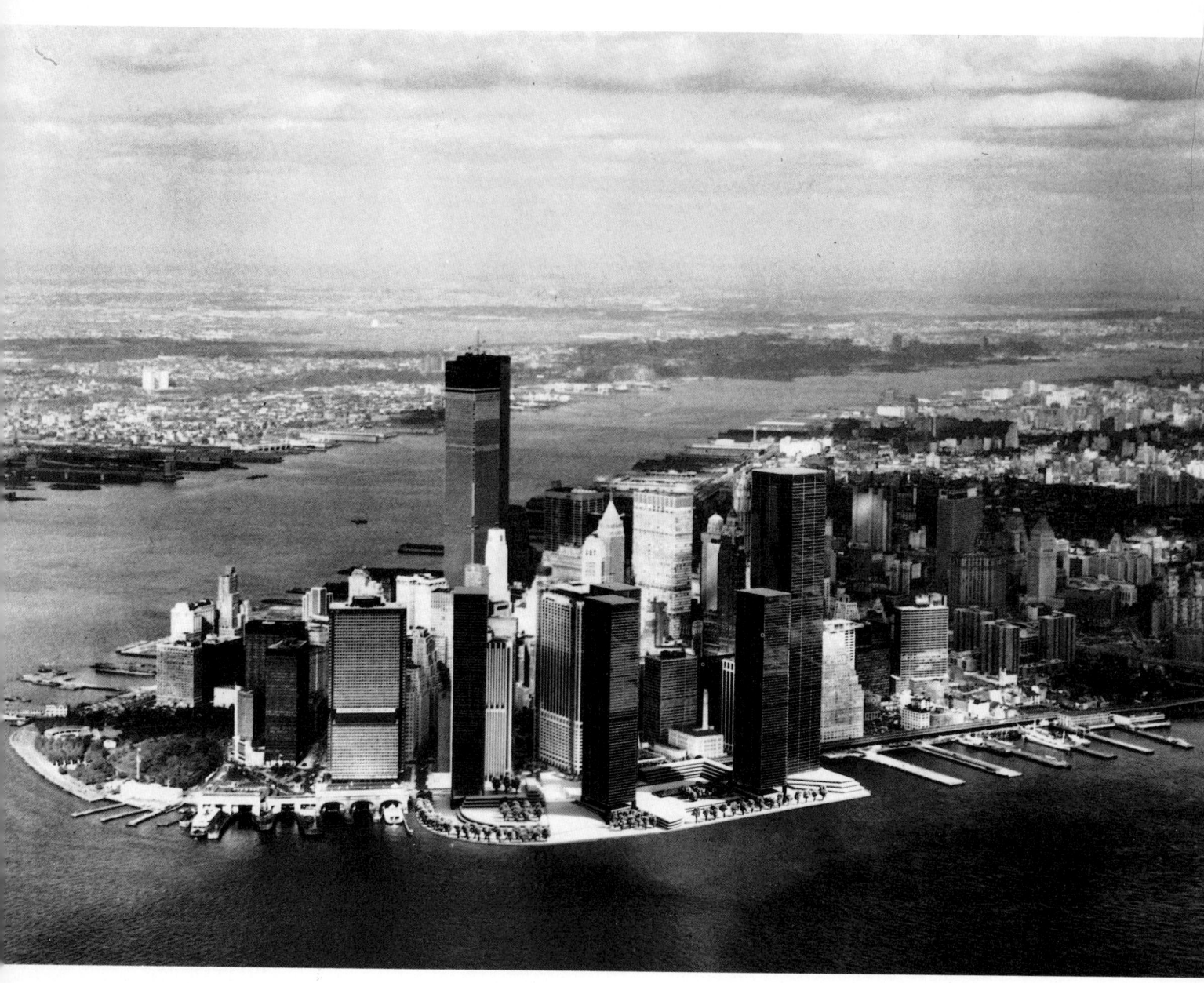

Manhattan Landing, platforms in the East River, Broad Street to
Gouverneur Lane. Davis, Brody & Associates, Horowitz & Chun and
Edward Larrabee Barnes, 1972. Photographic montage showing view
to the northwest. DBA

and informal meeting places as well as, in accordance with a municipal project requirement, permitting unobstructed river views from the west side of South Street.

Though the project would have been undeniably spectacular in technological terms, its visual and spatial complexity might have produced an effect more cacophonous than compelling. Furthermore, because of the building's height and bulk, its design seemed to take on a menacing or at least daunting aspect. The project was never realized, in part, Safdie contended, because "other developers were very keen to put office buildings on the prime lands that had been designated to us." Moreover, Safdie charged, Gordon Bunshaft and the New York Stock Exchange, planning to build a structure on an adjacent site (see below), were unhappy about their prospective neighbors: "A residential community did not appear to them compatible with America's highest financial institution; they could envisage mothers with baby carriages strolling in the stock exchange plaza at lunch time."[62]

Manhattan Landing

The dream of transforming lower Manhattan into a vital, round-the-clock, mixed-use neighborhood received a shot in the arm on April 12, 1972, when Mayor Lindsay and David Rockefeller jointly revealed a plan for a mile-long, $1.2 billion development to be built over the East River on platforms, effectively extending Manhattan's landmass by eighty-eight acres from the island's bulkhead line to the limits of its pierhead line.[63] The proposal called for the construction of six million square feet of office space, 9,500 upscale apartments, stores and restaurants, a 1,000-car municipal parking garage, a new park equal in size to Washington Square Park, a 400-room hotel equipped with indoor and outdoor tennis courts as well as a skating rink, a 500-berth marina, an oceanographic museum and a restored South Street Seaport area (see chapter 16). The plan also called for a new 1.3 million-square-foot building to house the New York Stock Exchange. A network of parks, including a redesigned Jeannette Park, was to be augmented by a 150-foot-wide public promenade extending along the East River from the Battery to the Brooklyn Bridge; the promenade was to be realized by requiring all riverfront builders to include a segment of the public amenity in their building plans. "Scenic corridors" of open space traversing the development and penetrating existing blocks were to ensure that the new buildings would not cut off the rest of lower Manhattan from river views.

The first half of the development was slated to be complete by 1976, with the entire complex finished by 1985. The architects initially commissioned were the firm of Davis, Brody & Associates for housing near Jeannette Park; Horowitz & Chun for the parking garage, as well as for housing to be erected above it; and Edward Larrabee Barnes, whom the Trump Organization commissioned to conduct a feasibility study for a mixed-use building to be located on the site of the Staten Island Ferry Terminal. A photomontage indicated the proposed development's mix of high- and low-rise buildings and the establishment of visual corridors providing clear sightlines from lower Manhattan's existing streets to the East River, despite the project's abandonment of a traditional street plan in favor of a superblock *parti*.

Whatever potential the project had for attaining a high level of design quality, its complex financial and bureaucratic underpinnings constituted perhaps its most noteworthy feature. Under the leadership of Richard Weinstein, the Office of Lower Manhattan Development worked directly with David

Rockefeller and the Downtown–Lower Manhattan Association on the Manhattan Landing project, forging what the editors of *Architectural Record* called "a unique and heartening alliance."[64] The project relied heavily on private-sector financing, orchestrated principally by Rockefeller, who Lindsay characterized as "the spark plug and the adhesive tape that has pulled together so much of [the] project."[65]

The most economically problematic aspect of the project was the housing. High-income families, it was believed, would not be attracted to the downtown location; rather, the housing was pitched to young, single Wall Street workers with annual incomes of less than $15,000. In order to reduce the unmarketability of apartments with $180-per-room rents, which would result from following conventional financial formulas, an alternate mortgage system was devised. Seventy-five percent of the necessary funds was to be provided by private lenders at below-market interest rates, perhaps as low as 7 percent; 20 percent was to be provided by the public-sector Housing Development Corporation, which, at the time of the project's announcement, had yet to be established by the City Council; and the remaining 5 percent would come from the developer's equity. The funds generated by the public sector would be derived from the sale of bonds that would eventually be paid back; in essence the transaction amounted to a loan and not a subsidy. Municipal tax abatements would be utilized to help make apartments affordable and the project as a whole feasible. The decision to construct the development on platforms rather than landfill had been economically motivized: platforms were, from a legal point of view, considered part of the buildings they supported and thus could be depreciated for taxes.

Though not enough about the architectural aspect of the project had been revealed to elicit serious comment, Ada Louise Huxtable's reaction to the project's planning aspect, and to the ability of public- and private-sector interests to work together in the service of good urban design, was highly favorable:

> What is involved in lower Manhattan is not just a billion-dollar development plan but the skilled manipulation of one of the highest density areas in the world and the most expensive real estate for a particular goal: the quality of the environment. That is usually not a component of real estate packages. There are two kinds of glue that hold together a proposal of this magnitude: money and planning. It is no secret that the resources [David] Rockefeller commands or influences can make things happen, and that he is personally selling the city's financial institutions on the desirability of providing the necessary investment.[66]

Huxtable lauded the proposed provision of a riverside promenade and "scenic corridors," noting that negotiating such amenities was not easy in bottom-line-oriented New York: "Everything relates to everything else—functionally and esthetically—something no New York development does voluntarily. The city does not just pull these features out of a hat. It is done through a kind of creative horse-trading with builders."[67]

The consistently liberal Citizens' Housing and Planning Council endorsed the project, despite the fact that it made no provision for low-income residents. The editors of the group's newsletter noted:

> An important market for the Manhattan Landing apartments may be found among the workers in the downtown financial district. These workers, in the middle echelons as well as among the clerical ranks, include a considerable and a growing number of non-whites. The age-old overlap between low-income and dark skin having greatly narrowed, Manhattan Landing should contain a significant number of non-white indi-

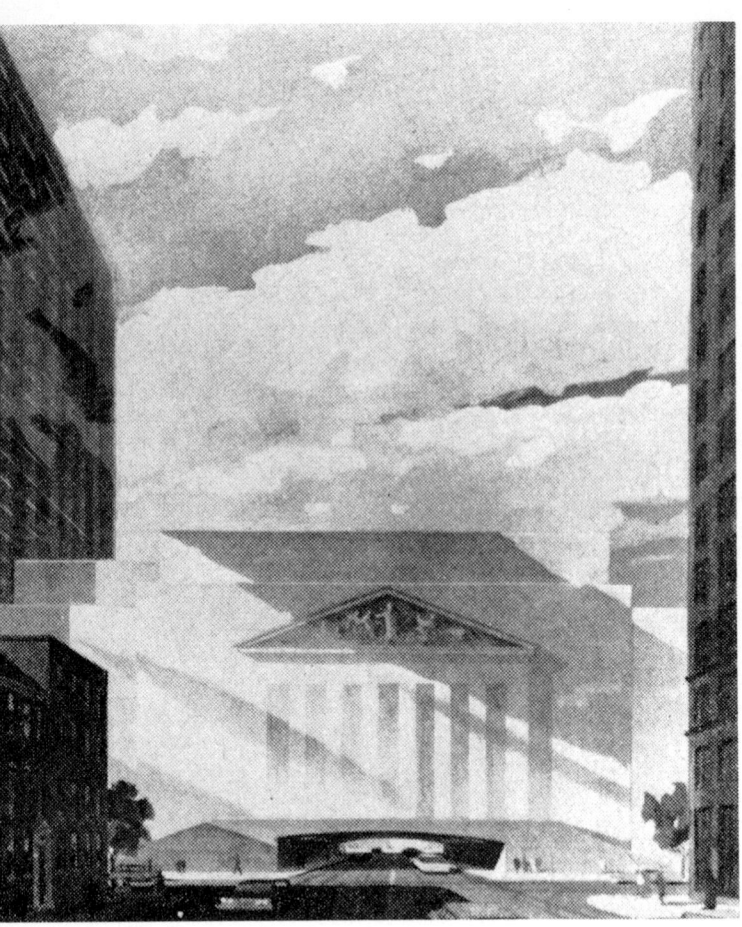

Proposal for New York Stock Exchange Building, Whitehall Street to Coenties Slip, Water to South Street. O'Connor & Kilham, 1963. Rendering of view to the southeast with Broad Street tunneling through the proposed building. PA. CU

viduals and families even without low-rent housing. . . . Those who view Manhattan Landing with favor will have to run the risk of appearing to slight the immediate needs of the poor in order to advance the economic interests of the city as a whole.[68]

Unfortunately, the elaborate network of financial support did not materialize and the project died.

New York Stock Exchange

At one time or another, plans for key lower Manhattan projects, including the World Trade Center and Battery Park City, as well as the unrealized Manhattan Landing, incorporated a major new facility for the New York Stock Exchange. The exchange's abortive search for a new home reflected several critical currents in the city's economic and urbanistic evolution: the increasing reliance on finance and service industries, as opposed to manufacturing, to provide the city's economic foundation; the city's struggle to maintain its traditional role as the nation's, and one of the world's, leading financial capitals; and the city's steadily intensifying battle against decentralization, as suburbs and new "satellite cities" threatened to etiolate New York's power.

In January 1960 the Downtown–Lower Manhattan Association issued a plan to build a vast mixed-use complex focused on an international trade mart to be built on a podium in the East River (see above). The association hoped that the New York Stock Exchange, having outgrown the headquarters it had occupied at 8 Broad Street (George B. Post, 1903; Trowbridge & Livingston, 1923), would relocate to a new building within the development. As delineated in a master plan drawn up by the firm of Skidmore, Owings & Merrill under the direction of Edward James Matthews, the building was to be an eight-story truncated cone. By the fall of 1961, with the fate of the overall project—by that time known as the World Trade Center—uncertain, the stock exchange began to consider other possibilities.[69] On April 1, 1963, the exchange publicly revealed preliminary drawings for a new building to be built on two blocks of the six-block, 12.8-acre Battery Park Urban Renewal Area.[70] The building was to occupy a site bounded by South, Whitehall and Water streets and Coenties Slip; Broad Street, which traversed the site, was to tunnel through the building. Triangular Jeannette Park, bordering Coenties Slip, was to share the eastern portion of the site. Designed by the firm of O'Connor & Kilham, the building was to be composed of a rather squat six-story section bridging Broad Street that was to house a 56,000-square-foot trading floor, more than double the size of the old facility's floor; to the east, an adjacent twenty-story slab was to contain offices.

The proposal immediately raised several concerns. The editors of *Progressive Architecture* noted that "some New York architects" thought the site was too far from its traditional place at the heart of the financial district. In addition, the editors said, "In its preliminary form, the design and massing of the Stock Exchange seems quite eclectic and heavy-handed."[71] The editors seemed to object to what they considered the traditionalism of the design, even though the only overtly historicist elements were fragments from the old building: the executive boardroom was to be installed inside the new building, and the 110-foot-long pediment sculpted by John Quincy Adams Ward and Paul Bartlett (1903) was to be placed on the new building's principal facade above the Broad Street tunnel.[72] The editors of the *New York Times* also voiced aesthetic concerns, placing the proposal within a broad civic context: "Facing the Battery and the downtown harbor [the proposed site] is a location of such excellence and potential urban beauty that the design responsibility of the

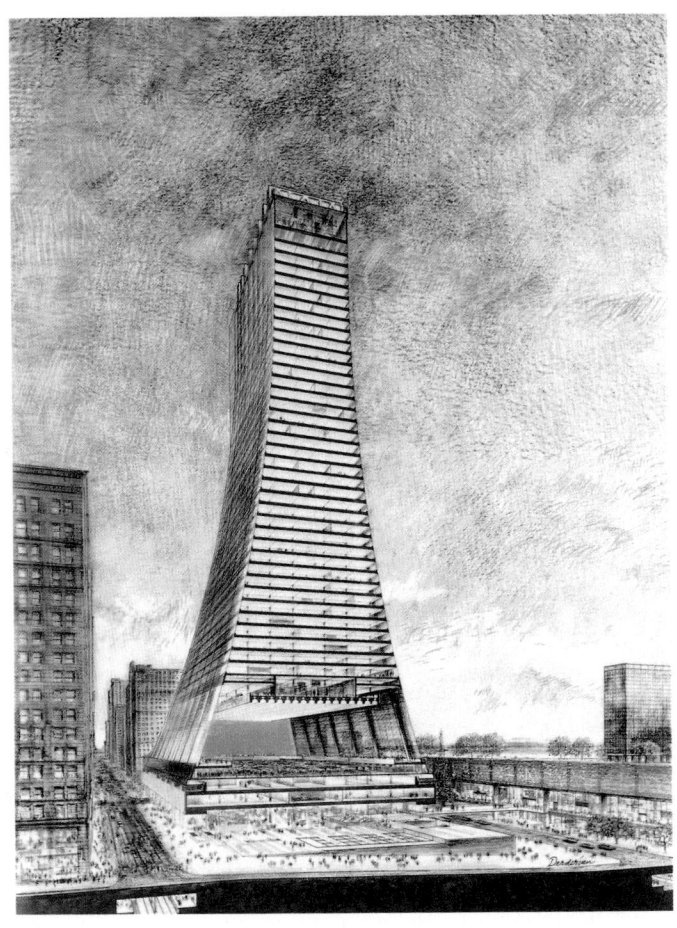

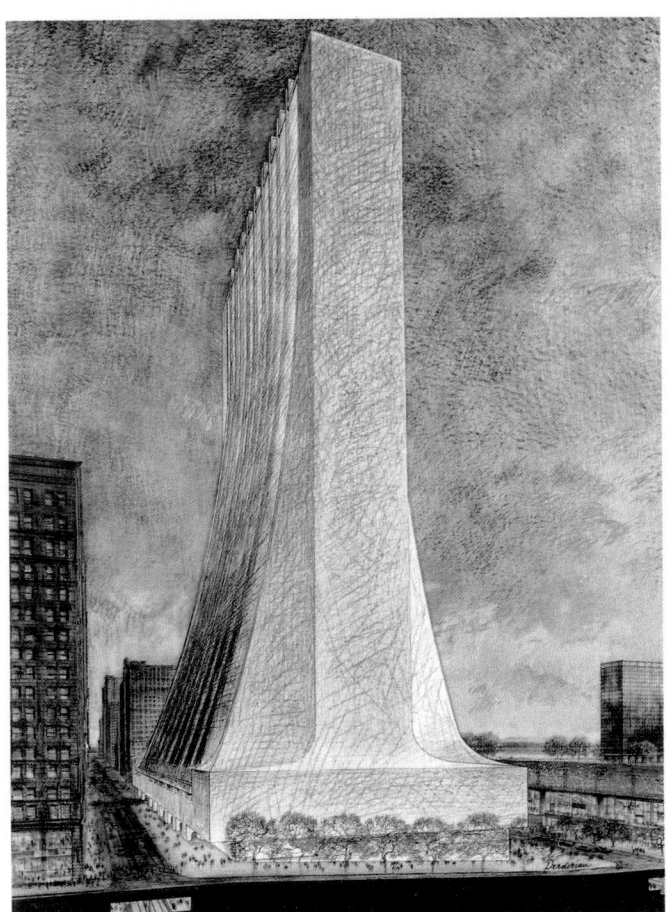

Finance Place, Cedar to Cortlandt Street, Church Street to Broadway.
I. M. Pei & Associates, 1963. Section perspective. PCF

Finance Place. PCF

Exchange becomes civic, as well as private. These buildings will inevitably be a landmark. The obligation is clear; the possibilities are immense. The published proposal, admittedly no more than a schematic suggestion, doesn't even hint at their fulfillment."[73]

In July 1963 the developer William Zeckendorf announced that he was interested in building a home for the exchange, either as part of his projected Finance Place, to be located on the site bounded by Broadway, Cortlandt, Church and Cedar streets, then occupied by Ernest Flagg's Singer Tower (1908), or on another site in the financial district.[74] According to the New York Times, the exchange immediately rejected the possibility; according to Zeckendorf, who recounted the history of the project in his autobiography, the stock exchange's response was somewhat more complex. Zeckendorf approached John Coleman, an influential member of the exchange, outlining his plans for the area: "The axis between the Trade Center and Chase Plaza, with its access to parking and subways, will make for a year-round people passage. We will have covered walks, malls, shops and restaurants. Set the Stock Exchange on our site, and it will be the very heart and core of the entire financial district." According to Zeckendorf, Coleman replied, "O.K., Bill, you deliver those buns, and we'll buy them." Zeckendorf then turned to the architect Henry Cobb, a partner in I. M. Pei's firm, who, as the developer would later state, "came up with one of the most ingenious building designs I have ever seen."[75]

Though the building was arguably more technologically than aesthetically significant, it was undeniably impressive. Cobb developed an effective solution to the problem of accommodating on a relatively constricted site both a 270-foot-wide trading floor and a tall office building that would contain 75 percent as much space as the Empire State Building. He combined the two elements in a forty-five-story slab, the long exterior walls of which sloped in from its 270-foot-wide base to a width of 90 feet at its pinnacle, creating a tapering tower. The shape of this tower would later influence Gordon Bunshaft in his work at 9 West Fifty-seventh Street and the Grace Building (see chapter 5). Zeckendorf described the dramatically swooping form as being "something like a beautifully tapered Mayan temple."[76] Along the tower's long facades, immense concrete piers, each nine by eighteen feet, were to originate four levels below the street and rise to the base of the exchange's cavernous trading floor, three levels above the street. Rising from the piers, eighteen curved steel beams—nine on each side—would climb the building's full height. A group of twenty-eight-foot-deep steel trusses, set in pairs and braced to be laterally stabile, were to span the building's top, approximately 650 feet above the street. The building was to be constructed in a conventional manner, with steel girders rising incrementally up the building's center; with the completion of the roof trusses, however, the central vertical supports were to be acetylene torched and removed, transforming the overall structure from a traditional compression type to a tension mode. The office floors would be hung, in effect, from the network of rooftop trusses, leaving the vast ground-level stock exchange trading floor completely free of columns.

Despite the fact that Zeckendorf had, as he would later state, "a fabulous and distinctive design, and an ideal location," and furthermore "had, or thought we had, unofficial but powerful backing within the exchange," the exchange declined Zeckendorf's offer.[77] By fall 1963 Zeckendorf would admit that his goal of attracting the exchange was "a lost cause."[78]

The day before Zeckendorf was scheduled to take title to the Finance Place site, the stock exchange announced that it would move to the Battery Park Urban Renewal Area site that it had been trying to acquire while in discussion with Zeckendorf. But the Battery site's location within a municipally organized district be-

came increasingly complicated. The city was to acquire the proposed site through condemnation and then sell it to the exchange; the exchange was in turn to pay either the city's cost of land acquisition or the site's so-called reuse value, whichever was higher. Although the exchange would not receive a write-down on the land's resale, a customary incentive for a commercial developer, its acquisition of the property through urban renewal strategies would be considerably simpler and less expensive than if the property were acquired on the open market. Zeckendorf, who had once advocated a similar strategy in behalf of his interests in the area to the west of the United Nations (see chapter 7), claimed the procedure was unlawful. The city justified using the urban renewal process in aiding a private-sector enterprise on the grounds that the exchange played an integral role in the life of the city and that its continued presence in New York was for the public good; in bottom-line terms, the exchange carried a $370 million payroll. Concern over the appropriateness of the acquisition process was exacerbated by the decidedly lukewarm reception that had been given O'Connor & Kilham's design and that continued to haunt the project. By October 1963 the city's Housing and Redevelopment Board suggested that the exchange, as Ada Louise Huxtable put it, "aim higher." A plan that an internationally recognized architect be brought in as a consultant, in an effort, in Huxtable's words, "to enlarge the range of design possibilities," was predictably enough not received enthusiastically.[79]

Two other thorny concerns were the preservation of some of Manhattan's last remaining eighteenth-century houses, threatened by the renewal program's proposed widening of Water Street, and the projected construction of a parking garage adjacent to Fraunces Tavern. The editors of the New York Times strongly stated, "It is unthinkable that the area's historic past would be omitted from plans for its future development."[80] Vehemently opposed to the garage proposal, Huxtable noted that "everyone," including the Housing and Redevelopment Board, which initiated the plan, agreed "that this is an appallingly bad land use." Underscoring the sometimes daunting aspect of realizing civic improvements in New York, Huxtable pointed out that the abandonment of the garage proposal would require a federally approved amendment to the encompassing urban renewal plan and an inevitably "tortuous trail of hearings."[81] Alternately, the exchange could acquire the garage site, leaving it undeveloped, and remove the threatened houses from harm's way, preserving them as executive club facilities.[82] "But," Huxtable concluded, "no one at present is interested in providing designs or cash for preservation. The Stock Exchange would be the biggest new building in Manhattan since the Pan Am and it is already as controversial. It offers a classic demonstration of how urban renewal functions, or fails to function, in New York."[83]

The city's efforts to introduce a modicum of planning to the area through the vehicle of urban renewal were further hampered in June 1964, when Sol G. Atlas, a developer, and his partner, John P. McGrath, a lawyer and former New York City Corporation Counsel, brought suit against the city, with the intention of preventing it from assembling the proposed Battery Park Urban Renewal Area. The real-estate entity of Atlas-McGrath owned 90 percent of the privately owned properties within the exchange site. The plaintiffs charged that their case was distinguished from others involving urban renewal efforts because so much of the land belonged to a single owner, one who, furthermore, was willing to upgrade the property of its own accord. Contending that the city was overstepping its legitimate bounds, Atlas and McGrath testified in New York State Supreme Court that "municipal intervention under the guise of urban renewal is unnecessary . . . when private enterprise is ready and able to rehabilitate a blighted area."[84] Atlas-McGrath soon reached an agreement with the New York Stock Exchange that did not require that the property be designated an urban renewal area. But the arrangement was contingent on the city altering the proposed site's street patterns. Atlas-McGrath's progress with the project was stymied when a group of individuals and business interests owning land within the proposed site brought charges against the developers, the city and the New York Stock Exchange, alleging a conspiracy. The plaintiffs were particularly critical of the plan to widen Water Street and in the process acquire and demolish some of the historically significant houses lining the street; the plaintiffs' attorney, Raymond Schaffer, stated that "under the sham and pretext" of widening the street, private property was to be seized for "private enrichment."[85]

Following the New York State Supreme Court's dismissal of the case, the New York Stock Exchange went forward with the development of the Battery Park site proposal; replacing O'Connor & Kilham, which had conducted the initial design study, the exchange handed the design of its new building over to Skidmore, Owings & Merrill, with Gordon Bunshaft serving as chief designer.[86] Designs were not released, however, before another twist occurred in the increasingly complex story. On March 4, 1966, Mayor Lindsay proposed a 50 percent increase in the municipal stock transfer tax, and the exchange responded by playing a trump card it had threatened to use earlier: it suggested leaving New York.[87] Two weeks later the exchange publicly canceled its Battery Park plans, intensifying its search for a new home outside the city.[88] The exchange received offers from places as far away as Ohio and California, as well as the village of Tyonek, located on a Moquawkie Indian reservation near Anchorage, Alaska.

Amidst this somewhat antic backdrop, the exchange more seriously considered four New Jersey sites: Hoboken, Jersey City, Newark and Weehawken. These options clearly revealed, at least to sensitive observers, the steady transformation of postwar New York from a discrete metropolitan city to merely a node, albeit an important one, within a sprawling megalopolis. Lamenting New York's potential loss, Russell Baker facetiously spelled out the consequences for the city of Hoboken:

Who but the most devout Communist-hater has not, at one time or another, silently condemned his creditors as "tools of Wall Street"? New York can absorb such abuse. It is a big city, and Wall is a very small street. But what about Hoboken? Once we are confronted with the Hoboken Stock Exchange, Hoboken will become the symbol of everything odious about capitalism. . . . Debtors will begin cursing their creditors as "tools of Hoboken." This is not a pleasant thing to happen to a town like Hoboken.[89]

Not surprisingly, the exchange decided to stay in New York. Rejecting Robert Moses's proposal to relocate to the World Trade Center, the exchange chose a site within what would become the Manhattan Landing project.[90] The building was still to be designed by Skidmore, Owings & Merrill. The demise of the Manhattan Landing project, however, seemingly doomed the construction of a new home for the Stock Exchange, which had to make do with its old trading floor and the additional office space it had acquired with the completion in 1956 of an architecturally undistinguished twenty-seven-story building at 20 Broad Street, designed by Kahn & Jacobs and Sidney Goldstone (see "Downtown," above). The entire saga of the exchange's efforts to expand and relocate ironically came full circle in 1977 when the management of the by-then completed World Trade Center offered to house part or all of the exchange's operations; the exchange did not accept the invitation.[91]

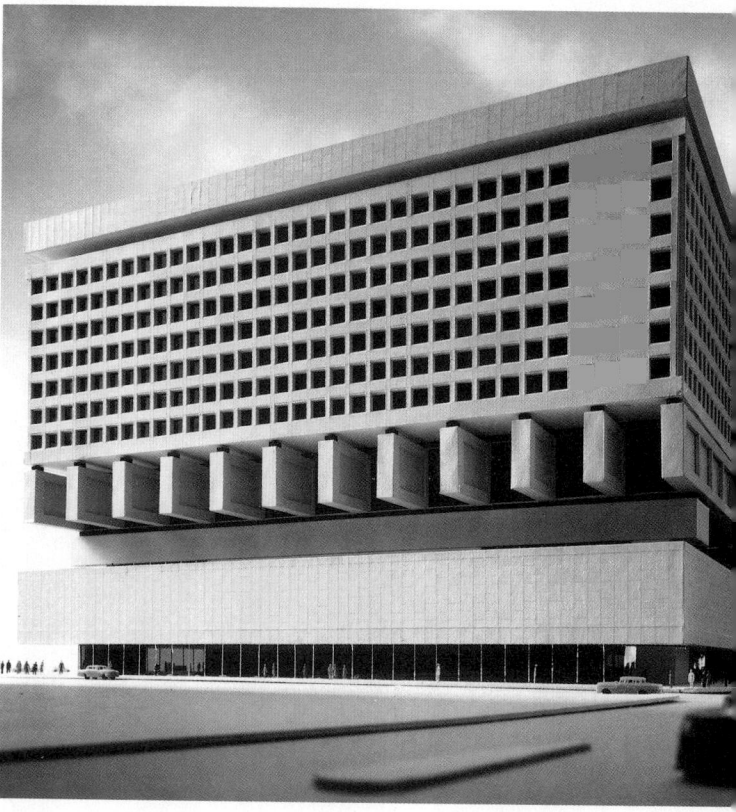

Proposal for New York Stock Exchange Building, Manhattan Landing, platforms in the East River, Broad Street to Gouverneur Lane. Skidmore, Owings & Merrill, 1966. Stoller. ©ESTO

219

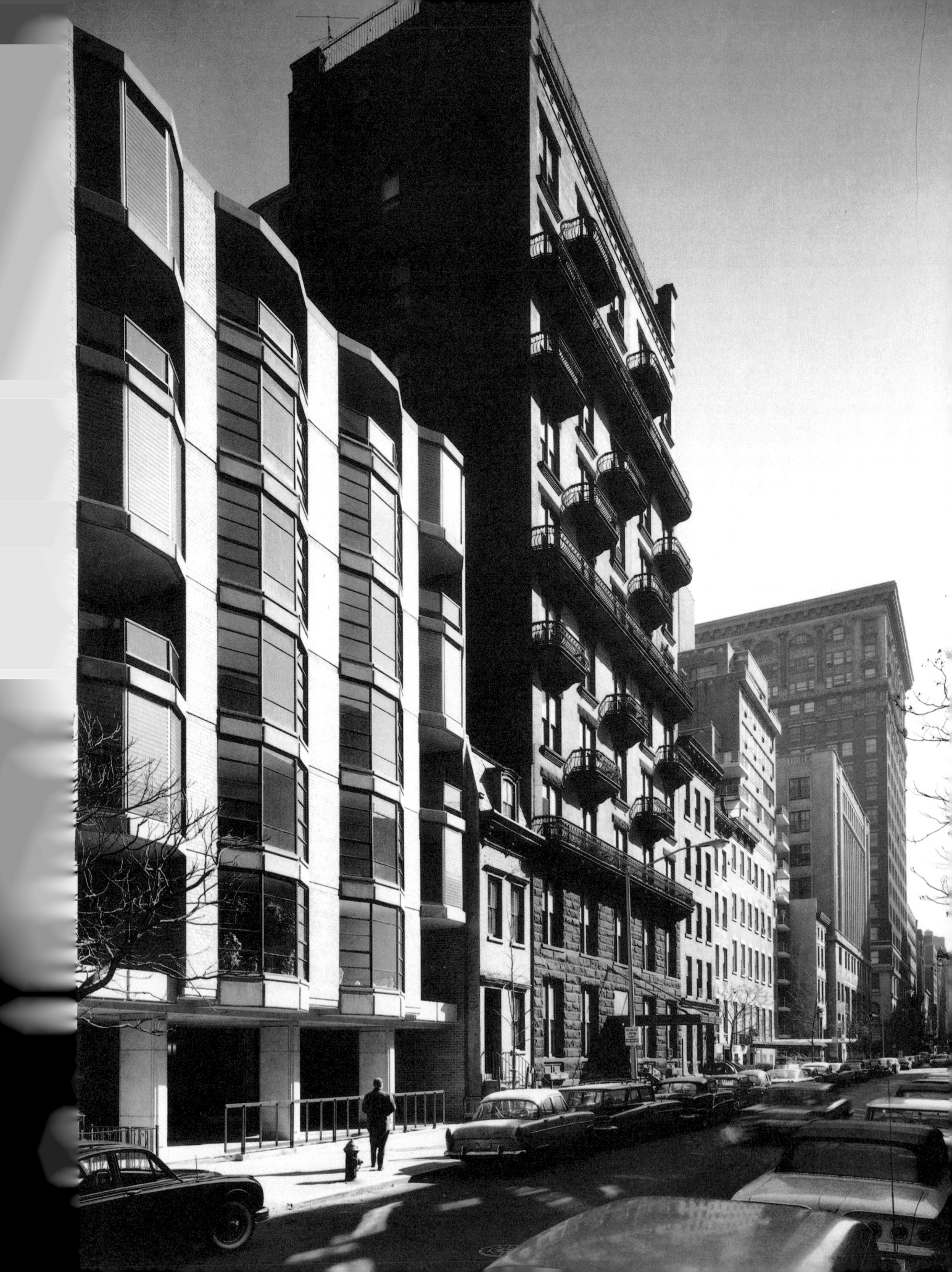

Chapter 4

Greenwich Village and SoHo

GREENWICH VILLAGE

Greenwich Village [is] the internment camp of Manhattan nonconformity. . . . The district still attracts artists, but for every artist it attracts a hundred civilians, so that the secret garden is ridden with vagabond neurotics and trampled underfoot by tourism. Desperatively, it retains a distinct local personality.
—*Kenneth Tynan, 1967*[1]

The postwar era brought sweeping social and architectural changes to what was indisputably the city's oldest and most preeminent artistic quarter, Greenwich Village, typically referred to as "the Village."[2] These changes had been set in motion in the 1930s, when a new, younger group of residents began to replace the bohemian artists—clearly identifiable by their clothes as well as their causes—who had lived in the Village since before the First World War. Following World War II another wave of "immigrants" reached the Village, and now the shift reflected not only changing currents in American culture but also changes in the New York real estate market. In an ironic twist that would increasingly become a hallmark of the city's ever-evolving urbanism, the very qualities that drew people to the area—intimate physical scale, architectural richness and the slightly offbeat charm of its residents—would be threatened by redevelopment undertaken largely to satisfy the fundamentally conventional tastes of the newcomers. The philosopher William Barrett, who lived in the Village and was an associate editor of the *Partisan Review*, discussed the changing nature of his neighborhood in a 1954 essay titled "The Village: Bohemia Gone Bourgeois." He noted that many of "the generation that came up in Bohemia with World War II" moved out of the Village, "driven elsewhere in search of cheap flats." Barrett went on to describe the new breed of Village resident:

On its most domesticated and bourgeois level, the Village has become a popular haven for young marrieds who prefer its informal—they still call it "Bohemian"—atmosphere to the featureless neighborhoods uptown. In the typical couple, both husband and wife have their separate careers, or just plain jobs, at least until the babies come. She may be in something like publishing, got to know the Village during leaves from Bennington or Vassar, and still finds the place a continuation of the adventures of college. . . . The young husband is probably a "Bohemian" because he is in publicity rather than advertising, but when the babies come and he wants more security, it will be advertising and our young couple will disappear into a suburb.

In the meantime, home may be a whitewashed basement apartment with a couple of African masks on the wall, Swedish glassware and wrought iron lying around, an elaborate hi-fi set ("Bohemian" because its mechanism is unhoused by a cabinet), and a studio couch still a principal article of furniture.[3]

The social transformation of the Village was, from the outset of the postwar period, accompanied by massive rebuilding. Underlying the public controversies that soon surrounded many building projects was a widespread concern that the Village as it had long been cherished as both a social and architectural enclave within the city would be lost. The first challenge to the Village's self-image was made in December 1944, even before the war's conclusion, when a nineteen-story apartment house was announced for the northwest corner of Washington Square North and Fifth Avenue, which would replace a half-block of Greek Revival townhouses, the so-called Rhinelander row at 14–18 Washington Square North, as well as obliterate MacDougal Alley.[4] The project was to be sponsored by Joseph Siegel, the builder in 1926–27 of the widely admired One Fifth Avenue, located across the street (Helmle & Corbett, in association with Sugarman & Berger).[5] By 1945 Siegel's plans had grown in scale, constituting what he described in January as a twenty-eight-story building[6] and what a subsequent report described as a thirty-story building housing 1,000 people,[7] a proposal that had an explosive effect on the community. While no substantial concerns for community preservation had been raised when One Fifth Avenue was built, perhaps because the Village of the

Butterfield House, 37 West Twelfth Street, between Fifth and Sixth avenues, West Twelfth to West Thirteenth Street, left. Mayer, Whittlesey & Glass, 1962. View to the northeast also showing the Andrea apartments (J. B. Snook & Sons, 1895, 1901), in the center. Stoller. ©ESTO

Jazz Age was largely comprised of transient bohemians and disenfranchised Italian immigrants, by the end of World War II Greenwich Village was beginning to be regarded as hallowed ground. As the editors of *Architectural Forum* observed, "How clearly the Washington Square district feels itself a neighborhood was apparent last month when its [sic] mobilized for blocks to fight portended postwar building of a thirty-story apartment building on one of the Square's Fifth Avenue corners."[8]

The argument against Siegel's project combined preservationist sentiment with concerns about community services, in particular inadequate school and transportation facilities to handle the new population density. The protest was spearheaded by Morris L. Ernst, the famous lawyer and supporter of liberal causes, whose campaign was based on the notion that, as he said, "People cannot take root when they live more than six or eight stories off the ground."[9] This position would become a benchmark in many discussions concerning the Village's future in the next thirty years and would run as a continuous thread through virtually all discussions of housing and urban redevelopment in the city as a whole. Exasperated with the protests, Siegel declared to the editors of the *New Yorker*: "I try to do a great big thing for Greenwich Village, and all that happens is letters to the editor. It's going to be the beginning of a new era for those poor people with hardly any closets at all. In my building they're going to have closets they can walk into and stomp around in."[10]

Claiming that the building would cast a seven-block-long shadow, the community took its case to Robert Moses in his dual roles as Park Commissioner and City Planning Commissioner. In March 1945 Moses responded on the community's behalf, questioning the prevailing zoning, which awarded a double-height bonus to park-facing sites. Moses stated: "We mean to revoke the double bonus which accrues at present to people who put Chinese walls around New York's little open spaces."[11] Moses drafted an amendment to the zoning that would limit the height of park-facing buildings to the width of the streets, in effect confining the buildings facing Washington Square to about seven or eight stories. Siegel, who was just about to file plans, seemed prepared for a fight: "I'm pretty sure Mr. Moses can't do this to me because I saw him coming and rolled up my sleeves. I've got the Real Estate Board in one pocket and a bankroll in the other."[12] Nonetheless, though demolition of the property began in November 1945 to make way for a scaled-down version of the original scheme, it stopped soon thereafter and the project did not go forward.[13]

In January 1950 a different developer, Samuel Rudin, came forward with new plans for the same site.[14] Rudin's project called for a new twelve-story, 300-family apartment house designed by Emery Roth's sons, Julian and Richard, to reflect some of the Greek Revival character of the five-story Rhinelander row. As proposed, Rudin's building would cover only 60 percent of the site, 10 percent less than the maximum permitted under the zoning, MacDougal Alley would not be affected and a garage for 250 cars would be provided to mitigate congestion. "We recognize and respect the sentiment of the neighborhood with respect to preservation of the old-time atmosphere, and our plans are in keeping with that feeling," Rudin averred.[15]

In April 1950 the City Planning Commission considered three zoning amendments based on Moses's earlier proposals that would restrict to five or six stories the height of buildings facing the north and south sides of Washington Square.[16] Intended to thwart Rudin's project, these amendments were opposed as spot zoning by the Citizens' Housing and Planning Council,

whose executive vice president, Ira S. Robbins, suggested instead that the city condemn Rhinelander row and offer it for resale with restrictions that would ensure its preservation and appropriate reuse.[17] A compromise was reached in May 1950: Rudin would clear the site, but the Roths' new building would be reconfigured so that it would appear as two separate structures, a nineteen-story gray-brick building facing Fifth Avenue, and a five-story red-brick Greek Revival–inspired building facing the Square in emulation of the Rhinelander row.[18]

In forging this compromise, the Roth firm was assisted by Harvey Wiley Corbett, in his capacity as chairman of the committee on architecture of the Municipal Art Society, and Arthur C. Holden, consultant architect to the Washington Square Association. As one of the architects of the towering One Fifth Avenue and an advocate of urban concentration, Corbett might not at first glance have seemed very sympathetic to the community's point of view, yet he was no dogmatic ideologue. According to the *New York Times*, he fought to come up with a solution that, as he put it, "may not make all the critics of the project happy, [but] may make some of them less unhappy."[19] Richard Roth, who appears to have taken over principal responsibility for the design, reported to the *New York Times* that the 343-unit building, completed in 1952, went through numerous revisions in an effort to take into consideration "circumjacence [sic] esthetics and building economics."[20] Though hardly a great work of architecture, the result was quite successful from the point of view of neighborhood planning: while its detailing failed to evoke the grandeur of the Greek Revival and Italianate townhouses of the original Rhinelander row, or of its existing neighbors, the modest scale and red brick of the five-story wing on Washington Square North softened the effect of the main building's bulk and maintained the overall impression of unity on the square's north side.

The leasing success of Two Fifth Avenue, as Rudin's building was called, seemed to open up the floodgates of development for the northeastern fringe of the Village, where most of the land belonged to the Sailors' Snug Harbor charitable trust. As dictated in 1801 by the will of the land's original owner, Revolutionary War privateer Robert Richard Randall, the trustees of the estate were obligated to retain ownership of the land but could negotiate leases for its redevelopment in order to generate income that would support a home on the property for "aged decrepit and worn-out sailors." Instead, in 1833 the trustees established the home, known as Sailors' Snug Harbor, on less developed and less valuable land on Staten Island along the Kill van Kull.[21] The trustees had never undertaken a coordinated plan for their Manhattan holdings, preferring to enter into long-term leases with individual private developers.

In early September 1950 plans were announced for the redevelopment of an entire block located in the heart of Snug Harbor's twenty-one-acre holding. Bounded by Eighth and Ninth streets, Broadway and University Place, the new development would replace a diverse collection of forty buildings with a landscaped platform containing shops and a parking garage surmounted by a mixture of six- and twelve-story apartment buildings designed by H. I. Feldman to house 750 families.[22] The developers, a syndicate headed by Harry Landes, had already commissioned Feldman to design a 123-unit, six-story apartment house, 50 East Eighth Street (1951), located on the opposite blockfront between Greene and Mercer streets.[23] At the end of September 1950 Landes proposed to raise the height of the six-story buildings in the group to eight stories, thereby increasing the number of units on the block to 850, but this plan was not implemented.

222

Construction did not begin until December 1952, when work commenced on 60 East Ninth Street, a six-story building housing 216 families, with 235 feet of frontage on both Eighth and Ninth streets and 188 feet on the west blockfront of Broadway.[24] By October 1954 it was complete, with a second building, 30 East Ninth Street, under construction at the opposite end of the block (along University Place) and the site for 40 East Ninth Street, a twelve-story building to rise in the center of the block from a raised garden terrace, ready to be cleared.[25] Influenced, perhaps, by the Roths' Two Fifth Avenue, Feldman used red brick on the low-rise buildings at each end of the block, suggesting an effort to respond to the Village context and offset the mass of the higher building, which the architect clad in a light-colored tan brick and set back from the street in the center of the block.

By the mid-1950s new construction on Snug Harbor land had spread to encompass ten blocks between Fourth and Fifth avenues, Waverly Place and East Tenth Street, or most of the charity's twenty-one acres. A real estate writer in the *New York Times* heralded the construction boom in the northeastern village as the "promise of rebirth in a neighborhood that may become one of the most fashionable in Manhattan," despite the increasingly widespread concern over the anonymous character of the new buildings and the loss of familiar landmarks.[26] These fears were intensified in 1952 when plans were announced for the destruction of the Hotel Brevoort, a century-old landmark comprising four connected townhouses on the east side of Fifth Avenue and on Eighth and Ninth streets, and its replacement by a "tall, ultramodern apartment building" sponsored by builders Sam Minskoff & Sons.[27] Minskoff's plans called as well for the demolition of ten townhouses adjoining the hotel, including the historic Mark Twain house, at 21 Fifth Avenue. The hotel's management, unable to comply with building department regulations, had been forced to close the Brevoort in 1949, but its famous dining room and sidewalk café, the first such café to open after the repeal of Prohibition in 1933, functioned until 1953, when the building's demolition began.

Designed by Boak & Raad and completed in 1955, the buff-colored brick-clad Brevoort apartment house rose fourteen stories over the Fifth Avenue blockfront, culminating in a series of five setback penthouse floors, with low-rise wings extending along both Eighth and Ninth streets.[28] The 301-unit building included a restaurant operated by William Lowenstein, whose promises to recapture the culinary glory and atmosphere of the old hotel's dining room and café were not fulfilled.[29]

Yet another tear in the Village's historic fabric occurred in March 1956 when the architect Arthur Weiser announced his intention to replace an East Village landmark, the north building of the former Wanamaker department store, with two nineteen-story apartment buildings housing 478 families.[30] The six-story, cast-iron store occupied the entire block bounded by Broadway, Fourth Avenue, Ninth and Tenth streets, which was owned by Sailors' Snug Harbor. Wanamaker's, consisting of its original cast-iron building at the Ninth Street location designed for the pioneering retailer A. T. Stewart (John Kellum, 1862)[31] and Daniel H. Burnham's masonry-clad, steel-framed fourteen-story annex (1907) on the block immediately south,[32] had closed its Manhattan store in December 1954 in order to concentrate on its growing suburban operations. This event shocked not only Wanamaker's employees, who reported that the store's business was good, but also most competing New York merchants, who until then had worried that business at Wanamaker's could only get better, given the number of large-scale apartment houses planned or newly constructed within walking distance of the

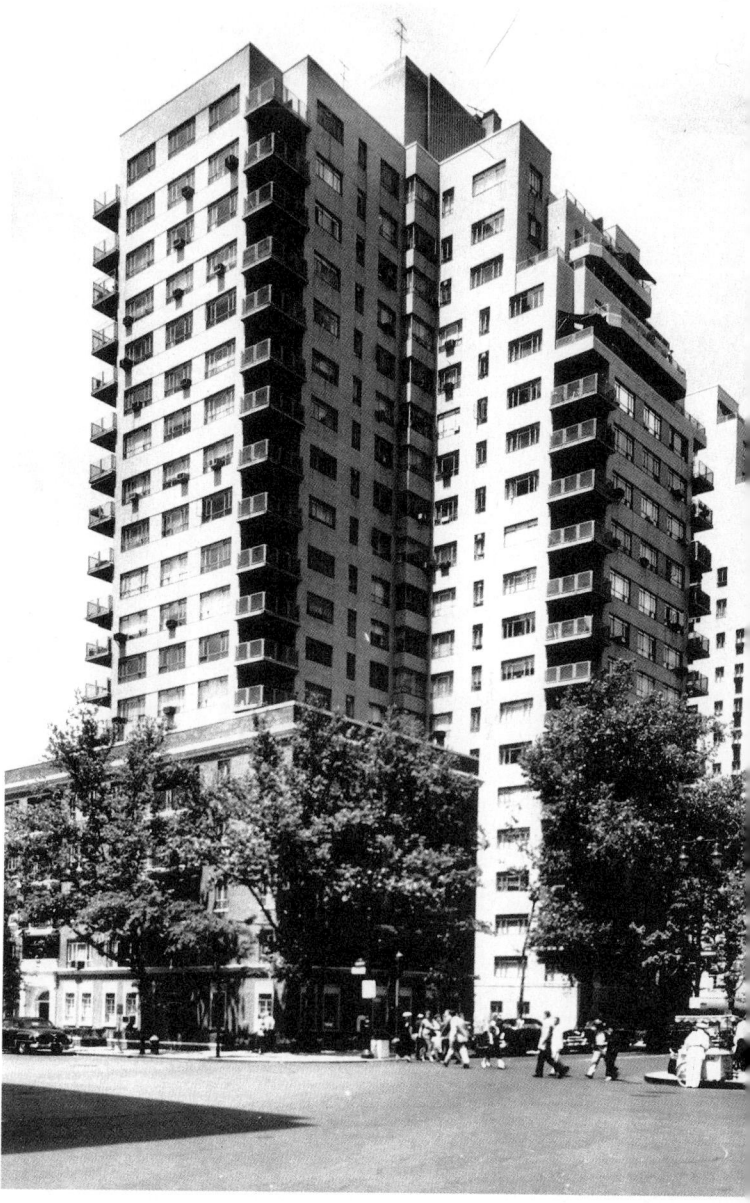

Two Fifth Avenue, Washington Square North to West Eighth Street. Emery Roth & Sons, Harvey Wiley Corbett and Arthur C. Holden, 1952. View to the northwest. Lincoln. PENN

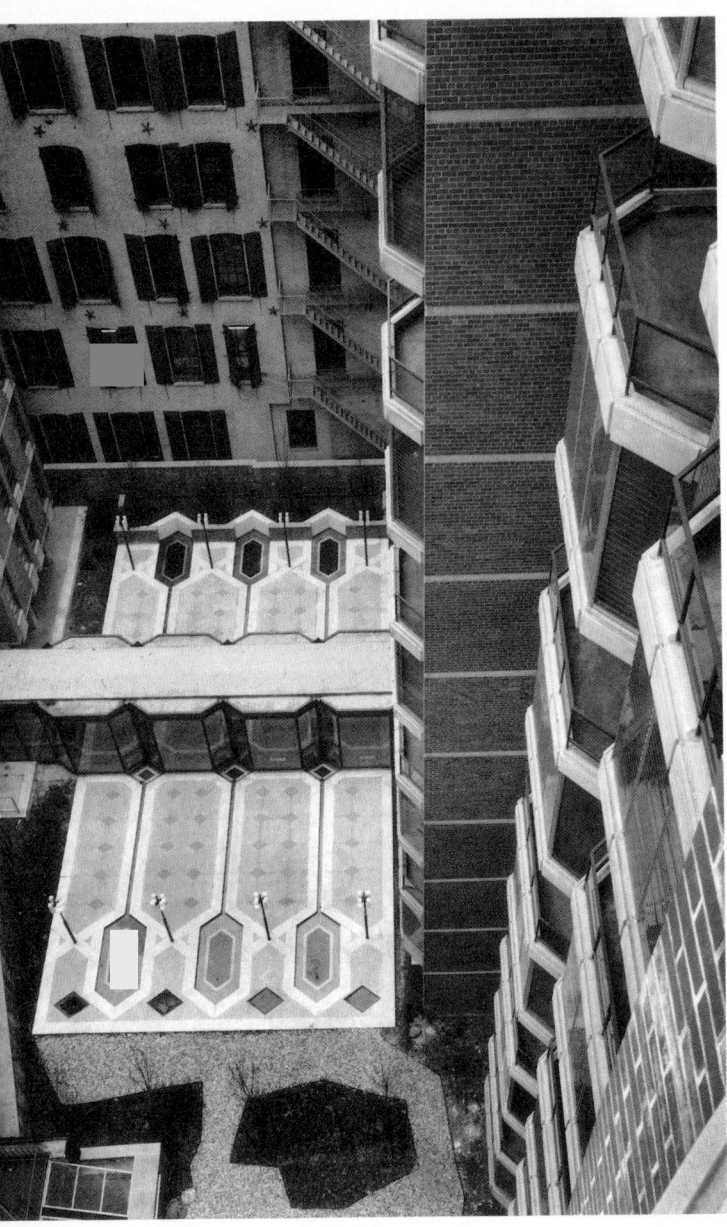

Butterfield House, 37 West Twelfth Street, between Fifth and Sixth avenues, West Twelfth to West Thirteenth Street. Mayer, Whittlesey & Glass, 1962. Interior courtyard. Stoller. ©ESTO

store. The journalist Meyer Berger, writing in the *New York Times,* said that New Yorkers "had come to love the place, its soft-spoken salespeople, its suave—but not too suave—floor-walkers, its mellow indoor bells, the concerts in the great Wanamaker Auditorium, the air of quiet gentility that always lay, sort of reverent and hushed, over its well-stocked counters."[33] Nonetheless, while the preservation of the south building had been determined by the start of renovations in 1955 for its conversion to office space,[34] the north building, although leased on a short-term basis to the American Telephone and Telegraph Company, seemed destined for destruction.

The store, with its grand central rotunda culminating in a glass skylight, represented one of the greatest achievements of cast-iron architecture in New York, but Weiser felt that its destruction was justified given the quality of his proposed replacement. "Our plan for the site directly opposes a concept of apartment-block planning that has persisted for the past 30 or 40 years," he asserted. "Instead of being enclosed on all four sides, thereby wasting the space in the center, the two blocks will be parallel and open at each end. It is a plan that has been in my mind for several years, awaiting the right spot to implement it."[35] Though perhaps not quite as innovative as Weiser claimed, his plan made an interesting transition between the courtyard apartments of the prewar era and the undifferentiated parallel slabs typical of the large-scale, high-density middle-income housing projects of the late 1950s and 1960s. As with the courtyard apartments, the apartment lobbies of Weiser's buildings were entered off the interior garden, with only service ways accessed from the street. And like prewar buildings, Weiser's proposal honored the street grid, closing the open ends—at least for the lower stories—with commercial frontage on Broadway and a head house on Fourth Avenue that would contain access to underground parking for 325 cars.

On July 14, 1956, however, shortly after demolition began to make way for the new apartments, a disastrous fire broke out in the building.[36] The fire was one of the worst in New York's history, not only requiring the efforts of approximately 600 firemen but nearly destroying the Astor Place subway station below the site and completely paralyzing both the Lexington Avenue IRT between Grand Central Station and the Brooklyn Bridge and the Broadway BMT between Thirty-fourth and Canal streets. Though the fire burned out of control for almost twenty-four hours, much of the building's cast-iron facade and interior system of columns and girders remained intact.[37] There were no second thoughts about the building's future, however, and it was demolished. Weiser's plans seemed to have derailed after demolition was completed, and the site was left vacant. In 1958 a second proposal for the now-cleared site emerged: a 369-family, twenty-story cooperative apartment building to be called Stewart House—an homage in name only to the previous building and its initial owner.[38] Despite the objections of some observers, most notably architect Arthur Holden, who suggested that the site be used instead for an underground parking garage covered by an open park,[39] foundation work for Stewart House had begun by April 1959 and the project was completed in 1960. Designed by Sylvan and Robert Bien, Stewart House was a twenty-story, white-brick, H-shaped building on the scale of Sylvan Bien's Schwab House (see chapter 9) or Emery Roth & Sons' Imperial House (see chapter 11). Encompassing only one-fourth of the site, the building incorporated a landscaped entrance court on Tenth Street and a landscaped rear court on Ninth Street.

According to a count by the *New York Times* in November 1959, twenty apartment houses were planned or under construction in Greenwich Village at the time.[40] Few of the new buildings, which were going up amid some of the oldest and most historic buildings in the city, were architecturally distinguished and most were oversized. A notable exception was Butterfield House (1962), at 37 West Twelfth Street, between Fifth Avenue and Avenue of the Americas.[41] This 103-unit apartment house of glass and brown brick was designed by Mayer, Whittlesey & Glass, with associate partner William J. Conklin and James S. Rossant in charge of design. It was divided into two buildings, a seven-story building facing Twelfth Street and a twelve-story building behind it that fitted in with the large-scale loft buildings lining Thirteenth Street. The two buildings were linked by a glass-enclosed corridor that traversed a decoratively paved interior courtyard. The Twelfth Street facade successfully evoked the massing and detailing of the neighboring nineteenth-century residential buildings with a lively rhythm of bay windows and limestone spandrels. As the Landmarks Preservation Commission put it in their *Greenwich Village Historic District Designation Report* of 1969: "Contemporary architecture, in such cases as this seven-story apartment house, where scale, form, and use of materials harmonize with their surroundings, need not necessarily introduce a note of discord into the street scene. . . . The delicacy of form and elegance of detail, inherent in the design, make [Butterfield House] as one with its residential neighbors."[42]

Of the other nineteen apartment houses reported as planned or under construction in Greenwich Village, most were on land leased from Sailors' Snug Harbor: between 1951 and 1966 construction on the Snug Harbor properties alone amounted to a total of ten new skyscraper apartment buildings with 2,445 units. Among these was Boak & Raad's Brevoort East, completed in 1965 on the west blockfront of University Place, between Eighth and Ninth streets, a building that was a taller version of the new Brevoort, which occupied the rest of the same block, but to many observers was in no other way distinguished from it or from any other new apartment building in the area.[43] Although the new buildings had diverse owners and lacked an overall plan, the ownership of the land on which they stood remained singular, as did the essential banality of their stripped-down architectural vocabulary. The result was a transformation of the ten-block neighborhood that looked almost as if it had been planned, but badly.

Built by Rose Associates and designed by Leo Stillman and John Pruyn, the thirty-five-story, beige-brick Georgetown Plaza, at 60 East Eighth Street, between Broadway and Mercer Street, reflected the impact of the 1961 zoning at its worst.[44] By allowing developers to construct towerlike buildings on low podiums, thereby breaking the continuity of height and character of the traditional street wall, this zoning confounded the Village's traditional small scale in a way that the 1916 zoning had not. The public and the media became increasingly concerned for the Village's fate in the face of such development. Writing for the *New York Times* in July 1966, William Robbins lamented that such buildings were "closing in" the Village and observed that the ten-block section owned by Sailors' Snug Harbor, in particular, "is more notable for the new apartment houses that have made it an island of uniformity amid the diversity of Greenwich Village than for the remaining vestiges of a faded era."[45]

Though the aggressive economic policies of Sailors' Snug Harbor were a spur to massive redevelopment, the organization's preference for numerous individual leases led to piecemeal demolition and rebuilding of its properties—ensuring at least a small measure of urbanistic and architectural variety, no matter how uniformly bland the new buildings. The damage they wrought to the Village's traditional idiosyncrasy was minor

compared to the bold plans that Robert Moses, in his capacity as chairman of the Mayor's Committee on Slum Clearance, announced in January 1951.[46]

Calling for the complete reconstruction of the southeast Village in order to create a new residential high-rise enclave to be called Washington Square South, Moses set out to level most of the forty or so acres bounded on the north by West Fourth Street; on the south by Spring Street between Avenue of the Americas and West Broadway and by West Houston Street between West Broadway and Mercer Street; on the east by Mercer Street; and on the west by Avenue of the Americas. Working with the architects Eggers & Higgins, Moses proposed for the site two high-rise housing projects that would have the effect of destroying the dense urban fabric characteristic of lower Manhattan's historic development, consisting in the southeast Village of closely packed tenements and some 200 loft buildings. The first, called Washington Square Gardens, would house 1,956 families in thirteen privately financed, middle-income towers, each nineteen stories tall, to be located between West Third and Bleecker streets; the second, Houston Houses, between Bleecker and West Houston streets, Mercer Street and Avenue of the Americas, would house 900 less-advantaged families in eight fourteen-story units built by the New York City Housing Authority, which also agreed to provide a site within the precinct for a public school and a playground. Working with Voorhees, Walker, Foley & Smith, Moses also called for an additional 14.5 acres between Avenue of the Americas and West Broadway, West Houston and Spring streets to be transformed into South Village, a residential enclave of seven fifteen- and twenty-story buildings housing 792 moderate-income families. Paying lip service to the Village's traditional role as an arts center, South Village was to be developed by the Foundation for the Improvement of Urban Living, Inc., a group proposed as a nonprofit venture that would assist in providing studio quarters and gallery space for craftsmen on the site.

A few neighborhood landmarks were to be retained in Moses's plans, including New York University's buildings along Washington Square and West Fourth Street, which would be supplemented by new buildings for the university, St. Anthony's Church on West Houston Street, the Sullivan-MacDougal Gardens and a few prewar apartment houses along Avenue of the Americas.[47] As controversial as the entire proposal was, one feature would prove particularly irksome to Villagers: Moses's call for the widening of West Broadway and its rechristening as Fifth Avenue South, which would link lower Manhattan directly to Fifth Avenue via a new roadway to be cut through Washington Square (see chapter 16).

The reaction to Moses's proposal was at first guarded. The *New York Times*, which generally tended to favor development, was positive but not uncritical. In "Topics of The Times" for March 13, 1951, the *Times* editors said that although Moses's plan called for "a transformation which will remove every familiar landmark—save only one—and will even abolish streets like Macdougal [sic] and Sullivan which gave the quarter color and access to the square," the prospect it presented was "pleasing—especially in contrast to what now meets the view."[48] The editors of the *American City*, while applauding the bold scale of the proposal, felt it posed "a unique challenge to citizen groups and the City Planning Commission." They also pointed out that "the area's considerable human, as well as financial values" were reflected in the anticipated land-acquisition costs, which at $14.16 to $19.54 per square foot were roughly $10 higher than the costs for three other projects proposed by Moses in other parts of the city.[49]

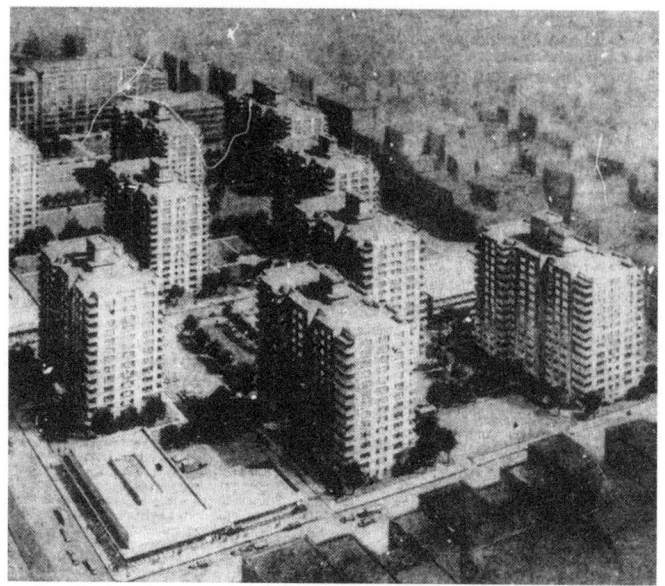

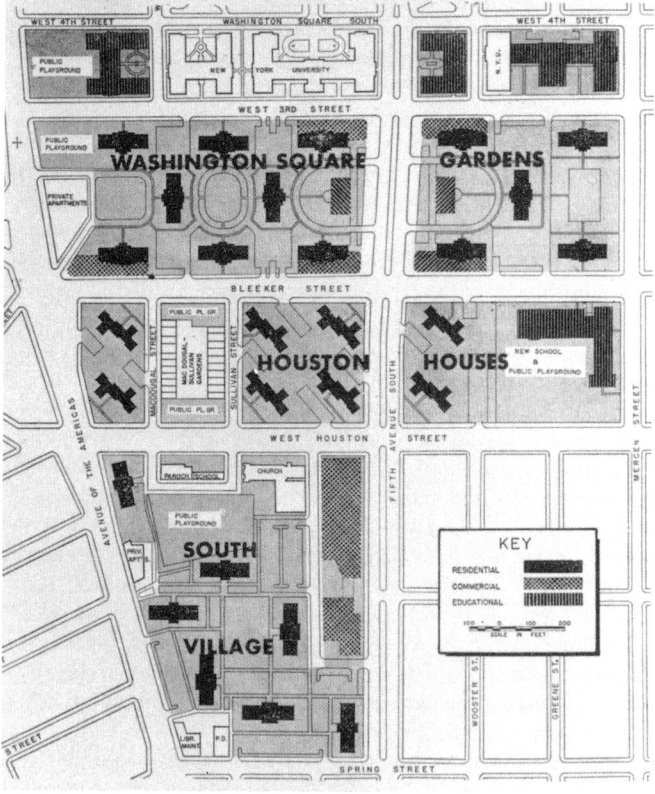

Top: Proposed redevelopment of area from West Houston to West Third Street, West Broadway to Mercer Street. Eggers & Higgins, 1953. Perspective of view to the northeast. NYT

Bottom: Map showing proposed redevelopment of area from Spring to West Third Street, Mercer Street to West Broadway and Sixth Avenue. AC. CU

Despite some positive press, Village residents were not happy about the plan and began to organize forceful opposition. The project gave impetus for the creation of a local newspaper, the *Village Voice*, founded in 1955, which was to become an important platform for this and other community-based attacks on urban redevelopment. The protest was also taken up by the professional design press. In August 1951 *Interiors* asked "Whither the Village?"—citing the potential loss of an area that though overcrowded was full of vitality, had excellent restaurants and shops, and featured old streets that did double duty as playgrounds for the neighborhood children. *Interiors* observed:

> Whatever it lacks in streamlined convenience, this picturesque section has one thing to distinguish it from the six other "slums" with which it was grouped for demolition purposes: it is a *community*, with a strong group sense which is quite unrelated to literary clichés about the Village bohemia overrun with impecunious Mimi's and Rodolfo's. It is a neighborhood settled by a homogeneous, self-supporting and self-sufficient group, bound by its own culture and traditions.[50]

These issues were crystallized when five architects and planners living in the Village—Robert Weinberg, Huson Jackson, Edgar Tafel, Joseph Neufeld and Bob Tieger—took the matter up with George De Martini, president of the Lower West Side Civic League. While there was no clear consensus against redevelopment per se, what emerged was a sense that the neighborhood was not a slum, although its housing was substandard, and that the Moses towers-in-the-park plan was, as Tafel put it, "an arbitrary and inhuman" proposal. "The buildings are years out of date, products of 'stock' planning, and the plan based on the questionable assumption that the whole area must be demolished rather than selectively rehabilitated."[51]

Moses was undaunted by the criticism. As he wrote to a friend:

> I realize that in the process of rebuilding south of Washington Square, there would be cries of anguish from those who are honestly convinced that the Sistine Madonna was painted in the basement of one of the old buildings there not presently occupied by a cabaret or speakeasy, that Michangelo's [sic] David was fashioned in a garret in the same neighborhood, that Poe's Raven, Don Marquis' Archie the Cockroach, and Malory's Morte D'Arthur were penned in barber shops, spaghetti works and shoeshine parlors in the purlieus of Greenwich Village, and that any one who lays hands on these sacred landmarks will be executed if he had not already been struck down by a bolt from heaven.[52]

As late as August 1953 Moses persisted in his approach and still had the support of the *New York Times*.[53] Nonetheless, he began to give ground to community objections by eliminating the area west of West Broadway and north of West Houston Street, though he extended the South Village project to include the area bounded by Avenue of the Americas and West Broadway, Spring and Broome streets. In his 1953 report to Mayor Impellitteri and the Board of Estimate, Moses presented conceptual plans for housing projects for the redefined area: 2,184 middle-income apartments were proposed for the 14.53-acre site immediately south of Washington Square and east of West Broadway; on the other housing parcel, south of Houston Street, with state aid, the New York City Housing Authority would construct the Mary K. Simkhovitch Houses for 1,440 lower-middle-class families—named for the widely respected pioneer settlement worker, who died in 1951 (see chapter 3).[54]

Although this drastically reduced Washington Square South project was considered by its sponsors not to "prejudice the character of Greenwich Village and Washington Square" nor "infringe" upon the "historical concepts of these areas," the communities concerned increasingly thought otherwise.[55] By October 14, 1953, the project, estimated to involve over $28 million in land acquisition and construction costs, was under attack by tenants, property owners and civic organizations who argued against it at the City Planning Commission's public hearing. Castigated as "government by stampede," the project was opposed on the surprising grounds that the housing proposed for demolition did not constitute a slum.[56] Hortense Gabel, representing seventeen civic groups opposing the project, demanded that before making any approvals, the Board of Estimate carefully study a City Planning Commission minority report that she helped prepare on tenant relocation. Though she claimed it was "the first major relocation exposé" and "the first official report by any governmental agency, that even hinted obliquely that Moses wasn't God," it had little influence.[57] Robert Caro, in his book *The Power Broker: Robert Moses and the Fall of New York*, described it as "an exposé without exposure."[58] Moses had his way, despite the vigorous opposition of local residents and merchants and the Citizens Union. In January 1954 the Board of Estimate adopted the renewal plan following the approval one month earlier of the City Planning Commission.[59] But the community was not so easily discouraged; a group of businessmen, organized as the Washington Square Neighbors, took the city to court in an attempt to hold on to their buildings, fighting a three-year battle, only to be rebuffed by the U.S. Court of Appeals in 1956.[60]

Even after the project finally emerged from the courts, its troubles were far from over. The first phase of the Washington Square South project to be implemented, dubbed Washington Square Village, got off to a shaky start when its developer, Morton S. Wolf, and builder, Paul Tishman, drew Moses's ire for delays in clearing the site.[61] Moses was eager to get started—he realized that community opposition was by no means quelled by the court's decision. Taking advantage of the developer's sluggish performance, the housing committee of the Greenwich Village Association was demanding that new sponsors be found and that the project be recast to provide more affordable middle-income housing.[62] So anxious was Moses to give the appearance of victory that with construction still in its early stages, Washington Square Village was formally dedicated in December 1957.[63] Replacing the original Eggers & Higgins proposal for a more or less regular grid of towers in a continuous park, Washington Square Village (1960), designed by Paul Lester Weiner in association with S. J. Kessler & Sons, called for three parallel "superslabs," each nearly 600 feet long, stretching from a vastly widened West Broadway to Mercer Street, and housing 2,000 families in all. Fifty-one-foot-long trusses carried the slabs across the rights-of-way of the former Wooster and Greene streets, which were kept open as pedestrian ways as much to save the cost of relocating their subsurface utilities as to retain prevailing north-south neighborhood pedestrian circulation patterns.

The vast open spaces between each slab only seemed to make the colossal scale of the buildings more apparent. The design was based in part on the so-called *lotissements à redents* which constituted the near-continuous wall of housing that Le Corbusier proposed for Paris in the 1920s. Cut up into singular slabs and more than doubled in height, however, they related more directly to Le Corbusier's aggressively massed Unité d'Habitation at Marseilles.[64] Weiner, who in his beginning work as a New York architect was associated with the gentler Viennese Modernism of Josef Hoffmann in the late 1920s and 1930s,[65] had changed direction as a result of his collaboration with Le Corbusier and José Luis Sert in various South

American projects in the 1940s and 1950s. Because Weiner was considerably fettered by the utilitarianism of the Kessler firm, not to mention the project's developers, the Corbusian exuberance was confined to the limited use of blue, yellow and red glazed brick, which enlivened the otherwise largely undifferentiated building envelope of light gray glazed brick; the sculpturally massed thirty-foot-tall rooftop shapes; and the lifting of the buildings above the ground on pilotis. The effect of this last device was diminished, however: because the area beneath the slabs was largely glazed in to create lobbies, there was little sense of a continuous "liberated" ground plane except where the two north-south streets ran through.

Weiner's design was enthusiastically embraced in some quarters for the explicit Modernism of its form, but other observers were troubled by its impact on the Greenwich Village context, and by its implications for future urban redevelopment in general. To compensate for the superscale of the slabs and their comparative anonymity, Weiner and the landscape architects, Sasaki, Walker & Associates, attempted to humanize the open spaces with lavish plantings as well as fountains and ingeniously designed street furniture. Although the open space was legally available to all citizens, the location of much of it between the slabs and on the platform above the garage suggested a private reserve for the project's tenants rather than a public park. Despite its size, Washington Square Village was surprisingly suburban, with shops clustered along West Broadway in a kind of "strip center."

While the Village itself was well established as a cultural amenity of New York, it was not clear that new construction on this scale would attract tenants, particularly given the scruffy character of Washington Square Park, and the shops were seen as one way of drawing people. To this end, special attention was also paid to creating exciting model apartments to reflect various life-styles, as well as a dramatic lobby, which was put in the hands of Weiner and his collaborator Ala Damaz, who designed it in a sparely minimalist style. The model apartments designed by five leading interior designers—Edward J. Wormley, William Pahlmann, Frederick V. Gerstel, Ellen Lehman McCluskey and Melanie Kahane—were rather conventional. The two model apartments by Weiner and Damaz, however, because of the highly aestheticized minimalism of their approach, far more aptly reflected the spirit of the building's design and forged a connection to contemporary artistic tastes in the Village. For the first of the two-and-a-half-room apartments Weiner and Damaz were assigned, they imagined a young couple as the tenants, for whom they specified low, delicately scaled furnishings that "modern-minded young marrieds" could afford. To achieve a bold effect Weiner and Damaz relied on a highly keyed paint job: varied hues of white and off-white, and two accent walls, one in the living room painted vermilion and another in the kitchen pass-through painted sky blue. In the second apartment, to be occupied by a single person, the designers sought a more lavish effect. In both apartments Weiner concealed lighting sources and used his own aluminum-channel, glass-and-marble shelf system to create what Olga Gueft described as an "exercise in juxtaposed and disappearing planes."[66]

Like the model apartments of the other designers, however, Weiner and Damaz's were based on idealized life-styles. In a letter to the editors of *Interiors*, one observer suggested that the editors visit typical apartments in the complex and see them as they were actually inhabited to assess the difference between ideal and reality: "They may not be as stylish as the decorators', nor as pure as Mr. Weiner's, but they might be an object lesson in the necessary domestic arrangements for people with limited living space and limited incomes."[67]

Perhaps because of their juxtaposition of ideal life-style and real, almost affordable, living space, the model apartments proved to be an instant hit with the public, attracting 1,500 viewers a day during the first three weeks they were on view and helping to make the project a success, despite the developer's initial nervousness. With more than two-thirds of the units in the first building rented by October 1958, Tishman exulted: "Since we have come, the section south of Washington Square is not 'the other side of the tracks' any more. . . . We believe we are leading the way for future growth of the entire Washington Square area."[68] Moreover, the stylishly Modernist buildings were deemed an artistic success by some observers, if not by the Village locals. Indeed, the buildings drew international attention when they were published in the influential French magazine *L'Architecture d'Aujourd'hui*, along with an essay written by Sigfried Giedion, the Swiss historian and apologist for Modernism, who extolled Washington Square Village as the introduction of "a different scale, a reflection of what Europe produces best in that domain."[69] Moses, too, was quick to expound on the merits of Washington Square Village. A fire in an old loft building at Great Jones Street and Broadway in March 1959 served merely to reinforce his point that the project helped reverse blight: he claimed in a press release that the lofts were "of the same type of inflammable buildings that were cleared to make way for the Washington Square Southeast or Washington Square Village Title One project."[70]

After the initial euphoria, however, the apartments rented more slowly and the project seemed in continual jeopardy. By the time the second building of the group was completed in 1960, the developers were anxious to be relieved of their obligation to create a third slab on the southern portion of the site. But New York University was willing to take this area over for educational use and for the development of middle-income cooperative housing known as University Village (see below).[71] The failure of the second Washington Square Village building to quickly attract tenants was not a matter of its urbanism or aesthetics, but one of quality: the low level of the first building's construction and finish had by now become a widely debated problem. What had been touted by the developers as an ideal—a "new conception of city living"—all too quickly revealed itself to be a slicked-up, pricey version of the typical postwar "luxury" apartment. *Time* magazine reported tenant complaints about "'tinny' stoves, faulty air-conditioning, erratic elevators, bugs in the basement, cracks in the plaster, rips in the corridor wall covering."[72]

Unlike many other disgruntled tenants of the period, who merely put up with postwar "luxury" housing that was somewhat less than what its label suggested, those at Washington Square Village demanded that their grievances be heard and that their complaints be satisfied. As a result, two protest groups emerged, an association of 324 tenants organized under the leadership of tenant Fran Weiss and a rival group called Faction for Action. In 1962 the tenants took Morton S. Wolf (the president, director and principal stockholder of the corporation that owned the project), the project's rental agent, Edna Manoville, and New York University (which owned the land) to court, seeking $9 million in damages. They alleged that they were induced to sign leases with promises of "luxury living" in three buildings bordered by "gardens on all sides," when instead, the tenants asserted, "the project has old-fashioned refrigerators, dangerous stoves, inadequate lighting fixtures, under-sized bathtubs, no sheltered parking, and gardens only between the first and second building."[73] Moreover, the tenants claimed that New York

University "for unworthy and selfish purposes," and disregarding community needs, "induced the corporation to delay and withdraw from tenants' use approximately five acres of Washington Square Village south of Bleecker Street."[74] Not even the commercial portions of the project would emerge unscathed: by 1962 the shopping center along West Broadway was virtually vacant, with only a Grand Union supermarket and the developer's rental office as tenants.[75]

Though Greenwich Village's identity as a charming and somewhat bohemian residential district was, by the time of World War II, firmly ensconced in the popular imagination, its alternate role as a home to major educational institutions was also fortified during the postwar period, largely through the expansion of New York University (NYU).[76] Founded in 1831, NYU, by the 1950s the nation's largest private institution of higher education, maintained two campuses, one in the University Heights section of the Bronx (see chapter 13) and the other at Washington Square in the Village. In contrast to "NYU Uptown," a campus of more than fifty acres laid out in 1894 by Calvert Vaux and containing a core building ensemble completed in 1900 to the designs of McKim, Mead & White, NYU's Washington Square facilities were housed largely in loft-type buildings that were not built for that purpose and lacked any distinct architectural presence or cohesion. In the late 1940s Eggers & Higgins drew up plans for an extensive building group on Washington Square to be rendered in a Georgian vocabulary.[77] The complex was never built but in 1951 the firm did realize its design for NYU's Vanderbilt Law School, the first building the university had erected on Washington Square since the completion in 1895 of the Main Building, which had been designed by Alfred Zucker as a mixed-use building only partially dedicated to the school.[78]

Located on Washington Square South between Sullivan and MacDougal streets, Vanderbilt was an unabashed essay in historicism. Eggers & Higgins's five-story Georgian building incorporated Harvard brick cladding, limestone trim and a pitched copper roof. Adopting an H-shape plan, it was organized around two courtyards. In front, an elevated entrance court maintained the street wall facing Washington Square Park with an arcaded walkway. No one complained about the building's Georgian design, which was competent if somewhat watery. But some did protest the fact that it replaced part of "Genius Row," a series of townhouses and apartment buildings that had been home to such notable figures as Willa Cather, Theodore Dreiser, Eugene O'Neill and Adelina Patti. By the late 1960s most observers had forgotten about Genius Row but had come to find the building a less than charming anachronism. Norval White and Elliot Willensky, writing in 1967, said, "One can sympathize with the desire to place this building in context with its neighbors on the square, but the solution chosen seems a bland and unnecessarily derivative approach."[79]

Throughout the 1950s NYU continued to respect its neighborhood. It did not go forward with Harrison & Abramovitz's proposed complex of two-story buildings to be linked by elevated passageways.[80] It also chose not to replace but to preserve a cherished bit of historic architectural fabric, hiring the French architect Lucien David in 1957 to orchestrate a rather utilitarian interior renovation of a nearly 150-year-old, two-story, stucco-clad house on the northwest corner of University Place and Washington Mews to serve as the Maison Française.[81] Continuing with its program of architectural traditionalism, NYU realized the eight-story red-brick Hayden Residence Hall (Eggers & Higgins, 1957) at 35 Washington Square West.[82] The

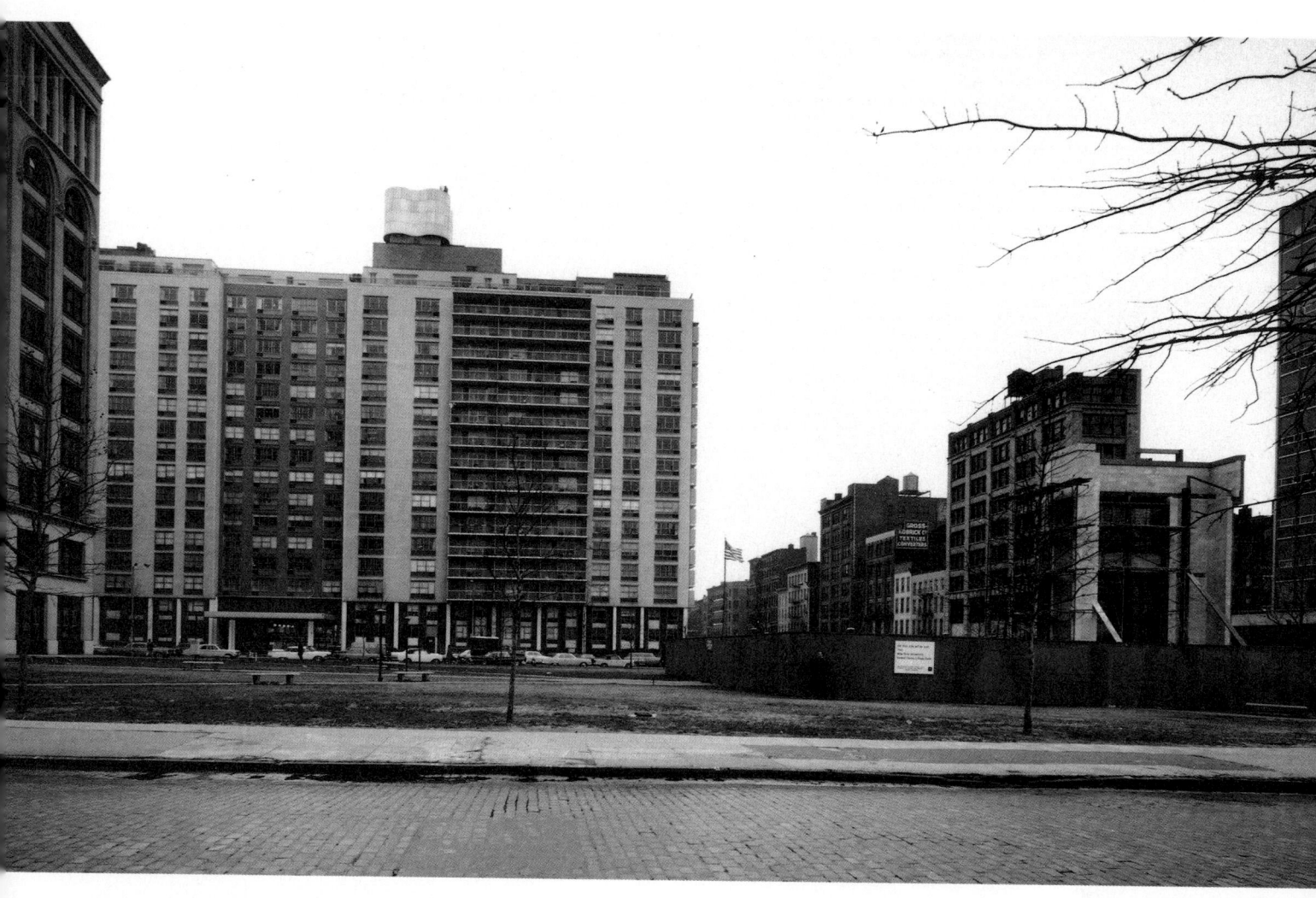

Above: Washington Square Village, Bleecker to West Third Street, La Guardia Place to Mercer Street. Paul Lester Weiner in association with S. J. Kessler & Sons, 1960. View to the south. NYU

Overleaf: View to the south of Greenwich Village. Washington Square Park is in the center foreground. NYU

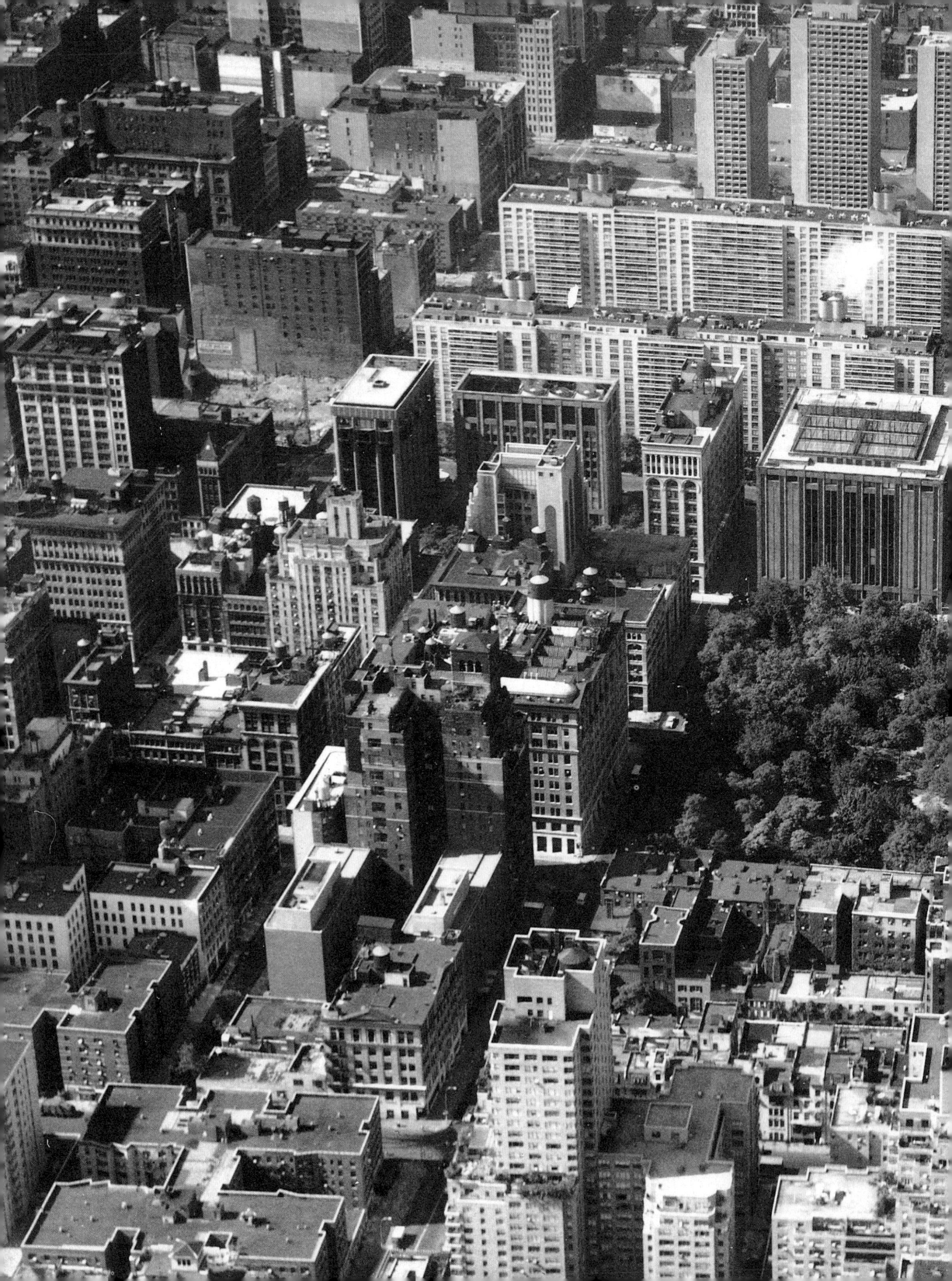

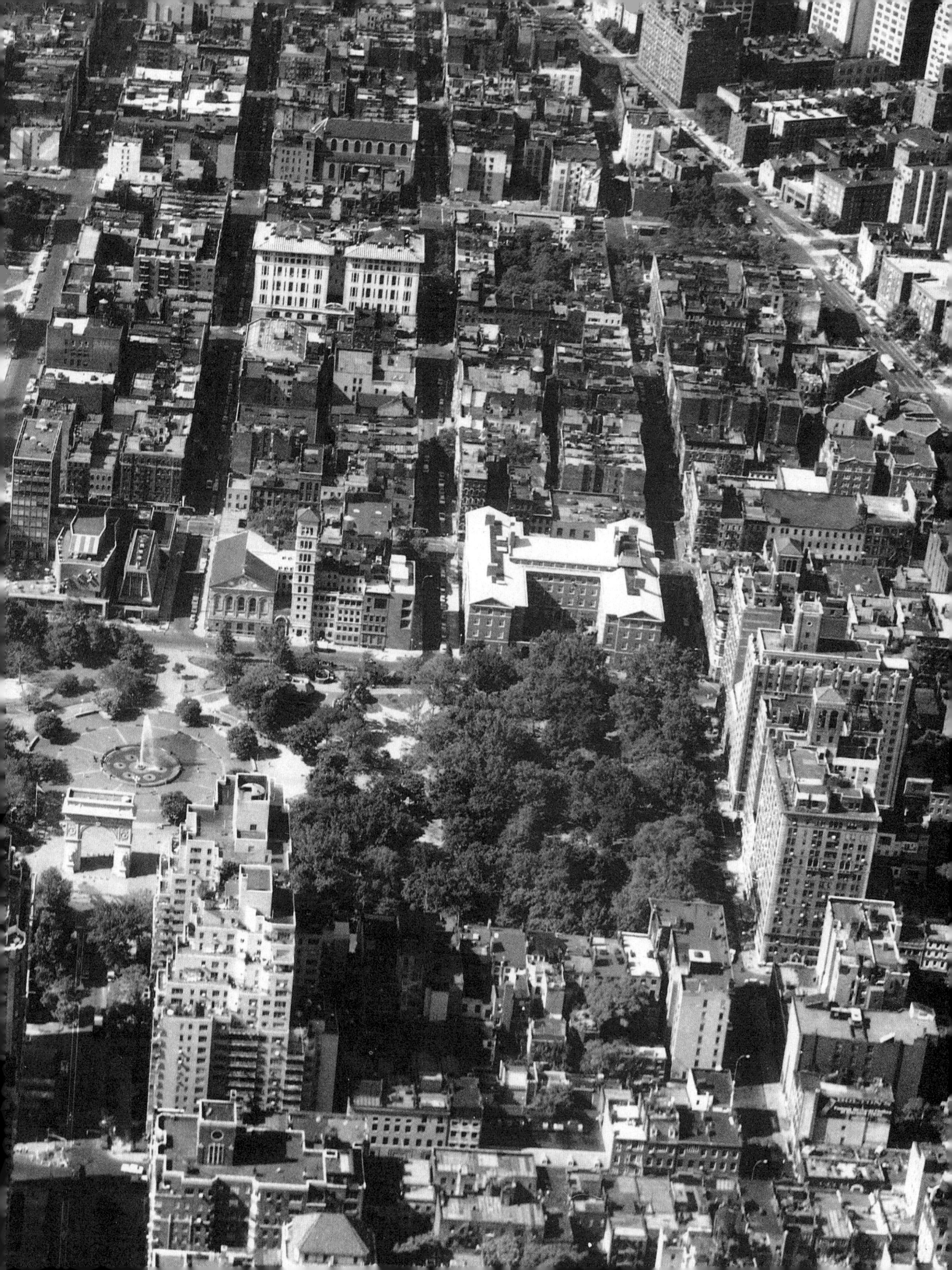

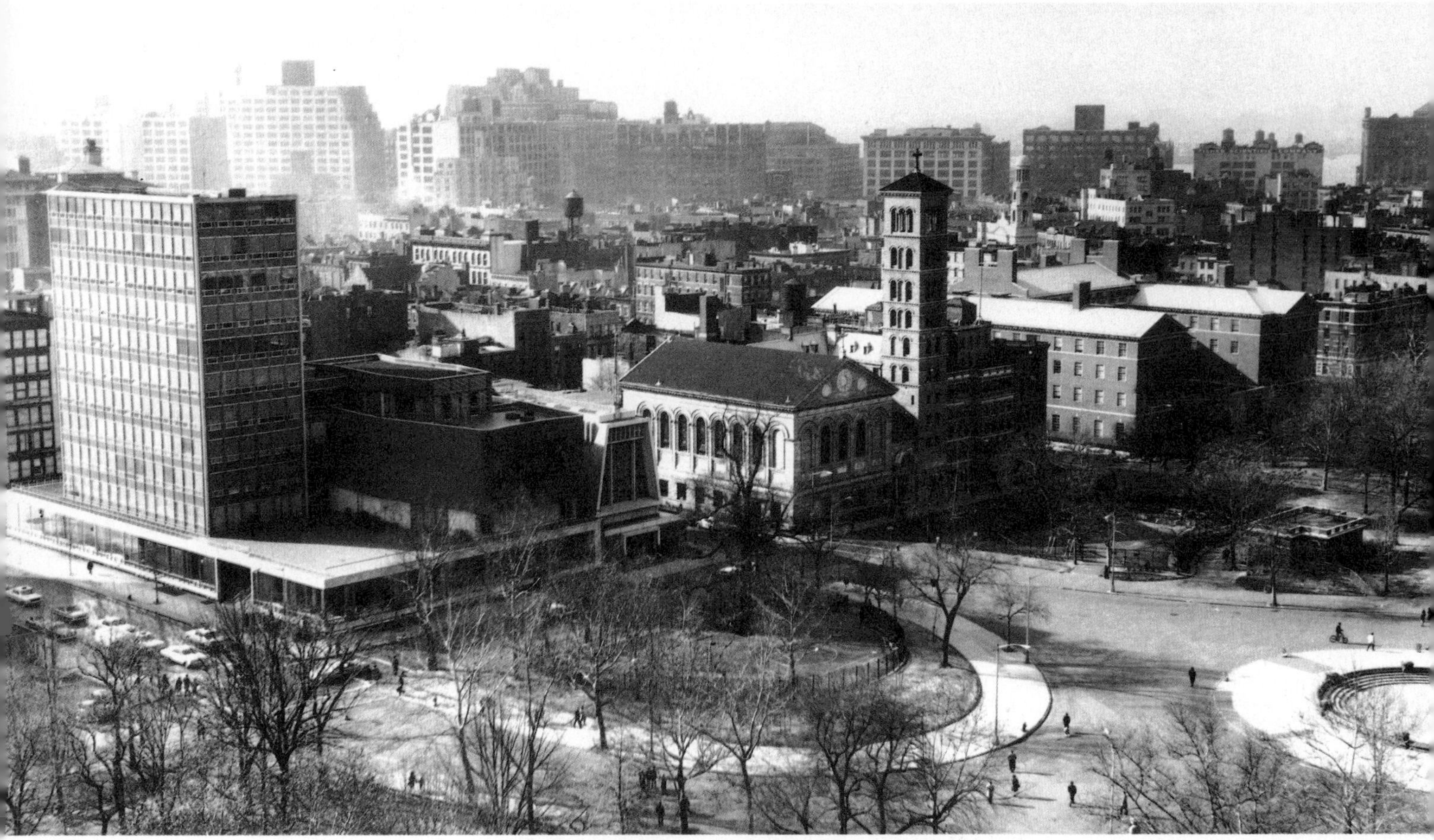

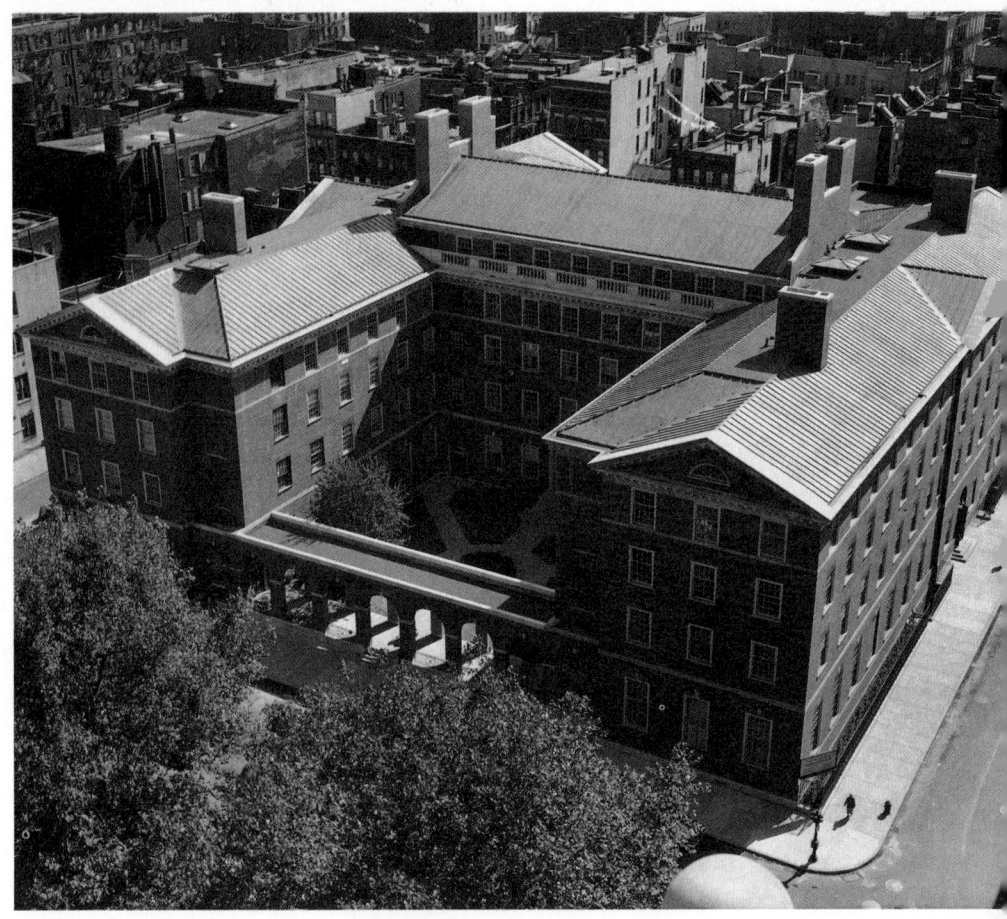

Above: View to the southwest of Washington Square South showing, from left to right: Loeb Student Center (Harrison & Abramovitz, 1960), Generoso Pope Catholic Center (Eggers & Higgins, 1964), Judson Memorial Church (McKim, Mead & White, 1892) and Vanderbilt Law School (Eggers & Higgins, 1951). NYU

Right: Vanderbilt Law School, Washington Square South, Sullivan to MacDougal Street. View to the southeast. NYU

vaguely Georgian red-brick building was internally integrated with the first eight floors of the Holly Chambers (C. F. Winckleman, 1930), directly to the east. Though Hayden Hall's design was serviceable at best, the building effectively maintained the street wall facing Washington Square Park and was sympathetic with its context. But with the coming of the 1960s, the university's attitudes to the neighborhood changed. Harrison & Abramovitz's Joe Weinstein Residence Hall of 1962, which occupied part of the block bounded by University and Waverly places, Greene and Eighth streets, replaced a rowhouse group at 5–11 University Place.[83] Consisting of two internally linked nine-story slabs, which shared a courtyard and collectively housed 564 students, the Weinstein buildings incorporated minimally detailed facades which, in their use of red brick, only very weakly referred to the elegant Greek Revival townhouses located nearby on Washington Square North.

In 1960 NYU completed the Loeb Student Center, the university's first postwar building to both decisively break with the Village's prevailing architectural traditions and adopt an explicitly Modernist approach.[84] Also designed by Harrison & Abramovitz, the building occupied most of the block bounded by Washington Square South, West Broadway, Thompson and Third streets; replacing more of Genius Row, the building stood east of McKim, Mead & White's Judson Memorial Church (1892), at the southwest corner of Washington Square South and Thompson Street, the profile of which continued to exert a strong presence along the square's southern boundary. Complexly massed, the Loeb Center seemed an attempt to reinterpret in strictly Modernist terms the campanile and basilica of the Judson Memorial. From its one-story glass-and-limestone base rose a narrow, rectilinear ten-story glass-and-aluminum slab set perpendicular to the principal Washington Square South facade and set back slightly from the West Broadway frontage; it also included an irregularly shaped, virtually windowless five-story brick volume housing an auditorium.

To relieve the austerity of the windowless facade facing the park, Harrison & Abramovitz proposed a wall-affixed sculpture, eventually choosing an untitled, abstract work by Reuben Nakian that consisted of carved aluminum plates clustered in three groups, all set along a diagonal visually linking the wall's lower left corner to its upper right.[85] The individual elements of the sculpture, which was installed in 1961, seemed randomly placed on the larger structure, as if they were held against the building by nothing more than shifting air currents. Nakian said the plates were meant to evoke students who, "once they are educated and civilized . . . fly away," liberated by "the freeing of the spirit" achieved through learning.[86]

The Loeb Center's interiors were designed by George Nelson. Ground-floor lounges were crisply Modernist and enlivened by bright colors; to service the estimated 6,000 students expected to use the building daily, Nelson employed durable synthetic materials, including white fiberglass curtains designed by Marie Nichols. In addition to office space in the tower for student organizations, the building housed a basement cafeteria, which extended slightly above grade to allow natural light to enter through sidewalk-level windows. The double-height Eisner-Lubin auditorium, which was the principal room in the building's five-story brick element, incorporated serpentine, red-brick walls and an undulating ceiling covered in natural birch veneer. A fourth-floor restaurant above the auditorium was called Top of the Park and featured white bucket chairs upholstered in gold vinyl designed by Charles Eames. The restaurant opened onto a terrace with commanding views of Washington Square and the city beyond.

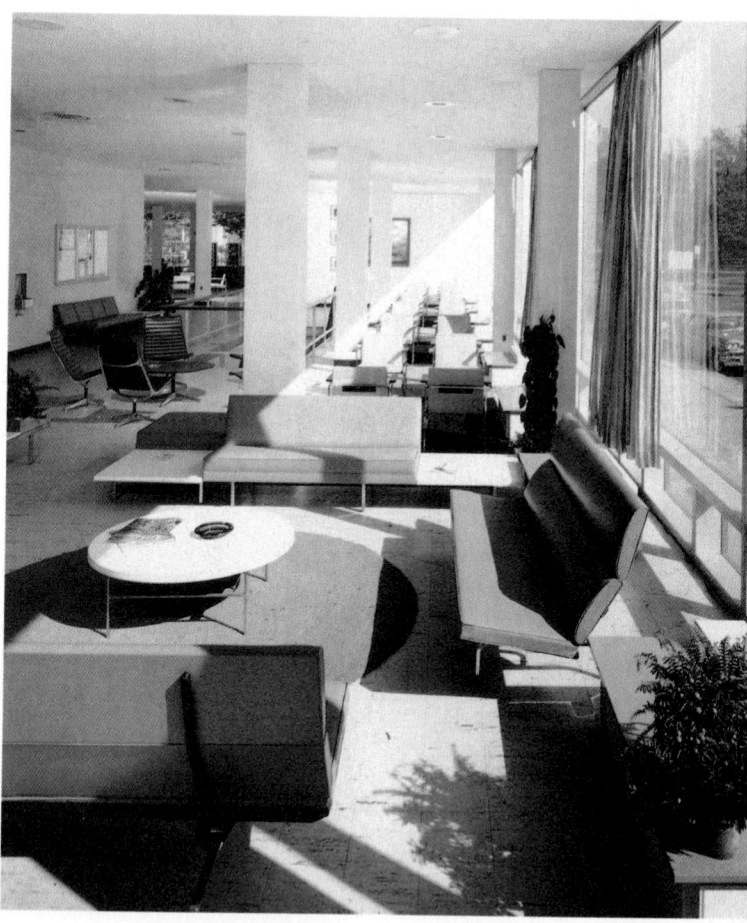

Loeb Student Center, southwest corner of Washington Square South and La Guardia Place. Ground-floor lounge designed by George Nelson. Stoller. ©ESTO

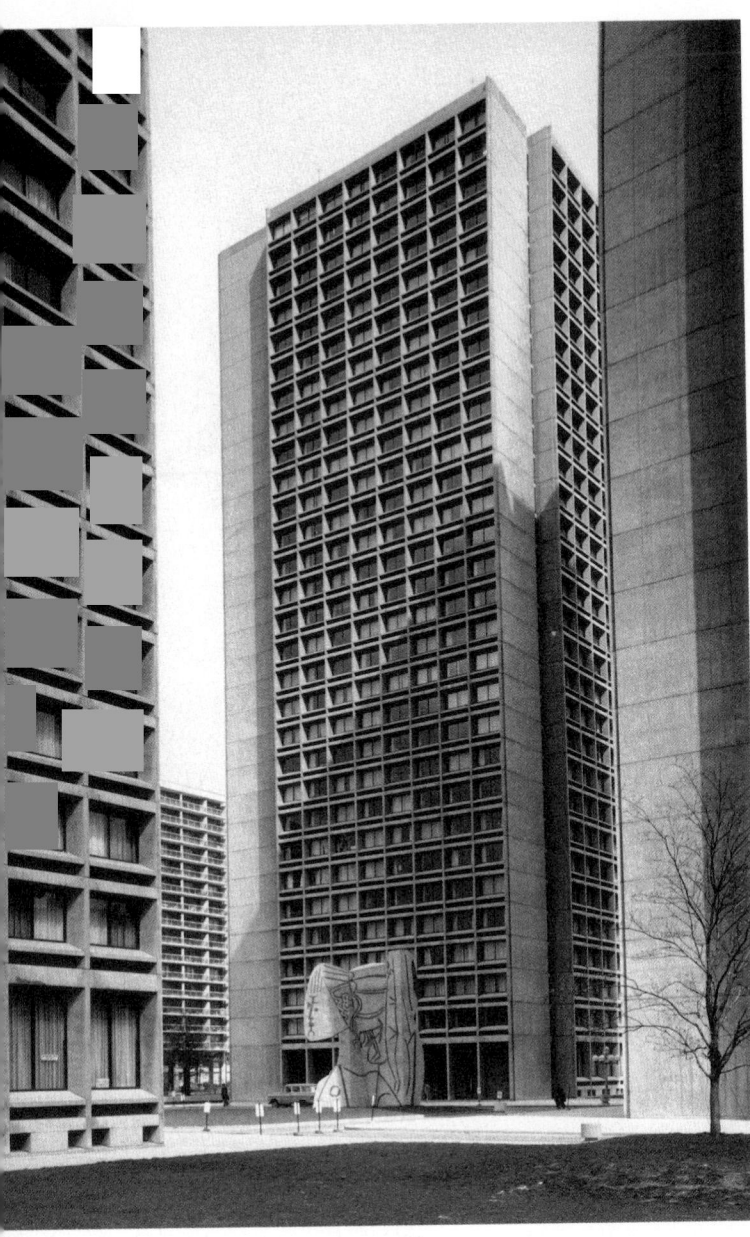

Above: University Village, West Houston to Bleecker Street, West Broadway to Mercer Street. I. M. Pei & Partners, 1966. View to the northeast showing the sculpture *Portrait of Sylvette* (1970) by Pablo Picasso and Carl Nesjar. NYU

Right: University Village. View to the northwest. Fred W. McDarrah. FWM

Critical assessment of the Loeb Student Center was positive, if somewhat restrained. The journalist Thomas W. Ennis, writing in the *New York Times*, characterized the building as "sleek and luxurious,"[87] while the editors of the *Village Voice* described it as having a "rigorously modern, glass look."[88] The editors of *Interiors* praised what they considered to be the center's sensitive relationship to the surroundings: "The Center . . . while unmistakably contemporary inside and out might be compared to a well-bred child who knows when to respect its elders, and impressive elders they are."[89]

The Holy Trinity Chapel and Generoso Pope Catholic Center (1964), designed by Eggers & Higgins and located directly west of the Loeb Center on the southeast corner of Washington Square South and Thompson Street, added yet another disparate stylistic note to the streetscape.[90] The aggressively Modernist building, a far cry from the same firm's genteel, thirteen-year-old Georgian law school just a few hundred feet farther west, was even more than the Loeb Center an attempt to update the Judson Memorial Church. It consisted of a windowless one-story base surmounted by a white granite-clad structure with inwardly inclined walls suggesting a temple on a podium, but one given a structurally determined trapezoidal shape. The north face was dominated by an abstract stained-glass window. Near the top of the building a series of louvers punctuated by narrow windows defined a clerestory, and an openwork flêche crowned the composition. Mannered at best, the building soon seemed very out of date, a victim of its own stylishness. In 1967 Norval White and Elliot Willensky said, "Walking down Fifth Avenue one is delighted with Washington Square Park, announced by the Memorial Arch—and then the eye looks through the arch and framed in the middle is this incongruous chapel."[91] By 1978 White and Willensky were significantly harsher in their critical assessment, characterizing the Loeb Student Center and the chapel as "two awkward attempts at 'modern architecture.'"[92] Writing a year later, Paul Goldberger dismissed the chapel as "a pitifully weak building to close the vista through the Arch."[93]

In 1963 NYU took title to the vacant five-and-a-half-acre parcel that was to have been the site of the last of the Washington Square Village superslabs and set out to develop a middle-income housing project, ultimately called University Village.[94] Mounting community pressure against Moses's renewal plan had resulted in an agreement worked out in 1960 by Mayor Robert F. Wagner by which NYU, as designated developer, would reserve one-third of the apartments in the new complex for people who either lived or worked in Greenwich Village, with first preference being given to former on-site residents who had been relocated from their apartments when the urban renewal project was initiated ten years before. The rest of the units would be reserved for NYU staff and their families.

In a bold move toward creating a high-quality project, I. M. Pei was retained as architect. Initial plans called for two thirty-story towers and an adjacent seven-story building; ground was broken in April 1964. But by the time University Village was completed in 1966 the third building had grown in height to match the other two towers. Despite their claim that "housing is no place for monuments," Pei and his design collaborators, who included James Ingo Freed, as well as A. Preston Moore and Theodore Amberg, organized the towers to create a monumental plaza, and the towers themselves, with their bold concrete structural grids and deep-set windows, furthered the impression of grand scale. Whereas Pei's previous housing had tended to emphasize the regularity of the structural grid, creating almost

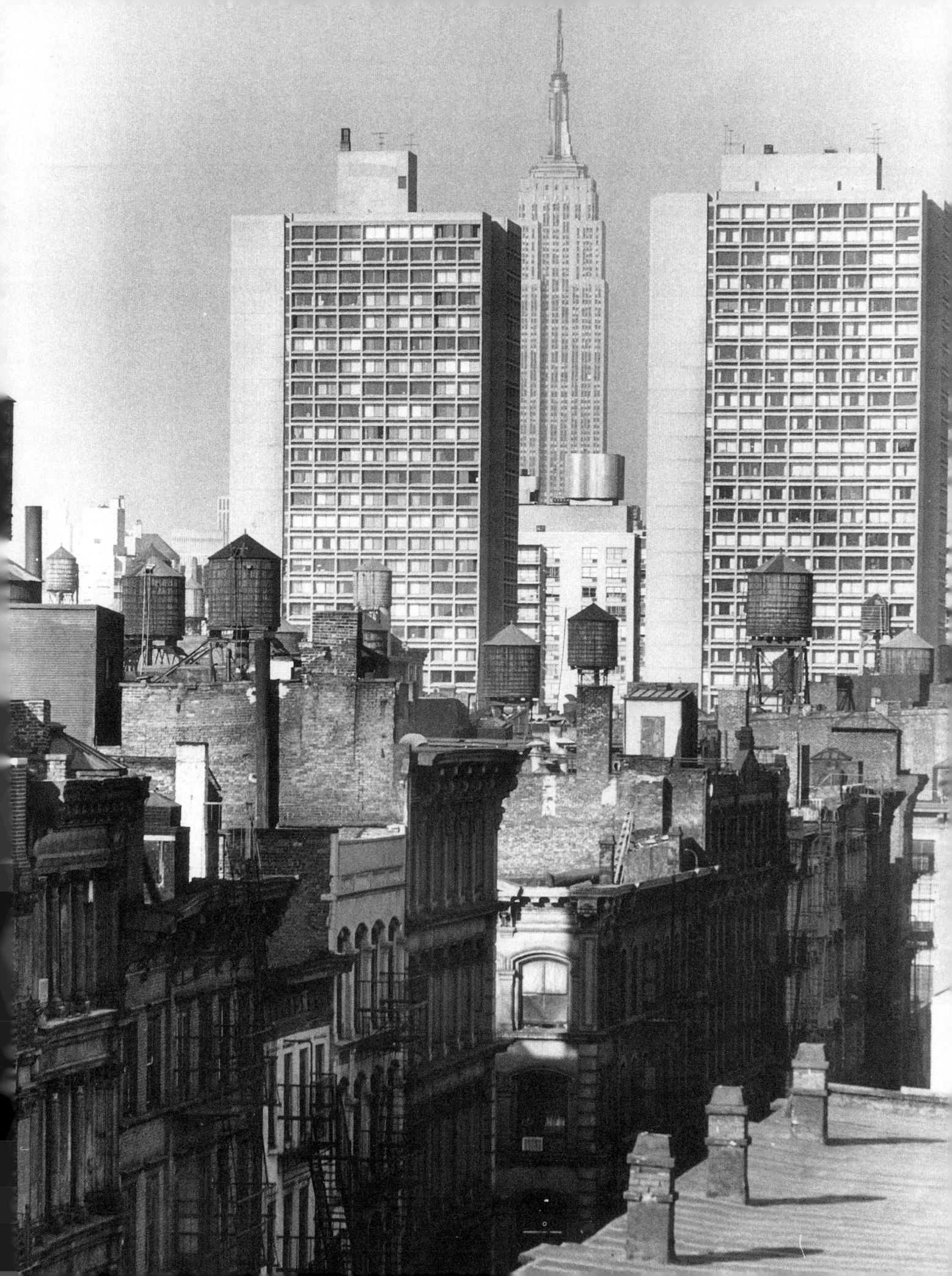

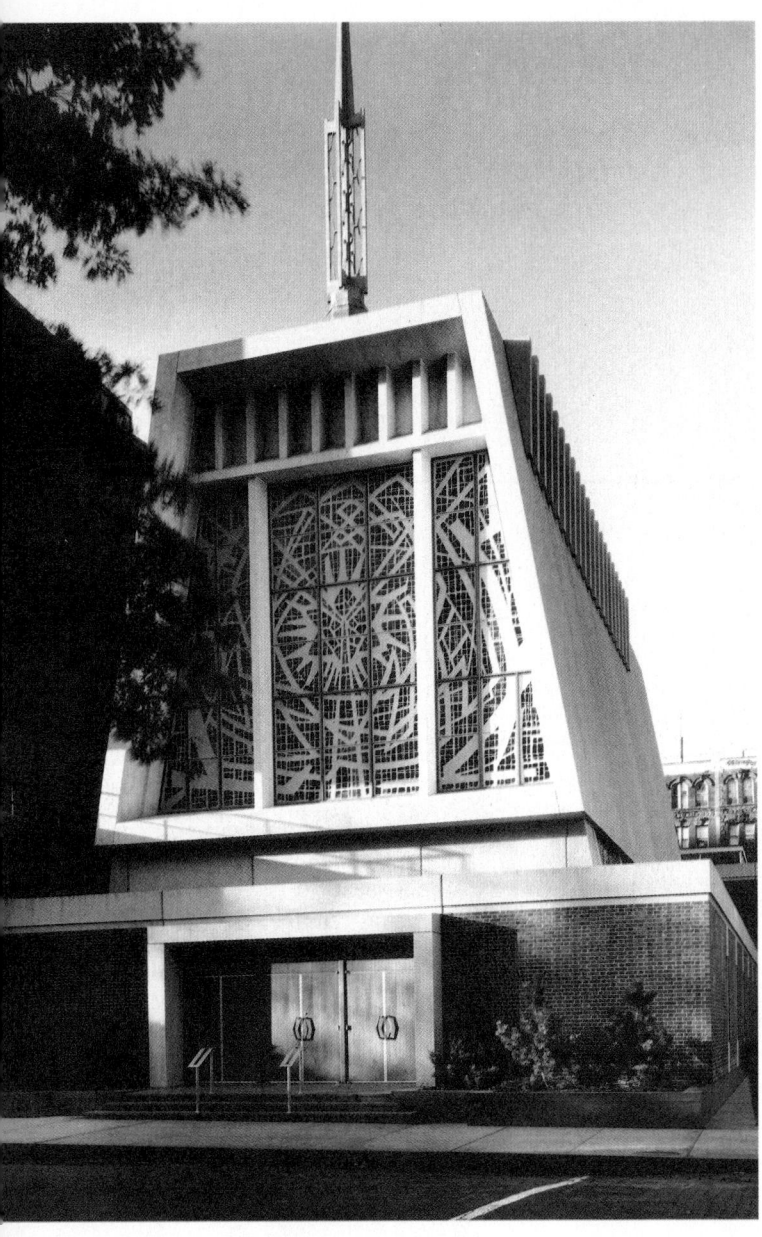

Generoso Pope Catholic Center, southeast corner of Washington Square South and Thompson Street. Eggers & Higgins, 1964. View to the southeast. Schnall. NYU

endlessly repetitious, impersonal facades, at University Village he pursued a counterbalancing impulse toward dynamic asymmetry based on a pinwheel-plan composition of the towers, juxtaposing the window grids with concrete sheer walls to create an animated, sculpturally vigorous yet human-scaled design. The placement of the buildings on the site furthered the sense of active composition by playing the long facade of one tower against the short facade of the other. The complex gathered its entrances around an internal plaza, deliberately turning its back on Houston Street, which, in accord with Moses's notion of superblocking and peripheral street widenings, had been condemned to a role as a crosstown truck route rather than a busy city street. The landscaping of the site considerably softened the transitions between the housing precinct and the neighborhood to the south.

As the focus of his plaza, Pei wanted a monumental sculpture by Pablo Picasso, who agreed to have his sometime collaborator, Norwegian sculptor Carl Nesjar, reinterpret his *Portrait of Sylvette* (1934), originally a two-foot-tall metal construction, as a thirty-six-foot-high, sixty-ton sculpture.[95] Working in situ, Nesjar executed *Sylvette* in concrete with a Norwegian black stone aggregate that was sandblasted to recreate the etched black lines of the original. Picasso was involved not only in the translation of the small construction to its new scale and material but also in its placement in the plaza. Despite the planarity of the composition, the construction in concrete, rather than the original metal, gave *Sylvette* a forceful, gestural presence that held its own amid the surrounding towers.

In 1964, in an effort to establish a cohesive and compelling architectural identity for the still rapidly expanding school, NYU hired Philip Johnson and Richard Foster to devise a coordinated plan encompassing both existing and proposed buildings.[96] The $100 million development plan was to be realized over a five-year period. The complexity of the problem was widely acknowledged. As the editors of the *Village Voice* put it, Johnson had "his job cut out for him," since "Alice in Wonderland never devised a greater variety of wonderment than that represented by the architectural styles of NYU."[97] The editors of *Progressive Architecture* were even more esoteric in their choice of metaphor: "To Philip Johnson has fallen the appalling task of cleansing the Augean Stables of New York University's Washington Square campus. To continue the bucolic metaphor, this is like locking the door after the livestock has been stolen, for NYU's 75-year record of design and planning in Greenwich Village invariably has been characterized by blundering, poor taste, and poorer community relations."[98]

Johnson's plan was a synthesis of conservation and construction. Its principal features were the preservation of the fine townhouse specimens of Georgian architecture along Washington Square North, the recladding in red sandstone of the existing Commerce and Main buildings along Washington Square East, and the construction of a new classroom building on the northeast corner of Washington Place and Washington Square East. This building would be of a style and a height (ten stories) consistent with the existing Commerce and Main buildings and would be physically linked to the Main Building by a glass canopy over Washington Place, transforming the three-block-long street, as well as the flanking blocks of Greene and Mercer streets, into an enclosed, landscaped pedestrian galleria terminating in an open piazza. Johnson's plan also called for the construction of a ten-story library at the square's southeast corner on a site that had stood vacant for several years and had previously contained a sixteen-story apartment building and a parking garage.

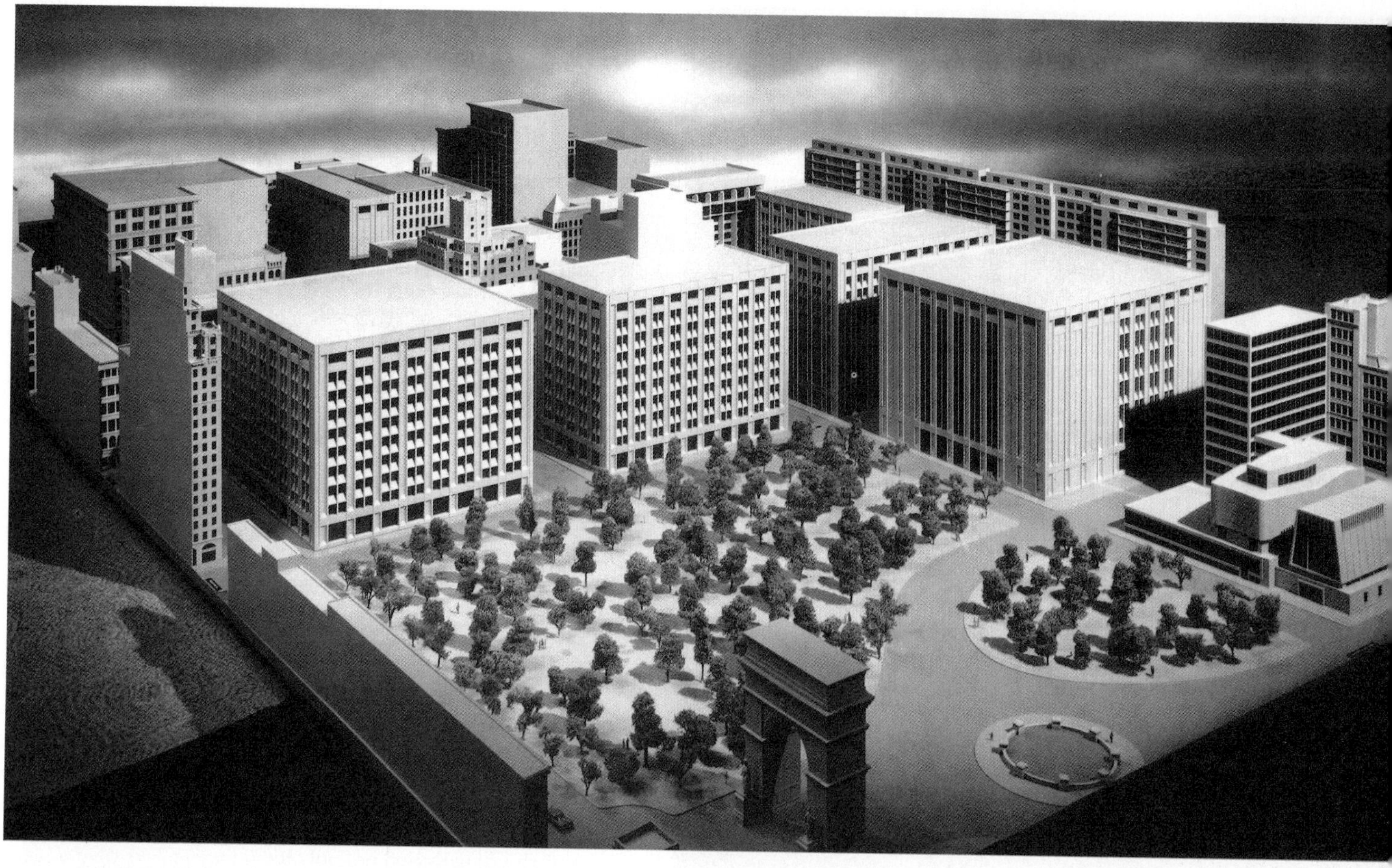

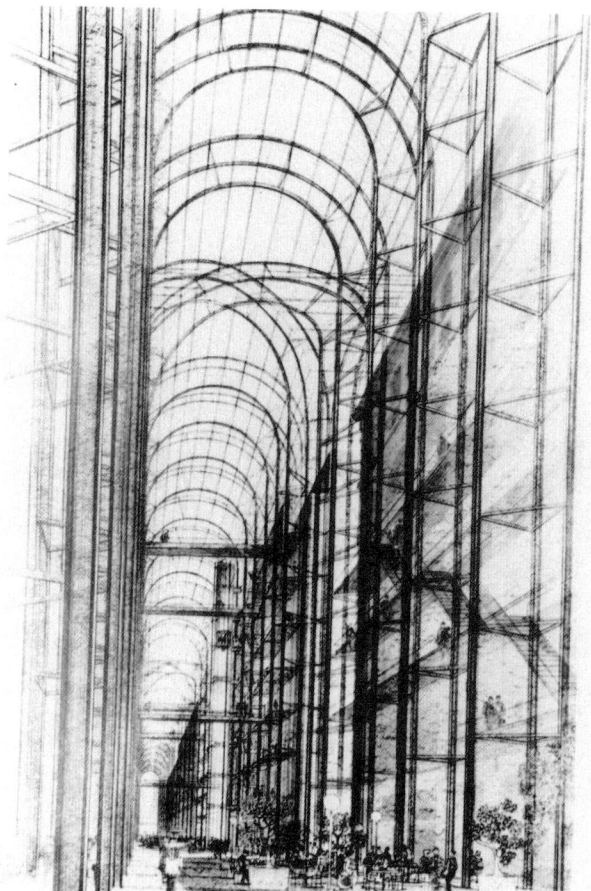

Above: Proposal for redevelopment of New York University's Washington Square campus. Philip Johnson and Richard Foster, 1964. View to the southeast. NYU

Left: Proposed pedestrian galleria, Washington Place from Washington Square East to Broadway, Greene and Mercer streets from Washington Square South to Waverly Place. Philip Johnson and Richard Foster, 1964. Perspective of view to the east. PJA

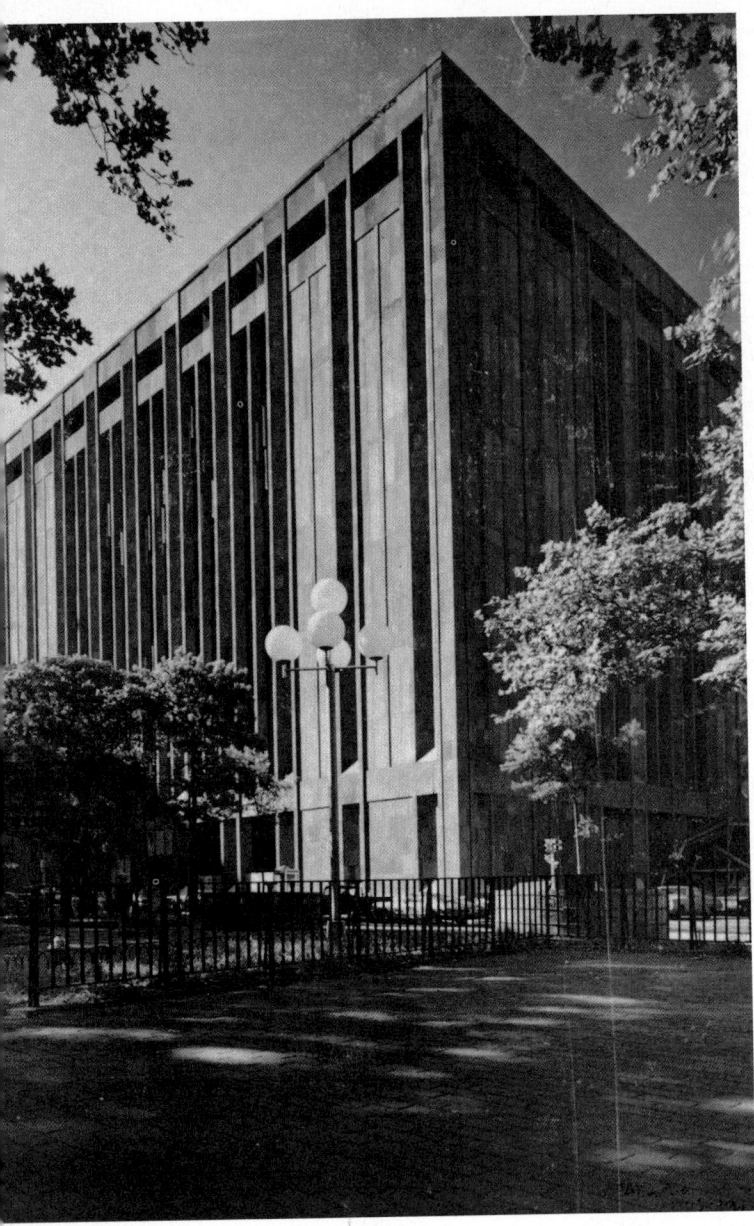

Above: Elmer Holmes Bobst Library and Study Center, southeast corner of Washington Square South and La Guardia Place. Philip Johnson and Richard Foster, 1973. View to the southeast. RF

Right: Elmer Holmes Bobst Library and Study Center. Interior court. NYU

The architect claimed his goals were simple: "Our primary aim is preservation of the park, instead of building individual monuments to architects or to the University."[99] Johnson somewhat disingenuously elaborated:

My whole aim is to quiet the square down; I want a single image, the way things used to be. . . . The whole idea is to preserve the park, to contain it; and with this homogeneity, to give the Washington Square campus an identity it hasn't had before. . . . We can't do anything about the 18th-Century scale at the north side of the square, but a square this size isn't hurt by height. And we wouldn't touch other buildings on the square. Some of them—on the south side—even have a certain folkloristic interest: Loeb and the Catholic Center.[100]

Of his own proposed buildings, Johnson commented, "They are fairly anonymous buildings, maybe even dull, but I'd rather have it that way than have them be pushy."[101] The architect went so far as to claim that he had intentionally made his projects as "boring" as the Washington Square North townhouses to "calm" the area "rhythmically."[102]

Regardless of Johnson's intentions, the proposal immediately sparked controversy and intense debate. Foreshadowing the violent conflict that would erupt several years later over Columbia University's relationship to the surrounding Morningside Heights and adjacent Harlem communities (see chapter 9), NYU, with Johnson in charge of its architectural destiny, was seen by many Greenwich Village residents as an increasingly self-interested and unwanted institutional intruder threatening the snug comforts of the historical residential bohemia and effectively appropriating Washington Square Park as its own campus. At the heart of the animosity between NYU and Greenwich Village stood not only the university's evolving identity and traditional town/gown conflicts, but an increasingly widespread concern for what constituted the nature of a livable city. While NYU president James M. Hester said that the plan "developed a concept that will preserve the traditional serenity and beauty of an important landmark in New York City,"[103] critic Ellen Perry, writing in *Progressive Architecture*, noted: "To other professionals (planners), Johnson is an aesthetician who lacks the knowledge of how a living urban campus can be realized. To some citizens, Johnson's plan is only a glossy cover-up for what is described as the same lack of regard for community values and community needs that NYU has repeatedly shown in the past. Several fear it as the cover-up for further expansion that will emerge as a *fait accompli* before long." Citing urbanistic issues, Perry said that the Johnson proposals "have thus far created only one more ugly situation. . . . The problem is not whether these buildings are 'good' or 'bad,' beautiful or ugly, but whether, in the complex way that a city grows and changes, the expansion of this urban university is creating more than it destroys, or is destroying more than it creates."[104]

Opposition to the plan focused on the first building to be realized, the Elmer Holmes Bobst Library and Study Center.[105] The library site had been the subject of public debate long before Philip Johnson and Richard Foster's plans were announced. In 1953 NYU announced that it had made a bid to acquire 3 of the total 17.68 acres south of Washington Square that were slated for Title I redevelopment. Some Village residents argued that NYU's acquisition of the land in question would constitute a gift of taxpayer money to a private institution; despite this objection, the plan was approved and NYU became the owner of the library site. In addition to overcoming informally expressed community opposition, NYU needed legislative action to realize its library plan: the City Planning Commission had to

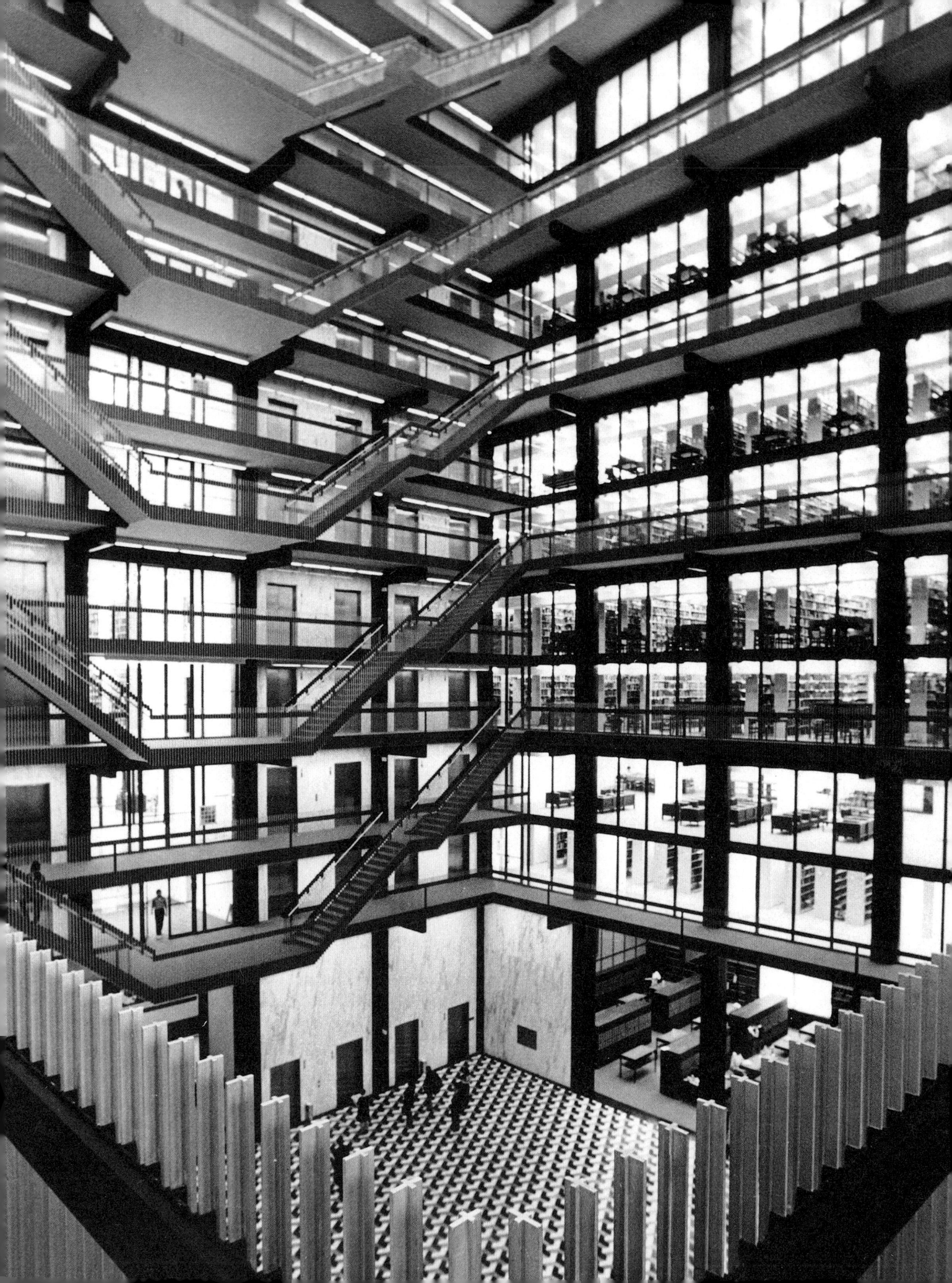

approve the narrowing of West Broadway by forty feet, returning it to its pre-Moses dimensions, as well as the compensatory widening of Third Street between West Broadway and Mercer Street; a Housing and Redevelopment Board ruling stipulating that all new building along Washington Square South maintain a sixty-foot cornice line with additional stories set back forty feet had to be waived; and the Board of Standards and Appeals had to grant a zoning variance to permit a building of the size and bulk proposed. Local Planning Board 2 of the City Planning Commission opposed both the narrowing of West Broadway and the granting of the zoning variance, though the board's power was only advisory, not legislative. The board was concerned about the park being overcrowded by NYU students and the profile of Washington Square South being overwhelmed by the proposed library's 150-foot height. Perhaps the board's most significant objection was to the shadows the building would cast across the park.

The activist–urban planner Jane Jacobs, whose participation on the Save the West Village Committee had been pivotal in blocking development in that part of the Village (see chapter 16), asserted, "All the glamour of Philip Johnson won't save that corner of the park from gloom."[106] Johnson countered that the library would not damage the park but indeed enhance its spatial integrity. The proposed narrowing of West Broadway would prevent the square from remaining "without a shape" and its space "leak[ing] away like water out of a bathtub."[107] Noting community opposition to the plan, Ellen Berkeley (née Perry) took a rather belligerently antivisual stance: "What happens when space develops an 'unsightly leak'? And when does the flow of space (usually a Good Thing) become space that leaks (always a Bad Thing)? These matters are never defined in terms that are intelligible to the citizen who just likes grass. Or is it possible that some people have figured it out and just like their space leaky?"[108]

In what would be widely viewed as a strategic move in the face of mounting opposition, rather than a seriously considered alternative, NYU presented designs for a twenty-two-story, progressively setback tower that filled the site's maximum allowable building envelope. Labeled "Hester's Revenge," the plan was not further developed. Another proposal, suggested by some opponents to Johnson's scheme, was to realize Johnson's design on the site then occupied by the temporary facilities of the ANTA theater, located two blocks from Washington Square, on the north side of Third Street between Washington Square East and Mercer Street. This plan was also not pursued.

By the time the Board of Estimate approved the vigorously debated library plan on August 25, 1966, twenty-nine community groups opposed the proposal. Describing the board's "four-hour, three-ring" public hearing, Berkeley reported that when "a bored and impatient Mayor John Lindsay [stated] his reasons for an aye vote, he seemed to grasp little of the complexity of the argument. He appeared to understand only one side well, as if he had made up his mind early in the game, and had only paid attention when his team was at bat."[109] Whatever the mayor's involvement, the plan was approved, albeit by a close twelve to ten vote. On December 29, 1966, New York State Supreme Court Justice Owen McGivern dismissed a suit brought by Jane Jacobs, City Councilman–elect Edward I. Koch, and two other Greenwich Village residents, Rachele Wall and Charlotte Natale, against the city and the Board of Estimate. The complainants charged that the city had dispensed of public land without auctioning it off. They also argued that when NYU provided funds for the city to conduct planning studies of the Washington Square Title I project, the architects hired by the city had ongoing professional relationships with the university and thus could not be relied on to render impartial judgments. Justice McGivern ruled that without proof of corruption or bad faith, the municipality's actions were permissible.

The controversy revolving around the urbanistic ramifications of the library obscured discussion of its architecture. As finally completed in 1973, after what the New Yorker described as "a difficult ten-year gestation that included postponements caused by suits by neighbors; interminable filing for variances and letting out of bids for construction; a need to switch contractors, to the tune of a nine-month delay; a six-month elevator-construction-worker strike; and a little trouble with the flow of sandstone," the library was realized largely as originally planned.[110] A massive 150-foot-high volume clad in Longmeadow red sandstone, the library rose sheer from its site, which included the annexed forty-foot-wide strip of West Broadway. A rather chaste composition that reflected Johnson's continuing efforts to marry Classical and Modernist vocabularies, initially expressed in New York eleven years earlier in his design for the New York State Theater at Lincoln Center (see chapter 9), the library was ringed by concave piers that rose the building's full height, dividing each of the building's facades into nine bays, and were punctuated by a band course above the first floor. The building incorporated windows only within the principal facade's center five bays, where they were arranged in vertical rows, and on the penultimate floor, along all four sides, bringing further definition to the minimally defined cornice.

In contrast to its rather austere and diagrammatic exterior, the building's interior had a decidedly theatrical aspect. Again recalling Johnson's design for the New York State Theater, the library was dominated by a grand interior space, 100 feet square and rising the building's full 150-foot height. The interior court or atrium was surrounded by glass-enclosed floors, which contained open stacks as well as specialized libraries. Gold anodized-aluminum picket railings were punctuated by what the editors of the New Yorker described as "chevron-shaped flying staircases."[111] Five double-height reading lounges overlooking Washington Square were flanked by balconies. Lacking a central reading room, the library, which could seat approximately 4,000 people and house about 2.5 million books, relied on the atrium not only as an organizational device but as a means of visually relieving the massive structure's bulk and providing a sense of communality. The space effectively served as the building's, and in large measure the university's, town square, a miniaturized version of Washington Square, "a campus built into the interior" of the library, as James Hester put it.[112]

Noting Johnson's references to the work of the sixteenth-century Italian architect Andrea Palladio, and in particular to Palladio's Church of San Giorgio Maggiore (1565) in Venice, the critic C. Ray Smith said:

As Palladio had superimposed one scale of order on another in the church . . . so Johnson has juxtaposed the vast interior twelve-story-high atrium, which feels like an exterior space, adjacent to glass-walled library and study spaces on the perimeter. Looking across the atrium from the south side and through the glass-walled interior spaces out to the open-air atrium of Washington Square to the north of the building is as mannered a view as Palladio strove for. This is witty, grand allusion by a witty architect imbued with the force of architectural history.[113]

To carry the historical reference further, Johnson's atrium contained a floor of black, white and gray marble arranged in a trompe l'oeil geometric pattern directly inspired by the flooring in San Giorgio Maggiore. John Tauranac called the atrium "one of the city's great interior spaces,"[114] but Paul Goldberger was far less impressed. He found the atrium "fussy and pretentious," explaining, "New York needs grand space and N.Y.U. certainly needed a monumental centerpiece, but how much better this would have been if the architect had been content to leave it alone and not fuss it up! Glitter is everywhere, with only the trompe l'oeil floor pattern . . . an element with enough strength for a room of this enormous scale—and even it clashes with the other details."[115]

One of Johnson's goals for the Bobst Library was to design, as Tauranac noted, "a library to do for NYU what Low Library had done for Columbia—set the tone for the buildings to come and act as the university's focal point."[116] While Johnson acknowledged that McKim, Mead & White's library (1895–98) suffered from functional inadequacies,[117] he felt that library planners had gone too far in the opposite direction, valuing functional considerations over all others: "You need something more than utility in the design," Johnson said, "something to make you think more of the library. The utilitarian aspects of the library will adapt themselves."[118] Whatever the building's functional success, it failed to fully realize its symbolic role, in part because Johnson's comprehensive plan for NYU was not adopted, thus robbing the university of a cohesive architectural identity and the library of a convincingly defined campus to dominate over.

Nonetheless, two similarly articulated buildings clad in red sandstone and designed by Philip Johnson and Richard Foster were realized, providing some measure of visual unity. Though begun after Bobst Library, the buildings were completed before it. The André and Bella Meyer Physics Hall (1971), on the southwest corner of Broadway and Washington Place, was located at the eastern boundary of NYU's "campus," a full four blocks from Bobst Library, where it seemed stylistically out of place.[119] Tisch Hall (1972) was closer—on the south side of Fourth Street, between Mercer Street and the cobblestone-paved pedestrian walkway that flanked Bobst and continued the axis defined by Washington Square East one block south to Third Street—and benefited from its proximity to the library.[120] But because Tisch Hall was set far back from the street, on an elevated, landscaped podium, its impact was diminished. The landscaped area, a weak substitute for the type of clearly delineated piazza originally called for in Johnson's master plan, contained the Gothic finial from NYU's first building, demolished in 1894 to make way for the Main Building at 100 Washington Square East. Rather than honoring the school's past, the stranded finial seemed unintentionally to memorialize NYU's long-standing failure to create a sense of place. Norval White and Elliot Willensky characterized Meyer and Tisch halls as "two more 'redskins,' this time *without* meaningful inner spaces."[121]

The Hagop Kevorkian Center for Near Eastern Studies (1972) was the fourth and last building designed by Philip Johnson and Richard Foster for NYU.[122] Located on the southeast corner of Washington Square South and Sullivan Street, the five-story-high, dark-granite-clad building faced the park with a stark, narrow facade, windowless up to the third-floor level, where a vertically arranged row of three deeply recessed windows was pushed to the building's corner. The fenestration visually wrapped around to the longer Sullivan Street facade, where it became part of an asymmetrical composition incorpo-

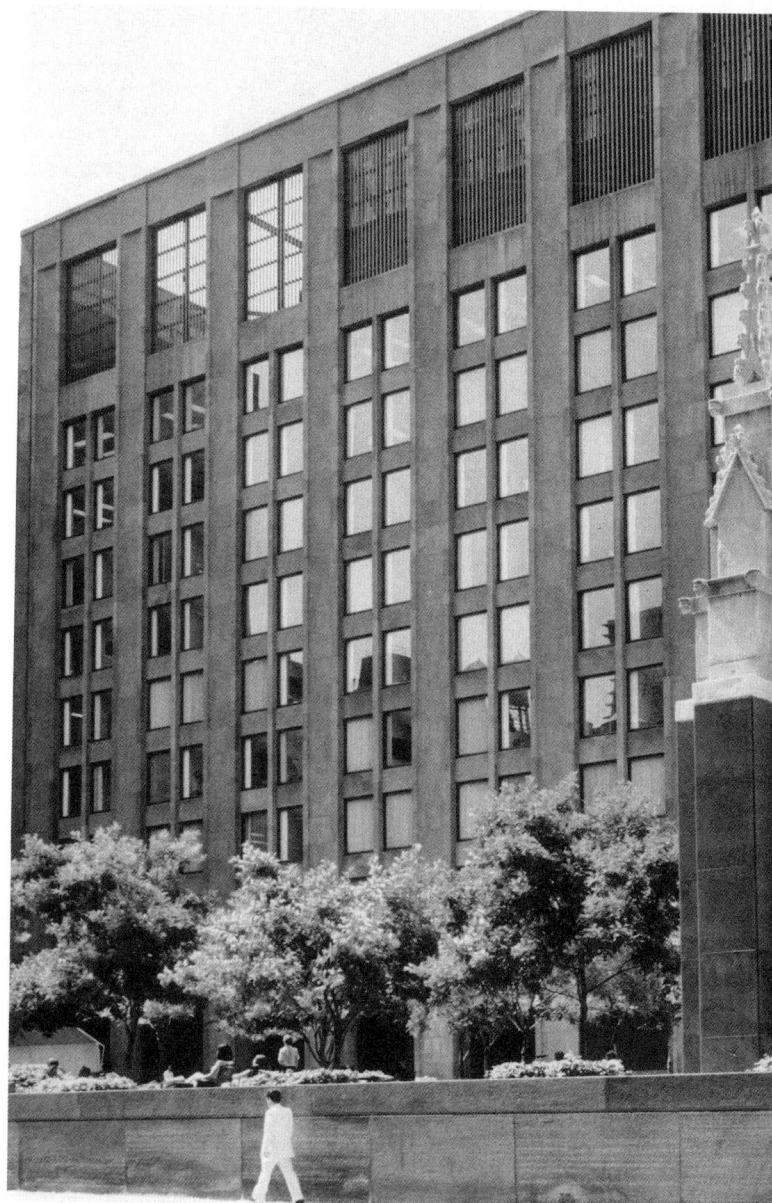

Tisch Hall, East Fourth Street, between Mercer Street and La Guardia Place. Philip Johnson and Richard Foster, 1972. View to the south. NYU

241

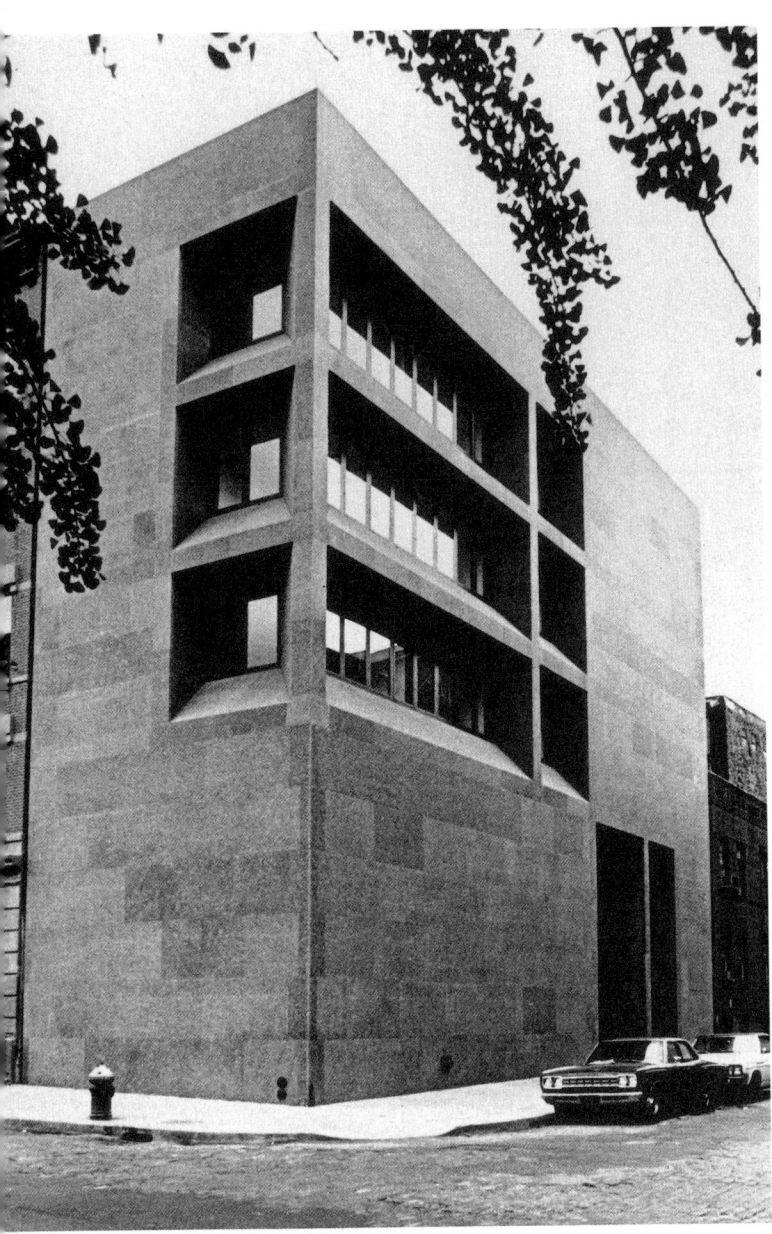

Hagop Kevorkian Center for Near Eastern Studies, southeast corner of Washington Square South and Sullivan Street. Philip Johnson and Richard Foster, 1972. View to the southeast. Rodriguez. NYU

rating the building's recessed principal entrance. Resembling a gargantuan minimalist sculpture, Kevorkian Center was undeniably effective in establishing a powerful presence and providing a visual antidote to the decorative Modernism of its earlier NYU neighbors. Characterizing the center as "a crisp, clean building that achieves urbanistic success through its streetside scale," Paul Goldberger pointed to the irony of so small a building yielding "a monumentality that is at least as powerful, and surely less strained, than that of the [Bobst] library."[123]

Weaver Hall (Warner, Burns, Toan & Lunde, 1965), completed after Johnson's appointment as master planner but prior to the completion of any of his buildings, was a soft-core version of the tough monumentality Johnson would propose.[124] Housing the Courant Institute of Mathematic Sciences, the building, which was elevated on a rough stone-paved podium, occupied the full western blockfront of Mercer Street between Third and Fourth streets. Weaver Hall consisted of a fourteen-story freestanding tower flanked on its northern and southern ends by single-story, modified octagonal pavilions, respectively housing an auditorium and two large classrooms. The podium extended to the lot line along the cross streets but was set back from Mercer Street behind a curbside landscaped area. Wedge-shaped tan- and red-brick piers, which housed most of the building's mechanical functions, ran the building's full height, terminating in a pronounced brick cornice. The spaces between the piers were filled in with dark glass windows and spandrels detailed with matte-finish metal frames. On the twelfth floor, which housed a library, glass-enclosed bays supporting top-level terraces were cantilevered between the piers. The *Progressive Architecture* editor James T. Burns, Jr., lamenting what he considered to be the dearth of postwar buildings in New York worthy of attention from out-of-town visitors, called Weaver Hall "notable" and stated that "we at P/A are thankful that we have another building to point out to the visiting designer from Des Moines."[125]

NYU was Greenwich Village's largest and most powerful educational institution, but its rival for prominence, the much smaller New School for Social Research, also expanded during the postwar period with reasonably felicitous results. In 1955 the New School, located on the south side of Twelfth Street between Fifth and Sixth avenues, announced plans to enlarge its facilities. In 1960 two buildings designed by Mayer & Whittlesey were completed: a nine-story, metal-and-glass International Style building, housing classrooms and offices, that was set back from but connected to the existing school building (Joseph Urban, 1930); and a similarly articulated, five-story building, housing a library, cafeteria and offices, fronting Eleventh Street.[126] The two new buildings were connected by a double-decked pedestrian bridge, supported in part by welded pipe trusses arranged in a repeated "X" pattern that crossed over the vacant rear lot between them. Mayer & Whittlesey walled off the area from the adjoining yards and landscaped it to function not only as an open passageway but as a "campus," or at least as an appropriate venue for both planned social events and impromptu meetings. A two-part, rough-hewn granite sculpture by Isamu Noguchi titled *Garden Elements* provided a grace note.[127]

In 1970 Frost Associates transformed the three-story Lane clothing store (Cordes, Bartos & Mihnos, 1952), occupying the full eastern blockfront of Fifth Avenue between Thirteenth and Fourteenth streets, into the New School's Graduate Faculty Center.[128] Though the design of the original building, clad in white brick and polished red granite and blandly detailed, was

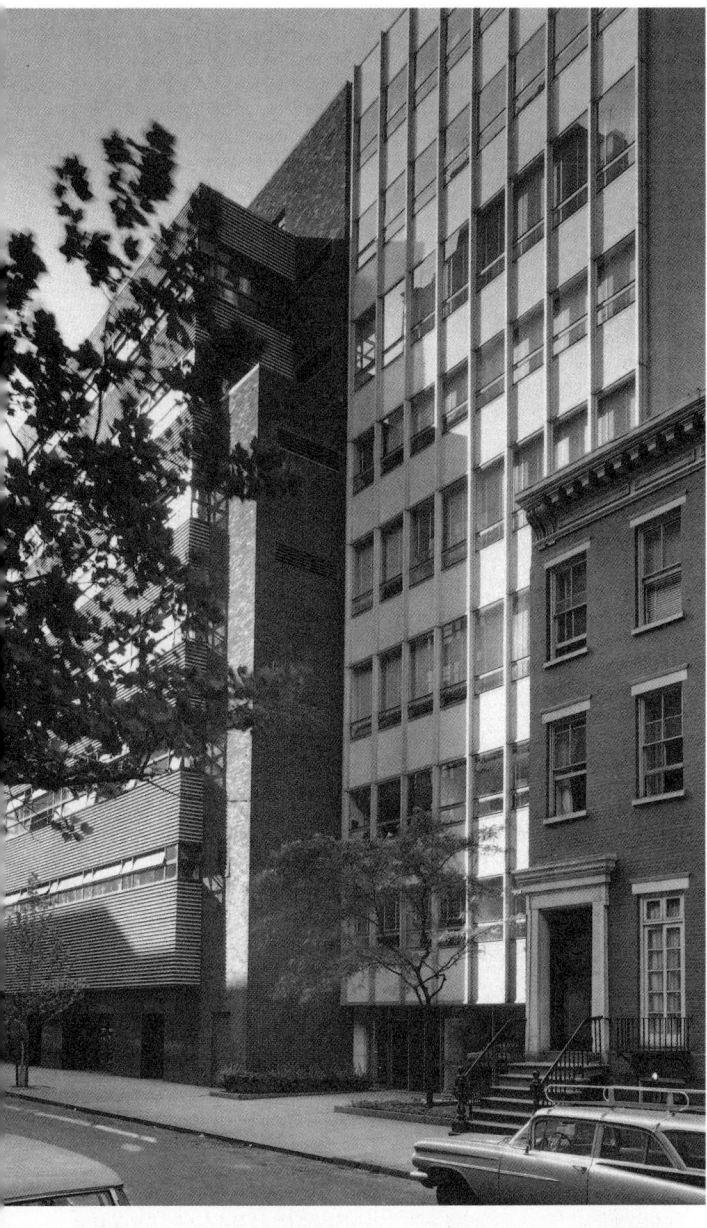

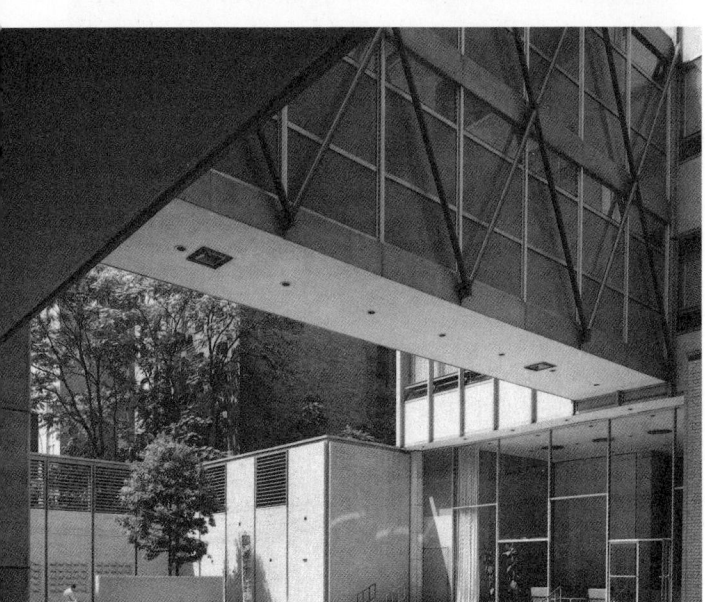

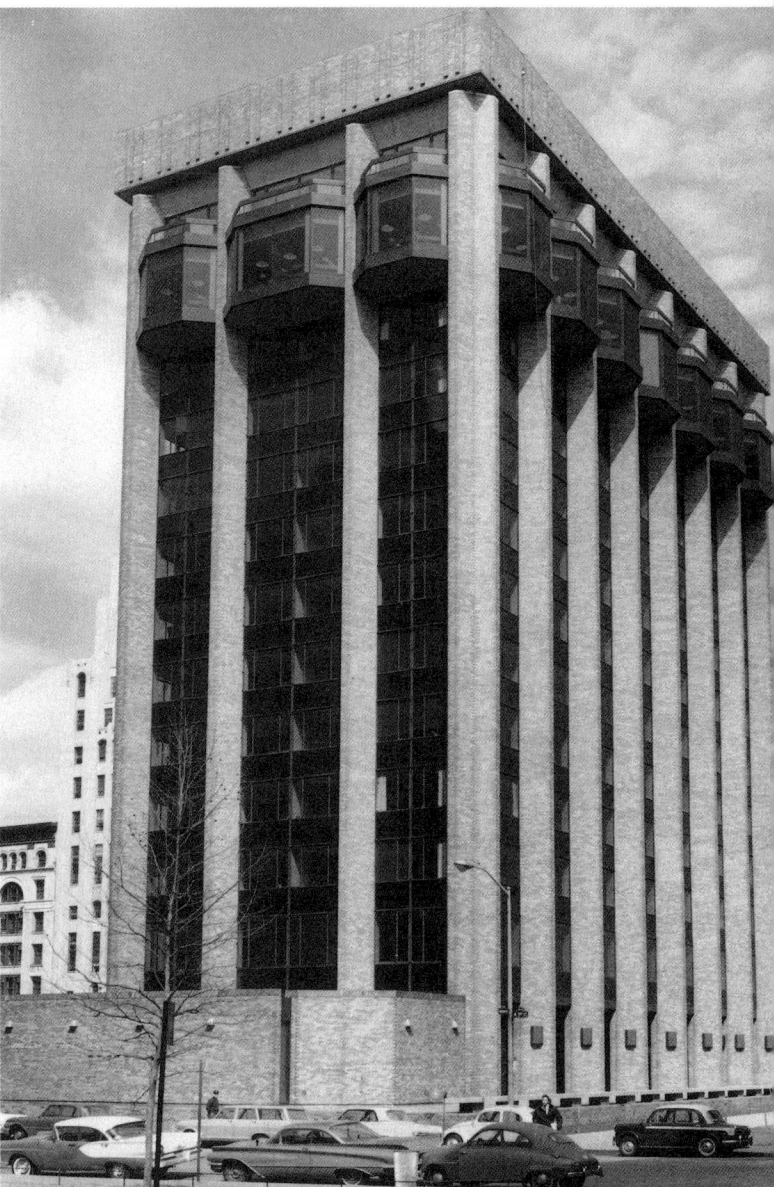

Top left: New School for Social Research addition, East Twelfth Street, between Fifth and Sixth avenues. Mayer & Whittlesey, 1960. View to the southeast showing original New School building (Joseph Urban, 1930) on the left. Stoller. ©ESTO

Bottom left: New School for Social Research addition. Courtyard. Stoller. ©ESTO

Above: Weaver Hall, Mercer Street, between East Third and East Fourth streets. Warner, Burns, Toan & Lunde, 1965. View to the southeast. NYU

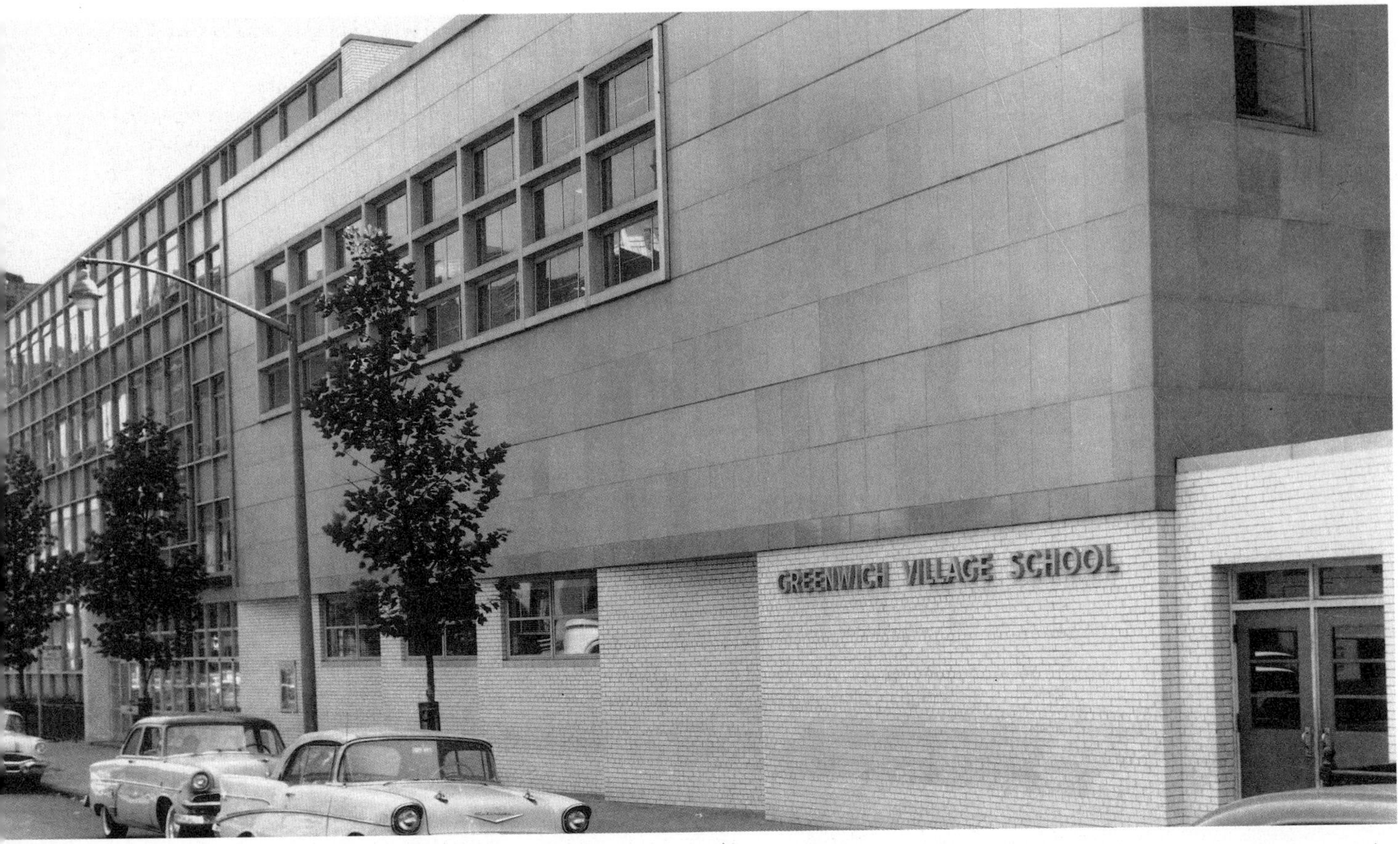

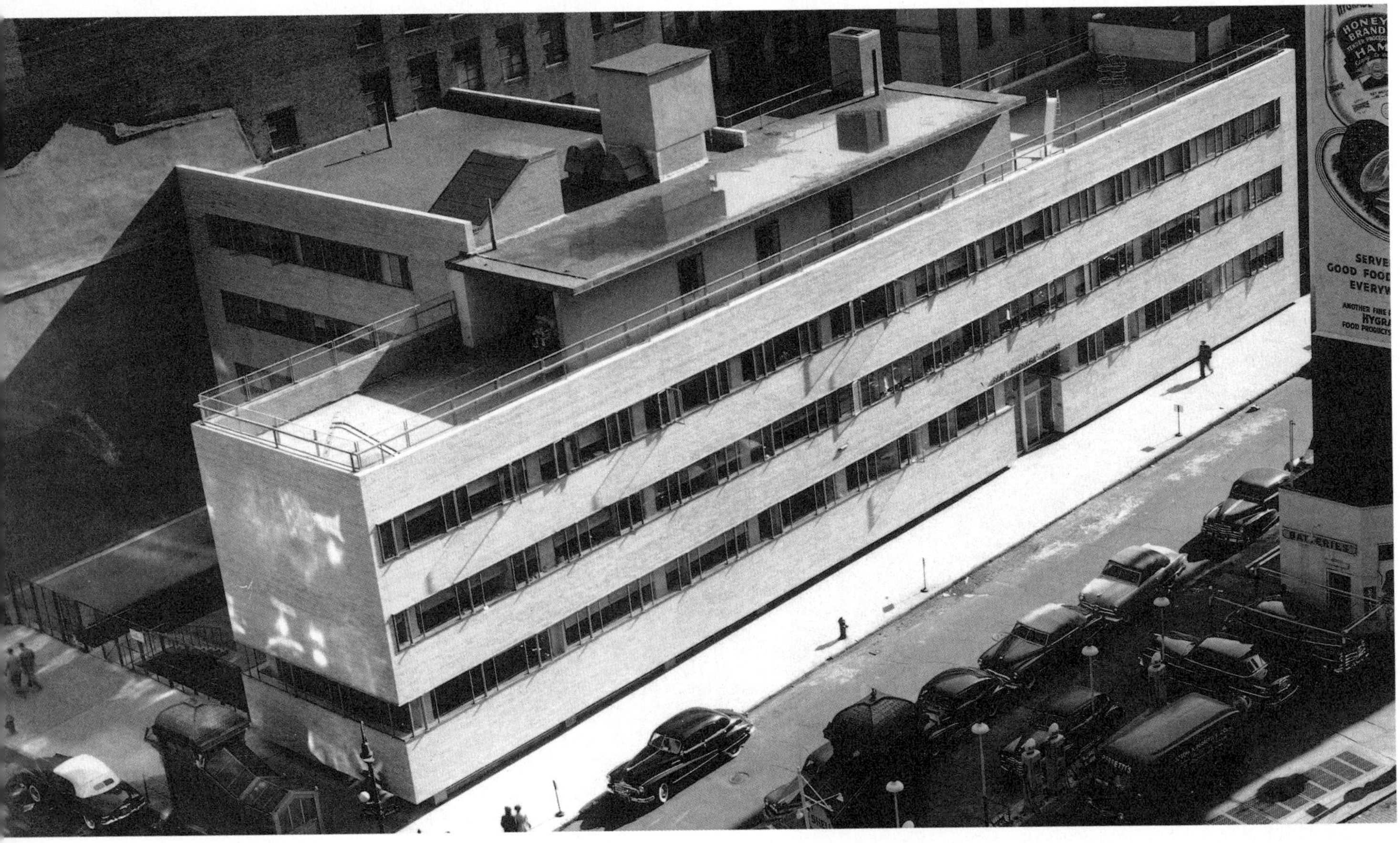

Top: Public School 41, West Eleventh Street, between Sixth and Seventh avenues. Michael L. Radoslovich, 1959. View to the southeast. NYCBE

Bottom: St. Barnabas House, southeast corner of Bleecker and Mulberry streets. Ketchum, Giná & Sharp, 1949. View to the southeast. Freedman. LF

modest in both its concept and execution, it received lavish praise from the ardently Modernist critic Lewis Mumford. In 1952 he said, "The total effect of the exterior . . . is simple, straightforward, and handsome; i.e., conspicuous without being vulgar. In a neighborhood where business is accustomed to shout at the top of its voice, this bit of urbane manners should be rewarded by recognition and approval."[129] By 1970 the building, significantly altered when its ground-level arcade was enclosed with showcase windows, was described by the critic John Anderson, writing in *Interiors*, as a "tawdry fashion store" and a "Greenwich Village eyesore."[130] As part of their renovation Frost Associates added narrow windows, arranged in groups of two and four, to the previously windowless upper two floors, but otherwise maintained the exterior. Inside, the interiors were gutted, with the principal exception of the building's centrally located escalators. An auditorium, an exhibition area and several offices were located on the first floor, along with glassed-in lounges and reading areas; the second and third floors contained classrooms and offices. In keeping with the school's history of stressing progressive and sometimes nonmainstream thought, the architects, as John Anderson put it, made "tidiness a far secondary consideration to an informal atmosphere of easy livability. Thus chairs are permissive types for young adults to slop around in, and they are often movable or swivelable to create impromptu groups."[131]

Much less visible than the institutions of higher learning but nonetheless significant was Public School 41 (1959), on the south side of Eleventh Street between Sixth and Seventh avenues.[132] Demolished to make way for the school was James Renwick's so-called Rhinelander Gardens, at 110–24 West Eleventh Street, a row of houses deeply set back from the street and incorporating delicately articulated, continuous cast-iron balconies on all three stories. Designed by the city's Bureau of Construction, with Michael L. Radoslovich serving as chief architect, P.S. 41 was a slightly better than usual, glass-and-metal building incorporating brightly colored, porcelain-enameled spandrels. In a weak nod to the site's past, some of the ironwork from the Rhinelander Gardens was used to create a trellis in a landscaped area outside the school's cafeteria.

Although there was comparatively little new construction outside the areas dominated by Sailors' Snug Harbor and NYU, a few interesting smaller institutional buildings were built to house church-sponsored agencies. In 1949 the New York Protestant Episcopal City Mission Society completed St. Barnabas House, on the southeast corner of Bleecker and Mulberry streets, which offered temporary shelter to homeless women and children.[133] As designed by Ketchum, Giná & Sharp, the four-story, buff-brick building, incorporating long strips of industrial sash, was a crisp essay in minimalist Modernism. Inside, the building housed a chapel and a fourth-floor nursery, which opened onto a rooftop play area. In 1964 another playground, on the northeast corner of West Houston and Mulberry streets, was built by St. Barnabas House.[134] Intended for resident children as well as neighborhood youngsters, it was designed by the landscape architect Robert Nichols and featured nontraditional play equipment.

In 1960, after some of Greenwich Village's most architecturally significant buildings had been lost and many others stood threatened, the architect Edgar Tafel designed a church house for the First Presbyterian Church on the west side of Fifth Avenue between Eleventh and Twelfth streets (Joseph C. Wells, 1845; south parish house, McKim, Mead & White, 1893) that reflected an increased sensitivity toward architectural precedent and con-

text.[135] The new church house was clad in a dark brown brick whose color related to that of the stone church. In addition, Tafel reiterated the quatrefoil motif of the Gothic church's cornice on both the cornice and the second- and third-story balconies of his building. The building was widely ignored by American architectural critics, but it was written about by the British critic Nicholas Taylor in *Architectural Review* in 1965: "Current English suspicions about the aggressive, personal architecture of leading American architects . . . [are] unlikely to be allayed much by the first gropings towards our own self-effacing ideals of harmonious townscape. It is perhaps not surprising that one of the attempts to express a common vernacular tradition comes from a former pupil of Frank Lloyd Wright." Noting the visual continuities between the original First Presbyterian Church and Tafel's addition, Taylor said that although the bold use of the quatrefoil motif "may paradoxically jar English eyes," the architect's decision was based on a strong argument: "the church has twice before been extended. . . . Both times the quatrefoil parapet was faithfully extended. On purely aesthetic grounds the parapet can be said to lighten the [new] structure's appearance."[136]

In 1964 the Village gained one of its most distinctive buildings, the National Maritime Union of America Building, filling the west blockfront of Seventh Avenue between Twelfth and Thirteenth streets.[137] The highly idiosyncratic three-story building was designed by the New Orleans–based architect Albert C. Ledner, who was influenced by the late work of Frank Lloyd Wright. Above a curved glass-brick base, windowless white concrete walls (later covered with small white tiles) were punctuated by nearly continuous horizontal openings incorporating scalloped edges in a vaguely nautical motif. The walls, which functioned as a series of cornices, were progressively cantilevered in small increments as they ascended. Recessed behind the openings were walls containing portholelike windows. The nautical theme was continued inside, where rooms were decorated with blue walls and green rugs. The journalist Mary Perot Nichols, writing in the *Village Voice*, called the building "palatial and highly tasteful," and described the cornices as giving "the impression of either portholes or waves." Nichols added that the "whole thing has a Moorish quality recalling, possibly, the rollicking days of the Barbary pirates."[138] Referring to the cornices, Norval White and Elliot Willensky were less positive in their judgment, calling the building a "huge double-dentured monument."[139] If at the time of completion the building seemed forward-thinking, by 1979 it appeared painfully contrived to many observers. Paul Goldberger damned it as "pretentious claptrap," explaining:

> Maybe this white building with round holes and round versions of sawtooth cornices is trying to make us think of ships; maybe it is trying to make us think of space travel; maybe it is trying to make us think of how nice the Village used to look before it got modern architecture. At the latter it succeeds; it is the sort of arrogant building that leads one to take on an unnatural degree of sympathy for its opposite number, a banal but good-mannered building like N.Y.U.'s Vanderbilt Law School on Washington Square.[140]

The so-called Battle to Save Washington Square (see chapter 16) was without doubt the most important and highly publicized park-oriented issue affecting Greenwich Village in the postwar era, but Union Square Park also drew widespread concern. The park, which defined part of the area's northern boundary along Fourteenth Street, was increasingly threatened not by

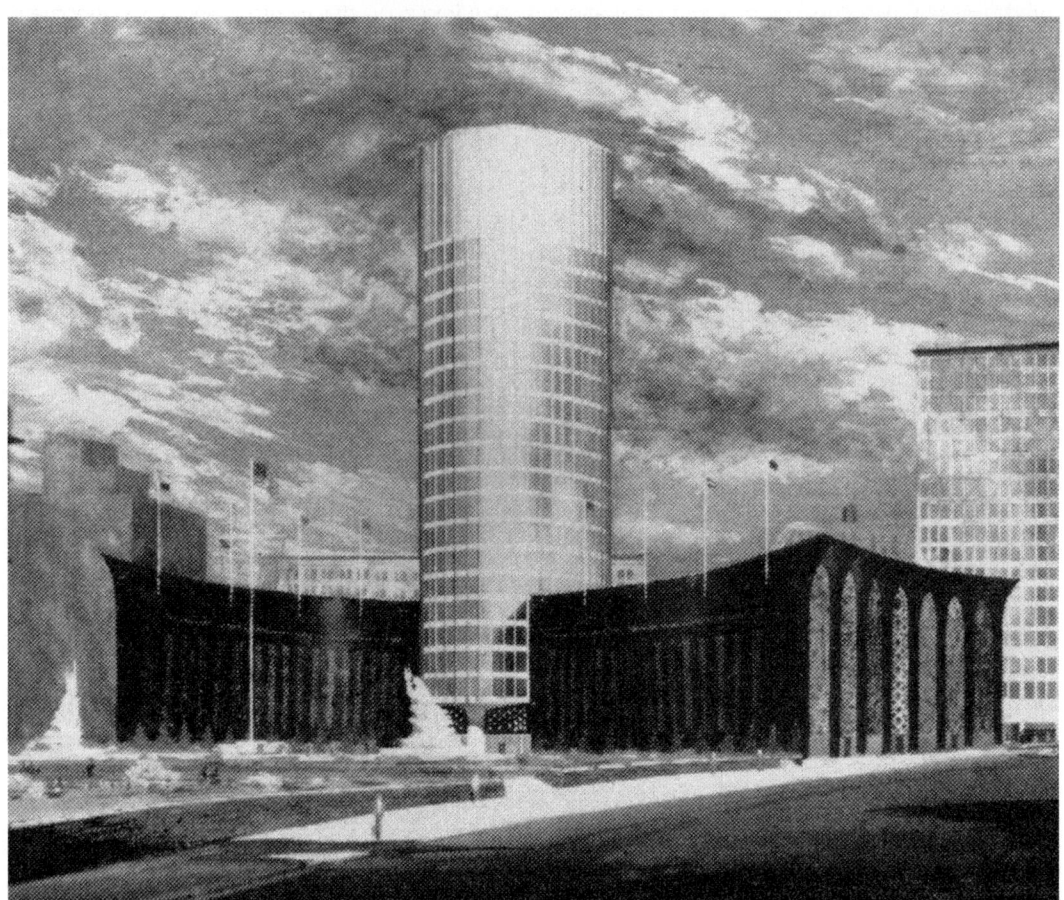

Right: Proposed veterans memorial and office building, Union Square Park. Maurice Warder Bacon, 1962. AF. CU

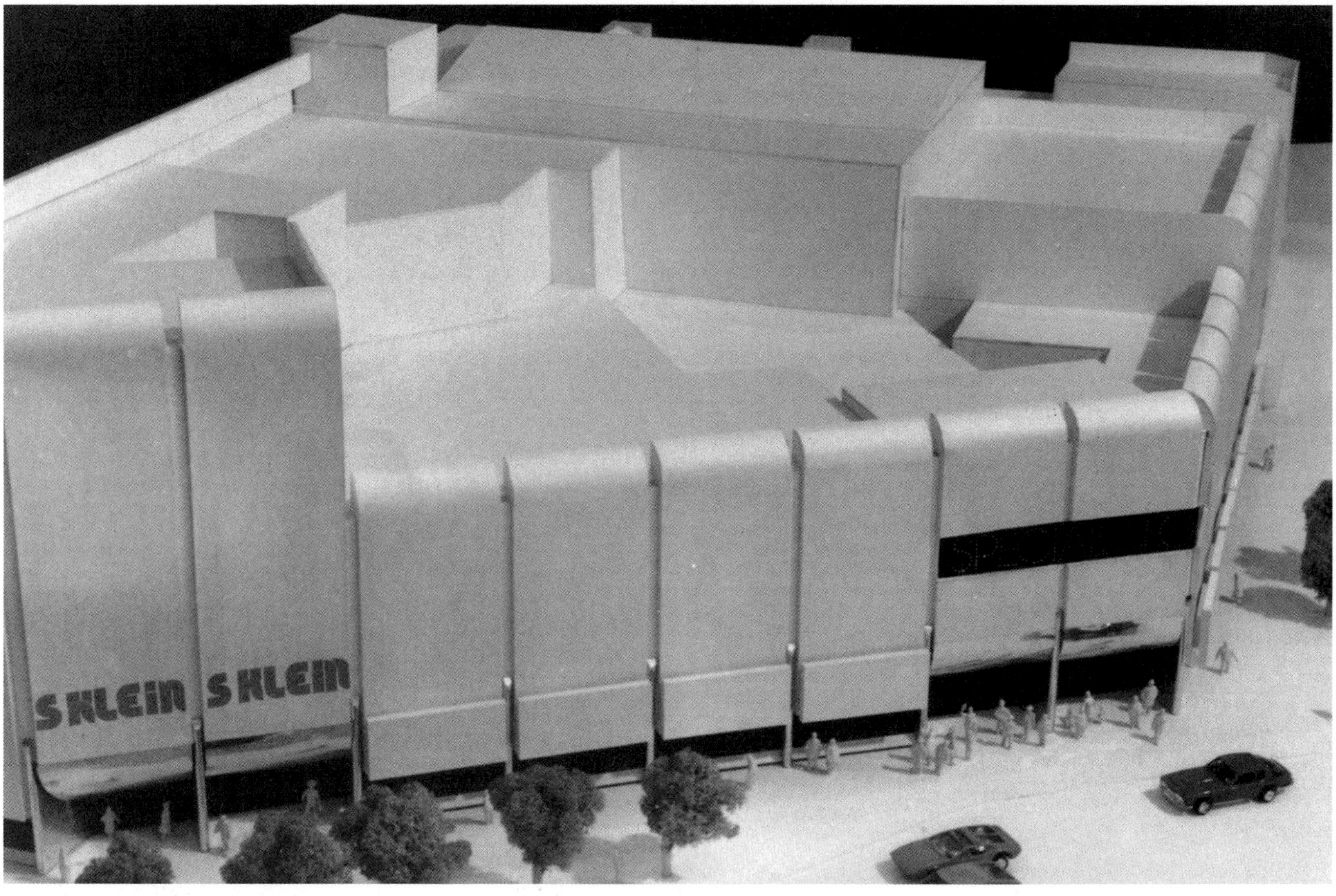

Below: Proposed renovation of S. Klein Department Store, east side of Park Avenue South, East Fourteenth to East Fifteenth Street. Andrew S. Blackman Associates with Stephen Lepp & Associates, 1975. View to the east. ASB

bulldozers but by a slow social decline that was turning it into a seedy and menacing corner of the city. In 1962, in an effort to create both a public memorial and private office space as well as, perhaps, to clean up the area, eight veterans organizations—the American Legion, the Army and Navy Union, the Catholic War Veterans, the Disabled American Veterans, the Jewish War Veterans, the Marine Corps League, the Military Order of the Purple Heart, and the Veterans of Foreign Wars—proposed to erect a tower facing south from the northern end of the park.[141] Architect Maurice Warder Bacon's design was for an eighteen-story, elliptical, glass-and-stainless-steel office tower flanked by two five-story, arc-shaped, arcaded wings clad in polished black granite. In addition to office space, the tower was to contain an auditorium, a library, a lounge, a meeting hall, a museum, a restaurant and an observation deck, as well as a subterranean parking garage accommodating 300 cars. The wings' principal facades were to be inscribed with the famous passage from Abraham Lincoln's Gettysburg Address of 1863: "It is rather for us the living to here dedicate ourselves that these dead shall have not died in vain." Vehement opposition to the plan arose immediately. The editors of *Progressive Architecture* noted that the building was "described by one observer as resembling two U.N. Assembly Buildings bisected by one Marina City tower."[142] Labeling the building an "atrocity," the editors of the *New York Times* argued that it would reduce the park to an insignificant forecourt and urged that it not be built.[143] The project was never realized.

In 1973 the McCrory Corporation, the parent company of the S. Klein Department Store, which was housed in a collection of several internally connected seven- and eight-story buildings that stood across from the southeast corner of Union Square Park, funded a study of the area executed by students at the Parsons School of Design.[144] Design proposals resulting from the study focused on the reconfiguration of the park's pathways, the repainting of the Union Square–Fourteenth Street subway station and the redesign of Klein's cast-iron exterior. Three alternatives were suggested for the Klein store: the addition of a sidewalk arcade consisting of a steel space frame filled in with triangular plastic panels; the restoration of the store's original display windows; and the painting of a "supergraphic" version of the store's name, stretching diagonally across the principal facade. The store management explored these possibilities but did not follow through with any of them. Three years later, in 1975, Julio Tanjeloff, a real estate developer with holdings on Fifty-seventh Street as well as on Fifth Avenue, announced plans to transform Klein's, which had closed the previous year, into a new store.[145] As redesigned by the architectural firm of Andrew S. Blackman Associates, with Stephen Lepp & Associates serving as associated architects, the buildings were to be wrapped in a continuous facade composed of a steel structure supporting polystyrene and fiberglass panels resembling stucco; curved soffits above the entrance and other details were to be made of polished stainless steel. This plan was never realized, and the boarded-up department store, along with Union Square Park and the surrounding area, continued to languish.

West Village

Nowhere in Greenwich Village did sentiment against cataclysmic urban renewal run higher than in the so-called West Village, bounded by West Houston and Fourteenth streets, Seventh Avenue and the Hudson River. On February 20, 1961, the Housing and Redevelopment Board, which had been created by Mayor Wagner in 1960 as a way to make the urban renewal process more responsive to community sentiment, announced its intention to study a fourteen-block area of the West Village, bounded by Eleventh, Hudson, Christopher, Washington, Morton and West streets, with the intention of eliminating blighting influences and augmenting the supply of middle-income housing.[146] Even though a plan had not yet been prepared—only a request to the Board of Estimate for funds to conduct a survey of the area had been put forward—West Village residents were immediately incensed by the announcement. For many observers it seemed to herald the arrival of bulldozers and the transformation of their neighborhood—which was characterized by old- and new-law tenements and nineteenth-century houses jumbled together with warehouses—into a tabula rasa for the construction of endless blocks of regimented high-rise housing projects.

A principal feature of the West Village neighborhood was the elevated structure along West Street that since 1934 had carried the New York Central's freight operations south to its St. John's Park terminal.[147] In early 1960 the terminal was closed and sold to a group of investors, spurring rumors about the imminent destruction of the elevated structure, which would open up large parcels for redevelopment.[148] William Zeckendorf, acting on behalf of the railroad's president, Robert R. Young, was known to be exploring the area's future as a real estate asset to the financially troubled company. Although city officials denied that anyone had been promised sponsorship of a large-scale project or commissioned to execute a plan, architect and planner Victor Gruen explained otherwise to the *New York Times* on March 4, 1961. He said not only that he had been asked by the city to conduct a preliminary survey of the area and to propose a redevelopment plan—albeit contingent on the approval of funding by the Board of Estimate—but also that a group known as Mi-Cove (the Middle Income Cooperators of Greenwich Village) had expressed an interest in sponsoring a project in the West Village.[149] The latter revelation was particularly troubling to West Villagers because it came in the wake of Mi-Cove's sweeping housing proposal, designed by Gruen, for the so-called South Village, located south of Houston Street and later considered part of SoHo (see "SoHo," below). Mi-Cove's chairwoman, Charlotte Schwab, stated that while her organization sought to secure a site in the South Village, they would be willing to transfer their plan to a site in the West Village.

Despite Gruen's comments to the *New York Times*, he echoed the city's repeated assertions that West Village residents had little cause for alarm. Referring to the takeover in May 1960 by the new Housing and Redevelopment Board of Robert Moses's duties as chairman of the Mayor's Committee on Slum Clearance, Gruen said, "We live in a new era marked by the change from Mr. Moses to this board of men who are more idealistic. They have come to the conclusion that wholesale demolition is not the answer. . . . They would like to try to save what is good, to improve what can be improved and to tear down only those structures which are incompatible."[150] Walter S. Fried, vice chairman of the HRB (as the new board quickly came to be known), also tried to discredit rumors of "bulldozer approach" renewal by citing a report of the City Planning Commission, which said: "The proposal would involve a combination of spot clearance of deteriorated old-law tenements and various industrial and commercial buildings and rehabilitation of structurally sound brick three and four story houses. It would be accomplished with a minimum of tenant relocation."[151]

West Village residents remained skeptical and apprehensive. Fearing large-scale renewal that would destroy both the neighborhood's intimate scale and its unique economic and social diversity, they formed the Save the West Village Committee, with Jane Jacobs, a resident of the study area (at 555 Hudson Street), and Dr. Donald Dodelson as its co-chairs.[152] Jacobs, the committee's most vociferous spokesperson, was already known as a critic of postwar urban renewal and was nearing the completion of her book *The Death and Life of Great American Cities*, which would become the literal *vade mecum* of a new ideology of urban planning and renewal (see chapter 1). She told the *New York Herald Tribune*: "We like having mixed up incomes and nationalities. Our children play with the Puerto Ricans a few doors down and the rich kids next door. In housing projects people tend to get classified by income. It's socially destructive, and what's more, it's dull."[153] The Save the West Village Committee was soon joined by other groups and individuals from the greater Greenwich Village area who protested the proposed study on principal.[154] When Mi-Cove formed its own group, known as the West Village Site Tenants' Committee, in favor of the proposal, Jacobs proclaimed it a "puppet" organization formed by the HRB or its "handpicked site sponsor" to create the false appearance of local support.[155] Schwab denied the accusation: "We had hundreds of applicants for housing from the West Village who desperately needed moderate-priced housing, so we decided to support it. Mi-Cove would like to become a sponsor of low-cost housing."[156]

At the end of March 1961 the nonpartisan Citizens' Housing and Planning Council (CHPC) joined the side of the city and Mi-Cove, releasing a policy statement that supported the proposed study: "In no sense, we believe, does the Housing and Redevelopment Board intend to level the area, to destroy its notably good housing, to tamper with that neighborhood character of which the residents are justifiably proud. By choosing a renewal plan that depends on, in the Board's own words, 'Conservation, rehabilitation, and redevelopment,' guidelines are given to the planners." They added, "We tread warily in the face of the outcry from the neighborhood. Yet, we feel that if the Housing and Redevelopment Board did not plan in the light of city-wide trends as well as local developments, the Board would come under the same attack, by the same voices, as now aimed against it for accepting this responsibility."[157]

On April 27, 1961—after two postponements, the day set by the Board of Estimate to decide on the allocation of funds for the proposed survey—fear and suspicion of the city's intentions culminated in what Susan Goodman, writing in the *Village Voice* in 1963, described as a "dramatic riot at City Hall, complete with balloons, and many political machinations."[158] In response to the Board of Estimate's announcement that they would refer the proposal back to the City Planning Commission, several members of the Save the West Village Committee delivered a New York State Supreme Court order to Mayor Wagner that obligated the city to "show cause" for its continued support of renewal in the West Village.[159] Jacobs, calling attention to the illegality of designating an area "blighted" without a public hearing, declared over the din of the crowd: "Every day this is held over, they are depriving us of our legal rights."[160]

The West Village Committee's demand to shelve the project was nonetheless ignored by the City Planning Commission, who maintained that the eight-block section of the study area east of Washington Street "would seem particularly desirable" for renewal. The commission also suggested that a section west of Washington Street be "decked over" in order "to foster the residential extension of the Village westward, and to protect and encourage the private rehabilitation which has already taken place in the area in recent years."[161] James Felt, the commission chairman, announced the recommendation on April 30 as part of a renewal program encompassing eighteen city sites and the citywide construction of 20,000 to 22,000 housing units in areas of low population density.[162] In an effort to distinguish the commission's "slum clearance" methods from those of Robert Moses, Felt's proposal called for mandatory hearings and increased public participation in the designation, survey and planning of potential renewal areas. The *New York Times* welcomed what it saw as a positive shift in renewal policy with a commentary that no doubt referred to the West Village:

> It would take some of the political heat out of urban rebuilding if the public could be brought to understand one thing: the designation of an area for study does not automatically set it aside as an area that will be leveled off and rebuilt, either in its entirety or even in part. If people immediately mobilize, with all apparatus of demonstration and vilification, when even an area is mentioned for study—protesting and refusing all possible change for the better without even knowing what may later be decided upon—there is no hope for a better way.[163]

But the hostility and protest of West Village residents continued unabated.[164] Responding to the *Times* commentary, community activist Rachele Wall pointed out the distinction made in the general municipal law between conservation renewal and clearance renewal: "Such unblighted areas as West Greenwich Village are under Section 10—clearance renewal," she wrote in a letter to the editors. "There are only nineteen acres in the fourteen-block village area, but the commission states there are twenty-four. To their way of thinking this is correct—there are twenty-four if you throw the blocks together and tear out the streets—and the houses on them, of course."[165] The journalist Mel Most, writing in the *Village Voice*, lashed out against developers and the city: "The whole concept of Greenwich Village is that it consists of houses and not housing. . . . We don't want houses in uniform there. Get out—you're not wanted. We're getting mad enough to picket your housing, write on the walls, insult the tenants, boycott your shops. We're all heartsick and fed up at the conquest of Greenwich Village by every economic interest that comes along and sees a desirable prize."[166]

As late as August 1961, only one month before the mayoral primaries, Mayor Wagner still supported a renewal program that would conform, as he put it, to "Village tradition."[167] But by mid-August enraged Village residents had one last great hope of putting an end to the study before it could begin: State Controller Arthur Levitt, Wagner's opponent for the Democratic nomination for mayor, turned the controversy into a key campaign issue, claiming during a tour of the West Village that the mayor had "invented a make-believe slum here" and that if elected he would drop the proposed renewal study. Levitt told the press: "I will not permit this area to be bulldozed and replaced with a vertical ant-hill in the form of a massive Title I project."[168] As his chief supporter, Tammany Hall leader Carmine DeSapio put it, "there are vast slums where redevelopment is needed, but Greenwich Village is not a slum area."[169]

The politically astute mayor, who was the first to call the area "blighted," did the expedient thing and withdrew support for the project, claiming that he was "deeply concerned and sympathetic with the people of the West Village neighborhood in their desire to conserve and to build constructively upon a neighborhood life which is an example of city community life at its finest."[170] Wagner urged the City Planning Commission to scrap the project and to include a greater section of Greenwich Village in the broader three-year, citywide renewal study that had been proposed a year earlier. But in its public hearing at City Hall on October 18, 1961, less than one month before elections, the City Planning Commission, emphasizing that the request of the mayor "does not destroy the independence of the commission," released an alarming twenty-nine-page report that described the West Village as "appropriate for urban renewal," "characterized by blight" and, worst of all, "suitable for clearance, replanning, reconstruction or rehabilitation."[171] The reaction was a near riot. As Edith Evans Asbury, writing for the *New York Times*, described it:

> The villagers, led by Mrs. Jane Jacobs . . . leaped from their seats and rushed forward. They shouted that a "deal" had been made with a private builder, that the Mayor had been "double-crossed" and that the commission's action was illegal. James Felt sought vainly to restore order by pounding his gavel. Then he called on the police to remove the unruly from the room. Despite that, the shouted protests increased. Mr. Felt then called a recess, sent for more police and left the room. . . . The villagers remained in their seats, chanting "Down with Felt!" until the meeting resumed nearly an hour later. They began shouting their accusations again as the commission secretary resumed the reading of the calendar. Policemen escorted several from the room and carried one man out feet first.[172]

Louis DeSalvio, an assemblyman speaking on behalf of the protesting Villagers, called the action a "reprehensible and strange decision" and declared that the commission had "sent the Urban Renewal Program of this city, state and Federal Government back to the dark ages of Robert Moses and his arbitrary and inhuman procedures."[173]

Jane Jacobs, fiercely determined to have the last word on the fate of her neighborhood, offered the following day an architect's résumé dated October 1960—five months before Mayor Wagner proposed that the area be studied for possible renewal—as proof positive that the private interests of a developer had dictated the City Planning Commission's continued support for the project. It said: "as consultant to Rose Associates Urban Renewal Dept. . . . I prepared sketch plans and perspectives for three large development areas" including "a renewal plan for West Greenwich Village."[174] David Rose, president of Rose Associates, told the *New York Times* that his firm "has never been and will not be interested in this project in any way" and that although the architect had "made sketches for some of the pipe dreams the boys had," he had "definitely not drawn any West Village sketches."[175] The architect, Barry Benepe, scoffed at the allegation as well, claiming not only that the project was merely a freelance assignment, paid for personally by Roger Schafer, Rose Associates' director of urban renewal, and executed for Schafer's own personal interest, but that the date on the résumé should have read October 1961.[176] Nonetheless, according to a later report, the plan included three fourteen-story and one twenty-one-story high-rise towers as well as low-rise units.[177]

Jacobs also alleged that the Neighbors Committee, a group that supported the proposed study, was just another "puppet" organization, in this case invented by Rose Associates to create the appearance of grass-roots support for renewal. James Kirk, the group's president and former president of the Greenwich Village Association, spoke out both to deny that he had ever heard of Rose Associates and to defend his backing of the study: "For the past ten years, dock workers, truckmen, longshoremen

and people like that who lived in the Village near their pier work have had to move away because of evictions. Their buildings were torn down to make way for new luxury-apartment buildings, or they were converted into smaller apartments which are too expensive and not large enough for their families."[178] Kirk, a resident of Stuyvesant Town (see chapter 5), the product of one of the city's largest slum-clearance efforts, told the *Village Voice*: "After living sixty two years in Village dumps, and then to be told that Stuyvesant Town is no good—that it is a jail—is nonsense. Believe me, I wish the poor people in the West Village could have something as good."[179]

On October 24, 1961, the Housing and Redevelopment Board announced that they would drop the project. "So far, so good," said a pleased but not fully satisfied Jacobs: "But this is incomplete. The next step is for the Planning Commission to remove the slum label from our area. We must judge the city's good faith by whether it proceeds to this next step."[180] The decision was not taken lightly by some city officials, particularly City Housing Authority Commissioner Ira S. Robbins, who described the West Villagers opposing the study as "ignorant, neurotic, dishonest, slanderous, disorderly and disgusting," and their efforts as "one of the oldest violations of the democratic process known to man—the attack of a collection of skillfully organized groups and or unorganized individuals who are misled and inflamed by emotional and calculated misrepresentations of the functions, powers, and goals of the Planning Commission."[181] Only one month later Felt expressed on television hopes of reviving the project, though he promptly abandoned the idea.[182] In accord with Mayor Wagner's decision, he agreed instead to remove the West Village from the city's slum-clearance map. As Felt put it, "it will serve no purpose to prolong this situation."[183]

In 1963 Jacobs and her committee came forward with their own plan for middle-income cooperative housing, designed by Perkins & Will to embody, as the West Village Committee put it, "a public example, a practical means of adding harmonious planned housing *into* an existing community without sacrifice of the people already there."[184] According to the committee, their plan would create housing for 1,300 people in 475 new apartments without residential demolition and relocation. The new buildings would occupy seven parcels of vacant land along the west side of Washington Street between Morton and Bank streets, where most of the overhead spur of the New York Central Railroad had recently been demolished. The apartments would overlook the public streets and interior mewslike courtyards. Some street frontage would be reserved for shops, and car parking would be provided in a central garage to be built under a narrow, block-long public park that paralleled Washington Street between Charles and West Tenth streets. Most important, the buildings would be appropriately low-scaled five-story walk-ups with fireplaces, exposed brick walls and flexible layouts throughout. "People will have a lot of leeway to fix the apartments the way they want," said Jacobs, who went on to moralize: "We don't believe in running people's lives."[185]

The press was enthusiastic about what seemed to be a harbinger of a new age in urban planning. The editors of *Progressive Architecture* lauded the plan: "Many aspects of the proposal are refreshing—not the least of these is the determination of a neighborhood to have a say in its own future; and the care with which the plan balances the appropriate with the feasible."[186] But for many of the observers who had supported the study proposed by Mayor Wagner two years earlier, praise was mixed with resentment. As James Kirk wrote to the editors of the *Village Voice*:

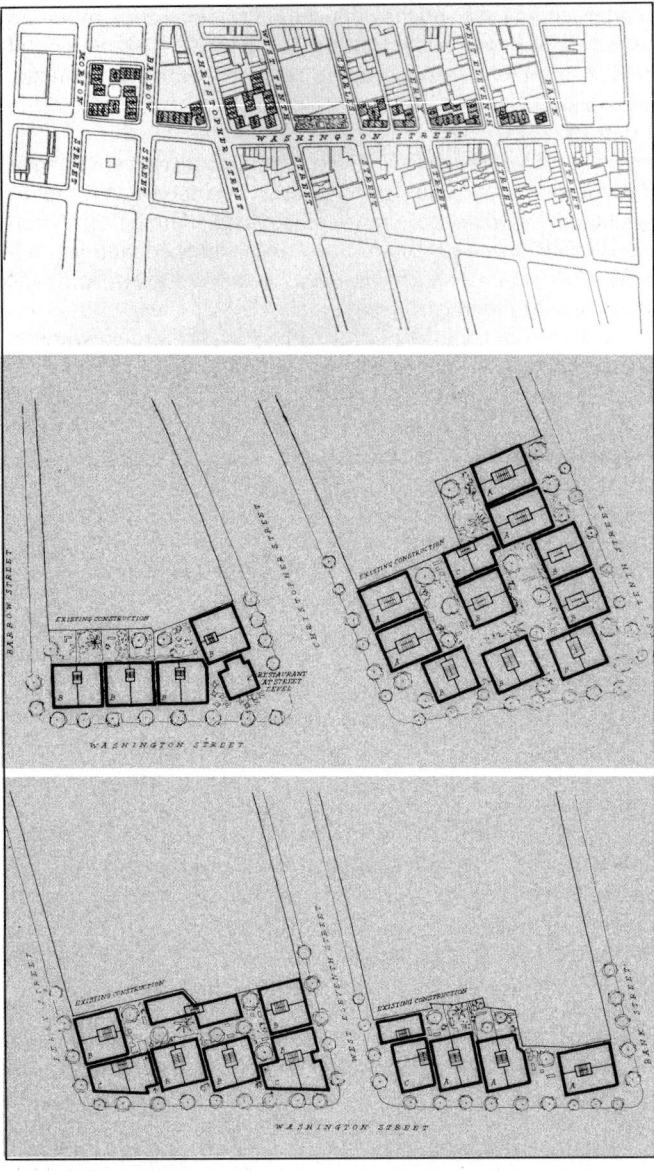

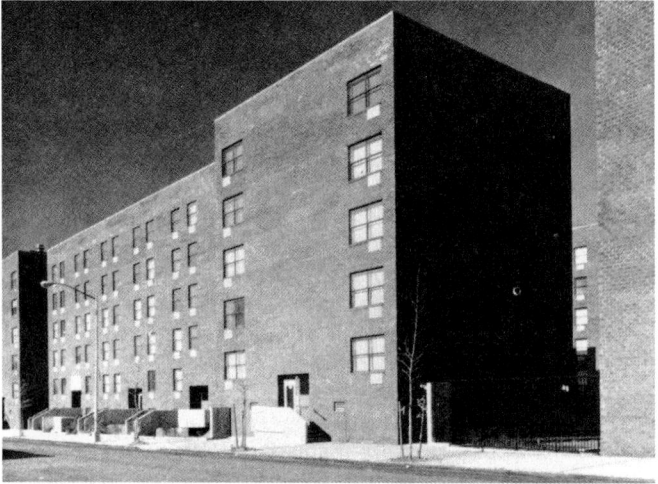

Top: Proposed West Village Houses, west side of Washington Street, Morton to Bank Street. Perkins & Will, 1963. Three site plans. PA. CU

Bottom: West Village Houses, west side of Washington Street, Morton to Bank Street. Perkins & Will, 1974. View to the northwest. Lieberman. PA. CU

In 1961, at the time we were supporting the proposed study to help clean up the miserable rat-infested slums of the West Village, Mrs. Jacobs fought and said there were no slums in "her" beautiful neighborhood, and that nothing was wrong with it that the people couldn't take care of themselves. Now, suddenly, she claims that for more than two years she has been trying to "enforce the laws against violations and illegal conditions" in the West Village, which the Study she fought against would have healed.[187]

The city did its best to bury Jacobs's plan. The City Planning Commission moved very slowly in processing the committee's applications, which would lead to the securing of a Mitchell-Lama loan, and stalled on necessary approvals. But the West Village Committee maintained a tenacious faith in its plan. When Samuel Ratensky was temporarily leading the Housing and Redevelopment Board, the scheme at last began to be moved along. The momentum built under Jason Nathan, Lindsay's housing administrator, who pushed the project forward beginning in late 1966, although the technicians kept picking away. Still no real progress was made, and in late 1967 rumors of the developer William Zeckendorf's interest in the site surfaced. At first the community dismissed the possibility; because Zeckendorf's financial empire had collapsed and he was at the time a defendant in a $50 million damage suit, charged with having mismanaged his assets, the prospect of his financing a major project struck many observers as preposterous. Nonetheless, Zeckendorf was still a formidable force in the development community, and when it became known that he had bought properties on twelve different blocks in the West Village, including the vacant strip along Washington Street intended for the new housing, and publicly called the area a "slum," the community began to take the rumors seriously.[188] Moreover, Zeckendorf, who would later characterize the West Village plan as "the triumph of eggheadedness," claimed to have the city's support for a bulldozer-driven reconstruction of the area funded with the proceeds of tax-exempt municipal bonds.[189]

The General Properties Corporation, a real estate concern that was organized by Zeckendorf, together with his son and son-in-law, but that the legally entangled Zeckendorf served officially only as a consultant, commissioned the architect Richard Meier to design an extensive residential development to be located along West Street south of Bank Street.[190] The project was to be financed by the widow of Robert Young and named after the late railroad millionaire. Meier's 1969 design called for high-rise buildings facing the river and low-rise units to the east that would relate in scale to the surrounding context. A mid-block park between West and Washington streets would extend southward the open space that Meier had just created at the Westbeth housing complex (see below). The Robert R. Young Housing was never realized; in 1984 Meier would somewhat simplistically state, "Unfortunately, local interest groups pressured the city to develop the site in another way, without any idea of its potential uniqueness."[191]

In January 1968 the city, through its Housing and Development Administration spokesman Woody Klein, strongly announced that the community-supported plan would be realized, although given Meier's developing plans, the announcement was perhaps premature. Klein acknowledged that the community's fears regarding the large-scale development, which had previously gone officially unrecognized, had been well founded, but that those fears should be put aside: "The Zeckendorf plan is dead. Forget about it. The administrator [Jason Nathan] has authorized me to state that he approves the West Village Housing

Plan in principle and looks forward to working out the details."[192] The approval came, as *Architectural Forum* later reported, despite the objections of Nathan's staff.[193]

In January 1969 the West Village housing plan was crystallized and ready for submission to the City Planning Commission in the next month. The plan was a landmark in a process that Jacobs had described as "unslumming," whereby a neighborhood was improved without cataclysmic changes and without such large expenditures of money that only high rentals could be charged for the new product. The plan was, as Mary Perot Nichols put it, "revolutionary in its modesty,"[194] a realization of the West Village Committee's rallying cry that "not a sparrow shall be moved."[195] The projected cost for the 457 new apartments to be provided was $8.5 million—compared to the $30 million price tag estimated for 300 units in a previous tower-in-the-park scheme. Perkins & Will's design called for forty-two five- and six-story buildings on a series of open lots, currently used for trucking, strung in an irregular pattern along Washington Street. Just north, Westbeth, which had been a key parcel in the Zeckendorf plan but was now being converted into artists' housing (see below), complemented the West Village plan. A diner at the southwest corner of Christopher and Washington streets was to be torn down to make way for a plaza, and a small shopping center was planned for a site next to Charles Lane, in addition to small stores scattered throughout the development intended to be run on a mom-and-pop basis.

Perkins & Will attempted to give the essentially modest brick buildings some personality by varying the shapes of the rooftops, which would also be exploited as cathedral ceilings in the designs for the upper units. Another innovative feature was to be a system of interchangeable rooms, whereby neighboring residents could buy or sell extra bedrooms as their family requirements evolved. This strategy, a dream of architects in New York at least since Howe & Lescaze proposed it for their Chrystie-Forsyth Street project (1932), was as troubling to officialdom in the 1960s as it had been in the 1930s.[196]

West Village Houses was the premiere exemplar of another cherished dream, that of an urban community working with its own architects to solve a housing problem. As Ray Matz, the designer/project manager for Perkins & Will, put it, "usually the architect is ahead of his clients. Here we were perfectly tuned in because they were able to articulate their feelings about the neighborhood and the kind of thing they wanted to preserve."[197] Nonetheless, city officials voiced several objections to the plan that were valid and could not be easily dismissed as bureaucratic harassment. For one thing, the nonfireproof construction chosen, a type usually confined to the outer boroughs, would reduce costs but was considered unsafe. In addition, many officials questioned the wisdom of using public funds to condemn land for Mitchell-Lama apartments; burdening a housing project with public spaces that would no doubt require special attention and incur unusual maintenance costs; and building and operating a wide scattering of five-story walk-ups. To the last concern the West Village Committee responded that "it is extremely marketable to Villagers by whom walking upstairs is considered a sound and healthy diversion."[198] *Housing and Planning News* pointed out the plan's key drawback: "If the Committee is correct, the project would be a delightful bit of variety in the Mitchell-Lama program; if it is wrong, and costs run out of hand, the City, alas, will be alone on the risk."[199]

The project continued to drag on. As late as October 8, 1969, the City Planning Commission refused to act on the plan, preventing its consideration by the Board of Estimate, where it faced its critical test and the opposition of a number of important real estate professionals including Zeckendorf.[200] At the end of 1969 the project was at last approved by the Board of Estimate, but soaring costs required a second vote by the board in 1972. Construction began soon after.

When after eleven years West Village Houses were opened to residents in 1974, economic inflation and the years of political and bureaucratic foot-dragging had resulted in the escalation of costs to $25 million. Worse still, New York's economic vitality was nearing a low ebb and the demand for housing was weak. In order to save on construction costs many of the "extras" planned by Perkins & Will had been sacrificed: mansard-style roofs, floor-to-ceiling sliding windows with balcony rails, exposed-concrete floor slabs and, as the project neared completion, even landscaping. Sales of the units moved very slowly during the summer of 1974, warming the hearts of "I-told-you-so's."[201] Unit costs were cited as a reason for the lack of buyer interest, as was the project's controversial walk-up design. But, as Joseph P. Fried pointed out in the *New York Times*, other, more conventional city projects such as Washington Plaza and Manhattan Plaza were experiencing similar difficulties.[202] So poor was the overall marketing process that prospective tenants' deposits were refunded. By the summer of 1975 West Village Houses was in serious financial trouble, and the buildings were totally vacant. Roger Starr, Housing and Development Administrator, soon foreclosed on the property and converted the apartments to rentals priced according to what the market would bear.[203]

As a result, the buildings were soon inhabited: the *New York Times* reported in August 1976 that apartments in West Village Houses were renting at an average of twenty per week with fewer than fifty units remaining.[204] City officialdom tended to regard the project as the greatest failure in the history of the middle-income housing program, but in 1976 Suzanne Stephens offered a more objective interpretation of its significance:

> West Village Houses played a historic role, for it paved the way toward current housing and urban planning thinking. . . . If it faltered along the way, the problem was less with the concept than with the not fully acknowledged gaps in client-sponsor-builder equation. But these difficulties were also due in large part to the players' being caught in a historical moment that created irreconcilable conflicts. The West Village Houses is still a pawn in a larger game; only now economic issues have replaced housing ones. It still stands as a metaphor for unresolved housing questions that confronted us in the 1960s and continue to confront us in the 1970s.[205]

If, as Stephens contended, the West Village Houses reflected unanswered questions regarding housing, then Westbeth (Richard Meier & Associates, 1969), an artists' housing complex located at the western edge of the Village, indicated that creative solutions to the city's housing problems could indeed be envisioned and achieved with a modicum of frustration and disappointment.[206] In 1967 the laboratory complex at 463 West Street that the Bell Telephone Company had abandoned for greener pastures in New Jersey was purchased for $2.5 million by the West-Beth Corporation, a joint consortium of the J. M. Kaplan Fund and the National Council for the Arts. The intention for the project was to renovate the building for artists' housing, related gallery space and performance spaces for dancers and theatrical facilities for filmmakers and theater people. Ambitions were high when Richard Meier was commissioned to design the renovation. The 725,000-square-foot complex, some

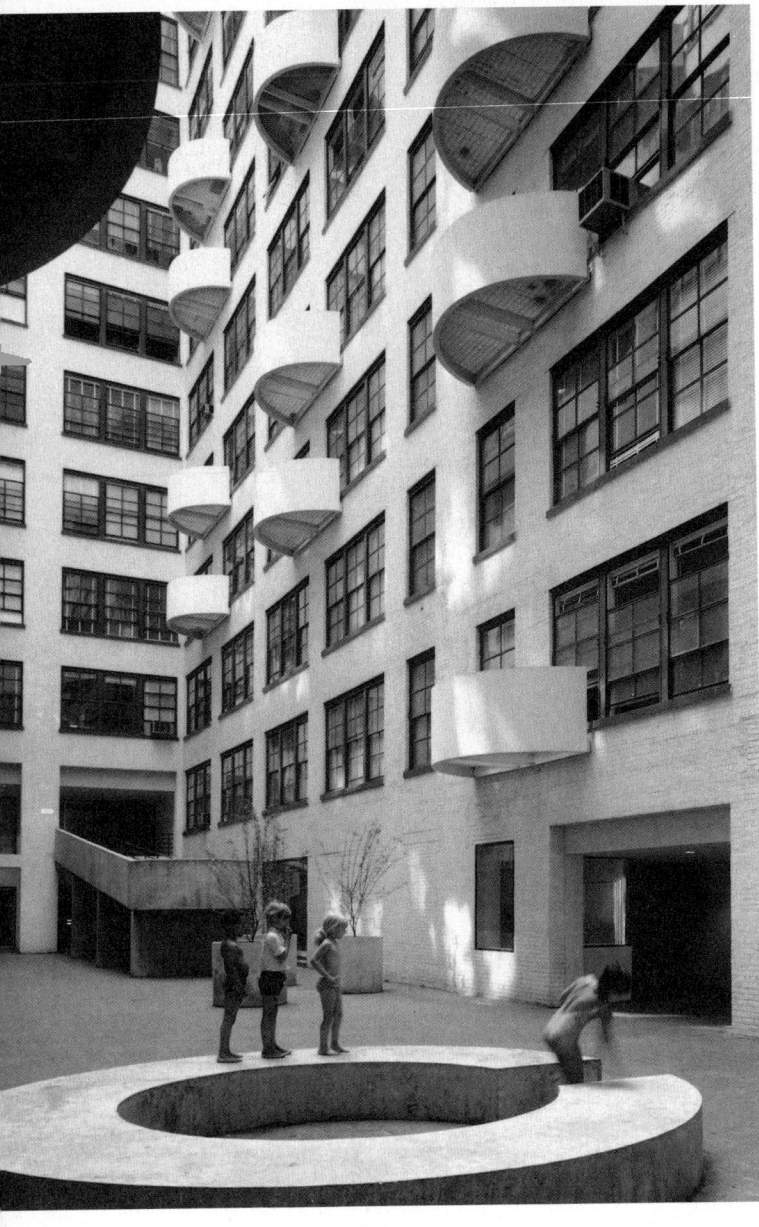

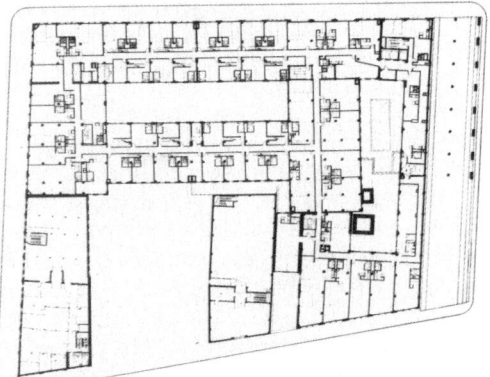

Top: Westbeth, Washington to West Street, Bank to Bethune Street. Formerly Bell Telephone Laboratories (Cyrus L. W. Eidlitz, 1900), renovated by Richard Meier, 1969. Interior courtyard. Stoller. ©ESTO

Bottom: Westbeth. Typical floor plan. RM

Right: Westbeth. Interior courtyard. Stoller. ©ESTO

of which had originally housed the Western Electric Company, dated back to 1900 (Cyrus L. W. Eidlitz)[207] and comprised the entire block bounded by West, Bank, Washington and Bethune streets. It consisted of a group of interconnected buildings ranging in height from three to thirteen stories, with an easement running along the Washington Street side allowing for the elevated tracks of the New York Central Railroad to run through the building. Before the Bell Labs had decamped for the suburbs, the facility and its scientists had given birth to the first talking movies, the first television and the first transistor.

The complex, originally projected to be called the National Artists' Center, was by the time of its completion in 1969 known as Westbeth, after two of the surrounding streets, West and Bethune. Westbeth was the largest residential rehabilitation project ever undertaken in the United States, as well as the largest artist community in the world and the only such community in the United States. In order to make residential use of the previously industrial complex possible, the City Planning Commission was forced to create its first special zoning district, a concept later applied to much larger areas including the theater district and the Lincoln Center area. Westbeth also benefited from a municipal tax abatement. The buildings not only had a distinguished history but seemed well suited to their new function, with high ceilings and generously proportioned, evenly spaced windows. Richard Meier's design was inspired by Le Corbusier's Unité d'Habitation at Marseilles, which combined living and working spaces, shopping and public services to create a vertically integrated, reasonably self-sufficient community. The unit planning was inventive, with ninety-six floor-through duplexes. There were high hopes as well for retail stores tailored to artists' needs, for performance spaces and for specialized studios for sculptors, printmakers and the like.

Meier's task was difficult, given the comparatively limited funds to create affordable apartments and at the same time ameliorate the somewhat grim superscale of the complex. His strategy consisted of removing two floors within the building's central well to form a tall, narrow courtyard open to the sky. The sheer walls surrounding the courtyard were modulated by delicately detailed curved steel balconies painted white, which provided secondary egress from the apartments. Meier was able to carve out 383 apartments ranging from 700-square-foot efficiency units to 1,300-square-foot family units. Only the bathroom and kitchen were fixed in place, permitting the occupants to fit out their space according to their own needs, thereby bringing to a planned community the flexibility of unstructured loft living.

Despite the best intentions of Meier and the sponsors, however, conflicts arose almost immediately. The root of the problem lay in the fact that though the West-Beth Corporation bought the building and administered its renovation, the actual funding for construction came from the Federal Housing Authority (FHA), which viewed it as a middle-income housing project. The FHA funding helped keep rents down, but it brought with it a host of constraints that flew in the face of the flexible interiors most artists wanted. Another important element affecting the organization of the Westbeth project was the decision to include "non-visual" as well as "visual" artists. While the sponsors saw this as a positive step against homogeneity within the Westbeth community, the visual artists saw it as a waste of precious resources on artists who did not have specialized space needs for their residences. Although Meier worked miracles in dealing with the bureaucracy, in the final analysis the units in most cases were too small for visual artists to work in and carry

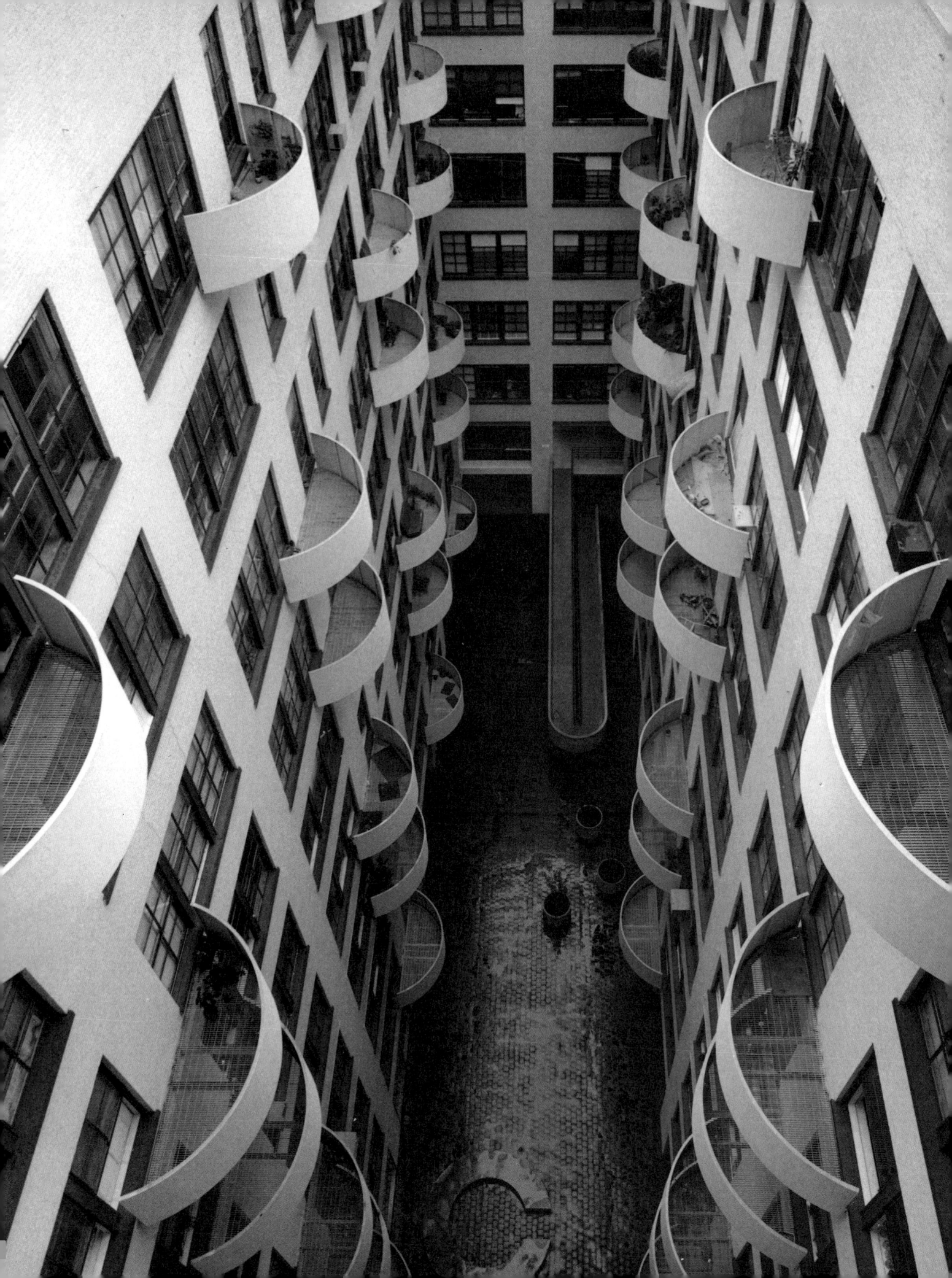

on a routine domestic life. It was mostly the painters and sculptors who were unhappy, partly because they felt their entitlement had been usurped by other artists, partly because the units were too small for them.

By 1972 tensions between the residents and the management had developed into a state of full-blown hostility. The Kaplan Fund, which had never intended to do more than provide seed money and the organization to see the project through construction, wanted to withdraw from the project and turn it over to its residents. But as the art critic Barbara Rose put it: "The concept that Westbeth could ever be self-supporting was naïve to begin with, but when the commercial space on the ground floor, designed to bring in additional revenue to be used for paying off the mortgage, could not be rented, it became clear that the project was in real trouble."[208] Some tenants held the Kaplan Fund to blame for this, claiming that they had not properly finished the commercial space, so that it could never attract storekeepers. One commercial tenant, Jacques Mourlot, the son of the celebrated French lithographer, did set up a shop in Westbeth, but was forced to return to France in 1972 after being evicted for nonpayment of the rent. Similarly, the Theater for the New City was unable to meet its financial commitments. In 1972, while seeking to distance itself from Westbeth, the Kaplan Fund, acting with Westbeth's board of representatives, imposed a 17.5 percent increase in rent to cover expenses. A rent strike ensued, spurring a move to make Westbeth a cooperative.

Though financial problems had in large measure transformed the dream into a nightmare, Westbeth continued in its original function of providing reasonably affordable work and living spaces for artists. It also stood as a pioneering example in the adaptive reuse of architecturally and urbanistically significant buildings. Despite its shortcomings, by 1979 Paul Goldberger could accurately write that Westbeth was a "distinguished relic by now . . . the spiritual father of all the commercial loft conversions that have created a whole new housing type for Lower Manhattan in the last decade."[209]

East Village

By the 1960s the transformation of Greenwich Village was so extensive that many of the area's most bohemian, least-well-heeled residents, displaced by "young, snap-brimmed men carrying attaché cases," as the journalist Eli Waldron put it, had migrated east of Broadway.[210] That exodus led to a new name, the East Village, for part of what had traditionally been considered the Lower East Side. At the beginning of the twentieth century the area, particularly the neighborhood between Third Avenue and Avenue A, was known as "Little Germany"; it later became a center of activity for Yiddish theater as well as home to a thriving Ukrainian-American community. In 1956 the destruction of the Third Avenue Elevated dramatically opened the area to redevelopment. Edmond J. Bartnett, writing in the *New York Times* in 1960, said that as a result of the demolition, "this area is gradually becoming recognized as an extension of Greenwich Village. Village guide books now include East Side high spots as Village territory—thereby extending New York's Bohemia river to river. . . . Although there is no real concentration of Village atmosphere at this time, there are scattered islands of Bohemia. Artists and students—even beatniks—are taking up new living quarters in a spotty pattern."[211] The transformation of the formerly run-down area into an increasingly chic artistic quarter was not without its ironies. As Bernard Weinraub noted in the

New York Times in 1963: "One of the more curious results of the influx of students and young persons is the fact that many of their immigrant parents once lived in the area, and then moved uptown or to the Bronx or Brooklyn."[212] By the end of the 1960s the Village's self-proclaimed bohemians were followed by "hippies" who were drawn to the East Village not only from around the city and its suburbs but from across the nation.[213] Along with the hippies, an increasing number of blacks and Puerto Ricans came to the East Village, transforming it into an extremely heterogeneous area, albeit one rife with social and racial tensions.

Though postwar changes in the East Village were more societal and commercial than strictly architectural, the area was nonetheless the site of large-scale planning proposals as well as some building activity. In 1956 the venerable, ninety-seven-year-old, tuition-free Cooper Union for Advancement of Science and Art embarked on an extensive building program, adding to the swift changes that were reverberating throughout the East Village.[214] As announced in 1957, the first building to be planned as part of the newly expanded Cooper Union was to house the School of Engineering. Designed by Harrison & Abramovitz, with Esmond Shaw, the head of Cooper Union's department of architecture, serving as associate, the building was to occupy the full block bounded by Third and Fourth avenues, Astor Place and Ninth Street and consist of three distinct but connected elements: along Fourth Avenue, a narrow, eight-story, glass-and-metal slab terminating in short, windowless, masonry walls and partially raised two stories above ground level on pilotis; along Ninth Street, a similarly articulated six-story slab; and projecting south from the lower slab, a two-story, wedge-shaped, masonry-clad pavilion housing two 160-seat lecture halls. The remainder of the site was to be left open and landscaped.

Harrison & Abramovitz's scheme would have provided New York with an early example of Le Corbusier–inspired Modernist architecture and urbanism. As realized in 1961 with a new design by the firm of Voorhees, Walker, Smith, Smith & Haines, the building was far less elegant and no more urbanistically sensitive to the surrounding urban fabric, which incorporated such architecturally significant buildings as the Cooper Union Foundation Building (Frederick A. Peterson, 1859) and Grace Church (James Renwick, Jr., 1845). The new engineering building, clad in buff brick and trimmed in stone, was five stories high along Fourth Avenue and six stories high along Ninth Street; both wings incorporated vertical strips of windows. A one-story projection containing the building's principal entrance partially filled in the intersection of the two wings, while covered walkways parallel to but set back from St. Mark's Place and Third Avenue helped to define a courtyard.

In 1963 Cooper Union revealed plans for further expansion, proposing that a classroom building, a library, a gymnasium and a student-faculty social center be built on the east side of Third Avenue between Seventh and Ninth streets. Though no specific plans were released, the school's administration announced that the buildings would not exceed five stories and would be set amid plazas. The plan immediately elicited protest from the community, including the management of McSorley's Old Ale House, at 15 East Seventh Street, a 109-year-old, all-male bastion of drinking and camaraderie that would have been demolished to make way for the proposed facilities.[215] The controversial plan was never realized. In 1967 plans were released for a six-story building to house many of the previously proposed facilities.[216] To be located on a trapezoidal site bounded on the west by Lafayette Street, on the north by Astor Place and

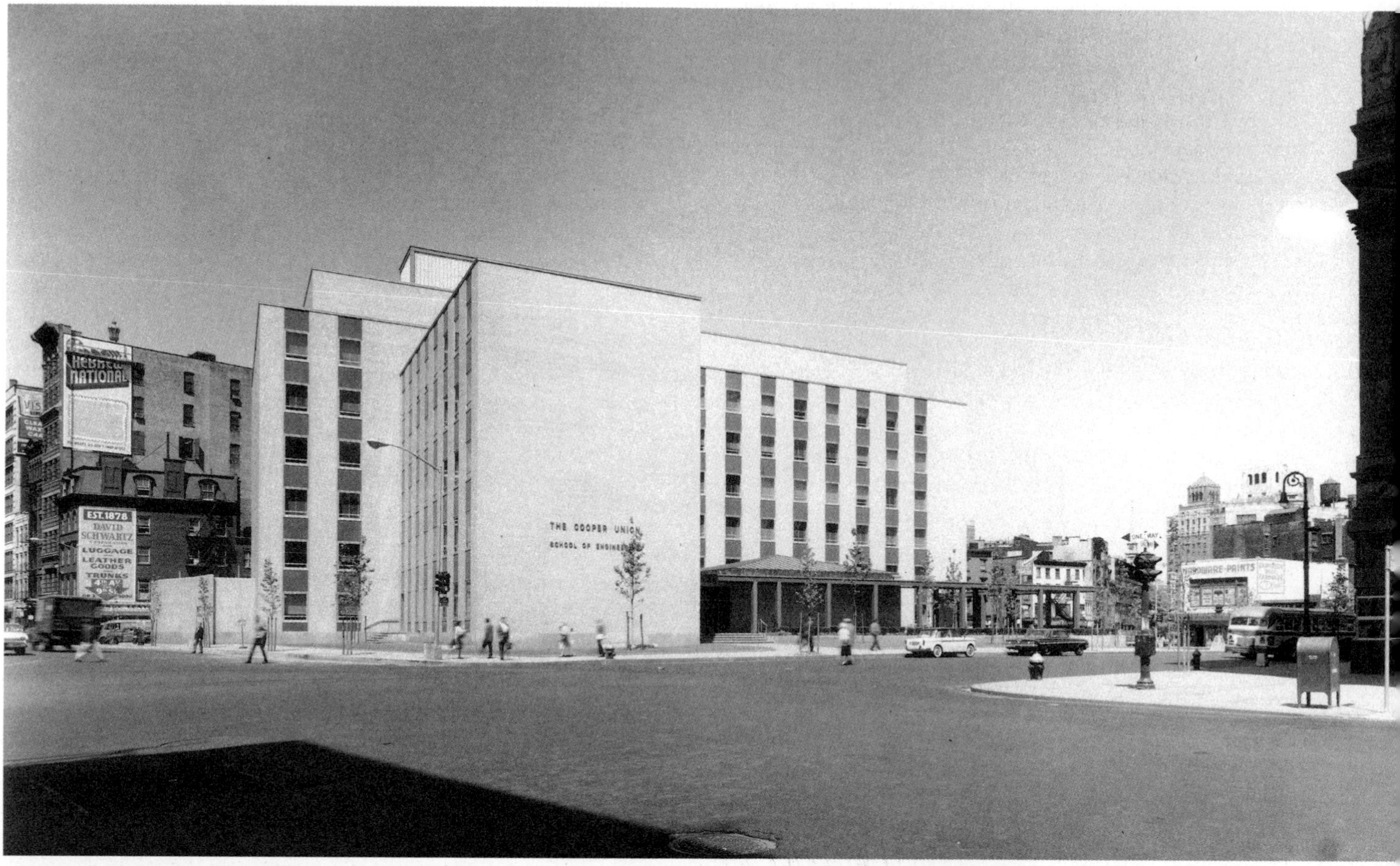

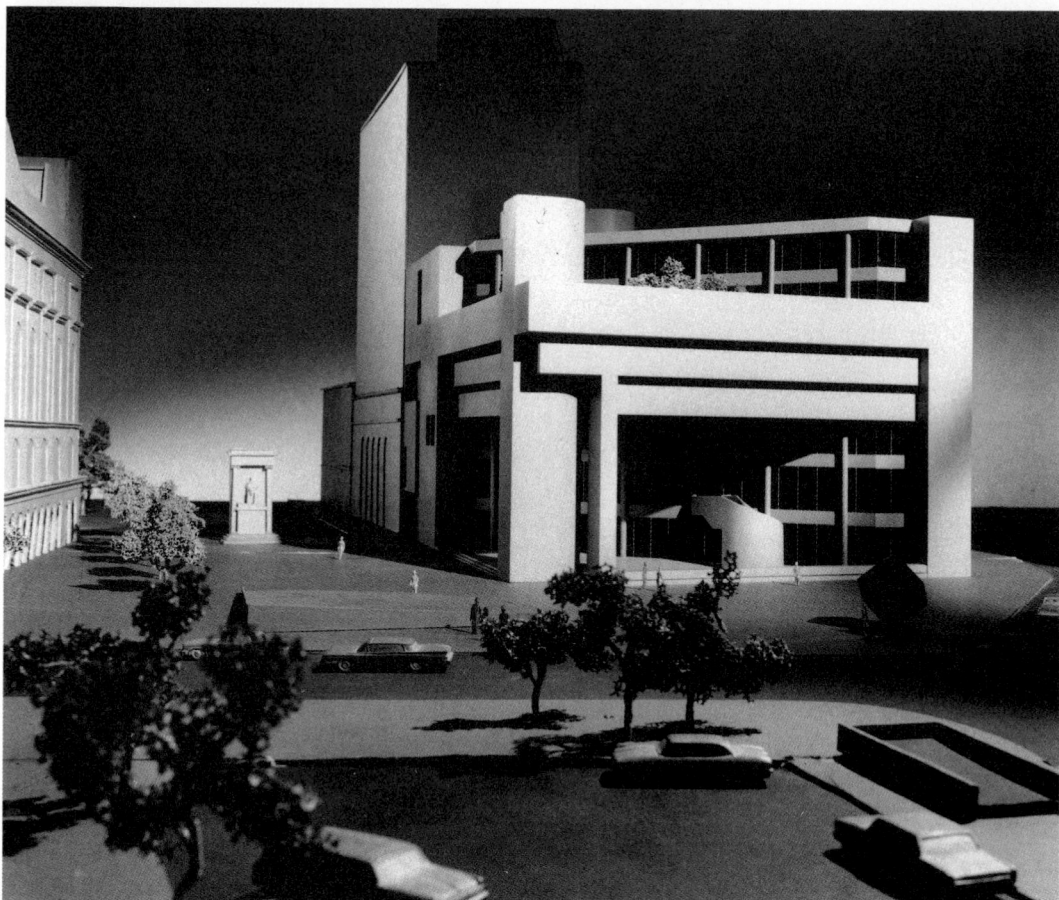

Above: Cooper Union
School of Engineering,
Third to Fourth Avenue,
Astor Place to East Ninth
Street. Voorhees, Walker,
Smith, Smith & Haines,
1961. View to the north.
HLW

Left: Proposed Cooper
Union building, south side
of Astor Place, Lafayette
Street to proposed plaza
over Fourth Avenue. Ulrich
Franzen, 1967. Model.
View to the south.
Freedman. UF

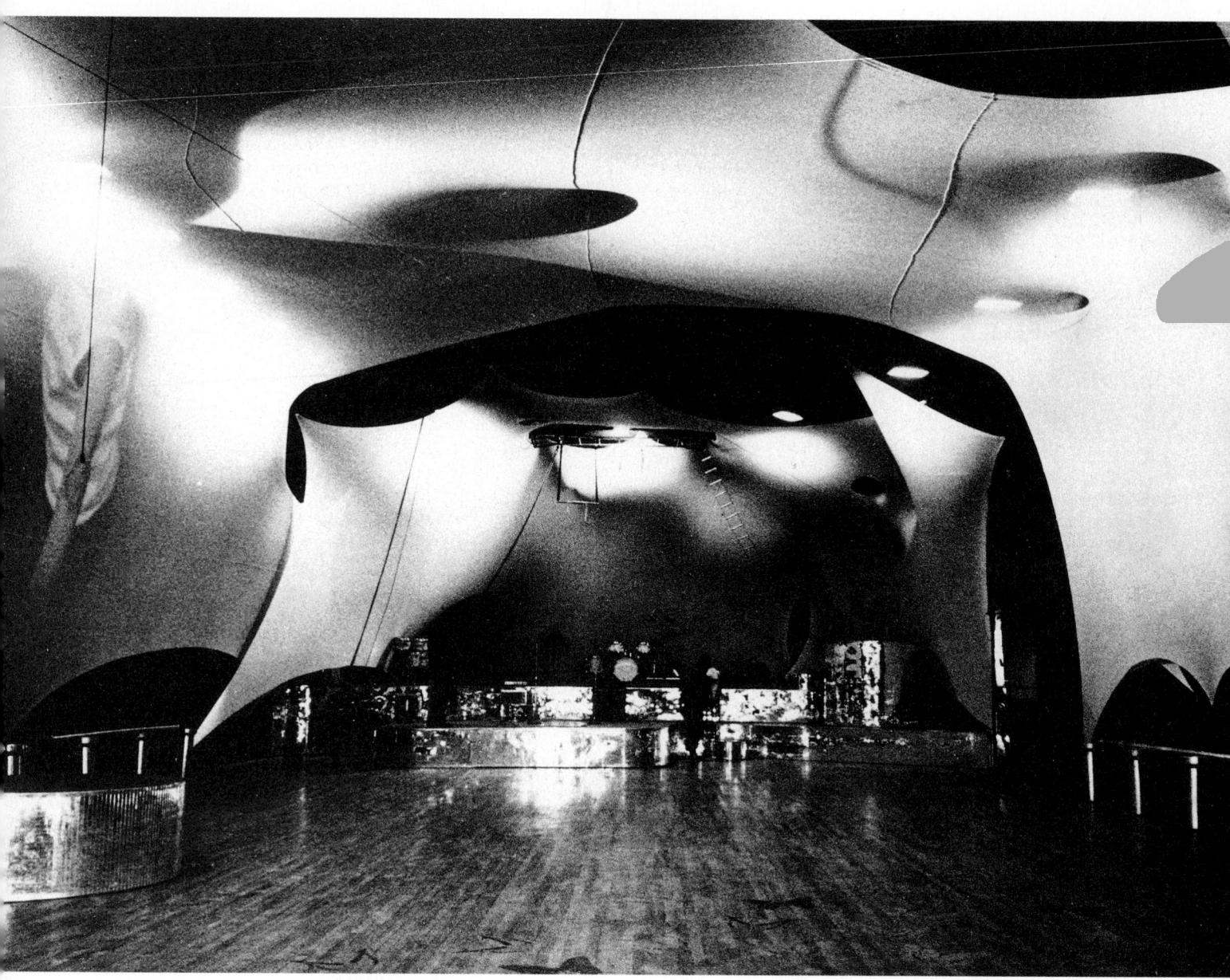

Electric Circus, 23 St. Mark's Place, between Second and Third
avenues. Chermayeff & Geismar, 1967. Dance floor. CG

on the east by Fourth Avenue, this building was designed by the architect Ulrich Franzen, who proposed to link it with the flanking buildings to create a campus setting, although a rather constricted one. To the west, an elevated pedestrian plaza would cross Lafayette Street, connecting to the brick-and-cast-iron Astor Place Building (Griffith Thomas, 1876), partially occupied by the school; and to the east, Fourth Avenue would tunnel beneath a new plaza fronting the school's Foundation Building and incorporating Augustus Saint-Gaudens's monument to Peter Cooper (1894), which was to be moved from Cooper Square.[217]

The massive, six-story building, though starkly abstract in its vocabulary, reflected contextual concerns not only in its height, scale and physical linkages but also in its complex massing and intricate geometry, which incorporated both the dominant orthogonal street grid and the diagonal axis defined by Astor Place. The proposed building's principal facade was aligned with the grid, while the remaining triangular portion of the site was utilized as a three-story entrance court, sheltered by a two-story projection that was held up, in part, by an imposing structural support marking the site's northeastern corner. The courtyard was to be punctuated by an exterior spiral staircase leading to the building's second floor. The sophisticated, boldly sculptural building was never realized.

Though Cooper Union failed to establish a spatially or stylistically coherent campus, in 1976 it enhanced its existing architectural fabric by realizing an innovative renovation of its Foundation Building (see chapter 16). Nine years earlier the Park Department had made a minor gesture toward creating a sense of place at the institution's front door when it erected *Alamo*, a sculpture by Bernard (Tony) Rosenthal, on the triangular traffic island northwest of the Foundation Building.[218] Originally exhibited as part of the Park Department's "Sculpture in Environment" series, held at various sites throughout the city during the fall of 1967, the minimalist, black-painted steel sculpture, which later became a permanent feature of Astor Place, consisted of a cube pivoting on one point. A participatory artwork, it could easily be rotated by passing pedestrians. The art historian and critic Sam Hunter observed that neighborhood youths "descended on it in droves, gayly straining, pushing and shoving against its ponderous bulk. . . . At times, weary of the pushing routine, young people simply collected at the platform base and fraternized in a subdued manner, converting the sculpture box's steep sloping side into a windbreak and retreat."[219]

The year 1956 saw not only the initiation of Cooper Union's expansion, but the proposal, issued by Robert Moses's Slum Clearance Committee, for a major Title I project to be undertaken in the East Village.[220] The plan called for the wholesale destruction and rebuilding of a 21.5-acre area bounded on the south by East Houston Street, on the west by the Bowery, on the north by St. Mark's Place and on the east by Second Avenue. Several months after the plan was initially announced in April 1956, an additional 8.5 acres extending south from East Houston Street to Delancey Street between the Bowery and Christie Street was slated for redevelopment.[221] Under the amended plan, 2,400 tenants, 450 residents of single-room-occupancy dwellings and 4,000 homeless men utilizing shelters, along with more than 500 businesses, were to be displaced by the construction of 2,900 middle-income apartments as well as industrial facilities.

The plan was controversial from the first. Community opposition focused on the problems of relocating both tenants and the area's large homeless population.[222] In 1960, in response to the protest, the newly established Housing and Redevelopment Board shelved the plan. The following year the Independent Cooperators Committee for the Renewal of Cooper Square Cooperative Housing revived support for the Title I project, conducting a survey that indicated that half of the local residents preferred to leave the area and would welcome an opportunity to move given the availability of viable accommodations elsewhere.[223] At the same time, the Cooper Square Community Development Committee and Businessmen's Association hired the urban planner Walter Thabit to devise an alternative to the Title I project.[224]

The proposal, which was intended to cause significantly less displacement and upheaval than Moses's plan, relied heavily on rehabilitation, restricting new construction to six blocks, three of which, bounded by the Bowery, Second Avenue, Houston and Third streets, were to be unified into a single superblock. The new buildings, of varying heights and irregular shapes, would be scattered across their sites, leaving a significant amount of open space. The plan also considered the future possibility of extending Third Avenue from Fifth Street, where it was absorbed into the Bowery, south to Delancey Street, and the simultaneous transformation of the corresponding stretch of the Bowery into a pedestrian mall. Industrial development in the district's southern portion was also advocated.

In 1962, at a New York State Association of Architects convention, the firm of Eggers & Higgins presented yet another alternate redevelopment scheme for the East Village.[225] The plan called for the unification of midblock yards and open areas to create communal landscaped courts based on the model of Sullivan-MacDougal Gardens.[226] Several lots on each block were to be cleared, providing street access to the interior spaces, which were to be traversed by winding walkways. The lower stretch of Fourth Avenue was to be closed to traffic and incorporated into a campus for Cooper Union; several side streets, including diagonally oriented Stuyvesant Place, were to be closed and utilized as pedestrian malls. New housing for artists was to harmonize with the surrounding low-rise tenements and rowhouses in both height and exterior materials, although they would have a reductivist, Modernist design.

In 1963 the City Planning Commission issued a "rehabilitation report" that called for a mix of renovation and new building within a thirty-three-block area that stood in sharp contrast to what Mary Perot Nichols called "the neighborhood-be-damned, bulldozer clearance, one-income ghetto philosophy of former planning czar Robert Moses."[227] Taking its cue from Thabit's alternate proposal, the commission recommended the rehabilitation of 85 percent of the area's buildings, including loft buildings to serve as artists' housing, as well as new "vest-pocket" public housing projects. Despite support from John Lindsay during his mayoral campaign of 1965, the plan languished for another six years, mired in bureaucratic red tape, before the City Planning Commission issued a radically reduced plan, concentrating on the area bounded by the Bowery, Second Avenue, Christie, Stanton and Fourth streets.[228] Finally, in 1970, a plan calling for 1,000 units of housing—half low-income and half middle-income—to be built within the smaller renewal area was approved by the City Planning Commission and subsequently by the Board of Estimate.[229] This approval came despite protests from area artists who argued that the transformation of industrial lofts into studio spaces had spearheaded a private-sector renaissance that publicly assisted renewal efforts would overturn. Yet even after more than a decade of debate and compromise, the plan proceeded slowly and was ultimately defeated by the recession of the early 1970s and the city's increasingly disastrous financial situation.

While the East Village failed to become the site of a large, public-sector renewal plan, its transformation during the post-war period was nonetheless decisive. St. Mark's Place, the portion of Eighth Street stretching between Third Avenue and Avenue A, unquestionably served as the area's "Main Street." It not only contained the highest density of commercial development but acted as a gathering place for a vibrant if uneasy mix of ethnic locals and outside youths, consisting of bohemians, political radicals, motorcycle gang members, hippies and by the late 1960s "teeny-boppers," identified in 1967 in the *New York Times* by J. Kirk Sale and Ben Apfelbaum as "the newest, and liveliest, subdivision of New York's teen-age world."[230] In the same year, John Kifner reported in the *Times* that "the psychedelic art shops, coffeehouses and antique stores began to shoulder their way in and among the Hungarian and Kosher groceries and Puerto Rican bodegas about three years ago, and have multiplied rapidly in the past year."[231] Among the new businesses that moved into the area and reflected the residents' tastes and values were the Diggers Free Store, which distributed used clothing, a coffeehouse called Something! and the Psychedelicatessen. On August 24, 1967, local merchants staged what the *New York Times* described as "a psychedelic block party" on St. Mark's Place between Second and Third avenues in an ultimately unsuccessful effort to gain support for a daily moratorium on automobile use from 7 P.M. to 12 A.M. The *Times* noted that "beneath the flow of balloons, daisies, lights and music came grumbles from some older residents and merchants on the block":

> "I'm too old for this stuff," said Jerry Polk, manager of St. Mark's Baths, as he handed turkish towels to middle-aged men on their way to the steam room. "St. Mark's Place has been the same way for, lo, these 30 years and it doesn't make sense to change now." "This is the destruction of the 20th century," said a woman huddled in the doorway of 10 St. Mark's Place as she watched youths dance in the street under bobbing umbrellas. "The merchants aren't speaking for the average person on this block."[232]

The merchants were, however, clearly responding to the needs of the 1960s freewheeling "younger generation" who flocked to the street's boutiques and cafés.

There was perhaps no greater emblem of the street's new-found role as a magnet for youth than the Electric Circus, a discotheque located on the second floor of a former ethnic social club known as the Polish National Home building, at 23 St. Mark's Place, between Second and Third avenues.[233] Designed by Chermayeff & Geismar and opened in 1967, the Electric Circus capitalized on the new hallucinogenic sensibilities principally associated with San Francisco's hippie movement. As the editors of *Progressive Architecture* described it:

> The Electric Circus has come to town with a psychedelic blend of showmanship, big beat music and pulsing projections. . . . It has a little of the look of a high-school gym, transformed beyond the wildest dreams of the prom committee. It is an almost total environment. Playing in the wash of an apricot-colored light, the band bangs out an electronically amplified beat. On the inside of a white wool canopy, draped beneath the ceiling . . . projections appear. The room is lit only by their dancing colors, which flow like a gigantic mass of protoplasm exploded against the ceiling. Occasionally, a circus performer appears and does his act—juggling, escape, trapeze work—by strobe light.[234]

In addition to the cavernous dance floor area, more intimately scaled spaces sheltered an in-house astrologer, a puppet theater in which a continuous show featured a self-immolating Buddhist

monk puppet, and the Electric Circus Store, a women's clothing boutique where patrons could purchase outfits, leave their street clothes in a checkroom, and go directly from the dressing room to the dance floor. Inside the so-called Great Expectations Room, also known by patrons as "the playpen," the adventurous could get their faces elaborately painted.

Located beneath the Electric Circus, several steps below street level, was the Dom, a threadbare neighborhood bar that began to attract a predominantly black clientele in 1965, when the block was home to the Black Arts Theater and the black poet and playwright LeRoi Jones. Following the opening of the Electric Circus, racial tension emerged between the young blacks and whites flocking to 23 St. Mark's Place. John Leo, writing in the *New York Times,* noted, "The Electric Circus is basically an expression of hippie culture, which professional youth-watchers find to be a movement by the sons and daughters of upper-middle-class white families. There are few Negro hippies. Waving his arm toward the Electric Circus, Sam Johnson, a Negro, said: 'Man, do you think we're running away from middle-class culture? That's a scene we never made!'"[235]

Despite the neighborhood's problems, the Electric Circus continued to draw crowds. Ironically, despite its pointedly counterculture ambience, the discotheque's $3.50 cover charge kept out most of the area's wandering flower children in favor of more well-heeled patrons seeking to temporarily experience, but not adopt, an alternative life-style. As Leo observed in 1967, "Hippies are almost as scarce as Negroes at the Electric Circus. . . . The hippie community is enthusiastic about the Electric Circus but can't afford the admission price."[236] In an effort to attract more of the genuine article and to maintain the commercially successful, offbeat atmosphere, the management instituted a policy that admitted barefoot patrons for fifty cents.

By 1969 the Electric Circus, which attracted such a young crowd that it did not serve liquor but only beverages such as egg creams and milk shakes, had become so firmly established as the center of New York's teen culture that its owners decided to transform it, perhaps to suit the tastes of their patrons as they became more mature. To do this they turned to a young, innovative pair of architects, Charles Gwathmey and Richard Henderson, whose Le Corbusier–inspired houses on Long Island were just beginning to attract wide attention.[237] According to *Progressive Architecture*, Gwathmey and Henderson's new Electric Circus was

> beautiful, sculptural, permanent, and formal in tone. But in spite of lasers slicing through space, slides flashing on all surfaces, and music pulsing every atom, the tactility quotient of space defined by such formal perfection is zero. . . . The owners feel that with changing slides, music, and kids, the place will constantly update itself. This would be true if the architecture itself were not such a strong statement—and one incapable of changing. In other words, the Electric Circus is a beautiful total environment, only not a totally total one.[238]

Though undeniably elegant, Gwathmey and Henderson's design perhaps reflected a misreading of the essentially de-architectural nature of the era; in any case, it stood in sharp contrast to the neighborhood's seedy and increasingly menacing aspect. On March 22, 1970, the violence that had plagued the East Village penetrated the Electric Circus's posh environment, literally tearing it apart: a bomb, reportedly planted by a member of the radical Black Panther party, which had been publicly supported by the discotheque's management, exploded and injured fifteen people. In August 1971, the club, seemingly unable to overcome either its violent past or the economic collapse of 1969, closed its doors for the final time.

SOHO

Getting to SoHo . . . is an ordeal . . . and the walk there through rubbish-strewn streets lined with dour warehouse buildings inside which the artists have staked out their glittering white lofts is not calculated to lift the spirits. . . . Nevertheless, after a period of fluctuating fortunes the new downtown art community seems launched. . . . From now on a regular trip to SoHo is pretty much obligatory, another in the expanding list of inconvenient pleasures New Yorkers are heir to.
—John Ashbery, 1971[1]

While the post–World War II era saw many distinctive parts of New York literally bulldozed and replaced by massive developments and projects that failed to evolve into successful neighborhoods, economically and sociologically meaningful urban renewal did occur through the more traditional process of area reclamation. While most of the reclaimed areas were once fashionable residential neighborhoods that had fallen into decrepitude, there was one notable exception: the area south of Greenwich Village, eventually known as SoHo (south of Houston Street), a former warehouse district that almost overnight in the late 1960s was transformed into the world's most vibrant artists' quarter. Beginning in the 1850s, the area bounded roughly by Sixth Avenue, Lafayette, Houston and Canal streets, which had served post-colonial New York as the nation's most celebrated red-light district, was rebuilt as an extensive warehouse district that by 1900 evolved into a vital center for light manufacturing, which it remained until after World War II.

In a fashion typical of New York's postwar development, the birth of SoHo began not with an act of creation or even of appreciation but with a threatened act of destruction: a vast highway project, the Lower Manhattan Expressway, promised to completely obliterate much of lower Manhattan's industrial loft district.[2] An expressway linking the Holland Tunnel with the Manhattan and Williamsburg bridges had been envisioned since the 1920s, when the Holland Tunnel was under construction. As advocated by the Regional Plan Association, the highway was conceived of as an essential and wholly inevitable part of an emergent megalopolitanism. Manhattan was a key way station along the Northeast corridor, and the new road was essential to moving traffic between New Jersey and Long Island. Despite the presumed logic, even inevitability, of the megalopolitan vision, from the project's inception, according to the journalist Vicki Hodgetts, writing in 1969, "Manhattanites, who believe that the earth is flat and drops off on either side of their island, regarded the proposed road as some awful sea creature rising from the deep to devour and destroy the city."[3]

In 1940 Robert Moses, chairman of the Triborough Bridge and Tunnel Authority, suggested the highway to Mayor La Guardia, who liked the idea; one year later the roadway was included in the City Planning Commission's master plan for arterial highways and major streets. In 1944, a year after Manhattan Borough President Edgar J. Nathan, Jr., delivered an engineer's report to the Board of Estimate calling for the highway, the State Legislature included the project in its official listing of the State Arterial Highway System. In 1946 Moses and Manhattan Borough President Hugo Rogers submitted a report advocating the construction of the highway, and the following year working drawings were completed by Madigan-Hylan, an engineering firm long associated with Moses's projects. By 1949 responsibility for the project had been taken over by the Triborough Bridge and Tunnel Authority, which, under Moses's leadership, had a

reputation for getting things done; nonetheless, funding remained scarce and the project's future cloudy. In 1956, when Congress passed the Interstate and Defense Highways Act, providing 90 percent funding on certain interstate highways, Moses seized the opportunity, quickly proposing four elevated interstate highways traversing Manhattan at Broome, Thirty-fourth, Fifty-ninth and 125th streets. The Broome Street Expressway, also known as the Lower Manhattan Expressway or LOMEX, was to displace 1,972 families and 804 businesses, and cost approximately $100 million. In December 1962 LOMEX was officially defeated by the Board of Estimate, but a year later Mayor Wagner suggested that Moses issue another plan, and the project was drawn on the official city map, allowing the city to begin condemning buildings along the proposed route.[4]

Thrillingly futuristic multilevel inner-city highways had been romantically portrayed by architects such as Harvey Wiley Corbett and Hugh Ferriss during the 1920s and later brilliantly realized by Moses along the East River and under Brooklyn Heights (see chapter 13). But by the 1960s projects such as the Cross-Bronx Expressway (see chapter 13) had made the public wary of new highway construction, no mattter how provocatively designed. Although LOMEX was, not surprisingly, supported by the construction unions, the expressway was opposed by such public figures as Congressmen John V. Lindsay and Leonard Farbstein, Assemblymen William F. Passannante and Louis DeSalvio, State Senator Joseph Marro, City Councilmen Theodore Weiss and Theodore Kupferman, *New York Times* reporter Gilbert Milstein, and the director of the Congress on Racial Equality (CORE), James Farmer, as well as Jane Jacobs, fresh from her fight to preserve the West Village. The New York Society of Architects, along with the Bronx and Brooklyn chapters of the American Institute of Architects (but not the New York chapter), opposed the project and suggested the construction of a tunnel linking Long Island and New Jersey with a single Manhattan connection to the West Side Highway; the proposal was never developed.[5] In addition, LOMEX was opposed by 200 community groups, including the Lower East Side Businessmen's Association, led by Hy Harmartz, who ran Ratner's Dairy Restaurant, a local gastronomic landmark.

LOMEX was also opposed by artists who in the late 1950s had begun to live and work in the area's nineteenth-century cast-iron loft buildings. Jim Stratton, an area resident who would document what became the nationwide phenomenon of loft living in his 1977 book *Pioneering in the Urban Wilderness*, claimed that the artists had played a catalytic role in blocking the expressway's construction, though other publicly voiced opposition seems to have preceded any official action by the artists' community. In any case, it was clear that the artists constituted an important lobby group. Stratton recalled that the area's first community organization, the South Houston Artist Tenants Association, founded in 1968, as well as the Artists Against the Expressway, "worked separately but pulled many of the same strings in the art world. 'The expressway was a certainty until the artists stepped in,' said the head of the local planning board years later. 'Opposition to the expressway was going nowhere. Our whole planning board couldn't even slow it down. Then a handful of artists stepped in and stopped it cold.' The expressway was the first hint of the loft artists' power."[6]

As early as 1962 Stephanie Gervis, reporting in the *Village Voice*, noted the range of motivations among those protesting the expressway:

> For city-planning expert Jane Jacobs and her roving warriors in the great fight against City Hall, it's another trench in their

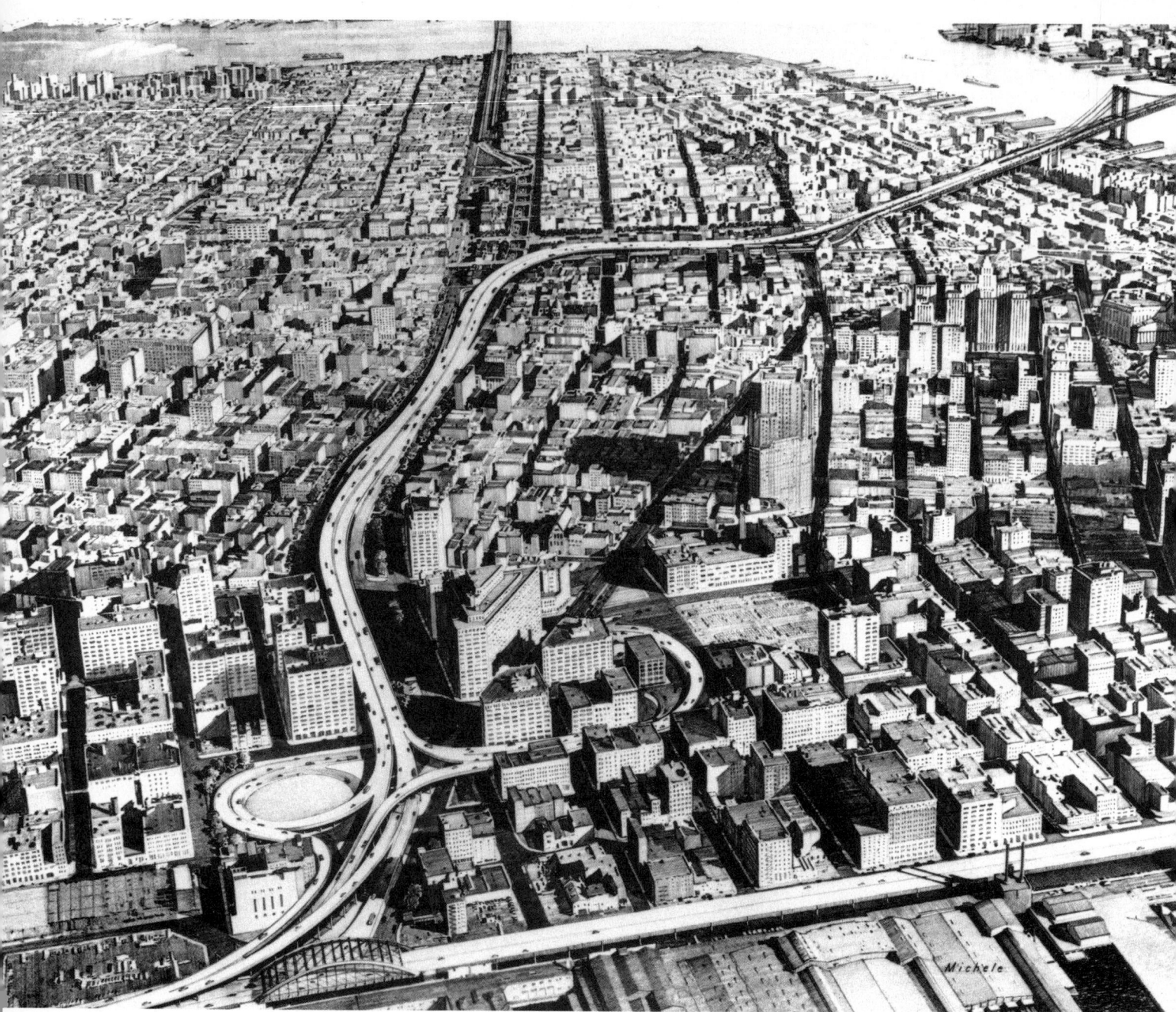

Proposed Lower Manhattan Expressway, connecting the Holland
Tunnel and the West Side Highway, in the foreground, with the
Manhattan Bridge, on the upper right, via Broome Street and the
Bowery. Rendering of view to the east, 1950. TBTA

Maginot Line against the dehumanization of the city. For the artists, it's a battle to hang onto their low-rent lofts, which would be eliminated by the Expressway. For the neighborhood kids it's a holiday, a chance to hop a ride on a bus or a truck and make some noise at City Hall. For their parents it's a desperate struggle to preserve their community, their way of life, from the blessings of automotive progress. In the long view of history, it will probably go down as just another battle in the endless Holy War against the spirit of Robert Moses.[7]

Congressman John Lindsay, who had proclaimed his opposition to all cross-Manhattan expressway proposals in his successful 1965 bid for mayor, advocated an alternate route running around the southern tip of Manhattan that became known as the "Lindsay Loop."[8] In April 1966, without the prior knowledge of Lindsay, who was now mayor, Deputy Mayor Robert Price told the press: "The project is out as far as the Lindsay administration is concerned." But despite Price's proclamation that "the city is for the people, not for cars," Lindsay, in a controversial move, rejected a proposal to demap the project.[9]

On April 10, 1968, Jane Jacobs, who had previously asserted that "the Expressway will Los Angelize New York," attended a public hearing on LOMEX.[10] When about a dozen anti-LOMEX members of the audience walked onto the stage and tore the stenotype record of the hearing to shreds, Jacobs announced that since there was no record, there could not have been a hearing. Jacobs was then arrested and charged with rioting, inciting to riot, committing criminal mischief and obstructing public administration. The charge was later reduced to disorderly conduct. Jacobs pleaded guilty during a short proceeding in which issues concerning LOMEX itself were not debated. Anticipating the trial, newly elected Manhattan Congressman Edward I. Koch called it "the first real public hearing we have been able to obtain on the Expressway."[11] Labeling Jacobs's action "stenocide," the architecture critic Peter Blake found the charge of disorderly conduct "a pretty ridiculous charge; *of course* Jane Jacobs is disorderly—that's her job!"[12]

When the federal government offered in 1968 to underwrite the construction of new buildings and parks deemed necessary components of highway projects, the Lindsay administration quickly devised a new proposal, to be federally funded, in which LOMEX would be submerged below grade—at some points beneath the subways that crossed its path—and surrounded by apartment and commercial buildings, as well as by warehouses, schools and parks. Ada Louise Huxtable found the proposal not significantly better than its predecessors:

> The in-and-out, over-and-under proposal that has come out of this attempt to defang the monster makes no one very happy. Ducking subways, utilities and the water table, it struggles above and below ground in a series of curious compromises of tortuous complexity, complete with enough entrances, exits and connections to turn Lower Manhattan into a concrete no man's land. Displaced people will now number in the low thousands rather than the high thousands. It is a question of degree: do you kill a city or maim it?[13]

In 1967 the Ford Foundation commissioned the architect Paul Rudolph to conduct a study of LOMEX as part of a larger project, later published as a book by the urban planner Peter Wolf titled *New Forms of the Evolving City: Urban Design Proposals by Ulrich Franzen and Paul Rudolph*.[14] Rudolph's proposal, "City Corridor," completed in 1972, called for a largely submerged expressway serving as the spine of a megastructure that would constitute a Y-shaped linear city-within-the-city connecting the Holland Tunnel with both the Williamsburg

and Manhattan bridges. Rudolph's proposal included separate levels for motor and pedestrian traffic as well as for parking; the plan also included accommodations for both private and public modes of transportation. Flanking this central transportation core were multiuse structures composed of dramatically cantilevered, trapezoidal slabs connected by a network of horizontal and vertical supports. Straining to establish a historical precedent for Rudolph's superscaled project, Wolf noted: "The multi-use building type integrated with transportation system is not really a new idea. In fact, the centuries-old Ponte Vecchio in Florence is one of the most attractive examples of such a building type. There, a pedestrian way and a road are flanked by shops and apartments."[15]

Reflecting much of the preceding debate over LOMEX, the proposal was presented as contextually responsive, although it was, in essense, an inhabited viaduct that would present a fairly uniform wall to the various neighborhoods it plowed through as it crossed the island. Nonetheless, there was, given Rudolph's predisposition to a purely tectonic ahistorical aesthetic, an effort to respond to particular situations: for example, the building and transportation complex was not to replace Broome Street, as was originally the case with LOMEX, but to be slipped between the backs of the buildings fronting Broome and Spring streets, thus leaving at least the existing cast-iron facades fully intact. In addition, the linear city was to be appropriately modulated in height. "The scale of the surrounding city," Wolf wrote, "is taken as a guide in massing the architecture along the corridor." He continued:

> One can say, with some exceptions, that the intention has been that if nearby buildings are relatively tall, the buildings along the expressway are relatively tall. (Bridges can, of course, be seen as rather tall buildings.) Where the highway traverses a low district, such as along Broome Street, buildings of low scale are proposed. So even though the proposed structural system lends an unusual appearance to the buildings, the scale of the buildings is in fact related to the city which would surround them, and of which they would become a part.[16]

Though undeniably spectacular, particularly in its technological bravura and the complexity of its functional organization, the overall Brobdingnagian scale and uniformity of architectural expression of Rudolph's uninterrupted linear city gave it a nightmarish aspect quite out of keeping with the period's increasingly preservation-minded contextualism. Urban designers Raymond Gindroz and David Lewis, analyzing the project as presented by Wolf in a second book, *The Future of the City*, stated:

> As a recommendation for an urban environment it appears to us to be incredibly limited in its vocabulary and horrendous in its inhumanity. We can't help wondering how much of the design would be left if it were subjected to the community and political process . . . if the citizens, the white-collar lawyers and corporation men, the Jews, the Puerto Ricans, and the blacks, who live in those areas shown so vaguely on each side of the expressway corridor and who would be expected to use it and make it part of their everyday city, were to be truly enfranchised in the process of designing this major infrastructural element driving its way through their inherited environment; and if the new inhabitants were allowed a chance to demonstrate the intricacies of their need in contrast with the repetitive trapezoid pigeonholes which they are offered in this design.[17]

In 1969 the Lindsay administration hired the architect and urban planner Shadrach Woods to study the area affected by LOMEX and propose a plan for its growth.[18] The choice was an

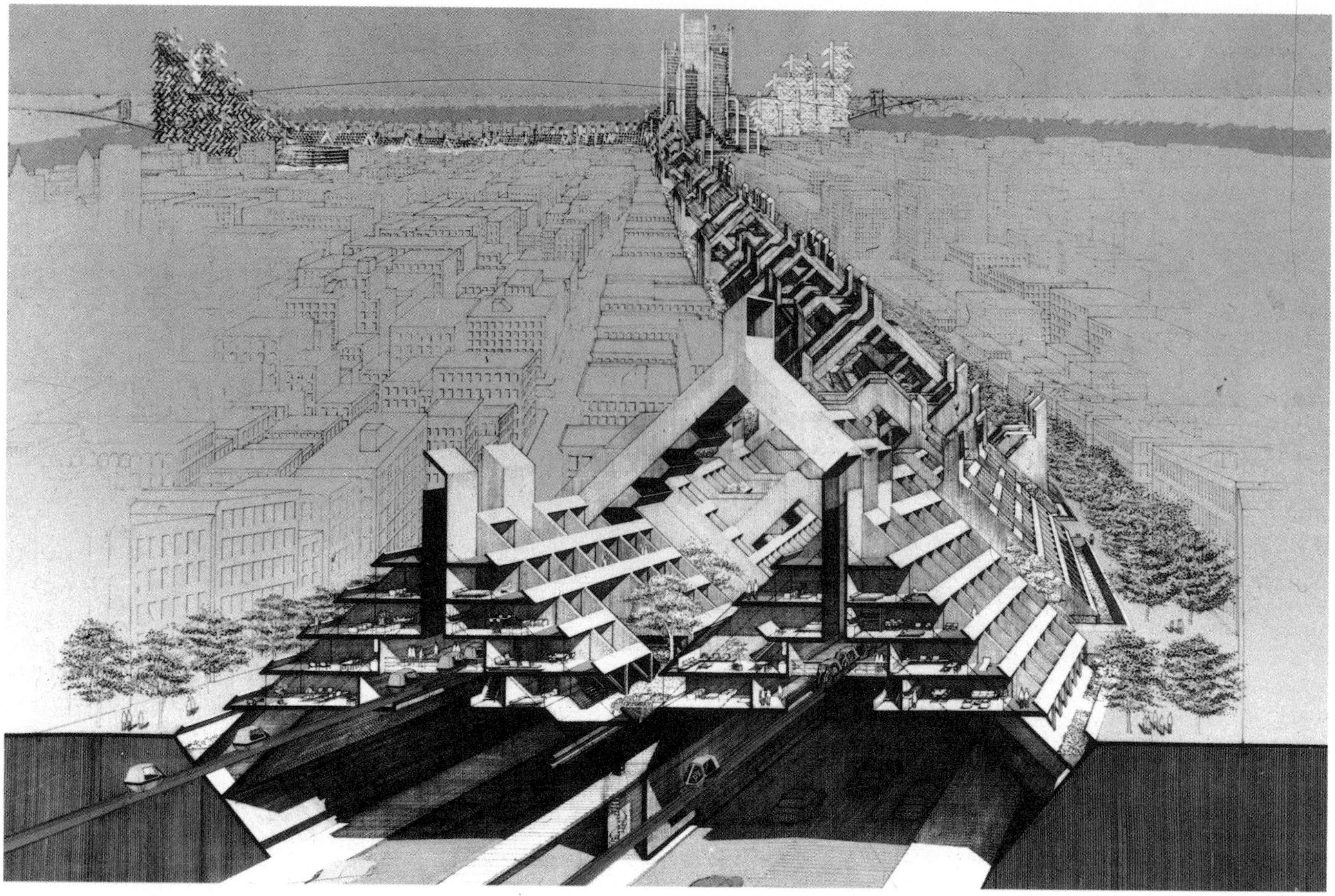

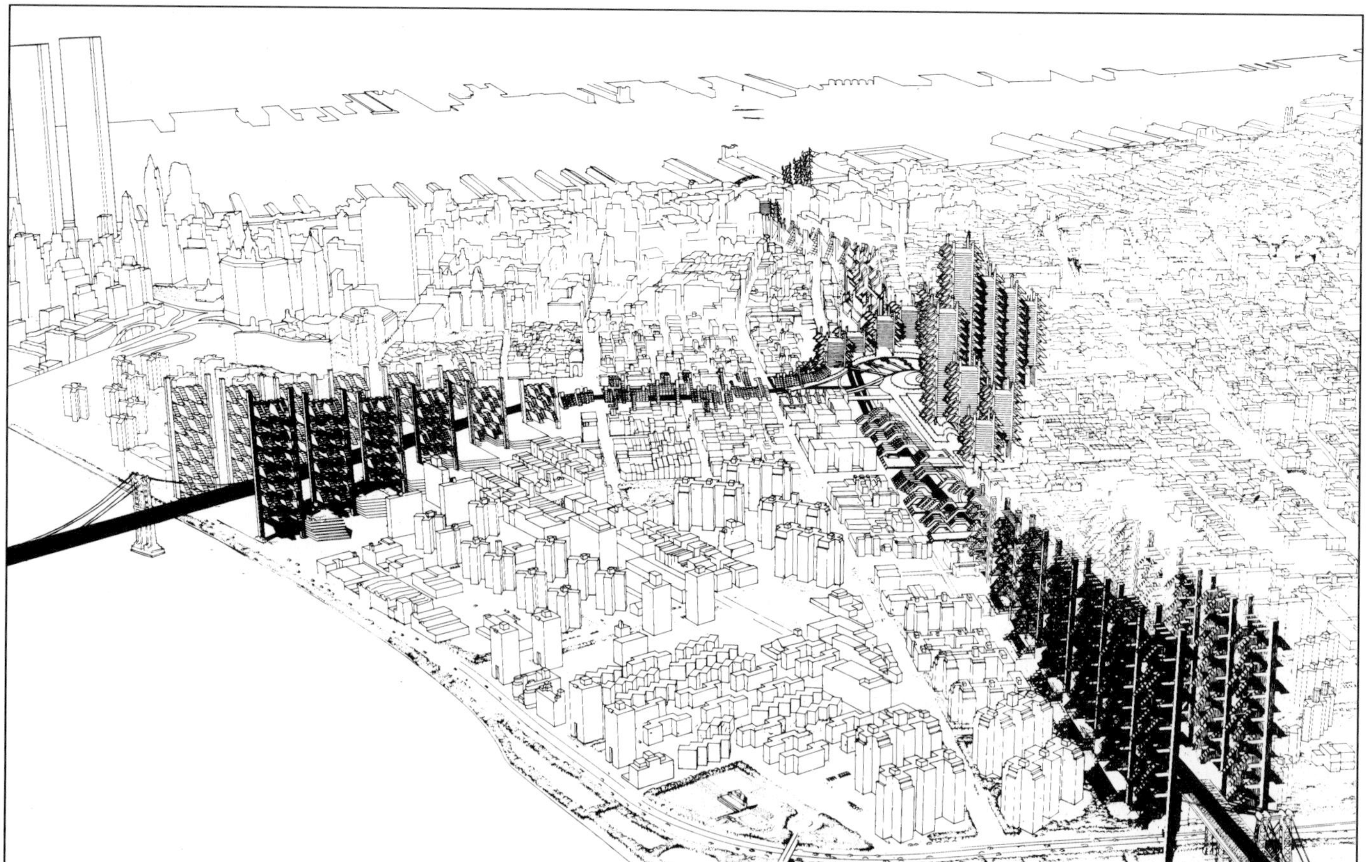

odd one given Woods's long association with Le Corbusier, whose destructive urban plans—the City for Three Million Inhabitants (1922) and the Plan Voisin for Paris (1925)—were the very models for the type of urban renewal so many New Yorkers were against.[19] Woods contended that LOMEX would improve the area by reducing congestion and thus encouraging light industrial concerns to stay in Manhattan and continue to provide much-needed, low-skill employment. Woods also argued that the area's artists, who sought legalization of their studio/homes, were working against their own best interests and that changes in zoning laws to permit residential use would simply pave the way for upmarket apartment-building construction that would displace the existing buildings and their artist tenants. In August 1969 the Board of Estimate sided with those who contended that LOMEX would increase congestion and air pollution, unanimously voting to remove the project from official city maps; finally, after more than four decades of debate and negotiation, LOMEX was defeated.

For Marshall Berman, the defeat of LOMEX marked the beginning of the end of Robert Moses's power. The expressway was defeated not only because a strong coalition of heterogeneous composition was organized against it but also because the protesters did not come off "as mere selfish opportunists, promoting their particular private interests against the welfare of 'the Public.'" Rather, they were appealing "to a general public on behalf of a coherent and striking public philosophy. Their basic idea, expounded most cogently and convincingly by Jane Jacobs, was that the street and the neighborhood were the very heart of city life, and that the destruction of streets and neighborhoods menaced the energy and integrity of the city as a whole. The new combination was too much for Moses."[20]

The battle over LOMEX decisively transformed the relationship between local communities and centralized planning agencies, but it also focused great attention on the political and economic implications of historic preservation. Its most powerful outcome was the preservation of lower Manhattan's nineteenth-century cast-iron commercial loft buildings, which, though widely admired by foreigners, had been largely neglected by New Yorkers, both inside and outside the architectural profession. In 1973 the area bounded by West Houston, East Houston, Crosby, Howard and Canal streets and by West Broadway was legally protected as the SoHo–Cast-Iron Historic Landmark District.[21] A principal proponent of landmarking was the indefatigable preservationist Margot Gayle, who, with the Friends of Cast-Iron Architecture, which she organized, bombarded Mayor Lindsay and other city officials with letters extolling the area's architecture and advocating its preservation.[22]

Ada Louise Huxtable had been one of the first American observers to publicly call attention to the architectural merit of the area.[23] In 1961 she pointed out that the English journal *Architectural Review* had featured the district eight years earlier, and said that "If urban renewal is not to turn into urban devastation, which it shows signs of doing, the officials of New York would be well advised to take a course in the history of the city's architecture."[24] Peter Blake was one of the Americans awakened by European interest in the area's architectural wonders. In 1968 Blake identified it as "one of the most spectacular museums of modern architecture to be found anywhere in the world."[25]

By this time the fact that the area was home to large numbers of artists was becoming widely known. While to many observers the phenomenon of artists living in New York's industrial lofts seemed new, in reality it dated back to the end of World

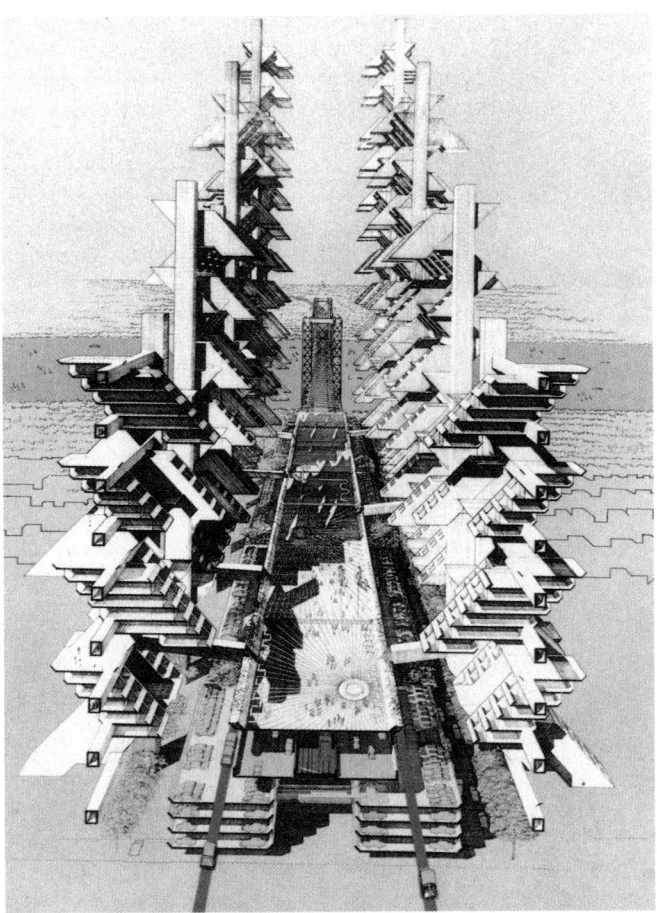

Top left: City Corridor proposal, connecting the Holland Tunnel with the Williamsburg and Manhattan bridges. Paul Rudolph, 1967. Section perspective of view to the southeast. PR

Bottom left: City Corridor proposal. Perspective of view to the west. PR

Above: City Corridor proposal. Section perspective of view to the east. PR

War II. In the mid-1950s Coenties Slip, in the Wall Street area, began to attract a number of artists (see chapter 3), and it was but one of several small clusters of artists' lofts beginning to be established around Manhattan; others included the Bowery and the stretch of Broadway just below Fourteenth Street. But the greatest concentration of artists was in SoHo, which began to be colonized in the late 1950s. When the artists first arrived in the manufacturing district, which constituted a significant portion of Manhattan's total industrial area, it was by no means a derelict one. In fact, Manhattan's manufacturing employment, which during the Depression had decreased only moderately as compared with that of the nation as a whole, expanded significantly during World War II. But the postwar era brought decline, and by the late 1960s the pace of that decline began to accelerate at an alarming rate.

According to Emmanuel Tobier, the downturn in manufacturing could be traced to a number of factors, including federal urban renewal, which led to the demolition of many buildings to make way for the Washington Square Urban Renewal Area, and the construction of public improvements, in particular the creation of improved vehicular access to the Brooklyn Bridge, which began the systematic destruction of loft buildings just east of City Hall.[26] But for the most part it was the free-market economy that drove industry from Manhattan, as changes in production techniques as well as the metropolitan area's transportation systems made suburban sites increasingly attractive to management. As far as the city was concerned, the district was increasingly a no-man's-land. As the writer Stephen Koch would later note, "Throughout most of the 20th century . . . Soho was known to city officials as 'the Valley'—a grey blur of low industrial buildings that nobody wanted to visit or look at, a flat region, rather like a gap in a comb where the teeth have broken, between the skyscrapers of Wall Street and the skyscrapers of Midtown."[27]

By the 1960s the area's artists, despite harassment by well-intentioned, safety-conscious building and fire department officials, clung tenaciously to their loft studio/homes. As Jim Stratton has pointed out, the redevelopment of the district as an artists' quarter did not constitute the first utilization of industrial lofts by artists, but it was the first instance of the emergent community organizing itself to withstand both the legal and the developmental forces threatening to thwart its growth. The area's development, said Stratton, "generated a new militance among the harried artist-tenants and, simultaneously, started the juices flowing in their middle-class pursuers. Tired of being chased out of their corners by more affluent adversaries, tired of capitulating to those who need artists but do not want them, this neighborhood drew its wagons into a circle."[28]

In 1961 *Newsweek*, reporting on the Manhattan loft situation, observed that "The artist's life in New York, once carried on in romantic garrets, has moved to the commercial loft."[29] Michel Duplaix, a photographer and a loft resident, clearly described the evolution of loft living in *Vogue*:

> Over the years the number of studios in New York has been decreasing steadily as old buildings are torn down and new ones go up. In the Village, high rents are driving out the artist and studios are at a premium. The demolition crews, architects and city planners of our utopian society make little or no allowance for artists, and the skylight is fast becoming a thing of the past. The modern beehives replacing the brownstones offer no promise to painters, poets, writers and photographers, etc. . . . There is only one answer:—a loft; a floor of unbroken space originally intended for commercial use.[30]

Among the first leading artists to move into the area below Houston Street were George Sugarman, Lee Bontecou and Romare Bearden. According to Stratton, Bearden was evicted after "being fleeced by a landlord," a not uncommon practice in which property owners turned a blind eye toward their illegal tenants and then, following the implementation of significant improvements at the renter's expense, exposed the illegality to city officials.[31] Bearden fought his eviction; his appearance in municipal court in March 1961 galvanized attention within the artists' community and culminated in a meeting at the Washington Irving High School auditorium attended by 800 area artists united as the South Houston Artists Tenant Association. The association members listened as the editor of *Art News*, Alfred M. Frankfurter, the art critic Clement Greenberg, the sculptor Isamu Noguchi and State Assemblyman Mark Lane spoke in defense of artists' rights to use loft space. At the meeting the beleaguered but well-intentioned fire commissioner, Edward F. Cavanagh, explained: "I'm all for artists and their creative talent. . . . I have absolutely no objection to an artist working in a loft—if the loft is safe. . . . But what I object to is this slander of the Fire Department. We're not unsympathetic, and we're not anti-art!"[32]

Taking matters a bit further, the South Houston Artists Tenant Association threatened an artists' strike to commence in September 1961. The tenant association proposed an "Artist Studio, Residence" building-occupancy category that would allow artists to legally live and work in loft buildings deemed reasonably safe.[33] The strike never occurred, but the city began to reconsider its policies and relax its enforcement program.[34] At the same time, pressure began to mount for the wholesale demolition of the loft district.[35]

As a result of the artists' protests, Mayor Wagner implemented a citywide, so-called Artist-in-Residence (AIR) program that permitted artists to take over the top two floors of a commercial or manufacturing building; typically, these were the least desired by commercial and manufacturing tenants and, because of skylighting and generally better lighting, the best suited to artists and their families. The lofts had to meet minimum standards of egress and sanitation; in addition, to alert firemen in emergencies, the artist had to declare his or her presence with an eight-by-ten-inch sign at the street door declaring in two-inch block letters "AIR" and the number of the studio.

The battle of the lofts continued throughout the 1960s. In 1963 twenty artists protested the city's loft policy at the opening of the exhibition of Leonardo da Vinci's *Mona Lisa* at the Metropolitan Museum of Art.[36] The picketing artists were tenants of the notorious Seymour Finkelstein, "King of the Lofts," a landlord and resident of Coney Island whose buildings were rife with violations. The picketers' placards were witty and to the point: "Space for Art, Not for Artists," "Leonardo Had a Place to Paint, Why Don't We?" Perhaps the wittiest of all read: "Mona Is Not the Only One Who Needs a Leasa." The struggle dragged on.[37]

In 1964 Governor Nelson A. Rockefeller signed a bill that permitted artists to live on all floors of a loft building, but it carried with it stringent fire and building safety requirements that would force many of the present illegal lofts to be abandoned by their artist residents.[38] More important, because the city's newly enacted zoning ordinance strictly separated residential from commercial and industrial zones, the passage of the state law created a period governed by what Ron Rosenbaum described as a "gentleman's agreement" among the officers of the Buildings Department, the Fire Department and the Police

Department "under which there was no active enforcement of the zoning prohibition against living in a manufacturing area. Nonetheless, the artists were vulnerable to landlords who could threaten them with eviction unless they paid hush money or exorbitant rents or both. Moreover, banks couldn't lend money for necessary improvements."[39]

Just as the artists were beginning to establish their right to legally inhabit the lofts, some Greenwich Village politicians and activists began to eye the adjacent loft district as an area that could be redeveloped for housing without requiring massive relocation. This idea was put forward by the Village Liberal Club in 1960 after a disastrous fire in an industrial loft took the lives of three fire fighters, indicating in the minds of some observers the obsolete nature of the area's buildings as industrial work spaces. In a letter to acting Borough President Louis Cioffi, club chairman Edward Doremus argued, "The plan we propose would make available a large tract, allowing the advantages of the 'bulldozer approach' without its disadvantages of dislocation . . . or architectural monstrosities."[40] A group calling itself Mi-Cove (the Middle Income Cooperators of Greenwich Village) proposed a specific plan for middle-income housing in the district. Designed by Victor Gruen in 1960 and supported by Mayor Wagner, Mi-Cove's proposed development was to replace the nineteenth-century cast-iron warehouses of the twelve-block, thirty-two-acre site bounded by West Broadway, Broome Street, Broadway and Houston Street with housing for 2,500 families accommodated in forty-one six- to fourteen-story apartment buildings, as well as a community center, a three-block extension of Washington Square Village's shopping promenade and a 500-car garage.[41]

Mi-Cove's founder, Charlotte Schwab, had started the group in an effort to bring to the area "a reputable middle-income cooperative" that would ease the problem of displacement caused by the widespread construction of high-rent apartment houses in nearby Greenwich Village and the anticipated destruction of housing stock to make way for the proposed Lower Manhattan Expressway. Schwab justified her proposal not on the basis of a detailed study of the area but on the overwhelming response—from over 2,000 people—to an advertisement she placed in the papers, which said simply, "Anyone interested in a true middle-income housing project write Box 460."[42] At least one observer, however, saw Schwab's goal as unrealistic: "If Mrs. Schwab believes this will happen through some city-sponsored, low-cost housing project," a woman wrote in a terse letter to the editor of the Village Voice, "we suggest she visit Washington Square Village."[43]

On November 30, 1961, Mi-Cove submitted Gruen's design to the Board of Estimate for approval.[44] Despite the support of Manhattan Borough President Edward Dudley, as well as some community leaders, the project sparked yet another debate, as Mary Perot Nichols described it in the Village Voice, over "the suitability of the site, who is to be the sponsor, the aesthetics and planning-wisdom of super-block developments, and the question of whether ideal objectives are more important than the urgent need for such housing."[45] Jane Jacobs said bluntly, "I think we've had enough demonstration in this city that large projects are neither safe nor interesting nor good neighbors for those adjoining them."[46] Jacobs's essentially conservative point of view was seen as obstructionist not only by old-guard housing officials but by a young generation of social activists such as the lawyer-planner Robert Abel, who was critical in a letter to the editor of the Village Voice: "While I do not dispute the lady's right to fight to preserve her own home, I re-

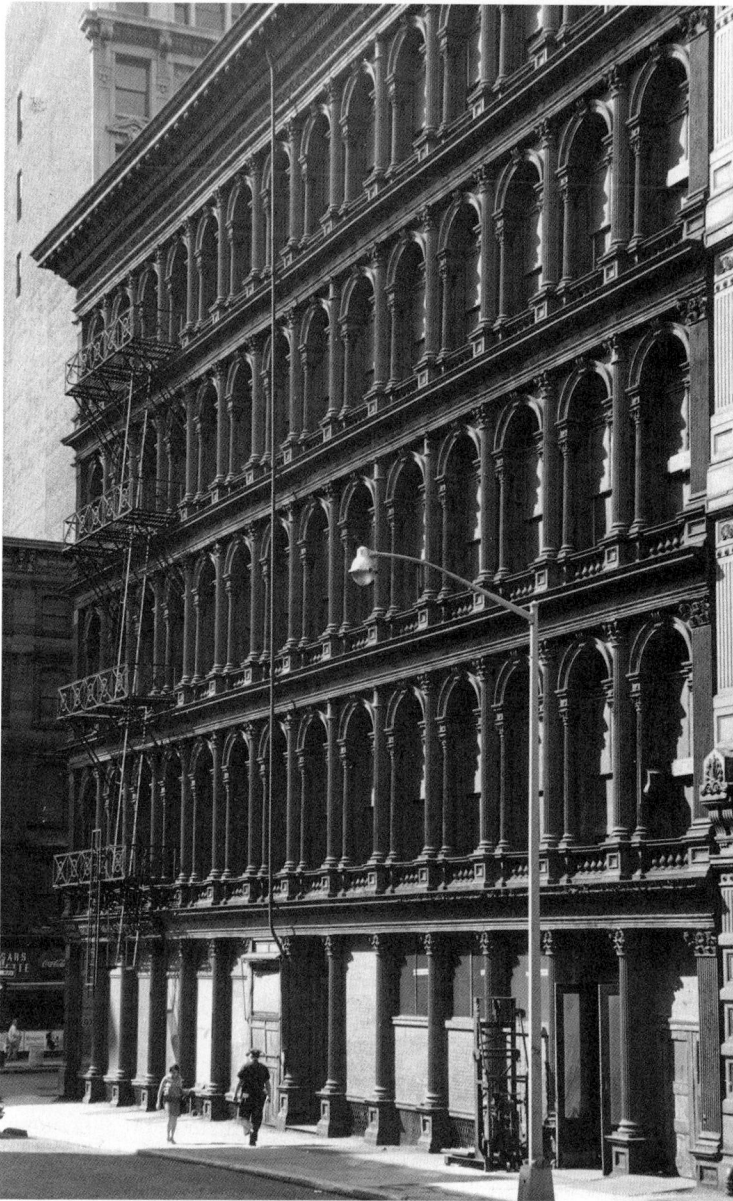

Haughwout Building, 488 Broadway, northeast corner of Broome Street. John P. Gaynor, 1857. View to the northwest, 1964. Fred W. McDarrah. FWM

sent her efforts to prevent 2,500 families from obtaining decent, attractive housing at prices they can afford. Let's have facts to support some of those so very attractive theories!"[47]

The city decisively rejected Mi-Cove's housing proposal when the City Planning Commission released an area study prepared by Chester Rapkin, an urban planner and economist, which described the area as an "incubator" for new businesses and a major source of employment for unskilled and semiskilled workers.[48] While Jane Jacobs praised Rapkin's study, I. D. Robbins, president of the City Club, which in 1962 published *The Wastelands of New York City*—a report on what it called the city's "commercial slums"—denounced as "folk concepts" Rapkin's arguments in defense of the neighborhood.[49]

In January 1966 the fifth floor of 427 Broadway, a cast-iron warehouse building (Robert Mook, 1872), collapsed, fueling arguments that SoHo was rife with unsafe buildings that should be torn down. But closer inspection proved, as the editors of *Architectural Forum* reported, that "the facts of the incident make the buildings seem all the more worth saving." It turned out that the collapsed floor was not an actual floor but planks that had been laid over a lightwell decades earlier without approval of the Buildings Department. The planks collapsed under the weight of 70,000 pounds—four times the permissible load. *Forum* went on to observe: "Through it all, the beautiful cast-iron facade remained standing in perfect shape. What was apparent before the disaster became even more obvious afterwards: this remarkable group of cast-iron buildings could easily and safely be rehabilitated to provide a handsome new residential section for New York—one that could have all the charm, without the coyness, of such areas as New Orleans' Vieux Carré and Washington's Georgetown."[50]

Though the legal groundwork of the area's transformation had yet to solidify, throughout the late 1960s manufacturers continued to be replaced by artists. In 1967 the J. M. Kaplan Fund, which had in part financed Westbeth, a pioneering artists' loft complex in the West Village (see "Greenwich Village," above), converted the industrial loft building at 80 Wooster Street into an artists' cooperative; a principal tenant was the so-called Cinematheque, run by avant-garde filmmaker Jonas Mekas.[51] Following the conversion of 80 Wooster Street, a colleague of Mekas's, George Maciunas, founded a development company known as Fluxhouse, a name that referred to Fluxus, the well-known group of experimental artists that included Maciunas, Mekas, Joseph Beuys, John Cage, Emmett Williams, Charlotte Moorman, Nam June Paik and Yoko Ono, among others.[52] By 1968 Maciunas had purchased more than ten buildings and turned five others into co-ops: 70 Grand Street (George DaCunha, 1887),[53] 16 Greene Street (Samuel A. Warner, 1895),[54] 131 Prince Street (Buchman & Deisler, 1894),[55] 451 West Broadway (James Dubois, 1884)[56] and 465 West Broadway (John H. Whitenach, 1889).[57]

It was at this time, according to Jim Stratton, that the painter and engineer Aaron Roseman gave the area, unglamorously identified by the City Planning Commission merely as the South Houston Industrial District and previously known, during its heyday as a manufacturing district, as "Hell's Hundred Acres," the new sobriquet SoHo. It was a catchy name because it was the same as that of the familiarly raffish London neighborhood. Stratton asserted that when Roseman thought of the name, "We all chuckled," thinking of "images of Holmes and Watson seeking clues in the murky fog of our local warehouse. From time to time over the next months, when adversity nibbled at our shanks, we would utter the new name and laugh. So.Ho.—a

joke, but it seemed appropriate. The rising dust, after all, could easily be mistaken for fog and we were certainly doing our best to outwit Scotland Yard."[58] Not all people living in the area were equally amused by the new name; as the *New York Times* art critic Grace Glueck noted, "Many SoHo residents object to the name, suggestive as it is of the grubby Bohemian district in London that the area does not resemble."[59] The art dealer Ivan Karp complained, "It's just another example of the American inferiority complex about European names."[60]

Complete with its undeniably hip if controversial name, SoHo drew increasing numbers of artists, driven out of other areas by the building boom elsewhere in Manhattan.[61] As Ron Rosenbaum put it: "Artists in New York—their loft buildings all over the city demolished to make way for high rise projects—have been trekking like shell-shocked refugees to the last loft area in the city, the South Houston manufacturing district." The issue was not necessarily the cost of space but its availability. Rosenbaum explained:

> The situation has become so serious that many artists are moving out of New York. Jim Rosenquist, who has no need for rent control, was simply unable to find any adequate loft space in New York at any price. He left New York for East Hampton. Jack Beal has been in a six-year-long court fight with the city to establish the legality of his living loft. He hasn't been able to invest any money in renovating his place for fear he'll be out on the street any moment. Barnett Newman has said that twice, during the most creative periods of his life, he was forced out of his loft and made to suspend his work to look for another one.[62]

The situation was worse for younger, financially more vulnerable artists. For the young SoHo artist, dodging municipal inspectors became a common and, at least in retrospect, romanticized pastime. Michael T. Kaufman, reporting in the *New York Times* in the mid-1970s, after residential lofts had been legalized, stated: "One artist remembers a friend who would greet a building inspector on the stairs saying, 'Wait just a minute I have a nude model posing.' Then he would go inside and using pulleys hoist beds above a false ceiling and camouflage the refrigerator, range and bathtub."[63]

As Rosenbaum pointed out, the artists' need for loft space was a direct corollary of the era's tendencies in painting and sculpture: "In the '20s and '30s artists could live in the Village because they didn't need huge studio space. By the late '40s and early '50s, after De Kooning and Kline met Kandinsky and Gorky and began doing their own thing, the Village was too expensive and the space too small, so painters and sculptors began moving into industrial lofts."[64] The journalist Stephen Koch saw in the art community's gravitation to SoHo's industrial landscape more than practical and economic considerations. Relating the growth of SoHo to artists' distaste for the bourgeois, Koch postulated that "For the avant-garde, a classically modernist contempt for everything merely middle-class and pretty, a love of an industrial look and style, a taste for incongruity, have all united to make SoHo an ideal landscape. In fact, SoHo's industrial resonance is a prime element of style, from the smallest detail of decor to the grandest esthetic theorizing."[65]

While artists poured into the area, the City Planning Commission was slow to officially recognize the trend, rejecting in 1969 a plan to create a special artists' district in SoHo and

---

392 West Broadway (1872), between Broome and Spring streets. View to the west. Fred W. McDarrah. FWM

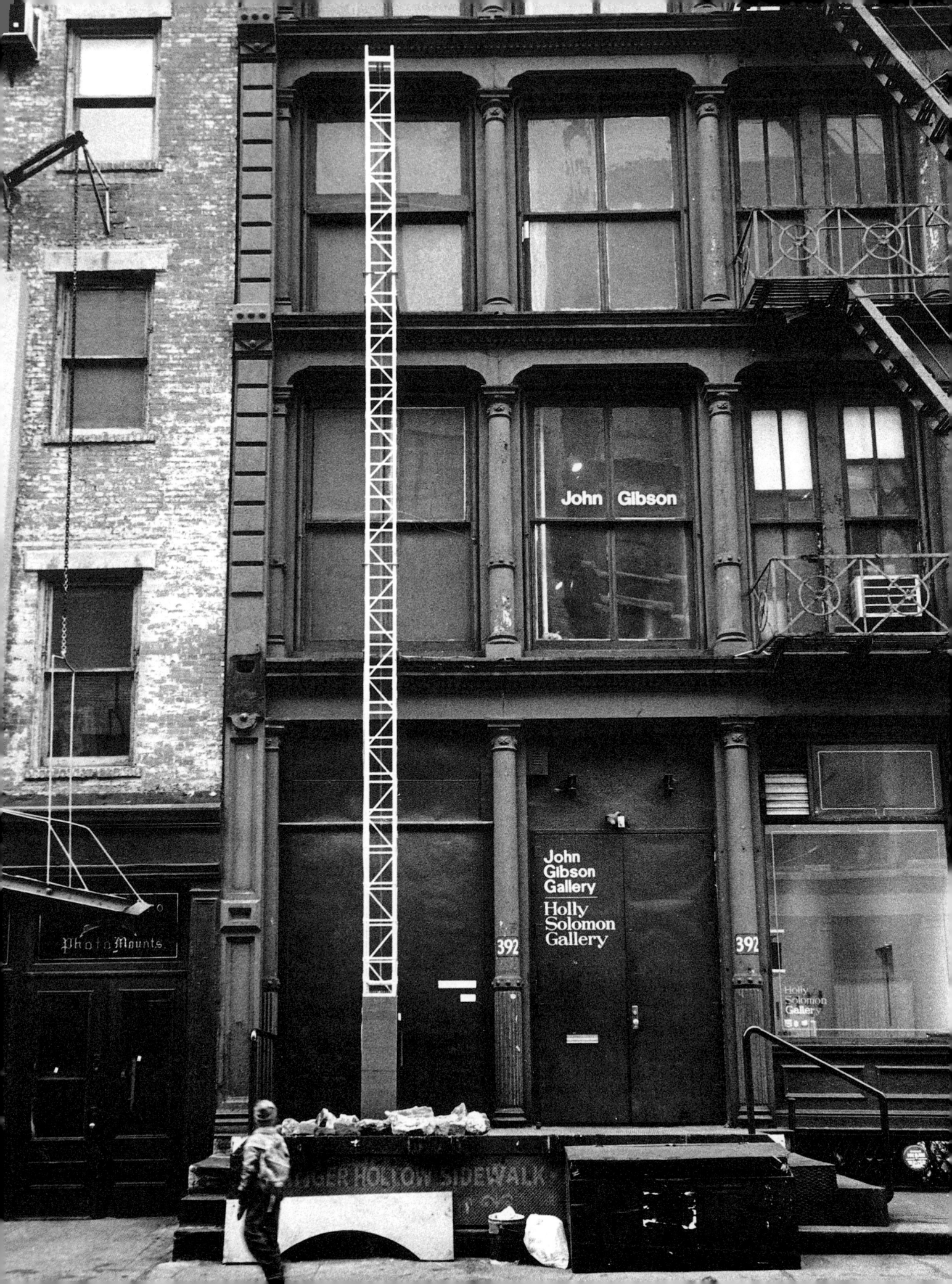

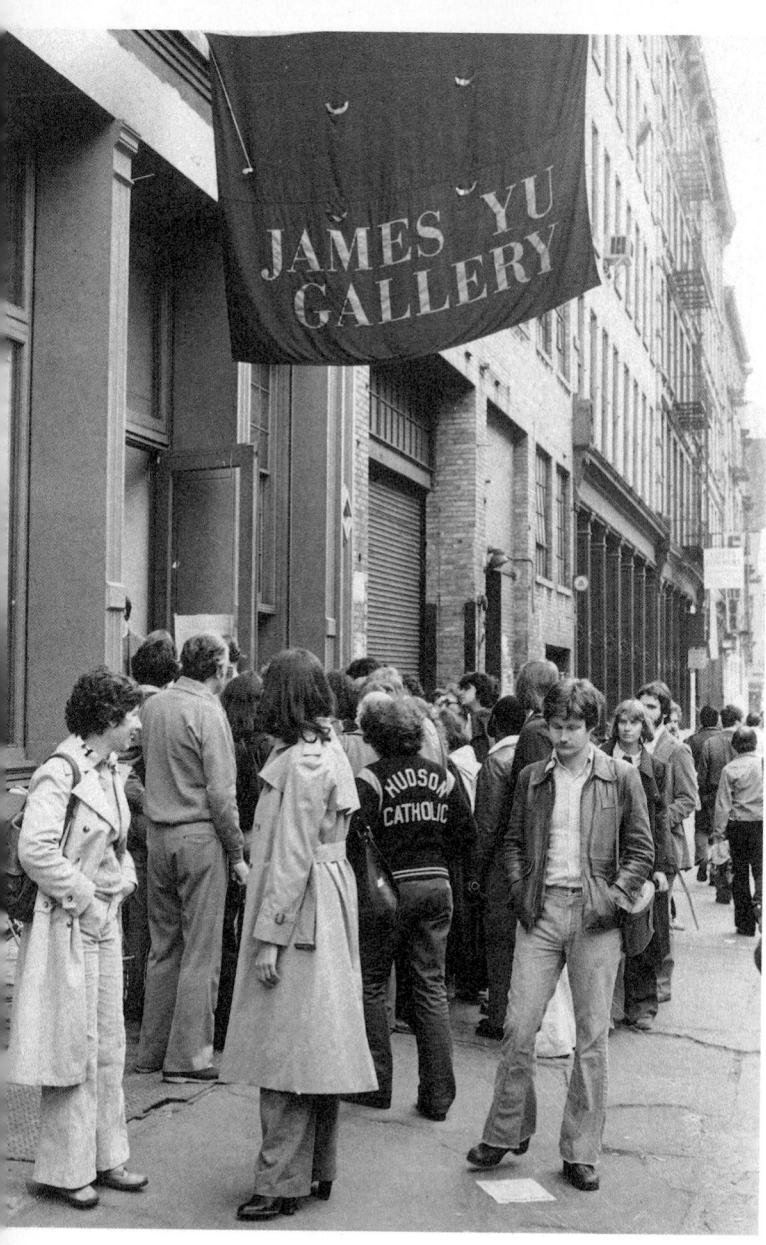

West Broadway. View to the southeast, 1977. Fred W. McDarrah. FWM

proposing instead a full study of the area that would take the artists' needs into consideration as it also looked into the area's continued vitality as an industrial "incubator."[66] A three-day arts festival held on May 8–10, 1970, sponsored by the SoHo Artists Association with help from the city itself, was intended to draw attention to the still threatened area.[67] More than 100 artists planned to open their studios to the public and stage performance and environmental art pieces in the streets. National events cast a pall over the festival, however: on May 4, 1970, four students were killed at antiwar demonstrations on the campus of Kent State University in Ohio, sending shock waves across the country and eliciting particularly strong reactions from New York's artists. Despite the misgivings of some SoHo artists and the participation of others in simultaneously held antiwar demonstrations in Washington, D.C., the festival was held, albeit with modifications: at the last minute, swathes of black bunting augmented the multicolored paper streamers that covered the facades of the area's cast-iron buildings. The dancer Yvonne Rainer led a funereal march through SoHo's streets in, as she stated, a "silent demonstration of solidarity," for which the dignified cast-iron loft buildings served as a powerful visual backdrop.[68] Whatever the impact of the political statements, the event succeeded in drawing a crowd. The editors of Time noted that "thousands of visitors trudged up and down endless flights of stairs to see paintings, sprayed-water 'street sculpture,' light shows and dramatic performances that ranged from the inspired to the inane. Above all, they saw evidence of the hard work and ingenuity that have transformed 40 blocks of bleak, empty spaces into home, work space and playground all in one."[69]

The festival's success struck many SoHo residents as a mixed blessing; though it undoubtedly swelled the ranks of support for SoHo among the population at large, it also seemed to seal the area's fate as yet another outpost of the trendy. As Mike Leff, an artist, put it: "This type of event tends to create a Bohemian environment; I'm down here strictly for the space and not to see it turn into a little old artistic colony."[70] The painter David Diao similarly stated: "Pretty soon we'll have boutiques here and see-the-artist tours. I came here because there was lots of space and it was close to Chinatown so I could eat cheaply. It was a great place for young artists starting out. Now it's becoming another Establishment area."[71] Diao's fears were soon realized. In 1971 Doris Friedman, a former New York City cultural affairs coordinator, led a group of women on a $125-per-ticket "Afternoon in SoHo" tour; proceeds were to be donated to the American Jewish Congress's women's division. Rita Reif, reporting for the New York Times, described the incongruous scene: "Many of the women seemed dressed for Broadway or a visit to uptown galleries. They wore hats and tiny veils and although a few had come in pants suits, most wore minks, tiger and seal fur coats. . . . Sam Schor, a truck driver, yelled . . . : 'Hey, lady—what are they giving away?' He howled with laughter when he heard the women were on a house tour."[72]

Not surprisingly, SoHo's pioneering artists were followed not only by curious onlookers but by powerful uptown art dealers. The area's commercial explosion was not, however, without its share of failures and what the poet and art critic John Ashbery called "a period of fluxuating fortunes."[73] The Park Place Gallery at 542 West Broadway, for instance, was short-lived, but following its closing in 1968, Paula Cooper, the manager of the ill-fated gallery, opened her own gallery on Prince Street. The inaugural show, which included work by the minimalist artists Dan Flavin, Donald Judd, Sol LeWitt and Robert Mangold, helped to establish SoHo as a setting for serious art, at the same

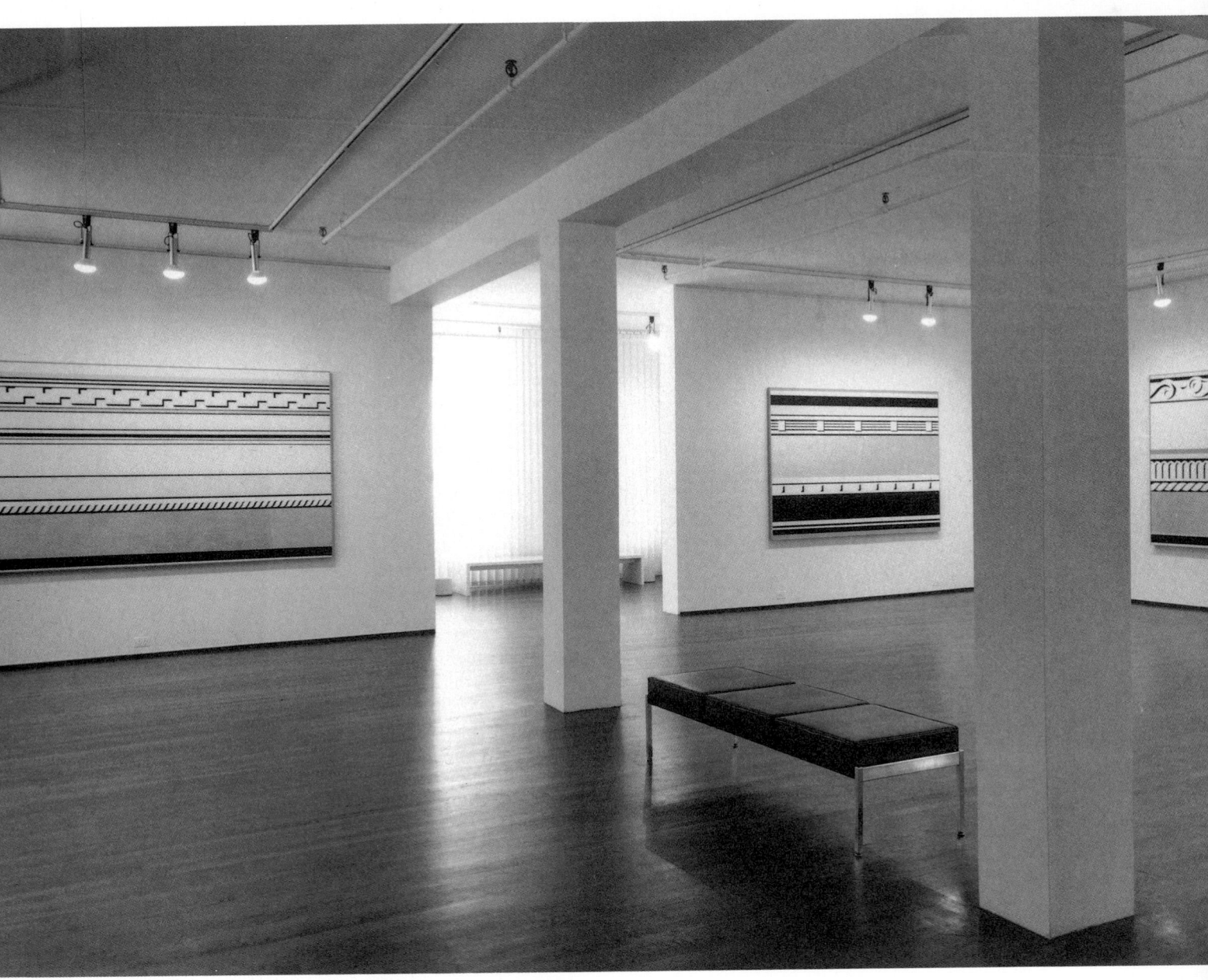

Leo Castelli Gallery, 420 West Broadway, between Spring and Prince
streets. John Bedenkapp, 1971. Main exhibition space. LCG

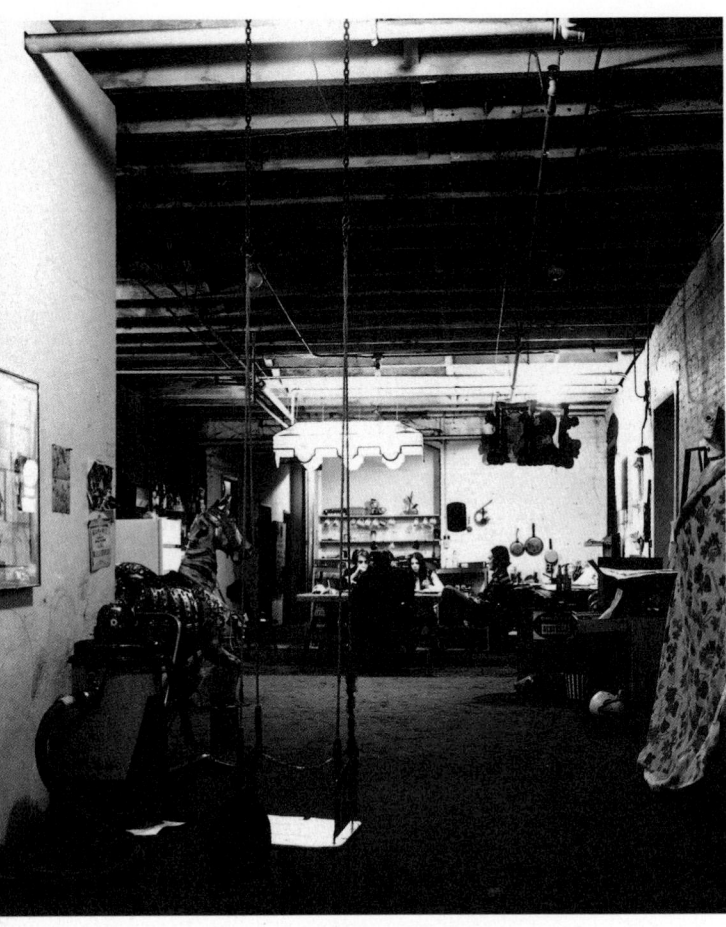

Above: Larry Rivers loft, 404 East Fourteenth Street, between First Avenue and Avenue A, 1967. Dining area. Moore. PM

Top right: Louise Nevelson residence, 29 Spring Street, northwest corner of Elizabeth Street, 1972. Dining room. Suttle. PG

Bottom right: Frank Stella loft, 84 Walker Street, between Cortlandt Alley and Lafayette Street. Richard Meier, 1965. Dining and living areas. RM

time that it marked the area's emphasis on youth and experimentation in contrast to the "establishment" orientation of the art galleries that lined Fifty-seventh Street and Madison Avenue. In 1969 Ivan Karp, who previously had worked with Leo Castelli, opened the O.K. Harris Gallery at 383 West Broadway. The number of SoHo galleries soon soared: in 1970 the publication *Gallery Guide* listed three galleries in SoHo; by 1973 there were over forty; by 1976 the number surpassed seventy.

It was clear that SoHo was firmly on the art world map by 1971 when, as Grace Glueck put it, "The invasion of SoHo, the grubby artists' neighborhood downtown, by a group of elegant uptown galleries was rousingly celebrated in a refurbished loft building at 420 West Broadway."[74] The five-story cast-iron building that had formerly housed the A. G. Nelson Paper Company was co-purchased and renovated by the Hague Art Deliveries company and the art dealers Leo Castelli and André Emmerich. Castelli and Emmerich had orginally conceived of using their SoHo spaces merely for storage but decided to transform the lofts into exhibition spaces. Each owner occupied a floor, as did the art dealers Ileana Sonnabend and John Weber. After visiting the gallery building, which John Corry, writing in the *New York Times*, would later describe as "something like the Macy's of SoHo,"[75] John Ashbery noted: "One's first impression is how good the work looks away from the East Side with its wall-to-wall carpeting, pallid walls and built-in reminders of the duller aspects of success."[76]

As domestication and gentrification were aggressively pursued, the artists' legal claim to their lofts remained tenuous at best. Finally, on January 11, 1971, the City Planning Commission approved the right of artists to live and work in industrial lofts within a forty-three-block area defined as SoHo; the plan was upheld by the Board of Estimate on January 18, 1971.[77] Though the plan had long been supported by Mayor Lindsay, its adoption was delayed by discussions as to the size and number of lofts permitted. City planners, finding that it was primarily the area's smaller lofts that were being abandoned by manufacturers, limited the size of the lofts available to artists to 3,600 square feet. Approximately 1,000 lofts came under the zoning. In order to qualify as an artist, residents were required to be certified by a twenty-member committee composed of artists, gallery owners and members of the local planning board; the committee was supervised by the Department of Parks, Recreation and Cultural Affairs. At the Board of Estimate hearing, Assemblyman Louis DeSalvio objected to the mixed composition of the proposed board, favoring one composed exclusively of artists. Despite this sentiment, the board unanimously approved the rezoning plan as proposed.

Stephen Koch, in an *Esquire* article titled "Where the Avant-Gardest Work the Hardest," noted that "SoHo may be the first neighborhood in the history of the Western World to *require* (it is an article of municipal law) that prospective residents make some plausible claim to the title 'artist.'"[78] The reversal of the age-old unwritten law that artists made undesirable neighbors struck some as absurd; many artists never bothered to register, and by 1976 it was estimated that about 15 percent of the area's loft dwellers were not artists or related to the arts at all but merely in search of space and, perhaps, the trappings of a chic life-style. Some artists were disappointed that the city had not more liberally opened all the loft buildings in the area to residential use. While the city's planners argued that the area was still serving manufacturing purposes, the artists suspected that, as Ron Rosenbaum stated, the City Planning Commission was "under pressure from real estate interests and developers to keep

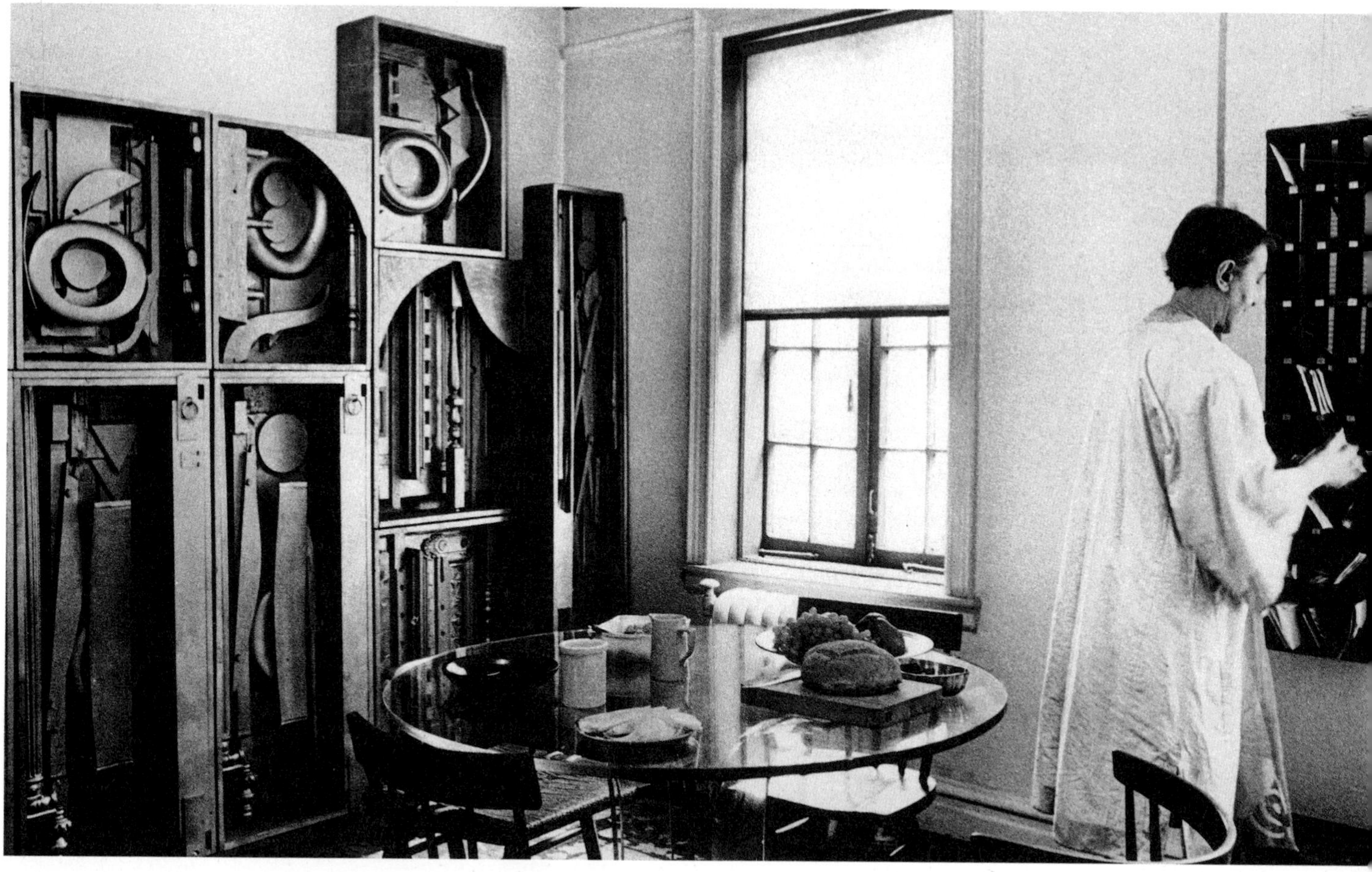

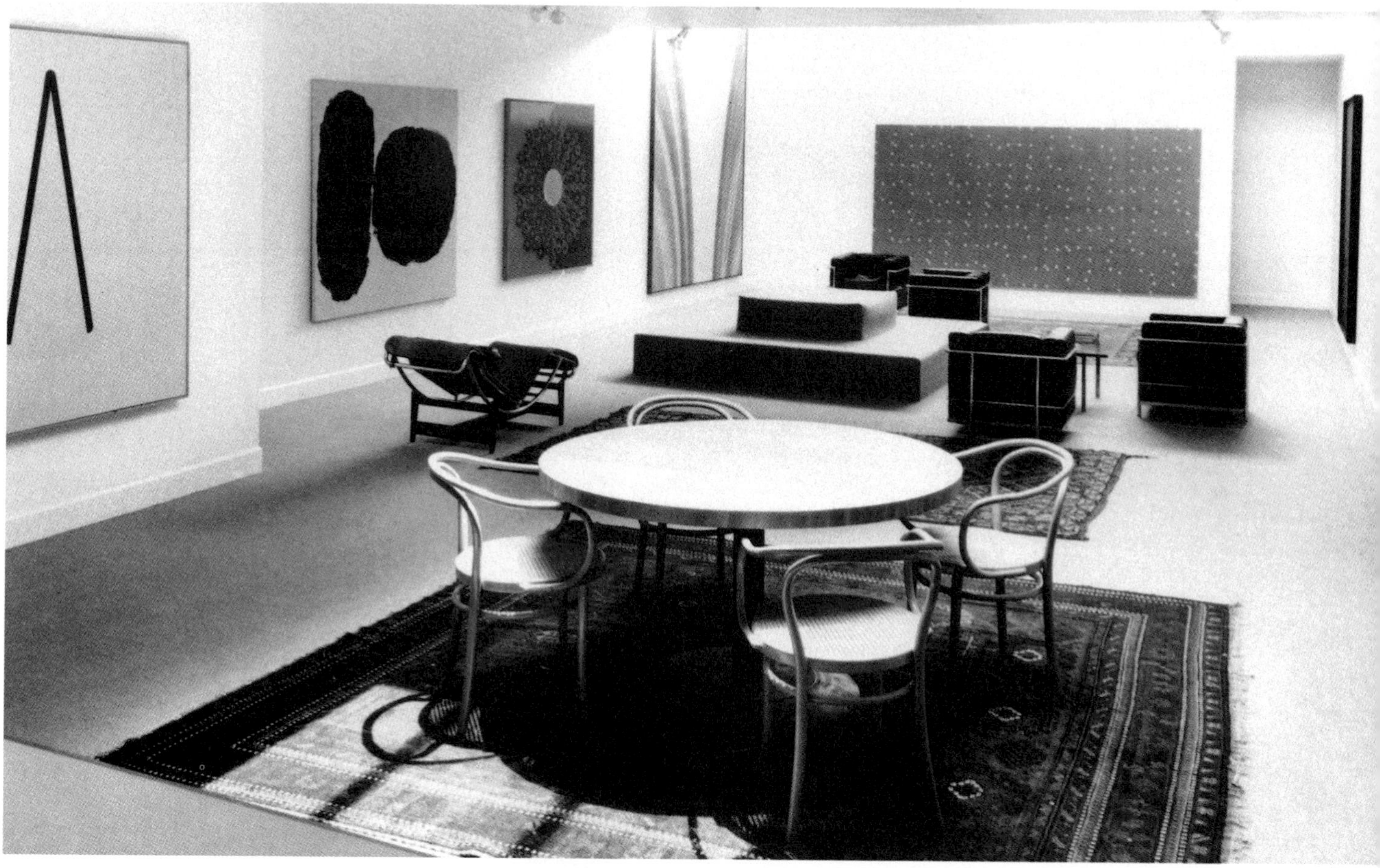

the area marginal so it will be available for some future large-scale demolition and renewal projects."[79]

Amid the dramatic flowering of galleries, shops and restaurants, there was perhaps no greater symbol of SoHo's changing character than a twenty-one-story sports center proposed in 1972 by the real estate developer Charles L. Low.[80] The building, to fully occupy a 100-by-200-foot site at 311 West Broadway between Canal and Grand streets, was to consist of a windowless concrete tower housing a vast array of facilities, including an Olympic-size swimming pool, four skating rinks, fifteen tennis courts, six squash courts, two handball courts and a 6,000-square-foot gymnasium with a jogging track, as well as health-food restaurants, sports-equipment shops, a child-care center and a 225-car parking garage. The SoHo Artists' Association immediately protested the project, known to opponents as "the slab," on the grounds that its massive scale and bulk would visually brutalize the neighborhood as well as cast long shadows across the surrounding low-lying buildings. The group was also concerned that the proposed sports center would attract an upscale Wall Street clientele, further boosting rents and exacerbating congestion. Despite these fears, other local residents, particularly in nearby Little Italy, favored the project, arguing that the center would fulfill long-overlooked recreational needs, particularly those of the area's youth. Their support for the project may also have stemmed from a dislike of the growing presence of artists and a sense that the sports center might engender large-scale, municipally sponsored projects. When the Board of Standards and Appeals approved a requisite zoning variance for the project, the SoHo Artists' Association, represented by the attorney Charles Jurist, filed a suit against the board charging that it had violated its own operating procedures. Apparently because of the strength of Jurist's arguments, Low withdrew his proposal before the case ever went to trial.

As SoHo developed, the press was eager to document the lives and life-styles of the artists settling there and in nearby areas.[81] The editors of *House and Garden* reported on Louise Nevelson, who occupied a mazelike studio on the northwest corner of Spring and Elizabeth streets east of SoHo in Little Italy.[82] Nevelson projected the image of the artist as a mysterious and glamorous figure and the artist's living and working environment as intensely personal. Though Nevelson's house, formerly a sanitarium, was large by city standards, it was anything but open, with virtually every wall of the numerous rooms lined by her intricate constructions. Robert Indiana's 3,000-square-foot loft on the west side of the Bowery near Prince Street was as personal as Nevelson's, though perhaps more gemütlich.[83] With thirty windows on four sides, it was an astonishing contrast to the typical uptown apartment. Filled with Victoriana and plants, as well as the artist's own agreeable LOVE paintings, the space seemed ideal to many members of a young generation reacting against suburbia and uptown alike.

In 1965 the painter Frank Stella and his wife, the art critic Barbara Rose, asked Stella's close friend Richard Meier, with whom he had once shared studio space, to design their loft south of Canal Street at 84 Walker Street.[84] Meier combined living and dining in a cleanly detailed rectangular room, with white-painted walls and ceiling and a floor covered with gray industrial carpeting. A carpeted seating platform provided the principal focus, around which an arrangement of Le Corbusier's furniture was grouped. Paintings by Stella's friends provided the principal decoration.

Robert Indiana loft, Bowery, between Prince and East Houston streets, 1969. Hans Namuth. CCP

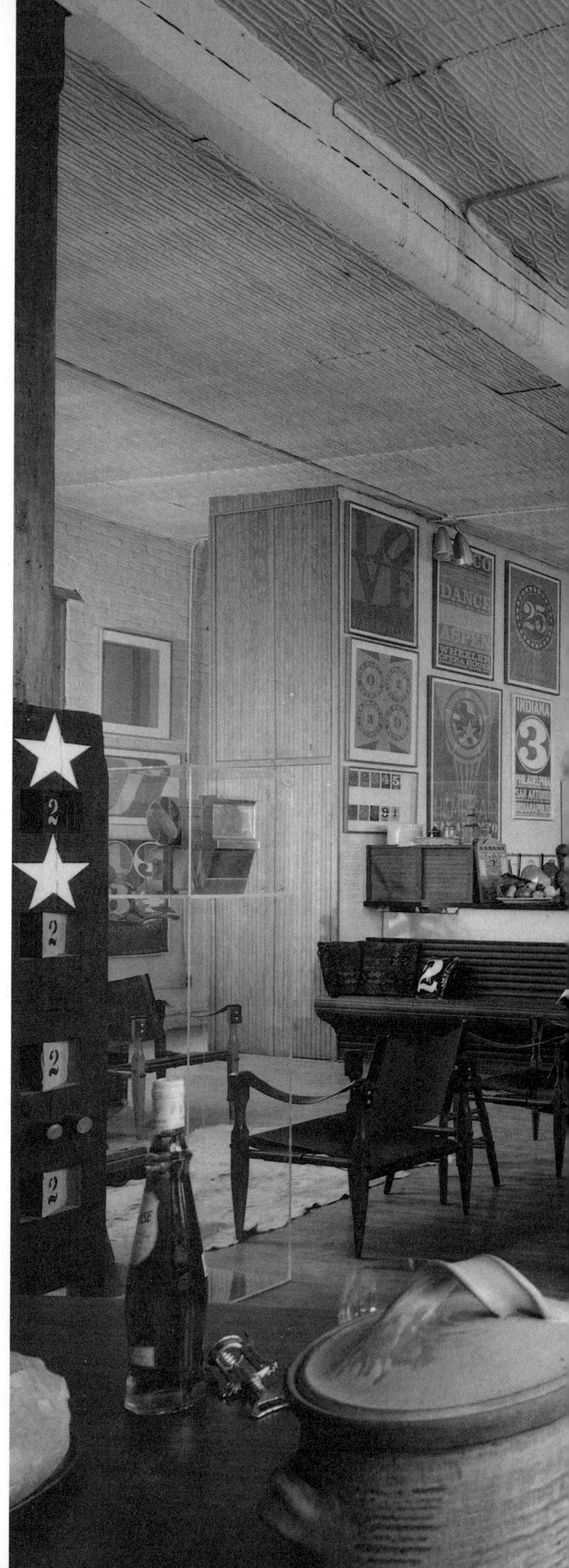

272

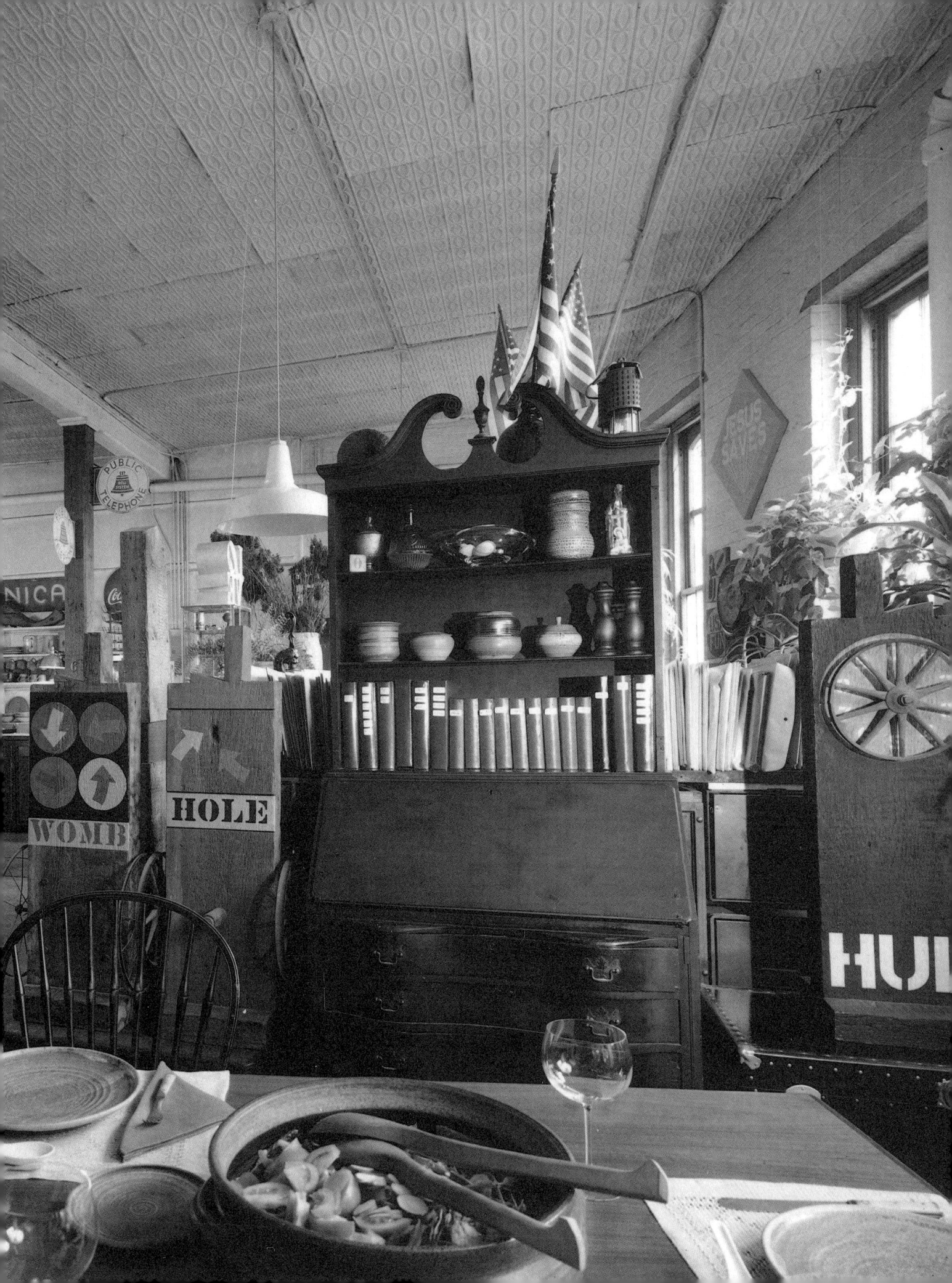

Following the legalization of loft living in SoHo, artists became preoccupied with fixing up their own lofts to the point that the journalist Joan Kron, writing in *New York* magazine, could legitimately claim that "they have ceased resisting the bourgeois life-style. Instead, they're putting time, money, and creative energy into their environment, often neglecting their art to concentrate on construction."[85] A number of artists such as Red Grooms and Arman had two lofts, one for working, one for living. Claes Oldenburg, Donald Judd and Robert Rauschenberg owned whole buildings which they entirely occupied.

Larry Rivers, a "family man" who mixed a career as a painter with a talent for jazz music, was a high-profile exemplar of a loft dweller, though he eschewed the increasingly fashionable SoHo precinct in favor of a loft at 404 East Fourteenth Street. Rivers was profiled for a mass audience in *Look* magazine in 1967, which presented him in his loft living room, replete with conventional, comfortable sofas and tables, a grand piano and a saxophone, extolling the virtues of vast, undifferentiated space: "I even take the baby for a walk in it."[86] As *Look*'s Mary Simons put it:

> Larry Rivers' pad, like his paintings and sculptures . . . has strong personal character. In order to live and work at home, this perpetually avant-garde artist rented a block-deep floor, with great space and light, in a Manhattan loft building, added a few head-high partitions to divide it into bedrooms, bath and living room. Only his studio at the back of the old building . . . has a ceiling-high partition and a door that locks. Living, dining and kitchen areas are really all one room.[87]

Following the artists, art patrons brought the idea of designed interior loft environments with them to SoHo; art dealers and architects would quickly follow. In 1966 the art historian and collector William Rubin, impressed by Meier's work for Stella, retained the architect to design a residential loft where he could effectively exhibit his extensive art collection, representing a veritable "who's who" of the contemporary art scene.[88] Though Rubin was quick to seize on the SoHo style of loft living, he was perhaps reluctant to actually live in the still rather scrappy industrial district, locating instead in a loft building at 831 Broadway on the northern fringe of Greenwich Village. As configured by Meier, assisted by Carl Meinhardt and working very closely with Rubin, the loft featured freestanding partitions defining private areas and ample wall space for the art. Within the dramatically skylit space, living, dining and kitchen areas were open to each other, but in contrast to the typical artist's loft, Rubin's incorporated a rather conventional sense of distinct although not completely enclosed rooms. Still, despite its conventional aspects, the loft struck some observers as being on the cutting edge of fashion. The art critic Annette Michelson rather breathlessly wrote in *Vogue*:

> William Rubin lives in an amazing new Manhattan apartment in an old loft building. . . . A large, light, fluidly composed space, designed for the living and working activities of a scholar and connoisseur, suggesting a life style predicated upon a complex and intimate professional involvement with one of the grander and more sumptuous of imaginable work tools: a collection of contemporary painting and sculpture which constitutes, as well, a constantly regenerative source of visual and intellectual refreshment.

Michelson added that "Mr. Rubin's studio . . . evokes—and quite consciously so—the atelier as it developed in Europe and flowered in the Paris of Impressionism."[89]

In 1970 Charles Cowles, whose parents were just completing the renovation of their Fifth Avenue apartment under Paul Rudolph's direction (see chapter 6), decamped from uptown to a loft at 59 Wooster Street.[90] Cowles was publisher of a provocative new art journal, *Artforum*, founded in 1962. His 75-by-100-foot loft had previously been divided up into twenty small workrooms. Assisted by Mark Hampton, a young decorator who had begun his practice in New York as representative of the Englishman David Hicks and was now working for McMillen, Inc., Cowles cleared the space to reveal its elegant columnar grid, erected one L-shaped freestanding partition to screen the more private areas, sanded the floors and sealed them in their natural color, painted the walls white, installed tracks for lighting, bought a jungle's worth of plants, placed his art and moved in.

By 1974 the architects had discovered SoHo. Hanford Yang, who was a collector as well as an architect, together with five other investors, bought a 35-by-80-foot cast-iron building at 112–114 Prince Street (Richard Berger, 1889–90). He encouraged City Walls to commission Richard Haas to produce one of his most memorable murals, carrying the building's street facade around to its exposed, undesigned party wall (see chapter 17).[91] Yang occupied the ground floor for his own use as an office and took the severely dilapidated second floor, which had once been a toy factory, for use as an apartment. Although Yang used the customary white partition walls, he arranged them to define a diagonal grid that enlivened the space. Instead of the Mies and Le Corbusier tubular furniture typically preferred by New York architects, he used the warmer, lighter, bleached-wood designs of Alvar Aalto. Another architect, Michael Schwarting, working with much less space and money—he did his own construction—ingeniously organized his loft at 471 Broome Street to accommodate his family and provide studio space as well, in essence creating a spatially particularized house within the space.[92] Schwarting's play of curving free-plan elements against more conventionally gridded walls provided a lively complement to the dialogue between the closed volumes of the "house" and the four monumental Corinthian columns that bisected the loft.

Like many New York neighborhoods, SoHo's success proved to be, at least in the eyes of most of its pioneers, its undoing. In discussing the pricing out of artists from the Greenwich Village brownstone market, the editors of *Time* noted, "New Yorkers, being neurotically fashion-addicted, not only use artists as their Seeing-Eye dogs but promptly use their kennels."[93] To a large degree this turned out to be the case in SoHo. In January 1972 Michael Kaufman found that three months after it opened in the airy ground-floor space of an industrial loft building located on the northwest corner of Prince and Wooster streets, a restaurant called Food, originally intended by its owners to serve inexpensive, hearty meals to local artists, was attracting people "coming from as far north of Houston as Larchmont. The place is now regularly crowded, with mink sheathed matrons sharing tables with paint besplattered artists. While business is great, there are some workers in the restaurant who do not think that is so good. . . . While the new popularity of the area has made it more comfortable for many of the artists to live there, many are aware of new threats more pernicious to their life-styles than building inspectors."[94]

Indeed, SoHo increasingly became home to stockbrokers, lawyers and dilettantes, all young, all affluent—the group that would later be dubbed yuppies (young urban professionals).[95] As Emmanuel Tobier has pointed out, "as this group took over more and more of the lofts, the industrial character of SoHo became less and less noticeable, allowing the market to expand

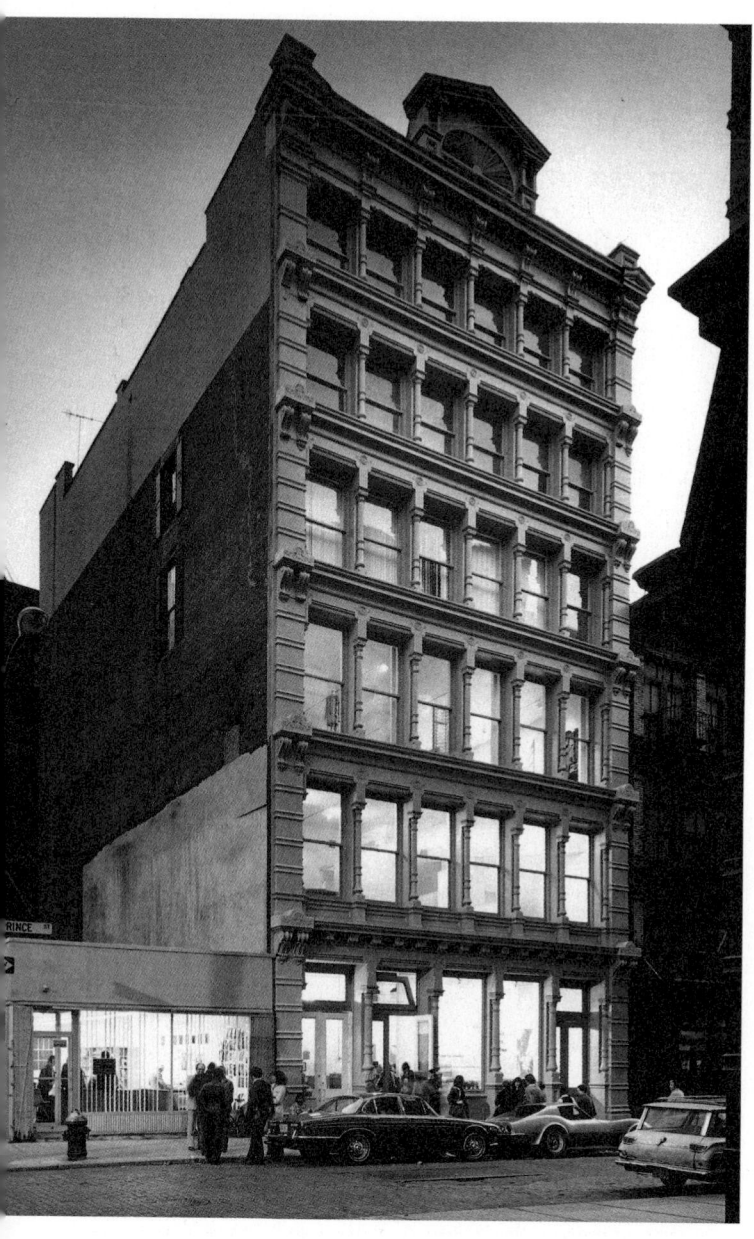

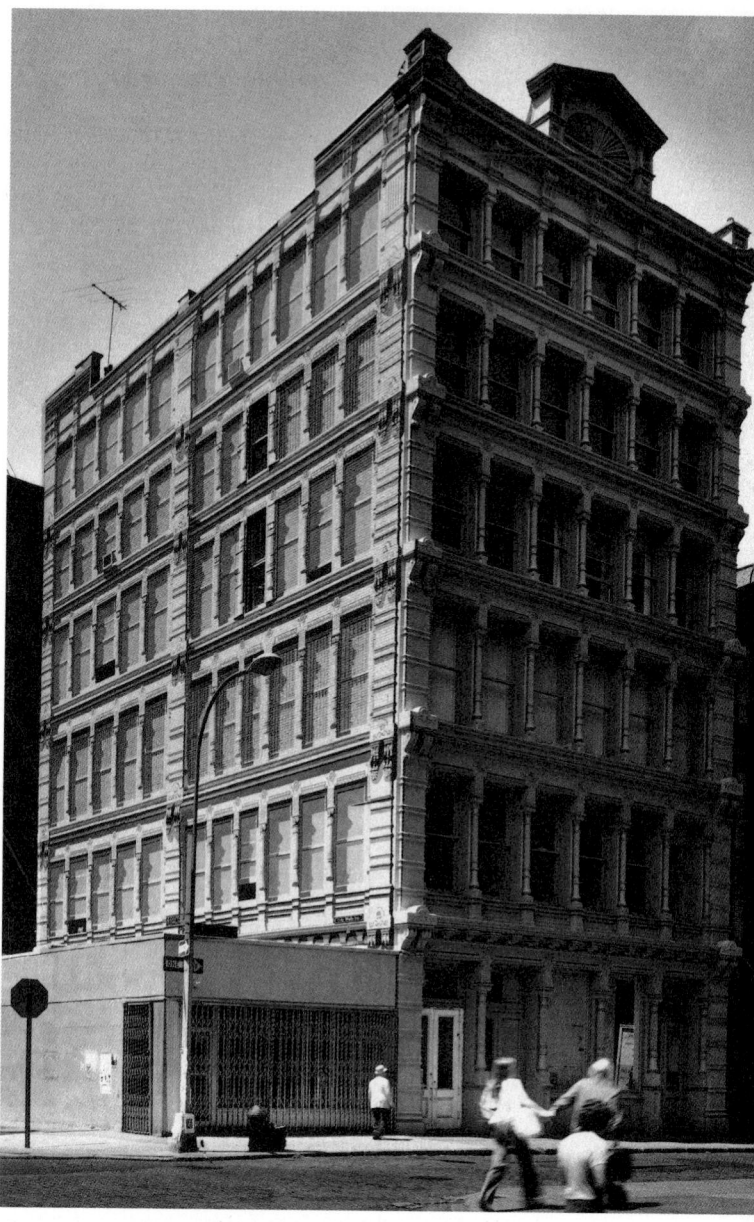

112–114 Prince Street, between Greene and Wooster streets. Richard Berger, 1889–90. View to the southwest. Maris. HY

112–114 Prince Street. View to the southwest showing mural (1974) by Richard Hass. Rosen. HY

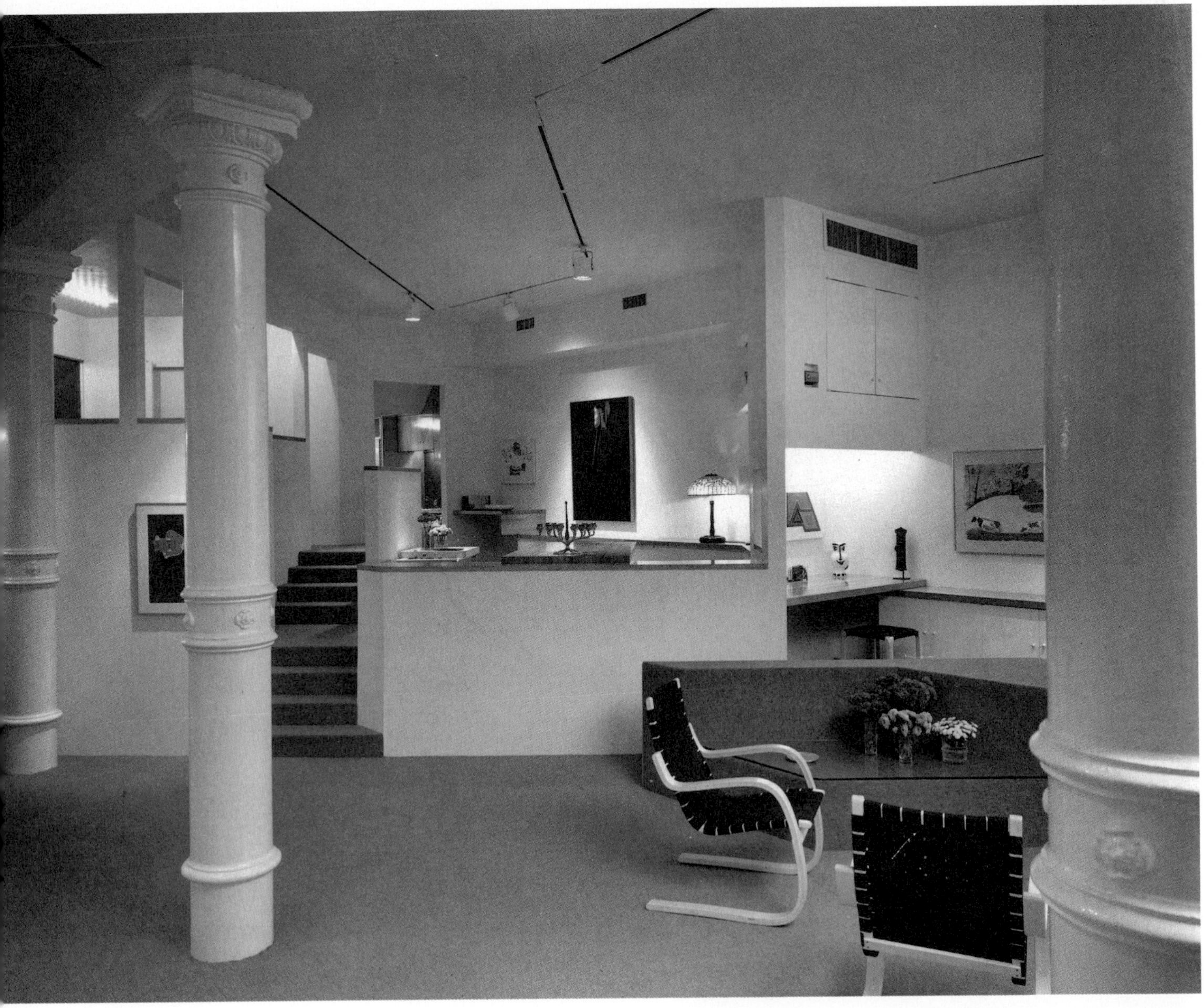

Above: Hanford Yang loft, 112–114 Prince Street, between Greene and Wooster streets. Hanford Yang, 1974. HY

Right: Hanford Yang loft. HY

Far right: Michael Schwarting loft, 471 Broome Street. Michael Schwarting, 1974. Silva. MS

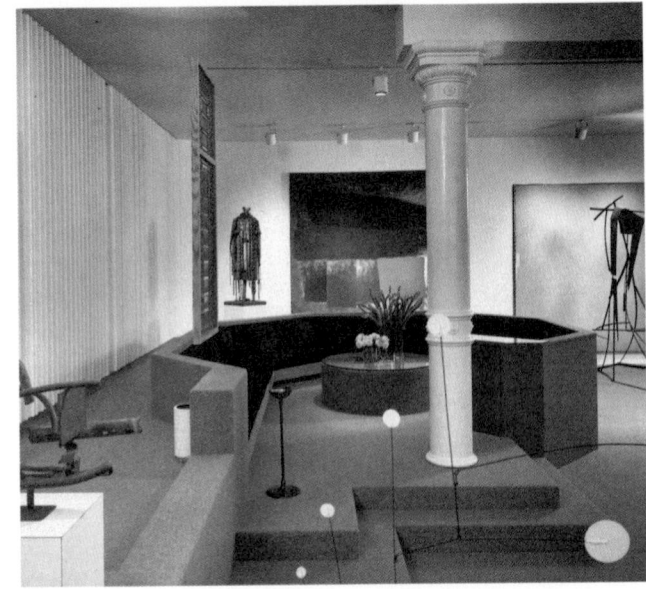

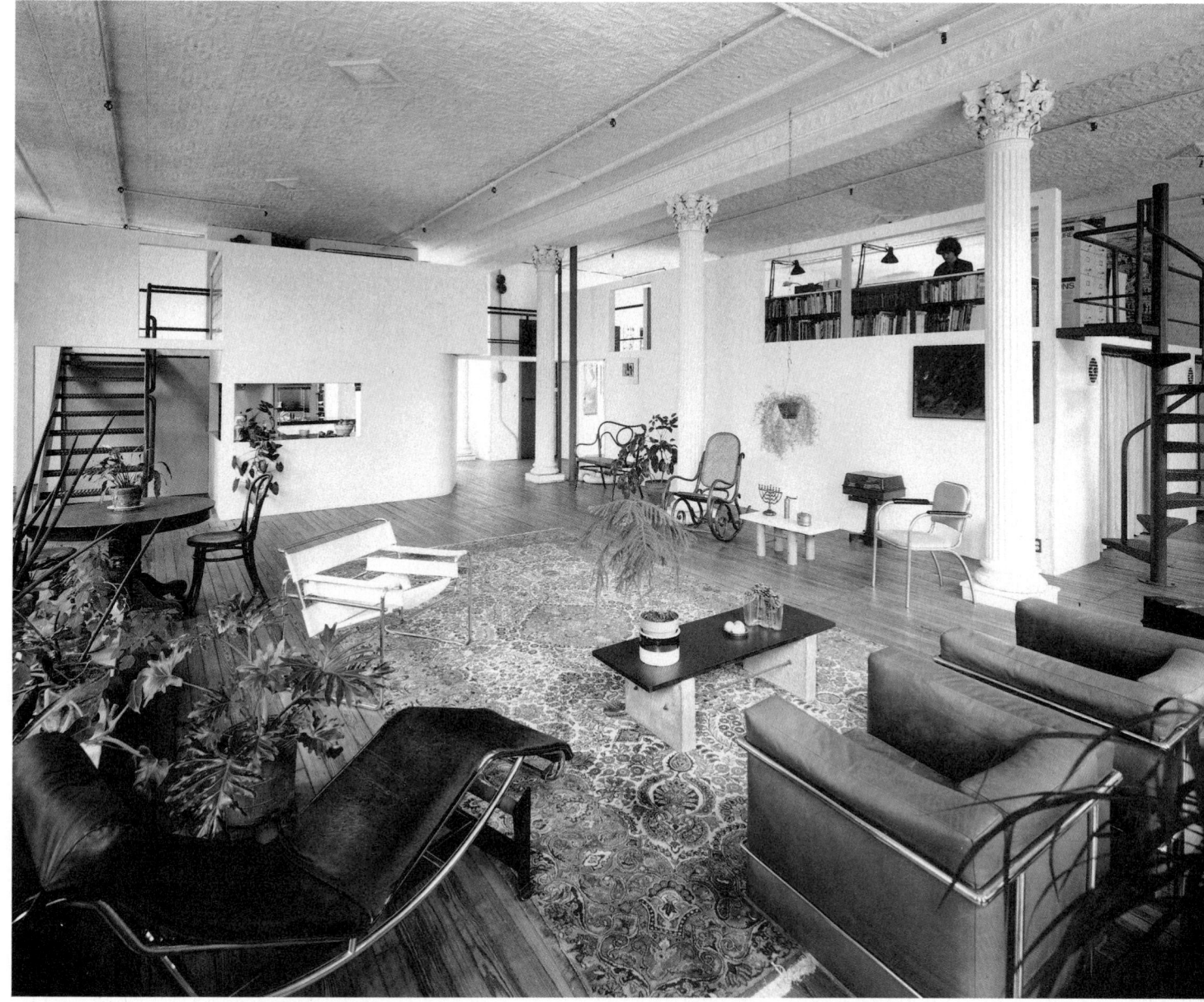

still further in a step-by-step fashion. By the second half of the 1970s, SoHo's lofts had definitely moved upmarket in terms of the prices they were commanding."[96] To some contemporary observers, however, the area seemed not to have changed so radically and to have remained fertile ground for artists. Walter Karp, writing in *Horizon* in 1974, observed:

> The truck-clogged streets are still almost as dismal as ever, making SoHo the ugliest art center in history, yet future historians may find in the local symbiosis between artists and corrugated boxmakers more than a marriage of convenience. That contemporary art, with its penchant for welding, wiring, plastics, and styrofoam, should thrive in an environment of rag processors and junk shops may well signify a final coming to terms between art and industrial civilization. Both, at any rate, are alive and well in SoHo.[97]

Julian Weissman, writing in *Art News* at about the same time, was less optimistic. Reporting that some SoHo artists had moved to Williamsburg and other parts of Brooklyn, and an even greater number to TriBeCa, Weissman questioned SoHo's future: "Is the SoHo artist really becoming an 'endangered species'? Some say yes. Others say no. This much is certain: while SoHo is still the most vital art community in New York, its prohibitive rents are keeping the vast majority of young artists out, while others are being forced out."[98]

Whatever SoHo's success or failure as an economically viable, working bohemia, its value to the city in terms of both its cultural and urbanistic vitality was undeniable. At the close of the period, the critic Jason Epstein tellingly assessed SoHo's significance: "Artists driven southward by the redevelopment of Greenwich Village . . . accomplished, without having intended to, what decades of urban renewal had failed to do. They restored a neighborhood and became its taxpayers. . . . SoHo's revival suggests that the spontaneous generation which once characterized New York's growth remains a possibility."[99]

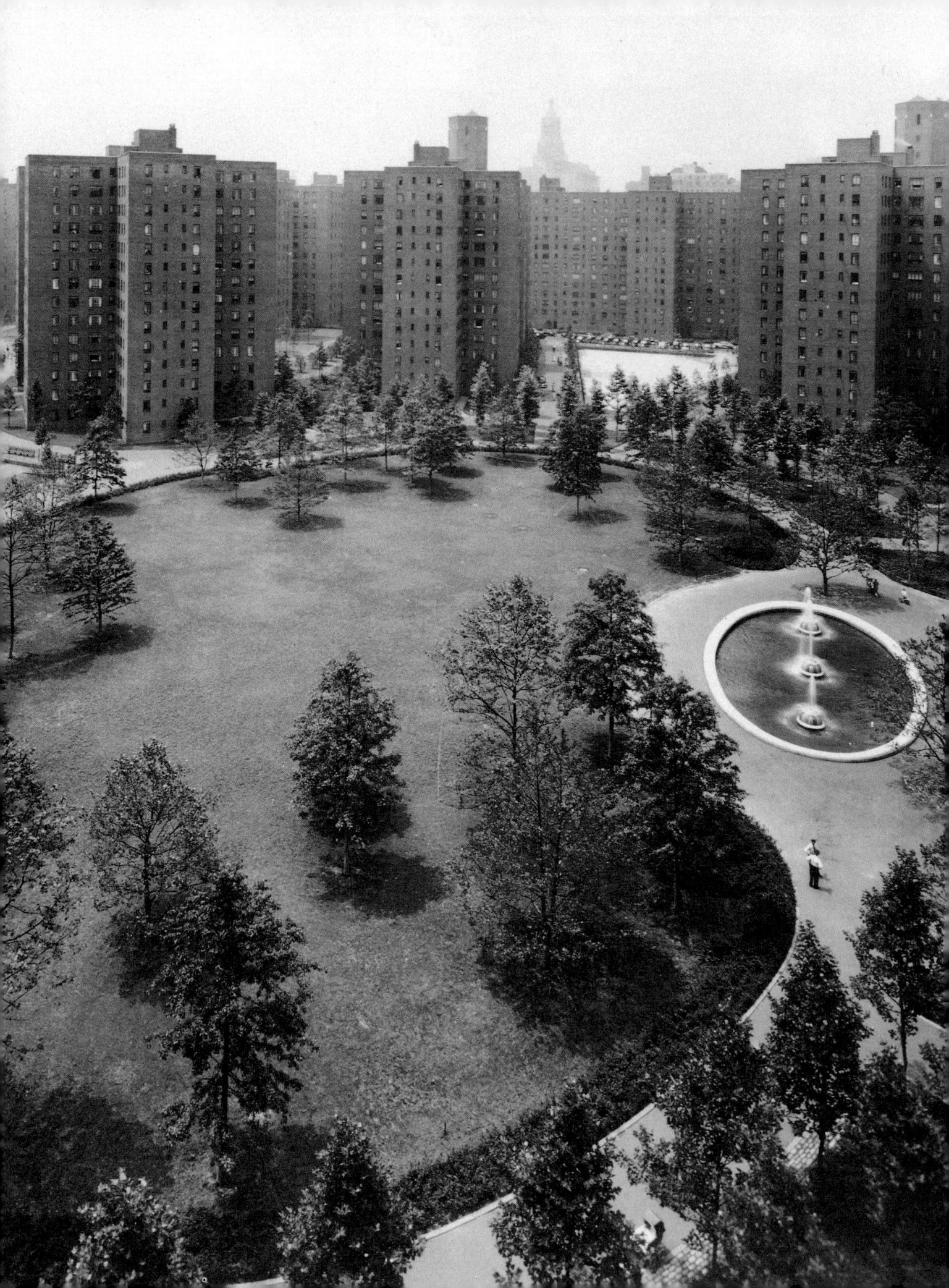

Chapter 5

Midtown

One was continually being jostled, yet longed,
at the same time, for the sense of others, for a human touch;
and if one was never—it was the general complaint—
left alone in New York, one had, still, to fight very hard
in order not to perish of loneliness. This fight, carried on in
so many different ways, created the strange climate of the city.
—James Baldwin, 1962[1]

EAST SIDE:
FROM STUYVESANT TOWN TO TURTLE BAY

Stuyvesant Town

The transformation of east midtown, the area bounded by the East River, Third Avenue, Fourteenth and Fifty-ninth streets, from an area dominated by industrial uses and tenements into one of the world's major concentrations of apartment houses and public institutions, including three major hospitals and the United Nations, was the first significant postwar manifestation of the city's revitalization.[1] This process of transformation had its roots in the redevelopment in the early 1920s of Sutton and Beekman places, and in the establishment of a co-ordinated housing group at Turtle Bay Gardens between Forty-eighth and Forty-ninth streets, Second and Third avenues.[2] The area's transitional nature was best exemplified by the fact that Fred F. French's Tudor City (1925–28), a development of upper-middle-class apartment houses on either side of Forty-second Street east of Second Avenue, had no windows opening to the east because of the abattoirs that filled the land between First Avenue and the East River.[3]

Stuyvesant Town, initiated by the Metropolitan Life Insurance Company in April 1943 as a result of new amendments to the Urban Redevelopment Companies Law, was not nearly as fancy as Tudor City. But its scale and its transformation of the nearby waterfront would effect even more catalytic changes

on the area's demography and urbanism. This development, the pet project of Frederick H. Ecker, Metropolitan's chairman, was the company's second superscale apartment complex in New York, following Parkchester in the Bronx, completed in 1942.[4] In return for agreeing to limit its profit to 6 percent on investment, for the next twenty-five years Metropolitan Life's taxes to the city were to be based on the area's assessed valuation in 1943.

The largest superblock yet undertaken, Stuyvesant Town called for the relocation of 10,000 residents from about 600 buildings in Manhattan's gashouse district. Thirty-five twelve- and thirteen-story buildings would be constructed to house 24,000 people on an eighteen-block, seventy-two-acre site bounded by First Avenue, Avenue C, East River Drive, East Fourteenth and East Twentieth streets. As conceived by a board of design chaired by Richmond H. Shreve, and with members including Andrew J. Eken, George Gove, Gilmore D. Clarke, Robert Dowling and Irwin Clavan, who is credited as the project's architect, Stuyvesant Town was not predominantly oriented to family living; over half of the 8,755 apartments contained only one bedroom.[5] Access to the site from peripheral streets was limited to eight places. The heart of the site was reserved for a quiet, traffic-free park called Stuyvesant Oval. Only 25 percent of the site was occupied by buildings, and garage parking for 3,000 cars was provided. Street-level shops were located along the perimeter streets, which were widened to provide limited-access service lanes. Despite the use of isolated tower slabs, the overall plan maintained the cohesion of traditional streets and courtyards to a remarkable extent: the perimeter buildings reinforced the existing urban grid and the inner buildings, although more loosely arrayed, still managed to define the central oval.

Stuyvesant Town was a controversial project from the beginning, raising objections early on because of its density. With 333 people to the acre, the project's density was only marginally lower than that prevailing on the site during its heyday as a slum in the early 1920s, when 75 percent of the apartments lacked central heating, 66 percent lacked bathrooms and 20 percent lacked private toilets.[6] The proposed population density was only one of the concerns, however; other issues included Metro-

Stuyvesant Town, First Avenue to Avenue C and East River Drive, East Fourteenth to East Twentieth Street. Irwin Clavan, 1947. View to the west of Stuyvesant Oval. MLI

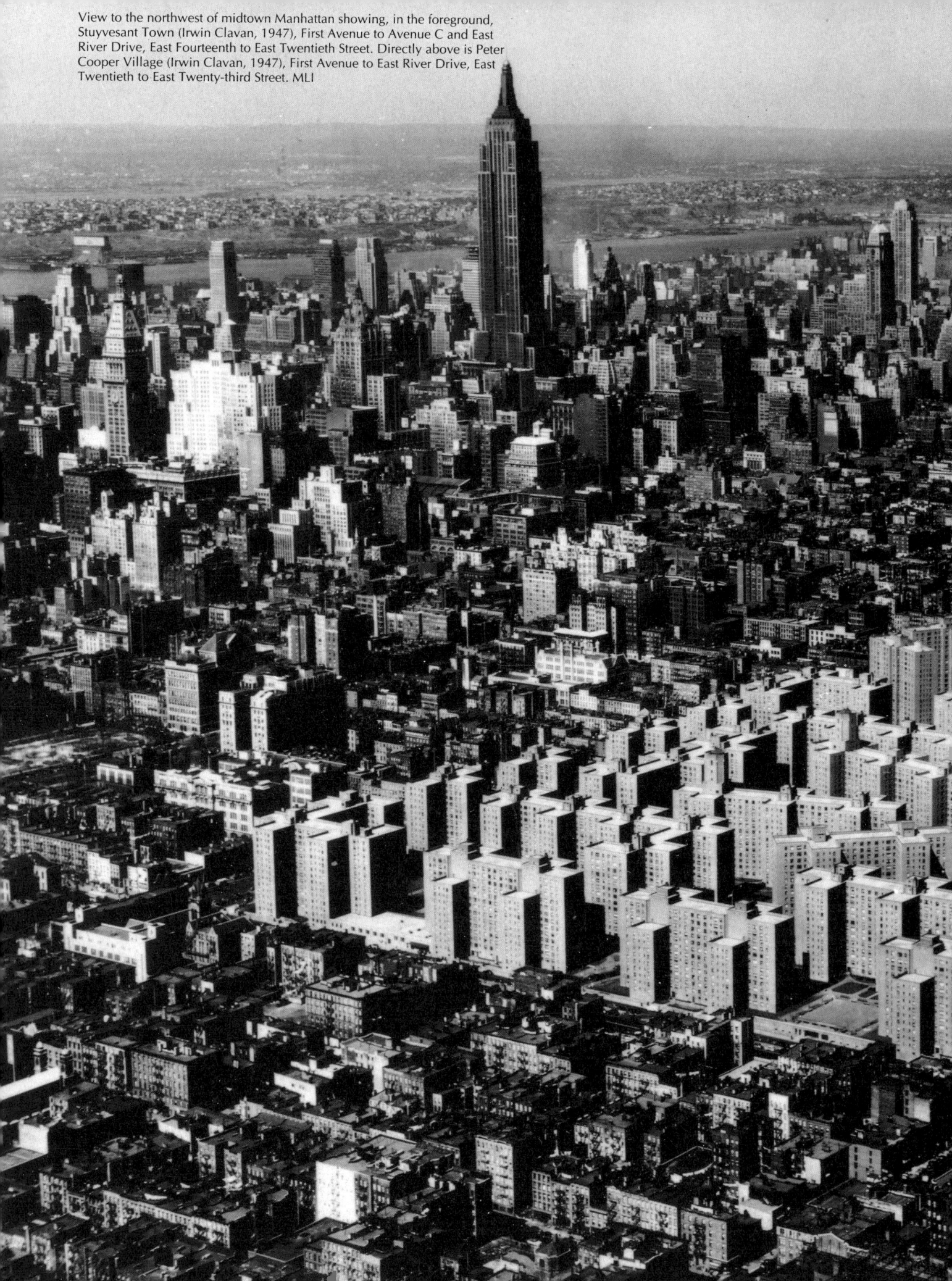

View to the northwest of midtown Manhattan showing, in the foreground, Stuyvesant Town (Irwin Clavan, 1947), First Avenue to Avenue C and East River Drive, East Fourteenth to East Twentieth Street. Directly above is Peter Cooper Village (Irwin Clavan, 1947), First Avenue to East River Drive, East Twentieth to East Twenty-third Street. MLI

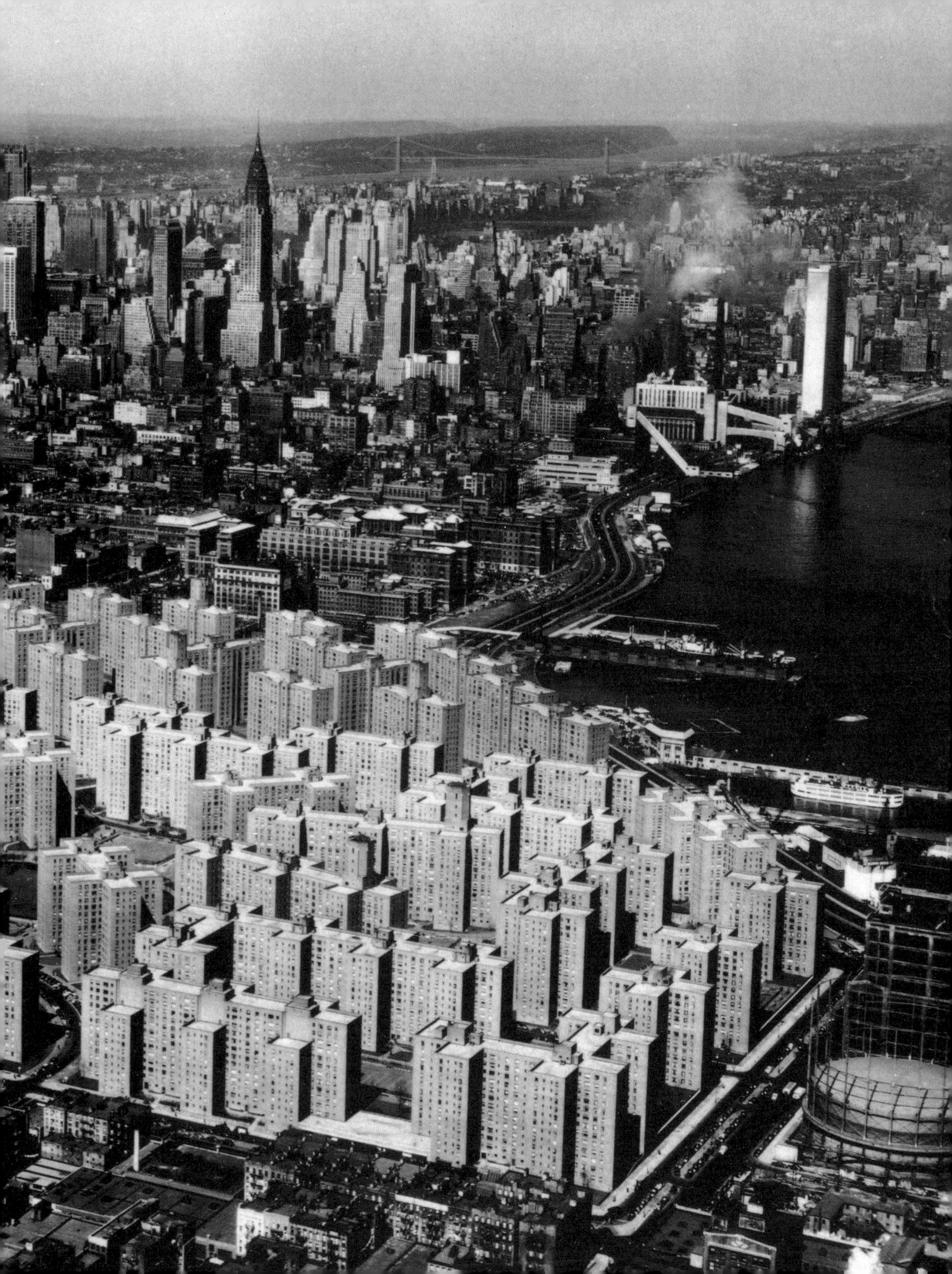

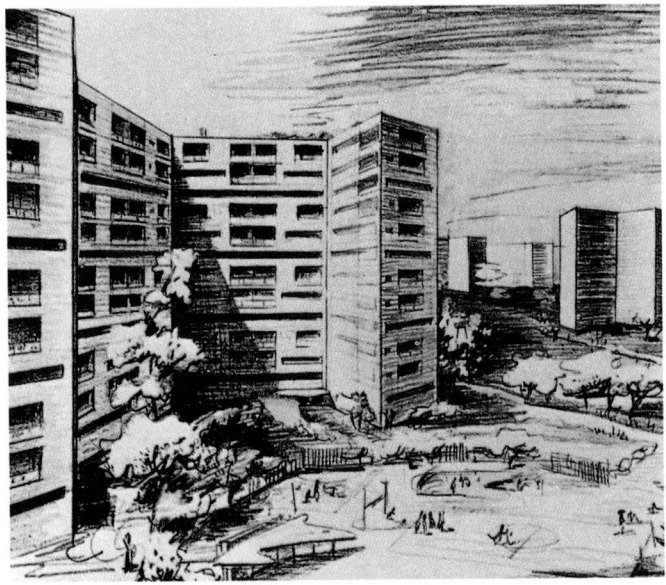

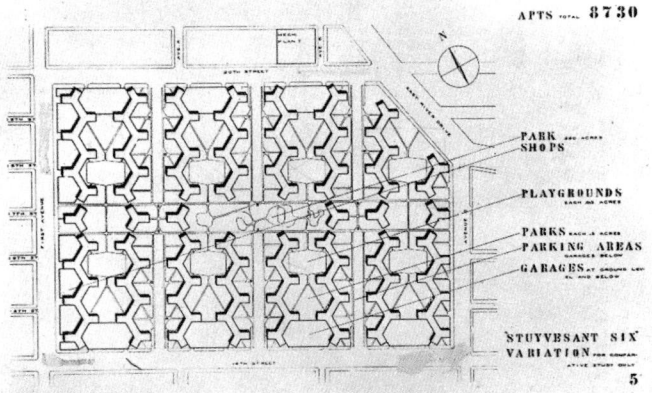

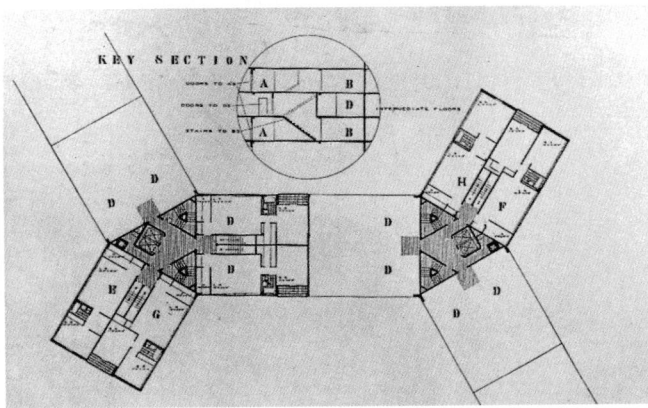

Top: Proposal for Stuyvesant Six, First Avenue to Avenue C and East River Drive, East Fourteenth to East Twentieth Street. Marcel Breuer, 1944. Rendering. PP. CU

Center: Proposal for Stuyvesant Six. Site plan. PP. CU

Bottom: Proposal for Stuyvesant Six. Plan of typical floor. PP. CU

politan Life's tax break, the rights of dispossessed families and the possibility of racial discrimination in tenant selection. Nonetheless, in June 1943 Stuyvesant Town received the support of the City Planning Commission, despite the dissenting vote of one member, Lawrence Orton, who bemoaned the failure to provide for a public school on the site, and the objections of twenty-three architects who protested the high population density.

The Board of Estimate also approved the project in June 1943, although the president of the City Council, Newbold Morris, and Manhattan's borough president, Edgar J. Nathan, Jr., cast dissenting votes and there had been considerable pressure from individuals and civic groups not to make haste. Immediately after the board's approval, the Citizens' Housing Council of New York took the city to court, objecting to the project as "a walled town" with private streets, too few community facilities, too high a population density, no safeguards against racial discrimination, no provision for commercial users along the waterfront and unlimited profit possibilities for the sponsor.[7] According to Architectural Forum, the protests were "ineffectual and disorganized," but they did raise issues that would become critical ones for urban redevelopment in the postwar era.[8] Even the normally prodevelopment editors of the New York Times cautioned the city to take its time,[9] as did the venerable housing expert Loula D. Lasker. In a letter to the New York Times dated May 28, 1943, Lasker argued that "to all intents and purposes [Stuyvesant Town] will be a company-walled town" and objected to the fact that although its population would be as large as that of Jacksonville, Florida, it would not contain a public school or other facilities, "with the exception of grossly inadequate park and playground space." Lasker also went on to criticize the project's discriminatory policies: "The Metropolitan Life has indicated that it will not consider applications from Negroes for apartments. As has been pointed out, the right of any citizen, regardless of race, creed or color, to share the benefits of public-aided projects has long been accepted in this State."[10] A few days later the New York Times published a defense by Robert Moses, which marshaled a barrage of technical arguments in behalf of the project and avoided the critical issue of racial discrimination.[11] The discriminatory policy was not without its defenders: the editors of Architectural Forum baldly stated, in response to a letter to the editor, that "not until the U.S. Government admits Negroes to all of its public housing projects does it seem rational to transfer this problem to the Metropolitan Life Insurance Company."[12] By late 1943 the argument over Stuyvesant Town was so intense that the National Association of Housing Officials described it as "a battle up to now lacking only in beer bottles and murder."[13]

In 1944 Tracy B. Augur published a full-scale analysis of the debate and a sympathetic assessment of the plan in the Journal of the American Institute of Planners. Augur's assessment of Stuyvesant Town as "the most dramatic project yet announced for the redevelopment of an American city" reflected the prevailing wisdom that sound urban renewal in the postwar era required projects of such scale. As Augur put it: "Little islands of redevelopment in a big sea of blight have little chance of survival." Finding virtue in many of the features that so antagonized Lasker and others, Augur observed that "there is a distinct unity to Stuyvesant Town derived from the fact that all of the building facilities will be of one kind and under one management, and that they will differ from those of surrounding areas." He applauded the central park and the "strong boundary in the form of widened streets and an outer wall of garages," claiming that "these are features that build neighborhood strength."

Taking pains to argue that Stuyvesant Town must be understood in terms of New York and not judged by the standards of rural America, Augur defended the development in a manner typical of many such statements that would be made on behalf of large-scale projects in the next few years: "If it is built as planned . . . there will be a living experiment in urban rehabilitation that will have inestimable value. It will be worth the price if for no other reason than to induce and keep alive the kind of argument that has already been generated by it, argument that makes it the excuse for probing the imponderables of urbanism."[14]

While the courts found for Metropolitan Life in the various suits brought against the project, many architects continued to be troubled by the design. In June 1944 *Pencil Points* published a counterproposal prepared by the Bauhaus-trained, Hungarian émigré architect Marcel Breuer, then in practice in Cambridge, Massachusetts, where he was a professor at Harvard's Graduate School of Design.[15] In one design, Breuer chose not to question the fundamental premises of Metropolitan Life's planning strategy, instead carrying the superblock idea even further, completely clearing the site of automobiles and, for purposes of "comparative study," proposing a regular pattern of continuous bent slabs. In a second proposal, which Breuer named Stuyvesant Six, he called for a 19 percent reduction in density; diagonal slabs that incorporated a "skip-stop" organization, with elevators stopping on alternate floors, would guarantee cross-ventilation to all apartments. In discussing the project, Breuer came down hard on the "country-suburban romanticism" of contemporary planning, applauding as a central feature of urbanism "the concentration, the nearness of a great many things to each other; the choice, or the illusion of a choice between many possibilities," and arguing against decentralization: "I do not believe that dissolving our metropolises and giving everybody, say, a half acre of land, would solve the problem. . . . The standards of an urban area cannot be expressed by the figure of its population per square acre."[16]

Despite public reservations over many key aspects of the project, no changes had been made to the original plan over the two years since the Board of Estimate had approved the project in June 1943, thereby sending to war-weary New Yorkers as well as to planning professionals an alarming signal about the character of the postwar development process. As Edwin S. Burdell noted in the *Journal of the American Institute of Planners* in 1945:

> The contract between the City and the Company was approved and there appears to have been no modification of the original plan involving from the standpoint of the public good such questionable features as the gift of some sixteen acres of former public streets, elimination of existing churches and public schools without provision for new ones within the project area, the apparent intention of discrimination as to type of tenant and, finally, freedom from responsibility of rehousing present occupants on this site or elsewhere. This project, which involves a cost of approximately $55,000,000 and is to house 24,000 persons, appears to have weathered all the storms. It will be the first tangible fruit of the several different varieties of urban redevelopment legislation enacted in the United States in the last five years.[17]

By the spring of 1945 plans began to be drawn up for the relocation of the families occupying the Stuyvesant Town site.[18] While Metropolitan Life was not required to help with relocation, it did undertake to do so on a voluntary basis, locating apartments in the open market and in public housing. As Burdell and other planners noted, despite deplorable conditions and the long-term threat of redevelopment, the gashouse neighborhood that was to be eliminated constituted a viable community. For the first time, perhaps, planners and elected officials were confronted with a new reality: that healthy communities existed, even thrived, in physically degenerated environments.

When Stuyvesant Town finally opened in 1947, despite the bleak uniformity of the buildings and the as yet immature landscape, middle-class New Yorkers welcomed it with enthusiasm as an appealing and distinctly affordable alternative to suburban tract houses.[19] Even *House and Garden*, the bible of upscale suburban living, took note, profiling a typical family, the Landmans, who found in a $76.50 per month Stuyvesant Town apartment their "first real home."[20] The critic Lewis Mumford, acknowledging the acute postwar shortage of affordable housing in New York, was quick to point out, however, that "any truly critical appraisal" of the city's new housing developments "will have to come . . . from a non-tenant. Those who are lucky enough to be accepted by the landlords will probably view their new homes through a rosy haze, as a Displaced Person might."[21] In a follow-up article on Stuyvesant Town Mumford asked important questions about the viability of skyscraper living for middle-income families:

> For mothers who have neither nursemaids nor governesses, nor even grandmothers and aunts, to aid them in looking after their children, life in the Stuyvesant Town barracks poses many difficulties. . . . Tall apartment houses are adequate for bachelors and childless couples, but children and the aged need quite different quarters, in houses and in low apartment buildings, arranged around greens where young children may still be under the eyes of their mother while she is at work about the flat. These new housing projects are not cut to fit the requirements of family life; family life must be cut to the requirements of large-scale building.[22]

Mumford tried to be gracious in acknowledging letters he had received from tenants who were pleased with their new surroundings: "Quite properly," he admitted, "they declare that their quarters are the equal of anything Manhattan can offer elsewhere at two or three times the rental, and they feel that they are in heaven." But, he continued, "Like almost all New Yorkers, who have spent most of their lives in cramped, sunless, dusty and even garbagy blighted areas, they have no proper basis for judging Stuyvesant Town. . . . They praise Stuyvesant Town only because they do not know how much is missing from its design."[23]

Mumford left no doubt as to his feelings about the quality of the project, castigating it as "an unrelieved nightmare" that epitomized "the architecture of the Police State, embodying all the vices of regimentation one associates with state control at its unimaginative worst." Mumford went on to say: "As things go nowadays one has only a choice of nightmares. Shall it be the old, careless urban nightmare of post-Civil War New York. . . . Or shall it be the new nightmare, a great super-block, quiet, orderly, self-contained, but designed as if the fabulous innkeeper Procrustes had turned architect—a nightmare . . . of impersonal regimentation, apparently for people who have no identity but the serial numbers of their Social Security cards?" He also severely criticized the project's population density and site planning, arguing that despite the seemingly large amount of open space, "instead of easing the general deficiency of parks and playgrounds in Manhattan . . . Stuyvesant Town actually adds to this chronic shortage." Furthermore, Mumford charged, "Once you are inside the super-block, you are walled in. . . . Even the pool of quiet green at the center of the development—the hap-

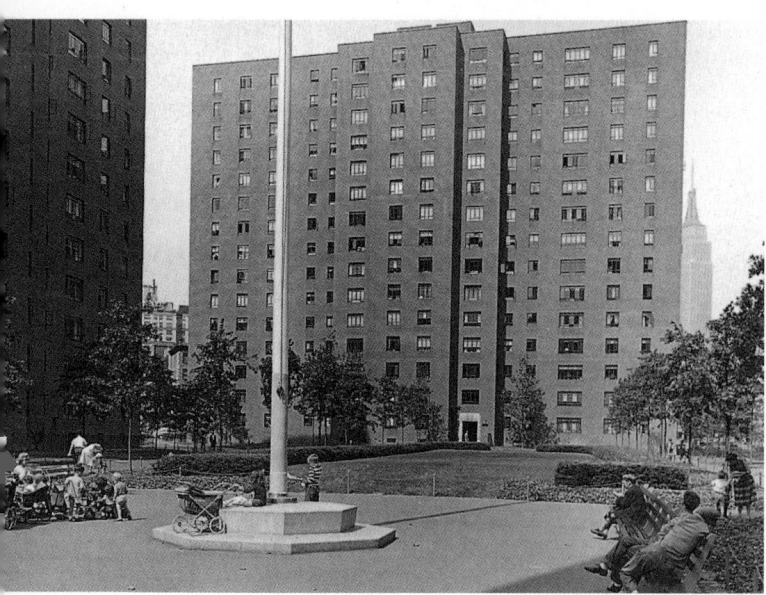

Peter Cooper Village, First Avenue to East River Drive, East Twentieth to East Twenty-third Street. Irwin Clavan, 1947. Gottscho-Schleisner. LOC

piest part of the whole plan—loses a good part of its repose through the inhuman scale of its architecture."[24]

Mumford found a bit more to like inside the buildings. "Except for a few skyscraper apartments, which temporarily have uninterrupted views from their upper stories," he stated, "nowhere in the more expensive residential districts in Manhattan will you discover any comparable access to sunlight, air, and vista." In addition, Mumford observed, "The standards of interior space throughout . . . are generous; even the minimum accommodations are more spacious than is usual in the prewar public housing projects of the same order, and the kitchens . . . are marvelously convenient." But even in this aspect of the design Mumford found fault, noting that "about a hundred and twenty square feet of costly space is wasted in each apartment on a windowless anteroom, called the foyer."[25]

Whatever Stuyvesant Town's architectural and urbanistic shortcomings, or the irreversibility of the patterns it established, to many contemporary observers the project's most troubling and potentially divisive aspect was the social one of racial segregation. In 1948, after Joseph Dorsey and two other black war veterans brought suit against the Stuyvesant Town Corporation and the Metropolitan Life Insurance Company for racial discrimination, the Appellate Division of the New York State Court affirmed the decision of the lower court in which Judge Felix C. Benvenga had said that the plaintiffs had confused "public use" and "public purpose" with the term "public project."[26] His decision had said that though Stuyvesant Town had benefited and continued to benefit from serving a public purpose—slum clearance—it was not in fact a public project. To help deflect charges of discrimination, Metropolitan Life permitted about a dozen white families to live in its 1,232-unit Riverton project in Harlem.[27] This satisfied no one, however, and pressure against the policy continued to build; the United Nations Secretariat, for example, refused to lease apartments for its staff in the development.

Where the courts had failed, public pressure on the mayor and Metropolitan Life eventually prevailed. Threatened by a bill against discrimination pending in the City Council, in 1950 Metropolitan Life admitted three black families, claiming that its admission of "some qualified Negroes" represents "no change in the company's policy."[28] Nonetheless, the legal case against Metropolitan Life was eventually taken to the United States Supreme Court, which announced its refusal to hear the case, thereby propelling action through legislation, a route that the New York courts had deemed legal.[29] Despite Metropolitan Life's opposition, the Brown-Isaacs bill barring discrimination in all publicly assisted housing, widely viewed as landmark legislation, was passed by the City Council.[30]

As work got under way for Stuyvesant Town, Metropolitan Life began to prepare plans for Peter Cooper Village, a 1,500-family development that was to occupy the site immediately to the north.[31] Bounded by First Avenue, East River Drive, East Twentieth and East Twenty-third streets, Peter Cooper Village was significantly different from its neighbor both in its economics and its site planning. Architect Irwin Clavan's plans for Cooper Village were filed in January 1946 and construction was well under way by early 1947. Because Cooper Village was built without tax exemptions or city land assembly, its rents were nearly double those of Stuyvesant Town. As a result, tenants were drawn from the ranks of the middle and upper-middle classes. In designing Cooper Village, Clavan abandoned the last vestiges of the traditional, mass-positive urbanism that had infused Stuyvesant Town with a hierarchy of open spaces and a true sense of a village clustered around a green. Instead, he favored a total lack of interior streets and an abstract, self-referential arrangement of un-differentiated slabs, shifted off Manhattan's orthogonal grid to minimize north-facing apartments and to take advantage of the best river and skyline views. In effect, this grid shift was Cooper Village's principal distinguishing feature, except for the larger apartment units, whose size and detail in no way reflected the high rent they commanded.

In the same October 1948 article where Lewis Mumford initially examined Stuyvesant Town, he turned his attention toward Cooper Village "with relief," as he said. Despite the latter project's greater height—the buildings were fifteen stories high—Mumford found that the overall "effect is not so tight and closed-in." The slabs' diagonal orientation, he noted, "seems to form a series of receding steps, like a Cubist demonstration of the relation of color and tone to distance." This quality constituted "almost the only effect that can be called aesthetic or architectural" at either Peter Cooper Village or Stuyvesant Town. Mumford concluded that "Peter Cooper Village is, aesthetically at least, a little less prisonlike than Stuyvesant Town."[32] Despite the features that distinguished it from its neighboring development, however, Cooper Village felt particularly anonymous, encapsulating the impersonal ambience of a "project" as much as any undertaking of the Housing Authority. With the completion of the Stuyvesant, Cooper and Riverton projects, the Metropolitan Life Insurance Company, now landlord to 2 percent of Manhattan's residents but discouraged by rising land-acquisition and construction costs as well as by the increasingly aggressive role of tenants and other civic groups, removed itself from the housing field.

At the outset of the postwar period Bellevue Hospital (McKim, Mead & White, 1908–39) represented the largest public health facility in the city. In 1944 plans were made for its expansion by the construction of a residence and school for nurses to occupy the entire block bounded by Twenty-fifth and Twenty-sixth streets, First Avenue and East River Drive.[33] Designed by Alfred Hopkins & Associates and finally completed in 1956 by its successor firm, La Pierre, Litchfield & Partners, the complex consisted of three slablike units organized around a south-facing, campuslike court.

In 1944 New York University (NYU) announced plans to develop a medical-dental center in conjunction with a proposed expansion of Bellevue Hospital.[34] By 1945 Skidmore, Owings & Merrill (SOM) had been retained to plan the so-called New York University–Bellevue Medical Center, at first proposing an idiosyncratically organized six-unit facility for the site, bounded by Twenty-fifth and Thirty-fourth streets, First Avenue and East River Drive.[35] In a gesture of approval, the city agreed in 1947 to permanently close to traffic Thirtieth, Thirty-first, Thirty-second and Thirty-third streets between First Avenue and East River Drive. This enabled NYU to revise plans for the medical center in 1949, resulting in an asymmetrically disposed, five-building complex encompassing eleven acres.[36] The plan called for a twenty-story, 600-bed University Hospital, a horizontally banded slab set perpendicular to the river. Low wings on either side were to house the College of Medicine, the Post-Graduate Medical School, the Institute of Rehabilitation and the University Clinic. A second tall slab, the sixteen-story Hall of Residence, would also run perpendicular to the river. A building to be called Alumni Hall, principally housing a 500-seat auditorium, would serve as the main entrance to the group.

A pure expression of scientific medical care as the product of unsentimental modernity, the complex marked a bold departure from the red-brick Classicism of the McKim firm's

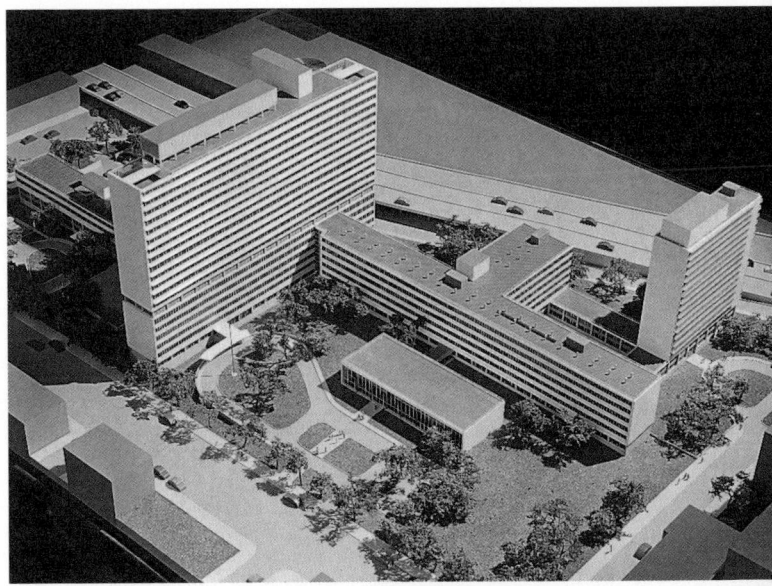

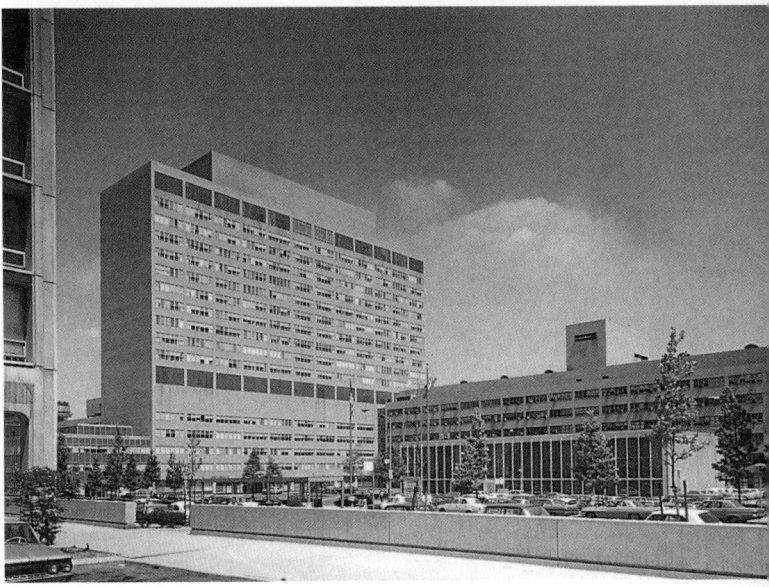

Top: Proposed New York University–Bellevue Medical Center, First Avenue to Franklin Delano Roosevelt Drive, East Twenty-fifth to East Thirty-fourth Street. Skidmore, Owings & Merrill, 1949. Model. View to the northeast. Stoller. ©ESTO

Bottom: New York University–Bellevue Medical Center, First Avenue to Franklin Delano Roosevelt Drive, East Twenty-fifth to East Thirty-fourth Street. Skidmore, Owings & Merrill, 1950. View to the northeast. Stoller. ©ESTO

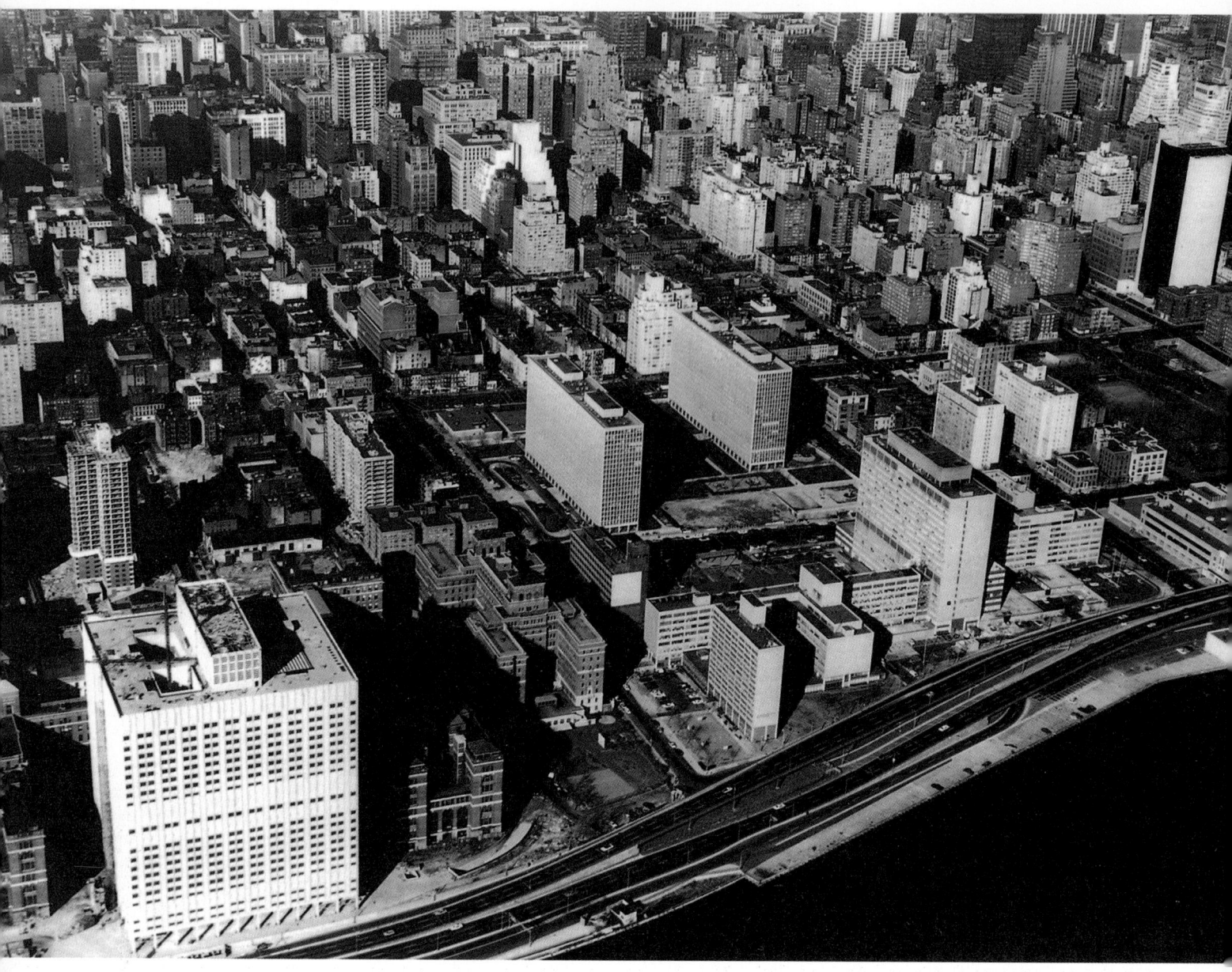

View to the northwest of New York University–Bellevue Medical Center, First Avenue to Franklin Delano Roosevelt Drive, East Twenty-fifth to East Thirty-fourth Street, with the New Building (Pomerance & Breines; Katz, Waisman, Weber, Strauss; Joseph Blumenkranz; Feld & Timoney, 1974) on the lower left. Kips Bay Plaza (I. M. Pei & Associates in association with S. J. Kessler & Sons, 1958–66) is in the center. The New York Telephone Building (Kahn & Jacobs, 1967) is on the upper right. NYU

Bellevue, as well as from the dense, Romanesque-inspired verticality of James Gamble Rogers's Columbia-Presbyterian Medical Center (1928)[37] or Coolidge, Shepley, Bulfinch & Abbott's Gothic-inspired New York Hospital–Cornell Medical Center (1932),[38] hitherto regarded as the two most successful hospital groups in the city. NYU-Bellevue's severe buildings, clad in white glazed brick and aluminum sash, were widely spaced, covering only 31 percent of the site. As initially designed by Gordon Bunshaft, the University Hospital was a strong, diagrammatically clear statement, with service spaces located on the north, and south-facing patients' rooms shaded by a continuous *brise soleil*, an arrangement similar to the one SOM pursued at the Veterans Hospital in Fort Hamilton, Brooklyn (see chapter 13). But, with the decision to rely on air conditioning, the building was redesigned to house two parallel corridors, with patients' rooms located along both the north and south walls and a nursing core between. This resulted not only in a lower building and shorter floor runs, but also in a fatter, stubbier mass. Even so, the sun shades, which gave the earlier scheme its character and could have been retained on functional grounds, were eliminated to save money.

The new medical center was not, as some observers charged, a one-off example of "spot planning" but part of a large-scale plan for the complete reconstruction of east midtown from Stuyvesant Town at Fourteenth Street to the United Nations. Other parts of the plan included the construction of hospital-employee housing intended for a site ultimately occupied by Kips Bay Plaza (see below); the construction of the brutally scaled, crudely detailed, nineteen-story Veterans Administration Hospital on the block bounded by First Avenue, Avenue A, Twenty-fourth and Twenty-fifth streets (Eggers & Higgins; Charles B. Meyers, 1954);[39] and the ongoing reconstruction of Bellevue Hospital itself. This began in earnest in the 1960s with the construction of the "New Building" (1974), a superscaled, 250-by-250-foot, twenty-five-story, 1,500-bed facility facing the Franklin Delano Roosevelt (FDR) Drive (formerly the East River Drive) between Twenty-seventh and Twenty-eighth streets.[40] Designed by Pomerance & Breines, in association with Katz, Waisman, Weber, Strauss, and Joseph Blumenkranz, and the engineeers Feld & Timoney, the "New Building" was a behemoth by any standard: the beige-colored, concrete-clad cube enclosed one-and-a-half acres of space on each floor, representing more space in one building than was encompassed by the total twenty-acre Bellevue property. With patients' wards wrapping the exterior, and the laboratories, kitchens, offices and service areas confined to the vast windowless interior, the structure in effect combined the facilities of fourteen buildings into one. Bernard M. Weinstein, Bellevue's executive director, declared: "If the devil himself had been commissioned to build a hospital facility, this is how he would have designed it."[41]

The "New Building" was only the most visible part of Bellevue's renovation, which continued to erode the clarity and eventually the identity of the original hospital group. A concrete parking garage (Pomerance & Breines; Katz, Waisman, Weber, Strauss; Joseph Blumenkranz; Feld & Timoney), built on what had been a courtyard facing First Avenue, was quite elegantly detailed by project designer John Jay Stonehill; but it was as disturbing to the pedestrian scale along the avenue as it was contradictory to the complex's overall urbanistic integrity.[42]

After the expansion of the NYU-Bellevue hospital complex, the construction of Kips Bay Plaza apartments in 1958-66 constituted the next significant step in the rebuilding of midtown's east side.[43] In 1957, when the property allocated for Bellevue South, a ten-acre superblock site bounded by First and Second

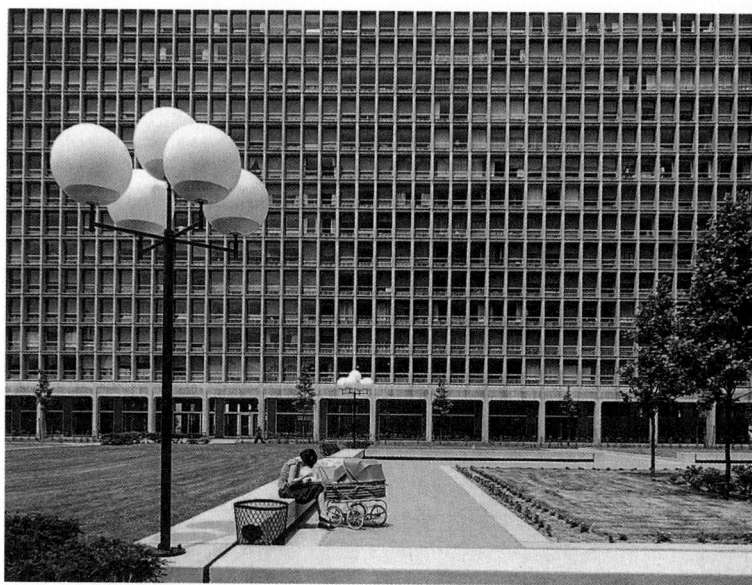

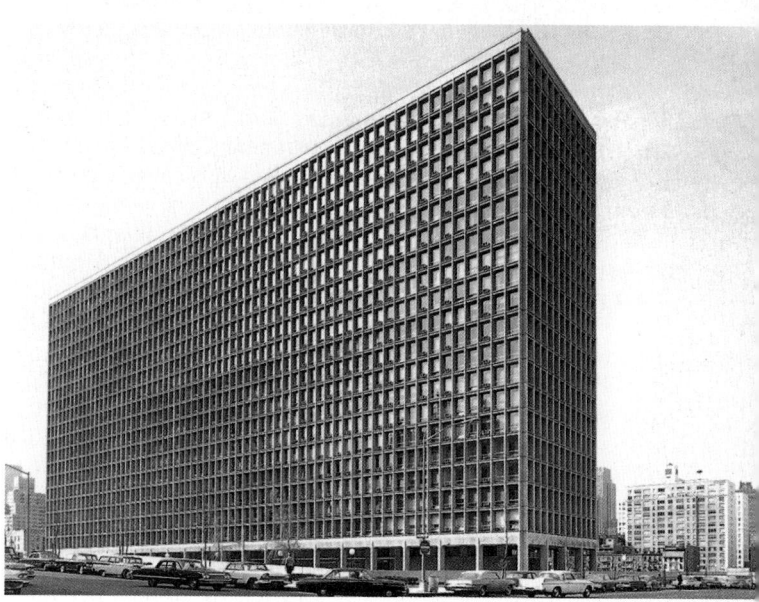

Top: Kips Bay Plaza, First to Second Avenue, East Thirtieth to East Thirty-third Street. I. M. Pei & Associates in association with S. J. Kessler & Sons, 1958–66. Interior courtyard. Cserna. PCF

Bottom: Kips Bay Plaza. View to the northwest. OMH

avenues, Thirtieth and Thirty-third streets, seemed destined to be taken over by the city due to unpaid taxes, Robert Moses approached William Zeckendorf of Webb & Knapp, which quickly bought majority control and paid the back taxes. Skidmore, Owings & Merrill, led by Gordon Bunshaft, had begun to develop a master plan for the Bellevue South project. Bunshaft discouraged I. M. Pei of Webb & Knapp's architecture department from taking on the project, and Pei himself initially seemed to agree, suggesting to Zeckendorf that he not assume the development and dismissing it as "just another housing project." Despite Pei's negativism, Zeckendorf assigned him the commission for the project, renamed Kip's Bay Plaza. The architect immediately reduced the number of buildings in the complex from the six called for by SOM to two large slabs, thus increasing the amount of continuous open space and, Pei contended, helping to "take the project-itis out of it."[44] In addition to the housing, the overall plan included a strip shopping center along Second Avenue and a ten-story medical-office building convenient to the New York University–Bellevue Medical Center across First Avenue.

The two 410-foot-long, twenty-one-story, parallel east-west apartment slabs that dominated the project contained a total of 1,136 dwelling units. Pei's design reflected an ambivalent attitude toward its context. With their boldly scaled concrete grids and extensive glazing, the buildings were a deliberate departure from the prevailing neighborhood fabric of brownstones and tenements. But the rectangular apartment slabs to some extent reinforced the city's grid, although the decision to offset them from each other and to create, with the other components of the development, a pinwheel plan contradicted traditional spatial closure. Space for 250 cars was provided underground, but surface parking provided along the site's perimeter further compromised the closure of the street wall as well as the utility of the sidewalks. Though the slabs defined a central landscaped park and the east-west street walls, the offset plan undermined these elements with a spatial dynamism resulting from the overlapping, shifting placement of the buildings with respect to each other. Nonetheless, the resulting courtyard space did provide, to some extent, a quiet, green oasis in which Pei hoped to install a large sculpture by Pablo Picasso. While Zeckendorf was willing to pay for either saplings or public art, he was not willing to pay for both, and Pei opted for greenery, waiting for another opportunity to commission the sculpture (which he did, at NYU's University Village [see chapter 4]).

Pei's design for the apartment slabs was developed in association with S. J. Kessler & Sons, a workhorse firm specializing in apartment houses. Kips Bay was notable for its imaginatively arranged unit plans, its dauntingly long interior corridors and the elegantly detailed exposed-concrete grid framing the large recessed plate-glass windows that made up the facades. In their reaction against the ad hoc planning and aesthetic banalities of typical postwar apartment house construction, Pei and his associates were influenced by the work of Mies van der Rohe, especially his reinforced-concrete Promontory Apartments on the south side of Chicago of 1946-49.[45] The architects set out, as Pei's associate Edward L. Friedman put it, to work within a design philosophy in which "a disciplined column spacing was mandatory, but not achieved at the expense of rooms inferior to those produced by the scatter column system."[46] The efficiency of repeated formwork in reinforced-concrete construction was the principal generator of the gridlike facade—in effect the grid was a load-bearing wall with a column at every window. The effect was softened only by the introduction of radiused corners at the window heads, which took advantage of the inherent plasticity of concrete, and by the

reduction of the column depth at the fifth and again at the tenth floor to express the diminished structural loads and give the composition some sense of vertical lift. Inside, the facades dictated that rooms be narrower and longer than many tenants would have liked. Nonetheless, the articulation of the facades constituted not only an aesthetic success but a bureaucratic one as well; exploiting his experience as a member of the Federal Housing Authority's advisory board, Pei configured the window recesses so that they legally qualified as balconies and the apartments were thus eligible for FHA subsidies (see chapter 2).

Pei's ability to achieve so much in the way of structural innovation and aesthetic consistency at Kips Bay was no mean feat. As Walter McQuade pointed out in 1961:

> The thicket of preliminaries facing the apartment-house designer is frightening. The first thorn in the thicket is the fact that construction costs of apartment houses are expected to be startlingly lower than those of office buildings built in the same cities by the same workmen. . . . Next is the matter of the FHA, the stern and complicated parent of American residential construction. Architect Pei says about his first essays into apartment-house design for urban renewal: "It's a science, not an art, but not a logical science, at that . . . a strange arithmetic. It took me six months even to begin to understand it."[47]

Despite all efforts to prove that superior design was economically competitive with the standard products of the marketplace, Pei was the first to admit that the cost of his design was "about seven percent above the cost of an ordinary project," much of which he attributed to the higher cost of the mechanical-ventilation systems required by the extensive use of glass.[48] But excess cost was only part of the story. The building's financially troubled sponsors, Webb & Knapp, skimped on quality in specifying the mechanical equipment, theorizing that it could be replaced later. Within a few years this caused considerable problems, which were inherited by the Alcoa Corporation when they took over the development in 1962.[49] William Zeckendorf was nonetheless proud of Webb & Knapp's sponsorship of the project: "Here we created something new in city housing—a sense of place and unity with buildings, gardens, and play areas—and have ever since been proud of what resulted. Kips Bay, being something new, had its flaws, but it was the prototype for any number of other developments." Anticipating the near compulsion for development that would characterize New York's growth, Zeckendorf predicted that "the builder or politician who moves to tear down Kips Bay will have some angry citizens' groups on his hands. Kips Bay was no surrender, but a genuine advance in quality of city living."[50]

Kips Bay did not stimulate other projects around it, perhaps because it was surrounded on the east by medical institutions, on the south by renewal projects already under way and on the west by a fairly stable, desirable neighborhood. On its northern border, at the southeast corner of Second Avenue and Thirty-fourth Street, one new apartment house was built, 300 East Thirty-fourth Street (1973), a thirty-three-story, 351-unit building designed by Max Wechsler & Associates and Henry Kibel, who was also its developer.[51] The building was a mediocre design, but it achieved a certain notoriety when, nearing completion, it was discovered that Kibel had built a larger building than zoning permitted. Kibel, who had previously petitioned the City Planning Commission for a zoning variance but had yet to be granted one, stated that he had taken a "calculated gamble."[52] Buildings Commissioner Theodore Karagheuzoff charged that Kibel had acted with "blatant indifference" and ordered that construction be halted.[53] The city subsequently allowed the building to be completed following Kibel's agreement to rent twenty-seven apartments to elderly tenants at substantially below-market rates, as well as to renovate, at a cost of about $50,000, an adjacent brownstone for use by community groups.

In 1959 Robert Moses, as chairman of the New York City Committee on Slum Clearance, proposed that the three "substandard" blocks bounded by Twenty-fourth and Twenty-seventh streets, Second and Third avenues, be designated the Gramercy Park Urban Renewal Area and thereby made eligible for assistance under the Title I provision of the National Housing Act of 1949.[54] Moses's plan, which required the approval of the City Planning Commission and the Board of Estimate, called for the construction of five sixteen-story buildings housing 1,275 middle-income families. When residents of the area protested that the neighborhood wasn't a slum, it was revealed in the press that their area had been so designated, at least in part, because their district assemblyman, who in public opposed the project, was in private the organizer of the real estate syndicate designated by Moses to redevelop it. This incident marked the first time an elected official was implicated in a Title I scandal.

By 1968 Moses's Gramercy Park project had been transformed into Bellevue South. The plan for this development employed new rent-subsidy techniques to provide for a variety of lower- to middle-income families, and new techniques of urban design and urban housing design intended to create a sense of neighborhood comparable to that of the substandard tenement districts it replaced.[55] From the point of view of design, the principal feature of Bellevue South was Davis, Brody & Associates' East Midtown Plaza, which filled the southern end of the renewal area, occupying the entire block between Twenty-third and Twenty-fourth streets, Second and First avenues, as well as a connected midblock parcel that extended north to Twenty-fifth Street.[56] Traffic on East Twenty-fourth Street was interrupted at the center of the block by the creation of two culs-de-sac so that the pedestrian space could flow uninterrupted to the northern block, where one low-rise building and one tower, also designed by Davis, Brody, were completed in 1974.

The plan called for some existing buildings on Twenty-third Street to be retained, including a clinic belonging to the Institute for the Crippled and Disabled, and St. Sebastian's Roman Catholic Church (1918), which was to become a focus of the midblock plaza, designed by M. Paul Friedberg & Associates, created as part of the project. The architects worked to make their design sensitive to its context, selecting brick color sympathetic to that of the existing church. In their 1968 master plan for the area, prepared under the direction of Lynda Simmons, who would serve as project architect, Davis, Brody wrote that the older buildings had a "permanent lease on life and a vital function—to guard insofar as possible the spirit of the old community while the new community is being erected."[57] Everyone involved was surprised and disappointed when St. Sebastian's was demolished without warning and the site was sold to a developer, who built a banal apartment house on it.

With their expressed concrete slabs, chamfered corners and low brick parapet walls (instead of the more typical glass-and-metal railings), the buildings of East Midtown Plaza had considerable sculptural presence, yet their overall massing never got out of hand and was never disrespectful to the street wall. Norval White and Elliot Willensky praised the complex as "urbane street architecture, with the terraces of Babylon," and called it "an ode to brick."[58] For Paul Goldberger, the project was "assertive, yet welcoming," and the brick towers felt "like

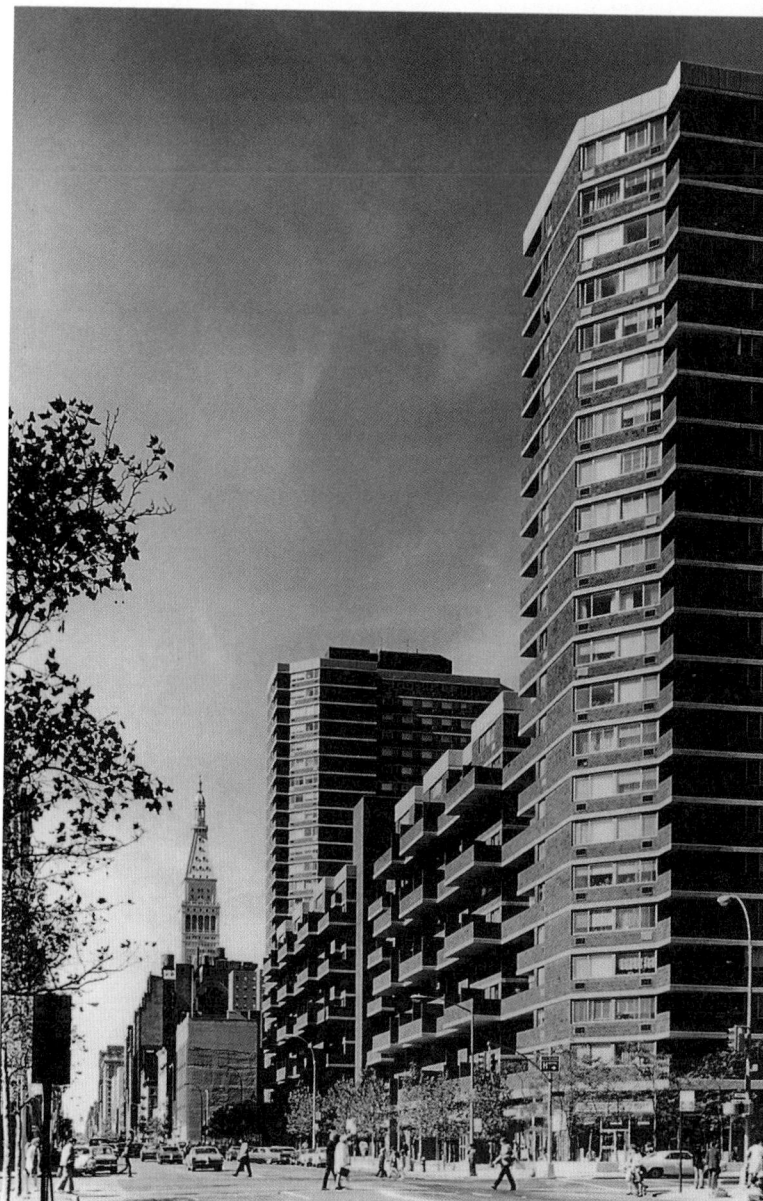

East Midtown Plaza, First to Second Avenue, East Twenty-third to East Twenty-fifth Street. Davis, Brody & Associates, 1974. View to the west. ©Norman McGrath. NM

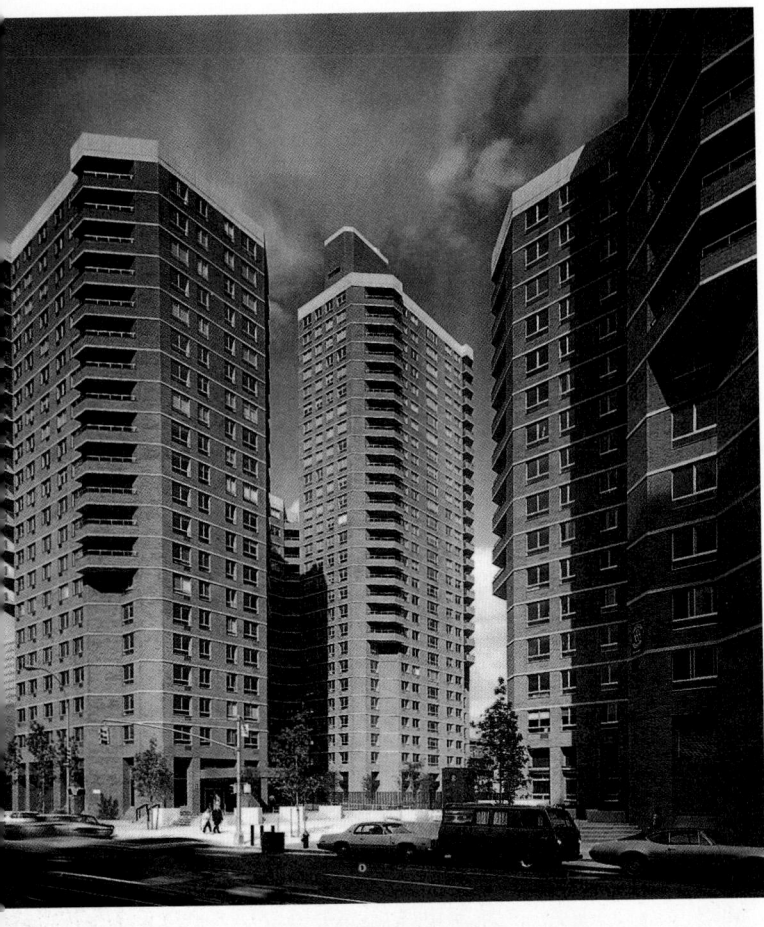

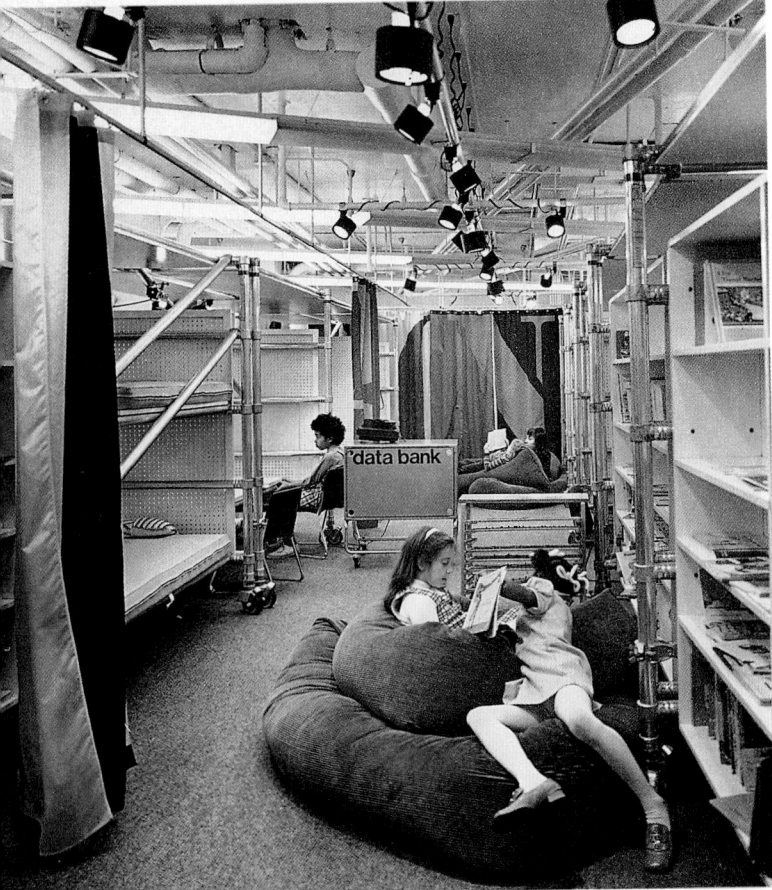

houses, not like institutions, for all their size." He explained: "At East Midtown Plaza, the relatively low wing along Twenty-third Street, the anchoring corner towers and the good central space all show a real willingness to recognize context. The exposed concrete reads as ornament here, not as structure, a further plus in that a utilitarian aspect of the building has been contorted into a happily nonutilitarian role."[59]

For Frost Associates' 1,600-unit Henry Phipps Plaza West, occupying a superblock site on the east side of Second Avenue between Twenty-sixth and Twenty-ninth streets, Davis, Brody's design for East Midtown Plaza was adapted with considerable sureness to the constraints of a tighter construction budget.[60] The red-brick complex incorporated numerous diagonal facades that contributed to an overall lively effect, although it failed to respect the street wall as conscientiously as its aesthetic progenitor had. Completed in 1976 as a Mitchell-Lama cooperative, Phipps Plaza West responded to the Phipps Foundation's program, which called for a landscaped "outdoor living room," easily accessible from the ground-floor laundries, as well as maximum sunlight and, wherever possible, cross-ventilation in the apartments.

In 1972 the architectural firm of Mayers & Schiff transformed 5,100 square feet originally intended for law offices on the ground floor of Phipps Plaza West, facing Twenty-sixth Street and accessible from a landscaped midblock plaza, into the Acorn School, a cooperatively run, private elementary school. In keeping with the school's experimental educational approach, Mayers & Schiff designed two movable aluminum scaffoldings, divided into 4'6"-by-6'0" modules, to provide a framework onto which partitions and countertops could be attached to create an endless variety of spaces. Janet Bloom, writing in *Architectural Forum*, noted: "Perhaps the more we have to suffer as part of a migrating horde, the more we need to enjoy flexible, individualized space; the more we need spaces of our own, doing with them what we will on a provisional basis. The provisional aspect of these scaffoldings is in tune with the current do-your-own-thing attitudes about life."[61] To complete their design, the architects incorporated a centrally located circular curtain track from which banners could be hung to form an impromptu theater in the round, as well as soft, free-form upholstered furniture and numerous boldly painted images, called, in the jargon of the day, supergraphics.

In 1963 the ninety-three-year-old Lombardic-style Roman Catholic Church of the Epiphany (Napoleon Le Brun, 1870), at 1373 Second Avenue, on the southwest corner of Twenty-second Street, burned down. This austere monument was replaced in 1967 by Belfatto & Pavarini's freely composed, mildly expressionistic church clad in purplish brown brick and set behind a 3,000-square-foot elevated forecourt.[62] Viewed from the street, the turreted building seemed quite modest in size; but inside, the visitor discovered a large, seemingly too low, flat-ceilinged nave that occupied space behind an existing school facing Twenty-second Street. As the editors of *Architectural Forum* described it: "The forecourt and the forms around it are undoubtedly positive contributions to the cityscape—at least as long as this intersection remains solidly built up."[63] Norval White and Elliot Willensky praised the church as "the most positive modern religious statement on Manhattan Island to date."[64]

Less successful was St. Mary's Catholic Church of the Byzantine Rite, on the southwest corner of Second Avenue and Fifteenth Street (1964).[65] Designed by Cajetan J. B. Baumann, the boxy, concrete-framed building was filled in with semi-abstract, Modernist stained-glass windows and articulated with rather weak historicist detailing. Steinmann & Cain's St. Vartan

Cathedral of the Armenian Orthodox Church in America (1967) was more convincing in its use of an historicist vocabulary.[66] Set back from and elevated above the surrounding streets, the domed brick building dominated its site, which was bounded by Second Avenue, Thirty-fourth and Thirty-fifth streets, and to the east by an access road to the Queens-Midtown Tunnel. A somewhat austere version of Romanesque churches of Asia Minor, St. Vartan's transcended the ersatz quality of St. Mary's to establish a more imposing and dignified appearance. A monumentally scaled bronze sculpture by Reuben Nakian, *Descent from the Cross*, provided a grace note to the church's otherwise barren plaza.

Waterside

By the 1960s it was clear that the tradition of slum clearance characteristic of postwar urban renewal was no longer tolerable, or even desirable, and the search for alternative means for creating new housing began in earnest. Key to any strategy that sought to eliminate tenant relocation was the availability of empty sites, sites with abandoned buildings or outmoded commercial sites, or, barring these, the creation of new sites by offshore landfill. As early as 1961 the developer Richard Ravitch, of the HRH Construction Corporation, had proposed an offshore landfill project to James Felt, chairman of the City Planning Commission. According to Ravitch, Felt handed the proposal back, saying "Don't waste your time."[67] In 1963, encouraged by a news report about the ideas of William F. R. Ballard, the new Planning Commissioner, who believed the opportunity was "ripe to build middle-income housing to open up windows on the waterfront so that the public can enjoy water-oriented parks and recreational areas,"[68] Ravitch revived his proposal, which he called Waterside. The architectural firm of Davis, Brody & Associates, working in conjunction with Ravitch and the Longstreet Corporation, an affiliate of the investment bankers Lazard Freres & Company, identified a potential site on the East River between Twenty-fifth and Thirtieth streets. Here development could replace abandoned city-owned piers by transforming the area between the existing bulkhead and pierhead lines into new land, much as lower Manhattan had often expanded to the river during the nineteenth century (beyond the pierhead line the U.S. Army Corps of Engineers forbade any construction). Though the site was physically cut off from the streets and traditional Manhattan neighborhoods to its west by the superblocks of Stuyvesant Town, Cooper Village, Kips Bay Plaza and the New York University–Bellevue Medical Center, as well as by the FDR Drive, it did enjoy sweeping views of the East River.

Informally unveiled in 1965—though not officially unveiled until December 1966, when the new regime of John V. Lindsay expressed a commitment to its realization—Davis, Brody's design for Waterside consisted of four towers totaling 1,470 apartment units and twenty-five duplex townhouses set on a platform built on pilings over the river.[69] Key to the development was the organization of this platform, which was in effect two levels of parking for over 700 cars, surmounted by the townhouses and towers. The architects conceived of the resulting open space as an urban plaza. Samuel Brody stated that "we want to make the area a 24-hour sort of place," serving upland neighbors as well as Waterside residents.[70] In contrast to Stuyvesant Town and Cooper Village, a school was to be provided, although it was not intended for Waterside's residents. Located at the south end of the plaza, the United Nations

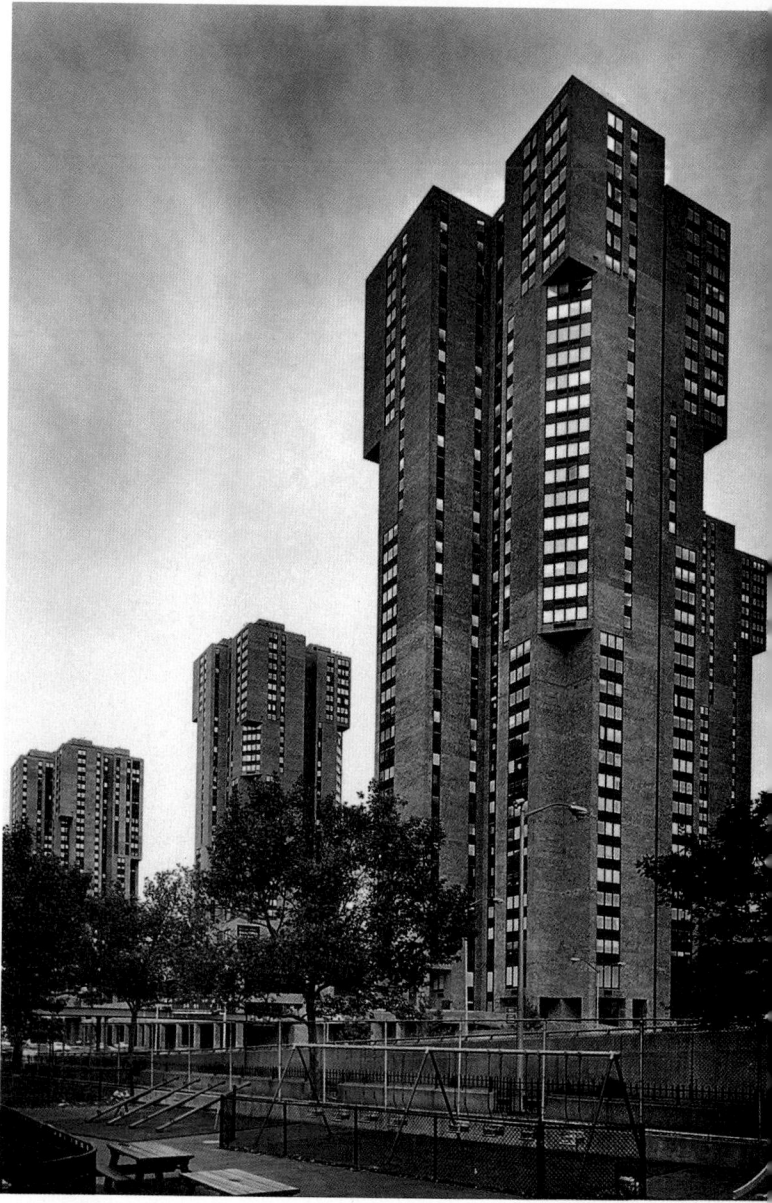

Top left: Henry Phipps Plaza West, east side of Second Avenue, East Twenty-sixth to East Twenty-ninth Street. Frost Associates, 1976. View to the northeast. ©Norman McGrath. NM

Bottom left: Acorn School, Phipps Plaza West, facing East Twenty-sixth Street between Second and Third avenues. Mayers & Schiff, 1972. Interior. Maris. M&S

Above: Waterside, platform in the East River, East Twenty-fifth to East Thirtieth Street. Davis, Brody & Associates, 1963–74. View to the north. ©Norman McGrath. NM

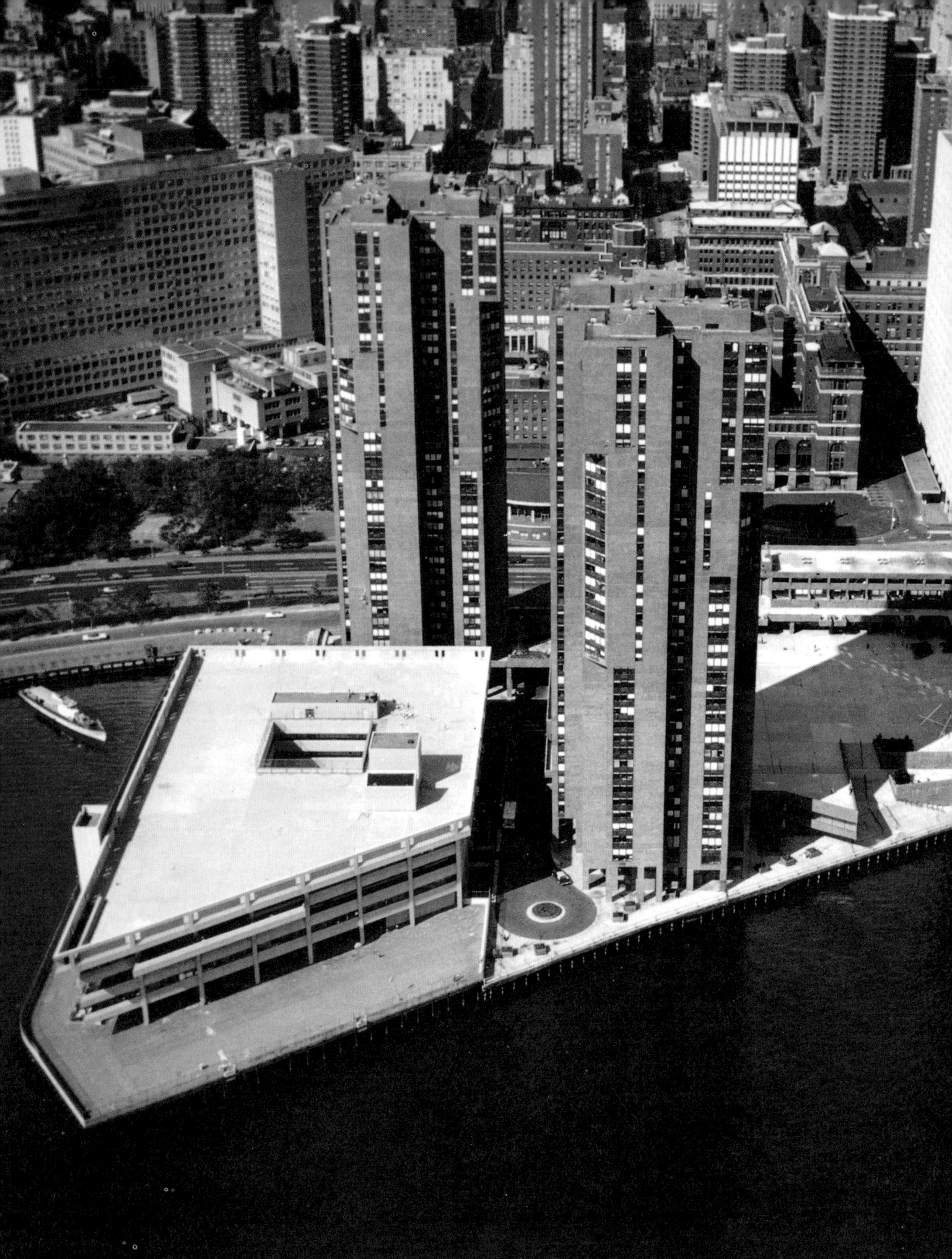

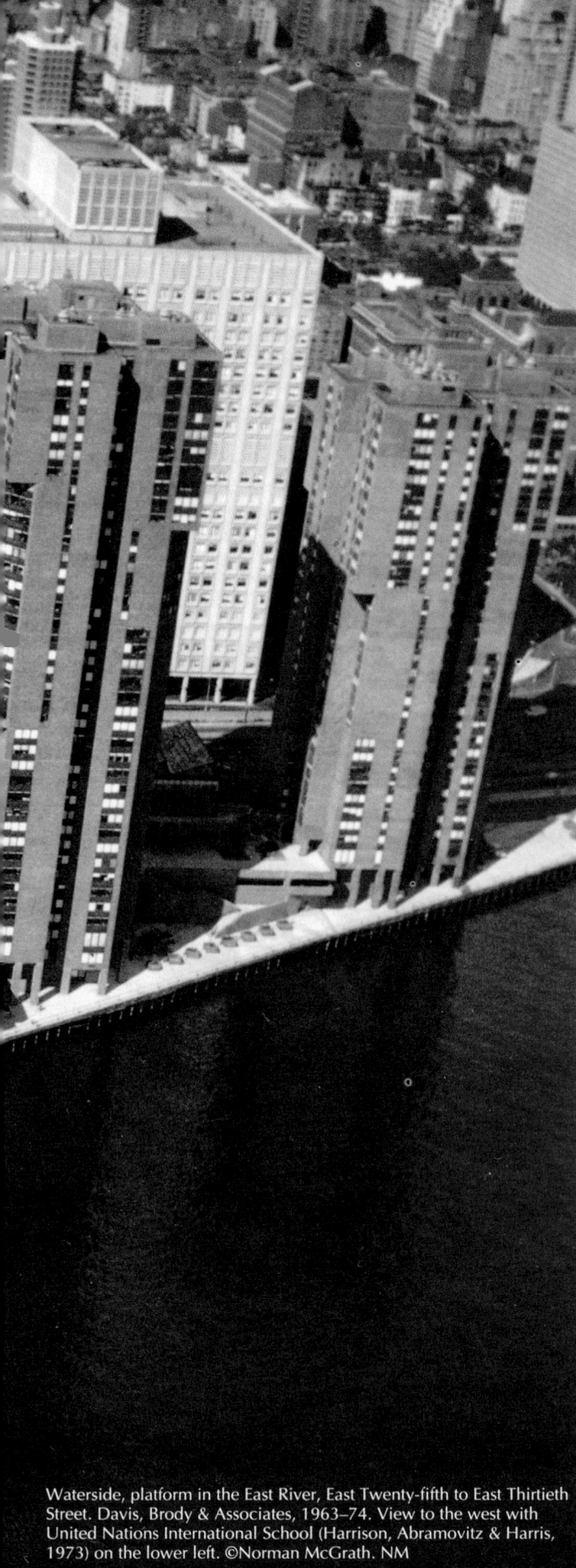

Waterside, platform in the East River, East Twenty-fifth to East Thirtieth Street. Davis, Brody & Associates, 1963–74. View to the west with United Nations International School (Harrison, Abramovitz & Harris, 1973) on the lower left. ©Norman McGrath. NM

International School (Harrison, Abramovitz & Harris, 1973) was created for the children of United Nations employees.[71]

In order to foster social and economic integration in the Waterside neighborhood, one of the towers, containing 370 apartments, was to be financed under the FHA 221-d-3 program, which made the apartments affordable to moderate-income families; 20 to 25 percent of these units were further subsidized to reach public housing levels. In addition, the rents for the remaining units were to be skewed in complex ways to assure the widest possible spread of tenant incomes. When the complex was actually built, these ideals were somewhat compromised, although considerable economic diversity was achieved.

What at first seemed a relatively straightforward undertaking, providing new housing in a central location without tenant relocation, was, of course, immensely complex. Not all the blame for the project's long gestation—work began on the design in 1963 and construction was completed in 1974—can be laid at the doorstep of the Wagner administration, which was frequently viewed as bureaucratic and insensitive to planning and architectural experimentation. Because federal law stipulated that the government would not have to pay any damages to the owner should it require the use of the navigable water at a future date, thereby making it impossible for the developers to obtain a mortgage, the water had to be declared non-navigable by an act of Congress. (Such an act was introduced by Representative Emmanuel Celler.) In addition, the community issues of access to the upland, the relationship to the New York University–Bellevue Medical Center complex and the search for a site for the United Nations International School all played their part in slowing the process. But by late 1966 Waterside at least seemed a realistic prospect, even though the City Planning Commission and the Board of Estimate had yet to consider it.

When the plan for Waterside was announced, Ada Louise Huxtable was enthusiastic. It was, she said, "trend-setting for New York in every sense of the term. It is an urban concept that utilizes the waterfront for housing and recreation in a distinctly urban way. The design is able, sophisticated and creative." Huxtable also pointed out that the standard of amenities and design proposed for Waterside was remarkable for New York: "This could be the city's first large-scale breakthrough from the norm of sterile housing cliches and arid open space that has been the bureaucratic or easy-profit formula. Waterside would be a standard-setting development for any waterfront city in the world." Despite the serious communication problems associated with so isolated a site, and the lack of landscaping on the plans, Huxtable believed that the plaza and its amenities were not merely "detached gimmicks with easy eye-appeal, but . . . sound instruments of the highest level of comprehensive planning. These stylish amenities are set into a solid functional framework of pedestrian and vehicular circulation, parking and servicing." Contrasting the Lindsay administration's more enlightened approach to urban renewal with that of the Wagner administration, Huxtable said: "Although New York has a clear score of zero to date in realizing its more progressive proposals, there is a good chance that this one can be more than paper planning."[72]

Waterside was by no means perfect. From the beginning, the decision to accept the existing configuration of the FDR Drive, instead of taking a bolder position as had been earlier recommended in a plan prepared for the city by Whittlesey, Conklin & Rossant, doomed Waterside to a kind of half life as an isolated project: its only connection to Manhattan at large by direct access and egress was via the northbound FDR Drive, or by a pedestrian overpass at East Twenty-fifth Street. To the south,

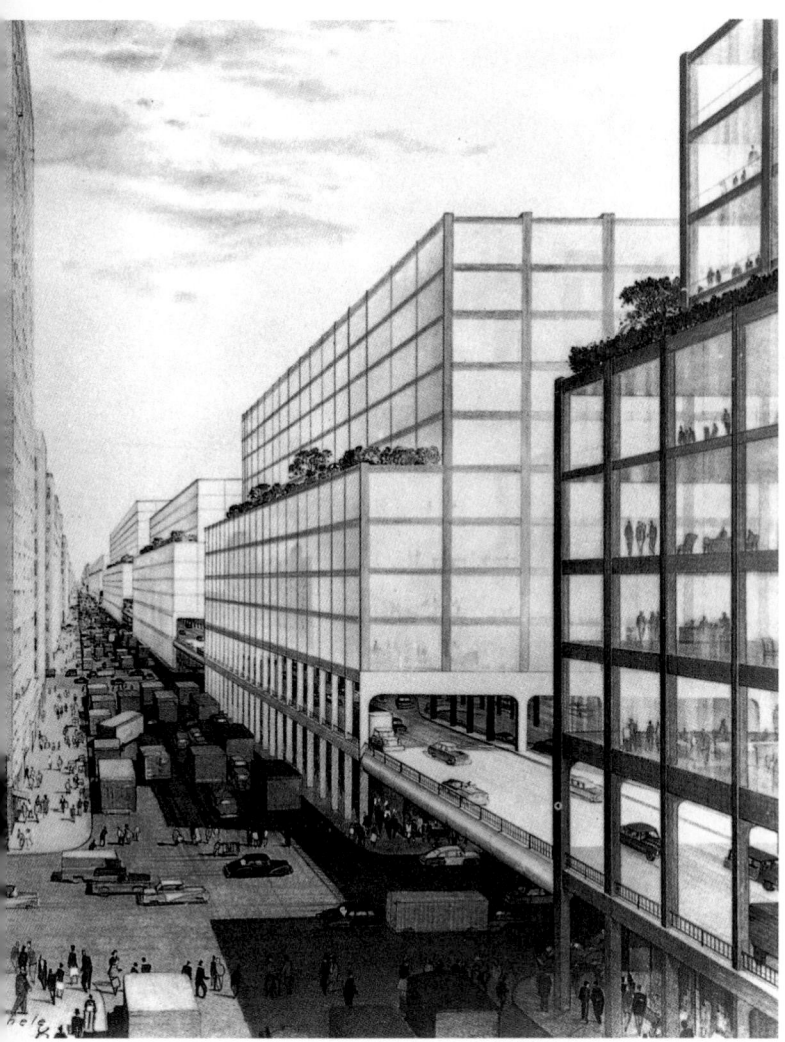

Above: Proposed mid-Manhattan crosstown expressway, Thirtieth Street. Triborough Bridge and Tunnel Authority, 1950. Rendering by Michele showing potential development of air rights above expressway. TBTA

Right: Proposed mid-Manhattan crosstown expressway. Rendering by Michele looking to the east. TBTA

the United Nations school was built without continuing the pedestrian promenade past it to hook up with walkways further downtown. In addition, though the four towers were kept slender to protect the upland views to the river, the buildings, clad in brown "jumbo" brick, had an aggressive sculptural force, in part because of the cantilevered upper floors that were necessary to accommodate the larger apartments, but also because of the designers' preference for Brutalist aesthetics.

In early 1971, ten years after the project was first proposed, Waterside's construction began.[73] Even with Mayor Lindsay's enthusiasm, the going had been tough. Recalling the mayor's press conference announcing Waterside in December 1966, Ravitch confessed in 1971 that he had "to chuckle looking back on it, because I don't know what the Mayor was announcing. What he really was saying was, 'We have this cockamamie proposal that we don't have any money for, and we don't know if it's legal.'"[74] By the time Mayor Lindsay announced in late January 1971 that Waterside was to go ahead, he had a solid project behind him, with nine major commercial banks lined up to lend $72 million as a result of his personal intervention. According to an anonymous housing expert quoted by the *New York Times*, the banks had lent the money "to ingratiate themselves with the Mayor, and there is a relatively small risk on this project."[75] Furthermore, the money was only a construction loan, and given the city's increasingly shaky finances and the absence of funds in various programs like Mitchell-Lama, which had sustained the city's housing programs in the 1960s, the project still had a cloudy future. But finally, on September 17, 1973, Mayor Lindsay and other dignitaries sailed to the site on a fireboat to start the dedication ceremony.

In a 1975 assessment of Davis, Brody's impact on housing in New York, Paul Goldberger praised Waterside, the firm's best-known project, as being "a visually exciting form, a powerful anchor to the skyline at water's edge." Although he acknowledged that there were some problems with the complex, such as its isolation from the rest of the city, he felt that they were "relatively minor liabilities in a city so used to mediocrity in housing that it accepts the appellation of 'luxury housing' for Third Avenue sheet-rock sheds. Waterside was conceived as something more than that, and it is a piece of architecture that, whatever its flaws, truly ennobles both the city and its riverfront."[76] By 1979 Goldberger's judgment was harsher, particularly with respect to the plaza, which he found "psychologically cold on even the warmest summer's day" and in "desperate need for landscaping." He again raised the issue of isolation: "One feels all too much on an island, cut off from the very city life these buildings presumably exist to enrich."[77]

Mid-Manhattan Expressway

As early as 1931 Thomas Adams, as part of his work for the Regional Plan Association, had called for a tunnel to traverse Manhattan beneath Thirty-eighth Street.[78] The call for a midtown tunnel would be made again by Manhattan Borough President Samuel Levy in 1936, by which time the Lincoln and Queens-Midtown tunnels were nearing completion.[79] Robert Moses took up the idea and, before the outbreak of World War II, began to plan for a mid-Manhattan expressway to cross the island at either Thirtieth or Thirty-sixth Street. In 1944 Manhattan Borough President Edgar J. Nathan, Jr., and Alfred B. Jones, chairman of the New York City Tunnel Authority, announced a plan for a complex of crosstown tunnels, with a tube beneath

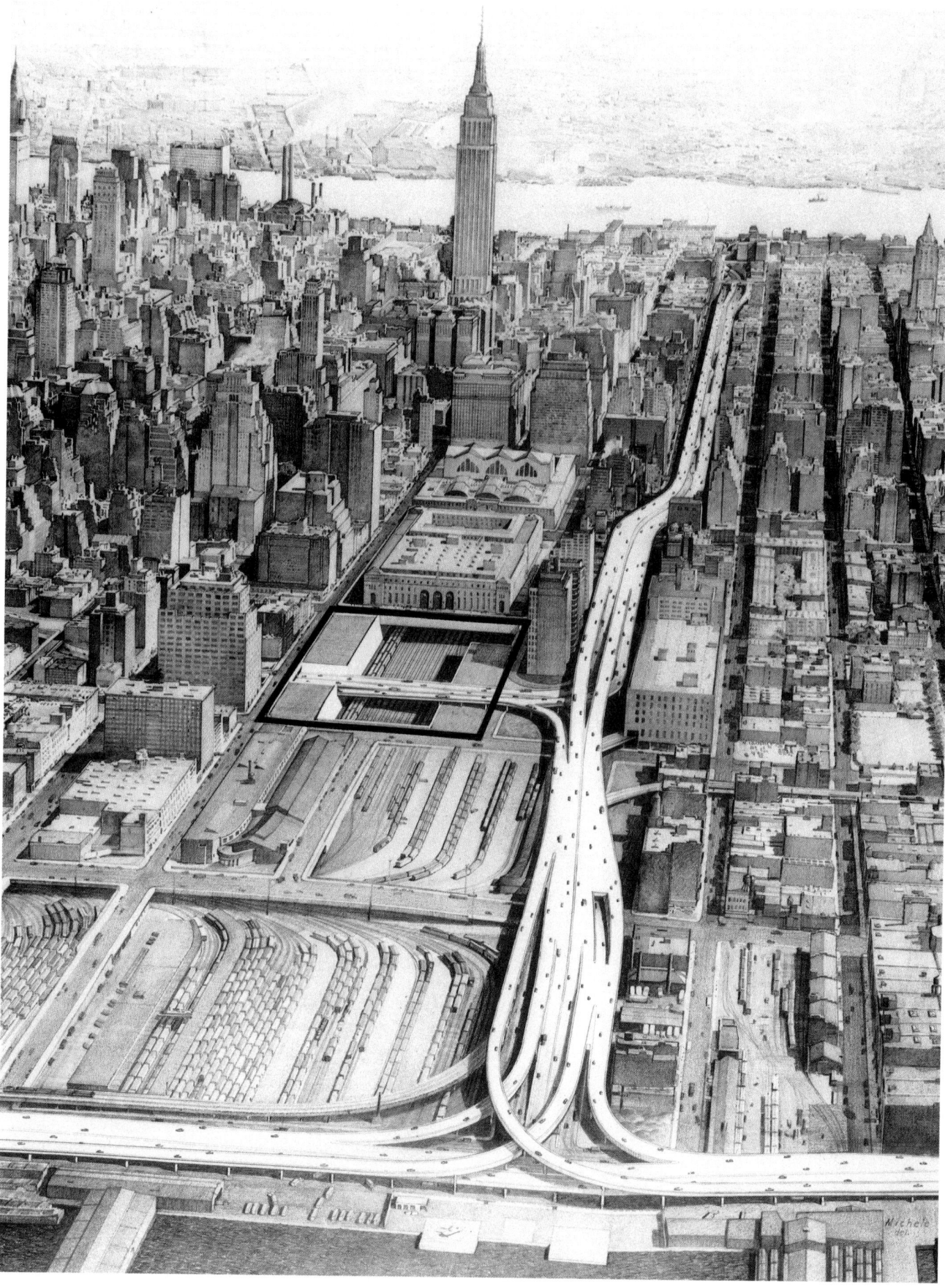

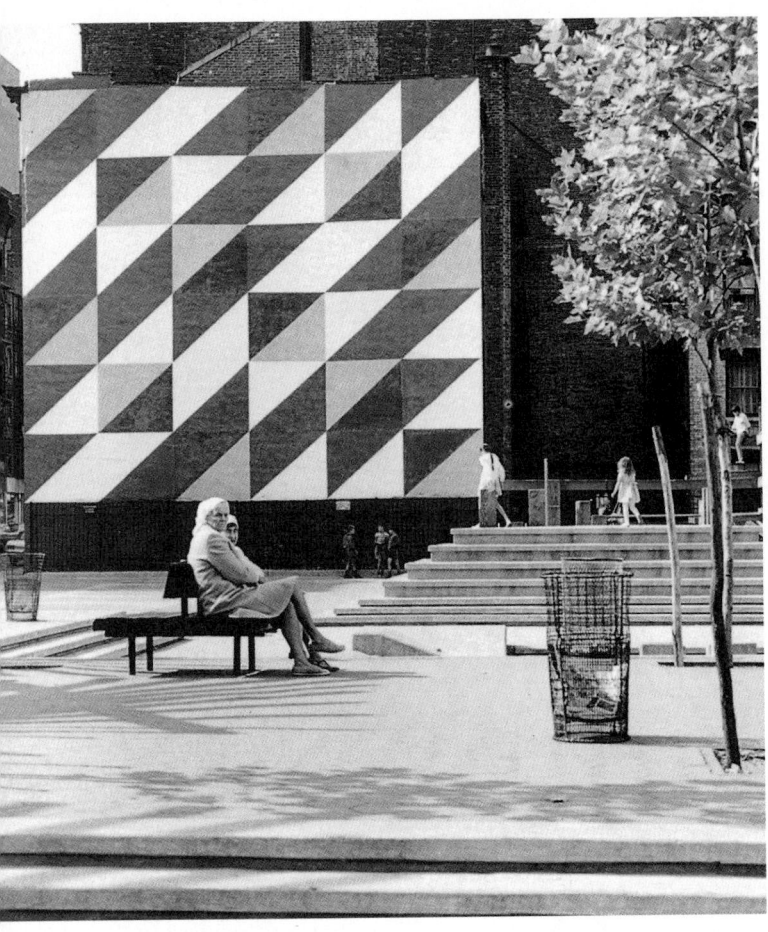

Vest-pocket park, northwest corner of Second Avenue and East Twenty-ninth Street. M. Paul Friedberg, 1966. View to the west showing untitled mural by Jason Crum. MPF

Thirty-sixth Street handling eastbound through traffic, a tube beneath Thirty-eighth Street handling westbound through traffic, and a third tube between them to serve local traffic.[80] The plan also included a large subterranean terminal for buses, taxis and chauffeur-driven automobiles to be located on the blocks between Fifth and Sixth avenues, Thirty-sixth and Thirty-eighth streets, connected by means of elevators to street level, where it would be surmounted by a skyscraper housing booking offices for all of the major airlines serving New York. As designed by Harvey Wiley Corbett, the massive building incorporated numerous setbacks and a roof structurally equipped to serve as a helicopter landing.

In 1946 Moses approached Mayor O'Dwyer with a new plan for the midtown crossing: a 100-foot-high elevated highway to run river to river, snaking past skyscrapers and tunneling directly through the Empire State Building's sixth or seventh floor. O'Dwyer responded enthusiastically, agreeing to Moses's offer to have the Triborough Bridge and Tunnel Authority pay for the project if it was operated as a toll road. In 1947 Cleveland Rodgers, in his capacity as a member of the City Planning Commission, advocated a modified version of the previously presented plan, with the addition of a new north-south avenue bisecting the blocks between Fifth and Sixth avenues, Thirty-fourth and Thirty-ninth streets.[81] Moses characteristically dismissed those supporting the alternate plan, including his highly sympathetic biographer, Cleveland Rodgers, as "crackpots."[82]

In 1950 Moses announced that he had persuaded the federal government to pay the cost of plans for a 160-foot-wide elevated road that would use the 60-foot-wide right of way of Thirtieth Street as well as a 100-foot swath to the south that would be created by tearing down the buildings lining the street's south side.[83] The Port Authority, Moses said, would pay for the new road's connections to the Lincoln Tunnel, and the Triborough Bridge and Tunnel Authority, which he headed, would foot the bill for the highway itself. The *New York Herald Tribune* ran an ecstatic editorial, praising Moses, Port Authority Chairman Howard Cullman and Mayor O'Dwyer as "big men [who] got together and made a big decision for the common good."[84] But civic and trade associations were angered by the plan and O'Dwyer reversed his position, professing that he didn't like overhead structures and that there was little chance that funding for a tunnel could be found. When protests continued to mount, O'Dwyer authorized the City Planning Commission to officially study alternatives, whereupon Moses withdrew his support for the project and turned his attention to the Lower Manhattan Expressway (LOMEX) across Broome Street (see chapter 4).

Despite Moses's disaffiliation with the project, support for a midtown expressway did not completely evaporate, and in 1957 the City Planning Commission proposed an elevated highway at Thirtieth Street. By this time, however, changes in the city's transportation network, including a proposed bridge linking Brooklyn and Staten Island across the Narrows, called the need for the expressway into doubt. As the Citizens' Housing and Planning Council pointed out, "current transportation thinking throughout the country emphasizes circumferential traffic movement, not the carving of super-expressways through the core of the City."[85] In 1958 Mayor Wagner and Manhattan Borough President Hulan Jack dropped their support of the project, concentrating instead on LOMEX and thus nearly ensuring that any midtown expressway would remain forever on the drawing boards.[86]

Given the cloudy fate of the expressway, in 1966 the Triborough Bridge and Tunnel Authority, which had begun acquiring land for the highway years earlier, agreed to lease a site on the northwest corner of Second Avenue and Twenty-ninth Street to the Park Department to serve as a so-called vest-pocket park.[87] The arrangement was contingent on the Park Department's agreement to dismantle any facilities and return the site to the authority should the highway project ever be realized. Designed by M. Paul Friedberg in consultation with local residents, the multilevel park and playground incorporated a fountain and wading pool, children's climbing equipment that resembled trees, a snack bar and a mural by Jason Crum.

Murray Hill

The postwar era brought significant changes to Murray Hill, bounded by Thirty-fourth and Forty-second streets, Third and Fifth avenues, and historically among Manhattan's most architecturally cohesive and socially desirable residential neighborhoods. The area had reached its pinnacle as a fashionable residential district around 1900 when great mansions, as well as slightly more modest houses, lined Madison and Park avenues. After the turn of the century the neighborhood began to change, with Fifth Avenue residences giving way to specialty and department stores. As its western edge became more commercial, the area's eastern fringes began to be gentrified, with former carriage houses being converted to residences, such as Sniffen Court (ca. 1850-60), which was transformed into a charming residential enclave during the 1920s.[88] Of the many apartment houses built in Murray Hill during the interwar years, none were as luxurious as those built uptown, though some were as interesting. The area acquired a cultural focus when J. P. Morgan built his library on East Thirty-sixth Street in 1906 (McKim, Mead & White),[89] which in 1927 was enhanced by Morgan's son, who commissioned an addition from Benjamin Wistar Morris, thereby creating a major public museum and research institution.[90] Murray Hill was also home to a variety of important professional groups and social clubs. During the 1920s the long-established tradition of converting old mansions to clubhouses continued with the recycling of several area landmarks.

Early signs of the neighborhood's decline as a fashionable residential area could be seen by the 1930s, when the Murray Hill retail stretch of Fifth Avenue became increasingly focused on a middle-class rather than a carriage-trade clientele. Gorham's (McKim, Mead & White, 1905),[91] on the southwest corner of Thirty-sixth Street, and Tiffany's (McKim, Mead & White, 1906),[92] on the southeast corner of Thirty-seventh Street, had decamped to uptown locations by the end of the decade, and the side-street townhouses began to be converted to small apartments. After the seeming stability of the immediate postwar years, the area began to change dramatically in the mid-1950s, at which time Thomas W. Ennis, a real estate reporter for the New York Times, was able to write: "Old Murray Hill, which lived in its elegant and exclusive past for as long as it could, is going through the biggest change in its history."[93]

After the war many of the best properties were assembled to form sites suitable for large-scale apartment houses, particularly along Park Avenue. In 1945 plans were announced to demolish three houses at 39, 41 and 43 Park Avenue to make way for an apartment house designed by George F. Pelham, Jr.[94] The project was never realized, but in 1955, 41 Park Avenue, a nineteen-story apartment building designed by Emery Roth & Sons,

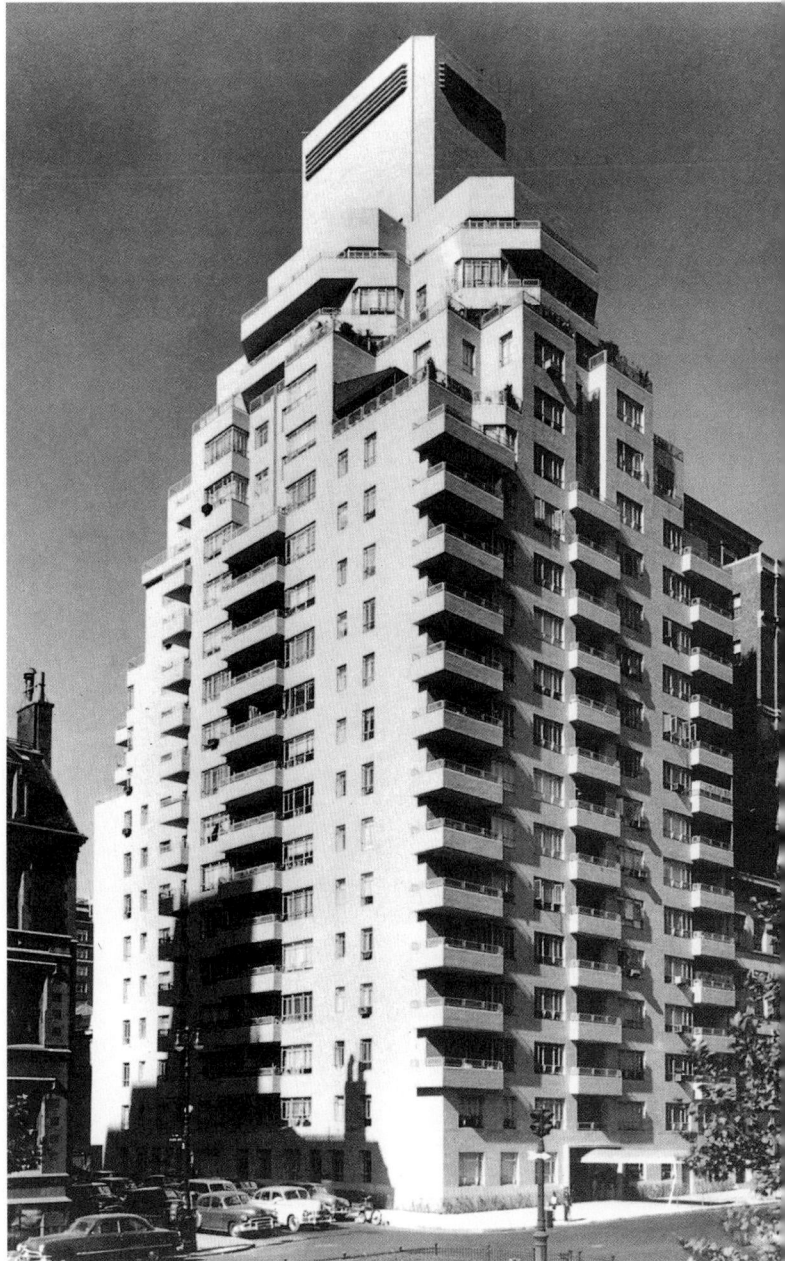

40 Park Avenue, northwest corner of East Thirty-sixth Street. Emery Roth & Sons, 1950. View to the northwest. Studly. ERS

297

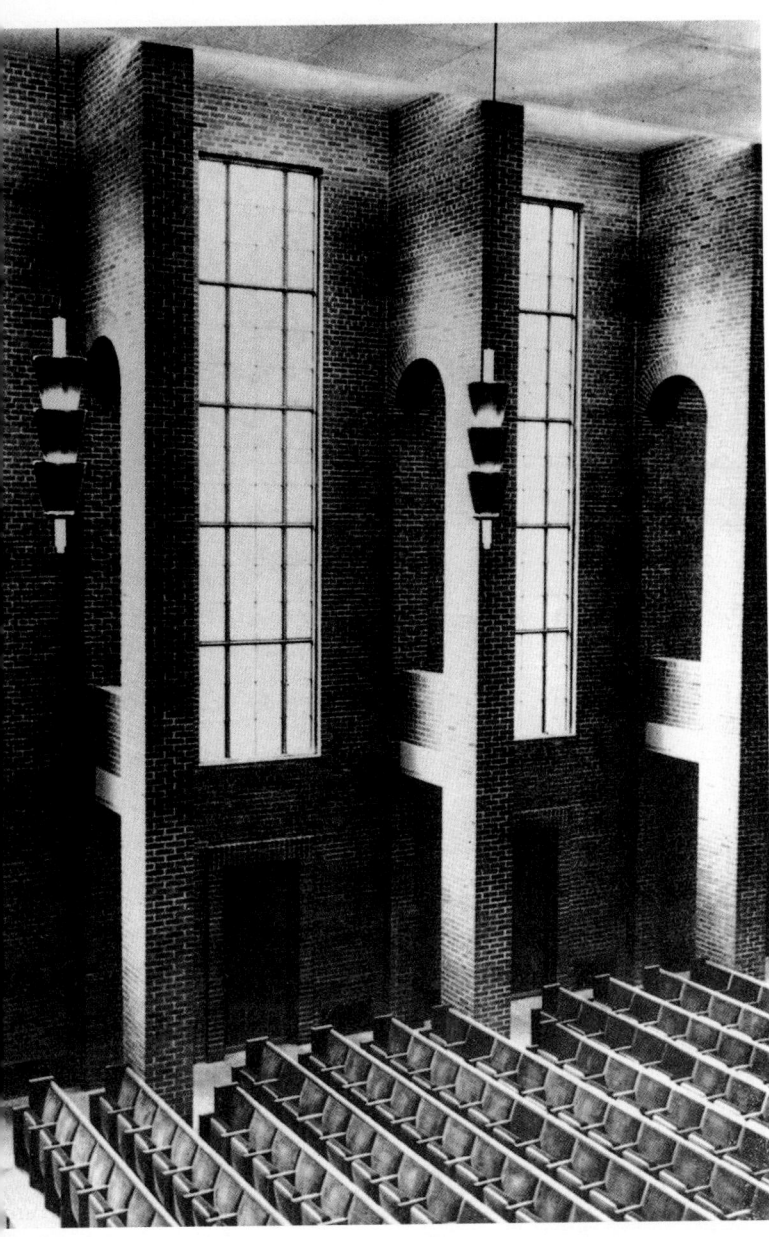

Community Church of New York, 40 East Thirty-fifth Street, between Madison and Park avenues. Magoon & Salo, 1948. Sanctuary. Alden. CNY

was completed on the site, which occupied the northeast corner of Thirty-sixth Street.[95] In 1950 a group of rowhouses as well as a mansion occupied by the Harvard Law Club gave way to 30 East Thirty-seventh Street (Emery Roth & Sons), between Madison and Park avenues, a subtly detailed, vaguely Georgian red-brick building overlooking the Morgan Library.[96] To the east of the Morgan Library, the Roths' eighteen-story apartment building at 40 Park Avenue, on the northwest corner of Thirty-sixth Street, was also completed in 1950 and replaced several brownstones as well as a vacant lot;[97] four years later, the Roths' nineteen-story apartment building at 30 Park Avenue, on the southwest corner of Thirty-sixth Street, replaced Gambrill & Richardson's townhouses for Jonathan and Frederick Sturges (1869–70). David Moed's seventeen-story Seven Park Avenue (1954), on the northeast corner of Thirty-fourth Street, replaced the Bacon Mansion, a Gothic-style vestige of pre–Civil War New York.[98] An eighteen-story apartment building at 35 Park Avenue (Sylvan and Robert Bien), on the southeast corner of Thirty-sixth Street, was completed in 1956 and replaced rowhouses.[99] A twenty-story apartment building at 80 Park Avenue (Kahn & Jacobs, with Paul Resnick, 1956), on the southwest corner of Thirty-ninth Street, replaced a group of rowhouses as well as a Venetian Gothic corner house (1870) designed for D. Willis James by the firm of Renwick & Sands.[100]

Magoon & Salo's Community Church of New York, at 40 East Thirty-fifth Street (1948), which stood on a site that had been vacant since 1930 and previously had been occupied by rowhouses, was Murray Hill's first postwar religious building.[101] Partially built out to its lot line and partially recessed from the street on an elevated entrance court, the flat-roofed, five-story-high building eschewed a traditional architectural vocabulary in favor of highly reductivist red-brick facades. Four narrow, vertically arranged strips of windows dominated the principal facade, illuminating the simply articulated sanctuary that was wrapped in the same red brick as the exterior. The architects, one of whom, Herbert Magoon, had designed the campanile at Jones Beach,[102] noted that the nondenominational orientation of the congregation had helped to determine their design solution. "It is a liberal church," they said, "with a membership including all creeds, races and colors. This freed us considerably from traditional stipulations."[103] The editors of *Interiors* praised the building for its simplicity of line and its sensitivity to the surroundings: "Using bold brick surface treatment, it is designed with an awareness of its background of tall buildings and skyscrapers."[104] At the building's opening, John Haynes Holmes, who headed the congregation, noted that while the church was being built he had been "terrified lest this building be mistaken in the end for a factory, a fire station, or a storage warehouse. But as the structure neared completion, all those forebodings disappeared. . . . When you look at this church, you behold not a replica of what has been, but a prophecy of what is yet to be."[105]

Another church in the area, the Church of Our Saviour (1959), on the southeast corner of Park Avenue and Thirty-eighth Street, boldly flew in the face of prevailing Modernist taste.[106] The architect, Paul W. Reilly, employed an archaeologically accurate Romanesque style to create a compelling image of aspiration that also recalled the neighborhood's glory days. The church replaced a mid-nineteenth-century townhouse. Noting that "stone carvers are a vanishing breed in New York," Meyer Berger told the readers of the *New York Times* in 1957 about seventy-one-year-old Araldo Perugi, who had come out of retirement to realize the limestone-clad church's extensive carving program, the largest such commission in New York since St. Bartholomew's Church (Bertram Grosvenor Goodhue, 1919;

Mayers, Murray & Phillip, 1927).[107] In 1967 Norval White and Elliot Willensky characterized the building as "remarkably correct Romanesque for its date" but noted, as if to suggest a failure of design, that air-conditioning equipment was housed where the church's carillon would traditionally be located.[108]

While Park Avenue remained residential between Thirty-fourth and Thirty-ninth streets, the 1916 zoning permitted commercial uses between Thirty-ninth and Forty-seventh streets. To the already existing Pershing Square Building, on the southeast corner of Park Avenue and Forty-second Street (York & Sawyer, 1914–23),[109] and the Architect's Building, at 101 Park Avenue, on the northeast corner of Fortieth Street (Ewing & Chappell and La Farge & Morris, 1912),[110] were added several postwar skyscrapers. The first of these, and in many ways the most interesting, was Kahn & Jacobs's 100 Park Avenue (1949), the first skyscraper erected in the Grand Central Terminal zone since the early 1930s.[111] The thirty-six-story building was built on the site of the Murray Hill Hotel (Stephen D. Hatch, 1883), on the west blockfront between Fortieth and Forty-first streets. Construction began in 1948 after months of legal battles with the hotel's residents, who were reluctant to move. Unlike the same firm's two-year-old Universal Building, 100 Park Avenue utilized a rather more traditional vertical aesthetic. It consisted of a large base containing 32,000-square-foot floors stepping back to a slender tower with 8,000-square-foot floors that emerged free at the twenty-first floor. The introduction of deep floors at the base, where some of the office space was sixty feet from the nearest window, was justified by the installation of air conditioning, a novelty at the time. Kahn & Jacobs had hoped to clad the building in metal and glass, but compromised on a scheme with facades consisting of expressed columns clad in white brick, between which ran a vertically continuous glass-and-aluminum window wall. From the point of view of real estate economics and functional accommodation, 100 Park Avenue set the standard for postwar office buildings. The building was rented from plans before it actually opened; it provided flexible, well-lit, climate-controlled office space; and it offered large floors for major tenants as well as accommodations for smaller companies.

The aesthetics of 100 Park Avenue, however, were less decisively contemporary. Lewis Mumford described the design as "halfway between the ticker-tape and the layer-cake styles," but he also had praise for it: "This structure by no means tries to tell its whole story in glass, as the United Nations Secretariat Building does, but it nevertheless has a sort of white, ethereal elegance that gives it an even greater air of lightness." Perhaps sensing that this encomium would raise a few eyebrows, Mumford went on to explain the building's aesthetic success:

Plainly, it is not just because the architects have followed Sullivan's dictum that a skyscraper should be a "proud and soaring" building. . . . The most plausible explanation, perhaps, is that while the over-all design of 100 Park Avenue is rigorous, making no attempt at decorative emphasis, there are nevertheless many little departures from uniformity—subtle contrasts of brick, metal, and glass, the sharp, staccato effect of white interior lights against the duller white of the bricks. . . . These touches are a form of, so to speak, self-ornamentation, to which architects in general should give greater heed, since, by current convention, they are about all that is left to the architect to relieve the emptiness of modern design.

Mumford also praised the building's entrance, with its "large amount of sheltered off-street space before one enters the lobby proper," and the "coldly admirable" juxtaposition of polished travertine walls and scalloped indirect-lighting troughs.

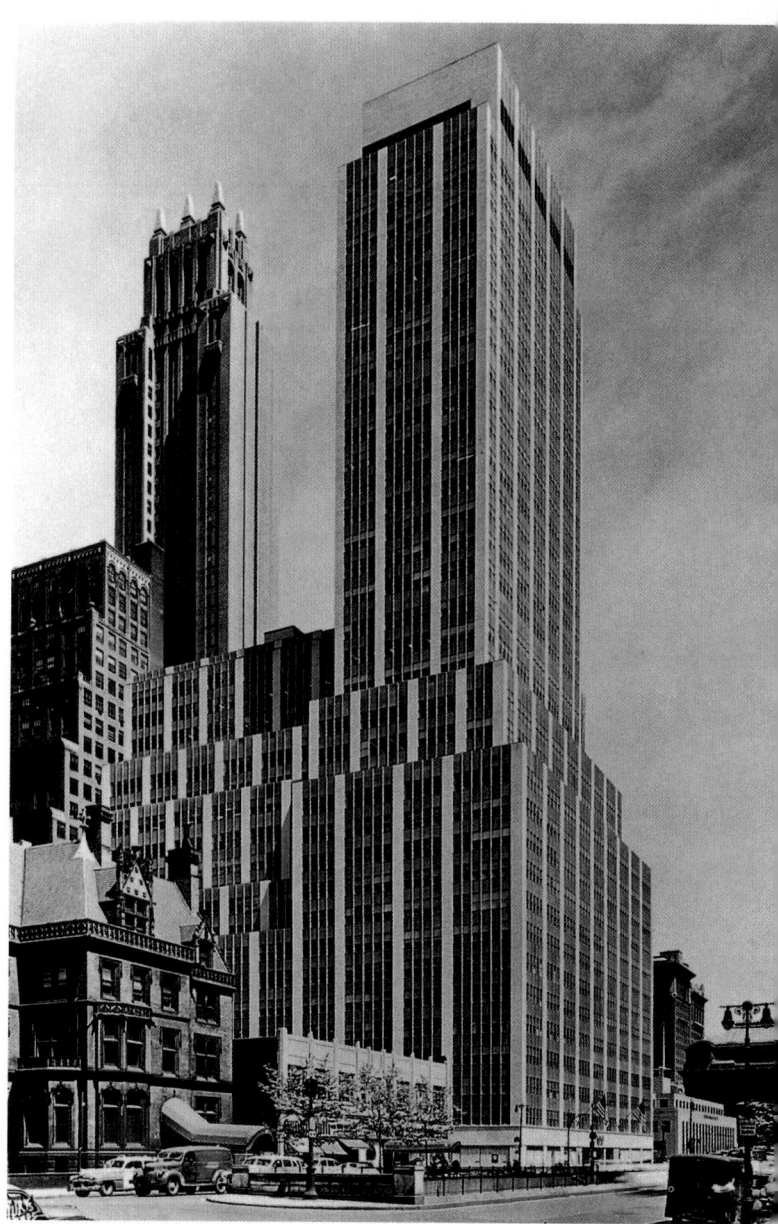

100 Park Avenue, East Fortieth to East Forty-first Street. Kahn & Jacobs, 1949. View to the northwest showing the original Princeton Club (Aymar Embury II, 1923), northwest corner of East Thirty-ninth Street and Park Avenue, in the foreground. Wurts. MCNY

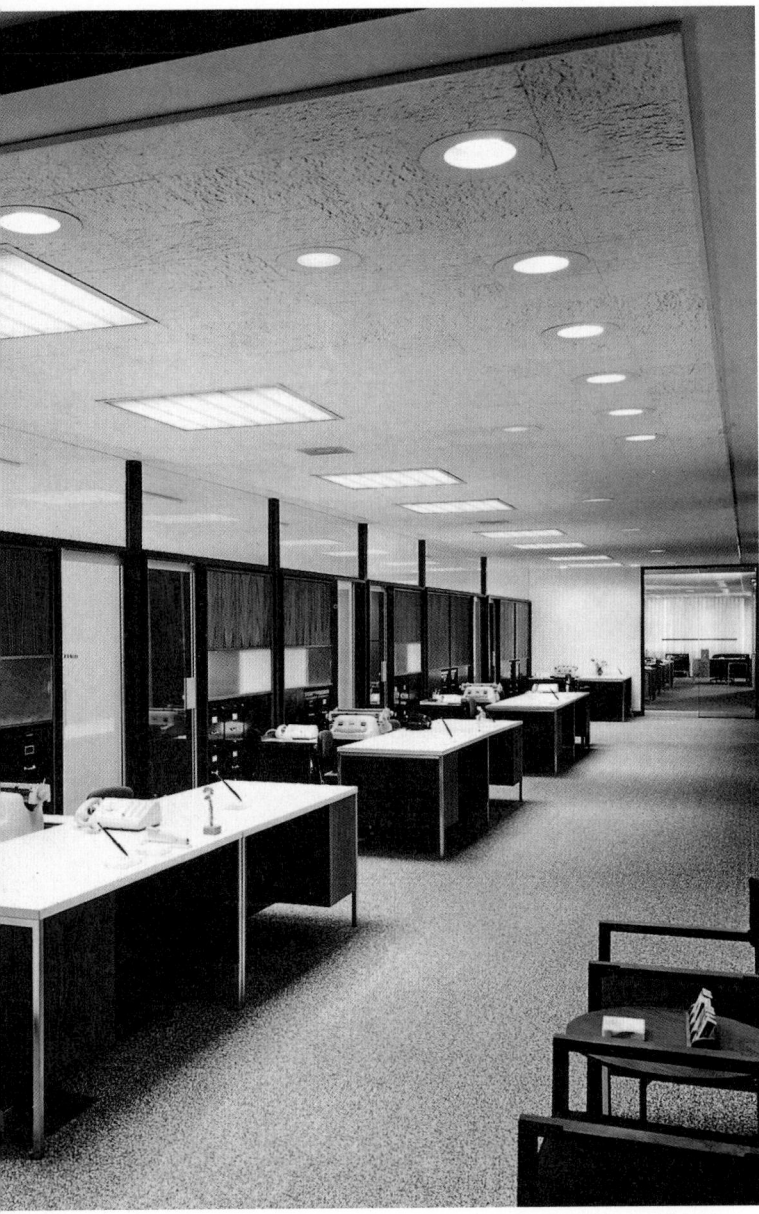

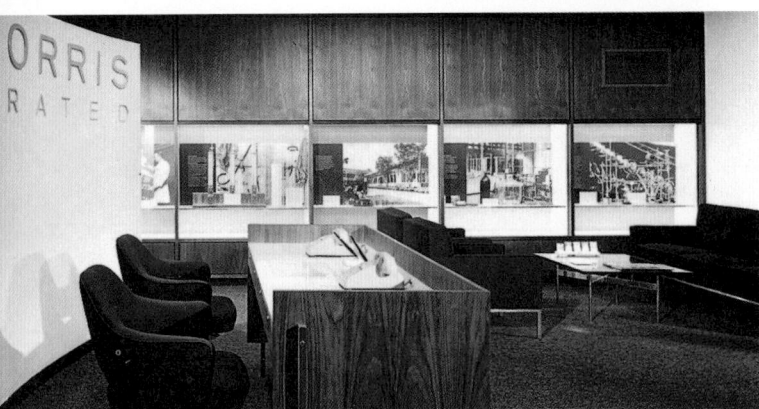

Top: Philip Morris offices, 100 Park Avenue. Ulrich Franzen, 1959. Secretarial pool. Stoller. ©ESTO

Bottom: Philip Morris offices. Reception area. Stoller. ©ESTO

"Indeed," he concluded, "almost the sole aesthetic flaw in the entrance is the overmassiveness of the bronzework in which it is framed."[112]

Although built as a speculative venture by Samuel D. Leidesdorf, 100 Park Avenue had Philip Morris & Co., Ltd., the tobacco-products company, as an important tenant from the beginning. The company's initial installation, also designed by Kahn & Jacobs, included a recreation area and an employee canteen on the third floor. The entire fourth floor was devoted to corporate offices, with numerous executive offices along the perimeter, many of which employed glass walls to allow access to light and view for lower-level employees located nearer the core. The design of the office space demonstrated the potential for efficient use by large companies of the deep, air-conditioned floors. In the building's tower, Skidmore, Owings & Merrill installed a small company, George Fry & Associates, consulting management engineers, in a suite of offices furnished with elegantly detailed, tablelike desks, a far cry from the "standard-issue" utilitarianism of Philip Morris's offices on the lower floors. In 1959, still occupying the same 30,000 square feet it had since the building was completed ten years before, Philip Morris retained Ulrich Franzen to renovate the space that had once been so up-to-date but was now outmoded and overcrowded.[113] Under Franzen's direction, the once open plan gave way to many small offices grouped into departments and gathered around secretarial pools. Franzen also provided such necessities of corporate life as a stylish reception area and a vaulted conference room that could be subdivided.

In 1952 Emery Roth & Sons drew plans for the National Distillers Building (1954), at 99 Park Avenue, a twenty-six-story, 445,000-square-foot building on the east blockfront between Thirty-ninth and Fortieth streets.[114] The new building filled several long-vacant lots, including one on the northeast corner of Thirty-ninth Street that during the Depression had served as the temporary site of two exhibition houses: a Georgian-style house designed by Roger Bullard and Clifford Wendehack and an all-steel house designed by William Van Alen.[115] The National Distillers Building also replaced several mid-nineteenth-century rowhouses, including one at 93 Park Avenue, occupied by the Navy Club, and one at 99 Park Avenue, on the southeast corner of Fortieth Street, which had been occupied by the Nurse's Club.

The Roths' design marked a significant achievement in technology: the prefabricated curtain wall, comprising 1,800 two-story-high panels, was the first in the city; and it was erected in six-and-a-half working days, a remarkable feat compared with the eight weeks or more that a conventional masonry facade would have required. Although masonry was originally specified, the decision to switch to aluminum was made after plans were begun. The change was triggered by executives of Tishman Realty & Construction Company, the building's developers, who had been impressed with the facade of the Aluminum Company of America's Pittsburgh headquarters, designed by Harrison & Abramovitz (1953).[116] Though the Roths' window wall was ingeniously designed, it was not particularly handsome. A four-faceted pattern was introduced on each panel to provide strength and reduce glare. Lewis Mumford found some value in the "effective contrasts of light and shade" that resulted from the curtain wall's faceted surface, but he cautioned against overuse of the material: "A whole avenue of aluminum walls would be dismal, and as grime overlaid the surface, it might likewise become dingy, too." Although Mumford felt that the "dour" quality of unwashed metal might suit the grimy industrial atmosphere of Pittsburgh, he noted that "in New York, which has hitherto lifted a bright, almost feminine face to the sky, this material can be welcomed only as an occasional note of contrast."[117]

Work was completed in 1964 on the Roth firm's 90 Park Avenue, on the west blockfront between Thirty-ninth and Fortieth streets, a forty-one-story, 895,000-square-foot, tower-on-base building clad in brown aluminum and glass and including a 150-car garage.[118] It replaced several buildings, including a group of townhouses that had been combined and remodeled by Aymar Embury II in 1923 to serve the Princeton Club.[119]

In 1976 Clinton & Russell's medieval-style Seventy-first Regiment Armory (1905), long one of Manhattan's notable structures, gave way to Three Park Avenue, on the east blockfront between Thirty-third and Thirty-fourth streets, a thirty-four-story tower that incorporated office space above the eleven-story Norman Thomas High School.[120] The mixed-use building was a project of the Educational Construction Fund, which sponsored mixed-use towers combining schools with revenue-generating facilities. Designed in a bright orange brick by Shreve, Lamb & Harmon Associates, the tower was turned at a forty-five degree angle to the street and its top was brightly illuminated at night, creating a prominent if not aesthetically distinguished landmark. Although Paul Goldberger was not impressed by its "garish orange" nighttime glow, he did admire the "attempt to create *some* sort of pinnacle in a flat-topped age." But he went on to ask whether it was intended as "a statement against the monotony of the standard uptown International Style tower" or "a statement against the rigid order of the street grid itself." He concluded that it was difficult to know for sure, and "harder still to make any sort of absolute judgment about this building," since "it is both too somber and too garish, and the arrogant break it makes at ground level away from the corner of Thirty-fourth and Park is inexcusable."[121] In 1975, as part of his annually presented "Cityscape Awards," the critic Peter Blake, writing in *New York* magazine, presented "One Bit of Dust" to the architects of the building, "one of the most grotesque Instant Eyesores to have gone up east of the Palisades in at least three weeks—an eleven-story school, topped or jostled by an askew 34-story office tower which (like all other Manhattan office towers) will soon stand empty staring blandly across town at the increasingly remarkable Empire State Building."[122]

Significant postwar building activity could also be found at the still-industrial fringes of the neighborhood near the East River. In 1951 plans were announced for the East Side Airlines Terminal, to be built on a large plot adjacent to the Manhattan approach to the Queens-Midtown Tunnel, running along the west blockfront of First Avenue between Thirty-seventh and Thirty-eighth streets and stretching 400 feet to the west, where the tunnel access road formed its fourth boundary.[123] The new facility was designed by John B. Peterkin, whose Modern Classical Airlines Terminal (1940) across from Grand Central was, in its way, a fit complement to the train station's monumentality and sense of place.[124] Ten years later the architect had a less ambitious design agenda, although his building program was more complex, consolidating bus and limousine services bound for La Guardia and Idlewild airports that were then housed at eleven different Manhattan locations. His design was a white-brick curved-corner box set on a base of dark gray brick laid vertically and pierced by regular grillwork that provided ventilation for the bus station within. As at the Port Authority's terminal on Eighth Avenue, the roof was used for parking. The principal public space was a 25,000-square-foot, horseshoe-shaped, second-floor lobby accessible by escalators from the main entrance on First Avenue. This concourse, distinguished

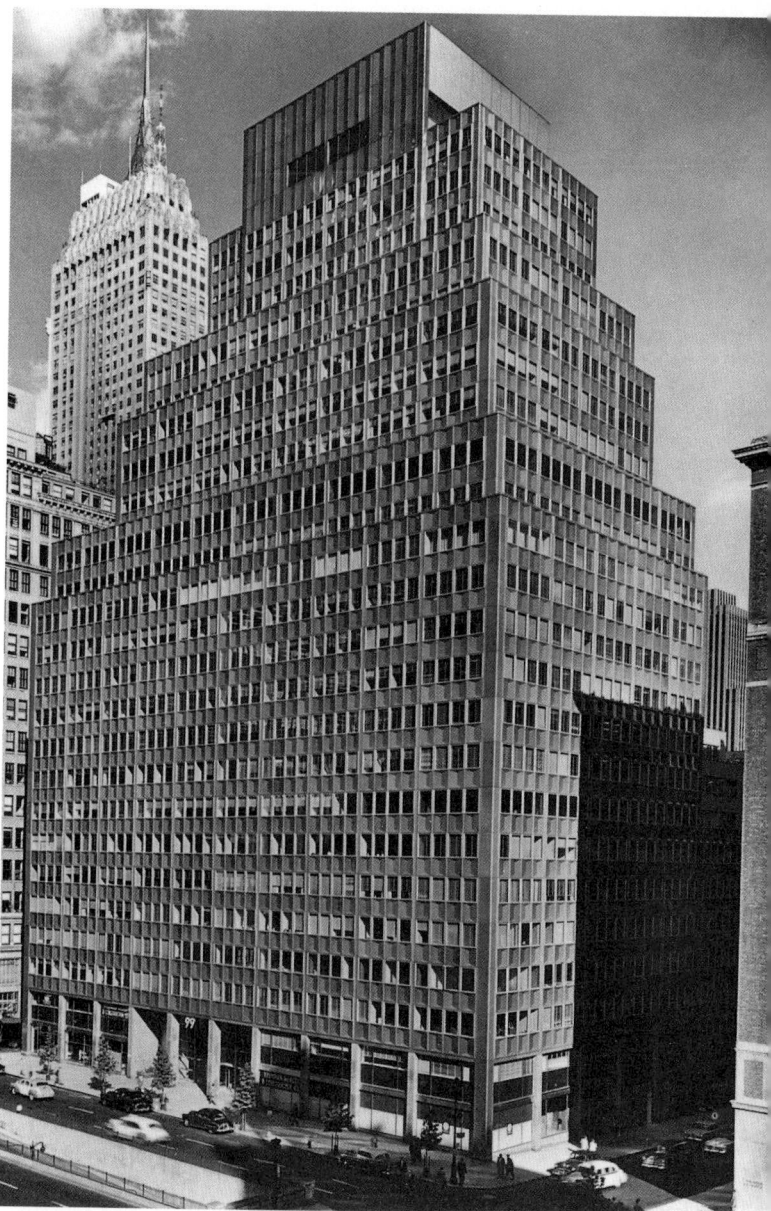

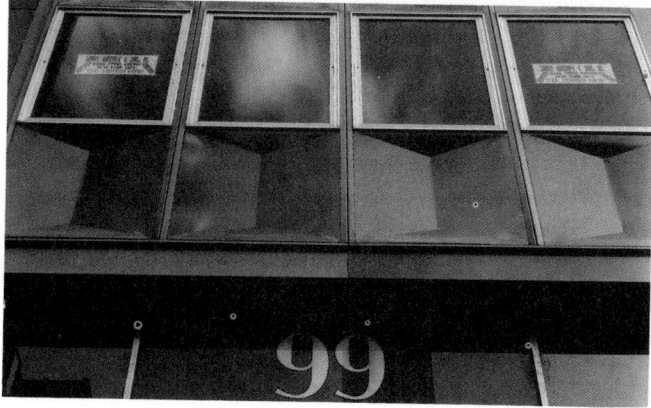

Top: National Distillers Building, 99 Park Avenue, between East Thirty-ninth and East Fortieth streets. Emery Roth & Sons, 1954. View to the northeast. Wurts. MCNY

Bottom: National Distillers Building. Detail of curtain wall. Lincoln. PENN

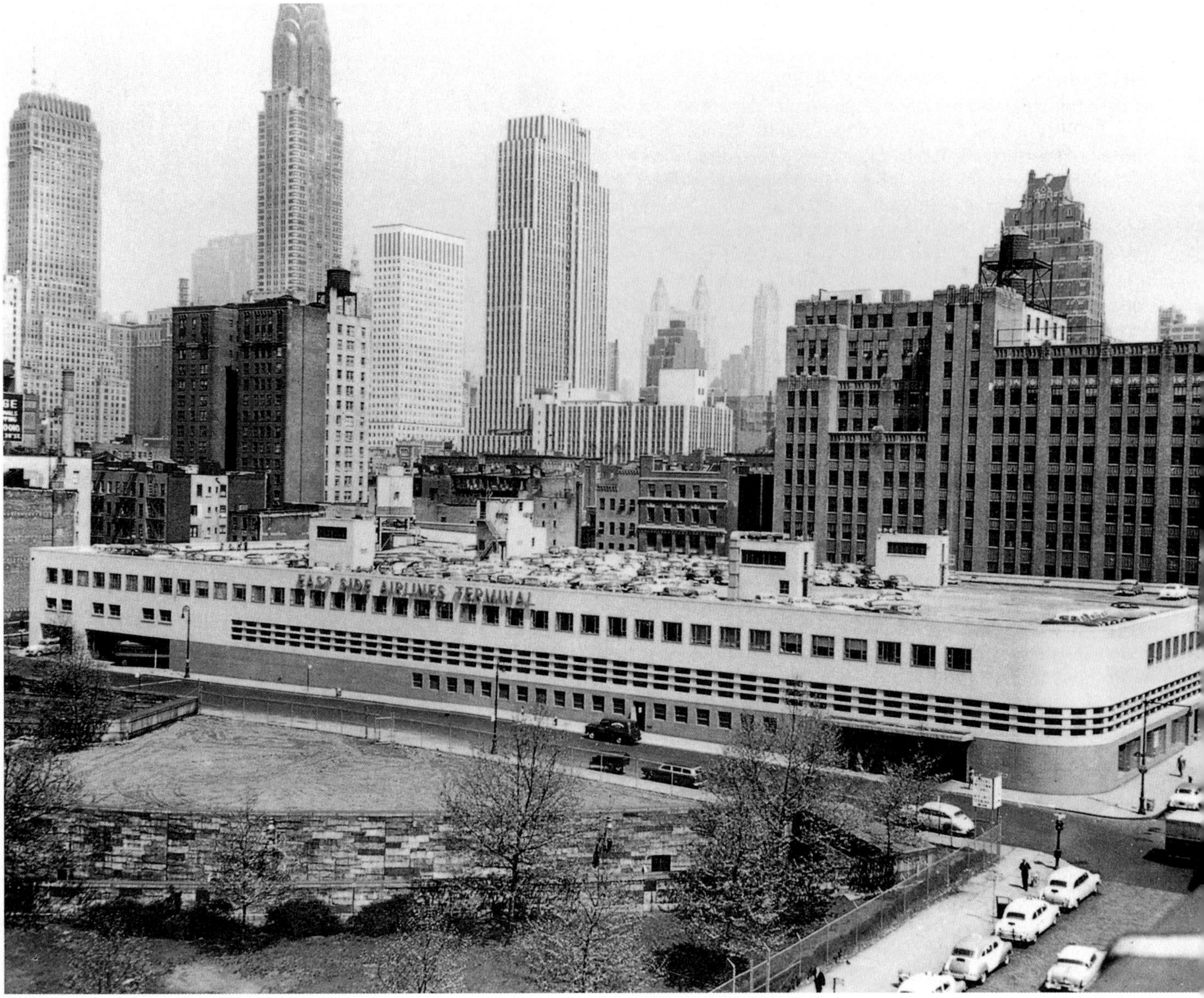

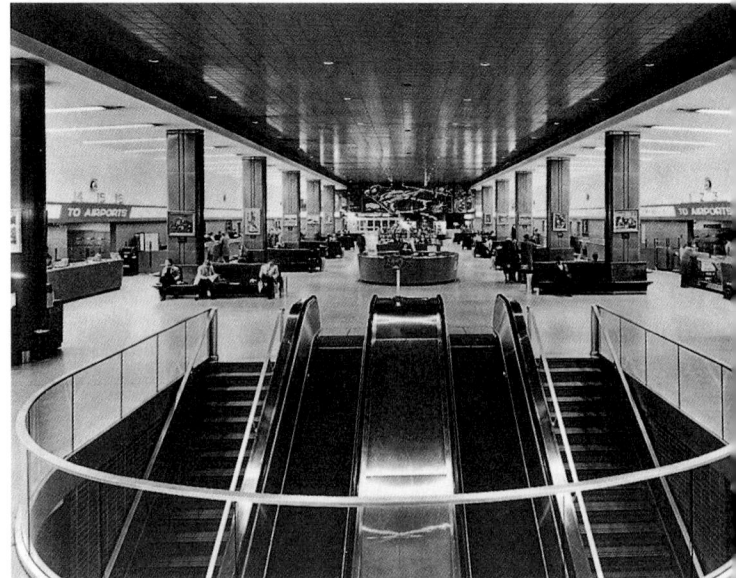

Above: East Side Airlines Terminal, west side of First Avenue, East Thirty-seventh to East Thirty-eighth Street. John B. Peterkin, 1951. View to the northwest. TBTA

Right: East Side Airlines Terminal. Second-floor lobby. Wurts. MCNY

Top far right: Amster Yard, 211 and 215 East Forty-ninth Street, between Second and Third avenues. Remodeling, James Amster and Harold Sterner, 1944. View to the north. OMH

Bottom far right: Amster Yard. View to the east of interior court. OMH by indirect fluorescent lighting, columns finished in red baked enamel to contrast with blue tile dadoes, and light gray-blue and creamy white painted ceilings, drew the admiration of Lewis Mumford, who praised "the handling of light and dark tones, the quality of lighting, to say nothing of the convenience and simplicity of the plan."[125]

Mumford preferred the east side terminal to the Port Authority's west side bus facility, "in that there is a greater unity in the exterior and a more serene handling of the inner space." The critic admired Peterkin's avoidance of the monumental: "The terminal is so emphatically inexpressive, so ostentatiously neutral, that a motorist in search of it, approaching from the south, might easily whiz past it under the impression that it was merely a supermarket or a parking garage." But, despite his enthusiasm, Mumford found the building "aesthetically incomplete" and said that "its design appears to have been halted before it was finished, in terms of both visual pleasure and identification. The neutrality of the building is better than the stale, effortful rhetoric of the old Airlines Terminal, but it is not enough. There is a time to be silent and a time to make oneself heard."[126]

While the East Side Airlines Terminal sought to establish the area near the Manhattan terminus of the Queens-Midtown Tunnel as a convenient if not grand gateway to the city, the district continued to maintain its gritty character. In 1967 the New York Telephone Company completed a twenty-four-story combined equipment and office building at 233 East Thirty-seventh Street, between Second and Third avenues.[127] Designed by Kahn & Jacobs, the limestone-clad building was distinguished by a monumentally scaled dark-glass bay. The building, which extended through to Thirty-eighth Street, was the first to benefit from the 1965 revisions to the 1961 zoning ordinance (see chapter 2).

Turtle Bay

Though the postwar development of the area known as Turtle Bay, roughly bounded by Third Avenue and the East River, Fortieth and Forty-eighth streets, was dominated by the United Nations (see chapter 7), as well as a myriad of banal high-rise apartment and office buildings, the neighborhood also acquired some architecturally distinguished low-rise residential development. In 1944 James Amster, a young, successful, Boston-bred decorator, happened upon a collection of buildings on the north side of East Forty-ninth Street, between Third and Second avenues, that suited his vision for an enclave of apartments and shops that would evoke the scale and character of the flats below Boston's Beacon Hill.[128] The site for Amster Yard, as the complex came to be called, was an L-shaped plot of land with two run-down brownstones at 211 and 215 East Forty-ninth Street and, behind them and directly to the east, a collection of back buildings that may once have been stables. By the 1940s the irregularly shaped property contained a working-class boardinghouse and shops for a cobbler, a plumber and an electrician, as well as a garbage-strewn and vermin-infested courtyard. It also housed the studio of the sculptor Isamu Noguchi until just before Amster took possession of the land. As the editors of *Architectural Forum* put it, these buildings, "together with overhead clotheslines and volunteer ailanthus trees, gave the courtyard a general atmosphere of genial if slatternly charm."[129]

When he first saw the property, Amster was advised by friends to demolish the buildings and construct a fifteen-story

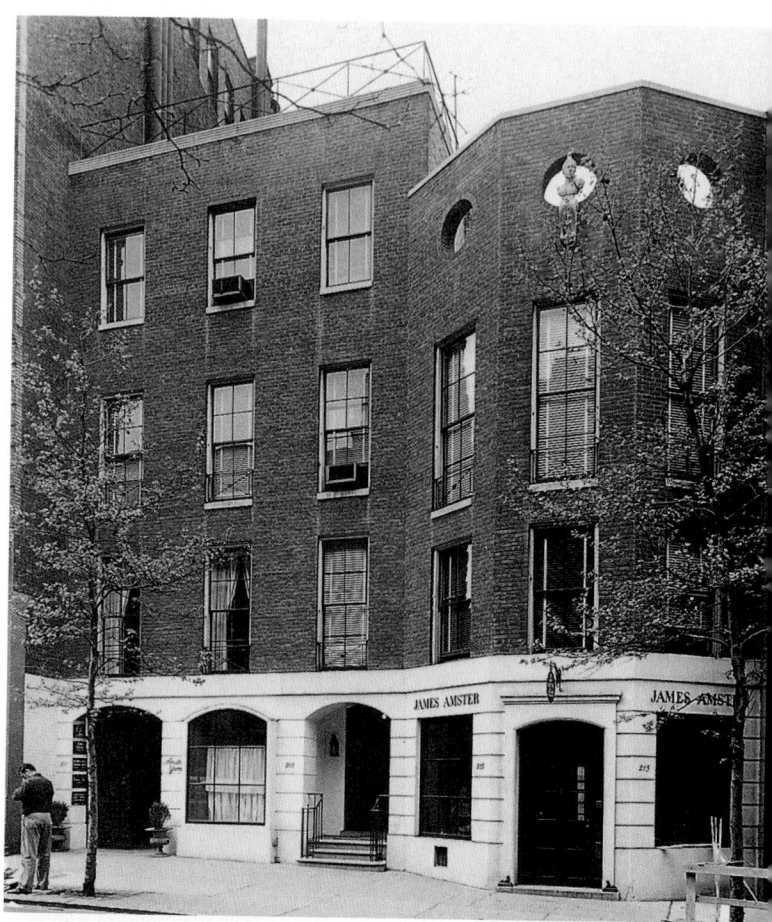

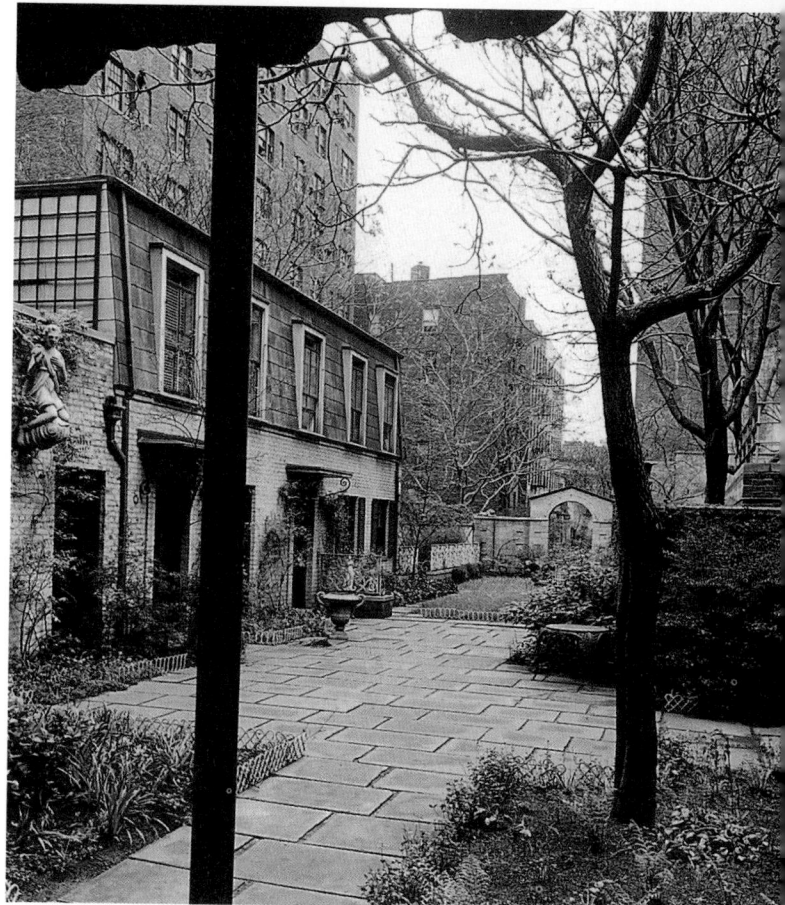

303

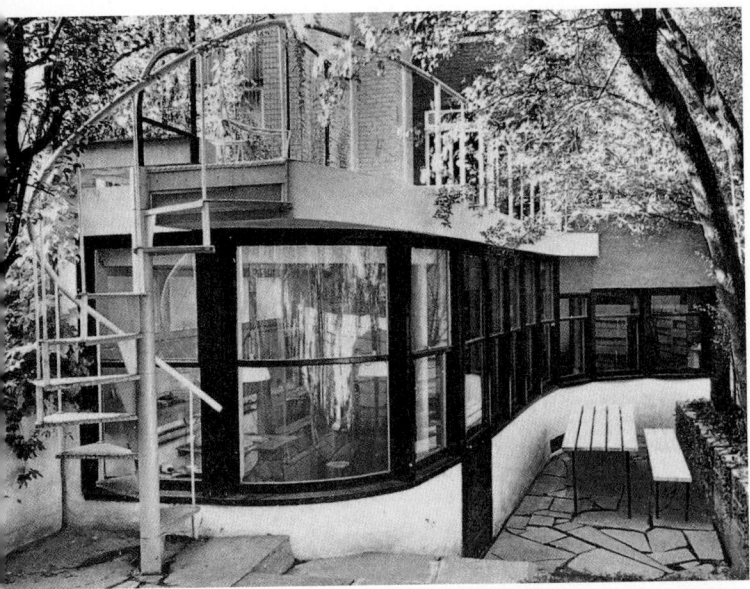

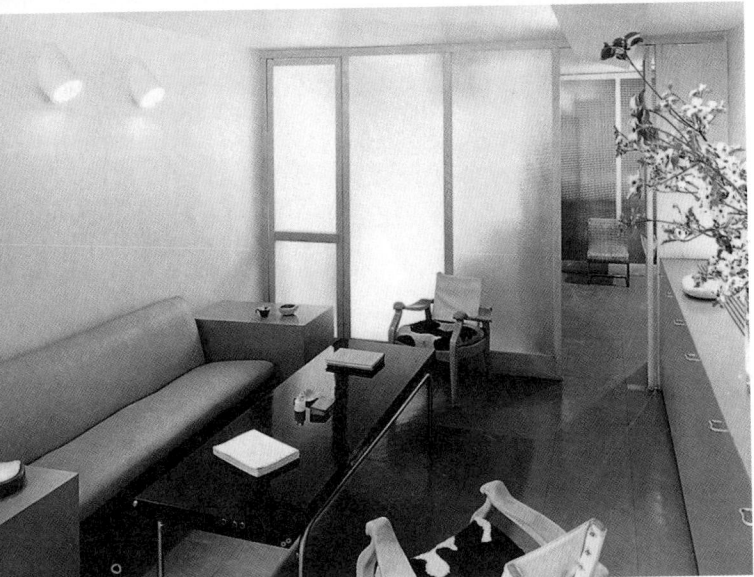

Top: Russel Wright studio and residence, 211 East Forty-eighth Street, between Second and Third avenues. Russel Wright, 1949. View to the south from the backyard of the ground-floor studio. Gottscho-Schleisner. IN. CU

Bottom: Russel Wright studio and residence. Conference room. Gottscho-Schleisner. LOC

Top right: Mrs. John D. Rockefeller III guest house. 242 East Fifty-second Street, between Second and Third avenues. Philip Johnson, 1950. View to the south. OMH

Center right: Mrs. John D. Rockefeller III guest house. Atrium garden and bedroom. Gottscho-Schleisner. LOC

Bottom right: Mrs. John D. Rockefeller III guest house. Living room. Gottscho-Schleisner. LOC

apartment house; but on the advice of the financier Bernard Baruch, a friend of his father's, he took a chance and retained the buildings to create his ideal community-enclave. Although the buildings were in poor condition, the choice to save and renovate them would avoid the imposition of a twenty-one-foot rear-yard setback required by zoning for new construction. In order to comply with zoning regulations requiring that two-thirds of the complex be devoted to shops and offices, Amster came up with the idea of a mixed-use community focused on the decorating trade, which made excellent sense given the proximity to Third Avenue, then the city's center for antiques and upholstery fabrics.

Amster worked with architect and painter Harold Sterner, who with his wife, Paula, soon occupied one of the back buildings as a combined office, studio and residence. Ted Sandler, an art director, was another tenant who collaborated on the development of the complex. Six residential tenants and two commercial tenants signed up before construction began; the decorator Billy Baldwin was an early tenant. The yard became quite fashionable when, at the suggestion of the songwriter Cole Porter, the Ohio playboy and patron of the arts Leonard C. Hanna, Jr., moved in, installing an elevator in his duplex. Amster himself did not feel financially secure enough to live there until 1955, when he took over the Sterners' unit.

Amster Yard was part of a long New York tradition of creating small-scale residential enclaves within the city's grid—just to the south of it lay one of the most complete examples of the type, Turtle Bay Gardens[130]—but it was the only such complex to be realized in the postwar era. Whereas Turtle Bay Gardens evoked Italy, Amster Yard, rather like Sniffen Court, suggested London by way of Boston. The complex as a whole was organized like a *petit hôtel particulier* in Paris, with the back buildings entered from a small courtyard, which appeared longer because of a mirror Amster added in a relieving arch. The street-facing brownstones were completely rebuilt in limestone and brick, with a passageway cut under one to access the yard and a bowed front on the other to give the brownstones greater visibility from Third Avenue. Amster occupied the shop under this bow window. The plans of the houses were organized to maximize light and privacy (most bedrooms faced the rear court). Every detail was carefully studied, including Classical moldings that were sensitively scaled to the small rooms. Throughout the complex, architectural fragments and sculpture were combined with landscaping to create an environment that seemed frozen in time.

Given the growth of midtown's appeal as an office center, there were only a few new or substantially renovated townhouses completed there after the war. In 1947, unable to find suitable space in an office building, the architect Morris Lapidus bought and remodeled a townhouse for his company's use (see chapter 6). In 1949 the designer Russel Wright and his wife, Mary, moved from their Park Avenue penthouse triplex to a brownstone at 221 East Forty-eighth Street.[131] Unlike Lapidus, who completely eradicated his brownstone's original identity, Wright went about the task of renovation on a more modest basis. He made changes to the top two floors, converting them to apartments, some of which he populated with high-style, moderately priced Modernist furniture by Hardoy and Knoll, among other prominent designers; others he designed in a Victorian manner that recalled the Wrights' first apartment (1931), but in a less theatrical way.[132]

The lower floors were occupied by the Wrights. Mary Wright's bedroom and the small dining room were also in the

Victorian style, but the living room, with its unadorned walls and soapstone fireplace, was decidedly contemporary. Russel Wright's offices were on the ground floor, where the principal feature was the new one-story-high drafting room that was built as an el to one side of the rear garden to which it opened through a nearly continuous, S-curve wall of double-hung windows. The studio's roof served as a terrace opening off the Wrights' living room; at the narrow end, an open metal circular stair led down to the garden. Overall, the addition managed to evoke the architecture of transportation, bringing to mind either the deck of an ocean liner or, as draftsmen in William Lescaze's neighboring office waggishly described it, "A Streetcar Named Desire."[133]

In 1947 the brownstone at 217 East Forty-ninth Street was transformed into the showroom and offices of the House of Italian Handicrafts, a nonprofit company founded by Max Ascoli, a professor of political philosophy at the New School for Social Research.[134] As adapted by Gustavo Pulitzer, who had designed the interiors of numerous European hotels as well as several ocean liners, the brownstone's exterior was painted white with green trim but otherwise left as if it was. Inside, the house was largely gutted and reorganized to accommodate large open spaces dominated by colorful murals by the painter and sculptor Constantino Nivola, who illustrated craftsmen at work.

In 1950, a few blocks away at 242 East Fifty-second Street, Philip Johnson completely transformed a carriage house to serve as a guest house for Mrs. John D. Rockefeller III.[135] Johnson's facade of dark brown iron-spot Roman brick, black metal and unpolished plate glass was startling yet understated. With its single central doorway, strong base and vertically proportioned three-bay facade, brilliantly made to seem as if it was raised off the base by the introduction of a band of clerestory windows, Johnson's composition was distinctly Classical in inspiration, though the vocabulary reflected the reductivist Modernism of the architect's mentor, Mies van der Rohe.

Inside, Johnson created a continuous, loftlike interior, with a combined living and dining room in front and a bedroom in back, each looking through fully glazed walls to a water-filled, landscaped, open-air atrium garden that lay between. Here Johnson revealed a debt not only to Mies's so-called courthouses of the 1930s and to George Nelson's 1941 Fairchild townhouse on East Sixty-fifth Street,[136] which featured a garden separating front and back rooms, but also to the sources for both in ancient Roman architecture. Whereas Mies's courtyards were largely places to be contemplated from within, and Nelson's was crisscrossed by enclosed circulation ramps, Johnson required that guests go out-of-doors to cross the pool, stepping on three travertine "pads" as they made their way. The critic John Jacobus noted that "Johnson has deliberately sacrificed a considerable area of interior space in favor of the court. In doing so, he has created spatial expansiveness despite the severe limitations of the site. . . . In addition to providing an outdoor room, this design opened up the otherwise thoroughly closed-in living spaces of the Guest House, providing them with an unexpected sense of airiness and flow."[137]

Johnson's handling of the interiors was far more spartan than one would expect not only of a Rockefeller but also of a disciple of Mies, who, though a minimalist, luxuriated in marbles, fine silks and supple leathers. The party walls were stripped of their plaster and the exposed brick was painted white, providing a sympathetic but not characterless backdrop for Mrs. Rockefeller's modernist art, which included a specially commis-

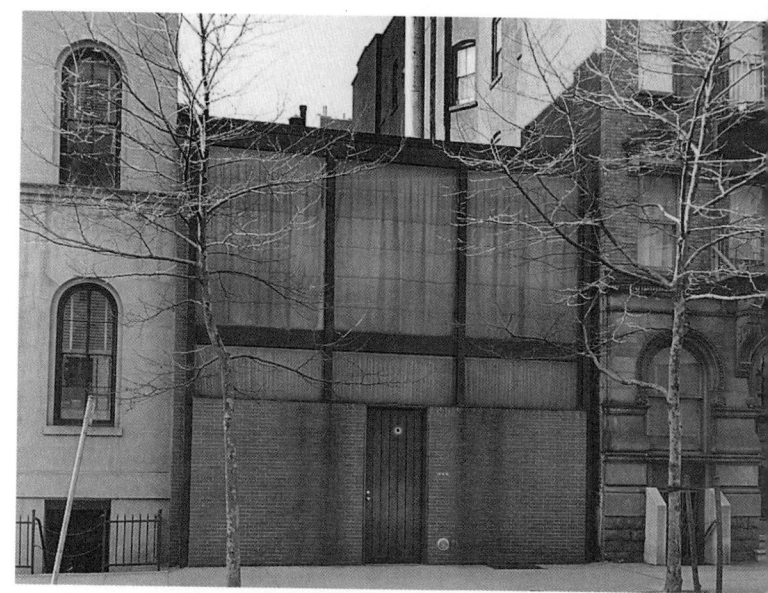

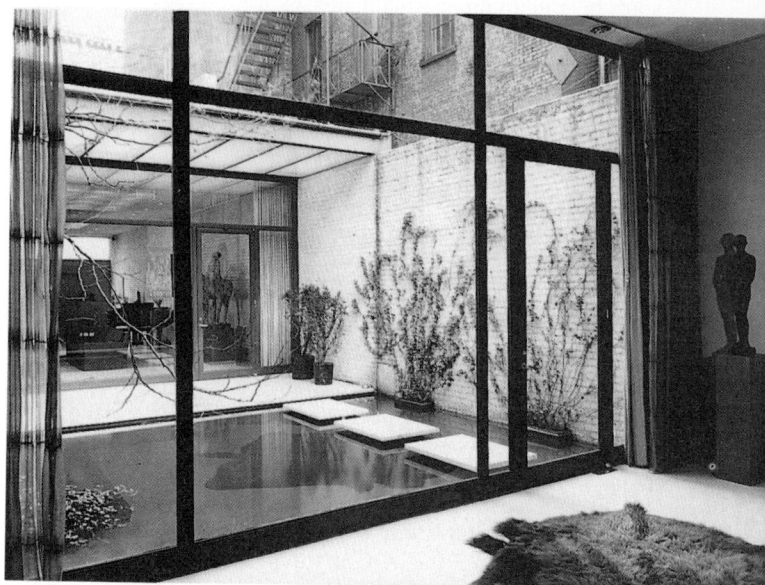

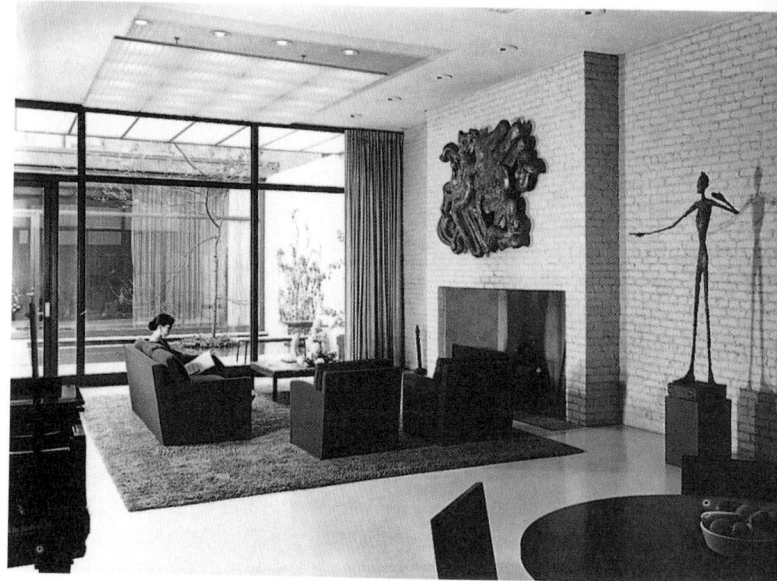

sioned relief, *Birth of the Muses*, by Jacques Lipchitz. The floors were covered with white linoleum; the few furnishings, principally upholstered pieces specially designed by Johnson, sat before the fireplace on a raftlike living room rug. Copper-laced goat's-hair curtains could be drawn across the atrium windows for privacy. The interior was a startlingly direct interpretation of the idea of continuous space so dear to architectural Modernists in the 1920s; and with its exposed brick walls and the presence of art, as the Pop artist Andy Warhol observed in 1974, it also anticipated the loft living that would emerge a decade or more later.[138]

For as long as the Rockefellers owned the house, it was used for parties, mostly given on behalf of the Museum of Modern Art. In 1958 the art was removed and the house was given to the museum for use as a guest house. In 1964, with the opening of the museum's new wing, designed by Johnson and containing extensive party facilities, the house was sold. The buyers were Mr. and Mrs. Robert Leonhardt, for whom Johnson had designed a house in Lloyd's Neck on Long Island and who kept the townhouse as a city pied-à-terre. After Robert Leonhardt's death, his widow remarried, and in 1972 she asked Johnson's help in finding a suitable tenant. Johnson decided to move into the townhouse himself, with his companion, the art curator and exhibition designer David Whitney. Johnson stripped the design even further, removing most of the curtains and replacing the furniture with foam scoop chairs designed by the Italian sculptor Gaetano Pesce, creating a livelier effect and bringing the house closer than ever to the mood of a loft.

Summit Hotel

Just beyond Turtle Bay's boundaries, on the southeast corner of Lexington Avenue and Fifty-first Street, the Summit Hotel, designed by Morris Lapidus and completed in 1961, dramatically reflected the evolving character of east midtown.[139] The city's first all-new, large-scale hotel in thirty years, the Summit was noteworthy in part because it represented a watershed in the postwar resuscitation of the city's hotel industry. It was also important in the architectural community, its unabashedly theatrical interpretation of International Style Modernism hitting a raw nerve and eliciting more numerous and more emotionally charged responses than the building would, in only a few years' time, seem to merit. In an era when most architects followed Mies van der Rohe's dictum "less is more" and stripped their buildings of virtually all ornamental elements and historical references, Lapidus's obvious delight in ornate decoration was highly controversial.

The Summit was intended as the first of several Manhattan hotels to be built by the enterprising thirty-five-year-old developer Preston Robert Tisch and his older brother Laurence, who, as *Business Week* noted in 1961, "have been unerringly right about the hotel markets they've entered."[140] To build the first of their proposed hotels, originally to be known as the Americana East but called the Summit by the time of its completion, the Tisches demolished the Loew's Lexington Theater and commissioned Lapidus for the design. The architect had gained prominence during the interwar and postwar years as the designer of eye-catching stores and had later received international recognition for the design of extravagantly decorated resort hotels including the Fontainebleau (1954) and the Eden Roc (1955) in Miami Beach and the Americana (1956) in nearby Bal Harbour, Florida. In his 1979 autobiography, *An Architecture of Joy*,

Lapidus described how he first brought his experience as a store designer to bear on the problem of hotel design: "I was convinced that just as a store had to be designed to make people want to buy what the merchant had to sell, so a hotel had to sell something also. What was that something? A home away from home? Absolutely not! Who wants a homey feeling on vacation? . . . forget the office, the house, the kids, the bills. Anything but that good old homey feeling that the old hotels use to sell."[141]

In his design for the twenty-one-story, 800-room Summit, Lapidus adapted many of the techniques and motifs he had used in his highly successful Florida hotels. For example, at the Fontainebleau, Lapidus had utilized a dramatically curved slab which, in its striking rejection of the ordinary boxlike forms of most apartment and office buildings, powerfully evoked the fanciful spirit of a vacation, despite the fact that it closely resembled Affonso Eduardo Reidy's low-income housing project of 1950 in Rio de Janeiro. At the Summit Lapidus would once again eschew strictly rectilinear form in favor of a gently undulating mass, placing an elongated S-shape building on the constricted site, which was seventy feet wide along Lexington Avenue and extended back for half a block along Fifty-first Street. While the Summit's curving mass ensured, as the editors of *Interior Design* said, that it would "never be mistaken for one of the monotonously-same new apartment houses or office buildings rising throughout the city," Lapidus justified the unorthodox shape on practical rather than aesthetic grounds.[142] Explaining that, given the site's zoning restrictions, a conventional footprint would render only 500 guest rooms, not the 800 required by his clients, Lapidus reasoned: "Why not bend the hall, in other words, create a squiggle or an S-shaped building with an S-shaped hall. Why not? An S-shaped building would achieve the greatest length and, therefore, more rooms per floor. The final building plan did achieve the 800 rooms. My clients were happy."[143]

The hotel's massing was but one feature that gave it a Florida-resort look and made it immediately recognizable. The curving facades were clad in pale turquoise glazed brick and dark green Italian tiles; the color of the tiles was repeated in the draperies visible in every guest room window. In the color choice for the building's exterior, Lapidus was inspired, he said, by "that eminent architect of the past, Raymond Hood," who in his McGraw-Hill Building of 1931 chose "fresh blue and green for its exterior."[144] The narrow end of the building fronting Lexington Avenue contained the principal entrance, above which a windowless expanse of white Vermont marble streaked with pale green veining was decorated only by the hotel's name, dramatically spelled out on vertically arranged, internally illuminated white plastic ovals held by triangular metal brackets. To one side of the entrance, in front of a molded-concrete wall studded with stained-glass fragments, a planting area contained palmlike plants, making explicit the reference to Lapidus's previous hotels in Miami Beach; among the foliage were egg-shaped lights elevated on tall metal rods.

Inside the Summit, Lapidus pulled out all the stops to convey a sense of accessible luxury, as well as to mask the severe spatial constraints imposed by the building program. As Lapidus put it, "Within the limited area of the first floor, I was asked to squeeze in . . . a reception lobby, a cocktail lounge, a dining room, a coffee shop, a men's wear shop, a barbershop, and even some meeting rooms. I finally shoehorned in all these spaces. I satisfied my clients' requirements, although, in my own mind, I called the lobby a dentist's waiting room because it seemed so small to me."[145] To conceal the lobby's size, Lapidus used a broad palette of bright colors, and clear plastic chairs as well as built-in furniture. The lobby also contained columns sheathed in East Indian rosewood and marble and decorated with gold anodized wreathlike sconces, an illuminated ceiling composed of gold cylindrical forms, wall panels covered in blue-green batik-patterned fabric, area rugs incorporating multicolored, swirling patterns, and white venetian terrazzo flooring with blue and green inserts shaped like bow ties, Lapidus's sartorial signature. Recalling, or more precisely recycling, techniques he had used to create a sense of drama in his Miami Beach hotels, Lapidus installed an open staircase that served as a visual focal point as well as leading to the lobby's public restrooms and to a ballroom. The staircase was highlighted by a colorful mosaic mural designed by Lapidus, "an abstraction," according to the architect, that was supposed to suggest "some sense of heading for a summit, but nothing more specific than that."[146] The glass-topped registration desk was also covered with colorful mosaics.

Throughout the lobby Lapidus used numerous highly decorative lighting fixtures. "Man has always achieved emotional comfort from being able to see the source of light—the moon, the sun or a burning fireplace," he argued. "There is also what I call the 'moth complex.' People are impelled to walk towards light. That is why in the elevator lobby of the Summit I have made the lighting especially bright. It leads people to that area."[147] The lighting was in fact so powerful that a separate air-conditioning unit was required to compensate for the heat it generated. Just in case the light failed to attract people's attention, the elevator doors were faced with blue, green, black, purple and turquoise designs rendered in porcelain enamel.

The hotel's restaurants all featured South American–inspired names and decorative themes. The Casa de Café coffee shop incorporated cast-stone wall panels designed by James Seeman to resemble pre-Columbian carvings, as well as a sculpture by Jordan Stechel that used machine parts in a modern interpretation of a pre-Columbian calendar. The Carioca Lounge contained sandblasted redwood walls, wooden bead curtains and decorative calf-hide wall panels. The Gaucho Room included gold Naugahyde-covered walls, ceiling beams decorated with porcelain enamel cattle-brand motifs and hand-hammered metal light fixtures that took the shape of steer skulls. "Here," Lapidus said, "I have created an image of Latin America which doesn't actually exist.. It is an area of fancy and whimsy."[148] In explaining his overall approach to interior design, Lapidus claimed that, although architects are "supposed to be through" once they put up the structure, "I can't help myself, when it comes to interiors, I get carried away."[149]

The Summit drew overwhelmingly negative critical responses from almost everyone who took the time to comment (and one way or another, most New Yorkers did). Only Olga Gueft, editor of *Interiors*, had some kind words. Arguing that the Summit was "an important addition to the New York scene and perhaps to the whole American scene," she felt it deserved a more conscientious response than the "gales of laughter" and "facetious rejoinders" with which it had been greeted. In her even-handed review, Gueft found that although Lapidus had "performed superbly" in many respects, the result of his "frantic effort to confuse the eye is simply: confusion."[150] The critic Walter McQuade, writing in the *Nation*, was more representative of smart New York chat when he quipped that the best comment he'd heard about the new hotel was "strictly nonprofessional: 'It's too far from the beach.'" He continued: "Soon, perhaps, we shall know whether a tropic sun leaning on the white sands is essential to sustain this manic architecture, whether a New York winter may not drive it desperate and

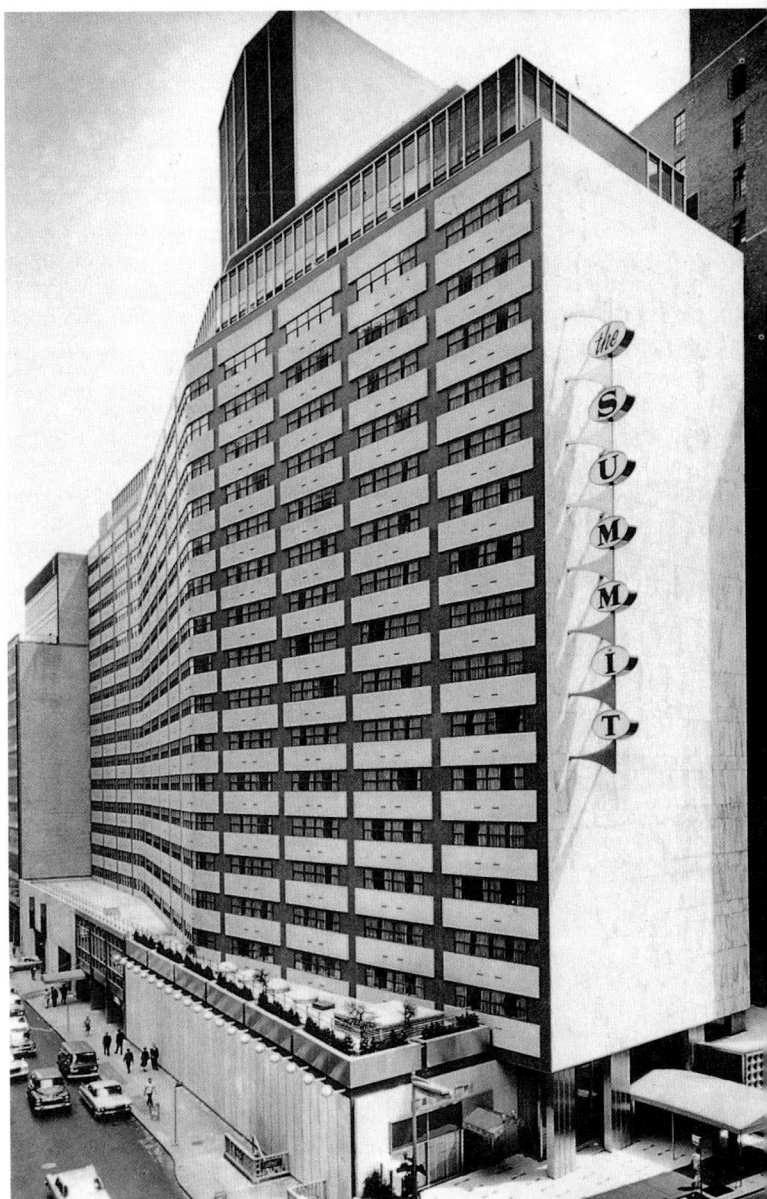

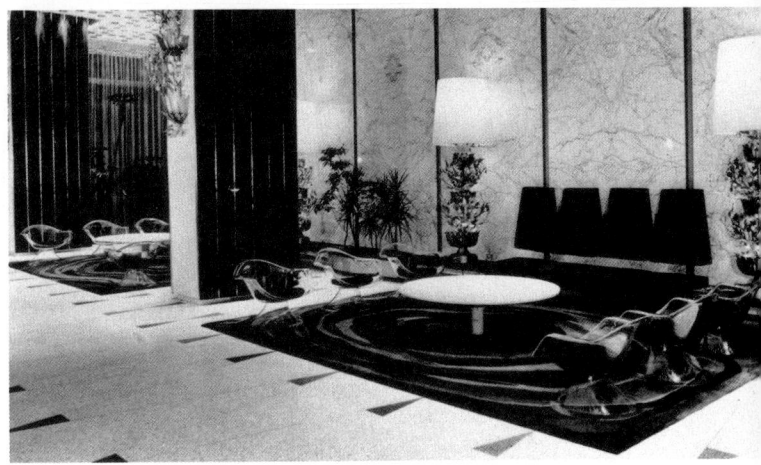

Top: Summit Hotel, southeast corner of Lexington Avenue and East Fifty-first Street. Morris Lapidus, 1961. View to the southeast. ML

Bottom: Summit Hotel. Lobby. ML

dreary. It is entirely possible that loud-speakers in the palm trees are an indispensable part of the act."[151]

To Russell Lynes, the matter was not open to question. "We are snobbishly intolerant in New York of the subculture of Florida," he wrote, "and we wish they would keep everything but their pompano and oranges down there where it belongs and not foul our nest with their taste. Ours is bad enough already; we need no help from the provinces." Lynes criticized the Summit's vertical sign, which he said "would do justice to any motel on the road from Dallas to Fort Worth or any bowling alley in Paramus, N.J." and went on to condemn the entire exterior: "It has a slightly greenish, underwater look about it, as though the sun were shining through a swimming pool on a body whose contours are made to undulate by the ripple of the water's surface. Somehow its knees look slightly detached from its thighs; it might almost be the old Beaux Arts of the '30s trying to do the twist."[152] The editors of *Time* were somewhat kinder in their appraisal, observing that the "graceful, serpentine curve of the long exterior wall . . . is a welcome change from Manhattan's orange-crate regularity," but adding that "the sea-green color of that wall mocks the eye."[153]

When it came to assessing the Summit's interiors, the critics were equally harsh. The editors of *Time* stated that "the decor can be described as something between Bronx baroque and Mexicali modrum."[154] McQuade commented, "It is generally agreed in the trade that Lapidus must cultivate the materials salesmen almost as assiduously as they certainly cultivate him."[155] The editors of the *New Yorker* took a perhaps more appropriately lighthearted stance, sharing Lapidus's own sense of delight and play:

How rarely in life does one get to announce the birth of a new style, whether in millinery, painting, or what you will! Imagine our pride, therefore, in being granted the privilege of announcing a brand-new style in architecture. Its name is Tongue-in-Cheek Aztec, and the inventor of both the style and the name is our old and gifted friend Morris Lapidus. . . . The interior features a bouillabaisse of mosaics, travertine, rare woods, vinyl tile, textiles and formica, and has—we were about to say it has as many colors as a rainbow, but that would be doing it an injustice, because it has a lot more colors than any rainbow *we've* ever seen, and nearly all of them are to be found within an inch or so of all the rest. The Summit is supposed to have cost twenty-five million dollars, and we wouldn't be surprised if a good half of this sum had gone into pigments.[156]

Ada Louise Huxtable was less amused, stating that "the Summit is a glittering display of gaudy confusion. Mosaics, marbles, woods, enamels, fabrics, synthetics, colors and crafts have been poured forth and combined with profligate abandon and aggressive insensitivity."[157] Issues of taste aside, the critics pointed out that though the Summit was hyped as a major hotel, it was very cramped. As Russell Lynes wrote: "The lobby, I had heard, was a whizzer, but I was struck with how small it was. I expected empty space to tower above my head, to awe me with its wasteful opulence, but it was only big enough (or so it seemed to me) to serve as the ante-room of an old fashioned palace hotel lobby."[158]

Three months after the Summit's opening the widespread criticism convinced the hotel's management that an interior redesign was required. While defending Lapidus and arguing that innovation inevitably met with criticism, Laurence Tisch ordered that the lobby be modified. Lapidus, who claimed that the majority of the criticism had come from "sidewalk critics" and

not guests at the hotel, would later say that the "color was just too much for New Yorkers accustomed to the dirty, grimy grays." Accordingly, Lapidus redid the design "using somber tans, and browns, and getting rid of the floating, clear-lucite furniture. New York was just not ready for that sort of thing."[159]

Some of the criticism of the Summit bordered on the personal, addressing Lapidus's general approach to design, not merely his work at the hotel. Walter McQuade described Lapidus as "an interesting architect with a strange specialty— bad taste." McQuade went on to state that Lapidus's "justification is that his buildings put people at ease, even make them happy, and he may well be right. By standards of commercial success, he certainly is right. At any rate, he is the architect who can best inhale the sweet smell of excess and build it a monument. When other architects try to design in his flashy style, they miss the essence that Lapidus uncannily captures."[160]

Lapidus acknowledged such criticism, but he argued that the Summit was appreciated much more by outsiders than by native New Yorkers. Not only that, he said, but those same New Yorkers loved his hotels in Florida: "Putting it bluntly, it's something like a businessman enjoying a cutie doing a striptease on a stage—but if his wife ever tried it, he'd holler bloody murder."[161] Years after the controversy, Lapidus would explain his goals at the Summit and in his architectural work in general:

I'm trying to create good architecture. I feel that I have done my utmost to design a fine building. . . . I resolved early in my career that, since I probably would not leave my mark, I might as well enjoy what I'm doing and have the people who use my architecture enjoy it as well. . . . I feel architecture in the 1950's . . . [seemed] to say to people, "If you don't understand it, you're stupid." I felt my role was to please people, allow them to get involved. They loved it or they hated it, but nobody just walked by my buildings. Maybe a few stood in front of the Summit and said, "My God, who the hell did that?" Maybe that was my way of trying to find status for myself.[162]

WEST SIDE: FROM CHELSEA TO CLINTON

Chelsea

Like nearly every Manhattan neighborhood, Chelsea, bounded by Fourteenth and Thirtieth streets, Sixth Avenue and the Hudson River, shared in the changes that came with postwar life. Yet despite a considerable amount of building activity, some of it on a rather large scale, the area managed to retain much of its prewar character. Chelsea first began to be developed around 1830 as an upper-middle-class residential enclave laid out on land inherited by the Reverend Clement Clarke Moore, author of the famous Christmas poem "A Visit from St. Nicholas." Moore donated the tract of land extending from Ninth to Tenth Avenue and Twentieth to Twenty-ninth Street to the General Theological Seminary, which established on it the city's first campus (East Building, 1827; West Building, 1836; expanded by Charles C. Haight, 1883–1900).[1] With the seminary as its focus, a neighborhood of fine houses, such as the Greek Revival–style London Terrace development (Alexander Jackson Davis, 1845), began to be built, gradually spreading to include a mixture of modest townhouses, working-class tenements and, along the river, warehouses and abattoirs.

For a time after the Civil War, Fourteenth and Twenty-third streets were premier entertainment and shopping streets, and

Sixth Avenue from Fourteenth to Thirty-fourth Street was the city's principal center of large department stores catering to the middle class.[2] But with the construction of Macy's at Herald Square in 1901 and Gimbel's at Greeley Square in 1911, the city's shopping center began to move northward and eastward along Thirty-fourth Street toward Fifth Avenue, where Benjamin Altman built his palace of consumption in 1906.[3] Beginning in the late 1920s Chelsea enjoyed something of an architectural renaissance, with the demolition of the original London Terrace houses to make way for Farrar & Watmaugh's apartment complex (1930) of the same name[4] and the construction of the highly functional yet stylishly modern Starrett-Lehigh Building (Russell G. and Walter M. Cory, with Yasuo Matsui, 1931).[5]

Chelsea's prime residential area had been cut in half in 1870 by the completion of the city's first elevated line, running from Battery Place in lower Manhattan along Greenwich Street and Ninth Avenue to Thirtieth Street; the discontinuation of service in 1940 and the subsequent demolition of the El in 1941 stimulated residential construction in the area.[6] In 1942 Elliott Houses was announced as one of the first postwar projects to be undertaken by the New York City Housing Authority.[7] Completed in 1947, the housing project was named for John Lovejoy Elliott, a social worker who was for many years the driving force behind the programs of the Hudson Guild, a neighborhood community center that was retained on the six-acre site that ran along the east side of Tenth Avenue between Twenty-fifth and Twenty-seventh streets. Twenty-sixth Street was not altered and was left to traverse the project, while Twenty-seventh Street was closed between Ninth and Tenth avenues and partially replaced by a narrow service road that ran around two of the towers and connected midblock to Twenty-sixth Street.

Designed by Archibald Manning Brown, William Lescaze and Morris & O'Connor, Elliott Houses consisted of four eleven- and twelve-story pinwheeling slabs that covered 22 percent of the site. Oriented with their long sides on a true east-west axis, the buildings were twenty-three degrees off Manhattan's grid. With the exception of the Wallabout Houses, a national defense housing development completed near the Brooklyn Navy Yard in 1941, Elliott Houses was the first publicly funded housing project composed exclusively of high-rise buildings. Though the complex's site planning reflected prewar precedents, several cost-cutting construction features were introduced at Elliott Houses that would soon become hallmarks of Housing Authority projects, including the employment of a concrete-column-and-slab structural system, red-brick cavity walls and unfinished concrete-slab ceilings. The project was thus a harbinger of the architectural mediocrity and callous attitude toward human needs that would increasingly dominate public housing. Nonetheless, usually thoughtful observers rationalized its banality and brutality. While Lewis Mumford criticized Elliott Houses as a "hulking" complex, "one of the most overcrowded and dismal examples of public housing in the city," he added that they were "a paradise compared to the earlier tenements they replaced."[8] Although Mumford failed to take into account the fact that the Elliott Houses thwarted the social cohesion that the tenements had fostered, in one way he was right. The development was a paradise, if not in comparison to the tenements it replaced, then in comparison to later municipal housing projects such as Chelsea Houses (New York City Housing Authority, 1961), two supremely banal twenty-one-story brick slabs containing a total of 424 units, located nearby on a site west of Ninth Avenue between Twenty-fifth and Twenty-sixth streets.[9]

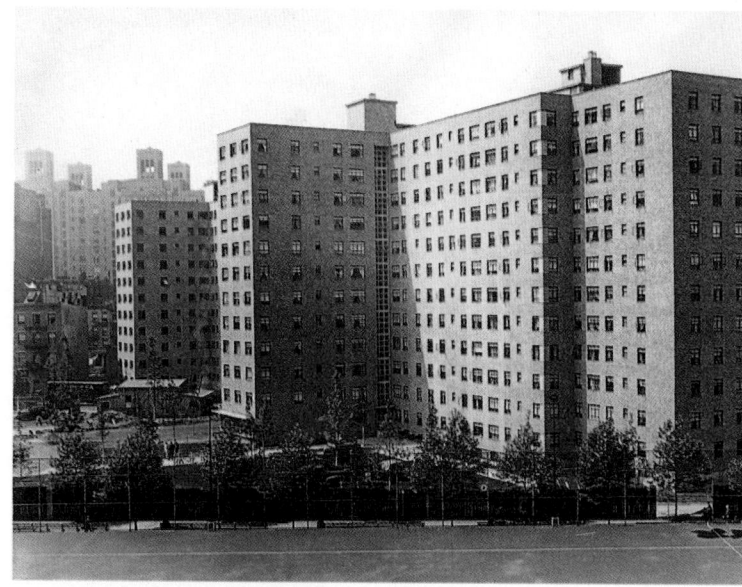

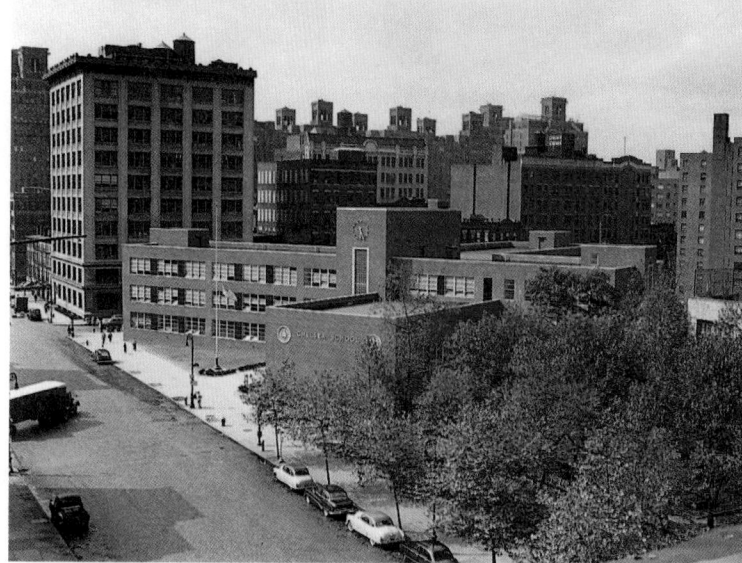

Top: Elliott Houses, east side of Tenth Avenue, West Twenty-fifth to West Twenty-seventh Street. Archibald Manning Brown, William Lescaze and Morris & O'Connor, 1947. View to the south. Marinoff. NYCHA

Bottom: Chelsea School, Public School 33, northwest corner of Ninth Avenue and West Twenty-sixth Street. Eric Kebbon, 1951. View to the southwest. NYCBE

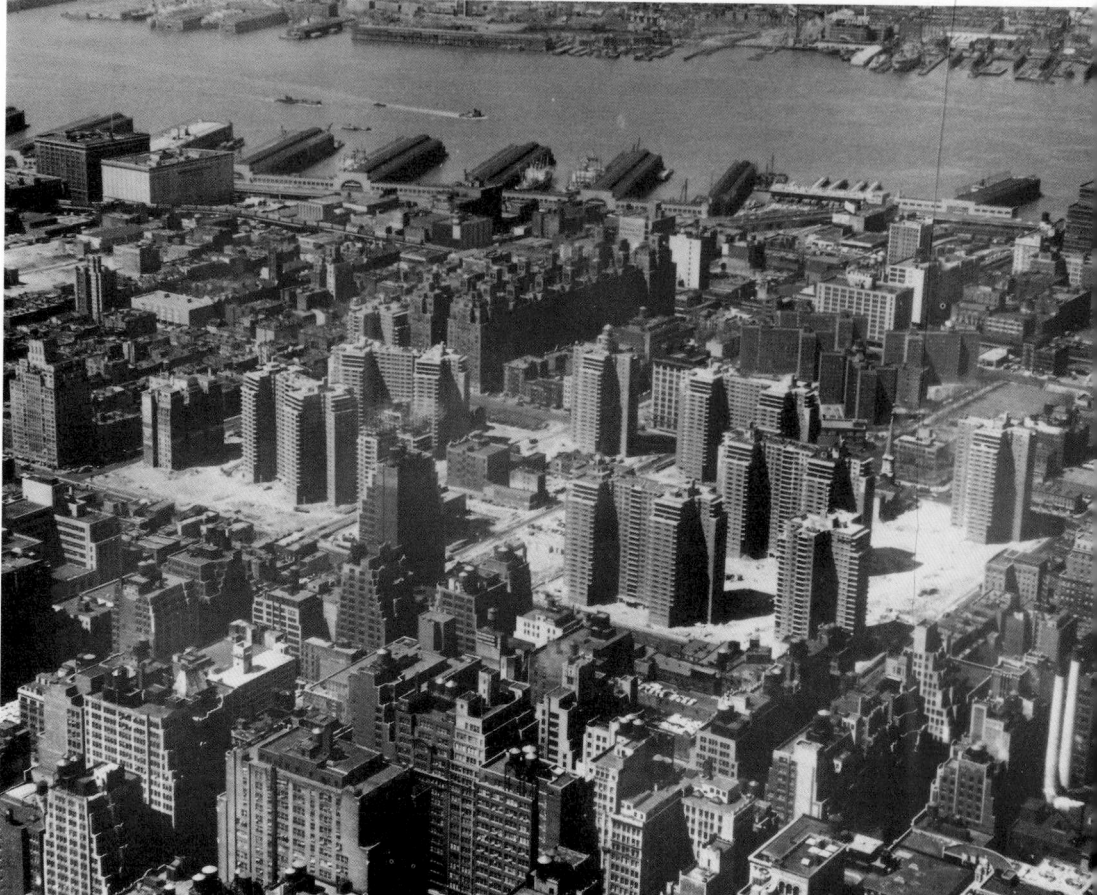

Right: Penn Station South, Eighth to Ninth Avenue, West Twenty-third to West Twenty-ninth Street. Herman Jessor, 1963. View to the southwest. Berinsky. ILGWU

Below: Proposal for redevelopment of Penn Station South. Lawrence Halprin, 1968. Proposed site plan. *A History of Housing.* RP

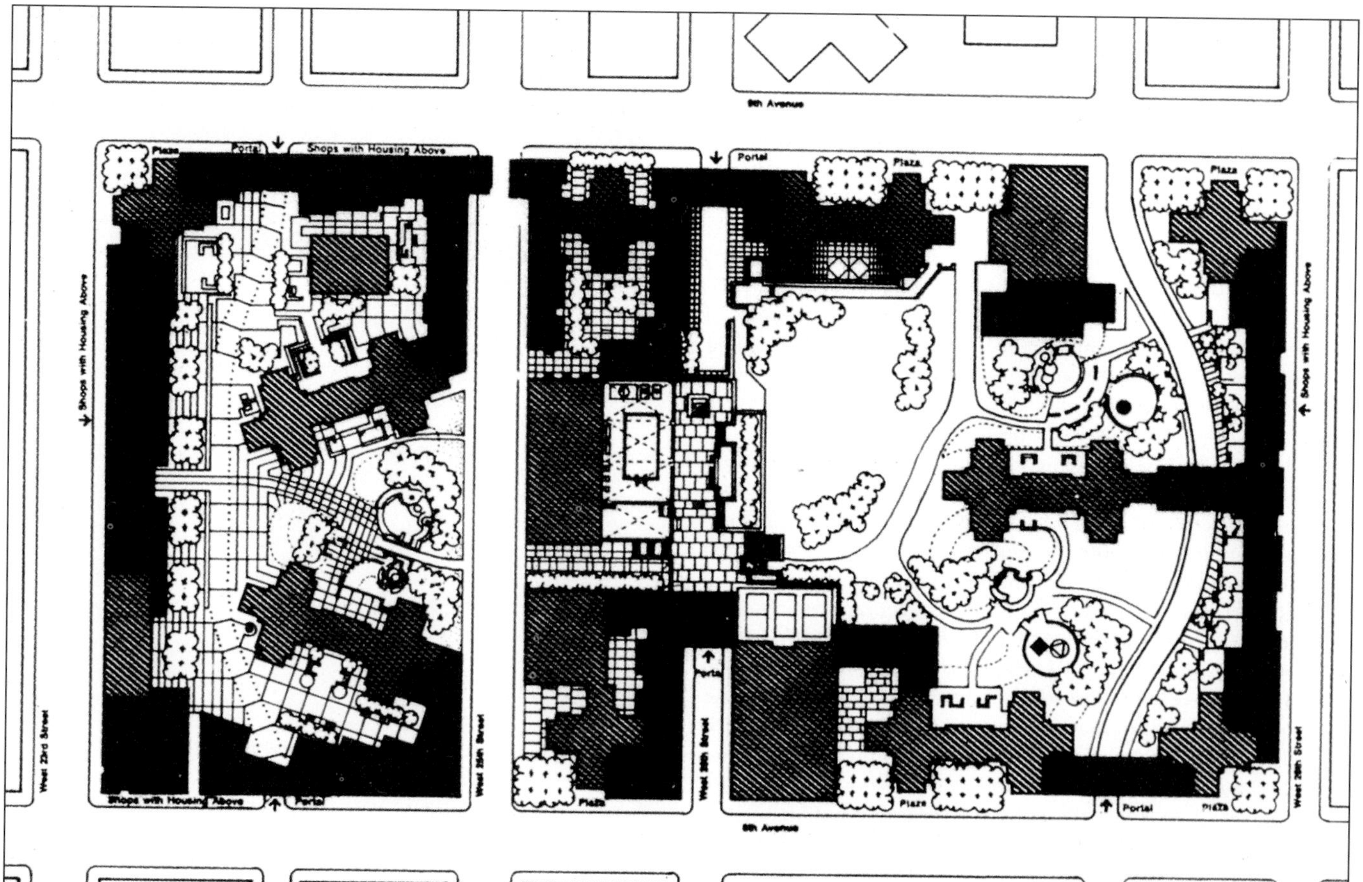

The area's renewal was augmented by Public School 33 (Eric Kebbon, 1951), located within the shadows of Elliott Houses and ultimately flanked by the Chelsea Houses as well.[10] The school replaced a four-story Dutch gabled facility (1857) located on an adjacent site. By closing Twenty-seventh Street, the school yard of P.S. 33 was linked with Chelsea Park, which extended north to Twenty-eighth Street. Kebbon's design adopted a modified cruciform plan, which, as in the Elliott Houses, was rotated to the cardinal points for the best solar orientation but had the effect of furthering the sense of urbanistic dislocation. The school contained three three-story-high arms and one two-story arm (the northeast) forming a triangular courtyard facing Ninth Avenue.

Mumford admired the "continuous dynamic movement of the planes of the building as one walks around it—and miraculously, one *can* walk all the way around it—that is entirely lacking in buildings conceived as uniform slabs." Though he also praised the "lively quality of the plan," he found the school's facades, made up of great panels of glass brick filling the stair towers above the entrances and red-brick walls, "severe to the point of bleakness," relieved only by the panels of metal casement windows and black-glazed terra-cotta spandrels that tied them together in vertical bands. Mumford found more to praise inside the school. He especially liked the well-equipped auditorium, which could serve the community at large, and the teacher's lunchroom, which could also function as a community room. By providing such facilities, Mumford said, P.S. 33 represented a new conception in which schoolhouses "are neighborhood centers as well as educational buildings."[11] Mumford also commented on the extensive use of low-maintenance vinyl tiles for floors and ceramic tiles for walls, as well as the use of movable furniture in the classrooms in place of the typical fixed benches and desks lined up in rows. He was particularly taken with the use of glass-paneled showcases in every corridor for exhibiting student artwork: "There is nothing so deadly to the imagination of youth as a finished and perfect building. And if the architect leaves more room for art, there may be less temptation to vandalism."[12]

The western fringes of Chelsea acquired yet another large-scale public housing project in 1965 with the completion of the 944-unit Robert Fulton Houses, which consisted of eleven buildings spread out between Ninth and Tenth avenues, Sixteenth and Nineteenth streets.[13] Designed by the firm of Brown & Guenther, Fulton Houses included eight seven-story, street-defining buildings clad in brown brick and three twenty-five-story slabs clad in brown and white brick that were set back from the street and isolated amid parking lots, fenced-off landscaped areas and playgrounds paved in asphalt. Though through streets were retained, the project had a rather menacing character due to the dullness of the buildings' facades, the bareness of the open spaces surrounding them, and the fact that the low-rise buildings were partially raised on stilts, creating dark, hard-to-patrol ground-level spaces.

Herman Jessor's Penn Station South (1963), a cooperative sponsored by the International Ladies Garment Workers Union's United Housing Foundation, was Chelsea's largest superblock housing enclave, with 2,820 apartments in ten twenty-two-story buildings.[14] Though not particularly distinguished as a work of planning or architecture, compared to the area's public housing it had a slightly more positive relationship to the surrounding neighborhood and incorporated a notable midblock park opening south to Twenty-third Street. Unlike other properties developed by the United Housing Foundation that were far away from

the garment district where so many union workers were employed, Penn Station South was virtually next door, occupying a vast site bounded by Eighth and Ninth avenues, Twenty-third and Twenty-ninth streets. The superblock plan was broken up by four streets that crossed the project: Twenty-fifth and Twenty-sixth streets, which ran uninterrupted through the site; and Twenty-fourth and Twenty-eighth streets, which were remapped to follow mirror-image curves, with the southern street arching to the south and the northern street arching to the north. While this gesture added some measure of visual interest, the failure of the buildings to define enclosing street walls made the undulating street pattern seem rather arbitrary and faintly suburban.

Penn Station South incorporated within its boundaries several interesting buildings, including Minard Lafever's Church of the Holy Apostles (1848), which had been added onto ten years later by Richard Upjohn & Son, and the Saint Columba Church (1845) and School (Thomas H. Poole, 1911), located at 343 and 329 West Twenty-fifth Street respectively.[15] Holy Apostles contributed a welcome scale and figuration to the vast complex, although it looked rather forlorn among its towering neighbors. The area's other historical buildings did not fare as well: the small-scale Manor Community Church seemed particularly alienated, sandwiched between a playground and an apartment tower and located across Twenty-sixth Street from a vast parking lot; nonetheless, the church provided a note of visual interest and charm.

Though Penn Station South was viewed by many observers as an architectural and urbanistic disappointment, from the start it was acknowledged not only for successfully providing acceptable, middle-income apartments but for reflecting organized labor's commitment to satisfying the needs of its constituents. At the project's opening-day ceremony, held on May 19, 1962, President Kennedy, accompanied by Governor Nelson A. Rockefeller and Eleanor Roosevelt, among others, addressed a crowd of 10,000. Calling the housing project "impressive," he praised union members: "It is the task of every generation to build a road for the next generation. I hope others will follow your example."[16]

In 1968 Mayor John V. Lindsay's newly formed "superagency," the Housing and Development Administration (HDA), commissioned the San Francisco–based landscape architect Lawrence Halprin to prepare proposals for the redevelopment of several tower-in-the-park housing projects, including Penn Station South. Halprin felt that the project's open space, which constituted 50 percent of the entire site area, was amorphous and that the perimeter streets, as well as those traversing the site, were lacking in "intimacy, interest and humanity." To counter these problems, he went beyond conventional landscape design by proposing to increase the project's density with a nearly continuous six-story-tall ring of new apartment buildings encircling the site as well as bridging the traversing streets. Halprin also proposed to raise the ground plane within the project so that the open space could span the intervening streets. The proposal to increase the residential density flew in the face of prevailing planning wisdom, which saw high population densities as a source of urban ills. Halprin argued that "the issue is less one of density than of land coverage, less of land coverage than of what facilities are provided in open space."[17] Halprin recognized that the project's unbounded open spaces not only were subject to adverse wind conditions, rendering them less inviting, but also served as potential breeding grounds for crime. The proposals were not implemented.

Mediocre though it was, by the 1970s Penn Station South was considered something of an achievement compared to most

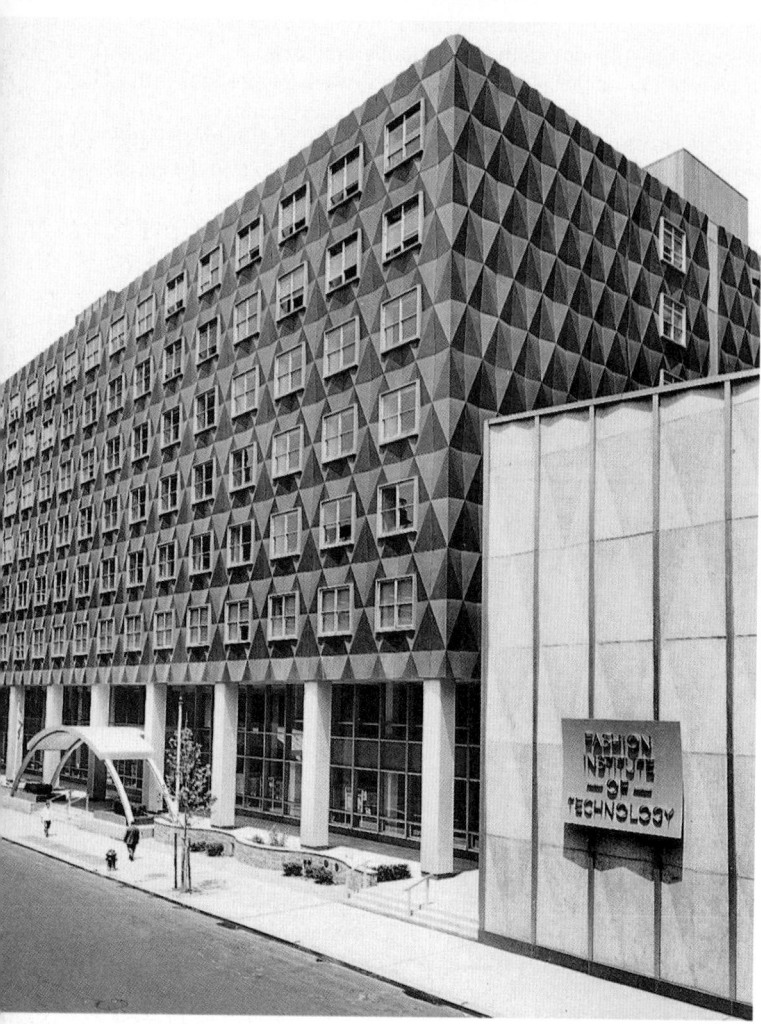

Administration and Technology Building, Fashion Institute of Technology, north side of West Twenty-seventh Street between Seventh and Eighth avenues. De Young, Moscowitz & Rosenberg, 1959. View to the northwest. FIT

postwar housing. In 1979 Paul Goldberger judged it "the best" of the post–Stuyvesant Town superprojects, a "Corbusian scheme . . . helped enormously . . . by the casual placement of the towers off a grid, and by the reworking of the street plan." Goldberger also found the design of the towers "decent," singling out for notice the vertical slats used as parapets for the balconies, "a tiny detail that makes a vast difference."[18] He also admired the setbacks near the top that gave the tower slabs some distinction at the skyline while providing broad terraces and unusual plans for the top floors of the apartments.

In 1960 the General Theological Seminary, long Chelsea's most important institutional presence, built a four-story mixed-use building that closed off the Ninth Avenue end of the full-block campus.[19] Designed by the firm of O'Connor & Kilham, the building housed a 125,000-volume library, as well as offices and a dean's residence. Clad in brick and rough-hewn stone, the structure weakly echoed the robust Gothic architecture of Charles C. Haight's buildings. Goldberger ridiculed the "cutesy little pointed windows [that are] supposed to be Gothic. This is not serious historical allusion; it is crudeness."[20] Along the Ninth Avenue frontage, the ground story of O'Connor & Kilham's building was recessed behind a covered, flagstone-paved forecourt that was visually shielded from the street by trees and shrubbery. The overall effect was of a suburban public library, an impression at odds not only with the campus as a whole but with its broader urban context.

In 1958 Chelsea became home to a very different kind of educational institution, the Fashion Institute of Technology (FIT), established in 1944 and reconstituted in 1956 as a fully accredited two-year community college under the auspices of the Educational Foundation for the Apparel Industry, the New York City Board of Education and the State University of New York.[21] FIT was as accurate a reflection of Manhattan's mid-twentieth-century character as the General Theological Seminary had been of the city's nineteenth-century character. The first buildings built for FIT's specific purposes, the up-to-the-minute if highly derivative Administration and Technology Building and the Morris W. and Fannie B. Haft Auditorium, were designed by the firm of De Young, Moscowitz & Rosenberg and completed in 1959 on midblock sites on the north side of Twenty-seventh Street. Stylistically related to the aluminum curtain-wall designs of Harrison & Abramovitz, the nine-story Administration and Technology Building incorporated facades clad with faceted aluminum panels in two tones of blue and punctuated by windows framed in a gold color; the principal entrance was marked by a sweeping arc-shaped canopy. The 300-seat auditorium, seemingly inspired by the work of the Brazilian architects Oscar Niemeyer and Alfonso Reidy, was enclosed in a boldly sculptural shell. Two decades after completion, the design of the two buildings seemed as dated as poodle skirts. To Paul Goldberger the "origami-fronted" administration building looked as if it "might be the best hotel in Dubuque."[22] Also designed by De Young, Moscowitz & Rosenberg, FIT's ten-story, 292-unit Nagler Hall dormitory, completed in 1962 on a midblock site on Twenty-seventh Street between Seventh and Eighth avenues, was clad with cross-shaped precast-concrete units, reflecting changing architectural fashions and setting the campus on a course leading to cacophony.

In 1967 a master plan was prepared for the college's expansion from three buildings into a full-blown campus occupying two blocks between Twenty-sixth and Twenty-eighth streets, Seventh and Eighth avenues. While the plan kept Twenty-seventh Street open, it called for a bridgelike megastructure to span its eastern end. The first phase of the plan included a six-story arts building at the southeast corner of the site and the Shirley Goodman Resource Center at the northeast corner, each completed in 1977 to designs by Youssef S. Bahri of the De Young firm, now working with the firm of Lockwood & Green. Bahri's buildings were a tailored version of Corbusier-inspired Brutalism, as was the De Young firm's David Dubinsky Student Center, also completed in 1977, on the east side of Eighth Avenue between Twenty-seventh and Twenty-eighth streets. Surveying the overall campus, Goldberger said that it appeared "at first glance not only as though every building were designed by a different architect, but as though every architect was forbidden to look at any of the other buildings before he set out to design his own. . . . The buildings themselves are dreary at best, silly at worst. They are a mix of Neo-Nursing Home, Downtown Parking Garage, Middle-American Convention Center, and Fancy-Pants Brutalism."[23] To Norval White and Elliot Willensky, FIT's architecture was a perfect if not necessarily intentional mirror of the fashion world it served, adopting a "change every season."[24]

Issues of historic preservation became increasingly important during this period, and in 1970 the Chelsea Historic District was established, incorporating the area between the south side of Twentieth and the south side of Twenty-second streets, Ninth and Tenth avenues, and some properties east of Ninth Avenue between those cross streets.[25] In addition, some noteworthy neighborhood landmarks were given the protection of law, including the eclectically detailed townhouse row at 437-459 West Twenty-fourth Street (1849–50),[26] the Chelsea Hotel, at 222 West Twenty-third Street (Hubert, Pirsson & Co., 1884)[27] and the Starrett-Lehigh Building.[28]

Though many of Chelsea's townhouses were not deemed of landmark quality, a slow but steady process of gentrification began to transform the area's residential streets. While most people preferred to restore the old houses, there were a few dramatic renovations, such as Robert Ostrow's reconstruction of 365 West Nineteenth Street (1970), a vandalized, abandoned, three-and-a-half-story rowhouse transformed into a seven-unit dwelling by building out to the maximum in the rear garden and adding an additional floor.[29] Ostrow commissioned the artist William Tapley to create an orchestrated painting for the public halls. Tapley's painting began at the outside vestibule and continued inside, where it swept down to the ground level and up through the three floors before terminating in a skylight.

Just across from Chelsea's northern border, directly behind McKim, Mead & White's Pennsylvania Station (1904–10) and General Post Office (1913), lay the subsurface, open-air yards of the Pennsylvania Railroad, extending west from Ninth Avenue between Thirty-first and Thirty-third streets.[30] In 1954 an option on the air rights over the yards had been granted by the railroad to William Zeckendorf for his Webb & Knapp company. Zeckendorf intended to include these sites in the vast West Side Redevelopment Project he was then planning (see below). But when his company went into bankruptcy, the air rights behind the Post Office were sold in 1967 to Lazard Freres, a prominent investment banking firm that was among the first in its industry to engage in real estate investment. At that time, Lazard Freres, with Mayor Lindsay's support, unveiled plans for the site, to include a high-density, high-rise apartment house project called Chelsea Walk[31] and a warehouse and distribution facility called Westyard.[32]

Designed by Philip Johnson, in association with the apartment house specialists Samuel Paul and Seymour Jarmul,

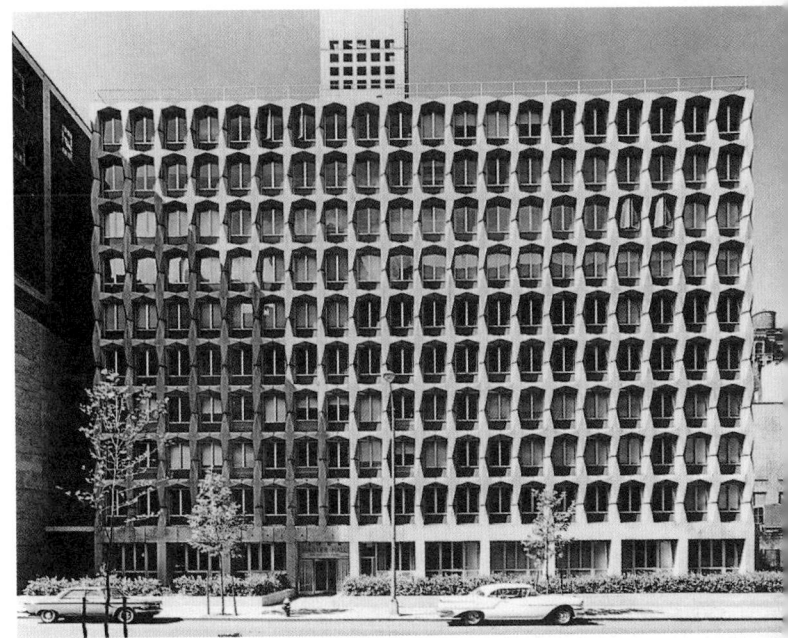

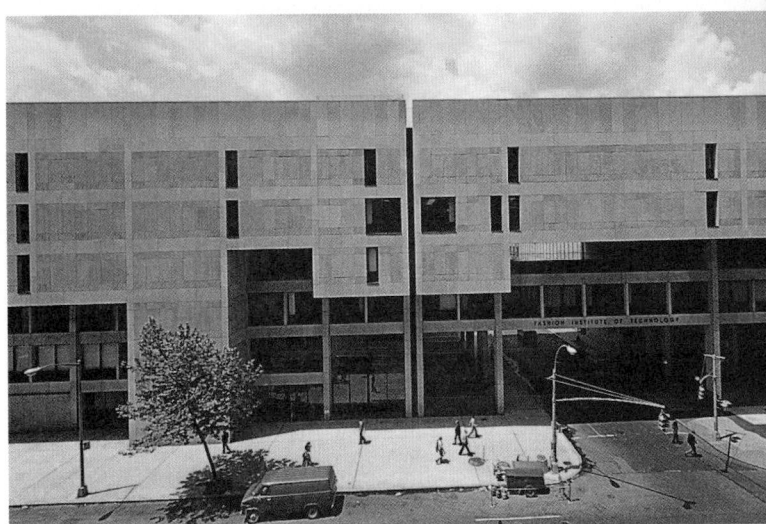

Top: Nagler Hall, Fashion Institute of Technology, south side of West Twenty-seventh Street between Seventh and Eighth avenues. De Young, Moscowitz & Rosenberg, 1962. View to the south. Wurts. MCNY

Bottom: Shirley Goodman Resource Center and Arts and Design Center, Fashion Institute of Technology, west side of Seventh Avenue between West Twenty-sixth and West Twenty-eighth streets. De Young, Moscowitz & Rosenberg and Lockwood & Green, 1977. View to the west. FIT

313

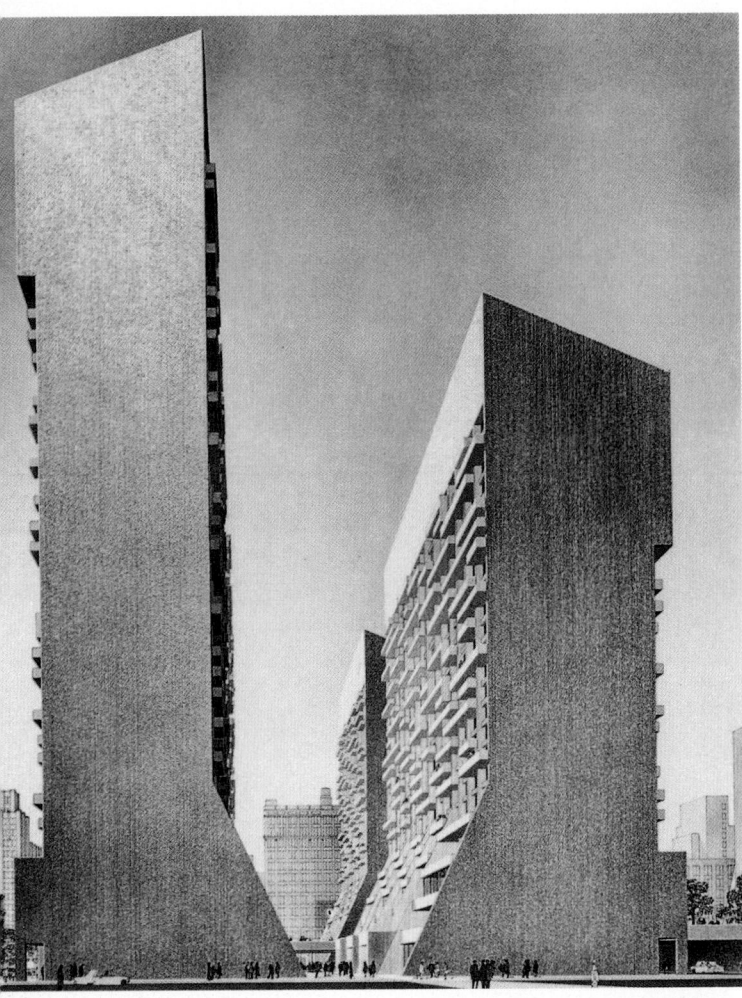

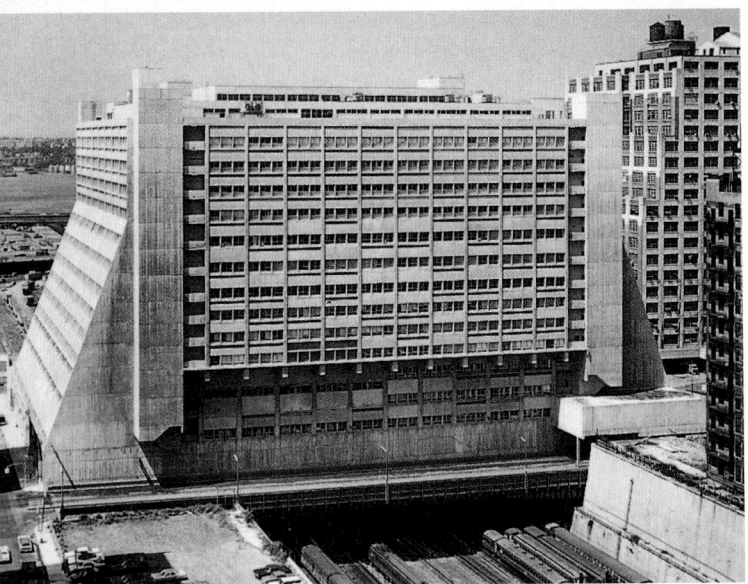

Top: Proposed Chelsea Walk, midblock between Ninth and Tenth avenues, West Thirty-first to West Thirty-third Street. Philip Johnson in association with Samuel Paul and Seymour Jarmul, 1967. View to the south. PJA

Bottom: Westyard Distribution Center, east side of Tenth Avenue, West Thirty-first to West Thirty-third Street. Davis, Brody & Associates, 1970. View to the west. ©Norman McGrath. DBA

Chelsea Walk consisted of two rows of slabs, oriented north-south along a new pedestrian street, with those on the west twenty-five stories tall and those on the east thirty-eight stories. To provide the essentials of community life for the residents, who would be surrounded largely by industrial and warehousing facilities, the ground floors of the buildings were devoted to shops, with the next two floors above reserved for professional offices. The buildings were deliberately brutal in their design, superslabs of white concrete with blank end walls and contrasting long facades enlivened by a seemingly random pattern of boldly sculptured projecting balconies. The slabs were glazed at the bottom to create a more intimate feeling of closure at the pedestrian level, while toward the top, they cantilevered forward to suggest a cornice; their roofs were also sloped. All in all the design reflected Johnson's interest at the time in the New Brutalism of contemporary English architecture and the diagonal geometries associated with the so-called Philadelphia School of architects.[33] The slabs' aggressive silhouettes and insistent directionality diminished the gracious effect of the wide space between the buildings. Although the city offered substantial tax abatements in order to ensure that apartments at Chelsea Walk would be priced for middle-class tenants, rising interest rates rendered the project economically unfeasible and it was ultimately abandoned.

But the site did not remain completely undeveloped: on the west end of the superblock a warehousing and manufacturing loft building, Westyard Distribution Center (1970), designed in an equally brutal architectural vocabulary by Davis, Brody & Associates, was built straddling the railroad tracks as well as a vehicular ramp leading to the Lincoln Tunnel. Supplying 1.4 million square feet of space, the fourteen-story Westyard was clearly a blockbuster. The exposed-concrete building had, as *Architectural Forum* put it, the "look of a pyramid that changed its mind."[34] In order to fit the building into the zoning envelope without using costly setbacks and to complement Johnson's Chelsea Walk, the architects developed a design that incorporated sloping walls: between four corner towers wrapped by a continuous one-story base, the street facades sloped back for eight floors before rising vertically for another five; along the site's eastern edge, where the sky-exposure plane of the zoning did not apply, the building rose sheer. The building's sculptural presence was enhanced by an internal organization of alternating warehouse and office floors. To express this on the facade, the architects devised an invertible concrete-and-glass panel that placed the window as high as a clerestory on the warehouse floors and at seated eye level on the offices floors, yielding a lively exterior effect that helped break down the building's colossal scale. Despite the generous twenty-six-foot columnar grid, the structure was strong enough to take on light manufacturing. Though it was intended to function as a distribution center for the garment center, Westyard attracted many more tenants seeking cheap office space for back-office operations. The bold structural scale of the design allowed for a clear area at the top for Skyrink, a private ice-skating rink, which, curiously, was windowless, failing to exploit the skyline and river views.

Regardless of its spectacular scale and size, Westyard was outclassed in certain respects by the Joseph Curran Annex of the National Maritime Union Building (1966), designed by the New Orleans architect Albert C. Ledner, in association with Furman & Furman of New York.[35] Housing recreational and medical facilities, the building complemented the union's headquarters on Seventh Avenue between Twelfth and Thirteenth streets, also designed by Ledner (see chapter 4). The annex anticipated some of Westyard's features and carried them out with rather more surface panache. Occupying a block-through site extending between Sixteenth and Seventeenth streets, the twelve-story building was deeply set back from the east side of Ninth Avenue on a raised plaza, approachable by means of stairs from either cross street. Like the union's main building, the annex adopted materials and motifs evoking naval architecture. Four entrances facing the plaza were recessed within sweeping concrete archways. The long facade facing the avenue was clad in white tile and was pierced by a regular grid of portholelike windows. Further contributing to the building's distinctive appearance, the Seventeenth Street facade sloped 8.5 degrees off the vertical to stay within the confines of the sky-exposure plane dictated by the 1961 zoning; here the rows of portholelike windows were syncopated. Despite the building's high-spirited aesthetics, reminiscent of some of Frank Lloyd Wright's last and zaniest projects, the editors of *Architectural Forum* felt the Curran Annex did not possess the "éclat" of Ledner's earlier building. It resembled, they wrote, "a gigantic pin-ball machine board," where steel balls would roll out of its eyebrow arched entry portal.[36]

Just beyond the northeastern corner of Chelsea stood Herald Square, which since the beginning of the twentieth century had been one of the city's great middle-class shopping districts and solidly remained so in the years after World War II. The increasing lure of the suburbs and the opening of suburban branches of New York's leading department stores, however, pressured midtown retailers to keep pace. In 1947 Robert D. Kohn, who had designed the 1924 addition to Macy's,[37] replaced a number of the store's escalators, including three in the original building (De Lemos & Cordes, 1902) that were among the first ever built.[38]

During the Second World War, McCreery's, occupying an undistinguished building on the north side of Thirty-fourth Street between Herald Square and Fifth Avenue (with a finger connection to the avenue), with a ground-floor arcade that had been smartly renovated by Starrett & Van Vleck in 1930,[39] attempted to update its outmoded shopping floors on a piecemeal basis.[40] The store retained the services of Williams & Harrell, who specialized in shop and department store design; Harrell had been associated with Norman Bel Geddes and Walter Dorwin Teague and Williams had been store architect for Altman's. Williams & Harrell's redesign of the fourth floor resulted in a bold spatial reorganization and a great simplification of the merchandising techniques. This could best be seen in the fur department, where an almost-white neutral space, sectioned off with gray sheer curtains, was punctuated by a few carefully placed chairs and sofas upholstered in green, magenta and blue. In 1947 McCreery's opened a completely renovated furniture floor designed by Lester Tichy, purportedly the first architect ever asked to redesign an entire floor of a department store.[41] Tichy successfully avoided visual clutter by creating a series of brightly lit "vignetted" areas separated from each other by pools of comparative darkness and sometimes further defined by swags of fabric. He augmented the floor's structural columns with glass fins pierced with holes. In an effort to save money, only a portion of the ceiling was furred down, with the rest simply painted black for dramatic effect. Despite its innovative merchandising, McCreery's business declined and it closed its doors in 1953.[42] The following year Ohrbach's, upgrading its image, relocated from Fourteenth Street to Thirty-fourth Street, moving into McCreery's former premises.[43]

By the late 1960s it was clear that the most interesting directions in merchandising were emanating from small bou-

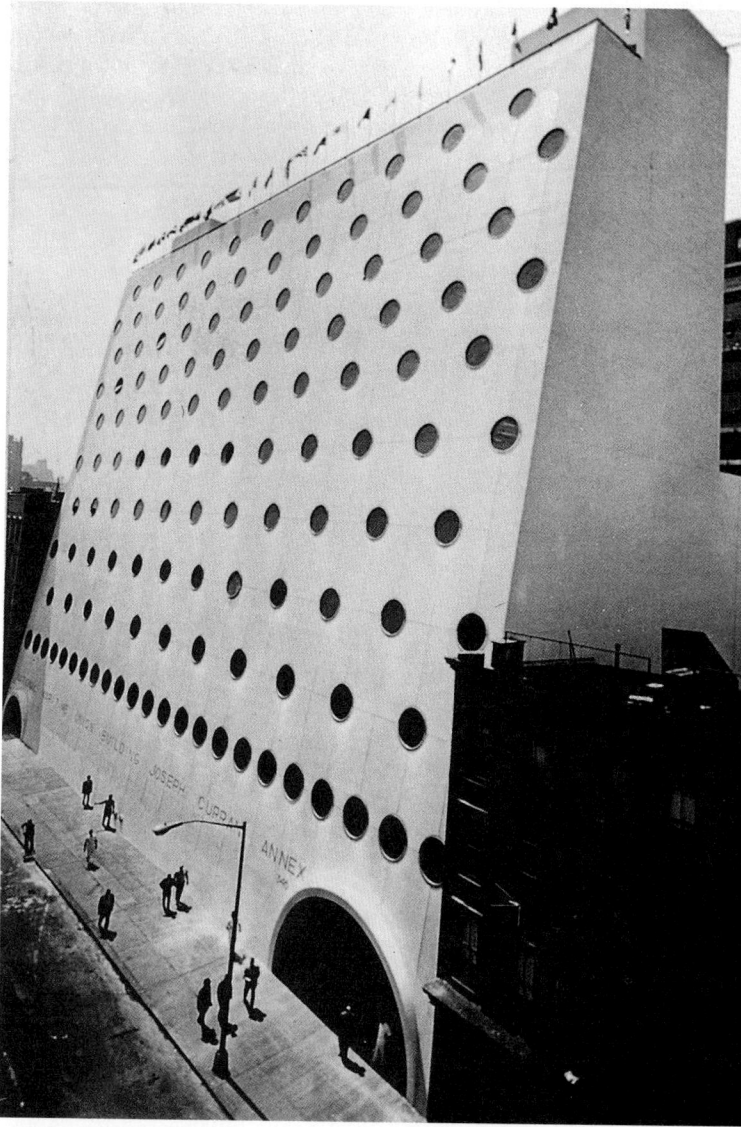

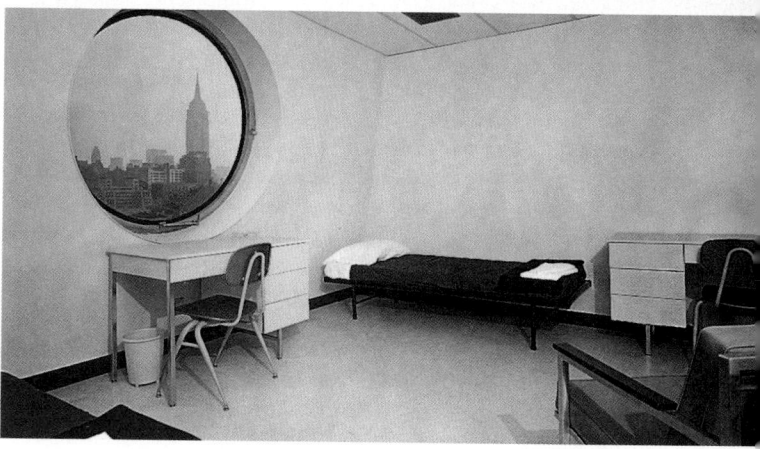

Top: National Maritime Union Building, Joseph Curran Annex, east side of Ninth Avenue, West Sixteenth to West Seventeenth Street. Albert C. Ledner in association with Furman & Furman, 1966. View to the southeast. ACL

Bottom: National Maritime Union Building, Joseph Curran Annex. Dormitory room. OMH

tiques, not department stores (see chapter 6). Even the traditional rivalry between Macy's and Gimbel's had fallen flat when in the fall of 1967 the stores mounted nearly identical Mediterranean promotions.[44] In 1976, seeking to regain some of its former allure, Macy's remodeled its basement level, where narrow aisles had cut through departments selling bargain goods. The floor was transformed into the Cellar, a cluster of shops lining an internal, tile-paved street that, to a *Newsweek* reporter, looked "like a Scandinavian village."[45] Departments selling everything from fresh produce to pots made by an on-premises potter were enclosed by picturesque storefronts facing the "street." A branch of P. J. Clarke's, the quintessential Third Avenue bar, re-created the nineteenth-century decor of the original, complete with a tin ceiling. Clarke's, which had successfully fought for its survival on Third Avenue only to be rendered a somewhat trivialized architectural ornament to one more banal, windswept plaza (see "Third Avenue," below), was in its incarnation in Macy's truly deracinated. Those seeking to recall the New York of the past could now do so not by visiting their favorite old haunts but by going to Macy's former bargain basement, where history was domesticated and hawked like one more household product.

Clinton

Known as Hell's Kitchen for generations, the area bounded by the Hudson River, Eighth Avenue, Thirtieth and Fifty-ninth streets was renamed in the 1960s to meet the realities of increasing gentrification. The new name, Clinton, came from that of DeWitt Clinton Park (1905), a two-block oasis located at the neighborhood's western edge, between Eleventh and Twelfth avenues, Fifty-second and Fifty-fourth streets. DeWitt Clinton High School (C. B. J. Snyder, 1906) stood on the west side of Tenth Avenue between Fifty-eighth and Fifty-ninth streets, but the school itself had moved to the Bronx in 1929 and the building was used to house its less academically prestigious successor, Haaren High School, until it closed in 1978.[46]

Punctuating the neighborhood's nondescript residential fabric of nineteenth-century rowhouses and tenements were a number of interesting projects, including Ernest Flagg's Model Tenements, at 506 West Forty-second Street and 569 Tenth Avenue, built in 1900 for the New York Fireproof Tenement Association.[47] To serve a theatrical clientele and later a lower-class population, most of the area's rowhouses had been broken up for single-room occupancy, although a few were still in private hands. Particularly near its northern boundary, the area also included a number of architecturally interesting, solidly middle-class apartment houses such as the Windermere (Theophilus G. Smith, 1880), at the southwest corner of Ninth Avenue and Fifty-seventh Street;[48] the Parc Vendome (1931), two buildings separated by a landscaped court, at 333-353 West Fifty-sixth Street and 330-360 West Fifty-seventh Street;[49] the streamlined Westmore (Boak & Paris, 1941), also two buildings separated by a landscaped interior courtyard, at 333 West Fifty-seventh Street and 340 West Fifty-eighth Street;[50] and, on the somewhat surprisingly elegant residential block of Fifty-fifth Street between Eighth and Ninth avenues, Emery Roth's 320–328 West Fifty-fifth Street.[51] The public baths (1906) at 232 West Sixtieth Street, for which the firm of Werner & Windolph had employed an imposing Classical architectural vocabulary, reflected a civic presence in the area; during the postwar period, however, the facility was increasingly rundown.[52]

West of Ninth Avenue, the area contained a large number of industrial structures, including McKim, Mead & White's powerhouse for the Interborough Rapid Transit (1900-1902) at Eleventh Avenue and Fifty-ninth Street;[53] a complex of buildings serving the Sheffield Farms Dairy (Frank Rooke, 1907), on the south side of Fifty-seventh Street west of Tenth Avenue, which were renovated in 1961-62 to serve as broadcast studios for CBS;[54] and the General Tire Building (Francisco & Jacobus, 1935), at 602 West Fifty-seventh Street.[55] The area's industrial character was augmented in 1963 by the construction of a commodious handling center for the United Parcel Service (Levy & Levy), at 643 West Forty-third Street, occupying the full block bounded by Eleventh and Twelfth avenues, Forty-third and Forty-fourth streets.[56] The pink building featured a curved principal facade and a monumentally scaled facade mural by Max Spivak depicting an abstracted interpretation of a conveyor-belt system.

Most postwar buildings in the area had even less architectural interest and made little contribution to Clinton's stability as a residential quarter. The neighborhood's first architecturally distinguished postwar project was Kelly & Gruzen's 2,727-student High School of Printing (1959), at 439 West Forty-ninth Street, intended to train students for the city's printing and publishing industries, which were experiencing personnel shortages.[57] The midblock site of the 327,000-square-foot school, west of Ninth Avenue, ran through to Fiftieth Street. A bold, imaginative interpretation of International Style Modernism, the steel-framed building consisted of a seven-story workshop and academic wing containing forty-seven shops, twenty-two classrooms and two laboratories, deeply set back from Forty-ninth Street behind an asphalt-covered playground. An adjacent free-form wing, housing an auditorium and a gymnasium, was built out to the lot line. The first five floors of the main block contained the shops, a large portion of which was sheathed in glass block interrupted by metal-louvered panels inserted for ventilation and by horizontal strips of clear glass set above each floor at eye level. At the ground floor, clear glass revealed the building's columnar structural grid, suggesting pilotis. The two academic floors above, articulated by a setback, were sheathed with double-hung windows. Inside, escalators were installed to handle the traffic generated by the large student body, attending in three shifts. The brick-sheathed auditorium and gymnasium were given separate entrances and lobbies so that they could be used by the community at large. An untitled, eleven-by-sixty-foot mosaic tile mural by the Abstract Expressionist artist Hans Hofmann adorned the wing's principal ground-floor facade; it depicted boldly colored forms derived from printer's symbols, offset by rectilinear color fields. Though the editors of *Progressive Architecture* felt that the mural provided "a vibrant note on a depressing street," they found that its "ruler-sharp edges sacrifice spontaneity and interest."[58]

Max O. Urbahn Associates' Park West High School was completed in 1977 at 525 West Fiftieth Street, running through the block to Fifty-first Street, between Tenth and Eleventh avenues.[59] The fundamentally pessimistic feeling communicated by the school's fortresslike exposed-concrete walls, in contrast with the optimism exuded by Kelly & Gruzen's glassy Modernism, reflected the public's changing perceptions about the city's schools. On the eastern end of the block, at 747 Tenth Avenue, an equally brutal, exposed-concrete apartment tower, also designed by Urbahn, was built by the city's Educational Construction Fund to help generate revenues that could be used to offset the cost of Park West's building.[60]

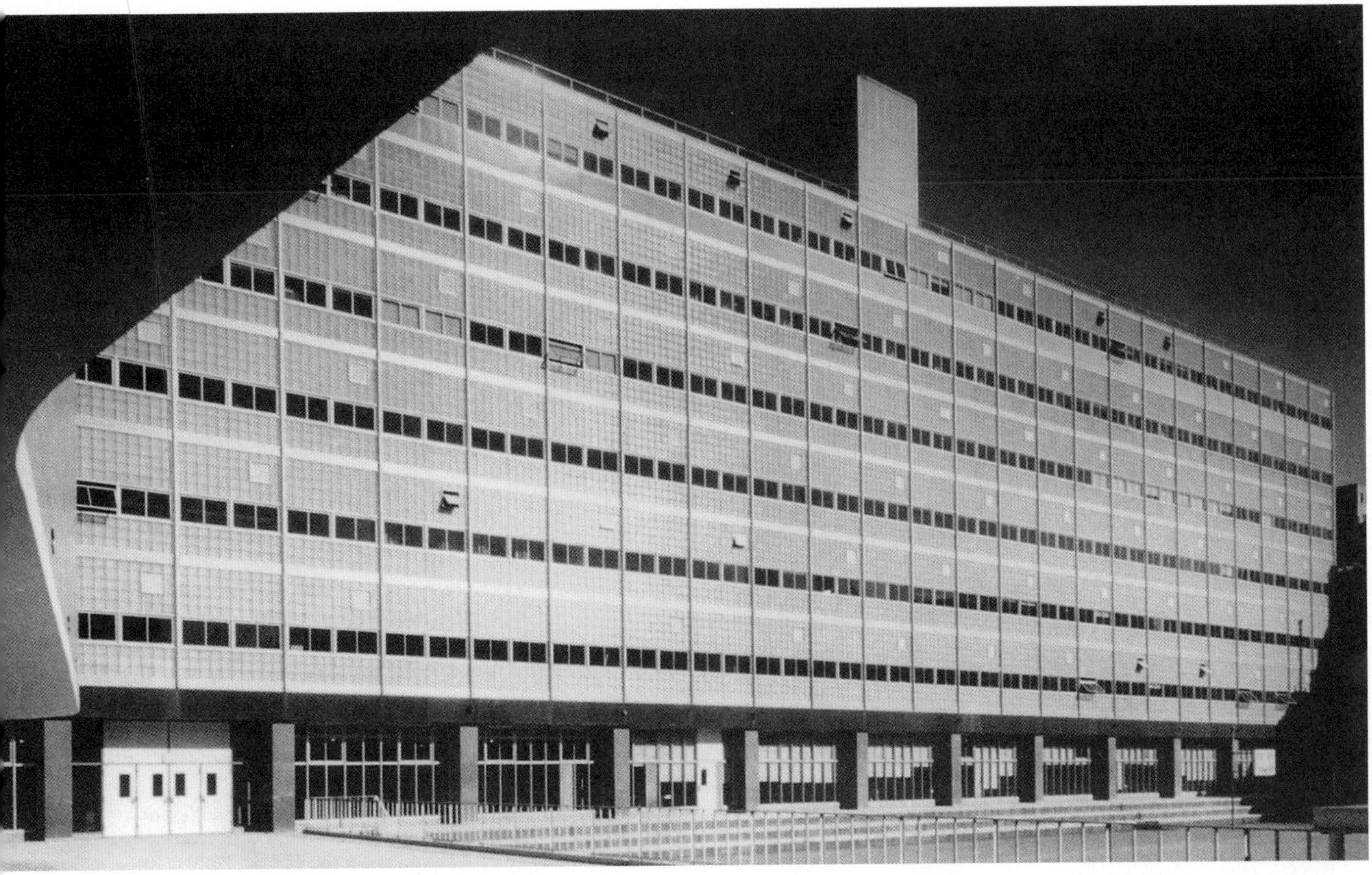

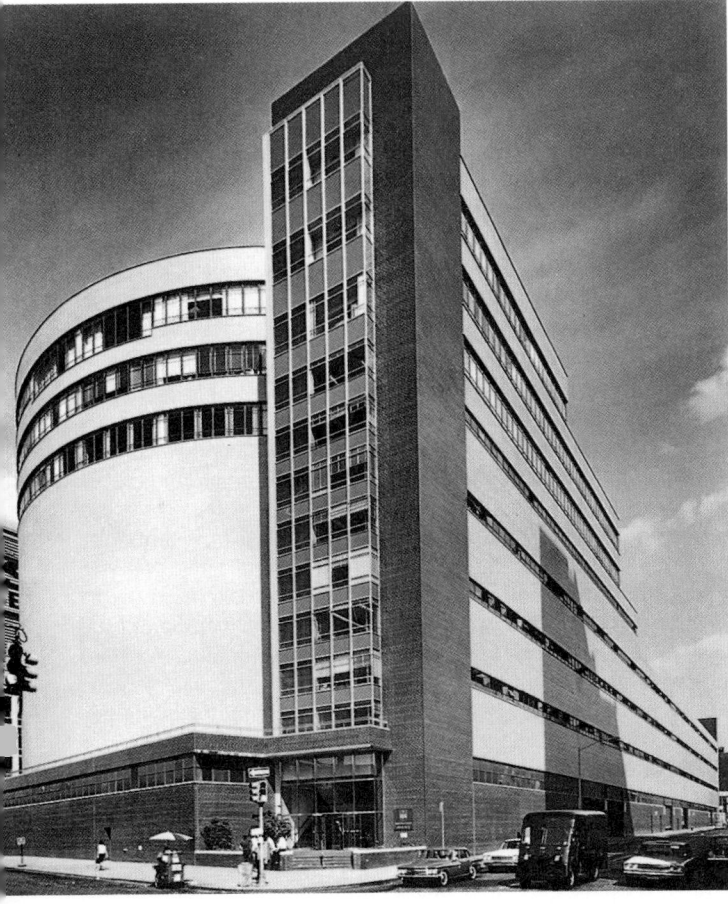

Above: High School of Printing, 439 West Forty-ninth Street, between Ninth and Tenth avenues. Kelly & Gruzen, 1959. View to the northeast. GS

Left: United Parcel Service handling center, 643 West Forty-third Street, between Eleventh and Twelfth avenues. Levy & Levy, 1963. View to the northeast. Wurts. MCNY

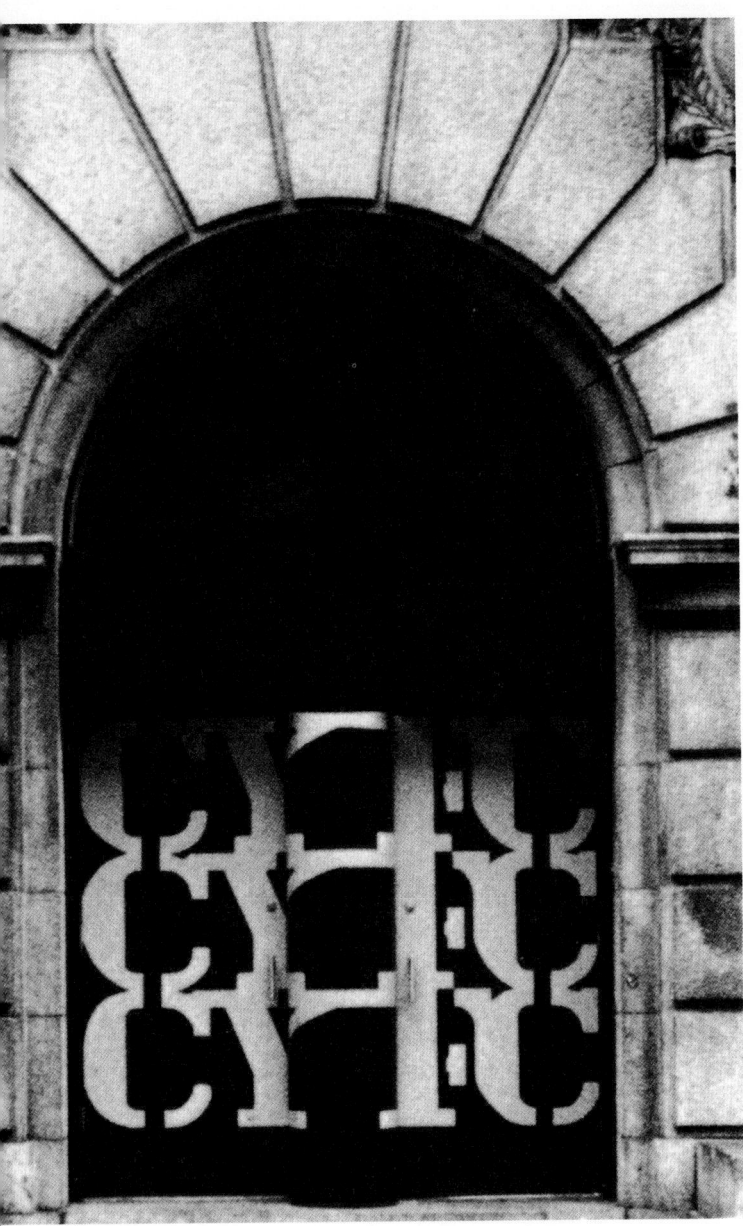

In 1970 James Stewart Polshek, an architect who specialized in projects involving the adaptive reuse of historic buildings, completed the transformation of the nineteenth-century Seventh District Police Court Building, at 314 West Fifty-fourth Street, into the Clinton Youth and Family Center, operated by the YMCA of Greater New York and the Rotary Club of New York.[61] Working with the architect Walfredo Toscanini and the graphic designer David Bliss, Polshek restored the building's original limestone facade, expressing its new purpose with boldly painted doors, windows and air-conditioning intake pipes. As the critic Robert Jensen noted in *Architectural Record*, these elements, "fitted within the orderly stonework of the past," implied that "we need not insist on historically accurate restorations to provide a necessary feeling of continuity with our roots, nor do we need to level old architecture to make cities better."[62] Inside, several brick walls constructed in ill-conceived previous remodelings were removed to restore the original dimensions of the vaulted lobby. Supergraphics were dramatically employed inside and out, with painted "shadows" from imaginary trees decorating the walls of the building's rear court. The former main courtroom became a gymnasium and basketball court, and its coffered ceiling was retained and equipped with recessed lighting. An existing Classical portico was used to frame a basketball backboard, while a new maple floor was added and the room's exposed brick walls were decorated with stylized murals depicting the repeated arcs of a bouncing ball. The critic C. Ray Smith praised the project as being "exemplary for the decade's recycling of static old buildings for new social uses, of preserving our architectural heritage with economical and imaginative means."[63]

The new building in Clinton that made the strongest statement was one of its most banal, the brutally scaled, crudely detailed New York Telephone Company Switching Center (Kahn & Jacobs, 1964).[64] During the interwar period the New York Telephone Company had distinguished itself as a sophisticated client whose architects were capable of elevating even the most utilitarian programs to the level of grand civic architecture.[65] But after World War II the company seemed to lose its architectural way. The new switching center, at 811 Tenth Avenue, occupying the full west blockfront between Fifty-third and Fifty-fourth streets, was one of three buildings designed by Kahn & Jacobs for the company in Manhattan (see "East Side: From Stuyvesant Town to Turtle Bay," above, and "Forty-second Street," below). Though the building contained only twenty-one stories, it had an overall height equivalent to forty stories because the height of each floor was increased to accommodate the telephone company's mechanical equipment. The building's most striking architectural aspect was the complete absence of windows, a feature justified by the telephone company on three grounds: a 50 percent savings in air-conditioning and heating costs; protection for the equipment from dirt and dust; and, most important, protection from fallout in the event of a nuclear war. The building was designed to be able to withstand a nuclear explosion up to fifteen miles away and was equipped with a two-week supply of food, water, fuel and bed linens. The visual monotony of the massive concrete building, clad in vertical strips of black granite and white enamel bricks, was relieved only to a negligible degree by a series of setbacks. Norval White and Elliot Willensky described the completed building as a "monster which looks, from a distance, as though it's covered with glistening mattress ticking."[66]

In addition to Manhattan Plaza (see "Forty-second Street," below), a number of other apartment houses were built within

Above: Clinton Youth and Family Center, 314 West Fifty-fourth Street, between Eighth and Ninth avenues. Renovation, James Stewart Polshek with Walfredo Toscanini and David Bliss, 1970. Remodeled main entrance. JSP

Top right: New York Telephone Company Switching Center, 811 Tenth Avenue, West Fifty-third to West Fifty-fourth Street. Kahn & Jacobs, 1964. View to the southwest. Acs. SA

Bottom right: Clinton Towers, 790 Eleventh Avenue, West Fifty-fourth to West Fifty-fifth Street. Hoberman & Wasserman, 1975. View to the northwest. JW

Clinton's core neighborhood to meet the needs of lower- and lower-middle-income families. Hoberman & Wasserman's Clinton Towers consisted of a high-rise tower, at 790 Eleventh Avenue, on the northeast corner of Fifty-fourth Street, and a low-rise, street-defining wing, at 590 West Fifty-fifth Street, on the southeast corner of Eleventh Avenue (1975).[67] Both elements were clad in a combination of smooth and striated pink concrete block. Occupying a 1.2-acre site, the buildings were originally envisaged as part of the six-block Clinton Park Housing Plan orchestrated by Hoberman & Wasserman and sponsored by Clinton Housing Associates and the city's Housing and Development Administration. The plan, which covered the area bounded by Tenth and Eleventh avenues, Fiftieth and Fifty-sixth streets, stressed neighborhood preservation. It called for the concentration of new development along the avenues rather than the more intimately scaled crosstown streets. The new apartment complex gathered up unused midblock density, resulting in a thirty-nine-story, 397-unit tower that loomed over its immediate neighbors. The abrupt transition was in part eased by an L-shaped, seven-story building that contained ground-floor shops stretching along Fifty-fifth Street, as well as a play area on Fifty-fourth Street and a generously proportioned midblock plaza. The complex's effectively articulated open spaces, designed by the landscape architect M. Paul Friedberg, went a long way toward establishing a convincing sense of place.

Clinton Towers was not only the first project realized under the Clinton Park Housing Plan but the first public housing built in the neighborhood in thirty years. Built on the most expensive land ever used for subsidized housing, it was completed as federal support for housing began to languish and just before the city's own political and economic fortunes reached a crisis point. Acknowledging Hoberman & Wasserman as "a firm that has made a reputation in New York as a designer of sensitive, if unspectacular, housing," characteristics that "apply precisely to the design of Clinton Towers," Paul Goldberger wrote that the project's "warm color and careful use of materials make it far more attractive than other high rise buildings," including high-end, market-rate apartments.[68]

Despite the aesthetic and urbanistic success of Clinton Towers and the strength of community support for affordable housing, by the time of the project's completion, popular opposition to virtually all area development had intensified. This sentiment was reflected by the Board of Estimate's enactment on November 21, 1974, of the Special Clinton Zoning District, which indicated the growing perception that the zoning ordinance of 1961 was not sufficiently fine-tuned to deal with distinct neighborhoods and that the densities it planned for were frequently far in excess of what individual communities were prepared to tolerate.[69] It particularly called attention to the helplessness of communities at the edges of "hot" real estate markets, which had hitherto been ineffectual in their efforts to counteract the pressures of New York's commercial developers. The new zoning district virtually ensured that new buildings would relate in height to their surroundings. Far more extensive in scope than the Clinton Park Housing Plan, the zoning district was bounded by Eighth Avenue and the Hudson River, Forty-first and Fifty-ninth streets. Intended to protect the existing community, consisting largely of elderly and lower-income tenants living in rent-controlled buildings, from the advent of upscale, high-rise buildings expected in the wake of the Convention Center (see below), the legislation had been drafted after two years of meetings with neighborhood representatives. The plan allowed high-rise construction along Eighth Avenue but barred

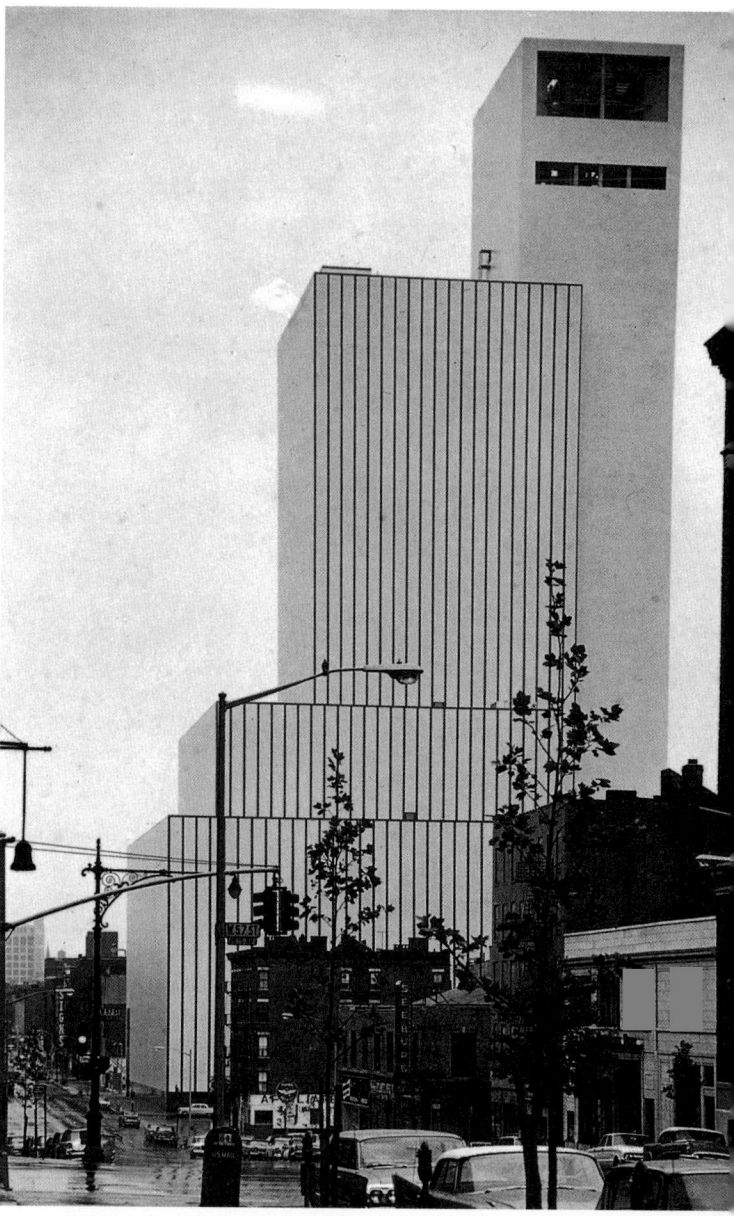

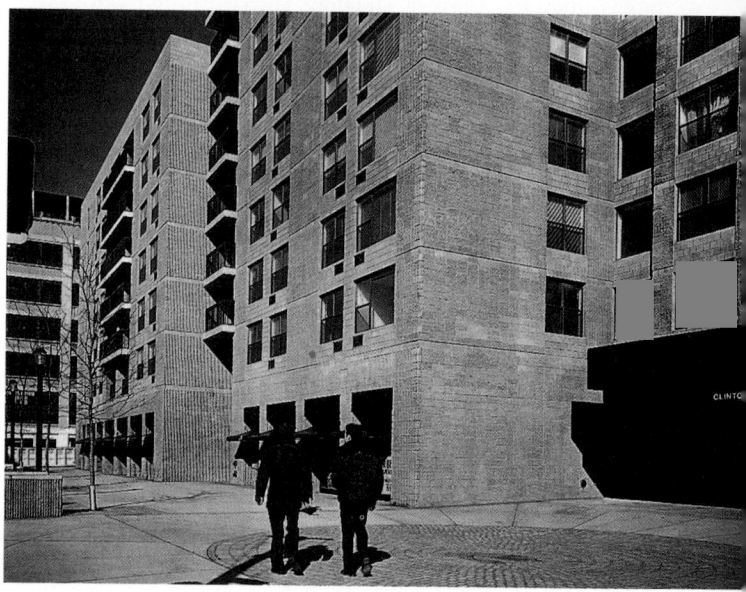

it from the heart of Clinton, where a further stipulation barred any replacement of structurally sound residential buildings, except by issue of a permit granted by the City Planning Commission. A system of bonuses further encouraged the preservation of existing buildings; developers would be granted extra floors in apartment towers built at the district's perimeter in exchange for the renovation of low-rise buildings located in the heart of Clinton. Though aimed at renewing the area, the zoning ordinance, together with a downturn in the economy, initially stymied building activity.

Convention Center

When William Zeckendorf's proposal for a "Palace of Progress" atop the site of Pennsylvania Station encountered economic and engineering obstacles in 1956 (see chapter 16), he began to create an even more ambitious scheme for what he called the West Side Redevelopment Project, which would utilize the air rights over the forty acres of open track that took up the area bounded by Thirtieth Street, the Hudson River, Thirty-eighth Street, Seventh Avenue, Thirty-fourth Street and Ninth Avenue.[70] Zeckendorf's plan, developed by his company's architectural division, headed by I. M. Pei, was dependent on the cooperation not only of the city but also of both the New York Central and the Pennsylvania railways, as well as the major television networks. It called for a convention hall, a merchandise mart with buyers' offices, a "permanent world's fair," and a "television city" with 400,000 square feet of production studio space and an additional 1.6 million square feet of support space. The television studio complex would provide "large horizontal areas for TV studios hitherto unavailable in Manhattan," and would help to slow the industry's move to California.[71] There would also be a heliport, a 2,000-room hotel, an apartment building and garage space for 7,500 cars that would be tucked under the buildings in below-deck areas, a natural by-product of the site's topography, which sloped steeply toward the river.

West of Tenth Avenue, Thirty-fourth Street would be interrupted by a Gramercy Park–like square; west of Eleventh Avenue would be Freedom Tower, a 1,750-foot-tall, freestanding shaft that would provide broadcasting transmission facilities and include a glass-enclosed elevator for tourists to ride high above the city. West of Freedom Tower, Thirty-fourth Street, having maintained its upland elevation, would open to a broad, Tudor City–like grouping, with the television center, apartment building, hotel and world's fair structures grouped around a narrow park and pedestrian bridges leading over the West Side Highway to more development and the waterfront heliport beyond. Twelve million square feet of space would be provided in the overall complex of buildings, which, it was rumored, would be designed by leading architects. But Zeckendorf's own financial crisis doomed the ambitious project.

While transatlantic passenger ship travel declined with the coming of jet planes in the 1950s, the Hudson River passenger piers remained quite active, catering especially to cruise ships. In April 1967 the Port Authority, responding to a request of Mayor Lindsay's, released preliminary designs for a central passenger ship terminal on the Hudson River between Forty-sixth and Fiftieth streets.[72] The Port Authority's proposal, prepared with the help of their chief architect, A. Gordon Lorimer, called for a six-berth facility replacing piers 86, 88 and 90. The five-story complex would separate activities that were hopelessly jumbled at the city's existing facilities: a continuous head house

combining a cafeteria and shipping-line offices would tie the three piers together. On the street level would be facilities for cargo and ship's stores; on the second level would be car, taxi and bus drop-offs, linked to Twelfth Avenue by ramps; baggage would be handled on the third level; the fourth level would contain climate-controlled waiting rooms; and, on the roof, there would be parking for 1,850 cars as well as public parks at the west end of each of the piers. Circular pedestrian ramps at each end of the head house would provide the principal architectural gesture of the otherwise utilitarian design.

The proposal was greeted with guarded optimism, given the declining status of the passenger ship business. George Horne, reporting in the New York Times, estimated that the new piers, though a boon to passengers, would increase the costs of ship turnarounds significantly. Nonetheless, Horne optimistically wrote, "Calling for modern and luxurious waiting spaces, baggage examination halls, ramps for taxicabs and automobiles, rooftop parking and a fancy waterside restaurant, the plan would provide the city for the first time with a berthing complex comparable to those abroad."[73]

The City Planning Commission's Urban Design Group saw the Port Authority's plans as a stimulus to Clinton's development as a "back-up area for the midtown business district," despite its lack of convenient rapid transit.[74] To help plan for Clinton's future in relationship to the piers, the Urban Design Group hired James Stirling, the English architect, to work with them in preparing a master plan for west midtown, covering the forty-two-block area bounded by Ninth Avenue, the Hudson River, Forty-first and Fifty-fifth streets.[75] Mayor Lindsay explained the choice of Stirling, who was a renowned architect but had virtually no planning experience, as an effort "to symbolize the international character of the terminal we are planning."[76] Stirling assembled a team in New York, directed by Arthur Baker and including Craig Hodgetts, Mary Jane Long and Michael Wurmfeld.

The principal features of the extensively documented plan, which was to be implemented in four phases, were a mixed-use waterfront development including between 1,000 and 3,000 low- and middle-income apartments; a linear office development along Forty-seventh or Forty-eighth Street accompanied by a small-scale elevated transportation system; the eventual expansion of that "spine" to include commercial and residential development and cover a width of three blocks; the creation of riverside parkland; and the construction of approximately 15,000 apartments housing an estimated total of 45,000 people. The plan also advocated the construction of a convention center, a maritime museum, a public high school and an extensive array of commercial facilities catering to tourists. In regard to the proposed housing, the report emphatically stated, "The objective should be to make possible a way of life consistent with middle-class family existence in an attempt to halt the well-documented tendency for middle-class families to leave the city. A city without a middle-class majority cannot hope to maintain standards, nor can the 'ideal city' be built unless through the compulsive desire of its citizens to live in it."[77]

The Stirling study was subsequently taken over by the Urban Design Group and the Office of Midtown Planning and Development, with principal contributions made by Jaquelin Robertson, Lauren Otis and Wolfgang Quante. The new team focused on the Forty-eighth Street corridor, now three blocks wide and tied into a crosstown transportation system that would connect the ocean liner terminal to Grand Central and the United Nations.[78] Major stations would be built at Eighth and Third avenues, where there would be connections to subway and commuter rail lines. The city originally intended to take advantage of rising property values that the new transit line would generate by condemning the land along the route's right-of-way and, after the new Forty-eighth Street line was built, selling the land to developers, reaping profits while demanding as a condition of the sale that the developers provide public improvements such as underground service tunnels and pedestrian concourses. Planning for the project began in 1969 at a time when the city's growth was slowing down. With an overbuilt office market, development pressure waned and the Metropolitan Transit Authority, itself strapped for cash and becoming less and less interested in the full-scale system initially proposed for Forty-eighth Street, began to advocate a "people-mover," a vague term that could mean either moving sidewalks or a mini-rail system.

Just as interest in the subway project was waning, interest in a new convention center grew intense. A convention center was first officially proposed by Mayor Lindsay on March 25, 1970, for a site bounded by Tenth and Eleventh avenues, Forty-fourth and Forty-seventh streets, and straddling the deep cut containing the Penn Central's freight line.[79] The proposal had strong backing in the business community, especially from the Midtown Development Council, a new consortium founded in May 1970 and chaired by G. S. Eysell, president of Rockefeller Center, Inc. Keen to compete with Chicago, whose McCormick Place was the world's largest convention facility, and recognizing the increasing role tourism was playing in the city's economy, boosters argued that New York was losing business because it lacked a building large enough to host a presidential nominating convention or a large trade show. At 750,000 square feet, the proposed center was to contain twice as much space as the Coliseum at Columbus Circle.

The Clinton community immediately opposed the site, and on February 24, 1971, Mayor Lindsay announced that the project would be relocated to an offshore location where a platform would extend into the Hudson River, from Twelfth Avenue to the pierhead line, and from Forty-third to Forty-seventh Street. At the same time, Lindsay expressed the city's intention to proceed with a radically reduced version of the ocean liner terminal; the project ultimately was completed in 1976.[80] With the site selected, the Urban Design Group proceeded with their study of the Forty-eighth Street corridor. They projected a new avenue-scaled Forty-eighth Street, which would pick up extra width from the closing of Forty-seventh Street; between Forty-sixth Street and the new Forty-eighth Street wider than usual blocks would be created on which new midrise apartment houses would be built. Additionally, platforms would span Forty-ninth Street to create superblocks suitable for high-rise and mixed-use commercial and office buildings in the blocks between Forty-eighth and Fiftieth streets, including the empty block where Madison Square Garden (Thomas Lamb, 1927) had stood until 1967. The Garden site and an adjacent full-block site were slated for another superscale redevelopment in 1971, when plans were released by Stephen Klein, a developer, for Katz, Waisman, Weber, Strauss's Merchants Convention City.[81] This project, consisting of a superblock complex of department stores, offices, hotels and a convention center seating 50,000 people, was never realized.

The new convention center was to be completed by 1976, presumably in time for the presidential convention of either the Democratic or the Republican party. A quasi-public group, the New York City Convention-Exhibitions Center Corporation, was created in 1971 by the New York State Legislature to build the project; hotelier Preston Robert Tisch was chairman of the cor-

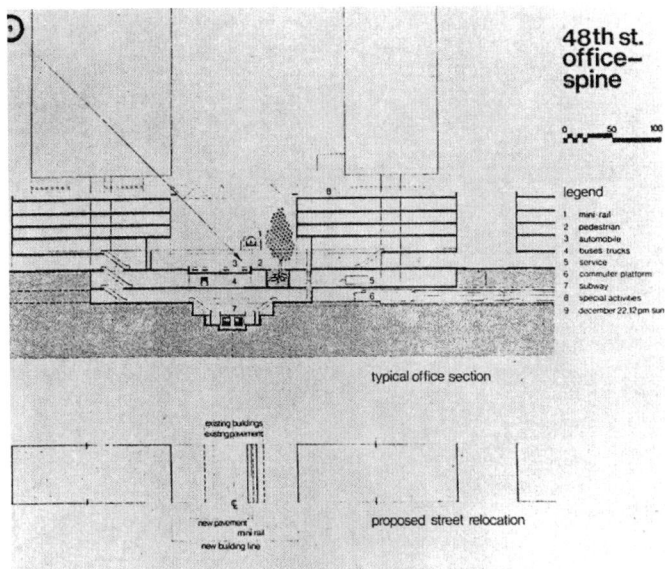

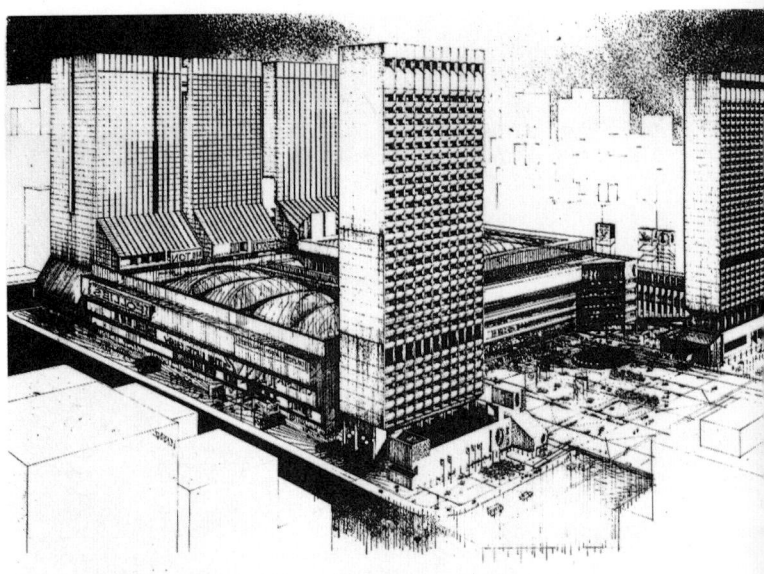

Top: Proposed redevelopment of Forty-eighth Street with mini-rail system. Section. James Stirling, 1968. NYC

Bottom: Proposed Merchants Convention City, Eighth to Ninth Avenue, West Forty-eighth to West Fiftieth Street. Katz, Waisman, Weber, Strauss, 1971. Rendering by Lorenz of view to the northeast. ©Gil Amiaga. GA

321

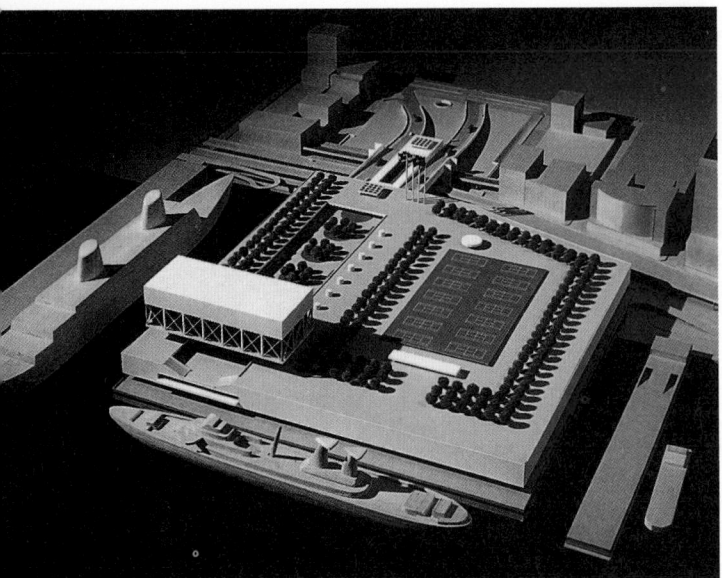

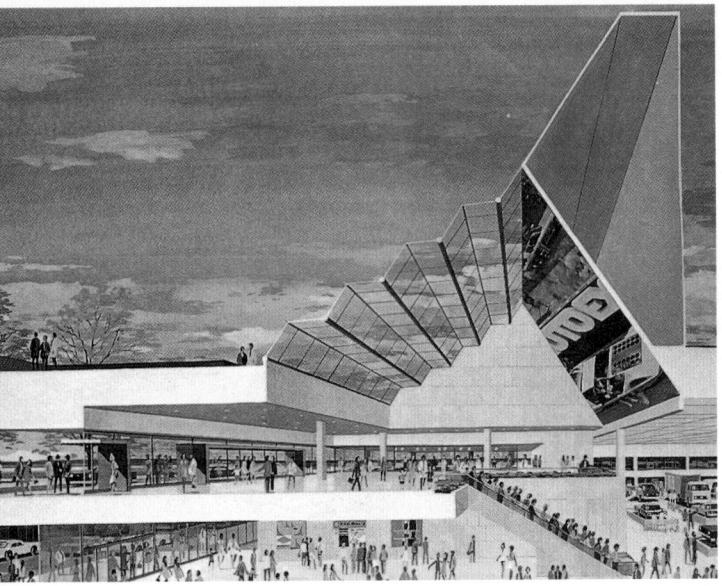

Top: Proposed convention center, on platforms in the Hudson River, West Forty-fourth to West Forty-seventh Street. Skidmore, Owings & Merrill, 1973. Model. View to the northeast. Checkman. LC

Bottom: Proposed convention center, Eleventh to Twelfth Avenue, West Thirty-fourth to West Thirty-ninth Street. Gruzen & Partners and Poor, Swanke, Hayden & Connell, 1976. Cutaway rendering by Mutin of view to the north. DSA

poration, and an architect, Thomas F. Galvin, was made its executive vice president. Galvin was put in charge of managing the architects, and Carl A. Morse, of Diesel Construction Company, was responsible for managing the construction. Out of the almost thirty architectural firms submitting credentials in April 1972, Skidmore, Owings & Merrill's New York office was selected from a short list of six that included Philip Johnson and John Burgee, I. M. Pei, and the Chicago firm of C. F. Murphy, which had designed McCormick Place.

Skidmore, Owings & Merrill was charged with preparing enough documents so that construction could begin in late 1973. Its team, headed by Gordon Bunshaft and J. Walter Severinghaus, developed a design for the forty-acre site, now extending only from Forty-fourth to Forty-seventh Street, that consisted of an almost anonymous, seventy-foot-high, four-level facility west of Twelfth Avenue. The roof would be developed as an eighteen-acre community park, with restaurants and with tennis courts that could be converted to skating rinks in winter. A comparatively small three-story building, carried over the sunken entry court on trusses, housed 150,000 square feet of meeting rooms and some restaurants while concealing a good deal of the building's mechanical equipment behind a floor-high rooftop parapet. The center, which would also provide parking space for 2,000 cars in a grade-level garage, was to be entered at its fourth or top level via a ramp bridging the West Side Highway. The forty-eight-foot-high exhibit area on the second level was to be surrounded by a two-lane service road so that trucks could load and unload displays with minimum inconvenience. Only sixteen columns were to support the ten-foot-deep, thirty-by-thirty-foot coffers of the exhibit hall's eight-acre roof. The west end of the center was to be developed as a quay-type pier so that exhibitions could be delivered by ship. Bunshaft described his design for the convention center as a "non-building" that would present as low a profile to the river as possible.[82] But the effect was dreary, as Ada Louise Huxtable observed, and the center was "not saved from concrete bunkerism by rooftop tennis courts."[83]

By early 1973 the projected costs of the building had doubled, in part due to escalation in the construction industry. Despite the $200 million price tag, experts felt that the center was still a worthy undertaking which would bring $151 million annually to the city, employ up to 2,800 full- or part-time persons and generate an additional 12,000 new jobs in the city itself. In April 1973, in anticipation of a May Board of Estimate hearing and vote over the convention center, Theodore Kheel, a lawyer specializing in labor mediation and an outspoken advocate of public transportation, wrote an article criticizing the lack of transportation planning he believed was necessary to accompany construction of the center. He pointed out that a report prepared for the city by Anthony Downs and the Real Estate Research Corporation in Chicago, which advocated coordinated planning for the project and for west midtown in general, had been ignored and seemingly abandoned. Kheel saw the congestion the center would produce as inherently destructive to the city's economic growth: "The convention center is the paradigm of an accounting system singularly responsible for the city's decline. What is touted as giving the city's economy a shot in the arm ultimately produces a loss of jobs, taxes, and business to the city."[84] Jack Newfield, the *Village Voice*'s muckraking reporter, attacked the center two weeks later, claiming it would "take funds away from housing, schools, day care centers, and hospitals. It will open up another working-class community to the real estate speculators. It will cause transportation chaos. It will cause a dangerous increase in air pollution."[85] This last claim was first made by the city's outspoken former Air Resources Commissioner, Robert Rickles, who, testifying at the Board of Estimate hearing, stated that "the effect of carbon monoxide on human beings is not a matter of conjecture" and warned that "the operation of the Convention Center will kill people in Clinton."[86]

The City Planning Commission approved the center on March 29, 1973. But with the Board of Estimate's vote not due until May 24, Newfield went on with his campaign, attacking Tisch, a prominent Lindsay supporter, as a self-serving member of the real estate community whose hotel empire would gain from the center's construction. Newfield raised for the first time for widespread discussion a proposal initially advocated by the Clinton community, to build the center above the Penn Central rail yards between Eleventh and Twelfth avenues, Thirty-third and Forty-third streets. While the Lindsay administration claimed that the cost of condemning this site would be prohibitively high, Newfield charged that the alternate location was opposed by real estate interests that had banked on the impact the Forty-fourth Street site would have on west midtown values. Opposition to the center ran strong; community leaders marshaled elected officials, who had increasing doubts about the project's feasibility, given the declining economy, and about its desirability, given the city's growing problems. Bronx Borough President Robert Abrams, who opposed the project, said that "in the final analysis the city will be judged as a place to live and work or a place to visit, not by the size and scope of the public monuments we build, but by the quality of life and safety we provide residents and visitors alike."[87] Nonetheless, the Board of Estimate approved the project in a vote of fourteen to four.

In May 1974 the editors of *Engineering News-Record* reported that the center, which had been stalled because of temporary funding problems, was on track again, with Skidmore, Owings & Merrill beginning working drawings and a contract for test borings awarded. Meanwhile, Galvin had left the Convention-Exhibitions Center Corporation to begin work as general manager of the Battery Park City Corporation.[88] Newfield continued to report on seeming improprieties, but, like other concerned observers, he began to raise a more essential question: "Why is the city government willing to spend $200 million—plus $186 million in debt service—for a boondoggle like the convention center, at a time of what everyone calls the most serious fiscal crisis in the city's history?"[89] Despite the lack of a clear answer or proof of a popular mandate, the Board of Estimate approved funding for the project so that it could begin in earnest.

By December 1975, after the projected cost of the center had escalated to $231 million, two new proposals were advanced. One, put forward by the city, state and the Port Authority, called for building the center on landfill at Battery Park City, an idea that met widespread opposition because of that project's own financial problems and because of its remoteness from midtown.[90] A second proposal, offered by a twenty-seven-year-old real estate promoter, Donald Trump, was more enthusiastically received. Trump, the son of a successful house and apartment builder working in Brooklyn and Queens, having decided to make the leap into big-time Manhattan real estate in the summer of 1973, obtained an option to purchase the Penn Central rail yards at West Thirty-fourth Street for use as middle-income housing.[91] But the project faltered as the New York State Urban Development Corporation defaulted on its bonds in February 1975 and the city's own fiscal problems grew, leading Mayor Abraham D. Beame to suspend financing of all city-built

housing the following September. Trump, however, began promoting the site, which ran from Thirty-fourth to Thirty-ninth Street, as "ideal for a convention center."[92]

In the same deal Trump had also obtained options for the Central's Sixtieth Street yards, which, ten years later, he would try to develop as Trump City. Asked why the New York Central had given Trump the option over others who had expressed interest in the sites, Victor Palmieri, the railroad's representative, later told *Barron's*, the financial magazine: "Those properties were nothing but a black hole of undefinable risk. We interviewed all kinds of people who were interested in them, none of whom had what seemed like the kind of drive, backing, and imagination that would be necessary. Until this young guy Trump came along. He's almost a throwback to the 19th century as a promoter. He is larger than life."[93]

On July 29, 1974, Trump announced that his options on the two rail yard sites were secure. He began to aggressively seek support for his plan, realizing on the one hand that the Forty-fourth Street site still had many advocates and that the city had already invested $13 million in taking the project as far as it had, and on the other hand that there were many who saw the Battery Park City site as an opportunity to help get that project moving. At a press conference called to announce his own "Miracle on Thirty-fourth Street," Trump claimed he could build a convention center on the site for $100 million. Theodore Kheel, who had come to support the Trump plan, effectively canceled the Battery Park City competition when he said that building a convention center in Battery Park would be "like putting a nightclub in a graveyard."[94]

Trump found that he had to promote not only his site but the very idea of the center itself, which many people felt should be dropped because of the city's fiscal crisis. But, as Trump has written, "that was classic shortsightedness. . . . Building [a convention center], I argued, was critical to reviving the city's image and, ultimately, to putting its economy back on track."[95] To make his point, Trump commissioned a master plan for the fifty-acre site from Gruzen & Partners, working with Der Scutt of Poor, Swanke, Hayden & Connell Architects. Scutt's design was for a faceted glass pavilion set atop a mammoth 800-foot-square box, modified somewhat with sculptured corner terraces and lounge lookouts that would break up the mass when viewed from outside and provide glimpses of the outdoors to conventioneers within. According to Scutt, "the message of the building" was "an electric environment of activity which says 'I am a Convention Center, come in and enjoy me.'"[96] The *New York Times* seemed persuaded. A January 1976 editorial on the "park-fronted crystal palace" stated that "in terms of cost, convenience, speed of completion, existing features and accessibility to the city's stores, hotels, restaurants and theaters . . . the 34th Street site wins hands down."[97]

By sheer persuasive force, and by directly confronting the city's real estate establishment—many of the same figures Newfield had been attacking from a different perspective in the *Village Voice*—Trump finally persuaded Mayor Beame, who had come out for the Battery site, to reopen the issue in 1977. That year the mayor and Governor Hugh Carey appointed a four-person committee to study the site alternatives. Reflecting both city and state interests, the committee consisted of Osborn Elliott, the Deputy Mayor for Economic Development; Victor Marrero, the chairman of the City Planning Commission; John G. Heimann, the New York State Commissioner of Housing and Community Renewal; and Felix Rohatyn, the chairman of the New York State Municipal Assistance Corporation. In May 1977

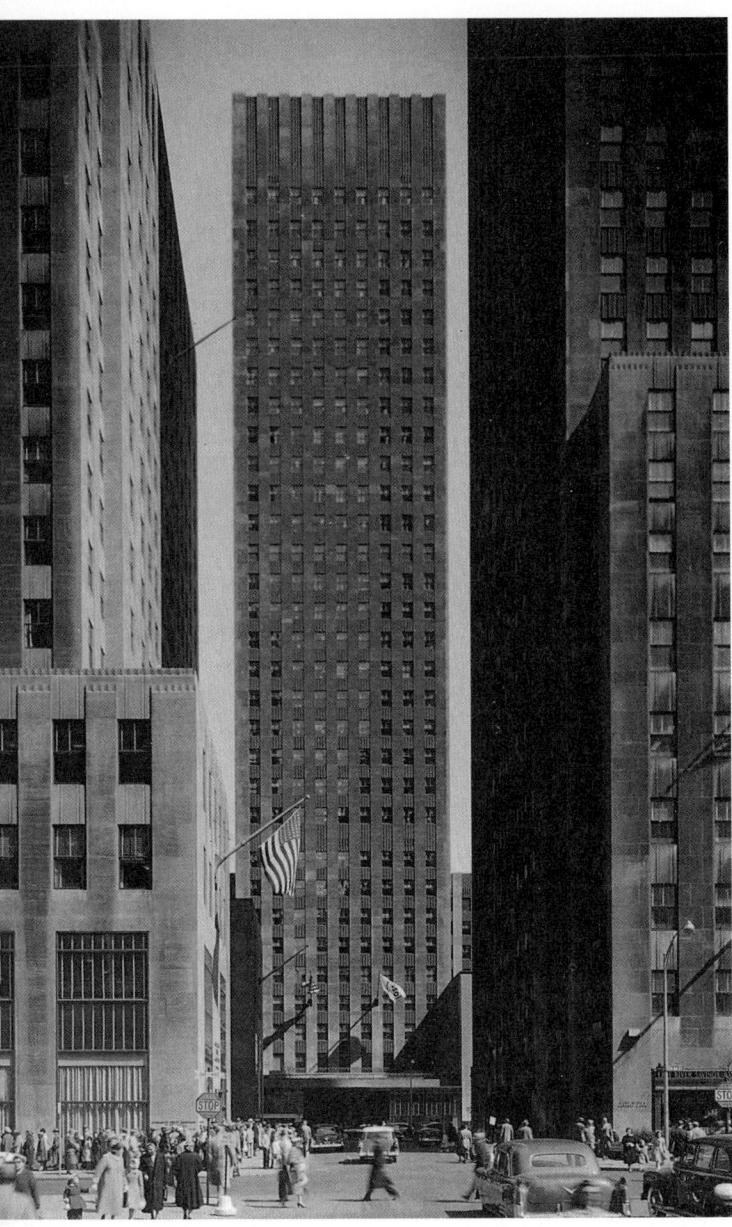

Esso Building, 15 West Fifty-first Street, between Fifth and Sixth avenues. Carson & Lundin, 1947. View to the north. Stoller. ©ESTO

Steven R. Weisman reported that after several months of study, the committee was "leaning" toward the Forty-fourth Street site.[98] Seven months later, following the election of Edward I. Koch as mayor, lame-duck mayor Abraham Beame publicly supported the Thirty-fourth street site.[99] Finally, on April 28, 1978, after eight years of development and negotiation, Mayor Koch and Governor Carey announced their intention to build a completely redesigned, $257 million convention center on a site bound by Eleventh and Twelfth avenues, Thirty-third and Thirty-ninth streets.[100] Foreshadowing the pivotal role in the city's evolution that Trump would play in the next decade, Charles Kaiser, writing in the *New York Times*, called the decision "a personal triumph" for the young developer.[101] With his signature flair for hyping his own achievements, Trump crowed that the mayor and governor's announcement was "perhaps the most significant economic decision made in New York City since the building of the United Nations."[102]

ROCKEFELLER CENTER

Rockefeller Center was officially completed when the "last rivet" was driven at a ceremony held on November 1, 1939.[1] Although at first it was reviled for its architecture and urbanism and for the techniques used to lease its space, Rockefeller Center soon became a beloved landmark for New Yorkers and tourists alike; after 1947 it was also a financial success. By the mid-1940s the complex occupied a unique place in the mythology of modern life. Sigfried Giedion, in his epochal polemic on behalf of architectural Modernism, *Space, Time and Architecture*, praised it as a "great urban development," explaining: "It introduces for the first time into a contemporary city the large scale that is to be found in the parkways and great engineering works. Its buildings, which . . . are conceived in coordination as a unit, introduce correspondingly new and original plastic elements."[2] The popular press hailed it as well, extolling its architecture and praising it as "a city within a city," a city in every aspect except its lack of a permanent residential population.

With its village-green-like plaza and evolving rituals reflected in elaborately orchestrated seasonal displays, Rockefeller Center came increasingly to represent a simpler, more benign form of urbanism as midtown on the whole took on a bigger scale and a more impersonal character. The lighting of the Christmas tree and the annual opening of the skating rink became major events in the city's calendar—an irony since neither the rink nor the tree, as Joe Alex Morris told the readers of the *Saturday Evening Post* in 1949, were part of the initial plan. The 125-by-95-foot sunken plaza culminating the axis of the Channel Gardens was originally planned as a fashionable shopping area leading into an underground avenue of stores stretching the length of the center. But, as Morris put it, the shopping area "flopped," and the management decided to install two restaurants and make the plaza into a "colorful and quaint Skating Pond in the shadow of New York's skyscrapers." The rink became one of Rockefeller Center's main attractions, drawing "hundreds of skaters a day who happily contribute a yearly total of $80,000 for the privilege of putting on a free show and salvaging the Center's biggest architectural mishap." In the summer, when the plaza was planted, it functioned, somewhat less successfully, "as a sort of glorified village green" with carefully staged dog shows, fashion shows and other public events.[3]

The lighting of the Christmas tree, the focus of the center's most spectacular season, was the year's principal event. According to Morris, it too came about more or less by accident: "The origin of the Center's Christmas tree is attributed to a group of workmen who set up a tiny pine and strung a few lights on it while they were excavating for the first buildings."[4] The management picked up on the workmen's action, and what began in 1934 with a sixty-foot tree draped with 1,200 colored lights had become by 1936 an eighty-foot tree with 4,000 lights. In 1948 the tree was ninety feet tall and required seven miles of wire to connect its 7,500 lights. By the 1970s the average height of the tree was similar to that of the original, with sixty-five-foot trees in 1971 and 1972 and a sixty-foot tree in 1974; they were, however, brighter, averaging about 12,000 lights. In 1973, with the energy crisis a major concern, the center contemplated cutting the tree's illumination by 25 percent but instead decided to eliminate the center's other exterior lighting, add thousands of multicolored reflecting disks to the tree and reduce the number of miniature bulbs.[5]

The final touch to the plaza came on February 24, 1942, with the installation of the flags of the twenty-six nations who joined in the Declaration by the United Nations, a resolution pledging to continue the war effort and not to sign a separate peace. This gave the great limestone- and glass-bordered outdoor room some desperately needed color and, when the wind was blowing, the snap and clatter of a full-dress military parade. As the commuter culture of the 1960s was at its peak and central cities in their most desperate state ever, the architectural historian Vincent Scully would celebrate the plaza as "one of the few surviving spaces in America that look as if they were designed and used by people who knew what stable wealth was and were not ashamed to enjoy it. Flags snap, high heels tap: a little sex and aggression, the city's delights. Jefferson would have hated it all."[6]

With its radio and television studios, Radio City Music Hall, a skating rink, innumerable restaurants and shops, as well as the offices that were its bread and butter, Rockefeller Center seemed to deserve the sobriquet of "Eighth Wonder of the World," bestowed upon it by Meyer Berger,[7] and membership among the "Seven Wonders of American Architecture," as established by a 1958 survey of 500 American architects.[8]

The center was modestly expanded in the 1940s with the construction of a building for the Standard Oil Corporation at the northern terminus of Rockefeller Plaza, at 15 West Fifty-first Street (1947).[9] The site had originally been intended for the plaza's northward extension to the Museum of Modern Art on West Fifty-third Street. The construction of the Esso Building, as 15 West Fifty-first Street was called, forever put to rest plans for a complex of cultural facilities—including at one time the proposed Guggenheim Museum—lining an extension of Rockefeller Plaza north to West Fifty-fourth Street. This dream of the 1930s had enjoyed the support of Mayor La Guardia and Robert Moses but was ultimately thwarted by the Rockefeller family's inability to acquire, at a reasonable price, the property at 21 West Fifty-second Street, which housed a former speakeasy that had evolved into the city's quintessential "power" restaurant, The 21 Club. The collapse of a hope for the Rockefeller Plaza extension paved the way for the construction of the New York Public Library's Donnell branch on Rockefeller-owned land on West Fifty-third Street and, across the street, the extension of the Museum of Modern Art, both of which lay in the proposed plaza's path.

Designed by Carson & Lundin, the center's staff architects, who had worked with the Associated Architects and with

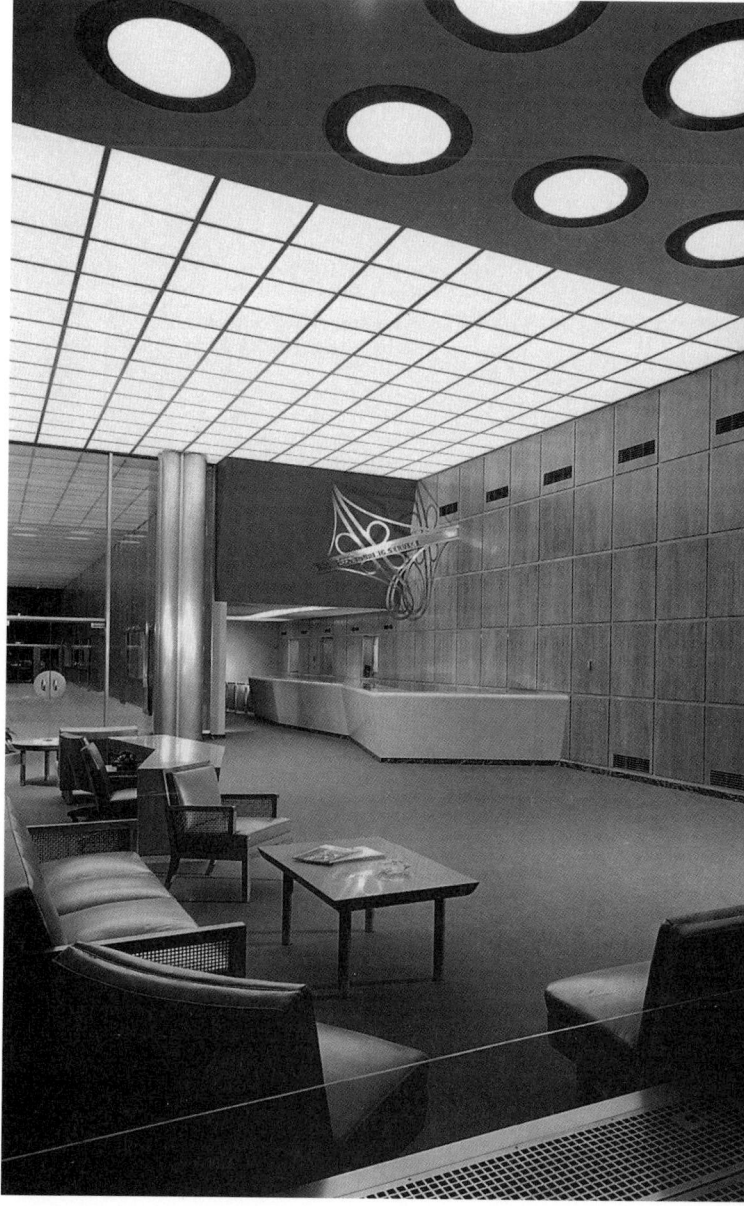

Esso Building. Touring Center. Gottscho-Schleisner. LOC

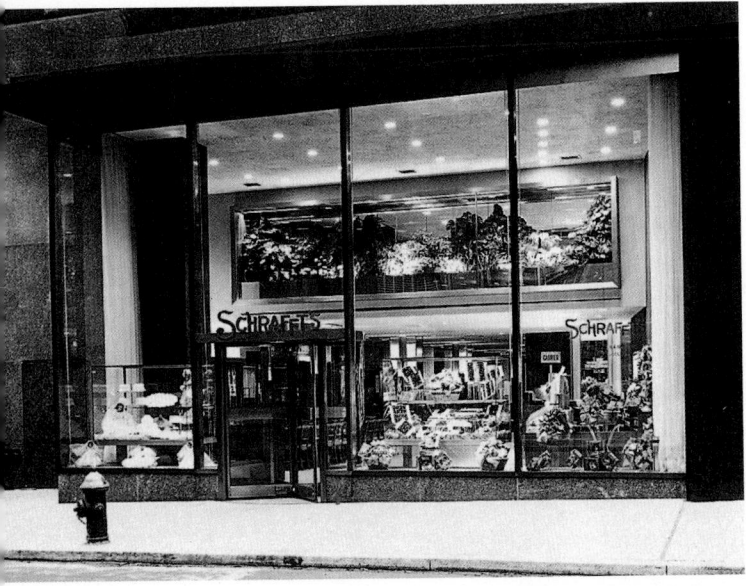

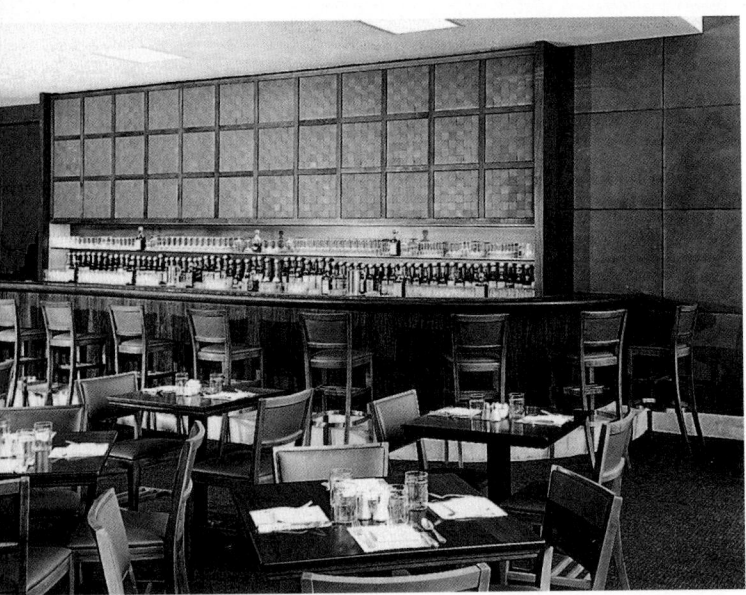

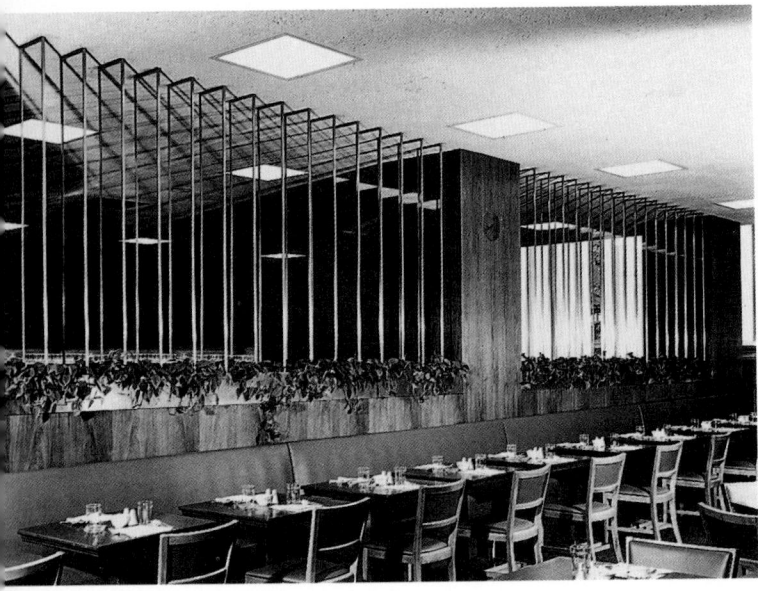

Wallace K. Harrison as consulting architect, the Esso Building picked up on the center's aesthetic of uninterrupted limestone vertical piers to accentuate the bold, slablike thirty-two-story tower that rose from a low base to close the axis of Rockefeller Plaza. Along Fifty-second Street the tower was intersected by two ten-story wings forming a T shape. The Esso Building was the first building in Rockefeller Center and the tallest building in the city to be completely air conditioned. The axis of Rockefeller Plaza was carried through the building by means of a high-ceilinged, austerely detailed, marble-sheathed lobby concourse entered from the street at either end through revolving doors set within large, virtually unbroken walls of glass. The principal decoration of the lobby was the ingenious wavelike pattern of the ceiling. To one side of the lobby, a Touring Center, top-lit by a gridded luminous ceiling concealing cold cathode-ray tubes, provided information and maps to motorists. Half of the building's ground-floor space was occupied by a block-long Schrafft's restaurant, also designed by Carson & Lundin. Described by the owner as "the world's largest service restaurant," it could accommodate 1,283 patrons at one sitting.[10] In contrast with the traditional decor of the typical prewar Schrafft's, this installation featured mirrored surfaces and extensive use of plants. The two-story-high, south-facing windows lighting the leather-paneled men's grill were particularly distinctive, "ridding this Schrafft's," as *Architectural Forum* put it, "of any vestige of the Helen Hokinson feeling."[11]

Although the center's architecture seemed increasingly old-fashioned when compared to the postwar metal-and-glass curtain walls, it did set the tone for some new buildings in the immediate vicinity, most notably Leonard Schultze & Associates' limestone-clad Crowell-Collier Building and Carson & Lundin's Sinclair Oil Building, both located on Fifth Avenue. The center evolved within its own boundaries as well. Over time, the original buildings were renovated to provide sophisticated air conditioning and wiring for new tenants. In 1960, with the relocation of Time, Inc. to its new building across Sixth Avenue (see "Sixth Avenue," below), the original Time & Life Building, completed in 1937, was overhauled for its new principal tenant, General Dynamics.[12] Although these renovations on the whole were done with little compromise to the center's artistic integrity, the loss of the Center Theater in 1954 to make way for expanded office space in Harrison & Abramovitz's addition to the western end of the original U.S. Rubber Company Building was more serious.[13]

In January 1974 Rockefeller Center, Inc. released plans for a new addition that provoked widespread concern: the RCA Management Conference Center was proposed to replace the twelfth-floor rooftop garden of the RCA Building.[14] As designed by Marlys Hann and James Maguire of Ford & Earl, industrial and interior designers from Detroit, the RCA Center would be the first commercial structure in New York and one of the first in the United States to use solar energy. Essentially a pavilionlike greenhouse surrounded by two stories of conventionally constructed meeting rooms, the facility, to be completed in 1977, was to be a pilot project in energy technology. The use of the rooftop for an enclosed space was controversial from the first. Many objected to the elimination of the landscaped rooftop gardens that had originally been one of the center's principal features, although the elaborate planting programs for these gardens had gradually been modified since the death of the center's resident landscape architect, Aart Marius Van den Hoek, in 1950[15] and the departure of horticulturist Homo Hagemeister in 1952.[16]

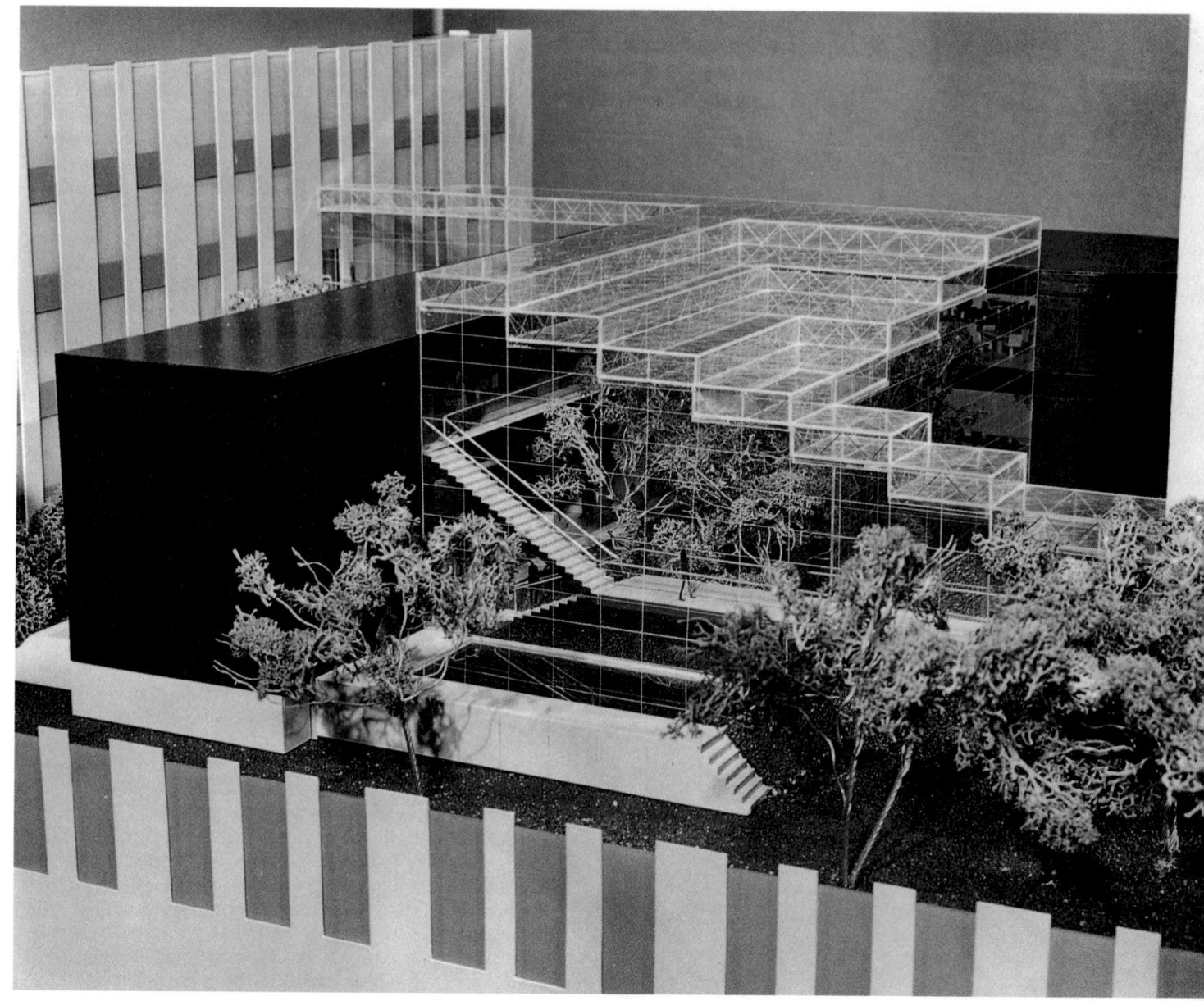

Top left: Schrafft's, Esso Building, 15 West Fifty-first Street, between Fifth and Sixth avenues. Carson & Lundin, 1947. Exterior. Gottscho-Schleisner. LOC

Center left: Schrafft's. Interior. Gottscho-Schleisner. LOC

Bottom left: Schrafft's. Interior. Gottscho-Schleisner. LOC

Above: Proposed RCA Management Center, twelfth-floor rooftop of RCA Building (Associated Architects, 1933), between Rockefeller Plaza and Sixth Avenue, West Forty-ninth and West Fiftieth streets. Ford & Earl Associates, 1974. FE

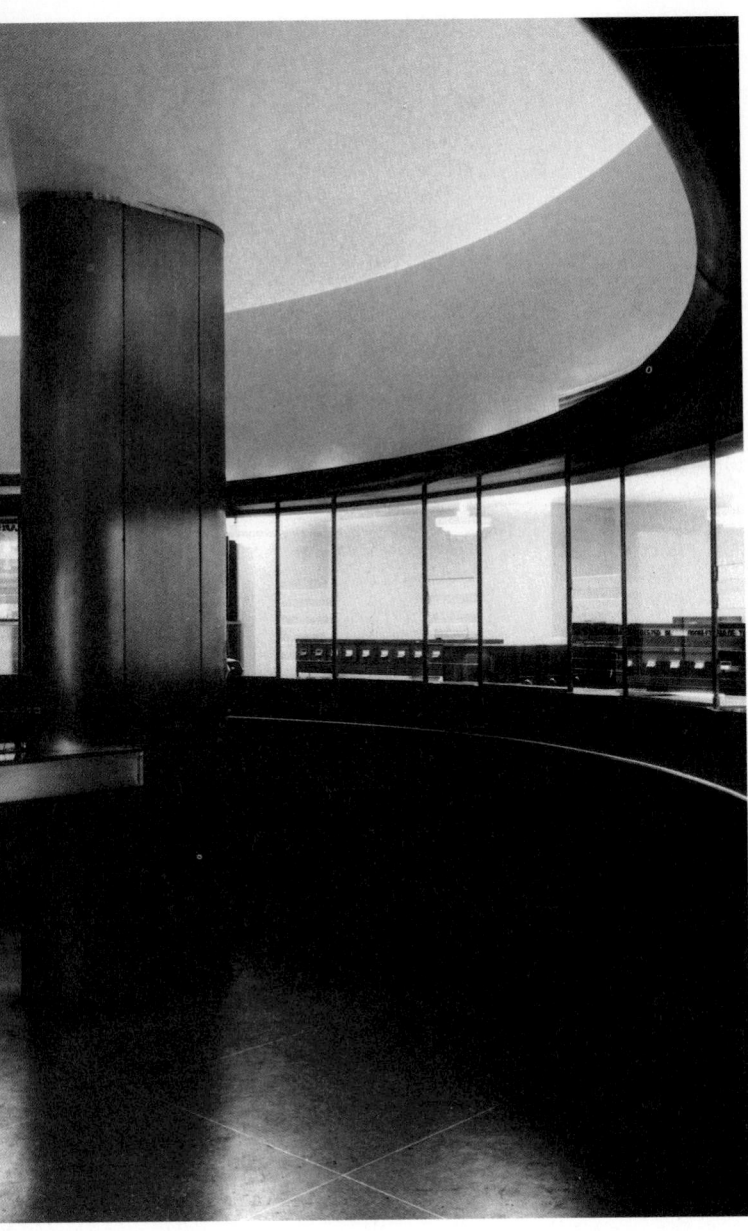

Above: First Federal Savings and Loan branch, 30 Rockefeller Plaza, between West Forty-ninth and West Fiftieth streets. Carson & Lundin, 1944. Banking floor. Gottscho-Schleisner. LOC

Top right: National City Bank of New York, 9 West Fifty-first Street, between Fifth and Sixth avenues. Walker & Gillette in consultation with Aaron G. Alexander, 1945. Banking floor. Gottscho-Schleisner. LOC

Bottom right: Bankers Trust Company branch, 51 Rockefeller Plaza, between West Fiftieth and West Fifty-first streets. Shreve, Lamb & Harmon Associates, 1946. Banking floor. Gottscho-Schleisner. LOC

The construction of the 24,000-square-foot management center was initially presented as an essential factor in RCA's decision to remain headquartered in New York; retaining 9,000 jobs in a declining economy was deemed so important that the project was announced jointly by Governor Nelson A. Rockefeller, Mayor Abraham D. Beame and Robert W. Sarnoff, RCA's chairman and chief executive officer. But in December 1975 RCA announced that it was canceling the project for economic reasons, explaining that estimated construction costs had nearly doubled since the original proposal. A key to the project's demise was the fact that Sarnoff, its strongest supporter, had been forced out of power the previous month.

Meanwhile, amid rumors that Radio City Music Hall faced demolition, the facility's reputation as a consummate work of architecture was increasing among a new generation of critics, architects and laymen. With its grand public spaces and extraordinary synthesis of Classical mass and Modernist ornament, the hall had come to be seen as a remarkable representation of a style that, after having been dismissed as confused and false, was now being celebrated as "Art Deco."[17] Just as RCA's plans to alter its rooftop were being announced, the Music Hall, beginning on January 30, 1974, was home to the New York Art Deco Exposition, which combined a five-day program of films from the 1930s with a flea-market-like bazaar in the lobby where Deco-style posters, ashtrays and other objets d'art were sold.[18] The exposition was an extraordinary success, with some 13,000 people attending in the first three days alone.

While Rockefeller Center attracted its share of retail shops, it failed to materialize as the successful shopping complex it was originally intended to become.[19] Instead, its ground-floor spaces were largely taken up by banks, many of which were housed in stylish facilities.[20] Banks clustered around the center's edges as well. Just before war restrictions put a halt to building, Chemical Bank & Trust Company completed a major facility at 11 West Fifty-first Street, directly opposite the center.[21] Designed by Walker & Gillette, who made something of a specialty of banks, the three-story-high building clad in limestone and granite reflected the architects' sure mastery of Modern Classicism, with a boldly scaled central wall of aluminum and glass set between sheer walls rising to visually support a cornice carved with the bank's name. Inside, the grandly proportioned banking hall was underplayed, with indirect lighting and waist-high partitions separating bank offices from the public. Next door, at 9 West Fifty-first Street (1945), to create two banking levels equally visible from the entrance, Walker & Gillette, working in consultation with Aaron G. Alexander, doubled the width of the original structure, their 1937 National City Bank branch building, reorganizing the interior on a split-level plan.[22] Carson & Lundin's First Federal Savings and Loan (1944), at 30 Rockefeller Plaza, was sleekly modern, with a round banking room interrupted by two bronze-clad, bull-nosed columns.[23]

After the war, Shreve, Lamb & Harmon Associates picked up on the Carson firm's circular theme in their Bankers Trust Company branch, at 51 Rockefeller Plaza, warming up the vocabulary with curtained windows, venetian blinds, white oak, blue-green plaster walls and Lillian Christiansen's colorful mural map of the United States.[24] By 1952 Chase National's Rockefeller Center branch, originally opened in 1932 and its busiest in midtown, had been remodeled five times, most recently by Carson & Lundin.[25] The architects erased the last vestiges of its original institutional look—its dark paneling, wrought-iron gates and dim lighting—and replaced them with light butternut plywood paneling, low, unfenced counters, recessed fluorescent lighting and white ter-

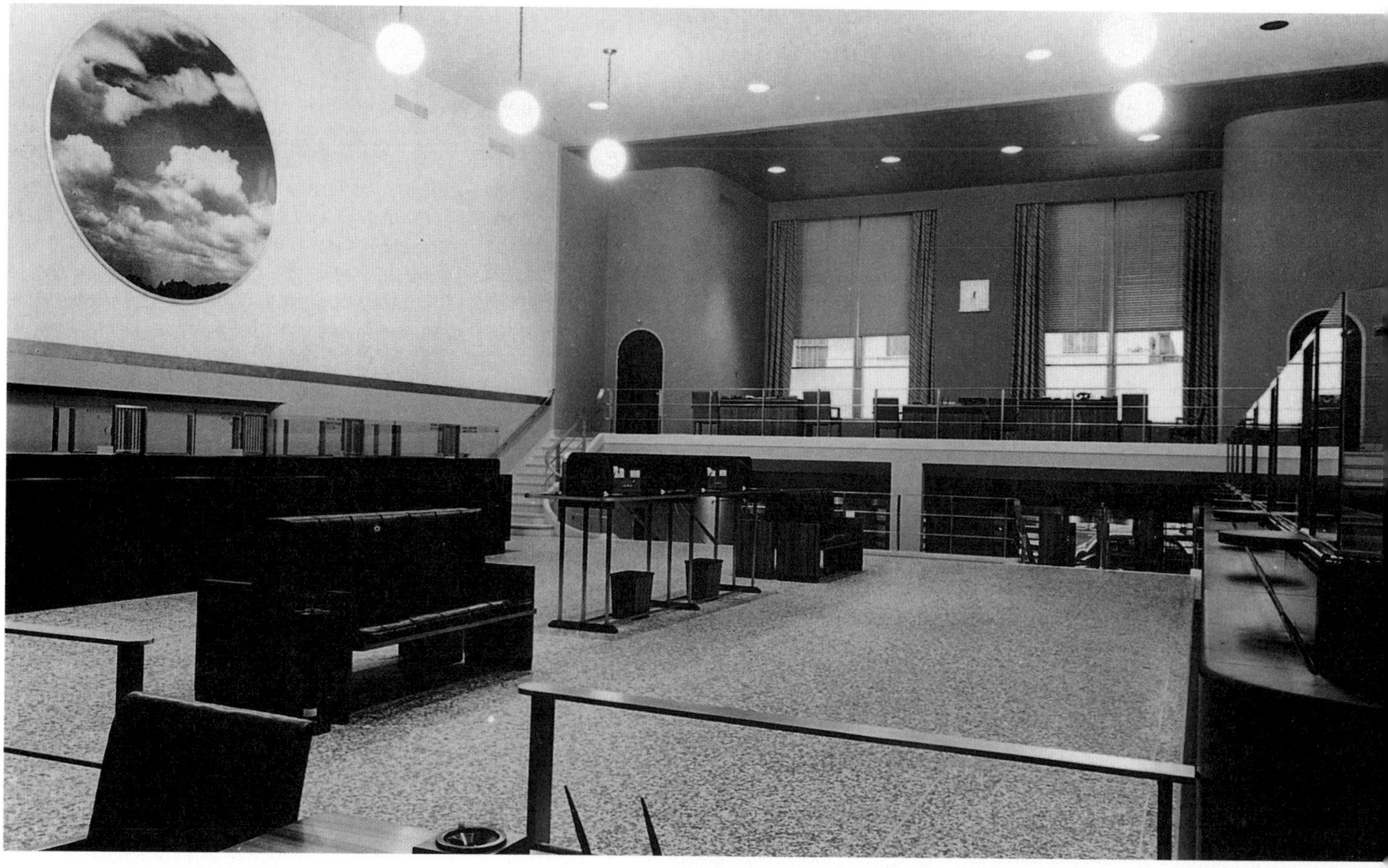

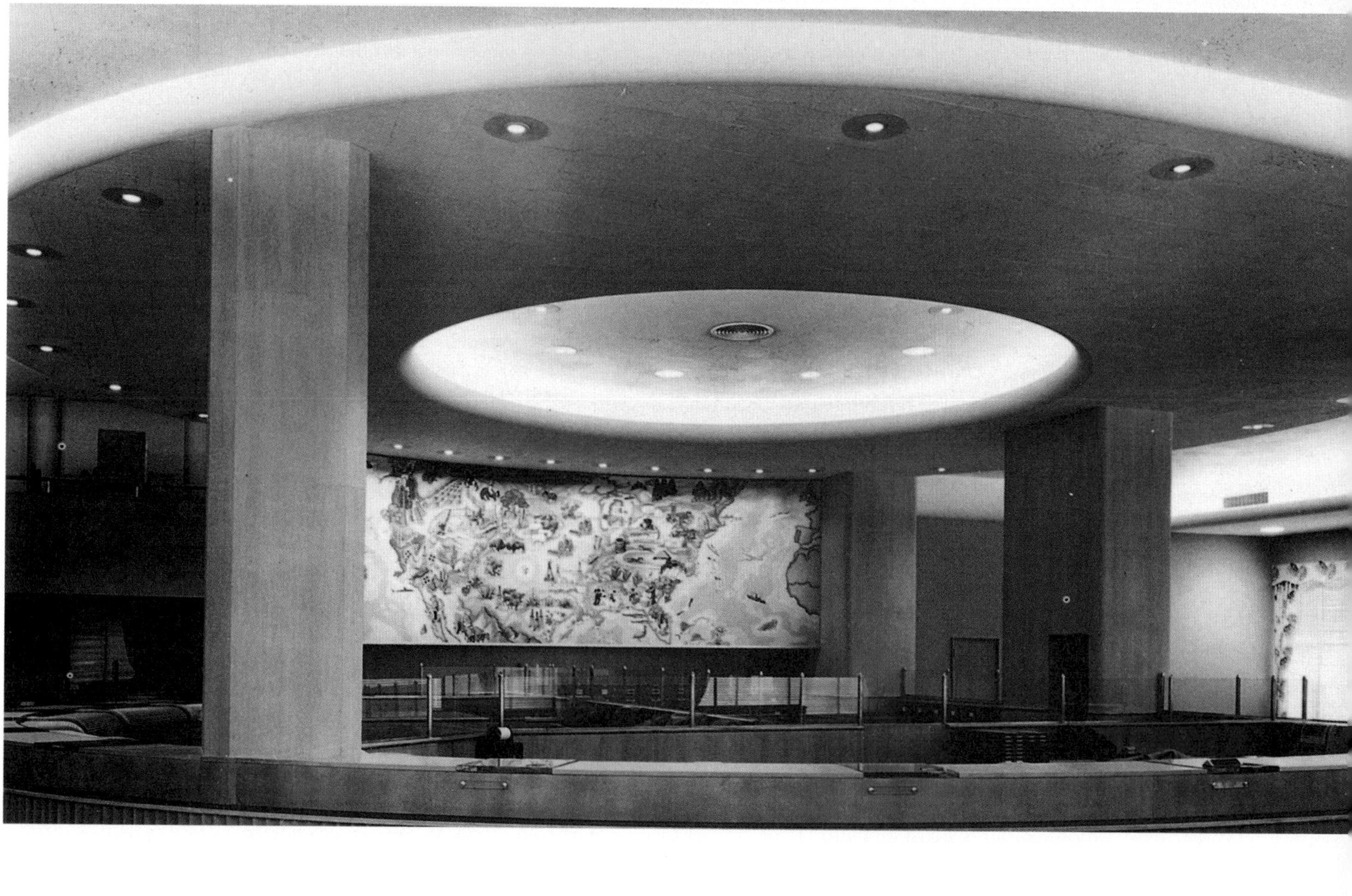

razzo floors. The Radio City branch of the New York Savings Bank (1955), the work of interior designer Eleanor Lemaire and architect John R. Weber, was designed to be "cheery, familiar and friendly."[26] The floor-to-ceiling backlit screen of sparkling, bronze-anodized, perforated aluminum, the blue-gray terrazzo floor and the rosewood-faced, white-marble-topped counters arranged in a saw-toothed pattern created a bold effect quite different from that of traditional banking facilities.

By the time the Irving Trust Company decided to open a Rockefeller Center branch at 1290 Avenue of the Americas (1963), a block-through facility that could be entered from either Fifty-first or Fifty-second Street, the area was almost saturated by its competitors. To create a distinct impression for the bank, Carson, Lundin & Shaw capitalized on the era's interest in fluid, sculpted shapes and designed what *Interiors* described as "a pavilion-like ceiling of dropped concave acoustic plaster sections which hang like tents between tapered white columns."[27]

PARK AVENUE

The reasons for the postwar transformation of the midtown stretch of Park Avenue from a swank residential boulevard to the urban equivalent of a corporate office park were complex; the changes cannot be attributed simply to "the basic rules of supply and demand," as architect Richard Roth, who was so much involved in the process, claimed in 1963.[1] The story of Park Avenue's postwar evolution has a prehistory that begins in 1929, when the avenue's first phase of development as New York's preeminent boulevard was drawing to a close. In that year Manhattan's zoning map was altered to permit retail shops along the avenue below Fifty-ninth Street.[2] But the stock market crash thwarted activity until 1936, when Robert Goelet, one of the city's leading landowners, began to replace the block-long row of brownstone houses on the west side of the avenue between Fifty-third and Fifty-fourth streets with a one-story taxpayer (Rosario Candela and Eric Gugler), completed in 1938, that included shops and the Normandie movie theater (Rosario Candela and Ben Schlanger).[3] The lingering Depression and the war prevented further change.

With the war barely over, William Zeckendorf's company Webb & Knapp, Inc. announced in July 1945 that it had taken a sixty-three-year lease on the Marguery Hotel at 270 Park Avenue from the New York Central Corporation with the intention of replacing the twelve-story courtyard apartment house (Warren & Wetmore, 1918) with a new office building.[4] *Architectural Forum* was quick to see the importance of Zeckendorf's announcement for Park Avenue's future: "The postwar razing of the Marguery to make way for business may presage a wide-scale answer to the problem which has longer [sic] plagued Park Avenue's biggest landlord, the N.Y. Central Railroad: lush apartment buildings, although fully tenanted, are no longer profitable."[5] These buildings were no longer profitable primarily because of rent control. According to the prominent realtor Douglas L. Elliman, rent control institutionalized the negative results of a chain of factors that made midtown apartment buildings financially undesirable. The controls were based on 1943 price levels, which, because apartment rents in midtown had dropped during the Depression by as much as 25 percent, were ridiculously low.

Even as the economy rebounded in the late 1930s, upper-class families who did not leave Manhattan for the suburbs moved farther uptown or farther east along the river, so that the rents in some of Park Avenue's grandest buildings never returned to anything near the true value of the real estate. One example cited by Elliman was the case of 300 Park Avenue, Sherry's Hotel, where eighteen-room apartments that had rented before the Crash for $25,000 per year were forced down to $6,000 or $7,000 per year during the 1930s and then frozen by rent control.[6] Though the building and its land had represented an investment of nearly $8.5 million in 1922, saddled as it was with 100 rent-controlled apartments, it was worth only $3.5 million when it was sold to the Uris Brothers in 1951 to make way for an office building. The system of rent control that allowed for such a situation could be avoided in two ways: the building could be sold to the tenants as a cooperative, or it could be demolished when alternate uses were permitted. In the 1950s cooperatives were the typical solution for luxury buildings on the Upper East Side and along Central Park West, areas that were suited only to residential use. But along the midtown stretch of Park Avenue, where the zoning had been changed and much more lucrative new office buildings could be built, demolition was common.

From the beginning, the new Park Avenue, lined with office buildings, was unpopular with critics. Lewis Mumford was the first to sound the alarm, in 1954 alerting his readers to the impact of Park Avenue's redevelopment on the midtown district as a whole. At the same time, he lamented the destruction of one of the twentieth century's great urban ensembles:

> As a result of . . . recent encroachment, the splendid scale of Park Avenue set by its early hotels and apartment houses is disappearing as one substantial building after another gives way to a new pile of offices. There is no longer in the heart of the city as much as half a mile of buildings—Park Avenue once boasted two or three consecutive miles—that combine coherence and civic dignity. . . . The mischief the city is now facing in midtown Manhattan is twofold—first, the density of occupation is increasing, and thus increasing the density of traffic; and second, this area . . . is being disrupted by the growing invasion of office buildings.[7]

Three years later, in 1957, Ada Louise Huxtable took in the scene with a New Yorker's characteristic blend of fatalism and irony:

> Today the old Park Avenue is being buried with remarkable and ruthless efficiency. Pedestrians pick their way through dust and debris, past temporary fences put together out of discarded (and still oddly personal) apartment house doors, while musty rubble thunders down chutes from ghosts of buildings stripped to shabby, naked steel. For we no longer just bury the past, we destroy it to make room for the future. Monuments and memories are demolished with the same cheerful, irreverent violence. As the old buildings disappear radical new ones rise immediately in their place, and the pattern of progress becomes clear: business palaces replace private palaces; soap aristocracy supplants social aristocracy; sleek towers of steel-framed blue, green, or gray-tinted glass give the avenue a glamorous and glittering new look.

But, unlike Mumford, Huxtable, who was just beginning her career as a critic, took a decidedly optimistic view of the changes: "Park Avenue still has its upper-class aura, its special air of privilege and prestige. The passing of the stately old apartments and hotels—most of which were thoroughly undistinguished buildings—has not eliminated this special brand of elegance from New York. It has merely changed its locale. In a surprise shift, elegance has moved from domestic to professional life, from the apartment house to the office building."[8]

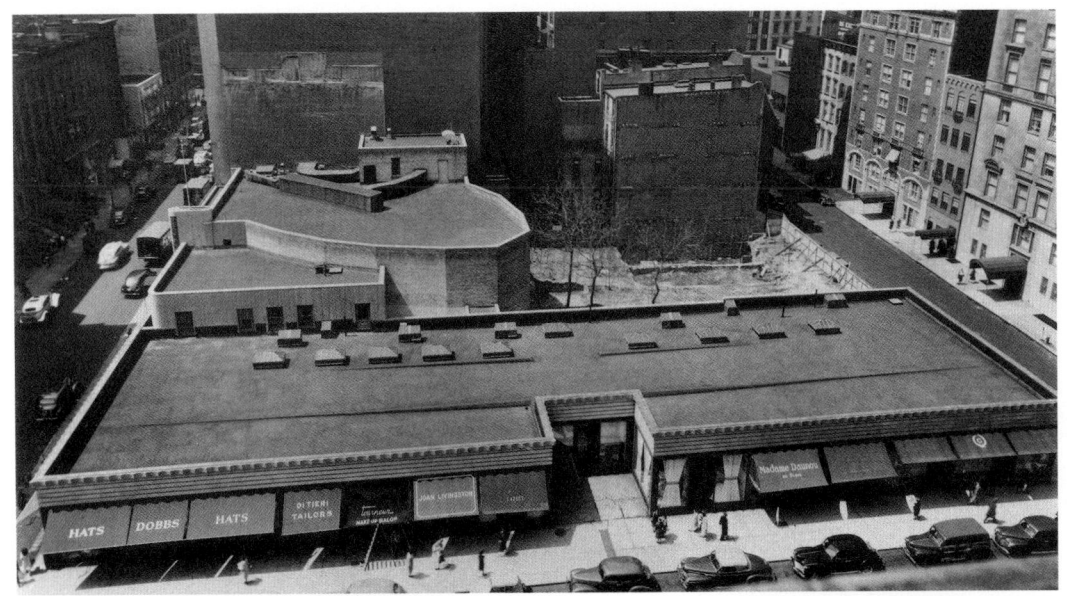

Left: Taxpayer building, west side of Park Avenue, East Fifty-third to East Fifty-fourth Street. Rosario Candela and Eric Gugler, 1938. View to the east showing the Normandie movie theater (Rosario Candela and Ben Schlanger, 1938) on the upper left. Wurts. MCNY

Below: View to the south of Park Avenue from East Fifty-fifth street showing, from left to right: 417 Park Avenue (Emery Roth, 1916), 405 Park Avenue (Herbert Tannenbaum, 1957) and Seagram Building (Ludwig Mies van der Rohe, Philip Johnson and Kahn & Jacobs, 1958). Gottscho-Schleisner. LOC

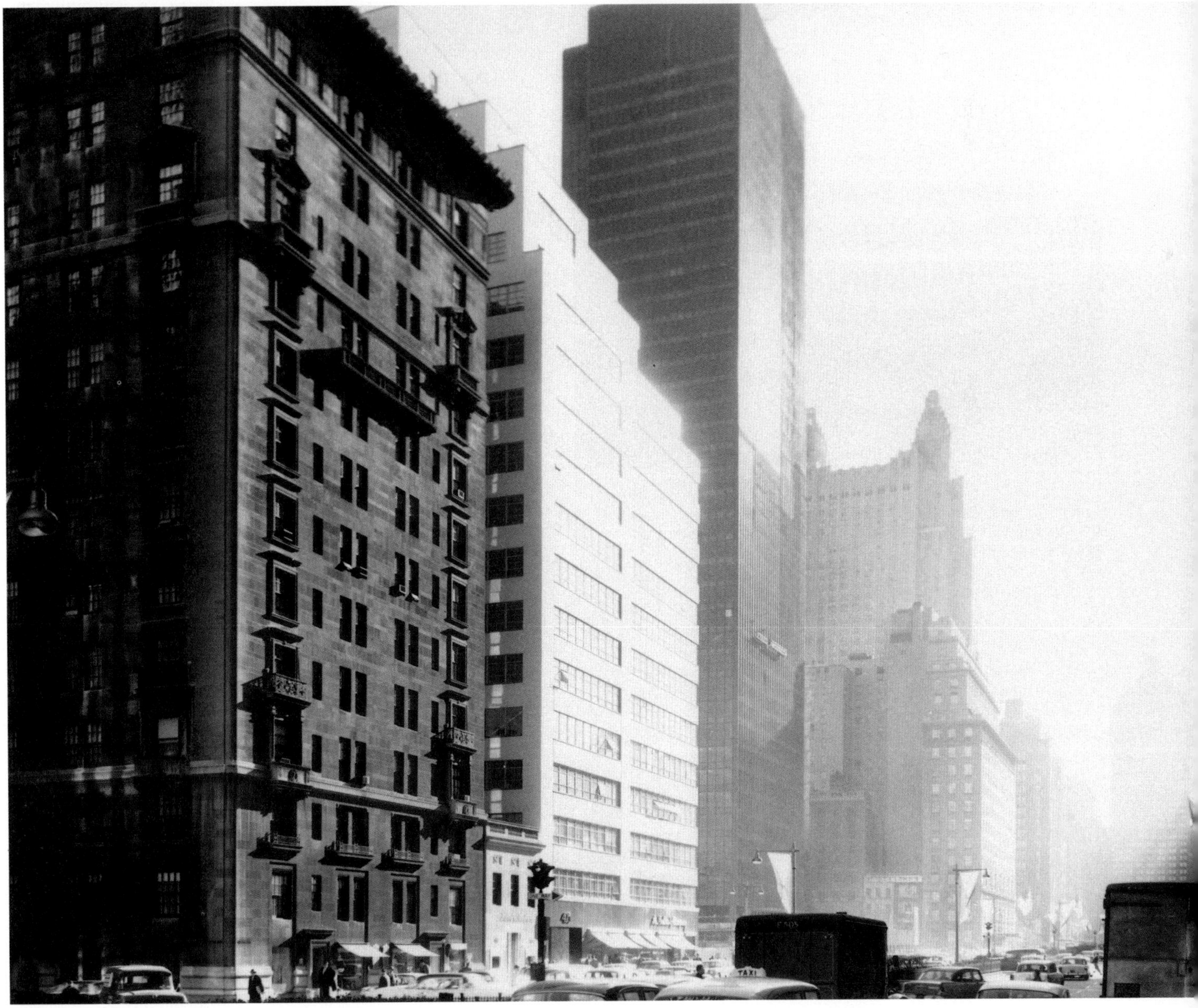

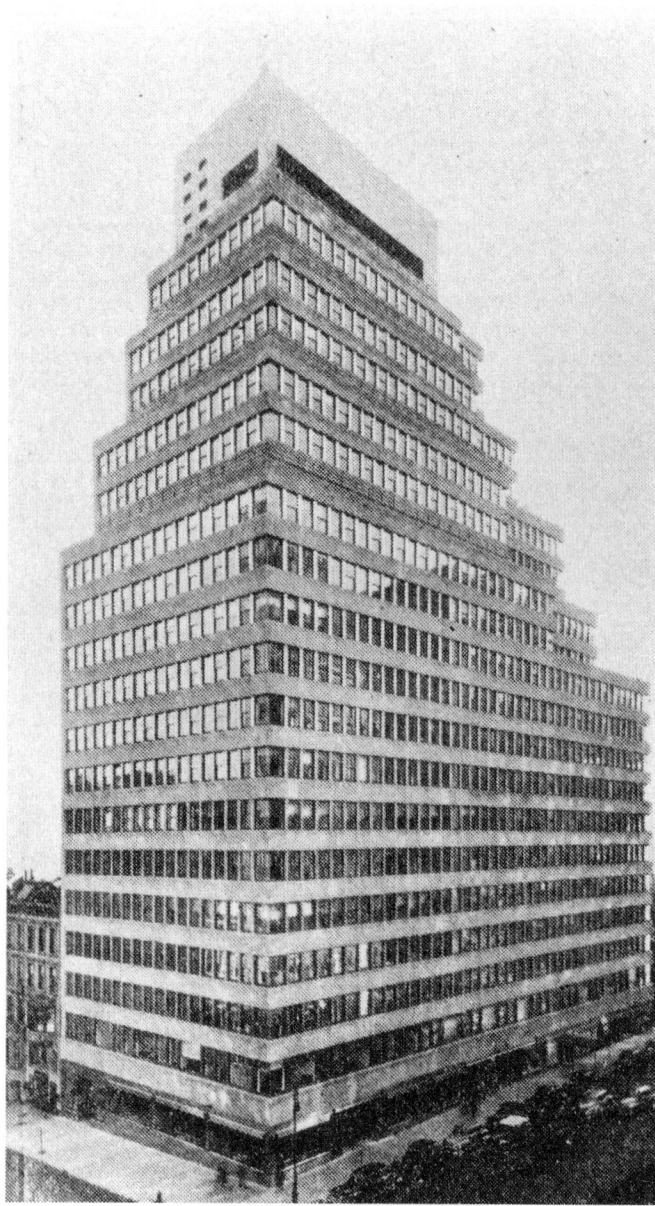

Universal Pictures Building, 445 Park Avenue, East Fifty-sixth to East Fifty-seventh Street. Kahn & Jacobs, 1947. View to the southeast. RERG. CU

The transformation of Park Avenue marked the corporate world's near-total repudiation of traditional architecture in favor of International Style Modernism. But, as Huxtable reported, though business welcomed the new minimalist style, the general public did not: "As in all matters of art, the public may not know much about architecture, but it definitely knows what it likes. What it does not like are those 'stark glass boxes.' They are shocking and strange. There is considerable gloomy talk of 'monotony' and 'uniformity' and tears shed for the passing of 'ornament' and 'character.'"[9]

Though Huxtable had virtually nothing positive to say about any of Park Avenue's new buildings, except for Lever House and the Seagram Building, she accepted the new minimalist aesthetic as a positive force. She seemed to see the transformed Park Avenue in quasi-messianic terms, claiming that it created "order out of existing civic chaos," despite the fact that pre-1945 Park Avenue was generally held to be America's most coherent boulevard. For Huxtable, then, Park Avenue's importance was as a positive symbol of architectural evolution, even if its actuality was disappointing. "Significant in spite of their faults, handsome in spite of their esthetic inadequacies, New York's new buildings," Huxtable concluded, "signal one of the most important structural and stylistic changes in the history of architectural design."[10]

Four months after Huxtable's assessment, the urbanist Jane Jacobs viewed the scene through less rose-colored glasses. In discussing "the handsome, glittering stretch" of Park Avenue, she pointed out that it was missing something: "People simply do not walk there in the crowds they should to justify this elegant asset to the city. . . . The office workers and visitors who pour from these buildings turn off, more often than not, to Lexington Avenue . . . or Madison Avenue. . . . Assuming that the customer is right . . . it is obvious that Lexington and Madison have something that Park doesn't."[11]

In a talk delivered in 1961 at a special meeting of the Architectural League devoted to the avenue's transformation, and subsequently published as "The Death of the Street," Vincent Scully, the historian and critic, saw the new Park Avenue as the fulfillment of Le Corbusier's vision of a city of broadly spaced, skyscraping towers. But where Le Corbusier's skyscrapers were conceived within a framework of Cartesian regularity and aesthetic uniformity, on Park Avenue competing architects, encouraged by their clients, were lining the street with highly individualistic monuments: "The skyscrapers fight each other: their own worst enemies, but the Avenue's most of all." Scully shared Mumford's sense of loss over the destruction of the old avenue, which he described as "a good street, one of the few splendid ones in America, in its own way noble and unique."[12]

In 1962, the year before the completion of the Pan American Building signaled the irretrievable loss of the old Park Avenue, the New Yorker devoted one of its "Notes and Comment" columns to the situation. The editors found that the avenue's "new architectural mode . . . leaves one with little to say. It glossily sheds human content. . . . The new buildings on Park Avenue . . . have not so much arrived as seeped through, and they hover on their thin stilts, slightly darker than the sky, like boxy clouds that, the next moment, may shrug and be gone." The magazine's editors went on to describe the effect of the new glass-skinned buildings:

> Not that they are transparent. No, they are curiously opaque, considering they are made of glass. The old skyline, the jagged continuum of rosy-ochre stone, was airier, really; its even ground of tint made the individual buildings appear to have

more silhouette than mass. Perhaps the opacity of the glass buildings has to do with their refusal to accept atmosphere, to melt as it were, into a landscape. For while it is true that they reflect, it is also true that they reflect only each other, like actors at a cocktail party who will speak only to other actors.

In conclusion the editors wrote:

> What we miss is some sense of monument. These new skyscrapers do not aspire to scrape the sky; at the point of exhaustion, where the old skyscrapers used to taper, gather their dwindling energy, and lunge upward with a heart-stopping spire, these glass boxes suffer the intense architectural embarrassment of having to house air-conditioning apparatus and the ascent of windows ends in an awkward piece of slatted veiling. A pity, perhaps, but well suited to our age of anticlimax. Glassy-eyed from contemplation of these buildings made entirely of windows, we walked west feeling oddly empty, as if we had dined on a meal of doughnut holes.[13]

The Setback Type

Before the influx of the tower or slab-type office buildings along Park Avenue, exemplified by Lever House and the Seagram Building, the prewar setback or "wedding cake" type was given a new lease on life, dressed in the new minimalist aesthetics of the International Style. Though the glazed exterior cladding of the structures built in this first phase of the typological evolution of the office building might have looked totally different from the brick-and-limestone apartment houses they replaced, they maintained the fundamental structure of the avenue, holding to the street wall that defined it. In fact, one Park Avenue office building, 430 Park (see below), was no more than a new skin applied to the frame of an old apartment building. Despite the extensive use of glass, these buildings appeared remarkably solid, especially in the daytime when the greater amount of light on the street rendered the glass opaque rather than transparent.

In January 1946 plans were announced for 445 Park Avenue, the avenue's first postwar office building and the exemplar of the minimalist setback type.[14] Completed a year later, the building occupied the east side of the avenue from Fifty-sixth to Fifty-seventh Street. To make way for the new building, the original 100-unit apartment building, designed by Charles Rich in 1907, was demolished. First named the Tishman Building after its developers, 445 Park Avenue was soon renamed the Universal Building in honor of its lead tenant, the Universal Pictures Corporation. Designed by Ely Jacques Kahn and Robert Alan Jacobs, the twenty-two-story building filled the block for twelve stories before taking on a rhythmic pattern of setbacks that reflected the different zoning controls applicable on each of the three streets it faced.

The design combined a traditional sense of tectonic solidity with the liberating dynamism of stressed horizontals and syncopated setbacks. The facade's alternating continuous bands of limestone and glass, which also alternated between fixed and double-hung windows, suggested Mies van der Rohe's Concrete Office Building project of 1922[15] and, even more, the streamlined minimalism of Erich Mendelsohn, particularly his Columbus Haus office building in Berlin of 1929–31.[16] While Mies and Mendelsohn achieved the effect of continuous horizontality through structural means, Kahn & Jacobs, by cantilevering the floor slab beyond the columns, employed slender, mullionlike columns at the building's edge, holding only the

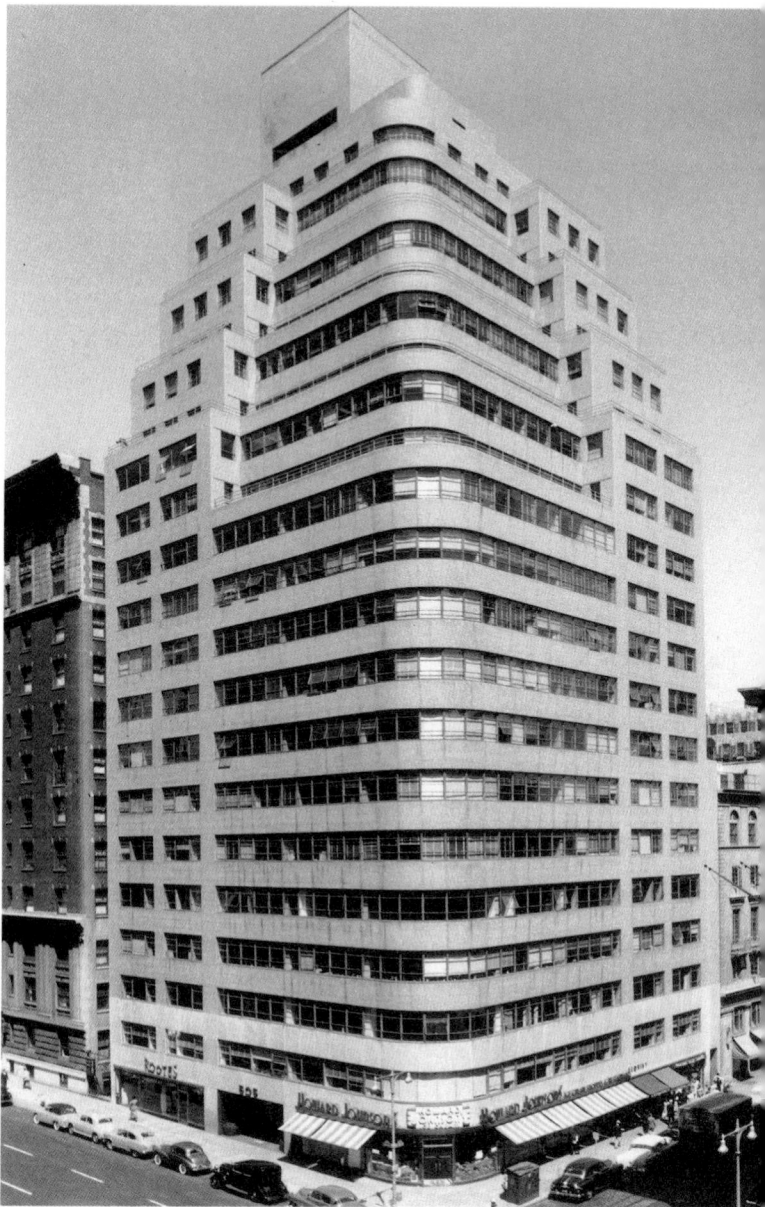

505 Park Avenue, northeast corner of East Fifty-ninth Street. Emery Roth & Sons, 1949. View to the northeast. OMH

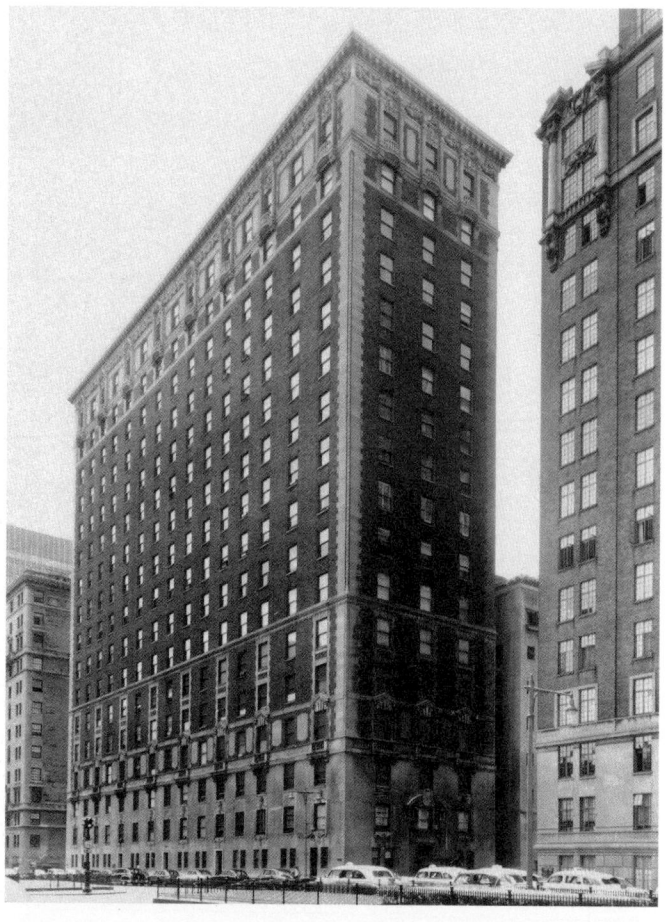

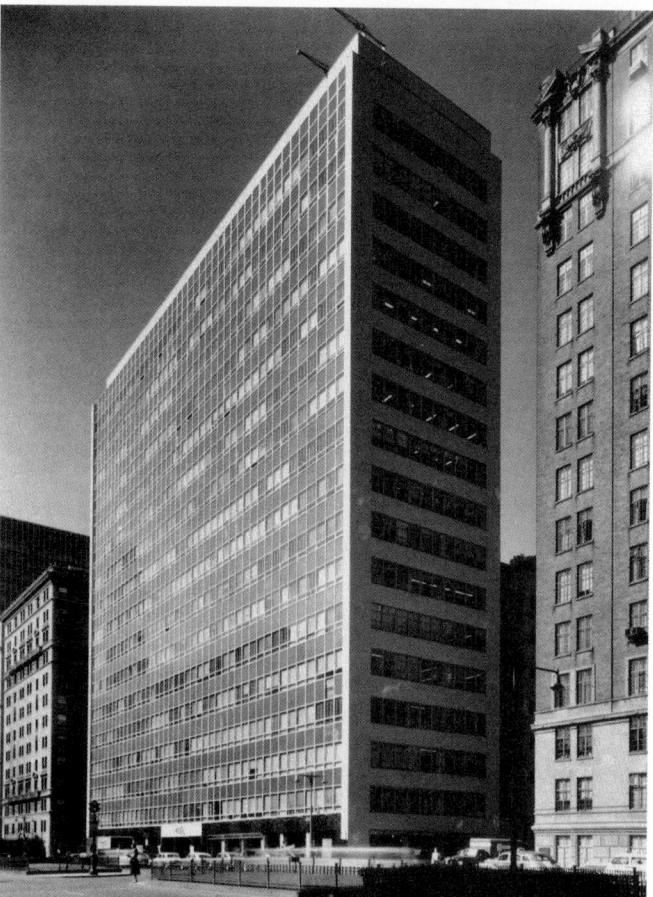

corners open. *Architectural Forum* considered this arrangement impure: "While slender outside columns contribute a certain lightness, heavy masonry facing disguises the true structural pattern of the building in a horizontal counterpart of the still persistent vertical style." The *Forum* article went on to say that though the alternation of dark and light stripes "creates an impression of continuous fenestration," the building was much less open than it appeared to be.[17]

The Universal Pictures Building was soon followed by Emery Roth & Sons' 505 Park Avenue (1949), a twenty-one-story building clad in yellow brick and located on the northeast corner of Fifty-ninth Street.[18] In this design the horizontal aesthetics of European Modernism were juxtaposed with the verticality of the traditional New York skyscraper: the dynamics of Mendelsohn-inspired continuous horizontal windows and spandrels that swept around a tightly radiused curved corner were bookended by two bays at each end that expressed the building's structural frame and reinforced the traditional sense of a street wall.

A few blocks south, the Davies Building (1952–54), at 460 Park Avenue, on the northwest corner of Fifty-seventh Street, contributed little to the public's appreciation of the new aesthetics.[19] Kahn & Jacobs were initially selected to be the architects of this 264,000-square-foot, twenty-two-story building, which was financed by the actress Marion Davies. But so powerful was the impact of Emery Roth & Sons' aluminum curtain wall for 99 Park Avenue (see "East Side: From Stuyvesant Town to Turtle Bay," above) that sometime in 1953 the Kahn & Jacobs firm was replaced by the Roths, who clad the frame with a similar wall. The aluminum-paneled curtain wall was erected in fourteen hours on June 21, 1954. The twenty-three-foot-high, four-and-a-half-foot-wide panels, each with two windows in them, were bolted to steel brackets already affixed to the steel frame. Finished with a grayish tint, they were intended to be glare-free.

While the Davies Building replaced comparatively insignificant buildings, the new building at 430 Park Avenue (Emery Roth & Sons, 1954), on the west blockfront between Fifty-fifth and Fifty-sixth streets, marked the first instance of the destruction of an impressive stone-clad apartment house to make way for a glass-and-metal office building.[20] The original apartment house, completed in 1916 by Warren & Wetmore for the William Waldorf Astor estate, had been one of midtown's most luxurious buildings, with many seventeen-room units. But instead of being torn down, the building was stripped to its steel frame and refitted for offices. The decision to renovate rather than replace the old building was based on a complex set of factors: for one thing there would be cost savings; for another, given material shortages due to the Korean War, the use of the existing structural frame would speed the project along, as would the avoidance of building a new foundation. But most important, a new building on the site could not duplicate the sheer mass of the original structure, built before New York's first zoning laws. The new 430 Park Avenue, with its green-tinted glass-and-aluminum curtain wall along the avenue, and its end elevations punched with horizontal window bands, was a coarse and compromised version of the U.N. Secretariat and Lever House. In the ground-level retail space at the north end of the building, Frank Lloyd Wright designed an automobile showroom for Maximilian Hoffman (see chapter 6).

The conversion of number 430 was so successful that a second apartment building, Cross & Cross's 405 Park Avenue (1915), on the northeast corner of Fifty-fourth Street, was converted into offices by the William Kaufman organization in association with Weiler and Swig.[21] The developers retained a little-known architect, Herbert Tannenbaum, whose design (1957) was a timid version of the Roths' 505 Park Avenue of a decade before.

The most imposing of the avenue's setback office buildings was 300 Park Avenue, the Colgate-Palmolive Building (1954–56), designed by Emery Roth & Sons for the Uris Brothers.[22] Occupying the block-long site of the former Sherry's Hotel (Warren & Wetmore, 1921), on the west side of the avenue between Forty-ninth and Fiftieth streets, and utilizing air rights leased from the New York Central Railroad, the 555,000-square-foot office building rose fourteen stories in a sheer cliff above Park Avenue before setting back to reach its ultimate height of twenty-five stories. Except for its red granite base, the Colgate-Palmolive Building was entirely sheathed in a curtain wall of aluminum and glass, with the spandrel panels painted a warm cream that complemented the buffs and yellows of the Waldorf-Astoria Hotel across the street. Inside, the office space was conventional, but it attracted a number of important tenants, including Kaiser Aluminum—which retained Welton Becket & Associates to design a suite of offices that would take full advantage of aluminum—and Knoll Associates, manufacturers of high-style Modernist furniture, who set up showrooms there.

Roth quickly followed 300 Park with another step-back design—this time for the Fisher brothers—a few blocks up the street at 400 Park Avenue (1955–58), occupying the northwest corner of Fifty-fourth Street, where it overlooked Lever House.[23] The twenty-one-story, 210,000-square-foot office building replaced an apartment house designed by Warren & Wetmore that had been the first in the city to have a central air-conditioning system when it was remodeled by Walker & Gillette in 1936.[24] Above its one-story granite base, 400 Park Avenue was sheathed in a glass-and-aluminum curtain wall. Next door, at 410 Park Avenue, the Roths erected a quite similar building (1957–59) for Francis J. Kleban, replacing Julius Harder's 1914 superluxurious apartment house.[25] The principal interest of the new building lay not in the curtain wall designed by the Roths but in the subtle changes effected on it by Skidmore, Owings & Merrill, who modified it to suit an important tenant, the Chase Manhattan Bank. The bank's interiors, with the principal banking hall raised to the second floor to form a piano nobile, were a distinguished suite of minimalist spaces embellished with high-quality art.

Some setback buildings occupying blockfront sites were big enough to support towers that, in accordance with zoning, could rise to unlimited height provided they occupied no more than 25 percent of the site area. The first of the tower-on-base office buildings on Park Avenue was Kahn & Jacobs's crudely detailed, 500,000-square-foot building at 425 Park Avenue (1954–57).[26] The new building, which occupied the entire east blockfront from Fifty-fifth to Fifty-sixth Street, replaced the oldest blockfront improvement on the avenue's midtown stretch, a row of brownstones that had been renovated by Casale & Witt in 1920.[27] Taking the exact opposite tack to their Universal Pictures Building of ten years before, which sat on the next block, Kahn & Jacobs designed an insistently vertical curtain wall, vaguely reminiscent of Raymond Hood's Daily News Building but with the white-glazed brick confined to thin piers and with enameled-glass spandrel panels.[28] Filling up the building envelope as a sheer block for twelve stories, the building stepped back twice before reaching the twenty-first floor, where a ten-story tower rose free.

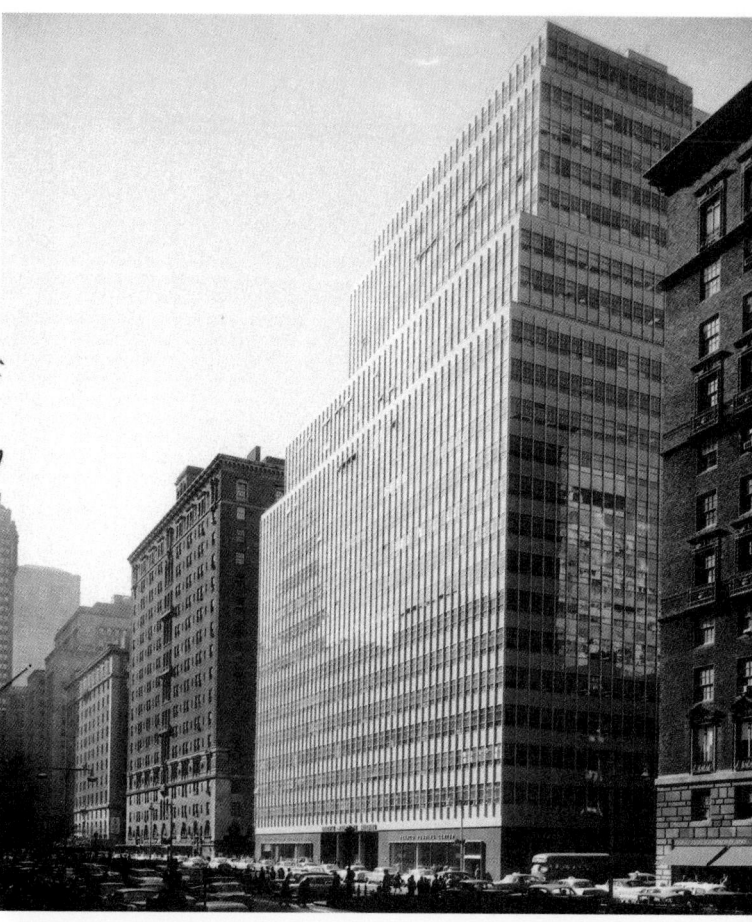

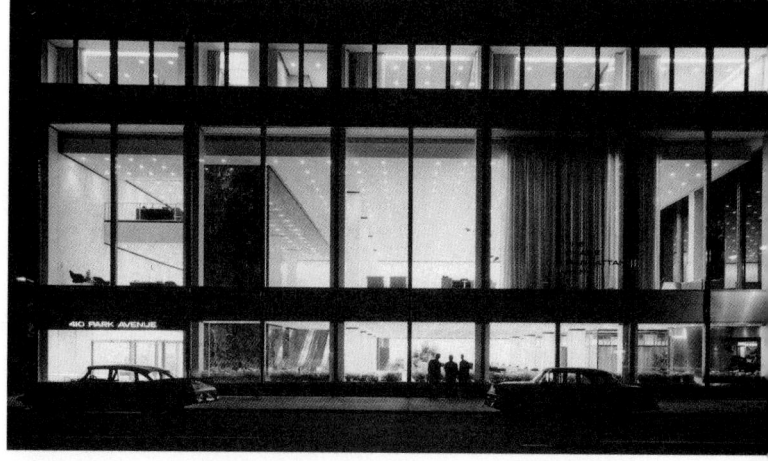

Top left: 430 Park Avenue, East Fifty-fifth to East Fifty-sixth Street. Warren & Wetmore, 1916. View to the southwest. Studly. ERS

Bottom left: 430 Park Avenue. Renovation, Emery Roth & Sons, 1954. View to the southwest. ERS

Top: Colgate-Palmolive Building, 300 Park Avenue, East Forty-ninth to East Fiftieth Street. Emery Roth & Sons, 1954–56. View to the southeast. Gottscho-Schleisner. LOC

Bottom: 410 Park Avenue, southwest corner of East Fifty-fifth Street. Emery Roth & Sons, 1957–59. View to the west showing Chase Manhattan Bank (Skidmore, Owings & Merrill, 1959). Stoller. ©ESTO

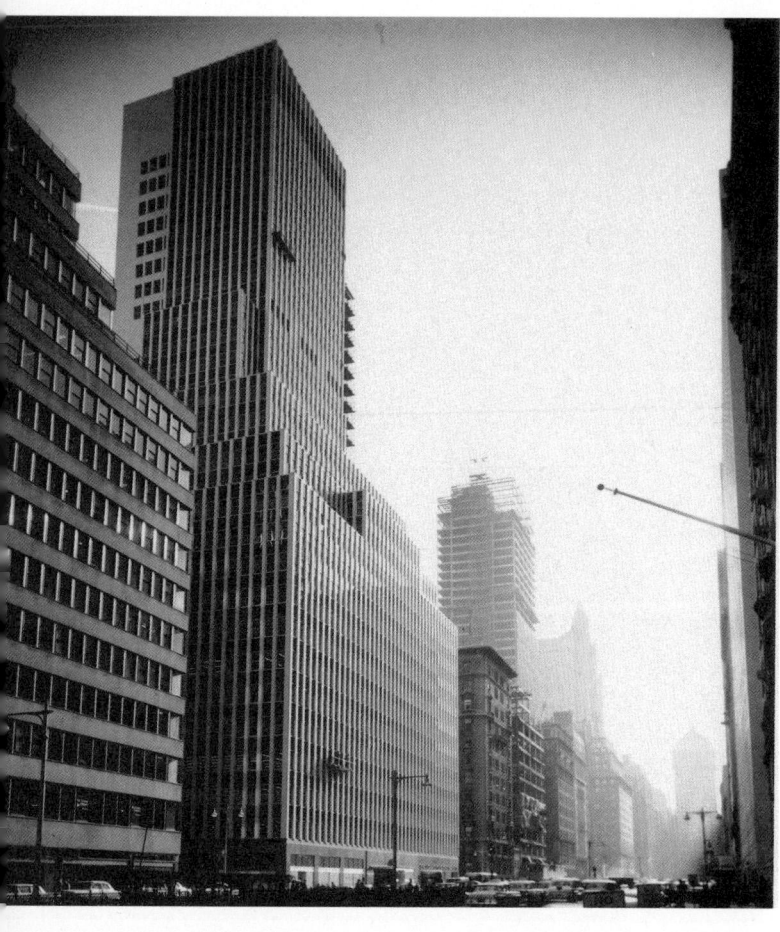

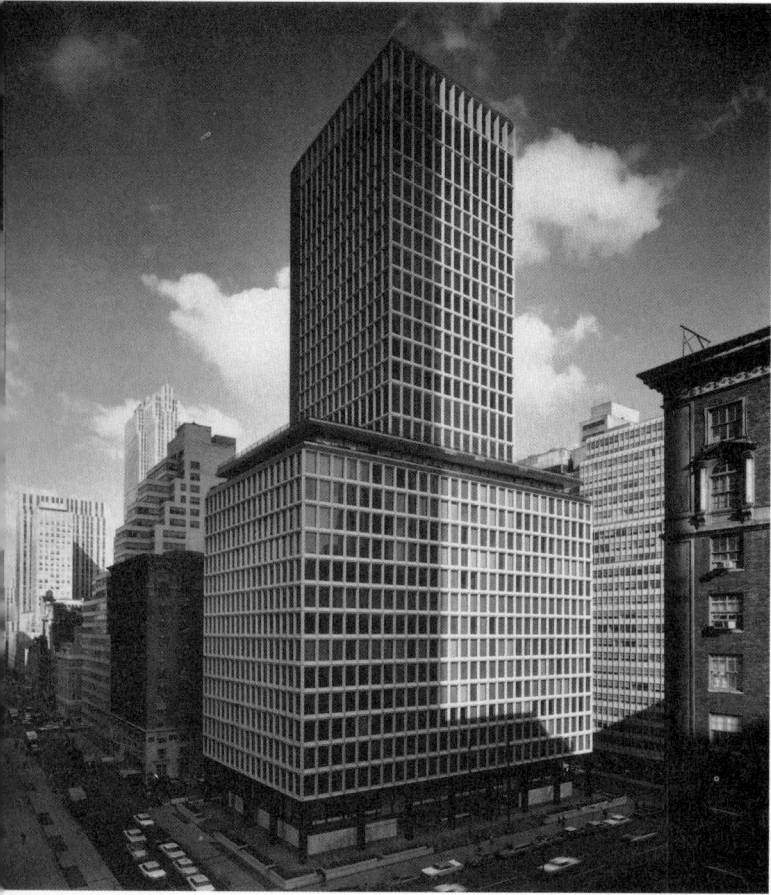

The Roth firm pursued a similar arrangement for the Uris Brothers at 350 Park (1958–62), on the west side of the avenue between Fifty-first and Fifty-second streets, a thirty-story, 400,000-square-foot building that replaced Warren & Wetmore's 1915 apartment building, 340–350 Park Avenue.[29] At the same time, the Roths, again working for the Urises, replaced another apartment building by Warren & Wetmore (320–330 Park Avenue, 1916), on the west blockfront from Fiftieth to Fifty-first Street, with a tower-on-base design that rose thirty-four floors.[30]

The last tower-on-base office building to be built on Park Avenue and the most diagrammatically pure exemplar, with only one major setback at the sixteenth floor, was the Bankers Trust Company Building, at 280 Park Avenue.[31] The building was designed in 1960–62 by Henry Dreyfuss, the industrial designer, in collaboration with Emery Roth & Sons, who were the architects, and Shreve, Lamb & Harmon, who were the interior architects. Following the lead of First National City Bank, Bankers Trust was establishing an important administrative presence in midtown while maintaining central offices in a headquarters building on Wall Street. The thirty-story, 412-foot-tall, 400,000-square-foot building, which replaced Warren & Wetmore's seventeen-story apartment house (1921),[32] occupied a comparatively small, 125-foot-deep blockfront site on the west side of the avenue between Forty-eighth and Forty-ninth streets. The Hotel Chatham (Warren & Wetmore, 1917), occupying the parcel to the west of the site, was held for future expansion, which took place in 1965.[33] In order to give the building a unique presence on the avenue, and to break with the thin-skinned glass-and-metal curtain-wall aesthetic of the previous decade, which was coming under severe criticism from the press and the public, Dreyfuss adopted a system of precast-concrete frames surrounding six-by-twelve-foot, floor-to-ceiling windows.

The Bankers Trust site, sitting above two levels of railroad tracks, presented unusual problems: in order not to block the tracks, elevator pits had to be at ground level. As a result, the principal lobby was located on the second floor, where it was accessible from the street by escalators. Influenced by Mies van der Rohe's Seagram tower as much as by the need to clear the railroad tracks below, the building was raised on a three-foot-high podium that formed a not very clearly articulated plaza wrapping around the building, which was set back from the street on three sides. The lobbies were set behind a double-height colonnade, also suggestive of Seagram's, although the use of granite and light buff precast panels was surely not.

With its sixteen-floor base surmounted by a nearly equal fourteen-floor tower, the design came out of an elemental approach that eschewed the smoother transitions of its wedding-cake predecessors, which, in amassing as much space as possible within the constraints imposed by zoning, had achieved a certain compositional fluidity. In its massing as well as its overall design Bankers Trust seemed to be making a statement; yet, as Ada Louise Huxtable observed, the building was actually "more conservative than trend-setting." She did, however, feel the design raised several important issues: "its bland, competent consistency raises pertinent and challenging questions of architecture as an industrial product, and the role of the non-architect in building design."[34]

Built under the old zoning but in effect a base without a tower, Skidmore, Owings & Merrill's Pepsi-Cola Building (1956–60), at 500 Park Avenue, was ambiguous in its urbanism but quite distinguished in its aesthetics.[35] Located at the south-

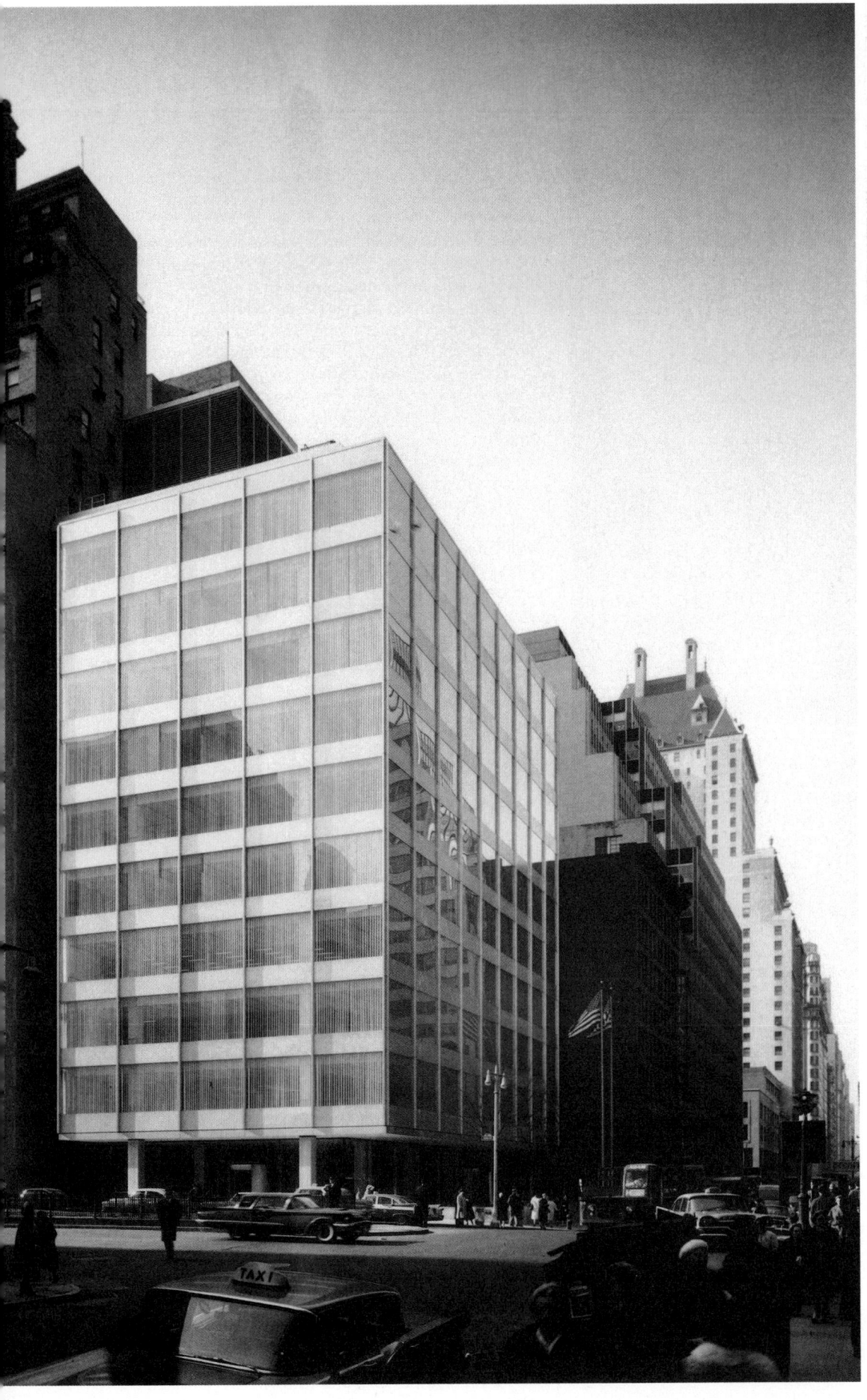

Top far left: 425 Park Avenue, East Fifty-fifth to East Fifty-sixth Street. Kahn & Jacobs, 1954–57. View to the southeast. Gottscho-Schleisner. LOC

Bottom far left: Bankers Trust Company Building, 280 Park Avenue, East Forty-eighth to East Forty-ninth Street. Henry Dreyfuss in collaboration with Emery Roth & Sons; Shreve, Lamb & Harmon, interior architects, 1960–62. View to the northwest. Stoller. ©ESTO

Left: Pepsi-Cola Building, 500 Park Avenue, southwest corner of East Fifty-ninth Street. Skidmore, Owings & Merrill, 1956–60. View to the southwest. Stoller. ©ESTO

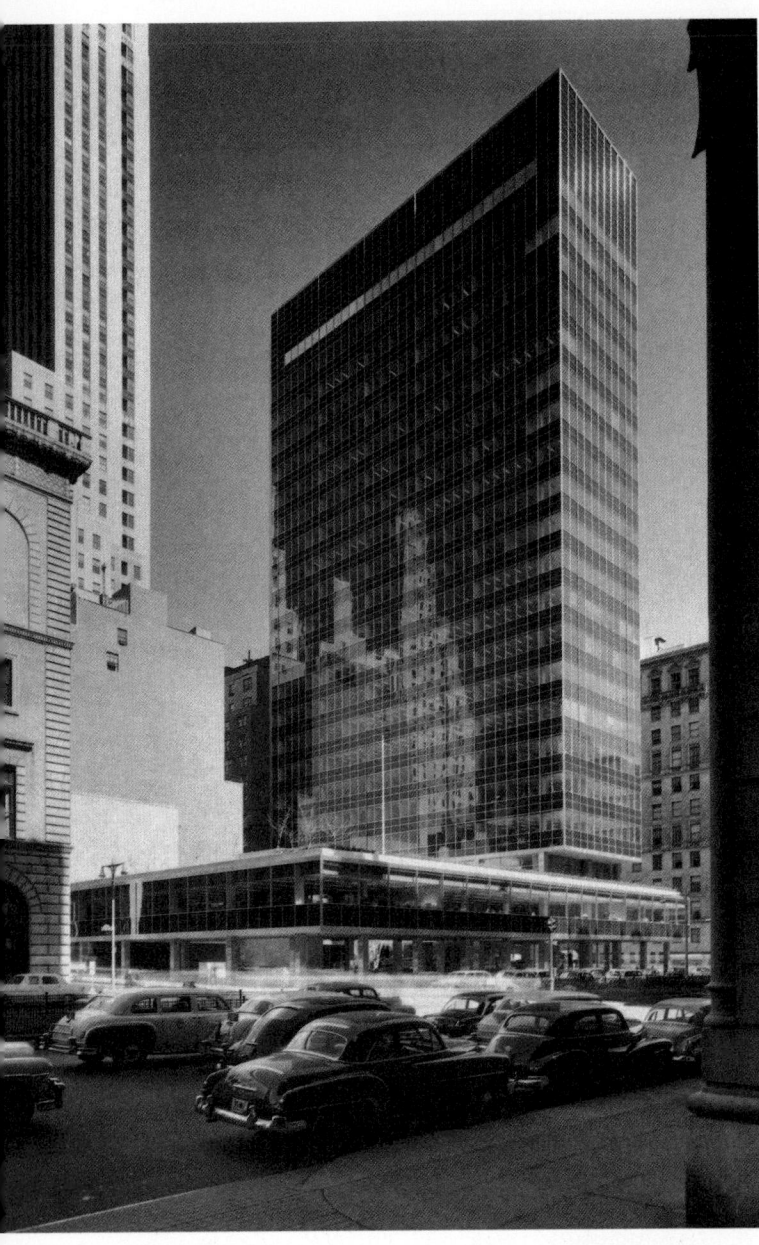

Lever House, 390 Park Avenue, East Fifty-third to East fifty-fourth Street. Skidmore, Owings & Merrill, 1952. View to the northwest. Stoller. ©ESTO

west corner of Fifty-ninth Street, it replaced the building designed by Napoleon Le Brun that had served as the headquarters of the Board of Education between 1893 and 1940. Though its base-mass was similar to that of typical prewar buildings, the eleven-story, 120,000-square-foot structure with a curtain wall of matte-finished aluminum and glass was detailed to appear as towerlike as possible, set off from its immediate neighbors by an L-shaped, black-granite-clad recessed service core that formed shadowy notches. The towerlike effect was reinforced by recessing the lobby and creating setbacks along Fifty-ninth Street. Because the 100-by-125-foot site sloped down to the west, the building plaza took on the character of a podium, furthering the illusion of a stand-alone tower set on a base.

Pepsi-Cola's design was marked by simplicity, both inside and outside. The bare lobby, intended to be used as an exhibition hall, and the office floors above epitomized the anonymous corporate design typical of the era. On the eleventh floor, a sparely detailed boardroom was presided over by the actress Joan Crawford, the widow of Pepsi-Cola chairman Alfred Steele, playing in real life a role she excelled at in the movies: tough corporate executive.[36] The building's curtain wall was notable for its elegance: with alternating horizontal bands of glass and metal that seemed to be pinned in place by thin vertical mullions, it was pure and crisply detailed, the quintessential essay in reductionism. The curtain wall was also technically innovative, with half-inch-thick, nine-by-thirteen-foot polished-plate-glass windows, the largest panes then available, set within a silver-anodized aluminum frame to create a powerful impression of transparency and weightlessness. This was particularly true at night, when the building, lit from within, positively glowed. The proportions of the structural bay and the cladding were beautifully scaled. What could have been diagrammatic and banal in the hands of lesser designers was here masterful. Twenty-one years after its completion Ada Louise Huxtable praised the building as "a kind of Pazzi Chapel of corporate design."[37]

Lever House

On April 29, 1950, a new era in the relationship between commercial enterprise and architectural expression was inaugurated when the Lever Brothers Company, a large multinational corporation famous for its soap products, made public its plans to build a headquarters building on a blockfront site on the east side of Park Avenue between Fifty-third and Fifty-fourth streets.[38] The one-story taxpayer structure that had been built on the site by Robert Goelet twelve years before (see above) was demolished to make way for the new twenty-one-story, 302-foot-high, 280,000-square-foot building, which would house 1,200 employees and consolidate company operations in New York as well as bringing jobs to the city from such locations as Cambridge, Massachusetts, and Chicago. Lever House was a remarkable oddity among skyscrapers in that the owner wanted only to house the company's staff, choosing not to build excess space to let out to tenants. It was a corporate headquarters pure and simple. In addition to approximately 150,000 square feet of office space, the building included an employees' dining room, an auditorium and an underground garage for fifty-five cars.

The design of Lever House announced the transformation of the aesthetics of American corporate architecture. With the building's completion the thirty-year-old utopistic ideas of Mies van der Rohe and Le Corbusier were at last realized at full scale. No longer an art of solid and void, of mass displacing and defining space, architecture was now a play of light and shadow on glass, an art of literal transparency and surface reflectivity. The construction of Lever House marked not only the fulfillment of an architectural but also an urbanistic vision: with the building slab lifted on a base and turned at a right angle to the grand axis of Park Avenue, the traditional street—the *rue corridor* so loathed by Le Corbusier—was no longer an exalted standard. The old order of the ensemble was replaced by a new urban order of individual, objectlike buildings "liberated" in space and set apart from one another.

In the mid-1940s Nathaniel Owings, of the firm Skidmore, Owings & Merrill (SOM), had prepared for Lever's management a sketch model of a slablike scheme for a site opposite Chicago's Drake Hotel; and in 1949 SOM's Charles D. Wiley had prepared a design for a downtown Chicago site that consisted of a slab on pilotis locked into a low mezzanine that wrapped around a small open-air courtyard. But Lever Brothers decided to build their headquarters in New York rather than Chicago because, as a company representative stated, "The price one pays for soap is 89 percent advertising . . . and the advertising agencies of America were there."[39]

At the time Lever Brothers undertook to build its headquarters, Charles Luckman, an architect who during the 1930s had practiced with some distinction in the Midwest as partner of William Pereira, was president of the company. Later, when the new building was being completed, Luckman left the company to return to architectural practice, giving rise to the false impression that he had been fired from his job because of the building's startling design.[40] Jervis J. Babb, an executive at Lever Brothers and eventually Luckman's successor, was sympathetic to the project and played an important role in its development. Babb had been indoctrinated to Modernist architecture while serving as vice president of the S. C. Johnson Company in Racine, Wisconsin, whose headquarters were designed by Frank Lloyd Wright.

SOM's design effort was led by Gordon Bunshaft, who had become a partner in the firm in 1949. At Lever House, Bunshaft created a dynamic composition of horizontal and vertical planes that expressed, as one writer pointed out when the building was still a project, "the striving of all modern architects to make visible pure geometric shapes so unlike earlier skyscrapers with their street-to-street mass and their ziggurat-like setbacks."[41] The horizontal element was a one-story-high slab containing 22,000 square feet of space—used for mail and stock rooms, offices and business machines—raised one story above the street on columns and punctured to create a courtyard. The vertical element, an eighteen-story slab with 8,700 square feet of office space on each floor, was set perpendicular to the avenue, and seemed to float above it because of a deep shadow recess at the third floor, where the cafeteria overlooked a landscaped roof terrace. The elevators were located at the west end of the tower where they could link up with a future tower should the company decide to expand its operations. Both horizontal and vertical elements were entirely sheathed in blue-green glass; unlike the United Nations Secretariat, whose north and south facades were solid, all of Lever House's exposed surfaces were wrapped in glass. At night, Lever House appeared to be at once an illuminated jewel and a transparent cage, an extraordinary effect against the solidity of traditional Park Avenue.

Had the site been developed in a conventional fashion, it could have supported a much bigger building: as built, Lever House was equal only to an eight-story building covering the entire site. The proportions of the slender, fifty-three-foot-wide slab

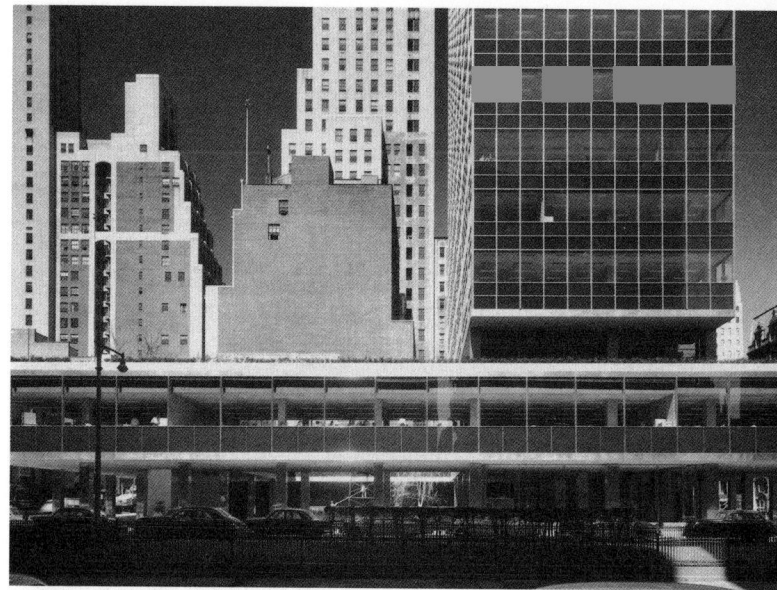

Top: Lever House. View to the west from Park Avenue. Stoller. ©ESTO

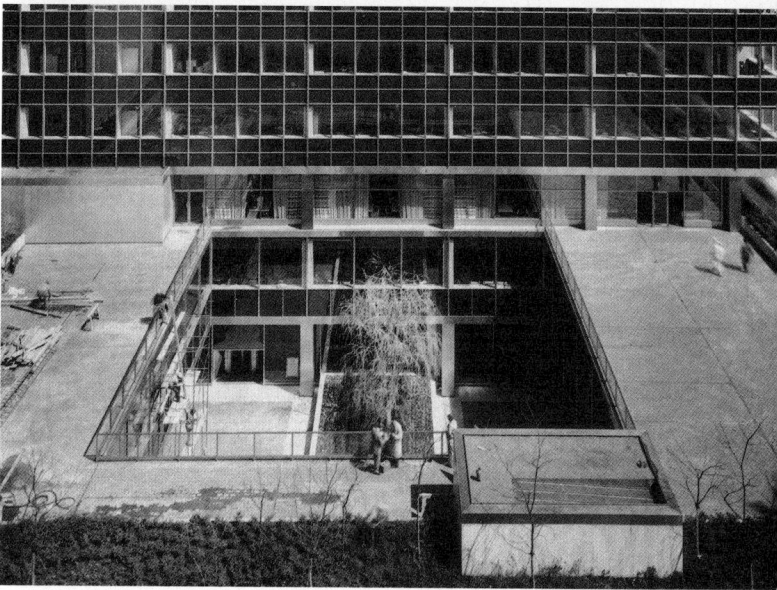

Bottom: Lever House. View to the north of interior courtyard. Stoller. ©ESTO

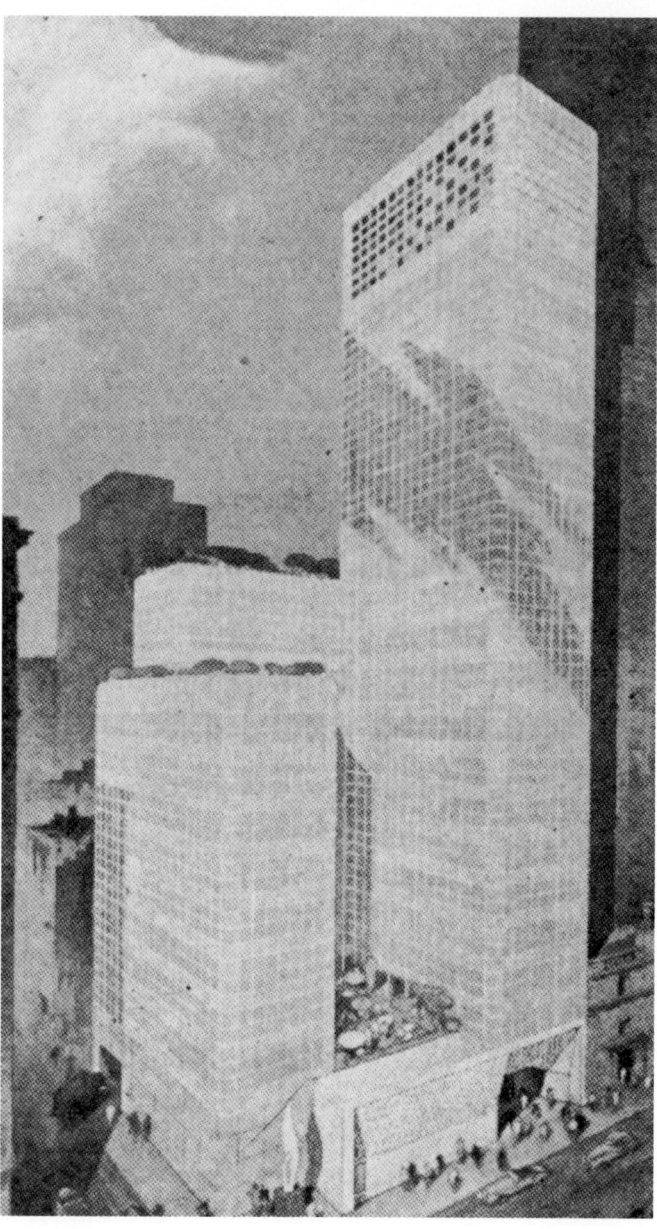

Proposed Alcoa Building, southeast corner of Park Avenue and East Fifty-eighth Street. Harrison, Abramovitz & Wiggins, 1946. View to the southeast. AR. CU

took advantage of the provision in the zoning ordinance which stipulated that a tower of unlimited height could be built without setbacks provided the footprint of the tower occupied no more than one quarter of the site's area at the tower's base. The relatively small size of the tower floors was, of course, incomparably more humane for the workers, who had great access to light and views. Even though the tower was to be completely air conditioned, its plan met the standards of office planning developed by Rockefeller Center in the era before air conditioning, wherein every desk was to be located no more than twenty-five feet from a window. This was in sharp contrast to postwar trends. As *Architectural Forum* explained when the design of Lever House was released:

> With space-starved tenants ready to pay $5 a ft. for offices 90 ft. deep, why worry whether the deepest areas were really worth building and paying their way? . . . Overnight New York forgot the vision given substance by Rockefeller Center. . . . Promoters bade their architects fill every inch of the city's lopsided zoning envelope in typical pre-Rockefeller Center fashion. . . . Now at last [with Lever House] New York is getting a fine office building that carries on from Rockefeller Center, a tower built on pride and the desire to build a name rather than the chance for a quick profit.[42]

Several aspects of Bunshaft's design for Lever House had precedents in previous buildings. Lever was not, for instance, the first postwar proposal for a building that would break dramatically with the street wall on Park Avenue. In 1946 Harrison, Abramovitz & Wiggins proposed for the Alcoa company a complexly massed stepped slab office building to occupy the southeast corner of Park Avenue and Fifty-eighth Street, where it would replace a fourteen-story apartment house, 471 Park Avenue, designed by Charles W. Buckham in 1908.[43] The design called for three slablike elements, of different heights, combined to form a U-shaped structure that enclosed a second-level open-air terrace facing Park Avenue. Instead of allowing for the usual street-level shops, the Alcoa company intended to treat the ground floor as a "display hall" to promote its products. The Alcoa Building was not realized, and in 1958 the frame of the original apartment house was stripped of its facades by Charles N. and Selig Whinston and reskinned in white brick.[44] The basic organization of Lever House, with its thin slab on a massive base, was also presaged by an earlier building, Howe & Lescaze's Philadelphia Saving Fund Society Building of 1932.[45] But whereas at PSFS the columns were located at the outside edge of the slab to create a contrast between vertical support and horizontal spatial enclosure, at Lever the columns were pulled into the building mass to create the opportunity for a sheer curtain wall of glass.

The decision to keep the ground floor of Lever House open was carefully considered in architectural and public relations terms. When asked about this decision by a writer from the *New Yorker*, a Lever Brothers spokesman stated that "The trees and flowers were more important than any quick return on some shops." He did add, however: "The fact is shops don't rent for much on Park Avenue. People buy on Fifth or Madison. All they do on Park is walk."[46] Not only was the ground floor largely reserved for public use—even the glassed-in lobby was to function as an exhibition hall during building hours—but the planted rooftop of the horizontal slab was also to be a recreational and visual amenity for the building's workers, in the manner of Rockefeller Center.

Taking advantage of year-round air conditioning, the building's windows were fixed to save on installation as well as on energy costs. The use of so much fixed glass presented one problem that fascinated the press: how the windows would be washed. After six months' study, Kenneth M. Young of the SOM staff designed exterior gondolalike rigs that moved up and down the facade on cables suspended from the roof and were shifted around the tower's perimeter on a system of rails. Two men would be employed full-time to wash the windows, utilizing this system, which would become a standard feature of curtain-wall buildings. Even Lewis Mumford could not resist extolling the ingenuity of the window-washing machine and the public relations value of an all-glass building: "For a company whose main products are soap and detergents, that little handicap of the sealed windows is a heaven-sent opportunity, for what could better dramatize its business than a squad of cleaners operating in their chariot, like the *deus ex machina* of Greek tragedy, and capturing the eye of the passerby as they performed their daily duties? This perfect bit of symbolism alone almost justifies the all glass facade."[47]

Particular attention was also paid to the building's interiors, which were designed by Raymond Loewy. A Lever Brothers spokesman claimed that one of the objectives in the interior design was to create spaces "women would enjoy working in," since most of the employees in the headquarters building were female. Although, according to the spokesman, the women were "crazy about" the interior design,[48] the New York Times art critic Aline B. Louchheim was less than enthusiastic. Relating Loewy's interiors to his long association with the Lever company as a packaging design consultant, she found the spaces too colorful and too visually cluttered. "I question such details as desk chairs with two aluminum legs and two wood legs," she wrote, "the chi-chi bent pipe divisions in the cafeteria and its animated patterned floor." Most of all she was dismayed by the lavish executive offices and boardrooms on the twenty-first floor, which she described as "esthetically vulgar" examples of "conspicuous consumption."[49]

Despite the building's seeming profligacy with usable space and its expensive detailing, the business community was quick to embrace Lever House as an appropriate expression of self. *Business Week* praised it as "spacious, efficient, and washable," a building that had "gone a long way toward making a work of art out of office space."[50] Architectural critics and pundits were slower to accept it. Lewis Mumford described it as "more package than Pyramid . . . curiously transitory and ephemeral."[51] Frank Lloyd Wright, in a lecture delivered before the American Institute of Architects in 1952, castigated it as a "box on sticks."[52] In his March 1, 1952, radio broadcast over the CBS network, Edward P. Morgan, taking issue with an article in *Fortune* that had praised the building as "a monument to American architectural enterprise,"[53] called the design simpleminded, telling his audience that some observers would "contend that a 10-year old boy could have done better with a Mechano set."[54]

Although Aline Louchheim criticized the interiors of Lever House, she was impressed with the structure itself: "Standing luxuriously in space and sparkling like some sea-colored jewel, it is our one building which takes full esthetic as well as practical advantage of modern means of construction." She admired the building for the clarity of its design and detail: "There are no decorative clichés, such as the aluminum waffle irons which mask mechanical devices at the U.N." Louchheim found the building's scale "legible" and the handling of the glass wall "neither monotonous or slick." Most significantly, she recognized that for all the talk of new construction techniques and the role

of structure as a determinant of contemporary architectural form, what made Lever House remarkable was its "'coloristic' and poetic" qualities. "What saves these effects from being contrived, merely picturesque, or anti-architectural," Louchheim said, "is the fact that we know and can always see (when we consciously or subconsciously seek that reassurance) that they are logically dependent upon the structural scheme of the building, visual effects neither denying, contradicting nor confusing the constructive facts."[55]

One aspect of the building, however, seemed to disappoint virtually everyone: the handling of the "liberated" ground-floor space. Although, as *Architectural Record* pointed out, SOM considered the gesture "an answer to city planning problems,"[56] Louchheim felt that it left much to be desired: "There seems to be a need for some arresting element to give the spatial area human as well as architectural meaning."[57] She particularly lamented the absence of the garden that had initially been designed by Isamu Noguchi and shown on the early models, which would have provided naturalistic shapes to relieve the structural rectilinearity. The architect Frederick Woodbridge was also troubled by the open space at street level: "The 'noble' sacrifice (presumably offset by public relations value) of rentable area seems to fall flat. All the open spaces and even the court with its little garden seems lifeless. What a difference it would make if there were a small cafe, a florist, a jeweller's shop or a smart modiste to give gaiety and animation to this little 'galleria.'"[58]

Vincent Scully's disapproval of Lever House was extreme. Putting aside issues of style and detail, he concentrated on the profound effect the building had on the character of Park Avenue as a great urban street. In his previously mentioned Architectural League speech of 1961, Scully unleashed a reaction against it that would become the dominant assessment of the building from that time on. The process of Park Avenue's death as a coherent street, Scully said, began with Lever House:

> Lever's attempted to acknowledge the Avenue's direction with its first two floors, which were themselves almost as high as the building it replaced. But in turning its tower and leaving much of its defined air-space free, it cut a hole in the wall that defined the Avenue. Instead of being trapped by a facade which wholly respected the street . . . the eye was . . . led out of the Avenue above the second floor to fall upon the undesigned walls of the buildings on the cross streets to the west. So Lever's broke up the street by breaking its facade, and, in so doing, questioned the validity of the concept of the street facade. It is true that, seen against the incoherent masses westward or against the older solid buildings to the north, Lever's was an elegant, pristine object, and might have been considered a special adornment to the Avenue, the breaking of whose continuity might thus have been condoned. But when the building to the north of it was reclad in a glass and plastic skin imitating Lever's, it became apparent that Lever's itself owed everything to the preexisting civility of the street. No longer seen against the contrasting solid backdrop which the older buildings had made, Lever's cool cube instantly lost something of its elegance and most of its point.[59]

Notwithstanding what many came to view as its fundamental anti-urbanism, Lever House was a triumph of Modernist aesthetics, setting a standard for postwar corporate architecture. The English critic Reyner Banham assessed the impact of Lever House in 1962, just when the formal and urbanistic ideals it represented were beginning to be widely challenged: "It gave architectural expression to an age just as the age was being born, and while the age lasted, or its standards persisted, Lever House

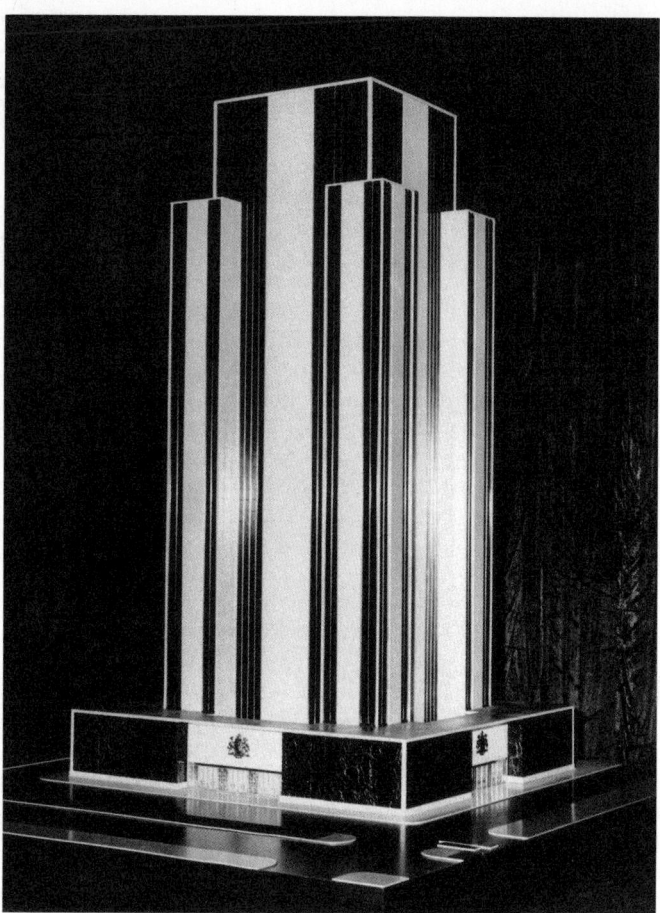

Above: Proposed Seagram Building, 375 Park Avenue, East Fifty-second to East Fifty-third Street. Pereira & Luckman, 1954. Model. View to the southeast. JES

Right: Seagram Building, 375 Park Avenue, East Fifty-second to East Fifty-third Street. Ludwig Mies van der Rohe, Philip Johnson and Kahn & Jacobs, 1958. View to the southeast. Stoller. ©ESTO

was an uncontrollable success, imitated and sometimes understood all over the Americanized world, and one of the sights of New York."[60]

Seagram Building

In 1954 the distillers Joseph E. Seagram & Company, taking their lead from Lever Brothers, announced their intention to build a corporate headquarters on Park Avenue.[61] The company had acquired the east blockfront between Fifty-second and Fifty-third streets, a site diagonally opposite that of Lever House. It was occupied by Rouse & Goldstone's Montana apartment house of 1913 and a number of smaller buildings, including a nine-story apartment house at 116 East Fifty-third Street, also by Rouse & Goldstone, and two rowhouses on Fifty-second Street.[62] One of the Montana's principal tenants was the notable restaurant Voisin, which was located on the Fifty-third Street side and, according to a spokesman for Seagram's, would be invited to occupy quarters in the new building. Seagram's hired the reconstituted firm of Pereira & Luckman to design the building, presumably because of Charles Luckman's role in the design of Lever House. They proposed a design consisting of a massive four-story base sheathed in marble, glass and bronze surmounted by a thirty-story vertically accented tower clad in glass and marble and visually buttressed at each corner by twenty-six-story square tourelles sheathed in the same combination of materials.

As a result of Lever House's success, Luckman was at the pinnacle of his fame and self-confidence. When asked by the *New Yorker* about his work on the project, he said: "Mr. Samuel Bronfman, president of the parent company in Canada, wanted us to do something memorable to celebrate the company's hundreth anniversary in 1957. I feel he has one of the finest minds I ever met, and coming from me, that's a compliment, because I have met some fine minds. He wants a building that will reflect character and integrity, and I think for a pretty good reason, because that's what Seagram's represents in the industry." In discussing his philosophy of architecture, Luckman said that he firmly believed it was "a business, and not an art." Luckman concluded the interview on a highly upbeat note: "I think we are adjusting our art to the realities of life. I've never had a better time. I am personally very happy to come back to Park Avenue for a repeat performance."[63]

But the Pereira & Luckman design was greeted with something less than universal enthusiasm. *Architectural Forum* said that it looked like an "enormous cigarette lighter" and that "others thought it resembled a big trophy."[64] But the most important critic of all, as it turned out, was Phyllis Bronfman Lambert, the twenty-seven-year-old daughter of Samuel Bronfman. Lambert was living in Paris when she saw a picture of the Luckman scheme in the international edition of the *Herald Tribune*. Recalling the incident in 1958, Lambert remembered "boiling with fury" over the mediocrity of the scheme. She wrote to her father that he should build a really fine building and that "he was lucky to be living in a period when there were great architects."[65] Samuel Bronfman listened to his daughter and authorized her to undertake a search for a new architect. To save embarrassment for all parties, Pereira & Luckman's scheme, which had been widely publicized as the accepted design, was now described as a preliminary model that had been prepared to pave the way for permits required to evict the tenants living on the site. But as Olga Gueft pointed out, regardless of the revised story, the newspapers implied that Pereira & Luckman "had been dumped overboard."[66]

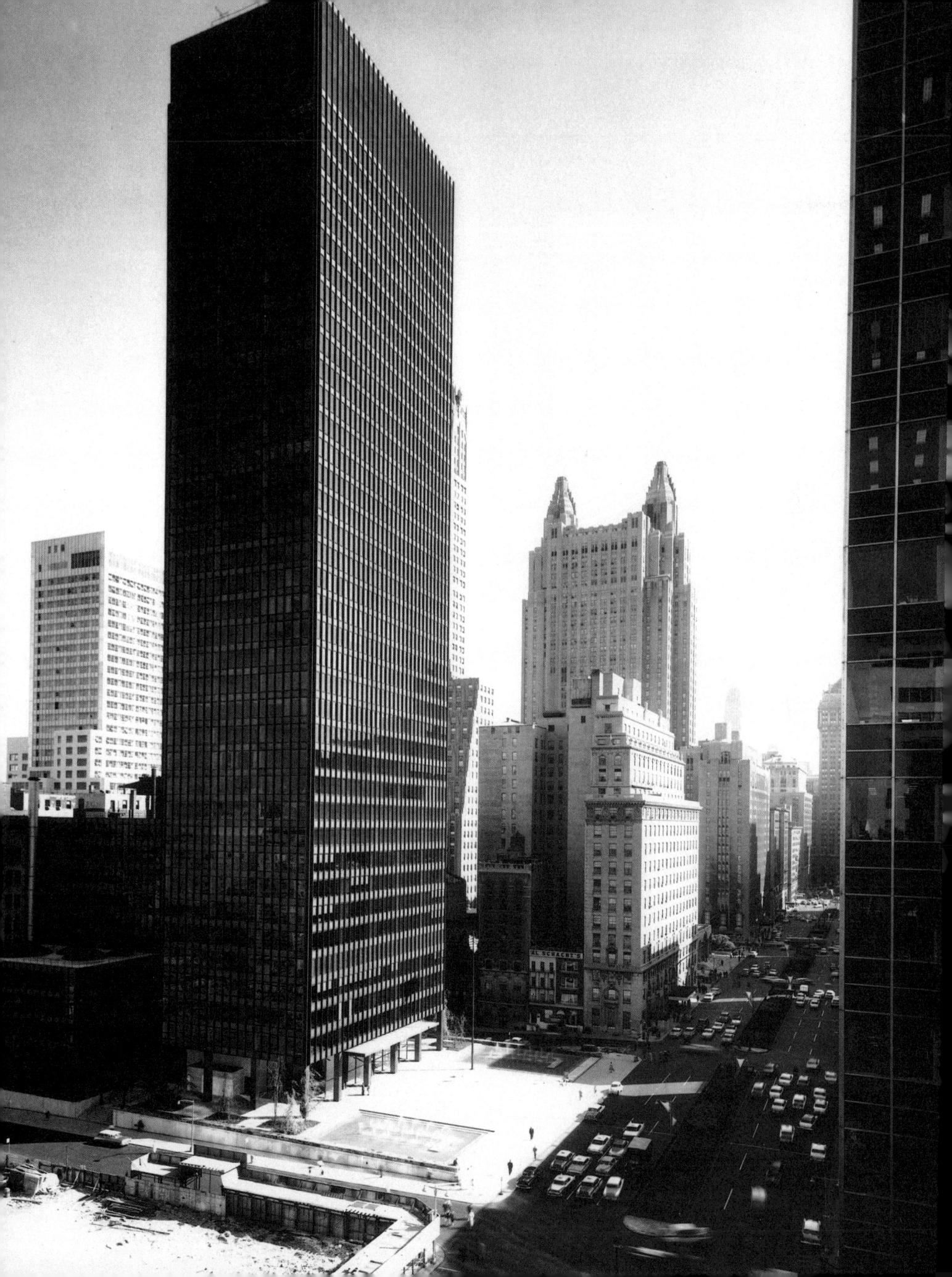

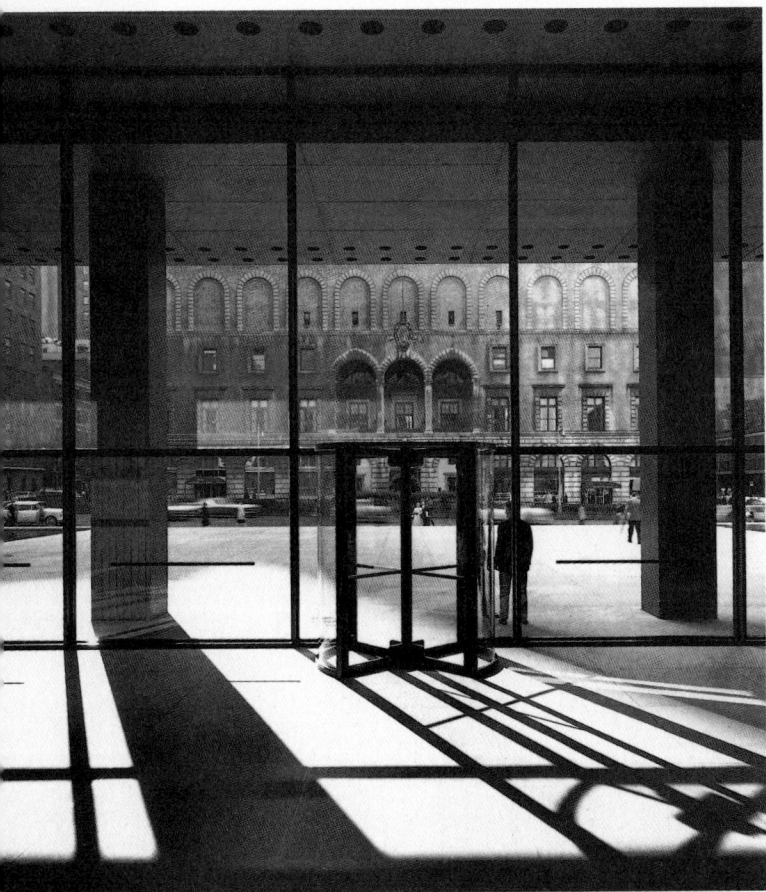

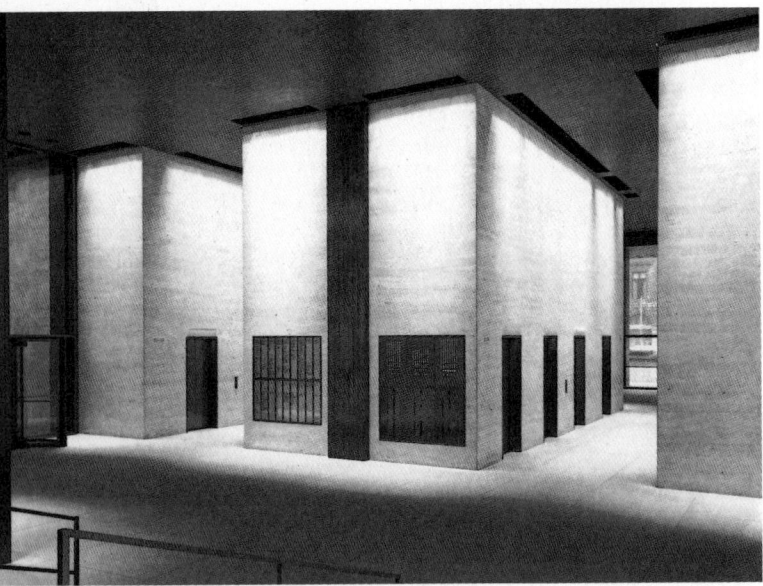

Top: Seagram Building, 375 Park Avenue, East Fifty-second to East Fifty-third Street. Ludwig Mies van der Rohe, Philip Johnson and Kahn & Jacobs, 1958. View to the west of the plaza from the lobby, showing the Racquet & Tennis Club (McKim, Mead & White, 1916). Stoller. ©ESTO

Bottom: Seagram Building. View to the northeast of lobby. Stoller. ©ESTO

In Lambert's search for an architect, she was introduced to Philip Johnson, then director of the Museum of Modern Art's Department of Architecture and Design. Taking Johnson's advice, she studied the work of leading Modernist figures of the day, including Walter Gropius, Marcel Breuer, George Howe, William Lescaze, Eero Saarinen, Louis Kahn, Minoru Yamasaki, I. M. Pei, Frank Lloyd Wright, Le Corbusier and Ludwig Mies van der Rohe. She interviewed a number of architects, and finally her search led to Mies van der Rohe, whom she had heard a lot about even before Johnson introduced them. In comparing Mies to some of the other architects she had considered, Lambert said:

> The younger men, the second generation, are talking in terms of Mies—or denying him. . . . They talk of new forms—articulating the skin or facades to get a play of light and shadow. But Mies has said: "Form is not the aim of our work, but only the result". . . . He has articulated the skin at the same time creating a play of depth and shadow by the use of the basic structural steel member, the I-beam. This ingenious and deceptively simple solution is comparable to the use of the Greek orders. . . . It is not a capricious solution; it is the essence of the problem of modern architecture that Mies stated in 1922: "We should develop the new forms for the very nature of the new problems."[67]

By late November 1954 the Pereira & Luckman scheme was a thing of the past and Mies van der Rohe had been retained to design the new House of Seagram.[68] The decision to hire Mies was not surprising, given his stature and renown, as well as the fact that Philip Johnson had been his leading American advocate for twenty-five years. Along with Mies, who was not licensed to practice architecture in New York State, Johnson was retained as co-architect and Kahn & Jacobs as associate architects. The choice of Mies as principal designer was widely applauded. In the lead sentence of her story in the *New York Times*, Aline B. Saarinen (who had been Aline B. Louchheim until her second marriage, to the architect Eero Saarinen) bubbled over: "New York is finally to have a skyscraper designed by one of the great leaders of modern architecture, Mies van der Rohe."[69]

Mies, ever laconic, explained his approach to the building's design in purely material and instrumental terms:

> My approach to the Seagram Building was no different from that of any other building I might build. My idea, or better, "direction," in which I go is toward a clear structure and construction—this applies not to any one problem but to all architectural problems which I approach. I am, in fact, completely opposed to the idea that a specific building should have an individual character. Rather I believe I should express a universal character which has been determined by the total problem which architecture must strive to solve. On the Seagram Building, since it was to be built in New York and since it was to be the first major office building which I was to build, I asked for two types of advice for the development of the plans. One, the best real estate advice as to the types of desirable rentable space and, two, professional advice regarding the New York City Building Code. With my direction established and with these advisers, it was then only a matter of hard work.[70]

Three weeks after the contracts with Mies and Johnson were signed, Mies was immersed in a study of the neighborhood. As Phyllis Lambert wrote to a friend:

> I can't wait to see what Mies comes up with for this building—he has a cardboard model made of Park Avenue between 46th and 57th streets with all the buildings on the Avenue and some going in the blocks and then he has a number of towers for dif-

ferent solutions that he places in the empty place of the old 375 and this model is up on a high table so that when he is sitting in a chair his eye is just level with the table top which equals the street—and for hours on end he peers down Park Avenue trying out the different towers.[71]

Mies wanted to avoid the setbacks that he felt compromised the design of the typical New York skyscraper, and he explored three schemes for freestanding towers: a square tower along the lines of the one Luckman had proposed; a rectangular one in a seven-to-three ratio, with the three-bay side parallel to Park Avenue, echoing the strategy of Lever House; and a five-by-three tower with the longer side parallel to Park Avenue, the direction he preferred. Lambert wrote enthusiastically about the third scheme: "This solution for the building has promise for terrific things—set back you hardly see it from the street coming up or down the Avenue . . . you don't know what is there and then you come upon IT—with a magnificent plaza and the building not zooming up in front of your nose so that you can't see it, only be oppressed by it and have to cross the street to really look at it, but a magnificent entrance to a magnificent building all in front of you."[72]

Despite Mies's reputation as a slow, deliberate designer, plans for the building were filed with the New York City Department of Buildings on March 29, 1955, just three months after his selection as architect, although the starting date for construction was uncertain because 20 of the 250 tenants who once occupied buildings on the site still remained in residence. The design was received with guarded enthusiasm by most commentators. A description of the scheme in Architectural Forum seemed slightly unsure of itself:

[It] proved to be a no-setback building but a building all set back, on a plaza stretching from 52nd St. to 53rd along the east side of New York's Park Ave.—a heady expenditure of dollar-laden ground area for an effect remarkably monumental. Like Lever House . . . the new squarish 38-story tower is to be clad in a restrained curtain wall of metal and glass, but the metal will likely be other than aluminum and steel (perhaps, like the model, brass) and the glass is certain to be all in color—but warm-toned, not blue. And the tower . . . will have the same panelized wall treatment all the way around, marble where not glazed.[73]

Architectural Forum was wrong in one respect: the model was made not of brass but of bronze. By late spring of 1955 the exact materials had been specified: the tower would be clad in bronze and topaz-tinted glass.

When the Seagram Building was formally opened on May 22, 1958, it was hailed in the artistic and popular press and praised by everyday New Yorkers as well. Mies's design was a profound bid to recapture, with the technology-inspired vocabulary of the International Style, the authority of the best skyscraper designs of the 1920s and early 1930s, to create a monumental corporate architecture out of the modular techniques of factory production. One significant element in creating this monumentality was the broad, half-acre plaza that resulted from the tower being set back ninety feet from Park Avenue. To the Seagram Company, the plaza was an expression of corporate power as well as a manifestation of their willingness to sacrifice short-term profits in return for long-term gains in prestige and good will. Probably a bid to rival the plaza that formed the forecourt of Raymond Hood's RCA Building, Mies's design, unlike Hood's, was not intended as a festive square but as a temenos, a sacred enclosure surrounding a holy place.[74] Its simplicity relieved only by two reflecting pools and a few trees, it was meant above all to be the exterior portion of the monumental entrance sequence, which continued in the equally austere lobby inside and culminated in the grandly broad shallow stairs leading up to the palatial Four Seasons restaurant at the rear. No benches were provided on the plaza, but New Yorkers soon found that the low, verd antique marble parapets that lined the side streets were suitable for sitting and ideal for sunbathing in good weather.

Mies had originally proposed sculpture for the plaza, suggesting complementary abstract sculptures flanking the central axis. But, unable to find a suitable artist who was interested in the problem, he and Johnson opted to have two reflecting pools with fountains instead, along with some trees (Karl Linn and Charles Middeleer consulted on the landscape design). Before the building was completed, the issue of the plaza sculptures was reopened when Picasso suggested placing his Bathers in the pools and Brancusi offered to enlarge his sculpture The Cock for the plaza, although neither was deemed appropriate. In 1964 Mies returned to the problem, considering the placement of Henry Moore's Reclining Figure on the plaza, a sculpture similar in mass and silhouette to the abstract forms the architect had drawn in early plans and sketches for the building. But after preparing large study drawings and mock-ups, both the architect and the sculptor rejected the idea. As Phyllis Lambert explained, Moore said that because the plaza was not particularly large, any sculpture placed there "would not be part of the plaza or the building" but would become "part of the environment to the north and south of the plaza." Moore felt that in this way the sculpture would be devalued and would detract from the quality of the plaza and the building. Mies reached the same conclusion, and was content with the fact that the plaza without sculpture was "a quiet serene space for people to be in or pass by in the busyness of New York."[75]

While some observers had misgivings about the austerity of the plaza design, others were critical of the tower because it was not pure enough. The thirty-eight-story slab was connected to a complexly massed lower building to the east that provided for more generously sized floors: the tower floors were 14,933 square feet each, but those at the base ranged from 31,955 square feet on floors two through four to 22,225 square feet on floors five through ten. Thus the Seagram Building was not the singular, simple pure tower shape Modernist architects had been calling for since Mies himself had proposed a glass skyscraper in 1919. In addition to providing large, lucrative office floors, the base visually screened out the undesigned rear elevation of the Central Branch of the Young Women's Christian Association (Donn Barber, 1920),[76] on the northwest corner of Lexington Avenue and Fifty-second Street, thereby integrating the new building into Manhattan's block pattern. Even the building's Park Avenue facade, a pure shaft, rigidly rectilinear, was criticized for its lack of purity. The architect Louis Kahn saw this rectilinearity as somewhat false: its failure to express the diagonal wind bracing, Kahn said, contradicted claims for the building's structural rationalism, making it like "a beautiful bronze lady in hidden corsets."[77] Even the compositional purity of the Park Avenue side was illusory, for the tower itself was also not "pure": its plan consisted of two parts, a five-by-three-bay principal section parallel to Park Avenue and a three-by-one-bay wing at the rear. Failing to understand the building's subtleties, some observers derided Seagram's as the "building with the bustle," but here, as in other aspects of the design, Mies separated himself from those of his followers who took his idea of purity to the level of oversimplification.

After the decision to leave half an acre of the site open as a plaza, the choice of bronze for the exterior cladding was the project's most unusual feature. The material, which had never before been used so extensively, was selected principally for its color, but also because it could be extruded with great precision to produce the crisp edges and high tolerances required for the exposed T-shaped mullions of the curtain wall. For the first time in curtain-wall design, the metal played a role as great as that of the glass, if not greater. Mies liked bronze, he said, because "it is a very noble material and lasts forever if used in the right way,"[78] a point elaborated on by William Jordy, who observed that Seagram's was "the first major metal-and-glass skyscraper consciously designed to age as masonry buildings age—an architectural property as appropriate for Seagram's whisky as sheen for Lever's soap."[79]

In his search for architectural essences—Mies was best known to the larger public for his aphorism "less is more"—he rethought every aspect of conventional skyscraper design. Not since Howe & Lescaze's pioneering Modernist skyscraper for the Philadelphia Saving Fund Society on Market Street in Philadelphia (1932) had the design of every aspect of a tall building been so carefully considered. Although money was lavished on the structure and its detailing—the Seagram Building cost twice as much as the typical office building of its time—it was not carelessly spent. The fifth-floor offices occupied by the top executives of the Seagram Company were elegantly appointed and largely furnished with Mies's classic furniture. But confined as they were to the nine-foot height of the typical tower floor they seemed rather modest, if not self-effacing, especially when compared with the spacious, brilliantly lit, twenty-four-foot-high lobby, with its travertine floor, travertine-clad walls and glass-tiled ceiling. All of the interior fittings were custom designed to complement the building's overall aesthetic: door handles, mail chutes, fire alarms, sink and toilet fittings. Much of the work involved in this enormous task was directed by Philip Johnson, who was as passionate as Mies in his pursuit of a perfected minimalism. As Henry-Russell Hitchcock wisecracked, "I've never seen more of less."[80] To which Phyllis Lambert added: "From the framing of the windows to the total building, love has gone into it—love for every detail."[81]

While the building was well received by the public and by the newspapers and newsmagazines, Lambert and the architects were nervous about Lewis Mumford's assessment because of his long-standing antipathy to aesthetic minimalism and high-density urbanism. But in his article, titled "The Lesson of the Master," Mumford disarmed the designers with high praise for the building. He began his essay: "There is a quick but accurate way of describing the new skyscraper office building at 375 Park Avenue. It is everything that most of the office buildings that have been going up in the midtown area in the last few years are not." At a time, Mumford said, when other contemporary architects continued to imitate "Mendelsohn's innovation of unbroken horizontal bands of wall and windows or van der Rohe's all-glass facade boxed by steel, van der Rohe himself has gone back to Louis Sullivan's concept of the skyscraper as a 'proud and soaring thing' and has designed one with unqualified emphasis on the vertical. . . . To make the departure even more unmodish, van der Rohe has also rejected the now standard thin, slab-shaped building."[82]

Mumford was quick to grasp the essential quality of Mies's window-wall design: "The faces of the building, instead of being an expression of the structure, are frankly and boldly a mask, designed to give pleasure to the eye and to complement, rather

than to reveal, the coarser structure form behind it. This is, after all, a logical treatment of the curtain wall, for the very nature of a curtain is to be detached from the structure, not to support it."[83] Confessing to initial skepticism about the use of bronze on the facade, Mumford explained that he had come to see it as an appropriate choice given the context: "If one accepts the fact that this is not just another business building but a singular monument, that its aloof, aristocratic qualities are not likely to be often repeated in a city where—to resort to that classic confession of the realty financier—'money does not look ahead more than five years,' this choice of dark bronze, meant to deepen in tone but not change, even under our heavy soot fall, is justified."[84]

Mumford also expressed admiration for the plaza, with its "human scale," and for the adjoining lobby: "The noble scale of the entrance is not just an outside pretense but an inside reality; again the clients showed themselves ready to sacrifice rentable space to achieve an esthetic effect that does more to set this building apart than the lavish murals or the most exuberant horticultural display. The serene effect of pure space itself . . . has once again been recaptured." But Mumford did object to the detailing of the plaza, beginning with the weeping beeches planted to the sides, which he described as being "closer to the spirit of Salvador Dali than to that of Mies van der Rohe." (The beeches did not do well in New York's air and were replaced with ginkoes in November of 1959.) He also objected to the absence of benches but pointed out that with the long marble parapet walls, the designers had unintentionally provided "a natural seat for those who would enjoy the play of water and air and green branches." The one "gross defect" Mumford found in the plaza design was the materials and execution of the pool and its fountains. Not only did he characterize the detailing of the stone, cement and mortar joints as slipshod; he described the pipes used to feed the fountains as "just so much raw plumbing. Where close contemplation demands perfect craftsmanship," he wrote, "such a failure becomes an esthetic enormity."[85]

But these were minor cavils, and Mumford's summation was extremely positive:

> What Mies van der Rohe has demonstrated in this building is how to do, with superb esthetic aplomb and with all but unerring taste, what his colleagues do coarsely and clumsily, in a spirit of tepid compromise with forces they have surrendered all too complaisantly in advance. For once, an outstanding human personality got the better of a system that places a premium upon self-effacing conformity and impersonality. . . . Taken with all its inherent limitations, this seems to me the best skyscraper New York has seen since Hood's Daily News Building; in classic execution it towers above the doubled height of the Empire State Building, while its nearest later rival, Lever House . . . looks curiously transitory and ephemeral when one turns from one to the other. Sombre, unsmiling, yet not grim, 375 is a muted masterpiece—but a masterpiece.[86]

Though the architecture of Seagram's continued to be held in high regard, the building's relation to its surroundings was viewed more critically. In a radio interview broadcast over WNYC (New York) on August 1, 1957, the English architect Sir Hugh Casson, after praising the Seagram plaza, voiced some reservations about Seagram's and other glass-faced buildings: "Very often you find if you look at a building like the new Lever House, for instance, or some of the new buildings around there, it's not always the case that you can see into it. What you see is a reflection of cars and sky and the buildings opposite it, which has its own attraction. But you could almost call it parasitic architecture, in that it lives by what it does for its neighbors. . . . [These buildings] depend very largely for their beauty on the contrast which they have with more permanent buildings."[87] One visitor from Chicago, in a 1959 letter to the editor of *Interiors*, raised some interesting points about the plaza that would also concern subsequent observers:

> The Seagram Building . . . is set so far back that if the trend continues a point of infinity will be reached. Buildings will be set further and further back until eventually New York becomes a great plain and all buildings will be in New Jersey. This of course would be a fitting memorial to Frank Lloyd Wright. . . . The idea that the open plaza enhances the building is not true in a city. In a city buildings should be jam-packed and cheek by jowl. There is plenty of open space in the country for people who want plazas.[88]

Vincent Scully was the first critic of stature to seriously and significantly qualify Mumford's extravagant praise for the project, and his criticism centered on the building's urbanistic effect. In discussing the transformation of Park Avenue, Scully described Seagram's relationship to the street:

> Seagram's could be set behind its own plaza, which opened on a decisive cross-axis. The building became a freestanding presence, while, by flattening its slab, it attempted to echo the Avenue's north-south direction. But Seagram's, too, owed much to pre-existing structures, that is to say, if visual chaos rather than the arches of the Racquet Club had been mirrored in its entrance doors, it would have been a much less successful building itself. . . . Seagram's . . . was conceived as a freestanding monument on its own, an aggressive statement of the special talent of its architects, dependent upon the pre-existing civil design of the Avenue but taking a step toward its destruction.[89]

By the early 1970s what had initially been admired as aloof perfection began to be seen as disconnected, antiurban, even antisocial. In their interpretative history, *Modern Architecture*, first published in 1976, the Italian historians and critics Manfredo Tafuri and Francesco Dal Co wrote:

> Here the absoluteness of the object is total. The maximum of formal structurality is matched by the maximum absence of images. The *language of absence* is projected on an ulterior "void" that mirrors the first void and causes it to resonate: the small plaza paved in travertine that separates the skyscraper from Park Avenue contains two symmetrical fountains. This is no place for repose or contemplation: Mies said that the two basins should be filled right up to their brims to prevent the public from sitting on their edges. The plaza is intended to be the planimetric inversion of the significance of the skyscraper: two voids answering each other and speaking the language of the nil, of the silence which—by a paradox worthy of Kafka— assaults the noise of the metropolis. The double "absent structure" stands aloof from the city in the very act of exposing itself to it.[90]

Counteracting such critics, Lambert argued that "the wonderful living quality about the Seagram plaza is that it changes all the time": "It looks wonderful when it is empty, then it changes as people go in and out of the building or just wander on the plaza. . . . Because of its intimate size the trees, the pools, the fountains and other people make a living environment and relate directly to the building, nothing is needed to make a transition."[91] From time to time the Seagram management did make the plaza available for temporary displays of sculpture. In 1965

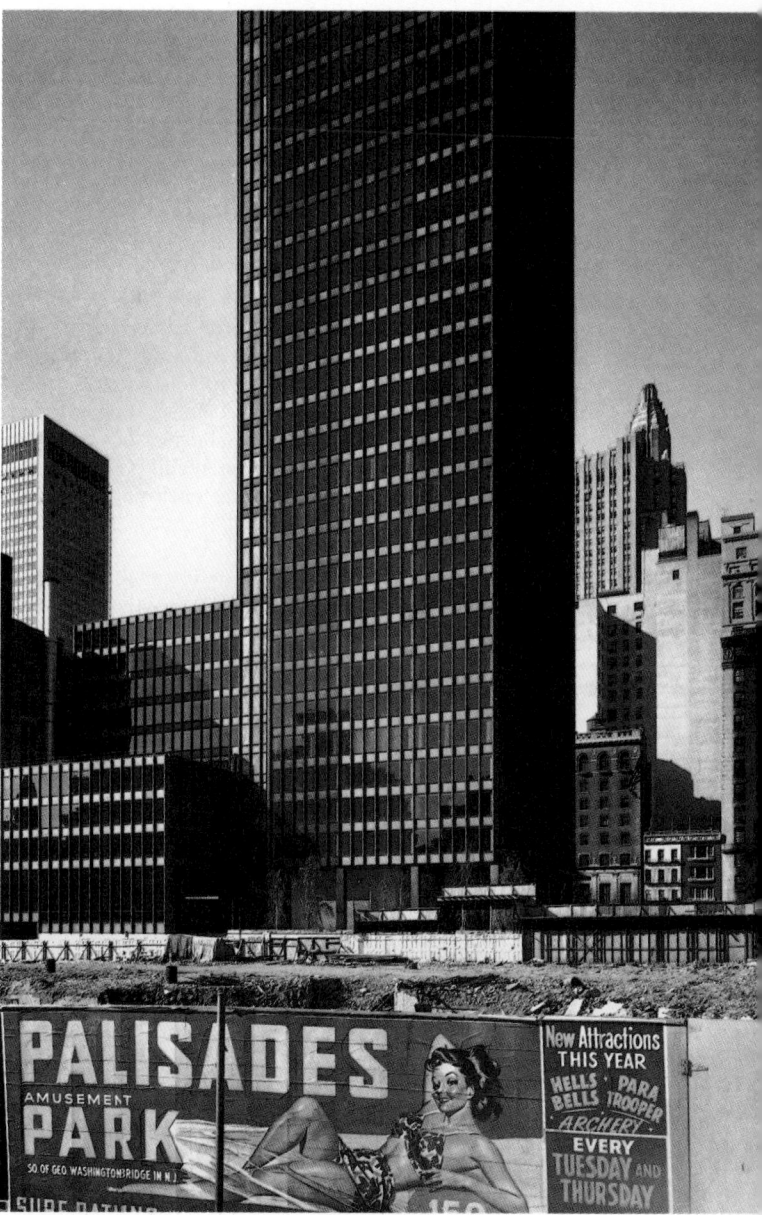

Seagram Building, 375 Park Avenue, East Fifty-second to East Fifty-third Street. Ludwig Mies van der Rohe, Philip Johnson and Kahn & Jacobs, 1958. View to the south from East Fifty-fourth Street. Stoller. ©ESTO an enormous Olmec head, brought to New York by the Mexican government for the World's Fair, was displayed on the Seagram plaza for six weeks in May and June before making the last leg of its journey to Flushing Meadows.[92] Although the newspapers had publicized the arrival of the colossal, nine-foot-tall, eight-foot-diameter, carved basalt sculpture, the strength of its presence was unexpected. As Olga Gueft described it:

> Even those who were on the lookout were electrified as they turned into Park Avenue. . . . It was no longer the same . . . no longer the familiar arid expanse of oversized glass boxes. The cold of the Seagram bronze had taken on a warm gleam. The ineffectual fountains had taken on a sumptuous grace. No longer were the passers-by mere human ants scurrying to escape the asphalt emptiness. They had acquired human dignity: none was in a hurry to leave. A colossal center of gravity had unified the uncoordinated, unsuccessful would-be civic space, as though the builders of the structures enclosing that space had worked together in the first place.[93]

Similar in feeling but less spectacular was the eight-foot-high, five-ton stone head from Easter Island that glowered down at passers-by from a twelve-foot-high podium set up in November 1968.[94] Barnett Newman's *Broken Obelisk*, a twenty-five-foot-high sculpture in Cor-ten steel, was installed on the plaza in the summer of 1967 as part of a program called Sculpture in the Environment (see chapter 17).[95] Thomas B. Hess, editor of *Art News*, described it as a "masterpiece . . . given a perfect setting."[96] Jean Dubuffet's twenty-four-foot-high, 5,000-pound, towering stainless steel figure *Milord la Chimarre*, displayed on the plaza in 1974, was described by one observer as an "eye-catching statement of anger and scorn for automation in our industrial society."[97]

The extraordinary capacity of the Seagram Building and its plaza to function together as object and void, backdrop and stage was highlighted by an intermedia theatrical event presented on the evenings of September 29 and 30, 1972, by Marilyn Wood.[98] For this "celebration," 1,000 bleacher seats were set in the northbound lane of Park Avenue to permit spectators to watch a ballet for sixteen dancers, as well as other events including a twelve-minute film documenting the comings and goings of life on the plaza.

Even without special events on the plaza, New Yorkers took to it as to a town square. Perhaps they were drawn there simply because no other public place in the area was appealing—the open space under Lever House, for instance, was empty most of the time. But more likely the public appreciated the wonderful backdrop provided by the tower's ineffable grace and the clear, sun-drenched lucidity of the space itself. In 1971 William H. Whyte, the sociologist and urban apologist, began to study the plazas that had sprung up all over Manhattan, inspired by the Seagram Building and the subsequent 1961 revised zoning ordinance, in an effort to understand why most of them were empty and lifeless. Despite the designers' seeming indifference to the needs of potential users, Whyte said, Seagram's plaza continued to be one of the few successful examples of its type. Whyte felt that because the entire periphery was "sittable," it was eminently approachable rather than aloof. The plaza, he said, conveyed an air of "genial permissiveness," enhanced by the absence of conventional fixed seating, which gave people a sense of choice: they could sit or lie along the parapet, sit on the broad shallow steps, or retreat under the trees to read or nap. Most important, he felt that in the plaza there was always a sense of

"something going on": "Sculpture sometimes, or maybe other events—the choreography of people moving across the plaza—vendors set up at the corner of 53rd Street—people put up their pictures along the granite walls—people just watching other people—there is always activity. This is a hallmark of a great urban space."[99]

The popularity of the Seagram Building's plaza was rivaled only by that of the twin dining rooms of the luxuriously appointed Four Seasons restaurant, occupying the plaza-level space of the lower building at the rear of the tower.[100] The Brasserie, at 100 East Fifty-third Street, a lower-priced, twenty-four-hour bistro, designed by Philip Johnson and William Pahlmann, occupied the ground-level space in the northeast quadrant of the building's podium.[101] The Four Seasons was largely the work of Johnson, although he collaborated with a variety of designers, including Pahlmann and Ada Louise and L. Garth Huxtable. The restaurant could be entered either through a street-level lobby at 99 East Fifty-second Street that led past coat check and toilet facilities to a stair rising to the bar room, or, more grandly, up broad shallow steps at the east end of the Seagram Building lobby, through glazed bronze walls and into a cross passage. The restaurant itself was made up of two grandly proportioned, sixty-by-sixty-foot, twenty-foot-high, column-free rooms. To create the column-free space, Mies had instructed the engineers to transfer the loads of the upper floors, yet another example of his willingness to sacrifice structural purity to aesthetic effect.

The Four Seasons was the crowning ornament of the chain run by the Restaurant Associates (see chapter 6). In keeping with the theming of the management's other luxury restaurants, this one featured a menu that changed with the seasons, as did aspects of the decor; permanent plantings of grape ivy and striped green nephthytis were supplemented by seasonal varieties such as firethorn in autumn, blue cedar in winter and azaleas in spring; the linen and even the staff uniforms were also changed seasonally.

The restaurant was lavishly appointed with beautiful materials as well as works of art, including a twenty-two-by-twenty-foot stage curtain that Pablo Picasso had designed for the Diaghilev ballet *Le Tricorne* in 1919, which was hung in the passage between the two dining rooms; tapestries by Joan Miró, hung in the Fifty-second Street lobby; and a number of notable paintings from the New York Abstract Expressionist school, including Jackson Pollock's *Blue Poles*, hung in the north private dining room, and one by Grace Hartigan, hung in the Pool Room. In addition, Mark Rothko was commissioned to paint a series of canvases. Rothko told John Fischer, the editor of *Harper's* magazine, "I hope to ruin the appetite of every son of a bitch who ever eats in that room."[102] Over the course of two years he produced approximately forty paintings, constituting three series, though he probably intended to install only seven pieces in the restaurant. Rothko ultimately found the setting inappropriate, and the paintings were never hung in the Four Seasons; eventually many of them were acquired by museums, including the Tate Gallery in London, which displayed the collection in a room of its own. A Constructivist-inspired pendant sculpture designed by Richard Lippold was specially commissioned to hang over the bar in the South Room, popularly known as the Grill or Bar Room.

Although Paul Goldberger claimed that the Four Seasons was the "first consciously modern design" for a restaurant in New York,[103] Johnson had more in mind: the point of the design,

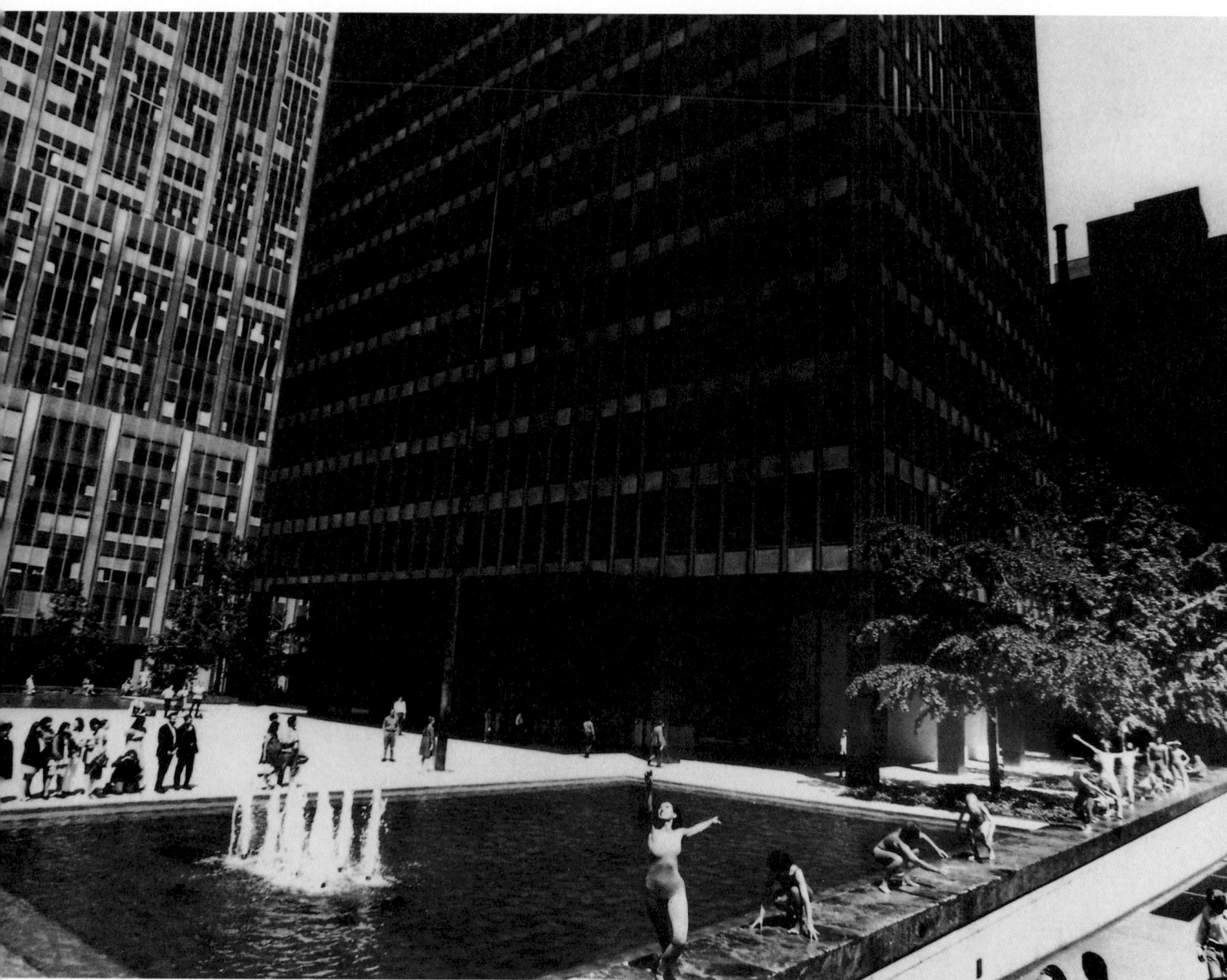

Rehearsal for "Celebrations in City Places: The Seagram Building and Its Plaza," presented by Marilyn Wood and the Celebration Group, 1972. Project of the Experimental Intermedia Foundation, sponsored by Joseph E. Seagram & Sons, Inc. and the New York State Council on the Arts in cooperation with the New York City Department of Cultural Affairs. Wood. JES

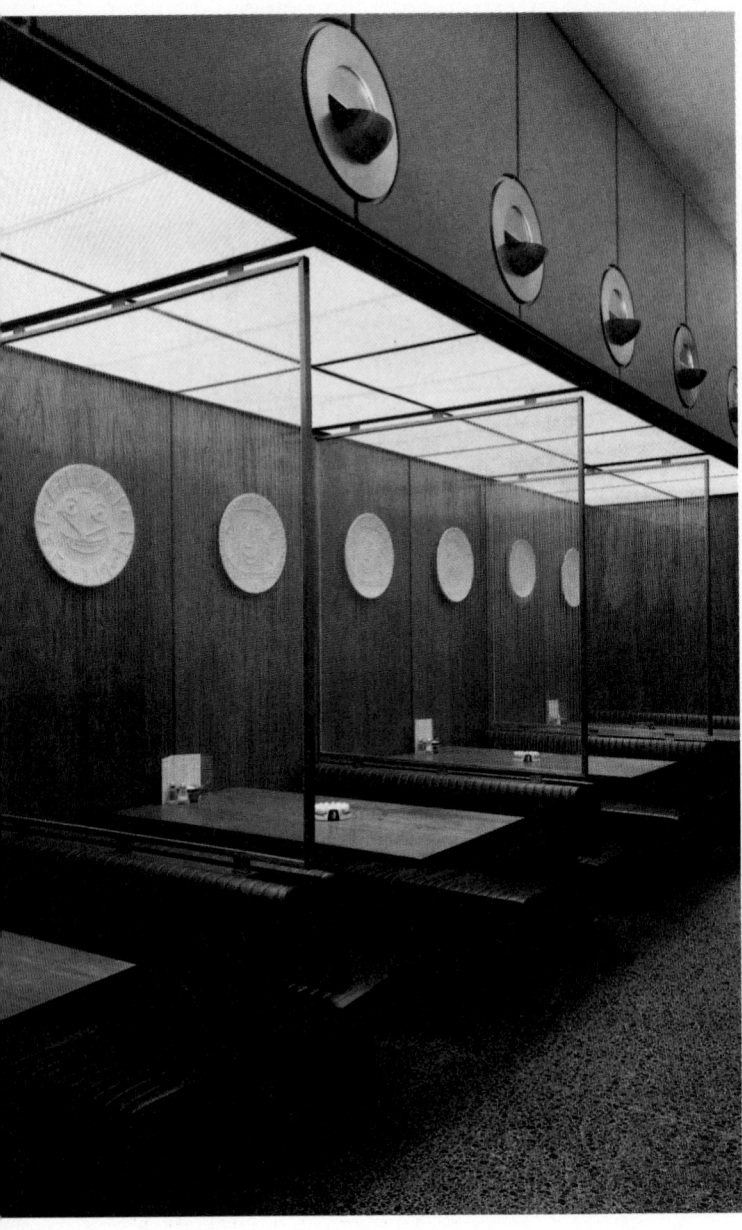

Above: Brasserie, Seagram Building, 375 Park Avenue. Philip Johnson, 1958. Interior. Reens. LR

Top right: Four Seasons, Seagram Building. Philip Johnson, 1958. Grill Room with sculpture by Richard Lippold above bar. Stoller. ©ESTO

Bottom right: Four Seasons, Seagram Building. Philip Johnson, 1958. Pool Room. Stoller. ©ESTO

the architect said, "was to be modern and yet get away from the austerity, the sterility, of the International Style."[104] More than any other single feature of the design, the white marble reflecting pool in the center of the Pool Room—an idea attributed to Pahlmann—established the restaurant as a spectacular setting for dignified dining. Seventeen-foot-tall ornamental fig trees, placed at the pool's corners and also suggested by Pahlmann, gave the room a more intimate scale. Seasonal plantings designed by the landscape architect Karl Linn, which included hanging baskets along the windows, further softened the effect. The glazed west and north walls were hung with festooned chains resembling Vienna curtains and designed by Marie Nichols in three tones of gold-anodized aluminum; as the result of a happy accident, these fluttered rhythmically as currents of air rose from the concealed ventilating ducts to create an effect of shimmering golden light. According to *Architectural Record*, even this rippling went through seasonal changes, with movement greater in summer and winter than in fall or spring, as the differential between inside and outside temperature varied.[105] The other walls were paneled in French walnut and natural rawhide, and the ceiling was broken up into cofferlike panels to accommodate Richard Kelly's sophisticated lighting scheme, which could be adjusted to complement the time of day and the season. To compensate for its distance from the windows and the pool, the seating along the east wall was raised to form a dramatic balcony from which diners could overlook the patiolike scene. The principal feature of the Grill Room was the Lippold construction, made up of narrow rods suspended on nearly invisible wires; the *New Yorker* said the piece seemed to hang "like golden strokes of rain."[106] The mood in this room was more austere, a minimalist version of a traditional gentleman's club. As in the Pool Room, a balcony was created along the eastern edge.

The restaurant exuded high-style design at every turn, including the logo of four trees, colored pink for spring, green for summer, red for fall and brown for winter, designed by Emil Antonucci for use on menus, matchbooks and staff uniforms. Less successful were the tabletop items: a fruit bowl designed by the Huxtables proved wobbly and was quickly taken out of service, as was their specially designed glassware with the Four Seasons logo. But the silver holloware they designed for tableside cooking, as well as their service wagons and place plates bordered in matte black, proved enduring features. Both rooms were furnished with Mies's amply proportioned Brno dining chairs, upholstered in black leather, and simple but generously sized tables designed by Johnson.

Interiors captured the essence of the Four Seasons' success: "One singular paradox of the design is that despite the exceptional richness of its materials and workmanship, it is essentially colorless and unobtrusive. It is not a stage setting; rather it is a theater that is not to date, nor tire the audience, but to focus on a perpetually changing *mis-en-scene*, an endlessly improvised drama—of the four seasons of nature, of the world's greatest metropolis, and of the pleasant rituals of serving and being served, eating, drinking, and conversing."[107]

Just a few years after opening, the Seagram Building was embroiled in a controversy that no one anticipated. In order to achieve the spectacular purity of his tower within the prevailing New York zoning law, Mies had pushed the building back ninety feet from Park Avenue, thereby creating the plaza and sacrificing rentable square footage that a more conventional setback massing would have permitted. Mies had also designed the most expensive office building of the time: the estimated cost was $36 million, in addition to the $5 million spent for land acquisition and the $4.5 million spent on the Four Seasons restaurant. When in 1960 a city tax assessor, Samuel Krasnoff, came to evaluate the building, he had what Anthony Bailey has described as an "epiphany": "This building of Mr. Bronfman's is not like other buildings. That slender tower! That costly bronze! That open, unused, *empty* space! Krasnoff consults his notebook. Assessed at $19 million! Clearly an idiotic sum, based on obsolete procedures. A new, revolutionary, beautiful building needs a new, revolutionary and beautiful assessment, based on cost rather than income."[108] Krasnoff argued that the failure to build the maximum allowable space the site could support and the decision to spend vastly more than was usual for a commercial office building were depriving the city of a potential extra $300,000 in annual tax revenues. The city's attorneys argued, in essence, that the "taxable value" formula, which assessed only what was built, neglected to take into account the "prestige value" of the plaza and the building. The result of this thinking was that although the Colgate-Palmolive Building across the street was taxed at $17.74 per square foot of office floor space, the Seagram Building should be taxed at $33.98 per square foot. This decision was fought by the Seagram Company, and the case eventually reached New York State's highest court, the Court of Appeals. In 1964 the court ruled in a four-to-three decision in favor of the city, determining that taxation should be based on the building's "real replacement value." In other words, the building would not be assessed on the basis of the capitalization of rental income, which would have established a value of $17 million, but on the basis of the building's lost potential, which set the value at $21 million.

As many observers noted at the time, the court's decision was a serious blow to architectural quality in New York. The *New York Times* editorialized: "With such a penalty attached, anyone putting up a superior, more costly building, like a Seagram Tower or a Chase Manhattan plaza, would indeed be a patsy or a fool. Architecture of quality could not have been more effectively eliminated from the New York scene by a law directly prohibiting it. The city may gain some additional revenues temporarily, but ultimately the city is a disastrous loser."[109] Architects and critics were shocked by the case: before the final decision was handed down, Ada Louise Huxtable had argued that special tax categories for prestige buildings would result in New York's "architectural annihilation."[110]

One solution to the tax problem was for Seagram's to sell the building and lease its space back from the new owners, who could be taxed at the usual rate because their name would not be attached to the building and they would therefore not gain any prestige from it. In 1972, while the company pondered its options, it moved 600 of its 983 employees to cheaper space in other locations, many outside New York, taking the opportunity to complain to Mayor Lindsay about the difficulties of doing business in New York.[111]

In 1976 Edgar Bronfman, who had succeeded his father, Samuel, as the company's president, surprised city officials with a request that the Seagram Building be designated a landmark. Being only eighteen years old, the building was far too young to be entitled to such status: the law required that buildings be at least thirty years old to qualify. In arguing his position, Bronfman emphasized the company's "resolve to preserve for New York City, in perpetuity, the building's architectural and esthetic integrity."[112] Although the company had received a number of attractive offers from potential buyers over the years, it had decided to retain ownership of the building, "the prestige of which," as Paul Goldberger put it, "has been a major source of

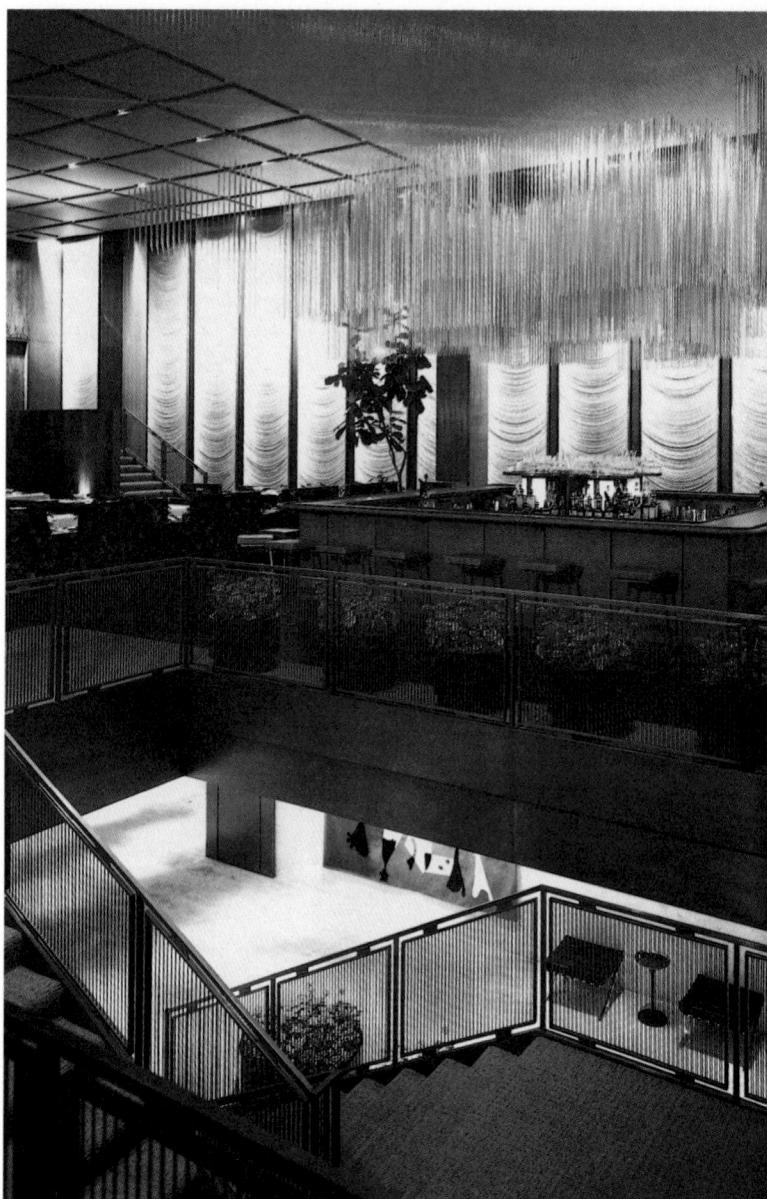

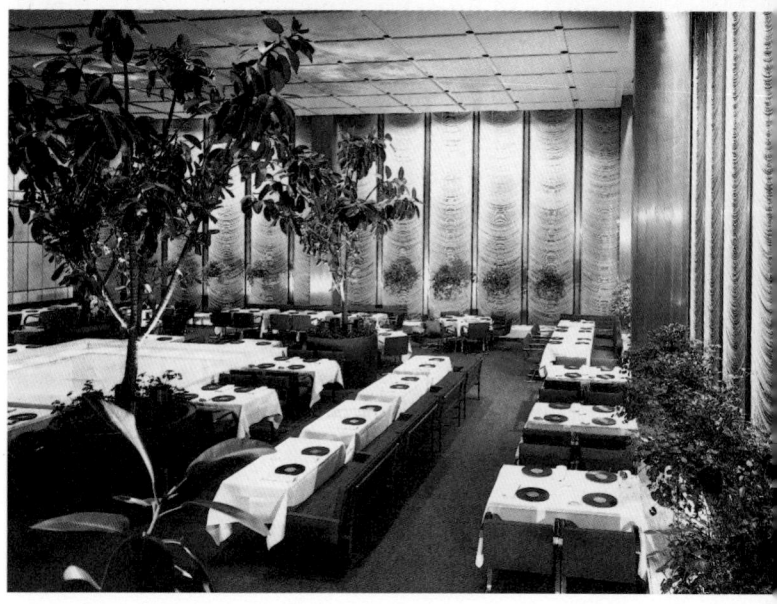

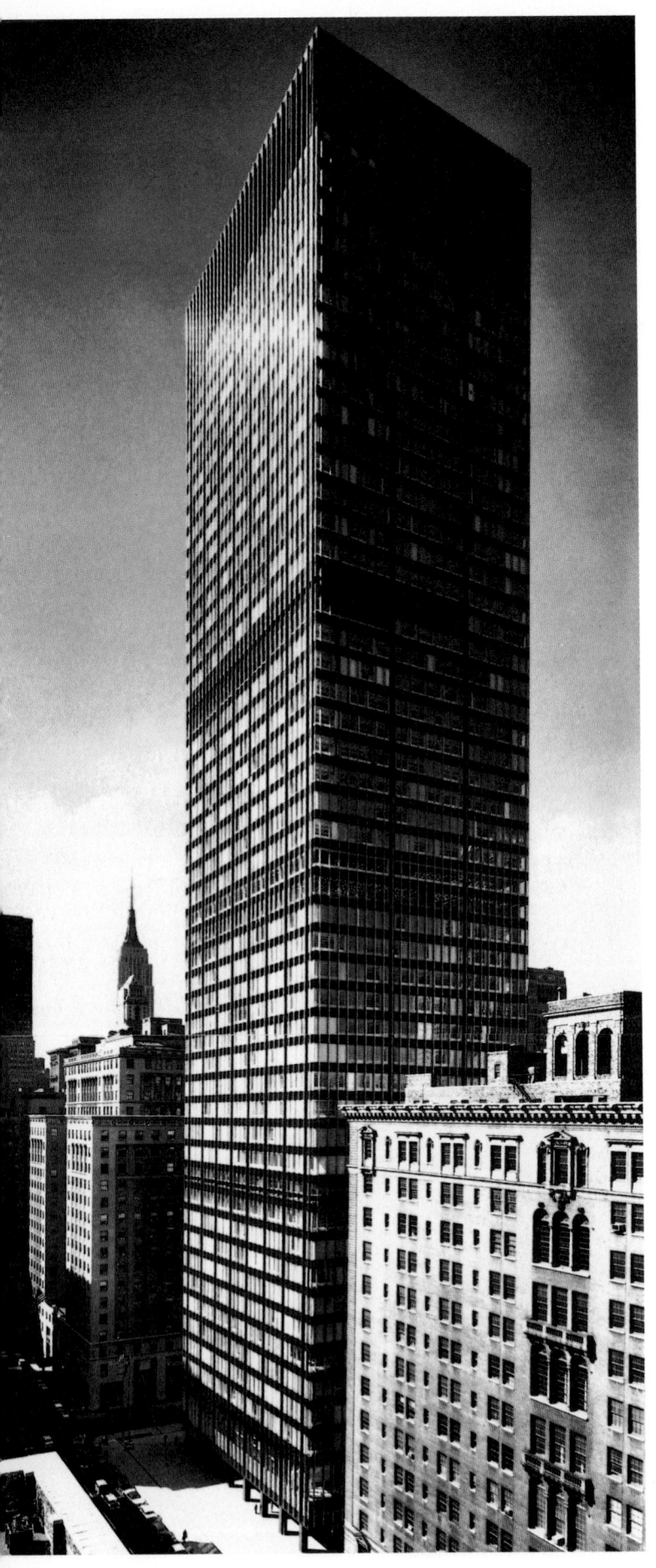

publicity for the company."[113] Acknowledging the fact of the building's "youth," Bronfman proposed that the landmarks law be revised to permit owners to request designation before their properties came of age. Mayor Beame turned the proposal over to Beverly Moss Spatt, chairman of the Landmarks Preservation Commission, who eventually denied Bronfman's request, pointing out that such a provision in the law "could cause problems in terms of our legal right to designate what we choose."[114] In 1979 the Seagram Company changed its policy and sold the building to the Teachers Investment & Annuity Association.[115]

After Seagram's: Progeny or Parody?

The work of Mies van der Rohe in general and the Seagram Building in particular had an extraordinary impact on office-building design during the 1960s. The architecture of Skidmore, Owings & Merrill, whose approach to Modernism had tended to be eclectic in the 1950s, shifted dramatically toward Mies after the publication of the early Seagram studies. Regrettably, few of SOM's Miesian office towers had the tectonic force or intellectual clarity of Seagram's, and the increasingly successful firm began to crank out more and more diluted versions of the original.

SOM's first Seagram-style building, and in some ways the best interpretation of it, was the Union Carbide Building (1955–60) at 270 Park Avenue.[116] Plans for the building were first announced in August 1955. The two-acre, full-block site, which stretched from Forty-seventh to Forty-eighth Street and from Park to Madison Avenue, was that of the former Hotel Marguery. A decade earlier William Zeckendorf had proposed a project for that same site that was rumored to be a complex of offices "tailor-built to the requirements of three big-league customers," with separate entrances for major corporate tenants and a department store facing Madison Avenue.[117] In the middle of the block, a 300-foot-high tower would rise without a setback from a fifteen-story base that would cover the entire site. To provide unbroken floor space in the tower, the elevator core would be placed to one side and not in the center. Zeckendorf's plan never materialized, however.

Union Carbide had in 1952 contemplated a move to suburban Westchester County but had later reconsidered, deciding on the Park Avenue site.[118] Unlike the Seagram Building, in which the owner occupied only a portion of the total floor space, Union Carbide was to be the sole tenant of the vast 1.2 million-square-foot complex (at the time the building was completed, however, ten tower floors were leased to outsiders). SOM's design team, headed by Gordon Bunshaft and assisted by project designer Natalie de Blois and interior designer Jack G. Dunbar, had proposed several schemes: a conventional nine-story-tall base topped by a forty-eight-story tower occupying 25 percent of the site (this was like Zeckendorf's scheme); a block-filling ziggurat that yielded 200,000 more square feet than the one finally chosen, but with floors that would have been too deep and dark; a tower at the Madison Avenue end of the site, which would have simplified construction by avoiding the complex subsurface conditions presented by the railroad tracks nearer Park Avenue, but seemed to contradict the prevailing urbanism; and a forty-one-story tower rising without setback along Park Avenue and a thirteen-story wing filling up the rest of the block. This last scheme was the one chosen, although by the time construction began in 1958, the Madison Avenue wing had lost a floor, and the tower, set back fifty feet from Park Avenue at the client's request and twenty-three feet from each of the side streets, had grown to fifty-two stories and a total of 1.5 million square feet of space. This made it not only the tallest building along Park Avenue but also the tallest building erected in New York since 1933. While Seagram's inspired a demand for zoning reform that would encourage the creation of plazas and would eliminate the ziggurat-type building, it was the far more "realistic" Union Carbide that actually influenced the proposed law, which was being considered as the building was being finished. But, as *Architectural Forum* warned in 1960, although buildings set back from the street were "infinitely preferable to the ziggurat 'cake molds' now in effect," they should not be overused: "Union Carbide's tower is set back, especially along Park Avenue; but while one or two setbacks of this sort along a street might offer welcome relief, an entire street of variously set-back buildings is likely to be an urban disaster."[119]

Although Union Carbide was proportioned similarly to the Seagram Building, its sheer size combined with the thinness and "black-and-white" graphic quality of its skin yielded a completely different and less favorable impression. As William Jordy put it in 1972: "Whoever would measure the difference between the architecture of genius and the best of the architecture of bureaucracy can do so nowhere more conveniently than here on Park Avenue, weighing the respective virtues of these two buildings. The advantages, especially when both buildings are considered as corporate expressions, are not wholly in favor of the Seagram; but . . . the Seagram is a greater architectural achievement than Union Carbide."[120]

Union Carbide's impression of top-heavy bulk was reinforced by the shallowness of its plaza and a low, thirty-eight-foot-deep arcade along Park Avenue. Such bulk was permitted under the zoning because the building was set back along three of its four property lines (it held to the line on Madison Avenue) and also provided a sixty-foot-wide, street-level pedestrian arcade extending Vanderbilt Avenue northward through the midblock. The arcade led to a small glazed lobby along Park Avenue and escalators that took visitors to the building's principal lobby, located one level above. This piano nobile arrangement was devised so that the elevator pits would penetrate as little as possible below street level in order to keep clear of the train tracks below. Provision was made for a future underground pedestrian passageway to Grand Central Terminal. The twenty-five-foot-high raised lobby was used as an exhibition hall, although its remoteness from the street and the seemingly private quality of the space failed to attract significant numbers of the general public.

Some of the building's most notable features were technical, including the stainless-steel curtain wall, which, except for the natural-colored mullions, was colored black by a new process, Permyron, developed by one of Union Carbide's divisions. Inside the building, a highly sophisticated integrated partition-and-ceiling system incorporated lighting, air conditioning and sound control. The typical office floors of Union Carbide accommodated an unprecedented degree of modular design in the ceiling grid, furniture, filing and storage systems, and introduced clustered workstations with low dividers.

On April 23, 1955, a few months before Union Carbide declared its intentions to build, Vincent Astor announced plans for Astor Plaza, at 399 Park Avenue, an office building on the block bounded by Park and Lexington avenues, Fifty-third and Fifty-fourth streets.[121] In 1953 Astor had begun assembling the site, which held twenty-one buildings, including such large apartment houses as 381 Park Avenue (Litchfield & Rogers, 1925), 383 Park Avenue (James Brite, 1912) and 399 Park Avenue

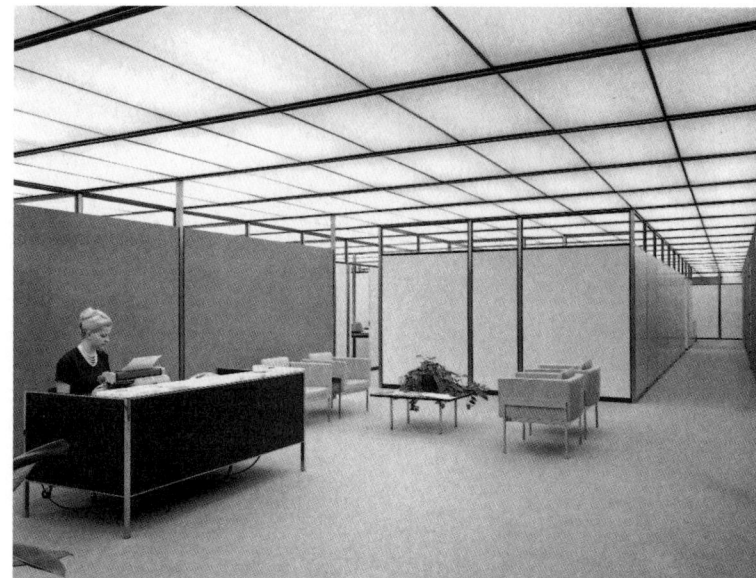

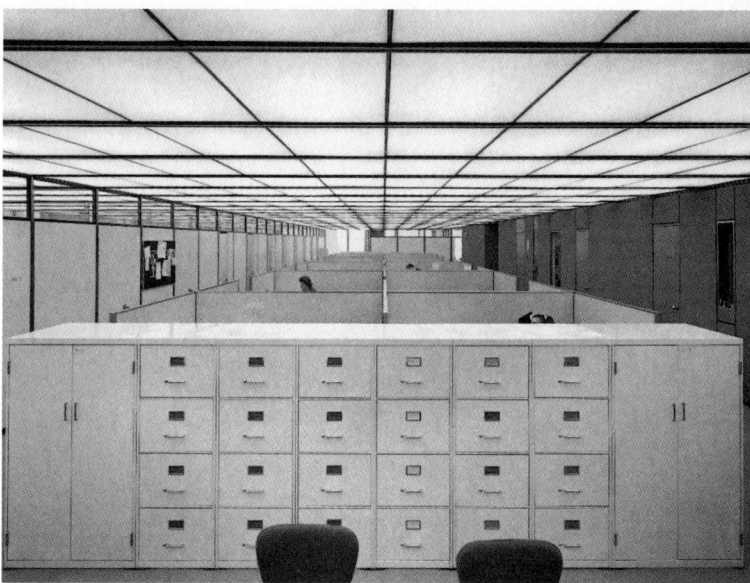

Left: Union Carbide Building, 270 Park Avenue, East Forty-seventh to East Forty-eighth Street. Skidmore, Owings & Merrill, 1955–60. View to the southwest. Stoller. ©ESTO

Top: Union Carbide Building. Interior. Stoller. ©ESTO

Bottom: Union Carbide Building. Interior. Stoller. ©ESTO

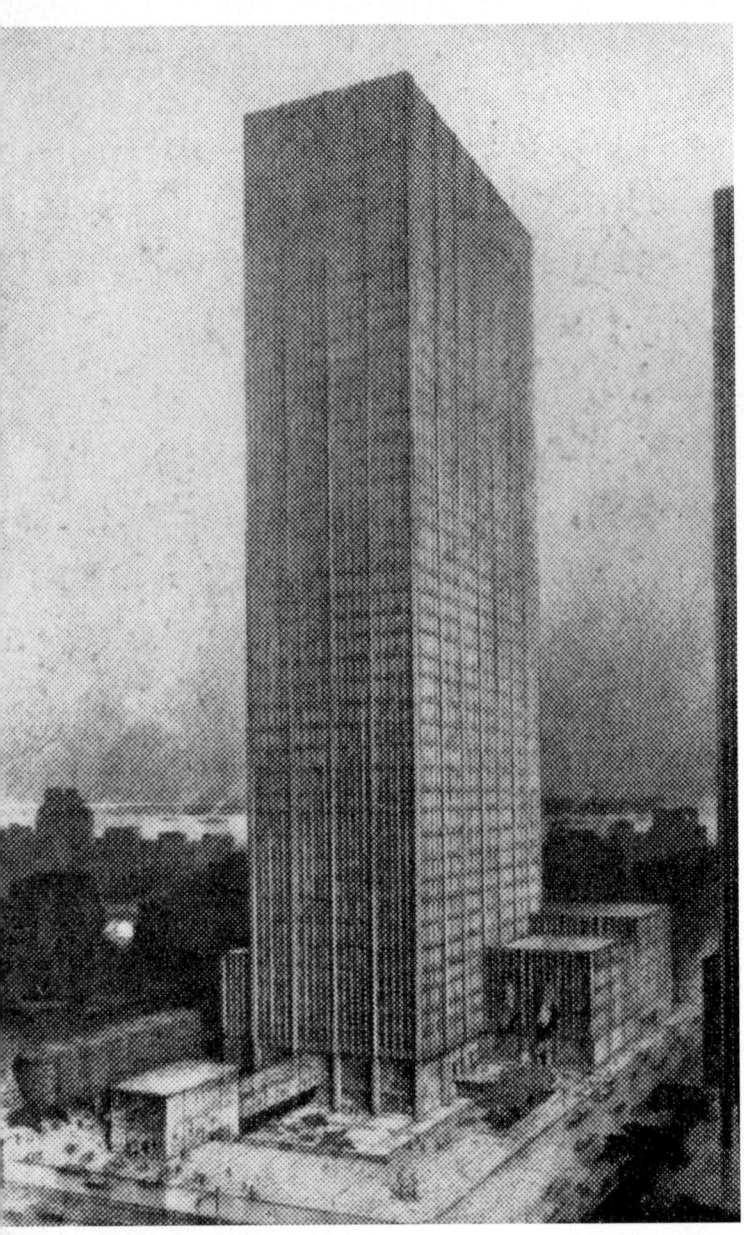

Above: Proposed Astor Plaza, 399 Park Avenue, East Fifty-third to East Fifty-fourth Street. Carson & Lundin in association with Kahn & Jacobs, 1957. Rendering. View to the northeast. AF. CU

Right: First National City Bank, 399 Park Avenue. Carson & Lundin in association with Kahn & Jacobs, 1961. View to the northeast. Stoller. ©ESTO

(Schwartz & Gross, 1915) and three nine-story apartment houses on East Fifty-third Street (number 105 by Walter Haefeli; numbers 115 and 123 by Cross & Cross). Astor and his associate investors, William S. Paley and Frank Stanton, retained the firm of Carson & Lundin, who proposed a forty-six-story tower slab, set well back from Park Avenue. The resulting open plaza would be comparable to Seagram's, but a large portion of it would be sunk below grade and lined with shops, restaurants and a bank, presumably in emulation of the original plan for Rockefeller Center. A two-story glass-enclosed exhibition pavilion at the street's edge would be connected to the tower via a bridge over the sunken garden. On the tower's roof there was to be a helicopter pad, and parking for 400 cars was to be provided. As at Rockefeller Center, underground pedestrian passageways would be built to link up with neighboring buildings and the subway. Astor's project was stalled, however, not only by financing but by a real estate holdout: Michels Pharmacy, whose proprietors, Mr. and Mrs. Jacob A. Michels, refused to sell their five-story rowhouse on Lexington Avenue even after Astor had offered $400,000. The problem was not solved until Astor gave up and the project was turned over to the First National City Bank, who managed to depersonalize the negotiations, meet the Michels' price and relocate their pharmacy in the neighborhood.

The decision of the First National City Bank to locate its national and overseas divisions, as well as its operating departments and the administration of its New York City branches, on Park Avenue initiated a significant trend in the banking community, which had hitherto remained firmly entrenched in the financial district. While the decision to some extent recognized the growing preference among employees for a midtown location, it more importantly acknowledged the presence of many of the bank's international clients in the area. Upon taking over Astor's project, the bank had the building redesigned by the same architects (in association with Kahn & Jacobs). One significant change was the drastic reduction of the plaza on Park Avenue, which thereby reinforced the closure wall for Seagram's that would have disappeared with the previous scheme. William Jordy praised this aspect of the "bulky money-maker," which was completed in 1961: "For once, greedy coverage deserves applause."[122]

Less innocuous was Emery Roth & Sons' 277 Park Avenue (1958–64), occupying a site between Park and Lexington avenues, Forty-seventh and Forty-eighth streets, replacing the grand courtyard apartment house of the same address that was designed by McKim, Mead & White in 1925.[123] On a lot the same size as that of 399 Park Avenue, the fifty floors of the new 277 Park Avenue supplied 1.5 million square feet of office space in a tower that was a near parody of the Seagram Building, but without the plaza or the tectonic finesse. In 1965–67 Emery Roth & Sons produced designs for yet another version of the Seagram Building: 299 Park Avenue, a forty-two-story black-glass-clad tower erected on the site of the Park Lane Hotel.[124] Because the site was much smaller than that of Seagram's, Union Carbide or 277 Park, extending only 150 feet east from Park Avenue to Park Lane, the service street that separated the hotel from the Barclay Hotel, the Roth office chose to build a tower that rose without interruption, creating an almost suffocating impression of bulk.[125]

The Roths followed these buildings in 1967–69 with 345 Park Avenue, occupying the block bounded by Park and Lexington avenues, Fifty-first and Fifty-second streets, previously home to the Hotel Ambassador (Warren & Wetmore, 1921) as well as a number of townhouses and tenements.[126] The twenty-

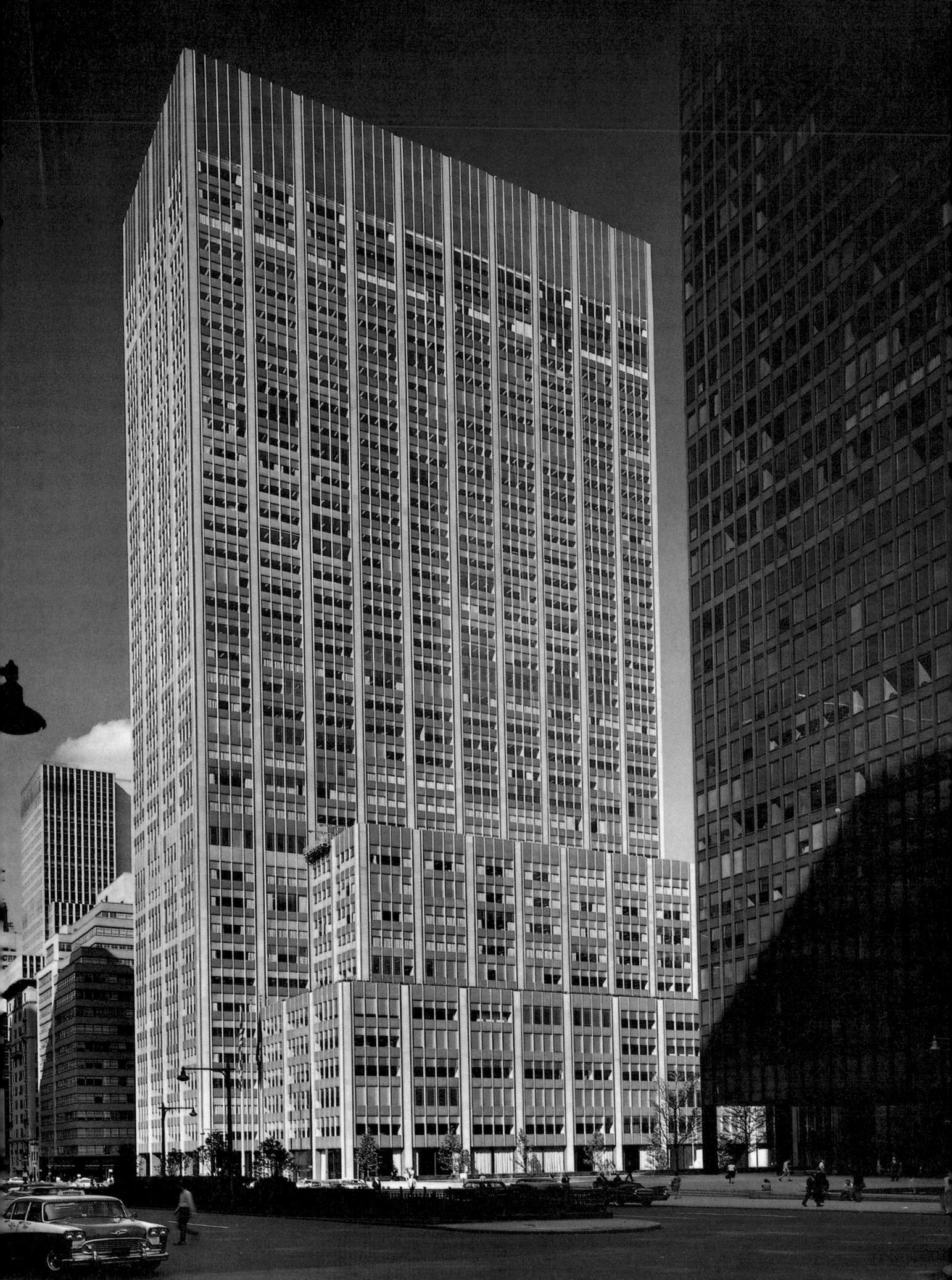

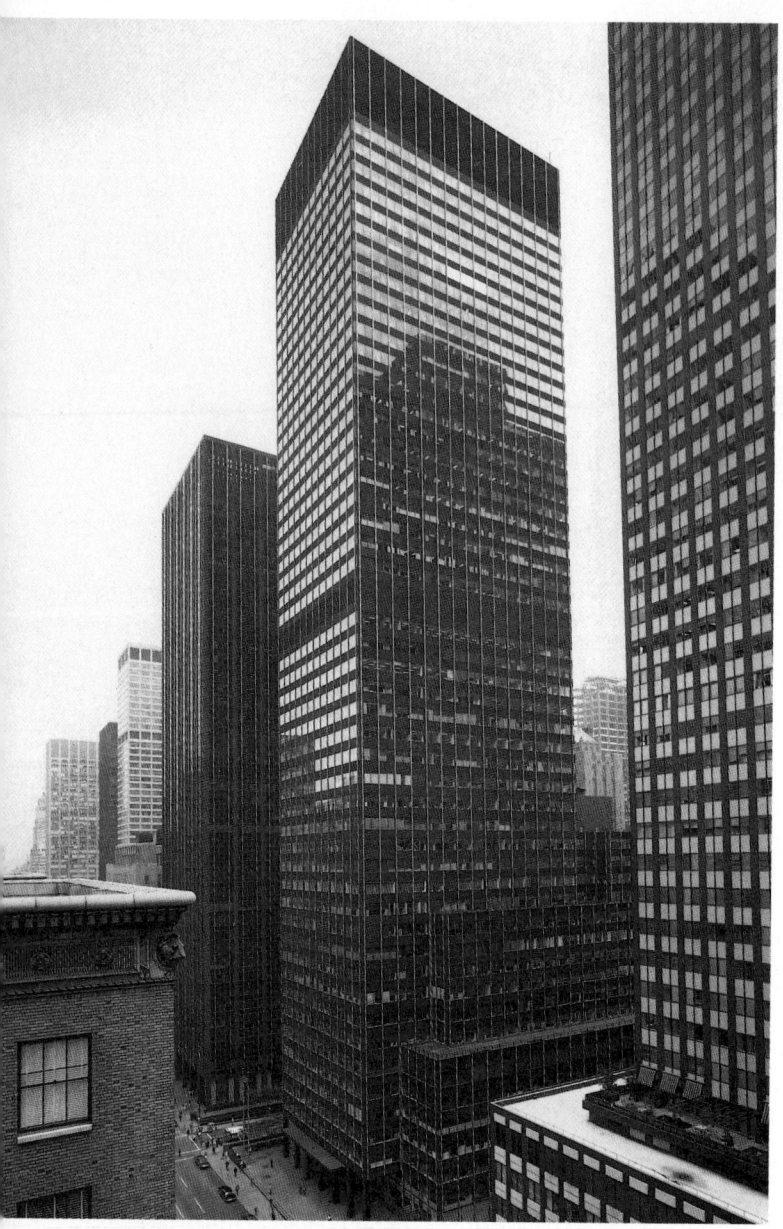

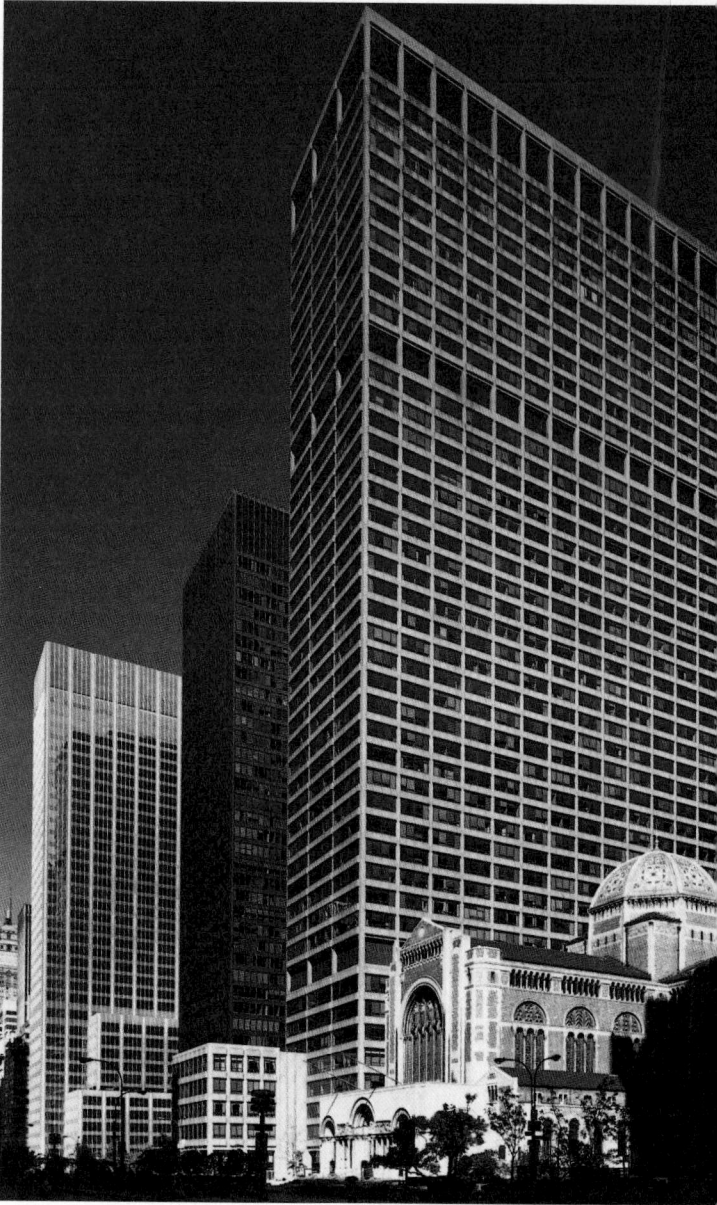

View northeast of Park Avenue showing 277 Park Avenue (Emery Roth & Sons, 1958–64), in the center; 299 Park Avenue (Emery Roth & Sons, 1965–67), to the left; and 245 Park Avenue (Shreve, Lamb & Harmon, 1967), to the right. OMH

Above: 345 Park Avenue, East Fifty-first to East Fifty-second Street. Emery Roth & Sons, 1967–69. View to the northeast showing St. Bartholomew's Church (Bertram G. Goodhue, 1919) in the foreground. ERS

Top right: Proposed 245 Park Avenue, East Forty-sixth to East Forty-seventh Street. William Lescaze, 1961. View to the southeast. PA. CU

Bottom right: 245 Park Avenue. Shreve, Lamb & Harmon, 1967. View to the southwest. Molitor. JWM fifth office building to rise on Park Avenue since 1946 and the fourteenth to have been designed by the Roth firm, it was not a version of Seagram's but a forty-four-story slab modified at its base by a vestigial five-story element projecting forward to within twenty-five feet of the Park Avenue building line on the Fifty-second Street side. This element was intended not only to complete the closure of the 23,000-square-foot plaza formed at the Fifty-first Street corner but also to provide appropriate closure and low height opposite the Seagram plaza to the north. While he was working on the Seagram design, Mies had hoped that the Ambassador would "build a whole new wing of rooms to look out" on his plaza, thereby creating an approximately seventeen-story-high "palisade."[127] But as built, the low wing of 345 Park robbed the northbound pedestrian coming upon the Seagram plaza of that extraordinary sensation of spatial release that had thrilled Phyllis Lambert from the very earliest stages of the design. The Roths did, however, make other attempts to defer to the Seagram Building: they kept their slab back from Park Avenue in line with Mies's tower and, in a departure from the dark colors adopted by many architects in emulation of the Seagram Building, they clad their building in buff-colored precast concrete, the rough texture and lightness of which helped reinforce the distinctiveness of Seagram's.

The next Park Avenue site to be redeveloped—a full block on the east side of the avenue, between Forty-sixth and Forty-seventh streets, Park and Lexington avenues—was a particularly choice one. Considered for a time by CBS for its new headquarters, it contained 247 Park Avenue, an office building built as part of the original Terminal City development, and the Grand Central Palace, which, with the construction of the Coliseum on Columbus Circle, had lost its standing as the city's principal exhibition facility.[128] In September 1961 plans were announced for a metal-and-glass-clad tower designed by William Lescaze.[129] The tower was to be set back from the street on all four sides and rise in a single mass to fifty-five stories. This design, along with Shreve, Lamb & Harmon's for 1301 Avenue of the Americas and Skidmore, Owings & Merrill's 140 Broadway, were the first supertowers proposed under the city's new zoning law. The 247 Park Avenue project faltered, however, and when it was revived in 1963, a more mundane design by Shreve, Lamb & Harmon was substituted.[130] When completed in 1967 under the name 245 Park Avenue, it filled two-thirds of the site with a five-story base and carried a forty-seven-story tower above it to provide 1.5 million square feet of office space.

Pan American Building

Despite all the changes Park Avenue had gone through in the 1950s and early 1960s, the stretch from Forty-sixth to Fifty-seventh Street managed to retain its essential character. The landscaped malls continued to be its principal distinguishing feature, and several of the prewar monuments remained: Phelps Barnum's Postum Building, Bertram Grosvenor Goodhue's St. Bartholomew's Church, McKim, Mead & White's Racquet Club, Schultze & Weaver's Waldorf-Astoria, Emery Roth's Drake Hotel, and a few apartment houses, including Emery Roth's 417 Park and Mott B. Schmidt's 450 Park (although this would be replaced in 1972 by a thirty-three-story, virtually all-black tower by Emery Roth & Sons).[131] Even with the new buildings, the street wall was remarkably intact; given the compression of forms viewed in perspective, the amount of building mass which defined the street far exceeded that which withdrew from it.

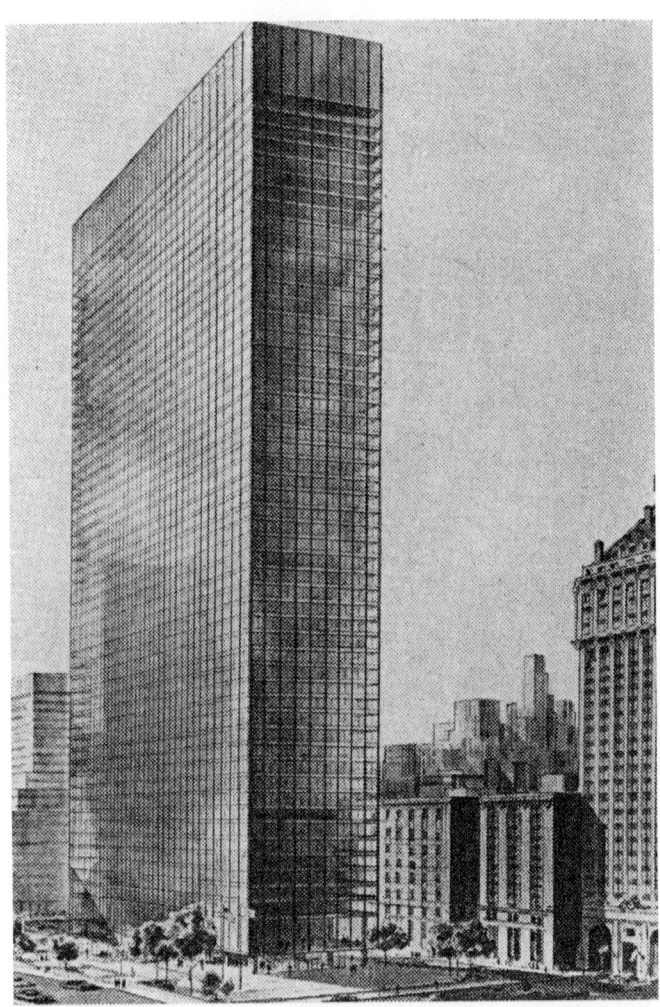

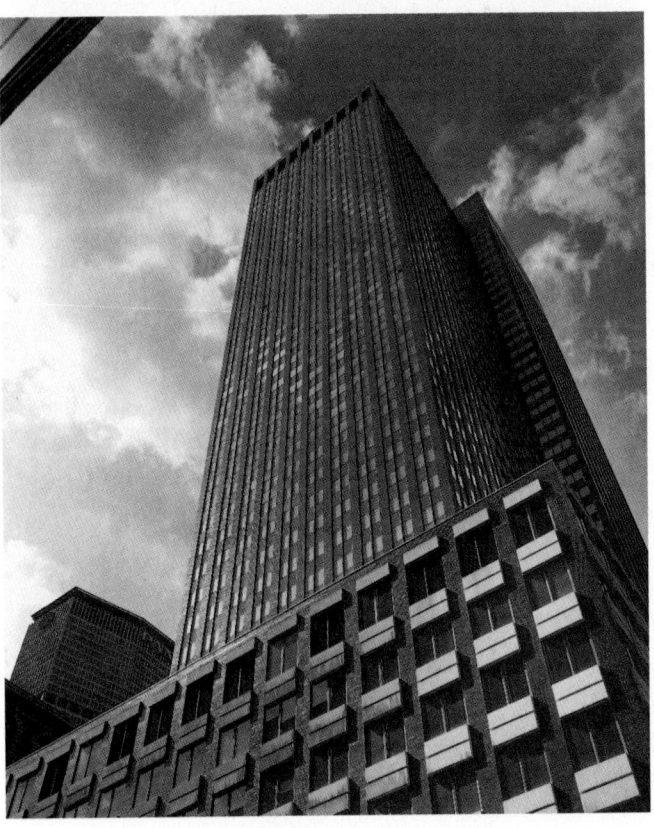

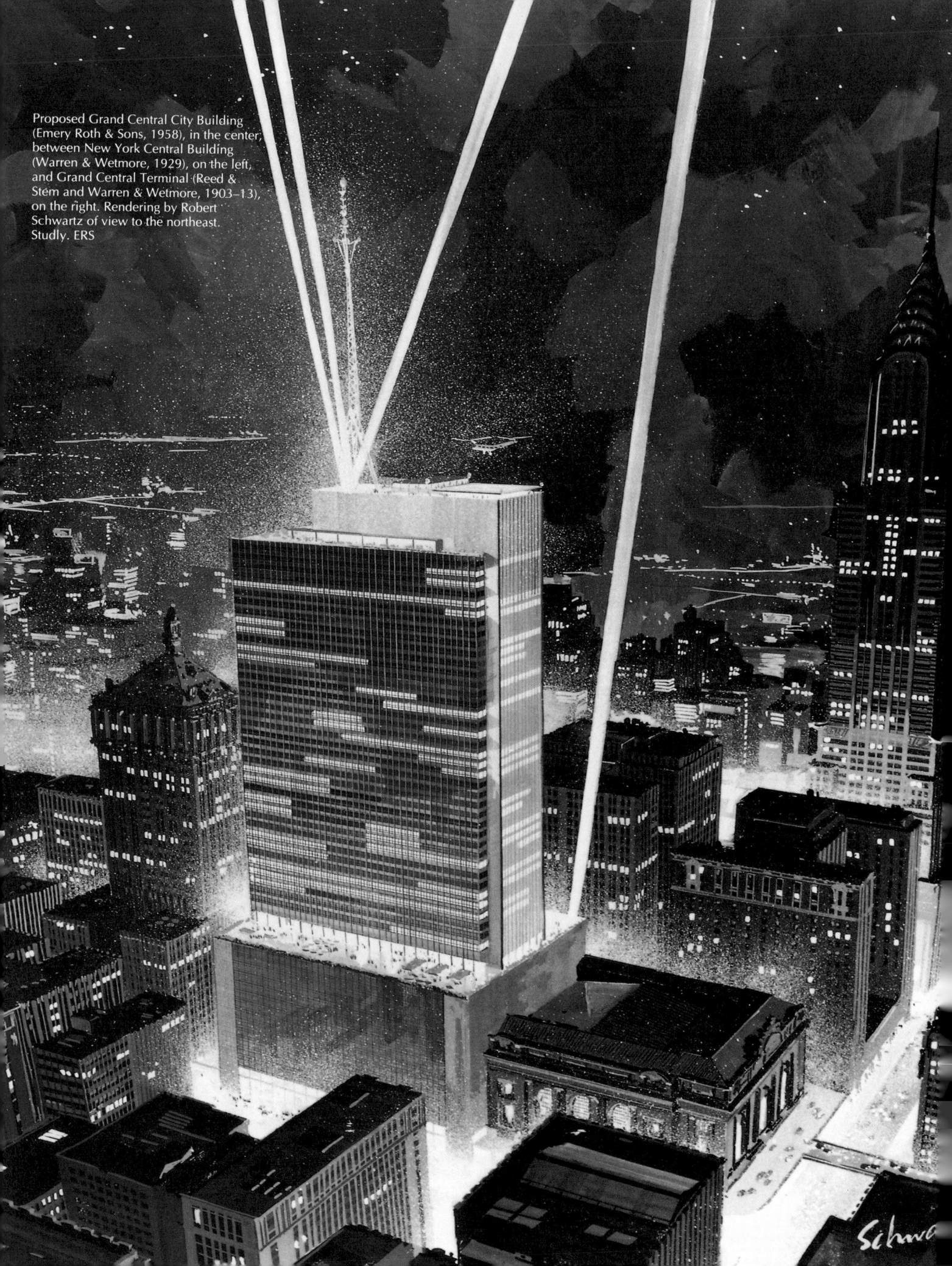

Proposed Grand Central City Building
(Emery Roth & Sons, 1958), in the center,
between New York Central Building
(Warren & Wetmore, 1929), on the left,
and Grand Central Terminal (Reed &
Stem and Warren & Wetmore, 1903–13),
on the right. Rendering by Robert
Schwartz of view to the northeast.
Studly. ERS

Moreover, because a considerable amount of the rebuilding of the 1950s had been just that—recladding rather than new construction—and because a lot of new buildings had been constructed under the old zoning, the traditional cornice line remained in vestigial form as the place where the base elements of individual buildings concluded and the setbacks began. Most important, especially when viewed from the north, above say Fiftieth Street, the avenue continued to be defined by the great campanile-portal of Warren & Wetmore's New York Central Building of 1929, which at once framed and closed the axis of the street while beckoning the eye around and beyond it and the pedestrians and automobiles through it.[132] But this all changed in 1963, with the completion of the Pan American Building; what had been a gradual transformation of the avenue became transmogrification.

The story of the Pan Am Building should be considered in relationship to the plans advanced for the reconstruction of Grand Central Terminal (see chapter 16). In 1954 Robert Young, chairman of the board of the New York Central Railroad, advised by William Zeckendorf, proposed a 1,600-foot-tall, eighty-story, 4.8 million-square-foot office tower, designed by I. M. Pei, for construction above a rebuilt Grand Central Terminal.[133] Pei's scheme, ballyhooed as the world's tallest building, was to be surmounted by an observation tower. Before any sketches had been released, Webb & Knapp, Zeckendorf's company, announced that the proposal was being "restudied."

In September 1954 Patrick McGinnis, president of the New York, New Haven and Hartford Railroad, which had a half interest in Grand Central Terminal, offered his own proposal, developed with the advice of the builder Erwin Wolfson. Designed by Fellheimer & Wagner, architects specializing in railroad buildings and successors to the firm of Reed & Stem, co-designers of the original terminal, it called for the construction of four million square feet of office space in a fifty-story H-plan mass straddling the axis of Park Avenue.[134] According to this plan, East Forty-third and East Forty-fourth streets, now interrupted by the existing terminal structure, would be permitted to continue across the site and the Park Avenue viaduct would be straightened so that traffic would run directly north-south. The existing terminal, which Alfred Fellheimer dismissed as "in effect, a 'Chinese Wall,'"[135] would be demolished; built in its place would be six connected low-rise structures surmounted by roof gardens, as well as a double-cruciform tower. At the tower's base were to be stores and restaurants adjoining the elevated, landscaped spaces, while at the building's summit was to be a heliport; the building would also contain indoor parking facilities for 2,400 cars. Although little appears to have happened to either of these plans for several years, while the two railroads struggled for economic survival, in 1958 plans were announced for what was first called Grand Central City but would become the Pan Am Building.

Although the New York Central and the New Haven railroads were unable to resolve their dispute over the extent of their joint ownership of the terminal and its facilities, they agreed to work together with McGinnis's development adviser, Erwin Wolfson, knowing that neither entity would profit because the revenues would be used exclusively to maintain the terminal and its operations. Wolfson selected Emery Roth & Sons as his architects, who proposed a massive fifty-story tower containing three million square feet of office space, almost half again as much as that contained in the Empire State Building.[136] The new building would replace the nearly invisible six-story Grand Central Terminal Office Building that sat behind the terminal proper. It would rise over the railroad tracks, with a lobby lifted to the level of the Park Avenue auto ramps and connected to street-level passageways by escalators. These passageways, in turn, were connected by more escalators to the terminal's concourse level below. Parking for 2,000 cars on four levels was to be provided; helicopters would be permitted to land on the roof. In addition, the new building would contain two 1,800-seat, live-performance theaters as well as a movie theater seating 1,200. An open-air restaurant on the seventh-floor roof would also be provided. In keeping with current planning theory, these features were proposed to minimize tenants' need to travel in the course of their typical business day and to expand the value of the office building to the community.

As designed by the Roth office, the Grand Central City building was to be sheathed in aluminum and glass, creating, as much as a structure so vast could, a backdrop to the elaborate architecture of the older surrounding buildings. The design was sympathetic to the context in at least one important way: its "base" was comparable in height to that of the New York Central Building (in some versions the base was lower); and the north-south tower rising from the base would not be significantly wider than that of the New York Central Building. The new building would thus cause a minimal disruption of the vista up and down Park Avenue.

But Wolfson felt uncomfortable with the modesty of the Roth design. Convinced that such a prominent site demanded something more, Wolfson asked Richard Roth to suggest a few possible design collaborators. Roth suggested Walter Gropius, who in turn suggested Pietro Belluschi. In July 1958 the two architects were hired to team up with the Roth office on the Grand Central City project.[137] Gropius was the founder of the Bauhaus in Germany in 1919 and its director until 1928, and had been a leading proponent of architectural Modernism in the United States since 1938, when he became chairman of the Department of Architecture at Harvard University's Graduate School of Design, a post he held until 1952. He was also active as an architect in his capacity as senior partner of the Architects Collaborative of Cambridge, Massachusetts. Although Gropius had little experience with commercial buildings, he had been the leading designer of the Boston Back Bay Center plan (1953) for the mixed-use redevelopment of a large site in Boston, a project that had a great influence on architects and planners in their urban redevelopment work in the 1950s.[138] Pietro Belluschi, dean of the School of Architecture and Planning at the Massachusetts Institute of Technology from 1951 to 1965, was the designer of the elegantly minimal Equitable Life Assurance Building in Portland, Oregon (1944–47).[139] Belluschi was currently developing designs for the headquarters of the Juilliard School of Music at Lincoln Center (see chapter 9). In announcing the appointment of Gropius and Belluschi, Wolfson claimed that they would assist in both "esthetic and functional" aspects of the design but would not significantly alter the glass-and-aluminum envelope the Roth firm had planned for the building.[140] Such claims notwithstanding, in February 1959 an entirely new design for the building emerged.[141]

Gropius and Belluschi's revised plan, prepared in association with Richard Roth of Emery Roth & Sons, was unveiled on February 18, 1959. It was not the modest revision that Wolfson had promised but a radical redesign. The tower was turned ninety degrees and ran east-west, along the axis of Forty-fourth Street. It was five stories taller than the original proposal, rising to fifty-five floors; but the base was lower, only six floors, lower than any other building around it, including

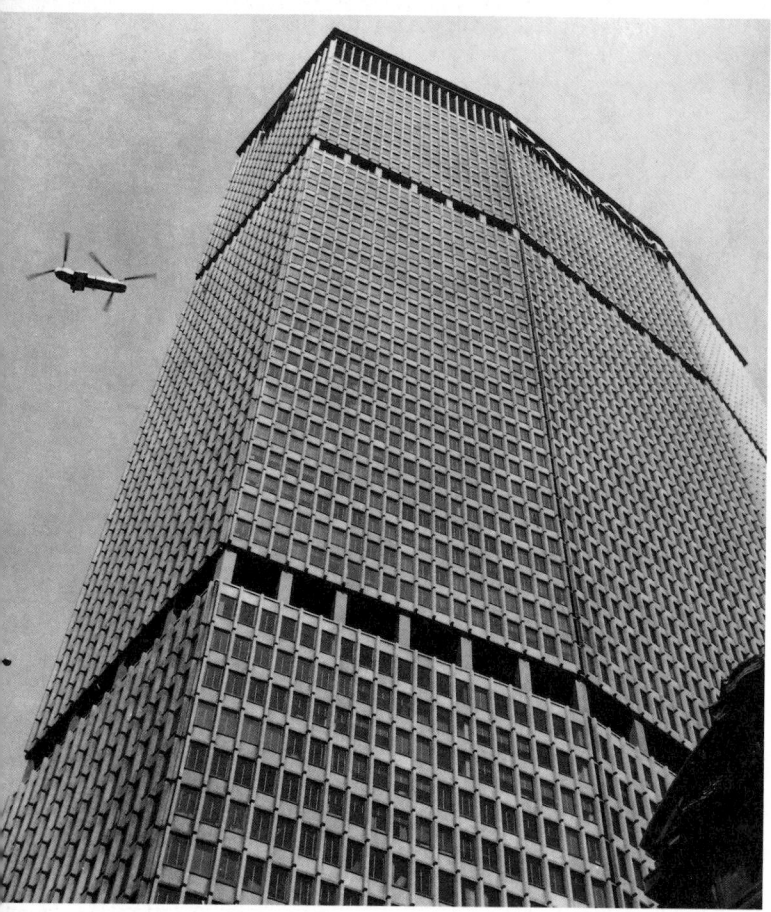

Above: Pan Am Building, 200 Park Avenue, East Forty-fourth to East Forty-fifth Street. Emery Roth & Sons, Walter Gropius and Pietro Belluschi, 1963. View to the northeast from base. ERS

Right: View south on Park Avenue from East Fifty-first Street showing Pan Am Building, with New York Central Building (Warren & Wetmore, 1929) directly in front. Molitor. JWM

Grand Central Terminal itself. (As finally designed, the base building was raised to eight stories to align with the terminal's cornice.) The new design supplied 2.4 million square feet of space, 600,000 fewer than the earlier design. Unlike the Roth design, this slablike tower, which covered 25 percent of the site, had no setbacks, but it was not without a unique sculptural presence. For one thing, its plan was that of a highly elongated octagon, with very narrow east and west ends and three broad planes along the north and south facades. It was broken into three horizontal sections, with bold shadows created by setting the curtain wall back behind the outside columns at the twenty-first and forty-sixth floors, where mechanical equipment was located. The neutral, silvery glass-and-aluminum skin of the previous design was replaced by a facade of precast concrete and glass.

Many reasons were given for the changes to the building. Richard Roth said the facets of the building would pick up "different planes of light as on a diamond,"[142] while Gropius argued that the new orientation would allow for more efficient air conditioning. Part of the motivation for the redesign may also have been the proposed changes to the zoning law, which were released in draft form only one month after Gropius and Belluschi had been hired. In addition, the tower's more slender profile improved the ratio of window wall to leasable office space. But it would seem that the main reason for the redesign was, as Wolfson claimed, to improve the building's appearance. The new look of the project, though daring, was hardly original. It was, in fact, based on a well-known prototype, Le Corbusier's unrealized skyscraper for Algiers (1938–42).[143] It also related to Gio Ponti and Pier Luigi Nervi's technologically innovative, far more sveltely proportioned Pirelli Building, then under construction in Milan.[144]

No sooner was the new design released than it became the center of heated controversy. Even the drawings failed to charm: Walter McQuade said that the drawings "go so far as to make it look pretty, but in the way . . . of those towering nightclub showgirls who don't perform, but just stand there and smile."[145] Sybil Moholy-Nagy, the widow of Gropius's Bauhaus colleague László Moholy-Nagy and now an architectural historian, was among the first to speak out against the new design, attacking the building for its destruction of a certain kind of urbanism:

> Esthetically, there was one moment of relief for the eyes in the linear wasteland of our avenues. The Grand Central Tower had an outline, *a profile*, a play of light and shadow that reminded the weary senses that someone once had cared to provide a solid substance as a syncope in the amorphous mass of indifferent shapes. So modest have we become in our claims for visual identification that even the eclecticism of 1929 has been gratefully received. Together with the [Grand Central] Terminal building, the tower provided *human* scale and architectural personality: something even to attack, but of its own character. This now will be lost.[146]

Natalie Parry, writing in response to Moholy-Nagy's critique and articulating a point of view that would become crucial to the subsequent battle for the preservation of the station itself, praised the scheme because it left intact "the spacious, star-studded Concourse of the Grand Central Terminal": "This otherwise wasteful monument to our past was originally destined for destruction, but in Wolfson's plans it has been preserved, together with the precious air space above it, as foreground to the faceted curtain wall of the Grand Central City Building which will rise behind it."[147]

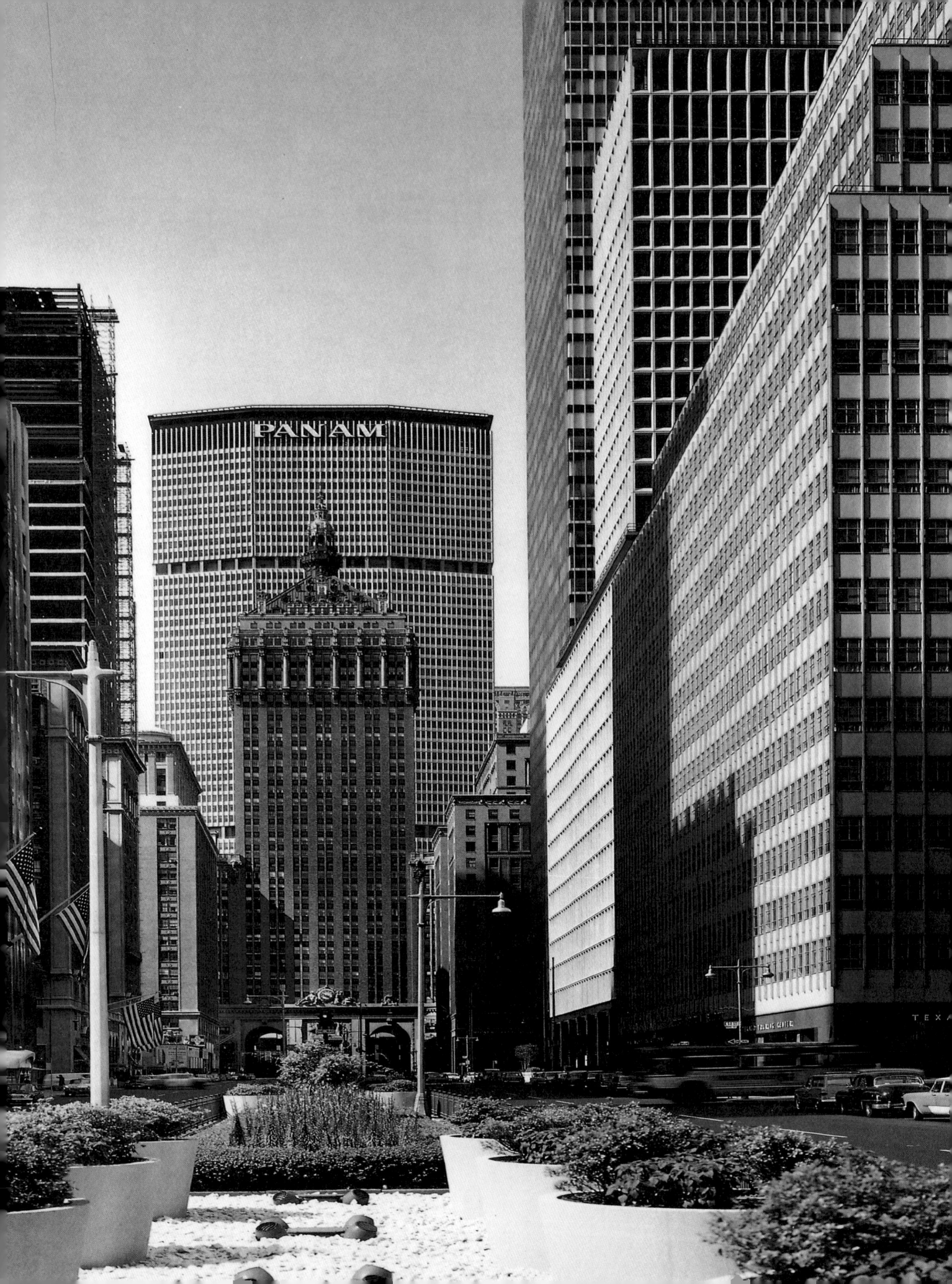

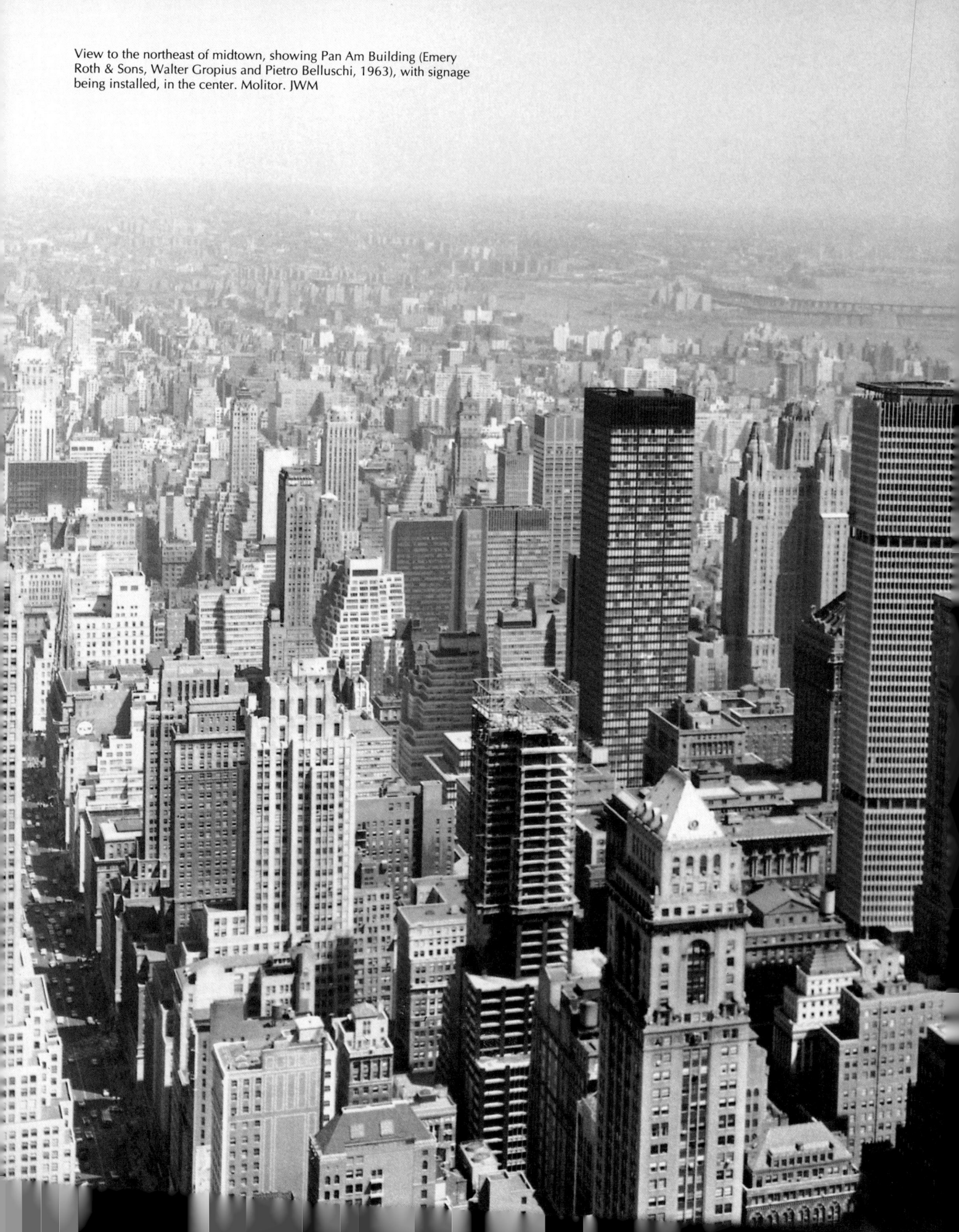

View to the northeast of midtown, showing Pan Am Building (Emery Roth & Sons, Walter Gropius and Pietro Belluschi, 1963), with signage being installed, in the center. Molitor. JWM

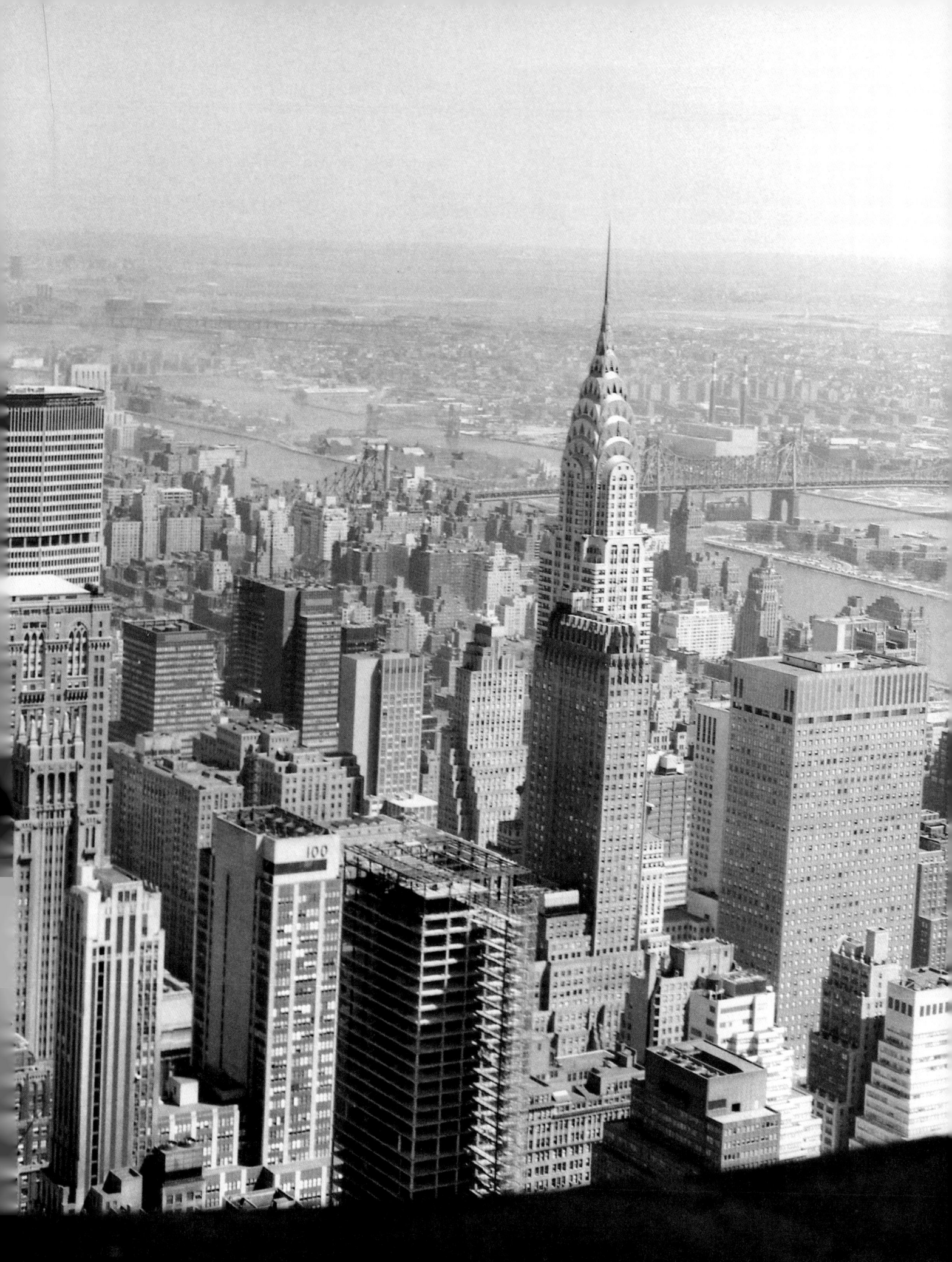

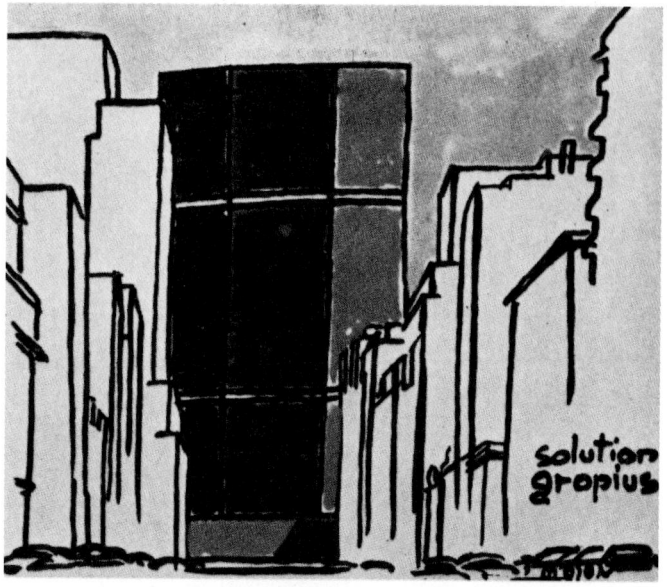

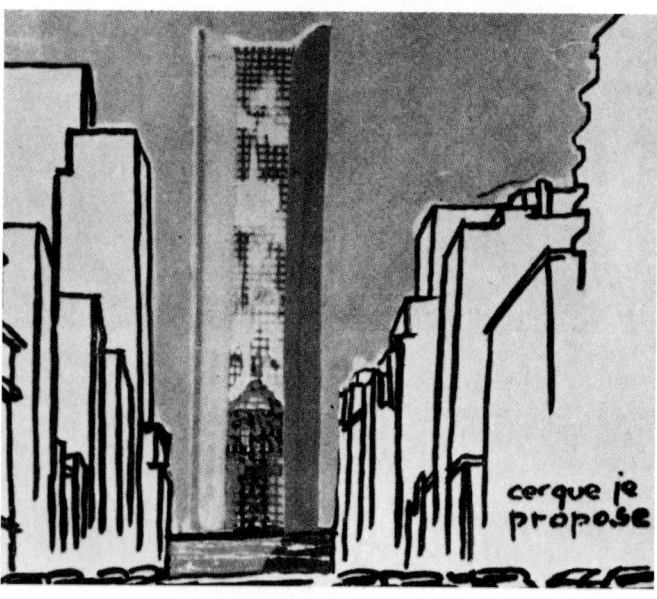

Above: Renderings by Martin Pinchis, 1960, showing, top: view to the north on Park Avenue with proposed Grand Central City Building by Emery Roth & Sons, Walter Gropius and Pietro Belluschi; bottom: same view with alternative building proposed by Pinchis. PA. CU

Top, center and bottom right: Alternative building proposals for the same site by Martin Pinchis. Views to the northeast. PA. CU

Disappointment in the revised design was expressed internationally. The Italian critic Gillo Dorfles, comparing Grand Central Terminal with the new project, said: "In place of a unique and unmistakable shape keeping . . . the fantastic mark of its origins, thus almost giving a seal to the important thoroughfare, Park Avenue, we shall have a building which lacks such fantastic and balancing characteristics of space, and appears instead—for all the rigorous harmonies of its masses and volumes—stylistically 'neutral.'"[148] In November 1959 a Rumanian architect, Martin Pinchis of Bucharest, published in *L'Architettura cronache e storia*, an influential Italian journal, two drawings illustrating an alternate solution for the tower that would not block Park Avenue's axis. Pinchis also submitted the drawings to the editors of *Progressive Architecture*, along with additional views hitherto unpublished. In a letter accompanying the drawings, he wrote:

> From the point of view of urbanism, one must realize that a building of monumental character, located on the axis of the most important major artery and the center of gravity of the city, imposes certain requirements of composition. At the same time the size of the building demanded by the program calls for a height which will make it a spire as well as the dominant element of a gigantic composition, and in this way will surpass the silhouette of all the skyscrapers existing in New York. It is necessary to bear in mind that the Avenue is on the average only 45 meters wide while some of the existing skyscrapers bordering it rise to a height of 200 meters. Between these two cliffs of glass and steel there is only the sky and the horizon which are free. Hence, there is the necessity of preserving the characteristic endlessness of New York avenues and not to create opaque screens which would obstruct them. . . . The plan should have considered equally important both the skyscraper tower and the Avenue which passes on both sides of the building.[149]

Pinchis, perhaps naively, proposed a building with a transparent center and two lateral wings, in essence a version of the H-shaped plan initially proposed by Fellheimer & Wagner, but turned so that the end bars of the H ran north and south.

Gropius was quick to reply to Pinchis's proposal. "Its plan is not workable, for while the modern tendency in office buildings aims at very large undivided areas on one floor . . . he offers only 2 very slab-like tall towers connected by a glass passageway." Gropius also responded to Pinchis's general theory of the site. "I am unable to follow the critic's argument that the tremendous traffic of this region's trade center must be expressed by a 'dynamic solution.' On the contrary, it appears to me to be desirable to close within this labyrinth of traffic movements the super-long Park Avenue view from both sides, with a quiet, imposing building mass of a strong prismatic form."[150]

The controversy over the building raged on. On January 15, 1960, a symposium was held in the auditorium of the New School to discuss the new design. Hans Simons, the school's president, was the moderator, and the speakers included Roth, Belluschi, Gropius and Wolfson as well as the architect-planner Victor Gruen, the architect-journalist Peter Blake, Thomas H. Creighton, editor of *Progressive Architecture*, and Paul Zucker, the historian. Surprisingly, Zucker voiced an eloquent defense of both the building and its urbanism:

> In city planning a certain minimum amount of conformity, of mutual relationship, of integration, is absolutely necessary. This does not exist on Park Avenue. . . . The buildings are solutions of specific problems, economic solutions, commercial solutions, and also very good aesthetic solutions. However, they have nothing to do with each other. . . . [Grand Central City]

offers the opportunity, the possibility, of a point of reference to which and with which all of these individual buildings are connected.[151]

It was issues of urbanism that seemed to be most on the minds of the forum's participants. Victor Gruen questioned the decision to park 2,000 cars on a central site immediately adjacent to the world's greatest concentration of public transportation. Thomas Creighton, saying he was "appalled by the fact that we seem to accept the statement that there must be a building on this site," disingenuously asked: "Wouldn't it be possible to leave the space completely open as one of the great plazas of the world?"[152] At the end of the evening, as if in response to the general sense that the problem with the project lay in its size, Belluschi said: "I'd like to put in a good word for urban congestion. . . . It's an excitement you can find only in New York City."[153]

Other voices were also raised on behalf of the building's urban effect and on behalf of high-density development in city centers. The planner Charles Abrams defended the scheme,[154] as did Emerson Goble, editor of *Architectural Record.* Goble persuasively suggested, as the building was under construction, that its size might be considered an asset, "not as a visual focus . . . but as a contribution to the working of the city life." Explaining that he was not discussing the building's aesthetics, Goble argued that "the business community works best in a vertical city, a three-dimensional city." He believed that buildings like this, which were centrally located and increased the convenience of business calls made on foot, helped push the city away from a dependence on cars. Although many observers had criticized the project because of its contribution to congestion, Goble continued, "a calm look" at the plans revealed ample circulation spaces for pedestrians to and through the building. Goble concluded his argument in favor of concentration by calling for a new way of looking at city planning controls: "I think the time has passed when we can simply hold out for the height-limit type of zoning and planning which brings us the horizontal city. . . . [Grand Central City] is a great big proponent of the vertical city. And I believe that the vertical city, in reasonable chunks, is what the necessities of the times would indicate."[155]

Richard Roth, writing in 1963, reinforced this point, placing the building squarely within the tradition of the congested city that Harvey Wiley Corbett had so eloquently advocated in the 1920s: "I have for over two decades advocated the intense, high density city plan for the business sections of New York City. The argument of course could be carried to the point of the ridiculous: how high can a vertical city go! But large scale urbanistic effects are achieved by verticality. A truly urbanistic city is composed of vertical areas, self-contained but continuous." His building, he believed, was a perfect example of how to create high-density urbanism without losing sight of humanity: "The proximity to public transportation is obvious. . . . It is a bustling building in the center of a busy, bustling district. Within the confines of its three acres, a complete, if narrow, life could be lived."[156]

In Ada Louise Huxtable's initial assessment of the project, she tackled issues of both urbanism and aesthetics. Claiming that "by virtue of its size and location, Grand Central City will inevitably be New York's most important structure," Huxtable explained: "There is no doubt that Messrs. Wolfson, Roth, Gropius and Belluschi have designed a major landmark. Whether it is monster or marvel, however, is being hotly debated in architecture and building circles." Although Huxtable felt that the building would do nothing to ameliorate the urban

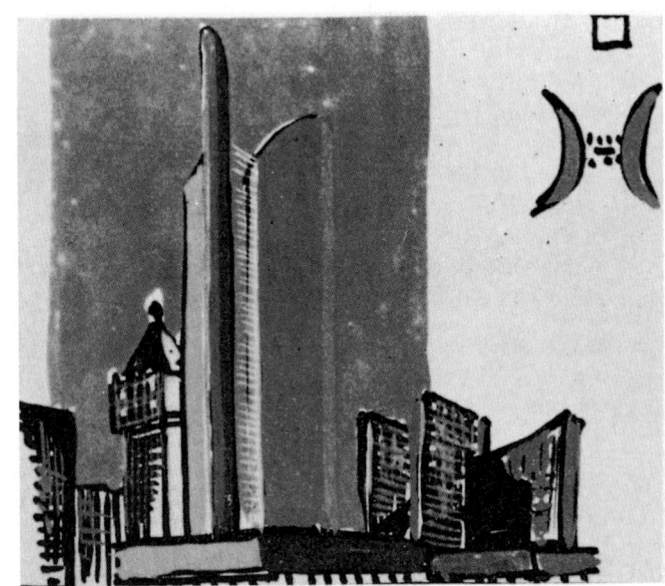

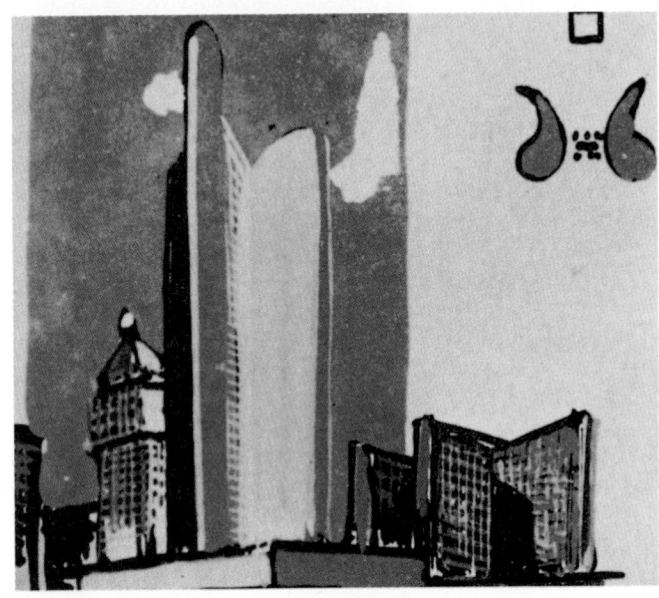

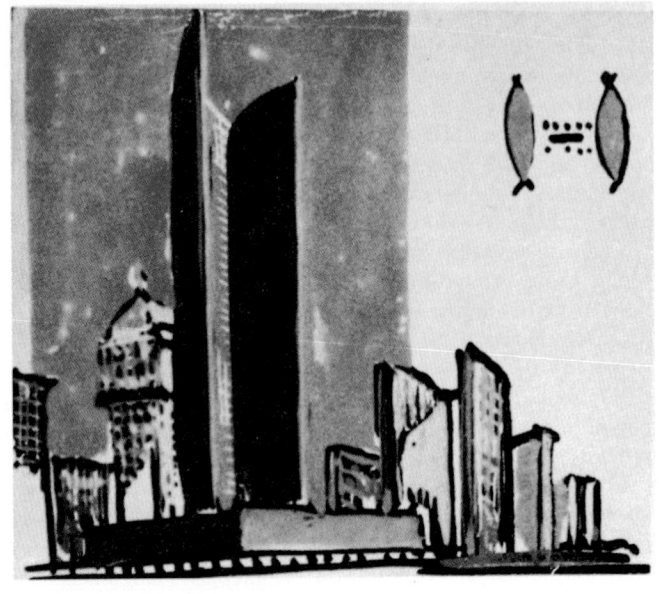

horrors of New York, she did see "one bright spot in the picture . . . the serious consideration that this major commercial edifice attempts to give to architectural esthetics," regardless of whether the result would be "monumentality or megalomania."[157] Edgar Kaufmann, Jr., had a much stronger opinion:

> Unlike most recent skyscrapers, this building . . . will be a white cliff of rough quartz, sharply patterned by vertical and horizontal shadows. Thus the colorful, generally feminine sleekness of the glass canyon to the north will be closed by a great, grainy, masculine slab. From the south this same slab will arise in strange contradiction to the sumptuous academic stone arcades of the station. Seen from either main approach, [the building] will sit adamantly eccentric among its neighbors. . . . Grand Central City is generally careless of its influence on the crowded Grand Central district, taking more from it than contributing to it. It expresses itself regardless of its neighbors, it blocks the view, it shares no whit of style. . . . [It] is a sincere effort, but in the very middle of the ruins of a short-lived grandeur it has failed to grasp the spirit of what is grand. Infinitely larger than any work that stood or stands nearby, its design shows none of the scale of urban grandness that is still exemplified in the station next door. The great architecture of New York at mid-twentieth century, it seems, has yet to be imagined.[158]

Construction of Grand Central City was delayed by a steel strike in 1960 that lingered well into the summer, giving Wolfson time to raise $25 million of the building's $100 million cost from Jack "King" Cotton, a flamboyant British entrepreneur. With this deal clinched, the new partners were able to sign Pan American Airways on for 600,000 square feet of space, and in December 1960 the building acquired its new name. Now the Pan Am Building, it would carry its corporate name aloft with two large signs, one atop the north facade, the other atop the south, and two of the company's logos at the top of the thin east and west walls—a kind of blatant advertising that had hitherto been absent from important New York towers. With Pan Am on board, Wolfson's early dream of a rooftop heliport was pushed forward, and by March 1961 New York Airways was ordering helicopters to provide regular service from the building to local airports. (This service went into effect with the completion of the building but was terminated in 1977 after a disastrous accident when a landing strut collapsed, resulting in the death of four passengers as well as one person in the streets below.)[159]

The steel strike also gave James Ruderman, the structural engineer, more time to develop drawings for the building, his most challenging project ever. Ruderman had worked on several high-rise buildings over the New York Central's railroad tracks: he was the structural engineer for the buildings at 290, 300, 320, 350 and 410 Park Avenue. This project, however, was more complicated: not only was the work to be done without disrupting scheduled train service, but it also involved two separate structural systems—the eight-story lower base building, which would use the columns of the old Grand Central Terminal Office Building, and the forty-seven-story tower, which would have its own independent structure.

Demolition of the Grand Central Terminal Office Building began in August 1960. By the fall of 1961 the tower frame was rising above the granite-sheathed base building (the recessed eighth and ninth floors were sheathed in aluminum), and tan precast-concrete "Mo-sai" panels—the first ever to be used in a major New York skyscraper—were being installed on its lower floors. At a brass band ceremony, on March 7, 1963, the building made its official debut with the hoopla, as Ada Louise Huxtable reported, "worthy of a Presidential inauguration."[160]

The first tenants began moving into the Pan Am Building in April 1963, but Erwin Wolfson was not there to greet them; he had died almost a year before.[161] Had he been alive, Wolfson would have been pleased. Contrary to the predictions of naysayers in the real estate industry, 93 percent of the office space was leased. Its financing was secure, with a $70 million mortgage taken by the New York State Employees Retirement Fund, the largest ever made in the city for one commercial property.

The building's public lobbies featured sixty-six elevators (five of them for freight) that transported tenants and visitors to the offices, four escalators that smoothed the way between the building's concourse and that of Grand Central, and fourteen escalators that took tenants and visitors up one level from the building concourse to the lobby (like at Union Carbide, the elevator pits had to be kept above the basement-level railroad). In keeping with Gropius's belief that artists should supply the decorative embellishment that contemporary minimalist architecture lacked, the public spaces were treated as a permanent art gallery, with work by his longtime collaborators Josef Albers, Gyorgy Kepes and Richard Lippold.

Kepes provided a mural composed of two aluminum screens made up of concentric squares. This two-sided piece was placed in two column bays behind the lobby information desk, where it could also be seen from the double-height north concourse below. Albers's contribution, a twenty-eight-by-fifty-eight-foot laminated tile mural with colors mixed in a complex abstract pattern, was affixed to the broad wall that lay straight ahead as one descended the escalators from the building's concourse to the railroad station. Both the Kepes and the Albers murals seemed overwhelmed by the architecture and the crowds. Most disappointing of all was Richard Lippold's wire construction, originally called *The Globe* but renamed *Flight*, specially constructed for the Vanderbilt Avenue lobby. Despite its name, this construction, with its forty-foot span and its cables attached to the balcony, seemed decidedly earthbound and stagy. As he was working on the piece, Lippold, concerned that the building's upbeat Muzak system would be incompatible with his work, invited the composer John Cage to create a suitable aural environment. But when Cage proposed that Muzak be used in a scrambled version, its sounds released by the to-ings and fro-ings of pedestrians who would activate photoelectric cells in the lobby, the management balked. They reached a compromise when the management agreed to play classical music through the sound system.

Despite the architects' efforts to soften the effect of the minimalist interiors, the lobby spaces were not well received. As James T. Burns, Jr., put it: "Moving past the colonnaded entry and into the lobby of Pan Am, one sees that the taste for monolithism did not desert the designers here. The spaces are much too big and heavy-handed. Surfacing materials are too numerous and varied, and lighting elements for general illumination and lighting of art works are too prevalent."[162] Ada Louise Huxtable was particularly critical of the lobby art program, which she denounced as "a face-saving gimmick," an "architectural cover-up . . . turning good art into a bad joke."[163] A more successful interior was the ticketing office that Pan American Airways opened in 1963 in the northwest corner of the building, designed by Charles Forberg Associates and Edward Larrabee Barnes Associates.[164] Influenced by the interiors of Eero Saarinen's TWA facility at Idlewild Airport, the team created a monochromatic interior with sculpted columns and curving seating units.

The Pan Am Building garnered more extreme criticism once it was built than it had when the revised design was presented four years earlier. Even before it was quite finished, Wolf Von

366

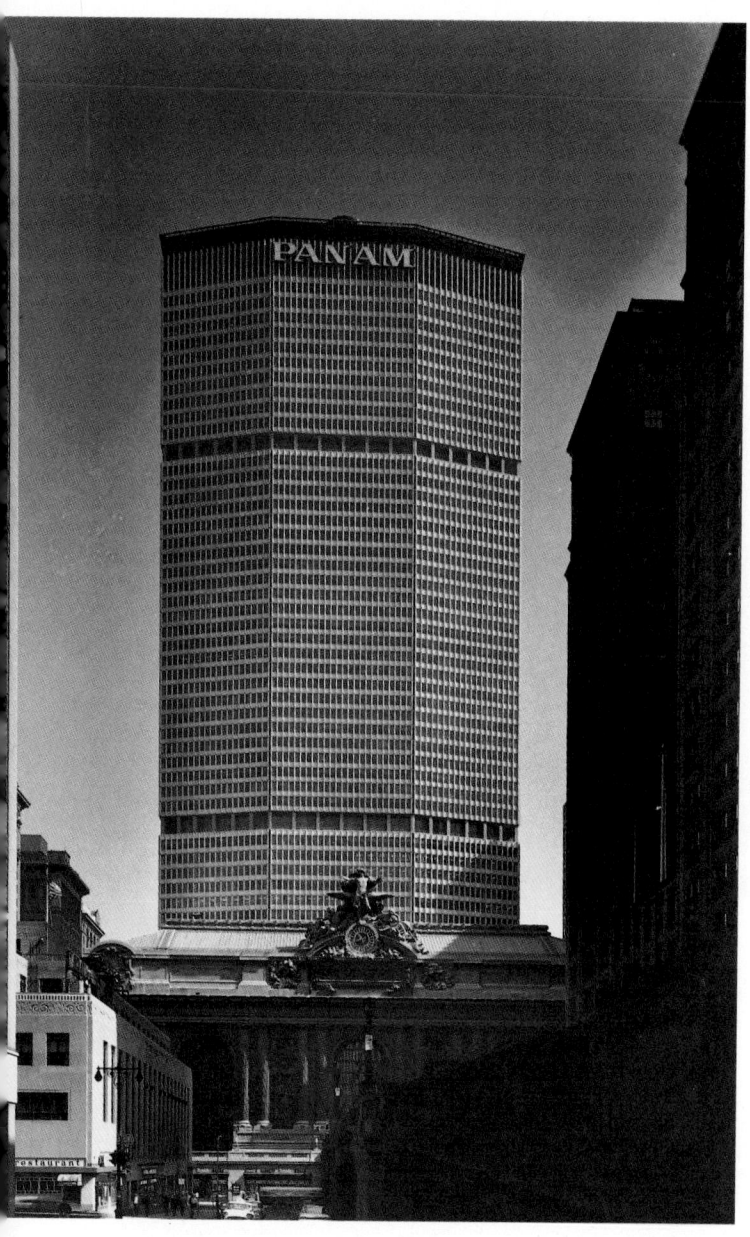

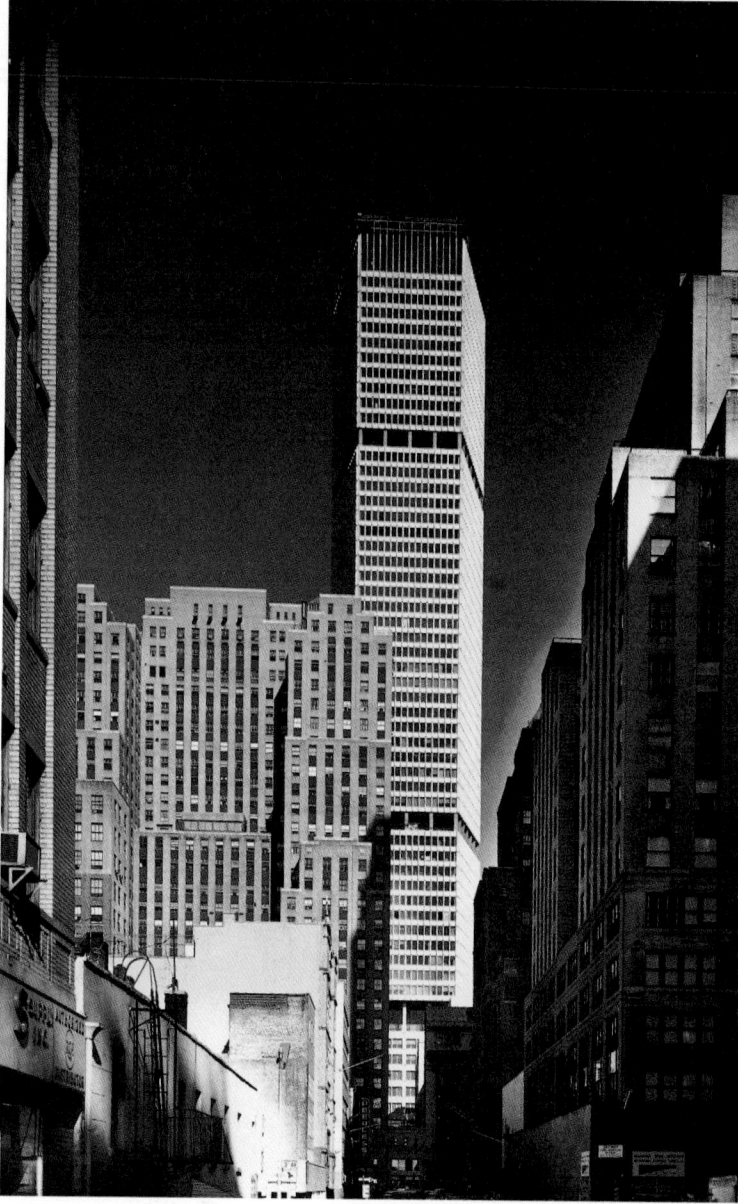

Pan Am Building, 200 Park Avenue, East Forty-fourth to East Forty-fifth Street. Emery Roth & Sons, Walter Gropius and Pietro Belluschi, 1963. View to the north with Grand Central Terminal (Reed & Stem and Warren & Wetmore, 1903–13) in the foreground. Molitor. JWM

Pan Am Building. View to the west from East Forty-fourth Street between Third and Lexington avenues also showing Graybar Building (Sloan & Robertson, 1927) in the foreground. Molitor. JWM

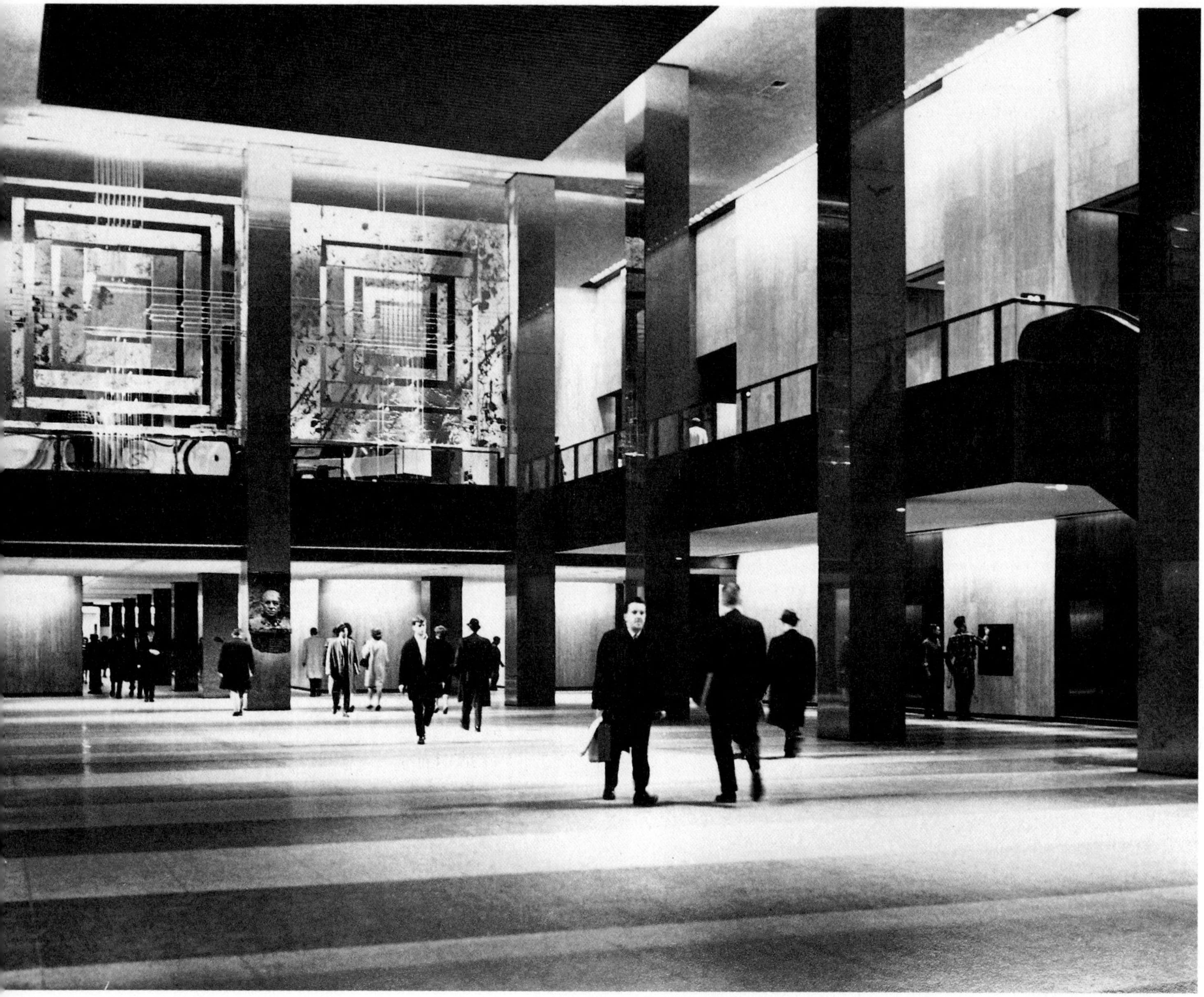

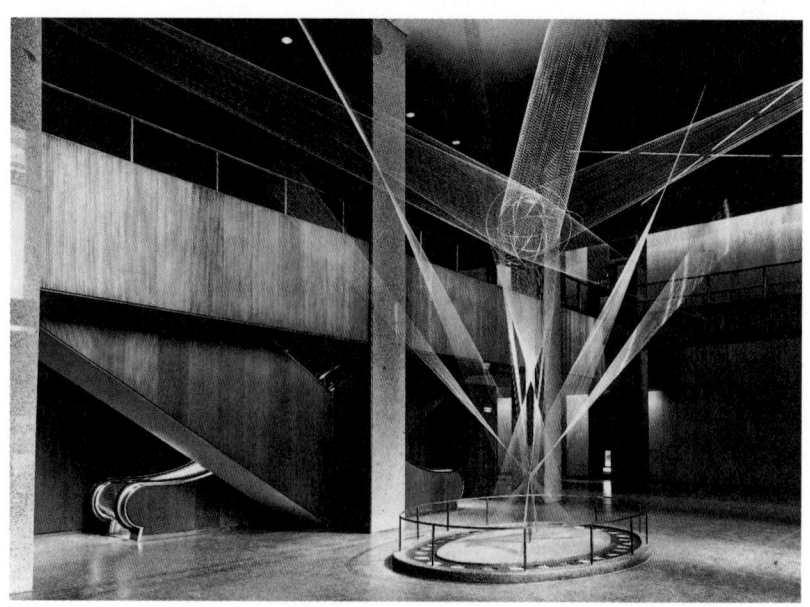

Above: Pan Am Building, 200 Park Avenue, East Forty-fourth to East Forty-fifth Street. Emery Roth & Sons, Walter Gropius and Pietro Belluschi, 1963. View of concourse showing, on the upper left, aluminum screens designed by Gyorgy Kepes. Molitor. JWM

Right: Pan Am Building. Vanderbilt Avenue lobby including sculpture *Flight* by Richard Lippold. Leeser. ERS

Top far right: Pan Am Ticket Office in Pan Am Building, southeast corner of Vanderbilt Avenue and East Forty-fifth Street. Charles Forberg Associates and Edward Larrabee Barnes, 1963. Cserna. GC

Bottom far right: *Proposed Colossal Monument for Park Avenue, NYC: Good Humor Bar.* Claes Oldenburg, 1965. Finkelman. Collection Donna and Carroll Janis. DCJ

Eckardt, writing in the *New Republic*, pronounced it a colossal failure: "So there it stands, bang! A $100 million slab which looks as though some malicious seven-league monster had nailed up one of our finest avenues with Gargantuan boards just to spite us." And he felt that the octagonal plan did nothing to ameliorate the effect: "As seen from the avenue, the reclining angles . . . are too shallow to be readily discernible." Lamenting the building's impact on Park Avenue, Von Eckardt pointed out that "Seen from downtown, it appropriates the . . . facade of the Grand Central station as though it were its own."[165]

Von Eckardt's was not the only attack on the building's relationship to Park Avenue: this aspect of the design was unanimously derided. Although the building's design was said to have been a true collaboration between Gropius and Belluschi, the crucial decision in determining how the building would affect the avenue—the decision to change the slab's orientation from north-south to east-west—was laid squarely on Gropius. The architect argued that it made "a strong point of reference for the unbalanced building masses that are situated north and south of Grand Central Station."[166] But for Vincent Scully, Gropius's decision to cross the street's axis and block the vista dealt Park Avenue "its fatal blow"; the building, he said, "visually denies the continuity of the Avenue beyond Grand Central, deprecates the length of the Avenue's movement, and smothers its scale. In any terms other than brute expediency it should not have been there at all."[167] Claes Oldenburg mocked the building's blockage of the avenue with his *Proposed Colossal Monument for Park Avenue, NYC: Good Humor Bar* (1965),[168] which consisted of a monumental sheath over the existing Pan Am Building, with traffic routed through a "bite" in the ice-cream bar.

Ada Louise Huxtable's assessment was also damning:

Bigness is blinding. A $100,000,000 building cannot really be called cheap. But Pan Am is a colossal collection of minimums. Its exterior and its public spaces, in particular, use minimum acceptable quality executed with a minimum of imagination (always an expensive commodity), or distinction (which comes high), or finesse (which costs more). Pan Am is gigantically second-rate. . . . For its bulk, its importance, its effect, and its ballyhoo, it had an obligation to be much better. Size is not nobility; a monumental deal does not make a monument.[169]

Perhaps the *New York Times* had the last word in its editorial, which, judging from the style of it, was written by Huxtable:

Now that we have the $100,000,000 Pan Am Building, just what have we got? We have gained the world's largest private office building. We have lost some of the world's most impressive urban views now that Pan Am's massive bulk blots out the sky and reduces the silhouette of the New York Central Building to an ineffectual shadow. We have also lost an opportunity to plan the city's most congested area sanely and efficiently. In sustaining these losses we have, alas, not gained an architectural masterpiece.[170]

Gropius, of course, thought otherwise, believing not only that his building was the proper solution to the problem but that it would prove its ultimate rightness when the New York Central Building was pulled down, a fate he seemed to think desirable and, apparently, inevitable. To this end he proposed a park for the site to create a proper forecourt for the Pan Am Building.[171] Yet almost twenty-five years later, when *New York* magazine surveyed more than one hundred prominent New Yorkers to come up with a list of the ten buildings they'd most love to see destroyed, it was the Pan Am Building, not the New York Central Building, that ranked first among their choices.[172]

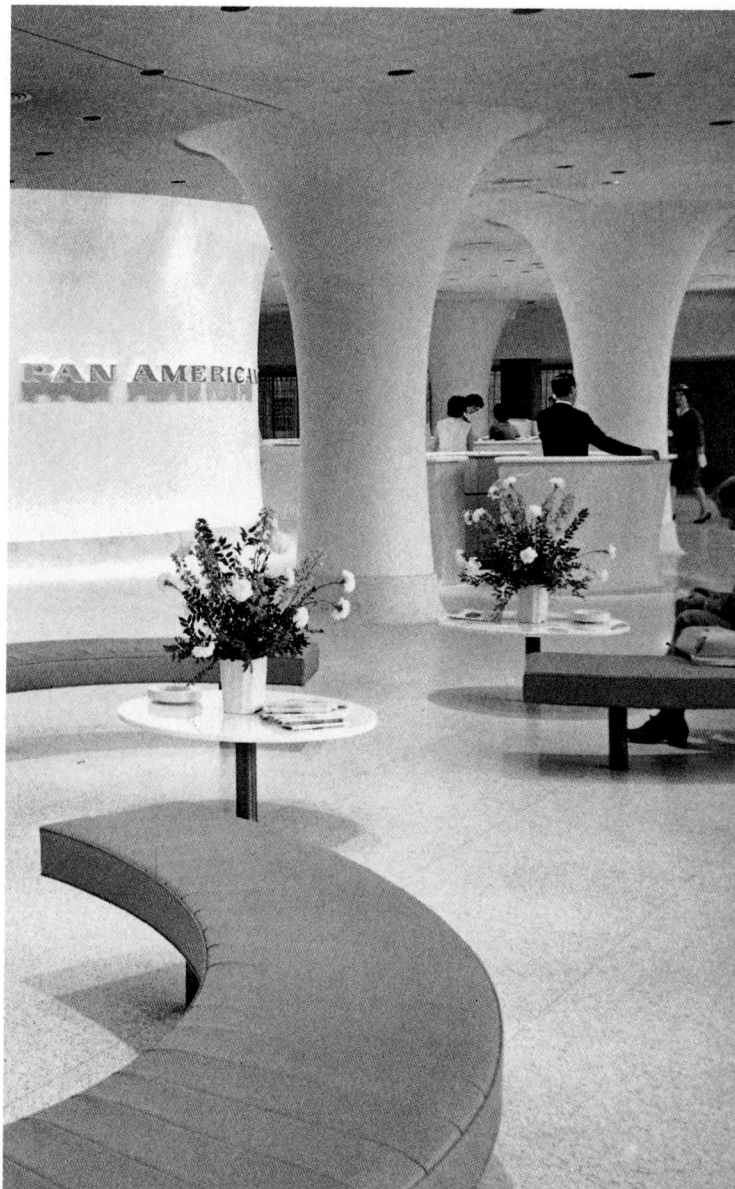

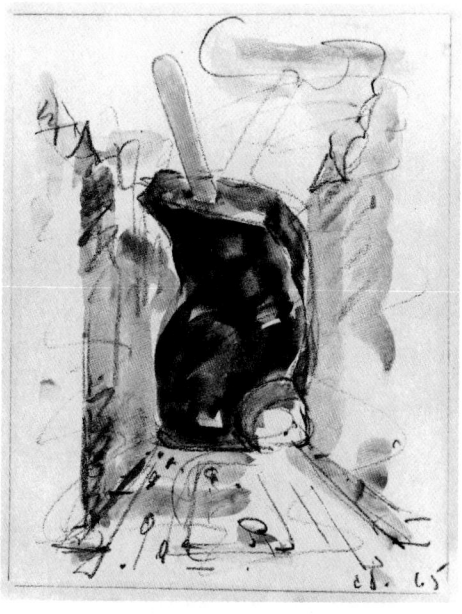

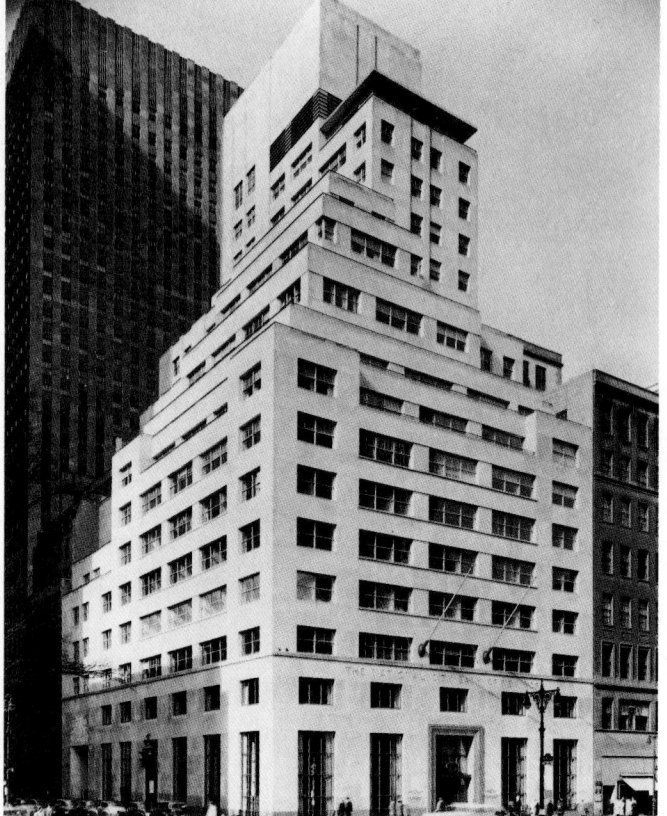

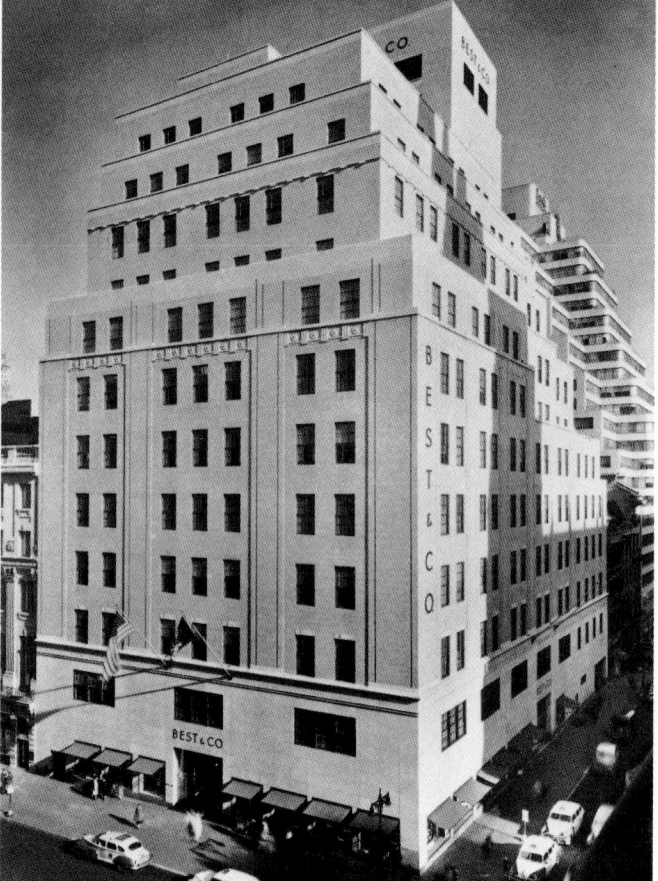

The postwar evolution of the midtown stretch of Fifth Avenue reflected the ebb and flow of the city's struggle to maintain the traditionally high standards of its commercial architecture as well as its ambience as a cosmopolitan environment.[1] In 1947 the Fifth Avenue Association tentatively proposed to establish a Board of Experts to review the design of new buildings.[2] The suggestion met with widespread alarm among leading architects and designers, however, and was soon dropped.[3]

Fifth Avenue's first significant postwar building was not an office building but a department store, Shreve, Lamb & Harmon's Best & Company.[4] Founded in 1891 as the Lilliputian Bazaar, the city's first store specializing in children's clothing, Best's had diversified into a specialty store featuring conservative, expensive clothing for men, women and children. The pioneer of suburban branch stores (see chapter 15), it had kept its 1910 store (Townsend, Steinle & Hackell), on the northwest corner of Thirty-fifth Street and Fifth Avenue, in good repair and it prospered.[5] But, in 1944, in keeping with the general uptown movement of fashionable shopping that had begun with Saks settling at Fiftieth Street twenty years before, the president of Best's, Philíp Le Boutillier, acquired the long-abandoned former headquarters of the Union Club, designed by Cass Gilbert in 1902.[6] In January 1945 demolition began to make way for a new twelve-story facility. As completed in 1947, the stripped-down, sparely but elegantly detailed Modern Classical building clad in white brick and marble rose seven stories before the first of a series of setbacks that culminated in a small twelfth floor. Fronting 113 feet on Fifth Avenue and 192 feet on Fifty-first Street, it had a 28-foot-wide "outlet" that extended through the block to Fifty-second Street, where there was space for off-street loading for six trucks.

Two office buildings were built almost simultaneously with Best's. Both, in their way, attempted to reflect the architectural style of their immediate neighbor, Rockefeller Center. The first of the two to be completed was Leonard Schultze & Associates' Crowell-Collier Building (1950), at 640 Fifth Avenue, on the northwest corner of Fifty-first Street, which replaced John B. Snook and Charles Atwood's house for William Henry Vanderbilt (1879–82).[7] Built to house the publishing company's offices, the Crowell-Collier Building was comparatively small, with an eight-story base filling the site and eight setback floors. An earlier scheme by Walker & Gillette (1944) had called for a thirteen-story building with continuous horizontal window bands above a fairly solid three-story base.[8] To Lewis Mumford, Schultze's limestone-clad design was "an example of eclecticism without conviction," an attempt to reconcile the traditional and the modern that managed "to combine the saddest features of each." Although Schultze had tried to relate the design of his building to that of Rockefeller Center, Mumford felt his facades lacked "visual relation" to the older complex; he was particularly critical of the "extremely depressing ornamental sculpture" over the side entrance. Yet he found that "viewed a few blocks away, from the south, the profile of the building is rather handsome."[9]

Fifth Avenue's second postwar office building, the Sinclair Oil Building (1952), replaced the St. Nicholas Collegiate Reformed Protestant Dutch Church.[10] The proposed destruction of this church initiated a stormy battle between, on the one side, the minister and his parishioners, who favored preservation, and, on the other side, the Consistory of the Reformed Protestant Dutch Church in the City of New York, which advocated demolition and held the power to make the final decision (see chapter 16). Where the architects of the Crowell-Collier Building may not have succeeded in their effort to capture the character of Rockefeller Center, the Sinclair Building's architects, Carson & Lundin, did, so much so that the building seemed to be an extension of the complex. Plans for the 350,000-square-foot, twenty-eight-story building, initially undertaken by the Massachusetts Mutual Life Insurance Company as an investment property and subsequently named for its principal tenant, Sinclair Oil, were unveiled in 1949. Carson & Lundin had been chosen to design the building because, as staff architects for Rockefeller Center, they would most likely be sympathetic to it. In return for sacrificing buildable area to prevent blocking any of the center's windows—the tower was pushed as close to Fifth Avenue as possible while still honoring the seven-story setback of the center's Fifth Avenue buildings—the architects were allowed to hook the new building into the center's network of underground concourses and its subbasement-level delivery system. The Sinclair Building consisted of a small tower—its 5,400-net-square-foot floors of rentable space were the smallest tower floors erected anywhere in the United States since 1930—sitting atop a seven-story base that filled the site. The principal portion of the building lay along Fifth Avenue and Forty-eighth Street, but a wing extended behind E. H. Faile's Goelet Building (1931) to Forty-ninth Street.[11]

While the effort to make the bulky, squat Sinclair Building a good neighbor to Rockefeller Center was commendable, to Modernist-minded observers the building's greatest success was its handling of the ground-floor lobby, "just where," as the editors of *Architectural Forum* put it, "Rockefeller Center obviously failed." The editors praised the building's column-free entrance as "one of the smartest small lobbies in the city."[12] Its most notable features were a sloped ceiling, intended to create a greater sense of space by forcing the perspective, and enameled metal lighting coves suggesting coffers. The lobby was entered from Forty-eighth Street so that the Fifth Avenue frontage could be reserved for shops, a distinctly different approach from that pursued by Rockefeller Center's architects in, for example, the British and French buildings, which sacrificed most of their narrow Fifth Avenue frontages to monumental entrances. The Sinclair Building's most important retail tenant was the venerable men's clothing store Rogers Peet & Company, which, in an effort to modernize their image, hired Raymond Loewy & Associates to design their ground-floor and concourse-level space.[13] Pan American Airways also occupied a store, representing the growing trend for airlines to establish ticket offices at prime Fifth Avenue locations (see below).

In 1952 the International Style Modernism anticipated by unrealized wartime proposals at last came to Fifth Avenue in the form of Emery Roth & Sons' nineteen-story 555 Fifth Avenue, on the southeast corner of Forty-sixth Street.[14] Only the third new office building to rise on the avenue since the war, 555 Fifth Avenue replaced six buildings from four to six stories in height, including one that once contained Richard Haviland Smythe's 1928 shop for John Ward, a men's shoe store.[15] In December 1952 plans were announced for another Roth-designed office building, this one occupying a modest 7,500-square-foot site at 720 Fifth Avenue, on the northwest corner of Fifty-sixth Street, replacing Rene Sargent and Horace Trumbauer's Duveen Brothers art gallery of 1911 (see chapter 16).[16] In a gesture toward the site's past and the traditionally high-class tone of this stretch of the avenue, the Roths proposed a stone-clad facade; as completed in 1954, however, the sixteen-story building re-

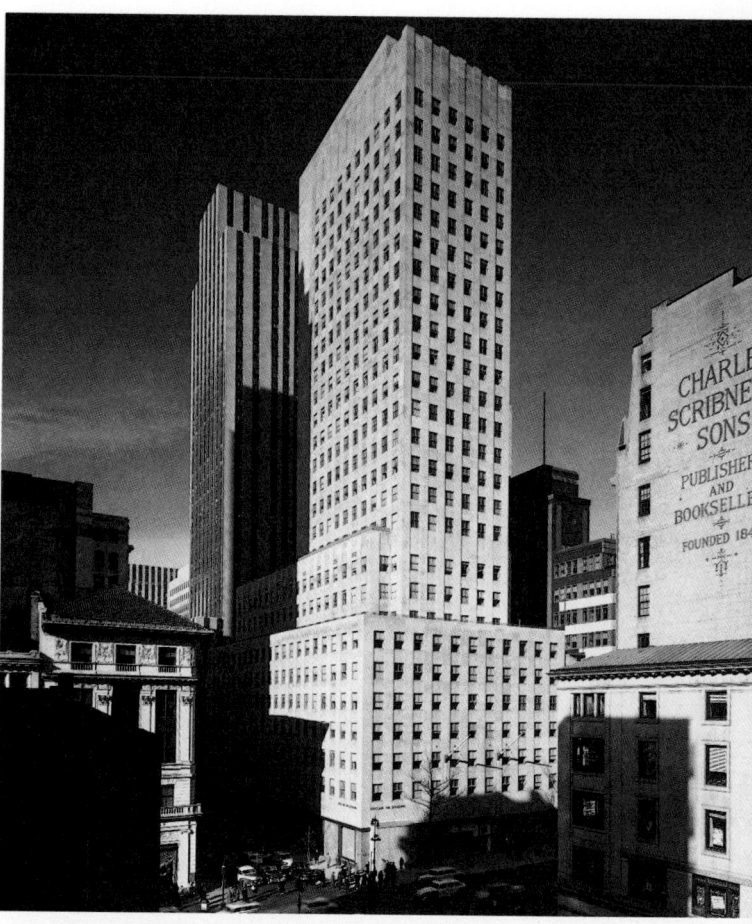

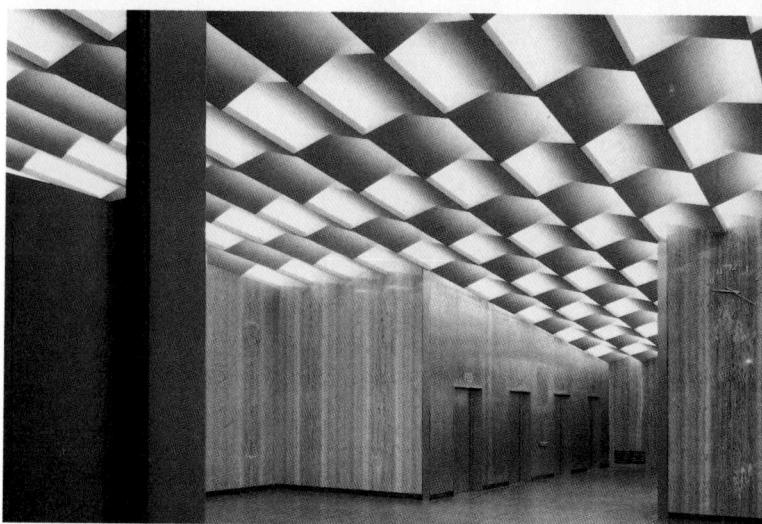

Top left: Crowell-Collier Building, 640 Fifth Avenue, northwest corner of West Fifty-first Street. Leonard Schultze & Associates, 1950. View to the northwest. Wurts. MCNY

Bottom left: Best & Company, northeast corner of Fifth Avenue and East Fifty-first Street. Shreve, Lamb & Harmon, 1947. View to the northeast. Wurts. MCNY

Top: Sinclair Oil Building, northwest corner of Fifth Avenue and West Forty-eighth Street. Carson & Lundin, 1952. View to the northwest. Stoller. ©ESTO

Bottom: Sinclair Oil Building. Lobby. Stoller. ©ESTO

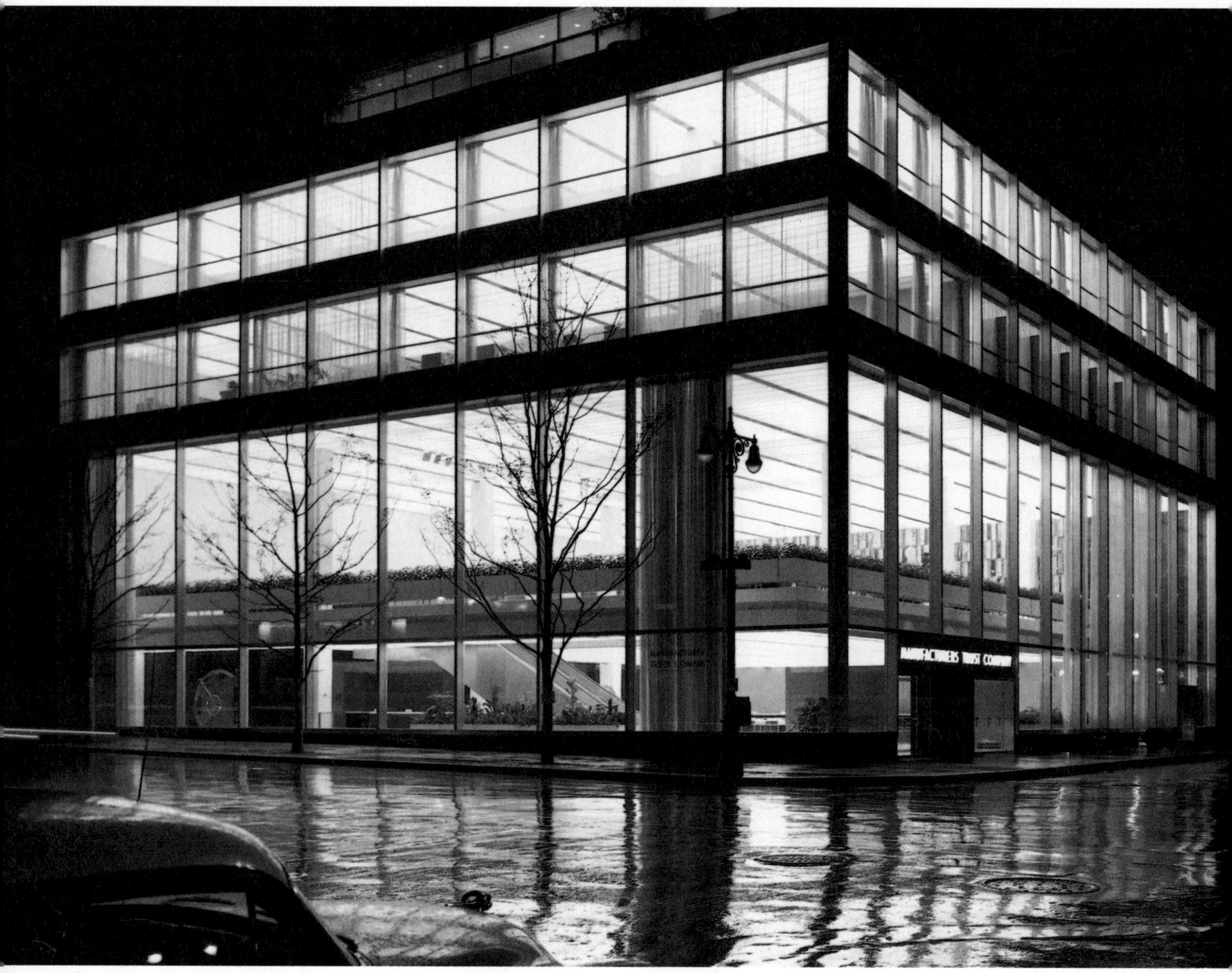

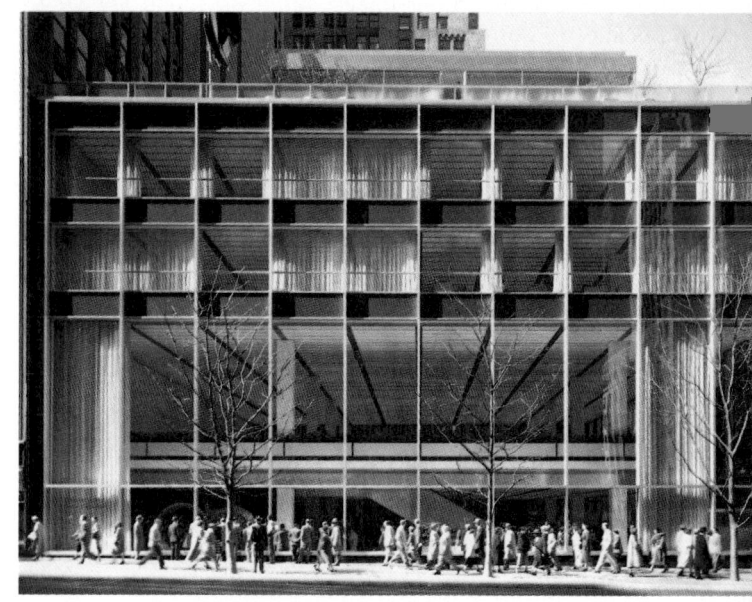

Above: Manufacturers Trust Company, 510 Fifth Avenue, southwest corner of Fifth Avenue and West Forty-third Street. Skidmore, Owings & Merrill, 1954. View to the southwest. Stoller. ©ESTO

Right: Manufacturers Trust Company. View to the west. Stoller. ©ESTO

peated the firm's typical formula of alternating horizontal bands of near-white brick and glass. Emery Roth & Sons' 579 Fifth Avenue, on the northeast corner of Forty-seventh Street, completed the same year, was a sixteen-story, 133,000-square-foot office building replacing the Jay Gould residence (Stephen D. Hatch, 1869), which had been torn down the year before.[17]

The midtown branch of the Manufacturers Trust Company (1954), at 510 Fifth Avenue, was not only the street's most architecturally distinguished postwar addition but also one of the canonic statements of corporate International Style Modernism.[18] Designed by Skidmore, Owings & Merrill, the Manufacturers Trust bank was also a public favorite. When it opened on October 4, 1954, 15,000 visitors jammed its halls to experience inside what could be so clearly seen through its virtually unbroken glass walls from outside. In its first year twice as many new accounts were opened as were ever opened in any Manufacturers Trust branch in a single year, and management began to notice that employees dressed better because they were more visible.

The bank was built on the 100-by-125-foot site of Clarence Luce's Hotel Renaissance (1894), on the southwest corner of Forty-third Street.[19] Manufacturers Trust had purchased the site in 1941, but wartime restrictions prevented construction and the hotel was not demolished until 1952. Rising from a low granite base, SOM's "crystal lantern," to use Lewis Mumford's term rather than the description of "goldfish bowl" more popularly resorted to, was a building of four stories and a penthouse, almost completely sheathed in a curtain wall of half-inch-thick, nine-foot-wide and twenty-two-foot-tall clear plate-glass panels held in place by aluminum mullions. "We had an idea that it was time to get the banks out of mausoleums," Louis Skidmore stated, and to emphasize that point SOM located the safe deposit vault facing Fifth Avenue just behind the glass wall.[20]

The radically different design not only gave physical expression to the client's self-image as a forward-thinking organization but also symbolized a dramatic change in banking practice. As the editors of *Architectural Forum* observed: "Banks used to sell *security*. But now, with their deposits federally insured, they are selling *service*. Today's bankers are an aggressive new breed of financial merchandisers . . . and they are out to lure every passing pedestrian into opening a special checking account."[21] "This is a store type of operation," SOM's chief designer, Gordon Bunshaft, proclaimed, "open, departmentalized, efficient."[22] The basic concept for the project came from SOM's Charles Evans Hughes III, who developed it over a weekend in an in-house competition, a practice the firm had developed in the late 1930s when, as coordinating architects for the New York World's Fair, they had to design many buildings on short notice. Bunshaft developed Hughes's design. Horace C. Flanigan, who became president of Manufacturers Trust Company in 1951, also played a strong role in the evolution of the design. Increasingly convinced that traditional bank architecture expressed outmoded banking conditions, Flanigan wanted something special for the new building, which replaced an existing branch diagonally across the street.

Behind the sixty-foot-high glass wall, cantilevered from the building's structural frame, lay a 9,300-square-foot, 14'6"-high first-floor hall, where the safe was located as well as the busy special checking division. The first floor was topped by a twenty-two-foot-high piano nobile containing the principal 6,000-square-foot banking floor that was set back, like a mezzanine, twelve feet from the glass along Fifth Avenue to visually connect it with the ground floor. The decision to treat this floor

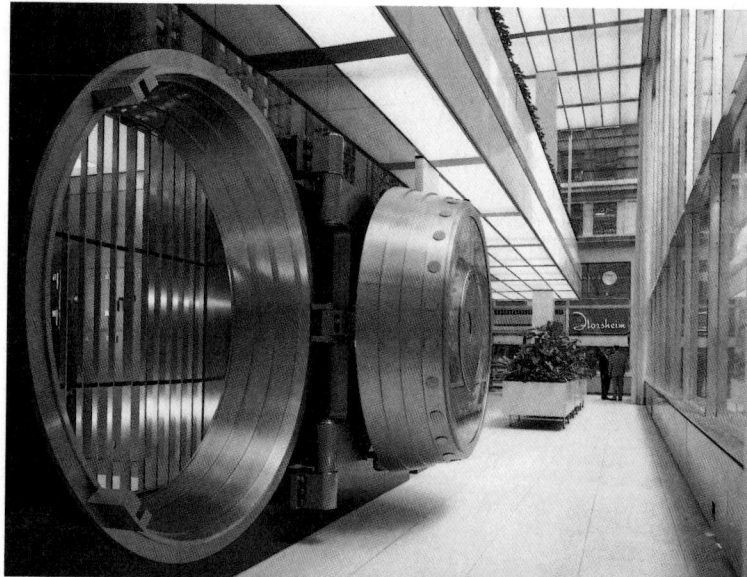

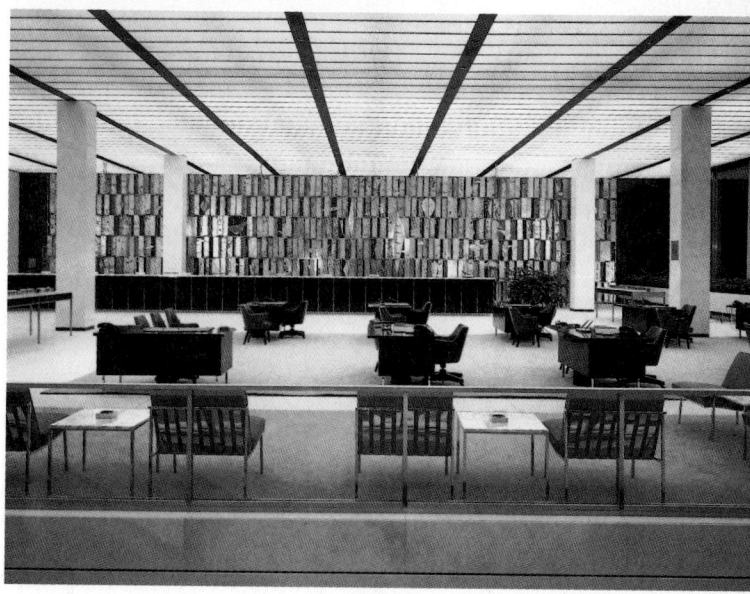

Top: Manufacturers Trust Company. Interior by Skidmore, Owings & Merrill in collaboration with Eleanor Lemaire, showing the safe deposit vault designed by Henry Dreyfuss. Stoller. ©ESTO

Bottom: Manufacturers Trust Company. Main banking floor showing decorative screen designed by Harry Bertoia. Stoller. ©ESTO

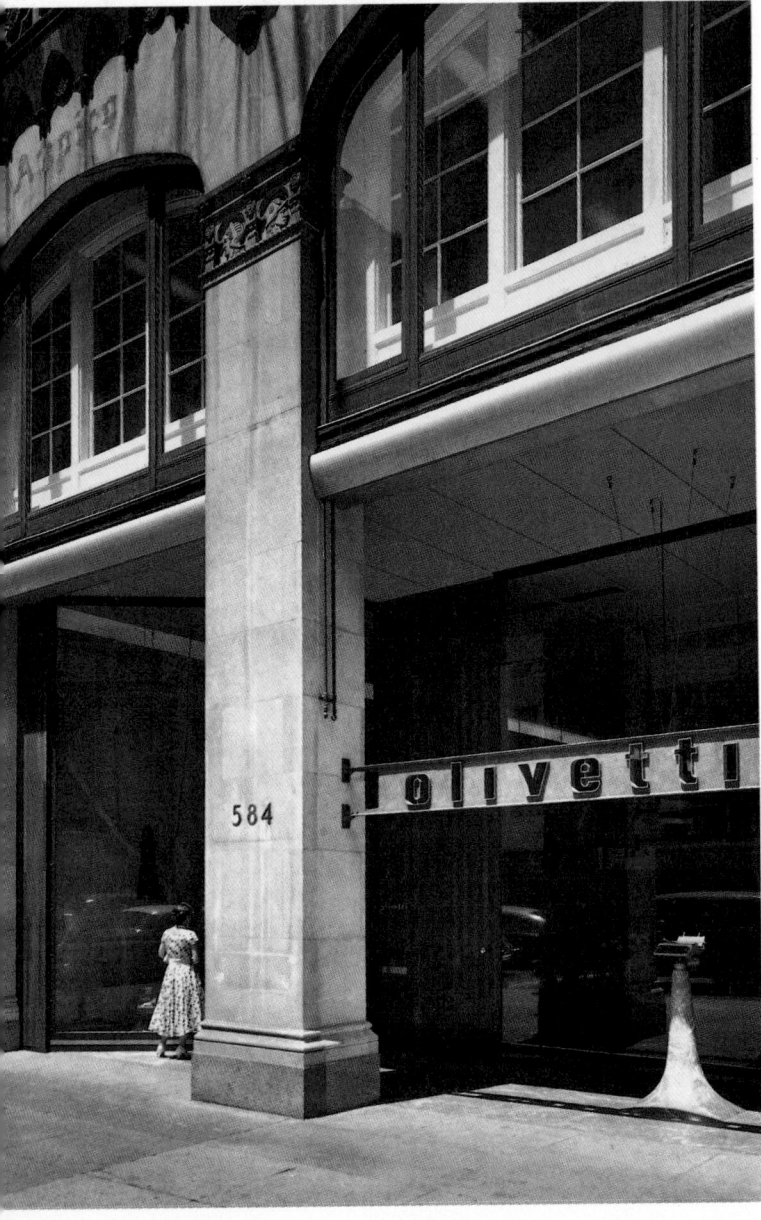

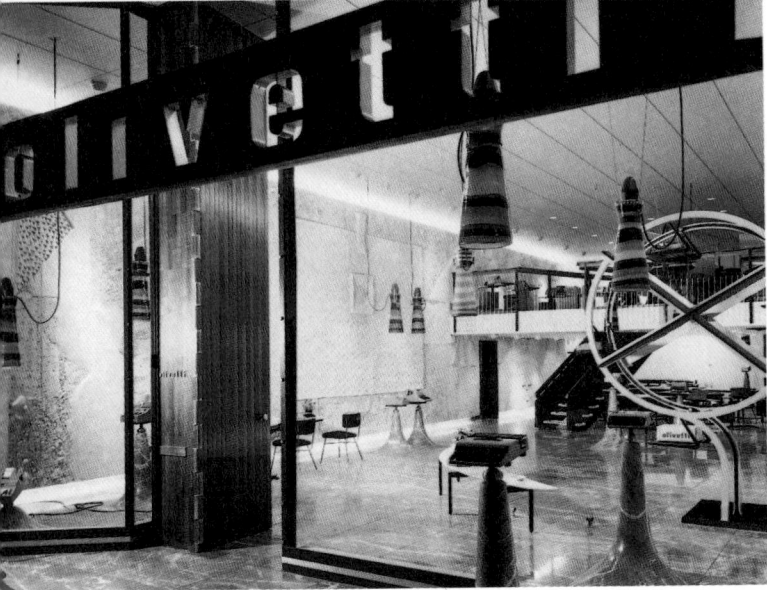

as a mezzanine enabled the designers to maximize the proportions of the glass wall, which suggested those of a Classical palazzo. Two 12'6"-high office floors were located above, along with a penthouse, which was set well back and contained reception, dining and lounging rooms for use by the bank's president, whose main office was downtown.

The extensive use of clear glass shaded only by gauzy curtains was environmentally sound because the site was so completely surrounded by tall buildings that virtually no direct sun penetrated the building's walls. The hefty mullions required for the big sheets of glass gave the building a traditional feeling of mass, despite its transparency. At least one observer, however, found the quality of the building to be somewhat ethereal. As Ada Louise Huxtable wrote: "In the Manufacturers Trust Building the glass is colorless and clear, and because of the even illumination inside, material walls disappear. Spandrels and mullions become mere frames for the arrangement of the interiors. The whole, viewed from the outside, is no longer architectural in the traditional sense: it is a design, not of substance, but of color, light and motion."[23]

The bank may have declined to build a larger office building on the site because, given the small size of the plot, the setback requirements, the requirement to provide off-street loading, the high ratio of core to rentable space and a deed restriction that ensured a neighboring building's light above sixty feet, the result would have been a structure of only marginal profitability. In the final analysis, the Manufacturers Trust bank was a rare example of a building shaped purely by the architect's vision of the site and its context and not by the zoning laws that typically controlled most buildings.

One of the principal features of the interior, which was designed by the architects in collaboration with Eleanor Lemaire, was the thousand-ton safe held back ten feet from the Fifth Avenue glass line. The safe had been styled for the job by Henry Dreyfuss, the industrial designer. The other outstanding element was Harry Bertoia's six-ton, eighteen-foot-high, seventy-foot-long decorative screen made of wire holding together 800 bronze and gold metal panels. Located near the west end of the second floor behind the tellers' counters, the screen was the butt of many jokes, causing one observer to report, "They must have cleaned out every junkyard in the city to build that thing."[24] Although Huxtable said it introduced "a note of Byzantine splendor in an otherwise austerely elegant interior," she regretted that its "delicacy" was "somewhat lost against the powerful glow of the luminous ceiling," which, however "clever" and "effective," could not overcome the deficiencies she saw in fluorescent lighting.[25]

Lewis Mumford placed the bank's design in a broad historical context. Citing precedents such as the glass-roofed Arcade Building that George Pullman built in his model town outside Chicago and the utopian ideas of Ebenezer Howard and H. G. Wells, he saw it as a revival of "the dream of building a whole city of glass that haunted the Victorian imagination." But he placed it in a contemporary context as well, citing similarities with Philip Johnson's Glass House in New Canaan, Connecticut, Mies van der Rohe's Lake Shore Drive Apartments in Chicago and Frank Lloyd Wright's S. C. Johnson & Sons Laboratory in Racine, Wisconsin, not to mention other work of SOM. He made direct comparison with the firm's Lever House (see "Park Avenue," above), drawing attention to the difference between that building's "almost opaque" sheath "stretched taut, like a film, over the frame it conceals," and the Manufacturers Trust building's "paradoxical combination of transparence and solidity—crystalline, yes, but not in the slightest frail or filmlike, for, if anything, it is both rugged and monumental." Mumford went on to praise the building for its "classic qualities of dignity, serenity, and order."[26] Taking credit for first broaching the idea of a glass bank as a deterrent to crime in a "Sky Line" column of the 1930s,[27] Mumford concluded that "nowhere have both interior and exterior been conceived more effectively as a whole, or treated in a more forthright manner, at once businesslike and elegant."[28]

After the glass wall itself, the single most notable innovation was that of the gridded luminous ceiling. Despite Huxtable's reservations about the choice of fluorescent lighting, the general reaction to this feature was favorable. The editors of *Architectural Forum* went so far as to say that the "building's lucid grace, which contradicts the steely quality of most metal-and-glass architecture, can be traced to one physical fact behind the sheer glass walls—the glowing ceilings." The ceilings, they said, accomplished two things:

> From outdoors they reduce to nothingness the apparent weight of the floor slabs hung from interior columns. . . . But even more important, the tremendous wealth of illumination which these vast plaques pour down from overhead does nullify the shine and reflectivity of the glass wall. It is an old merchandising trick—if you have a store window and you want the contents seen from outside, you have to put more foot-candles inside the glass than there are foot-candles of natural light outside the glass, or it mirrors. But doing this to a five-story building is new and surprising, a true landmark in delineation of space. It makes a glass wall into something it has not been before, an invisible control instead of a mysterious barrier. At last the deeply sculptural feeling of a steel frame under construction has been retained in the completed building.[29]

At night, when the building glowed like a lantern, it was at its most spectacular but also its most problematic, revealing its ambiguities all too clearly. As John Anderson pointed out in *Interiors*: "The columns, since they penetrate each of the luminous ceilings, seem to be supporting weightless planes of light. This impression of a false relationship of weights and masses may be liable to criticism, but it appears necessary if the dynamic cantilever construction and the unbroken luminosity of the ceilings were to exist simultaneously."[30]

Twenty-five years after the completion of the Manufacturers Trust bank, when its ideas had long been absorbed into mainstream practice and were now being challenged by a generation far more sympathetic to the stone-clad buildings of the 1920s than Bunshaft's had been, it began to be seen differently. In 1979 Paul Goldberger wrote that it "was built to create an image, as surely as any York & Sawyer Renaissance palace was a bank built to create an image, and to be fair, this bank is successful at it, too. It is best, indeed, as a stage set; as a great Miesian statement it comes off as second-rate and ordinary."[31]

The year 1954 saw the completion not only of the landmark Manufacturers Trust bank but also of a stylish and much-discussed combination showroom and retail outlet for the Olivetti Corporation, an Italian company specializing in typewriters.[32] The showroom-store at once boosted Fifth Avenue's role as the city's principal pedestrian promenade and clearly indicated that the street's future, even as far as retailing was concerned, would have a decidedly corporate cast. Occupying the ground floor of 584 Fifth Avenue (Warren & Wetmore, 1929), between Forty-seventh and Forty-eighth streets, Olivetti's was designed by the Milanese firm of architects Banfi, Belgiojoso, Peressutti & Rogers (BBPR), whose Torre Velasca skyscraper in Milan (1957–60)

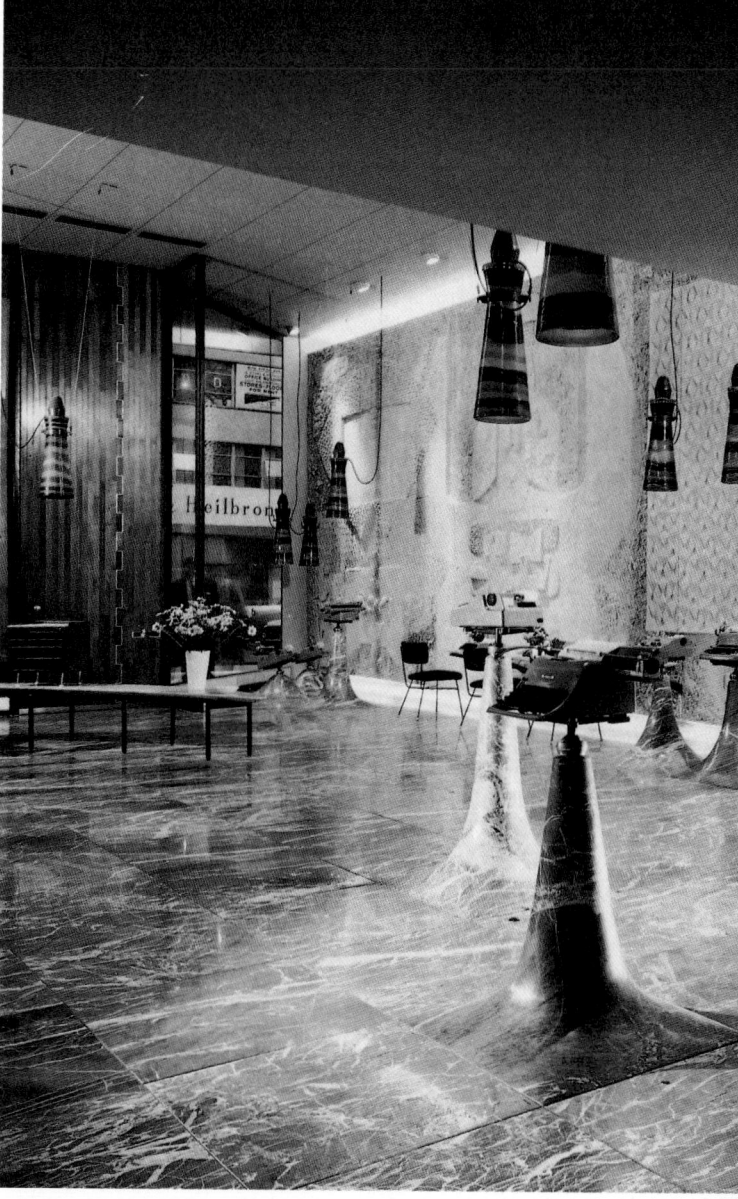

Top left: Olivetti Corporation showroom and store, 584 Fifth Avenue, between West Forty-seventh and West Forty-eighth streets. Banfi, Belgiojoso, Peressutti & Rogers, 1954. View to the southwest. Stoller. ©ESTO

Bottom left: Olivetti Corporation showroom and store. View to the southwest. Stoller. ©ESTO

Above: Olivetti Corporation showroom and store. Interior. Stoller. ©ESTO

would become a controversial landmark in the stylistic evolution from Modernism to Post-Modernism.[33] The Olivetti project was principally the responsibility of Enrico Peressutti, who visited New York frequently in the course of its construction. In keeping with the prevailing fashion of open-front shops, BBPR created an arcade behind the Fifth Avenue facade. In front of the glass, a bannerlike green-bronze sign, stretched between a limestone-clad structural column and the shop's northern wall, proclaimed the company's name. In the protected area formed by the recessed glazing, a green marble pedestal rising from the green marble paving supported a typewriter, available at all times of day and night to the public, who quickly adopted it as a beloved plaything. The poet Frank O'Hara used it to type many of the verses later collected in *Lunch Poems*; O'Hara would note on the jacket copy of the original publication, "Often this poet, strolling through the noisy splintered glare of a Manhattan noon, has paused at a sample Olivetti to type up thirty or forty lines of ruminations."[34] The glass wall was interrupted only by a sixteen-foot-high solid Italian walnut door carried on exceptionally large brass piano hinges.

Pushing open the door, which moved with amazing ease, the visitor crossed the floor, covered in the green marble used outside, moving under a blue-painted plaster ceiling toward a back wall filled with Constantino Nivola's seventy-foot-long cast-sand mural-like sculpture, *Hospitality*. Brightly colored Venetian glass pendant lights hung throughout the space, their warm glow supplemented by spot and cove lighting above and below the Nivola mural. Eight marble display pedestals similar to the one outside rose from the floor.

The showroom's construction proved a difficult feat of coordination. The contractor was Murphy-Brinkworth, with Natalie Hoyt in charge of the project, the city's only woman field executive. Hoyt described the construction process to the *New Yorker*: "Italians don't have as strict a notion of measured drawings as Americans do. . . . And I think Italian architects enjoy ad-libbing more than ours do. Peressutti would come over from Milan to see how things were going, have an inspiration, and make a drawing of what he wanted on a patch of bare wall. The next day, a painter would come along and paint over the patch, and nobody—not even Mr. Peressutti—would be able to remember precisely what the drawing had called for."[35]

Throughout the construction process, the New York City Department of Buildings proved to be demanding and, from the architects' point of view, obstructive. The department would not allow wood ceiling panels that had been fabricated in Italy to be installed for reasons of fire safety, necessitating a last-minute redesign. Again citing fire-prevention requirements, the department demanded that steel reinforcement be added to the marble stair, which moved up on a diagonal to the mezzanine where staff offices were located, and determined that a conveyor system designed for delivering typewriters up from the basement could not be used. Just as the building showroom was about to open, Peressutti complained: "How much more beautiful this room would have been without your Building Department! What we like in Italy is the natural. What you like in America is to imitate the natural. Stone is not stone, it is decalcomania of stone. Here, in this long, narrow cube, we wished to give a sense of natural richness and interpenetration, like stalagmites and stalactites in some imaginable cave. If we have succeeded at all, it is in spite of your forbiddings."[36]

The Olivetti showroom pleased professionals and the public alike. By the time *Architectural Forum* published the project in August 1954, it had, as the editors noted, "already proved to be box office along the world's broadway of merchandise. . . . Olivetti here attains popular success not by going down to the mythical infantile level of public taste, but by attracting the public up to a professional design level." *Forum* went on to place the showroom in the context of American architectural practice:

> [It] has cast a chunk of richly veined Italian marble into the recently placid surface of New York advanced design. . . . Against the current preference for sharp, staccato, surfacey, angular shop design, emphasizing lightness and transience, this new Olivetti showroom opposes weight and hearty exuberant voluptuousness. . . . Some would like to dismiss this finished design as a baroque retrogression, but they cannot. For this showroom, bold, intricate and exciting, clearly is a step, perhaps a leading one, into the uncertain future of U.S. shop design, which must always be changing to keep the customers interested.[37]

Olga Gueft, writing in *Interiors*, was equally enthusiastic, finding Olivetti's to be "a great piece of showmanship, a stupendous display, and wonderful theater." Rather than Peressutti's analogy to a cave, Gueft described the showroom in terms of water: "The passerby comes upon a sudden gap in the continuous stone and glass surface of Fifth Avenue, to find himself peering *beyond* a big pillar and *through* a sign, into a world astoundingly remote from the street. Marble the color of water, flecked with foam and golden bubbles, surges from the depths of the interior right out under his feet. A Mediterranean sky inside also ignores the steel-rimmed glass boundary." She continued the water images in discussing the interior: "The sand mural must go with a beach. There is some kind of balcony or deck further inside. From it falls a stair with solid sides like a gangplank. The deck rail is walnut as strong and smooth as a ship's rail. There is a knobbed metal picket fence below it—as sparkling white as the edge of the deck itself."[38] But, she pointed out in a later discussion, "Peressutti never for a moment forgot what the fantasy was for. Each sea-colored marble wave carries a typewriter on its crest. . . . The space is punctuated by these waves, each attended by a jewel of a lantern which hovers to pour down its own pool of brilliance. . . . For all its unbridled hedonism it is appropriate to the precision product on sale, being in itself an expression of perfectionism and ingenuity."[39]

Lewis Mumford was one of the few critics who was not at all impressed with the "slightly preposterous" showroom. "Among contemporary Italian works of industrial art," Mumford said, "Olivetti typewriters and adding machines, by consensus, deserve a high place and they also deserve a showroom that has some of their qualities and is correspondingly free of affectation and of visual violence. That is what the newly devised Olivetti foothold . . . is not." No aspect of the Olivetti design, he said, gave "so much as a hint of the technical skill, productive efficiency, aesthetic taste, and social responsibility that makes this firm one of the most interesting industrial enterprises in the world." Though he admired the exterior sign and typewriter, he did not approve of the bowed-in show window and complained that the walnut door was hidden from view by the exposed column. Like Gueft, Mumford saw sky and ocean in the interior, but, he asked, if analogy was intended, what was its meaning? He did not like the pendant lamps, which he castigated as "large glass sugarloaf shades" bearing "broad smudgy horizontal stripes." He also disliked the staircase, and while he did admire

Nivola's wall; he felt that it did not contribute to the overall design, but rather "puts the rest of the room in its shadow."[40]

Mumford was, however, somewhat encouraged by the direction of BBPR's work: "It could indicate the uneasy belief—becoming more and more widely shared by at least the younger generation—that no architectural design is complete that does not recognize certain feelings which are omitted by the calculus of the machine." But, he concluded,

> Unfortunately the human touch cannot be achieved with a simple slice of decoration. . . . To find the human key to the Olivetti design, the architects would have had to say to themselves, "If I were buying a typewriter or an adding machine, what would make it easy for me to try out the various models and come to a decision?" There is presumably a pleasant architectural answer to that problem, and I am confident it involves neither colored lamp shades nor conical display stands nor sophisticated sand modelling.[41]

In 1956 Benjamin Coates, president of the 118-year-old W. & J. Sloane Company, once the city's premier purveyor of fine furniture, announced that he would replace the store building (Warren & Wetmore, 1912), on the southeast corner of Fifth Avenue and Forty-seventh Street, with a thirty-four-story tower designed by Sylvan and Robert Bien, and seek a temporary location elsewhere in midtown.[42] Coates's plan was not immediately realized and the store remained in place until 1961. By that time Sloane's had been adversely affected by the increase in mass-market discounting, as well as by the growing influence of interior designers on the tastes and shopping habits of the well-to-do, who now preferred to buy fabrics and home furnishings directly from wholesalers. In 1961 Sloane's was taken over by the City Stores Company, owners of Franklin Simon, and under the new owners, the custom operations of the venerable retailer were scaled back as the new management sought a more middle-class market. The store was moved to smaller quarters in the former Franklin Simon store (Necarsulmer & Lehlbach, 1902), on the southwest corner of Fifth Avenue and Thirty-eighth Street.[43] Franklin Simon, also a faltering enterprise, was similarly downscaled; it absorbed another old retailer, Oppenheim Collins, and took over their building (Buchman & Fox, 1914) on West Thirty-fourth Street between Fifth Avenue and Herald Square.[44]

The most startling part of this process, and a point that caused many to begin to wonder about the fate of Fifth Avenue itself, was the decision of the pioneering discount retailer E. J. Korvette to take over the former Sloane's.[45] Although Korvette's architects, Neumann & Taylor, radically stripped Sloane's interior and installed escalators and modern climate control, they left the building facade more or less intact, though introducing some rather tinny-looking perforated aluminum screens between the Ionic colonnade. Korvette's impact on Fifth Avenue's architectural character was not as dramatic as many had feared, but it did further erode the avenue's traditional role as an exclusive shopping street, accelerating a process of democratization that had begun in the 1930s on the lower end and was now spreading north.

Carson & Lundin's Tishman Building (1957), at 666 Fifth Avenue, was a 1,245,000-square-foot, thirty-nine-story office tower located on the avenue's west blockfront between Fifty-second and Fifty-third streets.[46] The site, which once contained nine buildings, including Richard Morris Hunt's William K. Vanderbilt house (1882), replaced in 1927 by a five-story commercial building (Springsteen & Goldhammer), and McKim,

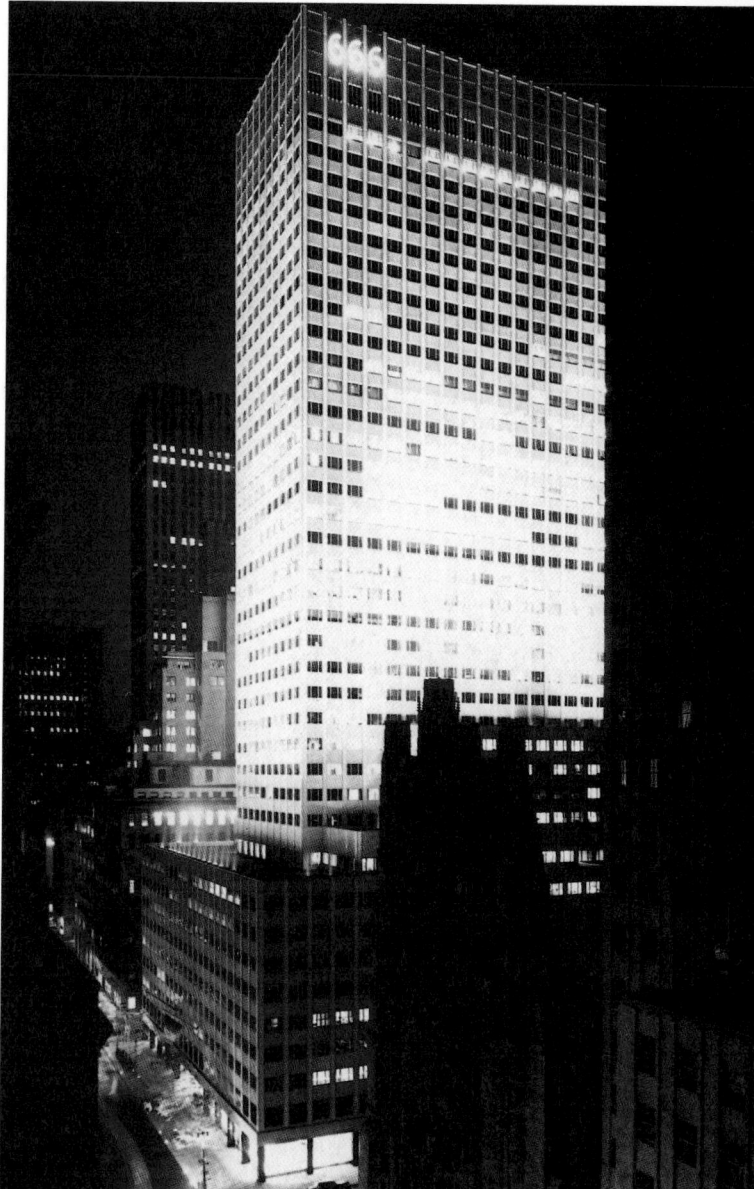

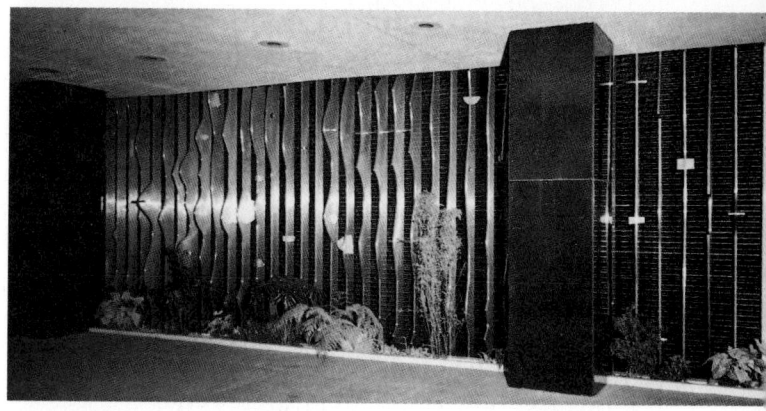

Top: 666 Fifth Avenue, West Fifty-second to West Fifty-third Street. Carson & Lundin, 1957. View to the southwest. Gottscho-Schleisner. LOC

Bottom: 666 Fifth Avenue. Ground-level arcade showing fountain designed by Isamu Noguchi. OMH

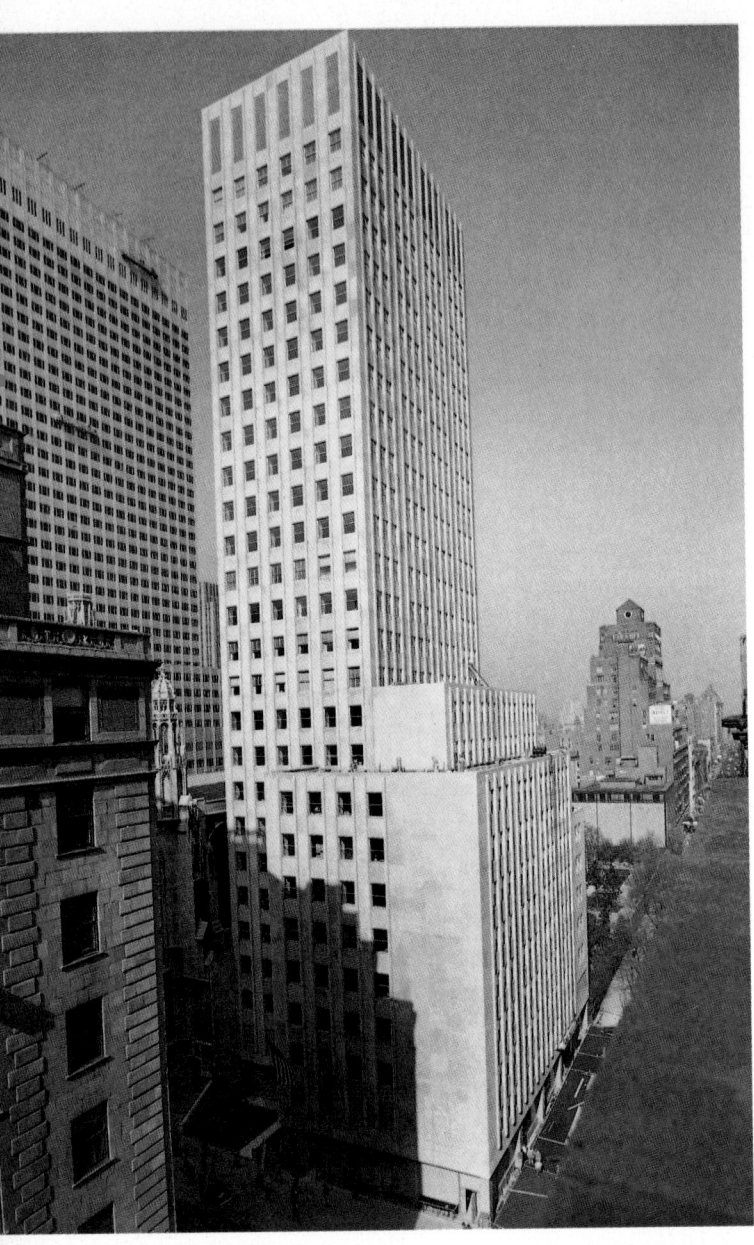

Above: Canada House, 680 Fifth Avenue, southwest corner of Fifth Avenue and West Fifty-fourth Street. Eggers & Higgins in association with Marazio & Morris, 1957. View to the southwest. OMH

Right: Corning Glass Building, 717 Fifth Avenue, southeast corner of Fifth Avenue and East Fifty-sixth Street. Harrison, Abramovitz & Abbe, 1956–59. View to the southeast. Stoller. ©ESTO

Mead & White's Mrs. William K. Vanderbilt, Jr., mansion (1905–6), had been assembled for a new Lord & Taylor department store.[47] Carson & Lundin were hired because Tishman initially wanted a stone-clad building sympathetic in design to Rockefeller Center. But by September 1956, when construction was well under way, new plans for the building were released that showed a curtain wall featuring patterned aluminum spandrel panels, a redesign that provided the city's largest aluminum-clad building and featured the widest windows, which at six feet were one-and-a-half feet wider than normal.

A principal feature of the building was a thirty-foot-wide, open-air, shop-lined arcade that ran 100 feet back under the building from Fifth Avenue, where it joined a north-south arcade connecting the two side streets. Isamu Noguchi, the sculptor and designer, put in charge of the lobby decor, created a strong connection between indoors and outdoors with a fountain that featured water cascading over metal strips on one side of a forty-foot glass wall. The wavy pattern of the metal strips was repeated in fins that separated the translucent panels of the lobby ceiling. According to Noguchi, Robert Carson, one of the building's architects, had retained an earlier model for "a sculpture of contoured louvers" that Noguchi had created for an unrealized bank wall in a Texas building Carson had designed. When he began working on 666 Fifth, Carson told Noguchi that he wanted to adapt the earlier design for an elevator lobby ceiling and asked the sculptor to create a waterfall wall "to go with it." Noguchi, "horrified at the idea of such arbitrary use," offered to redesign the ceiling for the cost of the waterfall alone.[48]

A widely praised twenty-minute film, *Skyscraper* (1959), directed by Shirley Clarke, in collaboration with Willard Van Dyke, Irving Jacoby, D. A. Pennebaker and Wheaton Galentine (see chapter 17), documented the building's construction, which was completed in November 1957. But it was not until June 4, 1958, when Abe Feder's extraordinary exterior lighting system, using seventy-two reflector-type lamps, transformed it into what the *Real Estate Record and Guide* called a "Tower of Light," that the building became a landmark that received wide comment.[49] So bright was the night lighting that it was turned off between September 18 and November 1, 1959, to prevent disorienting migratory birds; the same restriction was also placed on the illuminated stationary beacon on the Empire State Building. At the top of the building's slab, the numbers "666" glowed a bright red, contrasting with the icy coolness of the illuminated skin. Just below this sign, on the building's thirty-ninth floor, Stouffer's, the Ohio-based, middle-priced restaurant chain, opened a glamorous, upmarket cocktail and dining aerie called the Top of the Sixes, the first such facility since the Rainbow Room had opened atop the RCA Building in 1934.[50] The Top of the Sixes featured French cuisine that contrasted sharply with the simple Yankee fare of the typical Stouffer's restaurant, one of which was located on the building's ground floor and basement level. To complement the cuisine, designer Raymond Loewy cooked up a French-inspired mélange of elements including Paris bistro furniture, paneling from an old Norman chateau and primitive French paintings from the Napoleonic era, a far cry from the modern-minded sophistication of Elena Schmidt's Rainbow Room.

For Canada House (1957), on the southwest corner of Fifth Avenue and Fifty-fourth Street, the architects, Eggers & Higgins (in association with Marazio & Morris of Toronto), used tradi-

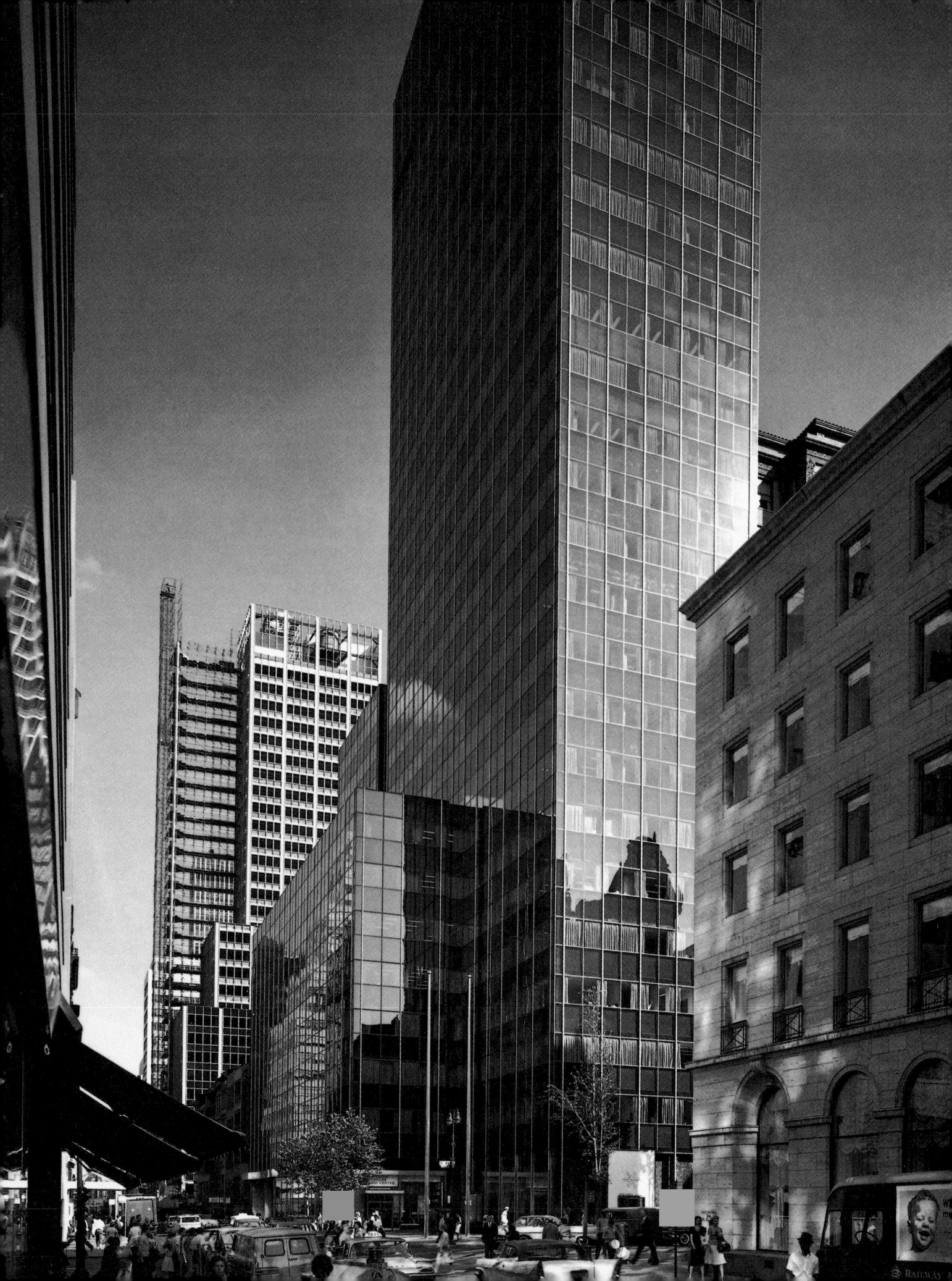

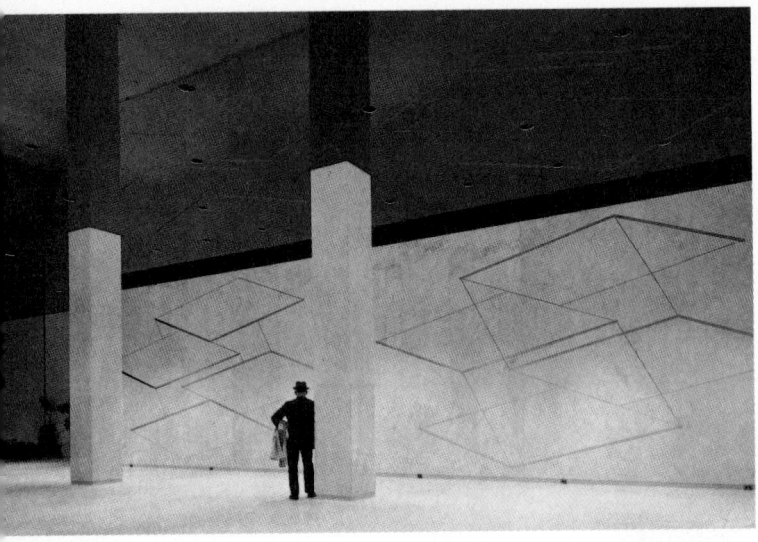

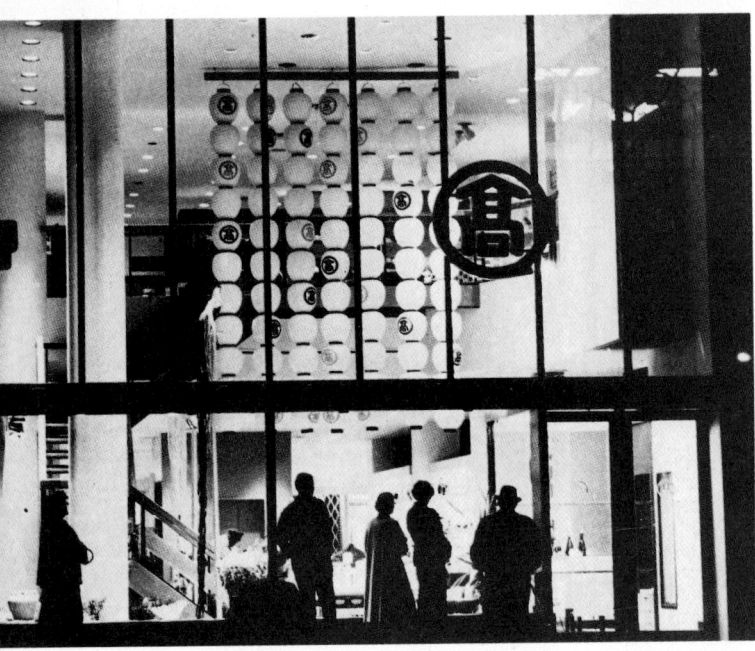

Top: Corning Glass Building, 717 Fifth Avenue, southeast corner of Fifth Avenue and East Fifty-sixth Street. Harrison, Abramovitz & Abbe, 1956–59. View of lobby showing mural by Josef Albers. Stoller. ©ESTO

Bottom: Takashimaya, 562 Fifth Avenue, northwest corner of Fifth Avenue and West Forty-sixth Street. Junzo Yoshimura in association with Steinhardt & Thompson, 1958. View to the west. MA

tional limestone cladding and the vertical proportions that characterized the avenue's typical office buildings to combat the blatant commercialism of Emery Roth & Sons' buildings and the brash 666 Fifth.[51] The site had two buildings on it, 680 and 684 Fifth Avenue. The first of these, a French Provincial building designed by William Welles Bosworth for John D. Rockefeller in 1914, had replaced the home (John B. Snook, 1882–84) of Lila Vanderbilt Webb, a daughter of William Henry Vanderbilt.[52] The site of number 684, at the corner, had been purchased from another Vanderbilt daughter, Florence Vanderbilt Twombly, whose four-story house (also John B. Snook, 1882–84) was torn down in 1927 and replaced with a six-story commercial building.[53] That building was eventually sold to Georg Jensen, whose silver and jewelry shop was located there from 1946 until the company sold the site to Canada House in 1956 and moved across the street to number 665, on the southeast corner of Fifty-third Street (see chapter 6).

Rising from a small landscaped midblock plaza, Canada House was designed to be a twenty-seven-story campanile to Bertram Grosvenor Goodhue's St. Thomas' Church, immediately to its south, a strategy that echoed—but with rather less panache—Cross & Cross's handling of the much taller RCA Victor Building (1931), to the east of Goodhue's St. Bartholomew's Church (1919; completed by Mayers, Murray & Phillip, 1927).[54] A nine-story mass occupied the Fifty-fourth Street corner, helping to define the plaza and making the block a symmetrical composition with the new tower in the center. To further complement the church, Canada House was clad in limestone, and a system of vertical limestone fins was devised to help slim the building's profile and give it a Gothic-like verticality. The northern third of the Fifth Avenue facade was left unfenestrated and unarticulated by fins. Covered in limestone, it carried a sculpture by Otto Thielemann of the seals of Canada and her provinces to give the building a further measure of institutional dignity.

With 717 Fifth Avenue, the 450,000-square-foot Corning Glass Building (1956–59), the architects Harrison, Abramovitz & Abbe achieved a high point of refinement in the design of glass curtain-wall office towers and the avenue gained a second undisputed landmark of postwar International Style Modernism.[55] The building occupied an awkward, L-shaped, 30,000-square-foot plot and replaced the four-story Fiberglas House (Skidmore, Owings & Merrill, 1948) (see chapter 6). It was designed by Wallace K. Harrison to function as a demonstration of his client's principal product and as a step forward from his U.N. Secretariat to represent the most advanced use of glass in a commercial building. A skin of green-tinted glass and aluminum wrapped the principal twenty-six-story east-west slab that interlocked with a twelve-story intermediary mass at the rear and a seven-story projection along Fifty-sixth Street containing the building's main entrance. Given the complexities of the site, the massing was ingenious. Rising from the small plaza at the site's corner, Corning Glass presented a slender mass to Fifth Avenue and seemed to soar above the city to a far greater height than it actually enjoyed.

In the building's broad, coolly impressive, sixteen-foot-high lobby that ran north-south through the block, a mirror ceiling of black Carrara glass contrasted with white marble walls and white terrazzo floors; the lines of a large mural by Josef Albers were cut into one wall and highlighted with gold leaf. Upstairs, the Corning Glass Company's offices were designed by Gerald Luss, who created what John Anderson described as "stately, breathtaking, and well-nigh 'perfect' interiors."[56] It was not the

380

corporate offices, however, but the company's Steuben Shop that, after the curtain wall itself, was the building's highlight. Since its opening in 1937 the shop had been located across the street in Platt & Platt's Corning Glass Building, at 718 Fifth Avenue, which in 1959 was renovated to suit the jeweler Harry Winston.[57] In the new Steuben Shop, John M. Gates, who had also designed the interiors of its predecessor, used highly figured dark-lacquered mahogany to panel a suite of rooms that showcased the ice-cold sparkle of the glassware and objets d'art it specialized in. A crystal fountain by George Thompson was the focus of a foyerlike room formed by freestanding partitions that described an oval.

Though corporate towers threatened to overshadow Fifth Avenue's traditional role as a shopping street, stylish retail concerns continued to be attracted to the avenue. The increasingly international nature of the city, as well as the remarkable revitalization of Japan's postwar economy, became dramatically apparent in 1958 when Takashimaya, a 137-year-old department store with outlets in Tokyo, Osaka and Kyoto, opened a three-story branch in an existing building at 562 Fifth Avenue, on the northwest corner of Forty-sixth Street, where Leighton's, a men's store designed by Victor Gruen (see chapter 6), had previously been located.[58] Intended to showcase high-quality Japanese merchandise, including antiques, lacquerware and fine china, the store was one of many to feature, as *Business Week* put it, the "growing tide of imports from many nations that have shown up on U.S. store shelves, in 'boutiques' the country over."[59] Designed by Junzo Yoshimura, who worked in association with Steinhardt & Thompson, Takashimaya's was entered through a two-story-high entrance hung with a banner of lanterns. Its glassy storefront, which was brightly lit at night, revealed the openwork wood stair that led to a mezzaninelike second floor. Yoshimura used mass-produced American materials rather than traditional Japanese ones; Armstrong Corlon took the place of tatami on the floors and Owens Corning Synskin suggested rice-paper shoji. Though the wood store fixtures looked custom-made, Shigeru Kawakami, the store's display director, designed them to be made out of standard parts. "Inside," *Architectural Record* reported, "the total impression is of luxury and serenity," fostered by even lighting, neutral colors on the walls and floors, and spaces carefully articulated by posts and screens to capture the scale of traditional Japanese house design.[60]

In 1964 the Italian publishers Rizzoli established a New York presence at 712 Fifth Avenue, between Fifty-fifth and Fifty-sixth streets.[61] Along with Charles Scribner's Sons, which had occupied an Ernest Flagg building at 597 Fifth Avenue, between Forty-eighth and Forty-ninth streets, since 1913, and Brentano's, which had occupied a store designed by Oswald C. Hering at 586 Fifth Avenue, between Forty-seventh and Forty-eighth streets, since 1925, Rizzoli helped define the avenue in the upper forties and fifties as a neighborhood of booksellers.[62] Renovated by Ferdinand Gottlieb, Rizzoli's new home, in a building that had first served Cartier's (A. S. Gottlieb, 1907), consisted of a series of single- and double-height wood-paneled rooms.[63] In 1966 the store expanded into the building at 2 West Fifty-sixth Street to create an L-shaped interior space. To Paul Goldberger, the store came "closer to being a club than a retail establishment." Goldberger would later recall that "Rizzoli was at its best in its early days . . . when one could stop there late at night, sip coffee and hear baroque music."[64]

In 1965 Brentano's expanded, adding a three-level wing at 6–8 West Forty-eighth Street designed by Danforth Toan of the architectural firm of Warner, Burns, Toan & Lunde.[65] At the same time, the store broadened its commercial activities, becoming, as its president, Leonard Schwartz, called it, "a cultural department store" that sold a wide variety of goods including art objects, antiques, games and sweatshirts.[66] In 1967 Doubleday moved its administrative headquarters to a seven-story building at 763 Fifth Avenue, on the northeast corner of Fifty-third Street.[67] Renovated by the Dallas-based architectural firm of Arch Swank Associates, the Doubleday Building incorporated a double-height bookshop on its first two floors in what had previously been the Salon Lenthéric (see "Fifty-third Street," below). Doubleday's also opened a store at 724 Fifth Avenue, between Fifty-sixth and Fifty-seventh streets.[68] Designed by Danforth Toan, it was a brightly lit, impersonal environment that revealed itself behind large plate windows.

Airline Alley

By the late 1960s two decades of strenuous building and real estate activity had significantly transformed Fifth Avenue from Forty-second to Fifty-seventh Street. By 1967, when Eugene K. Denton, a redoubtable seventy-nine-year-old merchant, closed the Tailored Woman specialty store, which he had owned and managed since 1919, he reminisced: "I remember when I opened here. There were little English shops and little French shops. They're all gone. Now we have plane ticket offices and banks."[69] Airline ticket offices began to arrive on Fifth Avenue soon after the end of World War II, a contemporary equivalent to the operations run by ship and railroad companies that since the nineteenth century had aggressively competed for passengers. While the railroads had been able to incorporate their sales and ticketing facilities in their stations, steamship lines had to set up sales offices in convenient business locations rather than at remote piers. The airlines faced a similar problem.

At first, air travel was confined to a handful of domestic carriers who, in 1940, set up their offices in a consolidated facility, John B. Peterkin's Airlines Terminal, on the southwest corner of Park Avenue and Forty-second Street, which also served as a principal station for limousine service to the city's two airports.[70] After the Second World War the rapid growth of transatlantic air travel dramatically changed the situation, with foreign and domestic carriers competing for overseas routes, and the foreign carriers fulfilling a second role as emblematic representatives of their nations. As *Interiors* observed in 1948:

> Half a dozen nations are competing to sell American travelers the swiftest, most modern, and most expensive of all forms of transportation. In addition to precious U.S. dollars, the prizes they seek are international prestige, good-will, and subsidiary trade. Needless to say, they put every effort into the selling, including—in the heart of New York—the standard sales practice of attracting the passerby on the street. . . . That is the reason why so many new open-front airline offices are springing up in the swankiest shopping districts.[71]

Air France was the first major foreign carrier to open an office on Fifth Avenue, locating at number 610, La Maison Française, in 1946.[72] In 1948 the airline leased a thirteen-story building at 683 Fifth Avenue, which housed the elegant, French-inspired two-story shopfront originally designed for the Dorothy Gray beauty salon (Kohn & Butler, 1928).[73] The ground floor

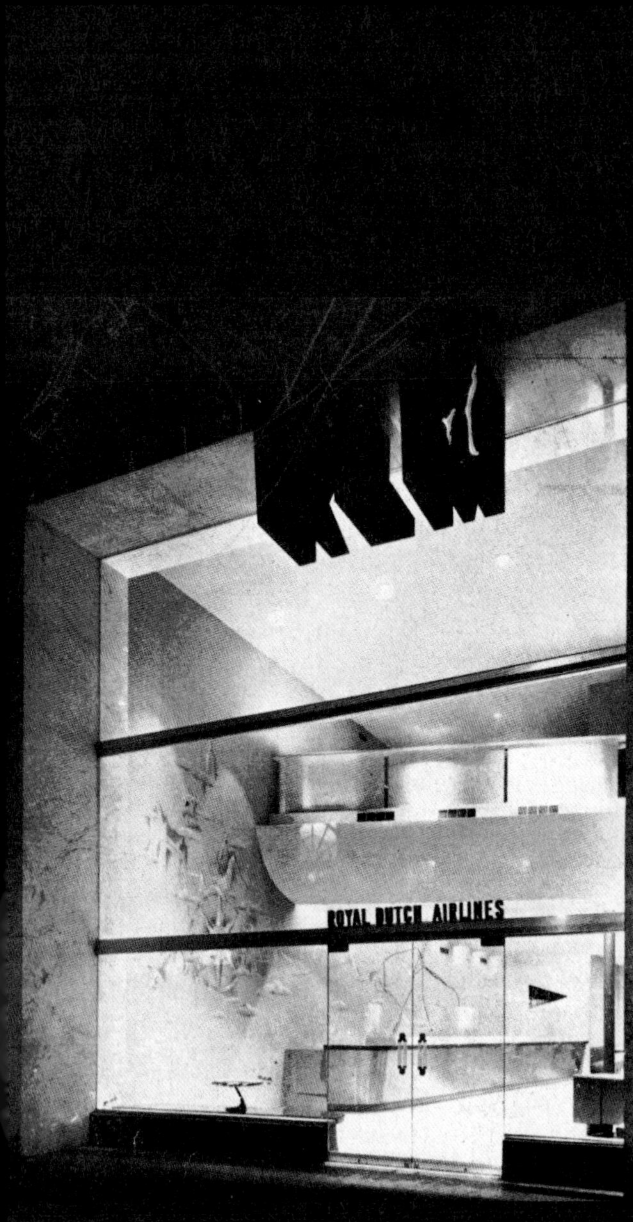

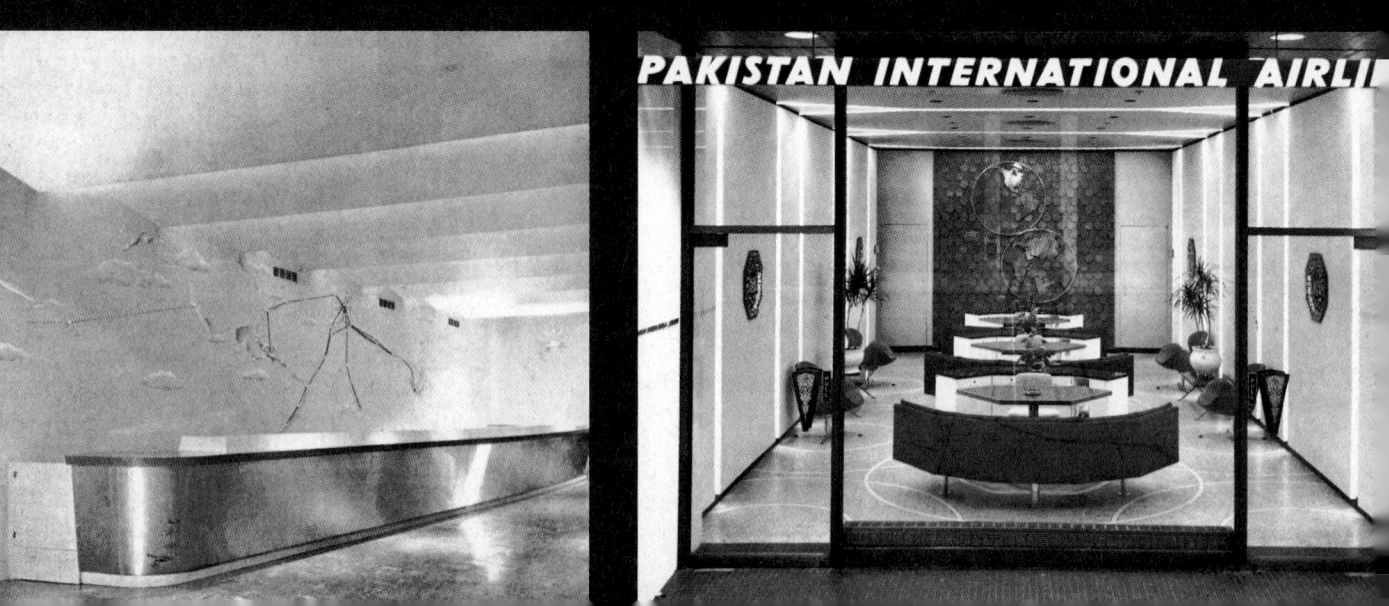

KLM ROYAL DUTCH AIRLINES

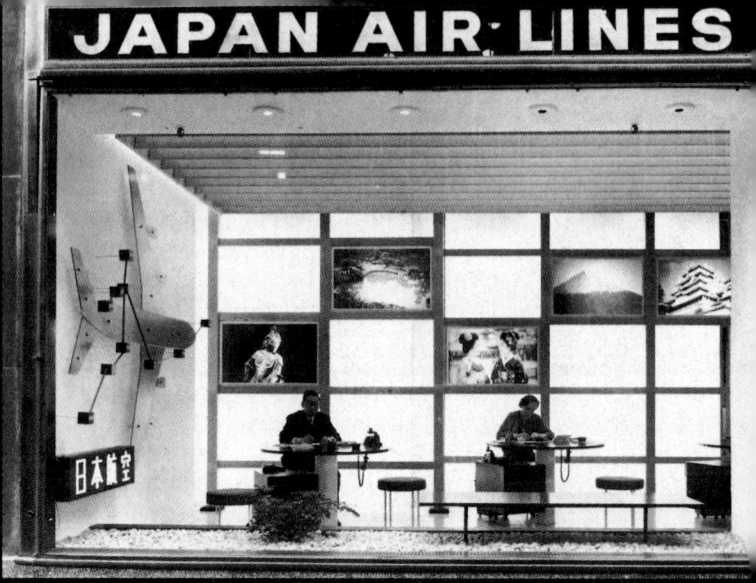

JAPAN AIR·LINES

日本航空

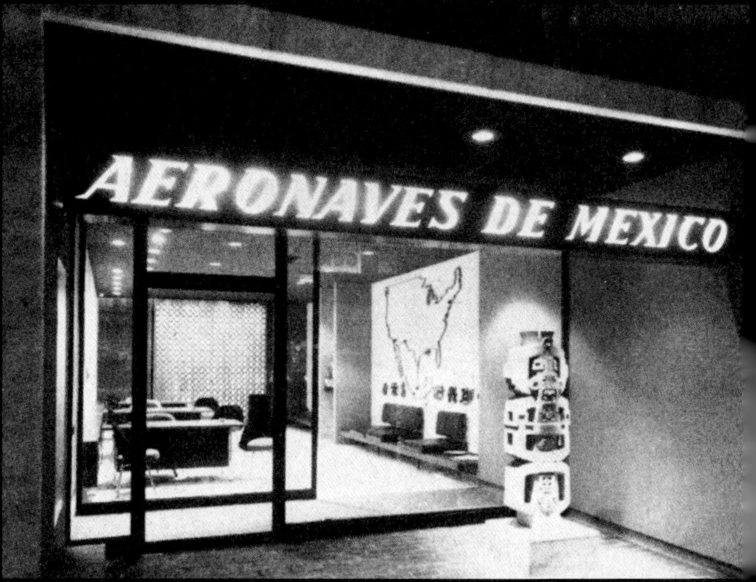

AERONAVES DE MEXICO

PAKISTAN INTERNATIONAL AIRLI

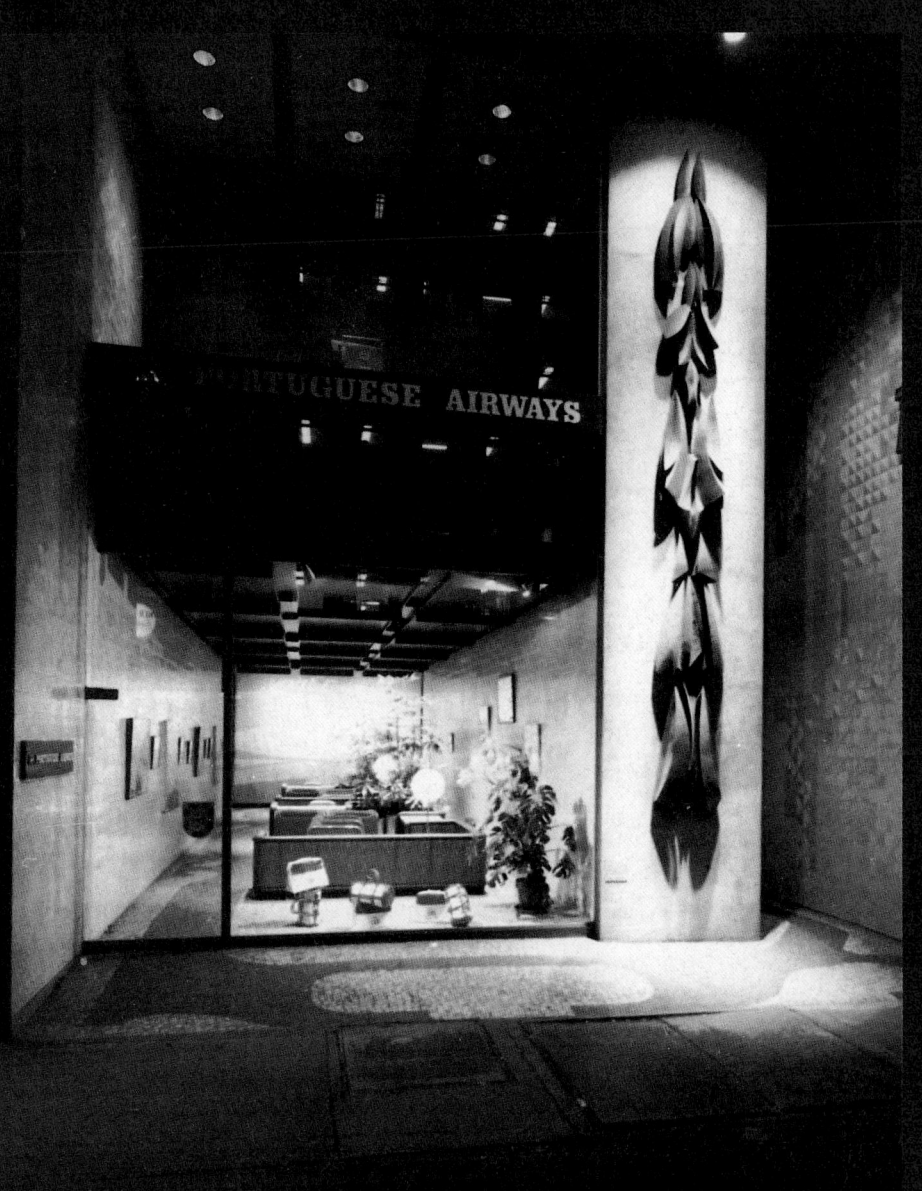

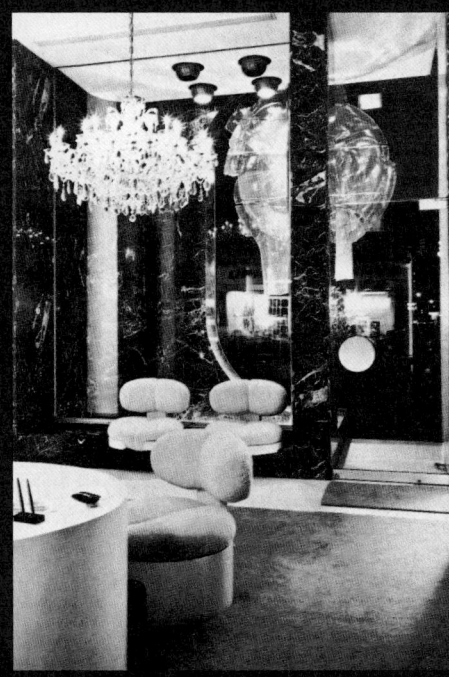

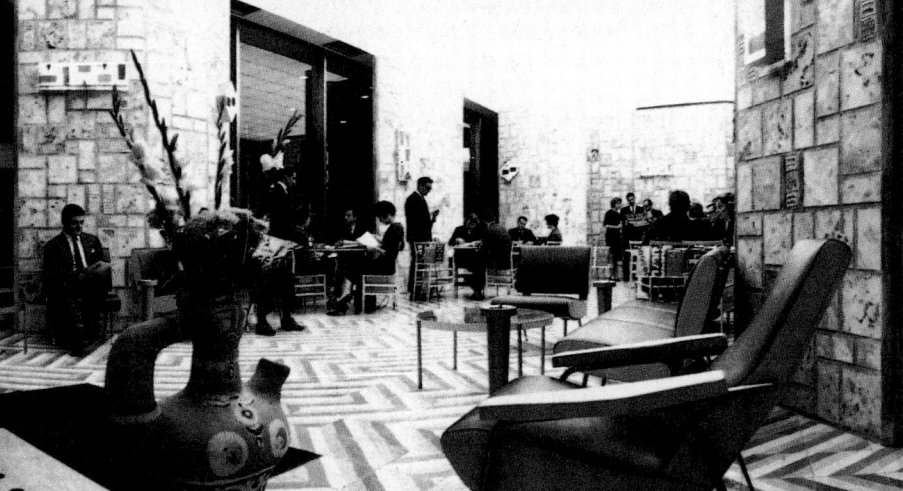

Facing page:
Top left: KLM Royal Dutch Airlines, 572 Fifth Avenue, between West Forty-sixth and West Forty-seventh streets. Louis Shulman, 1948. View to the west. Schnall. AR. CU

Bottom left: KLM Royal Dutch Airlines. Interior. Schnall. AR. CU

Top right: Japan Airlines, Rockefeller Center promenade. Junzo Yoshimura and Genichiro Inokuma in association with L. L. Rado and Antonin Raymond, 1956. Ticket office. JA

Center right: Aeronaves de Mexico, 500 Fifth Avenue, between West Forty-second and West Forty-third streets. Freidin-Studley Associates, 1957. View to the west. Schnall. IN. CU

Bottom right: Pakistan International Airlines, 608 Fifth Avenue, between West Forty-eighth and West Forty-ninth streets. Space Design Group, 1962. View to the west. Liebman. SDG

This page:
Top left: TAP Portuguese Airways, 601 Fifth Avenue, between East Forty-eighth and East Forty-ninth streets. Wilke-Davis in association with Luis F. Pinto and Vito J. Tricario, 1968. View to the east. MF

Bottom left: Alitalia, 666 Fifth Avenue, between West Fifty-second and West Fifty-third streets. Gio Ponti, 1958. Ticket office. AGP

Above: CSA, 545 Fifth Avenue, southeast corner of Fifth Avenue and East Forty-fifth Street. Jiri Louda, Ivan Skala and Freidin-Studley Associates, 1970. Entrance area. IN. CU

was renovated for use as a ticket office and the upper floors for business offices.[74] Meanwhile, KLM Royal Dutch Airlines established an independent booking agency in the storefront of 572 Fifth Avenue, between Forty-sixth and Forty-seventh streets, a building that also housed the headquarters of Swiss Airlines.[75] Louis Shulman, a young architect, opened the shopfront to almost two stories, framed it in Carrara marble and glazed it in horizontally proportioned bands carried on slim, finlike glazing bars of aluminum and stainless steel, designed with the help of engineer Peter Bruder. Lewis Mumford described the result as "the kind of composition that the Dutch architect, J. J. P. Oud, formulated in the twenties," whose possibilities designers "have not even begun to exhaust."[76] Inside, Shulman created a single room, double height at front but lowered farther back to accommodate a mezzanine, where an ingeniously profiled ceiling concealed cold cathode lighting above a long ticket counter.

BOAC, the British airline, also opened a retail facility in 1948.[77] Pamela C. Colgate's design was nowhere as stylish as that of KLM. As Mumford observed: "Plainly, the British have tried to impart to this terminal for their air service that aura of dependability that is characteristic of their mercantile navy. The light blue of the linoleum floor and the darker blue of the counters and the upholstered chairs have the same smart, seamanlike touch. I can't say as much for the zig-zag walls and the echeloned counters flanking them."[78] The following year Argentine Airlines opened offices, designed by Reisner & Urbahn, on the ground floor of the Savoy-Plaza Hotel, on the northeast corner of Fifty-eighth Street, that were far more spirited, conveying a sense of what Interiors called "the excitement and spontaneity of life in Argentina."[79]

Pan American World Airways was the first American carrier to open a significant independent sales office (1952), occupying the corner shop in the Sinclair Oil Building (see above), and retaining the building's architects, Carson & Lundin, to design its installation.[80] The space was sparely detailed with fine materials including a door and window frames in bronze; its principal feature was a large black-and-white map of the world illustrating Pan Am's routes in gold, designed by Robert Foster to fill the wall above the counter. In 1954 Northwest Orient Airlines, which occupied a narrow, rather poky office designed by the Chicago architects Holabird & Root (1945) at 535 Fifth Avenue,[81] expanded into the space next door at number 537.[82] On the exterior of the new ticket office, designed by Carson & Lundin, two horizontal bands of glass were separated by a wide spandrel that served double duty as a signboard. In recognition of the airline's status as the leading American carrier serving Japan, the architects designed the waiting and ticket-selling area to subtly reflect the character of Japanese architecture: walls were paneled to suggest shoji, and the massive scale of existing columns was broken up by plastering two planes and covering the other two with black-lacquered wood and space dividers made up of bamboolike wood dowels.

The arrival of jet travel in the late 1950s and the increased affluence, leisure time and cosmopolitanism of Americans resulted in an extraordinary growth of foreign travel. Consequently, many new foreign airline ticket offices were opened, and some of the earlier installations were expanded. In 1956 Japan Airlines chose a location in Rockefeller Center's promenade to showcase their national culture as well as sell tickets.[83] Designed by Junzo Yoshimura and the Japanese painter Genichiro Inokuma, working in association with L. L. Rado and his partner, Antonin Raymond, who had practiced in Japan during the 1920s and 1930s, the ticket office interpreted traditional Japanese themes far more convincingly than Carson & Lundin had been able to do

for Northwest. According to Interiors, the "main idea" of the design, which was based on classical Japanese forms but utilized American materials, was "the buoyancy of light," expressed as much in the almost seamless flow of space between the exterior and interior as it was in the ingenious handling of luminous panels hung from the ceiling.[84] Yoshimura also designed the furniture, which, combined with Inokuma's abstractly shaped fountain set in a pebble basin and the shoji- and bamboolike handling of the walls, created a delicate yet highly evocative effect. Louise Sloane, writing in Progressive Architecture, said that the ticket office, when viewed from the promenade, seemed "suspended in space, since no element touches another. . . . Comprised with the taste and simplicity characteristic of the best Japanese work, the total design is entirely modern in its lightness, brightness, and elegance."[85]

In 1957 Israel's El Al airlines established itself in Rockefeller Center, where it served, as Interiors put it, "as a semi-official propaganda agency for all kinds of travel to Israel."[86] The ambivalent nature of the agency's mission was effectively mirrored in the design by Tel Aviv architects Dvora and Yeheskiel Gad, who used a change in ceiling height to articulate a low-ceilinged entrance devoted to tourist attractions, primarily emphasizing culture, and a higher area for ticket sales. In the same year, BOAC moved its ticket offices into the Bank of New York Building (see below), at 530 Fifth Avenue,[87] and Aeronaves de Mexico established a New York presence with a stylish office at 500 Fifth Avenue, where designer Jack Freidin of Freidin-Studley Associates transformed a single-story shop into a patiolike salesroom that reflected the influence of the Mexican architect Luis Barragán.[88] Freidin pushed the shop's glass wall well back from the street and placed a six-foot Aztec-inspired clay sculpture by Enrico Arno on the outside. Red-brick paving flowed from outside to inside, as did a pepper-red wall along one side of the shop; on the other side of the interior, an adobelike wall with deep niches showcased typical native craft objects.

Two years later KLM took over 609 Fifth Avenue, on the southeast corner of Forty-ninth street, a thirteen-story building that had formerly housed the James McCutcheon & Co. store (Cross & Cross and Starrett & Van Vleck, 1925).[89] Working with Raymond & Rado, who also designed the airline's departure lounge at Idlewild, KLM completely demolished the first two floors of the limestone-clad building to create a glassy ticket office and extensively renovated the remainder of the building above to house its American office operations. (An early plan to strip the entire facade, including the cornices, was not carried out.) The new ticket office was boldly scaled but conventional in design, distinguished only by Gyorgy Kepes's fifty-one-by-eighteen-foot gray aluminum screenlike mural, conceived as an expression of, in the artist's words, "the experience a person has flying in an airplane at night and looking down on a panorama of city lights."[90]

Alitalia, the Italian airline, commissioned one of Italy's most distinguished architects, Gio Ponti, to design its facility (1958) on the ground floor of 666 Fifth Avenue.[91] For the ticket office, Ponti combined walls and floors of blue and white ceramic tile with furniture by Giordano Chiesa and ceramic sculptures and decorative panels by Fausto Melotti; six large pilasters, also covered in ceramic, conveyed a bold prismatic effect. "I chose this ceramic," Ponti wrote, "because such a mood didn't exist in New York . . . it represents something quintessentially Italian, or at least more Italian than an installation in wood, metal, glass, etc."[92]

In 1959 Iberia Air Lines of Spain announced that it would open ticket offices on Fifth Avenue, replacing the John Jarrell men's retail shop at number 518, between Forty-third and Forty-fourth streets.[93] The replacement of yet another Fifth Avenue retailer with an airline ticket office irked not only the Jarrell store's former manager, who complained that "banks and ticket offices don't enhance a shopping area," but also at least one nostalgic observer, who suggested that the ten or twelve blocks of Fifth Avenue above Forty-second Street be renamed "Airline Alley" or "Bankers' Boulevard."[94]

One year later Air India opened an office at 666 Fifth Avenue, a narrow shop which the architect and interior designer George Brelich opened to the street with plate glass, revealing a room largely illuminated by backlit white Sculpta-Grille panes.[95] A plexiglass interlayer suggested screened enclosures like the ones Edward Durell Stone had used so effectively in his United States Embassy building at New Delhi. Pakistan International Airlines followed in 1962 with a small office at 608 Fifth Avenue designed by Marvin B. Affrime, director of the Space Design Group; the office attempted to convey an impression of the home country through the sparing use of traditional tiles to form a mural that concluded the vista through the glass-fronted shop.[96] In 1961 Air France dramatically renovated its facility at 683 Fifth Avenue, replacing the shopfront with a thirty-foot-high glass front set back three feet from the building wall.[97] Designed by a Parisian, Robert Pontabry, who worked with Marvin B. Affrime, the new ticket office featured an abstract backlit mural, *City of Lights*, executed from a painting by Danielle Dhumez in Gemmail colored glass, an equally abstract Aubusson tapestry by Henri-Georges Adam and slick surfaces of painted plaster and dark mahogany. While the office was the perfect expression of prevailing French Modernism, its new glass front was hardly a compensation for the subtle elegance of the thirteen-year-old American proto-Modernist facade it replaced.

By the late 1960s it seemed that Fifth Avenue would be lined by nothing but airlines. In 1965 Trans-Caribbean Airways purchased the five-story building at 714 Fifth Avenue, between Fifty-fifth and Fifty-sixth streets, and Eastern Airlines leased the ground and second floors of 685 Fifth Avenue (Sloan & Robertson, 1926).[98] In 1968 TAP Portuguese Airways opened a ticket office at 601 Fifth Avenue, between Forty-eighth and Forty-ninth streets.[99] They employed New York interior designers Wilke-Davis, in association with Portuguese architect Luis F. Pinto and New York architect Vito J. Tricario, to create a dramatic, double-height facility featuring a sidewalk of stone mosaic that continued beyond the recessed glass wall into the shop, where tiled walls evoked typical Portuguese house facades. South Africa Airways followed in 1970 with a renovation of their sales offices at 605 Fifth Avenue by Wilke, Davis, Mitchell Associates.[100] CSA, Czechoslovakia's airlines, also joined the Fifth Avenue throng in 1970 with a provocatively designed facility at 545 Fifth Avenue, on the southeast corner of Forty-fifth Street, conceived by Czech architects Jiri Louda and Ivan Skala and implemented by the architect Joseph Kleiman, a partner of Freidin-Studley Associates.[101] Inside the scant seventeen-by-thirty-five-foot shop, the designers created a delightful mix of smooth stripped-down wall surfaces and hard-edge furnishings with craft objects such as a crystal chandelier from Bohemia and lamb coverings from the Tetra region.

Bankers' Boulevard

Concurrent with the proliferation of airline ticket offices in the 1960s and early 1970s, a steady growth in the number of banks on Fifth Avenue further jeopardized the street's retail character.

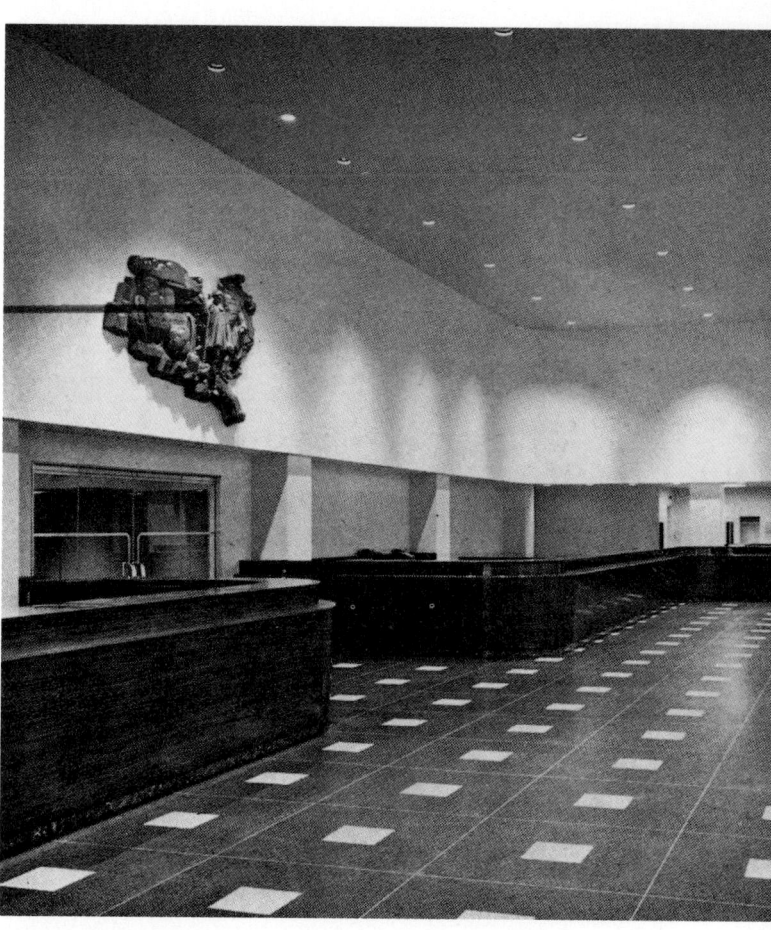

Bank of the Manhattan Company, 535 Fifth Avenue, northeast corner of Fifth Avenue and East Forty-fourth Street. Walker & Poor, 1952. Interior. Gottscho-Schleisner. PA. CU

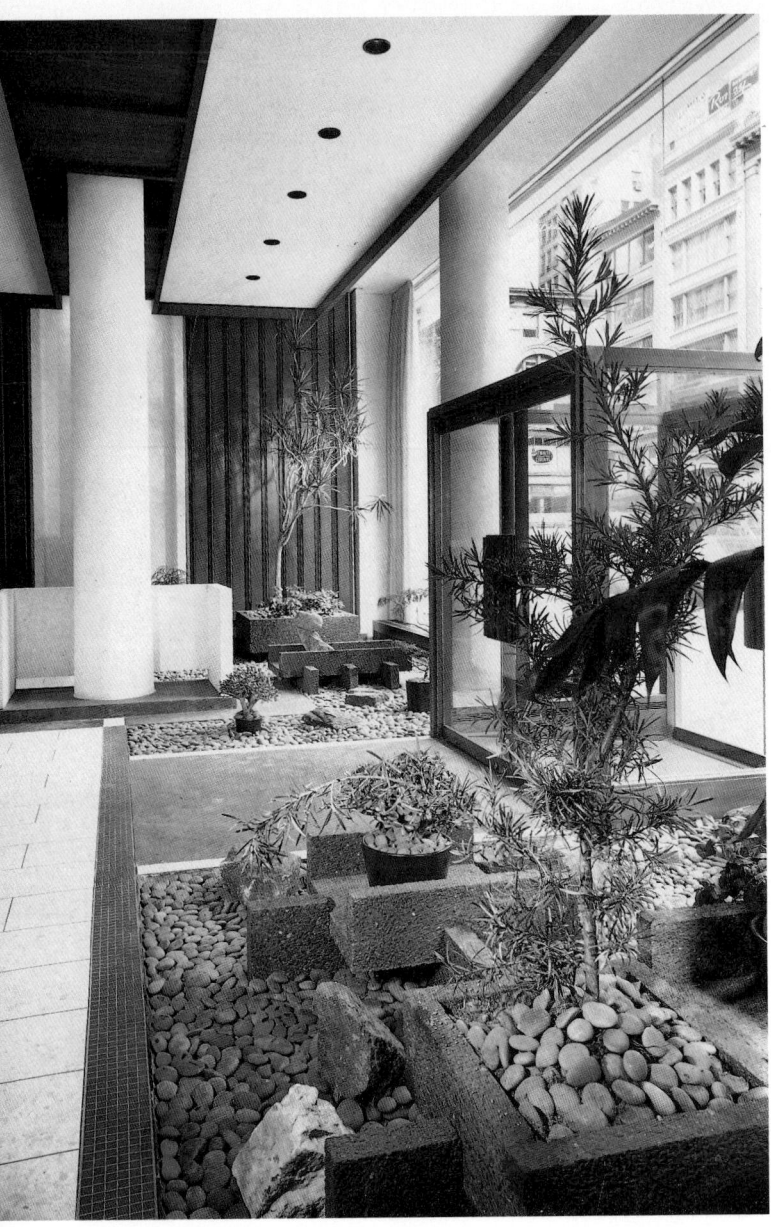

Bank of Tokyo Trust Company, northwest corner of Fifth Avenue and West Thirty-second Street. Carl J. Petrilli and Alexander Kouzmanoff, 1963. Entrance area. KP

Even more than airline ticket offices, banks compromised the avenue's function as a promenade because of the limited number of hours they were open to the public: banks were closed not only on Saturdays, as were airline offices, but also during the late afternoon. Moreover, whereas most airlines created interesting shop windows, banks presented the pedestrian with little more than placards advertising prevailing interest rates.

Among the first postwar banks on Fifth Avenue was the Bank of the Manhattan Company's branch on the ground floor of 535 Fifth Avenue (H. Craig Severance, 1926), variously known as the Delmonico Building, the Ruppert Building and the Central Mercantile Bank Building, and located on the northeast corner of Forty-fourth Street.[102] Walker & Poor's 1952 design was exceptionally tentative, presenting a new facade to Fifth Avenue that was dominated by three widely spaced, tall and narrow steel-framed expanses of glass—the northern two incorporating the bank's principal entrances—surmounted by a row of five comparatively small, horizontally composed windows. The portions of masonry wall between the main windows were blank except for two sculpted aluminum eagles that served as the base for flagpoles projecting out over the avenue. Inside, the double-height banking space, which incorporated a mezzanine level, contained white walls, white-marble-clad columns, a black and white terrazzo floor and open teller counters. Lewis Mumford offered extravagant praise for the bank, characterizing the remodeling as "from first to last, a handsome job." He went on to say:

> The whole job has been carried out with such consummate refinement that even when one winces—as is natural at the sight of eighteenth-century ladder-back chairs in a modern office— one feels not too unsympathetic with the architects' and the bankers' intentions. . . . In all this, there is little more effort to imitate the past than there is in the new Lever House, but the interpretation of the present is conspicuously different. With a wistful glance at its own historic beginnings, the bank has provided for its higher officers mahogany chairs and desks that exhale the conservative odor of wealth and genteel ease that is part of the backgrounds of Rowlandson prints. . . . If I had to choose between the Bank of the Manhattan Company's quarters and those of the top executives of Lever House, I would take the first on the ground that they are rather less stuffy.[103]

In 1956, two years after the completion of the Manufacturers Trust bank (see above), reflecting the lingering stylistic traditionalism that in part defined the nature of Fifth Avenue as well as that of many banking institutions, the venerable Seamen's Bank for Savings expanded its branch at 546 Fifth Avenue, on the northwest corner of Forty-fifth Street.[104] The architect Adolf Lancken Muller, of Halsey, McCormick & Helmer, continued the Classical vocabulary of the existing building in a new three-story building replacing 548 Fifth Avenue. The ground floors of the two buildings were united to jointly serve the bank.

By 1961 the intersection of Fifth Avenue and Forty-fourth Street had gained the distinction of containing banks on all four corners. On the northeast corner, at 535 Fifth Avenue, was the Bank of the Manhattan Company branch. On the southeast corner, number 529, a nineteen-story wedding-cake-type office building, designed by Emery Roth & Sons (1959), contained a branch of the Bankers Trust Company on its first three floors, which were articulated on the exterior to serve visually as the building's base.[105] The architecturally banal glass-and-aluminum building was somewhat noteworthy for its construction, which had completely engulfed an existing eleven-story building (Henry Ives Cobb, 1906) serving the bank; the bank maintained its branch operations during the entire construction process.

Occupying the west blockfront between Forty-fourth and Forty-fifth streets was the massive, twenty-six-story Bank of New York Building (Voorhees, Walker, Smith & Smith, 1959), at 530 Fifth Avenue.[106] To realize its new headquarters, the Bank of New York tore down what the *New Yorker* described as a "mansard-roofed, many-chimneyed trio of remodelled private houses" in which the bank had housed its midtown office.[107] The Voorhees design was a conservative, limestone-clad mass punctured by a regular rhythm of squarish windows and by a metal-and-glass-clad notch that formed a visual cornice at the tenth floor. Though arguably more dignified than its contemporaneous neighbors, the building's bulk and asymmetrical massing, including a twelve-story tower, rendered it rather awkward. On the Forty-fourth Street corner, the banking facility itself occupied an austere, monumentally scaled double-height space, lit by tall windows set deep within quirkily detailed stone embrasures.

Completing the intersection's quartet of banks in 1961 was 522 Fifth Avenue, on the southwest corner of Forty-fourth Street, which housed a street-level branch of the Morgan Guaranty Trust Company.[108] Designed by Eggers & Higgins, the limestone-clad building incorporated an arcade along Fifth Avenue behind which a predominantly glass facade contained the principal entrances of both the office building and the bank. The new Morgan Guaranty Building was in part a renovation; it consisted of twelve stories built on top of the eleven-story frame of a much-admired landmark, the former Louis Sherry's restaurant and hotel (McKim, Mead & White, 1898), which had become the Guaranty Trust Building in 1919.[109] The new design replaced the building's old granite skin with a limestone cladding punctuated with a grid of tall windows set in marble frames. The space given over to the two-story, 115-foot-long, 25-foot-deep, street-level arcade, carved out of the building's volume, was more than compensated for with the additional floor area created by filling in the original building's inner court.

The same internationalism that brought foreign shops and airlines to the avenue brought international banking facilities as well. This trend was pioneered by the Bank of Tokyo Trust Company, which opened a branch on the northwest corner of Fifth Avenue and Thirty-second Street in 1963, designed by the architects Carl J. Petrilli and Alexander Kouzmanoff.[110] Marian Page, writing in *Interiors*, observed that while "nothing has become more of a Manhattan cliché in recent years than the sleek and glassy bank which turns up on practically every corner," the Tokyo bank struck her as a "fresh departure from this shiny repetition."[111] Kouzmanoff stated that he and Petrilli had eschewed a conventional Modernist bank design in favor of one that reflected their corporate client's national origins, although they also honored the client's request that the design not be traditionally Japanese. To this end, the architects synthesized architectural vocabularies, contrasting the space's exposed-concrete structural columns with teak wall paneling. Five abstract wood sculptures, placed against the bank's fabric-covered rear wall, evoked the ornamental towers that adorn shrines in Kyoto. More explicitly referential was the interior, Japanese-inspired rock garden that flanked the bank's principal entrance and was clearly visible from Fifth Avenue through the glazed facade. Exotic plants, including bonsai, some in U-shaped, precast-concrete planters designed by Kouzmanoff and Petrilli, were dis-

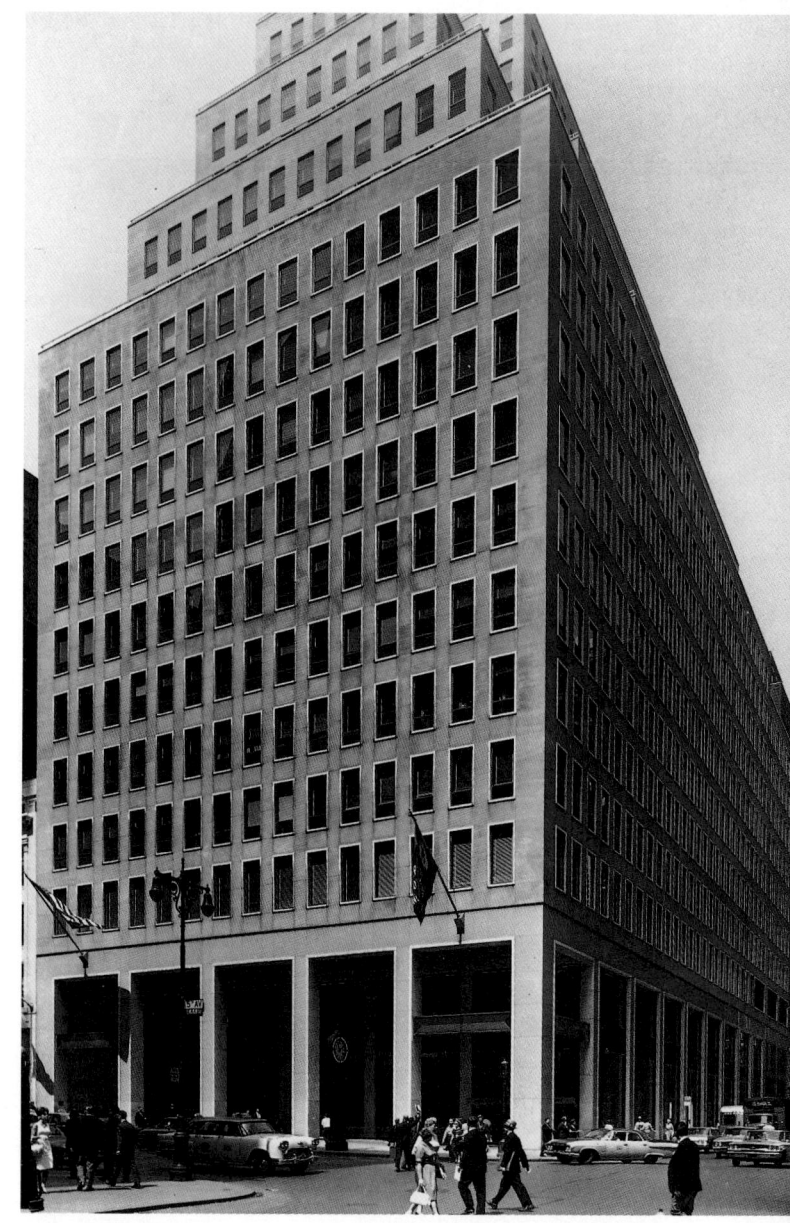

522 Fifth Avenue, southwest corner of Fifth Avenue and West Forty-fourth Street. Eggers & Higgins, 1961. View to the southwest. OMH

387

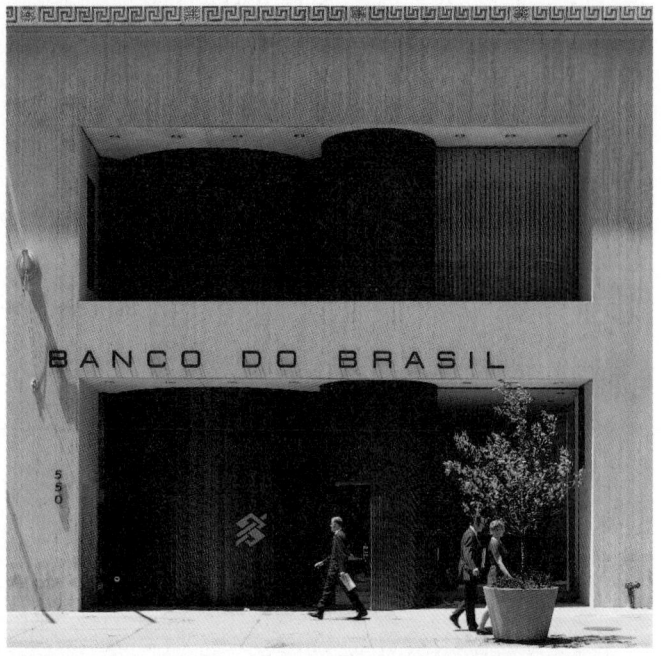

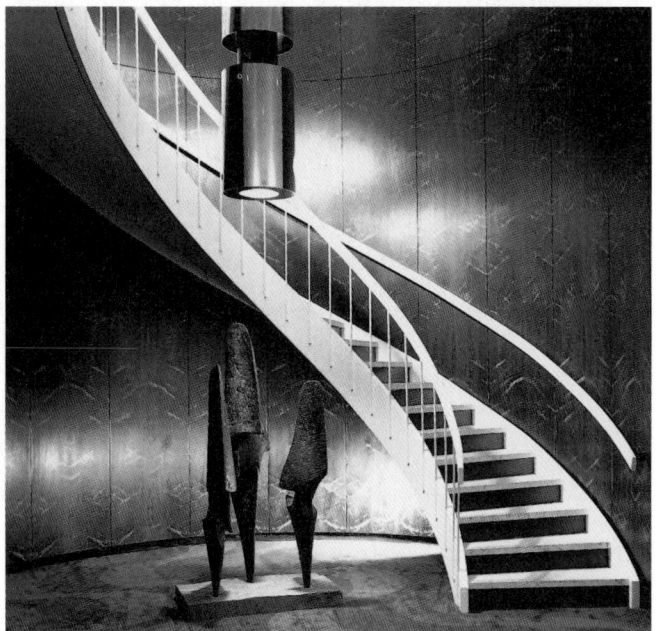

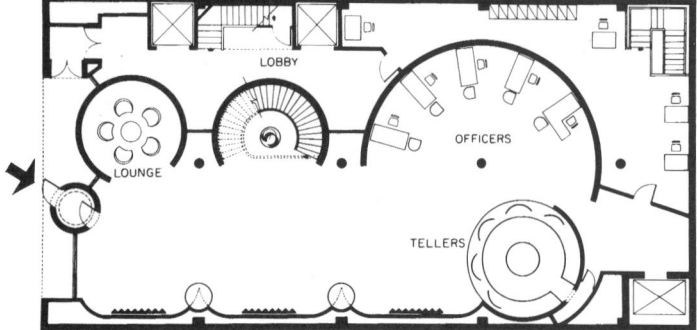

played against expanses of Japanese river rocks, punctuated by larger stones found on the grounds of Kouzmanoff's Westchester home.

In 1969 Latin America's largest bank, the 700-branch Banco do Brasil, opened an operation at 550 Fifth Avenue, between Forty-fifth and Forty-sixth streets, that constituted not only its first branch in New York but its first one in the northern hemisphere.[112] The design by Paul Damaz, a principal in the firm of Damaz & Weigel, did not attempt to transplant traditional Brazilian architecture, but it powerfully embodied the glamorous, somewhat theatrical interpretation of Corbusian Modernism that had been a hallmark of Latin American architecture since the 1930s.[113] Though distinctly Modernist, Damaz's design marked a departure from the glassiness that had been de rigueur in New York's bank architecture since SOM's Manufacturers Trust bank. The beige travertine facade, which suggested considerable depth, was interrupted by two asymmetrically placed cylinders sheathed in dark brown corrugated, anodized aluminum and separated by a sliver of glass; one cylinder contained the bank's principal entrance and functioned as a vestibule. Inside, the facade's curvilinear forms were repeated in a circular desk containing five tellers' booths as well as in a sweeping alcove clad in Brazilian rosewood and housing officers' desks. The entire floor was covered with carpeting decorated with dramatically undulating stripes that evoked typical Brazilian paving patterns. The bank's emphasis on large corporate accounts rather than individual accounts was reflected not only in the small number of tellers' booths but in the generously scaled second-floor executive offices, reached by a spiral staircase that encircled an abstract bronze sculpture by Alicia Penalba. Abstract wood wall sculptures by Sergio Camargo also decorated the main space.

In 1971 the firm of Poor & Swanke, formerly the Office of Alfred Easton Poor, designed a branch for the First Israel Bank and Trust Company at 579 Fifth Avenue, on the northeast corner of Forty-seventh Street.[114] The neatly detailed interior incorporated charcoal gray slate paving and columns clad in black-anodized aluminum. Behind the tellers' counters, a tapestry by the artist Maria Teresa Celinska depicted Jerusalem in abstracted, graphic forms. The editors of *Architectural Record* judged the bank's interior to be "exceptionally appealing" and noted that the nationalistic art was "the bank's principal identifying feature—a responsibility it shoulders with notable distinction."[115]

Olympic Tower

In 1970 Best & Company closed its doors and plans were announced for the replacement of its twenty-three-year-old facility with a forty-five-story office building to be developed by the Greek shipping magnate Aristotle Onassis working in association with Arlen Properties.[116] In the youth-oriented 1960s Best's "carriage trade" business had suffered, and efforts by new owners, the McCrory Corporation, to revitalize the store's image as a smart, upscale store had faltered in the economic downturn that began in 1969. As McCrory's president, Samuel Neaman, put it: "It is all a matter of economics. Best's has not responded to the full potential of capital that we have invested. . . . It is a matter, too, of retailing—or real estate values."[117] The fact of the matter was that Best's real estate, and in particular its Fifth Avenue property, was worth more to the shareholders than the potential profits of retailing. In one of the era's notable ironies, Fifth

Avenue retailing, which had given the street its distinction and prestige, was threatened with extinction by the very values it had created.

For a time Best's had considered constructing an office building above their existing store, but their plans did not crystallize until they were able to enter into an agreement with Onassis that called for combining their site with the air rights over the five-story 647 Fifth Avenue (Hunt & Hunt's George W. Vanderbilt house, 1902–5; addition, 1917) just to its north, which housed offices of the Greek magnate's Olympic Airlines.[118] In addition, in order to allow for a new building that would be big enough to justify the project, the developers purchased the air rights to the former Morton F. Plant residence (Robert W. Gibson, 1905; addition at 4 East Fifty-second Street, C. P. H. Gilbert, 1905), at 651–653 Fifth Avenue, on the southeast corner of Fifty-second Street.[119] Since 1917 this building had served as the six-story home of Cartier's, the exclusive jewelers (store remodeling, William Welles Bosworth, 1917), and it had been a designated landmark since July 1970. It was rumored that the development team tried to buy the air rights to St. Patrick's Cathedral as well.

Before the decision to close Best's was made, designs were developed by Morris Lapidus for a building that would be built above the store, wrapping around the Olympic and Cartier buildings in a slender L and connecting it with Fifty-second Street.[120] Lapidus saw the commission as heralding "a whole new direction" in his forty-year career. To get the job Lapidus had pleaded "for two long years" with Arthur Levien and Arthur Cohen, partners in the Arlen Company, for whom he had been designing housing and whom Onassis and the Rapid American Corporation, the conglomerate that controlled the McCrory Corporation, had chosen to manage their project.[121] It was Arlen's idea to include apartments as well as shops and offices in the new building. Lapidus's scheme called for a 200-foot-tall east-west midblock slab and included a shop-lined pedestrian arcade. The arcade would be built on other acquired properties to the east of Best's, linking Fifty-first and Fifty-second streets. The scheme also included a midblock plaza facing Fifth Avenue set on a portion of the 37'6"-wide site of the Olympic Airlines building, which would be demolished. The new building would not be built above Best's or Cartier's but only on the Olympic site.

Arlen had been reluctant to hire Lapidus because of his lack of experience with office-building design, but after six other firms failed to deliver suitable designs, they gave him one week to show what he could do. Anticipating such a turn of events, Lapidus had already been at work on a scheme in his Miami office and, with the help of his son Alan, who ran the firm's New York office, was able to meet the schedule. His proposal was for a twenty-story shaft clad in black granite, topped by a twenty-story mirrored cube "that bloomed like a lovely flower on its stem." Inside the cube were to be the most prestigious offices, as well as executive apartments and a full-floor art gallery, requested by Meshulam Riklis, chairman of Rapid American. The twentieth floor was to serve as "a huge sky plaza, an unrivaled display area for sculpture, a spacious reception area for visitors, and a congenial lunch-hour meeting place for people employed in the building."[122]

The scheme was favorably received by Onassis and Riklis, and Lapidus was authorized to develop plans. At about the same time, the exhibition of Lapidus's work at the Architectural League (see chapter 17), intended as a vindication of his pop-

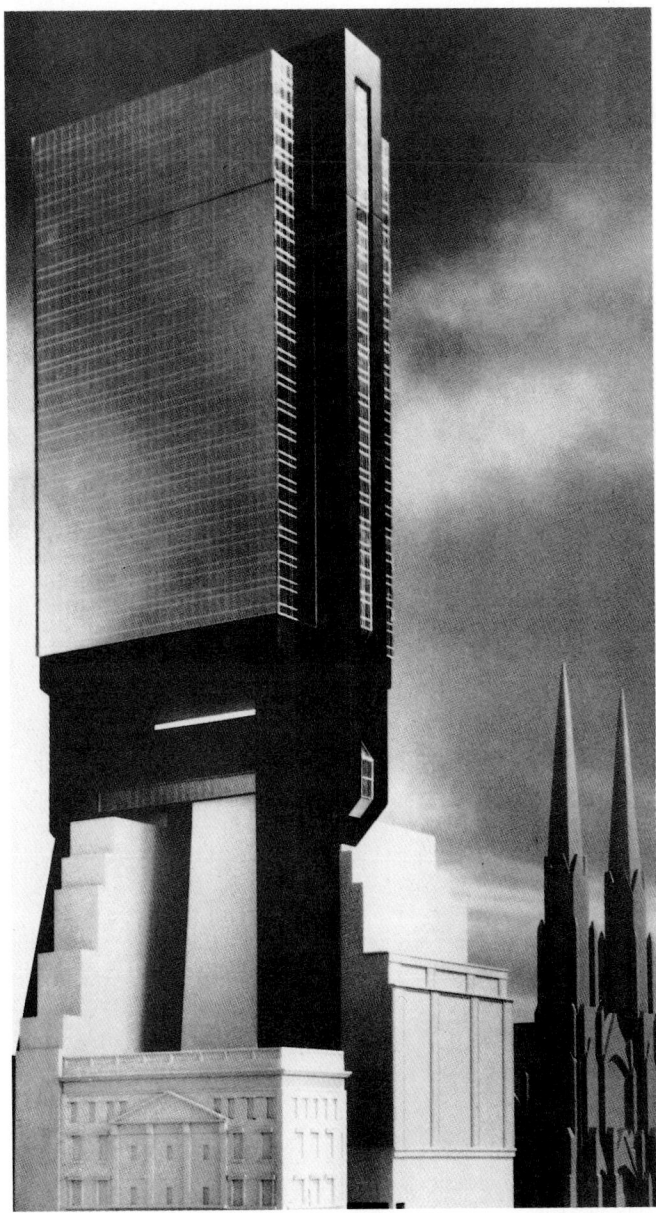

Top left: Banco do Brasil, 550 Fifth Avenue, between West Forty-fifth and West Forty-sixth streets. Damaz & Weigel, 1969. View to the west. Cserna. GC

Center left: Banco do Brasil. View of stairwell showing sculpture by Alicia Penalba. Cserna. GC

Bottom left: Banco do Brasil. Plan. AR. CU

Above: Proposed Olympic Tower, east side of Fifth Avenue between East Fifty-first and East Fifty-second streets. Morris Lapidus, 1970. Model. View to the southeast with former Morton F. Plant residence (Robert W. Gibson, 1905; addition at 4 East Fifty-second Street, C. P. H. Gilbert, 1905) below. ML

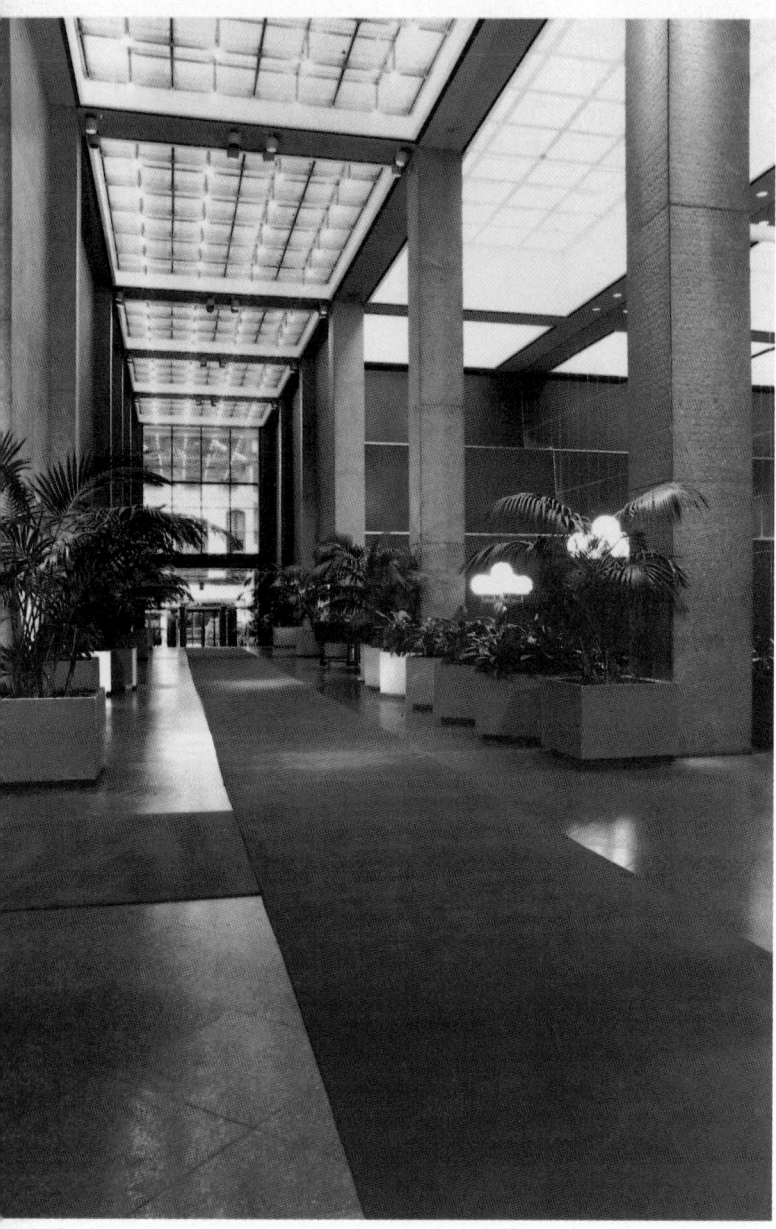

Above: Olympic Place, 645 Fifth Avenue, east of Fifth Avenue from East Fifty-first to East Fifty-second Street. Chermayeff, Geismar & Associates; and Zion & Breen; and Levien, Deliso & White, 1977. View to the north. OTA

Right: Olympic Tower, 645 Fifth Avenue, northeast corner of Fifth Avenue and East Fifty-first Street. Skidmore, Owings & Merrill, 1976. View to the northeast. Parker. SOM

ulist approach, opened to the less than enthusiastic praise of Ada Louise Huxtable. Worse still was an editorial in the *New York Times* (probably written by Huxtable) entitled "Good-by to Fifth Avenue?"[123] In a discussion of the street's role as a retail center, the editorial singled out Lapidus's involvement as a sign of the avenue's decline. Lapidus attributed subsequent troubles with the Onassis-Riklis-Arlen project in part to that editorial.

As project planning proceeded, work was also going forward on a new Special District plan, voted into law by the Board of Estimate on March 25, 1971, which was established to preserve Fifth Avenue's unique blend of retail, hotel and office uses.[124] Merwin Bayer, president of the financially troubled Arnold Constable department store, had described the situation five years earlier: "Rents have tended to push out stores, and store space has gone to others willing to pay the premium— banks, airlines, Government offices, travel agencies, showrooms. These changes . . . do not represent a positive step that bodes well for stores."[125] The new law grew out of a collaboration between city planners, retailers and the real estate community, led by Harry G. Huberth, who saw that the avenue's transformation into a corporate office center would have a negative impact on midtown's future as a whole. Surveying the avenue between Thirty-fourth and Fifty-seventh streets, Huberth found that only 5,296 feet, or 57 percent, of the street frontage was being used for retail; banks occupied 1,108 feet and airline ticket offices another 810. Huberth argued that if the trend were to continue unchecked, it would result in at least a doubling of banks and ticket offices by 1975, a phenomenon that "could mark the end of Fifth Avenue as a gracious pedestrian promenade and major tourist attraction. After all, no one wants to stroll in order to look into bank windows. Park Avenue is our major corporate avenue. Pedestrians veer off Park Avenue to window shop on Madison and Fifth. Our fear is that Fifth Avenue is going the way of Park Avenue."[126]

Encouraged by the Urban Design Group and the City Planning Commission, the city recognized the validity of Huberth's claims and introduced the Special District plan, the first zoning law in the United States that encouraged a mix of residences, offices and shops in single buildings. Jaquelin Robertson and his staff at the Office of Midtown Planning and Development analyzed the midtown stretch of Fifth Avenue, dividing it into three separate districts. They found that the blocks from Thirty-fourth to Forty-second Street, once the city's most fashionable retail area and until the 1950s one of its most vital, were now in trouble; those from Forty-second to Fiftieth Street, which had never been as strong for shopping, were now almost totally devoted to banking and travel on the ground floor; and those from Fiftieth Street to the Plaza were still very successful as a retail corridor but were showing signs of decay.

Rather than attempting to make the avenue less attractive to office development through rezoning, a process likely to anger real estate interests, Robertson's proposal called for space-bonus incentives that would encourage developers of new office buildings to include small stores and intimate restaurants in their plans and to further mix uses by including apartments. The Special District plan called for new structures on the east side of Fifth Avenue to be built flush with the avenue's building line and to provide, where possible, midblock, north-south, roofed pedestrian ways located at least fifty feet back from Fifth Avenue. Though buildings on the west side had to be lined up along the property line at their bases, they were required to be set fifty feet back above the eighty-five-foot line to give the avenue a greater sense of width, as it had around Rockefeller

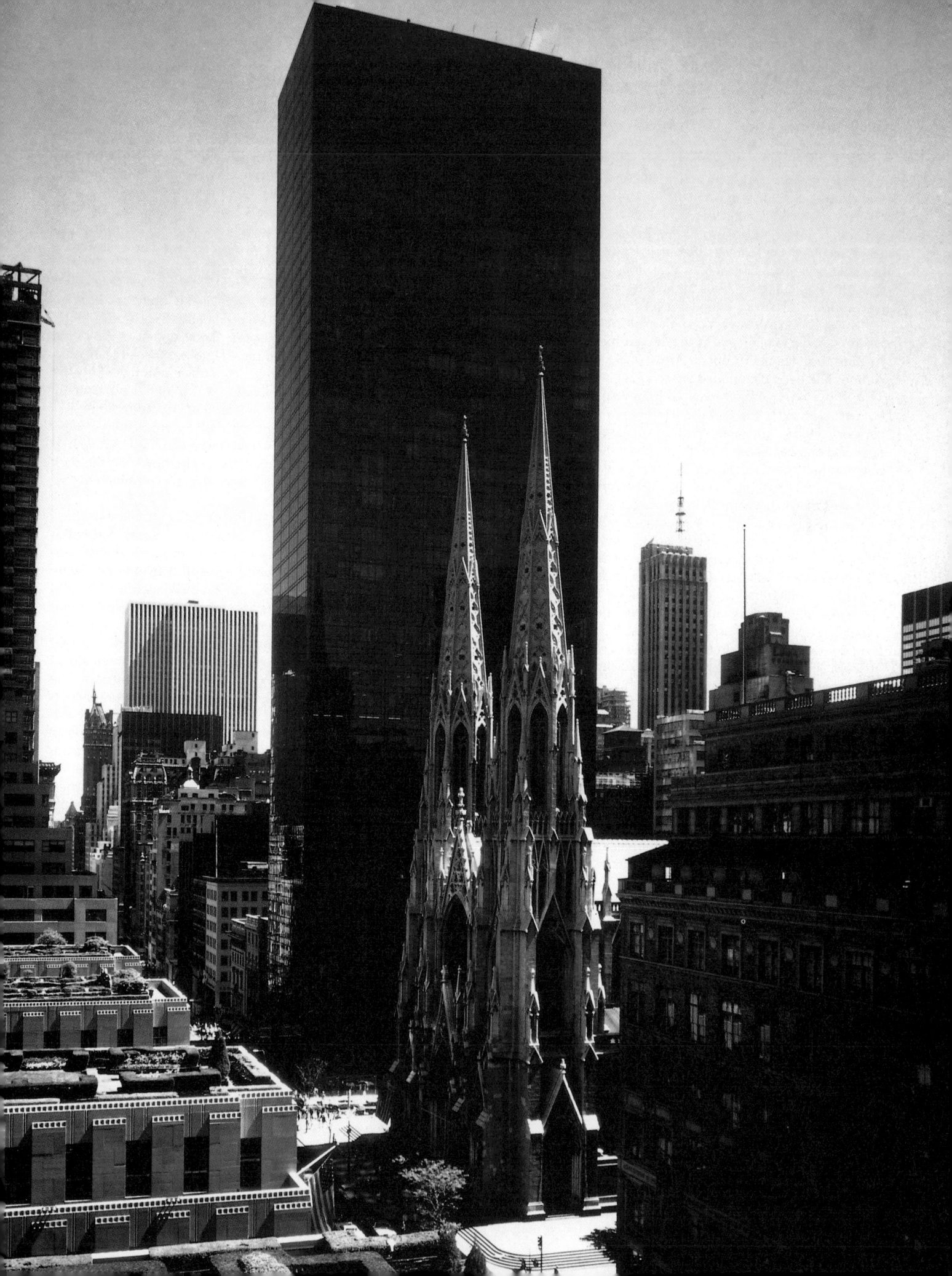

Center. Streetside plazas were banned on both east and west sides. A fixed percentage of retail space was required in any new building, but if a larger percentage was included, bonuses would be forthcoming. The kinds of retail uses were strictly controlled; airline ticket offices and banks were not permitted.

Just two weeks before the zoning proposal received final approval, American Airlines signed a lease for the ground floor and basement of 665 Fifth Avenue (C. P. H. Gilbert, 1912), recently vacated by Georg Jensen, which relocated to Madison Avenue.[127] Despite Robertson's opposition, the airline eventually convinced city officials that their lease should be exempt from the new regulations, citing a previously signed letter of intent. "It's particulary onerous to be told we can't move in after we've closed two Fifth Avenue ticket offices that belonged to Trans-Caribbean Airways," complained Richard Lempert, the airline's lawyer, referring to the recent merger of American Airlines and Trans-Caribbean Airways.[128] Though American Airlines had been determined to secure a Fifth Avenue address, its stay would prove short-lived. In 1974, in an effort to concentrate its sales and promotional activities in smaller and more dispersed facilities, American Airlines subleased the space to the Spanish National Tourism office. By this time, the eleven-story building had been purchased by Sam Minskoff & Sons, which stripped off Gilbert's walls and had the frame reclad in a dark-glass-and-metal curtain wall designed by the Eggers Partnership.

In the case of Olympic Tower, as the Onassis-Riklis-Arlen project came to be called, it seemed it was not the ground-floor ticket office for Onassis's airline that really irked Robertson and his colleagues; it was Lapidus's overblown design. But because Robertson's office had no power to review the aesthetics of a given design, it worked with the building's developers to create a more complex mix of uses for the site and to make the project a model for the future. In so doing, they argued for a less aggressive, more urbanistically conventional design, suggesting that Lapidus was not the appropriate choice, an idea that was reinforced by Huxtable's diatribe. To Lapidus's unending bitterness, Onassis fired him as architect. Kahn & Jacobs were brought in, but they too were fired; finally Skidmore, Owings & Merrill were given the job.

Although SOM was able to deliver a more sophisticated product, on the basis of the firm's previous urban buildings, they seemed less suited than Lapidus to the concept of mixed use and the functional and contextual complexities of the new zoning and the site. This impression was confirmed by the final product, an undifferentiated slab clad in brown-tinted glass.[129] Olympic Tower contained one million square feet of space packed in a rectangular slab rising sheer from its site for fifty-one stories. Incorporating ground-floor shops, a midblock enclosed pedestrian mall and twenty floors of offices topped by thirty floors of luxury apartments (230 apartments in all), SOM's design gave no visual clues to the mix of uses it contained and made almost no effort to project a welcoming image to the public at large that was expected to populate its galleria and enter its shops. This mixed use yielded a building that was not only unimaginably mute but also significantly bigger than the site would have permitted before: its floor area ratio (FAR) was 21.6, the highest ever.

SOM's Whitson Overcash claimed that sheathing the building with bronze glass created a "mirror for reflecting St. Patrick's cathedral, across the street."[130] But Olympic Tower's surfaces did little to enliven the street, and even though the building hugged the street line, the absence of detail and the dark glass made the shop doors difficult to find. Clear glass was eventually substituted at street level and the stores were leased to sophisticated merchants including Roberta di Camerino, an Italian shop selling handbags, the venerable leather goods purveyor Mark Cross, and H. Stern, the jewelers. The original intention was to extend the building's skin over Onassis's Olympic Airlines building, but after Paul Goldberger, Ada Louise Huxtable and others protested, the limestone facade of Hunt & Hunt's original building was maintained. (The building was designated a landmark on March 22, 1977.)

The developers seemed to do everything in their power to play down the public nature of the 8,700-square-foot, thirty-foot-high galleria, called Olympic Place, a public amenity mandated by the city in exchange for allowing more leasable space to be built on the site. Serving as the lobby to the office building (apartment dwellers entered under a separate canopy located to the west of its Fifty-first Street doors) as well as a midblock passageway, Olympic Place was invisible behind the dark-tinted glass; its presence was announced only by minute signs, and its interior lighting was so dim that passersby could not easily see into it at any time of day. Intrepid pedestrians who managed to enter the galleria were treated in daytime hours to filtered natural light and a waterfall that spilled down to a below-grade restaurant; at night, however, the dark stone floors and walls and the reflective glass combined to create a lugubrious effect.

Olympic Tower's curtain wall not only concealed its functional complexities, it also covered up an unusual structural system consisting of a thirty-floor cast-in-place reinforced-concrete-frame apartment building atop a twenty-one-story steel-framed office structure. Apartment dwellers were provided with a high level of amenities, including a concierge, a restaurant, barber and hairdressing salons, emergency electric power, and saunas and exercise rooms. The two highest floors consisted of large duplex apartments. In one apartment the international arms merchant Adnan Khashogi installed a swimming pool. The apartments, which offered superb views through the nine-foot-high floor-to-ceiling glazing, were gobbled up mostly by foreigners, "an indication that," as Paul Goldberger observed in 1976, "if the image of New York is in trouble so far as Americans are concerned, it still holds sway over the world at large."[131] Stanley Thea, an Arlen vice president, explained: "We merchandised the apartments to a select core of 80,000 people around the world. It has been extraordinarily successful in the face of the worst market in a century."[132] Jaquelin Robertson, now working for Arlen, boasted: "Finally we are building in the 1970's what was shown in the movies of the 1940's—penthouses on the 50th floor. Up to now the tops of the high towers have been given over to offices."[133] Model apartments were designed by leading decorators such as Mac II and the architect Robert A. M. Stern. The building was marketed with a brochure written in French, German, Spanish and Japanese, making it the first to take advantage of New York's emergence as a major international city.

The critical reception to Olympic Tower was not favorable. Goldberger characterized the building's "ice-cold dignity" as "pure Skidmore, Owings and Merrill." The tower, he said, "bears little difference from the average glass office tower—indeed, its plain skin is not as refined as Skidmore, Owings and Merrill's best work." He did have praise for the apartments, however, which he found "simple and straightforward" and "uncommonly well-detailed—there is none of the Sears Roebuck French Provincial cabinetry that one sees in most new apartments."[134]

Ada Louise Huxtable also had her doubts about the design. "The huge Olympic Tower," she lamented, "is no design triumph. It is about as nondescript as anything that size can be."[135] Huxtable particularly disliked the design of Olympic Place, which she labeled a "cop-out." Although the galleria, she said, had been "pictured in glossy brochures as bustling with elegant stores and restaurants, alive with a spectacular waterfall and other public amenities," a scaled-down waterfall was the only feature that survived the cost-conscious and fundamentally anti-public redesigns the owners imposed on Olympic Place. Noting that twenty-two wire chairs, five tiny tables, an "endless number of ordinary plants," and a party wall and service doors were "the dominant features of the blank bare tunnel," Huxtable argued that the space was "useless to anyone." It was all executed "so conspicuously on-the-cheap," she said, that "it could even be argued that this minimal effort and lack of retail space flouts the law's requirements and intent. . . . Olympic Tower has given the city the back of its hand."[136] Suzanne Stephens summarized the building's attitude most succinctly in her 1975 assessment: "Olympic Tower stands today, awkward in form, but slick in style, a solution that conveys signs of urbanity rather than creating a sense of urban place."[137]

As Olympic Tower was being planned, plans were also being drawn up for a new building to replace the nine-story DePinna's, on the southwest corner of Fifty-second Street, which closed in 1969.[138] DePinna's, which had begun as an upmarket men's and boys' clothing store in 1885 and later grew to include women's wear as well, moved from its original site at Fifth Avenue and Thirty-sixth Street to Fifth Avenue and Fiftieth Street in 1916. Twelve years later it settled on the site formerly occupied by the house Margaret Vanderbilt Shepard and Emily Vanderbilt Sloane shared with their families (John B. Snook and Charles Atwood, 1879–82).[139] This house was built for them by their father, William Henry Vanderbilt, whose own house, designed by the same architects at the same time, stood directly to the south and was connected to his daughters' mansion by a glazed atrium that served as a common entrance. At one point the developers, the Minskoff organization, who had owned the building since 1966, working with Lehman Brothers, the investment bankers, sought to find a user for the DePinna building. Eventually they demolished the building and sold the site to the Pahlavi Foundation, a New York organization set up by the Shah of Iran, some said to help sequester capital in the United States. Given the collapsed New York economy, the proposed 336,000-square-foot Pahlavi office building was greeted with enthusiasm. While Olympic Tower was in part a prototype for the new Special District, 650 Fifth Avenue was the first building to be completely conceived under its rules.[140]

Designed by John Carl Warnecke & Associates, the twenty-nine-story tower of 650 Fifth was set back forty feet from its seven-story base in accord with the Special District's mandate for buildings on the avenue's west side. Though its horizontal window bands were clichéd, the use of granite for the spandrels added a rather dignified note. This effect, however, was somewhat undercut by the rather overblown two-story entrance loggia around the corner on Fifty-second Street, populated with exposed escalators leading up to the 30,000-square-foot mall-like retail area and down to a future subway connection. The building was not completed until 1978, by which time the Shah's fall from political power had frozen the lavish funds originally designated for its construction. Nonetheless, as Paul Goldberger wrote, the building, still owned by the Pahlavi Foundation but developed to standards established by the Minskoffs, was "a

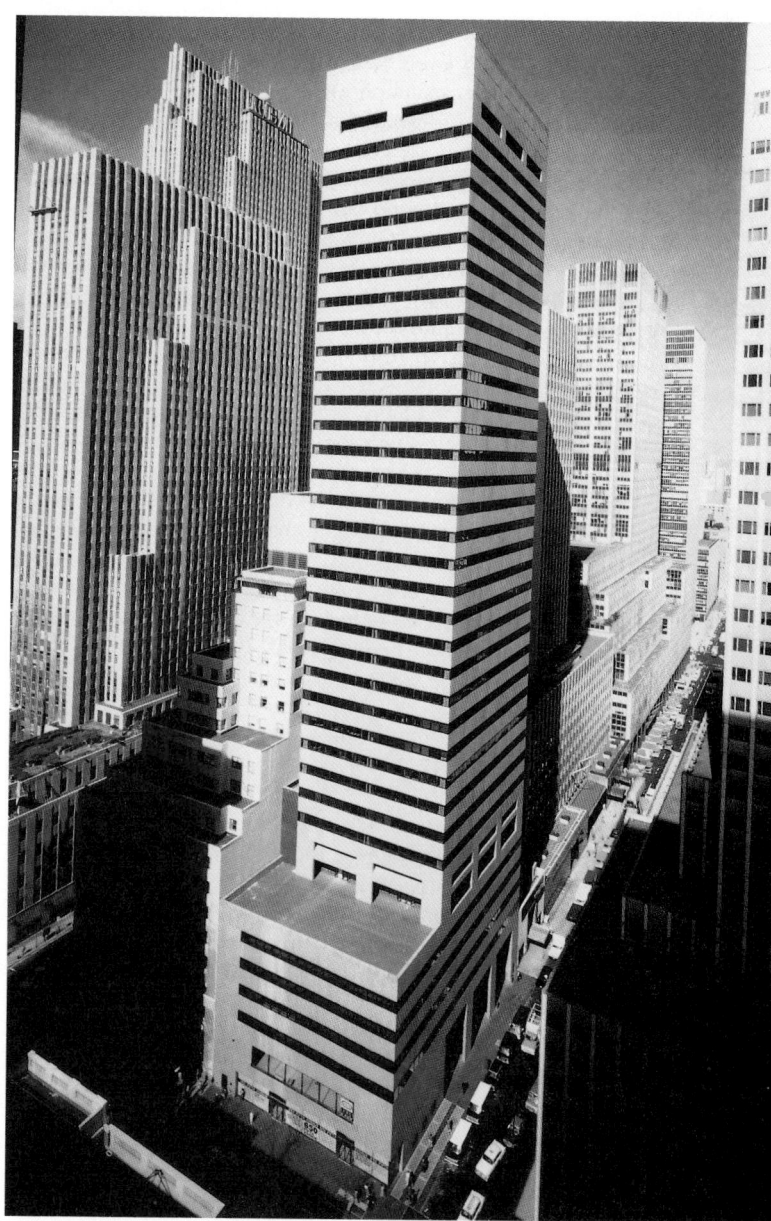

650 Fifth Avenue, southwest corner of West Fifty-second Street. John Carl Warnecke & Associates, 1978. View to the southwest. JCW

decent, sensible, dull" design, just the kind needed on Fifth Avenue, which had been "taken over . . . by loud, mirrored shopfronts and glass skyscrapers like Olympic Tower." With the replacement of the old image of Fifth Avenue by what Goldberger called "creeping Third Avenue-ism," Warnecke's building was a welcome, if banal, addition to the avenue. "Not every building can be a foreground building," Goldberger concluded, "some must be willing to stay in the background if the city is to work as a civilized amalgam of structures."[141]

To whatever extent the Fifth Avenue Special District plan set the stage for a revitalized, mixed-use urbanism, the city's declining economic health resulted in a shortage of high-quality retailers to fill the available space, opening the way for fly-by-night "discount" and "bargain" operators who further denigrated the avenue. In addition, with the national economic recession encouraging corporations to cut expenses, many closed their promotional showrooms, leaving even more street-level space vacant. Perhaps it was appropriate that the avenue's character could not be guaranteed by legislation alone. On Fifth Avenue, as so often seemed to be the case in New York, money talked; the street would simply have to wait for an economic upswing and a changing attitude toward urban life to turn its fortunes around.

SIXTH AVENUE

More than any other street in New York, perhaps more than any other in a major city in the world, the midtown stretch of Sixth Avenue, especially the twelve-block stretch north of Forty-third Street, was the representative street of twentieth-century Modernist urbanism, the most direct if not necessarily the purest expression of the ideas put forward by Le Corbusier during the 1920s. Sixth Avenue's birth as New York's preeminent Modernist street can be precisely dated: the completion of Rockefeller Center in 1939 and the removal of the avenue's elevated railroad that same year marked it as the prime candidate for redevelopment as a commercial thoroughfare.[1] When its manifest destiny was put on hold by wartime restrictions, architects and planners used the avenue as a model for postwar urban reconstruction. The El's demolition had been a pet project of Colonel V. Clement Jenkins, president of the Sixth Avenue Association, even though he realized that its removal would make all too obvious the avenue's threadbare reality as the street's largely neglected nineteenth-century buildings would be fully revealed for the first time. As Ernest La France described the avenue in the *New York Times Magazine*: "Flanked by smartness and gayety, crossed and recrossed daily by millions of people in search of amusement and merchandise, it has stood for thirty years dark, dirty and vacant. . . . It has been the Cinderella of Gotham, the unlovely sister of the bright and thriving streets beside it."[2]

Contrary to popular belief, the El had not originally been a source of blight. Its construction had initiated a period of prosperity along Sixth Avenue, bringing with it in the 1880s and 1890s the major department stores, theaters and restaurants that lined its right-of-way from Fourteenth to Thirty-third Street. But, as La France noted in 1939, the avenue had been "frozen in time" when the construction of subways before the First World War lured people to other locations where rapid transit was combined with an unblemished streetscape.[3] Now the construction of a new subway line under Sixth Avenue would at last make the street's rebirth possible.

Although "futuristic" proposals illustrating the avenue's potential were being circulated as early as 1938, it was not until 1941, when the United States Gypsum Company sponsored Edward Durell Stone to prepare a master plan, that a comprehensive vision for redevelopment was published.[4] Working with New York University architecture students, including Fred M. Ginsbern (son of apartment house architect Horace Ginsbern) and Stanley Torkelson, Stone called for a tree-lined avenue bordered by six-story-high buildings acting as podiums for high towers set back from the street wall. Recognizing that the short-term demand for office space was limited, he proposed a phased development: construction of the six-story buildings, which "would create an immediate improvement," would precede the construction of the higher setback portions.[5] Stone's plan concentrated on the stretch between Forty-second and Fiftieth streets, where buildings to house representatives of the twenty-one democracies of the Americas were to be located, each containing exhibition halls in addition to the office space needed to conduct international trade. Hotels, department stores and theaters would also be located there. The plan called for the construction of apartments on the avenue above Rockefeller Center; a concert hall, an art gallery, a health museum and a music museum with studios were also proposed. In the blocks south of Forty-second Street, the avenue would be lined with shops and showrooms, capitalizing on the strengths of Herald Square and the garment district.

In addition to the base-and-tower massing, there were two other key features of Stone's design, as illustrated in the drawings by Hugh Ferriss, that would become characteristic of the avenue's postwar architecture: the presence of plazas, and the buildings' total lack of ornamentation. The only decoration on these stripped-down versions of the International Style, with stressed horizontal bands of glazing, were the national flags that projected from their principal facades. As Stone described his design goals: "Unity in exterior design is achieved by expressing the usually concealed column and beam construction of New York's commercial buildings in the facades; creating an impression of large scale design with full flexibility in fenestration, but without the small scale effect of large walls, perforated with thousands of double-hung windows."[6]

Ely Jacques Kahn imagined a similar future for the avenue. In 1943, stimulated by the Museum of Modern Art's exhibition of recent Brazilian architecture, he wrote: "Conceive, for example, the possibilities of a new Sixth Avenue . . . [with] buildings on stilts. . . . Stores could be reached under a protected space. In the middle of the blocks west of Sixth Avenue, certain green parked areas might provide breathing spaces . . . and at the same time immensely improve the value of the cross streets."[7]

Sixth Avenue was renamed the Avenue of the Americas in 1945, six years after the idea was first proposed by V. Clement Jenkins, who envisioned a redeveloped avenue that would be the "commercial capital of the Western Hemisphere," a "central marketplace for the Americas."[8] From the first, the new designation was regarded as an awkward mouthful, which some New Yorkers reluctantly adopted but most refused to even acknowledge. In 1945 plans were announced for the Good Neighbor Building, a fifty-seven-story skyscraper designed by Leonard Rappaport, but it was never realized.[9] In 1946 Harvey Wiley Corbett prepared designs for a "hemisphere trade center," a complexly massed, seven-story building with a small landscaped courtyard as well as a skylit rooftop restaurant.[10] Again, nothing came of the project.

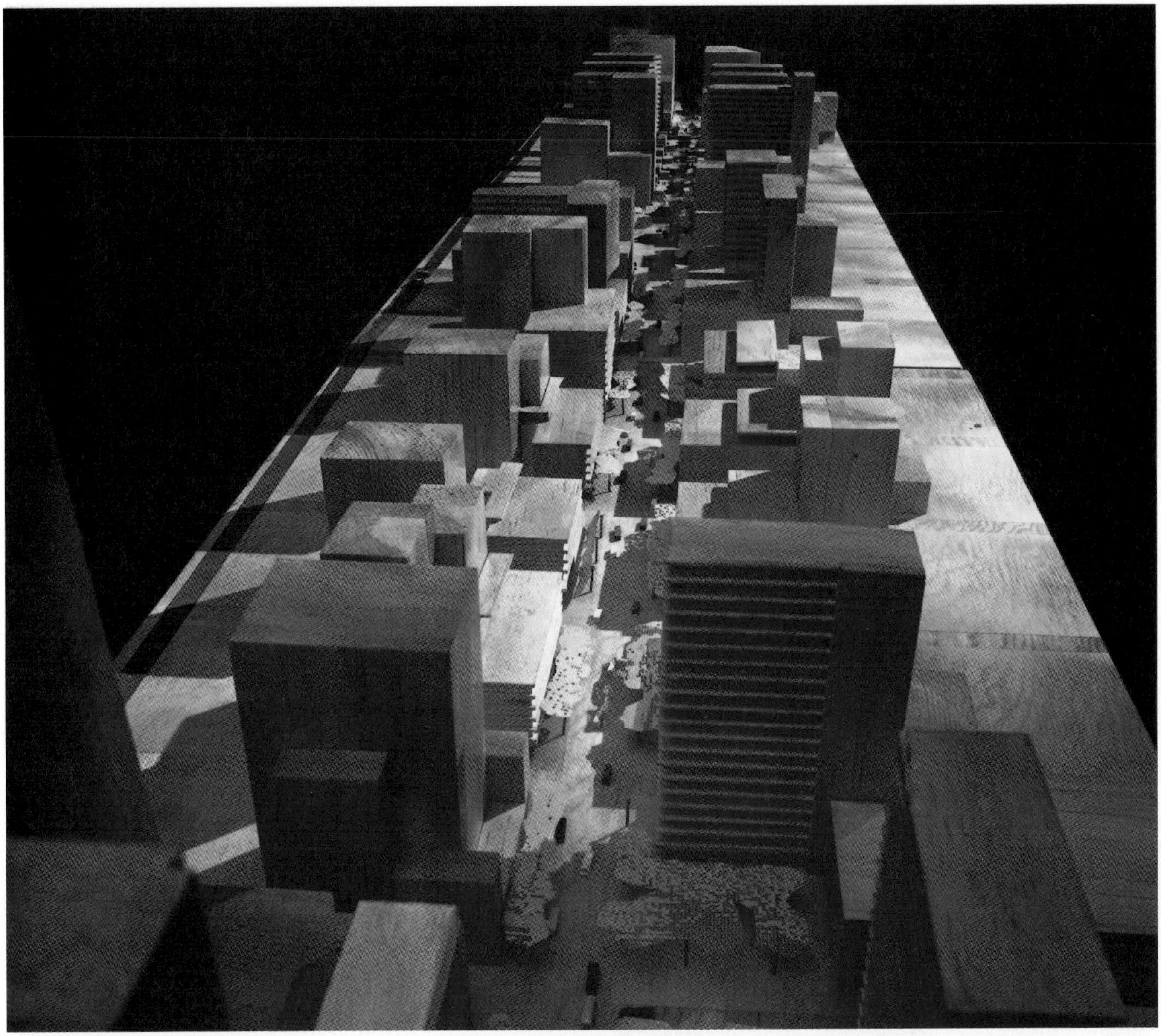

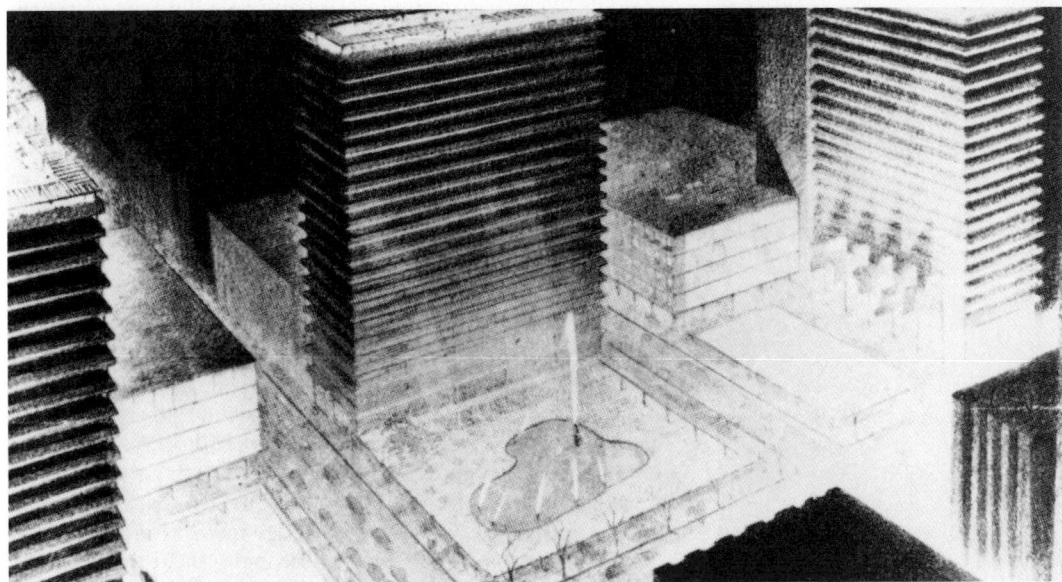

Above: Master plan for
Sixth Avenue between
West Forty-second and
West Fiftieth streets.
Edward Durell Stone, 1941.
Model. Stoller. ©ESTO

Left: Master plan for Sixth
Avenue between West
Forty-second and West
Fiftieth streets. Rendering
by Hugh Ferriss showing
proposed international
trade buildings. AR. CU

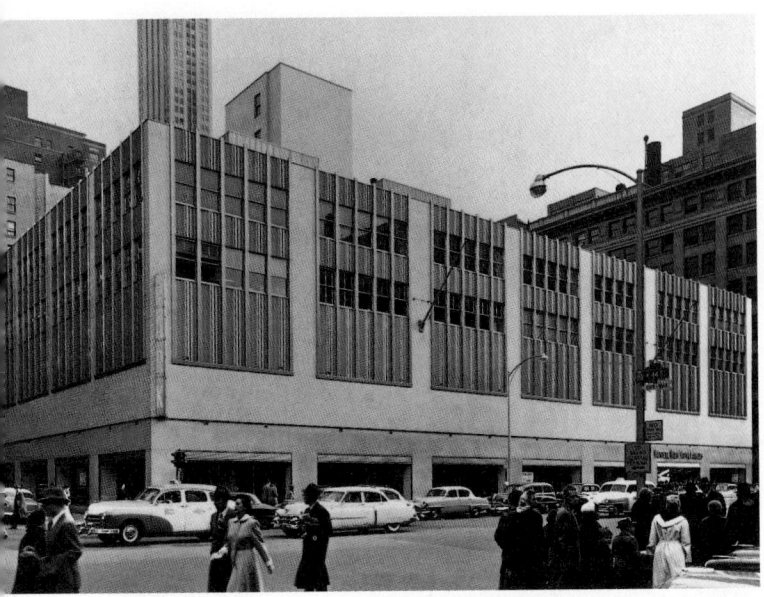

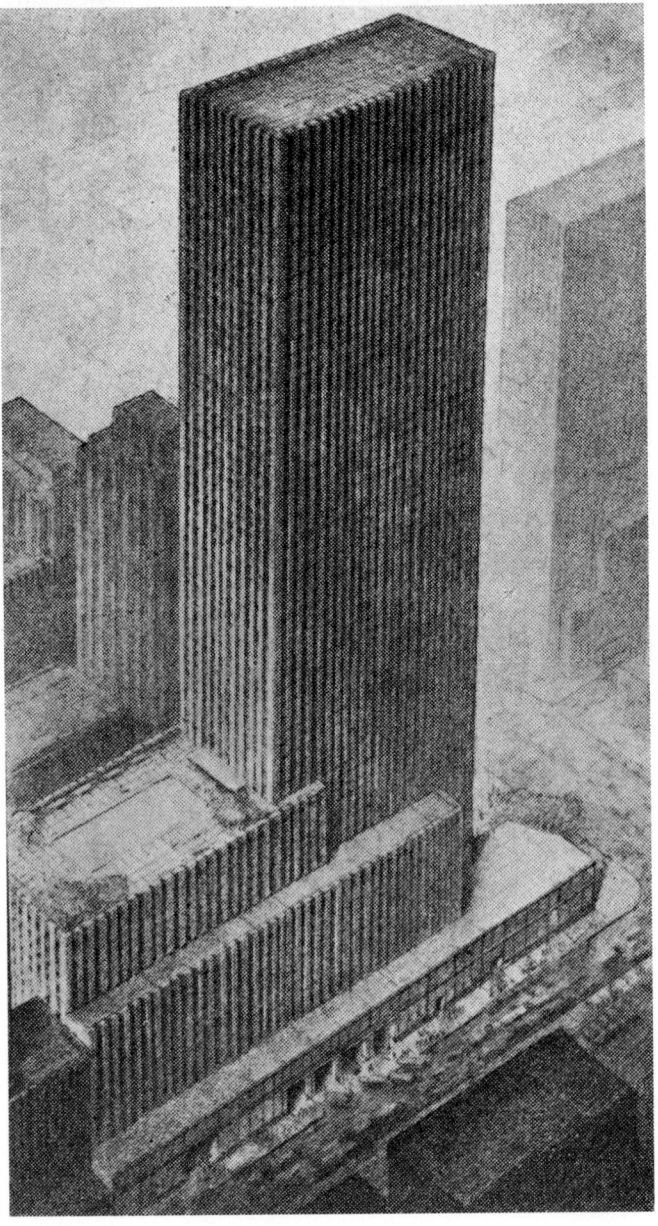

In 1947 Edward Durell Stone and the Avenue of the Americas Association took up the street's future again, this time working with Yale University architecture students.[11] In this plan the avenue would be lined with low buildings housing the consulates of the various American states, while slablike towers would contain revenue-producing hotels and offices. Definition of the avenue's street wall would be minimal. A below-grade north-south landscaped pedestrian promenade was proposed to run through the midblocks west of the avenue; it would be lined with shops, outdoor cafés, theaters and exhibition areas while also providing access to the hotel and office buildings.

Sixth Avenue's first postwar building had nothing to do with such grandiose plans: a parking garage was erected in 1951–52 on the vacant site of the former Hippodrome (Frederic Thompson, 1905), on the east side of the avenue between Forty-third and Forty-fourth streets.[12] In 1944 plans had been filed by Eggers & Higgins for a forty-two-story office building to rise on the site of the once-great theater, which had been acquired by the City Bank Farmers Trust Company at foreclosure in 1932 and demolished in 1939 to make way for a parking lot. In 1949 new plans were drawn up for the site by McKim, Mead & White, in association with Edward James Matthews, which called for a garage surmounted by a 240,000-square-foot office tower.[13] But the stylishly Modernist, well-proportioned tower, presumably the work of Matthews, was not built. As finally realized in 1951–52, with Kahn & Jacobs as architects, the site was developed with a building that contained street-level shops, one basement level and two floors of garage space topped by two more floors of offices, all packaged in an envelope that, though not distinguished as architecture, did at least camouflage the fact that the building was mostly garage.[14] In 1956–57 three more floors of office space were added on top of the existing building, and in 1961 work began on a twelve-story minitower set atop that.[15]

The avenue's next building didn't arrive until after November 1954, when Rockefeller Center's Center Theater was demolished to make way for an expansion of the U.S. Rubber Building.[16] Although the theater, together with Radio City Music Hall, had been the avenue's principal public ornament, and despite nine years as home to Sonja Henie's ice shows and serving as NBC's biggest television theater, it had suffered financial problems for many years.

At last, in 1955, plans were announced for a major new building that would eventually be realized: a thirty-four-story office building at 111 West Fortieth Street, on the northwest corner of Sixth Avenue through to Forty-first Street, which replaced the main office of the Union Dime Savings Bank (Alfred H. Taylor, 1910).[17] The new building, designed by Kahn & Jacobs and Sydney Goldstone, featured a facade of vertical white terra-cotta bands rising from a granite-clad base, the first major use of terra cotta on a skyscraper since Raymond Hood's McGraw-Hill Building (1931).[18] In order to maintain the bank in continuous operation, the project was built in two stages, with the first section constructed on the site of a parking lot at Forty-first Street.

Also in 1955 the Equitable Life Assurance Society and the builder Peter B. Ruffin, of Ruffin-Galbreath, announced plans for a sixty-story design by Harrison & Abramovitz for the east side of the avenue between Fifty-first and Fifty-second streets.[19] The site had begun to be assembled in 1949 by Equitable for a thirty-story, 400,000-square-foot speculative tower that could also serve as overflow space for the building the company was thinking of constructing across the street (see below).[20] Equitable did not go forward with this project but held on to the property. Because the Avenue of the Americas was not yet considered a desirable address, even in the vicinity of Rockefeller Center, Harrison & Abramovitz's building was to be known by its address at 33 West Fifty-first Street. Although the Sixth Avenue frontage was vacant and being used as a parking lot, the future of the project depended on the demolition of a number of buildings on West Fifty-second Street that housed such popular night spots as the Famous Door, Club Samoa, Club Del Rio and Club Pigalle. The landmark restaurant Toots Shor's, at 51 West Fifty-first Street, was also slated for demolition.[21] But when Shor proved intransigent, refusing to leave his famous restaurant, which had been on the site since 1939 in a building he had leased until 1967, plans were drawn to build around the restaurant.

Along with the Chase Manhattan Bank's headquarters building, announced for a site in lower Manhattan in the same year, 33 West Fifty-first Street was the boldest building yet proposed in the postwar era; at sixty stories, it would be one of the city's tallest. Although published accounts suggested that the building was to be clad in stainless steel in a manner similar to the same architects' Socony-Mobil Building (see "Forty-second Street," below), the renderings seemed to indicate a masonry cladding. An east-west slab would be set back forty feet from the avenue to create a landscaped forecourt, further defined by the embracing arms of a three-story base that covered most of the site. Echoing Raymond Hood's RCA Building, the tower was locked into lower, setback masses at its sides and rear, rising free only above the sixteenth floor.[22] By 1957 Equitable, heavily invested in the building it was undertaking for its own use across the street and in the building for Time, Inc. (see below), decided to abandon the project. With its departure went Ruffin as well, and the site was eventually sold in 1961.

In 1958 the Avenue of the Americas at last began to fulfill its promise with the construction of its first architecturally notable new office building, Carson & Lundin's 145,000-square-foot Deering Milliken Company Building, at 1045 Sixth Avenue, on the northwest corner of Thirty-ninth Street.[23] Deering Milliken consisted of a fat seven-story slab sitting on a slightly recessed, largely unfenestrated base clad in black granite. The slab presented windowless Georgia white marble end walls to the side streets and a principal facade of bands of gray-tinted vision and spandrel glass set between vertical fins clad in white marble. Inside, Florence Knoll Bassett's minimalist interiors lent a sophisticated note that was a far cry from the typical utilitarianism of the surrounding loftlike buildings. Just to the west of the avenue, a rival textile firm, Springs Mills, became the principal tenants in Harrison & Abramovitz's twenty-story 104 West Fortieth Street (1962).[24] Clad in green glass similar to that of the firm's Corning Glass Building (see "Fifth Avenue," above), the structure consisted of a base that occupied most of the building's midblock site and a slender slab above. Although the bulk of the building faced Thirty-ninth Street, it was entered across a narrow plaza on Fortieth, where the slab projected forward with tapered sides to convey an image of slender verticality.

The postwar destiny of the Avenue of the Americas as a grand corporate boulevard was ensured in December 1956, when Rockefeller Center, Inc. made a bold move, proposing a new headquarters for one of the center's prime tenants, Time, Inc., on a large site between Fiftieth and Fifty-first streets on the west side of the avenue and extending 410 feet toward Seventh Avenue.[25] For about ten years Time, Inc. had been considering a move from its 1937 Rockefeller Center building. In 1946 it had worked with William Zeckendorf to develop the site of the Marguery Hotel, at 270 Park Avenue, with a new building, retaining Harrison & Abramovitz, who proposed a three-story

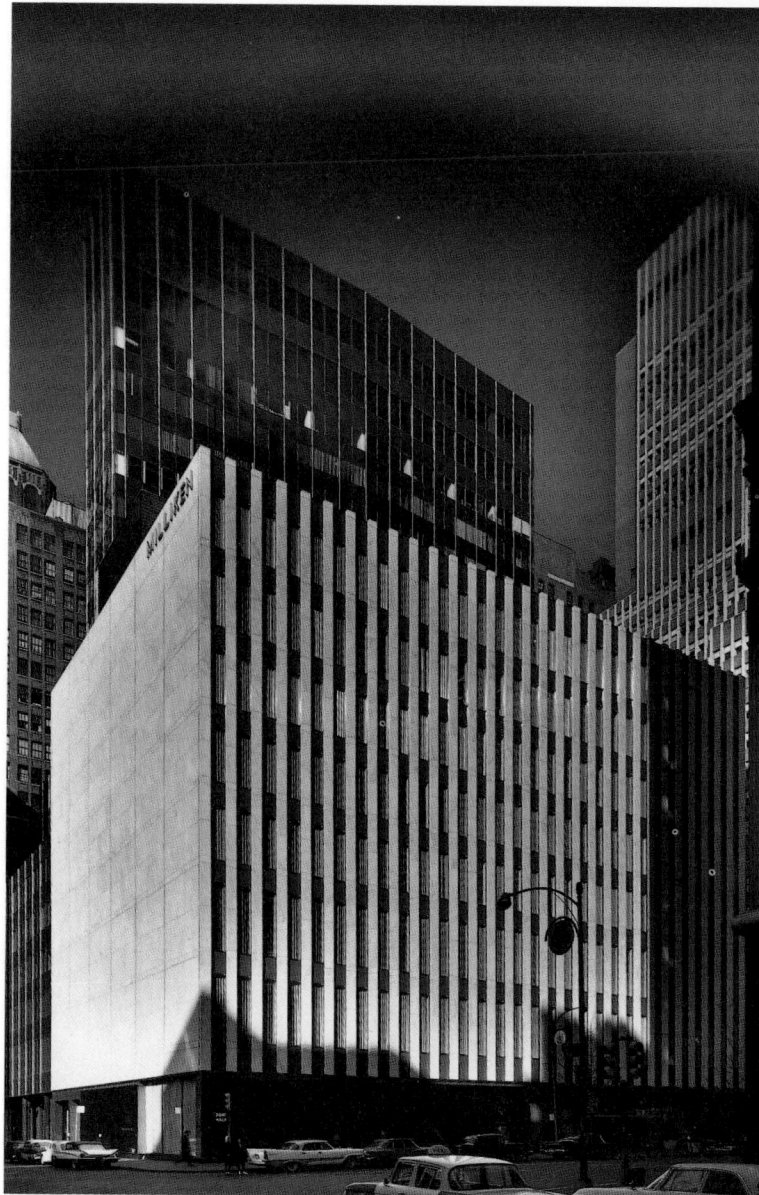

Top left: Office building and garage replacing Hippodrome, 1120 Sixth Avenue, east side of Sixth Avenue between West Forty-third and West Forty-fourth streets. Kahn & Jacobs, 1951–52. Wurts. MCNY

Bottom left: Proposed building at 33 West Fifty-first Street, east side of Sixth Avenue. Harrison & Abramovitz, 1956. Perspective showing view to the southwest. AR. CU

Above: Deering Milliken Company Building, 1045 Sixth Avenue, northwest corner of West Thirty-ninth Street. Carson & Lundin, 1958. View to the northwest showing 104 West Fortieth Street (Harrison & Abramovitz, 1962) in the background. Molitor. JWM

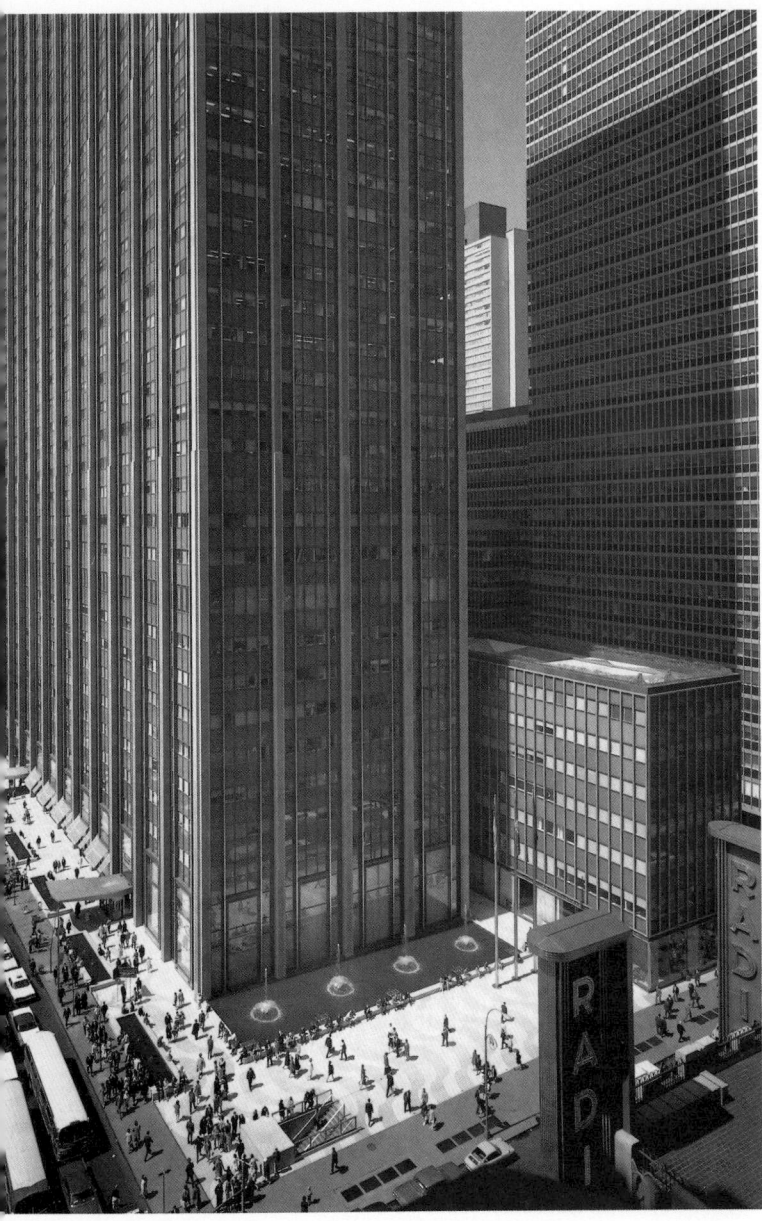

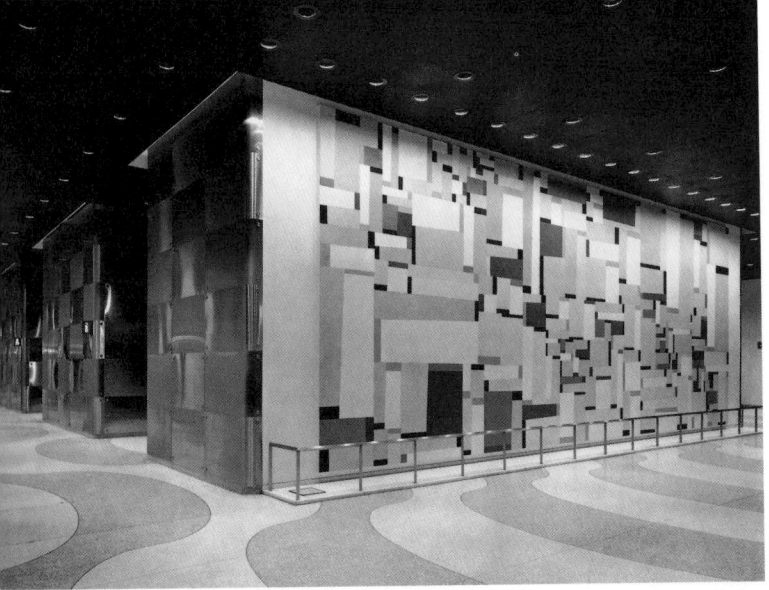

podium filling the site, surmounted by an aggressively massed thirty-five-story superslab running east-west and a series of shorter wings set at forty-five degree angles to the grid. The concept and the site were rejected.

Time, Inc. later considered moving to a suburb of Philadelphia or to Westchester County in New York but decided to remain in Manhattan because of the city's transportation and communication facilities. The company continued to consider relocating to Park Avenue, which Rockefeller Center's management felt would be an even greater blow to the prestige of the aging complex than a move to the suburbs. To avoid such a fate, a new corporation, Rock-Time, Inc., was formed in 1956 whereby Time, Inc. and Rockefeller Center, Inc. became equity partners in a new building to be built on the Sixth Avenue site, which Rockefeller Center, Inc. had acquired in 1953. Once home to a long-since-demolished trolley car barn, the site now consisted of a motley collection of small buildings housing offices, restaurants and shops, as well as a parking lot. Construction of the building began in May 1957 and it was opened in December 1959.

The Time & Life Building, named after the company's best-known publications, was designed by Harrison, Abramovitz & Harris. It contained 1.4 million square feet of space and rose without setbacks for forty-eight floors, making it the city's tallest single shaft. An 83-foot-wide, 170-foot-long landscaped plaza at the site's southeast corner was defined along its north edge by an eight-story, L-shaped base structure that wrapped around the tower's north and west sides; on the west, the tower was also set back thirty feet from Fiftieth Street to create a sidewalk mall. The new building was provided with an underground connection to the subway as well as a link to the original Rockefeller Center concourse system.

The tower's sense of height was enhanced by the use of tapered, buttresslike limestone-faced exterior structural columns that framed the gray-tinted windows and the aluminum-mesh-backed spandrels. This arrangement of exterior perimeter columns, ultimately derived from Howe & Lescaze's Philadelphia Saving Fund Society Building (1932), was part of a daring structural system that permitted largely column-free, 28,000-square-foot office floors, far and away the largest tower floors built in New York since World War II. In order to achieve the Time & Life Building's tremendous bulk in an undifferentiated tower, Rockefeller Center had acquired and demolished the Roxy Theater, which shared the block. By adding to the total size of the site, not only was more square footage permitted, but, under the zoning, it could be packaged as a sheer tower as long as it occupied no more than 25 percent of the combined lot.

On July 2, 1957, Marilyn Monroe opened the Time & Life Sidewalk Superintendents Club, which gave the already glamorous Time, Inc. even more public relations value. But unlike at Lever or Seagram's, corporate identity was not a principal factor in Time, Inc.'s decision to build; this was a working office building and a bottom-line investment far more than a corporate statement. This point was emphasized by *Architectural Forum*:

> Rockefeller Center built it, Time & Life gave it its name. The building's character reflects a joining of partners, a marriage of uses, a meld of design, a union between New York's two generic office-building types. Unlike the early postwar architectural pace-setters, such as the Seagram Building or Lever House, the Time & Life Building is not a posh institutional job with small floors, with architecture honed Seagram-sharp at fancy cost, and with or without extra space for rent to make

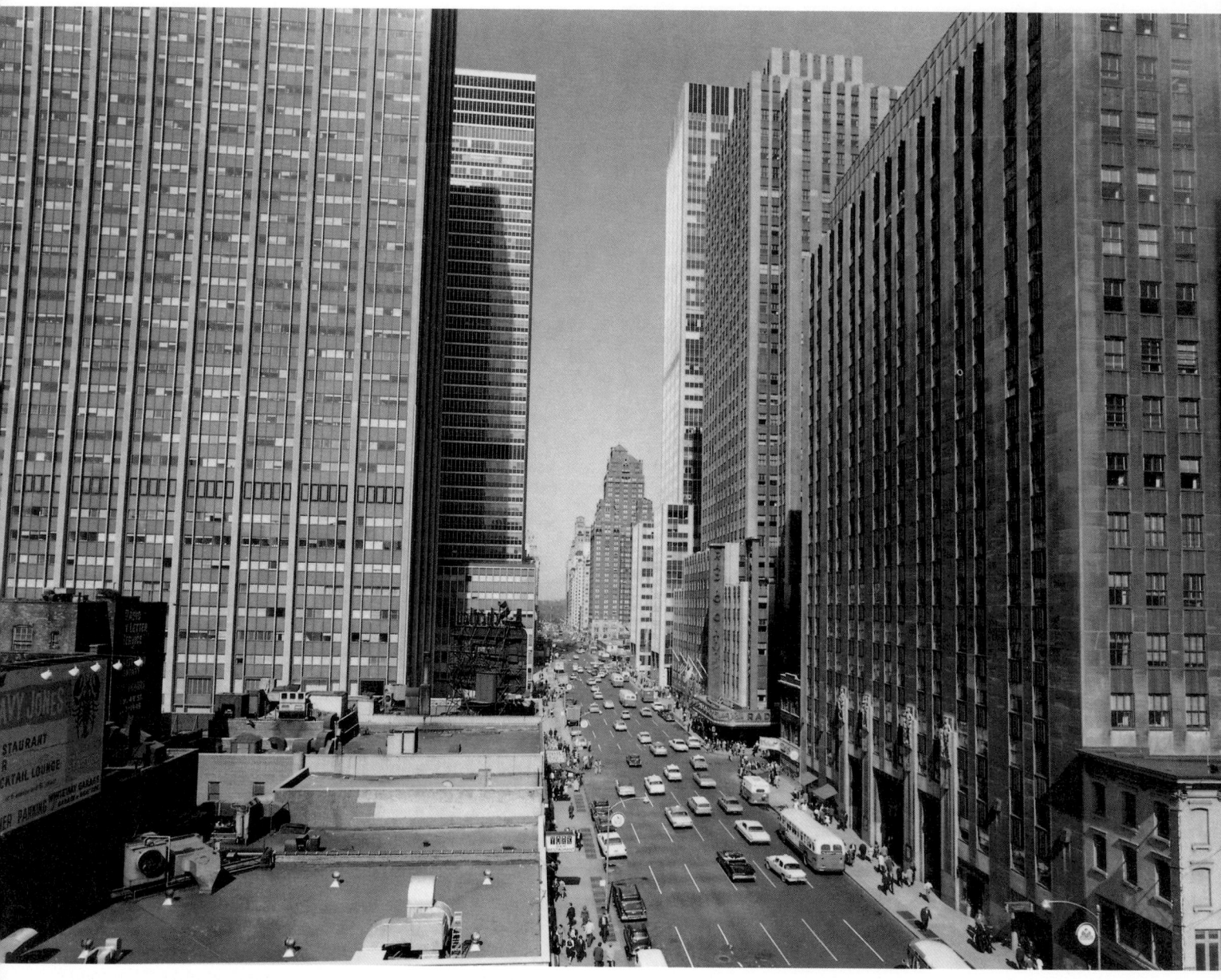

Top left: Time & Life Building, 1271 Sixth Avenue, West Fifty-first to
West Fifty-second Street. Harrison, Abramovitz & Harris, 1959. View to
the northwest. Stoller. ©ESTO

Above: View to the north on Sixth Avenue from West Forty-ninth Street
showing Time & Life Building on the left. OMH

Bottom left: Time & Life Building. Lobby showing the mural *Portals* by
Fritz Glarner. Stoller. ©ESTO

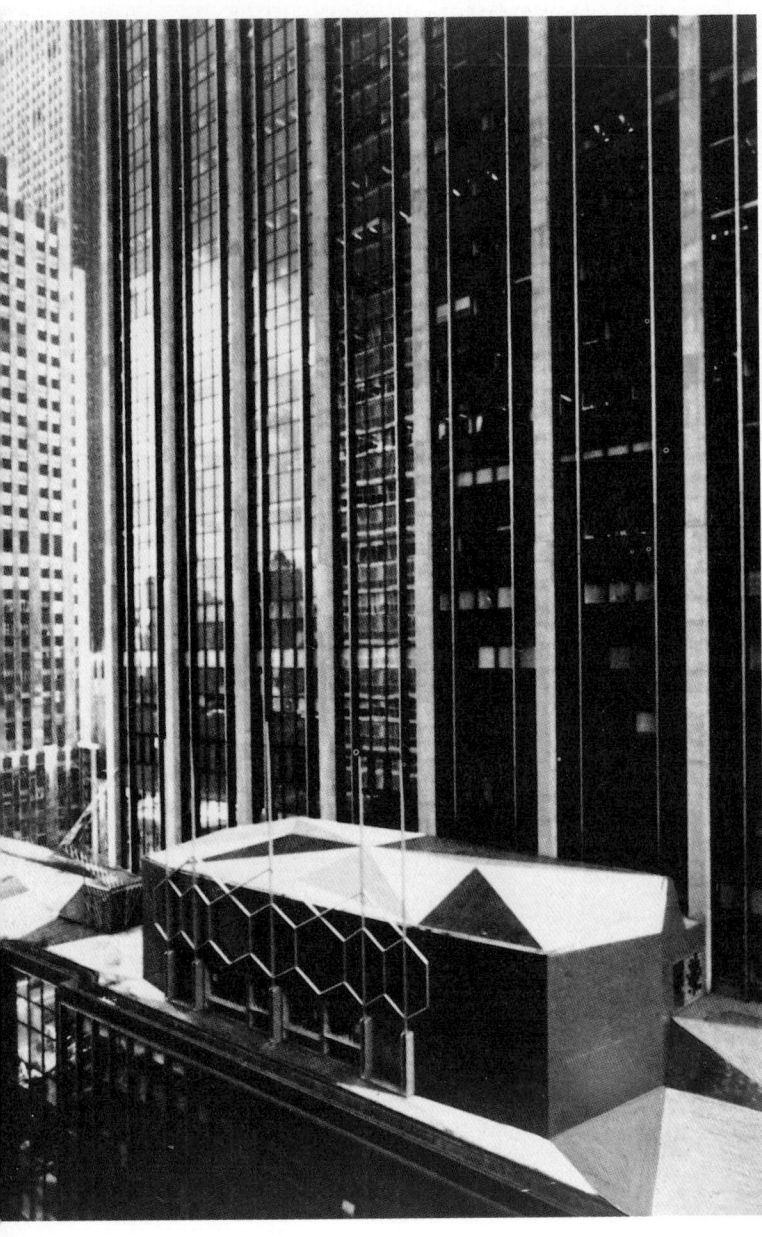

Pavilion housing the Time & Life reception room, bar and auditorium, eighth floor of the Time & Life Building (Harrison, Abramovitz & Harris, 1959), 1271 Sixth Avenue, West Fifty-first to West Fifty-second Street. Gio Ponti, 1959. View to the southeast. AGP

ends meet. Nor is it a cheap, crowded rental building by an operative builder, dressed in the biggest tenant's name. In skyscraper society, the Time & Life Building is upper-middle-class.

In keeping with this status, the building's design was not daring. As *Forum* said: "The architecture is conservative and in places wandering, but it is sturdy, and unquestionably the building is handsome. Originality was sacrificed to a more effective marriage with the Center."[26]

The building's plaza, its principal public feature, was welcoming rather than formidable, with four mushroom jets splashing water into a basin that was surrounded by a low parapet providing seating, as well as other seats and planting. Wallace K. Harrison's decision to pave the plaza and the building's lobby with undulating waves of dark gray and white terrazzo, a design idea he borrowed from the Copacabana district of Rio de Janeiro, seemed more justifiable as an illustration of the "good neighbor" ideals of the Avenue of the Americas Association than as a complement to the building's otherwise strict geometry. The Cariocan floor pattern inside the grandly scaled, sixteen-foot-high lobby also seemed out of place. Echoing the practice at Rockefeller Center, contemporary artists were called upon to help decorate the public spaces: at the eastern end of the elevator core, Fritz Glarner provided a mural that recalled Piet Mondrian's work, and at the western end was Josef Albers's geometric work *Portals*.

Time & Life's offices, filling twenty-one floors, were planned by Gerald Luss of Designs for Business, Inc. To test the new offices before they were installed in the building, a full-sized working mock-up was built in a warehouse in Astoria; even more remarkably, another mock-up, demonstrating many but not all of the features of the new space, was built inside the existing Time & Life Building in Rockefeller Center, where it was put to use by the advertising, promotion and public relations departments of *Sports Illustrated*, the company's newest magazine.

Although elevator lobbies were individually designed to signal the personalities of the various company publications, the typical office spaces were anonymous, crowded but pleasant, with glass-topped partitions that could be moved easily as requirements changed. Window space was reserved for the offices of top executives. The organization of the 350,000 square feet of space for 2,500 employees was a notable departure from the double ring of corridors typical of large-floor New York office buildings—one around the core for public circulation, and one inside the actual office space to separate outside offices from inner areas devoted to secretarial pools, filing and other back-up services. For the first time, this double-ring plan was eliminated in favor of an open network or "bay plan" that provided short transverse passages running out from the central core corridor to the perimeter, creating an orderly if somewhat congested arrangement. Wallace Harrison was later to criticize the result, claiming that the client had taken too strong a role in the interior planning: "They took the idea and carried it to the bitter end. Everything was so efficient, but there was no space. They took the space and divided it so you were cramped; their system produced a factory."[27]

The eighth floor was reserved for a set of rooms for corporate and sales meeting, specially designed by the Italian architect Gio Ponti.[28] These consisted of a dining room, a small meeting room and a lounge area that were located within the tower envelope and a reception room, a bar and an auditorium housed in a pavilionlike structure that sat on the roof of the building's base. Using a loose geometry of angled planes, Ponti synthesized the two elements so that the tower spaces and those in the

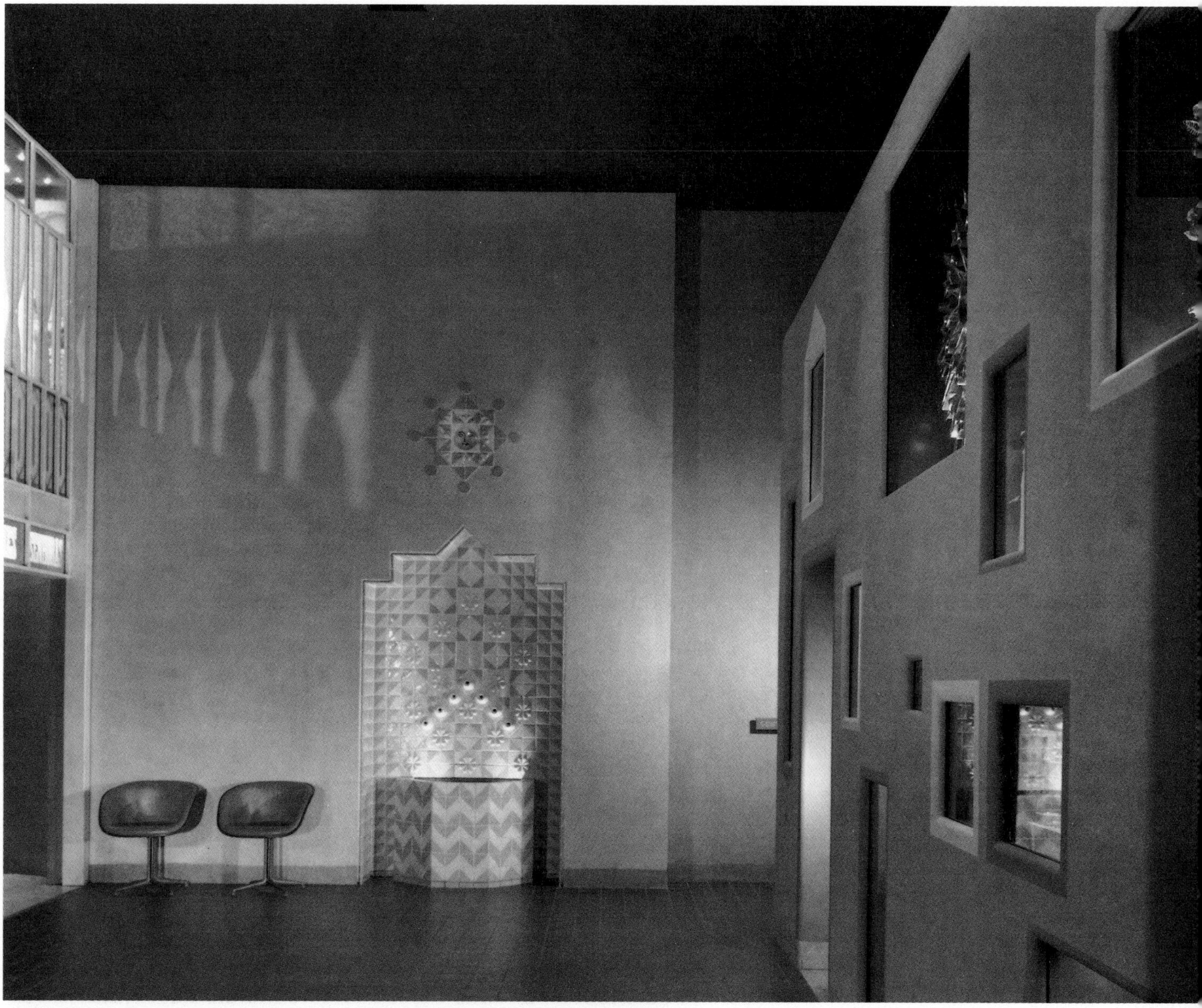

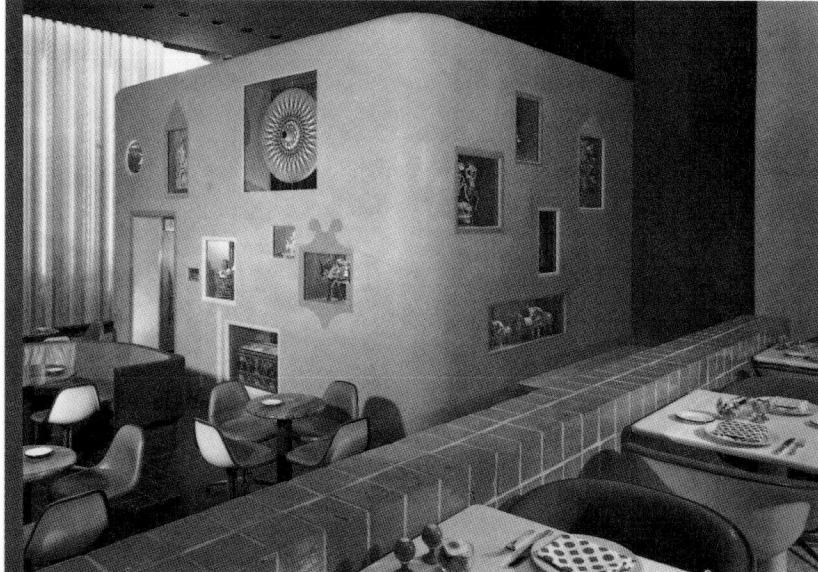

Above: La Fonda del Sol, Time & Life Building. Alexander Girard, 1961. Lobby. Reens. LR

Left: La Fonda del Sol. Dining area and enclosed bar. Reens. LR

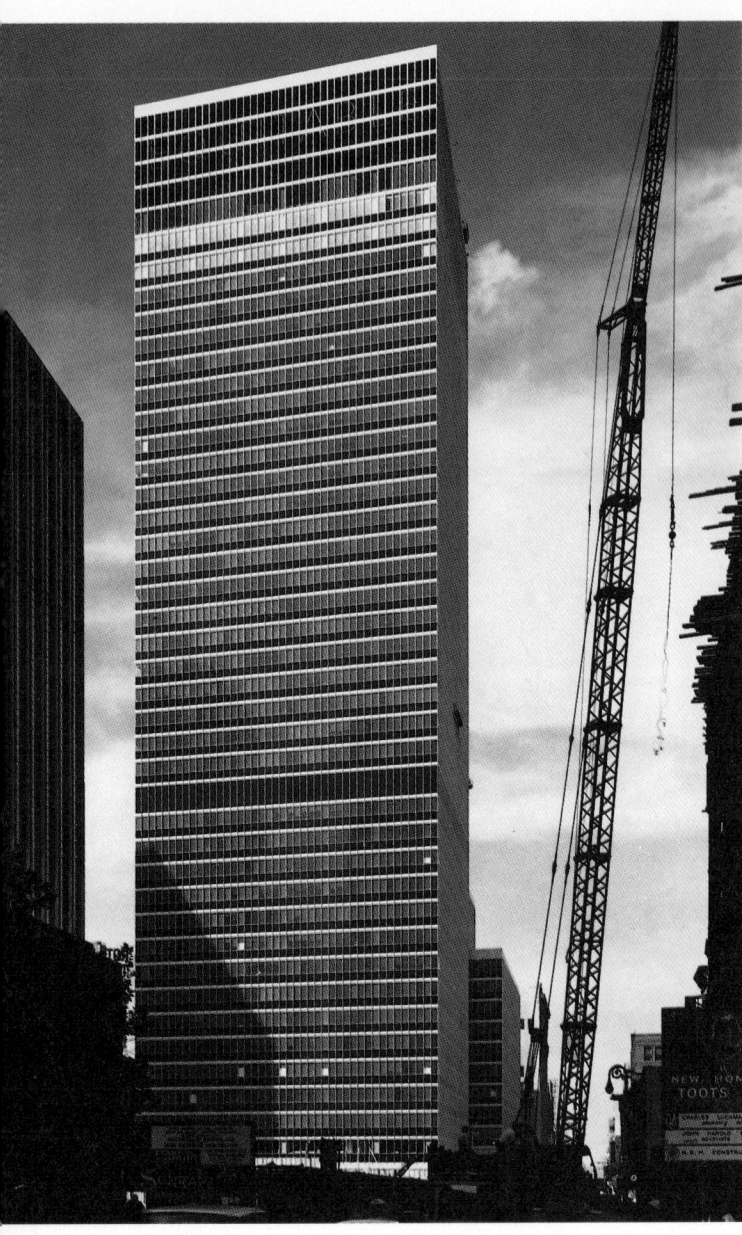

Equitable Building, 1285 Sixth Avenue, West Fifty-first to West Fifty-second Street. Skidmore, Owings & Merrill, 1959–61. View to the west. Molitor. JWM

pavilion flowed together. In contrast to the buttoned-down, right-angle corporate offices, the Ponti suite was ebullient and personal, with intricately designed biomorphic lighting fixtures and bold floor coverings—including marbleized sheet rubber in yellow streaked with green and dark blue—and walls punctuated with panels of glass block and hung with Sicilian fantasy paintings and daggers.

At the western end of the ground floor, a restaurant called La Fonda del Sol carried out the Latin American themes implicit in Sixth Avenue's official name and in the Brazilian-style paving of the building's sidewalks.[29] Buoyed by their success with the enormously expensive Forum of the Twelve Caesars (see chapter 6), located in the U.S. Rubber Building at Rockefeller Center, restaurateur Jerome Brody and his collaborators returned to the center with a larger, more reasonably priced restaurant whose gastronomical and architectural approach was perfectly suited to the first high-style restaurant on the Avenue of the Americas. When it opened in 1961, La Fonda del Sol was, after the Four Seasons (see "Park Avenue," above), the most completely integrated restaurant design in New York. Designed by Alexander Girard, who in the 1940s had left New York for permanent residence in Santa Fe, La Fonda was a remarkable evocation of Hispanic American themes down to the very smallest detail. But because it eschewed specific historical representations, it was also, as Girard said, "of our time."[30] The design was influenced by the rigorous yet sensuous simplifications of the great Mexican Modernist architect Luis Barragán, which were evoked here in a lighter key, with bright colors punctuating rough plaster walls carved with deep niches for displaying crafts as well as concealing lighting.[31]

Occupying a long, rambling area that stretched through the block from Fiftieth to Fifty-first Street, La Fonda unfolded like a village. The diner passed a dramatically lit lobby with a tiled fountain, the windowlike display niches and the sun symbol, which established the restaurant's theme. The feeling was largely that of being outdoors, an effect enhanced by Richard Kelly's lighting scheme. To one side the bar was contained in what looked like an adobe house. A series of individual dining areas formed a spatial sequence not unlike the passage through a collection of light-filled plazas and rooms, culminating in the largest space, a circular dining room. For Olga Gueft, this sequence, and the elements used to enliven it, provoked "an unorthodox emotional reaction best described as a *slow surprise*." She found La Fonda easy to take after the austerities of the Four Seasons: "There are works of art, yes!—but none are obscure or challenging. . . . There is up-to-date industrial design on every hand, but nothing of the cold feel, rigidity, or sharp edges that alert human flesh against machine products. . . . [Girard's] performance is two ways enchanting: for the *setting*; for the *details*."[32] According to Gueft, La Fonda's pièce de résistance was the ladies' room, which, like a mirador in traditional Spain, occupied a balcony over the entrance plaza. She admired its scale, its sparkling lighting and the skillful way in which it visually opened to the space below without compromising privacy.

Though splendid, La Fonda was not an enduring success, and in 1971 Carson, Lundin & Shaw renovated the space it had formerly occupied into a new branch for the Seaman's Bank for Savings.[33] It was a particularly stylish essay in Modernist minimalism, with round columns clad in mirror-finished stainless steel and white-flecked deep green marble counters that formed a continuous, exuberantly proportioned curve along one side of the main banking room. The design was so popular with the public that within three weeks of opening, the bank had achieved the business volume it had projected for its first six months at the location.

Gordon Chadwick, a member of the industrial design firm of George Nelson & Company, designed a dining facility on the forty-eighth floor of the Time & Life Building that, like the Rainbow Room atop the RCA Building, functioned during the day as a men's luncheon club, the Hemisphere Club, and at night as a luxurious restaurant, the Tower Suite.[34] To overcome the comparatively narrow column module that split the spectacular view into so many stripes, Chadwick mirrored the window embrasures, a device that had also been used in the Rainbow Room. But in Chadwick's hands the overall effect was not glamorous, merely corporate. When the view from the restaurant became blocked by other high-rise buildings, the Tower Suite's business declined and the room's design was modified by Fred B. Shrallow so that it could function at night as a catering hall. Most of the changes were minor, but glitter was added to the existing ceiling lights by capping the bottoms with pierced metal disks holding cut crystal. "You can't have a wedding or a Bar Mitzvah without crystal chandeliers," explained Shrallow.[35]

The construction of the Time & Life Building had profound repercussions on the westward expansion of midtown and the future of Sixth Avenue. As *Architectural Forum* put it, "The Time & Life Building's decisive beachhead across the avenue clears the way. It opens wide a frontier for the expanding city."[36] In August 1958 the Equitable Life Assurance Society broke ground for its long-contemplated new headquarters, located immediately to the north of Time & Life, on a blockfront lot between Fifty-first and Fifty-second streets that stretched 400 feet west toward Seventh Avenue.[37] Skidmore, Owings & Merrill's design (1959–61) was based on the firm's almost concurrent design for the Union Carbide Building (see "Park Avenue," above), at 270 Park Avenue. Like Union Carbide, the Equitable's 546-foot-high, forty-two-story tower rose uninterrupted from a small plaza; though 166 feet shorter than the Park Avenue building, the Equitable enclosed 200,000 more square feet of office space. In the midblock section to the west was a fourteen-story wing.

In contrast to the coal-like blackness of Union Carbide, the Equitable was clad in silvery aluminum. It was also less detailed than its Park Avenue counterpart, its lobbies and plazas less gracious, and its curtain wall thinner. Where Union Carbide captured some of the tectonic force of Seagram's, at Equitable the curtain wall seemed no more than what its name implied. It was this very simplicity that appealed to Ada Louise Huxtable: "Its immense size and streamlined simplicity are a reflection of the complex, impersonal business organization of our time. Equitable does not try for the luxury, prestige image . . . it stresses a no-frills kind of efficiency in a shell of simple dignity. Its esthetic effects are limited to fine points of structural design and to dramatically coordinated color inside."[38] But, as *Architectural Forum* pointed out, the building had one overwhelmingly negative aspect to it, a characteristic it shared with Union Carbide: "Both Equitable and Union Carbide . . . sit on their lots in almost complete indifference to their surroundings. They largely ignore the street and the neighbors—for both street and neighbors are subject to erratic change without notice or forethought."[39]

As the Equitable Building was being planned, William Zeckendorf had taken an interest in a blockfront lot across the street between Fifty-first and Fifty-second streets, the site of a proposed project that Equitable had abandoned in 1957 (see above). Backed by David Rockefeller's Chase Manhattan Bank, Zeckendorf planned not an office building but, as he pro-

claimed, "the greatest hotel ever built."[40] Zeckendorf succeeded in buying off Toots Shor simply by offering half a million dollars more than the million that had been repeatedly refused, as well as offering assistance in finding a site for a new restaurant. On September 9, 1958, the deal was complete and the Zeckendorf-Chase venture was on its way, with the Prudential Life Insurance Company actually owning the land in consideration of a construction loan. Plans for the 2,000-room, forty-eight-story hotel, designed by Harrison & Abramovitz, were announced in February 1959.[41] Although digging on the site began in the spring, Zeckendorf was unable to raise enough capital to see the project through to completion. With just a large hole in the ground to show for his effort, the property was sold in January 1961 to the Uris Building Corporation, which formed a joint venture with Rockefeller Center. Once again, Zeckendorf's dreams had exceeded his capacity to finance them. As Percy Uris put it: "Zeckendorf . . . knows as much about building as I know about being an aviator. I said it made no sense to put up a hotel on the site."[42]

The Urises brought in their favorite architects, Emery Roth & Sons, to redesign the building but retained Harrison & Abramovitz as consultants.[43] The bulky new design for 1290 Avenue of the Americas, with precast-concrete vertical piers infilled by glass and aluminum, was somewhat sympathetic to Rockefeller Center's architecture. The forty-three-story building was named after its lead tenant, the Sperry-Rand Corporation, which occupied eight floors of space, amounting to 400,000 of the 1.7 million square feet of floor area in the building.

But Zeckendorf had the last laugh, even if he didn't make any money on it, because the Uris Brothers entered into a joint venture with Rockefeller Center to build not only the Sperry-Rand Building but also, contrary to Percy Uris's previous stance, a large hotel, the New York Hilton Hotel, two blocks farther uptown on the west side of the avenue between Fifty-third and Fifty-fourth streets.[44] In September 1960 *Architectural Forum* reported that hotel specialist Morris Lapidus and Kornblath, Harle & Liebman, with Harrison & Abramovitz as consulting architects, were preparing preliminary plans for a thirty-eight-story, 2,200-room luxury hotel. Their proposal called for a gently curving narrow slab perpendicular to and set back from Sixth Avenue, with a semicircular driveway as the means of approach. But by year's end, when Lapidus's work on the nearby Americana Hotel (see "Times Square," below) seemed a conflict of interest with the Hilton, the project was handed over to another hotel specialist, William B. Tabler, who would also work in consultation with Harrison & Abramovitz. Tabler's design called for a four-story, masonry-clad base filling the site, above which would rise a 60-foot-wide, 392-foot-long, forty-five-story slab clad mostly in metal and blue glass. "The first blue skyscraper to be added to the New York skyline," as the developers described it, would accommodate 2,200 "outside" rooms.[45] Taking as a point of reference Schultze & Weaver's Waldorf-Astoria, completed thirty-two years earlier, the New York Hilton at Rockefeller Center, as the hostelry was officially designated, contained a midblock drive-through and motor lobby near the site's west end.[46] Whereas the Waldorf had a direct connection to a private siding of the New York Central Railroad at its basement level, the Hilton would have a 350-car garage.

Construction began on March 25, 1961, and the hotel opened on June 26, 1963. Over 2,200 identical baylike windows lined the slab's north and south facades, while the solid slab ends were clad in limestone. This arrangement, reminiscent of Wallace Harrison's U.N. Secretariat (see chapter 7), demon-

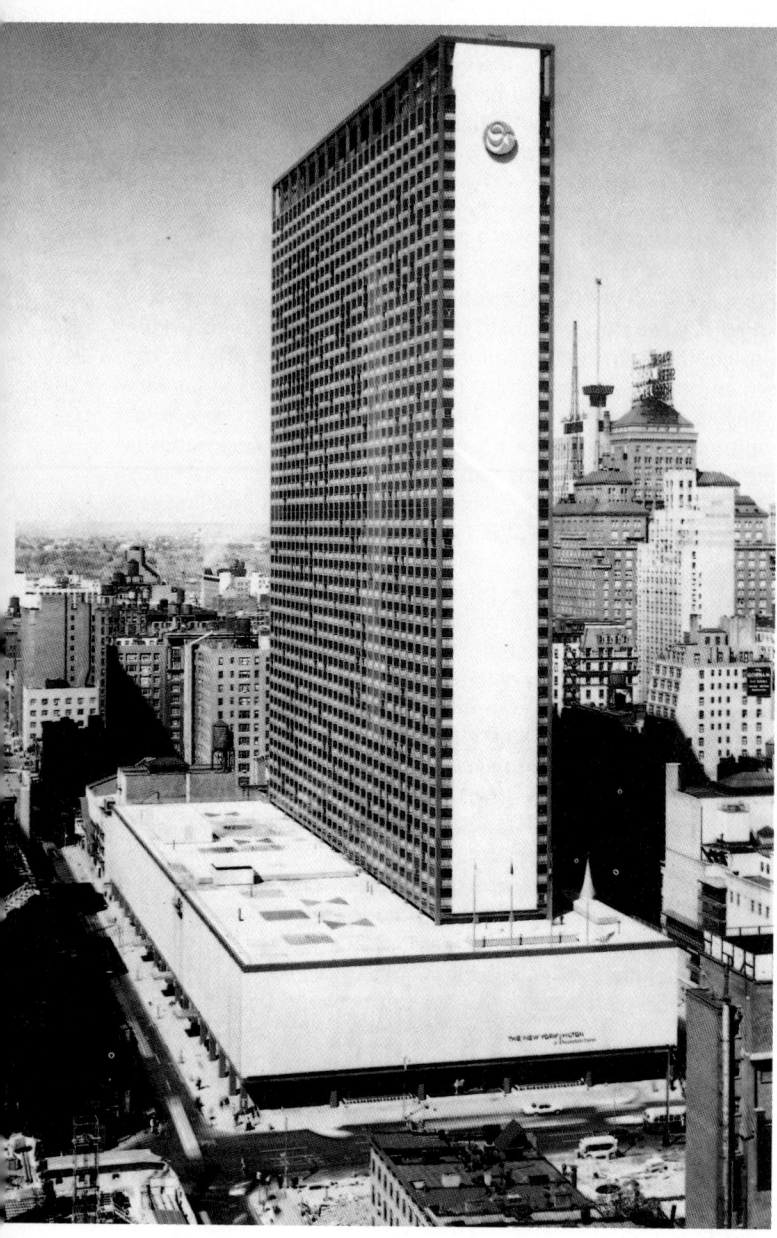

New York Hilton, 1335 Sixth Avenue, West Fifty-third to West Fifty-fourth Street. William B. Tabler, 1963. View to the northwest. WBT

strated how much more inspiring its stylistic prototype was, and how formulaic commercial Modernism had become in less than a decade. According to the Hilton's architects, the problem was "to take two 400-foot-long by 400-foot-high exterior walls and make them congruent with their neighbors, and residential in character in a way that avoided monotony." In describing their solution, the architects said: "First we stretched the structural frame to its maximum within the esthetic and building code requirements. Then we projected the windows out beyond the structure to form an apex at each room. This permitted the heating and air-conditioning system to run beyond the face of the structural frame. By so doing, the size of the room was increased and a window was formed which is residential in scale, includes a window seat, and offers an expanded panorama."[47]

Despite its hulking immensity and its repetitious faceting, the New York Hilton was treated kindly by most critics. While Huxtable found its facade "glossily impersonal,"[48] she went on to say that "within its business-like limits, the directness of the concept, the expertness of the plan, and the quality of execution are commendable."[49] Walter McQuade commented on the relationship between the base and the slab of the building: "The contrast of its simple bulk with the beehive above is not logically convincing, but quite graceful. Its massing has at any rate, a straightforward, diagrammatic feeling, and that seldom happens in hotels, or in other Manhattan buildings." McQuade also praised the building's fenestration: "Unlike the usual dull and endless expanse of flat, factory-fabricated glass facing, this curtain is pleated. The wall is folded in and out, so that its reflections are not blankly staring, in the reptilian way, but diverting."[50] The editors of *Progressive Architecture* called the building "an appropriate hotel for New York," and described its cavernous porte cochere along the Sixth Avenue blockfront and its midblock drive-through as reminiscent of "grand hotel days."[51] Only Russell Lynes was not favorably impressed. The Hilton's "tremendous glass slab," he said, "is set upon a rectangular base, very much like a tombstone. One would not be surprised to see in enormous letters across it:

> The International Style
> b. ca. 1920–d. 1963
> *Requiescat in Pace*"[52]

No matter what they thought about the building's exterior, most critics disliked the interior decorating, particularly the restaurants that occupied the hotel's Fifty-second Street side. There was general agreement, however, that Lydia and Harry de Polo's lobby promenades encircling the building on its second and third floors, where the ballrooms were located, represented a fairly spirited interpretation of Miesian Modernism. The four theme restaurants, the cocktail lounge and two secondary ballrooms were designed by William Pahlmann Associates, who were also responsible for the duplex VIP suites on the forty-fourth and forty-fifth floors; the principal ballroom was designed by stage designer Jo Mielziner. The restaurants, reached by means of a corridor called the Rue des Gourmets, were the Old Bourbon House, inspired by the New Orleans Vieux Carré; the bistrolike Place Lautrec; the somewhat Spanish night spot Valencia; the exotic Kismet lounge; and the luxurious Seven Hills, incorporating trompe l'oeil murals by René Boucher that seemed to open the room up to views of the Roman campagna. The ballrooms also had themes. Pahlmann's Mercury Ballroom, intended to accommodate the trade shows that the management hoped to attract, was a glitzy design with ceiling-mounted concave mirrors that suggested giant rearview mirrors on a car. In contrast to this space-age modernity, the Trianon Ballroom, also by Pahlmann, was decorated in a fairly straightforward interpretation of the typical French-inspired hotel ballroom of the 1920s. Mielziner's Grand Ballroom, on the other hand, was stylistically indefinable. Olga Gueft, writing in *Interiors*, characterized its design as "chop suey decor" and called the ballroom "the major flop of the vast Hilton enterprise."[53]

Ada Louise Huxtable criticized the contrast between the hotel's exterior and its interior: "From the outside this is clearly the world of tomorrow, as promised by Messrs. Conrad Hilton, Laurance Rockefeller and Percy Uris. . . . Inside the world of tomorrow gives way to never-never land, and it would have been better if it never had. For the fact is that the New York Hilton has barely let the architect through the door. Beyond that point the designers of the interiors have figuratively and esthetically thumbed their noses at him and vertigo sets in." She lambasted such elements as "stone walls made of plastered aluminum" and "paneled doors made of painted plywood," saying that these "parodies of antiquity" "deride and denigrate the structure they camouflage." The Rue des Gourmets, she predicted, "will please people who equate pretentious confusion with charm. It will give others esthetic indigestion." As for the Kismet Lounge, Huxtable said that the visitor could prepare for it only with "a few years in an MGM harem or a fortification of preliminary cocktails."[54]

Huxtable found the guest rooms, designed by the Statler-Hilton Studios under the direction of Ernest Wottitz, no more to her liking. While praising Tabler for creating "a better room, with 8-foot ceilings and bay-window walls, than most New York hotels or apartments can boast," she argued that "on the lower floors, they are defaced by motel modern colors that assault the senses" and that "in the top echelon suites, the rejection of the architecture is total." The interior treatment of the hotel, she concluded, was "not just an opportunity missed" but "a design disaster."[55]

Under the guiding hand of B. H. (Bob) Friedman, vice-president of the Uris Buildings Corporation, and a committee consisting of Seymour Levine, a member of the Uris organization, Gustav Eysell, the president of the Rockefeller Center Corporation, Wallace Harrison and Ernest Wottitz, the hotel's public spaces were lavishly embellished with contemporary art, much of it specially commissioned. Like that of the Chase Manhattan Bank Building of 1961, the Hilton's art program was a pioneering attempt to use contemporary art, particularly nonrepresentational art, as a decorating tool in a commercial building. The pieces included Philip Pavia's sculptural group *Ides of March*, which stood under the Sixth Avenue porte cochere, a six-by-six-foot black cast-iron sculpture by James Metcalf in the lobby, and Ibram Lassaw's delicate fused-metal hanging sculpture, *Elysian Fields*, in the promenade space. Gueft, who characterized the Pavia piece as a "big nothing" and the Metcalf as "a huge tar lollypop on a stick," questioned the basic premise of the art program: "The practice of commissioning important works of art has become so prevalent that some of our more acerbic critics have come to suspect it as a gimmick to mask mediocre architecture."[56]

In addition to the sculptures, nearly 8,500 signed, limited-edition prints adorned the guest rooms. Among the artists represented were Stuart Davis, Helen Frankenthaler, Jane Freilicher, Grace Hartigan, Jasper Johns, Lee Krasner, John Marin, Marisol, Robert Rauschenberg and Larry Rivers; the photographers Ansel Adams, Edward Steichen and Edward Weston were also represented. While the art unquestionably added a dimension of visual interest and quality to the hotel, Russell Lynes found the

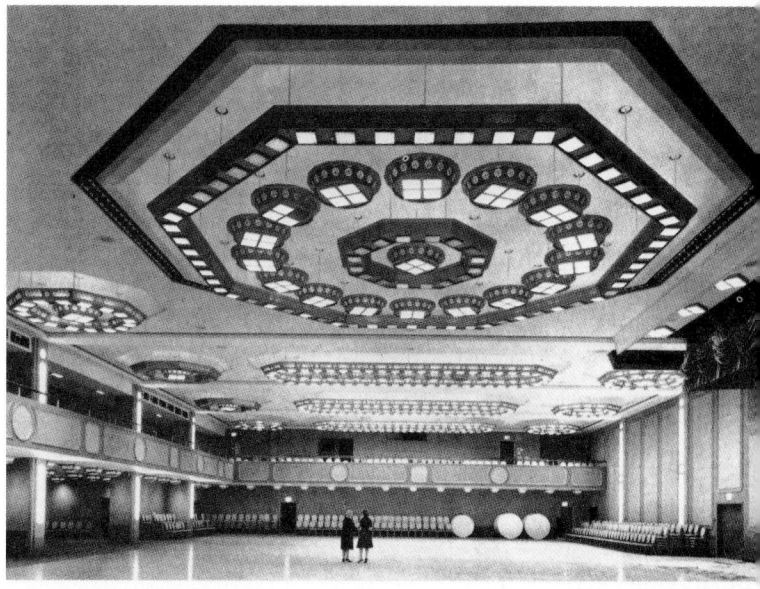

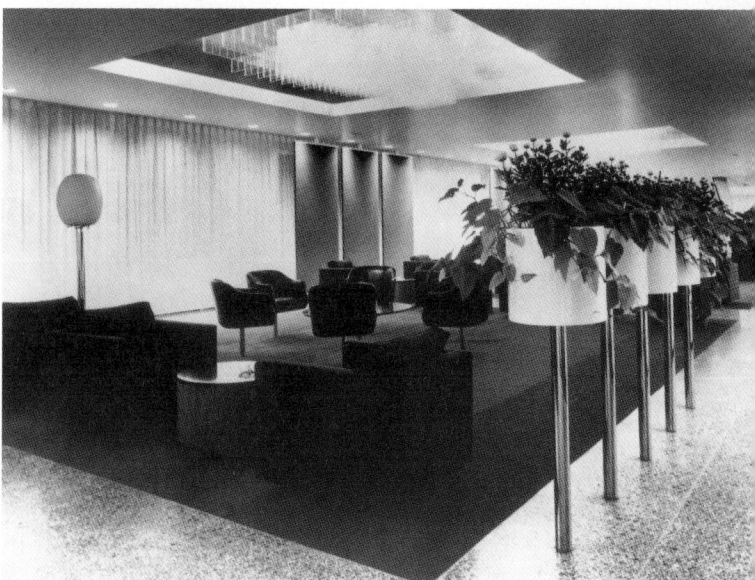

Top: New York Hilton. View of the Grand Ballroom. Jo Mielziner, 1963. Hirsch. IN. CU

Bottom: New York Hilton. Lobby promenade. Lydia and Harry de Polo, 1963. WBT

work more disconcerting than stimulating: "The selection of prints was made by a committee and it is therefore of sufficient catholicity to be unlikely to offend anyone in the world, but heaven knows what a sleepless guest may think. It may be perverse of me, but I have always found the non-art of hotel bedrooms rather restful; they do not ask one to react."[57]

In September 1961 designs were released for 1301 Avenue of the Americas, the J. C. Penney Building (1964), another Uris project.[58] Located on the west blockfront of the avenue between Fifty-second and Fifty-third streets, the forty-six-story tower containing over 1.4 million square feet of floor space was designed by Shreve, Lamb & Harmon Associates. The building was one of the first significant examples of the impact of the new zoning on large-scale construction. Published drawings illustrated how the building would have looked under the old rules as well as how it would look under the new rules. Under the old zoning, the relatively slender tower, covering 25 percent of the site, would have sat on a base that, with minor setbacks along the side streets, would have filled the entire site to twelve stories. Under the new zoning, though the building's overall height remained unchanged, an additional 200,000 square feet of floor area was permitted in a thick slab covering 40 percent of the site as a bonus for the provision of a street-level plaza and arcade spaces.

CBS Building

In July 1960 the Columbia Broadcasting System announced its intentions to build a headquarters office building on the east blockfront of Sixth Avenue between Fifty-second and Fifty-third streets.[59] Designed by Eero Saarinen just before his death in 1961, the CBS Building (1961–65), 51 West Fifty-second Street, was the most artistically ambitious of all the buildings built along Sixth Avenue in the postwar era. The 40,000-square-foot site, formerly home to five four-story apartment buildings and a 25,000-square-foot parking lot, had been assembled by William Zeckendorf and his Webb & Knapp organization and sold to CBS during one of his periodic cash crunches.

CBS had occupied space in a relatively undistinguished building at 485 Madison Avenue since 1929; although the construction of a grand, stylish headquarters designed by William Lescaze for the east side of Park Avenue between Fifty-eighth and Fifty-ninth streets was contemplated in 1935, the project did not go forward.[60] Postwar plans for a new headquarters building on other sites on Fifth Avenue, near the East River and even in the New Jersey Meadows had also been rumored. CBS had originally considered combining its offices with its broadcast facilities, which were scattered around Manhattan in custom-designed buildings and in various converted theaters. The site of what became the Pan Am Building was seriously contemplated, as well as a building intended for 247 Park Avenue. But eventually the company decided to rehouse the broadcast center in a former dairy distribution facility on West Fifty-seventh Street, between Eleventh and Twelfth avenues (see "West Side: From Chelsea to Clinton," above). According to William S. Paley, the network's founder and the company's chairman of the board, Sixth Avenue was chosen for the headquarters building because it would be "more stimulating" than Park Avenue.[61] Besides, the site was only three blocks away from the Rockefeller Center headquarters of its archrival, NBC.

In designing the CBS Building Saarinen explored a number of schemes for slabs and shaped towers before arriving at the final proposal, a thirty-eight-story reinforced-concrete tower

sheathed in black granite rising without setbacks from a plaza sunk approximately two feet (five steps) below the sidewalk grade. As the design unfolded, according to Ada Louise Huxtable, "It served as a demonstration model for the new zoning . . . with the Saarinen office helping to develop realistic land coverage ratios to permit the plaza-surrounded sheer tower. As such, CBS set the shape and standard for New York building today."[62] Saarinen was particularly concerned about the building's urban impact:

> We tried to place the building on the site so that we could have a plaza and still not destroy the street line. A tower should not be tied in with lower street buildings. It should stand alone with air and light around it. A plaza is a very necessary thing in a city. It lets people sit in the sun and look at the sky. A plaza allows a building to be seen. Our buildings should be seen, because they are monuments of our time. But a plaza can be a dangerous thing. We have to remember the street line and we have to remember the space between is as important as the towers. These arrangements should be orderly and beautiful so the streets do not look like torn things and the towers like isolated teeth sticking up from a gaping mouth.[63]

Nonetheless, Saarinen placed his building more or less in the center of the site, and the plaza had little spatial significance and provided no seating.

The 135-by-160-foot, 800,000-square-foot tower, occupying 60 percent of the site, was set back twenty-five feet from the building line on each side and by the same distance from a two-story service block located at the eastern end of the site. It constituted the purest skyscraper tower ever, a fulfillment of Saarinen's desire to create "a building that would stand firmly on the ground and could grow straight up."[64] Perhaps thinking of Mies's Seagram Building, and of the critics who viewed it as impure because it was not a sheer tower but rose from lower masses, Saarinen wanted CBS to be "the simplest skyscraper in New York."[65] According to John Dinkeloo, one of Saarinen's closest collaborators, who with other associates in the firm, including Joseph N. Lacy and Kevin Roche, took over the project after the architect's death on September 1, 1961, Saarinen had been "especially excited about this design. He felt he was going back to the tradition of Louis Sullivan and making a step forward from that dramatic and optimistic moment in the design of tall buildings."[66]

The 490-foot-tall tower was unusual for New York not only because of its singleminded simplicity of mass but also because it was the first in the city to be built in reinforced concrete rather than the steel frame typically used for high-rise office buildings. The five-foot-wide, V-shaped structural columns alternated with five-foot vertical bands of gray-tinted vision glass to minimize the sense of transparency; together with the granite spandrels, they conspired to give the building the appearance of rocklike solidity that would later earn the building the nickname of "Black Rock." Under the direction of Kevin Roche, the final refinements of the proportion of window to pier were resolved after Saarinen's death. The closely spaced V-shaped perimeter columns carried floor beams tying back to the central core, as well as a continuous, L-shaped haunch beam running against the inner face of the columns, leaving the floors free of columns for their thirty-five-foot depth. The open sides of the structural V's housed chases for electrical wiring, heating and air-conditioning ducts.

William Paley took credit for the decision not to use steel, while Dr. Frank Stanton, the president of CBS, claimed responsibility for the decision to have a sheer tower. As Eric Larrabee pointed out, "Where CBS left off and Saarinen began is now dif-

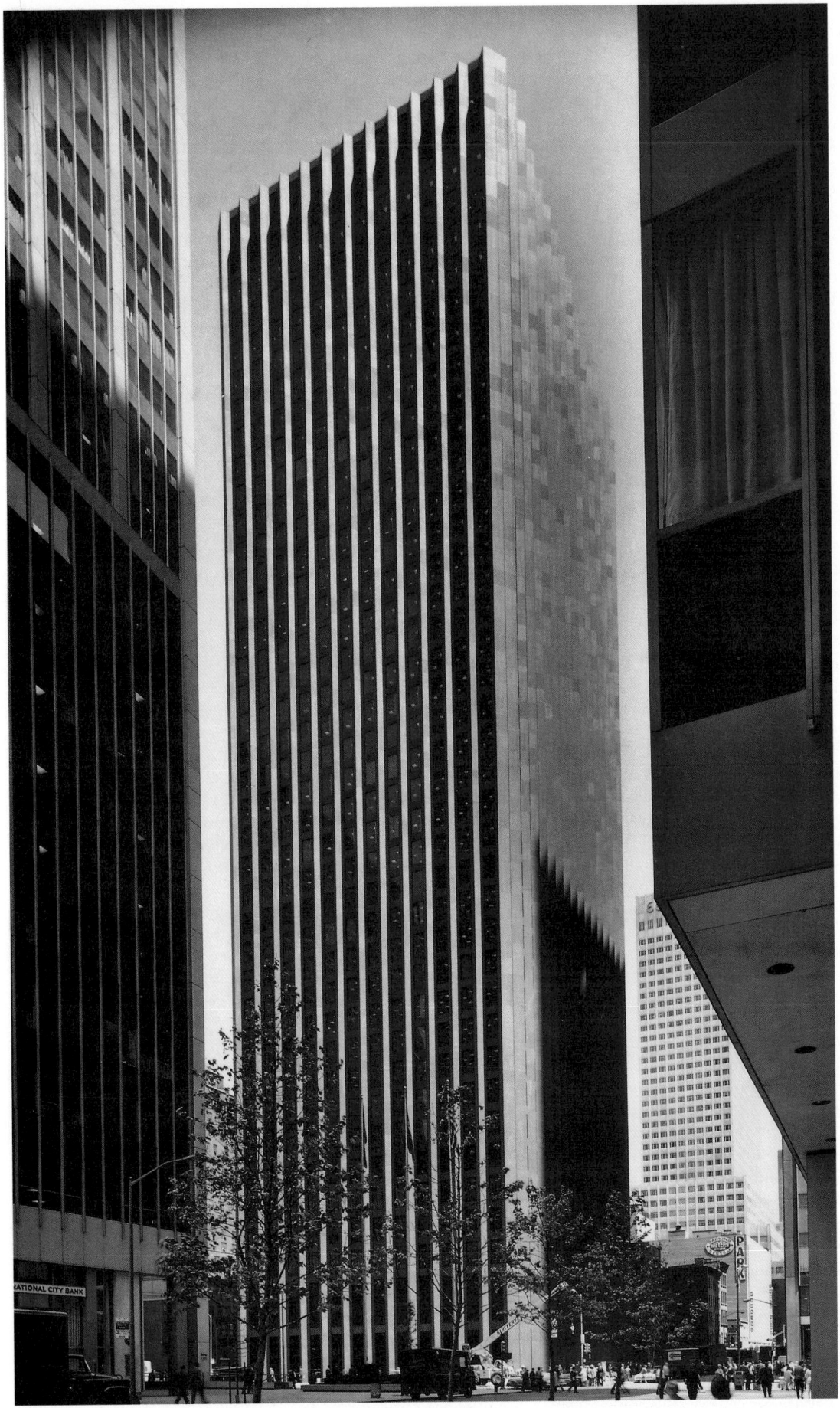

CBS Building, 51 West
Fifty-second Street,
northeast corner of
Sixth Avenue. Eero
Saarinen & Associates,
1961–65. View to the
northwest. Molitor.
JWM

ficult to determine, especially since he was the kind of architect . . . who . . . cared less who got credit for an idea than whether his own ideas prevailed." According to Larrabee, "Saarinen wanted to break the mold" of the rectangular cagelike skyscraper "and so did his client."[67] "After all," as Aline B. Saarinen, the architect's widow, pointed out, "that's why they came to Eero and not to Skidmore."[68]

Saarinen returned to the skyscraper the sense of solidity and mass that had been its principal characteristic before the advent of Modernist minimalism. But he did this in a completely Modernist way, by "restoring function to the masonry pier," as Larrabee put it: "By using concrete he could take vertical columns on the outside wall and make them do something for a change; by thickening them and deepening them he could set the windows in such a deep recess that, from an angle, you would see no glass at all."[69] The effect was distinctly Gothic, though philosophically derived from a consideration of Louis Sullivan's work. But it also had just as much to do with the work of Raymond Hood, most notably his black-brick American Radiator Building of 1924, and, as Larrabee was to point out, with the work of Sullivan's Chicago colleague, John Wellborn Root, whose Monadnock Building (1891), designed in partnership with Daniel H. Burnham, was a paean to soaring verticality executed in traditional masonry.[70]

While Saarinen's eclectic vision was intended as an explicit criticism of the typical postwar skyscraper, its isolated position on the site and its abstract form, which denied any strong sense of frontality or clear expression of entrance, made CBS a hypertypical exemplar of Modernist urbanism. Given that the end of traditional urbanism was taken as a desirable consequence of Modernist architecture, CBS was generally assessed in terms of its architectural rather than its urban impact. During the building's construction in 1964, for instance, Larrabee ignored the building's relation to its surroundings, simply characterizing it as "a radical challenge to a stagnating contemporary cliché."[71] Saarinen felt that with the CBS Building he would take the skyscraper to a level of architectural refinement even beyond the standard established by Mies van der Rohe. To his office collaborators Saarinen boasted: "It's even going to make the Seagram building look gaudy."[72]

The complex structural system necessary to realize Saarinen's puristic vision was designed by Paul Weidlinger with the help of computers, in an early demonstration of their usefulness to architects and engineers. The actual construction of the building was also complex. Because the site was above the IND subway where the Sixth Avenue line curved into the Fifty-third Street crosstown line, the construction of the foundation was difficult. The subway also influenced the location of the tower, which had to be placed in the center of the block to rise free of the tunnel. Despite such complications, and despite the lavish use of Canadian black granite and the seemingly experimental structural system, the CBS Building proved to be quite economical. Although costs were never officially released, Dinkeloo claimed it was less expensive to build than any other major New York office tower including the Seagram, Chase Manhattan or Union Carbide buildings.

When the CBS Building opened in 1965, it was widely admired, but not without qualifications. In 1966 Ada Louise Huxtable discussed the public's reaction to the building: "The dark dignity that appeals to architectural sophisticates puts off the public, which tends to reject it as funereal." But she did not blame the architect for the public response: "Thoroughly corrupted by what might be called the American Product Esthetic—applied equally to buildings and possessions—[the public] takes

bright and shiny as synonymous with new and good. Surrounded by tinsel and tinfoil, it finds CBS's somber restraint gloomy, and gloom is not part of the admired American way of life. The spurious glitter of much of the new Sixth Avenue surrounding CBS eclipses Saarinen's sober subtleties."[73]

Bethami Probst, writing in *Progressive Architecture*, saw the CBS Building as "a dignified, pertinent rebuke to its more strident high-rise neighbors," but said that in the "inevitable comparison" with the Seagram Building, it "fares less well." Probst observed that an "irreconcilable contradiction" was at the heart of the building's design: "Saarinen's longing to soar is repeatedly sacrificed in order to communicate permanence, strength and pride. Like Icarus yearning to fly higher and higher, Saarinen struggled consciously against being earthbound: 'All the time one works,' he said, 'one concerns oneself with the fight against gravity. Everything tends to be topheavy and downward-pressing unless one really works at it.'" She also pointed out that though CBS and Seagram's had the same number of floors, Mies's building was thirty-four feet higher and rose from a podium rather than from a plaza sunk beneath street level. In comparison with the "grand monumental approach" to the tower at Seagram's, as Probst put it, the CBS plaza was "a bravura declaration of apartness."[74]

Though many critics quibbled about the building's lack of structural integrity—in such details as the false columns and the uniformity of their mass despite the reduced loads of the upper floors—it seemed to represent a renewed sense of permanence and dignity in skyscraper design. Peter Blake extolled the building's virtues: "One may argue about the precise detailing of CBS; but there can be no argument over the fact that this is really a BUILDING, not speculative cubage wrapped in exterior wallpaper. . . . It is, in its way, not unlike the Washington Monument—a single event, a fine piece of sculpture, freed from the surrounding chaos. . . . CBS—Eero Saarinen's final pot-shot—stands aloof, alone, serene." In Blake's opinion this stance was a positive one, given what he viewed as the unsatisfactory urbanism of the renewed Sixth Avenue: "By its very presence, it offers a mute but unmistakable commentary on the slaughter on Sixth Avenue, the slaughter that is our cities today."[75]

David Jacobs was perhaps the most perceptive observer, describing both the building's strengths and its weaknesses:

The CBS Building is at its top precisely what it is at the bottom. It is not organic, it does not sweep or hover, it makes no implications about the space volumes it encloses; its surface is everything. It has been placed, or plunked, perpendicular to the ground; and because it is neither spare nor weightless, the plaza on which it sits has sunk, as though strained, below ground level. It seems to gather itself out of that ground and overpower it. . . .

It is possible that Saarinen used stone and a lower-than-eye-level plaza in an attempt to reintroduce a relationship between architecture and people. Stone is much less cold than steel; and while steel always seems a machine-made thing, stone is something that somebody had to cut and set. Therefore, CBS looks like a built building in a city where even the best new skyscrapers look manufactured, and the mediocre ones mass-produced. . . . Yet despite the human touches, it would seem that if humanizing was Saarinen's game, he would have done a better job of it. CBS is not a warm building. It may be neither inhuman nor sterile, monotonous nor manufactured, but it is impersonal and forbidding and from close by, downright overwhelming.[76]

Even more than Lever House or Seagram's, CBS was the embodiment of Modernist "total design" in the service of corporate image making. Although Saarinen had hoped to be asked to design the office interiors, the commission went to the Knoll Planning Unit, led by Florence Knoll Bassett, whom Saarinen had recommended and with whom CBS had worked before. Knoll worked in association with Carson, Lundin & Shaw, who served as interior architects. Lou Dorfsman, CBS's director of design, also took an active role, overseeing the art program, along with Bassett and Frank Stanton, and designing an innovative sidewalk construction bridge. Dorfsman also created a forty-foot-long bas-relief using food-related words in the employee cafeteria and designed the corporate typeface, a variant on the seventeenth-century French Didot face. Employees were not permitted to decorate their desks with personal items or even to display personal photographs, "unless," as Dorfsman joked, "it was an Avedon portrait."[77] CBS was a company known to be finicky about details—"I'd hate to work for us," Paley was quoted as saying about this point—and Stanton was the company's principal spokesman in matters of corporate taste.[78] A confirmed minimalist, the company president saw in the new headquarters building an opportunity to create in corporate terms a landmark comparable to Mies van der Rohe's Barcelona Pavilion. Even before moving to the new building, Stanton had two Mies-designed Barcelona chairs placed in his office and he "had rather hoped that there might some day be a CBS chair."[79]

Bassett's design was, as *Architectural Record* put it, a marvel of "coordination and attention to detail."[80] She developed the most fully articulated program of design control ever attempted by a corporation: employees worked in a stylish environment in which paintings, vases of flowers and pots of plants were virtually the only elements, aside from the furniture, that might compromise the purity of the architecture; and the furniture was so conceived to conceal most of the miscellany of office life and to make what was visible as invisible as possible. Bassett's approach was highly studied, with each interior thought out as if by a collagist, each vista composed as if by a graphic designer asked to render fully spatial a two-dimensional design. Her role was that of designer, curator and editor; as she put it, "My real job was the proper assembly of everything."[81] "Everything" included the total design of thirty-five office floors, as well as the selection of 899 species of plants and the drafting of a year-round order for flowers that stipulated the varieties and hues to be used in each color area.

The design of key public areas such as reception lounges and viewing rooms suggested a three-dimensional synthesis of Piet Mondrian's de Stijl compositions and the purist designs of Le Corbusier or Amédée Ozenfant. To some observers, like Patricia Conway, writing in *Industrial Design*, the effect was contrived:

> The interiors rely on self-consciously placed ashtrays, authorized plants, and 3,000 pieces of sanctioned art. The collection, assembled not for its inherent greatness but for its ornamental value, includes . . . lithographs, framed fabrics, blow-ups of posters, pieces of carpeting, wrapping paper, and beads in a shadow box. A few pieces have charm but, for the most part, there is a preponderance of hard-edge, straight-line compositions, obviously hung to pick up the color on this wall or complement the texture on that couch.[82]

Although Bassett's interiors met Stanton's objectives, they did not please everyone in the company: Paley hired Jansen, a Paris-based firm of high-style, traditional decorators, to design his

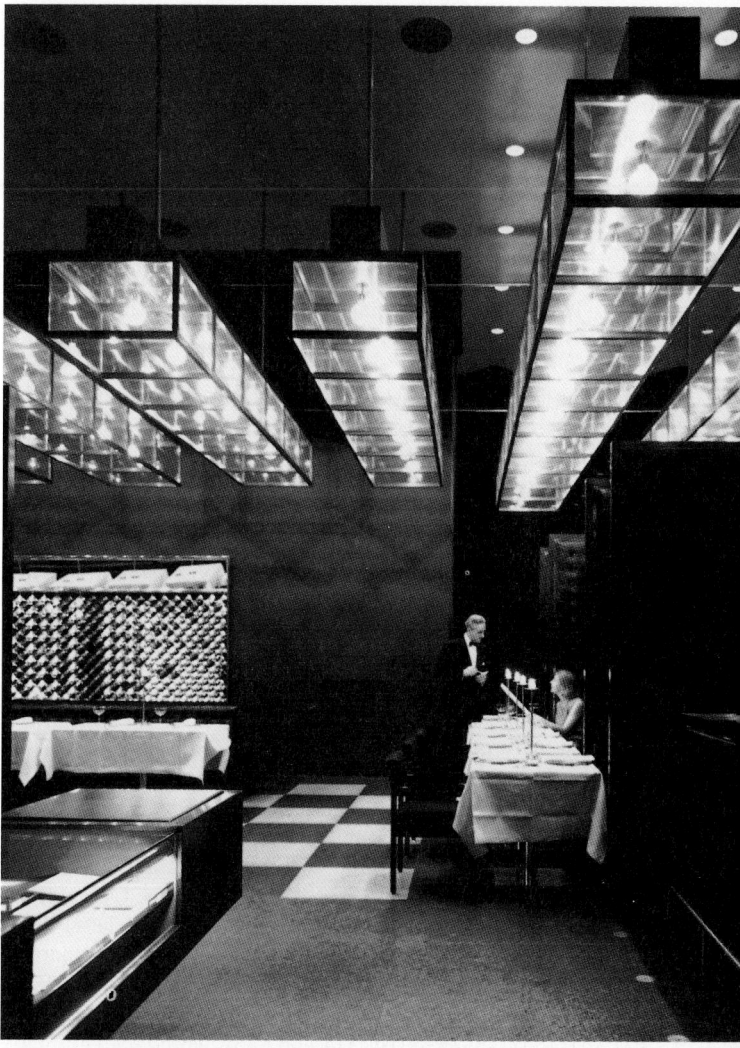

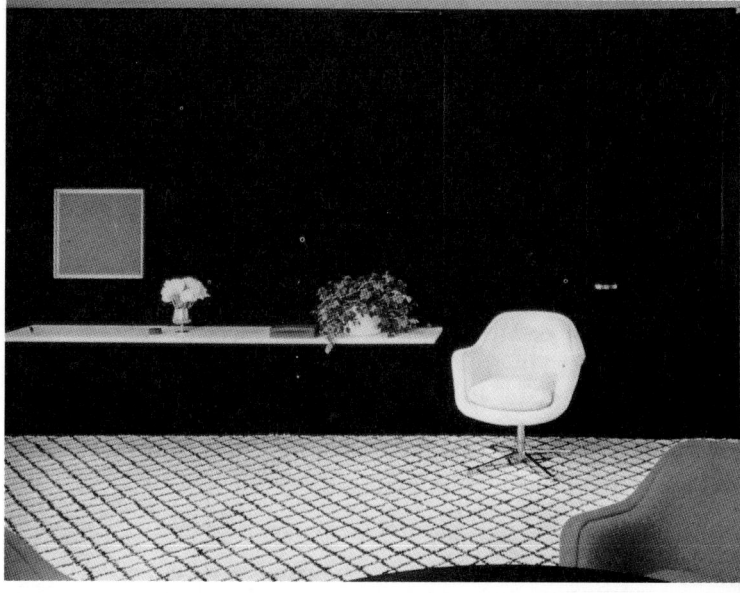

Top: Ground Floor restaurant, CBS Building. Warren Platner, designer, 1965. WPA

Bottom: Executive office, CBS Building. Knoll Planning Unit, 1965. KGA

own thirty-fifth floor offices in the manner of Napoleonic France, using mahogany furniture and, for fabrics, paints and wallpapers, a palette of dark green, Paley's favorite color. Further down the pecking order, some members of the rank and file were not so pleased either, but, unlike the chairman of the board, they couldn't do much about it. As David Jacobs reported, "Mothers complained about the rule against putting up the home art they had proudly displayed at 485 Madison Avenue. Nobody felt a serious obligation to replace tables and chairs precisely on the floor markers provided to insure maintenance of the décor."[83] Ada Louise Huxtable was harsh in her description of the building's interior: "The inside of CBS is a solid gold corporate cliché; a lavish cocoon, complete to standardized concealed wastebaskets and accredited and almost as equally standardized abstract art—interchangeable from Sixth to Third avenues. The building has been turned into the anonymous, vacuum-packed commercial shell that it was never meant to be."[84]

Even more problematic than the offices were the public spaces. The building's lobby, designed by Saarinen's office, was austere to the point of lugubriousness. "The combination of white travertine walls, floors, and ashtrays with dark granite columns and tinted glass gives the space a somewhat cold, monolithic appearance," Patricia Conway wrote. "The only points of visual interest in the lobby area are the graphics which identify the elevator banks and the directory mounted behind a sectional wall. This simplicity and functionalism serves to speed traffic but, at the same time, creates a rather Kafkaesque atmosphere."[85]

The western portion of the ground floor was taken up by a blandly fitted out branch of the Bank of New York.[86] The area to the east of the lobby was earmarked for a restaurant, a favorite project of Paley's, who was a well-known gourmet. Operated by the Brody Corporation, an offshoot of Restaurant Associates, CBS's Ground Floor restaurant was designed by Warren Platner, an architect specializing in interiors who had worked in the Saarinen office.[87] The CBS restaurant was meant to rival the Four Seasons and, like its predecessor, the Ground Floor would exemplify the building's spirit. As Olga Gueft put it: "Since the building has a monolithic power, unequivocal masculine strength was called for, a total abjuration of the phony; a menu both hearty and international; uncompromised quality in food, service, and decor, with commensurate prices; an open kitchen and stand-up bar; no apeing of period decor, but traditional luxuries—fine mahogany, leather, velour, brass, crystal, silver, china; what *looked* expensive would be expensive."[88]

The restaurant was large, with a seating capacity of 220 for dinner. Beyond the bar, located just inside the Fifty-second Street entrance, the narrow throat of the space balanced a continuous banquette set against the building's elevator core with an open kitchen (the preparation kitchens were in the basement). The principal dining room was at the rear, facing Fifty-third Street. The lighting was the room's principal ornament: an open structure of mahogany-framed glass coffers, each holding a single large, clear-filamented bulb. The top of the coffer was lined with red brass to give a rosy reflection. Although Gueft described the Ground Floor as New York's "most glamorous" restaurant, many other observers found it a cold environment, particularly at night when, despite a profusion of candles, the granite floor and columns conspired with the dark leather and the blackness of the windows to create an effect of cavernous gloom.[89] "No matter how much one recognizes the purity and meticulous elegance of the design," *Progressive Architecture* said, "no matter how much one recognizes that black velvet is the traditional foil for silver and glassware in shops, a doubt still lingers about whether a powerful black tomb, regardless of its handsome orchestration of textures, can ever be a suitable, psychologically acceptable atmosphere for pleasant dining."[90]

XYZ

In 1963 Rockefeller Center inaugurated the second phase of the avenue's transformation by undertaking an expansion plan to construct three new superscale office towers on the west side of the avenue south of the Time & Life Building, one each on the blockfronts that extended from Forty-seventh to Fiftieth Street.[91] Wallace Harrison's initial plan for the three blocks, known as the XYZ plan, called for towering slabs grouped in a pinwheel formation that created a large open plaza on the blockfront between Forty-eighth and Forty-ninth streets as well as a smaller, Seagram-like plaza between Forty-ninth and Fiftieth streets. This plan, which oriented the central of the three proposed towers on a north-south axis, also included a private street defining the western boundary of the principal square, which would transfer at least some of the urbanity of the original Rockefeller Center to its western extension. The central square—conceived by Harrison's partner Max Abramovitz—would also create a forecourt to the original complex's clifflike western edge, which had been designed to block out the El but now acted as a barrier against westward expansion. The plaza was to be sunk below street level to provide traffic-free pedestrian access to each of the new buildings and to connect with the Rockefeller Center concourse across Sixth Avenue. This plan, however, was rejected in favor of a more typically Modernist vision, also by Harrison, of nearly uniform parallel slabs running east-west, each rising from a large plaza. This Le Corbusier–inspired composition not only went back to Edward Durell Stone's early plans for the avenue (see above) but also referred to Lucio Costa's master plan for Brasília (1957), the new capital of Brazil, which was widely published and admired.

As the XYZ buildings were being planned, the City Planning Commission's Urban Design Group worked behind the scenes to salvage the spirit if not the letter of Harrison's initial scheme.[92] Although the center's plan called for much larger public open spaces than were required, a zoning variance was necessary because the buildings exceeded the maximum bulk permitted by zoning. In exchange for permission to build more square footage than the law allowed, the Urban Design Group's 1968 plans proposed pushing the three superslabs east toward the Sixth Avenue building line, more or less in the manner of Time & Life, and creating a shop-lined, glass-enclosed pedestrian promenade running north-south behind the towers, with a multilevel cross section achieved by carving out several of the buildings' rear, lower floors. Also proposed was a theater in the southernmost building of the group, to be occupied by the Celanese Corporation; this unusual programmatic element was intended to tie the Sixth Avenue corridor in with the theater district, which was also being studied by the Urban Design Group at the time (see "Times Square," below). Even though the Urban Design Group was able to interest the prominent theatrical impresario Robert Whitehead in running the proposed theater and managed to commission a preliminary design from Mitchell-Giurgola Associates, they failed to persuade the Rockefeller Center management of the virtues of the plan.

Without Nelson Rockefeller, who had embarked on a political career, Rockefeller Center, Inc. lacked a leader committed to architectural excellence. In a last-ditch effort, the Urban Design Group "leaked" its proposal to Ada Louise Huxtable, who discussed it in the *New York Times* in May 1968. Huxtable spared no feelings in her commentary:

> The corporate investors are determined to follow the same tried and true, catastrophic course of construction that has made New York a less and less viable place: the familiar, neolithic pattern in which a specific number of square feet of self-contained, totally depersonalized office space replaces a variety of small, necessary local facilities and functions, with the corporate giants hermetically sealed off from their surroundings by a few more pointless, windswept plazas and a dull clutch of ground-floor banks.

In advocating the Urban Design Group's plan Huxtable said: "This would be the kind of unified design that Rockefeller Center practiced but no longer preaches."[93]

As realized, the XYZ group was but a shadow of the ideals represented by Harrison's initial scheme or the Urban Design Group's proposal.[94] The idea of a midblock north-south street survived only as a grade-level pedestrian way running behind the three buildings, occupied by the Exxon, McGraw-Hill and Celanese corporations. An extension of Rockefeller Center's below-grade concourse system was built to link the three new buildings, the subway and the center, and its design was more successful than the concourse at Time & Life, with glass-wall corridors opening onto the sunken plazas that lay between the McGraw-Hill and Exxon buildings and Sixth Avenue.

The Exxon Building (1967–71) was the first of the XYZ buildings to be constructed.[95] As designed by Harrison, Abramovitz & Harris, with Welton Becket & Associates acting as consultants to the client, the building sat on a 98,000-square-foot site between Forty-ninth and Fiftieth streets, extending more than halfway back toward Seventh Avenue. The new building replaced a variety of one- to five-story structures, as well as the sixteen-story Plymouth Hotel (H. I. Feldman, 1929), and displaced fourteen of the twenty-three restaurants on the block.[96] The huge, 2.1 million-square-foot, fifty-four-story, 784-foot-high tower slab rose sheer from a street-level plaza on three sides. At the rear, it was locked into a seven-story wraparound base. The tower consisted of limestone-clad structural columns alternating with vertical bands of windows, in effect the same system Saarinen had introduced at the CBS Building, although here, because the columns were flush with the plane of the wall, it yielded no sense of mass.

The McGraw-Hill Building, a joint undertaking of the publishing company and Rockefeller Center, Inc., was the second of the buildings to be announced.[97] In 1965 McGraw-Hill had considered expanding its operation on Forty-second Street by building above a new bus facility proposed by the Port Authority for the west blockfront of Eighth Avenue between Forty-first and Forty-second streets.[98] But with the declining status of Forty-second Street, the company began to consider other locations, including the suburbs. Eventually, though, the lure of a location in Rockefeller Center became irresistible, and the company agreed to occupy the twentieth building in the center complex. McGraw-Hill's decision not to relocate to the suburbs was crucial to Mayor Lindsay's efforts to bolster New York's sagging economy and reassure the world at large of the city's continuing importance. As plans for the building were announced in December 1967, Shelton Fisher, McGraw-Hill's president, stressed the fact that it was the requirements of the company's creative people that tipped the balance in the city's favor: "Whatever their needs or inclinations, they can better satisfy them in New York than anywhere else. It's true that New York has its problems. But we feel it has the strength, the perma-

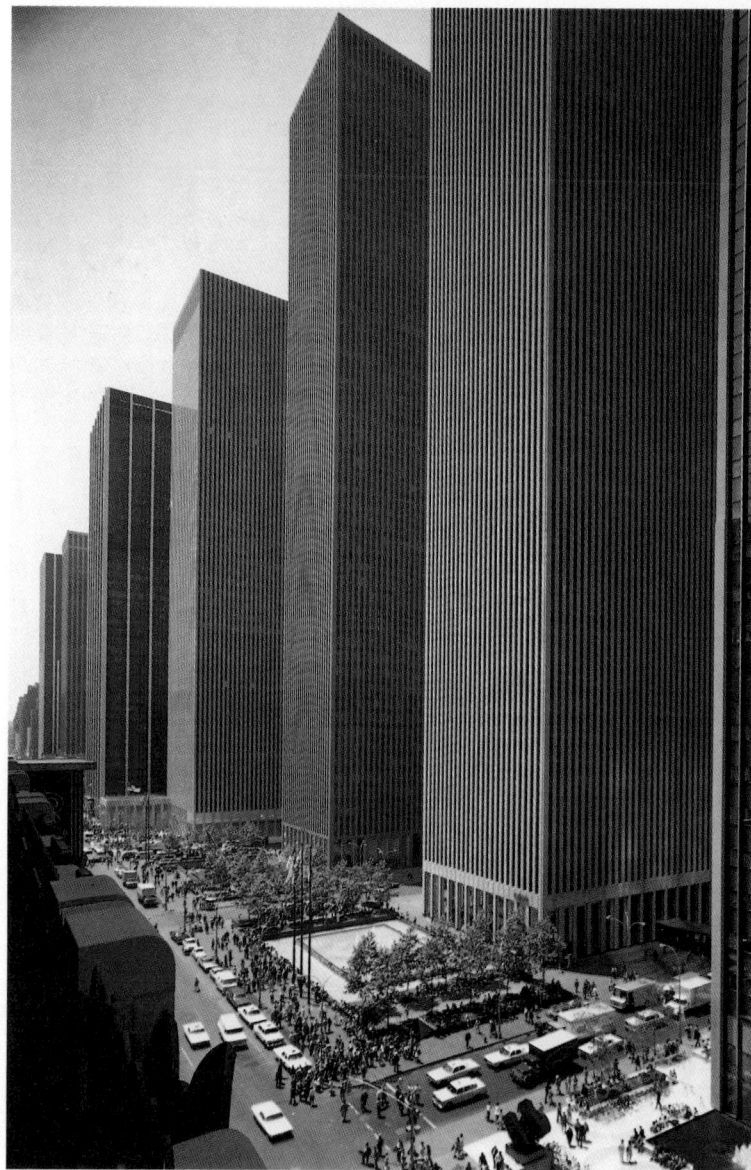

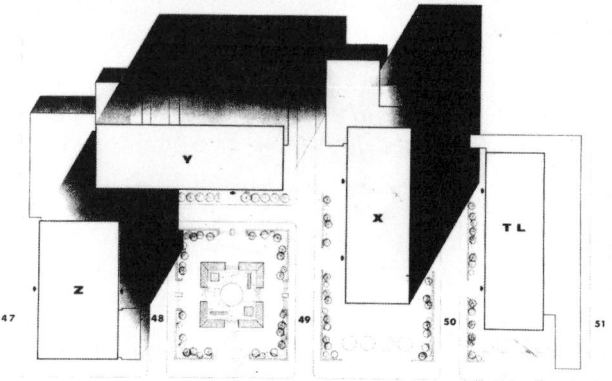

Top: View to the southwest of Sixth Avenue from West Fifty-first Street showing, from left to right: J. P. Stevens Tower (Emery Roth & Sons, 1971), Celanese Building (Harrison, Abramovitz & Harris, 1973), McGraw-Hill Building (Harrison, Abramovitz & Harris, 1972), Exxon Building (Harrison, Abramovitz & Harris, 1971), and a corner of Time & Life Building (Harrison, Abramovitz & Harris, 1959). Stoller. ©ESTO

Bottom: Proposed XYZ Buildings. Wallace Harrison, 1963. Site plan. TL is the Time & Life Building. Checkman. LC

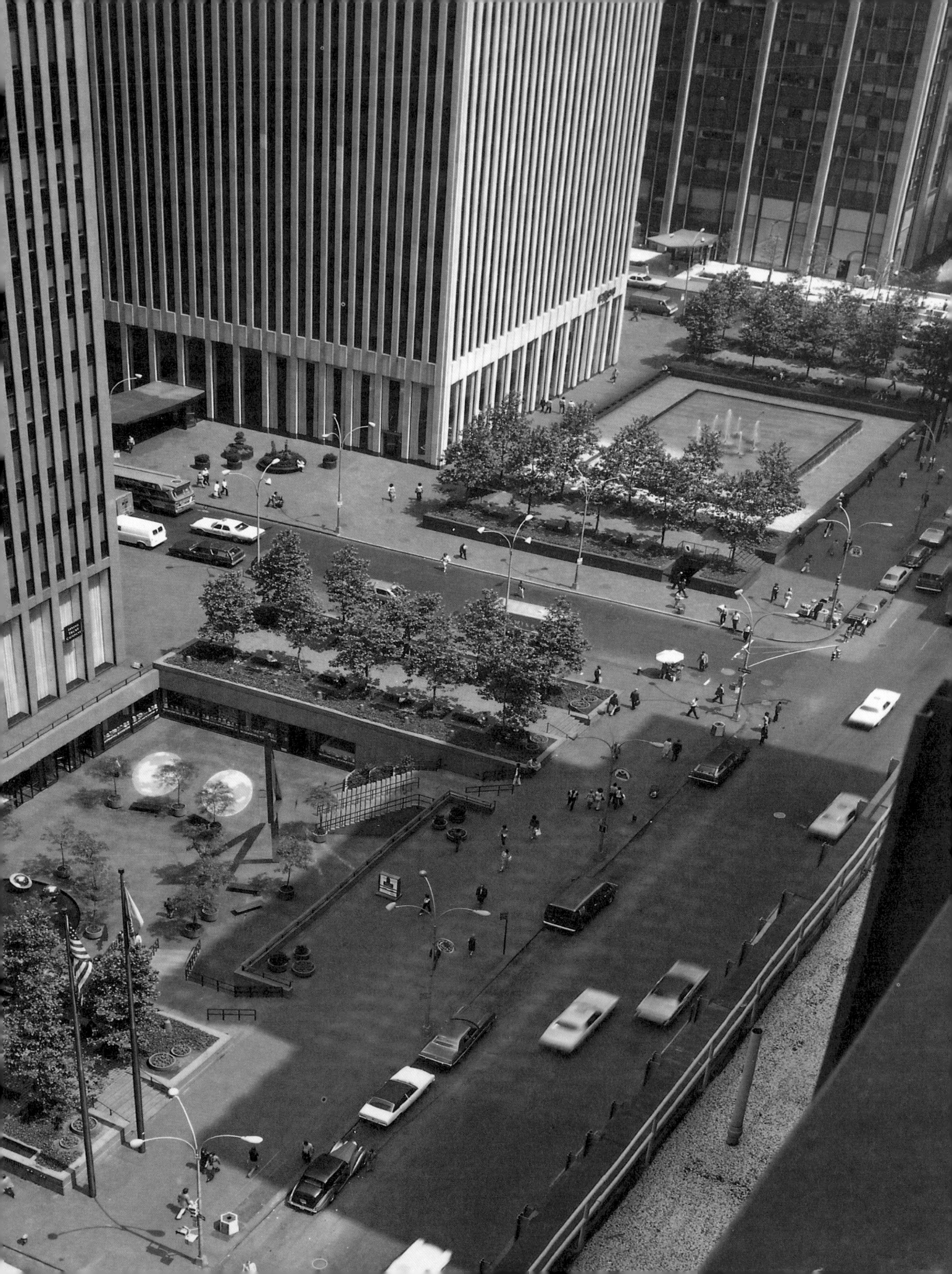

nence, and the compelling interest to overcome its difficulties that will keep it the Number One city of the world."[99]

The new building, a 1.8 million-square-foot, fifty-one-story, 645-foot-tall tower slab, would provide space for 5,000 office workers, most of whom had previously been squeezed into the landmark office building designed in 1931 by Raymond Hood at 330 West Forty-second Street; the remainder were drawn together from seven other locations in New York.[100] Designed by Harrison, Abramovitz & Harris, the red-granite-clad building occupied the blockfront on the west side of Sixth Avenue between Forty-eighth and Forty-ninth streets, a 100,000-square-foot site that extended approximately 500 feet west toward Seventh Avenue. The tower was set back 117 feet from Sixth Avenue to provide space for a plaza, sunk twelve feet below grade; off the plaza was a company-operated bookstore. A 152-seat planetarium originally planned for the plaza was abandoned when McGraw-Hill sold the company that was to run it. In its place a theater was built to house the multiscreen slide presentation *The New York Experience*, which, when it opened in 1973, was the first of a series of paeans to the city that poured forth in the 1970s and early 1980s as municipal fortunes ebbed and then began to flow again.[101] The principal feature of the plaza was Athelstan Spilhaus's stainless-steel-clad sculpture, *Sun Triangle*, which described the relationship between sun and earth at the solstices and the equinoxes. Wags interpreted the triangular sculpture rather differently—as an arrow pointing to the McGraw-Hill bookstore.

The exterior envelope of the McGraw-Hill Building, with its neutral, vertically striped window-wall system, was less than distinguished, as were the interiors reserved by McGraw-Hill for its own use (the company occupied about two-thirds of the building) and designed by the Office of Alfred Easton Poor. In 1973 James D. Morgan, an architect-journalist, evaluated the building in relationship to the company's former headquarters.[102] Castigating the company for accepting a predesigned building rather than commissioning one for its specific requirements as it had done in 1931, Morgan argued that the building was not well suited to the company's needs. It required not only that the offices be shoehorned into a predetermined configuration but also that such special corporate facilities as a cafeteria and an auditorium be squeezed into the limiting confines of the slab. In fact, a tower column had to be shifted five feet to accommodate the auditorium, which was located on the second floor of the seven-story "skirt" that surrounded the tower's western end.

As the building was under construction, a 1,225-square-foot mock-up of the new interiors was built in a Queens warehouse for employees to test. According to Morgan, many of the workers, who were used to the "unadorned and open spaces" of the Forty-second Street building, were disappointed with the model, which conveyed "too much of the anonymous feeling associated with the standard contemporary corporate office." Their doubts were confirmed when the twenty-three floors of interiors were installed, setting "a new standard of mediocrity for interior design." With its seemingly endless enclosed public corridors around the core, as well as a parallel system of corridors in the office areas themselves, the environment was, as Morgan put it, "Kafka-esque." For the top executive suite, on the nineteenth floor, and the executive dining rooms, on the fiftieth (designed by Ellen Lehman McCluskey Associates), the obsessive regularity of the typical floors and the "imposed privacy" of the office cubicles were abandoned in favor of lushly carpeted, generously proportioned spaces filled with comfortable seating and traditional-style furniture.[103] The new building's enormous lobby lacked the bravura and charm of Hood's modestly scaled, jukeboxlike

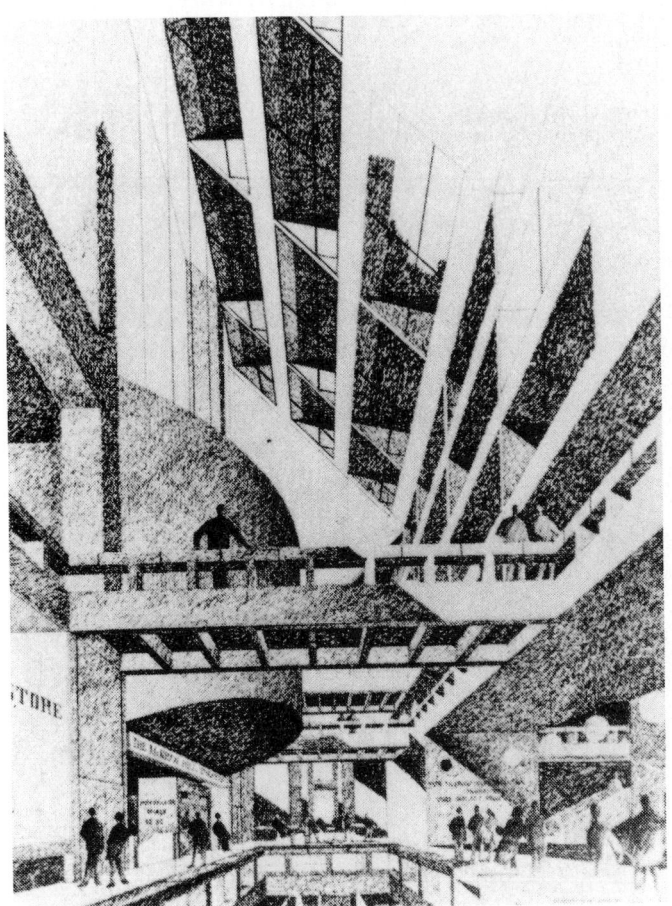

Left: View northwest of Sixth Avenue from West Forty-eighth Street showing, from left to right: McGraw-Hill Building (Harrison, Abramovitz & Harris, 1972), Exxon Building (Harrison, Abramovitz & Harris, 1971) and Time & Life Building (Harrison, Abramovitz & Harris, 1959). Stoller. ©ESTO

Above: Proposed pedestrian promenade west of XYZ Buildings. Urban Design Group, 1968. JB and NYC

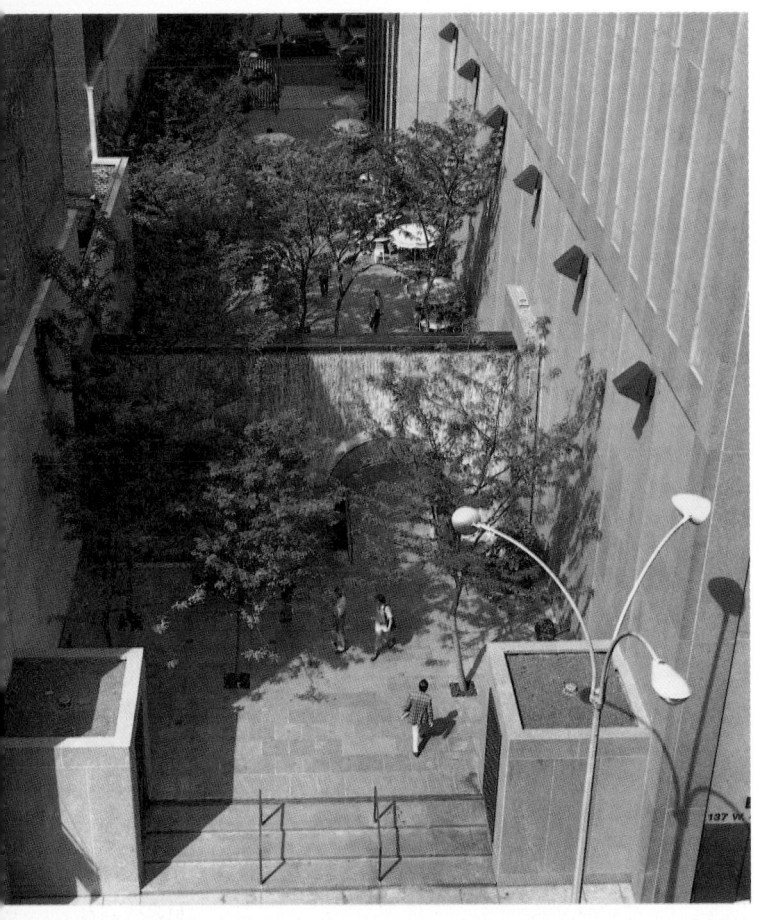

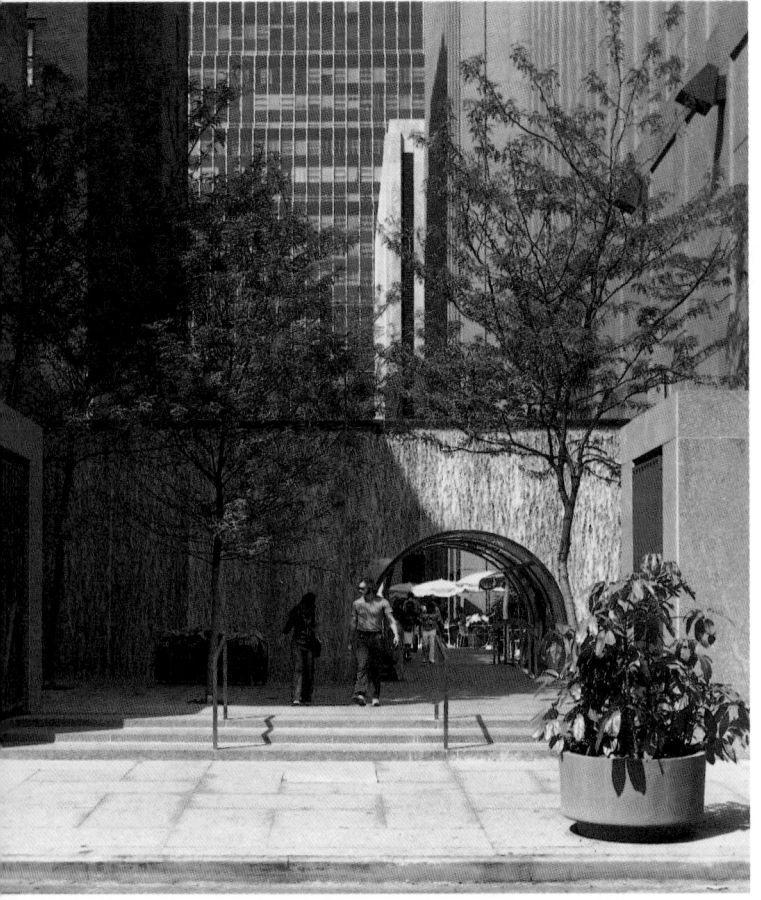

lobby. To contrast with the bright, icy whiteness of the Exxon Building's lobby across the street, the walls and floors of the McGraw-Hill Building's lobby were finished with a special dark red terrazzo, relieved here and there by strips of red Levanto marble decorated with quotations from Plato and John F. Kennedy.

Morgan felt that the new building was more than anything else "an expression of centralized authority," a tribute to the managers, who, producing no tangible product, felt the need to monumentalize themselves in order to assert their indispensability to the enterprise as a whole. "No longer is the building most important as a place where ideas are prepared for communication to the world," Morgan wrote. "These soaring office buildings are . . . management's playthings."[104]

In 1973 the third of the XYZ towers, 1211 Avenue of the Americas, between Forty-seventh and Forty-eighth streets, was occupied by the Celanese Corporation.[105] As anonymous as the McGraw-Hill Building, this 1.6 million-square-foot, forty-five-story building, designed by Harrison, Abramovitz & Harris, featured a projecting pavilion that closed its plaza along Forty-seventh Street and thereby marked the southern conclusion of the expansive, plaza-oriented urbanism of Rockefeller Center's westward expansion. Construction of the Celanese Building, which had been expected to get under way in 1967, was delayed by the refusal of several tenants to leave their apartments. William A. Reuben, an author who lived at 132 West Forty-eighth Street, claimed that he could not move until he finished the book he was working on—a study of Alger Hiss. Although he reveled in his "chance to hold up, even for a few minutes, a giant proposition" like the Celanese Building, Reuben finally agreed to move after he was paid $22,375.[106] The building was also delayed by Charles Dun Leavey, a doctoral candidate at New York University who occupied a two-room apartment at 117 West Forty-seventh Street. At first Dun Leavey said simply that he wanted to stay on the same piece of land where he was living, and that he would like an apartment in the new building. Later, in keeping with the spirit of late 1960s social activism, Dun Leavey said that he had no intention of vacating because he was "setting a good, pugnacious, stubborn example of social effectiveness, social usefulness for the needy, ignorant, insecure, helpless tenants throughout the city of New York."[107] Rockefeller Center, Inc. ultimately prevailed before the city's Rent Control Commission, however, and Dun Leavey was forced to move.

Although the Urban Design Group did not succeed in creating the new shopping street it had hoped for, a network of midblock pedestrian ways near the western end of each site was incorporated in the final plan. The first, running behind the Exxon Building, was designed along the lines of Robert Zion's Paley Park (see "Fifty-third Street," below). But where Paley Park was a destination point, Exxon's park was a passageway, lacking intimacy or spatial coherence. McGraw-Hill's minipark, with its circular tunnel cut through a waterwall, was far more appealing; its clear sense of spatial closure made it an immediate success as an outdoor lunchroom. Celanese's passageway, which featured an oddly scaled, vaguely anthropomorphic construction by Ibram Lassaw entitled *Pantheon*, was extremely bleak.

While the final result of the XYZ plan was in no way comparable to Rockefeller Center's complexly orchestrated spatial, functional and aesthetic synthesis, it was nonetheless a bold, distinct and vital achievement. As Gerald Allen observed in *Architectural Record* in 1974, the plazas and the buildings that abutted them "are not—as some people have hastily concluded—inept examples of architecture and urban design, though some may not like them." The plazas, he pointed out, "are certainly not unpeopled," and the buildings "make a powerful and perhaps even unique impression on the mind; together they make a *place* in the city that is not the same as any other place." Allen was not blind to the weaknesses of the new complex: "True, there is no sense of comfortable enclosure here, as there is at Rockefeller Plaza, and these buildings make minimal accommodation to the street or the people on it; their towers seem simply to crash into the ground. All of the imagery, too, is rigorously impersonal." But he ventured an explanation as to why the group worked: "Perhaps the key to success here is that whatever these buildings are doing to the public space of the city they are doing it together. They are not breaking up an urban fabric. Whether or not we like it, they are making one all their own."[108]

Alan Balfour, in his 1978 book on Rockefeller Center, took a much more negative view of the buildings:

The contrast between the original development and the extension west of Sixth Avenue invites numerous comparisons: benign paternalism to the east, bureaucratic imperialism to the west; a unified family on one side, a row of caricatured corporate headquarters on the other; to the east a powerful yet humane architecture sensitive to light, to air, to scale, a product of romantic functionalism and creative opportunism, in contrast on the west to a one-dimensional, good taste, gift-wrapped architecture, developed to contain the greatest amount of space permissible and through improved technology able to ignore all natural constraints. The buildings to the west satisfy broad commercial functions. Even though developed and owned in partnership with major tenants, corporations of widely different natures, this is simply the architecture of the retail space trade, recognizing no idiosyncratic needs. Each building is a general-issue product of bureaucracies that differ only in name, unconstrained by history or nature.[109]

The XYZ buildings were perhaps viewed most negatively by Nelson Rockefeller, Wallace Harrison's life-long patron, who criticized their design and virtually broke off what had been one of this century's most productive collaborations between architect and patron.[110]

Though the XYZ buildings were uniformly bureaucratic, together with their plazas they constituted the liveliest and most "user-friendly" stretch of the entire rebuilt avenue. This was abundantly clear when the complex was compared to the rash of buildings that had been constructed in a burst in the late 1960s and early 1970s. These buildings, while strengthening the avenue's status as a corporate address, did little to enliven its appearance or its street scene. Emery Roth & Sons' 1.5 million-square-foot Burlington House (1969), a fifty-story building at 1345 Avenue of the Americas, on the west blockfront between Fifty-fourth and Fifty-fifth streets, replaced Joseph Urban's Ziegfeld Theater of 1927.[111] Burlington, the textile firm, was the principal tenant on fourteen of the blockbuster building's floors. A sheer tower clad in glass tinted dark gray, Burlington House sat behind a block-long plaza facing Sixth Avenue, ornamented by two reflecting pools, each holding a golf-ball-like sphere that sent out streams of water. To its west, a midblock passageway separated the tower from a new 1,151-seat movie theater, the Ziegfeld, the first such large-capacity facility built since Radio City Music Hall.[112] Just south of the building's main lobby was the Mill, a promotional exhibition sponsored by Burlington and designed by Chermayeff & Geismar, the graphic and exhibition design firm.[113] The exhibition, occupying three floors, was divided into three sections—the first showing the raw materials used in textile production; the second focusing on the machines that did the weaving; and the third displaying the products

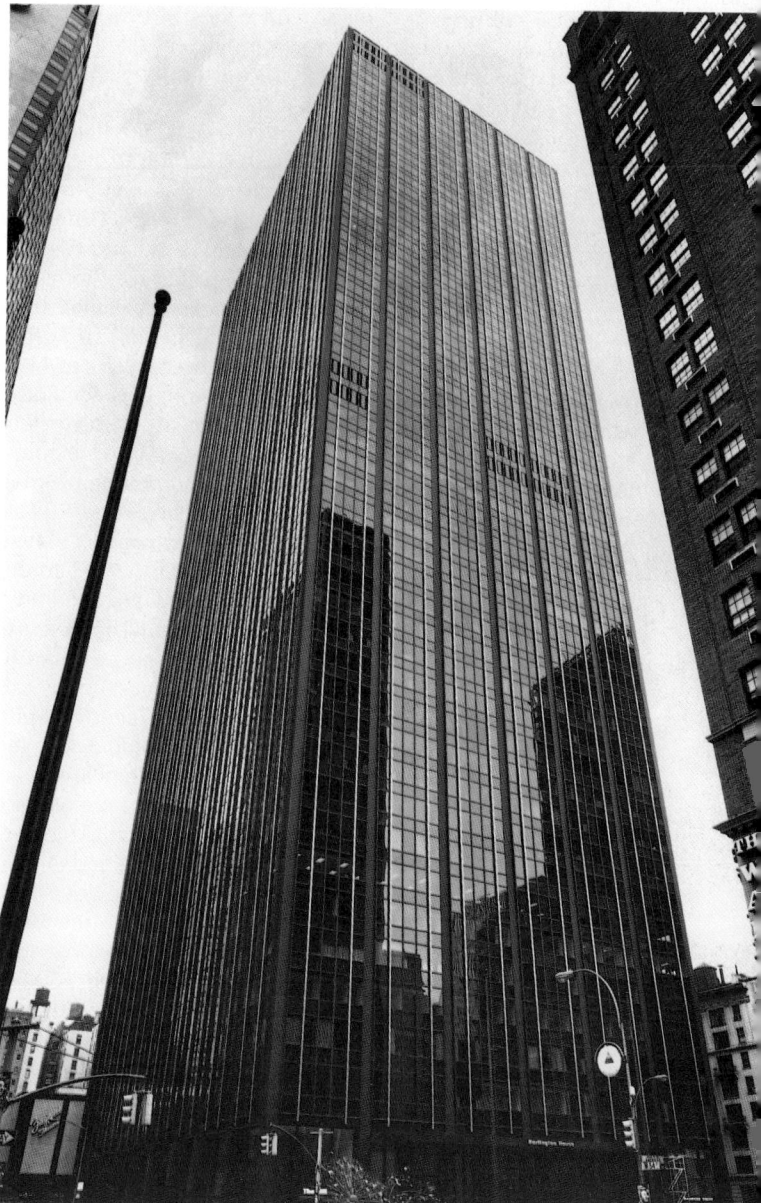

Top left: Pedestrian passageway west of McGraw-Hill Building, between Fifth and Sixth avenues, West Forty-eighth to West Forty-ninth Street. Harrison, Abramovitz & Harris, 1972. View to the north. Stoller. ©ESTO

Bottom left: Pedestrian passageway west of McGraw-Hill Building. View to the north. Stoller. ©ESTO

Above: Burlington House, 1345 Sixth Avenue, West Fifty-fourth to West Fifty-fifth Street. Emery Roth & Sons, 1969. View to the northwest. Wurts. MCNY

themselves—all presented on sixty-nine rear-screen slide projectors flashing hundreds of images on different-sized screens. Visitors passed from phase to phase on the longest moving walkway east of the Mississippi.

In 1971 Emery Roth & Sons completed the thirty-five-story, 293,000-square-foot Capitol-EMI Building, at 1370 Avenue of the Americas, on the southeast corner of Fifty-sixth Street.[114] Another Roth banality, 1133 Avenue of the Americas (1969), on the west blockfront between Forty-third and Forty-fourth streets, consisted of an 878,000-square-foot tower that rose forty-five stories.[115] The building's principal entrance was framed by a one-story base housing a bank, a recording studio and a photography gallery. The Roths' J. P. Stevens Tower (1971), at 1185 Avenue of the Americas, on the west blockfront between Forty-sixth and Forty-seventh streets, was a forty-story tower that yielded 850,000 square feet of rentable space for its developers, the Fisher Brothers, and also contained two auditoriums for the American Place Theater (see "Times Square," below).[116]

Plans were announced in 1967 for yet another speculative office colossus on Sixth Avenue, number 1166 (1974), to occupy the east side of the avenue between Forty-fifth and Forty-sixth streets.[117] Skidmore, Owings & Merrill's all-black forty-four-story building, based on the same firm's successful 140 Broadway (see chapter 3), was designed as a pure tower, almost square in plan, slightly set back from the avenue but with a generously sized plaza running through the midblock to the east. The decision to place the plaza in the midblock was arrived at not for aesthetic or environmental reasons but as a solution to a problem of real estate: the Tishman Realty & Construction Company's need to go forward with the building, despite their inability to come to terms with the owners of a small five-story loft building at 56 West Forty-sixth Street, who refused an offer of $1.34 million in 1969 for a building they had paid $140,000 for in 1963. Tishman instructed SOM to move the tower to the western part of the site and to design a plaza that kept the holdout building isolated in its midst. The delays caused by the negotiations proved very expensive: when 1166 was ready for tenants in 1974, none were to be found except at a rental rate below Tishman's break-even costs. After one significant potential corporate tenant, General Telephone & Electronics, changed its mind about the building and even about New York, moving its offices to Stamford, Connecticut, the building became the city's most notable white elephant, sitting empty for two years and draining its developer of $1 million a month. In the spring of 1976, with no significant potential tenant on the horizon, Tishman and its bankers, Citibank, abandoned the building, a glaring reminder of the city's sorry state of affairs. The project reverted to the New York State Employees' Retirement System, which held the mortgage on the land.

When the city's fortunes began to rise in the late 1970s, the new owner was ultimately able to attract tenants, including the International Paper Company, which became the building's principal tenant and undertook the completion of the plaza after the owners of the holdout building settled in 1978 for a mere $850,000. By this time architectural tastes had changed, and the company hired landscape architect Hideo Sasaki to transform the plaza, originally conceived by SOM as an austere and scantily landscaped space, into a park called International Paper Plaza. Although little planting was possible because most of the plaza was built over a deep basement, the site of the demolished holdout building provided a significant area that could be filled with earth to support large trees.

Before World War II the midtown stretch of Madison Avenue featured a broad but sophisticated mix of uses. The structures ranged from office buildings such as Starrett & Van Vleck's Canadian Pacific Building (1921), which contained A. D. Pickering's Fifth Church of Christ Scientist (1922) in its base, to LaFarge & Morris's Brooks Brothers men's specialty store (1917), on the northwest corner of Forty-fourth Street, to large hotels like George B. Post & Sons' Roosevelt (1924), on the east blockfront between Forty-fourth and Forty-fifth streets, and Warren & Wetmore's Ritz-Carlton (see below).[1] In the late 1940s this mix was dramatically altered by redevelopment that also robbed the avenue of some notable landmarks. By 1961 a survey of Manhattan corporations conducted by the real estate firm of Williams & Company, Inc. revealed that Madison Avenue, though still home to some of the city's most important men's clothing shops, was ranked behind only Park and Fifth avenues in terms of its desirability as an office location.[2] Ten years later Ada Louise Huxtable would warn of the potential effect of this increased corporate building: "What is threatened by the inexorable course of New York real estate is one of the finest pedestrian streets in the world and a fortuitous example of first-rate urbanism."[3]

In 1951, when William Zeckendorf established himself as the leader of Webb & Knapp, the developers, he renovated the company's headquarters, the Knapp Building, at 383–385 Madison Avenue, a stolid office building designed by Cross & Cross (1922–23).[4] Demonstrating his philosophy of "adding ideas to real estate," Zeckendorf renovated the lobby to include a sloping ceiling honeycomb of light containing 1,920 bulbs that could "produce 500 slowly rotating colors, and spell out such complex visual symbols as the cancer sword."[5] The lobby redesign was the work of Albert W. Lewis and Rudolph C. P. Boehler of Webb & Knapp, architects, and Paxton, Krueger & Associates, in association with the design firm of Norman Bel Geddes, and Rollo Gillespie Williams, who invented the "Rollo-Color" illumination system. Lewis Mumford found the lighting an example of "studied irrelevance": "If this were the lobby of a motion-picture theater or a night club, these lights would be charming and their use functional, but what they are doing in an office building I cannot begin to guess, since at night, when the lights are at their best, few people make use of the building or even pass by."[6] Despite Mumford's reservations, the lighting proved an enormous attraction, turning the combined buildings, according to Architectural Forum, into "the most talked-about, stared-at buildings" in New York.[7] Also part of Zeckendorf's renovation was the redesign of his own offices by I. M. Pei (see chapter 6).

The works of Emery Roth & Sons, while ubiquitous throughout postwar midtown, thoroughly dominated Madison Avenue. In 1950 the Roths completed the Look Building, at 488 Madison Avenue.[8] Perhaps the firm's best postwar work, it not only defined the aesthetics and economics of market-rate office-building design, but established the Roths, and the building's developers, Percy and Harold Uris, as the premier exponents of the new approach. Occupying a west blockfront site between Fifty-first and Fifty-second streets—the former home of Cathedral College, which had taken over the Boys Orphan Asylum (1893)—the twenty-three-story Look Building, with its symmetrical setbacks and strip windows, was instantly seen as a marketplace victory for International Style Modernism. As Architectural Forum put it when the project was announced in 1949, "Advocates of the strip window can chalk up another recruit to their ranks."[9] It was also a victory for construction efficiency in the service of economics: three seven-men riveting gangs rushed to erect the steel framework, topping the steel out in twelve weeks, despite the complexities of the building's curved corners.

While the Roths' earlier 505 Park Avenue had explored the aesthetic possibilities of horizontal strip windows, the designers had hedged their bets by bracketing them with strong vertical elements. The emphasis of the Look Building, however, was purely horizontal, with columns suppressed behind alternating bands of metal-framed glass and white brick. Lewis Mumford argued that the use of strip windows, which had originally been developed by factory engineers and early Modernists largely to bring light evenly into the full depth of a workplace, was compromised here by floors so deep that much of the space in the building was without benefit of natural light at all. Moreover, the structural implication of the strip window—that there was a column-free perimeter and a cantilevered exterior wall—was also falsified in the Look Building; Mumford acknowledged, however, that without this bit of visual chicanery an inflexible perimeter space would likely result from cantilevers of just a few feet. Although Mumford characterized it as a "white whale of a building . . . that raises its hump," he said the Look Building offered "some photogenic passages in compensation." He praised, for example, the effect of the "curving waves of black and white" dashing against the smooth unbroken rear wall of Best's department store in bright sunlight, but concluded that, "like so many good subjects for photography, it is almost innocent of architectural intention."[10]

In 1949, with construction under way on the Look Building, plans were announced for the Roths' 575 Madison Avenue, on the east blockfront between Fifty-sixth and Fifty-seventh streets.[11] This building was a variation on the Look design, but it had square corners and asymmetrical setbacks, which resulted from the fact that Fifty-seventh was a wide street and Fifty-sixth was not. The twenty-six-story office building replaced J. D. Leland & Company's American Art Association and Gallery, which had housed the auctioneers Parke-Bernet from 1937 until they moved to their new headquarters farther up Madison Avenue at Seventy-sixth Street (see chapter 11).[12] In 1950 plans were announced to demolish Warren & Wetmore's Ritz-Carlton Hotel (1910), on the west blockfront between Forty-sixth and Forty-seventh streets, to make way for another Roth building, 380 Madison Avenue (1953).[13] The new 600,000-square-foot, twenty-five-story building was built above a five-level garage with space for 600 cars. Again the Roths came close to repeating the Look Building, but squaring the corners. The building's symmetrical elevation on Madison Avenue, with broad recessed center and projecting wings, rose past three setbacks to a stubby three-story tower.

The diagrammatic formula of the Look Building became stale very quickly as the Roths repeated it in building after building. In 1954, for the developer Samuel Rudin, the Roth firm developed plans for the awkwardly massed, twenty-four-story, 200,000-square-foot 415 Madison Avenue, on the northeast corner of Forty-eighth Street, replacing a two-story taxpayer erected in 1937.[14] In 1956 the Roths were at work on 635 Madison Avenue, on the northeast corner of Fifty-ninth Street, a building for developer Joseph P. Blitz that replaced a four-story building with nineteen stories of offices housing 130,000 square feet of rentable space.[15] In the same year, again for Blitz, the Roth office designed the seventeen-story, 114,000-square-foot 545 Madison Avenue, on the southeast corner of Fifty-fifth

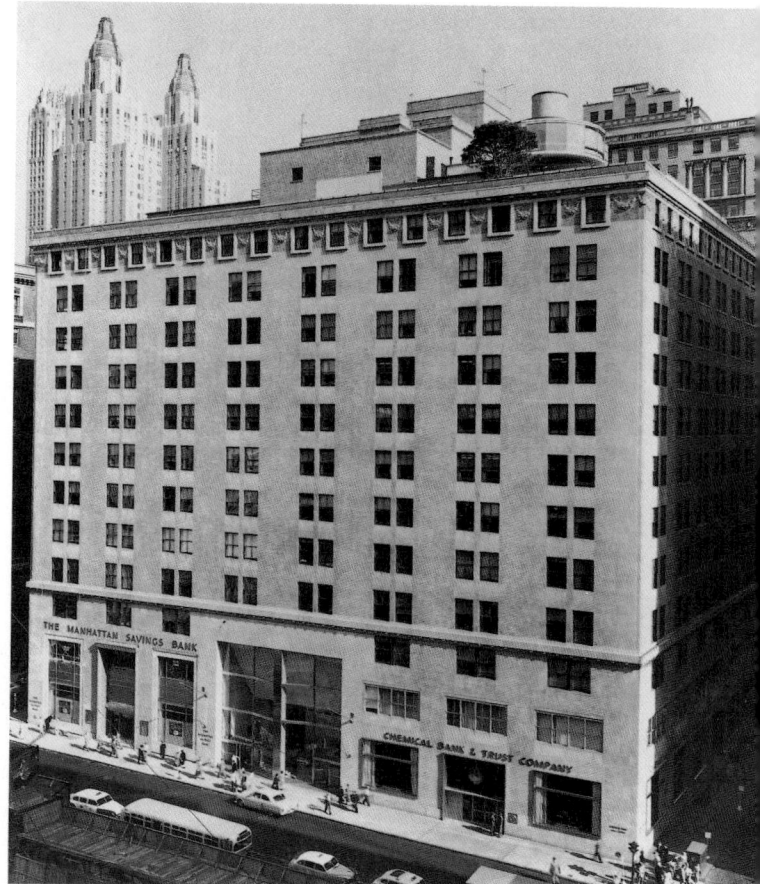

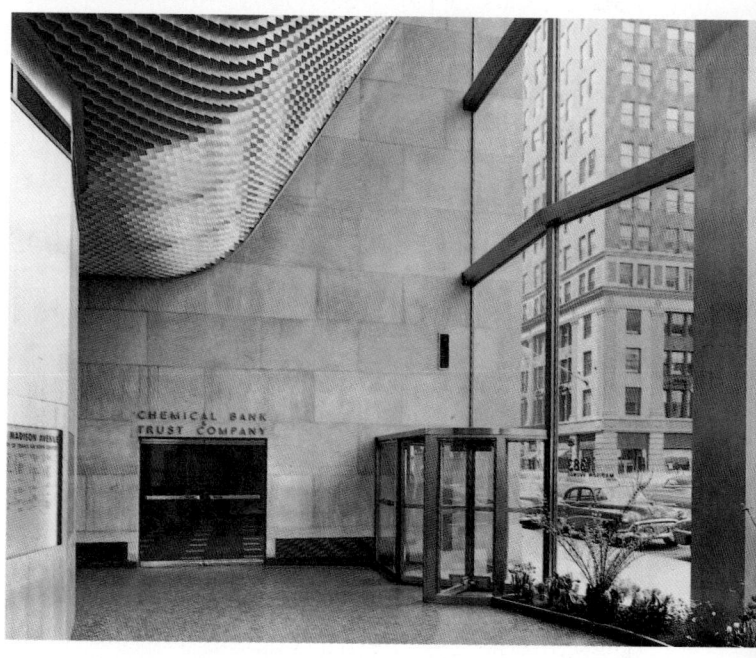

Top: Knapp Building, 383–385 Madison Avenue, East Forty-sixth to East Forty-seventh Street. Cross & Cross, 1922–23. View to the northeast showing entrance and lobby renovation (Webb & Knapp; Paxton, Krueger & Associates in association with Norman Bel Geddes; and Rollo Gillespie Williams, 1951) and Webb & Knapp offices (I. M. Pei in association with William Lescaze, 1952) on the roof. Wurts. MCNY

Bottom: Knapp Building. Entrance and lobby renovation. Wurts. MCNY

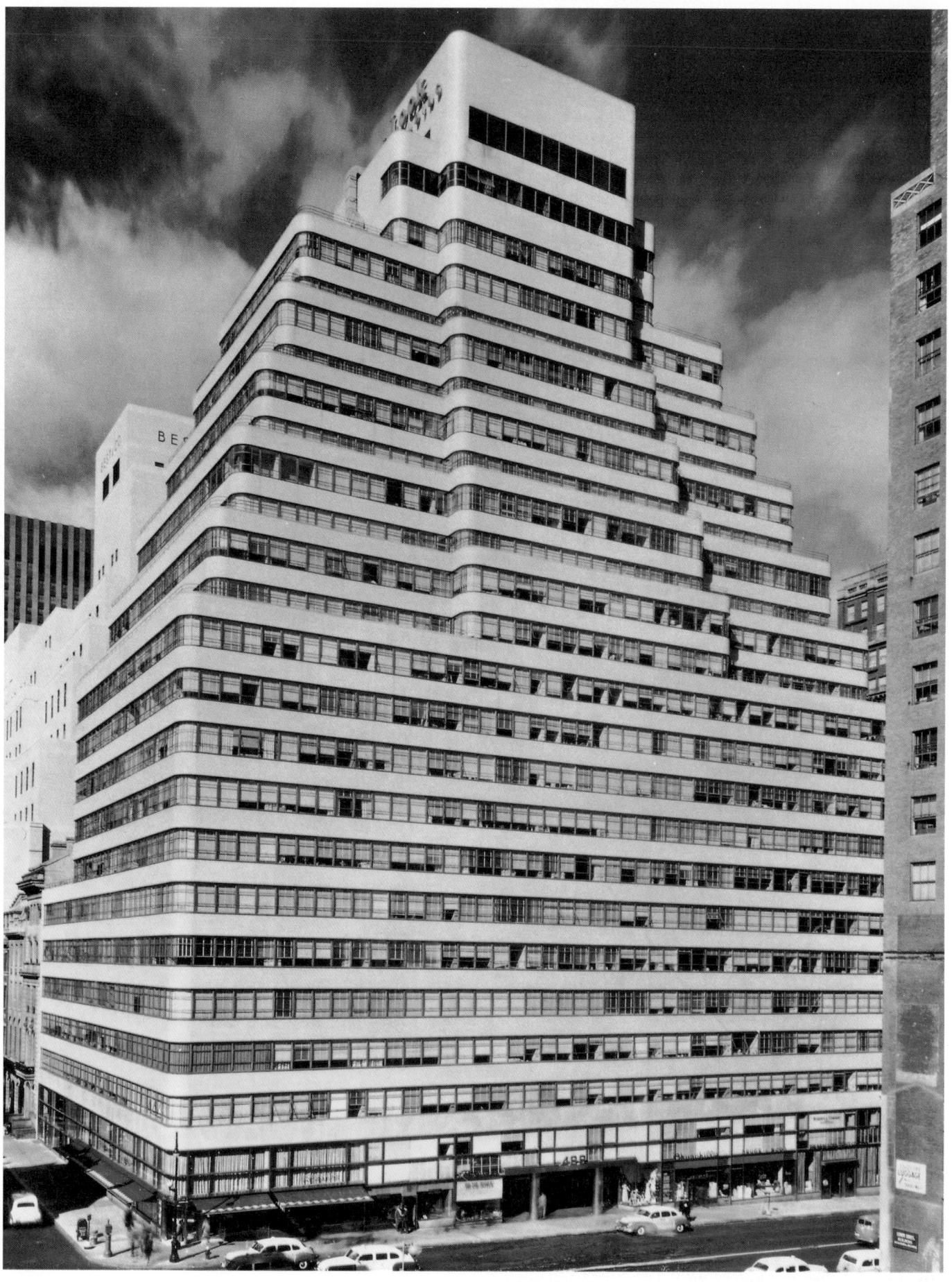

Street, a horizontal composition that featured alternating bands of strip windows and white brick.[16] In 1958 they completed 660 Madison Avenue, a twenty-two-story building at the southwest corner of Sixty-first Street.[17] It was developed by J. Paul Getty, who owned the adjoining Pierre Hotel, to which it was connected at the ground, second and third floors, providing the hotel with expanded catering facilities, including a new ballroom.

In the late 1950s the Roths, no doubt sensing that the banded International Style box was becoming a cliché, tried a new direction. Their 600 Madison Avenue, on the southwest corner of Fifty-eighth Street, a twenty-five-story, 315,000-square-foot building, featured an aluminum-and-glass curtain wall that reflected the influence of the Seagram Building.[18] By the time the building was completed in 1965, however, this approach also seemed old hat. The Roths followed this with 437 Madison Avenue (1967), a forty-story, 712,000-square-foot skyscraper that occupied the east blockfront between Forty-ninth and Fiftieth streets.[19] It replaced a number of buildings, including Robert W. Lyons's Hotel New Weston, on the southeast corner of Fiftieth Street, built in 1930 on land that had been part of Columbia College's midtown campus.[20] The 700-room New Weston, particularly popular with British visitors and with the literary crowd, had also been home to the Vassar Club. For 437 Madison, the Roths placed a twenty-four-story tower on a fourteen-story base that was set back from the building line on all four sides. Here the architects not only departed from the strip window of their postwar work but also eschewed Miesian prototypes to venture a signature statement: they employed a curtain wall that alternated dark bands of glass with vertical concrete strips and created a lobby facade that suggested the International Style Classicism of Lincoln Center's principal buildings. With their twenty-two-story, 138,000-square-foot Pan Ocean Building (1971), at 645 Madison Avenue, on the southeast corner of Sixtieth Street, the Roths returned to a less self-conscious Seagram-inspired curtain-wall formula.[21]

The Roth firm's principal rival was the office of Sylvan and Robert Bien, whose even more formulaic designs included the boxlike 625 Madison Avenue (1956), on the east blockfront between Fifty-eighth and Fifty-ninth streets, in which six stories were added to the ten-story Plaza Building (Sloan & Robertson, 1930) and the entire structure reclad with a gridded aluminum-and-glass curtain wall.[22] A more typical effort of the Biens was 655 Madison Avenue (1950), on the northeast corner of Sixtieth Street, a twenty-four-story, 170,000-square-foot, aluminum-and-glass design that rose sheer from a base of Norwegian granite for eleven stories before beginning a series of setbacks.[23] Exceptions to the firm's typical level of competent mediocrity were 260 and 261 Madison Avenue, on the west and east blockfronts between Thirty-eighth and Thirty-ninth streets.[24] Designed by Sylvan Bien in 1952 and 1954, these buildings formed a pair that, although not identically massed, gave the street an unusual consistency. So quintessentially "corporate" was number 260 that the editors of *Life* magazine chose it as the subject of a profile on New York office life.[25]

Madison Avenue's four other remaining new buildings were 477 Madison Avenue, 330 Madison Avenue (see "Forty-second Street," below) and 540 Madison Avenue, all designed by Kahn & Jacobs, and 555 Madison Avenue, designed by John M. Kokkins and Morris Lapidus. The twenty-three-story, 227,000-square-foot 477 Madison Avenue (1953), on the northeast corner of Fifty-first Street, replaced five townhouses that once belonged to William K. Vanderbilt, Mrs. O. H. P. Belmont, Mrs. Louise Dickey and Arthur Brisbane.[26] By the 1940s these

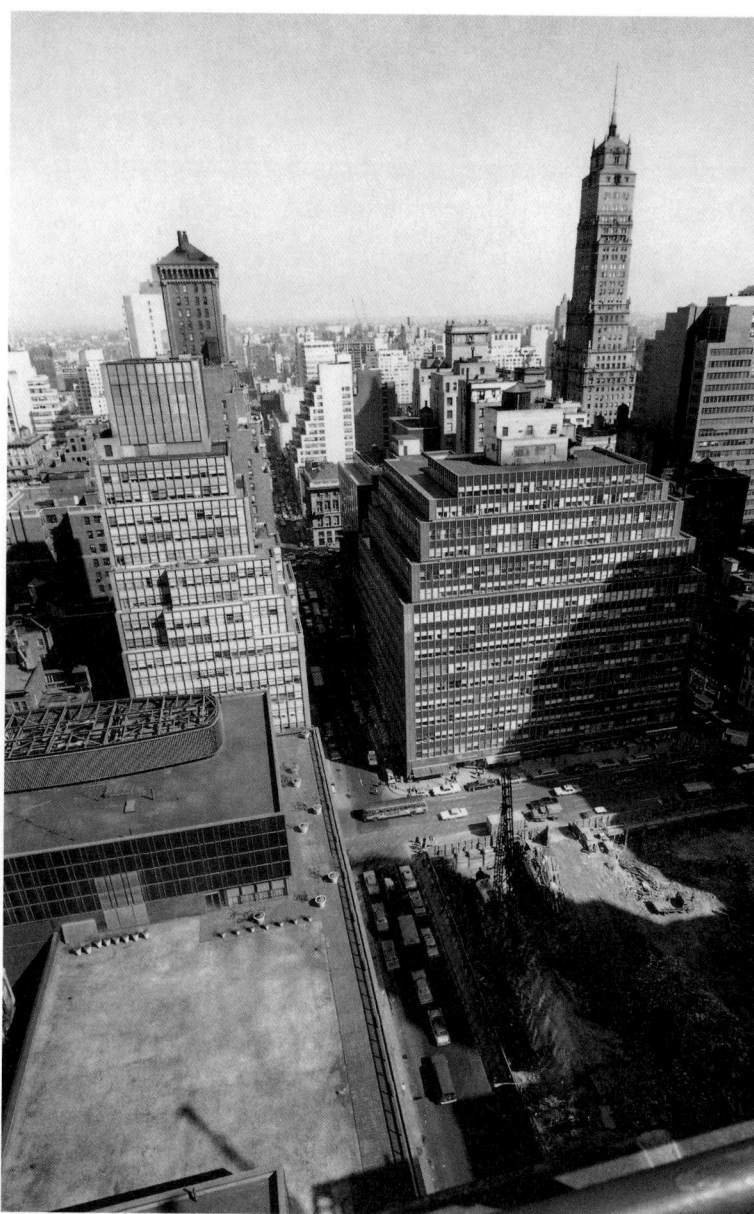

Left: Look Building, 488 Madison Avenue, East Fifty-first to East Fifty-second Street. Emery Roth & Sons, 1950. View to the northwest. Wurts. MCNY

Above: View to the west of east midtown showing 635 Madison Avenue (Emery Roth & Sons, 1956), on the left, and 625 Madison Avenue (Sylvan and Robert Bien, 1956), on the right. In the foreground is the roof of the CIT Building (Harrison & Abramovitz, 1958). OMH

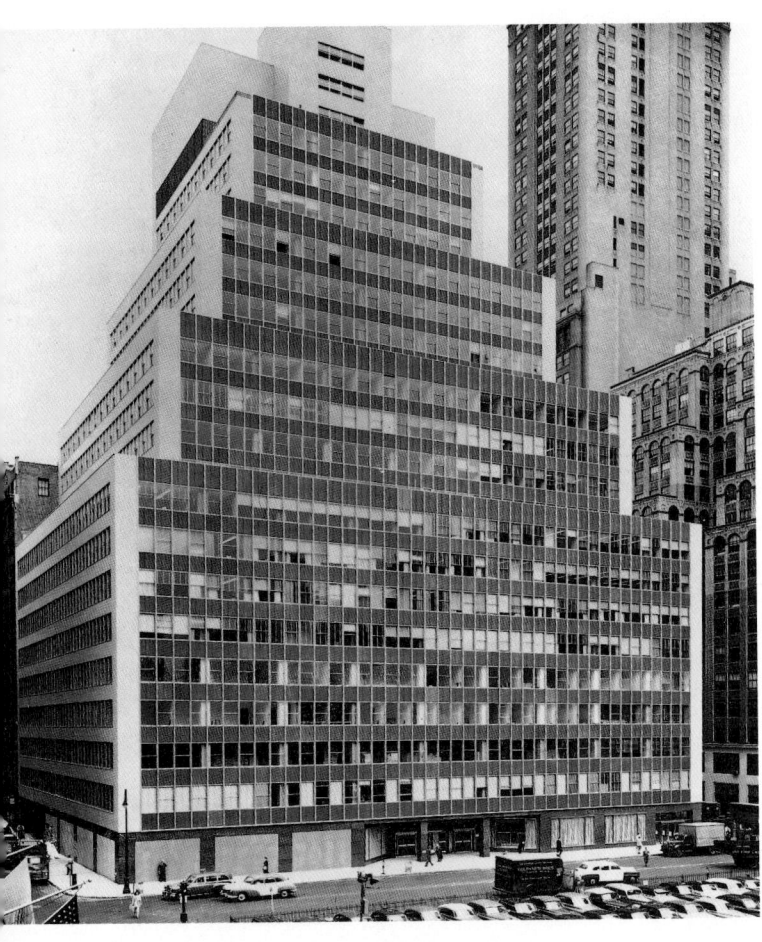

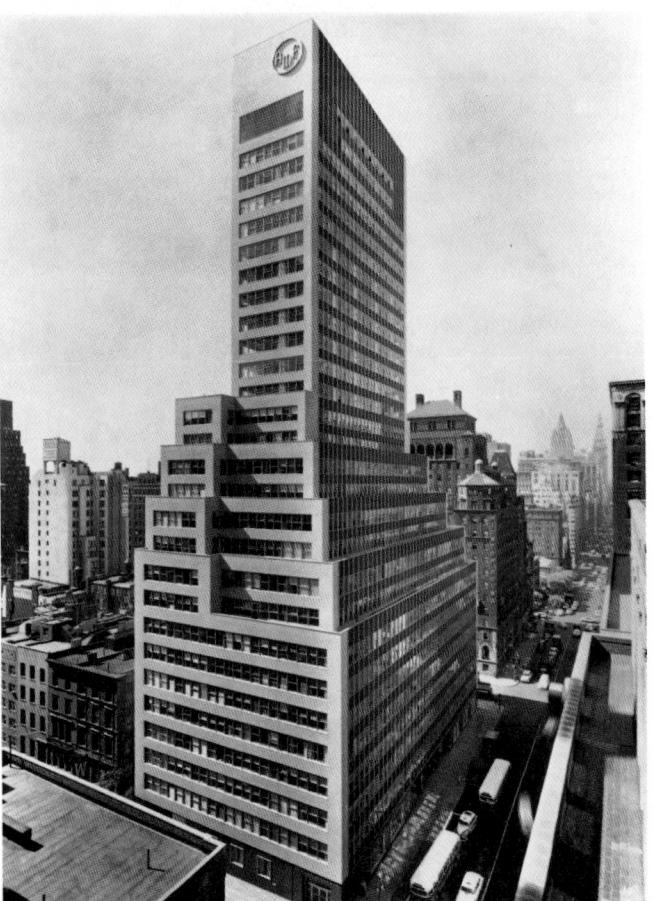

properties belonged to the Archdiocese of New York, which moved into the Villard Houses (see chapter 16) after the townhouses were demolished in 1950. The Korean War delayed the project and the site was used as a parking lot for two years. Kahn & Jacobs's design, distinctly inferior to the firm's earlier postwar office buildings, awkwardly combined a base building clad in a grid of vertical structural elements and suppressed spandrels with a ribbon-windowed wedding cake and a setback upper element. The same firm's 540 Madison Avenue (1970), on the southwest corner of Fifty-fifth Street, was a conventional thirty-seven-story, 231,000-square-foot, slablike shaft clad in dark-tinted glass and featuring black-colored mullions and spandrel panels.[27] Another conventional, anonymous office block, despite the participation of the normally flamboyant Morris Lapidus, was 555 Madison Avenue (1961), on the southeast corner of Fifty-sixth Street.[28] The thirty-two-story, 354,000-square-foot building occupied an L-shaped parcel that wrapped around the seventeen-story Winslow Hotel, which occupied the northeast corner of Fifty-fifth Street; the building also had frontage on Fifty-fifth Street.

Madison Avenue Mall

In 1971, reflecting widespread concern about the increasing pedestrian and vehicular congestion plaguing midtown Manhattan and the decline of Madison Avenue as a sophisticated shopping street, the Office of Midtown Planning and Development, headed by Jaquelin Robertson, proposed the creation of a permanent pedestrian mall extending along the avenue from Forty-second to Fifty-seventh Street.[29] The plan, which would prove highly controversial, had been preceded by several similar planning efforts and proposals, including one directed by the urban planner Robert C. Weinberg in 1961, which called for the creation of a pedestrian mall between Fifth and Sixth avenues from Forty-second to Fifty-ninth Street; the mall was to be named 5½ Way.[30]

But the idea of the Madison Avenue Mall did not come from the unrealized plan for 5½ Way. It was inspired by the first celebration of Earth Day, April 22, 1970, when for two hours Fifth Avenue between Fourteenth and Fifty-ninth streets was transformed into a pedestrian mall.[31] The public response was overwhelmingly positive; the avenue's retailers, however, were divided as to whether the ban on motor traffic helped or hindered business. Prompted by the public's response, Mayor Lindsay extended the moratorium in restricted form, closing the avenue to traffic between Forty-second and Fifty-seventh streets during four consecutive Saturdays in July. The following April, in observation of Earth Week, Mayor Lindsay imposed a motor traffic ban on Madison Avenue between Forty-second and Fifty-seventh streets to be in effect daily between noon and 2 P.M.[32]

Merchants gave the lunchtime pedestrianization program mixed reviews; in response to the allegation leveled by some merchants that many of the people who flocked to the mall were not the type to spend money, the editors of *Progressive Architecture* quipped, "they do—on Frisbees."[33] Whatever the effect on retail business, Mayor Lindsay pronounced the program "a spectacular success."[34] Two years earlier Lindsay had requested that the Office of Midtown Planning and Development conduct a study of area traffic; in 1970 Van Ginkel Associates of Montreal, who had been hired as consultants, published their findings in a report titled *Movement in Midtown*.[35] The report bluntly stated: "The cumulative effect of overloaded systems is

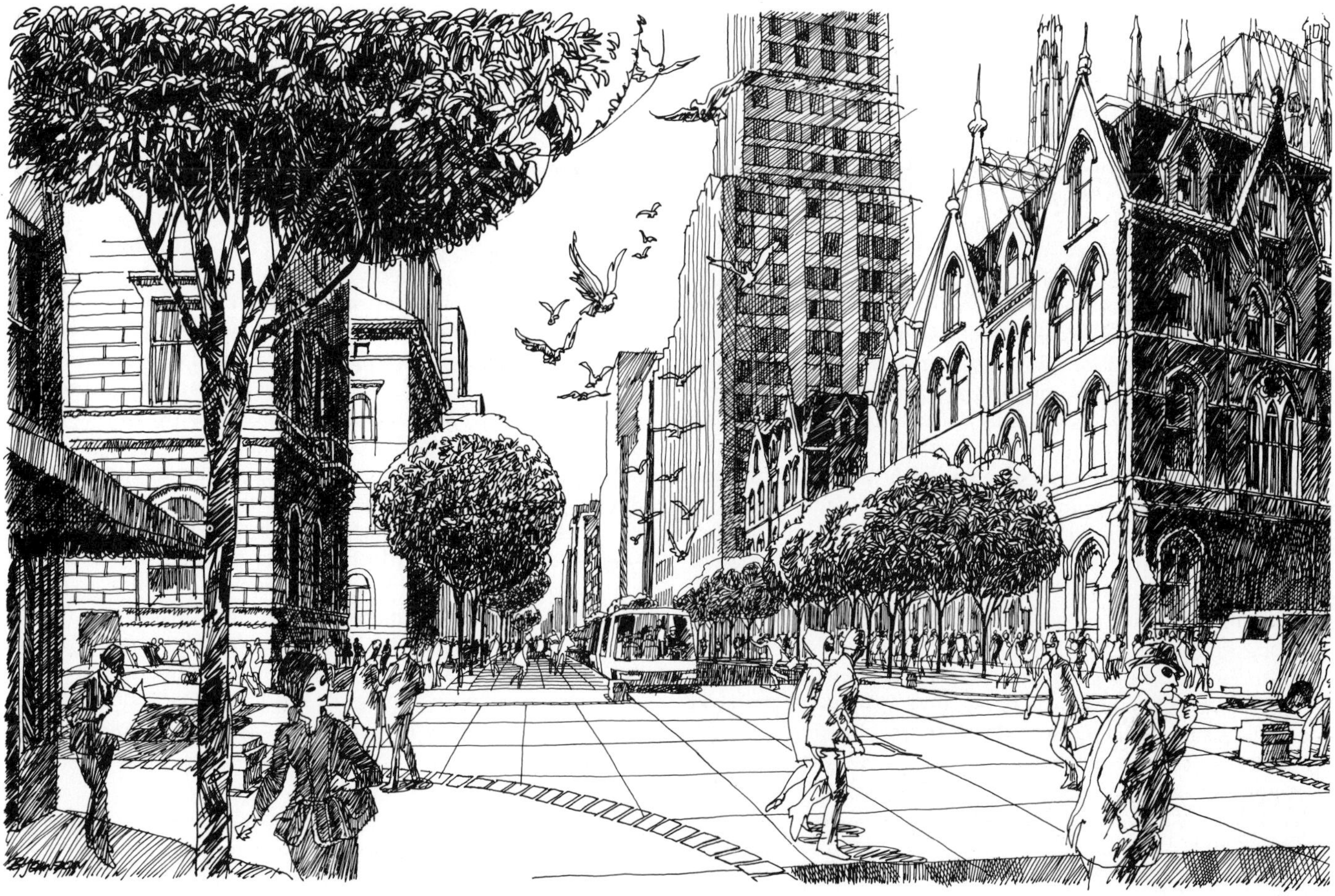

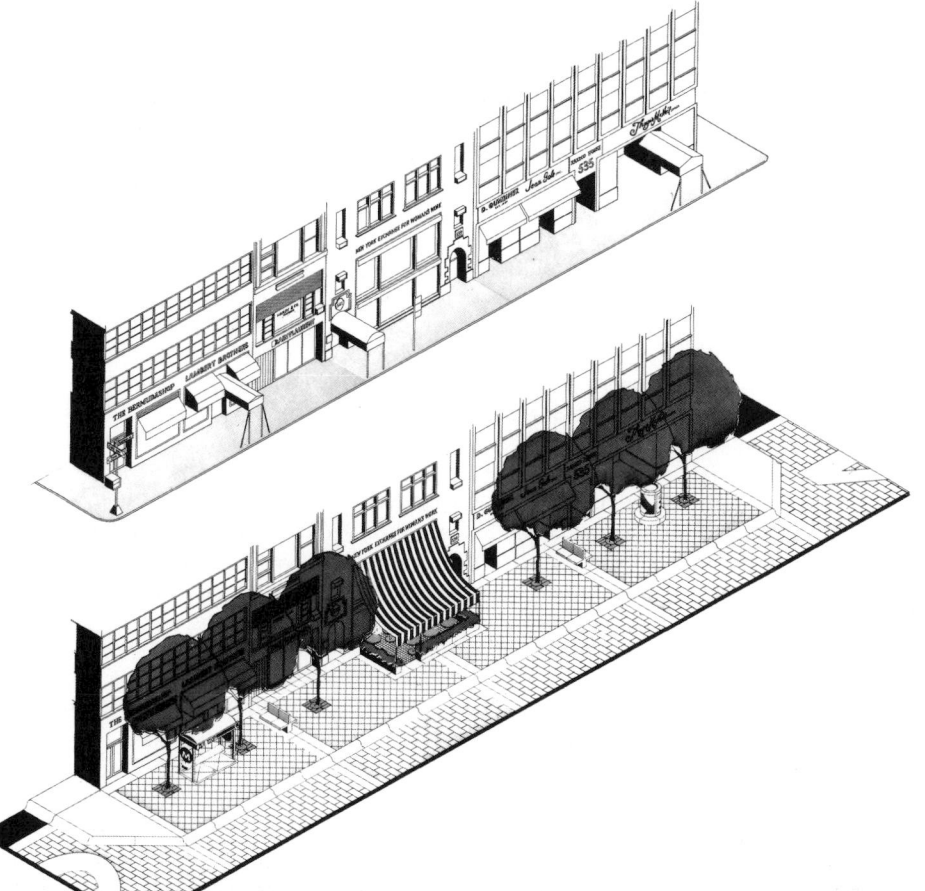

Top far left: 260 Madison Avenue, East
Thirty-eighth to East Thirty-ninth Street.
Sylvan and Robert Bien, 1952. View to
the northwest. Wurts. MCNY

Bottom far left: 261 Madison Avenue,
East Thirty-eighth to East Thirty-ninth
Street. Sylvan and Robert Bien, 1952.
View to the southeast. Wurts. MCNY

Above: Proposed Madison Avenue Mall,
East Forty-second to East Fifty-seventh
Street. Office of Midtown Planning and
Development with Van Ginkel
Associates, 1971. View to the south from
East Fifty-first Street. Sketch by B. Johnson
for Van Ginkel Associates. Prepared for
the City of New York, Office of Midtown
Planning and Development. NYC

Left: Proposed Madison Avenue Mall.
Axonometrics showing existing east
blockfront between East Fifty-fourth and
East Fifty-fifth streets, above, and same
blockfront with completed mall, below.
Drawings by Don Miles, City of New
York, Office of Midtown Planning and
Development. NYC

felt by millions of New Yorkers whose daily life is a long sequence of hypertension, frustration and wasted energy. The task of dealing with congestion in Midtown Manhattan, therefore, has considerably broader implications than those of increasing traffic flows and assigning more space to pedestrians. The real work is to make the city habitable and humane."[36] To that end, the plan set forth numerous proposals intended to ameliorate congestion, including the coordinated development of Forty-eighth Street and the transformation of the midtown stretch of Madison Avenue into a pedestrian mall.

Following Earth Week 1971, the Office of Midtown Planning and Development released its plans for the Madison Avenue Mall, designed by Don Miles, a senior designer for the New York City Planning Commission, working with Van Ginkel Associates. The avenue's sidewalks, which had been narrowed in 1921 from nineteen to thirteen feet, would be widened to twenty-nine feet and the street accordingly reduced from five traffic lanes to two, one in each direction; both lanes would be reserved for exclusive use by buses, emergency vehicles and, during specified morning hours, delivery trucks. Double rows of trees would punctuate the broad sidewalks, as would benches, kiosks and bus shelters. Both the street and the sidewalks would be repaved, perhaps in Belgian block. Supergraphics indicating the numbers of the cross streets were to be painted on the avenue itself, boldly filling each intersection. Minibuses capable of accommodating fourteen seated passengers would traverse the mall; the buses were quickly dubbed Van Ginkelvans after their designer.

In May of that year the editors of the New York Times said that although they were sympathetic to "any idea that promises to improve the condition of urban life," plans for the mall needed to be examined: "To subject the Mayor's proposal to realistic scrutiny is not to deny the ultimate appeal of urban malls, it is rather to prevent such plans from turning into illusory daydreams or diversions from the immensely difficult task of resuscitating business, commerce and livability in midtown New York."[37] Seven months later the Times came out in favor of the mall, which it said was "not just a pretty idea. We believe the merchants of Madison Avenue would benefit from the proposal, as would the shoppers."[38]

As Glenn Fowler reported in the New York Times, by this time the proposal had engendered a "showdown."[39] Mayor Lindsay and numerous civic groups, including Community Board 5, supported the plan. Area merchants were split: the Fifth Avenue Association was "firmly against" it,[40] and a newly formed group, Businessmen for the Madison Mall, which included over eighty real estate industry representatives, was in favor of it. The Association for a Better New York, founded in 1971, took the middle ground, advocating that the plan be instituted on a temporary basis before being made permanent. The Office of Midtown Planning and Development claimed that in a survey it conducted, nearly 70 percent of the 513 businesses questioned were in favor of the mall; but Jean Gale, owner of a linen shop, and Henri Bendel, owner of the famous boutique bearing his name on Fifty-seventh Street just west of Fifth Avenue, disputed the claim. According to the editors of the New Yorker, Gale said that those who supported the mall were mostly businesses located upstairs in office buildings and that ground-floor shops like hers, which depended on the carriage trade, "would be hurt by the presence of long-haired office workers attracted to a mall outside her doors."[41]

In September 1972, when Lindsay announced he would conduct a three-month-long test on Madison Avenue from Forty-fourth to Fifty-seventh Street, the Fifth Avenue Association immediately responded by filing a suit against the city, charging that it could not effect the proposed changes without the approval of the Board of Estimate. On March 5, 1973, New York State Supreme Court Justice Abraham J. Gellinoff ruled in favor of the association. When the court's Appellate Division subsequently upheld the ruling, Lindsay presented the plan to the Board of Estimate. The mayor's support of the project had remained steady throughout, and during his final six months in office it became a major focus. Defending his project in somewhat hyperbolic terms, Lindsay said: "I think the question comes down to this: What is a city for? Is it for people, or is it for automobiles and the gasoline engine? Unless people win out in this struggle, the city won't be livable, and no place will be livable. Because, after all, the cities are the only places left that aren't dependent on automobiles. The suburbs are completely dominated by them—you can't do anything out there without a car. But the cities have to be saved for people."[42]

Despite Lindsay's efforts, on July 11, 1973, in a vote of twelve to ten, the Board of Estimate defeated the proposal. Ultimately, the taxicab industry, which feared that the mall would exacerbate rather than reduce midtown motor traffic, proved instrumental in blocking the plan. The editors of the New York Times called the plan's defeat "a setback to the idea of progressive city planning for the long-range public good," concluding that while the plan "was not without problems, as all change is disruptive in an impacted city . . . it had great promise."[43]

THIRD AVENUE

The postwar transformation of Third Avenue was in some ways even more dramatic than that of Sixth Avenue, not because of the quality or density of the new development, or even because of the almost tawdry state in which the presence of the Third Avenue El had kept the street for so long, but because it happened so quickly. Though at first glance as architecturally undistinguished as Sixth, prewar Third Avenue, dotted with bars and restaurants that came close to resembling English pubs, had a distinct, raffish and quintessentially New York charm about it. The street also sprouted secondhand and antique stores that attracted a picturesquely broad range of patrons, from those on genuinely modest budgets to well-heeled bargain hunters and high-end decorators; according to some estimates, Third Avenue dealers were responsible for 15 percent of the nation's antiques trade.[1] The demise of the El changed all that.

The Third Avenue El was the best-known and longest-lived line of Manhattan's venerable system of elevated trains, but by the end of the Second World War its future was doomed. The El did not die all at once, however; rather, it succumbed to "progress" in stages. On December 31, 1953, service was terminated between Chatham Square and South Ferry.[2] Then, on May 12, 1955, the El made its last trip after seventy-seven years of service, with a trainload of 850 sentimentalists as well as 40 reporters and photographers, on a journey from Chinatown to the Bronx.[3] Harrison Salisbury reported in the New York Times: "Above Forty-second Street the ride turned into more of a salute than a wake. All along Third Avenue upper story windows were crowded and throngs emerged from the taverns and drinking establishments to raise glasses of beer in a friendly toast."[4] By February 16, 1956, the Manhattan stretch of the El was a thing of the past, although service was maintained in the Bronx until

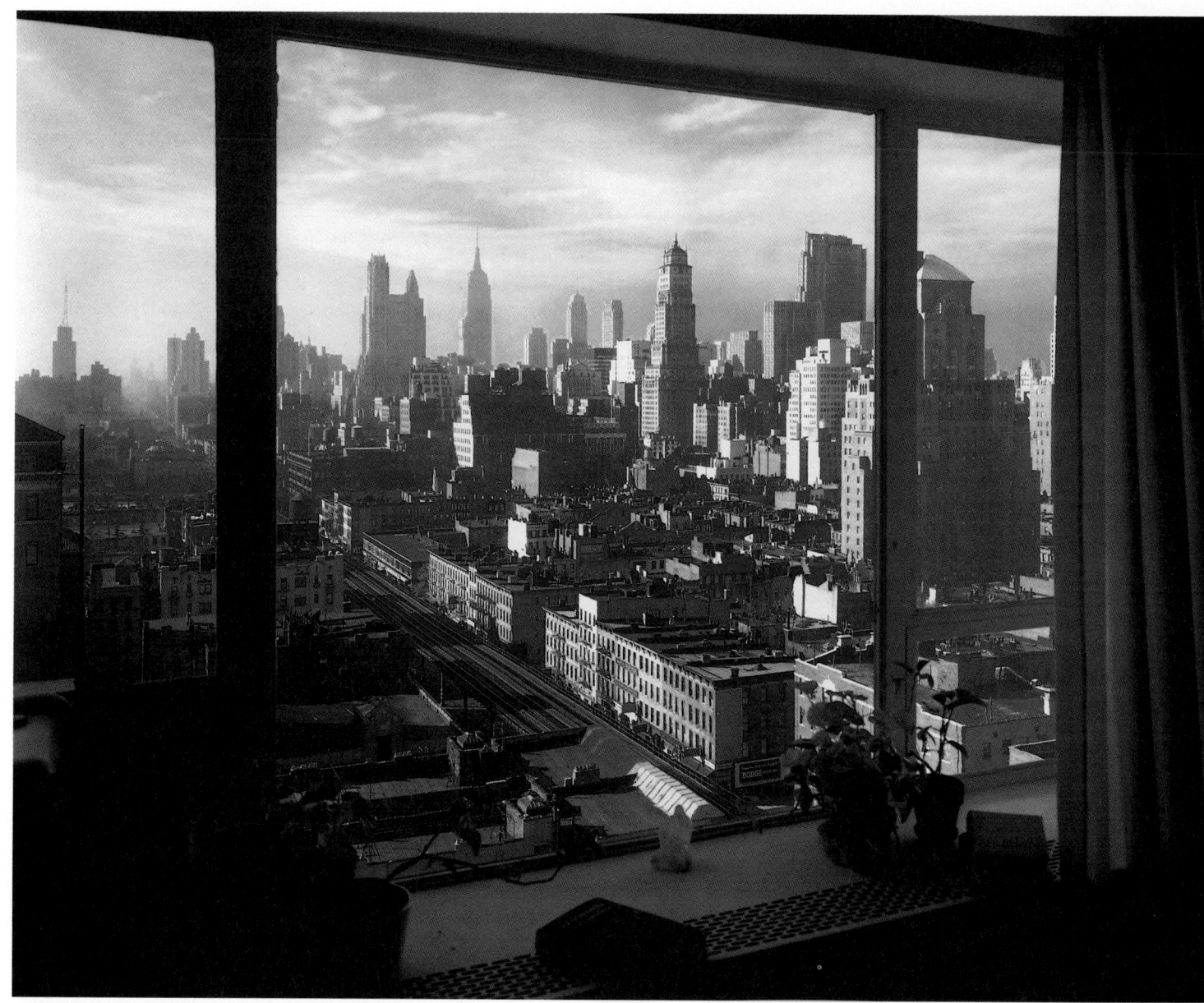

View to the south along Third Avenue from Manhattan House
(Skidmore, Owings & Merrill and Mayer & Whittlesey, 1950). Stoller.
©ESTO

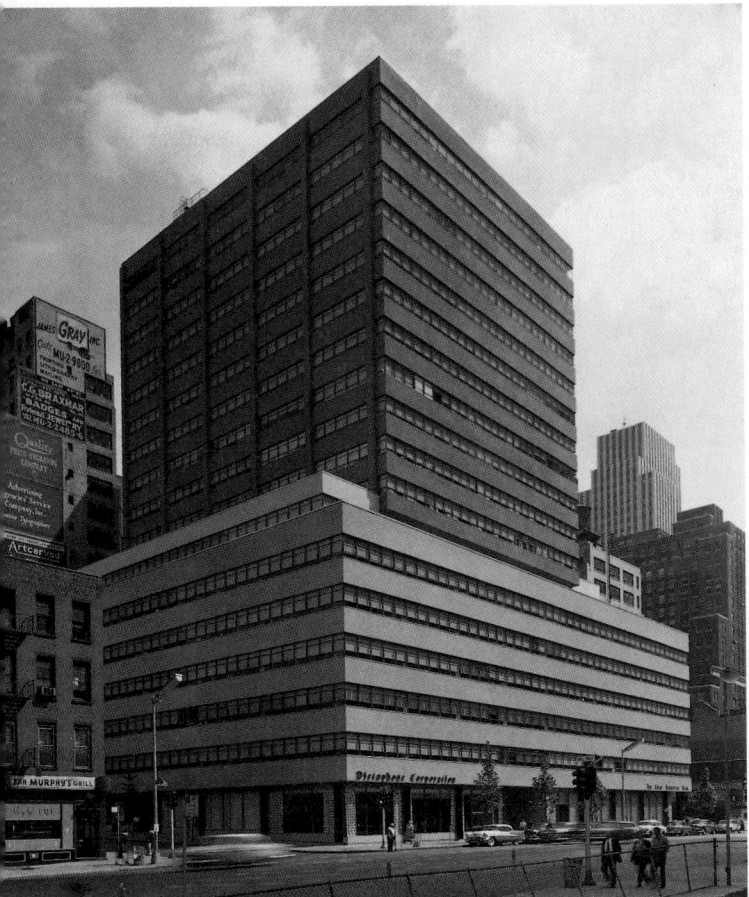

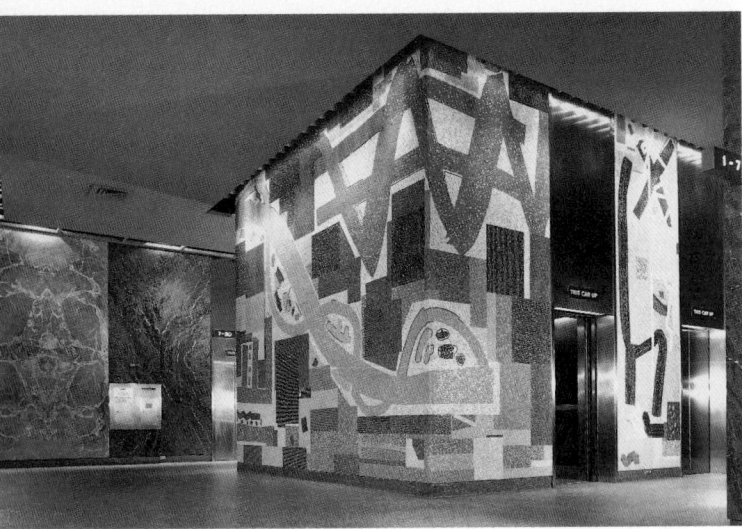

Top: 711 Third Avenue, East Forty-fourth to East Forty-fifth Street. William Lescaze, 1956. View to the southeast. Molitor. JWM

Bottom: 711 Third Avenue. Lobby showing mosaic mural by Hans Hofmann. Molitor. JWM

Top right: Girl Scouts Building, 830 Third Avenue, southwest corner of East Fifty-first Street. Skidmore, Owings & Merrill, 1957. View to the southwest. Stoller. ©ESTO

Bottom right: 750 Third Avenue, East Forty-sixth to East Forty-seventh Street. Emery Roth & Sons, 1958. View to the northwest also showing 485 Lexington Avenue (Emery Roth & Sons, 1956) to the left. Wurts. MCNY

1973. Its metal framework was sold for scrap by Morris and Julius Lipsett, demolition experts who would later enjoy the dubious distinction of having destroyed Pennsylvania Station. Some of the El's scrap metal was used to make girders for a third tube of the Lincoln Tunnel.

Unlike the demise of the Sixth Avenue El in 1939 as the city was still struggling to get out of the Depression and that of the Second Avenue El in time of war, the Third Avenue El came down just as New York's midtown economy was expanding. This point was not lost on *Newsweek*'s editors and photographers, who mercilessly contrasted the newly naked street with the sun-dappled undercroft of the old El and illustrated schemes for some of the bland office buildings that would soon line it. Their observation that "nostalgia in 1966 may sigh for the old Third Avenue, now coming down,"[5] was echoed by the editors of the *New Yorker*: "We doubt whether we ventured to ride on the dirty, dying 'L' more than three or four times in the past ten years; perhaps in another ten years we will begin to miss it sorely. Twenty more years and a brand-new 'L,' the 'L' of recollection, will go darting among the rooftops, at a speed the old 'L' never reached, through a city fairer than any of us has ever seen."[6] Though most of those who had lived and worked amid the shadows of the El were glad to see it go, its loss was not without a price. The expense of demolition was shared equally by the city, the borough and the local residents and businesses; because the Manhattan Elevated Railroad Company had financially compensated Third Avenue property owners for the loss of air and light in 1878, area residents in 1955 were required to return the favor.[7]

The El's removal not surprisingly engendered a flurry of real estate activity. Even before any changes were palpable, however, some proposals were set forth in anticipation of the avenue's new identity. In February 1956 the president of the Real Estate Board of New York, Clinton W. Blume, suggested that the avenue's name be changed to The Bouwerie, after the farm that Peter Stuyvesant bought in 1650 from the Dutch West India Company. He preferred the archaic spelling to the contemporary Bowery because, as Charles Grutzner put it in the *New York Times*, he felt that with the latter name, "the ghosts of too many broken dreams and alcoholic derelicts might haunt the bright, rebuilt avenue." But the alternative spelling was not sufficient to prevent that association in the popular imagination, and the proposed name change was never adopted. At the same time, the architect and photographer G. E. Kidder Smith, concerned that the avenue would develop, as Grutzner put it, "as a string of slums between clusters of modern buildings," emphasized that Third Avenue constituted Manhattan's last opportunity for coordinated urban planning.[8] Smith suggested that a moratorium on all construction be instituted until a comprehensive plan was formulated, but his recommendation was ignored. The city did, however, upgrade the avenue by widening its roadway from sixty to seventy feet, making it ten feet wider than Madison and Lexington avenues, as well as by installing new lights and planting trees along its length.

Even before demolition of the El began, construction of one major new Third Avenue office building had been completed: Reinhard, Hofmeister & Walquist's 1952 Chrysler Building East (see "Forty-second Street," below). Although the building's construction was a sure sign of faith in Third Avenue's commercial future, the optimism was qualified: not only did the building's management call it Chrysler Building East, but they used 161 East Forty-second Street as its official address. The completion in 1956 of William Lescaze's 711 Third Avenue offered a more unequivocal vote of confidence in the avenue's future.[9] This awkwardly massed, even lumpish, tower-on-base building, which occupied the entire east blockfront of Third Avenue between Forty-fourth and Forty-fifth streets, marked the fulfillment of a design concept that began with Howe & Lescaze's Philadelphia Saving Fund Society Building (1932) and was proposed in 1935 by Lescaze for the CBS headquarters in New York but never realized.[10] Unfortunately, compared with the crisp detailing and technological sheen of the PSFS Building, the white and blue brick skin of 711 Third Avenue was a letdown.

An early design for 711 Third called for a building with horizontally banded windows shaded by continuous two-foot-wide porcelain enamel eyebrows facing south on the Forty-fourth Street side; along Third Avenue an egg crate of three-foot-nine-inch-wide porcelain enamel hoods, set at a sixty-five degree angle to the windows, would take the west sun. This proposal would have resulted in a building with a twelve-story base that filled the 40,000-square-foot plot with setbacks at the twelfth and then the fifteenth floor, from which a slablike mass running east-west rose sheer to the twenty-eighth floor. As built, Lescaze's design consisted of a six-story base filling the site, two floors constituting a transitional "notch" and an eleven-story tower above. Continuous strip windows wrapped the building's base with alternating bands of gray brick; the columns on the north and south faces of the squarish tower were pulled to the outside of the building's skin. The relationship of columns to spandrels was as it had been in the PSFS Building, but 711 Third was chunky, not slender like its prototype.

The building's principal developer, William Kaufman, turned to artists as well as his architect to give the building a distinct character. Advised by Lescaze, Kaufman commissioned works by the sculptor José de Rivera and the painter Hans Hofmann, both artists who passionately advocated and pursued abstract visual vocabularies. Explaining his two-part, Brancusi-esque stainless-steel sculpture, *Continuum*, which was affixed to one wall of the building's entrance, Rivera said, "The beauty and source of excitement in this work is found in the interdependence and relationship of the form. . . . My idea was to integrate a form with a wall; to provide pleasurable animation for the area."[11] Hans Hofmann's contribution was a huge, 1,200-square-foot Venetian tile mosaic wrapping the lobby's elevator core. Hofmann's approach was rather more programmatic than Rivera's: "I thought of the people working there and I wanted to make it as spring-like as possible."[12]

The Girl Scouts Building, at 830 Third Avenue, on the southwest corner of Fifty-first Street (1957), was a small building that represented a high level of design sophistication.[13] Designed by Roy O. Allen of Skidmore, Owings & Merrill, as consultant to the architect William T. Meyer, the building deliberately eschewed any show of extravagance, in keeping with the desires of the cost-conscious clients. The thirteen-story building was clad with a super-refined curtain wall of clear glass and white structural glass spandrel panels set in a black anodized-aluminum grid.

Three more buildings rounded out the redevelopment of Third Avenue during the 1950s, though none were artistically distinguished. As designed by the firm of Emery Roth & Sons, which would come to play its characteristic role in the avenue's future, the rather squat, twenty-two-story 630 Third Avenue (1958), on the southwest corner of Forty-first Street, adopted wedding-cake massing with two setbacks.[14] The Roths' thirty-four-story 750 Third Avenue (1958), occupying the full west blockfront between Forty-sixth and Forty-seventh streets, incorporated several setbacks but managed to establish a more grace-

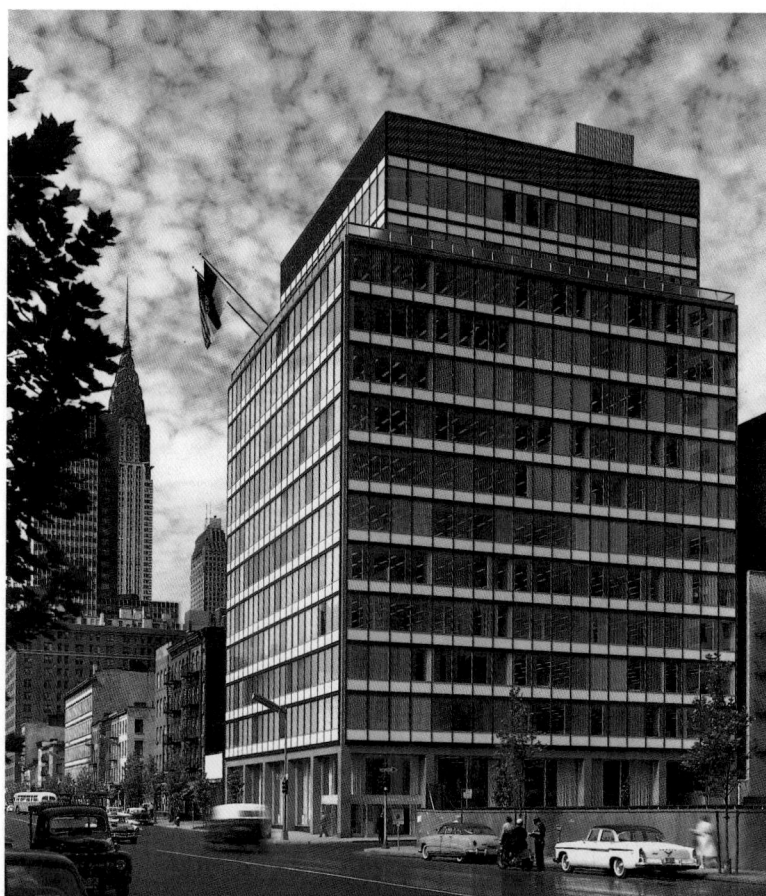

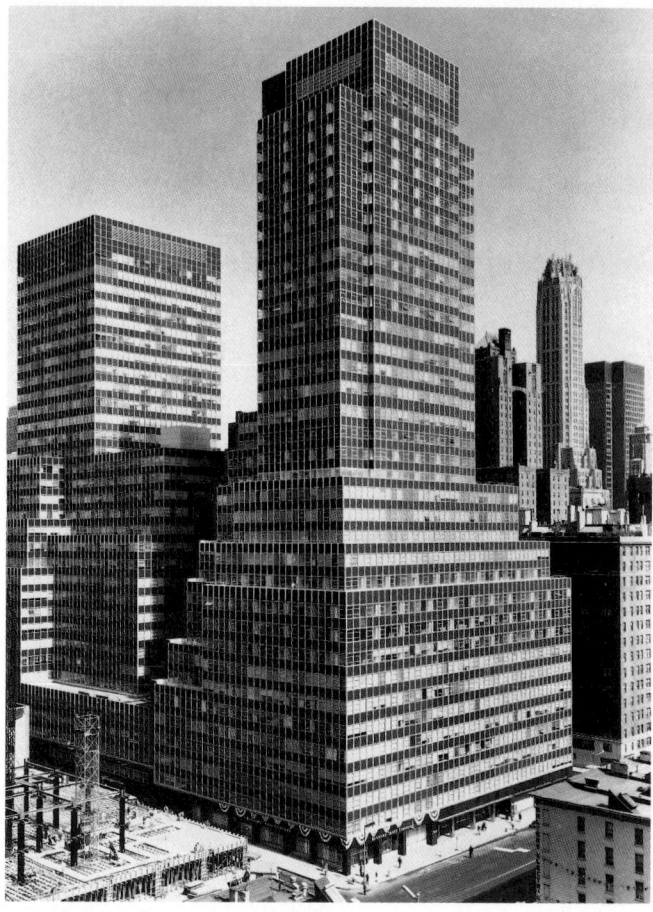

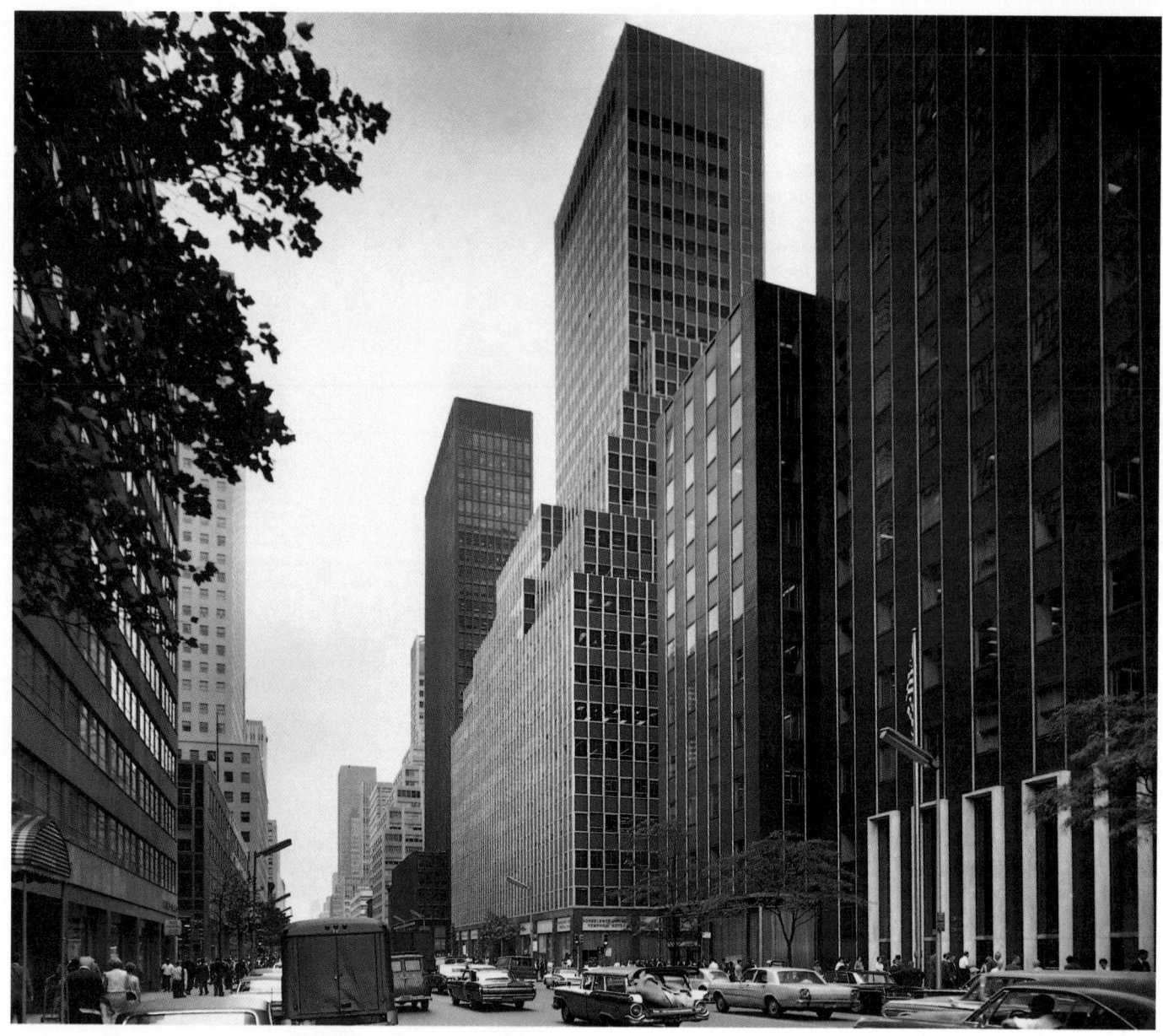

Above: View to the north along Third Avenue from East Fortieth Street showing, on the east side of the avenue, from left to right: 201 East Forty-second Street (Emery Roth & Sons, 1965), 200 East Forty-second Street (Emery Roth & Sons, 1959) and Continental Can Building (Harrison & Abramovitz, 1961), 633 Third Avenue, between East Fortieth and East Forty-first streets, on the far right. OMH

Top right: U.S. Plywood Building, 777 Third Avenue, East Forty-eighth to East Forty-ninth Street. William Lescaze, 1963. View to the southeast. Stoller. ©ESTO

Bottom right: U.S. Plywood Building. View of entrance loggia showing the sculpture *Contrapunto* by Beverly Pepper. Stoller. ©ESTO

ful profile, with interlocked volumes defining the tower.[15] One block south, 730 Third Avenue (1959), designed by Carson & Lundin, consisted of an eleven-story base filling the west blockfront between Forty-fifth and Forty-sixth streets, surmounted by a slender, centrally located eighteen-story tower.[16]

The transformation of Third Avenue from a slightly second-class office location into a prestigious corporate address began in earnest in the early 1960s, by which time the extensive rebuilding of Park Avenue from Forty-sixth to Fifty-ninth Street had forced developers to find sites to meet the seemingly limitless demand for new office space. By 1961 the business community's perception of Third Avenue had clearly changed; according to a poll conducted by the real estate firm of Williams & Company, Inc., Third Avenue ranked as the fourth most desirable Manhattan location, topped only by Park, Fifth and Madison avenues.[17]

The year 1961 saw the completion of four major office towers on Third Avenue. The Continental Can Building, at 633 Third Avenue, on the east blockfront between Fortieth and Forty-first streets, rose forty-one stories to enclose 800,000 square feet of leasable space.[18] While certainly not among the most distinguished works designed by the firm of Harrison & Abramovitz, the building's brick cladding made it, as the editors of the *New York Times* said, "an architectural rarity in this age of glass and metal."[19] Between the building's soaring piers of dark-green-glazed brick were vertical rows of green-tinted windows and green-glass spandrels. Robert L. Bien's American Home Products Building (1961), at 685 Third Avenue, on the east blockfront between Forty-third and Forty-fourth streets, was comparatively small, rising twenty-five stories and containing 200,000 square feet of office space.[20] Emery Roth & Sons' two buildings of the same year were blockbusters: the twenty-four-story, 340,000-square-foot Diamond National Building, at 733 Third Avenue, on the southeast corner of Forty-sixth Street;[21] and 850 Third Avenue, on the west blockfront between Fifty-first and Fifty-second streets, a twenty-story, 470,000-square-foot building.[22] Though all four buildings were less than distinctive essays in corporate International Style Modernism, each was fully rented by the time of its completion—a sure sign that Third Avenue had arrived as a sought-after business address. Also completed in 1961 was Emery Roth & Sons' 235 East Forty-second Street, occupying the northeast corner of Third Avenue (see "Forty-second Street," below). The editors of *Real Estate Record and Guide* commented on the avenue's swift transformation, noting that the developer Seymour Durst, who actively participated in the rejuvenation, "points out that a remarkable aspect in the growth of Third Avenue as an executive office center is the fact that the thoroughfare . . . wasn't even a contender before 1956."[23]

Third Avenue's new corporate persona could be seen clearly in William Lescaze's thirty-eight-story U.S. Plywood Building, at 777 Third Avenue (1963), on the east blockfront between Forty-eighth and Forty-ninth streets, one of the first office buildings to be built under the 1961 zoning.[24] The Plywood Building replaced a row of tenements as well as 751 Third Avenue, a small "back" house behind them that was accessible only via a narrow passageway; renovated and occupied by Philip Johnson in 1940, the building had been dubbed Hidden House by the architect's sister Theodate.[25] The tower left intact but dwarfed the low-lying enclaves of Turtle Bay Gardens[26] and Amster Yard (see "East Side: From Stuyvesant Town to Turtle Bay," above), both located immediately to the east. Had the building been built under the old zoning, it could have been 15

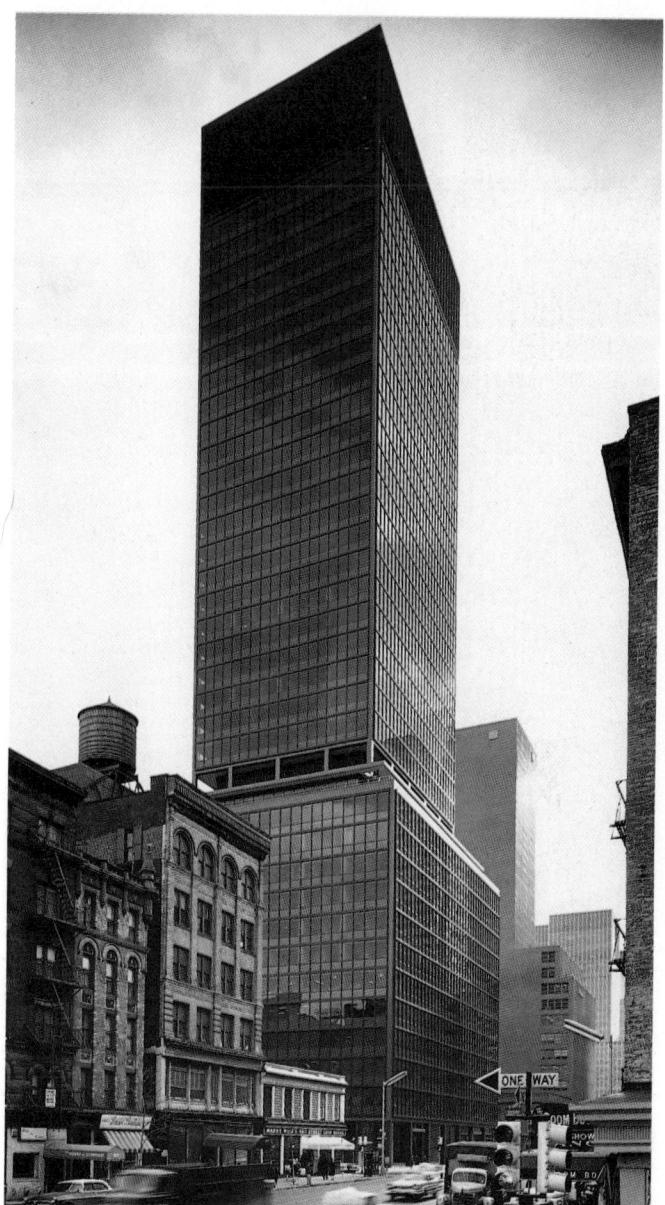

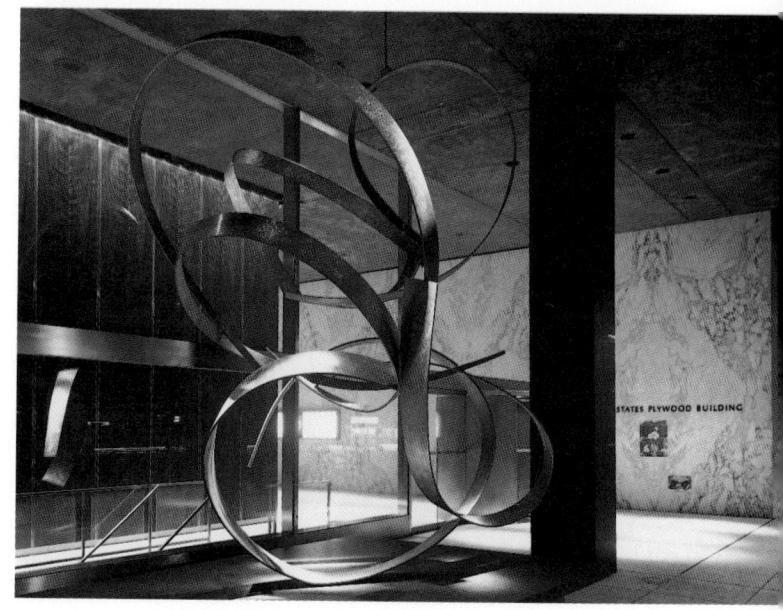

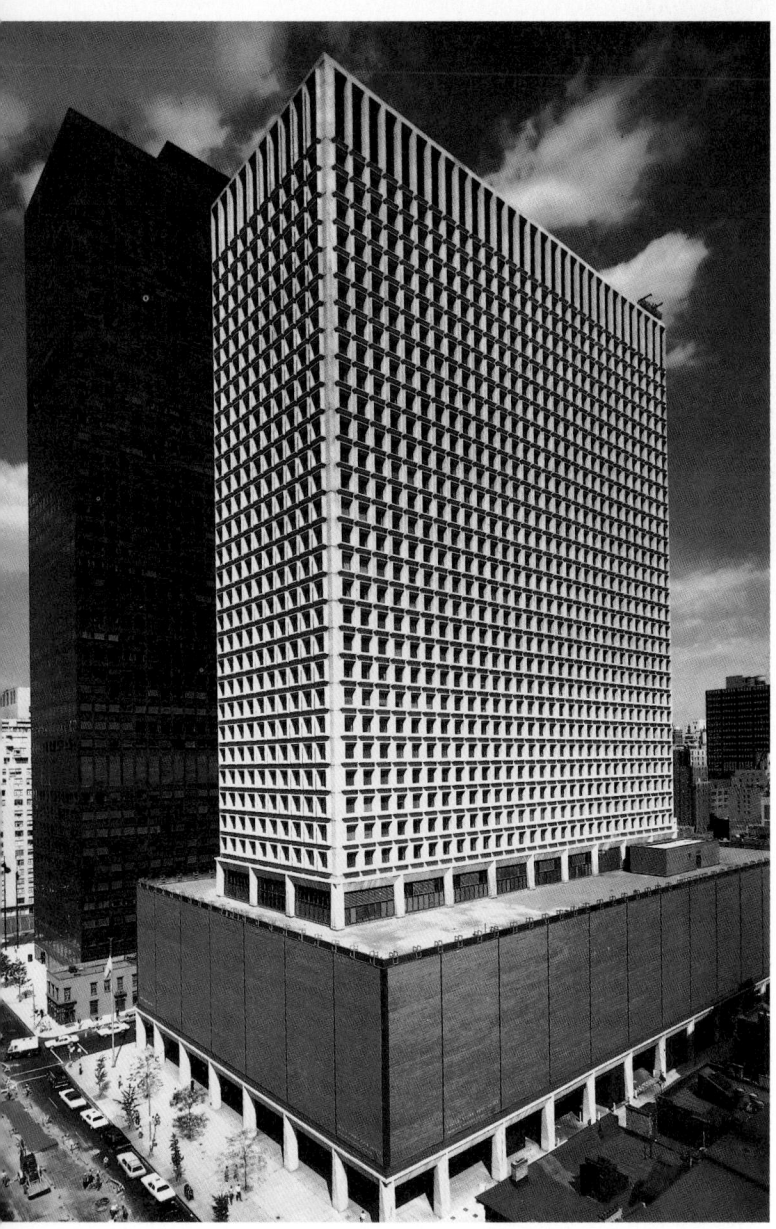

View to the northeast on Third Avenue showing, from left to right: 919 Third Avenue (Skidmore, Owings & Merrill, 1970), southeast corner of Third Avenue and East Fifty-sixth Street, with P. J. Clarke's at the base on the northeast corner of Third Avenue and East Fifty-fifth Street, and 909 Third Avenue (Max O. Urbahn & Associates in collaboration with Emery Roth & Sons, 1967), East Fifty-fourth to East Fifty-fifth Street. Stoller. ©ESTO.

percent larger than it was under the new; as built, the structure realized additional bulk by sacrificing 6,400 square feet of ground space to create a wraparound plaza formed by setting the structure sixteen feet back from the building line on three sides.

Working with an architectural vocabulary evocative of that used by Mies van der Rohe at the Seagram Building, Lescaze created an aluminum-clad, twenty-six-story tower set on pilotis resting atop a twelve-story base. Perhaps for the first time in a modern office building the idea of lobby art was carried out-of-doors to the public realm of the loggia, where Beverly Pepper's specially commissioned kinetic sculpture consisting of eighteen-foot-tall ribbons of hammered stainless steel rotated to entertain passersby. William Kaufman, one of the building's owners, described Pepper's design as a "counterpoint" to the building's austerity, hence its name, *Contrapunto*. The opinionated Kaufman, also the principal client for Lescaze's 711 Third Avenue, told the editors of the *New York Herald Tribune* that he was responsible for this "marriage of art, modern art and modern architecture," an achievement that "neither the architect nor the artist could render, and that only the builder could render, because he has the ear to hear what the audience wants."[27]

In 1963 two more wedding-cake-type buildings were completed: Emery Roth & Sons' straightforward, twenty-one-story building at 845 Third Avenue, on the east blockfront between Fifty-first and Fifty-second streets,[28] and David and Earl J. Levy's more distinctive, L-shaped Decoration and Design Building, at 979 Third Avenue, on the northeast corner of Fifty-eighth Street.[29] The D & D Building, as it was widely known, seemed in some ways a throwback to an earlier form of corporate Modernism, with an intricate pattern of setbacks and continuous horizontal strip windows separated by brick spandrels. Norval White and Elliot Willensky would later find in its design a clear demonstration of "the ziggurated New York zoning envelope . . . capitalized into a positive architectural statement (if you look skyward)."[30]

Compared to its predecessors, 909 Third Avenue (1967), a thirty-three-story building occupying the east blockfront between Fifty-fourth and Fifty-fifth streets, was Brobdingnagian in scale.[31] Designed by the firm of Max O. Urbahn & Associates, in collaboration with Emery Roth & Sons, the building incorporated a windowless, four-story, gray-brick-clad base housing a branch of the Post Office and, above it, a twenty-nine-story, 1,145,000-square-foot tower. The entire building was set back from the Third Avenue lot line and contained a recessed arcade on the ground floor that was defined by massive concrete columns. Unlike most of the avenue's glass-and-steel postwar high rises, the tower of 909 Third was clad in a somewhat grossly proportioned, cofferlike precast-concrete facade that seemed to reflect the influence of the Bankers Trust and Pan Am buildings (see "Park Avenue," above).

Well-established publishing houses, long a distinguishing feature of New York's business scene, added a measure of prestige to the "new" Third Avenue. The fact that they were merely principal tenants in speculative ventures, however, was reflected by the Roth-designed corporate containers in which they were housed: the Harcourt Brace Jovanovich Building, at 757 Third Avenue, on the northeast corner of Forty-seventh Street, completed in 1963;[32] the Macmillan Building, at 866 Third Avenue, on the west blockfront between Fifty-second and Fifty-third streets, completed three years later;[33] and the Random House Building, at 825 Third Avenue, on the northeast corner of Fiftieth Street, completed in 1969.[34] Random House, which was to occupy one-third of the new building, at first planned to retain offices in its former headquarters in the Villard Houses; when the company abandoned the plan, the fate of the historic complex was left in question (see chapter 16).

Although by the 1960s most of the antique shops and tenements that had lined the street only a decade before were now gone, a handful of restaurants and bars managed to hold out against the real estate juggernaut. One of these was the venerable Joe and Rose Restaurant, owned by Rose Resteghini, who also owned the five-story building in which the restaurant stood. In 1972, when 747 Third Avenue, a thirty-eight-story, 360,000-square-foot building designed by Emery Roth & Sons, was completed on the east blockfront from Forty-sixth to Forty-seventh Street, its structure spanned the restaurant, which was located near the middle of the Third Avenue frontage; in an arrangement worked out between the restaurant's owner and the new office tower's developer, William Kaufman, the existing building was reduced to a single floor and structurally stabilized, allowing the restaurant to operate continuously while large-scale construction was taking place all around it.[35]

Kaufman's son Melvyn, who was increasingly active in the family firm, added his own touch to the project. Pursuing similar tactics to those he had employed in 77 Water Street and 127 John Street (see chapter 3), Melvyn Kaufman hired Pamela Waters to design the lobby of 747 Third Avenue, as well as the plaza and sidewalks surrounding the building. Waters organized the paving as a series of undulating, three-dimensional curvilinear patterns in brick that formed planting boxes and seating areas, the latter sheltered by translucent striped awnings carried on simple metal frames. Explaining her work, Waters said she wanted people to walk "as if they were swept by the wind." The building was entered through a wooden front porch—a "reminiscence of the country."[36] Waters changed the mood considerably in the lobby, where the guts of the building's mechanical and electrical systems were exposed to view.

Kaufman's lobby was a prime example of a new phase of development that had been initiated several years before. What for ten years had been a virtually unbroken series of banal, conformist buildings began to break up around 1970. Pomerance & Breines's 443,000-square-foot Architect's and Designer's Building (1969), at 964 Third Avenue, occupying only a portion of the west blockfront between Fifty-seventh and Fifty-eighth streets and more prominent on Fifty-eighth, was conventional in most ways except for its use of an unusual palette of manganese-flecked brick, aluminum and bronze-tinted glass.[37]

Skidmore, Owings & Merrill's immense, darkly colored 919 Third Avenue, completed in 1970, added a measure of understated sophistication, if not visual excitement, to the avenue.[38] A tombstone mass not unlike the firm's 1166 Sixth Avenue, this forty-seven-story, glass-wrapped slab was set back from the avenue, filling the entire east blockfront between Fifty-fifth and Fifty-sixth streets except for the southwest corner. This corner was occupied by the well-known watering hole P. J. Clarke's, founded in 1908 and frequented over the years by a diverse and notable clientele, ranging from the playwright Eugene O'Neill to the eminent jurist Nicholas Katzenbach. The tavern occupied a four-story red-brick building that incorporated the wood-and-cut-glass facade of a structure built in 1884 to house a ground-floor retail store run by the George Ehret Brewery and apartments above. In 1967, when the Tishman Realty & Construction Company was in the process of assembling the property for SOM's tower, they were blocked by Daniel Lavezzo, who at that time owned the building housing Clarke's as well as another building on the block. Eventually

Lavezzo sold both buildings, but on the condition that Clarke's be preserved and a ninety-nine-year lease granted. In a widely publicized arrangement, the Tishmans agreed to these terms, though in 1968 they removed the tavern building's top two stories so that it would fall within the twenty-three-foot height mandated by zoning for a plaza bonus.

Even though the reconfigured building now looked atrophied and was absurdly small in relation to SOM's superslab, P. J. Clarke's survived as both a colorful neighborhood gathering place and a reminder of the avenue's gritty past. Paul Goldberger scoffed at the "tiny nineteenth-century remnant [that] now sits on the plaza of 919 Third like a piece of sculpture" and noted that "for all the fuss about Clarke's preservation, Skidmore, Owings & Merrill was not prepared to do anything to take the old building into account in its design." Perhaps, as Goldberger observed, the architects' real attitude toward the tavern could be surmised by the design of the new building, "with travertine spread around its base as if it were insect repellent keeping the old honky-tonk Third Avenue at bay."[39]

Between the end of World War II and 1971 a staggering thirty-one buildings had been completed on Third Avenue between Thirty-ninth and Fifty-seventh streets.[40] While the recession of the early 1970s slowed the avenue's phenomenal growth, it failed to completely stop new construction projects. Though in part this was because of the long lead time required for large-scale projects, it was also a reflection of the marketplace's continued faith in the avenue's desirability as a corporate address. Kahn & Jacobs's slablike Greenwich Savings Bank Building, at 950 Third Avenue, on the southwest corner of Fifty-seventh Street, was completed in 1971, the first in the city to employ the newly perfected, darkly reflective "mirror" glass that raised architectural minimalism to near absurdity.[41] Emery Roth & Sons continued to be a ubiquitous presence on the avenue with their 600 Third Avenue (1971), on the west blockfront between Thirty-ninth and Fortieth streets;[42] 800 Third Avenue (1972), on the west blockfront between Forty-ninth and Fiftieth streets;[43] and Blue Cross Building (1973), at 622 Third Avenue, on the west blockfront between Fortieth and Forty-first streets.[44] The first two were unremarkable, but the third was distinguished by a ploy that was surely one of the more notable abuses of the zoning law's plaza bonus provisions: the thirty-eight-story slab of 622 was located well west of Third Avenue but was reached by means of escalators ascending to a 7,000-square-foot landscaped plaza set on the rooftop of a single-story base.

By the mid-1970s the transformation of Third Avenue was largely complete, though construction projects would continue to be realized, most notably Hugh Stubbins's much-discussed Citicorp Center, completed in 1977, which occupied the full block bounded by Lexington and Third avenues, Fifty-third and Fifty-fourth streets (see "Fifty-third Street," below). In 1979 Paul Goldberger reflected a widely held popular opinion when he delivered his judgment on the rebuilt street, flatly stating that "when the El came down, Third Avenue boomed, and while that may have helped the economy, it did nothing for the quality of urban design." Goldberger described Third Avenue between Fortieth and Forty-ninth streets as "midtown's worst avenue—the one with the poorest individual buildings and the weakest sense of any ensemble," and went on to explain: "Here, nothing much is good on its own, and the buildings fail to make any effort to work together; Sixth Avenue is a picture of order by comparison. If it proves anything, it is that the Miesian mode, the stranded glass box, isn't so neutral as is often pretended. It can be an aggressive, unpleasant presence."[45]

Dry Dock Country

The new corporate identity was not the only one emerging in the mid-1960s to replace the traditional character of Third Avenue. One small stretch of the avenue, around the area of Bloomingdale's department store, which occupied two buildings that filled the block bounded by Third and Lexington avenues, Fifty-ninth and Sixtieth streets, became the focus of a lively retail and entertainment district. The area acquired a nickname, Dry Dock Country, derived not from the worlds of retail or entertainment but from the name of a local savings bank. The area's new character was initiated when several new, intimately scaled movie theaters were built, setting the neighborhood in competition with the city's premier nighttime and weekend magnet, Times Square. When the neighborhood's own picture palace, Proctor's New Fifty-eighth Street Theater (Thomas Lamb, 1918), was torn down in 1958 to make way for Alexander's, the void was quickly filled by the new theaters, which showcased the increasingly sophisticated films from Hollywood and abroad that were helping to reverse a decade-long decline in theater attendance. The wave of renewed attendance coincided with a change in municipal building law that permitted the inclusion of large auditoriums in mixed-use buildings as well as the stacking of theaters.

The double-decker movie theater Baronet-Coronet, at 993 Third Avenue, on the east side between Fifty-ninth and Sixtieth streets (1961), was the first of the new Third Avenue theaters.[46] Designed by John McNamara, the 600-seat Coronet crowned the existing 432-seat Baronet, a onetime nickelodeon that had been known as the Arcadia until 1951, when it was taken over by the Walter Reade chain. McNamara renovated and expanded the Baronet and sheathed the new building's Third Avenue facade with a terra-cotta honeycomb punctuated by tinted glass. Located at 1001 Third Avenue, on the same block as the Baronet-Coronet, was the much more distinguished Cinema I and Cinema II (1962), designed by Abraham Geller and Ben Schlanger and with interiors designed by Marion Geller, Abraham's wife.[47] The theater consisted of Cinema I, located on the upper level and seating 700, and Cinema II, set behind the entrance lobby and slightly below grade, seating 300. It was the first theater in New York with an open facade; the glass set between the posts of the marble-sheathed, concrete-framed structure revealed to passersby the warm glow of Cinema I's lobby, with its copper chandeliers and the flux of moviegoers milling about. Above the windows, on the exterior, six panels of blue Venetian mosaic tile contributed to the sparkling image. At street level, a covered arcade extending the length of the building provided shelter for patrons. The auditoriums of Cinema I and Cinema II were simply detailed, the first to have so-called "continental seating," in which the rows of seats were spaced widely enough to also serve as aisles. Four artists were commissioned to create art for the public spaces; the most distinguished piece was Ilya Bolotowsky's forty-five-foot-long, two-foot-high, De Stijl–inspired mural that curved along the rear wall of Cinema I's lobby. Norval White and Elliot Willensky praised the theater for its "simple elegance," asserting that in contrast to "escapist entertainment in escapist environments, movies here are serious business."[48]

Restaurants and casual eateries followed the theaters, although most of them were not memorable. One exception was a well-designed, moderately priced soup bar, La Bonne Soupe East, located on the east side of Third Avenue between Fifty-eighth and Fifty-ninth streets (1976).[49] Designed by Charles Mount, it synthesized the cuisine and visual charm of a French country inn with the streamlined efficiency of a typical New York coffee shop. La Bonne Soupe East continued design and culinary ideas first explored in La Potagerie (1971), on which Mount had collaborated with George Nelson, and Pot Au Feu (1974) in Rockefeller Center's Exxon Building, which Mount had worked on with Judith Stockman (see chapter 6). At La Bonne Soupe East, the tight space combined with the vocabulary of blond wood, tile and natural colors to produce a warm and intimate atmosphere, saved from claustrophobia by a glass-enclosed cocktail bar in the front and by Mount's ingenious manipulation of the ceiling plane to increase the illusion of height.

In 1965 Alexander's, the established discount department store that had branches in the outer boroughs and the suburbs but no "mother" store, opened a mammoth facility occupying the site of the former Proctor's New Fifty-eighth Street Theater and almost all of the remaining block bounded by Lexington and Third avenues, Fifty-eighth and Fifty-ninth streets.[50] Located directly opposite Bloomingdale's, the new Alexander's was an early indication that the central city was staging a comeback, and that though the suburbs were still vital, their rate of growth was slowing. George Farkas, the chairman of Alexander's, explained that they had opened the Third Avenue store because "we weren't able to achieve an image with no store in Manhattan to identify us."[51]

The new store was hard to miss; at 486,000 square feet, it was the largest store built in Manhattan since 1925. The editors of Business Week claimed that at $20 million (ignoring inflation), it was also the most expensive department store ever built anywhere.[52] Designed by Emery Roth & Sons, the five-story, marble-clad building was windowless, with the exception of a near-continuous strip of ground-floor display windows. Incorporating a rooftop parking lot, the building offered customers on-site parking, a rare service in a Manhattan store. Inside Alexander's, crystal chandeliers and other appointments more typically found in traditional high-end retail establishments were scattered about ordinary selling floors that were otherwise perfectly attuned to the bargain merchandise the store specialized in. Devoid of exterior decoration, the bland commercial container stood in stark contrast to the Modern Classical exterior of Bloomingdale's. To decorate the facades of its new store, Alexander's management had commissioned the surrealist painter Salvador Dali to create murals on the theme of fashion, but they later decided, as Angela Taylor reported in the New York Times, that "customers might not understand giraffes with drawers opening out of their bodies."[53] Works by the artist later adorned the building's executive offices. Despite the exterior banality of its new building, Alexander's was confident it could give Bloomingdale's, its once-middle-class but now-chic neighbor, a run for its money, and the store erected a rooftop billboard that aggressively announced, "Time is running out on higher prices." Although Alexander's was designed to be able to carry another six stories, these were never built.

The most important feature of the area's revitalization was not new restaurants, stores or theaters, but the gradual transformation of one of the city's oldest large-scale retailers, Bloomingdale's, from a rather dowdy mass-market emporium to a citadel of chic.[54] By 1972, the store's centennial year, Bloomingdale's had become the undisputed champion of all things trendy and tony. The story of Bloomingdale's transformation began in the 1950s, when the change in Third Avenue's fortunes, as Marilyn Bender put it in the New York Times in 1974, "enabled Bloomingdale's to come a long way out of the shadow of the Third Avenue El."[55] In 1967 Bloomingdale's added to its efficiency if not its allure by building a fourth-floor pedestrian bridge between the store's eight-story Lexington Avenue building (Starrett

& Van Vleck, 1930)[56] and an eleven-story building on the north side of Sixtieth Street in which it had office space. More apparent to customers was the 1972 installation of new escalators and an expanded, two-level, 50,000-square-foot men's store accessible directly from Third Avenue by a new street entrance at Sixtieth Street.

It was not so much the permanent physical upgrading of the store that reflected its new image, however, as its aggressive marketing strategies. These included a new corporate identity program orchestrated by the designers Massimo and Lella Vignelli and, even more important, a nearly constant interior building program in which "boutiques" were assembled and reassembled as quickly as fashion trends emerged and became obsolete. In 1972 the editors of *Business Week* described the store's atmosphere: "Hordes of real Beautiful People, would-be Beautiful People, long-legged girls wearing halter tops, boys sporting the layered look, and coiffed Park Avenue matrons swarm through Bloomie's endless shops, buying, bumping into friends, and chasing away depressions. Even the nonstop sawing, hammering, and drilling noises of boutiques being torn down and rebuilt fade into the background."[57]

In the 1970s Bloomingdale's became the city's nearest equivalent to the great department stores of the nineteenth century, where a visit took on social and even cultural implications. It gave rise to an active dating scene among young white-collar types in their twenties and early thirties who met while shopping there in the evenings or, especially, on Saturday, before going to a nearby movie and dinner. As Bender noted, "On Monday and Thursday evenings and all day Saturday there are the young materialists trooping in fond embrace toward the racks of Levis and answering the call of the advertisements that christened them 'Saturday's Generation.'"[58] Jill Robinson, writing in *Vogue* in 1976, characterized Bloomingdale's as "sort of like a Saturday-afternoon singles' bar," explaining, "If you're lucky, you come out through the Men's department with a date for standing in line at the theaters across the street, which play Bloomie's People movies."[59]

Barbara D'Arcy, the store's design director, exerted wide influence on interior design tastes with her popular model rooms on the furniture floor. Blending fantasy environments, such as a cavelike stucco-walled room, with glitzy but achievable ideas, D'Arcy paved the way for members of Saturday's Generation to personalize the anonymous apartments they were inhabiting. When D'Arcy stopped designing the displays in 1973, as Rita Reif wrote in the *New York Times*, it brought an end to the "semiannual pilgrimage of her fans to the decorated model rooms she made so famous."[60]

In 1973 the store installed a column of clocks at the principal Third Avenue entrance. Five of the clocks announced the time in New York while the others told the time in London, Paris, Rome, Tokyo and Rio de Janeiro. If the clocks rather boldly reflected management's claim to commercial hegemony, they also suggested that typical Bloomingdale's customers, even if only coming in from Forest Hills, liked to imagine themselves members of the jet set.

Paul Goldberger enjoyed the area's new vitality, noting that "the corner of 59th and Third has become the focus for the powerful attraction this neighborhood exerts on moviegoers, shoppers and voyeurs alike." But he lamented that the neighborhood had no distinctive urbanistic quality, as did Times Square, with its definitive interruption of Manhattan's relentless grid. At Fifty-ninth Street and Third Avenue, Goldberger wrote, "there is no center, no traditional sign that you are in a special place; you just feel it as you glide up the avenue into it, and when you pass you know that it is gone."[61]

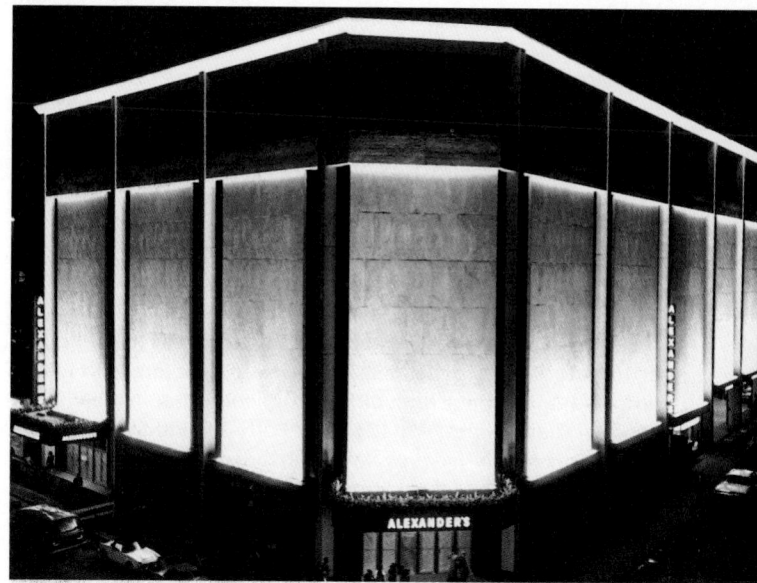

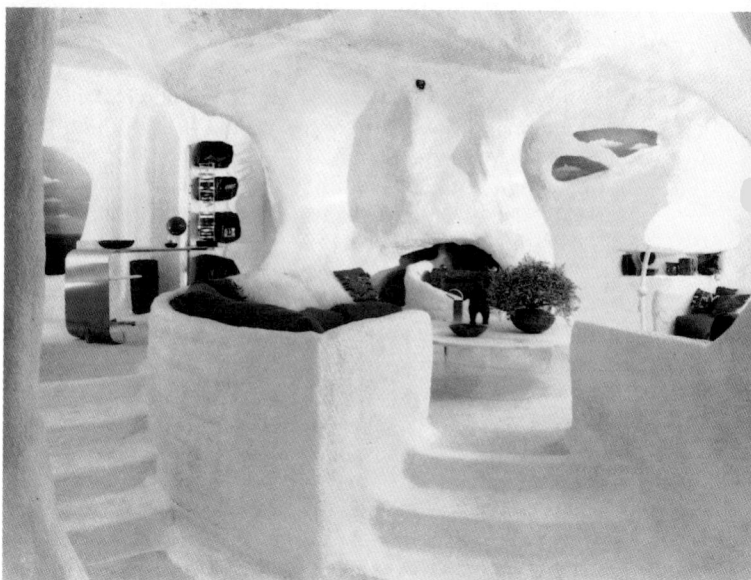

Top: Alexander's, northeast corner of Third Avenue and East Fifty-eighth Street. Emery Roth & Sons, 1958. View to the northeast. OMH

Bottom: Model room, Bloomingdale's, 1000 Third Avenue, East Fifty-ninth to East Sixtieth Street. Barbara D'Arcy, 1969. BDW

TIMES SQUARE

At the outbreak of World War II the Times Square district had returned to its pre-Crash prosperity, despite its somewhat tarnished glamour. The world's most democratic entertainment mecca, Times Square was declared in 1943 to be the "most densely populated place in the world at night."[1] Over six million people entered the area every week, five million of them to eat meals in its restaurants, 1,779,408 to go to the theater and 225,000 to fill the dance floors of its nightclubs. No new theaters had been built since 1927, but some of the older movie houses had been freshened up. Among these was the Criterion, at 1514 Broadway, where Eugene de Rosa, working with the interior designers Battisti Studios, reconfigured the interior along Modern Classic lines.[2] At 121 West Forty-second Street, just off Times Square, Ely Jacques Kahn converted a restaurant, which ran through to Forty-third Street, into a stylish theater called the Pix, with decor suggesting both Kahn's previous collaboration with Winold Reiss for Longchamps restaurants and Scandinavian Modern Classicism.[3] Entered through a long silver and salmon lobby and foyer, the 1,000-seat auditorium of the Pix, which specialized in foreign films, featured flame red and dubonnet-colored walls decorated with white plaster masks set between strips of warm gray. Specially designed white metal columnar fixtures set in niches concealed the source of the fluorescent lighting; this was one of the earliest uses of fluorescent lighting for decorative purposes.

One notable new restaurant enhanced the ever-more-democratic Times Square, Toffenetti's (1940), at 1482–1490 Broadway, on the southeast corner of Forty-third Street, built on the site of George M. Cohan's Theater (George Keister, 1909–11), which was torn down in 1938.[4] Designed by the fledgling Chicago-based firm of Skidmore, Owings & Merrill in association with Walker & Gillette, Toffenetti's, a popular round-the-clock eatery featuring potatoes, was a stylish essay in streamlined Modernism. It was the first restaurant equipped with escalators, which transported customers to the basement-level dining room.

With America's entrance into the war, Times Square became the port of call for virtually every GI en route to Europe. Its bright lights, its shops, its restaurants and nightclubs, and the extraordinary vitality of its street life was for many of them the first experience of big-city life. This dynamism was sapped somewhat by wartime restrictions when a midnight curfew was imposed by the War Mobilization Board in 1941. In response to the subsequent complaints of nightclub owners, Mayor La Guardia stepped in and arranged for the curfew to begin an hour later, explaining that, after all, "New York is still New York." The flamboyant club owner Toots Shor took the curfew in stride: "Any crum bum who can't get drunk by midnight just ain't tryin'."[5] The square also lost a bit of its spectacular brightness when war emergency blackouts required that its giant signs be left off beginning on the night of April 29, 1942, the first such dimming since the lightless nights of 1917.[6]

Even more dismal than the blackouts was the 1943 proposal to build a victory arch across Broadway and Seventh Avenue just north of Forty-third Street.[7] Sponsored by the Broadway Association, who commissioned Lucia Willoughby, the daughter of one of its members, to design it, the proposed temporary monument consisted of two giant palm fronds spanning the street and supported on decorated pedestals and pylons. Joseph M. Robinson, an irate reader of the New York Times, denounced it as "horse feathers sprouting from a metro-

nome,"[8] while the paper's art critic, Edward Alden Jewell, found the proposal "unspeakable."[9] A host of other citizens quickly joined the attack on the design, which was never built.

Times Square reached the apogee of its national prominence on the late afternoon of August 14, 1945, when it became the scene of an extended vigil as crowds gathered beneath a miniature version of the Statue of Liberty and the Times Tower's news ribbon in anticipation of an announcement of peace (see chapter 1). Blocking all traffic along Broadway between Fortieth and Forty-eighth streets, the crowd swelled from 200,000 in late afternoon to 750,000 by seven o'clock, when the message came across in lights, silencing those gathered there: "Official—Truman Announces Japanese Surrender." Afterwards, a joyous pandemonium broke out, and the crowds grew even larger: it was estimated that by ten o'clock two million people were packed into the area between Fortieth and Forty-eighth streets, Sixth and Eighth avenues. As the New York Times put it the next day, the "victory roar" they created "beat upon the eardrums until it numbed the senses."[10] A few months later, on New Year's Eve, Times Square witnessed a second such demonstration, when 1.5 million celebrants crowded the outdoor room to ring in America's first year of peace after World War II.[11]

After the war Times Square began to experience a decline, but the area's slide was not immediately noticeable.[12] What did seem quickly apparent was that Times Square would not continue to survive solely as an entertainment district, that its future health depended on its ability to attract other uses, most notably offices. The construction of office buildings in the area was hardly new: it was, in fact, the arrival of the New York Times headquarters there in 1904 that caused the renaming of Longacre Square, the southern end of the bowtie-shaped intersection of Seventh Avenue and Broadway.[13] Even important theaters like the Loew's State (1920) and the Paramount (1927) were built as part of major office buildings.[14]

The area's most likely path for growth lay to the square's northern end, where "soft" real estate suggested an expansion of the midtown core westward from Rockefeller Center. While Rockefeller Center was home to one television enterprise, the National Broadcasting Company (NBC), other important companies were without adequate studio facilities; Times Square seemed a logical location for a "television city" to complement the center's "Radio City." In the 1940s the Columbia Broadcasting System (CBS) converted a number of theaters in the area for television broadcasting before moving the bulk of its production facilities to Los Angeles in 1951.[15] In 1947 John Sloan Associates and Edward Durell Stone Associates prepared a design for a thirteen-story building to fill the block bounded by Broadway and Seventh Avenue, Fifty-first and Fifty-second streets.[16] On the Fifty-first Street end of the site stood the seven-story Healy Carriage factory building (Henry J. Hardenbergh, 1892), now converted to use as an office building, while on the Fifty-second Street side stood the Newport Flats (1876), one of the city's earliest multiple dwellings intended for prominent families. Also on the block were the Republic motion picture theater, built as the Piccadilly Theater in 1924 by Newton Schloss and Joseph Orlando, as well as the Roseland Dance Hall. The Sloan and Stone building, possibly intended to serve the newest network, the American Broadcasting Company (ABC), was to contain a 3,600-seat theater fully equipped for television production yet convertible to motion pictures and live theatrical performances, as well as office and retail space, a second-story restaurant reached from the street by escalators, and an elaborate roof garden and restaurant at the top. The design called for facades with

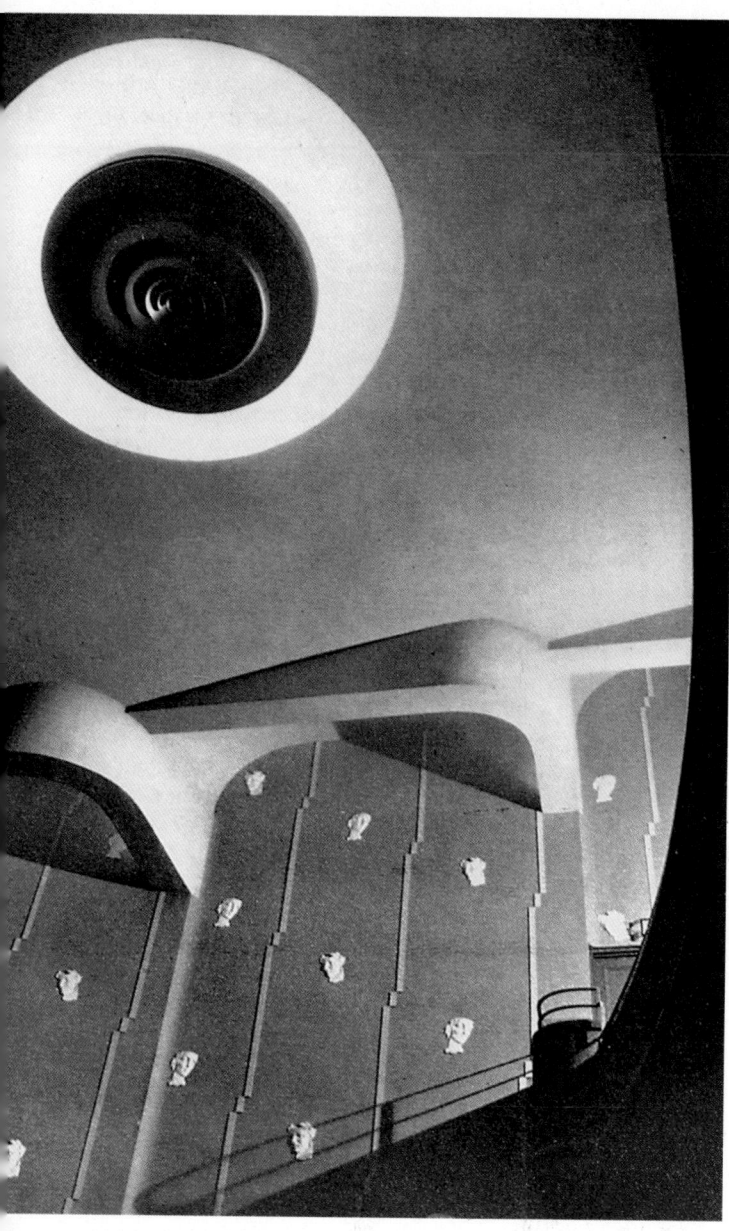

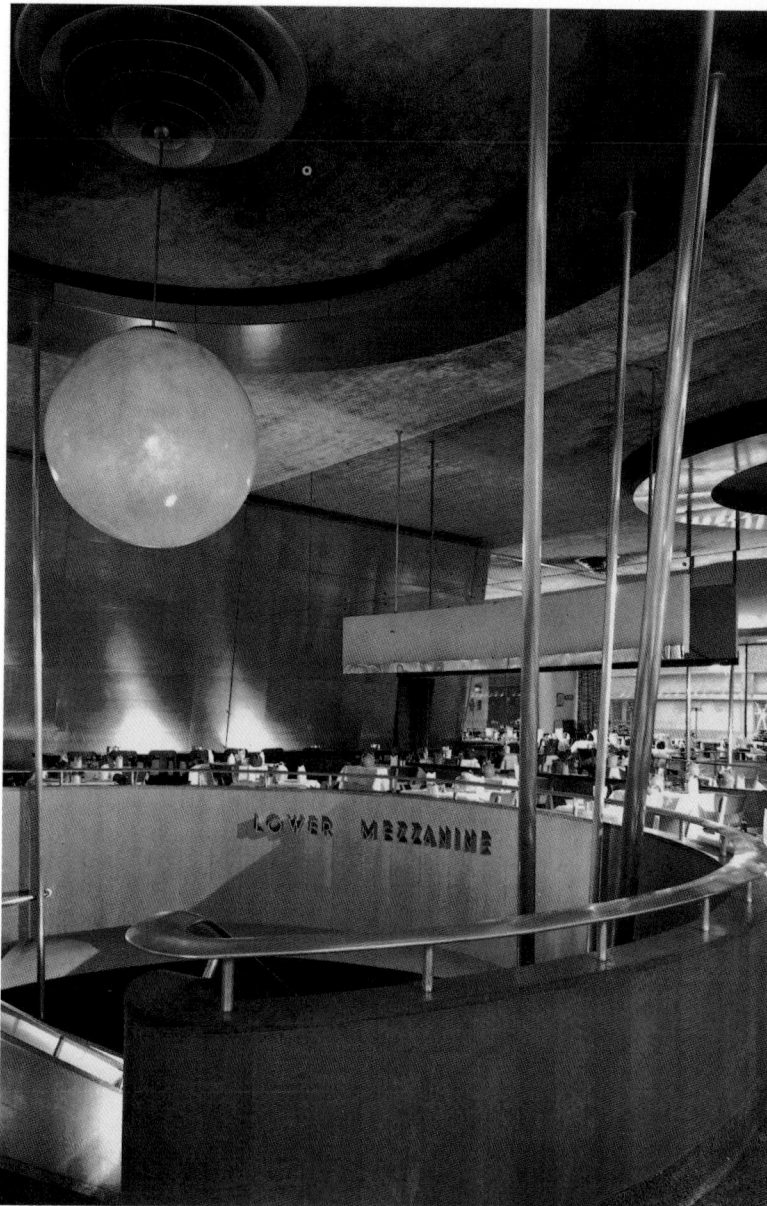

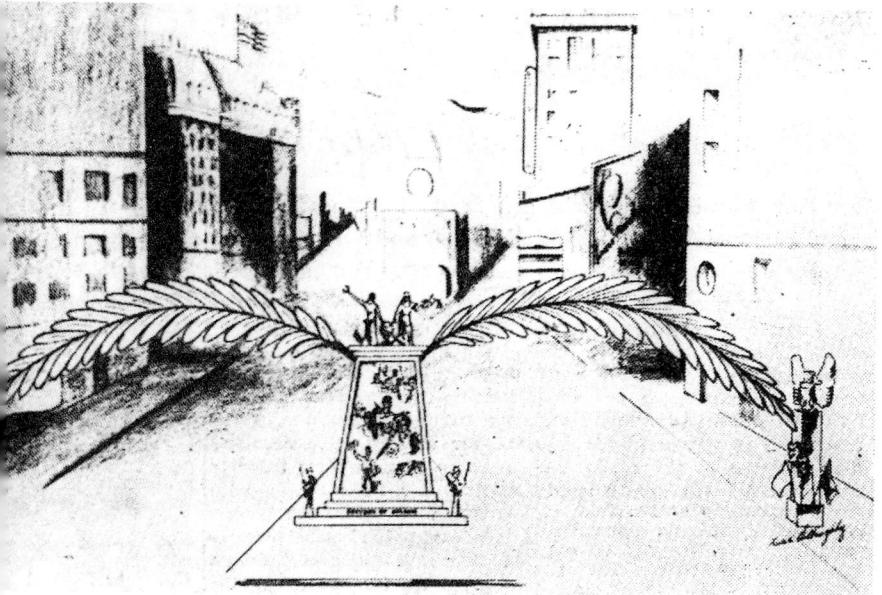

Top left: Pix Theater, 121 West Forty-second Street, between Times Square and Sixth Avenue. Ely Jacques Kahn, 1940. Auditorium. IN. CU

Bottom left: Proposed temporary victory arch, Broadway and Seventh Avenue just north of West Forty-third Street. Lucia Willoughby, 1943. Rendering. View to the north. NYT

Above: Toffenetti's, 1482–1490 Broadway, southeast corner of West Forty-third Street. Skidmore, Owings & Merrill in association with Walker & Gillette, 1940. Interior. Stoller. ©ESTO

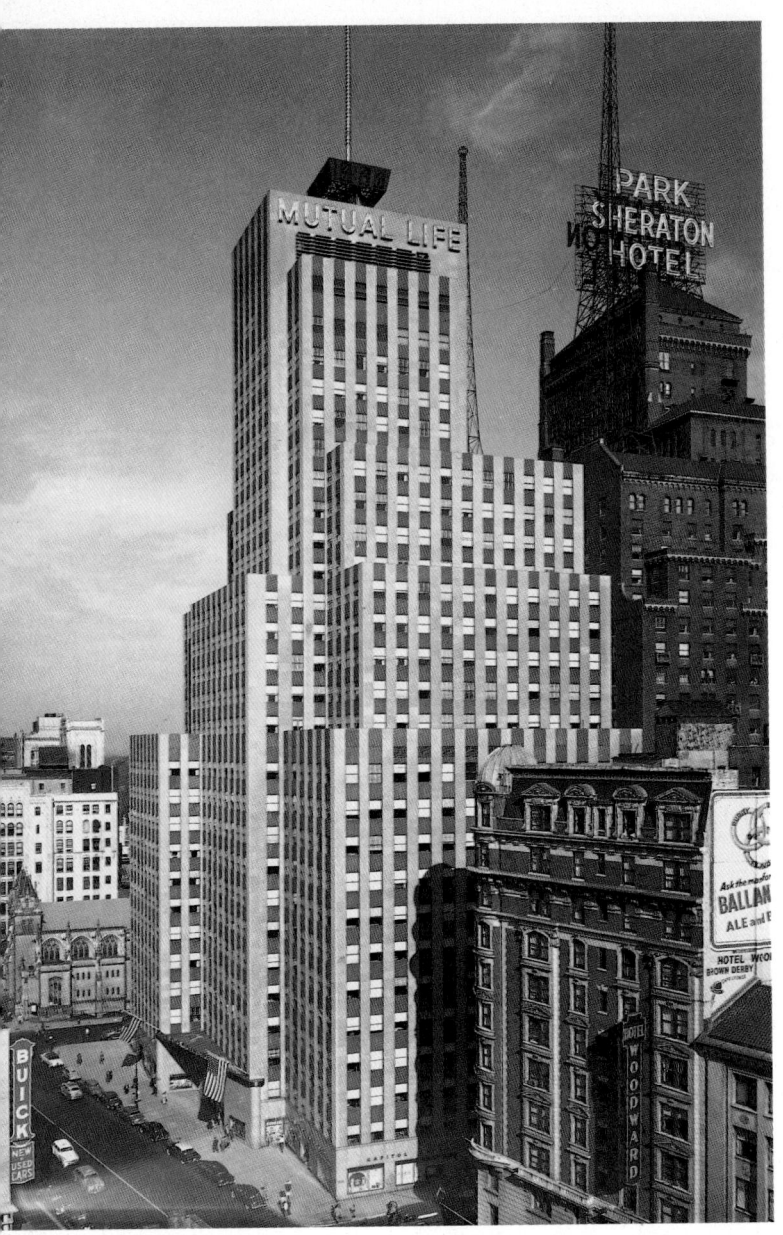

Above: Mutual of New York Insurance Company Building, 1740 Broadway, West Fifty-fifth to West Fifty-sixth Street. Shreve, Lamb & Harmon Associates, 1950. View to the north. OMH

Right: 1407 Broadway, Broadway to Seventh Avenue, West Thirty-eighth to West Thirty-ninth Street. Kahn & Jacobs, 1950. View to the south. Wurts. MCNY

alternating horizontal bands of aluminum-framed windows and marble. The rooftop garden would be sheltered by a cantilevered plane punctuated by "cheese holes" similar to those used at the Members Penthouse of the Museum of Modern Art.[17] The project was never built.

The first important building to be realized in the area after the war was a corporate office building that had no connection to the entertainment business: Shreve, Lamb & Harmon Associates' headquarters for the Mutual of New York Insurance Company (1950).[18] A holdover from before the war, the twenty-five-story, 421,000-square-foot building, vertically banded and clad in limestone, reflected the aesthetic perfected in Raymond Hood's Daily News and RCA buildings. The building was located on the east blockfront of Broadway between Fifty-fifth and Fifty-sixth streets, a site that was largely occupied by a parking lot but was once the home of the Sonoma apartment house (Thom & Wilson, 1885) and Stephen D. Hatch's Rockingham apartments (1876). Shreve, Lamb & Harmon's design received cautious praise from Lewis Mumford. He admired the composition of the building's traditional exterior walls, which consisted of vertical ribbons of stone alternating with vertical ribbons of windows, saying that they reflected the "plunging-ticker-tape style" of the prewar era. He was less favorably disposed to its overall massing, which virtually ignored Broadway's diagonal, and to its illuminated, star-topped rooftop mast rising from a four-sided black pedestal to announce the weather and the time. About the mast he wrote: "This crown doesn't crown and the decoration doesn't decorate . . . a little more freedom of design, a touch of imagination, even though it entailed extra expense, would have been welcome." Mumford proposed that Shreve and his associates should have taken their cues from the "inanities of Times Square; that dizzying whirl of lights," and suggested an electric signboard atop the building "whose aspect and message could be varied from season to season, or, for that matter, from day to day."[19]

While the Mutual of New York building was a prewar design, Kahn & Jacobs's 1407 Broadway (1950), a forty-two-story, million-square-foot skyscraper occupying the full block bounded by Broadway, Seventh Avenue, Thirty-eighth and Thirty-ninth streets, was strictly contemporary.[20] The site of 1407 Broadway had belonged to the Wendell sisters, fabled eccentrics, and was acquired in the early 1940s; the buildings on it were demolished and the lot partially excavated before the war put a stop to the work. Kahn & Jacobs's postwar design was geared to accommodate textile manufacturers who wanted to relocate from Worth Street to the garment district so they could be near their principal clients. The architects adapted the facade of their Universal Building (see "Park Avenue," above) to the requirements of a skyscraper, creating a remarkably vivacious building. Sacrificing several hundred thousand feet of potential leasable office space, the architects persuaded William Zeckendorf and Samuel M. Hirsch, the developers, to begin the setbacks at the fourth floor rather than the tenth floor mandated by zoning. In addition, at the developers' request, they provided an elaborate off-street loading facility for deliveries to the building. The building's most notable feature, aside from its size, was the exclusive use of horizontally banded windows, with frames painted vermilion to contrast with the serpentine green-colored brick that clad the alternating bands. Lewis Mumford did not like the building. Despite the sacrifice of buildable area, he saw developer greed in the *parti*, with its massive tower rising from a base. He did, however, find pleasure in the building's contrasting color scheme: "This is almost the first touch of real color in

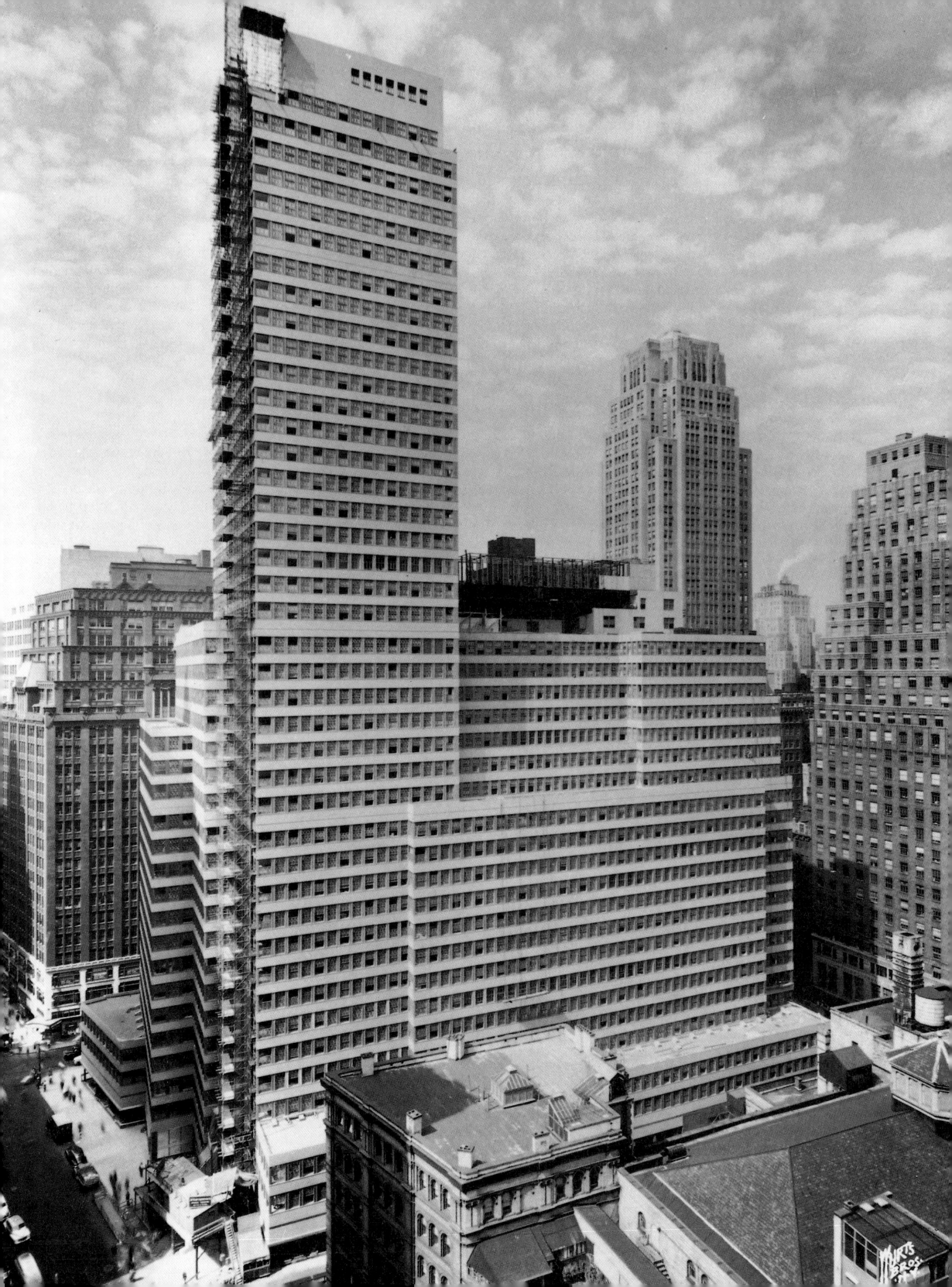

a big structure since the McGraw-Hill Building was put up, nineteen years ago."[21]

The apparel industry was the city's most important; in 1939, 35 percent of the nation's clothing was manufactured in New York. But even before the war the garment district's overcrowded conditions and its inappropriateness as a manufacturing center had become apparent. In 1930 Harvey Wiley Corbett's scheme for a new garment center to be built in the West Bronx gave architectural form to a trend that many knowledgeable observers believed inevitable—the relocation of clothing factories to suburban sites where they could be accommodated in low, well-lighted, horizontally organized buildings.[22]

Mayor La Guardia, sensing that the war offered an opportunity to maintain New York's leadership as a garment-manufacturing center and to supersede Paris as the world's fashion center, decided to assemble a committee to formulate plans for what would be called the World Fashion Center.[23] The committee, headed by Grover Whalen, the city's official greeter, included representatives of leading department stores; ex-governor Alfred E. Smith; realtor Peter Grimm; Frederick H. Ecker, chairman of Metropolitan Life Insurance Co.; Edna Woolman Chase, the editor of *Vogue*; and David Dubinsky of the International Ladies Garment Workers Union. In January 1944 the committee issued its report, which called for a large-scale complex of buildings to be built to house showrooms, design studios and executive offices; manufacturing would be left in the garment district or moved to the suburbs. The new complex would be built by developers, but as part of the project the city would build a combined war memorial and convention auditorium to seat 25,000, a 5,000-seat opera house, a school for industrial design, a rooftop heliport and an underground garage. The report contained proposals for ten sites ranging from six to eleven blocks each. One proposal called for a new Rockefeller Plaza–like avenue running between Thirty-fourth and Fortieth streets, lined by massive stone-clad buildings; another scheme proposed a glass-enclosed municipal auditorium and exposition hall surrounded by a colonnade with tapered columns. A third proposal called for the buildings to line the west side of Sixth Avenue from Thirty-eighth to Forty-second Street, with the convention auditorium located south of Bryant Park and a new opera house on the site of the Metropolitan Opera House on the block bounded by Broadway, Seventh Avenue, Thirty-ninth and Fortieth streets. Parking for the sites was to be located below either Bryant Park or Madison Square Park. Though many of its components would be realized in the postwar era, nothing came of the World Fashion Center itself.

In 1952 a new project was announced for the site of the Sloan and Stone proposal, the block bounded by Broadway and Seventh Avenue, Fifty-first and Fifty-second streets.[24] This scheme, for a 336,000-square-foot building that included 16,000 square feet of television studios, was designed by Emery Roth & Sons. They proposed a two-story base that filled the block and contained the television center, atop which twenty-three floors of glass-and-metal-encased office spaces were organized as two slabs joined together to form a right angle. The configuration, though it surely reflected that of Lever House, somehow suggested a hotel rather than an office building. This proposal was not realized, but in 1962 the site was at last developed, not as studios or offices but as a hotel.[25] The twenty-two-story, 724-room Loew's City Squire Inn, designed by Kahn & Jacobs, was a kind of plebian companion to Loew's larger, more imposing Americana (see below); the City Squire would serve to boost the Americana's business by adding to the area's reputation as a hotel district convenient to Times Square.

The 2,000-room Americana Hotel (1962), developed by Laurence and Preston Robert Tisch, was located on the east blockfront of Seventh Avenue between Fifty-second and Fifty-third streets, a site that had been occupied for sixty-five years by the fortresslike Italianate Manhattan Storage and Warehouse Company (James E. Ware, 1892), which was torn down in 1957 to make way for a parking lot.[26] The Americana was designed by Morris Lapidus, who also designed the Summit Hotel for the same developers (see "East Side: From Stuyvesant Town to Turtle Bay," above) and was working on the Uris hotel on Sixth Avenue (see "Sixth Avenue," above) when he was offered the new commission. The Urises initially accepted the fact that Lapidus was working on both hotels, but they later informed him that they had entered into a partnership with Laurance Rockefeller and Conrad Hilton and that Rockefeller insisted the architect resign from the Americana project. Although reluctant to forfeit the Hilton project, Lapidus decided to go with the Americana commission.

As realized by the firm of Morris Lapidus, Kornblath, Harle & Liebman, the Americana consisted of a three-story base containing the hotel's public rooms surmounted by a forty-seven-story east-west slab running as close to Fifty-second Street as zoning would permit. The slab was slightly angled in plan at its midpoint, forming a wide V; positioned at right angles to it, a twenty-five-story strip extended north toward Fifty-third Street. The building's long facades were composed of horizontal strips of stainless-steel-framed windows separated by bands of glazed yellow brick; its short blank facades were white Vermont marble. Commenting on the tower's shape, Lapidus said: "I don't design for shock. . . . And if I bent the Americana like a folded book, it's more than design; it's for added strength. A straight line takes a beating in the wind."[27] Whatever the imperative for the shape, the building had a lively, memorable presence, especially as it rose from the striped pavement of its Seventh Avenue plaza, where a semi-rotunda formed the slab's base. It was also structurally daring. The tallest reinforced-concrete-framed structure in the city, it combined three framing systems: from the ground floor to the fifth, the wall load was transferred to composite-steel-core columns; from the fifth floor to the twenty-ninth, reinforced-concrete sheer walls provided vertical support for the slabs, in addition to supplying wind resistance; from the twenty-ninth floor to the top, the slabs were supported on columns.

Although the hotel was primarily intended to meet the needs of business travelers and conventioneers, Lapidus, following his experience at the Summit, also tried to respond to the tastes of, as he put it, the "New Yorker at home."[28] In contrast with the exuberant interiors he designed for the Summit, Lapidus approached the Americana's interiors, as the editors of *Interior Design* noted, "with considerable reticence."[29] The main entrance was set back from Seventh Avenue and bordered on one side by a two-level, glass-enclosed, semicircular rotundalike projection containing restaurants and other public rooms. The lobby, which was enclosed by floor-to-ceiling expanses of glass along its street-facing wall and was thus clearly visible from the street, lacked Lapidus's usual kaleidoscopic mix of materials, colors and motifs. Instead, the lobby featured a comparatively reductivist scheme containing simply articulated furniture in gold and white as well as teak, white Alabama marble floors, and a colonnade of white marble veined with gold, supporting a series of gold-leafed domes leading to the registration desk. An open staircase providing access to a lower lobby was supported by concrete arches. The hotel was equipped with five restau-

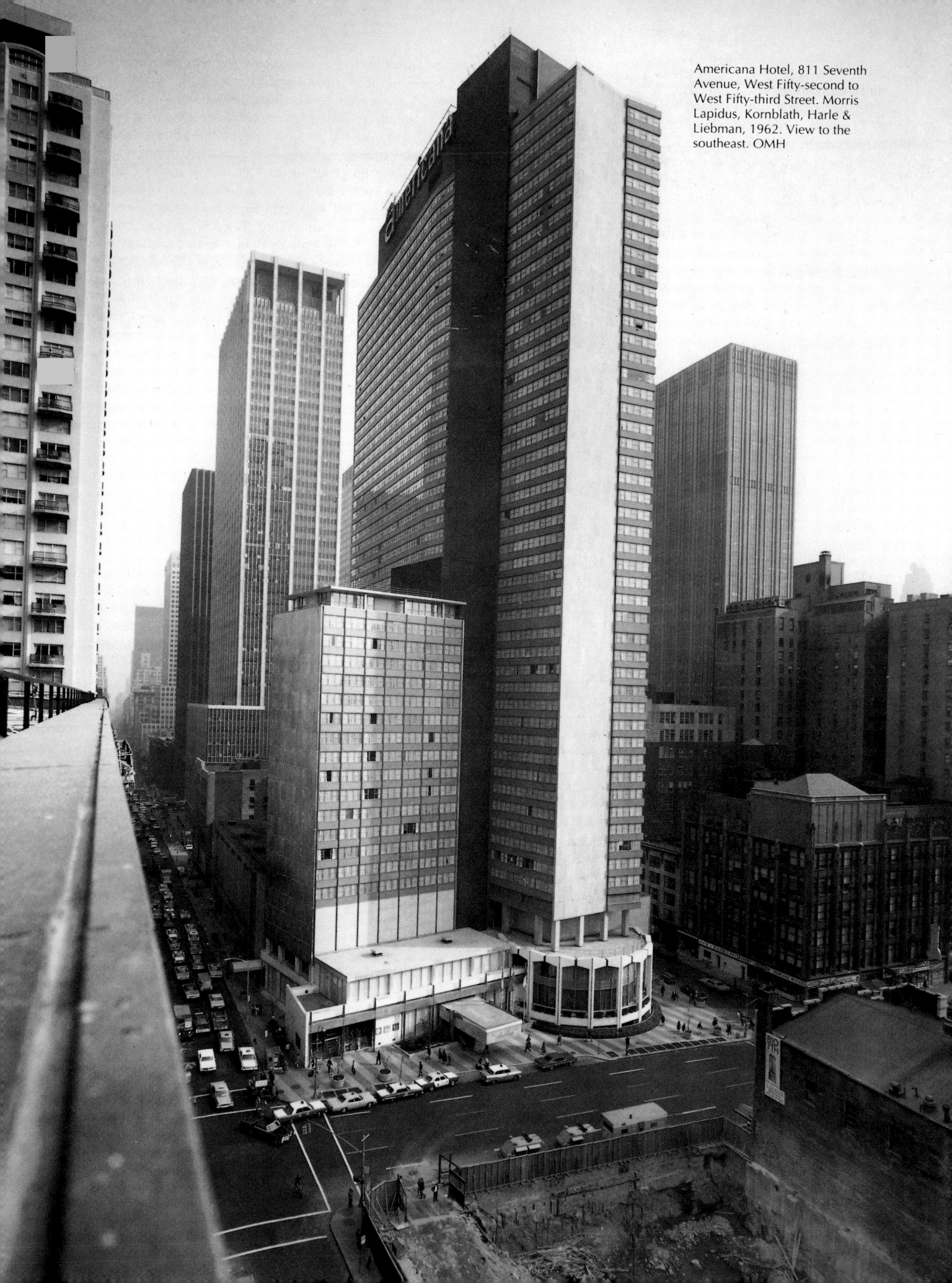

Americana Hotel, 811 Seventh
Avenue, West Fifty-second to
West Fifty-third Street. Morris
Lapidus, Kornblath, Harle &
Liebman, 1962. View to the
southeast. OMH

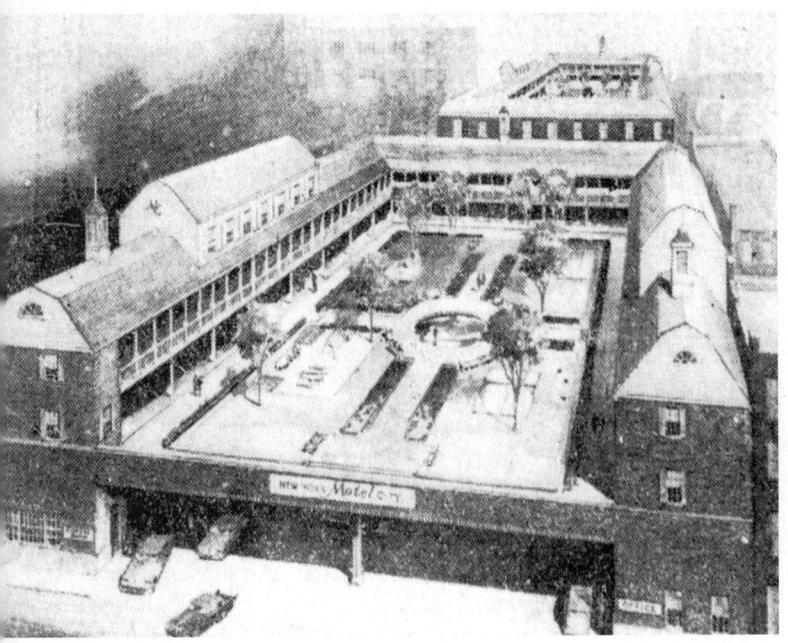

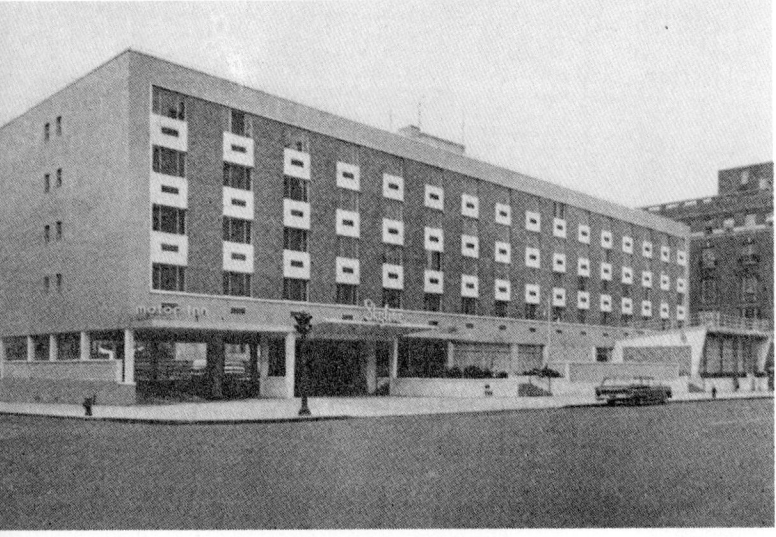

Top: Proposed Motel City, between Tenth and Eleventh avenues, West Fortieth to West Forty-fourth Street. Wechsler & Schimenti, 1958. Perspective showing view to the south with West Forty-fourth Street facade omitted to show central courtyard. NYT

Bottom: Skyline Motor Inn, west blockfront of Tenth Avenue, West Forty-ninth to West Fiftieth Street. Leo Stillman, 1959. View to the northwest. IN. CU

rants, ten ballrooms, an exposition hall and nearly an acre of kitchen facilities, which could serve 11,290 diners at once. The editors of the *New Yorker* described the hotel's 195-by-100-foot main ballroom: "The room is . . . done up in gold leaf, bronze, and marble, with a fifty-thousand-dollar chandelier attached to a winch, so that it can be raised and lowered; an electrically operated stage that can rise in four sections, seven or eight feet above the floor level; and a projection booth, equipped with movie camera and television apparatus, that disappears, when it's not in use, into the ceiling."[30]

Each public room was decorated according to a theme vaguely evocative of other times and places. Russell Lynes ridiculed this pretension, asserting that the hotel "appears to have no more reason to be called The Americana than The Summit has to be called The Summit. The banquet rooms and restaurants in the Americana are named La Ronde, The Royal Box, The Imperial Ballroom, The Royal Ball Room [*sic*], The Princess, The Versailles, The Regency, and so on. If this is Americana, we lost the Revolution." The single exception to the Eurocentric nomenclature was a men's bar called the Wooden Indian that contained, as Lynes put it, "a collection of the kind of cowboy-and-Indian mementos that looks as though they were bought by the yard." Lynes concluded that the building was "Americana only in the same way that a service station fluttering with pennants for a tire sale is Americana."[31] In response to such criticism, Lapidus said that the Americana and his other New York hotels had been "built for fun; the only trouble is, people take them seriously."[32]

In contrast with the large hotels built around Broadway and Seventh Avenue, the western reaches of the Times Square area became home to marginal motel-type projects of the kind usually associated with provincial cities. In 1958 plans were announced for the construction of a sprawling, 400-room motel on a 2.5-acre site stretching from Fortieth to Forty-fourth Street, between Tenth and Eleventh avenues, located above the New York Central Railroad's sunken tracks.[33] In order to raise capital, the financially troubled railroad had leased the property's air rights to Motel City Inc. for twenty-five years and further negotiated a percentage of the motel's gross receipts. The low-density building complex would be not only Manhattan's first motel but also the world's largest. Designed by the architectural firm of Wechsler & Schimenti, Motel City was to consist of four separate four-story buildings in the Dutch Colonial style, complete with gambrel roofs. Together the buildings would enclose a large, landscaped central courtyard lifted one story above a street-level parking lot; arcaded, open-air passageways were to surround the courtyards, which contained gardens, wading pools, children's play areas and shuffleboard courts.

The project represented a somewhat successful attempt to equip the moderately priced motel with resort amenities and, more important, to give it the distinct sense of being a series of cloistered retreats set apart from the turmoil of the surrounding city. The urban context, however, rendered kitsch the use of so specific a traditional architectural vocabulary. In a letter to the editor of the *New York Times*, one observer noted, "If a colonial motel, well designed for a country landscape and in scale with its surroundings, looks well on the road, it does not follow at all that a similar 'design' ten-times larger, plunked in the middle of a metropolis, is an esthetic solution to an architectural problem."[34] When the scaled-down complex of only two buildings was built, a decidedly more banal if more contextually appropriate Modernist vocabulary was adopted in place of the Dutch Colonial style initially called for. The two buildings of Motel

City, located between Forty-first and Forty-third streets, contained a total of 258 rooms: the first building, occupying the northern site, had three stories and was completed in 1962; the second building had seven stories and was completed the following year.

By the time Motel City was built, the Skyline Motor Inn, on the west side of Tenth Avenue between Forty-ninth and Fiftieth streets, had already achieved the distinction of being New York's first inner-city motel.[35] Completed in 1959, it was, according to the editors of *Real Estate Record and Guide*, a first not only for the city but for the nation.[36] As designed by the architect Leo Stillman, the 130-room motel consisted of a block-long, four-story, gray-glazed-brick rectangle elevated above a largely glass-enclosed lobby and restaurant, as well as a car ramp leading to a basement-level parking garage. The motel's rather austere principal facade was enlivened by white spandrels containing centrally located black air-conditioning units. With the exception of the motel's restaurant, which projected forward close to the lot line, the Skyline Motor Inn, in keeping with its suburban scale and aesthetic, was set back from the street by a sparsely detailed plaza landscaped by David Engel in "the Japanese style," as the *New York Times* put it.[37] The motel was convenient for motorists: guests arriving by car could drive into the free parking garage, confirm their reservations by loudspeaker, park, and then take an elevator to the ground-floor lobby, where they would check in. As in the prototypical suburban house, the "front" door became functionally secondary, if not altogether obsolete, while the "back" door, closest to the garage, became the principal entrance.

Inside, the motel adopted what the *New Yorker* described as "the sunniest Amurrican Modern style," with stripped-down interiors designed by Frederick Fox, best known not as an interior designer but as a designer of sets for the stage and television.[38] An executive suite containing an office/living room complete with desks, filing cabinets, multiple telephones and a typewriter was located on the main floor. Harold Steinberg, president of the Downing Management Corporation, which developed the motel, said, "We believe this is the coming hotel room for business men. A man coming to New York for a week's business can work and live here at the same time. If the demand is great enough, our next hotel of this type will have one-third of its rooms as executive suites."[39]

From the first, the Skyline Motor Inn was a highly successful business venture that inspired competition. It was quickly joined by the Sheraton Motor Inn, a much larger motel located nearby at the northeast corner of Twelfth Avenue and Forty-second Street, near the Lincoln Tunnel and adjacent to an exit of the West Side Highway.[40] Completed in 1962 and designed by Morris Lapidus, Harle & Liebman, the Sheraton Motor Inn was, as the editors of the *New Yorker* described it, "a startlingly classy pioneer in a somewhat déclassé neighborhood."[41] The twenty-story reinforced-concrete building consisted of a four-story parking garage surmounted by two attached sixteen-story slabs arranged in an L. Each of the 448 guest room windows was canted to maximize views of the river and midtown as well as to add visual interest to the otherwise austere facades. The editors of *Progressive Architecture* noted that the architects seemed to be "in a strangely subdued mood" and that the Sheraton compared with the Summit was "like a Weimaraner with a French poodle."[42] Despite its categorization as a motel, the Sheraton Motor Inn contained a wide variety of hotel-quality facilities, including a bar evocative of an English pub, a coffee shop designed to resemble a French country inn, two ball-

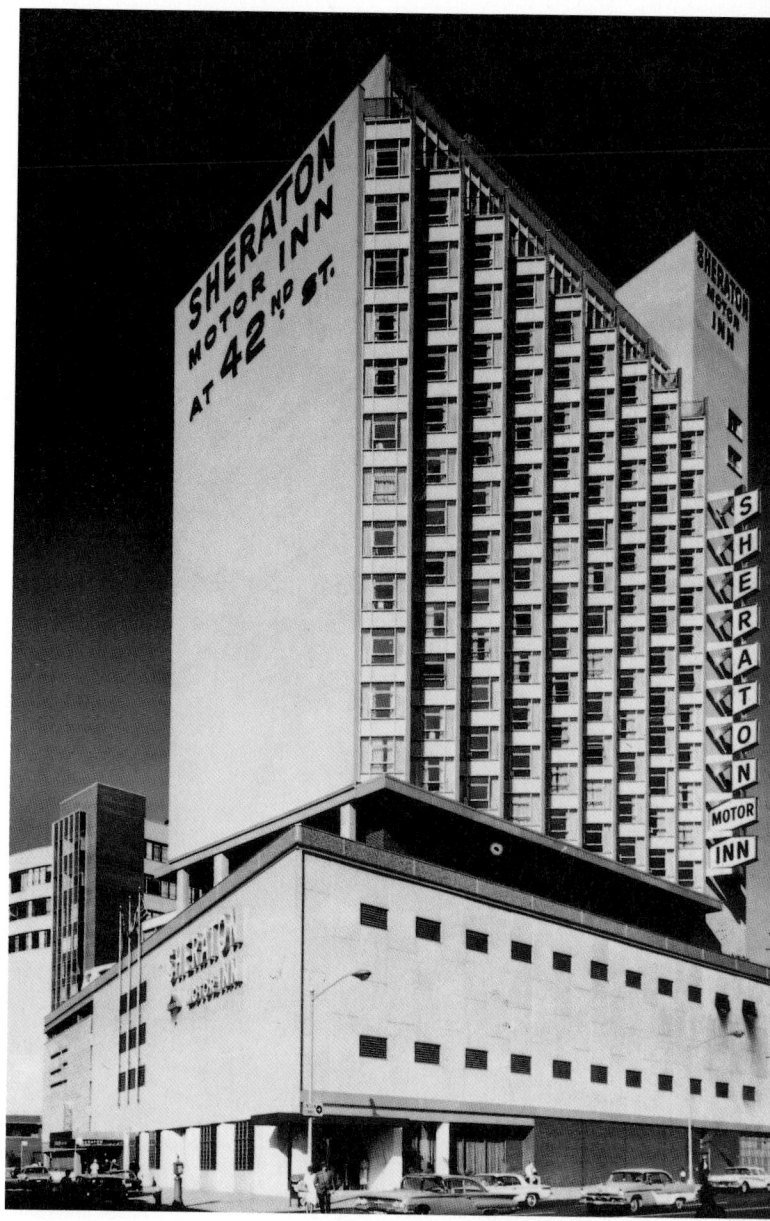

Sheraton Motor Inn, northeast corner of Twelfth Avenue and West Forty-second Street. Morris Lapidus, Harle & Liebman, 1962. View to the northeast. ML

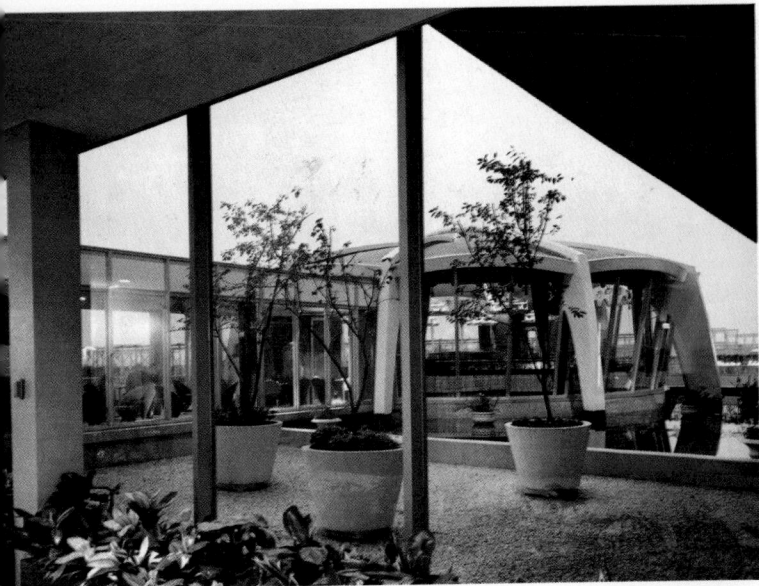

rooms, a rooftop swimming pool called "Surfside 20" and, on the roof of the parking garage, a restaurant called the Carousel Café, complete with banquettes that revolved to fully exploit the river views.

Several other motels were built in the area during the early 1960s. The Riviera Congress Motor Inn (1961), owned by the real estate developer and theater enthusiast Irving Maidman, was designed by Wechsler & Schimenti and located on the east blockfront of Tenth Avenue between Fortieth and Forty-first streets.[43] The eight-story building was surfaced in multicolored brick set in a pattern described by the editors of *Real Estate Record and Guide* as "an Indian primitive design." Inside, the motel contained 182 guest rooms and adopted an overall decorative theme based on Latin American motifs. The motel also incorporated a two-level enclosed parking garage as well as a rooftop restaurant and adjacent recreational area with badminton and shuffleboard courts. The *Real Estate Record and Guide* hyped the Riviera Congress as "the most recent development in the conversion of the area centered around Tenth Avenue and Forty-second Street from a drab neighborhood of warehouses and tenements to a modern resort area." The article continued: "The attraction of the area as a mushrooming vacation haven lies in its location. Situated near the Lincoln Tunnel, an important gateway to the city, [it] . . . obviates the necessity of battling the midtown traffic. Then, too, with the motor lodge offering the facilities and accommodations of a country-type resort, guests are able to enjoy a unique combination of country living and the excitement of a visit to the big city."[44]

In 1963 the Holiday Inn chain opened its first component in New York, timed to capitalize on the upcoming World's Fair; the ten-story, 260-room motel, designed by Max S. Simon, was located on a block-through site extending from Fifty-sixth to Fifty-seventh Street, between Ninth and Tenth avenues.[45] In the same year, the city welcomed the fourteen-story, 370-room Loew's Motor Inn, located nearby on the east side of Eighth Avenue between Forty-eighth and Forty-ninth streets,[46] and the Howard Johnson Motor Lodge, on the west side of Eighth Avenue between Fifty-first and Fifty-second streets, which was to be operated by the Loew's corporation in cooperation with the restaurant chain, long a symbol of reliable, family-oriented service.[47] And two blocks to the north, a seventeen-story motel and apartment building designed by the architectural and engineering firm of Herbert Fluscher Associates occupied a full-block site on the west side of Eighth Avenue between Fifty-fourth and Fifty-fifth streets, replacing Stillman's Gym, a venerable institution cherished by generations of athletes.[48]

The success of these west side motels depended not only on the short-term, fair-induced boom, or even on automobiling out-of-towners and suburbanites, but to a surprisingly large degree on New Yorkers, who sought a weekend refuge close to home. In August 1963 the journalist Gay Talese, writing in the *New York Times*, reported that the management of the Sheraton Motor Inn claimed that on some summer weekends, when the temperature soared, as many as a quarter of the motel's rooms were occupied by New Yorkers. Talese wrote:

> Twelfth Avenue is a neighborhood of warehouses and hash houses, and few New Yorkers think of it as an ideal place for spending a summer weekend. But it is. It is because such resort-like motels as the Sheraton Motor Inn—possessing an outdoor pool, fine restaurant and lively cocktail lounge—have recently given a kind of Atlantic City-on-Hudson touch to 12th Avenue and 42nd Street. On hot weekends the Sheraton—and other luxury motels built on Manhattan's West Side during the

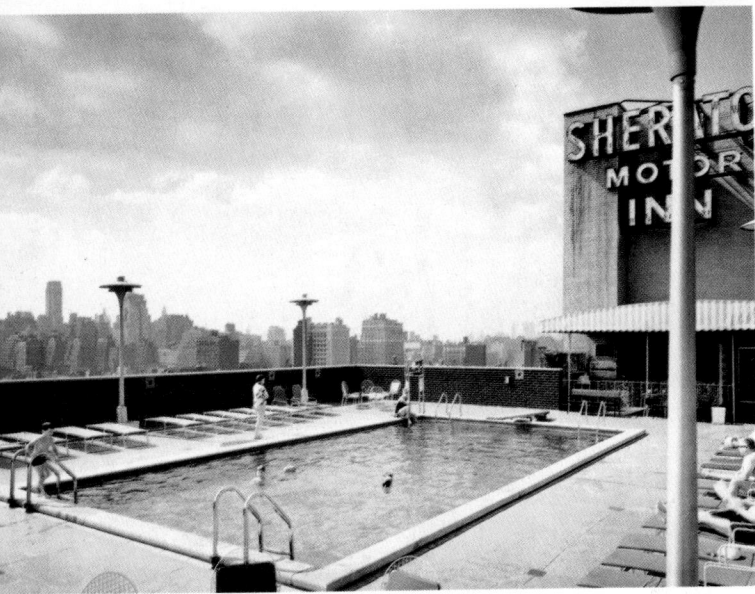

Top: Sheraton Motor Inn, northeast corner of Twelfth Avenue and West Forty-second Street. Morris Lapidus, Harle & Liebman, 1962. Carousel Café. ML

Bottom: Sheraton Motor Inn. View to the southeast of rooftop swimming pool. ML

last year or so—have been renting rooms to dozens of New Yorkers who do not wish to battle highway traffic, to gamble on cloudy skies or to eat inferior food in some overcrowded restaurant near the beach.[49]

In addition to hotels and motels, the west side gained a new private club facility in 1963 when the Princeton Club moved into its own building in the heart of clubland at 15 West Forty-third Street.[50] The club had been housed in a townhouse on the northwest corner of Park Avenue and Thirty-ninth Street until 1960, when it was sold to make way for an office building, 90 Park Avenue. Its new location was diagonally across the street from the Columbia Club, housed in the former Hotel Renaissance (Clarence Luce, 1894; Howard & Cauldwell, 1898);[51] next door to McKim, Mead & White's Century Association (1891);[52] down the block from the back of Cyrus L. W. Eidlitz's Association of the Bar of the City of New York (1895);[53] and just a block downtown from both McKim, Mead & White's Harvard Club (1902)[54] and Warren & Wetmore's New York Yacht Club (1899).[55]

Designed by Voorhees, Walker, Smith, Smith & Haines, with interiors by Chandler Cudlipp Associates, the Princeton Club was the first new clubhouse to be built in New York since the completion of the Union Club and the Cosmopolitan Club (both 1932).[56] It replaced a parking lot where the Academy of Medicine, designed by R. H. Robertson in 1889, had stood until 1936.[57] The club's bland limestone-clad facade, rising from a smooth granite base punctured only by the building's main and service entrances, conveyed very little of the sense of aggrandized domesticity characteristic of the best of its predecessors. Inside, according to the grumbles of one or two members, the club had a faint resemblance to "a Howard Johnson motel."[58] This was said to be the result of an effort to make the club a "family" institution, particularly geared "to please the girls," as the *Princeton Alumni Weekly* bluntly put it.[59] "Gone are all the ancient appurtenances of the Man's World," *Time* observed, "the big leather chairs, the massive standing lamps, the gloomy high ceilings and rich carpets. Instead, the rooms are low-ceilinged (more floors) and cheerily antiseptic, with light furniture and artificial plants, bathed in the flat shadowless lighting of fluorescent panels and inset ceiling lamps."[60]

Saving the Theater District?

Despite the significant amount of building activity in the area, the Times Square entertainment district failed to retain its wartime prosperity or glamour. As box office revenues declined, less investment was made in the theaters' physical plant, creating a dangerous downward spiral. No new theaters were built, although a few were renovated to keep up with changing tastes and developing technology. In 1952 the Broadway Theater (Eugene DeRosa, 1924), at 1681 Broadway, was converted by William Lescaze to accommodate Cinerama, a new film system that created startling impressions of three-dimensional reality by projecting the images captured by three cameras on a wide, curving screen.[61] Though the Broadway Theater had been designed for motion pictures, it had been converted for use as a legitimate theater in 1930 and reconverted to movies a few years later, only to be converted to live theater again in 1942. Lescaze's renovation was necessarily minimal, involving the insertion of the sixty-four-by-twenty-three-foot screen, set on a radius of twenty-five feet, and three projection booths under the balcony. Although Cinerama was, as *Architectural Forum* put it,

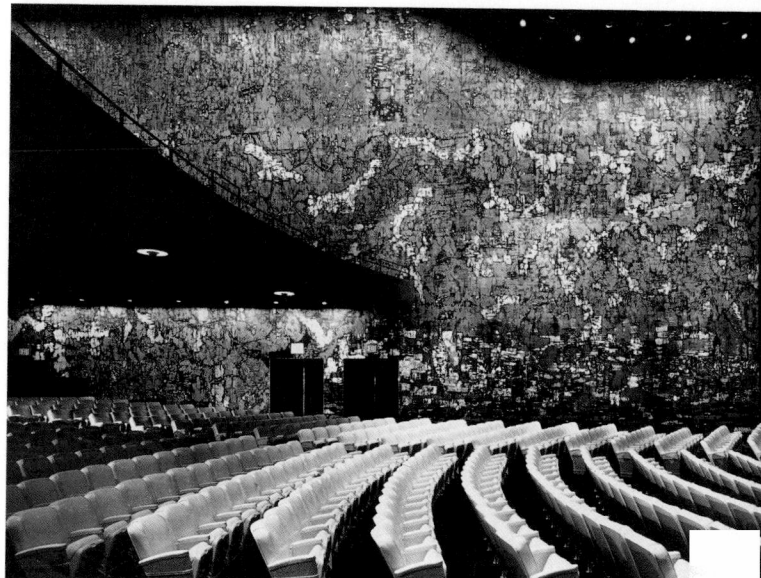

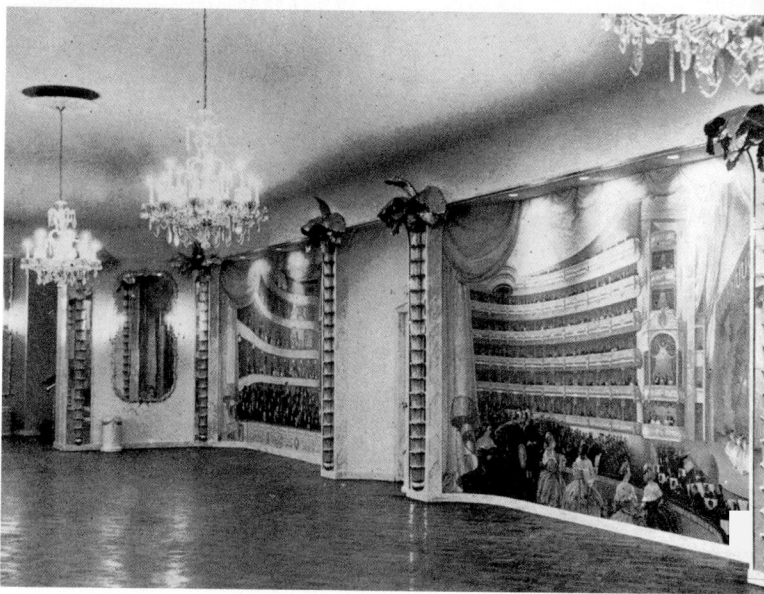

Top: Astor Theater, 1537 Broadway, northwest corner of West Forty-fifth Street. George Keister, 1906; renovation, John McNamara and Buffie Johnson, 1959. Auditorium showing part of Johnson's mural *New York Summer Night*. Freedman. BJ

Bottom: Lunt-Fontanne Theater, formerly Globe Theater (Carrère & Hastings, 1909), 205 West Forty-sixth Street, northwest corner of Broadway. Interior by Arthur Boys, 1958. Promenade showing murals by Cosmo di Salvo. Mazza. IN. CU

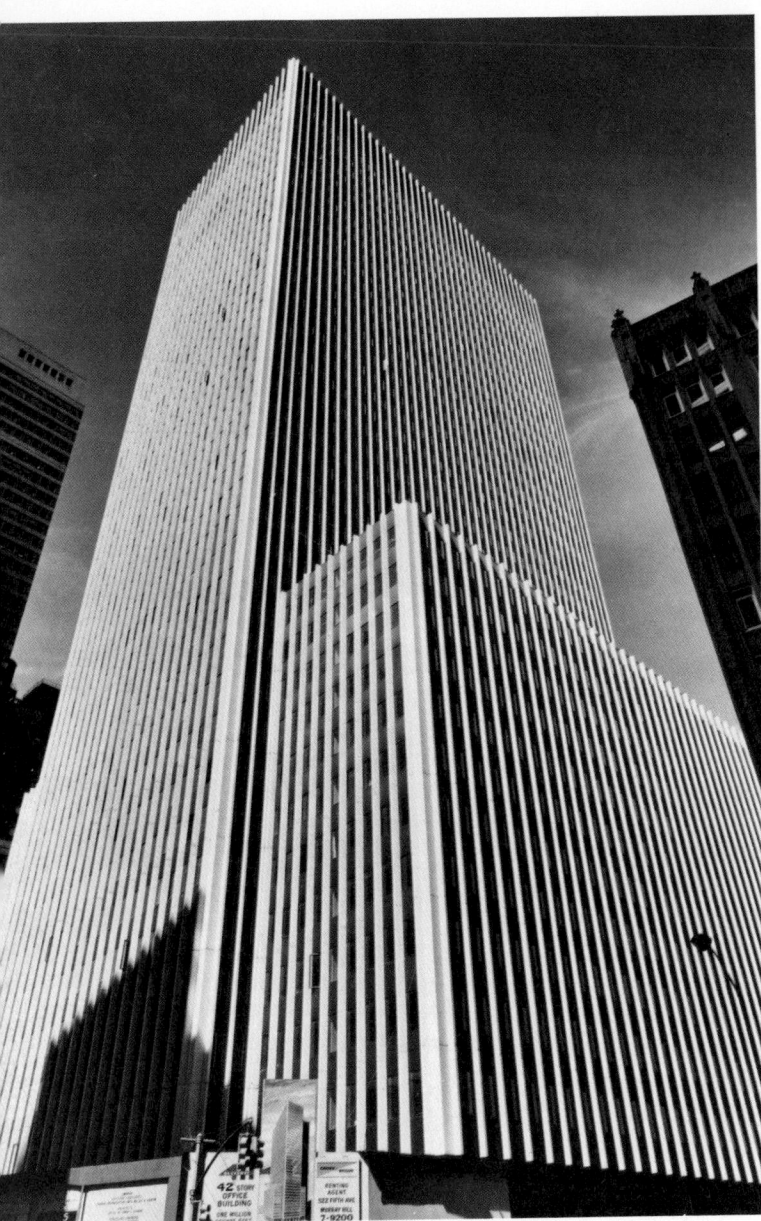

Above: 1411 Broadway, Seventh Avenue to Broadway, West Thirty-ninth to West Fortieth Street. Irwin S. Chanin, 1969. View to the southwest. Wurts. MCNY

Top right: One Astor Plaza, also known as the W. T. Grant Building, 1515 Broadway, West Forty-fourth to West Forty-fifth Street. Kahn & Jacobs, 1969. View to the northwest showing Minskoff Theater at the base. OMH

Bottom right: One Astor Plaza. Cross-section. TDT. CU

"Hollywood's first 'smash' answer to TV," it did not prove to be an enduring attraction.[62]

On December 17, 1959, the fifty-three-year-old Astor Theater (George Keister, 1906) was reopened after undergoing a million-dollar renovation to transform it into what was described as a "complete composition in abstract art."[63] The Astor was one of the few legitimate theaters built directly on Times Square; after 1913, when it showcased the film *Quo Vadis*, it alternated between films and live attractions, a policy that remained in effect until 1925, after which only films were shown. As redesigned by John McNamara, the veteran theater architect, and the artist Buffie Johnson, the theater now presented Times Square with a marquee of tiny, twinkling white lights that brought to glittering life a sidewalk of Venetian glass terrazzo squares. The same flooring was carried through to the lobby, which also contained a twenty-five-by-ten-foot continuation of Johnson's *New York Summer Night*, a huge abstract oil painting covering both side walls of the auditorium. Forty-five feet high and ninety-seven feet long, it was made up of 209 sections executed in a range of blues intersected by a network of black lines and white, yellow and red splotches. The remodeled interior featured a cantilevered mezzanine in place of the old boxes and balconies as well as an acoustically inspired curved ceiling and a new proscenium installed to accommodate the fifty-by-twenty-foot wall-to-wall screen, which could be configured as either flat or curved in accordance with the projection requirements of a given film.

Some existing legitimate theaters were renovated as well, most notably the former Globe (Carrère & Hastings, 1909), which became the Lunt-Fontanne in 1958.[64] As part of the redecoration, the theater's original entrance at 1555 Broadway was abandoned; the new entrance, at 205 West Forty-sixth Street, had formerly been a secondary entrance. Once the most luxurious of Broadway playhouses but used for movies since the 1930s, the theater was redecorated by the British designer Arthur Boys, who was asked by the new owner, Robert W. Dowling, to base his work on the music room of Frederick the Great's Sans Souci Palace and on Venice's Fenice Theater. Because, according to Dowling, "going to the theater should be like visiting a charming and gracious home," he wanted the redesign to have "a new elegance and comfort."[65] Marya Mannes said that the original Globe had been considered "the most beautiful" theater of its day, "with Grecian pillars and a balcony promenade that drew such phrases as 'commodious and handsome.'" Although she acknowledged that this style was "no longer supported by public taste," she found the renovation showy, lacking the dignity required for serious drama: "Mr. Dowling has spent millions in painting the reconditioned house pale-blue and white, encrusting it with rococo, stringing it with crystal chandeliers, upholstering it with damask and carpeting it in deepest pile; and what is his idea of a gracious home is my idea of an inflated powder room."[66]

In 1953 the announcement of the replacement of the historic Empire Theater, on the southeast corner of Broadway and Fortieth Street, with Emery Roth & Sons' conventionally clad, twenty-two-story, 340,000-square-foot 1430 Broadway office building (1956) foreshadowed a trend that would begin to alarm the theater world in the mid-1960s.[67] In 1967 the Paramount Theater (Rapp & Rapp 1926), a great motion picture palace that seemed secure by virtue of its location in a revenue-producing office building on the west side of Broadway between Forty-third and Forty-fourth streets, was closed and its vast interior space refitted for use by the *New York Times* as eight floors of offices that connected to the newspaper's headquarters in the Times Annex directly to the west.[68]

Shocking though the loss of the Paramount Theater was, it could be explained as a result of television's impact on the entertainment industry as a whole. Far less understandable was the 1965 rapelike renovation of the Times Tower (Cyrus L. W. Eidlitz, 1904), long the symbolic heart of the area if not the city as a whole (see chapter 16). Another significant loss was the 1967 demolition of the Metropolitan Opera House, which to many people was the city's most splendid theater interior ever (see chapter 16). The opera house, occupying a full block bounded by Broadway, Seventh Avenue, Thirty-ninth and Fortieth streets, was torn down to make way for Irwin S. Chanin's 1411 Broadway (1969), a bland forty-two-story office building clad in stone, bronzed aluminum and glass.[69]

But it was the closing of the Hotel Astor (Clinton & Russell, 1909) in 1966 that received the most attention. One of the world's great hotels, the Astor had been a landmark of New York since its completion. The configuration of the office building proposed to replace it, Kahn & Jacobs's One Astor Plaza (1971), was inextricably intertwined with the Special Theater District Zoning Amendment, which created the city's first special zoning district, devised to couple the construction of office buildings in the Times Square area with the construction of new theaters.[70] One Astor Plaza also marked the dramatic acceleration in the shift from Times Square's principal role as a nighttime world of entertainment to its hitherto secondary daytime role as an office district.

One Astor Plaza, also known as the W. T. Grant Building, was the fulfillment of a development concept for the site that had been considered as early as 1947, when plans were announced to convert the hotel to offices for Metro-Goldwyn-Mayer. Kahn & Jacobs's design for the site, the first building to be realized under the new zoning district, included the 1,621-seat Minskoff Theater, suitable for large-scale theatrical presentations such as musicals. The Minskoff, named for the building's developers, was built above a ground floor that contained shops facing Times Square and a covered arcade well to the west, which connected Forty-fourth and Forty-fifth streets. The musical theater was entered from this arcade; a second, 1,500-seat movie theater, located in the building's basement, had a separate entrance on Forty-fourth Street. Originally intended for the roof of the musical theater was a restaurant overlooking Times Square; although this was never built, a restaurant on street level, located at the western end of the site, where the new building backed up onto Shubert Alley, was built. At one point in the design process, Shubert Alley was intended to be redesigned as a glazed galleria.

The 1.4 million-square-foot, fifty-four-story office tower, largely sheathed in glass, was set atop the base containing the Minskoff Theater and was placed 135 feet back from Broadway. It was entered at the two Broadway corners, where escalators lifted officegoers up past the theater's edges to the second-floor-level lobby at the rear of the site. Der Scutt, Kahn & Jacobs's lead designer for the project, had studied and worked with Paul Rudolph, whose sculptural approach he admired. Scutt attempted to give the building presence and sculptural force by expressing the mechanical shafts as if they were superscaled pylons. Clad in granite and set at quarter points of each facade, they established a syncopated rhythm that suggested a pinwheel pattern, which was emphasized by the fact that the shafts were extended above the bulky tower to break the flat skyline as wedge-shaped sculptural planes. For C. Ray Smith, this gesture,

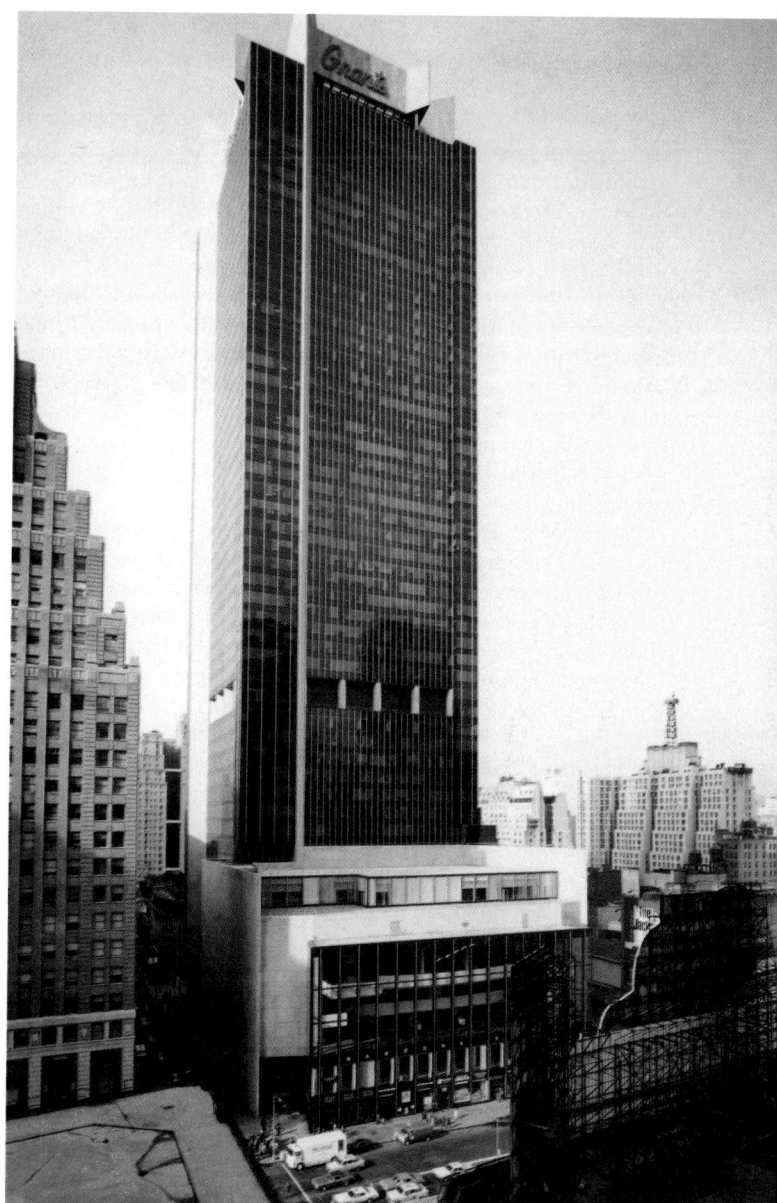

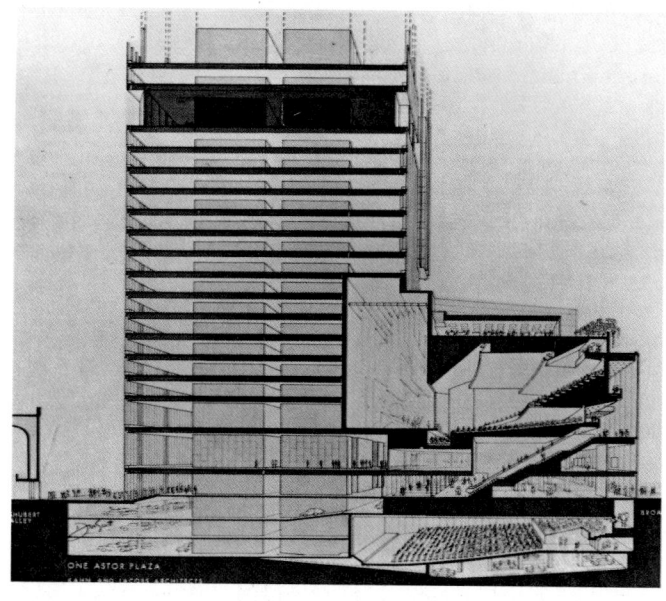

by altering the historic center-peaked crowning features of earlier skyscrapers, symbolized "the new design" spirit of the 1970s, with its ironic, mannerist sensibility.[71]

The construction of One Astor Plaza proved highly complex; the juxtaposition of an office building with a theater was technically demanding. As Thomas Connolly, the Bethlehem Company's supervising engineer in charge of the building's structural steel, explained: "Without that theater, this building would have been a snap from an engineering point of view. With this theater, it's become a humdinger of an engineering feat. This building has the largest beam, the largest truss and the heaviest girder of any building in New York."[72] To accommodate the theater in its base, the supporting structure of the building's east facade had to be supported by the roof of the theater wing, necessitating the construction of two massive girders carrying a Vierendeel truss. Despite the complex structural engineering, the final product was decidedly uninteresting. The musical theater proved too large for most shows and very costly to operate. In addition, its bland, detail-less design failed to spark the imagination of theatergoers. Viewed from Broadway, the theater's lobby—a cavernous glass box lifted above street-level shops—was the building's principal feature. Although it was illuminated at night, it came to life only during the short periods when theatergoers filled the space.

The city government's struggle to convince the developers of One Astor Plaza to build a mixed-use office and theater facility was based on certain assumptions widely held at the time. In the mid-1960s, when talk of the Hotel Astor's imminent demise was common, city planners were still not sensitive to the precarious future that New York's entertainment industry faced. The prevailing notion in city hall was that the westward expansion of the midtown office-building district was a good thing for the city as a whole. Moreover, few people, even those who struggled to preserve the theater district, saw the existing theaters as inherently worth saving. Richard Weinstein, a cofounder of the Urban Design Group and a key figure in the efforts to guarantee the theater district's future, believed that most of the remaining Broadway theaters were "uncomfortable and obsolete" and "not of sufficient architectural distinction to qualify for retention as landmarks."[73] For Weinstein and others, the area's future lay in the construction of new office buildings that included theaters, which would make Times Square a round-the-clock neighborhood of both work and pleasure. One Astor Plaza seemed to represent the beginning of a trend toward office development in the theater district, which had lost forty-five theaters since its heyday in the 1920s. In response to this perceived trend, the City Planning Commission, guided by its Urban Design Group, set out to develop special zoning provisions that would encourage developers working in the area to incorporate theaters in their new buildings, in return for which they would be granted bonuses in the form of additional leasable office area.

The process began when the Minskoffs applied to the commission for a zoning change so that the Hotel Astor site could be used for an office building—a change that, given the location, the scale and the commercial nature of both enterprises, would normally have been given more or less routinely. The Minskoffs also sought a special permit to modestly penetrate the sky exposure plane so that they could get the kind of large floor plates they wanted for their tower floors. In return for these favors, in accord with the 1961 zoning resolution's provisions, they initially proposed to provide a triangular, street-level public plaza, which they instructed their architects to locate inconspicuously to the side so that the building's lucrative Broadway frontage could be maximized. In making these requests, the Minskoffs never suspected that they would become embroiled in a tug-of-war with city officials over Times Square's future. Indeed, as Richard Weinstein later recalled, nothing out of the ordinary would have happened if someone in the City Planning Department had not brought the application to the attention of the newly formed Urban Design Group, whose somewhat vague mission was to maintain, as Weinstein put it, "the attractiveness of city sites."[74] Even then, things might have gone as the Minskoffs planned, had it not become known to the Urban Design Group that Mayor Lindsay, himself an avid theatergoer, was concerned that an office-building boom might lead to the theater district's destruction.

Once they grasped the circumstances, the Urban Design Group saw an opportunity to trade with the Minskoffs for a better design and requested that a legitimate theater be included as part of the project. The developers and their architects greeted the idea with derision, saying that the inclusion of a theater was technically and economically unfeasible. This contention was at least somewhat disingenuous, since Kahn & Jacobs had designed an unrealized mixed-use theater complex for an undisclosed site in the west fifties in 1953 at the behest of another client, Howard S. Cullman, a theatrical angel who was also chairman of the Port Authority.[75] The real source of the Minskoffs' objections was not, in all likelihood, the economics of this specific instance. Rather, they saw the Urban Design Group's intrusion as a threat to the investments they had made in theater properties throughout Times Square in the expectation that the district would cease to exist as an entertainment center and that the theaters would be torn down to make way for much more lucrative office buildings. Treating the Urban Design Group as little more than a nuisance, the Minskoffs took their arguments to the City Planning Commission. When its chairman, Donald Elliott, made it clear that he supported the theater idea, they went over his head to the mayor, who not only backed up the chairman, the commission and the Urban Design Group but also used his considerable charm to persuade the developers to rethink their position in the interests of the city as a whole.

The Minskoffs did so, returning with a proposal that included a theater located at the rear of the site and an office tower twice the size permitted under zoning. They also presented their first, theater-less scheme as well as another scheme, described by Weinstein as "a mindless, ominous, faceless structure, legal under existing zoning, with two low, clawlike appendages (doubtless both of them would have been banks) pinching a small plaza between them."[76] According to Jonathan Barnett, another principal of the Urban Design Group, the meeting when the new scheme was presented was a "tough" one, with the developers insisting that this proposal was their last word and that, even with the huge increase in floor area, it was only barely feasible. "I remember feeling very depressed as Donald Elliott and I took the elevator down from this meeting," Barnett recalled. "Donald, however, was elated. 'Well,' he said, 'I think you guys have got your theater.' I expressed doubt: it was impossible for the Planning Commission to grant anything like the floor area the developer was asking for. 'Oh that,' said Elliott, 'that just shows they're ready to negotiate.'"[77]

In the end, the Minskoffs included a theater in the front of their building, a 20 percent bonus of floor area was negotiated, and a special zoning district was created to permit similar bonuses for new office buildings between Fortieth and Fifty-seventh streets, Sixth and Eighth avenues, that incorporated theaters. Elliott's hopes for the new district zoning were high. In 1967, the year the new zoning was passed, he said:

> The tide of new office construction is sweeping westward, and the Great White Way lies directly in its path. We could stand by and see the theater district obliterated, or take the initiative to coordinate the planned redevelopment of the area with private capital. Office buildings and stores produce greater financial return than theaters. This means that every theater in the district is a potential target for redevelopment. Now, with the added economic incentive to build new theaters under planning supervision, the area can be enhanced and protected.[78]

Thus, when Mayor Lindsay led the group of city officials and business leaders in the groundbreaking for One Astor Plaza in October 1968, they were not merely celebrating the construction of an office building but proclaiming the triumph of a new partnership between the public and private sectors to achieve desired planning goals for which public funds were unavailable. In addition, they believed they were celebrating a new era of economic stability for Times Square as an entertainment center. The celebration, growing out of a heady mixture of high ideals and bottom-line economics, did not prove long-lasting, and Times Square somehow seemed all the more tawdry for its overscaled, underembellished corporate guest. And unfortunately, although the new Special Theater District Zoning Amendment, drafted by planners who believed that new office buildings in the district were both inevitable and desirable, did encourage the construction of new legitimate theaters, it made no provision for the preservation of existing theaters.

In addition to One Astor Plaza, two other office buildings providing theaters were built before the collapse of the city's office market: the Uris Building, incorporating two theaters (see below), and Emery Roth & Sons' J. P. Stevens Building (1971), at 1185 Sixth Avenue, incorporating two auditoriums for the American Place Theater in a largely below-grade space at the building's southwest corner. The American Place Theater opened with its first production on December 21, 1971. Ada Louise Huxtable praised Richard D. Kaplan, the theater's architect, for fitting the complex of auditorium, office and rehearsal spaces into the Stevens Building "as compactly and beautifully as a fine Swiss watch."[79] The theater was located to the west of a fifty-foot-wide midblock pedestrian street that was also part of the Stevens Building design. A second-floor restaurant formed a bridge between the office tower and the theater block. Entering from street level through a small glass lobby, theatergoers took a stair down past a series of levels, one of which served as a miniature gallery, ultimately reaching the 290-seat theater and 100-seat cabaret. In contrast with the lavish decor of the prewar era, the theaters' interiors were stripped down, with an open-grid ceiling of catwalks and lighting.

In 1968 the city's first great movie palace, Thomas Lamb's Capitol Theater (1919), fell to the wrecker's ball to make way for Emery Roth & Sons' Uris Building, at 1633 Broadway.[80] On the west blockfront of Broadway between Fiftieth and Fifty-first streets and extending 450 feet toward Eighth Avenue, the forty-eight-story, 2,240,000-square-foot behemoth rose as a sheer tower clad in dark gray glass and separated from Broadway by a sunken plaza. Two theaters were located behind the tower: the huge, 1,933-seat Uris Theater, intended for musicals, and the 650-seat Circle in the Square Theater. The Uris, designed by Ralph Alswang, had as its principal feature its size, a quality that

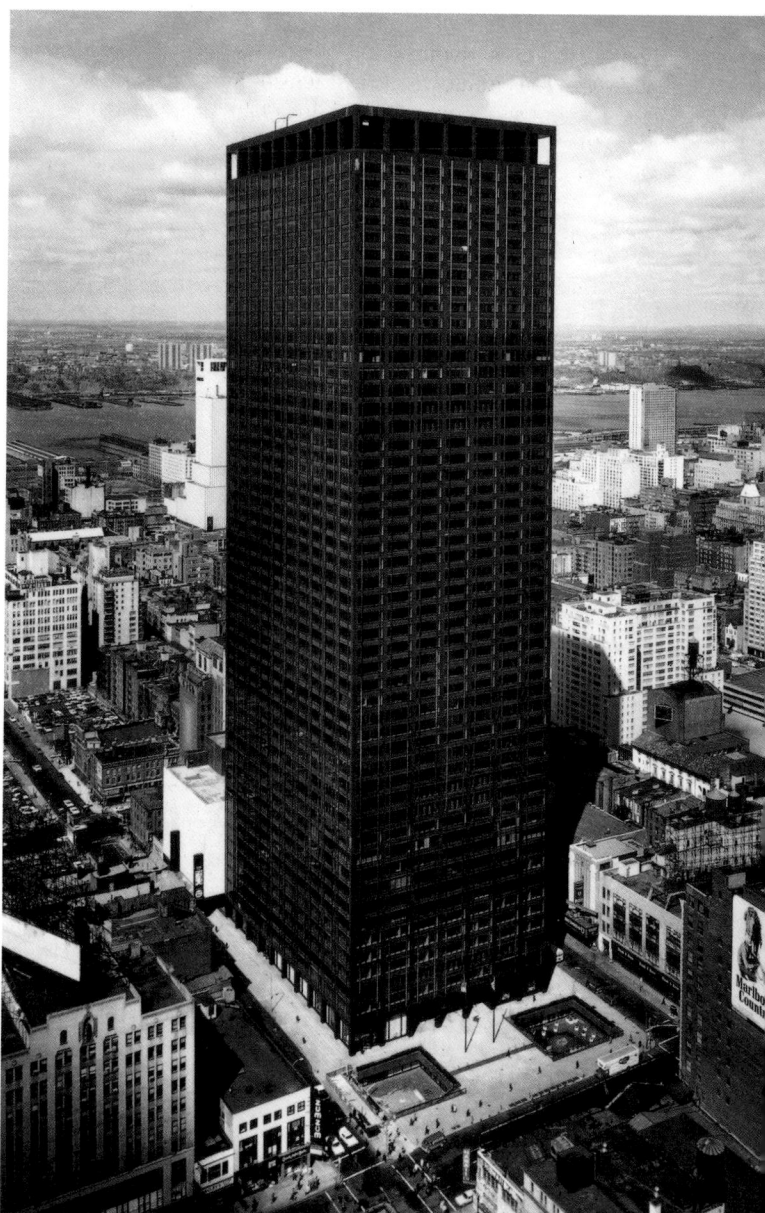

Uris Building, 1633 Broadway, West Fiftieth to West Fifty-first Street. Emery Roth & Sons, 1968. View to the northeast. ERS

445

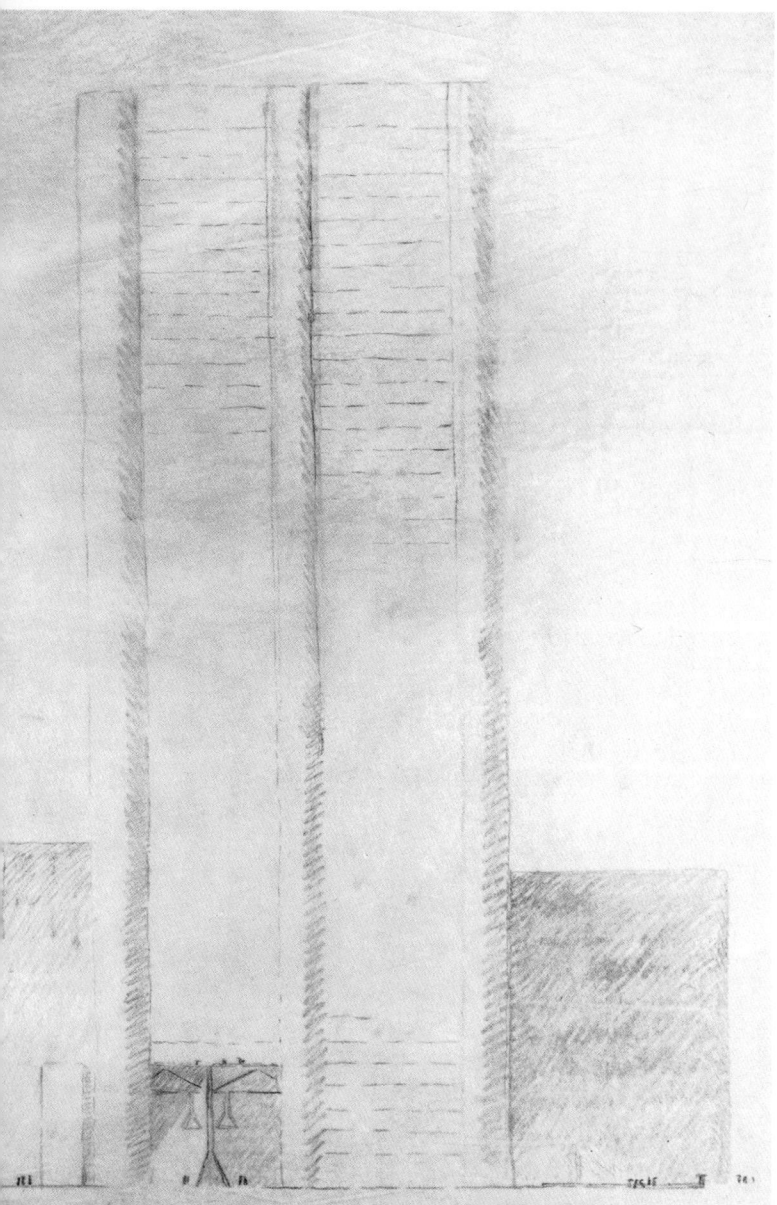

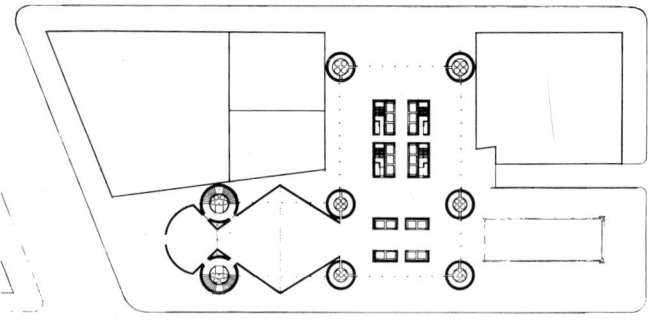

was also viewed as a disadvantage. As Richard Pilbrow, a British theater designer, observed: "The Uris is too large and spacious for my taste. . . . The success of many of our best old theaters in London stems from the ingenuity with which our ancestors crammed people in every nook and corner."[81] The Circle in the Square–Joseph E. Levine Theater (its official name), designed by Robert Alan Sayles along the lines of its predecessor in Greenwich Village, also received little praise. Playwright Tennessee Williams, saying that the auditorium was like a "gymnasium," complimented the actors in a revival of his play *The Glass Menagerie* for their ability to cope with its inadequacies.[82] Many other observers criticized the new facility, finding fault in particular with the long, narrow configuration of the auditorium.

There was little to admire about any of the new theaters except that they existed at all. In *New York* magazine Robert J. Schroeder voiced his concerns: "The pattern has become clear. The new Broadway theater will be plush, polished, safe theater, run by Off- and On-Broadway's theater establishment. It will be sanitarily housed and scientifically organized. Its tickets will be sold by computer. Its product will please any sound and right-thinking sales manager or foundation disbursement officer. Its aura will be that of affluence, affability and unstudied, effortless applause." Schroeder feared that the new theater would even influence the kinds of plays being written: "It will spawn ever-more-elaborate musicals, sponsored by the film, TV and recording establishment, along with foundation-backed multi-media theater pieces, mounted by the established 'avant-garde'—both of which forms will become the standard for theater across the nation and abroad." Clearly not content with this prospect, Schroeder issued what may have been the first cry for the preservation of the theater district as it was:

> When the last obstacle to progress has been removed—when the last many faceted block has been razed for another faceless, block-through office complex; when the last of Broadway's office-free oases has become a pool in an office patio—will we wish that we had made many times the kind of urgent and implacable stand that saved Carnegie Hall, a stand this time for a district rather than a building? Will we come to realize, when it is too late, that the existing Broadway theaters were not too expensive to keep, but instead too dear to lose?[83]

Not every new building in the entertainment district incorporated a theater: Emery Roth & Sons' bland, vaguely Miesian forty-two-story 1700 Broadway (1968), on the east blockfront between Fifty-third and Fifty-fourth streets, was strictly an office building, with approximately 500,000 square feet of rentable space.[84] As that building was being completed, construction began on the Roths' 888 Seventh Avenue, which replaced the Broadway Tabernacle (Barney & Chapman, 1904) and some lesser properties assembled to create an L-shaped site that faced Seventh Avenue, Fifty-sixth and Fifty-seventh streets as it wrapped around the Rodin Studio Building (Cass Gilbert, 1918), at 200 West Fifty-seventh Street, on the southwest corner of Seventh Avenue.[85] Completed in 1972, the Roths' building rose forty-six stories and contained 860,000 square feet of space, with floor sizes ranging from 16,000 to 19,000 square feet. In 1966–67 the Broadway United Church of Christ, together with an independent real estate developer, had proposed to build a mixed-use building on the site, as well as on an adjacent parcel extending west along Fifty-sixth Street to Broadway. Louis Kahn designed two schemes, both of which were far more daring, technologically and aesthetically, than the eventually realized

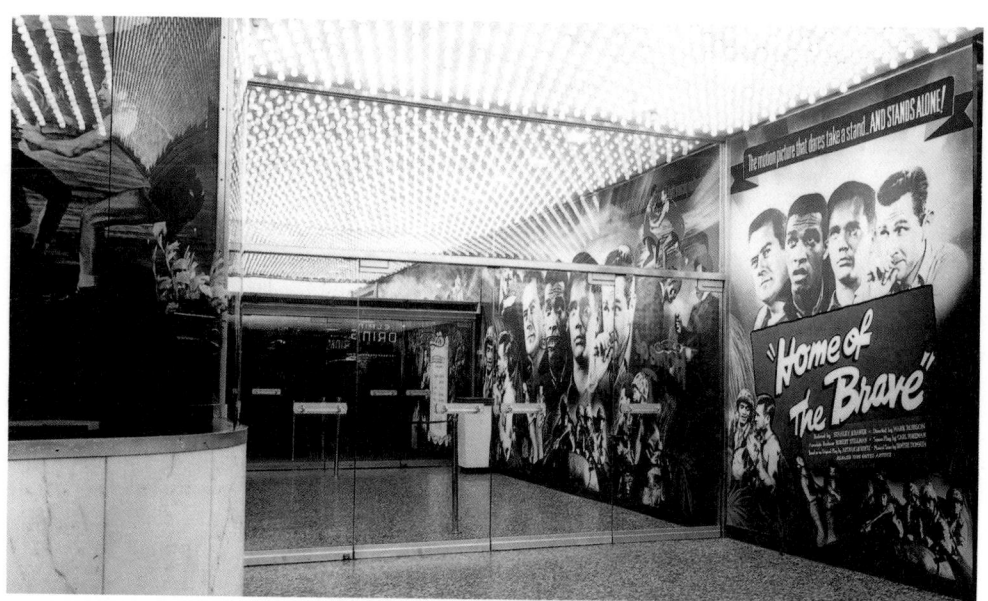

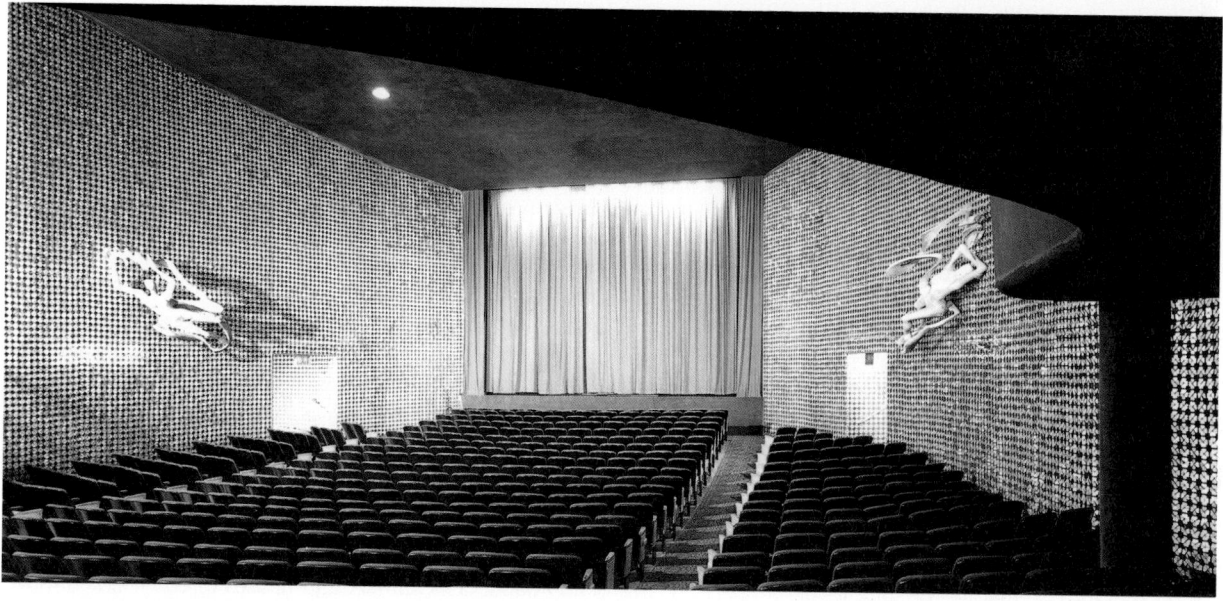

888 Seventh Avenue.[86] Both unbuilt projects called for a forty-six-story tower supported by cylindrical, slip-form columns, with every floor suspended from a surmounting head structure treated visually as a monumental cornice. At street level, a boldly massed church was to be situated near the corner of Broadway and Fifty-sixth Street.

Leo Kornblath's thirty-three-story 1500 Broadway (1972), on the east blockfront between Forty-third and Forty-fourth streets, was a banality, especially in comparison to what it replaced: Daniel H. Burnham & Company's Modern French Hotel Rector (1910–11), which had been operated as the Hotel Claridge since 1914.[87] The new building's most interesting feature was also its most transient: the developers hired the artists Nassos Daphnis and Tania to paint the structural frame as construction proceeded, a unique approach to architectural embellishment that was rendered all the more absurd by the fact that no money was set aside to adorn the completed building with works of art. The transitory nature of their work did not seem to bother the collaborating artists: "This is art in process. It's environment in process," said Tania, who claimed that she didn't

Top left: Proposed Broadway Church Apartment Tower, northeast corner of Broadway and West Fifty-sixth Street. Louis I. Kahn, 1966–67. Rendering of southern elevation. LIK

Bottom left: Proposed Broadway Church Apartment Tower. Site plan. LIK

Top: Victoria Theater, west blockfront of Broadway, West Forty-sixth to West Forty-seventh Street. Formerly Gaiety Theater (Herts & Tallant, 1908–9). Renovation, Edward Durell Stone, 1948–49. Main entrance. Freedman. LF

Bottom: Victoria Theater. Auditorium showing wall-mounted sculptures by Gwen Lux. Freedman. LF "like to make objects for the stock market, to create paintings so they can be bought and sold." Daphnis intimated that the best thing about the building was its painted frame: "It is beautiful now, but it is going to be very ugly."[88]

Preliminary plans were announced in 1972 for a new $75 million, 2,000-room, twin-towered, fifty-six-story midtown hotel.[89] Even more important in terms of the city's future development than the hotel's cost and size was its location: the west side of Broadway between Forty-fifth and Forty-sixth streets—in the once-glittering, now-tawdry and, to many people, menacing core of a Big Apple turning rotten. The hotel was conceived in conjunction with the controversial and never-realized convention center proposed for platforms in the Hudson River adjacent to the blocks between Forty-fourth and Forty-seventh streets (see "West Side: From Chelsea to Clinton," above). It was to be located directly north of One Astor Plaza on a site containing five theaters: the Astor Theater (see above); the Helen Hayes Theater, originally the Folies Bergère Theater (Herts & Tallant, 1911);[90] the Morosco Theater (Herbert J. Krapp, 1917);[91] the Bijou Theater (Herbert J. Krapp, 1917);[92] and the Gaiety Theater (Herts & Tallant, 1908–9),[93] which had been converted to a movie house called the Victoria after burlesque was banned by Mayor La Guardia in 1943. In 1948–49 Edward Durell Stone remodeled the Victoria, increasing its capacity from 700 to 1,100 seats by extending the proscenium arch, removing the stage and enlarging the auditorium by twelve feet by enclosing the passageway that had separated it from the adjoining Bijou Theater; the new screen was thereby located on the Bijou's outer wall.[94] In Stone's shimmering decorative scheme for the reconstructed auditorium, purplish red walls were covered with an aluminum mesh curtain or "coat of mail," actually parts of motion picture reels strung together and hung in semi-rigid fashion on the walls. The artist Gwen Lux designed two wall-mounted sculptures for the auditorium.

In 1972 Jaquelin Robertson, head of the Office of Midtown Planning and Development, said city officials were "extremely interested" in and "optimistic" about the hotel project, which he felt signaled "the renaissance of Times Square" and its future as "the next major development area in the city."[95] But Robertson, as well as spokesmen for Mayor Lindsay and the building's designer and codeveloper, the Atlanta-based architect John Portman, stated that important aspects of the project were unresolved and that its public presentation was thus premature. Despite its preliminary nature, however, by 1972 the project already had behind it a rather long and complex history. The real estate developer Peter Sharp, who owned the Carlyle Hotel and other important New York properties, had assembled the site in the mid-1960s and hired Emery Roth & Sons to design an office tower.

In 1970 Robertson persuaded Sharp to hire Robert Venturi as a consultant to work with the Roths to redesign the project so that it would enhance rather than obliterate Times Square's traditional character. Venturi, Denise Scott Brown and Steven Izenour conducted a feasibility study and proposed the addition of huge signs wrapping around the building. According to the architects, who published their unrealized scheme after Portman's had been announced: "Preliminary investigation . . . suggested a decorated shed, a traditional Times Square configuration rather than the megastructural bridges, balconies, and spaces that have been proposed for the area. Times Square is not dramatic space but dramatic decoration. It is two-dimensional, decorated by symbols, light, and movement." Venturi deliberately set out to create a complex containing "low public spaces" that would "derive their impact from beautiful surface decoration and advertisement, that is, from ornament on simple spaces

rather than from the penetrating forms of complex spaces." As for the interiors, they would be modeled on "the Art Deco surfaces in Rockefeller Center."[96]

Venturi's project fell through not only because of a glut in midtown office space but also because of its failure to capture Sharp's imagination. Nonetheless, Robertson continued to pursue the project. In 1971 he took Sharp to Atlanta to visit the Regency Hyatt Hotel, designed by Portman and completed in 1967.[97] Portman's undeniably spectacular, headline-making design, the opposite of Venturi's approach, impressed the developer. Robertson would later recall that Sharp "walked into the hotel and could only say 'Wow' . . . he stayed up half the night looking around."[98] Sharp immediately resolved to hire Portman to design a hotel on his Times Square property and soon reached an agreement with the architect-developer. Portman had long expressed interest in building in New York and had previously met with Robertson to discuss the possibility of erecting a merchandise mart in the Times Square area. In addition to serving as the building's architect, he would provide approximately 90 percent of the backing for the hotel.

Even before preliminary plans were presented, the project was controversial. Portman had a reputation as the leading designer of "gee-whiz" interior spaces that may have thrilled traveling salesmen or visiting realtors from New York, but did not go down so well with architectural critics. Furthermore, his combination of architectural showmanship and entrepreneurial acumen raised the hackles of fellow practitioners, some of whom were envious of his financial success, while others were offended by his refusal to honor the long-established separation of architecture from real estate development. As Paul Goldberger explained, "Portman's greatest sin in the eyes of the architectural establishment seems to be his decision to go into the development business himself—for there he rejects the traditional role of the architect as gentleman adviser to clients, a man hired to make his money by providing a physical design, not by involving himself in the nitty-gritty of the economics or the politics of a project."[99]

Unlike most critics, Goldberger, who acknowledged that Portman's "flashy, spatially extravagant designs tend to offend many architects and critics who were weaned on the spare, elegant purity of orthodox modernism," was sympathetic to Portman's approach: "His architecture refuses to come down to the low, vulgar level as many critics ascribe to such popular successes as Morris Lapidus's Miami Beach hotels, yet neither does it deliberately remain aloof. Portman provides vast spaces, unusual geometric forms and other devices which are not subtle, but which are sophisticated enough to create in the observer . . . the sense that he is in some sort of extraordinary place."[100] The architectural historian Vincent Scully also praised Portman's skillful manipulation of space: "When you are in them, Portman's worlds are completely convincing."[101] Weaving together influences as broad as St. Peter's in Rome, Tivoli Gardens in Copenhagen, Brasília, Rockefeller Center and the Guggenheim Museum, Portman created spaces that were undeniably memorable and crowd pleasing, returning to the time-honored conception of a big city hotel as a grand public place. According to Philip Johnson, "Portman has proved that it's good business to 'waste space.' The jury is still out on whether he's a great designer, but he gets people into his buildings and, more important, his buildings work."[102] Johnson also claimed that Portman's "analysis of what people want and his ability to get it done are second to none."[103]

As first released in 1972, preliminary drawings of Portman's Times Square hotel revealed two slabs, each approximately fifty-

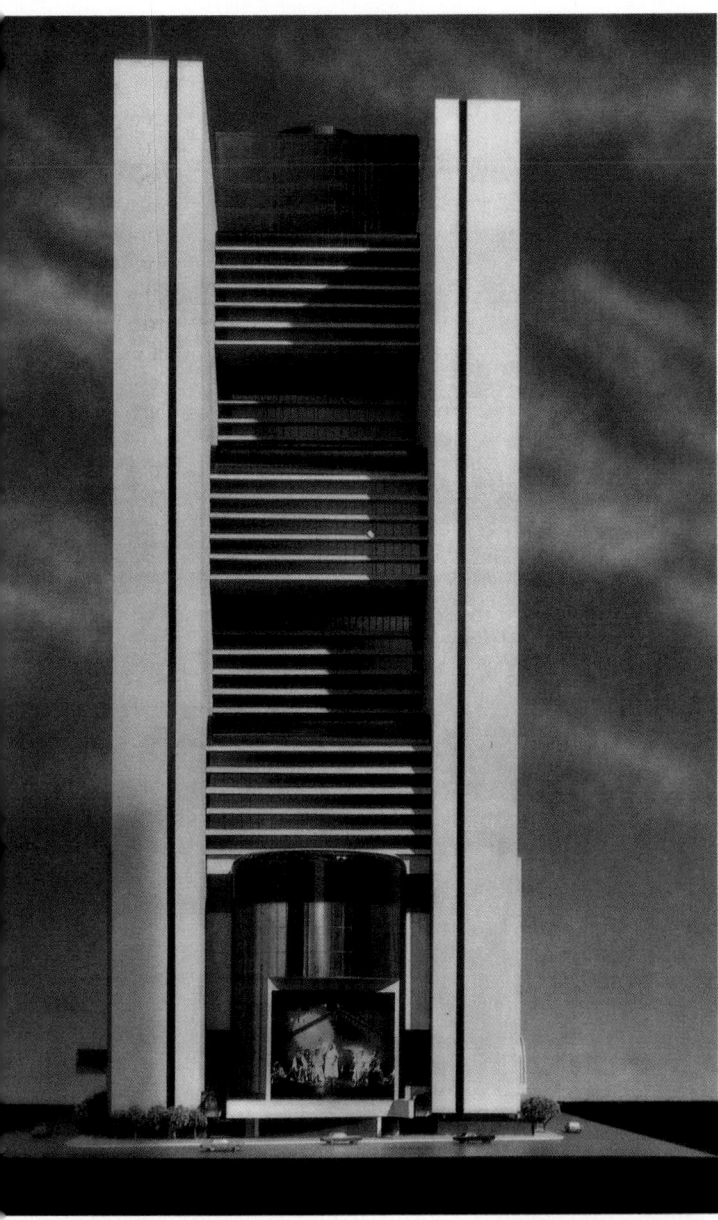

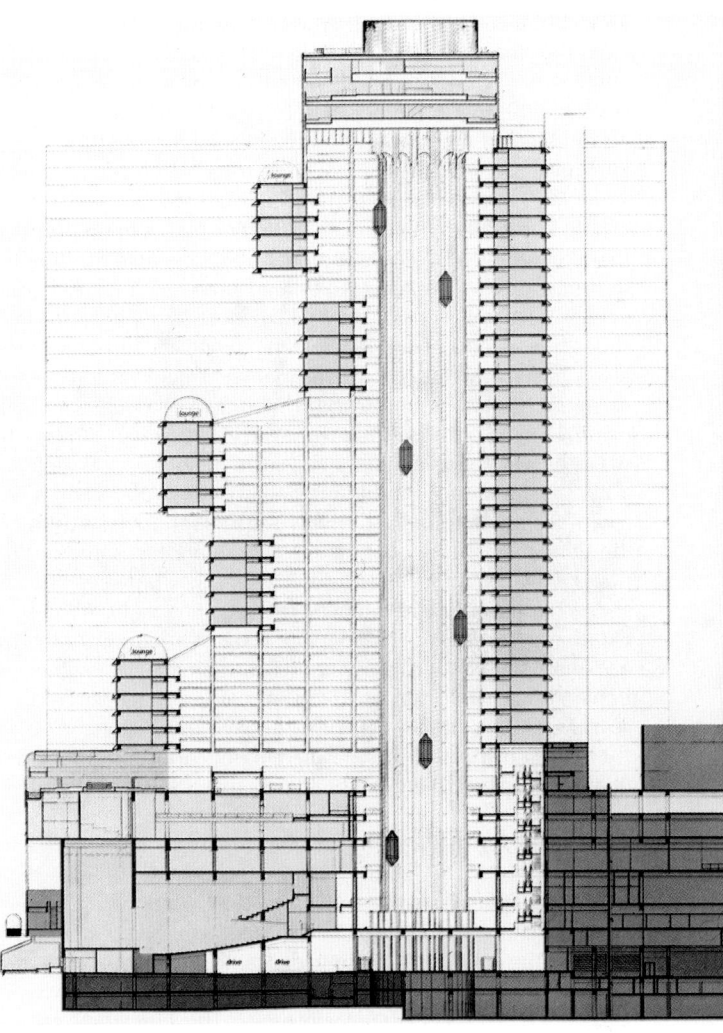

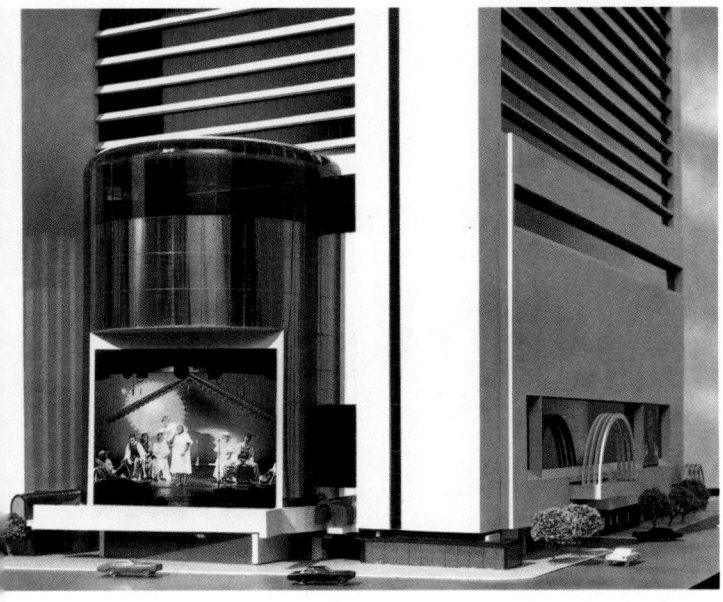

Top left: Proposed Times Square hotel, west side of Broadway, West Forty-fifth to West Forty-sixth Street. John Portman, 1973. Model. View to the west. JP

Bottom left: Proposed Times Square hotel. Model. View to the southwest showing Broadway facade, on the left, with signage and revolving cocktail lounge. JP

Above: Proposed Times Square hotel. Section. View to the south. JP

six stories high, connected by several five-story-high bridges. The space between the slabs and the bridges was left open to the air in order "to give the ladder-like structure a light, airy look."[104] As presented the following year, more developed plans called for the replacement of the open space between the towers with two soaring atria—Portman's most famous trademark—stacked one on top of the other. Here Portman was drawing on an established tradition in American hotel architecture: the inclusion of an enclosed, open area, often a "palm court" but sometimes a much larger glassed-in courtyard.

In addition to the stacked atria, Portman's hotel promised to include a 400-car underground parking garage and a 1,050-seat theater. On Broadway, Portman placed a 240-seat, glass-enclosed sidewalk café, above which were to be seven stories of shops, restaurants and a 400-seat movie theater surrounding the lower atrium. Above this arrangement a bridge was to contain a revolving cocktail lounge, from which patrons could survey the passing scene both on Broadway and in the lower atrium. The tenth, eleventh and twelfth floors were to contain, respectively, a 24,500-square-foot exhibition hall, meeting rooms and a ballroom. Stacked around a thirty-five-story-high lobby starting on the thirteenth floor would be 2,020 hotel rooms, some of them placed on 112-foot-long trusses suspended between the two slabs. The trusses were arranged toward or away from the street like drawers in a filing cabinet, the walls of which were the two east-west slabs. The staggered trusses dramatically defined the upper atrium while, as the editors of *Interiors* noted, "freeing the skyscraper of its traditional curse of boxed-in interiors."[105] Guest rooms faced the streets, and the single-loaded corridors were open to the atrium. On the building's exterior, sloping skylights enclosed the setbacks, creating a highly activated composition while allowing natural light to enter the upper atrium. The first twelve stories of the building's long side walls were to be punctuated by several large, irregularly placed windows; commencing at the thirteenth floor, horizontal strip windows extended for virtually the full length of the facades. Rising through the atria, both richly landscaped with full-size trees, were to be twelve glass-enclosed, high-speed elevators. The elevators, entered from the street level, were to emerge into the lower atrium through a reflecting pool or "lake" and again into the upper space through another pool before running the full height of the fifty-four-story building to arrive at a revolving restaurant on the top floor. The hotel, which by 1973 was budgeted at $150 million, was scheduled for completion in 1977.

At a City Hall press conference held in July 1973, Mayor Lindsay enthusiastically described the project as "one of the most solid pieces of urban planning I've ever seen. It will be more than a hotel, it will be a neighborhood, a city, bringing together the past, present and future of Times Square. Bringing John Portman to New York is the most exciting thing that's happened to us in a long, long time."[106] The editors of the *New Yorker* captured the blend of boosterism and bottom-line economics expressed at the conference:

> Mr. Portman . . . said that every architect wanted to do a major structure in New York. He said that New York was the No. 1 city in the world. He said that New York would continue to be the No. 1 city in the world. . . . He then went on to say that in the past too much emphasis had been put on welfare and low-cost housing, and things like that, which didn't pay for themselves. He compared the city to a garden. He said that the city government should tend its garden, because it was the fruit from the garden that paid for all the things that don't pay for themselves. He talked at some length about what goes into a healthy garden. He said that a city should lure private enter-

prise into the garden to make it healthy. On the whole, he seemed to think that New York Needed Help.[107]

Initial responses to the 1973 design were varied. The editors of *Architectural Forum* noted that observers had compared the building to a "wishing well, a bottomless pit [and] your mother's old washboard." But, they continued, "From our standpoint, *any* Portman in a storm (especially that of Times Square) will do just fine."[108] The editors of the *New Yorker* stated simply, "The hotel looked like fun."[109] Ada Louise Huxtable dismissed Portman's work in general as "flashy, corned-up, badly detailed,"[110] but characterized the proposed hotel as "the right building in the right place," explaining: "Its flamboyance can bring back the kind of theater district glitter that the new theaters, understated to the point of dullness, conspicuously lack. . . . For Times Square, it can be the promise of appropriate new life."[111] She later added: "In size and scale, in design bravura, in its ability to attract the middle class tourist and be an environmental catalyst, it would provide an essential stability for Times Square, in character with its traditional functions and style."[112]

The critic Stanley Abercrombie, writing in the journal *Architecture Plus*, took a different view of the hotel's relationship to its surroundings:

> For all its vigor and rich mix of uses . . . the hotel threatens to effect, at street level, a weakening rather than a strengthening of Times Square vitality. A revolving drum of tasteful graphics (with a bar inside) at the eighth floor level is a minimal concession to the square's tradition of flamboyant advertising; the building's legitimate theater is underground; the shopping facilities, while surprisingly abundant . . . are lifted an escalator ride above the street level; and a single ground-floor restaurant in the block facing Broadway will hardly be as lively as the funky jumble it is to replace—two movies, the Victoria Camera Shop, the Plaza de Athena Greek-Italian Restaurant, the Broadway Book Shop, Gaiety Music, The Spot ("souvenirs, gifts, cutlery"), Arrowsmith Shoes, and Queen's Snacks. The hotel project demonstrates some very welcome faith in the future of Times Square on the part of its developers; that faith would be more strongly evident if the design did not hedge its bets by being so introspective and by so cautiously raising itself above the street.[113]

Portman, who readily acknowledged the fortresslike approach, justified it by saying, "We knew we had to overcome the negative image of Times Square."[114] To do so, Portman said, he had "created a design that looks to security, though not in a negative way," placing "control points" at ground level and arranging elements so that most of the hotel's facilities would not be readily accessible to passersby. The sidewalk café, for instance, would be contained within a glass box, "revealing Times Square in a protected environment."[115]

Although Portman had professed a desire to create a building that was aesthetically and urbanistically in keeping with its surroundings, he rejected many of the area's most basic qualities. In attempting to create a sanitized, internalized version of Times Square, he denied the features that Venturi's study had stressed: the brilliant neon signs and other decorative flourishes that distinguished Times Square's architecture. Where Venturi had celebrated the two-dimensional, decorative quality of Times Square, Portman believed that "the signs really aren't enough to provide substance" for the "unique, fascinating, animated place" he wanted to create.[116] Members of the Office of

TKTS pavilion, Duffy Square, West Forty-seventh Street, between Broadway and Seventh Avenue. Mayers & Schiff, 1973. View to the north. Maris/Semel. M&S

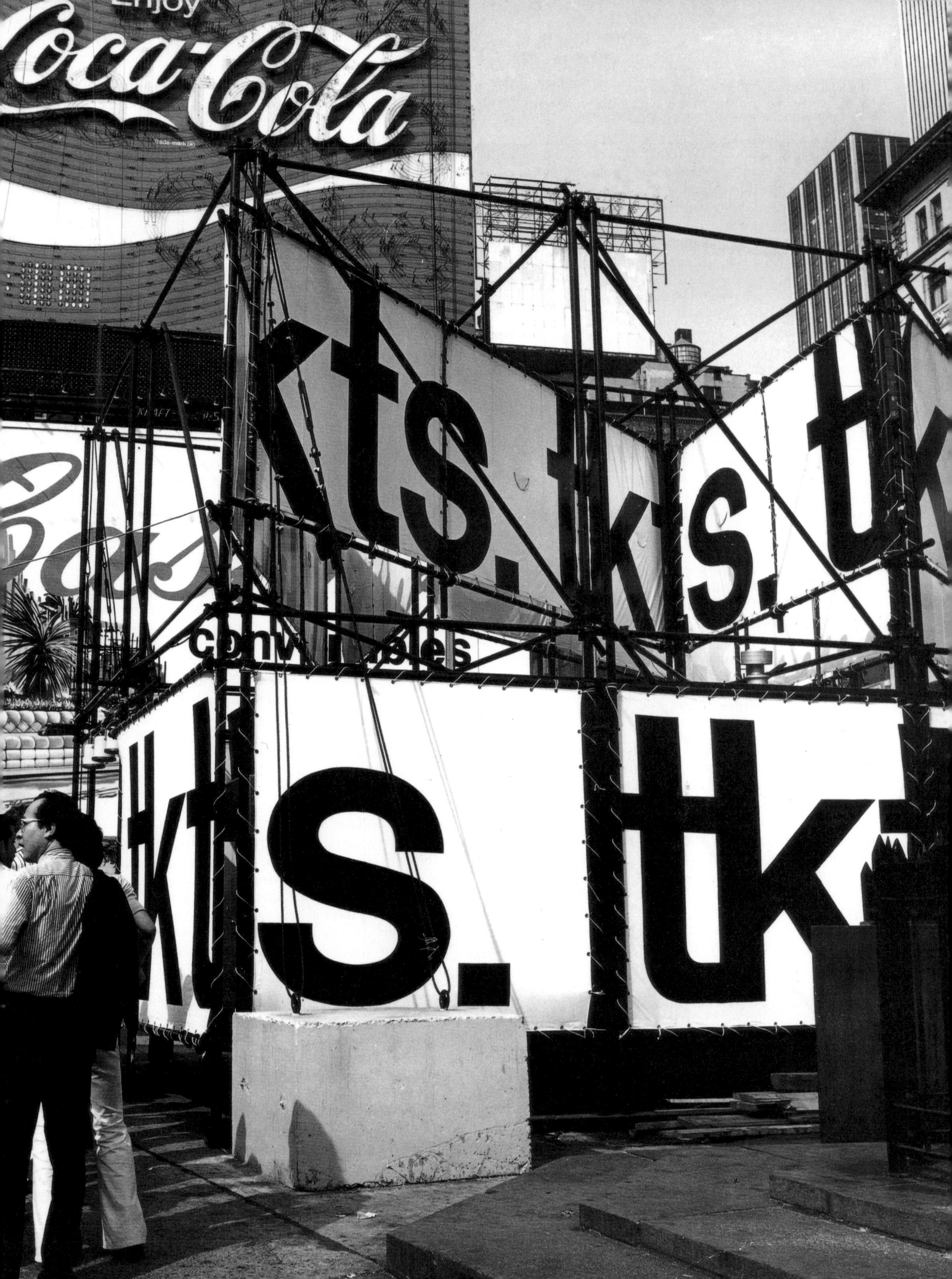

Midtown Planning and Development who worked with Portman favored the visual integration of the building with its surroundings. As William Bardel, who served as acting director following Robertson's departure, said, members of the office felt that it was "enormously important that the building reflect the special mood of Times Square" and encouraged Portman "not to restrict the public experience to the inside of the building." The office, Bardel said, wanted to show Portman that "you won't ruin an expensive, classy building with signs."[117]

Whatever the merits or shortcomings of Portman's design, economic recession and bureaucratic red tape delayed the project's realization until 1985. Even the benefits of the Special Theater District Zoning Amendment were not enough to realize Portman's hotel: it required a zoning remapping, a permit granting a 20 percent bonus in floor area, as well as modifications of setback and height regulations and a permit allowing the construction of a public parking garage. And although Portman included a legitimate theater and a movie theater in the complex, and was committed to renovating the existing Forty-sixth Street Theater (Herbert J. Krapp, 1924),[118] the protection of the Helen Hayes and the Morosco would become a major preservation issue in the 1980s.

Despite increasing crime, declining box offices, rampant prostitution and blatant sales of pornography, Times Square remained a powerful attraction.[119] As Ada Louise Huxtable put it, Times Square was "the greatest of all Pop Art displays . . . a better environmental show than anything in the galleries." For a visitor, she said, "The streets are rivers of every kind of life, and he comes to be part of it."[120] Two new signs of life appeared in 1973: Philip Johnson and John Burgee's renovation of the BMT division's Forty-ninth Street subway station, now clad in bright orange tile,[121] and Mayers & Schiff's TKTS, a pipe-and-canvas pavilion dispensing discount same-day theater tickets, which not only complemented the vitality of Times Square but also helped introduce a new generation to the pleasures of seeing live performances in its theaters.[122]

FORTY-SECOND STREET

Despite its problems—indeed perhaps because of them—at midcentury Forty-second Street was Manhattan's nearest equivalent to the archetypal Main Street. A journey along its two-mile length from river to river, short enough to be comfortably traversed on foot in an hour, presented a microcosm of the city at its best and its worst. Like Main Streets all over America, Forty-second Street brought together all the representative functions of its town, showcasing its commerce and its culture, its places of work and play, with offices at the center and manufacturing at the fringes. It had representative government buildings as well—not only a post office, but also the United Nations complex at its eastern end (see chapter 7). It was the welcome mat to out-of-towners, arriving either by train, by bus or via limousine from the airport. And like most American Main Streets, it began to lose ground in the postwar era, its role as a shopping and entertainment center diminished by suburbanization and the increasing impact of television, which kept people home at night.

While mid-Manhattan's other important crosstown streets were long established—Fourteenth and Twenty-third streets had their heydays in the post–Civil War era, and Fifty-seventh Street was thriving by the 1890s—Forty-second Street was a comparative newcomer, taking on its identity as an entertainment center on its west end around Times Square and a high-class commercial neighborhood on its east end around Grand Central only after the turn of the century.

Forty-second Street had thrived during World War II, its theaters and sidewalks so busy that no one seemed to notice how shabby it was becoming. But with peace came a clearer vision, and West Forty-second Street revealed itself as something troubled, tarnished, even tawdry. The beginning of Forty-second Street's dramatic postwar decline can be pinpointed at exactly 6:45 A.M., November 18, 1946, when buses replaced the crosstown electric streetcars that had run along its right-of-way since 1899.[1] For a while streetcars of the Broadway line continued to run along Forty-second Street from First Avenue to Seventh Avenue, where they turned to go uptown, but the loss of the very same thirty-two wooden trolley cars that had been used for crosstown service since 1908 was a sure signal of a new but not necessarily better order of things. That it would require forty new buses to replace the thirty-two trolley cars hinted at the diminished future which lay in store for the street. The buses were officially scheduled to do their round-trip runs in forty-nine minutes, a few minutes more than the streetcars had taken; and whereas the streetcars had seated fifty-five, with no limit on standees, the buses seated only forty-four people, with room for twenty-two standees.

Postwar decline on Forty-second Street was largely confined to the entertainment district between Seventh and Eighth avenues, though it had some effect on almost all the street's west side blocks. But east of Sixth Avenue, and particularly east of Third Avenue, Forty-second Street prospered as a business center, largely as a result of the proximity to both Grand Central and the United Nations. In 1949 plans were announced for 161 East Forty-second Street, the Chrysler Building East (1952), Reinhard, Hofmeister & Walquist's thirty-two-story addition to the Chrysler Building (William Van Alen, 1930), to be erected on the west block of Third Avenue between Forty-second and Forty-third streets.[2] The building was the first to take advantage of the impending destruction of the Third Avenue El (the spur to Grand Central had been demolished in 1923)[3] by locating its principal entrance on Third Avenue, although it hedged its bets by using a Forty-second Street address. A self-contained unit, it was connected to the Chrysler Building only by an underground passageway that also linked up with the subway. The blandly detailed, white-brick-clad building, no doubt intended to complement its big brother, ended up looking more like a poor relation. Lewis Mumford was appalled by the design, which he said had "the sophistication of a six-year-old's drawing of a skyscraper." He went on to explain: "It is no more than a little house with plain walls and small, simple, rectangular windows that, like Jack's beanstalk, keeps on growing and growing and growing. . . . Except for the mere fact of height and bulk, it doesn't even belong to the machine age. From a distance, its flat facade seems painted in two dimensions on a transparent backdrop."[4]

The announcement in July 1953 of plans to build Harrison & Abramovitz's Socony-Vacuum Building, at 150 East Forty-second Street, the largest office building undertaken in the city since the construction of Rockefeller Center, was front-page news in the *New York Times*.[5] The building's principal tenant, the Socony-Vacuum Company, renamed Socony-Mobil Oil Company in 1955, did not own the new forty-two-story building but had agreed to lease 500,000 of its 1.3 million square feet of space for twenty-five years. The fact that the company was relocating to midtown from its landmark headquarters building at 26 Broadway, designed by Carrère & Hastings, helped solidify the widely held belief that the downtown financial center was in decline and that midtown had usurped its role as the city's premier office location.[6]

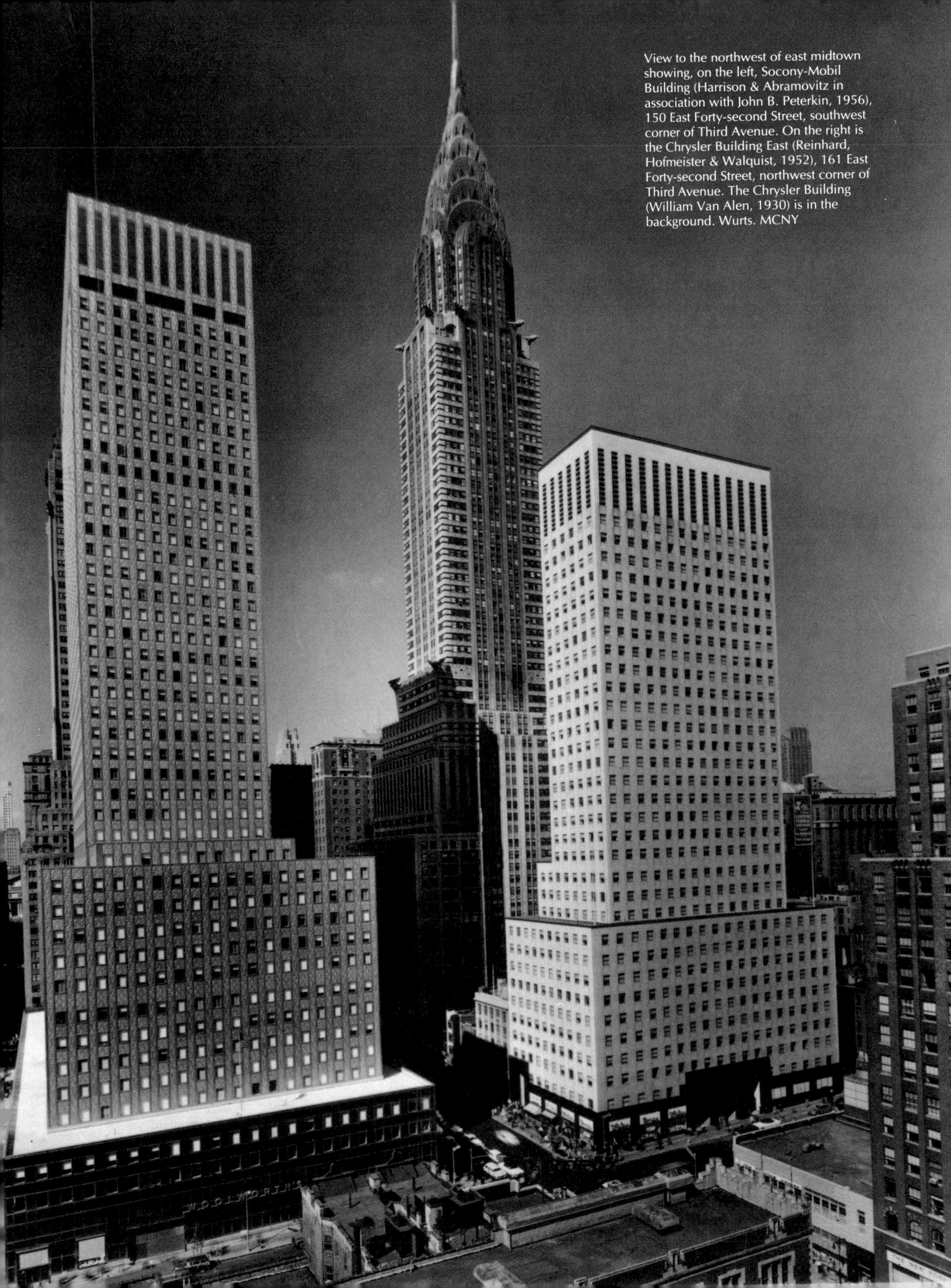

View to the northwest of east midtown showing, on the left, Socony-Mobil Building (Harrison & Abramovitz in association with John B. Peterkin, 1956), 150 East Forty-second Street, southwest corner of Third Avenue. On the right is the Chrysler Building East (Reinhard, Hofmeister & Walquist, 1952), 161 East Forty-second Street, northwest corner of Third Avenue. The Chrysler Building (William Van Alen, 1930) is in the background. Wurts. MCNY

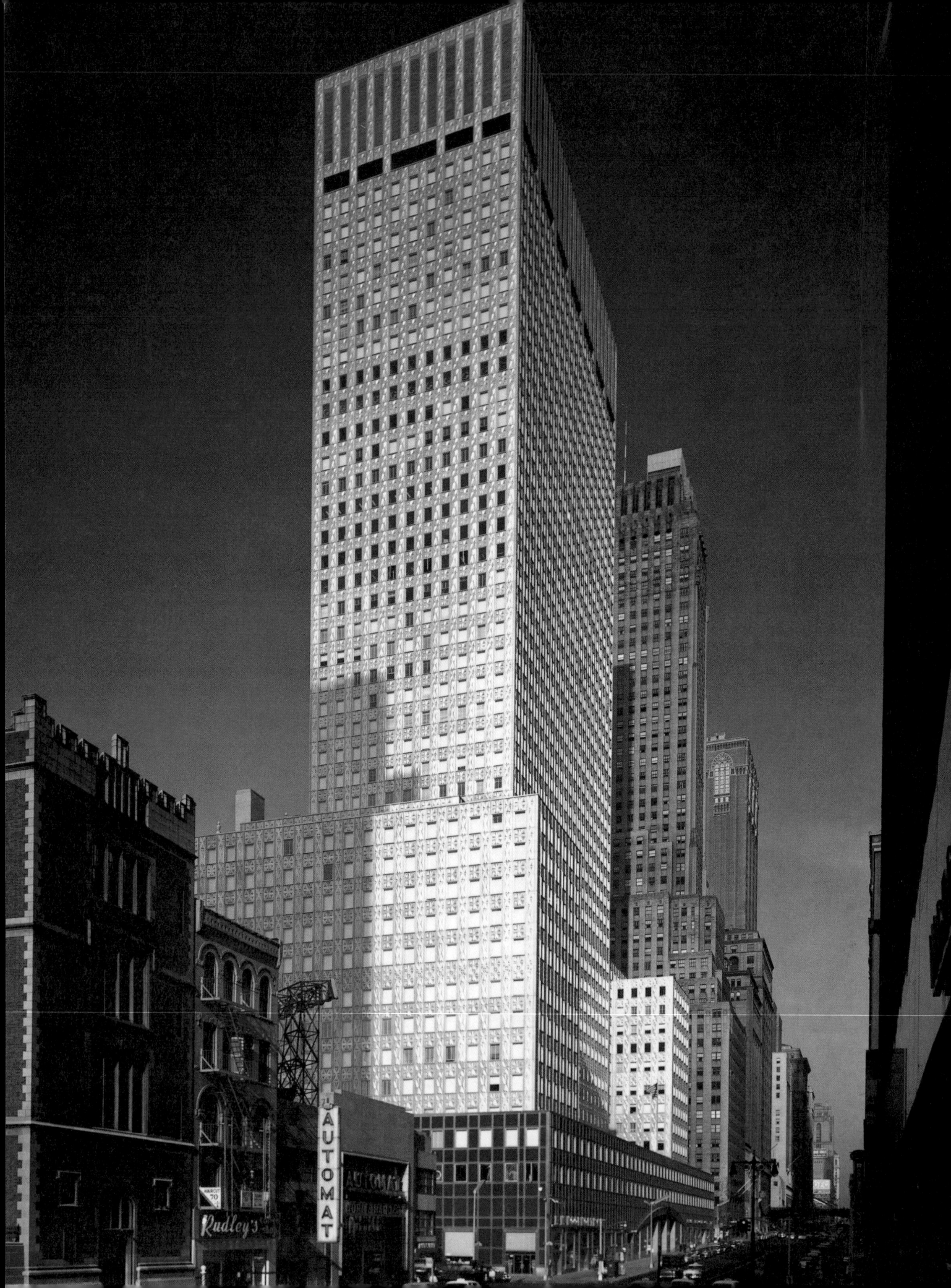

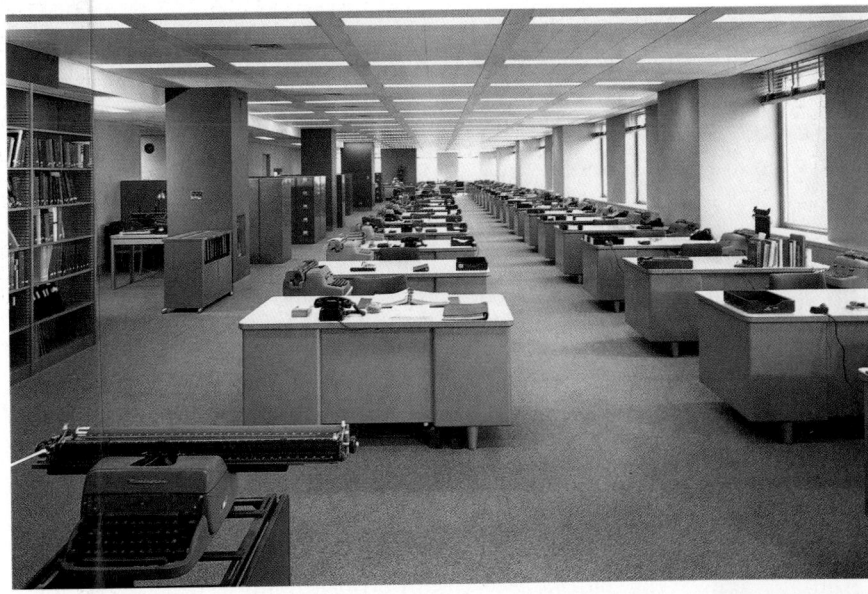

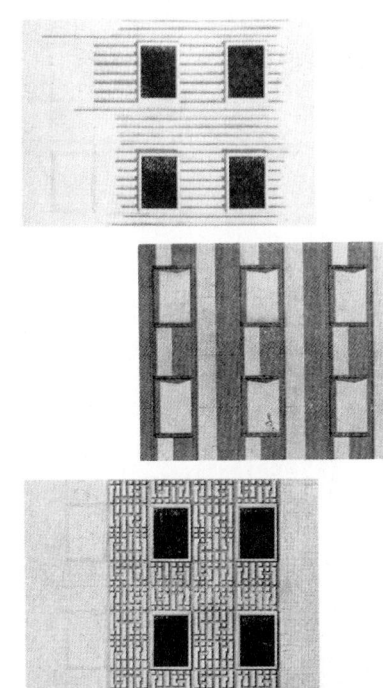

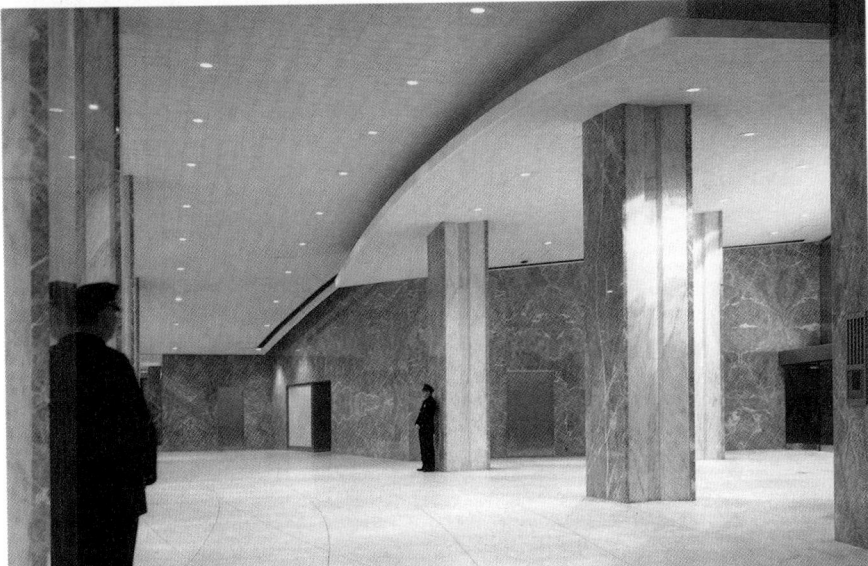

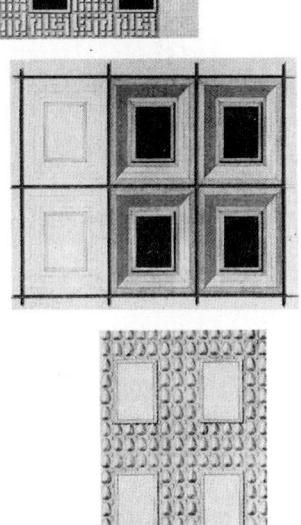

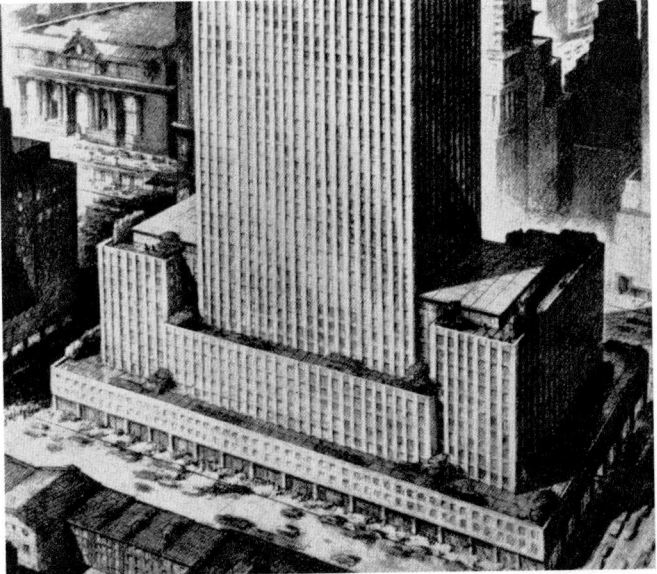

Far left: Socony-Mobil Building, 150 East Forty-second Street, Lexington to Third Avenue, East Forty-first to East Forty-second Street. Harrison & Abramovitz in association with John B. Peterkin, 1956. View to the southwest. Stoller. ©ESTO

Top left: Socony-Mobil Building. Secretarial pool. Stoller. ©ESTO

Center left: Socony-Mobil Building. Lobby. Stoller. ©ESTO

Bottom left: Socony-Mobil Building. Preliminary massing study. Rendering. View to the northwest. AR. CU

Above: Socony-Mobil Building. Preliminary studies for treatment of stainless-steel cladding. AR. CU

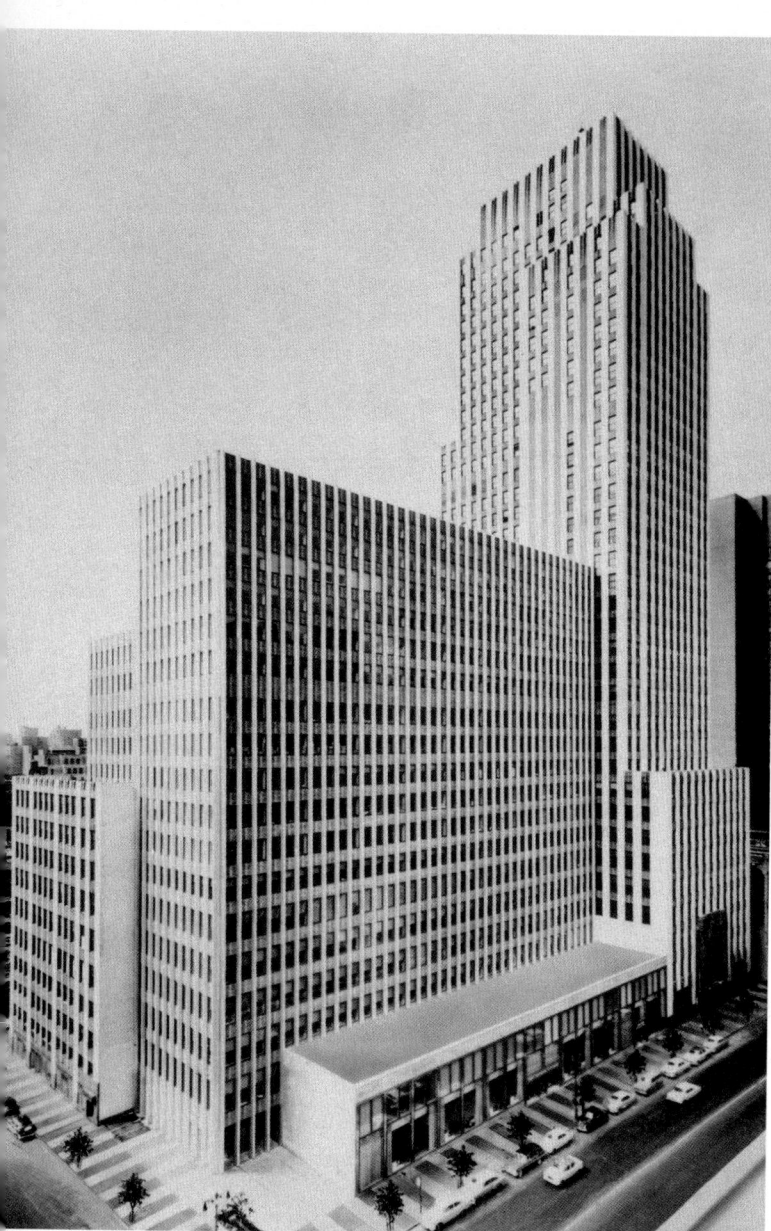

Daily News Building addition, southwest corner of Second Avenue and East Forty-second Street. Harrison & Abramovitz, 1958. Original Daily News Building (Howells & Hood, 1929) is on the right. View to the southwest. MA

The new building, completed in 1956, was developed by John W. Galbreath and associates including Peter B. Ruffin. Designed by Harrison & Abramovitz, in association with John B. Peterkin, it was the largest metal-clad office building and the largest centrally air-conditioned commercial building in the world. Its 75,000-square-foot second floor constituted the largest amount of enclosed office space on one floor in the city. The earliest designs called for a brick-clad building, detailed similarly to the limestone walls of Rockefeller Center's postwar buildings. It was no accident that the building took Rockefeller Center as a kind of model, given the role Wallace K. Harrison had played in the center's design as well as the fact that the Rockefellers were principal shareholders in Socony-Mobil. But Harrison, who had pioneered the aluminum curtain wall in his Alcoa Building in Pittsburgh and had previously proposed a similar design for Park Avenue, redesigned the Socony-Mobil Building to be clad in aluminum. Even though stainless steel was ultimately chosen after the steel industry matched the cost of aluminum, the design of the .037-inch-thick panels was the same as the one Harrison had proposed for the original material. The intricate, even fussy, "carved" effect that resulted was, as *Architectural Forum* correctly predicted, "sure to arouse controversy."[7] Lewis Mumford characterized the stainless-steel curtain wall as an aesthetic "disaster," explaining: "Seen close at hand, this sheathing reminds one of nothing so much as the pressed-tin ceilings that were popular fifty years ago in cheap shops and restaurants. . . . From the street, this new building looks as if it were coming down with measles."[8]

Although Harrison was the building's principal architect, John B. Peterkin, who had designed the Airlines Terminal Building (1940) a few blocks west on Forty-Second street and had long served as consultant to the Goelet family, owners of the land, had developed preliminary designs that established the building's basic massing.[9] In addition, in a process orchestrated by Galbreath and Ruffin, the building's exterior expression was developed as a joint effort between Harrison and Peterkin, with each preparing designs every step of the way and then meeting to select the best features for the final synthesis.

The building's three-story, block-filling base, sheathed with dark blue glass, was punctuated by glass-fronted shops and shallow eyebrow vaults marking the building's principal entrances, which led to a glistening vaulted lobby in white marble and terrazzo that connected Lexington and Third avenues, Forty-first and Forty-second streets. Above the base sat an H-shaped structure that was set back at the thirteenth floor to create a slightly stubby slab. *Architectural Forum* said that "the new cliff of offices will not be distinguished in the way UN and Lever House are, in slender striking mass," but that the building's "robust personality will be keyed by the soundness of the space for rental, and its impact will be made by the great exterior wall of stainless steel."[10]

The destruction of the Third Avenue El opened up development opportunities not only along that avenue's length but also east of the avenue. The midtown business district's Third Avenue barrier had already been broken by Starrett & Van Vleck's 205 East Forty-second Street (1929) and by Howells & Hood's Daily News Building (1929), at 220 East Forty-second Street, which was so located because zoning forbade manufacturing west of the avenue.[11] The Daily News Building was more than doubled in size in 1958 by a new eighteen-story wing, stretching east along Forty-second Street to Second Avenue.[12] The design, by Harrison & Abramovitz, was sympathetic to the original on the exterior; it was clad in a similar curtain wall but with different proportions to provide for wider windows. It was less sympathetic on the interior, where the dark, intricately shaped, dramatic lobby of the original was cut through and relit. As Paul Goldberger later put it, the Daily News extension was a "thoughtful but inadequate companion," a "weak echo" of the original.[13] As well as providing more office space, much of it available for lease to outside tenants, the expansion included a five-story addition to the nine-story newspaper printing plant, which faced Forty-first Street and formed the rear of the original structure.

By the late 1950s Forty-second Street between Third and Second avenues had begun a process of almost total transformation. In 1959 Emery Roth & Sons were busy at work on a thirty-three-story glass-and-aluminum-clad building at 235 East Forty-second Street, leased by Charles Pfizer & Co. as its world headquarters.[14] The building, replacing tenements, was completed in 1961. Neither its architecture nor its interiors, designed by Leonard-Colangelo-Peters, were distinguished. Other new office buildings on East Forty-second Street were even less so. Emery Roth & Sons' twenty-eight-story 200 East Forty-second Street (1959), on the southeast corner of Third Avenue, located on a site that once contained Hector Hamilton's Foltis-Fischer Building (1932), was a conventional aluminum-and-glass-walled wedding cake piling up to a stubby tower.[15] The young children of Seymour Durst, the developer, paralleled the building's realization with the construction of a scale model in the Durst family home in Scarsdale. William Lescaze's banal seventeen-story aluminum-and-glass-walled 300 East Forty-second Street (1963), replacing a two-story taxpayer and tenements, pushed the eastern edge of office row to the southeast corner of Second Avenue.[16] The Roths' thirty-one-story 201 East Forty-second Street (1965), on the northeast corner of Third Avenue, was a slab locked into a complexly massed base, clad with a bronze-toned aluminum-and-glass curtain wall to yield a slightly more stylish effect.[17] It replaced a miscellany of low buildings, including two-, three- and five-story tenements, and was the fourth big office building to be built at the intersection since the war.

The ground-floor corner space of 200 East Forty-second Street was occupied by an Automat, the last to be erected by Horn & Hardart. It exhibited little of the streamlined modernity of the grand freestanding Automats of the 1920s and 1930s, such as those at Sixth Avenue and Forty-fifth street or 104 West Fifty-seventh Street,[18] or of the Foltis-Fischer Building it replaced. But it had enough of the food-dispensing gadgetry to convey some of the magic of the earlier stores, offering, as Paul Goldberger put it, a recollection of "the place where a child is brought to lunch in the shadow of a great stone skyscraper, to be awed at the technology of the little boxes that take his nickels and dimes. That is the substitute for the awe he would feel at the skyscraper and the city itself, were he able to express it; the Automat takes its place, in a way that McDonald's and Burger King will never equal."[19]

By 1965 the stretch of East Forty-second Street from Park to Second Avenue had become, as a writer in the *New York Times* put it, "industry row," with more industrial corporations based there than in any city in America except Chicago or Pittsburgh.[20] The prominence of East Forty-second Street, as the *Times* article noted, was not just a reflection of the postwar boom but also the logical outgrowth of solid planning decisions made before World War I when the new Grand Central Terminal (Warren & Wetmore; Reed & Stem, 1903–13) was accompanied by the imaginative concept of Terminal City.[21]

Just to the east of industry row, but west of the elegantly medievalesque apartment houses of Tudor City and its green park (H. Douglas Ives, 1925–28), stood York & Sawyer's five-story Hospital for Ruptured and Crippled Children (1911), later renamed the Beth David Hospital.[22] In 1963 the hospital sold its

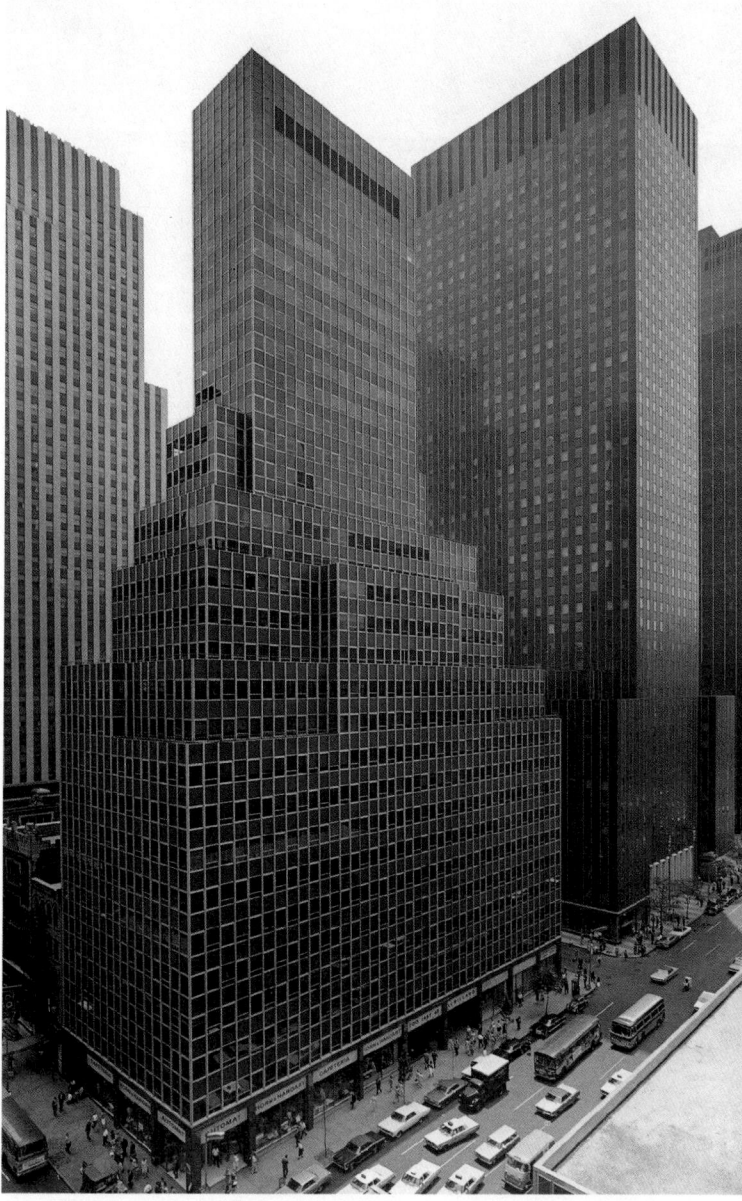

200 East Forty-second Street, southeast corner of Third Avenue and East Forty-Second Street. Emery Roth & Sons, 1959. View to the southeast. OMH

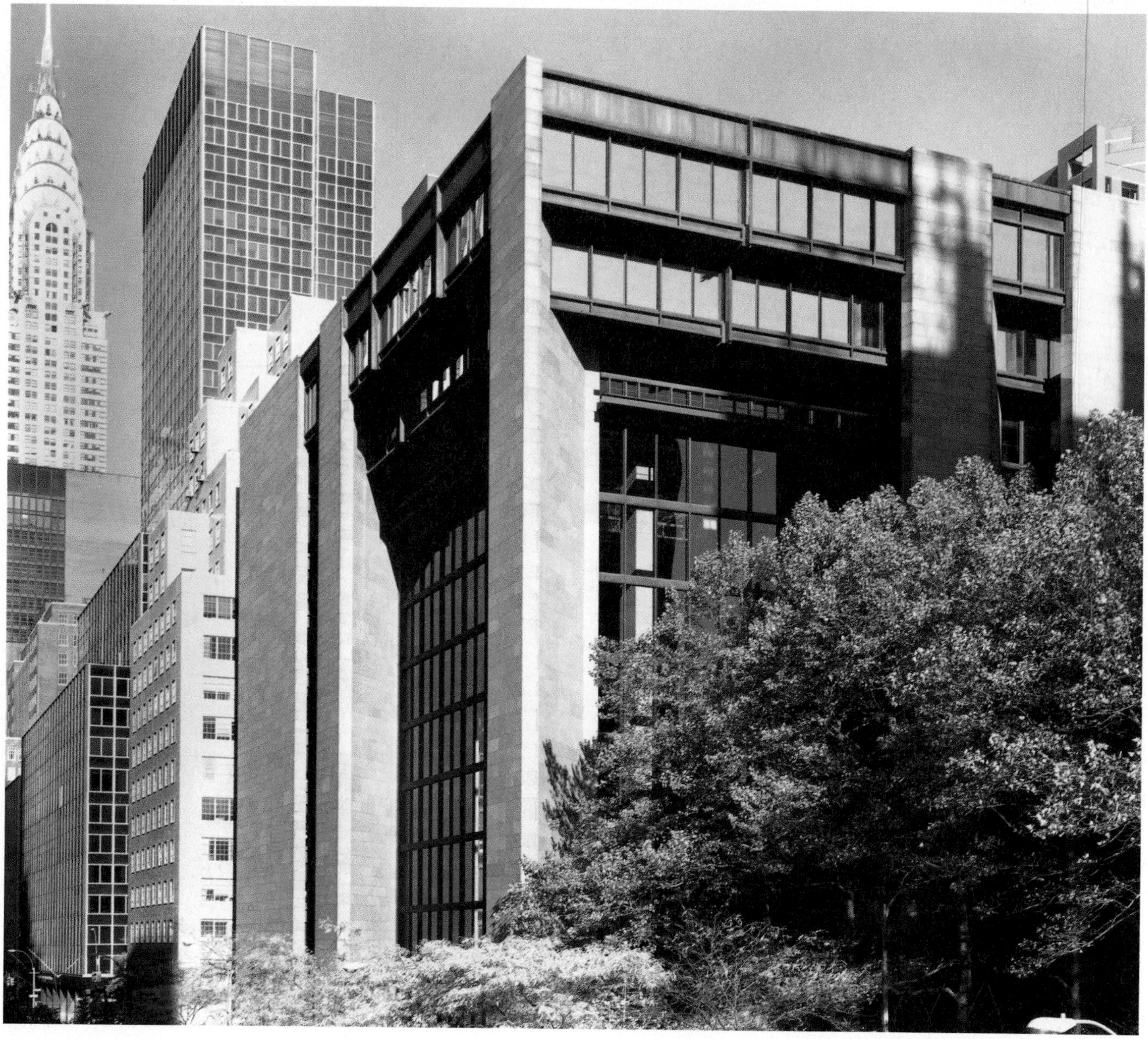

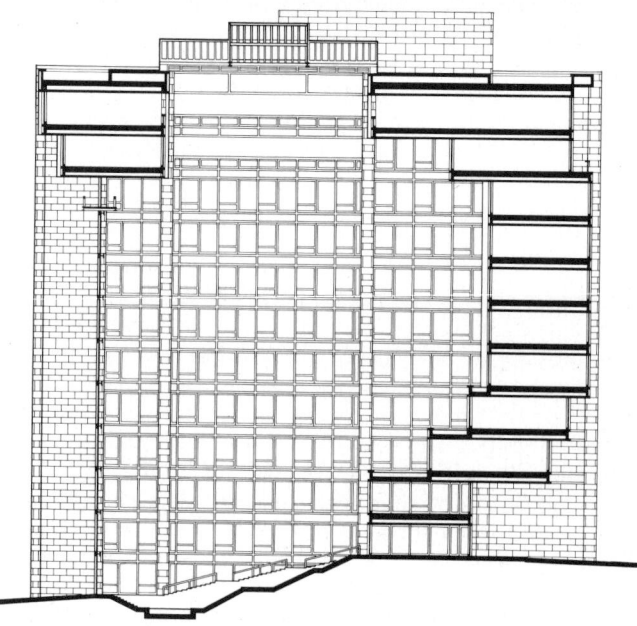

Above: Ford Foundation Building, 321 East Forty-second Street, between First and Second avenues. Kevin Roche and John Dinkeloo, 1967. View to the northwest. KRJDA

Right: Ford Foundation Building. Section. View to the west. KRJDA

Far right: Ford Foundation Building. Winter garden. KRJDA

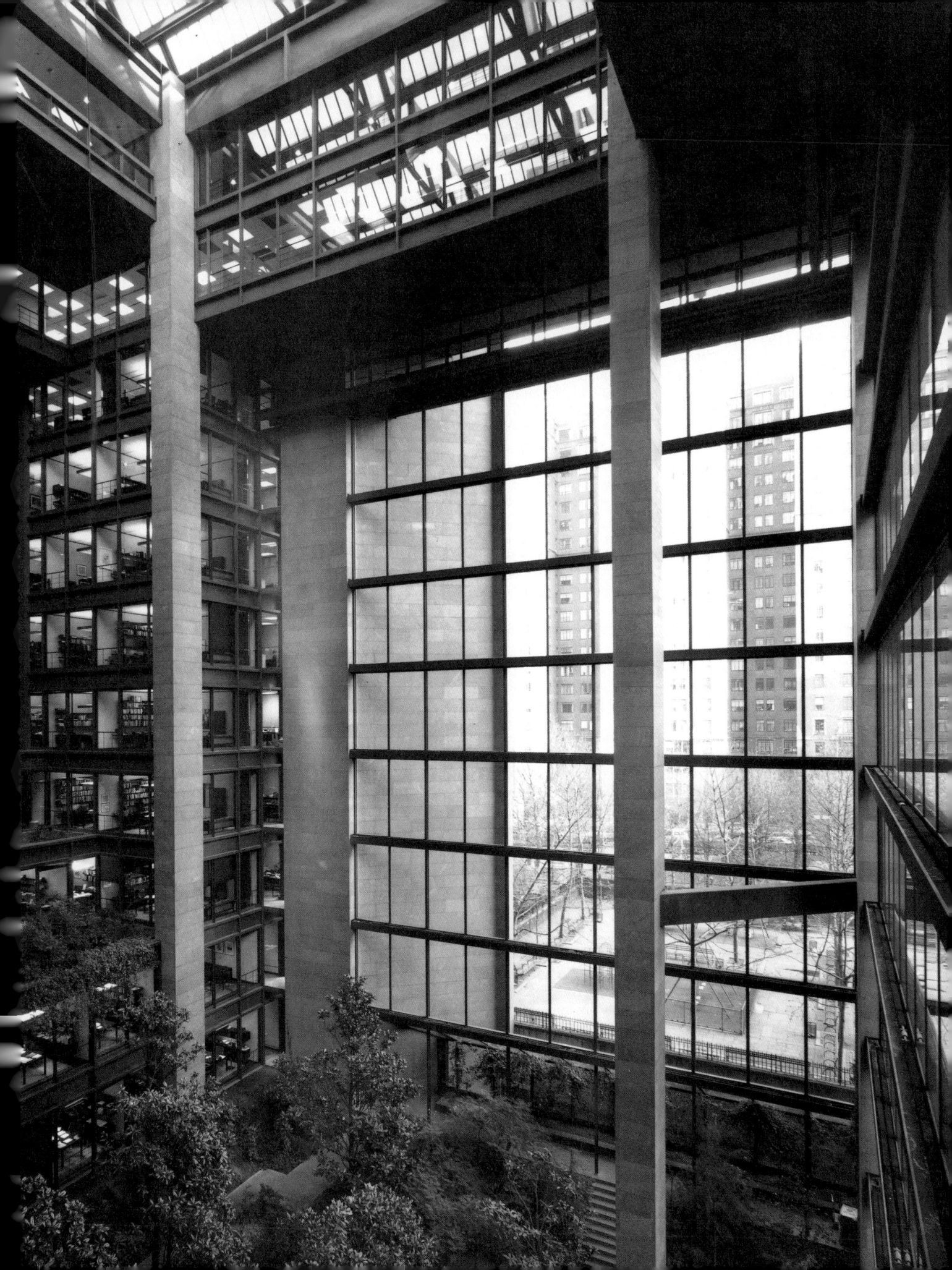

land to the Ford Foundation, setting in motion the design and construction of the foundation's headquarters building (1967), at 321 East Forty-second Street.[23] Designed by Kevin Roche and John Dinkeloo, the Ford Foundation Building was one of two buildings of unquestioned distinction erected along Forty-second Street in the postwar era, the other being the Socony-Mobil Building. The foundation's twelve-story office building was located on a 200-foot-square midblock site that sloped upward toward Forty-third Street. Just to its west stood Pomerance & Breines's 1957 office building, 800 Second Avenue. The 400-employee Ford Foundation, one of the world's richest philanthropies, had previously occupied ten floors in a conventional office building on Madison Avenue. The idea of building an architecturally innovative headquarters originated with Henry Heald, the foundation's president, who understood the prestige value of high-profile architecture from his days as president of the Illinois Institute of Technology, where he had been instrumental in seeing Mies van der Rohe's campus implemented. Ralph Schwarz, the foundation's director of building and planning, was brought in to supervise the project.

The initial proposal called for reinforced-concrete construction, but its high cost led to the decision to use exposed Cor-ten controlled-rusting steel as well as conventional framing sheathed with warm-toned brownish gray Canadian granite flecked with orange and pink. Other than the change in structural systems, the initial design, which was greeted with almost universal enthusiasm, was realized with only minor amendments. An L-shaped, 260,000-square-foot office block bordering the site's west and north boundaries, the building cradled within its arms a 160-foot-high, ten-story, 100-foot-square atriumlike winter garden. The skylit and glazed space was landscaped by Dan Kiley, a longtime collaborator of Eero Saarinen's (Roche and Dinkeloo had been associates in Saarinen's office before the young master's death at age fifty-one, in September 1961). The terraces of the garden were lushly planted with 17 full-grown trees, 999 shrubs, 148 vines, 21,954 ground-cover plants and 18 aquatic plants in a still-water pool.

Though the office building and its garden were oriented to the south and east, that is to Forty-second Street and to Tudor City Park, and though the garden could be entered from Forty-second Street, the principal approach to the Ford Foundation was on the north, along Forty-third Street, where a porte cochere was tucked within the building's mass. The building's weakest side was its western elevation. Writing in *Progressive Architecture*, James T. Burns, Jr., said that "the building perhaps turns its back *too* emphatically on its western neighbors who need the prospect of an interesting building more than those to the east," but that it redeemed itself nonetheless: "The Foundation headquarters does tie in with its commercial neighbors in one way however: the two upper floors, which ring the court on all four sides and contain executive office and dining areas, will carry on the 'cornice' line of 12th-story setbacks of New York's old zoning code."[24]

The building, though set on a seemingly unprominent midblock site, culminated a dramatic processional approach for visitors arriving by car. As Jonathan Barnett explained:

A visitor does not simply drive up to the Ford Foundation, he approaches it by a carefully planned processional way, which turns the mundane requirements of a one-way street system into a ceremonial journey of surprise and discovery. Traffic regulations require that every car headed for the 43rd Street entrance . . . must first drive east on 41st Street, and turn left to Tudor City Place, which crosses 42d Street on a bridge, affording a highly interesting three quarter view of the Foundation building . . . not visible again until the car pulls into the entrance way of the 43rd Street facade, a closed composition of granite and glass.

Part of the appeal of this view, according to Barnett, was that it afforded "no hint of the light and spacious garden court within."[25]

After reviewing the initial model and drawings, Ada Louise Huxtable reported that the "dramatic court design" would provide "one of the city's largest and most spectacular interior spaces as well as a humanized kind of office plan that New York lacks, and could learn from." The design, she said, "turns conventional office construction inside out. Instead of windowless interiors, with a perimeter of windowed offices that look out into windows across the street, the building turns in on itself, creating its own view." Huxtable compared this aspect of the design to late-nineteenth-century precursors, relatively low office buildings with "elaborately balconied office floors" surrounding full-height skylit interior courts.[26] Kevin Roche, the building's principal designer, explained that the building's inward perspective embodied the foundation's sense of itself as a community: "It will be possible, in this building, to look across the court and see your fellow man or sit on a bench in the garden and discuss the problems of Southeast Asia. . . . There will be an awareness of the whole scope of the foundation's activities."[27]

In her 1964 review Huxtable made a point that would continue to be invoked in subsequent discussions of the building: "It is a small addition to a big town, in New York's way of measuring landmarks by size, but it is a large potential dose of design quality in a city that matches its extraordinary vitality with the deadliness of its building cliches."[28] She elaborated on that observation in a second assessment of the building, published a few weeks before its dedication on December 8, 1967: "The Ford Foundation has built itself a splendid, shimmering Crystal Palace. More important, it has built a significant addition to the New York scene. It is one of the small handful of buildings released from the exigencies of commercial construction to rank as architecture at all." She praised not only the building's "original, highly romantic beauty" but also "the effective way it opens up a closed corporate group into a communicating organization focused on that great garden court," a space she called a "horticultural spectacular and probably one of the most romantic environments ever devised by corporate man."[29] Huxtable also admired the refined detailing of the building and especially its interior appointments, almost wholly designed by Warren Platner, an architect specializing in interiors who worked in the Roche and Dinkeloo office.

When the building was completed, many observers, expressing the politics of the moment, criticized the building as an inappropriately extravagant gesture, given the "waste" of space devoted to the garden, which, at the owner's request, had no benches and was not open during off-hours, making it in effect a lobby and not a public place. One unidentified neighborhood resident said a few weeks before Ford moved in: "They're building a damned temple to themselves."[30] But as Norval White and Elliot Willensky, grudgingly echoing the era's newly emerging environmentalism, pointed out: "The scheme is less extravagant than it seems when the value of the garden as a waste air chamber and thermal buffer is considered."[31] Huxtable also refuted the anti-Establishment arguments raised against the design by liberal and radical commentators:

Every inch of the Ford building's "waste" space works in terms of design, function and corporate or urban purpose. It is a humanistic rather than an economic environment. In the twentieth-century city, space and humanism are luxuries that we can no longer afford. Therefore architecture is something that we can no longer afford. It is . . . ridiculous to argue as to whether the Ford Foundation has built a monument to itself or whether the money might not be better spent on the problems of the world. Certainly the building could come under the heading of one of the foundation's more valid contributions to the arts. It is also certain that Ford will never give most New Yorkers anything except this civic gesture of beauty and excellence, and that is a grant of some importance in a world where spirit and soul are deadened by the speculative cheapness of the environment. . . . It is a social and urban tragedy that those who recognize the urgency of our human problems see their solution only in terms of the total sacrifice of style.[32]

Other objections to the Ford Foundation Building were perhaps more specific to the design solution. Jonathan Barnett struggled to come to terms with the designers' failure to achieve intimacy, tracing the problem to the symbolic implications of the space: "Roche has made the building essentially four-square; that is the building's height, length and width are very similar. The four-square building with an interior court is a traditional symbolic representation of the universe, and as such is an ancient symbol of power, used in religious buildings and palaces. The palace of the king of kings, the temple of the New Jerusalem, the house of the world, are the concepts this shape connotes."[33] The English journal *Architectural Review* addressed the building's monumentality even more directly: "It is another instance of the [Roche and Dinkeloo] firm's preoccupation with the simplified structural statement leading to a kind of giantism in architecture."[34] Vincent Scully, Yale's influential architectural historian and critic, in his *American Architecture and Urbanism* of 1969, criticized the building's "military scale on the street" and its "sultanic inner garden."[35] Robert Stern, in his *New Directions in American Architecture*, also published in 1969, said that the building was "an awesome shrine" that revealed "the ritualistic bureaucracy of private benefaction," and he described the monumentality of its exterior: "As a work of street architecture, the Ford Foundation Building, though it respects the lines and planes of the surrounding buildings, is without scale. Because it is inward in orientation, the exterior walls are composed without reference to the sizes of openings and floor levels."[36]

When Paul Goldberger assessed the building in 1979, he characterized the Ford Foundation headquarters as the "city's modern Medici palace, an appropriate housing for an organization whose philanthropic largesse rivals that of a host of beneficent dukes," and noted that it "has been perhaps a bit overpraised by critics who, despairing the virtual absence of anything decent in Manhattan in the years following its completion, pointed to it again and again." But, he concluded, "that should not get in the way of the fact that this is very distinguished architecture indeed—one Ford Foundation philanthropy that, by its very presence on the streetscape, benefits the entire city."[37]

Although most of East Forty-second Street west of Lexington Avenue had been redeveloped as high-class commercial real estate in the 1920s, some opportunities remained for postwar developers. The Emigrant Savings Bank built a new building at 5 East Forty-second Street in 1969, designed by Emery Roth & Sons.[38] It had little to offer compared with the building it replaced, Voorhees, Gmelin & Walker's 1933 renovation for the same client, a design inspired by Howe & Lescaze's never realized 1931 proposal for the company.[39] Kahn & Jacobs's 330 Madison Avenue (1962), a 720,000-square-foot building that

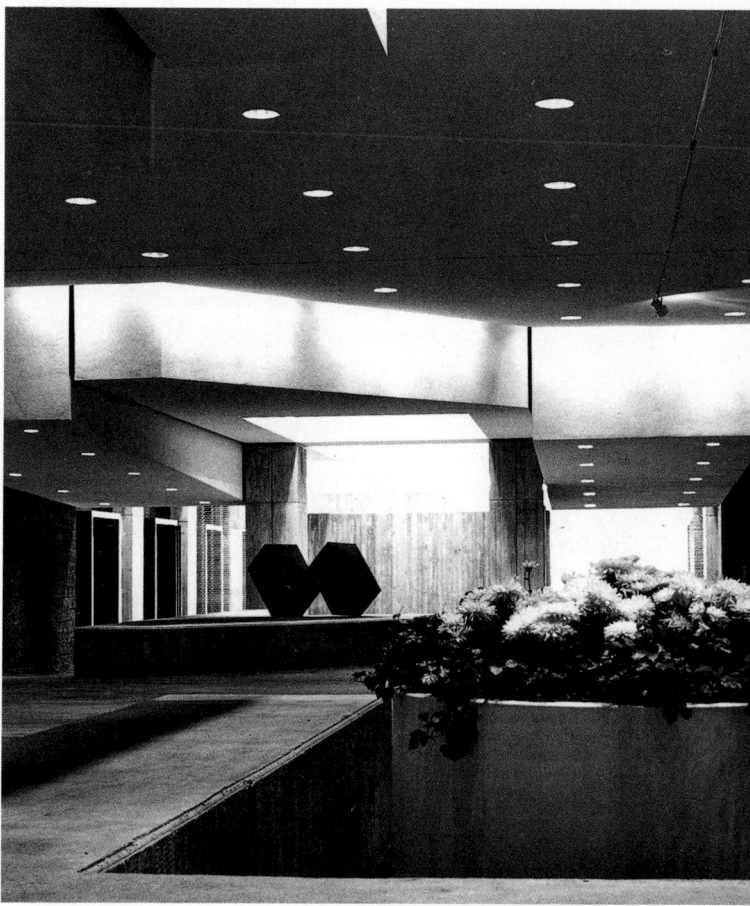

New York Graduate Center, 33 West Forty-second Street, West Forty-second to West Forty-third Street, between Fifth and Sixth avenues. Formerly Aeolian Hall (Warren & Wetmore, 1912). Renovation by Carl Petrilli and Samuel J. DeSanto, 1970. View to the south of passageway between West Forty-second and West Forty-third streets. Petrilli. CJP

Overleaf: View to the northwest of west midtown. The two towers in the lower right are the New York Telephone Company building (Kahn & Jacobs, 1974), on the left, and the Grace Building (Skidmore, Owings & Merrill, 1972), on the right. Acs. SA

461

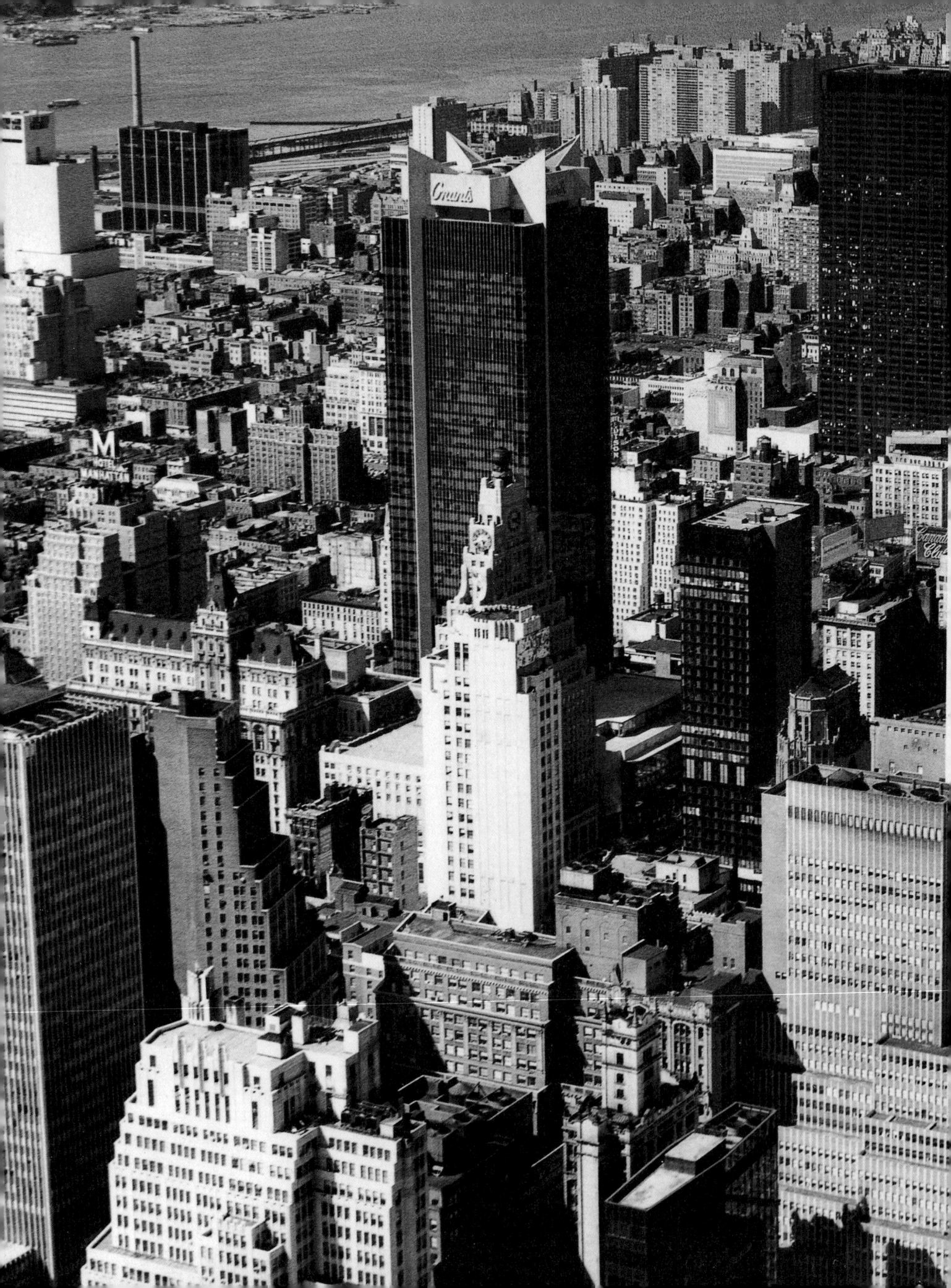

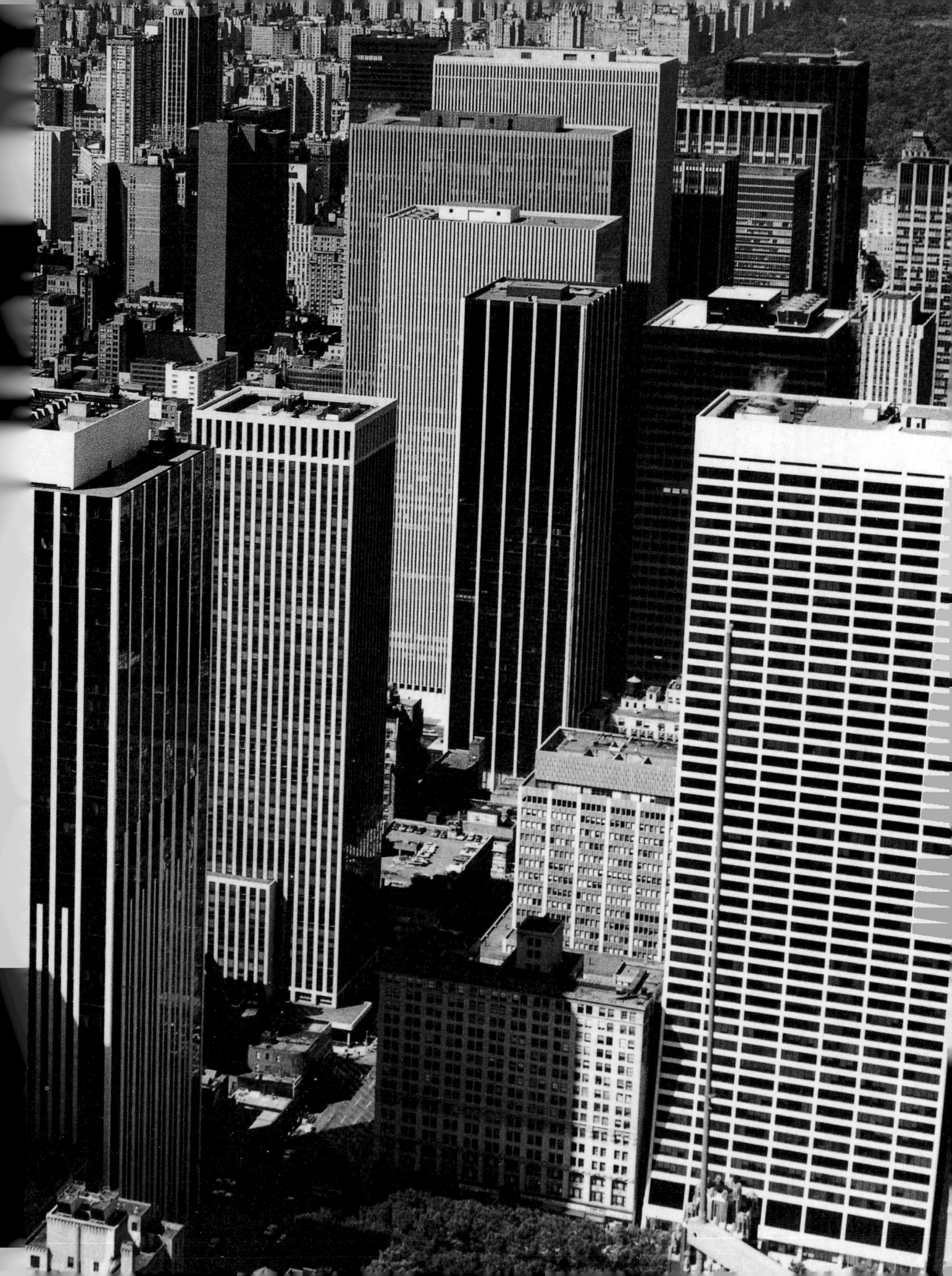

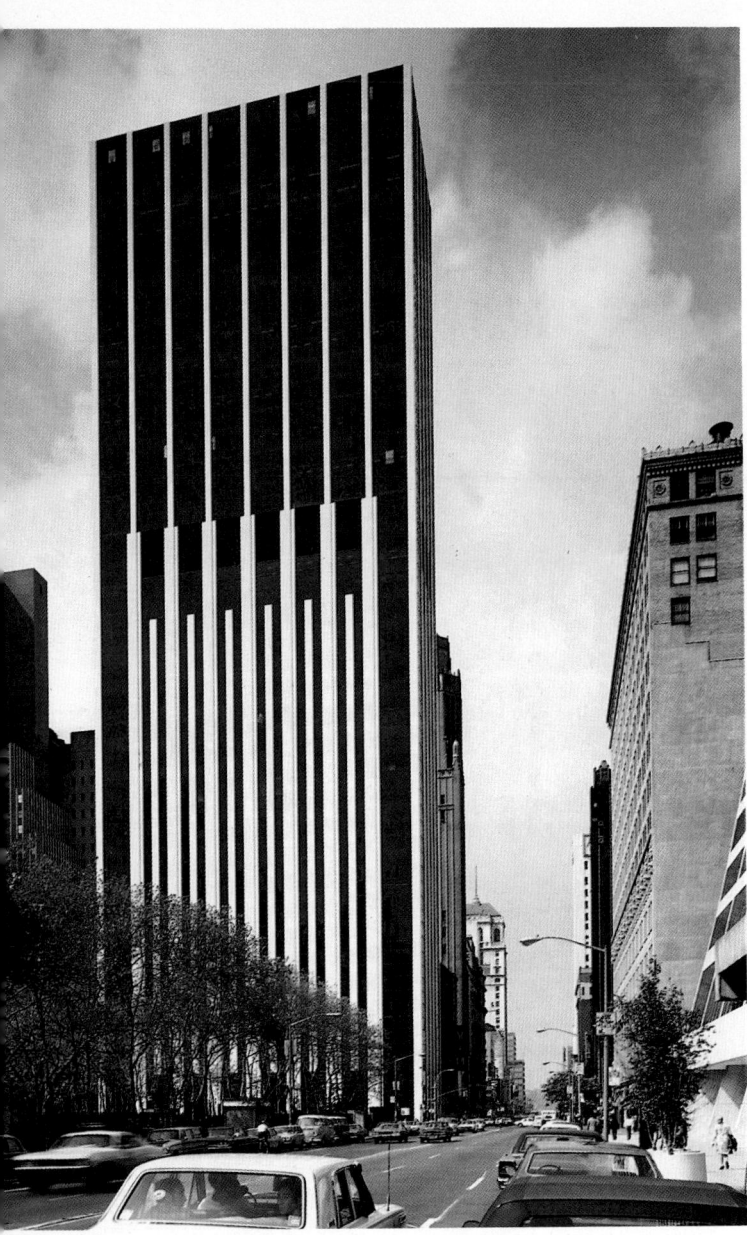

New York Telephone Company building, west side of Sixth Avenue, West Forty-first to West Forty-second Street. Kahn & Jacobs, 1974. View to the west. Acs. SA

occupied the west blockfront between Forty-second and Forty-third streets, was also not a worthy successor to its predecessor.[40] The new forty-one-story building, with a facade that consisted of three- and four-window-wide sections separated by vertical bands of dark brick, replaced Henry J. Hardenbergh's richly ornamented sixteen-story Manhattan Hotel (1897; remodeled for office use in 1922), which incorporated in its parapet a number of sculpted reclining Indian maidens.[41]

At Fifth Avenue stood Forty-second Street's most venerable anchor, the great public library (Carrère & Hastings, 1897–1911).[42] Although it faced the avenue, it belonged as much if not more to the crosstown street because of its access from the subways and suburban trains. With the closing of Warren & Wetmore's Aeolian Hall (1912) in 1924, the library was the street's sole cultural magnet until 1966, when it was joined by the City University's newly constituted New York Graduate Center, located in the former Aeolian Hall building, at 33 West Forty-second Street.[43] The hall had never prospered, despite the fact that it was sometimes home to distinguished music making, including the 1924 concert organized by Paul Whiteman that introduced George Gershwin's *Rhapsody in Blue*.[44] After the hall was closed, it was replaced by a Woolworth's store. The City University had selected the building because of its central location and its proximity to the library.

The renovation of the seventeen-story Aeolian Hall building, by Carl Petrilli and his project architect, Samuel J. DeSanto, was completed in 1970. One feature of the project could be described as memorable: a through-block, all-weather passageway the architects created by completely opening the space that had been Woolworth's and eliminating all street-level closure. The cavernous, seventy-five-foot-wide open-air concourse was paved with bluestone and lined with board-formed concrete and stucco. Although described by Ada Louise Huxtable as a "vest-pocket campus," it was less a gathering place than a shortcut for pedestrians traveling between two busy streets and a lobby to the classrooms and offices above as well as the auditorium beneath. Huxtable praised the concourse as the "kind of sophisticated urban and architectural design that most New York builders, lovers of pretentious schmaltz, shun like the plague."[45]

With the completion of the City University's New York Graduate Center, the block facing Bryant Park, which contained two major office buildings, 500 Fifth Avenue (Shreve, Lamb & Harmon, 1930) and the Salmon Tower (York & Sawyer, 1927), suddenly became a center of activity.[46] In 1969 the Stern Brothers department store closed its flagship store (J. B. Snook & Sons) after fifty-six years on the block.[47] Plans were immediately announced for its replacement, a fifty-story superslab, the W. R. Grace Building, at 41 West Forty-second Street, extending to Sixth Avenue by virtue of a plaza at the southeast corner of Forty-third Street.[48]

As designed by Gordon Bunshaft of Skidmore, Owings & Merrill, the shape of the Grace Building closely resembled that of the firm's previously designed 9 West Fifty-seventh Street (see "Plaza District," below). But whereas 9 West could be defended as providing a desirable break in Fifty-seventh Street's relentless street wall, the Grace Building broke the wall where closure was most needed, opposite the formal parterre of Bryant Park. As Norval White and Elliot Willensky put it: "An insult to the street, its swooping form nominally bows to zoning requirements for setbacks but was, in fact, an opportunity for some flashy architectural ego."[49] A similar assessment of the building's urbanism was expressed by Paul Goldberger, who said that, to the observer, both Grace and 9 West "destroy the pleasurable effect of a wall of buildings, similarly scaled, aligned evenly along a dignified street. To the passerby, they replace the traditional pedestrian experience of small-scale shop windows with massive columns, which come down at an angle onto the sidewalk to support the curved facade."[50] According to Bunshaft, the curving walls allowed more floor space in the lower nineteen floors without having to interrupt the vertical sweep of the design by introducing a setback—the very device that would have helped relate the building to its immediate context. Although the details of the Grace Building, including horizontal bands of windows on four sides, were a bit cruder than those of its uptown cousin, the new building nonetheless exhibited enough of the characteristic SOM finesse to pass as a distinguished if miscast effort. As at 9 West Fifty-seventh Street, travertine covered all surfaces that were not glass; but the facades of the Grace Building were structurally articulate, with a clear expression of stories and bays that made it seem more human in scale.

Executives of W. R. Grace & Co. professed satisfaction with the building, but from the first they were forced to admit that the plaza was a failure. It was a chillingly bare, football-field-sized expanse of travertine, punctuated with a planter and a bench, both also sheathed in travertine. Because it faced north, the plaza was shaded through many hours of the day; and because it was cut off from the building, which had no doors on to it, it quickly became a haven for layabouts. "Next to Grace Plaza," Goldberger wrote, "the mediocre plazas in the new buildings a few blocks up the Avenue of the Americas, which at least try to serve human needs, seem almost uplifting."[51] The plaza was so seriously flawed that simultaneous with the celebration of the building's completion, Grace announced a $10,000 student competition to develop a more appropriate design. Elevations and sketches were submitted by 187 students across the country. The first prize was awarded to Janis Eric Reiters, a student at Pratt Institute in Brooklyn, who called for a structural space-frame spanning the plaza to serve as a high-tech pergola.[52] This was not executed.

Despite the fact that two first-class office buildings, Helmle & Corbett's Bush Terminal Building (1918) and the sixteen-story Wurlitzer Building (Maynicke & Franke, 1919), had been built on the block of Forty-second Street west of Sixth Avenue, that avenue's El, together with the marginal character of the entertainments that lined the block, thwarted continued high-class development during the interwar period.[53] The sole postwar effort to counter the downward spiral of this block was made by the New York Telephone Company, which commissioned Kahn & Jacobs to design a combined equipment and office building for the Sixth Avenue block between Forty-first and Forty-second streets.[54] The new building replaced five old structures, including the nine-story Hart Building (Sidney Daub, 1925) and a Horn & Hardart's Automat.[55] Plans called for a building sheathed in gray-tinted glass that would be isolated from buildings to the west by a 15,000-square-foot plaza built on land to be acquired when the Wurlitzer Building, as well as three other buildings to the west along Forty-second Street, were torn down.

The project was initially conceived in the late 1950s by Joseph Bernstein, an independent real estate broker who had never built a building. Bernstein originally commissioned Skidmore, Owings & Merrill to develop plans for a forty-story, million-square-foot tower. The size of the building was contingent on the City Planning Commission's approving Bernstein's request to use the air rights of the low buildings he owned on Forty-first and Forty-second streets west of Sixth Avenue. When Bernstein was unable to complete negotiations with a major corporate office tenant, the New York Telephone Company came to him with a proposal to combine equipment and offices in a single building. To design the building the company brought in Kahn & Jacobs, who had designed two other buildings for them in Manhattan. Completed in 1974, the building was equivalent in height to a conventional fifty-three-story office building, with floors of 28,000 square feet piled up in a sheer tower. It was set back ten feet from the Sixth Avenue building line to create a wide sidewalk, which weakened the street wall bounding the west side of Bryant Park. In return for permission to build such a tall and unarticulated design, the architects included a seventy-five-foot-wide plaza at the rear that would extend between the two cross streets. Bernstein contributed $500,000 toward the improvement of the Sixth Avenue and Forty-second Street subway station, making possible a long-planned connection between the crosstown Times Square–to–Queens line and the north-south Sixth Avenue line.

Although Kahn & Jacobs's design featured, as Paul Goldberger observed, "a certain amount of structural innovation," it exhibited "none of the design quality one might expect from the headquarters building of the state's largest building-user, and particularly from the concern that once built 140 West Street," Ralph Walker's so-called Barclay-Vesey Building (1923–26), one of the quintessential skyscrapers of the 1920s.[56] Although Goldberger praised the massing of the building, which varied, he said, "slightly, though attractively, from the standard box," he criticized the facade as "a dull pastiche of windows and glaring white marble." He was particularly critical of the use of vertical marble stripes on the equipment floors, which, though it "suggests an echo of the vertical striping of the rear of the public library across Bryant Park . . . is rather decorative looking and, esthetically at least, too weak to be convincing."[57] In a second look at the building, Goldberger was even less kind: "The New York Telephone Co.'s headquarters . . . is a pretentious white-marble box whose vertical lines make a shrill and unpleasant echo to the vertical windows of the west facade of the public libary." He also castigated the "dark, awkward, and thoroughly unappealing plaza," as well as questioning the system that allowed such a trade-off for extra height: "Who really wins in such cases—the public or the real estate developer?"[58]

While individual projects perhaps testified to west midtown's growing role in the city's economy, many observers felt that even more important for the area's future was the health of the entertainment district, Forty-second Street's portion of which lay in the so-called Rialto block, between Seventh and Eighth avenues. For decades the central location of Forty-second Street and its principal focus, Times Square, had made it the city's nerve center and its greatest mixing valve. During World War II prosperity blinded most observers to the area's increasing seediness. But the rise of television and the general emphasis on family entertainment that accompanied widespread suburbanization in the postwar era conspired to drain the street of much of its life, leaving its increasing physical dilapidation all too visible. In 1954 Business Week reported that "Times Square . . . is not what it used to be," explaining that "the small stores fronting on the Square and along 42nd St. near the Square have been taken over more and more by penny arcades, pinball arcades, souvenir stores, outlet bookstores, auction rooms, open-front stores selling hot dogs or spaghetti or soft drinks—to the point where Times Square, close up, looks more like a carnival than anything else."[59] New regulations, adopted by the City Planning Commission early in 1954, prohibited carnival attractions but did not force those already in operation to close.[60]

In the early 1960s one enterprising realtor, Irving Maidman, recognizing the changing nature of the theater business, devel-

465

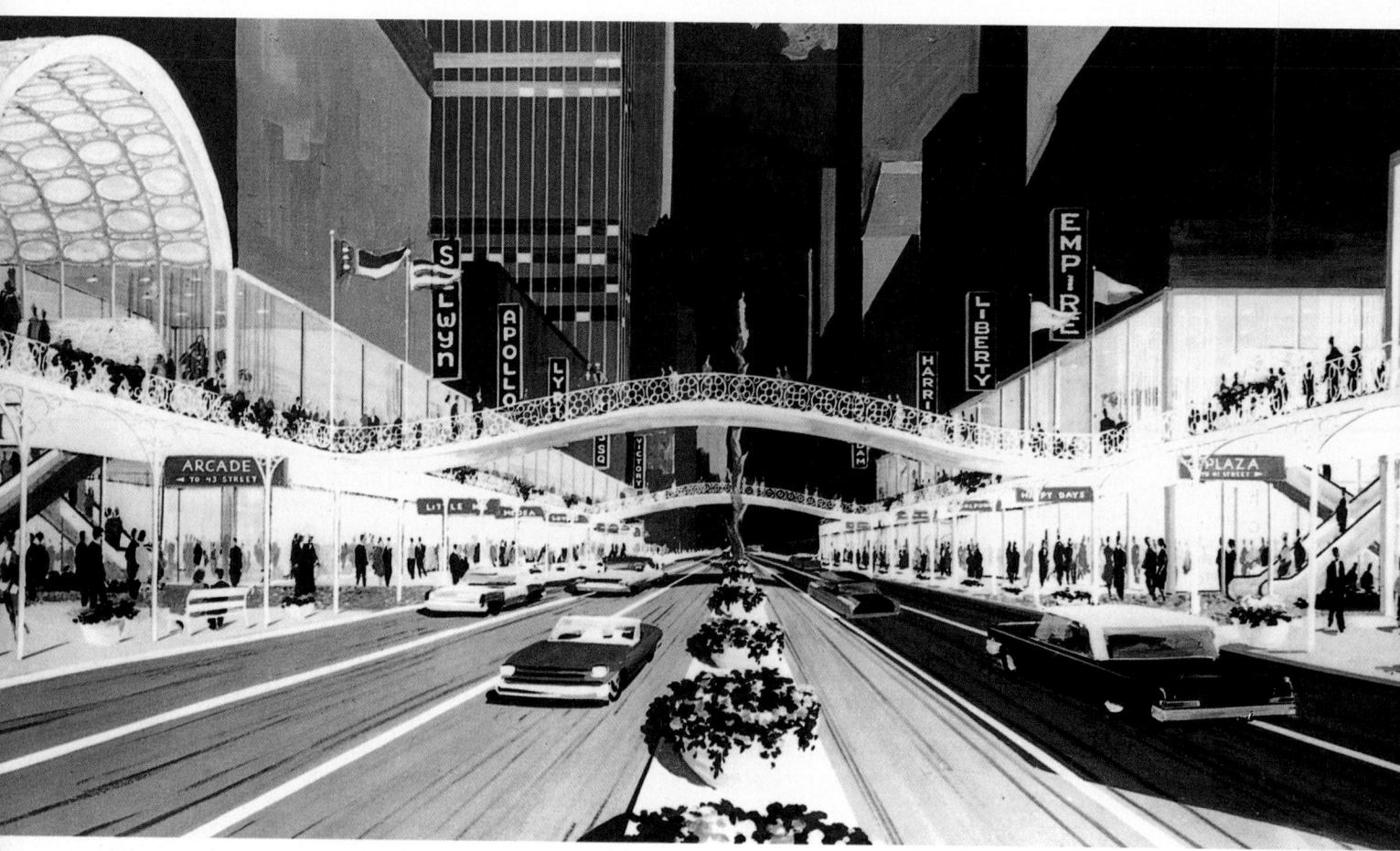

West Forty-second Street redevelopment plan. Richard W. Snibbe,
1962. View to the east. RWS

oped a series of small theaters and rehearsal halls geared to the more experimental "Off Broadway" theater, traditionally located in the vicinity of Greenwich Village.[61] Maidman's theaters, none architecturally notable, opened up a new era for the street, even bringing high-level experimental drama to the area on occasion, although his theaters were all in the 400 block between Ninth and Tenth avenues, considerably west of Forty-second Street's troubled, historical center near Times Square. The 199-seat Maidman Playhouse, at 416 West Forty-second Street, was constructed inside the building that once housed the now-defunct Bank of the United States. The theater opened in 1960 with the illustrator Russell Patterson's *Sketchbook,* a nostalgic review. Patterson had helped to design the theater, incorporating a cocktail lounge and a restaurant as well as offices for the Institute for Advanced Studies in the Theater Arts, a nonprofit group. The opening of Patterson's show was the first such theatrical event on Forty-second Street since 1937, when *Othello,* starring Walter Huston, had opened at the New Amsterdam. Though Patterson's review bombed, the theater was a hit. As Louis Calta, a *New York Times* theater critic, put it: "The seats and carpets are plush, the sight-lines are excellent, the L-shaped foyer is smartly decorated with paintings, the bar is strategically situated and the over-all theater design by Mr. Patterson is tasteful."[62]

In 1961 Maidman opened two more theaters on Forty-second Street, the Mermaid, at 420 West Forty-second Street, and the Midway, at 422 West Forty-second Street, each with a seating capacity of 149, which was 50 fewer than the Maidman Playhouse. The Mermaid opened with a revival of Eugene O'Neill's 1921 play *Diff'rent,* the Midway with a double bill of satirical plays by a young Polish playwright, Slawomir Mrozek. Maidman also opened the Mayfair in 1961, at 235 West Forty-sixth Street, between Broadway and Eighth Avenue, in a space within the Paramount Hotel that had previously housed the Diamond Horseshoe nightclub;[63] and in 1962 he opened the Mainline, at 442 West Forty-second Street. Patterson designed all of Maidman's theaters, which also contained workshops for building and storing sets, props and costumes, as well as extra rehearsal rooms, facilities that were in short supply in the theater district as a whole.

Maidman based his theater-building program on the concept of showcasing Off-Broadway-type productions in theaters that were more comfortable for and more convenient to the theatergoing public than those typically scattered around Greenwich Village. He also hoped to bolster the value of his other real estate holdings in the neighborhood, which included the West Side Airlines Terminal (see below) and the Riviera Congress Motor Inn (see "Times Square," above). But in 1965 Maidman was forced to convert the Maidman Playhouse, as well as the 300-seat Garrick, at 152 Bleecker Street, one of three small theaters he owned in Greenwich Village, into film houses, citing the lack of appropriate scripts for live plays. In addition, the attraction that year at his Mayfair was *The Wonderful World of Burlesque,* hardly the high-minded Off-Broadway fare he had originally promised.

By 1962 the decline of West Forty-second Street was widely regarded as a serious threat to the theater district as a whole, and that year the Broadway Association retained the architect Richard W. Snibbe to prepare a redevelopment plan to reclaim the street for the cause of "legitimate" theater.[64] Snibbe's study, preceded by one prepared by urban design students at Harvard in 1955,[65] called for the restoration of ten auditoriums and the construction of light metal Victorian-inspired sidewalk arcades as well as two second-story pedestrian overpasses that would cross the street at third points in the block. He also called for a central concrete island down the length of the block, with potted plants providing seasonal horticultural displays. With its mix of planning ideas

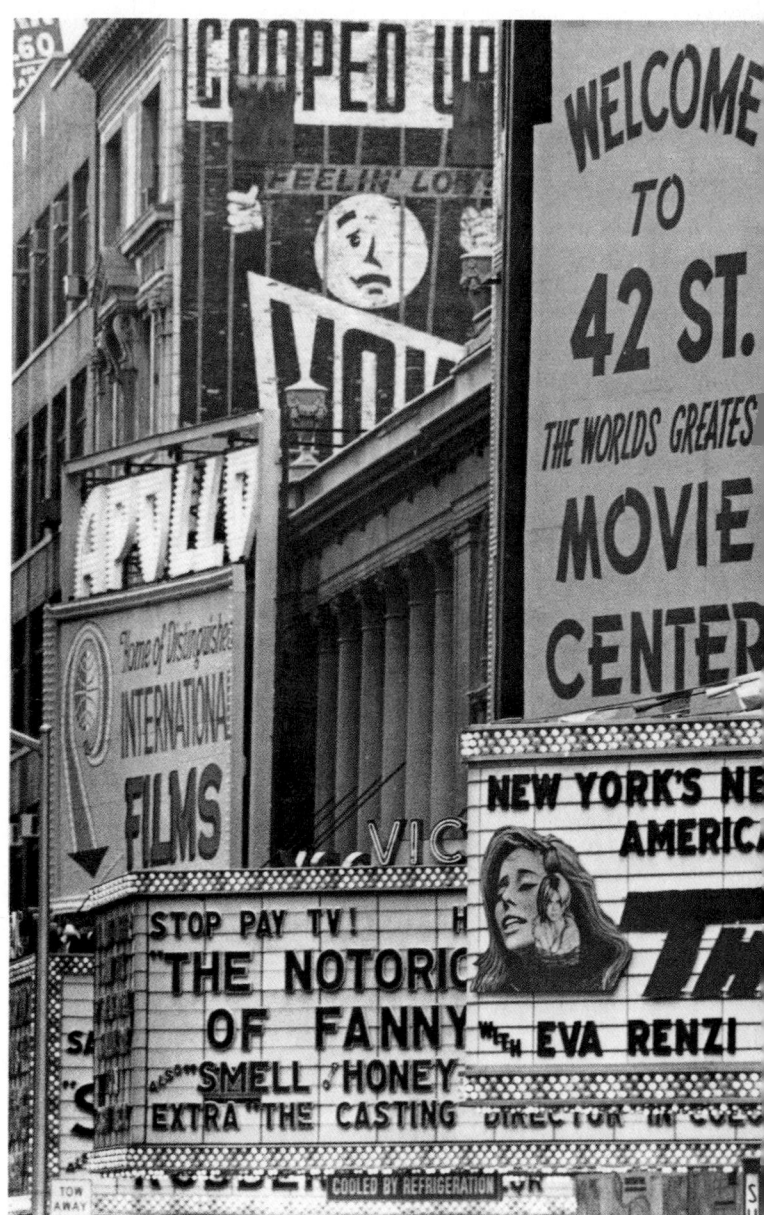

West Forty-second Street between Seventh and Eighth avenues. View to the northwest showing movie marquees, 1968. NYT

taken from suburban shopping malls and a sense of glittering urbanity that was difficult to reconcile with the street's ugly realities, Snibbe's unrealized scheme was at least provocative.

Meanwhile, conditions declined even more precipitously, despite patchwork efforts such as Douglas Leigh's 1963 sale of the Times Tower to the Allied Chemical Corporation, whose plan to boost the area by converting the building into a "showcase for chemistry" proved to be yet another step toward mediocrity (see chapter 16). The venerable seven-story Crossroads Cafe Building (Henry Ives Cobb, 1910), on the south blockfront between Seventh Avenue and Broadway, now owned by Irving Maidman and Douglas Leigh, was also remodeled to the point of oblivion in 1965.[66] To add yet another sad note to the street, the Franklin Savings Bank demolished its pristine landmark-quality headquarters building (York & Sawyer, 1899), on the southeast corner of Eighth Avenue and Forty-second Street, and relocated to a far less compelling new bank building designed for it by Poor, Swanke, Hayden & Connell (1974).

The empty lot left by the demolition became a highly visible symbol of the area's near collapse. Though not totally banal, the new bank building, at 661 Eighth Avenue, on the northwest corner of Forty-second Street, was but small consolation. Peter Blake described the bank's one-story concrete box sheathed in orange brick as a "Laundromat-type branch."[67] The two corners, diagonally across from each other, poignantly illustrated the failure to either preserve the best of the past or to create contemporary work of commensurate quality. To make matters worse, the bank branch was surmounted by a monumentally scaled trompe l'oeil mural on the reentrant walls of the adjacent building, the Corn Exchange Bank Building (Fellheimer & Wagner, 1927), at 303 West Forty-second Street, a twelve-story structure that wrapped the underdeveloped corner site. When viewed from a distance, the mural resembled uninspired, ribbon-window-type Modernist high rises. In addition, the parking garages built west of Eighth Avenue, despite some interesting gadgetry and the convenience they offered to suburbanites coming to see a show, were a blight to the street (see chapter 1).

When the United States Supreme Court upheld the First Amendment rights of those engaged in the publication and sale of pornographic literature and the presentation of pornographic theatrical entertainments, Forty-second Street was debased to serve an even lower level of public taste than before. The pornography trade encouraged prostitution, frequently involving homosexual men and young boys; and with prostitution came the drug trade. In 1970 yet another planning study was undertaken to help upgrade the troubled area, this time by Arthur B. Zabarkes, a twenty-six-year-old architect and planner.[68] He called for more office buildings and a major retail shopping center along Forty-second Street, as well as more intensive development of Times Square, including the construction of a top-grade cinema center and the expansion of the garment center northward. In 1972 Lewis Rudin, head of the Association for a Better New York, and one of the city's more enlightened realtors, made yet another call for a massive cleanup of Times Square and its environs: "To move New York forward, we must drive the dregs of society from the Great White Way. . . . Broadway and Times Square is the frame of reference of New York to the world. We cannot afford to tolerate the degrading atmosphere that pervades the area. It is debilitating and self-defeating to all New Yorkers."[69]

Part of West Forty-second Street's troubles lay in its increasingly lopsided function as a vehicular and pedestrian highway leading to trans-Hudson crossings. While the Weehawken Ferry

had for a long time made Forty-second Street a gateway to the west, the opening of the Lincoln Tunnel in 1937 vastly escalated the scale of traffic using the street as a passageway to and through midtown.[70] Through traffic increased with the opening of the tunnel's second tube in 1945 and its third tube in 1957. The street's function as a regional transit corridor was intensified with the opening of the Port Authority Bus Terminal in 1950 (see below).

With the development of interstate bus travel in the late 1920s, west midtown had become the destination point for suburban and interstate bus lines. From the outset bus travel was socially stigmatized, first in contrast to train travel, and then to air travel. Increasingly, more affluent long-distance travelers came to town on airplanes, while commuters from prosperous suburban areas traveled by train. In part this was because buses did not provide the amenities that trains had. Not only were buses confining and lacking in toilet facilities, but bus stations tended to be of unremarkable design and located in marginal areas of big cities, areas usually associated with trucking and warehousing activities, not to mention crime and prostitution. The first architecturally notable bus terminal constructed in New York was William Lescaze's short-lived Capitol Bus Terminal of 1927, at 230 West Fiftieth Street, but compared to the city's two railroad stations it was hardly a paragon of luxury or aesthetics.[71] The bus terminal incorporated in Emery Roth's Hotel Dixie (1930), at 251 West Forty-second Street, was another effort to lift the building type beyond banality.[72] In 1935, three years after the destruction of the Capitol Bus Terminal, Thomas W. Lamb echoed Lescaze's pioneering Modernism in the Greyhound Bus Terminal he designed for a midblock site that ran from Thirty-third to Thirty-fourth Street between Seventh and Eighth avenues.[73]

In 1941 the City Planning Commission, in an effort to relieve the west side of the major traffic nuisance caused by the bus terminals scattered all over the area, approved the construction of a terminal that would concentrate all the buses in one building.[74] The proposed site was just west of the McGraw-Hill Building (Raymond Hood, Godley & Fouilhoux, 1931), on the western end of the block bounded by Forty-first and Forty-second streets, Eighth and Ninth avenues, a location that was chosen because of its proximity to the recently completed Lincoln Tunnel.[75] The proposed 300,000-square-foot, sleekly streamlined terminal, ten times larger than any other in the world, was to be connected with the tunnel's Manhattan approach by an underground roadway that would allow buses from New Jersey to reach the station without using city streets. The corporation undertaking the new terminal was headed by the publisher Harold W. McGraw, who undoubtedly selected Harrison & Fouilhoux to design the building because, as successors to Raymond Hood, they could be counted on to be sympathetic to his company's headquarters building.

The terminal project was stopped by the war, and it was not until 1947 that it was once again taken up, this time by the Port Authority.[76] By the time the planning for the new terminal began in earnest, there were 125,000 daily bus commuters to and from New Jersey, over half of whom were served in small terminals scattered hit or miss in west midtown. The new terminal (1950), designed by Walter McQuade, chief architect in the Port Authority's engineering department, occupied a different site from the one considered in 1941, filling the entire block lying between Eighth and Ninth avenues, Fortieth and Forty-first streets. The four-level structure, which could accommodate as many as 2,500 buses per day and 450 cars in its rooftop parking lot, was connected by ramps to the Lincoln Tunnel entrance plaza to the west.

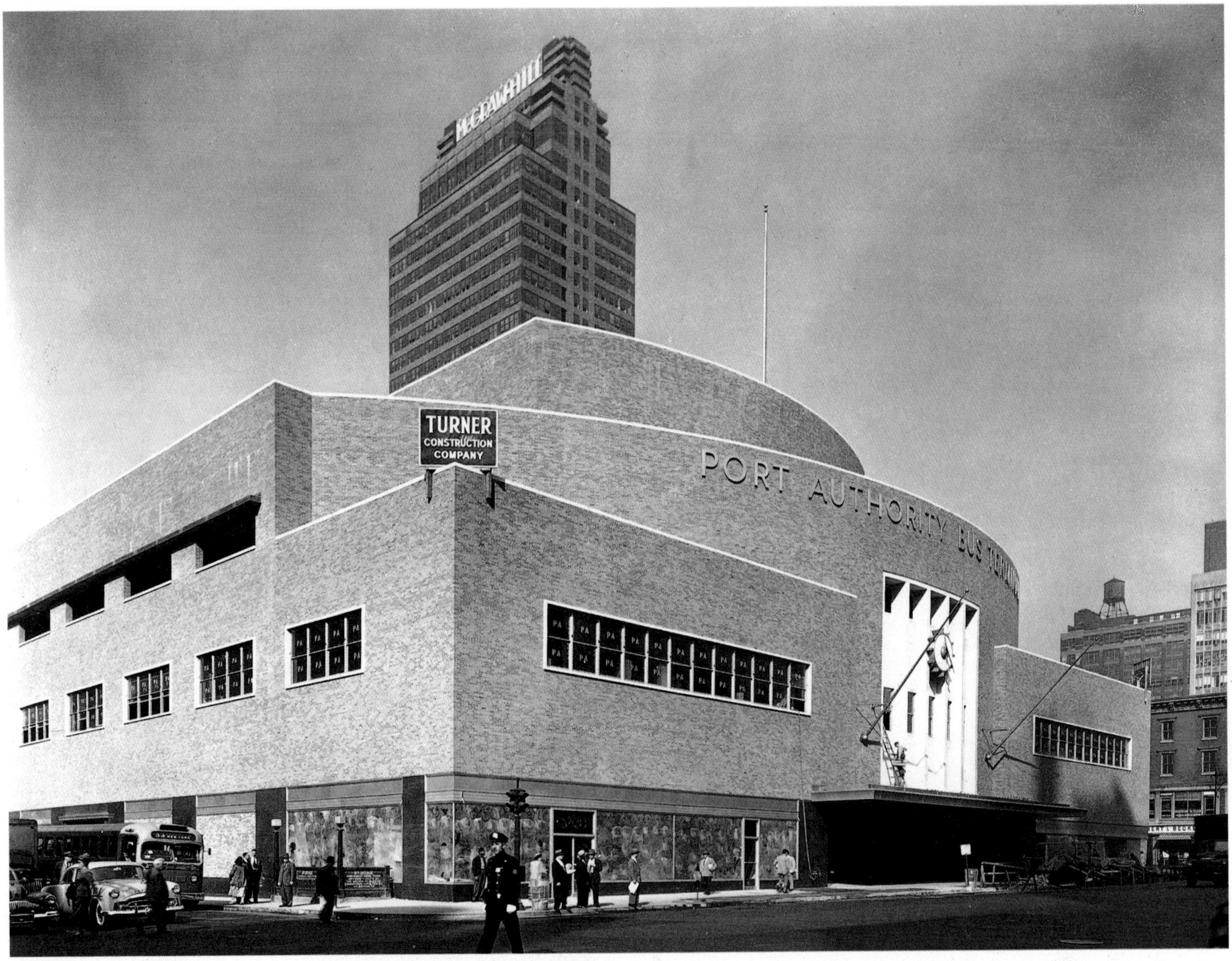

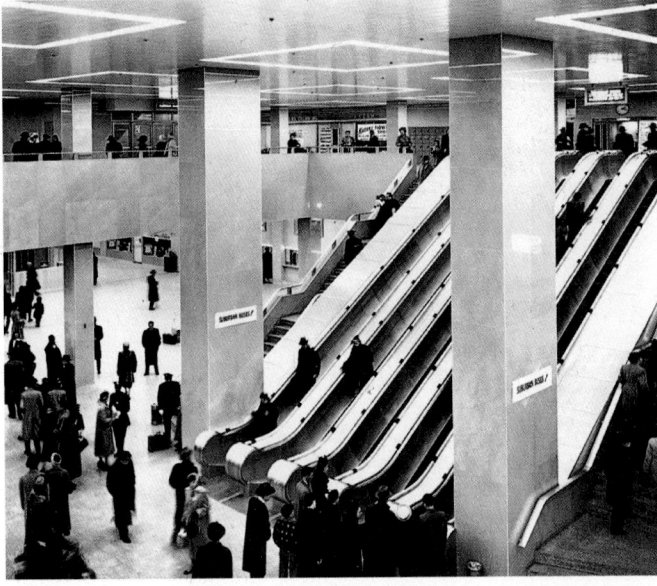

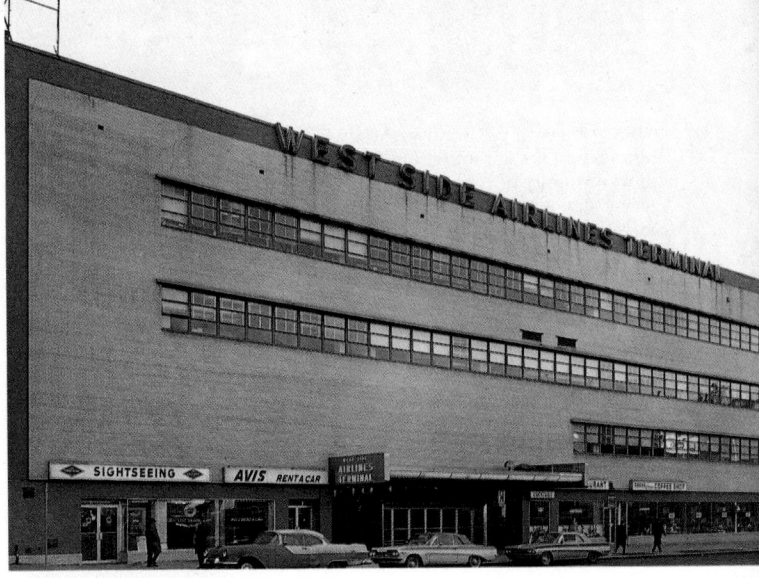

Top: Port Authority Bus Terminal, Eighth to Ninth Avenue, West Fortieth to West Forty-first Street. Walter McQuade, 1950. View to the northwest showing McGraw-Hill Building (Raymond Hood, Godley & Fouilhoux, 1931) in the background. PANY

Bottom left: Port Authority Bus Terminal. Interior. Wurts. MCNY

Bottom right: West Side Airlines Terminal, east side of Tenth Avenue, West Forty-first to West Forty-second Street. Port of New York Authority staff architects, 1955. View of West Forty-second Street facade. OMH

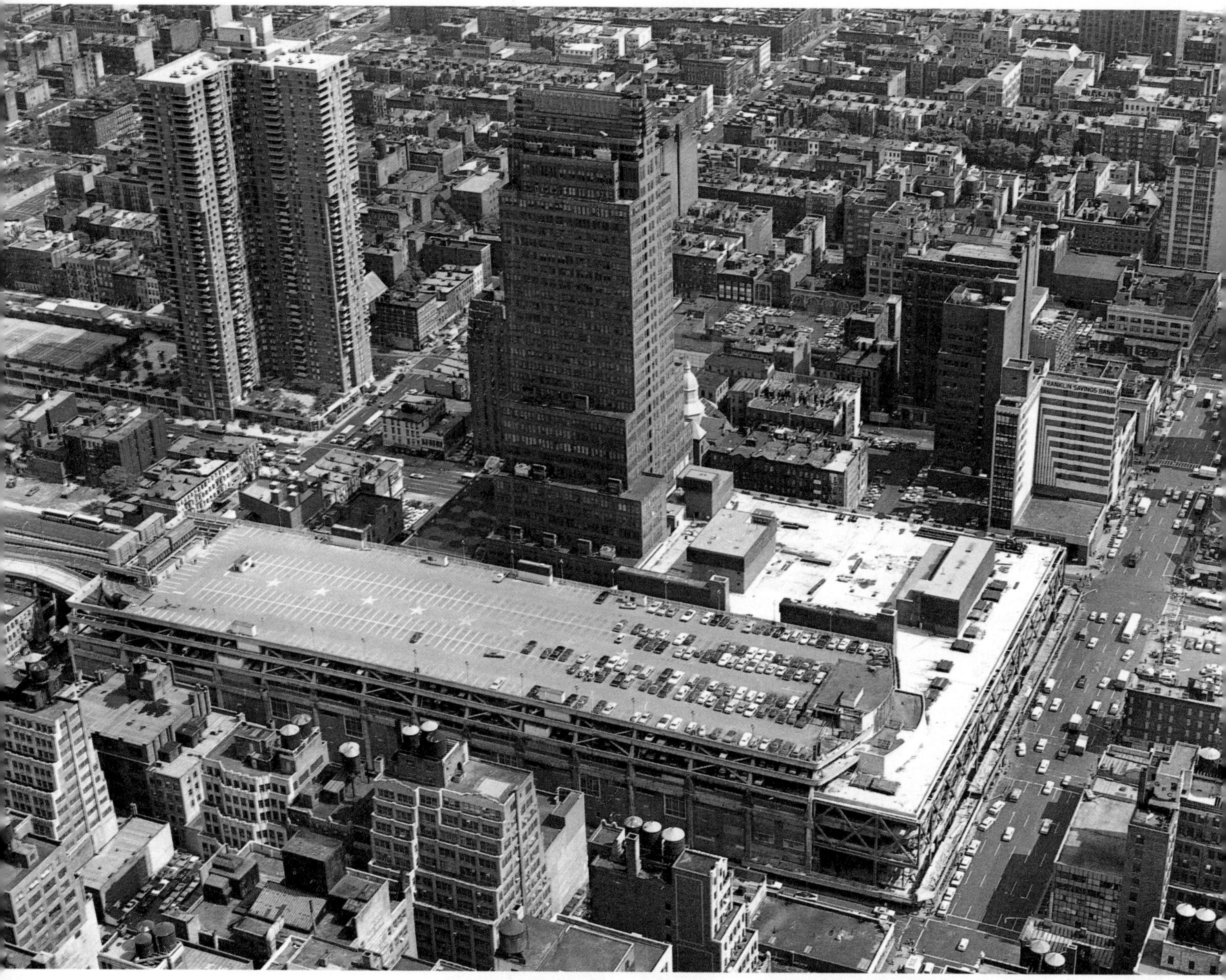

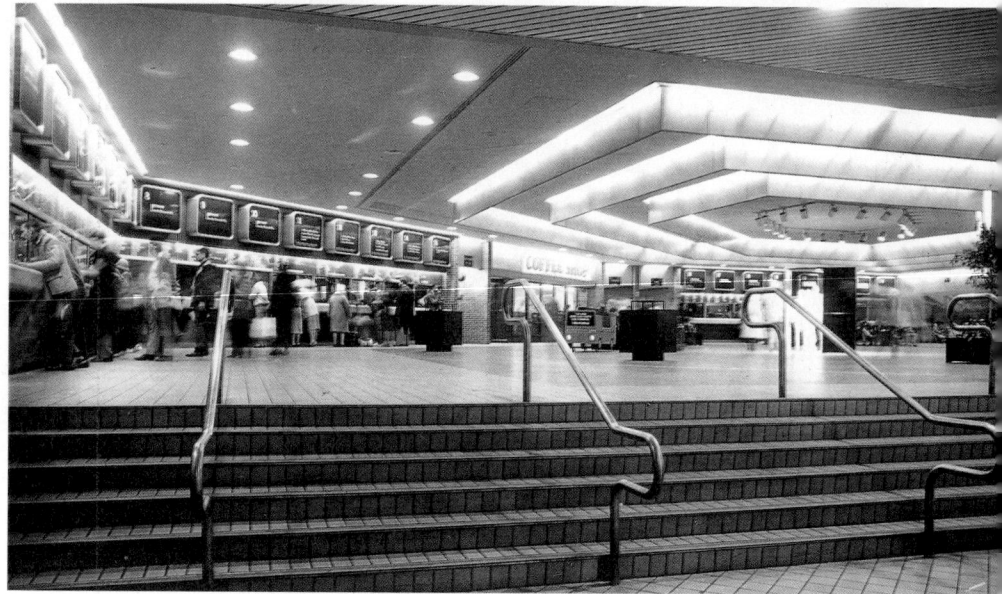

Above: View to the northwest showing renovated Port Authority Bus Terminal (Port Authority of New York and New Jersey staff architects, 1981), in the foreground; Manhattan Plaza (David Todd & Associates, 1977), on the upper left; McGraw-Hill Building (Raymond Hood, Godley & Fouilhoux, 1931), in the upper center; and Corn Exchange Bank Building (Fellheimer & Wagner, 1927), with trompe l'oeil mural on reentrant walls wrapping around Franklin Savings Bank (Poor, Swanke, Hayden & Connell, 1974), on the upper right. PANY

Right: Port Authority Bus Terminal. Main waiting room. PANY

The terminal was organized so that long-distance buses, only some of which arrived through the Lincoln Tunnel, occupied the street level, entering and departing at Ninth Avenue. Suburban buses, all of which used the Lincoln Tunnel, went directly to the terminal's third level via elevated ramps. The second level, which because of the site's slope was entered at grade on the building's Eighth Avenue end, was devoted to ticketing areas and waiting rooms, as well as a shopping arcade that featured a supermarket and the city's biggest soda counter. On a mezzanine level there were administrative offices and a bowling alley. While elevators and stairs were provided, most passengers used the thirty-one escalators, which also led to the subway concourse under Eighth Avenue.

The building's steel frame was clad in a warm red brick trimmed with limestone. On the Eighth Avenue side the turning radius of the suburban bus right-of-way was expressed as a curving mass cleaving the building in two to mark the entrance and aggrandize the scale of an enterprise that many people saw as inherently ignoble in comparison to the great railroad terminals. *Architectural Forum* said that although the structure was "not apt to win any building beauty contests," it represented "a carefully thought-out answer to both internal and external traffic-routing problems—motor and pedestrian."[77]

In 1955 West Forty-second Street was further transformed into a transit corridor with the opening of the West Side Airlines Terminal, designed by the Port Authority's own architects.[78] Occupying the east side of Tenth Avenue between Forty-first and Forty-second streets, the building was not inspiring. "The best one can say about it," Lewis Mumford wrote, "is that it is admirably placed in relation to the destination of its passengers—the Newark Airport." In Mumford's view, the four-story, mostly off-white brick building was bland, sinking "without protest, a nonentity, into the dismal swamp of buildings around it." Inside, Mumford was pleased to find a two-story-high rectangular room, "much pleasanter than the waiting room in the Port Authority's Bus Terminal." With a powdery indigo blue ceiling, pale yellow walls, light gray terrazzo floor and light spruce green counters, the room suggested "airiness," even though it was illuminated exclusively with fluorescent lighting.[79]

Despite the construction of the Port Authority Bus Terminal, and the authority's efforts to ban suburban and long-distance buses from Manhattan streets, some companies held onto their independent locations. Nonetheless, by 1961 the terminal was working at full capacity, and in 1963 the Port Authority provided more bus docks in a new addition, at which time all bus lines were consolidated in the facility.[80] The new terminal featured trusses that spanned the existing structure and thereby created three levels of parking, bringing the total capacity to 1,000 cars and freeing up the three-acre roof of the existing building for service as an additional all-weather suburban bus terminal. The fifteen reinforced-concrete Vierendeel trusses required to span the 200-foot-wide terminal were carried on thirty new steel columns placed along the building's outer edge. Sixteen of the original escalators were removed and twenty-five new ones added, raising the total to forty. In the process, the building lost what little pretense to dignified monumentality it once had. It also managed to seem more congested than before, as well as more confusing to use.

By 1975 even the augmented facility had become inadequate and the Port Authority released drawings for an expanded and renovated facility that would increase by 50 percent the capacity of what was already the world's busiest bus terminal.[81] The five-level extension, finished in 1981, filled the eastern half of the block immediately to the north of the existing terminal. A common facade, dominated by a forty-foot-high steel truss that spanned the two buildings and the intervening street at a point twenty-five feet above grade, completely obliterated the original building's identity. A new tunnel under Ninth Avenue eliminated even more surface bus traffic. The extension was designed so that a high-rise structure, initially projected at fifty-four floors, could be built above it. Along the Eighth Avenue streetfront, the expanded terminal's lobby spaces were set back behind glass walls to create a high arcade and greater sidewalk area to accommodate the sixty million passengers who used the bus terminal each year—twenty-one million more than in 1950, when the original facility opened. Inside, the public spaces were designed in a cheap, glitzy style typical of the worst kind of suburban shopping mall.

The construction of Manhattan Plaza, twin apartment houses occupying the block bounded by Forty-second and Forty-third streets, Ninth and Tenth avenues, was symptomatic of the city's perilous state of affairs in the 1970s as well as its cunning and self-confidence in the face of disaster.[82] The idea of Manhattan Plaza was hatched in the early 1970s as part of the Lindsay administration's efforts to shift development from the east to the west side of midtown Manhattan. The site, which mostly consisted of parking lots, had been assembled by Seymour Durst, who was contemplating the construction of an office building there but lost interest in the project after the office boom collapsed. He sold the site to the HRH Construction Company in 1973. Originally intended as upper-middle-class housing, Manhattan Plaza's two towers, one forty-five and the other forty-six stories tall, contained 1,690 one- and two-bedroom and studio apartments, most with balconies. The towers were set on a continuous one- and two-story podium containing stores and elaborate sports facilities, including an Olympic-sized swimming pool, squash and rooftop tennis courts (covered by an air-inflated bubble for winter play), as well as a 1,000-car garage. By the time the plans for the project were crystallized in 1974 and construction was under way, Manhattan Plaza had begun to look like a very risky undertaking, given the city's inability to effectively clean up West Forty-second Street's theater block, the reluctance of most commercial office-building developers to show any interest in the street's potential west of Sixth Avenue, and the shaky finances of the city in general. Richard Ravitch, executive vice president of HRH Construction, claimed that "a lot of people say I'm nuts to be doing this."[83]

While some cynical observers seemed all too anxious to see the project fail as a symbol of the city's larger problems, a growing number of people began to appreciate the stable social values and physical charm of the neighborhood that extended north from the site—so much so, in fact, that the area's historic name, Hell's Kitchen, was abandoned in favor of Clinton, a new name with a much more upmarket ring to it (see "West Side: From Chelsea to Clinton," above). It was believed that by creating so much housing with almost no residential relocation, Manhattan Plaza would ease the pressures brought on the existing Clinton neighborhood by gentrification; it would also provide the area with a new infusion of affluent residents. Moreover, the construction of Manhattan Plaza also involved a promise to provide blacks and other nonwhites with a larger-than-usual percentage of construction jobs, many of them high-paying. According to Ravitch, whose company was as enlightened about hiring policies as it was daring in its choice of projects, "Several years ago we decided that, whether or not the law required it, we wanted to offer equal opportunity, and we've done so ever since."[84]

The complex was planned by David Todd & Associates, with Robert Cabrera in charge of design, in a manner highly rem-

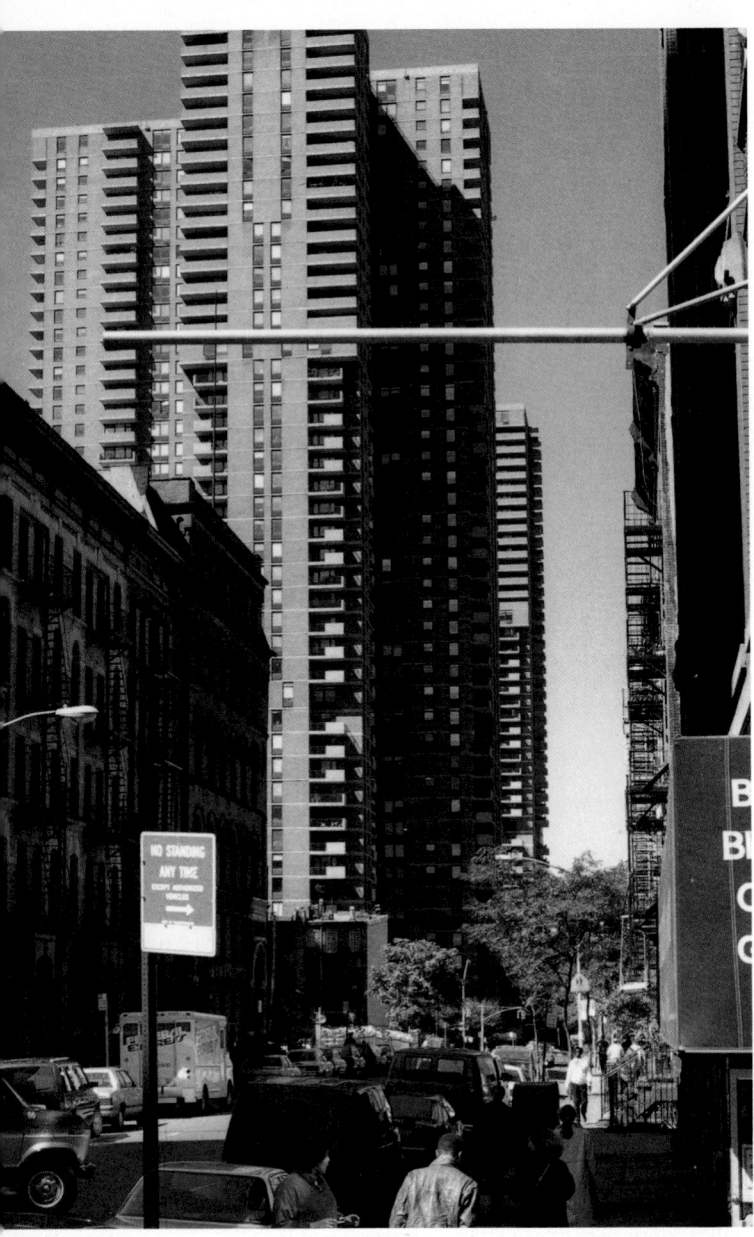

Manhattan Plaza, Ninth to Tenth Avenue, West Forty-second to West Forty-third Street. David Todd & Associates, 1977. View to the west. Cabrera. DT

iniscent of Davis, Brody & Associates' Waterside, also developed by Ravitch (see "East Side: From Stuyvesant Town to Turtle Bay," above). The decision to pack the apartments into two widely spaced towers, which Paul Goldberger characterized as "an approach to urban planning that . . . is generally considered traditional today," had its advantages.[85] According to Todd, "Larger structures in mid-block would have cut the sunlight and would have destroyed the small scale of the mid-block area as well."[86]

Ravitch compared Manhattan Plaza with the Tudor City development of the 1920s at the east end of Forty-second Street, expressing hope that his project would "do for West 42d Street what Tudor City did for East 42d Street."[87] From any distant perspective the project seemed overwhelming and impersonal, and hardly comparable to its pedestrian-oriented, intimately scaled predecessor. Yet from the pedestrian's point of view, Manhattan Plaza, with a block-filling podium that stepped back from the building line on West Forty-third Street, creating small plazas, was far and away more user-friendly than the isolated, plaza-bound Waterside.

As the buildings were rising, the city's fiscal plight worsened. With apartments in established neighborhoods going unoccupied, it was unlikely that affluent New Yorkers would choose to pioneer the marginal fringe of midtown even if it was being called Clinton. By May 1975, with the project more than half completed, the city was convinced that the complex, financed with a $90 million Mitchell-Lama mortgage loan, was doomed and that the buildings might have to be rented to poor and moderate-income families. This would not only compromise the capital investment but would also thwart the effort to turn Clinton into a mixed-income neighborhood.

In 1976, as the construction neared completion, federal rent subsidies valued at $11.5 million per year for forty years were obtained by the city's Housing and Development Administration, and Manhattan Plaza's future seemed relatively secure. However, the surrounding community did not welcome the socioeconomic mix that such subsidies usually implied, and their opposition was intense. The plan was also denounced as a "bailout" for the developers. But in an inspired move, the city, acting on the suggestions of Fred Papert, who was then president of the Municipal Art Society, and Daniel Rose, the developer who had been retained as the project's managing agent, persuaded the federal authorities to let the subsidies be confined to low- and moderate-income tenants engaged in the performing arts. Manhattan Plaza would thereby become not one of the city's least suitable settlements for disadvantaged families but one of the most provocative experiments in large-scale socially integrated housing ever undertaken. The idea was turned over for study to the Settlement Housing Fund, which, in reporting its findings in 1976, estimated that 100,000 households in New York had members engaged in the performing arts, about two-thirds of whom had incomes that made them eligible for federally assisted housing. Moreover, the report argued that confining the federal subsidies to performing artists was serving not only a local need but a national one as well. As Lynda Simmons, chairman of the fund's study committee, put it, "New York is the nation's incubator city for the theater, since it is where young performing artists from all over the country come to start their careers. By using Federal funds to subsidize housing for the performing arts we are helping the entire country."[88]

In January 1977 the subsidy plan was accepted and tenants began moving in, with about 70 percent of the apartments rented to performing artists, who agreed to pay 25 percent of their annual income in rent. Thus, an actor having a good year could conceivably pay rent that exceeded market rates, while in a bad year he would be required to pay only 25 percent of his unemployment benefits. Early notable tenants included the playwright Tennessee Williams and William Hamilton, the novelist and *New Yorker* cartoonist. The remainder of the apartments were leased to senior citizens from Clinton and Chelsea and to residents from those neighborhoods who had been inadequately housed. Successful though the subsidy plan was in providing housing for a class of tenants who could effectively cope with the project's colossal scale, Manhattan Plaza was hardly a model for the future. As Paul Goldberger put it, "Architecturally, the towers are decent, with somewhat more flair than the average new apartment skyscraper on the East Side. But that is it—there is no real innovation here, and no real style, and good as the success of the development is for this troubled area, a neighborhood full of such buildings would be no neighborhood at all."[89]

FIFTY-THIRD STREET

Fifty-third Street occupied a unique position in the architecture and urbanism of postwar midtown. Despite the fact that it was not a wide, two-way thoroughfare like Fourteenth, Twenty-third, Thirty-fourth, Forty-second and Fifty-seventh streets, it became a rather important crosstown conduit for traffic because the southbound East River Drive emptied onto it and because the crosstown subway ran beneath it. It also acquired a remarkable collection of architecturally significant buildings, many for leading public institutions. Among the buildings that distinguished Fifty-third Street were thirteen large-scale office and hotel buildings located between Third and Tenth avenues which, though they faced various avenues, usually could be entered from Fifty-third Street. These included Citicorp Center and the Harper & Row Building (see below); 399 Park Avenue, the Seagram Building and Lever House (see "Park Avenue," above); 666 Fifth Avenue (see "Fifth Avenue," above); the CBS Building and the New York Hilton (see "Sixth Avenue," above); 825 Seventh Avenue (Russell M. Boak, 1967) and 810 Seventh Avenue (Kahn & Jacobs, 1970);[1] the Americana Hotel and 1700 Broadway (see "Times Square," above); and the New York Telephone Company Switching Center (see "West Side: From Chelsea to Clinton," above).

While the presence of so many large buildings helped define Fifty-third Street as a darkened commercial canyon, it was the informally defined cultural center extending from Fifth to Sixth Avenue that gave the street its greatest prominence. That block, with its aggregation of important institutions—the Museum of Modern Art, the Museum of American Folk Art, the Museum of Contemporary Crafts and the Donnell Library—more accurately expressed the nature of the city's postwar cultural life, where commerce and art were so intertwined, than did Lincoln Center (see chapter 9), which was conceived along the lines of an earlier model, that of a campus dedicated to culture. Unlike the more cohesive but more sanitized confines of Lincoln Center, West Fifty-third Street between Fifth and Sixth avenues somehow managed to suggest a distinct precinct without interrupting either Manhattan's dominant and unifying street grid or midtown's characteristic commercialism.

Museum of Modern Art

West Fifty-third Street was established as a cultural center with the completion of Philip L. Goodwin and Edward Durell Stone's 1939 building for the Museum of Modern Art, which had begun nine years earlier in rented space in the Heckscher Building (Warren & Wetmore, 1922).[2] The new building, at 11 West Fifty-third Street, contributed greatly to the museum's popular

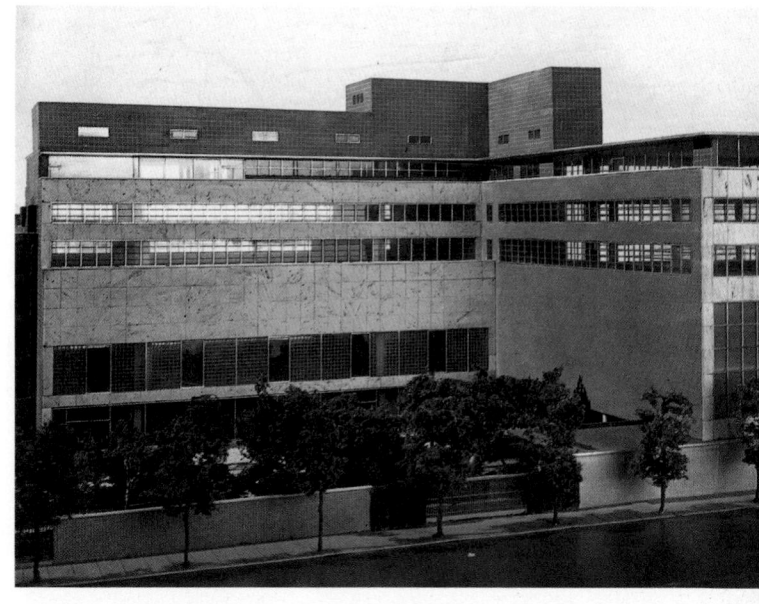

Proposed Museum of Modern Art wing, south side of West Fifty-fourth Street, between Fifth and Sixth avenues. Philip L. Goodwin, 1946. Model. View to the south. Checkman. LC

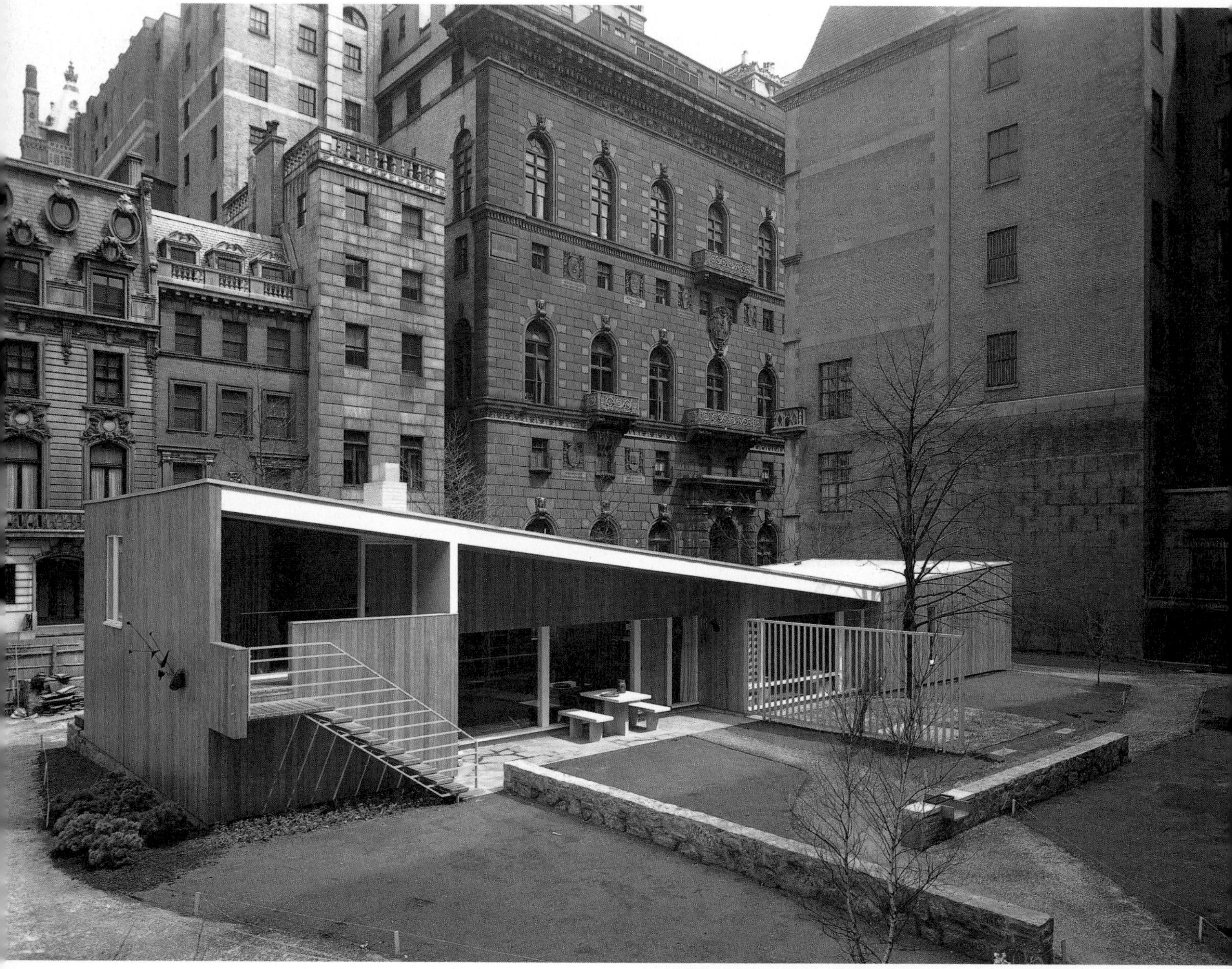

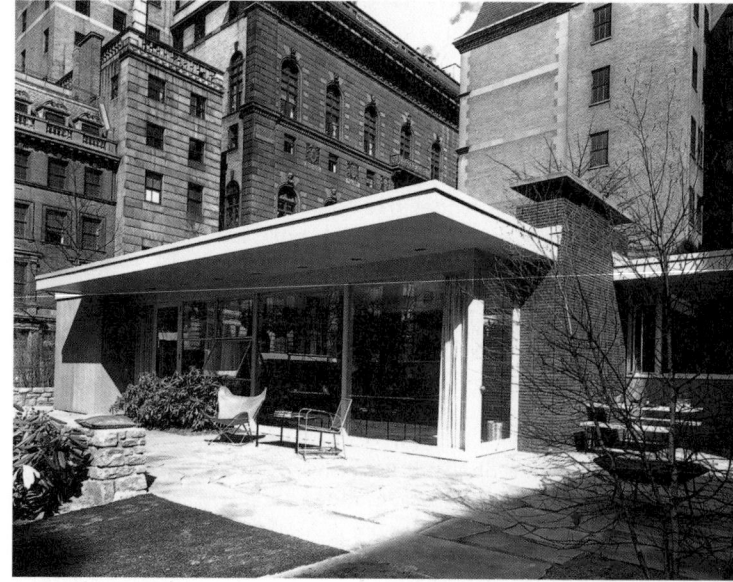

Above: Demonstration house, Museum of Modern Art, 11 West Fifty-third Street, between Fifth and Sixth avenues. Marcel Breuer, 1949. View to the northeast. Stoller. ©ESTO

Right: Second demonstration house, Museum of Modern Art, 11 West Fifty-third Street, between Fifth and Sixth avenues. Gregory Ain, 1950. View to the northeast. Stoller. ©ESTO

Top far right: Demonstration house. Marcel Breuer, 1949. Living area. Stoller. ©ESTO

Bottom far right: Demonstration house. Marcel Breuer, 1949. Ground floor. Stoller. ©ESTO appeal, so that by 1946 plans were being drawn by Goodwin for a new wing that would occupy the site of John D. Rockefeller's townhouse at 4 West Fifty-fourth Street, which had been torn down in 1938 (with important rooms donated to the Brooklyn Museum and the Museum of the City of New York). The decision to build the new wing was made possible by Rockefeller's gift of the site, valued at $1 million. A model of the expanded museum, which used the same architectural vocabulary as the original building, was unveiled early in 1946 and a fund-raising campaign was begun a year later.[3] The new wing's first floor was to be 3,847 square feet, a little more than twice the area of the main floor of the 1939 building; the additional gallery space would allow for more than 10 percent of the permanent collection to be put on view at any one time.

Not able to go forward with its new wing as quickly as had been hoped,[4] the museum took advantage of the expanded garden space the Rockefeller gift created to build a full-size demonstration house designed by Marcel Breuer, which was on display from April 14 to October 30, 1949.[5] According to *Arts and Architecture*, Breuer's house was "an up-to-date solution for the commuter, intended to be built for $25,000.00 by a local contractor."[6] Like Roger Bullard and Clifford Wendehack's "America's Little House" and William Van Alen's "House of the Modern Age," both built in the 1930s on a vacant Park Avenue lot, and Edward Durell Stone's "House of Ideas," built on a rooftop terrace in Rockefeller Center in 1940, Breuer's house extolled the virtues of surburban living to an urban population grappling with its housing problem and looking longingly to life in greener pastures.[7] But Breuer's sprawling, one-story design, with its inverted "butterfly" shed roofs and its loose-fitting interior spaces that "flowed," to use a buzzword of the day, into one another and visually spilled through large plate-glass walls to the out-of-doors, was not the Colonial stereotype most middle-class Americans had in mind. It was nonetheless quite upmarket, intended for an acre or two of land, presumably to be occupied by what Frederick Gutheim described as "that shadowy figure of metropolitan life, the well salaried junior executive and his young family."[8] Breuer's house was meant to illustrate a new, more accommodating form of Modernism, as well as to capitalize on the suburban trend and its deep roots in Anglo-American values. As Breuer put it: "Modern architects don't like severity in a house. Perhaps we did once, but we don't any more. Little by little we've learned how to use the old materials—stone, unpainted wood—in fresh ways. We've learned to make houses that grow gently out of the land and will weather and become more beautiful with age."[9]

In reviewing the house, Gutheim praised its aesthetics: "Its natural treatment of wood and stone surfaces, the wide glass areas and unified design of indoor and outdoor living areas, the sense of continuous space . . . these will etch themselves in the imagination." But he claimed that the organization of the plan, which placed the parents' bedroom at the opposite end of the house from the children's, with the living spaces in between, reflected "parental ignorance or worse, an immaturity and reluctance to accept the responsibilities of parenthood that can only be described as 'Greenwich Village moved to the country.'" Gutheim also criticized the openness of the plan, its combination of living and dining in one room, and the small size of the kitchen, which neither allowed young children to spend time there with parents nor permitted meals to be taken there. In short, he concluded, "This house has one thing that will be seen in few other exhibition houses—good taste. It is a work of art. But it is also a house, and it has been called a house for family

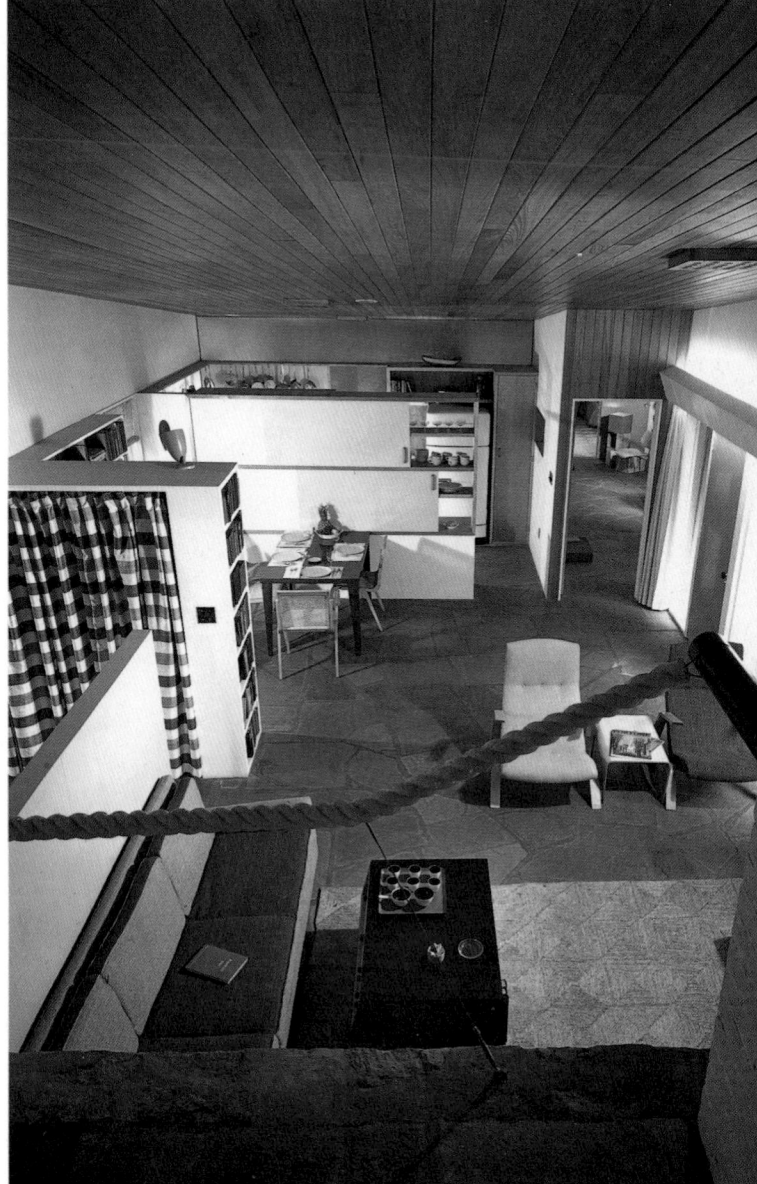

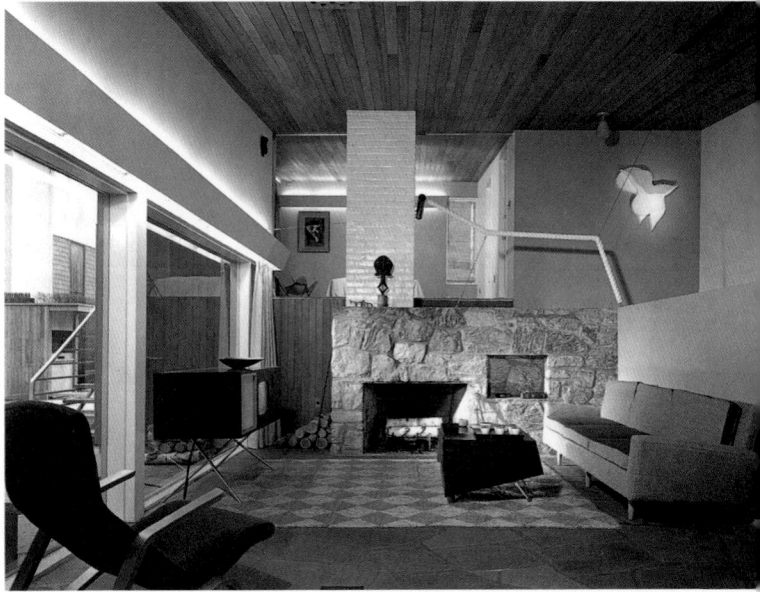

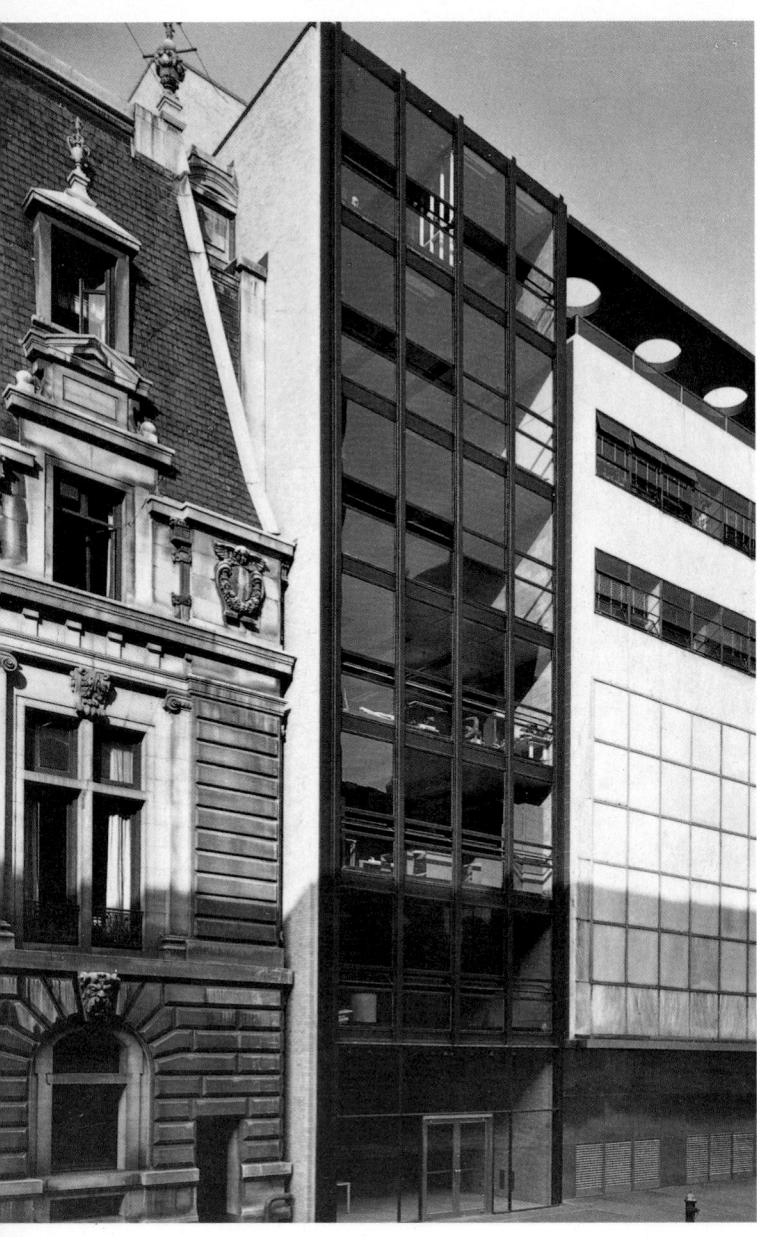

Grace Rainey Rogers Memorial, Museum of Modern Art, north side of West Fifty-third Street between Fifth and Sixth avenues. Philip Johnson, 1951. View to the northeast. Georges. MOMA

living. By that standard it falls short of other houses, perhaps not as handsome or as well built but better planned."[10]

In response to Gutheim's criticism, Philip Johnson, director of the museum's Department of Architecture and Design, and Peter Blake, its curator, refuted his basic premise: "The museum did not act in the role of a client. We did not tell the architect what to do in building his house, any more than we would have told Picasso what colors to use had the museum commissioned him to paint a mural. . . . The museum is a museum of art, and it did not ask Mr. Breuer to solve problems of living in sociological terms (although he also did that), just as it would not ask Picasso to select his colors for their therapeutic value."[11]

So immensely popular was the house—an estimated 75,000 people visited it during the summer of 1949—that the museum, with a co-sponsor, the popular magazine *Woman's Home Companion*, commissioned a second house, which was exhibited in the summer of 1950.[12] Designed by the California Modernist Gregory Ain, this house was geared to a much less affluent customer than Breuer's was, and the uncompromising Modernism of the flat-roof design made it seem even more remote from the typical suburban landscape for which it was intended. Eliot Noyes, the architect and industrial designer, said that the house was neither cheap enough nor small enough to function as a prototype for the kind of speculatively built housing William Levitt was building on Long Island, nor was it experimental enough to point the way to new artistic directions in the field. As a result, he said, the house was "agreeable as a design but pointless as a project," and the exhibition "interesting but without much significance."[13] Lewis Mumford accepted the diminution of artistic quality that the more modest budget and more restricted suburban setting implied, but he quarreled with the lack of privacy in the open plan, the lack of sound internal planning and the lack of adequate ventilation. "All in all," he said, "one wonders what service the Museum thought it was performing when it lent its prestige to a model with so many demerits." Mumford said that although fifteen years ago such a house might have been welcomed, now that Modernist domestic architecture was no longer unprecedented, standards were higher: "The beautiful, as Emerson said, rests on the foundations of the necessary, and the modern house that does not do justice to both the requirements is hardly worth placing on exhibition."[14]

In July 1950 the museum began construction on a new wing, much smaller than the one planned by Goodwin in 1946.[15] Located on a narrow lot immediately to the west of the museum, it was designed by Philip Johnson, who had returned to the museum's staff in 1946, after an absence of twelve years, during which time he pursued interests in politics, studied architecture at Harvard, where he received his Bachelor of Architecture degree in 1943, and served in the U.S. Army.[16] The new seven-story wing (1951), or annex as it was called, replacing a townhouse at 21 West Fifty-third Street (C. P. H. Gilbert, 1905), was built to house staff offices as well as the museum's People's Art Center, a program for children and amateur adult artists that had been operating out of leased space at 681 Fifth Avenue.[17] Johnson's design for what was to be officially designated the Grace Rainey Rogers Memorial was notable for its uncompromising Miesian facade of glass and steel, the first of its kind to be seen in New York. Henry-Russell Hitchcock found the facade even "more Miesian in its vocabulary" than Johnson's famous Glass House of 1949 in New Canaan, Connecticut.[18] The editors of *Architectural Forum*, writing in 1955, said that with this addition Johnson had proved his mastery of what they called Miesian "Modern Classicism." The Rogers Memorial, according to *Forum*, completed "a striking vignette of changing taste and technology," in which tradition and modernity were contrasted as well as various strategies within Modernism itself: the early International Style of Goodwin and Stone's building "had turned the emphasis to volume defined by a thin, smooth-looking envelope hiding the skeleton that holds it off the ground," while the addition, "evolving from its parent, is today's pure expression of structure: the steel skeleton holding either glass or brick panels, its rhythm held as quiet as possible."[19]

Although Johnson was not given charge of the annex's interiors, his personal office there was a demonstration of how he would have liked all the staff offices to be; with simple slablike desks covered in white plastic laminate, along with lounge chairs and a sofa that resembled cat's cradles of wrought iron upholstered in black transportation cloth, designed by Darrell Landrum, the office could also function as a conference room for staff meetings. As *Interiors* observed: "It's all in line, yet because the axial formality is as unstuffy as it is precise, it comes off with a kind of residential ease."[20]

The success of the Rogers annex established Johnson as the museum's preferred architect, which he was to remain through the early 1970s. In 1952 he renovated the Members Penthouse, the restaurant and lounge located on the top floor of Goodwin and Stone's main building.[21] Having become shabby after more than a decade of heavy use, the penthouse was expanded and reconfigured to handle far vaster crowds than had originally been anticipated. Johnson banished the lounge proper to a small area at the end of what was reorganized as a cafeteria-style dining room. In keeping with his tasteful machine-inspired minimalism, but justifiable on functionalist grounds such as easy maintenance, Johnson eliminated the carpets, wood-framed chairs and upholstery of the original design, replacing them with gray and taupe plastic Eames chairs with metal legs set around simple wood tables. The floor was covered in gray corklike tile; to soften the light and modulate the din, the windows were hung with airy fishnet-type curtains designed by Marie Nichols.

As work progressed on the Rogers Memorial, which did not occupy the full through-block site that Goodwin's original design had been planned for, an arrangement was entered into with the Whitney Museum of American Art whereby the two museums would share the rear or Fifty-fourth Street portion of the site, enabling them to construct a new museum to replace the Whitney's outmoded facility at 8–12 West Eighth Street (see chapter 11). The east facade of the new Whitney would face the Modern's garden, and much of its ground floor would be occupied by a new cafeteria for the Modern's patrons. The Whitney had been anxious to relocate for quite some time. A previous effort to merge with the Metropolitan Museum of Art had broken down in 1948, as had a subsequent attempt at cooperation between the Whitney, the Metropolitan and the Modern (see chapter 10). Under the new plan, the Whitney would become, in effect, the Modern's tenant, as the Modern owned the land upon which the new facility would stand. Alfred Frankfurter, the editor of *Art News*, characterized this arrangement as "more a common-law marriage than a King James Version one."[22]

The new Whitney Museum (1954), at 22 West Fifty-fourth Street, was designed by Augustus L. Noel of Miller & Noel, the architects who had designed the museum's Eighth Street facility, a continuing association that could in part be traced to the fact that G. McCullough Miller, one of the firm's partners, was married to Gertrude Vanderbilt Whitney's daughter Flora.[23] Though Noel was the architect, the basic concept for the exterior and, indeed, the building's entire east wall were designed by Philip Johnson. Thus, in effect, the Whitney's identity was confined to its Fifty-fourth Street facade, and even there Johnson was asked

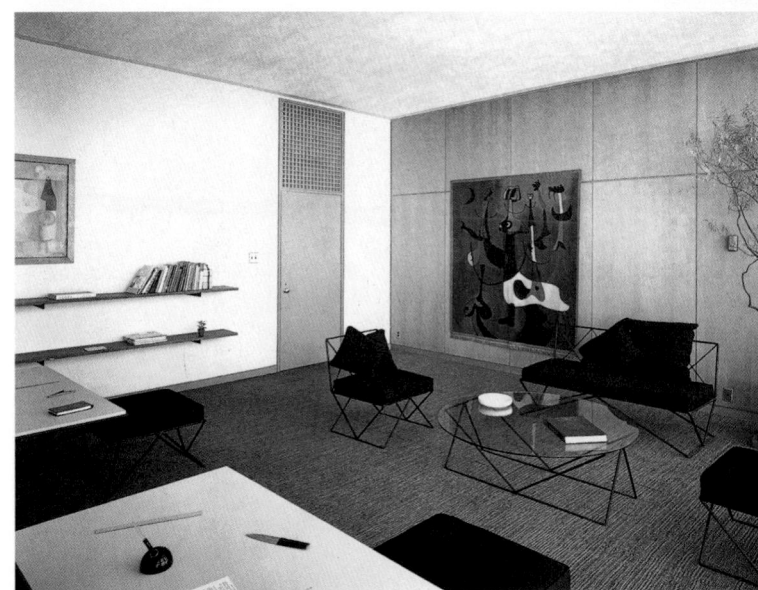

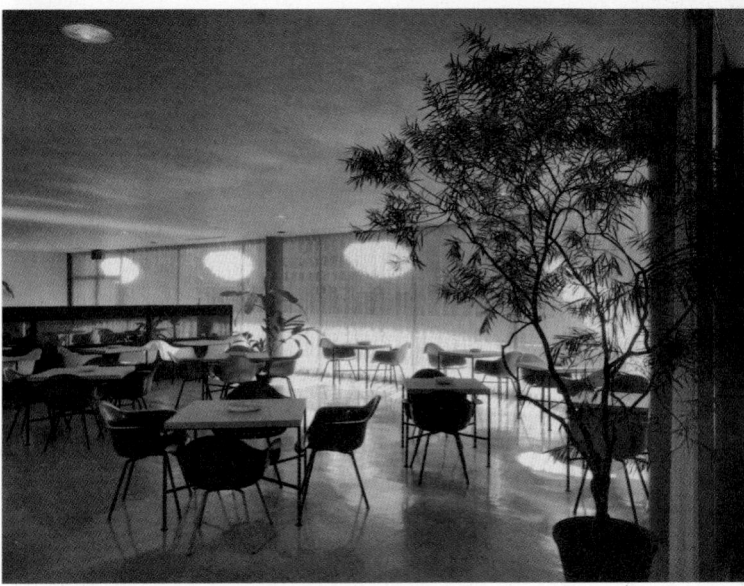

Top: Philip Johnson office, Grace Rainey Rogers Memorial, Museum of Modern Art. Philip Johnson, 1951. Stoller. ©ESTO

Bottom: Members Penthouse, Museum of Modern Art, 11 West Fifty-third Street, between Fifth and Sixth avenues. Philip Johnson, 1952. Stoller. ©ESTO

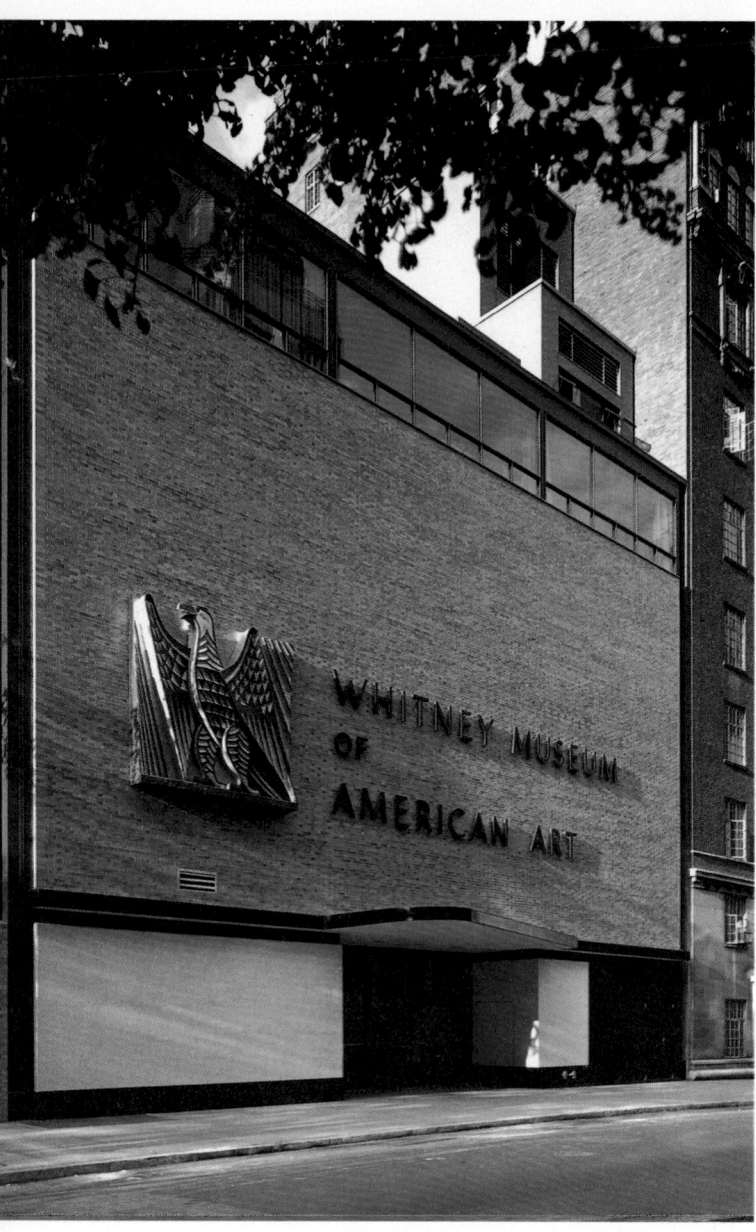

Whitney Museum of American Art, 22 West Fifty-fourth Street, between Fifth and Sixth avenues. Miller & Noel, 1954. View to the southwest. Stoller. ©ESTO

to consult on the design to ensure a coherent result. Inside, Noel collaborated with Bruce Butterfield, the same designer who had worked on the Eighth Street building.

The principal ornaments of the steel-framed, gray-brick facade were the large letters spelling out the museum's name and a rather fierce-looking eagle, the Whitney's traditional emblem, vastly enlarged and interpreted in bronze by Lewis Iselin. The physical relationship of the Whitney to the Modern was curious, not only in the way the facades were handled but also in the way the interiors functioned. For one thing, entrance to the Whitney was free, while the Modern required the purchase of a ticket; the ticket booths that separated one from the other interrupted the seemingly easy flow back and forth between the two museums at ground-floor level. Providing a further break was the contrast between Johnson's Miesian Classicism and Noel and Butterfield's somewhat dowdy attempt to evoke the mood and the look of the Eighth Street facility both on the facade and inside. Noel and Butterfield did, however, experiment with innovative lighting techniques inside the Whitney, creating the illusion of skylighting with glass-panel ceilings that concealed cold cathode tubes, and providing dramatic highlights with incandescent spots. Also of note were the freestanding movable partitions on detachable wheels, which had flanged bases that made them satisfactory as fixed walls.

Lewis Mumford found the Whitney's Fifty-fourth Street facade its least compelling feature. He complained of not being able to read the lettering from down the street and was disdainful of the white mosaic, black metal and highly polished marble that made up the entrance area. The combination, he said, suggested "Funeral Home elegance" or, worse still, "the facades of cheap shops and provincial movie palaces." Mumford was not fond of Butterfield's interiors either: "Except for a few slight touches, such as the volute termination of the stair rail, he has obeyed the law of modern design to the letter, but has defied its spirit." Mumford was particularly critical of the "dismal" lighting, and he questioned whether "overhead light, diffused and directed," was appropriate for a gallery.[24] Robert M. Coates, the *New Yorker*'s art critic, also criticized the lighting, saying that he found himself longing "for something warmer, more varied, less chillingly impersonal. It's an odd feeling, after all, when you find you don't even cast a shadow yourself."[25]

At the same time that the Modern's west wing and the Whitney's new headquarters were being realized, Johnson redesigned the Abby Aldrich Rockefeller Sculpture Garden.[26] The original garden, designed by John McAndrew in 1939, was highly informal, little more than a gravel-covered yard separated from Fifty-fourth Street to the north by a wood stockade fence. Johnson's redesign, first proposed in 1950, was undertaken in collaboration with the landscape architect James Fanning, the architect Landis Gores, and George Hopkinson, who was the architect of record. When completed in 1952, it marked a total transformation of the 107-by-200-foot garden from a casual, near-suburban yard to a sophisticated, De Stijl–inspired outdoor room. As Johnson put it: "The old garden was a collection of trees in which we served food. We showed some sculpture there, but after the war we all felt there were ways of showing sculpture to better advantage than in a back yard."[27]

To replace the stockade fence, Johnson called for a wall of gray-glazed brick, some of it ivy-covered, some left blank to serve as a background for sculpture. The wall was interrupted by two slatted wood gates to Fifty-fourth Street, which were needed to service the garden. Their open grillwork provided passersby with a sense of the garden and gave museumgoers what Johnson described as an "emotional release from the inside." The floor of the

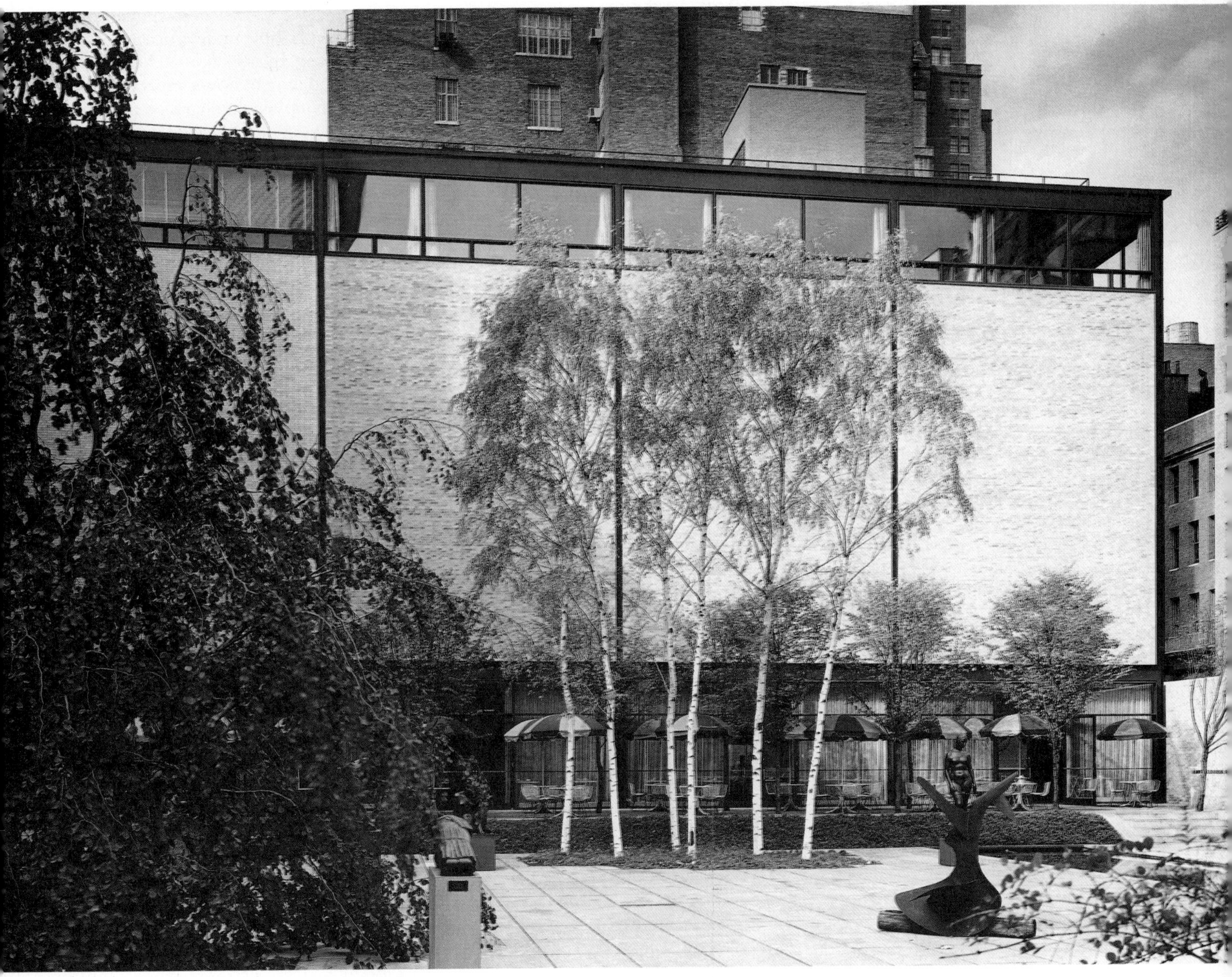

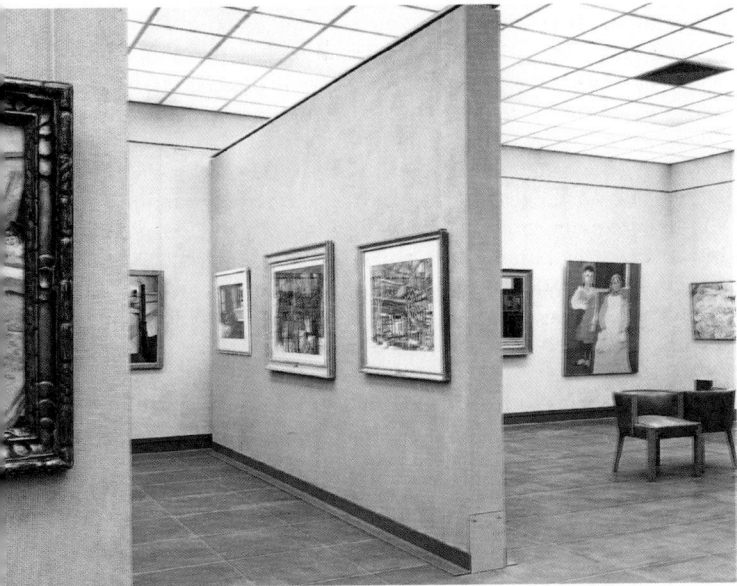

Above: Whitney Museum of American Art. Garden facade with Abby Aldrich Rockefeller Sculpture Garden (Philip Johnson, James Fanning, Landis Gores and George Hopkinson, 1952) in the foreground. Stoller. ©ESTO

Left: Whitney Museum of American Art. Galleries. Stoller. ©ESTO

garden was set two feet below grade to maximize its impact when viewed from the museum's lobby and to permit a greater illusion of height for the outdoor room, whose "ceiling" plane was defined by the fourteen-foot-high brick wall on Fifty-fourth Street. At the west end, a street-level terrace separated outdoor dining from the garden itself, which was paved in large slabs of unpolished gray Vermont marble, thick enough to form bridges over the two watercourses or canals that helped articulate the room into four distinct areas. Clumps of trees—Hankow willows, European birches, European hornbeams and ailanthus—and some sloping vine-planted topography helped soften the effect. "My conception was a piazza," Johnson stated. "I have always loved the Square of St. Mark's in Venice. . . . It's really a sort of outdoor room, a roofless room, with four subrooms formed by the planting and the canals, to provide four space backgrounds for the sculpture."[28]

The garden enclosure was weakly defined along the east, where the verticality of Canada House and St. Thomas' Church seemed at odds with its horizontal sweep. But on the west, Johnson was able to maintain control by designing the east-facing facade of the Whitney Museum as four steel-framed bays infilled with the same gray brick he used for the Fifty-fourth Street garden wall. Extensive glazing at the ground floor revealed a quite austere restaurant, which he also designed to face the garden, and at the top level the same pattern of glass was repeated. Overall, the tripartite vertical organization of this facade and the regularity and proportions of the bays revealed, even more than the elevation of the Rogers Memorial, Johnson's mastery of Modern Classicism.

Lewis Mumford summarized the overall effect of the redesigned garden: "It serves a manifold purpose—as an outdoor display space for sculpture (always best seen under natural light), as a resting place for those who have acquired 'museum fatigue' or the 'Surrealist blues,' and as a foreground for people eating outdoors." He was generous in his assessment of the design: "The architecture of this garden, severe and formal, is an excellent pedestal and background for the sculptured figures, especially those in bronze, and the living part of the garden provides an almost romantic contrast with its variety of exotic species. . . . The total effect . . . is a happy one, and it gives the buildings of the Museum a grace and completeness that they sorely lacked."[29]

The new garden plan did not include the easternmost, "dogleg" parcel of land on Fifty-fourth Street, directly behind Canada House. In the summer of 1954 this site, which had been home to the exhibition houses by Breuer and Ain, was turned over to an exhibition house of a very different kind, a contemporary version of a traditional aristocratic Japanese house of the sixteenth and seventeenth centuries.[30] Given to the museum by the American Japan Society of Tokyo, the house had been built in Nagoya, Japan, disassembled and shipped to New York in 636 crates. Under the supervision of its architect, Junzo Yoshimura, who worked on the site with a dozen or so American carpenters, plasterers and laborers as well as two carpenters, a gardener and a plasterer he brought with him from Japan, the house was reassembled in the garden. In the summers of 1954 and 1955 it was visited by over 223,000 people, who glided across its floors in paper slippers. While at first the house seemed an oddity amid the museum's collection of twentieth-century art, on closer inspection the elegant spareness of the detailing, the modularity of the parts and the flowing spaces seemed the ultimate expression of modernity. When the exhibition was over, the house was dismantled and reerected as a permanent display in Philadelphia's Fairmount Park.

Mumford wrote extensively about the Japanese house in his Sky Line column in the New Yorker, where he praised it as "a consummate piece of work." "The greatest lesson the Museum house teaches," he wrote, "is how much beauty can be achieved merely by quiet repose, by selection and elimination, by stripping every human requirement down to its essentials." Relating the house to contemporary Western architectural practice, Mumford cautioned:

> Many architects think they have achieved a modern form merely because they use plastics and steel and don't waste any of their clients' money on ornament. They mistake lack of imagination for "the contemporary touch," and they take refuge in the fashionable slogan "less is more" without realizing that their particular less is less indeed. But the fact is that the more one eliminates, the more important it is to refine every detail and to measure with the eye every proportion as meticulously as Mies van der Rohe does. The Japanese have had long experience with these refinements.[31]

On April 15, 1958, a devastating lunchtime fire swept through the museum's second floor, forcing the evacuation of about 500 people, mostly visitors, killing one workman, injuring three visitors and twenty-eight firemen, and seriously damaging numerous works of art, a few beyond repair.[32] The fire began on the second floor, where a project to air condition the museum was under way. The blaze began when a tarpaulin caught fire, presumably started from a workman's discarded cigarette, and flames quickly ignited several open cans of paint. The fire was exacerbated by the nonfireproof materials used by the museum in violation of codes to create display partitions throughout the building.

As the editors of the New York Times observed, the fire brought forth the realization that the museum had grown beyond the status of an ideological provocateur to become a major institution held in wide esteem: "The fire threw much light on the affection New Yorkers feel for the museum, plainly showing that it is not merely the interest of a few dedicated enthusiasts."[33] The museum was closed for repairs until October 8, 1958, during which time new air-conditioning and smoke-detection systems, as well as brighter lighting, were installed and the wooden partitions were replaced by new partitions built with fireproof steel studs and plasterboard. At the same time, the original lobby—since its completion an emblem of the high-style, streamlined modernity of the interwar years—was reconfigured, substituting plate glass for the now distinctly unfashionable glass block, so that passersby on the street could see through to the sculpture garden beyond.

In November 1959 the museum announced plans for a new wing, a bulky eight-story addition that would provide for maintenance shops and parking on two basement levels, five floors of column-free gallery space totaling 31,000 square feet, one floor of offices above the galleries and a trustees' penthouse.[34] On the ground floor, a new entrance to the museum on Fifty-fourth Street would free up the ground floor of the Goodwin and Stone building to house temporary exhibitions. The addition, which was to be sited on the 100-by-113-foot dogleg parcel located on Fifty-fourth Street to the east of the museum's garden, would result in a vastly expanded facility but would demote the internationally recognized principal building to backdoor status. Designed by Philip Johnson, who had left the museum staff to form his own independent practice, Philip Johnson Associates, the addition was a massive, boxy building. Its two principal unfenestrated travertine-clad facades, one facing Fifty-fourth Street, the other looking west into the museum garden, were to be broken up into narrow bays articulated by pilasterlike elements whose fussy details seemed to rob the structural columns of their tectonic force.

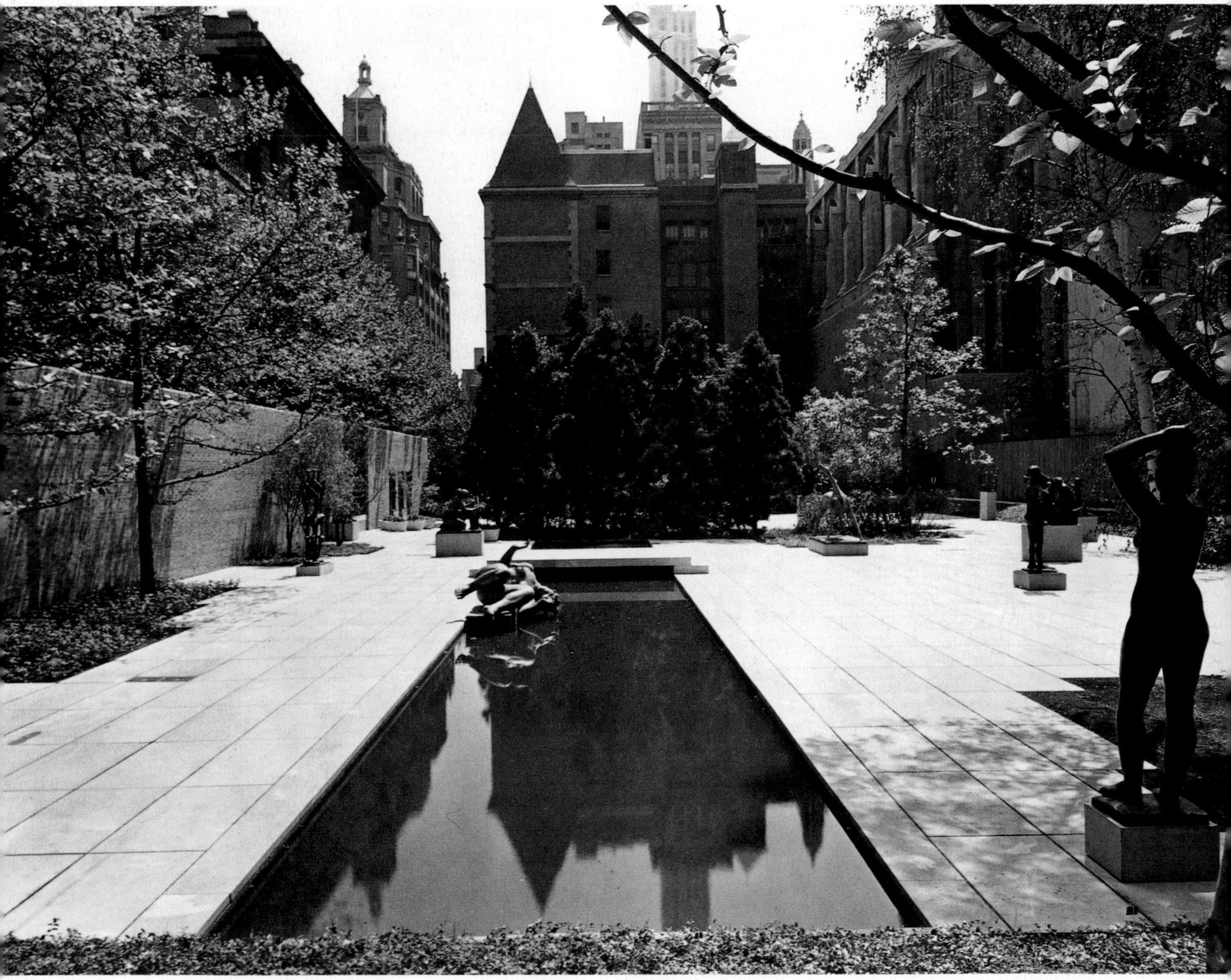

Above: Abby Aldrich Rockefeller Sculpture Garden, Museum of Modern Art, between Fifth and Sixth avenues, West Fifty-third and West Fifty-fourth streets. Philip Johnson, 1953. Sunami. MOMA

Left: Japanese House, Museum of Modern Art, 11 West Fifty-third Street, between Fifth and Sixth avenues. Junzo Yoshimura, 1954. View to the northeast. Stoller. ©ESTO

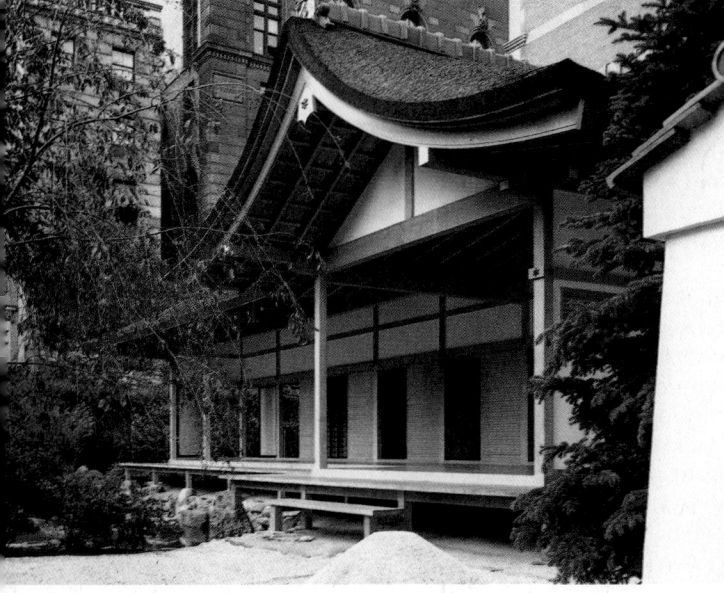

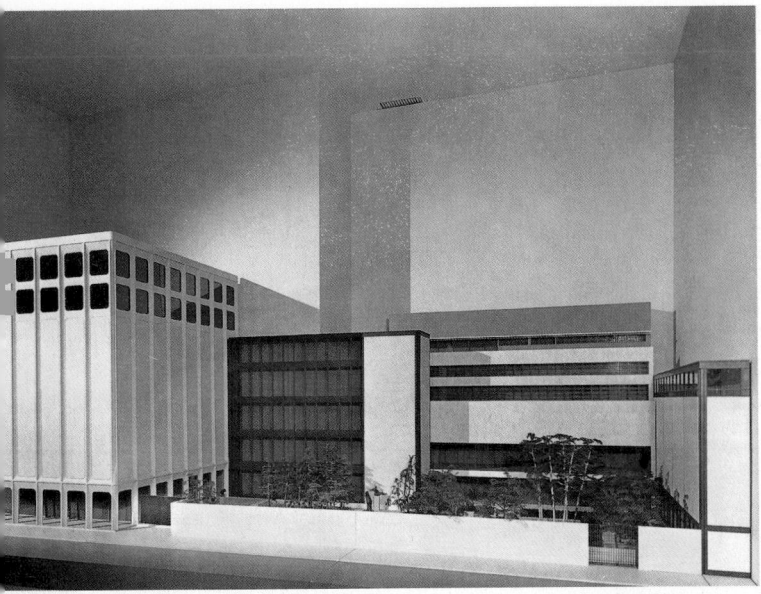

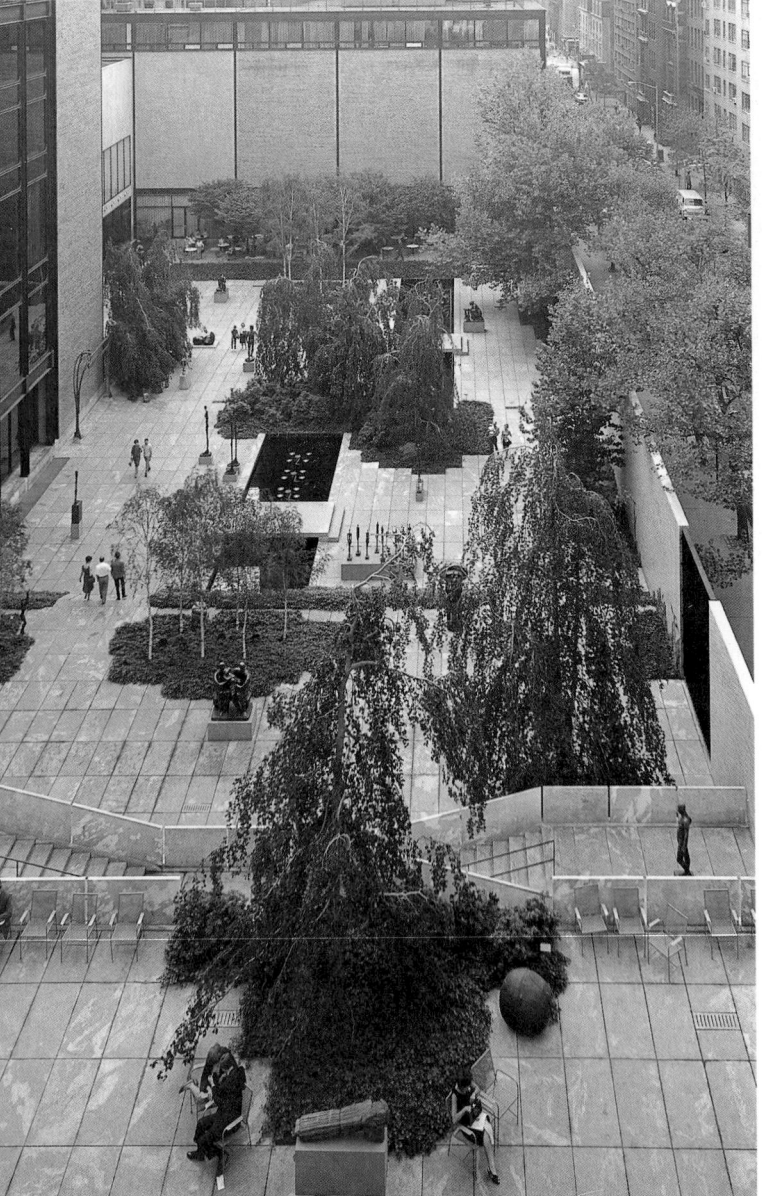

The glass-enclosed ground-floor lobby was to be set back under the building to create a sidewalk arcade. The trustees' penthouse at the top, also set back from the building line, was to be invisible from the street and garden. To connect the new building with the old, a steel-and-glass corridor building would be built leading to a new windowless brick stair tower.

The museum did not go forward with this ungainly scheme and in 1961 announced plans for the construction of a reduced facility (1964), in part built on the Fifty-fourth Street site and in part expanding the Goodwin and Stone building to the east, filling in the space between it and the rectory of St. Thomas' Church.[35] Rather than combining all elements of the expansion in one blockbuster building, a plan that had raised considerable objections, especially because the tall building would have cast the garden in shade, this plan, also designed by Johnson, included three distinct components. On the Fifty-fourth Street site, a so-called garden wing would be built, in effect a two-story exhibition building with one grade-level fifty-by-seventy-five-foot display hall as well as below-grade space intended for the Art Center, an outgrowth of the museum's People's Art Center. The roof of this building, just sixteen feet above the level of the museum garden, would be developed as an extension to the garden, and connected to it by two broad flights of shallow stairs.

Johnson's plans also called for the existing Rogers building to be almost tripled in size, expanded to the west by demolishing 23 West Fifty-third Street, Hunt & Hunt's George Blumenthal house of 1905, as well as a remodeled brownstone next door. Though this aspect of Johnson's proposal was never realized, the upper floors of the Blumenthal residence were renovated for use as administrative offices, and the ground floor was later transformed into a series of rather anonymous rooms serving as a book store (Abraham Rothenberg Associates and Thomas Lowrie, 1973–75).[36]

To the east of the Goodwin and Stone building, Johnson proposed that a fifty-foot-wide new building be constructed on the sites of 7 West Fifty-third Street, a rowhouse designed by Jardine & Jardine (1868), and 5 West Fifty-third Street, a rowhouse designed by Steven D. Hatch (1871); the two houses had served as the lifetime home of Mrs. E. Parmalee Prentice, the sister of John D. Rockefeller, Jr. In addition, the modified but still largely intact lobby of the Goodwin and Stone building, now inadequately sized for present needs, would be completely rebuilt to form a glazed concourse leading directly on axis from the street to the garden. The new east building would contain three gallery floors, two office floors and one floor for receptions. Beginning in 1966, when the Whitney Museum moved into its new building on Madison Avenue (see chapter 11), the Modern would also have full use of the building it had shared with the Whitney since 1954. The net effect of these changes was that the exhibition space was doubled. The garden was also expanded and somewhat redesigned by Johnson in collaboration with the landscape architects Zion & Breen. Ground was broken for the east building and the garden wing in November 1962.

While the design of the garden building was notably quiet, a great podium presented a wall-like facade to Fifty-fourth Street, broken only by simply detailed recessed steel-and-glass entrance doors. The Fifty-third Street facade was more dramatic, with Johnson reinterpreting his Mies-derived facade for the Rogers Memorial on a much bigger scale and tinting the window and spandrel panels, which were set in black-painted steel frames that featured rather arbitrarily curved fillets at their corners. Nonetheless, the new facade, with its street-level arcade, managed to complement the Goodwin and Stone building even as it came close to overpowering it. The east building presented a similar face to the garden, where it abutted the brick stair tower, the only portion of Johnson's 1959 expansion plan to have been realized.

Ada Louise Huxtable hailed Johnson's east building as "one of New York's most subtly effective structures, its refined simplicity quietly understating the care of its detailing and the sensitivity of its relationships to older buildings and commercial and residential neighbors. It is successful not only as architecture, but also as cityscape." She particularly admired the building's facades: "If steel can be said to be subtle and sensuous, it is here. Painstakingly detailed, with curved corners against the glass, projecting and recessed sections and stiffening beams as elegant as marble columns, the effect is a tasteful enrichment of the museum's earlier flat facades. . . . The all-glass and metal facade has not been handled in such handsome fashion since the vogue for cast-iron fronts in the late 19th century." Huxtable also praised the redesigned entrance lobby: "It is expansive and impressive with a glass wall to the garden—a good demonstration of the Johnsonian talent for entrances and exits."[37]

Most significant, Huxtable said, was the fact that "the museum has not 'modernized' itself in the conventional sense—one of the most atrocious of architectural practices—but shows a clear, consecutive, compatible sequence of evolving tastes within a period of dynamic architectural change. . . . It provides a lesson in proper relationship through scale and detail rather than through refacing the old and 'frosting' the new with matching materials." In summary, she said: "The word for all this is professional, in its highest and most knowledgeable sense; the ultimate compliment in a field rife with uneasy dilettantism."[38]

In 1967 Johnson completed work on the Founders Room, located on the top floor of the east building. Designed to accommodate the overflow from the Members Penthouse and to provide a place for board meetings as well as opening-night receptions, the room was part of a suite of three that could be combined for very large events. The walls and ceiling of the square, twenty-six-foot-high Founders Room were articulated by exposed decorative I-beams that suggested structure and were disposed in an ABA rhythm to define a large square at the center of the plan. On the ceiling, high pointed plaster vaults were set within the I-beam grid, lightened with strips of exposed unfrosted light bulbs. Ever the Modernist at play, Johnson made sure no one was fooled by the structural framework by holding the pilasters one-and-a-half feet above the floor. C. Ray Smith said the Founders Room was a "classic room in Miesian idiom [sent] sky high"; although the joke may have been "sick architectural sacrilege," he said, it was "irresistibly funny." Smith described the overall effect of the room as "a combination of Mies, Gothic, and a carnival midway of the [18]90's and . . . somewhat Turkish."[39]

Despite the profundity of the changes wrought by Johnson, they would pale in comparison with those that followed. The winds of change were first felt on February 9, 1976, when the museum announced its intention to erect a forty-story condominium tower atop its existing building, as well as to double the size of its exhibition spaces and add an auditorium and educational facilities.[40] At a museum press conference, Mayor Abraham D. Beame, besieged by the city's mounting fiscal crisis, indulged in old-fashioned boosterism, pledging his support for enabling state legislation that would grant the tower real estate tax-exempt status and confidently identifying the plan as a "vivid demonstration of New York's vitality."[41] Museum officials outlined several key aspects of the new building program: the tower was to be built over the southwest corner of the building, minimizing the shadow it would cast over the garden; the main building's north wall would be pushed several feet into the garden to allow for a

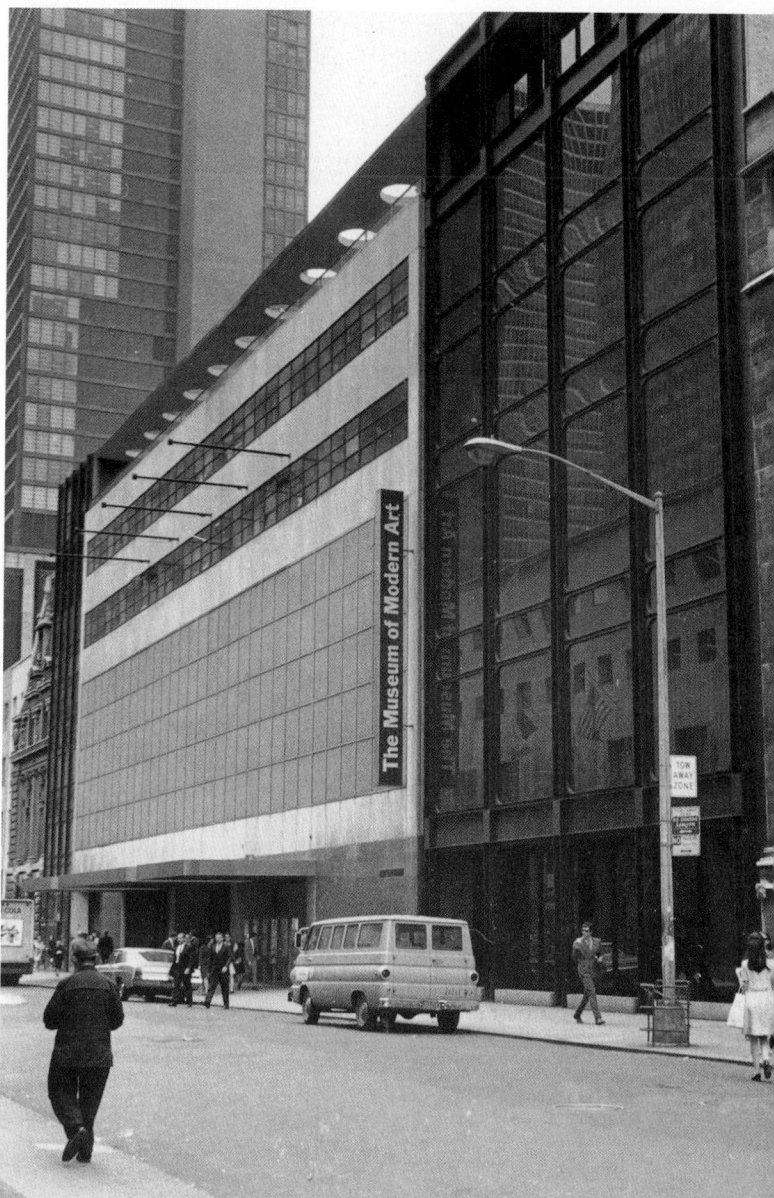

Top left: Proposed Museum of Modern Art wing, between Fifth and Sixth avenues, West Fifty-third to West Fifty-fourth Street. Philip Johnson Associates, 1959. Model. View to the south. Checkman. LC

Bottom left: Museum of Modern Art, 11 West Fifty-third Street, between Fifth and Sixth avenues, West Fifty-third to West Fifty-fourth Street. View to the west showing remodeled sculpture garden and, on left, building addition. Philip Johnson Associates, 1964. Stoller. ©ESTO

Above: Museum of Modern Art addition, between Fifth and Sixth avenues, West Fifty-third to West Fifty-fourth Street. Philip Johnson Associates, 1963. View to the northwest showing original Museum of Modern Art (Philip Goodwin and Edward Durell Stone, 1939) on the left. Budnick. MOMA

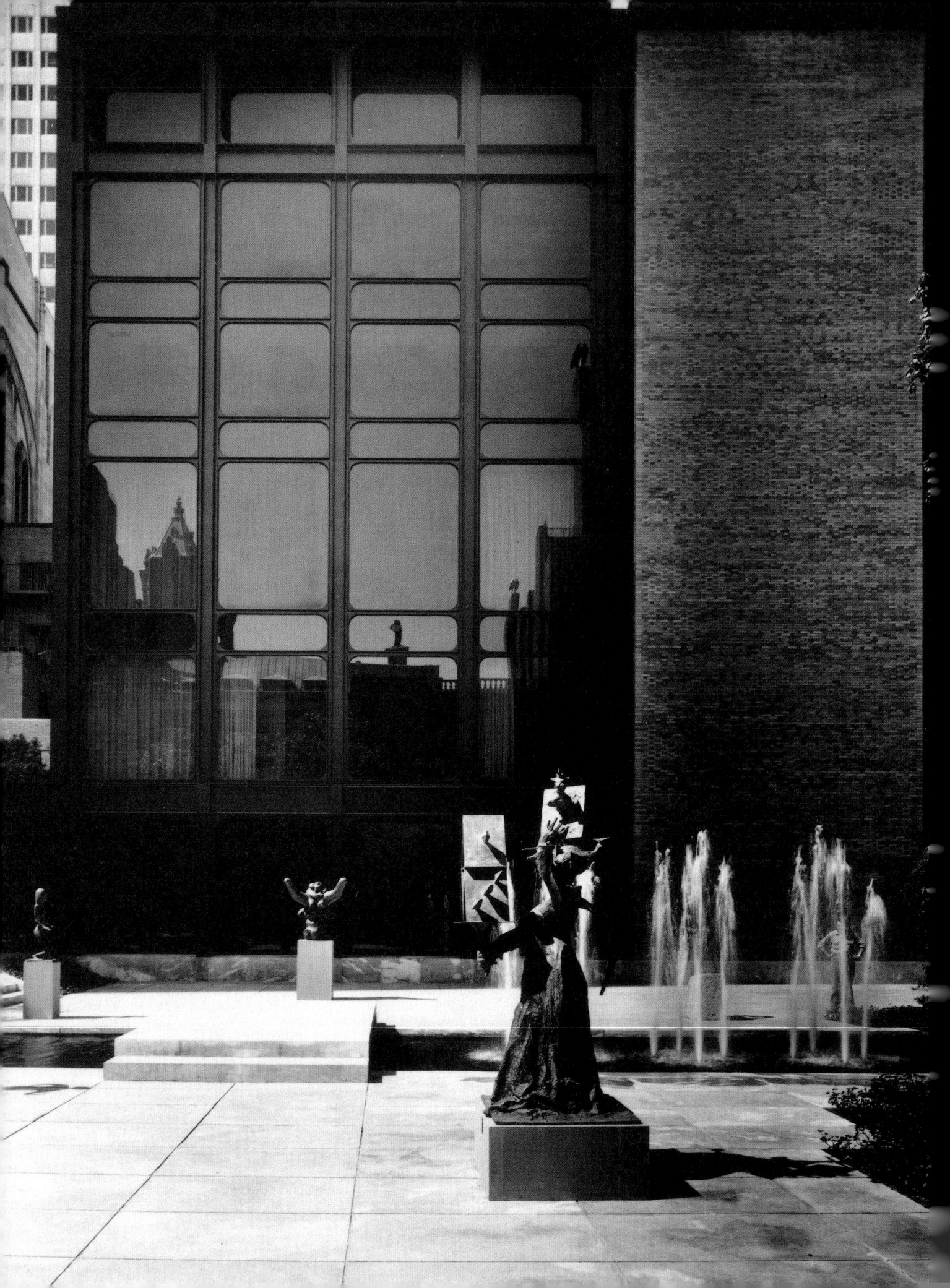

glassed-in circulation area crisscrossed by escalators; the in-door-outdoor restaurant would be moved from the garden's western end to its eastern end.

Although the museum's press release was specific about the program, the architect was not announced, leading to intense speculation as to who had been chosen. Paul Goldberger noted in November 1976 that the recession may have slowed building activity but that it seemed to intensify gossip in architectural circles: "Now, with almost no buildings going up at all, no one is any longer able to make a full-time job out of setting odds on likely architects for each new project. But that has served to concentrate talk even more on the few projects that are in the serious planning stage . . . and expansion for the Museum of Modern Art has emerged as the major plum of this scant season."[42] Following a pronouncement by the architect Kevin Roche, who had been considered a strong possibility for the job, that he was not interested, the museum, according to Goldberger, narrowed the selection to three firms: I. M. Pei & Partners, Mitchell/Giurgola Associates, and Gruen Associates, whose chief designer, Cesar Pelli, had just been appointed dean of the Yale School of Architecture. On February 3, 1977, Pelli was given the prestigious commission.

Though the Museum of Modern Art was unquestionably the dominant cultural presence on Fifty-third Street, the block between Fifth and Sixth avenues gained another important institution and its first truly public building in 1955, when the Donnell Free Circulating Library and Reading Room, a component of the New York Public Library system, opened at 20 West Fifty-third Street.[43] Designed by Edgar I. Williams in association with Aymar Embury II, the four-story building clad in Indiana limestone occupied a 175-foot-wide, 100-foot-deep plot opposite the museum. The site was donated by John D. Rockefeller, Jr., who had acquired it as part of the ill-fated plan of the mid-1930s to extend Rockefeller Plaza north to the Museum of Modern Art.[44]

The library was the bequest of Ezekiel J. Donnell, who came to America from Ireland as a boy, prospered as a cotton merchant and died in 1896. Donnell stipulated in his will that upon the death of his last child, which occurred in 1924, when Florence Donnell died, his estate be assigned to the New York Free Circulating Library (which had been incorporated with the New York Public Library) for the construction of "a reading room . . . which shall be open every day in the week . . . from noon until ten o'clock . . . in which young people can spend their evenings profitably away from demoralizing influences."[45] As a result, the Donnell was the first library in New York to provide regular extended hours for teenagers (other sections of the library would have more restricted hours of service). Litigation over the will followed the death of Florence Donnell, and it was not until 1943 that the site was acquired from Rockefeller. As costs kept rising, the building was twice redesigned to make it smaller, and only after Rockefeller returned the cost of the land to the library was the project able to go ahead.

The editors of *Interiors* described the building's exterior as "unobtrusively contemporary."[46] Lewis Mumford was intrigued by its stylistic evasions and found the facade suggestive of "a Renaissance front cleansed of ornament and stretched on a steel frame." He went on to say: "In its use of standard building units, in its rejection of traditional forms and ornaments, in its assiduous anonymity, as in its general flatness and lack of contrast in light and shade, this building is quite as 'modern' as the Museum. But it is modern, as it were, by default." Mumford found the overall effect of the Donnell Library "unsatisfactory" because "it does not aesthetically come together. This building

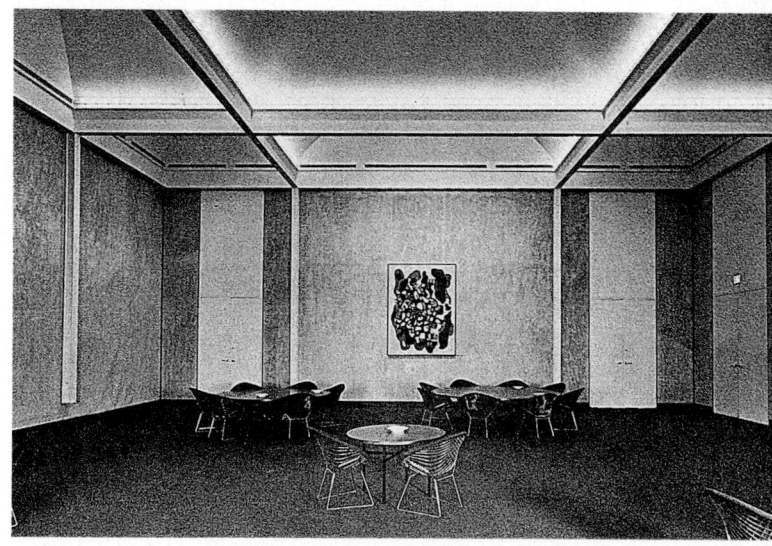

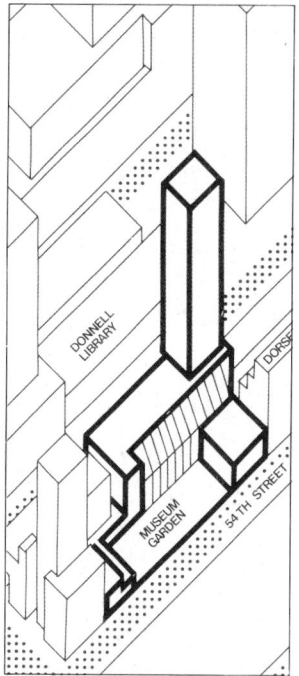

Far left: Museum of Modern Art addition, between Fifth and Sixth Avenues, West Fifty-third to West Fifty-fourth Street. Philip Johnson Associates, 1964. View to the south from sculpture garden. Georges. MOMA

Above: Founders Room, Museum of Modern Art, 11 West Fifty-third Street, between Fifth and Sixth avenues, West Fifty-third to West Fifty-fourth Street. Philip Johnson Associates, 1967. PA. CU

Center: Museum of Modern Art expansion and condominium tower, between Fifth and Sixth avenues, West Fifty-third to West Fifty-fourth Street. 1976. Axonometric showing view to the southwest. MOMA

Bottom: Donnell Free Circulating Library and Reading Room, 20 West Fifty-third Street, between Fifth and Sixth Avenues. Edgar I. Williams in association with Aymar Embury II, 1955. View to the southwest. Garber. NYPL

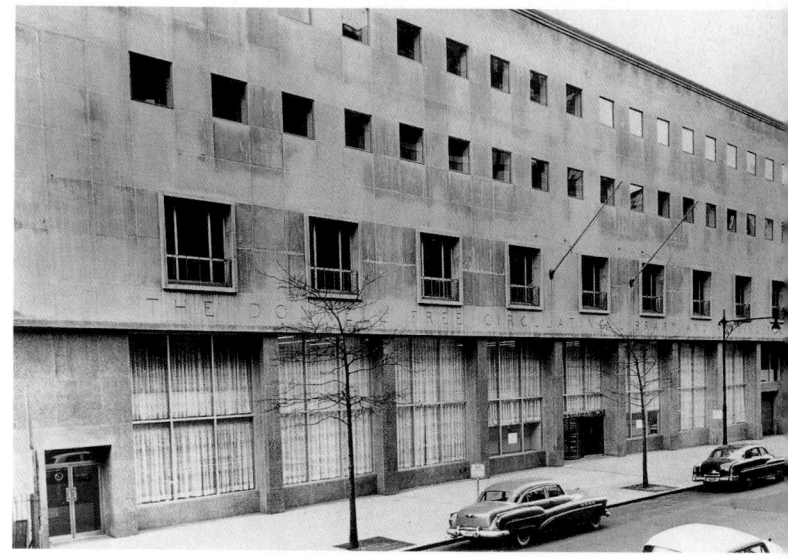

485

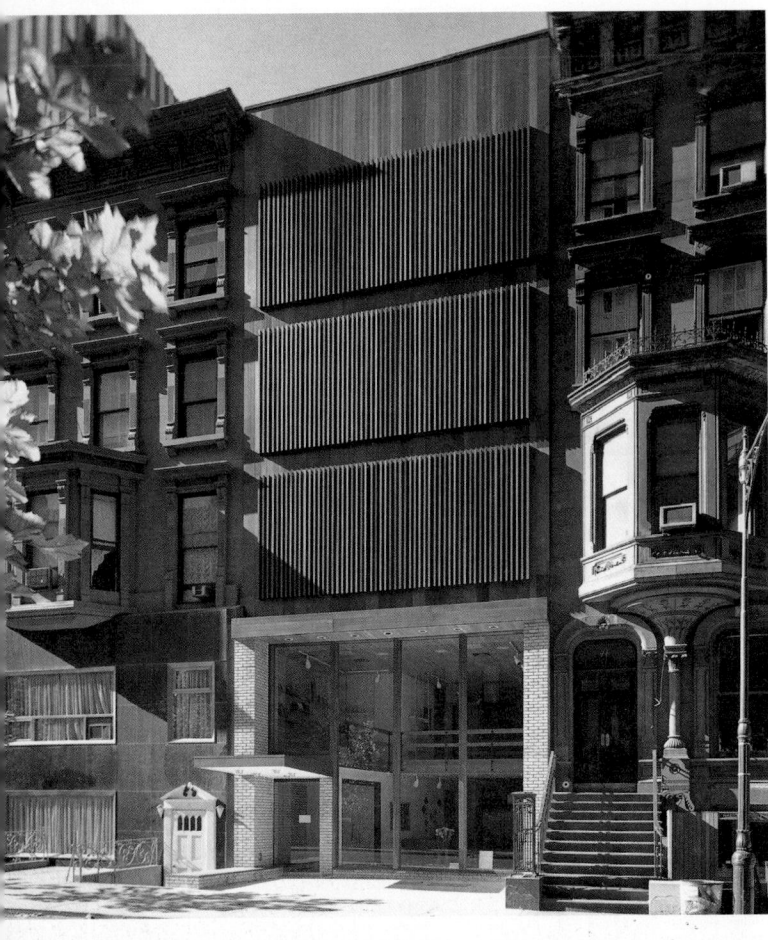

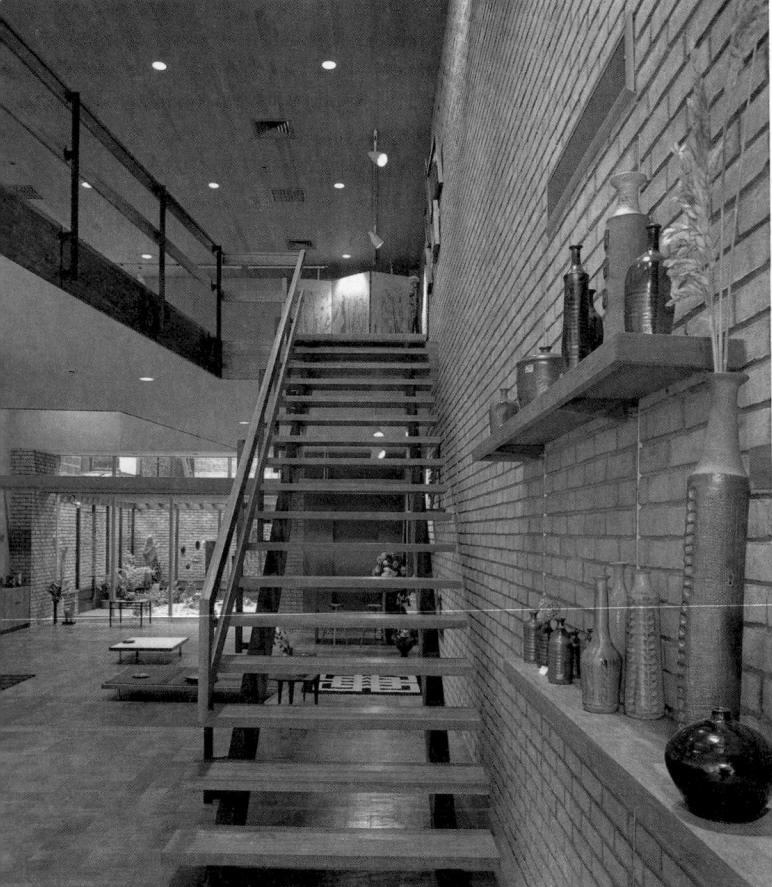

is neither the old nor the new, neither functional usefulness nor aesthetic purity, and still less an effective synthesis. Instead, it is a little of everything, indecisively assembled, without even the satisfaction that a clean miss, if well aimed and done with style, sometimes gives."[47]

Mumford did, however, have high praise for the Donnell's interiors:

> The chilling reserve of the exterior has given way to an unusually gracious interior, thanks to the good proportions achieved by the architects and the excellent taste, at least at this point, of their design. The front part of the room at once envelops the visitor in its hospitable air. . . . One may sink into a comfortable seat at either side of the entrance, or sit at one of the tables beyond it with a sense of palatial leisure and peace—a sense that has almost been lost even in luxurious hotels. . . . This room should prove to anyone with open eyes, if proof be needed, that light and color and texture, discreetly employed, do not require stale symbolism or factitious ornament to achieve effects comparable to those of Robert Adam.[48]

In September 1956 Fifty-third Street became home to yet another cultural facility, the Museum of Contemporary Crafts, at 29 West Fifty-third Street.[49] The new museum was housed in a former brownstone turned rooming house, which was twenty-five feet wide by seventy-five feet deep. The brownstone was dramatically renovated by the architect David R. Campbell to contain a ground floor and mezzanine devoted to exhibitions, a second floor housing a library and a members' lunchroom, and a third and fourth floor for staff offices. The museum, the administration of which served as a principal activity of the American Craftsmen's Council, was devoted to advancing the appreciation of artistic handicrafts. By placing the museum directly opposite the Museum of Modern Art, the council sought to counteract that institution's bias in favor of industrial design. The crafts museum was also intended to complement America House, a shop marketing the work of American craftsmen, which the council ran nearby at 485 Madison Avenue (see chapter 6).

Campbell stripped the upper facade of ornament and covered it with white-painted stucco; at the entrance, he added a slablike canopy projecting out from a plane of granite. The facade, according to the editors of *Interiors*, was "warmly attractive rather than awe-inspiring." Inside, they continued, "there is a space that is surprisingly vertical though interrupted by a suspended balcony with a curved edge, and the additional surprise of cream-colored walls, floor and ceiling, a large expanse of natural brick, and a sculptured railing of thick, handsome wood curving expansively up the stairs and around the balcony."[50]

In 1961 the American Craftsmen's Council brought America House to the block from Madison Avenue, locating it in a converted brownstone at 44 West Fifty-third Street, once again hiring Campbell to orchestrate the renovation.[51] Working with a very tight budget, he opened up the building's two lower floors, treating the second floor as a mezzanine floating between a double-height space just behind a new plate-glass wall and an open-air, trellised courtyard in the rear. Dark-bronze-colored aluminum shutters were used to blank out the upper floors of the facade, a gesture that disrupted the scale of the street wall in a disquieting way. Inside, the brick party walls were exposed to create a rough-textured backdrop suited to the merchandise on display.

In 1962 coffee manufacturer Joseph B. Martinson founded the Museum of Early American Folk Art, which mounted its first show in the exhibition hall of the Time & Life Building.[52] The following year the fledgling museum moved to Fifty-third Street. But while it shared the prestigious locale of the Modern and the Museum of Contemporary Crafts, its quarters were not only vastly less distinguished, they were minimal by nearly any standard. With the expectation that it would serve as a temporary home, the museum rented an architecturally undistinguished second-story space in a former rowhouse at 49 West Fifty-third Street. In 1970, by which time the museum had dropped the word "Early" from its name, becoming simply the Museum of American Folk Art, it chose a former townhouse at 136½ East Seventy-fifth Street, where it had maintained administrative offices, to serve as its permanent home. Economic woes would soon stymie the museum's operations, however, and in 1974 the New York State Attorney General's office began an investigation of the museum's financial dealings. The museum's problems were exacerbated when its dynamic director, Bruce Johnson, died at the age of twenty-seven in 1976. Under Johnson's direction the museum had become, as the *New York Times* noted in his obituary, "one of the city's liveliest and more controversial" museums.[53]

While the block west of Fifth Avenue was dominated by cultural enterprises, the block between Fifth and Madison avenues featured several small-scale commercial projects that were also of architectural interest. In 1948 Harrison & Abramovitz's design for the Salon Lenthéric brought a measure of cool sophistication to the northeast corner of Fifth Avenue and Fifty-third Street.[54] Although not quite as opulent or distinguished as the cosmetician's 1929 shop in the Savoy-Plaza Hotel (Paul Chalfin), the new store was a worthy successor.[55] Its facades were clad in smooth sheets of American travertine and punctuated by square windows framed by minimally detailed moldings made of the same material. Inside, the architects, working with the interior decorator Ruby Ross Wood and the lighting designer Abe Feder, boldly combined unornamented walls, lighting fixtures recessed into coves and cofferlike ceiling grids with eighteenth-century French furniture to create an ambience of understated luxury that was at once traditional and up-to-date.

In 1961 the furniture manufacturer Herman Miller opened the Textiles & Objects shop at 8 East Fifty-third Street.[56] Designed by Alexander Girard, the store was jam-packed with textiles he designed as well as toys and crafts he selected in his world travels. The shop's principal effect was, as the editors of *Architectural Record* described it, that of "a life-size showcase" presenting "wares in an atmosphere of gaiety and liveliness."[57] Overlapping panels wrapped in fabrics were hung to modulate the shop's narrow, deep and irregular space, partially revealing, partially concealing the myriad of brightly colored objects on display in the otherwise pristine white environment. The ceiling sparkled with 350 silvered reflector light bulbs set on strips that ran parallel to the street. A notable departure from the recessed downlights typical of the high-style interiors of the period, Girard's lighting would have a strong influence on the designers of the late 1960s.

In 1970 a retail outlet for Creative Playthings, a CBS-owned manufacturer of innovative children's toys, opened at 1 East Fifty-third Street.[58] Designed by the graphic designer Keith Godard and the architects Craig Hodgetts, Robert Mangurian and Les Walker, this high-spirited, free-form model play environment became a destination point for sophisticated parents and their young children. Eschewing traditional store design, the designers transformed the 15-by-100-foot interior space of an existing brownstone, ingeniously deemphasizing the needs of the adults

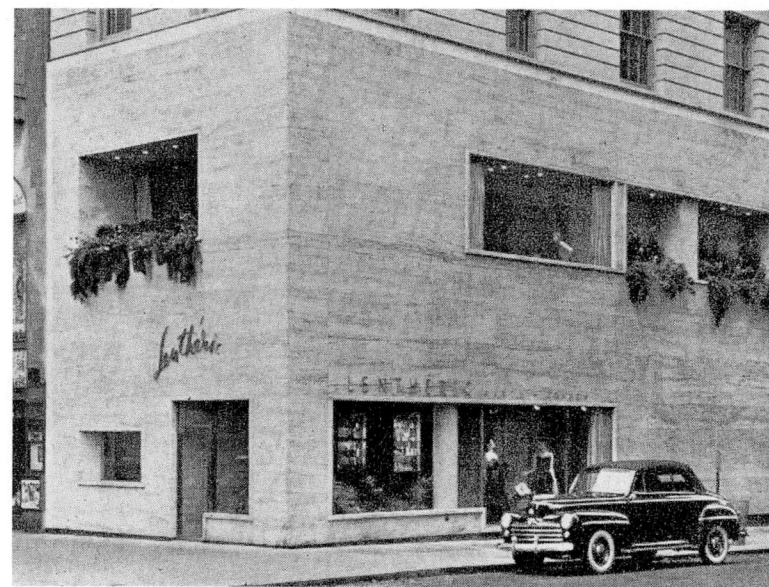

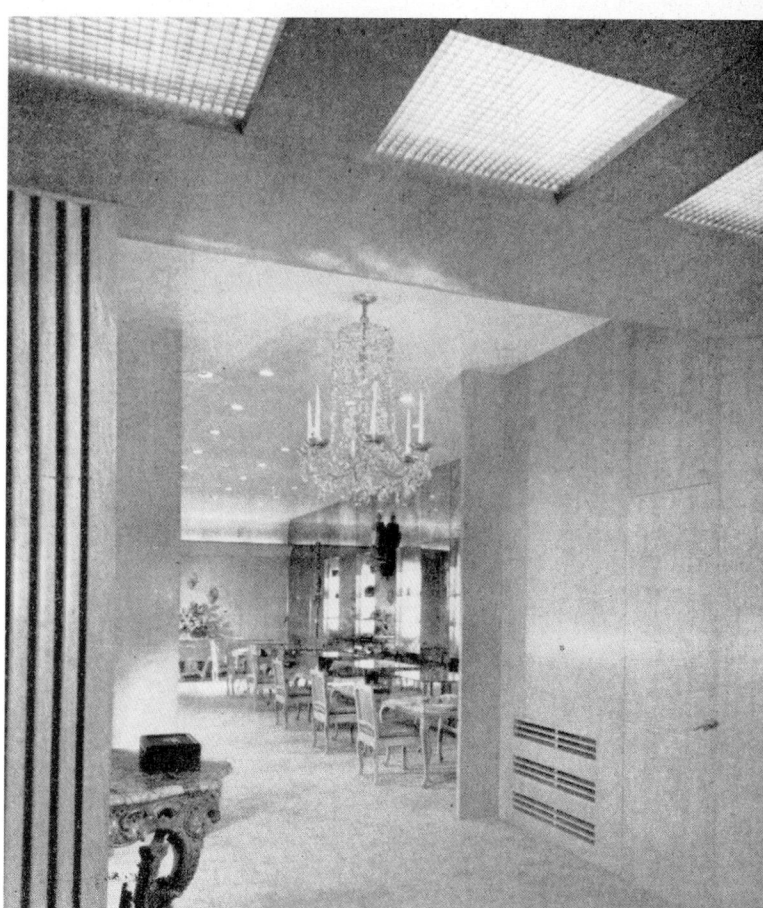

Top left: America House, 44 West Fifty-third Street, between Fifth and Sixth avenues. David R. Campbell, 1961. View to the south. Reens. LR

Bottom left: America House. Interior. Reens. LR

Top: Salon Lenthéric, northeast corner of Fifth Avenue and East Fifty-third Street. Harrison & Abramovitz, 1948. View to the northeast. Schnall. AR. CU

Bottom: Salon Lenthéric. Interiors by Harrison & Abramovitz with Ruby Ross Wood and Abe Feder. AR. CU

487

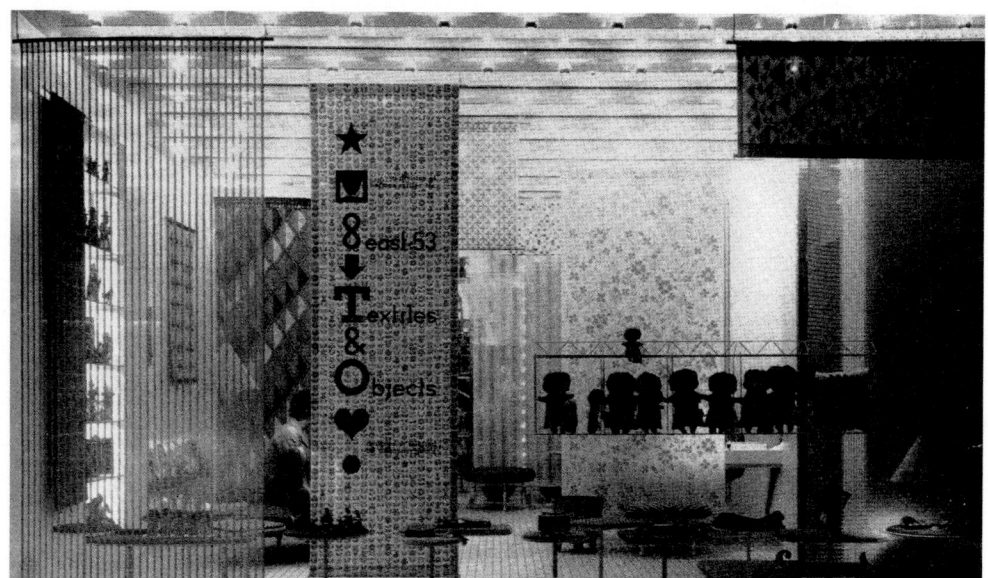

Right: Textiles & Objects, 8 East Fifty-third Street, between Fifth and Madison avenues. Alexander Girard, 1961. Webb. AR. CU

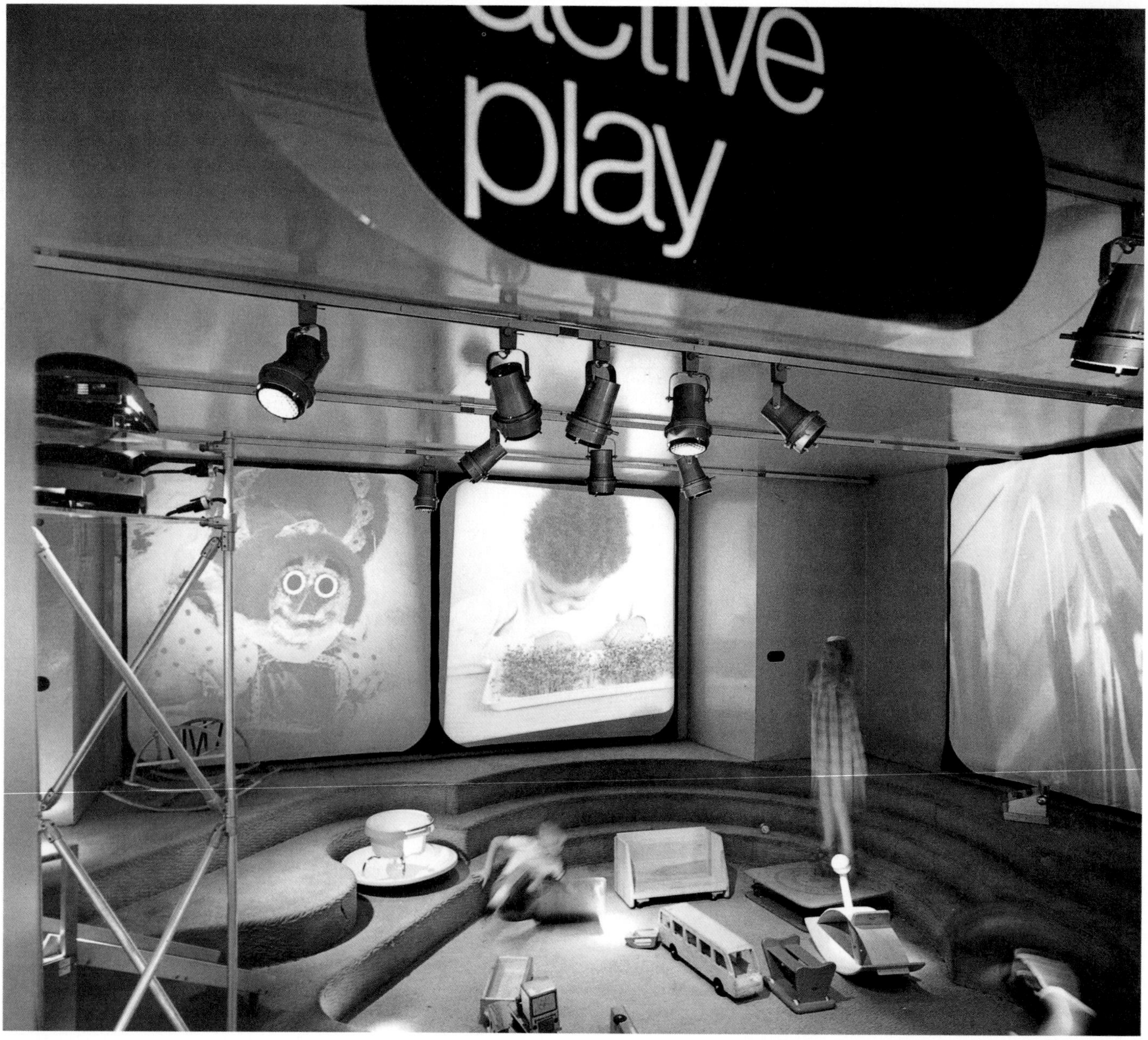

Below: Creative Playthings, 1 East Fifty-third Street, between Fifth and Madison avenues. Keith Godard, Craig Hodgetts, Robert Mangurian and Les Walker, 1970. ©Norman McGrath. NM

who purchased the toys in favor of the children who used them. When approached from the street, a large neon sign with the store's logo dominated the expansive floor-to-ceiling display window. Inside, orange-painted walls enclosed a carpeted, multilevel space containing movable display units made of riveted aluminum air-conditioning ducts. Bold, color-coded graphics identified not only different types of merchandise but the age group for which the toys were intended. Children were encouraged to try out the toys, as well as to push the levers and buttons located on the display cases that set off banks of blinking lights and activated recordings of electronic music. Multiple slide projectors presenting an ongoing show further contributed to the participatory and theatrical qualities of the store.

In 1966 the block quite literally received a breath of fresh air with the creation of Samuel Paley Plaza, the first of the city's so-called vest-pocket parks.[59] William S. Paley, chairman of the board of CBS, acquired the site at 3–5 East Fifty-third Street, formerly occupied by the Stork Club, Sherman Billingsley's glamorous and exclusive nighttime haunt, and established a foundation to build and maintain a park, named in honor of his father, who had died in 1963. As designed by the landscape architect Robert Zion, a principal in the firm of Zion & Breen, working in association with the architect Albert Preston Moore, the park's line of closure was set back behind the building wall to form an inviting forecourt to the outdoor room within, which was elevated by a few steps to enhance its special character as a destination. Zion planted the 42-foot-wide, 100-foot-deep site with twelve honey locust trees, paved the floor with gray granite sets and lined the sides with ivy-covered brick walls. To further establish the park as an outdoor room, Zion placed a gate along the street side, a feature that also served a security function. He also transformed the back wall of the park into a twenty-foot-high water wall, providing a compelling visual grace note as well as a clever means of muffling traffic noise. To furnish the outdoor room Zion selected casual, white-painted openwork metal chairs designed by Harry Bertoia.

From the first, Paley Park was an extraordinary success, attracting 2,000 to 3,000 people a day. Perhaps referring to the aquatic landscape designs of Luis Barragán, Paley said that Zion's ideas were based on what the landscape architect had seen in Mexico.[60] Whatever the park's aesthetic sources, to many observers it was more than an articulate design statement; it was nothing short of an urbanistic revelation. The author John Tauranac wrote:

> Olmsted and Vaux showed that 840 acres of landscaping could create a major urban park. Andrew Haswell Green showed that trees planted on sidewalks and median strips could create parkways. Lillian Wald showed that a patch of concrete with a swing or a slide stuck into it could make a playground. Raymond Hood showed that landscaping just a few open spaces and rooftops could create the vernal oasis that is Rockefeller Center. And Zion & Breen have shown that one waterfall, a dozen trees, a little ivy, and a few tables and chairs can make a vest-pocket park that is an island of tranquility in a sea of activity.[61]

Though Paley Park struck some New Yorkers as startlingly new, the idea of vest-pocket parks had been germinating for quite some time. In 1962 Robert Zion responded to a broadside against small neighborhood parks written by the critic Jane Jacobs and published in *Architectural Forum*. In a letter to the magazine's editors, Zion took issue with Jacobs's argument: "Jane Jacobs' explanation of what kills city parks was extremely interesting and valid, but if she implies that parks have no place

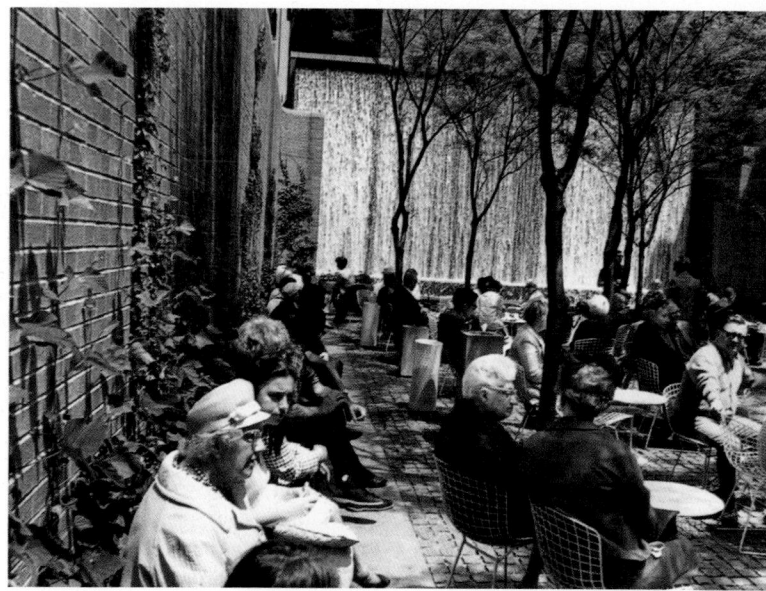

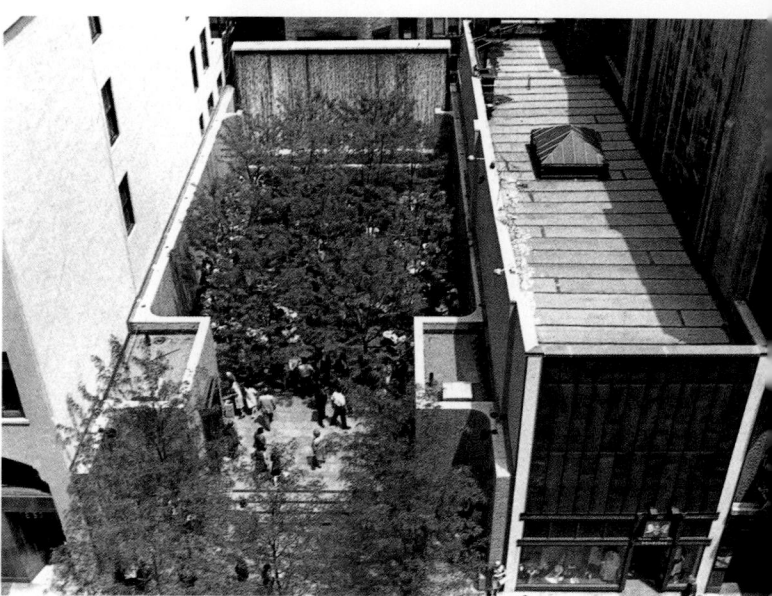

Top: Paley Park, north side of East Fifty-third Street between Fifth and Madison avenues. Zion & Breen in association with Albert Preston Moore, 1966. View to the north. ZB

Bottom: Paley Park. View to the north. ZB

in midtown because they are taken over by 'bums and perverts,' then I *do* object." He favored a system of "parklets" running throughout commercial areas, where "the leveled site of an old brownstone, cobbled and packed with plane trees," would provide sufficient space.[62] In an exhibition titled "New Parks for New York," prepared jointly for the Architectural League of New York and the Park Association, Zion pointed out that New York's Park Department administrators were under the mistaken impression that a site of at least three acres was necessary for an urban park—clearly an unaffordable luxury in a vital central business district.[63]

Zion contended that "the dignity of the human being" could be reaffirmed by a midtown park as small as 50 by 100 feet, and he explained the benefits of such an open area: "It is a part of space removed from the flow of traffic (including pedestrian traffic), enclosed, protected and sheltered from noise. Preferably it is a space between buildings, benefitting from the shelter of neighboring structures; the type of space which is now most commonly used as a parking lot." He saw the midtown parklet as an oasis that would provide "rest for the office worker who has finished lunch and seeks a place to spend the remainder of the lunch hour; rest for the shopper . . . ; rest for the tourist or passerby who will be refreshed visually by the scale of the place, by the dense green growth and, hopefully, by the quiet of the tiny place." Zion called for vine-covered walls to create "vertical lawns"; ceilings framed by a canopy of closely planted trees; light, portable furniture rather than fixed, inflexible park benches; "sitting walls and steps to accommodate the more hardy"; and "bold, simple waterworks to refresh the spirit, providing restful sound as well as vigorous movement."[64]

Zion illustrated his ideas by developing sketches for three midtown sites being used as parking lots and suggested that the cost for the acquisition, development and maintenance of these parklets be taken on by abutting property owners who would benefit from such amenities. In 1964 Zion received just such a commission when the Franklin National Bank hired Zion & Breen to create a parklet setting for their proposed Millinery Park Branch in the garment district; the firm of Eggers & Higgins was to design the kiosklike banking structure.[65] But the project was not built, and it was not until 1966, when Paley approached Zion, that he was able to realize his dream.

The product of Zion and Paley's vision, Paley Park went on to inspire similar projects in turn. The most notable of these was Greenacre Park (1971), a 60-foot-wide, 110-foot-deep park at 217–221 East Fifty-first Street between Second and Third avenues, sponsored by Mrs. Abby Rockefeller Mauzé.[66] The designers, Sasaki, Dawson, DeMay Associates, in consultation with the architects Goldstone, Dearborn & Hinz, adopted a complex composition incorporating numerous levels, pergolas, planting beds, an abstract sculpture and a sculptural cascade of water that emptied into a deep pool. Though directly related to Paley Park in concept, its far more convoluted design rendered it less of a room in spatial terms and less of an oasis in urban terms.

The block between Fifth and Madison avenues also featured a major corporate tower, Emery Roth & Sons' thirty-seven-story Harper & Row Building, at 10 East Fifty-third Street, occupying a midblock site extending south to Fifty-second Street.[67] Completed in 1972 on a site that previously contained Alexander Girard's Textiles & Objects shop (see above), the otherwise banal steel-and-glass box, set back from Fifty-second Street on a small sunken plaza and from Fifty-third Street on an elevated plaza, was distinguished on both streets by the presence of a mirror-surfaced column, designed by the graphic designers Chermayeff & Geismar. A through-block open-air passageway connecting the cross streets provided access to Harper & Row's bookshop, a stylish, two-story-high store designed by Chermayeff & Geismar in association with the architectural firm of Smotrich & Platt. Inside the shop, double-height columns were decorated with the latest book covers.

Citicorp Center

The unique architectural and urbanistic character that made Fifty-third Street at once an enclave within midtown and a microcosm of midtown itself was powerfully encapsulated in Citicorp Center, completed in 1977.[68] Designed by the Cambridge, Massachusetts, firm of Hugh Stubbins & Associates, architects with comparatively little experience in skyscraper design, what had begun as a conventional office building was transformed into a lively mixed-use facility that reflected a particular moment in the evolution of architectural Modernism and of the city's fortunes. Occupying the block bounded by East Fifty-third and East Fifty-fourth streets, Lexington and Third avenues, Citicorp displaced the usual east midtown mixture of seedy buildings whose ground floors typically housed the mass-market shops that catered to the lunch-hour needs of office workers, as well as some upper-end restaurants, including the renowned Café Chauveron. On the southeast corner of Lexington Avenue and Fifty-fourth Street stood the block's one institution, St. Peter's Lutheran Church, a local landmark since 1903. As the realtors were buying up the block in 1968 they offered to buy the church's property as well. The church had considered relocating to the United Nations development district, but the young pastor, Ralph E. Peterson, objected to the move. He had developed an active program directed to the area's office workers, including Theater at Noon, along with jazz-accompanied vesper services each Sunday, activities that had dramatically raised church attendance and encouraged the congregation to stay put.

Donald Schnabel and Charles McArthur, the real estate brokers who began the land assemblage, approached the First National City Bank in the hopes of interesting them in establishing new corporate headquarters on the site, supplanting the dull building they occupied at 399 Park Avenue (see "Park Avenue," above). Not only did the bank need additional office space; despite recent growth that had made them a rival to Chase Manhattan, they still lacked a strong public image, which a dazzling new building could help establish. Even after the bank agreed to move their headquarters to the site, the process of assemblage moved slowly if steadily forward. One structure, 880 Third Avenue (Herbert Tannenbaum, 1965), a banal office building on the southeast corner of the block, at Fifty-third Street and Third Avenue, remained on the site because it was too new to justify acquisition and demolition.[69] The key parcel on the block, St. Peter's Church, was finally acquired in 1970 when Citicorp (the new name of First National City Bank) agreed to pay the church a fee of $9 million for the building and to construct the shell of a new 40,000-square-foot church on the site. Thus the bank, as Andrew Alpern and Seymour Durst were to put it, was allowed "to obtain its new headquarters building in a sympathetic setting, ecumenically joining God and mammon to the benefit of both."[70]

By the time the entire site was assembled in 1973 at a cost of $40 million—the most expensive site ever—Stubbins and

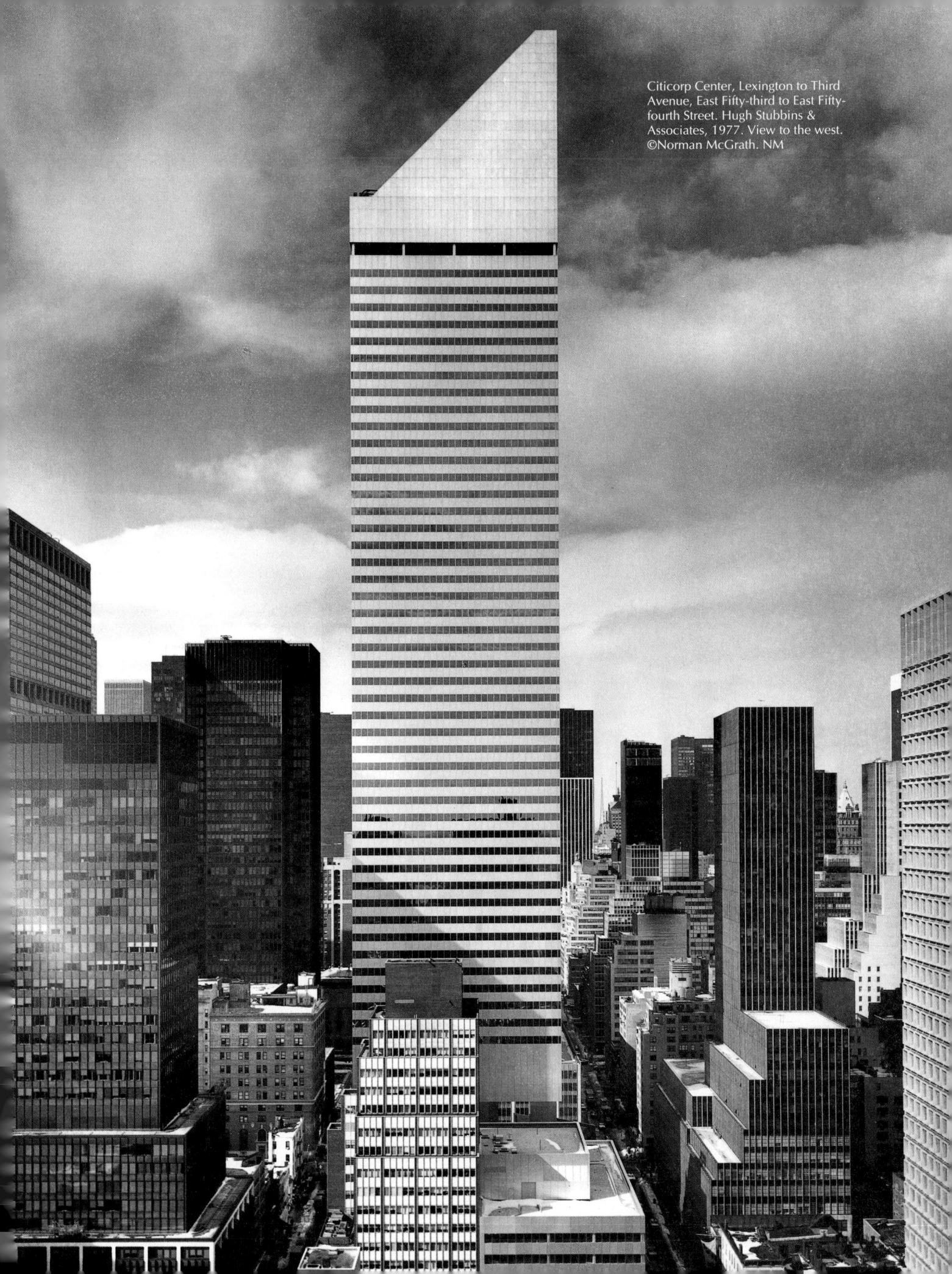

Citicorp Center, Lexington to Third Avenue, East Fifty-third to East Fifty-fourth Street. Hugh Stubbins & Associates, 1977. View to the west. ©Norman McGrath. NM

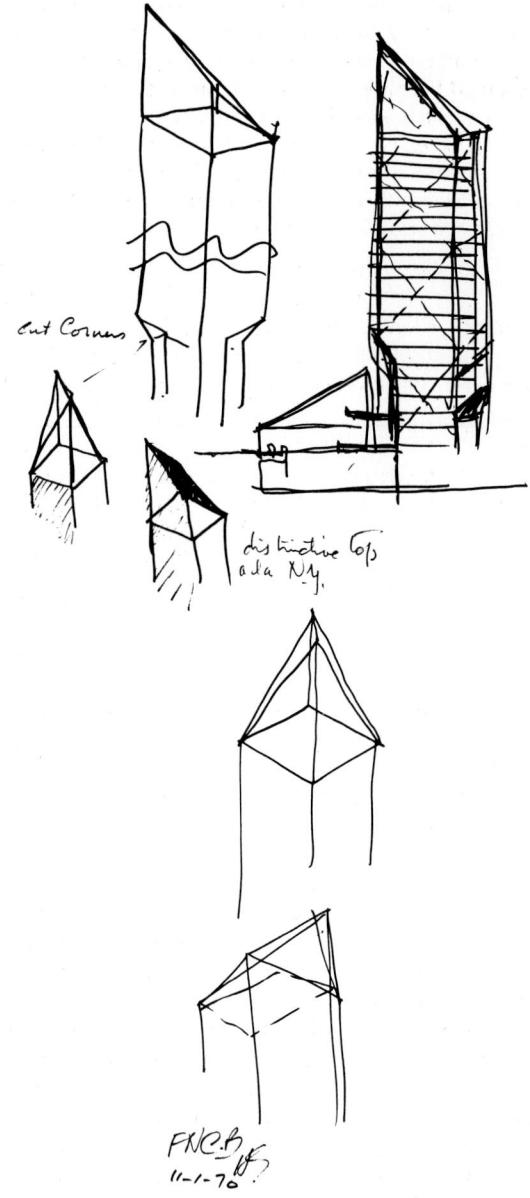

cut Corners

distinctive top
ada NY.

FNCB
11-1-70

Preliminary sketches for Citicorp Center. Hugh Stubbins, 1970. HS

Peter Woytuk, his associate, in association with Emery Roth & Sons, and in consultation with Edward Larrabee Barnes, who had been advising St. Peter's, had developed designs for the $128 million, fifty-nine-story, 1,780,000-square-foot building. The slender tower, clad in aluminum and reflective glass, was to be lifted above a new St. Peter's on four ten-story-high, 112-foot-tall, 24-foot-square colossal pylons or "supercolumns." The design also called for a seven-story building that filled the easternmost portion of the site and included offices as well as a maze of shops gathered around an atrium. The entire complex came to be known as Citicorp Center, the shopping portion as the Market at Citicorp Center.

From the first, Stubbins planned Citicorp Center as a critique of prevailing New York skyscraper design. In a 1970 letter to Henry J. Muller, a senior vice president of the bank, Stubbins set forth his early thoughts about the project:

> The new, slick, slab buildings that march up the avenues of New York and other U.S. cities are symbolic expressions of the Machine. They are anonymous—cool and inhuman. We must use the resources of big business, reinforced by moral and social ideas, to develop a new generation of office buildings planned for the community and expressive of the humanity of the individuals who use them. By revitalizing urban development with an emphasis on people, we could produce a more enjoyable place in which to live and work. Such a building might even be a source of inspiration for other cities.[71]

In return for a development bonus, the building included a two-level pedestrian plaza at the southwest corner of the block that led down to an improved subway concourse below. The plaza also connected to the Citicorp tower's stacked lobbies, which provided access to the double-deck elevators that served the one million square feet of office space located on forty-six floors. (The double-deck elevators were the first used in New York since those installed in the Cities Service Building in 1932.)[72] The open space was sufficiently articulated to mitigate the colossal scale of the supercolumns and the sheer tower above.

The facade of the Citicorp tower, which featured alternating bands of glass and aluminum, was ordinary, but its slender proportions, shiny surfaces and the bold concluding element—a 160-foot-high roof with a forty-five-degree slope—gave it a memorable skyline presence. Its columns were placed at the midpoints of each side, creating open, cantilevered corners that further enhanced the tower's sense of dynamism. Six other schemes for the building were studied, including one with an offset core that sported two pitched rooftop elements, in opposing directions. The final scheme, with its south-facing sloped section, was chosen in the belief that it would contain 100 apartments under a terraced greenhouse facade in order to qualify for a zoning bonus. Although this did not come to pass, the sloping crown was retained as part of a solar energy experiment to be conducted by a research team from the Massachusetts Institute of Technology and funded by the National Science Foundation; a flat-plate collector was to be installed on the tower's surface that would operate a solar-powered dehumidifier in the air-conditioning system. The experiment did not go forward, however, and the collectors were never installed. Regardless of the initial justifications for it, the sloping top gave the building a strong image; as Stubbins explained in his autobiography: "The angled roof plane—with its potential for solar energy collection—expresses the technology of our time. In so doing, a new concept emerges identifying Citicorp within the New York skyscraper hierarchy. It also relieves the uniformity of flat-topped towers proliferating in the center of the city."[73]

At 914 feet Citicorp was the seventh tallest building in the world. Its advanced structural system, designed by the Boston-based engineers William LeMessurier & Associates, allowed not only for the tower's combination of slenderness and great height but also for the cantilevered corners that extended seventy-two feet from each of the four supercolumns. The cantilevers were created to provide St. Peter's with sufficient space around its new building so that its identity as an institution distinct from the bank would be absolutely clear. The tower employed a chevron pattern of diagonal bracing that created interesting window shapes on the inside but was rendered virtually invisible from the outside by the banded skin. One of Stubbins's associates, W. Easley Hamner, would later comment that the decision to camouflage the structural system might have been a mistake, robbing the building of an expressive, scale-giving feature comparable to the diagonal bracing on Skidmore, Owings & Merrill's John Hancock Center (1970) in Chicago.[74]

Citicorp was the first tall building to employ a tuned mass damper (TMD) to slow building movement in the wind and minimize tenant discomfort caused by building sway. The principle of the TMD, a 400-ton, thirty-by-thirty-by-six-foot mass of concrete, as *Architectural Record* reported, was "to place a large mass at the top of the building, to leave the mass 'free' to remain still as the building moves, to transmit this tendency to remain stationary to the building through connections to the structure, and, further, to tune the machinery so that the period of the mass's movement equals the period of the building's movement."[75]

Responding to the "moral clout" exerted by St. Peter's Church, as well as pressure from the Office of Midtown Planning and Development, Citicorp and the building's architects concentrated their resources on the public realm. Inside the low, seven-story, 277,000-square-foot Market building, the bank, working with marketing consultant Michael Buckley and food consultant George Lang, planned a vast food hall to supply the shopping needs of the 40,000 people living in the immediate neighborhood along with the lunchtime needs of the 100,000 people working in the area. Buckley and Lang proposed an eclectic mix of thirty restaurants and retail shops featuring the world's leading cuisines as well as equipment and literature devoted to cooking; the naturally lit atrium, with plants and a fountain, would thus function as a gathering place built exclusively on the theme of food. In an article in the *New York Times* in 1976, when the city's self-image was at a low ebb, Alfred E. Driscoll, Citicorp's vice president in charge of the project, said that the Market was an image-maker for the bank, "an opportunity for us to demonstrate our commitment to New York, to have something fine connected with our corporate name, to have something with a tourist potential."[76] The Market concept was based on two similar centers Driscoll and his colleagues had visited, Crown Center in Kansas City and the Hartford Civic Center, both planned by Buckley.

A month before ground was broken for Citicorp in February 1974, Ada Louise Huxtable described the project as "very strong on urban design and very weak on architecture. . . . What happens at and below ground, in terms of subway circulation, pedestrian movement, the provision of commercial and recreational facilities, and the promise of community activity and amenity is outstanding, and what happens in the air, shouldn't." Huxtable characterized the tower design as "quite simply, awful," and went on to explain:

It reaches weakly after image in its ill-advised, slide-off-and-angled top, arrived at for obvious identity and public relations purposes, in an unlikely combination of disturbing gimmickry and denatured Bauhaus blandness. It has neither romanticism nor structural rationalism but, instead, appears to have been painstakingly invented with a tortured logic through a series of pragmatic esthetic compromises. Alas, this tower just doesn't come off as an architectonic expression of one of the great structural developments of our time.[77]

Citicorp was topped out on October 6, 1976. As Carter Horsley reported in the *New York Times*, the topping-out ceremony of a major skyscraper traditionally marked "an occasion of a certain civic gravity." But this one, he said, was "more meaningful than most" since the new Citicorp building would be the only major office construction to be completed in the following year.[78] There was a distinct note of sadness at the topping-out party. As one construction worker, Ronnie Adams, put it, "I wish it would go another 100 floors; I'd be employed another three years."[79]

In June 1977, as the building neared completion, Huxtable still found the tower's sloping roof a "most disconcerting sight," but she admired the facade, with "all that brute strength . . . encased in the thinnest, flattest, sleekest panels of softly glistening, silvery aluminum. . . . It is steel muscle in a silken glove." She also found much to like on the ground: "What is emerging from the hoarding, dust and rubble on an avenue grown increasingly shabby and honkytonk . . . is a singularly suave blockbuster that comes down to the street with innovative drama." She praised the four-column design as "one of the most impressive—if somewhat disquieting—architectural acrobatic acts in the world," the result of an "extraordinary" engineering scheme.[80]

Huxtable's biggest concern about the building was its "overwhelming" bulk, an example of the "awesome and sometimes disturbing results of the bonus zoning that allows larger buildings in return for special pedestrian features." She warned of the effects of such zoning: "Like other new structures that take full advantage of the new zoning, Citicorp is a bruising lump in the skyline. Even with its finesse, it brutalizes the eye. The trade-off, supposedly, is inhumanity in the air for more humanity in the street. But the new scale that has been established—and will inevitably take over when construction resumes—is becoming a frighteningly measurable reality in terms of the mass and concentration with which New York customarily builds."[81]

When the complex was dedicated on October 12, 1977, Paul Goldberger described it as "a remarkably intelligent synthesis of a number of architectural themes that have been in the air for a number of years." He saw the building as a positive addition to New York: "If in recent years the movement away from the boredom of the glass box has achieved more success in other cities, Citicorp puts New York back in the running as a place where new skyscrapers stand for something more than just rentable square feet." And he placed Citicorp in the vanguard of contemporary architecture: "The image is what architects have come to call 'high-tech'—smooth, sleek, utterly cool. If the elaborate facade of the Woolworth Building suggests a draftsman's anguished hours of meticulous drawing, Citicorp's outside looks as if it could have been designed only by a computer."[82] To the critic Suzanne Stephens, however, the building, "despite its stylish coat of shiny aluminum and tinted glass," was "little more than a modern Fifties high rise in drag."[83]

Citicorp's Market, occupying the first three levels of the complex's low-rise building, proved a tremendous success. Its principal tenant was Conran's, the first American branch of an

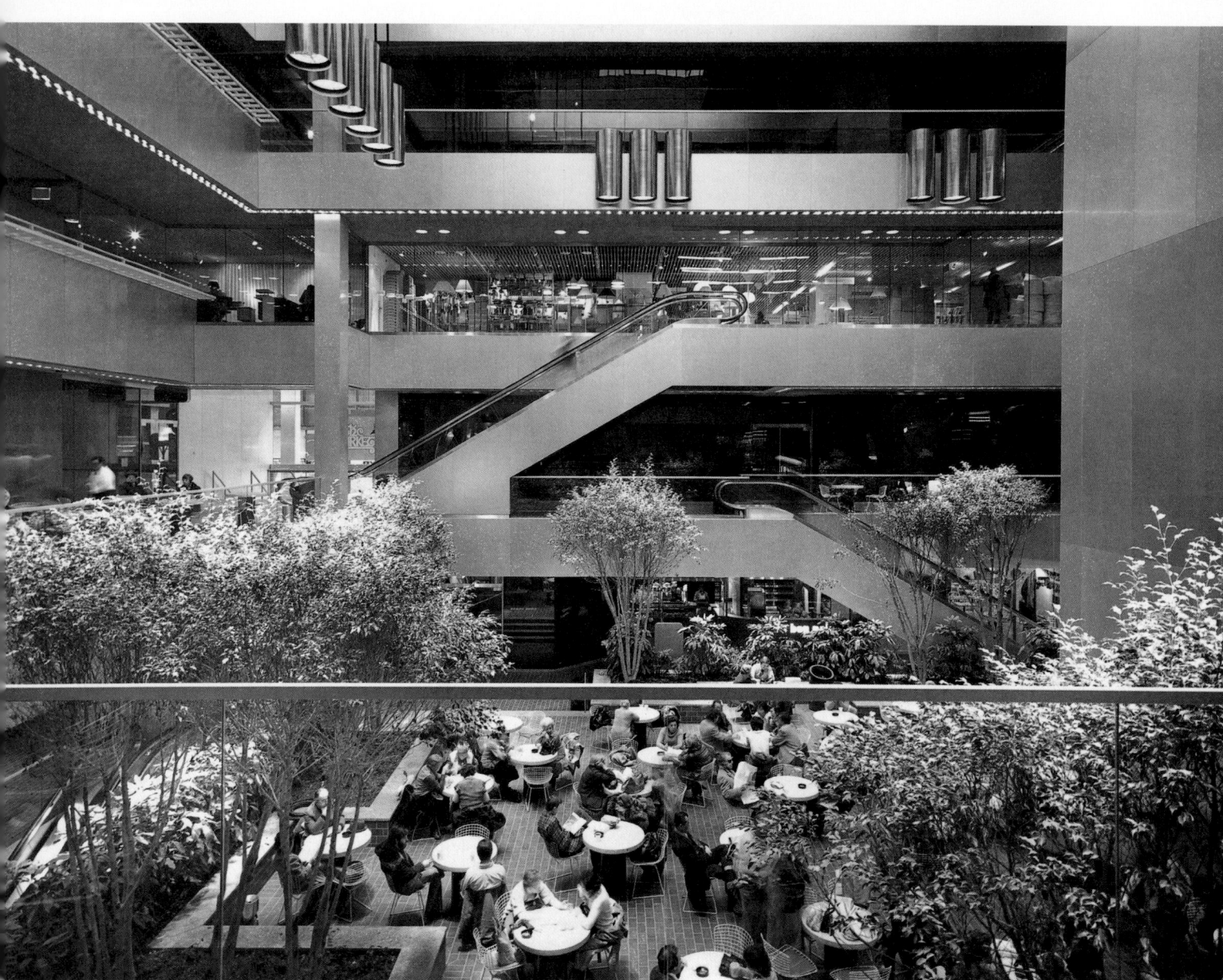

Citicorp Center, Lexington to Third Avenue, East Fifty-third to East Fifty-fourth Street. Hugh Stubbins & Associates, 1977. Market. ©Norman McGrath. NM

English chain specializing in stylish but inexpensive products for the home. Conran's was only part of the carefully orchestrated mix that quickly made the Market a part of the city's daily life. Rather than serving as a midblock passage, the 85-foot-high, 90-by-100-foot skylit atrium, surrounded by a combination of shops, was designed as a destination place. August Heckscher, an early enthusiast of the Market, wrote: "It is an amenity in which we can all rejoice. It fulfills one of the deepest needs of urban life—a place where men and women can gather, can make of the chores of their existence something of a ceremony and a celebration, and germinate on any day the feeling of being at a fair." Heckscher did feel, however, that the space had shortcomings, notably the "silver skin, so handsome on the building's exterior," which "seems cold at the atrium's more intimate scale," and the cylindrical lighting fixtures, which suggested "an indoor space rather than creating the illusion of an exterior cityscape."[84]

The Market had other critics as well. In September 1977 Suzanne Stephens described the Market's exterior as "just one more anonymous glass-and-aluminum wall, smack at the end of the sidewalk," which she felt was "a dull substitute for the old small-scale townhouses and brownstones containing boutiques, theaters, and restaurants that once made the 54th Street block one of the more special urban settings in midtown."[85] A year later, Stephens was even harsher in her criticism. She categorized the Market as a "'stratified success'—meaning a commercial success that does *not* cut across class lines." It was "functionally an enclave," she said, deriving its popularity from "what it keeps out as well as what it offers within." She saw the Market as representing a dangerous trend in which public amenities were moving away from "the true public domain, the street, to inner sanctums where private and public domains blur," becoming "staked out territories where it is not unusual that persons find themselves inadvertently paying for this amenity through the price of a cup of coffee even if access is 'free.'" Stephens discussed the ramifications of this trend:

> This interiorization and privatization process reveals not a world of the "real," the subconscious, and true self of the city, but a world that is an idealized projection of how the city would like to see itself viewed. Thus, this oasis is a simulation of a New York street or plaza, kept clean under tight control. Restrained enough for a corporate world, safe enough for out-of-towners, clean enough for New Yorkers tired of the "real" world, this is a consumer's fantasy of internationalism and of New York. . . . But in the end, the space becomes claustrophobic: Not being able to see the outside world, or be aware of the weather, one finds this oasis, for all its milling people, free concerts, and chocolate-covered strawberries, begins to take on a deathly pall.[86]

The new St. Peter's Church and the Chapel of the Good Shepherd, donated by Erol Beker, a Turkish immigrant who was a parishioner, were the most successful parts of the Citicorp complex. The chapel, located within the office tower's mass, was a twenty-eight-foot-long, twenty-one-foot-wide, five-sided, all-white room. Its principal features were the white-painted wood elements created by the sculptor Louise Nevelson, including a large, abstract version of a traditional cross depicting Christ as the Good Shepherd. Nevelson also contributed five wall reliefs, a candle holder and three hanging columns representing the Trinity. To the art historian Jean Lipman, the pieces were "unquestionably the masterwork of Nevelson's architectural sculpture." The re-

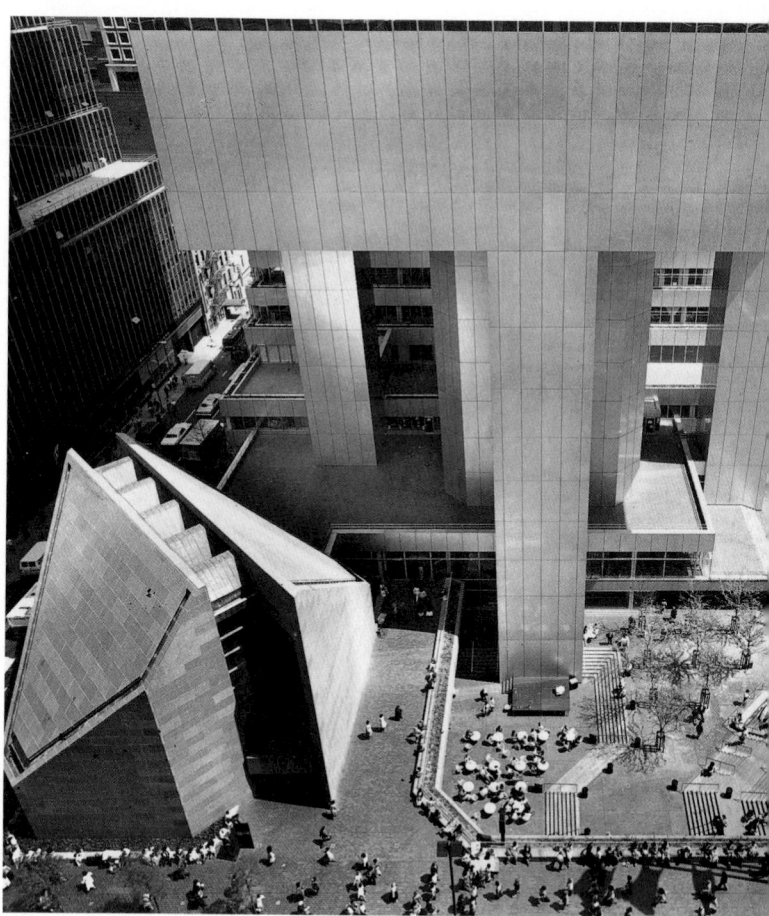

Citicorp Center. View to the east showing St. Peter's Church on lower left. ©Norman McGrath. NM

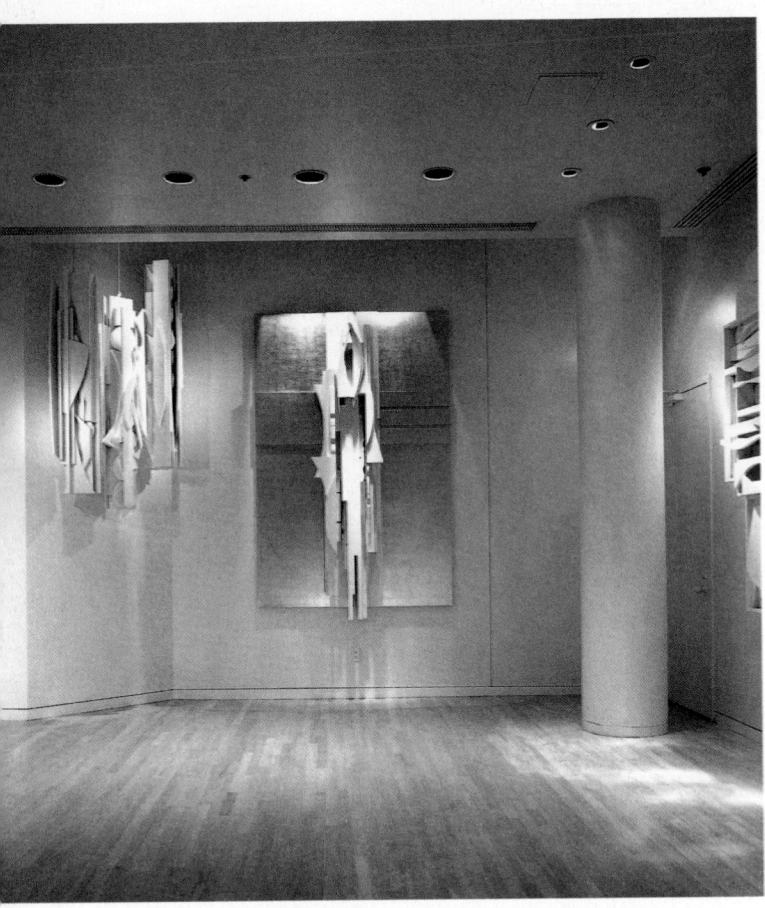

Above: Citicorp Center, Lexington to Third Avenue, East Fifty-third to East Fifty-fourth Street. Hugh Stubbins & Associates, 1977. Chapel of the Good Shepherd with sculpture by Louise Nevelson. Crane. PG

Right: Citicorp Center. St. Peter's Church sanctuary showing furniture and objects designed by Lella and Massimo Vignelli. ©Norman McGrath. NM

liefs, she said, "create an environment both aesthetically exciting and psychologically serene."[87] Nevelson described her intentions in terms that were broadly spiritual, not specifically religious or Christian: "The Chapel was designed to be universal; it's a symbol of freedom. . . . If people can have some peace while they are there, and carry it with them in their memory bank, that will be a great achievement for me. . . . I meant to provide an environment that is evocative of another place, a place of the mind, a place of the senses."[88] To whatever degree the piece succeeded as abstract art, its ability to communicate religious content and to function within the traditions of ecclesiastical art remained in question. Hilton Kramer, the art critic for the *New York Times*, asked, "In what respect, if any, does the chapel differ from an ordinary museum installation of Mrs. Nevelson's work?" According to Kramer, the answer was "none whatever." He went on to generalize about the relationship between art and religion: "Social observers have said in recent years that the art museum in America has in some respects tended to take the place of religious institutions as a center of community life. One can imagine that this would be a vexing problem for these religious institutions. But is the answer to turn such institutions into art museums?"[89]

The church itself, located at the site's northwest corner, was a prismatic form, clad in dark gray granite, that emerged distinctly from the tower above it. Set at a forty-five-degree angle to the street to emphasize its independence, the church was entered from the plaza level; it was also connected to the tower via passageways on two levels. Inside, worshipers found an eighty-five-foot-high sanctuary, lit from a skylight that ran across the top and from vertical strip windows at the front and back. The ivory-painted terraced room, with its boxy red oak furniture designed by Lella and Massimo Vignelli, was spare, although color was effectively used in the seat cushions and in the clergy's vestments. The center pews were designed so that they could be removed when the church was used for concerts and other special events. Paul Goldberger characterized the sanctuary as being "like an immense, angular tent," but he felt its design was lacking: it was neither an "irrational, brilliant, subtle interior" like Le Corbusier's Ronchamp chapel nor "a perfectly proportioned, totally direct and rational space" like Louis Kahn's Unitarian Church in Rochester, New York.[90]

In 1978, a year after its completion, Citicorp Center added another touch to the surrounding streetscape with the installation of three black-finished, cruciform pylons incorporating street lights, traffic signals and signs indicating street names and parking regulations; seven visually harmonious lampposts were also installed at midblock locations. Designed by Designetics, a New Jersey–based lighting and graphic design firm, the pylons added a measure of visual simplicity and sophistication to the typically cluttered New York street scene and seemed at home with the sleek facades of Citicorp. The pylons recalled an earlier design for multipurpose posts devised in 1969 by Massimo Vignelli and the lighting consultant Seymour Evans (see chapter 2).

Citicorp posed serious questions for the future: did the tax abatements and zoning waivers and the beau geste of building a new church adequately compensate for the building's colossal size, the overwhelming scale of its pilotis and the constrained razzle-dazzle of its indoor market? Was the building a grand gift to a city struggling to recapture its self-esteem, or was it a sugar-coated grab for real estate profit?

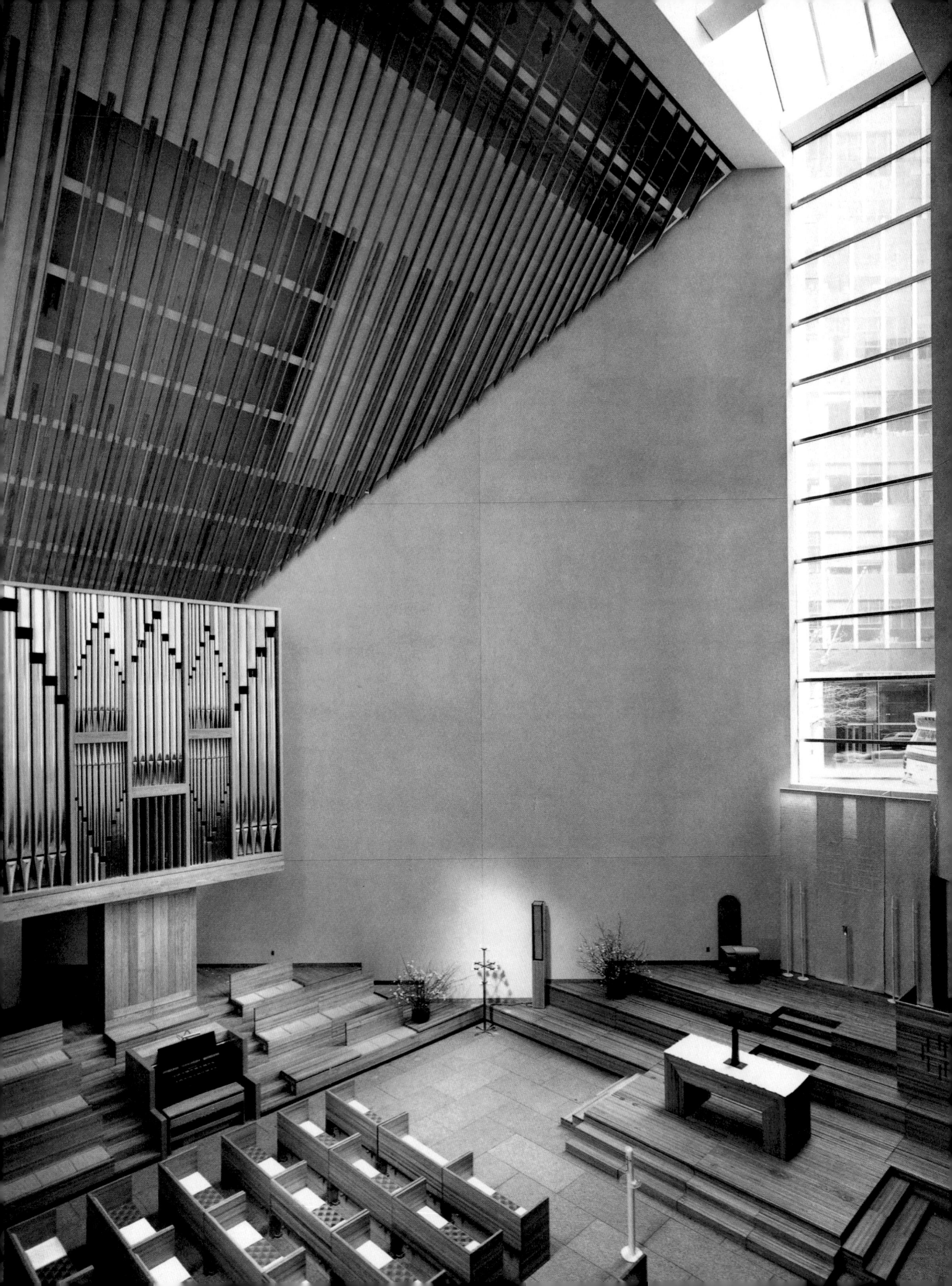

At the end of World War II the upper part of midtown, extending from Third to Sixth Avenue, and from Fifty-sixth Street to Central Park South (west of Fifth Avenue) and Sixtieth Street (east of Fifth Avenue), constituted a special area unto itself.[1] It was a small town for the rich, as it were, incorporating a remarkable array of exclusive clubs, top-end hotels, apartment houses and shops as well as high-quality office buildings. If Fifty-seventh Street and Fifth Avenue was the principal crossroads of this exclusive village, then the Grand Army Plaza was its village green and Central Park its open country.

One of the Plaza district's first postwar buildings was Emery Roth & Sons' sixteen-story 4 West Fifty-eighth Street (1948), a traditionally styled and functionally urbane structure that combined offices with Warner-Leeds's Paris Theater, the city's first postwar movie theater.[2] Located on the basement, ground-floor and mezzanine levels, the Paris Theater was the first to take advantage of a change in zoning that allowed auditoriums of more than 299 seats to be located in mixed-use buildings; previously theater auditoriums had to be built as freestanding structures, though they were often entered through lobbies located within office buildings. The theater's sponsor, the French Pathé syndicate, was seeking to increase their share of the American market by starting a chain of so-called art theaters; the Paris was built as their test case. Touted by the architects as "more visually conceived than the conventional type of motion-picture theater," on the exterior it featured a restrained canopy projecting from an equally restrained, almost unbroken limestone facade.[3] A large window at street level showcased the lounge, where patrons could be seen sitting on Scandinavian-inspired furniture not eating popcorn but drinking coffee, tea and, on chilly days, bouillon. A restaurant was located at the basement level. The 571-seat auditorium was simplicity itself, with plain walls and smooth ceiling planes that subtly modulated the boxlike space to suggest an oval.

In 1950 the Lighthouse, the flagship building of the New York Association for the Blind, a charitable organization benefiting the visually handicapped, completed a five-story building at 110 East Sixtieth Street that was connected to its original six-story building (1913) at 111 East Fifty-ninth Street.[4] The architects for the combined facility, Clay, Potter & Coulter, retained the main entrance on Fifty-ninth Street. Despite their attempt to establish a gentle presence on Sixtieth Street through the use of brick and limestone, the horizontal window bands and almost unfenestrated base disrupted the scale of the brownstone-lined block. In 1962 the association vacated the original building to make way for Kahn & Jacobs's new headquarters, a fourteen-story, 125,000-square-foot office building, clad in gray-tinted glass and precast-concrete panels, at 111 East Fifty-ninth Street.[5] Zoning required that the new building be set back sixteen feet from Fifty-ninth Street to create a plaza; in order to allow for sufficient floor space, the north facade was hung from a fourteenth-floor truss to cantilever sixteen feet over the fifth floor of the 1950 building. The new building's Fifty-ninth Street facade, as Norval White and Elliot Willensky put it, would have been "unassuming background architecture" had it not, by its placement, formed a tiny plaza peopled by four metal stacks, which released air-conditioning exhaust "without subjecting pedestrian passersby to the usual blasts of warm, stale 'air.'"[6]

Across the street, William Lescaze's 110 East Fifty-ninth Street (1969), which ran through to Fifty-eighth Street, had 465,000 square feet of office space packaged in a thirty-seven-

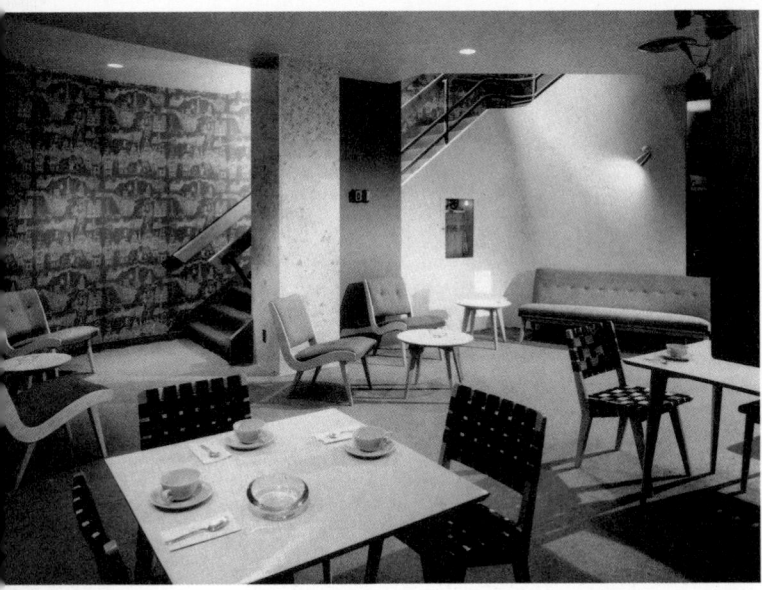

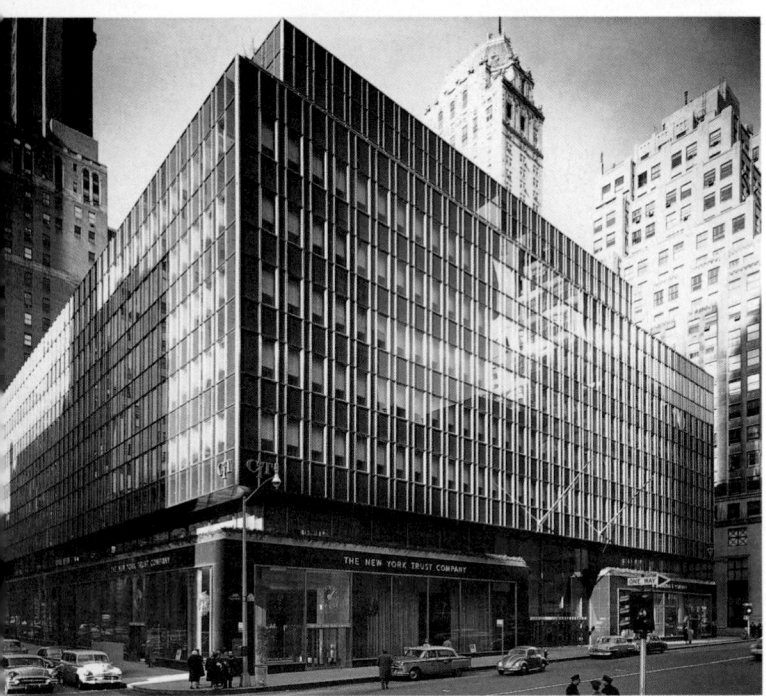

Top: Paris Theater, 4 West Fifty-Eighth Street, between Fifth and Sixth avenues. Warner-Leeds, 1948. Lounge. Freedman. LF

Bottom: CIT Building, 650 Madison Avenue, between East Fifty-ninth and East Sixtieth streets. Harrison & Abramovitz, 1958. View to the northwest. Stoller. ©ESTO

story building that consisted of a twenty-story tower set atop and to the side of a seventeen-story base.[7] For this building's plaza, placed on Fifty-eighth Street, where it would get the most sun, the sculptor Bernard (Tony) Rosenthal created *Rondo*, an eleven-foot-diameter, four-foot-thick, revolving bronze disk set on its end, like a coin in the course of being flipped.

The area's first distinguished work of corporate Modernism, the headquarters of the CIT Corporation (1958), occupied the west blockfront of Madison Avenue between Fifty-ninth and Sixtieth streets.[8] CIT was one of midtown's most intriguing postwar office buildings and also, at only eight stories, one of its smallest. Designed by Max Abramovitz, of Harrison & Abramovitz, the squat building was sheathed in polished black granite set within a stainless-steel grid, the first such use of stone. The result was a sleek if brooding presence, not unlike that of the Daily Express Building (Ellis, Clarke & Gallannaugh, in collaboration with Sir Owen Williams, 1930-32) on Fleet Street and Shoe Lane in London, a similarly proportioned mass.[9] At street level the building consisted of a central entry lobby serving the building's single tenant, flanked by rental spaces suitable for banks. The second floor, which was recessed to help visually float the office floors above, contained dining and meeting rooms as well as a 228-seat auditorium. Top executives occupied the eighth-floor penthouse, which looked out on broad landscaped terraces. As with the Manufacturers Trust Forty-third Street branch (see "Fifth Avenue," above), the decision to limit the building's height came from the client, who preferred not to lease space, and the architects, who realized the aesthetic impact a carefully detailed, low, blocky building would have amid the area's ragged landscape of coarsely detailed, crudely massed curtain-walled infills and towers. But while the cramped site of Manufacturers Trust could yield very little in the way of leasable office space and the building therefore represented minimal economic sacrifice, the CIT site was an entire blockfront and the size of the building was thus a grand gesture. Inside this custom-made corporate palazzo, the company's message about quality was somewhat less clearly delivered. Although the 9'3" ceiling height was more generous than the norm and the use of full-height doors fostered the sense of spaciousness, the interior fittings and furnishings, specified and designed by Eleanor Lemaire, failed to achieve a strong image.

To the west, CIT was soon joined by the controversial Playboy Club (Oppenheimer, Brady & Lehrecke, 1962), at 5 East Fifty-ninth Street, a dining and drinking facility that served the middle-class corporate crowd.[10] The Manhattan branch of the Playboy Club, which originated in Chicago, was a seven-story building, previously home to the Savoy Art Galleries, which was remodeled to suggest a glamorous Modernist movie set of the 1930s. The principal feature of the facade was a spiral stair that rose through a glass cylinder, affording pedestrians spectacular glimpses of the 125 so-called Bunnies, women staff members scantily clad in rabbit costumes whose business it was to help the guests. (In the winter of 1963 one of the Bunnies was a young graduate of Smith College, a journalist named Gloria Steinem; her essay about her experiences at the Playboy Club, "A Bunny's Tale," published in *Show* magazine, became a foundation stone of the women's liberation movement.) The building's entrance, which the architects hoped would be "a fitting gateway to a palace of lusty but innocent fun," led to six different entertainment areas, most designed by Playboy's director of design, Art Minor.[11] These rooms were connected by a second, mesh-trapped staircase that called to mind nothing so much as the chicken-wire covering of a rabbit hutch. Despite the Bunnies

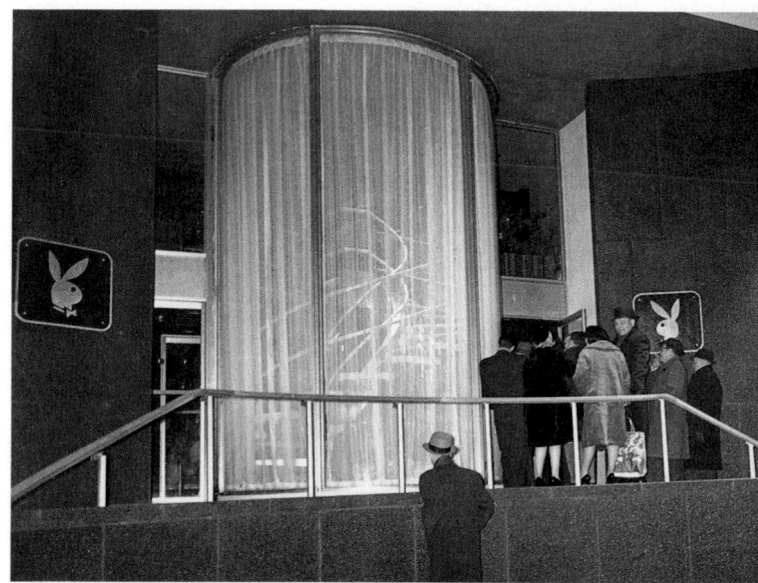

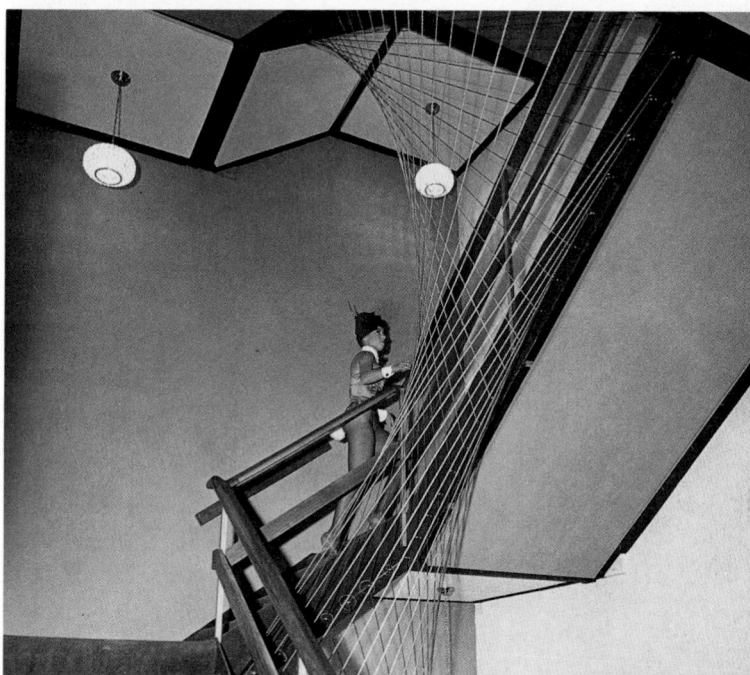

Top: Playboy Club, 5 East Fifty-ninth Street, between Fifth and Madison avenues. Oppenheimer, Brady & Lehrecke, 1962. Entrance. Hopkins. OBV

Bottom: Playboy Club. Staircase. OBV

499

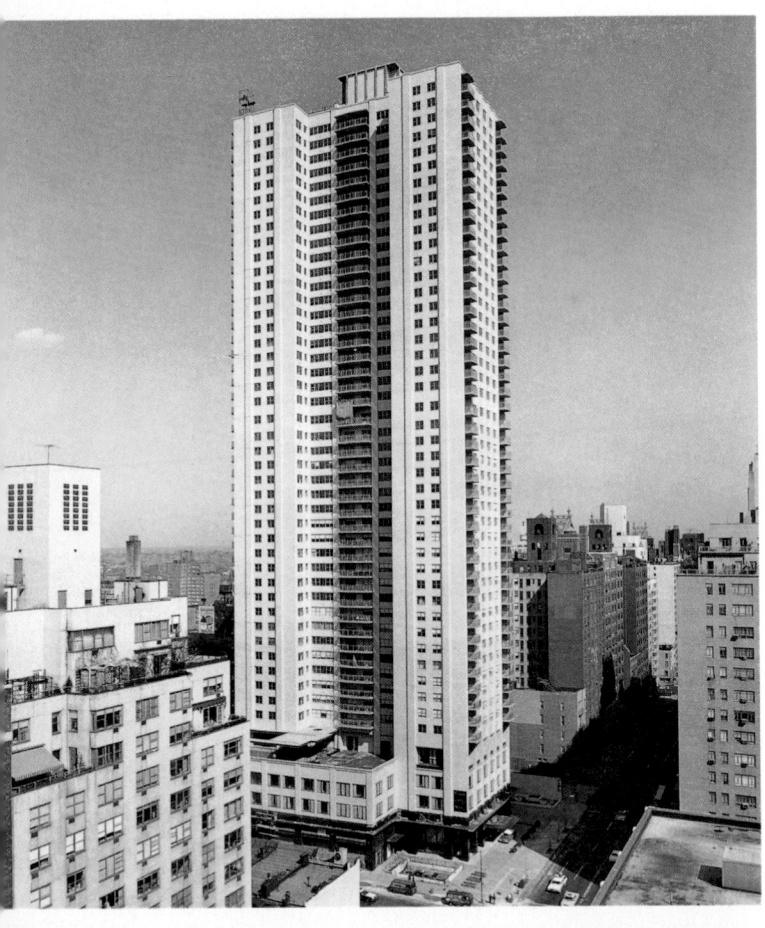

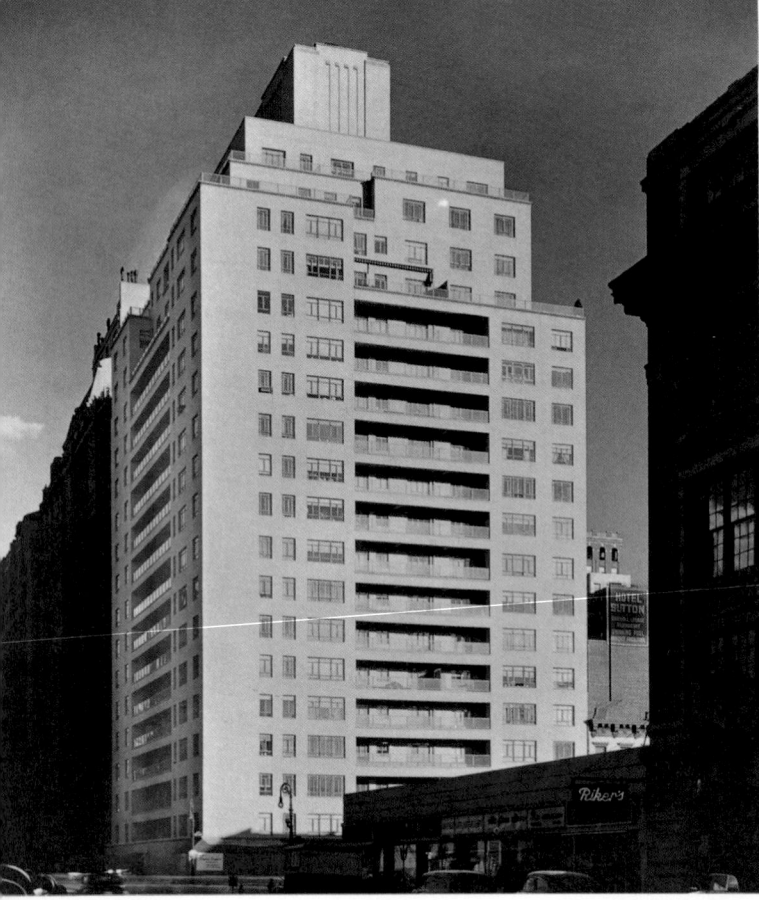

and the attempts at high style, the Playboy Club was relatively tame stuff—tepid even for tired businessmen and out-of-towners on a spree.

Fifty-seventh Street, stretching to the East River, was the Plaza district's Faubourg Saint-Honoré, a quintessential representation of the high-priced ingredients that characterized the area as a whole.[12] In the immediate postwar era, development activity on Fifty-seventh Street, the only east-west thoroughfare in mid-Manhattan extensively zoned for residential purposes, was concentrated east of the Plaza district's boundaries, where a number of high-rise apartment houses were built.[13] The first and the most distinguished of these was announced in 1946: Emery Roth & Sons' eighteen-story building, with a penthouse, at 300 East Fifty-seventh Street, on the southeast corner of Second Avenue, completed in 1948.[14] With 165 apartments, 115 of which had balconies, the tan brick building was not only simply detailed but also well planned. By 1961 four more apartment buildings had been realized on East Fifty-seventh Street and three more were being planned.

The character of new apartment construction on the street dramatically changed with the implementation of the new zoning controls in 1961, which led to the construction of two supersized apartment towers. The first of these was Philip Birnbaum's banal forty-seven-story Excelsior (1967), at 303 East Fifty-seventh Street, on the east blockfront of Second Avenue between Fifty-seventh and Fifty-eighth streets, which had 371 balconied apartments.[15] The city's tallest apartment house and its tallest concrete-framed structure, the Excelsior, clad in glazed white brick, was set behind a south-facing plaza, designed by M. Paul Friedberg and used as an automobile drop-off, which led to a double-height lobby decorated with the theatrical glamour usually found in Miami Beach hotels. A swimming pool was located at the foot of the tower on top of the building's four-story base.

Five years later plans were announced for a second apartment tower, the Galleria (1975), at 117 East Fifty-seventh Street.[16] Designed by David Kenneth Specter in association with Philip Birnbaum, the Galleria would become one of the city's most talked-about apartment houses. It was originally planned as an office building, but when the market for such space slumped drastically, the developers, unable to justify the site's exclusive use for apartments, entered into negotiations with the city to develop a mixed-use facility. The city was represented by Jaquelin Robertson, the architect and urban designer who was head of the city's Office of Midtown Planning and Development, and Walter McQuade, the architectural journalist who was then serving as a member of the City Planning Commission. The fifty-five-story Galleria, which usurped the Excelsior's status as the city's tallest concrete-framed building, comprised a forty-seven-story tower on an eight-story base set to the north side of the midblock site. The tower, barely visible from Fifty-seventh Street, formed an important addition to the area's skyline, particularly when viewed from uptown. The building's two components, offices and apartments, were treated as independent entities, each with its own mechanical, electrical and other basic systems.

In contrast to Olympic Tower (see "Fifth Avenue," above), the city's other major legislated mixed-use tower, the Galleria made all the right urbanistic moves. Not only was it built out to the street line, it was also articulated into functionally expressive components culminating in a dramatic skyline feature. Yet, as Paul Goldberger wrote, it still didn't succeed: "The differentiation of uses on the facades would be more convincing . . . if the facades themselves were better. As they are, the combination of

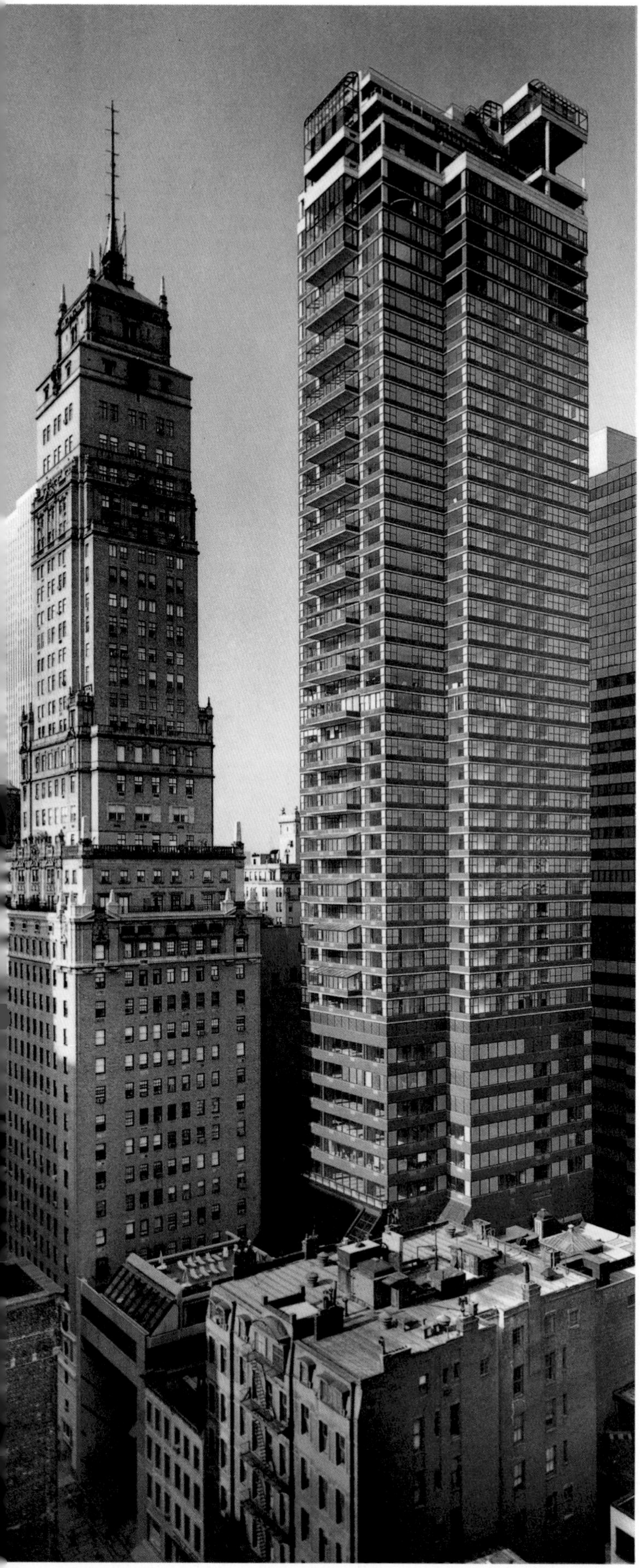

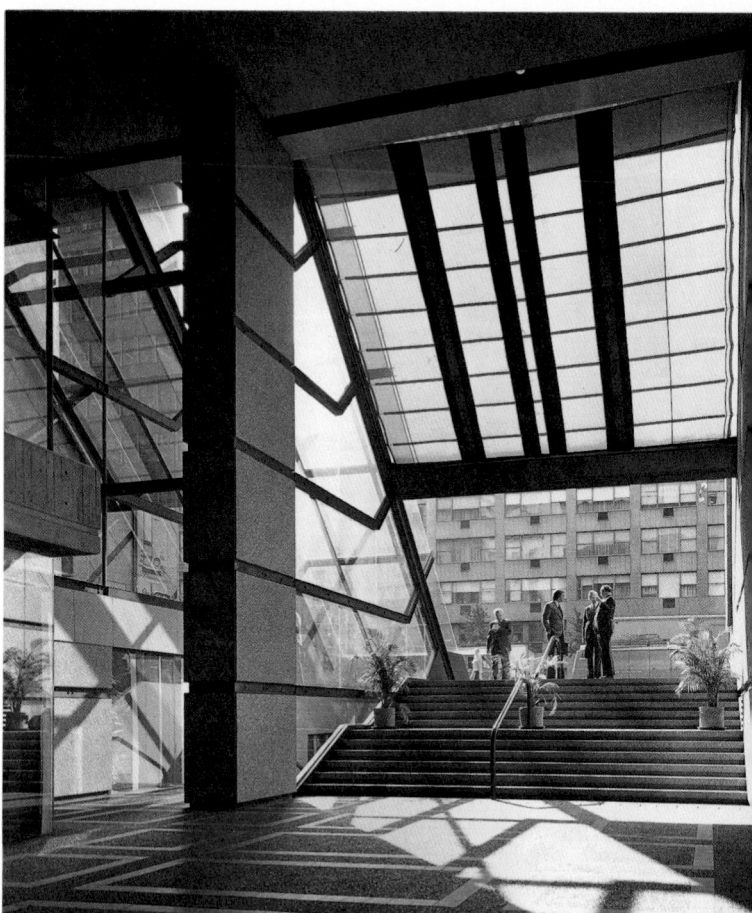

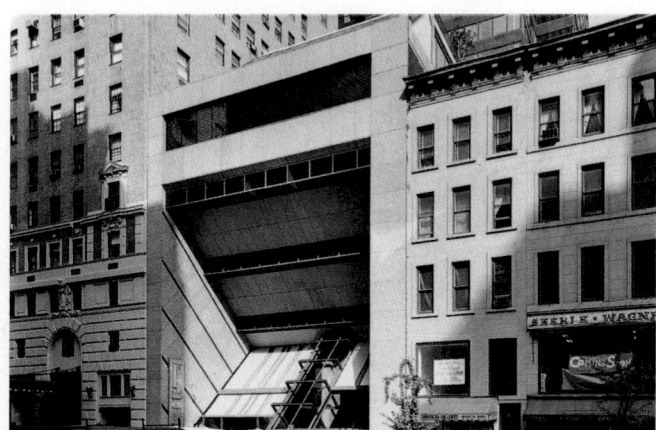

Top far left: Excelsior, 303 East Fifty-seventh Street, east blockfront of Second Avenue, East Fifty-seventh to East Fifty-eighth Street. Philip Birnbaum, 1961. View to the northeast. OMH

Bottom far left: 300 East Fifty-seventh Street, southeast corner of Second Avenue. Emery Roth & Sons, 1946. View to the southeast. ERS

Left: Galleria, 117 East Fifty-seventh Street, between Lexington and Park avenues. David Kenneth Spector in association with Philip Birnbaum, 1975. View to the northwest, also showing Ritz Tower (Emery Roth and Carrère & Hastings, 1925) in the background. ©Norman McGrath. NM

Top: Galleria. View to the south from atrium. ©Norman McGrath. NM

Bottom: Galleria. Main entrance. ©Norman McGrath. NM

Right: 9 West Fifty-seventh Street. View to the southwest showing, from left to right: 4 West Fifty-eighth Street (Emery Roth & Sons, 1948), 9 West Fifty-seventh Street and Plaza Hotel (Henry J. Hardenbergh, 1907). Parker. SOM

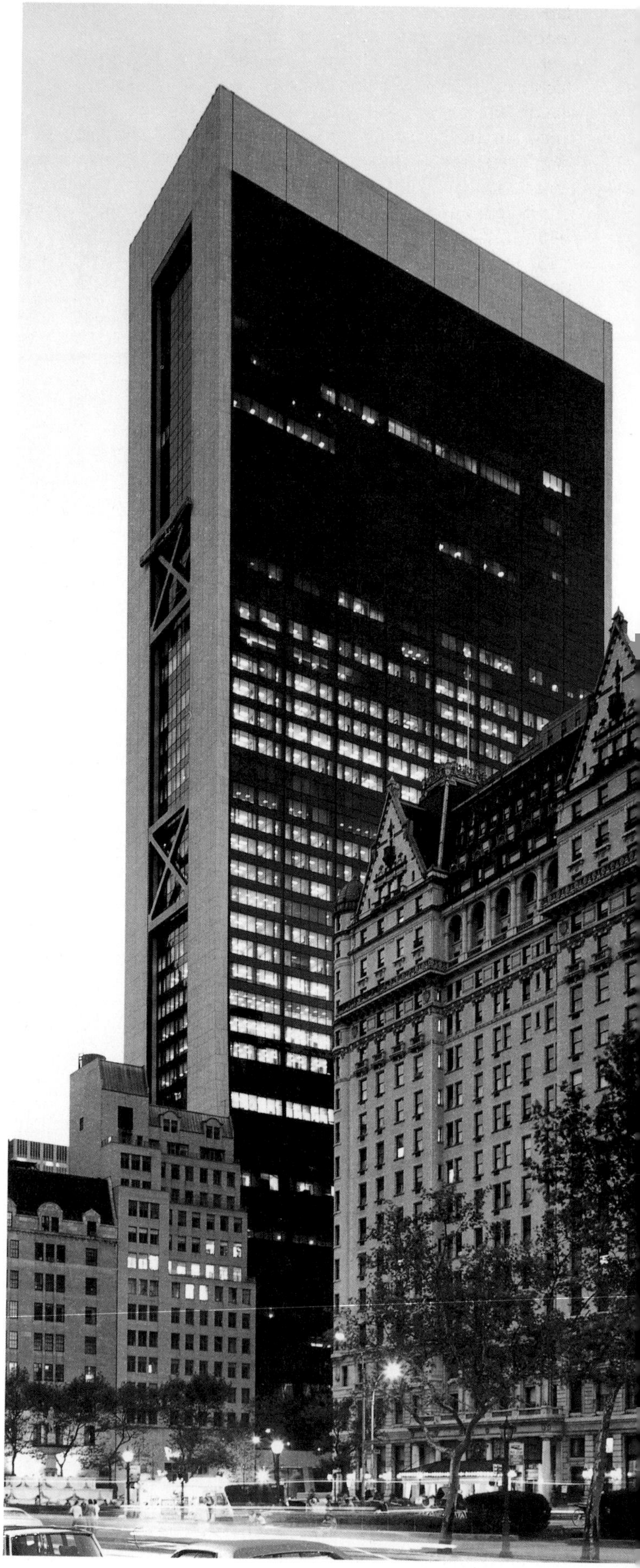

Below: 9 West Fifty-seventh Street, between Fifth and Sixth avenues. Skidmore, Owings & Merrill, 1974. View to the west of plaza including sculpture of number nine by Ivan Chermayeff. ©Norman McGrath. NM

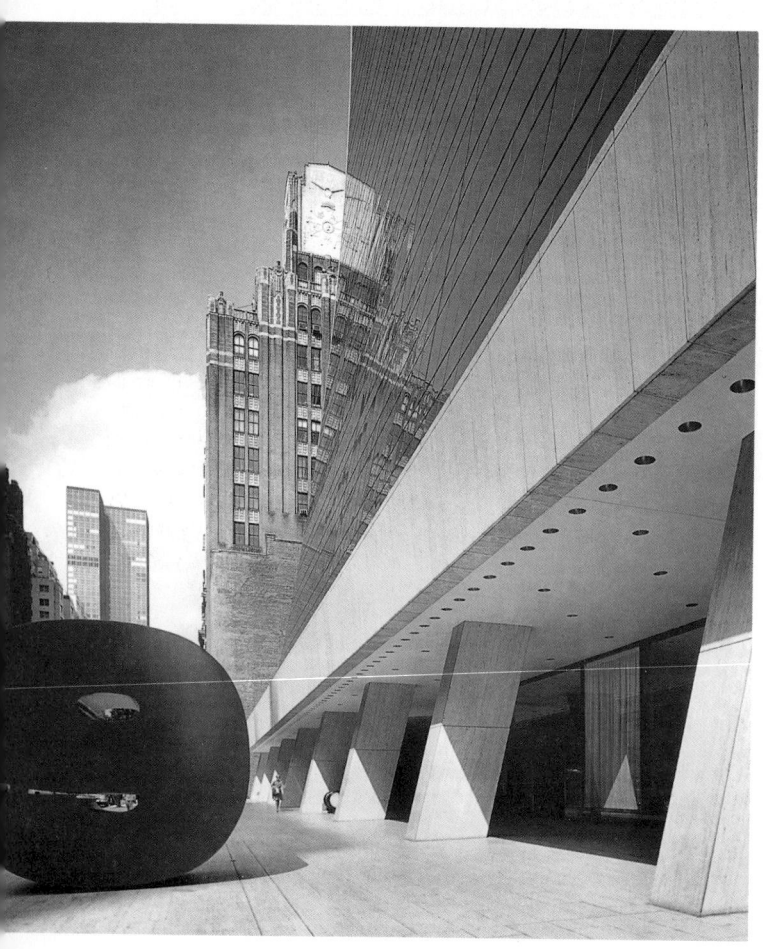

dark brick and double-hung windows, with wall cutouts for air conditioning units, bears an uncomfortable resemblance to the average Third Avenue high-rise apartment building upon which this structure is supposed to be an improvement."[17] Not even the use of winter gardens, in effect fourteen-foot-square glassed-in balconies that protruded halfway beyond the setback line, a device suggested by Robertson, could redeem the crude repetitiousness of the facade.

In return for permission to build 253 condominium apartments on thirty-eight floors, nine floors of offices and a private club, as well as service floors, the developers provided a dramatic ninety-foot-high skylit atrium whose image was based on Milan's Galleria. Specter's soaring, cleverly mirrored space was sixty feet higher than required by the law, which allowed fourteen square feet of additional leasable floor space for one square foot of covered pedestrian space, provided that the space was at least thirty feet high, thirty feet wide, 3,000 square feet in area and contained some retail space. Because the building was under design as the new legislation was being written, the developers, uncertain of what would be required for the full bonus, only added eleven square feet for each foot of public space they built. While Skidmore, Owings & Merrill created a separate lobby for residents of Olympic Tower, the atrium in the Galleria complex was designed to be used by all tenants in an effort to activate the space. To clarify circulation within, Specter devised a series of platforms and bridges to articulate the paths leading to the various functions, such as the club, offices and apartments.

Although the Galleria was intended by the city planners and by Specter to be a midblock pedestrian passage linking Fifty-seventh and Fifty-eighth streets, it seemed to discourage the public's use. According to Suzanne Stephens, pedestrians entering the atrium from Fifty-seventh Street were forced to "descend 12 steps (six feet) to the main lobby then go up again before coming out at grade." Furthermore, she said, "the passageway jogs enough so that the route is hardly direct." Moreover, the very choice of finishing materials and details made the public feel unwelcome: "As attention-riveting as the entrance is, its design concomitantly gives off signs of a self-contained world within, not immediately perceptible to the unknowing public. The dark granite walls of the atrium and the reflectivity of the glass doors make it well nigh impossible to peer inside; the canvas awnings further cut down on the visibility of the interior (and limit the amount of natural light entering the atrium)."[18]

The Galleria's most celebrated feature was not its atrium, however, but the four-story penthouse commissioned by Stewart Mott, an heir to a fortune made in General Motors and an idealistic philanthropist who proposed to live and work atop the building as well as to grow his own food on the 7,500 square feet of terraces that were part of the suite. Mott was already established as Manhattan's leading farmer, having converted much of the rooftop of 800 Park Avenue, where he lived, into a small livestock and crop-producing farm; his activities evoked the ire of his fellow co-op owners, who took him to court.[19] The new penthouse, intended as the ultimate in self-sufficient urban living, as well as an educational model, was designed by Specter and his associate Gerald Jonas as a highly articulated composition of concrete-framed, mostly glazed volumes enclosing 10,000 square feet of space that would permit Mott to live heliotropically, rising in the morning to the sun in the East Solarium and watching it set in the evening from a desk facing west. The project got out of hand, however, and in 1975, Mott,

a thirty-eight-year-old bachelor, abandoned it, amid disputes over the purchase price and change orders brought on during construction. The building itself, caught in the city's severe economic downturn of 1973–74, went bankrupt in 1976 and the project was sold to the real estate subsidiary of Morgan Guaranty Trust, which successfully marketed the apartments when the city rebounded.

While Fifty-seventh Street saw almost no office construction before 1961, the new zoning encouraged the construction of two major office buildings: Jack Brown's Squibb Building (1972), at 40 West Fifty-seventh Street, and Skidmore, Owings & Merrill's remarkably profiled and detailed 9 West Fifty-seventh Street, both of which threatened to alter the street's character as a luxury shopping area.[20] Begun in 1968 but not completed until 1974, 9 West Fifty-seventh Street occupied a 62,000-square-foot site that ran through to Fifty-eighth Street, incorporating the unused air rights over the Paris Theater and replacing among others the six-story loft building at 26 West Fifty-eighth Street that housed Paul Rudolph's spectacular architectural office (see chapter 6).[21] Designed by Gordon Bunshaft, 9 West was the most provocatively shaped skyscraper New York had ever seen. The swooping, tapered slab had north- and south-facing walls sheathed in gray-tinted glass and sloping inward from a wide base to a more slender top, and end walls sheathed in travertine, relieved by a broad vertical window band crisscrossed by exposed diagonal structural bracing. The structure itself was lifted on columns to form a false arcade behind which shops would be located. Two additional shopping levels were to be located below grade and connected to street level by escalators. The building was set back thirty-six feet from West Fifty-seventh Street on a travertine plaza and forty-nine feet behind a parklet along West Fifty-eighth Street, dramatically breaking with the street-defining building wall. Because it rose so high above its neighbors and broke free of the city's traditional urbanism, it was seen by many observers as an act of unbridled architectural arrogance.

Popularly described as a glass ski jump, 9 West was also referred to as one of the "bell-bottoms,"[22] together with Skidmore, Owings & Merrill's Grace Building (see "Forty-second Street," above). Bunshaft argued that his design was the result of a direct reading of the zoning code: it filled the zoning envelope yet avoided the conventional ziggurat massing of most buildings by smoothing out the setbacks into a continuous curve that followed the angle of the sky exposure plane. But, as the editors of Progressive Architecture argued shortly after the design was released, Bunshaft's solution was "facile," a demonstration of a "block-buster approach to architecture."[23] Using zoning as his justification, Bunshaft was in fact following a pattern that had its origins in the work of Corbusier-inspired Modernists of the 1930s and, more recently, in C. F. Murphy's First National Bank Building in Chicago, which was nearing completion as work on 9 West began.[24]

In his introduction to a compendium of SOM's work, Arthur Drexler, while not defending the building, did much to explain it:

9 West 57th Street is controversial . . . not because it is tall but because it does not rise straight up from the street (as architects have taught everyone to expect). Ostensibly the result of interpreting the zoning envelope to avoid setbacks, without trading off too much ground area for a "plaza," the building pitches back in a sweeping curve . . . and then rises vertically. This disrupts the continuity of the street and leaves the sides of adjacent buildings exposed; their intersection with the curved glass plane is politely described as unfortunate.

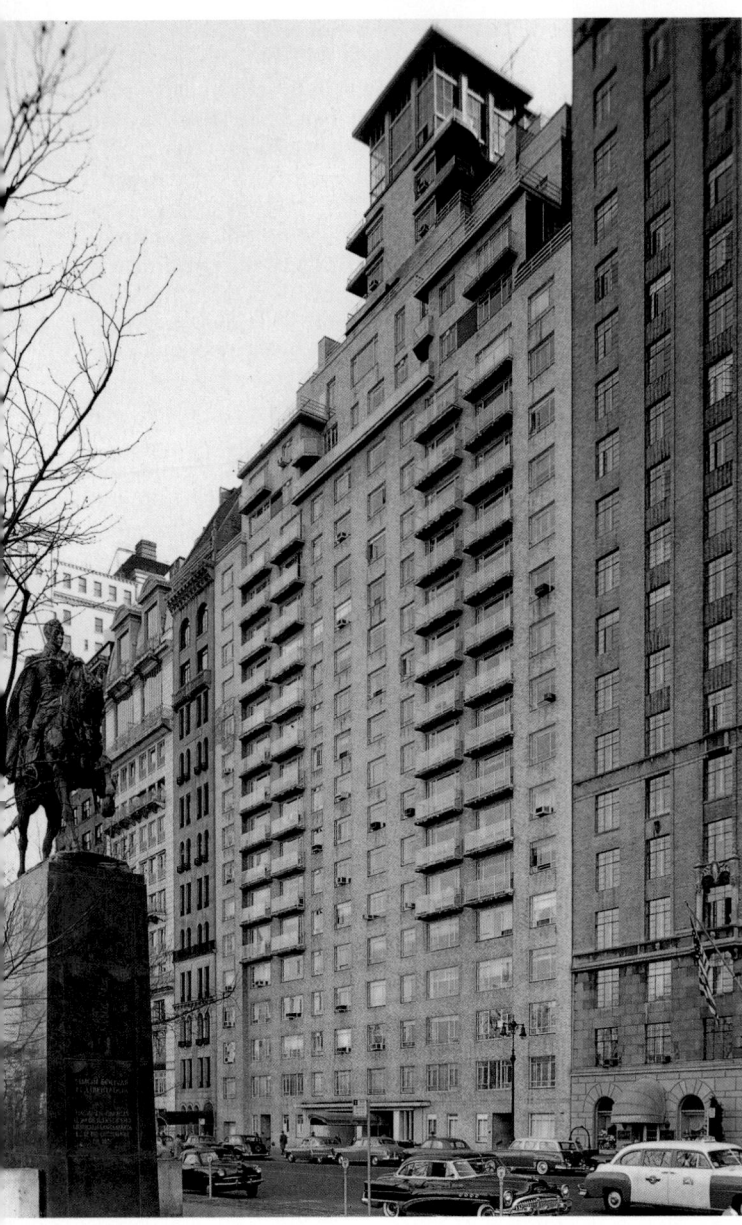

40 Central Park South, between Fifth and Sixth avenues. Mayer &
Whittlesey, 1941. View to the southeast. OMH

Drexler praised the building's entrance, where "the bottom of
the glass wall is terminated by an enormous trough extending
across the full width of the building, carrying off rain water
and at the same time providing a generous and explicit . . .
canopy. . . . Perhaps it is just this contrast, between the agreeable scale at street level and the glass ski-jump looming overhead, that disturbs critics more than the conjunction with
buildings on either side." Drexler noted that, regardless of its
critical reception, the public was quite positive about the
building: "The layman's response is disarmingly contrary to
learned opinion. Indeed this building quite literally stops people in the street; the immense curved glass wall is an exhilarating spectacle, not as architecture but as urban theater, as
fascinating as a fountain."[25]

The reaction to the building among the city's leading architects was varied. Wallace K. Harrison felt that "the sloping wall
comes very naturally—it gives a smooth line that appears to give
added height by disappearing perspective."[26] Henry Cobb, the
partner in I. M. Pei's firm who specialized in the design of tall office buildings, and who had experimented with a slope-walled
approach in his design for the New York Stock Exchange (see
chapter 3), which served as another influence on Bunshaft, contended that "tapered buildings have a very strong, hostile and
aggressive visual impact in the psychological sense and architects should consider the feelings of the man in the street."[27]
Jaquelin Robertson was a particularly outspoken critic of the
bell-bottom approach: "The rather odd knife-shape of the slope
leaves horrible scars on the face of the party walls of the adjoining building."[28]

In 1974, when Robertson was a member of the Fifth Avenue Association's biennial architectural awards jury, he helped
turn their report into a criticism of the building and its urban impact. The report compared 9 West unfavorably to Jack Brown's
aesthetically banal Squibb Building, diagonally across the street,
which had a tall midblock arcade, respected the street wall and
featured, instead of empty plazas, a two-story-high base filled
with shops.[29] When Sheldon Solow, developer of 9 West, was
informed by the Fifth Avenue Association that his building had
"urban bad manners," he replied that it "may have bad manners
but it has good foresight," explaining: "In twenty years that
whole block will be developed at this scale and I think my building will set the standard."[30]

Ada Louise Huxtable saw 9 West as a harbinger of a negative trend at the Skidmore firm:

> Something has gone wrong at SOM, and to say so is a little like
> attacking the pope. But what professionals are saying in pri-
> vate, and what should be aired in public, is that there has been
> an evolution of design needs and philosophy that has some-
> how passed the firm right by. SOM's consistently quality-con-
> scious buildings are also the increasing source of a persistent,
> monumental form of environmental abuse that is a growing
> cause of critical concern. I think, personally, that it is a simple
> case of hardening of the arteries of architectural ideas. The less
> kind call it arrogance; the more tolerant see it as an inability to
> respond to changing perceptions of urban experience. But the
> basic fact is that the firm's practitioners are singlemindedly in-
> tent on the building as a monument, or as a splendid piece of
> technology, with near-total blindness to its environmental side
> effects, which are often disastrous.[31]

Despite its critical reception, 9 West was a brilliant real estate success, with Avon Products agreeing to lease 500,000 of its
1.5 million square feet of office space before construction began.
But the retail spaces were not so successful: because the area

504

proposed for shops was set so far back from the street, it did not attract retailers; nor did the below-grade areas, which had been intended for dealers in antiques and art, as well as a restaurant. Even Solow realized that the plaza created too much open space, and to ameliorate the situation he retained the graphic designer Ivan Chermayeff, who had designed the optically dazzling graphics for the building's construction fence, to create a sculpture in the form of a ten-foot-high, five-foot-wide bright red-orange number 9.

If Fifty-seventh Street was the Plaza district's Faubourg Saint-Honoré, then Central Park South, with its cliff of elegant apartment houses and hotels facing north to the park, was its Gold Coast. First developed in the 1870s and 1880s, Central Park South was redeveloped beginning in the late 1920s when the so-called Spanish Flats (Hubert, Pirsson & Company, 1882) were demolished to make way for York & Sawyer's New York Athletic Club, completed in 1930.[32] Although the Plaza Hotel had anchored the street's eastern end since 1907, there was no imposing western terminus until 1941, when Mayer & Whittlesey's 240 Central Park South was completed.[33]

Mayer & Whittlesey's twenty-two-story 40 Central Park South (1941), similar to number 240, stood on the site of the Dalhousie (1884), a pioneering apartment house.[34] Where 240 Central Park South occupied a spacious if geometrically complex through-block corner site, number 40, which also ran through to Fifty-eighth Street, was built in the middle of the block a bit west of the Plaza Hotel. The development in fact consisted of two buildings, one facing Central Park and one facing Fifty-eighth Street, with a garden between the two. The south-facing building was built as a comparatively low, eleven-story structure to protect the view and light for the rear-facing apartments in its companion. As at 240 Central Park South, the windows were very large; the *New York Times* described them as "picture windows," a phrase increasingly associated with suburban houses.[35] Forty Central Park South consisted of small apartments, although many had fireplaces in their living rooms, and extensive hotel services were provided. The upper floors, where zoning prescribed setbacks, consisted of penthouse-type apartments that piled up to the building's crowning feature, a glass-enclosed elevator penthouse. Together with the extensively glazed lobby and the simple vocabulary of gray brick and white-painted steel sash, the penthouse gave the design a sense of the restrained, nonpolemical Modernism that distinguished not only 240 Central Park South but also Wallace K. Harrison and J. André Fouilhoux's style-setting Rockefeller Apartments of 1936.[36]

In 1954 Mayer & Whittlesey, now joined in partnership with M. Milton Glass, designed 220 Central Park South for a site that also ran through to Fifty-eighth Street.[37] Replacing three nineteenth-century rowhouses and an apartment building, all built by the Appleby family, number 220 had as its immediate neighbor to the west Charles Buckham's Gainsborough Studios (1908), one of the most distinguished examples of the "artist's studio" apartment house type that flourished before the First World War.[38] Unfortunately, neither the character of its neighbor nor the previous efforts of Mayer & Whittlesey influenced the design. The twenty-story building had coarsely detailed rows of double-hung aluminum windows set in white brick, corner balconies and a blocky elevator penthouse; a similarly dismal building faced Fifty-eighth Street and was separated from its companion by a garden. The setback base of the building on Central Park South compromised the street wall that was so critical to the framing of the park.

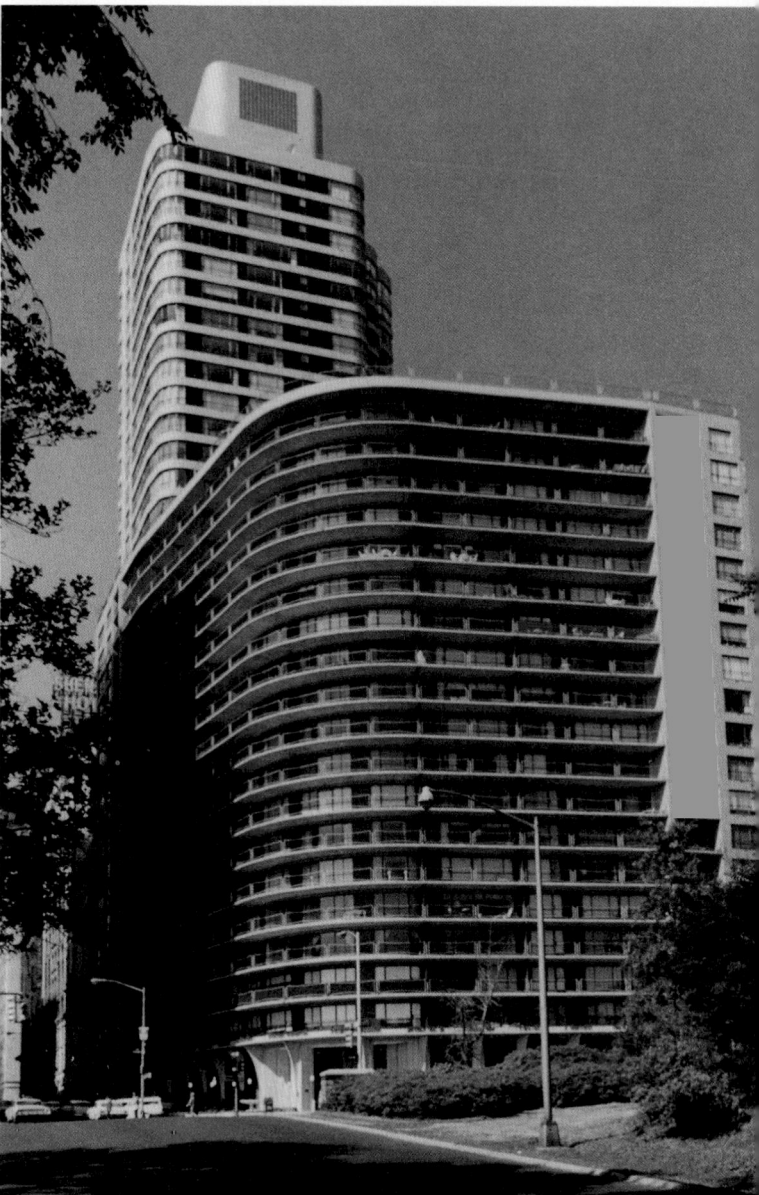

200 Central Park South, southwest corner of Seventh Avenue. Wechsler & Schimenti, 1964. View to the southwest. BS

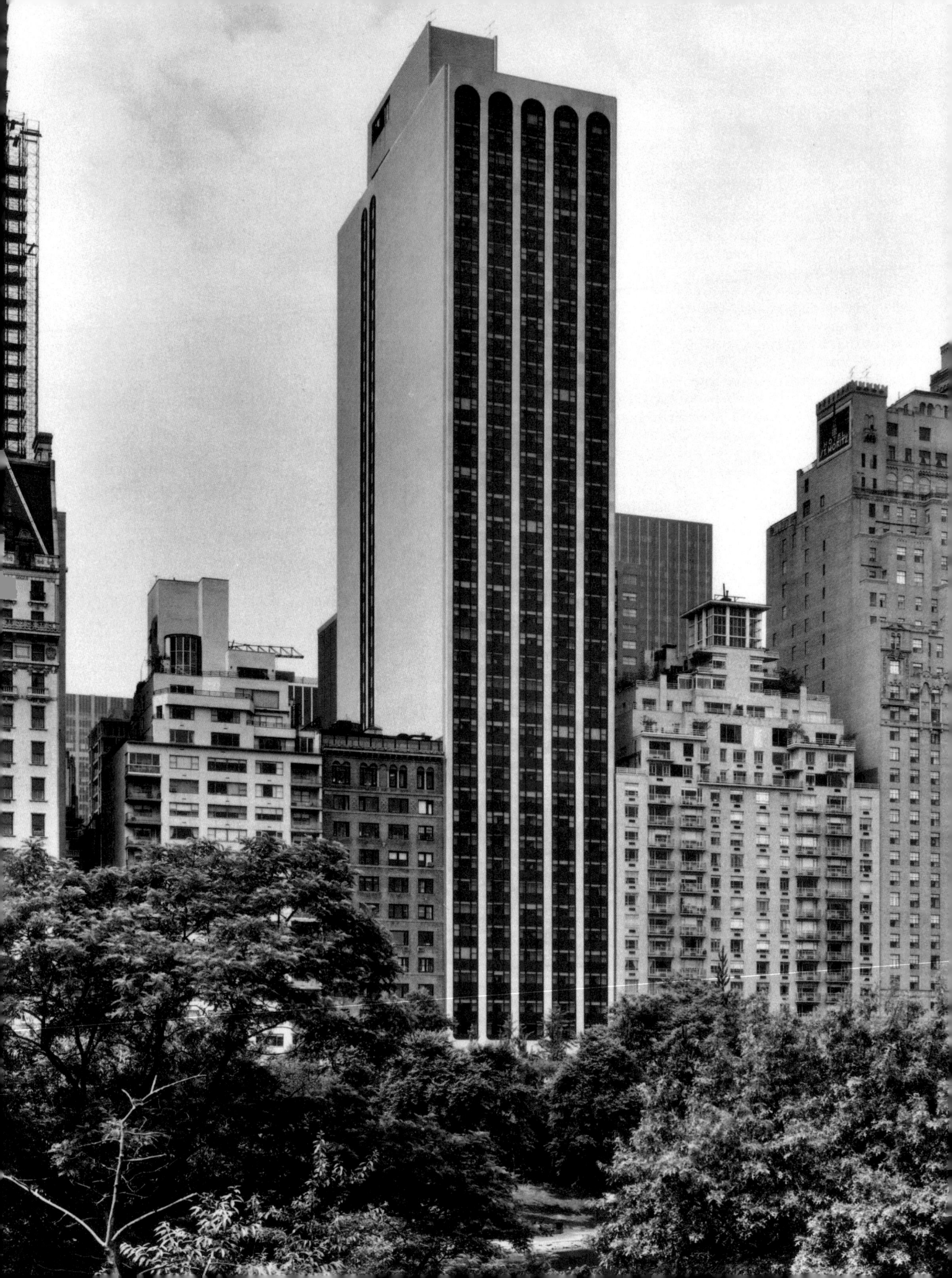

By 1961 the value of a Central Park address had soared, and four buildings were reported in planning or construction for Central Park South, which was described in the *New York Times* as "Luxury Lane," with "more doormen, limousines and poodles per square foot than any other part of the City."[39] Philip Birnbaum's 24 Central Park South, a rather narrow infill building cheek by jowl with the Plaza Hotel, contained a five-room duplex penthouse among its thirty-seven apartments.[40] With its white-glazed-brick facade rising from a black-granite base, it was noticeable if not notable. Further west, at 116, Zareh Sourian designed an eighteen-story white-brick building filling the astonishingly narrow twenty-five-foot frontage on the park and a thirteen-story, 116-foot-wide building to the rear along Fifty-eighth Street.[41]

On the southwest corner of Seventh Avenue, a small apartment house and a number of brownstones were torn down to make way for Wechsler & Schimenti's 200 Central Park South (1964), which abandoned the synthesis of traditional urbanism and Modernist architecture exemplified by the work of Mayer & Whittlesey in favor of a kind of aggressive, self-referential Modernism that had hitherto been largely absent from Manhattan.[42] With its 308 apartments, 200 Central Park South consisted of a bold mass set back forty feet from the intersection and sweeping around the corner from Central Park South to Seventh Avenue with a 225-foot-long, twenty-one-story stack of continuously curving balconied apartments supporting a fourteen-story tower. To complement the sweeping curve, which increased the number of park-facing apartments in the building's base, a "plazetta" was created at the corner entrance—essentially a tiny landscaped taxi drop-off of a type virtually unknown in New York apartment house design, where corners had traditionally been filled with solid building. Shocking though the building's shape was, so reminiscent of Morris Lapidus's Fontainebleau Hotel (1954) in Miami, Florida, it had its admirers.[43] In 1979 Paul Goldberger praised its "swooping curve," saying it was "not a bad way at all for a large avenue to meet Central Park."[44] The same architects' twenty-two-story 210 Central Park South (1968), which replaced four brownstones after a bitter battle, also featured continuous balconies, but the use of dark brown brick to clad the spandrels of the first three stories, and the elimination of superfluous details, gave the design a bit more dignity.[45]

Amid the boom in office buildings in the Plaza district in the late 1960s, and in the face of the loss of the Savoy-Plaza Hotel (see below), the City Planning Commission took steps to preserve the status of Central Park South as a hotel district.[46] Prevented from constructing an office building by the commission's rezoning of the immediate area, the real estate mogul Harry Helmsley decided instead to construct the Park Lane Hotel, a forty-six-story, 640-room tower on a block-deep site on Central Park South between Fifth and Sixth avenues.[47] The project required the demolition of a twelve-story and a fifteen-story apartment house as well as five-story commercial and residential buildings. Helmsley's hotel (Emery Roth & Sons, 1971), the tallest building on Central Park South, constituted a forceful if banal flat-topped addition to the skyline. Its construction was a big financial gamble not only because of its $30 million budget but also because, instead of relying on convention-based business like the era's other skyscraper hotels, it pursued the affluent individual traveler.

The building was designed as a slab with travertine piers separating vertically arranged rows of windows, running nearly the full height of the principal facade to culminate in arches; at the bottom of the window bands were reversed arches. The hotel's principal entrance was on Central Park South, but there was also a porte cochere approached by a semicircular drive-

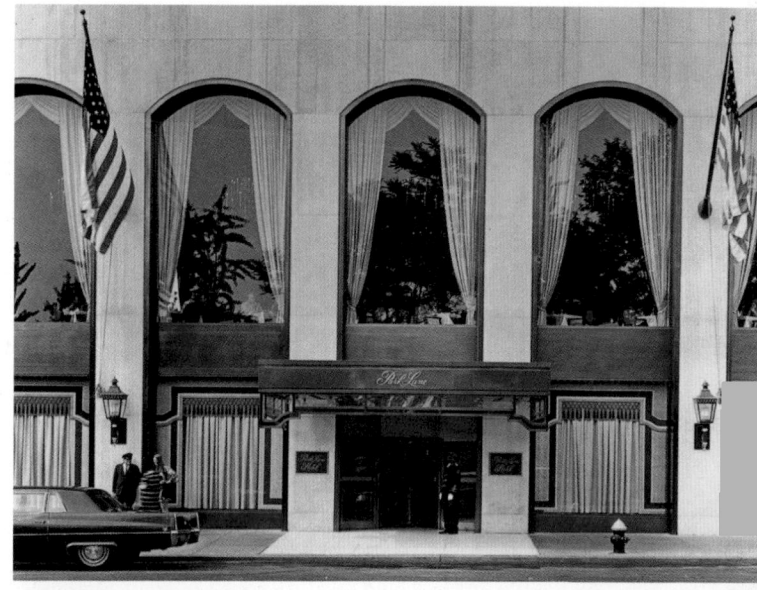

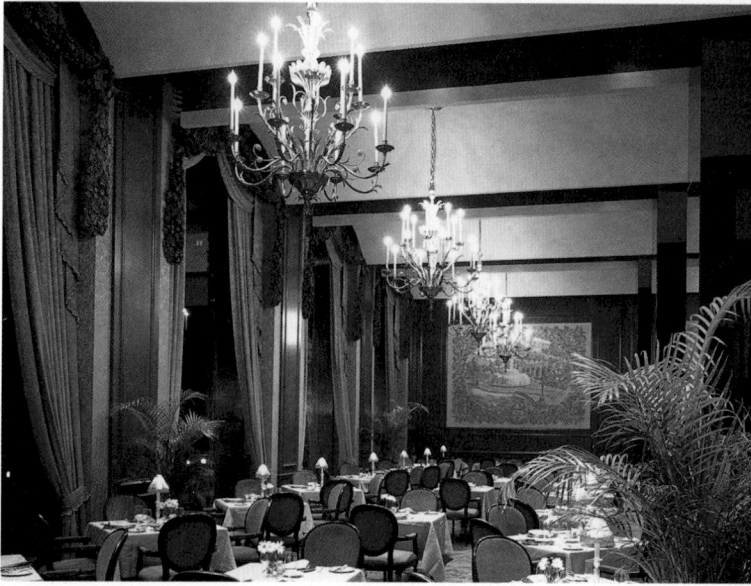

Left: Park Lane Hotel, 36 Central Park South, between Fifth and Sixth avenues. Emery Roth & Sons, 1971. View to the southwest showing 40 Central Park South (Mayer & Whittlesey, 1941) on the right. Wurts. MCNY

Top: Park Lane Hotel. Entrance. Wurts. MCNY

Bottom: Park Lane Hotel. Main dining room, designed by Tom Lee. Georges. BBB

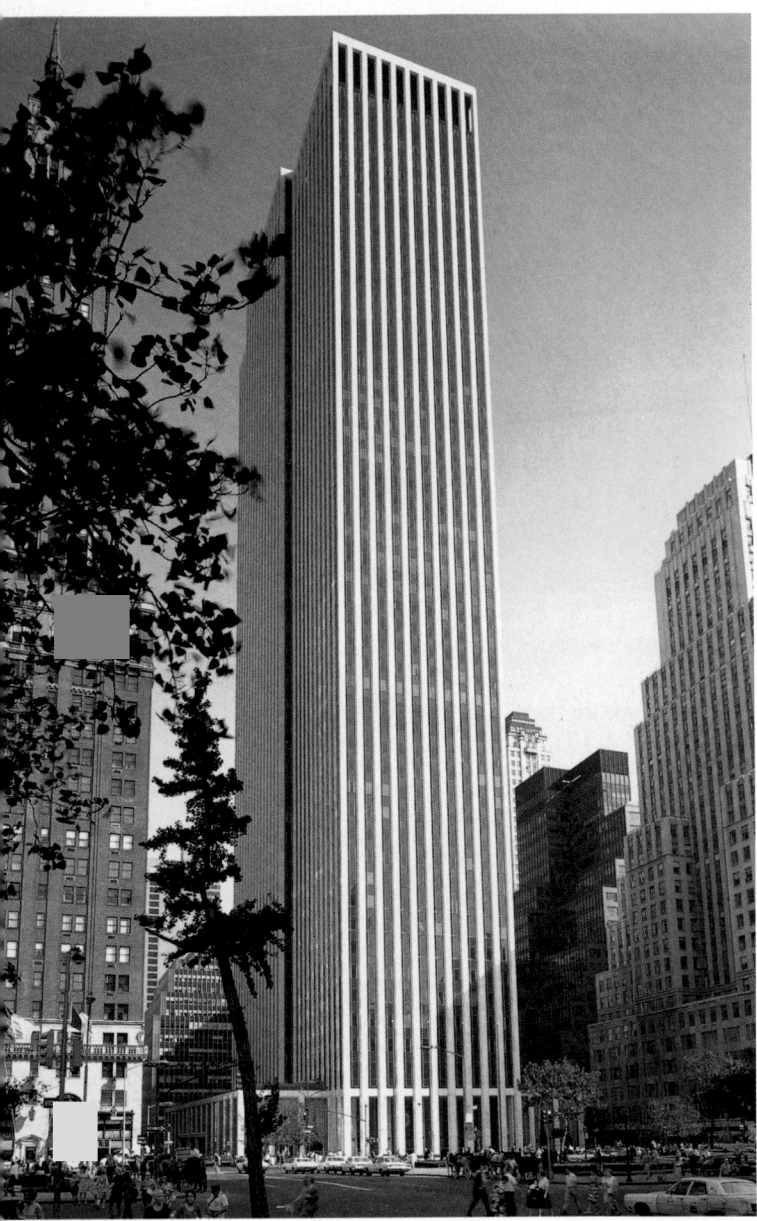

Above: General Motors Building, 767 Fifth Avenue, East Fifty-eighth to East Fifty-ninth Street. Edward Durell Stone in association with Emery Roth & Sons, 1968. View to the southeast. Stoller. ©ESTO

Right: View to the southeast from Central Park showing, from left to right: Hotel Pierre (Schultze & Weaver, 1930), Parc V (Emery Roth & Sons, 1963), Sherry-Netherland Hotel (Schultze & Weaver and Buchman & Kahn, 1926), General Motors Building and Squibb Building (Buchman & Kahn, 1930). Leeser. ERS

way on Fifty-eighth Street. Inside, the public rooms, designed by Tom Lee, an interior designer who specialized in hotels, struggled to marry the designer's taste for a lighthearted contemporary approach with the client's request for traditional decor. Lee, who had designed for the stage, said that "designing a hotel is like producing a play," and his interiors for the Park Lane were infused with a sense of drama.[48] The lobby had marble floors and walls and nontraditional crystal chandeliers; some of the public areas featured carved valances fashioned after the designs of the English Baroque woodcarver Grinling Gibbons. The hotel's main dining room, on the second floor overlooking Central Park, was distinguished by nineteen-foot-high ceilings and walls papered with a design based on decorative motifs used in the sixteenth-century royal chateau at Fontainebleau.

At the heart of the Plaza district lay the Grand Army Plaza, at Fifth Avenue and Fifty-ninth Street, which had attained its present form in 1916 (Pulitzer Fountain, Carrère & Hastings; sculpture by Karl Bitter).[49] With the exception of McKim, Mead & White's Metropolitan Club (1894), the plaza-facing landmarks of the nineteenth century had almost all been torn down or remodeled.[50] The ensemble that had taken their place, beginning with Henry J. Hardenbergh's Plaza Hotel (1907) and including Schultze & Weaver and Buchman & Kahn's Sherry-Netherland Hotel (1926), McKim, Mead & White's Savoy-Plaza Hotel (1927) and Schultze & Weaver's Hotel Pierre (1930), was a remarkable one.[51] The announcement in 1964 that the Savoy-Plaza would be demolished to make way for an office building, coming on the heels of the decision to demolish Pennsylvania Station, sent shock waves through the city (see chapter 16). Although the proposed new building, the General Motors (GM) Building (1964–68), 767 Fifth Avenue, was impressive as an exemplar of the direction America's older generation of Modernists were taking in their attempt to enrich the vocabulary of contemporary architecture, it did not outweigh the concerns many had for the preservation of the plaza's integrity as a great urban place.[52]

The fifty-story building, designed by Edward Durell Stone in association with Emery Roth & Sons, occupied the full block between Fifty-eighth and Fifty-ninth streets, Fifth and Madison avenues, replacing, in addition to the Savoy-Plaza, the four-story Emmet Arcade (in which was located a notable Longchamps restaurant),[53] at the southwest corner of Madison Avenue and Fifty-ninth Street, and the fifteen-story Madison Hotel (1919), at the northwest corner of Madison Avenue and Fifty-eighth Street. Since 1927 General Motors, the building's prime tenant, had been leasing space in a building bearing its name at 1775 Broadway,[54] but the company had come to regard the Broadway location as shabby. The English real estate wheeler-dealer Max Rayne, head of London Merchant Securities Ltd., the Savoy-Plaza's new owner, believed that the city's hotel market would drastically soften after the closing of the World's Fair, and felt the moment was opportune for the hotel's destruction.

Although Stone had prepared schematic designs for skyscrapers, including, in the late 1950s, preliminary plans for two versions of a proposed twenty-nine-story tower for an undisclosed site on Third Avenue and, earlier, projects for Sixth Avenue and the theater district, he had never built one.[55] In December 1964 Stone presented his design, which called for a vertically banded, marble-clad slab emerging from a one-story, site-filling podium and embraced by twenty-one-foot-high wings along the side streets. The slab itself was to rise for a sheer leap of forty-eight stories, vastly outstripping its near neighbors in mass and height. It would also be much brighter: clad in white marble, it would emphasize "the salient characteristic of a skyscraper . . .

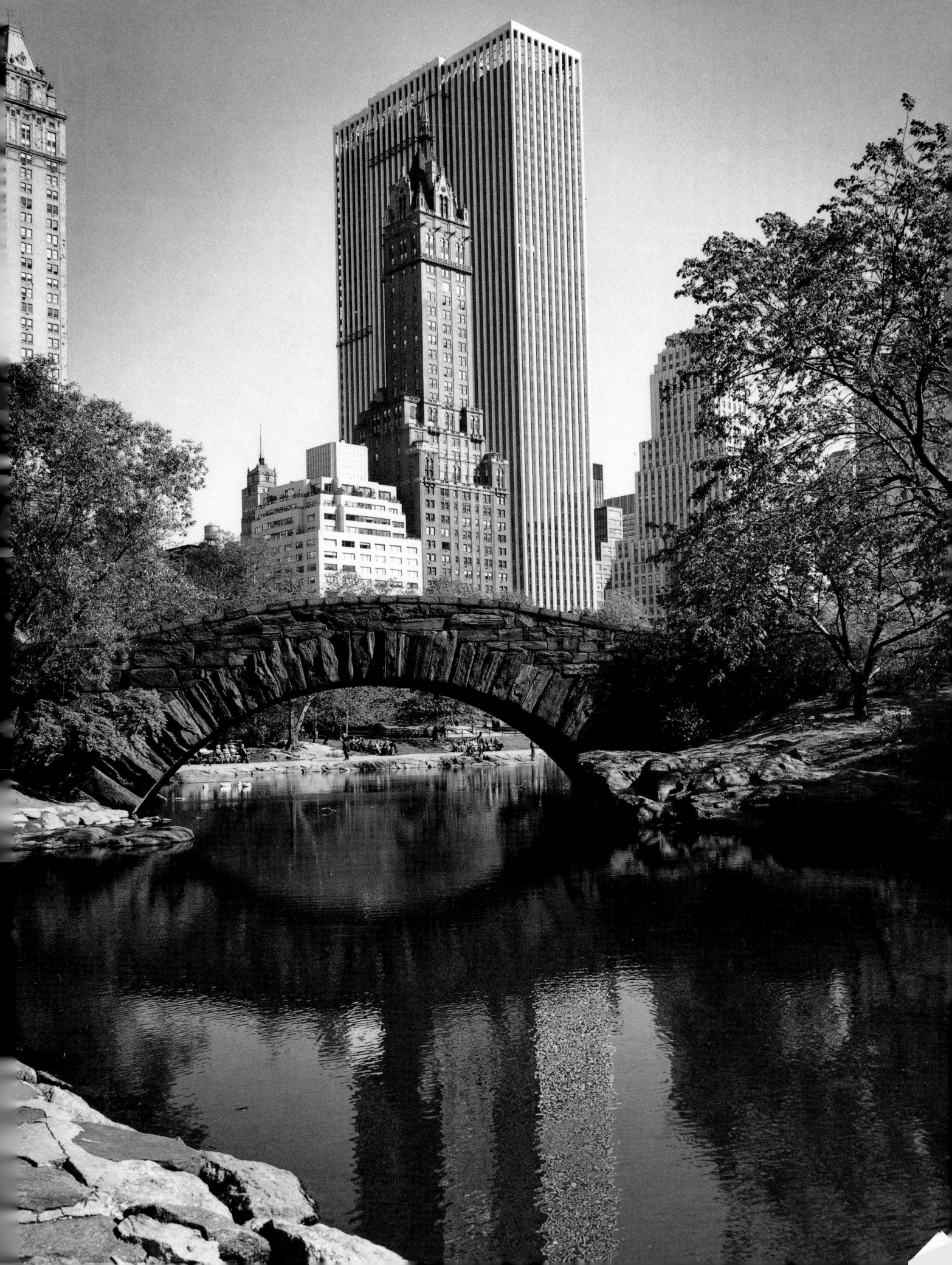

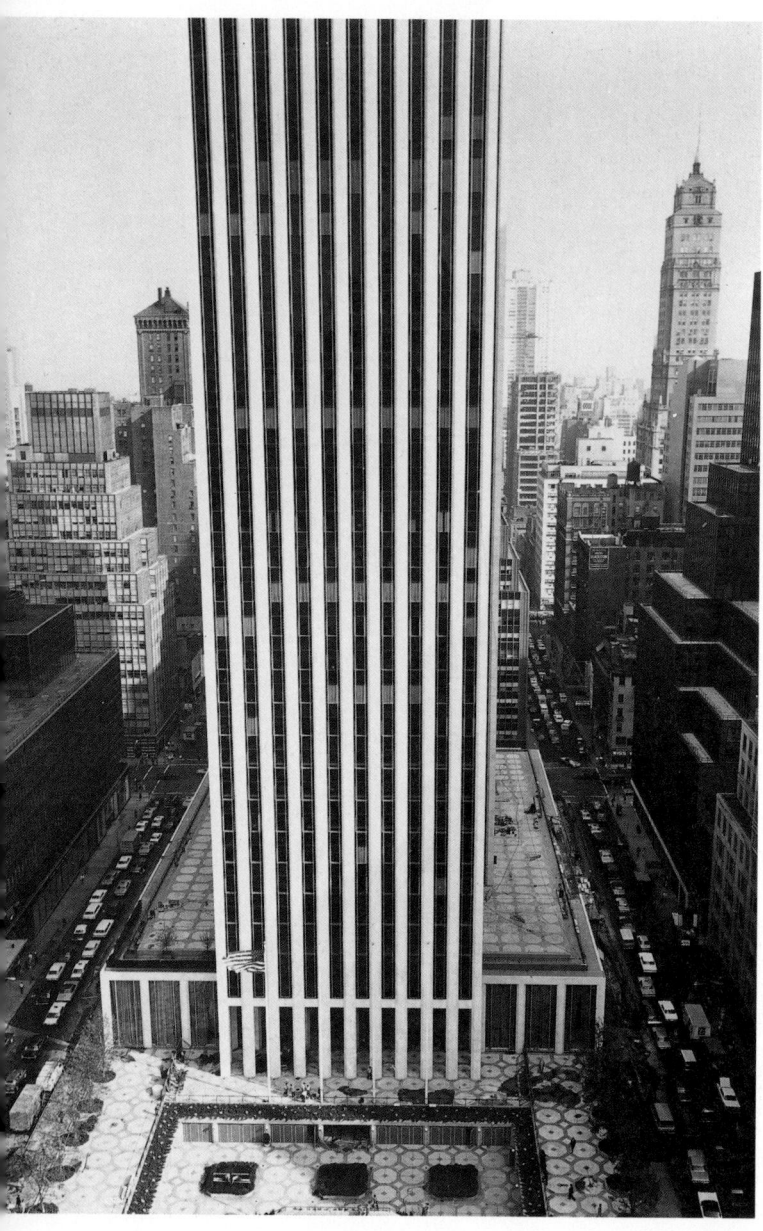

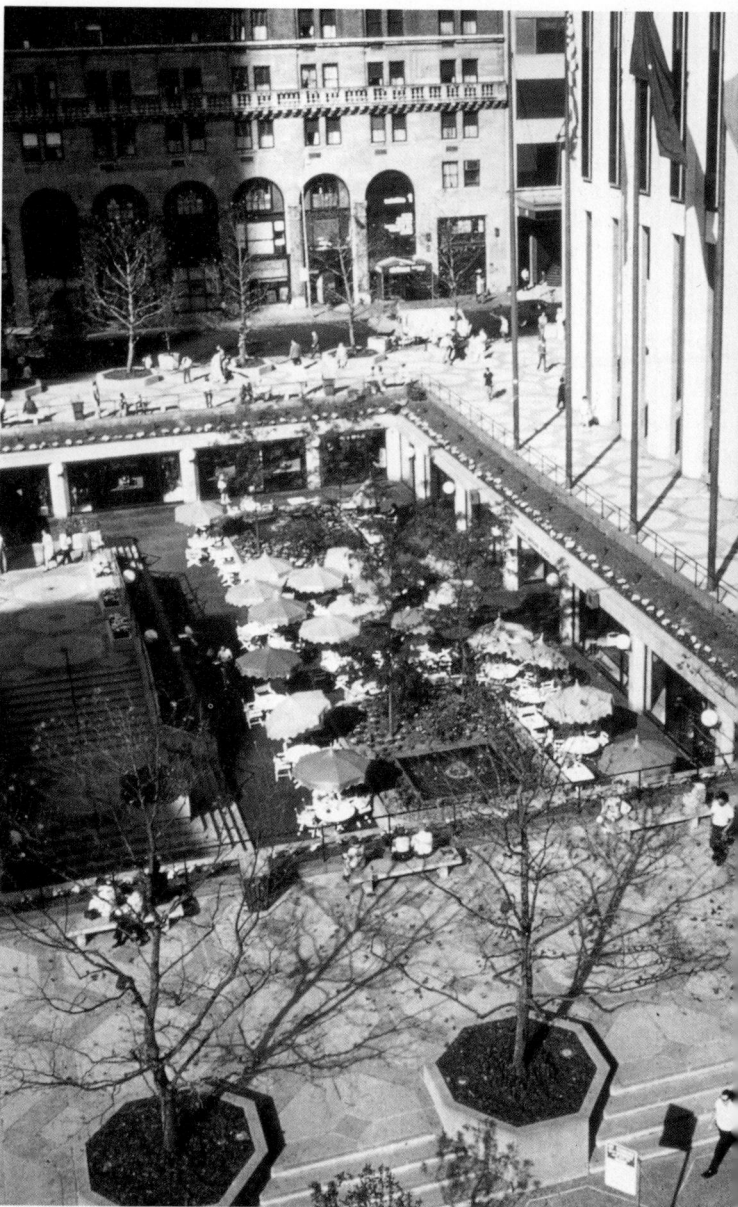

General Motors Building, 767 Fifth Avenue, East Fifty-eighth to East Fifty-ninth Street. Edward Durell Stone in association with Emery Roth & Sons, 1968. View to the east. EDS

General Motors Building. View to the northeast of sunken plaza. EDS verticality," to become a dominant player on the Central Park skyline.[56] Stone said that he set out "to create a building that will salute the skyline and enhance one of New York's finest neighborhoods," a building with "the quality of permanence . . . designed for the future as well as the present and the past."[57] Stone believed that white marble was contextually appropriate to the surrounding buildings, many of which, he pointed out, were clad in marble at least on their lower floors. Moreover, he hoped it would "start off a new trend toward buildings that look more permanent and have a light color." Probably thinking of the new building's Madison Avenue neighbor, CIT (see above), Stone went on to say that "those black buildings that have been modish in the past look perfectly horrible."[58]

From the first, Stone was put on the defensive. Not only had there been a lot of bad publicity about the demolition of the Savoy-Plaza, but a committee of three architects had been named by the Fifth Avenue Association to confer with the developers over the building's "conformity with the character and dignity" of the area. For whatever reason, they were not consulted prior to the public announcement of Stone's design. Ada Louise Huxtable, after an interview with Stone, observed that though quality was "the key to the design," it was "being held within a tight commercial framework." She was encouraged by early study models for the new building; the scheme of alternating vertical bands of marble and bay windows suggested to her "a color, scale, plasticity and contemporaneity that could be a definite addition to the area." Huxtable argued that "the straight-sided new tower could be an excellent backdrop for the earlier, more nostalgic" Sherry-Netherland skyscraper, which it would dwarf.[59]

The editors of *Progressive Architecture* were far less optimistic about Stone's proposal. They compared its arrival opposite the Plaza Hotel to that of a "*nouveau riche* nephew come to visit his genteel relations" and said that the building would "drastically alter one of the city's few areas of Old World charm." They were particularly critical of its lack of contextuality: "In a group of sedate older buildings, it is liable to be as conspicuous as Gulliver in Lilliput." Its "statement of vertical strength," they pointed out, was inappropriate "in an area whose major statement is not strength but dignity. Its crispness and rigidity are more suited to the corporate parade field of Park Avenue than the formality of the 'parlor' where it finds itself."[60]

By early 1965 the design had been refined and the one-story podium had given way to a 200-by-100-foot plaza along Fifth Avenue, an outdoor room slightly larger than Grand Army Plaza itself, lined with shops on three sides and sunk twelve feet below grade in emulation of the sunken court at the heart of Rockefeller Center. The building was intended to make its mark as a prestigious corporate symbol, but with no sacrifice to bottom-line economics. As Cecilia Benattar, a spokesman for the owners put it, "We wanted to carry out the spirit of the new zoning concept. We provided the maximum amount of open space encouraged by the zoning law and this earned us the right to take the maximum amount of interior space allowed."[61]

Huxtable was now extremely critical of the design she had earlier praised: "Its contribution to the rape of the [Grand Army] plaza is a clear demonstration of how the new zoning, like the old zoning, is to be used exclusively as a tool for profit." She went on to describe the folly of the building's plaza, its most egregious urban design failure: "To achieve the most bulk possible under the new law, it will have an open plaza facing the existing plaza. Ever heard of a redundant plaza? This is it. Something like having two heads. Not only does it provide extra

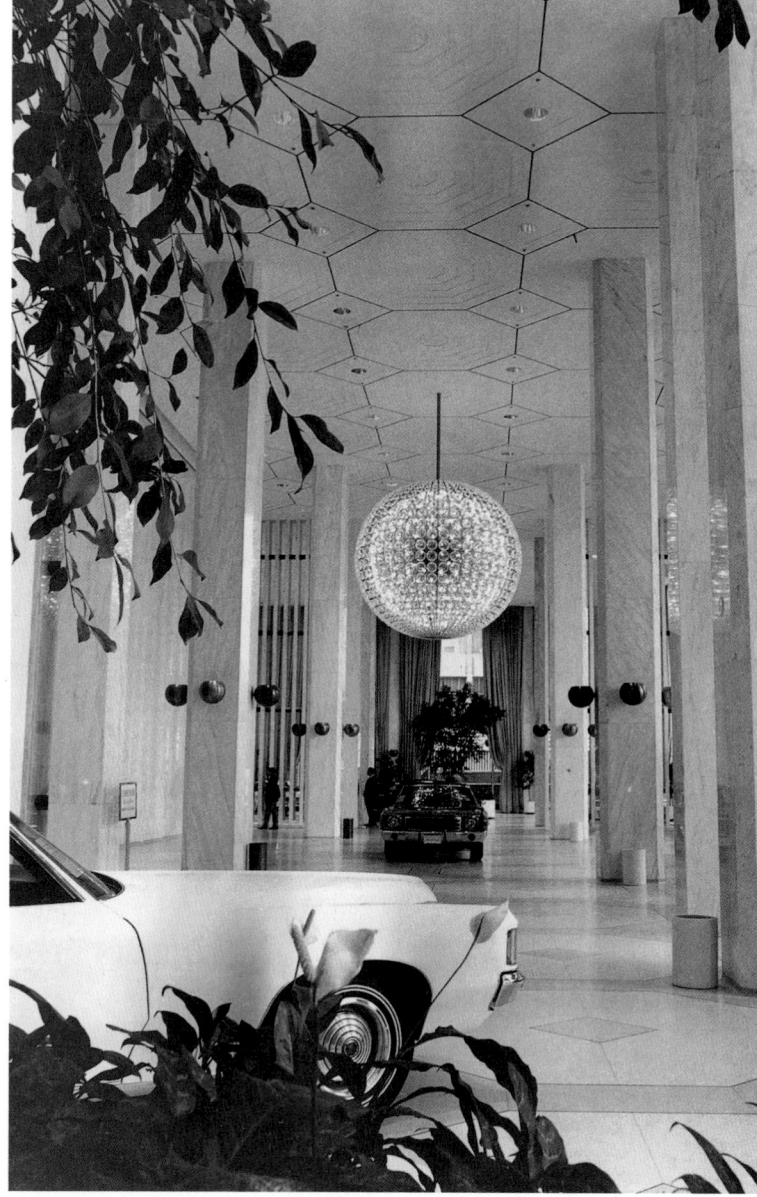

General Motors Building. Exhibition rooms designed by LeRoy Kiefer. EDS

511

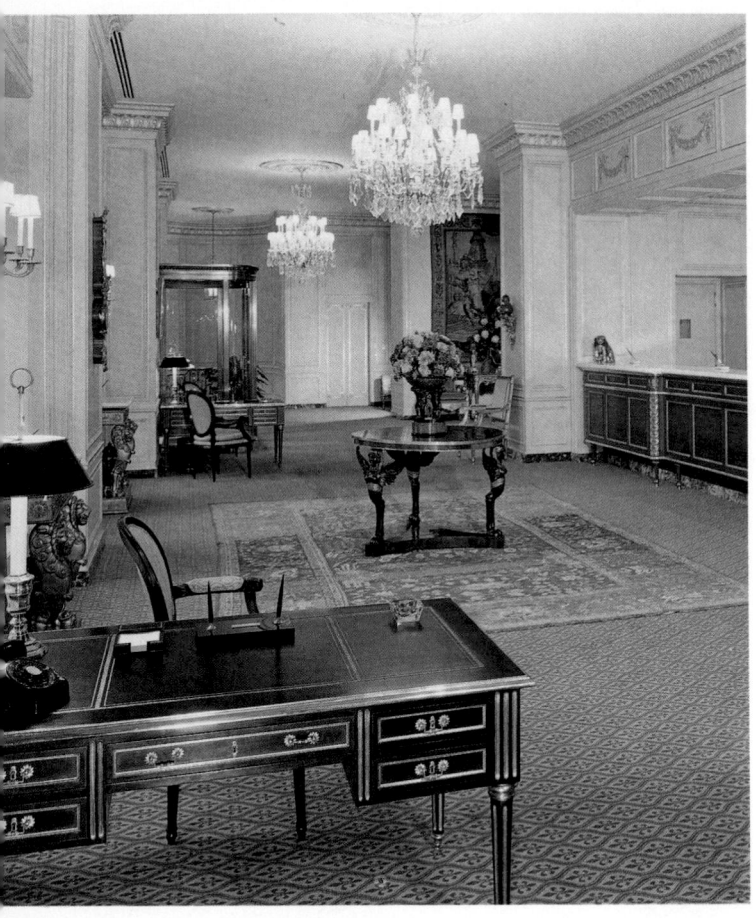

Above: La Banque Continentale, 785 Fifth Avenue, between East Fifty-ninth and East Sixtieth streets. Eggers & Higgins and Ellen Lehman McCluskey, 1963. Main banking floor. EMC

Top right: Proposed design for 800 Fifth Avenue, between East Sixty-first and East Sixty-second streets. Ulrich Franzen, 1976. Model. View to the northeast. Freedman. UF

Bottom right: 800 Fifth Avenue. Ulrich Franzen, 1978. View to the northeast. Aaron. ©ESTO

space at the one spot in New York where it is not needed, but it breaks the building line where enclosure is desirable." Nor was Huxtable pleased by the piazzetta formed along Madison Avenue, because, she said, the avenue's "best feature, urbanistically, is the intimacy of its small, closely connected, luxurious specialty shops that unroll the treasures of the world for the pedestrian. Why destroy that scale and continuity?"[62]

The building's completion in late 1968 brought a fresh round of commentary. Peter Blake pointed a finger not at the building's economic underpinnings but its banal design: "Seagram built its skyscraper under the same system and the same speculation; and Seagram built a bronze Rolls-Royce. General Motors . . . built a high-rise Schrafft's."[63] Huxtable continued to find fault with the building: "Behind the marble cladding and bay windows, architecture, like the proverbial thin man in the fat man's body, is signaling wildly to get out." She also lambasted the "small-town department store and styling section décor" of the building's public interior spaces, especially its grandly proportioned exhibition rooms, designed by LeRoy Kiefer of GM's Detroit styling staff, where the latest GM cars were displayed. She concluded her final assessment by saying: "General Motors has brought a new style and a new kind of abundance to Fifth Avenue. What it lacks, unfortunately, is class. It has the best address in town. It has not given the city its best building."[64] Though the critics had their way with it, four years after it opened, Stone was convinced that the public had the final—and approving—word: "There isn't a taxi driver in New York who won't say that the General Motors Building is the most beautiful thing in the city."[65]

In 1959, five years before the decision to tear down the Savoy-Plaza was announced, plans were formulated to demolish several other buildings facing the plaza to make way for a thirty-five-story office building designed by H. I. Feldman.[66] It would replace Henry J. Hardenbergh's Fifth Avenue Estates Building (1903); an apartment building at the southeast corner of Sixtieth Street and Fifth Avenue, and Jardine & Jardine's Park & Tilford Building (1884; Fifth Avenue facade remodeled 1905; Fifty-ninth Street frontage remodeled 1920), an L-shaped building with a Fifth Avenue frontage directly north of the Sherry-Netherland. The office building was not realized, but in 1963 the Parc V, 785 Fifth Avenue, an extremely bland apartment house with eighteen stories and a penthouse, designed by Emery Roth & Sons, was completed on the site.[67] On the building's ground floor, facing Fifth Avenue, the Franklin National Bank, a Nassau County–based institution, established a facility called La Banque Continentale catering to the superrich.[68] Designed by Eggers & Higgins, architects, and Ellen Lehman McCluskey, decorator, the bank's interior evoked an eighteenth-century private townhouse in Paris; the staff included a liveried footman.

Just north of the Grand Army Plaza, one last townhouse of the pre–World War II era remained: a rather dreary red brick Georgian mansion designed by R. S. Shapter in 1922 for Mr. and Mrs. Marcellus Hartley Dodge at 1 East Sixty-first Street. After the war Mrs. Dodge, who lived on an estate in Madison, New Jersey, kept the property because she liked to use the large side yard, which was protected from Fifth Avenue by a high brick wall, for her dogs when she came to town for business or shopping. While the house was dull, the structure and its garden created a remarkable ensemble with the much more distinguished Knickerbocker Club (Delano & Aldrich, 1914), at the northern end of the block.[69] After Mrs. Dodge died in 1973, the house was torn down and replaced by a thirty-three-story apartment slab, 800 Fifth Avenue (1978).[70]

As originally proposed for the site, 800 Fifth Avenue was to take advantage of bonuses recently made available to park-fronting property owners, awarded not for the inclusion of plazas but for financial contributions to the maintenance of Central Park. In order to facilitate the bonus application, the City Planning Commission urged Bernard Spitzer, the developer, to retain a design architect to rework the plans drawn by Max Schimenti, who had also worked with the developer on 200 Central Park South (see above). Spitzer chose Ulrich Franzen, who eventually presented a design he described as "a stern, proper bottom breaking into a 'joie de vivre' top."[71] It consisted of fourteen floors built up to the Fifth Avenue street wall and, set slightly back, a nineteen-story slab punctuated by bay windows and topped by an ornamental copper roof loosely suggesting the mansard roof of the Hotel Pierre, its immediate neighbor to the south. A low wing containing offices was proposed to run along Sixty-first Street, set back behind a small plaza.

Despite the support of the editors of the *New York Times*, Franzen's design was rejected on May 8, 1976, by Community Planning Board 8, which objected to its height, its midblock plaza and the use of brown brick for the facade instead of the limestone or light tan brick typically used along Fifth Avenue. By late June, Franzen had come up with a second proposal, which Paul Goldberger called an "impressive improvement over the old."[72] In this scheme, Franzen pushed the tower back twenty feet from the avenue and lined the base up with the street, treating it as a Classically inspired limestone screen wall that echoed the base of the Pierre and the total mass of the Knickerbocker Club. The east facade of 800 Fifth Avenue, which overlooked a still quite intimate, low-lying landscape of townhouses, featured boldly staggered ranks of balconies that were meant to complement the area's residential scale but did not quite succeed. In July the revised scheme was approved by the City Planning Commission, and demolition on the Dodge house was completed by February 1977, when construction on the new building began.

When the building was completed in late 1978, the first tenants were appalled by the shoddy workmanship inside, the low (8'2") ceilings, the inadequate ventilation for kitchens and a host of other details that belied its claims to luxury accommodation. Other observers, like Ada Louise Huxtable, were critical of its exterior. Reflecting on the process that led to the final design, she wrote:

> [Franzen's] first revised design was full of references to the surroundings so abstract that only the architect could know for sure. . . . The next version . . . was negotiated to death by the city and the community. The result is a pitiful compendium of watered-down mannerisms that are supposed to maintain the integrity of the avenue and relate to adjacent buildings, but speak more clearly of the inflation of costs and impoverishment of crafts in our own times. . . . If there is any achievement here, it is making the bland grotesque.[73]

In 1979 Paul Goldberger characterized the design as one that "rejects the modernist principle" of a building as a "pure object" and seeks an accommodation with the context, "at the price of consistency or even at the price of any rigid ideology at all." While Goldberger found this approach fine in theory, in reality the building was "so big that ideas and principles don't matter." Though he found the limestone front along Fifth Avenue handsome, "and a welcome attempt at craftsmanship in a day when putting a chandelier in the lobby is considered fancy apartment-house design," it was not enough to "offset the immense mass behind it."[74]

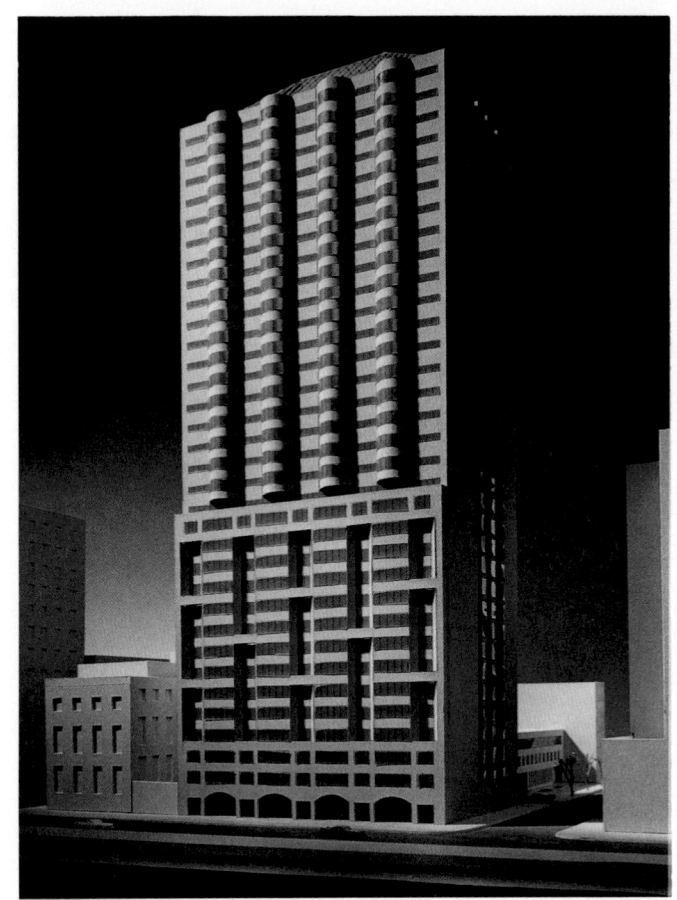

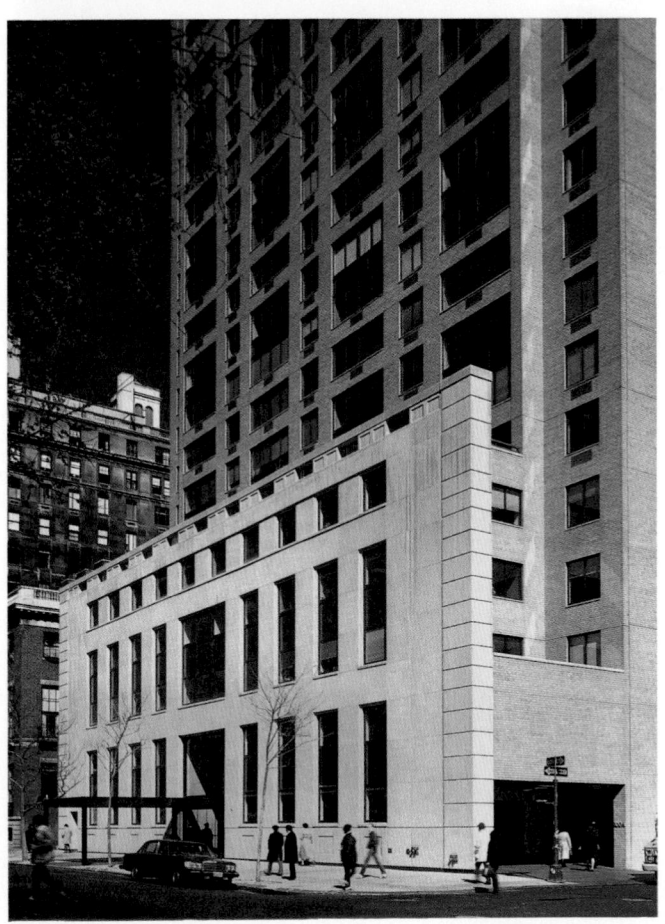

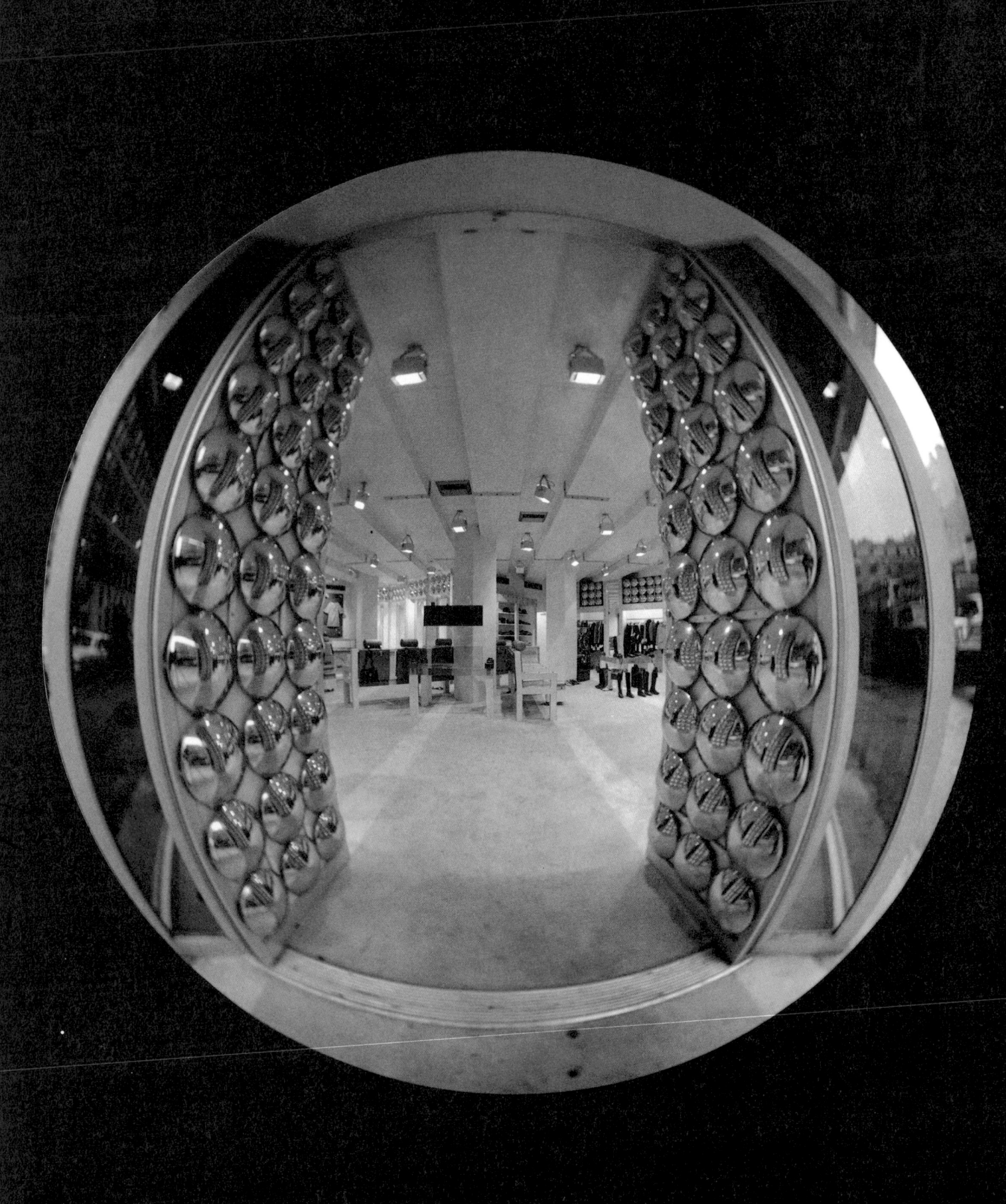

Chapter 6

Interiors

It is a myth, the city, the rooms and windows . . .
for anyone, everyone, a different myth.
—Truman Capote, 1950[1]

ART GALLERIES

The art gallery was perhaps the most interesting and problematic category of interior space to be systematically undertaken by Modernist architects. Because such architects often considered themselves artists, they frequently found themselves in conflict with painters, sculptors and collectors who, in seeking to surround their art with a near-sacred aura of self-referential individuality, were contemptuous of any effort to create a total environment of art and display.

On October 20, 1942, Solomon Guggenheim's niece Peggy opened Art of This Century, a gallery devoted to the most avant-garde examples of contemporary art.[1] Located in two former tailor shops at 30 West Fifty-seventh Street, existing townhouses that had been renovated by the firm of Gronenberg & Leuchtag in 1921, the gallery was designed by the Austrian émigré Frederick J. Kiesler. When he arrived in New York in 1926 Kiesler had been an exponent of De Stijl, but he went on to design, among other things, Cubist-inspired show windows for Saks Fifth Avenue, Surrealist-inspired stage sets for the Juilliard School of Music and the provocative Space House for the Modernage furniture company.[2]

Art of This Century was not quite an art gallery, not quite a museum. It displayed portions of Peggy Guggenheim's collection of painting and sculpture, but while the collection was growing it also provided an opportunity to showcase new artists, some of whom were not able to gain access to the commercial galleries. Guggenheim wanted to create, as she put it, "a research laboratory for new ideas," and said that the undertaking would serve its purpose "only if it succeeds in serving the future

instead of recording the past."[3] Even more striking than the art on display was the gallery space itself and the display techniques devised by Kiesler, whom Guggenheim asked to develop "some new method . . . for exhibiting paintings, sculpture, collages, and so-called objects."[4] Guggenheim, in a direct critique of the outrageously overscaled silver frames favored by her uncle Solomon's curator, Hilla Rebay, said that she felt frames were "wrong" because they "kill a picture."[5] Kiesler agreed:

> Today the framed painting on the wall has become a decorative cipher without life and meaning, or else, to the more susceptible observer, an object of interest existing in a world distinct from his. Its frame is at once symbol and agent of an artificial duality of "vision" and "reality," or "image" and "environment," a plastic barrier across which man looks from the world he inhabits to the alien world in which the work of art has its being. That barrier must be dissolved: the frame, today reduced to an arbitrary rigidity, must regain its architectural spatial significance.[6]

Art of This Century consisted of four rooms. The most conventional of these was the "painting library," a daylit room that contained a series of combination storage and display stands for small pictures, where visitors seated on folded stools made of wood and ultramarine canvas could study the art. As seen in Kiesler's published sketch, they may have anticipated Frank Lloyd Wright's proposed method of displaying art in her uncle's museum (see chapter 11).[7] In a second, tunnel-like room devoted to the Surrealists' work, Kiesler created concave plywood walls from which the unframed art projected on rods—actually sawed-off baseball bats—another display technique that would influence Wright in his work for the elder Guggenheim. The room's ceiling consisted of plywood panels pierced with holes and hung fifteen inches below the actual ceiling to allow for interchangeable lighting units. For the center of the room, Kiesler designed free-form plywood-sheathed shapes that could be used as seats, chaise longues or sculpture stands. The lighting scheme was also novel; it called for alternating the illumination of the two sides of the room for two minutes each, separated by a three-and-a-half-second pause of total darkness. Kiesler coordinated this pattern with sound effects that simulated the roar of an

Latinas, 769 Madison Avenue. Bill Hock, 1966. View through entrance. Reens. LR

515

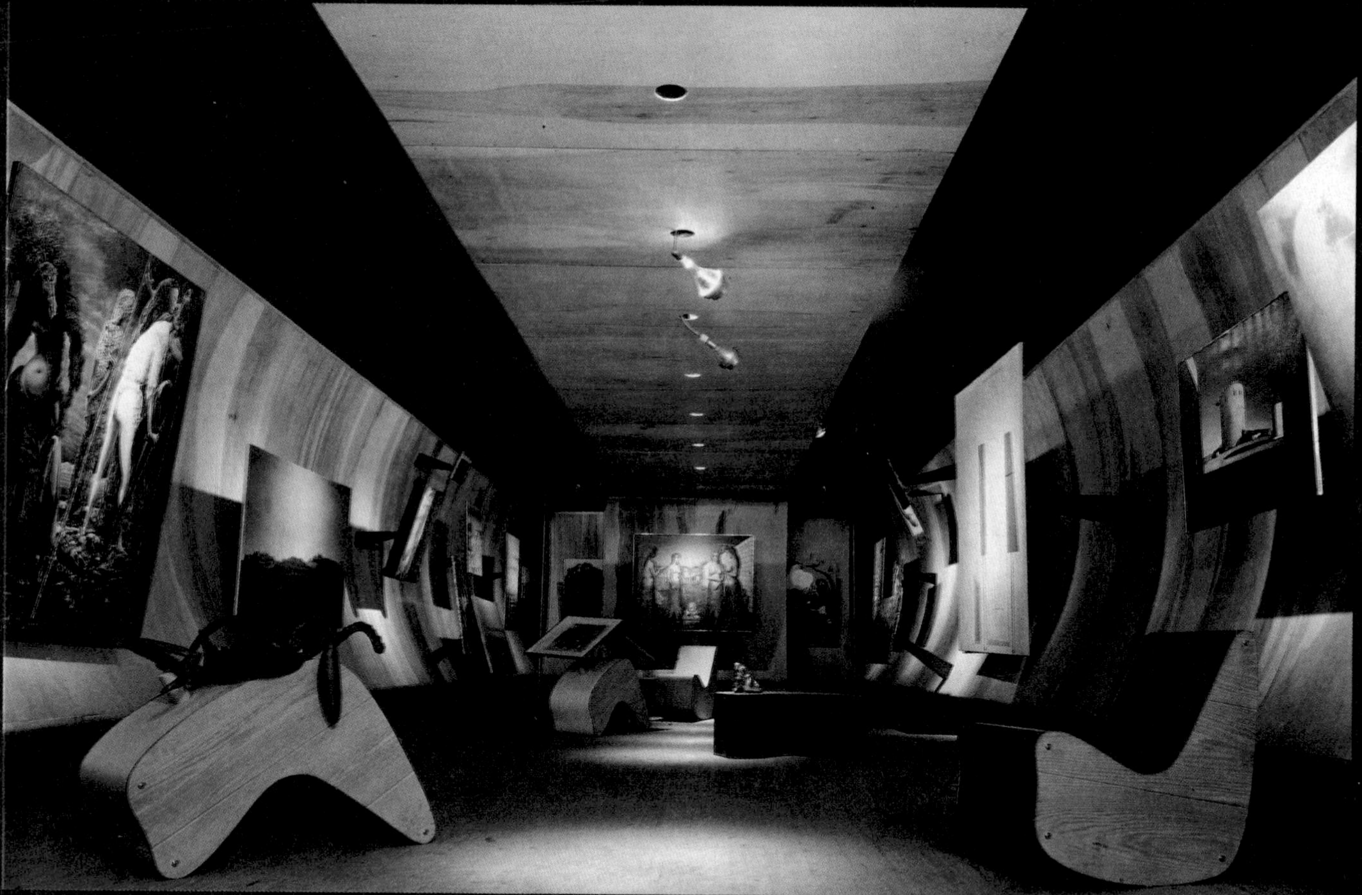

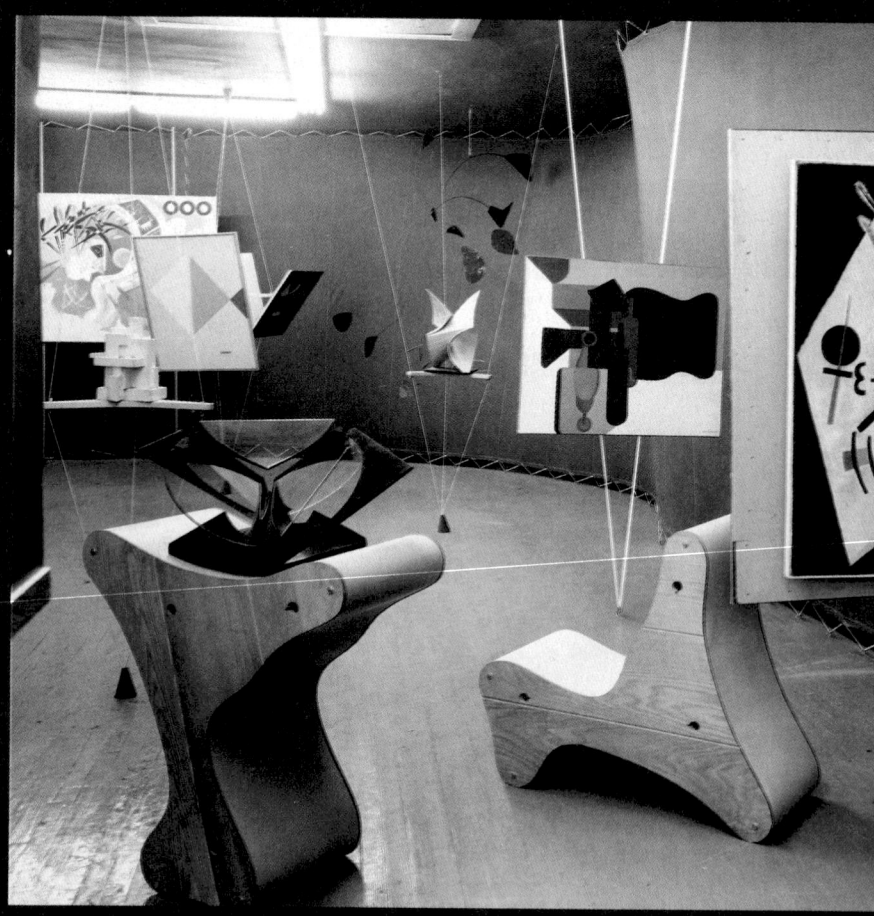

Top: Art of This Century, 30 West Fifty-seventh Street.
Frederick Kiesler, 1942. Abbott. COGR

Bottom left: World House Gallery, 987 Madison
Avenue. Frederick Kiesler, 1957. Stoller. ©ESTO

Bottom right: Art of This Century. Abstract Gallery.
Abbott. COGR

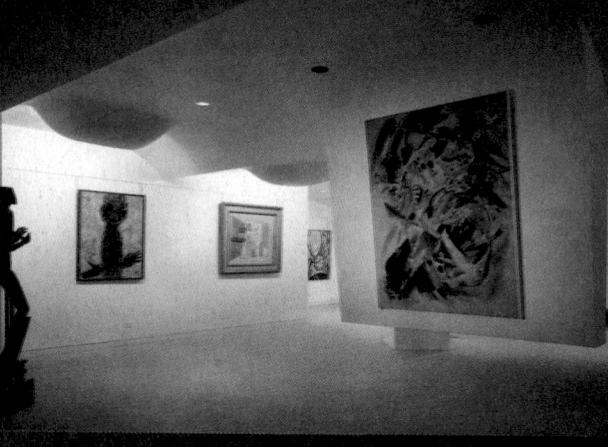

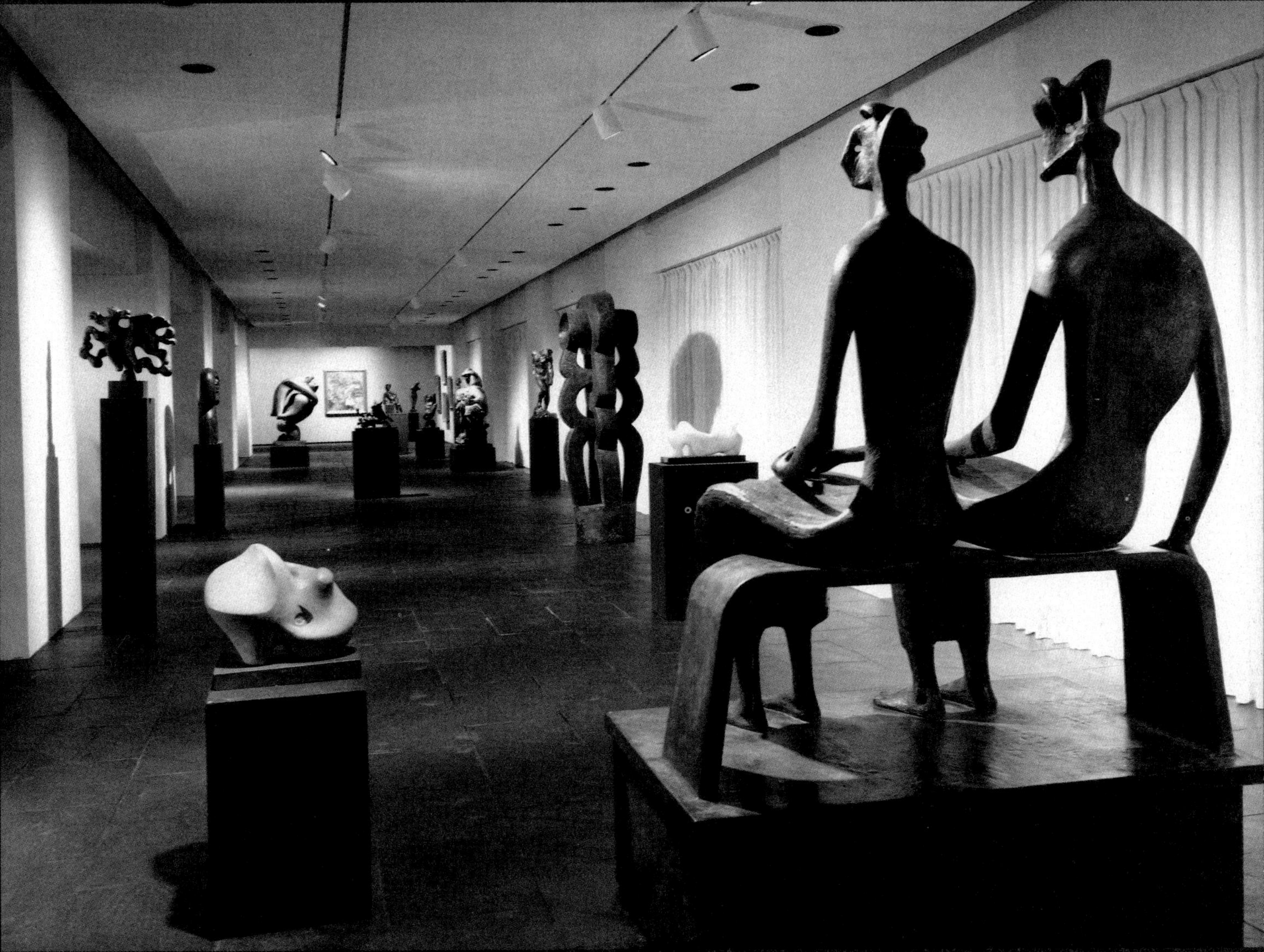

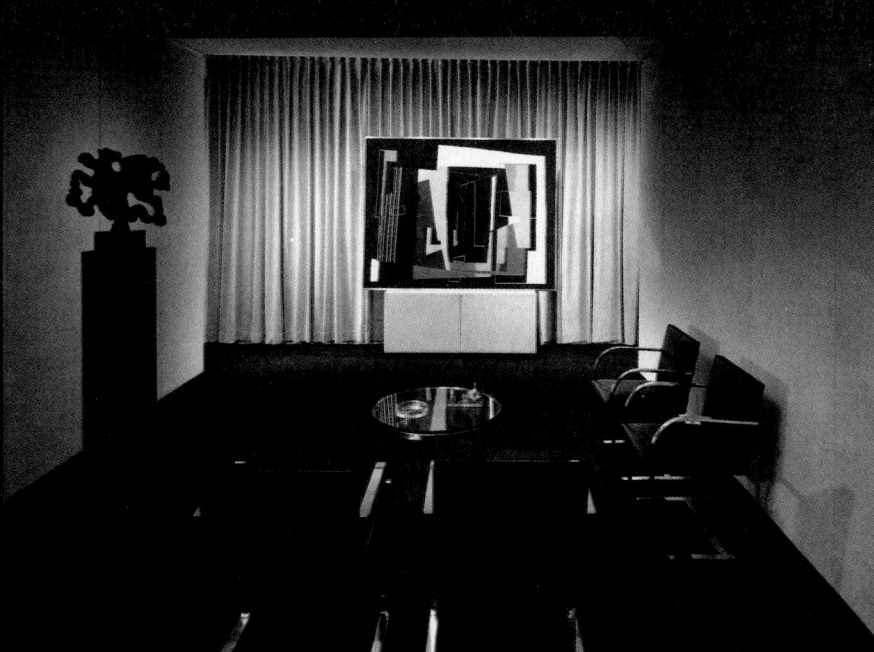

Above: Marlborough-Gerson Gallery, 41 East Fifty-seventh Street. Wilder Green, in association with Justin Henshell, 1963. Georges. WG

Left: Marlborough-Gerson Gallery. Georges. WG

approaching train. Although he said that, in contrast to ordinary museum lighting, which "makes paintings dead," the gallery's lighting "pulsates like your blood," it was found to be irritating and was soon eliminated.[8]

The third room, known as the Abstract Gallery, was equally dramatic. As the editors of *Architectural Forum* reported, it showcased "paintings in boxes with peepholes, paintings suspended in mid-air, paintings bewilderingly framed in mirrors."[9] Kiesler modified the boxlike room by lining it with an inner wall of ultramarine canvas that described a free-curving shape. The resulting space was dramatically punctuated by frameworks of cloth, tape and rope with wooden wedges that held each painting in space; a universal-joint fastening on each wedge allowed the pictures to be tilted in any direction.

The fourth room, known as the Kinetic Gallery, was, as Kiesler put it, "devoted to an automatic method of showing paintings."[10] *Architectural Forum* reported that one group of paintings on a motor-driven belt "appeared only when the visitor interrupted a beam to a photo electrical cell" and that "sculpture was displayed in a similarly unconventional manner."[11] Among the works in this gallery were fourteen reproductions from Marcel Duchamp's *Boîte en Valise*, which could be seen only through a peephole as they were carried on a conveyor belt that the visitor moved by turning a large wooden wheel. A second such construction displayed paintings by Paul Klee. To experience André Breton's *Portrait of the Actor A.B.*, the gallery-goer lifted a lever, whereupon a portrait of the artist swung around and a shutter opened to reveal the poem-object inside.

Kiesler's installation was so extraordinary that it almost overwhelmed the art. As the *New York Times* art critic Edward Alden Jewell observed, Kiesler had "built the museum in a truly miraculous way and with such inventive thoroughness that if anything had been overlooked it won't be missed, by the general public at least, for a long while." Jewell was especially intrigued by Kiesler's innovations in methods of display: "Taking the frames off the pictures, Mr. Kiesler has framed the exhibition instead. Walls have ceased to be functional . . . for in this rebel arrangement art moves out into the open. Sometimes, thus liberated, it looks faintly menacing—as if in the end it might prove that the spectator would be fixed to the wall and the art would stroll around making comments."[12] The painter-critic Manny Farber was equally impressed:

> What Kiesler has done essentially is to take the frames off the paintings, the paintings off the walls, and the walls away from the gallery. The result is a view of painting which is uninfluenced by spurious devices—such as the frame, which is cursed by making any bad painting look at least official. Kiesler, by taking his paintings off the wall, has further shown that the wall was another burden to the spectator's eye. Without either frame or wall, the spectator gets a clearer shot of the picture image and can see it immediately for what it is.[13]

Kiesler's gallery was a landmark in the history of modern art and architecture. In her monograph on the artist, Lisa Phillips explained his achievement: "Kiesler accomplished three important things in 'Art of This Century.' First, he manipulated real space to create a sculptural environment. Second, he assigned viewers an active role, as they moved through space, exploring and interacting with it. And finally, he underscored the quality of art objects as real things in real space, thus completing his triangular correlation between space, spectator and art object."[14] Art of This Century was an environmental event that would stimulate an entire generation of American artists who absorbed the lessons of European modernism and created new, highly per-

sonal work—later called Abstract Expressionist—that Guggenheim would in turn display in the gallery.

In 1947 Kiesler transformed Alexander Iolas's Hugo Gallery, at 26 East Fifty-fifth Street, into a highly charged environment for an exhibition called "Blood Flames." Among the many artists inspired by this show was the incipient hyper-minimalist Ad Reinhardt, who saw it as a "unique, imaginative experiment" that attempted "to reorganize the field of vision according to rules of sympathetic magic to achieve an integration of architecture, sculpture, and painting."[15] Kiesler's World House Gallery (1957), designed in collaboration with the architect Armand Bartos, occupied a two-level shop in the Carlyle Hotel (Bien & Prince, 1929–30), on the east side of Madison Avenue between Seventy-sixth and Seventy-seventh streets.[16] The gallery, commissioned by Herbert Mayer, a lawyer and businessman from Greenwich, Connecticut, featured a new shopfront with cutaway slits and peepholes that revealed the marble, plaster and aluminum interior. Wall planes flowed into ceilings that, as *Time* put it, "billowed" to house controlled artificial light.[17] Inside the entrance, an aluminum-covered ceiling sloped toward a marble island set within a jet-fed black glass pool. An open stair just beyond a Brancusi-like column led to additional gallery space on the second floor.

Writing about the design as he was working out its details, Kiesler said that the commission was an opportunity "not to design a specific gallery, but a *new type.*" The "first consideration in conceiving the gallery," he said, "must be a design that would make conducive a meeting between painting and visitor." He described the effect further:

> To help the "unbiased" approach to art (and architecture, if possible), the fundamental hiatus between art and nature had to be unmistakably and immediately demonstrated. This was achieved by making the visitor step (as soon as he entered) on to an island of white marble—a square-area of the main exhibition hall. This island was actually separated from the surrounding wall by a river-bed of several feet (3 or 4), a trough filled with water (not deep) and bordered on the far edge with green foliage. From there rose the walls of a double-height space, three of which serve as carriers of paintings. Thus the visitors were first kept at bay from them, not only physically but through the unexpected shock of seeing the separating water-bed. It set them (invariably) aback, wondering, and actually stopped them in their customary run-through of galleries and museums.

The artists whose work was on display, Kiesler said, objected "most violently to the water," which they thought was "an advertising trick, slick, a decor, to detract from their work." But to Kiesler it was a representation of nature, a confrontation with "the very source of origin."[18]

Kiesler's greatest challenge was to tie the two floors of the gallery into a continuous whole, which he set out to do by wrapping them "into a single elliptical enclosure." He explained how he achieved this result:

> Floors of lower areas continued in hyperbolic curvatures upward into the ceiling of the upper floor, sliding down and rising partly again, falling suddenly, as into air-pockets. They rose upward again, and finally downward, becoming a bent-wall at the other end of the long, long room; and did not stop in their flow there either; near the floor, the flow of the total elliptical enclosure suddenly protruded into a bench, curled backwards (underneath), swung rapidly forward again into the floor, becoming actually the floor itself, rolling on and on thus concluding a new geometry of space.[19]

In November 1963 the entrepreneurial art dealer Frank Lloyd opened the Marlborough-Gerson Gallery, a sumptuous, museum-like branch of London's Marlborough Gallery and by far the most luxurious and seemingly permanent setting for the sale of contemporary art New York had ever seen.[20] The party celebrating the opening of the 12,000-square-foot art emporium was an event of unaccustomed proportions in the art world; it signaled, as *Newsweek*'s Jack Kroll put it, "an epic crossbreeding of culture and commercialism."[21] The party drew such a crowd—an endless stream of what *Women's Wear Daily* described as "Lively Young Naturals and Everywhere First Fashionables"—that the Fire Department temporarily barred entry to the gallery.[22] The architect Wilder Green, working in association with Justin Henshell, designed the new gallery's headquarters on two floors of the Fuller Building (Walker & Gillette, 1929), at 41 East Fifty-seventh Street, the lower five floors of which had been specially designed to accommodate such enterprises.[23] Green, who for some years had been on staff at the Museum of Modern Art, including a position as assistant director of its Department of Architecture and Design, was experienced in museum installation.

Marlborough-Gerson was one of the largest commercial galleries in the world, in essence a small museum. Its principal room, a 170-foot-long hall with boldly scaled columns and waxed dark gray slate floors, conveyed a sense of gravity, an effect that *Progressive Architecture* described as "solid and heavy, a bit of a combination of Egypt and the 30's."[24] Parallel to this hall, and separated from it only by freestanding columns, were low-ceilinged alcove galleries that could be partitioned off from the main space. The real selling was done at the end of the gallery, in small salons with carpeted floors and fabric-covered walls. Despite the minimalism of plain walls and ceilings, Green felt the gallery established "a sense of place." He explained his intentions: "I wanted visitors to remember the galleries as well as the works of art. It was important that the galleries be architectonic. . . . The attempt was to design a space that would have a distinct architectural character but would also be an excellent background. In the Marlborough Galleries I was attempting to balance the two."[25] As *Business Week* pointed out in 1965, the size and success of the Marlborough-Gerson Gallery was "a symptom and a product of a twofold revolution that has been sweeping the world of art": New York's ascendancy over Paris as "the creative center of contemporary art," and the upsetting of "old myths and economic patterns" brought about by the culture boom, with prices for avant-garde art skyrocketing along with those for more established work.[26]

Charles Gwathmey and Richard Henderson's small, by-appointment gallery for Marjorie Neikrug (1964) brought gallery design back to the surrealistic spatial games of Kiesler, yet here held in check by a strict geometry.[27] Gwathmey described the Neikrug Gallery, which specialized in pre-Columbian art, as being composed of abstract, "three-dimensional, sculptural articulations" derived from the cubist work of Le Corbusier. It occupied the basement of a townhouse at 224 East Sixty-eighth Street, but the architects also renovated the ground floor as part of the spatial sequence patrons would experience. Despite very low ceilings and a limited area, Gwathmey created an "illusionary" space. He took elements that human beings normally relate to visually and threw them "into a dimension that was unfamiliar," as he explained: "Not having vertical planes meet with a line at the ceiling point, and situating all structural lines at levels unfamiliar to the common visual situation, makes the space completely unarticulated and continuous."[28] The editors of *Progressive Architecture*, noting "a formal, detached air of the

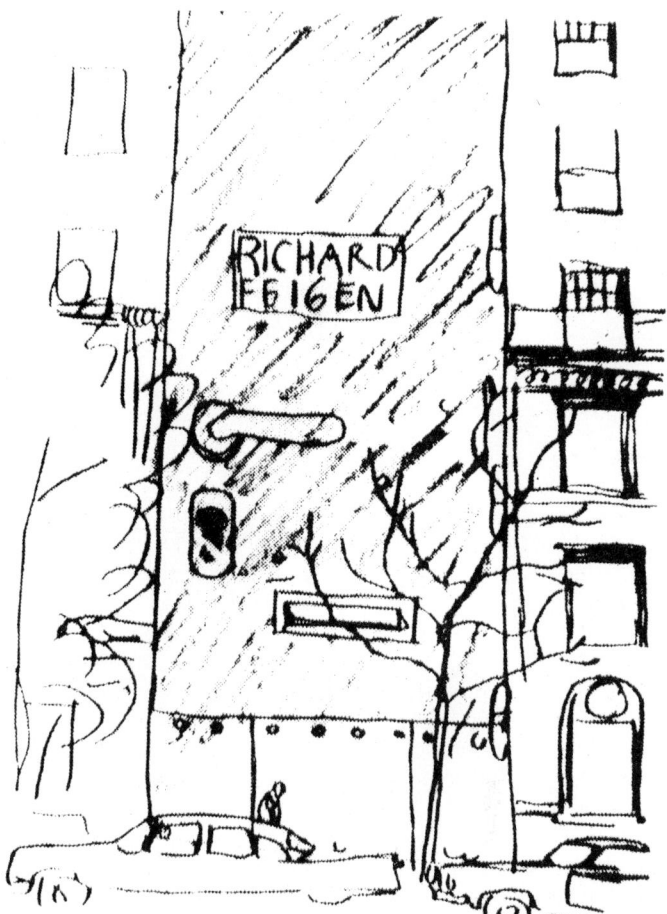

Feigen Gallery, 27 East Seventy-ninth Street. Hans Hollein, 1970. Preliminary sketch. AHH

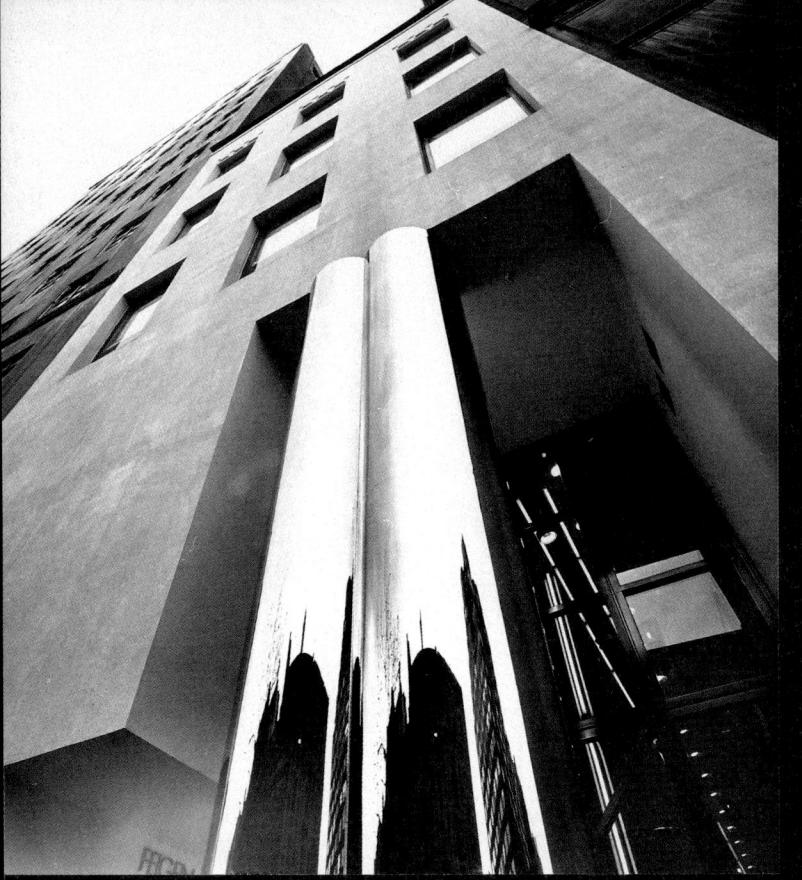

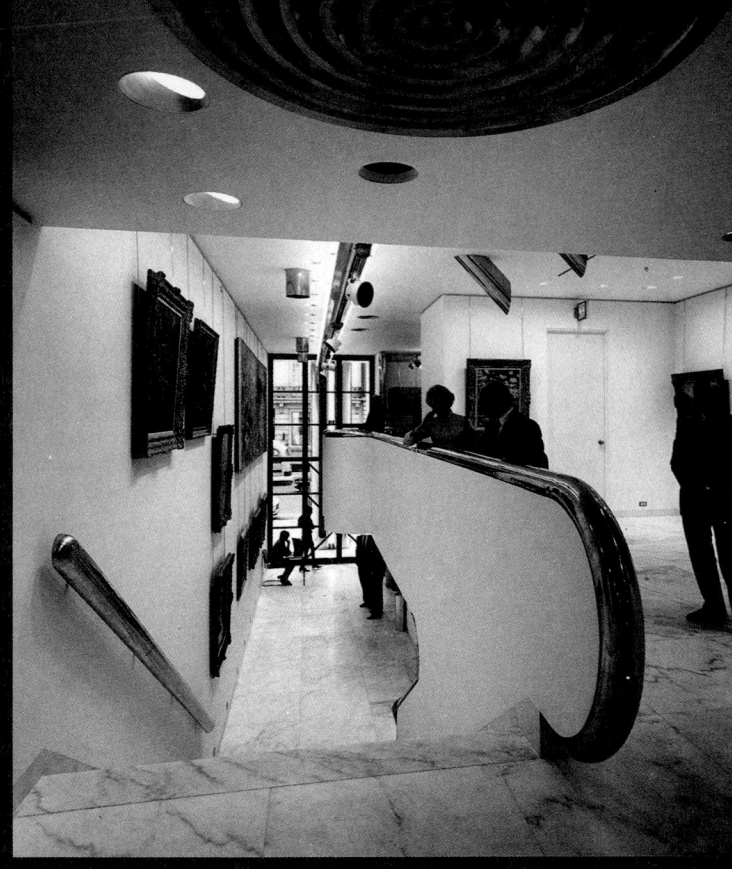

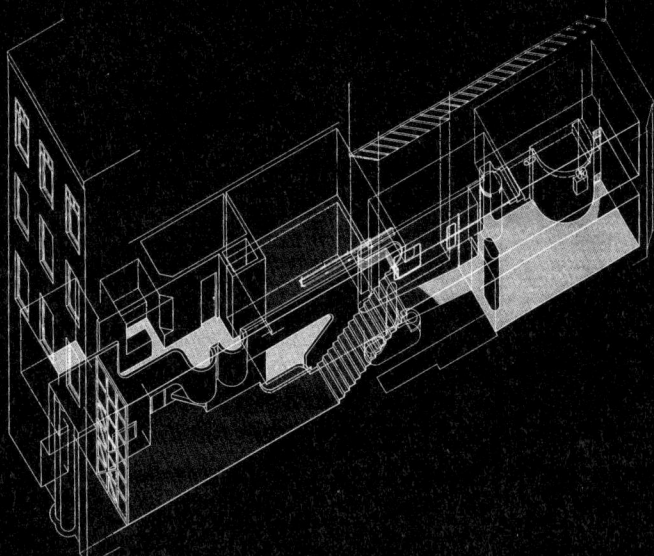

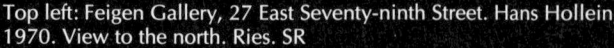

Top left: Feigen Gallery, 27 East Seventy-ninth Street. Hans Hollein, 1970. View to the north. Ries. SR

Bottom left: Feigen Gallery. Isometric. AHH

Top right: Feigen Gallery. Hubmann. AHH

Bottom right: Feigen Gallery. Entrance detail. Ries. SR

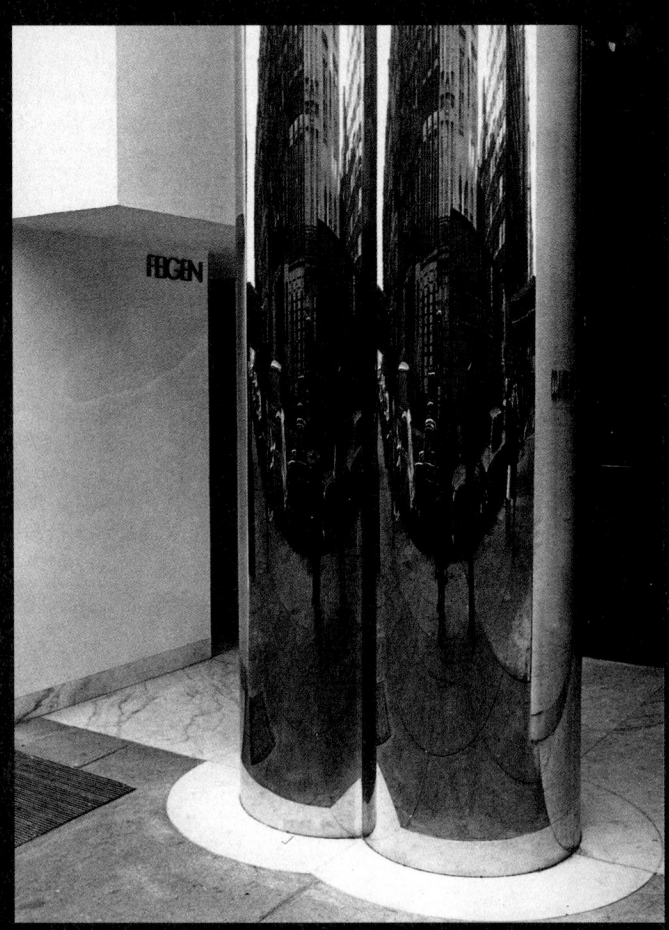

abstractionist in Gwathmey's approach," concluded: "The resulting spatial ambiguity, which is a product of this abstract formalism as well as of more romantic approaches, seems to give proof
that this ambiguity is a major design direction of our day."[29]

Richard Feigen's gallery (1970), at 27 East Seventy-ninth
Street, between Fifth and Madison avenues, was designed by the
young Austrian architect Hans Hollein, working in association
with American architects Peter Blake, Julian Neski and Dorothy
Alexander.[30] It was daring in conception, yet, like Parke-Bernet
two decades before (see chapter 11), it was also linked to an underlying Classicism and severity as well as an intention to monumentalize the art marketplace. The gallery was confined to the
ground, first and second floors of a 21-foot-wide, 100-foot-deep
converted brownstone, but the architect redesigned the building's entire facade, behind which was also an apartment for the
owner. Just as his fellow national Frederick Kiesler had a quarter
century before, Hollein proposed a design that was based on
prevailing art trends. In his first sketches, Hollein explored an
approach akin to that of Pop Art. But as the project evolved, he
changed directions: in one of the pioneering gestures of the historicizing formalism that would characterize architecture in the
1970s and 1980s, Hollein turned to sources in architectural history, basing his design on the work of yet another Austrian,
Adolf Loos's Goldman & Salatsch office building of 1909–11.[31]

Hollein's design called for a plain white stucco facade punctuated by a near-neutral grid of single-light windows, the topmost
capped by an abstract version of a Doric frieze. A recessed log-
gialike entrance to the gallery and upstairs apartment was interrupted by paired stainless-steel columnar shafts intended to convey the same iconic power as the Doric columns Loos used to
mark the entry to his building. The asymmetrical erosion of the
Feigen building's mass and the enormous Schinkel-inspired
bronze entrance doors created a definitive separation between
the public street and the intimate, extraordinary and rather contradictory spaces within. Hollein treated the second-level gallery
as a mezzanine balcony overlooking a vertical slice of space that
ran along the building's east wall. The impeccable detailing recalled the nautical streamlining of the 1930s.

In his discussion of the gallery, the architect-critic Kenneth
Frampton expressed deep concern about the commercialization
of art that the plush interior represented. Hollein's design, he said,
embodied the values of "the 'show biz' stage of the art market":

> The medium is, naturally, *opera buffe*. Transcendental notions
> are out of court, for this is the hall of illusions, the forbidden foyer
> of delights, an arena for immediate sensation and gratification.
> Those who unconsciously resist the imagery, will indulge their
> senses in the baroque materials; the honey pile and vivid pink
> plush that might have graced an ageing Schönbrun; the white,
> lined marble under foot, suggestive of cavalry trousers and crino-
> line seductions; the continuous chrome "art deco" handrail; an
> ostentatious bearer of *luxus* too fat for the hand. The sexuality
> implicit in Hollein's forms is surely inescapable.[32]

Though the space was dazzling and the imagery provocative, in
the end the gallery's size and proportions were ill suited to the
display of art. Feigen soon sold the building to the Japanese fashion designer Hanae Mori.

With the opening of the Feigen Gallery, upper Madison
Avenue reached its pinnacle as a center of the art world. This
development was celebrated, in its way, by the seventy-five-
foot-long, fifteen-foot-wide stretch of black and white terrazzo
sidewalk that Alexander Calder designed for the west midblock
between Seventy-eighth and Seventy-ninth streets, where his
dealer Klaus Perls was headquartered along with such other no-

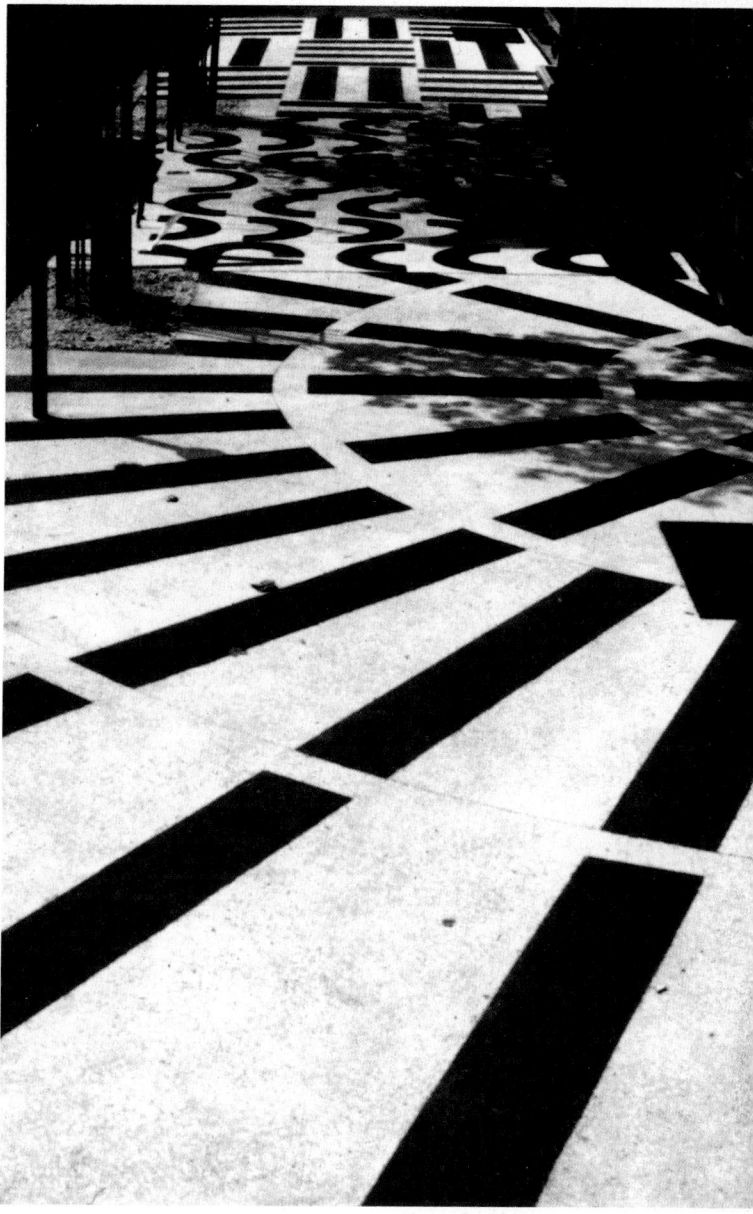

Sidewalk in front of 1018 Madison Avenue, between East Seventy-
eighth and East Seventy-ninth streets. Alexander Calder, 1970. PEG

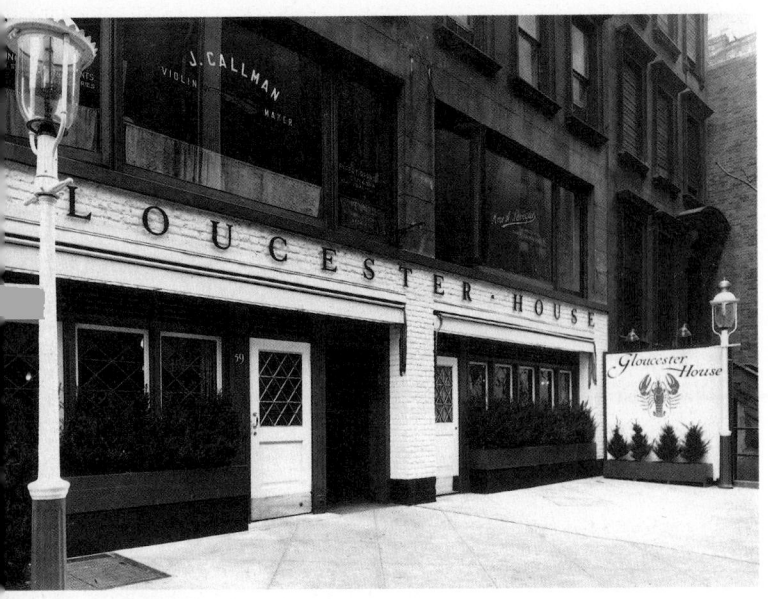

Above: Gloucester House, 59 West Fifty-first Street. Francis Keally, 1948. View to the northeast. Gottscho-Schleisner. LOC

Top right: Al and Dick restaurant, 151 West Fifty-fourth Street. George Nemeny and Abraham Geller, 1948. View to the north. Stoller. ©ESTO

Bottom right: Al and Dick restaurant. Stoller. ©ESTO

table dealers as James Graham & Sons.[33] Morton Rosenfeld, owner of number 1018, commissioned the design, which consisted of a syncopated pattern of parallel lines, crescents and radiating diagonals executed in black terrazzo and set in a field of white terrazzo. The design seemed less a reflection of Calder's characteristic approach than of the Op Art geometric pattern-painting then fashionable on the international art scene.

Calder's design for so fundamental an element of city life as a sidewalk can be said to have marked the full acceptance of Modernism by a long-wary New York public. But just as Hollein's Feigen Gallery offered a challenge to the self-referential aesthetics of the Modernists, the too-cozy relationship of art and money that the Madison Avenue art scene represented was being challenged by a new generation of dealers who were following artists downtown to the lofts of SoHo, where a community of artists and dealers flourished as never before in New York (see chapter 4).

RESTAURANTS AND NIGHTCLUBS

Restaurants

While wartime rationing inhibited restaurant business, postwar prosperity, combined with the shift in taste from austere Modernism to a rich eclecticism that combined modern and traditional themes, encouraged many restaurateurs to redecorate. In 1947 one of Alice Foote MacDougall's Italianate coffee shops, the Firenze (H. Drewey Baker, 1926), at 6 West Forty-sixth Street, which had been serving as a restaurant known as the Fishery for several years, was completely renovated.[1] According to *Interiors*, the designer, Seymour Joseph, was asked "to eradicate the last traces of pseudo-Sienna, increase the seating capacity, improve air-conditioning and circulation—always important in a fish restaurant—and give the whole a Joseph's coat of many colors."[2] Above the continuous banquette seating that lined the Fishery's dining hall, Joseph created a series of backlit portholes that contained marine-inspired three-dimensional still lifes designed by Robert Borgatta. In contrast to Joseph's comparatively restrained effort at the Fishery, Dunhall's, at 1440 Broadway, just below Times Square, was remodeled by Herman H. Seigel to convey a sense of excitement.[3] A 600-seat facility that included counter service as well as dining rooms, the new Dunhall's featured blue, white and yellow glass mosaic murals and elaborate suspended ceilings in free shapes combined with traditional chandeliers and furnishings.

At the other end of the economic spectrum was the socially exclusive, pricey Colony restaurant at Madison Avenue and East Sixty-first Street, whose reputation was built on a combination of fine food and plain decor, including simple bentwood chairs. In 1942 the owners decided to renovate the restaurant—but without closing.[4] In response to the challenge, the designer Vinicio Paladini, working in collaboration with C. Valentino, devised a solution that could be effected over the weekend, between Saturday's and Monday's lunch, when the Colony was normally closed. Their solution was to slipcover all the bentwood furniture and the room as well, using striped canvas to transform it into a delightful garden tent.

The master of mixed metaphor for gastronomic architecture was Zareh Sourian, whose Sea Fare restaurant (1944), at 25 West Fifty-sixth Street, combined parts of the interior of a 175-year-old barn from Litchfield, Connecticut, with a program of sculpture by eight Modernist artists including Rhys Caparn,

Reuben Nakian and Arline Wingate.[5] Sourian's white-painted clapboard facade aimed at the New England look, and an oddly proportioned entrance porch sheltered a wire sculpture of a plunging fish that served as the restaurant's only signboard. A checkerboard arrangement lining one of the dining room walls featured the work of all eight sculptors; the rope-bound, freely curving bar was presided over by three reliefs by John Hovannes. *Architectural Forum*, not entirely enthralled with the total ensemble, commented that "the end result, which is charmingly interlaced with some discreet plant life, is about as close to the Aquarium as any restaurant we know."[6] Sourian seemed more in control with his Simplon restaurant (1946), at 112 Central Park South, where he covered the curving walls with murals by Norwood Patton.[7]

At another seafood restaurant, Gloucester House (1948), at 59 West Fifty-first Street, near Radio City, the traditionalist architect Francis Keally approached the problem of a fish house with a more consistent vocabulary. As *Architectural Record* put it, no doubt with Joseph's Fishery and Sourian's Sea Fare in mind, "New York City . . . boast[s] a seafood place designed to resemble an aquarium and another with swaying portholes intended, evidently, to test the seaworthiness of its customers at critical dietetic moments. Gloucester House, by comparison, is a staid and conservative Inn."[8] Not only was Keally asked to design the restaurant, he was also consulted on its name, as well as incidental details like menu cards and staff uniforms, which contributed to the total effect. As a result, Gloucester House came off as a convincing evocation of a particular character if not a specific place, much as Mrs. MacDougall's coffee shops had in the 1920s. For many of the up-and-coming gray-flanneled organization men for whom the restaurant was intended, this thematic, conservative approach was a refreshing contrast to the helter-skelter, eclectic Modernism of most of the competition.

Postwar Modernist architects undertook a more naturalistic approach. George Nemeny and Abraham Geller's Al and Dick restaurant of 1948, at 151 West Fifty-fourth Street, presented a facade that was almost suburban in scale.[9] The interior was suburban-cozy as well, relying for its visual effects not on traditional detail but on a simple palette of rugged, natural materials. The restaurant occupied its own two-story building, which the architects faced with matched vertical boarding; an elegantly detailed canvas-and-pipe-rail canopy was hung above the entrance. The interior included exposed brick and fieldstone, as well as stained and waxed Douglas fir planks for the walls, an acoustical plaster vault and simple, custom-designed polished brass pendant light fixtures.

Al and Dick could be seen as a reflection of the vernacular-based Modernism of the Bay Area of California—a stylistic movement very much on the minds of New York's architects in 1948 as a result of a symposium at the Museum of Modern Art. But it may also have reflected the direction of Finnish Modernism, which many architects were first exposed to at Alvar Aalto's exhibit for the 1939 New York World's Fair, and which was given more permanent representation in a restaurant and art shop sponsored by the Finnish Consulate and located in Finland House, at 41 East Fiftieth Street.[10] Designed in 1948 by the Finnish architect Aarne Ervi, in association with the New York firm of Magoon & Salo, they consisted of simple interiors lined with natural unpainted pine and accented by Paavo Tynell's sparkling polished brass pendant light fixtures pierced to create pinpoints of brilliance.[11] The interiors were detailed and fabricated in Finland and shipped to New York for reassembly on the site. The craftsmanship was impeccable; as *Architectural Forum*

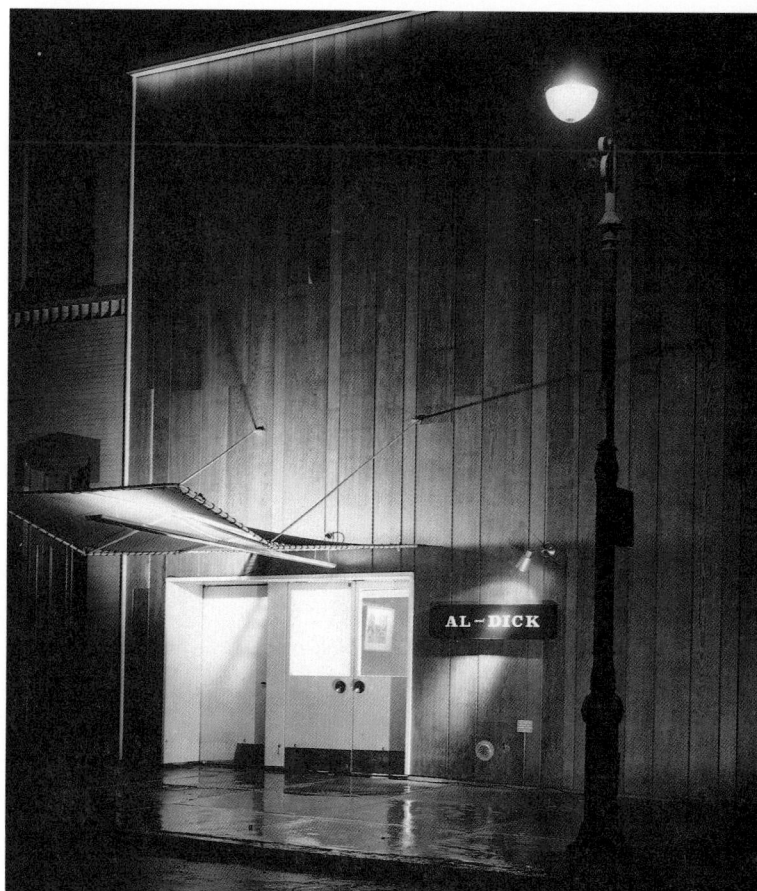

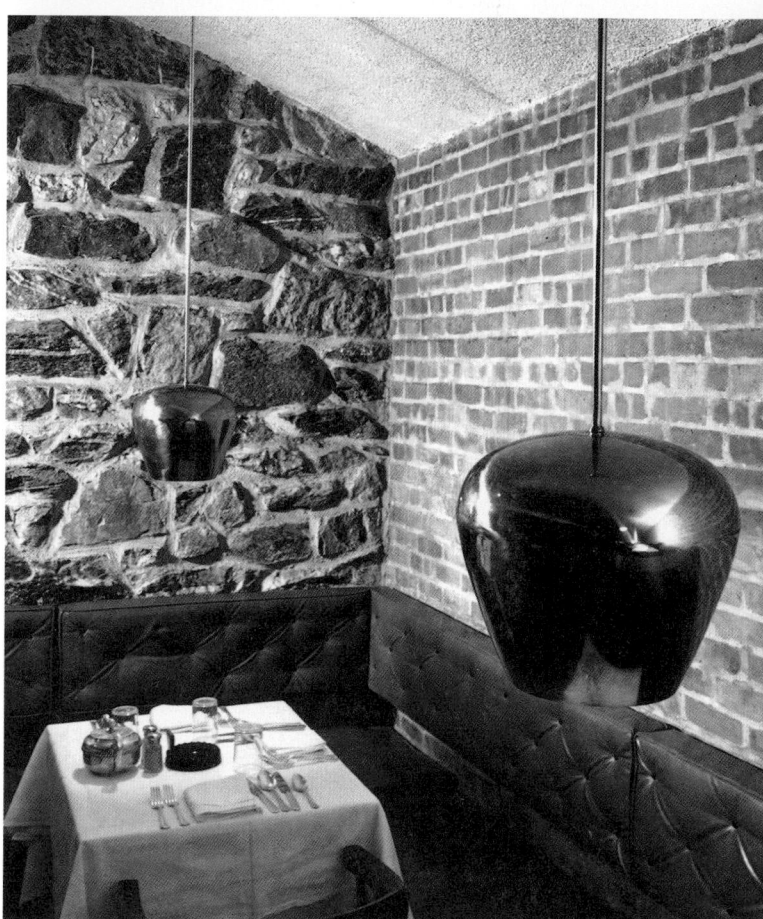

warned, however, it would be difficult to repeat such results in the United States, given the realities of American building practice.

In the 1940s and 1950s the top New York restaurants, most of which specialized in classic French cuisine, were elegantly appointed though not architecturally distinguished. When Henri Soulé's Pavillon restaurant, begun in 1939 as part of the French Pavilion at the World's Fair and located at 5 East Fifty-fifth Street, was moved to the Ritz Tower in 1957, he contented himself with a conventional sequence of rooms conventionally decorated.[12] The same was true for Soulé's principal competitor, the Chambord, which was founded in 1936 and occupied a distinctly déclassé location beneath the El at 803 Third Avenue between Forty-ninth and Fiftieth streets.[13] According to an article in Holiday, Chambord had "no 'décor,' as we have come to know the meaning of the word, no trace of stage setting or showmanship. You have to look sharply to notice the few decorative touches, like the ceiling-high mirrors, the arrangements of flowers in niches along the walls, the cloth-covered lamps found in comfortable suburban homes."[14]

The staid predictability of the best restaurants began to give way in the mid-1950s, perhaps in response to the increasingly sophisticated tastes of New Yorkers, who had begun to travel extensively after the war, visiting not only the capitals of Europe but also Mexico and the Far East. City residents began to enjoy more exotic food and seemed willing to pay very high prices for it if it was served in suitably exotic surroundings. Thus a new trend emerged, that of the theme or, as William Wilson Atkin and Joan Adler put it, the "festive" restaurant.[15] Restaurant "theming" was of course not new to New York: the precedent had been set by Mrs. MacDougall's coffee shops in the 1920s and, before that, by the splendid Murray's Roman Gardens of 1907, as well as ethnic restaurants, almost all of which featured a bit of the country's decor.[16] Some of these were quite charming and deceptively authentic, if not in detail, at least in overall character. Alexander McIlvaine and Minor Bishop's Trattoria Gatti, at 246 East Fortieth Street, with a fountain, reproductions of Italian statuary, rough plaster walls and gondolier-style waiters' uniforms, was a superior example of this type.[17] Others, like Chateau Henri IV, in the Alrae hotel at 37 East Sixty-fourth Street, which was based on a medieval castle, were essays in what Minor Bishop described as "frankly inaccurate opulence." Entered across a real moat on a real drawbridge, the restaurant included "a profusion of draped fabrics, wrought iron, armor, heavy chandeliers, and prodigious ornamentation."[18]

Perhaps the first, tentative sign that New Yorkers would support upmarket theme restaurants began with the 1954 renovation of Rockefeller Center's Restaurant Mayan (1935), located in the International Building. Remodeled by Carson & Lundin, the restaurant emerged as an almost undecorated, neutral environment subtly modified with a "Mayan color scheme" of earthy yellow, turquoise, terra-cotta and olive green that served as a counterpoint to predominantly off-white walls.[19] Reproductions of recently discovered ancient Mayan heads placed behind the bar were the only form of applied decoration and the only specific representation of the theme. Further west, in the former Hotel Lincoln, which the real estate entrepreneur William Zeckendorf had purchased and remodeled as the Hotel Manhattan, Melanie Kahane's appropriately stagy Playbill restaurant of 1958 took the theater world as its theme.[20] The Playbill, which replaced a dingy coffee shop, was intended to rival the long-established Sardi's as a fashionable pre- and post-theater restaurant. Whereas Sardi's had as its principal decor an ever-expanding collection of caricatures of prominent theater

people, Kahane, working with Howard Williams, another decorator, and Abe Feder, the lighting designer, chose to concentrate on the artifice of the theater itself. Beginning with the red-and-white carnival canopy at the entrance, the restaurant's two floors were, according to John Anderson, "thoroughly theatrical in metaphor, sheer theater themselves. . . . The restaurant is rich in the inventive and relishable details that keep a show sparkling: miniature stage sets built into alcoves of the cocktail lounge, a dividing wall of klieg lights, star cutouts in ceilings for lighting."[21] And in response to Sardi's caricatures, there were three giant murals by the famously inventive New York Times stage caricaturist Al Hirschfeld.

Theme restaurants began to be taken seriously after Jerome Brody, Joe Baum and their Restaurant Associates came on the scene in the 1950s.[22] Baum was committed to restaurants not merely as places to eat but also as places for public entertainment. The Forum of the Twelve Caesars (1957) was Restaurant Associates' first theme restaurant, and it was "so faithful to its name," as the New Yorker pointed out, "that the bartenders wear leather jerkins of authentically Roman cut and the menu features roast peacock, salmon baked in ashes, and other dishes worthy of a Petronius Arbiter."[23] The Forum, located in the U.S. Rubber Building at Rockefeller Center, was designed by William Pahlmann Associates. Pahlmann hit upon the theme when he discovered twelve portraits of Caesars in an antique shop; he used these to decorate the dining room. With George Thiele of his staff and with Daren Pierce, Pahlmann created a series of rooms that were suggestive but not really specific: there was just enough Roman-inspired Classicism to make diners forget that the basic vocabulary of the design was virtually identical to what one found in many red-flocked "high class" French bistros in New York.

Restaurant Associates' next theme restaurant was far more ambitious, taking on the motif of all nature itself: the Four Seasons, which alternated menus, plants and incidental decor four times a year but whose austerely luxurious ambience was far more the result of its location in the Seagram Building and Philip Johnson's interior design (see chapter 5). Buoyed by the success of the very costly Forum, Brody and his collaborators returned to Rockefeller Center with a larger, more moderately priced restaurant, La Fonda del Sol, the most festive of all, in which Modernist and vernacular architecture were brilliantly blended (see chapter 5).

In 1966 Alexander Girard, the designer of La Fonda del Sol, working in association with Lee Schoen, designed another theme restaurant, this time for Jerome Brody, who had left Restaurant Associates. Occupying the eastern end of the Sherry-Netherland Hotel (Schultze & Weaver and Buchman & Kahn, 1926) and opening onto Fifty-ninth Street, L'Etoile undertook to convey a French theme in a high-class restaurant without reverting to the typical "period" approach.[24] Girard's strategy was to combine the French moderne design of the late 1920s and early 1930s with strictly contemporary elements. This technique worked less well than it had in La Fonda, perhaps because the traditional icons at L'Etoile belonged not to a timeless vernacular style but to a relatively indistinct movement that seemed, at least to older diners, barely historical. Whereas the arte popular of La Fonda was totally exotic and could play well against Charles Eames's swivel dining chairs, at L'Etoile the Eames-like "Etoile" chair system looked awkward and just a bit futuristic, as though television's Jetson family had furnished a suite on the steamship Normandie.[25] The plan of the restaurant made for a rather static spatial sequence. In contrast to La Fonda's stroll through a

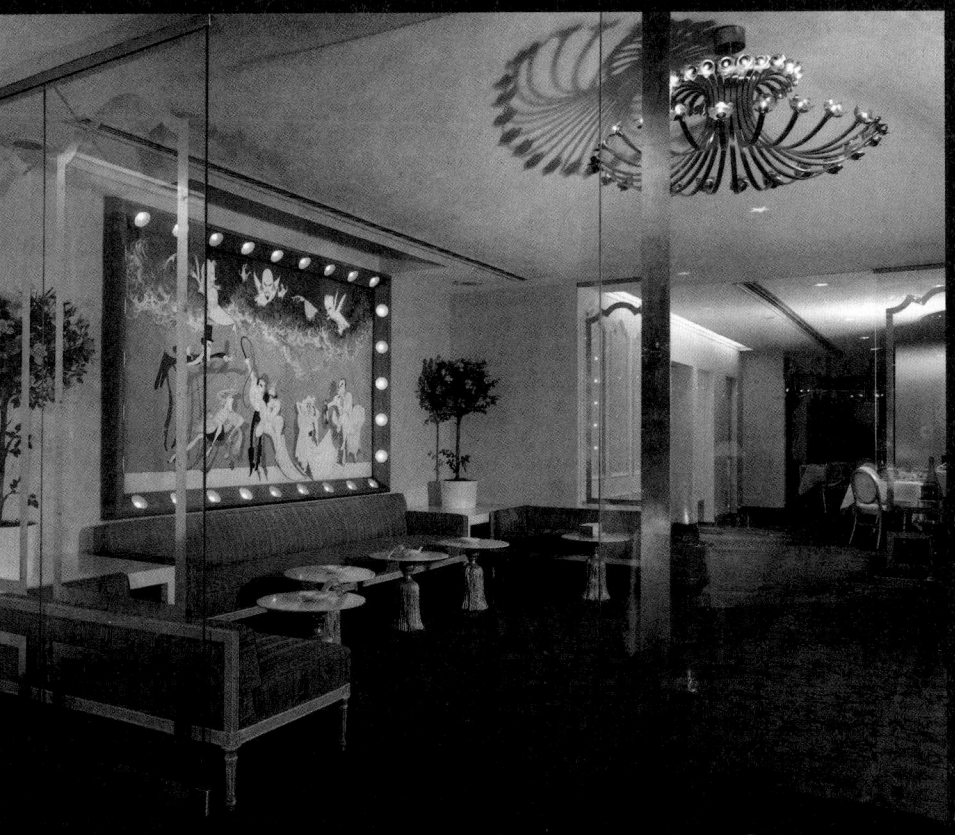

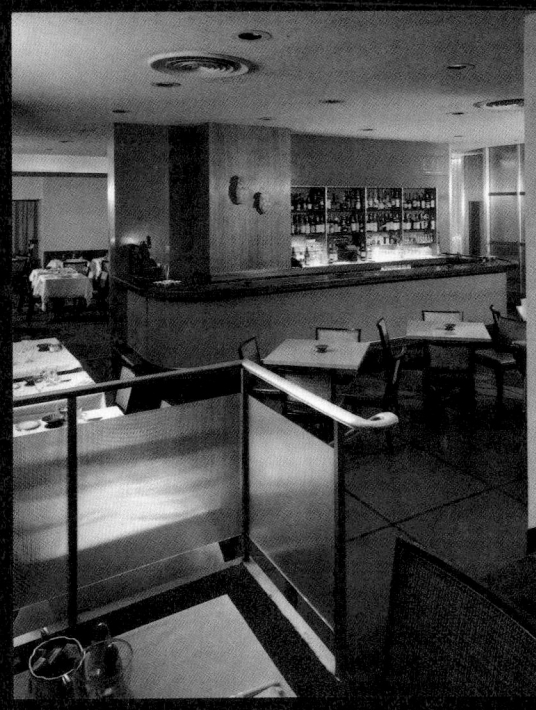

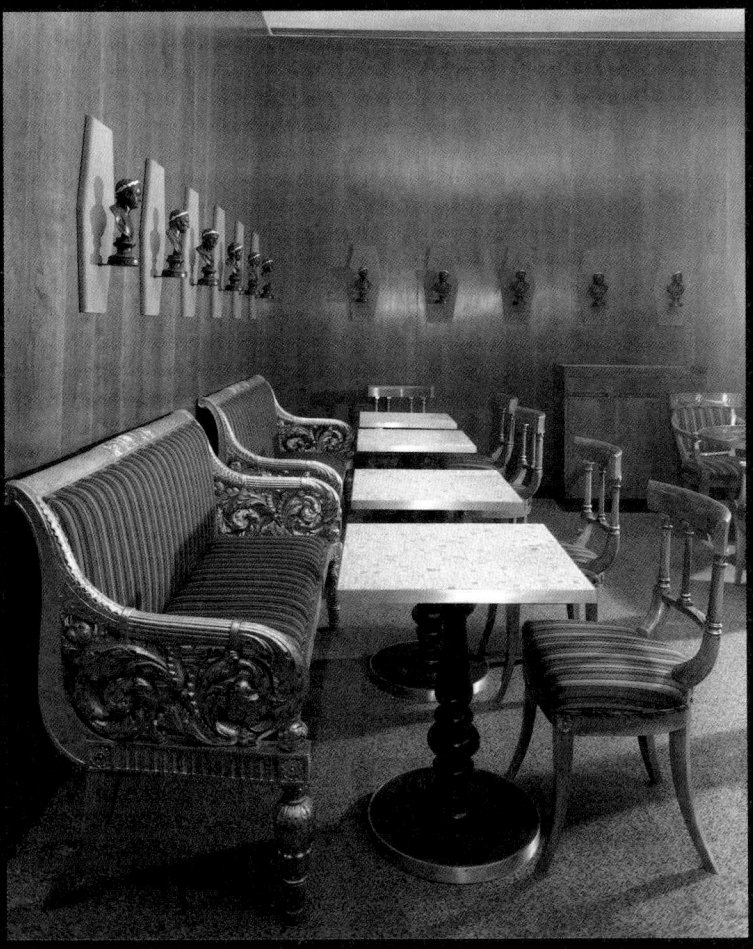

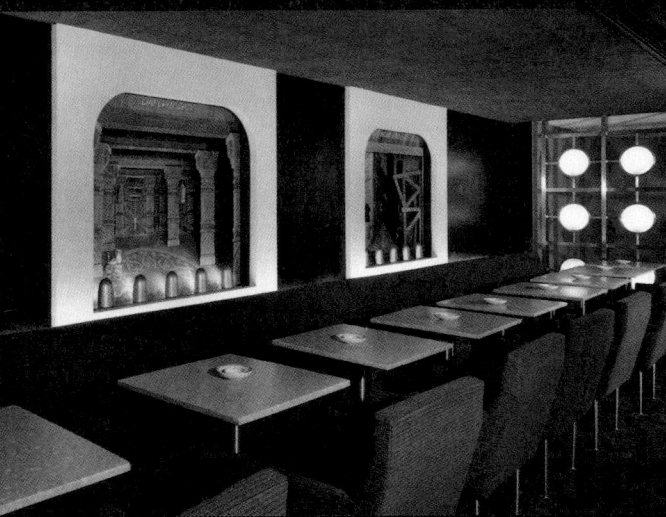

Top left: Playbill, Hotel Manhattan, Eighth Avenue, between West Forty-fourth and West Forty-fifth streets. Melanie Kahane, 1958. Reens. LR

Bottom left: Forum of the Twelve Caesars, 57 West Forty-eighth Street. William Pahlmann Associates, 1957. Reens. LR

Top right: Restaurant Mayan, 16 West Fifty-first Street. Carson & Lundin, 1954. Stoller. ©ESTO

Bottom right: Playbill. Reens. LR

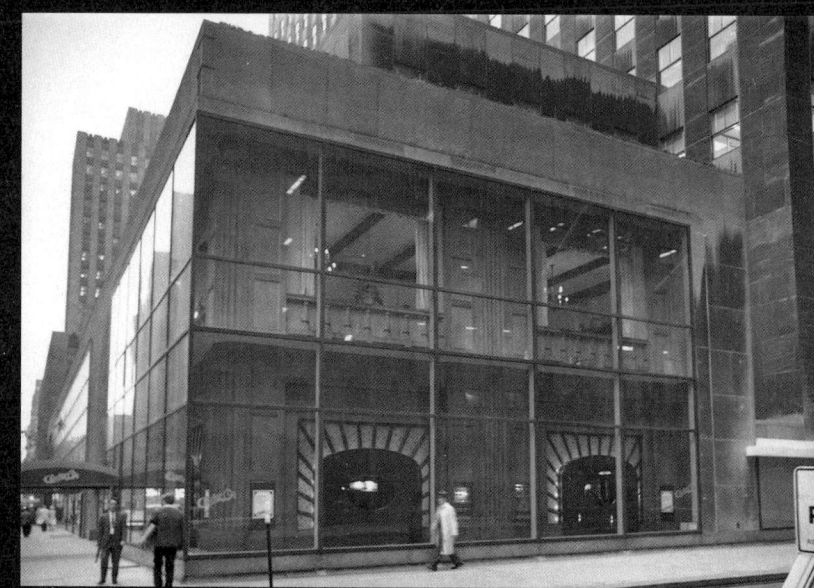

Right: Charley O's, 33 West Forty-eighth Street. George Thiele, 1966. View to the west. Reens. LR

Bottom left: Pearl's, 38 West Forty-eighth Street. Gwathmey Siegel, 1976. Maris. GSA

Bottom right: Pearl's. View to the south. GSA

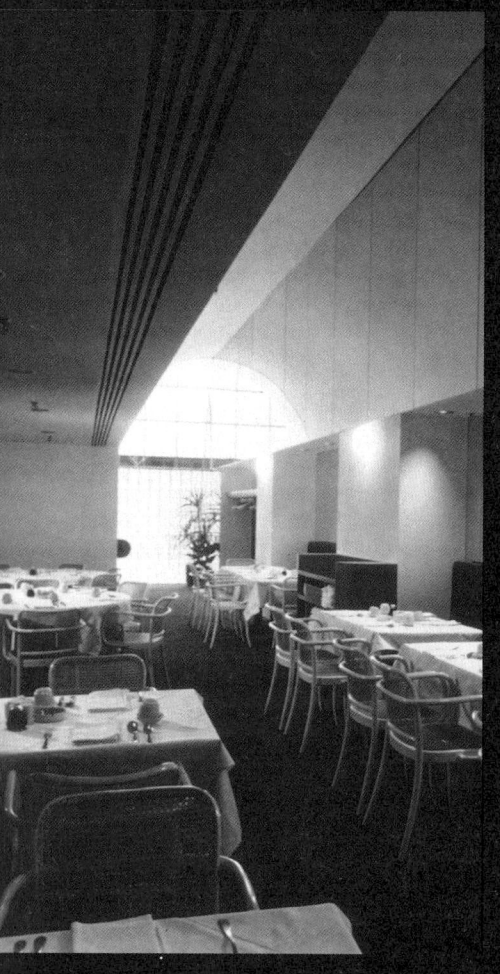

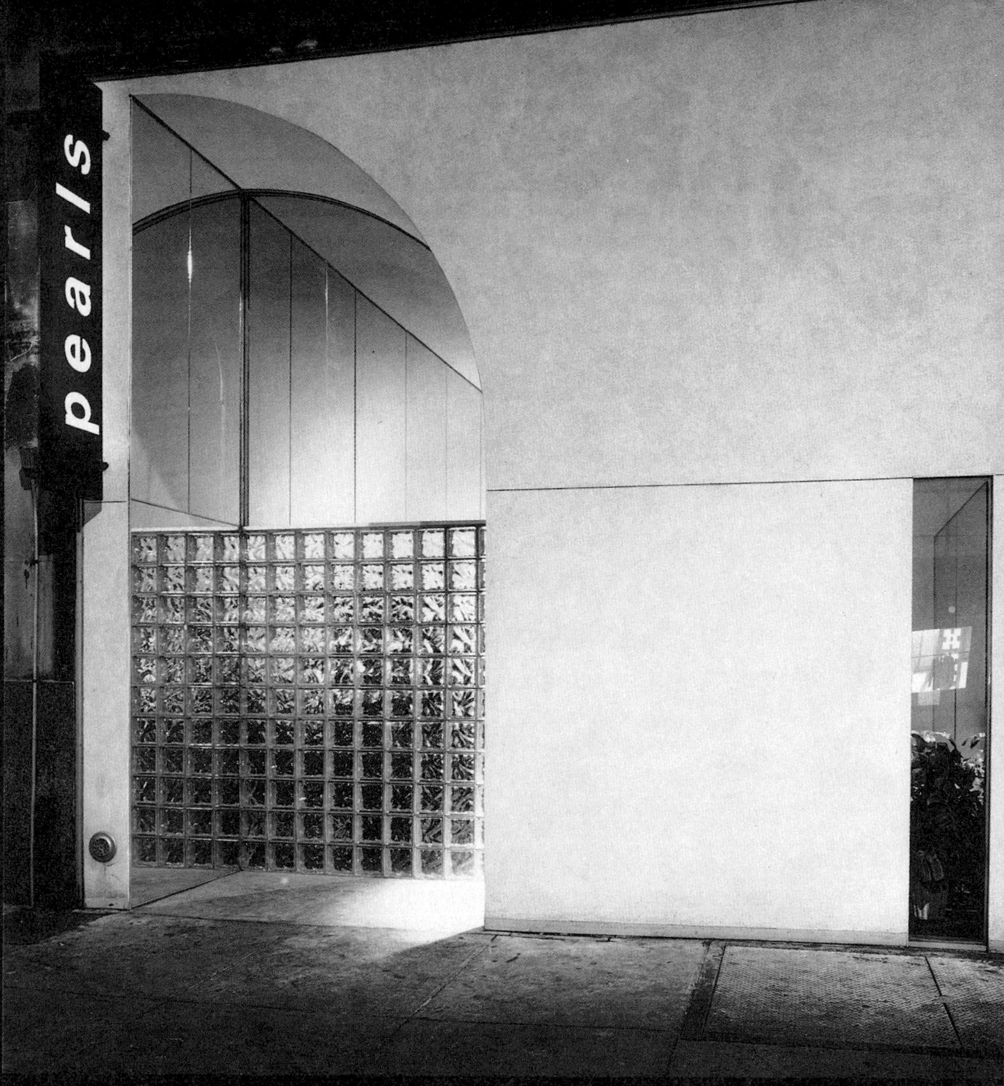

Latin American village, L'Etoile took diners on a procession through the lobby of a great hotel or a transatlantic luxury liner. But, as *Domus* observed, "One constant thing in Girard's approach to design is the pleasure he takes, every time, in introducing a new vocabulary of images, which the new theme suggests—a new key. This way each of his environments appears as a different and unique 'character,' the features of which are not to be forgotten."[26]

Simultaneously, Restaurant Associates reverted to a more conventional theme, but used in a very sophisticated way, with Charley O's, inserted behind one of the large glass walls that gave Rockefeller Center's Eastern Airlines Building a strong sense of European modernity.[27] Charley O's, designed by George Thiele (who had worked on the Forum), was set within the glass box at the northwest corner of Forty-eighth Street and Rockefeller Plaza, where the Holland House restaurant had been. The restaurant effectively evoked a turn-of-the-century Anglo-Irish pub and looked, as Olga Gueft noted, "much older than the glass wall of the Eastern Airlines Building, which seems to have been slipped over it when Rockefeller Center was built." Although atmospheric, the design was rather stagy, leaning toward the manner of Chateau Henri IV more than the freewheeling style of L'Etoile. Nonetheless, once diners got beyond the very shock of its setting, as Gueft observed, it "looks convincingly *undesigned*, though every detail is not only right, but very fine."[28]

The example of Girard's L'Etoile seemed to inspire others to create theme restaurants with a contemporary point of view. Nicos Zographos and Paul Sapounakis's Dionysos restaurant of 1970 placed diners on three levels, with the lowest level treated as a sunken garden and the upper levels as terraces.[29] A slate floor, rough plaster walls and simple fabrics furthered the illusion of an exterior environment, but the poor lighting and the general tightness of the space kept this restaurant from being a rival to La Fonda del Sol. In the hands of the Interior Concepts team, the facade of the Swiss Pavilion (1970), at 4 West Forty-ninth Street, with its Corbusier-inspired curving turret, may have been as "avant garde as a *Graphis* cover," but inside, its three-level dining room seemed a slightly chilly, cleaned-up version of La Fonda's Latin American villages.[30] Linear relief decoration, though adapted from traditional sgraffito of the Grison district, seemed mechanical, not primitive. Nonetheless, the giant cowbells (*treichlern*) gathered to form a space divider in the bar, along with various other craft objects, helped give the design a geographical focus, even if the architecture itself seemed a bit too universal.

While the Forum and La Fonda highlighted unfamiliar cuisines, one exotic cuisine, Chinese, was widely known to New Yorkers, typically through either pretentiously banal "Shanghai Palaces" or hole-in-the-wall quick-meal operations such as King Chuan in the theater district. In 1974, under the direction of the architect P. H. Tuan, who was called in by the owner to help save a failing enterprise, King Chuan was reborn as Cousin Ho's, with a design that was a witty synthesis of red-painted Constructivist forms and Times Square razzle-dazzle.[31] A nod was also given to Hollywood's view of China, represented in old movie stills of Charlie Chan and other celluloid Asians that lined the walls. The opening of Russel Wright's Shun Lee Dynasty (1966), at Second Avenue and Forty-eighth Street, made fine Chinese food available in a spectacular, luxuriously appointed setting.[32] In consultation with the architect Fred Liebman and the designer John King, Wright transformed a confining space into a dazzling, opulent if garish restaurant that marked a distinct departure from the Modernist-inspired industrial design which had characterized his work in the 1930s. While the design was no doubt based on Chinese precedent, the use of magenta, hot orange, royal blue, turquoise, torrid purple, bright green, soft light blue and chartreuse, in conjunction with gold, bamboo and bronze, was startling, and the final effect seemed overbearing for the delicate cuisine.

A few years later the subtlety of Chinese haute cuisine was to find its appropriate architectural counterpoint in Pearl's restaurant, a sliver of space transformed in 1973 by Charles Gwathmey and Robert Siegel.[33] Pearl's occupied a 14-foot-wide, 100-foot-deep shopfront at 38 West Forty-eighth Street. To increase the sense of width, Gwathmey Siegel combined a half barrel vault with mirrors to complete the shape. The interior, painted white, carpeted in gray and simply furnished with white-painted cane-seat Prague chairs, was the ultimate in stylistic minimalism. The light coming through the glass block at the entrance and the glittering crowd drawn by the proprietress, Pearl Wong, added just enough sparkle to ensure the project's success.

In 1976 Gwathmey Siegel followed the success of Pearl's with Shezan, at 8 West Fifty-eighth Street, a restaurant squeezed into the basement-level space formerly occupied by the Paris Theater's restaurant.[34] As Stanley Abercrombie pointed out, the main task of the architects was to manipulate and camouflage the subterranean location of the restaurant, which was entered at street level: "Gwathmey and Siegel contrive here to move diners to ever lower depths without their awareness. They achieve this by means of visual ambiguities and also by positive action: at each point where vertical movement occurs, they have provided an important horizontal attraction—an important wall, an important volume of space, or both."[35] Through the skillful use of reflective, polished aluminum, acoustic ceiling tiles, and mirrored and gray carpeted walls, the architects transformed the dining room, a low, featureless space, into a glittering chamber of "light and illusion," as Gwathmey put it.[36] Though the food was Indian, the architects insisted that "the environment . . . not be related ethnically to the food."[37] Paul Goldberger praised the architects for creating a room that "manages the remarkable trick of being sleek and cool, but soft and gentle at the same time."[38]

The most spectacular restaurant of the 1960s, Maxwell's Plum, at 1181 First Avenue, on the northwest corner of Sixty-fourth Street, was designed not by an architect but by its owner, Warner LeRoy.[39] Begun in 1965 in a space that for years had been a luncheonette, Maxwell's Plum was expanded three years later into an adjacent space that had been a movie theater. The final result was the ultimate Belle Epoque café, with painted and stained-glass partitions and chandeliers that were mostly ersatz; the spectacular custom-made ceiling over the upper-level dining room, however, was made entirely of Tiffany glass, illuminated from behind by 1,252 sixty-watt bulbs. There were also ten lanterns purchased from the Vanderbilt Hotel, the central portion of a Lalique fountain and two genuine Tiffany lamps. Maxwell's Plum was "like taking a ride through Disneyland," as one of the waiters put it. "It's totally removed from reality. . . . There's a feeling of age, right? But these are instant antiques. They're only *five* years old."[40] LeRoy was also responsible for the equally flamboyant renovation of the Tavern on the Green in Central Park (see chapter 10).

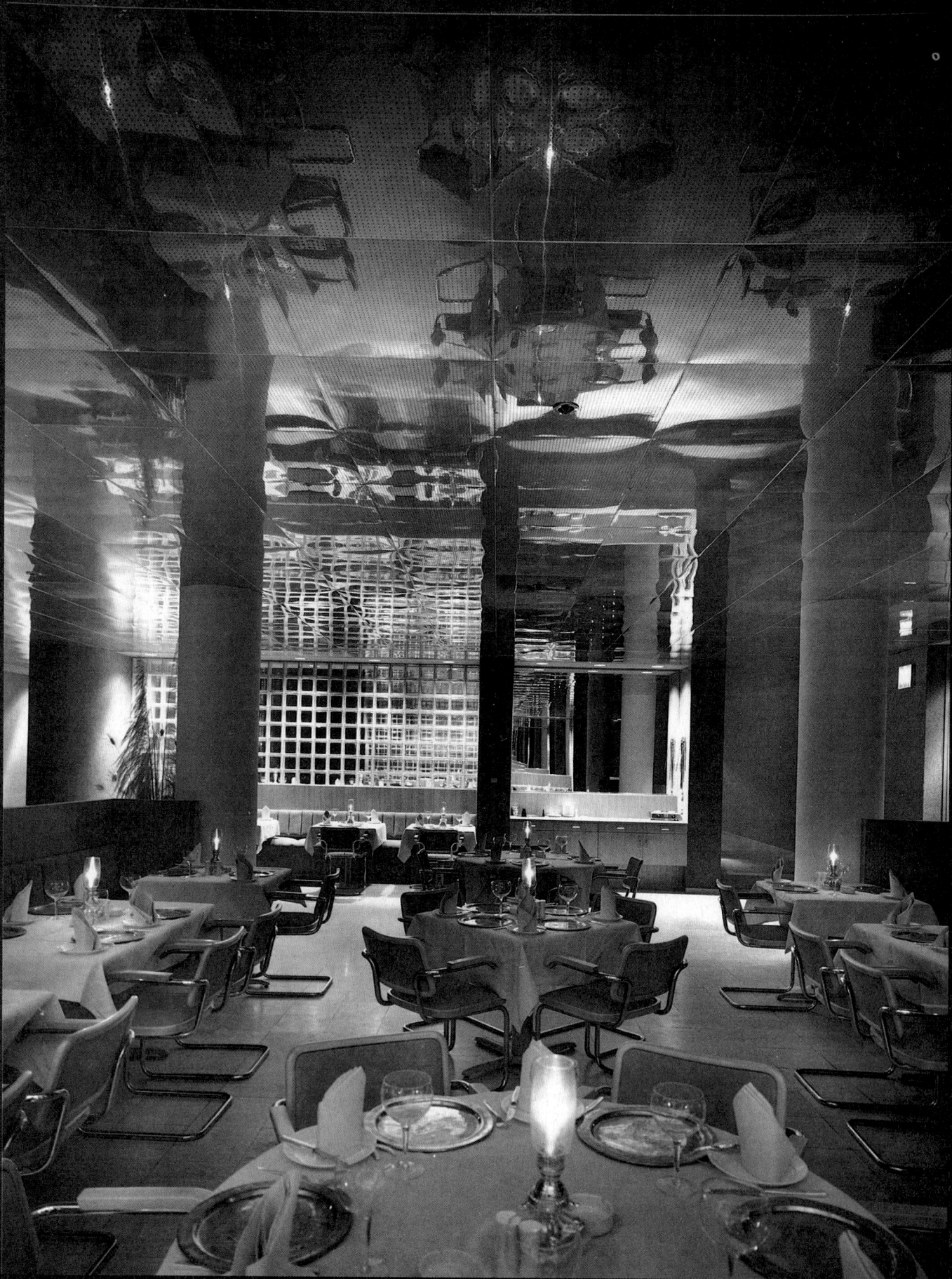

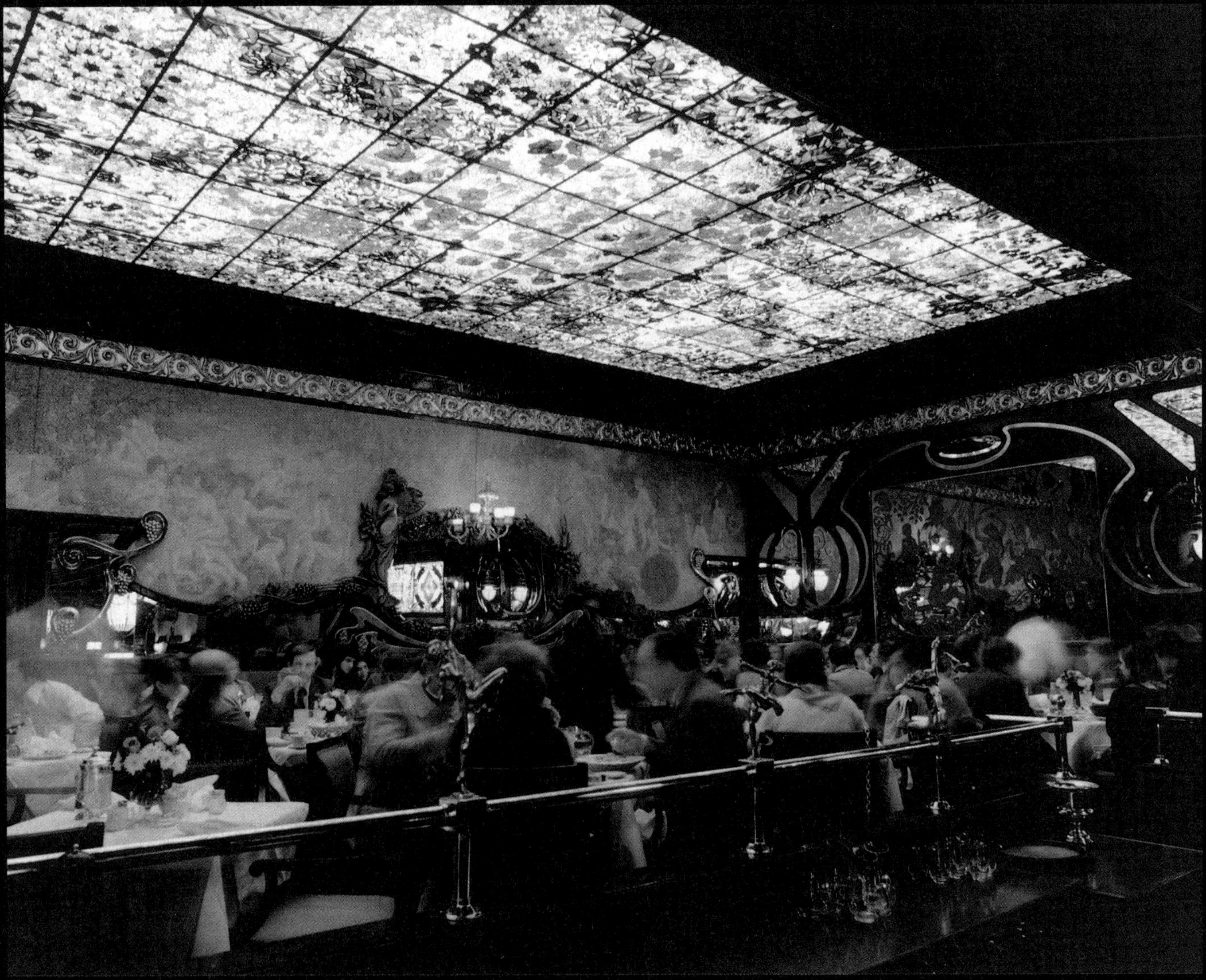

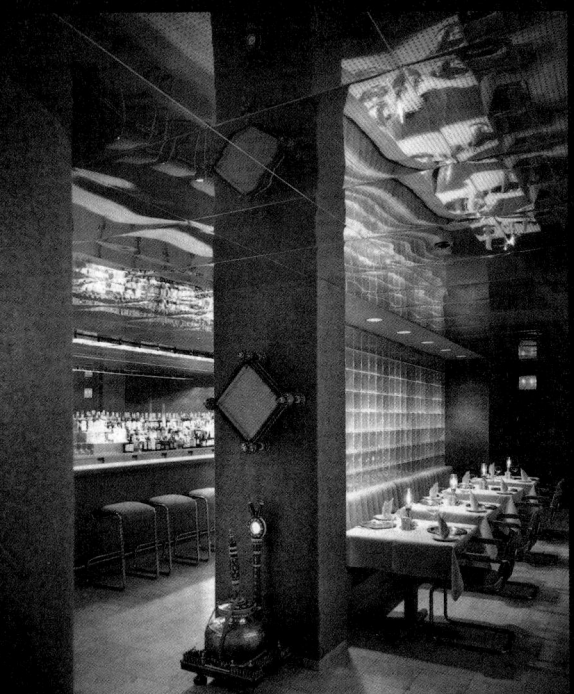

Far left: Shezan, 8 West Fifty-eighth Street. Gwathmey Siegel, 1976. ©Norman McGrath. NM

Above: Maxwell's Plum, 1181 First Avenue. Warner LeRoy, 1968. WL

Left: Shezan. ©Norman McGrath. NM

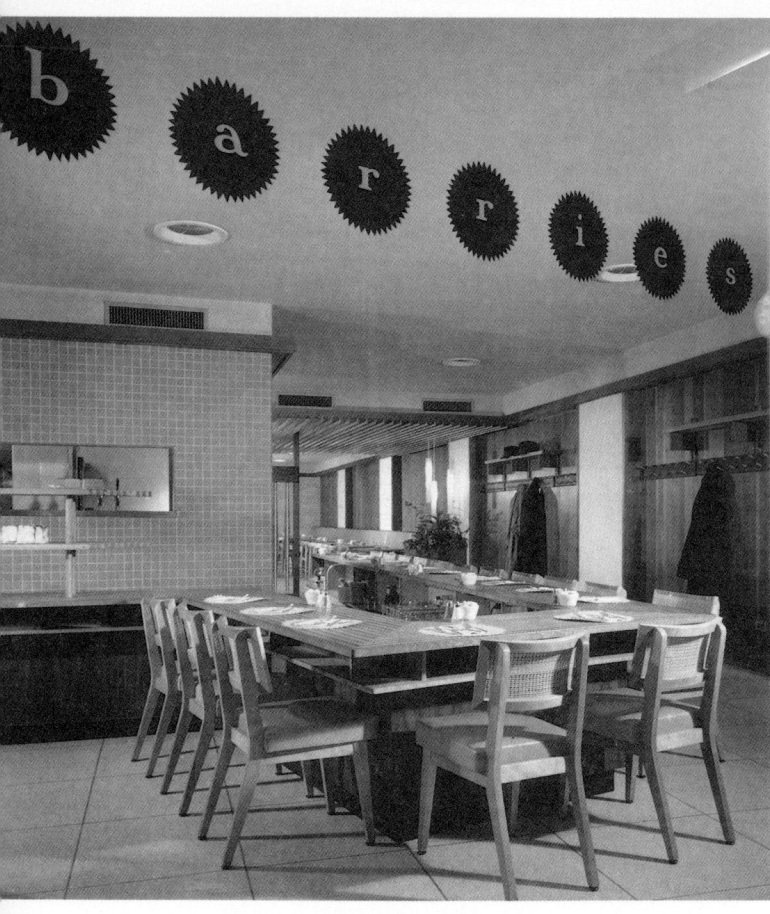

Barrie's, 65 East Fifty-fifth Street. Arthur Silver, 1956. Stoller. ©ESTO

Fast food served in a sophisticated setting became increasingly popular in the interwar years, when the plain, sanitary whiteness typical of the Childs restaurants began to give way to the International Style Modernism of such midtown landmarks as Hector Hamilton's Foltis-Fischer restaurant and the Automat chain.[41] The 1940s saw more colorful and more exuberant designs. The air-conditioned, twenty-four-hour Riker's shops, designed by Daniel Laitin, were notable for accommodating the desire of the chain's new owners to abandon the "white porcelain enamel stage" while still respecting the habitual preoccupation with hygiene-inspired design.[42] Laitin complemented the free curves of his plans with the abstract, surrealistic shapes of murals created by painter and mosaicist Max Spivak. The normally restrained Eugene Schoen also took on the fast-food problem with uncustomary brio in his Buitoni Spaghetti Bar, where plates of pasta were rolled out on a conveyor in the center of a U-shaped counter.[43] Here surfaces of stainless steel and mirror, which conveyed a sense of cleanliness, were juxtaposed with peach-colored walls and a dark blue ceiling in keeping with the new, softer sensibility.

With the notable exception of Chock full o' Nuts, by the 1950s most fast-food restaurants had begun to take on a warmer, less clinical, even homey image.[44] These new restaurants worked more or less within the boundaries of an easy Modernism, influenced in particular by contemporary Scandinavian design. Arthur Silver's Barrie's restaurant (1956), at 65 East Fifty-fifth Street, was a notable example of this trend in an individually owned facility.[45] The front portion of the restaurant was devoted to a free-form dining counter designed for chairs rather than bar stools, while more conventional table service was located in the rear. Natural-finished wood was abundantly used for architectural surfaces as well as tabletops and countertops. Both the scale and the character of the restaurant were residential. As Lois Wagner noted in *Interiors*: "The serenity of the solution, hardly typical of such eating places, was certainly indicated by the gloss of the neighborhood, but Silver's intent, more than this, was to free the restaurant from all the stigmatizing associations of a counter joint."[46]

George Nelson and Charles Mount's La Potagerie (1971), at 554 Fifth Avenue, used a brighter, cleaner palette more closely attuned to the corporate Modernism of the 1960s to pursue the same ideals—to put, as John Anderson observed, "character and occasion back into the snack."[47] The idea was to marry the cuisine of a French provincial inn—everything on the menu was a soup—with the efficiency of a New York luncheonette. The interior was completely revealed to the pedestrian through an enormous unframed, curved butt-glazed window. Quarry-tile flooring, glazed wall tiles, rough plaster walls and abundant plants suggested the country but with a distinct overlay of urbanity. At the end of the long narrow space, a raised dining area with a waterfall concluded the spatial sequence and reiterated the indoor-outdoor ambiguities of the design.

In 1974 Charles Mount, now working with Judith Stockman, returned to the same theme for the Pot au Feu, which occupied a somewhat twisted 7,000-square-foot L of space in the recently completed Exxon Building in Rockefeller Center.[48] Here the intimacy of La Potagerie was not possible, so Mount and Stockman created a multilevel space where the act of dining itself provided the principal visual drama. As the designers put it: "We tried to create the effect of a grandstand so that eating becomes something of a spectator sport. And since the main circulation takes place below the level of the tables, it does not disturb the diners."[49] Using simple, vinyl-coated metal garden furniture designed by Harry Bertoia, Mount and Stockman relied on the dynamics and intricate geometry of the space, as well as aggressive graphics, to enliven the scheme and to direct the attention of pedestrians to the restaurant's existence behind the closely spaced grid of the Exxon Building's facade. Mount returned to the Potagerie theme once again in 1976 for La Bonne Soupe East, on the east side of Third Avenue between Fifty-eighth and Fifty-ninth streets (see chapter 5).

No restaurant chain more perfectly exemplified the role of fast-food dining in mid-century American life than McDonald's, which originated as a suburban drive-in hamburger joint but by the late 1960s was making inroads on the urban market.[50] The chain's entry into New York, and particularly Manhattan, was stormy, with virtually every new franchise store bringing controversy—usually community protest over visual blight, litter, double parking, perceived and imagined issues of crime, homogenization and so on. When McDonald's tore down the building at the southeast corner of Eighty-sixth Street and Amsterdam Avenue in 1974, neighborhood protest was so intense that the company withdrew, leaving a lot that remained empty for twelve years.[51] Similarly, neighbors successfully opposed a facility proposed for the southwest corner of Sixty-sixth Street and Lexington Avenue.[52] Nonetheless, by 1975 forty McDonald's were open in New York, thirteen of those in Manhattan.

While most of the McDonald's shops built in New York conformed to the company's standard "townhouse" design, in a few "sensitive" locations the company introduced more individual themes. In 1975 McDonald's leading New York franchiser, twenty-five-year-old Irwin Kruger, who owned eighteen franchises in partnership with Howard Bass, opened a store at 966 Third Avenue, in the heart of the "design district."[53] For the store Kruger retained George Nelson to create something a little more sophisticated than usual. "We took on the McDonald's project," Nelson said, "as something of a challenge to see what it would be like to work with the largest of the fast-food chains. What we learned almost instantly was that specifications in most cases were already established, and no deviation was permitted."[54] Nonetheless, Nelson managed to take the standard repertoire of quarry-tile floors and fixed seating and give the three-story "townhouse" shop a distinct and pleasing character. Photo murals set a nature theme that was enhanced by baskets of plants hung under false skylights.

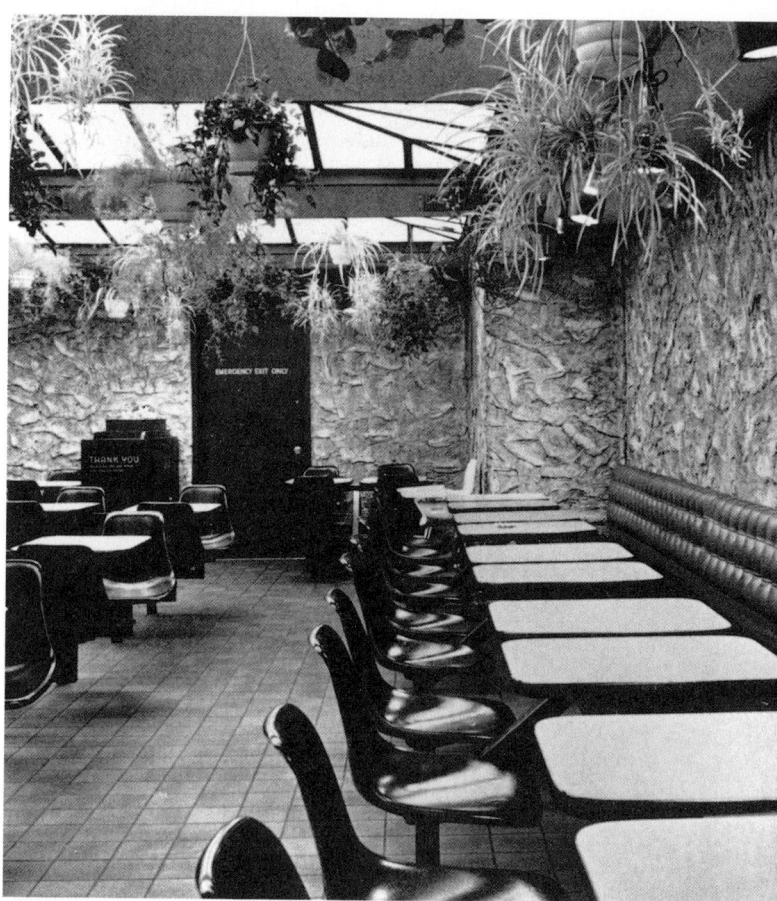

McDonald's, 966 Third Avenue. George Nelson, 1975. Cohen. IN. CU

Nightclubs

The early 1940s was the heyday of the New York nightclub. With Prohibition and the Depression behind them, New Yorkers escaped from the gathering war clouds and then from the realities of war itself by squeezing into crowded *boîtes* where they could share indifferent food, watery drinks and exuberant high jinks.[55] As Maurice Zolotow, the Broadway columnist, reported in 1942 to the readers of the *American Mercury*:

> Since the war began in 1939, the night clubs have gone through an erratic series of reactions. At first, there was the long-anticipated effect, what *Variety* called 'escapology,' as crowds jammed the nighteries in their eagerness to escape the headlines. Then, as the headlines caught up with America and escape was out of the question, club attendance became almost a barometer of the quality of the news: bad war news meant bad business, good news a surge of trade.

The nightclub era reached its zenith in 1942. Zolotow described the scene: "On every alley in every large American city, these palaces of pleasure are jammed today with seekers of release from war tension. Service men trying to press a twelvemonth of diversion into a short furlough. Holders of war contracts whose pockets bulge with extra cash. Wealthy refugees habituated to continental night life. Just men and women escaping the tom-tom insistence of war news." He saw the nightclub as a profound measure of the times:

> It may be rightly regarded as a special aspect of the modern cosmopolitan city, the city in which the individual human being is deracinated. Far removed from the neighborhood tavern, the night club offers the closest approximation in Megalopolis to a shared experience between man and man; it helps compensate for the loss of community feeling in the city of half a million or over. With its unique blend of entertainment and alcohol and closeness of humanity—table pressing against table and conversation running freely among strangers . . . the night club is, in a sense, the city's community festival, its substitute for the barn dance at harvest time.[56]

On the whole nightclub architecture was indifferent, although there were exceptions. Café Society Uptown (1940), at 128 East Fifty-eighth Street, was an essay in lighthearted surrealism, with two murals by Anton Refregier and an aluminum sculpture by Robert Cronbach depicting two free spirits that was suspended over the dining room.[57] Refregier's surrealistic murals, which owed something to both de Chirico and Joan Miró, served to visually expand two sides of an otherwise unarticulated box. After an unpopular renovation in 1945 by an unidentified designer, Refregier was called in again the next year to do new murals for the club, this time collaborating with the sculptor Paul Petroff.[58] Refregier's themes included the evils of greed and the sterility of education, but the designs were so abstract and the colors so bright that it's doubtful many of the club's pleasure seekers took much notice of the messages.

Dorothy Draper's Monte Carlo (1940), at 49 East Fifty-fourth Street, was far grander in scale and much more dramatic in decor.[59] One entered through a white marbleized foyer illuminated by sconces in the form of extraordinarily lush plants. Gliding across a boldly patterned black-and-white floor, the clubgoer could stop for a drink at a bar and glance across a balustrade at a night view of Monte Carlo shown in two murals, then go on to a meal and dancing in the dining room, which was draped entirely in chartreuse and red satin. In 1941 Franklin Hughes reworked Draper's scheme, adding more conventional, jungle-inspired murals, but also a spatially engaging awning cantilevered from a colonnade of thin white pipes.[60] Two years later, after William Zeckendorf became the club's owner, the Monte Carlo expanded into the former Harry Richmond Club next door as well as Helen Morgan's House of Morgan (Scott & Teegen, 1936).[61] Hughes was hired again, this time to take up Draper's original themes in the new bar. He also redecorated the main dining room with an even more effulgent palette. As *Interiors* reported, however, "Monte Carlo is becoming so enormous that old timers shake their heads dolefully over it,"[62] and by 1946 the size of the establishment and the public's growing disenchantment with nightclubbing led the management to call Hughes back to adapt the room for a dinner cinema.[63]

Perhaps the most glittering of all the clubs was Larue, at 45 East Fifty-eighth Street, which Norman Bel Geddes revamped in 1941.[64] The designer used mirrors to make two separate rooms appear as one, skillfully banking crystal flowers with gold and silver leaves against the glass to further dematerialize the space. By the early 1940s the club, which had been opened as a speakeasy in 1928, was something of an institution, catering to an affluent, young crowd who danced to Eddie Davis's band. The 1.2.3. Club (1942), at 123 East Fifty-fourth Street, with its largely brownish gray and white interior, was far more restrained, befitting an enterprise underwritten by such high-society types as Cole Porter, Dwight Deere Wyman, Mrs. Paul Mellon and Leonard Hanna.[65] Its piano-playing entrepreneur, Roger Stearns, an architect turned entertainer, entrusted the design of the club to Karl Noble and the lighting designer Abe Feder.

In 1945 Dorothy Draper remodeled the Versailles, at 151 East Fiftieth Street. According to her biographer, Carleton Varney, its reopening "was a symbolic relighting of Manhattan cabaret nightlife."[66] But it proved to be an economic disaster for Draper, who was left with her suppliers' unpaid bills when the club owners declared bankruptcy shortly after opening night, a sign of changing fortunes in the nightclub business, which began a slow decline ending in virtual death by the 1950s. With so many middle- and upper-class families decamping to the suburbs, the city's evening hours became increasingly governed by commuter timetables; even more significant was the emphasis on family "togetherness," which often centered on the newly widespread television that was bringing to the home the top-class variety-hall music and comedy that had previously been available almost exclusively in nightclubs. The communal camaraderie of the club was replaced by the introspective, privatized life of the family in its isolated house.

In the early 1960s, however, as the charms of the suburbs began to pall and the generation of postwar suburban families was maturing, many returned to Manhattan to live or at least to play. The era of good plain thinking that was represented by the Eisenhower presidency was giving way to a more urbane, even glamorous style of life, associated with the Kennedy administration. One of the first signs of a change was the relocation to larger quarters of El Morocco, one of the few clubs to have survived the postwar social slump. As Priscilla Ginsberg wrote in 1961: "For three decades El Morocco has been the plush mecca for such gaudy, tinseled and cut-glass personages as Liz, Eddie and sometimes Debbie, the Duke and Duchess of Windsor, Onassis and Maria Callas and even Greta Garbo." The new club, at 307 East Fifty-fourth Street, was designed by Valerian Rybar, a brilliant new figure on the decorating scene. "Elmo's" had become such an institution that Rybar maintained virtually all of the late Vernon MacFarlane's design for the old headquarters: not only the blue zebra-striped banquettes but also the cellophane palms, the Moorish courtyard and the starry sky over the tiny dance floor. Upstairs, Rybar gave the new Champagne Room his own personal stamp, with more than a whiff of nineteenth-century Viennese luxury, which, according to Ginsberg, left "the ladies with the gasping feeling of wanting to unlace their stays."[67]

The new El Morocco had a brief incandescence; it closed almost as soon as it reopened when its founder John Perona died in 1961.[68] El Morocco reopened again in 1964, only to close again five years later.[69] In 1971 the club had another glittery reopening. This time its by now traditional decor was refurbished by the decorator Ellen Lehman McCluskey. On opening night, all of society was there, including Aristotle Onassis, not with his opera star paramour, Maria Callas, but with his new wife, the former Jacqueline Bouvier Kennedy. The air was electric with excitement. As Mrs. Onassis told Charlotte Curtis, society writer for the *New York Times*, "Ari's been talking about this opening for three days."[70]

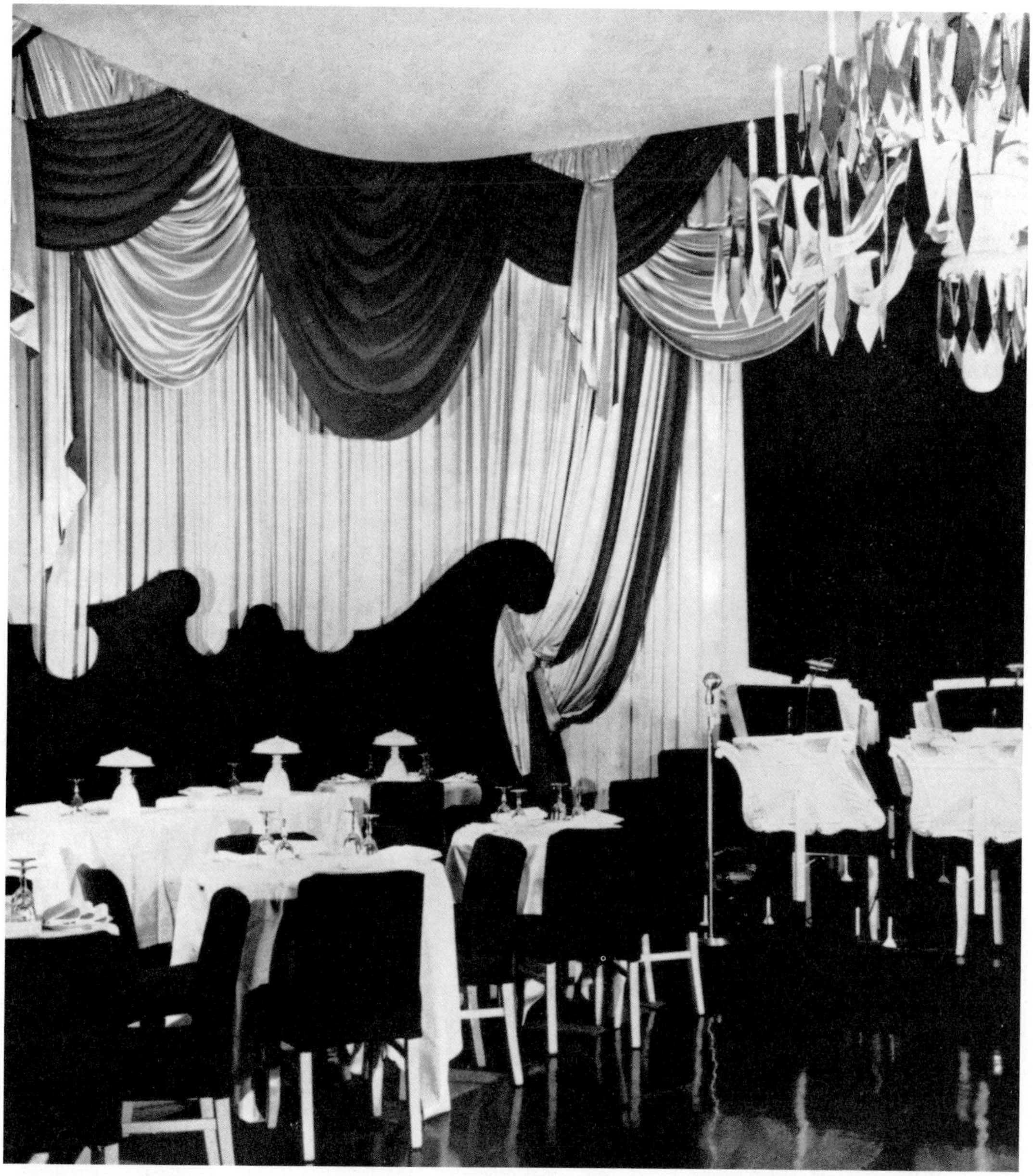

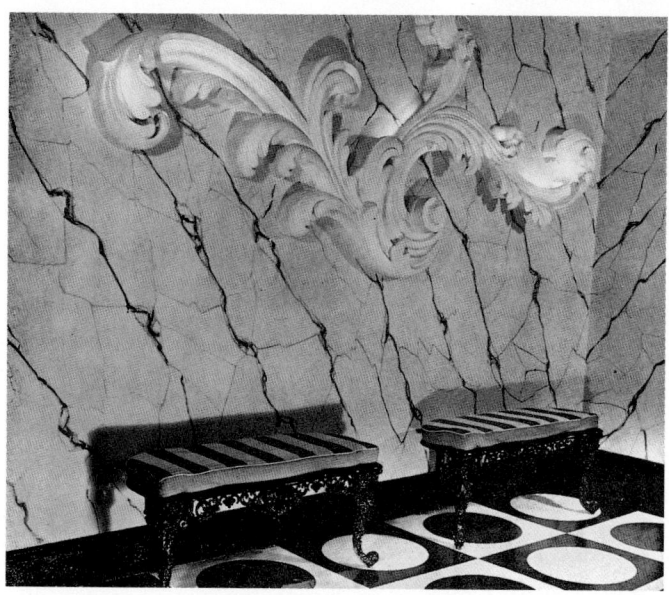

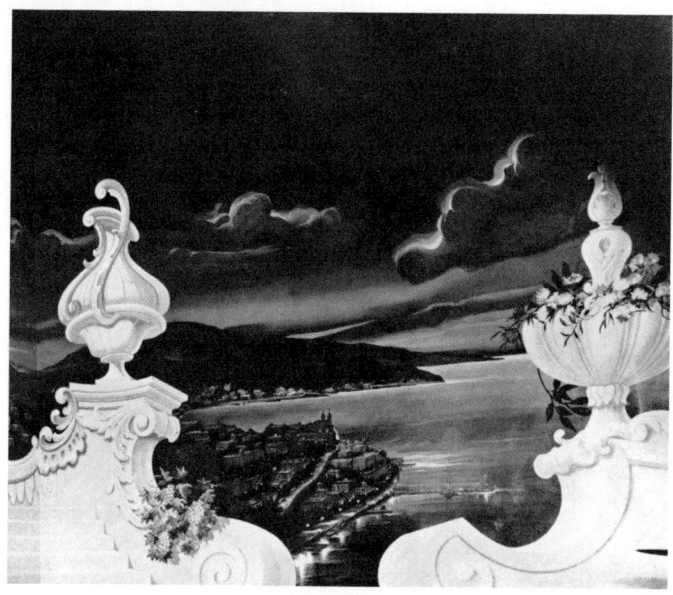

Left: Monte Carlo, 49 East Fifty-fourth Street. Dorothy Draper, 1940. Dining room. IN. CU

Bottom left: Monte Carlo. Entrance. IN. CU

Bottom right: Monte Carlo. Wall mural. IN. CU

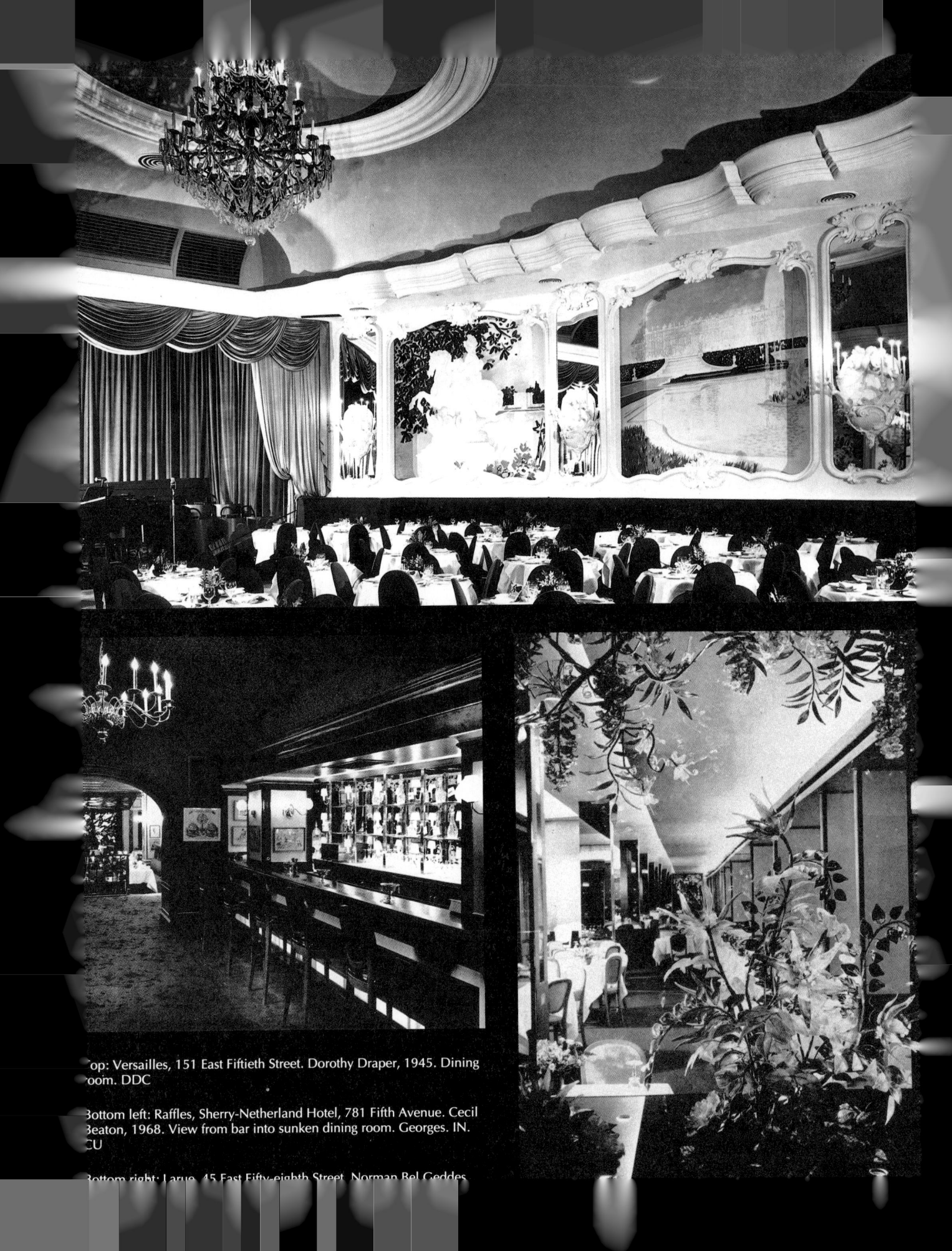

Top: Versailles, 151 East Fiftieth Street. Dorothy Draper, 1945. Dining Room. DDC

Bottom left: Raffles, Sherry-Netherland Hotel, 781 Fifth Avenue. Cecil Beaton, 1968. View from bar into sunken dining room. Georges. IN. CU

Bottom right: Larue, 45 East Fifty-eighth Street. Norman Bel Geddes.

By the late 1960s traditional nightclubs were giving way to a new form, the discotheque. Le Club and L'Interdit were fashionable versions of the type. L'Interdit, in the basement of the Hotel Gotham, featured a large-scale sculpture of a jazz combo by the artist Marisol as virtually the only embellishment in the otherwise characterless room.[71] Shepheard's, in the Drake Hotel, was another popular discotheque, catering to a young, monied crowd who pounded a twelve-by-twelve-foot dance floor beneath a pink silk tent; the overall effect of the room was characterized as "East 50's Pharaoh."[72]

From the point of view of design, Cecil Beaton's Raffles was the most interesting of the clublike discotheques.[73] Located in the basement of the Sherry-Netherland Hotel, Raffles opened in October 1968. It included a bulletin board for communications between the superrich and their hangers-on—"Will Mr. Capote call Mrs. Paley?"—as well as the usual bar, and dining rooms that featured one-way mirrors to overlook the dance floor without appearing to pry. The name Raffles suggested at once raffishly correct life in the British colonies and an English men's club, which Beaton chose as his point of departure: "Women always want to get into a place that looks as if it belongs to men," he opined.[74] Using dark flocked wallpaper, figured carpets of his own design, tufted black leather sofas and lots of brass and wrought iron, Beaton designed something more like the parlor of a swank bordello than a stuffy London club, an effect made all too obvious by the illuminated ceiling he created out of pieces of colored glass. Fashion and society columnist Eugenia Sheppard much preferred the highly polished, dark brown carved walnut arched entrance to the cocktail lounge, which she described as "a bit of Beaton genius," explaining: "Framed by the arch, Raffles is the image of security, permanence and tradition, not just one but at least a hundred years old."[75]

These discotheques were small and exclusive—Raffles and Le Club were membership clubs, as was L'Interdit intermittently. But some new clubs opened to serve a more middle-class crowd, an answer to the giant nightclub palaces of the 1930s. The first of these clubs, which featured live and recorded rock music, was Olivier Coquelin's Cheetah (1966), at 1680 Broadway, on the southeast corner of Fifty-third Street, located in what was formerly the Arcadia Ballroom.[76] The Cheetah included an 8,000-square-foot dance floor, which could accommodate 1,000 couples, a reading room, a television room, a movie theater where avant-garde short films were shown, and carts dispensing Nathan's hot dogs. But by the time the rock club era was in full swing, a younger generation of clubgoers had moved the action away from midtown, where the traditional club scene had developed near offices, hotels and restaurants, to a downtown venue where young bohemians lived and would-be hipsters congregated. The Electric Circus, located in a former Polish social club on St. Mark's Place in what was coming to be called the East Village, was the most spectacular of the new dance palaces (see chapter 4). It was followed by Cerebrum (1968), located at 429 Broome Street in SoHo. According to Time, Cerebrum was "a theater without a stage show, a cabaret without food or liquor, a party without an occasion."[77] Its owner, Ruffin Cooper, a former talent agent, described it as "an electronic studio of participation."[78] While traditional issues of architecture and interior decoration were no doubt far from the minds of the transparent-toga-clad participants in Cerebrum's highly exploratory program, the environment was unquestionably a reflection of the prevailing counter-cultural trend toward dematerialized space—what architect James Wines would come to describe as de-architecture.[79]

Between the 1940s and the 1970s interior decoration, previously characterized by a certain dilettantism, underwent a dramatic metamorphosis. By the end of this period it had emerged as a fully articulated approach not only to the embellishment but to the actual creation—in effect the architecture—of commercial and residential interiors, thereby fulfilling a long-held goal of Modernism. What had been known as decorating came to be known as interior design, space design and even interior architecture. Though this transformation began in fin-de-siècle France and Germany, and can be traced through the work of Frank Lloyd Wright, as well as that of Walter Gropius, Ludwig Mies van der Rohe and Le Corbusier—the principal formulators of canonical Modernism—the final phase, in which interior design was accepted as a fact of professional practice, was in large measure a New York story.

Despite this new development, traditional interior decorating continued to play an important role in the residential field. True, some of the old guard, like Eleanor McMillen Brown and Dorothy Draper, expanded the scope of their services and repositioned their firms so that by the 1950s they were serving as full-fledged interior designers providing traditional decorating as well as interior architecture for residential and commercial clients.[1] But, at least through the late 1940s, the stalwarts of the interwar period continued to hold sway over the New York scene: Nancy McClelland, who had established her decorating shop at 375 Fifth Avenue in 1922 and was active until the 1950s;[2] Elsie de Wolfe, who was semiretired but undertook occasional projects;[3] Diane Tate and Marian Hall, whose scholarly Adam-style room for Mr. and Mrs. Carl J. Schmidlapp showed no diminution in their ability to carry out traditional work with panache;[4] and Ruby Ross Wood, who reached her stride in the 1930s and, assisted by her talented protégé, Billy Baldwin, continued to work until her death in 1950.[5]

Even though the acerbic T. H. Robsjohn-Gibbings was increasingly involved in furniture design and writing, he too continued to decorate.[6] In 1950 Robsjohn-Gibbings treated his own apartment as an elegantly understated stage set for both public gatherings and private life. Gray walls and carpeting, as well as gray linen curtains and upholstery, were used throughout the apartment as a foil to sleekly modern dark walnut furniture of his own design.[7] In 1961 Robsjohn-Gibbings employed a similarly prudent approach in the design of a thirteen-room Park Avenue apartment for Victor Ganz, a manufacturer of costume jewelry who had amassed the largest privately owned collection of Pablo Picasso paintings in America. Attempting to balance the paintings' visual power, the decorator selected an array of antique furniture, including Spanish Gothic, Italian Renaissance and seventeenth-century English pieces. According to Time, the ensemble "created a remarkably effective multi-century effect that recognizes Picasso's presence but does not succumb to him altogether."[8]

A handful of significant figures would continue into the 1970s as traditional decorators and satisfy a select but highly influential clientele. Mrs. Henry Parish II, called "Sister" by her friends and colleagues, emerged in the 1960s as the undisputed master of quiet taste inspired by the English country house, frequently and skillfully adapting it to the scale and functional programs of New York apartment living. Her own maisonette apartment at 960 Fifth Avenue epitomized the approach.[9] Michael Greer, who had once worked for Nancy McClelland, steadfastly maintained the traditional point of view.[10] Greer's work from the late 1950s on, specializing in bold, even bombastic interpretations of the Directoire and Empire styles, continued the grand manner of decorating.

From the 1950s until his retirement in 1972, Billy Baldwin was New York's preeminent decorator. His strength was an ability to fuse paint, lighting and simple furniture into personal and fundamentally graceful dwelling places.[11] By the early 1960s Baldwin's interiors, exemplified by his own small Amster Yard apartment, demonstrated just how far interior decoration had been infiltrated by the impulses of architectural Modernism toward simplicity and ahistorical, abstract design.[12] Perhaps Baldwin's most inventive essay was the library of the apartment he designed in 1955 for the songwriter Cole Porter on the thirty-third floor of the Waldorf Towers.[13] The living and dining rooms were fairly conventional, using antique French furniture that Porter and his late wife, Linda, had collected in the 1920s. But the library was unique: a dark room highlighted by freestanding brass bookcases specially designed by Baldwin. By the mid-1960s Baldwin began to respond to the requirements of a new generation of clients whose point of view was self-consciously youthful and family oriented. For Mrs. Louise Savitt and her three-year-old son, Baldwin decorated a modest apartment at 21 East Sixty-sixth Street, painting the woodwork white and using lots of bright, clear-colored, flower-strewn fabrics and wallpapers. "The effect of the bedroom," Baldwin averred, is "deliberate pointillism, like a Seurat painting."[14] *Vogue* said that throughout the apartment "the unhesitant mixing of colours cuts through prettiness with zip."[15] Baldwin's apartments for Mr. and Mrs. Harding Lawrence, Mr. and Mrs. Leland Hayward and a host of other important business-oriented socialites testified to his influence and the range of his talent.[16]

The figure who best represents the transformation of interior decorating into interior design and whose work most consistently reflected the evolution of New York trends in the 1940s through the 1960s was William Pahlmann.[17] After studying art and interior decoration at the New York School of Fine and Applied Arts, including a sojourn in the school's Paris program, Pahlmann set up as a decorator in New York.[18] In 1936 he was hired by Walter Hoving as head of interior decoration at Lord & Taylor's department store, where Pahlmann's baroquely theatrical model rooms, offering versions of the English Regency and American Early Victorian periods, set a fashion in the late 1930s.[19]

In 1941 Lord & Taylor's sent Pahlmann to Peru to prepare for a promotion that resulted in a line of furniture and fabrics based on native themes.[20] Pahlmann's theme promotions at Lord & Taylor's were widely reported, influential events, comparable in their way to the opening of a Broadway play, making him, as *Interiors* noted, "the best known and most publicized interior designer in the department store field."[21] But because his work was largely in the area of "model rooms," it was criticized by some as overscaled, aggressive and stagy, a quality it shared with the flamboyant work of Dorothy Draper. These criticisms were softened with the completion in 1942 of Pahlmann's first apartment, a penthouse for Mrs. Marion Falk near Gramercy Park.[22] The Falk apartment was dramatic (and dramatically lit by Abe Feder). The owner's Oriental antiques were mixed with modular platform sofas that suggested a Scandinavian influence, but the voluptuous, tufted, Regency-inspired built-in banquette was pure Pahlmann.

After completing his military service, where he specialized in camouflage and rose to the rank of lieutenant colonel, Pahlmann established an independent practice as an interior de-signer, capitalizing on his commercial experience and his sense of drama to take on important assignments designing hotels (see chapter 5) and restaurants (see "Restaurants and Nightclubs," above), as well as residential work. His own apartment of 1955, with its twelve-foot-long blond leather sofa and its eclectic mix of decorative high art and craft objects, exemplified a cosmopolitan approach that would be the hallmark of much of the era's best work.[23] Pahlmann's apartment for Margaret Cousins, the prominent editor, combined smooth paneling around the fireplace with exposed bookshelves and simple wood furniture, synthesizing high sophistication and the down-home quality of a college professor's study.[24] His decorating of an apartment in Brooklyn Heights was subdued so as not to distract from the spectacular view of the lower Manhattan skyline outside the window.[25] Where typically Pahlmann's postwar work was intimate in scale, his firm did take on occasional residential commissions that were, as *Interiors* put it, "in the Grand Tradition."[26] Pahlmann's apartment for Mrs. Walter Hoving, for instance, was designed for formal entertaining.[27] The living room was dominated by a coromandel screen and furnished with gold and black Empire and Regency pieces that harked back to the model rooms he created in the 1930s at Lord & Taylor's. In 1965 Pahlmann relocated his own residence, from a large Park Avenue apartment he had moved to in the late 1950s and had done to the nines,[28] to a small apartment at 40 Central Park South.[29] Here he combined the Louis XVI fauteuils he bought in his student days in Paris with Japanese art and a scaled-down version of a tub chair he had first designed in the 1930s, creating an environment that, compared with the theatricality of his historicizing early career, seemed modern rather than stagy.

Beginning in the 1950s, architects became more involved in residential interior design; in addition, some interior designers, though usually not trained as architects, began to approach the problem from an architectural rather than a decorative perspective. The basis of the architectural approach can be traced to the introduction of European Modernism in the late 1920s, a movement that rejected the distinctions between architecture and decoration in favor of a unified approach sometimes called "total architecture," a phrase favored by Walter Gropius.[30] Economics also encouraged architects to take an interest in interiors: with very little new building, architects needed to find other ways to use their talents and to survive economically. Helping to furnish apartments was a reasonably lucrative way to explore ideas, especially since middle- and upper-class New Yorkers changed their apartments with great frequency during the 1930s and early 1940s, before wartime housing shortages and rent control laws began to limit mobility.

During the 1930s Philip Johnson, Jan Ruhtenberg, Donald Deskey, William Muschenheim, Paul Lester Weiner and Russel Wright designed notable apartment interiors in the Modernist style.[31] Although at first their work reflected the cool, machine-inspired aesthetics of Le Corbusier and Mies van der Rohe, by the 1940s they almost exclusively followed Le Corbusier's new, surrealist-inspired primitivism, which had eclipsed the influence of Mies (who had built almost nothing since 1931). But they were also beginning to take note of the Finnish architect Alvar Aalto, whose use of natural materials had more in common with American taste. Aalto became quite influential after his installation of the Finnish exhibit at the 1939 New York World's Fair gave architects a chance to study his work firsthand.[32] The primitive approach of Hungarian-born, Bauhaus-educated architect Marcel Breuer, practicing in Cambridge, Massachusetts, and teaching at Harvard, was also adopted for interiors, although

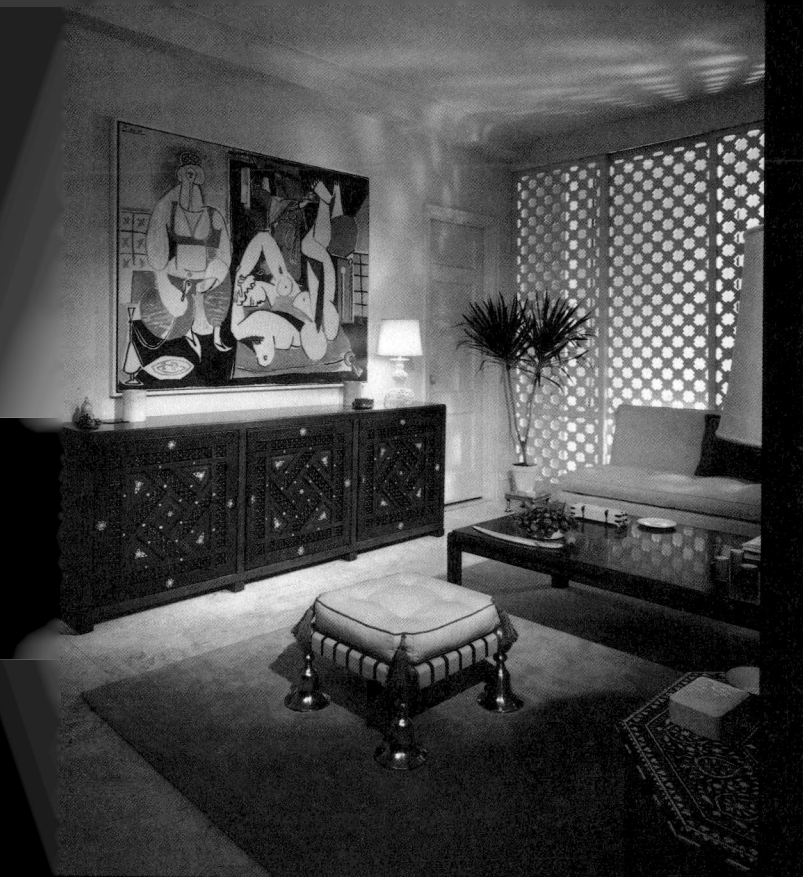

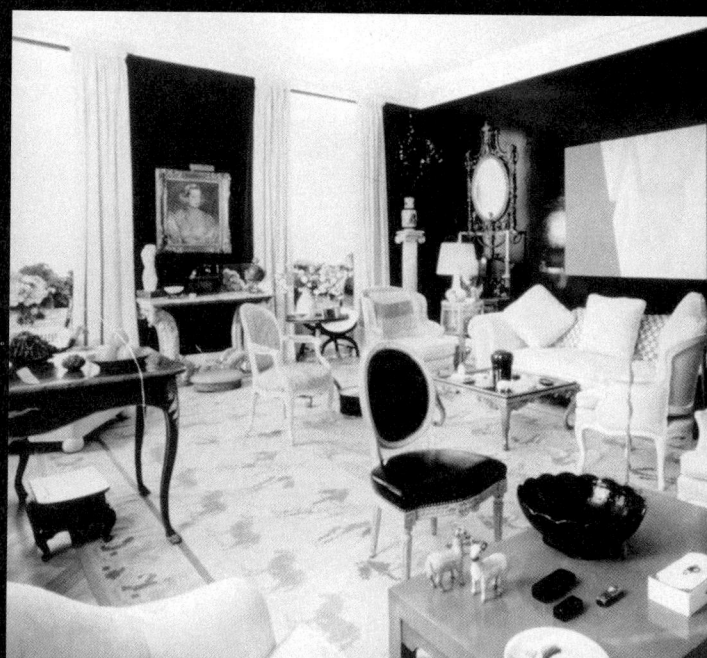

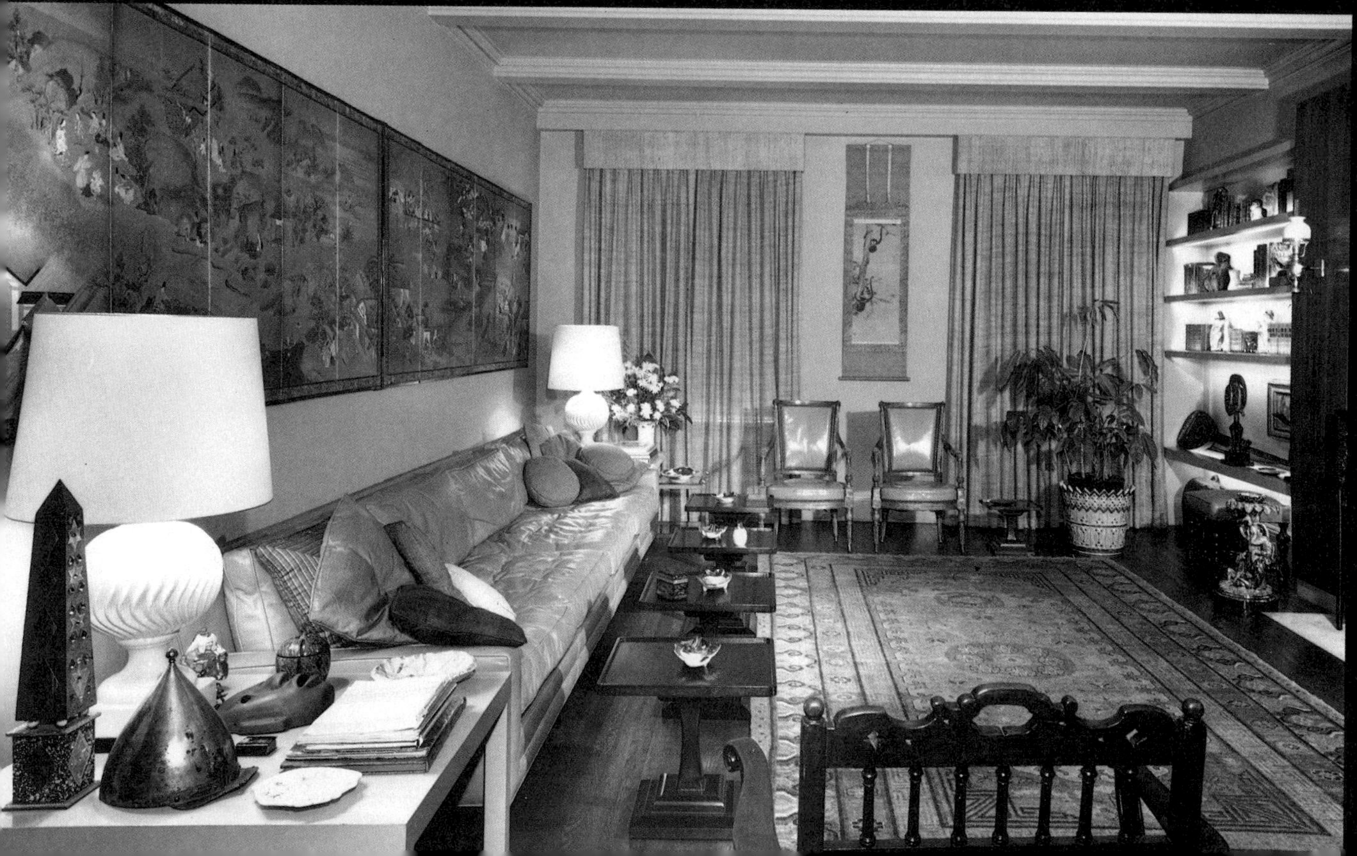

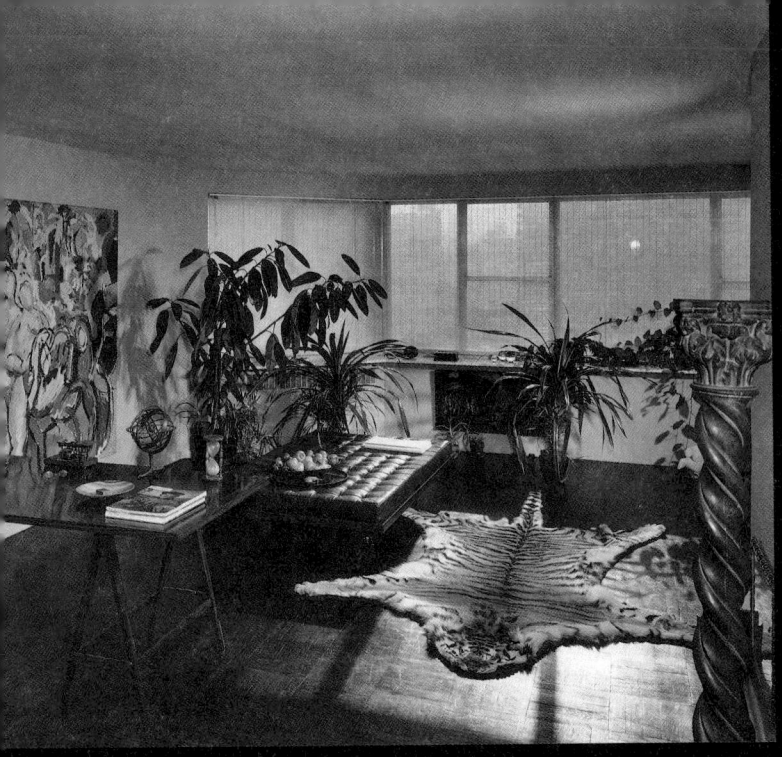

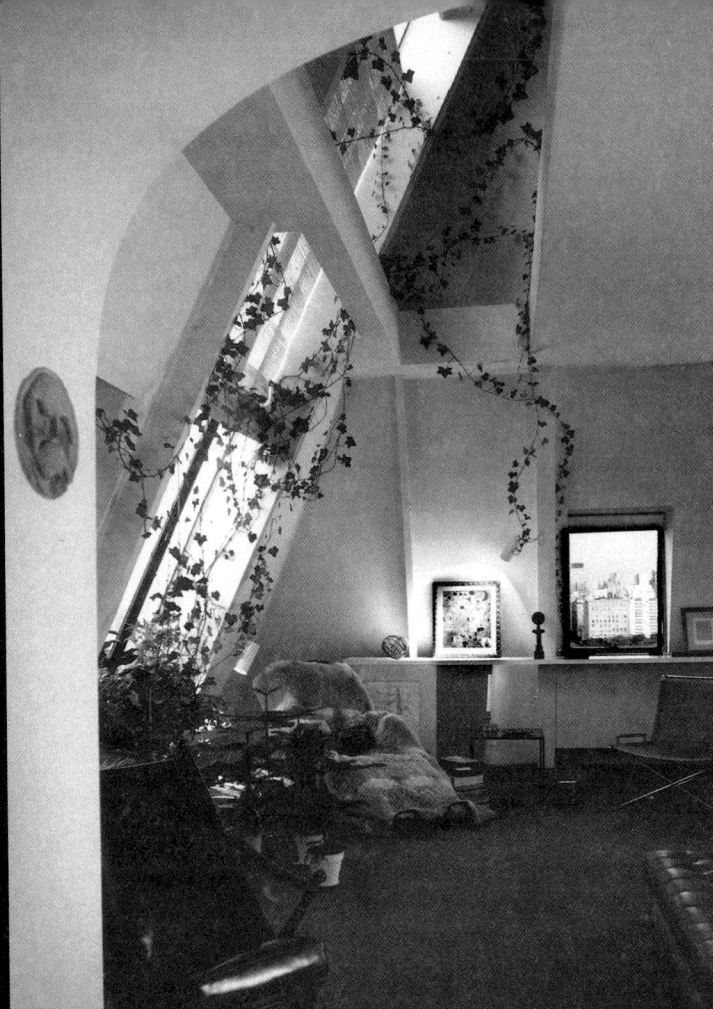

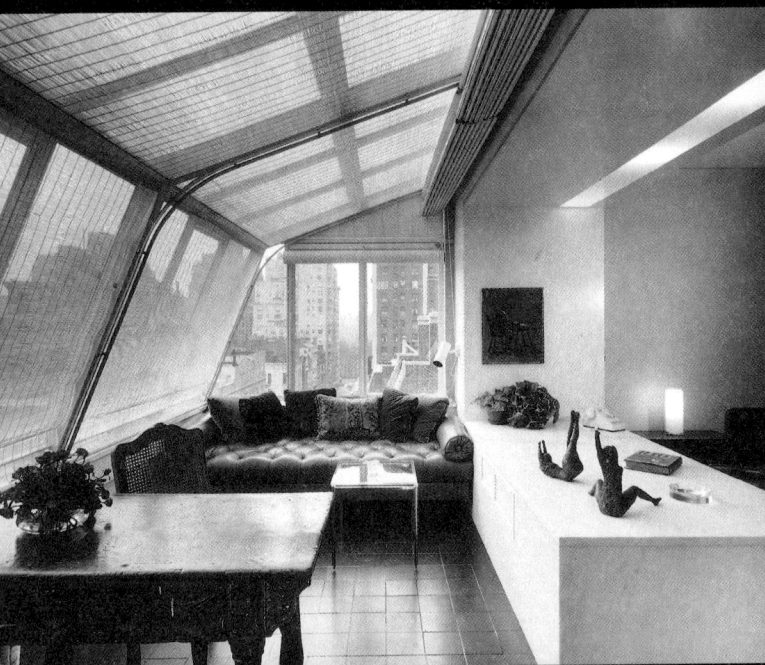

Top left: Ward Bennett apartment, 200 East Sixty-sixth Street. Ward Bennett, 1957. Georges. WB

Bottom left: Rubin apartment, 700 Park Avenue. Ward Bennett in association with Earl Pope, 1962. Reens. LR

Top right: Ward Bennett apartment, 1 West Seventy-second Street. Ward Bennett, 1964. Naar. WB

Bottom right: Ward Bennett apartment, 1 West Seventy-second Street.

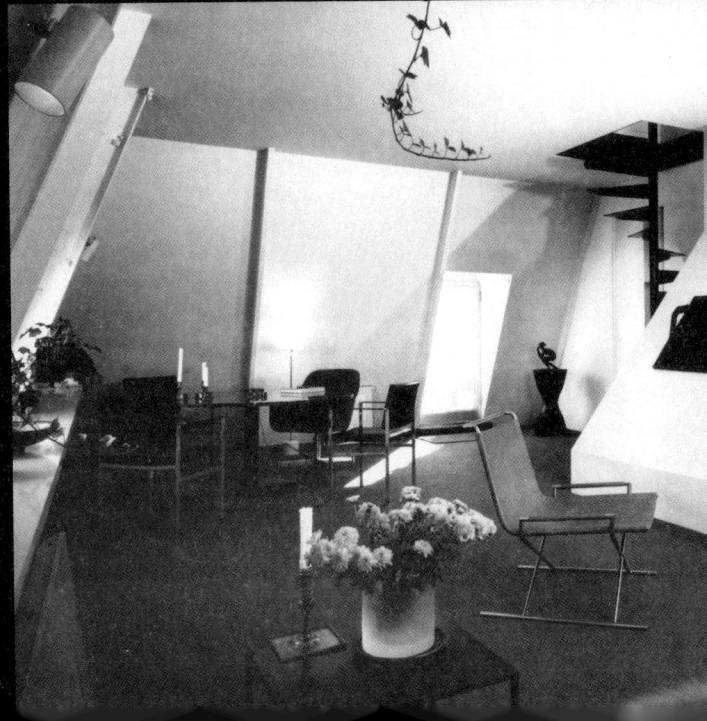

more in suburban house design—where natural materials, rough surfaces and curving lines would help win friends for a naturalistic Modernism—than in apartments.[33] The later work of Le Corbusier, the work of Aalto and Breuer, as well as that of Frank Lloyd Wright, whose career was once again in the ascendancy after several decades of decline, directed architects away from the mechanomorphology of 1920s International Style Modernism and toward a more personal, craft-oriented style.

This individualistic, sometimes eccentric approach to interior design was particularly characteristic of dislocated designers who settled in New York in the wake of the declining political situation in Europe and Asia. Felix Augenfeld, an Austrian who arrived in New York in 1939, received early commissions for the interiors of two identical apartments in a Central Park West building.[34] Aside from a striped tent that lowered the ceiling height and created a more festive atmosphere in the den of one apartment, and the furniture Augenfeld designed for both apartments, the interiors were relatively straightforward. In 1949 Augenfeld took on another apartment, a Park Avenue penthouse, which he filled with his own furniture designs.[35] In a letter to the editor of *Interiors*, S. G. Weiner, a design instructor at Brooklyn College and the Museum of Modern Art, took strong exception to Augenfeld's installation, and particularly to the specially designed mahogany bar cabinet, which he believed to be an "enormously expensive piece [that] has all the charm of a deep-freeze unit, all the vitality of a butcher shop refrigerator."[36] Augenfeld's 1954 design for a one-room apartment was simpler and less cluttered.[37]

The first New York apartment (1949) of the Chinese-born, American-educated architect I. M. Pei was an essay in what Arthur Drexler described as "planned surprises." As Drexler told the readers of *Interiors*, Pei was "regulated only superficially by the modern idiom," assembling "the ingredients of his living room with a slight backward glance at tradition."[38] Among Pei's aesthetic conceits were a wall of vertical unselected boards floating in front of a visually undesirable fireplace and chimney breast, a radio-phonograph cabinet cantilevered from the wall at a rakish angle, and a tan leather sofa visually connected to the ceiling by a single, slender pole. All of these elements paled in comparison to the room's principal focus, a single fish bowl carefully placed on a marble coffee table.

The first successful exploration of the highly keyed, Corbusian version of surrealist primitivism was undertaken by Benjamin Baldwin and his associate William Machado.[39] In their combined brownstone studio and living quarters of 1948, they used removable fiberglass shoji window screens, cocoa matting, a shaggy Moroccan rug, a pony-skin and leather officer's chair and a McCormick reaper tractor seat, which was mounted on four legs to serve as a stool, representing one of the earliest architectural uses of such an item. An unframed painting by Miró was directly incorporated as an end panel to the freestanding, built-in storage wall. Baldwin and Machado's modest collaboration was important in several ways: not only did it interpret the ideas of Le Corbusier and Aalto at a very sophisticated level, mixing motifs from preindustrial cultures with industrial "as-found" products; it also used painting and sculpture as an integral part of the decorating scheme. Moreover, the composition of the design team—Baldwin, the Princeton-trained architect turned interior designer, and Machado, the Harvard-trained fine artist turned interior designer—bespoke a totally new integrative approach within Modernism that was comparable in its vivacity if not its warmth to the work of traditional decorators.[40]

No one propounded this point of view with greater consistency than Ward Bennett, an autodidact born Howard Bennett Amsterdam.[41] At age fifteen, Bennett began his career as a stock boy at the fashion designer Hattie Carnegie's, eventually working his way up to a position in advertising and display before going off to Europe for travel, study and a brief stint in Le Corbusier's studio. According to Jane Fiske, in an article describing Bennett's first apartment commission, he was as anxious to depart from Modernism's moralistic stance against comfort as he was to reject its "School of Slab and Hairpin Leg" clichés of the 1940s.[42] While Bennett's early interiors succeeded in being spare without seeming empty or cold, they did not create strongly identifiable images. His Stafford apartment of 1954, designed for collectors who had previously lived in Paris, and whose eclectic tastes ranged from ancient Egyptian art to Goya to Braque, was located in an undistinguished contemporary apartment house which lacked the traditional proportions and details that could have provided a counterpoint to Bennett's reductionist impulses.[43] What emerged was a low-key, somewhat bland backdrop for the art, combining a few traditional French pieces with built-in bookcases, simple box sofas and tables designed by Bennett. The designer's own apartment of 1957 was also located in a recently completed apartment building.[44] To create a tension between old and new, smooth and textured surfaces, he juxtaposed objects he collected with those he designed. The apartment was sparsely furnished, with some of Bennett's commercially produced designs as well as a tufted leather settee that dominated the living room and an English Victorian chair drawn up to a rosewood desk slab supported by custom-designed sawhorses.

In an apartment for Jan Mitchell, the restaurateur and art collector, Bennett was able to go beyond decoration into what he described as interior architecture, removing walls and replacing them with sliding screens to open up and rearrange the space, removing cornices, enlarging windows and concealing lighting.[45] In a Fifth Avenue apartment for Mr. and Mrs. William A. M. Burden, which had been renovated by Philip Johnson in 1953–56 (see below), Bennett transformed the entrance into a white-painted gallery rotunda with a black-and-white marble floor and a "false" oculuslike skylight above a centrally placed Hans Arp sculpture, which stood on a pedestal lacquered in matte black.[46] In an apartment for Mr. and Mrs. M. O. Rothman, Bennett replaced the dining alcove with a raised lounging platform to take advantage of the view; in keeping with changing living patterns, he relegated dining to an interior wall where a desk doubled as a table for meals.[47] For the Rubin apartment (1962), located in a postwar apartment building on Park Avenue, Bennett, working in association with Earl Pope, not only reconfigured the plan but reorganized every detail of the fenestration, the lighting and the mechanical system, going so far as to enclose a terrace to create a solarium.[48] In the final analysis Bennett and Pope achieved a meticulously configured and detailed neutral container for the owner's antiques and works of art.

Bennett created his masterwork when he designed an apartment for himself in the Dakota (Henry J. Hardenbergh, 1882), at 1 West Seventy-second Street, where he reached a near-perfect balance between strongly modeled space and minimalist detail.[49] As *House and Garden* reported, Bennett "had a very definite idea of *how* he wanted to live, a manner which he termed 'purely in the twentieth century,'" yet he wanted to do so in a traditional studio environment.[50] The two clusters of servants' spaces in the Dakota's attic that he assembled as an apartment were an ideal situation. Separated by an air shaft, they afforded spectacular park views through small but strategically located windows; in one of the roof's pyramidal peaks the designer built a crow's-nest-like office. Surprisingly, Bennett, who was by now established as a leading contract furniture designer, banished freestanding furniture in favor of floor cushions, mattress-divans covered in glove leather and carpeted shelves that could double as window seats and serving buffets. A north-facing skylight was cut into the atelierlike living room, providing a diagonal view of the park and, more important, a view of the adjoining pyramidal roof turret, a grand yet benign sculptural presence that presided over the space.

After 1960, when Bennett completed his work on the Chase Manhattan Bank headquarters (see chapter 3), he concentrated on product design rather than interior decoration, but his influence could be seen in the work of a number of other designers, including his predecessor in reductivist Modernism, William Machado. In 1970 Machado completed the renovation of another set of former maids' rooms in the Dakota, a design that, though inspired by Bennett's apartment, drew upon a collection of books and art to create a richer, warmer effect.[51]

The designer who most successfully built upon Ward Bennett's contribution was John F. Saladino, who was trained in the fine arts at Notre Dame and at Yale.[52] Whereas Bennett's approach reflected the hard-edged minimalism of mid-century Modernism, Saladino's, while still spare, introduced a softer line and a greater feeling for natural materials. The debt to Bennett was particularly clear in Saladino's own apartment of 1969, which featured a low furniture grouping that included such Bennett staples as stacked floor cushions and stacked, leather-covered mattresses.[53] But Saladino added to them a natural wicker tub chair, and he retained traditional mantelpieces and dark-stained shutters that Bennett would probably have removed. For Ruth Campbell's apartment, designed on a tight budget, Saladino used simple furniture, and even an "as-found" wooden industrial spool made to serve as a cocktail table.[54] The giant graphic circle he introduced to magnify the visual importance of the fireplace reflected the new "supergraphics" that were influencing artists, designers and architects alike in the late 1960s.[55] The irregular configuration of Saladino's next apartment for his own use, where he had more space to work with, suggested to the designer a street, which he organized on a number of platforms; together with an imaginative manipulation of the ceiling plane, this device created a sense of vast space.[56]

While Saladino represented the earthier side of Bennett-inspired minimalism, there was another strain, a tougher, purer and more fundamentally architectural side that came to flower in the early 1970s with the work of Bennett's principal disciple, Joseph Paul D'Urso.[57] D'Urso first drew attention with a one-room apartment he renovated for Reed Evins, a twenty-year-old shoe designer. Here D'Urso laid out his vocabulary—a no-color palette, industrial materials, broad platforms carpeted in gray, spare use of select pieces of classic Modernist furniture. The overall sense was of the apartment as a silent backdrop for life. As D'Urso described his notion of design: "Most interior design today is based on a kind of fake individuality in which the designer seeks to 'interpret' his client's personality. . . . I try to create firm, clear backgrounds for my clients. They are then responsible for giving them life."[58]

D'Urso's first major commission was for the fashion designer Calvin Klein.[59] Faced with a banal space on the forty-sixth floor of the Sovereign, at 425 East Fifty-eighth Street, D'Urso and Klein agreed that the spectacular view had to be the main focus of the design, and that D'Urso's preferred palette of white walls,

black leather upholstery and chrome tubular furniture was very much on target. D'Urso gutted the three-bedroom apartment, reorganizing the plan and replacing the conventional boxlike rooms with two principal rooms for sleeping and living connected by wide pivot doors that could be opened to permit continuous flow for parties. The apartment was not a refuge from the city, but instead a platform from which to view it, a place to see it as a glittering work of art. "For me," said Klein, "this apartment is where New York is."[60]

For the most part, designers like Bennett, Saladino and D'Urso used painting and sculpture, just as they used freestanding furniture, to provide a counterpoint to their impulse toward spatial simplification. But there was another postwar trend in interior design in which the art became the central focus. When the art scene—both the creation and the collecting of contemporary art—shifted to New York from Paris, the problem of the collector's apartment became an important assignment for interior designers. This was clear as early as 1948, when Walter Rendell Storey, the veteran writer on the decorative arts, in his annual essay, "Interior Decoration," called attention to the new interest in art collecting and the impact paintings and sculpture could have on interior decoration.[61] The designer Bertha Schaeffer was quick to sense the importance of the interplay between the two, not only exploring that relationship in a series of interiors, but also devoting part of her time to the business of being an art dealer.[62] And, from time to time, exhibitions were organized to help the public see how contemporary art could find its place in the domestic environment. In 1961, for example, the Decorative Arts Center at 305 East Sixty-third Street mounted what House and Garden described as "one of the largest art exhibits the city has seen," transforming its furniture showrooms into thirty room settings for pictures and sculptures borrowed from local galleries by the artist Cleve Gray, who acted as curator.[63]

Many of the most interesting interiors of the 1950s and 1960s were built to accommodate important art collections. One of these was designed in 1950 by Edgar Kaufmann, Jr., who had studied painting in Vienna and had apprenticed as an architect with Frank Lloyd Wright before coming to New York to proselytize on behalf of Modernist interior and product design. For his own use Kaufmann renovated the abandoned quarters of the Montauk Yacht Club, which had been located at the base of the Campanile apartment house at 450 East Fifty-second Street until the construction of the East River Drive robbed the club of its waterfront.[64] After descending from the building's lobby, an arriving visitor to Kaufmann's apartment was confronted by a front door "so close to a glass wall that the rather startling view is made to seem like the first of the rooms." Beyond the glass, a gravel and ivy-covered terrace was built a foot or two above the highway. The former clubhouse was completely gutted and the intercolumniation of its stripped-down, brick-and-fieldstone exterior was infilled with glass. Inside and out, the space was organized to suggest a Mies courtyard house of the 1930s, with curtains strategically located to close down the space for privacy. Whereas Mies would have preferred refined materials, Kaufmann chose unpainted cinder block as his principal wall surface, no doubt a reflection of his interest in Frank Lloyd Wright's architecture as well as the apartment's location in what was essentially a basement. Richard Kelly designed the lighting, making extensive use of many of his pioneering concealed spot and flood lighting techniques. Every piece of furniture and every painting was exactly placed, yet the effect was one of casual openness. As Arthur Drexler observed:

Mr. Kaufmann's approach to design has produced a hierarchy of values which makes architecture an amplified, three dimensional picture frame, to be filled with objects which, though more important to him than the architecture itself, are equalized by the freedom they're given. It would be possible to add a Venetian bombe commode without disrupting a "style." It would become another ornament in an eclectic garden, according to the seasons of its owner's taste.[65]

In 1975 Kaufmann created another apartment, working with the designer Paul Mayen to transform a relatively ordinary nine-room apartment at 535 Park Avenue into an extraordinarily proportioned, subtly colored five-room showcase for fine art and furniture.

Between 1953 and 1956 Philip Johnson, whose residential work was largely confined to suburban houses, designed renovations in the Fifth Avenue apartment of Mr. and Mrs. William A. M. Burden.[66] Burden was president of the Museum of Modern Art, where Johnson was director of the Department of Architecture until 1954 and a trustee from 1958. In 1954 Burden had commissioned a house design from Johnson that was never built but was exhibited at Samuel Kootz's gallery.[67] The first part of the Burden apartment tackled by Johnson was the dining room, where, apparently under the influence of Mondrian, he devised with Richard Kelly a suspended grid of brass tubes that concealed tiny lights directed upward onto the ceiling. Within the grid, three light boxes full of pin-dot spotlights provided sparkle for the room's paintings and the dining table.

Arthur Drexler went from a brief stint at Cooper Union to a job as a writer for *Interiors* magazine, where his article on Philip Johnson's Glass House brought the young journalist to the architect's attention. He was subsequently hired as an assistant curator in the Department of Architecture at the Museum of Modern Art. While principally occupied with his growing responsibilities at the museum, Drexler occasionally undertook independent design commissions. In 1959, assisted by Poppy Wolff, he designed the apartment of Mrs. Elizabeth Bliss Parkinson, a museum trustee and a prominent art collector.[68] Drexler reorganized what was a conventional nine-room apartment at 205 East Seventy-second Street to create a continuous flow of space from the entry, past a gallery, through the living room and into a library. He covered the floor with blue glass mosaic tiles, an idea inspired by Mies van der Rohe's use of glass tiles for the ceiling of the Seagram Building's lobby. *Interiors* described the apartment as "a seascape, isolated, peaceful, whose mysterious limits are suggested rather than defined by white walls that seem less substance than light. The floor of this seascape is a shimmering surface of tiny vitreous glass mosaic. . . . Sunlight plays across the surface . . . transforming one of the flat dimensions of the apartment into a depth."[69] While Drexler was clearly the "space maker" for the Parkinson apartment, it was probably Wolff who arranged the owner's antique Italian, French and German furniture, which gave the design a surprising warmth. A sculptural arrangement of traditional furniture could be seen in Wolff's own apartment and in the apartment she designed for the actor Robert Loggia and his family.[70]

In 1964 Albert Herbert designed the apartment of Stella and William Copley, who had just returned to New York from France and who had assembled one of the world's more important collections of Dadaist art (Copley was an artist, painting under the name William Cpley).[71] Herbert began his professional career working on contract interiors for Michael Saphier Associates, but by 1955 he had set out on his own as an interior

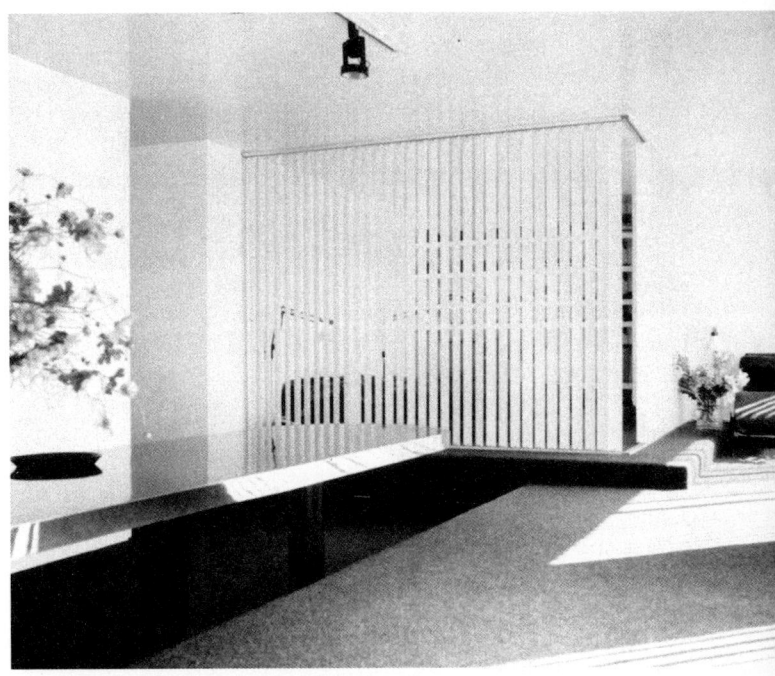

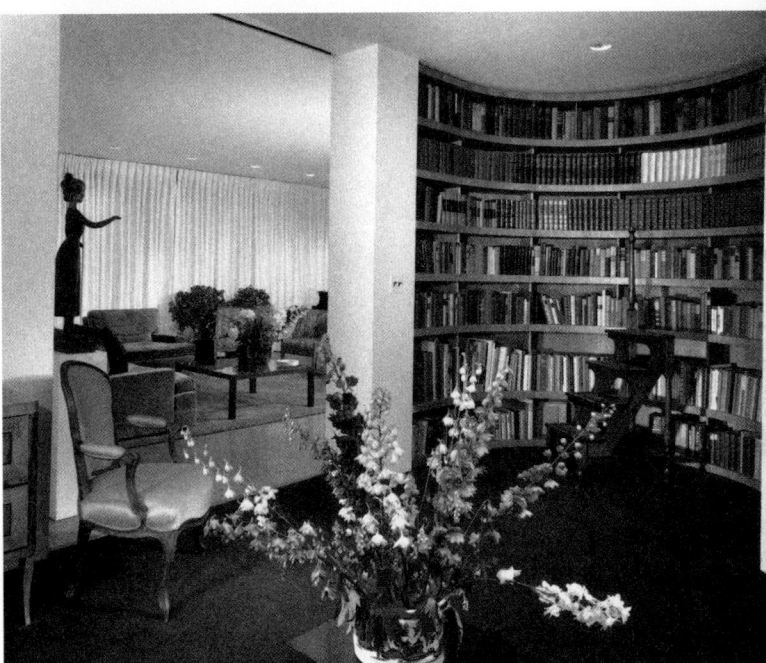

Top: Reed Evins apartment, 417 East Fifty-seventh Street. Joseph Paul D'Urso, 1975. Aaron. ©ESTO

Bottom: Elizabeth Bliss Parkinson apartment, 205 East Seventy-second Street. Arthur Drexler assisted by Poppy Wolff, 1959. Reens. LR

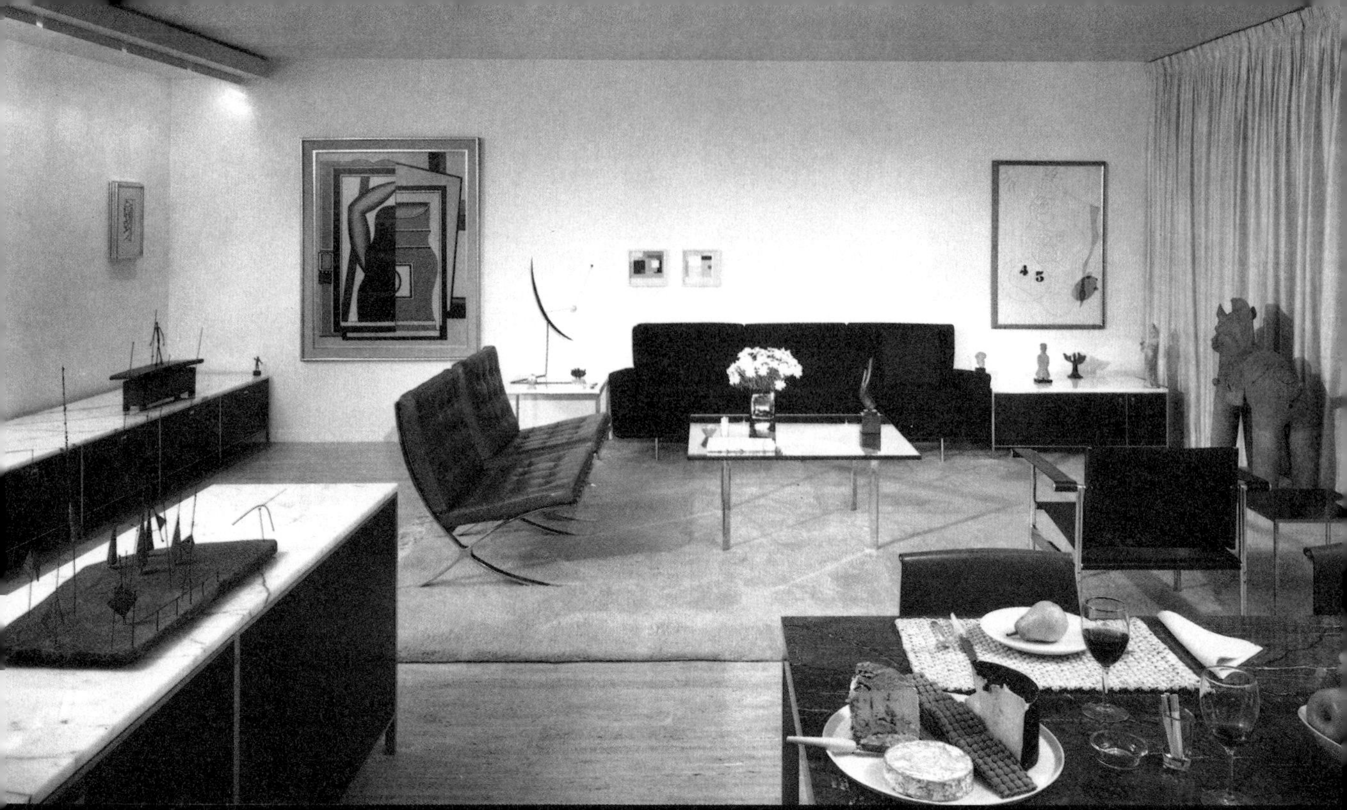

Above: Gordon Bunshaft apartment, 200 East Sixty-sixth Street. Gordon Bunshaft, 1956. Stoller. ©ESTO

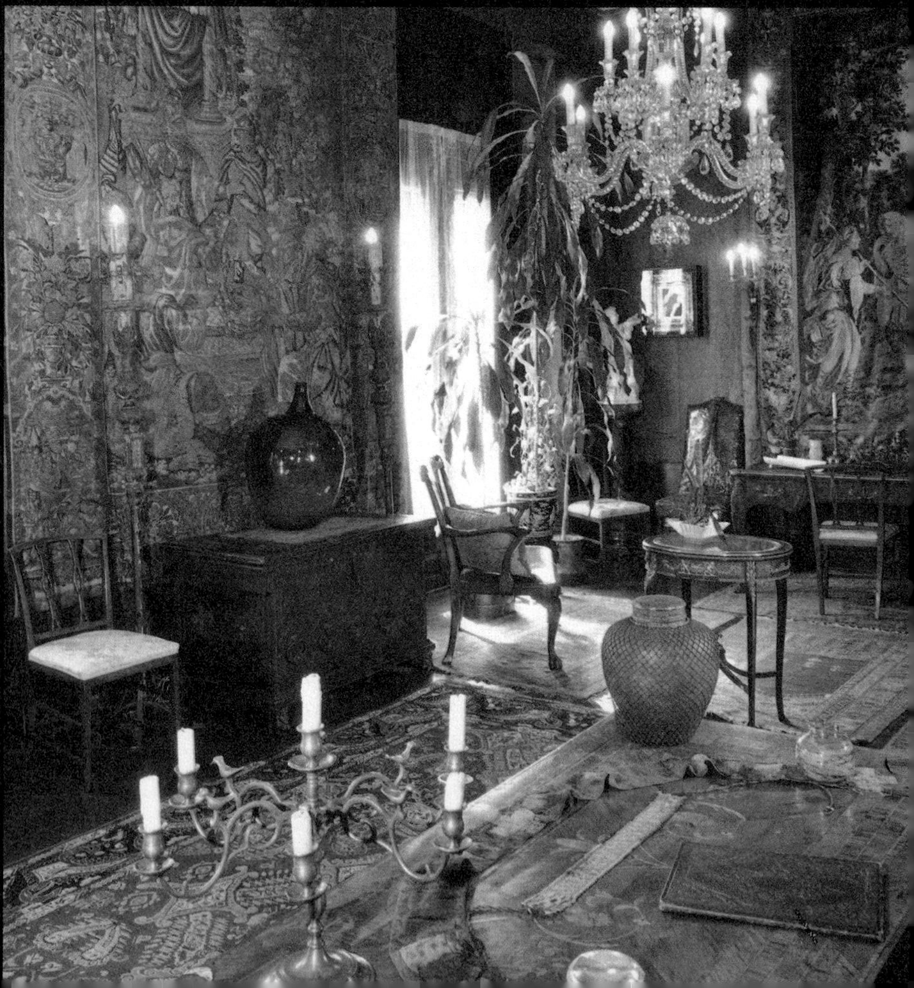

Right: Julian Clarence Levi apartment, 205 West Fifty-seventh Street. Julian Clarence Levi, 1962. Cserna. GC

designer concentrating on residential projects. An early small apartment, for his own use, was perhaps overly furnished,[72] but when he moved in 1962 to larger quarters on a penthouse floor of a typical postwar apartment building, he revealed a sure grasp of space and a finer editorial judgment.[73] Herbert's combination of white walls with strong accents of electric blue was influenced by Breuer. Herbert soon moved again and his new combined studio-apartment on the top two floors of 323 East Fiftieth Street, with its stripped-down, near-cubical double-height living room, painted white and furnished with a black piano and classic Modernist chairs by Le Corbusier and Mies van der Rohe, was in its way a restatement of Philip Johnson's own interior of 1934, sure testimony of the return to Bauhaus-inspired minimalism after the experiments with naturalism and surrealism.[74]

In renovating the living room of an apartment at 1125 Park Avenue for Mr. and Mrs. Donald Blinken, who began to collect the work of Mark Rothko and Philip Guston around 1950, John Bedenkapp, an architect who had worked for Philip Johnson, stripped away all extraneous detail, lowered the ceiling to accommodate recessed lighting and pulled the simple, boxlike upholstered furniture onto an island of carpet away from the walls, which were left free for Rothko's tall, iconlike abstractions.[75] For Fred Mueller, co-owner of the Pace Gallery, a leading showcase for contemporary art, Bedenkapp renovated a much more spacious apartment at 10 Gracie Square overlooking the East River.[76] Where the Blinken apartment had been tight, Mueller's penthouse was spacious and his collection, unlike Blinken's, was eclectic, including traditional Chinese furniture as well as a wide variety of contemporary art. The detailing was perfectly minimal, deferring to the space itself, the views and the objects and paintings.

The most architecturally coherent and, in some ways, the most curatorially consistent art collector's apartment belonged to Gordon Bunshaft, chief design architect of Skidmore, Owings & Merrill, and his wife, Nina.[77] Located on a high floor of Manhattan House, completed by SOM in 1950 (see chapter 11), the small apartment was conceived as a vessel for an art collection that contained paintings by Afro, Miró, Léger, Nicholson, Dubuffet and Picasso, and sculpture by Bertoia, Calder and Giacometti. In 1956 Bunshaft drastically renovated the apartment, further clarifying the already spare and reasonably well detailed spatial framework, introducing falsework to conceal lighting and laying a travertine floor in the living-dining room. Mies's classic Barcelona chairs, not yet in regular production when Bunshaft had his made, were combined with simple upholstery and a prototype chair from the Laverne collection.

Bunshaft's apartment was so perfect a representation of its moment that in 1962 the editors of Architectural Forum were moved to present it in juxtaposition to the eclectic apartment of Mr. and Mrs. Julian Clarence Levi, a preeminent expression of fin-de-siècle taste. Levi, who was then eighty-eight years old, had attended Columbia and the Ecole des Beaux-Arts in Paris before returning to New York to commence his practice in partnership with Alfred Taylor in 1907. The Levis' extraordinarily cluttered suite of high-ceilinged rooms in the Osborne (James E. Ware, 1885), at 205 West Fifty-seventh Street, was a record of their taste and their travels.[78]

Bunshaft's apartment apparently inspired other art-collecting architects to undertake significant renovations to showcase their treasures. In 1963 Armand Bartos, sometime partner of Frederick Kiesler, renovated a duplex apartment at 155 East Seventy-second Street to accommodate a collection of School of Paris Modernist paintings.[79] Like Bunshaft, Bartos simplified the details to create a neutral container that let the paintings provide the personality.

Not every collector demanded an austere setting. The movie mogul Sam Spiegel did not appear overly concerned about the integration of his collection of French Impressionist paintings when he asked Edward Durell Stone to duplicate the qualities of Stone's East Sixty-fourth Street townhouse (see chapter 11) in Spiegel's duplex penthouse on Park Avenue.[80] The operative word, according to John Anderson of Interiors, was "fantasy," but the plan was logical and carefully worked out.

Billy Baldwin's apartment for the publisher S. I. Newhouse, Jr., was a perfect response to the client's request for "comfortable furniture, but nothing with too strong a personality," so as not to detract from a fast-growing collection of contemporary paintings.[81] For some designers, the apartment itself could be the realization in three dimensions of certain graphic values from the canvas or printed page. Such, understandably, was the case with Alvin Lustig, the innovative graphic designer, who began to lose his eyesight in the early 1950s, when his career was reaching a new plateau. He had just begun the design of the Wilheim apartment, which he completed with the assistance of his wife, Elaine. Olga Gueft said that the apartment represented "the meticulous design of elevations and the conscious control of planes," with a "concentration on geometric 'found' forms or combinations thereof, to the exclusion of organic or manually-made forms."[82] Although Lustig was unable to reconfigure the apartment's plan, his design inventiveness found expression in the elevations: in the smoky gray fireplace wall of the living room, for example, or the Constructivist details, such as the vertical bar steel supports that carried the plane of the sofa bench, or the Brancusi-esque assemblage of metal that marked the otherwise invisible corner of the dining room. After Alvin Lustig's death in 1955, Elaine Lustig continued his practice in graphic design, occasionally turning to interiors.[83]

By the late 1960s a reaction was beginning to set in against the minimalist Modernism that so dominated the prevailing practice of interior design. Though this reaction manifested itself in several distinct directions, at its core was a reaffirmation of the positive attributes of strong as opposed to neutral space making, color and ornament. As C. Ray Smith wrote of this new trend, which he called "supermannerism," in 1967:

As soon as the present distillation of Minimal Interiors is achieved—the last refinement of the International Style—a counter approach waggishly raises its elaborately ornamented head. The new aesthetic happening evidences an interest in spatial ambiguities, confusion and distortion. . . . The new direction approves a permissive, realistic economy of means and a rigorous reverence toward established architectural principles. It corresponds to current psychedelic investigations, perhaps, by aiming at expanded spaciousness. If baroque man saw himself at the center of his universe, contemporary man has a double vision that also puts him above the earth—in orbit, as it were—looking down on it from the viewpoint of some extraterrestrial architect studying an earthbound model.

The iconoclastic work of the late 1960s and early 1970s corresponded in intensity to the Modernist innovations of the 1920s and 1930s. Although the new direction was not connected to a clear program of social action, as the earlier design revolution had been, it expressed, as Smith said, "strong statements—or as today's designers might say, strong non-statements. For it is a double-visioned, almost polarized view that is swinging into focus."[84]

Throughout the 1960s the fabric designer and decorator manqué Jack Lenor Larson decorated a series of brownstone floor-through apartments for himself, constantly pushing the limits of total design in search of a more provocative and satis-

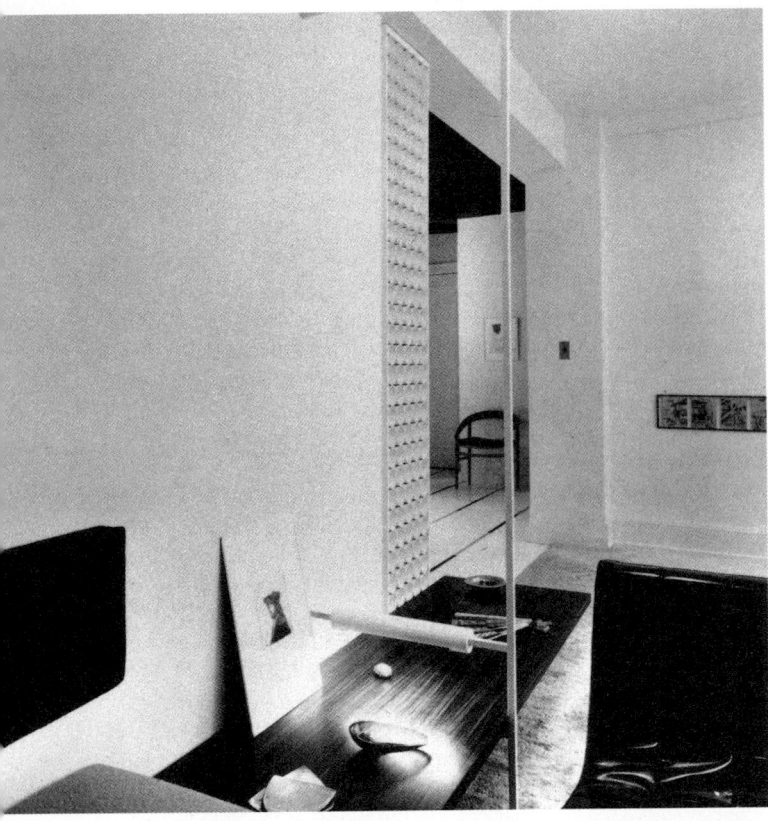

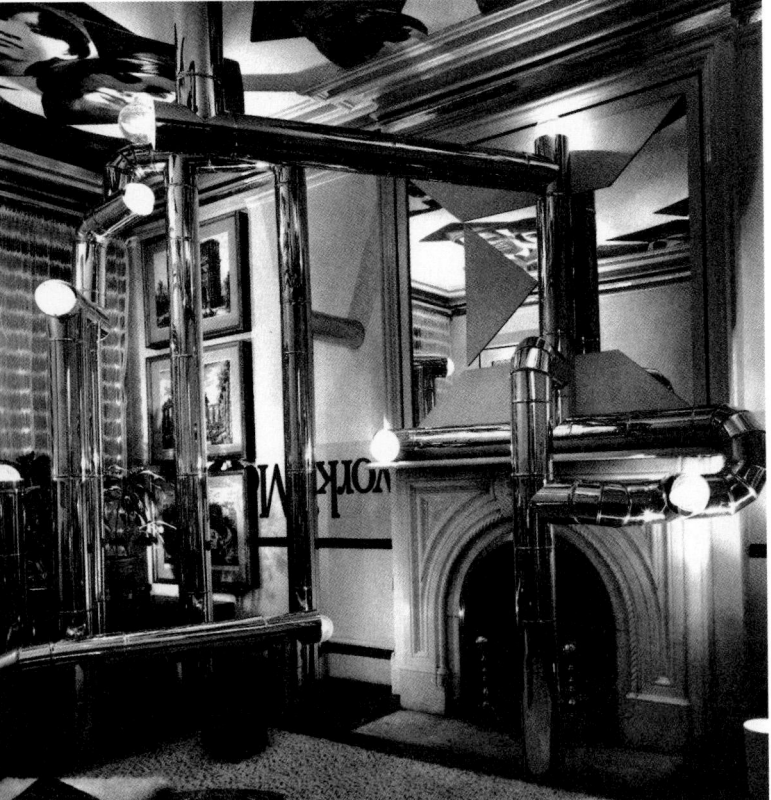

Top: Wilheim apartment, East Seventy-third Street, between Lexington and Park avenues, Alvin Lustig with Elaine Lustig, 1954. Georges. ELC

Bottom: Hugh and Tiziana Hardy apartment, 793 Lexington Avenue. Hugh and Tiziana Hardy, 1966. ©Norman McGrath. NM

fying balance between tradition and modernity than the prevailing minimalism provided.[85] In 1968, no longer content to merely rearrange the furniture, add another layer of fabric or place another collection of objects, Larson chose instead to dramatically modify one room of his apartment by stretching cloth vaults over it. He completed the effect with furniture also covered with stretch fabric and designed by Pierre Paulin. The use of stretch fabric, which related to experiments with similar materials at full scale by the German engineer Frei Otto, offered a perfect transition: a minimalist means to achieve the soaring complications of traditional vaulted architectural space. The effects that could be attained by combining stretch fabrics with "black light" illumination, which makes many materials glow and—as Larson used it—give off the quality of moonlight, fit in perfectly with the era's liberating, anticonventional, antiestablishment mood. As Larson put it, "In its way, it's psychedelic. . . . It's a string of moods I can walk through or sit in or lie down in or work in and be excited or calm or amused or remote. This is the way I've wanted to live for a long time."[86]

While Larson confined his stretch fabric environment to one room, Aleksandra Kasuba developed a similar environment for her entire brownstone apartment at 43 West Ninetieth Street. In a design that, according to Kasuba, "killed the square,"[87] she sought to "camouflage the hostile neutrality of flat surfaces." Echoing arguments offered by Frederick Kiesler in the 1940s, Kasuba explained: "In our present housing, the 90-degree angle serves efficiency above all, steadily depriving the senses. The square silently orders behavior, mechanizes body movements."[88] Kasuba's environment consisted of a series of eight distinct settings for eating, talking and sleeping (this last activity performed under a bower of woven yak hair), each separated from the others by a continuous warped fabric. Furniture was minimal and carpet was used to cover the floors and walls. In an attempt to allow for "privacy without alienation, privacy that doesn't interfere with your being," Kasuba did away with distinct rooms: "I am against the formal bedroom. A separate room just for sleeping is a waste of space. A room where a child can slam the door and be alone with his hostile feelings only makes the feelings grow worse."[89] Kasuba succinctly summarized her aims: "The environment was not designed to suit physical convenience as presently conceived, but the whole idea was based on sense and body movement needs."[90]

Rebellion against the prevailing minimalism took another direction, paralleling the rise of Pop Art and influenced by the work of Charles Moore, a California-based architect and academic who came east in the fall of 1965 to direct Yale's architecture program. Working with the graphic designer Barbara Stauffacher, Moore had created a raucous new kind of architectural decoration consisting of superscaled elements painted onto and superimposed over traditional architectural compositions. The architect Hugh Hardy and his wife, Tiziana, were early proponents of supergraphics in New York. Introducing a stripe to perk up the ordinary kitchen of their apartment (1966), they found, as Tiziana put it, that "the stripe went her own way," projecting a cone of space across the boxlike room, distorting its scale and even its apparent reality by confusing the viewer's sense of room enclosure. According to Hugh, supergraphics were not faddish. "It will be increasingly difficult to make a distinction between design and fad in the future," he averred. "It is academic to say that what is popular is not important. . . . Why can't something that is important for the present be important for all time? Anyway I suspect that 'for all time' will be an increasingly meaningless thing. Today, we are interested in the simultaneity of the two. And we recognize that the hierarchical establisher who says today that the popular is superficial is speaking from just as superficial a pose."[91]

The living room of the Hardy apartment, with its heavy Victorian cornice and carved marble fireplace mantel, featured a number of unusual elements, including a hanging construction that C. Ray Smith described as "a kind of modern whatnot composed of shadow boxes: the smallest possible angle irons were screwed to the wall and left exposed; similarly, the electric cables for the lighted boxes were strung loosely, spontaneously, as the function required. Hardy explained, permissively, 'Why not?'"[92] The room was overlaid with a huge billboard promoting VISTA, a government-sponsored social agency, cut into sections and glued to the walls and ceiling. A sculpture made of brightly polished stovepipe, with arms terminating in glaring lights, wrapped around the room.

Two young Yale-trained architects carried the new sensibility even further. Peter Hoppner covered the hallway walls of his small brownstone apartment, on East Sixty-fourth Street just off Madison Avenue, with silver Mylar, creating a psychedelic, funhouse effect. Hoppner closely followed developments in avant-garde art and saw the new trend as analogous to the aestheticism of the 1920s, even though its formal language was quite different: "The whole spirit of today is like the spirit of the 20's. And people are using silver because they are tired of all white and natural colors."[93] Frederick Romley was also recently out of Yale in 1966, when he and his wife, Elizabeth, took a floor-through apartment on the piano nobile of an imposing townhouse at 19 East Seventy-third Street and painted the walls matte silver. "What makes silver seem like a fad," Romley claimed, "is that silver or aluminum foil seems like a superficial throwaway material that is as quickly used up as the designs of Seventh Avenue." But, he said, "What we do lasts."[94] Upon the publication of the Romley apartment in *Progressive Architecture*, Sim Van Der Ryn, an architect on the faculty of the University of California at Berkeley, wrote the editors to offer them "kudos" for pioneering a first in the architectural press: "To wit: the gorgeous color photo of the Romley pot party. . . . Do I take it that the Zigzag cigarette papers on the table, the fellow on the right sifting grass, and the one on the left dragging his joint add up to a grass party?"[95]

Andy Warhol's silver-painted studio, called the Factory, was no doubt a big influence on the era's high-spirited interior decoration. According to a Warhol biographer, David Bourdon, it was not the artist but an assistant, Billy Lunch (later known as Billy Name), an off-Broadway lighting designer who became part of Warhol's entourage, who had first covered his own East Seventh Street apartment with aluminum foil. "Warhol thought the placed looked 'terrific,'" according to Bourdon. When, at the end of 1963, Warhol moved to his first Factory, a fourth-floor loft at 231 East Forty-seventh Street, between Second and Third avenues, he invited Lunch to design his new studio. Bourdon described the design process:

> He created the silver setting by covering the concrete walls and some of the three ceiling arches with aluminum foil. He sprayed a rough brick wall with silver paint, transforming it into a shimmering surface. He continued spraying until he had covered almost everything—desks, chairs, copying machine, toilet, dismembered mannequin, and pay phone—with a gleaming metallic silver. He even coated the floor with Du Pont aluminum paint—but the traffic was so heavy that he had to repaint it every two weeks to keep it shiny.[96]

In several New York apartments William Tapley, a painter trained at the Ecole des Beaux-Arts in Paris and the Royal Academy in London, created a series of room-sized, programmatic paintings that grew out of the clients' psychological requirements rather than the compositional demands of the architectural space.[97] For the playroom of the Perkel apartment in Manhattan, Tapley created a beachlike environment for the children; in the dining room, arcs and circles suggesting the work of painters Frank Stella and Kenneth Noland were splashed across the otherwise bland ceiling and walls. In the Levitt apartment, Tapley responded to the client's interest in nature by creating a representation of the night cycle from sunset to sunrise.

A significant corollary to the supergraphics movement was the development of large-scale modular furniture units, many of which created rooms within rooms: Les Walker's "supercube," a brightly painted, large-scale cabinet or "living machine" he built in his apartment that opened up to make separate areas for conversation, dining, dressing and sleeping;[98] Craig Hodgetts' "Rapid Assembly Total Floor," a version of the "living machine" that incorporated sophisticated electronic consoles;[99] or the more high-style suite of "superfurniture"—velvet-covered foam-and-plywood units—designed by the architect James Rossant (for whom Walker worked) to replace all conventional furniture in the elegant parlor of the Rossants' Greenwich Village brownstone.[100] A cube designed by Peter Hoppner provided a bed on top and storage inside; a desk and a sofa were cantilevered from it.[101] Tim Woods would refine the supercube idea, bringing a measure of Corbusier-inspired decorum to a seven-foot plywood cube he placed on angle in the one large room he shared with his wife, Ruth.[102] In 1975 George Ranalli, an avowed admirer of Louis Kahn as well as Gamal El-Zoghby (see below), designed a strictly geometrical supercube for his own small apartment at 100 West Fifteenth Street.[103] Michael Hollander pulled the cube apart to create in his eight-by-twelve-foot brownstone bedroom-study a series of room-width, traylike platforms that slid on wall-hung horizontal rails (1967). The topmost tray was reserved for sleeping, the middle tray was used for deskwork and the lower tray supported the conventional furniture and, according to Hollander, was needed "both compositionally and ritualistically" to manifest the system's liberation from the spatial boundaries of a conventional room.[104]

Romuald Witwicki, a young French architect who had worked for the master geometrists I. M. Pei and Skidmore, Owings & Merrill, carried the modular idea to the furthest reaches of obsession and finesse. In 1969 he devised a "systems room" that combined, as C. Ray Smith observed, "the weightlessness of the all-white environment with a bit of floating platform furniture—which pulls out, lifts up, spins around—and also with projected decoration." Witwicki set up his environment in the one-room apartment of Ivanka Mihailovich, an architect who worked for Pei and who lived at Pei's Kips Bay Plaza apartments. "Architect Pei may have waited this long for a model room to suit his own tastes so well," Smith waggishly observed.[105] The system consisted of sliding platform units and a ceiling-mounted beam that held lighting fixtures and slide projectors and pull-down roller shades needed for partitioning the space. The architect Douglas Kahn and his wife, the designer Stephanie Mallis Kahn, offered a less rigorous but more flexible variation on the modular theme in their own Kips Bay Plaza apartment.[106]

An Egyptian-born designer, Gamal El-Zoghby, recognizing the fundamental inertness of architecturally scaled furniture and cabinetwork, evolved a vocabulary of raised platforms and

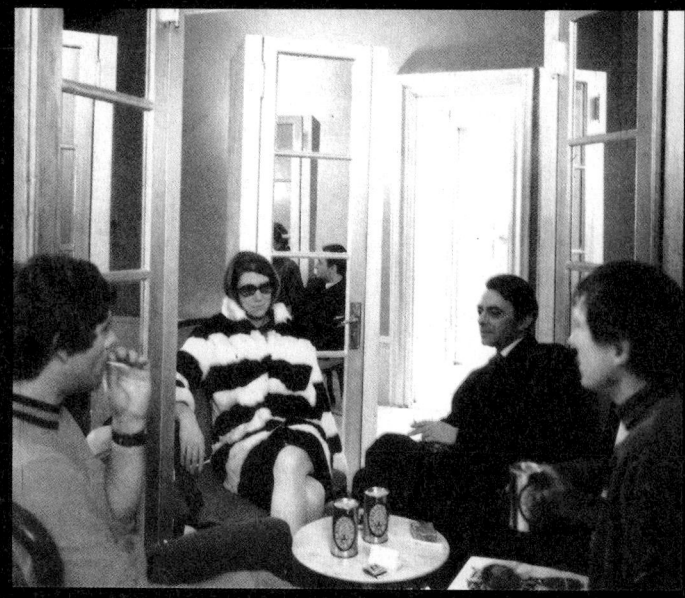

Top: Frederick Romley apartment, 19
East Seventy-third Street. Frederick
Romley, 1966. Reens. LR

Center left: Rapid Assembly Total Floor.
Craig Hodgetts, 1969. Reens. LR

Center right: Rapid Assembly Total Floor.
Reens. LR

Bottom: Rapid Assembly Total Floor.
HFDA

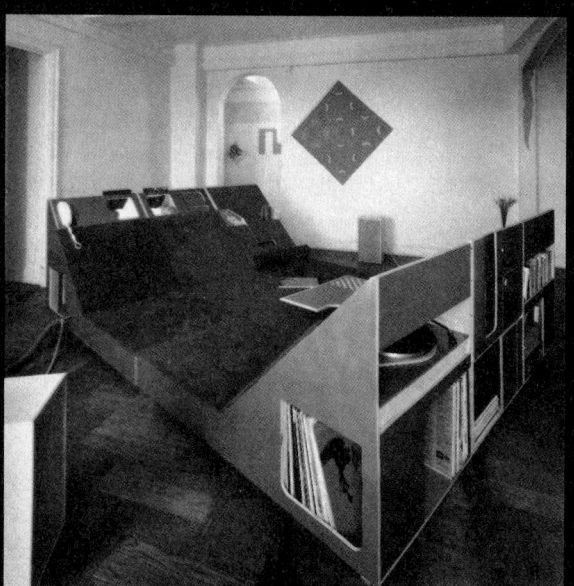

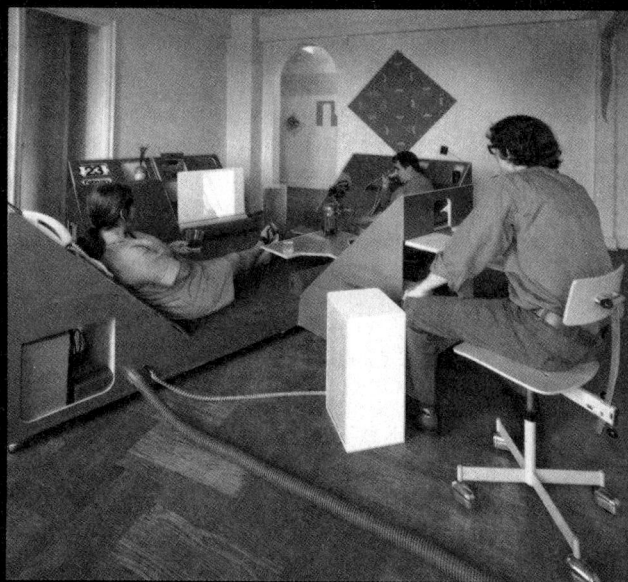

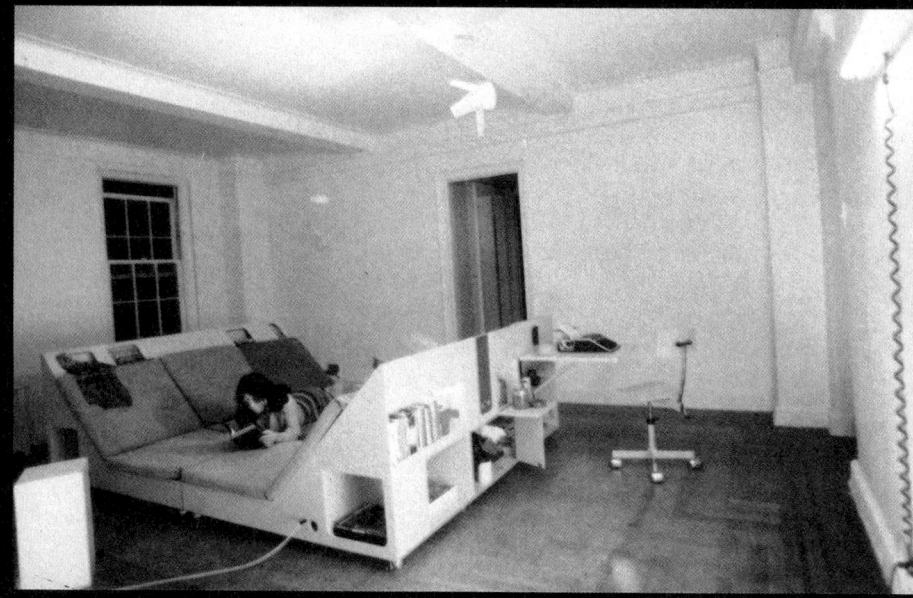

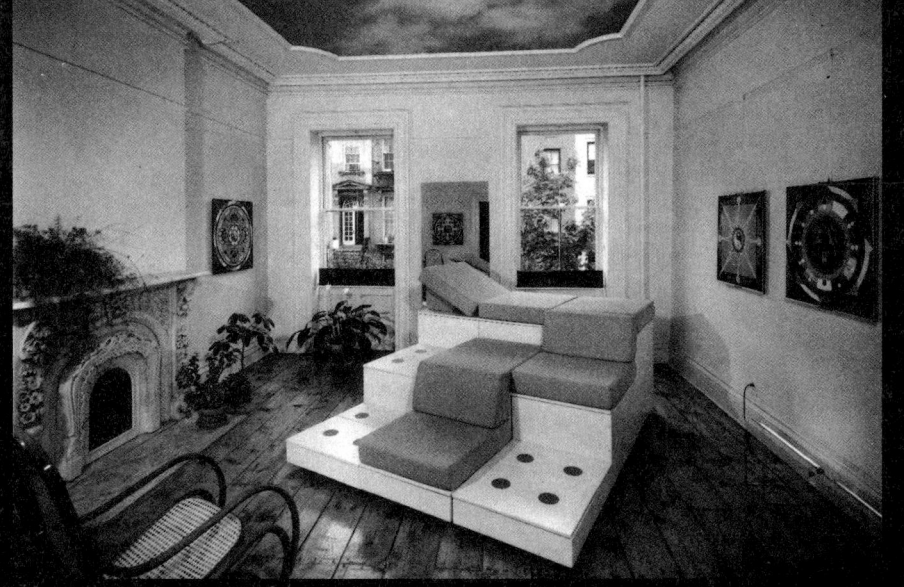

Top: James Rossant apartment, 114 Sullivan Street. James Rossant, 1972. Superfurniture. ©Norman McGrath. NM

Center: James Rossant apartment. ©Norman McGrath. NM

Bottom: James Rossant apartment. ©Norman McGrath. NM

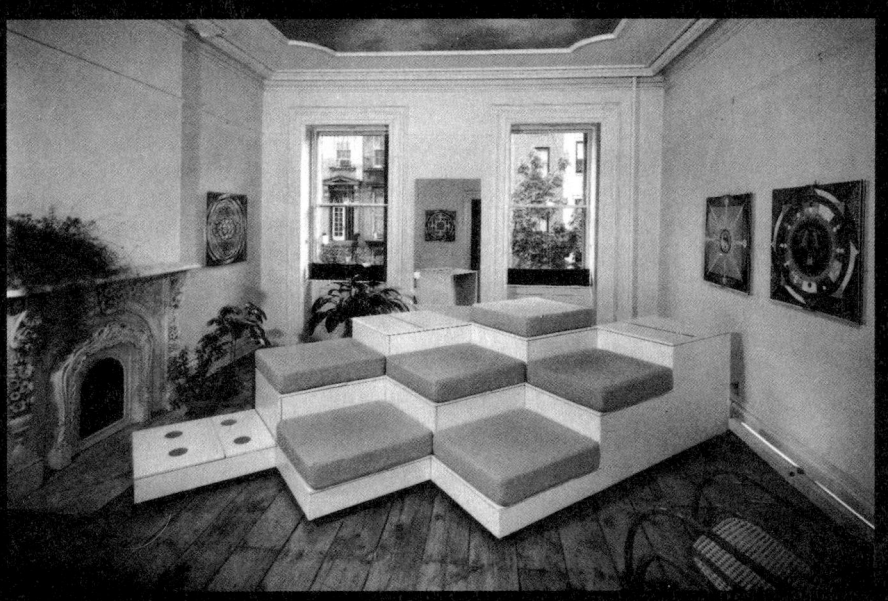

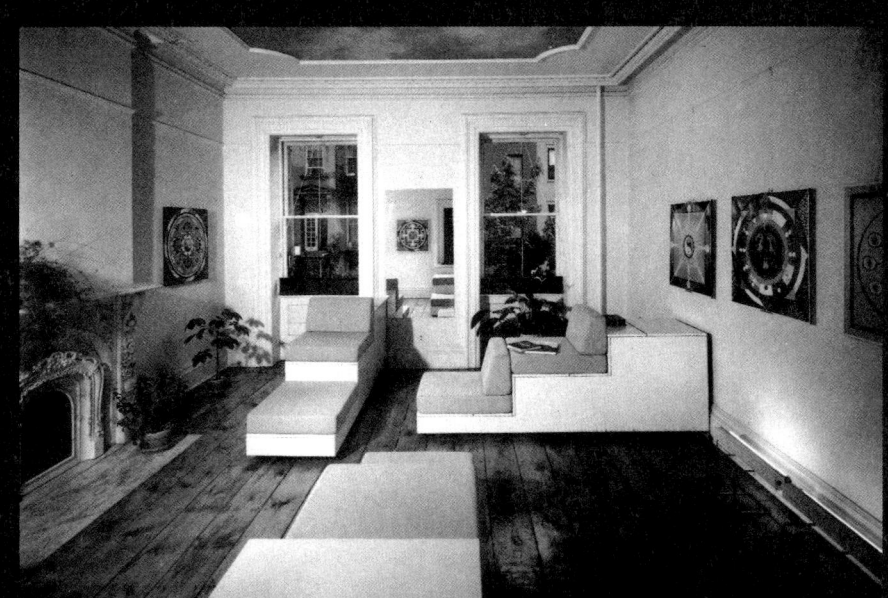

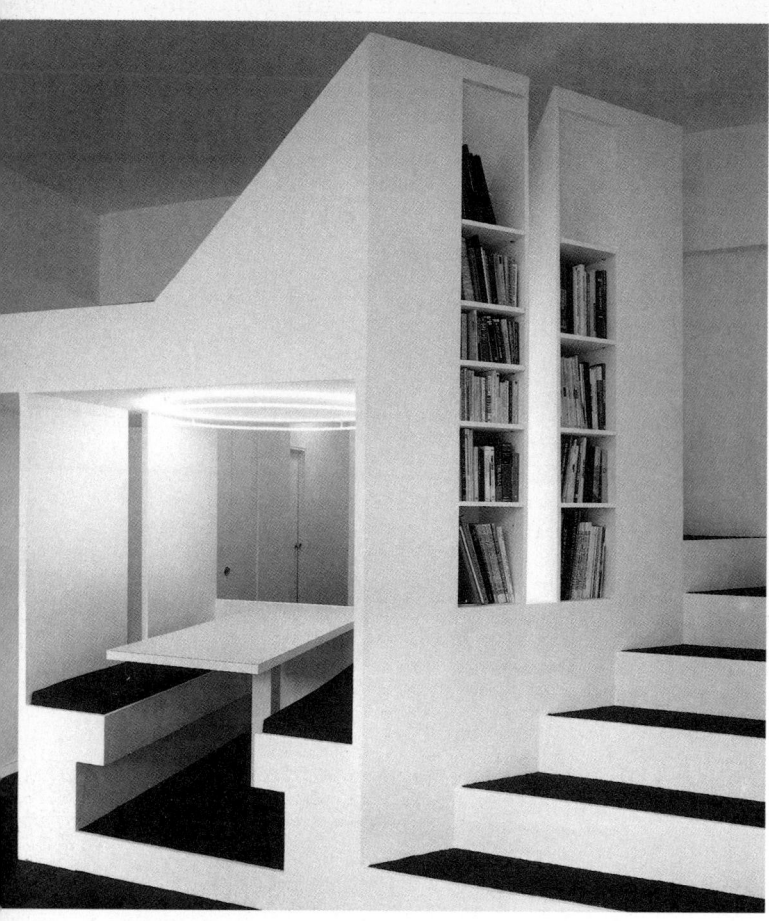

George Ranalli apartment, 100 West Fifteenth Street. George Ranalli, 1975. Cserna. GC

large-scale shadowboxes that he installed in a number of apartments to create a series of seemingly undecorated "home environments."[107] "The world has been cluttered for such a long time," said El-Zoghby. "I would like to help purify."[108] For the comedian and self-confessed video addict Jackie Mason, El-Zoghby designed a living room using platforms to create three sofas focusing, theaterlike, on the television.[109] For the same apartment El-Zoghby created a built-in dining table and chairs, all in effect wood platforms with carpet insets, and a bedroom in which only a mattress interrupted the scheme of raised platforms, which provided all the storage. According to Norma Skurka, this "remarkably pure 'anti-object' living environment" yielded a "sense of completeness and total serenity."[110] For the designer Josephine Rogers, El-Zoghby fashioned an apartment that included a "fur pit" lined in wolfskin and a sofa surrounded by carpeted platforms.[111] He created a highly abstract, rigorously ordered environment for his own use in which no one space was specifically assigned a function, an approach that he defended as an antidote to urban chaos: "Its restraint calms me; I feel reborn when I return to it."[112]

No matter how iconoclastic, each of these new trends in interior decoration and design resorted to traditional means to achieve their effects: architectural changes, or cabinetwork, or at least paint. One direction, however, was profoundly radical—the use of projected images to modify space and impose different styles or moods of decor. Described in the hip lingo of the day as "turned-on decor," it was developed as an art form by Earl Reiback, who sometimes worked with Jack Lenor Larson, and as a decorating device by C. Ray Smith, who outfitted his brownstone parlor with a system that projected environmentally scaled images of architecture or nature to visually transform the presumed boundaries of space.[113]

Supergraphics and supermannerism were short-lived trends. More enduring was the move toward spatial complexity and decorative richness that was initiated by the architect Paul Rudolph. After completing seven years as chairman of Yale's architecture department, Rudolph relocated his offices to New York in 1965 (see "Offices," below) and began a series of constructions, reconstructions and expansions in his living quarters overlooking the East River at 23 Beekman Place.[114] Rudolph had already begun work on his New York apartment while still living in New Haven, and by 1967 it had evolved into a remarkable essay in spatial dematerialization, using mirrors, curtains made of small plastic discs and exposed lighting. Rudolph covered one wall in his bedroom with a portion of a billboard and lined his kitchen with a wallpaper collage of gasoline-company posters. "This is how you can afford great gobs of color without the expense of paintings," Rudolph explained, "and each week you can afford a new one."[115] Rudolph's imaginative spatial composition was most apparent in his all-white living room, where a series of cantilevered "floating" platforms, with concealed illumination below, were combined with specially designed, leather-covered "club chairs," plaster casts of ornamental panels designed by Louis Sullivan and a glass dining table with wire-thin ice-cream-parlor chairs pulled up to it. To one side of the living room's glass wall, a door led outside to a long, narrow bridgelike balcony made of steel grating. In 1975 Rudolph redesigned the apartment, transforming it into a softer, more sensuous environment yet retaining the fundamental composition of floating platforms and walls mirrored to dematerialize the mass; so creamy white and shiny was the apartment that Rudolph joked it was "like living in a milk bottle."[116]

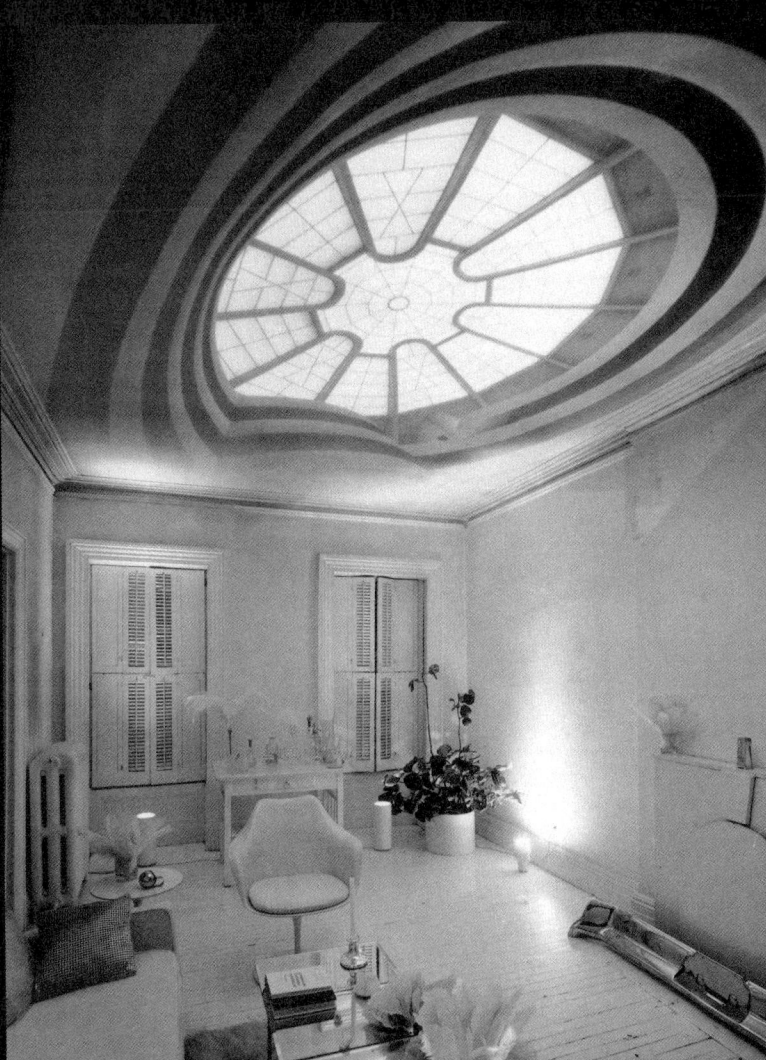

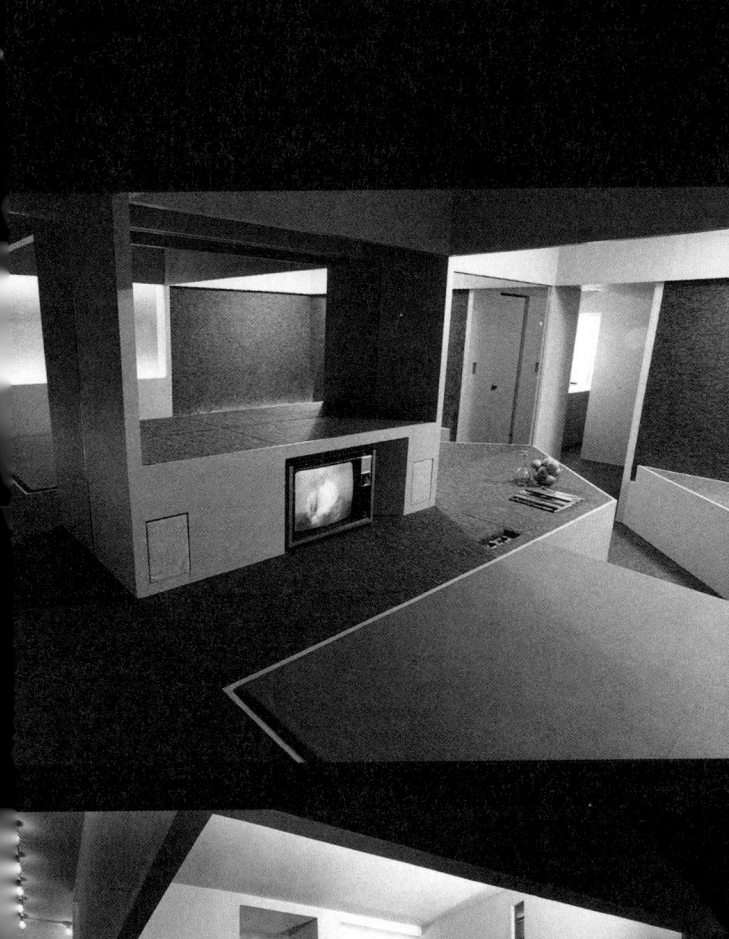

Top left: Jackie Mason residence, 200 Central Park South. Gamal El-Zoghby, 1971. GEZ

Bottom left: Gamal El-Zoghby apartment, 312 West Eighty-seventh Street. Gamal El-Zoghby, 1968. Propper. GEZ

Above: C. Ray Smith apartment, 411 East Fiftieth Street. C. Ray Smith, 1967. Reens. LR

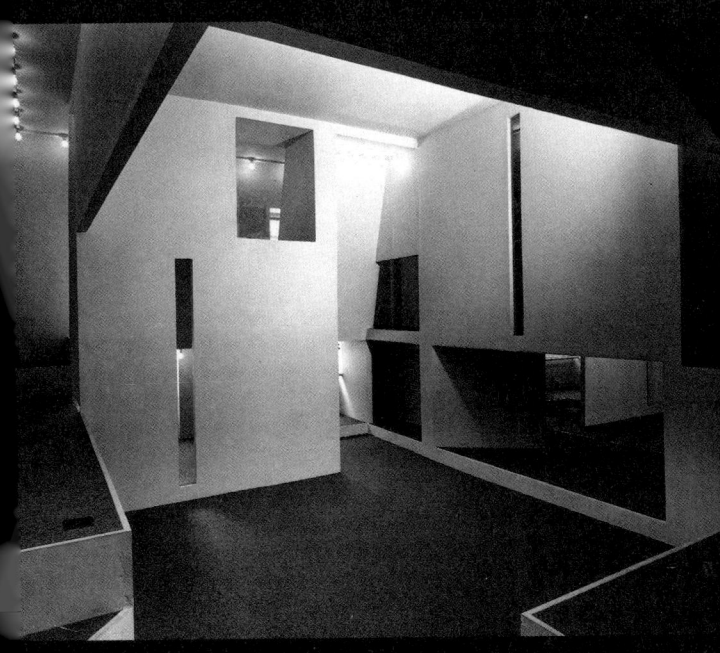

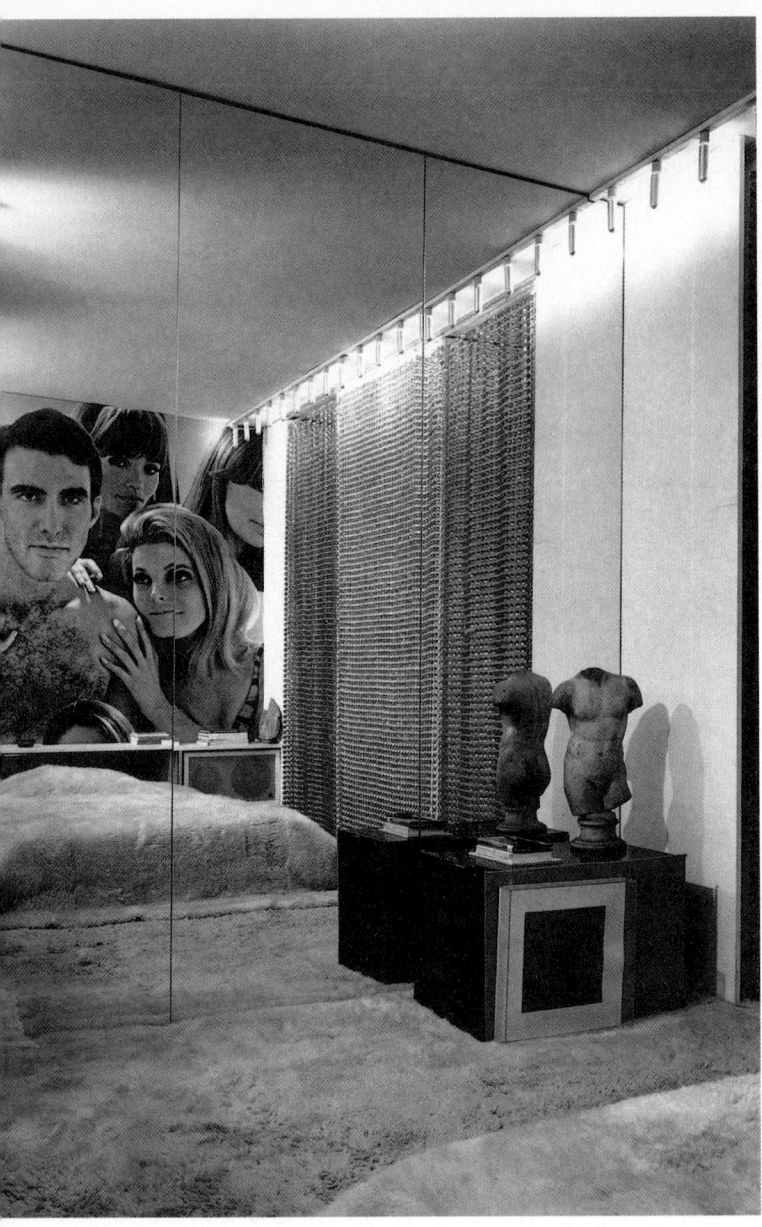

Above: Paul Rudolph apartment, 23 Beekman Place. Paul Rudolph, 1967. Bedroom. PR

Top right: Paul Rudolph apartment, 23 Beekman Place. Paul Rudolph, 1967. Stoller. ©ESTO

Bottom right: Paul Rudolph apartment, 23 Beekman Place. Paul Rudolph, 1975. Stoller. ©ESTO

The dazzling surface effects of Rudolph's apartment tended to obscure the structural logic of the spaces. This logic came out much more clearly in the double-story apartment Rudolph designed in 1973–74 for his friend Joanna Steichen, a psychotherapist and the widow of the photographer Edward Steichen, whose "Family of Man" exhibition had been installed at the Museum of Modern Art according to Rudolph's designs in 1955. Rudolph insisted that the design was a collaboration: "She is a friend, the remodeling was down the street from where I live. I just gave her practical advice, produced a few working drawings and dropped in from time to time to see how things were coming along."[117] According to *Vogue*, the apartment fulfilled a dream long cherished by Steichen: to live in a cliffside cave overlooking the sea.[118] The apartment was carved out of the double-height basement of a building on the East River; by inserting an L-shaped balcony, Rudolph created at the end of the room a cavelike seating area. The detailing of the space was very crisp, with thin planes acting as shelves forming the platforms for the seating. The design also featured a Corbusier-inspired, almost creaturelike internal stair.

In designing Dorothea and Lee Elman's apartment at 1 West Sixty-fourth Street, Rudolph worked within the confines of a fixed architectural plan to indulge in almost pure decoration.[119] He transformed the living room by ringing it with a curtain of light formed by small reflector spots hung from a ceiling track, and by painting and carpeting the room in white. Otherwise it was bare except for two specially designed, exceptionally low, carpeted seating clusters. The dining room was lined in silver Mylar and the entrance hall lit by four "light paintings." Rudolph also worked on a large apartment at 4 East Sixty-sixth Street for Gardner Cowles, a prominent publisher, and his wife, a former newspaper editor and a leading socialite. The *New Yorker* described the housewarming party in "The Talk of the Town":

> Paul Rudolph . . . used curved lacquered walls, Mylar walls, and many, many mirrors, and the guests of Mr. and Mrs. Cowles admired all these things. People wandered admiringly through the living room, where there was an enormous painting by Frank Stella on a curved brown-lacquered wall, and through the library, the floor of which was carpeted in goatskin, and many congregated in Mrs. Cowles' bathroom, which was a tunnel vaulted in silver Mylar and studded with hundreds (perhaps thousands) of tiny mirrors.[120]

Rudolph's search for a spatially enriched Modernism and his frank embrace of decoration to enhance that enrichment influenced a number of younger architects, many of them former students who settled in New York in the late 1960s. One former student was Robert Stern, whose first apartment (1966), at the Century, 25 Central Park West, transformed the "sunken" living room into a platformed living space arranged to take advantage of the view by raising the floor at the windows and at the same time creating a focus around the (fake) fireplace.[121] Stern used cabinetwork to deepen and rationalize the space and showcase art. In 1967 Der Scutt, another former student of Rudolph's, pursued similar themes in his apartment at 229 East Seventy-ninth Street.[122] Scutt raised his monochromatic carpeted platform in order to create an introspective sunken well of seating, the design's principal feature. Orange and yellow enameled metal tubes punctuated the space, directing circulation and manipulating the scale with their seeming monumentality.

In 1975, in designing Kay Unger's apartment, the architects Charles Gwathmey, yet another former Rudolph student, and Robert Siegel were faced with a stepped-down living room, as

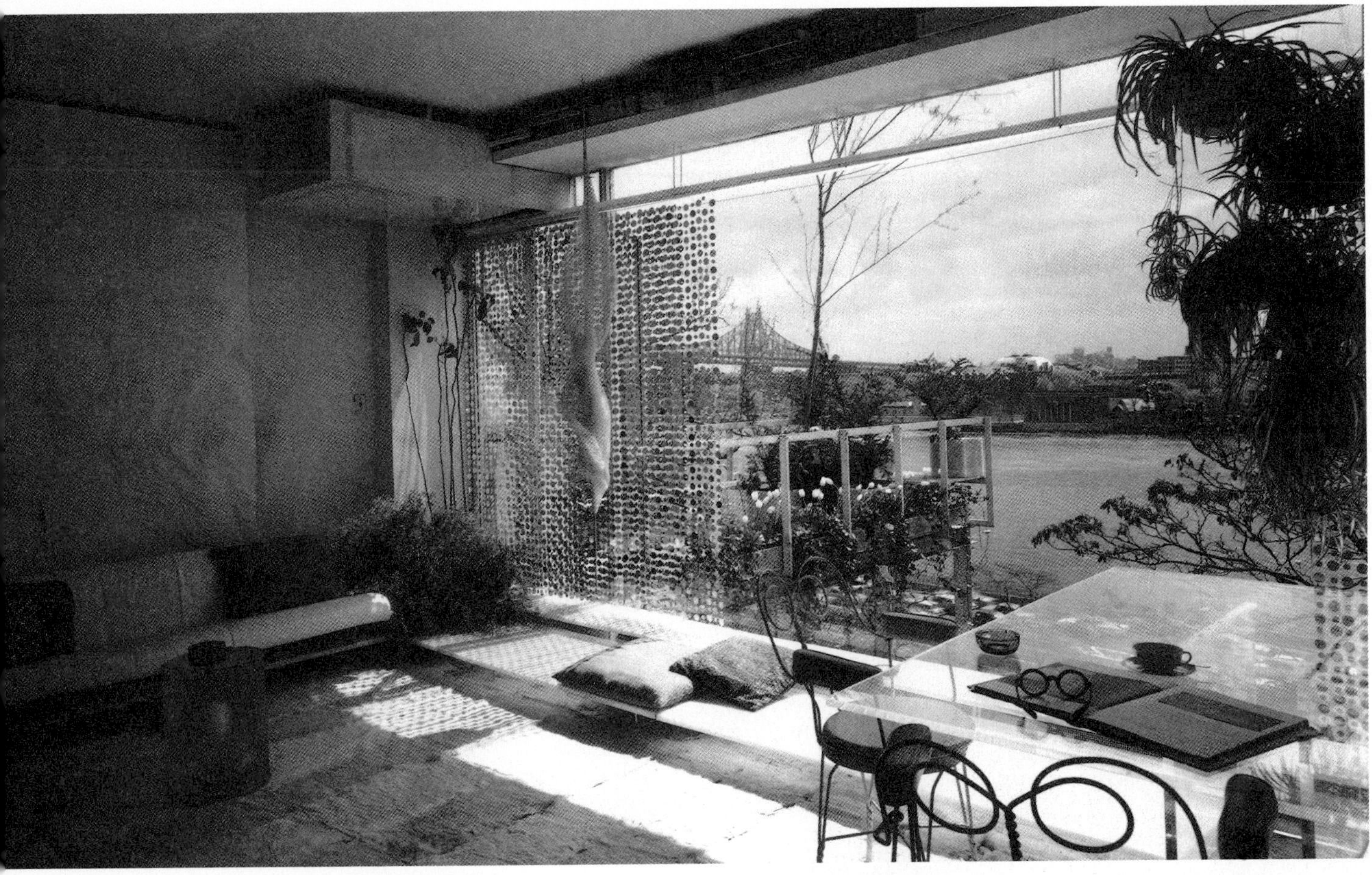

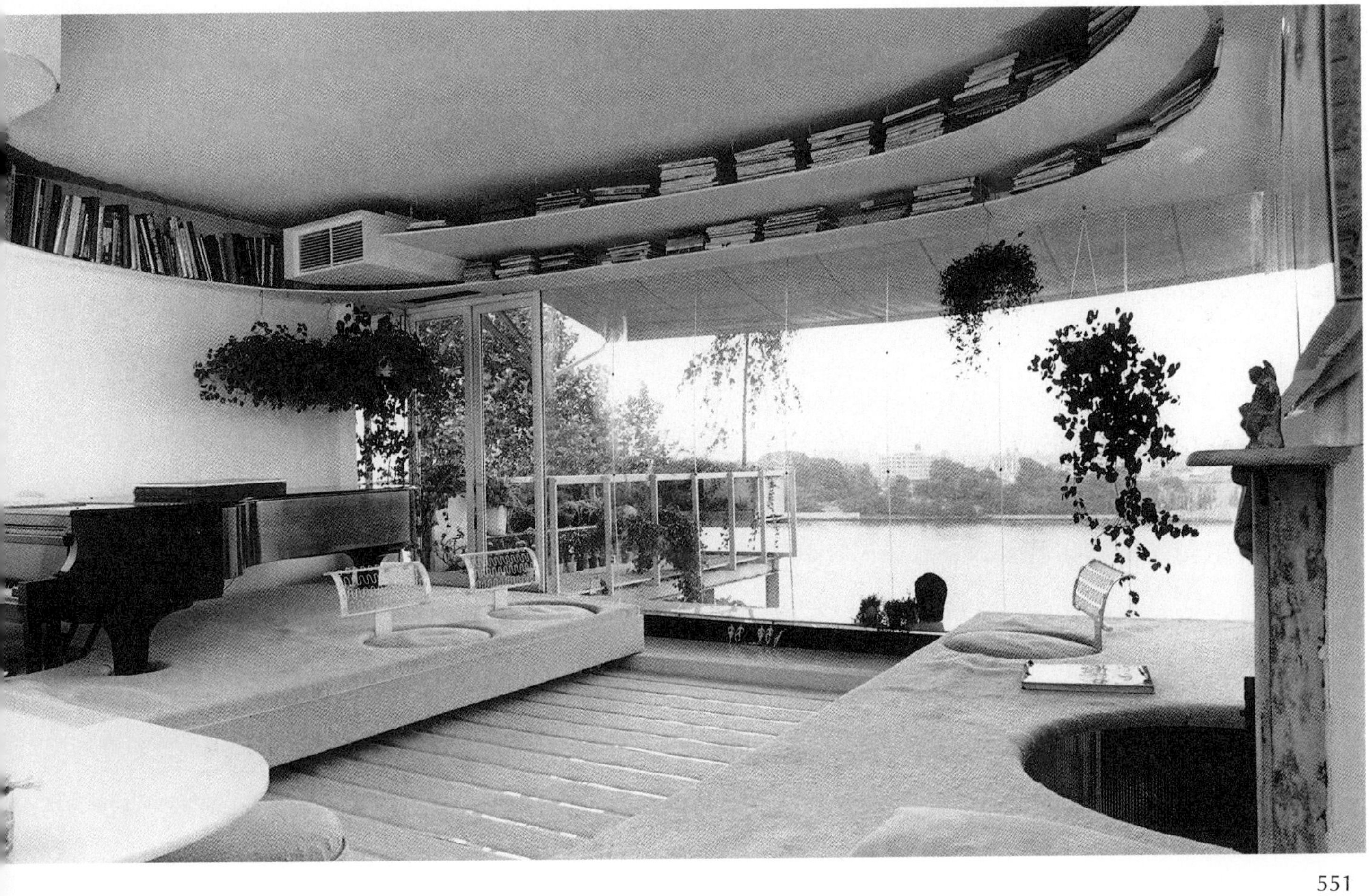

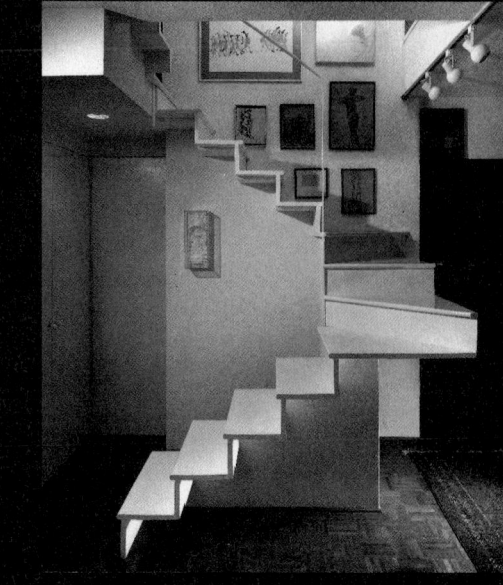

Right: Joanna Steichen apartment, 455 East Fifty-first Street. Paul Rudolph, 1973–74. Interior stair. Robinson. PR

Below: Joanna Steichen apartment. Living room. Robinson. PR

Top far right: Robert Stern apartment, 25 Central Park West. Robert Stern, 1966. Hans Namuth. RAMSA

Bottom far right: Der Scutt apartment, 229 East Seventy-ninth Street. Der Scutt, 1967. ©Norman McGrath. DSA

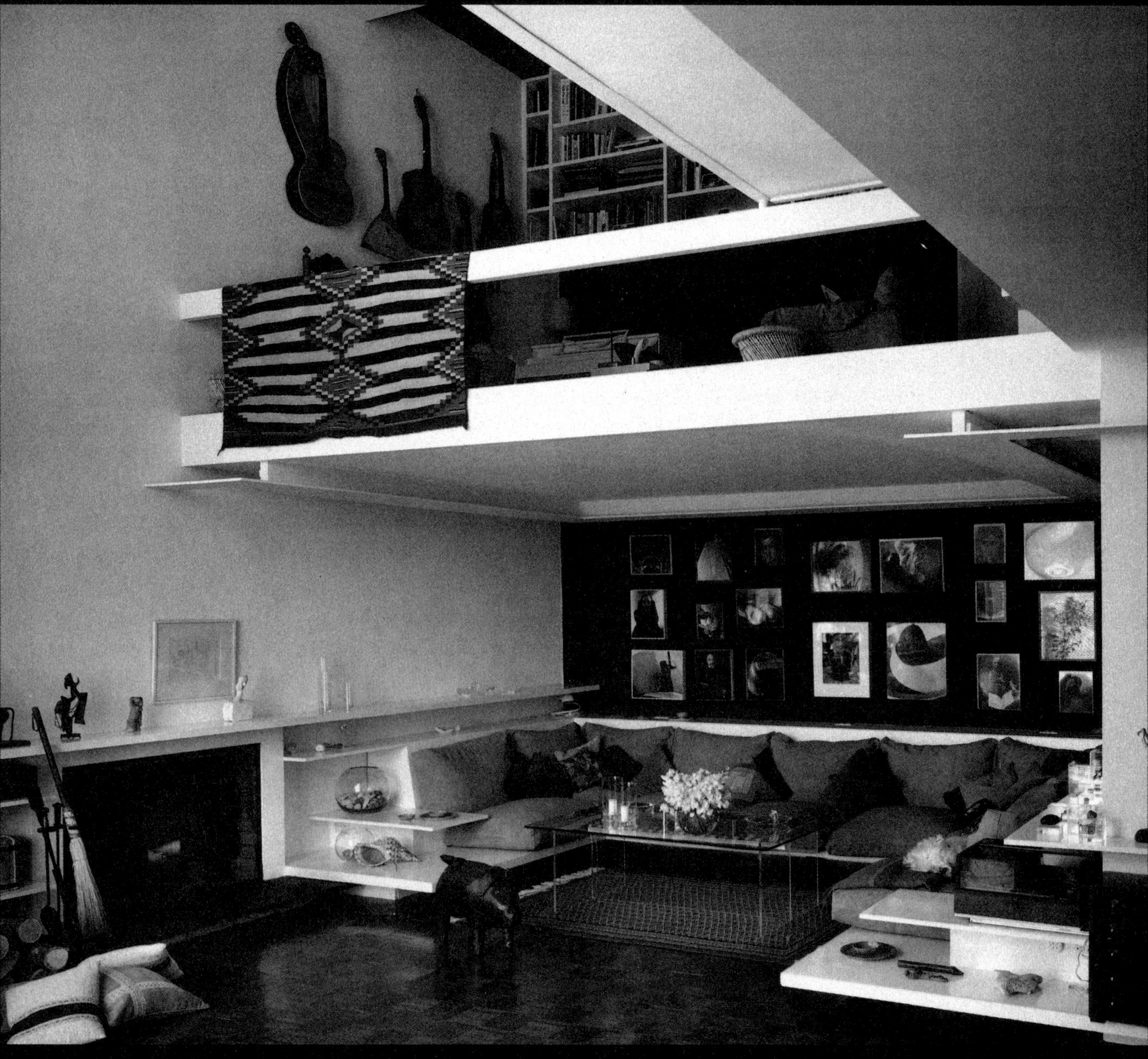

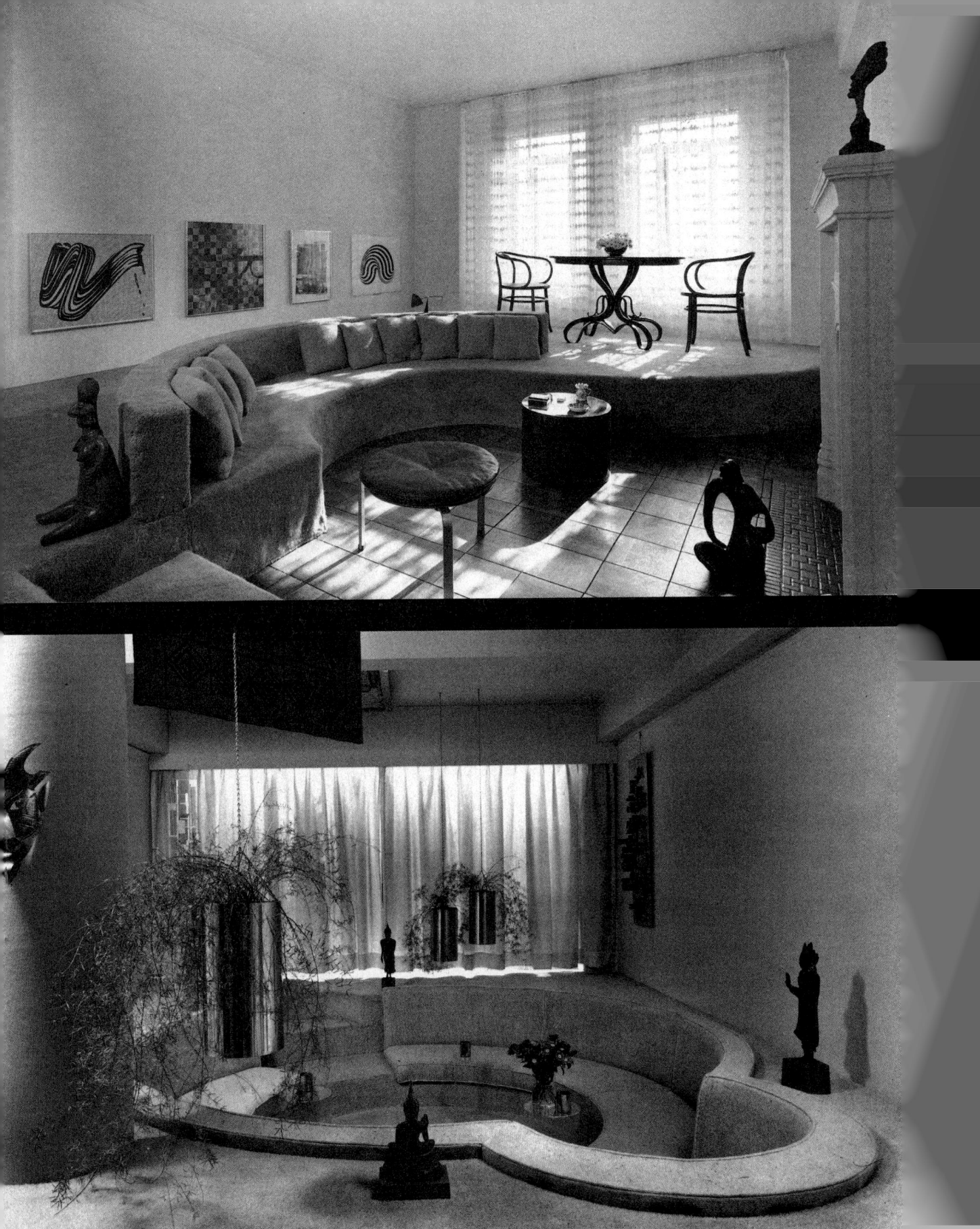

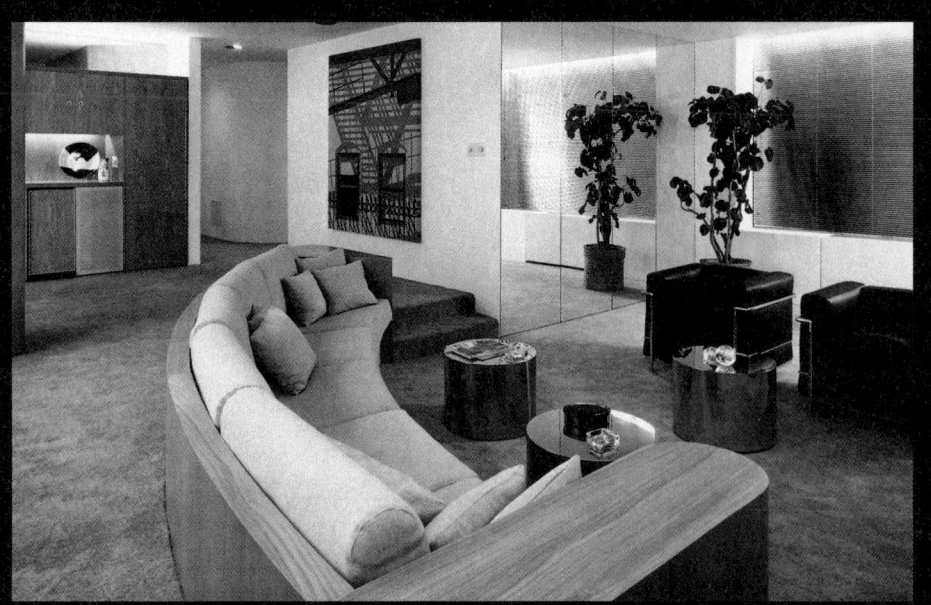

Left: Kay Unger apartment, 136 East Thirty-sixth Street. Gwathmey Siegel, 1975. GSA

Below: David Beer apartment, 131–135 East Sixty-sixth Street. David Beer, 1969. ©Gil Amiaga. GA

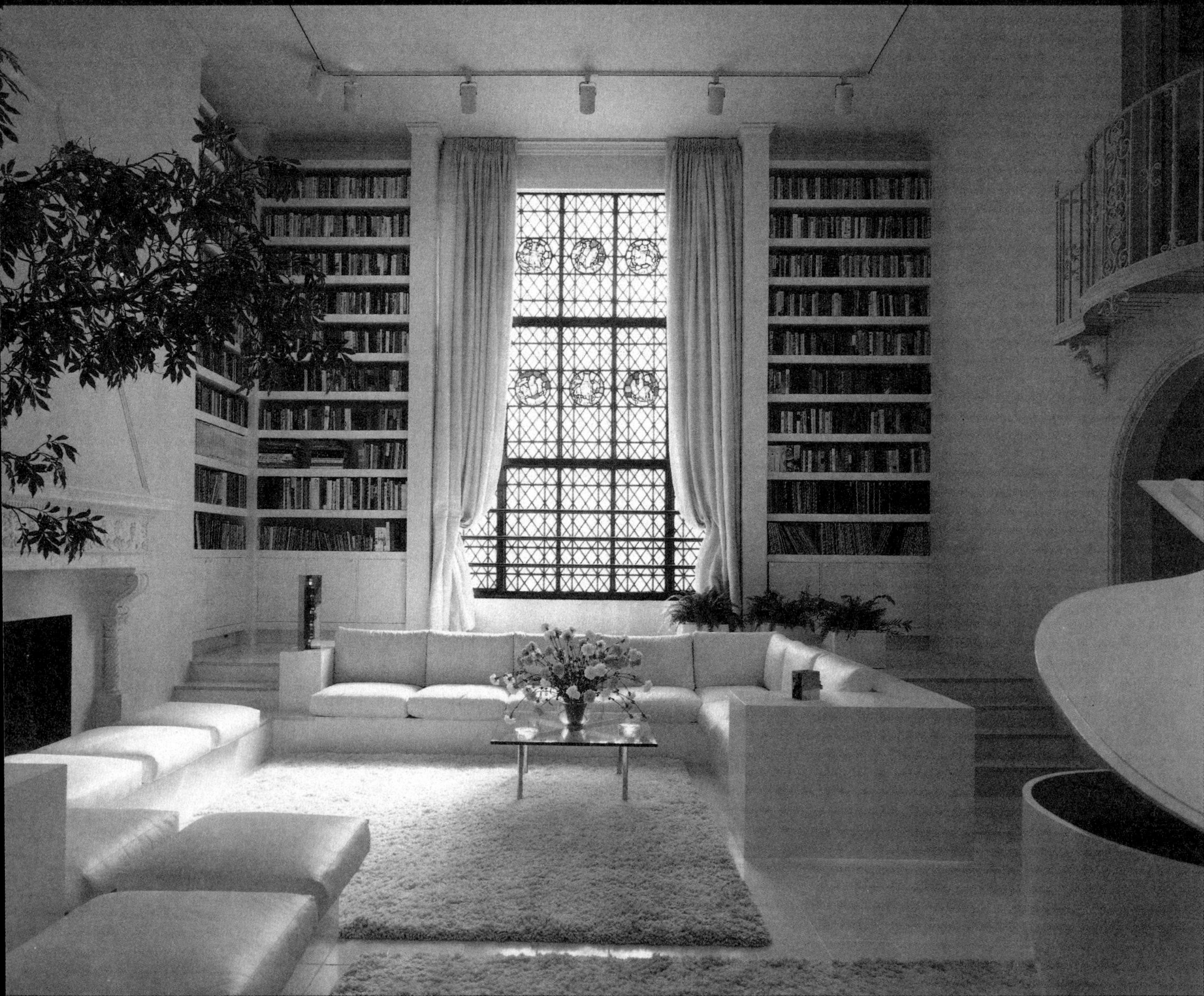

Stern had been.[123] Their solution was to reinterpret the platform theme with high sophistication and fine materials, including travertine and white oak as well as the by now traditional carpeting. In 1969 David Beer, renovating an apartment he had previously furnished with conventional Miesian furniture, also pursued this direction.[124] Beer's apartment was a grand, eight-room duplex that he occupied with his family in the apartment house Charles Platt designed in 1906 at 131–135 East Sixty-sixth Street.[125] Taking advantage of the nobly proportioned twenty-foot-high volume of space and its beautiful fireplace and leaded windows, Beer made a relatively conventional furniture grouping seem built-in by wrapping the living room with a continuous platform that was painted white to further distance the new insertions from their sixty-three-year-old environment. The most extensive exploration of the platform *parti* was made by the architect Norman Jaffe in his renovation of a three-room pied-à-terre.[126] Like Stern and Gwathmey Siegel, Jaffe was confronted with a dropped living room, which he saw as an opportunity to reorganize the apartment as a series of platforms and to use curving surfaces to ease the transitions between its principal rooms, which were reconfigured as episodes in a single spatial continuum.

A new generation of young married couples, eschewing the suburbia of their parents, began a relatively widespread trend in the late 1960s, commissioning architects to entirely and boldly reconfigure large apartments. These near palaces were likely candidates for major rebuilding for several reasons. First, though they were valued for their spaciousness, their interior plans often lacked the sense of "spatial flow" so ingrained in the postwar sensibility. Furthermore, they frequently had large areas devoted to ill-proportioned servants' rooms, which many younger clients wanted reconfigured for more general family use. In addition, most of these apartments were physically worn out—inadequately wired and without air conditioning, which had become standard equipment for Manhattan apartments built after 1950. Finally, these apartments—many of which were located on the once fashionable, then marginal and now revitalized Central Park West—could be acquired relatively cheaply, although they needed large amounts of capital for imaginative reconstruction.

In 1970 the architects Mayers & Schiff demolished three rooms of the Bruce Slovins' apartment at 285 Central Park West to create a sixteen-by-sixty-foot entertainment space with a thirty-eight-foot multipurpose party unit running down the length of the room, above which a light canopy of multicolored neon gave off quite a glow.[127] On the East Side, in River House, at 435 East Fifty-second Street, architect Yann Weymouth and decorator Merrill Scott gutted the first floor of a river-facing duplex to create a single loft space for Louis F. "Bo" Polk.[128] Only a structural column and a storage cabinet were permitted to interrupt the purity of the sixteen-by-sixty-seven-foot white-tiled room. The furniture was on wheels, creating an effect that was certainly casual, if not as gritty as that of SoHo.

Two architectural firms dominated apartment renovation in the late 1960s and early 1970s: Robert Stern and John Hagmann; and Gwathmey Siegel. In 1967, prior to establishing his partnership, Stern renovated for his family's own use an apartment at 101 Central Park West, reorganizing the plan by inserting bold, curving partitions to clarify the distinctions between public and private space.[129] Replete with cow wallpaper designed by Andy Warhol, Pop and Minimalist art, classic Mies and Le Corbusier furniture, as well as an English Chesterfield sofa and the soaring arc of a Castiglioni lamp, the apartment sought to synthesize the vitality of downtown loft living with the

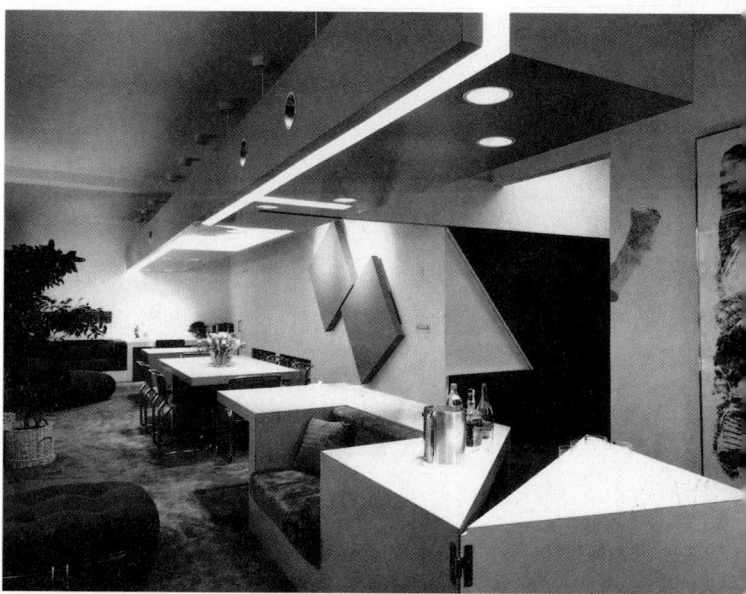

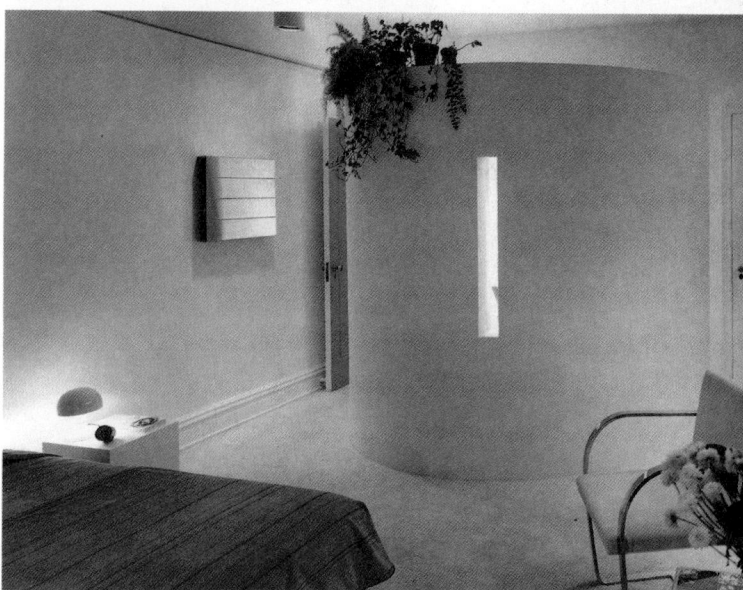

Top: Bruce Slovin apartment, 285 Central Park West. Mayers & Schiff, 1970. Maris. M&S

Bottom: Robert Stern apartment, 101 Central Park West. Robert Stern. 1967. Hill. RAMSA

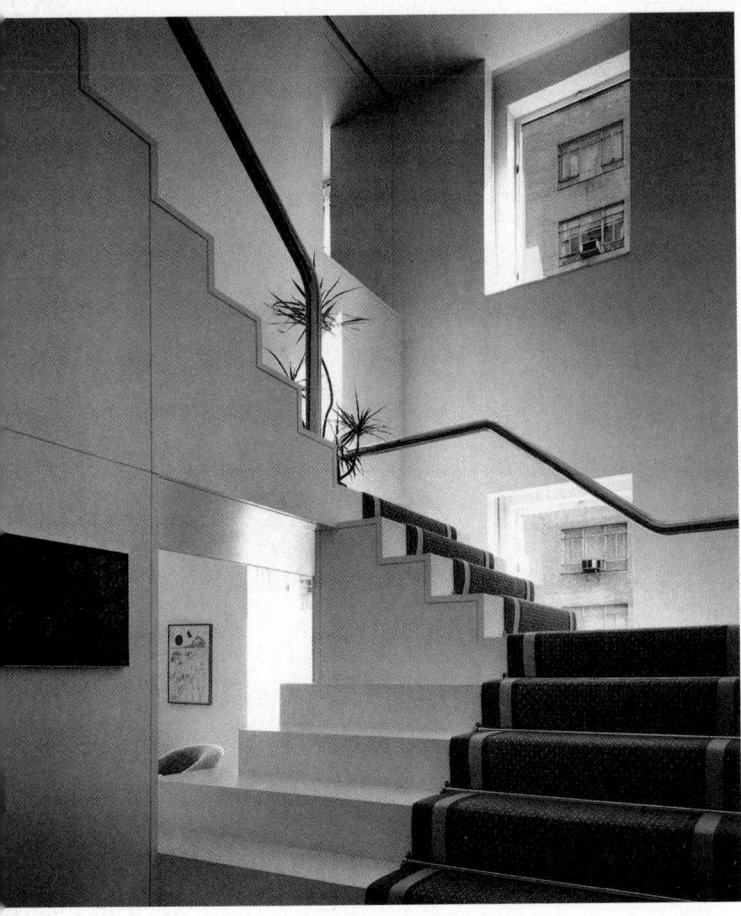

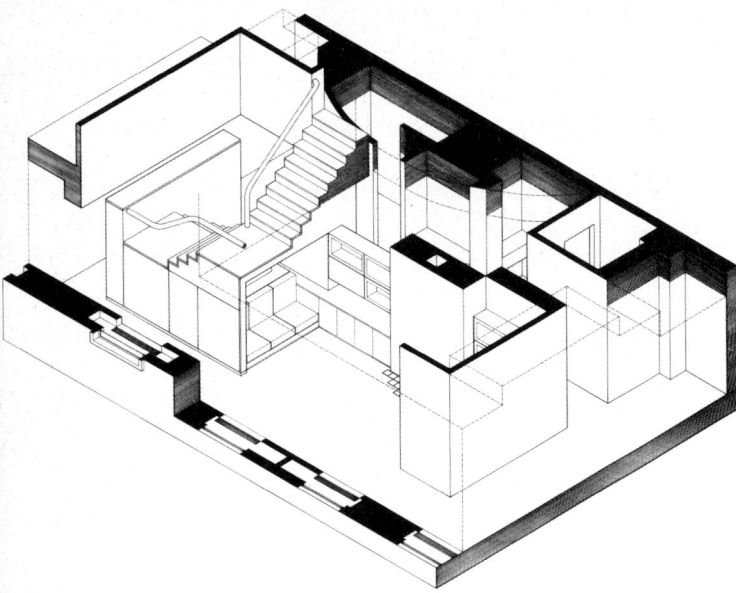

Top: Richard Danziger apartment, 950 Fifth Avenue. Robert Stern and John Hagmann, 1973. ©Norman McGrath. RAMSA

Bottom: Richard Danziger apartment. Axonometric. RAMSA

stability of conventional family living uptown. In 1971–72 Stern and Hagmann employed a similar strategy, substituting diagonals for curves, in renovating the apartment of Mr. and Mrs. Jerome Kretchmer at 262 Central Park West.[130] At about the same time, Stern and Hagmann completed the reconstruction of a duplex apartment at 101 Central Park West, removing a portion of the intervening floor to create a double-height room overlooking Central Park, with the master-bedroom balcony projecting over the space to produce a fireside cave effect in the manner of Paul Rudolph.[131] As Stern noted: "Buy a city apartment and you're probably buying a box. But you can make a totally personal world inside that space. The only place this world has to touch what's really outside is at windows."[132]

Stern and Hagmann's approach to the problem of the large apartment redesign reached its fullest expression in the renovation of Mr. and Mrs. Richard Danziger's duplex unit at 950 Fifth Avenue in 1973.[133] Here, a long narrow space was opened and made continuous, punctuated by a staircase incorporated into a large-scale, cabinetlike island, which separated the entrance hall from the living and dining rooms to either side and sheltered an intimate fireside seating area. In 1973 Stern and Hagmann also renovated a tiny rooftop apartment for an older couple, Mr. and Mrs. Lester Eisner, Jr., at 116 East Sixty-sixth Street, an ordinary postwar building.[134] Here the strategy was to tightly control the entrance sequence to maximize the impact of the apartment's exceptional view toward midtown. In order to gain some height and to capture terrace space, a greenhouse was used to enclose the dining room; it was sheltered from the sunlight by lightweight exterior blinds that could be rolled up at night for gazing at the stars and the skyline.

In contrast to Stern and Hagmann's spatially fragmented, eclectic interiors, Charles Gwathmey, at first on his own and then in his short-lived partnership with Richard Henderson and then with Robert Siegel, single-mindedly pursued a direction drawn from Le Corbusier's classicizing "purist" houses and apartment interiors of the 1920s and early 1930s. Gwathmey began his series of renovations with the apartment he rented for his family's use at 50 West Sixty-seventh Street in 1964, where only a few interventions were possible; the most notable of these was a vaulted ceiling in the hall leading to the combined living and dining room.[135]

In 1969 Gwathmey Siegel achieved their first fully resolved apartment interior for the actress Faye Dunaway.[136] Located at the base of the south tower of Emery Roth and Margon & Holder's Eldorado apartments (1931) on Central Park West, the Dunaway apartment consisted of two apartments that were gutted and reorganized with curves and diagonals to form one apartment with three main areas: for entertaining, sleeping and cooking. All detail was stripped away, and the white walls were contrasted with polished slate floors. Most of the furniture was built-in, and mirrors were extensively used to complicate the space and to reflect views of Central Park and the Fifth Avenue skyline. The master bathroom was spectacularly sybaritic, with a chaise and a tub based on designs by Le Corbusier. Gwathmey Siegel's sprawling Fifth Avenue apartment for Paul and Kay Breslow (1971) lightened the palette, with slate giving way to silver-gray carpeting, and with a curving wall of glass block and extensive light oak cabinetwork.[137] The owners' collection of African tribal art was sympathetically displayed in vitrines along a principal wall of the living room, and homage was paid to the geometrics of the art in the masklike plan figuration of the continuous built-in, room-dividing cabinet unit.

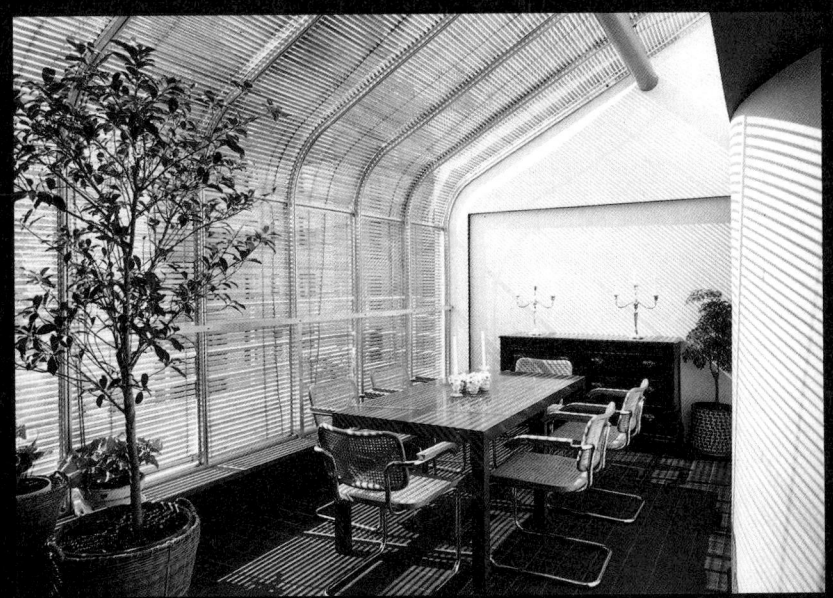

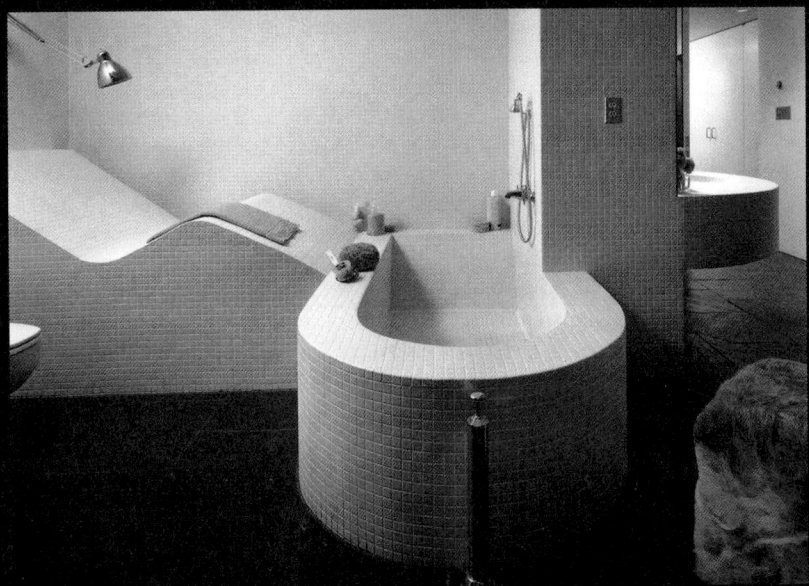

Top: Lester Eisner, Jr., apartment, 116 East Sixty-sixth Street. Robert Stern and John Hagmann, 1973. Stoecklein. RAMSA

Center: Faye Dunaway apartment, 300 Central Park West. Gwathmey Siegel, 1969. Master bathroom. Stoller. ©ESTO

Bottom: Faye Dunaway apartment. Master bedroom. Stoller. ©ESTO

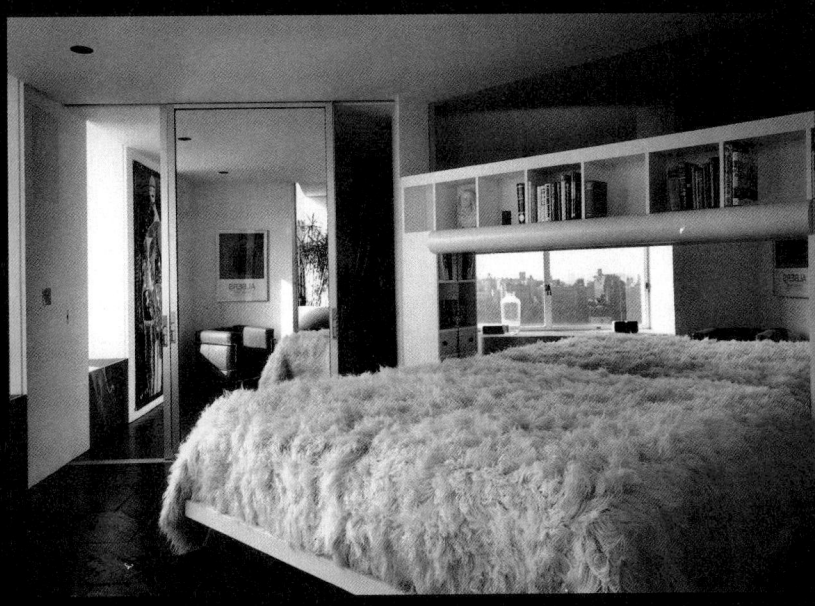

The postwar office-building boom was fueled not only by the growth of corporate activity but also by the increasingly sophisticated day-to-day operations that constituted business life. New machinery transformed the office, as did new management techniques, not the least of which was the increased emphasis on corporate identity and corporate culture. Before the Second World War, with a very few notable exceptions, such as Frank Lloyd Wright's total designs for the Larkin Company in Buffalo, New York (1904), and for S. C. Johnson & Son in Racine, Wisconsin (1939), the organization of office space and the selection of equipment had been the province of a purchasing agent, with only the occasional executive suite and reception areas turned over to a decorator or architect.[1] But beginning in the 1930s the growing size of office installations and their dependence on complex, constantly changing electronic technology demanded more sophisticated responses to the problem than merely furnishing a loftlike space with chairs, desks and filing cabinets. In addition, the effectiveness of "industrial design" in the marketplace, where it stimulated consumption, led many to believe that through design the worker could be encouraged to produce more. As a result of these developments, a new kind of designer emerged, the office space planner, who combined the functions of interior architect, decorator and purchasing agent.[2]

The large-scale involvement of design professionals in the organization and aesthetics of the office work space can be traced to the construction of Rockefeller Center. As the editors of *Interiors* pointed out in 1941, "Rockefeller Center provides, without a doubt, the most outstanding opportunity for the expression of appropriate interior design in the realm of the commercial world. Prosperous firms, large and small, establishing their offices on such premises require expert planning to make the most of the areas rented."[3] Typically, even in Rockefeller Center, the tenants who employed designers were those who were particularly concerned with marketing their services to a design-conscious clientele. The installation of the Bulova Watch Company in Rockefeller Center, for example, was one of the most integrated overall efforts in New York during the 1930s.[4] It was designed by Morris Lapidus, who treated reception and display spaces as well as executive and back-office spaces as a single problem. In addition to being elegant, the Bulova offices were technologically innovative, featuring one of the first large-scale installations of daylight fluorescent tubes. Also at Rockefeller Center were Ann Hatfield's designs for Time, Inc., developed under the direction of the architects Harrison & Fouilhoux; Ian Woodner's reception room and executive office for Yawman & Erbe; Carson & Lundin's office for Henry T. Ewald, of the Campbell-Ewald advertising agency; and Edward Durell Stone's particularly stylish, Scandinavian-inspired glassed-in penthouse office suite for the publishers Simon & Schuster.[5]

With the increase of women executives, Beryl Austrian, an interior designer who specialized in the decoration of apartment house and hotel lobbies, found herself with a new speciality: designing for top businesswomen, including Blanche Knopf, the publisher; Estele Hamburger, the advertising agent; and Katherine Gravens, the radio commentator.[6] Some of the most interesting wartime installations were for companies involved in the women's fashion business. For the cosmetics house of Northam-Wortham, Morris Lapidus took a provocative direction, combining an undulating ribbed wood wall, based on the work of the Finnish architect Alvar Aalto, with a desk uphol-

stered in tufted imitation pigskin;[7] and for Mangel's, a chain of dress shops, Lapidus (who also designed the shops) created a dramatic reception lobby in his characteristic syncopated Modernist manner.[8] Joseph Platt's interiors for Street and Smith, publishers of the fashion and beauty magazines *Mademoiselle* and *Charm*, filled two floors of the Chanin Building.[9] Eleanor Lemaire, whose Modernist interiors were among the most interesting of the 1930s, continued to prosper, increasing the scale of her projects and eventually expanding the scope of her practice in the 1950s to include large-scale office and banking interiors.[10] But in the 1940s Lemaire's work was still mostly small-scale: her reception room for Revlon, the cosmetics firm, dramatically combined chintz upholstery with slick wall planes and shadowboxes for product display.[11] Many women executives preferred a residential rather than a corporate atmosphere for their personal offices, and they frequently employed interior decorators: Joseph Platt put together a theatrical, eclectic combination of Victoriana and French furniture for Betsy Talbot Blackwell, editor-in-chief of *Mademoiselle*; Billy Baldwin installed Carmel Snow, editor of *Harper's Bazaar*, in a more restrained, French-inspired office. But some male executives also hired decorators: Harold K. Guinzburg, president of Viking Press, for instance, commissioned an utterly correct, Regency-inspired librarylike office from Hobe Erwin, of Erwin & Jones.[12]

Despite claims that the experience of the war would radically and immediately transform the character of the entire office, in the late 1940s most high-style design continued to be confined to reception and display rooms and the personal offices of top executives.[13] Lapidus's work for glassware distributor Irving W. Rice (1945) revealed a blend of surrealist-tinged Modernism and high drama.[14] But it seemed old hat compared with the suite of "experimental" offices designed in 1944 for *Look* magazine by their brilliant, twenty-nine-year-old graphic designer, or Visual Research Director (as he preferred to be called), Alvin Lustig.[15] Lustig's design was bold for an office, but its jumpy contrasts of planes, textures and colors was not particularly different from Lapidus's influential shop designs (see "Stores," below). In 1945 another publication, the recently founded magazine *The Reporter*, hired Lustig to design its offices in the Empire State Building along similar lines.[16] Forced to squeeze twenty-two people into a 1,600-square-foot space, Lustig designed storage walls and modular desks to create efficient workstations, and special pendant lighting fixtures that provided general illumination as well as task lighting. To minimize claustrophobia yet achieve some degree of privacy for individual writers, Lustig suspended three-quarter-inch-thick sheets of translucent plate glass between each of their desks, the same material he used for the work surfaces throughout.

Jedd Stowe Reisner's reception room for the publishers Reynal and Hitchcock (1945) was a bit calmer, reflecting the Scandinavian Modernist design showcased at the New York World's Fair of 1939.[17] It took advantage of a story-and-a-half-high studio space on the twenty-first floor of 8 West Fortieth Street, originally the drafting room of the building's designers, Starrett & Van Vleck.[18] Reisner devised a series of fixed louvers to shield the skylit room from direct light and dampen acoustics. To come to grips with the vast space, he arranged the furniture in groups and used movable screens to create private conference areas. In 1948 Reisner, in partnership with Max O. Urbahn, designed the offices for another publisher, Dial Press.[19]

Advertising agencies, like publishers, commissioned inventive office suites.[20] Most notable among these was the formidable J. Walter Thompson Company, which had employed

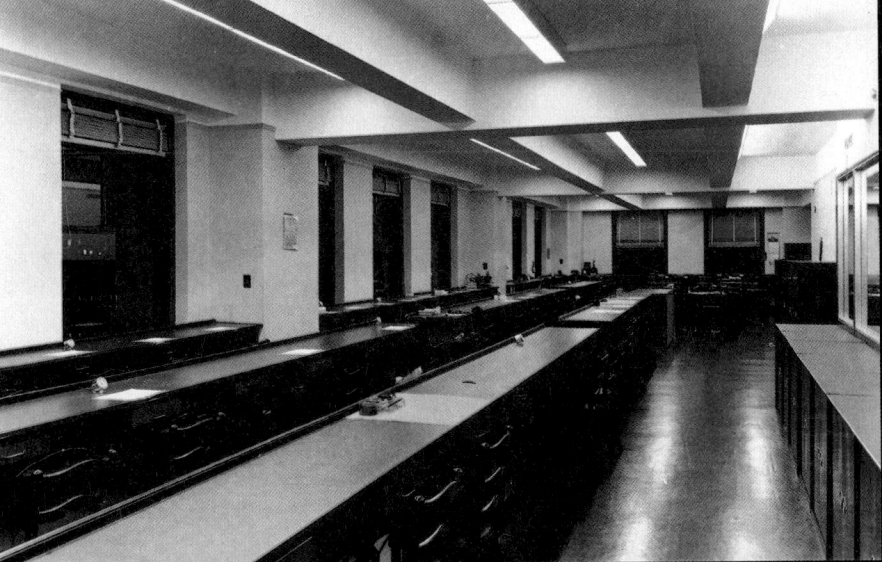

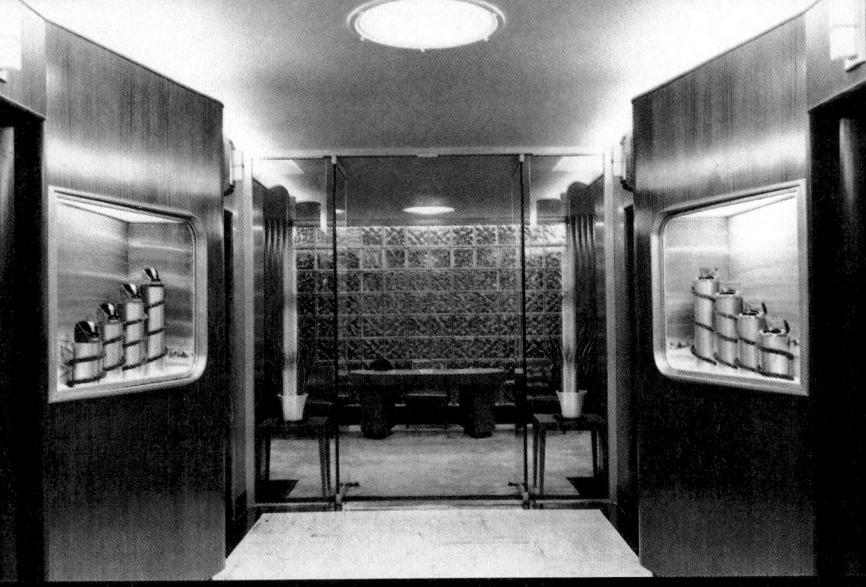

Top: Bulova Watch Company, 630 Fifth Avenue. Morris Lapidus, 1939. Gottscho-Schleisner. LOC

Center: Bulova Watch Company. Gottscho-Schleisner. LOC

Bottom left: Penthouse office suite, Simon & Schuster, 1230 Sixth Avenue. Edward Durell Stone, 1940. Stoller. ©ESTO

Bottom right: Office of Betsy Talbot Blackwell, *Mademoiselle* magazine, 122 East Forty-second Street. Joseph Platt, 1949. Gottscho-Schleisner. LOC

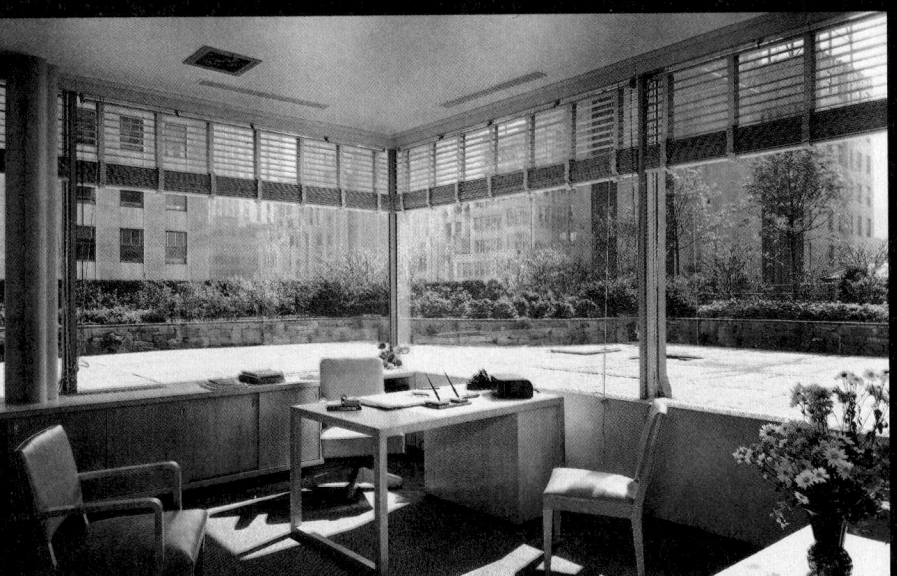

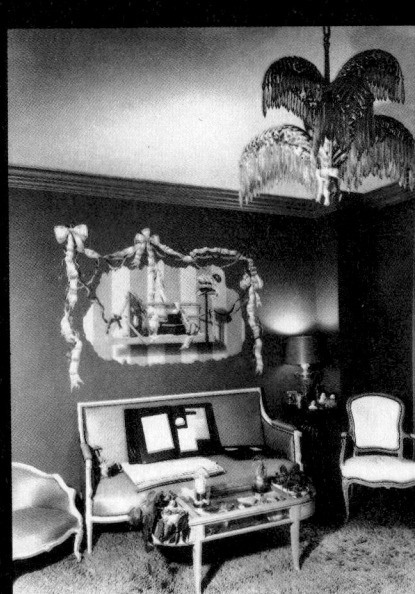

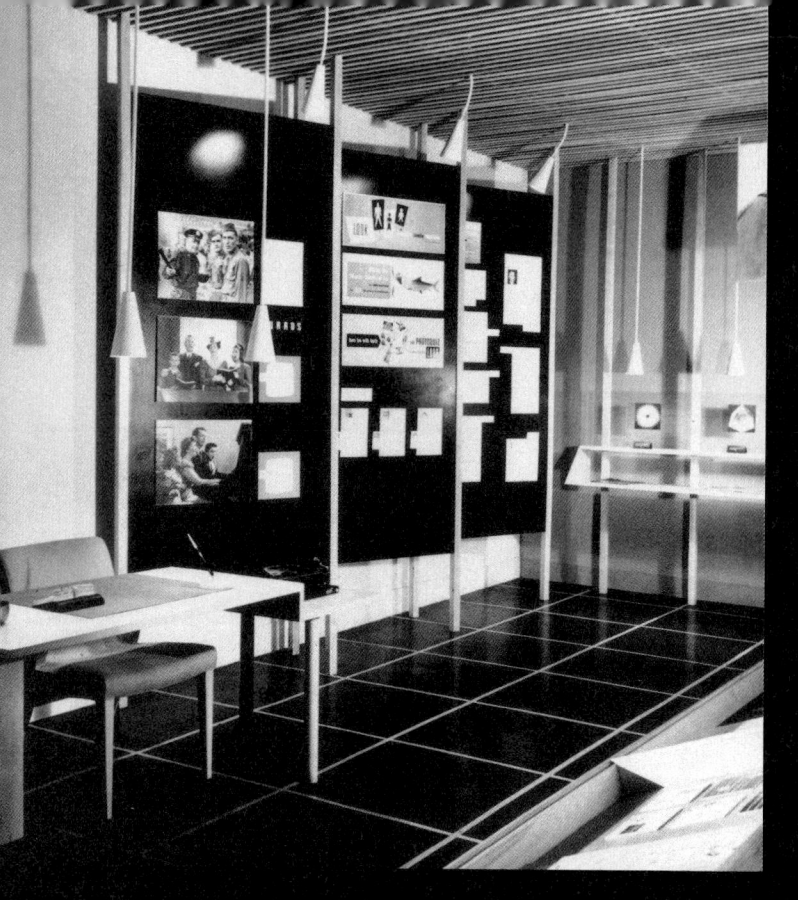

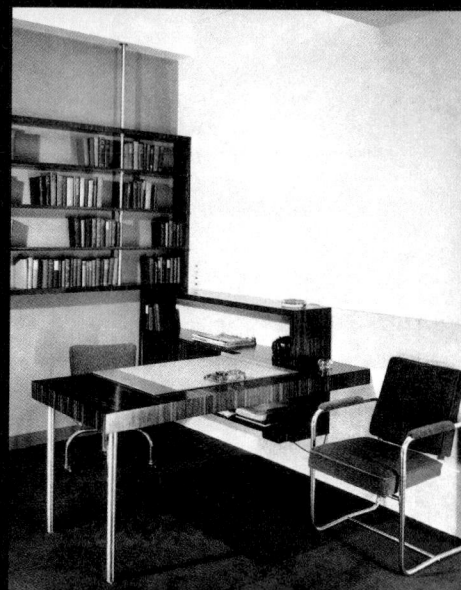

Top left: Offices of Look magazine, Look
Building, 488 Madison Avenue. Alvin Lustig,
1944. ELC

Top right: J. Walter Thompson Company, 420
Lexington Avenue. William Lescaze, 1945.
Executive office. SU

Bottom: J. Walter Thompson Company.
Secretarial pool. ©Gil Amiaga. GA

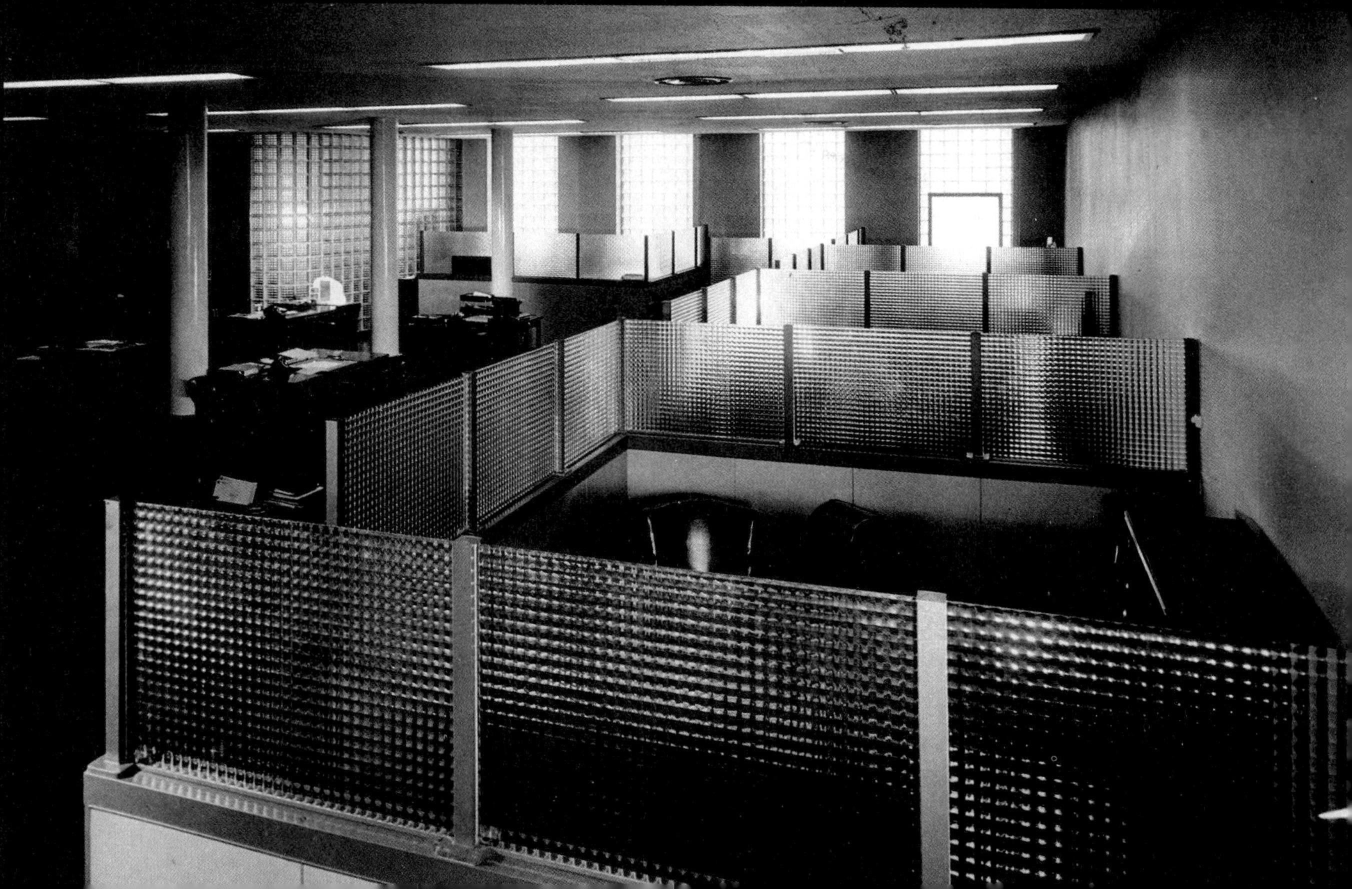

Norman Bel Geddes to great advantage in designing their Graybar Building offices in 1928[21] and in 1945 retained William Lescaze to redesign their offices on two floors of the Chrysler Building.[22] While some of the interiors were rather undistinguished, utilizing ordinary wooden office furniture, others were crisply detailed interiors making extensive use of glass partitions framed in blond wood. In one office Lescaze incorporated stylish tubular furniture into a scheme that evoked Ludwig Mies van der Rohe's 1930 apartment for Philip Johnson.[23] A stair connecting the two floors was opened up with a shipshape aluminum handrail. Donald Deskey's offices and conference areas for a smaller agency, Grey Advertising (1945), were also noteworthy.[24]

By the mid-1950s the growing scale of office operations, the increasing number and variety of office machines, especially electronic computers, and the quickening pace of growth and change in business demanded a new kind of response. This new discipline, which came to be known as space planning, went beyond promotional aesthetics to encompass the physical organization of entire companies, frequently occupying one or more floors of new office buildings. One firm, Designs for Business, Inc., founded in the 1930s by Maurice Mogulescu as Ad-Pro Displays and Interiors, pioneered office space planning.[25] Mogulescu's firm had its origin in exhibition display work, first prospering with projects generated by the New York World's Fair of 1939. After the war the firm continued to grow, turning its attention to showroom design and then to office interiors; it became Designs for Business in 1946. But it was not until 1948, when Gerald Luss, a twenty-two-year-old graduate of Pratt Institute's newly instituted interior design program, joined the firm, that it took off. By 1952 Luss was director of design, and the firm was generally acknowledged as the most successful practitioner of space planning, a holistic approach to commercial interior design that combined interior architecture, interior decoration and frequently project management as well as purchasing. Designs for Business profited by the managerial revolution of the 1950s and by the exceptional boom in office renovation, which could be attributed to three factors: the scarcity of rental space resulting from the wartime building freeze, which required that tenants use existing space as efficiently as possible; an excess profits tax, which encouraged businesses to invest in capital improvements; and a shortage of potential employees, which forced management to increase office amenities to attract workers.

Designs for Business began to make a name for itself in 1952 with three installations: 2,500 square feet of offices for the Knickerbocker Construction Company, a significantly larger installation for the Lawrence C. Gumbinner advertising agency, and the offices of the publisher Henry Holt and Company, three work environments more notable for a very efficient use of space than for any particular aesthetic feature.[26] Luss could achieve stylish effects, as in his design for Tower Fabrics, where rough cinder-block walls and exposed construction hardware created a perfect foil for the company product.[27] But the firm's typical work was far less dramatic, emphasizing flexible modular office partitioning, elegantly crafted cabinetry and straightforward, serviceable furniture.[28]

Luss was the first interior designer to realize the full potential of Modernist minimalism to satisfy the functional office programs of the postwar corporation. In 1957 he wrote:

Ever since the beginning of the postwar construction boom, large corporate firms have sought to utilize the advantages inherent in the new type of modern, air-conditioned office building—the opportunity to set up with technological advances,

automated procedures, new operational methods, new equipment, more efficient layouts, new concepts of furnishings and decoration for the human aspects affecting productivity, etc. No mere whim—this new concept of physical facilities and operational methods is of basic urgency to accommodate the vast expansion, the increased complexities accumulated by business and industry during the war.[29]

The firm's breakthrough came with the offices of the Olin Mathieson Chemical Corporation, where they performed comprehensive services that included advice on real estate as well as internal corporate organization.[30] Olin Mathieson, created by merging two companies, was one of the first important corporations in the postwar era to move their headquarters to New York, relocating in 1955 from St. Louis to four floors of Emery Roth & Sons' 460 Park Avenue, which had just been completed. Luss and his associates analyzed the new firm's space requirements and operational patterns and advised them to locate on the four 10,000-square-foot floors in 460 Park rather than on fewer larger floors that could have been found in a different building. Because the company was newly created, Luss realized that change would be an important aspect of their immediate future, so he devised a flexible, demountable partitioning system as well as a compatible ceiling system. The desks were also modular and demountable.

A slew of important corporate interiors followed the Olin job: Designs for Business installed Continental Grain Company in Two Broadway;[31] American Enka Corporation in 530 Fifth Avenue;[32] Corning Glass Works in its headquarters building, 717 Fifth Avenue (see chapter 5); Simmons, the mattress company, in 50 East Forty-second Street;[33] Coro Company, the costume jewelers, in 47 West Thirty-fourth Street;[34] Maritime Overseas Corporation in 511 Fifth Avenue;[35] Sperry & Hutchinson, Co. in 330 Madison Avenue;[36] and, most notably, Time, Inc. in their new Sixth Avenue headquarters (see chapter 5). The firm's own offices in the KLM Building on Fifth Avenue exemplified their mastery of modular partitioning and corporate organization.[37] Here a sophisticated system on a grid of extruded-aluminum posts framed modular, easily demountable, clear glass partitions that could be moved as office requirements evolved. The office was thus visually open yet acoustically private, juxtaposing drafting-room clutter with the far more orderly realm of conventional executive-suite design.

In 1965 Luss left Designs for Business and, together with Eli Kaplan, established Luss/Kaplan and Associates Limited, branching out into new fields, including hospital design, while continuing to design offices as well as a variety of provocative smaller projects.[38] Among these were the offices of the Minskoff real estate interests (1967) in One Astor Plaza,[39] and 2,139 square feet of highly unusual offices for Morton Globus (1970), an investment counselor, on the thirty-second floor of Burlington House.[40] Luss's design for Globus, recalling I. M. Pei's offices for William Zeckendorf (see below), set two circular enclosures within the rectangular grid of the leased space, eliminating conventional corridors and providing only two rectangular offices for the partners while establishing a dramatic sense of continuously flowing space. In place of Pei's refined minimalism, Luss employed a rich vocabulary of flashy materials, sheathing the outside walls of the conference room with small hexagonal ceramic tiles and lining its inside walls with the same dark brown carpet he used to cover the floors.

According to Olga Gueft, Globus's stylized offices greeted visitors with "vibrations of concentrated power as soon as they enter, vibrations that grow stronger as they move from the re-

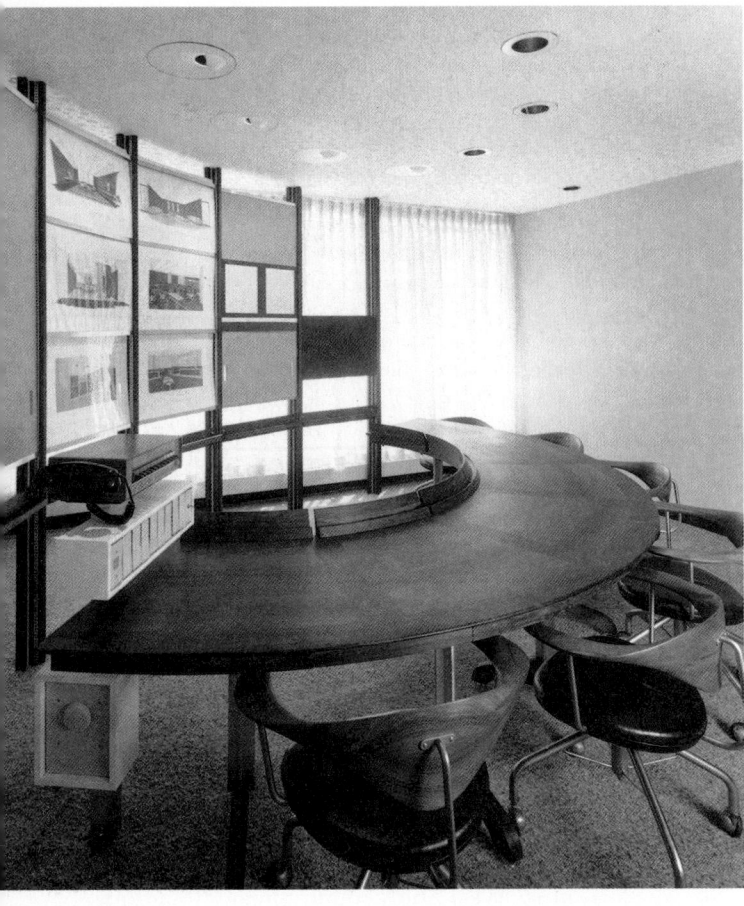

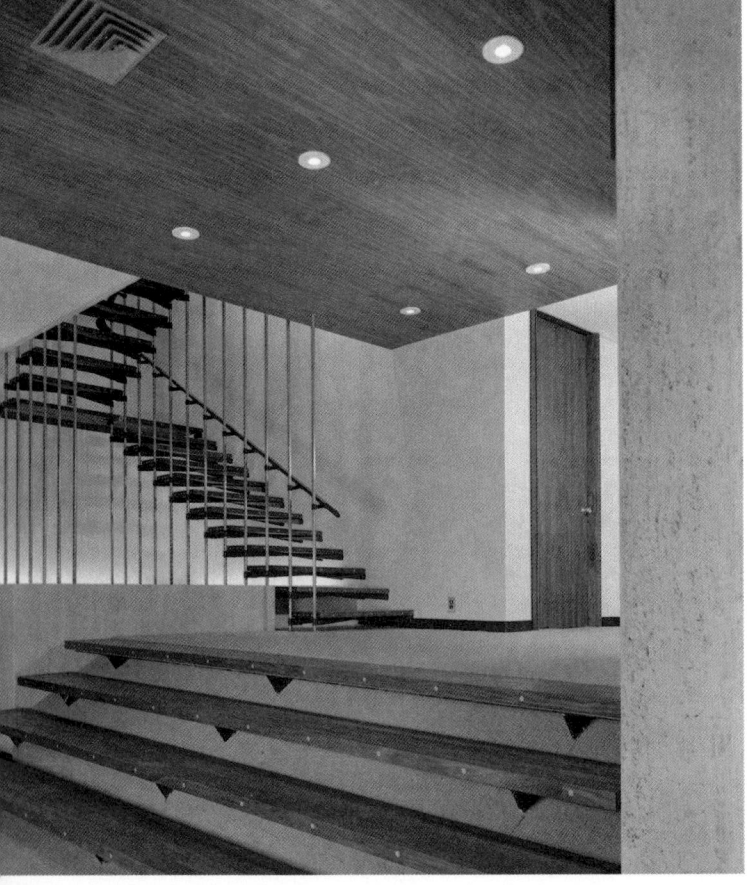

ception area to the partners' territory past an intriguingly mysterious conference room." Gueft continued:

The difficulties of the assignment were of two kinds—spatial and psychological. The space is actually modest in size and low-ceilinged, a close-fisted travesty of the volumetric grandiosity associated with finance since the high-ceilinged heyday of Wall Street. . . . As to the psychological problem: All organizations which handle other people's money wish, for reasons we need not dwell on, to look as permanent as the Rock of Gibraltar. Evanescence won't do, nor frivolity.[41]

Ada Louise Huxtable was not quite so smitten with the design. Quoting from Luss/Kaplan's publicity, which described the reception area as "starkly simple and understated to the point of no provision for reception seating since visitors are seen by appointment and immediately received into the offices," she went on to observe: "The reception desk stands alone, isolated and abstract, focused by a white plastic light shaft molded above it—an illuminated altar to the process of making and losing money. One of God's more responsible representatives will see you right away." She concluded: "The modern movement has come full circle from revolution against the Establishment to playing con games with its architectural symbols. It's a long way from Ronchamp."[42]

In less than a decade the power of the new space planners, who were specialists, as the *Architectural Forum* put it in 1957, "in the science of making interior office space work out logically, i.e. profitably," had become extraordinary.[43] Luss's chief rival for influence and clients was Lawrence Lerner of Michael Saphier Associates, a firm that established their reputation in 1955 with the design of their own offices.[44] Saphier, an industrial designer, began the firm in 1937, teaming up in 1947 with Bernard Schindler, an engineer. The firm took on a strong design direction when Lerner joined them in 1949. Lerner had studied design at Brooklyn College in 1946 and 1947, enrolling in an innovative program organized by the Russian-born architect Serge Chermayeff, who had worked in collaboration with Erich Mendelsohn. When Saphier and Schindler received their first important project, the space planning for 1407 Broadway, Lerner joined them as a renderer, and he quickly became the firm's chief designer.[45] Early important clients included the National Association of Manufacturers, at 2 East Forty-eighth Street,[46] and the realtors Herbert Charles & Company, at 545 Madison Avenue, where they collaborated with the decorator Melvin Dwork and commissioned the sculptor Constantino Nivola to design a wall.[47] One of the firm's most elegant corporate interiors was executed in 1964 for Century Theatres, Inc., at 1450 Broadway.[48] The firm also designed midtown offices for the Wall Street brokerage house Sutro Brothers, at 625 Madison Avenue;[49] and they installed the firm of Neuberger & Berman in offices at 120 Broadway that showcased the firm's museum-quality collection of twentieth-century art.[50]

The Saphier firm grew quickly, and in 1960 with the staff swelled to sixty, they moved into offices on the second floor of the Look Building, at 488 Madison Avenue.[51] In a futuristic style that anticipated the world of the Jetsons, the cartoon family created by Hanna-Barbera in 1962, the offices featured a play of circles and curves in the plan and exaggeratedly angular furniture in the reception room and presentation areas. Important clients at this time, when the firm began to refer to their design speciality as "environetics," included the Manhattan Shirt Company, for which they designed a showroom in the Time & Life Building,[52] and the Glickman Corporation, a real estate firm that was located in the two-story, vacated vault of the Bankers Trust bank at 501 Fifth Avenue.[53]

By the mid-1960s the firm, now known as Saphier, Lerner, Schindler, Inc., had adopted a cooler, more "corporate" aesthetic, which could be seen in the reception lobbies they designed for three companies located at 1290 Avenue of the Americas: the Fairbanks Whitney Corporation, the National Credit Office and Clairol, Inc.[54] In 1966 the firm, now known simply as SLS, moved their offices to even larger quarters (which were supplemented with branch offices in Los Angeles, San Francisco, Chicago and Boston). The new offices, 50 percent larger than their previous headquarters, consisted of 11,000 square feet of space in 600 Madison Avenue in which glass partitioning was used extensively to create a feeling of openness while maintaining acoustic privacy.[55] Also in 1966 SLS became part of the corporate world they served when they joined the Business Systems Equipment Group of the giant conglomerate Litton Industries. The firm was now the unchallenged technological leader in the field of office space design, and in making extensive use of computers to analyze client programs and to design actual installations, the office designers brought their techniques and character into remarkably close harmony with those of the clients they served.[56]

While SLS's bread-and-butter work was in space planning on a vast scale, they showed off their design skills in small projects for showrooms and corporate suites such as those of Muzak, the company that piped recorded music into public spaces.[57] For Muzak's principal space, at 100 Park Avenue, SLS provided a slick, stylized setting, updating the futuristic exuberance of their earlier work with a vocabulary of polished metals and cold cathode accent lighting. SLS could also work in the cool, Mies-inspired Modernism so beloved by corporate America, as demonstrated in the lobby and executive offices they designed as part of the advertising agency Leber Katz Paccione's 31,000-square-foot office suite in the General Motors Building.[58] But the offbeat 1975 installation of the Gilman Paper Company in 40,000 square feet of space on the fourteen-foot-high mezzanine of the Time & Life Building was more characteristic of SLS's aesthetics.[59] Lerner organized the Gilman office grid at a forty-five-degree angle to the building's structural grid. Medium-height, vinyl-covered gypsum-board partitions were installed to define major circulation routes, and low white walls were used to enclose work areas but to keep a sense of spatial openness throughout the vast space. Colorful partitions, combined with an intricate ceiling hung with exposed air-conditioning ducts placed below the building's structural frame, created a lively if somewhat chaotic effect that was a far cry from the geometric regimentation of the typical corporate environment that space planners had advocated for more than fifteen years.

Throughout the 1950s and 1960s, independent architects, interior designers and decorators played a decreasing role in corporate interior design as space planners came to the fore. But they did garner some of the plum commissions for boutiquelike office suites, which often set the aesthetic standard by which the space planners were measured. The era's most extraordinary offices, those of the developer William Zeckendorf, were created in 1952 by the architect I. M. Pei working in association with William Lescaze.[60] At the time, Pei headed the architectural division of Zeckendorf's firm, Webb & Knapp, where he assembled a team of talented, bright young architects that included Don Page, Carl Groos, Ulrich Franzen and Henry Cobb, who would later become Pei's principal design partner. Zeckendorf commissioned Pei to create a $500,000 duplex suite on the vast roof of Webb & Knapp's headquarters, the Knapp Building, at 383–385 Madison Avenue (Cross & Cross, 1922–23).[61]

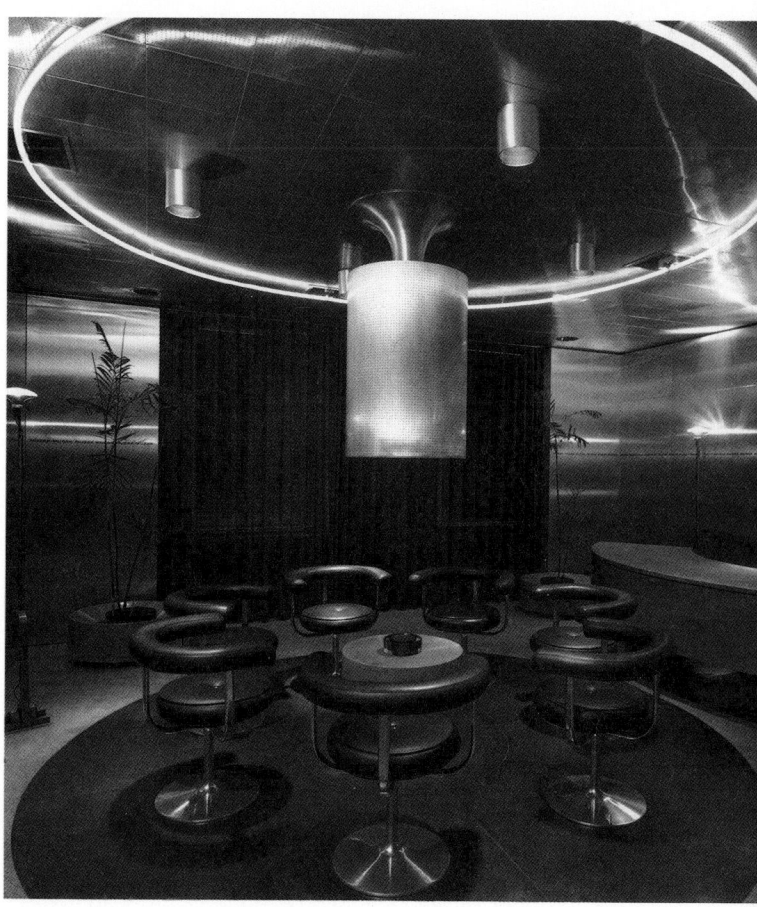

Top left: Offices of Michael Saphier Associates, 488 Madison Avenue. Lawrence Lerner, 1960. Reens. LR

Bottom left: Glickman Corporation, 501 Fifth Avenue. Michael Saphier Associates, 1961. Reens. LR

Above: Offices of Muzak, 100 Park Avenue. Saphier, Lerner, Schindler, Inc., 1972. Reens. LR

Pei's solution was a pioneering, uncharacteristically exuberant example of the emerging corporate Modernism. The arriving visitor stepped off an elevator directly into an expansive reception area that occupied about one-third of the penthouse's 12,000-square-foot main floor. To one side were the executive offices; above them, connected by means of a curving stair, were the work spaces of the staff architects and a conference room. Straight ahead, past the reception desk, a glazed wall opened onto a terrace, walled in marble and punctuated with planting and sculpture in a manner that recalled Mies van der Rohe's Barcelona Pavilion (1929) and Le Corbusier's Paris penthouse for Count Charles de Beistegui (1931).[62] Only one object interrupted this vast sea of visually continuous space—a circular, teak-covered, twenty-five-foot-diameter drum that sheltered Zeckendorf's private office. To combat the acoustical problems inherent in a circular shape, the inner walls of the silolike office were lined with faceted oak-veneer panels. Just beyond the office, a smaller cylinder contained an elevator that lifted visitors to Zeckendorf's lounge, a round conning tower cantilevered off the core and thrust into the mid-Manhattan skyline. Containing a private dining room and entertainment space, this "crow's nest," as Architectural Forum called it, was "the final flourish in this palace for a modern business Caesar."[63]

Zeckendorf explained that in describing his requirements for the offices, he had told Pei: "'I don't want to be buried away in some inaccessible corner.' Pei had already noted that the great majority of visitors to Webb & Knapp came to see me and then went on to see someone else. His solution, therefore, was to start visitors off directly beside the place most of them wanted to go—my office. Within the great open lobby and display area of the top floor of our building, he built . . . a headquarters within a headquarters—my office."[64] E. J. Kahn, Jr., the son of the notable commercial architect Ely Jacques Kahn, profiling Zeckendorf in the New Yorker in December 1951, as Pei's design was nearing completion, observed that Zeckendorf's "only outside view is of the sky, which he can glimpse by gazing through a handful of plastic skylights let into the ceiling of his cylinder."[65] Pei arrived at this unusual solution after analyzing Zeckendorf's character: "I came to the conclusion that he is a showman . . . and that it would be ridiculous to create any environment for him other than one consisting exclusively of himself. Why give him windows to compete with his own personality?"[66] Architectural Forum, picking up on Pei's analysis, characterized the office as Zeckendorf's "two-level rooftop palace, his showboat riding the crest of Manhattan."[67] Using a similar metaphor, Zeckendorf said that the new headquarters dominated its surroundings "as effectively as the lone turret of that famous Civil War ironclad, the Monitor, once dominated its own deck and the water for miles around."[68]

But Architectural Forum saw more in the Zeckendorf office than a stage set for power broking:

What Pei and associates achieved has three-fold significance. First, there was the opportunity here to . . . demonstrate the peculiarly modern art of floating small curved spaces, independent and self-enclosed, into the big rectangular space of the modern "loft." But, beyond that, the best values of the job may lie in the part least possible to convey in words and pictures: the sensitivity and art with which every last line, every last color—of room and furniture and painting and sculpture and planting—were harmonized to contribute an agreeable euphoria. And, finally, unlike some of the earlier "modern masters," Pei, the Chinese realist, has treated the sciences seriously too—of sound, of light, of temperature—without ever relaxing his

hold on overall design. Here the functionalist and the artist are in a rarely happy marriage [sic].[69]

At the time, Zeckendorf's rooftop offices were unique; most everyone else was content to work with the austerity of a typical office building. Yet high-style, custom office interiors for top executives began to become a regular feature of the New York commercial scene in the 1960s, when the impact of Ward Bennett's achievement at Chase Manhattan was felt by other clients (see chapter 3). In 1962 Bennett himself designed an executive suite for Louis J. Glickman, chairman of the Glickman Corporation. Glickman, who hired the designer on the basis of his work at Chase, had the recently installed work of Michael Saphier Associates (see above) ripped out to make way for Bennett's design, which was exceptionally elegant and refined.[70] By the mid-1960s the use of high-style designers and architects had become so prevalent, said Elaine Kendall in an article in the New York Times Magazine, that "bankers, brokers, and real estate men" were "tossing out the stuffed swordfish and calling in the decorators. . . . No one wants just a place to work any more. The office is becoming a kind of stage, from which one projects both a personal and a corporate image."[71]

In 1966 the small, "hot" advertising agency of Papert, Koenig, Lois, Inc., moved into 50,000 square feet of space on five floors of William Lescaze's U.S. Plywood Building, at 777 Third Avenue.[72] The firm had been formed in 1961, when the three founders took 3,000 square feet of space in the Seagram Building before they had a single client. The firm prospered, and in 1962 they moved to their second office, a single floor in the General Dynamics Building in Rockefeller Center, which was competently but not stylishly fitted out for them by the architect Donald W. Porter.[73] For their next move—to the Plywood Building—the firm hired Nicos Zographos, a romantic minimalist interior and furniture designer. Working with the architect Charles Koulbanis, Zographos turned the five floors of offices into an elegantly stripped-down working environment. The extraordinary absence of clutter and of color—the palette was confined to white, black, gray and brown—created an environment of Zenlike subtleties. Although, as John Dixon observed, such nuances were perhaps lost on many employees and clients, they kept "the visual discrimination of [George] Lois and his art staff sharply honed."[74] Lois's office was a quintessential essay in power, as Michael Korda noted in his widely discussed article on the subject:

The desk is small and simple, like a schoolteacher's, and faces a kind of enclosed sofa on which visitors sit, like schoolchildren, at some distance from teacher's desk. Their discomfort can only be increased by the fact that one ashtray on the small square table to the left is clearly out of reach, while the light from the window behind the desk shines directly in their eyes. Because of the high back and sides of the sofa, they might as well be locked in a box. Here, the clean desk is carried to its utmost refinement. No humanizing touch is present, and the only point of attention and interest is presumably Mr. Lois himself.[75]

The reigning experts of stylish corporate minimalism were the Knoll Planning Unit, headed by Florence Knoll Bassett, a designer and the widow of Hans G. Knoll, founder of the group's parent company, the world's preeminent wholesalers of high-style Modernist furniture.[76] The Knoll Planning Unit's design for the executive offices of their parent company, at 320 Park Avenue, represented a new attitude to the workplace.[77] The design featured a corridor lined with full-height flush doors concealing filing cabinets and office machines, an extensive use of

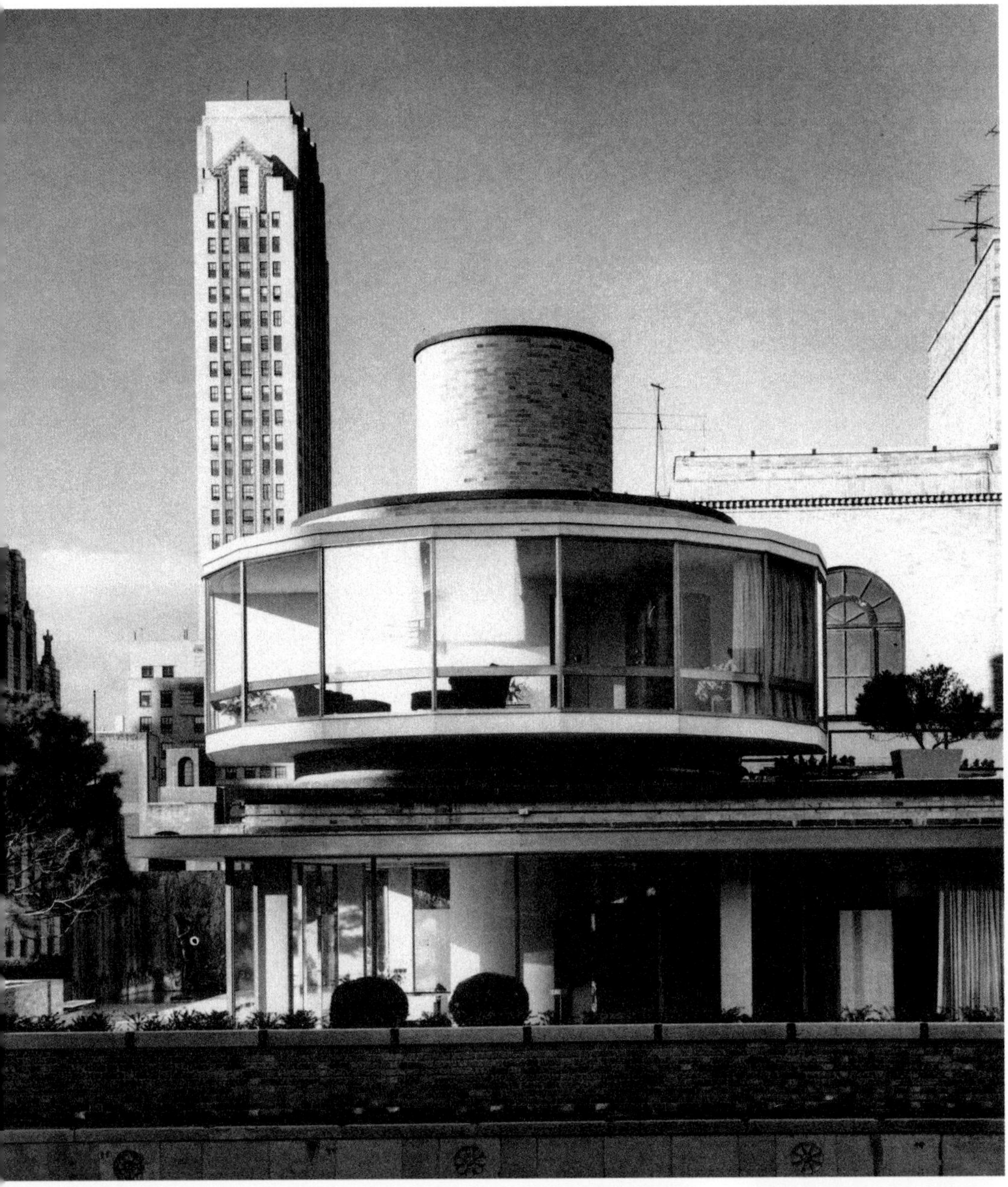

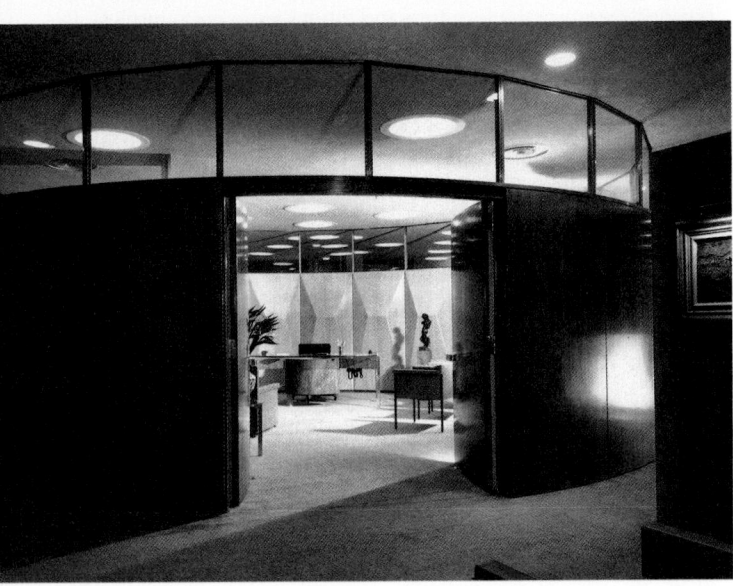

Top: Penthouse office suite, Webb & Knapp, 383–385 Madison Avenue. I. M. Pei in association with William Lescaze, 1952. View to the north of William Zeckendorf's lounge and private dining room. Stoller. ©ESTO

Bottom left: Penthouse office suite, Webb & Knapp. View from reception area into Zeckendorf's office. Stoller. ©ESTO

Bottom right: Penthouse office suite, Webb & Knapp. Stoller. ©ESTO

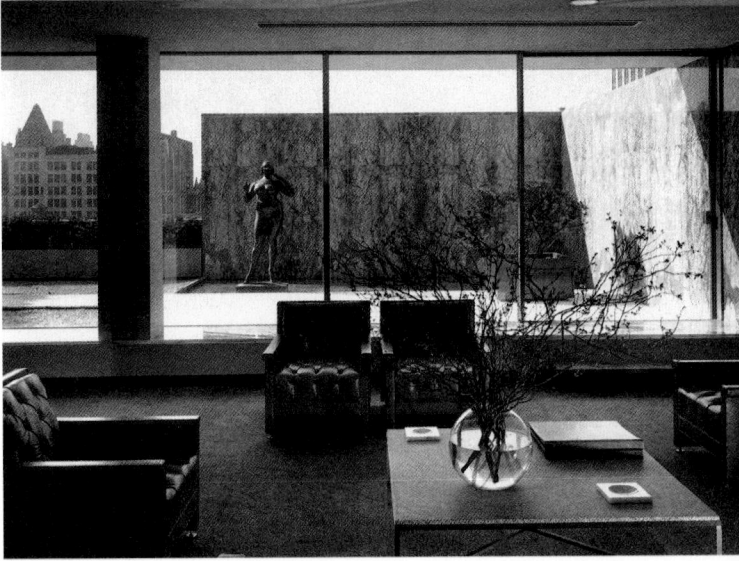

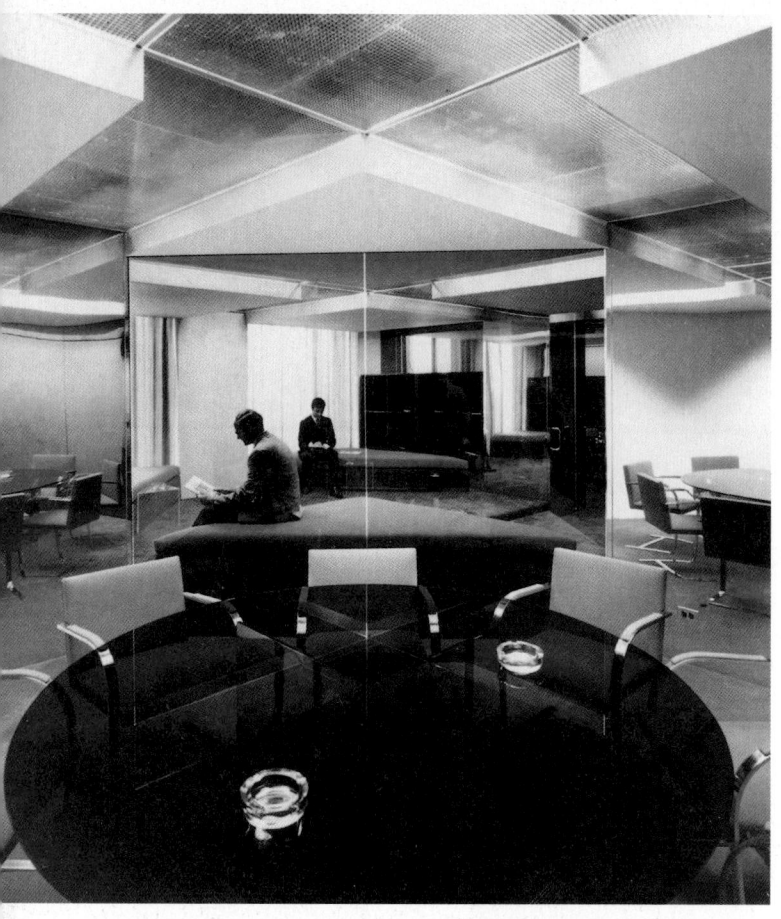

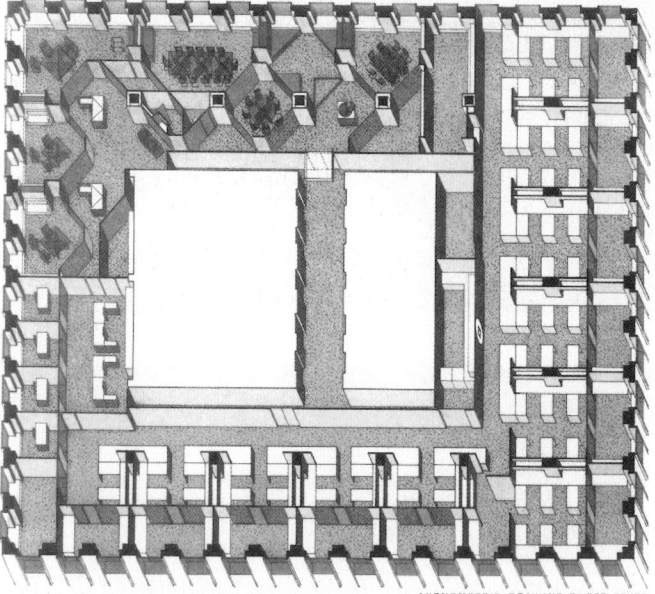

Top: W. A. DiGiacomo Associates, 1515 Broadway. Der Scutt, 1969. DSA

Bottom: W. A. DiGiacomo Associates. Axonometric. DSA

tables in place of traditional desks in executive offices, and sophisticated incandescent downlighting in place of standard fluorescent light panels. Other notable interiors designed under Bassett's guidance were offices for CBS at 485 Madison Avenue (1954)[78] and in their new building on Sixth Avenue (see chapter 5), for the Carnegie Endowment for Peace (see chapter 7) and for the Deering Milliken Company (see chapter 5). After she retired in 1965, the planning group was led by Peter Andes.[79]

In 1963 the Houston-based architect Howard Barnstone, assisted by Eugene Aubry, renovated the offices of Schlumberger, Ltd., a firm that had employed Philip Johnson to design their Mies-inspired, minimalist research headquarters building in Ridgefield, Connecticut.[80] Three years later Schlumberger moved from their offices, at 660 Madison Avenue, to larger quarters at 277 Park Avenue, where Barnstone and Aubry were hired again to develop a scheme that would set a trend for "liberated" corporate environments.[81] The new Schlumberger offices were at once very minimal in detailing and spatially active in plan, with diagonally placed glass partitions separating offices from circulation areas. The use of the diagonal—of "twisting, frugging, wiggling walls," as C. Ray Smith put it—reflected the influence of the so-called Philadelphia School of architecture. As Smith said, however, the walls were more than a stylish device: "They achieve, surprisingly, a leveling of spatial hierarchy—an equalization of the quality of light and spaces provided for executives and for secretarial staff."[82] The walls, which were developed, according to the architects, from a "squiggley doodle," expanded the space in unusual ways, producing "a crazy house of reflections" while transforming interior corridors into "a series of grand lobbies."[83]

Der Scutt, a young, Yale-trained architect, also explored diagonal partitions in his offices for W. A. Di Giacomo Associates, mechanical engineers, but in this case the scheme was disciplined to a forty-five-degree grid.[84] Installed within One Astor Plaza, which Scutt had designed for Kahn & Jacobs, the Di Giacomo offices were startling: bright colors, bold juxtapositions of shiny metal and plastic surfaces, gray-tinted glass partitions and modular built-in furniture created a working environment quite at odds with the utilitarianism of the typical engineering office. Prentice & Chan, Ohlhausen also used diagonals in their 1970 offices for the young advertising agency of Scali, McCabe, Sloves.[85] But their diagonals were in the form of comparatively small-scale zigzag partitions arranged to individualize each office. In keeping with the status of a beginning business venture, the furniture and fittings were quite modest. In 1973 Beyer Blinder Belle also used the diagonal as a rotated square with chamfered corners to form the conference room in their offices for Two Trees, Inc., a development firm located in the Harper & Row Building, at 10 East Fifty-third Street.[86] In an attempt to evoke the atmosphere of a SoHo loft, Jeff Byers, one of the company's principals, displayed examples of his large collection of contemporary art in the offices.

The use of the diagonal was but a tentative move in the search for environmental liberation, which reached its peak in supermannerism. This aggressive approach, inspired by graphic design, had comparatively little impact on the world of big business, with a few notable exceptions, including the extraordinary headquarters for the cosmetics firm Fabergé by the Dallek Inc. Design Group.[87] Godfrey Dallek, who had been an outspoken proponent of good design as a management tool,[88] had provided staid interiors for Fabergé since 1960, but for this 1971 project he put together a team of young designers, principally Stanley Felderman. Occupying the thirty-seventh and

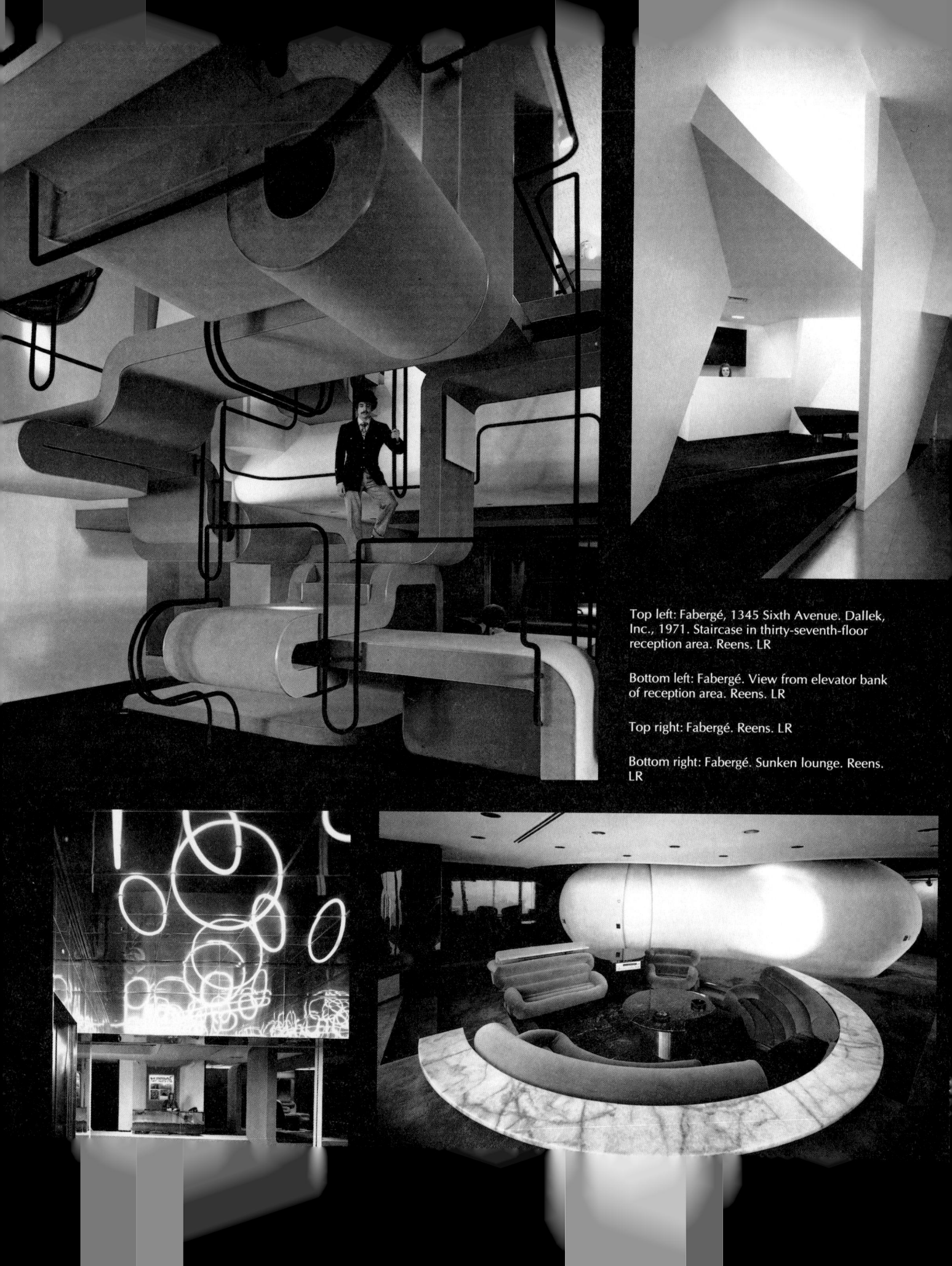

Top left: Fabergé, 1345 Sixth Avenue. Dallek, Inc., 1971. Staircase in thirty-seventh-floor reception area. Reens. LR

Bottom left: Fabergé. View from elevator bank of reception area. Reens. LR

Top right: Fabergé. Reens. LR

Bottom right: Fabergé. Sunken lounge. Reens. LR

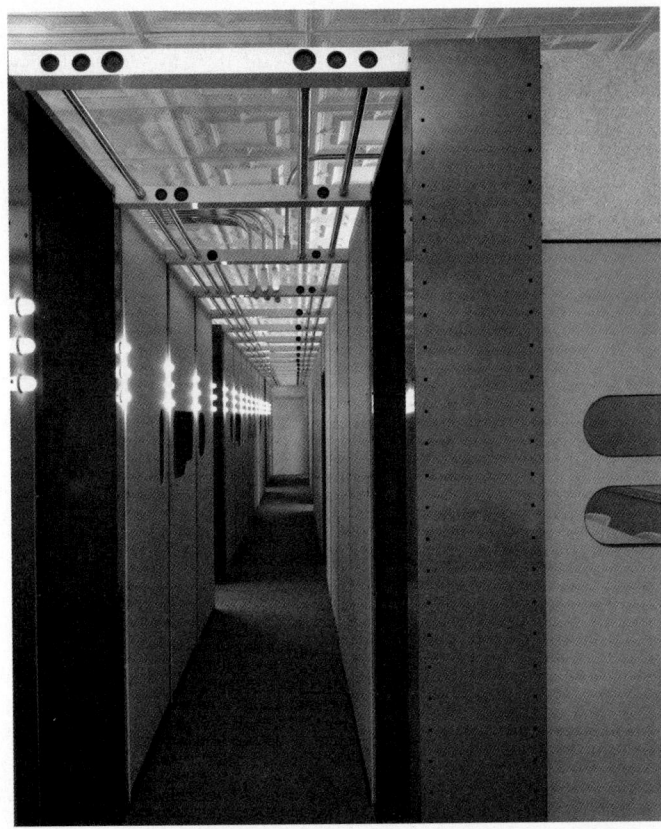

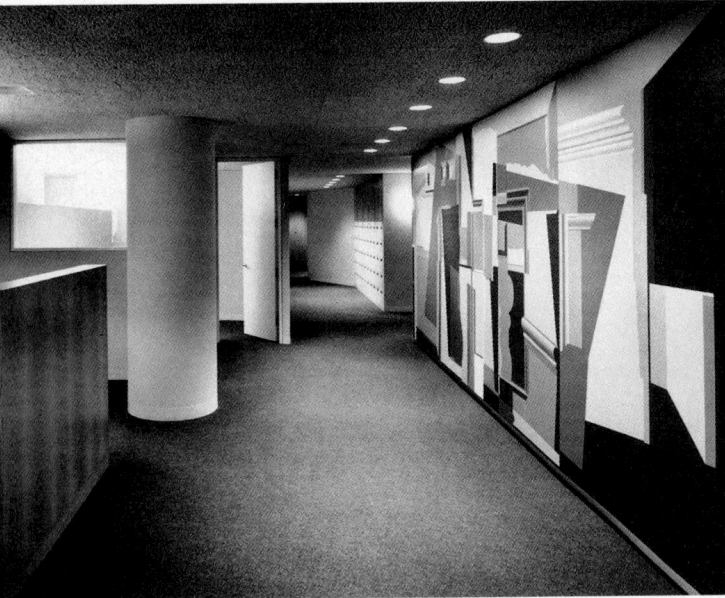

Top: Offices of Jules Fisher and Paul Marantz, 212 West Fifteenth Street. Works, 1975. Reens. LR

Bottom: Transammonia, 410 Park Avenue. Gwathmey Siegel, 1974. View showing mural by Michael Graves. Maris. GSA

thirty-eighth floors of Burlington House, the Fabergé offices constituted a remarkable, iconoclastic environment. The thirty-seventh-floor elevator lobby set the tone with polished chrome walls, black ceilings and coils of disembodied colored light. Just beyond was the reception area, a coal black and mouse brown room, as soft and fuzzy as the elevator hall was hard and metallic. The principal feature of this area was a superscaled sculpture that doubled as a stair to the upper floor of offices. The offices marked a radical departure from the pink and powdery environments traditionally created for the cosmetics industry, reflecting the philosophy of company president George Barrie, who felt that 1960s "liberation" had changed women's attitudes toward cosmetics and that the industry would have an increased market among men in the future. As Olga Gueft observed:

> Given this updated view . . . conditions were set for a design program radically different from any cosmetic corporation headquarters ever seen before. The result is, however, not merely different from any other cosmetic corporation headquarters, but different from *any* interior—corporate or residential. . . . Fabergé has an eye-boggling variety of Op-kinetic, Italianate space-age, angle-walled, architectonic, woodsy forties, and Paris-in-the-thirties decor—sprinkled with such accessories as motorized prismatic paintings, computerized projections, and cut-out life-size portraits of the executives stationed in the board room bar.[89]

Most firms experimented with supermannerism in a more modest way, usually employing graphic elements such as numbers and letters at vast size to manipulate the scale of ordinary rooms. On a near-shoestring budget, the Atlanta-based architects Heery & Heery in 1970 installed the publishers Grove Press in a renovated building on Mercer Street, part of a revitalizing neighborhood that was coming to be known as NoHo (north of Houston Street).[90] To enliven a fairly conventional set of offices, the architects used supergraphics as decoration and signage, even emblazoning bathroom doors with the increasingly common biological signs for male and female. The architects Smotrich & Platt, working with graphic designer Wade Zimmerman, used supergraphics representing various patents to animate the Rockefeller Center offices of a firm specializing in patent law.[91] The same architects combined wall-size photomurals with a diagonal plan in their installation for Harper & Row, the publishers, on thirteen floors of the office building bearing their name at 10 East Fifty-third Street.[92] Even Giovanni Pasanella, usually a fastidiously restrained architect, employed supergraphics to enliven the office he designed for Joseph E. Seagram & Sons when that firm consolidated its New York operations in new facilities at 800 Third Avenue.[93]

While supergraphics brought a new vivacity to the corporate office, their impact was necessarily superficial; designers tried other, more structured approaches to inject character into the anonymous loftlike workplace. In 1975 Jeffrey Hannigan of the design firm Works created an erector-set-like environment at 212 West Fifteenth Street for the lighting designers Jules Fisher and Paul Marantz.[94] The high-tech scheme consisted of an autonomous system of metal struts and panels defining offices and storage areas; the electrical conduit was left exposed, creating an openwork subceiling that visually framed the original pressed-tin ceiling. In the same year, the graphic designers Dorothea Elman and Robert A. Propper worked in collaboration with the architect Theodore Ceraldi to rig a partitioning system for their own office that was made out of awning canvas stretched across found industrial parts, creating wonderfully translucent walls.[95]

Supermannerism and high tech were short-lived trends. Beginning around 1970, architects and designers began to seriously reconfigure the office environment, overthrowing the rigidities of modular, Mies-inspired geometry in favor of the sculpted walls and spatial intricacies associated with Le Corbusier's Cubist-inspired work of the 1920s. It was easiest to pursue these ideals in small, almost domestically scaled offices, such as Christopher H. L. Owen's American headquarters for the London-based shipping firm Globik Tankers (1975).[96] But Charles Gwathmey and Robert Siegel, preeminent proponents of this style, were able to adapt it to comparatively large installations. They did so by confining their sensually curved partitions of wood, plasterboard or glass block to reception areas and important gathering points in the plan, and handling the necessarily repetitive aspects of the installations in a highly disciplined and fundamentally straightforward manner. Gwathmey Siegel's 1975 offices for the law firm Bower and Gardner and for the Barber Oil Corporation demonstrated the sophistication and refinement of their design approach.[97] For Transammonia Corporation (1974), at 410 Park Avenue, they pursued another dimension: for this client they commissioned the architect Michael Graves to decorate the walls along the principal circulation spaces with Cubist-inspired murals that drew their imagery from the immediate architectural context outside the company's offices and from the sculpted Modernism of Gwathmey Siegel's design.[98]

It was in the working environments of the architects and designers themselves that some of the era's most inventive, not to say kooky, office spaces were created. I. M. Pei, Philip Johnson, Ulrich Franzen and most other architects of the postwar Modernist generation housed themselves in the same type of office buildings that their clients found themselves in: Johnson's offices, for instance, were on the thirty-seventh floor of the Seagram Building.[99] But some members of that generation, as well as the majority of younger architects who began to establish themselves in the late 1960s, sought to express anticorporate ideals in settings distinct from the midtown business environment. Flushed with postwar success, one nonconformist, Morris Lapidus, transformed a twenty-foot-wide, fifty-foot-deep brownstone at 256 East Forty-ninth Street into duplex offices, housing his staff of twenty-five on the two lower floors and cellar and leasing two upper floors to another architect.[100] Lapidus completely demolished the facade, replacing it with a recessed and glazed ground-level entry, above which three identical floors of continuous glass were framed in a projecting brise-soleil-type element. Though the facade treatment paid homage to William Lescaze's townhouse office of 1934 and Morris B. Sanders's townhouse office of 1935, the interior of Lapidus's workmanlike office, with conventionally positioned private offices and conference rooms and loftlike drafting rooms, did not live up to its predecessors.[101]

It was not until 1965 that a New York architect created for himself a working space as personal and as challenging as Lescaze's. That year Paul Rudolph, who had been chairman of Yale's Department of Architecture and had designed that university's Art and Architecture Building (1963), completed his offices in New York, where he had relocated.[102] The triplex office suite was at the top of 26 West Fifty-eighth Street, an unremarkable six-story loft building located across from the Plaza Hotel. The exploding, light-filled space that Rudolph designed was a dream world of modernity where architects performed prodigious feats of office acrobatics as they moved about platformed drafting rooms that seemed to float and bridges that seemed to

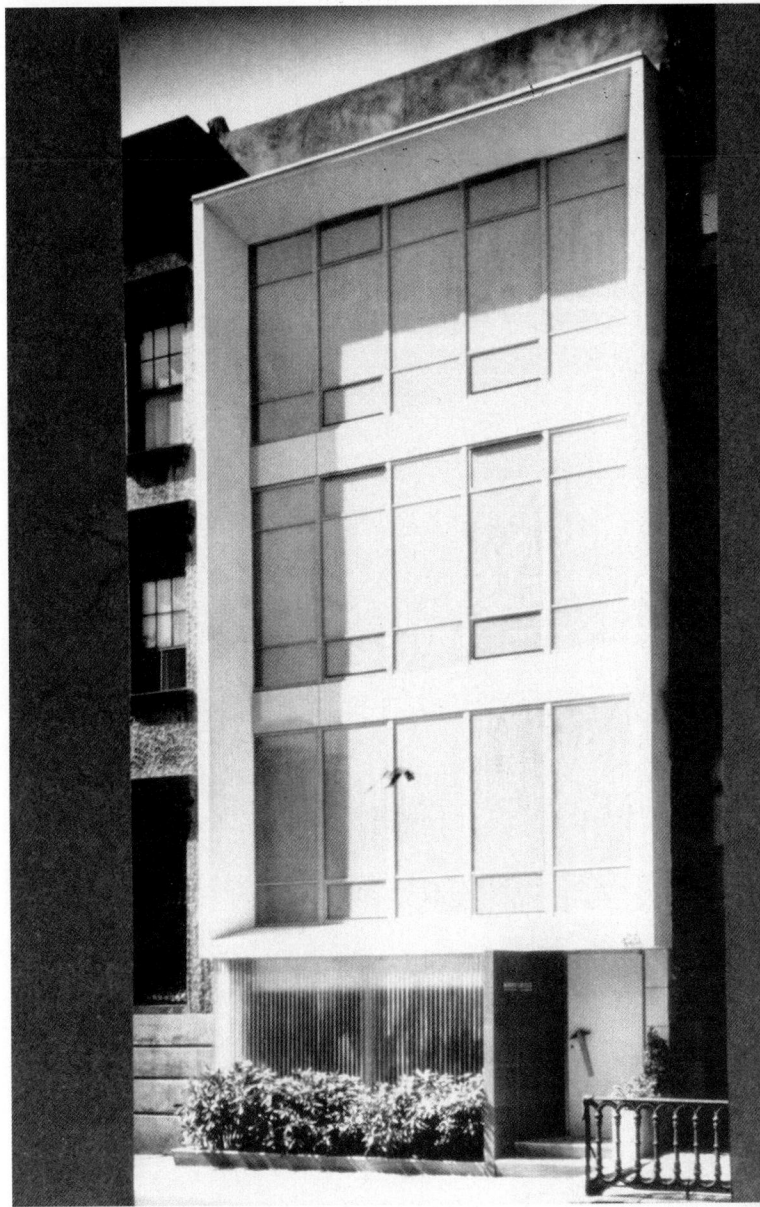

Architectural offices of Morris Lapidus, 256 East Forty-ninth Street. Morris Lapidus, 1947. View to the south. ML

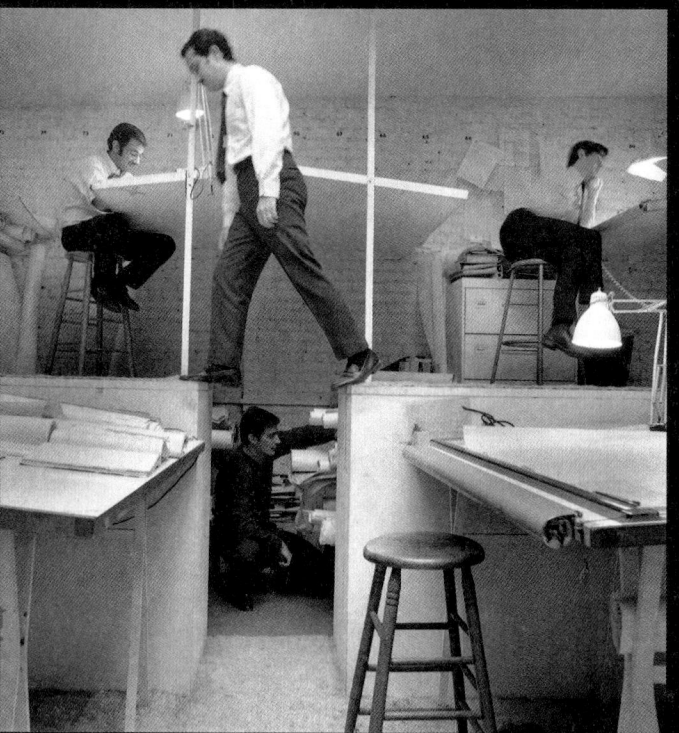

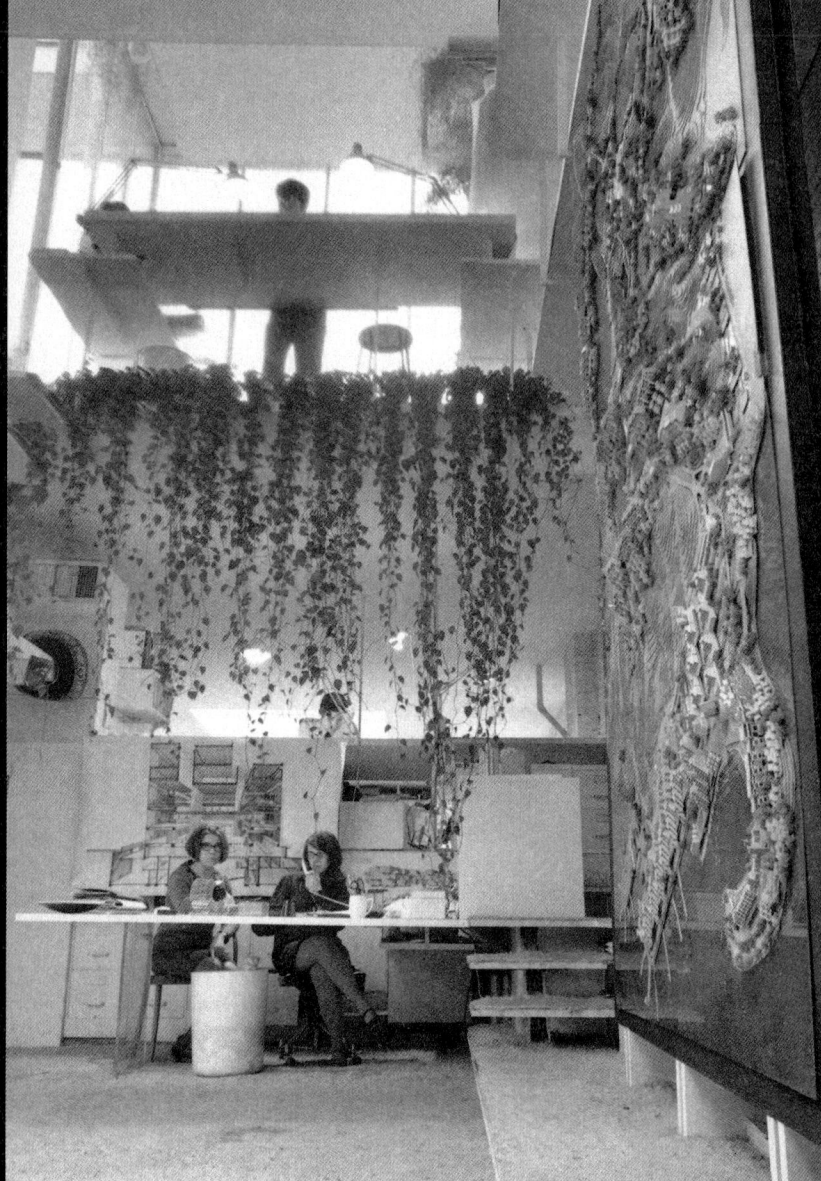

Top left: Architectural offices of Paul Rudolph, 26 West Fifty-eighth Street. Paul Rudolph, 1965. Platformed drafting room. Reens. LR

Top right: Architectural offices of Paul Rudolph. Reception area. Reens. LR

Bottom: Architectural offices of Paul Rudolph. Paul Rudolph at his desk. Reens. LR

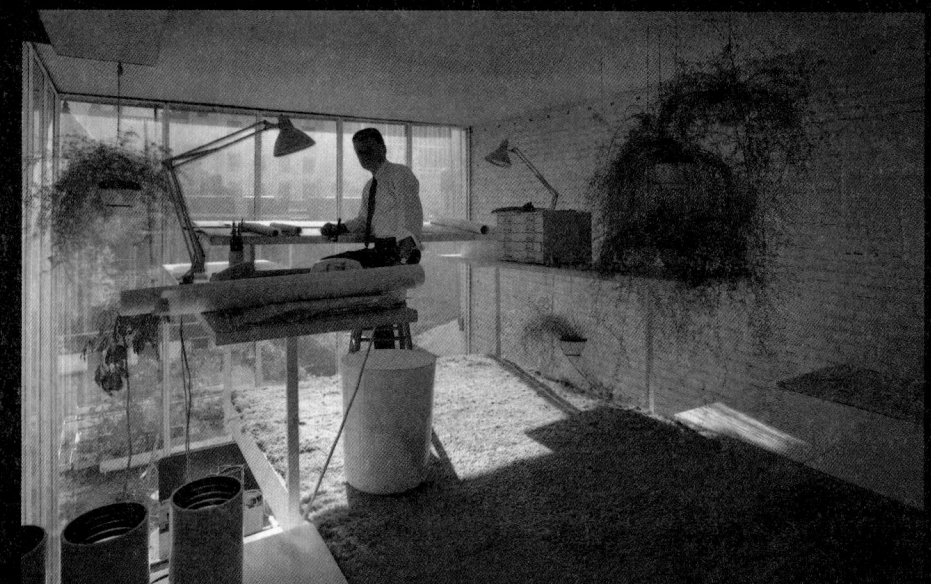

defy the laws of gravity. The effect, according to *Progressive Architecture*, was "confusing, disconcerting, and immediately impressive."[103] In some ways, the space was like the one Pei had designed for Zeckendorf thirteen years before, with a sequence of movement leading from the existing top floor of the building to a rooftop pavilion, in this case housing Rudolph's own office. But Rudolph's scheme was not about quiet good taste. His was a spatial free-for-all in which platforms seemed to slide through space barely attached to the building's brick party walls or to joists, maximizing a sense of instability. Although Rudolph said the office "was only slightly shaky," moving through the space was not for the faint of heart. The dizzying effect was enhanced by rope balcony rails, which were eventually replaced by more secure parapets after, as Rudolph put it, "the look on a certain mayor's face said that was one civic center I wasn't going to do."[104]

So daunting was the effect, *Progressive Architecture* observed, that "One might have thought that everything was arranged to put the client at a disadvantage in front of the master."[105] "It was usually disconcerting on first visit," Rudolph said, "because suddenly, after being in the elevator, the space was not defined. And when people know the definite limitations of a space they are more happy. This space was free flowing vertically, like a Mies plan turned on edge."[106] It was also a deliberate critique of Mies's work. Rudolph's decision to organize the platforms along a spiraling path, typical of his work at the time, was intended to repudiate Mies's "universal" spaces of "parallel horizontal lines of equal distance," which Rudolph deemed "a negation of the human spirit." With the clutter of drawings and scale models, the double-decked drafting tables, the tumbling vines of innumerable plants, the hum of typewriters, the buzz of telephones and conversation, and the bath of light pouring in from the rooftop monitors, the room was unforgettable—and almost impossible to work in. But the architect had made his statement: "There was a lot going on in that space. I have no pretensions about it not being a work space. The utilitarian and the notion of 'a sequence of spaces' are alien—at war with each other—-many people say. But that space was used in highly intensive ways, and for me it worked. Besides, that is what I think 20th-Century architecture is all about."[107] In 1969, after only four years in the place, Rudolph was forced to relocate to more conventional space at 54 West Fifty-seventh Street when the loft building was torn down to make way for Gordon Bunshaft's 9 West Fifty-seventh Street.

In 1964 the architects Richard D. Kaplan, Michael Zimmer and James Stewart Polshek, with his associate Walfredo Toscanini, banded together to create a shared office for their independent practices.[108] Polshek and Kaplan had for a year or so shared a studio on the attic floor of John H. Duncan's Knox Building (1903).[109] The new offices were on the forty-seventh floor of Charles F. Moyer's 295 Madison Avenue (1929), a hitherto unused space surrounding the building's water tower, one that met the architects' requirements for an office that would be both dramatic and cheap.[110] The 1,400-square-foot loft commanded views of Manhattan on all sides. Three of the four corner niches were converted to offices for the principal architects; the fourth housed a toilet. In the center of the space, to one side of the water tower, a freestanding cubicle with two sides of glass and two of concrete block served as a conference room, while the remainder of the minimally embellished space served as a drafting room.

Richard Meier's first office (1963), occupying half of one floor of a narrow rowhouse at 56 East Fifty-third Street, was perhaps the most austere of all: its unornamented, white-painted

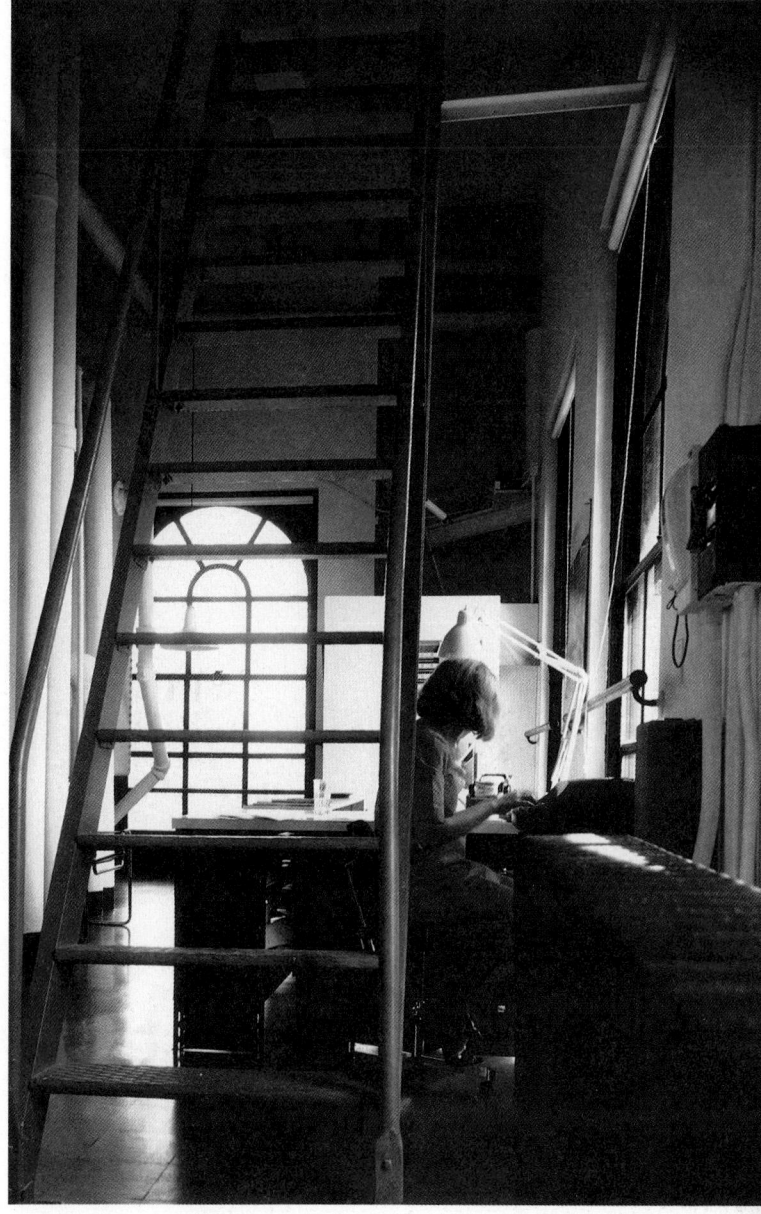

Architectural office shared by Richard D. Kaplan, Michael Zimmer and James Stewart Polshek, 295 Madison Avenue. Richard D. Kaplan, Michael Zimmer and James Stewart Polshek, 1964. JSP

571

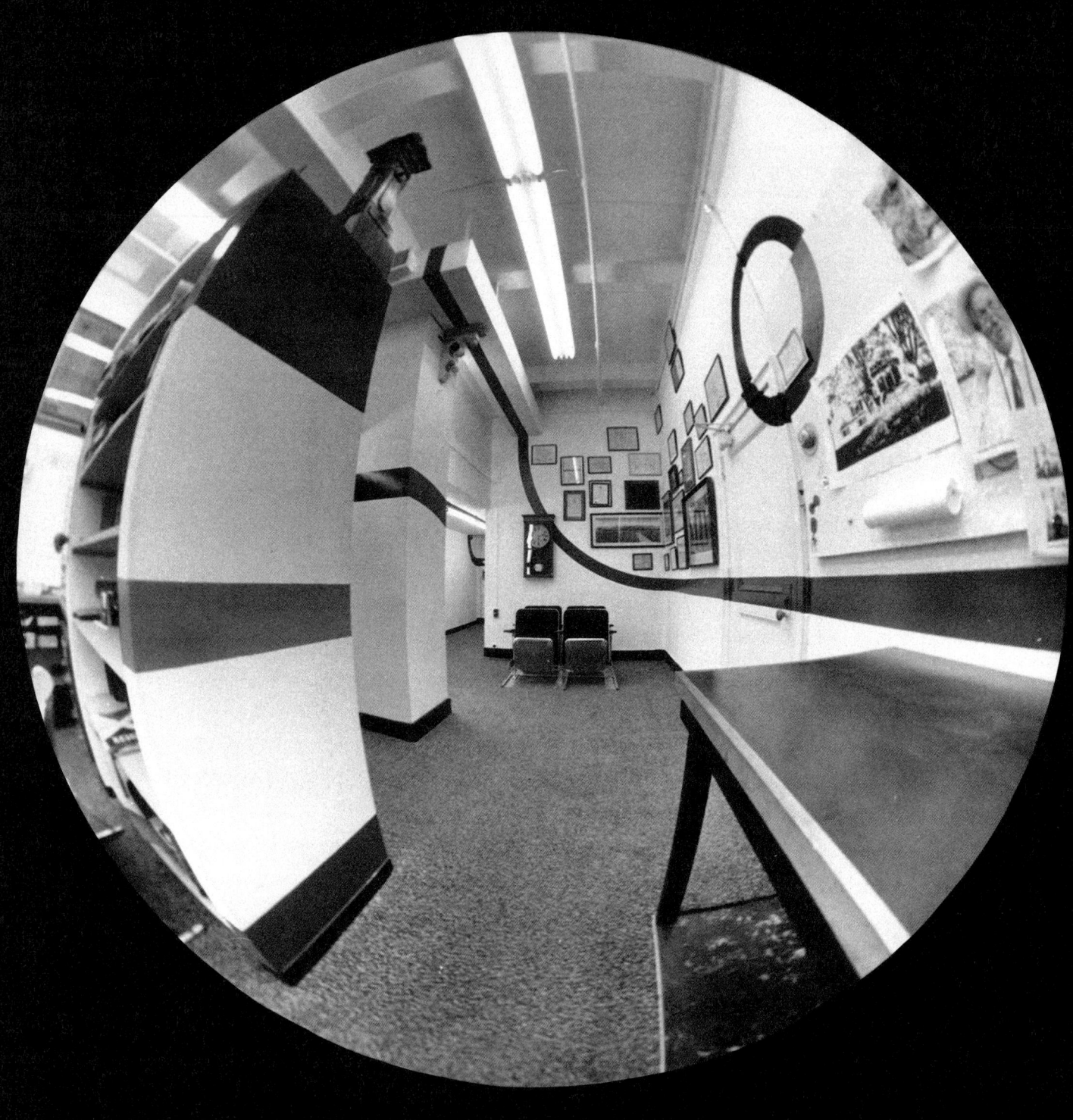

walls surrounded a reception desk and a single large butcher-block workstation at which Meier and his small staff worked.[111] In 1969 Meier moved to another spartan but much larger facility at 136 East Fifty-seventh Street.[112] Hobart Betts's office was a bit more complex, squeezing six workstations, a conference area, a reception area and storage into an L-shaped space on the twenty-third floor of the Fuller Building.[113] Charles Hughes established himself in a forty-by-ninety-foot loft space at 330 East Fifty-ninth Street, where he created a studio to provide room for receptionists and backup staff for himself and other small architectural and design practices in need of "start-up" space.[114] The straightforward plan of offices, providing shoulder-height cubicles for the various principals and one open drafting room for all their assistants, was designed by Hughes, a former partner at Skidmore, Owings & Merrill, in collaboration with his first tenants: architects Mary T. Hood and Christopher H. L. Owen and designers John Hughes Hall, Maria Ardena Radoslovich and Joseph Paul D'Urso.

In contrast to the stark minimalism of typical high-style architectural offices, Hardy Holzman Pfeiffer's office (1967), at 257 Park Avenue South, was bursting with color and clutter. As C. Ray Smith described the design:

> Down the hallway between the drafting room and the partners' offices, a cylinder or cylindrical paint stripe cut through the entire length and, in Hardy's view, implied that it went on forever. Another cylinder segment cut through the reception area perpendicular to the hallway; a bold green one blasted open the reception desk, and a red cylinder at the entry had fluorescent tubes fixed onto the cut line, exploding its intersection with the wall/ceiling. Diagonal lines bisected the entry, implying sections through the room. In addition, there was an assortment of objects isolated out of context and looking singularly new: a chrome-yellow traffic light sitting on a bed of pebbles like a Japanese lantern, a pair of detached theater seats, a moose head.[115]

In 1970 the architects Conklin & Rossant designed the office they shared with the engineers Zetlin, DeSimone, Chaplin & Associates to express their joint specialties. In keeping with the no-nonsense aesthetic of Brutalism, hung ceilings were eliminated to reveal the ductwork and electrical conduit; in keeping with the prevailing taste for liberated geometry, the centrally located square conference room was twisted on its axis to establish a forty-five-degree diagonal relationship to the orthogonal plan as a whole.[116] In 1972 Robert A. M. Stern and John Hagmann housed their expanding offices in a corner suite in the former Colonial Club on the slowly gentrifying Upper West Side, creating a freestanding superscale cabinet to house six drafting stations without compromising the circular geometry of the suite's corner turret.[117]

The Carnegie Hall offices of the young firm of Gwathmey Siegel were a superb representation of their sophisticated, stylish approach, which lay somewhere between minimalism and supermannerism.[118] The firm, which was founded in 1965 as Gwathmey & Henderson, became for a short time Gwathmey, Henderson & Siegel when it was located on East Eighty-sixth Street. In 1969 Gwathmey Siegel relocated to a more central spot in Carnegie Hall's studio building, inaugurating a trend that would bring Giovanni Pasanella as well as Robert Kliment and Frances Halsband to the same building. The small, ten-person office was located in a high, narrow space with windows at one end; a superscaled cabinet, at once reception desk and storage wall, articulated the transition between the

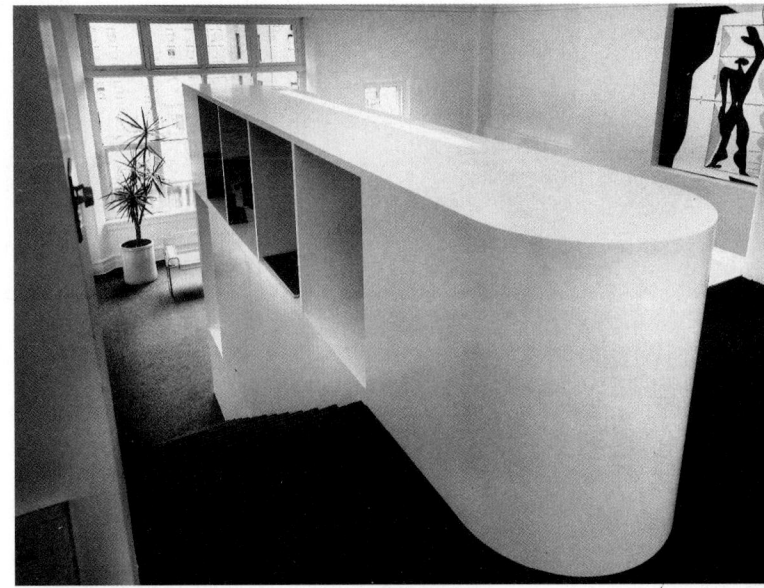

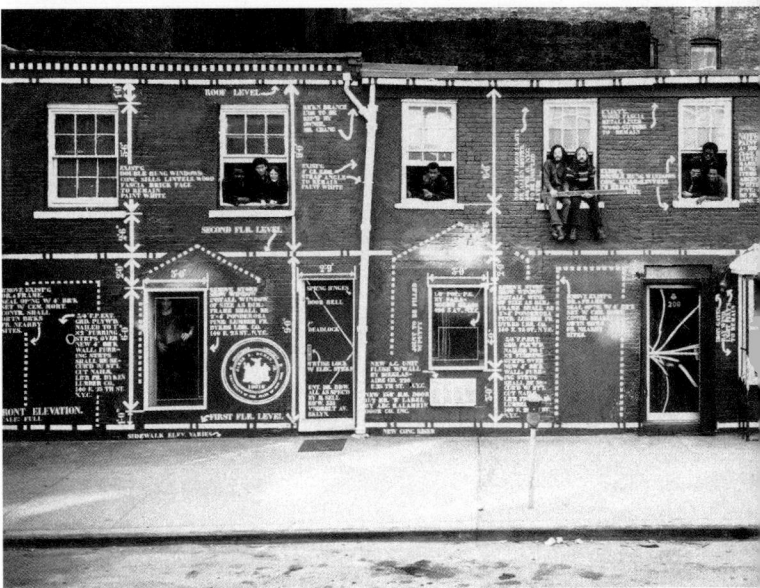

Left: Architectural offices of Hardy Holzman Pfeiffer, 257 Park Avenue South. Hardy Holzman Pfeiffer, 1967. Reens. LR

Top: Architectural offices of Gwathmey Siegel, Carnegie Hall's studio building, 154 West Fifty-seventh Street. Gwathmey Siegel, 1969. Maris. GSA

Bottom: Architectural offices of James Doman & Associates, 202 East Twenty-fifth Street. James Doman & Associates, 1971. View to the south. JDA

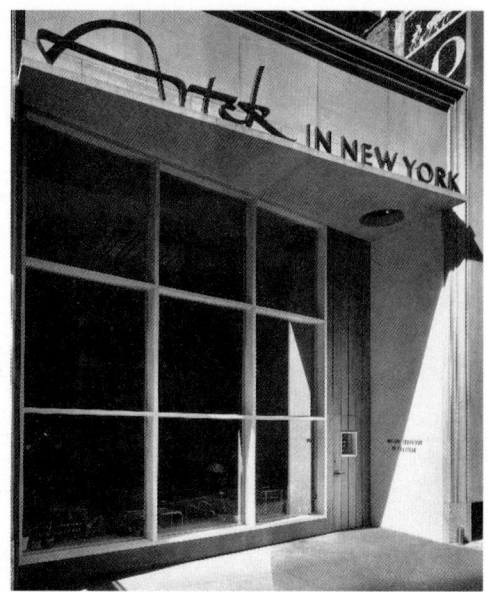

lower entrance level and the drafting room, a half level above, where the principal feature was an island of desks divided by low partitions.

The architectural office that best represented the antiestablishment iconoclasm of many young firms was that of James R. Doman & Associates at 202 East Twenty-fifth Street. The office filled a small building, the exterior wall of which was transformed into what *New York* magazine described as "the most readable facade in town."[119] By removing two bay windows, sealing two door openings and, under the direction of Glean Chase, one of Doman's associates, painting the brickwork to resemble the blueprint for the renovation, Doman created a professional sign as well as a conversation-stopper: passersby could not only marvel at the total effect but pause to read specific instructions. One read, "Br'kn branch l'dr to be rep'd by owner, Mr. Chang," a deliberate provocation to the landlord to make needed repairs, and another, "Cont'r shall obt'n br'ks fr. nearby sites," a reference to the rubble piles on languishing redevelopment sites to the east.

STORES

Shop design in New York during and immediately after the war was dominated by Morris Ketchum, Jr., and his partners, by Morris Lapidus and by José A. Fernandez. Morris Ketchum, Jr., graduated from Columbia University in 1926 and then spent two years studying at the School of Fine Arts at Fontainebleau and traveling on the Continent, during which time he was converted to the newly ascendant Modernism.[1] When he returned to the United States, he worked for a while in the offices of Mayers, Murray & Phillip (successors to Bertram Grosvenor Goodhue) and then set up shop as an independent. He shared offices with Edward Durell Stone, with whom he designed the Food Building South for the New York World's Fair of 1939.[2] At Stone's recommendation, Ketchum was asked to collaborate with Paul T. Frankl on the Mosse linen shop at 650 Fifth Avenue in 1938, which launched his career as a shop designer.[3] The next year Ketchum worked with Victor Gruenbaum, an Austrian émigré specializing in shop design (he later shortened his name to Gruen and became known as an architect of shopping centers), on the design of Lederer's, a shop specializing in leather goods, at 711 Fifth Avenue.[4] Ketchum also designed a shop for Ciro's jewelers in 1939, located next door at number 713.[5] Each of these stores was a landmark in its field, combining the open-front or arcade-type storefront introduced in the 1920s with clear lines and elegant graphics that had their origins in the *moderne* Parisian style and, to some extent, in the high Modernism of the International Style. More than any other building type, shops were the advance messengers of the new trends of European architecture.

Although Ketchum would expand the scope of his work, eventually building his firm of Ketchum, Giná & Sharp (1941–58) and its successors, Ketchum & Sharp (1958–61) and Morris Ketchum Associates, into a diverse architectural practice, shop design dominated most of his early career. In keeping with his Modernist predilections, Ketchum advocated glassy shopfronts that dispensed with traditional show windows to open up the entire store interior to the view of passing pedestrians. With Francis X. Giná, Ketchum designed the Finnish design shop Artek on East Forty-ninth Street as a demonstration of his open-faced concept, setting a nearly two-story-tall square grid of glass at a rakish angle to the building line.[6] In 1942 Ketchum designed

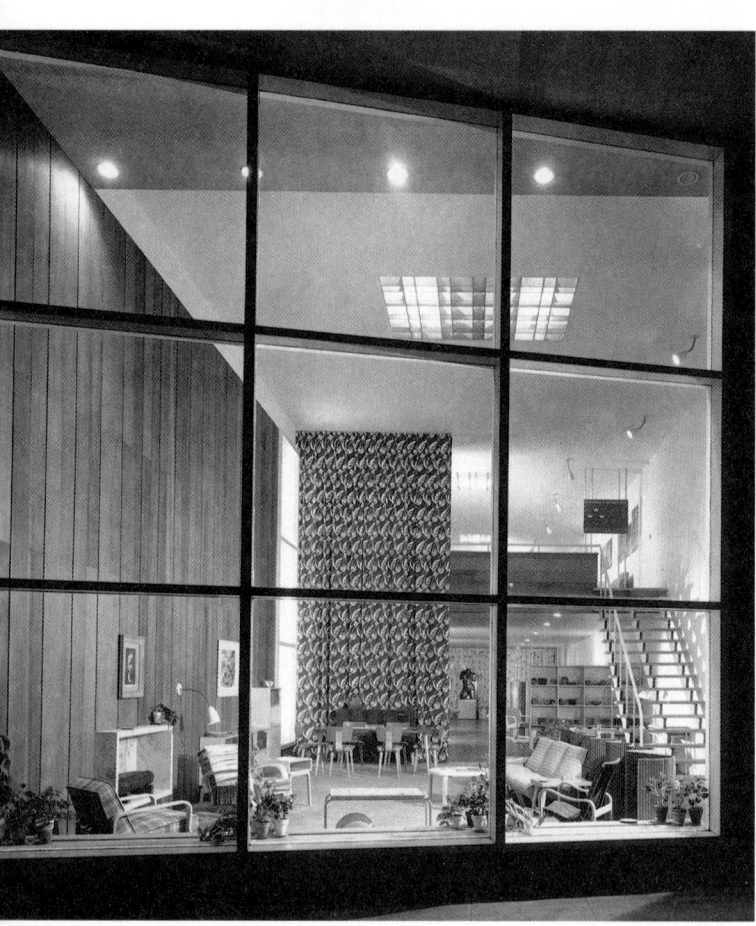

Top: Artek, 16 East Forty-ninth Street. Ketchum, Giná & Sharp, 1942. View to the south. Stoller. ©ESTO

Bottom: Artek. Stoller. ©ESTO

the Lillian Park Avenue shop, at 51 East Fifty-fifth Street.[7] Also in 1942 he designed the first of what would become a series of shops for Wallachs, the men's clothing store, on Brooklyn's Court Street (see chapter 13).

Store commissions for Ketchum poured in, including a haberdashery for Steckler at 2085 Broadway that he designed with Gruenbaum;[8] a children's shop in Forest Hills, Queens;[9] and America House, at 485 Madison Avenue, on which he collaborated with Giná and the decorator Dorothy Draper.[10] America House, the retail headquarters of the American Craftsmen's Cooperative (which would evolve into the American Craftsmen's Council), was entered through a solid, bright red door set within the glass storefront. The red door was but a prelude to the flag-waving color scheme of red, white and blue inside. The shop was treated as a display case, with all the merchandise visible from the sidewalk. At the back, a split section created a lower level and a mezzanine across the parapet on which was painted a bold mural showing an eagle and a banner carrying the shop's name. The simple wood display tables, brought from a previous location around the corner, were placed on a diagonal to enliven the space.[11]

Ketchum's Trade Winds Inc., a gift shop specializing in products made by refugees from Hitler's Europe, was squeezed into a nine-by-fifteen-foot basement space in a remodeled brownstone, at 56 East Fifty-fifth Street, yet its big front window, curvilinear cabinetwork and dramatic lighting gave it a considerable presence.[12] His Dana Festive Fashions shop of 1944 in J. E. R. Carpenter's 515 Madison Avenue (1931) was also quite narrow, but Ketchum enlarged the feel of the space by using a mirror wall on one side.[13] That same year Ketchum, Giná & Sharp undertook the first of a series of designs for shoe stores with the renovation of the London Character store at 205 East Fordham Road in the Bronx.[14] The principal decorations of the shop's interior, visible to passersby behind backless display windows, were the neat stacks of shoe boxes and the wide, simply detailed boxlike seating. At about the same time, Ketchum and his partners set a fully glazed shop for Florsheim's women's shoes behind an arcade created out of the base of 516 Fifth Avenue, on the northwest corner of Forty-third Street.[15] They illuminated the arcade with the same "egg crate" ceiling grid used inside the shops, rendering the glass wall nearly invisible in most light.

In Ketchum's designs for the Plymouth chain of women's specialty shops, he framed his trademark arcaded shopfront in wide bands of polished gray granite against which a raised bronze sign was silhouetted. A typical Plymouth shop, located at Parkchester in the Bronx (1941), maximized the small street frontage by using an arcade to lure the shopper to its front door, while the actual selling area was buried in the heart of the building block.[16] At Plymouth's 187 Broadway shop in the financial district, the problem was less complicated and the path of movement much less contrived.[17] In other designs for the same chain, such as that at Broadway and Eighty-second Street, the arcade was dispensed with, resulting in an even more elegant effect.[18]

In 1955 Ketchum and his partners completed a large store on Fifth Avenue for Wallachs.[19] Located in Emery Roth & Sons' recently completed 555 Fifth Avenue, the shop was almost suburban in scale, sprawling along its 125-foot frontage—the longest of any men's store along the avenue. At Giná's instigation, the entire frontage was glazed, a new idea in men's clothing stores, which tended to favor dignified, dressed show windows and imposing front doors such as those of Brooks Brothers (LaFarge & Morris, 1917), at Madison Avenue and Forty-fourth Street.[20] Though the

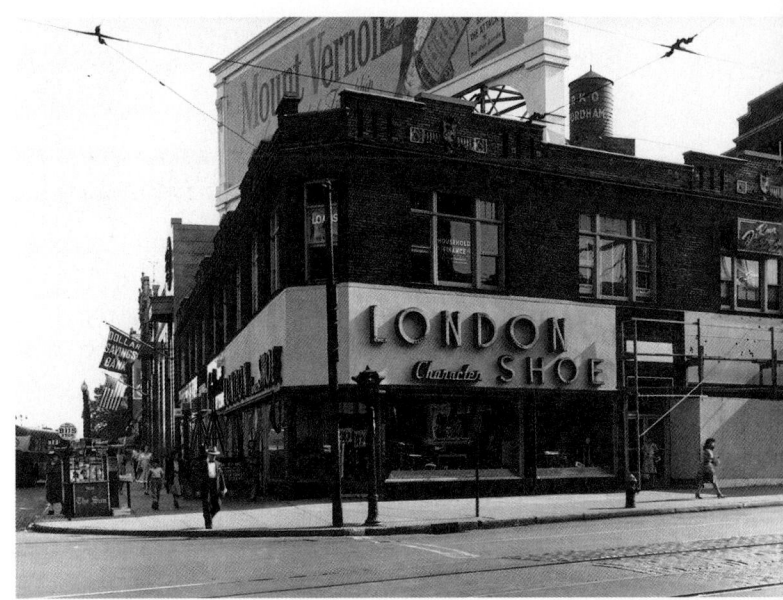

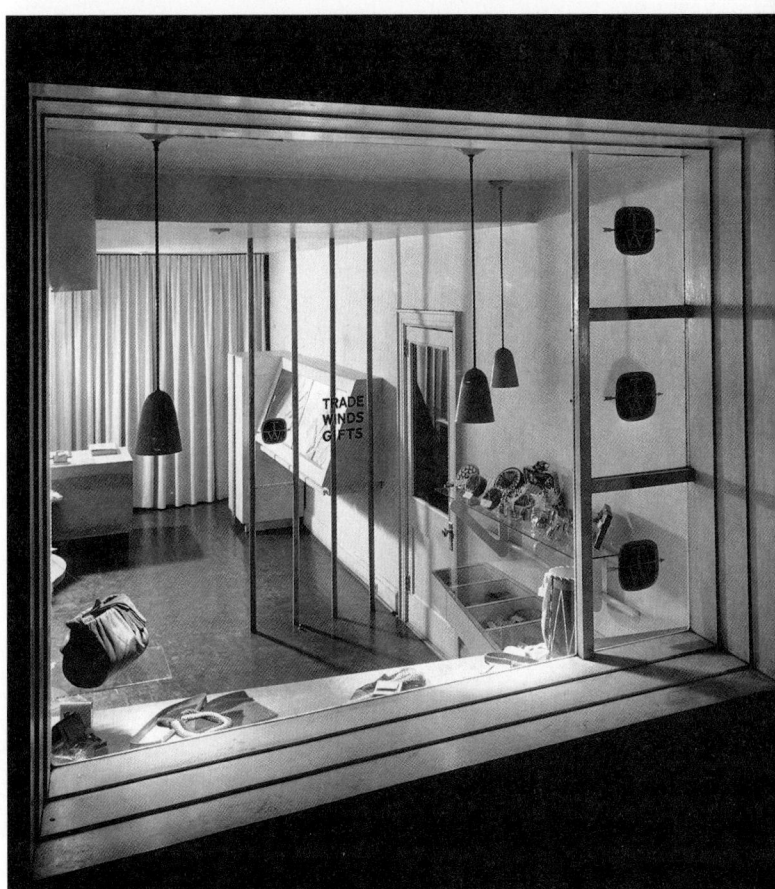

Top: London Character, 205 East Fordham Road, Fordham, the Bronx. Ketchum, Giná & Sharp, 1944. View to the northeast. Gottscho-Schleisner. LOC

Bottom: Trade Winds, Inc., 56 East Fifty-fifth Street. Ketchum, Giná & Sharp, 1942. Stoller. ©ESTO

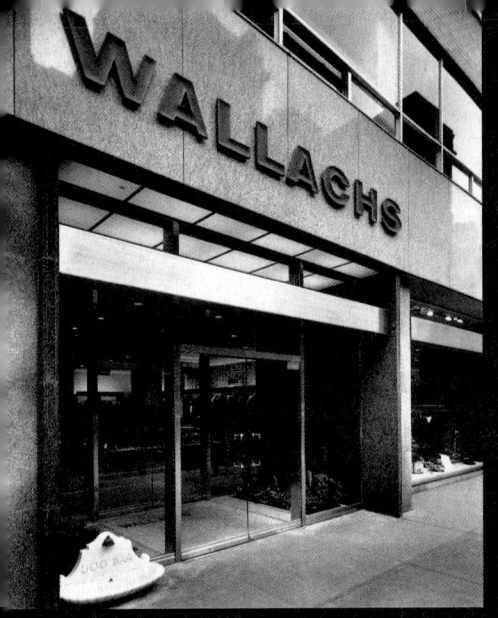

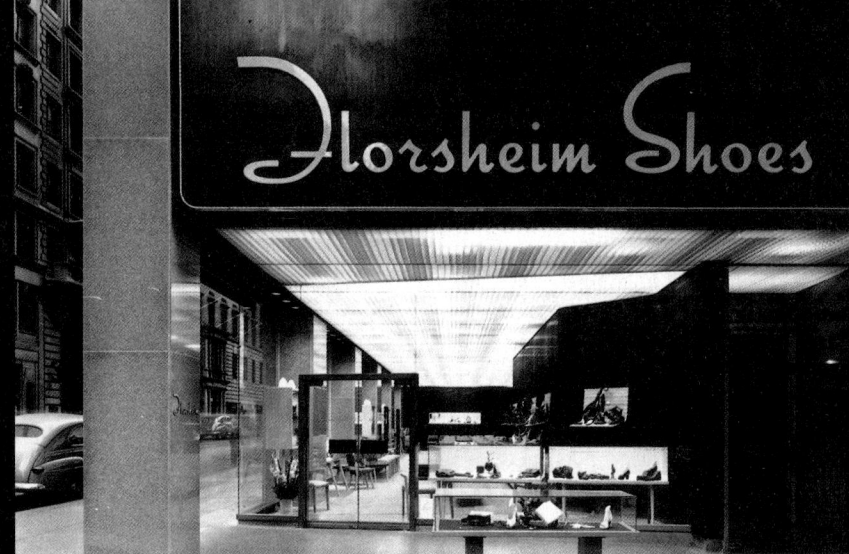

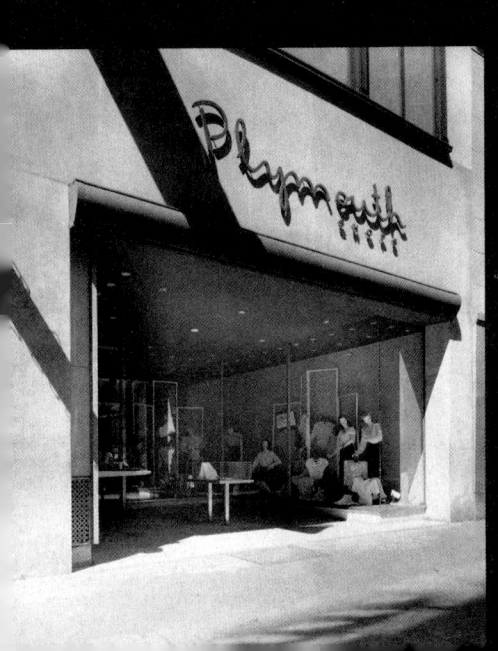

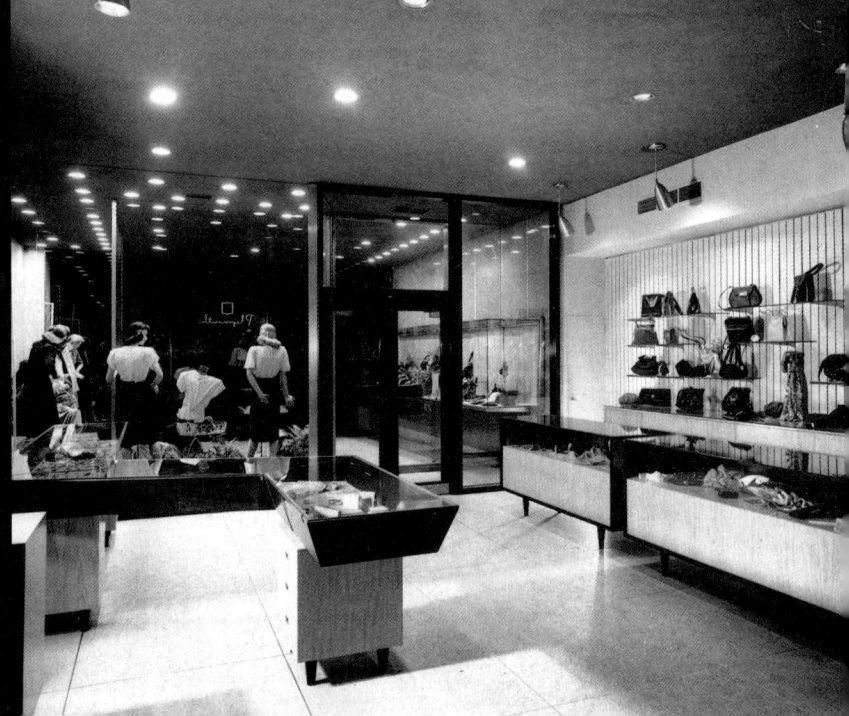

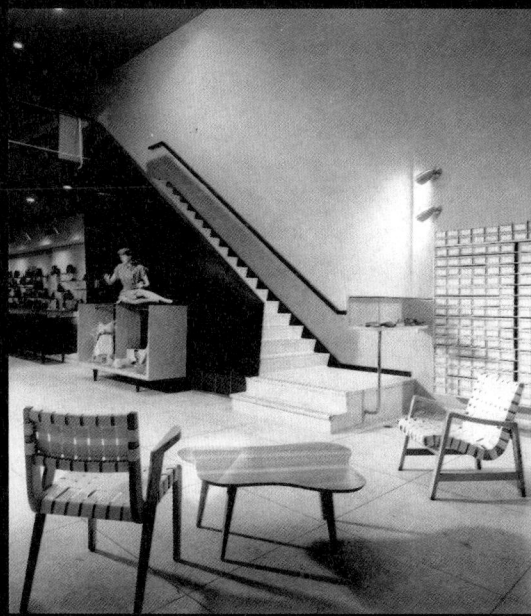

Top far left: Wallachs, 555 Fifth Avenue. View to the southeast showing dog bar on lower left. Ketchum, Giná & Sharp, 1955. Stoller. ©ESTO

Top left: Florsheim Shoes, 516 Fifth Avenue. Ketchum, Giná & Sharp, 1944. View to the west along West Forty-third Street. Gottscho-Schleisner. LOC

Bottom far left: Plymouth, 187 Broadway. Ketchum, Giná & Sharp, 1948. Freedman. LF

Bottom left: Plymouth, 187 Broadway. Arcade. Freedman. LF

Above: Plymouth, 187 Broadway. Freedman. LF

Right: Wallachs. Main stair. Stoller. ©ESTO

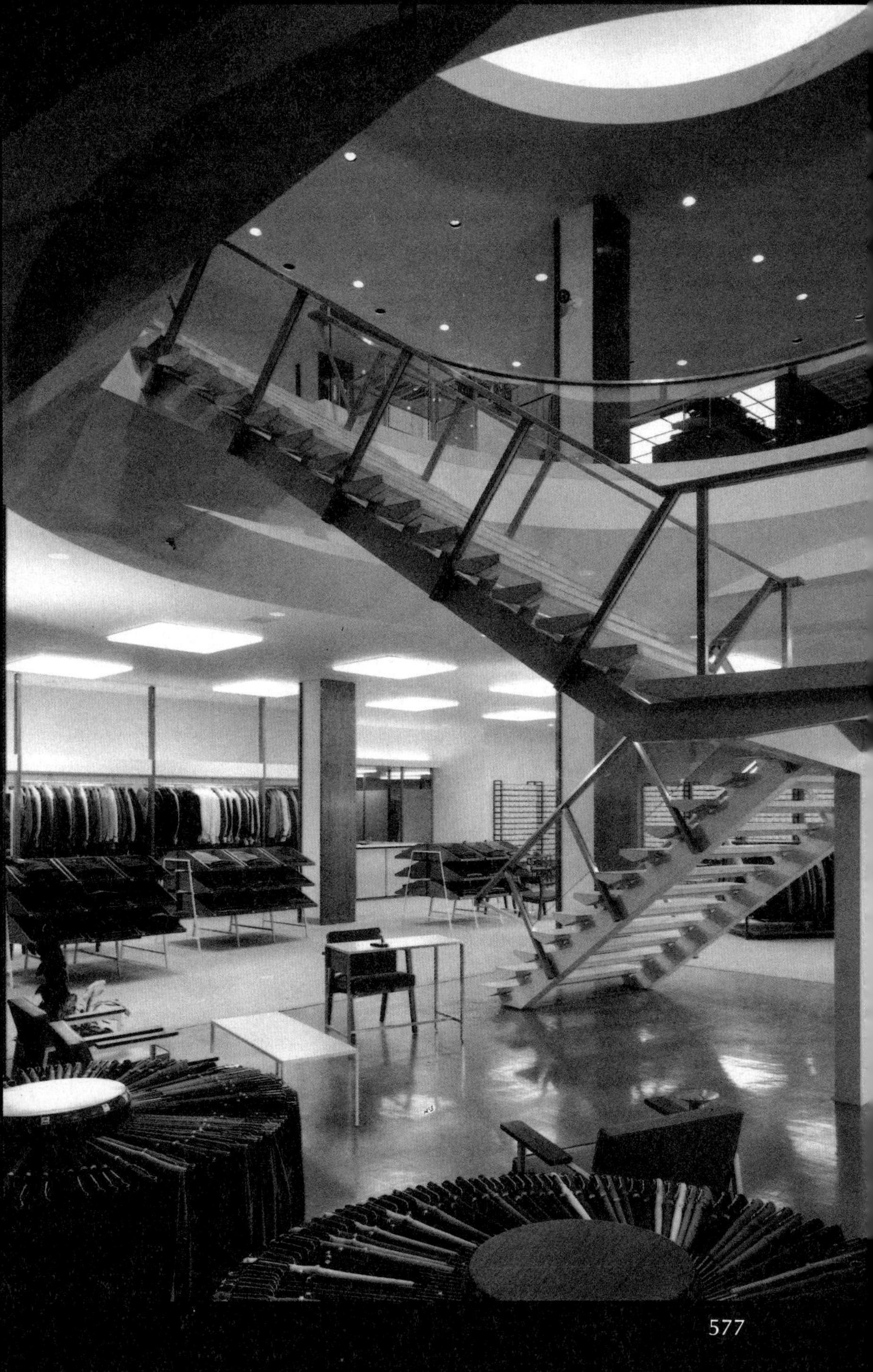

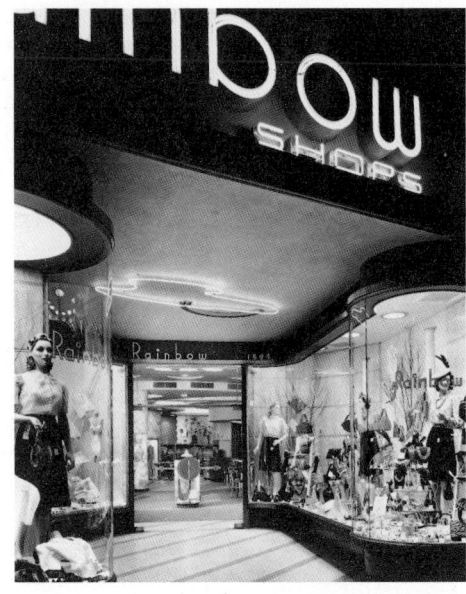

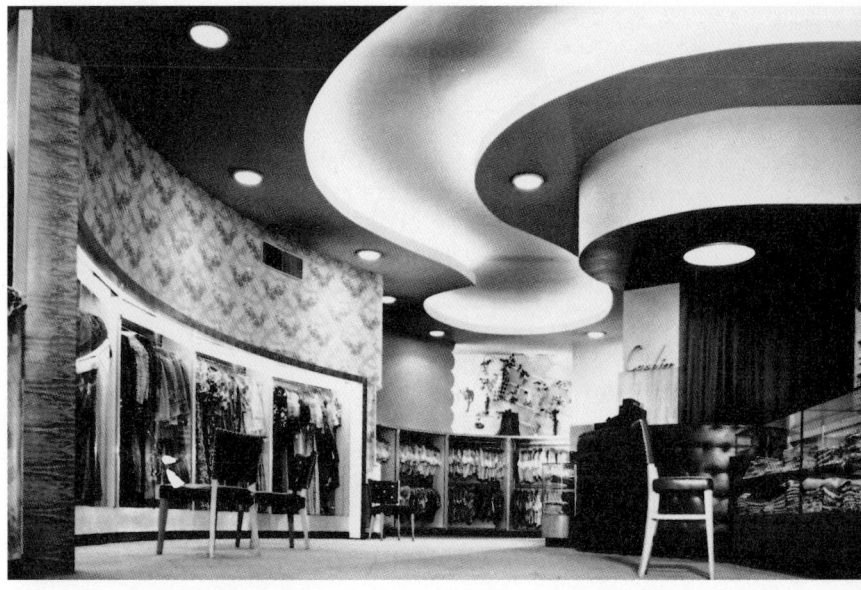

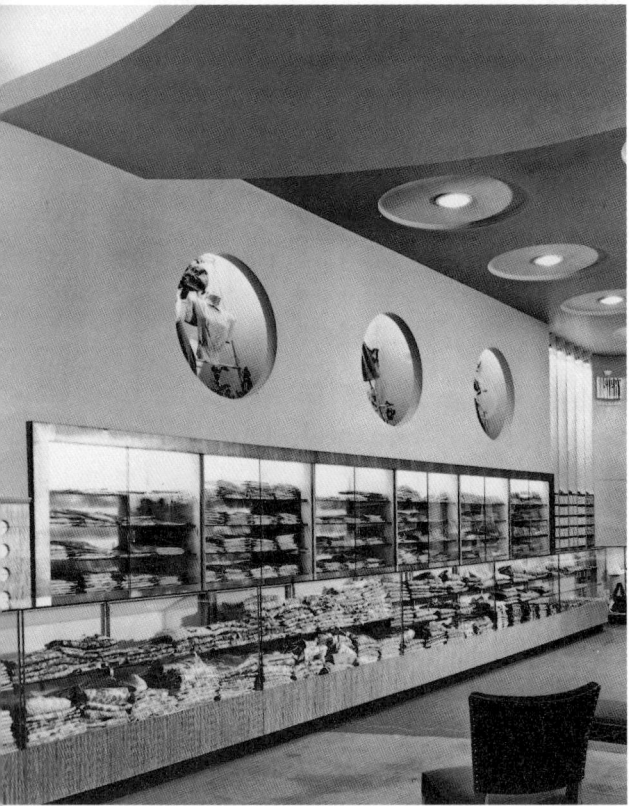

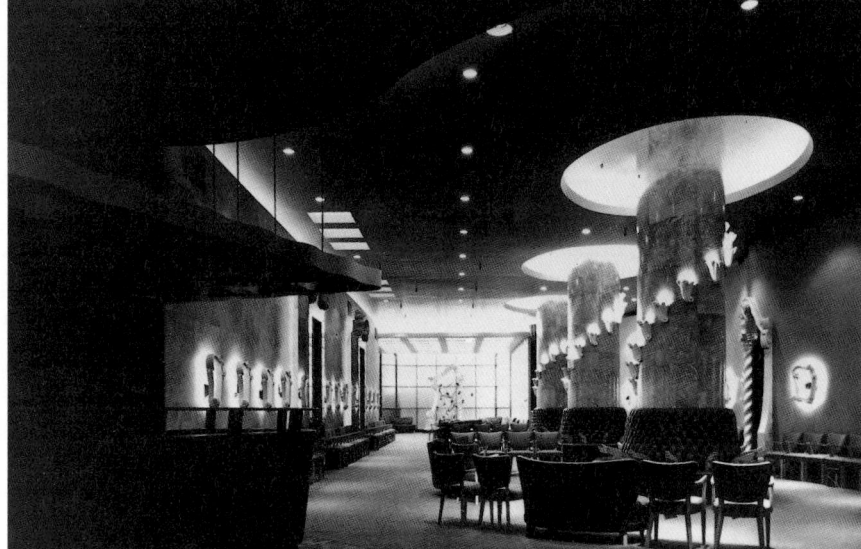

Top left: Rainbow Shops, 1524 King's Highway, Flatbush, Brooklyn. Morris Lapidus, 1941. View to the north. ML

Bottom left: Rainbow Shops. ML

Top right: Rainbow Shops. ML

Center right: Ansonia, 49 West Thirty-fourth Street. Morris Lapidus, 1943. ML

Bottom right: London Character, 1492 Broadway. Morris Lapidus, 1946. ML

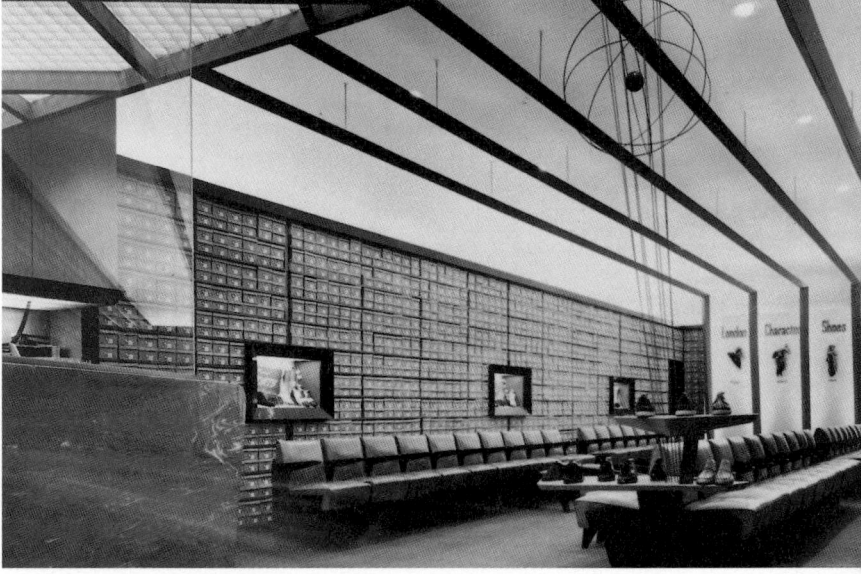

overall effect of the design seemed more suited to a suburban shopping center than to Fifth Avenue, one special gesture carried with it an appealing urbanity: the sidewalk dog bar, a low water fountain installed outside the Fifth Avenue entrance. The neutral-colored main floor, devoted to haberdashery, was suggestive of the banking hall of Howe & Lescaze's Philadelphia Saving Fund Society Building (1932) in the detailing of the columns; a dramatic, Corbusier-inspired, glass-railed stair led down through a large circular opening to the clothing floor below.[21]

Ketchum's work appeared positively restrained when compared to Morris Lapidus's efforts. Lapidus, who began to design storefronts in the 1930s, established himself as the undisputed master of zippy shop design.[22] Before studying architecture at Columbia, he had considered a career as a theatrical set designer. Working sometimes on his own and sometimes as designer for the storefront and interior packagers Ross-Frankel, Lapidus developed an influential prototype for the Regal Shoe chain and designed a Wallachs store on Fordham Road in the Bronx (although he seemed to lose that client to Ketchum, who worked for the chain throughout the 1940s and 1950s). Lapidus's Rainbow Shops chain exemplified his work of the 1940s and early 1950s—a highly theatrical rendition of the surrealistic Modernism suggested in certain projects by Le Corbusier and picked up with enthusiasm by his Brazilian disciples Lucio Costa and Oscar Niemeyer, whose work was widely published in America and promoted by the Museum of Modern Art.[23] Lapidus, who visited Brazil in 1949, later recalled that Niemeyer was "the one man I had to see . . . because he was a man who was doing things the way I thought they should be done."[24] Lapidus's Rainbow Shop at 1524 Kings Highway, Brooklyn, designed for Ross-Frankel, was entered through a deep arcade defined on either side by a free-form curving display window and lit from above by a free-form neon tube reminiscent of the amoeboid shapes favored by Niemeyer and by the Swiss surrealist sculptor Hans Arp.[25]

Lapidus believed his mission was to put architecture in the service of merchandising: "The aim of the modern architect is to change over the store into a better kind of merchandising instrument." He shared Ketchum's enthusiasm for the open storefront, adding to it a more positive emphasis on shop-window display and interior lighting, no doubt a result of his interest in theatrical set design. He felt that the new indirect lighting techniques, which he described as the "egg crate" and the "swiss cheese" or "cheese hole," "should be handled like the instruments in an orchestra." "One factor that should not be overlooked," he said, "is the possibility of using light not only as a source of illumination but as a decorative and planning medium."[26] Lapidus's theatricality was nowhere more visible than in his spectacular "Baroque Moderne" Ansonia shoe shop (1943), at 49 West Thirty-fourth Street.[27] With its dramatic, Borromini-inspired ceiling grid and its wall-display niches, in which Lapidus freely reshaped and backlit baroque molded frames to create a truly surrealist effect worthy of such European masters as Salvador Dalí and Christian Bérard, the shop was a dazzling architectural equivalent to the decorating of Dorothy Draper. Lapidus's curving plan, glamorous lighting and specially designed, luxuriously tufted furniture helped establish the unique synthesis of Modernism and Classicism that was to earn him his reputation as a scenographic master, a talent he would put to good use in Miami Beach, Florida, where he would become the postwar era's leading hotel architect. Better than any other architect of the period, Lapidus understood how to bring the pleasures of high style to the middle market.

Known as a flamboyant designer, Lapidus could also be restrained, as in his pattern department for Hearn's department store, at 20 West Fourteenth Street,[28] or his London Character shoe store (1946), at 1492 Broadway.[29] His A. S. Beck shoe store (1947) carried the melding of inside and outside about as far as it could go, with a continuous composition of free-form shapes on the ceiling penetrating the deeply recessed glass wall that separated the entrance arcade from the shop itself.[30] Also notable was Lapidus's work for Martin's, a Brooklyn department store (see chapter 13).

Though not nearly so prolific as Ketchum or Lapidus, José (Joseph) A. Fernandez was nonetheless able to establish his own distinct approach. Born in San Juan, Puerto Rico, Fernandez studied architecture at Syracuse University and then at Columbia, where he received his degree in 1925. After serving as an instructor at Columbia, he worked in a succession of firms, including the offices of Thomas Lamb and Aymar Embury II, and finally set out on his own in 1936. In the narrow, deep space of his shop for Rebajes (1941), the jewelers, at 377 Fifth Avenue, Fernandez took the open-front concept one step further than Ketchum or Lapidus, treating the arcade space as a lobby in which actual sales could be made: what at first seemed to be a curving low display case revealed itself as a sales counter.[31] Taking his cue from Ketchum's design for Ciro's, Fernandez sheathed the facade of Rebajes in flush marble panels with no carving; only the stylized raised letters of the store name served as ornament. Inside the shop, Fernandez struck out in a more original direction, creating what *Interiors* described as "one of the most interesting show cases in New York"—an S-shaped counter suspended from the ceiling on thin metal rods so delicate that it swayed when customers leaned against it.[32] The counter was top lit from a light trough that was also suspended and followed the S-curve plan. Counterbalancing this counter, in the manner of the surrealist abstractions of the 1930s, a second suspended, tapered, bull-nosed counter was cantilevered at a dramatic angle from the first to create a high-wire drama.

Fernandez was to return to the theme of suspension in his Kitty Kelly shoe shop in Grand Central (1959).[33] Built in "air space" rented from the railroad, the shop was suspended from an overhead structure in a space adjoining the busy ramp leading to the terminal from the corner of East Forty-second Street and Vanderbilt Avenue. The shop presented windows facing the ramp, and a short arcade led to the interior. Influenced by the compositional abstract frame-and-plane games that architects and designers such as Charles Eames were exploring to great effect, Fernandez produced a loftlike interior defined on the ceiling as well as the walls by a busy arrangement of asymmetrically placed panels.

Fernandez's other work included the Corsetorium shop in Rego Park, Queens (1942), and the Lucy Lynne shop (1944), designed for a Queens confectioner; with their ribbons and furbelows, both stores reflected Lapidus's baroque modern style, which here might more accurately be labeled rococo.[34] His Marjorie Lane shop in Flushing (1944), which featured blond wood cabinetry, was rather more restrained, although the plan was twisted on its axis to create a curved selling area at the rear of the shop, a compositional idea originated by Lapidus.[35] Quieter still was Fernandez's Kobrin Bros. jewelry shop (1945), at 3579 Broadway, where a large-scale, gridded, black-and-white linoleum floor provided the only strong relief from pickled oak walls and casework.[36] Fernandez's Richards (1944), at 392 Sixth Avenue, a twelve-foot-wide men's apparel shop, was stricter in its gridded geometry, with the now-ubiquitous open

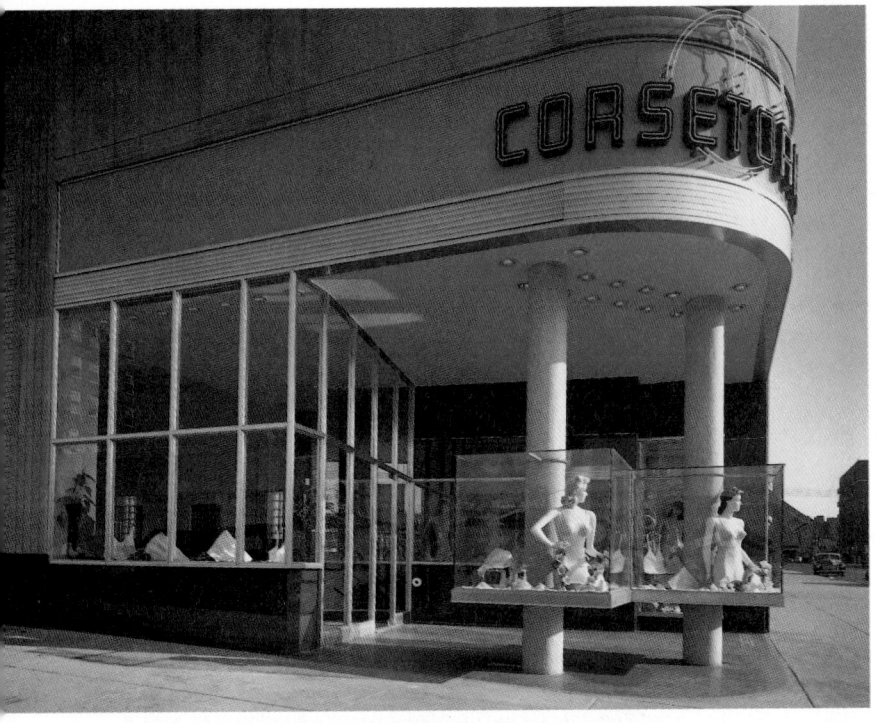

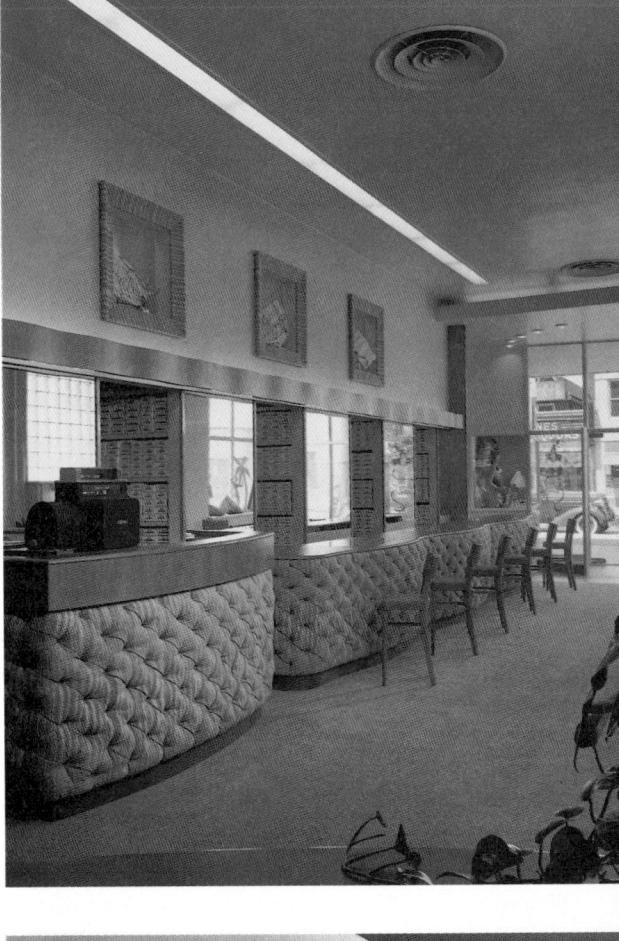

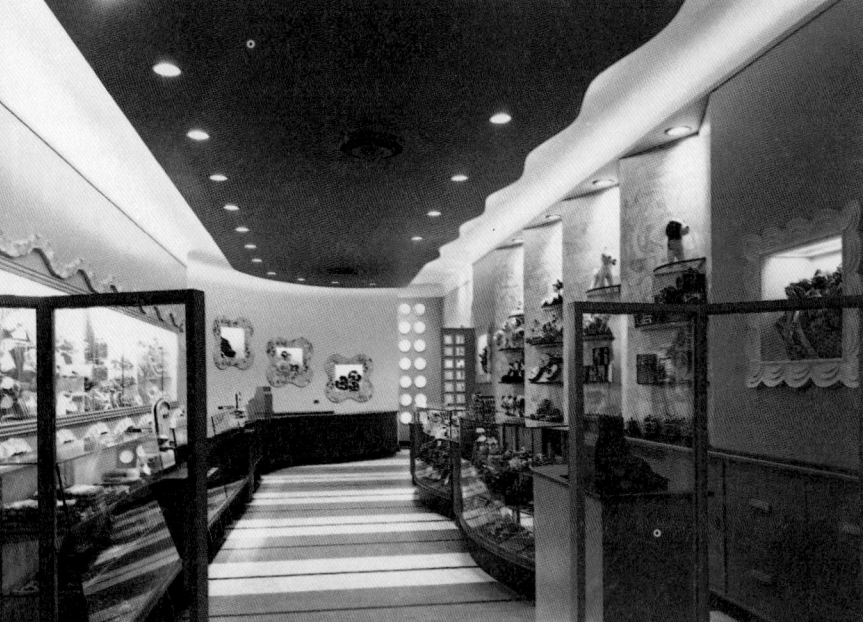

Top: Corsetorium, 94–24 Sixty-third Drive, Rego Park, Queens. José A. Fernandez, 1942. Stoller. ©ESTO

Bottom: Lucy Lynne, 95–07 Sixty-third Drive, Rego Park, Queens. José A. Fernandez, 1944. Gottscho-Schleisner. LOC

Top right: Corsetorium. Stoller. ©ESTO

Bottom right: Lucy Lynne. Gottscho-Schleisner. LOC

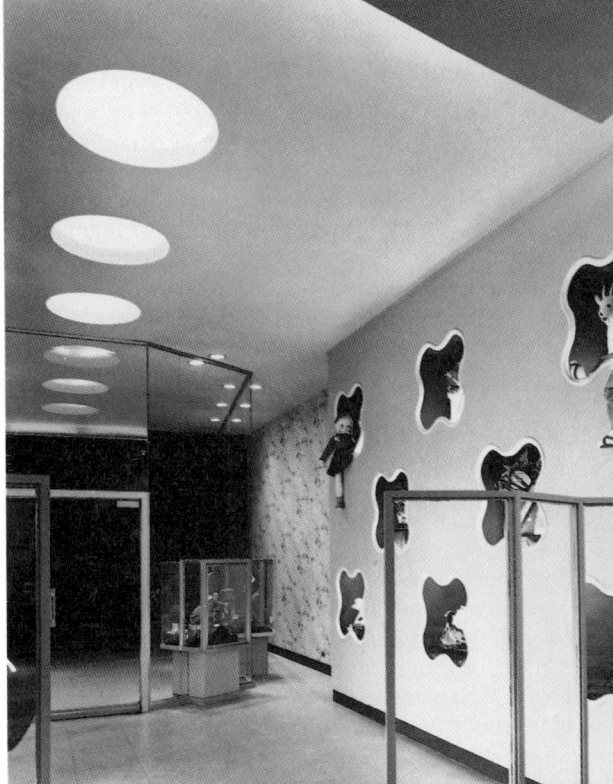

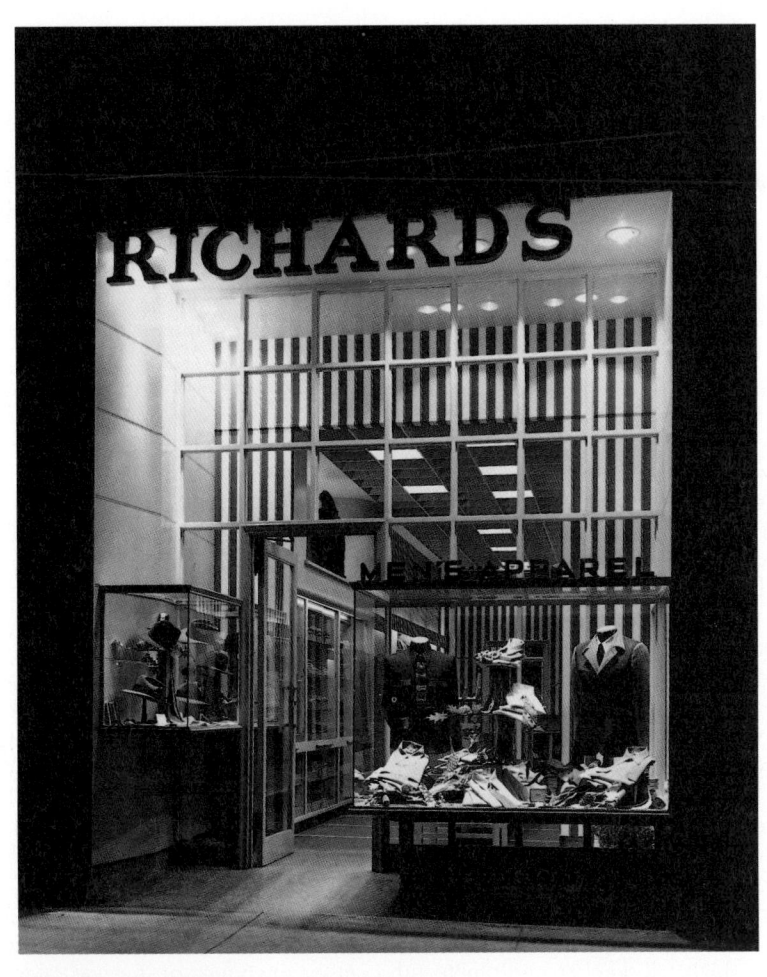

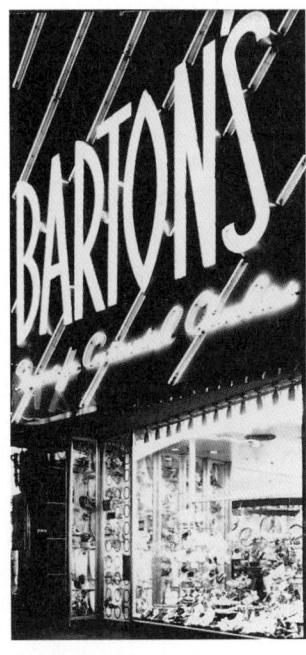

Top left: Richards,
392 Sixth Avenue.
José A. Fernandez,
1944. Gottscho-
Schleisner. LOC

Top right: Barton's,
29 Cordlandt Street.
Morris Lapidus,
1947. ML

Bottom: Barton's.
ML

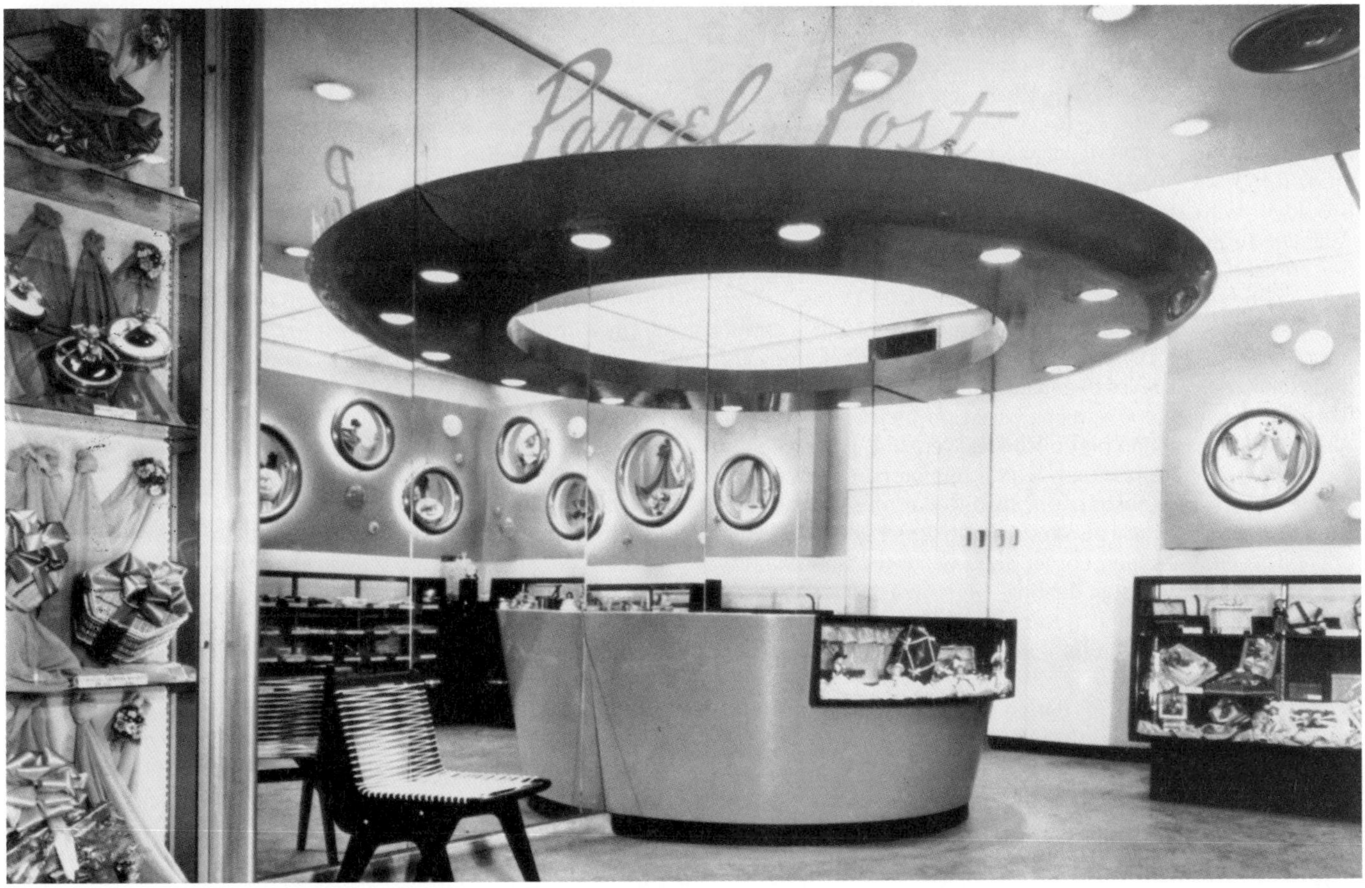

front modified by the inclusion of large glass display cases to achieve a delightful spatial ambiguity, especially at night.[37] His Paris shop (1942), at 417 Fifth Avenue, had as its principal feature a deep arcade in which examples of the furniture sold inside were displayed without cases (but wired down to prevent theft).[38] Also of interest was his Balch Price fur shop in Brooklyn (see chapter 13).

Fernandez's largest commission was the 1945 renovation of the Modernage shop, at 16 East Thirty-fourth Street.[39] In 1933 Modernage, New York's principal retailer of contemporary furniture, had commissioned Frederick Kiesler's Space House, and in 1948 it would present a four-room house designed by Paul McCobb, a young designer whose marriage of Bauhaus-inspired modularity with the natural woods and soft contours of Scandinavian Modernist work would make a deep impression on the middle-class suburban house market.[40] Fernandez's original designs, brilliantly delineated by the young architect Sidney Katz, proposed a bold open-front arcade entrance on Thirty-fourth Street that would lead shoppers to a continuous selling floor divided into departments by changing levels, plant boxes attached to upright poles and fluted wooden screens. Only the design for the front portion of the store was executed; the rear space, which extended through the block to Thirty-third Street, was used for a conventional installation of model rooms. The bold scale of the new opening and its smooth terra-cotta surround surely helped merchandise Modernism for the home to the middle-class shopper as never before.

Although Victor Gruenbaum would make his greatest contribution after relocating to California, for a few years he and his first wife, Elsie Krummeck, were an important force in New York design. Gruenbaum and Krummeck launched their independent career in 1939 after achieving quick success with their chaste Altman & Kuhn's candy shop and their shop for Lederer's, which they designed with Ketchum.[41] In 1940 they were joined by Michael Auer, a Hungarian trained in Budapest, Zurich and Michigan, and the firm quickly established offices in New York and Los Angeles and sought to establish a national practice.

The success of the exclusive Altman & Kuhn's confectioners attracted the attention of the management of Barton's, a growing chain of popularly priced candy shops based in Brooklyn, with stores at 790 Flatbush Avenue, 922 Flatbush Avenue, 1706 Kings Highway and 267 Wyckoff Avenue. For Barton's the new firm of Gruenbaum, Krummeck & Auer created a candy-striped prototype shopfront in 1941 that became the firm's distinctive signature for decades.[42] In a typical Barton's shop, the customer passed through a black door gridded with glass portholes to enter a brightly lit room whose walls were lined with wood screens based on the designs of Alvar Aalto. Gruenbaum and his colleagues were also responsible for the distinctive Barton's logo, which reinforced the candy-box theme with subtle abstraction. In one Barton's Bonbonnière shop in Manhattan, at 126 West Fiftieth Street, the interior was opened to view through corner glass windows, and extensive use was made of tungsten lighting—in contrast to the prevalent neon, cold cathode and fluorescent lighting of the day—in sixty-watt bulbs hung on thin rods from the ceiling to create a sparkling effect.[43]

Gruenbaum's work for Barton's was to have a wide impact. In 1947 Morris Lapidus designed a Barton's shop in lower Manhattan on Cortlandt Street, repeating Gruenbaum's porthole theme on the entrance but diverging in the interior with an extensive use of floor-to-ceiling mirrors.[44] Not only was the chain to build almost fifty installations along the Gruenbaum line over the next ten years, but rival chains adopted comparable approaches, as could be seen in Charles C. S. Dean's design for Loft's candy store, at 251 West Forty-second Street, which was the pacesetter for 175 new units in that long-established chain.[45] For another candy company, Henny Wyle Chocolates, Gruenbaum, Krummeck & Auer transformed a tiny shop into a delightful tent and located the sweets in round turntable counters based on their designs for Altman & Kuhn's.[46] For the shop they also designed scallop-edged shadowboxes and low tables supported on Roman-style X's executed in a white-painted metal grid typical of the work of the Viennese architect Josef Hoffmann. Abandoning the popular arcaded, recessed shopfront, the designers instead grouped Henny Wyle's shop window and glass door into one plane and shaped the opening to conform to the cross section of the tent within, thereby creating a memorable facade that literally rendered the interior on the exterior. For a fancy Danish delicatessen, Gruenbaum, Krummeck & Auer created a simple circular salesroom focused on a salad counter designed to resemble a gigantic salad bowl.[47]

Gruenbaum was absent from the New York shop scene until the 1950s, when, with his name shortened and free of his partnership with Krummeck and Auer, he returned to design two important installations, the Leighton's men's shop and a new Barton's. Leighton's, relocated from Times Square to the northwest corner of Fifth Avenue and Forty-sixth Street, was diagonally across from Ketchum's new Wallachs (see above). Its design was somewhat ponderous; *Architectural Forum* called attention to its out-of-scale two-story portico.[48] Just two years after its opening in 1956, Leighton's was replaced with a branch of Takashimaya, the Tokyo department store (see chapter 5). Barton's was a different story entirely. In 1952 the company requested a new design for the chain's fiftieth store, located in a derelict mid-nineteenth-century rowhouse on the east side of Sixth Avenue between Thirty-fifth and Thirty-sixth streets. Working in collaboration with Alvin Lustig, the graphic designer, and Stanley McCandless, the lighting designer, Gruen set out to create "a toy shop for adults."[49] He refreshed his palette by playing a Modernist vocabulary against the framework of the Victorian building. But he also gave the new shop some of the historical character of its host, a significant display of sympathy for the architecture of the Victorian era in a time when the typical tendency was to cover up the period's buildings if not to tear them down. In this the design was surely influenced by the innovative interpretations of Victorian typography that transformed the pages of the English journal *Architectural Review*. Another notable feature was the shop's lighting: recognizing that recessed downlighting, typically favored by Modernists who sought a look of sleek efficiency, was largely characterless, Gruen developed pendants, inspired by Alexander Calder, to stimulate the eye as they diverted attention from the workaday recessed lights.

Shop design, though dominated by a few specialists, attracted the interest of a wide variety of design professionals. In the hands of Dorothy Draper, master of spectacular overkill, surrealism was effectively married to the Classically inspired vocabulary of traditional decoration. No interior better revealed Draper's sensibility than that of the Coty beauty salon (1941), at 612 Fifth Avenue. As the editors of *Interiors* observed, "If Miss Draper had made the new Coty Salon on Fifth Avenue any more Baroque it would have bust!"[50] According to Carleton Varney, Draper's successor in the decorating business and her biographer, the store's opening in the summer of 1941 was a lavish affair: "It included the Rockettes and a squadron of Radio City

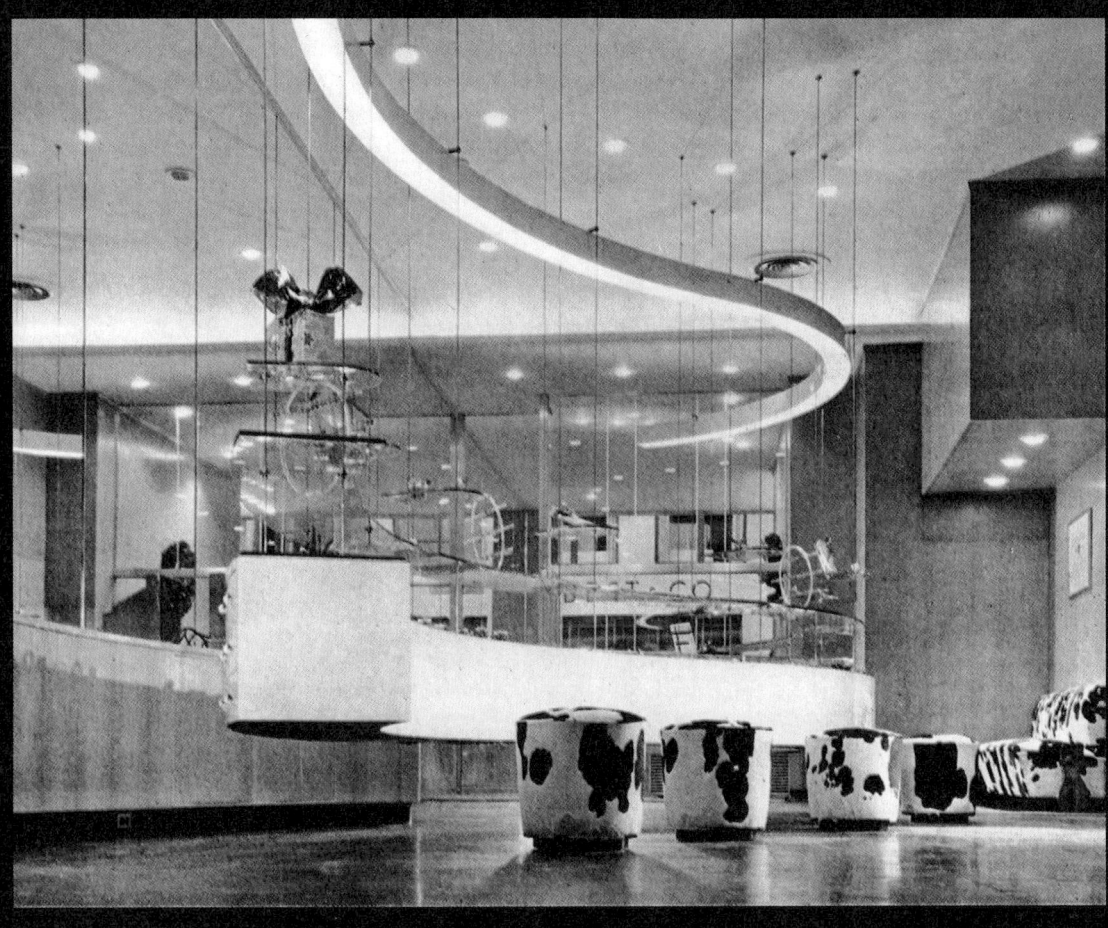

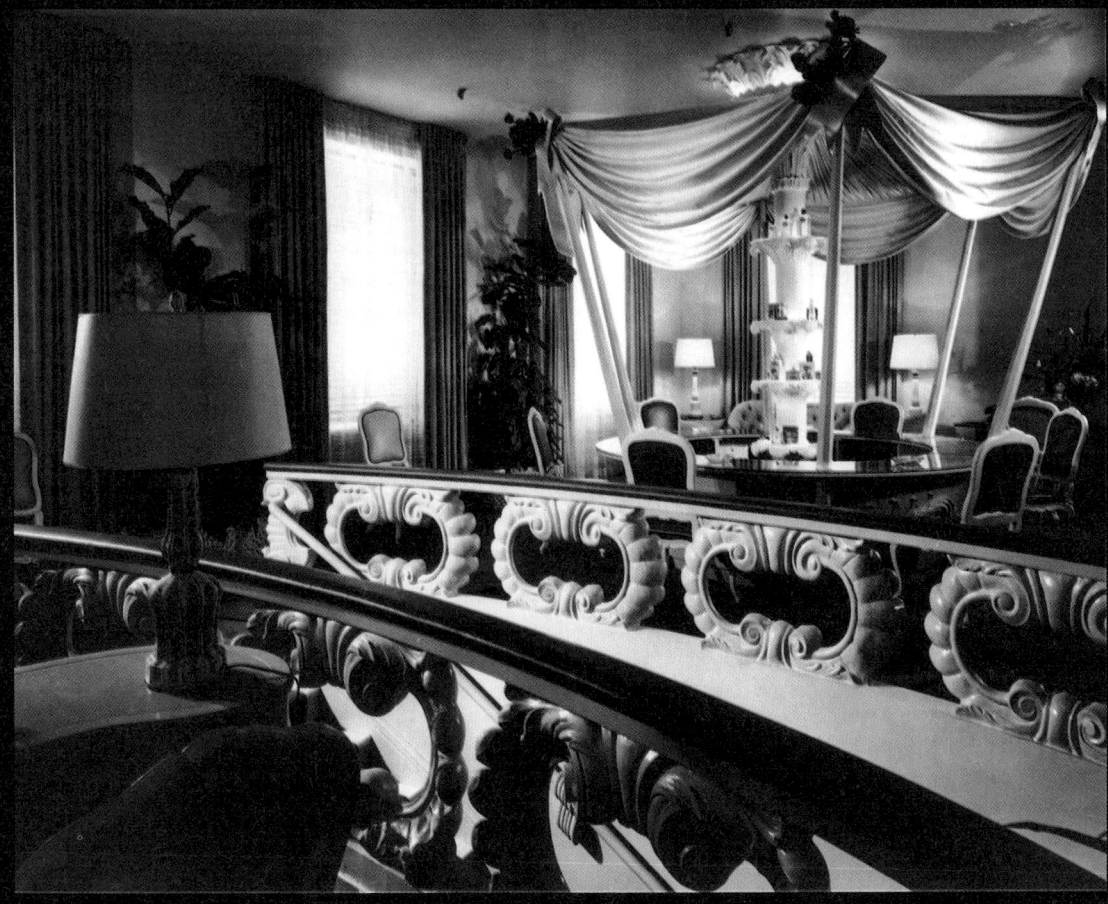

Top: Rebajes, 377 Fifth
Avenue. José A.
Fernandez, 1941. IN.
CU

Bottom: Coty, 612 Fifth
Avenue. Dorothy
Draper, 1941. DDC

Music Hall ushers. Thousands watched Mr. and Mrs. Al Smith dance to the 'Sidewalks of New York.' A bottle of perfume was broken on the steps of the salon, a Coty tradition." Varney said that "patriotism" was on the decorator's mind when she chose the salon's red, white and blue color scheme, and he went on to describe what he called "Draper's latest fantasy: Tall lacquered black screens with exotic red roses and mother-of-pearl leaves, a smoky blue carpet, tall white plaster trees, walls covered with massive roses, tulips, and lilacs. The columnists found a new name to describe it: 'Modern Baroque.'"[51]

The English decorator and furniture designer T. H. Robsjohn-Gibbings managed to interpret traditional styles with an essentially Modernist economy of line. Collaborating with the architect Edward Durell Stone and the lighting designer Thomas Smith Kelly, Robsjohn-Gibbings designed the elegantly understated Hunt & Winterbotham shop (1941), at 702 Fifth Avenue, whose interior combined natural materials, including an exposed-brick fireplace corner and cypress casework, with Belter-style furniture as well as furniture designed by Alvar Aalto.[52] Robsjohn-Gibbings, who had worked on the Lily Daché salon in 1937,[53] was to collaborate with the architect Rene Brugnoni on the shop of another milliner, the flamboyantly eccentric Mr. John, who headed John-Frederics (1940).[54] Located on the second floor of 53 East Fifty-seventh Street, the shop managed to be at once serene and wacky. Notable features included the gray harewood screen that formed the entrance, bird-cage-like fitting rooms for special customers, extraordinary tendril uplights that provided most of the room's illumination and mirrors used to expand the space and contribute sparkle.

Tommi Parzinger's shop for the exclusive jeweler Olga Tritt (1949), at 18 East Fifty-seventh Street, was as restrained as the John-Frederics salon was mad. Parzinger and Tritt were intent on avoiding what the *Interiors* critic Olga Gueft described as "the two design cliches which are alternately resorted to in most *bijouteries*": "Baudy House Baroque" and "bank-vault decor." Outside, the shopfront, with a white enamel studded door, plate-glass window and black Carrara glass signboard carrying the shop's name in raised letters, was almost as abstract as a work of Bauhaus-inspired graphic design. Inside, the effect of restrained elegance was conveyed by the simplest and most traditional means—fine materials, simple patterns and just enough visual clutter to keep things interesting, as Gueft said, "to knock the spectator's eye out—but gently."[55]

Paul Bry, a French émigré designer, made a specialty of shops catering to women. In 1941 he created a new facade and interior for Alfred Rainer's fur shop at 17 East Fifty-fifth Street.[56] A prowlike triangular display case was the facade's principal feature; inside, mirrors and loosely draped fabrics established a simple backdrop for the furs being shown. Bry's own women's clothing shop (1944), at 204 East Fifty-seventh Street, which had mullioned windows and a domestic scale, embodied his belief that small specialty stores must be individually designed and given a distinct personality to survive the competition of mass merchandisers.[57]

The tradition of restrained, almost classic Modernism was consistently upheld by Robert Carson of Carson & Lundin, who had worked on many of the interiors in Rockefeller Center, as well as on the elegant I. Miller salon (1939) at Fifth Avenue and Fifty-fourth Street.[58] Carson & Lundin's Gotham Hosiery shop (1944), in Rockefeller Center's International Building North, at 634 Fifth Avenue, reversed the normal organization of such shops, placing a series of freestanding storage units and kidney-shaped showcase counters in the center of the space, minimizing the walking necessary by sales help.[59] Because lighting was concealed in the top of the cabinets, the ceiling could be treated as a clean surface, making the small shop seem surprisingly lofty and spacious. In 1945 the firm designed a second shop for the company in an eight-foot-wide space at 627 Madison Avenue.[60] Using the same type of individual counters as in the earlier shop and lining one wall with continuous mirrors, they succeeded in fostering a remarkable sense of uncluttered space.

During the 1950s, as Manhattan merchants fretted over city dwellers fleeing to suburbia, there were few innovative designs for specialty stores, and little was done to update existing facilities. By and large this period of inactivity continued even through the early 1960s, with one notable exception, the spectacular and smothering interiors Victor Lundy created for the new shop of I. Miller (1961), the women's ' shoe emporium, in the Heckscher Building (Warren & Wetmore, 1922), on the southwest corner of West Fifty-seventh Street and Fifth Avenue.[61] Olga Gueft was enthralled by the design:

> It is breathtaking, this interior, where sinuous ribs of weathered wood rise to sheathe the walls and columns, swelling and ebbing like waves, growing into arches, soaring into vaults, interlocking with the fans that spray out of the lofty columns, curling to clasp the balconies in a tendriled balustrade. This drowned cathedral, worn into rills by the sea, encloses a space which appears immense. With great skill the architect has placed tinted mirrors that magnify it endlessly, but he has also hung panels of fabric to camouflage the mirror trickery, to parade solemnly as curtains merely screening the reflected vastness. The fact that the inner columns are complete in three dimensions and real to their towering tops makes the incalculable reach of mirrored space convincing. . . . Despite the *moyenage*, *art nouveau*, and pre-Raphaelite phantoms it summons, this interior is brilliantly original and a total integration of space, structure, and mood.

Gueft, however, had some reservations about the store. Complaining about its virtual invisibility from the street and Lundy's decision not to rip out the building's original windows, Gueft went on to question the design's appropriateness: "Should a fashionable shopper in need of shoes push open the door, the objects of her search are bound to appear out of place if not downright sacrilegious. Whatever her religious attitudes, her *instinctive* reaction will be to renounce the fripperies of this world and do penance in humble habit—with bare feet."[62] The I. Miller shop never functioned properly, despite the efforts of other designers to correct its shortcomings by flooding the merchandise with light and by removing the shields behind the windows to open the interior to the outside.

Lundy was given a second chance to explore his spatial ideal of treelike columns in 1965 when he completed the Singer Sewing Center on the ground floor of Rockefeller Center's Maison Française, on the south side of the Channel Gardens.[63] After visiting the Singer showroom, Gueft reported that although the vocabulary was the same as that of I. Miller, the rilled wooden structures were simpler. And, she said, "Lundy has now taken care to make the interior the cynosure of the pedestrian. Not only window obstructions but even metal mullions have been removed, with clear glass interior braces substituted."[64] From the outside looking in, the shop resembled a grove, but on the inside, the well-lighted interior made it easy to concentrate on the displays.

While little attention was being paid in the 1950s and early 1960s to traditional types of shops—those specializing in clothing, shoes, cosmetics—new types were emerging that seemed

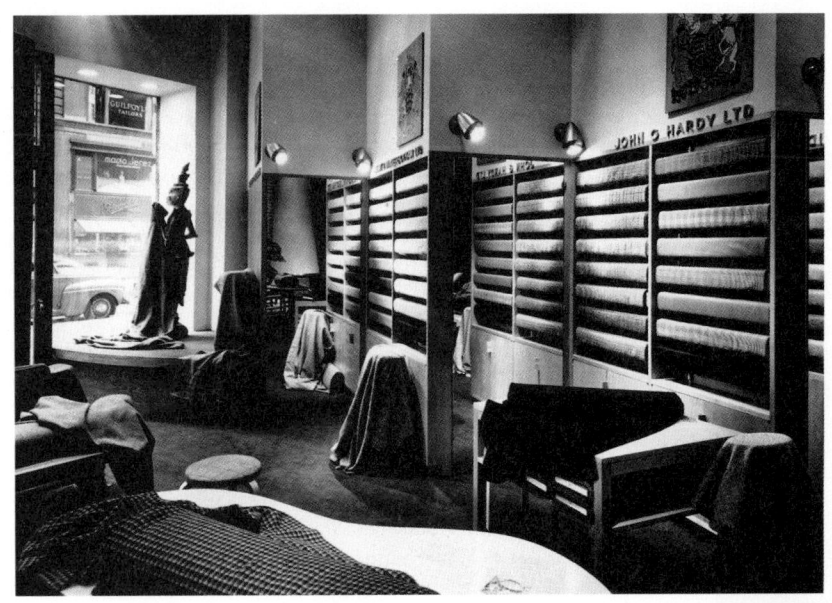

Top: Hunt & Winterbotham, 702 Fifth Avenue. T. H. Robsjohn-Gibbings and Edward Durell Stone, 1941. Lincoln. PENN

Center: Gotham Hosiery, 634 Fifth Avenue. Carson & Lundin, 1944. Gottscho-Schleisner. LOC

Bottom: Gotham Hosiery, 627 Madison Avenue. Carson & Lundin, 1945. Gottscho-Schleisner. LOC

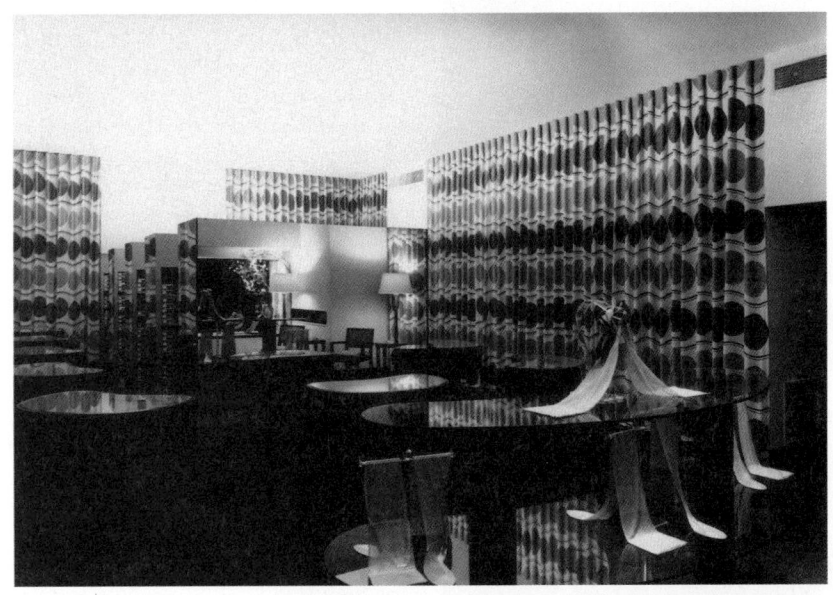

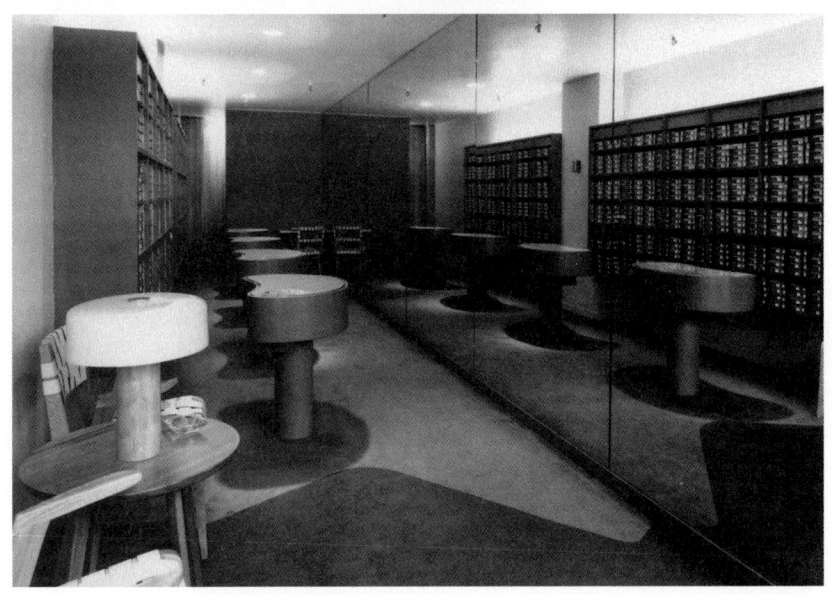

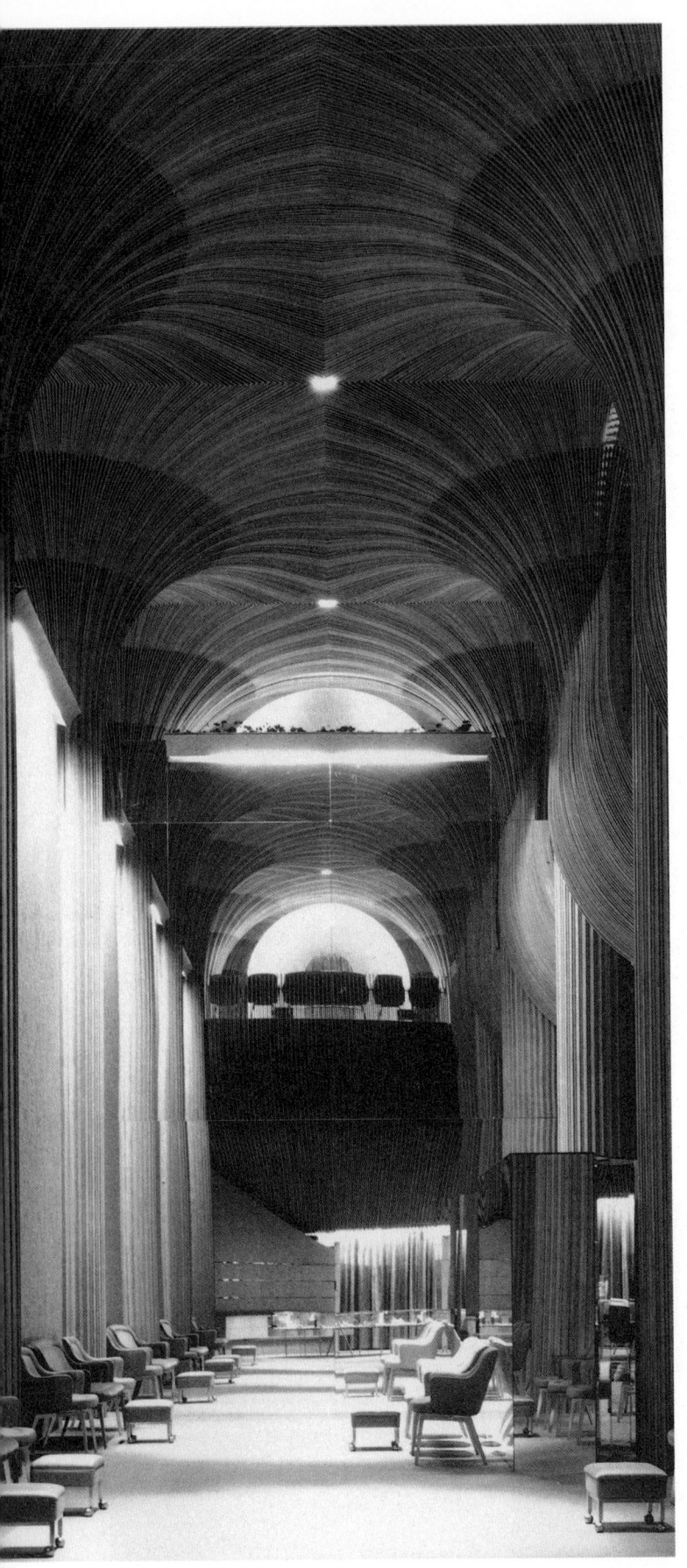

I. Miller, southwest corner of West Fifty-seventh Street and Fifth Avenue. Victor Lundy, 1961. Cserna. GC

ideally suited to high-profile design. One new category, of which Ketchum's America House was the progenitor, specialized in modestly priced high-style items for the home. The first of these was New Design Inc. (1948), occupying two floors of a brownstone at 33 East Seventy-fifth Street that were opened up to display modern furniture, crafts and household articles in a setting comparable to one the shopper might have at home.[65] Begun by three women with a limited budget, New Design was designed by Dorothy Q. Noyes and Robert H. Rosenberg.

It was quickly followed by Bonniers (1949), which was principally a bookstore but also sold other items and eventually evolved into an important distributor of contemporary design objects.[66] Located in a five-story building at 605 Madison Avenue (Walter Haefeli, 1915), Bonniers was widely regarded as "the best recent redesign in New York City."[67] Charles H. Warner, Jr., and Harold E. Leeds transformed the two bottom floors of the building into the selling area, expressed on the facade with a two-story plate-glass window. The rest of the facade received a coat of white paint. Inside, the two floors were visually integrated by the creation of an open stair, which permitted long diagonal vistas from floor to floor, and by the dramatic decision to hold the second level back from the facade. Bonniers quickly became a focus for young, modern-minded architects and designers in New York; with its success, the shop expanded to the rear in 1957 to accommodate more examples of Scandinavian design.[68] Cepelia (1960), at 5 East Fifty-seventh Street, a small shop featuring Polish handicrafts, was designed by two American architects, John Dodd and William Hall, in collaboration with W. Kawecki, a Pole.[69] The store's extensive use of natural materials set it apart from the prevailing sleekness of its neighbors.

In 1960 a boarded-up pizza joint on the ground floor of a tenement at 194 Third Avenue, between Seventeenth and Eighteenth streets, was transformed by Marvin B. Affrime's Space Design Group into Wilburt's, an elegant, airy shop selling contemporary bric-a-brac. Begun by Wilburt and Miriam Feinberg "to reflect the taste and care and talent which artisans and artists from all corners of the earth have put into [their] wares," Wilburt's became, despite its location on the shabby fringes of Gramercy Park, a mecca of sorts, as notable for its design as for its merchandise.[70] Using Fifth and Madison avenues as their standard, the owners and the designer created a simple rectangular volume of space, closed from the street by a wall of glass recessed three feet behind the building line. The large panes of glass were held in place by exceptionally thin metal frames. Inside, there were no fixed showcases. The floor, which consisted of four huge circles of oak strip flooring set in white marble chips, an abstract interpretation of Japanese garden design, helped articulate the space.

In December 1963 D/R International, the New York branch of Design Research, begun ten years earlier in Cambridge, Massachusetts, by architect Benjamin Thompson, was opened in a five-story-tall townhouse (1877) at 53 East Fifty-seventh Street.[71] The building had been renovated by a previous tenant, the Joseph Brummel art gallery, which had added a new limestone front with a distinctive Serliana incorporating flanking service and principal entrance doors (I. N. Phelps-Stokes, 1924–25). In the renovation by Thompson, the facade was maintained but the interiors were gutted to create uncluttered floors connected by a network of stairs and half levels. Although these allowed reasonably easy flow through the lower two floors, above the second floor, where only one staircase and one elevator were available, circulation was more difficult. The

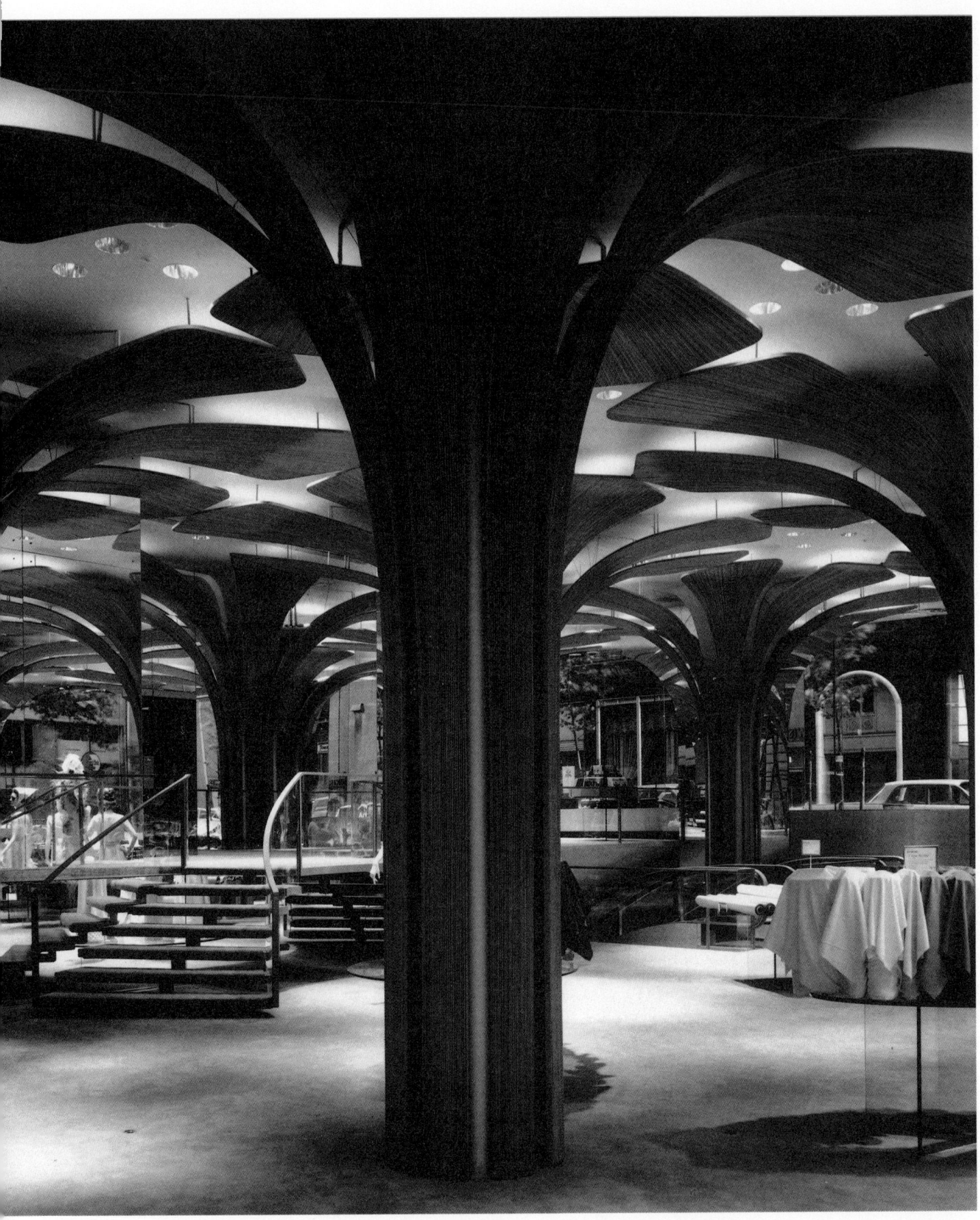

Singer Sewing Center, Maison Française, Rockefeller Center. Victor Lundy,
1965. Cserna. GC

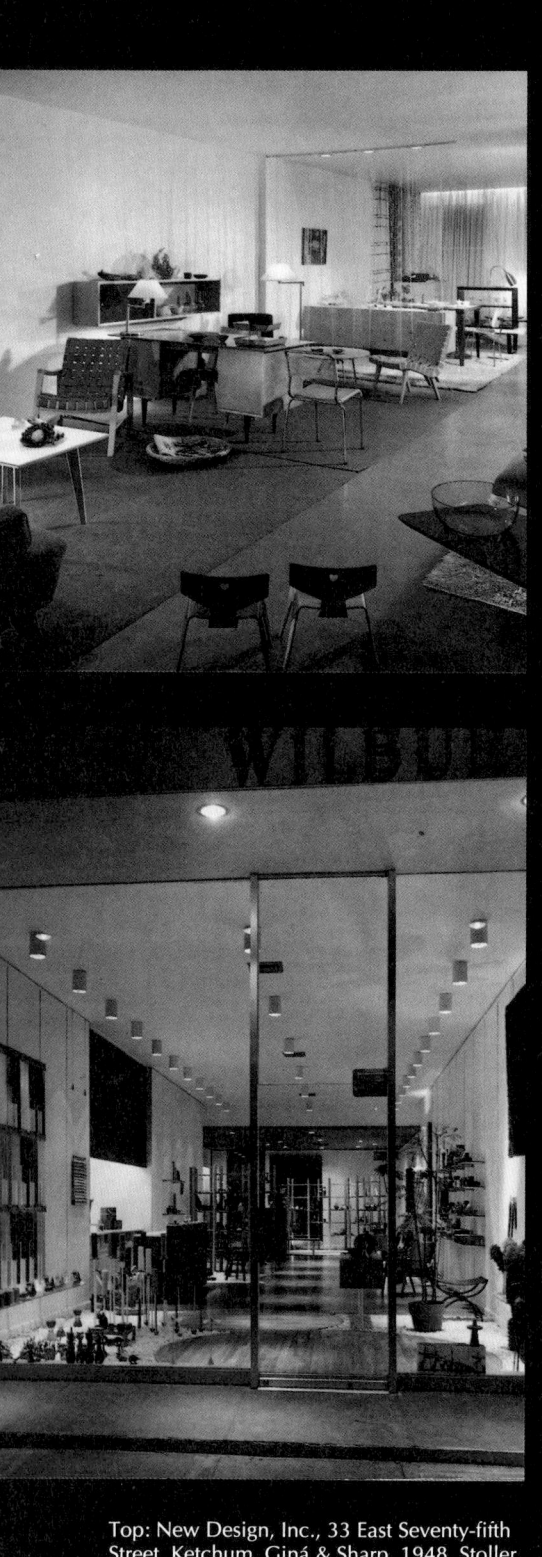

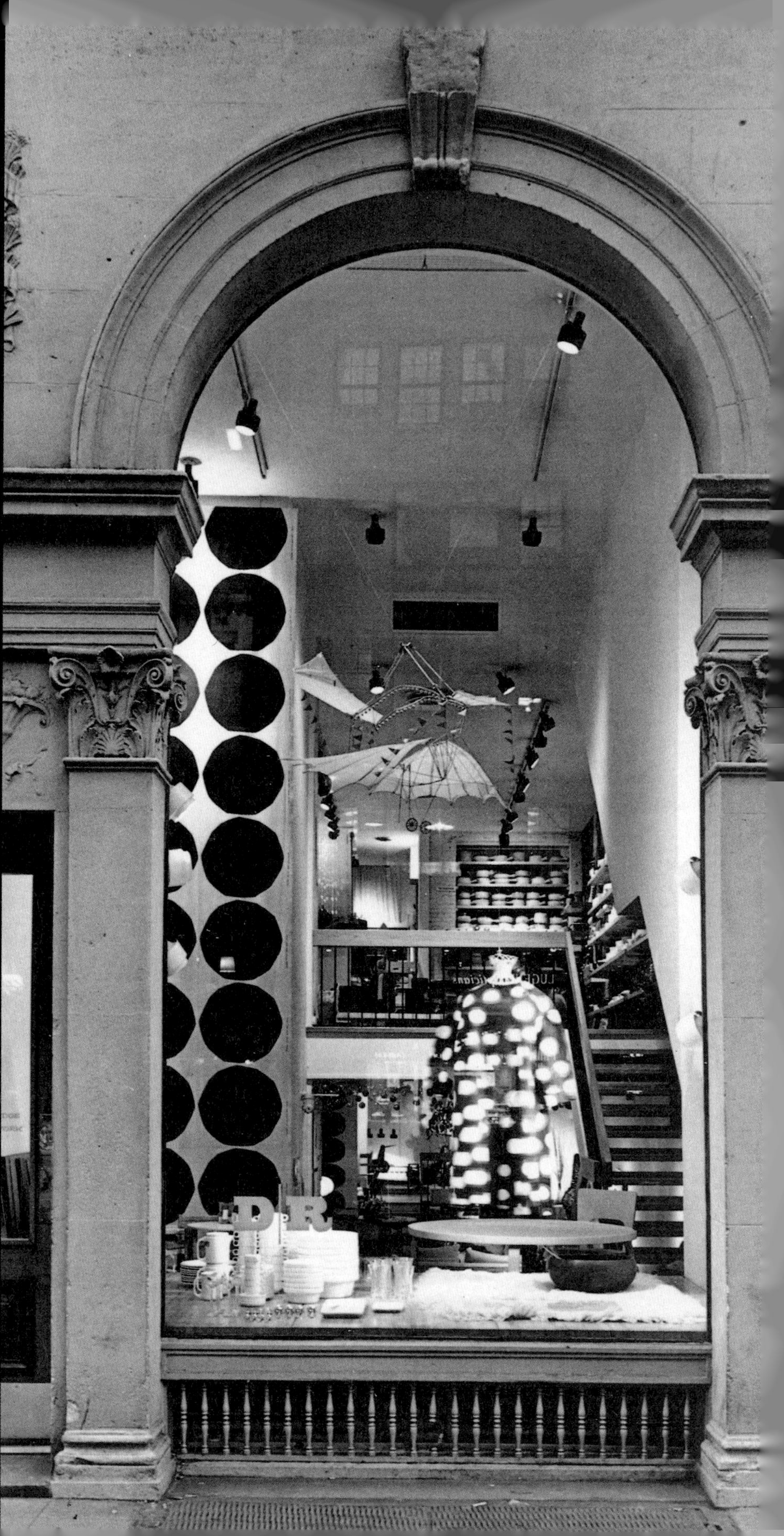

Top: New Design, Inc., 33 East Seventy-fifth
Street. Ketchum, Giná & Sharp, 1948. Stoller.
©ESTO

Bottom: Wilburt's, 194 Third Avenue. Space
Design Group, 1960. Liebman. SDG

Right: D/R International, 53 East Fifty-seventh
Street. Benjamin Thompson, 1963. BT&A

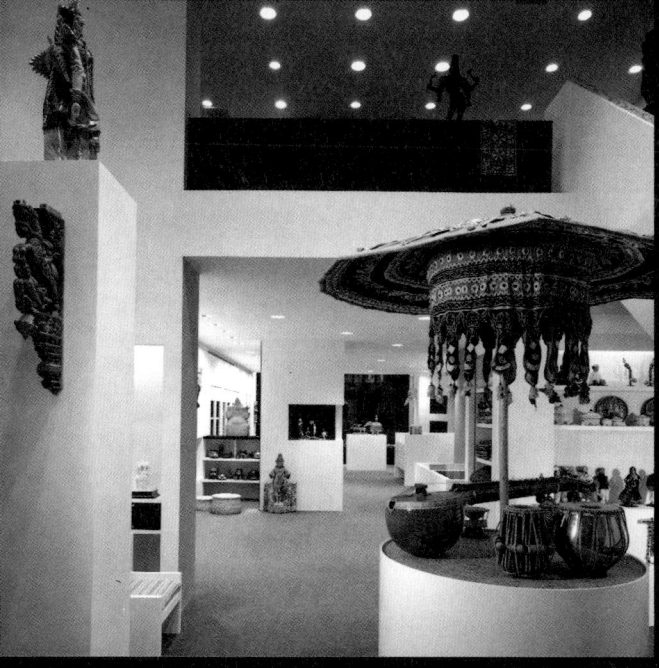

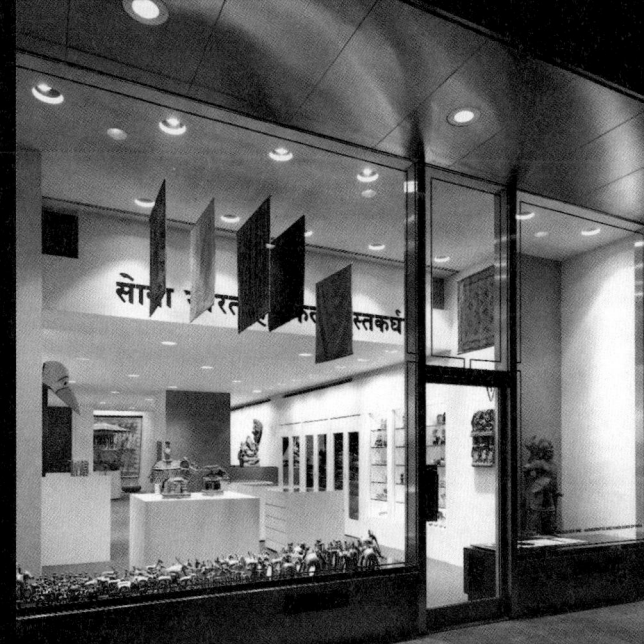

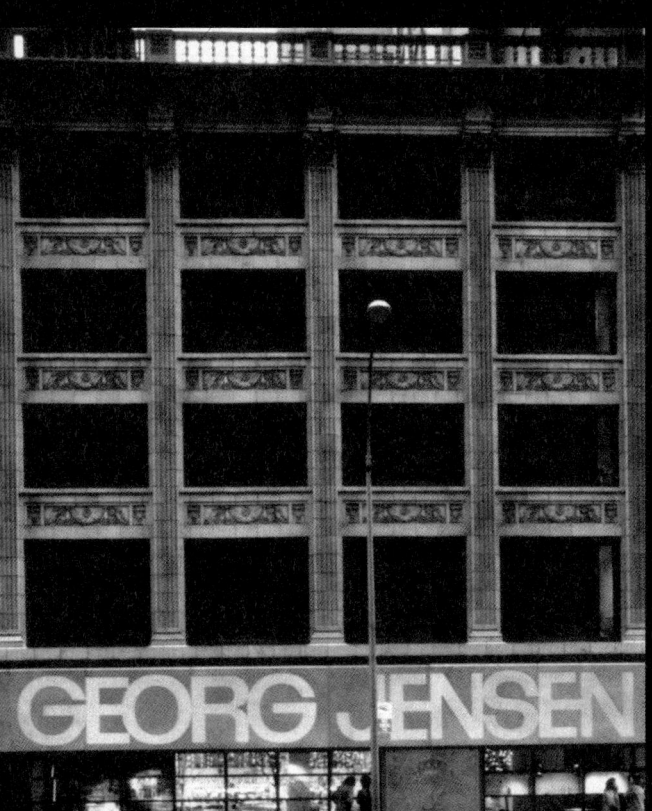

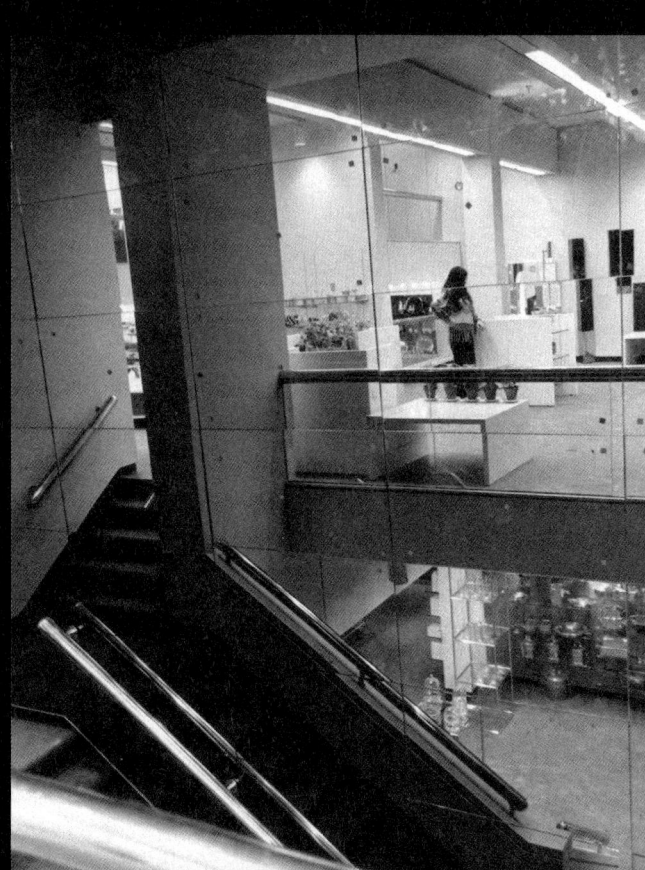

Top left: Sona the Golden One, 7 East Fifty-fifth Street. Richard Meier and Elaine Lustig Cohen, 1965. Stoller. ©ESTO

Top right: Sona the Golden One. View to the north. Stoller. ©ESTO

Bottom left: Georg Jensen, 601 Madison Avenue. James Stewart Polshek, 1970. View to the east. JSP

Bottom right: Georg Jensen. JSP

walls were covered in white-painted gypsum board and the sanded wood floors were given a clear finish. Thompson explained the modesty of the design: "D/R has the kind of feeling it does because we are treating the problem in context of its importance. We know we are not changing the face of the nation with our little store, nor is I. Miller with their shoe joint on Fifth Avenue, though you would think they intended to. We're not advocating that furniture become sculptural or architectural, nor would we want to live in a house pretentious or artificial or overwhelming."[72] Priscilla Ginsberg Dunhill, a reporter for *Interiors*, explained that what made D/R "such a pleasant experience and lifts it well above the level of most shops of good design" was its embodiment of Thompson's point of view, "that design is an all-encompassing world."[73]

In 1965 the fledgling architect Richard Meier and the designer Elaine Lustig Cohen, working with a very modest budget, created the elegant showcase Sona the Golden One, at 7 East Fifty-fifth Street, a shop directed by Pupul Jayakar of India's Handicraft and Handlooms Export Corporation to sell handicrafts similar to those that had impressed visitors at the World's Fair.[74] The nonprofit shop, which was part of the Corning Glass Building, was treated very simply by Meier, who created an all-white box punctuated by simple white cubes that served as display stands and by niches, shelves and glass-topped troughs that seemed to be carved into the thickness of the bounding walls. On the second floor, a conference room and offices carried out the theme on a smaller scale and demonstrated how effective the bright fabrics could be as upholstery and decoration in the white cubic world that Meier was instrumental in formulating as the leading style of the 1970s.

Of the shops specializing in high-style design objects for the home, Georg Jensen was the most established and the most famous. In 1956 the store, best known for its silver, moved from its home of ten years at 684 Fifth Avenue. Jensen's new location was across the street, at 665 Fifth Avenue, where the Danish architect Finn Juhl renovated the building's main floor by introducing modular lighting and display systems, and Warner-Leeds updated the building's exterior by threading a new, glassy facade behind the building's structural pilasters.[75]

In 1970 Jensen left Fifth Avenue for a trendier location at 601 Madison Avenue, next door to its rival, Bonniers.[76] Jensen's imminent arrival on Madison Avenue was announced by an elegant sidewalk construction bridge decorated by the graphic designer Deidi von Schaewen who, presumably influenced by the work of Christo, draped white vinyl over large letters spelling the store's name. The new store was squeezed into two townhouses (1869) that had been unified with a Classically inspired facade in 1928–29 (Bloch & Hesse). James Stewart Polshek, who was selected to undertake the renovation, redesigned the lower floor of the building's facade, creating a continuous band of modular mullioned display windows interrupted only by two unfenestrated cast-aluminum entrance doors with a bas-relief of Jensen's traditional crest. Above the windows, a fifty-foot-long recessed metal sign spelled out the company's name. Inside, Polshek opened up the low-ceilinged space by removing a portion of the second floor to create a double-height, atriumlike selling area and by adding a mirrored staircase luring shoppers down to a basement-level selling floor. Unfortunately, these gestures were not strong enough to overcome the inherent limitations of the cramped space. Olga Gueft pronounced the design "a disappointment, even a fiasco," explaining: "Those down-to-earth designing chores of coping with color, lighting, and display were hopelessly botched. Even the carpet is a flop; it is a 'practical' and 'unobtrusive' charcoal gray that manages to look grim while exaggerating the dust of every footprint."[77] *Progressive Architecture* found the lighting "often more dominant than the merchandise, particularly the levels that are lit by a series of bare filament bulbs on matte aluminum ceiling."[78] Polshek was not pleased with the results either. Almost twenty years later he would recall that "the project proved to be frustrating because of the exceedingly poor quality of workmanship caused by the pressure of time."[79]

Increasingly, booksellers who had been content with librarylike monumentality, as for example Scribner's, at 597 Fifth Avenue (Ernest Flagg, 1913), or Brentano's, at 1 West Forty-seventh Street (Oswald C. Hering, 1925), began to take a more aggressive sales-oriented attitude.[80] Part of this approach was the commissioning of brightly lit shops that had more in common with establishments selling jewelry or knick-knacks than with public institutions. In 1952 Antonin Raymond and L. L. Rado, in association with the graphic designer Ladislav Sutnar, designed the tiny, eleven-by-seventeen-foot Golden Griffin, at 611 Madison Avenue, opening the shop to a view of the street through broad glass walls and using the open bookshelves and a few specially designed display racks as the shop's principal decoration.[81] White walls, yellow ceiling beams and black-painted posts and table legs, as well as display racks in red, blue and yellow, made for a memorable color scheme. Even Ernest Flagg's cavernous yet elegant Scribner's bookstore was renovated by George Von Geldern to give it more zip. Michael Saphier Associates'· 1960 installation for the shop of Schirmer Inc., the music publishers, at 4 East Forty-ninth Street, seemed to be a complete updating of Scribner's monumentality.[82] Saphier's two-story-high barrel-vaulted room organized the array of items sold into a single statement. Among other notable bookstores of the period were several efforts on Fifth Avenue, including new shops for Rizzoli, Brentano's and Doubleday's (see chapter 5).

The interwar years saw the emergence of a new kind of facility that combined the street-level accessibility of a shop with the exclusivity of a wholesale showroom devoted to a single product line. Although company products could not be purchased at many such showrooms, manufacturers' representatives were on hand to answer questions and promote the line. The first of these showroooms were devoted to building products, particularly plumbing fixtures: a display hall occupied a large portion of Raymond Hood's American Radiator Building of 1924, and Crane plumbing operated an impressive International Style exhibition hall designed in 1937 by Landefeld & Hatch.[83]

In 1948 the firm of Skidmore, Owings & Merrill completed a display hall for the Fiberglas Corporation as one of its first postwar commissions in New York.[84] Located in a former brownstone at 16 East Fifty-sixth Street, Fiberglas House included offices on the upper three floors behind horizontally banded aluminum-framed windows set flush in an Indiana limestone facade. At street level, behind an eighteen-foot-tall window, a vestibule led to a large showroom set on the old parlor floor half a level above. Fiberglas products were used whenever possible throughout the project: the natural-colored walls, which resembled cork, were actually Fiberglas mat; ceilings were also Fiberglas, as were many of the upholstery fabrics, which were designed by Marianne Strengell of Cranbrook. Viewed from the street, especially at night, when the gridded corklike walls and the gridded luminous ceiling could be easily seen, the building exemplified uncompromised modernity as few New York buildings had since William Lescaze's townhouse of 1934.[85] Fiberglas House was torn down to make way for the Corning

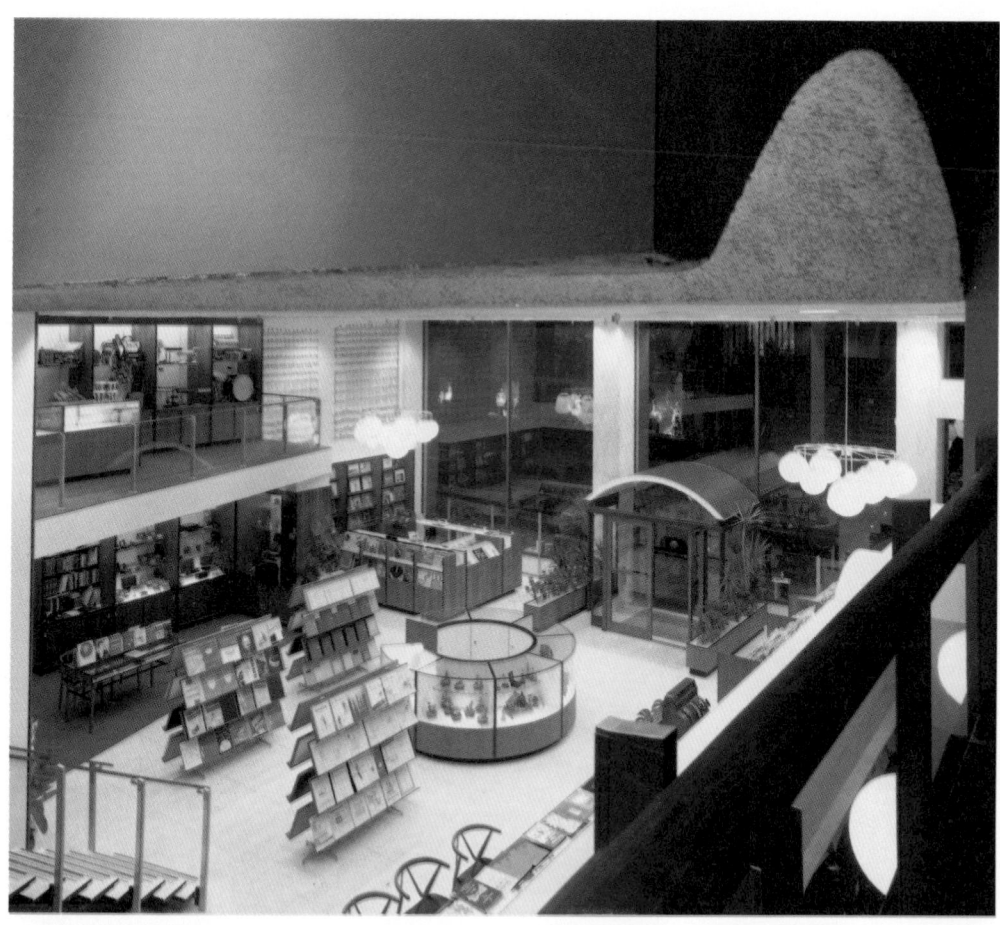

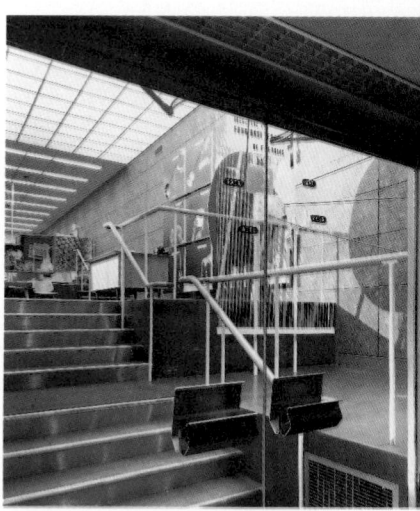

Top left: Schirmer, 4 East Forty-ninth Street. Michael Saphier Associates, 1960. Reens. LR

Bottom left: Fiberglas House, 16 East Fifty-sixth Street. Skidmore, Owings & Merrill, 1948. Stoller. ©ESTO

Top right: Fiberglas House. Entrance. Stoller. ©ESTO

Bottom right: Fiberglas House. Stoller. ©ESTO

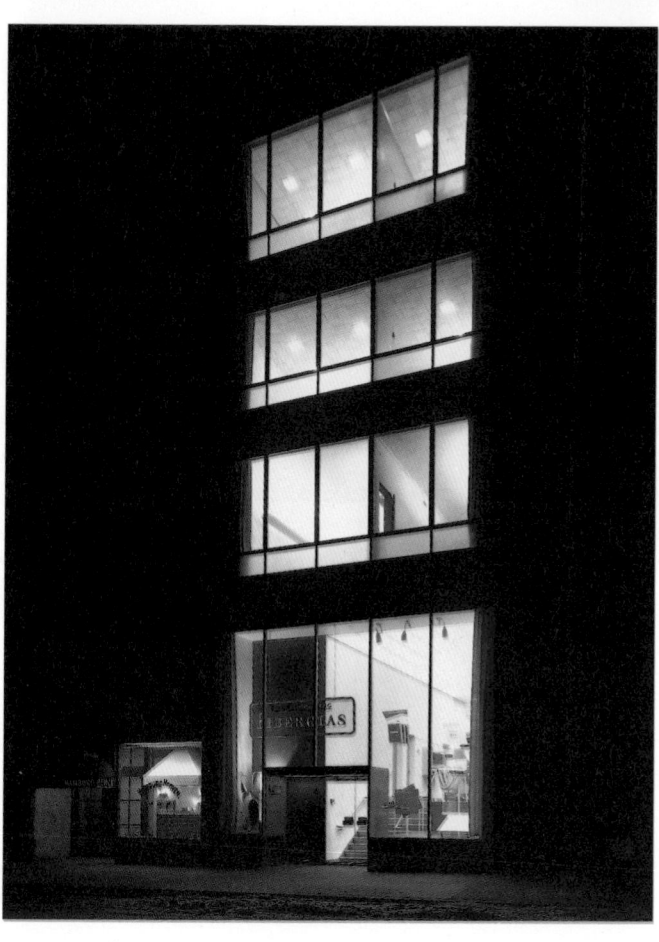

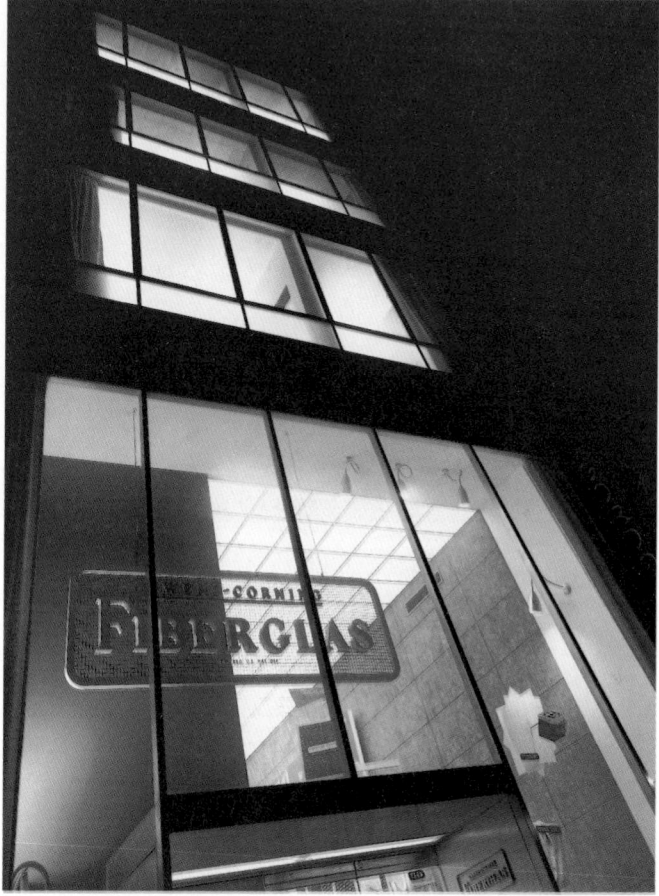

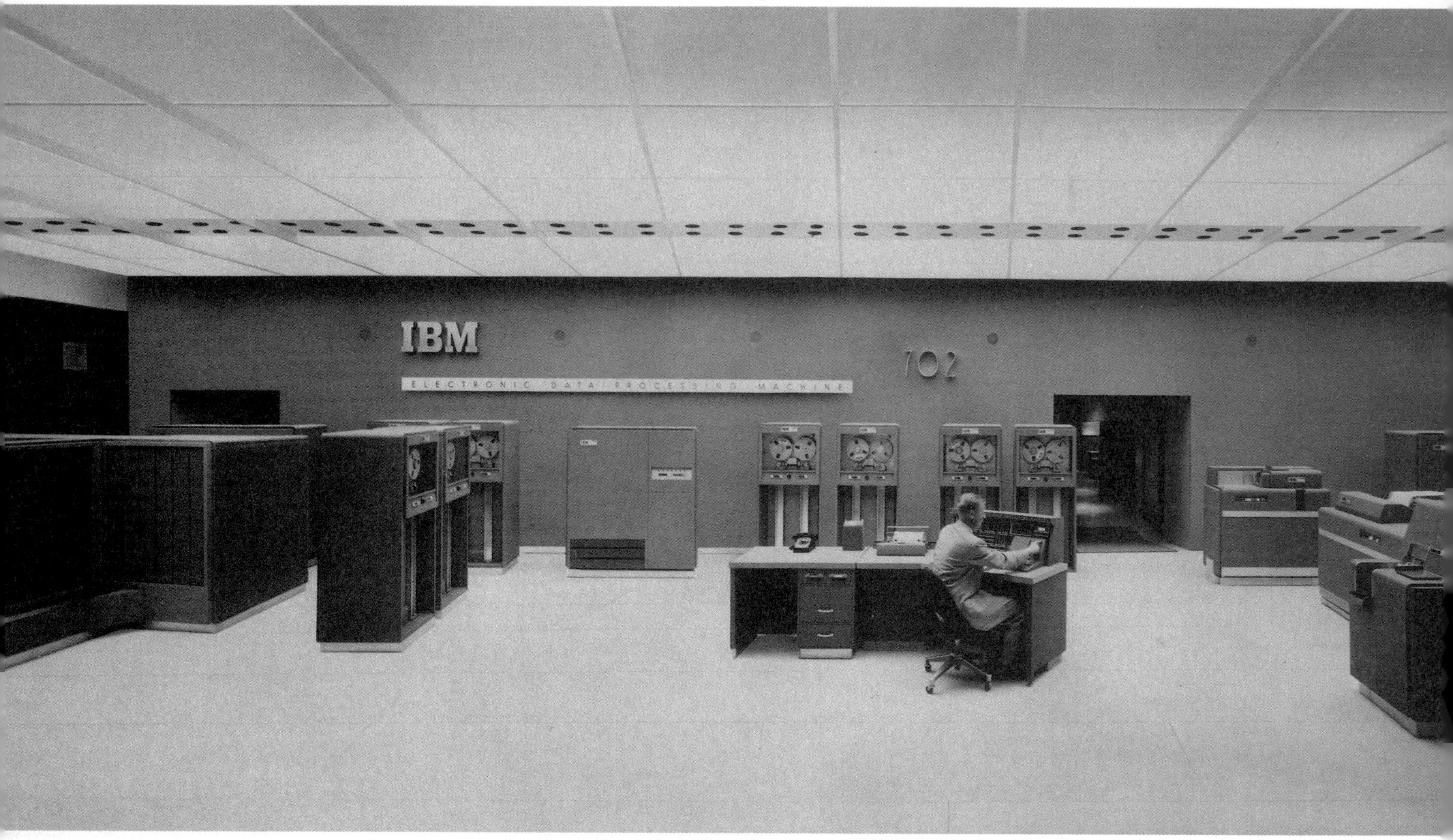

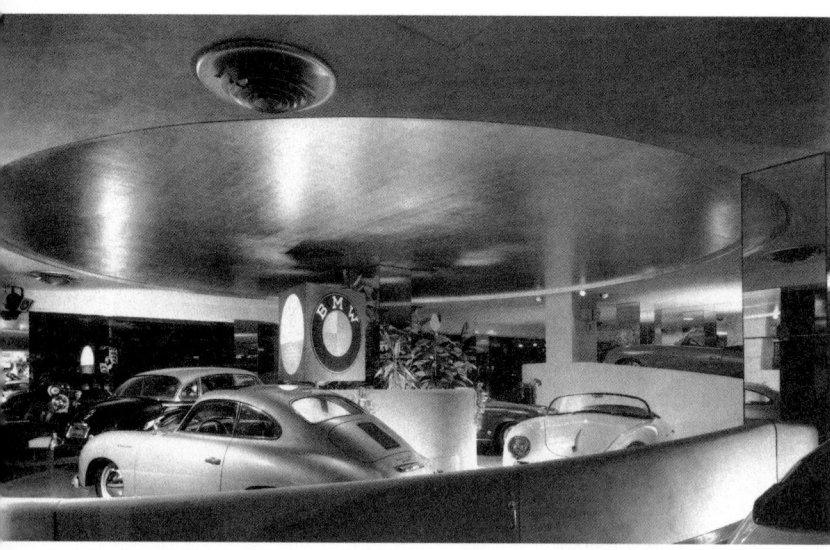

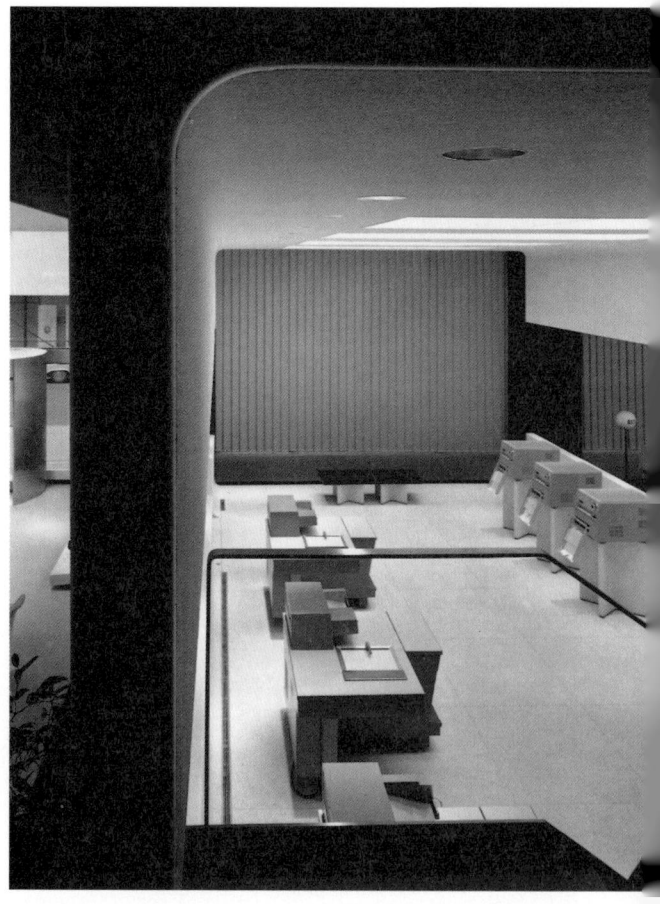

Top: IBM showroom, 590 Madison Avenue. Eliot Noyes, 1955. IBM

Bottom left: Maximilian Hoffman showroom, 430 Park Avenue. Frank Lloyd Wright, 1954. Stoller. ©ESTO

Bottom right: Xerox showroom, 1290 Sixth Avenue. Eliot Noyes, 1963. Stoller. ©ESTO

Top far right: Xerox showroom. Stoller. ©ESTO

Bottom far right: Elliott Industries, 281 Madison Avenue. Space Design Group, 1962. Liebman. SDG

Glass Building, which incorporated a new, scaled-down version of the showroom, designed by Maria Bergson for the ground-floor area just east of the plaza.[86]

A far more controversial Fifth Avenue showroom, which also served as a retail outlet, was completed in 1954 for the Italian corporation Olivetti, specialists in high technology office machines (see chapter 5). One year later Eliot Noyes designed a lobby showroom for the American leader in business machines, IBM, at 590 Madison Avenue.[87] In 1963 Noyes designed a showroom for Xerox that occupied a ninety-two-by-forty-seven-foot ground-floor space in the Sperry-Rand Building, at 1290 Sixth Avenue.[88] Noyes broke up the space with a series of elevated display islands, each surrounded by low parapets and demarcated above by similarly sized dropped fascias. In designing the showroom for Elliott Industries (1962), at 281 Madison Avenue, Marvin B. Affrime's Space Design Group replaced the building's original show windows, setting four large panes of glass in bronze frames in each opening.[89] Inside, they created a clean white cube of space, interrupted only by floating blue and purple panels hung from the ceiling that featured the company's logo on one side and outsized photographs of its products on the other. In 1969 Michael Saphier carried Noyes's ideas for Xerox a step further in his Dennison Copier showroom, at 230 Park Avenue, where he isolated each copier on a square rug set under a square tube suspended from the ceiling, inside which concealed fixtures flooded the machines with light for maximum drama.[90]

Automobile showrooms were seldom designed with as much care as the Xerox and Olivetti showrooms had demonstrated. One notable exception from the interwar period was Reinhard & Hofmeister's Chrysler Salon (1936), located in the Chrysler Building (William Van Alen, 1930).[91] In the postwar era new auto showrooms were more commonly constructed in the outer boroughs and suburbs than in Manhattan. But the stretch of Broadway in the Fifties retained its traditional identity as automobile row until General Motors left for the Grand Army Plaza in 1968 and Ford, which had offices and a showroom designed by Walter Dorwin Teague (1938) at 1710 Broadway,[92] moved in 1972 to a grossly proportioned, glass-clad, twenty-story, 460,000-square-foot building designed by the Eggers Partnership on the northeast corner of Fifty-seventh Street and Eleventh Avenue.[93] The new GM Building included a large showroom, but its design had an unfortunate quality of glamour gone awry (see chapter 5). Frank Lloyd Wright's design for Maximilian Hoffman's showroom (1954), which was intended for Jaguar but by the time of its opening was a showcase for Porsche and BMW, was similarly unsuccessful.[94] Squeezed into a low-ceilinged retail space at the north end of Emery Roth & Sons' 430 Park Avenue, the showroom lacked a strong presence despite the use of a turntable and the suggestion of a Guggenheim-like ramp.

The design of high-end emporiums catering to personal grooming seemed to capture the mood, and extravagant tastes, of both the well-to-do clientele and the city at large. While some of New York's most interesting early examples of Modernist design were hair salons, such as William Lescaze's Maison Bertie (1928), at 695 Fifth Avenue, Vahan Hagopian's Lantieri (1934), at 2123 Broadway, and Harold E. Sterner's Helena Rubinstein Salon (1937), at 715 Fifth Avenue, in the postwar era there was a return to traditional design.[95] Decorated by William Pahlmann, the extraordinary Prince Matchabelli Crown Room, at 711 Fifth Avenue, featured murals by Howard Pederson, dramatic lighting by Abe Feder, elaborate antique tables and objets d'art, tufted settees and painted, abstracted versions of eighteenth-century English breakfronts.[96]

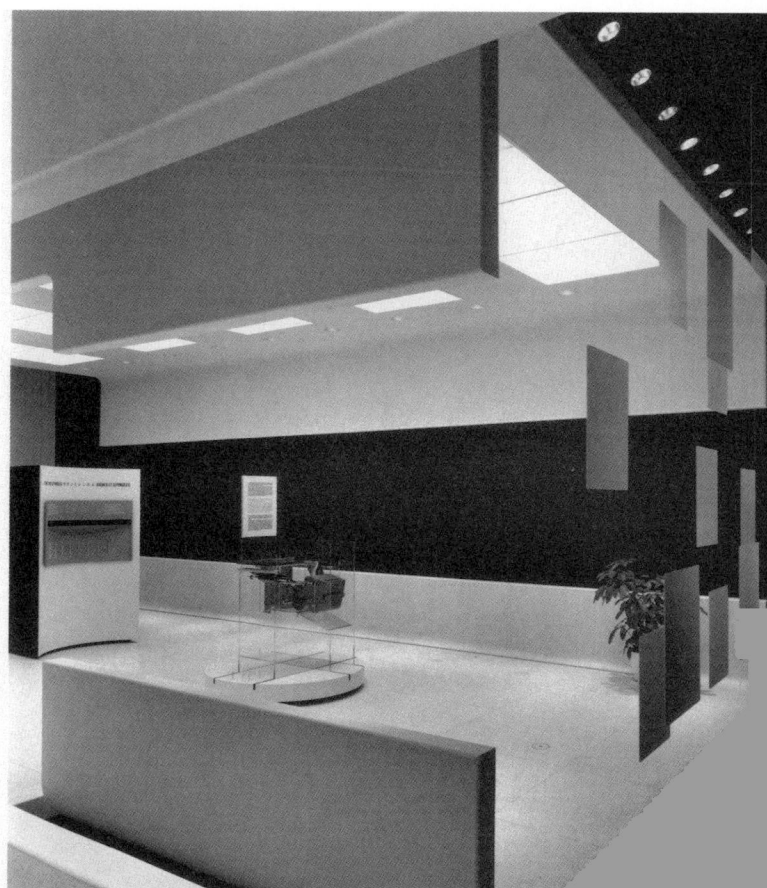

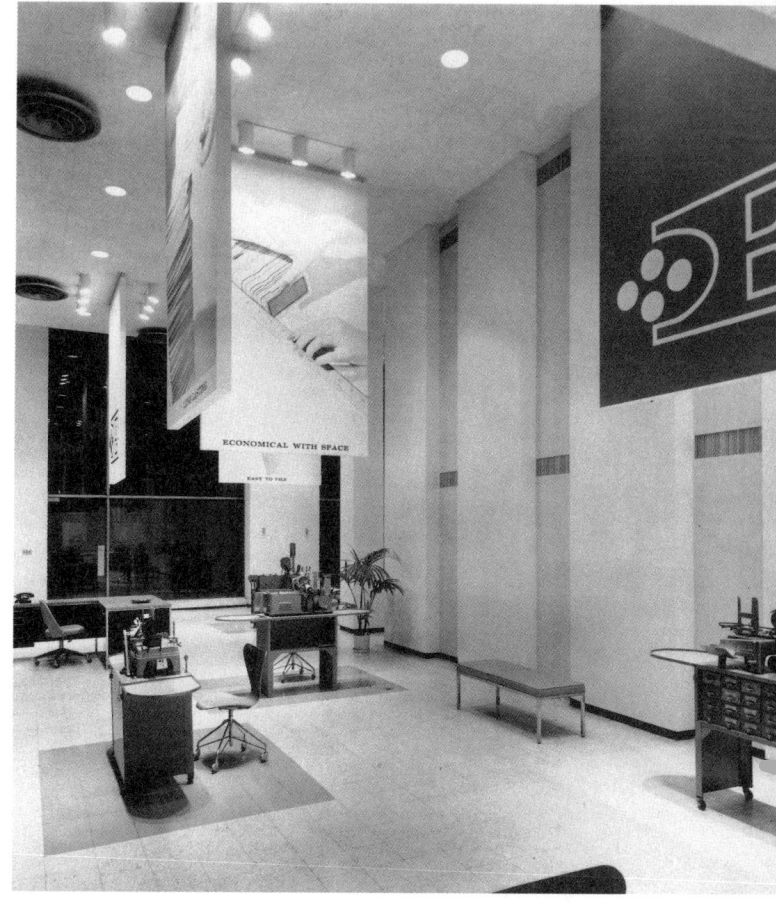

593

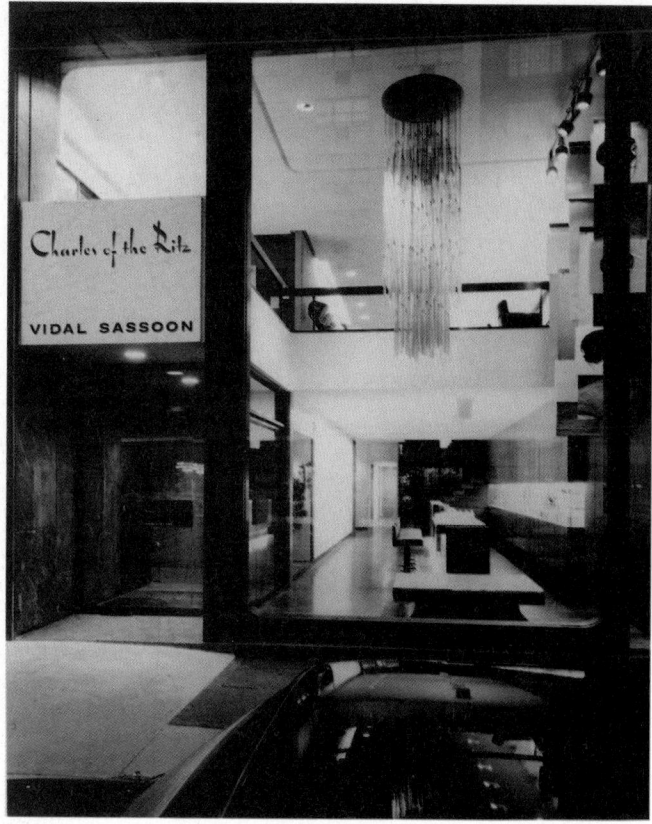

Above: Vidal Sassoon/Charles of the Ritz, 803 Madison Avenue. Gordon and Ursula Bowyer, 1965. Schnall. VDSS

Top right: Paraphernalia, 28 Greenwich Avenue. Ulrich Franzen, 1966. Entrance area with spotlit pedestal displays. UF

Center right: Paraphernalia, 659 Lexington Avenue. Ulrich Franzen, 1969. Projection system with images displayed on rear wall. UF

Bottom right: Paraphernalia, 659 Lexington Avenue. Clothing racks on sales floor. UF

Top far right: Paraphernalia logo. Ulrich Franzen, 1966. UF

Center far right: Paraphernalia, 795 Madison Avenue. Ulrich Franzen, 1966. Tractor seat. UF

Bottom far right: Paraphernalia, 659 Lexington Avenue. Plan. UF

The stylish but vulgar opulence exemplified by Prince Matchabelli reached its apogee in the House of Revlon (1960), the last of the great salons to be built before hair went natural in the late 1960s.[97] Located in a storefront of the Gotham Hotel (Hiss & Weekes, 1905) at 2 West Fifty-fifth Street, the House of Revlon was entered off Fifth Avenue through a black-granite-framed portal that reached as high as the hotel's third floor.[98] A glowing, backlit pyramidal glass canopy and two clusters of overscaled bronze carriage lanterns called further attention to the shop's presence, as did flanking windows shaded by red leather awnings welted with gold rope. The salon was decorated by Barbara Dorn, who worked closely with the company's owner, Charles Revson, to create a salon with "all the luxuries and niceties women always look for in beauty shops but can never find."[99] These included a therapeutic pool for pedicures, attractive hair driers that disappeared into the ceiling when not in use, a sunken Roman bath, crystal chandeliers, marble counters, and fine furniture selected to go with the color scheme of pink, gold, champagne and white, which the designer believed was "vibrant and eternal."[100]

Upon entering the House of Revlon, patrons encountered a boutique where the company's products were sold; the space was modeled on a shop of the Directoire period. They then moved into the oval, Empire-style reception room, which opened to the "Touch of Genius Pompeiian Plaza," a Roman atrium with a narrow, flower-strewn, rill-like foot-soaking pool, vaulted over by a shallow ceiling. Fluted columns with specially designed bases and capitals lined the edges of the narrow pool; curtains running between the columns provided privacy for patrons. The twenty setting and styling areas were also divided into cubicles, but the drying room was kept a big open space. The editors of Time magazine were dismissive of the design: "The U.S.'s latest most preposterous beauty shop is a designer's powder-puffed version of what Pompeii would have looked like if Revlon had been running things before Vesuvius decided to end it all."[101]

With the arrival in 1965 of the British stylist Vidal Sassoon, not only did the elaborate hairstyles of the 1950s and 1960s vanish but also the outrageous styling of the hair salons themselves. Sassoon's first salon, opened in association with Charles of the Ritz, at 803 Madison Avenue, was designed by Gordon and Ursula Bowyer, architects who had designed Sassoon's London salon in Grosvenor House.[102] A professed admirer of Mies van der Rohe and Eero Saarinen, Sassoon believed that "a building should complement what you're trying to do."[103] To match the severe, almost masculine hairstyles Sassoon favored, the Bowyers used black, dark brown and beige for the sleek surfaces of the salon. They exposed the space to public view through a two-story plate-glass window set in a heavy metal frame that was curved at the corners, like the frames Philip Johnson had designed for his recently opened Museum of Modern Art addition (see chapter 5). The Bowyers surrounded the window and the adjoining recessed entrance portal with dark gray natural-cleft Buckingham slate, which extended inside for ten feet. Large-scale photographs and silk banners in yellow and gold were the principal decoration on the interior, and a white marble sign incised with gold letters distinguished the exterior.

By 1966 Sassoon's would seem very staid compared with the pulsating colors and glittering effects of the high-fashion boutiques located nearby on Madison Avenue. Among these was Latinas, at 769 Madison Avenue, designed by Bill Hock, a former cabinetmaker turned fashion designer, who covered the

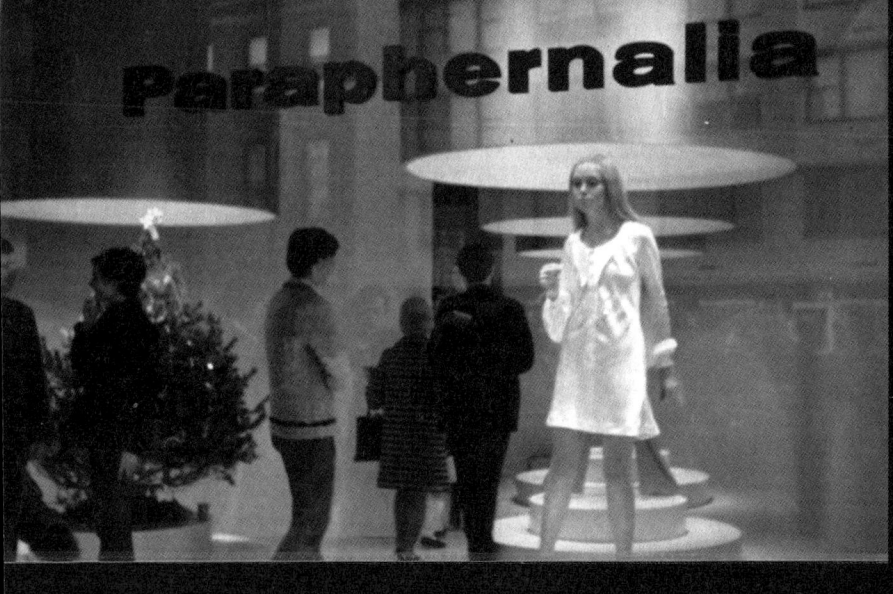

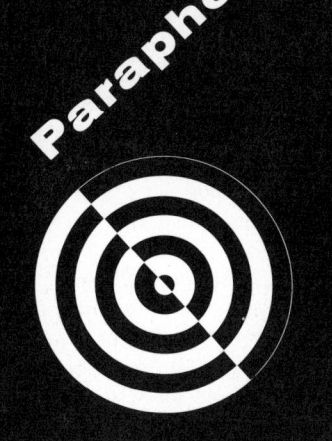

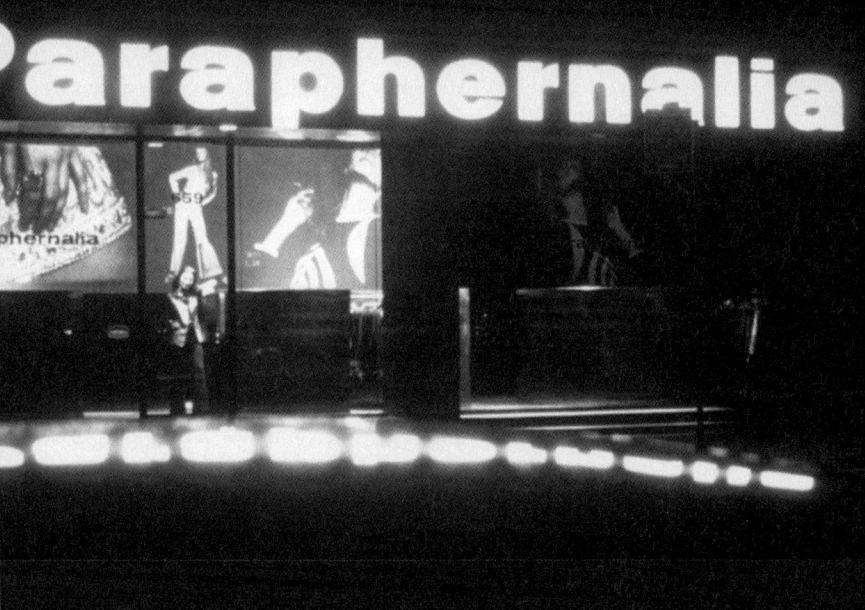

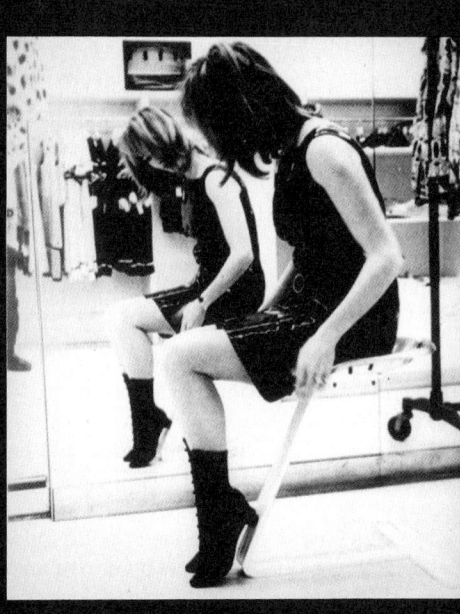

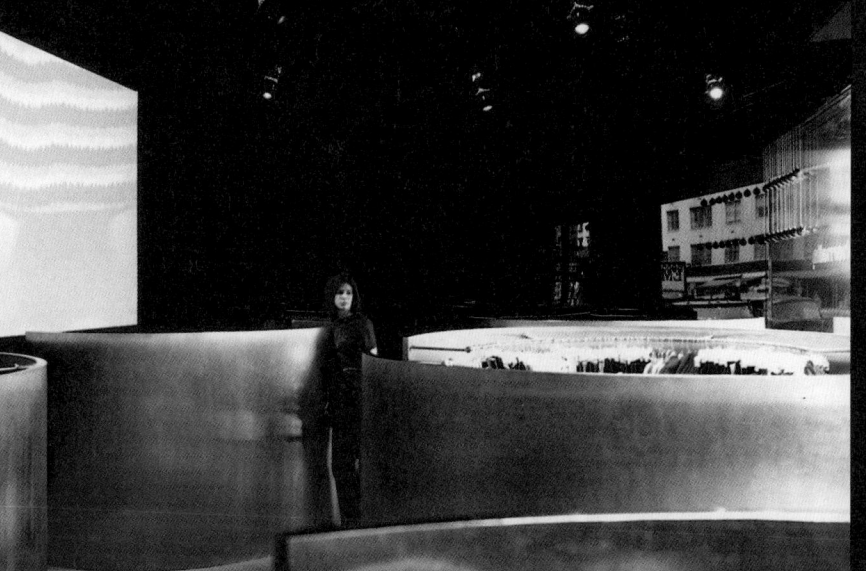

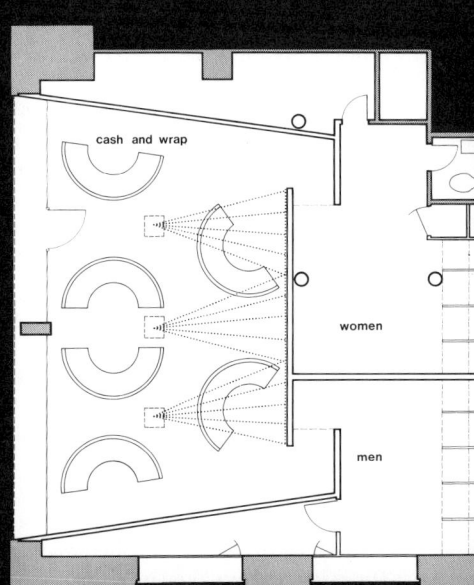

entry doors with "California Baby Moons" (standard hot-rod hubcaps).[104] The series of shops designed by the architect Ulrich Franzen for the nationwide boutique chain Paraphernalia included one at 795 Madison Avenue (1966) that Norval White and Elliot Willensky described as "a local center of jet-set fashion. A wood shell (barrel vault) recalls and continues, in friendly fashion, the brick-arched facade. Tractor seats for the weary, or those being adorned."[105] Paraphernalia specialized in cheap, trendy women's clothes, a controversial example of which was the heavily promoted "Nun's minidress" designed for the chain by Walter Holmes; in 1968 they added a men's line.[106] Franzen designed a second shop for Paraphernalia in 1966 in the West Village at 28 Greenwich Avenue. This store combined an entry area featuring spotlit pedestal displays, "all stark and uptown gallery-like," according to White and Willensky, with a back room "crammed with kicky boutique fashions, swinging chicks with boy friends, as well as curious grandmother types."[107]

In 1969 Franzen designed a much larger facility for Paraphernalia in midtown at 659 Lexington Avenue that was most notable for the slide-projector system, devised by Menell Associates, used to advertise its wares.[108] C. Ray Smith described the startling scene:

> Inside, all attention is focused on the rear wall: a projection screen on which splashily colored projections are flashed from three carousel units mounted overhead behind the exterior sign. . . . The side walls are sheathed in panels of shiny black acrylic plastic; the front window has minimal black framing and is set back from the building line so that the side walls seem to continue through the nearly invisible glass. A structural column is sheathed in black aluminum. The ceiling is black; the carpeting is dark tan, continuing the color of sidewalk into the interior.[109]

Six stainless-steel, four-and-a-half-foot-high half-circles, echoing the store's target logo, designed by Franzen, were positioned to hide the functions of the merchandise and service desks they contained. Franzen explained the appeal of the design: "The projected images, rather than the merchandise in the store, become the enticement, provide the impulse to look and to come in. Everything was done to create an environment and an ambience in which the people and the projections are the performance, in which the customers project themselves into a different context, into the ambience of a discothèque."[110] On the outside, the store's name was spelled out over the entrance in prominent white letters affixed to a black background. The letters were originally illuminated in a red and white chase sequence, but when the shop next door imitated the idea, Franzen lit the letters in an unblinking red. The architect Daniel Solomon saw the design of the store as a harbinger of things to come: "Franzen's Paraphernalia store with its architecturally scaled projections of clothing is probably the most fashion influenced space ever designed by a major architect. Electric architecture, with space defined by projections or light, is coming to be an everyday form of commercial building."[111]

Abracadabra (1967), at 243 East Sixtieth Street, designed by a display director who wanted anonymity, featured Marsha Weintraub's line of miniskirted women's clothing hung at the front of the shop in a mazelike area of mirrors and fluorescent lights attached to perforated metal columns that pulsated to a flicker flash sequence like the running lights on theater marquees. According to Abracadabra's lighting consultant, Marvin Gelman, "There is a tremendous swing-over today in all specialty shops to dramatic, theatrical, psychedelic lighting."[112] Peter

Gluck's Contessina Boutique (1967), at 798 Madison Avenue, reserved some of its more spectacular lighting effects for the dressing rooms, where bare bulbs were part of the clothes hooks.[113]

By 1969 the new bold, graphic approach to design dubbed "supermannerism" by C. Ray Smith, an editor of *Progressive Architecture*, could be seen in stores all over town. It was evident in two designs by Alan Buchsbaum: a modest neighborhood greeting card shop, the Paper Poppy, in upper Manhattan at 4801 Broadway and Dyckman Street, designed in association with Irene Grabowich, and Lucidity, a shop at 775 Madison Avenue that featured only objects made of plastic, a total repudiation of the craft aesthetic favored in typical high-style design shops such as D/R International (see above).[114] Supermannerism even invaded one of the model rooms designed by Barbara D'Arcy at Bloomingdale's, where color stripes streaked across a floor, over a chest of drawers, and up one wall and culminated in arrows.

The most elaborate demonstration of the new sensibility was a store called On 1st (1968), at 1159 First Avenue.[115] Conceived and masterminded by the photographer Bert Stern, it occupied the ground-floor shop and basement level of a bland brick thirty-five-story apartment house, the St. Tropez (Brown & Guenther, 1965), at 340 East Sixty-fourth Street, distinguished only by the fact that it was the city's first condominium.[116] To announce the shop, Stern, working with the artist Sven Lukin, spelled out the store's name in story-high letters; the "1st" was painted on the building's facade, but the letters "o" and "n" were three-dimensional. The shop's window, which contained nine closed-circuit television screens that showed changing views of the merchandise and customer activity inside, was recessed in the hollow of the "o," while the shop's doors were set between the uprights of the lower-case "n." The storefront graphics were illuminated at night to flash 580 red, green, blue and yellow incandescent bulbs in a preset series of primary, mixed color and pure white combinations. In designing both exterior and interior, Stern worked with a group called the American Thought Combine, Inc., which consisted of an architect, an art director, a physicist, a psychologist and light-and-sound technicians.

Inside, in a single rectangular room covered entirely with dark blue carpet and filled with flashing patterns and bouncing light, all meeting points between planes were rounded in coves to help destroy any sense of spatial boundary. As C. Ray Smith put it, the effect of the room was to render "scale and space . . . ambivalent, contradictory, and especially when the sound system [was] in orbit, completely disorienting. . . . Beams of lights pierce the gloom to single out objects in their weightlessness."[117] In this environment shoppers were offered such items as paper plates designed by the artist Gerald Laing, "wallpaper" silkscreened on silver Mylar by the painter Roy Lichtenstein, and unusual furniture, some of it designed by artists. A circular stair led to the downstairs shop, where clothes designed by artists were sold: scarves by the artists Jack Youngerman, Richard Anuskiewicz and Robert Indiana; dresses by Ken Scott and others. In this red-carpeted room, exposed concrete-block walls and exposed basement pipes were painted in horizontal stripes that rose vertically through the color spectrum from bright red to violet on the ceiling, where sparkling lights were hung from wires colored to match. "If this shop isn't the blast off," Smith concluded, "you'd better strap yourself in for the real thing."[118]

At the same time that supermannerism was making its greatest impact, the appetite for luxury goods seemed to grow, attracting many foreign retailers to the New York market. Many of these, particularly Italians, saw a New York location—either on upper Fifth or upper Madison avenues—as an important status symbol if not necessarily a significant source of profits.[119] The new foreign boutiques displayed an aesthetic of cool refinement that had been presaged by Sassoon's. It could be seen in the conventional Modernism of Yves Saint Laurent's Rive Gauche boutique (1969), at 855 Madison Avenue, designed by Isabelle Heby in association with Allen Cottrell,[120] or in the more interesting reconstruction of the brownstone at 801 Madison Avenue to accommodate the Italian designer Valentino (1970).[121] After completely gutting the eighteen-foot-wide, five-story brownstone, the Milanese architect Aldo Jacober, working with Cristina Annoni, Fiorella Butti, George Wasser and Carl Schwartz, used rounded glass and mirrors to create the impression of a five-story cylinder on the facade. At the third- and fourth-floor levels, the aluminum-trimmed facade was encased in panels of brown porcelain enamel. Inside, rounded walls, molded ceilings and the liberal use of mirrors, vinyl and chrome continued the dramatic effect. In 1974 Ferragamo, the Italian shoe designer, took over the ground-floor space formerly occupied by the Fiberglas showroom in the Corning Glass Building (see above).[122] The architects Giancarlo and Luigi Bicocchi and Roberto Monsani took advantage of the building's slick curtain wall by opening the interior to it, simply dividing the room into different areas with triangular white plastic-laminate partitions that created a sense of one single space. This shop was a far cry from the pulsating individualism that had rocked the design world only five years before.

Most department stores were slow to adapt to the new tastes of consumers for more individualized shops, but not Henri Bendel, the exclusive specialty department store at 10 West Fifty-seventh Street (Henry Otis Chapman, 1912).[123] Never a force on the scale of Saks or Bonwit's, Bendel's was transformed by Geraldine Stutz, who at age thirty-three had become the store's president in 1957. "It is my job to edit Bendel," said Stutz, whose background was more in fashion journalism than in merchandising.[124] The prevailing wisdom at the time was that the first floor of a store was to be kept wide open to lure the customer, an idea that Morris Ketchum, Jr., and other designers had borrowed from department stores and adapted to great commercial advantage for small shops beginning in the early 1940s. Stutz's innovation, the Street of Shops, ran counter to this trend, breaking down the department store into small, boutiquelike departments that were individualistic and introspective. Stutz felt that, rather than providing glimpses of the merchandise itself, each department needed to create a first impression for the shopper that consisted of an architectural or at least graphic representation of the character of the merchandise. The Street of Shops, which filled the main floor at Bendel's, and the numerous boutiques that were established on its upper floors returned the drama of stylish decor to large-scale retailing. Stutz hired talented interior decorators, including Edward Zajac and Richard Callahan, who were responsible for Bendel's Fancy on the second floor.[125]

Bendel's own store designer, McKim Glazebrook, created the store's new beauty salon (1965), intended to be the first phase of a "beauty floor" that would include exercise and steam rooms.[126] Dissatisfied with traditional American beauty salon designs, Stutz traveled throughout Europe searching for prototypes. "Slice it anyway you like," she said, "in all the years I've been sitting in those wretched salons, it all added up to one big agony. . . . So I had the hair shampooed off my head in Rome, London, Paris . . . to see what the truly great salons are like." Glazebrook responded to her request for "something eternally

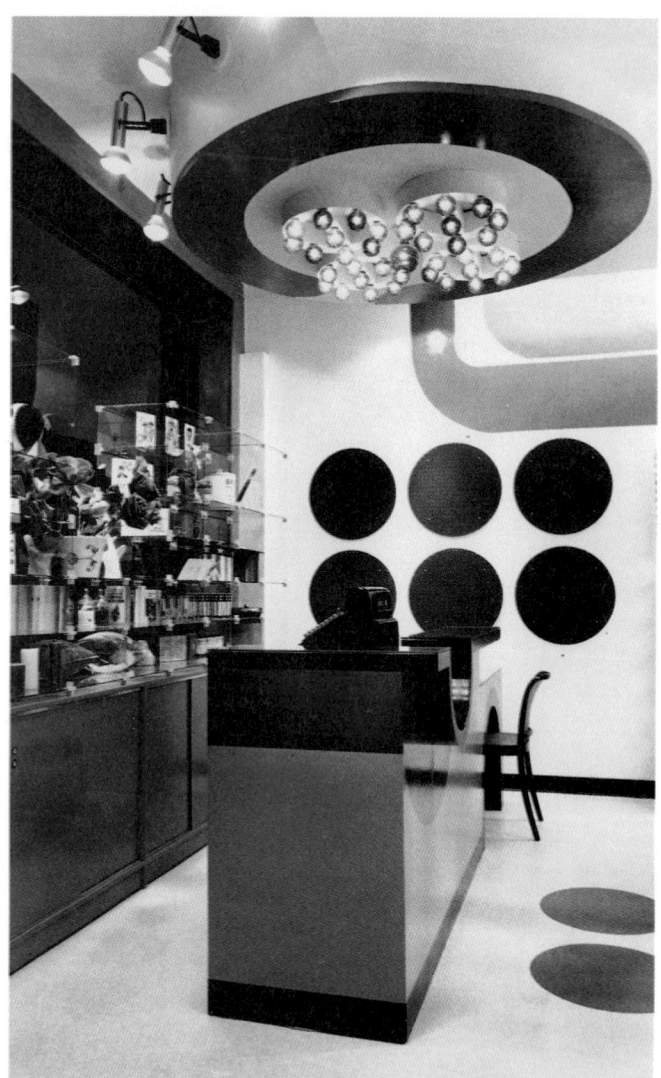

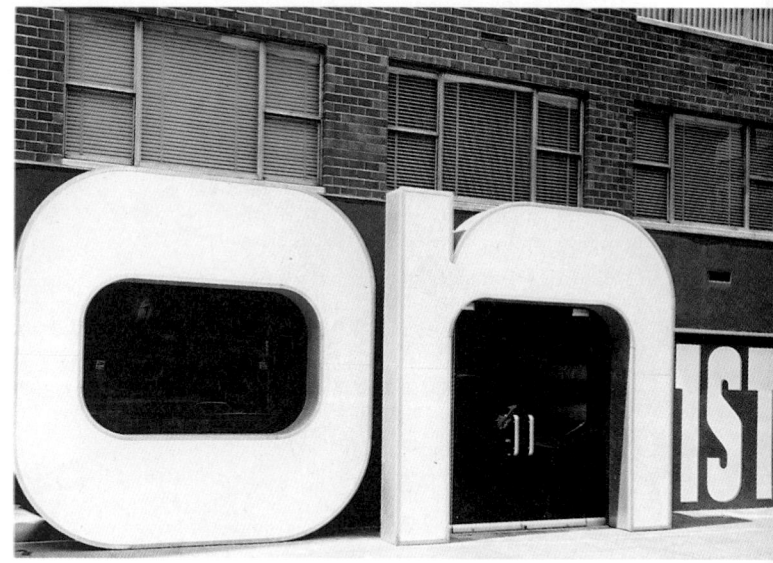

Top: Paper Poppy, 4801 Broadway. Alan Buchsbaum in association with Irene Grabowich, 1969. View to the west. Hujar. AB

Bottom: On 1st, 1159 First Avenue. Bert Stern, Sven Lukin and American Thought Combine, Inc., 1968. Stern. BST

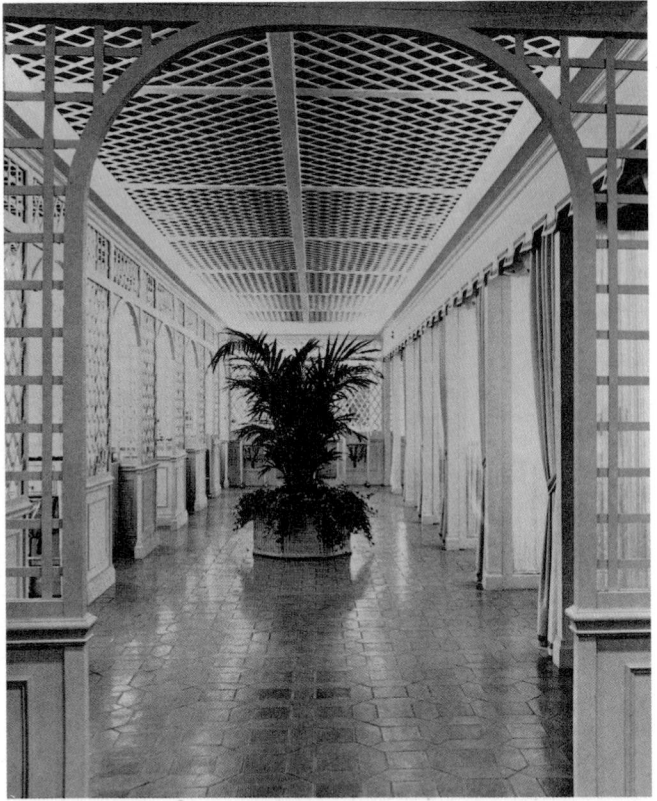

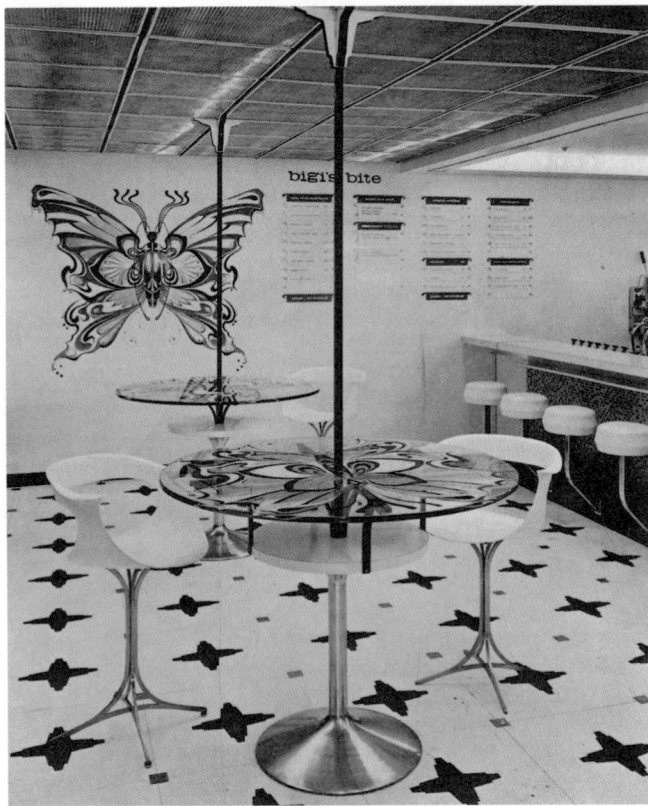

Top: Beauty salon, Henri Bendel, 10 West Fifty-seventh Street. McKim Glazebrook, 1965. Menard. IN. CU

Bottom: Bigi's Bite, Bergdorf Goodman, west side of Fifth Avenue, West Fifty-seventh to West Fifty-eighth Street. Tom Lee, 1969. Fullerton. IN. CU

sunny and springlike" by creating an *orangerie*—a pavilion of green and apricot latticework complete with terra-cotta flooring, chintz and gauze drapery, wicker furniture and potted plants. Glazebrook's scheme even extended to the design of the sinks and hair driers. Stutz approved of the results. "You see, everybody is comfortable on our great big summer porch," she remarked. "It's all here but the crickets."[127]

Inspired by Stutz's approach at Bendel's, the larger established retailers began to relearn the lessons they had forgotten, that presentation was as much a part of retailing as the merchandise itself. Bonwit Teller, which since 1930 had occupied space designed by Ely Jacques Kahn in the former Stewart & Company Building (Warren & Wetmore, 1929), on the northeast corner of Fifth Avenue and East Fifty-sixth Street, quickly added a number of boutiques, including the B. H. Wragge Room, designed by Sydney Wragge, the clothing designer, and Harry Hinson, Bonwit's director of store planning.[128] Replete with sculpture by Eduardo Paolozzi and Ernest Trova and classic furniture by Marcel Breuer, the shop exuded the machismo of much Modernist design of the period in a manner that was perhaps a bit strong for a dress shop. Working along the same lines, Billy McCarty more appropriately designed the store's Vidal Sassoon barber shop, seeking to evoke a "twenty-first-century men's club" with leather chairs, a lot of polished stainless steel and a dark chocolate and terra-cotta palette.[129] Yet none of these seemed to turn the store's financial tide.

In what was to prove a last-ditch effort to save the day with design, the young firm of Walker/Grad was hired in 1976 to transform the store's ground floor, a room that had remained virtually unchanged since Bonwit's had taken over the building.[130] Ken Walker had already helped redesign Bendel's Fifty-seventh Street shopfront and had designed their very successful "Shoe Biz" boutique, reviving the look of the late 1920s and early 1930s, when Bendel's and Bonwit's were in their heyday.[131] In an effort to enliven Kahn's design, Walker added mirrors on the columns, mirrors with half-round oak strips along the walls and new glass display cases that sat on bases made of the same oak. Paul Goldberger acknowledged that Walker's redesign was an improvement but felt that he didn't go far enough: "The problem is not in the basic concept, just in the fact that the design is perhaps a bit more spartan than it need be."[132] Whatever advantage Bonwit's received from its new ground floor was not enough to help the company's finances. In 1979 Bonwit Teller's parent company, Genesco Inc., sold the building to the developer Donald J. Trump.[133] The editors of the *New York Times* mourned: "Bonwit's lost its suave image when trendiness took over. . . . In this day of the boutique, a department store must know its onions—or its caviar—as well as its leather jeans, and, like Bendel's, out-boutique all the rest. Bonwit's helped make the area around 56th and Fifth the shopping mecca of the world. But real estate values are less ephemeral than fashion."[134]

Bergdorf Goodman (Buchman & Kahn, 1928), on the west side of Fifth Avenue between West Fifty-seventh and West Fifty-eighth streets, had survived the so-called youthquake of the 1960s not only by catering to an increasingly affluent older clientele but also by concentrating on those youngsters who wanted the assurance of the Bergdorf name. As early as 1955 it opened a boutique called Miss Bergdorf, designed by S. S. Silver Interiors.[135] The 10,000-square-foot space, formerly occupied by administrative offices, was divided into a series of intimately scaled departments that were traditionally appointed, complete with Louis XVI and Directoire furniture, silk wallcovering with a Chinese floral pattern and antique chandeliers. The store's management had expected the department to do, at best, $750,000 of business a year. A decade after its inception, Miss Bergdorf made $3 million in a year and was the store's most lucrative department.

So successful was Miss Bergdorf in bringing customers into the once intimidatingly highbrow store that in 1966 it opened Bigi, catering to an even younger and more daring clientele.[136] If Miss Bergdorf's customers ranged "from 18-year-old sophisticates to 80-year-old Edna Ferber," as Marilyn Bender, writing in the *New York Times*, said, Bigi was aimed at twelve- to seventeen-year-olds, as well as "some of those women who owe their nymphet figures to diet and exercise."[137] Bergdorf's hired the designer Tom Lee to create a "mod" environment, with a black-and-white vinyl tile floor, a mirror-finished gridded ceiling and exposed incandescent light bulbs. Lee continued the theme in the Bigi's Bite snack bar of 1969.[138]

In 1968 Bergdorf's doubled its selling space by taking over three neighboring buildings on the northwest corner of Fifth Avenue and West Fifty-seventh Street, 742 and 744 Fifth Avenue and 1 West Fifty-seventh Street, which it owned and had formerly leased to a specialty shop, the Tailored Woman.[139] In a redesign by the architect Perry Cashmore, with the store's planner, C. J. Breyer Associates, serving as coordinator of the design, the store was opened up to provide more spacious selling areas, particularly for the men's departments, and to accommodate traffic patterns that resulted from a new entrance on Fifty-seventh Street. The store's exterior underwent no significant changes.

Another venerable department store that remodeled to keep pace was Lord & Taylor (Starrett & Van Vleck, 1914), on the northwest corner of Fifth Avenue and Thirty-eighth Street.[140] In 1976 Ron Pavlik completed a redesign of Lord & Taylor's monumentally scaled ground floor, but he retained the basic structure because, as the designer stated, "you just could never replace that ceiling today."[141] Pavlik did, however, replace the wood parquet floor with travertine and the display counters with new cases made of travertine, glass and chrome. The room's already grand proportions seemed enlarged by bronze mirrors that ran around the perimeter and segmented mirrors that covered the room's grid of square columns. Perimeter shops were remodeled with dropped ceilings; walls were treated with a flexible system of suede-covered plywood slats that could accommodate changing display arrangements. Paul Goldberger, who thought that the main floor of Lord & Taylor was "one of New York's finest selling spaces," disliked the redesign intensely:

> The columns are mirrored (but in strips, not single panes of glass, as at Bonwit's), the floor is lit with the intensity and subtlety of a baseball stadium and there are . . . potted palms all over the place. All this has cost Lord & Taylor the dignity and graciousness for which it has always been known. Mirrors, mirrors everywhere—even between the elevators, where they overlap some of the old ornamentation—make the place look shiny and trendy, but it is more cheap glitter than genuine elegance.[142]

In the late 1970s the rivalry among New York's department stores and their competition with boutiques was vividly played out in the larger stores' display windows. Picking up on Salvador Dalí's 1939 windows for Bonwit Teller,[143] these new windows married a surrealist sensibility with topical black humor to become, as Rosemary Kent wrote in *New York* magazine, "a kind of street theater."[144] In 1973 Bendel's hired twenty-five-year-old Robert Currie, who had previously designed display windows for the Norma Kamali boutique on Madison Avenue but had no formal training as a designer.[145] In a series of windows that alternately confused, shocked and delighted observers, Currie put

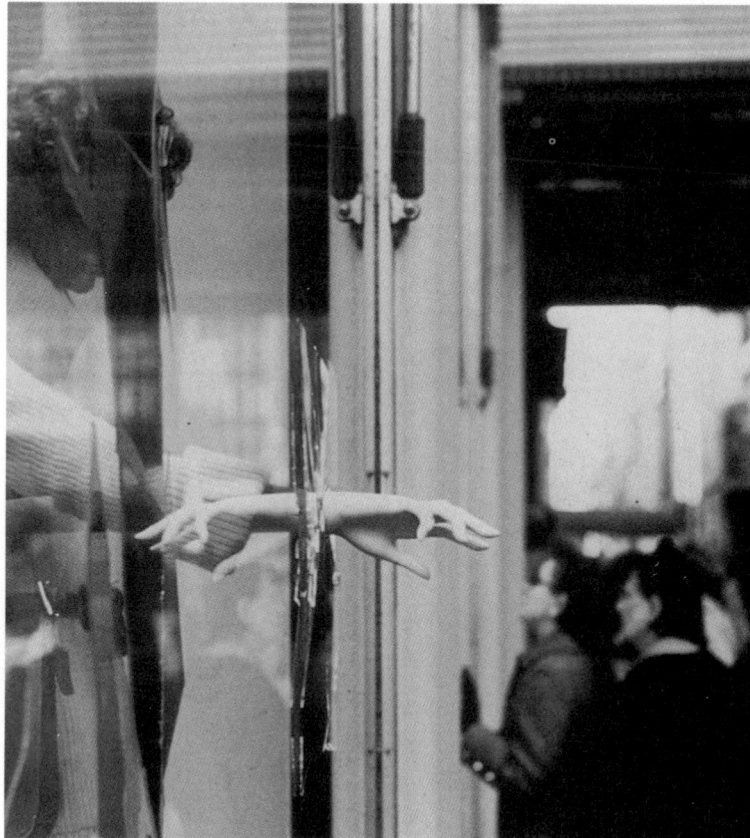

Bonwit Teller display window, northeast corner of Fifth Avenue and East Fifty-sixth Street. Lynn Hershman, 1976. ©Lynn Hershman, Courtesy Robert Koch Gallery, San Francisco. RKG

high-fashion mannequins into a variety of unlikely situations: snooty, Upper East Side types walking their pet fish; a deadly drama in which the corpse on the floor apparently chose the wrong vial; dressy ladies passing the time at a lesbian bar; well-heeled women standing amid piles of garbage. In a window titled "Home on the Range" and set in a kitchen, spaghetti-haired women in loungewear frolicked as champagne chilled in the background. Although Stutz gave Currie carte blanche, when the designer proposed a funeral scene complete with casket, she replied, "Over my dead body."[146]

Not to be outdone, Bloomingdale's hired Harlem-born Candy Pratts, who, like Currie, was young and without formal design training, although she had briefly studied merchandising at the Fashion Institute of Technology.[147] Pratts's window designs included a naked woman in a bathtub disappearing under a layer of sponges; a scantily clad man in a bathroom glimpsed through a partially open door; a drug bust being conducted in a U.S. Customs office; and a group of women playing dress-up.

At Bonwit Teller, the artist Lynn Hershman spent two years negotiating with the store's management before receiving approval for her window displays.[148] In one design, enormous disembodied mouths talked about the future while live speakers answered questions from passersby. Ultimately, the dimensions of a store window proved too confining: on October 28, 1976, a mannequin named Bonnie appeared to be breaking the glass of one of the store's Fifty-sixth Street windows, and for the following five days she could be seen in Central Park, at the Metropolitan Museum of Art, in a subway station and in SoHo talking to observers by way of a hidden cassette recorder.

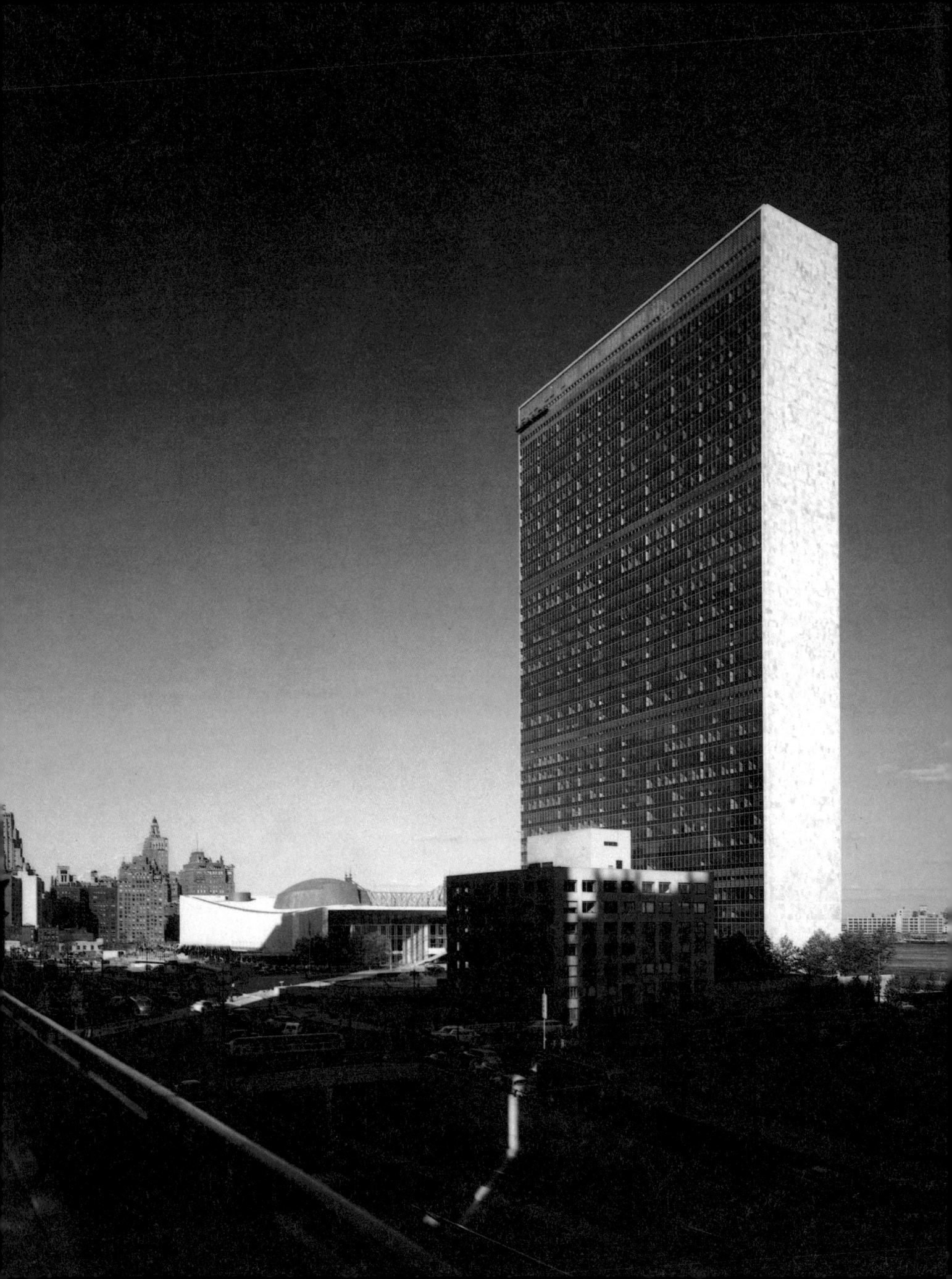

Chapter 7

United Nations

Along the East River, from the razed slaughterhouses of Turtle Bay, as though in a race with the spectral flight of planes, men are carving out the permanent headquarters of the United Nations— the greatest housing project of them all. In its stride, New York takes on one more interior city, to shelter, this time, all governments, and to clear the slum called war. New York is not a capital city—it is not a national capital or a state capital. But it is by way of becoming the capital of the world.
—E. B. White, 1949[1]

Following in the wake of the failed League of Nations (1919–46), which the United States never joined, the United Nations was established in 1945 to maintain international peace and promote cooperation in solving international economic, social and humanitarian problems.[2] The title "United Nations," coined by President Franklin Delano Roosevelt in 1941 to describe the Allied powers, was first officially used on January 1, 1942, when twenty-six governments signed a resolution pledging to continue the war effort. This event was commemorated in the United States when the flags of the signing nations were flown at Rockefeller Center. In a 1945 meeting in San Francisco, fifty-one member nations signed the U.N. Charter, the organization's governing treaty.

Early in 1946, at a United Nations General Assembly meeting in London, the Preparatory Commission determined that the new organization's international headquarters would be located in the United States and went on to establish the Permanent Headquarters Committee to consider both site and architecture. Consisting of delegates from all the member countries and led by Dr. Eduardo Zuleta Angel of Colombia as its chairman, the committee was broken up into two groups. One group, the Headquarters Commission, consisted of delegates, architects and other professional advisers who were led by Sir Angus Fletcher of Great Britain; a second group, the Committee on Sites and General Questions, was chaired by the Uruguayan

delegate, Juan Felipe Yriart. A third group, called the Headquarters Advisory Committee, was created later by the U.N.'s first secretary general, Trygve Lie, on January 2, 1947. It was chaired by former Senator Warren Austin, from Vermont, then Permanent Representative of the United States to the United Nations.

A variety of sites were considered, ranging in size from six to forty square miles and in location from New York City to Connecticut, Boston, Philadelphia and San Francisco. Robert Moses, in his capacity as City Construction Coordinator, encouraged the Permanent Headquarters Committee to locate the United Nations in Flushing Meadows Park, whose development had languished since the closing of the 1939–40 World's Fair.[3] In March 1946 the arrival of delegates, staff and journalists for the first Security Council meeting to be held in New York put a strain on the city, which was short of hotel and office space as well as permanent housing for those who would remain in New York, recently designated the interim headquarters pending a final site selection.[4] Moses succeeded in persuading Lie to use the New York City Building (Aymar Embury II, 1939), which had been built for the World's Fair, on an interim basis; it was converted in two months' time for use by the General Assembly.[5] Meanwhile, the Security Council met in the gymnasium of Hunter College's Bronx campus, which was hastily fitted out for the purpose by the architects Voorhees, Walker, Foley & Smith, who in fifteen days sheathed the rafters with acoustical tile, glued thick carpeting to the floor planks and covered the room's brick walls with 3,500 yards of sound-muffling, fire-flash fabric.[6] Later the Security Council, the Secretariat and other U.N. functions were housed in a converted manufacturing plant of the Sperry Gyroscope Company at Lake Success, nearby in Nassau County.[7] A master plan for a permanent facility in Lake Success was prepared by Clarke & Rapuano but never pursued.

As the search for a site was being conducted, the choice of an architect or architects for the new complex was also being debated. Journalists and professional groups called for an international design competition, as did many prominent architects. In the April 1946 issue of *Progressive Architecture*, the architects Ernesto Rogers (Italy), Alfred Roth (Switzerland) and the Americans John W. Root, Marcel Breuer, Morris Ketchum, Jr.,

United Nations Headquarters, First Avenue to the East River, East Forty-second to East Forty-eighth Street. Board of Design, Wallace K. Harrison, Director of Planning, 1947–52. View to the northeast. Stoller. ©ESTO

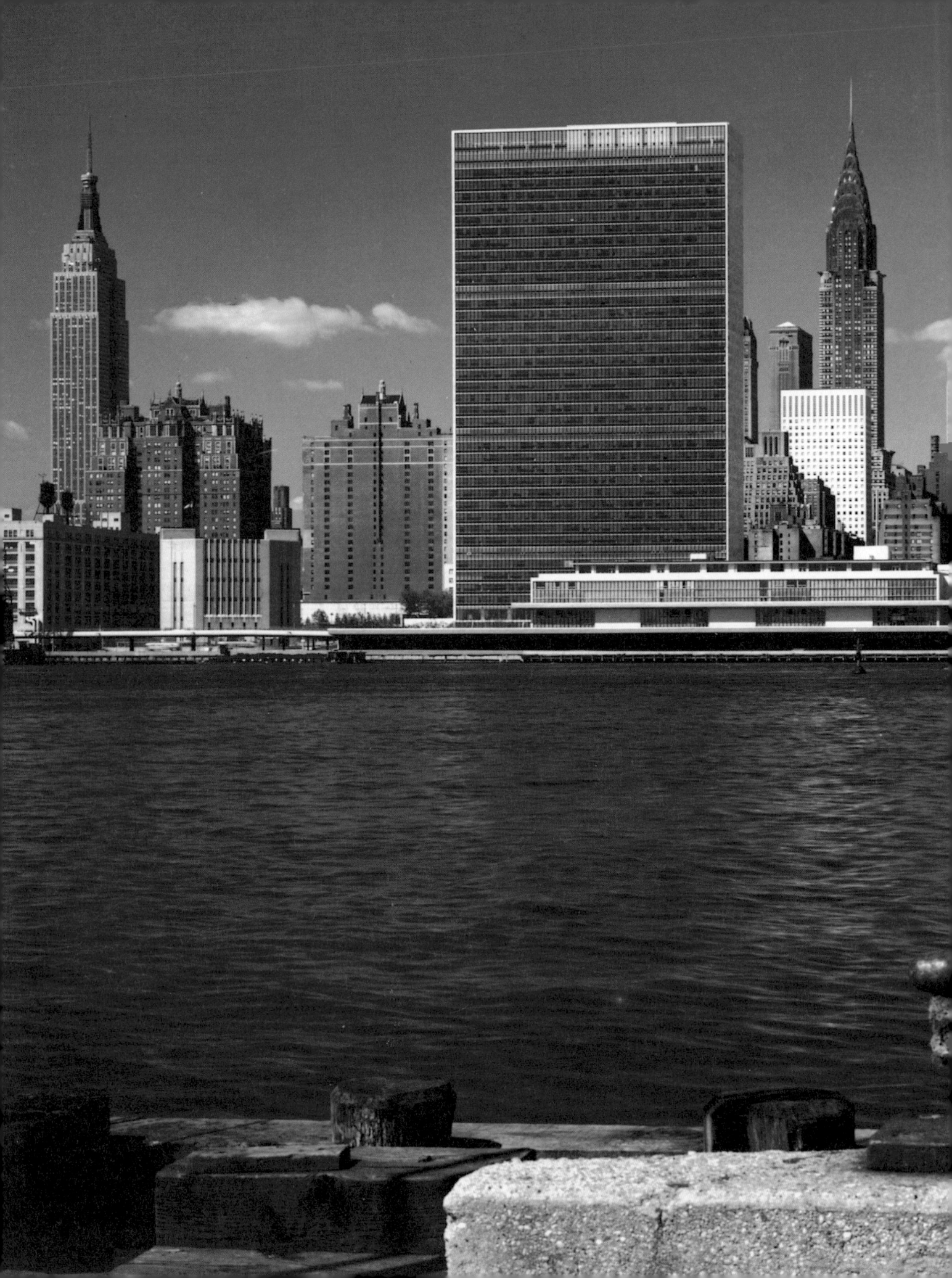

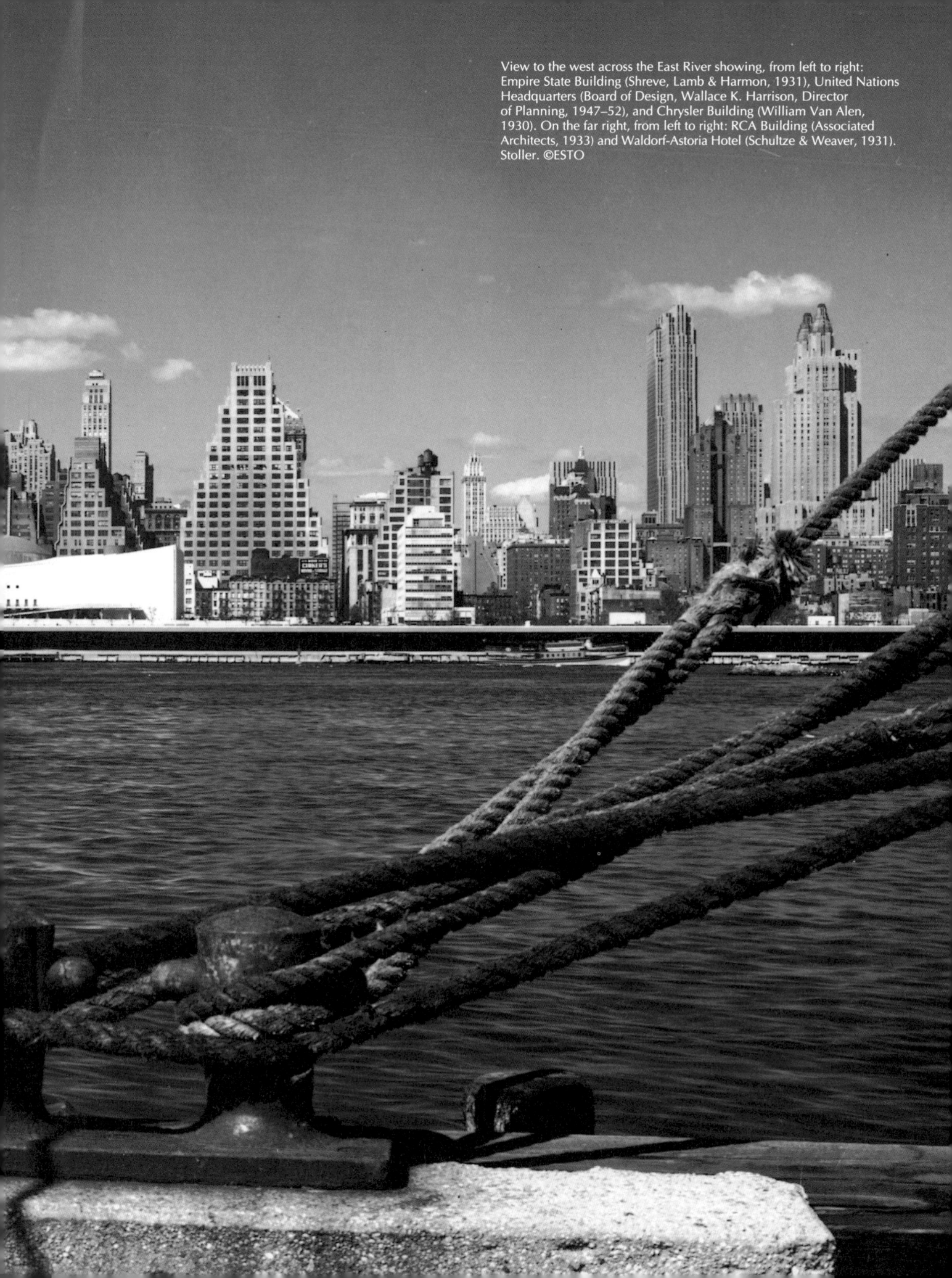

View to the west across the East River showing, from left to right:
Empire State Building (Shreve, Lamb & Harmon, 1931), United Nations
Headquarters (Board of Design, Wallace K. Harrison, Director
of Planning, 1947–52), and Chrysler Building (William Van Alen,
1930). On the far right, from left to right: RCA Building (Associated
Architects, 1933) and Waldorf-Astoria Hotel (Schultze & Weaver, 1931).
Stoller. ©ESTO

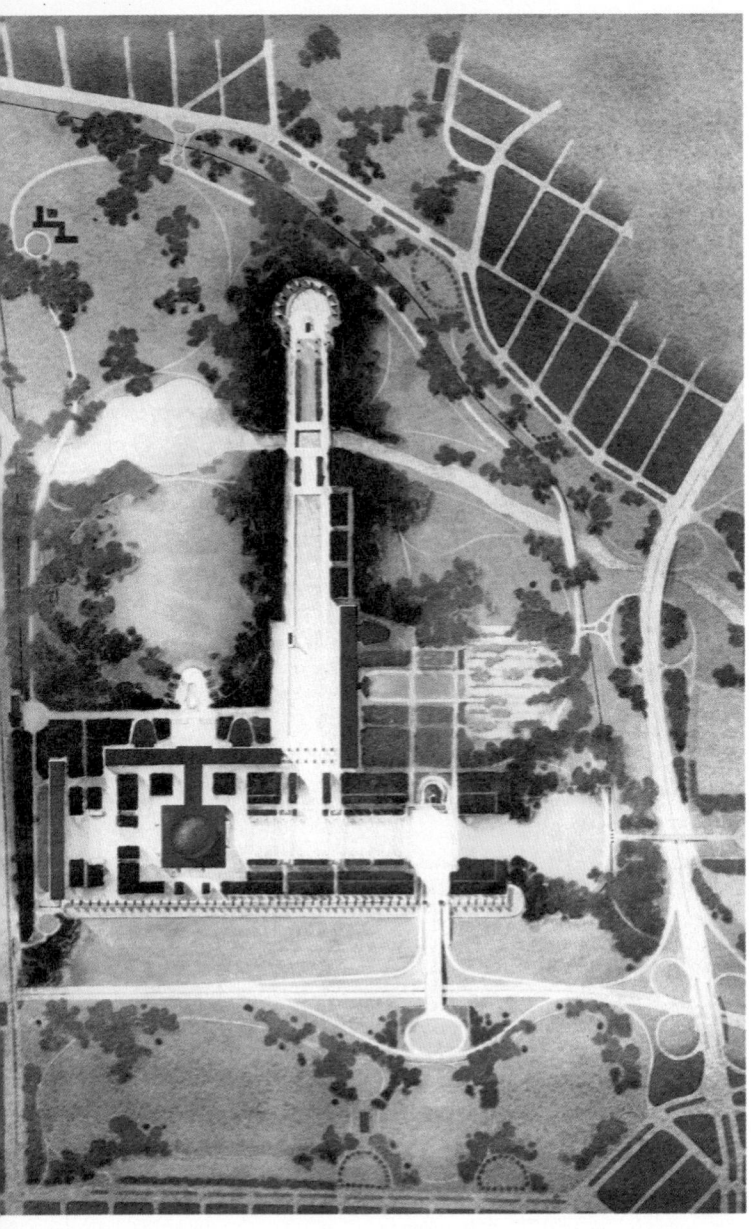

Above: Proposal for United Nations Headquarters, Lake Success, New York. Wallace K. Harrison, Aymar Embury II, Louis Skidmore, Earle Andrews and Gilmore D. Clarke, 1946. Plan. C&R

Top right: Proposal for United Nations Headquarters, Flushing Meadows, Queens. Wallace K. Harrison, Aymar Embury II, Louis Skidmore, Earle Andrews and Gilmore D. Clarke, 1946. Rendering by Hugh Ferriss of view to the northeast. CU

Bottom right: Proposal for United Nations Headquarters, Flushing Meadows, Queens. Rendering by Hugh Ferriss of central lagoon and statue depicting world peace. CU

Richard J. Neutra, Alden Dow and Ernest J. Kump submitted letters in support of a competition.[8] In addition, the trustees of the Museum of Modern Art lobbied for and offered to organize a competition. But Lewis Mumford cautioned against a competition, pointing out that the new enterprise had not even developed a functional program for its headquarters complex. For Mumford, and it would appear for many of those involved in the site selection, the "first matter to be decided [was] whether the United Nations will be served best by a small complex of buildings, such as those created at Geneva [for the League of Nations], or whether, in view of the scope and importance of this new organization, a whole urban community, resting like Washington within its own territory, must not be ultimately built."[9]

Frederick Gutheim also argued against the idea of a competition, calling instead for the creation of a permanent building committee and a permanent staff of architects. Gutheim mapped out a three-part system of management: "Obviously, there must be a chief architect. Then there must be a sizable group of principal architects. Finally, there should be many students, apprentices, draftsmen—call them what you please—to fill out the staff."[10] George Howe was one of the first practicing architects to raise a voice against the notion of a competition. In a letter to Eric Gugler, president of the American Institute of Architects, written on behalf of a group of architects and planners, Howe proposed that a strong coordinating architect be appointed—the group suggested the Hungarian-born Roland Wank, whose work with the Tennessee Valley Authority was widely admired. Of all the ideas put forward about how to go about designing the complex, Gutheim's and Howe's suggestions came closest to being acted on.

In the August 1946 edition of *Progressive Architecture*, Mumford discussed the subject of the U.N.'s future home in a preview of a paper he would soon read at a meeting of the Royal Institute of British Architects on the occasion of his receiving the Howard Memorial Medal. Mumford argued that the organization's global importance not only in the field of politics but also in terms of social conditions and culture automatically ruled out "the suggestion that the headquarters be small, inconspicuous, secluded, either lost in the urban mass of some great metropolitan area, or removed, for the sake of extra parking space, recreation grounds, and housing quarters to some suburban site within easy automotive access of a great city—as if it were an insurance company or a popular periodical." The requirements for a world organization demand "nothing less," he said, "than the building of a complete city."[11]

Mumford's proposal was bold: to make way for a new city "by a large-scale process of slum clearance, removal, and rebuilding, financed wholly by the United Nations, *within* an existing world metropolis"; to create a "balanced urban community, definitely limited in population and area, with all its land permanently owned and controlled by the United Nations, on the lines . . . of the garden city"; to use the new world center as a demonstration, in layout, design and construction, of the "very methods of cooperation we must now apply throughout the planet to preserve order, to keep the peace, to establish a decent minimum of living, and to make the maximum human use of the energies man now commands." While Mumford pointed to "a blasted city like Berlin or Leningrad" as a possible home, he acknowledged that "even in New York or Paris . . . it would not be difficult to find plenty of land, on the scale of two to three thousand acres, whose gradual clearance for a world center would immensely revitalize the whole city."[12]

By the time of his London talk, Mumford had both deepened his initial argument and reconsidered some of the more naive as-

pects of his proposal. He accepted Manhattan as an appropriate setting for the world center, suggesting that such a center might relate to New York the way Vatican City relates to Rome. More important, he strengthened his call for a grand gesture:

> We shall never do justice to the future, either politically or architecturally, if we let our imaginations be sterilized by the images of old St. Petersburg and Versailles, Karlsruhe, Washington and Whitehall. We must have something better to give the world than any of those cities have even hinted at; nor can that something better be expressed in terms of the modest suburban estate of which the present committee of the United Nations seems with pathetic modesty to be thinking. For the suburb is not a symbol of world cooperation but of romantic isolationism, of withdrawal and retreat. Whatever else the world center of the United Nations must be by way of accomplishing its political and cultural functions, it must at least be an adequate symbol.[13]

Meanwhile, as part of his effort to get the United Nations to permanently locate in Flushing Meadows, Robert Moses, acting on behalf of Mayor O'Dwyer, had assembled a blue-ribbon committee that included Nelson A. Rockefeller, Winthrop W. Aldrich, Charles Meyer, Grover Whalen, Arthur Hayes Sulzberger, Frederick H. Ecker and Thomas J. Watson. Moses also put together a team of engineers and architects including Wallace K. Harrison, Aymar Embury II, Louis Skidmore, Earle Andrews and Gilmore D. Clarke. In September 1946 this team produced plans for a headquarters complex on the site.[14] As depicted by Hugh Ferriss, Moses's scheme called for a ceremonial entrance drive leading motorists east from the Grand Central Parkway to a formal court that was the southern terminus of a monumental, pylon-bordered plaza culminating at its northern end in a domed assembly hall, located where the Federal Building (Howard L. Cheney, 1939) had been during the World's Fair.[15] The other U.N. functions were to be accommodated in two-story buildings, some of which would face a lagoon. Harrison's hand was felt strongly here: the basic arrangement was not a little like his Trylon and Perisphere for the fair, but it was somehow less compelling as an icon.[16] *Architectural Forum* said that the scheme revealed "a guileless admiration for pageantry" and was "faintly reminiscent of eighteenth century pomp." *Forum* was critical of the scheme's overly solemn tone:

> The dome of the General Assembly effectively dominates the site but the architectural simplicity of the building group as a whole is robbed of its native dignity and importance when wedded to planning and planting "in the grand manner." The theme of the United Nations is proclaimed, not by the obvious symbol of gaily fluttering flags, but by an austere row of pylons standing knee-deep in a moat-like reflecting pool. Though the solemnity of the undertaking cannot be over stressed, it seems hardly necessary to introduce the *memento mori* note struck by these masonry piers in their resemblance to . . . cenotaphs.[17]

In October 1946 the U.N.'s Headquarters Commission issued its 143-page report to the Second Part of the First Session of the General Assembly. The report included a history of the commission and its activities and enumerated basic criteria for site selection, as well as detailed descriptions of the five sites selected for further study. Designated numbers two, five, ten, twenty and forty after their approximate square mileage, these sites were all located in Westchester County, in the towns of Cortlandt, Harrison, Somers and Yorktown. The report also included a special section by the French delegate to the commission, Le Corbusier, which outlined his conception of the work to be done: "We will draw

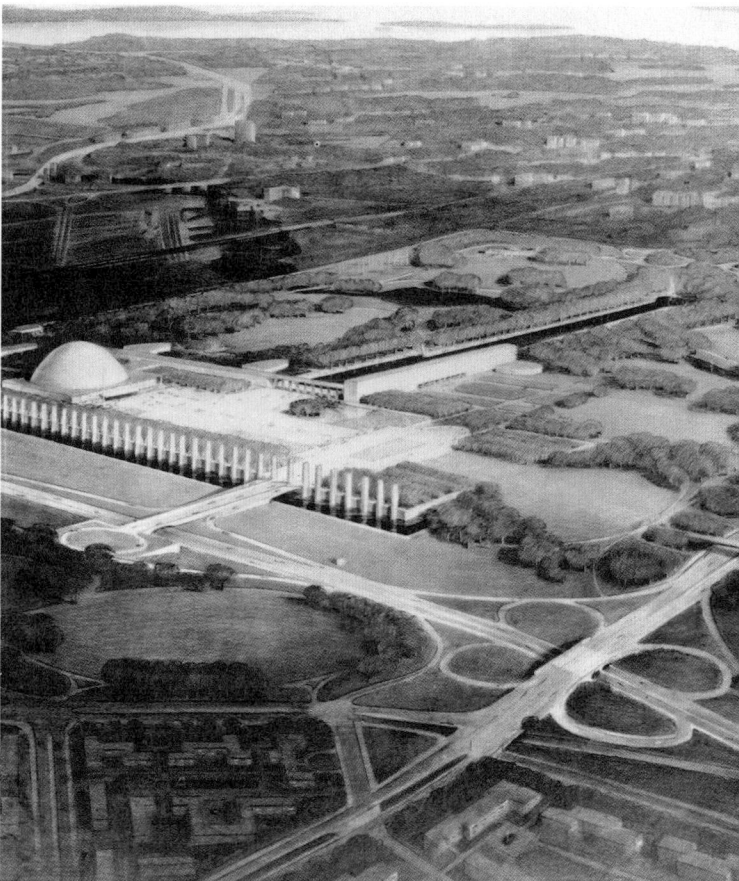

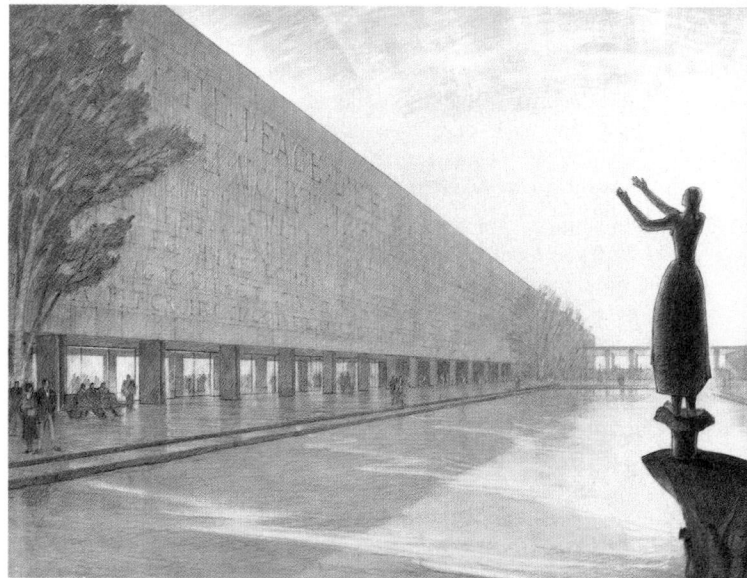

upon the prodigious resources of technical accomplishment, we will employ those forces that have been acquired by the mechanizing world during its first hundred years. . . . In these United States where everything already exists, yet where nothing really is finally determined, we will not waver as to what line to follow. We will look forward and not backward."[18]

To further the case for the Flushing Meadows site, Harrison and Rockefeller produced a one-reel film, but the delegates could not be persuaded: in fact, their antipathy to the location grew the more time they spent working in the New York City Building. The committee seemed prepared to recommend the selection of a ten-square-mile tract in the suburbs of Philadelphia, although there were some who favored a site straddling the Westchester County towns of White Plains and Harrison, and others who preferred a site in Fairfield County, Connecticut, that the Regional Plan Association endorsed.[19] Interest in the latter site was eliminated when, on an inspection tour, members of the Committee on Sites and General Questions were stoned by locals who wanted to keep their bucolic exurbia unimproved.

Trygve Lie was one of the few U.N. representatives who remained consistently in favor of locating the headquarters in New York. In his autobiography, Lie described the mood surrounding the issue of site selection:

A sour note began to sound in the Secretariat . . . where older employees from the San Francisco and London days, and particularly those from Geneva, began to contrast New York with those localities. The climate, housing troubles, higher costs as compared even to other metropolitan centers—all tended to broaden the spectrum of discontent. And I was hardly surprised at the number of staff members who were in favor of moving Headquarters anywhere—as long as it was away from New York. I would be the last to describe New York City as an ideal residential area for those not born and raised there. But just how important was all this? Were we not concerned with more basic factors? A train of hard political reasoning had decided me in favor of this city. Under the circumstances, I should have to continue to place these considerations first, regardless of deficiencies in climate, personal comfort, and the like. None of us was here on vacation.[20]

Surprisingly, some New Yorkers were against the idea of the U.N. locating in the city. Eight New York architects led by Talbot Hamlin, most of them on the faculty of Columbia University's architecture school, as well as the school's dean, Leopold Arnaud, argued against the U.N.'s location anywhere in New York in a letter to the New York Times.[21]

Recognizing that New York was in danger of losing the United Nations, Rockefeller, at Harrison's prompting, met with Lie and Senator Austin, who made it clear that only a site very near Manhattan, or one on Manhattan Island itself, would persuade the United Nations not to choose Philadelphia. With the deadline for site selection set for December 31, 1946, Rockefeller had to move fast. As luck would have it, a site of incomparable visibility in Manhattan was about to become available because William Zeckendorf, the prominent, visionary but undercapitalized developer, was unable to move forward with the development he had proposed for it.[22] The site was that of the abattoirs that lined the East River above Forty-second Street, which Zeckendorf had been assembling since 1945.

The East River shorefront in the lower forties had long been home to the abattoirs. When Tudor City (H. Douglas Ives, 1925–28) was designed, these noxious slaughterhouses seemed permanently ensconced; although east-facing windows in the complex would have offered spectacular river views, none were

provided because of the stench of freshly killed animals from First Avenue, popularly known as Blood Alley.[23] But by war's end the abattoirs were outmoded and their owners, the Swift and Wilson meat-packing companies, were ready to close them. Zeckendorf was attracted to the abattoir district because it offered the potential for vast development with virtually no tenant-relocation problems (only sixty families lived in the two apartment houses on the site), and he quickly acquired most of the land east of First Avenue between Forty-second and Forty-ninth streets, as well as considerable property in the upland area between First and Second avenues. The site east of First Avenue amounted to about seventeen acres.

Zeckendorf had a vision of the site's enormous potential: "Marion [Mrs. Zeckendorf] and I took to walking over to the edge of Beekman Place after dinner. There we would stare south toward the slaughterhouses, outlined by First Avenue and the welter of east-west cross streets, to the rising bulk of Tudor City. During the fifth or sixth of these visits, an idea came to me. I visualized a great, flat, rectangular platform stretching from the elevation of Tudor City east to the river and then north to where we stood on Beekman Place."[24] When he made a connection between his idea and the platforming that had transformed the railroad yards north of Grand Central Terminal into a hotel and office district called Terminal City,[25] Zeckendorf realized he "was no longer dealing with fantasy but with genuine possibility." At this point, Zeckendorf, who had not yet set up his own architectural department, called on Wallace Harrison, known for his work on Rockefeller Center. Harrison agreed to work on the East River project, which came to be called X City. Victoria Newhouse, Harrison's biographer, has written that Zeckendorf wanted to create "no less than his own Rockefeller Center; to describe the idea, he picked up the same terms that had been used in the first press releases for Rockefeller Center: 'A city within the city.' The only architects left from the original Rockefeller Center team were Harrison and Corbett. With Corbett now in his seventies, Harrison was the obvious choice."[26]

As portrayed in renderings by Hugh Ferriss, and most spectacularly in a night view drawn by A. Leydenfrost, Harrison's Le Corbusier–inspired design for X City was a boldly scaled vision of postwar urbanism that astutely married sound real estate principles with enthralling, futuristic aesthetics.[27] To be built on a platform raised forty feet above First Avenue, X City was to contain four identical, forty-story office slabs at the southern end of the site, three identical, cruciform-plan, thirty-story apartment towers housing 7,500 families at the northern end of the site and, more or less at the center, two fifty-seven-story slabs, curved in plan, with their circumferences facing each other in near tangents. One of these slabs was to contain offices, the other a 6,000-room hotel. Penetrating the slabs and extending out from them both north and south were to be a conventional hall for 6,000, as well as an opera and concert hall, probably the suggestion of Harrison, who had been involved in finding a new home for the Metropolitan Opera since the early days of Rockefeller Center's planning. In addition, there would be a yacht landing and a heliport on an enormous podium that would extend out into the river. Parking for 5,000 cars, to be accommodated in the podium, would be accessible not only from abutting streets but also from the East River Drive, which would run under the development. With land acquisition nearly complete, Zeckendorf released plans to the public in October 1946. Life magazine featured the scheme as part of its profile of Zeckendorf in the same month.[28] But because the developer was so short of cash, he could not go forward with the plan; instead, he offered to sell his land to the city.

Although the city could not afford to buy the land, Harrison's X City scheme was used to promote the East River location when the United Nations began to narrow down its search for a site in early December 1946. According to Newhouse, George Dudley, Harrison's chief assistant on the X City project and then one of his close collaborators on the U.N. job, "simply penciled in the words 'General Assembly' in place of the opera, and 'Security,' 'Economic and Social' and 'Trusteeship'" next to various other auditoriums that the proposal had contained.[29] Not only did X City make the U.N. selection committee aware of the site's possibilities, but it in many ways established the design character of the world headquarters.

When Nelson Rockefeller learned that the X City site was available, he lobbied heavily in its behalf as an alternate to the Flushing Meadows site. On December 9 he assembled a meeting to discuss the X City site as well as other possibilities. At the meeting were his father, John D., Jr.; his brother Laurance; a Rockefeller family lawyer, John Lockwood; his Pulitzer Prize–winning press assistant, Francis Jamieson; and Wallace Harrison. His other brothers, David, Winthrop and John D. III, were also consulted by telephone. At the meeting, Rockefeller, certain that the United Nations must remain in New York State, convinced his father and his brothers to offer the organization most of their land at Pocantico, near Tarrytown, Westchester County, some 4,000 acres in all. But when three members of the Permanent Headquarters Committee, including Le Corbusier, flew over the Pocantico site in a Rockefeller plane, their resolve to locate in the center of New York if they were to abandon Philadelphia was only hardened. By the evening of the next day, December 10, John D. Rockefeller, Jr., had decided that the best solution was to buy Zeckendorf's site and give it to the United Nations, an idea too costly for the city government to undertake on its own but well within the ability of one of the world's richest men. By December 11, less than seven months after Zeckendorf had started assembling the site, a deal between the Rockefellers and Zeckendorf had been made. The agreement was said to have been completed in the real estate mogul's unofficial office, the Monte Carlo nightclub, which he owned. According to a story told by Howard Myers, publisher of *Architectural Forum*:

> After Wallace Harrison had signed the history-making option, he started back to Rockefeller Center to report the news to Nelson Rockefeller. Realizing how much Rockefeller wanted to know the outcome, Harrison decided to telephone. When the word came through, Mr. R. was understandably delighted and shouted, "Wally, that calls for a celebration. See if you can't bring back a bottle of champagne." Entering a liquor store, Harrison, after deliberation, selected a vintage appropriate to the occasion. Carefully he withdrew his wallet from an inside pocket. In it were the executed options for $8,500,000 and two $1 bills.[30]

The Rockefellers' offer to donate the site to the United Nations was announced for the December 12 morning newspapers.[31] Negotiations with the federal government over a possible gift tax to be levied were in progress, as were discussions with the city over street closings and the like and with the U.N. Permanent Headquarters Committee, which had to approve the site.[32] By the next afternoon, Hugh Ferriss was busy at work on a two-by-three-foot drawing depicting how the new headquarters—a version of X City—might look on the East River site.[33] On December 14, the same day that the Manhattan site was finally approved, another New York site was offered by its owner, the eighty-nine-year-old architect Ernest Flagg, to serve as a supple-

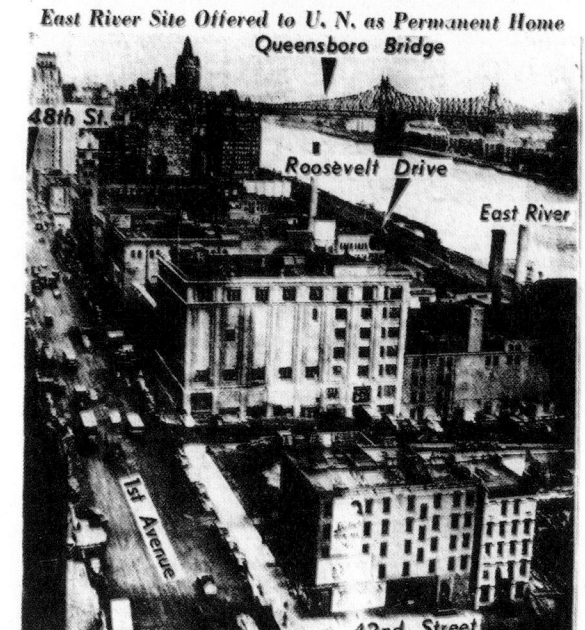

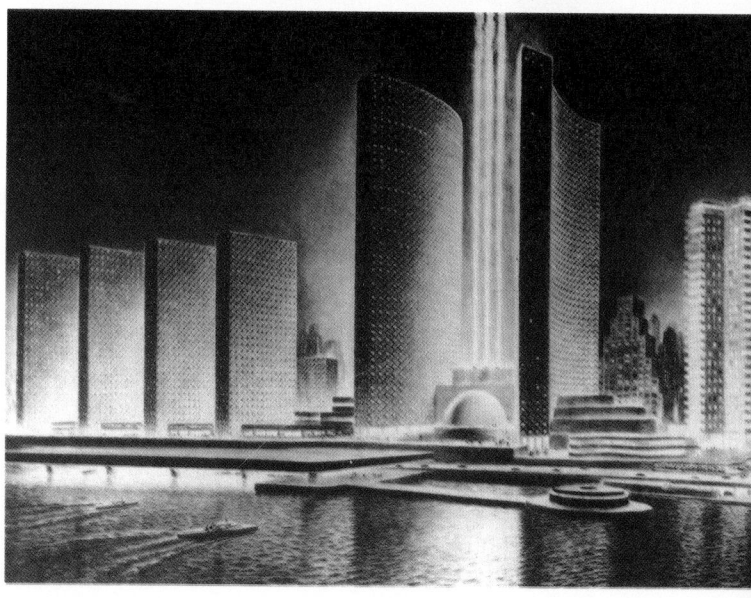

Top: December 12, 1945, announcement of John D. Rockefeller, Jr.'s gift of a site for the United Nations Headquarters. WZ

Bottom: Proposal for X City, First Avenue to the East River, East Forty-second to East Forty-eighth Street. Wallace K. Harrison, 1946. Rendering by A. Leydenfrost of view to the west. CU

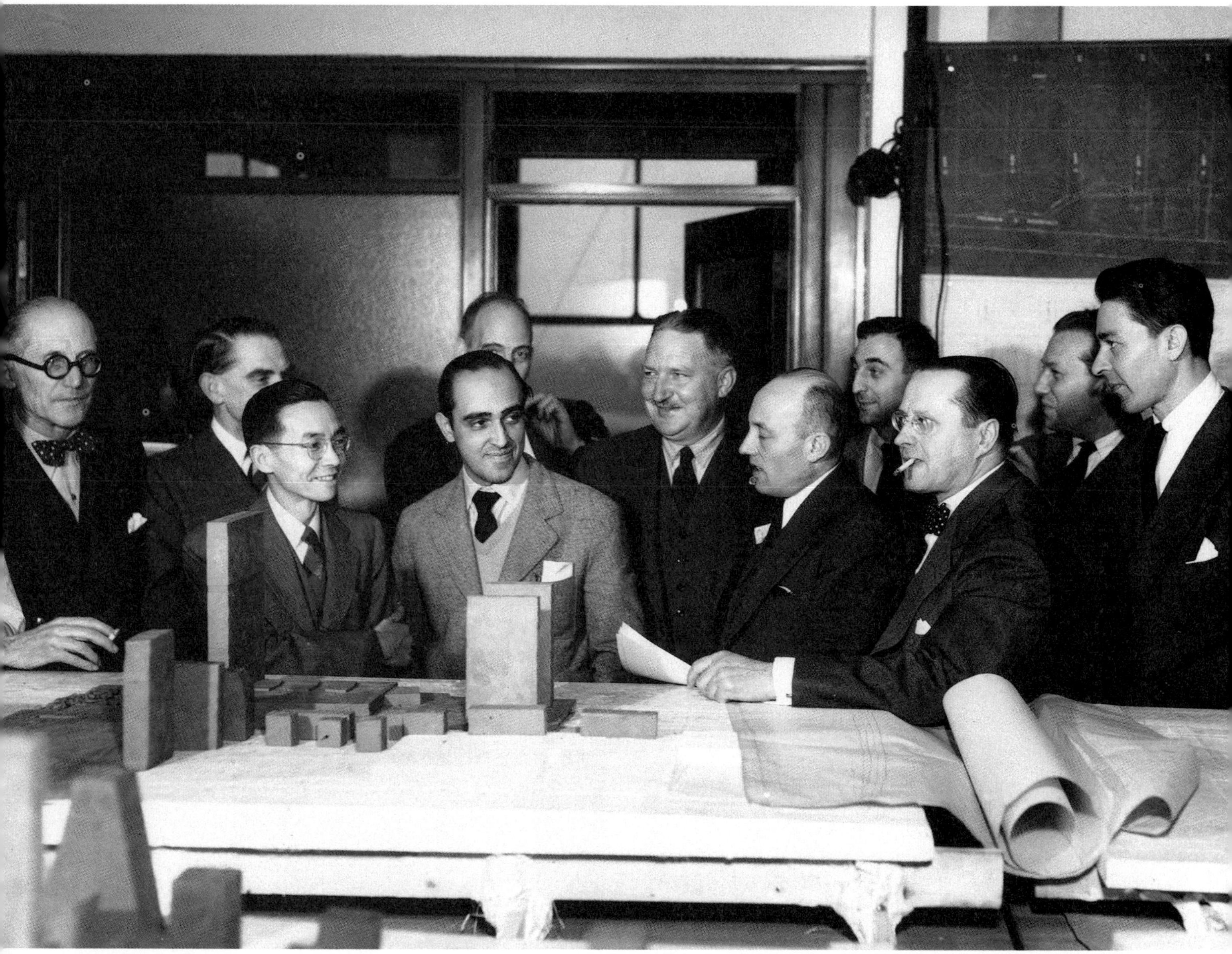

Above: Portrait of the United Nations Board of Design, showing, in the foreground, from left to right: Ssu-ch'eng Liang (China), Oscar Niemeyer (Brazil), Nikolai Bassov (USSR) and Ernest Cormier (Canada); in the background, from left to right: Le Corbusier (France), Vladimir Bodiansky (France), Wallace K. Harrison (United States), G. A. Soilleux (Australia), Max Abramovitz (United States) and consultants Ernest Weismann (Yugoslavia), and Matthew Nowicki (Poland). In the foreground is a preliminary model. UN

Right: Proposal for United Nations Headquarters, East River site. Wallace K. Harrison, 1946. View to the northwest. Rendering by Hugh Ferriss. CU

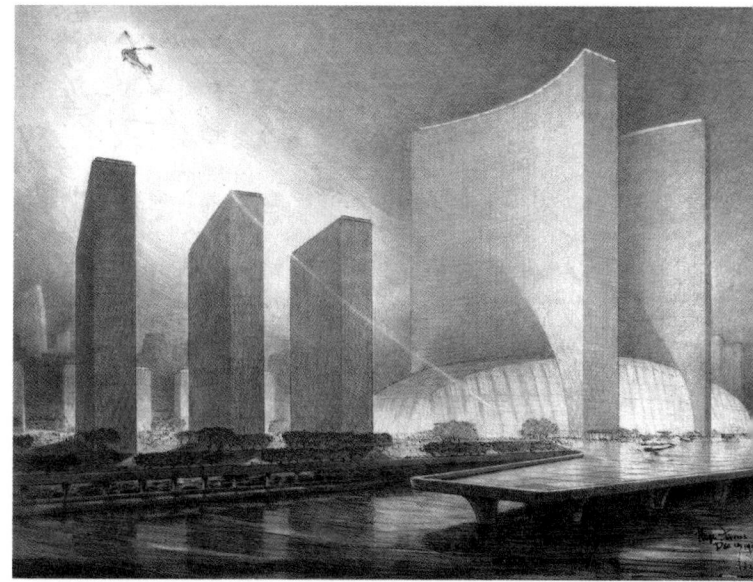

608

ment to the East River site to accommodate overflow functions from the principal building.[34] Flagg's property on Todt Hill, Staten Island, consisting of 300 acres overlooking the harbor, was not acquired by the world organization.

On January 6, 1947, Wallace Harrison was appointed Director of Planning for the United Nations' Permanent Headquarters, an overwhelming job that encompassed marshaling his colleagues to create a single design, meeting with the U.N. and city bureaucracies and dealing with the press.[35] Working closely with Trygve Lie, Harrison immediately set to work, at first tackling the selection of architects to serve on the Board of Design.[36] Certain obvious talents had to be bypassed: Alvar Aalto because Finland was not a member of the United Nations; Walter Gropius and Ludwig Mies van der Rohe because, though they now resided in America, their German birth and long careers in Germany made them politically unpalatable. Frank Lloyd Wright seems never to have been seriously considered.

The Board of Design that was finally chosen was hardly an all-star team, but on the whole it was made up of thoughtful and creative architects. Its one undeniably brilliant innovator was Le Corbusier, representing France; the other members were G. A. Soilleux (Australia), Gaston Brunfaut (Belgium), Oscar Niemeyer (Brazil), Ernest Cormier (Canada), Ssu-ch'eng Liang (China), Sven Markelius (Sweden), Nikolai D. Bassov (U.S.S.R), Howard M. Robertson (United Kingdom) and Julio Vilamajo (Uruguay). A number of special consultants were appointed, including Hugh Ferriss (U.S.A.), whose drawings document the schemes of some of the individual participants as well as the evolving collective scheme,[37] Vladimir Bodiansky (France), Ernest Weissmann (Yugoslavia) and the young, gifted Polish Modernist Matthew Nowicki. Louis Skidmore, Gilmore D. Clarke and Ralph Walker were also signed on as consultants.[38]

Harrison had pushed for Le Corbusier's participation, even though this choice was controversial. Although he contributed decisively to the final design, the cantankerous architect would prove to be a continuous thorn in Harrison's side. At about the time the East River site was chosen, Le Corbusier had already written a report of his own on the site selection process in which he voiced his preference for a location near Philadelphia, characterizing New York as "terrifying" and "menacing."[39] In the early part of his text, he explicitly advocated against locating the United Nations in New York: "In no case must the United Nations become a corollary to America. To implant its Headquarters in the very shadow of the skyscrapers of Manhattan is inadmissible. The Manhattan skyscrapers are by their nature too precarious; New York is a thrilling city but so disputable that it cannot take the Headquarters of the United Nations into its lap. This is a question of moral proportion. In fact a question of 'respectability.'"[40] But faced with the selection of the Manhattan site, Le Corbusier paved the way for his continued participation in the project by saying that the site would not be "the cradle of the United Nations" but merely its "Battle-Post." He went on to explain that New York, as the world's most modern city, would offer great convenience: "Here you can work out the solutions for our modern world without a single day of delay . . . avoiding what might have been too dangerous and too long an interval, were you to have attempted prematurely to build an ideal World Center. . . . It is too soon for a World Center. Therefore, accept in the meanwhile this Battle-Post which is offered to you."[41]

Le Corbusier had hoped for a suburban site, comparable in scale to the Cidade dos Motores being planned in Brazil by his disciples Paul Lester Weiner and José Luis Sert.[42] But once the East River site was settled upon, he squeezed several "supple-

ments" into his report, extolling the choice and pointing to his 1922 project, Contemporary City for 3 Million Inhabitants, as a model for the new complex. This project had had a profound influence on Raymond Hood, Rockefeller Center's principal architect, and on Harrison, as demonstrated by his X City proposal. Le Corbusier surely saw the East River site as a kind of promised land in which he might at last realize his great urban vision.

Approving of only five of the architects on the Board of Design (himself, Bassov, Robertson, Niemeyer and Harrison), Le Corbusier proposed a supplementary design group—staffed by Ernest Weissmann and Matthew Nowicki, both of whom were already hired as consultants, as well as Clive Entwistle (United Kingdom), Amancio Williams (Argentina), Stamo Papadaki (Greece) and Carlos Lazo (Mexico)—but this suggestion was not taken up. By the end of January 1947 Le Corbusier had arrived in New York, setting up shop in the U.N. Headquarters Planning Office on the twenty-seventh floor of the RKO Building in Rockefeller Center. Working more or less parallel to the rest of the design team, he produced sixty pages of sketches and notes by April.

Work on the official U.N. scheme began in February, even before the full membership of the Board of Design had been established.[43] Just as Harrison prepared to make his first report on the project, outlining a strategy for its phasing, forty-one architects and designers, members of the American Institute of Architects and the American Society of Planners and Architects, in a letter addressed to Trygve Lie, protested that the East River site was "seriously inadequate" and that the method of selection being used for the Board of Design was "professionally unworthy of such an important assignment."[44] The protesting architects included Thomas H. Creighton, editor of *Progressive Architecture*, a staunch advocate of an international competition. Despite their plea, the Board of Design began meeting on February 17 (and would meet daily for two or three hours through early June), and its membership was confirmed by early March. At the same time, Harrison, working with Dudley and another young architect, Harmon Goldstone, was busy developing a program for the new complex. Harrison also worked with his younger partner, Max Abramovitz, who organized a staff to begin site planning for the complex and the surrounding neighborhood.[45] Given that the world organization was new, evolving and bound to grow, this stage of the work was crucial. As the Board of Design developed ideas, and a cadre of staff architects and draftsmen, under the direction of Michael Harris aided by Hugh Ferriss and René Chambellan, drew them up and built study models, it fell to Harrison to develop a coherent unity. Soon Harrison would ask Abramovitz to serve as deputy director and Dudley as secretary of the Board of Design.

Each architect on the Board of Design had his own ideas about how to organize the three principal elements of the complex: the General Assembly, the Secretariat and a building to accommodate various smaller meetings and conferences. Sven Markelius, who was city planner for Stockholm, wanted to connect the complex to Welfare Island, where he proposed locating employee housing, and to Queens beyond, as well as to midtown via a mall-like boulevard terminating at Fifth Avenue. Howard Robertson piled the program up into one integrated mass facing a large plaza; Harrison proposed a north-south office slab and a free-form domed auditorium connected by a podium, a scheme like Niemeyer's and Ssu-ch'eng Liang's, which were fundamentally variations on Le Corbusier's ideas. Though there was input from the various members of the team, Le Corbusier's scheme, which he had been developing since January, was the basis of the final plan. Among the most important elements of his

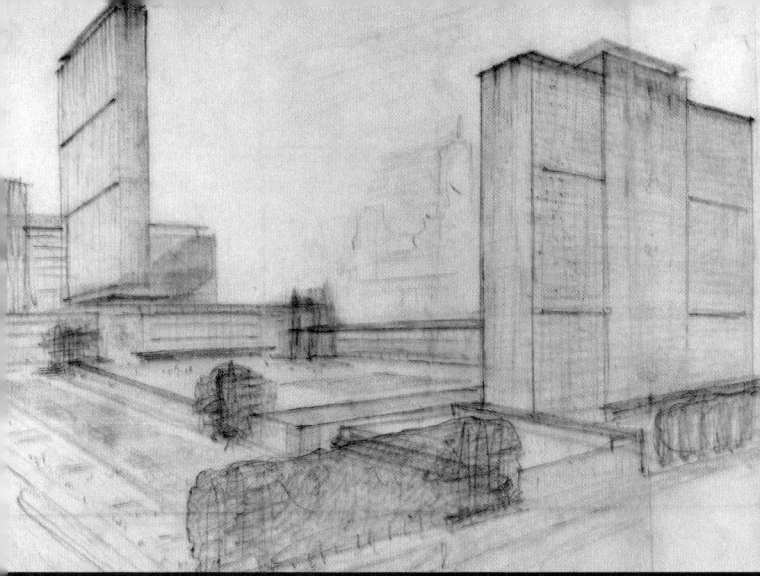

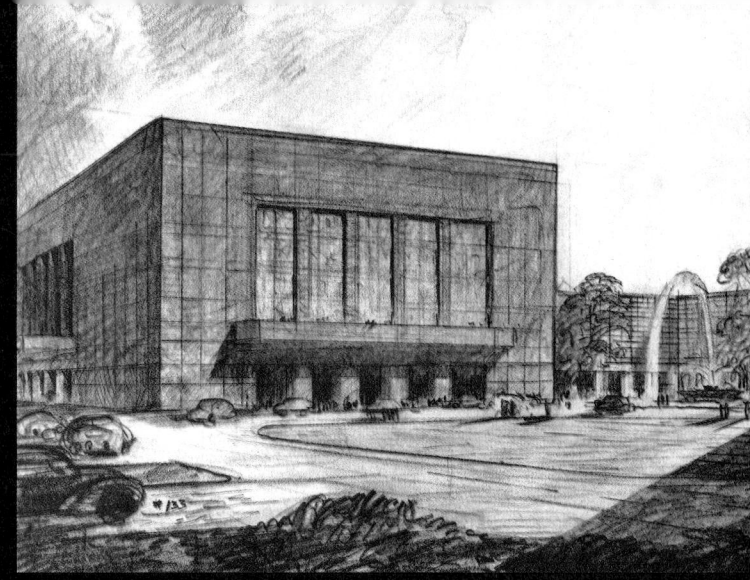

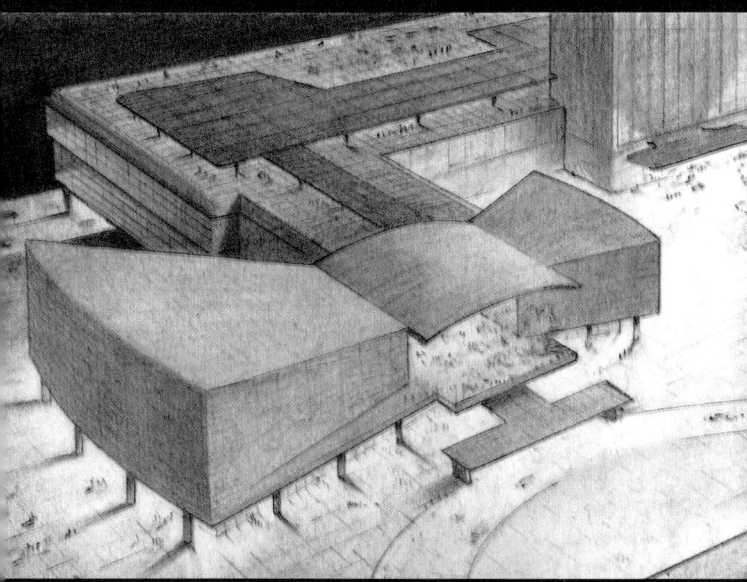

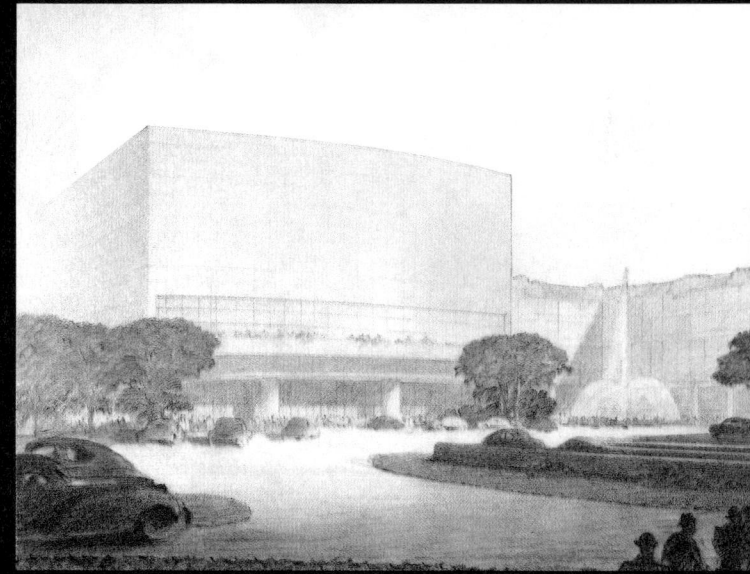

Top: Proposal for United Nations Headquarters, East River site.
Howard Robertson, 1947. Sketch. CU

Bottom: Proposal for United Nations General Assembly Building,
East River site. Le Corbusier, 1947. Sketch. CU

Top: Proposal for United Nations General Assembly Building, East
River site. Nikolai Bassov, 1947. Sketch. CU

Bottom: Proposal for United Nations General Assembly Building, East
River site. Wallace K. Harrison, 1947. Sketch. CU

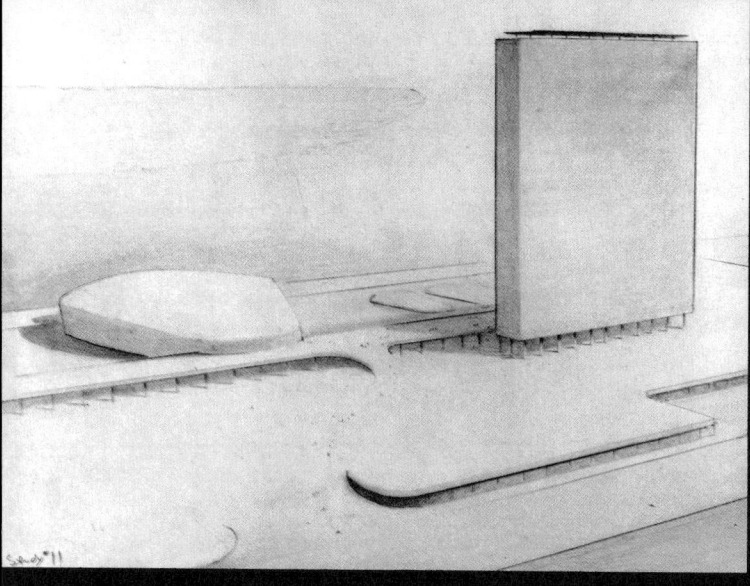

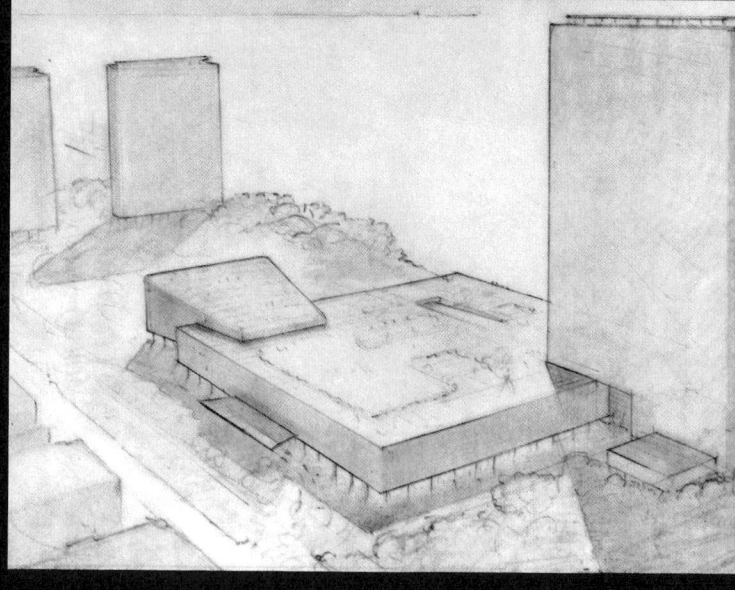

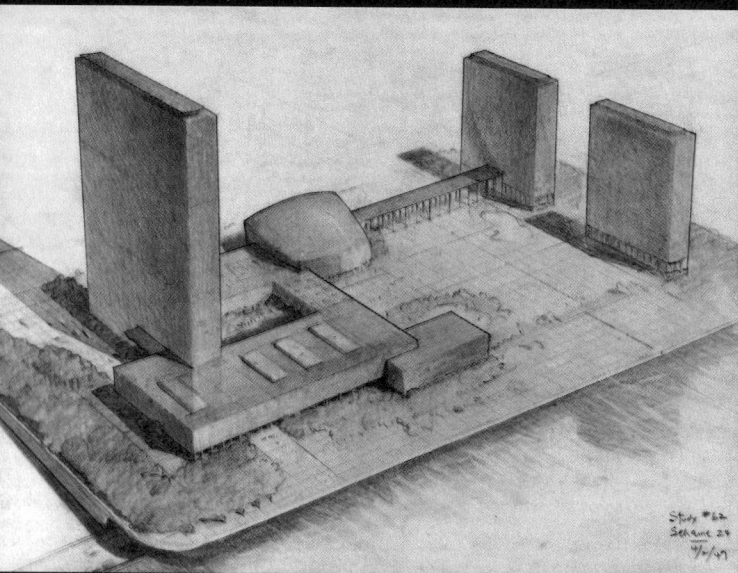

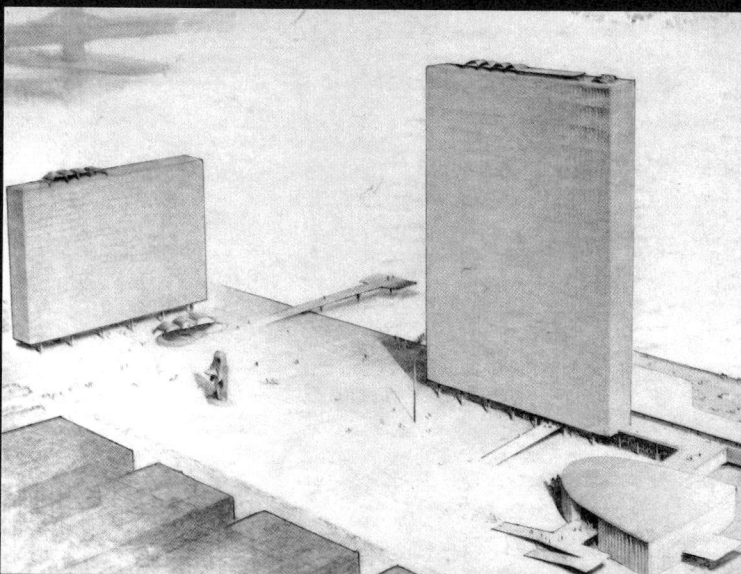

Top: Proposal for United Nations Headquarters, East River site.
Wallace K. Harrison, 1947. Sketch. CU

Bottom: Proposal for United Nations Headquarters, East River site.
Ssu-ch'eng Liang, 1947. Sketch. CU

Top: Proposal for United Nations Headquarters, East River site. Le
Corbusier, 1947. Sketch. CU

Bottom: Proposal for United Nations Headquarters, East River site.
Oscar Niemeyer, 1947. Sketch. CU

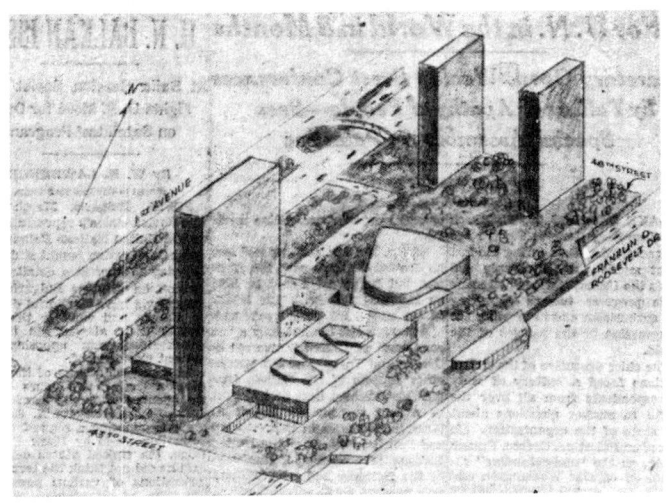

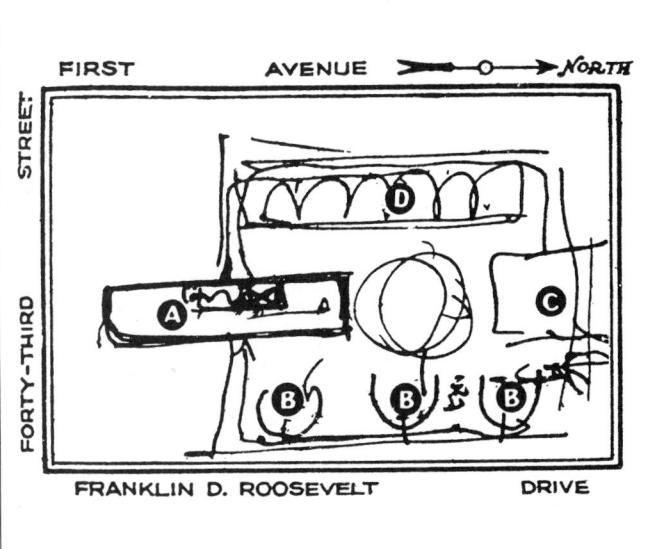

Top: Proposal for United Nations Headquarters, East River site. Board of Design, Wallace K. Harrison, Director of Planning, 1947. Sketch. NYT

Bottom: Proposal for United Nations Headquarters, East River site. Wallace K. Harrison, 1947. Doodle. NYT

plan were the buildings set above street level on a continuous podium, the ramps that would lift visitors to the podium from the widened Forty-seventh Street mall and the slablike office buildings set off from low amoebalike buildings that housed the meeting rooms and General Assembly. Harrison's point of view was present as well, but as X City had revealed, it was essentially Corbusian. Harrison's interpretation of Le Corbusier's approach was evident in a key drawing where the Secretariat was shown as a curved slab straddling the auditoriums in a manner very similar to that of the hotel building in X City.

By late March 1947, when negotiations with the city over the permits necessary to superblock the headquarters site were completed, and after a "doodle" by Harrison indicating the current status of the design had been published in the *New York Times,* the Board of Design felt sufficiently comfortable in their progress to release preliminary sketches illustrating two versions of a five-building scheme. Both featured a slablike Secretariat, locked into a low podiumlike building for the three council chambers, and a General Assembly building as well as two office buildings placed at the site's northern edge.[46] In one proposal, the two slabs were placed in a parallel formation, on the north-south axis; in the other they formed a near-solid wall along the East Forty-eighth Street boundary. One of these two buildings was to house the Delegations, the other Special Agencies (eventually delegations would establish off-site independent missions to the United Nations); other agencies were to locate elsewhere in New York as well as in remote U.N. centers in Paris (UNESCO) and Geneva (WHO).

On May 22, 1947, the day after the Board of Design formally presented its scheme to the General Assembly, Harrison was amazed to find a very different scheme from the one he had shown them published on page one of the *New York Herald Tribune* as the official proposal. What the *Tribune* ran was Le Corbusier's design uncompromised by the suggestions of others: a dynamic composition combining a wafer-thin, north-south slab housing the Secretariat, a low, podiumlike building for the meeting rooms slid to the north along the riverfront, and behind, facing First Avenue but extending even farther north, a mass with an asymmetrically sloped roof and raised on pilotis housing the Security Council and the General Assembly in separate chambers. As Harrison noted on the caption of his copy of the *Tribune,* this was "a lie, not at all [the] scheme chosen. . . . This is a photo of Corbu's modified scheme. How did he get a photog to take this?"[47]

The photo released was a variation of a proposal Le Corbusier had made on March 27, 1947, called scheme 23A. Citing this document and his notebook, which mysteriously disappeared shortly afterwards (it reappeared in 1948), Le Corbusier consistently claimed authorship for the U.N.'s design. But whether he was solely responsible or not, it is clear that his vision was essential to the final outcome. It is also clear from the X City drawings and from sketches by Harrison that he too made a significant contribution to the design. But despite some conciliatory gestures Le Corbusier made to Harrison during the summer of 1947 in the hope of obtaining the commission outright, by November 1947 he would acknowledge no contribution but his own: in a letter written to Harrison in the third person, he stated that "he wishes that his own name not be mentioned," but that the U.N. design was "100% the architecture and urbanism of Le Corbusier."[48]

Le Corbusier also proved difficult over the design of particular details of the complex, most notably the all-glass east and

west walls of the Secretariat, one of the principal features of the U.N.'s most memorable building. Le Corbusier argued for the *brise soleil* (exterior sunbreaker) he had devised in the 1930s as a solution to the environmental drawbacks of the glass wall he used at the Salvation Army Building in Paris (1929–33).[49] Harrison felt that the *brise soleil* would not only add cost but would also be difficult to maintain in winter because of ice buildup. He preferred the blue-green tinted double glazing called Thermopane, which was eventually chosen. The solar problem was not taken lightly: a four-story mock-up of a portion of the window wall was built on the roof of the Manhattan Building on East Forty-second Street to study the question.

Though flawed, the U.N. complex as crystallized in the spring of 1947 was the long-awaited, triumphant realization of interwar-era Modernist architecture and urbanism.[50] The dynamic composition of the buildings consisted of the unencumbered mass of the Secretariat slab, distinguished by the diagrammatic clarity of its cladding—two walls of glass and two of stone—and, as a foreground set piece, the Assembly Building with its hourglass plan. The shape of the Assembly Building was designed to provide a midsection lobby between the Assembly hall and a room for the Security Council. Because the shape was a particular favorite of Harrison's, and because it had been approved by the now-disbanded Board of Design, it was retained even after budget problems required the elimination of the council chamber. The rooftop dome was added at the request of Senator Austin, who felt it was a necessary design feature to convince Congress of the building's suitability and thus to obtain government funds for the building's completion.

By mid-summer 1947 the plan and building massing of the three principal elements was quite firm, although a fourth building, an east-west slab housing delegates, was still located at the north end of the site. At this point Harrison and his team, as well as many individuals and groups outside the U.N., began to focus on the world capital's relationship to its immediate environs. In terms of administration, this was the responsibility of Robert Moses, who was City Construction Coordinator at the time.[51] One of the first to call attention to the need for coordinated planning was a private citizen, Dr. Marcellus Bronk, an eighth-generation descendant of Jonas Bronck, for whom the Bronx had been named. In December 1946 Dr. Bronk proposed that the entire area facing the U.N.'s site be developed as a cultural and business center, with hotels, theaters and an opera house.[52] He advocated the use of a podium on both the U.N. and upland sites so that the two could be linked across First Avenue. In addition, the American Institute of Architects initiated studies of the upland area at the same time.[53]

Under Moses's leadership, the City Planning Commission had been developing proposals parallel to the design of the U.N. itself, beginning in January 1947.[54] According to William Zeckendorf, Moses never showed strong support for a meaningful master plan for the upland area. As early as March 1947, "when a UN spokesman chided the city for lack of boldness and vision in its share of the site planning, the city, in the person of Commissioner Moses, gave a soft reply, but paid no attention to these murmurs."[55] Typically, Moses's concerns were largely with traffic flow, not land use, and certainly not large-scale urban design. Under his direction, and with designs by Andrews & Clark, the City Planning Commission called for the replacement of the narrow forty-foot-wide tunnel that had carried the trolleys past Tudor City to the river along Forty-second Street with one

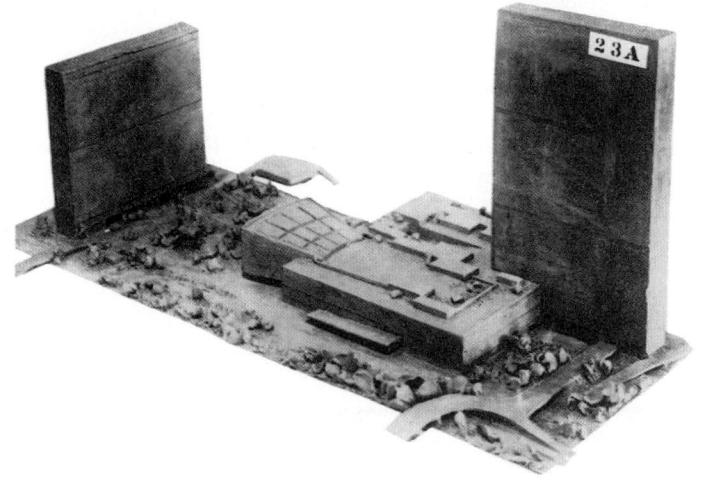

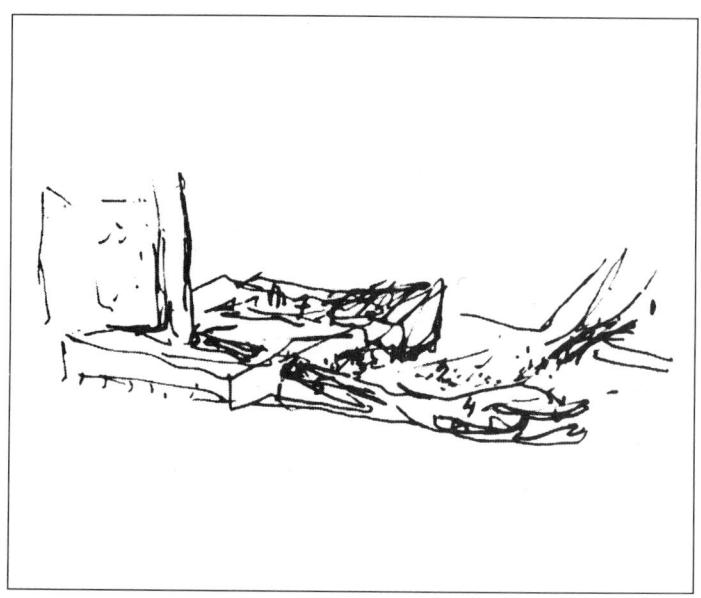

Top: Proposal for United Nations Headquarters, East River site. Le Corbusier, 1947. Model. View to the northeast of scheme 23A. *Le Corbusier: Oeuvre complète.* ©1994 Artists Rights Society, New York/SPADEM, Paris. ARS

Bottom: Proposal for United Nations Headquarters, East River site. Le Corbusier, 1947. Page from Le Corbusier's sketchbook depicting scheme 23A. *Le Corbusier: Oeuvre complète.* ©1994 Artists Rights Society, New York/SPADEM, Paris. ARS

sixty feet wider that would slip under a graceful bridge carrying Tudor City Place.[56]

Thus, as a result of solving a traffic problem, an appealing if less than monumental approach to the U.N. was established at Forty-second Street, far more monumental and more visible than the one at Forty-seventh Street that was intended as the grand entrance. The construction of a six-lane tunnel under First Avenue between Forty-first and Forty-eighth streets also enhanced the sense of ceremony at street level by eliminating through traffic.[57] The now comparatively quiet First Avenue was in 1952 renamed United Nations Plaza, initiating an annoying and confusing trend of street name changes that began to plague the city, particularly Manhattan's midtown business districts.[58] The granting of an aerial easement over the Franklin Delano Roosevelt Drive (formerly the East River Drive) allowed for the realization of several benefits of the high podium featured in the early schemes, an element that had been eliminated because it was too costly. Building over the FDR Drive enhanced the monumentality of the U.N.'s setting, provided some desperately needed extra land area and ameliorated the negative impact of the highway. Although the cost of rebuilding the highway across U.N. property was paid for by the world organization, the cost of the on and off ramps to the north and south of the complex was borne by the city.

The construction of a small park designed by Andrews & Clark (1948), on the west side of First Avenue at the foot of Forty-third Street, added a minor grace note to the area.[59] The nearest thing to a grand gesture that Moses was to include in his proposals for the U.N. district was a broad approach to the complex leading east from Second Avenue along Forty-seventh Street. Created by demolishing the northern half of the block between Forty-sixth and Forty-seventh streets, it was in many ways an empty gesture, since it led not to the U.N.'s buildings but to the park north of the Assembly Building. While most of the buildings slated for demolition to realize this plan were of no particular consequence, the destruction of St. Boniface's Roman Catholic Church (1858), on the southeast corner of Forty-seventh Street and Second Avenue, raised concern in the community; 2,000 people unsuccessfully petitioned the Board of Estimate to leave it intact. In 1965 the widened Forty-seventh Street and the strip of park along its southern edge was named in honor of Dag Hammarskjold, the Swedish-born secretary general (1953–61) who died in 1961 in a plane crash while on a mission to the Congo.[60]

Although Moses's viewpoint ultimately prevailed, other concepts for the development of the upland area were presented. On July 24, 1947, under pressure from Zeckendorf and a number of architects, planners and interested citizens, as well as the anti-Moses contingent in government, including City Planning Commissioner Goodhue Livingston and Councilman Stanley M. Isaacs, the Board of Estimate had withheld approval of Moses's plan.[61] This allowed time to consider plans prepared by Zeckendorf as well as by the New York Chapter of the American Institute of Architects for a more comprehensive development of the land west of First Avenue. Zeckendorf's plan, first presented to Moses in March 1947, was turned down by him on April 1, in a letter.

In late August the New York Chapter of the American Institute of Architects, which had been studying the U.N. environs since December 1946, presented the Board of Estimate with a plan for extensive redevelopment of the area.[62] It called for a below-ground artery surmounted by a 150-foot-wide mall connecting Lexington and First avenues and the redevelopment of sites between the north side of Forty-fifth Street and the south side of Forty-eighth Street, all the way east from Lexington Avenue to the U.N. The architects' plan had been developed under Robert C. Weinberg's direction out of frustration with what Frederick J. Woodbridge, chairman of the chapter's committee on civic design and development, called the City Planning Commission's "lack of coordinated planning" and its "piecemeal" proposals.[63]

On August 25 Zeckendorf hosted a lunch at his Monte Carlo nightclub that was attended by Livingston, Isaacs, and 150 architects, engineers, investment bankers and theatrical and musicians' representatives. They gathered to hear the details of a plan that involved the development of the six blocks bounded by the north side of Forty-sixth Street, the south side of Forty-ninth Street, and First and Third avenues.[64] As presented in a rendering by Earl Purdy, Zeckendorf's plan in many ways paralleled the ideas of Sven Markelius. It called for a 1,340-foot-long, 320-foot-wide concourse or mall that would be the principal focus of a mixed-use complex of buildings, including two forty-story east-west slab-type office buildings forming a monumental gateway at Third Avenue, an opera house, a concert hall and eight theaters and, between Second and First avenues, twin groupings of four sixteen-story, north-south slabs, the upper thirteen floors of which would house more than 1,000 families. At the end of the vista, where the axis of the U.N. site was crossed by that of the new mall, a vastly tall openwork steel pylon, guyed in place by cables, rose from a fountain and circular sunken plaza, a twentieth-century answer to the stone obelisks beloved by city planners at least since the time of Pope Sixtus V. To achieve his plan, Zeckendorf required that the city condemn the land for $13 million, the amount he was prepared to pay for it, and that land taxes be frozen for a period of time. Unlike the abattoir site, however, this site contained not only viable business properties but also housing for 2,000 people.

Zeckendorf's moves were viewed with suspicion by many observers, especially those who lived in Turtle Bay Gardens, which would be destroyed by his proposal.[65] The journalist Dorothy Thompson was incensed by the prospect of Zeckendorf's plan; in a letter to the editor of the New York Times, she threatened that the residents of Turtle Bay Gardens, "most of whom are highly socially minded people, may recall that the Constitution declares that the right to bear arms shall not be abridged!"[66] Zeckendorf quickly responded with his own letter: "Believing that the city will obtain such great benefits for its future world capital with an approach such as suggested by us [Zeckendorf's firm, Webb & Knapp] to the United Nations, we have not only offered the suggestion freely but have offered to underwrite it if necessary. Surely the City of New York could not think in less grandiose terms than those for the permanent approach to the United Nations. . . . We do not seek either profit or glory."[67]

While the New York Times remained neutral, merely suggesting that the Board of Estimate consider the American Institute of Architects' proposal,[68] the editors of Architectural Forum lambasted the mayor and the board for their shortsightedness.[69] As Zeckendorf put it almost twenty-five years later: "Moses, like all men, has certain weaknesses. One blindspot, for instance, is his seemingly inherent inability, or great reluctance, to step beyond the design and building restrictions that were imposed upon the city by the previous generation's intoxication with grid-patterned streets. Another weakness centers on his natural but extensive pride of authorship. Our plan clashed with his on both these counts." Because Moses had already convinced

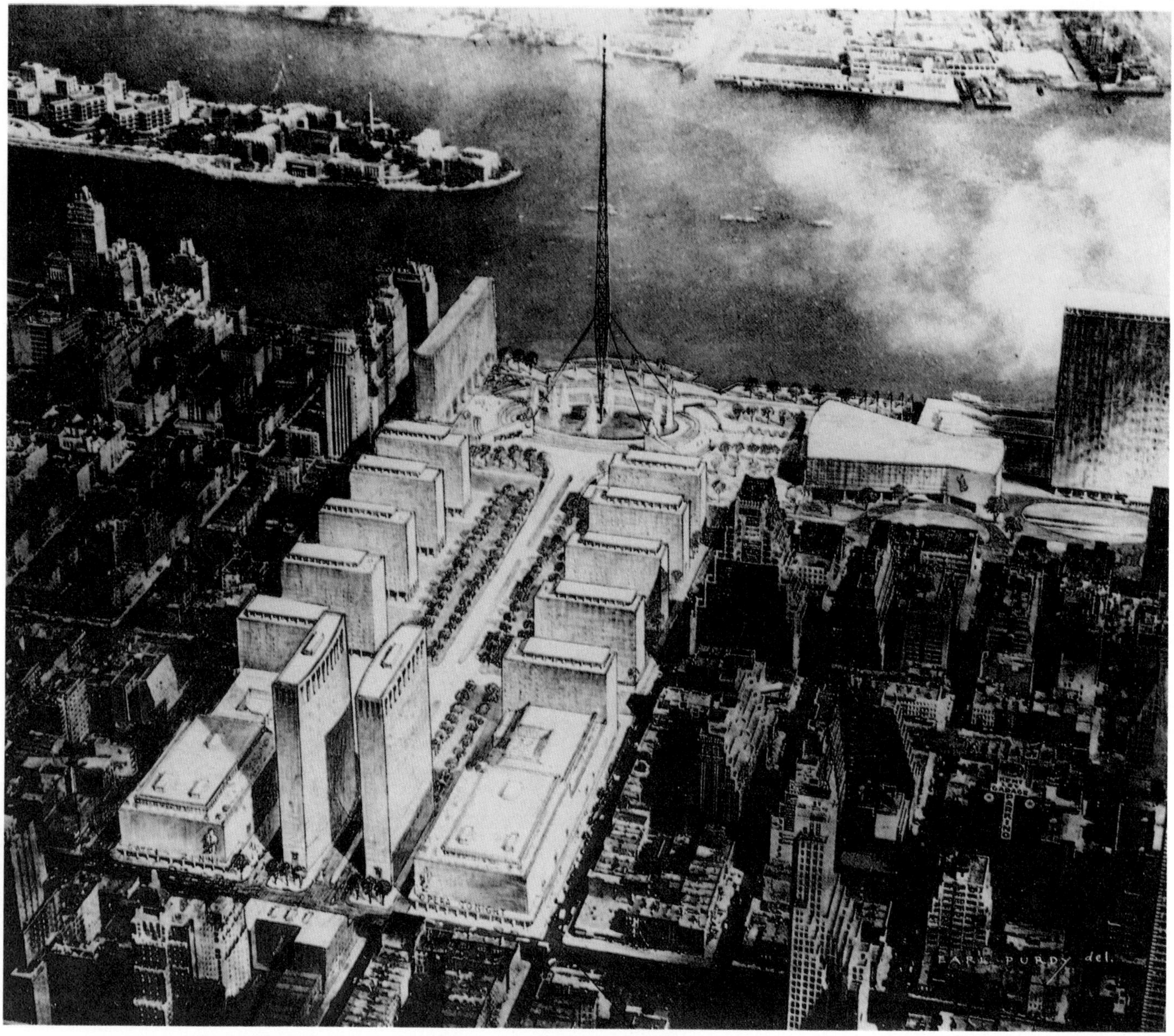

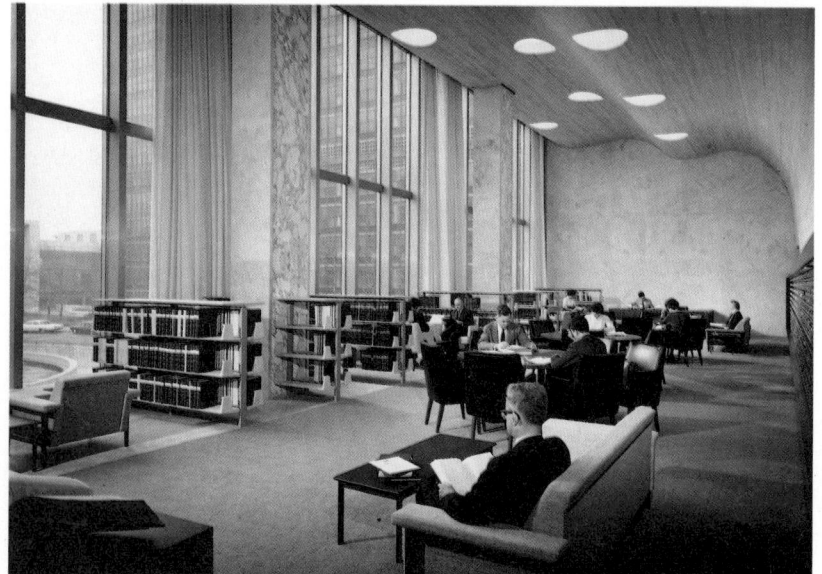

Above: Proposal for the area to the west of the United Nations, from First to Second Avenue, East Forty-sixth to East Forty-eighth Street. Proposal by William Zeckendorf, 1947. Rendering by Earl Purdy of view to the east. WZ

Left: United Nations Library, northeast corner of First Avenue and East Forty-second Street. Harrison, Abramovitz & Harris, 1963. Interior. Stoller. ©ESTO

Top: Proposal for United Nations Headquarters, from First Avenue to the East River, East Forty-second to East Forty-eighth Street. Board of Design, Wallace K. Harrison, Director of Planning, 1947. Rendering of view to the south showing, from left to right: Conference Building, Secretariat and General Assembly Building. CU

Bottom left: Proposal for United Nations Headquarters. Rendering of view to the southeast showing General Assembly Building, in the foreground, and Secretariat, in the background. CU

Bottom right: United Nations Headquarters. Rendering of view to the north showing General Assembly Building, on the left, and Secretariat, on the right. CU

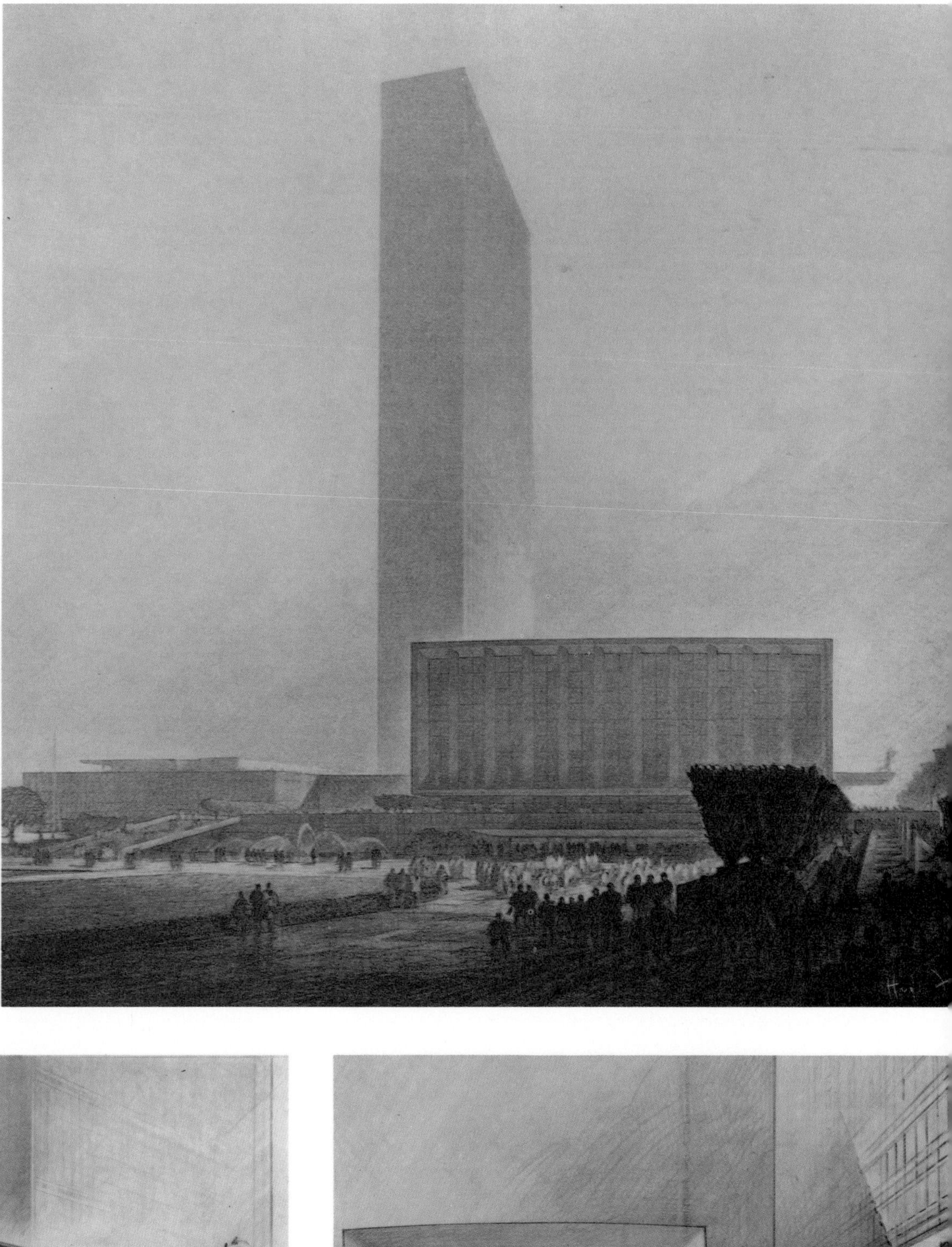

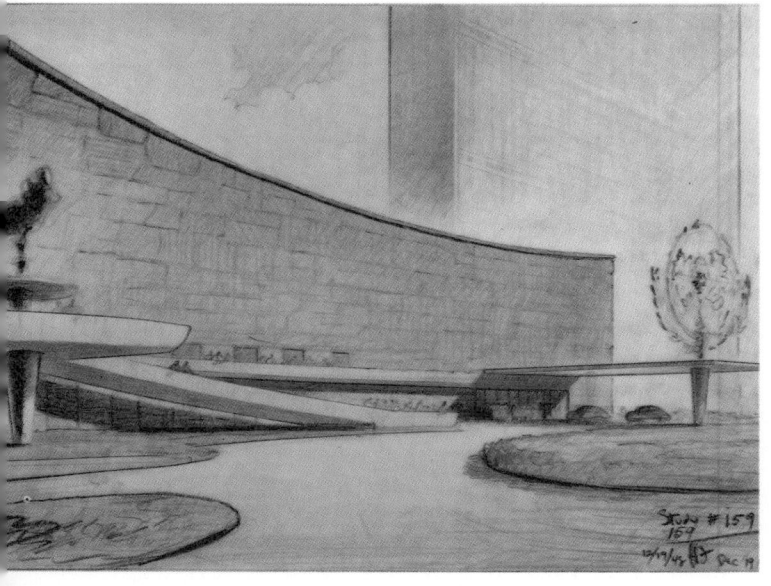

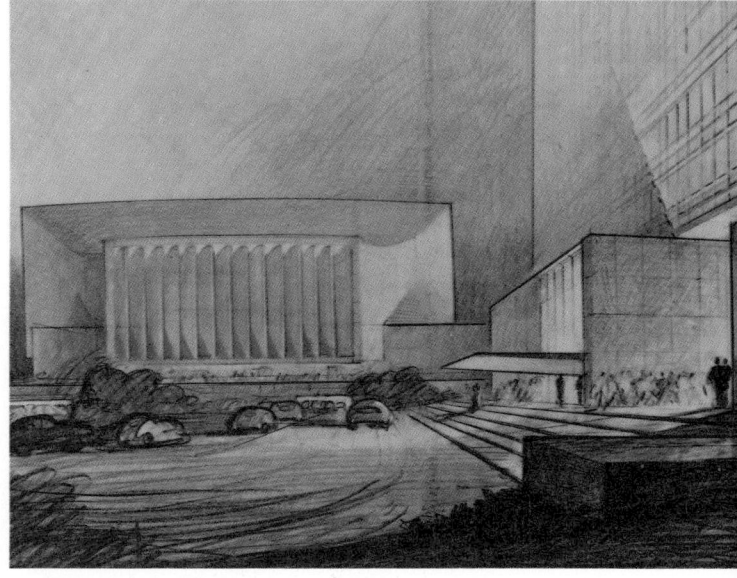

Mayor O'Dwyer that the Zeckendorf scheme was impractical, the special Board of Estimate hearing arranged to review it on August 28, 1947, was a foregone conclusion. Zeckendorf described the scene: "After great difficulties in getting the model, which covered several tables, through the crowded corridors and past various official guards to the doors of the main chamber, we found we would not be allowed to display it. Then, when I stepped into the chamber to testify, O'Dwyer looked over at me and snapped, 'What do you want?'" Moses implied that because Zeckendorf's plan required the city to condemn the land, he had conceived the project to make an enormous profit at the expense of the taxpayers. Zeckendorf, not to be publicly insulted, accused the Board of Estimate of abdicating its powers to Moses, a nonelected official, whom he challenged to testify "without the mantle of immunity."[70] Near pandemonium broke out, and Zeckendorf was ordered from the chamber. As he left, Zeckendorf said, "I know I am licked. I knew the decision was made before this meeting."[71]

In its report the next day, the New York Times described the meeting as "the bitterest debate in recent City Hall history";[72] according to Zeckendorf, "it was no debate, it was a cry in the wilderness."[73] The editors of Architectural Forum chided the board for its show of democratic process, New York style: "The Board of Estimate's hearing couldn't have been more like a highly colored demonstration of New York Planning-in-Action if it had been staged for the benefit of visiting nations."[74] A few months later, even after Zeckendorf's firm, Webb & Knapp, had divested itself of its Turtle Bay holdings, he continued to stump for a monumental approach to the U.N., going so far as to take out full-page ads in the New York Times to convince the public that his plan and that of the American Institute of Architects, unlike Moses's, were ones "New York could take pride in."[75] But Moses's mind was made up: neither Zeckendorf's nor the American Institute of Architects' plan was approved, and little was done to think in large-scale terms about the upland area for almost twenty years. As a result, as Zeckendorf gloated, "the city built a dark, narrow mall with dull, gray stones, lining its floor and walls. This drab vest-pocket park and bit of road were designated as the official approachway to the UN. The main vista for most of this 'approachway' consisted of the backsides of a series of tenements and factories on Forty-sixth Street. . . . An entranceway to the putative capital of the world it is not."[76]

Demolition of the fifty buildings on the U.N. site began in July 1947. Only one building on the site was not cleared to make way for the world headquarters, a seven-story, 70,000-square-foot, exposed-concrete building built for the New York City Housing Authority (1947) on the northeast corner of Forty-second Street and First Avenue; this was first used for offices and in 1951 was converted to use as the U.N. Library.[77] In 1959 plans were revealed for a replacement to the Housing Authority building. Designed by Harrison, Abramovitz & Harris, and completed in 1963, it was a miniature version of the Secretariat, consisting of a three-story, glass-sheathed slab running east-west along Forty-second Street.[78] Inside, the design borrowed details from such modern masters as Alvar Aalto and Marcel Breuer.

In September 1947 the General Assembly gathered to, among other things, approve the detailed report on the design of its new headquarters.[79] In addition to the ninety-six-page illustrated report, the delegates were shown a twelve-foot-long model of the complex and a technicolor movie with commentary prepared by Oliver Lundquist explaining the design. Initial reaction to the scheme was largely favorable. Philip Johnson, then architectural adviser to the Museum of Modern Art, pro-

nounced it "the best modern piece of planning I have seen"; Henry Wright, managing editor of Architectural Forum, deemed it "a completely workmanlike job." But there were naysayers as well, including the editors of the Washington Star, who criticized the "designers' diabolical dream" for "its isolation from historic thought, its independence of the accumulated feelings of centuries. They have sketched the 'new world capitol' as if it were something completely out of touch with the achievements, the hopes and the prayers of humanity since written records first were kept." Frank Lloyd Wright was just as negative, describing the design as "a super-crate, to ship a fiasco to hell."[80]

Lewis Mumford was not very impressed either. To begin with, he thought the design was old hat, a warmed-over combination of Le Corbusier's "breezy City of the Future and the businesslike congestion of Rockefeller Center, a blending of the grandiose and the obvious." Mumford was also critical of the site, saying that several other "magnificent" sites could have been chosen: "Perhaps the best, and the ripest (that is, the rottennest), would have been the area immediately south of Washington Square, a region almost destitute of tall buildings, let alone substantial ones. Imagine an assembly hall on the axis of Fifth Avenue. It would fill the eye, and if there were no skyscrapers near at hand to compete with it, it would look thoroughly important, too; indeed, no other big building in the city would be set off to better advantage." Mumford also came down hard on Moses's plans for the uplands west of the site: "The present approach to the United Nations is a sordid slum, and it cannot be left to the erratic beneficences of free enterprise to provide the only approach that would be aesthetically sound; namely, a group of related buildings, conceived in accordance with the function and purpose of the United Nations headquarters itself. To think that a strip of formal park will create the necessary atmosphere is not to think at all."[81]

As drawings for the U.N. complex were being developed during 1948, and the city was embarking on $20 million worth of improvements around the site, the very future of the undertaking seemed threatened because of Congress's failure to authorize the $65 million interest-free loan needed to construct the buildings.[82] But after Governor Thomas Dewey, Republican candidate for president, lent his support on July 2, it was clear that no matter who was elected that November, the project would go forward.[83] Groundbreaking for the Secretariat Building took place on September 14, 1948.[84] By October excavation for the first three buildings was well under way. Meanwhile, Le Corbusier, now back in Paris, called a press conference to complain that he hadn't been asked to supervise construction of the complex, which was being built from plans that, as he saw it, were "mainly my own work." But Harrison, replying on behalf of Trygve Lie, stuck by a masterly letter of conciliation he had recently written Le Corbusier: "I am delighted that you feel that you are the one who designed the United Nations Headquarters. It pleases me equally that other members of the Board have that same satisfaction. After all, the combined work was to be symbolic of the unity and selflessness of the United Nations."[85]

By June 1949, with the steel skeleton of the Secretariat rising, the thirty-nine-story glazed slab, 544 feet high, 287 feet wide and 72 feet thick, with 5,400 operable windows and 5,400 glass spandrels, began to take form.[86] It attracted the attention of architects, who marveled at its slender shape and technological innovations, and the general public, who hadn't seen a comparable large-scale construction project in New York since the completion of Rockefeller Center. To commemorate the founding of the world organization four years before, the Secretariat's ceremonial cor-

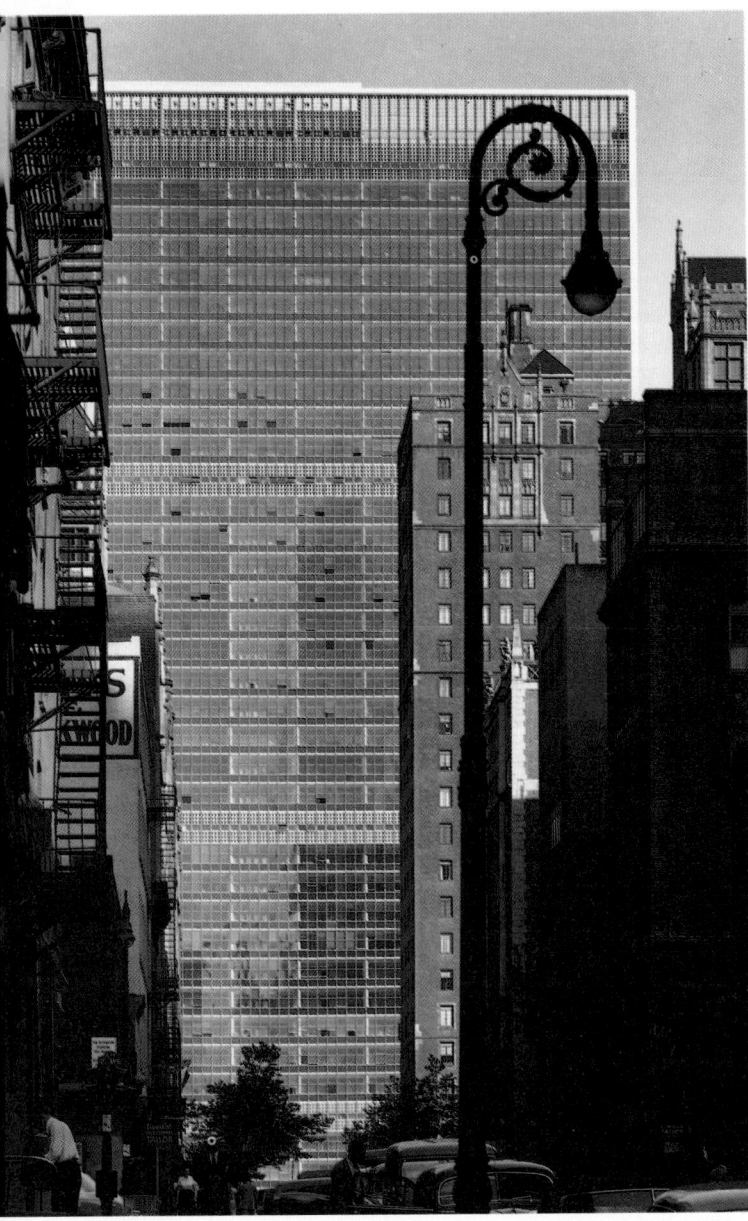

United Nations Headquarters, First Avenue to the East River, East Forty-second to East Forty-eighth Street. Board of Design, Wallace K. Harrison, Director of Planning, 1947–52. View to the east showing Secretariat. Stoller. ©ESTO

nerstone was laid on October 24, 1949, proclaimed U.N. Day by Mayor O'Dwyer.[87] Even as the building was under construction, Le Corbusier continued to rail against Harrison and his team; on December 7, 1949, he delivered another salvo:

> My plan was accepted and the Secretariat . . . is under construction. . . . But now I am refused permission to see what is being done. I have made official representations to the United Nations and I have been told I should be flattered my plan has been accepted. From a legal point of view I know they are right. I had no contract. I just gave my opinion as an expert. But it is a question of fundamental honesty. I should have been recalled to New York to supervise the construction of the palace.[88]

The construction details of the Secretariat were a revelation, especially for architects, who were impressed by the handling of the mechanical ventilation in pipe galleries at the sixth, sixteenth, twenty-eighth and thirty-ninth floors. Introduced to contain the building's sophisticated mechanical equipment, they were triumphantly expressed on the east and west facades of the building, where small-scale gridded intake grilles provided a distinct break with the otherwise uninterrupted curtain wall. (The pipe galleries were not ventilated at the ends, where the Vermont marble walls rose unbroken.) To achieve the effect of continuous glazing and near-weightlessness, the window walls were cantilevered 2'9" beyond the structural steel columns. The curtain wall itself, initially plagued by leaks, consisted of a four-by-twelve-foot aluminum grid into which was placed double-hung aluminum sash (seven four-foot divisions in each twenty-eight-foot-long bay). The blue-green heat-absorbing Thermopane glass was combined with Venetian blinds and a year-round air-conditioning system to provide brightly lit, workable interiors. The spandrels between window bands were of the same glass, but with the inner face of each panel painted black. Inside, the offices represented a high degree of integration as well, with movable modular metal partitions and a perforated metal pan ceiling that incorporated four-foot-long, three-tube troffer fluorescent light fixtures combined with square air-handling diffusers.

In the spring of 1950, with the Secretariat more or less complete, an avalanche of opinions was unleashed on its design and that of the U.N. as a whole, an outpouring that would not abate until all the buildings were completed in 1952.[89] Lewis Mumford, writing in September 1951, when the Secretariat was partially occupied, characterized the building as "a superficial aesthetic triumph and an architectural failure. A few more triumphs of this nature, and this particular school of modern design might be on the rocks." He objected to the sheer size of the Secretariat in relationship to the other U.N. buildings and he deplored the composition's lack of "spatial gradations between the midgets and the giant." He also found the Secretariat's tinted windows problematic, although he acknowledged the effectiveness of the great glass walls, which served "as a mirror in which the buildings of the city are reflected":

> No building in the city is more responsive to the constant play of light and shadow in the world beyond it; none varies more subtly with the time of day and the way the light strikes. . . . No one had ever conceived of building a mirror on this scale before, and perhaps no one guessed what an endless series of pictures that mirror would reveal. The aesthetic effect is incomparable, but, unfortunately, when the building is most effective as a looking glass it is least notable as a work of architecture.[90]

Only on dark days or at nightfall, said Mumford, did the Secretariat come alive; only when "the stabs of light on the ceilings of the offices add an unexpected liveliness to the west fa-

cade, making it almost the equivalent of a starry sky," did the building lose the sheer two-dimensionality of a mirror and take on a sense of three-dimensional space. At these times the building became "chaste, startling, fairylike in its cold austerity, a Snow Queen's palace, exhaling by night a green moonlight splendor." Although "paraded as pure engineering and applied geometry," Mumford continued, "this new skyscraper proves really to be a triumph of irrelevant romanticism. If anything deserves to be called picture-book architecture, this is it, for all the fundamental qualities of architecture seem to have been sacrificed to the external picture, or, rather, to the more ephemeral passing image reflected on its surface."[91]

Mumford took issue with the very idea of the slab, which he found functionally wanting, attuned more to the values of "a real-estate speculator trying to get the maximum possible amount of rentable space" than to the needs of the occupants: "A freestanding building can have light on all four sides, but the architects of the Secretariat have blanked out two sides of it with solid walls of marble." Mumford blamed this lack of attention to human needs on Le Corbusier, who, he said, was "hypnotized by the notion that the skyscraper is a symbol of the modern age." Skyscrapers "conceived without respect for human scale or insight into human requirements and values are indeed symbolic," Mumford said, but "they are symbols of the way specious considerations of fashion, profit, prestige, abstract aesthetic form—in a word, 'the package' of commerce—have taken precedence over the need of human beings for good working and living quarters." The Secretariat was thus, according to Mumford, a failure as both a conscious and an unconscious symbol, "since it symbolizes the worst practices of New York, not the best hopes of the United Nations."[92]

In a second assessment of the Secretariat, Mumford turned to the building's interiors. "So far from being the model office building it might have been," he said, "it is really a very conventional job." Except for a single bench at its south end, Mumford disliked every aspect of the building's lobby. He found it too low, providing unsuitable views through windows that opened to the river, where "the jeering, jangling hulk of the plant that ventilates the Queens Midtown Tunnel" was a prominent element. The west-facing wall was for Mumford the most blatant failure of the building's design. But he also protested the skyscraper type in general as a deterrent to communication between staff members, particularly those working on different floors, and he felt that it was especially ill-suited to the building's purpose: "A building to house an international personnel devoted to bringing about world cooperation and world peace should be more than a slick mechanical job. . . . It should be both a visual and an operational symbol, and its beauty should arise out of the due fulfillment of all its functions, graded in the order of their human importance. That is almost the last merit one could impute to the new United Nations Secretariat Building."[93]

Many other observers, however, felt the Secretariat was a meaningful symbol. The architect Henry Churchill, though he had his doubts about some of the details, particularly the top grille, which "does not hide the pent-house, which is actually a very simple shape and could very well have been left visible," nonetheless praised the building's symbolic qualities:

Visually it completely dominates the group: when one thinks of U.N. one thinks only of the vast green-glass, marble-end slab, although in plan it forms only a small part of the total building area. This visual dominance is probably as it should be, for in governmental organizations today the clerical worker with his

paper-shuffling and the permanent heads of departments, divisions, bureaus, sections are the people who get the work done. . . . It is somehow fitting that the Secretariat should become the symbol of the U.N.—an up-ended filing case for human beings, their hopes, their fears and their aspirations for a steady job. That is the new American Dream, a steady job, that is what we hope a United World will bring us, in the terms of peace and security; and of that the Secretariat is a just, if unconscious, expression.[94]

The editors of *Architectural Forum* devoted the better part of their November 1950 issue to the Secretariat. "Not since Lord Carnarvon discovered King Tut's Tomb in 1922," the editors opined, "had a building caused such a stir. Just as Carnarvon's discovery influenced everything from cigarettes to women's skirts, so the new Secretariat would change the face of every city in the Western World." Reviewing Le Corbusier's and Harrison's contributions to the complex, *Forum*'s editors observed:

So the Secretariat was plastically a work in the manner of Le Corbusier, and it was technologically, and as an organizational feat, an American product. In his justifiable fury against the Beaux-Arts mannerisms of American architects, Le Corbusier never acknowledged the degree to which an American architectural tradition underlay his own advance. Now, in the person of the Director of Planning, America had produced an architect in its own great tradition, capable of fusing the esthetic accomplishments of international modern architecture with the technological accomplishments which made it livable.[95]

The editors described the building as the first full-blooded realization of Mies van der Rohe's post–World War I glass skyscraper projects and as a descendant of Willis Polk's remarkably glassy Hallidie Building (1917) in San Francisco.[96] They also noted that glass, used at the scale of the Secretariat, would function less as a transparent skin than as a mirror, a point first made by Mies long before. Emphasizing the principal distinction of the Secretariat's design, the editors said the "shimmering veil" of the glass had "depth as well as surface."[97]

For this issue *Forum* had sent a questionnaire to leading architects soliciting their opinions about the Secretariat. These responses were then organized as a round-table discussion, labeled "A Great Debate." The discussion opened with George Howe's claim that "the Secretariat is a masterly example of the power of architecture to express monumentality by the use of the rectangle alone. It is a triumph of unadorned proportion."[98] Percival Goodman criticized this very monumentality, however, articulating in words and drawings two proposals: a continuous six-block-long, twelve-story-high, fifty-foot-wide office building; and a two- or three-story-high building covering the entire site, atop which could be placed three or four towers to house employees.[99]

The most interesting part of *Forum*'s debate focused on the Secretariat's impact on modern architecture. Howe believed that it would "justify architects, who now seem to be threatened by a romantic reaction, in the opinion that the possibilities of a reasoned expression of function through structure in unadorned proportional form, have not yet been exhausted."[100] Henry-Russell Hitchcock, the historian whose work with Philip Johnson and Alfred Barr had done so much to plant the seeds of European Modernism in American practice, offered a surprising assessment: "The building seems to me an end, not a beginning, and roughly speaking some twenty years out of date in terms of expression."[101] This was also the opinion of Rudolph Schindler, the Austrian-born Modernist who had been practicing in Los

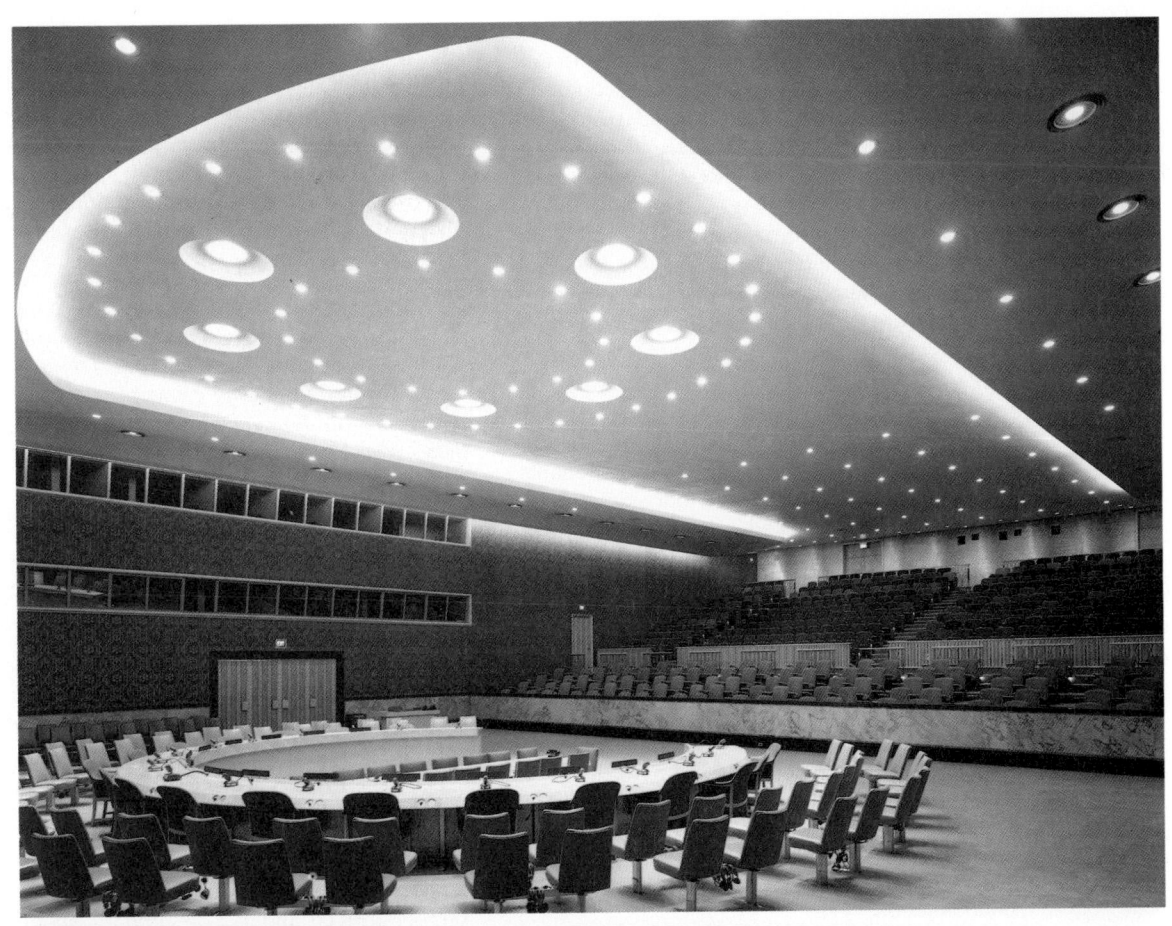

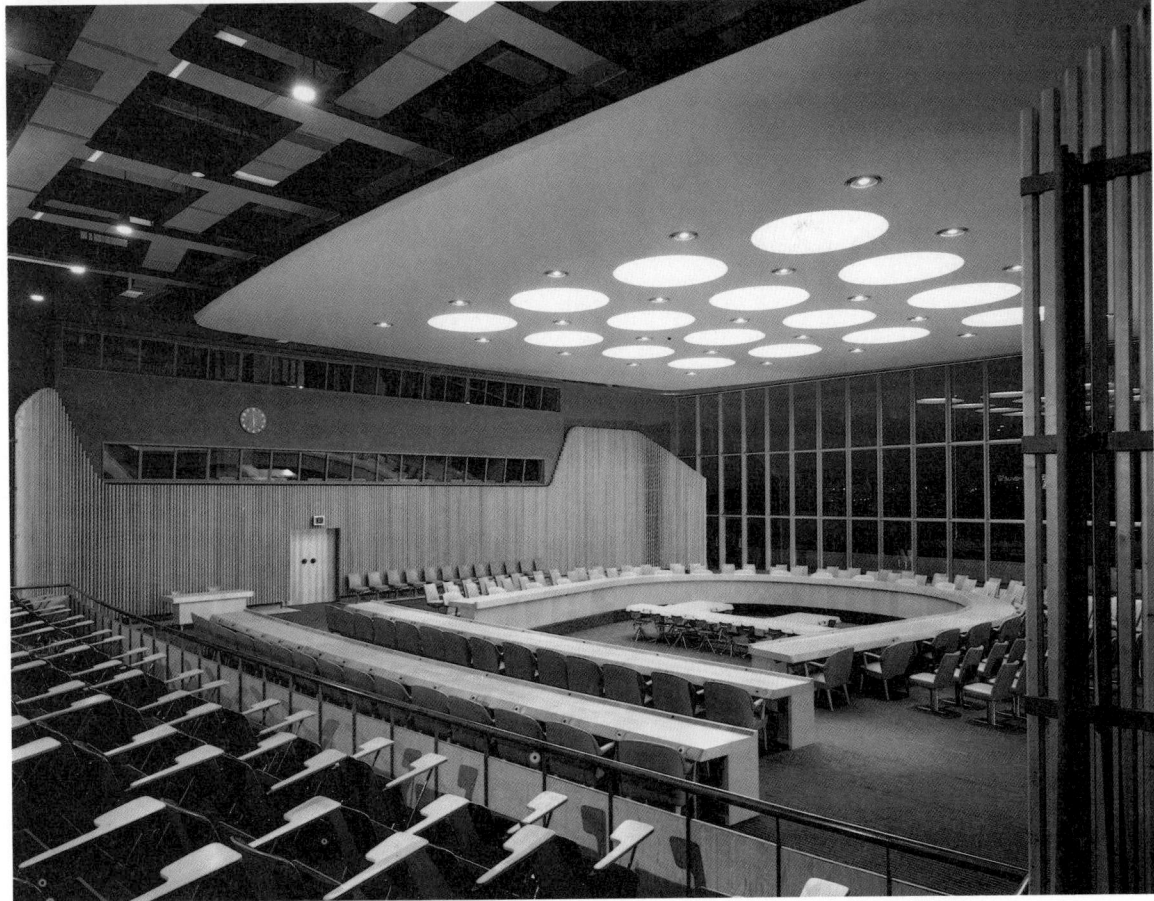

Angeles since 1920: "Let's hope that the UN buildings are the final apotheosis of the approach to architecture called the 'International Style' and that we will finally realize that 1 plus 1 equals 2 is true only in mathematics, but that in nature and art 1 plus 1 must become 3."[102] In their own conclusion, "Where Do We Go from Here?" *Forum*'s editors summed up their viewpoint:

> The new glass building on the East River had done a great many things: it had supplied a monumental symbol for the UN; it had produced a fine example of the free-hanging glass-and-metal curtain wall; it had given an impressive demonstration of the power of technology to control climate; it had proved that architectural collaboration (even among determined individualists) was not impossible. . . . Just as the modern Secretariat had supplied a monumental symbol for the UN, so the UN had, in turn, given modern architecture an aura of respectability, an association with world-wide prestige.[103]

The second component of the U.N., the 400-foot-long, five-story Conference Building, directly to the northeast of the Secretariat, was completed in February 1952.[104] The building, which *Architectural Forum* described as "both the most complex and the least visible" of the U.N. structures, contained three eighteen-foot-high principal rooms: one for the Security Council, one for the Trusteeship Council and one for the Economic and Social Council, each accessible to delegates, the press and the general public via secured passageways leading from the Secretariat and from the General Assembly.[105] Each council room faced east to the river, while a delegates' lounge was placed at the north end of the building, overlooking the formal garden. Conference rooms were located on the floor below, dining rooms on the one above.

Abel Sorenson, of the U.N. Planning Office, was responsible for the building's interiors, but each of the three council rooms was designed by a different Scandinavian architect. The Security Council, donated by Norway, was designed by Arnstein Arneberg, an architect of Oslo's town hall, who used a royal blue material embellished with gold decorations to cover the walls as well as for upholstery and drapes. This scheme, although more a simple "job of decoration" than the other two, as Olga Gueft observed and as Arneberg acknowledged, was still effective.[106] Henry Churchill found it "rich and consistent" yet "curiously antique; not 'old fashioned,' but reminiscent rather of the best late medieval decors."[107]

Finn Juhl's Trusteeship Council, a gift of Denmark, was quite different—"strikingly light and vibrant," as Churchill put it, with a ceiling that consisted of a series of fencelike wooden battens suspended below the network of structure and mechanical equipment.[108] These "floating screens," Gueft said, offered "lightness and freedom from the overhead pressure of a great dropped ceiling."[109] Juhl's ceiling would influence many designers in the 1950s, especially those undertaking shop renovations.

Sweden donated the Economic and Social Council, designed by the country's leading architect, Sven Markelius, who had also served on the U.N.'s Board of Design. Markelius produced what Churchill called "the boldest and most dramatic" of the three rooms, making a sharp distinction between the public gallery and the delegates' working area through a dramatic contrast of colors.[110] Overhead, Markelius reinforced the ceiling by painting the various beams and ducts in a pattern of grays, blacks and patches of off-white.

Despite his praise for the separate rooms, Churchill was not impressed with the overall ensemble: "Striking as all three principal Council rooms are, they do not speak the same language; they lack a common accord of dignity. They are vibrant, thin; their at-

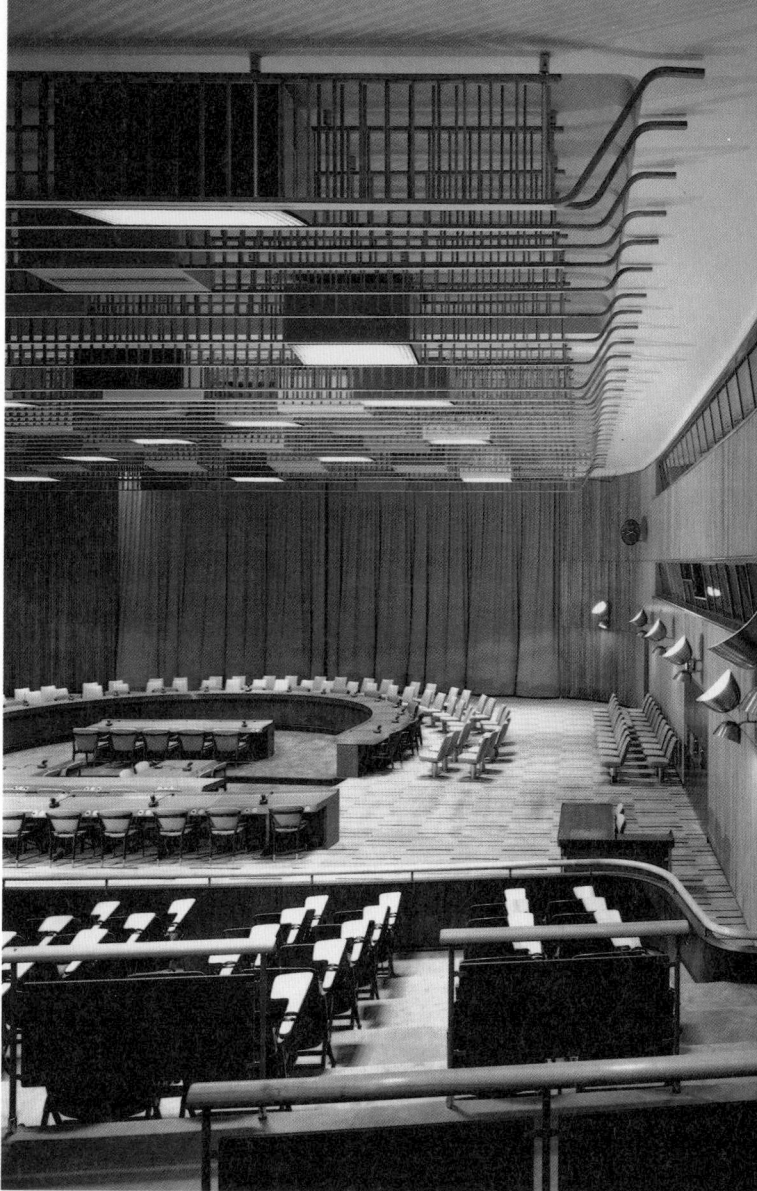

Top left: Security Council Chamber, Conference Building, United Nations Headquarters, First Avenue to the East River, East Forty-second to East Forty-eighth Street. Arnstein Arneberg, 1952. Stoller. ©ESTO

Bottom left: Economic and Social Council, Conference Building, United Nations Headquarters. Sven Markelius, 1952. Stoller. ©ESTO

Above: Trusteeship Council Chamber, Conference Building, United Nations Headquarters. Finn Juhl, 1952. Stoller. ©ESTO

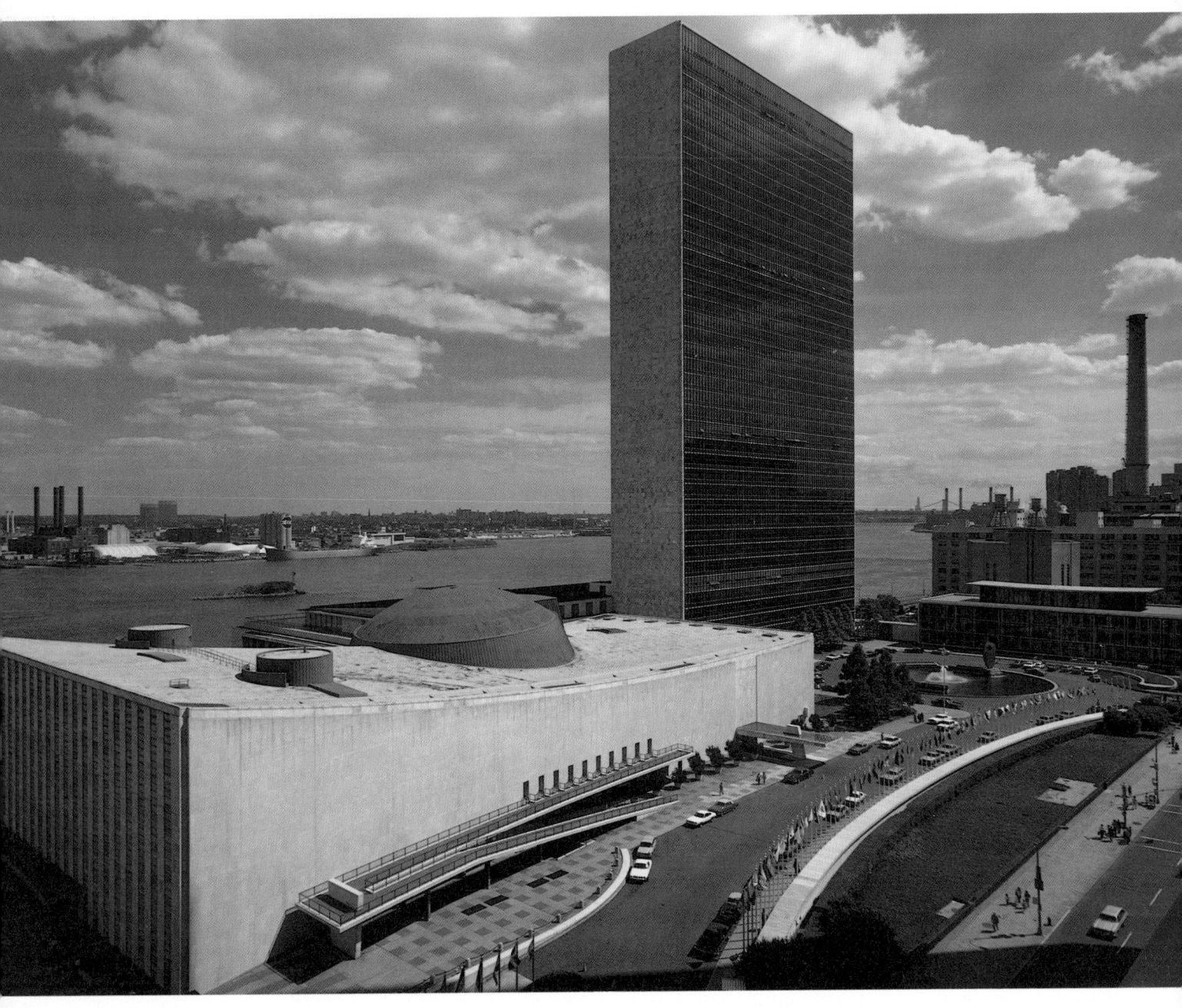

General Assembly Building, United Nations Headquarters, First
Avenue to the East River, East Forty-second to East Forty-eighth Street.
Board of Design, Wallace K. Harrison, Director of Planning, 1947–52.
View to the southeast showing Secretariat in the background. Stoller.
©ESTO

traction comes from and is on the surface, there is no depth. All three lack conviction; they are the expression of personal ideas of decoration, not the expression of an underlying and common culture. They are not, in fact, *architectural* decoration at all."[111]

The General Assembly Building was completed on October 9, 1952, and it quickly became a great favorite with the public, which valued the U.N. almost equally as an institution and as an exemplar of a new aesthetic order.[112] Perhaps the public liked the General Assembly because its form seemed familiar. This fact escaped Lewis Mumford, who lambasted the building, saying it resembled a motion picture palace, replete with two murals by Fernand Léger that he saw as comparable to the one Ezra Winter had created for Radio City Music Hall. As a "home for a great institution," Mumford concluded, "it is a painful simulacrum, the kind of thing Hollywood might have faked."[113]

The editors of *Architectural Forum* explained what they saw as the visual rationale for the Assembly Building's massing:

> The Assembly Building is the lowest of the major buildings in the UN group, and yet it is the climax. Eyes are drawn instantly to it by its central position, by the solidity of its unbroken stone walls—and above all by the powerful contrast with the surrounding rectilinear buildings of its sweeping curves. Being concave instead of convex gives the building the fresh impact of "the opposite"—as if an hourglass dress were to appear in a hoop-skirt society. The Assembly Building is therefore a mid-century lesson in architectural poetry, and what thoughtful men will discuss is the allowable degree of poetic license.[114]

The saddle-backed building, running north-south, turned a blank wall to First Avenue. This wall, clad not with the marble originally intended but a cheaper though lovely substitute, Portland stone from England, was relieved only by the delegates' entrance, a dramatic two-level ramp that recalled similar devices used in the New York World's Fair, and a dramatically shaped canopy. The all-glass south wall, tucked under a broad overhang, suggested an entrance but was in fact impenetrable; visitors entered at the north end, which was distinguished by a regular alternating pattern of flat, marble-clad, pierlike planes and translucent glass set above the doors. The overall effect was memorable, at least from some vantage points, as even Mumford had to admit: "Happily, viewed at one point—from the north, along First Avenue—the two visible buildings (the Conference Building is conspicuously absent) suddenly become a vision of delight, when the steep down curve of the Assembly roof, looking somewhat foreshortened from below, intersects the steep marble slab of the Secretariat, to the south. If one could stand permanently at that point, one could forgive all the architectural lapses."[115]

Inside, the Assembly Building encompassed two principal spaces, the visitors' lobby and the meeting room itself. The seventy-five-foot-tall lobby, lit from the north by vertical strips of marbled glass, had as its principal feature three dramatically cantilevered balconies and a ramp, supported on parabolic arches, which led from the lobby floor to the lowest balcony. Mumford noted that the effect of the room was comparable to a Meyerhold stage set of the 1920s and that the "billowing forms" of the balcony parapets recalled the black-and-white drawings of concrete structures that Erich Mendelsohn had published some thirty years earlier.[116] Paul Rudolph, the iconoclastic young architect, also saw the design in theatrical terms: "Of course the building is not really a product of the International Style but rather a background for a grade 'B' movie about 'one world' with Rita Hayworth dancing up the main ramp." Rudolph criticized the lack of "balance between the volume of the lobby and the extremely violent movement of the balconies and ramps, and the vertical movement of the prisonlike northern facade."[117]

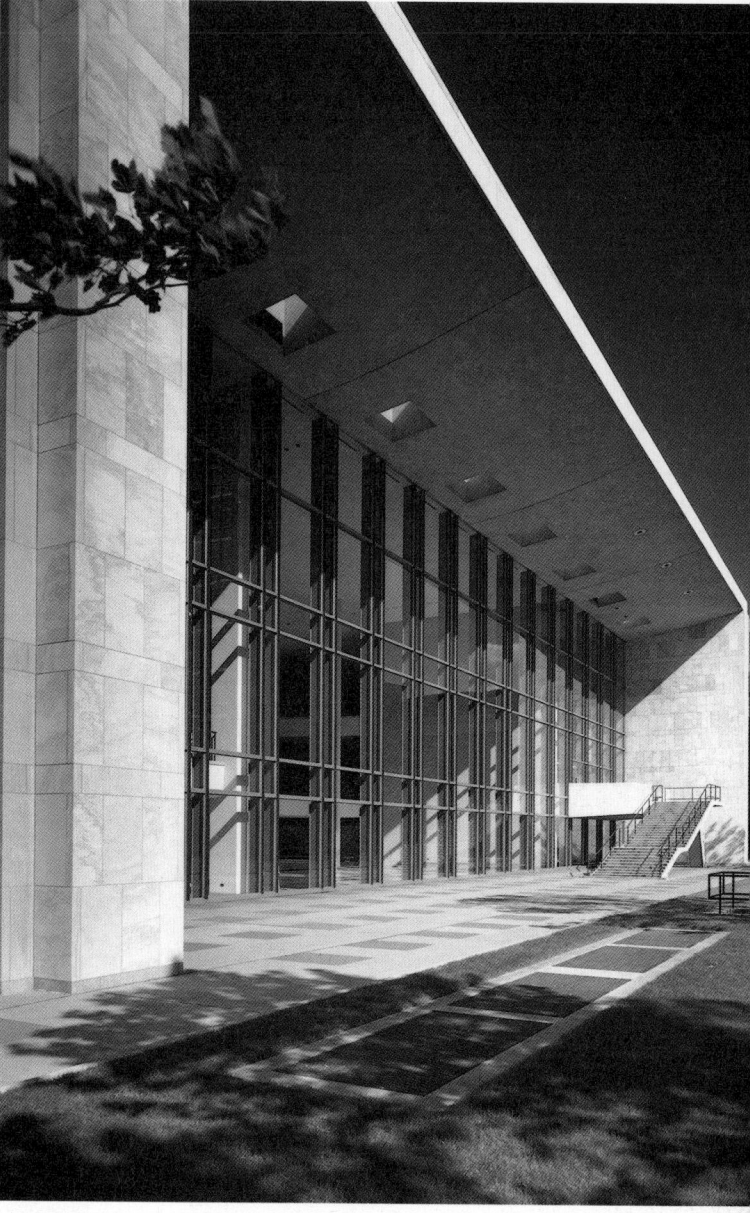

General Assembly Building, United Nations Headquarters. View to the northeast. Stoller. ©ESTO

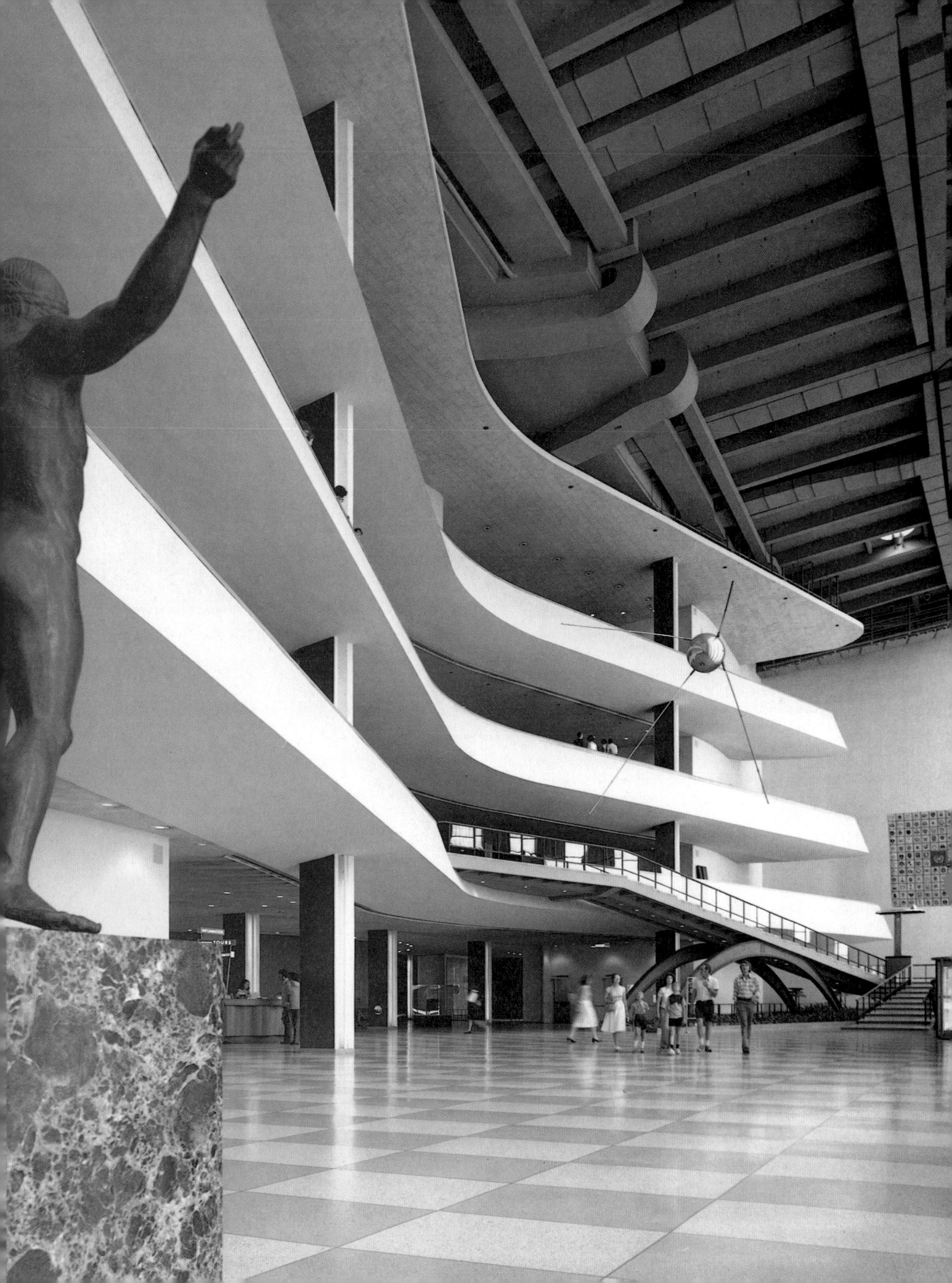

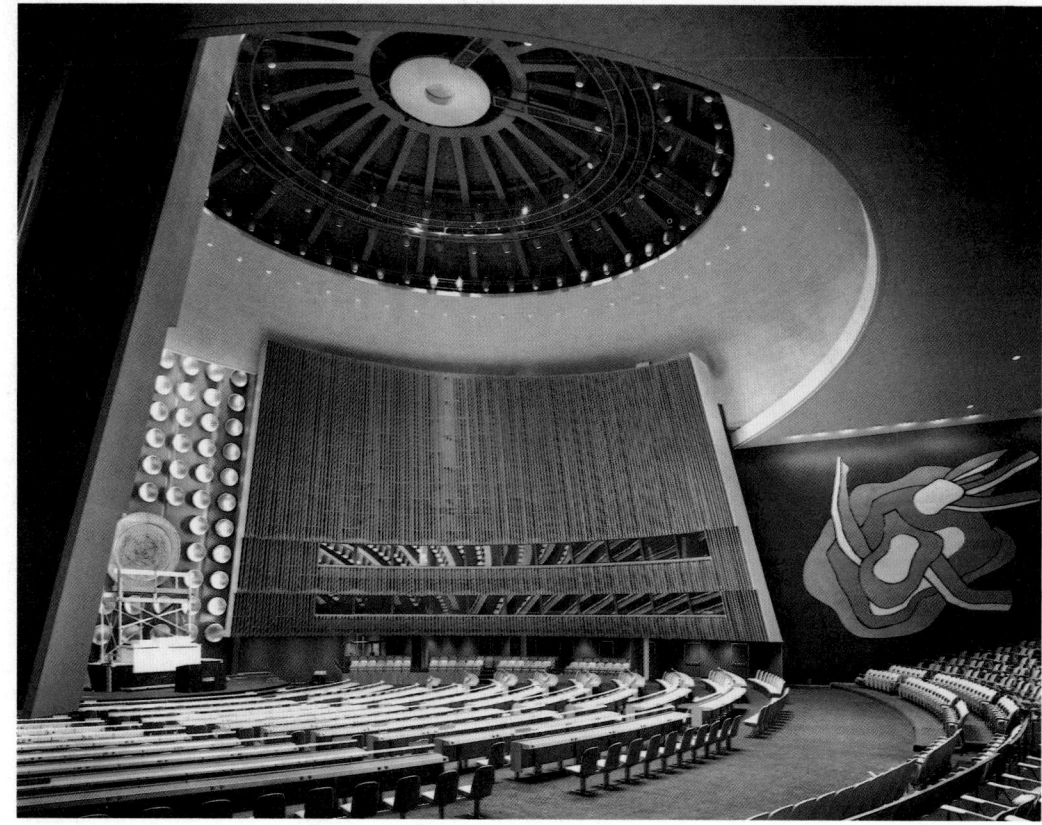

The General Assembly Hall, a circular room seating 850 people at gently terraced, continuous horseshoe-shaped desks, rose seventy-five feet to an open-ribbed dome painted powder blue. The semicircular wall of the south half of the room was dramatically canted inward and covered with gold-leafed wood strips to give the effect of fluting. The other half of the room was much more conventional, consisting of a tier of seats on the main floor and a balcony above. Paul Rudolph was even more critical of the Assembly Hall than he was of the lobby. Its most "disconcerting feature," he said, was "the lack of identification with the exterior form of the building," but he had other complaints as well: "The complicated intersections of the compound curved ceiling forms and the lack of a visual resting place for the exposed ribs of the center dome (it appears to rest on a curved plaster surface) is not to be excused. The sloping walls surrounding the timid dome seem to unwittingly symbolize a world which has indeed gone a long way toward crashing upon itself." All in all, Rudolph lamented, "The International Style has never been more misunderstood. Le Corbusier's diagram unfortunately did not indicate the way for the interiors of the UN Assembly Building."[118]

The editors of *Architectural Forum* defended the building against its detractors, arguing that its design had grown out of "a different temper and a different approach from some of the best known modern masters." They explained: "Here is a building that represents an intuitive series of treatments rather than development of a closely reasoned scheme; a series of episodes rather than a close-knit event; an empirical set of experiments rather than the compact exposition of a theory. *What is depended on to hold it all together is taste, judgment, personality.*" The editors placed the Harrison design squarely in "a continuing tradition" whose last great exponent was Harrison's mentor, Raymond Hood, "who used to hate what he called 'doctrinaire' modernism." The "em-

piricism" of Harrison's form making, they said, had resulted here in a work of "popular baroque, aiming at dramatic effect without too strong a regard for purity." *Forum* concluded its analysis on a cautionary note: "In the very act of damning the Assembly Building as a new version of Radio City Music Hall its critics have put their finger on something important. There may be here a closer relationship than in many a closely rational design to the hidden impulses that motivate the people: a subject worth thinking about."[119]

After their defense of the building, the editors of *Architectural Forum* canvassed the profession. Among the architects who responded were George Howe, who rejected the editor's suggestion that the design represented a "popular baroque" approach, and said he would "prefer a more analytical adjective": "One might call this interior, for example, the legislative phase of modern architecture. It seems like a well-meaning social statute adopted after a long debate and many compromises not always consistent." Howe went on to criticize the arguments in defense of the building: "I consider *Forum*'s fashion-style commentary as empty as a blown egg."[120] Pietro Belluschi, then dean of MIT's School of Architecture and Planning, was equally put off by *Forum*'s rationale, and asked: "How much rot can one contrive to serve up as a dish?" Belluschi found the *Forum* critique a "slick semantic exercise [which] tried not very successfully to make a case for Hollywood. If this is the fruit of 50 years' trial and error in architectural thinking, there is reason to be discouraged."[121] A young architect, Robert Woods Kennedy, lambasted the building, saying its style represented "eclecticism turned modern."[122] And finally, Landis Gores, a sometime partner of Philip Johnson's, wrote that "the ineptness apparent everywhere in the Assembly Building cannot be excused by a counteroffensive against architectural principle."[123]

In 1949, as plans for the design of the gardens and open

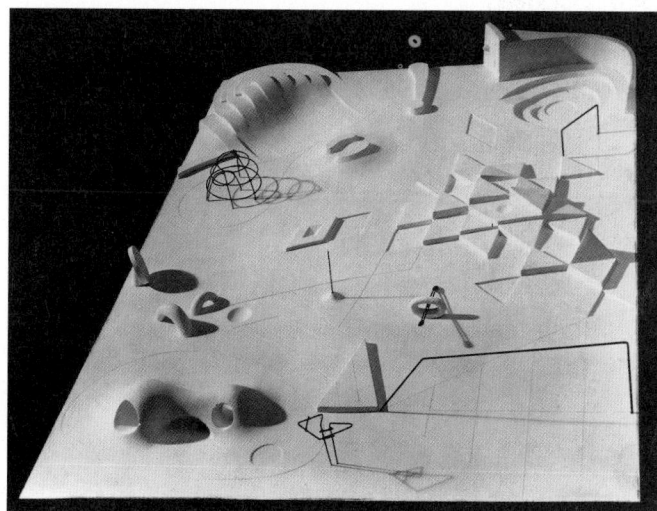

Left: Proposal for United Nations Playground, First Avenue to the East River, East Forty-sixth to East Forty-eighth Street. Isamu Noguchi, 1952. Model. INF

Below: United Nations Headquarters, First Avenue to the East River, East Forty-second to East Forty-eighth Street. Board of Design, Wallace K. Harrison, Director of Planning, 1947–52. View to the southeast showing park at northern end of site. C&R

space at the north end of the U.N. site were being advanced, Robert Moses proposed that a neighborhood playground be included.[124] When Trygve Lie reported that the delegates were opposed, Moses put the project temporarily aside. In 1951 Mrs. Thomas B. Hess, Mrs. John D. Rockefeller III and Mrs. David Levy, residents of Beekman Place, commissioned the sculptor Isamu Noguchi, collaborating with the architect Julian Whittlesey, to design an innovative playground for the 100-by-140-foot site at the northeast corner of the U.N. property that Moses had intended for his project. The three women planned to contribute $75,000 of the costs. Noguchi's interest in playgrounds went back nearly twenty years to his Play Mountain scheme (1933), also proposed for a site in New York. According to Aline B. Louchheim, a *New York Times* art critic, the model of the U.N. playground, which resembled "a contour or relief map," indicated that "much of the equipment would be built like sculpture" and would include tunnels, curved and step-like climbing areas, spiraling paths and a sloping area of multiple slides, as well as jungle gyms, swings and a wading pool.[125]

In March and April 1952 the model of Noguchi and Whittlesey's design was displayed at the Museum of Modern Art, which touted the playground as "the most creative and imaginative play area idea yet devised."[126] But Moses would have none of it. When shown the design, he stated: "If they want to build it, it's theirs, but I'm not interested in that sort of playground. If they want us to operate it, it's got to be our plans. We know what works."[127] With Moses so adamant, the playground's sponsors withdrew their support, but not without a final flurry of polemics, principally in the pages of *Art News*, where Mrs. Hess's husband, who served as managing editor, described the design as potentially "one of the most important integrations of modern art with daily life in recent years," and went on to berate Moses:

> The playground was killed by ukase from a municipal official who is supposed to run the parks in New York, and who somehow is the city's self-appointed guardian against any art forms except bankers'-special Neo-Georgian. The fact that he had no legal or moral right to dictate the U.N.'s aesthetics was of concern only to the many distinguished educators, child welfare specialists and civic groups who had seen the model and had hailed it as the only creative step made in the field in decades.[128]

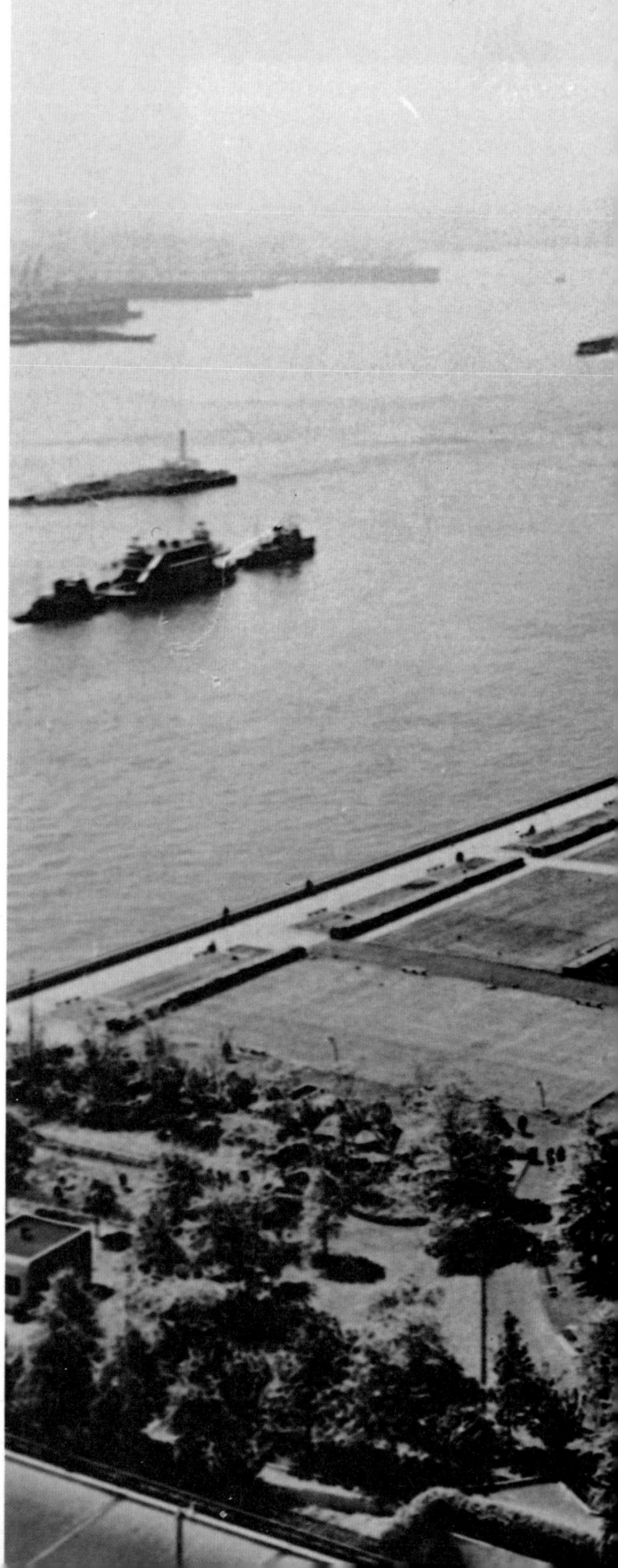

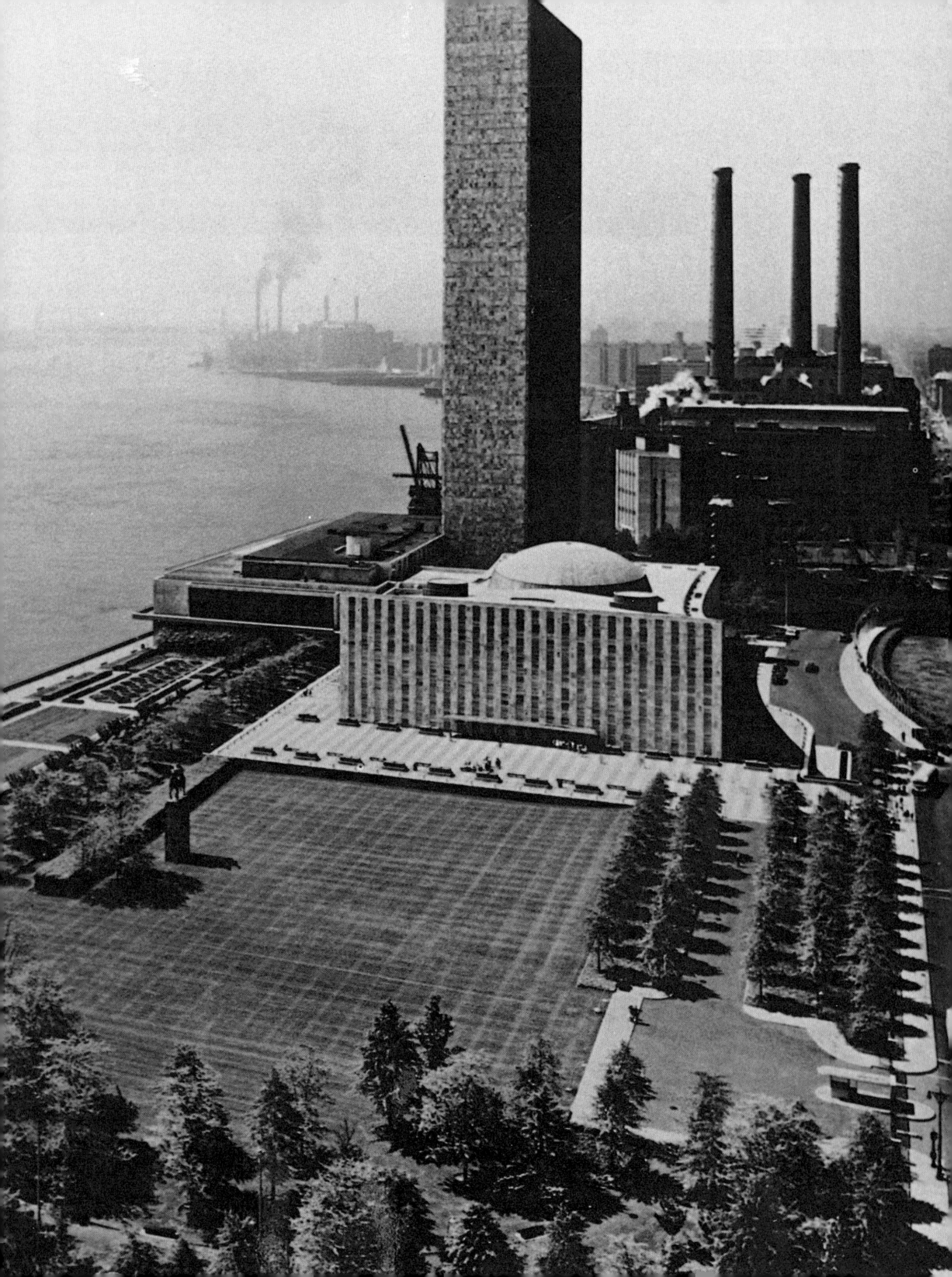

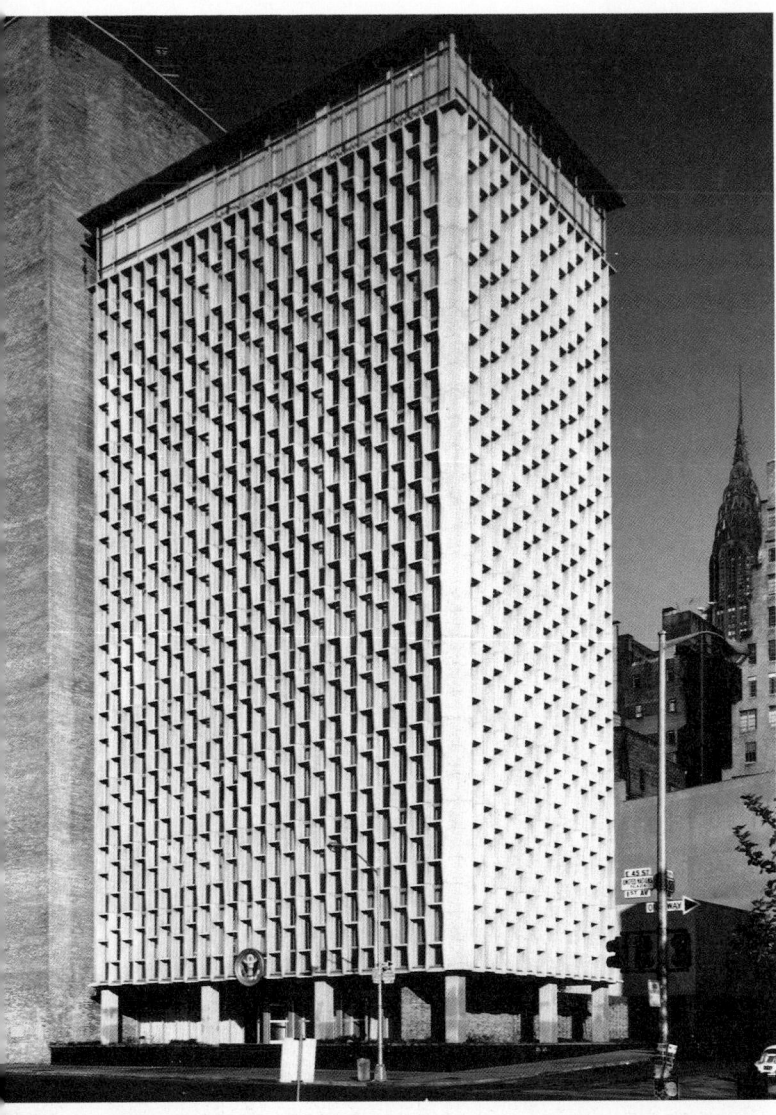

Although there was no coordinated planning of the area that lay between Second Avenue and the U.N. complex, redevelopment proceeded nonetheless, beginning in earnest in the late 1950s, when a motley collection of apartment houses, office buildings and some rather more imposing buildings designed for institutional clients began to replace what the *New York Times* characterized as "blighted tenements, scrubby sand lots and rows of dilapidated stores."[129] One of the first new buildings was 800 Second Avenue (1957), which occupied the entire east blockfront between Forty-second and Forty-third streets.[130] The site was formerly part of the Hospital for Special Surgery, which had occupied most of the block between First and Second avenues before selling its property to Beth David Hospital and moving to new quarters at 535 East Seventieth Street. It had originally been planned for an apartment house, but the demand for office space by U.N. delegations and by organizations doing business with the U.N. was so great that the developers decided to commission a design for an eighteen-story, 216,000-square-foot office building from Pomerance & Breines.

Some older buildings in the area were retained and recycled. In 1957 the American Institute of Physics occupied a renovated four-story warehouse, at 335 East Forty-fifth Street, facing First Avenue, once used as a furniture and upholstery factory.[131] But for the most part the existing neighborhood fabric was destined for replacement. The American Institute of Physics was joining two other important entities that had chosen to build new buildings close to the U.N.: the Carnegie Endowment for International Peace (Harrison & Abramovitz, 1953),[132] at 345 East Forty-sixth Street, on the northwest corner of First Avenue, and the I.B.M. World Trade Corporation (Harrison & Abramovitz, 1958),[133] on the southwest corner of First Avenue and Forty-sixth Street, which extended north to the as yet unrealized strip park the city was proposing along the south side of a widened Forty-seventh Street. The twelve-story Carnegie building featured limestone-clad lateral facades, while the east facade facing First Avenue was sheathed in metal and glass. The Carnegie Endowment occupied only the street, second, eleventh and penthouse floors of the building, leasing the rest of its space at favorable rates to other national and international nonprofit organizations that might have been accommodated in the unrealized north office building of the U.N. complex itself. Inside the building, the Knoll Planning Unit designed a number of the more important rooms, including the lobby and the penthouse lounge, depending extensively on the sculptural mass of furniture designed by Mies and other European Modernists to enliven the minimally detailed spaces. The design of the eleven-story, 66,000-square-foot I.B.M. building, located across the street from the Carnegie Endowment, was similar, although because it was clad entirely in limestone, the resulting building was much less interesting.

In 1961 the Engineering Societies Center was completed at 345 East Forty-seventh Street.[134] Consisting of a consortium of sixteen engineering societies, the center had been located at 32 West Fortieth Street (Whitfield & King, 1906).[135] Having outgrown that facility, the engineers unsuccessfully sought a number of other locations in the city, even threatening to leave New York, before settling on a prominent site running the block between Forty-seventh and Forty-eighth streets facing First Avenue. Shreve, Lamb & Harmon's design placed an eighteen-story slab clad in glass and stainless steel astride a two-story base sheathed in glass, steel and limestone. A large auditorium

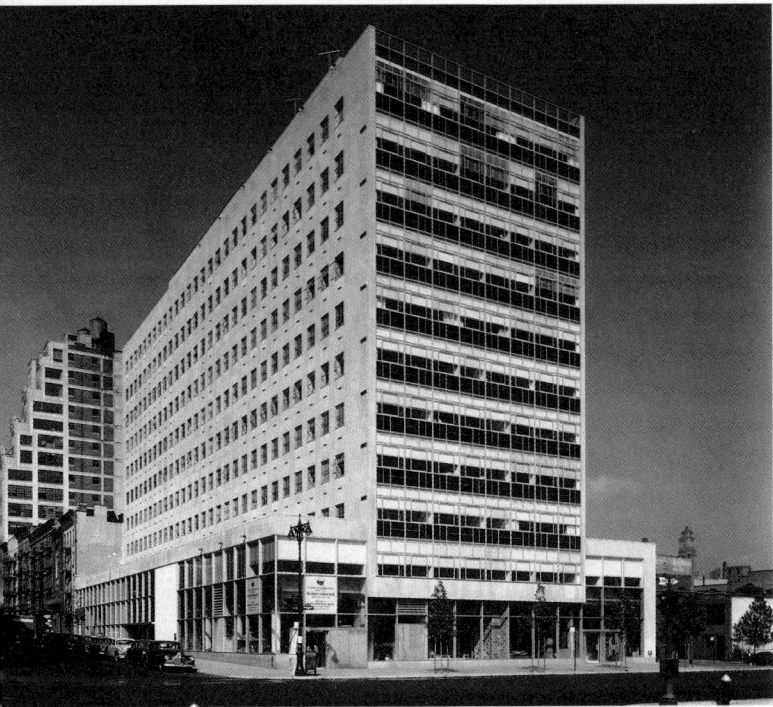

was located in the basement. The 258,000-square-foot building was entered from Forty-seventh Street, where the exterior structural columns supporting the slab formed a monumental porch approached across a small plaza.

The most important institutional entity to settle at the edge of the U.N. was the United States Mission to the United Nations, which occupied an unusual twelve-story slab jointly designed by Kelly & Gruzen and Kahn & Jacobs (1961).[136] Sited at the southwest corner of Forty-fifth Street and First Avenue, the building included a two-story auditorium wing along the north edge of the site that provided a transition between the main mass of the mission building and the remaining buildings on the block. This arrangement also guaranteed light to three sides, the fourth being occupied by a windowless service tower, clad in light gray-buff brick, at the west boundary. The most striking feature of the design was the cream-white cast-stone screen that was placed in front of the floor-to-ceiling glass curtain wall, justified as a sun-control measure but more likely an homage to the screenlike grille that Edward Durell Stone had in 1958 wrapped around his U.S. Embassy Building in New Delhi, then the jewel of the State Department's modern architectural crown.

The Methodist Board of Christian Social Concerns was another institution that chose to locate near the U.N.[137] Its twelve-story Church Peace Center (1962), designed by William Lescaze, was located at the southwest corner of Forty-fourth Street and First Avenue. Lescaze sheathed the bulk of the building in glass, concentrating his efforts on the base, which was separated from the superstructure by a recessed floor that formed a deep shadow intended to visually float the mass above. A stained-glass mural by the Belgian sculptor Benoit Gilsou was set back from the building line to identify the principal entrance feature along First Avenue. A virtually uninterrupted plane of travertine sheathed the base along Forty-fourth Street, isolating the building from pedestrians.

Harrison, Abramovitz & Harris's Institute of International Education (1964), on the west side of First Avenue between Forty-fifth and Forty-sixth streets, was a straightforward, fourteen-story, 100,000-square-foot glass-and-steel-faced structure that stretched one hundred feet along the avenue.[138] The institute was responsible for the administration of Fulbright Scholarships as part of its mandate to foster international exchange in education. Far more interesting than the building itself were the Edgar J. Kaufmann Conference Rooms on the twelfth floor, designed by the distinguished Finnish Modernist architect Alvar Aalto, whose only other work in the United States was the Baker House dormitory at MIT (1948).[139] Aalto's rooms were commissioned by Edgar Kaufmann, Jr., a curator, historian and critic of architecture who believed that the institute needed a ceremonial place to entertain important foreign guests and to hold meetings for about 300 people.

Aalto's scheme provided two conference rooms as well as a reception hall that could be used either as an auditorium or a large conference room. Movable partitions could be slid back into pockets to open up the space for even larger gatherings. The fan shape of the reception room, somewhat compromised due to considerations of acoustics and sightlines, was a signature of Aalto's, as were the undulating curves of the ceiling and the walls lined with birch rods ("spaghetti," as Aalto called them), which were gathered in one area to form shapes suggestive of tree branches or hockey sticks. Although the grouping was meant to suggest a stylized forest, it was, according to Ada Louise Huxtable, "reduced to a small stand of 'trees' by New York's fire laws."[140] At Kaufmann's request, the entire suite of

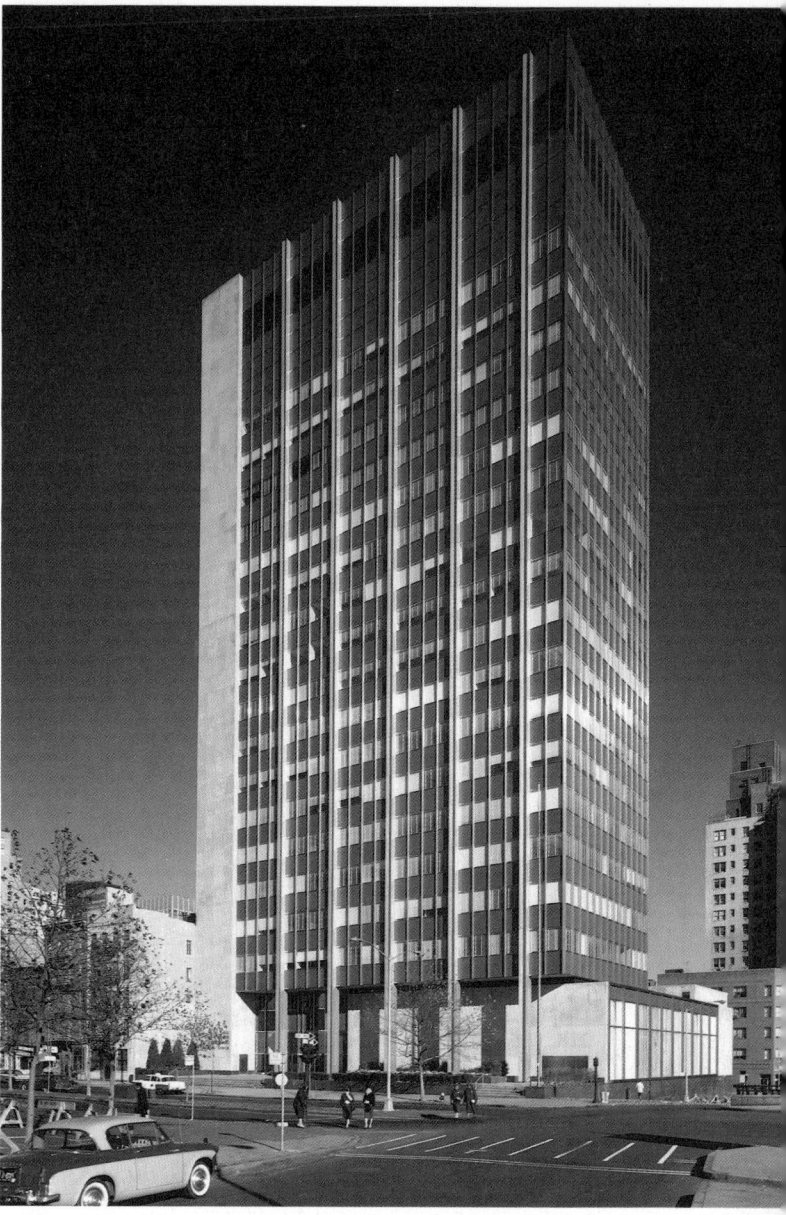

Top left: United States Mission to the United Nations, 799 First Avenue, southwest corner of East Forty-fifth Street. Kelly & Gruzen and Kahn & Jacobs, 1961. View to the southwest. GS

Bottom left: Carnegie Endowment for International Peace, 345 East Forty-sixth Street, northwest corner of First Avenue. Harrison & Abramovitz, 1958. View to the northwest. Molitor. JWM

Above: Engineering Societies Center, 345 East Forty-seventh Street, northwest corner of First Avenue. Shreve, Lamb & Harmon, 1961. Stoller. ©ESTO

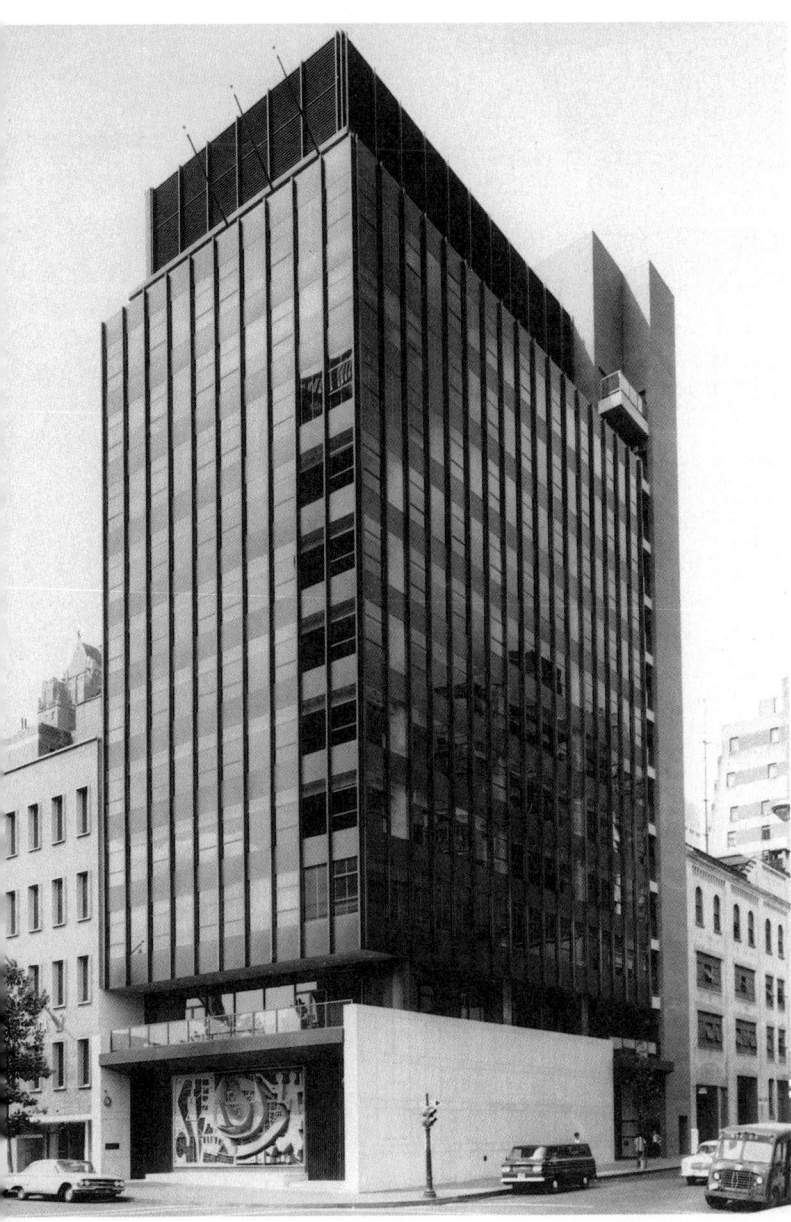

Church Peace Center, southwest corner of First Avenue and East Forty-fourth Street. William Lescaze, 1962. View to the southwest. SU

rooms was fabricated under Aalto's direction in Finland to insure unity of design and a high level of finish. To give some punch to the somewhat bland vocabulary of birch, ash and plaster, in the entry hall Aalto used dark, cobalt blue tile units to create frames around openings. Sparkle was added by specially designed light fixtures of filterlike screens made out of gold-plated copper and, in some fixtures, leather. Huxtable praised the suite as "the most beautiful and distinguished interior New York has seen in many years," saying that the rooms were "so far superior to corporate and institutional interior design here that they make the standardized, expensive ploys of teak-by-the-yard, carpet-by-the-vertical-inch and conference-table-by-the-ton seem flashy and cheap by comparison." She not only admired Aalto's superbly crafted details but also praised the "sensitive and loving manipulation" of the loftlike space, which "molds, instead of denying, the existing architectural shell. It is creative camouflage rather than destructive decoration. And it is frankly sensuous rather than severe."[141]

In 1963 Harrison's vision of towers at the north end of the U.N. site, dating back to his X City proposal of 1946, was at last realized when ground was broken for the two towers that would become 860–870 United Nations Plaza (1966).[142] The two thirty-two-story apartment towers were placed on a six-story base containing 336,000 square feet of office space, with a terrace floor atop the offices marking the transition between the two. (This terrace was initially proposed as a sun deck but was never used as such because it was felt that the sight of semiclad sunbathers would have an adverse effect on the value of the apartments on the towers' lower floors.) The apartments were entered through a common lobby off Forty-ninth Street, while access to the offices was from two lobby entrances on Forty-eighth Street. Set on 2.3 acres of land, the building housed 334 apartments, including fifty-six duplexes on the top eight floors, some as large as nine rooms and many with wood-burning fireplaces; their lavish size and logical plans represented a level of accommodation that was extremely rare in the postwar era. Harrison & Abramovitz's design, though unique for apartment houses in New York, was typical of Mies-inspired office buildings. Its principal subtlety was the difference in scale between the elements that made up the curtain wall wrapping the apartment towers and those of the wall enclosing the offices in the base.

Despite its hulking mass and the slightly brooding quality of its dark-tinted glassy facades, so much more like commercial office buildings than like the palazzoesque prewar apartment buildings that had set the standard of fashion along Fifth and Park avenues, the U.N. Plaza, as the development was commonly referred to, quickly became a fashionable address for the power elite, including many high-level corporate executives. This could be attributed to the level of amenities supplied the tenant-cooperators; the luxurious appointments within the apartments, which featured marble bathrooms; the convenience to midtown; the dramatic views of the East River, the U.N. itself and the midtown skyline; and the fact that the building was located at the foot of Beekman Place, long a fashionable address that had seen no new construction since the early 1930s. The building was favored by high society and the politically powerful as well as corporate types; the first wave of residents included the lawyer Christian Herter, Jr., the novelist Truman Capote, the philanthropist Mary Lasker, the former Attorney General William Rogers and Senator Robert F. Kennedy. Mrs. Lasker's apartment in the east tower was to serve not as her home—she was quite happy in her townhouse on Beekman Place—but as a kind of private art gallery for her growing col-

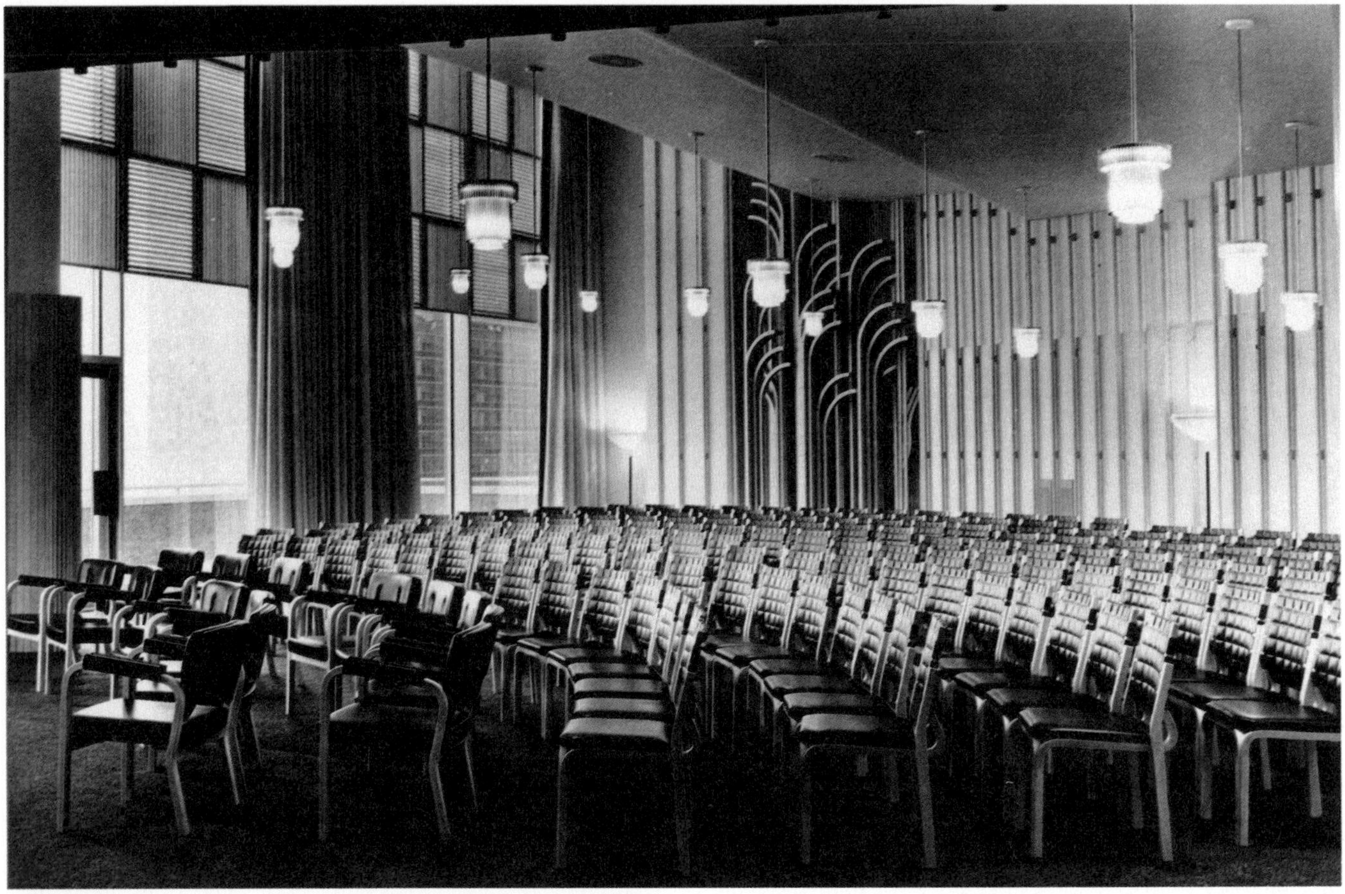

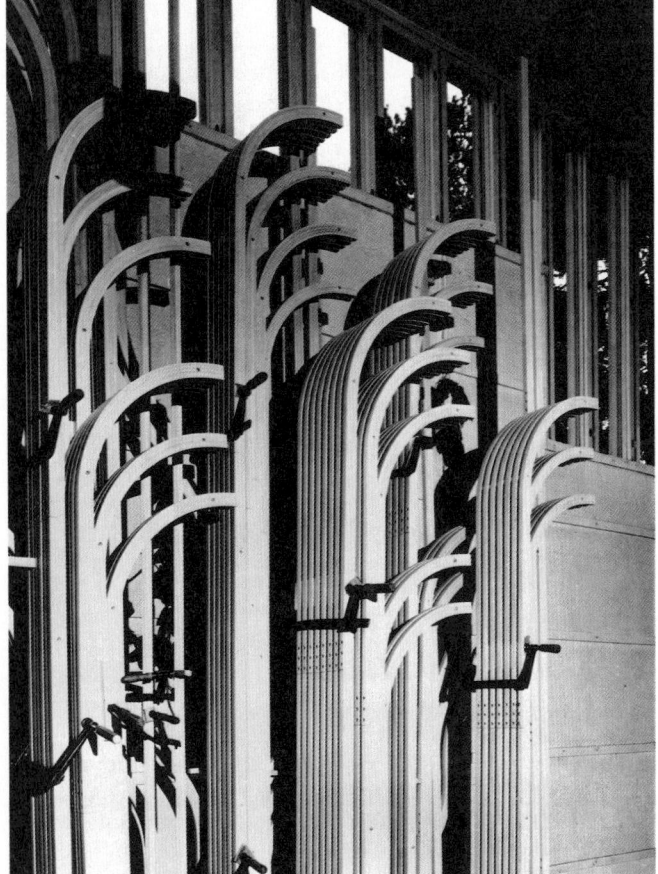

Above: Edgar J. Kaufmann Conference Room, Institute of International Education, 809 First Avenue, between East Forty-fifth and East Forty-sixth streets. Alvar Aalto, 1964. IIE

Left: Edgar J. Kaufmann Conference Room, Institute of International Education. Birch rods lining walls. IIE

lection of contemporary art. Some tenants, such as Bonnie Cashin, the fashion designer, chose not only to live in the project but also to take office space there.

U.N. Plaza became an instant landmark. In September 1966 *House Beautiful* chose a duplex apartment in the complex as the setting for a special decoration feature.[143] Emily Malino was asked to show the magazine's readers how there was room for plenty of "window treatments" and wallpapers, despite what the architects surely regarded as the building's principal asset, the continuous wall of glass. Many decorators tackling apartments for actual residents seemed to struggle against all that glass, but occasionally the interior design complemented that of the building. When Gerald Luss and Mart Gordon of Luss/Kaplan Associates designed a duplex for an art collector and his family, for instance, they combined marble floors, simple curtains and muted colors to create what Olga Gueft described as "less . . . a series of furnished rooms than . . . a pavilion, out of doors yet aloof from the soot and noise below."[144] An altogether different approach was taken by the designers Burt Wayne and John Doktor, hired by Stanley Schneider, president of Columbia Pictures, and his wife to decorate their apartment.[145] To avoid the clutter of table lamps that might block the view, the designers sprayed the walls and ceiling with a rough stuccolike surface and created stalactitelike protrusions from the ceiling to accommodate recessed downlights, creating an organic effect quite in contrast with the building.

Besides the challenge they presented to decorators, the all-glass facades of the "compound," as some of the building's denizens came to call it, presented other problems. *Time* reported that glare from the sun was so intense that some residents had taken to wearing sunglasses indoors.[146] For some residents, the building's glassiness was a privacy problem as well. One couple, enjoying cocktails across the street in the rooftop restaurant of Beekman Towers, discovered that the restaurant provided a perfect view of their U.N. Plaza bedroom. Another, Joyce Susskind, the wife of a prominent television producer, reported her amazement when, walking naked from her shower, she looked out at the view only to find a window washer looking in.

Although luxury apartments and office buildings were built in the new U.N. neighborhood, it lacked a cultural focus until 1971, when Japan House, headquarters of the Japan Society, was opened at 333 East Forty-seventh Street.[147] The only important building to face the widened street, Japan House replaced some small nondescript apartment houses on the midblock site, purchased by John D. Rockefeller III, the organization's president since 1952. The design of Japan House was entrusted to the Japanese architect Junzo Yoshimura, who had designed the Japanese house exhibited at the Museum of Modern Art in 1954–55 (see chapter 5). Yoshimura collaborated with George Shimamoto of Gruzen & Partners. The delicately detailed if somewhat dour four-story building married slick surfaces and continuous horizontal window bands with natural-cleft slate, shoji and bamboo screens, a combination that came off best at night, when the glow from the lights within emphasized the linear patterns of the various materials and the layers of enclosure. The intention was to create modern, minimalist equivalents for traditional elements of Japanese architecture, including a slanted, three-foot-tall fence that echoed the *inuyarai*, an "honorary bunker" insuring privacy in Japanese townhouses.

Raymond & Rado's sixteen-story, 100,000-square-foot office building, Two Dag Hammarskjold Plaza (1971), on the southeast corner of Second Avenue and Forty-seventh Street, was a quiet essay in minimalist aesthetics.[148] It was not the building, however, but the elevated plaza on which it sat that was important. In an unusual agreement, part of the relatively dreary and underutilized Dag Hammarskjold Park was leased by the city to the developer, Harry Macklowe, for 125 years, provided that he build and maintain a public sculpture garden integrated in the new building's arcade. In turn, Macklowe was allowed to build an extra 25,000 square feet of floor space. The plaza was designed to display outdoor sculpture in an ongoing series of changing exhibitions that helped to deinstitutionalize the neighborhood.

In 1966, with the cooperation of city, U.S. and U.N. officials, and the support of the Ford Foundation and the Rockefeller Brothers Fund, the East River–Turtle Bay Fund was established to help plan for the future of the U.N. neighborhood and provide office space as well as hotels and apartments needed to support the world organization's activities.[149] In 1968 schematic plans for the U.N.'s expansion were released and the organization changed its name to the Fund for Area Planning and Development.[150] The fund was headed by Ralph Schwarz, who had been director of building and planning for the Ford Foundation's own headquarters building, completed the year before. The plan proposed four major projects: a linear park along the East River; a United Nations office building; a mixed-use building combining apartments and a permanent home for the United Nations International School; and a visitors' center and hotel in conjunction with an office building for delegations. The park, which was to be built on a platform in the East River extending from Thirty-eighth to Forty-third Street, would include five tennis courts, two bocci courts and a basketball court; artificial grass was also a feature of the design. It was intended to compensate for the loss of a city-owned playground on the site just to the south of the U.N. Library, where the new office building, an eight-story, glass-clad structure designed by Harrison, Abramovitz & Harris, was to be built.[151] Connected by enclosed passageways to the Secretariat, the proposed building was to incorporate within its mass the ventilating shaft of the Queens Midtown Tunnel, which was the block's principal feature.

Designs for the mixed-use building that would house the U.N. International School were developed by Mitchell/Giurgola in association with Emery Roth & Sons.[152] Mitchell/Giurgola were also the architects for the school's temporary headquarters (1967) in a five-story loft building at 418 East Fifty-fourth Street.[153] The mixed-use facility was developed as an alternative to a waterfront site at East Twenty-fifth Street, which Harrison, Abramovitz & Harris were preparing designs for in conjunction with Waterside (see chapter 5). As the feasibility studies for the facility developed, the building was to combine 700 apartment units, parking for 300 cars and a school for 1,500 students on a site bounded by the west side of First Avenue and extending two-thirds of the way toward Second Avenue between Thirty-ninth and Fortieth streets. The apartments were meant to generate revenues for the school, which served on an equal basis children of U.N. employees and those of unaffiliated American families. Transformer stations and ventilating equipment for Consolidated Edison were to be incorporated on the street level of the project; the school would occupy the first four floors above; and the apartments were accommodated in an intricately planned slab set diagonally, from the northeast to the southwest corner of the site, in order to minimize the blockage of southern light to Tudor City.

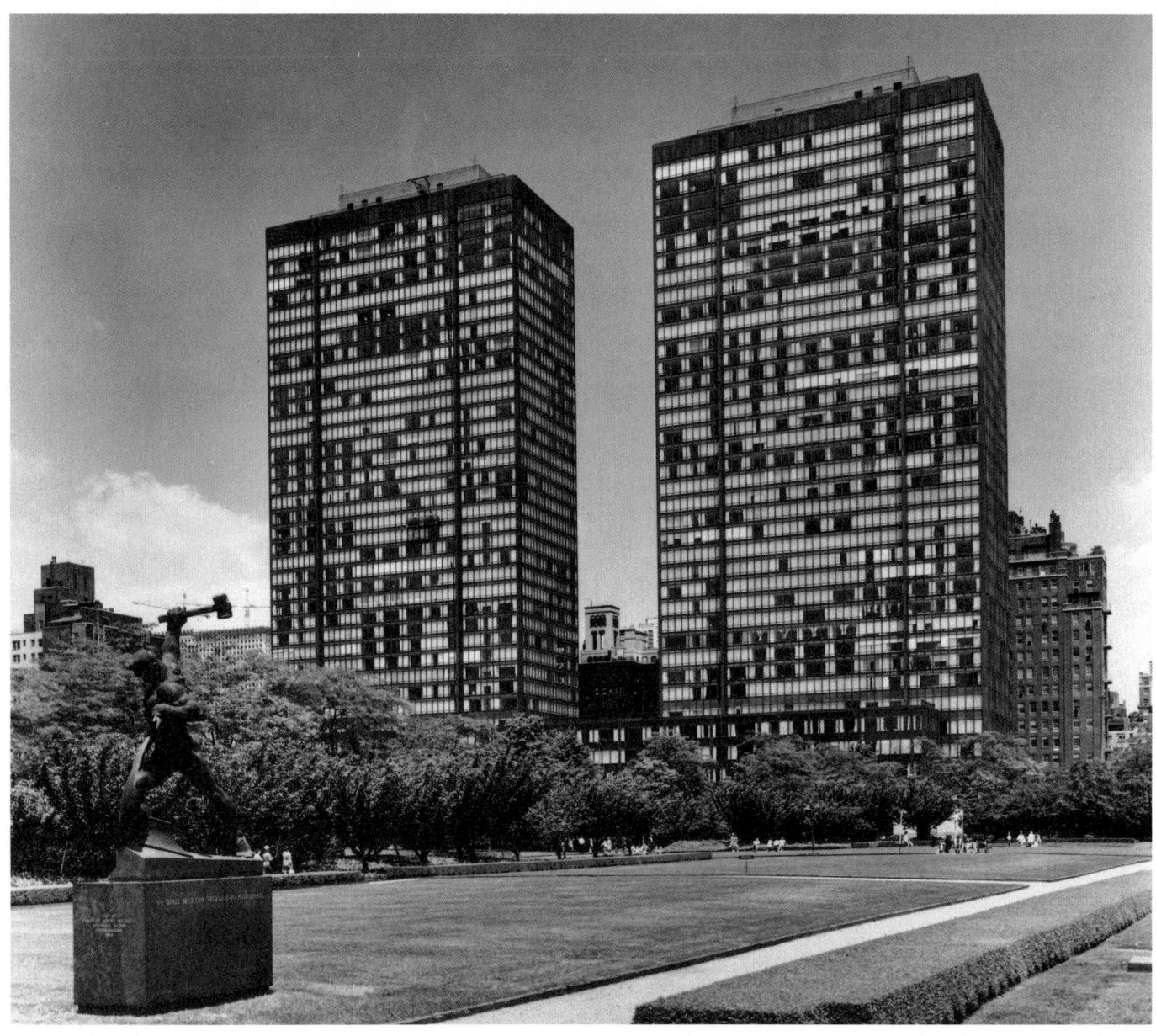

860–870 United Nations Plaza. Harrison & Abramovitz, 1966. View to the northwest showing sculpture *Let Us Beat Our Swords into Plowshares* by Evgeny Vuchetich, 1958. Wurts. MCNY

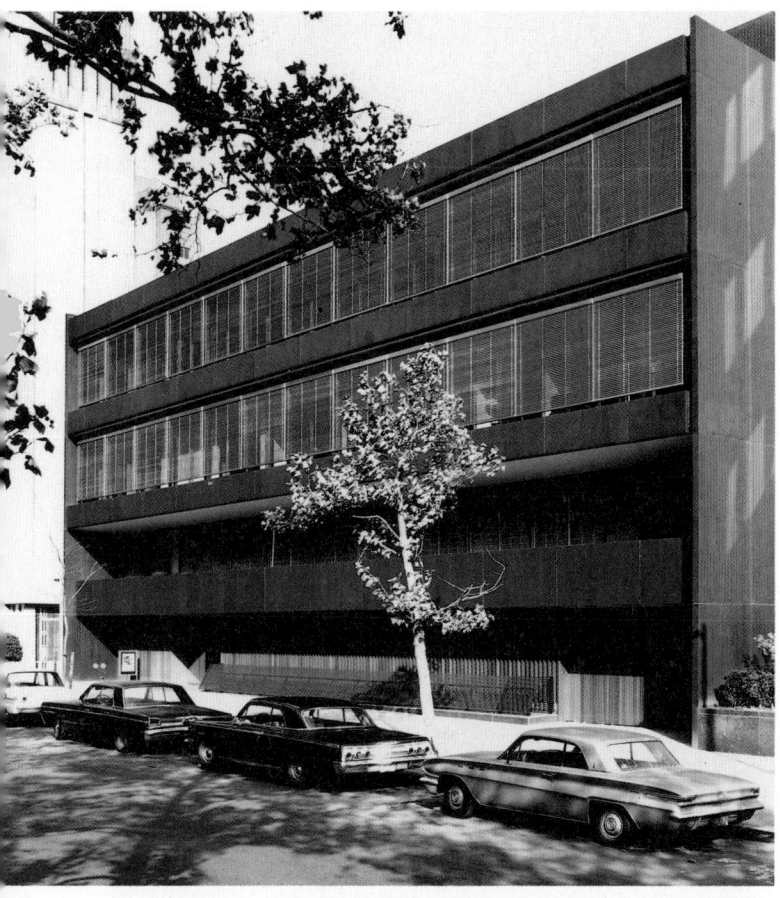

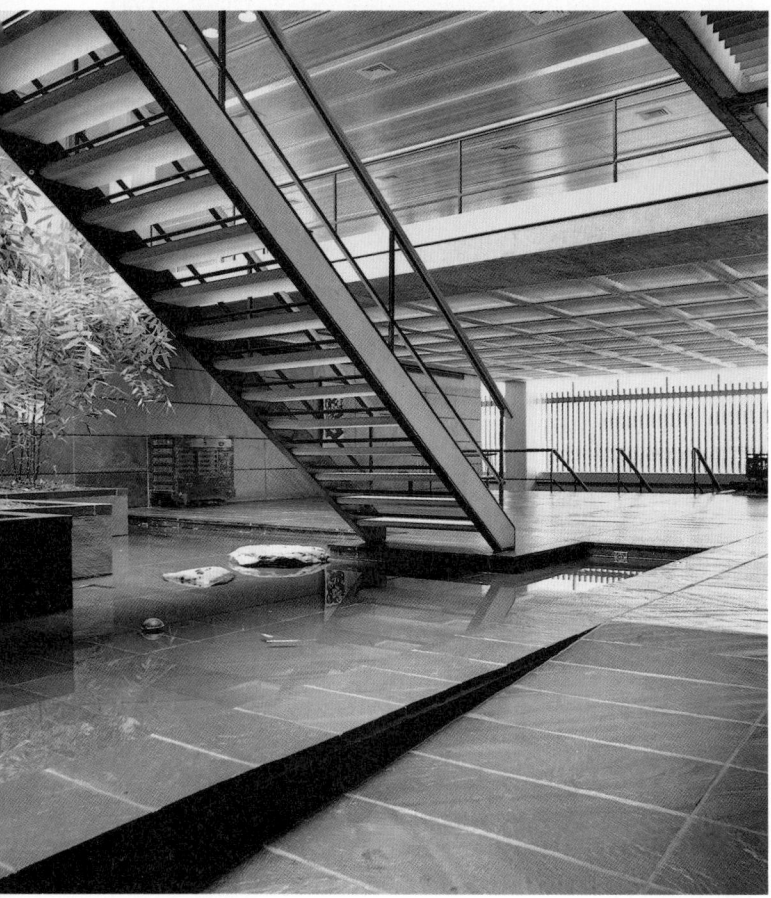

The final component of the plan, which proved the most interesting and controversial, was the only one to go forward. As originally conceived, it was a small urban renewal or redevelopment plan, calling for the creation of a more or less self-contained superblocked enclave bounded by First and Second avenues, Forty-third and Forty-fifth streets. The superblock would replace all existing structures, including Raymond Hood and Kenneth Murchison's landmark-quality Beaux-Arts Apartments, at 307 and 310 East Forty-fourth Street (1931), except for the U.N. Mission to the U.N.[154] Designs for this project were developed by Kevin Roche and John Dinkeloo, who had worked closely with Schwarz on the Ford Foundation Building. A preliminary version of the Roche-Dinkeloo design, released in the summer of 1968, called for a ring of eleven- to nineteen-story structures around the edges of the superblock, as well as twin forty-story towers on the axis of Forty-fourth Street.[155] Each tower would be square in plan but rotated forty-five degrees off the street grid. The boundary buildings were to provide almost two million square feet of space; the towers were to yield an additional one million square feet devoted to apartments and hotels.

The inner area of the superblock was to be developed as a podium that would house shops, restaurants and a visitors' center, as well as a terminal for tour buses and a parking garage. Because of the site's slope, the roof of the podium could be entered at grade at Second Avenue but would be one full story above First Avenue; thus it could be continued across the avenue as a plaza, which would enhance the approach to the U.N. complex. (Dag Hammarskjold Plaza was intended to perform this function but did not, because once the Secretariat was sited further south than early sketches had proposed, it led only to the park north of the U.N. complex itself.) A shop-lined walkway would penetrate the blocks to the north of the site to connect with Dag Hammarskjold Plaza.

By November 1969, of the four initial proposals, only the plans for the superblock were still being pursued.[156] As developed by Roche-Dinkeloo in 1968 and 1969 under a new entity, the United Nations Development Corporation (UNDC), a quasi-public organization whose majority shareholders were the City and State of New York, the plan emerged in a much larger form. Although it appeared to be a massive crystalline forty-story superstructure, to be sheathed in mirror glass, a material never before used in the city, it was in effect three buildings containing three million square feet of office space. Along the First Avenue frontage, a fourth building containing a 700-room hotel was proposed. The three office buildings were to surround a glass-roofed, 195-foot-square, 540-foot-high atrium, also forty stories tall, that opened to the southeast through its fourth wall, the only one to be sheathed in transparent glass. At the base of the well, a "rotunda" occupying the "backyard" space to the east was to be devoted to visitors' activities; a health facility was to be located at its top. An enclosed bridge would lead visitors over First Avenue to the U.N. complex itself.

The project, which needed City Planning Commission approval, had problems from the start. Although Mayor Lindsay and his City Planning Commission chairman, Donald H. Elliott, viewed it with enthusiasm, there was public resistance. Congressman Edward I. Koch was a leading opponent, questioning the project's bulk and density, originally with a floor area ratio of 12 and now pushed up to 18 FAR, the highest ever in the city. The populist columnist Pete Hamill attacked it on various grounds, ranging from the increased density it would bring to the neighborhood to its effect on air pollution to the dislocation of 700 resident families from the site. But, Hamill noted, his major

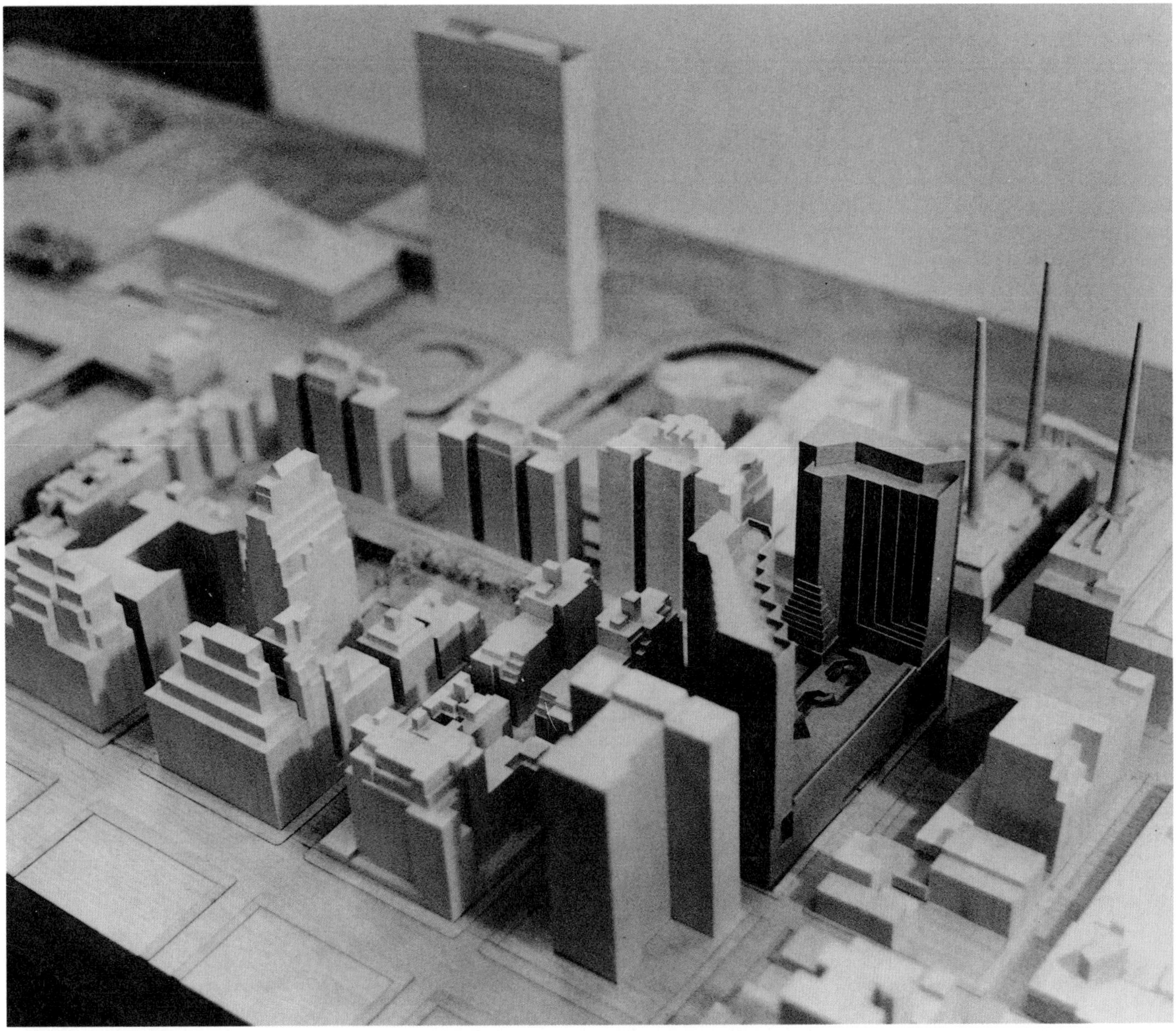

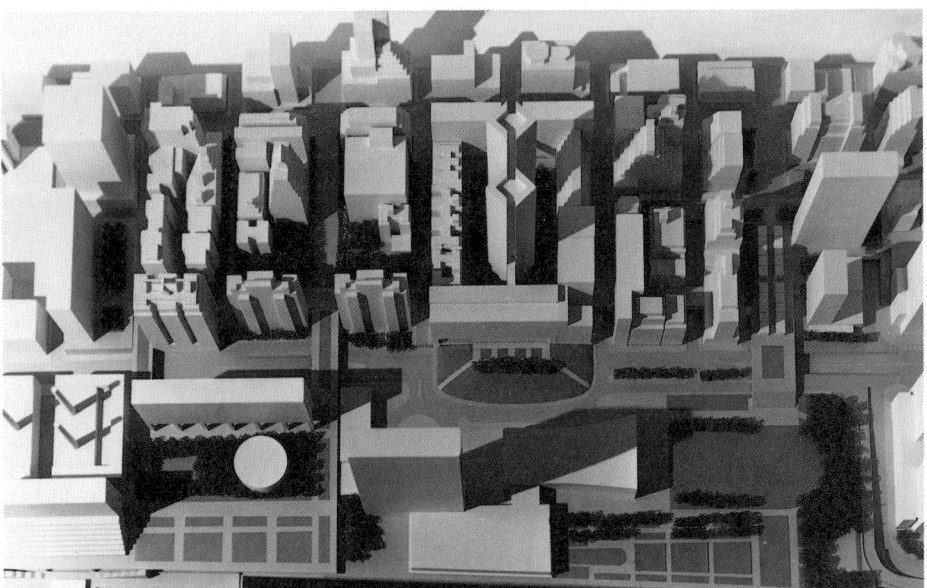

Top far left: Japan House, 333 East Forty-
seventh Street, between First and Second
avenues. Junzo Yoshimura, 1971. View
to the northwest. Steiner. GS

Bottom far left: Japan House. Interior.
©Norman McGrath. NM

Above: Proposal for United Nations
International School, between First and
Second avenues, East Thirty-ninth and
East Fortieth streets. Mitchell/Giurgola in
association with Emery Roth & Sons,
1967. Model. View to the northeast. MG

Left: Proposed mixed-use development
for the Fund for Area Planning and
Development, First to Second Avenue,
East Forty-third to East Forty-fifth Street.
Kevin Roche and John Dinkeloo, 1968.
Model. KRJDA

objection was "the assumption that it carries about this town; that somehow these free-loading diplomats assigned to the UN have some blessed right to live across the street from their job, while the rest of us have to come screaming into Manhattan on the subway cages."[157] A young assemblyman, Andrew Stein, urged that the development be relocated to Welfare Island, summing up the public's resentment neatly: "You can read the UN charter from end to end, and you will find nothing in that charter that guarantees to its personnel and officials the privilege of rolling out of bed directly into their offices."[158]

In late 1969 Ada Louise Huxtable expressed qualified enthusiasm for the design, emphasizing both the merits and the problems inherent in its scale. She called the Roche-Dinkeloo proposal an "architectural spectacular": "The immense, faceted forms of its three joined office towers and connecting hotel wing would be covered with a sleek skin of reflecting glass panels, giving the city back to itself in a kind of monumental architectural dissolve. The building is a superb tour de force, a giant trick with mirrors." But she felt that Roche's first plan, though rejected as financially unjustifiable, "was more successful in the resolution of the tie-up between the United Nations buildings and their immediate environs, to create what could truly be called a 'U.N. district.'" She went on to frame the issue more pointedly:

> The question being asked is whether the corporation, with its quasi-public status, tax-free bonds and substantial city tax abatement, is emphasizing the master planning job for which it was created, or putting up some elegantly speculative real estate. . . . The proposal raises this central issue: whether the development corporation is underwriting an extravagantly beautiful design that will be an international monument, but may not be the optimum solution in terms of urban design or rational economics.[159]

In a reassessment of the project three months later, in February 1970, Huxtable claimed to admire the design, though she never conveyed why. She went on to describe the "irony" of supporting the plan, which "does just about everything we know we should not be doing in New York":

> In the form it has taken—and the question being raised here is whether that form is right or inevitable, artistically or economically—it is inimical to the city's best environmental interests. It accomplishes its laudable objectives through a monolithic construction of crushing bulk and density and questionable community impact, total ghettoization of UN functions (at considerable convenience and security savings, to be sure) and the enshrinement—as urban design, no less—of the discredited real estate rule of "the highest and best use of land" being its most profitable use; that is, luxury office space in midtown Manhattan.[160]

Huxtable argued that "there is a lot more to 'public purpose' in urbanistic terms than wrapping up conventional investment economics in a smashing architectural package." She was uncharacteristically brutal in her attack on the high cost of the proposed building design, attributing the expense to extravagance and a desire for a grand gesture:

> What has pushed the price and the bulk of the project up is not just rising costs and the increased ratio of the commercial to subsidized space that this mandates—as claimed. It is also the cost of a kind of design grandeur that, to some observers, is as megalomaniacal as it is magnificent. . . . What is being subsidized, the UN's functional needs or the architect's esthetic needs? Or UNDC's edifice complex? . . . In the final analysis, the proposed building is a beautiful monster, created by monstrous economics.[161]

Despite critical objections, the project was approved by a slender five to four majority of the City Planning Commission in January 1970 and by the Board of Estimate three months later. Progress was delayed, however, when the UNDC failed to obtain federal loan guarantees. Eventually the UNDC turned to the New York State Legislature, and in 1971 an agreement was hammered out, but only after considerable compromise, including a reduction of the FAR to 15 and a $75 million limit on the amount of guaranteed bonds, enough to finance only the first phase of development.[162] Any future expansion would require another act of the State Legislature. With the new guidelines in place, the design was modified.

In 1975 the first portion of the Roche-Dinkeloo master plan was realized: One United Nations Plaza, a thirty-nine-story, 505-foot-tall slab that incorporated 360,000 square feet of office space on its first twenty-six floors and a 292-room hotel on the top thirteen floors; guest services and a restaurant were located at street level and a coffee shop and three small meeting rooms were on the second floor.[163] A health club with indoor swimming pool was located on the twenty-seventh floor and an indoor tennis court on the thirty-ninth. One United Nations Plaza occupied the north side of Forty-fourth Street, running one hundred feet west from First Avenue. The eccentrically massed building, the first in New York to combine hotel and office uses, was essentially L-shaped in plan, wrapping around two buildings, including the U.S. Mission to the U.N., so that at its western end it ran through the block to Forty-fifth Street.

In addition to two setbacks on its north side, which were sheathed with glass laid at a forty-five-degree angle to form shedlike roofs that enabled the building to be continuously wrapped, a twelve-story-tall portion of the building was cut away at its southeast corner, in deference to William Lescaze's Church Peace Center across the street (see above), which was also twelve stories high, and to create a greater impact from the northbound approach along First Avenue. A continuous glass canopy covering the sidewalk along Forty-fourth Street furthered the look of a naturally formed crystal, an impression not unlike that suggested by Hugh Ferriss in some of his drawings for the city of the future made during the 1920s.[164] To heighten the sense that the design was a phenomenon of nature rather than a mere building, the blue-green glass curtain wall was gridded in a pattern that denied any sense of the building's true scale. The 4'7"-by-2'7½" rectangles of glass, laid horizontally, did not relate to the floors of space behind them but divided the typical vertical unit into four equally sized panels.

Virtually all critics commented on the scalelessness and muteness caused by this facade treatment. As Paul Goldberger observed: "The glass covers everything like a great shining blanket, and its pattern offers no hint as to the goings-on inside."[165] In a later assessment, Goldberger said that the skin was so beautiful that one was tempted to overlook questions of scale, "to let this exquisite tower be the exception that proves the rule." The building, he said, "is an intelligent counterpoint to the U.N.'s Secretariat Building—the color relates well, the materials relate well, and the odd shape . . . provides an appropriate rhythm to play against the Secretariat's even slab."[166] John Tauranac, although troubled by the refusal of the designers to let the curtain wall suggest or describe the spaces behind it, also had praise for the facade: "When viewed from afar, say the FDR Drive in the twenties, One United Nations Plaza shimmers in the sun, like an oasis that is in reality a mirage. Fortunately, it is no mirage, and like all oases, its coolness is refreshing."[167]

Perhaps the most surprising aspect of the Roche-Dinkeloo

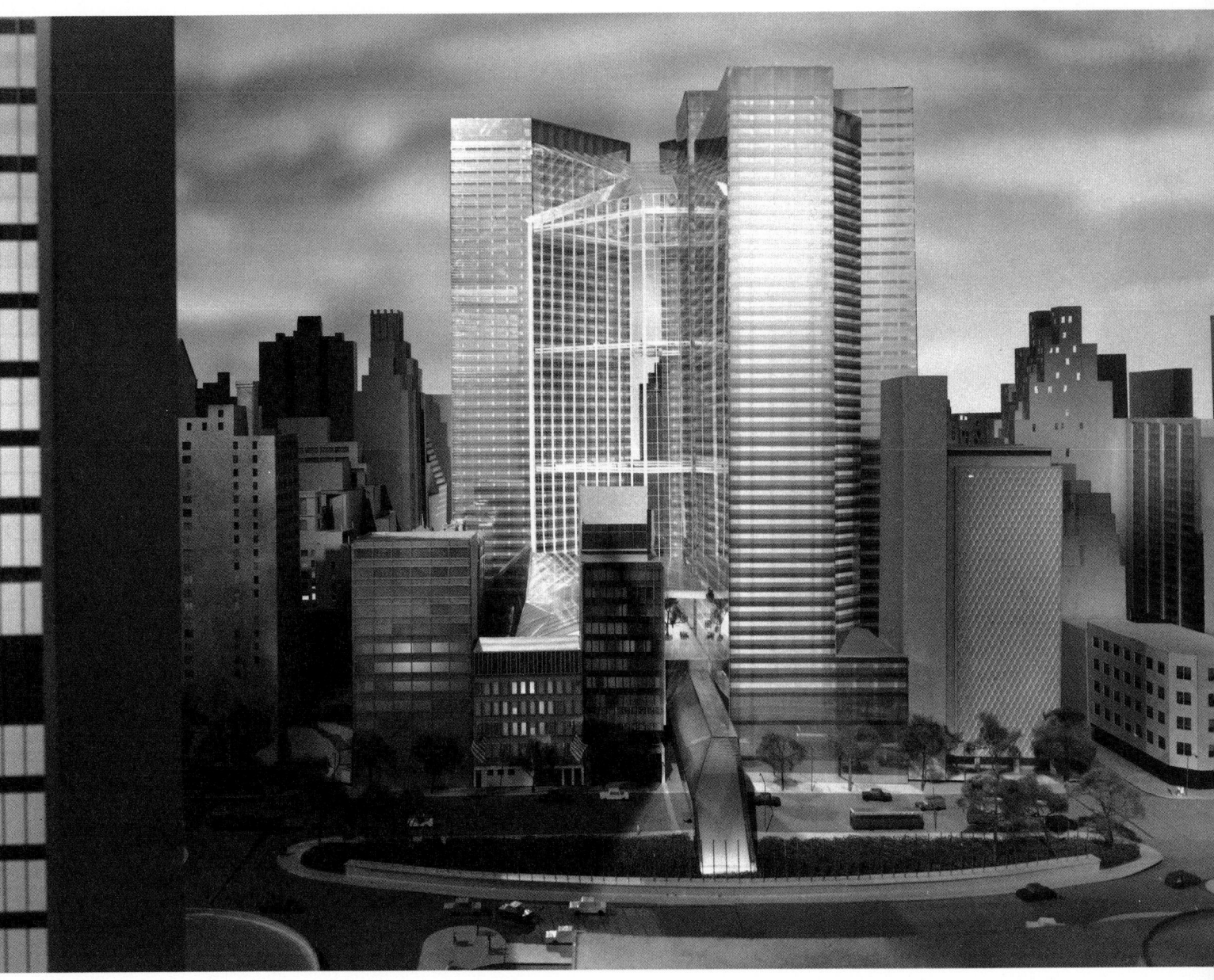

Proposed mixed-use development for the United Nations Development Corporation, First to Second Avenue, East Forty-third to East Forty-fifth Street. Kevin Roche and John Dinkeloo, 1969. Model. View to the west. KRJDA

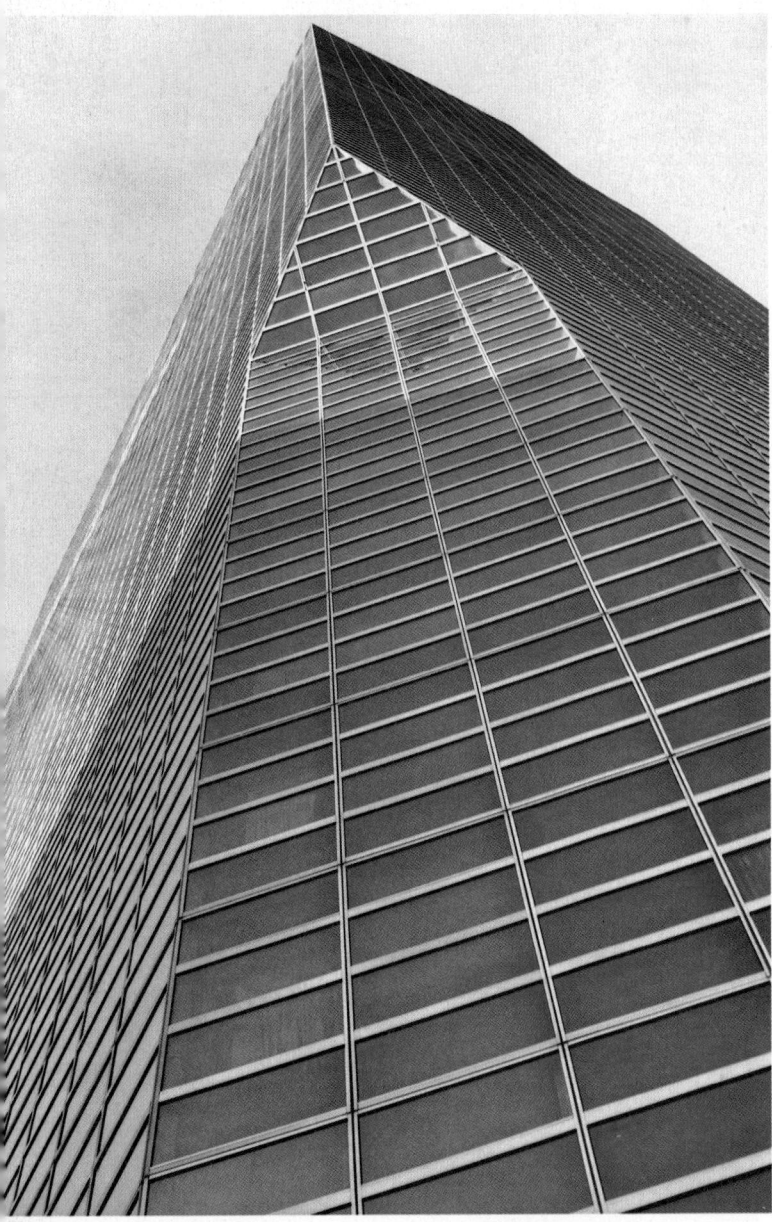

design was the fact that, despite the brilliant effects achieved, the building was almost as cheap to build as the typical spec office building—which definitively refuted Huxtable's earlier criticism that the UNDC development was extravagant. Though the quality of the office space was no better than average, and the interior fittings for the various U.N. departments housed in the building were rather dreary, the lobbies and corridors exhibited a higher level of detail and finish than was ordinarily the case. More spectacular by far was the hotel, for which Roche, in a departure from typical practice, was put in charge of the interior design; the result was characterized by Walter McQuade as a "hard edged hedonism."[168] The typical guest rooms were of average size and were furnished with stock pieces as well as some designed by the architects. Though the zolatone-painted walls and the faux fox fur bedspreads may not have been everyone's idea of glamour, Huxtable seemed to like the interior design, praising the use of "soft, unpatterned fabrics, in subtle, muted, nonstandard colors—taupe, grayed blue, rose beige." She also admired the architects' decision to replace "that universal hotel horror, the pictures on the walls," with high-quality framed embroideries, "from bold to delicate, chosen from every period and culture; many are of museum caliber."[169] More interesting were the suites, some of which were duplexes set behind the glass sheds, with double-height living rooms and open-riser spiral staircases. The swimming pool, with its magnificent skyline views, was tented over with white fabric, perhaps the most conventionally decorative touch. A corridor to the pool, slipped between the exterior curtain and the core, was lined with mirrors to heighten the dizzying view.

Best of all was the hotel's main floor, which could be entered from Forty-fourth Street or from a through-block driveway. Both the driveway and the lobby, which was small, were specially designed to meet the security needs attendant to a hotel catering to diplomats. The lobby was paved in Italian verd antique marble, which continued up the walls as wainscoting, above which a velvet-textured fabric was applied over panels. A wide chrome handrail set out from the wall held small incandescent bulbs, eliminating the visual clutter that table lamps would provide and washing the walls with what Huxtable described as "dark glitter."[170] Past the elevators, visitors climbed a few steps to the Ambassador Grill and Bar, where Roche created a spectacular setting using black and white marble squares on the floor. Overhead, above the circulation paths, was a false skylight, the panels of which were reversed mirror glass with pentagonal mirrors and a myriad of small lights behind, producing extraordinary reflections, especially at the points where the paths twisted around the Ambassador's subdued drinking and dining areas.

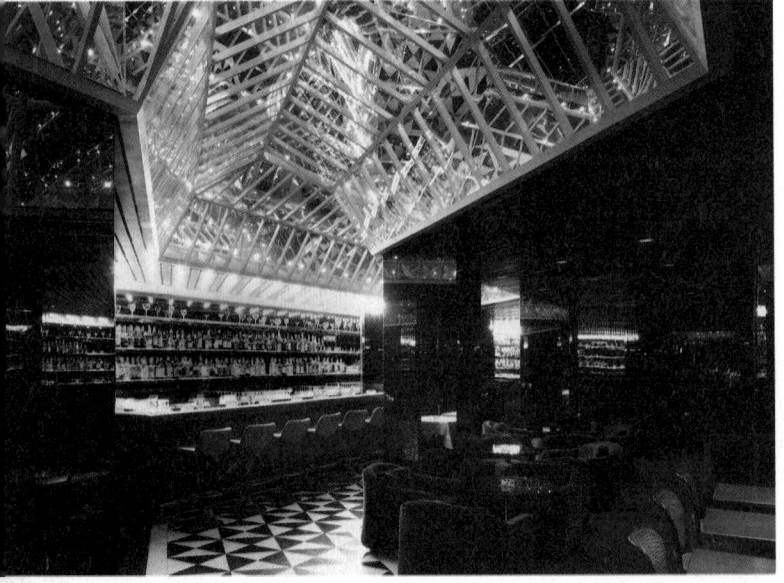

Top left: One United Nations Plaza, northwest corner of First Avenue and East Forty-fourth Street. Kevin Roche and John Dinkeloo, 1975. View to the northwest. Ries. SR

Bottom left: One United Nations Plaza. Bar. KRJDA

Right: One United Nations Plaza. View to the northwest. Stoller. ©ESTO

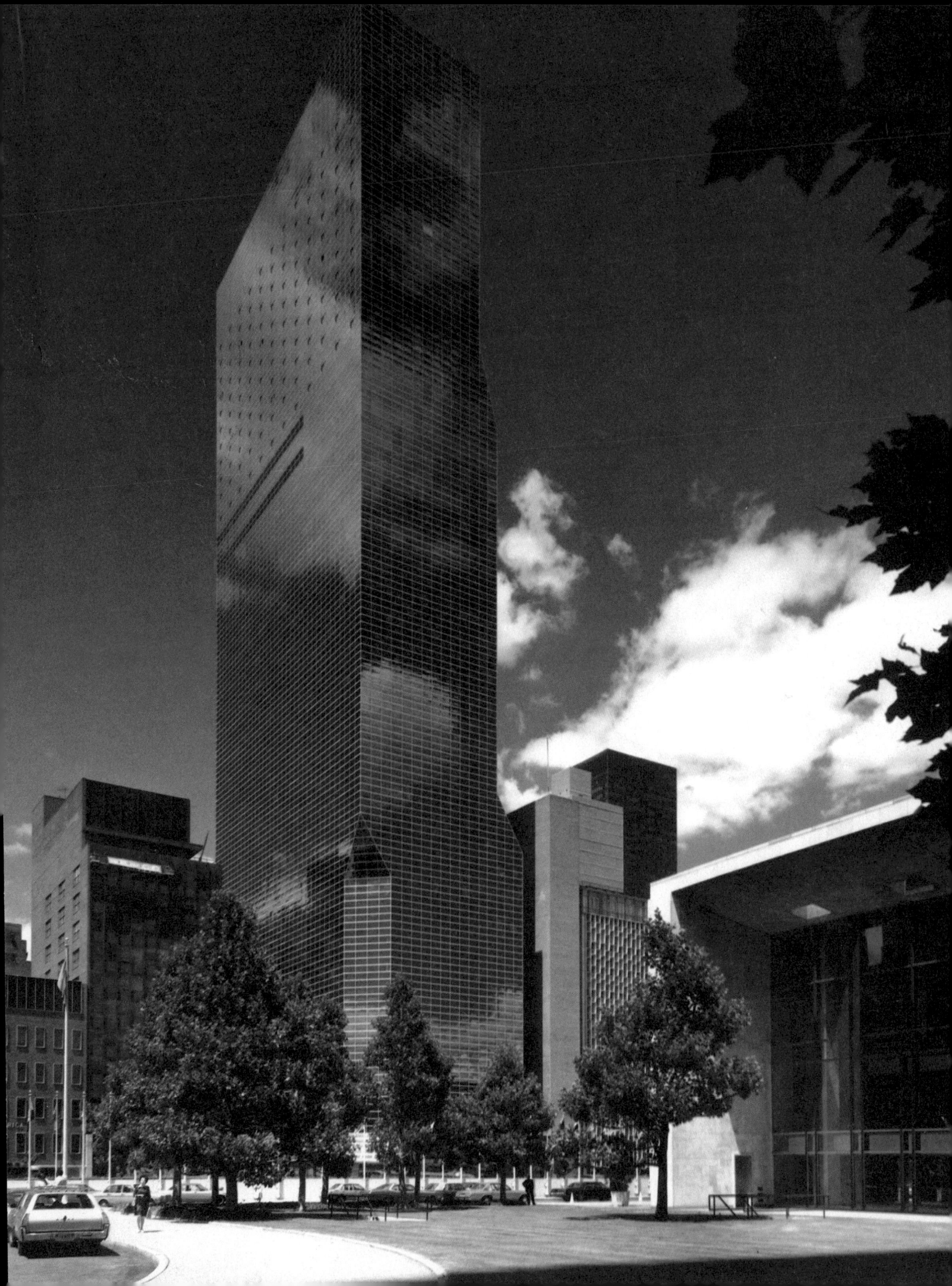

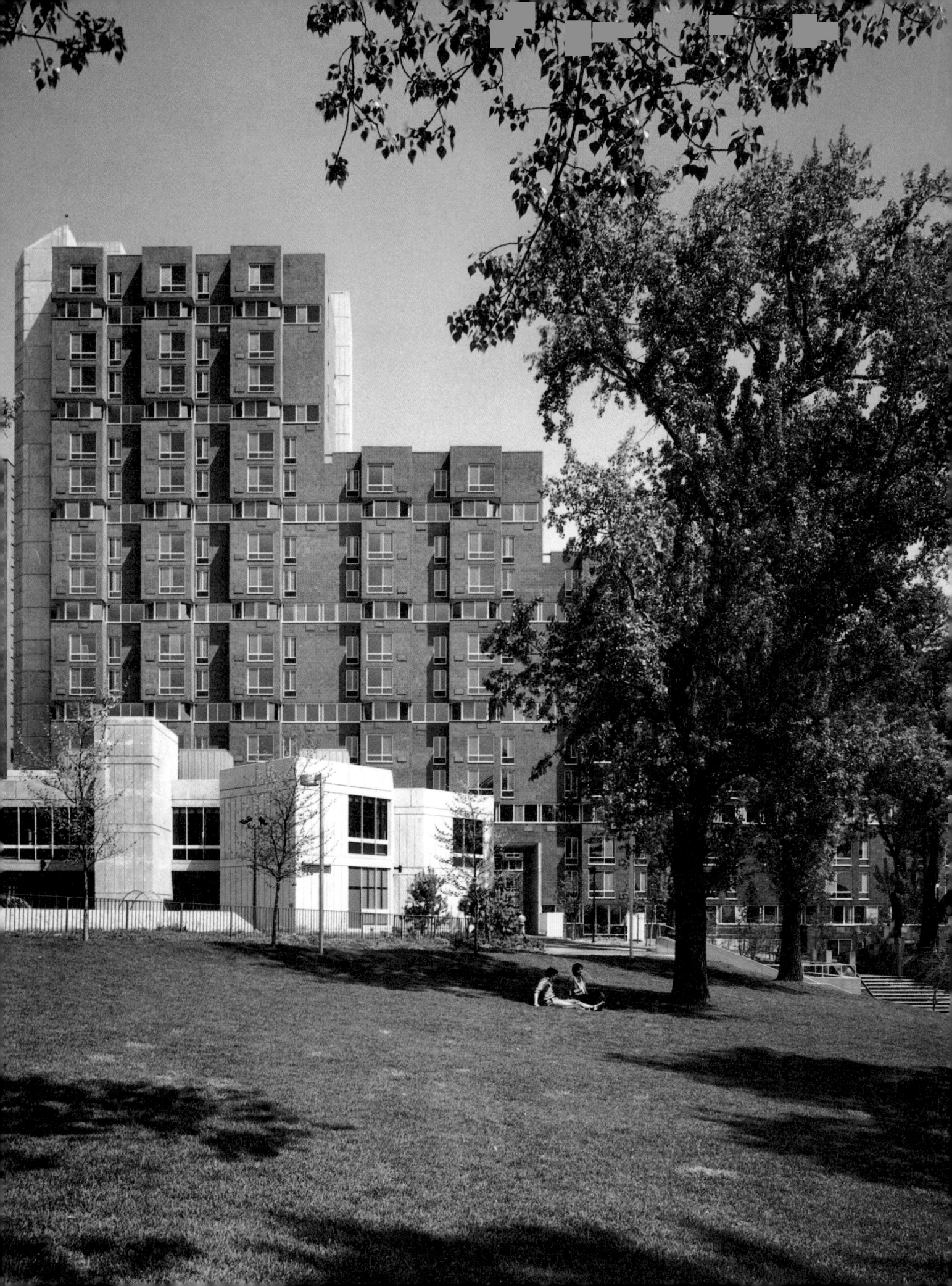

Chapter 8

Roosevelt Island

I can't think of a more exciting site for a new town anywhere in this country. If we botch this one, we might as well give up on urban design altogether.
—Peter Blake, 1969[1]

The development of Roosevelt Island, a 147-acre island lying 300 yards off Manhattan's shore in the East River between Fiftieth and Eighty-sixth streets, as a "new town," complete with extensive housing, stores, schools, a church and numerous public amenities, was one of the city's most self-conscious, serious postwar efforts to make a significant contribution to urbanism.[2] Two miles long and 800 feet wide at its widest point, the small island had an extraordinary history. It was called Minnahanonck by the Indians, Varcken (Hog) Eylandt by the Dutch and Ferkens or Perkens Island by the English. Later it was called Manning's Island when it was owned by Captain John Manning, the commander of British forces who tamely surrendered New Netherlands to the attacking Dutch in 1673, for which he was court-martialed and publicly disgraced. As Blackwell's Island—Robert Blackwell was Manning's heir—it became a convenient yet out-of-view depot for the city's poor, infirm and insane. It would retain this name for over two centuries, until 1921, when it became Welfare Island, which was changed to Roosevelt fifty-two years later.

When Philip Hone, former mayor and famous diarist of early-nineteenth-century New York, visited the island in 1828 he was impressed by the quality of the building stone it could supply for the penitentiary the city proposed to construct there. Soon after, the city paid $32,000 for the island, where in 1834 prisoners began to be housed. Charles Dickens visited its insane asylum in 1842, finding "a lounging, listless madhouse air which was very painful."[3] In 1872 a fifty-foot-tall lighthouse at the island's northern tip was reputedly built by John McCarthy, a purportedly insane inmate who worked under the supervision of architect James Renwick, Jr.

In 1907 the final report of the New York City Improvement Commission proposed that Blackwell's Island be transformed into a park, but nothing came of this plan.[4] Nine years later two truck-sized elevators were built to carry traffic down to the island from the Queensboro Bridge, supplementing ferry service that left from the foot of East Seventy-eighth Street in Manhattan. No direct connection was built to the island until 1955, when the New York City Department of Public Works completed the Welfare Island Bridge, a liftbridge constructed across the east channel to Vernon Boulevard and Thirty-sixth Avenue in Long Island City.[5] Two years later the last active trolley-car line in New York City, which had traversed the Queensboro Bridge and stopped at the island's elevator, ceased operating.[6]

The island continued to be home to the sick, and new hospitals were built to supplement and ultimately replace the increasingly outmoded nineteenth-century facilities. At the southern end of the island, Isadore Rosenfield's Goldwater Memorial Hospital, originally called Welfare Hospital for Chronic Diseases, was completed in 1939 and added on to in 1971; at the northern end stood the Bird S. Coler Hospital, a 1,890-bed facility for the chronically ill, designed in the 1930s but delayed by World War II and not completed until 1952–54.[7] But the new, well-lit hospitals could not overcome the "air of gloom" that hung about the island, which, as William Robbins wrote in the *New York Times*, seemed to be "a reminder of a wretched past, its abandoned buildings reminiscent of the miserable souls that have peopled it."[8] The ninety abandoned buildings that stood on the island served no larger purpose than to provide students at the city fire fighter's school with a place to set fires and practice putting them out.

In 1961 an elaborate plan was released for the conversion of Welfare Island into a community of 70,000 people, equal in population to New Rochelle, New York, or East Orange, New Jersey.[9] The plan was put together by architect Victor Gruen, industrialist Frederick W. Richmond and Roger L. Stevens, a real estate promoter and theatrical producer, who collectively formed the East Island Development Corporation to develop the island, which they proposed to rename East Island. The syndicate had been orchestrated by Richmond, who first conceived of the development in 1960 while gazing out from his Sutton Place apart-

Eastwood, Roosevelt Island. Sert, Jackson & Associates, 1976. View to the north from Blackwell Park. Rosenthal. SJA

ment at the spectacularly located but underutilized piece of real estate. City officials were kept informed of the plan as it evolved, but when it was released to the public in May 1961, they exhibited only cautious optimism for its success, recognizing the problems posed by the island's comparative inaccessibility as well as those associated with turning over so much land to one developer.

Gruen's plan called for the construction of a platform twenty-two feet above ground level, covering nearly the entire island and incorporating schools, shops and other public facilities, all connected by an air-conditioned pedestrian concourse. Slab and serpentine-shaped apartment buildings ranging in height from eight to fifty stories and containing a total of 20,000 units were to sit on top of the platform. To complement the existing hospitals, which were to remain on the island, Gruen proposed two large apartment buildings near the Coler Hospital to accommodate ambulatory elderly patients, thereby freeing up valuable hospital bed space. Private automobiles were to be banned from the island, which would be served by a conveyor-like system of cars running under the platform and along the island's length, stopping every 900 feet—in effect a system similar to that proposed for the Forty-second Street shuttle in 1951 (see chapter 2). Transportation to the mainland was to be provided by improved service on the existing elevators that ran from the island to the roadway of the Queensboro Bridge, by the lift-bridge leading to Queens, by ferry to various Manhattan landings and by the construction of a new station on the IND subway line, which ran under the island near its southern tip. Gruen touted his plan as "not just a big housing project" but "the first 20th century city." He explained: "We would really integrate housing with other facilities, avoiding the intermingling of transportation. It would mean unscrambling the melee of flesh and machine."[10]

But the plan failed to gain support, largely because high city officials were under growing pressure to consider the development of the island as a park, a proposal also supported by the editors of the New York Times, who argued: "Through the years Welfare Island has retained its pastoral tranquility more by virtue of inaccessibility than through enlightened planning. It is time to consider how this East River tract can best benefit the greatest number."[11] In addition, the park proposal was vigorously supported by the New York Chapter of the American Institute of Architects and the National Recreation Association as well as by various influential individuals like Lewis Mumford.[12]

The public announcement of Gruen's plan also elicited an angry response from the builder Francis J. Kleban, who two years earlier had presented to the City Planning Commission plans for what he called Sutton City, a smaller residential community on Welfare Island.[13] He had commissioned the architect William Lescaze, who devised a plan calling for four thirty-one-story apartment towers to be located south of the Queensboro Bridge and to contain a total of 2,400 units. Kleban asserted that Commissioner James Felt's response to the plan had been "unenthusiastic," and he demanded that his proposal be considered before Gruen's; whatever reconsideration his plan was given, the proposal was never realized.[14]

At the same time that Gruen was preparing his plan, a team of architecture students at Columbia University, working under the direction of Percival Goodman, developed a plan for the island based on Goodman's "Terrace City" concept, in which a platform for schools and shops was ringed by layers of terraced houses stepping back to a high central spine. The Columbia

team proposed their city as a home for 20,000 United Nations employees. According to Progressive Architecture, "the towers-on-hills concept" of the Columbia design offered "a lively, open silhouette when viewed from across the river, as contrasted with the more 'developmenty' look of the East Island proposal."[15]

The city's decision in 1963 to construct a new subway tunnel that would cross Welfare Island just north of the Queensboro Bridge as it linked Manhattan and Queens revived interest in the island, stimulating plans for the construction of a building designed by Harrison & Abramovitz (1965) to house the United Nations International School on a seventeen-acre site at the island's southern tip, a prominent site clearly visible from the U.N. headquarters.[16] Parents of the school's students successfully blocked the plan, arguing that Welfare Island was not sufficiently accessible and, with its large infirm population, not an appropriate environment for children. Earlier, United Nations Secretary General U Thant had reluctantly approved a school site at the northeast corner of the headquarters' property, but the proposal had drawn criticism from U.N. personnel as well as nearby Beekman Place residents, including Laurance Rockefeller, who argued that a school would crowd the constricted tract. The City Planning Commission subsequently approved a proposal to build a school on a platform extending five hundred feet into the East River directly south of Davis, Brody & Associates' Waterside development.

In June 1966 Mayor John V. Lindsay announced the city's intentions to plan for Welfare Island's future, at first seeming to favor new housing for physicians and nurses, though other proposals being considered at the time included an educational campus, an exhibition center and low- or middle-income housing.[17] Most significant, Lindsay announced that the city had condemned forty-five dilapidated and unused hospital buildings. At a "clean-up" ceremony on the island, Mary Lindsay, the mayor's wife, proposed that the island be called East River Island.

In February 1968 Lindsay appointed a twenty-two-member Welfare Island Planning and Development Committee, headed by Benno C. Schmidt, managing partner of the J. H. Whitney & Co. investment firm.[18] Other committee members included Mrs. Vincent Astor, William Bernbach, Ralph Bunche, Marcia Davenport, Philip Johnson, James Linen and Edward J. Logue, who would soon be appointed head of the newly established New York State Urban Development Corporation (UDC). City officials serving on the committee were Bernard Bucove of the Department of Health Services Department, Donald Elliott of the City Planning Commission, August Heckscher of the Park Department and Jason Nathan of the Housing and Development Administration. A year later, in February 1969, the committee issued its report.

The 141-page document, written by Woody Tate, favored expanding the two hospitals to accommodate ambulatory patients and additional medical staff; it also advocated extensive park and recreational facilities, an improved sewage-disposal system and a subway station in the Sixty-third Street tunnel and recommended building enough housing "to achieve the minimum size required to justify community facilities, shopping, and services needed to support this resident community."[19] The report rejected large-scale housing as well as other exotic schemes that had been proposed, including casino gambling. The committee conspicuously ignored Consolidated Edison's request that nothing be proposed for the island's southern tip, where, opposite the United Nations headquarters, the utility company was thinking of building a nuclear power plant.[20] Other ideas suggested for the island but not commented on in the report

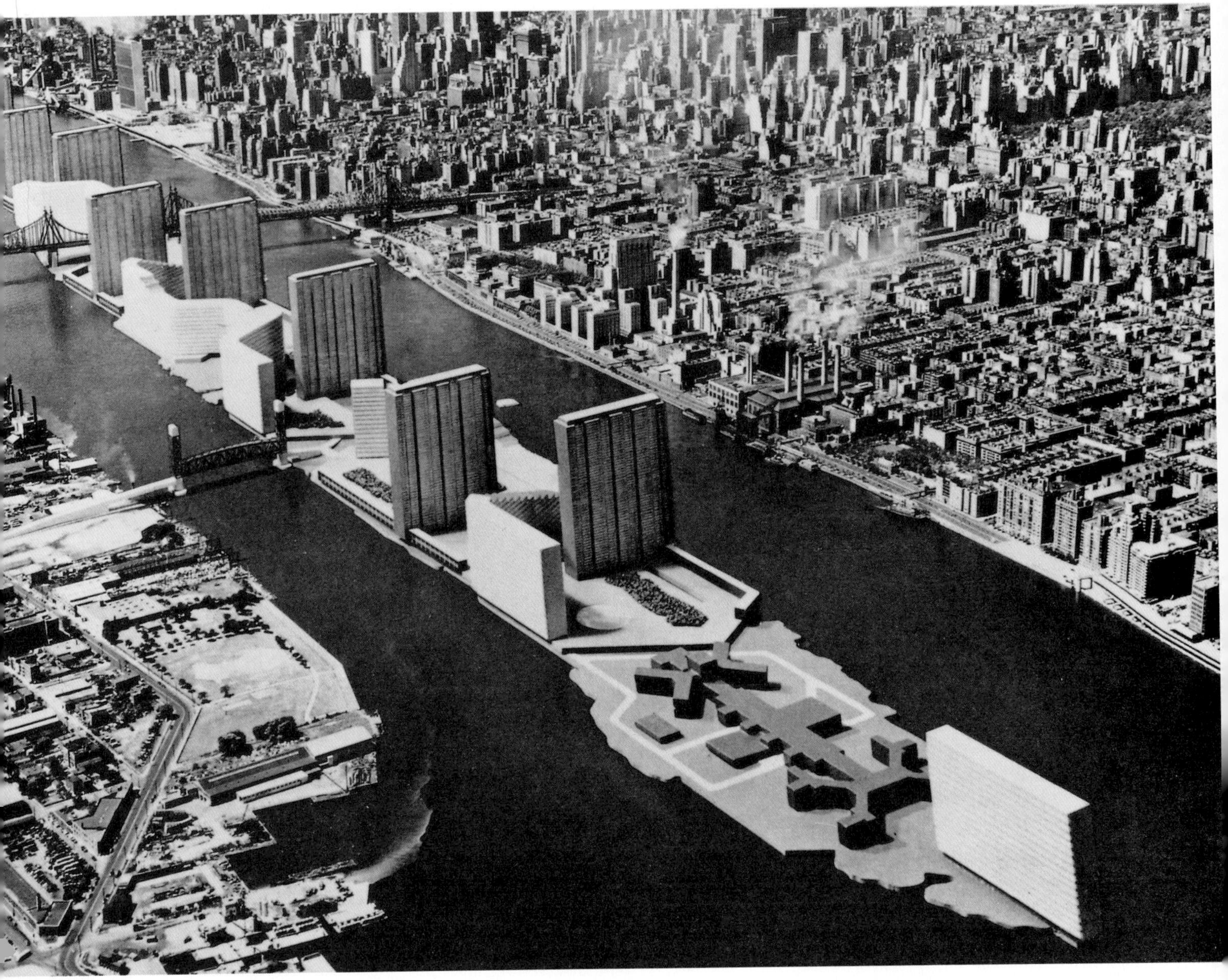

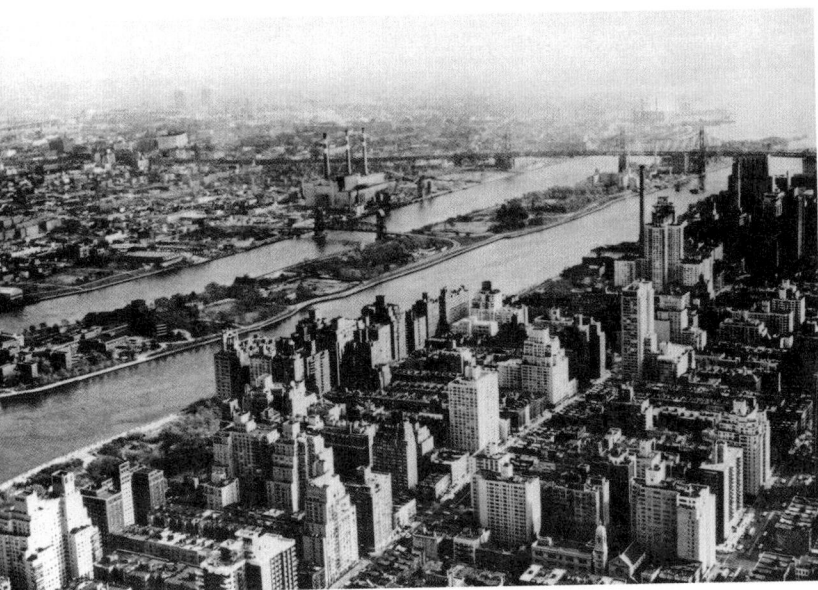

Above: East Island Proposal, Welfare Island. Victor Gruen, 1960. Photographic montage. View to the southwest. *East Island.* CU

Left: View to the southeast showing Welfare Island,1960. *Roosevelt Island Housing Competition.* UDC

643

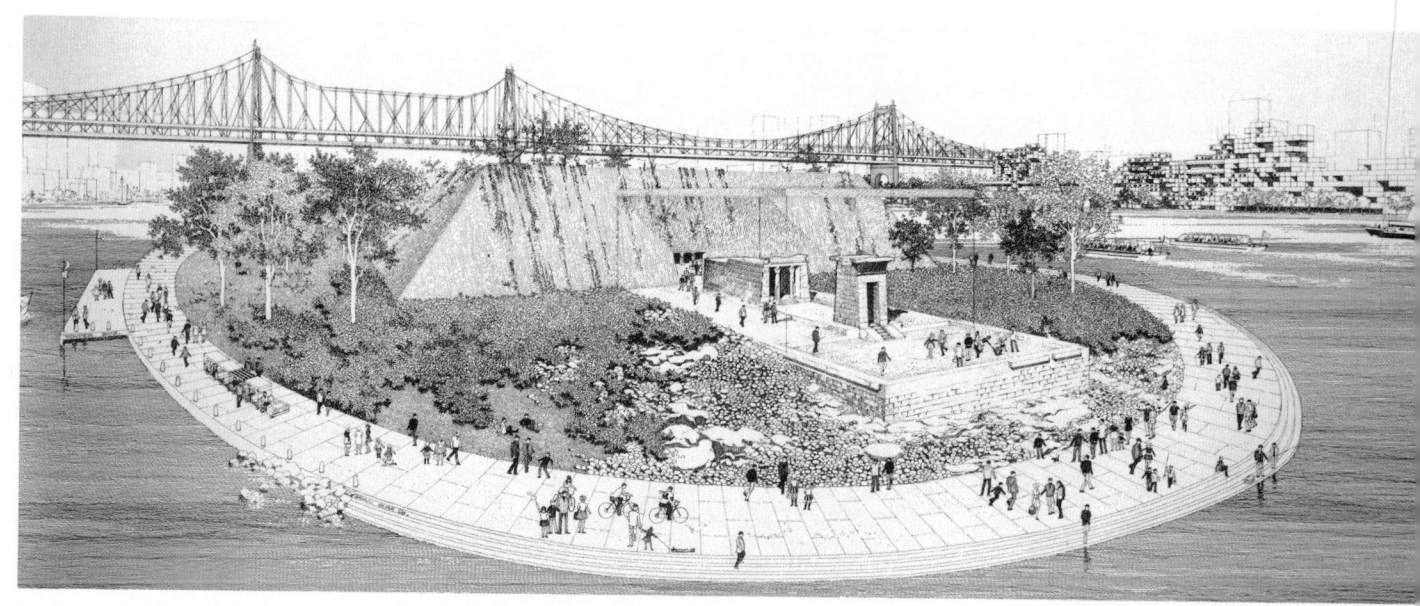

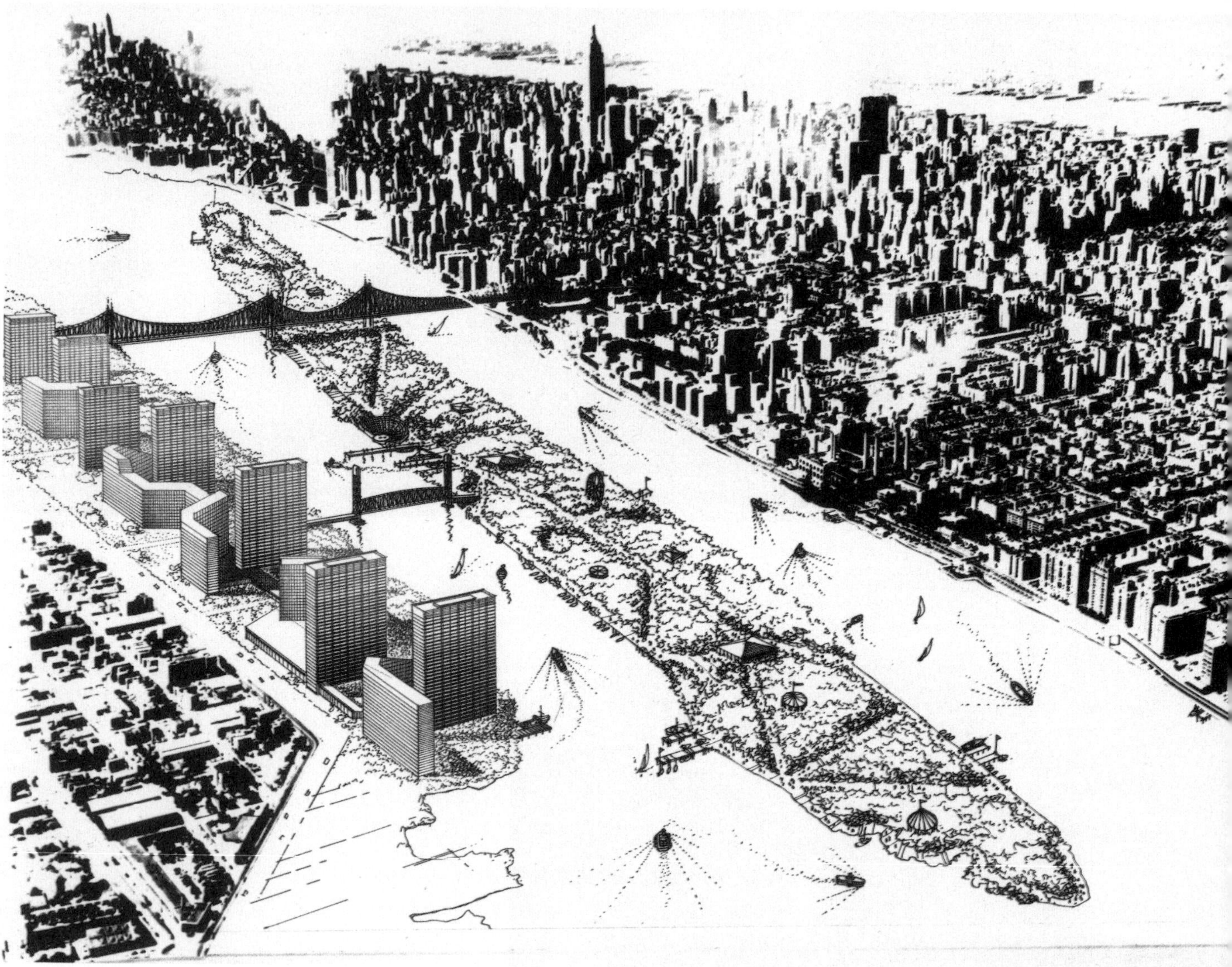

Top: Proposal for museum of Egyptian art, Welfare Island. Zion & Breen, 1968. Rendering of view to the north, including Temple of Dendur and Egyptian museum. ZB

Bottom: Proposal for park, Welfare Island. Zion & Breen, 1965. Rendering of view to the southwest, including proposed housing on the Queens shoreline. ZB

were the recommendation made by Roger Starr of the Citizens' Housing and Planning Council that the bodies interred in Queens and Brooklyn cemeteries be dug up and reburied on the island to make way for needed housing in those boroughs;[21] the proposal by futurist Herman Kahn that the island be linked to Manhattan and Queens with causeways and bisected by a canal to permit the river's continued use as a shipping corridor;[22] and a proposal presented by Robert Zion and Harold Breen calling for the placement of the Temple of Dendur adjacent to a museum of Egyptian art to be built at the island's southern end.[23] Zion & Breen also offered another proposal, to develop the island as a park reminiscent of Tivoli Gardens in Copenhagen and relocate the housing Gruen had planned to underutilized land on the Queens shore. Accessible from midtown Manhattan by subway or high-speed water bus, the new park was to feature tree-lined promenades, cafés, small theaters and a new home for the New York Aquarium, located since 1957 in Coney Island after its removal from Battery Park.

On October 9, 1969, a week after the contract for construction of the Sixty-third Street tunnel was let, Philip Johnson and John Burgee's master plan for the island's development, based on the findings of Schmidt's committee, was released to the public at the opening of an exhibition, "The Island Nobody Knows," shown in the Metropolitan Museum of Art's galleries until October 23.[24] Noting previously rejected plans to devote the island exclusively to high-density housing, public parkland or industrial use, Johnson and Burgee called for a $200 million mixed-use development that would incorporate the existing hospitals while providing housing for 20,000 low- and moderate-income people in two separate automobile-free "island towns" (Northtown and Southtown), a twenty-five-acre ecological park that would reproduce the natural features of the region, a four-mile-long waterfront promenade and a 2,000-car garage called Motorgate. The project would not be undertaken by private developers but by the UDC, which would lease the land from the city in return for $1 million in the first year and an adjusted amount in ninety-nine subsequent years, after which the land and its improvements would return to the city. The agreement stipulated that construction begin within eighteen months, something the UDC, with sweeping powers that enabled it to bypass local codes and bureaucracies, could achieve. The project was to be completed in eight years.

In the exhibition catalogue Johnson and Burgee said that the island contained "some of the most charming, tree-lined, paved and bench equipped promenades west of the river Seine" and some of "the most spectacular views east or west of anywhere: panoramic views of Manhattan that remind you of Feininger's photographs; perspectives of a high-flying bridge that recall Piranesi's drawings; glimpses of docks and of industrial plants that look like Charles Sheeler's paintings at their most dramatic; and, finally, the movement of tugboats, of cars on the multilevel highways along the Manhattan waterfront, of seagulls and of helicopters above."[25] To preserve the island's natural amenities and avoid long, monotonous strips of buildings, Johnson and Burgee's plan divided the island latitudinally into nine zones: five parks and four building groups. The island towns, consisting of four- to twelve-story-tall apartment houses that included shops and public facilities, projected a believable and appealing image of medium-density urbanism, comparable to that of prewar Forest Hills or Kew Gardens in Queens.

The brick-clad buildings of Northtown clustered around the Motorgate; those in Southtown were gathered around a "town center," a glassed-in galleria, which Johnson and Burgee com-

pared to the Galleria Vittorio Emanuele II in Milan. The galleria connected a waterfront "town square" on the Manhattan side with a waterfront "harbor square" on the Queens side that embraced the East River with a series of steps leading down to the water's edge, which Johnson and Burgee compared to the Ghats of Benares on the Ganges. In addition to apartments, the plan provided for a 2,000-student public school, a day-care center, swimming pools, police and fire stations, a post office, 100,000 square feet of commercial space, 200,000 square feet of office space and a 300-room hotel. A north-south road called Main Street would run most of the island's length, with traffic restricted to emergency vehicles, minibuses and bicycles. "There are no cross streets," Johnson and Burgee said. "Instead, there are tree-lined pedestrian walks that lead between apartment houses to the river, east and west—first leading the eye one way, then shortly after, the other. The main attraction of this narrow island, after all, is that glimpses to its waterfronts are so dramatic."[26] In addition to retaining the two hospitals—a decision based on expediency since their replacement would be too costly—the plan called for the preservation of the island's landmark structures, including Blackwell House (1796–1804) and the romantically ruinated New York Lunatic Asylum (1839; additions, 1847–48, 1879), with its spectacular octagonal stair tower.

Ada Louise Huxtable was impressed with the plan, and with the exhibition of "The Island Nobody Knows," which she felt was "in the fine tradition of London's public display and discussion of planning projects that makes that city a peculiarly civilized place."[27] Peter Blake, writing in New York magazine, also greeted the plan with enthusiasm, though he added a somewhat fatalistic twist to his appraisal: "It is a nice plan for a very nice community, and if it doesn't get built, more or less in its proposed form, New York will have just about had it so far as better-quality housing is concerned." Blake went on to point out that there wasn't "anything fancy" about the proposal, explaining:

> The housing . . . is almost non-architectural and nondescript and deliberately so: brick buildings of no particular formal composition, that meander around courts open to the waterfronts, and step down from a maximum height of 14 stories along the Main Street "spine" of the island to a low four stories along its shores. As these nondescript buildings step down toward the water, they create roof terraces for apartments higher up, and offer views of the East River to all and sundry.[28]

"This is my Jane Jacobs period," said Johnson, defending his uncharacteristically low-key approach.[29] Blake interpreted this position as "straight Pop," but cautioned: "The only danger is that Pop Island could, under the pressure of economics, degenerate into Lefrak Island—unless Johnson and Burgee remain in control."[30]

The proposed project and lease arrangements sailed through a review by the Board of Estimate, which on October 29, 1969, gave its full support; Edward Logue, in his capacity as head of the UDC, immediately took charge.[31] To flesh out the skeletal master plan, Logue hired ten New York and Boston architects: Johnson and Burgee were brought back for the town center; Giorgio Cavaglieri was given responsibility for historic preservation; Gruzen & Partners for systems analysis; Kallmann & McKinnell for the Motorgate, which would also include shops, a fire station and a post office; and the firms of Conklin & Rossant, John M. Johansen, Sert, Jackson & Associates and Mitchell/Giurgola for 3,000 units of low-, middle- and high-income housing that would accommodate 12,000 people in the project's first stage. The landscape architects Dan Kiley &

Partners and Zion & Breen were hired to study the parks, streets and promenades, and the engineering firm Gibbs & Hill was retained to develop the island's infrastructure of services and transportation.

On October 6, 1970, a first interim report was presented in the form of a second exhibition at the Metropolitan Museum of Art on the island's rehabilitation, featuring detailed designs for the buildings that would be built.[32] Like the Whitney Museum's survey of the UDC's work around the state, "Another Chance for Cities," this exhibition was timed to the upcoming gubernatorial election. Huxtable saw the project as the UDC's "showpiece and star performance," and the exhibition as much "more than a political event: it is a planning event of the first magnitude." She praised Johnson as "a late-blooming urbanist of notable sensibilities" who had created "a genuine urban environment in which the two elements consistently left out by the routine commercial developer are conspicuously present: the amenities of living through design." Noting that for the Boston Government Center Logue had hired I. M. Pei to produce a master plan and then had pursued a policy of "divide and conquer," parceling the buildings out to architects "who produced a full spectrum of humdrum to superior structures," Huxtable expressed her belief that for Welfare Island "any danger of chaos by coalition is offset by the kind of diversity that will prevent a 'project' look."[33]

In a second review of the Metropolitan exhibition, Huxtable expressed concern that "one of the plan's most felicitous features, the side views through to the water from the central, north-south main street, were lost, with the street turned into an almost solid wall of the highest buildings." But her major worry was that with each architect "conspicuously doing his own thing," the entire project might fall victim to "the purely practical matters of construction technology and economics [which] will ultimately determine whether any of this is built at all, the urbanistic esthetic and picturesque planning principles be damned." But, she mused, "That's New York."

Some architects, such as Conklin & Rossant, proposed a unique industrialized system of construction, an approach that Huxtable questioned, cautioning that such building techniques were usually more costly, required redesign and deflected attention from the basic task of providing good housing in a desirable setting: "The design answer will be found to be more commonality in such things as good, standardized apartments (just give everyone the best possible apartment and he will make his own kind of nest) and more attention to the relationships of views, walks, passageways, waterfront, public and private spaces and those things that create the amenities of environment."[34]

By May 1971 Huxtable was quite nervous about the island's future:

The Welfare Island plan started out to be but no longer is . . . a coherent shaper and binder together of disparate elements into a recognizable urban idea. The original Welfare Island plan by Philip Johnson is being tragically eroded; it is hard to tell whether from disinterest or default. The idea—a schematic set of principles that emphasized a quality of island life in shared public views and spaces—is taking a beating from a team of architects who have not communicated meaningfully once they began work, with no conceptual control for the agency or for the master planner, who was immediately dropped from the job. It is better to honestly scrap a plan than to mutilate it in this fashion.[35]

Though some observers contended that the problem was due in part to a strained relationship between Johnson and

Logue, Johnson was particularly magnanimous in his evaluation of the situation. "I think they're all doing very well," Johnson stated. "Force of events, money and the actual conditions have caused them to make changes in my master plan, but they're following it as well as they can. Ed Logue's got fine architects working on the job, and Logue's a genius. He's the only person who could get this done."[36] Anthony Bailey, writing in the New York Times, described Logue's participation: "Logue is to be seen a least once a week plunging in his bearlike way around the site—old corduroys, green Shetland sweater, shirttail hanging out and no hard hat covering his stack of grey hair; slow-speaking, fast-thinking, a mixture of charm and combativeness, fussing about the color of tiles and asking awkward, provoking questions of his staff. He is proud of what he is doing on the island."[37]

Construction began in June 1971, with the first phase—calling for 300,000 square feet of commercial and office space, 3,000 units of housing, and streets, sewers and water lines—scheduled to take two years.[38] By the end of 1972, though the schedule had slipped, 2,138 apartment units were under construction in four apartment buildings in Southtown: Eastwood Apartments and Westview, designed by Sert, Jackson & Associates; and Rivercross Apartments and Island House, designed by John Johansen.[39] Direct responsibility for the project had been put in the hands of the Welfare Island Development Corporation, whose first director, Adam Yarmolinsky, departed in a personnel shake-up in February 1972. That same year the UDC's chief consultant, Richard Ravitch, a leading builder specializing in housing, also resigned; he believed the introduction of low-income tenants in 30 percent of the housing would undermine efforts to attract upper-income residential tenants as well as good commercial tenants. Delays in constructing the subway station, by 1972 estimated to open in 1979 or 1980, five years after the first tenants were to move in, was also a rising cause of concern. In addition, many observers continued to feel that Johnson and Burgee's original plan had been disastrously tampered with. As Steven Weisman reported in the New York Times: "To many critics, the river vistas were the most distinctive feature of the plan—the aspect that proved Philip Johnson a master at complementing the island environment. But Mr. Logue defends the changes that were made, and calls them slight. And by heightening the buildings, he says, he has permitted more residents than before to enjoy the view." But most of all, as Weisman reported, the criticism focused on the architectural changes, perhaps because Johnson "has not bothered to hide his chagrin at being dropped as the overall planner."[40]

In addition to problems of design, Welfare Island's growth continued to be stymied by political and economic problems. Not only did the staff of the Welfare Island Development Corporation change repeatedly, but many of the original architects had discontinued their associations with the project as well. By 1973 only Sert, Jackson & Associates and John Johansen, now in partnership with Ashok M. Bhavnani, were designing the housing in Southtown. Lawrence Halprin & Associates had been hired as landscape architects for the plaza, and Dan Kiley was at work on the park setting for Blackwell House. Johnson and Burgee and Zion & Breen were out, as were Conklin & Rossant and Mitchell/Giurgola.[41] Kallmann & McKinnell were still at work on the Motorgate, now downsized to accommodate only 1,000 cars, as well as the firehouse, post office and shops that were part of the original plan.

On August 20, 1973, amid the UDC's increasing staff problems and its inability to produce an affordable project, Welfare

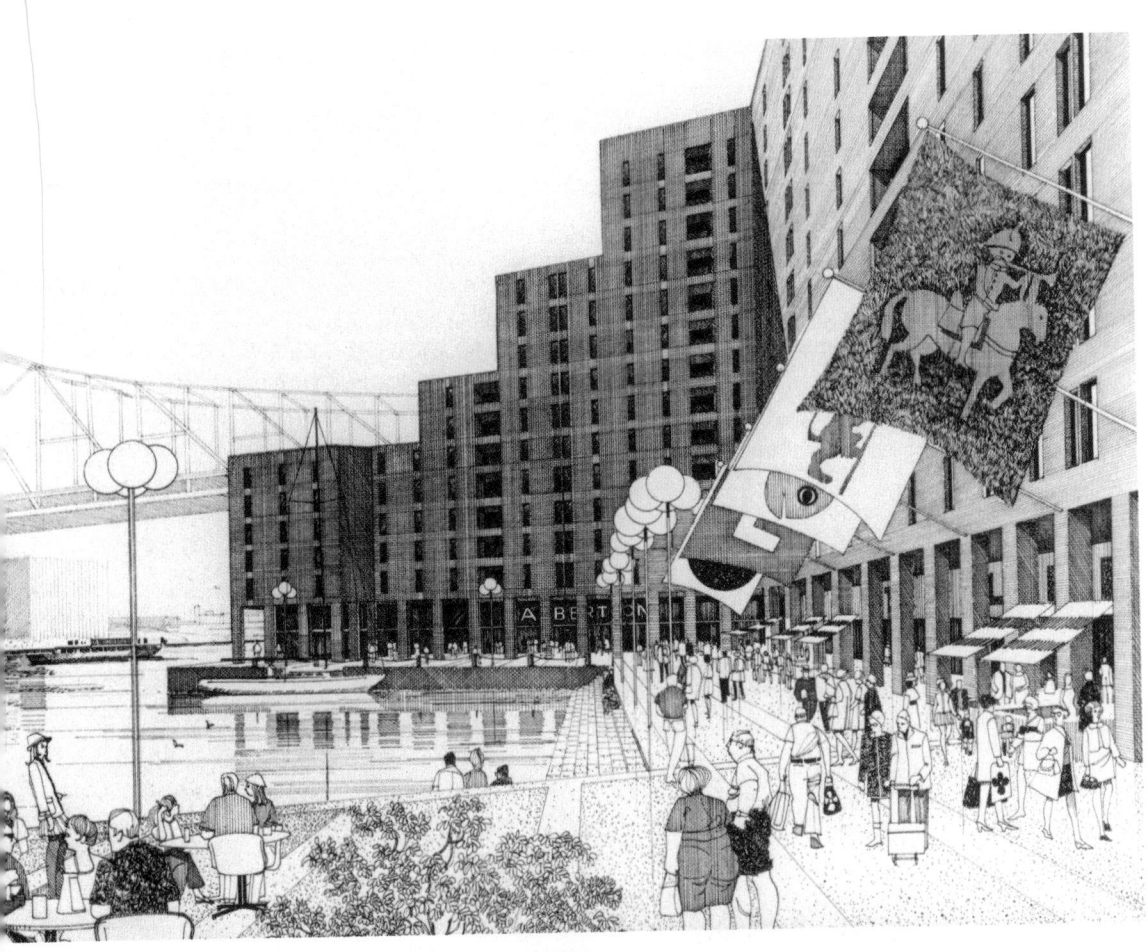

Top: Proposal for
Welfare Island. Philip
Johnson and John
Burgee, 1969.
Rendering by Ronald
Love of proposed
harbor. *The Island
Nobody Knows.* CU

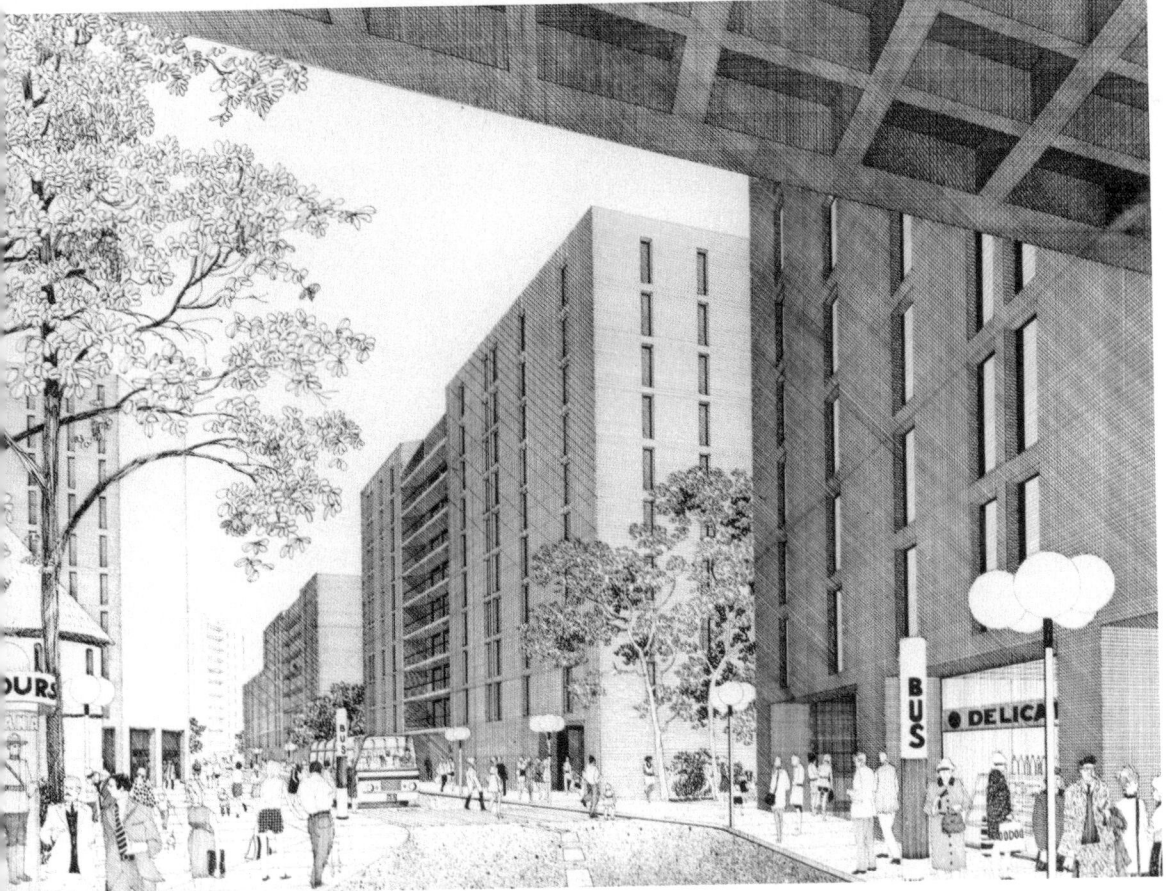

Bottom: Proposal for
Welfare Island.
Rendering by Ronald
Love of proposed Main
Street. *The Island
Nobody Knows.* CU

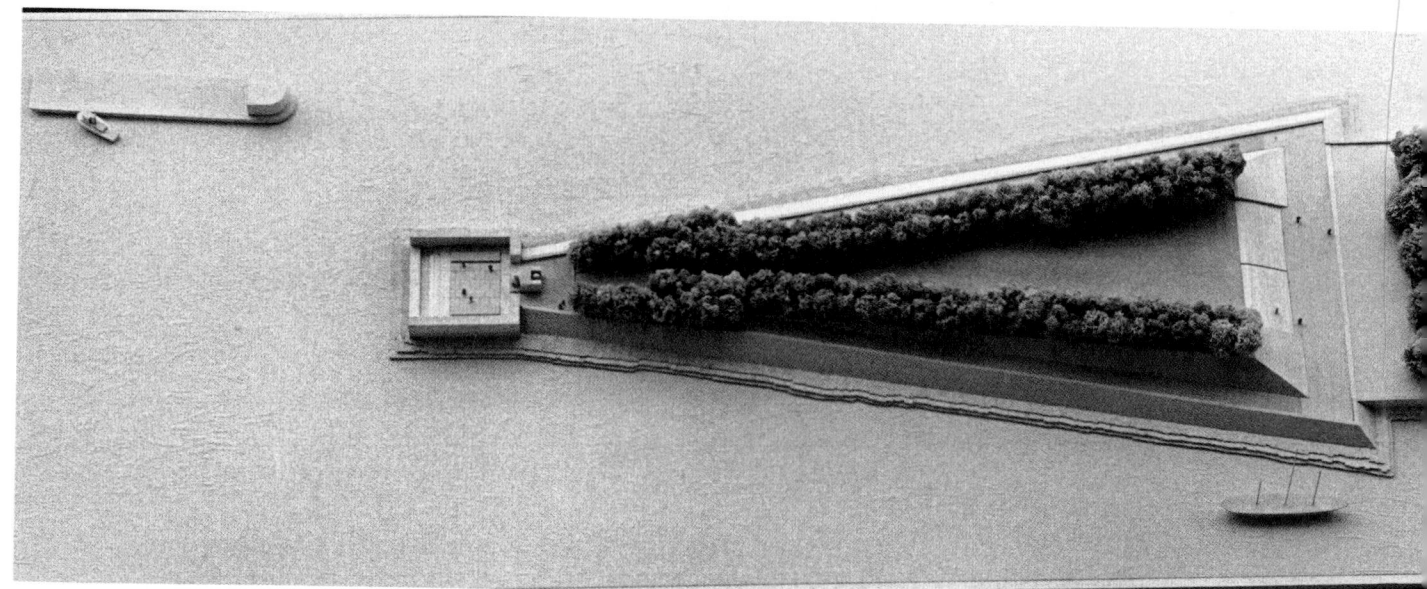

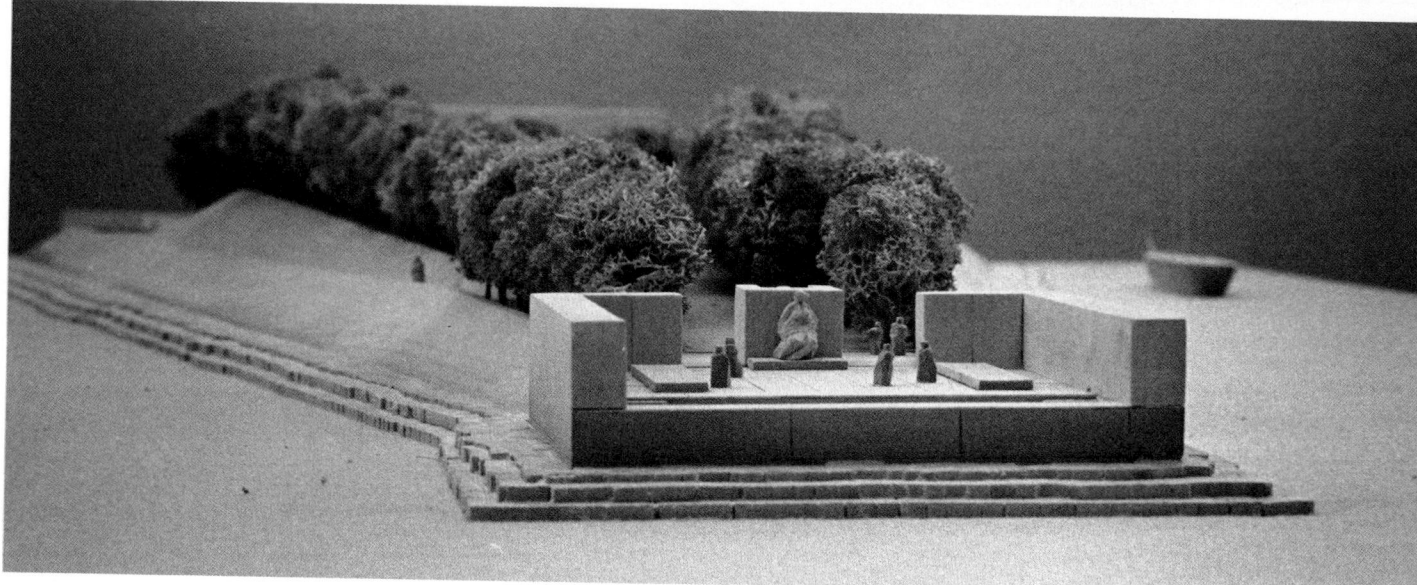

Top: Proposal for Franklin Delano Roosevelt Memorial, Roosevelt Island. Louis I. Kahn, 1974. Model. Aerial view. Pohl. LIK

Bottom: Proposal for Franklin Delano Roosevelt Memorial. Model. View to the north. Pohl. LIK

Island's name was changed to Franklin Delano Roosevelt Island at Mayor Lindsay's request.[42] At a ceremony marking the name change, held on September 24 and attended by members of the president's family, as well as by Mrs. Lindsay and the committee of distinguished sponsors of Franklin Delano Roosevelt Island Day, a model of the Four Freedoms Monument dedicated to FDR was unveiled.[43] Designed by the architect Louis I. Kahn, the memorial incorporated four sixty-foot-high stainless-steel pillars representing the "four freedoms" that Roosevelt had identified as the aims of World War II: freedom from want, freedom from fear, freedom of expression and freedom of worship. The design proved controversial, particularly because of its height. Early in 1974, before he died on March 17 at the age of seventy-four, Kahn prepared a second design, which was approved by the Roosevelt family. This design was publicly presented on April 25 at a dinner of the Four Freedoms Foundation, which was raising money to supplement the $2.2 million pledged by the state and the $2 million pledged by the city toward the realization of the $4.4 million project. Proposed for a location at the southern tip of the island on a 780-foot-long triangular site largely created out of fill from the Sixty-third Street subway tunnel, Kahn's Classically inspired design called for a subtly sloped park leading to a roofless "room." The fate of the 600-foot-high Delacorte Fountain (Pomerance & Breines, 1959), located just below the tip, was never resolved: the geyser, which the *New York Times* called "esthetic *juvenilia*" and money "literally down the drain," would presumably drown the memorial were it not for the fact that the vicissitudes of the East River—log-jammed waterways and careening tugboats—rendered the fountain inoperable much of the time anyway.[44]

In his design for the memorial, Kahn reduced his formal vocabulary to create what he called a "pre-Grecian temple space," framed with a virtually pure masonry architecture that defined a room, bounded by twelve-foot-high, medium gray granite walls on three sides; the roofless room opened to the south, looking down the river to the harbor.[45] A traditional bust of Roosevelt was to be placed facing north, greeting visitors; a more abstract sculpture was to be placed inside the room, where quotations from Roosevelt's writings were to be carved on the walls. In designing the memorial, Kahn created a spatial sequence that used the technique of forced perspective to concentrate the arriving visitor's attention on the bust of Roosevelt, and provided a vestibule for the austere memorial room and the sweeping view beyond.

Theodore Liebman, the Welfare Island Development Corporation's director of design, was obviously concerned about the fate of the design, given Kahn's death and the storm of controversy that surrounded two schemes for a Roosevelt memorial in Washington, D.C., one submitted in 1960 and one in 1966, both of which were rejected. Liebman said that Kahn "was pleased with his work—we're very fortunate that he lived long enough to see the design through to a stage he was satisfied with"—and that the memorial should be built "with complete integrity to Kahn's design." He added: "We're dealing with a piece of history."[46] The architect Michael Rubenstein, an associate at the firm of Mitchell/Giurgola, which took over the execution of the design following Kahn's death and prepared working drawings in association with the Philadelphia-based firm of David Wisdom Associates, viewed the proposed monument as a memorial to Kahn as well as to Roosevelt.

Thomas B. Hess, a passionately Modernist art critic who claimed friendship with Edward Logue and Louis Kahn and sympathy for Roosevelt, hated the design. In an open letter to Logue, which he published at the beginning of one of his regular *New York* art columns, Hess wrote: "Dear Ed, Please keep Lou's plans on the drawing board." He attacked the design as "a saddening astonishment," but put the blame neither on Logue nor on Kahn. "Kahn had pressed for another plan," Hess explained, "a highly architectural structure with a stately, if abstract, impact. But the Roosevelt family insisted that a bust of F.D.R. be included in his monument. This prerequisite caused all the grief. Kahn's solution was to propose an eclectic, almost parodic temple plan. . . . By opening the back wall, Kahn seems to make a wry comment on how the gods of modern civilization have gone public." Hess also disapproved of the use of granite, which, he said, "signifies brutal, centralized force, the dark magical omnipresence of the government and the demigods who command it and us." He continued:

> This is the sort of political edifice that the Italian fascists loved and Speer perfected for the glory of the Third Reich. . . . The site itself is treated heartlessly. What was a modest, picturesquely rugged shoreline has been disciplined to straight lines and symmetrical angles that have no significance beyond the alarming one of man's ability to impose a meaningless geometry on nature. The ultimate irony is that Roosevelt, who fought totalitarians to the death, is commemorated in the harsh style propagated by the dictators.[47]

Whatever the validity of Hess's criticism, the memorial remained unrealized not because of its perceived aesthetic shortcomings but because of a shortage of funds. As Martin Waldron reported in the *New York Times*, "A monument to the President who led the country out of the great Depression of the nineteen-thirties may become a victim of the recession of the seventies."[48] Acknowledging that the city could not afford to honor its initial pledge, municipal officials stated that $1.9 million were required in private donations. By October 1975 only $250,000 had been raised, and sufficient funds were not forthcoming. The rocky promontory remained, as Priscilla Tucker put it in *New York*, "a ragtag landscape of crumbling buildings, trees hemmed by underbrush, rubble, and wild flowers."[49]

In the late summer of 1974 eighty members of the Citizens' Housing and Planning Council toured Roosevelt Island, and they reported being impressed.[50] The pace of construction was frantic, with the UDC pushing for an opening of the entire first phase late in 1975.[51] At this point the architect Ulrich Franzen still favored the island's complete transformation into public parkland, though such a scheme was clearly more theoretical than practical.[52] At last, in April 1975, Roosevelt Island began to function as a town when thirty-four middle-income tenants moved into Johansen & Bhavnani's Island House, though the development still resembled an isolated island fortress more than a welcoming homestead.[53] Nonetheless, on June 24, 1975, Joseph P. Fried reported in the *New York Times* that "the inconveniences of being pioneer residents are relatively minor nuisances given the advantages they find";[54] and in November Richard F. Shepard wrote that there was "an extraordinarily upbeat mood among some of the newcomers."[55] But a stream of settlers was slow to materialize, partly due to the delayed completion of the tram (see below) and the subway stop and the initial lack of commercial facilities on the island. More important, however, were doubts about the UDC's financial viability, about the development's future should the agency collapse, and about the durability of the state's and city's commitment to maintaining an economically balanced community.

But as the buildings were completed, the public was at least reassured about one thing: the apartment buildings, if not ex-

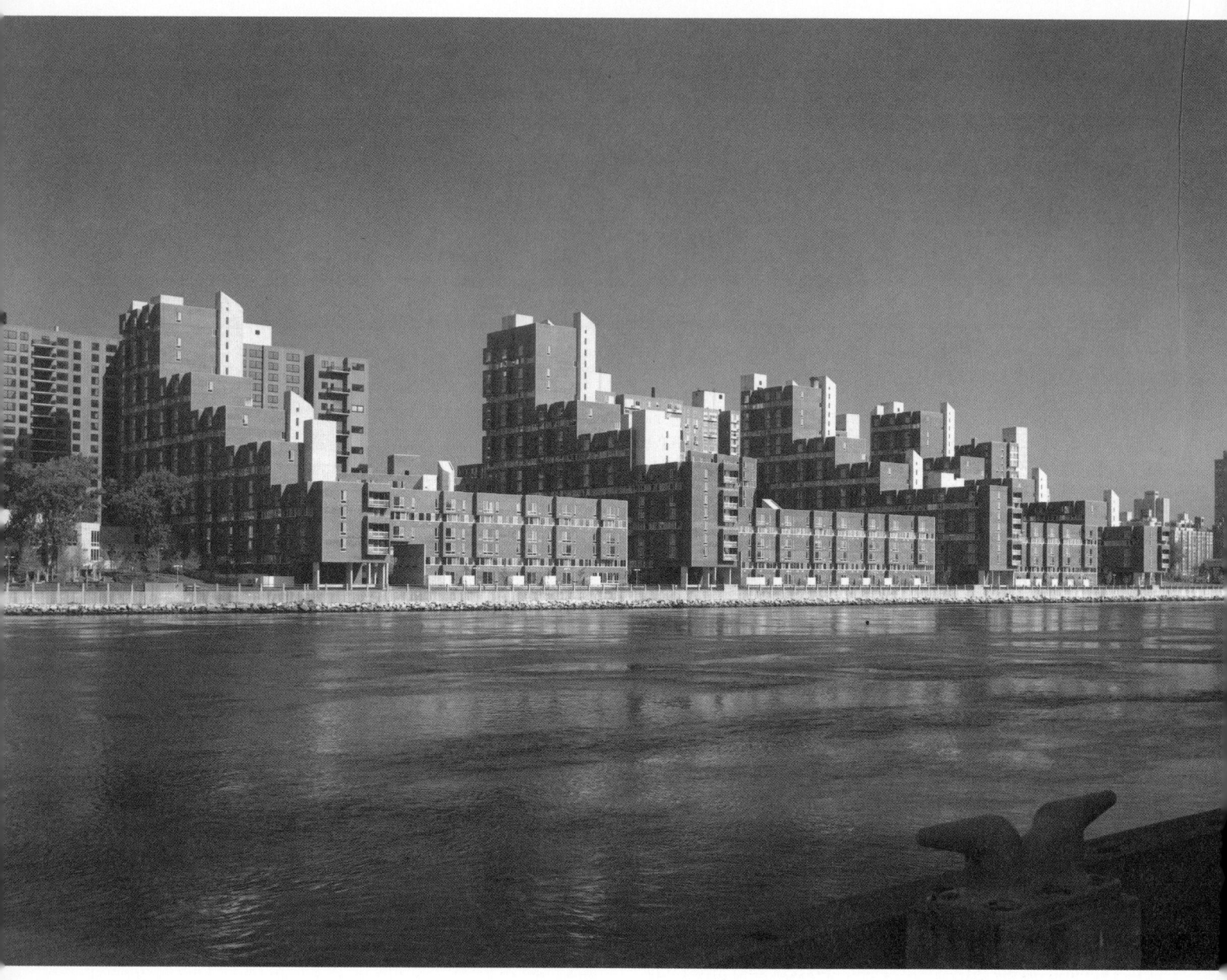

Eastwood Apartments, Roosevelt Island. Sert, Jackson & Associates, 1976. View to the northwest. Rosenthal. SJA tremely distinguished, were at least more successful as architecture than most built in the postwar era, and the level of accommodation they offered was more than adequate. In Southtown, Johansen & Bhavnani's middle- and upper-middle income Rivercross and Island House buildings enjoyed choice East River views.[56] Located opposite Manhattan's Rockefeller Institute, Rivercross's three reinforced-concrete-frame buildings, at 505, 513 and 541 Main Street, housed 850 families in all and were clad mostly in three-inch-thick dun-colored, cement-asbestos panels. The bland walls were given sculptural relief by the buildings' overall stepback massing, rising from the river to Main Street, and the punctuation of exposed painted vent pipes. The buildings, according to Johansen and Bhavnani, had an "unselfconscious industrial look," the only vestige of the UDC's initial desire to create a totally systems-built development.[57]

Though Paul Goldberger was not happy with the look of the cement-asbestos cladding of Island House and Rivercross, he understood, as the architects claimed, that the money saved by using the material enabled them to do much more in the design of the apartments and courtyards. Goldberger was particularly taken with a "well-planned" two-bedroom apartment in Island House, "with a bedroom that feels as if it were jutting out over the water, and has views up and down the river," making it "one of the most spectacular medium-sized apartments built in New York in years." He also praised the area surrounding the building: "The exterior open spaces are pleasing here, too, and one part of Island House—a landscaped and paved plaza with a restored church as its centerpiece—is as fine a civic square as any neighborhood in the city can claim."[58] Praising both buildings' generous communal spaces and amenities—which included a glassed-in swimming pool overlooking the East River at Rivercross, another notable benefit of the architects' efforts at cost cutting—the critic Stanley Abercrombie noted:

> This sort of housing design—seriously concerned with ennobling and lifting the spirits of those it houses, not just within their private apartments but throughout the buildings' whole progression of spaces—is the sort of housing most architects want to build. Most never have the opportunity. . . . The Roosevelt Island housing, therefore, (particularly "Rivercross") is cause for the architectural profession to rejoice: the UDC has provided a rare opportunity for experimentation, and Johansen & Bhavnani have taken full advantage of it. If in the short term context of the housing market (because the generous semi-public areas must be paid for by increased cost for the private areas), the scheme remains problematic, in the long-term context of evolving architectural forms that will satisfy man's need for civilized housing, the Johansen & Bhavnani designs constitute an important step.[59]

Sert, Jackson & Associates' contribution—the Eastwood Apartments (1976), housing 1,003 middle- and lower-middle-income families on a six-acre site along the east side of Main Street from numbers 510 to 580; and the 360-unit Westview Apartments (1976), 595–625 Main Street, on the west side facing Manhattan—had, as even Johansen and Bhavnani reportedly admitted, "more charm" than Rivercross and Island House.[60] In a series of housing and academic projects for Harvard and Boston universities, José Luis Sert had evolved a vocabulary of tile-decorated concrete buildings with skip-stop plans, glassed-in exterior passageways and sculptured penthouses that owed a good deal to the late work of Le Corbusier. At Roosevelt Island, Sert and his partner, Huson Jackson, added a new element: a composition of terraced finger buildings piling up in boxy increments from two stories at the water's edge to twenty-two stories

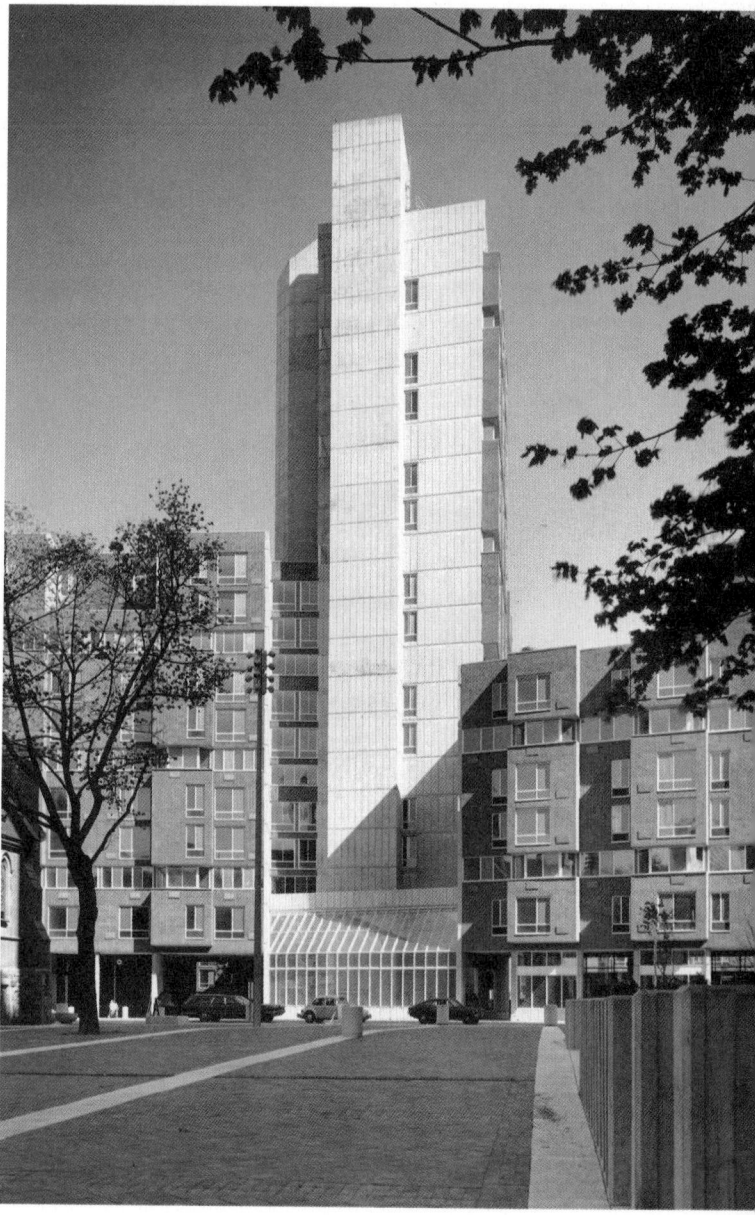

Eastwood Apartments, Roosevelt Island. Sert, Jackson & Associates, 1976. View to the east of Main Street facade. Rosenthal. SJA

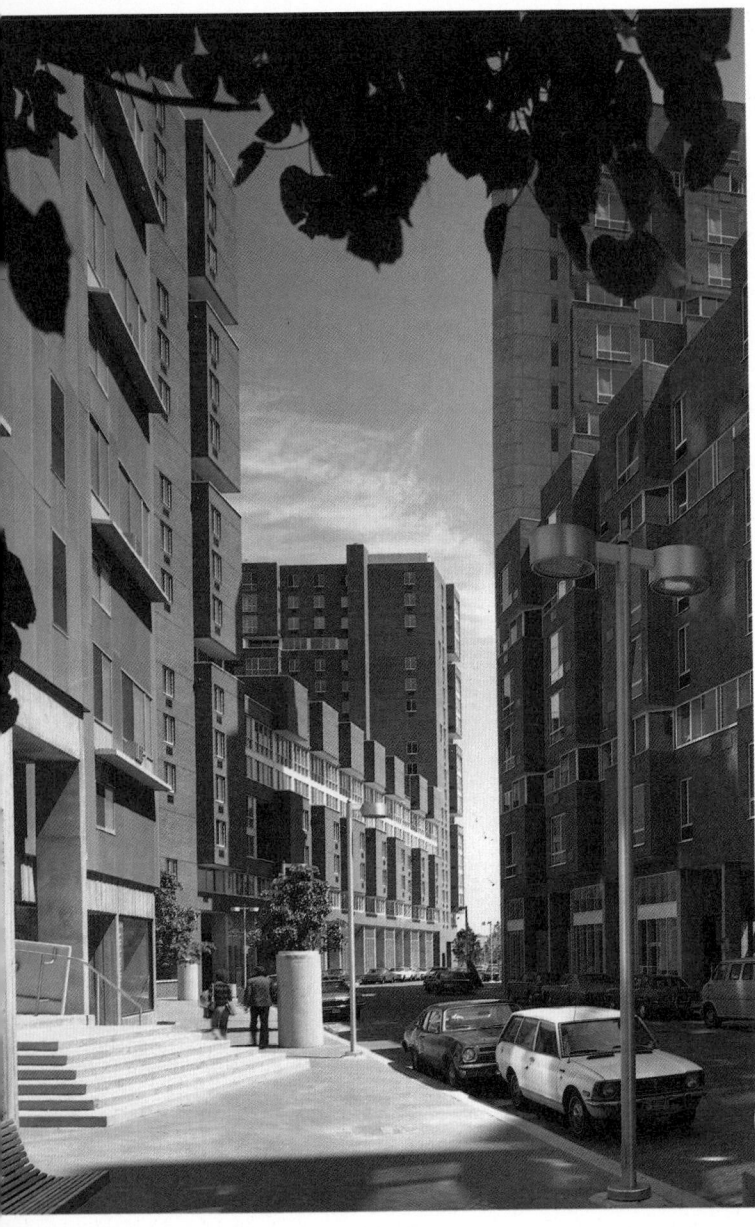

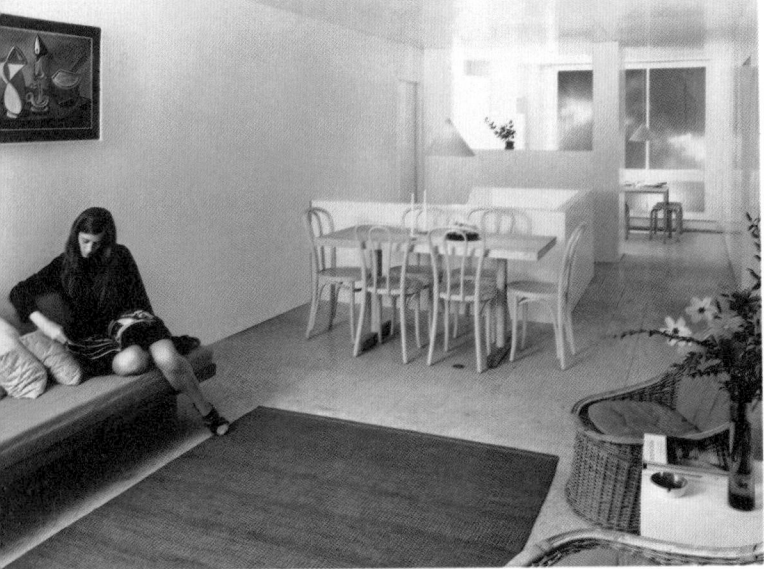

along Main Street. Sert and Jackson proposed that the roof terraces be used as children's play areas, but the UDC opposed the idea for reasons of both cost and security.

The buildings were grouped to form a series of courtyards, preserving some of the site's existing trees. Breaking with the Johnson and Burgee plan, which had called for courtyards open to the river, Sert and Jackson closed them with six-story buildings at the ends, although the structures were cut through with monumentally scaled open-air passageways that framed water views. Along Main Street they placed seven-story buildings between the four twenty-two-story slab ends, in an effort to realize some of the intimate scale Johnson and Burgee had proposed, which had been lost when Logue permitted much higher densities and much taller buildings. Still, the effect was somewhat canyonlike. Inside, the buildings' elevators stopped at every third floor, with corridors leading to individual apartments on that floor and internal staircases leading up or down to the other two floors. The apartments located above or below the corridor ran as "floor-throughs," with windows at both ends. Comparing the work of Johansen & Bhavnani and Sert, Jackson & Associates in 1976, Goldberger observed that though the Johansen buildings had the choicer views and catered to the wealthier tenants, the Sert buildings "have a certain edge."[61]

Kallmann & McKinnell's Motorgate (1974) constituted the island's only new freestanding public facility.[62] Residents and guests parked their cars in this structure; to reach their ultimate destination, they could take (for no charge) the specially designed, red-painted, battery-powered electric minibuses that tacked up and down Main Street. Drivers making deliveries could travel on Main Street, where short-term curbside parking was permitted. Goldberger described the 1,000-car reinforced-concrete garage, which incorporated shops, a fire station and a post office in a recessed sidewalk arcade, as "one of the finest buildings on the island—the same Brutalist concrete vocabulary that was overbearing in works by these architects such as the Boston City Hall is just right for a combination garage and symbolic entrance to a community."[63]

In 1976 Roosevelt Island finally became more accessible to Manhattan when the new tram was opened for service.[64] The idea began as a temporary solution to the island's access problem in March 1973, when William Chafee, one of the UDC's staff architects, proposed a gondola-type aerial cable car connecting the west side of Second Avenue between Fifty-ninth and Sixtieth streets to a site on the island north of the Queensboro Bridge at 300 Main Street. Designed by the engineering firm of Lev Zetlin Associates and built by the VSL Corporation/von Rolls Ltd. of Bern, Switzerland, the 3,100-foot-long tram, which was identical to the cableways in both Disney theme parks, took three and a half minutes and cost fifty cents per ride—the same cost as a subway ride. The tram carried two synchronized 125-passenger cars, one going in each direction, on cables hung 300 feet above the river at its highest point, where it crossed the openwork steel structure of Tower No. 2, just east of York Avenue. Tower No. 1 was located between Second and First avenues, and Tower No. 3 was just at Roosevelt Island's western shore. Twelve trips could be made per hour on what was billed as the world's first mass-transit tramway, moving 1,500 people each way. Although the system was managed and monitored from the Roosevelt Island terminal, each car had an attendant who could override the automatic controls. Passengers were lifted above the river, following a route just north of the Queensboro Bridge, where they could gaze through the wrap-around windows of the twenty-five-by-thirteen-foot cabin at the spectacular urban scenery and at the traffic on the bridge.

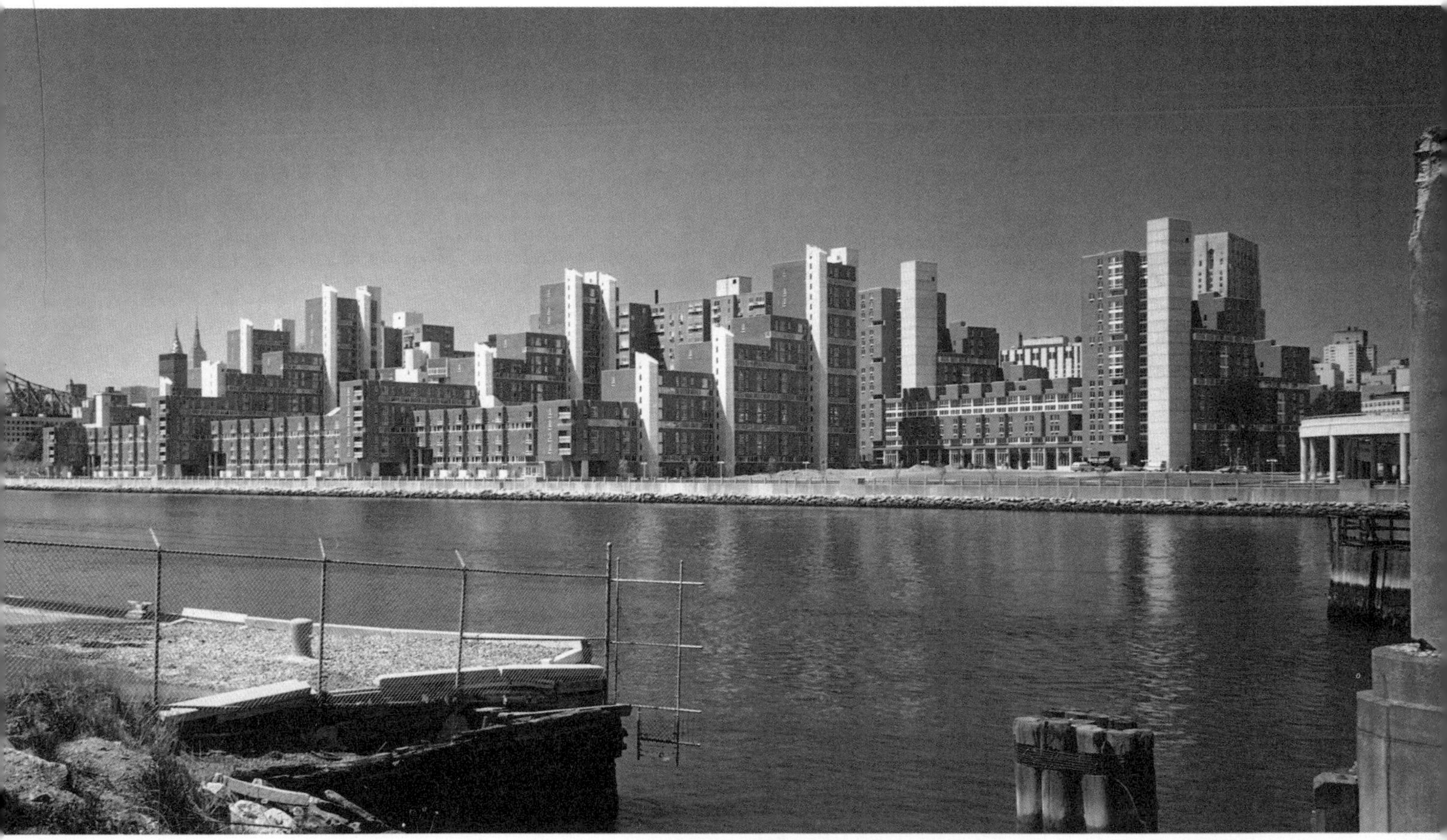

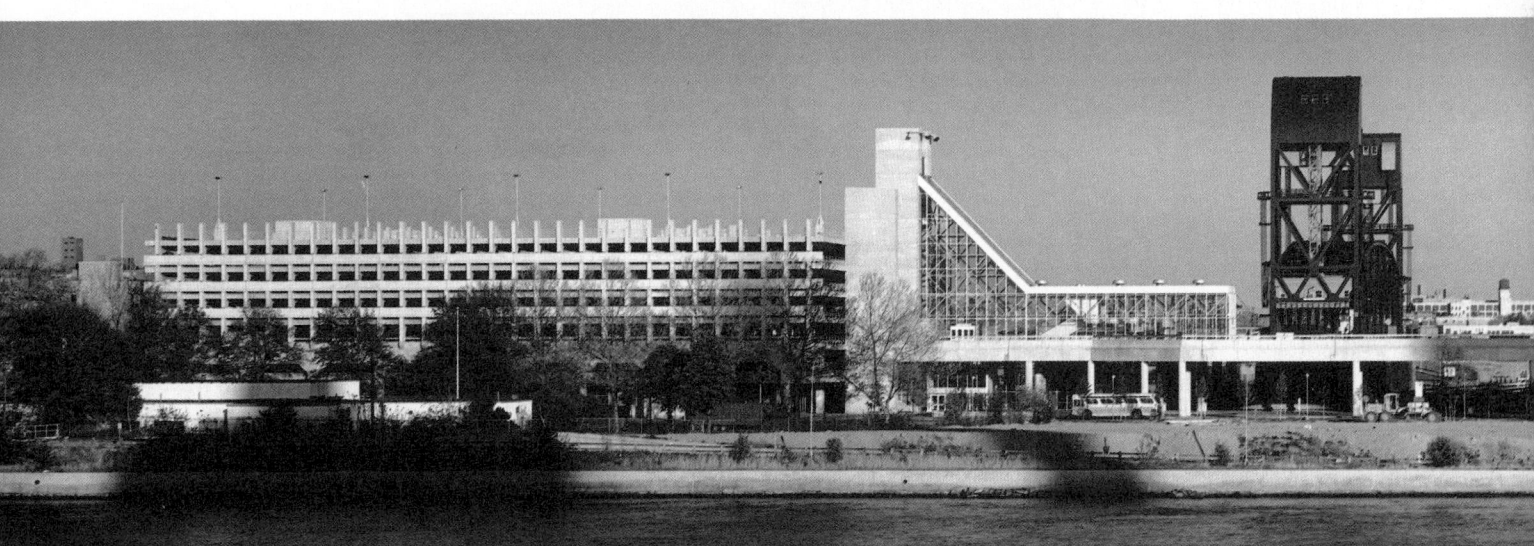

Top left: View to the north on Main Street, Roosevelt Island, showing, from left to right: Island House (Johansen & Bhavnani, 1975), Westview Apartments, (Sert, Jackson & Associates, 1976) and Eastwood Apartments (Sert, Jackson & Associates, 1976). Rosenthal. SJA

Bottom left: Mock-up of floor-through unit, Roosevelt Island. Sert, Jackson & Associates, 1971. Rosenthal. SJA

Top: Eastwood, Roosevelt Island. Sert, Jackson & Associates, 1976. View to the southwest from Queens. Rosenthal. SJA

Bottom: Motorgate, Roosevelt Island. Kallmann & McKinnell, 1974. View to the east. KMW

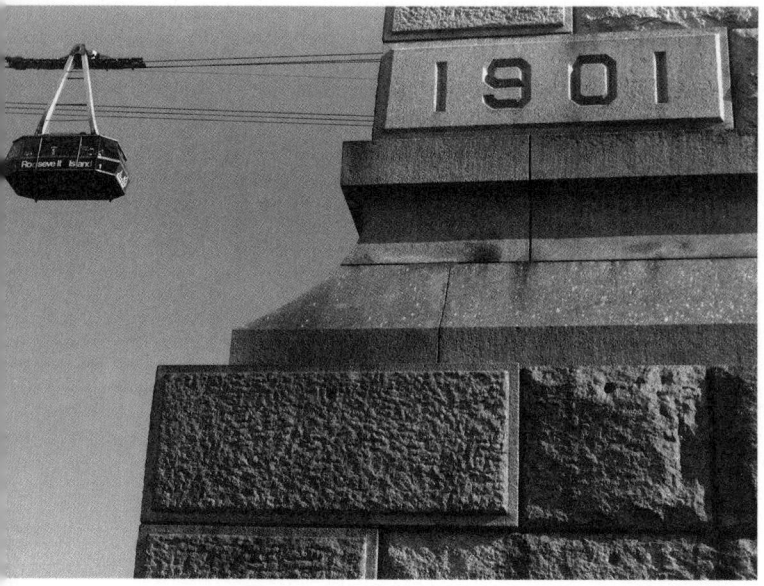
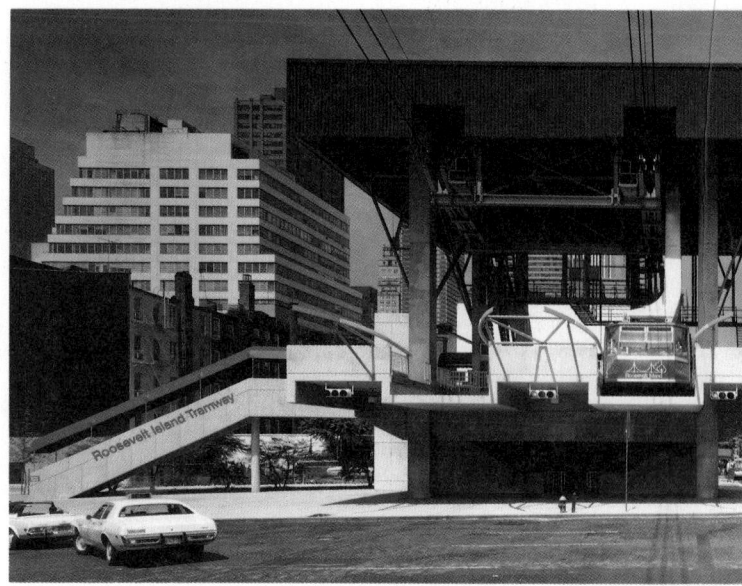
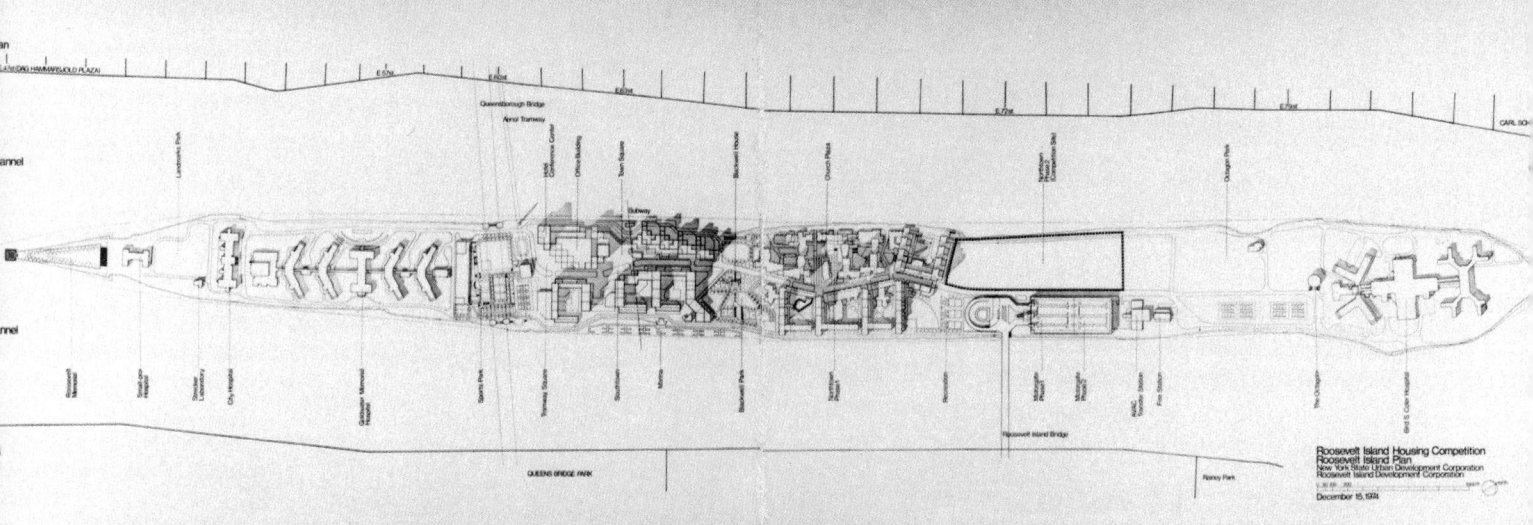

Top left: Roosevelt Island Tram, Roosevelt Island. Lev Zetlin Associates,
1976. View to the north from base of Queensboro Bridge (Henry
Hornbostel and Gustave Lindenthal, 1901–9). TT

Top right: Manhattan Terminal, Roosevelt Island Tram, west side of
Second Avenue, East Fifty-ninth to East Sixtieth Street. Prentice & Chan,
Ohlhausen in association with Lev Zetlin Associates, 1976. View to the
west. PCO

Bottom: Map of Roosevelt Island for Northtown Competition, 1974.
Roosevelt Island Housing Competition. UDC

On the Manhattan side, a six-story terminal was designed by Prentice & Chan, Ohlhausen in collaboration with Lev Zetlin Associates. The structure incorporated forty-inch steel-and-concrete columns, which were intended to support a thirty-two-story building, although the surmounting tower was never realized. The structure was also cantilevered along its eastern facade to accommodate the widening of Second Avenue and along its western facade to allow for an off-the-street bus stop, but neither plan was realized. Perhaps in part as a result of these elements, the tram station was a study in exaggerated contrasts. With rough, boldly massed concrete walls sheltering the brightly colored rotary machinery and tendril-like cables, it was, as Goldberger wrote, "a really lovely kindergarten version of *Modern Times* and absolutely the right beginning or end for a visit to the island, which is itself so much a combination of modern, industrial imagery and gentle game-playing."[65]

At its first test run on February 16, 1976, the tram ran into trouble near its Manhattan terminus, hitting the top of a streetlight pole that was to have been lowered. After a series of false starts and rescinded dates, its dedication was held on May 17. Despite the snags, not to mention the gloom that increasingly surrounded the Roosevelt Island project as the UDC, and then the city, fell victim to financial crisis, the tram was a bright, optimistic vision. As Michael Winkleman wrote in September 1975, prior to the tram's opening, "the three-minute ride is more than just another tourist attraction. Though it's sure to rival the old favorites—the Empire State Building, the Statue of Liberty, the Cyclone—the big news is that, as New York teeters on bankruptcy, a futuristic means of travel and a newfangled town, floating midstream, are becoming realities."[66]

The editors of *Time* said that, with the tram's opening, "convenience and mystique came together" in "the Little Apple," as they called Roosevelt Island. "Paris has its glittering Ile de la Cité on the Seine," they contended, "Budapest its merry Margaret Island on the Danube. New York City also has an island in the stream that may someday be an equally stimulating place to live or visit."[67] Michael Demarest, a senior writer for *Time*, described the tram ride:

> Cabin Two began its stately ascent noiselessly and almost imperceptibly. The 18,300-lb. C-2 reached a top speed of 16.3 m.p.h. and a peak altitude of 250 feet. . . . We touched down on R.I. after a flight of 3,134 ft. and 3½ min. . . . Wind speeds are constantly checked; service is stopped if gusts reach 45 m.p.h. On C-2's return trip, winds caused the tram to tilt 1° to starboard, according to the onboard inclinometer. "Not feeling seasick?" asked engineer Ozerkis. "Or airsick?" If we had said yes, he would doubtless have passed out Dramamine.[68]

Writing in 1979, Goldberger was also enthralled with the tram ride, calling it "extraordinary—gentle, soft, soaring," and saying "there could be no better way to traverse a river or a part of a city." He continued: "It is a symptom of our times, no doubt, that you think first that you are in Disneyland and that someone has deviously pasted a photograph of the Manhattan skyline across the window of your tram car, but if the illusion lasts no more than a split second, there is greater pleasure still in perceiving the reality: this is not Disneyland at all—it is New York."[69]

A significant component of the Roosevelt Island plan was the sequence of open spaces, ranging from Main Street to various parks and gardens as well as a waterfront esplanade, and the preservation of some of the island's historic structures. In Northtown, Blackwell House (1796–1804), a clapboard farm-house, was restored by Giorgio Cavaglieri, a process in which, according to Goldberger, "a modest, unpretentious farmhouse" had been "sanitized" to look "like a model house for a new suburban tract development." Although Goldberger praised Dan Kiley's work in creating Blackwell Park, the landscape setting for the house, he felt that it was ultimately a failure because of the impossibility "of bridging the visual gap between this poor, lonely little building and the huge housing blocks looming near it."[70] Goldberger much preferred the fate of Frederick Clarke Withers's Gothic-style Chapel of the Good Shepherd (1888–89), which Cavaglieri restored and recycled as the Good Shepherd Community Ecumenical Center; it was surrounded by a plaza designed by Johansen & Bhavnani and Lawrence Halprin & Associates.[71]

In 1974, with the work of the first phase nearing completion, the UDC announced a two-stage design competition for the completion of Northtown, with 1,000 units of housing on the 9.2-acre site opposite the Motorgate.[72] In his statement to the competitors, Logue attempted to justify the competition brief, which would inevitably bring forward high-density, high-rise solutions:

> It was only a year and one half ago that we announced our intention to build low-rise high-density housing as opposed to high-rise housing throughout New York State. . . . Why then, on Roosevelt Island, are we asking the profession to address a housing problem at twice the density of our stated low-rise housing policy? There are several reasons and in them lie the heart of this request. The first is the context. Roosevelt Island is a new community without an existing residential stock in a fixed configuration. It has excellent views and a dimension of water around it that affords the opportunity to create housing based on human scale without the cornice lines of neighboring buildings of another century as a constraint. The second is our genuine desire to go beyond conventional housing solutions to find ways in which families can be well housed in a diversity of situations. If we can be convinced that elevator dependent housing can serve families, as well as elderly and childless households, with maximum livability, it will give us much more flexibility in our housing program.[73]

The competition jury, chaired by José Luis Sert, included the architects Paul Rudolph, Joseph Wasserman and Alexander Cooper, as well as Sharon Lee Ryder, an architectural journalist, Franklin D. Becker, a sociologist, and Frederick P. Rose, a real estate developer. As originally proposed, the competition was to be held in two stages: eight finalists would be selected at the end of the first stage, and first-, second- and third-prize winners at the end of the second stage. But in February 1975 it appeared unlikely that the UDC would be able to pay the interest due on its previously issued bonds, and Governor Hugh Carey consequently asked for Logue's resignation, replacing him with Richard Ravitch. Because it was clear that the new units would not soon be built, the competitors were officially notified of the UDC's problems and the competition was called off in midstream.[74] With so much work already done by the entrants, however, the UDC resumed the competition as a single-stage undertaking that would probably not lead to a building commission. For some entrants this was a remarkable opportunity to focus on "ideas" as opposed to buildings. Joseph Wasserman would later explain: "This competition was a device to publicize among the professionals of this country the issues, objectives and methodology of UDC and to get literally thousands of architects thinking about these things on this kind of scale."[75]

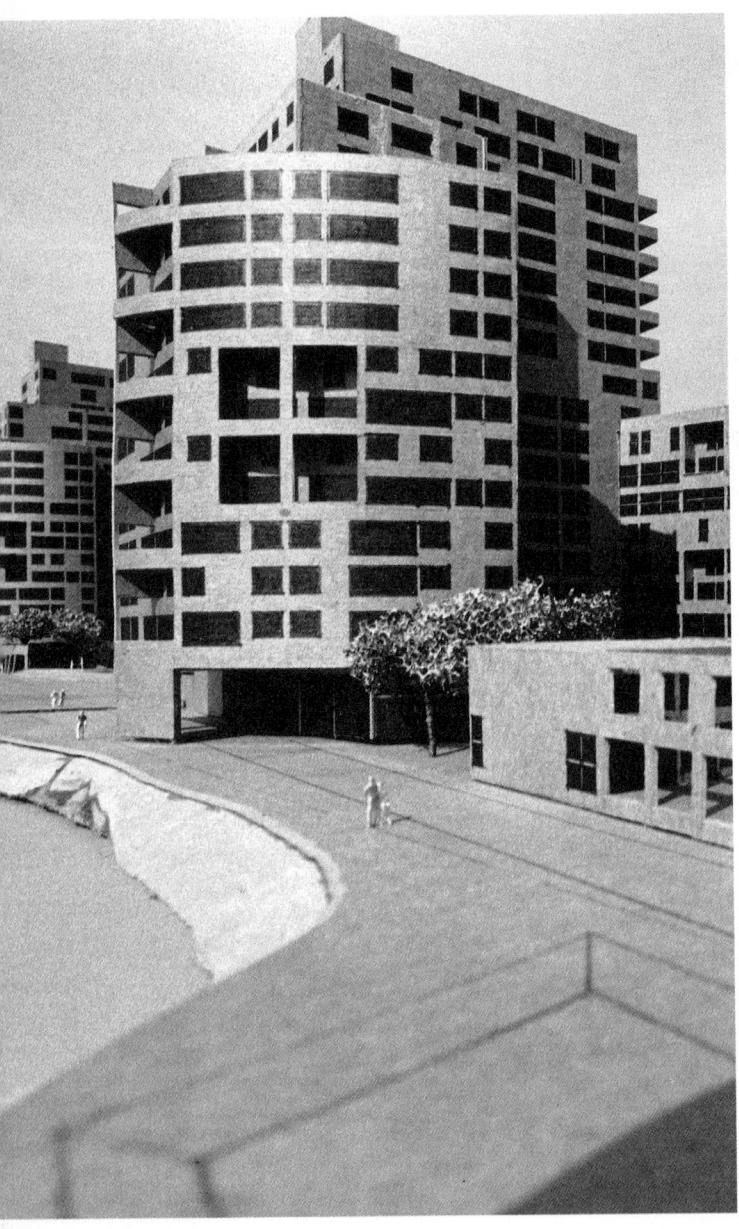

Above: Competition entry, Northtown Competition, Roosevelt Island. Stern & Hagmann, 1974. Model. View to the northeast. Stoecklein. RAMSA

Top right: Competition entry, Northtown Competition, Roosevelt Island. Sam Davis and ELS Design Group, 1974. Model. View to the southeast. Severin. SD

Bottom right: Competition entry, Northtown Competition, Roosevelt Island. Kyu Sung Woo, 1974. Axonometric. View to the southeast. KSW

Bottom far right: Competition entry, Northtown Competition. Kyu Sung Woo. Model. View to the east. KSW

Two hundred and fifty architects prepared schemes, and a divided jury split the prize between four young firms: Stern & Hagmann, of New York; Kyu Sung Woo, also of New York; Sam Davis and the ELS Design Group, of Berkeley, California; and Robert L. Amico and Robert Brandon of Champaign, Illinois. Sert dominated the jury, as Paul Goldberger noted in his report of the decision, so that many of the entries, including three of the four winners, were similar to the Sert-designed housing under construction on Roosevelt Island at the time. Goldberger described the fourth scheme:

> The one entry to depart from the Sert massing, and the most controversial one so far as the jury was concerned, was the one from Stern and Hagmann. It consisted of higher sections on the riverfront rather than inland, with curving facades facing downriver to take advantage of the views. The complex was planned around an irregular central open space, and its facade design recalls buildings by Robert Venturi, the controversial architect whose work has been a major influence on Robert Stern.[76]

In explaining his firm's competition entry, Stern said: "Our decision to enter the Roosevelt Island competition was based on our belief that the recent, revisionist housing theory of Jane Jacobs, Oscar Newman and others remains unfulfilled in formal terms, and that urban multifamily housing design, at least in this country, remains largely alienated from its American antecedents, mired in pseudo-technological pipe dreams."[77]

While the jurors remained mostly silent about the controversy, Paul Rudolph said of the Stern & Hagmann proposal: "I don't understand this scheme—it is so much in competition with what has already been built. The central space doesn't provide any sense of 'space' as I understand it. There is an arbitrary and picturesque turning of the interior mall."[78] Other members of the jury were far more sympathetic: Joseph Wasserman said, "It has a New York quality, a richness. I could spend a day here discovering a lot of interesting places. A lot of concern was given to the livability issues. It is a rich tapestry of ideas."[79]

A number of other provocative schemes were not premiated: Clinton Sheerr and Susana Torre's proposal for neutral slablike buildings in which individual tenants could, under professional guidance, tailor their own units;[80] Rem Koolhaas and Elia Zenghelis's re-creation of Manhattan;[81] and O. M. Ungers's even more extreme idea, a typological simulation complete with Central Park surrounded by a grid of streets and buildings.[82] Each of these schemes would become important benchmarks in the artistic rediscovery of Manhattan as an icon that would become prevalent in the late 1980s. The group Art Net, consisting of Peter Cook, Ron Herron, Ingrid Morris and six other English collaborators, as well as the American Peter Eisenman, presented an entry that called for three spiraling cylinders, looking a bit as if Frank Lloyd Wright's Guggenheim Museum had been merged with a gas-storage tank.[83]

Although the competition yielded no building commissions, the completed portions of Roosevelt Island nonetheless constituted a considerable achievement. By 1978, 5,500 people occupied the island's four apartment buildings. If the development's architecture failed to satisfy all critics, its plan did succeed in retaining the island's inherent advantages as a kind of *rus in urbe*, albeit a relatively high-density one. Robin Herman, writing in the *New York Times* in 1978, described the island in a Manhattanite's equivalent to bucolic terms: "Just three and a half minutes from Bloomingdale's by way of the Tinker Toy colored tram, it is yet a world apart from the

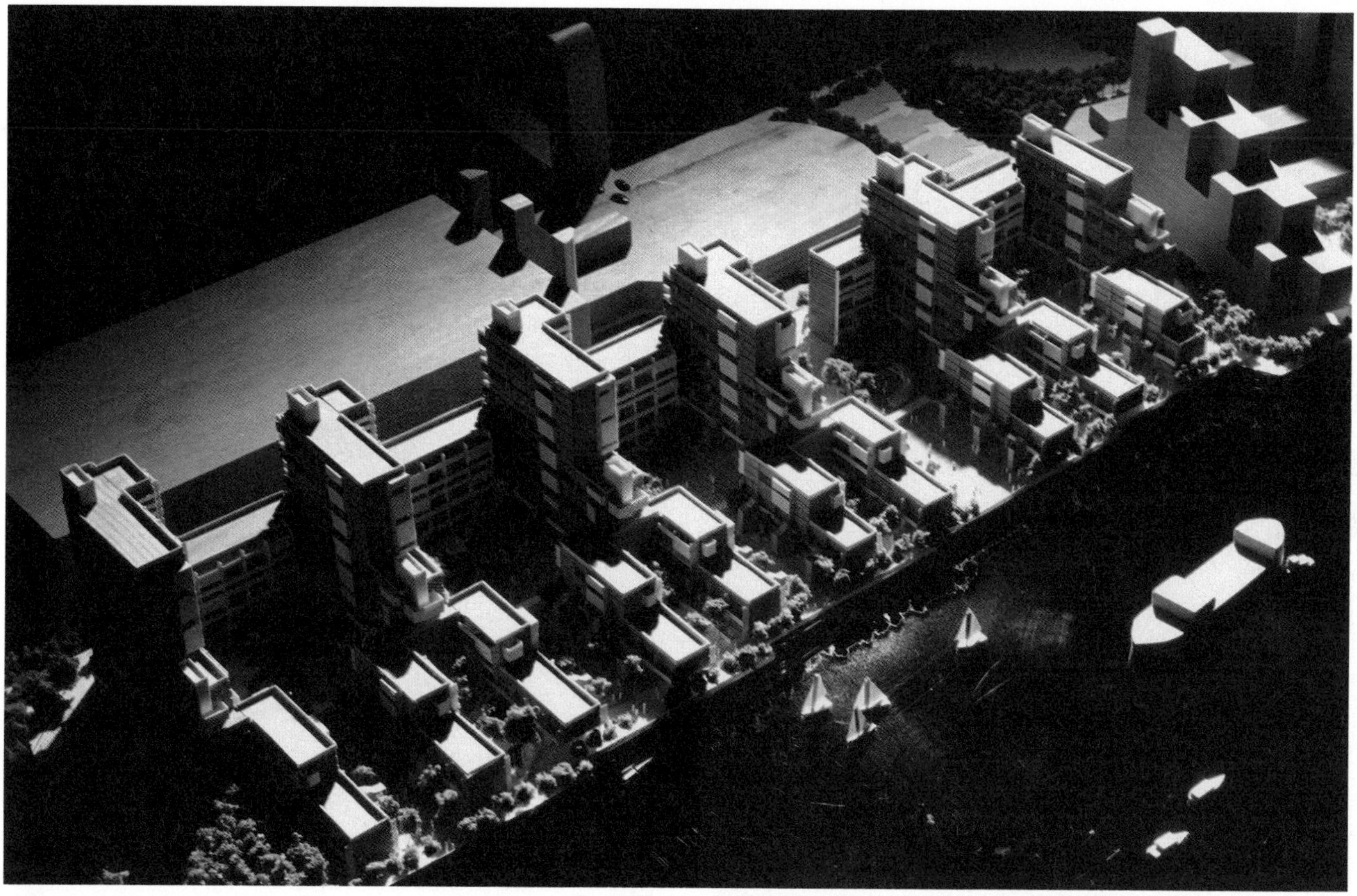

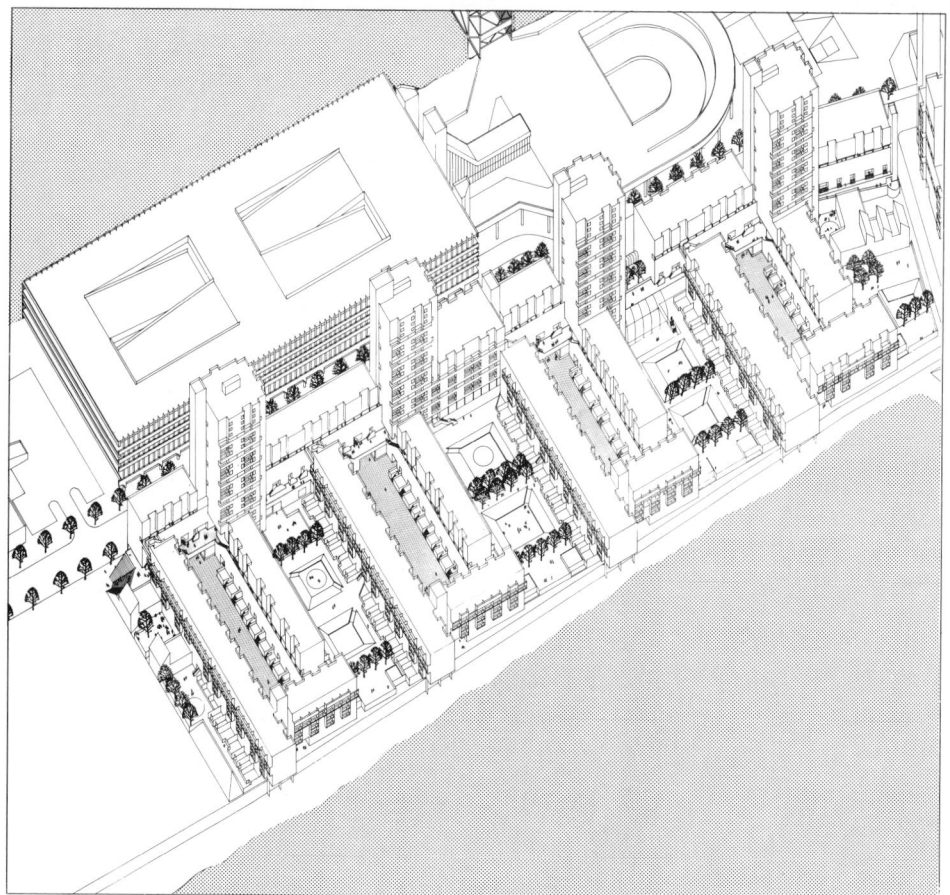

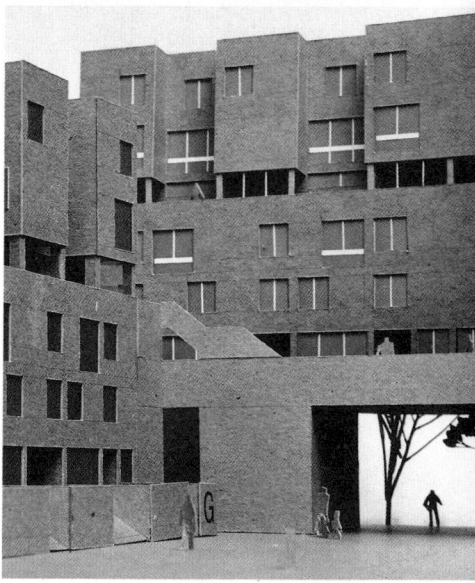

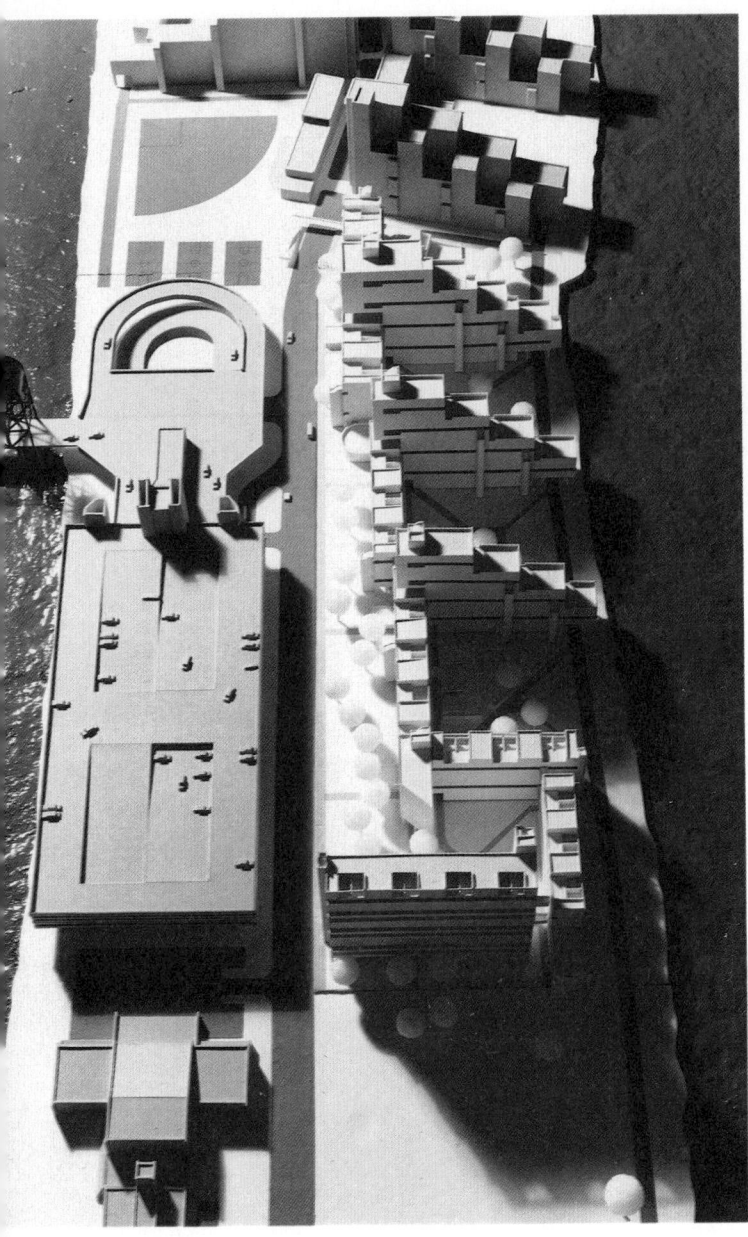

Above: Competition entry, Northtown Competition, Roosevelt Island.
Robert L. Amico and Robert Brandon, 1974. Model. View to the south.
Kaha. RLA

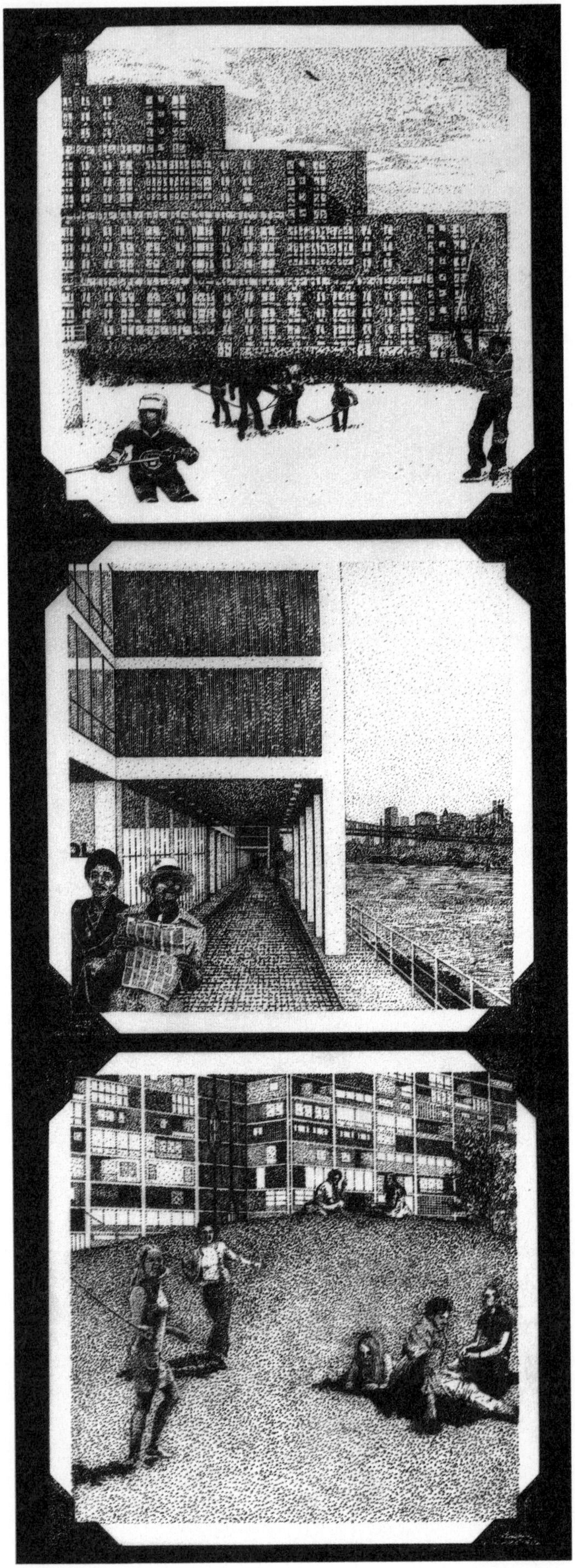

Right: Competition entry, Northtown Competition, Roosevelt Island.
Clinton Sheerr and Susana Torre, 1974. Three renderings of site in use.
ST

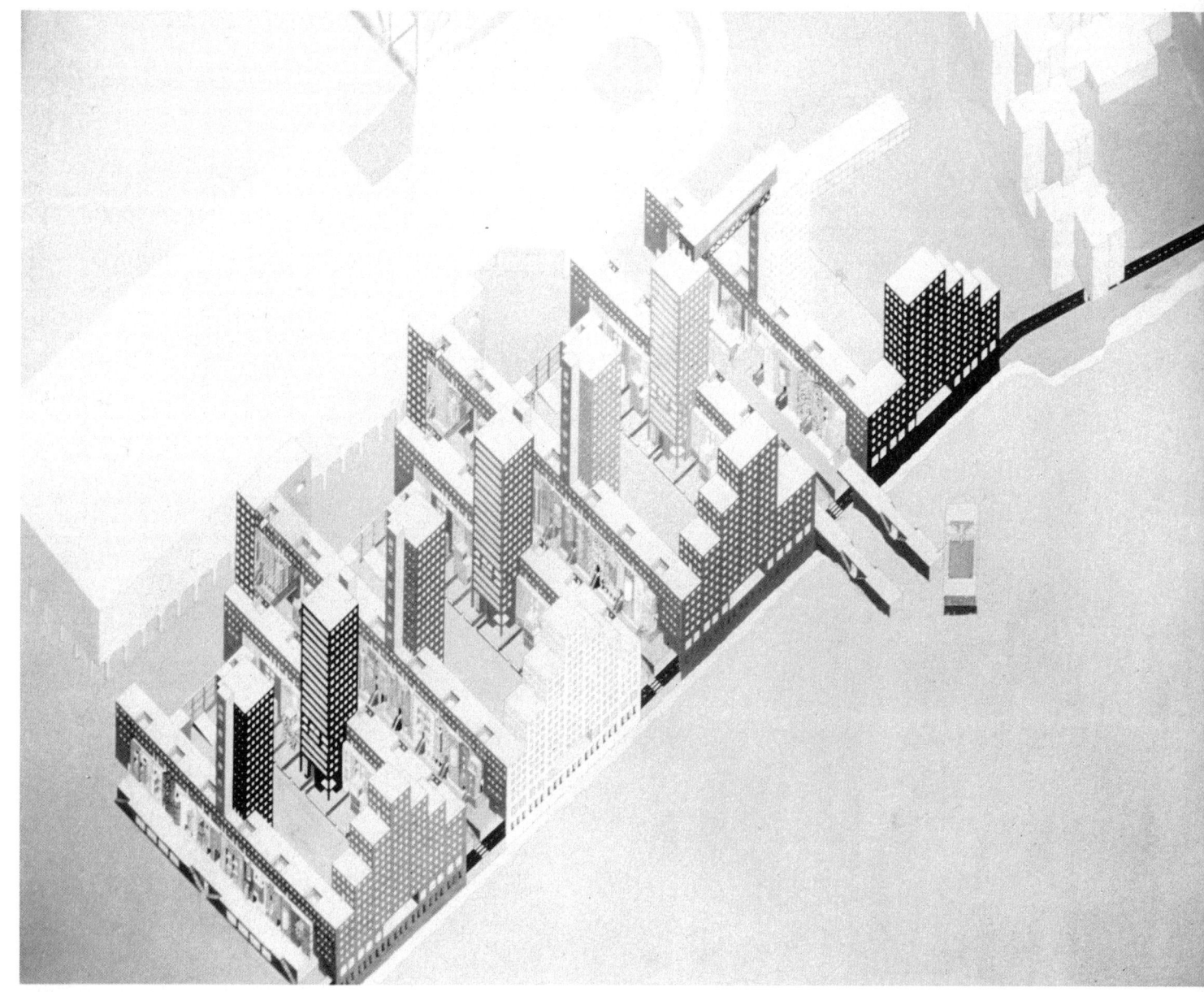

heat and bustle of Dry Dock country." In this "oasis of quiet carpeted in suburban green," Herman said, residents could enjoy "the constant breeze that keeps Roosevelt Island fresh smelling and always a few degrees cooler than the 'mainland.'"[84] Ironically, however, it was in part the island's ability to distinguish itself from the surrounding "mainland" that limited its success; while Roosevelt Island did indeed avoid some of the urbanistic chaos of Manhattan, it also lacked its vitality. As Barbara Goldstein put it in *Architectural Design* in 1975, "Although linked directly to Manhattan, Roosevelt Island has all the appearances of a new town, or a chunk of residential White Plains floated down the East River. It seems to be more of a hermetically sealed suburb than an integral part of New York City."[85] And not all of the island's residents were charmed either. Ron Aaron Eisenberg, a public relations executive, said that while the new town was "a place that people should see and that sociologists and urbanologists and a multitude of other 'ologists' should study," it was "depersonalization itself."[86] After living on Roosevelt Island for three months, he returned to Manhattan.

Competition entry, Northtown Competition, Roosevelt Island. Rem Koolhaas and Elia Zenghelis, 1974. Axonometric. View to the southeast. OMA

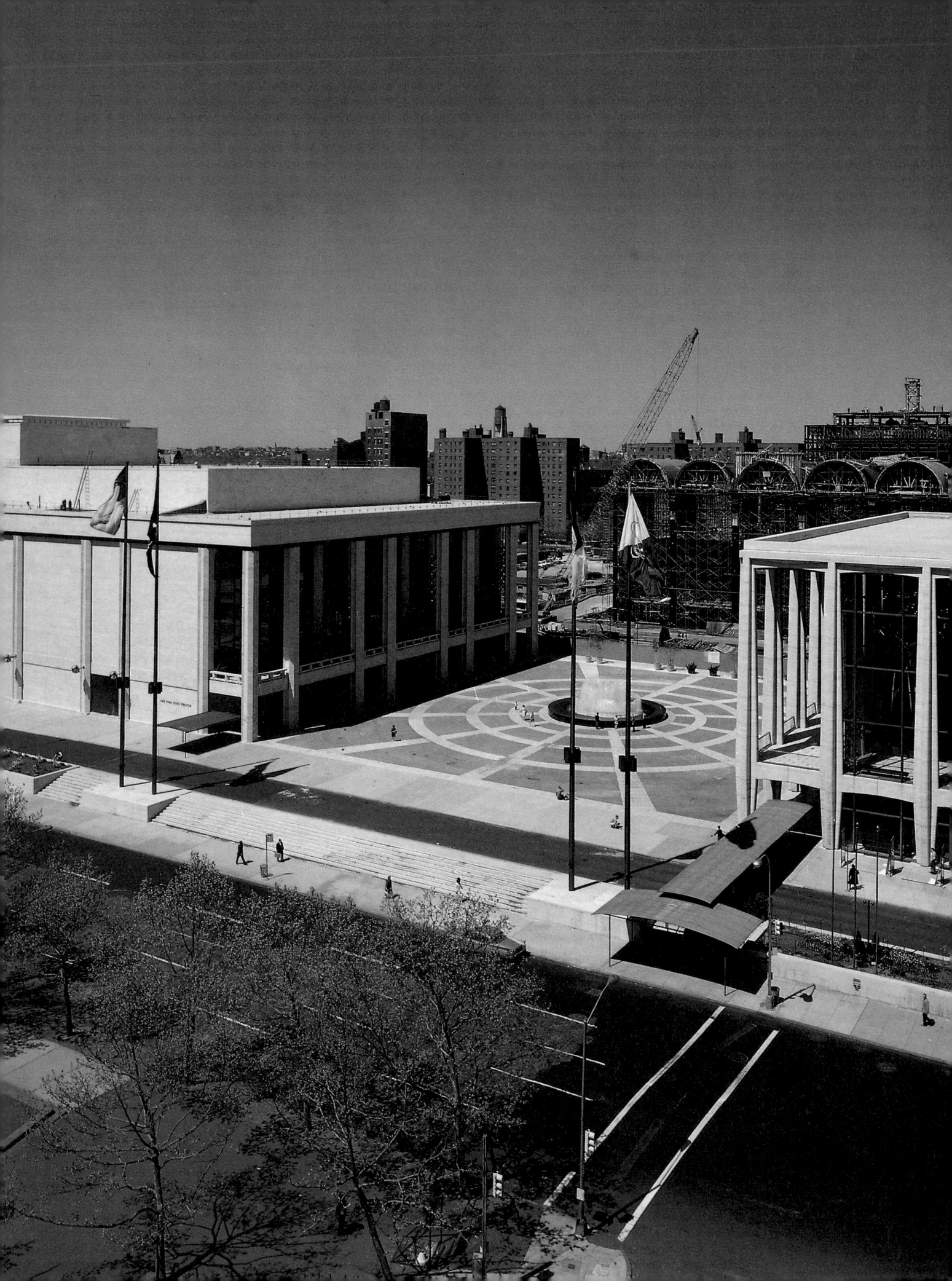

Chapter 9

Upper West Side

West Siders are convinced that theirs is the best of all neighborhoods. These are the people who have abandoned Greenwich Village to the tourists and the speculators, who shun the East Side as superficial, who abhor the suburbs as sterile, who regard themselves as connoisseurs of the city and are the stubborn zealots in the cause of urban life.
—Lawrence Van Gelder, 1969[1]

THE FALL

In 1940 the prominent developer Dr. Charles Y. Paterno offered an optimistic view of the future of the Upper West Side, based on its recent past as one of New York's premier apartment house districts. "The natural advantages already exist," Paterno told the *New York Times.* "The new parkway development and the George Washington Bridge have not only placed it foremost among the areas destined for improvement but guaranteed the beauty of its surroundings. . . . It is up to the investor, now, to capitalize on these advantages, to recognize that they alone are responsible for the profits he may enjoy, and build apartments that will provide new tenants with all the sunlight and healthy space that the location calls for."[1] What Paterno seemed to have in mind was a bold reconstruction of the west side along the lines of his own Castle Village of 1938,[2] with its tower-in-the-park site plan, influenced as much by the French master Le Corbusier as by the American rationalist tradition that had also informed the designs of the Wardman Park Hotel (Mesrobian & Wardman, 1918), Washington, D.C.,[3] the Alden Park Apartments (Edwyn Rorke, 1920), Germantown, Pennsylvania,[4] the Edgewater Beach Hotel (Benjamin Marshall, ca. 1920), Chicago,[5] and the Longwood Towers (K. M. De Vos and Company with George R. Wiren and Harold Field Kellogg, 1922–25), Brookline, Massachusetts.[6]

Despite Paterno's wishful thinking, the actual direction of the west side's post–Depression era evolution was very different.

Lincoln Center, between Columbus and Amsterdam avenues, West Sixty-second and West Sixty-sixth streets. View to the southwest showing New York State Theater (Philip Johnson, 1964) on the left, Metropolitan Opera House (Wallace K. Harrison, 1966) under construction, in the center, and Philharmonic Hall (Max Abramovitz, 1962) on the right. Stoller. ©ESTO

The Upper West Side, customarily defined as the area bounded by the Hudson River, Central and Morningside parks, West Fifty-ninth and West 125th streets, had undergone two major development phases before the 1940s. In the first phase, extending from the early 1870s through about 1910, the area's open land was built up mostly with block upon block of nearly identical rowhouses as well as many charming, individually designed townhouses.[7] Conceived by enlightened developers as New York's equivalent of London's fashionable West End, it was in reality more like that city's Bohemian Thames-side enclave, Chelsea, or the Pont Street area near Cadogan Square. Although some suburban-style villas were built along Riverside Drive and some apartment houses were built on West End Avenue, Central Park West and Broadway as part of this first wave of development, most of the land was reserved for attached single-family townhouses. The scale of the area was protected by covenants that prevented any other form of development for twenty-five or more years after the construction of the townhouses. But when these covenants began to run out in the first decade of the twentieth century, many of the area's townhouses, particularly those along the most desirable avenues—Central Park West, West End Avenue and Riverside Drive—as well as those along the wide crosstown streets, began to be replaced with large, luxuriously appointed apartment houses, a process that continued until the stock market crash of 1929.

In his book of 1899, *The New Metropolis*, E. Idell Zeisloft observed that the residents of the Upper West Side "are not as a rule of the old and historic New York families or very wealthy as a class, but all are people exceedingly well-to-do, a fair proportion of them are Hebrews and many are former residents of other cities who have found here the best value for their money."[8] By the turn of the century, so many German-Jewish families were located there that the Progress Club, previously located at Fifth Avenue and Sixty-third Street, relocated to a new clubhouse designed by Louis Korn (1904) at 1 West Eighty-eighth Street, on the northwest corner of Central Park West.[9] The most successful and most assimilated Jews, however, belonged to the Harmonie Club, which in 1905 relocated its headquarters from Forty-second Street to a palatial clubhouse designed by McKim, Mead & White at 4 East Sixtieth Street, across the street from J. P. Morgan's Metropolitan Club.[10]

661

By the mid-1930s, according to James Trager, "Jews constituted more than half the population of the area from 72nd Street to 96th Street between Central Park West and Riverside Drive."[11] This group, very different from the German-descended Jews of the late nineteenth century, had made their fortunes not in finance but in manufacturing—usually the garment industry—or in entertainment-related enterprises. Many of these Jews had themselves emigrated from Eastern Europe, mostly Russia or Poland. In 1939 *Fortune* would report in a special issue on New York:

> The West Side is inhabited chiefly, though by no means exclusively, by New York's foreign Jews, who have standards of their own, but whose interest in social prestige is practically nil. These people have behind them generations of city life, often originating in poverty. They are not only wedded to the city but know how to get the most out of it for their money. They take more pleasure than the Ivy Leaguers in cultural activities, even theater is a necessity; and they habitually cultivate a wide variety of taste from food to music.[12]

Some of the apartment houses built during the late 1920s rivaled in style, if not spaciousness, the great west side apartment houses of the fin de siècle. One of the most luxurious of these, replacing the hotel of the same name, was the Majestic Apartments (1930), at 115 Central Park West, developed by Irwin S. Chanin.[13] After the stock market crash, Chanin replanned the tower floors so that the single ten-room units on each floor were redesigned as one six-room and one four-room apartment. The Depression hastened the area's transformation, as many of the townhouses and apartments were broken up into smaller and more affordable units. A notable example of this trend was the renovation of the Clarendon Apartments, at 137 Riverside Drive, on the southeast corner of West Eighty-sixth Street. In 1941 the grand triplex suite at the top, maintained by William Randolph Hearst, the longtime owner of the building, was remodeled to create modest-sized units.[14]

At the same time, the area's two tenement-lined avenues, Columbus and Amsterdam, began to slide downward, as working-class Irish families moved out of Manhattan to better housing in the outer boroughs. With the demolition in 1940 of the seventy-two-year-old Ninth Avenue elevated train line, the first such rapid-transit system in the world, some tenements were upgraded as multiple dwellings.[15] The removal of the El fostered a hope that Columbus Avenue would be rebuilt, but with the lingering Depression and the subsequent outbreak of war, this did not occur. The area's decline was accelerated when in 1939 single-room occupancy residences were permitted for the first time, ostensibly to meet a surge in demand for housing in connection with crowds expected to flood the city for the World's Fair.[16] Single-room-occupancy not only affected the tenements on the less prosperous avenues as well as many side-street brownstones and townhouses, but it also led to the decline of at least one large, prominently sited apartment house: the seven-story Hudsonia (1902), at 321 West Seventy-ninth Street, on the northeast corner of Riverside Drive. Two years after the Hudsonia was converted to a single-room-occupancy residence hotel in 1941, it was demolished because of city officials' concern about the quality of its safety features.[17] Although the site was highly desirable, and real estate experts expected that a twelve-story apartment building would be built there soon after the war's end, it remained vacant until 1950, when work began on a banal, red-brick-clad, six-story building, designed by Horace Ginsbern, that was more typical of what one would find in either Brooklyn or Queens than in Manhattan.[18]

The Upper West Side did benefit somewhat from the comparative prosperity of 1939–41, with a few modest new six-story apartment houses being built along the side streets to replace townhouses. Like the somewhat taller side-street apartment houses of the 1920s, these upset but did not totally shatter the neighborhood scale. In addition, one major apartment house was completed in 1941, 295 Central Park West, on the southwest corner of Ninetieth Street, designed by Emery Roth as a restrained complement to the gloriously modernistic Eldorado immediately to the north, which Roth had designed in association with Margon & Holder ten years before.[19] In contrast to the lavishly sized and appointed suites of the Eldorado, 295 Central Park West contained 135 apartments of one to five rooms. Minimal detailing was promoted as an innovation: according to the architect, metal was used instead of the traditional wood for baseboards to provide for easier cleaning and better sanitation. Other notable apartment houses were the twin units at 175 West Ninety-second Street and 180 West Ninety-third Street (ca. 1940), on the east side of Amsterdam Avenue, designed by Kleban & Leader for the block-long site previously occupied by the Women's Methodist Home.[20] Immediately to the east was the Joan of Arc Junior High School (1940), designed by Eric Kebbon, the area's only significant new public improvement since the Depression, except for the opening in 1932 of the Independent subway line along Central Park West.[21]

Despite the general euphoria after the war, there were very few expressions of confidence in the Upper West Side's future. True, developers were at last able to complete and successfully rent the notorious Hudson Towers, on the northwest corner of West End Avenue and West Seventy-second Street.[22] It had been designed twenty years before by Arthur Weiser as a combination hospital and hotel, and although construction on the towers had begun in 1924, the building was left unfinished when financing ran out. It was still incomplete when the city took it over for nonpayment of taxes in 1940; even at that comparatively prosperous moment, the city was unable to auction the Hudson Towers off. It was not until 1945 that developers purchased it and completed it as a twenty-three-story apartment house.

Even small-scale commercial projects were rare. One exception was a branch of the popular, moderately priced Riker's restaurant chain, on the southwest corner of Broadway and 104th Street.[23] Designed by the architect Daniel Laitin, the restaurant, located on the ground floor of a prewar red brick apartment building, presented the street with sleekly Modernist facades dominated by large expanses of glass and a brightly colored, abstract glass-mosaic mural that extended inside to frame the entrance.

A major renovation of the American Museum of Natural History, one of the Upper West Side's greatest architectural landmarks, as well as one of the city's most cherished public institutions, was proposed in 1942.[24] One year earlier, Park Commissioner Robert Moses, who never lost an opportunity to take a swipe at New York's intellectual establishment, had attacked many of the city's museums, including the Museum of Natural History, saying they were "musty" and "exclusive," and had called for extensive physical and administrative changes.[25] Acting with the approval of the museum's board of trustees, the city engaged Moses's longtime collaborator on Park Department projects, Aymar Embury II, to remodel the building; acting with the approval of the Park Department, the museum trustees in turn hired the architect Eliel Saarinen to advise them concerning Embury's preliminary proposals. Embury was to pay the museum $1,000 out of his fee for

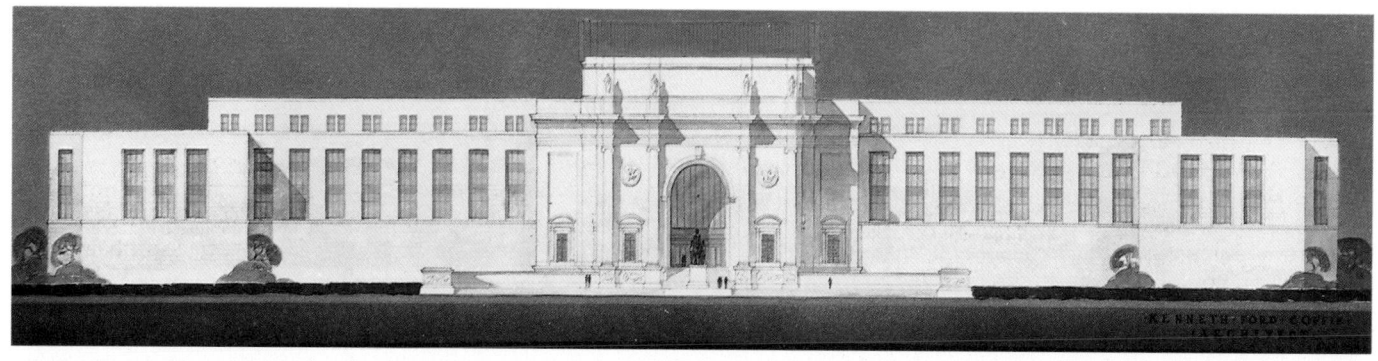

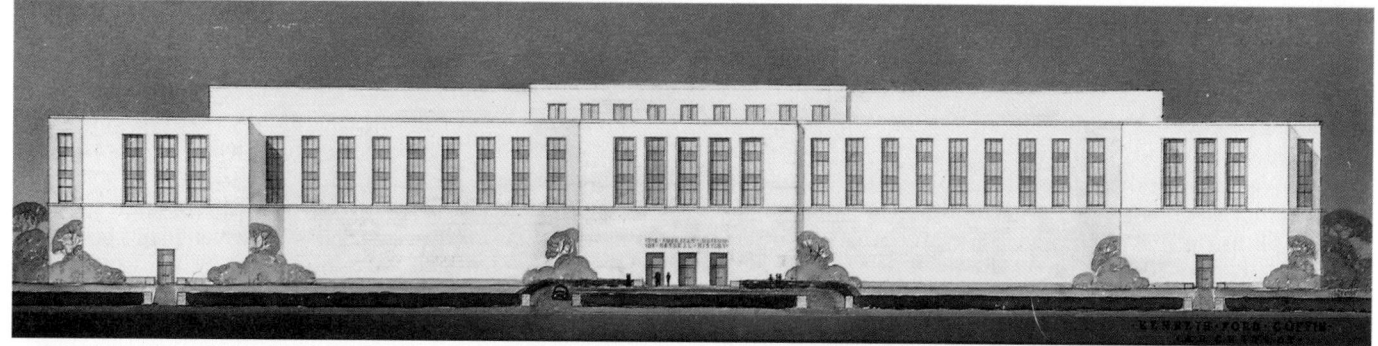

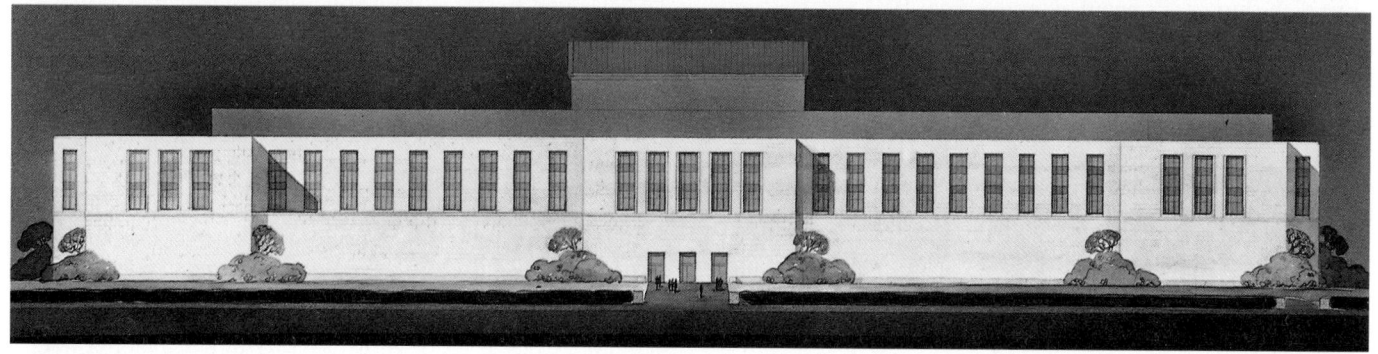

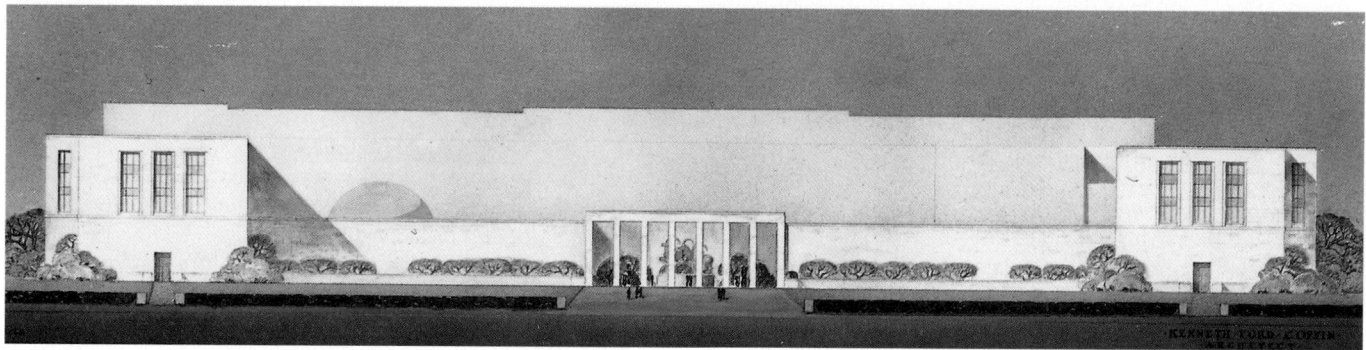

Proposal for alteration of the American Museum of Natural History, Central Park West to Columbus Avenue, West Seventy-seventh to West Eighty-first Street. Aymar Embury II, 1943. Elevations showing, from top to bottom: Central Park West facade, incorporating New York State Theodore Roosevelt Memorial (John Russell Pope, 1936); West Seventy-seventh Street facade; Columbus Avenue facade; and West Eighty-first Street facade. AMNH preparing preliminary plans to cover Saarinen's fee; he was to pay the museum an additional $5,000 to compensate Saarinen after completion of final plans. Embury called for the complete transformation of Cady, Berg & See's robustly articulated Romanesque composition of 1890, which extended along Seventy-seventh Street between Columbus Avenue and Central Park West.[26] Saarinen immediately objected to the basic proposal, arguing that instead of making the substantial financial investment required to remodel what he considered to be an essentially unworkable structure, the museum should erect a new building sometime in the future. Some members of the museum's board considered Saarinen's idea impractical and strongly urged revamping the existing building, but the museum kept open the possibility of retaining the Seventy-seventh Street facade as it was and reallocating the allotted funds for new construction on the northwest corner of the site, bounded by Columbus Avenue and Eighty-first Street. The museum subsequently decided to pursue the remodeling option. Embury proposed a highly reductivist design calling for the removal of the corner towers that broke up the skyline and helped articulate the facade. He also proposed to strip the facade of all its details and reorganize it, so that above a windowless two-story base housing exhibits, punctuated only by a symmetrically placed entrance, would be more floors of offices lit by vertical strip windows.

In response to the proposal, A. Perry Osborn, acting president of the museum's board of trustees from 1941 to 1946, said, "I do not like the innumerable Greek temples that have sprung up all over Washington nor many of the copies of old Gothic buildings that dot college campuses. I particularly dislike the brown granite pseudo fortress that composes the South facade of our Museum. After all, a fortress was designed to repel people, not attract them. . . . I think Embury has hit upon a simple, styleless type of architecture that looks very enduring to me."[27] Saarinen was more critical, writing to Embury that the design, "although good in proportion and mass distribution, is rather austere."[28]

If Saarinen was qualified in his praise, many observers simply disliked the proposal, which was publicly released in January 1943. Despite widespread and virulent opposition, the museum administration backed Embury's proposal on functional grounds, saying it would significantly improve both exhibition and storage facilities, and on aesthetic grounds, claiming it would serve as an effective element in an overall composition dominated by John Russell Pope's rigorously Classical New York State Theodore Roosevelt Memorial (1936), which now served as the museum's principal entrance on Central Park West.[29] In a letter to Albert E. Parr, the museum's director, Robert Moses, usually a supporter of Embury, said, "I was sure that you would run into criticism from old New Yorkers if the architects went too far with functionalism. Every now and then I have had to warn Aymar Embury about this, and he has always been good-natured about it. Saarinen is way over in that direction anyway. It is a thing to be careful of. Perhaps the conservatives are reactionary, but you can't get too far ahead of the procession in public work."[30]

In the course of developing the preliminary plans, Embury and Saarinen diverged in their recommendations. Osborn invited Saarinen to submit an alternate proposal, but the architect refused, stating that to do so would be to enter into direct competition with Embury, overreaching his role as consulting architect and betraying his responsibility as a "congenial member" of the architectural profession. Saarinen's "tentative

scheme," he said, "must by no means be considered a design-suggestion for the contemplated structure. It must be considered, only and alone, a design-analysis so as to enable me more intelligently, perhaps, to offer advice."[31] Whatever Saarinen's intent, some of his drawings were shown by Embury to Osborn and Parr. Saarinen called for the use of brick cladding, the incorporation of extensive fountains and reflecting pools, and the addition of entrance colonnades leading from Columbus Avenue to the museum's Seventy-seventh Street entrance and from Central Park West to the museum's Eighty-first Street entrance. While acknowledging the artistic merit of Saarinen's proposal, the museum's board of trustees endorsed Embury's design. In recognition of unanticipated costs accrued by Embury in the design process, and perhaps because of the conflict with Saarinen, the museum relieved Embury of his responsibility of covering the consulting fee. Though the museum was still officially committed to Embury's design in 1945, the controversial plan was never realized. In 1967 the museum's Seventy-seventh Street wing was designated a landmark.

Among the few institutional projects completed on the Upper West Side in the early 1950s was Sylvan Bien's boldly detailed International Style building (1950) for the Godmothers League, a service organization founded in 1918 to aid the children of World War I veterans and working mothers.[32] Located at 255 West Seventy-first Street, between Amsterdam and West End avenues, the three-story buff-brick building had a principal facade that incorporated deeply recessed balconies and horizontal strip windows, dramatically curved back away from the street to define a courtyard. The block's traditional street wall, defined by rowhouses and modestly scaled apartment buildings, was nonetheless respected by the inclusion of a low brick wall surmounted by a metal fence.

Eric Kebbon's far more conventional Public School 75 (1952), at 733 West End Avenue, on the west blockfront between Ninety-fifth and Ninety-sixth streets, was a mildly Georgian red-brick building, typical of his postwar work for the Board of Education.[33] In 1963 plans were advanced for the more stylishly ambitious Louis D. Brandeis High School, at 151 West Eighty-fourth Street.[34] Designed by Charles Luckman, the new midblock, 1,700-student facility, which ran through to Eighty-third Street, provided 254,000 square feet of space incorporating forty-two classrooms and related facilities in a rectangular doughnut, with a concrete frame exposed and infilled with vertical slitlike windows alternating with brick panels. Inside the doughnut, the courtyard began at the second-floor level so that the building's base, containing a gymnasium and an auditorium, could take up most of the available site.

Only one significant, large-scale project was undertaken on the Upper West Side in the immediate postwar years: the replacement of Charles M. Schwab's Riverside Drive mansion with a vast red-brick apartment house called Schwab House.[35] Schwab's site, mansion and furnishings had cost $8 million when they were put together between 1901 and 1907. Designed by the French architect Maurice Hébert, the seventy-five-room house sat on the entire block bounded by Seventy-third and Seventy-fourth streets, West End Avenue and Riverside Drive. It had been unoccupied since the death of Mr. and Mrs. Schwab in 1939. One of Manhattan's last freestanding mansions, and one of the grandest ever constructed in the city, the Schwab house was torn down in 1948, its passing largely unnoticed and completely unprotested. The new Schwab House (Sylvan Bien, 1950), a 654-unit, seventeen-story apartment house containing a subterranean parking garage, occupied 60 percent of its full-block site. Complexly massed into various wings separated by landscaped courtyards, which provided light and air for the apartments, it had the quasi-suburban appearance of Andrew J. Thomas's prewar garden apartments, but at a vastly greater density.[36]

In 1955 *House and Garden*'s decorating editors helped a young couple, Lee and Jim Cody, decorate their Schwab House apartment. Mrs. Cody was Lee Lewis, a fashion model; Mr. Cody was a special agent for an insurance company. The decorating scheme was spare, with simple upholstered and wooden furniture. Furniture was carefully selected with an eye to the Codys' sense that their time in Schwab House was going to be short because, as *House and Garden* put it, "Lee and Jim plan for a house of their own."[37] The Upper West Side, once a pinnacle in the search for a permanent city home, had now become a way station for young people on the way up and out. It had also become a "trap" for the financially insecure elderly and for the poor. By 1950 it was clear that the Upper West Side was not only declining as a desirable middle-class area but more seriously was in danger of slipping into a state of uncontrollable decay, of becoming a slum. The area's lack of appeal was reflected in the virtual absence of large-scale projects and even small-scale ones. A rare exception was Irving Brodsky's banal, six-story brick building at 711 West End Avenue (1952), on the west blockfront between Ninety-fourth and Ninety-fifth streets, which replaced tennis courts.[38]

One solution to the impending problem was to demolish the area and start again. In 1946 the real estate developer William Zeckendorf proposed a combination industrial center and airport to occupy a large part of the Upper West Side as well as a portion of the western part of midtown.[39] Scattered throughout the site, roughly bounded by Ninth Avenue, Broadway, the Hudson River, Thirty-fourth and Seventy-ninth streets, were to be thirty-five ten-story buildings housing industrial facilities and terminals for trucks and buses, as well as freight and commercial railroad lines. Forming a vast deck above was to be a 3,600-by-12,000-foot rooftop landing field that would loom 200 feet over a network of streets and moving sidewalks tunneling through the complex of buildings. Although Zeckendorf boldly asserted that "an airport must have the same ease of accessibility as a railroad, and must be in the center of things it serves," practical considerations made his vision unfeasible.[40]

Though the Upper West Side was no longer attractive to the upwardly mobile middle class, it proved a viable location for the Puerto Ricans who were pouring into the city. Some found cheap but relatively desirable accommodations in rent-controlled tenement apartments, while many more were forced to occupy virtually windowless basement apartments. By the mid-1950s a totally "new" Upper West Side had emerged; its social complexion was unlike any New York had ever seen before, with class conflicts dramatically exacerbated by issues of race.

The close juxtaposition of social classes was hardly new to Manhattan's neighborhoods. It had existed on the Upper East Side where Park Avenue and Yorkville intersected, and even more so along the East River where the towering luxury apartment houses of Beekman and Sutton places had squared off against the blight and tenements of the aging industrial district. But in these cases the juxtaposition of rich against poor, lace curtain against shanty, occurred in a city in which social hierarchies were more or less unchallenged. In the postwar era the social juxtapositions on the Upper West Side were far more com-

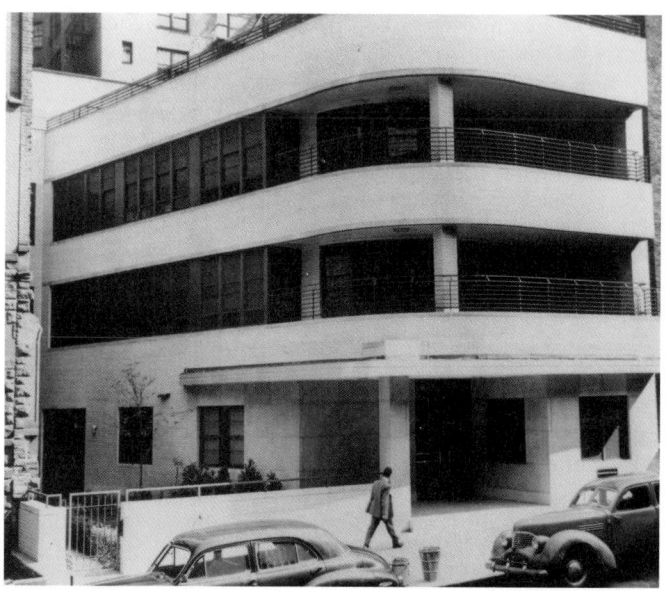

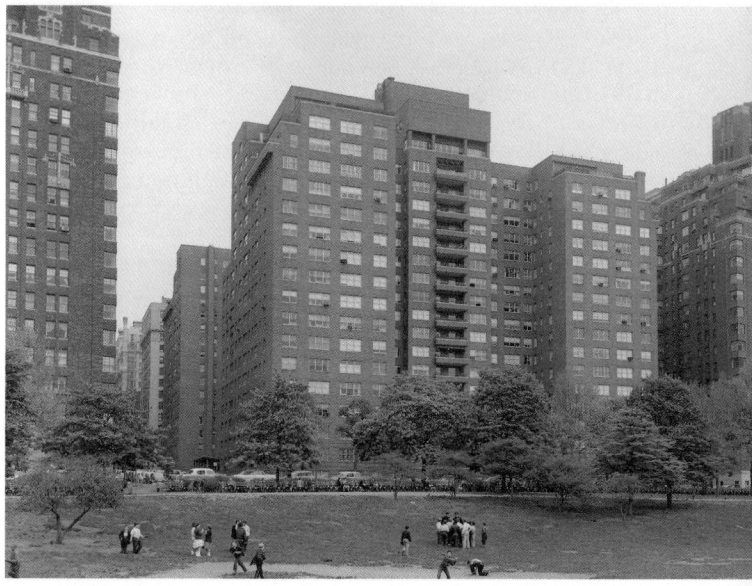

Top: Godmother's League, 255 West Seventy-first Street, between Amsterdam and West End avenues. Sylvan Bien, 1950. View to the northeast. EG

Bottom: Schwab House, West End Avenue to Riverside Drive, West Seventy-third to West Seventy-fourth Street. Sylvan Bien, 1950. View to the southeast showing Riverside Park in the foreground. OMH

plex, with much greater tensions created by differences in language, culture and especially race. As Russell Porter reported in the *New York Times*: "A characteristic of West Side life is the mixture of races and nationalities in run-down neighborhoods with integrated housing in close proximity to modern houses and apartments with all the comforts and conveniences. These contrasts of squalor living next to luxury have created frictions, resentments and fears."[41]

The political analyst Theodore H. White, in his memoir of 1978, *In Search of History: A Personal Adventure*, recalled that when he returned to New York in October 1953 after a five-year stay in Europe, he was warned that the Upper West Side was not what it had once been. "Obviously," White said, "that meant that blacks and Puerto Ricans were moving in." But White, like other Manhattanites of a new kind, politically liberal and committed to city life as a concrete representation of those political views, "believed in integration, would have felt like traitors to join 'White Flight,' if the term had been coined then, and wanted to live on the West Side." White and his family took a well-priced, spacious apartment with a park view on Central Park West and Eighty-fourth Street. White recalled that the situation was not ideal: he could not send his children to school in the neighborhood, nor were they safe playing in Central Park just below his window. Although he had lived "in Irish Boston, in warlord China, in darkling Germany," this was the first time he was afraid to walk the street outside his own house at night. "The problem," he said, "was one of compression—two kinds of culture contesting in the pressure of closed city apartment blocks." It took him six months to pass through the various reactions to the confrontation: "First, the blindness to the problem; then the bravado-disdain of the reality; then discomfort, and finally fear." After one year's residence, White and his family left the Upper West Side for what he called "the perfumed stockade" of the Upper East Side.[42]

The character of the Upper West Side was so dramatically changed that the essayist Marya Mannes could observe in 1959 that "the West Side I once knew is wholly dead, the tale of what has happened to it in thirty-five years a parable of decline, harshly tangible." The greatest change of all, Mannes said, was in the brownstones, "street after street after street of them running from River to Park," which "once provided, as do certain streets in European cities, the peace of maintaining the pattern of stability. . . . These houses, tenanted each by one family, polished and scoured by maids, the glass of the windows bright, spelled safety." Now, Mannes continued, "these same brownstones have an evil look, singly and corporately. Nearly all of them have become rooming houses, run by landlords who preside over their decay. So many of the windows are gray with grime, so many of the stoops and cornices are crumbled that the single clean window with flower boxes is a gesture of courage and gallantry, and the single painted facade a constant reproach to surrounding sloth and neglect." Mannes observed the new racial mix in the neighborhood:

"Nice" people still live in these brownstones—many of them refugees of the late 1930's . . . together with a number of American professionals, they form islands of decency in a brown sea of squalor. For greater poverty has moved in next to them: Puerto Ricans crowded ten in a room, spilling over the stoops into the streets, forced through no fault of their own to camp indoors as well as out, warming their souls on the television set and blanking out thought with the full volume of the ra-

dio. . . . They have taken over, without will or design but merely by numbers and poverty, those parts of the city doomed by avarice and abandonment to slums. Their only sin lies in their majority: they outnumber their white neighbors-in-squalor—the perverts, addicts, delinquents, criminals and failures who infest the city. . . . As for the rich and favored—and the West Side still has its share—they live in the big apartment buildings that face Central Park. . . . It is only a line one building thick that separates them from the rotting poor.[43]

In the early 1960s the decline and decay and the tensions White and Mannes alluded to were at the point of danger, reaching a peak on July 6, 1961, when a fight between a black woman and a Puerto Rican woman on the block of West Eighty-fourth Street between Columbus and Amsterdam avenues escalated into a full-fledged riot.[44] In the next summer another riot broke out on August 1, 1962, when blacks and Puerto Ricans clashed on West Ninety-fourth Street between Columbus Avenue and Central Park West. Things had gotten out of hand; the stage-play gang warfare of *West Side Story* had become an ugly reality.

Ten days before the July 6, 1961, riot on West Eighty-fourth Street, Don Ross, a reporter for the *New York Herald Tribune*, had begun a five-part series on the Upper West Side in which he described a new renewal program "to halt the flight of the middle-class residents from the upper West Side to outlying parts of the city and the suburbs." The neighborhood, Ross said, had become a unique but volatile "mixture of squalid and good housing, of well-cared-for, tall apartment houses next to shabby brownstones and old law tenements that had been converted to one-room-per-family occupancy. It is a place of considerable fear, racial tension and juvenile delinquency."[45] In a vivid description of the area's evolution, Ross traced the history of a single apartment building, the Hendrik Hudson, on the lower edge of Morningside Heights at 380 Riverside Drive, between 110th and 111th streets. When the building, designed by William L. Rouse, was completed in 1907, it contained seventy-two eight-room units; it was, at the time, one of the city's largest apartment buildings and one of the neighborhood's most lavish. By the 1950s the building had become a severely overcrowded rooming house, sheltering approximately 1,500 tenants; some rooms housed eight people, and as many as seven children and ten adults shared a single bathroom. In 1958, 150 building residents were arrested on drug, prostitution and theft charges. The following year the building was sold. Its new owners relocated most of the tenants, the vast majority of whom were black or Puerto Rican, and remodeled the building into 155 units. Ross described the new tenants as being "in the middle income range," with 20 percent affiliated with Morningside Heights institutions.[46]

The transformation of 380 Riverside Drive was a portent of the future. But the creation of a more stable and desirable environment would require drastic measures. Clearly, with 335,000 people living within its borders, the area's problems could not be tackled as a single unit. In the early 1950s four areas were targeted for study and future renewal: Lincoln Square, Manhattantown, the West Side Urban Renewal Area and Morningside Heights. Each was to become in its way a landmark in the history of urban redevelopment; even more important, the West Side Urban Renewal Area was to prove a critical testing ground for a new grass-roots urban political activism in which residents played a decisive role in determining the future of their neighborhoods.

COLUMBUS CIRCLE

By the end of World War II Columbus Circle, the Upper West Side's principal gateway, had become the slightly seedy northern terminus of the theater district, home to such theaters as the Cosmopolitan Theater (John Duncan, 1904; Joseph Urban, 1923).[1] Postwar activity began with a proposal for a new indoor sports arena in 1946.[2] A 25,000-seat facility intended to supplement Madison Square Garden, the arena was the brainchild of the Garden's president, General John Reed Kilpatrick, and Robert Moses, who proposed it in combination with a 200,000-square-foot exhibition and convention space. Difficulties in obtaining funding authorization in Albany, as well as the growth of television—which cut down the audiences willing to pay to attend sporting events—stalled the project.[3]

In December 1952 Robert Moses, in his dual roles as chairman of the Mayor's Committee on Slum Clearance and chairman of the Triborough Bridge and Tunnel Authority, secured federal funds for the redevelopment of two blocks immediately west of Columbus Circle, which were combined to create a site big enough for a major convention and exhibition facility to be known as the Coliseum.[4] The new building would fill the void left in 1951 by the conversion of the Grand Central Palace (Warren & Wetmore, 1911) into an office building.[5] Moses proposed to meet the site-acquisition costs with funds obtained through the new federal Title I program, which was intended to help clear slums and build affordable housing. Because the program required that projects receiving funding must be dominated by residential construction, Moses dedicated more than half the site to residential purposes, although he counted the land used for parking as part of the housing.

Acquisition costs for the site, bounded by Columbus Circle, Broadway, Columbus Avenue, West Fifty-eighth and West Sixtieth streets, were very high, in fact the highest ever in the nation, six times the average cost of a typical Title I project in New York. This aspect of the scheme particularly irked planner Robert C. Weinberg, who felt that without a large-scale master plan for the area—which he called "the basic purpose of Title I"—the project would set an unfortunate precedent.[6] The site also brought with it problems of tenant relocation: 243 families lived on the site, along with 362 hotel- and rooming-house occupants. And in addition to the former Cosmopolitan Theater, which was being used by NBC for some of its most popular television shows, the site included the twenty-two-story Gotham National Bank (Sommerfeld & Steckler, 1920). The Coliseum project was challenged in the courts when a pawnbroker named Kaskel sued the city, claiming that the site was not a slum. Despite expert testimony by William C. Vladeck, president of the Citizens' Housing and Planning Council, who claimed that only 10 percent of the tenements were substandard or unsanitary and only 2 percent of the site was a slum, New York State's highest court denied the plaintiff's objections by a vote of 5 to 2.[7]

Although Skidmore, Owings & Merrill were at one point rumored to have been selected to design the Coliseum, the job was ultimately awarded to Leon and Lionel Levy, who had been associated with the project since its conception, in consultation with John B. Peterkin, Aymar Embury II and Eggers & Higgins.[8] Preliminary designs called for a fluted, boxlike building that confronted the circle's concavity with a giant convex curve swinging from Fifty-eighth to Sixtieth Street. Joseph Addonizio, of the West of Central Park Association, characterized it as "an oversized salt box"; Albert S. Bard, of the City Club, called the

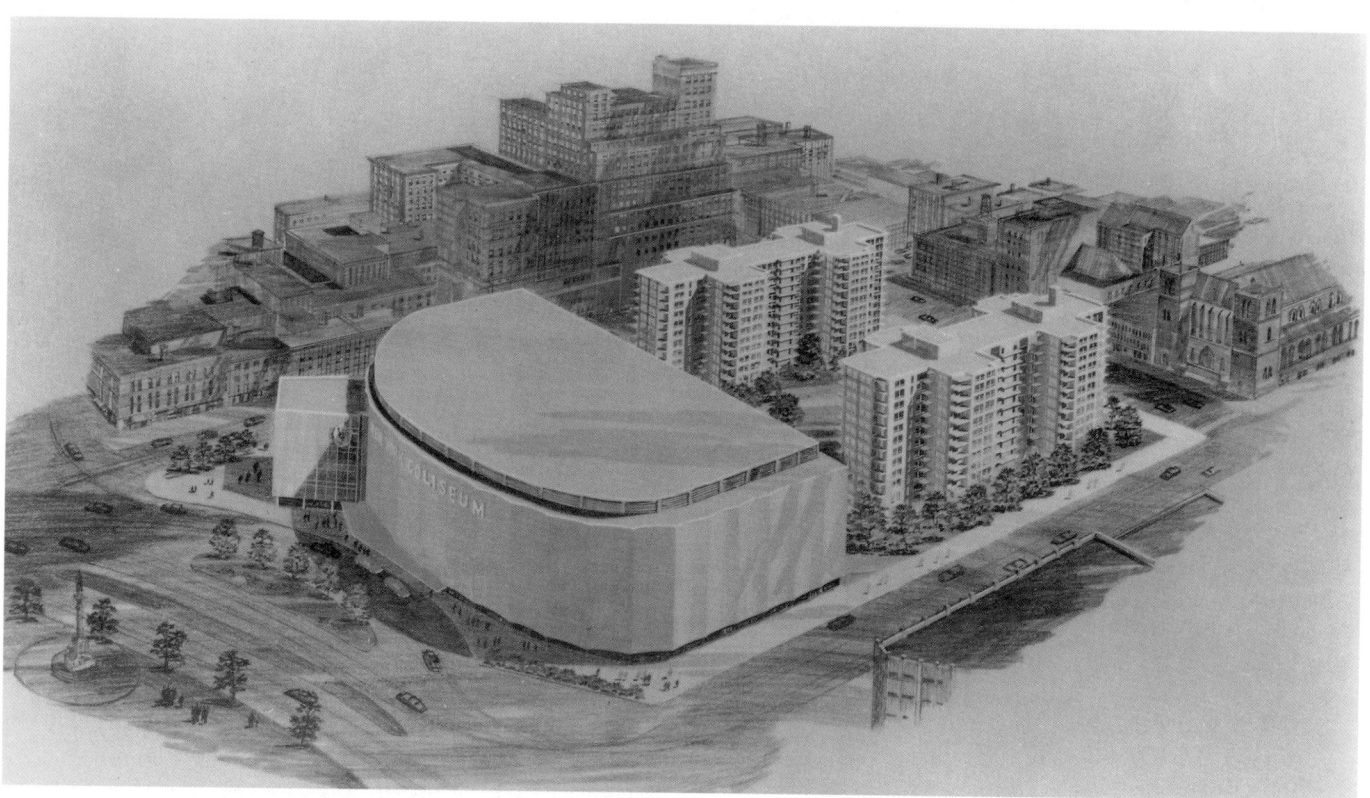

Proposal for Coliseum, west side of Columbus Circle, West Fifty-eighth to West Sixtieth Street. Leon and Lionel Levy, in consultation with John B. Peterkin, Aymar Embury II and Eggers & Higgins, 1953. Perspective of preliminary design showing proposed apartment buildings by Sylvan and Robert Bien on the right. TBTA

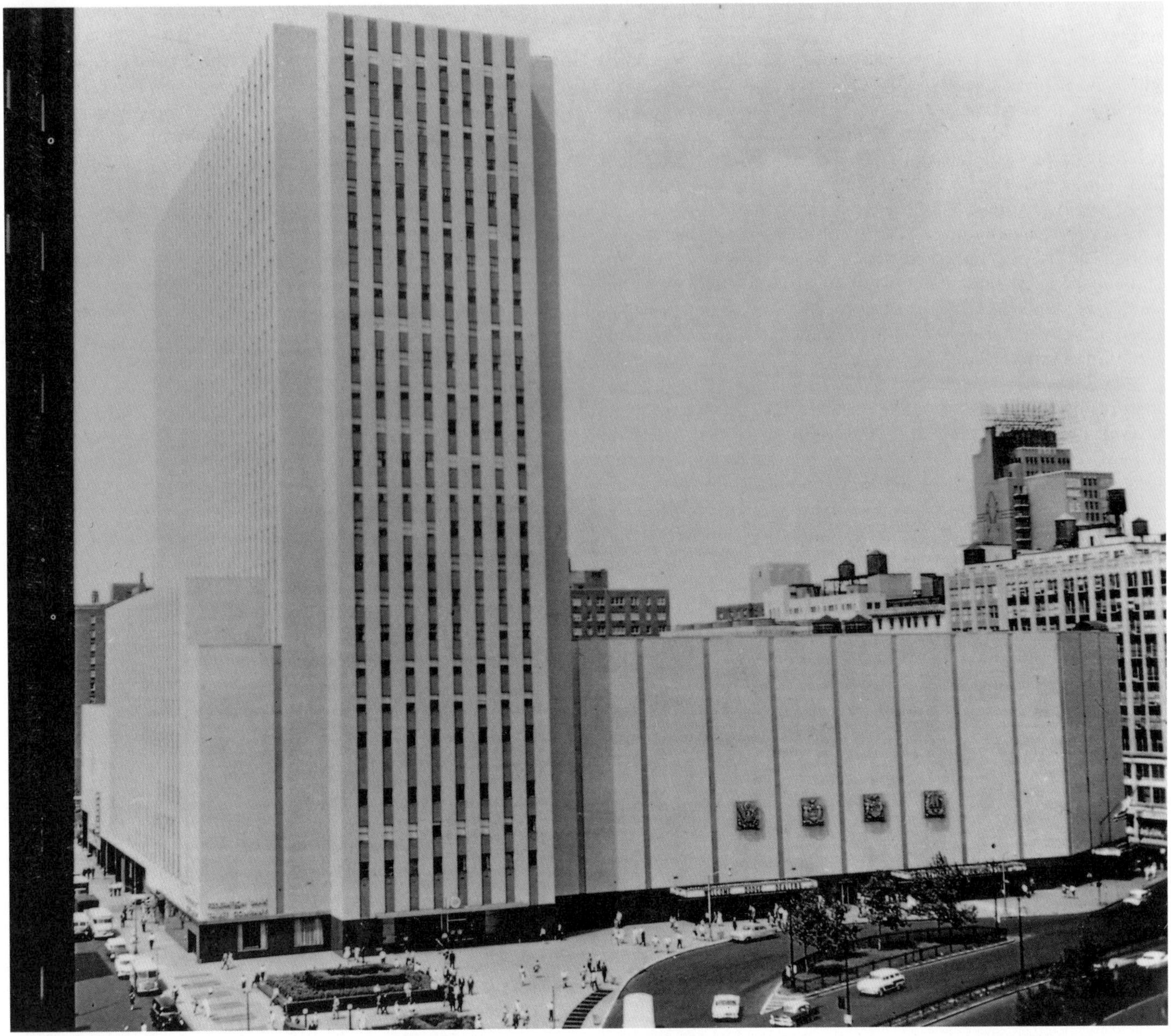

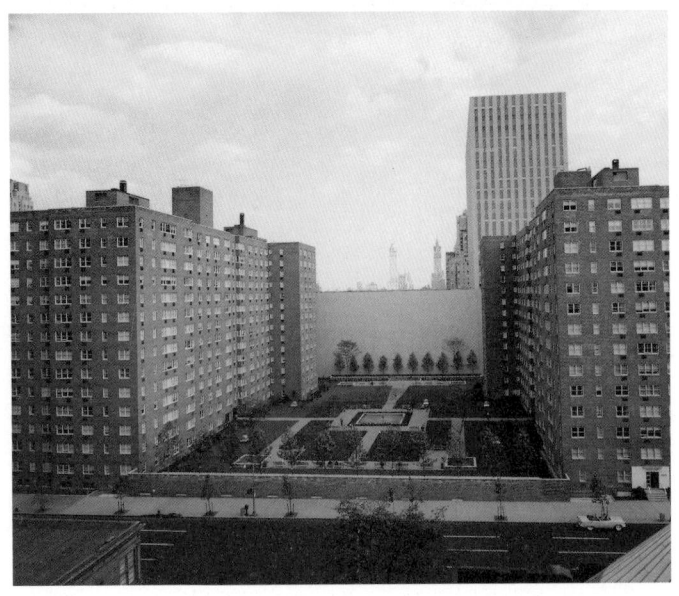

Above: Coliseum, west side of Columbus Circle, West Fifty-eighth to West Sixtieth Street. Leon and Lionel Levy, in consultation with John B. Peterkin, Aymar Embury II and Eggers & Higgins, 1954. View to the northwest. TBTA

Right: Coliseum Park Apartments, 345 West Fifty-eighth Street and 350 West Sixtieth Street, east side of Columbus Avenue. Sylvan and Robert Bien, 1957. View to the east. TBTA

design "just plain punk."[9] By May 1954, when construction got under way, the design had evolved into a facility combining a twenty-story, 241-foot-tall, 533,000-square-foot office tower running east-west along Fifty-eighth Street—a programmatic element not included in the original plan—with a four-story, 273,672-square-foot exhibition hall (half again as big as Grand Central Palace), an 850-car underground garage and two 300-family, red-brick-clad, slablike apartment houses designed by Sylvan and Robert Bien for the site's western end. The final design not only lacked the auditorium that such facilities usually have but also the 6,000 fixed balcony seats originally planned to overlook the exhibition hall's main floor, which would have helped it better function for the kinds of large meetings that were often key features of business and political conventions.

The Coliseum faced Columbus Circle with a 421-foot-long, 106-foot-high windowless wall, which was clad in light gray brick above a dark granite base and adorned only with four eleven-foot-square aluminum medallions, designed by Paul Manship to depict the coats of arms of the United States, New York State, New York City and the Triborough Bridge and Tunnel Authority. Not only did the broad, ponderous rectilinear mass disregard the circle's geometry, it also blocked the axis of Fifty-ninth Street, which was demapped through the site. To minimize congestion and compensate for the loss of this street, Fifty-eighth and Sixtieth streets were widened. The building's design allowed trucks either to drive directly onto the ground-level exhibition floor for loading and unloading or to ascend by ramp to the 82,000-square-foot second-floor exhibition hall; the large, forty-nine-foot-long elevators installed to further facilitate deliveries were big enough to handle semitrailer trucks.

The building's design, which Moses characterized as "conservative modern," satisfied few observers.[10] Just as construction was about to begin, Art News editor Alfred M. Frankfurter blasted the design in a curtain raiser delivered before 350 architects and their guests gathered for the annual dinner of the American Institute of Architects' New York Chapter, making public the content of his April editorial. Frankfurter felt the building's design was "pedestrian" and riddled with "hybrid pseudomodern detail." It was poorly sited, he said, and, worse yet, planned as "if it really disdained, as well as ignored, the arc of the circle on which it is to stand . . . as if it merely faced another shoddy loft building instead of, diagonally across the axis of Columbus Circle, the matching concave double entry into Central Park." Frankfurter castigated Moses for "the completely dictatorial way in which [he] is imposing the design upon the public without anyone getting in a word of dissent,"[11] and he went on to criticize Moses's choice of Embury, Eggers & Higgins and Peterkin as the design advisory committee, dismissing the group as "a unanimous roster of conservative, eclectic architects: it is as if the President appointed an advisory committee on foreign policy composed exclusively of isolationists."[12] Moses was handed a copy of Frankfurter's editorial as he arrived late at the dinner; as the event's principal speaker, he made indirect reference to the attack, telling his audience that public officials had no right to experiment on a big scale, a point he had made over and over again in the past: "The architect who looks forward but is no revolutionary or drawing board radical must depend on conservative public officials to save his profession from egotists, publicity seekers, iconoclasts and crackpots."[13]

No sooner had construction begun than questions were raised about the inclusion of the office building, a feature that Moses had neglected to point out to federal funding authorities before they had seen it published in the press. Until Mayor Wagner was able to intervene and smooth ruffled feathers, the project was in danger of being stricken from the Title I program because it contained too much premium commercial space.

A year into construction, progress on the exhibition building suffered a major setback when some 16,000 square feet of formwork and 8,000 square feet of freshly poured concrete, supported on a forest of four-by-four-foot timbers and steel jackposts, dropped twenty-two feet to the floor below, burying one workman and injuring fifty-one others. Despite six investigations, blame for the collapse was never fixed, but design standards for formwork were tightened.

The Coliseum opened on April 28, 1956. The day after its opening, the editors of the New York Times, while defending it as a functional solution to a problem, were certain that, unlike its Roman namesake, New York's Coliseum would not be the object of moonlight veneration by generations of tourists. Frank Lloyd Wright was rather more blunt: "It's a great utilitarian achievement, but architecture is something else again. . . . I think it's all right for New York"—a city he professed to despise—"but I hope it stays here."[14] From the first the Coliseum was a building New Yorkers loved to hate. As a taxi driver put it: "They should have got an architect to design it for them."[15] Nonetheless, it promised to have a positive impact on the city's tourist industry. With the opening of the Coliseum, the world's largest exhibition facility in terms of square feet (Chicago's Navy Pier had the most exhibition space on one level), the city's share of the trade-show industry was expected to grow: two months before the Coliseum's opening, contracts had been closed for eight new trade shows, with others signed and pending for as late as 1958.[16]

The residential component of the project consisted of the Coliseum Park Apartments (1957), at 345 West Fifty-eighth Street and 350 West Sixtieth Street, which overlooked a two-acre garden set between the two buildings and atop the complex's 300-car parking garage.[17] Though comparable in size to I. M. Pei's Kips Bay Plaza, Sylvan and Robert Bien's red-brick facades were unassuming, if not simply boring, but the thin slab entrance canopies carried on metal pipe were rather witty.

To many architects the most galling aspect of the Coliseum complex was not its bland and boxlike appearance but its complete disregard for the geometric challenge posed by Columbus Circle. Shortly before his death in an airplane crash in Egypt in 1950, the Polish-born Modernist architect Matthew Nowicki had proposed a shopping center for Columbus Circle that would be housed in an artfully sculpted concrete doughnut elevated above the street.[18] In 1957 John Barrington Bayley, an architect trained in Modernism under Walter Gropius at Harvard but now converted to the cause of a revived Classicism, proposed a scheme that ringed the circle with a colossal portico and enclosed galleries honoring the dead of World War II and the Korean War. The vast scale of Bayley's layered design, which stepped up in three terraces from north to south, was intended to convey "terrabilita, that sense of awe and power beloved by Michelangelo."[19] Bayley also proposed a new pedestrian plaza for the center, raised above the level of traffic, and a grand, Bernini-inspired stairway leading to a new concert hall and opera house, presumably sited at the southwest corner of Eighth Avenue and Fifty-eighth Street. Bayley's theater would be entered through a high-domed foyer, from which the audience would move onto a magnificent oval stairwell and at last to an auditorium that took its inspiration from Carrère & Hastings's interior for the Metropolitan Opera House. Though provocative, Nowicki's and Bayley's proposals were purely speculative. In

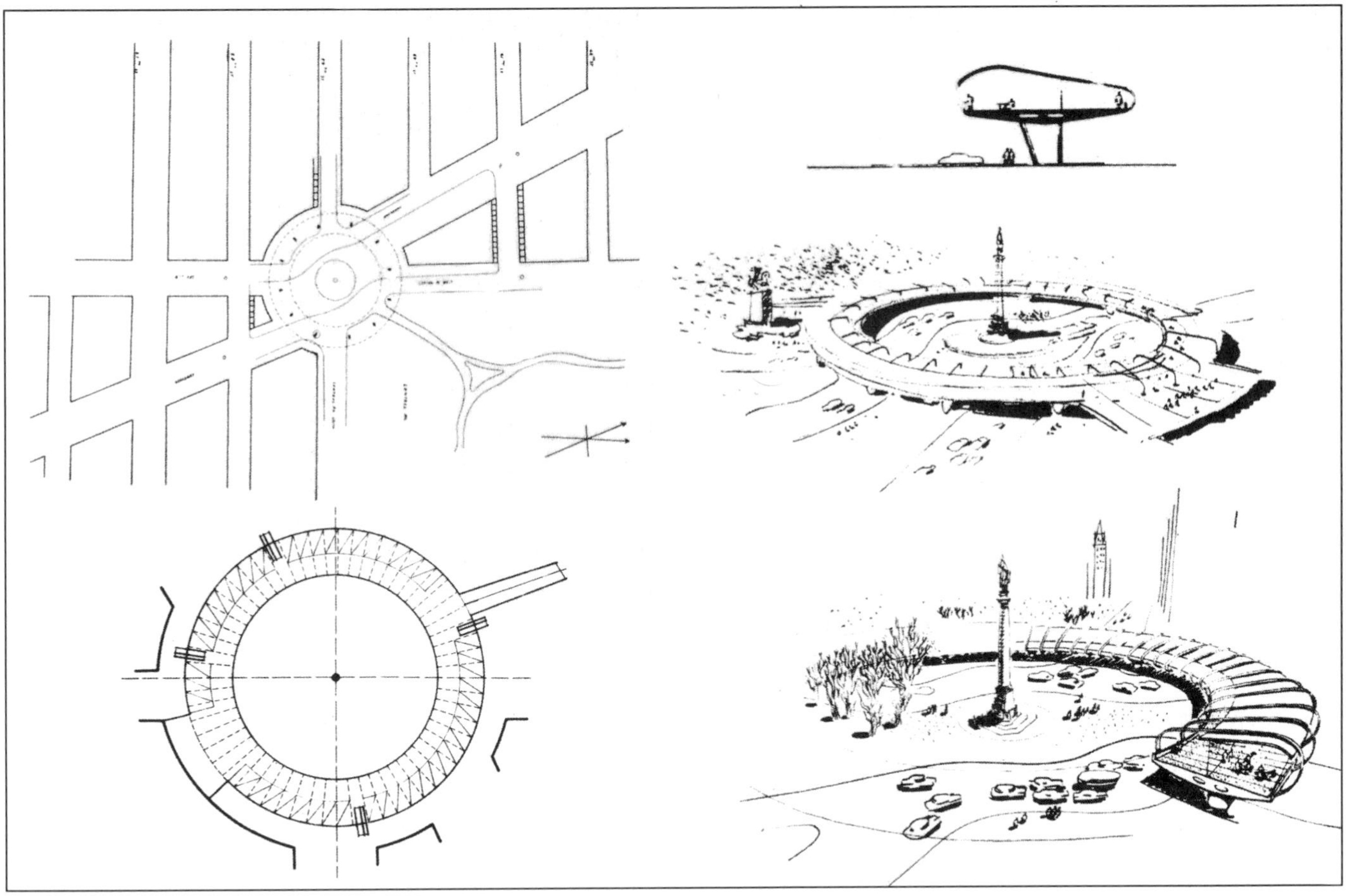

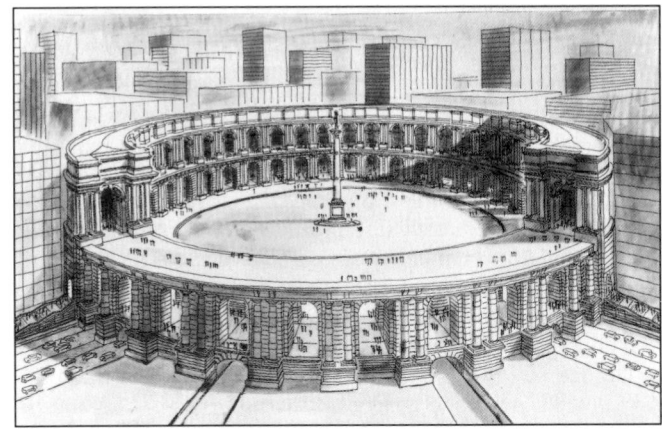

Above: Proposal for shopping center, Columbus Circle. Matthew Nowicki, 1950. Clockwise from upper left: site plan, section, aerial perspective, perspective section and plan. Hicks. UPV

Right: Proposal for concert hall and opera house, Columbus Circle. John Barrington Bayley, 1957. View to the southwest showing elevated pedestrian plaza with Gaetano Russo's statue *Columbus* (1892) in the center. HHR

Bottom right: Proposal for concert hall and opera house, Columbus Circle. John Barrington Bayley, 1957. Interior. HHR

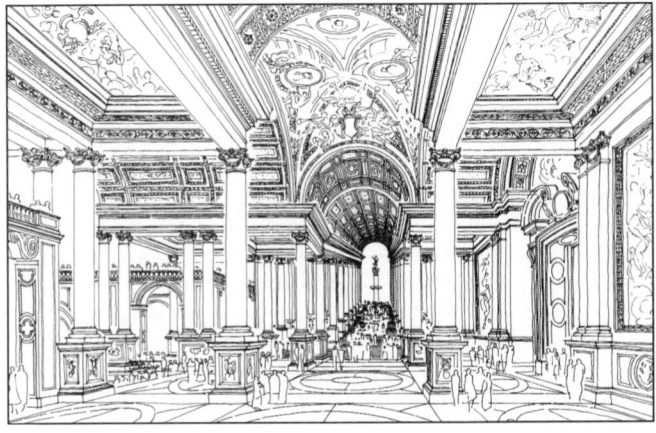

1961 the circle was modestly spruced up when Douglas Leigh, the creator of outdoor advertising spectaculars, contributed thirty-six fountains in two tiers to ring the base of the rostral column carrying Gaetano Russo's statue of Columbus.[20]

In 1968 the Triborough Bridge and Tunnel Authority proposed to augment the Coliseum complex by bridging Sixtieth Street with an expanded exhibition hall identical to the original and by constructing a new office building on the northwest corner of Broadway and Sixtieth Street, again nearly identical to its original counterpart. Contemplating the TBTA's aerial perspective drawing of the expanded scheme, Ada Louise Huxtable observed: "That is not a trick mirror image you see . . . it is merely the Coliseum doubling its bulk and banality." According to Huxtable, this new plan would "put the final stamp of spoilage on what could have been one of the city's handsomest public spaces, if anyone had cared."[21] The TBTA's expansion plans did not go forward.

Whatever its aesthetic faults or functional limitations, the Coliseum was the pivotal factor in the rebirth of the Upper West Side, attracting attention to the area as a whole and to the potential of Columbus Circle in particular. It inspired the grocery store heir, theatrical angel and art patron Huntington Hartford to choose for his Gallery of Modern Art (1964) a site at Two Columbus Circle, a small, wedge-shaped block bounded by the circle, Broadway, West Fifty-eighth Street and Eighth Avenue.[22] Before hiring Edward Durell Stone to design his museum, Hartford had worked with Hanford Yang, a Chinese-born architecture student at MIT but not a registered architect in New York, who proposed an evocative eleven-story building that consisted of interlocking concrete cylinders sheathed in opaque plastic.[23] Stone kept Yang on as project manager for a short time but redesigned the project in 1956 while Hartford struggled to evict a tenant on the site. Stone's first scheme called for blank facades, interrupted above a ground-floor arcade only by a single vertical strip of glass and by big windows wrapping the entire tenth floor. A second scheme, published in 1959, wrapped the building in a completely neutral meshlike grid, revealing the structural frame only at the base and the roof, where there was to be a landscaped terrace. In both schemes, Stone was searching for a Classical simplicity compatible with, and complementary to, Carrère & Hastings's United States Rubber Building (1912), located diagonally across from the site at the southeast corner of Broadway and Fifty-eighth Street.[24]

Later in 1959 Stone released the drawings for his final scheme, which squeezed galleries and other public spaces—including a 154-seat auditorium, an espresso and cocktail bar and a restaurant—as well as curatorial and storage spaces into a ten-story building, framed in reinforced concrete and clad with gray-veined white Vermont marble. The structure filled out the awkward geometry of the site, which measured ninety-seven feet at its broadest point. The walls of the Venetian-inspired vertical palazzo were perforated with portholelike openings at the corners, base and crown to suggest rustication inspired, according to Stone, by Saint-Germain-des-Prés, a Romanesque church in Paris.[25] At the ground floor, the building was carried on columns to form an arcade. The top two floors, where the restaurant was located behind a loggia, opened to a view of Central Park. Ada Louise Huxtable likened the overall effect to a "die-cut Venetian palazzo on lollypops,"[26] while Olga Gueft said that the building's "red-granite-trimmed, green-marble-lined colonnades, these rows of portholes like borders of eyelet hand-embroidered on a marble christening robe are too winsome for heavyweight criticism."[27]

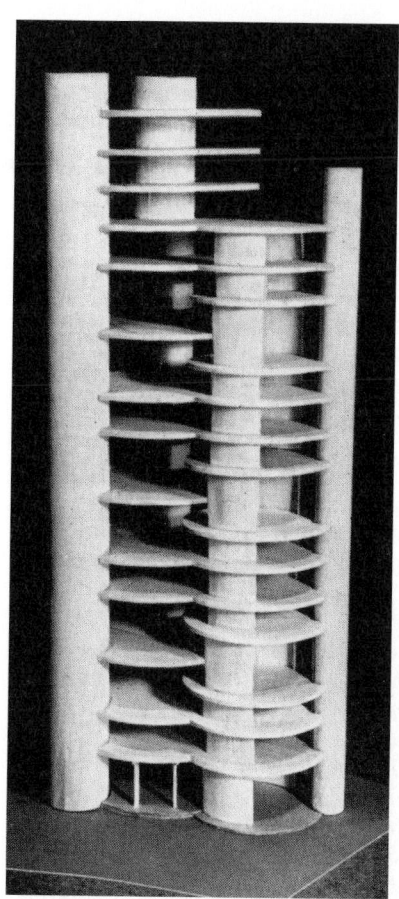

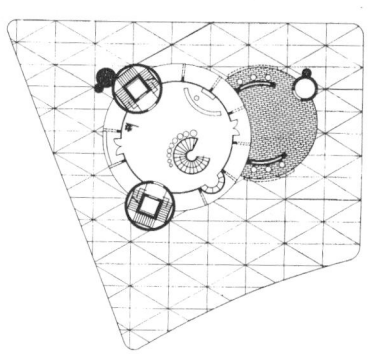

Top: Proposal for Gallery of Modern Art, Two Columbus Circle, bounded by the circle, Broadway, West Fifty-eighth Street and Eighth Avenue. Hanford Yang, 1956. Model. View to the southeast. HY

Bottom: Proposal for Gallery of Modern Art. Ground-floor plan. HY

From a curatorial point of view, the gallery was intended to rival the Museum of Modern Art, combatting its commitment to Modernism with a collection that favored representational art. Stone's design, with its Classical tripartite composition and distinct evocation of traditional form, seemed a perfect complement to the museum's mission. Like other observers, the art critic Stuart Preston noted this combination of contemporary and traditional in the design of the building, which he described as "a Venetian palazzo built in the streamlined terms of twentieth-century architecture."[28] But the avowed Modernist Alfred Frankfurter took issue with this assessment: "To attribute a 'Venetian' source to the design," he said, "is to libel on the grandeur of the Queen of the Adriatic."[29]

Inside, Stone organized the equivalent of three-and-a-half floors of galleries at half levels, like "a grand staircase, with the galleries serving as landings," creating two relatively grand double-height display rooms surrounded by more intimate viewing rooms with lower ceilings.[30] The arrangement of a stair gallery wrapped around a core was similar to that of Howe & Lescaze's Scheme Six, proposed for the Museum of Modern Art in 1931.[31] Filtered natural light was introduced through the glazed perforations at the corners, a technique that worked well with Abe Feder's artificial lighting while also producing tantalizing glimpses of Central Park without distracting the viewer from the art. The lobby floor was paved in terrazzo, into which were set the discs that had been cut out of the marble when the exterior arches were formed. In contrast to the white-painted anonymity of the Museum of Modern Art's galleries, Hartford's were paneled with walnut and other hardwoods and thickly carpeted or elaborately finished in *parquet de Versailles* and marble. A pipe organ was included in one of the double-height galleries. Though Hartford's collection did not include any paintings by Gauguin, the ninth-floor Polynesian restaurant, the Gauguin Room, included a tapestry based on one of the French master's paintings. The interiors were designed by Stone's staff under the direction of John Crews Rainey, who worked with Mildred Hill.

Ellen Perry described the atmosphere of the galleries as one "of paintings enjoyed in a private home with no sense of the museum as a mere storage or learning place."[32] Frankfurter, however, was no more pleased with the museum's interior than he had been with its exterior: "It has something of the cheap glamour of a shoe emporium on Main Street. The galleries have too much expensive tropical wood paneling . . . too much height to the ceilings of the galleries cramped by the dictates of the pre-shaped plot on which the building was raised; too little sense of respect for art, with too much awe for the jewel case that advertises the wealth and status of the owner." As for the restaurant, he said, it gave "a spurious South Seas atmosphere . . . that looks all too much as if strip-teasers, already conveniently reduced to grass skirts, were about to do a Polynesian floor show."[33]

Despite a bright young founding director, Carl Weinhardt, Jr., the museum was not able to find a secure niche in New York's art world. Always somewhat fickle in his enthusiasms, and surely troubled by the operating costs of his ambitious enterprise, Hartford transferred the museum building to Fairleigh Dickinson University in 1969, which turned it into the New York Cultural Center in 1970; the following year Hartford, who had retained ownership of most of his art, sold the collection. The museum's failure came as no surprise to art critic Hilton Kramer, who was perhaps the cruelest commentator on the building, which he called "one of the worst designed museum

structures in the world," with an interior that "resembled more than anything else a rest home for retired bankers." In a post-mortem discussion of the museum, Kramer noted that Hartford's objective had been "ill-conceived" from the start:

> There was never sufficient money or sufficient intelligence— or, for that matter, sufficient art—in the operation of the Gallery of Modern Art to make it, even remotely, a plausible rival to the Museum of Modern Art, or even to the lively 57th Street galleries a few blocks away. Some of the artists favored by Mr. Hartford—Pavel Tchelitchew, Lovis Corinth and Salvador Dali—had long been represented in the permanent collection of the Modern, and no roster of newly discovered talent was forthcoming. The Gallery of Modern Art very soon became something of a joke, a comic irrelevance to the city's busy art life. Even the guards there seemed vaguely disconcerted and suspicious at the sight of visitors entering the premises to look at the more and more infrequent exhibitions.[34]

Another *New York Times* art critic, John Canaday, also found fault with Hartford's polemic: "In creating his own museum of what he called modern art, Hartford attacked the fortress with the puniest of weapons—or rather, with no weapon at all. He wanted to wipe out everything from Cubism to Fauvism right on through the New York School, which was then in its heyday, but he had nothing to offer as a potential gap-filler for the 50 years of invention that he wanted us to forget. . . . It was a collection without focus or unity." But Canaday attributed the museum's failure in part to Stone's design, saying that the structure's height, "under New York's building code, demanded so much elevator and stairway space that the exhibition galleries were reduced to boutiques clustered around palatial escape routes."[35]

The New York Cultural Center had a short, brilliant life under the directorship of Donald Karshan and then Mario Amaya, who was appointed director in 1972 and turned it into a Kunsthalle, mounting 150 different shows and attracting large crowds but also running up big, unrecoverable costs. In 1975 the museum was closed and the building was put up for sale by the university, an event that Hartford celebrated with a party for 500 guests. The closing of the New York Cultural Center was seen by critic David Bourdon as a sign of a "deepening economic crisis that is clobbering New York's cultural institutions." But, as he pointed out, the demise of the Cultural Center was hastened by the inappropriateness of Stone's galleries for a museum based on rotating exhibits: "A disaster before it left the drawing boards," Bourdon said, it was a "museum . . . paradoxically very short on gallery space. Fire stairs, public stairs and elevators left relatively little room for art." Although the "static, inflexible, oddly shaped, multi-storied galleries" may have been suited to Hartford's collection, they were impractical for a hip, contemporary Kunsthalle approach.[36] Hilton Kramer felt that Mario Amaya had been the only hope for making the Cultural Center "a valuable adjunct to the cultural life of the city." But, Kramer said, because Amaya was "saddled with an absurd and expensive building, in which every exhibition space has the character of a hallway, anteroom or lounge leading to a nonexistent center, and denied the imaginative support necessary for large operations of this sort, he has now been deprived of the opportunity to make good on a bright promise, and the city has lost something in the process. No doubt we shall all survive the loss, but it is anything but a cause for rejoicing."[37]

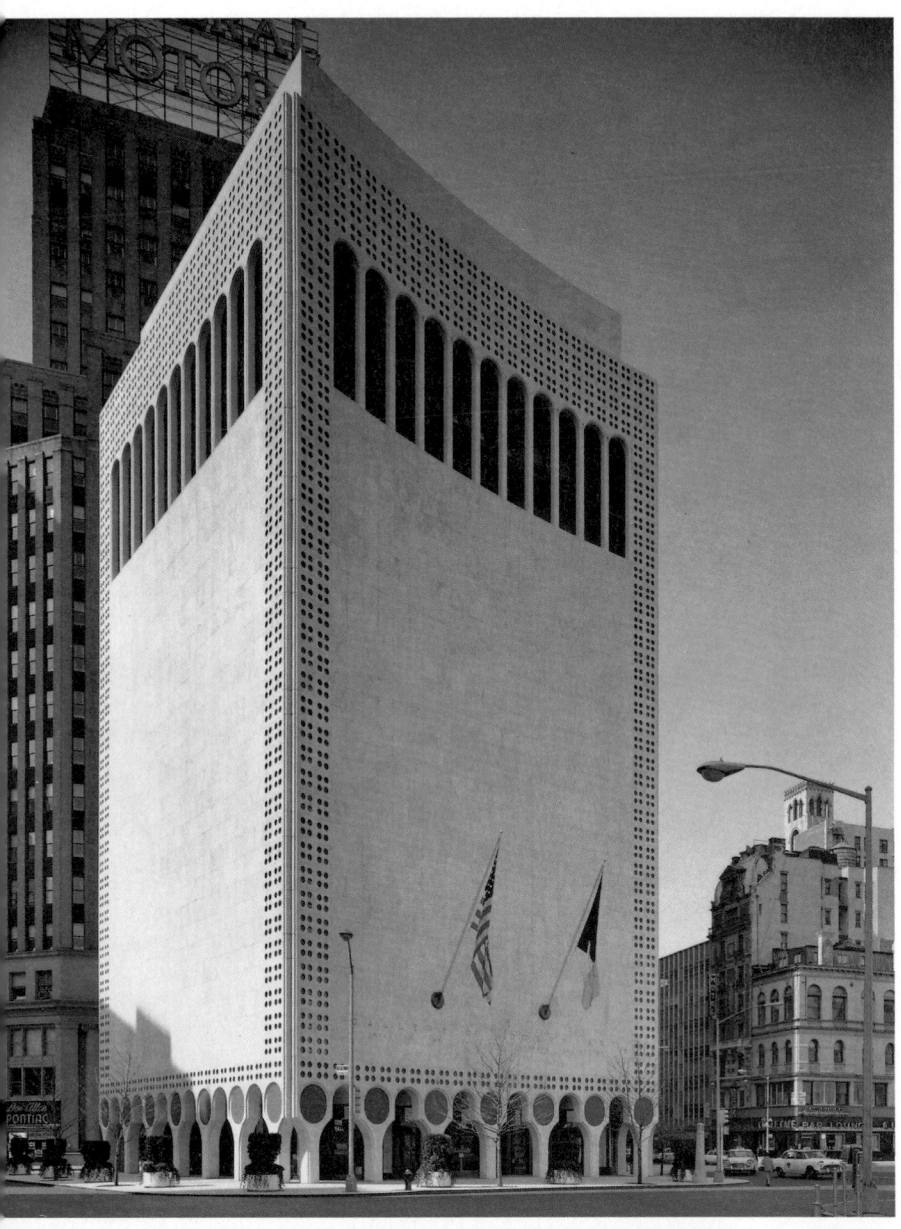

Left: Gallery of Modern Art, Two Columbus Circle, bounded by the circle, Broadway, West Fifty-eighth Street and Eighth Avenue. Edward Durell Stone, 1965. View to the southwest. Stoller. ©ESTO

Below left: Gallery of Modern Art. Gallery. Stoller. ©ESTO

Below right: Gallery of Modern Art. Gallery. Stoller. ©ESTO

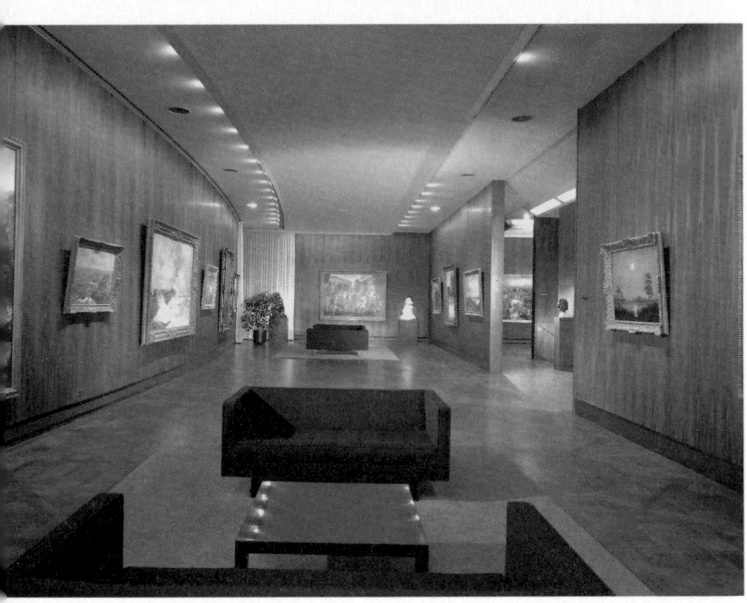

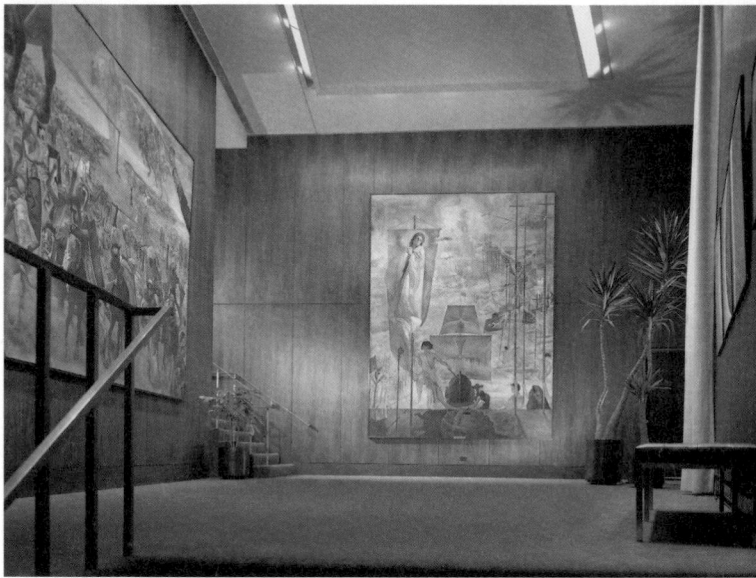

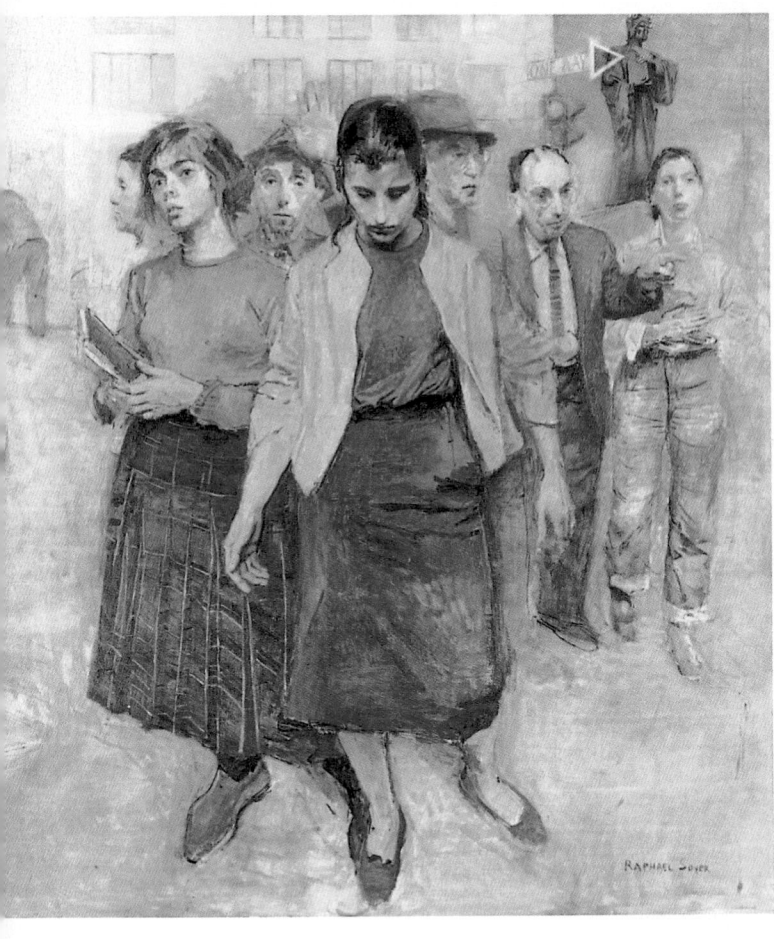

Farewell to Lincoln Square. Raphael Soyer, 1959. Oil on canvas. Stalsworth. HMSG

Lincoln Square, the bowtie-shaped intersection of Broadway, Columbus Avenue and Sixty-fifth Street, was the focus of a large area of mixed character that was bounded by Broadway, the Hudson River, Fifty-ninth and Seventieth streets. Never truly fashionable, the area had been developed, beginning in the 1870s, as a predominantly Irish middle- and lower-middle-class residential neighborhood that constituted, in effect, an extension of Hell's Kitchen to the south. Lincoln Square, which had been named, according to historian Peter Salwen, for a local land-owner, became home to a rather odd assortment of monuments.[1] Around 1902 the merchant William H. Flattau purchased a thirty-foot-high version of the Statue of Liberty, thought to be one of the prototypes produced by sculptor Frédéric-Auguste Bartholdi, and placed it on top of a warehouse he owned at 43 West Sixty-fourth Street.[2] In 1921 a larger-than-life-size likeness of Dante Alighieri by the sculptor Ettore Ximenes was erected on the square's southern triangular sliver of green open space, which was subsequently named Dante Park.[3] During the economic boom years of the 1920s, a site on the east side of Broadway between Sixty-second and Sixty-third streets had been chosen for the monumentally scaled Palais de France, a sixty-five-story complex containing consulate offices, commercial office space, a hotel and an exhibition hall; the complex would have provided the neighborhood with a significant measure of glamour, but the stock market crash abruptly tabled the scheme.[4]

The area flanking Amsterdam Avenue from the Upper Fifties through the Sixties, home to a large population of blacks and often the site of racial violence, had been known as San Juan Hill since the turn of the century.[5] Some sources said its name commemorated the heroism of black veterans of the Spanish-American War; others said it arose when New York City policemen subduing a race riot reminded observers of Theodore Roosevelt's troops charging the famous Cuban redoubt. Though the area suffered from economically depressed conditions and a high crime rate, it was also the scene of pioneering efforts at social reform. William Lewis Buckley, a former slave who earned his doctorate from Syracuse University, lived on San Juan Hill and established an adult night school, a nursery school and a kindergarten for the children of working mothers. For many years Mary White Ovington, a white journalist and social worker, sought to improve the area's living conditions, eventually convincing the philanthropists Elizabeth S. Clark and Henry Phipps to build model tenements there. Designed by Whitfield & King and completed in two stages in 1907 and 1911, the Phipps Houses, on Sixty-third and Sixty-fourth streets between Amsterdam and West End avenues, were rather routinely articulated red-brick six-story tenements, but they incorporated improved interior plans that became prototypes for enlightened working-class housing.[6] Clark and Phipps also aided the efforts of the City and Suburban Homes Company, a limited-dividend company sponsoring working-class housing, to erect other model tenements, including the Tuskegee, the Hampton Apartments and the Alfred Corning Clark Houses, all designed by Ernest Flagg and located on Sixty-eighth and Sixty-ninth streets between Amsterdam and West End avenues.[7]

Among the area's most colorful residents was Lillian Harris, known as Pig Foot Mary. Born in Mississippi, she moved to the area in 1901 and used the kitchen of Randolph's Saloon, located on Amsterdam Avenue near Sixty-first Street, to prepare pig's feet, which she sold on the street from a converted baby carriage. Harris invested her earnings in real estate and ultimately amassed holdings worth $375,000. By 1917 Harris, like many of the area's more affluent blacks, had moved to Harlem. With this exodus came a marked decline in the area's fortunes, and the transformation of many buildings into rooming houses patronized by both whites and blacks.

By the 1950s, with part of the San Juan Hill/Lincoln Square area functioning as a red-light district and 96 percent of its dwellings deemed substandard by the city, the neighborhood could be legitimately described as a slum. But, as Frederick Gutheim pointed out in *Harper's*, it was not "structural defects" that made the area a slum: "Rather it is the overcongestion, disease, delinquency, crime and scrambled population. . . . Perhaps the conflicting strands of violence and respectability are succinctly conveyed by the sign on a dry cleaning shop: 'Stain Specialists. Expert Removal of Blood, Ink, Nail Polish, Vomit.'"[8] Despite sensational reports of "white flight" to the suburbs and the flood-tide immigration of poor blacks and Puerto Ricans, in 1957, 73 percent of the neighborhood was white.

Though principally a working-class neighborhood, Lincoln Square was not exclusively so. Artists were attracted to the area as well; many of them moved into the Lincoln Square Arcade Building, on the west side of Broadway between Sixty-fifth and Sixty-sixth streets.[9] Built around 1902, the building was destroyed by fire in 1931 but then rebuilt according to the original plans. It housed an odd assortment of tenants, including a bowling alley, a theater, jewelry and millinery shops, law offices and detective agencies, as well as dance schools and studios for financially strapped artists. Some of these artists taught classes there, including, at one time or another, Alexander Archipenko, George Bellows (whose roomate in the building was the playwright Eugene O'Neill), Thomas Hart Benton, Stuart Davis, Joseph Floch, Robert Henri, Edward Hopper, Rockwell Kent, Yasuo Kuniyoshi and Raphael Soyer, who hired a number of young women working in the building as models, incorporating their likenesses into several of his paintings. In his *Farewell to Lincoln Square* (1959), which included a portrait of Floch and a self-portrait of the artist, all of the figures, whom Soyer would later describe as "dispossessed people," were depicted aimlessly walking through the neighborhood; in the background was a demolition worker bearing down on a jackhammer.[10] The Arcade Building was demolished in the 1960s to make way for the Juilliard School (see below).

Despite the neighborhood's colorful past and mildly bohemian flavor, it was widely viewed by city officials as a slum beyond rehabilitation except by means of total clearance and rebuilding. By 1947, when the city-sponsored Amsterdam Houses were completed, a portion of the neighborhood had already been transformed.[11] Occupying most of a terraced superblock site that sloped down from Amsterdam to West End Avenue between Sixty-first and Sixty-fourth streets, Amsterdam Houses were designed before the war by a team consisting of Grosvenor Atterbury, Harvey Wiley Corbett and Arthur C. Holden. The project represented one of the last such developments to define open space along Classically inspired lines and to exhibit brickwork that was carefully detailed to create simple ornament. Amsterdam Houses accommodated 1,084 families in thirteen buildings—ten six-story T- and H-shaped units and three thirteen-story towers adopting modified cruciform shapes. The three towers were pushed close to the building line along the west side of Amsterdam Avenue, and thus did significantly less damage to that street's traditional sense of scale and urbanism than would be typical of later "tower-in-the-park" schemes. In addi-

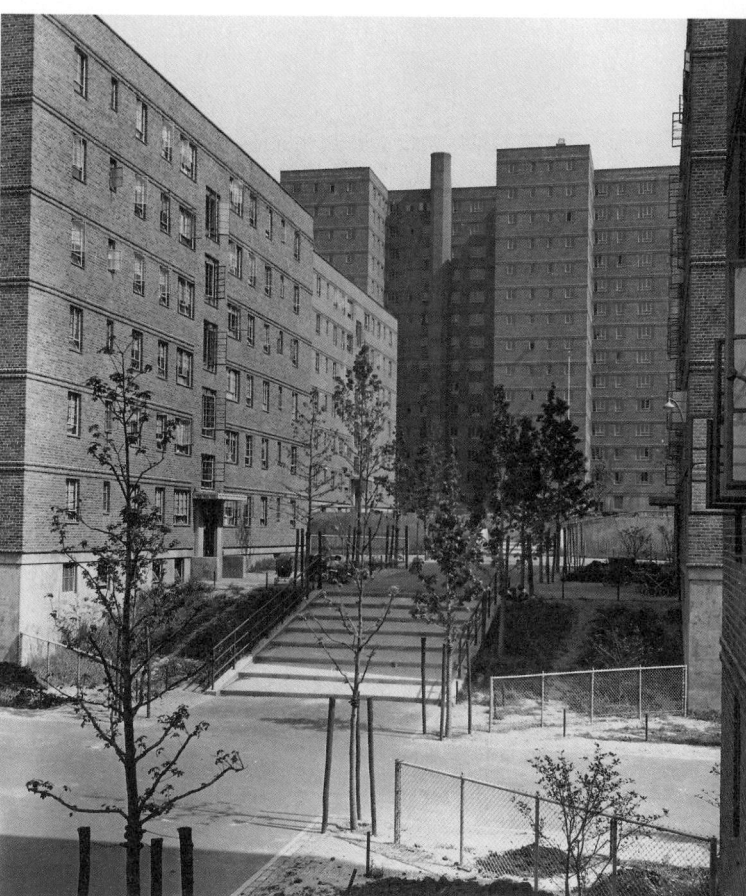

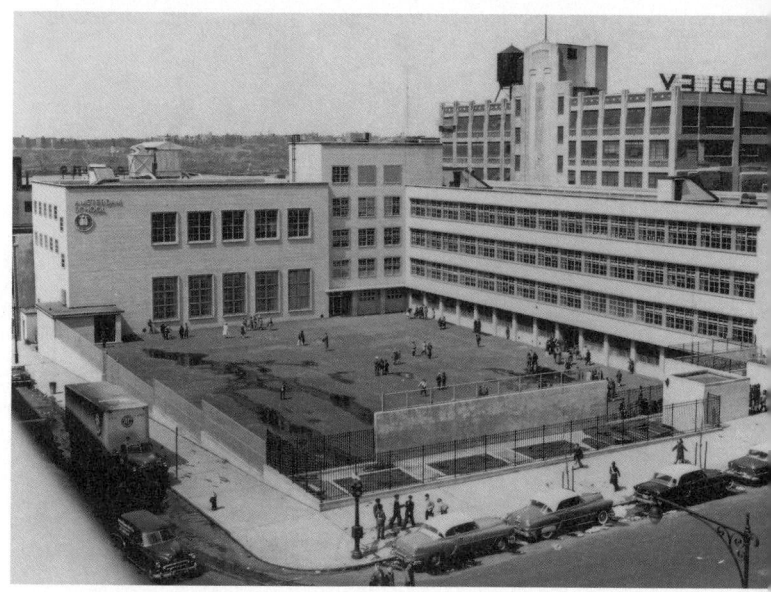

Top: Amsterdam Houses, between Amsterdam and West End avenues, West Sixty-first and West Sixty-fourth streets. Grosvenor Atterbury, Harvey Wiley Corbett and Arthur C. Holden, 1947. View to the northeast. NYCHA

Bottom: Public School 191, west blockfront of Amsterdam Avenue, West Sixtieth to West Sixty-first Street. Eric Kebbon, 1955. View to the northwest. NYCBE

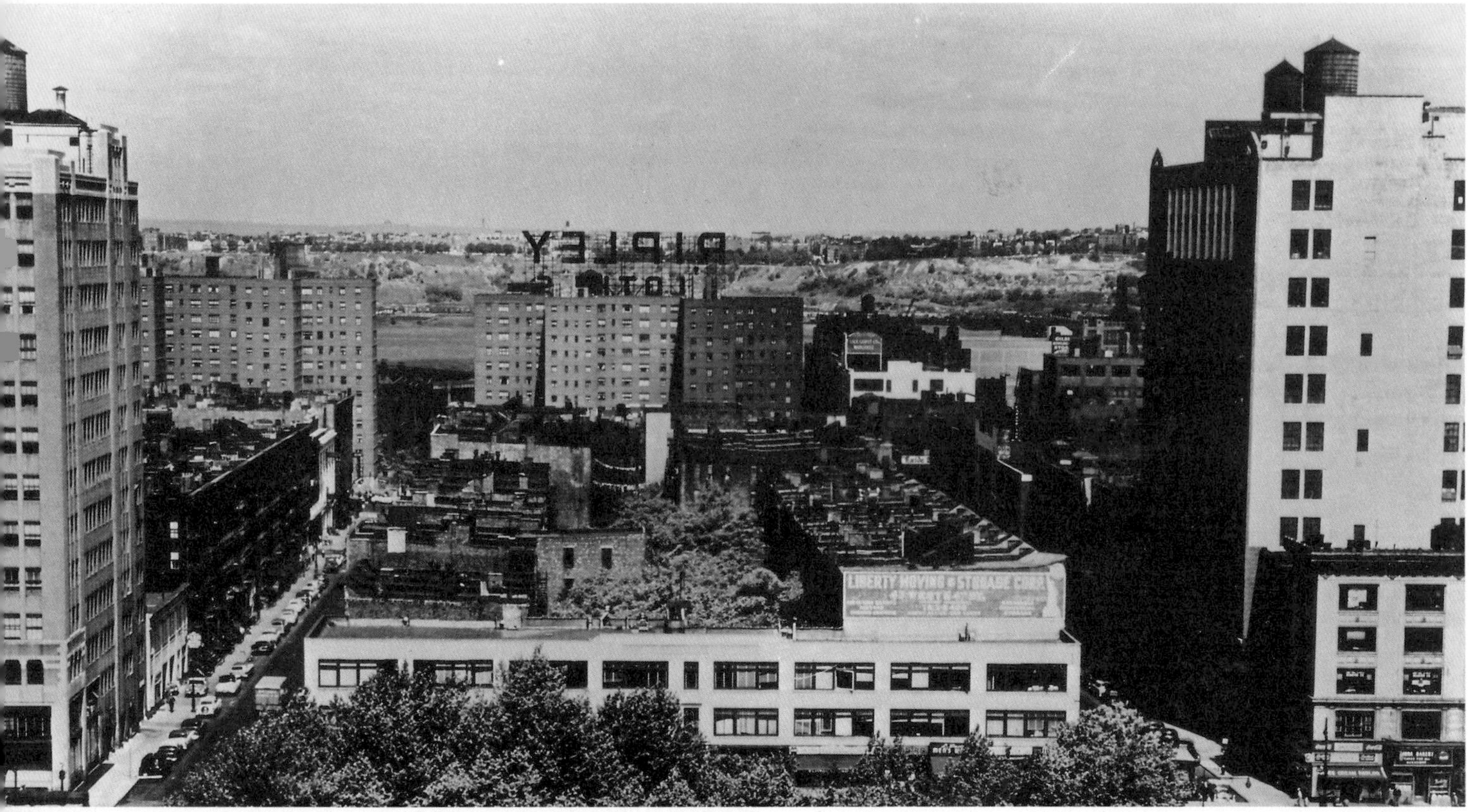

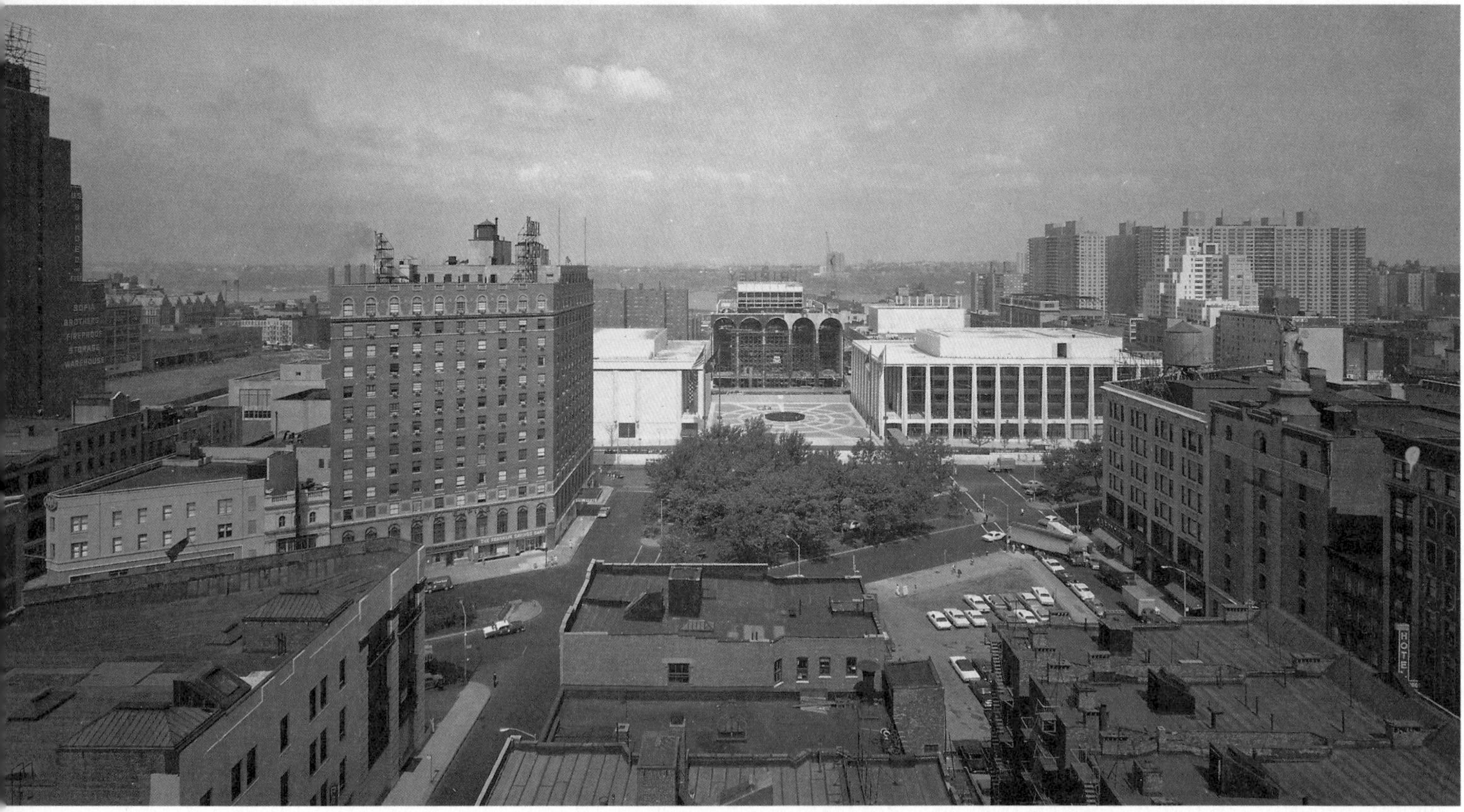

Top: Proposed site of Lincoln Center. View to the west from Broadway showing West Sixty-third Street on the left and West Sixty-fourth Street on the right. Amsterdam Houses (Grosvenor Atterbury, Harvey Wiley Corbett and Arthur C. Holden, 1947) are in the background. MOA

Bottom: Lincoln Center, between Columbus and Amsterdam avenues, West Sixty-second and West Sixty-sixth streets. View to the west showing New York State Theater (Philip Johnson, 1964) on the left, Metropolitan Opera House (Wallace K. Harrison, 1966) in the center, and Philharmonic Hall (Max Abramovitz, 1962) on the right. OMH

tion, an almost monumental effect was created by treating the axis of Sixty-second Street as a stepped pedestrian mall leading toward the river.

Except for Amsterdam Houses, the area saw little new construction during the immediate postwar period. In 1953 plans were announced for an addition to Power Memorial Academy, a Roman Catholic high school founded in 1931 for boys from poor and working-class families.[12] To be located directly south of the rather stolid, ten-story, brick-clad main building, on the southeast corner of Amsterdam Avenue and Sixty-second Street, the major portion of the annex was to house a gymnasium. For the addition Kelly & Gruzen designed an austere, utilitarian building set back from and elevated above Amsterdam Avenue on a landscaped podium. A glass-walled passageway linking the annex to the main building was to serve as the building complex's principal lobby; it would be approached by a broad granite stairway leading from the avenue. The project was never realized.

Public School 191 (Eric Kebbon, 1955), with its expansive playground, occupied the full west blockfront of Amsterdam Avenue between Sixtieth and Sixty-first streets. The L-shaped plan pushed the monumental elements to the rear of the site, leaving Sixty-first Street with a four-story buff-brick box, a utilitarian Modernist composition that eschewed the strong civic presence of the elaborately detailed Dutch Colonial-style DeWitt Clinton High School (C. B. J. Snyder, 1906) to its south, and of Kebbon's typical work of the 1940s.[13] But the design was elegantly detailed, with horizontal strip windows set in boldly projecting metal frames running most of the length of the school's principal facades. At the western end of the Sixty-first street side, a vertically arranged grid of small square windows surmounted the building's principal entrance to express its main stairwell. At the building's eastern end, a short Jeffersonian serpentine brick wall defined a small garden.

Lincoln Center

The Lincoln Square Urban Renewal Area project, the centerpiece of which was Lincoln Center for the Performing Arts, was announced in 1955.[14] Though the undertaking as a whole was significant, the decision to create a cultural center was what established the project as the era's most ambitious and successful attempt at traditional large-scale urban placemaking, as grandly conceived and executed as the preceding era's greatest urban ensemble, Rockefeller Center.[15] While Rockefeller Center clearly represented the accommodation of fin-de-siècle civic ideals to interwar economic realities, the functional program of Lincoln Center was in many ways much better suited to those same ideals. Lincoln Center was the shining ornament of a large, gritty slum clearance and redevelopment program that promised to revitalize the city's traditional urban fabric by destroying whole sections of it. But it was also a heroic and definitive attempt to refute the accusations of both outsiders and New Yorkers that the city, and with it the United States as a whole, was too focused on the bottom line to be a significant player on the international cultural stage. As the music critic Howard Taubman wrote, the center had the potential to "show that democracy has the determination and power to devote itself to things of the mind and heart as well as to creature comforts."[16] By building a cultural center of unsurpassed quality, size and diversity, the city would provide the means to fulfill the destiny that had fallen to it over a thirty-year period, beginning with

Europe's economic collapse after World War I and gaining extraordinary momentum as the politically and racially enforced out-migration of the 1930s and early 1940s depleted Europe's cultural storehouse.

True to the city's nature, even the loftiest dreams of culture were rooted in pragmatism. From its inception, the Metropolitan Opera had attempted to subsidize its operations with commercial leasable real estate. The 1883 opera house had included commercial space and an apartment hotel; various plans for a new home drawn up in the late 1920s that had included office buildings, a hotel and stores led to the development of Rockefeller Center, which eventually contained two large theaters, neither one of which housed the opera company.[17] The search for a new home for the Metropolitan was postponed during the 1930s as the Metropolitan Opera Company itself struggled to survive the Depression. After the war, with the company back on sure economic footing, management once again turned its attention to the problem of building a new opera house. Robert Moses became interested in the opera's search for a new home when he realized that the company's plight could help him realize his long-delayed municipal convention hall complex at Columbus Circle. Moses was also aware of the difficulties suffered by the New York Philharmonic orchestra at Carnegie Hall, where the renewal of its lease was jeopardized by increased efforts to develop the site for greater profit (see chapter 16). Moses invited the Metropolitan Opera Association and the New York Philharmonic Society to join together to build a music center on a portion of the site, "to assure the over-all development of a harmonious unit," as the editors of the New York Times put it.[18] The idea of two of the city's leading cultural institutions undertaking a coordinated construction project was, as the music critic Alan Rich put it in his history of Lincoln Center, "startling, to say the least, as if Macy's had gone into partnership with Gimbel's."[19] Moses made it clear that the music organizations would be fully responsible for the construction costs of their new buildings, offering them only the financial benefits of marked-down site-acquisition costs. In return, Moses's project, for which he would use Title I funds as a vehicle for realizing his "vision of a reborn West Side, marching north from Columbus Circle, and eventually spreading over the entire dismal and decayed West Side," would receive marketing assets of incomparable value.[20] When the negotiations failed to produce an agreement, the site was used for housing.

The Columbus Circle site, conveniently and dramatically situated at one of the city's most prominent crossroads, would have provided the institutions with an opportunity to create imposing civic monuments at the northern terminus of the theater district. But at the same time, Moses's invitation raised questions about the Metropolitan Opera's willingness to modify its traditional stance as a quasi-aristocratic group that was too "white glove" to cooperate directly with municipal government. Benjamin Boretz, writing in the Nation, observed that the Columbus Circle project "was so unequivocally public that the conspicuously privileged Metropolitan could hardly be slipped in without raising serious questions about propriety in the use of public funds."[21]

The Metropolitan Opera continued to search for a new site. In 1954 it placed an option on the block-long site on Park Avenue between Fifty-second and Fifty-third streets that would eventually become home to the Seagram Building, but the Metropolitan soon rejected it as too small.[22] Meanwhile, though the Columbus Circle site had not captured the imagination of members of the Philharmonic and Metropolitan boards, Moses continued to try to mastermind the concept of a cultural district, for a while considering Washington Square South before returning to the Upper West Side. There he focused his attention on Lincoln Square after receiving a commitment to participate in the project from Father Laurence J. McGinley, president of Fordham University, who had long sought a suitable location for a midtown campus to house the university's schools of law, business, education and general studies, then scattered throughout Manhattan in office and industrial loft buildings.

Moses then turned to securing the Metropolitan Opera's participation. He was aware that he would have a hard time convincing the Metropolitan Opera Association's Board of Directors, chaired by George Sloane, of the wisdom of locating in the slummy Upper West Side site. So, although he preferred to work with his own seasoned group of architects and engineers, including Aymar Embury II and Gilmore D. Clarke, over whom he could more easily exercise control, he began his campaign by convincing Wallace K. Harrison of the site's potential when he and Mrs. Moses were dinner guests of the Harrisons at their Huntington, New York, home early in 1955. Harrison, who was socially and professionally well connected—his wife, Ellen Milton Harrison, was the sister-in-law of John D. Rockefeller, Jr.'s only daughter, Abby—had been producing drawings of a new opera house for more than twenty-five years, since one had been planned as part of Rockefeller Center. With Harrison as his ally, Moses had the perfect entrée to the opera's board and many of its well-heeled patrons. Moses's strategy soon proved effective. Believing that here at last was a chance to get his opera house built, Harrison outlined the situation to Charles M. Spofford, a prominent corporate lawyer who had just become chairman of the opera's board. Spofford quickly approved of the proposed site.

The Metropolitan Opera was, however, far from the raison d'être of the Lincoln Square renewal project, as was often later assumed.[23] Rather, it was a by-product of a larger endeavor—slum clearance. Had the Metropolitan not been interested, Moses would still have cleared the site and rebuilt it, with Fordham University as its principal institutional tenant and much of the land given over to housing, probably along the lines of Lincoln Towers (see below).

By the spring of 1955 rumors were flying, and the renewal project was reported to include a new opera house, a concert hall, a two-block campus for Fordham University and a city-owned theater best suited for dance.[24] Also rumored to be part of the scheme were a ten-story building for the fashion industry, a headquarters building for the Engineering Societies, a twelve-story office and professional building, a skyscraper hotel, two public schools, a shopping center, at least one parking garage and 4,080 middle-income housing units, to be rented at $35 to $50 a month per room.

Following Spofford's approval of the Lincoln Square site, Metropolitan Opera representatives raised again the idea of a coordinated cultural complex housing both the opera and the symphony. Several Metropolitan and Philharmonic board members began to envision an even larger complex. Working together, the boards began in 1956 to set about finding someone to direct such a complex. Spofford, who was instrumental in the search, first considered Nelson A. Rockefeller, but his decision to enter politics as a candidate for governor of New York precluded the possibility. When Spofford ran into Nelson's older brother, John D. Rockefeller III, at a Council on Foreign Relations conference, he told him of the Metropolitan's and the Philharmonic's plans to relocate. Rockefeller expressed interest in the project, and eventually he was asked to be the president of Lincoln Center.

John Rockefeller seemed a somewhat curious choice, since he lacked a strong interest in either the performing arts or architecture, with which his brother Nelson was fascinated. Indeed, many observers, including Harrison, were surprised when he accepted the position.[25] The journalist Joe Alex Morris, writing in the Saturday Evening Post in 1958, noted: "It may seem preposterous . . . that the newest and most promising recruit to Broadway is John D. Rockefeller 3rd, who can't rumba and was once suspected of suppressing a yawn while seated in the Golden Horseshoe of the Metropolitan Opera House."[26] Rockefeller himself admitted, "I enjoy music, but I have no special background for it, unless you count a few years in which my parents unsuccessfully encouraged me to become familiar with a violin."[27] Morris also noted that Rockefeller's philanthropic activities had long been conducted under the shadow of his father's highly publicized efforts and that "except for his work in the Japan Society, he had not been able to plunge with zest and enthusiasm into personal projects as his younger brothers had plunged into almost everything from diplomacy to farming."[28] But Lincoln Center fit into Rockefeller's larger sense of purpose; it was an opportunity to shape the nation's cultural life and, more important, to influence America's international status. He argued that the country's lack of leadership in the arts "has been a handicap in our relations with other peoples and, for that reason, it is my hope that Lincoln Center may become a symbol before the world of America's cultural development."[29]

Once Rockefeller signed on, he threw himself into the assignment with enthusiasm, forming a group, incorporated in the spring of 1956 as the Exploratory Committee for a Musical Arts Center, that met regularly for lunch meetings at the Century Club to help plan the new center and strategize its fund-raising campaign. In addition to Rockefeller and Harrison, the committee was composed of Metropolitan Opera Association members Spofford, Anthony A. Bliss, Irving S. Olds (former chairman of U.S. Steel), C. D. Jackson (publisher of Fortune), Arthur A. Houghton, Jr. (president of Corning Glass Works) and Floyd Blair of the Philharmonic-Symphony Society, who was later replaced by David M. Keiser, a trustee of the Juilliard School; Lincoln Kirstein, co-founder and managing director of the New York City Ballet; Devereux Josephs, chairman of the New York Life Insurance Company; and Robert E. Blum, vice president of the Abraham & Straus department store and president of the Brooklyn Institute of Arts and Sciences. The committee, and Rockefeller in particular, struggled to justify the center's existence in the face of pressures to rebuild the city's educational and research institutions and its declining housing resources. Several years later Rockefeller would describe the center as "a new kind of city therapy," explaining: "Other things have been tried, other methods have appealed to private organizations. Medicine, museums, experimental housing—each one was the most pressing problem of its time. But we believe that this is the time for a more active form of help—a time for art."[30]

The most significant issue for the committee to resolve was which arts should be accomodated; opera and symphony were definitely to be included, as was ballet, which the committee viewed as musically based. The committee also felt that despite the plethora of commercial legitimate theaters in New York, there was a strong need for an American repertory theater, which could be provided with a permanent home in the new complex. In addition, committee members advocated the inclusion of a library and museum dedicated to the performing arts,

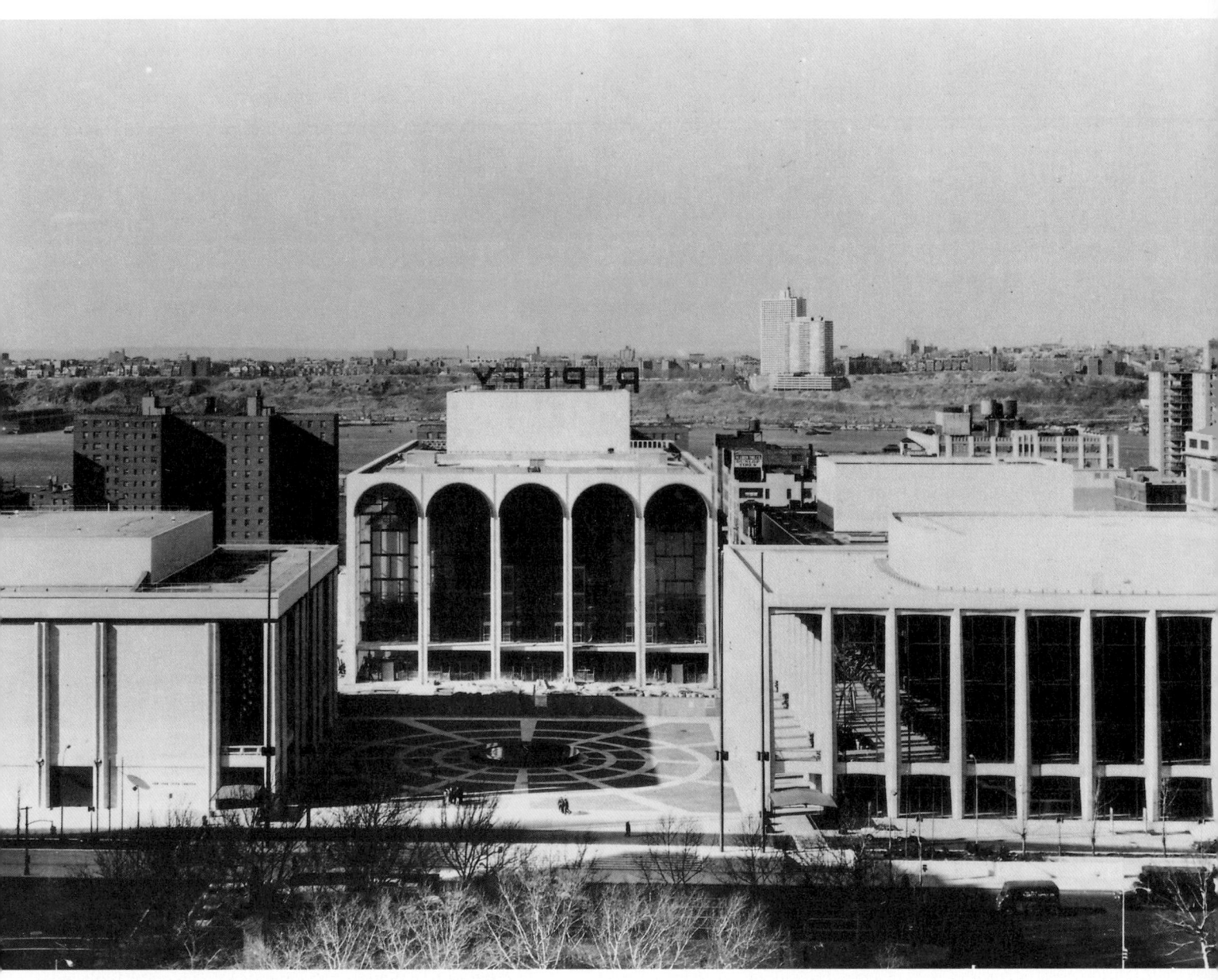

Lincoln Center, between Columbus and Amsterdam avenues, West
Sixty-second and West Sixty-sixth streets. View to the west showing,
from left to right: New York State Theater (Philip Johnson, 1964),
Metropolitan Opera House (Wallace K. Harrison, 1966), and
Philharmonic Hall (Max Abramovitz, 1962). MOA

as well as a performing arts school. Painting and sculpture would not be included, since ample facilities for the visual arts already existed in New York and only a limited number of disciplines could be effectively accommodated in a single complex. With the scope of the project having been focused, Rockefeller traveled to Europe in the spring of 1956 with Harrison; Anthony Bliss; Herman Krawitz, the founding manager of the Falmouth Playhouse on Cape Cod and a member of the Metropolitan Opera Building Committee; Walter Unruh, a German architect and stage designer; Herbert Graf, stage director of the Metropolitan Opera since 1935; and Alan I. Fowler of the engineering firm Day & Zimmerman. The group's mission was to study the architecture and the operating procedures of theater and music organizations including the Old Vic, the Comédie Française, the Vienna State Opera and La Scala.

On May 28, 1956, Moses presented his plan for the entire renewal area to Mayor Wagner and the Board of Estimate.[31] The area was to constitute a modified L-shaped site, bounded on the south and north by Sixtieth and Seventieth streets, on the west by the New York Central railroad yards above Sixty-sixth Street and Amsterdam Avenue below, and on the east by Broadway above Lincoln Square and Columbus Avenue below. As part of the plan, the Broadway producer and entrepreneur Roger L. Stevens proposed a mixed-use development to be built on a triangular superblock site bounded by Broadway and Amsterdam Avenue, Sixty-fifth and Seventieth streets (although Sixty-sixth street was to remain open).[32] Designed by Pereira & Luckman, who worked with the theater designer Jo Mielziner, Stevens's project called for three connected circular structures containing five theaters and commercial space. Alternate plans called for two circular buildings, one to contain five theaters and the other to be a freestanding theater-in-the-round for experimental productions. The Broadway site between Sixty-fifth and Sixty-sixth streets was to contain a circular building housing restaurants and shops and linked to the rest of the development by a pedestrian tunnel beneath Sixty-sixth Street. The virtually windowless buildings, set amid landscaped grounds and serviced through an underground parking garage, anticipated Charles Luckman's ungainly design for Madison Square Garden Center, realized in 1968.

By May 1957 Stevens's development had been dropped from the project due to budgetary limitations on federal land subsidies.[33] Even with this deletion, however, the development was the nation's largest Title I project undertaken to date, requiring an estimated $2,580,000 in land subsidies from the federal government, as well as a contribution of approximately $12,290,000 from the city. Moses reported that a land bid of $5.00 a square foot had been made by Fordham University, $8.00 by the Metropolitan Opera and the New York Philharmonic, and as high as $9.35 from what Moses described as "responsible private developers for the housing and commercial section."[34] In October 1956 the Board of Estimate unanimously granted preliminary approval of the project.

Opposition to the development arose immediately. Citizens' groups bemoaned the displacement of families occupying the tenements and subdivided brownstones that dominated the area, claiming that most residents could neither qualify for low-rent public housing nor afford the area's new middle-income rental units. A group representing local businessmen opposed the project as well. When a CBS-TV public affairs program was scheduled to televise a debate on the project, the city declined to send a spokesman, calling the topic "too emotional."[35] The Council on Housing Relocation, chaired by the attorney Harris L. Present, clearly seeking to block the project by any legal means, filed a petition with the Federal Housing and Home Finance Agency charging that the subsidized sale of land to Fordham, a Jesuit-run university, violated the constitutionally guaranteed separation of church and state. This brought the directors of Lincoln Center into the public debate, and their legal counsel filed an *amicus curiae* brief arguing that federal and state contributions to Title I projects were not issued as subsidies to individual sponsors per se but were intended to eliminate slum areas for the public good.[36] On December 23, 1957, New York State Supreme Court Justice Owen McGivern dismissed the case of *Sixty-fourth Street Residences, Inc. v. the City of New York*, stating, "In hard reality, to exclude Fordham or any other sectarian institution from great overall community planning efforts, such as the Lincoln Square project, would be to relegate such institutions to the other side of the tracks."[37] The case went all the way to the United States Supreme Court, which dismissed it on June 9, 1958.[38]

Not all civic groups disapproved of the project, however. The Citizens' Housing and Planning Council endorsed the plan but asked the City Planning Commission to undertake a neighborhood study and consider developing low- and middle-income housing projects in the area. The group's *Citizens' Housing News* editorialized: "Understandably, opposition has come from residents and businessmen who will be displaced. Moving to a new neighborhood, leaving friends and neighbors and changing schools, can be a difficult experience. This is worsened considerably when families are uprooted involuntarily and forced to find new quarters in times of a housing shortage."[39] The City Planning Commission denied the council's request, and ultimately 16,732 people would be relocated to make way for the enormous renewal project. Those who saw the project as essential to the city's cultural life tended to overlook the human issues. Harold Schonberg described the anticipated transformation of the area in dramatic, idealized terms: "Out of the most barren wastes, as poets since Chaucer have observed, come the most beautiful flowers. A barren urban waste is the Lincoln Square area. . . . Old-law tenements stand, blowsy and run-down, in silent shoulder-to-shoulder misery, full of filth and vermin. . . . Out of it will rise the Lincoln Center for the Performing Arts, a cultural fairyland."[40]

In contrast to national urban renewal policy, which placed the burden of responsibility for demolition and tenant relocation on the municipality, New York regulations stipulated that these responsibilities be borne by the sponsor. In this case the sponsor was Lincoln Center, Inc., founded on June 22, 1956, when it became the landlord of 188 existing buildings housing 1,647 families and took on responsibility for both tenant relocation and, until demolition was complete, management of the properties.[41] In addition to its residential property, Lincoln Center became landlord of 383 commercial and institutional properties. The most problematic of these was the twelve-story Kennedy Building, located on the west side of Columbus Avenue between Sixty-second and Sixty-third streets.[42] The building was owned by the Joseph P. Kennedy family and rented to the federal government, which used it, among other purposes, to house offices of the Unites States Immigration Service and the Atomic Energy Commission. Originally Moses had omitted the building from the project because it would be too costly to purchase, but he favored its inclusion at the right price. Rockefeller negotiated with the Kennedy family to buy the building for $2.5 million, which Moses agreed to on the condition that the Lincoln Center management pay $1.5 million of that and convince the federal government to include the property within the renewal area boundaries. Moses's conditions were accepted, and the site was eventually cleared and incorporated into the project.

From the beginning it was assumed that Harrison, assigned the job of designing the opera house, which was always recognized as the focal point of the entire Lincoln Center project, would also choose the other architects and coordinate all of their designs. But Harrison, who had participated in the team effort that resulted in Rockefeller Center, and had just emerged from a difficult experience as the head of an international team of architects for the United Nations headquarters (see chapter 7), turned down the opportunity. After recommending his partner, Max Abramovitz, as architect for the Philharmonic's building, he then drew up a list of names from which Rockefeller's committee could choose. Harrison's list consisted of his friend the Finnish architect Alvar Aalto; the Swedish architect and urban planner Sven Markelius, with whom he had worked on the United Nations design; the Hungarian-born, Bauhaus-affiliated architect Marcel Breuer, now working in the United States; the Italian-born architect Pietro Belluschi, now dean of the Massachusetts Institute of Technology School of Architecture; and his former mentor at the Boston Architectural Club, Henry R. Shepley, the most traditionally minded architect to be considered. Harrison also proposed Edward Durell Stone, I. M. Pei and the architectural firm of Skidmore, Owings & Merrill. In October 1956 Harrison's recommended group of architects, together with the American architect Philip Johnson; the German theater architect Walter Unruh; the American stage director Herbert Graf; the architect-renderer Hugh Ferriss; the acoustical engineers Hugh Bagenal, Richard Bolt and Richard Newman; the theater design consultant George Izenour; and Stuart Constable, representing Robert Moses's office, gathered in the offices of Harrison & Abramovitz for a two-week-long parley to discuss the proposed center.[43] At the start of the discussion the site was bounded by Columbus and Amsterdam avenues, Sixty-second and Sixty-fourth streets; by the time the conference convened, Harrison, with Johnson's help, had persuaded Moses to expand the site to Sixty-fifth Street. Moses's original renewal plan had proposed a site plan calling for a north-south mall bisecting the superblock site and linking Fordham University on the south with Stevens's proposed commercial theater complex on the north. Moses also proposed a public park on the southwest corner of the site, onto which the opera house would face.

The design panel immediately confronted a key issue: the relationship of the complex to the surrounding urban fabric. Some panel members advocated creating an introspective place apart from the turmoil of the city, citing the Piazza San Marco in Venice as a model.[44] Other members of the panel—Breuer in particular—accepted the superblock *parti* but favored a plan that would more fully embrace the city and proposed rearranging the buildings around a plaza opening onto Columbus Avenue and Broadway.[45] Along these lines, Belluschi and Johnson suggested arranging the buildings around the site's perimeter, leaving a large plaza in front of the opera house and open to Columbus Avenue, a plan that disregarded the park Moses had proposed. Markelius proposed a similar plan, though it preserved Moses's park and incorporated a north-south passage traversing the site; his plan also called for the entire complex to be elevated on a podium. Breuer subsequently changed his proposal, suggesting an asymmetrical arrangement of buildings around a plaza opening onto Sixty-fifth Street with a broad flight of stairs. According to this plan, a dominant opera house would terminate a secondary east-west opening onto Columbus

Avenue. Harrison and Abramovitz proposed a similar scheme, though they lined most of the Sixty-fifth Street frontage with a narrow building housing the library and the museum, as well as a separate repertory theater building. They placed the principal entrance to the north-south plaza at the site's northeast corner, where visitors would enter through a grove of trees.

Belluschi and Shepley collaborated on a more Classical arrangement, with a centrally located plaza, approached from Columbus Avenue through a narrower passageway framed by two buildings; in effect, the plaza was to be F-shaped. The scheme was largely symmetrical, with the exception of the open space in the site's southwest corner necessitated by Moses's park. Harrison and Abramovitz elaborated on this proposal, pulling the Columbus Avenue buildings back to create a larger, rectangular plaza. Aalto produced a design calling for an internally focused complex punctuated by narrow entryways. Building on this concept, Breuer proposed a narrow, continuous building elevated on stilts, with its bottom surface clad in acoustical tile to minimize the intrusion of street noise; the building would define a courtyard opening onto Columbus Avenue. Eventually Harrison and Abramovitz's last proposal served as the basis for the final elaboration of the complex. The final plan, proposed in March 1958, was glowingly described by Harold Schonberg: "The architectural emphasis will be on space and beauty, light and air, greenery and color. No buildings will try to poke through the clouds, skyscraper-style. Rather, they will be in a world's fair style, grouped around a plaza planned to be as big as the Piazza San Marco in Venice."[46]

As planning proceeded, it became increasingly clear that the site could not comfortably accommodate all of the proposed facilities. The planning team urged Moses to relinquish his park space, but he wouldn't budge, thereby in effect fixing the western boundary of the dance theater and the southern boundary of the Metropolitan Opera House and forcing into place all the principal structures. On the penultimate day that the committee convened, Moses announced, in typically dramatic fashion, that he would be willing to trade a portion of his Lincoln Center park for park space elsewhere. The announcement elicited a flurry of new proposals, including one by Johnson and Belluschi that called for two buildings flanking the opera hall and occupying the southwest and northwest corners of the site. Moses, however, subsequently withdrew his offer and insisted on maintaining the park's original boundaries. Recognizing that the performing arts school could not fit on the center's allotted site, he then agreed to support efforts to include the eastern half of the block bounded by Amsterdam Avenue, Broadway, Sixty-fifth and Sixty-sixth streets, which had previously been part of Roger Stevens's mixed-use development proposal, and suggested that a pedestrian tunnel or bridge link this site to the main complex. By October 1958 the property had been purchased and incorporated into the project.

The final selection of architects was made in 1958. Because they wanted to use only American architects, the Lincoln Center board rejected Aalto and Markelius. Breuer was eliminated because he was generally considered too rigid, and Shepley for being too conservative. Although Harrison had passed up the opportunity for overall control, he nonetheless played an important role, recommending Belluschi for the Juilliard School, Eero Saarinen for the repertory theater and Gordon Bunshaft, partner in charge of design at the New York office of Skidmore, Owings & Merrill, for the library and museum.[47] The opera house was to be designed by Harrison, and the commission for the symphony hall went to Abramovitz.

The selection of an architect for the theater that would be developed primarily for dance but would also function as a second opera house was undertaken in a different way.[48] Here Governor Nelson Rockefeller was brought into the decision-making process, since the theater would also serve as a venue for events celebrating New York State's tricentennial in 1966. He turned to the choreographer George Balanchine, whose New York City Ballet was to be a principal occupant of the theater. Balanchine chose Philip Johnson, a friend of Rockefeller's and since Harvard College days also a close friend of Lincoln Kirstein's, Balanchine's principal sponsor. Johnson had in 1946 renovated the lobby of Balanchine's School of American Ballet, at 637 Madison Avenue; his low-budget design included covering the walls with marbleized paper in a manner inspired by Mies van der Rohe's landmark Barcelona Pavilion of 1929.[49]

Each architect was given full control over his design, although John Rockefeller, fearing an aesthetic free-for-all, insisted on a series of meetings to be chaired by Harrison and attended by all of the architects as well as himself. Also attending were Edgar B. Young, Rockefeller's personal assistant, who later served as the center's acting president (1961), executive vice president (1962–65) and chairman of the Building Committee (1961–71), and René d'Harnoncourt, the director of the Museum of Modern Art, whom he invited to serve as an adviser to the Lincoln Center board on aesthetic issues.[50] The idea of these group meetings was perilous, as Harold Schonberg noted in 1959:

> Suppose six great pianists . . . were locked in a room and ordered not to come out until they had decided on the correct interpretation of Beethoven's "Hammerklavier" Sonata. How many eons would pass? How many wounds would be inflicted? How much blood would be shed? Yet, in another field, much the same thing is actually going on at the moment. Working on the building for the Lincoln Center for the Performing Arts on New York's West Side are . . . six of America's most prominent architects, six notable temperaments, each with strong ideas about design and esthetics.

Harrison's role, in terms of leadership, was minimal. Schonberg characterized him as "nominally presiding over the architectural symphony, but notably loath to act as the conductor," attributing perhaps some of Harrison's reticence to his complex nature, which allowed him to be "described as the Eisenhower of architects, a modernist, a reactionary, a maverick (his own description), an architectural tycoon, a tough construction man and a gentle-hearted aesthete who paints Légeresque abstractions for relaxation."[51]

Harrison's biographer, Victoria Newhouse, hypothesized that the architect's reluctance to take a more aggressive role in shaping the complex's design was due to a lack of support from John Rockefeller. She also suggested that Harrison's attitude was influenced by unpleasant memories of the United Nations headquarters project. Recalling that experience, Harrison said: "We got up to the last minute and ran into a dead end. One-half believed in one thing and one-half in another thing. I took the bull by the horns and made the decision. 'You'll hate me for this,' I said, and I was right. Le Corbusier hasn't spoken to me since. This time I have refused to take that position. I won't go through that damn thing again. It put me in the hospital for six months."[52] Newhouse described Harrison's detachment from the planning process for Lincoln Center: "As the meetings went on, Harrison seemed increasingly reluctant to participate. . . . He reminded his colleagues again and again that he could serve only in the

capacity of chairman and they 'had to make up their own minds.' Perhaps by this time he had already sensed that the prolonged debates of the different Lincoln Center groups were counterproductive."[53] Nonetheless, Harrison had strong diplomatic skills and an aura of calm, both of which proved invaluable. As Schonberg put it: "When the going gets a little rough, Harrison smooths things out. 'He tells us we're all artists,' one of the architects says. 'He explains how this is a meeting of the minds. He appeals to our better instincts. Somehow he manages to reconcile differences.'"[54]

Under the chairmanship, if not the leadership, of Harrison, the architects surveyed the proposed site plan and, after heated debates, approved the basic positioning of the plaza and the constituent buildings, rejecting Bunshaft's and Saarinen's efforts to resurrect Aalto's and Breuer's call for an all-encompassing single megastructure. The architects played with the idea of using the site north of Sixty-fifth Street for the dance theater; the site was enticing because of its remoteness and the fact that it was the only part of the complex fronting directly on Broadway. Eventually the original position of the dance theater was maintained. The repertory theater and the library and museum were located on the site Johnson and Belluschi had proposed for them at the northwest corner of the compound, where they shared a single building, to be designed jointly by Bunshaft and Saarinen.

The principal concern for the architectural committee was that of design unity. In achieving this, Philip Johnson clearly took the leadership role, as he had in fixing the site plan before the architects for the individual buildings had been chosen. Early on in the design process, Johnson arrived at a committee meeting with a complete master plan; he would later recall that when he "walked in with *that*, all the architects said, 'Well, Philip is trying to kill us all,' which of course I was."[55] Johnson may have been responsible for the placement of the three principal buildings, but the design team rejected many of his detailed suggestions, including his proposal for a curved-front dance theater and his subsequent proposal for a continuous, plaza-enclosing arcade (see below).

In an effort to establish cohesiveness, Belluschi proposed that all the buildings be clad in Roman travertine. The stone, formed from sulphur deposits in the natural warm springs near Bagni di Tivoli, outside Rome, was the primary building material used in ancient Rome and was employed at the Coliseum.[56] The architects quickly agreed, and according to Edgar Young, "of all the decisions required this was the quickest one they would make."[57] The material, which suggested the monolithic concrete that was closer to some of the architects' taste but would probably not have been approved by either the board or the public, was admired for its whiteness, its subtle markings and its ability to, as Philip Johnson claimed, "grow old . . . beautifully."[58] In this he was only partially right; it looked fine as it got older but proved to be overly susceptible to damage as a result of New York's alternately dry, wet, freezing and mild climate. Though the decision to use travertine was painless, the implementation of that choice was more problematic. First, the estimated cost of the material was 50 to 70 percent more than was budgeted. Second, the Limestone Institute, supported by several members of Congress, objected to the use of imported building-stone in a project that would receive federal funding. The institute submitted a lower bid for its American-quarried product, after which a competing supplier submitted an even lower bid for travertine if the stone were cut and finished abroad. While the architects continued to advocate the use of travertine, threats of labor demonstrations if American stonemasons were not employed resulted in a compromise: Italian travertine was used, but it was fashioned by American workmen, at a cost overrun of 25 percent.

Harrison, Abramovitz and Johnson, the architects of the three plaza-facing buildings, agreed that the principal facades of their structures should be mostly glass. According to Lincoln Kirstein, the decision also reflected other considerations:

> The early meetings of the corporation were held at the Century Club. Catty-corners, at 43rd Street and Fifth Avenue, shone a recently completed branch of the Manufacturers Trust, designed by Gordon Bunshaft. Its all-glass exposed frontal, with the vault door plain to all in a splendid symbol of armored candor, greatly impressed Mr. Rockefeller. He was taken with its frankness, its seasonal nocturnal warmth. Lincoln Center was bid to have a glass skin on every face, whether or not transparency had any function. In this he was seconded by Arthur A. Houghton, Jr., chairman of the board of the Philharmonic-Symphony Society, and its president. He was also chief of Corning Glass Works.[59]

Working with clay models of the proposed buildings, the group also agreed that the dance theater and the concert hall would be of equal height and similar massing, and that the two buildings would incorporate exterior balconies at the same promenade level. Despite a lack of total design resolution for the individual buildings, the complex's site plan was approved by the Lincoln Center board in February 1959, and construction began three months later.[60]

As construction got under way, a key change occurred in the Lincoln Center organization. Rockefeller proposed that Robert Moses and Mayor Robert Wagner be invited to join the board as ex-officio directors. Despite opposition from some of the board's members and its legal counsel, Rockefeller prevailed. This decision reflected Rockefeller's diplomatic skills, a feature of his personality that was indispensable in his dealings with Moses. As Joe Morris reported, "It took a great deal of Rockefeller's soft persuasion to keep [the group] on an even keel . . . but over the long run, his quiet, painstaking persistence seemed to complement the efforts of the fast-moving, fast-talking and temperamental Moses. They worked together with a minimum of friction, which was essential to success of the project."[61]

Lincoln Center's groundbreaking took place on May 14, 1959, and was celebrated as a media event, complete with the participation of President Eisenhower. According to the editors of *Business Week*, the ceremonies sought "to dramatize to the nation—and the world—the status achieved by the arts in this country."[62] To celebrate the occasion before the 12,000 people who gathered at the site, and the half million or so who watched the proceedings on New York–area television broadcasts, Leonard Bernstein conducted the New York Philharmonic, accompanied by the opera singers Risë Stevens and Leonard Warren. "This was the real beauty of yesterday morning's occasion," the editors of the *New York Herald Tribune* wrote, "the fact that a great vision suddenly took shape, a first audience was convened, a first performance given."[63] Eisenhower took a high-minded view of the project, characterizing it in sweeping, global terms: "Here will develop a mighty influence for peace and understanding throughout the world."[64] But the *New York Times* was more nationalistic: "It will be a beacon to the world, revealing that Americans know how to build the life of the spirit on its material bounty."[65]

The public attention garnered by the groundbreaking festivities was quickly and carefully exploited in a public relations campaign organized by the advertising guru David Ogilvy working with thirty-one other leading advertising executives and an

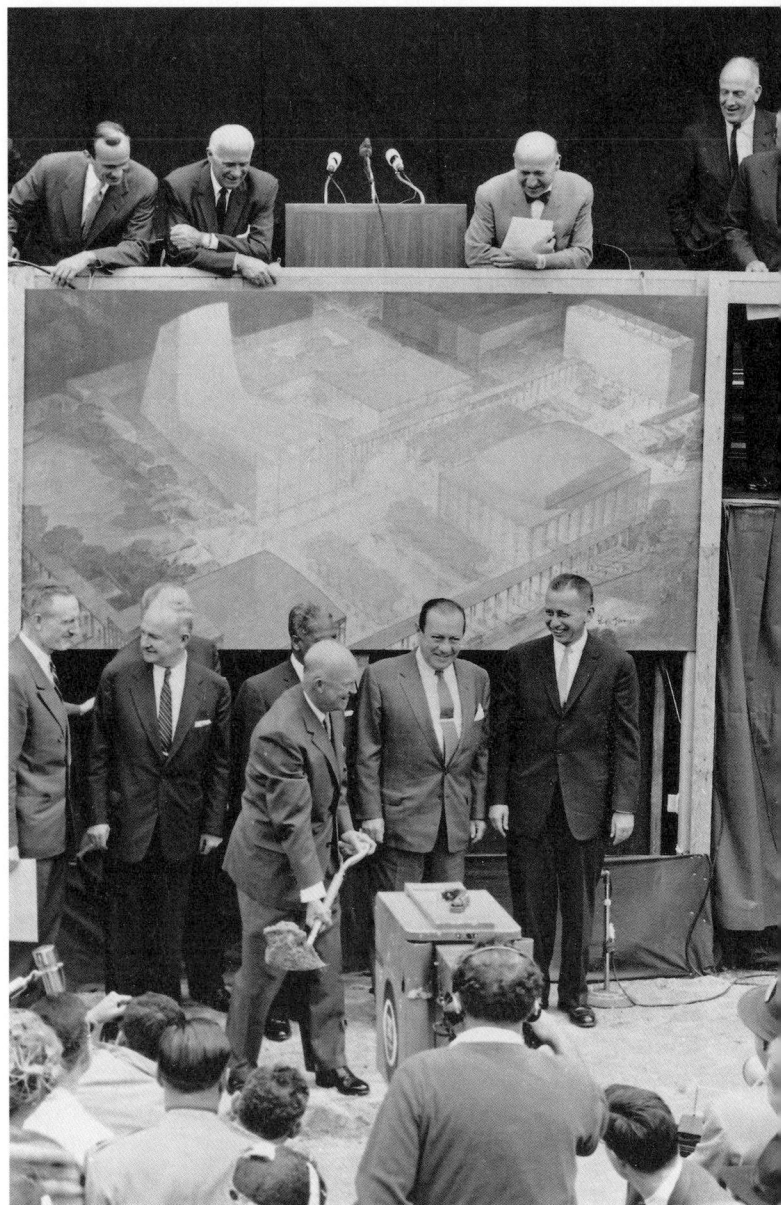

Lincoln Center groundbreaking ceremony, May 14, 1959. President Dwight Eisenhower is in the center holding a shovel. The rendering of a proposal for Lincoln Center is by Hugh Ferriss. CU

army of volunteers culled from prominent firms. Among the group's efforts were the installation of scale models of the center, accompanied by audio presentations, in public spaces such as City Hall and Grand Central Terminal; essay and art contests organized in over 800 schools; full-page advertisements run in local newspapers as well as nationally circulated magazines; radio and television spots featuring celebrities who volunteered their services; and direct mail contact with 100,000 people.

The tasks of organizing and constructing the vast cultural complex began to resemble a military campaign. In fact, military personnel figured prominently in the growing Lincoln Center bureaucracy. In December 1960, when Rockefeller became the chairman of the newly created Executive Committee, he was replaced as the president of Lincoln Center by retired Army Chief of Staff General Maxwell D. Taylor, who had played an important role in the formation of NATO and served on the faculty of West Point. Retired Major General Otto L. Nelson, Jr., vice president in charge of housing for the New York Life Insurance Company, had been brought into the project in 1956 by his boss, Devereux Josephs, chairman of New York Life and a member of Lincoln Center's board.[66] Nelson, who was not paid for his time, served the center until 1960, when he was replaced as the center's executive director of construction by his assistant, Colonel William F. Nelson, who had previously supervised major military and civil works programs for the Army Corps of Engineers. On April 21, 1961, President Kennedy requested that Taylor be released from his duties for a two-month period in order to participate in an assignment concerning the recent Bay of Pigs incident; Rockefeller immediately agreed.[67] Kennedy subsequently informed Rockefeller that Taylor was to be recalled to active duty for a White House assignment as a military adviser. He was replaced as president of the Lincoln Center board by William Schuman, a composer and president of the Juilliard School.

Philharmonic Hall

Philharmonic Hall was the first building at Lincoln Center to be completed, opening on September 23, 1962.[68] Following the execution of preliminary designs by the architect, Max Abramovitz, including one of 1958 that called for a broad, cantilevered, second-level terrace, details of Philharmonic Hall's design were publicly released five days prior to groundbreaking on May 9, 1959. The hall was to be a five-story, glass-walled building, surrounded by a travertine-clad concrete arcade composed of nine piers along the north and south facades and eleven on the adjacent sides. The piers, which were not solid but rather ladderlike structures, rose sixty feet and culminated in pointed arches twenty-two feet wide. Seven months later, after excavation of the site had begun, a new design was released, which was the one eventually built. It called for a higher and wider building; for an arcade only on the plaza side, where a promenade-level balcony was introduced; and for solid piers, now rising seventy feet, that were tapered at both ends and culminated in shallow, rounded arcs.

Inside, a low-ceilinged ground level contained restaurant areas that were separated from the circulation areas only by movable partitions. Concertgoers ascended by elevators and two escalators to the second-level Grand Foyer, a soaring, 50-foot-high, 25-foot-wide, 180-foot-long room overlooking the plaza. Three balconies leading to the hall's seating tiers and wrapping around the sides of the auditorium, where they incorporated staircases, formed the Grand Foyer's principal interior feature. On the building's northern side, where the backstage ar-

eas were located, the balconies terminated in floor-to-ceiling mirrors. Abramovitz arrived at the design of the auditorium itself after at least one more experimental scheme, influenced by Hans Scharoun's Philharmonic Concert Hall in Berlin (1956–63), that eliminated all sense of a proscenium and placed a portion of the audience behind the musicians. The *New York Times* described Abramovitz's working methods: "As a designer, [he] moves experimentally, from one kind of solution to another; he is not known for a specific 'style' or an identifying hallmark."[69] In its final form, the 2,162-seat, bottle-shaped auditorium was lined with plaster walls painted dark blue, contrasting with seats upholstered in shades of gold. Complexly shaped acoustical "clouds" hovered below the ceiling.

The interior of the building had a sense of spaciousness, a quality Abramovitz stressed. While he "wanted to create . . . the perfect concert hall, the pure concert hall," he told the *New Yorker*, what he wanted above all was space, "space for people to move freely about in, to breathe easily in." He went on to explain:

> In most halls, people sit in an inside place, the auditorium, and then, during intermissions, step out into another inside place. No freedom. Too cramped, too enclosed. I want a large percentage of open space in which the spirit can flourish. . . . I have often pointed out that in the Royal Festival Hall, in London, the public space amounts to 26.1 square feet per person, while the public space in Carnegie Hall amounts to 3.6 square feet per person. Here we will have 15.1 square feet of public space per person. . . . People can look out through the big windows, people can look in through the big windows. I want the building to be a pageant for the whole community.[70]

In assessing Philharmonic Hall upon its completion, Ada Louise Huxtable argued, like Abramovitz, that "such a building . . . unlike other buildings of a less special social and performance character, can be evaluated only when it is alive and in action." In that regard, Huxtable found the building laudable. It was, she said, "handsome at day" and at night took on "a remarkable beauty. From the outside, the drama of light, movement and color, seen through the glass walls, enclosed by the great tapered frame, makes the structure a spectacular success in action." She felt that the movement of the crowds was "the building's life blood" and, apparently ignoring such public gathering places as Pennsylvania Station and Grand Central Terminal, asserted that "only in the Guggenheim Museum can one see a similar union of people and architecture."[71] Before the building was completed, when the reinforced-concrete structure had yet to be clad in travertine, Huxtable had praised the exterior as "a timeless, classic design," particularly the "tall, graceful arches" that communicated "the dignity and scale appropriate to an important public building."[72] She continued her praise of the building after it opened. "The effectiveness of the building as a civic monument . . . is immediately apparent," she said. "It is beautiful, and its structure has a great deal to do with its beauty. The taper of the columns conforms to the lines of stress of their reinforced concrete, heaviest at the first-floor crossing, slimmest at the bottom and the top. . . . The scale, the proportions and the modeling of this exterior have unusual finesse and elegance as well as a delicate strength." Huxtable was equally impressed with the building's interior treatment, which created a "traditional theatrical air of rich and elegant architecture that somehow gives the vast hall a surprising intimacy. This air is difficult to create within the severe simplicities of modern design, and here Mr. Abramovitz just manages it."[73]

Less than a month after the opening, Huxtable reassessed the project, and again praised it highly:

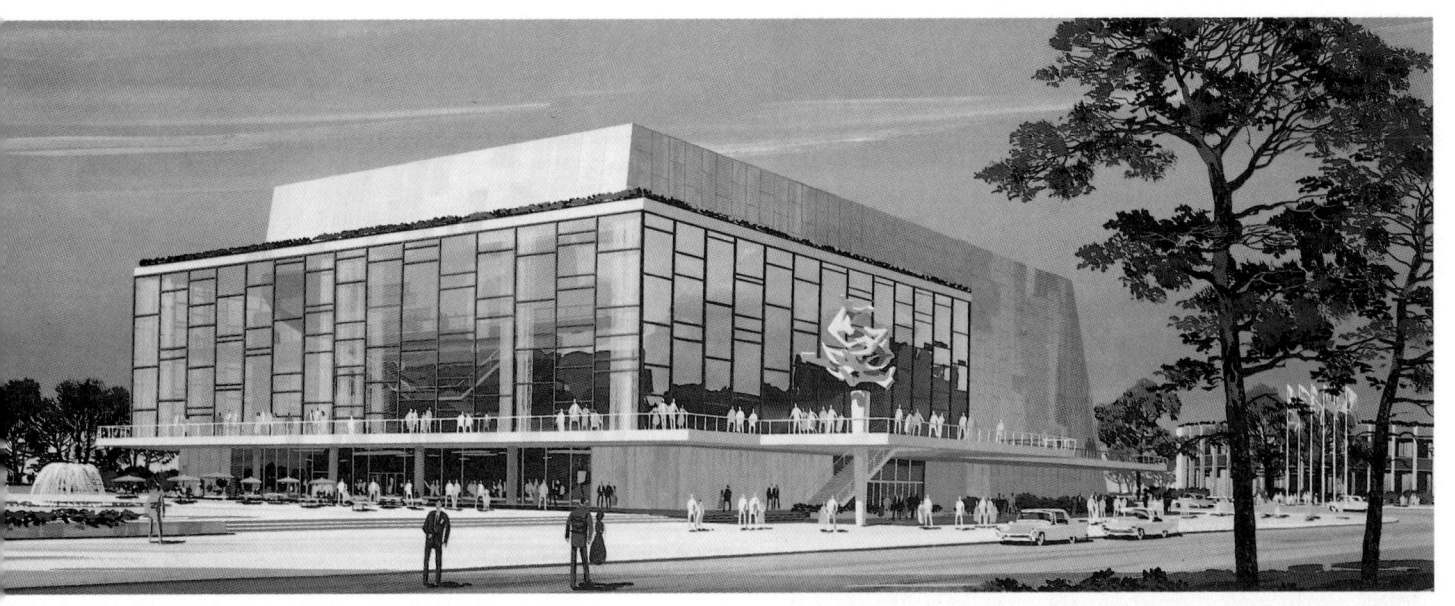

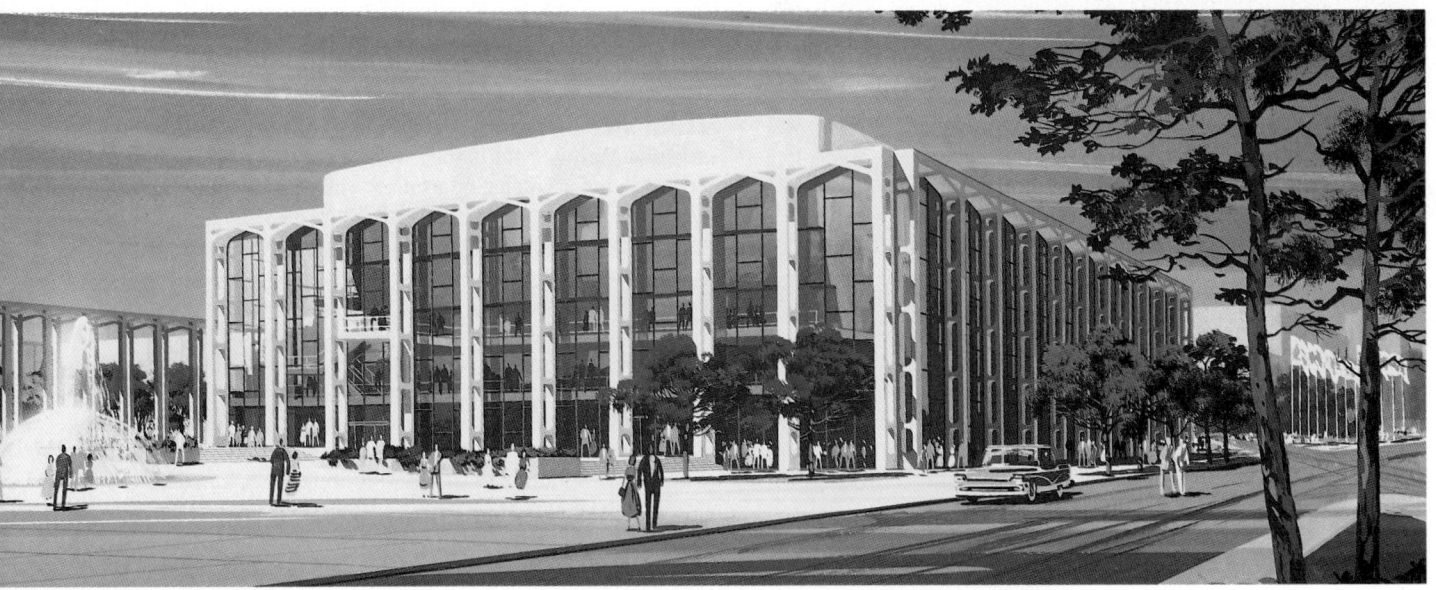

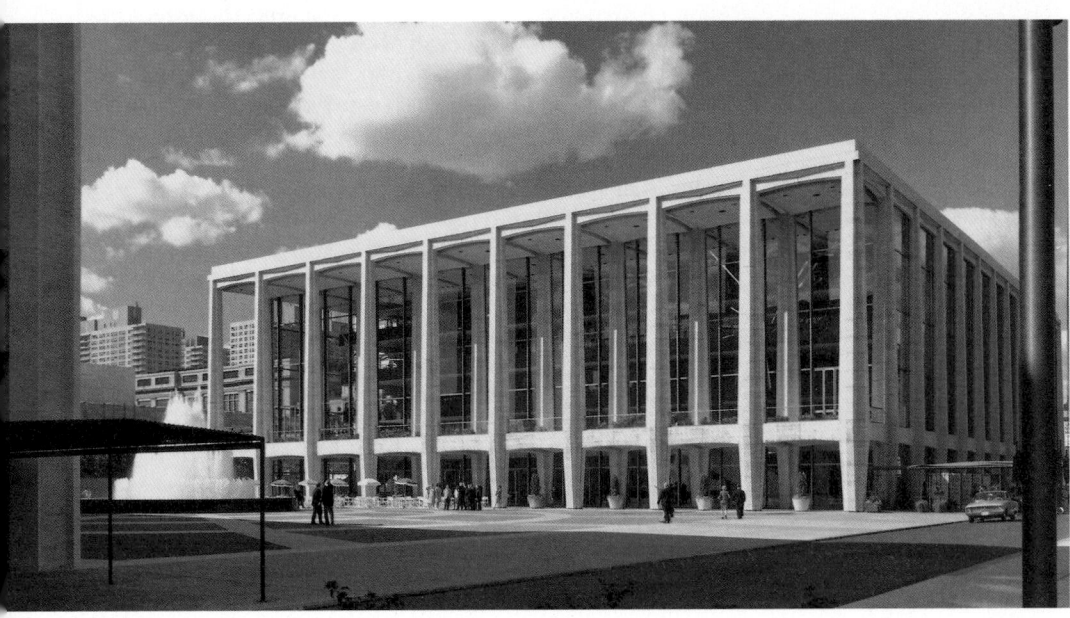

Top: Proposal for Philharmonic Hall, southwest corner of Columbus Avenue and West Sixty-fifth Street. Max Abramovitz, 1958. Rendering by Robert Schwartz of view to the northwest. ALC

Center: Proposal for Philharmonic Hall. Max Abramovitz, 1959. Rendering by Robert Schwartz of view to the northwest. ALC

Left: Philharmonic Hall. Max Abramovitz, 1962. View to the northwest. Stoller. ©ESTO

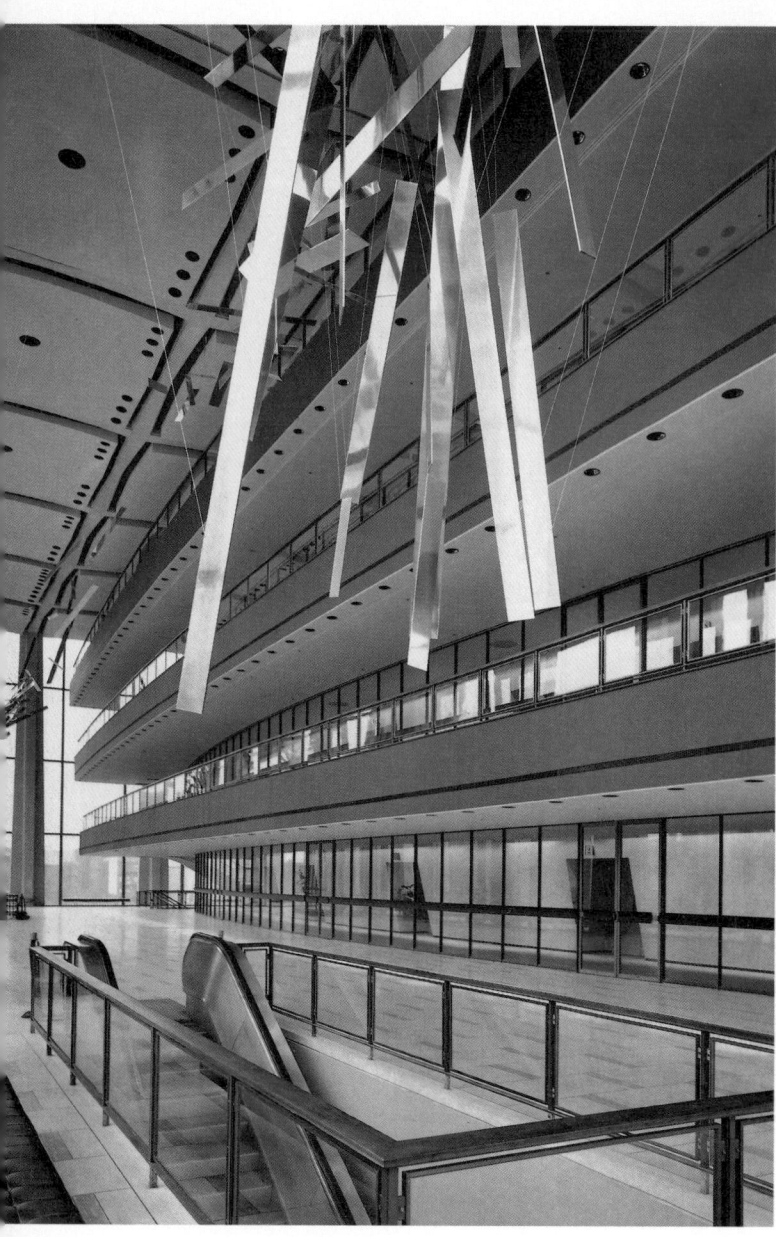

Philharmonic Hall, southwest corner of Columbus Avenue and West Sixty-fifth Street. Max Abramovitz, 1962. View of the grand foyer showing Richard Lippold's hanging sculpture *Orpheus and Apollo* (1962). Stoller. ©ESTO

The building has monumentality, and it is no less effective for being somewhat studied and contrived, for New York is rich in awkward architectural accidents and poor in calculated dignity. . . . It has elegant scale, color and surface—there is no more beautiful material than travertine and no more traditionally acceptable civic ornament than the formal colonnade. But the Philharmonic's most admirable feature is the manner in which its architect . . . has integrated the building's social uses with its design, so that the activity of its audiences, seen through the glass walls, brings the structure dramatically to life.

But she also reported on some of the "defects" of the hall that had become apparent since its opening: "Repeated visits develop an impression of confused and ineffectual interior spaces. The concertgoer enters crabwise from the plaza and virtually stumbles over a restaurant more suggestive of eat-and-run than haute cuisine, sidestepping it to escalators that ascend, department-store style, to the grand foyer above, so that the main public space is reached without appropriate psychological or visual impact." The foyer, she said, "suffers from the inauspicious entry and from the fact that it is narrow for its height and never capable of being grasped in its entirety from any of the balcony promenades that face out onto it." She continued her criticism: "Even the commendable use of audience color and movement as the building's most decorative effect suffers in proportion to the audience's drabness. Neutrality becomes negativeness. The design's most successful aspect remains its after-dark vitality, seen from the street."[74] Walter McQuade, writing in the *Nation*, was even harsher in his opinions, quarreling with Abramovitz's attempts at integrating Modernist minimalism with Classical composition as well as observing that, "despite its many layers and stairways," Philharmonic Hall failed to present "a really compelling sequence of spaces as you advance up on the lap of the escalators."[75]

Three months after Philharmonic Hall's opening, the sculptor Richard Lippold finished installing his monumental hanging work, *Orpheus and Apollo,* in the building's multistory Grand Foyer. "I wanted something light and airy and graceful," Abramovitz later recalled, "and naturally I thought of the great chandeliers that were always used in buildings of this kind in Europe. I made inquiries, and wrote to J. & L. Lobmeyer, in Vienna, a very old and famous firm, which supplied chandeliers to the Emperor Franz Josef. . . . Lobmeyer's did a lot of sketches . . . but they just didn't have the delicacy I wanted."[76] Abandoning the idea of chandeliers, Abramovitz considered a sculptural solution. He approached Lippold, who had already established a reputation for successful collaborations with architects, most notably with Philip Johnson at the Four Seasons restaurant (see chapter 5). Lippold received a letter from his New York art dealer, Marian Willard, extending Abramovitz's invitation to work on the hall. "It is suggested that two vertical Lippolds be suspended at some point above or just in front of the escalators, brilliantly lighted and visible from all eye levels from the balconies," Willard wrote. "Seen from the balconies, they will hang surrounded by glass and the city as a background. Does this perchance set your imagination to work?"[77] Lippold, having been infected by what he would later describe as "the Lincoln Center virus," answered with a resounding yes.[78]

As Lippold developed his project, he decided not to use metal rods, which had become his sculptural signature, but instead milled sheets made of a copper-and-zinc alloy called Muntz metal and cut to various lengths. The sheets were to be suspended in two large masses sweeping toward each other from either end of the foyer. While Lippold maintained his usual abstract formal vocabulary, the new material carried unexpected expressive implications: "Although I did not intend these

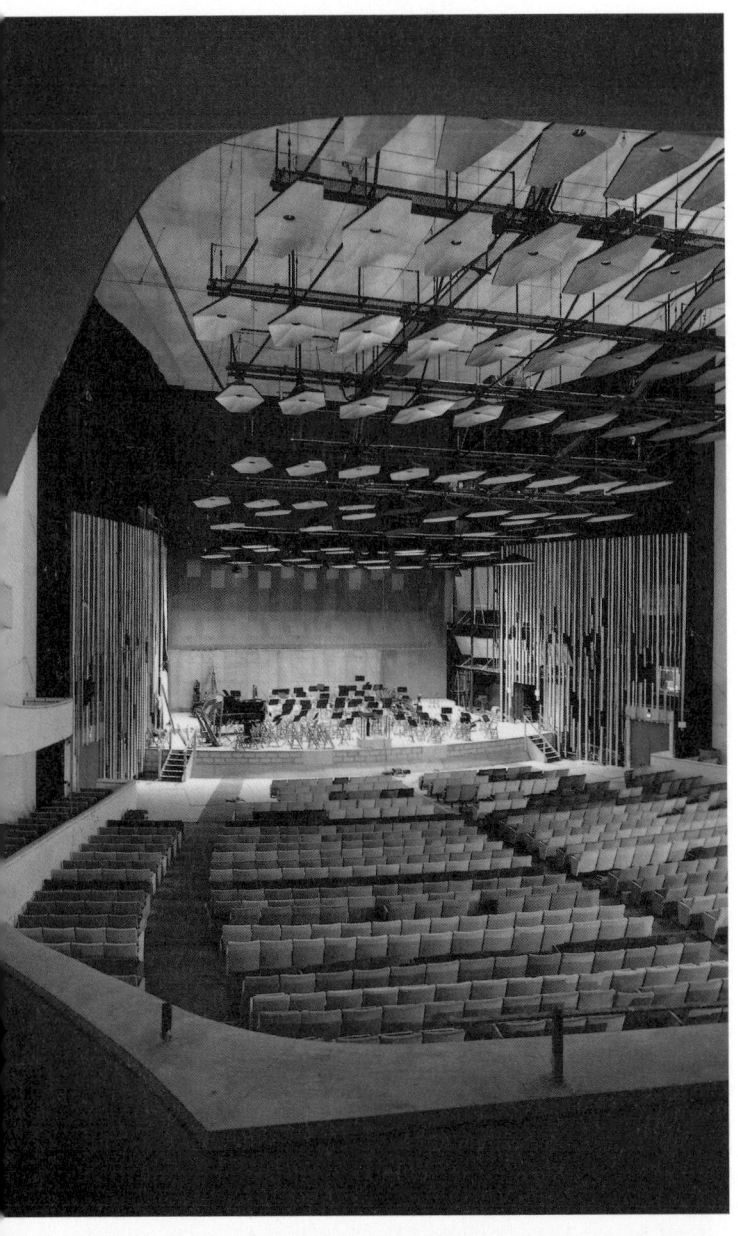

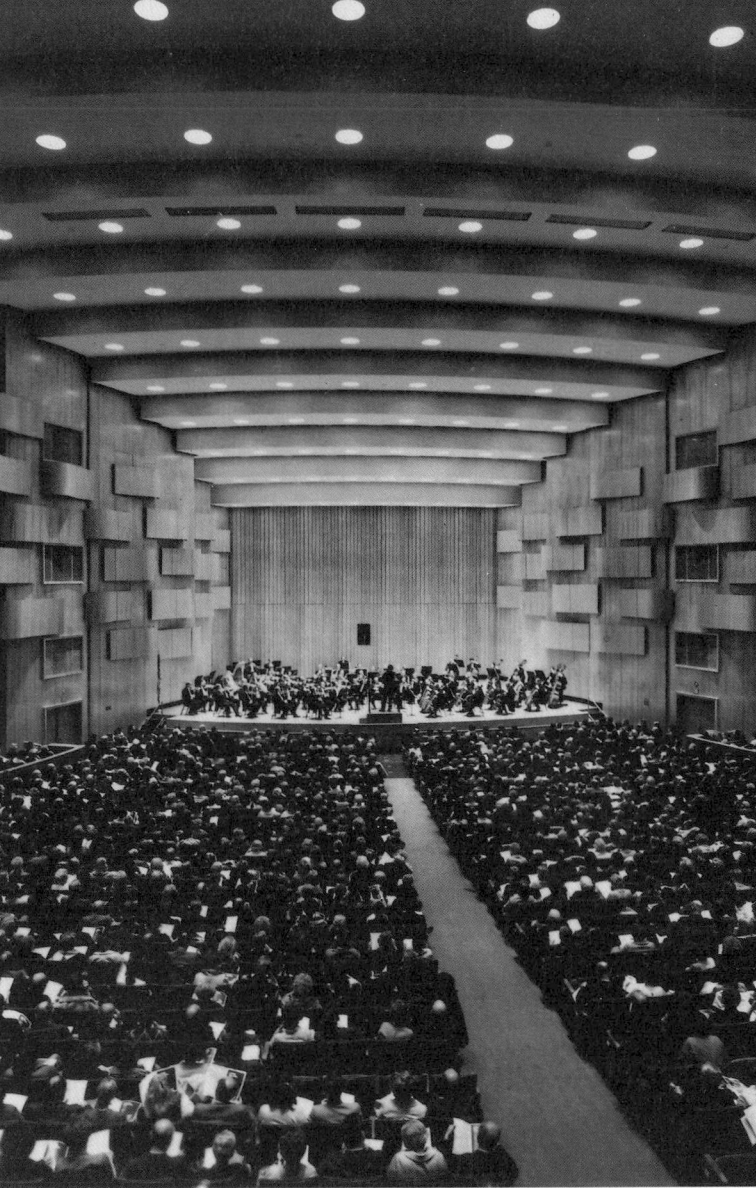

Top left: Philharmonic Hall auditorium. Max Abramovitz with acoustical engineering by Leo Beranek, 1962. Stoller. ©ESTO

Above: Philharmonic Hall, redesigned auditorium. Acoustical engineering by Heinrich Keilholz, Manfred Schroeder, Vern Knudsen and Paul Veneklasen, 1963. Acs. ALC

Bottom left: Proposal for Philharmonic Hall auditorium. Max Abramovitz, 1957. Rendering by Robert Schwartz. ALC forms to be figurative, they seem to be acting like people. By their gestures, these two figures seem to me like friendly gods (atomically conceived, like all of us), reflecting in their splendor the splendor of man, and identifying it with the spirit of the architecture which is in the spirit of music, thus including man as a part of the total spirit of life."[79] Lippold titled his work after the Greek god Apollo and his putative son, the musician Orpheus.

The sculpture consisted of 190 Muntz metal sheets individually suspended on two stainless steel cables; the work was estimated to weigh five tons. Once it was installed, Edgar Young noticed that both clusters contained one sheet, placed directly above each of the foyer's escalators, that was hung from a single wire. He alerted the artist to the risk of these bladelike forms falling and persuaded him to install auxiliary wires. Many observers would also question the work's aesthetic value. Hilton Kramer said that the piece was a prime illustration of the Lincoln Center directors' "distressing weakness for sculptural claptrap." He continued: "In a building that has not lost its capacity to depress one's spirit with its general flaccidity of design, this huge construction has remained a symbol of everything that one's taste as well as one's sense of intellectual rigor quarrels with in the whole Lincoln Center enterprise."[80] Clive Barnes said he found the sculpture "hard to take seriously."[81]

Whatever Philharmonic Hall's aesthetic strengths and weaknesses, the design of the auditorium was viewed by many people as a search for the acoustically ideal concert hall. Nearly all design decisions—including the hall's shape, its cubic volume, its seating capacity, the size and placement of its balconies, the choice of seating fabrics, and the floor and wall treatments—were subject to acoustical considerations. Five years of extensive research and testing, including in-depth study of fifty-four concert halls and interviews with about twenty-five of the world's leading conductors, concluded with a "tuning week," held from May 28 to June 2, 1962, during which various sounds—pistols, yachting cannons, clapping hands—as well as the Philharmonic Symphony Orchestra itself were heard and analyzed. Following the conclusion of what he called "a unique chapter in the annals of acoustical design," the acoustical engineer Leo Beranek said, "Whether history will award Philharmonic Hall a position among the world's finest environments for concert music is still too early for us to judge. But the understanding already engendered among musicians, architects, and acousticians should enrich the acoustical designs of the future and avoid many pitfalls of the past."[82]

This "understanding," however, did not prove sufficient: the hall's acoustical performance was a decided disappointment. "From Row R on the orchestra floor the sound was clear, a little dry, with not much reverberation and a decided lack of bass," Harold Schonberg reported. "It was good sound, but one had hoped for a more mellow quality." From the top rows, he said, "the tonal characteristics are altogether different. Here bass can definitely be heard . . . so full in sound that it almost appears amplified and too live. It is exciting, though, and in climactic movements . . . the effect lifts one off his seat."[83] John Molleson wrote in the New York Herald Tribune that "people who pride themselves in their hi-fi sets said the hall sounded like inferior stereo."[84] The composer and music critic Virgil Thomson said, "Either there is amplification or there is something wrong. I haven't heard a cello or a double bass yet."[85] The editors of Time summed up the situation in a telegraphic assessment:

Diffusion of sound so unbalanced that best vantage point is, ironically, cheapest seat in top balcony. New York Philharmonic musicians complain they cannot hear each other on-

stage, say hall is glorified $17.7 million pinball machine. Mood of pessimism pervades. Rumors circulate that visiting orchestras are going to boycott splenderous blue-and-gold hall in favor of mellow surroundings of Carnegie Hall. Soloists panic, talk of canceling performances.[86]

Winthrop Sargeant, the music critic for the New Yorker, was said to be so confused by the hall's acoustical effects that he could not clearly evaluate a given performance.[87] Two months after the building's opening, Time magazine noted that music critics had reported the hall's sound alternately as "confused, honest, unbalanced, weak, loud, intimate, percussive, dry, mushy, uncolored and artificial." The article continued: "The two faults most frequently noted at Philharmonic Hall are the swallowed bass notes and the bright, unorchestrated sounds of the violins and high woodwinds. Cellos, basses and harpsichords have gone unheard, and in soft passages, pianists sometimes sound as if they had no left hand."[88] Responding to such criticism, Beranek said: "I predicted in the beginning that it would take a year to get the hall into its ultimate condition, and I stick to that. We have to work very slowly and cautiously."[89]

After Beranek's initial response, Lincoln Center officials remained silent on the subject until April 1963, when president William Schuman announced that a $300,000 improvement program would be implemented in the auditorium. As outlined by a panel consisting of the German acoustician Heinrich Keilholz and Americans Manfred Schroeder, Vern Knudsen and Paul Veneklasen, the plan called for installing plastic slats to connect the individual sound reflectors that formed the acoustical "clouds" above the stage, enclosing the walls surrounding the stage with sound-reflecting surfaces, and simplifying the rather intricate series of vertical setbacks in the walls near the stage. "If we have learned anything from all of this," Abramovitz ruefully commented, "it is that acoustics is still an inexact science. . . . The original design of Philharmonic Hall was flexible enough to allow for changes, and now we are making them. If someone comes along five years from now with good ideas for further improvement, we will be able to use them, too."[90] But even after the alterations were made, the acoustics remained inferior. As conductor George Szell put it: "Imagine a woman, lame, a hunchback, cross-eyed and with two warts. They've removed the warts."[91] In 1964 and 1965 further changes were instituted by Keilholz, including the installation of new wood-backed seats that, although they resembled "those in cheap movie houses," according to Time, at least contributed to making the hall's acoustics bearable, if not ideal.[92]

When the building had opened, George Szell had cried, "Tear it down and start over!"[93] In 1972 a $10 million gift from Avery Fisher, the pioneering hi-fi equipment manufacturer, made it possible for Lincoln Center to do just that with its ill-fated concert hall. The auditorium was completely gutted and rebuilt in 1975–76 according to plans devised by Philip Johnson and John Burgee and the acoustician and Columbia professor Cyril M. Harris. The redesigned auditorium, renamed Avery Fisher Hall, was transformed from a bottle-shaped room to a rectangular one, with a gold-leaf-covered proscenium arch framing a stage and orchestra shell finished with English oak. A raised floor brought the musicians in closer contact with audience members, including those seated in the balconies. From the balconies hung rows of spherical lights; suspended from the ceiling was a flexible screen composed of hexagonal, gold-colored panels, each of which contained centrally located crystalline light fixtures.

Describing his collaboration with Harris, Johnson explained: "We are both fond of classic shapes and traditional ma-

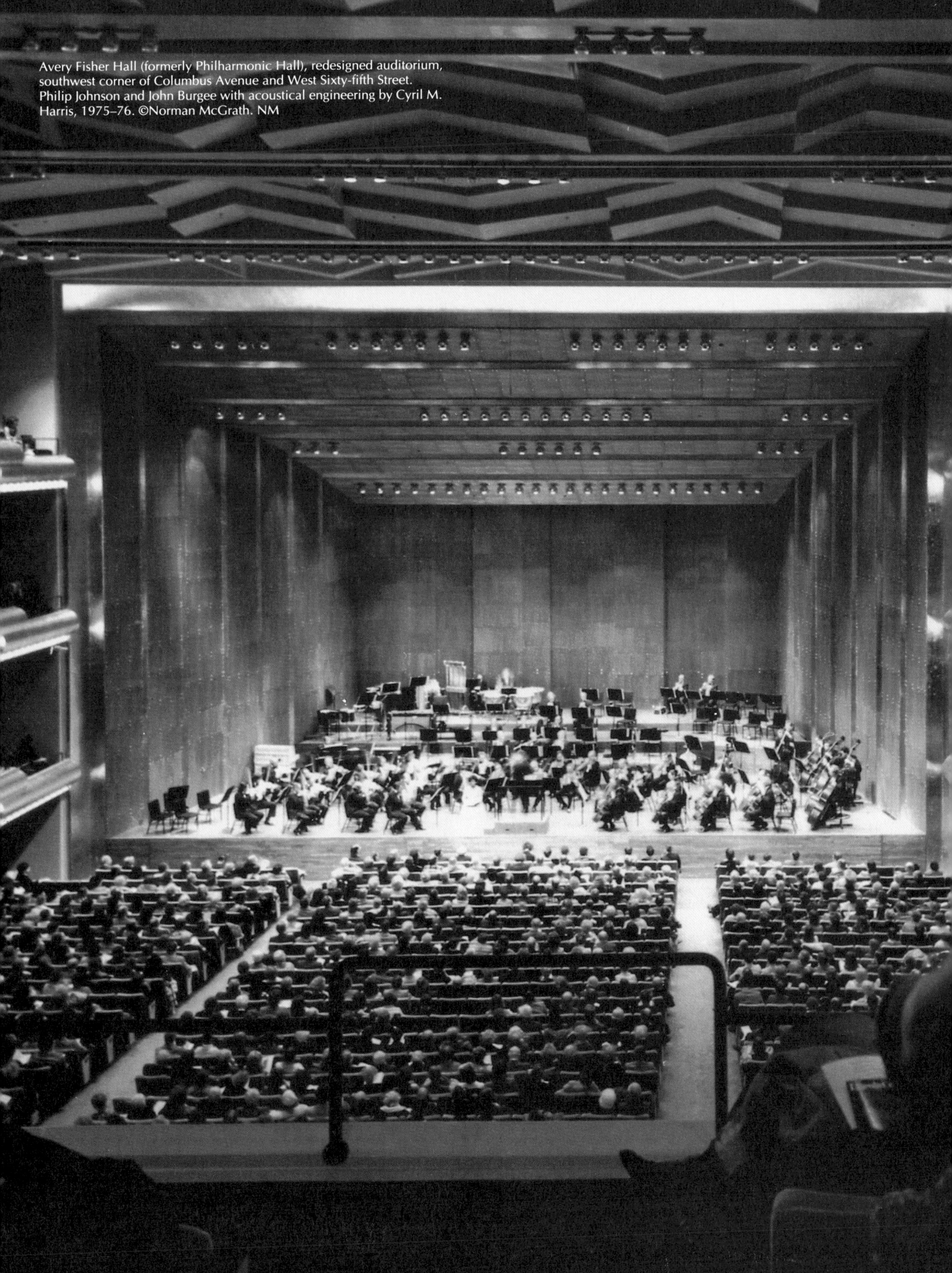

Avery Fisher Hall (formerly Philharmonic Hall), redesigned auditorium, southwest corner of Columbus Avenue and West Sixty-fifth Street. Philip Johnson and John Burgee with acoustical engineering by Cyril M. Harris, 1975–76. ©Norman McGrath. NM

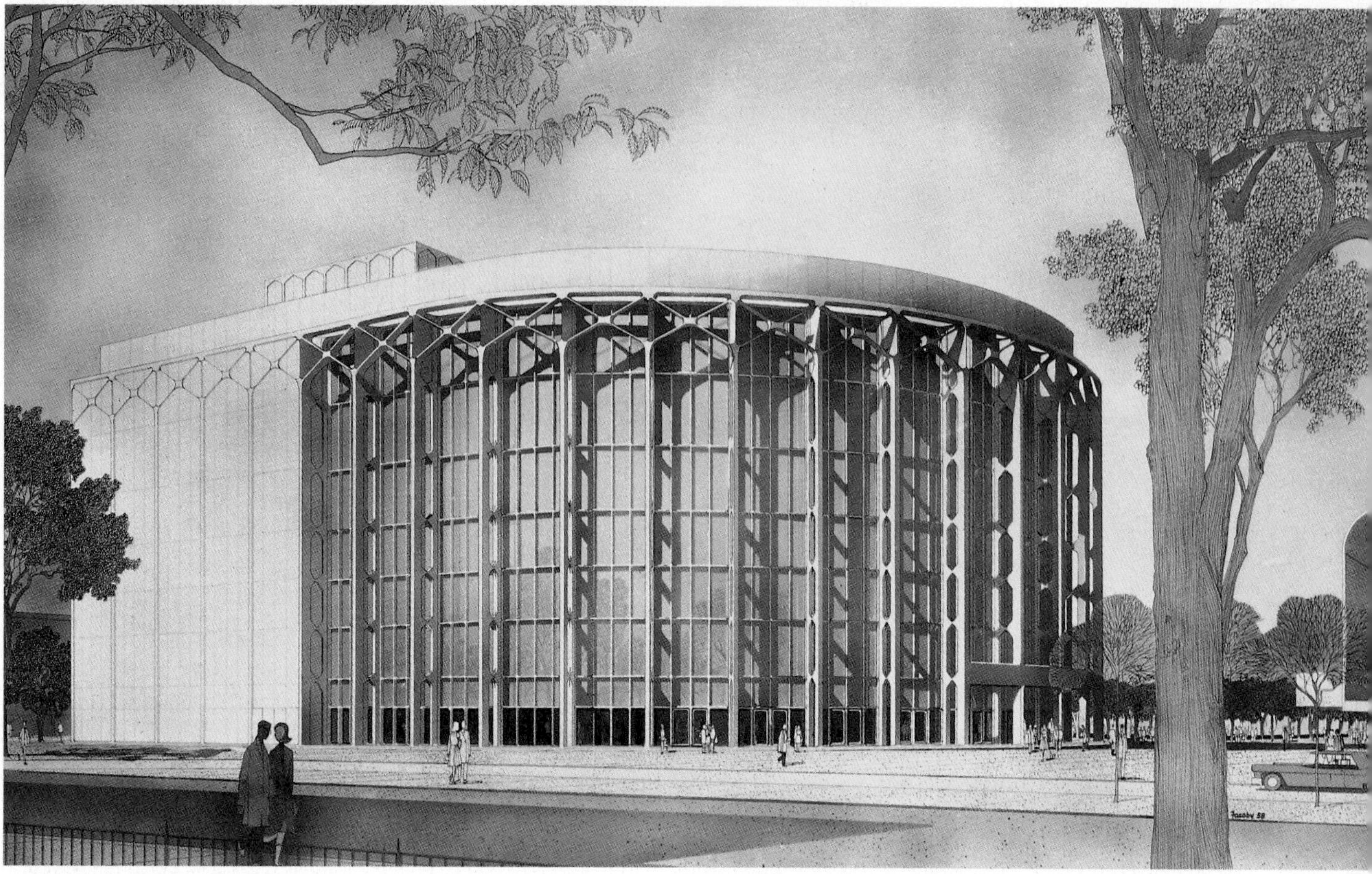

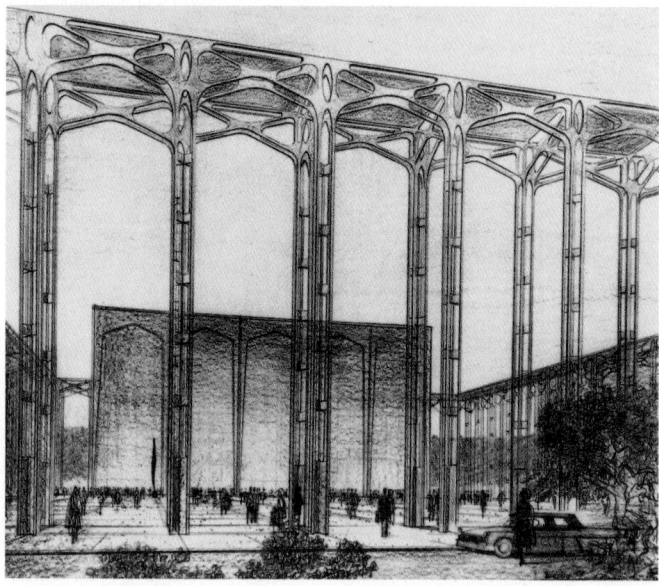

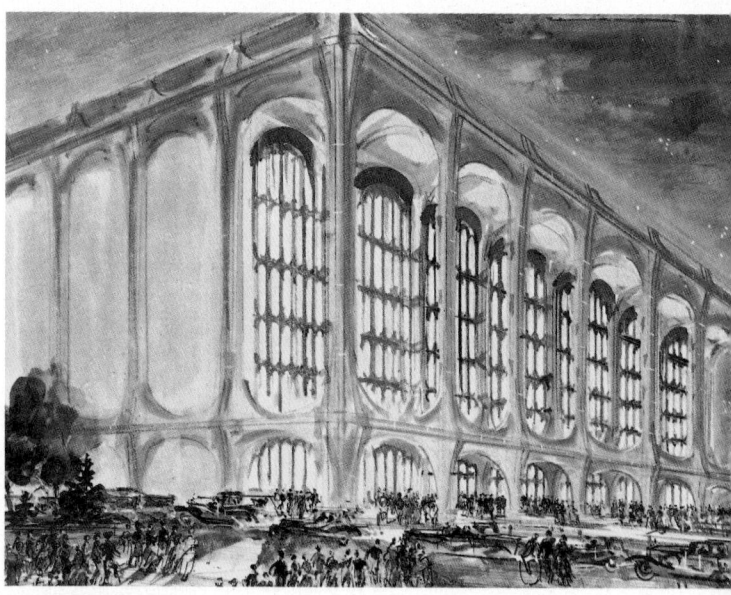

Top: New York State Theater, northwest corner of
Columbus Avenue and West Sixty-second Street. Philip
Johnson, 1958. Rendering by Jacoby showing view to the
southwest. Merit. ALC

Bottom left: Proposal for arcade to enclose the main plaza at Lincoln
Center, west side of Columbus Avenue, West Sixty-third to West Sixty-
fourth Street. Philip Johnson, 1958. View to the west. PJA

Bottom right: Proposal for New York State Theater. Philip Johnson,
1960. Rendering by J. Tagos of view to the southwest. ALC

terials, and are not afraid to admit it. And then, we get along well because Cyril understands everything I say about architecture, and I don't understand a word of what he says about acoustics."[94] The redesigned hall was praised as both an architectural and an acoustical success. The critic Hubert Saal, writing in *Newsweek* about the opening night, said: "Not only the music sounded better. . . . So did the applause."[95] Harris was pleased with his redesign, clearly a massive improvement, and commented: "I think my greatest pleasure comes from hearing the musicians say that they don't have to bow or blow so hard—that I've added ten or twenty years to their careers."[96]

New York State Theater

The second building to be completed at Lincoln Center, and the only one to be built within budget, was the New York State Theater, designed by Philip Johnson, with Walter Unruh serving as stage design consultant.[97] The initial plans for the theater, released early in 1959, called for a semicircular building, with a sweeping glass facade framed by a colonnade of girderlike, precast-concrete double columns. The columns were to continue as a blind arcade surrounding the back walls of the stage house. The architectural historian Vincent Scully said that this early design evoked "the revolutionary projects of Ledoux and Boullée" but also possessed "the taut, stretched, and rather nervous quality . . . characteristic of American work of the pre-Richardsonian period." Scully drew attention to "the conscious historicism of Johnson's method, seeking as it does to reverse the clearly outworn process of spatial continuity and to recapture the clarity of the first architectural intuitions of the modern age."[98] The design was rejected by the Lincoln Center design team not only because it compromised the symmetry of the entire ensemble and upstaged the opera house, but also because the decision had been made that the central plaza should be consistently bordered by rectilinear facades. Johnson then proposed a delicate arcade of tall slender columns to enclose the plaza, connecting the dance theater and Abramovitz's concert hall as well as forming the principal facade of both; later Johnson recalled that this hyperattenuated colonnade was inspired by his interest in precast concrete. The architectural historian William Jordy noted that if this proposal had been realized, "the theaters would have been visually subordinated to the outdoor room formed by the all-embracing portico."[99]

An alternate design for the New York State Theater was publicly released on June 26, 1961; this was the scheme that was eventually realized, with the building officially opening on April 23, 1964. Although it conformed to the dimensions of Philharmonic Hall, which it faced across the main plaza, the dance theater more openly paid homage to the Classical tradition. The principal facade of the travertine-clad concrete theater was divided into seven bays by four pairs of multifaceted columns. It confronted the plaza with a low arcade surmounted by an open-air promenade punctuated by hanging vertical clusters of faceted light fixtures. The critic C. Ray Smith described these as "looking like inverted 'sparkler' fireworks,"[100] the editors of *Time* called them "Cyclopean rhinestones,"[101] and the music critic Winthrop Sargeant said they were "about as functional as a Christmas tree, which—in case you haven't thought about it—is very functional indeed, since a Christmas tree lifts the human spirit and remains an unconscious symbol of rejoicing in many a psyche."[102] The theater's side and rear facades were virtually windowless and were punctuated only by minimally detailed pilasters and small clusters of lights like those on the principal facade's balcony.

John Morris Dixon, an editor at *Progressive Architecture*, praised Johnson's use of materials as well as his use of a Classical vocabulary: "Approaching the theater across the plaza, one gets the impression of a building of great strength and assurance. The colonnade is monumental but not overbearing—a design that is symbolically appropriate to the materials used."[103] But Ilse M. Reese, one of Dixon's co-editors, was not so impressed, charging that the design came "dangerously close to the pretentious Italian monumentality of the Mussolini era."[104] James T. Burns, in the same *Progressive Architecture* article, said that "the huge Pop Art chandeliers he hung in the colonnade seem to be Johnson arching a cynical eyebrow at the whole pretentious undertaking."[105]

In discussing his design for the theater's facades, Johnson revealed some of his sources and motivations: "I admit, as some critics have suggested, that the paired columns on my theater come from Perrault's facade at the back of the Louvre. I wanted to reduce the nine bays on the front of the Philharmonic Hall opposite, to three enormous bays divided by four double-clustered columns, all for the sake of clarity. I do not really object to the nine bays but I wanted my entrance to be so obvious—one door going only one way. The contrast with Philharmonic Hall is obvious."[106] Johnson would later admit to being disappointed in his own design: "*I* know that the outside of my theater is no good, but . . . what I had to do was to follow the 20-foot rhythm of [Philharmonic Hall], and by then I didn't *want* to follow a 20-foot rhythm. We'd all agreed years before to stick to it, and . . . since I had to follow the others, I made my baroque temple, or whatever it is. . . . I don't think it's a successful adaptation of the classical motif."[107]

Inside the building, Johnson presented a carefully orchestrated series of spaces. The low-ceilinged lobby was flanked at either end by staircases that were, as Forrest Wilson wrote in *Interiors*, "beautifully sculptural and sensitively detailed."[108] Johnson decorated the theater with works by the contemporary artists Edward Higgins, Jacques Lipchitz, Reuben Nakian and Francesco Soumaini; Lee Bontecou and Jasper Johns also contributed pieces that were specially created for the space. Johnson, who at around the same time had commissioned artworks for his New York State Pavilion at the World's Fair (see chapter 14), noted: "Commissioning decorative works of art for monumental buildings is dangerous in any age. In ours it is well nigh impossible. Artists are interested in their own expression, not in helping out mine. I in turn am more interested in space modulation than in wall decoration. Sometimes we can get together in spite of the difficulties. The New York State Theater was such a time."[109] The Bontecou work, an imposing, symmetrically composed abstract wall relief titled *1964*, was housed in the lobby's eastern stairwell; the Johns piece, a low-relief sculpture titled *Numbers*, was contained in the western stairwell.

The historian Henry-Russell Hitchcock observed that the commissioned works were formally installed, "almost as a nineteenth-century academic architect might have done, symmetrically on the stair landings."[110] The art critic John Canaday offered strong praise of Bontecou's work and its relationship to the surrounding space, despite what at first seemed to be a clash of visual idioms: "Word that Miss Bontecou had been commissioned for one of her highly individual constructions . . . gave a shaky feeling that in a theater devoted to ballet and operetta her contribution might look like a bit of exposed plumbing. But . . . she has risen above every connotative hazard to produce a vigorous and superbly balanced design perfectly adapted to the allotted space."[111] Johnson was also pleased with her work: "Her piece fits as well as a baroque statue in the niche of a baroque hall. The stair hall is a better stair hall for her efforts." The architect felt differently about Johns's piece: "Jasper Johns, certainly one of the geniuses of American painting, took the opposite path. His *Numbers* is one of his most sensitive pieces [but] it cannot 'carry' the stair hall."[112]

From the dark compression of the ground-floor lobby, the stairs led up to the light-flooded spaciousness of the unabashedly theatrical Grand Promenade, a 50-foot-high, 60-by-200-foot room capped by a gold-leafed ceiling that Johnson claimed was "the biggest gold-leaf job in the world."[113] More than an entr'acte gathering place, the promenade was designed to serve as a room for official receptions, a "parlor" for the state, to use Governor Rockefeller's term. The room could accommodate 600 diners and was augmented by extensive kitchen facilities. According to Russell Lynes, the idea of such a grand room arose when, during the first discussions of the new theater, Governor Rockefeller argued that the building should be more than just a theater and diverted funds from the temporary New York State Pavilion at the 1964 World's Fair to this permanent representation of the body politic.[114]

The entire room was ringed with three tiers of balconies enclosed by bronze railings, some of which incorporated faceted light fixtures and decorative gold-mesh panels in a pattern that Lincoln Kirstein said was "borrowed from Jackson Pollock's splashes."[115] As they passed the auditorium's rear wall, the balconies bowed out into the center space in a sweeping convex curve. The three walls of glass were hung with gold-anodized ball-link chain "curtains," evocative of those Marie Nichols had designed for the Four Seasons restaurant. Glass doors provided access to the building's plaza-fronting exterior balcony. Strips of red Rosso Merlino marble formed a grid pattern in the room's travertine floor, providing a visual warmth that contrasted with the cool effect of the room's ivory and gold tones.

Nineteen-foot-high, twelve-ton Carrara marble sculptures of paired female figures, adapted from small-scale papier-mâché originals designed by the Polish-born sculptor Elie Nadelman, graced each end of the room. As Lincoln Kirstein would later recall, the figures, "in their glowing metaphorical nudity," were immediately the focus of controversy for "a small but influential group in the Lincoln Center management, at a time when ultimate control of the theater was still in doubt." However, he said, "the large hole in the building's exterior wall, which alone was wide enough to admit them to a floor above the street, had been sealed on schedule, and the figures were safe."[116] Henry-Russell Hitchcock complained that the sculptures had perhaps been copied "not too happily";[117] Forrest Wilson also questioned the success of the translation but nonetheless deemed the results "a tribute to Nadelman's sculptural skill, and the talents of the Italian carvers."[118] Kirstein later explained that although there was criticism of the decision to enlarge in marble Nadelman's four-foot-high papier-mâché originals, "his own heroic figures in stone and bronze gave every indication that he was projecting an heroic scale, and was only deprived by circumstance."[119] Winthrop Sargeant, who thought the two sculptures looked as if they had been modeled in yogurt, was not sure they were great sculpture, "but they are at least very good substitutes for it, having substantial mass and weight, and reminding one that one is in a place where human beings are still important, namely a theater."[120] Canaday characterized the Nadelman sculptures as "the most satisfying ornaments serving a comparable function since Carpeaux's sculptures on the facade of the Paris Opéra nearly 100 years ago," and went on to explain:

These paired female figures have a combination of high style, sly levity and swelling monumentality that unifies them with the scale and elegance of the architecture and, at the same time, involves them in a kind of amorous badinage with its angularities. In this perfect marriage between sculpture and architecture, either would miss the other in a separation. But the sculpture is the dependent partner. As pure sculpture, these superb confections are not much more than deft and devilishly clever, but as architectural adjuncts they are brought to fulfillment.[121]

At once elegant and playful, the Grand Promenade was particularly distinctive because it cut to the heart of the self-imposed austerity of the prevailing architectural minimalism. "It is somewhat shameful to note," said Hitchcock, "that this is the handsomest, if not the largest, architectural 'room' created in New York since the concourse of the Grand Central Station by Reed & Stem and Warren & Wetmore of a half-century earlier."[122] The editors of *Time* called the room "the perfect place in which to pop a champagne cork."[123] Ada Louise Huxtable was moved to put aside her normally puritanical attitude toward architectural decoration and fully embrace the Grand Promenade's design:

This spectacular [room] promises to be one of the most impressive public spaces New York has ever seen and it may become the theater's star attraction. . . . Like the rest of the theater, the Promenade is sumptuous, elegant, sophisticated and seriously beautiful. And it is the key to the architecture. This is a design concept that doesn't give a hoot about structure, except to make things more sumptuous, elegant, sophisticated and seriously beautiful. . . . Architecture is a structural art, and its most sacrosanct objective, according to its philosophers, is to express structure visually and aesthetically. The building doesn't do that, and the architect doesn't care. He has used structure only to create splendid social areas and theatrical interior magic.[124]

Other observers were much less enthusiastic. Virgil Thomson thought the Grand Promenade looked like "a jail courtyard";[125] the dance and theater critic Clive Barnes echoed this idea when he said that the room had "a hint of the cold-steel, machine-gun-scrutinized terraces of Alcatraz."[126] A similar sentiment was voiced by the theater designer George Izenour, who said that the room's "cold megalomania" was "more in keeping with the Galleria between the main cell blocks at Sing Sing prison than a public space intended for New York's 'volks opera.'"[127] C. Ray Smith pointed out that such comparisons were not unjustified, since Johnson himself said that he had adapted the room's spatial arrangement from a jail he had seen and liked.[128] John Morris Dixon had other complaints about the room, particularly its detailing. "At the top of the stairs," he said, "comes the first big let-down. At this point, it seems, Johnson ran out of both steam and travertine. In this whole vast room, nothing above the red marble and travertine floor sustains the character established in the exterior and lobby. All is subdued tinsel and blunted glitter. The balconies that encompass the space look downright flimsy."[129] James T. Burns was equally critical: "This dichotomy of strong against weak, travertine against candy box frou-frou, is where Johnson's attempt to *épater les bourgeois* backfires. Had he carried it to the ultimate in one direction, the theater could have been a successful jab at a never-never-land bit of fluff; emphasized strongly in an opposite view, it might have achieved a significant monumentality. As it is, it falls between stools and becomes neither one nor the other."[130]

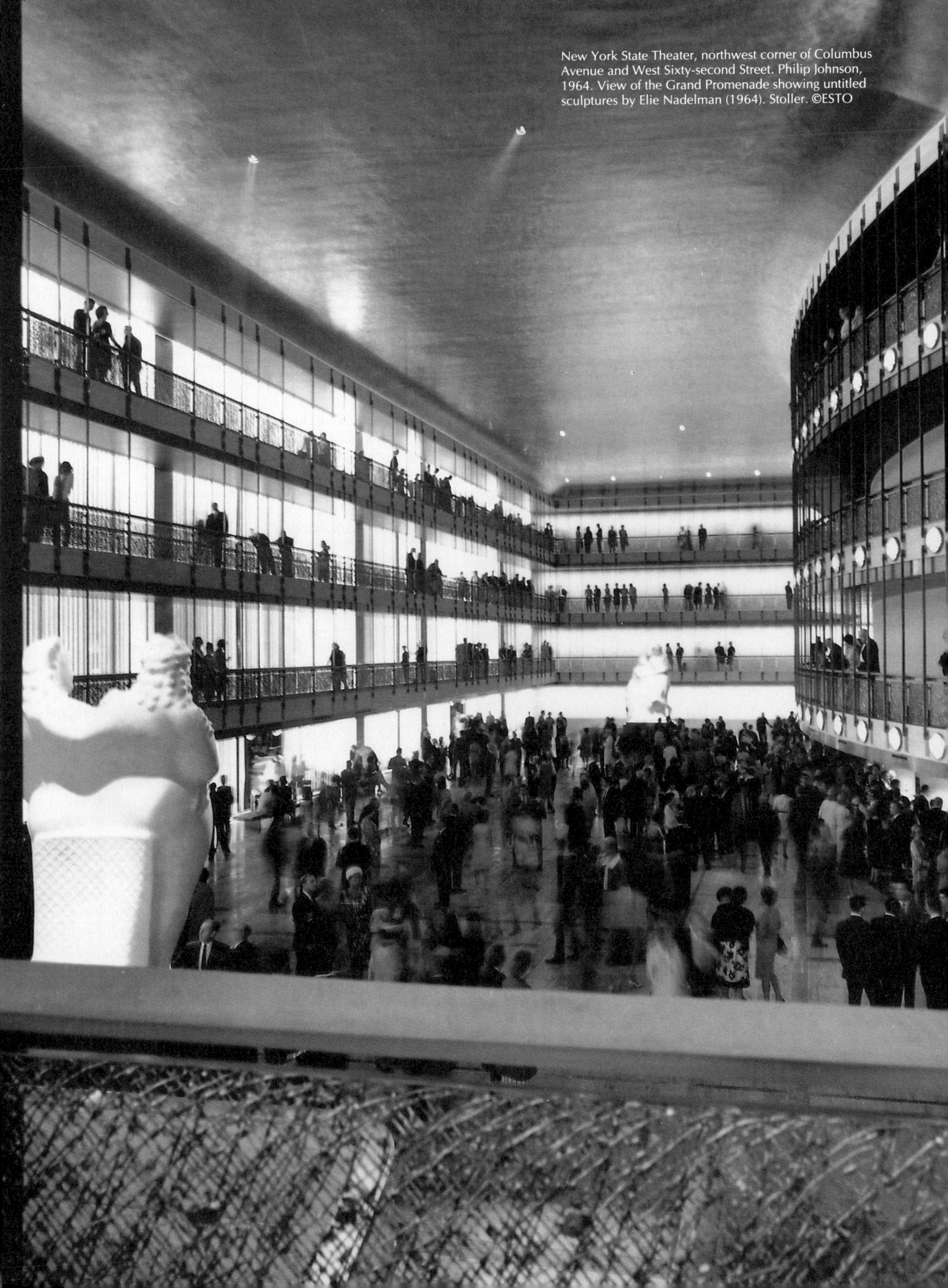

New York State Theater, northwest corner of Columbus Avenue and West Sixty-second Street. Philip Johnson, 1964. View of the Grand Promenade showing untitled sculptures by Elie Nadelman (1964). Stoller. ©ESTO

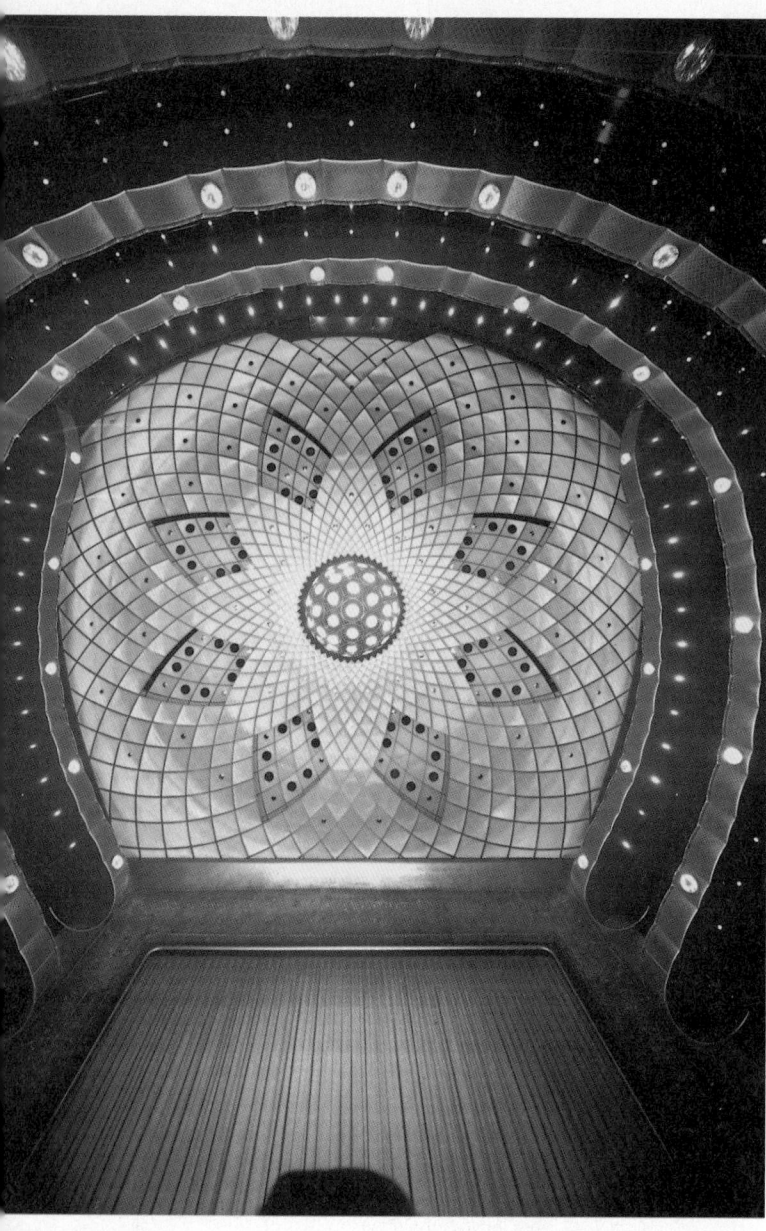

New York State Theater, northwest corner of Columbus Avenue and West Sixty-second Street. Philip Johnson, 1964. Auditorium. Stoller. ©ESTO

Despite the controversy over the flamboyant Grand Promenade, the ultimate value of the theater as a whole rested squarely on its principal room, the auditorium. According to the dancer and Balanchine biographer Moira Shearer, Johnson designed the auditorium's proscenium stage to meet the choreographer's specifications. Lincoln Kirstein saw the theater as an unqualified success, at least from a technical point of view, with a high proscenium arch and a springy stage floor of Balanchine's own invention that made it "the best theater for dance in the world." As Kirstein noted, however, the theater did have a major flaw. Because of the ease of construction, he said, Balanchine ignored a vital factor: "The orchestra pit, planned by Lincoln Center's computation, was to hold but thirty-five men, normal complement for Broadway musicals. If ballet failed, *Showboat* or *Oklahoma!* could pick up the tab." When he discovered the inadequacy of the pit for dance concerts, Balanchine's response was one of "astonished wrath," leading to a redesign.[131] In Kirstein's estimation, however, the sixty-five people who could be accommodated after Balanchine's alterations was still insufficient.

The auditorium adopted a traditional "court theater" design, utilizing a broad horseshoe plan with five tiers of shallow balconies carried around the side walls to meet the proscenium arch. Once again stressing the social aspect of theatergoing, Johnson noted: "In this room where everyone can see everyone, the walls will be animated by people in the side balconies."[132] Explaining the advantage of such an arrangement, Johnson said:

> If you sit somewhere in the back, you do see the stage, but around you, crowding around the proscenium, are people; the walls are paved, covered, wallpapered with people. . . . Your angle of vision from the rear includes much more than the proscenium; it takes in a lot of the side wall. And people sitting up there sometimes can't see well . . . but at least you say, "I'm in the midst of a wonderful place where something is going on." You get a sense of participation.[133]

The auditorium accommodated 2,801 people and was distinguished by an unusual seating arrangement: the rows of seats were spaced four feet apart, so that the generous intervals between them could serve as aisles; running the full width of the room without the interruption of a traditional center aisle, the rows were accessible through ten side entrances. This "continental" seating arrangement, rare in the United States but popular in Europe, had several advantages over more conventional plans: the best floor space was used exclusively for seating; significantly more leg room was provided than in most theaters, yet no seat was more than 140 feet from the stage; overcrowding in the aisles was minimized; and, according to Johnson, the room could be emptied in two minutes.[134] Johnson also felt that continental seating would "look more elegant."[135]

The critical response to the auditorium was mixed. The journalist Barbara B. Jamison reported in the *New York Times* that some theatergoers were not pleased with the seating arrangement. "Once seated I felt trapped," said one audience member. "And heaven help you if you're a few minutes late and have a center seat," said another.[136] James T. Burns objected to the plan on more intellectual grounds: "The concept of a large scale 'court-theater' for the democratic crowds that will throng here to see Rodgers and Hammerstein and the New York City Ballet is dubious at best. The attempt to force a square crowd into a round hole is unjustified, to my mind."[137] George Izenour also questioned the relationship of the theater's design to its intended audience and purpose. Izenour charged that Johnson seemed "somehow to have gotten the idea that his client was some hereditary Grand Duke of New York State instead of being its sovereign people. . . . The pity of it all is that someone of vision and authority with the power to act and, above all, gifted with a sense of modern theater design history did not sense the inappropriateness of this design."[138]

The decoration of the auditorium furthered the opulent tone established in the Grand Promenade. Gold leaf was used for the fifty-one-foot-high proscenium arch, as well as the ribbed surfaces of the balconies' gently scalloped parapets, which were further articulated with the same faceted lights used elsewhere in the building; gold leaf also embellished a sixteen-light cluster that served as the room's chandelier and the focal point of the decoratively gridded ceiling. The walls were dark red, as were the upholstered seats. Huxtable was as impressed with the auditorium as she had been with the promenade: "Every detail is classic theater in its function, freshly devised in its design. There is no false note, no wrong texture, no misstep in the complex relationship of surfaces and shapes. The key word is finesse." She even approved of the light fixtures, which others had dubbed "automobile headlights" but which she thought were "more like giant French paste brilliants, a contemporary version of traditional glitter."[139] Dixon, however, said that the lights lacked "the refractive effect associated with glitter, having only the oily transparency of aging plastic."[140] Forrest Wilson, noting that the lights had "elicited some harsh criticism," defended Johnson by noting that he had originally intended to employ cullet in the lenses, "an ingenious concept, thwarted because the instability of such glass renders it liable to unpredictable shattering."[141] Dixon felt that there was an essential gap between the concept and the execution of the auditorium design: "The choice of materials seems so wrong in some cases as to appear deliberate. . . . The ceiling, the chandelier, the proscenium, and the balcony fronts—all of the salient features of the space—are obviously related to the traditional opera house: specifically, the old Metropolitan Opera House. But is this homage or parody?"[142]

Speaking collectively of the theater's interiors, Dixon said, "We have here . . . a series of useful ceremonial spaces to rejoice about, decked out (above the promenade floor) in motel materials that are, after all, as nonessential as they look. Maybe this is what Johnson is telling us, but he hasn't made it a pretty story."[143] Perhaps some of the negative response to the interiors was due to the fact that such frankly decorative work had been created by Johnson, who had previously pursued the highly reductivist International Style with vigor and commitment. Ilse Reese, for example, was "surprised to see the distinguished collaborator of Mies van der Rohe, the advocate of understatement, simplicity, and purity in architecture, going so far in this building to cheapen his architecture with an overabundance of gilding in an obvious attempt to dazzle the audience."[144] But the critics' concern for the overall "look" and meaning of an architect's entire oeuvre contrasted strongly with the general public's lack of interest in such issues, a difference that was clearly reflected in the varied public and professional responses. As Olga Gueft explained, although the building received "applause" from the patrons and artists who expected "space, facilities, emotional stimulation, and identification with the traditions of the arts they serve . . . the reaction of the scholar-journalists who pronounce the profession's recorded judgement is more ambivalent." Johnson, she said, was "now accused of the heinous sin of abandoning his Miesian apprenticeship. Johnson's defection to romanticism is more annoying than Edward Stone's. In abandoning the Miesian faith, Stone, like a convert, proclaimed

that he had seen the new, the true light. But Johnson hints only that 'the Bauhaus is the tradition against which our generation had to revolt,' and reminds his critics of Emerson's evaluation of consistency—'the hobgoblin of little minds.'" In her own assessment, Gueft celebrated the inconsistency of the New York State Theater's design: "The exterior is neo-classic, massive, with beautifully spaced sets of pillars. Inside, a huge promenade is threaded by gold-laced balconies whose fine bronze uprights complete the pattern of the rouge marble plaiding on the travertine floor. And the auditorium is magnificent, baroque, a bit vulgar? Inconsistent! So what? . . . Johnson points out that our century has 'no decorative vocabulary, and no craftsmen.' *De gustibus disputamus*."[145]

What rendered Johnson's design ultimately satisfying was the architect's understanding that a successful theater design establishes a setting in which the act of theatergoing is exalted, in which the movement of the audience is as carefully choreographed as that of the dancers onstage; the patrons are thus elevated to the status of performers in a grand and entertaining ritual. "Architect Philip Johnson," the editors of *Time* noted, "fully shared Balanchine's notion of what a ballet theater's mood should be: he designed the building to make everyone in it feel formally dressed whether he is or not."[146] Even Dixon, who had offered sharp criticism of the building, said: "No matter what one may think of the visible surfaces of the interior, little fault can be found with the spatial organization of the building. All of the spaces promise to serve their complex functions very well, and all of them—considered solely as spaces—are handsome. . . . The interrelationship of these major spaces—lobby to promenade, promenade to balconies (both inside and outside the auditorium)—is ingenious and highly effective."[147] Johnson himself explained: "The New York State Theater, whatever stand one takes on its art works or decorative features, whatever one's views of Neo-classicism vs. concrete, is designed as a procession. The pop up the 'baroque' stair into the Mississippi-steamboat Promenade is of the essence. So are the side stairs up to and down from the upper balconies. So are the silhouetted moving people who form the living friezes to the space. This is all a question of procession."[148]

Vivian Beaumont Theater and Lincoln Center Performing Arts Library and Museum

The third building to be completed at Lincoln Center was in fact two buildings, one wrapped around the other, located in the northwest corner of the complex's superblock site.[149] Completed in 1965, these were the Vivian Beaumont Theater, designed by Eero Saarinen & Associates and the theater designer Jo Mielziner, and, surrounding it on the south and west sides as well as slipping over its top, the Lincoln Center Performing Arts Library and Museum, designed by Gordon Bunshaft of Skidmore, Owings & Merrill. Originally, two separate buildings had been proposed for the theater and for the library-museum, but after initial studies the two firms decided to combine their efforts in the design of a single building. Olga Gueft noted the rare element of voluntary cooperation on this project, particularly in light of the competitive spirit that had plagued the Lincoln Center enterprise as a whole. According to Gueft, Harrison, Abramovitz and Johnson "admitted that they could hardly resist the most overwhelming design temptation built into the Lincoln Center program: the temptation to compete with each other rather than to submerge their artistic egos

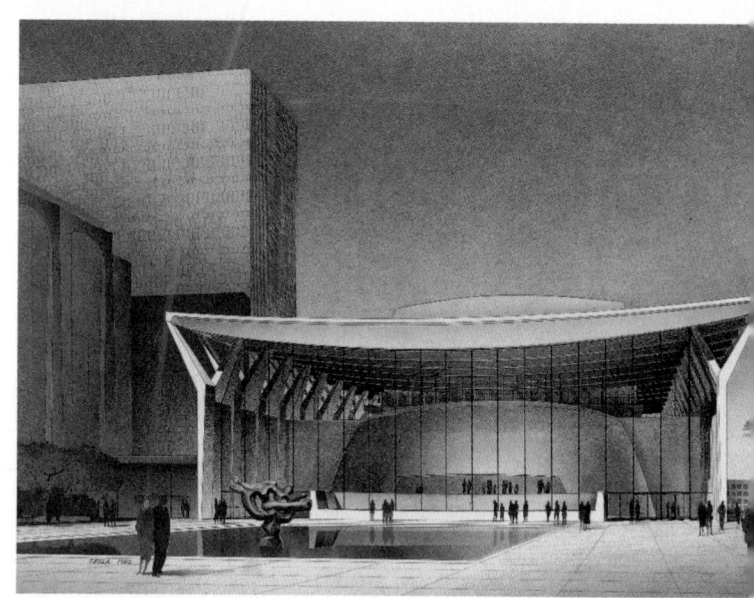

Right: Proposal for Vivian Beaumont Theater and Lincoln Center Performing Arts Library and Museum, Lincoln Center Plaza North to Amsterdam Avenue, south side of West Sixty-fifth Street. Skidmore, Owings & Merrill, Eero Saarinen and Jo Mielziner, 1965. Rendering by Tesla of view to the west. ALC

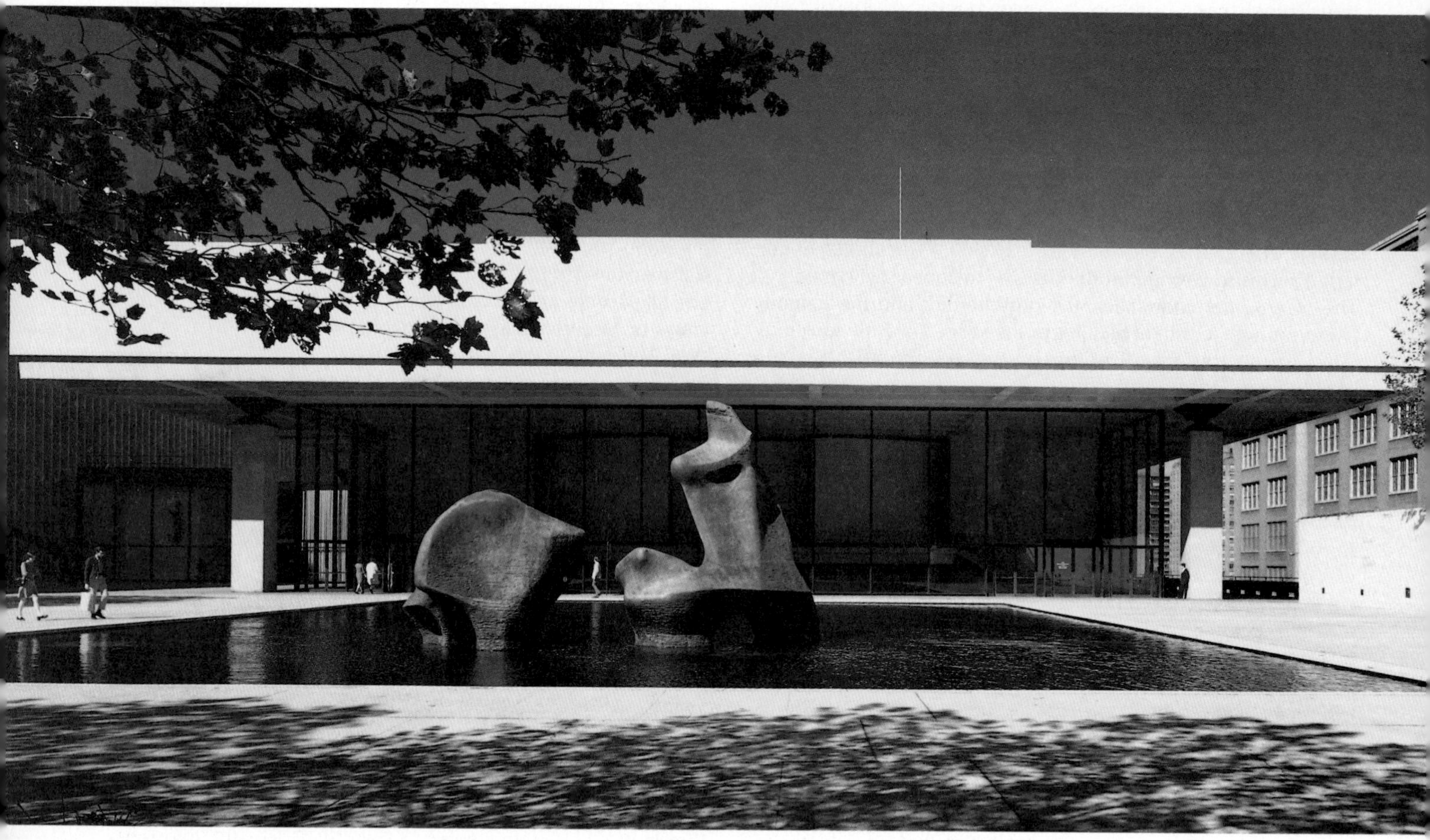

Below: Vivian Beaumont Theater and Lincoln Center Performing Arts Library and Museum. Skidmore, Owings & Merrill, Eero Saarinen and Jo Mielziner, 1965. View to the west showing Henry Moore's sculpture *Reclining Figure* (1965). Stoller. ©ESTO

in a presumably more desirable unity." In the case of Saarinen and Bunshaft, however, "the two firms decided not to go their separate ways, and that one building could house the two facilities better than two."[150] The firms entered into what C. Ray Smith called a "successful and seemingly selfless collaboration."[151] Saarinen wrote to his staff about the team effort: "This is the least likely marriage I have envisioned. But it might be very interesting. We can at least call it an affair."[152] The collaboration between Bunshaft and Saarinen, who died in 1961 at the age of fifty-one after working on the theater for three years, was surprisingly free of tension. There were, however, two bones of contention: the treatment of the theater's exterior corners, and the question of who would produce the project's lucrative working drawings. The two architects struck a bargain: Bunshaft agreed to sacrifice making the drawings when Saarinen gave up his three-column design in favor of Bunshaft's single-column scheme.

In contrast to a preliminary design of 1960, which called for a glazed principal facade surmounted by a gently concave roof hung between flanking arcades of Y-shaped piers, the final design presented an austere principal facade consisting of a bold, undecorated attic supported by two massive, exposed-aggregate-finish square columns that formed a peristyle surrounding the building's recessed glass walls. Enormous steel pins, sheathed in inverted pyramidal bronze covers, joined the columns to the attic. A deep, coffered, two-way structural grid was exposed inside and out. The scale of the facade was vast, far beyond that of its nearest neighbors.

The building fronted a large landscaped plaza, named Lincoln Center Plaza North, to be bounded on the south by the Metropolitan Opera House, on the east by Philharmonic Hall and, after 1969, on the north by a pedestrian bridge crossing Sixty-fifth Street and leading to the Juilliard School. On its southern edge, adjacent to the Metropolitan, the plaza incorporated rows of trees potted in travertine planters. Approaching from Broadway, across the great court, theatergoers came upon the smaller plaza, where, as Clive Barnes pointed out, "At dusk the trees are lit, campily but charmingly, and it is nice and human to walk through them. There are not many places in our city where you can walk among trees at night."[153] To the rear, the sloping site resulted in a far more brutal relationship to the pedestrian, the street and the neighborhood context.

The plaza was dominated by a 120-by-80-foot reflecting pool containing a monumental two-part bronze sculpture by Henry Moore, Reclining Figure, an abstracted sixteen-foot-high representation of a female figure; it was the largest work the sculptor ever created.[154] Like all of Moore's reclining figures, this one was inspired by pre-Columbian representations of the deity Chacmool. She appeared at once modern and ancient, brooding and contemplative, lounging in the reflecting pool, as Time put it, "mingling the domestic grace of a nude in her bath with the powerful, primitive presence of a goddess disturbed from sleep by Leonard Bernstein."[155] Although Moore preferred isolated, rural settings for his large-scale works, he was pleased with the Lincoln Center site; he liked the idea, he said, "of the space being surrounded by controlled building. . . . I didn't want my piece to stand there like a wooden soldier."[156] Apparently unaware that the sculpture was the first work erected on municipally owned land in New York that was not traditionally representational, Hilton Kramer said, "Though it was hardly daring or imaginative to invite Henry Moore to create a sculpture . . . the result was nonetheless a happy one, for this 'Reclining Figure' is one of the sculptor's major works."[157] Ada Louise Huxtable praised the north plaza group, particularly in light of what she

characterized as the retrograde nature of the building ensemble defining the main plaza: "Standing in front of the theater, with its strong, structural good looks and the fronting pool and Henry Moore sculpture, the visitor sees one of the few honestly contemporary vistas in the place. This is the sole moment [at Lincoln Center] that lifts the spirit of those to whom the twentieth century is a very exciting time to be alive and for whom the fleeting sensuality of lighting effects and matching travertine is not enough."[158]

Also contained in the plaza was a modern sculpture by Alexander Calder, placed near the entrance to the library-museum.[159] The blackened steel structure, twenty-two feet long and fourteen feet high, was made up of two sheets of steel intersecting at an obtuse angle, which connected in turn with four spindlelike forms to resemble a gigantic spider. Despite its animated quality, the sculpture was named Le Guichet, the French word for ticket window, because of an opening in one of its steel plates. The installation of Le Guichet, like that of Moore's sculpture, had required the approval of Park Commissioner Newbold Morris, since both would stand on municipally owned land and fall under the jurisdiction of his department. Morris disliked both works, and although he approved Moore's, he did not approve Le Guichet, explaining:

> My duty is to stick to certain standards which may be based in part upon my own taste, and to resist the use of park property for artistic experiments. Unlike private art collections, works cannot easily be removed or replaced once they are accepted by the City; many of these become outdated with the passing of time. Furthermore, we must select objects of art which will be most rewarding for the most people. . . . Whether this is art or not, it does not appeal to me for installation in a park area.[160]

To resolve the dilemma, Mayor Wagner ordered that both works be considered by the Municipal Art Commission, which, in June 1965, in a vote of 5 to 4, approved them. When the Moore sculpture was officially dedicated on September 21, 1965, Morris told Edgar Young, executive vice president of Lincoln Center, "I was wrong. It really is beautiful."[161] He did not, however, change his opinion of Le Guichet, although he entertained the possibility: "Maybe it will grow on me. If the Municipal Art Commission voted to accept the sculpture, I must be wrong. I'm a product—or maybe a prisoner—of the 19th century."[162] Hilton Kramer felt that the Calder was "first rate" but that it was "absurdly misplaced in relation to the Moore."[163]

The Vivian Beaumont Theater was named after its principal benefactor, whose father, E. J. Beaumont, had founded the May Company department store chain. Entering the theater at the plaza level, one could descend to a sunken lobby, which led directly to the principal level of the theater as well as to the underground parking garage, or ascend to an elevated gallery and the theater's loge. The two-level lobby, with its wall of glass, was austere to the point of bareness. So was the theater's auditorium, which was minimally decorated with wood paneling and red upholstery. But the Beaumont was notable for its physical adaptability and its technological innovations. Its 1,100 seats, with 770 in the orchestra and 330 in the loge, none more than sixty-five feet from the stage, were arranged in a sweeping semicircle set at a steep rake. The 10,000-square-foot stage, more than three times the size of the largest stage on Broadway, incorporated a forty-six-foot-diameter turntable encircled by an independently operated five-foot ring. Combining a traditional proscenium format with a small apron thrust, the stage had an expandable platform that could be transformed into a fully open apron thrust by lowering the first seven rows of seats into the

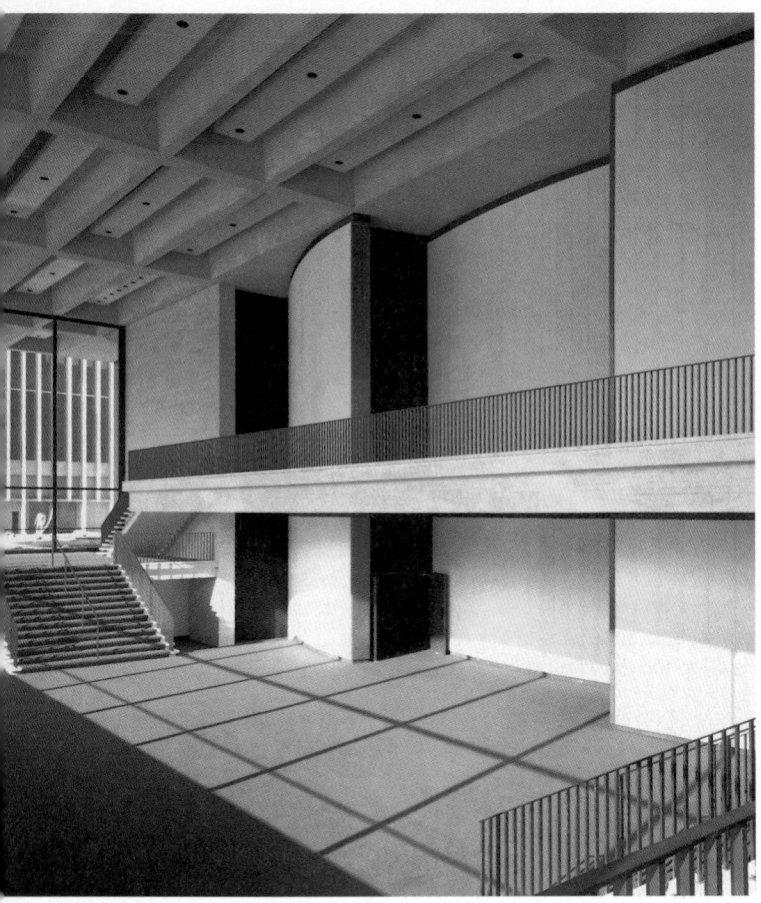

Above: Vivian Beaumont Theater, Lincoln Center Plaza North to Amsterdam Avenue, south side of West Sixty-fifth Street. Eero Saarinen and Jo Mielziner, 1965. Lobby. Stoller. ©ESTO

Top right: Lincoln Center Performing Arts Library and Museum, Lincoln Center Plaza North to Amsterdam Avenue, south side of West Sixty-fifth Street. Skidmore, Owings & Merrill, 1965. View to the northeast. Stoller. ©ESTO

Top far right: Lincoln Center Performing Arts Library and Museum. Circulation desk. Stoller. ©ESTO

Center far right: Lincoln Center Performing Arts Library and Museum. Reading room. Stoller. ©ESTO

Bottom right: Vivian Beaumont Theater and Lincoln Center Performing Arts Library and Museum, Lincoln Center Plaza North to Amsterdam Avenue, south side of West Sixty-fifth Street. Skidmore, Owings & Merrill, Eero Saarinen and Jo Mielziner, 1965. Section showing view to the north. SOM

basement. In this extreme form, the stage heightened the intimacy between actors and audience. Even the proscenium arch was flexible; it could be incrementally opened or closed by moving seven flexible panels. In order to establish clear sightlines when the deeply recessed proscenium stage was in use, the designers had modified the sweeping arc of seats so that the semicircle's ends were angled to more nearly approximate an egg-shaped plan.

Saarinen and Mielziner arrived at their final design only after rejecting fifteen preliminary plans over a three-year period. In order to test its viability, they built a full-scale mock-up of their scheme inside an abandoned movie theater in Pontiac, Michigan, on which Mielziner plotted out the stage sets of 150 plays he had previously designed.[164] Saarinen and Mielziner's theories were further tested in a temporary theater, opened in 1964 and housed within a prefabricated structure located on a site owned by New York University on West Fourth Street near Washington Square.[165] Despite a suggestion by the editors of *Progressive Architecture* that the university maintain the theater, it was torn down after the Lincoln Center project was completed.[166]

The Beaumont received rave reviews upon opening. The Hollywood film director and producer Otto Preminger described it as "the most beautiful theater,"[167] and the playwright Alan Jay Lerner called it "marvelous and effective."[168] C. Ray Smith stated unequivocally that the theater "and the building enclosing it are the finest designs at Lincoln Center."[169] The resident repertory company did not fare as well, floundering from the start and experiencing repeated personnel changes. Many people believed that the Beaumont's extensive facilities got in the way of creativity; some even complained that the theater was unworkable. The deep recess of the proscenium stage and the comparatively intimate scale of its peninsular extension proved difficult for actors to negotiate within a single production. In 1968 Clive Barnes said that the theater was "the least effective" one at Lincoln Center and that although aesthetically it was "a charmer," its technical aspects were "far less fortunate": "Under the artistic and technical advisement of Jo Mielziner— one of our more tedious if more respectable stage designers— the Beaumont falls short of excellence. The sight lines are not too good. . . . The dressing rooms are rather good, but technically the theater is no prize."[170]

In addition to its principal theater, the Beaumont contained a minimally decorated, 299-seat, amphitheater-type space, originally called the Forum and later the Mitzi Newhouse Playhouse. Also designed by Saarinen and Mielziner, this theater, which was for experimental productions, was accessible to the public only through the parking garage.

The library and museum were housed on the Beaumont Theater's roof in a rectangular doughnut-shaped space behind the windowless attic of the facade, with the doughnut's "hole" being filled by the Beaumont's stagehouse. The library-museum presented a plaza-level, two-story, glass-and-steel facade, adjacent to the Metropolitan Opera House's northern facade and rather awkwardly slipped beneath the Beaumont's monumental attic. A competent if undistinguished essay in International Style Modernism, the entrance facade was somewhat overwhelmed by its immediate context. The library-museum also extended behind the theater stagehouse, descending two floors to Amsterdam Avenue, where a second entrance was located.

Inside, Bunshaft's design presented a series of largely undistinguished if functional spaces. The most successful spaces were the plaza-level entrance area, which contained an eighty-foot-

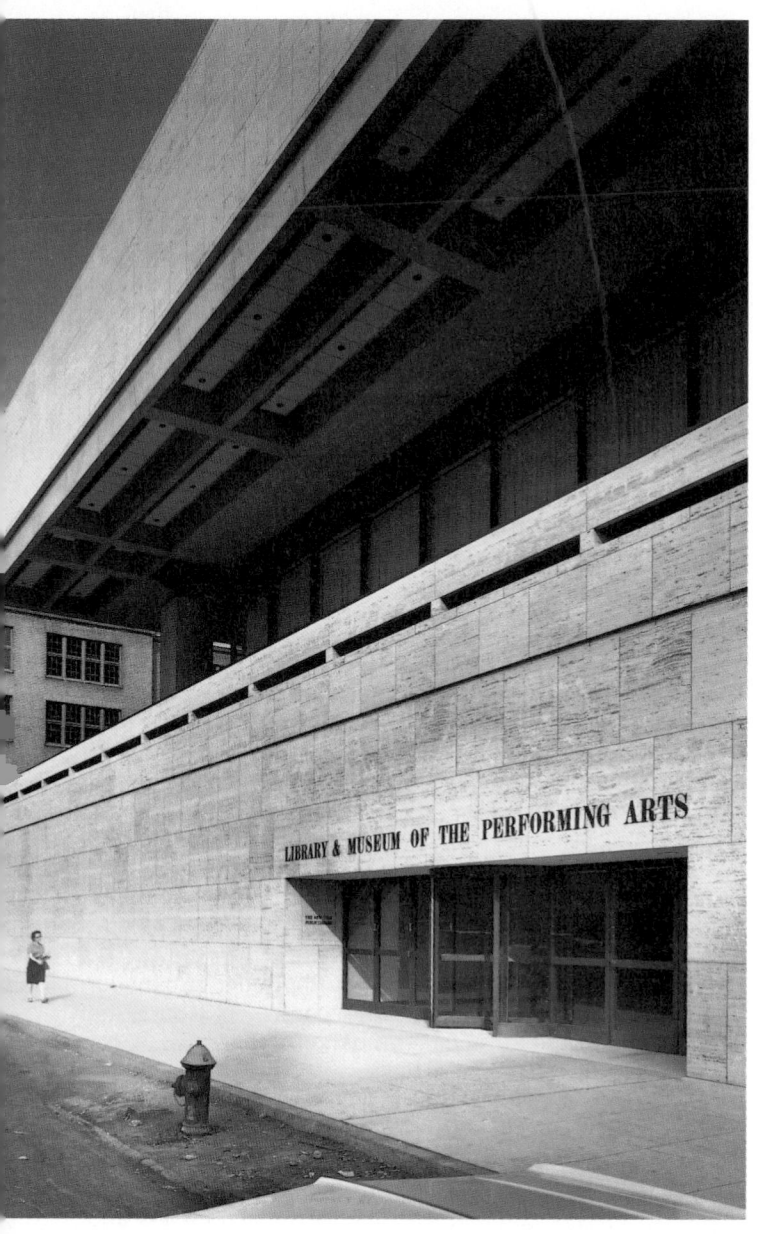

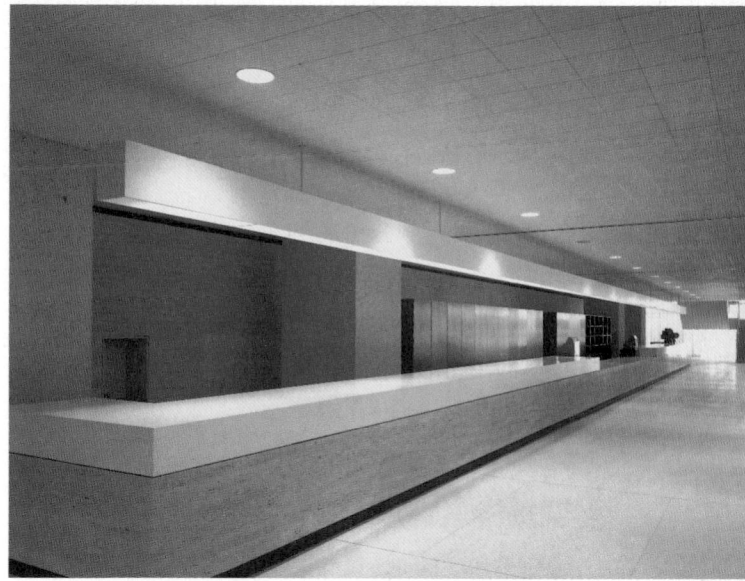

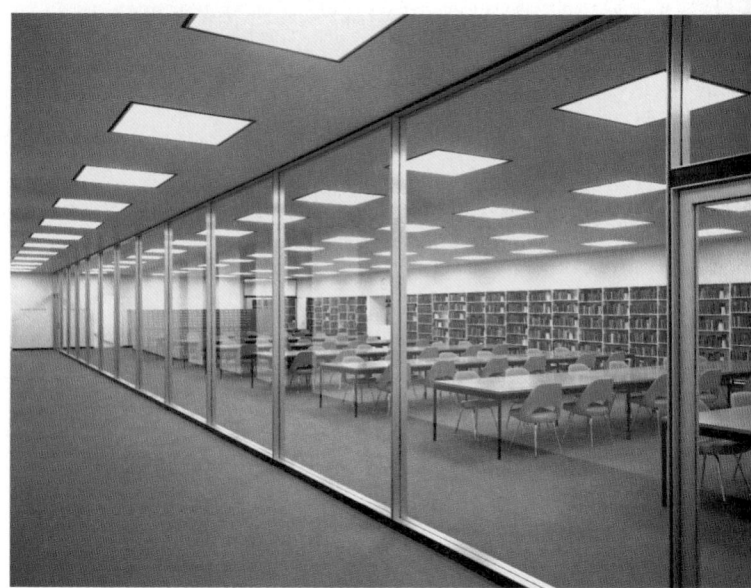

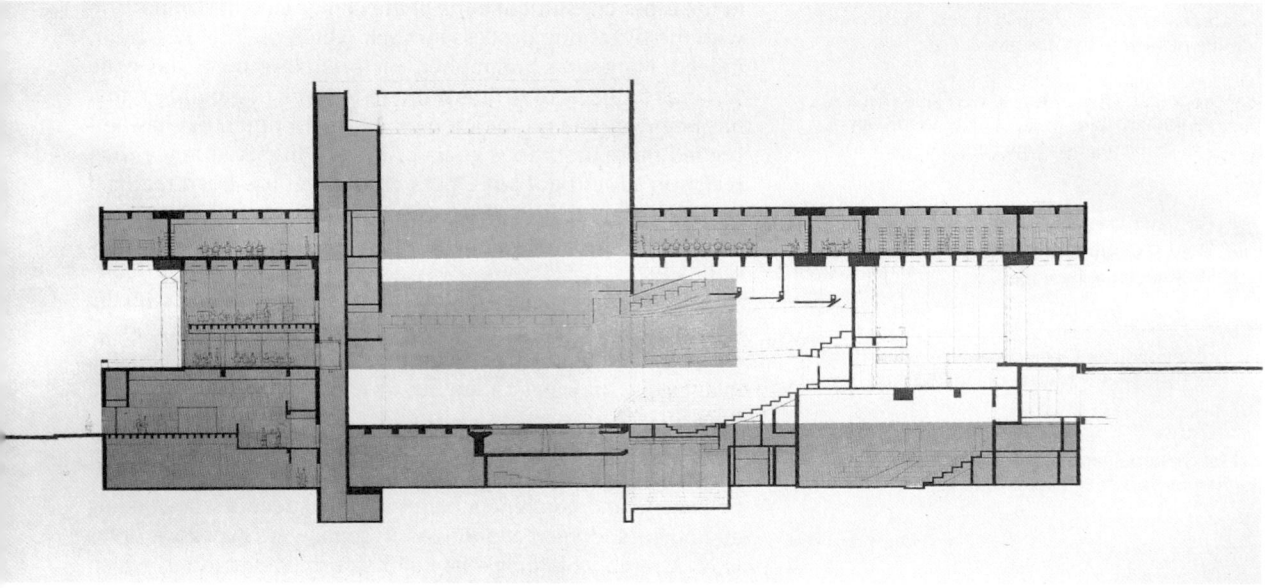

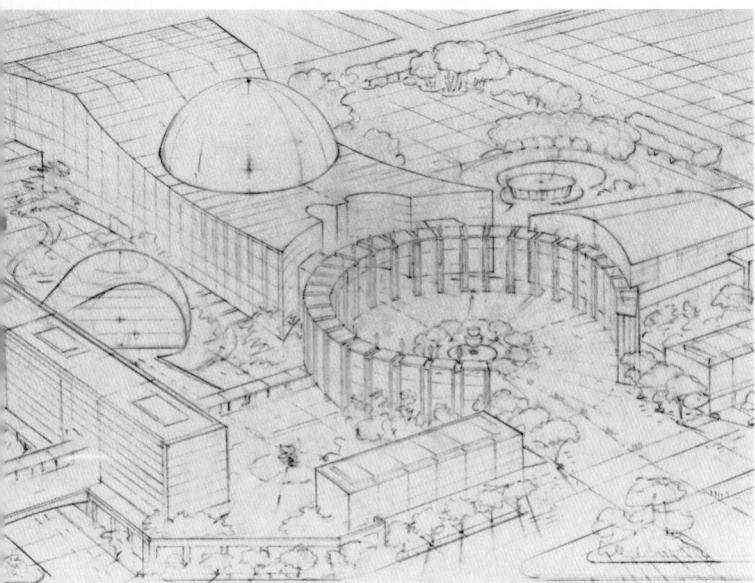

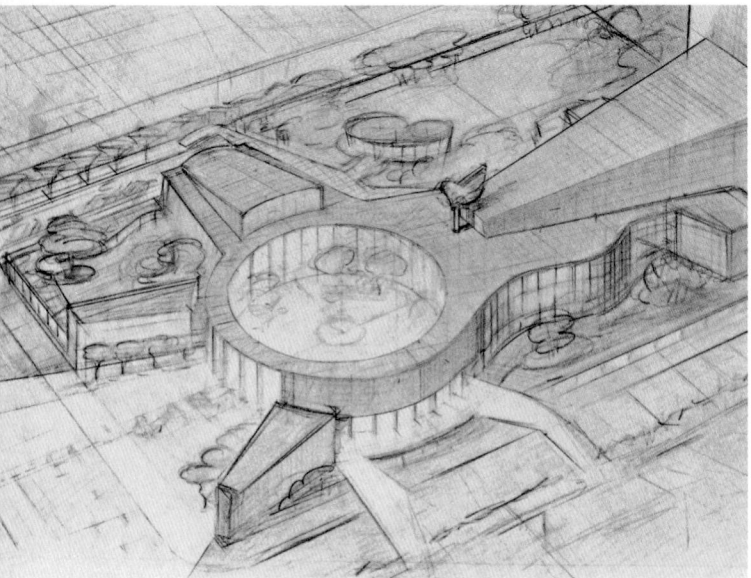

Top: Proposal for Lincoln Center, between Columbus and Amsterdam avenues, West Sixty-second and West Sixty-sixth streets. Wallace K. Harrison, 1955. Rendering of view to the northwest. CU

Bottom: Proposal for Metropolitan Opera House, west side of main plaza at Lincoln Center, West Sixty-third to West Sixty-fourth Street. Wallace K. Harrison, 1955. Rendering by Hugh Ferriss of view to the southwest. CU

Top right: Proposal for Metropolitan Opera House, west side of main plaza at Lincoln Center, West Sixty-third to West Sixty-fourth Street. Wallace K. Harrison, 1956. Rendering by Robert Schwartz of view to the southwest. ALC

Center right: Proposal for Metropolitan Opera House. Wallace K. Harrison, 1957. Rendering by Robert Schwartz of view to the southwest. ALC

Bottom right: Proposal for Metropolitan Opera House. Wallace K. Harrison, 1957. Rendering by Robert Schwartz of view to the southwest. ALC

long travertine circulation desk; a children's library, which included the freestanding Heckscher Oval, a theater defined by padded, fabric-covered panels of gold on the outside and blue and green on the inside; and the mezzanine-level gallery space, which incorporated the exposed-concrete, coffered ceiling of the Beaumont Theater lobby, as well as glass walls fronting Amsterdam Avenue and Sixty-fifth Street. C. Ray Smith drew a rather sweeping conclusion from the banality of the interiors and the circuitousness of the circulation patterns: "If Miesian designers cannot organize space with greater clarity and cannot detail with greater purity, then the dead end of that aesthetic is sufficiently proclaimed." But Smith also praised the library-museum, saying that "the calm and generous, clean and unsqualid atmosphere of this civic building, and its concept of making the background of the performing arts more readily available, can be received only with gratitude and acclaim by all the citizens of New York."[171] Olga Gueft was similarly impressed:

> It is the least luxurious component of Lincoln Center . . . and the least aloof, most amusing, most cheerfully housed cultural facility imaginable. People of every age and race and dress seemed completely appropriate in it, and they were all perfectly behaved, totally absorbed, and thoroughly delighted with the readily touchable, beautifully made, ingenious equipment that enabled them to listen to music as well as look and read and watch performances at will without disturbing their neighbors and fellow spectator-auditors. And it occurred to us that heaven on earth need not necessarily be pictured as a group of people playing harps, singing, feasting, or dancing, but by people happily together absorbed in quiet study.[172]

Metropolitan Opera House

The last of the three buildings to spatially define Lincoln Center's main plaza was the Metropolitan Opera House, the center's pivotal enterprise in terms of both its physical placement and the prestige and glamour it lent the entire undertaking.[173] Designed by Wallace Harrison, the Met, as the building came to be known, was completed in 1966. No project as complex and ambitious as Lincoln Center could ever be realized without a good dose of complications, delays, setbacks, changes, compromises, interpersonal fireworks and sometimes theatrical *Sturm und Drang*, yet the tales relating to the other constituent parts of the center pale in comparison with the Byzantine process through which the Met was built. Indeed, Harrison's biographer, Victoria Newhouse, has gone so far as to assert that "it is difficult to think of a building that has been worked on for a longer period of time, that has embodied more ambitious goals or greater flights of fancy than Harrison's Metropolitan Opera House, yet has been realized so unsatisfactorily. Many ambitious architectural designs have been compromised seriously, but none perhaps more radically."[174]

In 1955, when Robert Moses had approached him with the idea of a new Metropolitan Opera House as part of a coordinated arts center, Harrison had produced a series of dramatic, imaginative drawings calling for a central plaza encircled by a Bernini-esque double colonnade and a monumental Le Corbusier-inspired sculptural group opening toward Broadway. Harrison's opera house was to flank the western edge of the colonnade and combine a barrel-vaulted structure surrounding an immense, domed auditorium, in some ways evocative of his U.N. Assembly Building. The building's sculptural forms, which were to be clad with colored tiles arranged in bold geometric patterns, similar to his design of the domed Caspary Hall at Rockefeller University (see chapter 11), reflected the architecture of Iran, which had impressed Harrison on a recent trip.[175] The plan also called for a tower on the western edge of the site and a wedge-shaped concert hall south of the colonnade. Subsequent plans, issued throughout the fall of 1956, incorporated modifications, including the replacement of the opera house's dome with a steeply sloped wedge-shaped structure.

Harrison's first schemes were daring, disregarding the opera company's tradition of aesthetic conservatism, which was succinctly articulated by its imperious director, Rudolph Bing: "The Met is a museum, not an avant-garde theater or a place for try-outs."[176] Not surprisingly, Bing summarily rejected Harrison's suggestion that operas might be staged in the round, insisting on a proscenium stage. The opera company's conservatism, and the increasing rift between architect and client, was apparent in November 1955, when Francis Robinson, an assistant manager, suggested that the San Francisco War Memorial Opera House (Brown & Landsburgh, 1932) be viewed as a paradigm, as well as the Fox Theater (Marye, Alger & Vinour, 1929) in Atlanta, the Indiana University Auditorium (A. M. Strauss with Eggers & Higgins, 1939) and the Elliott Hall of Music (Walter Scholer, 1940) at Purdue University.[177] In October 1956 Harrison complained to Anthony Bliss, an influential member of the Metropolitan Opera Building Committee, that using these buildings as guides in designing the new opera house was "like comparing an autobus to a Rolls Royce."[178] Harrison continued to sketch sculptural shapes that resembled Matthew Nowicki's Livestock Pavilion (1952–53) on the State Fair Grounds in Raleigh, North Carolina, and Jørn Utzon's Sydney Opera House, first published in 1957. In one of these schemes, the soaring shapes surmounted a rectilinear building incorporating a second-level exterior balcony above which glass facades were punctuated by closely spaced louvers. In another scheme, a similarly articulated base, minus the balcony, was surmounted only by a horizontal slab that was separated from it by a clerestory and functioned visually as a cornice. In October 1957 Harrison sketched a complexly massed, angular, glass-walled building that resembled the design he was then working on for the First Presbyterian Church in Stamford, Connecticut.

By the following spring, with coordinated planning for Lincoln Center under way in earnest, the more understated and conventional tone advocated by opera officials seemed at last to have found its way to Harrison's drawing board. As released to the press by John Rockefeller in May 1958, Harrison's proposed design called for a 228-foot-wide facade defined by a double arcade enclosing five eight-story-high glazed arches. These were, in effect, the cross sections of the 225-foot-long barrel vaults that swept westward to their termination in a fourteen-story stage loft. Bays were to pierce the building's arcaded side walls. Behind the stage loft was to be a twenty-one-story slab—containing administrative offices as well as revenue-producing, leasable office space—that would confront the plaza with a sheer, windowless facade. The stage and auditorium were structurally independent elements, in essence a building within a building. Charles Grutzner, writing in the *New York Times*, called the design "imposing,"[179] and the editors of *Architectural Forum* deemed it "startling,"[180] later adding that "the whole structure [had] the appearance of a mammoth foot."[181] Harrison's fellow Lincoln Center architects were divided in their opinions: at the time of the design's release in 1958, Breuer called it "dignified,"[182] while Johnson found it "flamboyant."[183]

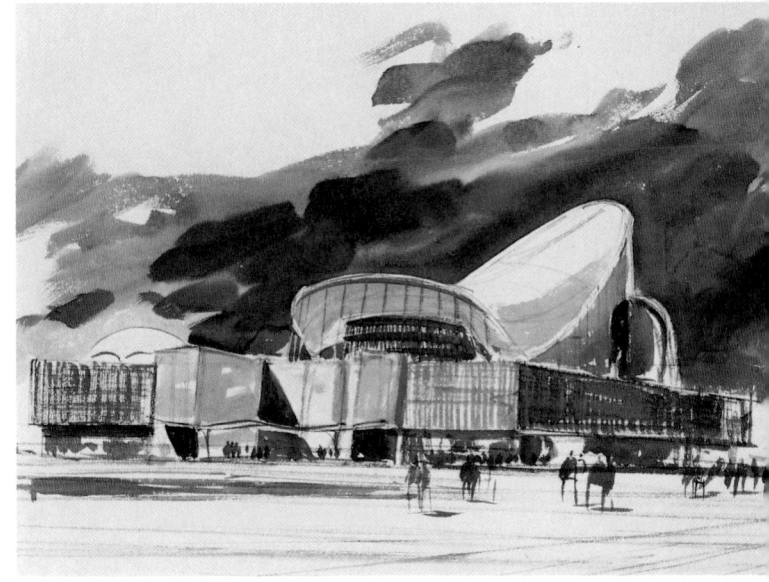

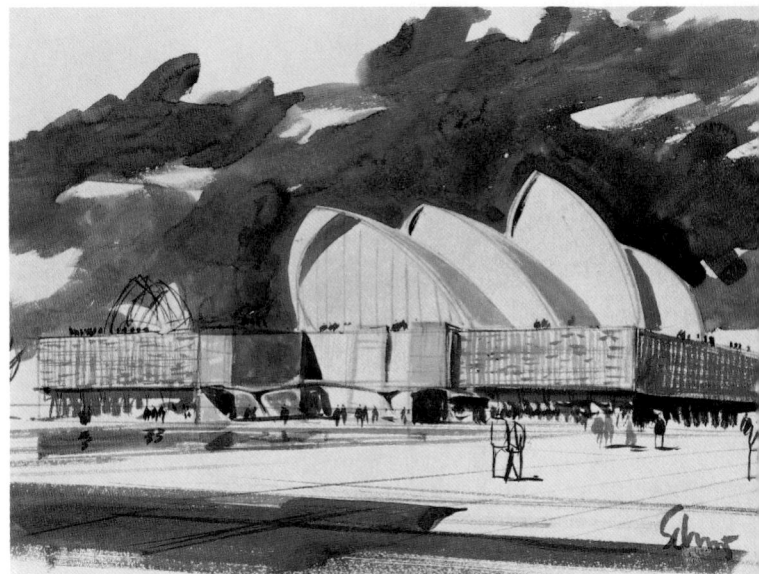

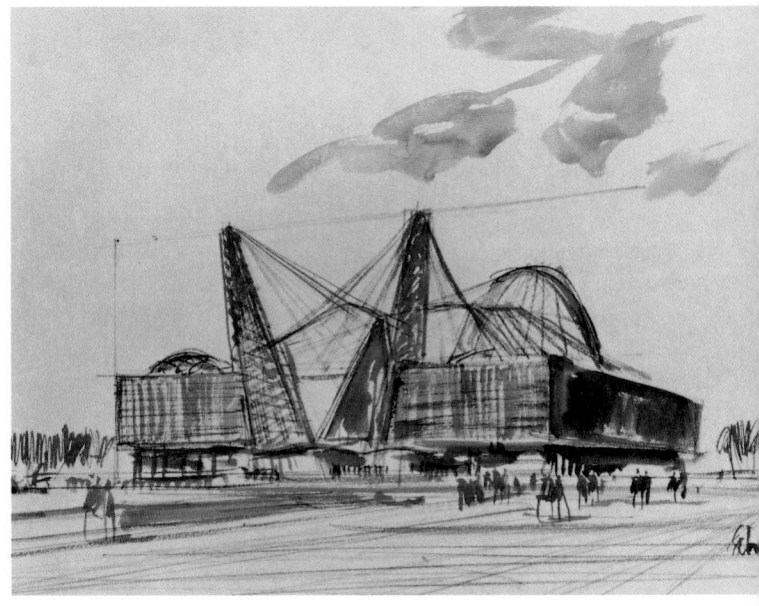

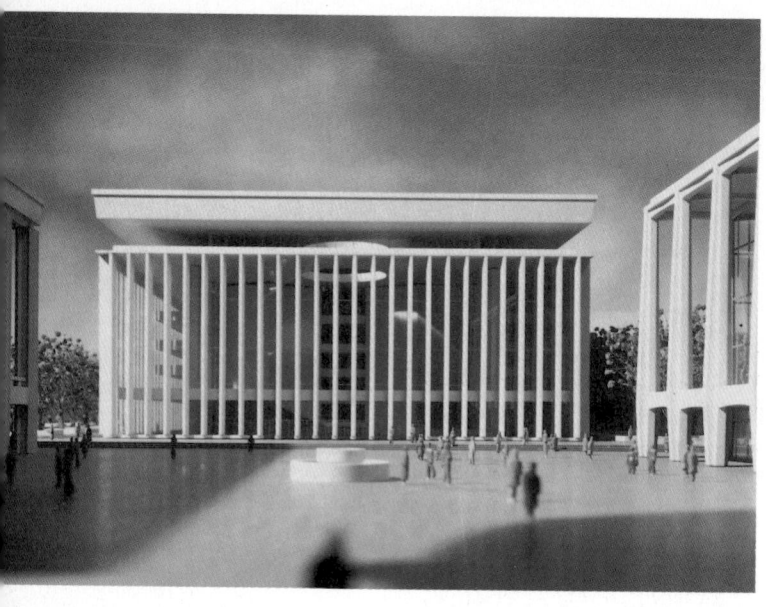
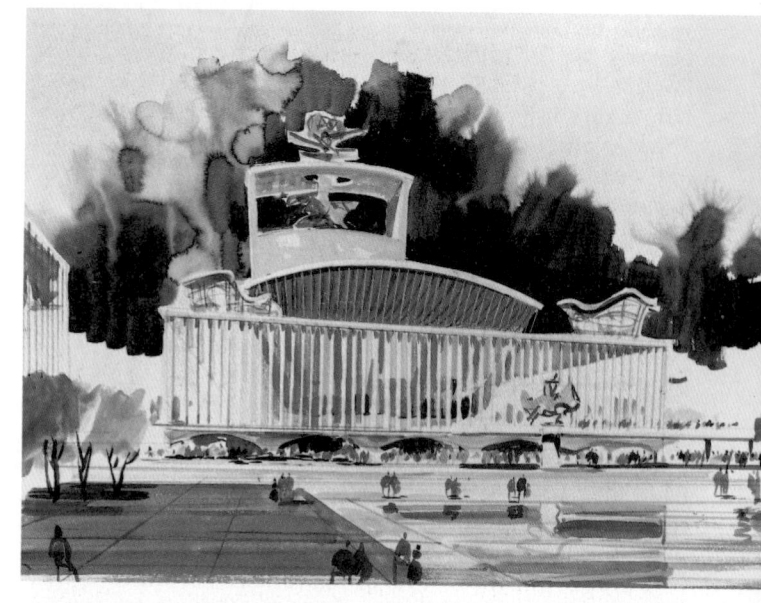
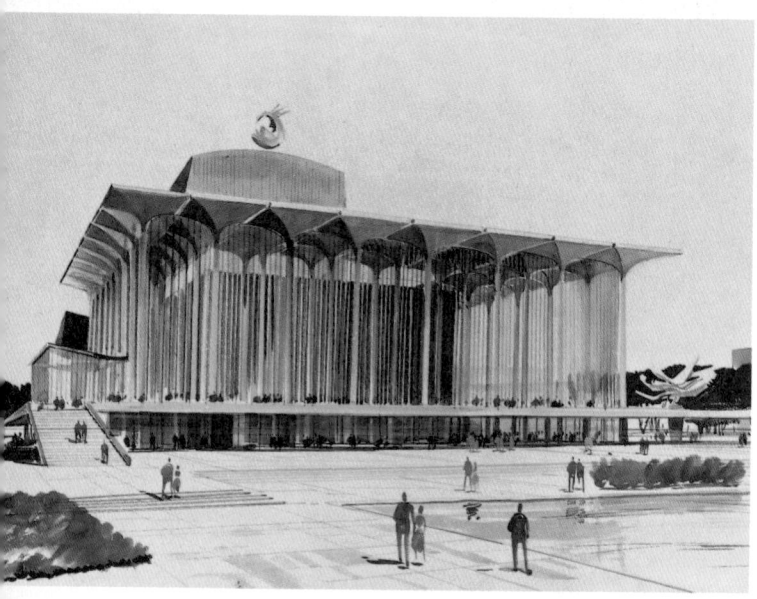
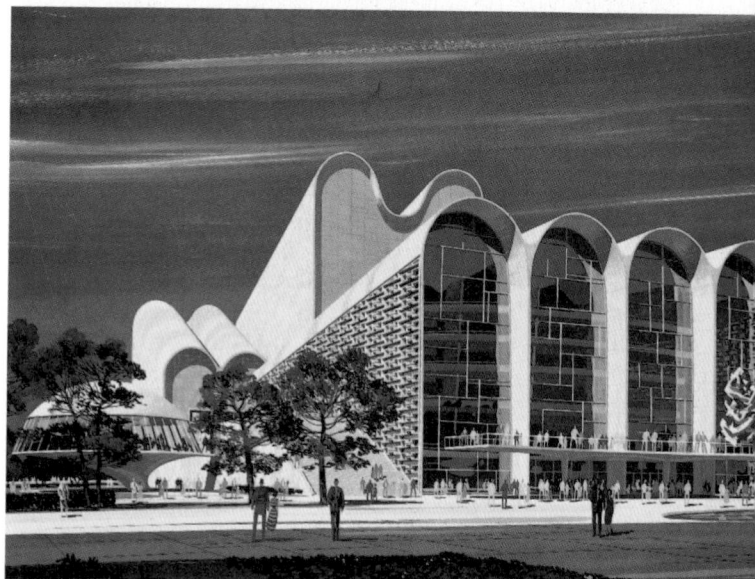
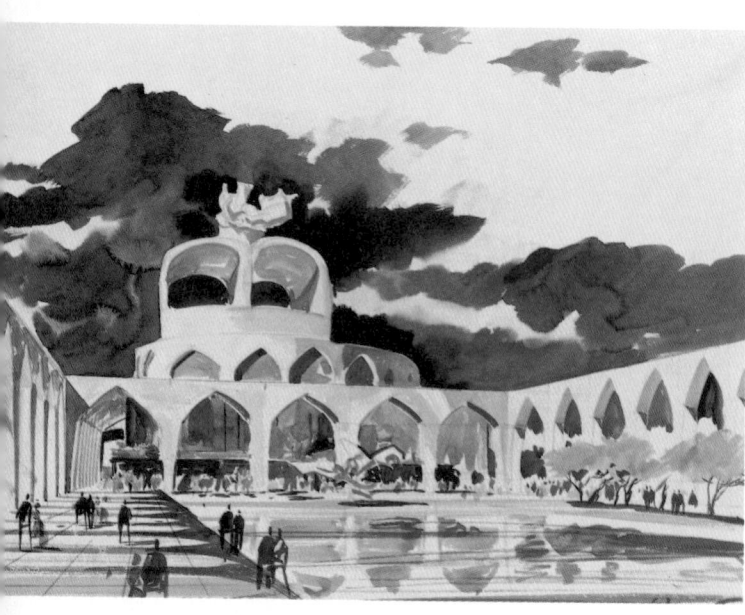
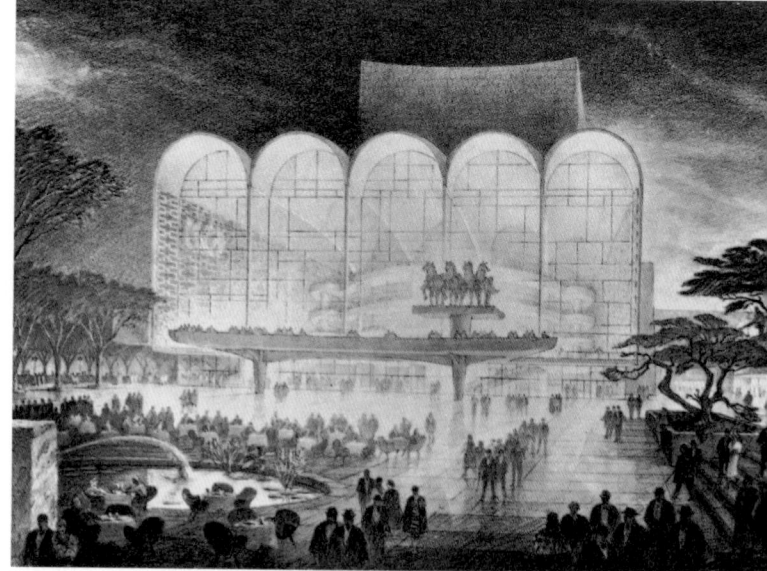

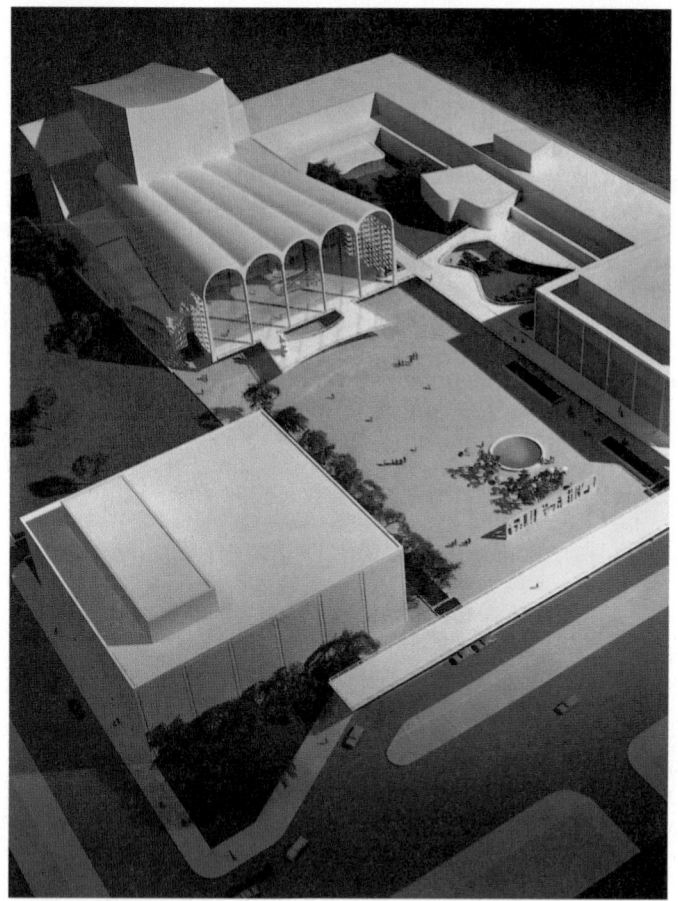

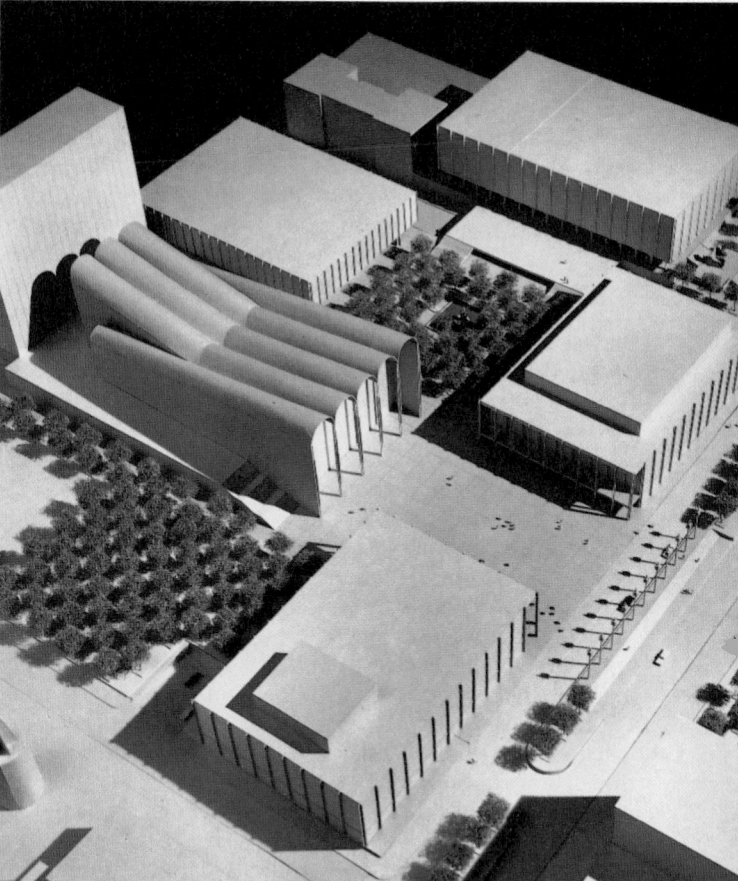

Top far left: Proposal for Metropolitan Opera House, west side of main plaza at Lincoln Center, West Sixty-third to West Sixty-fourth Street. Wallace K. Harrison, 1957. Model. View to the west. Stoller. ©ESTO

Center far left: Proposal for Metropolitan Opera House. Wallace K. Harrison, 1957. Rendering of view to the northwest. ALC

Bottom far left: Proposal for Metropolitan Opera House. Wallace K. Harrison, 1957. Rendering of view to the west. ALC

Top left: Proposal for Metropolitan Opera House. Wallace K. Harrison, 1957. Rendering of view to the west. ALC

Center left: Proposal for Metropolitan Opera House. Wallace K. Harrison, 1957. Rendering of view to the northwest. ALC

Bottom left: Proposal for Metropolitan Opera House. Wallace K. Harrison, 1958. Rendering of view to the west. CU

Above: Proposal for Metropolitan Opera House. Wallace K. Harrison, 1958. Model. View to the northwest. Stoller. ©ESTO

Top right: Proposal for Metropolitan Opera House. Wallace K. Harrison, 1958. Model. View to the northwest. Stoller. ©ESTO

Harrison's design was a refinement of the Hopkins Center (1955–62), a performing arts facility he had been commissioned to design for Dartmouth College at the suggestion of Nelson Rockefeller, an alumnus. The modified *parti* of the Hopkins Center, which also incorporated an arcaded principal facade, seemed to satisfy the Lincoln Center board. In November 1958, however, significant cost overruns moved John Rockefeller to request that all the architects revise their plans to achieve a 25 percent cost reduction. In response, Harrison vastly reduced the building's size and its array of facilities, sacrificing in particular much of the lobby and circulation space that had enveloped the auditorium. Herman Krawitz, a member of the building committee who had previously suggested that both Harrison and Abramovitz be fired,[184] described the revised plan as "adequate."[185] Rudolph Bing countered that "to build only an adequate and not the best opera house possible today in New York City would make the country the laughing stock of the world, and the opera a subject of Russian propaganda."[186]

Harrison spent the following year redesigning the building yet again. On October 28, 1959, he asked the team of architects, as well as Rockefeller and two of his associates, to choose between two designs: the previously presented barrel-vaulted scheme, and a proposal that set the arches within a rectangular structure. With the exception of Max Abramovitz, all of the architects chose the more restrained flat-roofed design; the majority's decision, supported by Rockefeller and his associates, prevailed. A year and a half later, with the entire Lincoln Center project still far exceeding its projected budget, Harrison was once again asked to radically modify his design. Several of his fellow architects suggested changes in the building's proportions and internal structure. Anthony Bliss, acting against Harrison's wishes and without the participation of the opera board members, many of whom were out of town, approved the changes. By this point, as Newhouse later noted, "Although Harrison was still nominally the architect for the Met, essentially his design had been obliterated."[187]

Other changes would diminish even further Harrison's contribution. Despite the fact that the eastern portion of the adjacent twenty-one-story office slab was to contain only conference and utility rooms, which were often windowless, the real estate consultant Gordon Braislin argued that windowless office space would not be rentable; Harrison rather feebly proposed to insert slotlike windows. By June 1961, however, Lincoln Center officials rejected the idea of a tower, on the grounds that a weak real estate market made it economically unfeasible. At the same time, the architect was summoned to meet with Rockefeller and Bliss. Nearly twenty years later, Harrison, who still recalled the incident with great bitterness, told his biographer that at the meeting he had been fired.[188] Harrison was not, in fact, fired, but he was given six weeks to come up with a design that met the budgetary requirements. He presented a revised plan, to which Bing objected that the reduced stage equipment was insufficient. In December 1961 Harrison presented yet another plan, his forty-third, which was approved of by his fellow architects, the building committee and the board of directors, but with one last proviso: Bliss insisted that the side arches be replaced by louvers set at 3'4" intervals, similar to the facade treatment called for in one of the early schemes. "Had Harrison known beforehand the extent of his design compromise," Newhouse later wrote, "he would perhaps not have accepted the Lincoln Center commission. As it was, only his strict sense of obligation can explain his ability to have persevered."[189]

But approval of the design did not mean the end of the design process, or of Harrison's troubles: still remaining was the articulation of the interior, including the resolution of thorny acoustical problems. Harrison willingly let Cyril Harris, the acoustician, take the lead in shaping the auditorium. Working closely with Harris, he devised a broad parquet, with rows of orchestra seats punctuated by two central aisles and surrounded by five levels of horseshoe-shaped tiers. The auditorium was fully separated from the surrounding shell; the walls were covered in West African Kewazinga wood; the gold-leafed ceiling, incorporating a series of curvilinear recesses, was hung from springs and the floor rested on a bed of cork and lead. Twenty-four starburst-form chandeliers, with a multitude of crystal clusters attached to spokes emanating from a central node, were a gift of the Austrian government as repayment for American help in reconstructing the Vienna State Opera after World War II. During performances, the chandeliers were mechanically elevated to avoid obstructing sightlines. Gold fluting decorated the angled, crescent-shaped surfaces that fronted the balconies and boxes.

Despite Harrison's objections, many of the auditorium's other decorative features, including the bright red mohair plush seat upholstery and the lights and satin swags that decorated the balcony fronts, were dictated by a decorating committee composed primarily of nonprofessionals and chaired by Mrs. John Barry Ryan. A gold broken-grid pattern adorned the "mix" panel bordering the proscenium arch, an effect John Canaday derisively characterized as looking like "gilded Nabisco Wafers."[190] Edmund Wilson, the literary critic who commented occasionally on architecture, also counted "the 'Nabisco area' around the proscenium" among the "horrors of the new opera house." Although he found the "Christmas-tree ornament" chandeliers to be the theater's "most successful feature," he was critical of the stage itself: "From the last row of the balcony, the stage looked almost like something seen through the wrong end of the telescope."[191]

Crowning the proscenium arch was a sculpture by Mary Callery that tried to bridge the gap between Modernist minimalism and Classical representation, a combination bound to antagonize the critics, most of whom were still caught up in the waning battle of the styles. The editors of *Interior Design* wrote: "In dead center above the proscenium arch is perhaps the most offensive element in the entire house—a specially commissioned work of art resembling antler horns intertwined [that] has no meaning on a literal or abstract level."[192] Canaday dismissed it as "a piece of junk jewelry."[193] Winthrop Sargeant suggested that the sculpture "represented a pair of intertwined shackles, symbolic of what I do not know, unless it is that once you become an opera fan you are chained to opera for life."[194] Hilton Kramer was unsparing in his attack on Callery's piece:

> This is not only a strikingly unlovely work in itself, but the kind of work that immediately identifies itself as an artistic nullity. Conceived as a sort of sculptural bouquet of bronze arabesques, it feigns an airy grace the sculptor has been conspicuously incapable of realizing. . . . Miss Callery's work is just contemporary enough to remind us of its borrowings, but its spirit is reactionary—an attempt to capitalize on the formal syntax of modernist sculpture while producing something that would look old enough, safe enough, above all perhaps, glittery and expensive enough, to fit comfortably into the atmosphere of prefabricated nostalgia that is the prevailing note of feeling throughout the Metropolitan's new home.[195]

Changes to Harrison's plans had radically reduced the size of the lobby, transforming it from a potentially spectacular space into a rather cramped one. Nonetheless, some of the architect's ideas for the lobby were realized, although not precisely in the

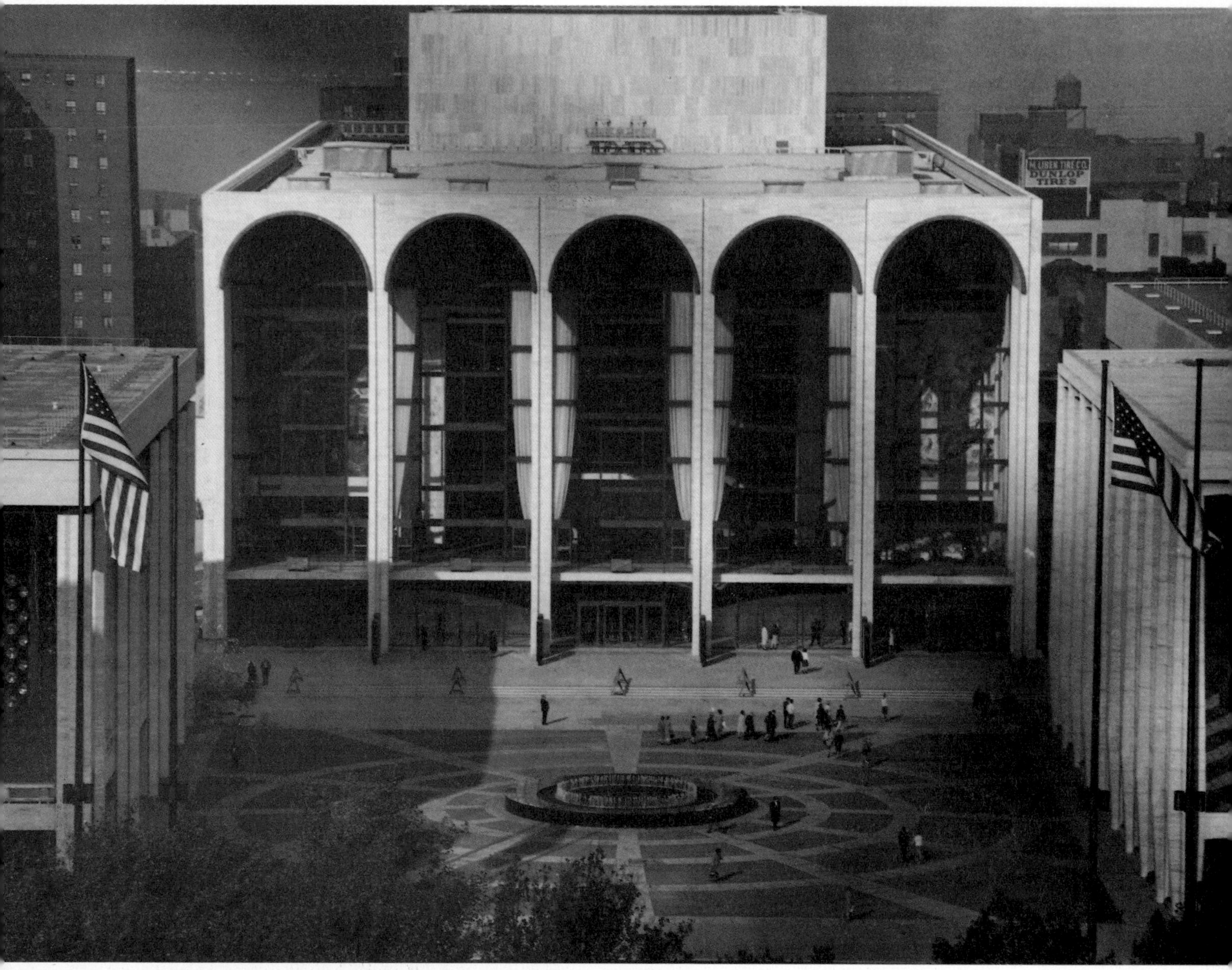

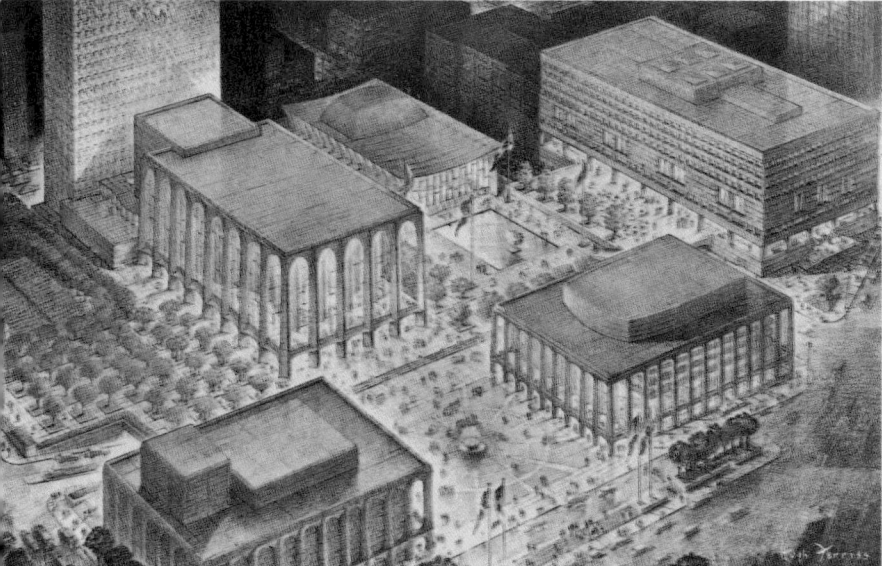

Above: Metropolitan Opera House, west side of main plaza at Lincoln Center, West Sixty-third to West Sixty-fourth Street. Wallace K. Harrison, 1966. View to the west. Mélançon. MOA

Left: Proposal for Metropolitan Opera House. Wallace K. Harrison, 1959. Rendering by Hugh Ferriss of view to the northwest of Lincoln Center with Metropolitan Opera House in center. MOA

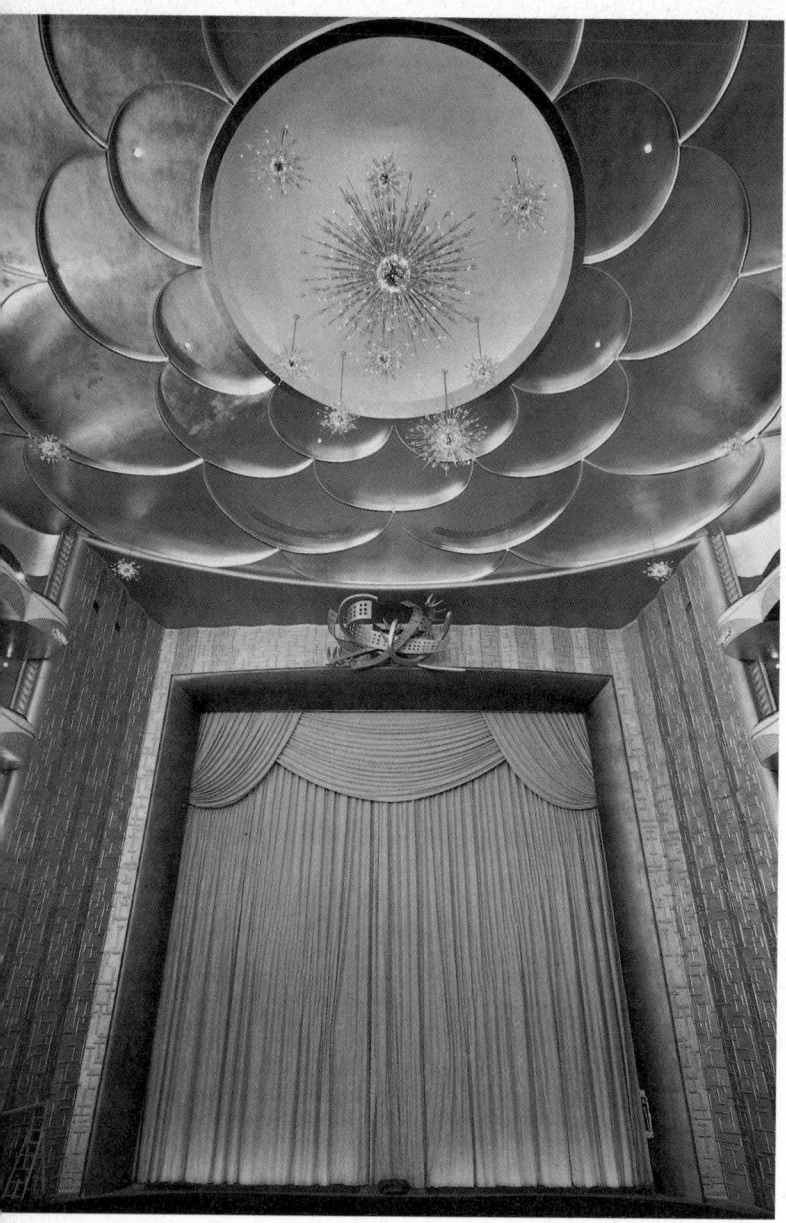

Above: Metropolitan Opera House, west side of main plaza at Lincoln Center, West Sixty-third to West Sixty-fourth Street. Wallace K. Harrison, 1966. View of auditorium showing untitled sculpture by Mary Callery above proscenium arch. Mélançon. MOA

Right: Metropolitan Opera House. Main staircase. Mélançon. MOA

manner he had intended. Clearly he had it in mind to evoke, albeit in contemporary terms, the grandeur of traditional opera houses, of which Charles Garnier's Paris Opéra (1875) was the preeminent examplar. He also had behind him the compelling spatial sequences of Radio City Music Hall and his own work at exploring the drama of crowd movement at the U.N. General Assembly Building. Despite the budget and space limitations at the Met, Harrison achieved considerable success in attaining his goals. The soaring but narrow lobby, with walls lined in dark red fabric, was overlooked by a series of balconies containing circulation space. It was dominated by a sensuously curvilinear double staircase, covered in red carpeting and illuminated by eight crystal chandeliers matching those of the auditorium. Although Harrison had intended to clad the balustrade in white marble, economic considerations forced him to leave its concrete structure exposed. The staircase swept up from the concourse level to the ground-floor entrance and again to the Grand Tier level. More successfully than any of the other Lincoln Center architects, Harrison was able to follow in the tradition of Garnier, using the staircase to gather together all classes of the audience—from those arriving in limousines to those entering from the subway via the underground concourse. The editors of *Newsweek* found that the staircase, "spiraling upward through the lobby in a winsome curve," was "perhaps more charming than grand."[196] Clive Barnes was more critical, charging that "the architects, with their strange view of circulating space, have provided [an] experience of claustrophobia for many of the social register's overachievers."[197]

The elimination of the original entrance hall, as well as other changes to Harrison's plans, had resulted in the placement of two immense blank walls on either side of the central stairwell, which were highly visible from the plaza through the building's glass facade. To ameliorate the negative impact of these walls, the Metropolitan Opera Art Committee, chaired by Agnes Belmont, commissioned Marc Chagall to paint two large paintings, each thirty feet wide and thirty-six feet high. The paintings, which shared the theme of music, were similar to the ceiling Chagall had recently completed for the auditorium of the Paris Opéra, furthering the connection with Garnier's masterpiece. One of the pair, *Le Triomphe de la Musique*, incorporated a portrait of Rudolph Bing as well as of the ballerina Maya Plisetskaya.

Harrison was not happy with the choice of Chagall, whose work he considered hackneyed: "I would have picked world-class artists like Léger but Bing was the boss, he ran the show."[198] Ada Louise Huxtable did not comment directly on the paintings but simply noted that they were the result of architectural necessity: "The offices, workshops and services . . . have been placed between the auditorium and the outer shell, muddling the design concept, filling the open area and creating two huge walls on either side, facing the glass facade, where there was to have been clear, soaring space. These walls were awkwardly placed, and blank. The solution of the Opera Committee—a reflex that seems to be automatic with any cultural group these days—was to commission the Chagall murals."[199] Edmund Wilson complained that the murals could not be properly seen "because the promenade where they have been put is too narrow to allow one to get far enough away from them."[200] Lincoln Kirstein dismissed them as "Chagall's Hallmark Chanukah cards."[201] John Canaday contended that the murals might have been painted by the artist "40 years ago, or [by] any person with a nimble wrist and access to a set of color reproductions of Chagall's recent (i.e. post 1950) work."[202] Winthrop Sargeant's assessment was mixed: "I have always regarded Chagall as the

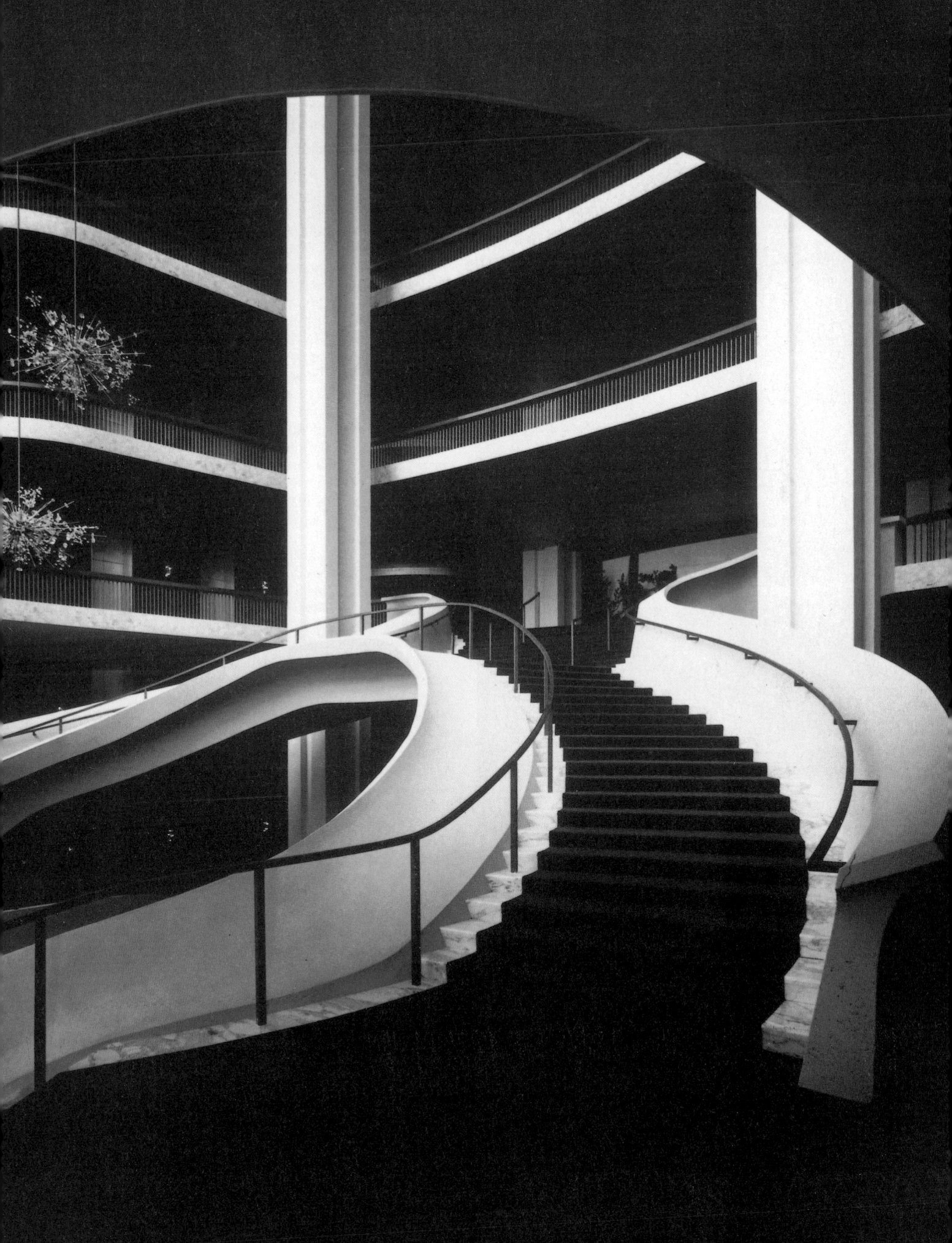

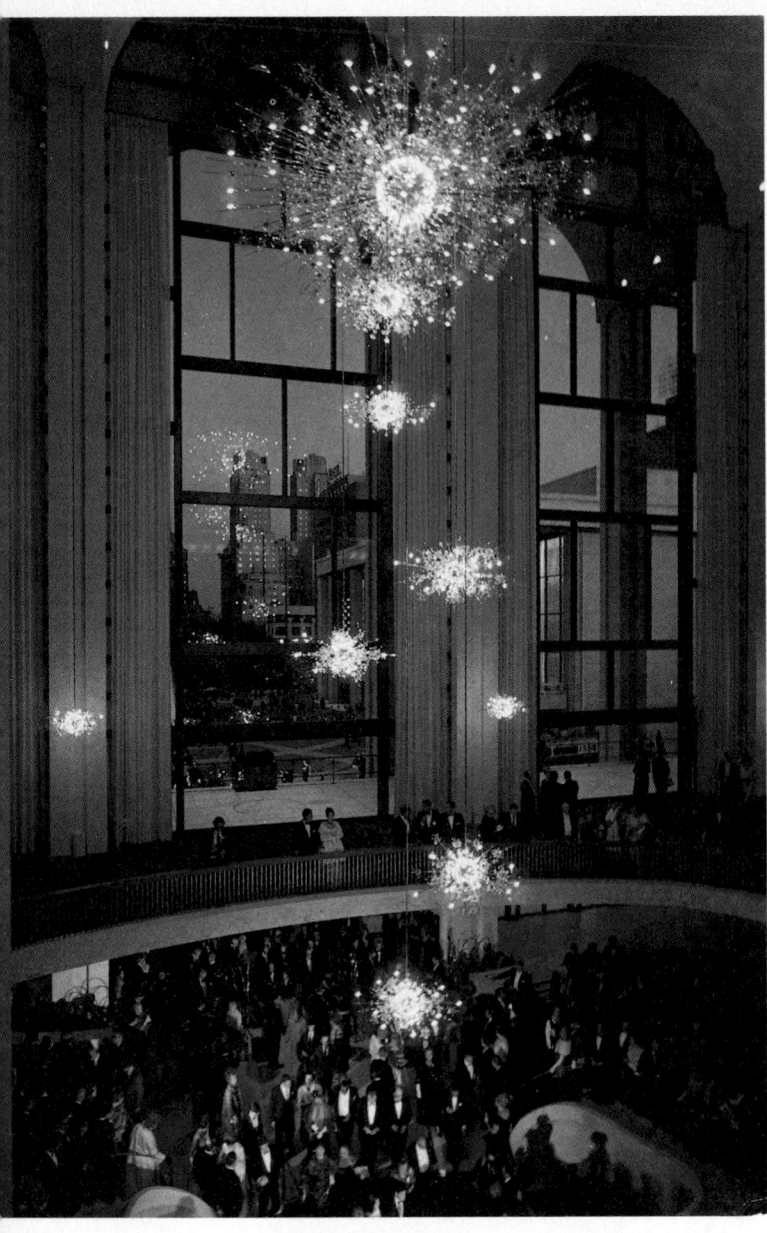

Metropolitan Opera House, west side of main plaza at Lincoln Center, West Sixty-third to West Sixty-fourth Street. Wallace K. Harrison, 1966. Lobby. Acs. SA

Harpo Marx of the Fauve movement in art. The murals are slightly silly, but they do have charm, especially at a distance of a hundred or two hundred feet."[203] To some observers, the murals were a metaphor for the aesthetic shortcomings of the opera house in general. In his savage critique, Clive Barnes argued that though "there may be a more vulgarly designed opera house in the world," he could not recall any that surpassed this one: "By night it is lit up like a Christmas tree—a monstrous Christmas tree whose incredibly rich owners have acquired two of the world's most unattractive and largest paintings by Chagall and spotlight them to the annoyance of sensitive passersby on nearby busses."[204]

In addition to the Chagall murals, the lobby contained two nudes by Aristide Maillol, titled *Summer* (1910) and *Venus without Arms* (1920), as well as a figurative work by Wilhelm Lembruck, titled *Die Kniende*, which was selected by Harrison. The editors of *Newsweek* found that as a whole the art at the Met suffered "in contrast to Philip Johnson's lively collection in his State Theater."[205] Sargeant, however, disagreed: "Generally, the art on the inside of [the Met] has a great deal more dignity than the junk sculpture and other avant-garde stuff that clutter the State Theater and Philharmonic Hall."[206]

Although design compromises had radically diminished many aspects of the Metropolitan Opera, the approach to the building from the nobly proportioned main plaza remained dramatic. It was slightly marred, however, by the presence of four shallow travertine steps leading up to the opera house; these were not only visually weak and fussy, but, because of their unorthodox riser/tread ratio of three inches to twenty-five inches, they were also a considerable physical menace, causing many people to trip. As the critic James Marston Fitch put it: "Those innocent little steps have gained a reputation as the most dangerous steps in New York. . . . They can trip people just as effectively as piano wire."[207] Two months after the building's opening, in response to a rash of reported accidents, police barricades were installed temporarily to act as railings and black tape was used to outline the treads. Five months later Harrison & Abramovitz designed lacquered bronze railings containing fluorescent lighting and had the treads resurfaced with an abrasive material. In 1982 the steps were removed completely and replaced by a gently graded slope.

By the time of the Met's completion, the project's budget had exceeded $45 million. Yet even that staggering amount proved, perhaps inevitably, insufficient to finance Harrison's dreams. The editors of *Newsweek* noted: "Wistfully, Harrison thinks of the let-'em-eat-cake Paris Opera, with its elegant arcades of waste space. 'That kind of house would have cost us $100 million,' he says, 'but after all, that was built by an emperor, and he put the whole empire into it.'"[208] In the end, Harrison was philosophical about the often frustrating experience of designing the opera house and seeing it through to completion: "Although I proposed some more romantic designs . . . the Met and the Lincoln Center people decided they didn't want too radical a break with tradition. The result is a conservative compromise. To me, it gives a feeling of a jewel box enclosed in a glass case. Others may think that it's just two boxes. However, they're two good boxes and that makes all the difference."[209]

Whatever Harrison's misgivings, many observers thought he had gotten the building's overall design just right. The editors of *Architectural Record*, for instance, were laudatory:

> The directors of the Metropolitan Opera Company, determined that the new Lincoln Center house should surpass the one built in 1883, told the architect: We do not want just an opera house

. . . we want a house for grand opera. And architect Wallace K. Harrison has given the Met that quality. Like opera itself, it is more flamboyant and more colorful than life; an elegant setting of gold leaf, red plush, and crystal; latter-day Baroque architecture for the most Baroque of the arts—grand opera.[210]

Olga Gueft, though considerably more qualified in her praise, also appreciated Harrison's achievement: "It is laughably easy to tear the design to ribbons. . . . The sculpture of the flowing promenade stairs is fractured by the variety of materials in which it is carried out. The cruciform pillars, marble screens, hammered bronze rails, and obese padded bars could be in a Miami hotel. . . . [But] for all its ineptitudes the grand stairway and lobby *are* grand—and in their unity with Lincoln Center's Fountain Plaza—exhilarating."[211]

Other observers were not so understanding. The editors of *Look* said: "Behind the new opera's gracefully arched facade, architect Wallace K. Harrison has erected a building that tries to appeal to every taste—and fails."[212] George Izenour noted: "This is but one more instance where covering up function with phoney (but expensive) architectural *kitsch* precluded an adequate stage for opera and created an auditorium that—like the New York State Theater—ignores the twentieth century."[213] Even the sympathetic Gueft noted the architect's confusion: "It is painfully obvious that Harrison could not make up his mind whether he wanted the Met to resemble Saarinen's TWA Terminal, Schönbrunn, St. Marks, or the RKO Orpheum."[214] Ada Louise Huxtable relieved Harrison of primary responsibility, noting that the Metropolitan Opera "knew what it wanted": "What it wanted were the gilded trappings of tradition and all the comforts of home. 'We couldn't have a modern house,' Mr. Harrison says with a gentle sadness. 'I finally got hammered down by the opera people. I personally would have liked to have found some way around it, but my client wouldn't have liked that at all.'" The Met, she continued, "got a good plan that works well in terms of circulation, bars, restaurants, and general social movement, and then proceeded to have it embellished in a style that is most notable as a curiously unresolved collision of past and present of which the best that can be said is that it is consistently cautious in décor, art and atmosphere. It is a sterile throwback rather than creative 20th-century design."[215]

In addition to the Met's principal public spaces, the building contained a variety of restaurants, clubs and offices. The Top of the Met restaurant, located on a sixth-level balcony, overlooked the building's soaring circulation space and the public plaza beyond. As designed by Harrison, it was enclosed on three sides only by a curving bronze-slat railing; its rather understated decor included red banquettes and carpeting, as well as silver upholstered chairs. Whimsical murals depicting both historical and contemporary banquet scenes, which Raoul Dufy had originally painted in 1950 to serve as backdrops for Gilbert Miller's Broadway production of Jean Anouilh's play *Ring Round the Moon*, decorated the restaurant's northern wall. Located on the south side of the building's fourth floor, the Cornelius Bliss Room, also designed by Harrison, incorporated luxurious materials—including oak paneling and furniture of Macassar ebony, Peruvian onyx and black leather—within a reductivist Modernist aesthetic that was deemed appropriate for a meeting room used by the opera's board of directors, as well as other opera groups and committees.

The Opera Café, designed by L. Garth Huxtable, also adopted a Modernist decor. Occupying a long, narrow room located on the north side of the building's ground floor, the café incorporated a semicircular dining area as well as a bar, the

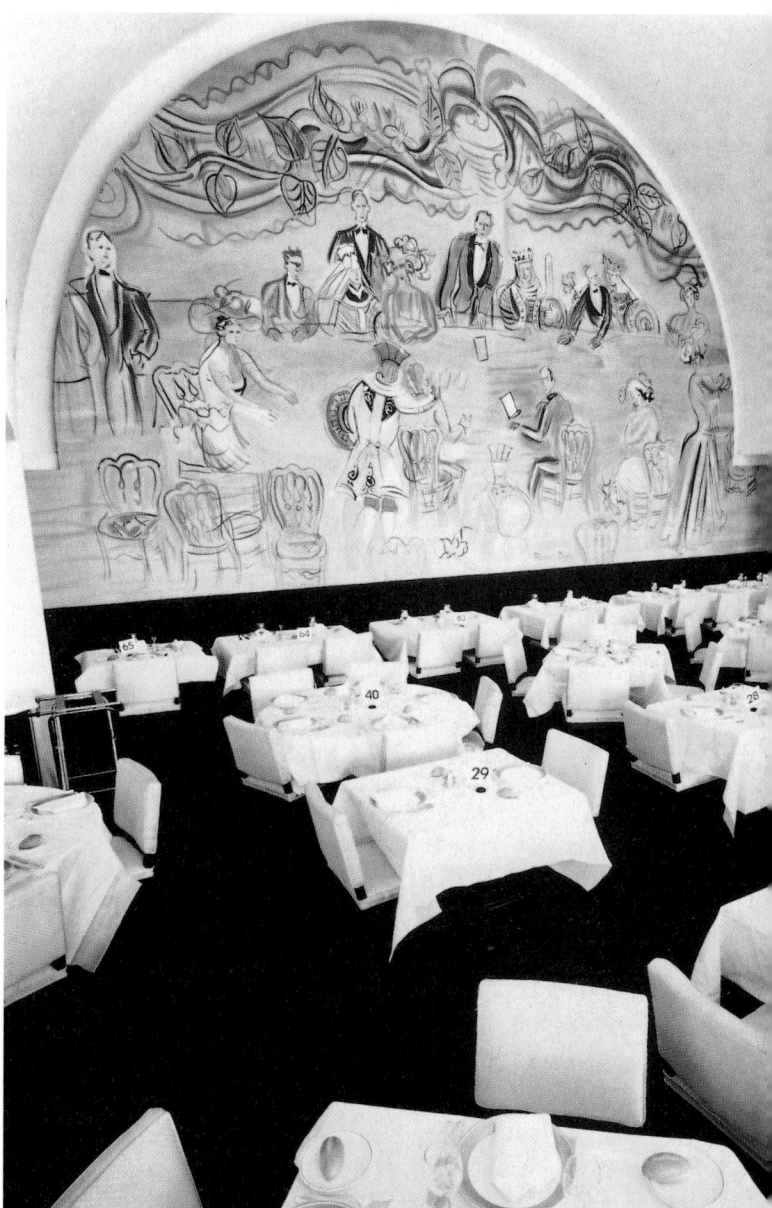

Metropolitan Opera House. View of Top of the Met including mural paintings (1950) by Raoul Dufy. MOA

walls of which were paneled in alternating strips of mirror and teak. In striking contrast to these rooms was the Belmont Room, which served as a reception and conference area for the Opera Guild and was named for the group's socialite founder, Eleanor Robson Belmont. Located on the south side of the third floor, the Belmont Room was designed by the fashionable decorator Billy Baldwin in a frankly historicist and residential style to convey a contemporary interpretation of a traditional drawing room.

The commissions for several other rooms were given to two young designers who would soon be establishment favorites. Angelo Donghia's design gave the Opera Club, on the north side of the sixth floor, a distinctly clubby atmosphere. The room contained a silver-papered ceiling, crystal chandeliers and wall sconces, black-and-gold-lacquered Regency-style chairs and a circular bar faced in black leather punctuated by stainless-steel strips. The effect it established, Huxtable said, was akin to the "Prohibition-nightclub Empire" style.[216] Mario Buatta was responsible for all of the executive offices, including Rudolph Bing's, as well as the press lounge. Bing's office, on the south side of the ground floor, contained traditional English furniture, including a custom-made double-pedestal desk made of walnut burl and topped in green leather.

The Met's opening night was September 16, 1966. "The operatic happening at New York's Lincoln Center last week," the editors of *Newsweek* reported, "was preceded by more flourishes and fanfare than any single similar occasion since Giuseppe Verdi wrote 'Aida' to commemorate the opening of the Suez Canal. 'No doubt about it,' drawled a bored matron with tired eyes and a $900 gold lamé evening dress, 'this is quite possibly the greatest social event since the Nativity.'"[217] The event, for which the least expensive ticket was $200, attracted the rich and famous, including the First Lady, Lady Bird Johnson, accompanied by Philippine President Ferdinand Marcos and his wife, Imelda; Ethel and Robert Kennedy, Joan and Edward Kennedy, and Rose Kennedy; Mayor John V. Lindsay and his wife, Mary; and Marian Anderson.

The opening performance was the world premiere of Samuel Barber's specially commissioned *Anthony and Cleopatra*, directed by Franco Zeffirelli and starring Justin Díaz and Leontyne Price in the title roles. Though the opera was almost universally panned, the acoustics of the hall were widely praised, in marked contrast to the fiasco at Philharmonic Hall four years earlier. "The stock thing to say about the new Met is that 'the acoustics are very good,'" Edmund Wilson would later write, "and the faults of architectural taste are sometimes said to have been made on the account of the acoustics."[218] The architectural historian James Marston Fitch made a similar point, observing that the opera house's "uniformly excellent acoustics . . . go far to compensate for its visual vulgarity."[219]

Although the opening-night performance was preceded by a few problems as performers and technicians became accustomed to the mechanics of the theater, which Zeffirelli described as "a strange planet," the Met's technical facilities, both on and behind the stage, were perhaps the building's most remarkable aspect.[220] Among the theater's dizzying array of features were seven sixty-foot-wide hydraulic lifts that could be operated, at speeds up to forty feet per minute, individually or in combination; two movable side stages; a backstage containing a fifty-seven-foot-diameter turntable; two orchestra lifts; 109 motorized battens; three motorized stage curtains; and a lighting control board so sophisticated that it was known by its users as "Cape Canaveral." To the editors of *Newsweek*, the building's synthesis of aesthetic conservatism and state-of-the-art tech-

nology made it a "magnificent hybrid, as if the Louvre were equipped to fire a Polaris missile."[221]

As Harold Schonberg noted: "Nobody is going to like [the Met] except the public. . . . But there are several things that cannot be taken away. The stage facilities are stupendous, and the auditorium is an acoustical success. Those are two not inconsiderable items in an opera house."[222] Ada Louise Huxtable was somewhat more cynical: "Like the rich man who has been a hungry child and keeps three refrigerators full of food, the Metropolitan can now gorge itself on turntables, elevators, raked, raised and lowered stages, moving footlights and scenery and a computer-style lighting system, all to make up for its deprivations in the old house. It is now possible as it has been demonstrated in the opening opera, to overproduce, overmechanize and overdesign." Huxtable went on to say that the technological achievements represented by the opera house could not offset the building's architectural shortcomings:

> The dream of both the architect and the client, was for the finest modern opera house in the world. The result, technically, is apparently just that. Architecturally, however, in the sense of the exhilarating and beautiful synthesis of structure and style that produces the great buildings of our age, it is not a modern opera house at all. . . . Since the new opera promises to be an excellent performing house, with satisfactory acoustics, it may not matter that the architecture sets no high-water mark for the city; that it is average, rather than adventurous or avant-garde. Performance, after all, was the primary objective. It is secondary, but no less disappointing, to have a monument *manqué*.[223]

Plaza

With the completion of the Metropolitan Opera House came the completion of the main plaza, designed by Philip Johnson. The plaza's dark aggregate pavement was inlaid with travertine arranged in a series of concentric circles and twelve spokes radiating from the centrally located Revson Fountain, a strikingly simple, thirty-eight-foot-diameter circle of polished Canadian black granite.[224] The fountain was internally illuminated by 88 lamps emitting 26,000 watts of light and contained a complex of 577 jets that could spew forth 9,000 gallons of water per minute in a wide range of patterns; perhaps its most spectacular effect was the emission of a thirty-foot-high, six-foot-wide column of water. The entire presentation was electronically orchestrated by computer-programmed tapes played in a control booth that was located beneath the plaza. The fountain could also be programmed from a console located on the New York State Theater's exterior balcony; Johnson had hoped that such artists as George Balanchine, Leonard Bernstein, Igor Stravinsky and Pablo Picasso would program the fountain, although this never came to pass.

Three years before the plaza's completion, Anthony Bliss had advocated using the open space as the site of a monumentally scaled porte cochere to provide a grand entranceway to the constituent buildings, but the decision was made to install a fountain instead. As realized, the plaza proved immensely popular with the public, not merely as an entrance court to the theaters, but as a destination, an architecturally and spatially coherent public square in a city with few such amenities. The placement of the center's three principal theaters around a nobly proportioned public space brought the enterprise a profound if not altogether planned democratic aspect. Even if you

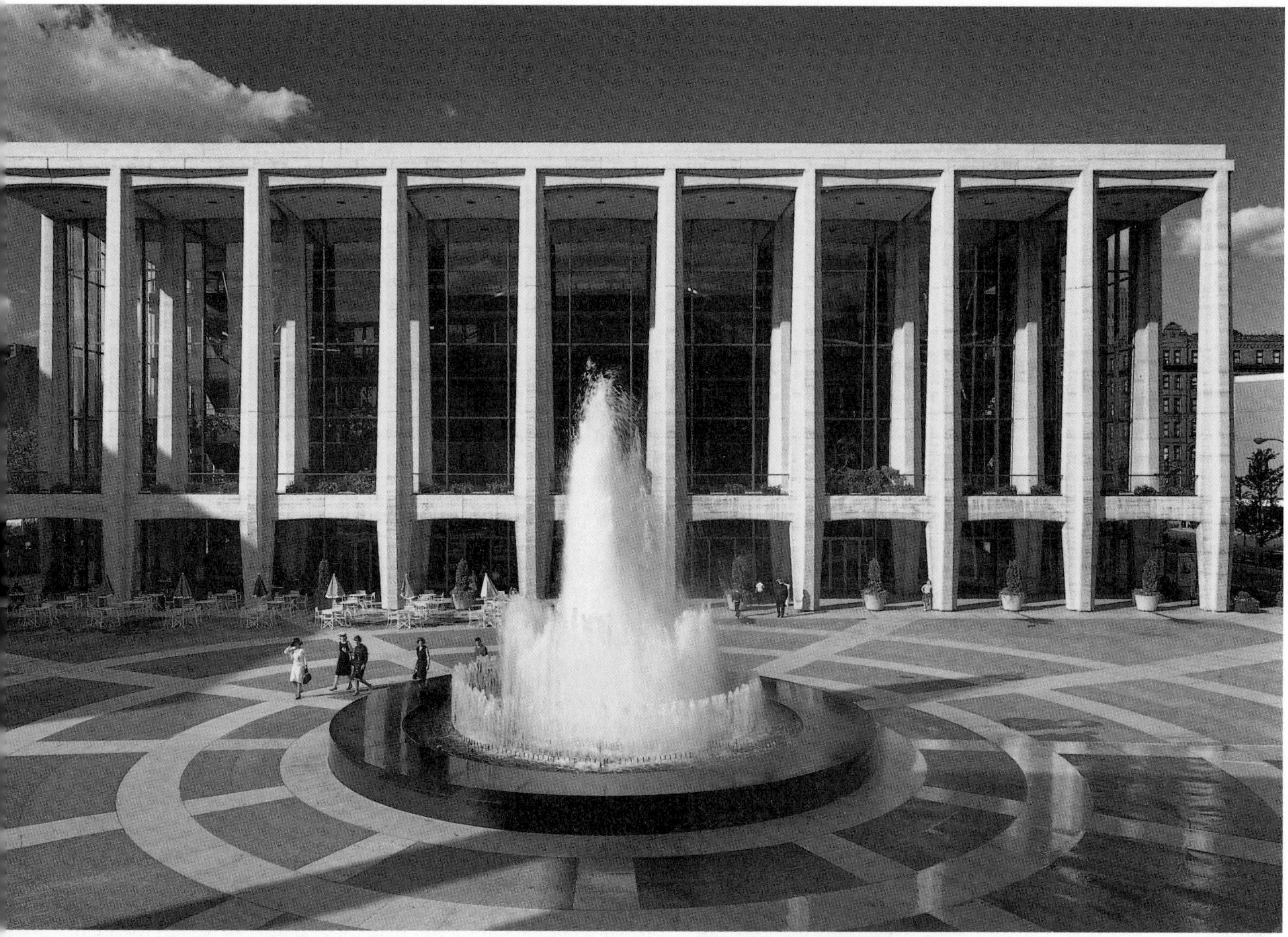

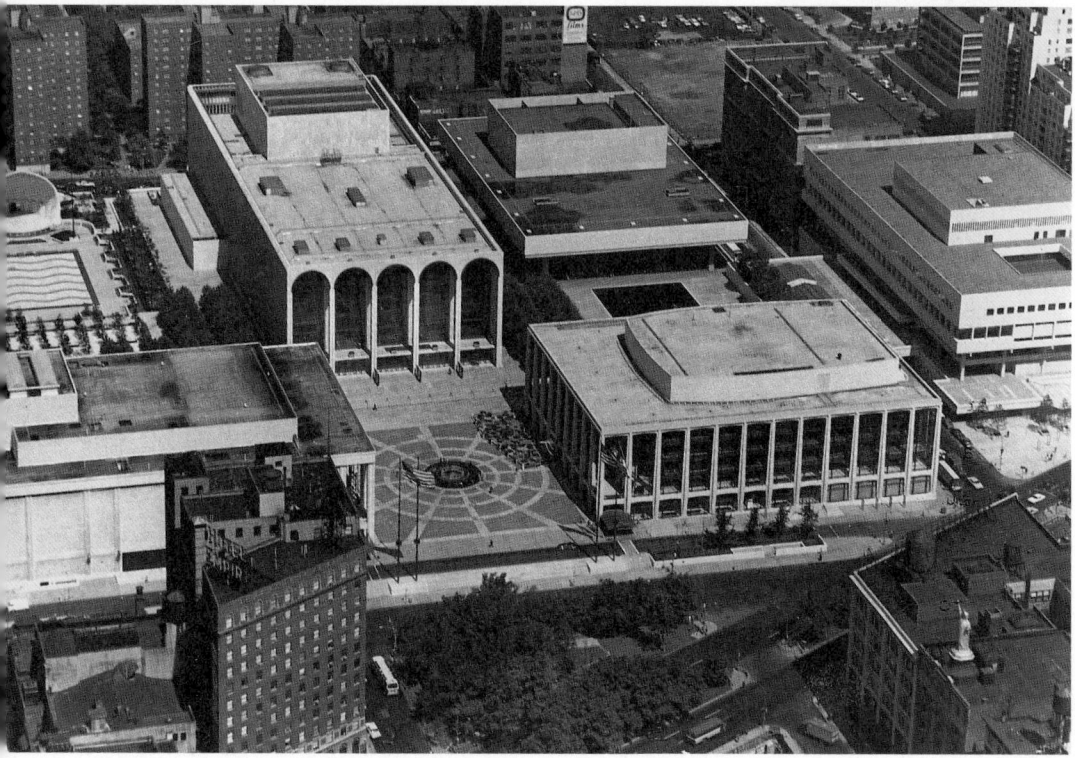

Above: Lincoln Center Plaza, between Columbus and Amsterdam avenues, West Sixty-third and West Sixty-fourth streets. Philip Johnson, 1966. View to the north including the Revson Fountain in the foreground and Philharmonic Hall (Max Abramovitz, 1962) in the background. Stoller. ©ESTO

Left: View to the northwest of Lincoln Center showing, clockwise from lower left: New York State Theater (Philip Johnson, 1964), Daniel and Florence Guggenheim band shell in Damrosch Park (Eggers & Higgins, 1969), Metropolitan Opera House (Wallace K. Harrison, 1966), Vivian Beaumont Theater and Lincoln Center Performing Arts Library and Museum (Skidmore, Owings & Merrill, Eero Saarinen and Jo Mielziner, 1965), Juilliard School Building (Pietro Belluschi in association with Eduardo Catalano and Westermann & Miller, 1969) and Philharmonic Hall (Max Abramovitz, 1962). ALC

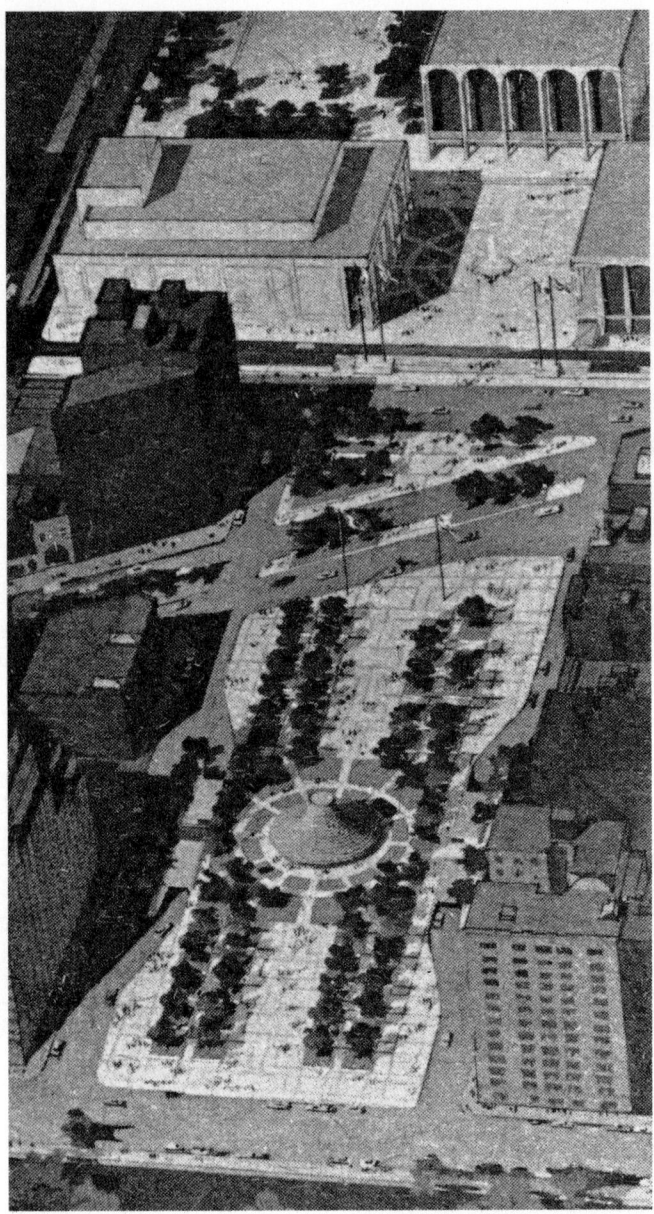

Proposal for monumental mall connecting Lincoln Center to Central Park, Columbus Avenue to Central Park West, West Sixty-third to West Sixty-fourth Street. William F. R. Ballard, 1966. Rendering of view to the west. AF. CU

could not afford a ticket, you could come and watch the show put on by the theatergoers as they entered and exited and as they gathered in the lobbies and terraces during the intermissions. Even some critics who were generally displeased with the center's architecture found the plaza satisfying. Clive Barnes rhapsodized over the fountain's "spurts, splurts, and splashes."[225] In 1966 Huxtable wrote, "Fortunately, the scale and the relationship of the plazas is good, and they can be enjoyed as pedestrian open spaces, a value that may well increase with use and age."[226] Not everyone, however, was satisfied. The sociologist and author William Whyte had recommended that the plaza be adorned with large trees, and both Hugh Ferriss and Philip Johnson had produced sketches of landscaped schemes.[227] In the end, though, it was decided that trees would detract from the center's architectural and spatial qualities.

In November 1966, following the completion of the Metropolitan Opera House, the architect William F. R. Ballard, who served as chairman of the City Planning Commission, proposed the construction of a monumental mall connecting Lincoln Center's main plaza with Central Park to the east.[228] The landscaped mall was intended to fully occupy the block bounded by Broadway, Central Park West, Sixty-third and Sixty-fourth streets; a 1,000-car garage would be located beneath it. The mall had the support of Wallace Harrison, who, along with other members of his advisory committee, had ten years earlier advocated the organization of Lincoln Center around a central plaza, which they hoped would ultimately be approached by a grand allée leading from Central Park. Even the urban planner Sven Markelius, the only committee member to oppose the center's organization along an east-west axis, had suggested lifting the complex five meters above street level and connecting his proposed principal entrance on the site's northern boundary along Sixty-fifth Street to Central Park by an elevated roadway spanning Broadway. The proposed mall linking Lincoln Center and Central Park mirrored the sweep of Daniel H. Burnham and Edward H. Bennett's 1909 plan for Chicago, as well as the Mall in Washington, D.C.

Ballard's plan, released shortly before he quit his municipal post, called on the city to acquire the property as parkland through eminent domain and would have necessitated the demolition of three architecturally significant buildings: the Ethical Culture Society School (Robert D. Kohn and Carrère & Hastings, 1902), on the northwest corner of Central Park West and Sixty-third Street;[229] the adjacent Ethical Culture Society Hall (Robert D. Kohn, 1911), on the southwest corner of Central Park West and Sixty-fourth Street;[230] and the West Side Branch of the YMCA (Dwight James Baum, 1930), at 5 West Sixty-third Street, just west of the Ethical Culture Society buildings and extending through the block to Sixty-fourth Street.[231] The initial response of Algernon D. Black, chairman of the Ethical Cultural Society, to the plan was measured and cautious: "I think there should be a tie between Lincoln Center and the green of Central Park," he said. "It is a visionary idea, and we have always backed progressive planning. But I think great care should be taken if it involves the removal of our meeting house."[232] More vehement opposition soon arose from the society, as well as from the YMCA and from the New York Academy of Science, which owned the western portion of the block and had already cleared the site to make way for a twenty-one-story headquarters building.

Shortly after Ballard's proposal was announced, the industrial design firm of Raymond Loewy/William Snaith, Inc. presented an alternate plan to Mayor Lindsay, although drawings were not publicly released. The Loewy/Snaith plan called for a complex of tall buildings to be erected between Broadway and Central Park West, Sixty-third and Sixty-fifth streets. Widely spaced to provide unobstructed sightlines between Lincoln Center and the park, the buildings were to be set amid landscaped plazas lined with stores and cafés and linked by second-level pedestrian walkways that would span Broadway and Central Park West as well as provide access to Central Park. Snaith noted that the threatened institutions could be rehoused in new buildings on the site or that the proposed complex could be constructed around the existing buildings.

Ada Louise Huxtable lambasted both plans:

Mr. Ballard's proposal . . . is a discouraging demonstration of the dated ideas of c. 1900 Beaux Arts *parti* planning. . . . In spite of constant references to Parisian boulevards, and the inevitable fountains and potted trees, the results, more often than not, have been lifeless voids with a half century of subsequent problems of how to fill them up appropriately . . . and how to make them work as urban spaces. . . . The Hoving-Snaith scheme would turn the Ballard-Harrison *allée* into a passaggiatta or activity-oriented mall with shops and stores. Any resemblance to the original, as they say, is purely coincidental. Pick your version; it is all window dressing. Both are innocent of even a basic bow to the neighborhood's real planning problems.

Huxtable contended that both schemes failed to effectively address the center's "catastrophic circulation pattern and the Kafkaesque street crossing" and further charged that the removal of the Ethical Culture Society and YMCA buildings, or the attempt to integrate them with "chic urban effects," would jeopardize the stability of a community already in the midst of significant social change.[233]

In response to Huxtable's article, Park Commissioner Thomas P. F. Hoving wrote to the editors of the *New York Times* to deny any connection on his or Mayor Lindsay's part with the Loewy/Snaith plan.[234] William Schuman, the president of Lincoln Center, also wrote a letter to the *Times* editors, explaining that the center's administration had not initiated the mall concept. While Schuman failed to take a definitive stance, his statement that the center objected to any changes that would "damage the present services or future mission of the institutions located in the area involved" clearly allied the center with the anti-mall forces.[235] These ultimately proved powerful enough to withstand even Nelson Rockefeller's support of the mall, rumored to be based on his desire for an unobstructed view of Lincoln Center from his apartment at 810–812 Fifth Avenue.[236] The editors of *Architectural Forum* provided the last word on the subject: "One eminent New York architect has . . . proposed an alternative plan, which surely deserves equal consideration by Mayor Lindsay. He suggests building a mall from the Y.M.C.A. *west* to the Hudson, and tearing down everything in *its* path."[237]

Although no monumental landscaped mall was built, Lincoln Center was provided with at least a bit of parkland: Robert Moses's Damrosch Park (1969), named after the renowned family of musicians, was located southwest of the main plaza, bordered on the east by the New York State Theater, on the north by the Metropolitan Opera House, on the south by a widened Sixty-second Street and on the west by Amsterdam Avenue.[238] Designed by the architects Eggers & Higgins and the landscape architects Dan Kiley and Webel & Westermann, the 2.34-acre park was visually dominated by the Daniel and Florence Guggenheim Band Shell, a curiously unprepossessing concrete structure whose shape was described by *Progressive Architecture* as "a halved onion with a point."[239] The Guggenheim shell could seat seventy-

five musicians and faced an open area large enough to accommodate 4,500 people. At its eastern end, Kiley created a bosk of London plane trees that mirrored a similar arrangement around the reflecting pool, providing welcome shade and an intimacy otherwise lacking in the complex.

Juilliard School

In 1969 the Juilliard School moved from its buildings on Morningside Heights, which were taken over by the Manhattan School of Music, to a new building at Lincoln Center, the last to be completed there.[240] Juilliard's construction had been delayed because it depended on the demolition of part of the High School of Commerce (William H. Gompert, 1925), which the Board of Education refused to relinquish until a replacement had opened. But in 1965 the new school, which would ultimately become the Martin Luther King, Jr. High School (see below), was still unbuilt, and the board agreed to close and demolish the existing school in two stages. Construction of the Juilliard School began that year but was plagued by further delays, including those imposed by labor strikes. Designed by Pietro Belluschi, in association with Eduardo Catalano and the firm of Westermann & Miller, Juilliard's building, physically linked to the rest of Lincoln Center only by a broad pedestrian bridge crossing Sixty-fifth Street, was completed after approximately seventy different sets of preliminary drawings had been produced over a period of twelve years.

Despite the fact that the building was clad in travertine (here a gift from the Italian government), Juilliard's design was distinctly different from the principal Lincoln Center structures. Eschewing the Classically inspired vocabularies of the center's three most prominent buildings, Juilliard's architects adopted a Brutalist aesthetic; the results suggested to the editors of *Newsweek* "a friendly fortress."[241] Although the school was the center's only building to face directly onto Broadway, the architects, in keeping with the aggressive stylistic stance, stayed with the orthogonal and rejected the avenue's diagonal street wall, creating a small triangular plaza as a forecourt. Rising five stories, with an additional four stories below grade, Juilliard incorporated a sweeping second-level terrace, cantilevered for most of its length, which was reached by a monumental staircase rising from the Broadway plaza; on the south, the terrace merged with the plazalike pedestrian bridge. The building's principal entrances were on Sixty-fifth and Sixty-sixth streets, and on the second-level terrace at the end of the bridge. Cantilevered above the third story, the building's upper portion contained double-height square windows surmounted by horizontal strips of smaller square windows. In 1971 *Three Times Three Interplay*, Yaacov Agam's thirty-two-foot-high abstract kinetic sculpture, consisting of three movable zigzag-shaped aluminum tubes, was installed on the southeast corner of the building's terrace. Agam claimed that his goal was "to give plastic and artistic expression to the ancient Hebrew concept of reality" and that his piece was "not a statement, but a constant becoming, not a sculpture but many possibilities for one."[242] He had intended for the piece to be participatory, with passersby arranging and rearranging the sculpture's parts, but viewers proved reluctant to do so, to the relief of the school administration.

Inside, the architects provided facilities for George Balanchine's independently organized School of American Ballet, as well as for a drama division and the famous music division of the Juilliard School, which claimed to be the world's first con-

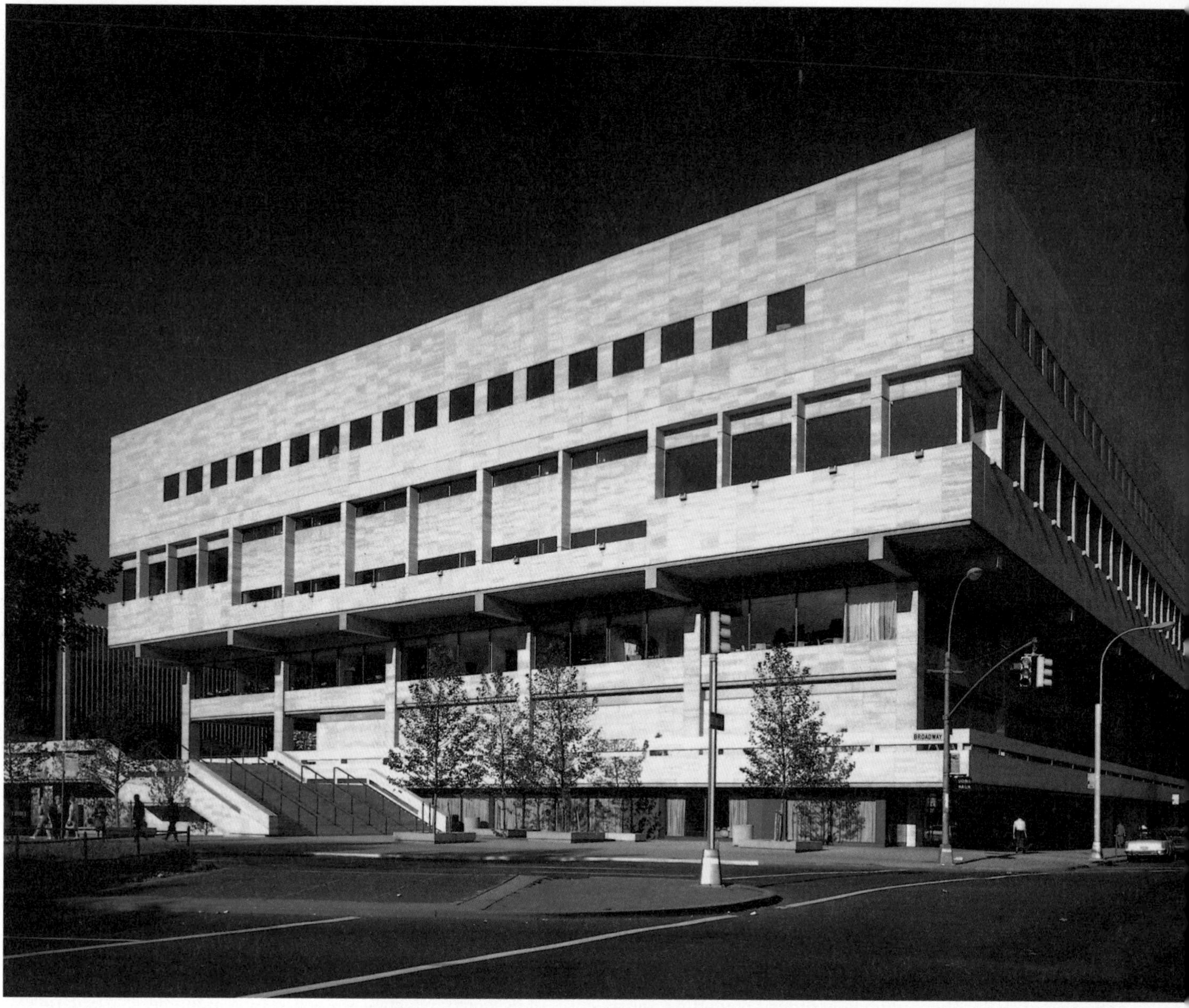

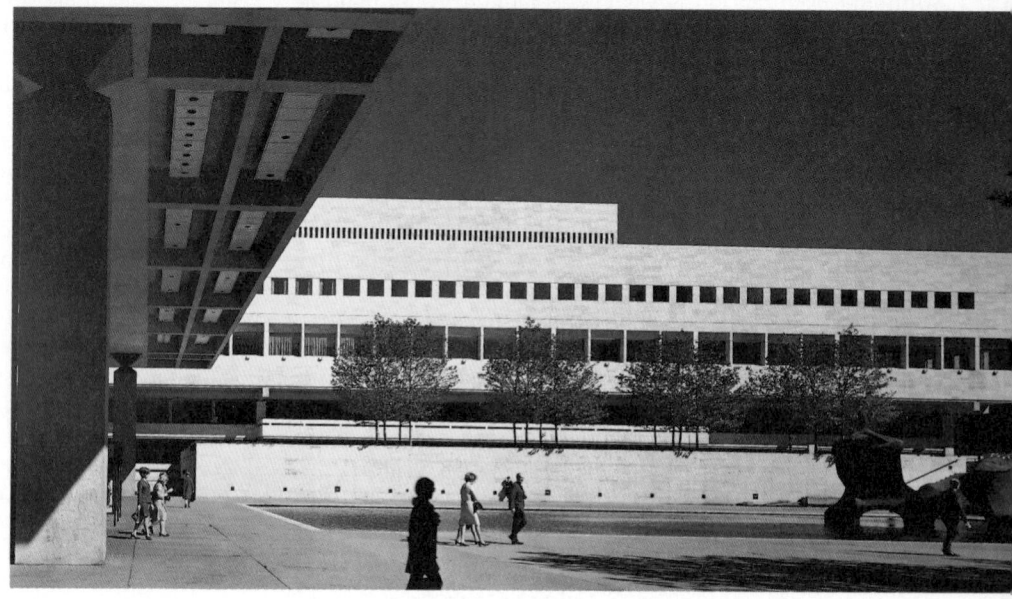

Above: Juilliard School, west side of Broadway, West Sixty-fifth to West Sixty-sixth Street. Pietro Belluschi in association with Eduardo Catalano and Westermann & Miller, 1969. View to the southwest. Stoller. ©ESTO

Right: Juilliard School. View to the north. Stoller. ©ESTO

servatory dedicated to all of the performing arts. Mildred Schmertz, writing in *Architectural Record*, noted that the architects "have managed to tuck and fit the assorted instructional and performance facilities of a good-sized campus into one integrated structure" and that "an almost infinite variety of spaces [have been] fitted together with a sorcerer's skill in an arrangement as intricate as a Chinese puzzle."[243]

The building contained three principal performance spaces, of which the Juilliard Theater and the Paul Recital Hall were reserved for use by the school. The 1,026-seat, oval-shaped Juilliard Theater contained a movable ceiling, designed by the engineer Olaf Soöt, which could be adjusted to create dramatically different acoustical effects for performances of opera, drama and dance. Both the ceiling and the walls were clad in cherry wood and basswood. The 277-seat Paul Recital Hall was paneled in cherry wood and incorporated sloped ceiling coffers; it also contained a Holtkamp pipe organ.

The building's largest auditorium, and its only public theater, was the 1,096-seat, wood-paneled Alice Tully Hall. Despite being given the only opportunity at the center to provide an imposing Broadway entrance, Belluschi chose to tuck the theater's principal public entry beneath the building's monumentally scaled exterior staircase. The sense of entering an important public space was further diminished by the theater's lobby, which, although generously proportioned, was depressed several feet below grade. The theater was designed primarily to accommodate recitals and chamber music performances, but because the first three rows of seats could be replaced by an expanded stage, it could also accommodate the needs of small orchestras. The hall's location within twenty-two feet of the subway tunnel under Broadway necessitated the insertion of a one-inch-thick, cork-lined asbestos pad between the theater's foundation and bedrock, as well as the isolation of the theater's walls from structural columns.

Alice Tully Hall proved to be a warm if slightly gloomy space ideally suited to chamber music events. The comparative simplicity of Juilliard's performance spaces was welcomed by critics who had lamented the acoustical problems and overdecoration in other buildings at Lincoln Center. "Juilliard's interiors are in some ways better than those of the other buildings," argued Mildred Schmertz. "Its beautifully shaped wood panelled auditoriums, for example, prove that it is possible to create elegant halls in contemporary terms without resorting to skimpy evocations of the gilt, plaster and crystal decor of the great halls of the past." Schmertz was impressed with the building's overall design: "The art with which the arts are housed affects them profoundly for the better. It is fortunate, therefore, that the incredible effort on the part of Belluschi and his team has produced such a fine building. Since Juilliard is a school for the musicians, actors and dancers of the future, it is appropriate that the best building at Lincoln Center should be theirs."[244]

Ada Louise Huxtable was similarly impressed, though she was somewhat harsher in her comparison of the building with the rest of Lincoln Center:

> The Juilliard is a good building, free of the uncertain pretentions and pomposities of the Metropolitan Opera House, the New York State Theater. . . . [Its] style, guided by Mr Belluschi, an architect of notable sensibility who has worked most beautifully, in wood, for almost 40 years, is a kind of restrained establishment modern. It is not avant-garde, but its refinements and simplicities are timeless. With the Beaumont Theater, Juilliard offers architectural and esthetic reality to the cultural confusions of Lincoln Center, ending 14 years on an upbeat.[245]

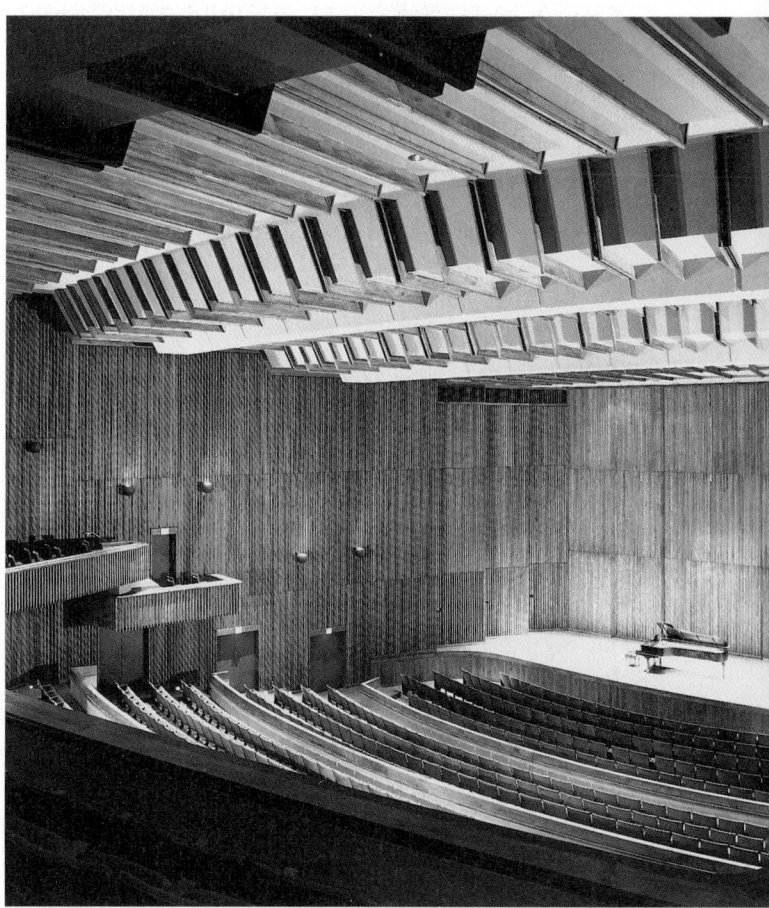

Juilliard School. Alice Tully Hall. Stoller. ©ESTO

In a later review Huxtable characterized the design as "a marriage of form and function in terms of rational simplicity and bare-boned solutions." She continued: "Juilliard, in fact, is an economy job. The richness of those theaters is in their sweep of space, the warmth of their exposed wood ceilings and walls, justness of colors and proportions, and the total absence of the gratuitous gimmicks of glamor—the romantic strainings of real or fake gold leaf and gift-shop crystal that have turned the rest of Lincoln Center into an overdressed dowager."[246]

Looking back on the school ten years after its opening, Paul Goldberger saw Juilliard as "probably the best building at Lincoln Center," but he qualified his praise: "This would be a ho-hum Brutalist building if it were done in concrete and located somewhere else; here, the travertine brings a warmer texture, and the determination of Pietro Belluschi not to play the same two-bit classicizing game as the architects of the buildings on the main plaza did is appealing."[247]

In 1966, when enough of Lincoln Center was built so that its success as an ensemble, a great urban set piece, could be assessed, Huxtable asked the "$165.4 million question": "What hath money, hopes, dreams and talent wrought?" Her answer: "lushly decorated, conservative structures that the public finds pleasing and most professionals consider a failure of nerve, imagination and talent. . . . By creative measurement, much of its product and most of its plant are an artistic failure. And that is why its expensively suave, extravagantly commonplace presence is making a great many people in the fine and performing arts profoundly uneasy."[248] Walter McQuade speculated that the center's trouble had been timidity: "Despite the massive wealth, force and fame of people on its top committees, they seem to have turned pale at the notion of finding a great architect and asking him for a great set of buildings."[249]

In 1979, twenty years after the center's groundbreaking, Paul Goldberger noted that its design had taken on a new significance as architectural fashions had changed. "Far from looking backward," he said, the center's buildings "seem now to be odd precursors of the current fashion for designing in classically inspired styles." He continued: "When the buildings were new, they appeared brazenly reactionary, but today, with a changing intellectual climate far more hospitable to buildings that allude to historical styles, this is no longer the case. But that does not make the buildings good, for their problem was never that they were classical, but that they were so badly classical."[250]

Writing in 1968, Clive Barnes emphasized the immensity of the Lincoln Center undertaking: "Only in America—or possibly in Russia—could the concept of Lincoln Center have arisen. Only in America—or possibly in Russia—do men dream such grandiose ideas, and having dreamed them bring them to reality. It is, after all, a grandiose idea. Almost ridiculous in its conception. The biggest and most brutish conglomeration dedicated to culture, culture and still more culture, that the world has ever seen." Its very grandiosity was what elicited such extreme reactions: "A Kubla Kahn pleasure palace, reviled, admired, tolerated, and now, inescapably and wonderfully, a part of New York City. No one seems to be indifferent to Lincoln Center. You either love it or you hate it. I love it." Barnes noted that although many people had derided Lincoln Center as "a cultural supermarket," there were sound economic and, "if one can put it this way, *emotional* reasons for grouping all these performing-arts units together like so many packets of detergents on a shelf. In a sense the *emotional* reason was the most important. Americans . . . desire the big and the visible. Lincoln Center was to be big and visible—and we can praise the Lord it was, for if it had not been so in concept it would never have come about in fact."[251]

Olga Gueft observed that, despite the critical response to the center, it was embraced by the general public:

Much of the criticism leveled at each new architectural debutante at Lincoln Center has puzzled the unpretentious New Yorkers who have been taking naive delight in their first grimeless cultural center. After the sooty, cramped 57th Street corner of Carnegie Hall and the dank lobby of The Metropolitan Opera House, the airy porticoes, fountains, and diamond lights of Philharmonic Hall and The New York State Theater have been seized with glee by audiences unwilling or incapable of discerning what highbrow critics have called "disastrous" acoustics and "fashionably mediocre neo-classic" design.[252]

One weakness in the Lincoln Center plan, however, affected critics and public alike: it was severely underserved by public transportation. In addition, despite a complex subterranean network of roadways, drop-off points, entrances and parking facilities, the center was insufficiently prepared to cope with motor traffic. On virtually any night when a performance was being presented, congestion was pushed beyond a comfortable level in what was already a heavily traveled area. To make matters worse, Columbus and Amsterdam avenues were the Upper West Side's only through truck routes. The music critic Alan Rich, writing in *New York* magazine in 1969, discussed the situation in detail:

The logistics problems are . . . tremendous. Trying to approach the area by car or taxicab any time after about 7:30 is a high-risk activity any night during the season; the parking spaces are pretty much gone by then, and the cabs are bumper-to-bumper five blocks away in any direction. Getting there by subway isn't much better; everybody knew when the Center was planned that having the area served by a single IRT station would be inadequate, and everybody was right. If you arrive from downtown, you have, furthermore, the problem of crossing the extremely hazardous three-way intersection of two major north-south avenues (Broadway and Columbus) and a major crosstown street (65th). . . . If the arriving-happy-at-Lincoln-Center problem is bad, the getting-away-in-one-piece situation is even worse. . . . People who, minutes before, have been wallowing in esthetic uplift are suddenly transformed into screaming monsters by the Great Lincoln Center Taxi Rush. Inside the halls, this leads to furtive but noisy departures during the last, climactic pages of symphony and opera, and to the fact that there is seldom enough applause at the end of an event to get a performer offstage, let alone back for a bow.[253]

Clive Barnes maintained that the center's sprawling, campuslike plan was at least partially responsible for the traffic problem, and he recalled the opinion of Frank Lloyd Wright, who perhaps more than any other American architect understood the impact of the automobile on architecture and planning. "At the beginning of 1956," Barnes wrote, "on hearing that the plans called for so many buildings," Wright "offered a little impromptu advice. 'It would be amusing,' he said, 'to put them one on top of the other and to leave three times as much space for parking.' I now wonder if he was joking."[254]

Aside from traffic problems, the consolidation of facilities at Lincoln Center also had the potential, especially in daytime or during performances, of creating an antiseptic environment devoid of the city's vital energy. In 1961 James Marston Fitch warned that the center was "not apt to yield the maximum of metropolitan excitement because its specialized use will lead to part-time, monochromatic activity. Traffic jams at curtain time will alternate with wasteland emptiness at other times."[255] Seven years later, Barnes made a similar point: "This great bag of buildings . . . runs the danger of becoming a separate precinct apart from the normal life of the city."[256] As early as 1958 Frederick Gutheim had anticipated the problem:

> The natural neighbors of concert halls, theaters, and artistic enterprises are not other institutions of the same sort. They are hotels, night clubs, bars, restaurants, bookstores, music shops, flower stores—all the services that are part of an evening out. What else does one do between leaving the office and arriving at the opera? Where to meet one's friends, to exchange views, to pass an agreeable hour (glass in hand) before an experience that one anticipates sharing? How to recapture its pleasure afterwards? Perhaps it was a mistake not to move the Russian Tea Room along with the Philharmonic to Lincoln Center. . . . What I am speaking of is not an after-thought or a detail that can safely be overlooked. The lack of attention thus far paid by Lincoln Center to the complete cultural and social experience means, in effect, sandwiching music in between rides on the subway. Unless it is remedied, it may finish off the audience as a working partner of the artist. If so, I am afraid, it will contribute a provincial tone to the performing arts in New York City, and be fatal to their serious acceptance.[257]

Around Lincoln Center

Critics like James Marston Fitch and Frederick Gutheim who worried that Lincoln Center would become an isolated cultural precinct had little to fear, for the center's impact on the surrounding area was profound and for the most part positive. By 1979, according to Lincoln Center's administration, 30 percent of the Upper West Side between Fifty-ninth and Seventy-second streets had been rebuilt; the new construction, with a total value of $600 million, increased the city's real estate revenues 400 percent. While the cultural center was the principal stimulus to the area's rebirth, by far the greatest amount of new construction came as a result of the Lincoln Square Urban Renewal Area project of which it was a part.

After Lincoln Center, the most significant element of the renewal project was Lincoln Towers (1962–64), an enclave of eight twenty-eight-story apartment buildings designed by S. J. Kessler & Sons.[258] The buildings collectively covered only 19 percent of their thirty-acre, landscaped superblock site, which was bounded by Sixty-sixth and Seventieth streets, Amsterdam Avenue and the abandoned New York Central railroad yards, and traversed only by West End Avenue. (One building on this site, Princess Towers, originally called Lincoln House, on the northwest corner of West End Avenue and Sixty-sixth Street, was developed separately.)[259] A new north-south street running between Sixty-fifth and Seventieth streets defined the development's western boundary. It was named Freedom Place to honor three young civil rights activists, Michael Schwerner, Andrew Goodman and James Cheney, who were murdered outside Meriden, Mississippi, in the summer of 1964; Schwerner and Goodman were both New Yorkers who had attended the Ethical Culture School.[260]

The complex's banal, beige-brick towers, punctuated by aluminum-sash windows and cantilevered balconies, were distinguished only by their size; two pairs of buildings were linked together to create immense slabs, one running along the west side of West End Avenue and the other between West End and Amsterdam avenues, roughly between Sixty-seventh and Sixty-ninth streets. Together the buildings contained 3,897 centrally air-conditioned apartments housing approximately 10,000 people. Space for 1,000 cars was provided on the site, some of it in two-level enclosed parking garages accessible from Freedom Place and West End Avenue; other parking areas were included on the site as features of the enormous landscaped courts defined by the superslabs. A one-story shopping strip on the east side of West End Avenue between Sixty-ninth and Seventieth streets and a two-story commercial and office space development that ran along the west side of Amsterdam Avenue above Sixty-seventh Street completed the ensemble.

Despite its size and the fact that it was even more impersonal than the increasingly ridiculed developments of the Housing Authority, Lincoln Towers managed to seem suburban in character, reflecting the sponsors' intention to attract middle-class tenants from other parts of the city, as well as returning suburbanites, who would value being located so near midtown and Lincoln Center. "A new community is rising in the West 60's and 70's," wrote journalist Bernard Weinraub in the *New York Times*, describing Lincoln Towers.

> Its residents are affluent and successful. Many are actors and musicians. Some are elderly couples who have moved in from the suburbs. There is also a sprinkling of widows, businessmen, prosperous young couples with children, groups of two or three girls living together, African diplomats and interracial couples. 'This,' declared Mrs. Gladys Quinn, holding her infant daughter in the hallway of an apartment house in Lincoln Towers, 'is the new *West Side Story*.'

The development proved an extraordinary success, but there were problems. Weinraub noted that "amid luxury and culture, fear still lingers," explaining that many of the residents viewed themselves as easy targets for criminals. "Perhaps the single most striking quality of the small city rising near Lincoln Center is the virtual obsession with protection. Guards abound; blue-uniformed doormen stand near building entrances like nightclub bouncers, interrogating visitors and demanding identification."[261]

Public School 199 (1963) was built in conjunction with the housing development.[262] Located at 270 West Seventieth Street, between West End and Amsterdam avenues, the school, designed by Edward Durell Stone, was a prominent example of the Board of Education's effort to go outside its own Bureau of Design and commission leading architects. The three-story elementary school building was set back from and slightly depressed below the widened street. Thin, glazed-white-brick piers incorporating decorative brickwork patterns rose to support a cantilevered roof, and recessed gray walls were punctuated with a near-uniform grid of windows. A distinct departure from the suburban-inspired designs of the 1950s and early 1960s, the school suggested the domesticated monumentality of Eric Kebbon's best efforts of the 1940s and was notable for a high level of finish and delicate details. As the editors of *Architectural Forum* put it: "This is one of Edward Durell Stone's most vigorous buildings, formal but not a bit fancy. Against a backdrop of apartment houses with their cliffs of punchcard windows and ledges of balconies, it stands free and clear, testifying to the dignity and seriousness of education, and to its rigors as well."[263]

Fordham University was also housed in the Lincoln Square development.[264] In addition to its Rose Hill campus in the Bronx, Fordham occupied a number of different Manhattan locations, which it proposed to consolidate at Lincoln Center. Initial plans for the Manhattan campus, designed by the firm of Voorhees, Walker, Smith, Smith & Haines, were published in

January 1959. They called for a cluster of low-rise buildings, with virtually continuous horizontal strip windows, surrounding two small courtyards located at the eastern end of a superblock site bounded by Amsterdam and Columbus avenues, Sixtieth and Sixty-second streets. A long, narrow, similarly articulated building, separated from the main complex by a third courtyard, ran north-south about midway through the block. A stylized circular campanile, composed of two tiers of soaring arches and occupying the northern end of that courtyard, was intended to be highly visible from Lincoln Center.

Only one component of the original plan, a building for the law school (Voorhees, Walker, Smith, Smith & Haines, 1962) facing Sixty-second Street, was realized. However, a second building, designed by the firm of Slingerland & Booss, was completed in 1969. The steel-framed, precast-concrete-clad building, named the Leon Lowenstein Center, housed a newly established liberal arts college, as well as the university's schools of education, business and social service. A long, narrow slab running parallel to Sixtieth Street, the building featured thin vertical strips of windows that, as the editors of *Progressive Architecture* reported, "one source describes as an attempt to complement the white travertine mullions of the Metropolitan Opera House."[265] The structure was elevated on a massive concrete podium that turned a sheer wall toward Sixtieth Street and contained the vast, rather barren Robert Moses Plaza. Reached by a broad flight of stairs that led from Sixty-second Street and the Lincoln Center plaza beyond, the Robert Moses Plaza contained a green marble slab decorated with a bas-relief of Moses by the sculptor Albino Manca.

In 1961 a residential complex, Litho City, was proposed by the Amalgamated Lithographers of America, Local 1, for a platform above Penn-Central's train yards that stretched along the Hudson River from Sixtieth to Seventieth Street.[266] Litho City promised to make Lincoln Towers look like a toy town. Edward Swayduck, the union's local president, asked Peter Blake, the managing editor of *Architectural Forum*, to recommend an architect for the immense project, and without hesitation he suggested Le Corbusier. Swayduck and several associates went to Paris to meet with the architect, but Le Corbusier would not see them. Blake would later write that "a rather wonderful opportunity was missed," explaining that "although Corbu's Litho City might not have met the standards newly established by Jane Jacobs, it might have been a superb prototype—if only one against which to rebel."[267] Ultimately the job went to the firm of Kelly & Gruzen; the project designers were Jordan Gruzen, Peter Samton and the Corbusier-influenced Mario Romanach. Swayduck, who said that the time had come "when enlightened public service must be recognized as a fundamental principle and responsibility of labor," approached August Heckscher, who was serving as the cultural adviser to the White House, for guidance.[268] Heckscher established and headed an advisory committee consisting of Blake; Edmund Bacon, the director of Philadelphia's City Planning Commission; Charles Colbert, the dean of Columbia University's School of Architecture; and Aline Saarinen, the architecture critic. A spirited one-day committee meeting produced a list of possible design consultants: Romaldo Giurgola, Philip Johnson, Paul Rudolph, Shadrach Woods and the office of the late Eero Saarinen. Despite these efforts, no consultants were brought in to work on the project.

Kelly & Gruzen's design consisted of nine apartment towers ranging in height from forty-one to forty-nine stories, placed amid landscaped grounds; enclosed parking facilities were located beneath. Schools—including the proposed United World Center, an international educational facility serving 1,000 students as well as foreign diplomats—a twenty-story motel, shops, a marina, a luxury-liner pier and a waterfront park were to complete the middle-income residential development, which was intended to accommodate 25,000 people. Though Brobdingnagian in scale, the scheme did show some degree of respect for the city's characteristic urbanism, calling for the extension of the street grid. Nonetheless, the plan was widely opposed; both the Citizens Union and the New York Chapter of the American Institute of Architects, fearing that the project would contribute to congestion in the area and further stress already overburdened services, urged the city to conduct a comprehensive area study before granting approval. The project died in 1966 when union leaders claimed that Penn-Central had impeded progress and railroad officials countercharged that the union had never delivered the requisite performance bond.

The following year plans were released for another Swayduck project, the vast Graphic Arts Center, designed by Paul Rudolph, also for a site fronting the Hudson River, this one near the heart of the New York printing trade on the west side below Canal Street.[269] The complexly massed development, containing industrial lofts as well as apartments, schools and recreational facilities, was to bridge the West Side Highway, occupying a site bounded by the Hudson River, Harrison, Greenwich and Laight streets, as well as extending on platforms into the river itself, where it would incorporate a marina. The futuristic, technologically bold scheme called for prefabricated apartment units to be hung from trusses cantilevered from cores containing elevators and fire stairs. The plan was never realized.

In 1974 the fledgling real estate developer Donald Trump announced his intention to erect a massive housing development on the former Litho City site, as well as on an L-shaped site owned by Penn-Central, extending from Thirtieth to Thirty-ninth Street, from the Hudson River to Eleventh Avenue at the site's northern end and Tenth Avenue at its southern end.[270] Two years later, with no construction begun, Trump called for the rerouting of the West Side Highway to the east of the Litho City site and the extension of Riverside Park south from Seventy-second to Fifty-ninth Street (see chapter 2). Neither that proposal nor Trump's general plans for the site progressed.

A headquarters building for the New York Chapter of the American Red Cross, on the northwest corner of Amsterdam Avenue and Sixty-sixth Street, was completed in 1963 in the renewal area.[271] Designed by Skidmore, Owings & Merrill, the building was a pristine gridded temple, perched dramatically on a platform that compensated for the sloping site; a retaining wall emerged from ground level at the site's northern corner and rose to a height of sixteen feet at the lower southwestern corner. The five-story building consisted of a precast-concrete superstructure that divided the long front and rear facades into thirty-five bays of equal size, and the side facades into twenty bays each; recessed five feet behind this grid were glass walls set into aluminum frames. Despite the architects' effort to carve out a site worthy of its institutional occupant, Norval White and Elliot Willensky said that the low podium, "surveying traffic-choked Amsterdam Avenue," was "hardly an acropolis."[272]

The travertine-clad walls of the Lincoln Square Synagogue (1970), located within the shadow of Lincoln Towers at 200 Amsterdam Avenue, echoed Lincoln Center's architecture to establish a tone of civic authority.[273] The firm of Hausman & Rosenberg designed the two-story-high building as a boldly

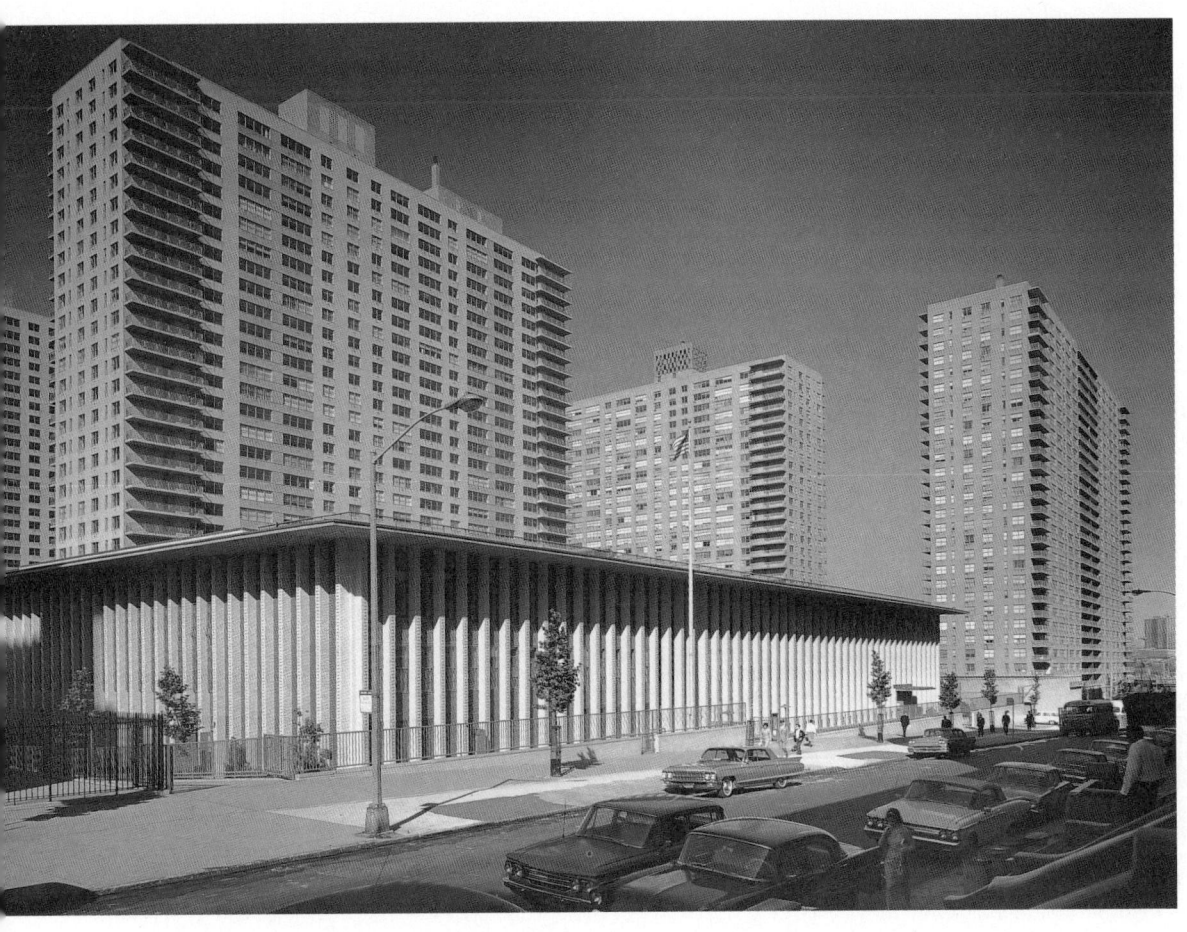

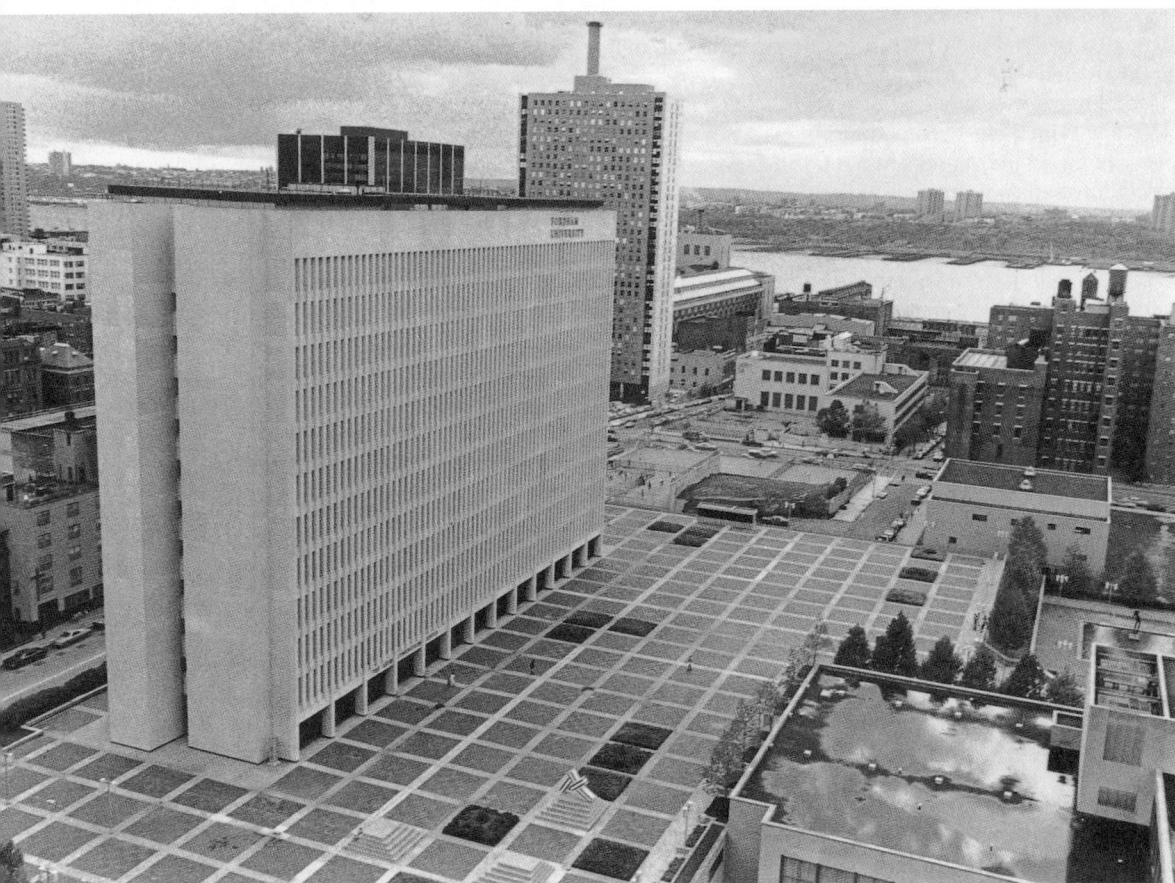

Top: Public School 199, 270 West Seventieth Street, between West End and Amsterdam avenues. Edward Durell Stone, 1963. View to the southwest. Stoller. ©ESTO

Bottom: Fordham University, between Columbus and Amsterdam avenues, West Sixtieth and West Sixty-second streets. Slingerland & Booss, 1961. View to the southwest. FUA

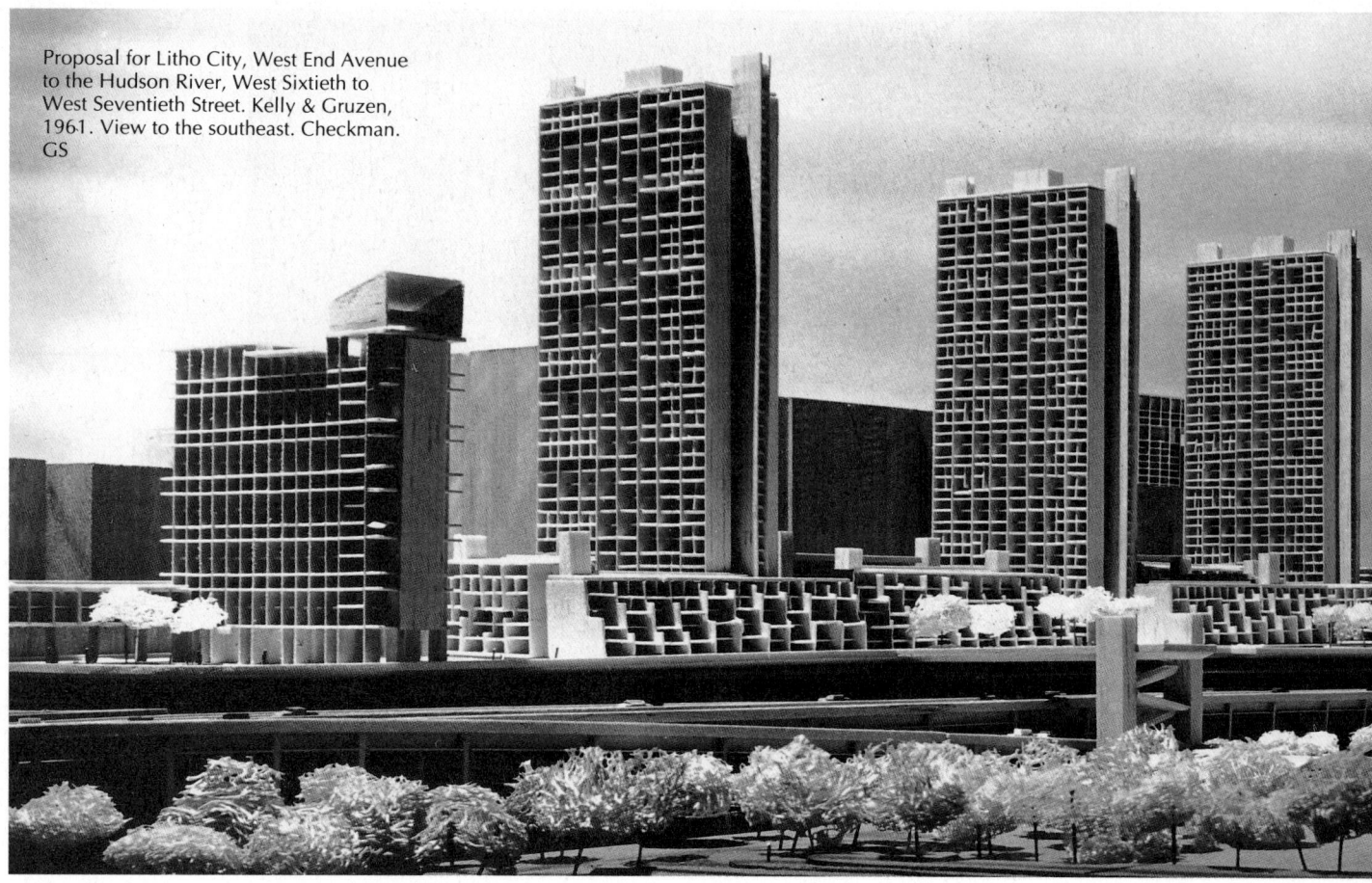

sculptural cylindrical shape set back from the street and flanked by V-shaped piers that extended beyond the roofline. Inside, a circular sanctuary contained an arenalike seating arrangement. While the synagogue's gleaming exterior powerfully reflected the area's renewal, the building nonetheless seemed more appropriate to the landscaped grounds of the World's Fair at Flushing Meadows than to heavily traveled Amsterdam Avenue.

The Martin Luther King, Jr. High School (1975), on the west side of Amsterdam Avenue between Sixty-fifth and Sixty-sixth streets, had been proposed more than a decade earlier as a replacement for the demolished High School of Commerce.[274] Designed by Frost Associates, the school added to the avenue's emerging civic identity but failed to maintain any sense of the traditional street wall or contribute to the pedestrian scale. Deeply recessed from the avenue on an elevated plaza paved in red-brown quarry tile, the building was clad in dark-tinted glass and self-weathering steel. As at Intermediate School 201 in Harlem (see chapter 12), classrooms faced inward and were surrounded by glass-wall corridors that allowed students to glimpse the outside world only between classes. The dark glass further severed the link between the building's interior and the outdoors. Internal activity was nearly invisible to passersby, except at night, when the empty, illuminated corridors cast a glow across the rather barren plaza. At the northeast corner of the plaza, a monumental sculpture memorialized Martin Luther King, Jr., the slain civil rights leader.[275] The sculptor William Tarr, who had originally been commissioned by the school's architects to design a fountain for the plaza, created a twenty-eight-foot cube of the same steel used for the school. Looming above the street, the cube was covered with quotations from King, as well as dates and initials relating to his life.

Even before the school's completion, some observers feared that its elevated plaza would prove uninviting and would be removed from the area's overall pedestrian traffic patterns. In 1969 the Housing and Development Administration released preliminary plans for the Lincoln-Amsterdam Urban Renewal Area, which called for the construction of an addition to the Amsterdam Houses, stores, a community center and the La Guardia High School of Music and Art.[276] As designed by Robert A. M. Stern and Alanne Baerson for the HDA, the plan took into consideration the heavy, swift-moving traffic patterns that the area's superblocks had introduced on the remaining superwide through streets, as well as the raised datum plane of the Lincoln Center development caused by the westward slope of the land. The proposed solution was to build two pedestrian bridges: one linking the plaza of the Martin Luther King, Jr. High School to the east side of Amsterdam Avenue, and another linking the proposed La Guardia High School to Lincoln Center. In addition, the plan attempted to help break down the superblock pattern with the creation of a midblock pedestrian bridge within the renewal area that would extend from the Sixty-fourth Street cul-de-sac penetrating the site of the Amsterdam Houses across Sixty-fifth Street to the Martin Luther King, Jr. High School; a fourth pedestrian bridge would cross Sixty-sixth Street, linking the school to the Lincoln Towers development. Although the proposal was never realized, it stimulated a redesign of the La Guardia High School, originally designed by Pietro Belluschi and Eduardo Catalano; when completed in 1985, long after the delay caused by the city's fiscal crisis, the design was credited to Catalano alone.[277]

Oppenheimer, Brady & Lehrecke's twenty-seven-story addition to the Amsterdam Houses (1974), at 240 West Sixty-fifth

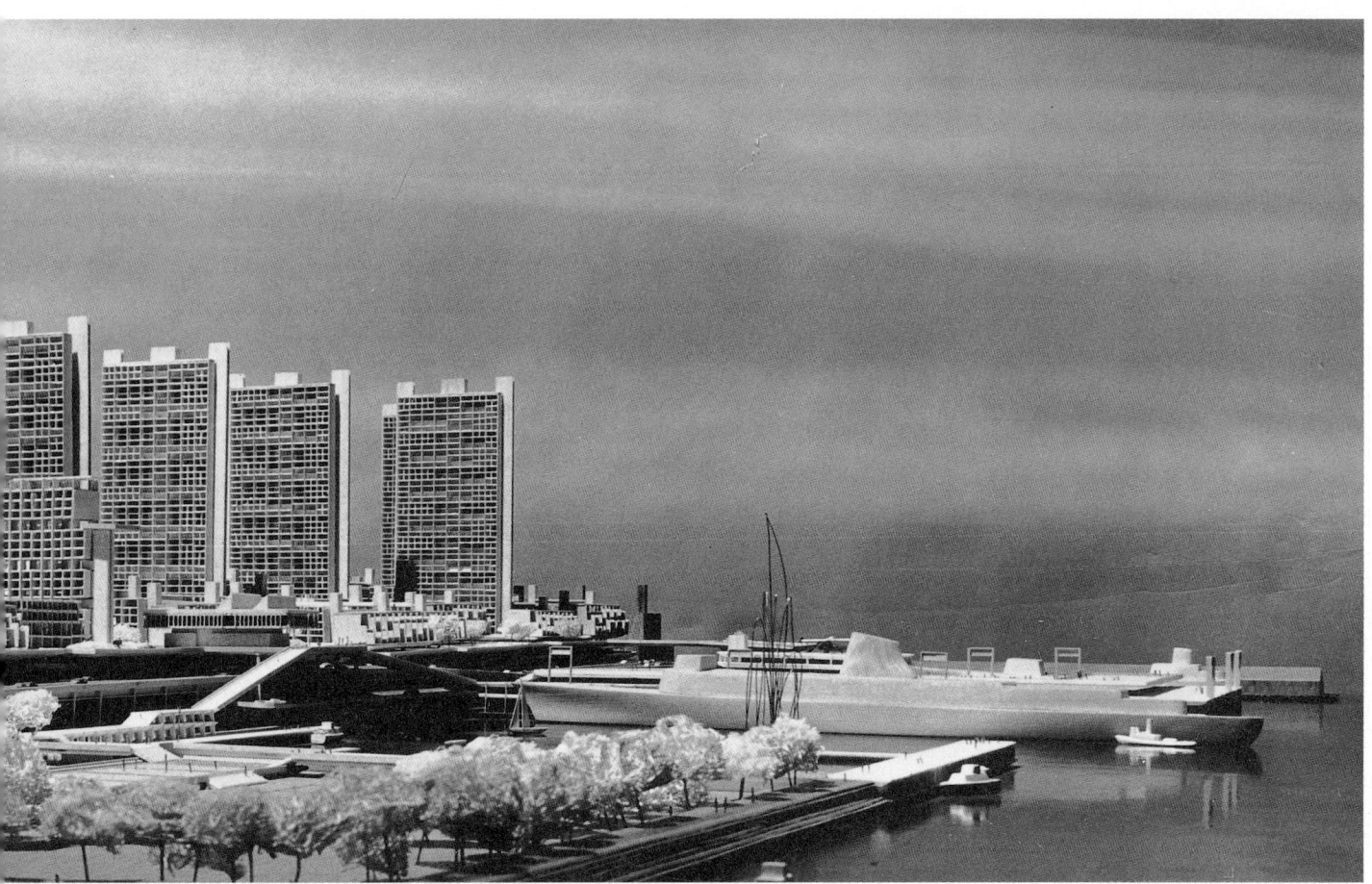

Street between West End and Amsterdam avenues, was one of the area's housing highlights, breaking out of the standard mold of publicly assisted housing.[278] The brick walls of the tower, which rose from a plaza bordered by low-rise buildings containing a day-care center and other community facilities, were interrupted by triangular concrete projections evoking the bay windows of brownstones. Two years later David Todd & Associates' Lincoln-Amsterdam Houses, at 110 West End Avenue, on the east side of the avenue between Sixty-fourth and Sixty-fifth streets, again presented an alternative to traditional public housing while elevating the general design quality of the area's new residential buildings, public or private. As designed by Robert Cabrera, the associate in charge of the project, the building's facades combined orange jumbo bricks and precast concrete in highly sculptural compositions incorporating multiple setbacks, projections and cantilevered sections. Norval White and Elliot Willensky noted that the building was designed "almost as heroic, nonrepresentational sculpture-in-the-round."[279]

The impact of privately sponsored building spurred by the completion of the Lincoln Square Urban Renewal Area projects could be most dramatically seen along Broadway. Not surprisingly, the construction of Lincoln Center stimulated a dramatic increase in the number and quality of restaurants in the area.[280] First among the new establishments was the Ginger Man, located at 51 West Sixty-fourth Street, opened in 1965 by the public relations executive Ned McDavid with the actor Patrick O'Neal and his brother Mike.[281] The restaurant's principal facade featured a large expanse of glass, shielded by an awning that also protected an outdoor sidewalk café. Inside, dark wood paneling established the informal, clubby atmosphere of an Irish pub.

Soon after, the restaurateur Herb Evans opened an estab-lishment bearing his name in a space formerly occupied by a supermarket on the northeast corner of Broadway and Sixty-fourth Street.[282] Working with the architect Samuel Arlen, Evans gave his restaurant an instantly recognizable identity on the street, putting up brick facades punctuated by a dozen floor-to-ceiling arched windows and Victorian-style light fixtures. Inside, Evans and Arlen created a gardenlike ambience, complete with freestanding lampposts and potted trees, in the large space enclosed by brick walls.

The Lincoln Square Motor Inn (1963), located on the north side of Sixty-sixth Street, between Amsterdam Avenue and Broadway, capitalized on the area's increased tourist trade while also reflecting a larger trend toward the provision of motel-style accommodations on Manhattan's west side.[283] Designed by Leo Stillman, with interiors by Leon Hegwood and Carlton Varney of Dorothy Draper & Company, the ten-story building was clad in red and white enamel brick. Its amenities included a subterranean parking garage and a rooftop swimming pool. In 1974, two years after the Lincoln Square Motor Inn was bought by the People's Republic of China to serve as their mission to the United Nations, the architect Henry Liu designed an elegant but severe new stone-clad entrance.[284]

S. J. Kessler & Sons' behemoth Dorchester Towers (1965) was the first privately developed upscale apartment building erected in the area after the construction of Lincoln Center had sent property values soaring.[285] Distinguished not by its overall design quality but by its setback massing along Broadway, which reflected the lingering effects of pre-1961 zoning ordinances, the building also had the somewhat dubious distinction of being the first white-glazed-brick apartment building constructed on the Upper West Side.

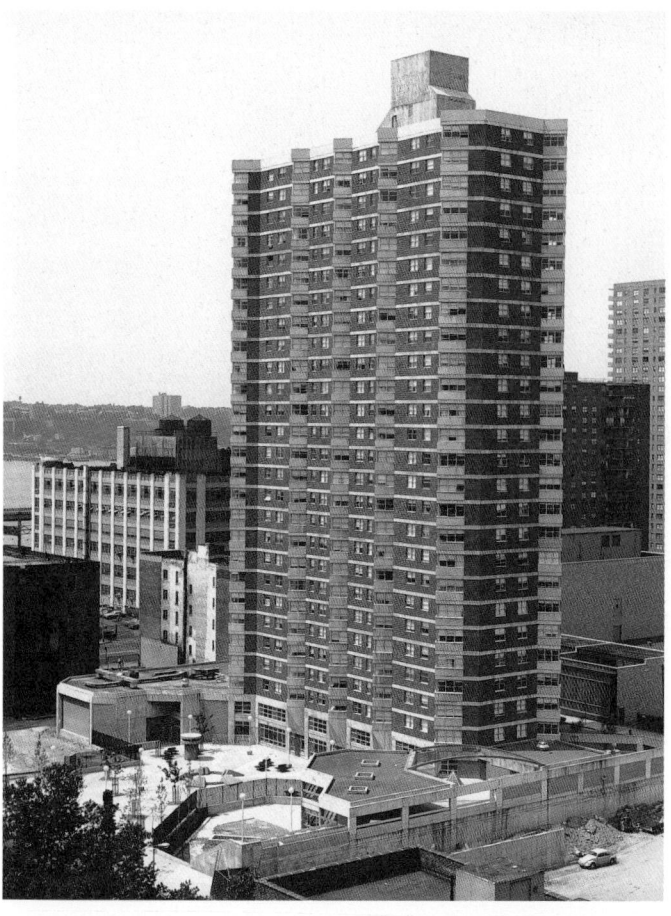

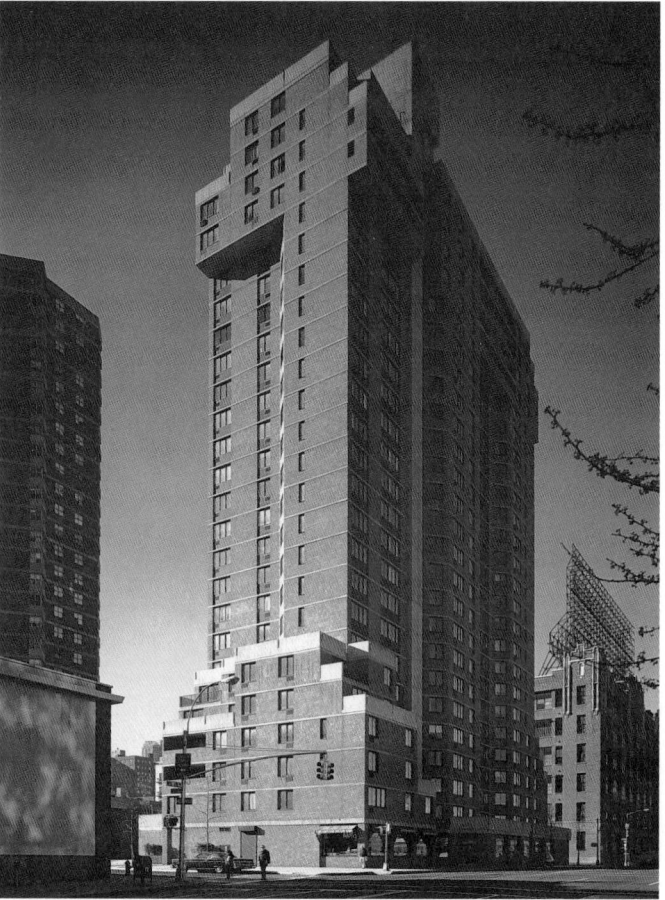

Private office development also took place in the area, but the quality of the products was distinctly second class. In 1963 the Bankers Trust Company completed a branch bank at 1960 Broadway, which occupied the prominent trapezoidal site just north of the parklet that was Lincoln Square but ignored the avenue's diagonal.[286] The two-story rectangular building, designed by Oppenheimer, Brady & Lehrecke, was a carefully articulated if rather meagerly budgeted essay in Miesian Modernism. Clad in black-anodized aluminum and glass, the building stood in sharp contrast not only to its ragtag nineteenth-century neighbors but also to the Classical buildings of Lincoln Center.

In 1966, a five-story office building with a curtain wall of aluminum, glass and gray porcelain, designed by H. I. Feldman, was completed on a site occupying the full blockfront on the west side of Broadway between Sixty-sixth and Sixty-seventh streets.[287] The Marie Antoinette Hotel (Julius Munckowitz, 1895) and an annex (C. P. H. Gilbert, 1903), which had become the Dauphin Hotel, stood on the site until they were demolished in 1961 and 1962 respectively.[288] The site served as a parking lot until 1964, when construction on the office building began.

Skidmore, Owings & Merrill designed 1865 Broadway (1966), on the northwest corner of Sixty-first Street, to serve as the headquarters of the American Bible Society, which also rented space to nonprofit arts organizations.[289] The exposed precast-concrete structure of the twelve-story building gave it a hulking presence. It was set back from Broadway, failing to fill its irregularly shaped site and leaving a rather miserly plaza along the avenue.

Certainly one of the area's most dramatic building sites, one that could have served as a symbolic gateway to the entire renewed Lincoln Square area, was the triangular plot bounded by Broadway, Central Park West, Columbus Circle and Sixty-first Street. Since 1915 it had been occupied by a two-story commercial structure known as the American Circle Building, which had been built by William Randolph Hearst as a temporary building, to be replaced with a skyscraper headquarters for his publishing empire.[290] Wartime shortages, however, stymied his plans. When the building was demolished in 1966, it was revealed that it contained a mysterious Gothic room, reputedly built as a private chapel for Hearst's longtime companion, the actress Marion Davies. In 1945 Emery Roth and Pomerance & Breines collaborated on a proposal for a sixteen-story office building to be erected on the site.[291] The building, which was never realized, was to fill its wedge-shaped site and, like the pioneering Flatiron Building (D. H. Burnham & Co., 1903), was to have gracefully curved corners.[292] While the facades were to be dominated by a grid of chastely articulated punched windows, the presence of Classically inspired decoration on the first floor, as well as a double-height recessed colonnade at the eleventh and twelfth floors, furthered the Modern Classical vocabulary that Emery Roth had pursued during the interwar period.

In 1965 it was announced that a forty-five-story, bronze-colored aluminum-and-glass office tower would be erected on the site, completing the postwar reconstruction of Columbus Circle.[293] The new office tower, designed by Harold M. Liebman & Associates, was to be surrounded by an open plaza elevated four feet above the street. The building's vertical service cores were to be housed in a narrow white marble tower flanking the building's west side. The following year the plan was abandoned in favor of an alternate design, also prepared by Liebman, that called for a far more distinctively massed building.[294] The proposal was for a ten-story triangular office building that completely filled its site, topped by a thirty-five-story circular apartment tower, planned to contain Manhattan's most expensive rental accommodations. Ada Louise Huxtable found the proposed building laughable: "The reasoning here seems to be that if a ship-shaped glass structure is a success in Hartford (the Phoenix Mutual Life Insurance Building by Wallace Harrison) and circular apartment towers made history in Chicago (Marina City by Bertrand Goldberg), New York can go two cities one better by building both, one on top of the other."[295]

Although the developers of the proposed building, the Forteyn Management Company, cleared the site, they could not secure the requisite mortgage financing. In 1967 they sold the property to the Investors Funding Corporation of New York, which leased it to the publicly owned Realty Equities Corporation. The latter corporation erected a forty-four-story office building, designed by the Dallas-based architect Thomas E. Stanley, and leased approximately half of the space to serve as the headquarters of Gulf & Western Industries.[296] The tower, clad in white marble and aluminum, sat on an elevated podium that terminated at the triangular site's apex in a circular sunken plaza, which contained an entrance to the building as well as access to the Columbus Circle subway station. This feature was introduced at the behest of the Urban Design Group, who were in the midst of preparing guidelines to channel the street's future in light of the dramatic changes they felt were about to take place along Broadway as a result of Lincoln Center's success (see below). Despite its forty-four stories, the building failed to convey a strong sense of height or maximize the site's potential for establishing a memorable skyline icon that would stand free of its immediate context. Instead, the highly visible building was at once a behemoth and a banality, and its contribution to the skyline was notable only as a memorial to a lost opportunity.

A top-floor restaurant in the Gulf & Western Building, located in a space used as an executive dining room during the day, did, however, take full advantage of the site's spectacular views. According to the designer, Ellen Lehman McCluskey, the restaurant's animal and plant motifs, which appeared on the room's wallpaper as well as on frosted-glass partitions, were inspired by adjacent Central Park and its zoo. The building also included a 532-seat movie theater, designed by Carson, Lundin & Shaw and managed by the Paramount Pictures Corporation, a subsidiary of Gulf & Western. The theater was virtually invisible at street level, its location marked only by a thirty-foot-diameter glass-walled structure—in essence a superscaled kiosk—based on a proposal by the Urban Design Group. The pavilion filled the northwestern portion of the triangular site and was surmounted by a continuously operated light-emitting-diode sign. It housed a ticket booth, as well as an escalator and a curved staircase that led to a subterranean lobby and auditorium; theatrical lighting illuminated the theatergoers' route. The staircase was evocative of Wallace Harrison's boldly sculptural intertwined staircases at the Metropolitan Opera House, and the lobby seemed to simultaneously pay homage to its high-culture prototype and parody it.

By 1969 widespread concern had arisen over the area's fate as it continued to be transformed by large-scale residential and commercial development. That year a fifteen-block special zoning district, an irregular, somewhat gerrymandered area bounded by Amsterdam Avenue, Central Park West, Sixtieth and Sixty-eighth streets, was proposed to encourage the maintenance of the area as a lively, mixed-use area.[297] The goal of the legislation was to establish a uniform cornice line and a continuous ground-level arcade for the buildings on the east side of

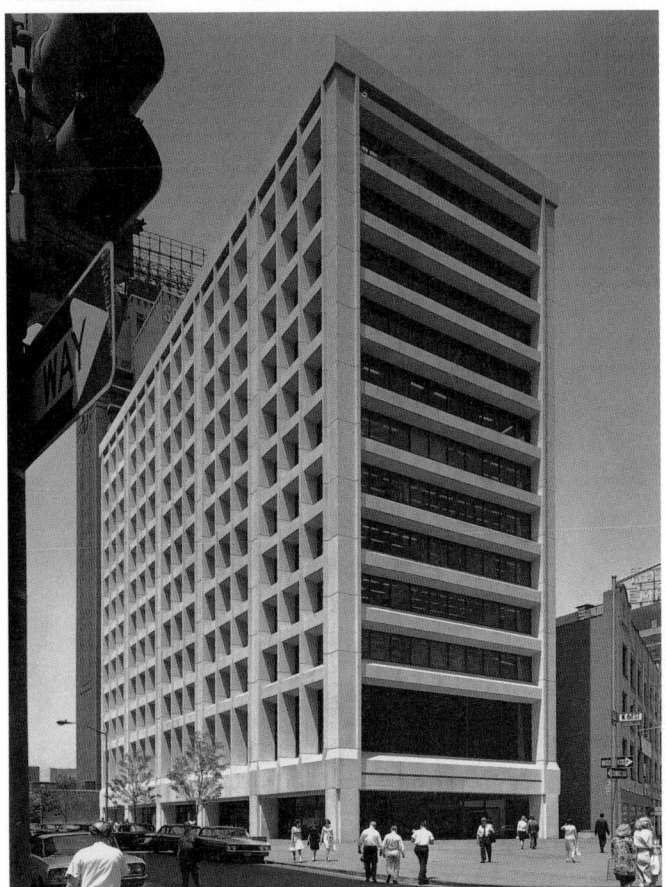

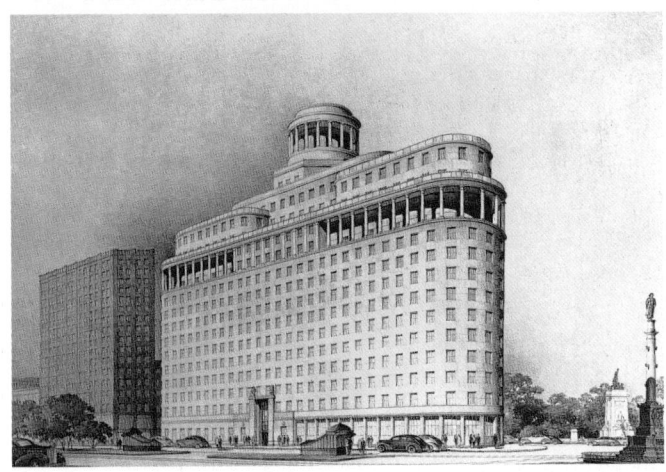

Top left: Addition to Amsterdam Houses, 240 West Sixty-fifth Street, between Amsterdam and West End avenues. Oppenheimer, Brady & Lehrecke, 1974. View to the northwest. NYCHA

Bottom left: Lincoln-Amsterdam Houses, east blockfront of West End Avenue, West Sixty-fourth to West Sixty-fifth Street. David Todd & Associates, 1976. View to the southeast. Hoyt. DT

Top right: American Bible Society, 1865 Broadway, northwest corner of West Sixty-first Street. Skidmore, Owings & Merrill, 1966. View to the northwest. Stoller. ©ESTO

Bottom right: Proposal for office building at Columbus Circle, bounded by Broadway, Central Park West and West Sixty-first Street. Emery Roth and Pomerance & Breines, 1945. Rendering of view to the northeast. Wurts. ERS

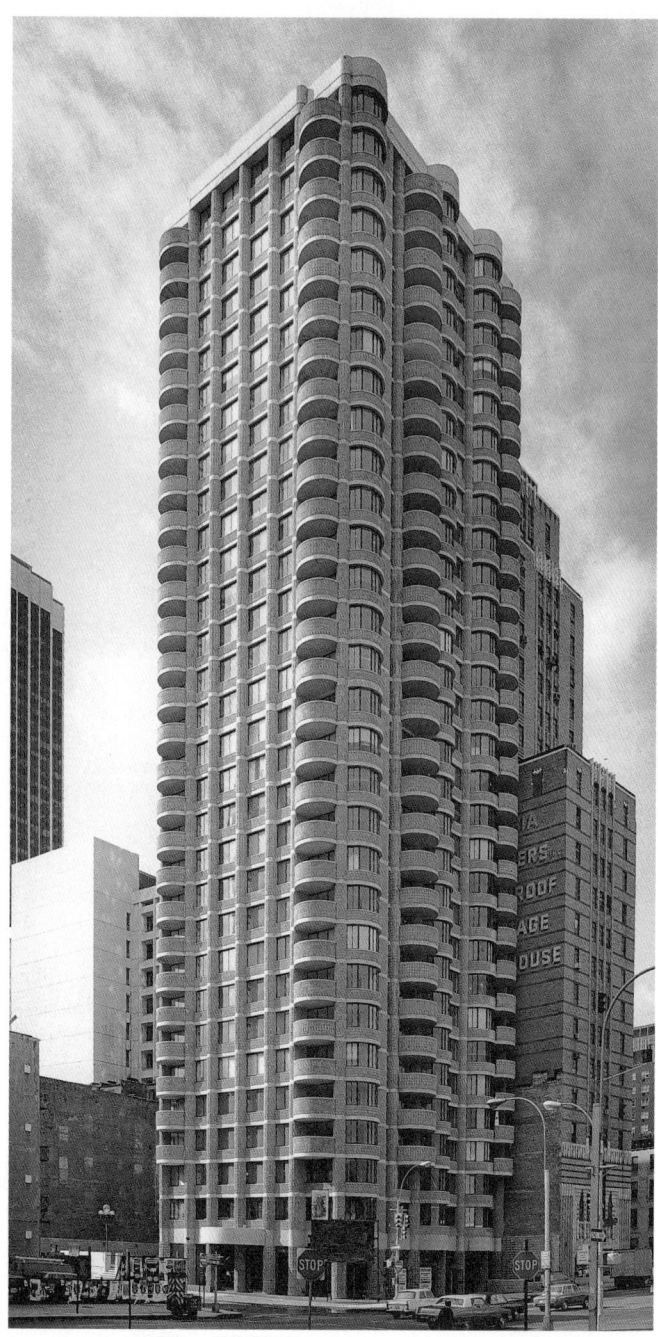

Lincoln Plaza Tower, southeast corner of Columbus Avenue and West Sixty-second Street. Horace Ginsbern & Associates, 1972. View to the southeast. ©Gil Amiaga. HASU

Broadway between Columbus Circle and Lincoln Center, mid-block plazas on the east side of these buildings, enclosed public spaces and improved subway entrances. According to Jonathan Barnett, one of the principals of the Urban Design Group, which formulated the district plan, "it contained the first language that specified a range of mandated or optional improvements in advance of any decision to build. Its purpose was to regulate the development of new buildings in the neighborhood of Lincoln Center for the Performing Arts. One of the subsidiary purposes had been to stimulate private real estate development; but there was no master plan for this development, much less any means of seeing that a plan was followed."[298] The Lincoln Square Special Zoning District was the second incentive district initiated by the City Planning Commission (the first was for the theater district). Walter McQuade, the editor of *Architectural Forum*, enthusiastically supported the resolution establishing the district: "Several years ago, Broadway became a pleased but uncertain link between Columbus Circle and that glorious new rich cultural event—Lincoln Center. She was like a mother without a high school diploma, whose daughter had just married a Rockefeller. . . . If [the legislation] works, this part of Broadway may become one of the world's pleasantest and best-looking avenues."[299]

The first building to reflect the impact of the new zoning was One Lincoln Plaza, designed by Philip Birnbaum and completed in 1971.[300] The building's site, on the east side of Broadway between Sixty-third and Sixty-fourth streets, had been purchased by the developer Seymour Milstein after the New York Academy of Sciences had abandoned its plans to build there. Milstein's mixed-use building filled in what would have been the western endpoint of the proposed mall and directly faced Lincoln Center, becoming in effect a powerful if oversized and stylistically inconsistent element of the plaza building group. According to Jonathan Barnett, it was Milstein's decision to develop the site that triggered the City Planning Commission's urgency in establishing the zoning district. Once the special district had become law, Milstein, "playing skillfully on the institutional jealousies between City agencies," convinced the Board of Standards and Appeals to give him an additional 20 percent floor area bonus over the bonus already allowed by the special district. This resulted in the City Planning Commission taking the Board of Standards and Appeals to court. Eventually the case was thrown out, and Milstein began construction of the building. "The developer followed the provisions of the special district," said Barnett, "but the building's additional bulk seriously distorts the Planning Commission's design intent. . . . All in all, the building was not the best advertisement for special design legislation; but the arcade and massing essential for the district concept are there."[301]

The facades of Milstein's forty-three-story tower were visually active though banal, combining beige and dark-brown brick; the building was far more significant as a reflection of the area's changing economic fortunes than as architecture. It was also a serious test of the city's willingness to hold to its own planning ideals. The City Planning Commission had imposed numerous restrictions on the project, including the provision of a public park east of the building, which Milstein accepted in exchange for the right to build additional stories. The commission then asked Milstein to develop the property on the block directly to the south in the same manner, calling for a larger park (though it would be divided by Sixty-third Street); again, the developer agreed. After excavation for One Lincoln Plaza had begun, the city tried to downgrade the zoning for both of Milstein's properties. Milstein sued the city for the right to complete the building as proposed and won the case. When the city succeeded in downzoning the adjacent site, however, Milstein withdrew his plan to develop it.[302] In the meantime, the developer was unable to acquire a property occupied by a five-story tenement on the north side of Sixty-third Street that he had intended to clear to make way for One Lincoln Plaza. After long and arduous negotiations with the tenement's owner, Colonel Elyachar, who refused to sell, Milstein went ahead with his building. Andrew Alpern and Seymour Durst would later claim that the presence of the holdout tenement contributed to the awkward massing and problematic interior planning of Milstein's building; it indisputably diminished the size and value of the adjacent park.[303]

One Lincoln Plaza incorporated an eight-story base containing office space for the American Society of Composers, Authors and Publishers (ASCAP), as well as other tenants, and a commercial arcade facing Broadway. Above this sprouted a thirty-five-story apartment tower that adopted a modified L shape. Angling back sharply from Broadway, the tower's western facade conformed neither to Broadway nor to the prevailing street grid. Norval White and Elliot Willensky called the building "a spastic work" whose "overwhelming skewed prism has no redeeming social significance." Commenting on the area's zoning regulations, the authors said that the building's public arcade "only allowed it to be bigger—what an urbanistic mistake!"[304] Paul Goldberger described One Lincoln Plaza as "one of the city's very largest apartment buildings, and one of its most disturbing: it towers over Lincoln Center, making the buildings of the cultural complex look even weaker and more fragile than they are, and it wreaks havoc with the Central Park West skyline as seen from Central Park."[305] Taking his criticism even further, Goldberger said that "the massive hulk of One Lincoln Plaza bearing down from across Broadway . . . is a sign to all that when it comes to planning and architecture in New York, culture may be important, but commerce ranks higher."[306]

The aborted Milstein project between Sixty-second and Sixty-third streets was replaced by 30 Lincoln Plaza, a crudely detailed but cleverly massed apartment building, also designed by Philip Birnbaum (1979).[307] Above the third story, the building's mass rose in an echelon; the curved corners of the facade were tangential to Broadway, creating the impression of bay windows while holding the street wall. The buff brick used here was far more sympathetic to the surroundings than the visually strident light and dark brick patterning of One Lincoln Plaza had been; the building's warm golden tone complemented the Modern Classic Century Apartments (Irwin Chanin, Jacques Delamarre and Sloan & Robertson, 1931), located directly to the east.[308] To comply with the area's zoning regulations, 30 Lincoln Plaza incorporated a midblock park containing a multilevel fountain, as well as a street-level commercial arcade and a subterranean movie theater complex that reflected the neighborhood's new identity as an entertainment center.

The area's most egregious new work of architecture was Two Lincoln Square, a thirty-six-story apartment tower on the east blockfront of Columbus Avenue between Sixty-fifth and Sixty-sixth streets (1975).[309] An undistinguished beige-brick slab designed by Schuman, Lichtenstein & Claman, it was sponsored jointly by a private development partnership and the Church of Jesus Christ of Latter-day Saints (the Mormon Church). The building was sited with its long walls running perpendicular to the avenue; the tower turned a windowless wall toward Central Park, denying its tenants spectacular views. Goldberger called

the building "as undistinguished as they come" and the blank wall "a frigid gesture to the building's surroundings," but he noted that the lack of windows had resulted from city building codes, which had strict requirements for fenestration on a building's property line but not facing a street. "Rather than reorient the building," Goldberger said, "the architects found it easier to build the windowless wall."[310] At the tower's base and extending the full block to Sixty-fourth Street was an eighty-five-foot-high, travertine-covered structure housing church offices, a chapel and an information center. To satisfy the special district's bonus requirements for ground-level arcades, a "public space" was included between the low-lying building and the tower, but it consisted of little more than a dreary and sometimes menacing cul-de-sac connected by a short passage to Columbus Avenue. A notable example of the abuse of the special district's provisions, the public space performed no useful social function and was quickly padlocked, despite protests from the City Planning Commission.

An even greater disappointment in its inability to realize the potential of its site was the Nevada Towers (1977), a single building occupying the triangular block bounded by Amsterdam Avenue and Broadway, Sixty-ninth and Seventieth streets and designed by Philip Birnbaum.[311] Not only did the rectilinear building, clad in dark brown brick, fail to adopt the dramatic triangular shape of its site, but its north-facing wall was nearly blank, punctuated only by small kitchen and bathroom windows, failing to take advantage of the unobstructed views up Broadway that the site naturally commanded. The site's apex was occupied by a one-story commercial building separated from the tower, which rose without setbacks.

A rare exception to the prevailing banality of apartment house design in the area was the Lincoln Plaza Tower, on the southeast corner of Columbus Avenue and Sixty-second Street.[312] Designed by Harold Sussman of Horace Ginsbern & Associates, the striated concrete building incorporated bay windows and rounded balconies. Goldberger praised the building, calling it "one of the few pieces of luxury housing built since World War II in New York that try." He went on to describe its architectural precedent: "It is straight out of Paul Rudolph—one of New York's best examples, in fact, of the trickle-down aspect of contemporary architecture, in which a good architect invents a form and it is copied in increasingly simplified, picturesque, and less rigorous ways."[313]

MANHATTANTOWN AND THE WEST SIDE URBAN RENEWAL AREA

In 1951 Robert Moses, in his capacity as City Construction Coordinator and chairman of the city's Committee on Slum Clearance, sent to the Board of Estimate a proposal for Manhattantown, a slum clearance project for the site bounded by Central Park West, Amsterdam Avenue, West Ninety-seventh and West 100th streets.[1] The plan called for the elimination of West Ninety-eighth and West Ninety-ninth streets, and the compensatory widening of the perimeter crosstown streets. In 1952 the site, consisting of dilapidated garage structures as well as run-down apartment houses, tenements and rowhouses, most of which had been converted to single-room occupancy, was acquired under Title I of the Housing Act of 1949. The relocation problems posed by the site were vast, yet Moses made light of them, as he did in most of his slum clearance projects. But in this case, after relocation had begun, civic groups, led by the Women's City Club, challenged him, pointing out that as a result of his policies people were living there in worse conditions than before, and that relocation was proving problematic for the economically disadvantaged families housed on the site because the market-rate housing offered them was too expensive and public housing was available only after long waits, if at all.

Manhattantown was the first massive renewal project to be scrutinized on a cost-benefit basis that took into serious consideration the plight of those living on the site. Opponents of the project argued that the site's current residents would not benefit from the renewal process because the 2,560 new dwelling units proposed for the seventeen twenty-story-high buildings would not only be too expensive but would also represent a significant reduction in the amount of housing presently available on the site. It was not statistical analysis, however, but charges of rampant corruption running throughout the entire Title I slum clearance program in New York that compromised Manhattantown. After charges of corruption led to an investigation by the Senate Committee on Banking and Currency in the fall of 1954, Mayor Wagner banned future work for five years on Title I projects for all initial private participants in Manhattantown, including the architect Melvin E. Kessler, of S. J. Kessler & Sons, who had taken an equity position in the development and whose fees had been misrepresented in the sponsors' public filings.[2] Moses's deals with developers had come to reek of cronyism, and he had let Manhattantown drag on for years as the first developers milked the project by collecting rents from on-site tenants living in condemned housing, which the temporary landlords were not obliged to maintain to any decent standard. As a result of the Title I scandals, and those surrounding the Manhattantown project in particular, Moses and his high-handed approach began to be carefully examined by the press: "It is not that Moses acts against the law," Stephen G. Thompson wrote in *Architectural Forum* in 1959, "but simply above it."[3]

By 1957 no construction had taken place and the original developers, Jack Ferman and Seymour Milstein, were replaced by Webb & Knapp, which developed the project along with the Aluminum Company of America (Alcoa). In July 1957 the name of the project was changed to West Park Apartments, and shortly thereafter Park West Village. As redesigned by Skidmore, Owings & Merrill and completed in 1960, it consisted of seven red-brick slabs, ranging in height from seventeen to twenty stories, with well-proportioned metal casement windows and balconies. The buildings, collectively containing 2,700 apartments, were set amid landscaped grounds that also incorporated above-ground parking lots and tennis courts, which were located at the northeast corner of Amsterdam Avenue and Ninety-seventh Street and were managed as a private club.

At the site's northern edge, along 100th Street between Columbus and Amsterdam avenues, a cluster of public facilities served both Park West Village and the public Frederick Douglass Houses development to the north, which consisted of twenty-nine buildings, including renovated four-story buildings and twenty-story brick high rises.[4] Located between Manhattan and Amsterdam avenues, 100th and 104th streets, and completed between 1957 and 1970, the Douglass complex, which was designed by Kahn & Jacobs, housed 2,462 families. At the project's southern border, adjacent to the Trinity Evangelical Lutheran Church (George W. Conable, 1909), at 164 West 100th Street, were two new civic buildings: a four-story building (Knappe & Johnson, 1960), 141–150 West 100th Street, clad in white-enamel brick and green metal panels, housed the

Eleventh Battalion of the Fire Department and the Twenty-fourth Police Precinct; across the street, a brick-and-concrete building (Harry M. Prince, 1960), 150–160 West 100th Street, set back from the street and organized around a landscaped open courtyard, housed the Bloomingdale branch of the New York Public Library and the Department of Health's Riverside Health Center.[5] Though together the buildings helped to create a village-scaled civic center, the bland, heavy-handed, vaguely Modernist designs were a telling testament to the collapse of standards in the area of municipally sponsored construction.

More successful was the Grosvenor Neighborhood House (1963), on the southeast corner of Amsterdam Avenue and 105th Street, the first privately financed settlement house to be built in New York City since 1928.[6] Despite its modest size and three-story height, the blocky mass of the Modernist building, designed by the firm of Moore & Hutchins, filled the corner site, establishing an appropriately monumental presence. On the first floor, horizontal strip windows were punctuated by dark brown brick piers and spandrels clad in a variety of earth-toned mosaic tiles. The two higher stories were clad in limestone-trimmed buff brick and incorporated large expanses of glass. At the top, a chain-link-fence cage enclosed a rooftop recreational area. Located directly to the east, at 150 West 105th Street, between Amsterdam and Columbus avenues, was Unger & Unger's Public School 145 (1961), the Bloomingdale School.[7] This ordinary structure was a low-lying, three-story, buff-brick mass accentuated by horizontal strip windows and relieved by vermilion piers that, although apparently intended to be playful, struck a shrill note instead.

In 1954 the Citizens' Housing and Planning Council proposed to Mayor Wagner a radically new approach to urban renewal that would combine new housing and open space with increased code enforcement to stem a further decline of existing housing stock, in essence establishing a policy of "neighborhood conservation" rather than conventional, cataclysmic urban renewal. "Deterioration of what were considered some of the city's soundest residential areas," the council pointed out, "is proceeding so rapidly and on so vast a scale that unless checked immediately and effectively, the city shortly will find itself with a slum problem many times greater than that which existed when present redevelopment and housing programs were initiated."[8] The council's report was based on an intensive pilot study of the eight blocks bounded by Ninetieth and Ninety-fourth streets, Central Park West and Amsterdam Avenue. There field researchers, led by Professor Sophia M. Robeson of Columbia University's School of Social Work and Elizabeth R. Hepner, Director of Research of Morningside Heights, Inc., discovered that neighborhood deterioration had resulted not from a population exodus but from a massive in-migration caused by the continual break-up of large dwelling units into smaller and smaller ones.

In October 1955 Mayor Wagner, testifying at the Astor Hotel before the Housing Subcommittee of the House Banking and Currency Committee, which was touring the nation's major cities to assess conditions, and responding to the Citizens' Housing and Planning Council's proposal, came forward with a plan of his own for the rehabilitation of sound buildings and the construction of vest-pocket housing projects, to be carried out over four or five years. Wagner's plan called for the concentration of city funds in small areas within the Upper West Side to create demonstration projects that would simultaneously get at the worst pockets of decay and stimulate the private sector to undertake further development in the surrounding areas. In his testimony, Wagner argued:

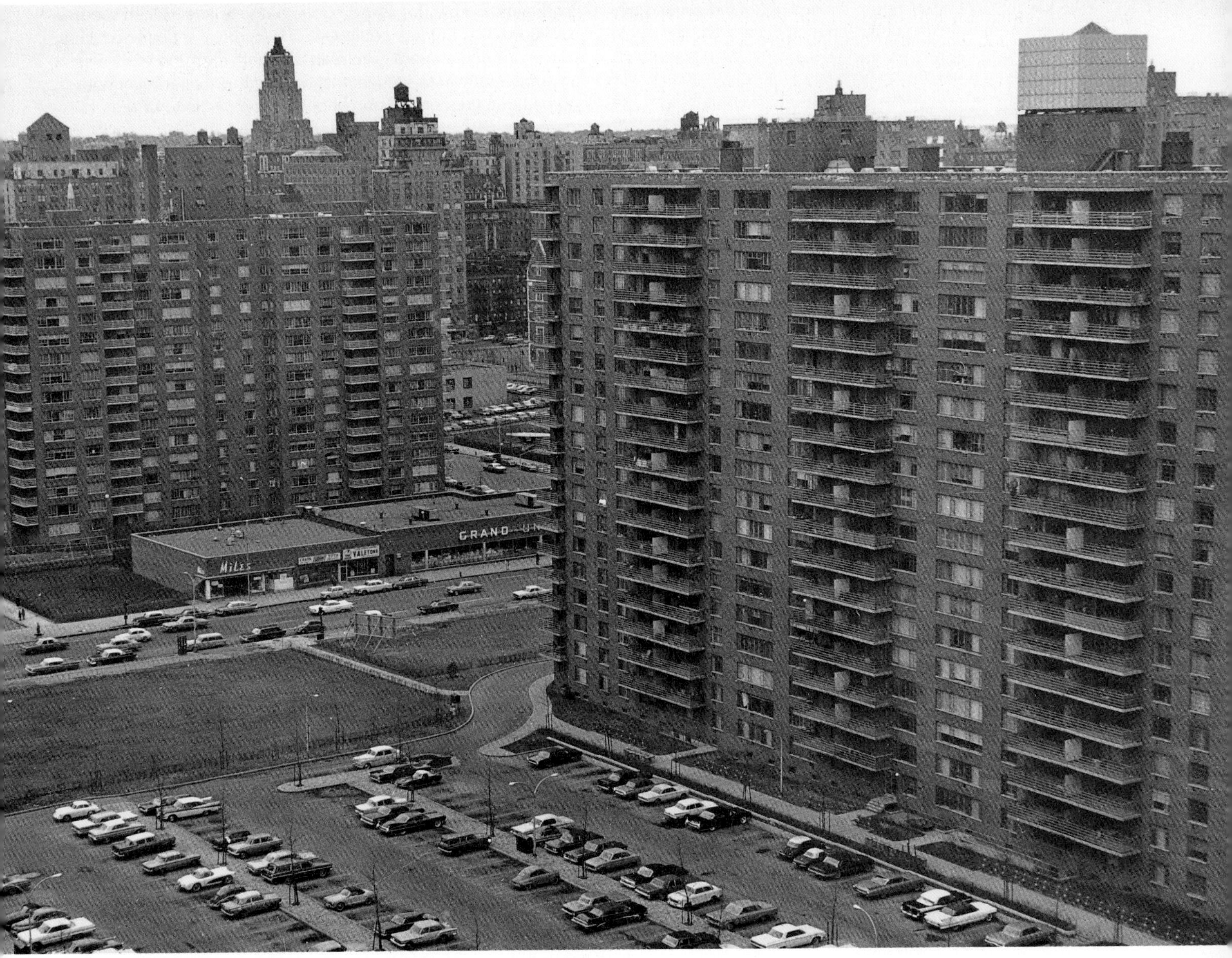

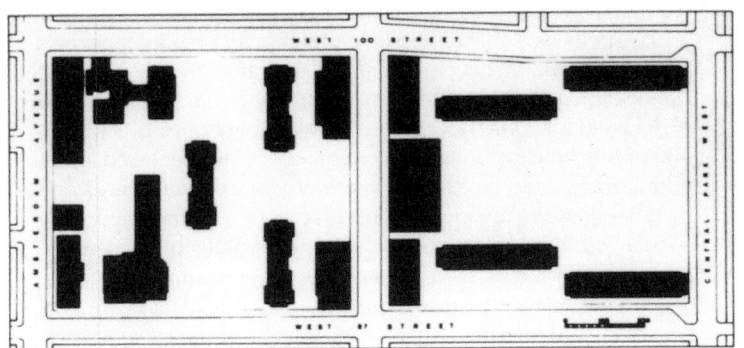

Above: Park West Apartments, Amsterdam Avenue to Central Park West, West Ninety-seventh to West 100th Street. Skidmore, Owings & Merrill, 1960. View to the northwest. Fred W. McDarrah. FWM

Left: Park West Apartments. Site plan. *A History of Housing.* RP

The key to success lies not in the amount of federal and city monies put directly into public housing in the area. The key to success lies in the way we operate to encourage private enterprise to go in. It has always been pardonably loath to risk substantial sums on real estate in an area of declining values. We feel that if we set the pace, as we reclaim a three-block section here and there, private enterprise, using the public credit under the urban renewal law, will go in and reconstruct the adjoining blocks, so the area will be on the way up again.[9]

Pinpointing another important factor of the renewal process, the Citizens' Housing and Planning Council editorialized, "A major element in the success of a broad-gauged program such as the Mayor has proposed, involves the participation and support of the local community."[10]

Even though he advocated a vest-pocket approach to demolition and reconstruction, Wagner's plan called for the designation of all 200 blocks of the Upper West Side as an urban renewal area in order to take advantage of various federal funding programs, which he believed would encourage private investment. But the City Planning Commission balked at the sheer size of the plan, despite the fact that its new chairman, James Felt, picked by Wagner to replace John J. Bennett, Jr., had also been instrumental in its framing. Nonetheless, Felt was able to work out a compromise in which the City Planning Commission would undertake to produce what the Citizens' Housing and Planning Council called a "practical plan," based on Wagner's vision of the West Side Urban Renewal Area as not just another "project" but a renewed and reconfigured neighborhood.[11] With the aid of a federal grant and the cooperation of twenty-five city departments and two state agencies, as well as advice from the Mayor's Committee on Urban Renewal, the commission went to work and in June 1958 presented its findings, published the following year in a volume titled *West Side Urban Renewal Area Preliminary Plan.*[12]

As seen in the publication, the scope of the plan had been severely curtailed. Instead of the 200-block area originally considered, the West Side Urban Renewal Area was a 20-block, clearly defined neighborhood lying between Eighty-seventh and Ninety-seventh streets, Central Park West and Amsterdam Avenue. The report was something of a landmark, including a notably thorough demographic survey that contradicted the conventional wisdom which held that the city was losing population; it cited statistics that revealed the population of the target area to have increased from 33,000 in 1950 to 39,000 in 1956. Although the white population had decreased, this loss was more than made up for by a major influx of Puerto Ricans, whose numbers swelled from 1,700 to 13,000 in the same time period. In addition, the population was extremely unstable: seven out of ten families in the area had moved there since 1950. Needless to say, given virtually no new construction in the area, the increased population brought with it overcrowding: of the 15,324 living quarters in the area, 17 percent consisted of one-room units (mostly furnished rooms) occupied by two or more persons, the majority of whom were paying almost twice as much per square foot of space as those living in the area's elevator apartment houses.

The report also contained a house-by-house survey of eight blocks in the area, pointing out specific areas of decay suitable for redevelopment as vest-pocket housing as well as a system of linked midblock parks and walkways. In addition, the survey determined that though most of the area's abundant rowhouses were in serious disrepair, 89 percent were suited to rehabilitation as affordable housing. Moreover, the report advanced a method to take advantage of the rowhouse resource, calling for public

condemnation, followed by public bidding, after which successful individual bidders could use FHA mortgage financing to reduce carrying charges. The plan also called for the replacement of some of the area's tenements with high-rise apartment houses, to be built, the commission hoped, by private enterprise.

The first and second plans differed in their geographic scope and the extent of public funds they required, but it was clear that both represented a new approach to the area and to urban renewal in general. And because the wholesale use of the bulldozer was eschewed in favor of preserving the Upper West Side's many small buildings, they also called for a transformation of the entire financial mechanism for urban renewal. As Charles Grutzner wrote: "The big difference between the new project and the current redevelopments under the city-Federal slum-clearance program is that the West Side program will not depend on Federal or city contributions to the resale of properties to redevelopers. Also, instead of turning condemned properties over to one or a few big developers, an attempt will be made to interest many smaller developers in building on cleared sites or rehabilitating the structures worth saving."[13]

The plan was not embraced by the Committee on Slum Clearance because the committee's chairman, Robert Moses, opposed large-scale rehabilitation in favor of the near-total reconstruction of slum areas. Thus, to implement the plan, Mayor Wagner created the interdepartmental Urban Renewal Board in 1958.[14] The seven-member board was chaired by James Felt, chairman of the City Planning Commission. Samuel Ratensky served as the board's director, proving to be a sympathetic, imaginative and resilient interpreter of its complex and innovative mandate, which included negotiating with the Urban Renewal Administration of the Federal Housing and Home Finance Agency for funding.[15] Ratensky, who had begun his career as an architect, had a vision of architecture as a social service rather than primarily an art. In 1946 he had joined the New York City Housing Authority, and six years later he became its planning director. In 1957 Ratensky was awarded the New York Chapter of the American Institute of Architect's Arnold W. Brunner Fellowship, enabling him to make an extensive study tour of European housing.[16]

Under Ratensky the Urban Renewal Board made real progress toward implementing the plan. In October 1958 he reported that the board had applied to the Federal Housing and Home Finance Agency for a $460,000 planning grant.[17] By May 29, 1959, he was able to release a preliminary plan for the area's rehabilitation and development. As prepared by the planners Candeub & Fleissig and the architects Brown & Guenther, the plan called for 7,400 new units of market-rate housing as well as 400 public housing units.[18] The remainder of the renewed area's population would be housed in elevator apartment houses and in rehabilitated rowhouses. The plan was accompanied by a 150-page report on the area's real estate values by the economist Chester Rapkin, who drew attention to the almost complete absence of new construction in the area, the drying up of support from institutional lenders, the growth of absentee ownership and the transformation of a major portion of the housing stock to single-room occupancy.[19] Rapkin also reported that the area's population had gone from 24,950 in 1925 to 38,950 in 1956, largely as a result of subdividing the existing housing stock, and that 27 percent of the population was living in overcrowded conditions, in circumstances reminiscent of late-nineteenth-century slums. Over 60 percent of the area's 1,037 residential structures were rowhouses, two-thirds of which were being used as rooming houses.

The Board of Estimate reviewed the plan at a public hearing on September 17, 1959. Although they supported the plan, many community leaders asked for more low- and middle-income housing. The Citizens' Housing and Planning Council advocated more affordable housing but pointed out that the high land costs, which required subsidies for middle-income housing, would make low-income housing even more difficult to realize. Such costs had already forced the Housing Authority to plan the state-subsidized, low-income, 400-unit Stephen Wise Houses (see below) at the highest density of any public housing project in the city.[20]

The plan called for the preservation of many but by no means all of the rowhouses. Battles to save individual rowhouses slated for demolition were largely unsuccessful, except for the efforts of the 9-G cooperative (see below) and of the residents of 325 Central Park West (George F. Pelham, 1900). This apartment house, believed to be supported partially on outmoded and dangerous wood timbers, was saved from demolition when residents invited the housing official Milton Mollen and several of his colleagues to a "progressive" dinner party that moved from apartment to apartment in order to reveal that the building was anything but a slum.[21]

On March 29, 1960, the Urban Renewal Board offered plans for a pilot project—for portions of West Ninety-fourth and West Ninety-fifth streets between Central Park West and Amsterdam Avenue—that would demonstrate its program for rowhouse rehabilitation.[22] Thirty-five rowhouses functioning as rooming houses, as well as two multistory apartment houses cut up for single-room occupancy, constituted the core of the pilot project. Brown & Guenther had been retained by the Urban Renewal Board to help select sites and develop preliminary plans for their redevelopment. As the project slowly ground its way through the arduous processes of public land condemnation and approval, as well as through what the Citizens' Housing and Planning Council described as "the fog of doubt and indecision," new techniques were developed to help potential homeowners finance their purchases and renovation costs.[23] Although financial institutions were reluctant to lend money, in 1961 Mayor Wagner persuaded a group of banks to help form a $3 million lending pool for the purpose.[24]

In the spring of 1961 the Citizens' Housing and Planning Council, increasingly sensitive to issues of race and civil rights, began to raise serious questions about the social consequences of the plan. Given the comparative poverty of a majority of the neighborhood's existing population, the council argued, "most of the present residents will be unable to afford the new nonpublic rents; the racial composition of the area, therefore, will probably be considerably different after renewal from what it is now." They asked: "If the public housing units in the area can take only 8% of the present residents, is it racial discrimination not to build more in the area? Is there an obligation to rehouse in the area the same population mix that lives in it at the present time? If a preponderance of non-white families cannot afford to make the down payment on middle-income cooperatives, are the cooperatives practicing racial discrimination?"[25]

In March 1961 Mayor Wagner issued a final version of the West Side Urban Renewal Area plan, which he hoped would be approved in April.[26] In his statement, Wagner claimed that the plan was the city's "most ambitious undertaking in urban renewal to date, and for New York City a revolutionary approach in the problems of blight and decay." It was, he said, "part of a coordinated plan for the renewal of the entire west side," an area stretching north from the Washington Street Market in lower Manhattan.[27] Wagner later said that the plan was one aspect of an "all-out war on the forces of crime, slum blight and poverty that have infected Manhattan's West Side," a battle "to get rid of all the rats—slumlords, pushers and true rodents."[28] J. Clarence Davies, chairman of the Urban Renewal Board, characterized the plan as "a triple threat attack," combining spot redevelopment, rehabilitation and neighborhood conservation "to retain desirable characteristics in the neighborhood."[29] It called for 1,000 low-rent public housing units, 2,800 high-rent apartments and 4,200 middle-income apartments.

Jackie Robinson, the black baseball star, hailed the proposal as "the first truly integrated project the city ever attempted," but not every minority leader agreed.[30] According to the historian James Trager, Puerto Rican leaders insisted that unless there were at least 2,500 low-income units, there would be a mass exodus of low-income groups from the area: "Few blacks or Puerto Ricans could afford the new middle-income housing, they said, and there were charges that urban renewal was in reality just a scheme to force blacks and Hispanics to vacate the upper West Side and move to less desirable parts of the city."[31] A public hearing of the City Planning Commission to discuss the project resulted in an argument between Jack E. Wood, the housing secretary for the National Association for the Advancement of Colored People (NAACP), and Aramis Gomez, a Puerto Rican leader. Wood's position was that to provide housing in the renewed area for every low-income family now housed there would be tantamount to giving "municipal sanction for a policy of containment and encourage the development of a community characterized by racial and economic balance." Gomez contended, however, that the project was "a massive piece of deception . . . the biggest hoax perpetrated on the neighborhood and the people of New York City."[32] Even as the plan progressed, strong objections continued to be raised, especially to the perceived lack of low-income housing. The Stryker's Bay Neighborhood Council and Father Henry J. Browne, a Roman Catholic priest at St. Gregory's Church, at 144 West Ninetieth Street, were particularly active advocates.[33]

On June 22, 1962, Mayor Wagner ordered that 800 of the proposed high-income units be replaced by 700 middle-income apartments and that the number of low-income units be increased from 1,000 to 2,500.[34] In a fifteen-hour public hearing held by the Board of Estimate the following day, Miguel Rubal, an area resident, asserted that the plan would greatly benefit Hispanics, but Joseph Monserrat, an official of the Migration Division of Puerto Rico, spoke for many others when he argued that the plan would fail to meet "the real needs" of New Yorkers.[35] The plan was also opposed by Percy Sutton, president of the NAACP's New York chapter, and the Reverend Patrick Rafferty of the Holy Name Roman Catholic Church, at 207 West Ninety-sixth Street, who said, "Let us poor people stay in New York."[36]

Amid the controversy, the City Planning Commission issued a report that painted what must have seemed an almost unimaginably optimistic picture of the area's future:

Old time New York residents still remember a quieter, more leisurely city: clean, attractive, good to look at, good to live in. That is essentially what the plan seeks to make out of these twenty crowded blocks with their rows of substandard houses and the squalid face of blight. When the plan has been carried out, new plazas will open unaccustomed stretches of sunlight and air. Traffic flow will be improved, trees planted, and attractive new stores will replace rundown shops. New community facilities will serve the neighborhood. Old community facilities—nine schools, two school playgrounds, ten religious

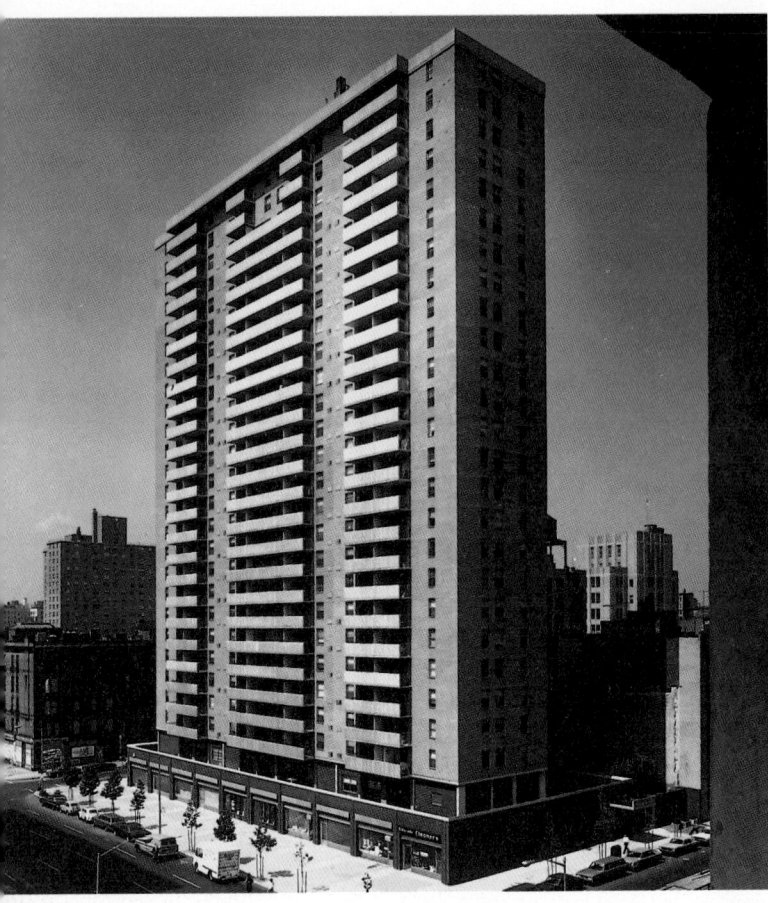

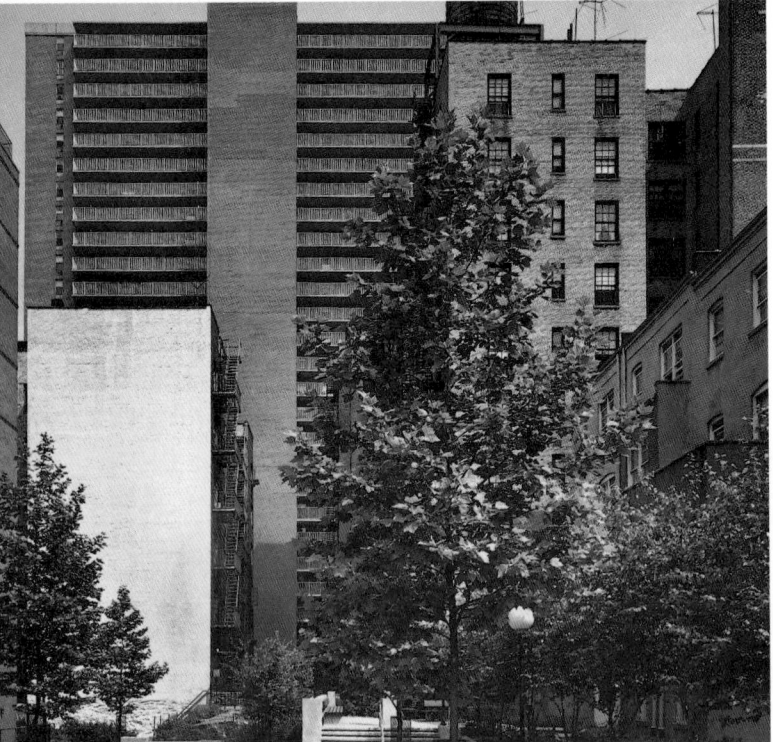

Top: Columbus Park Towers, east side of Columbus Avenue, West Ninety-third to West Ninety-fourth Street. Ballard, Todd & Snibbe, 1967. View to the northeast. Stoller. ©ESTO

Bottom: Columbus Park Towers. View to the west. Stoller. ©ESTO

structures, two community centers—will stay. There will be large areas of new building in the neighborhood. The good houses of today will still be there. In short, the neighborhood will keep the charm of diversity—the mixture of old and new, big and small, the variety of people and materials and buildings that has always attracted people to city living. It will be spacious, housing as many people as today, but in a far better way. Many of the buildings will be cooperatives, in which occupants will share ownership as well as pride in their neighborhood. There will not be the enormous population turnover of today. It will be, above all, a pleasant place to live.[37]

Although the final plan, which included the building of 7,800 new apartments, the rehabilitation of 350 brownstones and the conservation of some 3,600 existing apartments, was adopted by the Board of Estimate on June 27, 1962, implementation moved at a snail's pace, slowed by the perennial problem of tenant relocation.[38] The last wave of relocation was begun in late 1965 with Operation Consolidate, a program to move the remaining 1,000 tenants by placing those who wished to remain in the area in designated holding areas and those who wished to leave in desirable housing elsewhere.[39] Creative strategies, such as skewed rentals, were developed to help achieve the plan's idealistic economic mix.[40] But after five years, a high mortgage market and a general unease over the ultimate feasibility of the undertaking left most of the key redevelopment sites vacant.

Along with harsh economic realities, bureaucratic entanglements stymied the renewal project. In 1965 Milton Mollen, a lawyer and chairman of the Housing Redevelopment Board, resigned his municipal position to become Coordinator of Housing and Development, a post newly established by Mayor Wagner.[41] Two years later Mayor Lindsay created the first of his administration's so-called superagencies, consolidating nearly all city housing departments, including the Housing and Redevelopment Board, the Department of Buildings, the Rent and Rehabilitation Administration, the Department of Relocation and some of the functions of the Department of Real Estate, into a single entity called the Housing and Development Administration.[42] With these administrative changes in place, long-anticipated housing projects along Columbus Avenue began at last to be realized. In 1966 Jason Nathan, who, in his capacity as City Renewal Commissioner and chairman of the Housing and Redevelopment Board, served as Lindsay's "housing czar," offered a program to speed up the West Side Urban Renewal Area project. His plan recognized the inevitable: that the new high-rise apartments would require tax exemptions if they were to provide realistically priced middle-income housing.[43]

Despite the high social ideals represented by the project, and the unprecedented concept of an architectural integration of new and old, by and large the new construction was ordinary and distinctly at odds with the traditional character of the neighborhood. Most of the new apartment buildings were undifferentiated freestanding superslabs rising from ill-defined plazas that were mandated not only by zoning but also by even more stringent controls developed as part of the urban renewal plan, which hoped to transform Columbus Avenue into a kind of Modernist Champs Elysées for the middle class. Taken as a group, the new structures lacked a sense of coherent urbanism; individually, they were banal.

The 234-family red-brick-clad Strykers Bay Houses (1967), at 689 Columbus Avenue, between Ninety-third and Ninety-fourth streets, was among the first completed Columbus Avenue apartment complexes in the renewal area.[44] Designed by Holden, Egan, Wilson & Corser, the two towers—one seventeen stories, the other twenty-one—evoked the average public housing of the 1940s and 1950s; only the corner windows provided a more upmarket reference. The brown-brick facade of the twenty-seven-story Columbus Park Towers (Ballard, Todd & Snibbe, 1967), on the east side of Columbus Avenue between Ninety-third and Ninety-fourth streets, was somewhat enlivened by concrete balustrades enclosing the building's balconies.[45] Yet, like its less interesting companions, this building shattered the neighborhood scale in ways that pre-1961 wedding-cake designs never had. Edelbaum & Webster's RNA House (1967), at 150–160 West Ninety-sixth Street, between Columbus and Amsterdam avenues, housed 208 families in a structure reminiscent of I. M. Pei's Kips Bay Plaza. Although the building's front was described by Norval White and Elliot Willensky as a "concrete beehive of a facade," it rather effectively honored the wall of this important crosstown street, despite being slightly set back from the building line.[46] The twenty-story Jefferson Towers (Horace Ginsbern & Associates, 1968), on the eastern blockfront of Columbus Avenue between Ninety-fourth and Ninety-fifth streets, had a syncopated pattern of terraces that gave the facade a kind of aggressive charm.[47] West Side Manor (Kelly & Gruzen, 1968), a twenty-seven-story, buff-brick slab, was situated perpendicular to Columbus Avenue on the east blockfront between Ninety-fourth and Ninety-fifth streets, decisively rejecting any sense of traditional street wall.[48] The situation was exacerbated by a 20,000-square-foot landscaped plaza, fronting the avenue and bounded by the tower as well as a one-story commercial building.

Trinity House (1969), occupying the west blockfront of Columbus Avenue between Ninety-first and Ninety-second streets, took its name from its sponsor, the Trinity School, which incorporated an extension of its adjacent main building (Charles C. Haight, 1894) into the base of Brown, Guenther, Battaglia, Seckler's 200-unit, twenty-nine-story apartment tower.[49] At once bland and brutal, Trinity House had a gridded concrete structure filled in with brick and rose from a twenty-three-foot-high base that turned a blank wall to Columbus Avenue, establishing a rather menacing presence on the street. The architects successfully incorporated a vast array of educational facilities into the base—classrooms, a chapel-auditorium, an indoor swimming pool and an outdoor play area on the roof—in addition to a parking garage and a separate entrance and lobby for the apartment house.

Columbus House (1970), on the west blockfront of Columbus Avenue between Ninety-fifth and Ninety-sixth streets, was one of the few inventive designs to be realized.[50] Originally designed by Ballard, Todd & Snibbe, Columbus House was redesigned by the office of Horace Ginsbern & Associates as a thirty-three-story, brown-brick-clad tower with hefty concrete columns that projected forward beyond the brick walls to enclose large, recessed balconies. At its base, the typical pancake for commercial space was, owing to a sloping site, a bit taller, giving better than usual definition to the street wall. Both the one-story building and the tower were surmounted by sloped metal roofs. Liebman & Liebman's Columbus Manor (1971), on the east side of Columbus Avenue between Ninety-second and Ninety-third streets, epitomized the avenue's dull buff-brick towers.[51] Dominick Salvati's Leader House (1972), located directly across the avenue, was no more successful.[52]

Horace Ginsbern & Associates designed the six-story Town House West (1973), at 5 West Ninety-first Street; unlike most of the new buildings that transformed the renewal area into a brave new world of towers and plazas, this structure clearly reflected

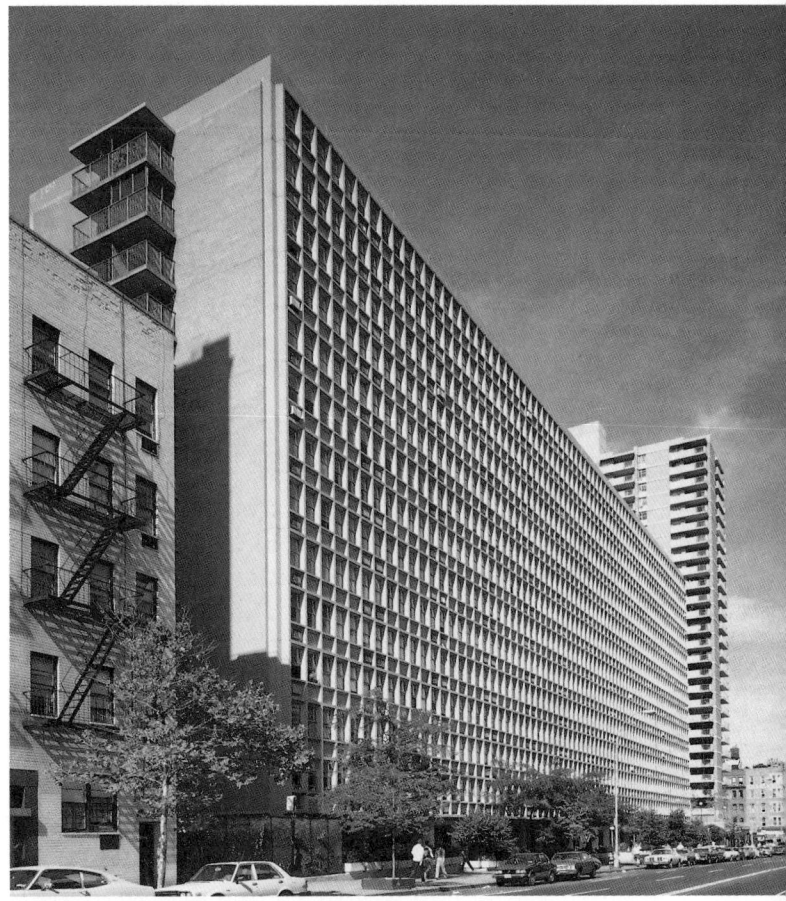

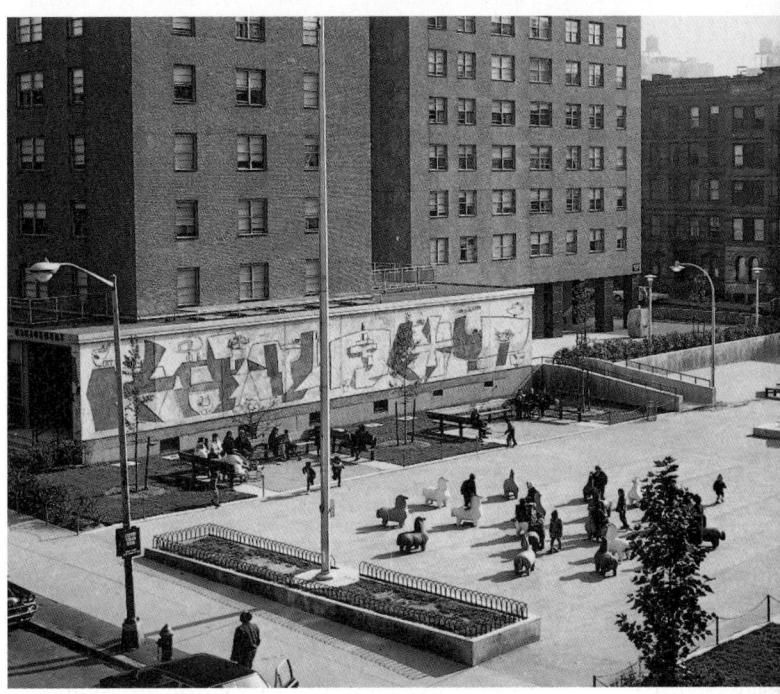

Top: RNA House, 150–160 West Ninety-sixth Street, between Columbus and Amsterdam avenues. Edelbaum & Webster, 1967. View to the southwest. ©Gil Amiaga. GA

Bottom: Stephen Wise Towers, 124 West Ninety-first Street, between Columbus and Amsterdam avenues. Knappe & Johnson, 1964. View to the southeast showing plaza by Richard G. Stein & Associates. NYCHA

the scale, and to a lesser extent the forms, of the area's traditional urbanism.[53] According to Frederick M. Ginsbern, the son of the firm's founding principal, the building was intended to form "an attractive balance between the three- and four-story reconverted brownstones and the 30-story towers which have dominated the renewal project to date." The building's height, he said, was "in scale with the human element of the four-story brownstones" and was further modified by a dormered roof line. The exterior was clad in dark brick with cast-stone accents that emphasized the cantilevered upper walls, "not unlike the bay windows of the brownstones across the street."[54] Norval White and Elliot Willensky described the building as a "modest six-story work which evidences in the development of its facade a clear desire to enrich the streetscape without heroic efforts or lavish budget."[55]

Ifill Johnson Hanchard's St. Martin's Tower (1971), at 65 West Ninetieth Street, on the east blockfront of Columbus Avenue between Ninetieth and Ninety-first streets, with its syncopated arrangement of balconies, had livelier facades than those of most Columbus Avenue towers.[56] Holden, Yang, Raemsch & Corser's nineteen-story Turin House (1972), on the east side of Columbus Avenue between Eighty-ninth and Ninetieth streets, seemed coldly impersonal because of its pink concrete-block walls.[57] Yet the imaginative planning of this building composed exclusively of duplex apartments, replacing conventional corridors with double-height open breezeways reached by skip-stop elevators, represented an important development in the evolution of the city's multifamily housing. Edward Durell Stone's twin-tower scheme for the west blockfront of Columbus Avenue between Ninety-sixth and Ninety-seventh streets was not realized, nor was a Ballard, Todd & Snibbe scheme for Columbus Avenue.[58] As the city's fortunes declined in the mid-1970s, a handful of Columbus Avenue sites remained vacant—some with boarded-up, abandoned buildings—strong symbols of the only partially fulfilled nature of this important urban vision.

Several renewal-area apartment towers were located on the east side of Amsterdam Avenue, where the disjunction between old and new styles in architecture and urbanism was particularly noticeable. Gruzen & Partners' New Amsterdam (1971), on the east side of Amsterdam Avenue between Ninety-fifth and Ninety-sixth streets, combined buff brick with exposed-concrete floor slabs, concrete balconies and floor-to-ceiling windows.[59] George Kaplan's Heywood Broun Plaza (1974), later renamed Heywood Tower, at 175 West Ninety-first Street, on the east blockfront of Amsterdam Avenue to Ninety-first Street, was a typical dark-brick slab whose banality was relieved only slightly by Ernest Trova's twenty-two-foot-high asphalt sculpture, *Profile Canto West*, located in the plaza behind the tower.[60] Seymour Joseph's Glenn Gardens (1975), on the east side of Amsterdam Avenue between Eighty-seventh and Eighty-eighth streets, consisted of a tower set back from Amsterdam Avenue on a large plaza and a five-story building fronting Eighty-eighth Street; it marked the southern boundary of completed renewal projects.[61]

In 1967, with many of the renewal sites at last under way, Jason Nathan and Samuel Ratensky, recognizing that the slab-and-base *parti* mandated by zoning for the new apartment buildings was potentially damaging to the area's urbanism, decided to take a second look at the plan. They asked Lawrence Halprin, the New York-born, San Francisco-based landscape architect and self-styled urbanist, to prepare a formal critique to guide the development of the remaining sites along Columbus Avenue south of Ninetieth Street. His study would be part of the

overall assessment of the open space and urban design of New York's redevelopment projects that the city's new superagency, the Housing and Development Administration, had commissioned. In his published report, *New York, New York*, Halprin proposed to ameliorate the vacant, ragtag quality established by the superscaled slabs and superwide sidewalks of the redeveloped Columbus Avenue by planting double rows of trees.[62] He also suggested that, contrary to the initial plan, the renewal area should be treated as a coherent and somewhat self-sufficient community; to foster that ideal, he proposed an elevated "cross-avenue" plaza at Columbus Avenue and Eighty-ninth Street. Halprin's recommendations were not followed.

While Columbus Avenue was slow to emerge as the landscaped boulevard the planners had hoped for, one open space within the renewal area was an instant success: the playground at Stephen Wise Towers (Knappe & Johnson, 1964), the Housing Authority's high-density vest-pocket apartment houses at 124 West Ninety-first Street, between Columbus and Amsterdam avenues.[63] Although the two nineteen-story, salmon-colored, brick-clad buildings housing a total of 400 families were bland, the playground was unusual. Instead of the standard equipment, the designer of the plaza, Richard G. Stein & Associates, with funds provided by the J. M. Kaplan Fund, installed eighteen cast-concrete, pastel-colored miniature horses arranged in a loose circle facing a twenty-foot-high, eighty-foot-long cast-cement bas-relief mural, both by the Italian-born sculptor Constantino Nivola.

Despite the lackluster quality of most of the new buildings and the spaces they defined, the West Side Urban Renewal Area gradually wrapped itself in the mantle of success, largely because of the enormous popularity the restored rowhouses enjoyed as part of the nationwide rediscovery of townhouse living. The four-and-a-half-story rowhouses, in a wide variety of historically derived styles, were typically divided into a duplex garden-level apartment reserved for the owner and, above, four smaller rental apartments. Most of the "brownstoners," as the new homeowners were generally called—although some of the grander houses were clad not in brownstone but in limestone or brick—were young professionals for whom the purchase of a derelict house was a golden opportunity to combine good housing with a promising financial investment. Not surprisingly, many of the buyers were architects. One couple, Mr. and Mrs. Yung Wang, both recent graduates of the Yale School of Architecture, undertook the renovations themselves;[64] other architects, such as Lee Pomeroy,[65] Stanley and Laurie Maurer,[66] as well as the designer Robert A. Caigan,[67] designed the innovative space but left its physical realization to others.

The success of the renovations within the renewal era spurred interest in the wealth of rundown townhouses throughout the Upper West Side, and by the late 1960s signs of construction could be seen on virtually every block.[68] Several leading young architects produced extremely imaginative designs, including Peter Samton, who renovated 161 West Eighty-eighth Street (1969),[69] and Robert Golder and his wife, the interior designer Poppy Wolff, who renovated 55 West Seventy-third Street (1970), one of the rowhouses designed by Henry J. Hardenbergh in 1885.[70]

Rowhouses also provided the opportunity for several socially innovative projects. The Housing Authority, for example, took on a group of four brownstones and renovated them to create a single building, 54 West Ninety-fourth Street (1968), one of the few demonstrations of low-rise public housing in the city that was free of the usual stigma of "project" design.[71] In another instance, the so-called 9-G Cooperative (1968), nine racially mixed middle-class buyers purchased a row of nine brownstones at 19-35 West Ninety-third Street, between Central Park West and Columbus Avenue, and converted them into thirty-one residential units with a common backyard and a common walkway along the top floor.[72] The brownstone row (Joseph H. Taft, 1888) had been saved from demolition by a group of area residents known as the Little Old New York Citizens' Committee, formed in 1962 to help families find rowhouses in the renewal area; it took the group eighteen months to convince the city that the row, made up of houses considered too small for rehabilitation and slated for replacement by a ten-story apartment house, should be preserved. Among the initial purchasers of apartments in the newly formed co-op were Jackie Robinson and his wife, Rachel.

The idea of a brownstone cooperative had first been proposed for the urban renewal area by Stanley M. Isaacs, the socially committed and feisty former Manhattan Borough President.[73] Basing his suggestion on the concept of "horizontal cooperative" housing established by architect Arthur C. Holden and on such imaginative coordinated rehabilitation efforts of the 1920s as Sullivan-MacDougal, Turtle Bay and Sunnyside gardens, Isaacs proposed the acquisition of two groups of ten houses located back to back and the development of a large garden yard between them.[74] Inside, the buildings could be renovated as stacked duplex apartments sharing a common stairway, a strategy that would circumvent the more stringent and costly requirements applied to multiple dwellings housing three or more families.

The 9-G Cooperative constituted only half of Isaacs's development module, a row of twenty-foot-wide, thirty- to forty-foot-deep houses originally built as a unit. The Little Old New York Citizens' Committee brought in architects Judith Edelman and Stanley Salzman as consultants to reconfigure the row. Edelman and Salzman helped find buyers for the co-op and eventually realized their design, removing all the stoops and replacing them with three small lobbies but otherwise keeping the street facade intact, with each house in the group maintaining its distinct visual identity. In the rear, an entirely new facade was created, emphasizing the unity of the buildings. Inside, the traditional spatial definition of individual rowhouses gave way to a complex interlocking of units, based in part on the plans Le Corbusier had devised for housing blocks in Marseilles, Nantes and elsewhere. The provision of one interior corridor as well as an exterior walkway on the top floor made it possible to create thirty-one custom-designed houselike units, each either directly accessible to the street or connected to it by elevator. When the project received a Bard Award in 1969, the jury, which was headed by the critic and historian Sybil Moholy-Nagy and included the architect Pietro Belluschi, praised the cooperative, saying that the "continuity of the street as the ligament of every true city has been preserved; and no attempt has been made to destroy the row house module of the front elevations." Their citation continued: "The most important aspect of the 9-G Cooperative is proof furnished that the city can be saved as a fit habitat for a highly differentiated society, and that it is the architect who must do the saving."[75]

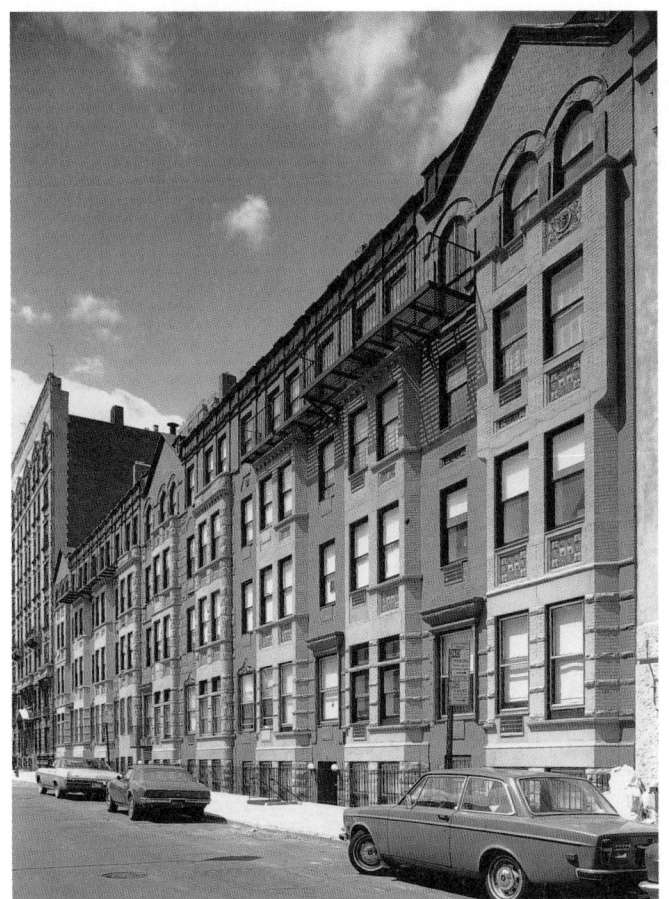

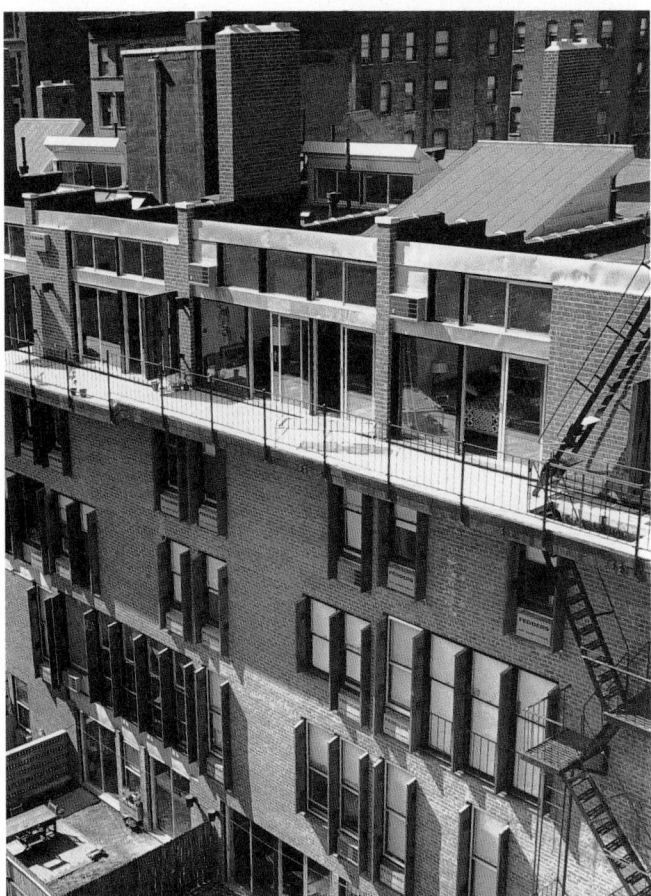

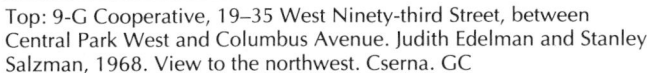

Top: 9-G Cooperative, 19–35 West Ninety-third Street, between Central Park West and Columbus Avenue. Judith Edelman and Stanley Salzman, 1968. View to the northwest. Cserna. GC

Bottom: 9-G Cooperative. View to the southeast showing common walkway. Cserna. GC

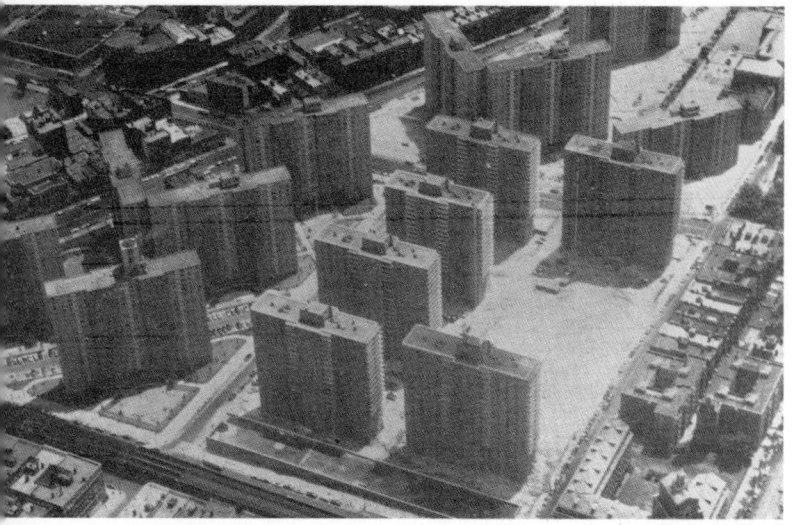

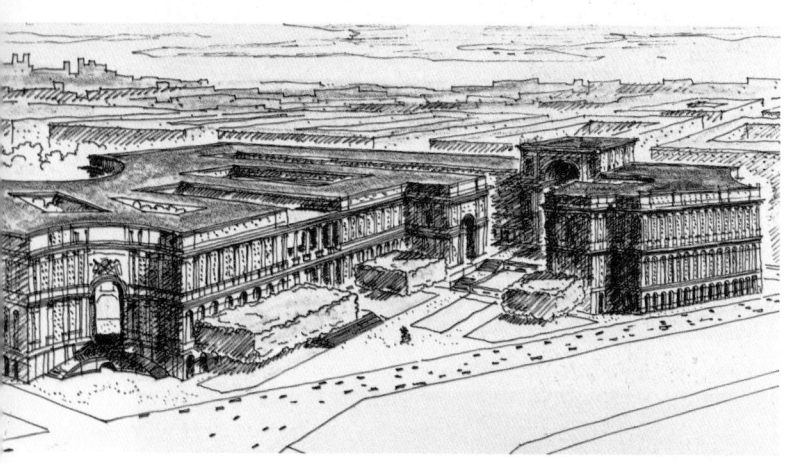

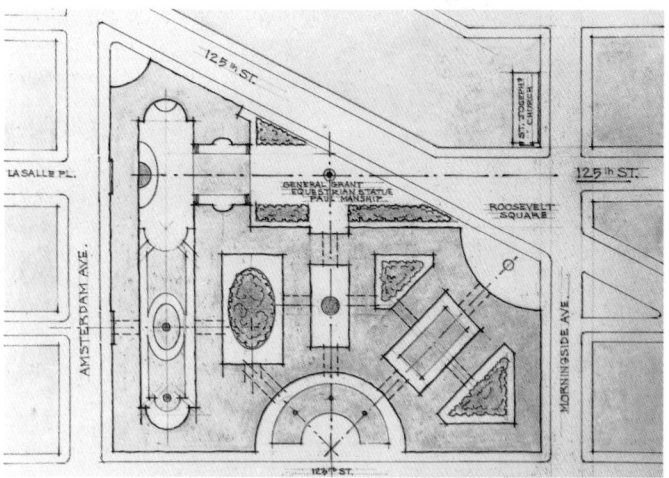

Top: View to the northeast showing Morningside Gardens (Wallace K. Harrison, 1957), Broadway to Amsterdam Avenue, West 123rd to La Salle Street, on the lower right, and the General Grant Houses (Eggers & Higgins, 1955), between Broadway and Morningside Avenue, West 123rd and West 125th streets, on the left and top right. AF. CU

Center: Proposal for General Grant Houses, Amsterdam to Morningside Avenue, West 123rd to West 125th Street. John Barrington Bayley, 1957. View to the southwest. HHR

Bottom: Proposal for General Grant Houses. Site plan. HHR

MORNINGSIDE HEIGHTS
Morningside-Manhattanville

Morningside Heights, bounded by 110th and 125th streets, Morningside Park and the Hudson River, experienced the same deterioration that plagued the rest of the Upper West Side after World War II. In 1947, hoping to reverse the neighborhood's declining fortunes, nine area institutions—Barnard College, Columbia University, Corpus Christi Roman Catholic Church, International House, Jewish Theological Seminary, Juilliard School of Music, Riverside Church, Teachers College and Union Theological Seminary—joined together to form Morningside Heights, Inc., a nonprofit agency promoting neighborhood conservation and redevelopment.[1] David Rockefeller, who had vigorously advocated the establishment of the group, served as its first president; the city planner Lawrence Orton served as executive director. The first project of Morningside Heights, Inc. was a public safety campaign that included securing better street lighting and establishing a foot patrol.

In 1951, when members of Morningside Heights, Inc. recognized in the Title I provisions of the 1949 Housing Act a way to promulgate physical change benefiting the middle-class constituency that was the backbone of the area's institutional employment group, the organization became the sponsor of the city's first Title I redevelopment project, Morningside-Manhattanville.[2] The project would replace ten acres of deteriorated buildings with 981 units of middle-income housing, accommodating approximately 3,500 residents. The site, bounded by Broadway and Amsterdam Avenue, 123rd and LaSalle streets, was densely packed with old-law tenements housing 735 persons per acre, three times the average for New York City and more than twice the number who would live in the six twenty-story buildings proposed for the project by Wallace K. Harrison. To accommodate some of the displaced low-income tenants, a new public housing project, General Grant Houses, would be constructed adjacent to the Title I development. Just to the north, on a site bounded by 129th and 133rd streets, Broadway and Amsterdam Avenue, a third housing project, known as Manhattanville Houses, would also be realized (see chapter 12).

From the first, Morningside-Manhattanville was touted as a potential showcase for what could be done to rebuild the city's slums. As Reverend Harry Emerson Fosdick, the pastor of Riverside Church, put it when he urged the City Planning Commission to approve the plan: "I am convinced that what you are considering today is not just the face of one housing project but the possible future of one of the city's most important neighborhoods. It is a pioneer neighborhood where the American city confronts some of its most characteristic problems and where, if we solve them at all well, the whole world will know it." Key to the plan was a commitment to racial integration. "These building projects," Fosdick said, "both public and cooperative . . . can be and will be—not in theory alone but in fact—interracial. We are pleading for inclusive housing—interracial, international, and meeting both low-income and middle-income needs."[3]

Despite vociferous opposition from the community, the Morningside-Manhattanville plan was finally approved by the Board of Estimate in January 1953. General Grant Houses (1955), which consisted of ten brick-clad, twenty-story buildings designed by Eggers & Higgins to cover only 12 percent of its site, was the first Housing Authority project to contain buildings exceeding seventeen stories.[4] The design of the project was so banal that in 1957 the architect John Barrington Bayley produced drawings for an alternate scheme, a single megastructure punctuated by numerous courtyards and articulated in a rigorously Classical vocabulary.[5] Bayley's visionary plan, which incorporated grand allées and formal vistas, stood in sharp contrast to the abstract geometry and anonymous aesthetic of the Housing Authority's towers-in-the-park approach.

With tenant relocation under way by late 1953, a final count revealed that 1,511 families would have to be displaced to make way for the Morningside-Manhattanville development. By early 1954 demolition had begun, and Harrison's design for Morningside Gardens, the new name of the Title I project, was released, showing six slabs, clad in red brick and containing balconies. Oriented north-south, the slabs were pushed to the north, east and west edges of the site to create a large parklike open space along LaSalle Street. When Morningside Gardens opened in 1957, it was widely hailed as a success. The youth programs and private street patrols sponsored by Morningside Heights, Inc. went a long way toward stabilizing the area, and the project reported a virtual absence of crime in its first five years of existence. Nonetheless, as E. J. Kahn, Jr., put it in 1965, the development still fell "somewhat short of becoming an acropolitan Eden."[6]

Columbia University

Many of the postwar problems on Morningside Heights lay in the neighborhood's historical evolution, in which residential areas had been pushed to the periphery by a huge, almost monolithic complex of institutional buildings more or less clustered around Columbia University's fortresslike campus, which at once defined and blockaded the enclave. Though unquestionably one of the world's great centers of learning, postwar Columbia was in many ways in disarray.[7] Led for forty-three years by Nicholas Murray Butler, who was succeeded in 1945 by acting president Frank D. Fackenthal and, after 1948, by Dwight D. Eisenhower, a much-beloved military hero with no university experience, Columbia became increasingly ill at ease with its identity as an urban university, to the extent that some university officials considered relocating the campus to a rural site. The physical plant was neglected, and almost no new building projects had been undertaken for some time. Even when plans were drawn for new construction, the university seemed unable to chart a coherent future. No longer feeling bound by the 1893 master plan developed for the institution by Charles Follen McKim, nor by the Classical language of his buildings, university officials were not prepared to embrace Modernism either. Instead, they drifted. During the Depression the university's requirements for additional space were met largely by renovating existing classroom buildings, usually creating additional floors by cutting down the original high ceilings.[8] The university's newest building, Eggers & Higgins's Brander Matthews Theater (1940), on the south side of 117th Street at Amsterdam Avenue, was a rather tepid, Classically inspired, two-story brick building with a principal entrance that adopted a Palladian motif.[9] Successfully planned for theatrical events, particularly experimental productions, the theater doubled as a lecture hall during the day. Long-contemplated plans to complete University Hall (McKim, Mead & White, 1893) lay dormant. During the war temporary one-story metal buildings were erected on the plaza behind Low Library; these remained in place until the 1960s.

In 1946 the university proposed to meet its housing shortage by establishing a "trailer campus" for student veterans and their families in Fort Lee, New Jersey, forty-five minutes from Morningside Heights; the plan was never realized.[10] Two years later, under Eisenhower, Columbia retained the stylistically conservative firm of Adams & Woodbridge to help prepare a long-range plan of architectural coordination and development, not only for the Morningside campus but also for the medical center in Washington Heights, for Baker Field in Inwood and for other remote Columbia properties.[11] High on President Eisenhower's priority list was the development of an engineering center, and in 1949 the university began to assemble a site for that purpose at the southeast corner of 125th Street and Riverside Drive.[12] In 1951 Voorhees, Walker, Foley & Smith released their design for the center, proposing a fourteen-story, 250,000-square-foot gridded slab that incorporated an existing four-story building, which the architects remodeled.[13] Although fund-raising was undertaken for the largely utilitarian new tower, it was never built.

In 1964 the university utilized the site instead for a twenty-one-story apartment building housing faculty members and their families, designed by Brown & Guenther, who created a four-story podium with a tower raised on stilts, establishing a ground-floor loggia.[14] The podium contained a 355-car parking garage and, on top, a landscaped terrace and playgrounds. Though the massive slab, containing 180 apartments, had undistinguished facades of concrete and buff brick, inside, the architects adopted a rather inventive plan that replaced conventional double-loaded corridors with wide, glass-enclosed, generously proportioned single-loaded hallways pushed to one side of the building. Windows punctuated the corridor's internal wall, encouraging their use as supervised children's play areas and transforming the conventional apartment building corridor into a high-rise version of the back alley or public sidewalk. In 1967 the original architects' successor firm, Brown, Guenther, Battaglia & Galvin, designed a similar twenty-six-story tower housing 100 apartments and office space, linking it to the earlier building by a glass-enclosed passageway.[15]

Many members of the university community felt that, given Columbia's location in New York, the university should stress the arts. With no studio building and only the Brander Matthews Theater, Columbia's commitment to the arts was in no way comparable to that of Harvard, Princeton or Yale. In 1948 the university announced that it would establish two new schools—the School of Painting and Sculpture and the School of Dramatic Arts—and erect an arts center building.[16] A fifteen-story building, to be designed by Leopold Arnaud, dean of Columbia's School of Architecture, was to rise on a block-long, university-owned site on the east side of Amsterdam Avenue between 116th and 117th streets, where the Brander Matthews Theater as well as several greenhouses were located. By 1955 the projected arts center had evolved into a ten-story building that would also house the architecture school, but the following year, when plans were released for a major campus expansion, the so-called East Campus superblock that encompassed the arts center site made no provision for such a facility.[17]

The East Campus was to be bounded by Amsterdam Avenue, Morningside Drive, 116th and 118th streets and would incorporate the President's House (1912); Johnson Hall, including the Women's Faculty Club (1925); the Men's Faculty Club (1925); and the Casa Italiana (1927), all designed by McKim, Mead & White.[18] The architect of the project, Wallace Harrison, called for the demolition of the Brander Matthews Theater, as well as the greenhouses, several apartment houses and a row of townhouses built by David Kennedy in 1899,[19] to make way for his "little vision of a future big city."[20]

The editors of the *New York Times* praised the superblock plan, stating that the anticipated agreement to close 117th Street "illustrated anew" the "happy relationship between city and university that has so long existed."[21] Not all observers, however, were pleased. The visually acute sociologist Nathan Glazer said in a letter to the *Times* that he found the proposal "depressing." He objected particularly to the elimination of part of 117th Street, which he considered "one of the pleasantest streets in the Columbia neighborhood," explaining that the "peaceful feeling given by the row of low city houses on the north side of the street, with the large trees in front bending over the roadway, is one of the rarest one may experience in New York." Glazer also lamented the potential loss of the Brander Matthews Theater, which he described as "one of the most delightful amenities of Columbia University—and the neighborhood."[22] He suggested that the completion of McKim's original scheme for the campus as a series of spatially tight internal courtyards would be a superior alternative to expansion. Nonetheless, the superblock plan proceeded.

Harrison's plan for the East Campus consisted of a raised podium similar to that of the main campus, atop which would be built three slabs: one for the Law School, one for faculty offices and one for a graduate-student residence hall; 117th Street would be demapped and 118th Street proportionately widened. A 100-foot-wide, platformlike bridge would be built across Amsterdam Avenue to help minimize the separation of the new area from the established campus complex. The main campus podium, formed largely of mounded earth, contained only service spaces and related passageways; Harrison's would hold classrooms, dining facilities and a parking garage.

In 1959, as designs were being developed for the Law School, the idea of an arts center was revived, this time planned for a block-long site on the east side of Amsterdam Avenue between 115th and 116th streets.[23] Designed by Moore & Hutchins, the center, which was to be connected to the East Campus complex by a pedestrian bridge over 116th Street, consisted of a twelve-story slab containing classrooms and laboratories set back from 116th Street. Along Amsterdam Avenue, a low glass-enclosed structure would have linked the main building to two virtually windowless theaters on the southern end of the site. Once again, the project went unrealized.

The first building of the East Campus to be completed was Harrison & Abramovitz's Law School (1961).[24] Connected to the main campus by a broad, sparsely landscaped pedestrian bridge over Amsterdam Avenue and set back from the southern and western edges of the podium, the reinforced-concrete building rose eight stories above the East Campus plaza. The plaza-level story was wrapped in glass and punctuated by the asymmetrically placed, west-facing principal entrance, which was raised on a short flight of steps and protected by a canopy. Above this level, the building's facades consisted of vertical concrete louvers separated by vertical strips of windows. The building stood in sharp contrast to the articulated Classicism of the historic campus. Moreover, it was odd. Given the enclosed balcony lounges that projected from either end of the boxlike mass, it was not surprising that the building earned the nickname of "the toaster." Though the new building was far more commodious than the Law School's previous home in Kent Hall (McKim, Mead & White, 1914), its design proved functionally problematic as well.[25] The podium was filled with large classrooms and broad, low-ceilinged corridors that gave the impression more of an airport than academic facility. Although the new library, a book tower with stack room for 300,000 volumes, doubled the

capacity of the library at Kent Hall, its placement at the building's core confined faculty offices to the perimeter. This arrangement substituted a traditional sense of collegiality for a streamlined efficiency typical of postwar office-building design, seriously compromising staff communication. The treeless platform bridge connecting back to the main campus was windswept in winter, scorching hot in summer, and the space underneath it was a dreary, threatening environment. Raised to a level high enough to permit trucks to pass below, the platform intersected Philosophy Hall (McKim, Mead & White, 1910) at an unfortunate place, robbing its rear elevation of dignity.

In a sweeping assessment of Columbia's new buildings published in *Columbia College Today*, Allan Temko, a Columbia College graduate and an associate editor of *Architectural Forum*, as well as the architecture critic of the *San Francisco Chronicle*, was critical of the Law School's new building, especially its color: "Its whiteness clamors for attention and detracts seriously from the centrality of Low Library. McKim's plan called for predominantly brick structures with the white Low Library as a campus focal point. . . . For no strong reason, the Law School has become a competing focal point. Low Library should have been left in its central glory. The architects, who went into a new idiom for the Law School, could have done it in compatible color." Temko also criticized the building's interior, which he found "lacking in serenity. It's bleak and cut up; the circulation is not what I would call successful." Temko concluded that the Law School was "a fine opportunity wasted," which came as no surprise, he said, because Harrison & Abramovitz had "missed great opportunities before. They are usually competent, but without final brilliance. The United Nations, where Wallace Harrison was supervising architect, and the new Time and Life Building, which they did, are also wasted opportunities. Still, the firm is of some distinction in the United States."[26] Ada Louise Huxtable gave the building "an A for effort" but found it wanting "in its relationships to its surroundings."[27]

Following the announcement of the Law School design, Harrison & Abramovitz revealed plans for the East Campus graduate-student dormitory and a building for the School of International Affairs, which were to complete the complex. The firm issued several designs for the dormitory, including schemes calling for a single building as well as groups of two and four towers, all set in the northeastern corner of the East Campus.[28] None were built. As originally designed, the School of International Affairs was to be housed in a thirteen-story slab located on 118th Street.[29] On its long north- and south-facing sides, the building was to include thin piers, similar to those of the Law School, but more widely spaced and punctuated by tripartite windows. The building was to sit on its own portion of the East Campus podium, which would be punctured by a rectangular sunken court at the base of the slab. It was redesigned in 1965 as a fourteen-story structure incorporating gridded facades with deeply recessed windows. The final version, as completed in 1971, was a fifteen-story building of limestone and poured concrete that retained the essential siting and massing of the earlier designs. The details of its exterior elements were so brutal, however, that the Law School seemed delicate in comparison, while the urbane, palazzolike Casa Italiana, stripped of its urban context, was set adrift.

After the adoption of the East Campus plan, attention was refocused on the main campus. One of the university's most effective postwar planning decisions was made in 1953 when, in anticipation of the institution's 200th birthday the following year, the right-of-way of 116th Street between Broadway and

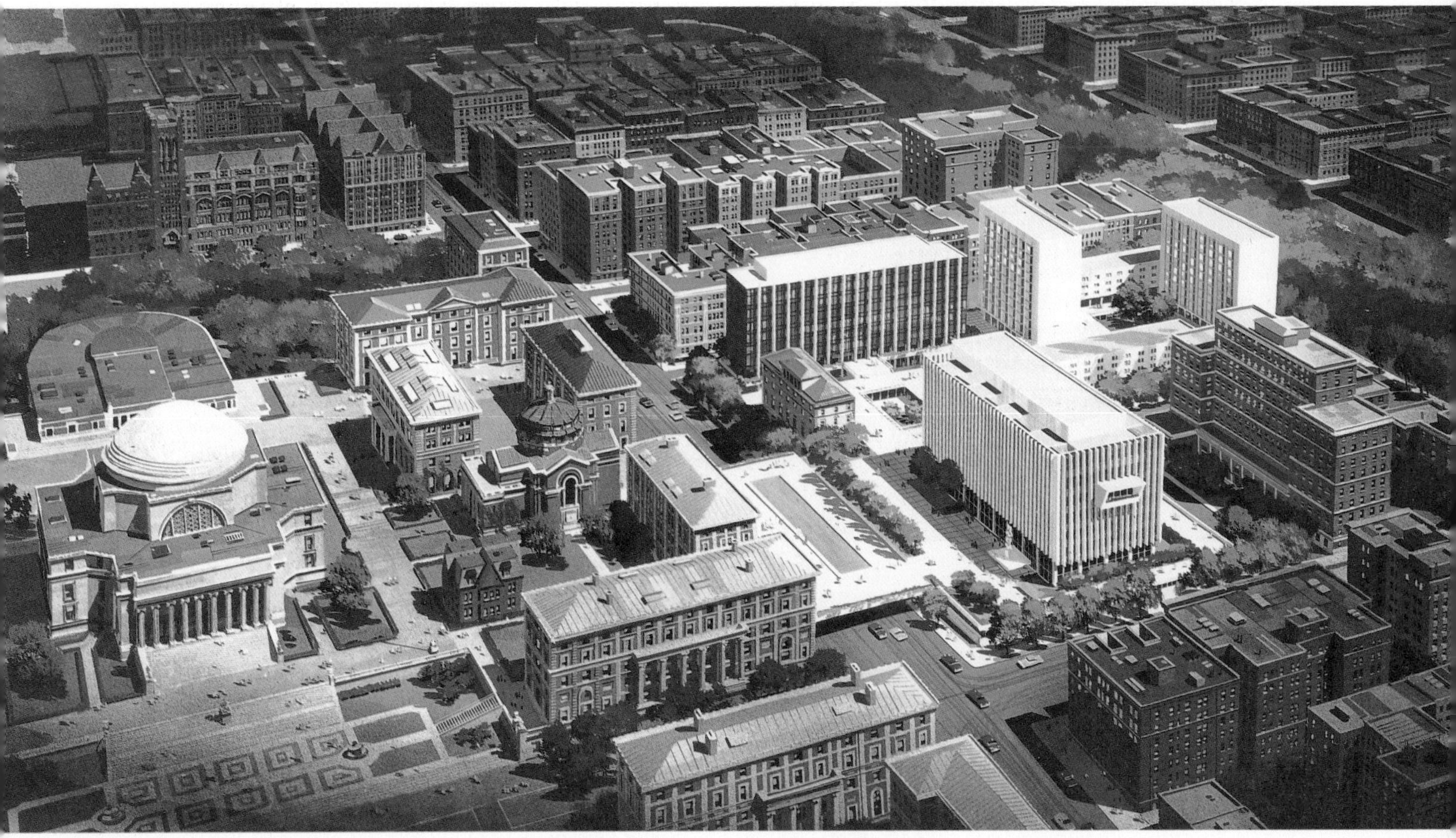

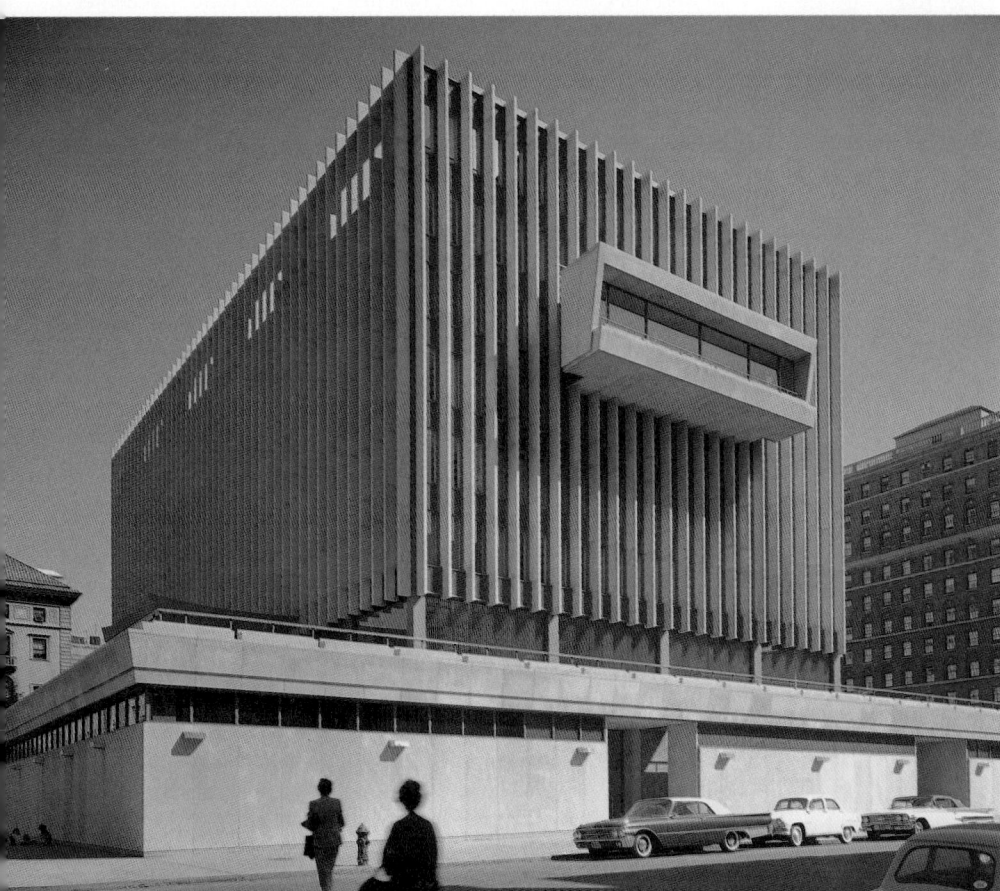

Top: Rendering by Robert Schwartz of view to the northeast of Columbia University with a proposal for the East Campus (Wallace K. Harrison, 1956) on the right. CCT

Left: Law School, Columbia University, northeast corner of Amsterdam Avenue and West 116th Street. Harrison & Abramovitz, 1961. View to the northeast. Stoller. ©ESTO

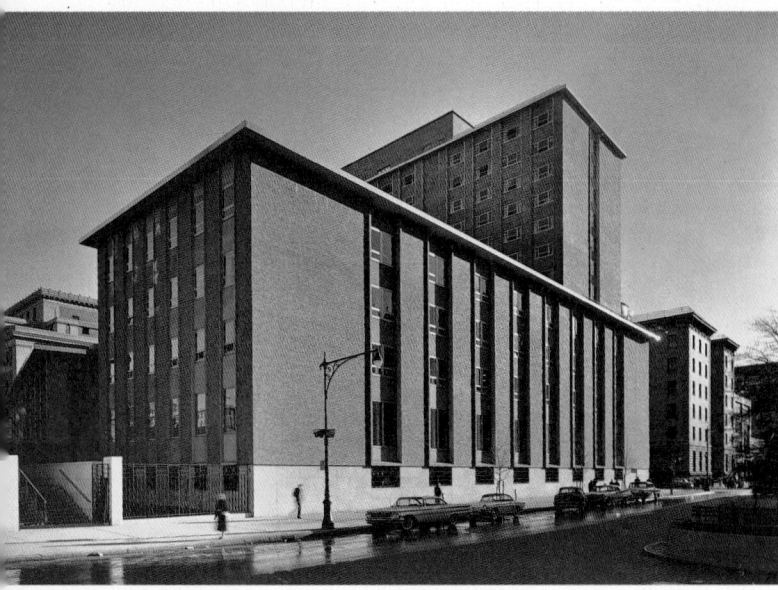

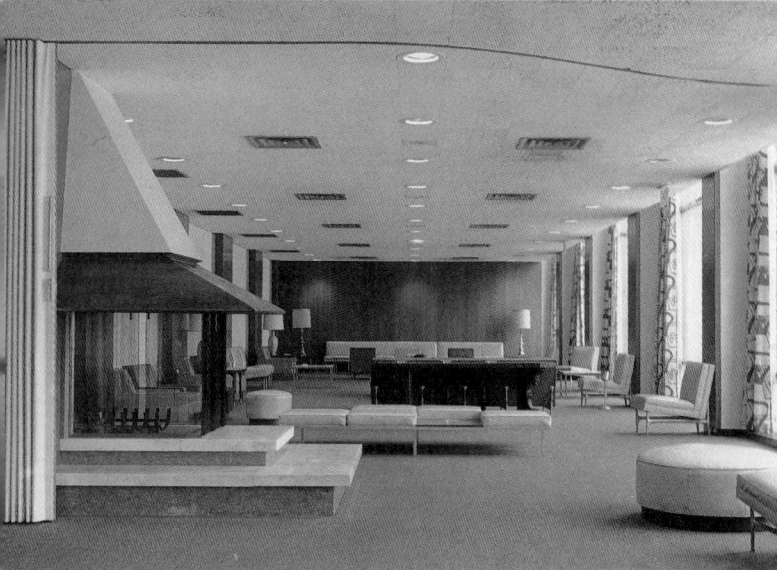

Top: Ferris Booth Hall and Carman Hall, Columbia University, northeast corner of Broadway and West 114th Street. Shreve, Lamb & Harmon, 1956. View to the southeast. Molitor. CCT

Bottom: Ferris Booth Hall. Lounge. Plowden. CCT

Amsterdam Avenue was purchased for a token fee of $1,000 and transformed into a landscaped walkway, renamed College Walk.[30] In 1967 ornamental gates were installed at the walkway's endpoints.[31]

In 1956 the Advisory Council on Architecture, replacing the office of the Consulting Architect to the University established eight years earlier, was created "to insure," as *Progressive Architecture* explained, "that new buildings planned . . . will receive aesthetic consideration."[32] The committee's membership consisted of the architecture school's dean, Leopold Arnaud, Professor Charles Reiger of the school and Arthur C. Holden, William Platt and Frederick J. Woodbridge—all in all a panel of not particularly distinguished, conservative designers. *Architectural Forum* reported that when Woodbridge asked the numerous firms who were then working on buildings for the university to bring together drawings of their schemes for review by the advisory panel, the confusion was "quite immense. Groans of laughter accompanied the discovery of one incongruity after another, as plans were unrolled for buildings that were intended to stand in close conjunction but had been worked out as if each were a military secret." While progress was being made to bring harmony to the individual efforts, *Forum* expressed doubts that these "last-minute rescue techniques" could "regain the distinction conferred on the core of her campus by . . . McKim, who was allowed to execute a coherent plan in which the total result exceeded the sum of the separate parts."[33]

That same year saw the release of Harvey Clarkson's less than inspired design for an undergraduate student center and an adjacent dormitory, which constituted the first major addition to the main campus since the completion of James Gamble Rogers's Butler Library in 1934.[34] Clarkson, who was the chief designer for Shreve, Lamb & Harmon, had first proposed a student center for the east side of South Field in the late 1940s.[35] In that scheme he had nearly eliminated the courtyard formed by McKim, Mead & White's Hartley Hall (1905), Livingston Hall (1905), Hamilton Hall (1907) and John Jay Hall (1926).[36] But the vocabulary in his earlier scheme was nonetheless far more sensitive to the McKim firm's buildings than was that of the 1956 student center and dorm. The site for the new buildings, in the southwest corner of the campus, bounded by 114th Street and Broadway, was cleared in 1957 of tennis courts as well as the oldest building on campus, an ivy-covered, dormer-windowed 1879 cottage that had served as the gatekeeper's lodge of the Bloomingdale Insane Asylum until the land was purchased by Columbia University in 1892. The building's demolition occurred despite some protest by students and by Dustin Rice, a professor of fine arts who argued that it possessed even greater architectural character than McKim's buildings, which he denounced as representations of an "emasculated Renaissance."[37]

Completed in 1960, Clarkson's Ferris Booth Hall was a four-story building that formed a podium for a thirteen-story slablike dormitory, originally designated New Hall but later renamed to honor a beloved Columbia College dean, Harry J. Carman.[38] Ferris Booth Hall was a monumentally scaled mass that opened through a two-story glassy facade to a raised flagstone patio. The zigzagged wall framing the patio seemed perhaps more appropriate to a suburban backyard than to McKim's imposingly Classical campus. The building's principal wall was placed at a diagonal to the campus grid, creating impressive views toward Low Library, but at the expense of McKim's master plan, which had been honored for sixty-four years. It contained a wide array of facilities, including a 780-seat auditorium, theater rehearsal and dressing rooms, an art gallery, a photographic dark room, a music library, studios for WKCR, the student-run radio station, a bowling alley, a rifle range, a lounge and a cafeteria-style restaurant called the Lion's Den. Looming above Ferris Booth Hall and set back slightly from 114th Street was New Hall, whose crude brick-and-limestone facades contrasted vertical piers with horizontal window bands in a misguided attempt to update McKim's Classicism. The dormitory was entered on the eastern facade from a pedestrian walkway that led to the main campus from 114th Street.

Though Allan Temko felt that the general location of the two buildings completed "the grand design for the South Field," he was extremely critical of their architecture: "They are heavy and pompous, without being rich. They are embarrassingly bureaucratic in mood. The massing is maladroit, to put it mildly. . . . The two new buildings look cheap beside the older ones. They seem almost unfinished, as if corners were ruthlessly cut. The details are skimpy and unimaginative. Yet we all know that the two buildings were far from inexpensive." Of the dormitory, Temko said: "The entrance and ground floor are poorly handled; the placement of the lounge shows a shocking ignorance of the flow of students. New Hall makes little provision for the two most important needs of College men, lively discourse and private study. I feel it's a rather mean building, like a Victorian reformatory."[39] Whatever the architectural shortcomings of the complex, however, the dormitory did succeed in providing much-needed student housing, and Ferris Booth Hall gave student life a useful venue.

In 1961 the School of Engineering at last moved into a new building, Seeley Wintersmith Mudd Hall, designed by Voorhees, Walker, Smith & Smith.[40] To many observers, Mudd Hall further testified to the disintegration of Columbia's architectural traditions. Rising from a base that occupied a sloping site at the northeastern corner of the main campus, bounded by Amsterdam Avenue and 120th Street, the banal, virtually detail-free brick slab provided a visual balance to Pupin Hall (McKim, Mead & White, 1926).[41] Alan Lapidus, a student at the School of Architecture and the son of the well-known shop and hotel architect Morris Lapidus, himself a Columbia graduate, dismissed Mudd Hall as "an unbelievable hunk," explaining that it was "just a storage house for students . . . shoved into the campus like a cork."[42] Allan Temko said the building was nothing short of "a disaster":

> Frank Lloyd Wright called buildings like the School of Engineering boxes with holes punched in them. Why, some low-cost housing developments look better! Beside the classical presence of the McKim, Mead & White buildings it looks ugly and cheap. . . . Columbia has a fine Engineering School, one which has helped advance modern technology considerably. Yet not a single significant structural advance of the 20th century appears in the construction of that building. The new Engineering School could have been built in 1900. How did a school working on the frontiers of applied science ever get such a reactionary building?[43]

Voorhees, Walker, Smith, Smith & Haines expanded the facility with a second undistinguished brick building, known as the Engineering Terrace (1966), which linked Mudd Hall to a plaza separating Schermerhorn Hall and the new business school (see below).[44] In 1963 the architects proposed a third building, known as the Engineering Tower, to rise on stilts perpendicular to Mudd Hall.[45] The building was never realized, and the Sherman Fairchild Center for the Life Sciences would eventually rise on its site (see below).

By the time Mudd Hall was opened, Columbia's students had become alarmed by the university's new building program. In 1962 they took an activist position, protesting the construction of Uris Hall (1964), Moore & Hutchins's building for the business school. Opposition to Columbia's new architecture had become so outspoken that when WKCR, the campus radio station, asked Percival Goodman, a Columbia professor of architecture, to comment on the university's new planning and architecture, the university administration seized the tapes, claiming that Goodman may have made libelous remarks.[46] George Charles Keller, the editor of Columbia College Today, noted the widespread dissatisfaction with the university's new architecture. Perhaps putting it a bit overdramatically, he warned that if negative "feelings continue to multiply, they could represent the greatest single detriment to growing alumni support in future years, as well as an obstacle for those who seek to continue to attract the nation's finest students and the world's greatest scholars to Columbia."[47]

Moore & Hutchins's design for Uris Hall, the building that first brought into the open student and faculty criticism of the new campus architecture, was minimally detailed.[48] A previous proposal by Eggers & Higgins, presented in the early 1950s, had used more traditional ornament and trim, but to a nonetheless paltry effect.[49] The final design was built on top of McKim, Mead & White's uncompleted University Hall, whose ground floor was demolished while the lower floor, containing the university's gymnasium, was preserved. Uris Hall was made up of a nine-story limestone-clad slab containing offices and seminar rooms, flanked by two lower wings housing classrooms, a cafeteria and administrative offices. A semicircular reading room capped by a folded-plate structure projected from the rear above the rusticated apsidal base of McKim's original design.

Uris Hall's design raised a storm of objections in the architecture school, located just a building away. In a widely reported protest staged at the ground-breaking ceremony on April 17, 1962, a group of students, led by Harry Parnass and Alan Lapidus, displayed signs with such slogans as "Ban the Building" and "No More Uglies." Parnass and Lapidus had numerous criticisms of the building:

> In terms of esthetics it looks backwards rather than forwards—it is mock monumentality, eclectic, manneristic and awkward, a junior skyscraper. Although it faces south it shows no concern for light nor does it utilize any of the technology developed in the last twenty years to reduce sun glare with shading devices. It ignores the master plan drawn up for the campus in the Eighteen Nineties by McKim, Mead and White, which prescribed a low building for that site. It will "crush" the Low Memorial Library by towering over it. . . . The building should have some image relating to the students who will work in it. This building looks no different from a post office or a branch office of an insurance company.[50]

Alan Spector, a first-year student at Columbia's School of Architecture, claimed that the "building contradicts everything we've been taught."[51]

Percy Uris, the real estate developer and Columbia University trustee who together with his brother Harold donated most of the funds for the building, responded that Columbia architecture students had not "learned their lessons properly" and that it was "a fine building."[52] The architect Robert S. Hutchins claimed that he was "not distressed" by the protest but acknowledged that he had read the demonstrators' signs: "I wrote down every single one," he said. "I'm going to show them to my partner."[53] The debate over the design of Uris Hall soon widened to include critics and commentators not intimately associated with the university. Peter Blake, managing editor of *Architectural Forum*, voiced his opinion to a *New York Times* reporter: "Many handsome buildings in the contemporary idiom are being built today. But all too few are on college campuses. If Columbia can do no better in this idiom than the drawing I've seen of its proposed School of Business, then it should go back to neoclassic prototypes and thus at least produce a coherent campus."[54] James T. Burns, an editor of *Progressive Architecture*, characterized Uris Hall in the *Columbia Daily Spectator* as an example of the "scholastic model office building" that business students would encounter once they graduated.[55] The problem, however, was that, in the hands of the mediocre architects selected, the design was clumsy, not nearly as fine a manifestation of corporate culture as the buildings of Lever Brothers, Seagram's or a host of other companies that prized high-quality architecture. And though the intention had been to erect a building that was architecturally sympathetic to the campus, the students wanted something uniquely modern, similar in spirit to the glamorous buildings that were going up around the Yale campus. William Platt defended the scheme as a "nonentity, an efficient building that fits in," one that "should not be the kind of building the architectural students have in mind."[56] But the critic Katherine Kuh, writing in the *Saturday Review*, disagreed, saying that the building recalled the "dreary fascist architecture from Mussolini's day" and that "somehow $7 million seems a lot to spend on a nonentity."[57]

In 1968, four years after the building's completion, the courtyard separating it from Low Library was adorned with an abstract monumental sculpture by the Australian-born artist Clement Meadmore. The 6,340-pound, black-painted object, titled *Curl*, took the form of a twisted square column placed horizontally on the ground in a posture that, according to *Progressive Architecture*, made it seem to be lying "helplessly" in the plaza.[58]

At the same time that Columbia College and several of the university's graduate schools were experiencing severe growing pains, Barnard College, an independent college for women within the university, located across Broadway from the main campus, was expanding its physical plant with virtually no protest, although with little more success. In 1957 Barnard announced plans to build a new dormitory and student center directly east of, and connected to, Brooks Hall (Charles A. Rich, 1907).[59] As initially designed by O'Connor & Kilham, the complex was to consist of a massive student center, sheathed with large vertical expanses of glass, and an adjacent nine-story dormitory, with each receiving light from a floor-to-ceiling vertical strip window as well as an eye-level horizontal glazing band. The student center was not built on the site, but the dormitory, named Helen Reid Hall and located on the northwest corner of Broadway and 116th Street, was completed in 1959. The building was architecturally undistinguished but more contextually appropriate than the earlier scheme, with brick exterior walls, a copper cornice and carefully proportioned individual double-hung windows.

In 1957 Barnard also announced plans to build an academic building, Adele Lehman Hall, north of Barnard Hall (Brunner & Tryon, 1917).[60] Designed by O'Connor & Kilham, Lehman Hall (1959), which housed the Wollman Library as well as other facilities, was a five-story building pushed to the property line along Claremont Avenue in order to save as much of Barnard's diminishing open space as possible. Facing east toward a grassy lawn and Broadway beyond, Lehman Hall was

dominated by a three-story, glass-enclosed volume cantilevered over an arcade of columns clad in green enamel. To shield the library from glare, the facade included an irregularly gridded concrete *brise soleil*.

In 1966 the college resuscitated plans for a student center, this time combining it with a classroom building in a complex north of Lehman Hall, on the former location of 119th Street, which had been closed and made part of the campus in 1951 in anticipation of future construction.[61] The two-story student center, Millicent McIntosh Hall, and the twelve-story classroom tower to its north, Helen Goodhart Altschul Hall, were designed by Vincent G. Kling, a Philadelphia-based architect and a Columbia University trustee.[62] Built into its sloping site, McIntosh Hall presented a windowless podium along Broadway, topped by a glass-enclosed upper story, which was surmounted in turn by a heavy slab that acted visually as a cornice. In striking contrast to this unobtrusive if less than graceful low-lying building, Altschul Hall towered over the campus. Horizontal bands of windows punctuated the tower's principal and rear facades; the windowless north- and south-facing walls gave the building a menacing aspect.

A 1966 lawsuit resulting from the purchase of the notorious Bryn Mawr Hotel at 420 West 121st Street, on the southeast corner of Amsterdam Avenue, by Remedco, a real estate concern representing Columbia University and nine other Morningside Heights institutions, reflected the growing tensions between the expanding university and the surrounding community.[63] Remedco argued that the so-called welfare hotel had become a hotbed of drug trade and prostitution; tenants countered with the allegation that the university had racist motives, seeking to push out the area's nonwhite residents. Despite the protests, the deal went through and the building was taken over and demolished by Barnard College to make way for a sixteen-story dormitory. During construction a group of demonstrators in black veils staged a "mourn-in" on Amsterdam Avenue to lament the buildings that had been destroyed to make way for university expansion.[64] The Barnard dormitory, named Plimpton Hall (1969) and designed by Slingerland & Booss, was a banal, 284-room brick-and-limestone tower set back from the street atop an elevated plaza that covered ground-level stores. It was noteworthy only for the arrangement of its rooms in apartmentlike units that shared kitchen and bathroom facilities.

Undoubtedly the most controversial architecture project ever undertaken by Columbia University—a gymnasium, intended for both Columbia College undergraduates and teenage boys from the nearby Harlem community, to be built on public property in Morningside Park—was at first glance both modest and imaginative, yet it would eventually threaten to tear apart the institution as it became a focus of student protest.[65] The proposal had already gone through a long and complex development prior to the initiation of the scheme for a building in Morningside Park: demands for the replacement of University Hall's inadequate gymnasium and swimming pool had been voiced as early as 1914, when that building was severely damaged by fire.[66] In 1941 the university abandoned plans to erect a gymnasium either at the southwestern corner of the campus, bounded by Broadway and 114th Street, or on the east side of Amsterdam Avenue between 116th and 117th streets. At that time Columbia's in-house architects proposed to complete University Hall based on a modified version of the original design, adding an extension, essentially a freestanding brick-and-limestone building connected to the existing hall by a narrow, three-level passageway. The annex's principal facade, facing 120th Street,

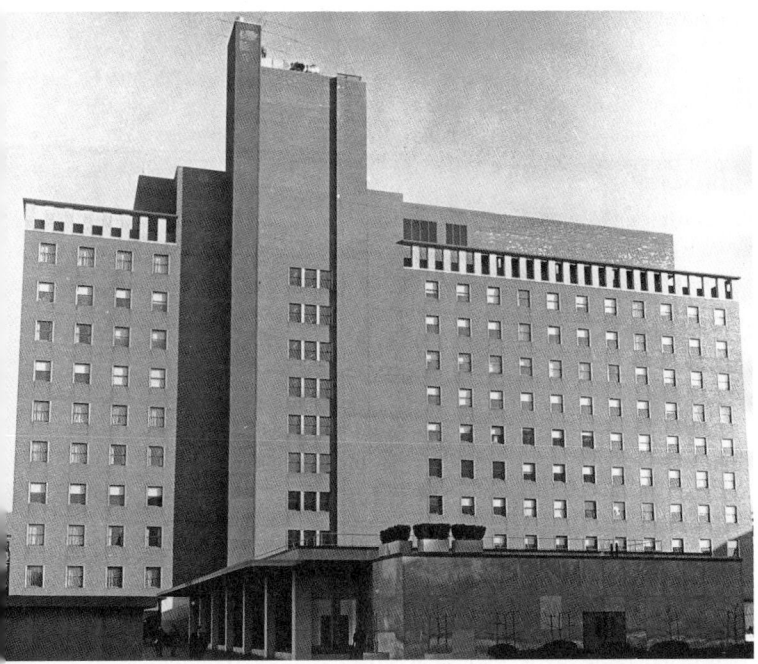

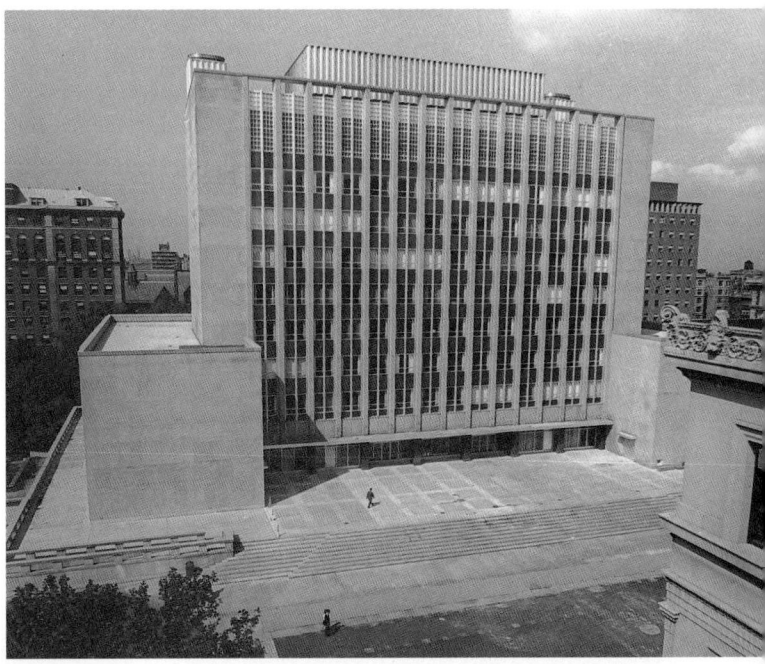

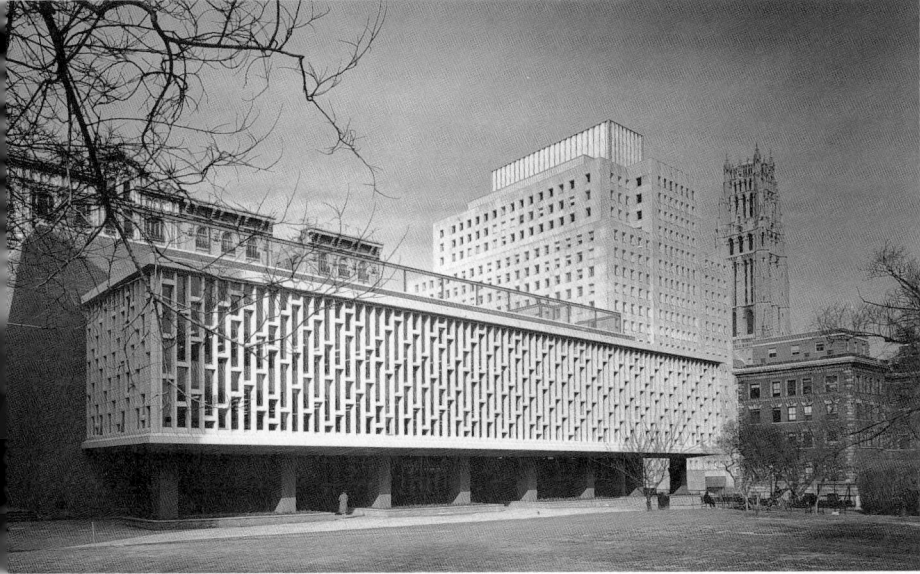

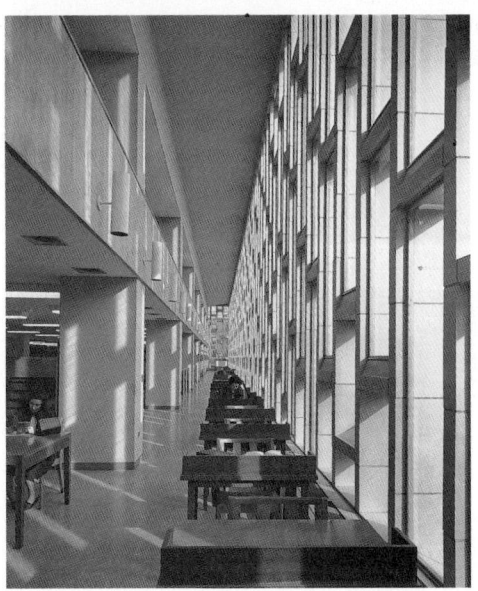

Top left: Seeley Wintersmith Mudd Hall, Columbia University, southwest corner of Amsterdam Avenue and West 120th Street. Voorhees, Walker, Smith & Smith, 1961. View to the north. CUOPI

Top right: Uris Hall, Columbia University, between Broadway and Amsterdam avenues, West 118th and West 119th streets. Moore & Hutchins, 1964. View to the north. CCT

Bottom left: Adele Lehman Hall, Barnard College, between Broadway and Claremont avenues, West 117th and West 119th streets. O'Connor & Kilham, 1959. View to the northwest. Stoller. ©ESTO

Bottom right: Adele Lehman Hall. View of Wollman Library. Stoller. ©ESTO

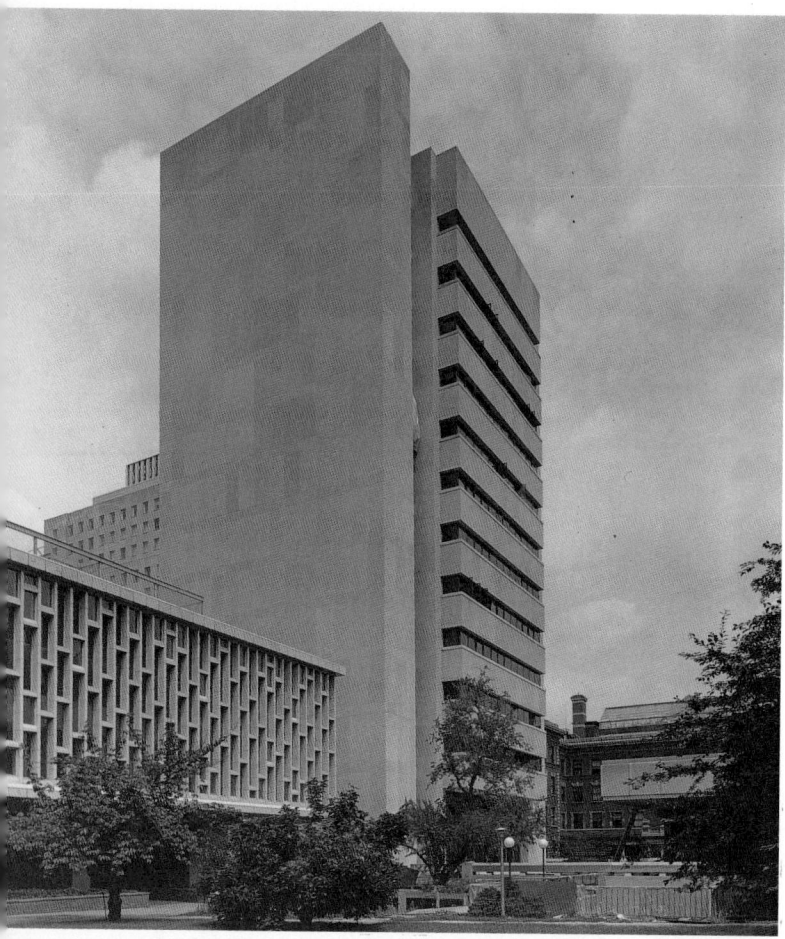

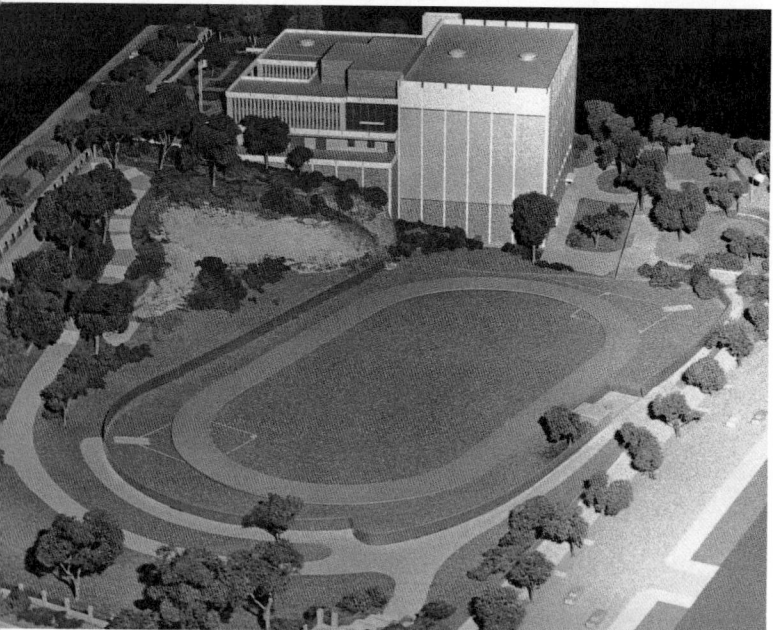

Top: Helen Goodhart Altschul Hall, Barnard College, between Broadway and Claremont Avenue, West 118th and West 119th streets. Vincent G. Kling, 1969. View to the northwest showing Lehman Hall (O'Connor & Kilham, 1959) on the left. OMH

Bottom: Proposal for Columbia University Gymnasium, Morningside Park. Eggers & Higgins and Sherwood, Mills & Smith, 1961. Model. View to the northwest. CCT

was to incorporate a centrally placed entrance surmounted by an arched window and flanked on either side by six large arched windows.[67] Between 1945 and 1947 Eggers & Higgins developed a scheme calling for a similarly traditional if slightly more stylish building at the same location that featured a rusticated stone base and, above, minimally detailed piers separating vertical strip windows.[68] Alternate schemes for an addition to University Hall were proposed by Reinhard, Hofmeister & Walquist in 1949, Columbia's in-house architects in 1950–54, Eggers & Higgins in 1955 and Adams & Woodbridge in 1957.[69]

In 1954 Columbia University president Grayson Kirk, who succeeded Eisenhower in 1952, and Park Commissioner Robert Moses had a conversation that laid the foundation for the gymnasium-in-the-park proposal. Kirk noted the university's severe lack of recreational space and Moses voiced his concern over the fact that the park was widely ignored. As the editors of *Columbia College Today* would later report, "Moses was worried because Morningside Park was woefully underused; hardly any white families had entered it in nearly a decade and Negro families were not especially attracted to rock climbing."[70] Out of this conversation grew what the *New York Times* called "an unusual agreement": Columbia University pledged to build 7.1 acres of playing fields, including three touch football fields, two softball diamonds and a soccer field; a storage building; and a combined field house and comfort station, all located at the southern end of Morningside Park.[71] In exchange for near-exclusive use of the fields on weekdays during most of the academic year, the university would provide trained supervision for community activities. The arrangement, which was to prevail for ten years, was revocable by the city but not by Columbia. The Columbia Community Athletic Field was completed in 1957.

The following year university representatives conferred with the Park Department about the possibility of building a university gymnasium in Morningside Park. Taking their cue from the previous agreement, Kirk and Moses reached an understanding that if Columbia built a public gym according to Park Department specifications, the city would permit the university to build its own gym above. Plans to build a gymnasium directly north of the playing field were announced in 1960. Built into the park's steep, rocky slope, the building was to occupy a 2.1-acre site along Morningside Drive at the terminus of 113th Street, extending east nearly the full width of the park toward Morningside Avenue. The budget was $6 million, a figure that would rise to more than $13 million by 1968. Columbia was to lease air rights in the public park from the city in exchange for the provision of the lower-level community gymnasium, which would be used by neighborhood boys for boxing, wrestling, playing basketball and handball and participating in other activities under the supervision of Columbia personnel. The major portion of the building, representing a little more than 85 percent of the total space, was to serve Columbia College students and encompass extensive athletic facilities, including a swimming pool, as well as classrooms and offices. The architect Max Abramovitz claimed credit for the concept of a "double facility" and the cross-sectional arrangement of the parts.[72] The actual commission, however, was awarded to two firms, Eggers & Higgins and Sherwood, Mills & Smith, whose joint design was approved by the Municipal Arts Commission in May 1961. Their scheme confronted Morningside Drive with three concrete-framed, brick-clad, boxlike volumes entered off a paved courtyard. Viewed from Harlem, the 150-foot-tall building loomed over the park, its mass punctuated by a small entrance to the community facility.

In the fall of 1961 Kirk signed a fifty-year lease with Park Commissioner Newbold Morris for the air rights to the parkland, to be rented annually for $3,000. The plan met with the approval not only of the university and the municipality but of the New York State Senate, Governor Nelson A. Rockefeller and, according to a 1966 article in Columbia College Today, "dozens of community groups." Looking retrospectively at a time when debate over the gym had not yet arisen, the article described the initial optimism about the project:

> On the surface the idea of constructing the gymnasium . . . seems remarkably lacking in controversy. If anything, it was designed to facilitate compromise. It is to be built on a huge rock outcropping; so almost no trees or grass will be disturbed. By using the park site instead of a city block, no residents of Morningside Heights will be displaced. Also by using the park site, Morningside Park, for decades an untended no man's land of broken bottles, crumbling, dangerous cement stairs, and unpruned trees and bushes, would be made clean, safe, and horticulturally lovely again. . . . And, the "Chinese Wall" effect of the deserted park between Morningside and Harlem will be partially eliminated and the park turned into an interracial meeting place full of activity. Perhaps best of all, the community would be given a fine indoor facility.[73]

But as early as 1964, as reported by the journalist Robert Alden in the New York Times, Columbia and its neighbors had become involved "in a controversy that grows more bitter each day. . . . The suspicion of some people in the neighborhood is so deep that every effort of Columbia is cast in an ugly light. The park projects are pictured as land grabs."[74] An Ad Hoc Committee on Morningside Park was formed in 1965 by the Parks and Playground Committee of the Morningside Renewal Council, which questioned the project's wisdom but expressed little doubt that it would be realized, despite the fact that John V. Lindsay, during his campaign for mayor, had objected to the gym project in the white paper on parks that Thomas P. F. Hoving, who would become Lindsay's Park Commissioner in 1966, prepared for him. Hoving objected to the proposal on several grounds: that local communities should be consulted regarding their public parks, that open parkland should not be built on, and that public parks should not be used for private purposes. State Senator Basil Patterson and Assemblyman Percy Sutton also objected to the project, introducing legislation to repeal the act that had enabled the university to rent the land. Patterson expressed his community's negative feelings toward Columbia, which was considered an increasingly insular institution, out of touch with urban realities. "I'm not against using park space if the community need is urgent," Patterson stated. "Parks are to be used, not just looked at. But I'm not sure that this gymnasium is going up under circumstances that are fair to the community." He continued: "We don't want to fight every expansion by the University. . . . But, Columbia must come before the community and the city and explain its needs and hopes in an open democratic way. Look, Columbia's neighborhood has changed. The mood of the Negroes has changed. I've reacted to it. Columbia hasn't."[75] Patterson and Sutton's legislation was not passed.

In 1965 Morningside Park became the site of another building project, Public School 36, but because the elementary school was built by the city for unrestricted use by the public, the project did not stimulate protest.[76] P.S. 36 (1966) occupied a hilly site on the "panhandle" of the park, bounded by Amsterdam Avenue, Morningside Drive and 123rd Street. The sophisticated design, by Frederick G. Frost, Jr. & Associates, consisted of four three-story buildings linked by second-story bridges. Between the buildings were terraced plazas, some of which incorporated playgrounds designed by the landscape architect M. Paul Friedberg. The three structures consisted of rough-hewn fieldstone bases, concrete facades and brick stair towers. Fieldstone was also used in a fence that partially enclosed the schoolyard, as well as in the terraces' retaining walls; the material served to relate the composition to the rocky outcroppings that were the park's outstanding natural feature. In the southwest corner of the site was a monumental, welded-steel sculpture, composed of letters and numerals, by William Tarr, which quickly became a neighborhood landmark.

Perhaps the public figure who was most outspoken in opposition to Columbia's proposed gym, and certainly the person who elicited the harshest criticism from the university, was Thomas Hoving. In defending the proposal, a university official complained that "once again it appears that Columbia must be a target for charges and implications that it is somehow a sinister organization scheming to defraud and deceive the people of New York."[77] "It sounds like they have a guilty conscience," Hoving responded. "Those are their words, not mine. . . . I certainly do not see Columbia as a 'sinister organization.' It is a great cultural and educational institution with severe problems of town and gown. All we want is that the community get a slice of the pie."[78]

In the fall of 1966 the mood surrounding the controversy seemed to be one of compromise, with an aide to Mayor Lindsay saying, "I think the University and the community and the city have turned the corner on this issue."[79] Lawrence Chamberlain, vice president of the university, who had been instrumental in the creation of the Columbia Community Athletic Field, was more cautious but nonetheless optimistic: "Most of the slow, cordial, intimate contacts between the University and the community that were carefully built up since World War II have been smashed in the last few years. Hopefully, the climate may be changing again."[80]

Columbia officials began to meet with community representatives and, encouraged by Hoving to give a bigger "slice of the pie" to Harlem residents, had agreed by 1967 to include a separate swimming pool for the community in the building.[81] They unequivocally stated, however, that they would make no further concessions and that the university would not share the entire facility, as some people had suggested. Though many observers felt that the revised proposal still smacked of racism, and despite the objections of fifteen of the sixteen Harlem organizations represented by the West Harlem Morningside Park Committee, which had taken over for the Ad Hoc Committee, the new scheme was supported by Patterson. On December 14, 1967, at a meeting sponsored by the West Harlem Morningside Park Committee, the black militant H. Rap Brown, who coined the phrase "Burn, baby, burn," suggested that any gymnasium in the park could be demolished by arson.

In what would prove to be a major tactical blunder, the university, sensing that time was running out for the project, began construction on February 19, 1968, with no prior announcement. The following day approximately twenty people staged a sit-in at the site; twelve people, including six Columbia students, were arrested. On February 29 about 150 demonstrators marched from a campus rally to the park, where some protesters attempted to tear down the chain-link fence surrounding the construction site. The subsequent clash with police foreshadowed the violent campus demonstrations that would soon follow.

743

In an article written the following month, Ada Louise Huxtable summarized the symbolic nature of the conflict over the gym:

> Architecture creates symbols; this is one of its functions. There is a symbol going up right now in Morningside Park: The new Columbia University Gymnasium. But this is not the kind of symbol anyone wanted. It stands for one of the more disturbing problems of our troubled times—the deep and bitter split and many-layered misunderstanding between a privileged urban university and an underprivileged community. . . . The real tragedy of the whole Columbia gym affair is that this dubious and even harmful project has been carried out in good faith. The institutional mentality is not diabolical. It is simply grossly imperceptive. It has meant well and behaved with consummate wrongheadedness.

Moreover, Huxtable commented, the gymnasium "is certainly not going to be a very sensitive building," pointing out that "the huge masonry bulk will never blend with its rustic setting. It is in conflict just by being there." She concluded that, "while thought and care have gone into the architectural treatment, the result cannot be characterized as either inspired or sympathetic to the site."[82]

The gymnasium became one of the touchstones of the "crisis at Columbia," the student strike that crippled the university in April and May of 1968 and set off tremors that would affect campuses across the country for the next few years. Many demonstrators contended that the university's plan to build the gymnasium represented its racist impulses. As Marta Gutman and Richard Plunz wrote, the gym symbolized "the University's failure to understand the problems of poverty and racism and its arrogant exclusion of the community from its planning policy." But, they continued, it was also "feared as a symbol of encroachment. For if Columbia were presented to Harlem as an Acropolis, then surely the gym could have become the gate, the Propylea of the complex on top of the Heights. Cruelly though, since the gate did not give Harlem residents access up the hill, it was feared as the University's first step on a march that would ultimately invade and occupy West Harlem."[83]

Even before the strike, various Columbia student groups, including the University Student Council, as well as the faculty of the architecture school had joined with the community in its opposition to the gym. Most of these participants, however, saw the protest as a symbolic one, since the gym's construction seemed inevitable and its value as a facility for both Columbia and the community seemed clear. Even as late as March 6, 1968, the editors of the *Columbia Daily Spectator* vigorously supported the gym in an editorial titled "Enough Is Enough."[84] But the strike crystallized opposition to the gym. On April 24, 1968, the faculty of Columbia College voted its opposition to the project and asked that construction be stopped. That same day students occupied President Kirk's office in Low Library, and protestors marched to the chant, "Gym Crow Must Go!" On April 26 Mayor Lindsay requested that work on the gymnasium be stopped and promised that work would not resume until community leaders had been consulted. Shortly thereafter the Morningside Park Preservation Committee, headed by Victor Crichton, a former Columbia College student board president, filed suit against Columbia and the City of New York charging both with improper use of public property. But the crisis was resolved before the suit was heard in court.

In May a five-member investigative commission that would bear the name of its chairman, the Harvard Law School professor and former Solicitor General Archibald M. Cox, was appointed by a faculty group to evaluate the campus disturbances.[85] Harold F. McGuire, a university trustee, reported to the commission that he believed Thomas Hoving "was the one who stimulated" opposition to the gym proposal and that Hoving's statements had functioned as "the germs and ideas" behind the student demonstrations.[86] John Wheeler, a lawyer representing the university, similarly reported to a City Council committee that Hoving's "calls for action" were "not unlike those we have been witnessing on the campus in recent weeks" and that "his cries to take to the streets did not go unheeded by those seeking to harass the university." Wheeler also asserted that the gym was a "completely phony issue" and that the real issue was "student power."[87] Hoving, who in 1967 had resigned his post as Park Commissioner to become director of the Metropolitan Museum of Art, labeled the charges leveled against him "tripe." He recalled that when, in January 1966, he had calculated that community space in the gym would be approximately 12.5 percent of the total, he was "amazed, annoyed and . . . angered." If a building were erected in Central Park opposite his home and significant restrictions were placed on public access, he said, "It would certainly bother me." He concluded that it was "a question of principle. It's the community's property and you just can't hand any of it over for exclusive use."[88]

While Hoving was busy refuting attacks against him, his successor as Park Commissioner, August Heckscher, began meeting with community leaders to study alternative plans for developing Morningside Park. In October 1968 the Architects Renewal Committee (ARCH), under the direction of the architect J. Max Bond, together with the West Harlem Community Organization, presented an ambitious plan to use the gymnasium site for a variety of public facilities, including a 1,200-seat amphitheater, a multipurpose skating rink/pool, a building for cultural programs, a playground, a "soul food garden" and outdoor parking space. While the plan's sponsors searched for funding, the fate of the stalled gym remained uncertain.

In August 1968 Grayson Kirk resigned as president, without, he asserted, any pressure from the university. Three months later Andrew W. Cordier, Columbia's acting president, retained I. M. Pei to plan for the university's future growth on Morningside Heights in what would be its first comprehensive attempt to address large-scale physical development issues since McKim's campus plans of 1893 and 1903.[89] At the announcement of Pei's appointment, Cordier promised "a new era" in the university's history, one that would be marked by greater emphasis on community participation: "There will be consultation—a great deal of consultation—with the people of the neighborhood."[90]

On March 3, 1969, after a mail poll of one hundred community leaders from Morningside Heights and West Harlem confirmed widespread opposition to the gym, and taking Pei's advice into consideration, the university's trustees unanimously approved Cordier's recommendation to permanently drop the project. The trustees also expressed their willingness to restore the site—which would prove difficult, given that the rock outcropping had been extensively blasted—or to work with the community on other park improvements. The trustees did not, however, endorse the plan developed by ARCH. Despite the university's pledge of support, the site remained in its partially excavated state for more than two decades.

Ten years after the initial agreement allowing its construction had been reached, the gymnasium project in Morningside Park was dead. In its remarkably even-handed report on the strike, the Cox Commission succinctly summarized the issues surrounding the project: "Whether the gymnasium was good or bad for Harlem, public property was being used for private purposes and the new spokesmen for the increasingly self-conscious black community of the mid-1960s had no share in the planning or decisions." The report concluded, however, that "there was no impropriety in the original project, and that the University acted in complete good faith in negotiating an agreement with the Park Department which was considered fair to both the University and the community." Dismissing one of the major complaints against Columbia during the protests, the report continued:

> Viewing the matter solely as a business transaction, there is no merit in the criticism that the community would receive the use of . . . 12 percent—while Columbia would receive . . . 88 percent. If the University had required much less gymnasium space—for example, an area no bigger than the portion of the building dedicated to the City, the University and the City would have equal shares, but the value of what the community would receive would be exactly the same as under the actual arrangement. . . . The size of the building the University constructs for itself has little or nothing to do with the adequacy of the facilities the community receives in return for the use of the land. We further find that the University officials were following accepted academic practices when they rejected the suggestion that the use of the entire facility be shared with the community by allocation of time. . . . We know of no University willing to surrender control over major facilities used by its students. Finally, on a purely pragmatic view, it would be reasonable to conclude that the community would benefit more from a swimming pool and gymnasium open to its young people summer and winter, with expert guidance, than from the 2.1 acres of rocky hillside that it lost.

But, as the commission concluded, "these points were not the real issue," and the arrangement could no longer be viewed as a business transaction, "a fact which the University officials utterly failed to grasp, or if they did indeed grasp it, utterly failed to acknowledge. As the Chairman of the Citizenship Council told us, the gym was a 'very visible symbol of something which is more serious, which is the expansion program that is going on in Columbia.'"[91]

In light of the charges that the Morningside Park gym proposal reflected Columbia's "imperialism," it was ironic that it was, perhaps, merely the most widely publicized, not the most potentially divisive, of several expansion plans. In May 1966 the Advisory Council on Architecture had pinpointed five areas for development and expansion, refocusing attention on existing and ongoing projects as well as outlining new ones. The North Campus, from 118th to 120th Street, between Broadway and Amsterdam Avenue, would include future engineering and science facilities; the South Campus, from 111th or 112th to 114th Street, between Broadway and Amsterdam Avenue, would include an expansion to the main library and new college housing and related facilities; the West Campus, from 112th to 116th Street, between Broadway and Riverside Drive, would include future graduate-student and staff housing and, perhaps, a new home for the School of Social Work; the East Campus, from 115th to 120th Street, between Amsterdam Avenue and Morningside Drive, would include future buildings for arts and architecture, international affairs, political science and a graduate housing complex; and the outlying campus would include various new facilities at remote locations, such as Columbia-Presbyterian Hospital and the Lamont-Oceanographic research laboratories.[92]

In November of that year Ada Louise Huxtable wrote in the *New York Times* that the proposed South Campus was potentially "even more explosive" than the proposed gym.[93] The complex was to consist of an addition to Butler Library spanning 114th Street, as well as dormitories and residential buildings, all built on land already densely developed with housing. A large platform was to cross 113th Street; 112th Street was to be eliminated completely between Broadway and Amsterdam Avenue. Columbia's in-house architects had drawn up the preliminary plans. Additionally, in 1963, a group of graduate students in Columbia's architecture school, including Jack R. Cosner, Daniel P. D'Oliveira, Arnold G. Henderson, Richard E. Kaeyer, Kirby M. Keahey, David A. Millard, J. Daniel Spears and Douglas Dean Telfer, had undertaken a South Campus design study.[94] Their proposal called for outlying groups of low buildings, some organized around courtyards, and a towering five-wing megastructure occupying the center of the site. The idea of developing a South Campus was ultimately abandoned, though the university's retention of the allotted property left open the possibility of realizing such a plan in the future.

In the May 15, 1968, issue of the *New Republic*, James Ridgeway, an associate editor of the magazine, wrote of another Columbia expansion plan: "The plans to build an apartheid gymnasium set off the siege at Columbia University, but this scheme is a minor facet of the enormous realty consortia the university is forming with private industry." Ridgeway claimed that between World War II and 1968 the educational institutions on Morningside Heights had been responsible for displacing 7,500 area residents, the majority of them poor and nonwhite, and that it was anticipated that an additional 11,000 people would be forced out in the ensuing decade. The author further charged that "a major renewal project affecting thousands of people in New York City is being undertaken by a small group of [Columbia] trustees operating behind closed doors," and that it constituted part of "a land grab, driving north into Harlem, east into the run-down slums around Central Park and south to 96th Street."[95] According to Ridgeway, Columbia began buying land between 125th and 130th streets, Broadway and the Hudson River, in 1967 with the intention of building a 3,000-unit apartment complex, one-third of which would be occupied by Columbia faculty. A waterside park and a marina would also be built. The apartments would be located on a massive platform stretching over the area, beneath which would be parking facilities and stores, as well as factories.

To meet its goals, Ridgeway reported, the university had entered into a complex agreement with the New York City Housing and Development Administration and the Negro Labor Committee, a coalition of AFL-CIO groups, formed in 1952. The university would finance the industrial area and the Negro Labor Committee would finance the housing complex; state aid would also be employed. The Negro Labor Committee hired Ifill & Johnson as consultants, Columbia hired Praeger-Kavanagh-Waterbury as consultants, and Clarke & Rapuano were approached to serve as the entire project's coordinating architects. The whole project was to be built by Percy Uris, who had agreed to work on his own behalf, not in conjunction with Uris Brothers, and without financial compensation.

Publication of Ridgeway's article motivated Courtney C. Brown, dean of the Columbia School of Business, to publicly outline the project, which he did "reluctantly," according to Peter Kihss, reporting in the *New York Times*.[96] Though the university denied many of Ridgeway's allegations, the volatile nature of the project was undeniable. Given the political climate, it was not surprising that the proposal was not pursued. An alternate scheme, designed by Richard Dattner & Associates and Henri A. LeGendre & Associates and sponsored by the Negro Labor Committee, was initially published in November 1968.[97] It called for a vast array of industrial, commercial and recreational facilities, as well as seven apartment buildings ranging in height from seven to fifty-four stories. The massive project was never realized. (The area had also been studied by a team of architects and planners from Princeton University as part of the Museum of Modern Art's 1967 exhibition, "The New City: Architecture and Urban Renewal.")[98]

The community and, it seemed, much of the press had become so hostile to Columbia that in the aftermath of the strike it was suggested that the university once again seriously consider relocating away from Morningside Heights. In 1968 the journalist Arnold Beichman, writing in New York magazine, posed the not-altogether-rhetorical question, "Will New York City be better off if the Columbia University site is transferred to its neighboring Harlem community and turned into an all-black university and educational complex?" Beichman went on to note that "It is difficult for some faculty members, and even some members of the administration, to believe that Columbia University, in some form or other, will move elsewhere. Yet the idea of moving has been considered by one official who told me: 'If it gets too rough, we'll move. After all, we've done it before.'"[99]

But Columbia did not relocate, and it remained an ineluctable fact that the community would effectively limit university expansion beyond the core campus. This was clearly acknowledged in I. M. Pei's master plan for Columbia, unveiled in May 1970, which called for a 50 percent increase in university construction but advocated more intensive development of existing real estate than ever before. One of Pei's principal responsibilities was the selection of a new site for the gymnasium, which he proposed to incorporate as part of a subterranean, 750,000-square-foot, five-level student center complex that would also accommodate an extension to Butler Library, a bookstore, a café and shops, all built beneath South Field. An underground concourse, at some points open to the sky, would connect the complex to existing campus buildings and also directly to the subway. In his optimistic report, which advocated design solutions that would promote the sometimes contradictory goals of improving the surrounding urban context and stimulating an internal sense of collegiality, Pei asserted that "the activities in the concourse might well spur the neighboring private sector to provide competitive services, shops and theaters. Such a result would make upper Broadway a much more exciting place—at least as lively as Harvard Square in Cambridge, Massachusetts."[100]

Pei's plan also called for extending the upper campus platform, filling in the remaining pockets of natural grade at the north end of campus and constructing three large buildings on the new podium to meet the expanding space demands of the science faculties. With the chance of an arts center being realized on Amsterdam Avenue increasingly remote, the report recommended that the architecture school and Avery Library be housed within an extension to Avery Hall (McKim, Mead & White, 1912). This would be created by burrowing east beneath the courtyard bounded by St. Paul's Chapel and Avery, Schermerhorn and Fayerweather halls—the only one of the courtyards realized in full accord with McKim's master plan—as well as west beneath the plaza that separated Low Library from Uris Hall. "We have exploited underground construction to the maximum," Pei said. "It has the advantage of no housing relocation and it gives us the chance to tie the whole university together."[101]

In a reflection of the report's spirit of sensitivity toward community needs, Pei proposed an apartment tower, containing approximately 320 units, to be shared equally by the university and the community.[102] The tower, which would be flanked by a park and would incorporate retail, day-care and parking facilities, was to be built on a site bounded by 121st Street, Amsterdam Avenue and Morningside Drive. The site had been purchased in 1962 by the College of Pharmacy, a Columbia University affiliate, which had begun to vacate and clear it but had sold the property to the university when it failed to raise the required funds to build. The partially demolished site had become a crime-ridden eyesore and a symbol to many observers of Columbia's callous attitude toward the neighborhood and its housing needs. Pei's plan also recommended the renovation of the existing six-story apartment building at 130 Morningside Drive, which would be used to house tenants relocated from the College of Pharmacy site. Despite completion of a feasibility study by the firm of Brown, Guenther, Battaglia & Galvin, and an endorsement by the university's administration, the project was never realized.

Most controversial of all was Pei's proposal to erect a pair of twenty-three-story towers facing South Field—one south of Journalism Hall, the other south of Hamilton Hall—which, Pei said, "will do much to improve the scale, proportion and definition of the open space."[103] Each tower was to incorporate a twenty-three-foot-high, ground-level open space that would provide access between South Field and the newly enclosed flanking quadrangles, as well as leading to the network of underground concourses Pei proposed to build below South Field. Though essentially rectangular in plan, each building was to incorporate a truncated southern corner facing South Field; the buildings would thus introduce a diagonal element to the otherwise rigorously gridded campus. Objections to the towers ranged from the students' sense that South Field, the principal undergraduate gathering place, would now suffer from "bad vibes" because of the looming towers filled with faculty, to the complaint that the towers would cast long shadows over the limited amount of open space on the campus. Plans for the towers and the construction under South Field were dropped; it was estimated that $27 million was needed just to excavate the bedrock-covered site for the subterranean complex, which William J. McGill, who became the university's president in 1970, described as "one of the craziest proposals I had ever heard in my life."[104]

In 1969 the firm of Warner, Burns, Toan & Lunde presented a design for a north-south-oriented Life Sciences Building, to be located at the northwest corner of the campus and linked by enclosed pedestrian bridges to Pupin and Chandler halls on either side. The building would rise several stories higher than its neighbors and would have a grid of deeply recessed windows along its Broadway frontage and, confronting 120th Street, a virtually windowless wall, punctuated by an angular indentation running nearly the full height of the facade.[105] A trapezoidal wing, elevated on a podium above what remained of the grassy, tree-covered portion of the campus historically known as "the grove," was to thrust the building toward Uris Hall.

The Life Sciences Building was not realized, however, and in the spring of 1971 the university announced that it would resurrect plans to build a gymnasium on the site, a location that had been considered suitable for such a purpose as early as 1896. Designed by the architect R. Jackson Smith of the Eggers Partnership, the successor firm of Eggers & Higgins, which had begun to work on designs for Columbia's gymnasium in 1945,

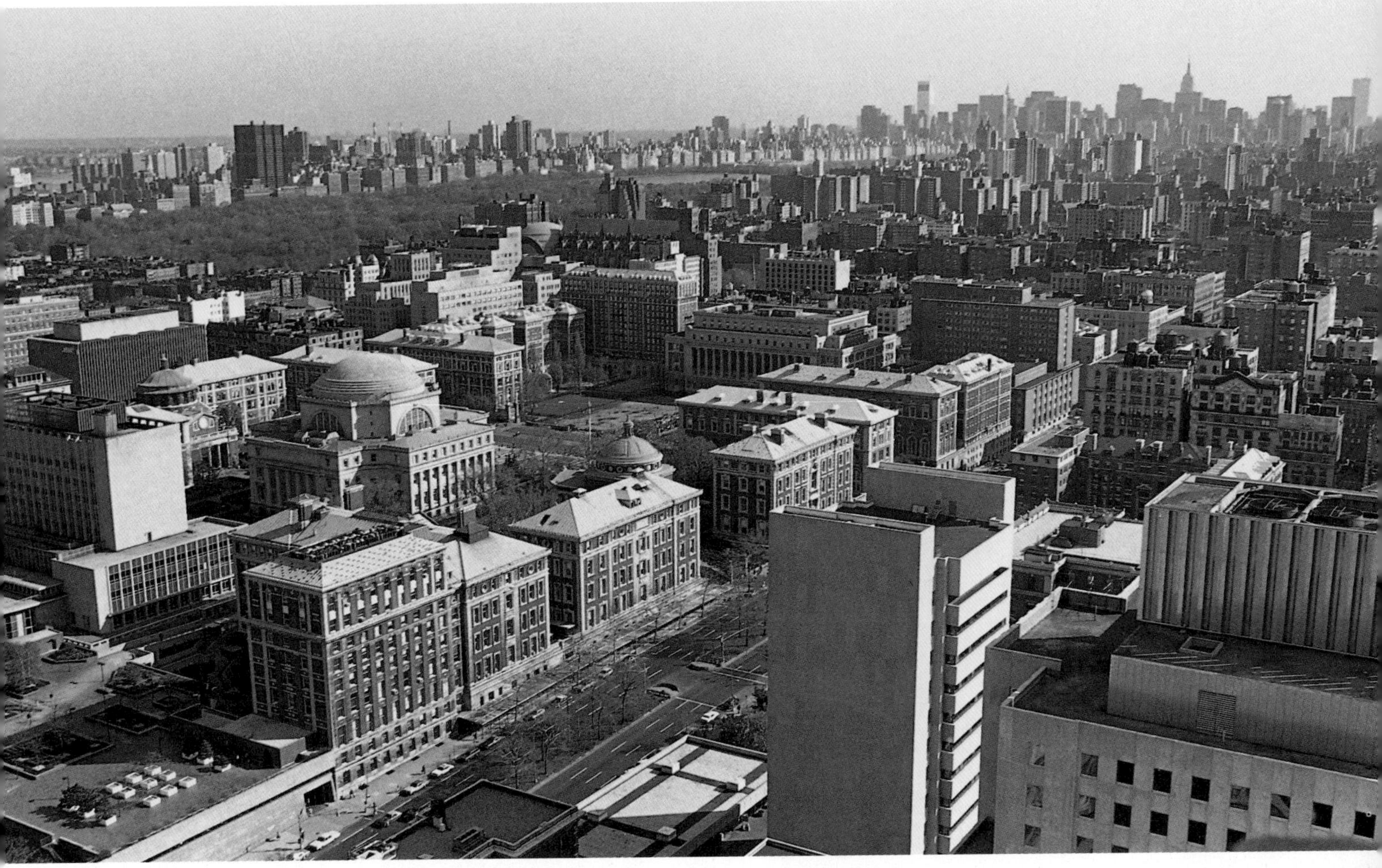

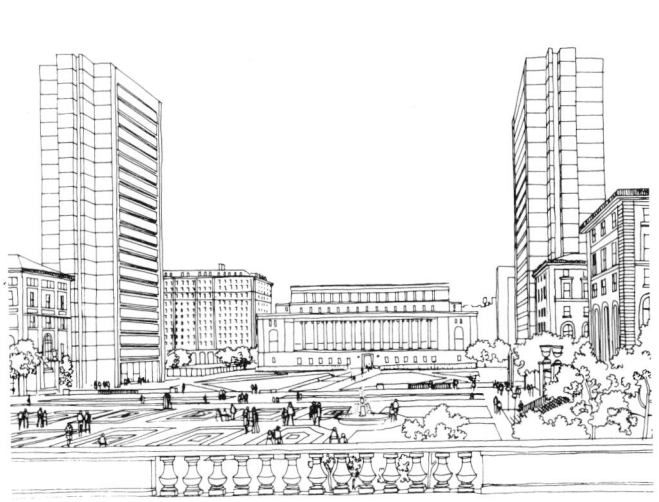

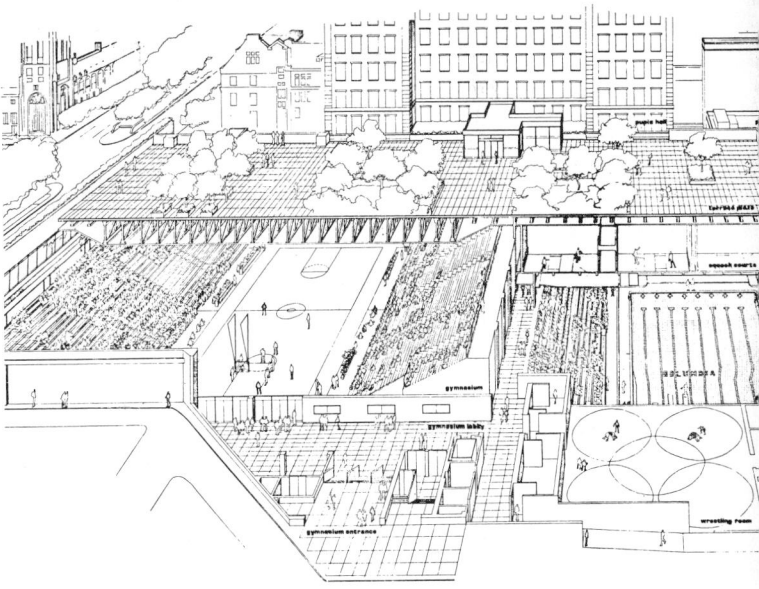

Top: View to the southeast of Columbia University showing Marcellus Hartley Dodge Physical Fitness Center (Eggers Partnership, 1974) on the lower left, Helen Goodhart Altschul Hall (Vincent J. Kling, 1969) and Interchurch Center (Voorhees, Walker, Smith & Smith and Collens, Willis & Beckonert, 1958), both on the lower right. CCT

Bottom left: Proposal for South Field towers, Columbia University, between Broadway and Amsterdam Avenue, West 114th and West 116th streets. I. M. Pei, 1970. View to the south. PCF

Bottom right: Marcellus Hartley Dodge Physical Fitness Center, Columbia University, southeast corner of Broadway and West 118th Street. Eggers Partnership, 1974. Cutaway perspective showing view to the north. CCT

747

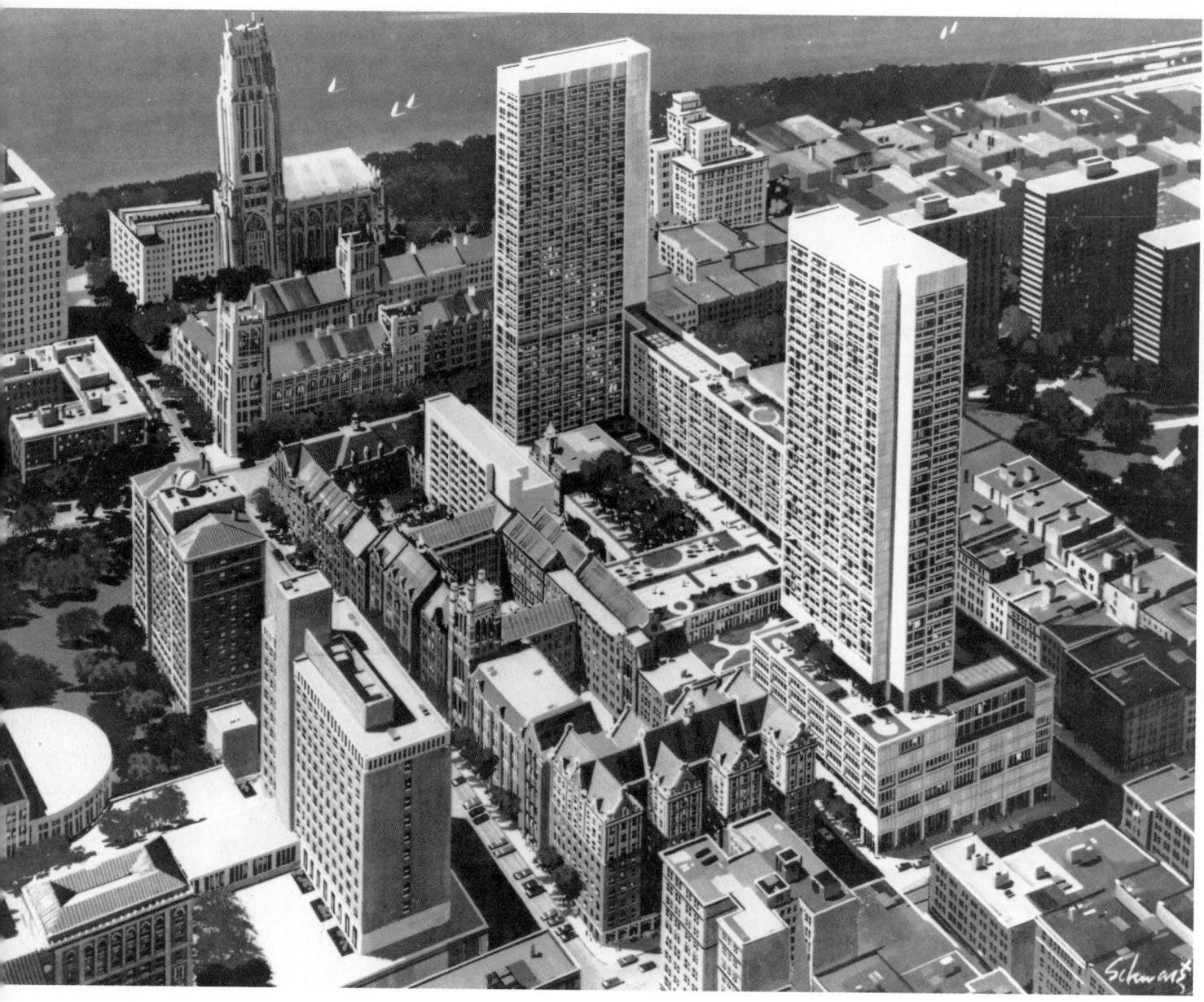

Proposal for housing and academic complex at Teachers College,
Columbia University, Broadway to Amsterdam Avenue, West 121st to
West 122nd Street. Hugh Stubbins & Associates, 1969. Perspective by
Robert Schwartz of view to the northwest. TC

the low-lying building featured a roof that was treated as a land-scaped plaza, extending the North Campus podium west to Broadway and north to Pupin Hall. The new gym, which extended twenty feet below grade and connected to the old athletic facilities in the base of University Hall, necessitated the demolition of a power plant whose tangle of smokestacks had long been a campus eyesore. Approached by an outside staircase leading down one level below that of the upper campus and by a bridge that spanned an existing service drive, the building's physical presence was minimal. Its nondescript, thirty-foot-high facade along Broadway, as well as another short facade set back from 120th Street, in effect continued McKim's podium wall. Officially opened on December 7, 1974, the facility was named the Marcellus Hartley Dodge Physical Fitness Center, in part because, as McGill put it, "the word 'gym' had an odorous quality in New York and we didn't want that term hanging around." Although McGill confidently proclaimed that the building was a "symbol of the university's commitment to the city," it contained no facilities specially built for the community; like the old gym in University Hall, however, it was available to community groups on a limited basis.[106]

In 1969 Teachers College, an affiliate of Columbia, unveiled Hugh Stubbins & Associates' master plan to demolish most of the block bounded by Broadway, Amsterdam Avenue, 121st and 122nd streets to build two forty-story tower slabs, housing both low-income families and graduate students.[107] The site-filling base of the towers would be used for college facilities, more than doubling the academic space on the existing campus. The blockbuster "omnibuilding" would be connected to the main campus via bridges. Stubbins also proposed an eleven-story building, Thorndike Hall (1973), the only portion of the scheme to be realized. At the heart of the academic complex, Stubbins and his co-designer, Peter Woytuk, provided space for the 500,000-volume Milbank Memorial Library, the world's largest collection of materials on education, which would be housed in a bridge over 121st Street and open onto a land-scaped plaza. A two-block-long, four-level mall or "inner street" was to be located in the complex as well. Though the plan was developed independently of Pei's, it also recognized that future development would have to be at a much higher density than in the past.

Early in 1969 Skidmore, Owings & Merrill were hired to design, in conjunction with I. M. Pei, a master plan for a complex of science buildings to occupy the northern end of Columbia's main campus.[108] A comprehensive plan was not followed, though, and instead plans were released in 1974 for a single building, the Sherman Fairchild Center for the Life Sciences, named for its major donor, who had attended Columbia in 1919–20 and subsequently developed the aerial camera.[109] The eight-story laboratory complex was designed by Mitchell/Giurgola Associates; Romaldo Giurgola was a member of the Columbia faculty and had been chairman of the architecture department from 1965 to 1971. The building occupied a site at once cramped and prominent; principally oriented along the north-south axis, it sent out a small but visually important east-west wing just behind Schermerhorn Hall (McKim, Mead & White, 1896), terminating a major walkway east of Low Library and blocking from general view the dismal blankness of Mudd Hall. The design of the building, completed in 1977, reflected the constraints imposed by the site, not the least of which was the column spacing of the five-story podium wing of Mudd Hall upon which it sat. "It is hard to imagine a more ungrateful location for any building," the critic Martin Filler wrote, but the site

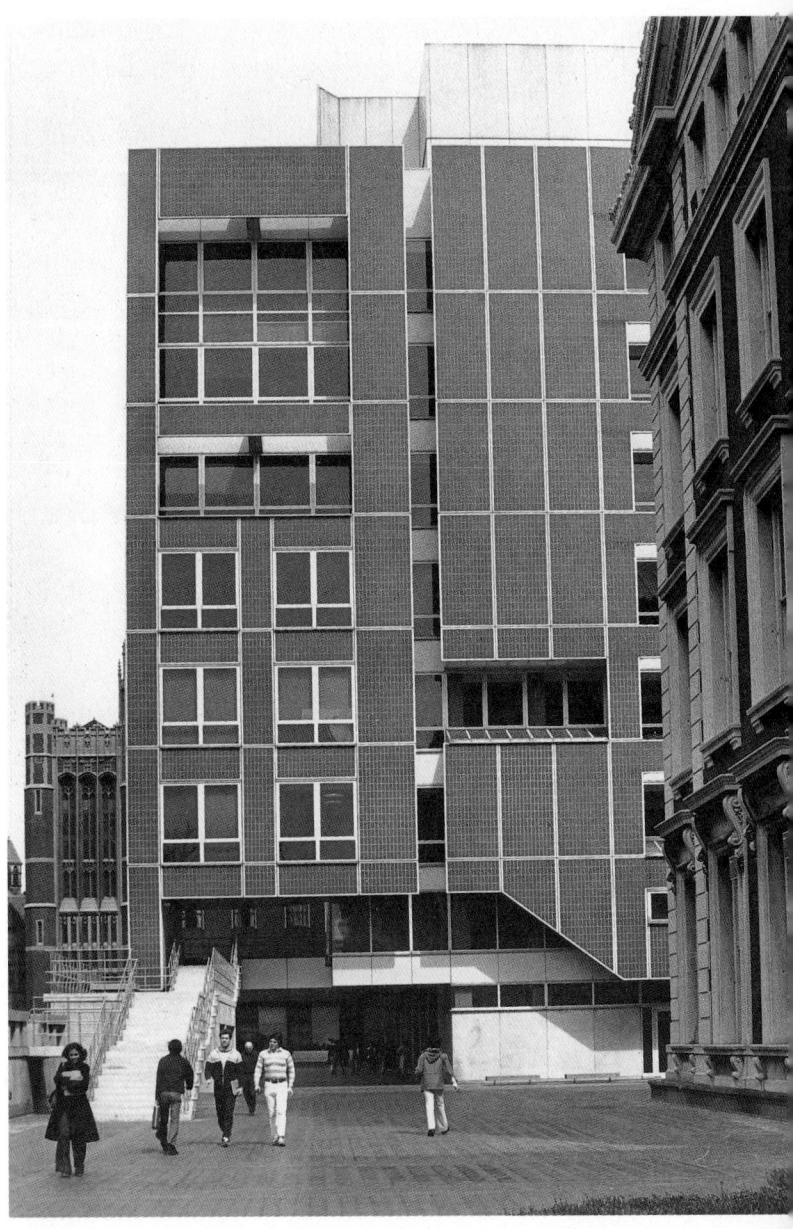

Sherman Fairchild Center for the Life Sciences, Columbia Unversity, between Broadway and Amsterdam Avenue, West 118th and West 119th streets. Mitchell/Giurgola Associates, 1977. View to the north. CUOPI

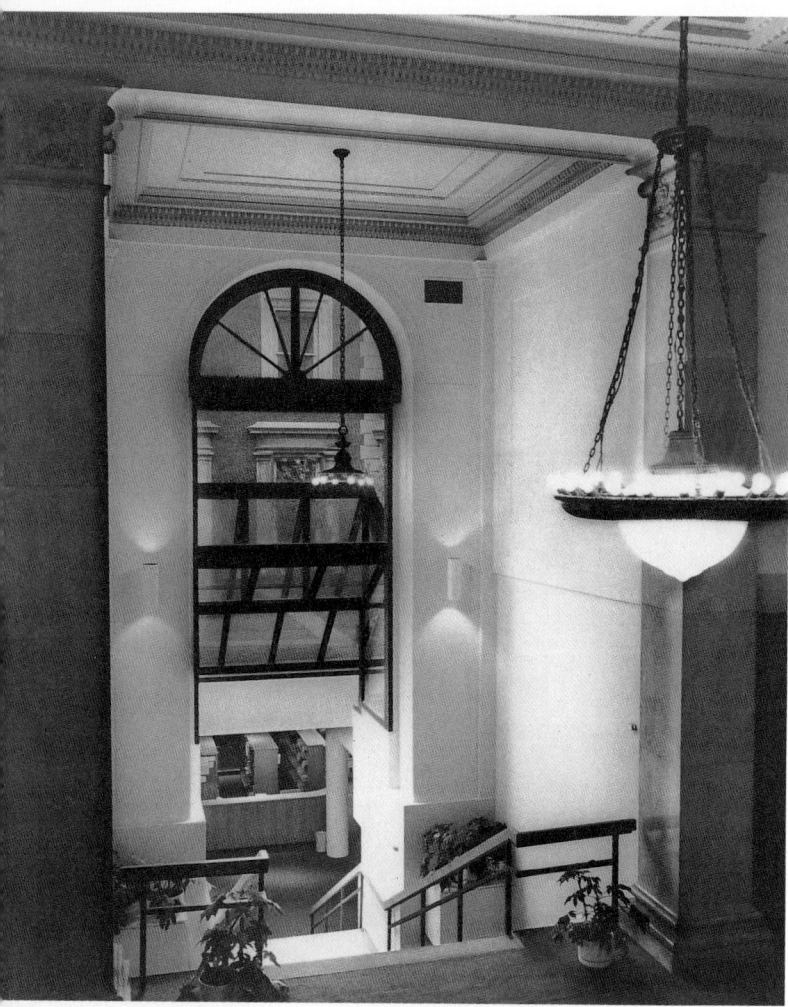

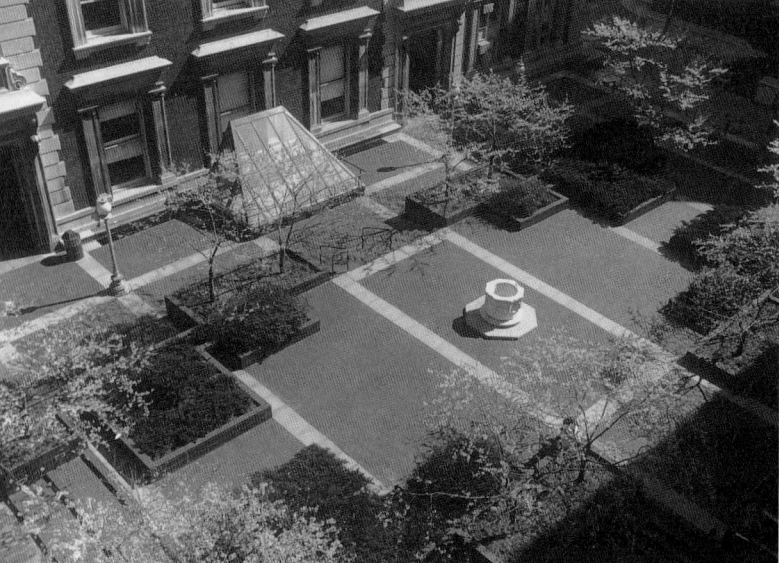

Top: Extension to Avery Hall, Columbia University, between Broadway and Amsterdam Avenue, West 117th and West 118th streets. Alexander Kouzmanoff & Associates, 1977. Staircase from Avery Hall to extension. KP

Bottom: Extension to Avery Hall. View to the southeast showing relandscaped courtyard. KP

"paradoxically offered the guaranteed prospect of making any new building that rose there look good if only by comparison with what surrounded it."[110] Giurgola chose to honor, albeit in a technologically advanced way, the campus vocabulary of brick and limestone by hanging concrete panels surfaced in red quarry tile from the glass- and metal-clad frame. The building's principal entrance was located on the second floor and reached by an exterior staircase and a bridge, leaving clear a ground-level passage leading to Mudd Hall beyond. Inside, the building's well-equipped laboratories were set in crisply detailed, pastel-colored interiors.

The building was lauded by the press, not only as the product of a distinguished firm, but as a turning point in Columbia's architectural fortunes. Paul Goldberger called Fairchild Hall "one of Mr. Giurgola's best works" and said that it reversed "a long-standing indifference to architecture that resulted in Columbia's erecting what are generally acknowledged to be the worst buildings in the Ivy League." He described the building's merits:

> It is an unorthodox and remarkably successful design, for it manages to be at once massive and light. The color and the material make the building strong enough to hold its own against the large structures beside it, yet the delicacy of the facade functioning as a screen brings lightness to the building at the same time. The facade has depth and texture, like the older McKim buildings nearby, and the patterns of the screen wall act in a way as latter-day equivalents of ornament.[111]

Ada Louise Huxtable was more qualified in her praise. "It is elegantly proportioned," she said, "but quite a lot too red (as yet) for the weathered brick around it, and the attempt to blend it in color and scale with its motley neighbors while maintaining the integrity of a 'skin' structure, has been of distinctly limited success. This effort has also led to some visual ambiguities; neither the rationale nor the articulation of the facade are immediately clear. It is not even easy to find the entrance."[112] The critic Suzanne Stephens discussed the architects' success in relating the building to its campus context: "A contextual approach . . . does not have to be limited to any orthodox kind of response, such as one grounded in literal allusions to a historical style. This is seen clearly at Fairchild Center where Mitchell/Giurgola has engaged in a structuralist form of contextualism—where the classical-style architecture nearby is referred to through proportions of the screen wall panels and the rhythmic progression of open and closed planes."[113]

Martin Filler addressed the building's more immediate stylistic sources:

> Much at Fairchild is strongly reminiscent of the work of Romaldo Giurgola's acknowledged master, Louis Kahn. The screen created by the hung wall paneling plays down the glazing behind it . . . and it creates the double layer effect—the "wall behind a ruin"—that was a favorite theme in Kahn's work. The so-called "served" and "servant" spaces are rigorously separated and defined. . . . But the building's light and friendly feeling has little spiritual kinship with Kahn's two laboratory buildings: the functionally disastrous Richards Laboratories of 1957–61 at the University of Pennsylvania, and the solemn Salk Institute of 1962–66 at La Jolla.

Filler also noted that the architects had seen a number of Alvar Aalto's works on recent visits to Scandinavia, and that "his general approach to design has been clearly, if nonspecifically, transmitted to the design of this building."[114]

In December 1974 the implementation of the last major element of the Pei plan to be realized was announced: Alexander Kouzmanoff & Associates' two-level extension to Avery Hall.[115] The Avery Library collection had been severely cramped for years; as early as 1944 Dean Arnaud had recommended to the university that a new building housing the library and the architecture school be erected.[116] As completed in 1977, the expansion stretched under the courtyard east of Avery Hall, connecting Avery Library's basement stacks with a new reading room placed on top of a new auditorium and exhibition space. The potential underground space Pei had identified to the west was left for the future. The new lower-level reading room was connected by a skylit stairwell to the original reading room; this element reduced the finely articulated McKim, Mead & White space to the status of, as Goldberger put it, "a sort of leftover corridor."[117] Although Stephens praised the "quiet serenity" that the extension's minimally detailed spaces provided, she felt that they did not measure up to the original's interiors: "While . . . changes in walls and ceiling planes are expressive, they don't *mold* the space the way McKim's coffers and niches do. Important design elements and details in the new reading room—such as the skylight ribs, handrails, and artificial lighting—lack the delicacy that the old work calls for. Even considering the budget, less was attempted here to refer to the neo-Renaissance palazzo upstairs than one might hope."[118]

Outside, the relandscaped courtyard was raised to allow for a higher ceiling in the library's new reading room, drastically altering the relationship of the surrounding buildings to the ground plane. The courtyard included new brickwork and architectural elements; lampposts and gates reclaimed from the original courtyard visually linked it to the surrounding campus. Nonetheless, as Goldberger noted, it was "fussed up," conveying "a bit of the air of a suburban shopping mall."[119]

Two other modestly scaled university building projects—Hogan Hall and Jerome L. Greene Hall—were completed in 1977. For Hogan Hall R. M. Kliment & Frances Halsband converted a former nursing home (Trowbridge & Livingston, 1898), on the southeast corner of Broadway and 114th Street, for use as offices and graduate-student housing.[120] The exterior of the building was left largely intact, although the architects did redesign the front and rear entrances and replace the building's deteriorated copper cornice with a patterned brickwork parapet.

In the mid-1970s the Columbia Law School, having long since succumbed to the near-constant, university-wide search for more space by transforming the lounges of its building into offices, commissioned Robert Stern to design a new building housing lounges, dining rooms and offices.[121] It was to incorporate the former Women's Faculty Club and link it with the Law School while serving as a focal point to Sulzberger Plaza, located between the two larger buildings. Budgetary cutbacks reduced the project's scope to a renovation of the former club, in effect a three-story wing of Johnson Hall. The renovated portion, renamed Jerome L. Greene Hall, was linked to the adjacent Faculty House (former Men's Faculty Club) with a second-story bridge. Drawing on popular associations with a refined, clublike law school atmosphere rather than the actual interiors of the Harrison & Abramovitz Law School building, Stern used moldings and a white and beige color scheme to rearticulate the strong architectural features of the double-height, Adam-style main space, which included a fireplace and four large arched windows. Red and brown vinyl chairs and sofas, as well as an Oriental-style rug, furthered the clubby look.

Columbia University and its affiliates were not the only institutions to build on Morningside Heights during the postwar period. In 1958 the Interchurch Center, sponsored by the Protestant and Eastern Orthodox churches, was completed on a site provided by John D. Rockefeller, Jr., and bounded by 119th and 120th streets, Claremont Avenue and Riverside Drive.[122] The limestone-clad building was designed by the firms of Voorhees, Walker, Smith & Smith and Collens, Willis & Beckonert to relate to the Rockefeller-sponsored Riverside Church (Allens & Collen, 1930), but its clumsily articulated, looming seventeen-story mass only seemed to muscle in on its elegant neighbor's turf, causing waggish observers to label the building "the God Box."[123] Collens, Willis & Beckonert's eight-story addition to Riverside Church, completed the following year, was more contextually sensitive.[124] The addition, located directly south of the church, was reductivist in its detailing, but the pointed arched windows were an appropriate if rather weak echo of its predecessor's Gothic vocabulary. More steadfastly Modernist was MacFadyen & Knowles's limestone-and-glass Mitzi Newhouse Pavilion (1970), an addition to the Manhattan School of Music.[125] Located at 120 Claremont Avenue, on the northwest corner of 122nd Street, the conservatory's main building (Donn Barber, 1910; Shreve, Lamb & Harmon, 1931) was formerly the Juilliard School of Music;[126] the Manhattan School of Music moved to Morningside Heights from its former location (Donn Barber, 1928) at 240 East 105th Street, between Second and Third avenues, when Juilliard moved to Lincoln Center in 1969.[127] The Manhattan School of Music's former building was purchased by the city and occupied by Park East High School.

The various additions to St. Luke's Hospital erected between 1954 and 1968 had the unfortunate effect of overwhelming and maiming the grand, mansard-roofed hospital (Ernest Flagg, 1892–96), which had formerly exerted a powerful architectural presence on the Heights.[128] Among the hospital's postwar additions were the nine-story Florence Stokes Clark Building (1954), designed by York & Sawyer, on the east side of Amsterdam Avenue and 113th Street, and an adjoining nine-story unit completed three years later;[129] the ten-story Women's Hospital (1965), on Amsterdam Avenue between 114th and 115th streets;[130] a seventeen-story staff apartment building (1968) designed by Harry M. Prince, on the southwest corner of Amsterdam Avenue and 114th Street;[131] and a thirteen-story service and research building (Harry M. Prince, 1968), on 114th Street just east of Amsterdam Avenue, that replaced the original hospital's western pavilions.[132]

In 1967 plans were announced for Morningside House, a nonprofit housing project for the elderly to be erected on the west side of Amsterdam Avenue between 111th and 112th streets.[133] The twelve-story, reinforced-concrete building, designed by Philip Johnson, was to be faced in light-colored stone and brick. The building's highly articulated exterior—according to the *New York Times*, it looked like "a group of castles"—reflected its distinctive interior plan; on each of the building's ten residential floors, which would be equipped to serve as infirmaries if necessary, a centrally located hexagonal room, functioning as either a sitting room or a nurse's station, was to be surrounded by other hexagonal rooms.[134]

In 1970 the building's construction was effectively blocked by squatters who occupied several tenements that had been slated for demolition on the site. Despairing of ever attaining affordable housing in the West Side Urban Renewal Area or adja-

751

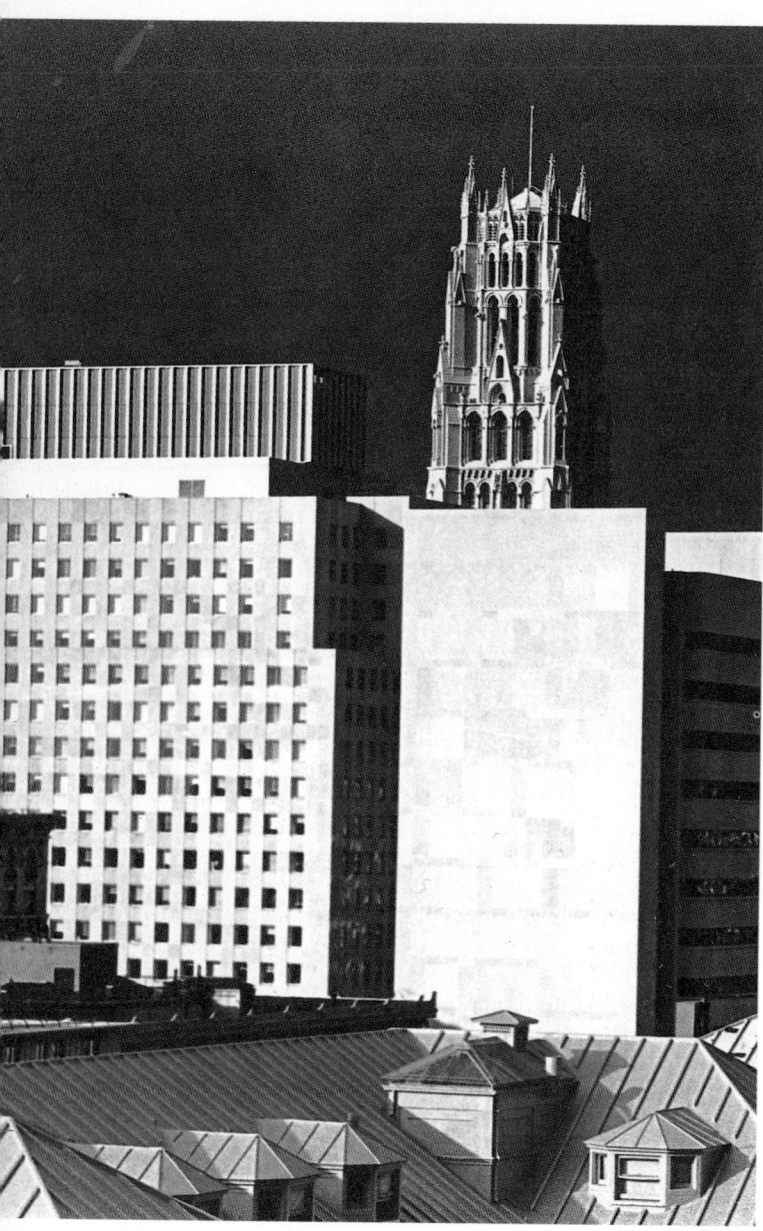

Interchurch Center, from Claremont Avenue to Riverside Drive, West 119th to West 120th Street. Voorhees, Walker, Smith & Smith and Collens, Willis & Beckonert, 1958. View to the northwest showing Interchurch Center on the left, with Helen Goodhart Altschul Hall (Vincent G. Kling, 1969) on the right and the tower of Riverside Church (Allens & Collen, 1930) behind. CCT

cent neighborhoods, and perhaps taking their cue from Columbia students who two years earlier had occupied campus buildings, squatters "liberated" condemned city-owned buildings throughout the west side, including Morningside Heights, as part of an effort known as "Operation Move-In."[135] The city initially responded by threatening eviction and removing kitchen and bathroom fixtures from vacant buildings. Despite official city opposition, the squatters received support from Congresswoman Bella Abzug as well as from local community groups and the Episcopal Diocese of New York. In the case of Morningside House, the squatters forced the project's sponsors to relocate the facility to 1000 Pelham Parkway South in the Bronx, where Philip Johnson and John Burgee's design for a pair of five-story serpentine buildings with conventional double-loaded corridors was completed in 1974.

In 1976 Amsterdam House (Kennerly, Slomanson & Smith), also a housing project for the elderly, was completed at 1060 Amsterdam Avenue, on the northwest corner of 112th Street, directly north of the former Morningside House site.[136] The gray brick facades of the thirteen-story slab were somewhat enlivened by natural wood window frames, although the building remained a tepid reflection of Philip Johnson's unrealized project. Nonetheless, Paul Goldberger characterized Amsterdam House as "far, far above the usual norm" of housing for the elderly.[137]

In 1971, the progressive Bank Street College of Education and Laboratory School, founded in 1916 and formerly located in a converted factory building at 69 Bank Street, moved to a new building at 610 West 112th Street, on a midblock site between Broadway and Riverside Drive that had once been slated as part of Columbia University's never-realized West Campus plan.[138] In the early 1960s the college had retained the firm of Mayer, Whittlesey & Glass to make recommendations for expansion; the architects advocated moving. College officials decided to abandon their Greenwich Village headquarters when Columbia, seeking to fortify the role of Morningside Heights as New York's academic acropolis, offered highly favorable financial terms. Bank Street College's new facility, designed by the Chicago-based firm of Harry Weese & Associates, was a twelve-story, red-brick building incorporating a single eighth-floor setback along 112th Street and a second-floor setback, which supported a play area, along its rear facade. The building's rather banal facades featured deeply recessed windows bordered by angled granite sills. Inside, a double-height skylit atrium rose from a basement-level cafeteria up through the main lobby.

The area's housing supply was supplemented in 1975 by the Cathedral Parkway Houses (Davis, Brody & Associates, in association with Roger Glasgow), at 125 West 109th Street.[139] Jointly sponsored by the Morningside Renewal Council and the Harlem Urban Development Corporation, the latter a subsidiary of the New York State Urban Development Corporation, Cathedral Parkway Houses occupied the former site of the Woman's Hospital (Allen & Collens, 1906), which had extended through the block to Cathedral Parkway.[140] An aesthetic cousin to Davis, Brody & Associates' Waterside (see chapter 5), Ruppert Towers (see chapter 11) and Harlem River Park Towers (see chapter 13), the 309-unit, moderate-income complex, consisting of one twelve-story and one twenty-story building separated by a multilevel courtyard, featured complex patterns of setbacks and cantilevered projections that established a strong sculptural presence.

Given that the most divisive architectural and urbanistic issue facing the Morningside Heights community during the post-

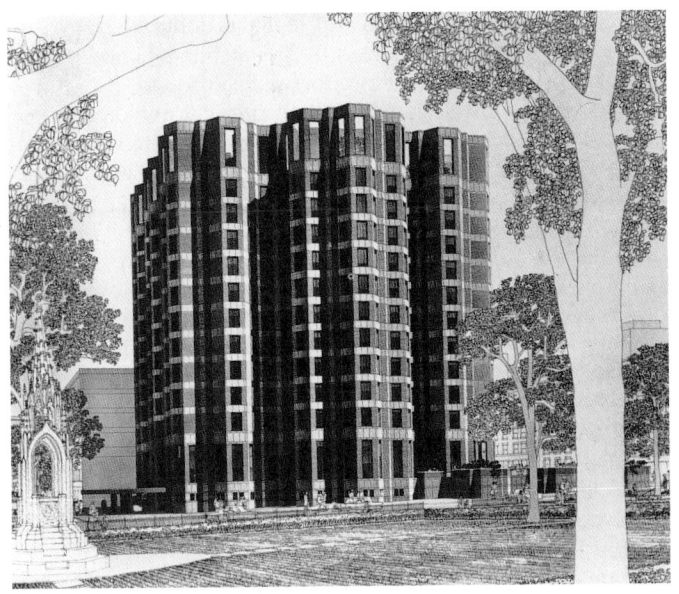

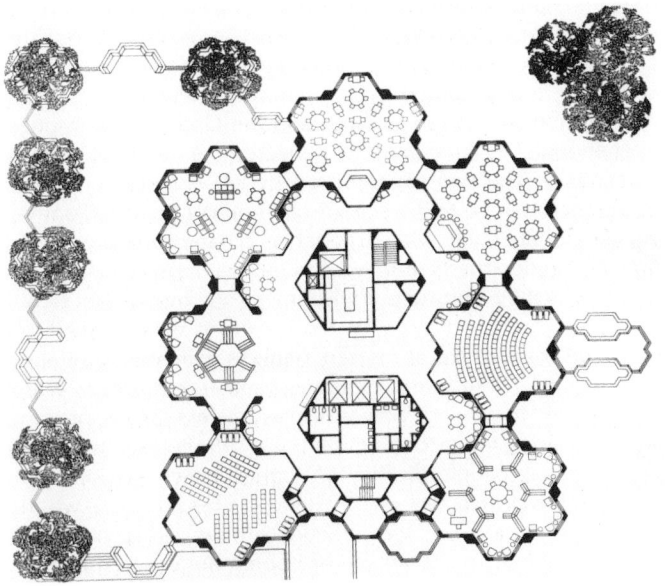

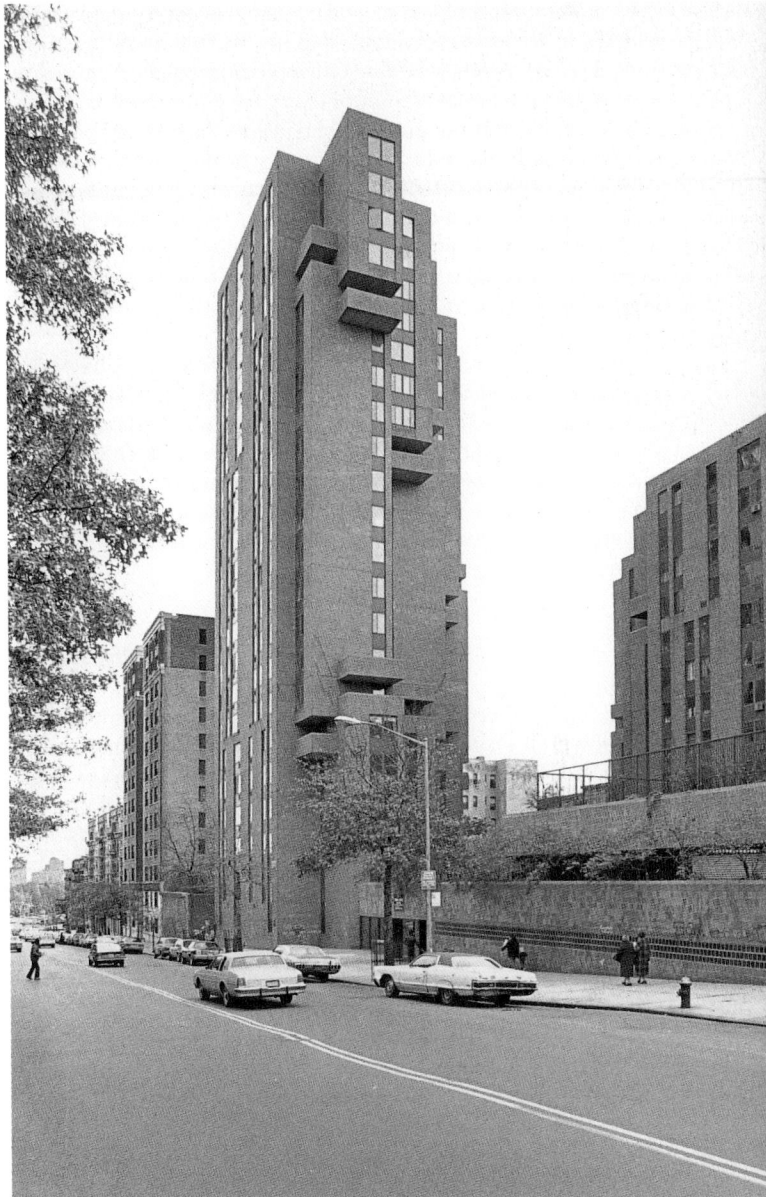

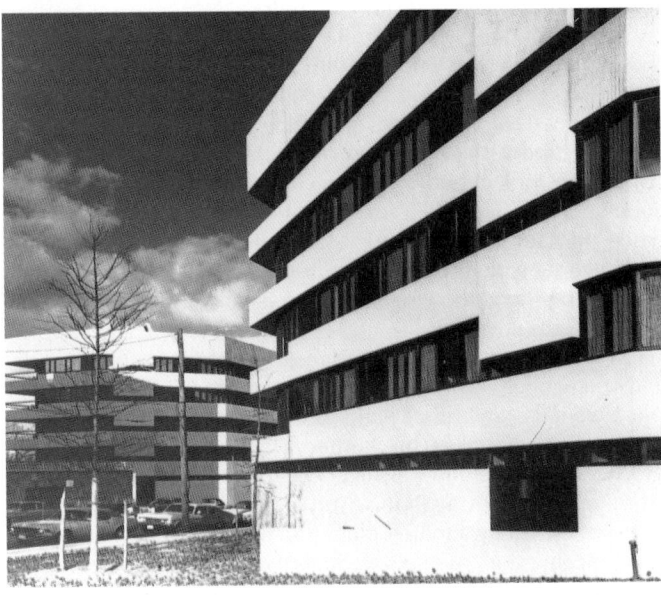

Top left: Proposal for Morningside House, southwest corner of Amsterdam Avenue and West 112th Street. Philip Johnson and John Burgee, 1970. Drawing of view to the west from the grounds of the Cathedral of St. John the Divine. PJA

Center left: Proposal for Morningside House. Ground-floor plan. PJA

Bottom left: Morningside House, 1000 Pelham Parkway South, between Lurting and Hone avenues, Morris Park, the Bronx. Philip Johnson and John Burgee, 1974. PJA

Above: Cathedral Parkway Houses, 125 West 109th Street, between Amsterdam and Columbus avenues. Davis, Brody & Associates in association with Roger Glasgow, 1975. View to the southeast. DBA

753

war era centered on what constituted the appropriate use of public parkland, it was fitting that one of the area's few completed park projects relied heavily on community participation. In celebration of its centennial in 1972, the National Park Service asked the nonprofit Cityarts Workshop to co-sponsor a public art project on the site of Grant's Tomb (John H. Duncan, 1897), administered by the park service as the Grant National Monument, at the northern end of the Morningside Heights stretch of Riverside Park.[141] Pedro Silva, a sculptor and the project's director, conceived of a free-form, 150-foot-long concrete bench running along three sides of the imposing, Classical monument and invited local residents to cover the bench with a continuous mosaic mural of their own design. To inspire the participants, Silva presented a slide show focusing on the works of the Spanish architect Antonio Gaudí and the sculptor Simon Rodia, creator of the Watts Towers in Los Angeles. The result, completed in 1973, was a jaunty composition, a diverse melange of images from street scenes to imaginary creatures, that translated the energy if not the forms of graffiti art into institutionally sanctioned public art.

St. John the Divine

The design and construction of one of New York's most revered and powerful institutions, the Cathedral of St. John the Divine, which had begun in 1892, continued well into the postwar period.[142] As was the case with many other architectural projects on Morningside Heights, the completion of St. John's was the source of major controversy, raising not only stylistic issues but also the question of what role the metropolitan cathedral should play in its increasingly troubled neighborhood. During the 1920s and 1930s construction had proceeded in accord with the plans of Ralph Adams Cram, who in 1911 had replaced Heins & La Farge, the original architects.[143] Conceived as a celebration of New York's Metropolitanism as much as an expression of religious devotion, the granite cathedral was designed as an eclectic mixture of Romanesque stylistic motifs and Gothic planning; it was recast in a purer French Gothic style by Cram. On Sunday morning, November 30, 1941, less than a year before Cram's death, the doors opened to reveal the finally completed 520-foot-long nave of the world's largest Gothic cathedral.[144] Ten thousand worshipers attended the services that day, the largest number ever assembled in the church.

The completion of the nave by no means marked the end of the massive construction project. Still missing were the transepts, the west towers and the flèche above the crossing where the terra-cotta dome, designed as a temporary feature, represented a stylistic and spatial discontinuity with the Gothic nave. Work was stopped with the outbreak of World War II, but it was resumed when peace returned. In June 1945 the carved wood reredos that stood behind the altar was removed to open up what was described as the "longest uninterrupted vista in Christendom," measuring one tenth of a mile from the rose window, the largest in the world, to the choir.[145]

By the mid-1950s, when the Episcopal Diocese began to find fund-raising for the project increasingly difficult, partially because of white flight to the suburbs, work began to slow on the cathedral. In 1954 Architectural Forum asked James Marston Fitch, a professor at Columbia's architecture school, to "open a broad inquiry" on the question of "whether the cathedral might not better be finished" in the modern style.[146] The discussion was stimulated not only by fund-raising problems but also

by claims (ultimately disproved) that the dome, designed by Heins & La Farge and realized by the architect-builder Rafael Guastavino in 1909, might be structurally unsound.[147]

Fitch argued that, given the estimated $5 million and five years of work that would be required to complete Cram's design, a "less costly, less time-consuming alternative would seem desirable."[148] But the real issue, he emphasized, was to determine the appropriate style for the cathedral: should it be completed in the Gothic or in the contemporary manner? Taking a cue from La Farge's own claim that "in the works of the medieval past it is not the few finished examples, in which the last word has been spoken to the point of dryness, that most excite our imagination" but rather those works "in which successive styles appear together," Fitch came down decisively in favor of developing a new scheme.[149]

Fitch's views provoked a wide debate. One architect, Major E. J. Peterson of Alexandria, Virginia, questioned whether it was fair to apply the stylistic aesthetic of Notre Dame or Chartres to St. John's. "The change in these cathedrals was a normal one, not one distinct style forced onto another," he said, whereas at St. John's "we have a building that is already 800 years old in style and half built to a pattern that is fixed. The problem at the crossing can be resolved with modern engineering, but the Gothic bulk remains." Peterson suggested that, to meet the challenge, a new cathedral be built on a different site, arguing that "St. John has been tortured and the Gothic style insulted long enough."[150] In an address delivered before the New York Chapter of the American Institute of Architects, Pietro Belluschi, dean of MIT's School of Architecture and Planning and an architect with wide experience in church design, argued that to abandon the Gothic was "to put in a most direct and intimate way the results of our wisdom, of our knowledge, of our maturity as architects, against a set of forms which have for a thousand years served as the very symbols of human inspiration to worship." These forms, he argued, may seem hollow when copied, but they were powerful nonetheless, "still speaking with endearing tones to the multitudes, still representing in the eyes of many people the highest expression of religious faith when faith was at its highest."[151] Belluschi felt that there was no simple answer and that the cathedral's future represented a serious challenge to the ability of contemporary architecture, with deep roots in a materialistic conception of culture, to achieve a spiritual dimension.

A little more than a year after Fitch's analysis, Architectural Forum presented its readers with a portfolio of Modernist-inspired designs for the cathedral's completion.[152] Four of the five schemes presented were developed by graduate students at MIT working under the direction of their visiting critic, Minoru Yamasaki, and advised by Canon Darby W. Betts, formerly of St. John's. Of the four MIT schemes, Manfredo Nicoletti's, given pride of place in the magazine, was the most resolved. In his search for "a structure which springs upward from the earth, creating a continued growth to the sky," Nicoletti proposed replacing the dome with a tentlike tower of metal and glass, held up on a triangulated structure that was resolved on the skyline as soaring openwork.[153] The triangular form and some of the details of Nicoletti's design clearly anticipated that of Skidmore, Owings & Merrill's chapel at the United States Air Force Academy (1956–63).[154] The fifth scheme, developed by Douglas Barker, a third-year student at Pratt Institute, called for a low, glassy transept roofed by a folded-plate structure, and a wall of stained glass closing the nave and lighting the altar, all crowned by a metal openwork flèche.

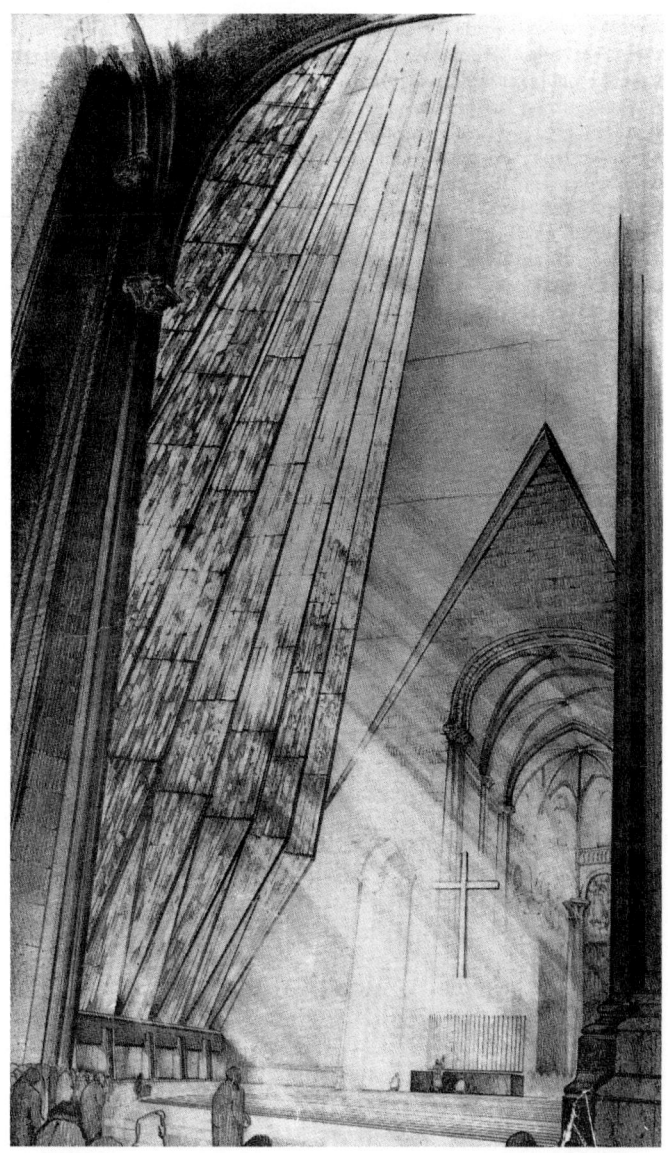

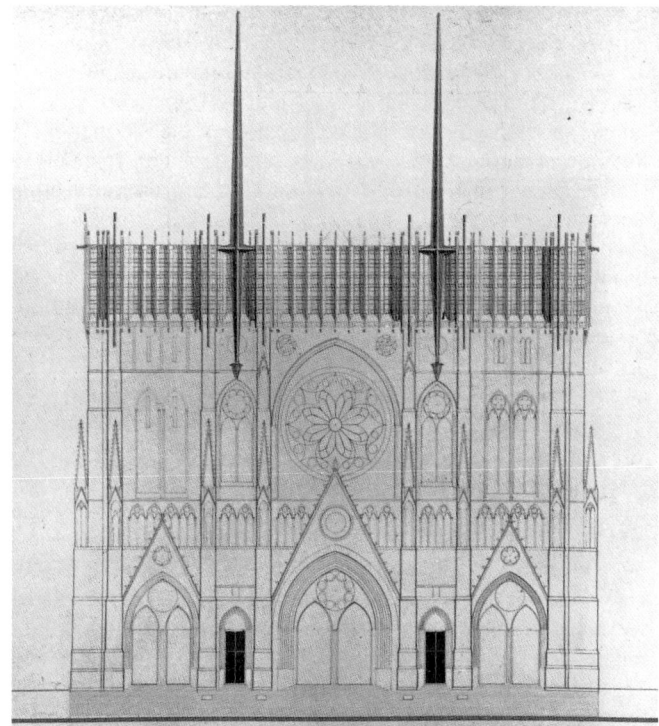

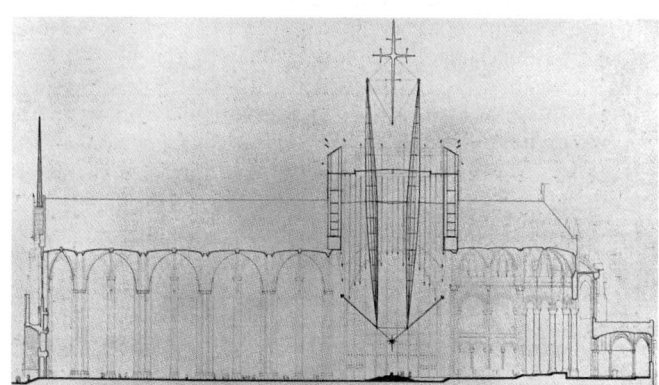

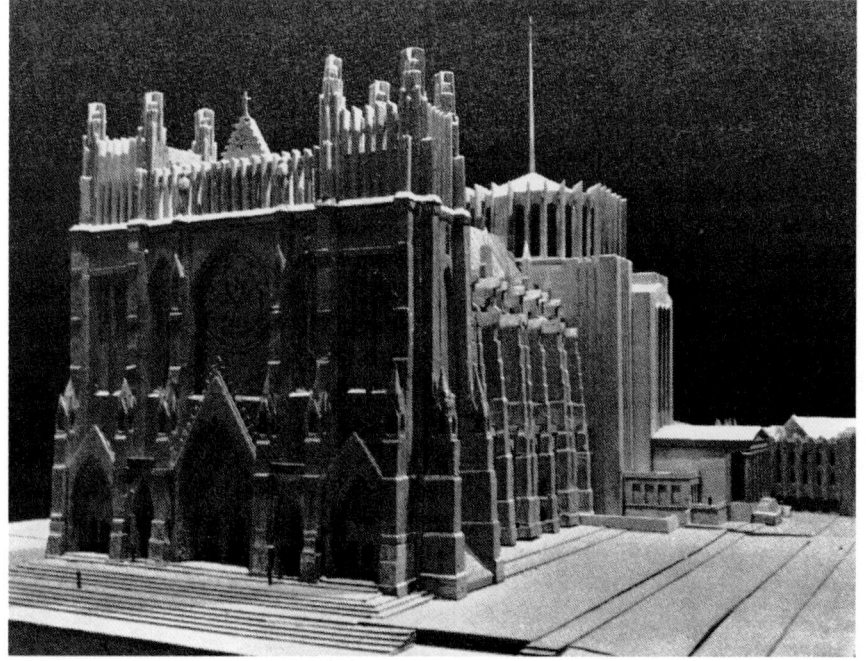

Top left: Proposal for the Cathedral of St. John the Divine, Amsterdam Avenue to Morningside Drive, West 110th to West 113th Street. Manfredo Nicoletti, 1955. Drawing showing interior of crossing. AF. CU

Bottom left: Proposal for the Cathedral of St. John the Divine, Amsterdam Avenue to Morningside Drive, West 110th to West 113th Street. Adams & Woodbridge, 1966. Model. View to the northeast. PA. CU

Top right: Proposal for the Cathedral of St. John the Divine. John M. Woodbridge, 1956. Elevation of principal facade. AR. CU

Bottom right: Proposal for the Cathedral of St. John the Divine. John M. Woodbridge, 1956. Longitudinal section. AR. CU

In June 1956, six months after the *Forum* article, *Architectural Record* presented a project for the cathedral, prepared as a master's thesis in architecture at Princeton University by John M. Woodbridge, the son of the architect Frederick Woodbridge, who was a partner in the firm of Adams & Woodbridge.[155] Retaining Heins & La Farge's great arches, which Cram had virtually ignored in his redesign, Woodbridge proposed a tower suspended over the crossing from diagonal ties, providing a focal point for the altar below without blocking the vista down the nave. The combination of old arches with a new structure created a vivid dialogue, and the use of a structural system based on tension rods and cables, expressing lines of force, suggested an approach that was Gothic in spirit, yet Woodbridge's scheme lacked the formal bravura of Nicoletti's.

In November 1966 the Right Reverend Horace Donegan, Episcopal Bishop of New York, announced that the diocese was scrapping Cram's plan in favor of a new, joylessly stiff scheme developed by Adams & Woodbridge for the cathedral, which had come to be known as "St. John, the unfinished."[156] In place of Cram's towering flèche, the new design called for a low octagonal tower that lit the interior through concrete louvers filled with colored-glass panels. Two elevators would be included to replace the winding, sixteen-story staircase that led to the roof. The stripped-down facades of the towers and transepts were to be built of concrete and sheathed in granite, a far cry from the tectonic purity and sacrificial craftsmanship of Cram's cut stone. The design represented a cutback in costs, necessitated at least in part by the drastic reduction in contributions to the church that had come as a result of Donegan's strong liberal positions on controversial social issues, particularly civil rights. Contrary to suggestions that the cathedral was an anachronism that should not be allowed to drain further funds from social programs, Donegan believed that its completion would express "the unifying center, the energizing force of the diocese. St. John the Divine is a symbol to the whole community of the sovereignty of God over the affairs of man."[157]

The editors of *Progressive Architecture* were critical of Adams & Woodbridge's design, which they said had a "massiveness reminiscent of U.S. office buildings in the 1930s," which would "overbalance the massiveness of the rest of the church."[158] Walter C. Kidney described the "mindless" proposal as "modernistic—of 1930—and not the best 1930 at that."[159]

Even as the new cathedral design was being revealed, young Episcopal priests and laymen were growing more vocal in their objections to spending precious funds on the cathedral's completion, no matter what style. Responding to their arguments in October 1967, Donegan announced that "the cathedral church will for the immediate future remain as it now stands, unfinished. There will be no fund-raising for its completion so long as I am bishop of New York, until there is greater evidence that the despair and anguish of our unadvantaged people has been relieved."[160]

THE NEW WEST SIDE STORY

By the late 1960s the vast amount of public and private investment in the Upper West Side had worked not so much to stabilize the previously declining area as to radically alter its social composition and physical appearance. This new socioeconomic entity was coming to be regarded as one of the few positive signs of growth in the postwar campaign to restore the health of New York's traditional neighborhoods. The area, as Mayor John V. Lindsay put it in 1969, was "enjoying more of a renaissance . . .

than any other single neighborhood of our city,"[1] and the journalist Nicholas Pileggi reported in *New York* that "the same kind of young, successful and relatively affluent middle-class families that moved to the suburbs 20 years ago and to the East Side 10 years ago are moving to the West Side today."[2] The neighborhood had begun to prevail not only as a middle-class alternative to the east side and suburbia but as a definite locus on the international cultural map. In 1969 Lewis Nichols of the *New York Times* even argued that "an excellent case" could be made that the Upper West Side had "taken over from the Village" as the city's literary center.[3] The neighborhood had become what its original promoters had dreamed of a hundred years before, a desirable address for families who were perhaps not quite as fashionable as those on the Upper East Side but were often more individual, more "artistic."[4] Crime was still a serious problem, but, as Pileggi noted, the area's new demographics were clearly effecting a change: "The bedpan, truss and traction medical supply stores that used to blanket the West Side have been replaced by youthful boutiques . . . bookstores, theaters, antique shops, and a proliferation of moderately priced Cuban, Japanese, Thai, Italian, French, Indian, Egyptian and Israeli restaurants."[5]

To the casual visitor, Broadway, the Upper West Side's traditional shopping and schmoozing center, looked much as it had, with its less-than-sophisticated mix of shops and groups of old people sunning themselves on benches at the ends of the central malls that formed the area's most important oases. But closer inspection revealed not only a new, younger crowd of shoppers but also here and there a few shops and restaurants that were a bit different from longtime favored hangouts such as Schrafft's, Steinberg's and the Tip Toe Inn. In 1970 Gamal El-Zoghby transformed an ordinary luncheonette at 2527 Broadway, between Ninety-fourth and Ninety-fifth streets, into a restaurant named Cleopatra.[6] El-Zoghby expanded it into an adjacent store and redesigned it, presenting Broadway with a bold, blue-glazed-brick facade and a 3'6"-high projecting red-painted metal sign proclaiming the restaurant's name. Deep shadows from the sign and the recessed door combined with the dark-tinted glass of the windows to heighten the sense of drama. Inside, a central aisle cleaved a path leading between flanking dining booths finished in plastic laminate to an illusionistic terminus—a mirror that convincingly destroyed the sense of closure which would otherwise be suffocating in so small a space. The illusion of space was further enhanced by the use of arrowlike cutouts between the booths, the staggering of each booth a step higher than the one in front, and an extraordinarily lush mural that filled the side walls above wainscot height.

Four years later El-Zoghby completed the curiously named Genghiz Khan's Bicycle, on the southeast corner of Columbus Avenue and Sixty-ninth Street.[7] The restaurant, which offered Turkish cuisine, was among an increasing number of stylish restaurants and boutiques that were transforming the once-shabby stretch of Columbus Avenue between Lincoln Center and the Museum of Natural History into one of the city's liveliest promenades, realizing in the free market what planners had hoped to encourage within the confines of the West Side Urban Renewal Area. Genghiz Khan's Bicycle was designed as a tiny but sparkling white Modernist interior executed largely in plasterboard and plastic laminate. The restaurant's space was increased by the addition of a glassed-in area that extended out onto the sidewalk beyond the building line. Individual booths were defined by plastic laminate partitions cut into bold geometric shapes and neatly fit together like the pieces of a puzzle, the "architectural equivalent," said Norval White and Elliot Willensky, "of a carefully tailored suit."[8]

As the Upper West Side continued to attract affluent new-comers, there was a scattering of new apartment construction, catering to the same "luxury" market that filled up apartments on Third and Second avenues. Horace Ginsbern & Associates' Mayfair Towers (1964), at 15 West Seventy-second Street, a 498-unit, twenty-seven-story pile clad in glazed white brick, occupied a site previously reserved for tennis courts belonging to the adjacent Dakota apartment building.[9] While the Mayfair was hardly an aesthetic rival to its neighbor, it was, like the Dakota had been in its own time, technologically innovative, featuring the city's first incinerator-less refuse-disposal system, which enabled tenants to send their trash down a chute leading to the basement, where it was collected in large containers that could be emptied daily by private sanitation services. Wechsler & Schimenti's 60 Riverside Drive (1965), on the northeast corner of Seventy-eighth Street, replaced seven townhouses with a twenty-story, white-brick-clad, fifty-five-unit building.[10] Completed in 1967, 80 Central Park West, on the northwest corner of Sixty-eighth Street, was a slender, twenty-five-story apartment tower housing 172 units, the fashionable avenue's first new apartment building erected south of Ninety-sixth Street since 1941.[11] Designed by the architects Paul Resnick and Harry F. Green, the buff-brick tower rose without setbacks from behind a mini plaza, breaking the street walls of both Central Park West and Sixty-eighth Street. It stood out from its neighbors because of its many projecting balconies, not to mention the bland banality of its facades.

The Upper West Side's rising fortunes also brought new life to some forgotten spots, such as the area in the Seventies that lay between the Lincoln Square and West Side urban renewal areas. The Gloucester (1975), at 200 West Seventy-ninth Street, was an eighteen-story apartment building filling the west blockfront of Amsterdam Avenue from Seventy-eighth to Seventy-ninth Street.[12] At the request of the developer, the architects Schuman, Lichtenstein & Claman broke with prevailing practice to clad the building in red brick and introduce a minimum amount of detailing to suggest a Georgian tone. Even more symbolic of the area's new vitality, even in its most downtrodden corners, was the March 18, 1969, announcement by Alexander's department store of its intention to build a six-level, 230,000-square-foot department store and a 1,000-seat movie theater on the west blockfront of Broadway between Ninety-sixth and Ninety-seventh streets.[13] Perhaps Alexander's was encouraged by the suggestion of Community Planning Board 7, made in 1968, that the site would be excellent for a department store, and by the results of a two-year-long study that statistically confirmed what seemed visible everywhere: that the trend away from the area had been reversed, and that Upper West Siders had a good deal of disposable income (the study showed the average was $3,970 per year, which compared favorably with the $4,410 available to the average Upper East Side resident). The store, to be Alexander's second Manhattan branch and the first major department store on the Upper West Side, was to replace the Riviera-Riverside theater complex, built in 1913 by the trailblazing movie producer William Fox, who founded the company that became the 20th Century Fox Film Corporation.[14] In addition to showing earlier silent "flickers," these theaters had been a prized stop on the vaudeville circuit and a setting for popular Yiddish theater.

The proposal set off a major public debate. Murray Siegel, a director of the West Side Chamber of Commerce, called the development "a shot in the arm for the area such as we have not had for 20 years."[15] But the Reverend Henry Browne, of St.

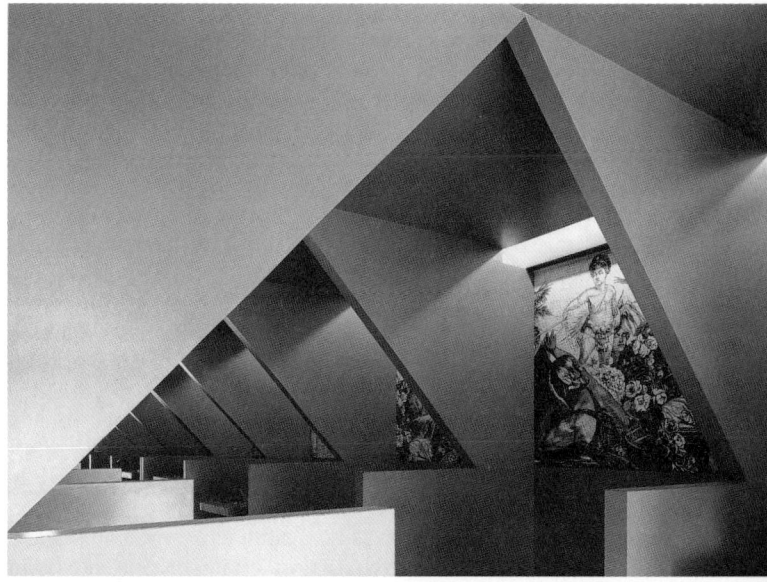

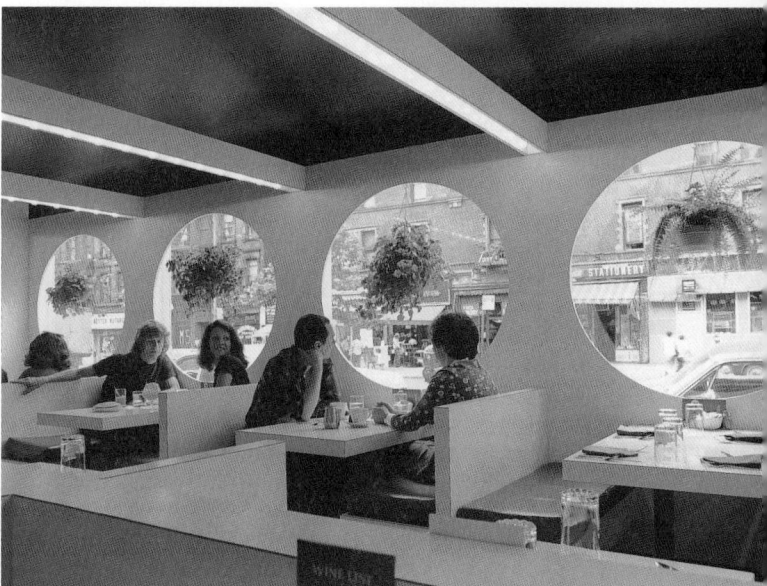

Top: Cleopatra, 2527 Broadway, between West Ninety-fourth and West Ninety-fifth streets. Gamal El-Zoghby, 1970. Interior. Cserna. GEZ

Bottom: Genghis Kahn's Bicycle, southeast corner of Columbus Avenue and West Sixty-ninth Street. Gamal El-Zoghby, 1974. Interior. Perron. GEZ

Gregory's Roman Catholic Church, argued: "So it will knock out a few hustlers, pushers and prostitutes. It will clean up the avenue. Big deal. The first reaction of the public is: 'That's terrific.' But this is the beginning of a grab by the real estate guys and banks."[16] Jeff Brand, an area politician, similarly stated: "They talk of a renaissance. But what they mean is a conversion to another luxury area like the East Side. . . . We want a neighborhood with small stores, boutiques."[17] Even Community Planning Board 7 raised objections to the plan, insisting that the store provide traffic guards to aid schoolchildren, finance subway improvements, incorporate truck bays, install high-intensity street lighting and employ minority construction workers. In June 1970, amid the controversy, the City Planning Commission indefinitely postponed its decision whether or not to grant the store requisite changes in the zoning laws governing the site. The following month Alexander's announced that it was dropping the proposal.

In 1974 the Riviera-Riverside was again threatened when Christopher Boomis, a Kansas-born contractor who had made a quick and big splash in New York real estate, proposed to build a thirty-four-story slablike apartment building, the tallest north of Lincoln Center.[18] The proposed 588-unit building, to be designed by Schuman, Lichtenstein & Claman, was squarely aimed at affluent single people and couples without children, as it was to be composed exclusively of one-bedroom apartments. To avoid some of the problems that had stymied the earlier Alexander's project, Boomis's building was designed to comply with existing zoning regulations. But the project drew the immediate ire of Upper West Siders, who organized the Ad Hoc Committee for the Preservation of the West Side to oppose the project and preserve the theater complex as an entertainment and cultural showcase. Despite such objections, demolition of the theaters began in December 1974, and in February of the following year Boomis announced that the apartment tower might incorporate a department store "like Alexander's or Korvette's"; the new dual-use plan would require zoning variances.[19] Even before tackling community objections, Boomis encountered other troubles: in June 1975 Manhattan District Attorney Robert Morgenthau and the New York City Department of Investigations began to look into allegations of bribery in connection with Boomis's contract with the city to erect a $37 million pier and warehouse complex in the Hunt's Point section of the Bronx.[20] Pending the outcome of these investigations, the City Planning Commission suspended its hearings on the requested zoning variances. Boomis subsequently charged that Bernard Beame, the son of Mayor Abraham D. Beame and his campaign manager, had offered him a major building project in exchange for a secret campaign contribution. This was never substantiated, however, and the negative publicity doomed Boomis's career and halted his Broadway apartment tower project.[21] The site remained vacant until 1982.

By the late 1960s established Upper West Side institutions that might have once considered relocation to more stable and desirable neighborhoods felt confident enough about the area's future to undertake significant new building projects. In 1968 Collegiate, the oldest operating private school in the country, located at 260 West Seventy-eighth Street, between Broadway and West End Avenue, built a rather severe, brick-clad addition designed by the firm of Ballard, Todd & Associates.[22] It had none of the visual interest of the Dutch-inspired Collegiate Dutch Reformed Church and School (Robert W. Gibson 1893) that stood directly to the south on an adjacent site, separated from the addition by a brick-paved courtyard.[23] In 1969, after two years of deliberation, another venerable Upper West Side institution, the Calhoun School, founded in 1896, decided not to decamp to Riverdale but to stay in the area. On May 19, 1969, Irving Stimmler, one of the school's trustees, said:

> We believe in the West Side. We feel that once more this is the coming place. This is where the future is. It would have been so easy to move to the suburbs, a marriage of convenience with instant expansion. But the question really was, "Do we want to give up the ghost and become just another exclusive school catering to the upper classes?" Most of our students are going to end up in the city, and how are they going to cope if they've been educated in the suburbs? We're a city school. A West Side school. We decided to stay and fight it out here.[24]

In 1975 Calhoun opened a new building called the Learning Center, at 433 West End Avenue, on the southwest corner of Eighty-first Street, designed by Costas Machlouzarides.[25] This scale-destroying five-story facility, which resembled a television set with "screens" facing both streets, replaced rowhouses by Clarence True (1898). Despite the school's civic-minded decision to stay in the area, its new building paid little respect to its neighbors, as Norval White and Elliot Willensky observed: "A more unsubtle and out-of-scale response to this urban-design challenge is hard to imagine."[26] Inside the Learning Center, curved walls punctuated the otherwise open floors, whose lack of traditional classrooms reflected the school's progressive approach to education. Edgar Tafel's four-story stucco- and brick-clad Andrew Goodman Building (1974), an annex to the adjacent Walden School, located at 1 West Eighty-eighth Street, on the northwest corner of Central Park West, was more sympathetic to its surroundings, relating relatively successfully to the grand Classicism of the school's main building, which had been built to house the Progress Club (Louis Korn, 1904).[27]

Working on a shoestring budget, Kaminsky & Shiffer transformed the West Eightieth Street Community Child Day Care Center (1971), at 223 West Eightieth Street, a three-story building of no particular distinction, into a whimsical structure housing classrooms and a rooftop play-cage.[28] Inside, the school was a bit drab, but the facade—with red- and blue-painted stucco covering over the old building, as well as deeply recessed window bands and swags on the rooftop parapet—was delightful.

Religious institutions also strengthened their ties to the community. Victor Christ-Janer's Church of St. Matthew and St. Timothy (1970), at 26 West Eighty-fourth Street, between Columbus Avenue and Central Park West, replaced an earlier church (William Halsey Wood, 1894) that was lost to fire in 1965.[29] Christ-Janer's new building also absorbed the church's community center (1962), designed by the firm of Neski & Neski.[30] Though it maintained the street's building wall, the boldly geometric principal facade of the new cast-concrete building and its deeply recessed entrance broke with the block's residential scale and established a rather strong presence in keeping with the principles of aesthetic Brutalism. Inside, a long, narrow, downward-sloping hallway led to a sanctuary distinguished by a colorful mosaic crucifix and wall hangings.

The preservation of the Upper West Side's open spaces became a key issue in the postwar era. In 1947 a nonprofit organization, the American Memorial to Six Million Jews of Europe, began to develop plans for a site in Riverside Park near Eighty-third Street.[31] In exchange for the parkland, the city reserved the right to approve the design. After installing a commemorative plaque in the park, the organization set out to build a more imposing memorial, at first approaching the sculptor Jo Davidson, who proposed a group of twenty-five-foot-high figures arranged in a circle fifty feet in diameter. As publicly presented at the Jewish Museum in 1948, Davidson's proposal, developed in collaboration with the architect Ely Jacques Kahn, had been revised to incorporate a fifteen-foot-high bronze figure placed on a forty-foot-high base. But the memorial organization's design committee rejected Davidson and Kahn's approach, going on to solicit proposals from the artists William Zorach, Chaim Gross and Leo Friedlander, and the architects Percival Goodman and Erich Mendelsohn. The group ultimately favored Goodman's scheme, which called for a flagstone plaza surrounded by cedar trees and flanked by a pylon surmounted by a monumental menorah.[32] Although Goodman claimed that his design had been accepted by the group but was later dropped at the insistence of Park Commissioner Robert Moses, the memorial group denied the allegation. Mendelsohn subsequently prepared two proposals.[33] In one, working with the sculptor Mitzi Salomon, he called for a circular, open-air platform defined by low walls from which a semi-enclosed passageway led to an assembly hall that was surmounted by a towering, latticelike representation of the stone tablets inscribed with the Ten Commandments. In the other, working with the sculptor Ivan Mestrovic, he called for a similar platform, but here, one side of the enclosing wall carried a solid representation of the twin tablets. Neither scheme was realized due to a lack of funds.

Following the group's failed efforts, two other organizations sought to realize similar memorials.[34] The Warsaw Ghetto Resistance Organization proposed two twenty-six-foot-high sculpted Torah scrolls upon which scenes of the Holocaust were to be depicted; the Artur Zygelboim Memorial Committee proposed a monumentally scaled, stylized representation of a figure surrounded by flames and thorns. Both memorials were designed by the sculptor Nathan Rapoport and, on February 11, 1965, both were rejected by the New York City Art Commission. Eleanor Platt, a sculptor and a member of the commission, commented that the scrolls were "excessively and unnecessarily large" and that the figure adopted so "tragic a posture" that it might disturb children.[35] Jewish community leaders objected to Platt's comments, but the commission did not reverse its decision. In 1965, perhaps attempting to finally put not only the two proposals but the entire long-debated issue to rest, the editors of the *New York Times* wrote:

> Inevitably the issue will be clouded and warped by the nature of the cause, the esthetics of the designs, and compassion for the victims of one of the most monstrous crimes in human history. But this is not the point. The point is the degree to which monuments and memorials should be put in New York parks, and, more basically, if they belong there at all. . . . Within the city's stone and concrete vise, the natural beauty of the parks is a spiritual gift to all, more than any monument devised by man.[36]

Despite the editorial, however, the issue was not dead: the next year Louis Kahn was asked to design a nonrepresentational monument to the Jewish victims of the Nazis for a site in Battery Park, and that proposal would continue to be developed and debated for years (see chapter 3).

In February 1964 another battle over open space erupted when plans were announced for the construction of a children's playground in a shrubbery-covered slope at the lower level of Riverside Park, between 101st and 103rd streets.[37] The bold and unconventional playground, to be jointly financed by the family and friends of Adele Rosenwald Levy, a philanthropist, was the

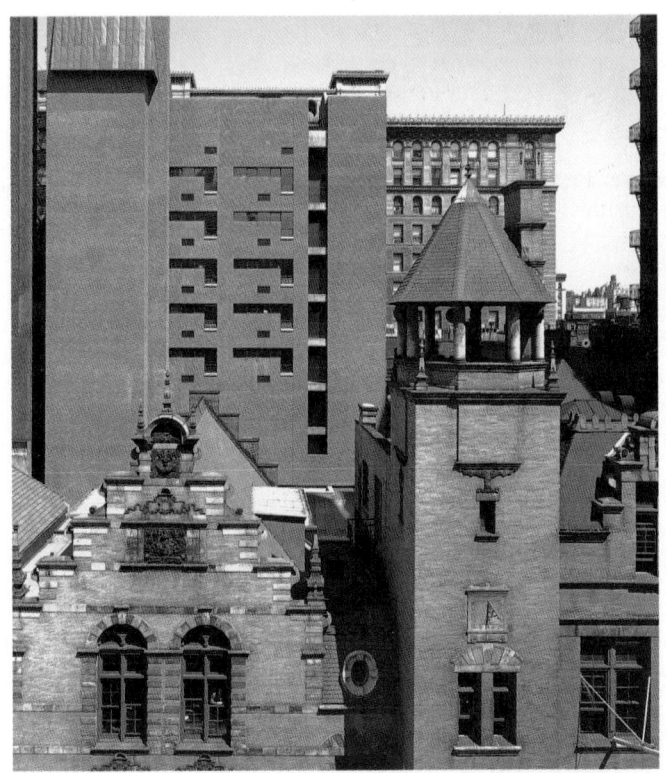

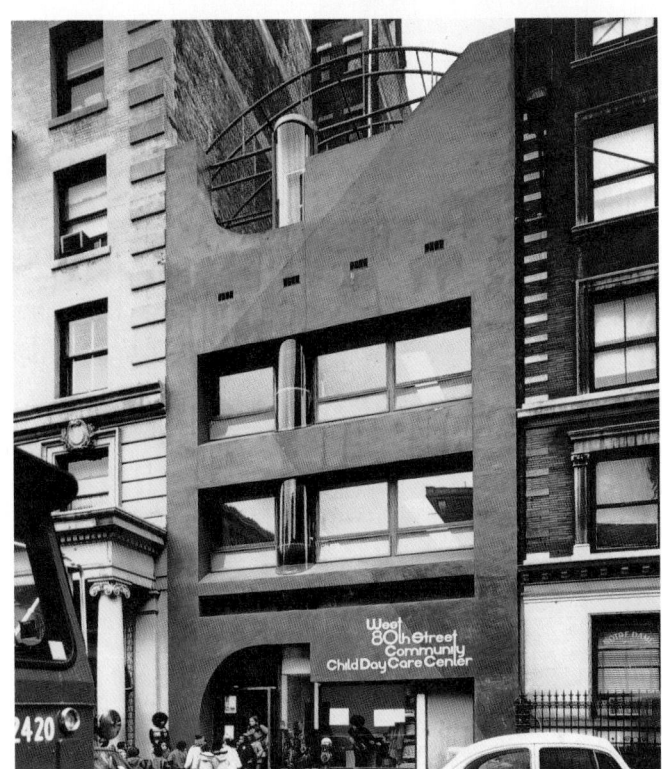

Top: Addition to Collegiate School, 260 West Seventy-eighth Street, between Broadway and West End Avenue. Ballard, Todd & Associates, 1968. View to the north showing Collegiate Dutch Reformed Church and School (Robert W. Gibson, 1893) in the foreground and addition in the background. Stoller. ©ESTO

Bottom: West Eightieth Street Community Child Day Care Center, 223 West Eightieth Street, between Broadway and Amsterdam Avenue. Kaminsky & Shiffer, 1971. View to the north. WK

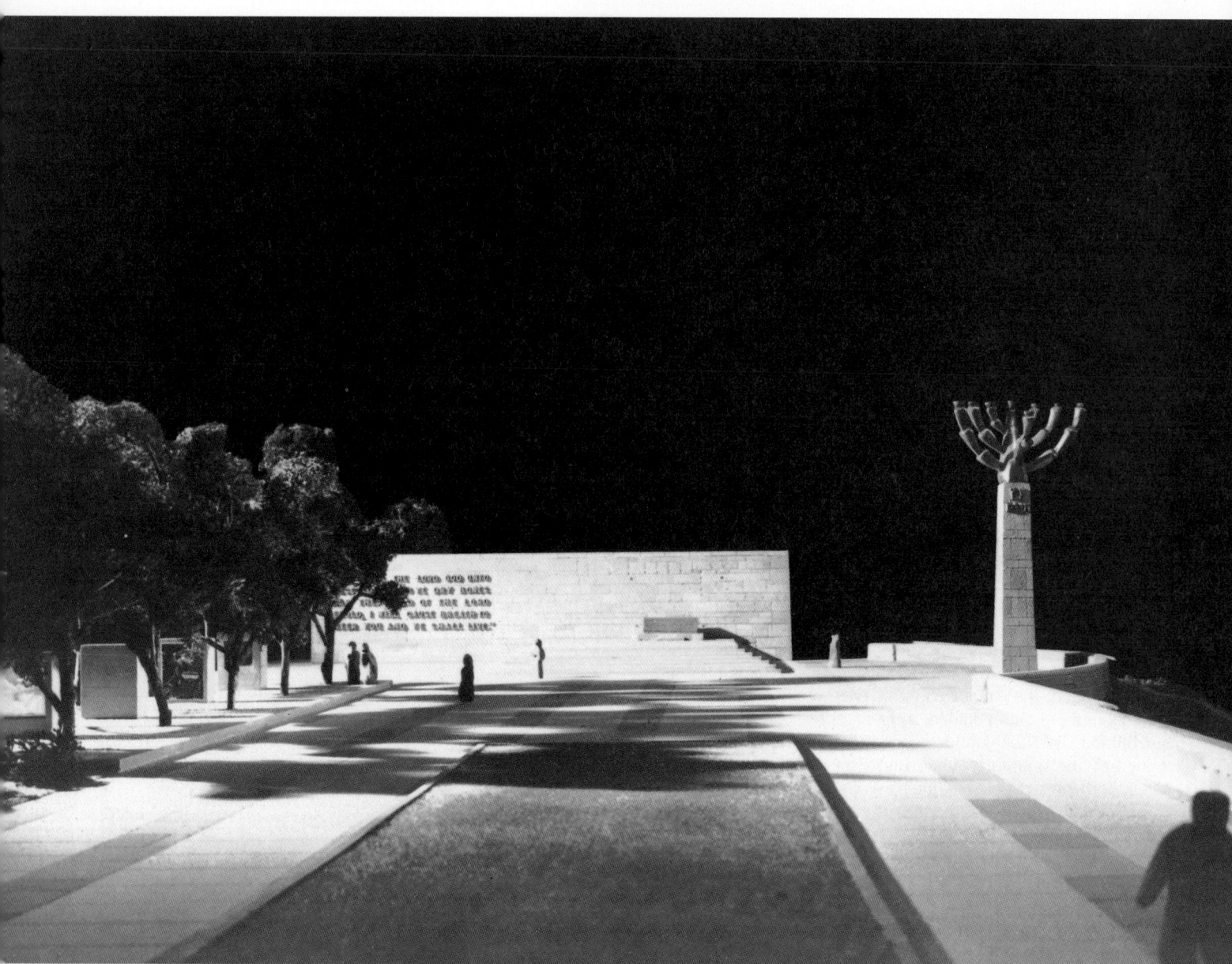

Proposal for the American Memorial to Six Million Jews of Europe,
Riverside Park near West Eighty-third Street. Percival Goodman, 1950.
Model. View to the south. CU

product of a collaboration between Louis Kahn and the sculptor Isamu Noguchi, who took the lead in the design. Proclaiming that "playgrounds haven't changed since the invention of the swing and the sandbox," Noguchi, who had previously designed a playground for the United Nations site (see chapter 7), proposed an imaginative landscape of water slides, a stepped pyramid for climbing, an amphitheater and, for rainy-day play, skylit underground rooms, whose roofs would be grassed over to minimize their intrusion on the park.[38] Of the collaboration, the often cryptic Kahn said: "I did not speak in terms of architecture, he did not speak in terms of sculpture. Both of us felt the building as a contour; not one contour but an interplay of contours so folding and so harboring as to make, by such a desire, no claim to architecture, no claim to sculpture."[39] Joseph Lelyveld, writing in the *New York Times*, said that the design "looks like an amalgam of ancient civilizations."[40]

But as inventive as the design was, it drew fire from many critics who saw it as an unnecessary incursion into valuable parkland, a point Kahn was clearly sensitive to when, at the model's unveiling, he said, "there is nothing here that doesn't say park."[41] Opposition to the playground swelled as part of a citywide feeling that the parks were becoming a dumping ground for memorials to individuals and special-interest groups. Noguchi would later claim that opposition to the project also came "from the 'better-advantaged' people of the community against what they thought might become an invasion of their quiet park by the rowdy Negroes and Puerto Ricans from the slums a few blocks east."[42] When demands were made that the proposed playground be realized on vacant lots in the area, Noguchi was at first sympathetic but later opposed to the idea.

In December 1965, despite strong opposition from Park Commissioner-designate Thomas Hoving, largely on the grounds that the community had not been involved in the design process, Mayor Wagner signed municipal contracts for the playground's construction. When John Lindsay was elected mayor in November 1965, he made his administration's opposition to the plan clear; but by February 1966, both he and Park Commissioner Hoving had come to back the plan because it had "simply gone too far down the line to stop."[43] Perhaps more to the point was the fact that the city was reluctant to offend the Levy family, which had donated $600,000 to the project. Nonetheless, in April 1966 the New York State Supreme Court ruled that the city did not have the right to realize the project because the amount of collected funds fell $99,553 below the lowest construction bid received. The unexpected court order suddenly turned a previously planned anti-playground demonstration in the park into a celebration, complete with a Dixieland jazz band.

Although the Kahn-Noguchi playground was never built, another innovatively designed recreational facility was: in 1967 the venerable Public School 166 (C. B. J. Snyder, 1898), at 140 West Eighty-ninth Street, was provided with a new 100-by-175-foot playground designed by the landscape architects M. Paul Friedberg & Associates.[44] When community protest had prevented the construction of a Board of Education design calling for four basketball courts and five standard pieces of play equipment protected from vandalism by a sixteen-foot-high chain-link fence enclosure, the Vincent Astor Foundation came forward with funds for an alternate design. Friedberg's playground was a Noguchi-inspired landscape that included a sunken court which could double as an amphitheater, movable and stationary play platforms, heavy wooden climb-over beams and cobbled sculptured climbing mounds, one of them big enough to incorporate a public rest room.

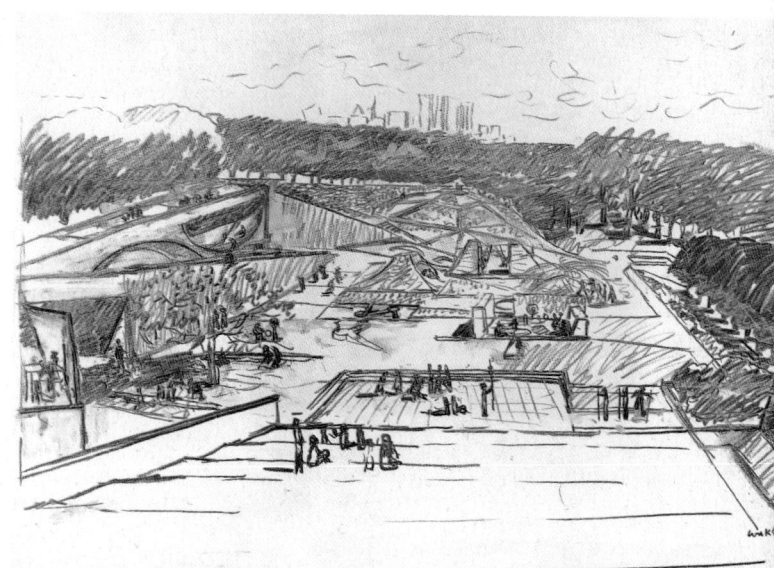

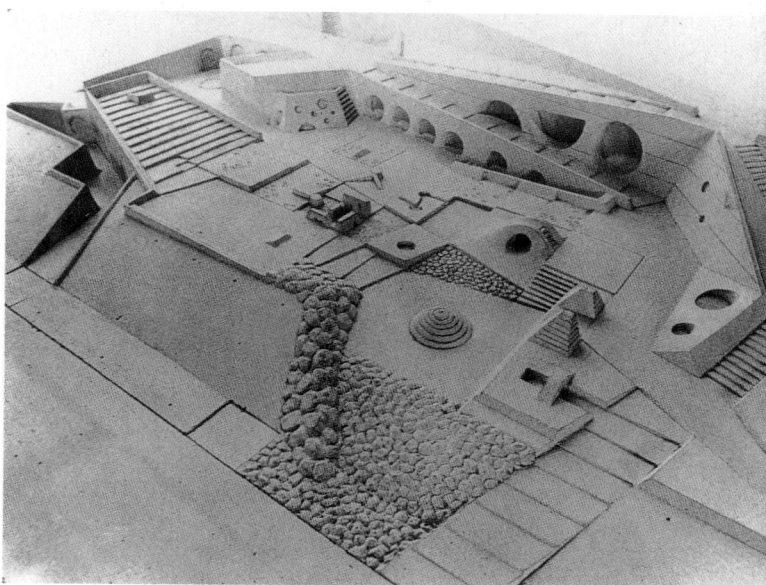

Top: Proposal for playground, Riverside Park, between West 101st and West 103rd streets. Louis I. Kahn and Isamu Noguchi, 1950. Drawing by Kahn showing view to the south. LIK

Bottom: Proposal for playground, Riverside Park. Model. View to the northeast. INF

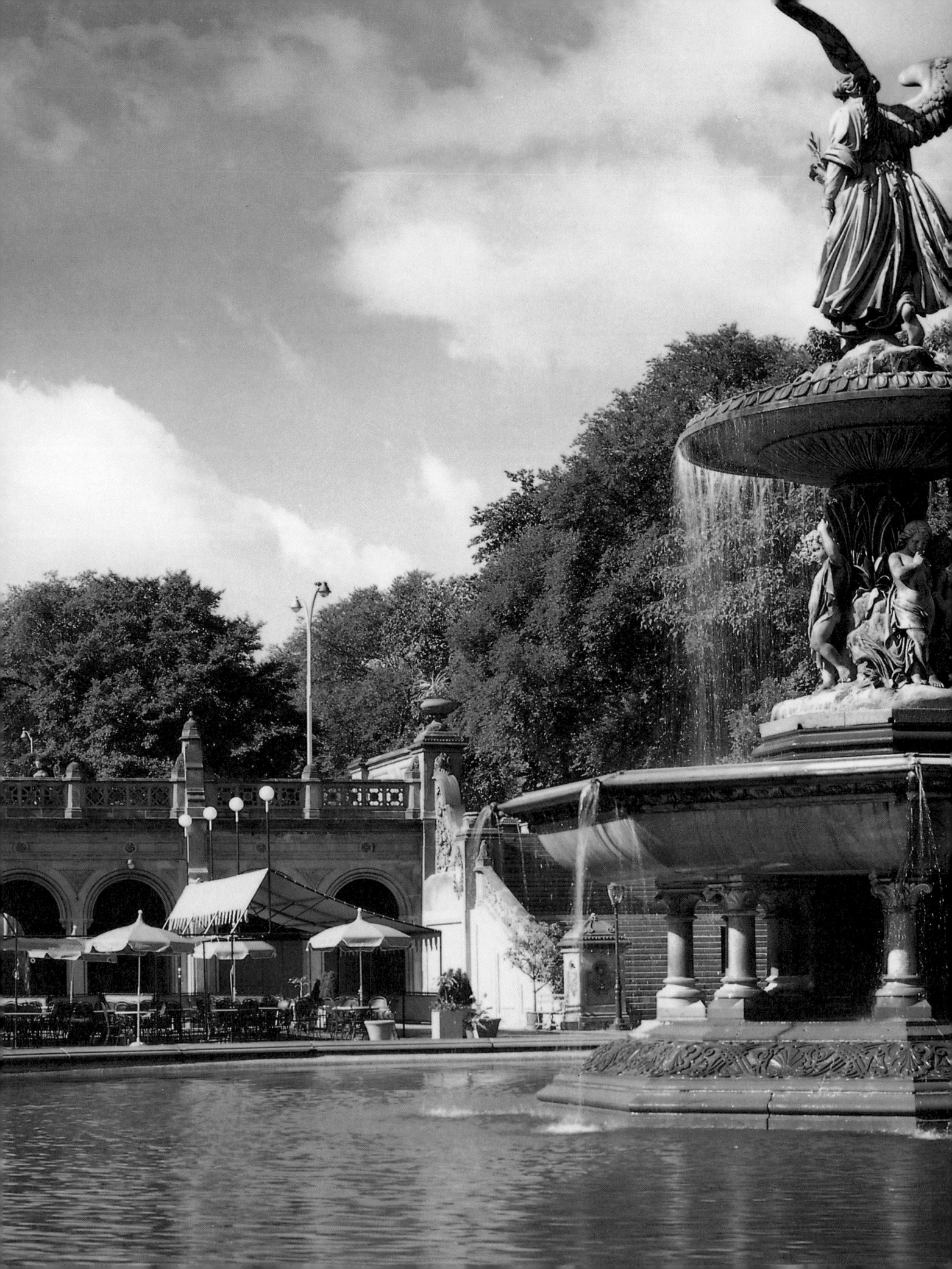

Chapter 10

Chapter 10

Central Park

Central Park . . .is the calm eye in the center of a hurricane. It is
the vision of men who knew man's needs. It is the measure of
seasons in a city which tries to insulate itself from them. It is the
refuge of wild things escaping stone. . . . It is the only sleeping land
in a sleepless city. And it is the only place . . . from which the
dream of Manhattan is wholly visible because the eye has room to
embrace it and the heart the distance to love it.
—Marya Mannes, 1960[1]

Moses Turns Pharaoh

In the fall of 1941 the *New Yorker* ran a three-part article on
Central Park (Frederick Law Olmsted and Calvert Vaux,
1858–73), reporting on its history and the complex interlocking bureaucracies that contributed to its daily operation.[2] Eugene
Kinkead and Russell Maloney's account, virtually the first comprehensive report on the park since the time of Olmsted, mixed
history, gossip and description to good effect. On the whole, the
writers felt that the park had not been in better hands since
Olmsted's day and that it was a far healthier environment than
the city that defined its boundaries. "Central Park today," they
said, "presents the rather tough and worldly-wise face of a winner in the metropolitan struggle for survival."[3] Much of what was
good about Central Park was attributed to Robert Moses, who
since becoming park commissioner in 1934 had restored public
confidence in the graft-infested Park Department.[4] Moses not
only built playgrounds both in Central Park and throughout the
city but also began a systematic program of modernization for the
park's neglected, technically outmoded and stylistically unfashionable Victorian-era facilities. In 1934 he transformed the rat-infested Menagerie, the nation's oldest zoo, by building a cluster of
small-scale, red-brick buildings designed by Aymar Embury II. In
the same year he created the Great Lawn on a site that had previously been occupied by a Hooverville and before that by a

Fountain Café, at Bethesda Fountain and Terrace (Calvert Vaux and
Jacob Wrey Mould, 1868–73; sculpture by Emma Stebbins), north side
of Seventy-second Street cross drive. James Lamantia in association
with Elizabeth Gordon, 1966. View to the southwest with Bethesda
Fountain on the right. Stoller. ©ESTO

reservoir. In 1936 Moses tore down the so-called Ladies
Refreshment Salon (Calvert Vaux, 1864), which had been glam-
orized in 1929 by Joseph Urban as the Casino but was in Moses's
eyes no more than a den of iniquity.[5] The Casino was replaced
within two months by the Mary Harriman Rumsey Playground.
Moses later established a new dining facility, the Tavern on the
Green, in the former sheepfold on the park's west side.

In keeping with his view of the park as an urban playground—a rather different conception from Olmsted's view of it
as an arcadian pleasure ground—Moses envisioned new active
recreational facilities for the middle class, but many of his boldest plans could not be realized until after the end of the Second
World War. One of the first of these was a skating rink, designed
in 1945 by Aymar Embury II and completed in December 1950
as the result of a $600,000 donation from the estate of Kate
Wollman, who had been left a fortune by her brother, William J.
Wollman.[6] Located on a two-acre site just north of the Fifty-
ninth Street lake and about 400 feet west of the zoo, the new facility, known as the Kate Wollman Memorial, was a 214-by-
175-foot artificial outdoor skating rink, the world's largest, set in
an amphitheaterlike depression. Atop a crescent-plan "skate
house," partially burrowed into the hill at its northern end, was
a children's playground. In the winter the rink could accommodate a thousand skaters on its acre of ice, and in the summer the
area could be used for roller skating, concerts or dancing.

The *New York Times* reassured its preservation-minded
readers of the project's value: "We suppose everyone is a little
apprehensive when a new project is going into the park, because
we are all—and Commissioner Moses foremost—determined to
keep the park unspoiled. We believe most critics will agree . . .
that this change has enhanced the usefulness of the park without
damaging its beauty."[7] One critic who did not agree was Lewis
Mumford. In his assessment of the design in 1951, Mumford was
perhaps the first important observer to criticize Moses's work at
Central Park, finding little to praise in the new facility or, for that
matter, in the "process that has been going on, sometimes ruthlessly, for the last twenty years." The area where the Wollman
Memorial was built, Mumford wrote, had been "one of Frederick
Law Olmsted's happiest pieces of naturalistic landscaping," featuring an "almost Japanese picturesqueness of quiet water and

arching rock, diminutive in scale and concentrated in effect." But now, he went on, "a mixture of consistent neglect, natural erosion, and artful improvement in the worst taste of suburbia has destroyed half the loveliness of the setting."[8]

Mumford was particularly vehement in his criticism of the skate house, which he felt was neither an extension of the landscape nor an elegant Modernist pavilion. If sheathed "entirely of glass as green and glacial as the United Nations Secretariat Building," Mumford said, it "would have looked like an ice grotto in winter and in summer could have been filled with tropical vines and trees." But as built it was "a conspicuous structure whose facade is a series of red brick piers alternating with wide windows that are topped by very flat arches. Contrasting bands of limestone and red brick form the arches, and two great brick pylons, which serve as a ventilator and a chimney, stand out like huge round blocks in the center of this composition." Mumford also had nothing nice to say about the rink itself, which he felt was designed "in a crassly utilitarian manner": "It is surrounded by a high fence of heavy woven wire, punctuated by tall poles of aluminum to hold floodlights. This stockade, designed to keep even youthful acrobats from getting into the enclosure without paying their nine cents, simply serves its purpose. It is also the final insult to the eye."[9]

Mumford went on to castigate Moses for his overall approach to the park's revitalization: "I am not grousing about bicycle paths in themselves or about such elegant formal gardens as the one that replaced the old conservatory at East 105th Street, nor do I quarrel violently with the menagerie buildings that replaced the hideous original zoo. I do complain about the system of piecemeal improvements that are in the spirit neither of the original plan nor of any new twentieth century one." Mumford boldly proposed, perhaps for the first time, that the park "be meticulously restored to Olmsted's design," noting that "both the Ramble and the wooded hill section above 100th Street are logical candidates for this treatment." The rest of the park, he said, "should probably be turned into open space, formalized to an extent with wide pleasances and gardens. If such a plan for the Park existed, a structure like the Wollman Memorial, which represents neither formalized elegance nor naturalistic self-effacement, would never have got beyond the preliminary sketches."[10]

Moses, of course, saw it differently. In the opening chapter of his retrospective career survey, *Public Works: A Dangerous Trade*, published in 1970, Moses defended his plans for Central Park. He contended that Olmsted and Vaux's "extraordinary, far-sighted, ingenious landscape plan for a park of 843 acres in what was then a wilderness of rocks, stagnant pools, goats, and squatters in the center of Manhattan but far north of the population of the time" had been "more or less religously followed by most of the commissions and commissioners," with alterations being made only "to meet the demands of the city growth."[11] Moses claimed that as park commissioner he fought off undesirable architectural intrusions into Central Park and that while all physical changes to the park's sacred ground generated controversy, most of his plans met with strong public approval. And though Moses may have lacked a plan to suit Mumford and clearly did not encourage the sort of architecture the critic advocated, the park commissioner did have a consistent vision of what the new park buildings should be like: sturdy in construction and traditional in form, with an evocative, playful character like that of Calvert Vaux's original park buildings. Though Vaux's structures were appreciated by Moses and his architects, they were deemed expendable because they were casually constructed and, more to the point, functionally and stylistically outdated. Furthermore, Moses's piecemeal approach to mending what by 1950 had begun to be regarded as the "deplorable condition" of the park was due at least as much to a lack of Park Department funding as it was to his lack of an overall plan.[12]

For better or worse, the Wollman Memorial seemed to set a precedent that would later earn Central Park the nickname "Memorial Cemetery" as somewhat heavy-handed designs for large-scale projects were proposed by the commissioner and frequently constructed through the well-intended generosity of an elite few.[13] When the Central Park Carousel burned in November 1950, the Michael Friedsam Foundation came forward the next year with a $75,000 donation to build a new one.[14] Completed in July 1951, the seventy-eight-foot-diameter brick octagonal structure housing the merry-go-round, apparently designed by Park Department engineer Gustave Chirlian, continued the vocabulary of the Wollman Memorial, although the pavilion's low-pitched roof rising to a broad cupola was far less whimsical than the vaguely Chinese- and French-inspired shapes synthesized at the rink. The charred remains of the old Central Park carousel were purchased by a school teacher, who had it restored and placed in the Bronx Beach Playland in September 1951.[15] In 1952 the Friedsam Foundation donated money to build an identical structure and carousel for Prospect Park in Brooklyn (see chapter 13).

For the Kinderberg, or children's mountain, a promontory situated between the carousel and the Wollman Memorial, an anonymous donor gave money to build a smaller version of the carousel pavilion to serve as the Chess and Checkers House (1951).[16] Although the editors of the *New Yorker* attributed the design of the thirty-five-foot-wide pavilion to its builder, Benjamin Leavin of the Great Eastern Construction Company, the basic concept seems to have been Gustave Chirlian's. Replacing a rustic wooden structure that had burned several years earlier, the Chess and Checkers House was to be, as the *New York Times* put it, "a resort of retired oldsters."[17] The donor, who turned out to be the financier Bernard M. Baruch, not only took pity on the old men he saw in a photograph playing chess on a park bench but also wished to commemorate the site where he first courted his wife, Annie Griffen. In gratitude, the Park Department labeled a bench in his honor "Reserved for Bernard M. Baruch."

In 1954 Moses went on to tear down the Seventy-second Street Boathouse, a rustic wooden structure built in 1924 (which had replaced the first boathouse in Central Park, constructed in 1873), to build in its place one designed by chief park designer Stuart Constable.[18] The gift of Adeline and Carl M. Loeb, for whom it was named, the new boathouse opened on March 12, 1954. Long and low, with red brick walls, white limestone trim and a swooping copper-clad roof similar to that of the Wollman Memorial, it was punctuated by pergolas and a black-and-white clock set in a gable. In 1954 Moses also opened the Kerbs Boathouse for model yachts, located on the east side of Conservatory Lake. Designed by Aymar Embury II, it also adopted a style similar to that of the Wollman Memorial, which Moses insisted was in keeping with "the traditional Victorian architecture of Central Park."[19] Further uptown, in 1947 Moses completed the reconstruction of the Harlem Meer, a project he had begun before the war, and a new boathouse.[20]

The impulse to litter the park with commemorative sculpture, and not the construction of functioning memorials, was a major problem. Olmsted had so regretted the proliferation of sculpture and memorials in Central Park that he banished them from the outset in Prospect Park, his next major undertaking.[21] In the Moses era, however, such memorials multiplied in Central Park, and though they intruded into the naturalistic landscape, some of

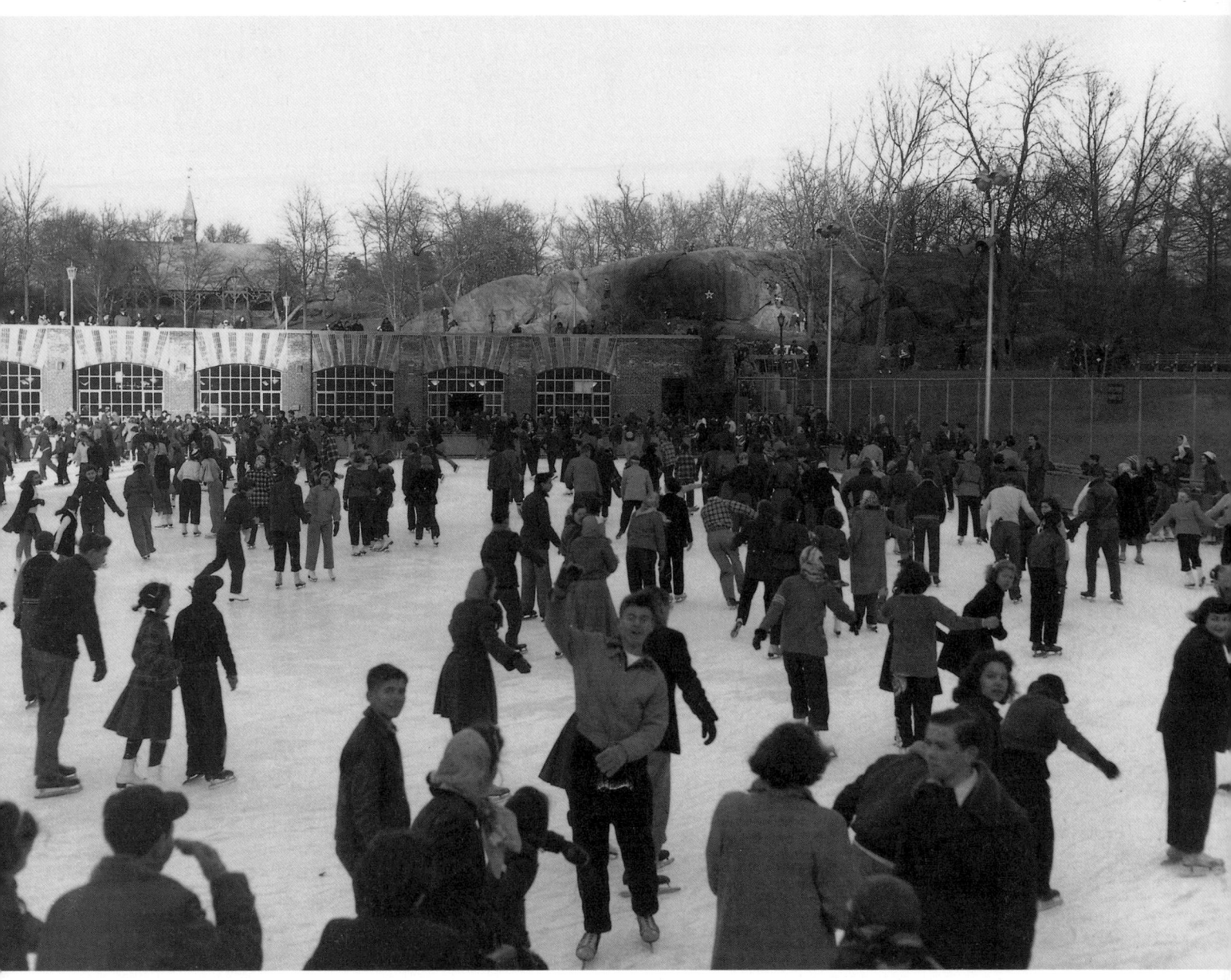

Wollman Rink, near East Sixty-third Street. Aymar Embury II, 1950.
View to the north. NYCPPA

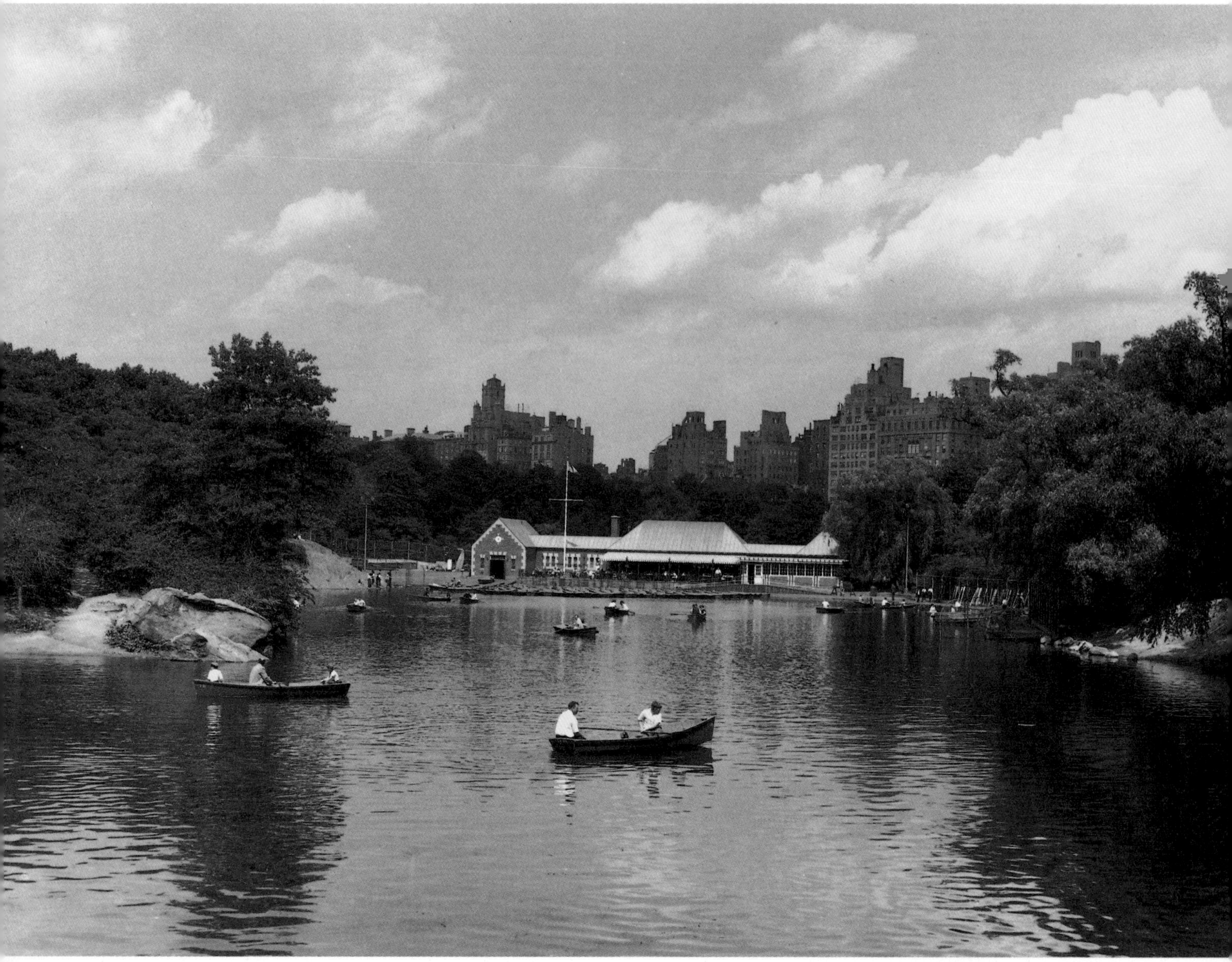

Above: Loeb Boathouse, near East Seventy-fourth Street. Stuart Constable, 1954. View to the northeast. NYCPPA

Right: Central Park Carousel, north side of Sixty-fifth Street Transverse Road. Gustave Chirlian, 1951. View to the northwest. NYCPPA

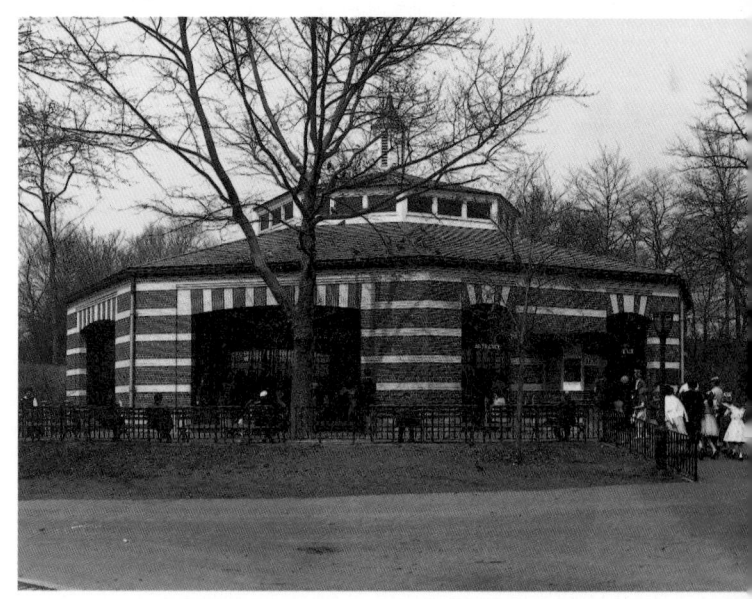

them were quite charming. In 1956 a larger-than-life-size bronze portrait by the sculptor George John Lober of the beloved Danish storyteller Hans Christian Anderson was erected on the west side of Conservatory Lake.[22] The figure was seated on a stone bench, designed by Otto F. Langmann, with a sculpture of the "ugly duckling" standing nearby. The casually composed monument was compelling, and children took to sitting in the figure's lap.

The character of the park's entrances had been a subject of considerable artistic debate and public controversy since the early 1860s, when Richard Morris Hunt, the first American architect to be trained at the Ecole des Beaux-Arts in Paris, proposed a series of monumental gateways for the barely completed facility.[23] The response to Hunt's proposed gateways was for the most part negative. Olmsted and Vaux, Hunt's strongest opponents, believed that his formal, French-inspired designs, with their elaborate terraces and fountains, would conflict with the rural, natural and democratic atmosphere of this most American park. As a result of the controversy over Hunt's designs, the park's entrances continued to have the modest, almost gardeny character that Olmsted and Vaux had originally intended, with the exception of the Maine Memorial (H. Van Buren Magonigle and Attilio Piccirilli, 1913) at the Columbus Circle entrance.[24]

Moses picked up on Magonigle's example when he added a second monumental gateway (1945–51) to the park at Sixth Avenue and Central Park South.[25] Doing his best to help establish Sixth Avenue as the Avenue of the Americas, Moses's designers, the landscape architects Clarke, Rapuano & Holleran, flanked the park's entrance at the end of that street with two heroic statues of South American political heroes: Simón Bolívar of Venezuela and José de San Martín of Argentina. Of all the postwar improvements undertaken in the park, only this pleased Mumford, who saw it as a demonstration of what could be achieved if even "a modicum of intelligence is applied to civic design."[26] The principal ornaments of the plaza were the statues. Simón Bolívar, by the American sculptor Sally Jane Farnham, had been executed in 1919 after she had won an international competition sponsored by Venezuela. In 1921 the widely admired statue was placed in the park near Central Park West and Eighty-third Street after an inferior 1883 statue of the hero had been ordered removed from a Broadway mall in 1897 by the city's art authorities. In April 1951 Farnham's statue was relocated to the Avenue of the Americas site, where it was joined a month later by a reduced copy of the French sculptor Louis Joseph Daumas's José de San Martín (1862), the original of which stood in Buenos Aires.[27] Both sculptures were placed on granite pedestals. In 1965 Anna Vaughn Hyatt Huntington's 1959 statue of the Cuban patriot José Martí was added to the group; it was placed farther north in the park, almost on axis with the Avenue of the Americas.[28]

Mumford hailed the new plaza for its "balanced composition," and observed that because the entrance to the park was slightly off the axis of the Avenue of the Americas, "there was no temptation to bring the statues closer together and to make them terminal points on that axis." He was lavish in his praise of the plaza: "The spacing of the statues, the dark granite bases, the paving between them, the curving wall that bounds the northern rim of the small plaza, all make this one of the best achievements of the Parks Department since it did over the site of the old Conservatory." But Mumford could not resist making another dig at the skating rink; he concluded his assessment of the plaza with the observation that it "redeems the severe damage that has been done the Park by the unappetizing Wollman Memorial."[29]

The park's most beloved sculpture, José de Creeft's Alice In Wonderland, was placed by Moses just north of the Conservatory Lake in a setting designed by Fernando Texidor with the landscape architect Hideo Sasaki.[30] Dedicated on May 7, 1959, the sculpture was the gift of the publisher George T. Delacorte as a memorial to his wife, Margarita, who, he said, "read Alice to all our children."[31]

On May 30, 1955, Moses released plans for the construction of an indoor and outdoor recreation center for senior citizens to occupy a fourteen-acre tract in the area known as the Ramble, where a tangled maze of paths, stairways and bridges wound through a rocky, wild landscape nestled between the lake and the East Drive, south of the Seventy-ninth Street transverse.[32] Working with a $250,000 gift from the Florina Lasker Foundation, supplemented with modest city funds, Moses proposed to build a recreation building at the north end of the site, which would be served by a new stop along the route of the Seventy-ninth Street crosstown bus. Designed by Moore & Hutchins, the center resembled in almost equal measure the so-called second Prairie Style work of Frank Lloyd Wright and a suburban ranch house. The facility was to include a food bar, a television room, a radio room, a music room with a piano and record player, a game room and a general social hall. Outside, Moses proposed to spend $200,000 reorganizing the Ramble's path system, clearing ground for horseshoe pitching, shuffleboard and croquet, as well as creating an area for game tables and umbrella-shaded tables for alfresco dining.

Almost immediately, the proposal raised a howl of protest. In a letter to the New York Times written on the day the project was announced, Jerome C. O'Brien accused Moses of "proceeding apace with his plan to surburbanize the park. A few years ago we saw one of its loveliest and most picturesque spots spoiled by the Wollman Memorial and now another memorial threatens the Ramble."[33] A few days later Robert Cushman Murphy, Lamont Curator Emeritus of the American Museum of Natural History's Department of Birds, and Richard Edes Harrison and Kathleen Green Skelton, members of the Linnean Society, attacked the plan as a dire threat to one of the park's most important bird sanctuaries. Daniel Chase, executive director of the Park Association, defended it, however, and said it was minimally disruptive. Moses responded to the plan's critics by pointing out that the decision to locate the senior citizens' center in the Ramble would allow him to meet a social need and to redevelop an area that had become a nuisance, attracting petty criminals who robbed and occasionally mugged bird-watchers. But the critics were not to be quashed. Harrison ridiculed the idea of devoting the site to the elderly, who would have to climb the equivalent of seven stories from the proposed bus stop to reach the hilltop recreation building. Eventually the Municipal Art Society joined the attack, asking that the project be replaced by a rehabilitation of the Ramble itself. On November 30, 1955, three days before the project was to come before the Board of Estimate, the "Battle of the Ramble" was won by the bird-watchers when the Lasker Foundation, acting on the advice of its counsel, withdrew its offer to construct the facility.[34] The Park Department decided to go ahead with the suggested rehabilitation of the area.

By this time Moses had other work to attend to: at Central Park West and Sixty-seventh Street, the commissioner was preparing to renovate the Tavern on the Green restaurant and expand its parking facilities.[35] Moses's plans for the restaurant, announced in January 1956, called for enlarging the Tavern's capacity from 600 to 720 persons and increasing its cocktail lounge and kitchen facilities. He also proposed to build an

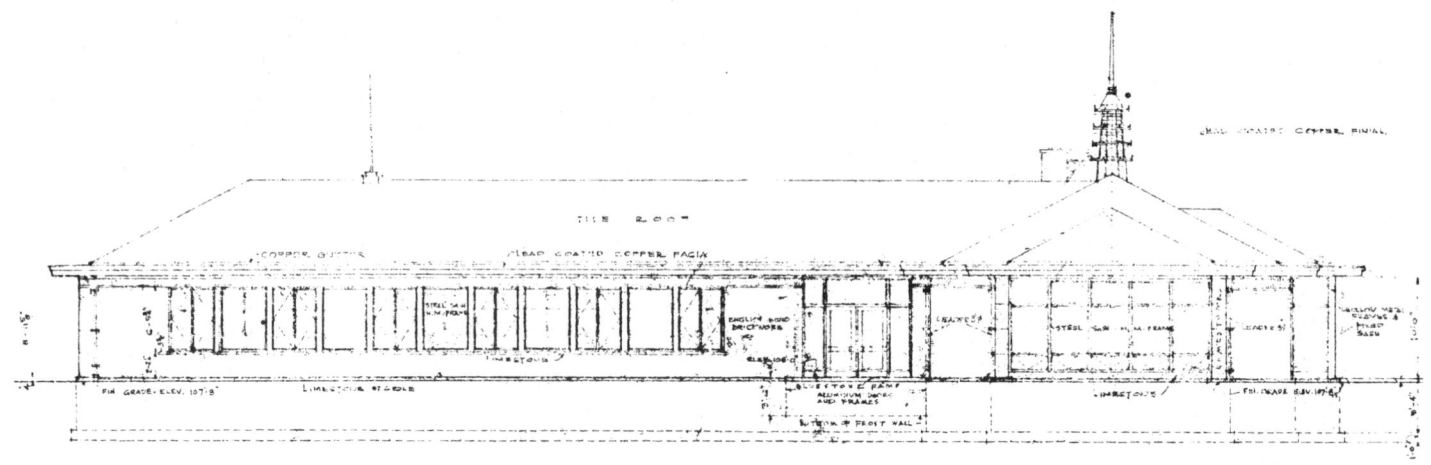

Above: Proposal for a senior citizens' recreation center, the Ramble, south side of Seventy-ninth Street Transverse Road. Moore & Hutchins, 1955. South elevation. NYCPPA

Right: Mothers and children protesting the building of a parking lot in Central Park, between West Sixty-seventh and West Sixty-eighth streets, April 1956. NYT

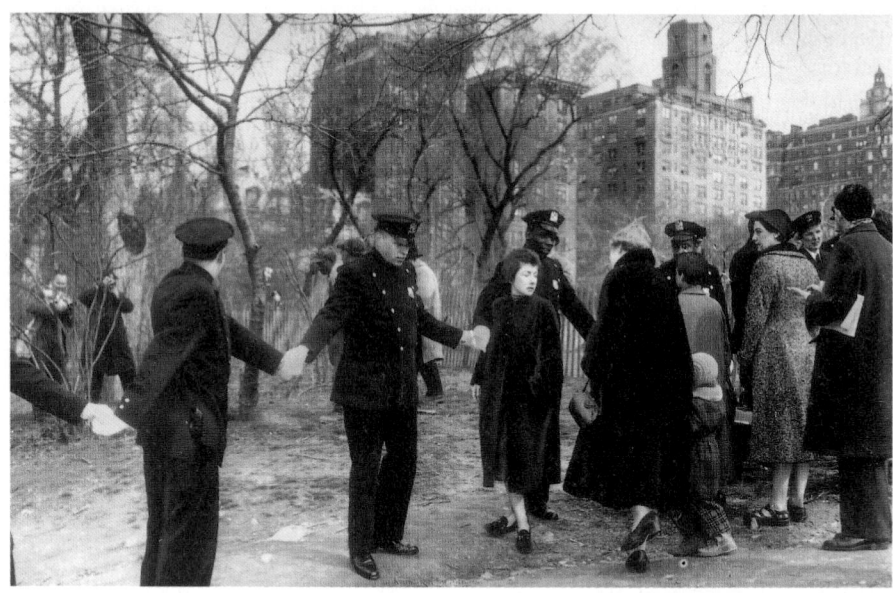

eighty-car parking lot north of the Sixty-seventh Street park entrance, thereby doubling the number of parking spaces at the restaurant. Though the plan was reported in a short article in the *New York Times*, there was no public response until April 9, 1956, when Roselle Davis, wife of the artist Stuart Davis, and one of the mothers who with their young children frequented the grassy glen about three hundred feet inside the park between Sixty-seventh and Sixty-eighth streets, noticed a group of men with blueprints and surveying equipment. When they had gone for lunch she noticed that their blueprints, spread out on the grass, bore the title "Detail Map of Parking Lot."

Davis and a few other mothers enlisted to their cause a neighbor, Fannie Hurst, a well-known novelist and social activist, asking her to help draft a petition to which signatures of some of the neighborhood's most famous residents could be added. Soon another neighbor, *New York Herald Tribune* staff writer Richard C. Wald, reported on the proposed project. On the same day twenty-three mothers, three fathers and eleven children met in the rain to dramatize their objection to the project, which would result in the loss of fifty trees. The group's spokesman, the photographer Arnold Newman (who ironically was later to take the most memorable portrait of Moses, see

chapter 1), urged a weekend campaign of doorbell ringing and passed out petition forms addressed to Moses and Mayor Wagner. When asked to meet with the protest group, Moses put off the encounter for several days.

At about seven o'clock on April 17, when Elliott and Elinor Sanger woke up in their twelfth-floor apartment at 75 Central Park West to find a bulldozer at work in the park below, they called their friend Stanley M. Isaacs, the former Manhattan Borough President and longtime Moses foe. He advised them to "Get the women out there, and call the newspapers and television."[36] Within minutes, thirty or forty women were on the scene with fifteen youngsters and ten babies in their carriages. The group's presence ground the operation to a halt, creating a tableau that when Isaacs arrived on the scene looked as if the bulldozer had been stopped in its tracks by the amassed protesters. The only difference between this confrontation and scores of other ones like it that Moses had previously experienced in his many controversial acts of urban clearance, particularly in the outer boroughs, was that this one received extensive newspaper, radio and television exposure. This controversy was in the heart of Manhattan, in Central Park, the city's most sacred preserve, and powerful people were involved. Within hours Moses's attack on the glen had been broadcast; by the next day the picture of mothers and children confronting brute force hell-bent on transforming parkland into a parking lot was all over the city.

Negotiations began as the mothers guarded the parking lot site from 7:00 A.M. until dark. Meanwhile, Isaacs sent a letter of protest to Mayor Wagner, saying that "not even the Lord High Park Commissioner should be allowed to destroy park beauty for the benefit of a commercial enterprise."[37] As negotiations dragged on, the story remained on the front pages of the papers. Even the *New York Times*, hitherto among Moses's most loyal advocates, questioned the project in an editorial entitled "Only a Half Acre—But":

> If this were land somewhere else there would be nothing to get excited about, but Central Park is different. To New Yorkers, and especially those who live near the park, it is sacred land. To use it for anything but park is like insulting the flag. After fighting all these years against all the causes that were offered to invade it, why should New York at this late date give up a half acre for the personal convenience of eighty carloads of people having chicken dinner in the Tavern? . . . Let the diners at the Tavern ride there in taxicabs.[38]

By the second week the confrontation was being called the "Battle of the Tavern on the Green." But Moses would not give in, and at 1:30 A.M. on April 24 he sent in workers to define the site's boundaries with a four-foot-high snow fence and then moved a bulldozer into position. By daylight, when the mothers got to the scene, one maple tree had been toppled. The media went wild, and the public continued to express its disgust in letter after letter published in the pages of the city's newspapers. In this single arrogant act of defiance, Moses had destroyed a public reputation that had been near inviolate for almost thirty years. As Robert Caro later put it: "For the first time he had been portrayed to the public at large not as a defender but as a destroyer of parks and as an official interested not in serving the people but in imposing his wishes upon them."[39]

The mothers obtained an injunction against Moses in the courts, with State Supreme Court Justice Samuel H. Hofstadter stating that it seemed "most doubtful if the benevolent and far-sighted genius of Messrs. Olmsted and Vaux, who laid out the park, envisaged a bucolic night club. Certainly it cannot be argued that there is any dearth of cocktail lounges, bars and cabarets in our city, and in this very vicinity." Hofstadter suggested that perhaps Moses regarded the half-acre in question as "de minimus," but the judge declared that "no foot, or even inch, of park space is expendable in our teeming metropolis."[40] The city appealed Judge Hofstadter's ruling, but it was rejected by the five-member Appellate Court on June 5, 1956. Meanwhile, opposition to the project continued to swell, with organizations ranging from the Citizens Union to the New York Southern Baptist Association issuing negative statements. Isaacs marshaled arguments against Moses and the project, looking into the Tavern lessee's highly favorable financial arrangement with the city, an arrangement that, although it did not benefit Moses directly, enabled the commissioner to use the Tavern's ambience as an extension of his personal power.

Moses did not grasp the gravity of the situation, and confident of victory, he went with his wife on a twenty-four-day cruise to Spain. The controversy continued to boil, fueled by the potential scandal involved with the concessionaire's contract and by rising public sentiment against Moses, which grew beyond the city's boundaries. Even Governor W. Averell Harriman

took a stand, saying, "If I had lived on the west side of Central Park, I'd have been out with the mothers and their prams."[41] When he returned from his vacation, Moses immediately held a press conference, blasting his opponents as a "small, noisy minority" largely consisting of "childless women howling about their non-existent children."[42] But this was pure bravura; by this time Moses had come to realize the battle's·potentially serious consequences, including the possibility of a public trial in which damaging evidence about his dealings with the Tavern's concessionnaire might be uncovered. As a result, Moses did what he had never done before: he backed down, agreeing on July 17, 1956, to drop the project. In addition, he agreed to build a new playground on the spot where he had proposed to park cars. The playground opened in April 1957.

The Battle of the Tavern on the Green marked a decisive point in Moses's career and in the relationship between New York's citizens, their elected officials and their appointed commissioners. "The public's best weapons," the *New Yorker* said, "turned out to be baby carriages and a battalion of brave mothers who stood off the Commissioner's bulldozers and sharp tongue in the early stages and eventually brought him to what the *New York Times* termed an unconditional surrender."[43] The conflict marked an important point in the evolution of the highly vocal participatory democracy that would dominate New York's politics for a decade or more beginning in the late 1960s.

In 1959 Moses made another serious blunder when he banned the New York Shakespeare Festival from Central Park.[44] The Shakespeare Workshop, as it was called when it was founded by Joseph Papp in 1953, consisted of a group of young actors who performed in the basement of the Emmanuel Presbyterian Church on East Sixth Street in Manhattan. Papp's leftist politics made him a controversial figure; even his practice of financing performances with donations and refusing to charge admission was seen by some observers as subversive. Nonetheless, Papp's Shakespeare Workshop attracted such enthusiastic audiences, including people who had never been exposed to the English classics, that it acquired the city's approval in 1956 to give free Shakespeare performances in the East River Park Amphitheater and later in 1957 in Central Park.[45] Only two years later, however, Robert Moses set new requirements for continued Shakespeare performances in Central Park, demanding not only that Papp charge admission but also that the workshop pay $10,000 to the Park Department to cover the expense of replacing grass eroded by the crowds.[46] When Papp announced that the workshop could not meet these demands, the situation escalated into a public debate staged in and out of court, as well as in the press ·and among the general public. When the future of Papp's Shakespeare-in-the-Park seemed blackest, Murray Handwerker, owner of the famous Nathan's hot-dog chain, offered a site in Oceanside, Long Island—a sure slap in the face to the city and a suggestion that made Moses's policies seem particularly ill-advised and the commissioner himself seem at once elitist and philistine.[47]

The editors of the *New Yorker*, like much of the media, came out against Moses in the debate:

> When . . . Robert Moses banned the free Shakespeare Festival in Central Park, he robbed the Bard of one of his few chances at an audience with no advance knowledge of the plots. And when Mayor Wagner, a great talking friend of public education, gave the Commissioner his way, he let an important kind of public education down badly. Thousands of children and adults came to the performances at the Belvedere who had nei-

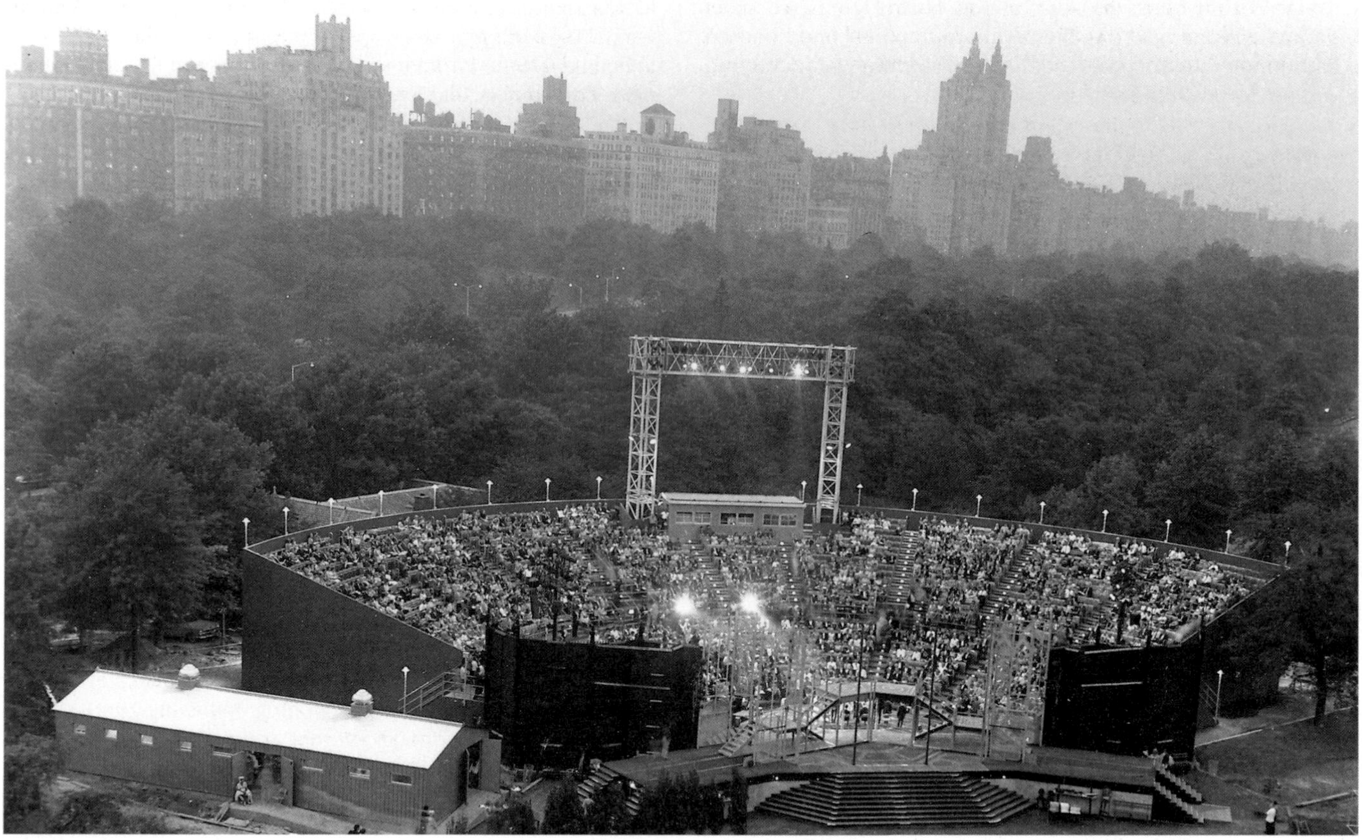

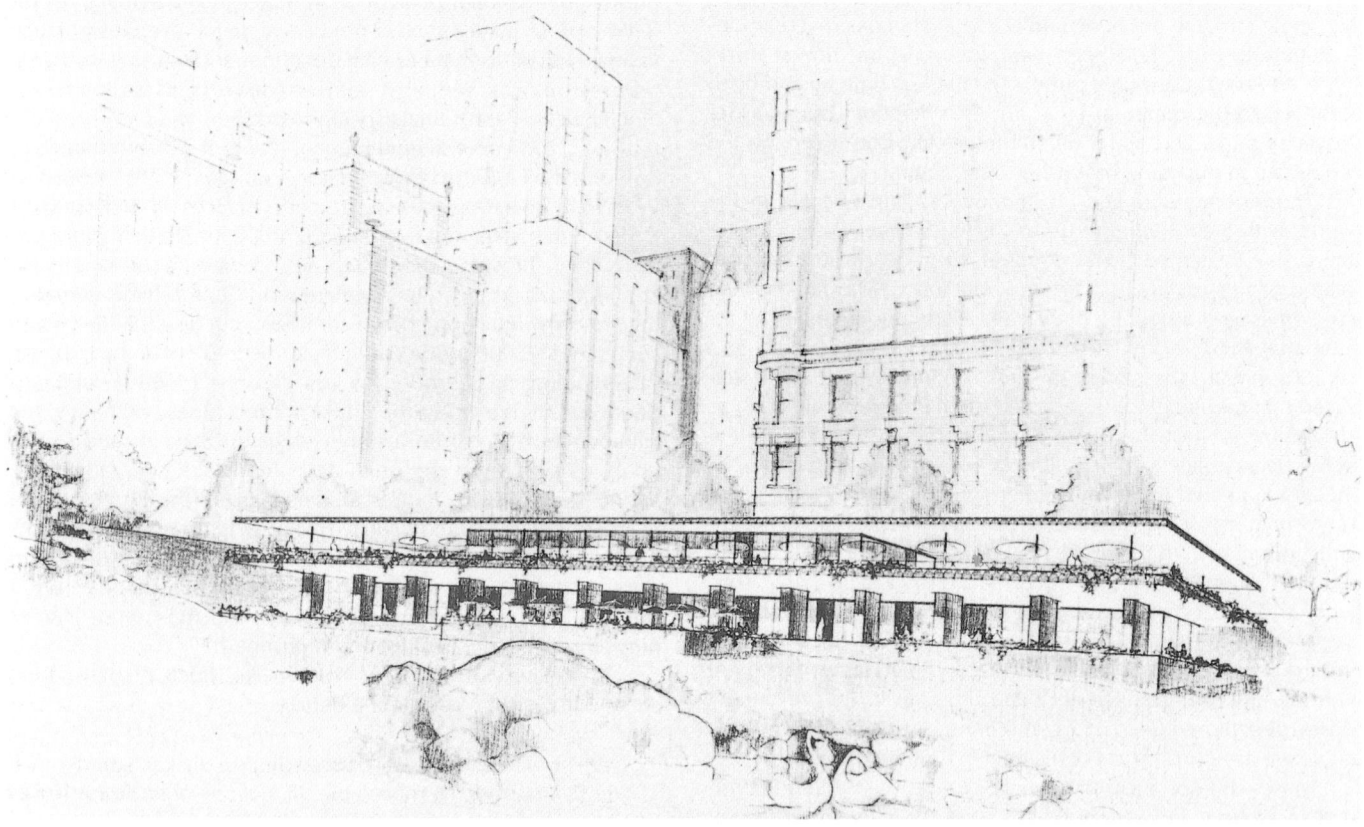

Top: Delacorte Theater, near West Eighty-first Street. Eldon Elder and New York City Park Department Design Staff, 1962. View to the northwest showing opening night performance of *Othello,* June 1962. NYCPPA

Bottom: Proposal for café sponsored by Huntington Hartford, Central Park South, west of Grand Army Plaza. Edward Durell Stone, 1960. View to the southeast. MA

ther read nor seen the plays, or even heard them talked about. The *ambiance*, the weather, the color and lights, and simple curiosity brought them out; some had never seen any sort of play in the flesh. Hundreds came back again and again.[48]

The case eventually reached the Appellate Court, which ruled in favor of Papp, calling Moses "clearly arbitrary, capricious, and unreasonable" in his decision to forbid free theater in the park.[49] The court suggested that a more reasonable compensation for the city's expenses would be a sum of $20,000 to be raised by Papp. The city then reconsidered its position, but only after Papp posted a $20,000 bond, which he was able to do when the Edward L. Bernays Foundation and the Louis K. Ansbacher Trust each came forward with $10,000. By August 1959, Moses, in a total reversal, requested $250,000 to construct a permanent home for the Shakespeare Festival. The *New York Times* supported the move,[50] as did numerous civic groups and individuals, although the Park Association objected to the theater as an encroachment.[51] George T. Delacorte ultimately came to the festival's financial rescue.[52] In June 1962 the festival theater was opened on a site below the Belvedere, where the original Central Park performances had been held. Named for Delacorte, it was designed by Eldon Elder, the festival's stage designer, and the Park Department's in-house staff. The facility consisted of a steeply raked steel-framed wood amphitheater facing west to take advantage of the Belvedere as a backdrop.[53]

In August 1974 plans were announced for a new theater to be built on the same site to replace Elder's theater, which after twelve years' service had begun to show serious signs of deterioration.[54] The new 2,500-seat facility, designed by Giorgio Cavaglieri, who had designed Papp's Public Theater (see chapter 16), met with opposition from several quarters. Henry Hope Reed, the coauthor of a 1967 history and guide to the park, protested its cost, while James Marston Fitch, the department's newly appointed director of historic preservation, preferred a site nearer Central Park West. As public opposition mounted, official support was withdrawn. Meanwhile, the *New York Times* editorialized that the $1 million needed to renovate the Delacorte Theater, or the $3 million needed to build a new theater, were both irresponsible sums given the city's financial woes and the fact that the total park budget was only $4.5 million.[55] Papp threatened to move his programs to the Vivian Beaumont Theater at Lincoln Center, an action he did not ultimately take.[56] In June 1976, the twentieth anniversary of the New York Shakespeare Festival's first free performances in the park, Papp unveiled a completely renovated Delacorte Theater, accomplished without the city's help.[57]

In March 1960 Moses released Edward Durell Stone's plans for a café to be built on parkland across the street from the Plaza Hotel.[58] A gift to the city from Huntington Hartford, the heir to the A&P supermarket-chain fortune who also commissioned Stone to design his Gallery of Modern Art (see chapter 9), the café was intended as a site-sensitive building that would be "gay, accessible, ornamental, and within the means of the average family and tourist."[59] Stone's design consisted of a two-story pavilion with sliding walls of glass deeply recessed beneath overhangs and cantilevered balconies facing the park. The 40-foot-wide, 240-foot-long building, accommodating approximately 500 diners, was to be pushed tight up against Central Park South, where it would be entered at grade; a lower level would open directly to the park. In a statement about his gift, Hartford said: "We are constantly asked why New York, the city of offices and indoor living, seems to be lacking in a certain leisurely charm, that atmosphere almost of country, which is so

characteristic of many of the older European capitals. With the current sprouting of skyscrapers on all sides . . . there is a pressing need in New York for renewed emphasis on the out-of-doors and the happy leisure which ought to go with it."[60]

Despite the donor's good intentions, the project caused an immediate furor. The day after the gift was announced, the *New York Times*, in a startling move, argued that "we are against any more invasions into Central Park, so beloved by the public that it has become something special, something almost sacred."[61] In a zealous and single-minded campaign, the *Times* followed this editorial with others on April 19, May 3, May 21, May 26 and June 17. The *Times* was quickly joined in its protest, not only by the usual group of park protectors and citizen groups, including the Citizens Union, Park Association, Fifth Avenue Association, Municipal Art Society, Lexington Democratic Club and Fine Arts Federation, but also by ordinary citizens, who wrote numerous letters against the café to the paper.

In addition, Walter Hoving's Tiffany & Co. went to court to prevent the city from accepting the gift. Sensitive to the impact that the area's increasingly democratic character was having on its "carriage trade" businesses, Hoving argued that the café would "cheapen" the neighborhood. To this charge Moses replied that the café's "clientele will not diminish the number of expense account executives who trade in the area."[62] For Hoving, as for many others, Moses had gone too far: "Some officials in office a long time seem to get a sovereignty complex. . . . Not only do they feel they know better than the rest of us taxpayers, but they ride roughshod sometimes, notably Mr. Moses, whose fine work for many years I have applauded, but whose habitual arrogance, particularly in this situation, I decry."[63] Moses accepted Hartford's gift on March 13, a few months before turning over his post as park commissioner to his handpicked successor, Newbold Morris. Initially doubtful about the café, Morris quickly rallied behind it, pointing out that the project could be easily realized, since all of the required money was already in the city's coffers. By the end of July Bergdorf-Goodman's, the exclusive specialty department store, had joined the protest, as had the New York chapters of the American Society of Landscape Architects and the Appalachian Mountain Club. Though no longer park commissioner, Moses continued to urge Mayor Wagner to go ahead with the pavilion. "The land involved is a neglected corner of the park," he said, "representing less than one-half of 1 per cent of the total area. . . . The original plans for Central Park included restaurants of just this kind and some of them were built."[64]

Meanwhile, the *New York Times* and others argued that the controversial gift be put to a vote of the Board of Estimate. After a hearing on July 28 at which twenty-two people spoke against the café and six rose in its defense, the Board of Estimate unanimously approved the gift of $862,500 from Hartford (including the fee of $112,500 for Stone's services). Tiffany's dropped its suit in September, but Hoving, joined by many civic groups, pursued it on his own behalf.

Design drawings, finished in February 1961, called for a 32-foot-wide, 160-foot-long building, smaller than the one originally announced. But the slow progress of Hoving's suit through the courts held construction up and costs spiraled, rising to $1.7 million by June 1961. In March 1962, at the behest of Moses and Morris, Hartford paid $5,000 to print a brochure promoting the project. Again the *New York Times* editorialized against the pavilion, asking that Hartford's money be used to acquire parkland in one of the city's slums. Hoving's suit reached the New York State Supreme Court in June 1963. On August 26,

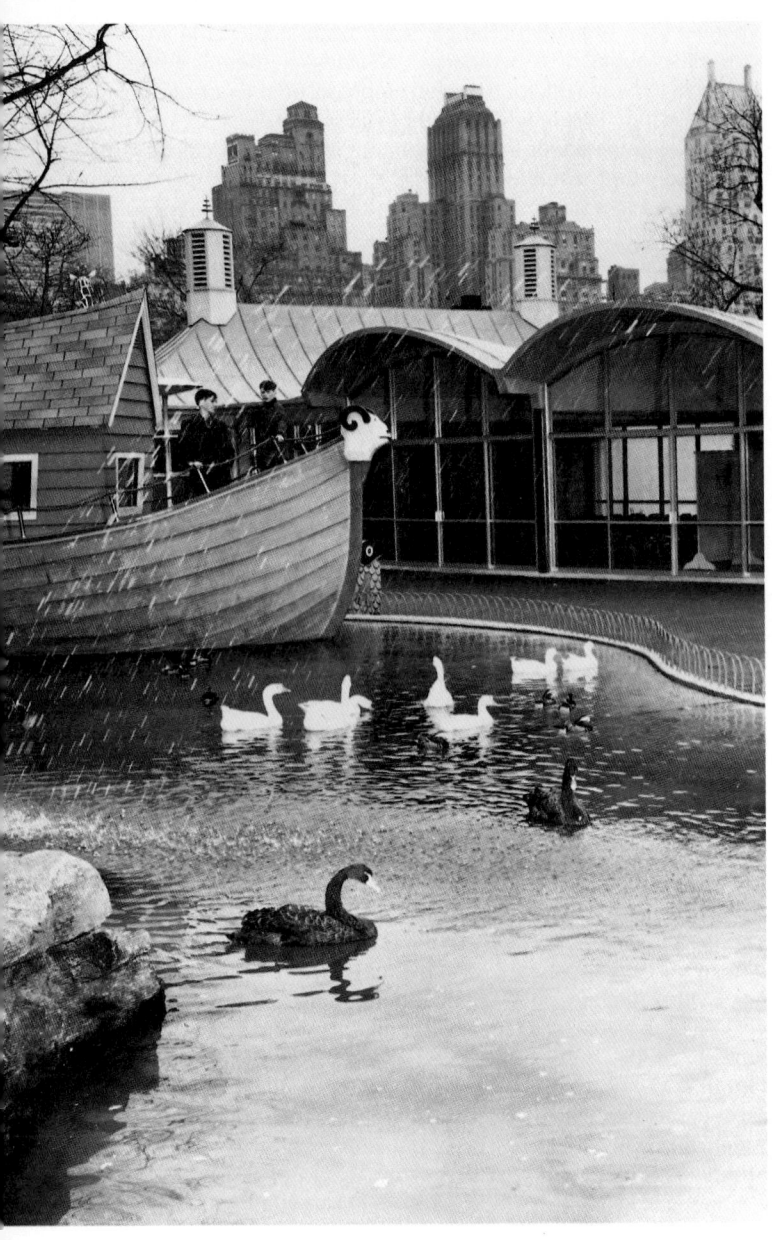

Children's Zoo, near Fifth Avenue, between East Sixty-fifth and East Sixty-sixth streets. Edward Coe Embury, 1961. View to the southwest. MA

1963, Judge Jacob Markowitz ruled in favor of the city, volunteering the opinion that the café would "extend the present dimensions of Central Park by a unique distinctive and cultural addition."[65] On March 26, 1964, after the Appellate Division also ruled in favor of the city, Hoving announced that he would seek a reversal of Markowitz's decision in the Court of Appeals, the state's highest court. A year later, on March 11, 1965, this court also supported the city in a 5-2 decision.

After this last ruling Ada Louise Huxtable lashed out against the café and Stone's proposed General Motors Building (see chapter 5) in an ongoing *New York Times* series called "How to Kill a City."[66] When in the spring of 1965 Huntington Hartford began to make noises about the swelling costs of underwriting his Gallery of Modern Art, the *Times* suggested that the city excuse him from his café gift, thereby freeing up additional funds for the museum.[67] In June 1965 the editors of *Progressive Architecture* reviewed the proposed pavilion in most unfavorable terms, calling it a saloon, a critique that Commissioner Morris labeled "a dreadful distortion."[68] In September 1965 opponents of the pavilion gained a new and ultimately important ally when Congressman John V. Lindsay, seeking the office of mayor, came out against it. In his white paper on the city's parks, prepared by Walter Hoving's son, Thomas P. F. Hoving, a curator at the Metropolitan Museum of Art whom Lindsay would later appoint as park commissioner, Lindsay said: "I will do everything I can to stop the construction of this restaurant, to which almost every citizen's group interested in the beautification of the city is opposed. . . . A certain type of restaurant is needed in Central Park, but not necessarily the complex structure Mr. Hartford envisioned."[69]

Lindsay was elected in November 1965, and in the following month, in an effort to save the project, Hartford asked Stone to modify the design, lowering the pavilion so that its roof was flush with street level. On February 15, 1966, Mayor Lindsay and Commissioner Hoving met with Hartford and Stone at City Hall, and the project seemed to be dropped, once and for all. But in August, in a last-ditch attempt, Hartford offered the city $1 million for the construction of recreational facilities in the Bedford-Stuyvesant area of Brooklyn, contingent on his being allowed to go forward with the café. Rejecting the offer, Hoving declared that Hartford was displaying "irresponsible philanthropy" and proffering a "carrot on a warped stick."[70] Later Hartford revised his position and offered money for the Brooklyn project with no strings attached, only to change his mind once again soon thereafter. In any case, the café was not to be.

Though many of Morris's efforts as park commissioner were failures, one or two of his projects met with some success, in particular the Children's Zoo (1961), which enlivened the pitlike space just west of Fifth Avenue between the redesigned access roads of the Sixty-fifth Street transverse.[71] The gift of former New York State Governor and Mrs. Herbert H. Lehman, the Children's Zoo, occupying one acre, was housed in an appropriately lighthearted if somewhat clumsy combination of Modernist and vernacular-inspired buildings designed by Edward Coe Embury, the son of Aymar Embury II. The zoo included a child-size Noah's Ark made of California redwood. The entrance to the zoo, which adults could visit only if accompanied by a child, was through an extensively glazed Modernist building, the roof of which incorporated a series of shallow vaults. Equally popular was the Delacorte Clock (1965), which surmounted a triple-arched, red-brick gateway, also designed by Edward Coe Embury.[72] Built along the path connecting the main zoo with the Children's Zoo, the gateway incorporated a cupolalike clock tower that rose through a wrought-iron loggia to support a bell rung on the half hour by two bronze monkeys, the work of sculptor Andrea Spadini and designer Fernando Texidor.

Not so successful was Morris's last major project for Central Park, the Loula D. Lasker Memorial (1966), a large-scale facility that accommodated swimmers in summer and ice skaters in winter.[73] Designed by Fordyce & Hamby, the Lasker Memorial sat at the south end of Harlem Meer, a location that some observers objected to because it implied de facto racial segregation, given that the skating rink component duplicated similar facilities at the Wollman Memorial, which was far more accessible to all citizens via public transportation and would become even more "lily white" than it already was. The Lasker Memorial's design was technologically ingenious: the floor slab beneath the 3'6"-deep oval swimming pool was served by refrigerant piping, which could transform it into a 28,000-square-foot skating rink in winter. Although the project was announced in 1962, the pool was plagued by technical problems and was not opened until after Morris had left office, at which time Ada Louise Huxtable dismissed it as "an oppressively jazzed-up military installation of saw-toothed trimmed concrete."[74]

In May 1964 the integrity of Central Park was subjected to perhaps its greatest threat ever when Frank L. Lazarus, commissioner of the Department of Real Estate, presented a plan to the executive committee of the Mayor's Housing Policy Board calling for the conversion of all parkland above 106th Street to public housing and the redistribution of the equivalent lost acreage to neighborhood parks in Central Harlem south of 123rd Street.[75] Lazarus's plan was motivated by the increasing difficulties his department was having in relocating tenants from sites designated for new housing. Greeted by widespread criticism in and out of government circles, the plan was quickly dropped.

The Hoving Happening

On December 1, 1965, Mayor-elect Lindsay announced that he would replace Park Commissioner Newbold Morris with Thomas P. F. Hoving.[76] The thirty-four-year-old Hoving had been trained in art history at Princeton, where he received his B.A. in 1953 and his Ph.D. in 1959. He immediately went to work at the Metropolitan Museum of Art, where he quickly rose to the position of curator of the Cloisters.

From the start of his appointment as park commissioner, Hoving was intent on changing the public's perception of what a park could be, proclaiming that "the old rinkydink, hand-me-down stereotype of park is out, OUT!"[77] Hoving viewed New York's parks not only as a vital aspect of the physical cityscape but as an integral part of New York's cultural life, a stance that would be reflected in 1968 in the Park Department's reorganization as one of the city's new "superagencies" and in its redesignation as the Department of Parks, Recreation and Cultural Affairs. (In 1976 the department would be reorganized once again, becoming the Department of Parks and Recreation.) While Hoving's principal commitment was to the idea that parks were public theaters, he was also sensitive to the fact that most of the facilities, though dilapidated, were incomparable works of art as much in need of conservation as any painting in a museum. Before taking office, Hoving announced the appointment of Henry Hope Reed as curator of Central Park, an idea first advanced in the white paper on parks he had put together for Lindsay's campaign.[78] Clay Lancaster, a historian who specialized in the architecture of Brooklyn Heights, was

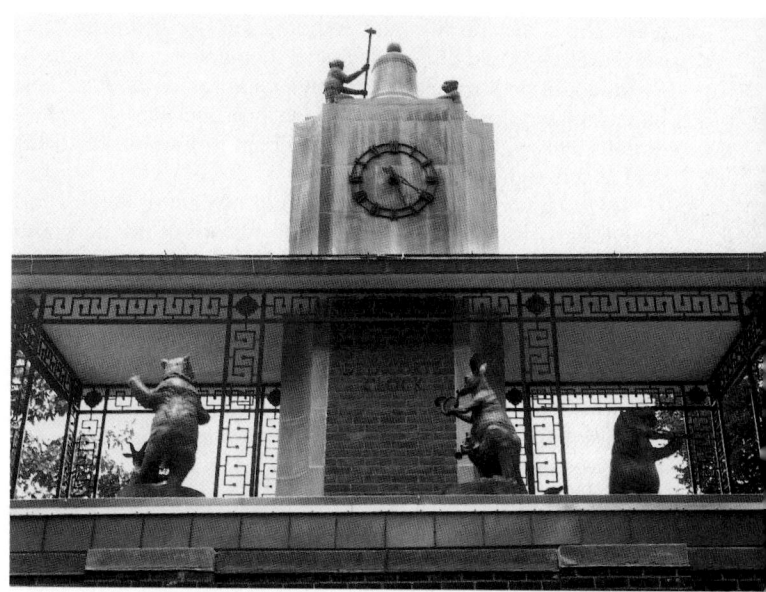

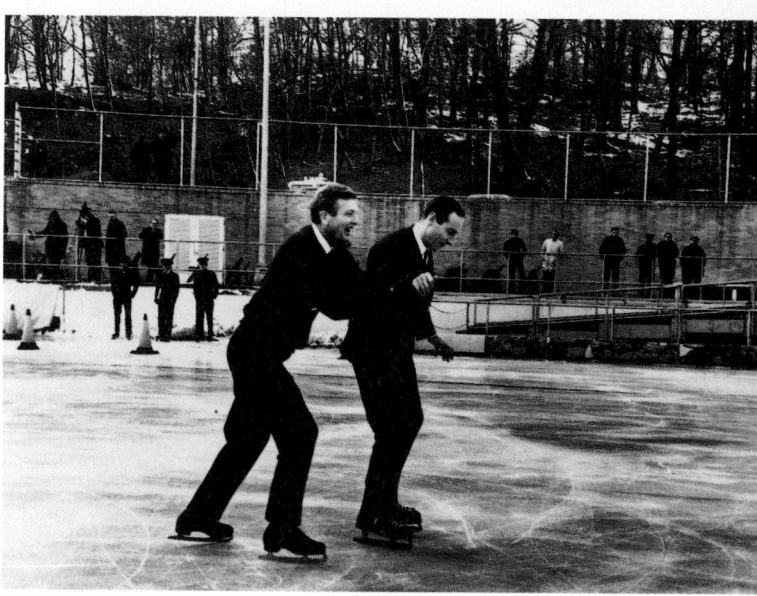

Top: Delacorte Clock, near Fifth Avenue and East Sixty-fifth Street. Edward Coe Embury, 1965. View to the north. NYCPPA

Bottom: Mayor John V. Lindsay (left) and Park Commissioner Thomas P. F. Hoving (right) at the dedication of the Loula D. Lasker Memorial, 1966. NYCPPA

given the same job title and responsibility for Prospect Park. The curators would bring a degree of scholarship to park affairs: Reed would help write a history and guide to Central Park, and Lancaster would publish a guide to Prospect Park.[79] Subsequently Hoving added Arthur Rosenblatt, an architect, to his staff as a design consultant.

Hoving had envisioned the curator of Central Park as "an individual who knows intimately the history of the park and who would be able to give professional advice on the repair and reconstruction of its original elements." In addition, Hoving said, the curator would "gather together all the sketches, plans, watercolors, and charts of the original plan of Central Park, in order to have exact reconstructions made of certain of the now missing elements, in the same accurate manner that Colonial Williamsburg has been brought to life."[80] Reed, an antiquarian and impassioned polemicist for the City Beautiful Classicism of fin-de-siècle New York, was an odd but interesting choice. His walking tours of the historic city had done a great deal to expand interest in and appreciation of architecture among middle-class New Yorkers, while his book, *The Golden City* (1959), was an influential polemic against architectural Modernism.[81] Some people, especially architects, were concerned about Reed's selection, described by the editors of *Progressive Architecture* as "hinting at the dangerous influence of a curator exclusively oriented toward the architectural past."[82]

After taking office on January 6, 1966, Hoving seemed to transform the city's park system—or, more accurately, the public's attitude toward parks—overnight. As *Newsweek* put it after less than six months of Hoving's stewardship, a "summer romance" was blooming between Hoving and the average New Yorker.[83] Taking a leaf from the art scene, and anticipating the participatory spirit that would sweep the younger generation in a year or two, Hoving initiated a series of "happenings" in Central Park that included an uninhibited mass "paint-out," a high-spirited game of capture the flag played by sixty youngsters and a colorful Gay Nineties costume party.[84] He gave a kite party, though kites had been officially banned in the park since 1906 because they scared horses.[85] "'Parks are for people' is the most leaden statement, but it's true," Hoving said after the madcap events of his first summer as commissioner. "Recreational facilities should have a flair. They should be spontaneous, offbeat, with a slight tinge of potlatch—letting everything go."[86] In keeping with his belief that Central Park, as a public work of environmental art, had to be experienced in as many different ways as possible by as many different people as possible, Hoving banned automobiles from the park drives on Sunday morning so that bicyclists would have a time all their own and trees could get a break from carbon monoxide. He also organized a music festival at the Wollman Memorial that featured leading pop and jazz entertainers. "A park is like a stage," he said. "If you leave it sitting, nothing good is going to happen. Parks . . . should teach and enrich and relax and inspire and be like works of art for the entire city to enjoy. We're trying to light up the city, and the more lights the better."[87]

By late summer 1966 Hoving began to give physical expression to his concept of the park as theater. In August, at a lively press brunch, Hoving dedicated the Fountain Café, a sophisticated alfresco dining place on the Bethesda Terrace.[88] By the 1950s the Bethesda Fountain and Terrace (Calvert Vaux and Jacob Wrey Mould, 1868–73), though much photographed and admired, had taken on an image of decayed magnificence that

was a far cry from the joyous pageantry originally intended.[89] In 1962 the fountain was scheduled for its first restoration since it was completed, with repairs slated for broken statuary and ornamental balustrades as well as its malfunctioning water system.[90] But the work was merely a stopgap measure. Hoving changed all that, first by raising $50,000 from park benefactor George T. Delacorte for an elegant and popularly priced restaurant, then by hiring the New Orleans architect James Lamantia to create the facility and luring the successfully stylish Restaurant Associates organization to run it.

Lamantia, who consulted with designer Elizabeth Gordon, created two seating areas: an area in the central panel of the terrace where 200 diners would be seated and waited on, and a more popular area to either side where diners could find their own seats after picking up food at two new lakeside kiosks. Kitchen facilities were neatly tucked away in the arcade that had originally been designed to lead pedestrians from the Mall to the water's edge. Lamantia's scheme was extremely simple. To provide shelter from sun and rain, he designed two tents draped in brown and beige canvas and asymmetrically massed to emphasize the central area. The tents' principal columns were extended upward through the fabric to support illuminated globes. The two kiosks, with their low-pitched copper roofs, deferred to the character of the historic architecture. Emma Stebbins's statue, *Angel of the Waters*, seemed to float above it all with more joy than ever. As Lamantia put it: "This microcosm of Classicism was our handsome background, giving us little to do but respect the setting and blend with it."[91]

The decision to quickly install a café at Bethesda Fountain was certainly affected by the ongoing battle against Huntington Hartford's café (see above), a battle that had been initiated by Hoving's father, Walter, and that was concluded only as final plans for the Fountain Café were being made. As James Burns observed: "Comparison will inevitably be made between this eating facility and the notorious Huntington Hartford Cafe. . . . It should be noted that Lamantia's plan utilizes with tact and sympathy an existing park landmark that needed such a solid *raison d'etre*, whereas the Hartford building would have been erected over virgin parkland right at the main entrance to the park, for all the world like a high-class Coney Island."[92] Ada Louise Huxtable also viewed the Bethesda restaurant in favorable contrast to the Hartford disaster: "Comparison with the abortive Hartford cafe, argued in and out of the park's southeast corner for years and finally quashed, is instructive. That pretentiously formal snack bar would have bulldozed a serene spot of rocks and greenery, where it is most necessary, to place the facility where it is least needed, bordering a congested avenue. The Fountain Cafe, on the other hand, uproots nothing."[93]

Not content with the Fountain Café, Hoving set out to create a prototypical facility he had called for in his white paper, a model for "a series of colorful restaurant kiosks surrounded by small tables and chairs" that could be built in various locations in any number of parks.[94] To generate ideas for this kiosk restaurant Hoving organized a design competition, the first to be sponsored by the Park Department since 1907.[95] The Horn & Hardart food company, which contributed the $2,000 prize money, was expected to build and operate one prototype. The winning proposal, by twenty-nine-year-old architect William Maurer, was described by Hoving as an "imaginative, pleasantly temporary, prefabricated, knock-down modular design."[96] It consisted of seven colorful building-block-like units—looking like dressed-up milk cartons—each containing separate refreshment facilities. "To contrast with the openness of the parkscape," Maurer

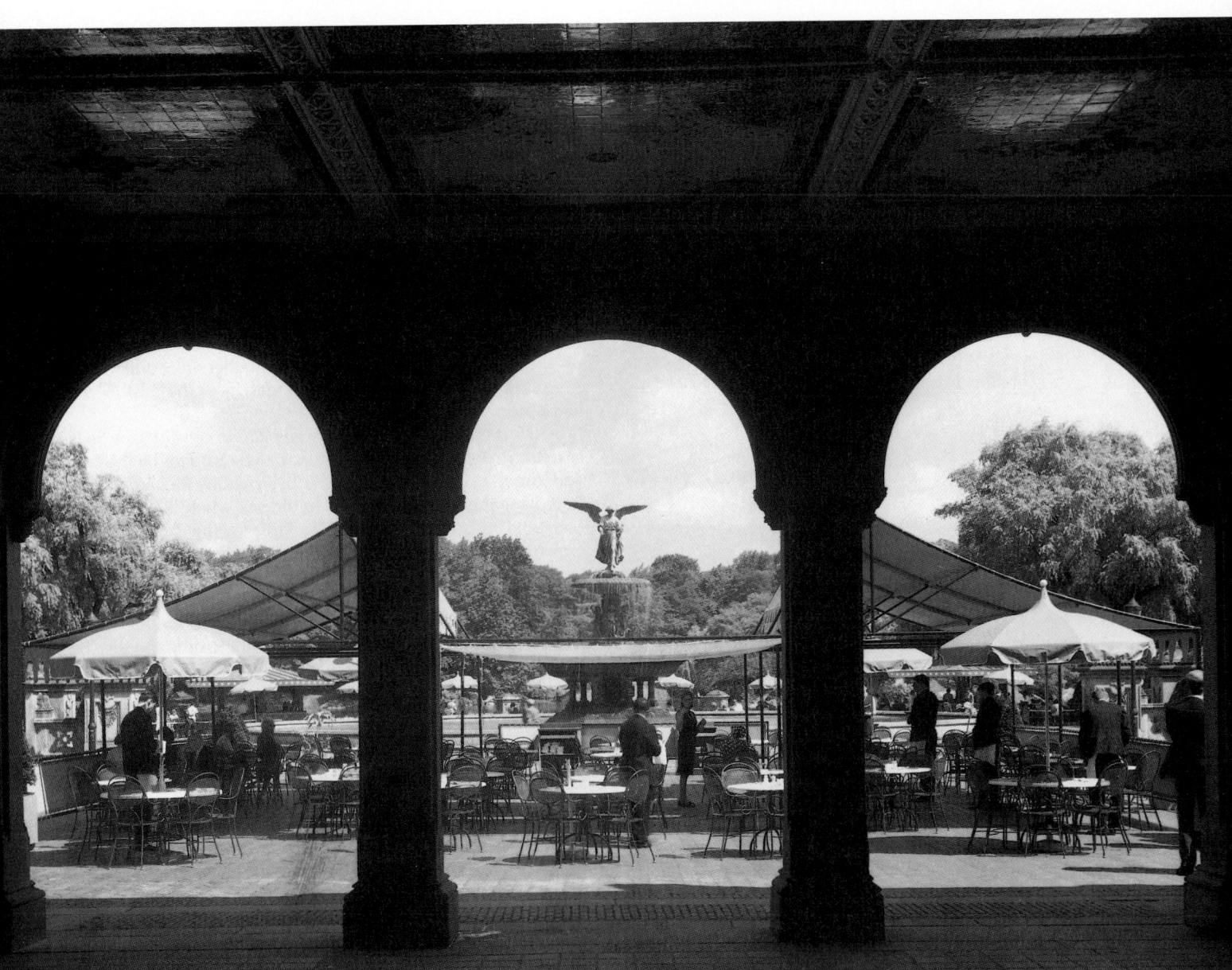

Fountain Café, at Bethesda Fountain and Terrace (Calvert Vaux and
Jacob Wrey Mould, 1868–73; sculpture by Emma Stebbins), north side
of Seventy-second Street cross drive. James Lamantia in association
with Elizabeth Gordon, 1966. View to the north with Bethesda
Fountain in center. Stoller. ©ESTO

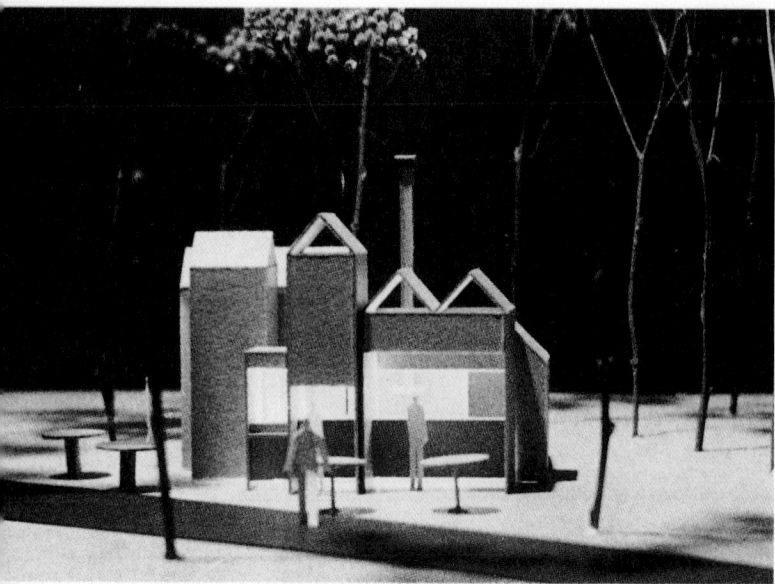

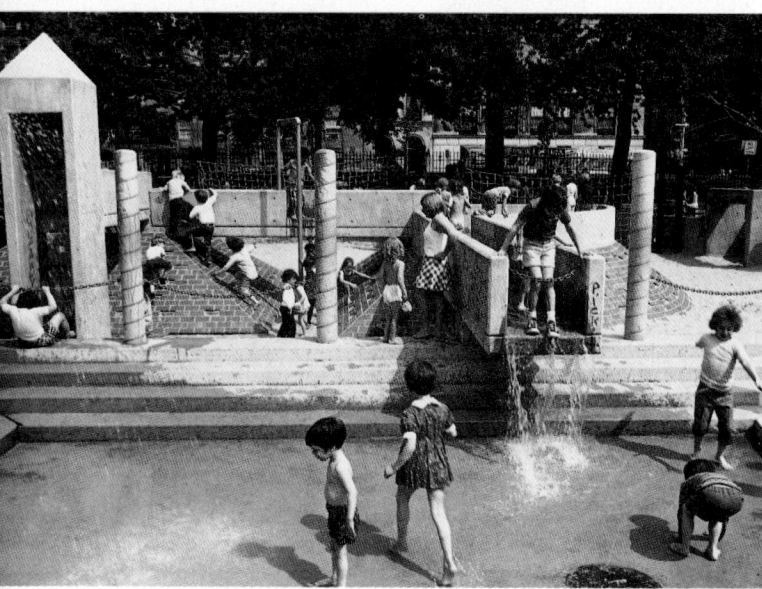

Top: Proposal for Central Park kiosk restaurant. William Maurer, 1966. Model. WM

Bottom: Ancient Play Garden, near Fifth Avenue, between East Eighty-fifth and East Eighty-sixth streets. Richard Dattner, 1972. View to the east. RD

explained, "I was led to a plan for small tower enclosures. The bazaar-like nature of the enclosures also expresses the individual functions of the kiosk and, therefore, gives the scheme aesthetic strength."[97] The kiosks were intended to be portable structures that could be set on asphalt or grass. Tables and chairs would be gathered around to complete the café facility. Huxtable liked Maurer's design, which she labeled "Toy, or Dollhouse Modern," and said it provided "charm without frills." But she questioned whether the competition jury, which included the Classicist Henry Hope Reed and the Modernist architect Paul Rudolph, fully recognized the spirit of the program, which called for a new design that would "re-establish" Olmsted and Vaux's "original design intent."[98] Hoving, however, was happy with this modest proposal, which he celebrated as "the end to the stereotyped, tired and rather rinky-dink type of structures which have marked park design in the past."[99] The kiosk proposal was never realized.

In June 1966 Hoving announced plans to construct the Sixty-seventh Street Adventure Playground, to be paid for by the Estée and Joseph Lauder Foundation.[100] Designed by Richard Dattner to replace the playground next to the site where Robert Moses had tried to create additional parking for the Tavern on the Green (see above), it marked a bold departure from the standard facility of swings, slides and climbing bars that Moses had introduced in 1934. Speaking on behalf of his parents, Leonard Lauder said that "the family had first wanted to do this several years ago when many of our friends were fleeing the city because they thought New York was not the place to bring up children. We decided to build several of these to give the city just this little lift."[101] The playground, which opened in May 1967, was based on the "adventure idea" of participatory play, which encouraged kids to build up and tear down environments, an idea first developed in Scandinavia and Britain, where bombed-out wastelands left over from World War II provided unprogrammed play opportunities for children. Central Park's version principally served the children of the Upper West Side, where the Mothers' Committee to Improve the West 67th Street Playground had lobbied for the project. These youngsters, who, according to *Progressive Architecture*, had "neither the wastes of Europe nor the alleys of Harlem to intrigue" them, were given a sanitized interpretation, with a splashing pool, a sailboat channel, climbing poles and mounds, a bumpy slide, cargo netting, a puppet theater, tree houses and pits, and a jumble of wooden poles.[102]

In 1972 Dattner completed a second adventure playground, the Ancient Play Garden, located near Fifth Avenue, between Eighty-fifth and Eighty-sixth streets.[103] The playground's child-scaled pyramid, sundial, river and amphitheater seemed very much at home on the site, which was slated to become the front yard of the Metropolitan Museum's expanded Egyptology wing housing the Temple of Dendur. In the same year plans were unveiled for yet another imaginative playground funded by the Lauders: Discovery Play Park, which was conceived by local mothers five years earlier and built at 100th Street and Central Park West to the designs of Ross-Ryan Jacquette Architectural Associates.[104]

Despite Hoving's innovations, he also fell victim to the memorializing impulses that had afflicted his predecessors. In October 1966 Hoving's announcement of a plan to erect a life-size bronze statue of Mary Poppins, the fictional nanny created in 1934 by the writer P. L. Travers and given a new lease on life in a 1964 film, drew hoots from the public and the *New York Times*.[105] Even more controversial was a proposal to designate

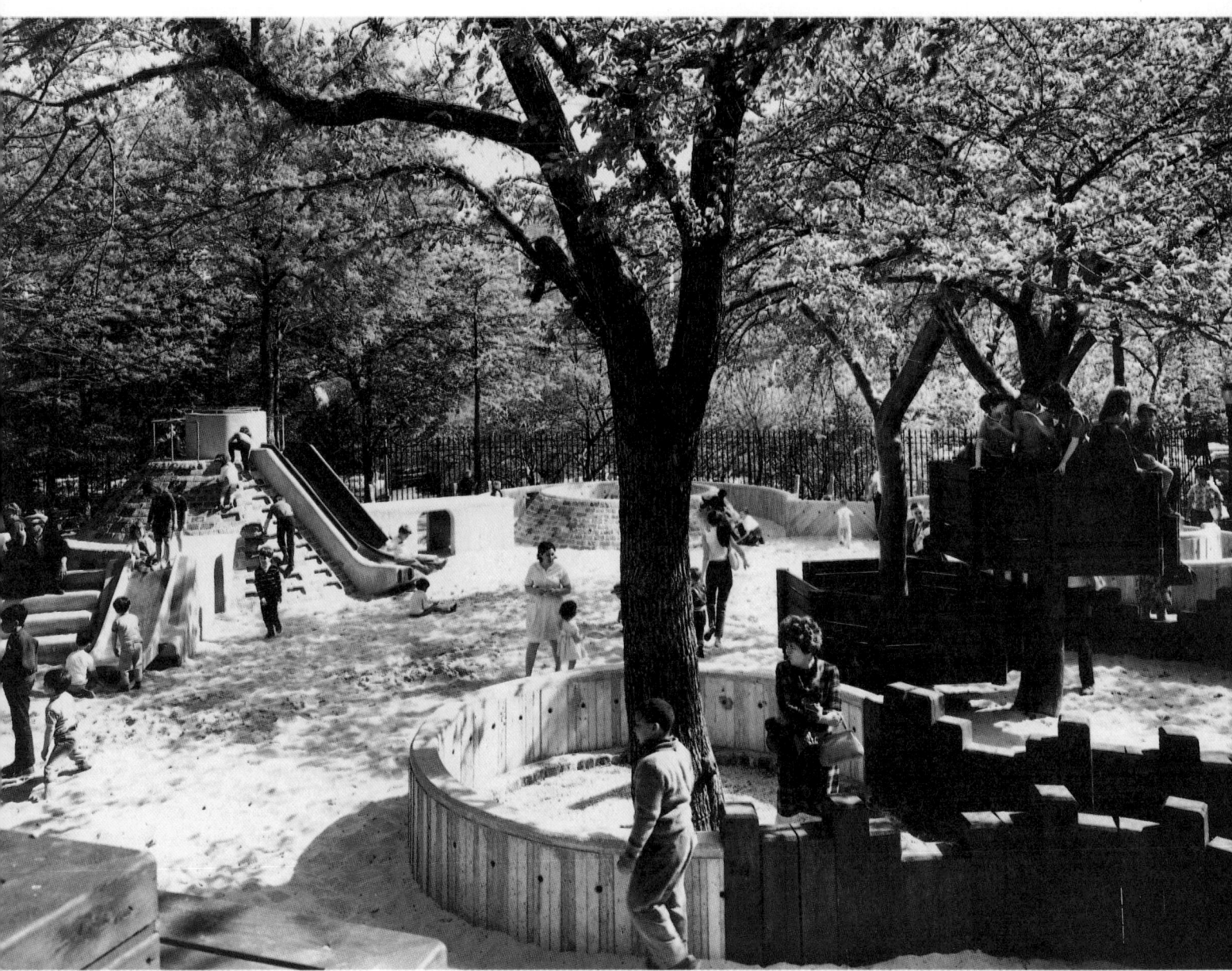

Sixty-seventh Street Adventure Playground, near Central Park West and
West Sixty-seventh Street. Richard Dattner, 1966. View to the
southeast. RD

an area in the park's northern reaches to function as a "sort of revolving world's fair."[106] Hoving announced the idea after a four-day visit to Mexico, where he was persuaded to help the country promote its bid to be host of the 1968 Olympic Games by allowing it to build a pavilion in the park that would include small refreshment kiosks and a restaurant, where diners would be serenaded by Mexican bands. The *New York Times* was not pleased:

> Central Park is not a handy Olympics tie-in. It is not a fairground, exhibition gallery, hall of fame or spawning ground for juvenile literary immortals in second-rate statuary. It is not Disneyland—yet. Mr. Hoving can breathlessly promote castle-building, flag-catching, and his other assorted energetic but harmless activities until exhaustion or ennui sets in. His parks-for-pleasure philosophy has been commendable; and until now we have admired his imaginative sensitivity in avoiding destructive installations to serve his roving festival needs.[107]

Hoving's plans for both projects did not go forward.

On October 1, 1966, Hoving announced plans for a combined police station house, stable and riding ring, the first and as it turned out the only important capital improvement he would propose for Central Park during his term of office.[108] Five firms were invited to compete for $100,000 in prize money, contributed by Stephen R. Currier, head of Urban America, Inc., a nonprofit organization interested in improving the quality of American cities, with the winner receiving the commission. The participating firms were Edward Larrabee Barnes; Marcel Breuer & Associates; Kelly & Gruzen; Philip Johnson; and Whittlesey, Conklin & Rossant. The site for the new facility lay behind the 22nd Precinct station house on the south side of the Eighty-sixth Street transverse. The new police complex would house stables and a riding school and would become home to National Guard Squadron A, known for its polo playing. The squadron had been housed in the 94th Street Armory until that building was largely torn down to make way for a school and playground (see chapter 16). Though the competition was the brainchild of Currier and Hoving, the stables project had been initiated by Newbold Morris, who had commissioned a banal design from Eggers & Higgins.

The jury consisted of Hoving, Currier, Police Commissioner Howard R. Leary, the landscape architect M. Paul Friedberg and the architects Peter Blake, William Breger, Lewis Davis, I. M. Pei, Arthur Rosenblatt and Paul Rudolph. While intended as an effort to raise the aesthetic quality of civic architecture, the competition was also calculated to defuse opposition to the project, which immediately raised objections among dedicated opponents of encroachment, who had been appalled by the previous administration's proposal. The competition program was drawn up by the architects Bentel & Bentel, who toured similar facilities throughout the world in preparation. Though a portion of lawn was to be sacrificed to provide space for a full-size spectator riding ring for horse shows, polo and the training of police horses, most of the facility would replace a parking lot and workshop buildings. In addition, competitors were required to incorporate Calvert Vaux's Central Park Stable (1870) into their design. The architects were allotted a total of eight acres of land on which to plan four acres of buildings and two and a half acres of access roads, loading areas and parking lots.

Even before the results of the competition were announced, Save Central Park, a newly organized committee chaired by Richard Edes Harrison, protested two "dangerous precedents" set by the project: the establishment of the park's first arena for indoor sports, and the building of its first structure for city services not related to the park.[109] In February 1967 the selection of Kelly & Gruzen's proposal was announced. The scheme, which took maximum advantage of the sloping site, accommodated the 110 horse stalls required by the police department and the 220 needed for private citizens under a three-acre roof covered by an orchard of flowering crab apple trees planted in three feet of earth. An outdoor riding ring, circled by a thirty-foot earth mound, would be directly to the west of the orchard; beneath the ring would be a similar facility. A new station house for the 22nd Precinct was to be burrowed into the hill north of the riding facility; to minimize the intrusion on the historic landscape, the building's one exposed wall was to be clad in the same granite as the walls that bound the Eighty-sixth Street transverse road. All in all, the architects claimed, the amount of building covered by landscape would equal 95 percent of the ten-acre site. At least one disgruntled member of the jury felt that the scheme had been selected for "negative" reasons—that is, because it was the least visible. That certainly could not be said of Whittlesey, Conklin & Rossant's second-prize winner, which hung a forty-foot-high roof structure from compression rings at the top of radial steel columns to create a "mountain-like landscape form." Philip Johnson's proposal, which aimed to preserve the site "to the greatest degree" so that "the buildings almost vanish," made a virtue of the vast roof expanse by creating a terrace level high enough to provide a view of the reservoir.[110]

Though Kelly & Gruzen's proposal promised a comparatively invisible building, it won no converts from among park preservationists, who were against the project no matter how it was designed. On February 12, 1967, five days before the designs were released, Save Central Park wired Mayor Lindsay to protest the construction of anything except the police precinct station; even Hoving's own appointee, Henry Hope Reed, was against it, as was Mayor Lindsay's political mentor, Bethuel M. Webster,[111] and the Park Association, whose president, Sheldon Oliensis, said, "A beautifully designed encroachment is an encroachment nonetheless."[112] In mid-March a mass protest was held on the Great Lawn, with elaborate signboards hoisted in the air by picketing children and adults. Richard Edes Harrison, who carried a sign saying "Repent. The end of the park is near," claimed that the stable's roof would be highly visible, especially from the Belvedere Terrace. "The architects claim their scheme is unobtrusive," he stated, "for the same reason the Park Department blanked out the word 'polo' on their drawings—salesmanship. Actually, this high building, whose top is more than an acre, will loom over the middle of the park like a Mayan pyramid."[113]

Ada Louise Huxtable, perhaps under some pressure from the management of the *New York Times*, which supported the scheme, neatly avoided the issue of the design, but not of the project's appropriateness, pointing out in detail the number of encroachments that had usurped park space over the years.[114] On March 12, just a few days before leaving his post as commissioner, Hoving grudgingly bowed to public pressure by modifying the project's scope: "We will take off the top ring and reduce the size of the one under it," he said, "so that those fools who call it a polo field can put an end to this mendacious piece of talk."[115] Though the *Times* editorialized in favor of the compromise scheme, the Park Association, among others, remained opposed. But on March 13, at the behest of the City Council and the Board of Estimate, Hoving's revisions were adopted.

Two years later, on February 17, 1969, Hoving's successor, August Heckscher, released revised plans, also prepared by the Gruzen firm, trimming the project back even further: gone were

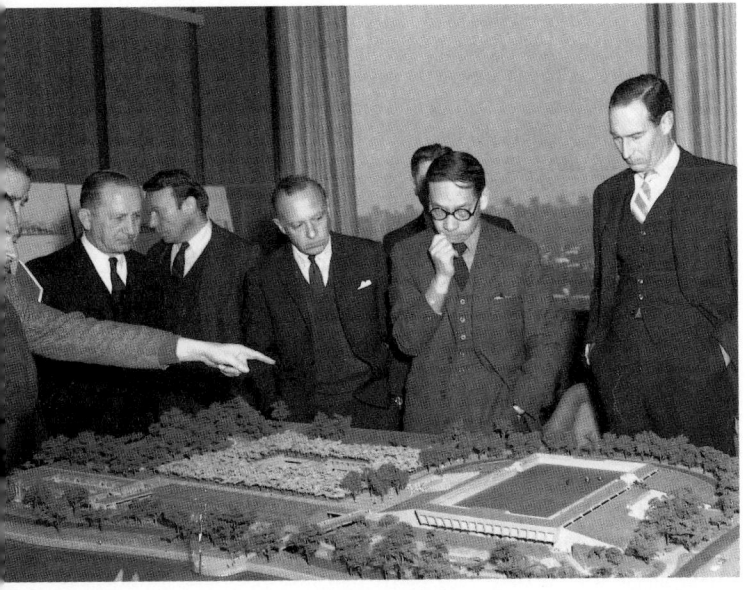

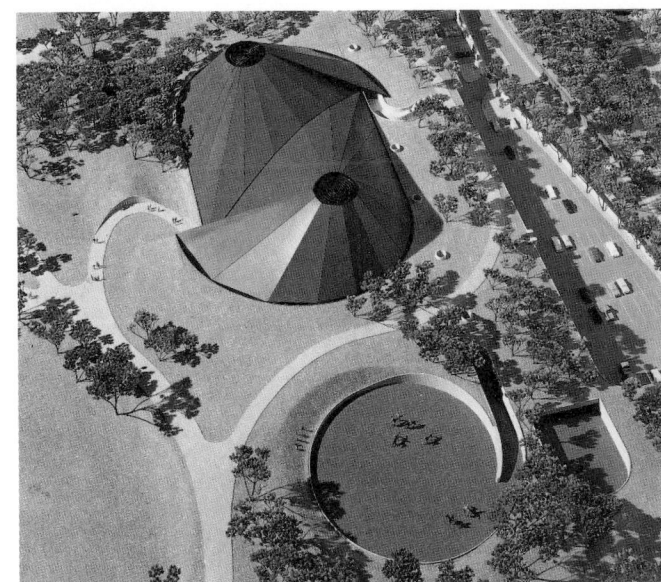

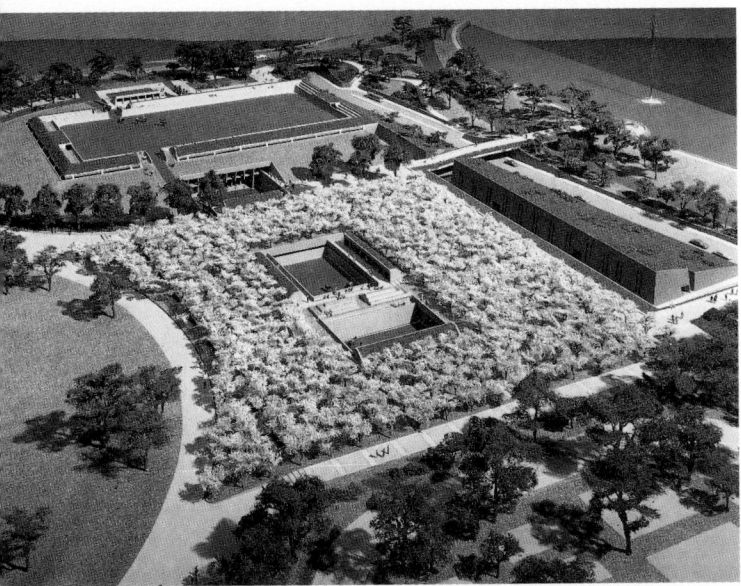

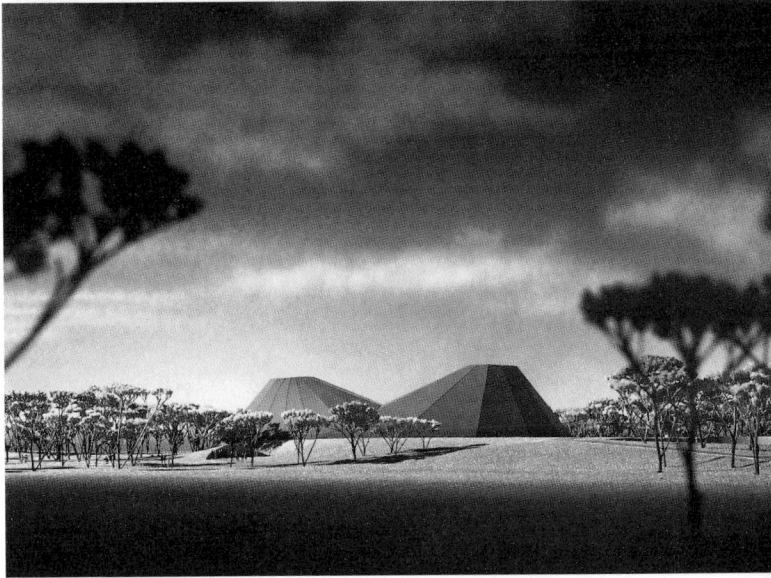

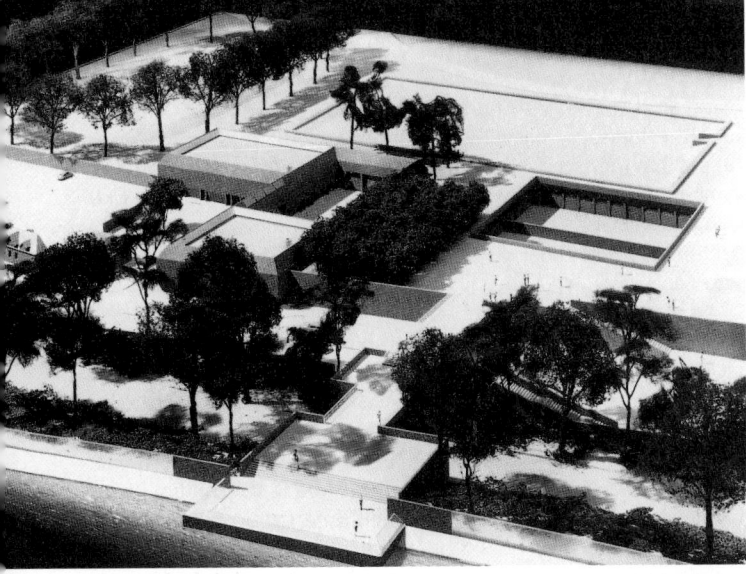

Top left: Design jury for Central Park stables competition showing Arthur Rosenblatt on the far left, Peter Blake in the center and I. M. Pei and Thomas P. F. Hoving on the right. A model of Kelly & Gruzen's winning proposal is below. NYCPPA

Center left: Proposal for Central Park stables, south of Eighty-fifth Street Transverse Road. Kelly & Gruzen, 1966. Model. View to the northwest. Checkman. GS

Bottom left: Proposal for Central Park stables, south of Eighty-fifth Street Transverse Road. Philip Johnson, 1966. Model. View to the southeast. Checkman. PJA

Top right: Proposal for Central Park stables, south of Eighty-fifth Street Transverse Road. Whittlesey, Conklin & Rossant, 1966. Model. View to the northwest. Checkman. CR

Center right: Proposal for Central Park stables. Whittlesey, Conklin & Rossant, 1966. Model. View to the north. Checkman. CR

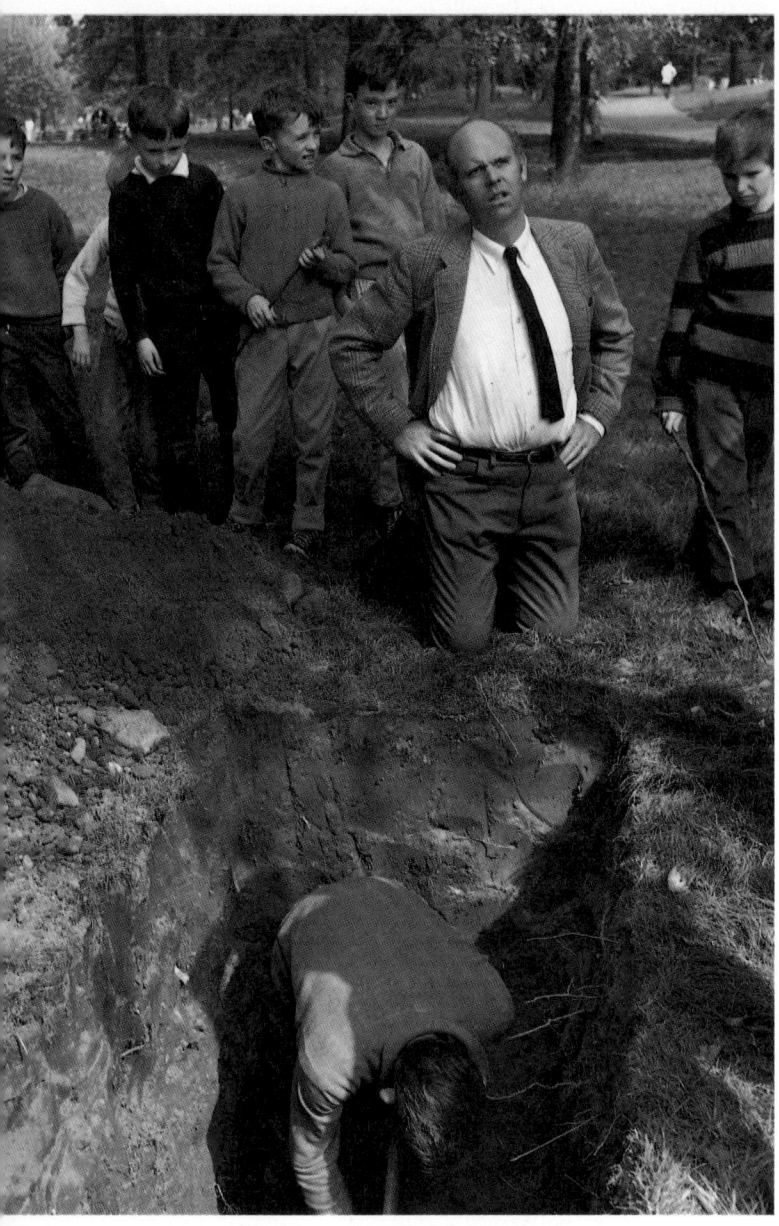

Buried Piece. Claes Oldenburg, 1967. Oldenburg at sculpture site.
NYCPPA

the outdoor ring, one of the two corrals for privately owned horses, and the 3,000 spectator seats; the Vaux-designed stables along the transverse road were preserved, perhaps to be rehabilitated as a museum. Groundbreaking for the revised scheme was scheduled for 1970. But the Park Association remained opposed, and the endorsement from the *New York Times* was far more qualified than it had been two years before, a reflection, perhaps, of the changed public mood. Though the Board of Estimate and the City Council continued to permit the stables to be carried as an item in the city's 1969–70 capital budget, $2.6 million was slashed from the $4.8 million initially approved. A year later the project came under political fire once again, and Gruzen's design was scuttled by the Board of Estimate and the City Council in favor of a new plan that would eliminate the public stables. Richard Edes Harrison rejoiced, pointing out that the revised project eliminated not only the public stables but also administrative offices for the mounted police, over 80 percent of the stalls for police horses and the riding school, which had been the principal functional feature of the "huge and objectionable" riding hall.[116] Meanwhile, the 185-rider mounted police corps continued to make do with temporary quarters in a converted taxi garage at West Fifty-fifth Street and Tenth Avenue, and the Claremont stables on West Eighty-ninth Street remained, albeit under threat of demolition for urban renewal.

Preserving the People's Park

In May 1966 Hoving's mentor, James J. Rorimer, director of the Metropolitan Museum of Art, died suddenly, leaving the way open for the commissioner to return to the museum as his successor. The museum's trustees appointed Hoving to the post in December 1966, a controversial decision given his short, flamboyant career in public life. Hoving's successor as park commissioner, August Heckscher, who took office on March 16, 1967, was a very different type of person: quiet, contemplative, something of a philosopher, a man of inherited wealth who also had a sense of public responsibility.[117] Asked at his swearing in whether he would follow in Hoving's footsteps, Heckscher replied: "I won't do exactly what Tom did. We had Hoving Happenings and now we will have Heckscher Occurrences."[118]

Heckscher's "occurrences" were surely more high-minded than Hoving's happenings, which were mildly spoofed by the artist Claes Oldenburg in 1967. As part of a program organized by Doris Freedman to place thirty-two sculptures throughout the city, Oldenburg lured two grave diggers to the park, where they excavated a six-by-three-foot rectangular space. Finished by lunch, Oldenburg used the mealtime to contemplate the work before having them fill up the hole in the afternoon. "This is a conceptual work of art and is as much valid as something you can actually see," Oldenburg said. "Everything is art if it is chosen by the artist to be art. You can say it is good art or bad art but you can't say it isn't art."[119]

Hoving had been publicly criticized by Henry Hope Reed, his curator of Central Park, for permitting the "commercial invasion" of the park, by which he meant corporate-sponsored "free" concerts, happenings and Shakespeare-in-the-Park. Reed was particularly upset about a concert given by the popular singer Barbra Streisand in 1967.[120] Though the concert, which was sponsored by a beer company, was free to the public, it was taped for future telecasting, at which time sponsors would advertise and Streisand would be paid. As Reed pointed out, such events exacted a physical toll on the park; the thousands of pounds of garbage left on the Sheep Meadow following the Streisand concert took three days to remove. Hoving had characteristically dismissed Reed as a "fuddy duddy," but Reed was not without his supporters.[121] Though the *New York Times* generally favored the public programs that had transformed Central Park into a nighttime entertainment center, they warned that "the public guard must be up constantly if the park's integrity is to be maintained. Two years ago the Federal Government declared Central Park a National Historic Landmark. It can remain so in fact forever—but only if it is not exploited, 'improved' or trampled to death."[122]

Despite such warnings, Heckscher supported popular corporate-sponsored events, explaining that "the various interests of all the people must be reflected in park activities."[123] With public funding drying up as a result of the city's increasingly dismal fiscal situation, Heckscher not only turned to corporations to sponsor public events but also to private benefactors to help with preservation and restoration efforts. Sometimes the best intentions backfired, as in 1972 when, to celebrate its one hundreth anniversary, Bloomingdale's department store offered to pay a large part of the money needed to restore the crumbling Mall.[124] The store got trapped in a controversy over one element of that restoration, a rather trivial design for a sunken outdoor pit housing a theater-in-the-round developed by the Park Department staff in association with Edward Durell Stone for the area near the band shell. The *New York Times* was quick to oppose the project:

> The money for this woefully miscalculated priority would go a long way toward repairing the artful Olmstedian balance of the formal and natural that is the abused and poorly appreciated beauty of Central Park. The "forces of good" persist in its aggressive destruction. Unpopular as the suggestion may be, it is probably time for the Parks Department to draw back a bit on its tireless promotion of culture, fun and games when it encourages irreversible changes in their name. . . . There could be no better activity for a sesquicentennial year than to restudy Olmsted's original great work and its subsequent erosions, for a new master plan with emphasis on restoration and maintenance of planting and features lost and threatened, and their appropriate uses today. And there could be no better place for the generously proposed donation than to fund such a program. No one needs a $300,000 hole in the ground.[125]

Bloomingdale's declined to fund such a study, however, and the project was eventually scrapped. Heckscher had more luck when he enlisted the support of Mrs. Lucy G. Moses and Mrs. Lila Acheson Wallace to rebuild one of Olmsted and Vaux's great glories, the Bow Bridge, which had begun to look, according to the *New Yorker*, "as if it had been mugged."[126] The bridge was reopened in 1974.[127]

With Heckscher as commissioner, the Lindsay administration's attitudes toward parks in general, and Central Park in particular, changed, moving away from mass entertainment and hullabaloo toward the more basic issues of maintenance and conservation. High-minded members of the public were only too willing to concur with this new emphasis. Groups of citizens had already begun to organize themselves to help not only preserve but maintain the parks. Primary among these groups was the Friends of Central Park, organized in 1967. According to Richard Edes Harrison, one of the founding principals of the Friends:

> We want to see more money spent on keeping the Park clean and green, on planting and landscaping. Most of the people who come here just want to walk or sit, to escape from the pavement, noise, and smells of the city. A natural park is its own magnet; it doesn't need Happenings, recreation centers, and all the contrived amusements that could easily be put elsewhere. Fortunately, Happenings come and go, but amusements converted into buildings have a way of remaining.[128]

The conservation effort was furthered by the publication of scholarly works, which helped citizens and administrators alike to better understand and appreciate the park. In 1967 Henry Hope Reed, working together with Sophia Duckworth, published *Central Park: A History and Guide*.[129] The centenary of the park's opening in 1869 inspired a flood of other books discussing Olmsted and the park.[130]

The increased interest in the park's preservation reflected widespread appreciation for the park as an integral, even necessary, aspect of life in New York City.[131] As public support for park conservation grew, fueled by widespread general concern about the ravages of air pollution and local dismay over the impact the city's budget crisis was having on park maintenance, Heckscher increasingly focused on park preservation, while trying to resolve controversies that swirled around the stables project initiated during Hoving's administration (see above), as well as the Metropolitan Museum of Art's plans for expansion (see below). A growing sense of the park's potential not as public theater but as a place for quiet contemplation or outdoor exercise became apparent in the increasing number of walking and jogging trails throughout the park. In fact, the park became the focus of a renewed national interest in physical fitness, most notably running. In 1970 the first New York City Marathon acknowledged the running fad with a twenty-six-mile and 385-yard-long course laid out on park roadways.[132] Of the 126 runners who competed in the first marathon, 55 finished. By 1976 the marathon had attracted a total of 2,002 competitors and the race's course had been extended to encompass all five boroughs, with the finish line in Central Park.

The Subway and Central Park

Late in 1963 the Transit Authority announced plans to build a new subway tunnel to Queens that would run under Sixty-fourth Street, as well as Central Park, in Manhattan.[133] Unlike most of the city's subway lines, which operated under busy, commercial avenues, the proposed Sixty-fourth Street tunnel was to run beneath the park, fashionable Upper East Side residential blocks and the 14.5-acre campus of the world-renowned Rockefeller Institute (see chapter 11). While many park groups and neighborhood residents seemed to accept the inevitable disruption that would accompany the tunnel's construction, officials of the Rockefeller Institute raised a storm of protest.[134] The Transit Authority's plan, news of which reached the institute only through the pages of the newspapers, called for construction of three vertical shafts linking the tunnel with the surface—two for emergency evacuation of passengers and one to be used as a construction shaft—blasted 100 feet down through solid granite on a site at York Avenue and Sixty-fourth Street, just south of the Rockefeller Institute campus. After conversations between institute staff members and the Transit Authority got nowhere, Detlev Bronk, the institute's president, delivered a report to Transit Commissioner John J. Gilhooley outlining the likely adverse consequences to ongoing experimental work and stating that it might prove necessary for the institute to leave New York should the subway plan go forward. By mutual agreement between the Transit Authority and the institute, a team of seismologists, headed by Father Joseph Lynch of Fordham University, was assembled to study the impact the tunnel's construction would have on the institute.

Meanwhile, other groups began to voice objections to the Sixty-fourth Street proposal. In December 1963 the Fifth Avenue Association urged that an earlier Transit Authority plan for a subway tunnel at Sixty-first Street be resuscitated, pointing out that it would provide more advantageous connections with the existing subway system, particularly the Lexington Avenue line.[135] The Sixty-first Street proposal had been abandoned because the East River was forty-two feet deeper at that point than at Sixty-fourth Street, a difference that would mean an estimated $5 million extra for tunneling costs. By February 1964 five other civic groups—the Citizens Budget Commission, the Citizens Union, the Commerce and Industry Association, the Downtown–Lower Manhattan Association and the Queens Chamber of Commerce—had joined with the Fifth Avenue Association in favoring the Sixty-first Street proposal, arguing that the Sixty-first Street site would result in better service and necessitate less damage to Central Park.[136] They also argued that because a Sixty-first Street tunnel would burrow 1,000 fewer feet beneath the park than the Sixty-fourth Street tunnel, at a savings of $3 million to $4 million, the overall cost would not be significantly greater. The groups described the Sixty-fourth Street alternative as a "disastrous mistake";[137] the Citizens Budget Commission ridiculed it as "leading from nowhere to nowhere."[138]

In December 1964 the Transit Authority announced that it would put the tunnel under Sixty-third Street instead of Sixty-fourth Street, which provided, as Richard J. H. Johnston put it in the New York Times, a "solution to the differences that have developed between the authority and the Rockefeller Institute."[139] While the Rockefeller Institute was satisfied with the location of the new tunnel, Manhattan City Councilman Robert A. Low argued that the city was "building a tunnel at the wrong time, at the wrong place and the wrong facilities."[140] The underwater portion of the project, which awaited only Board of Estimate approval before construction could begin, was estimated to require from six to seven years to complete. In 1965 the drawings for the Sixty-third Street tunnel were put out to bid. To the Transit Authority's shock, only one bidder responded, offering to undertake the project for 101 percent more than the $28.1 million the authority had estimated.[141] Even after the estimated cost for the tunnel had been reduced by substituting trench-type construction for the original shield-driven compressed-air method, it was still too expensive.[142]

By November 1967, when New York voters passed a $2.5 billion transportation bond issue that would make construction possible, the tunnel had been redesigned in a double-decked arrangement that could also accommodate traffic of the Long Island Railroad (which New York State had assumed control of in 1965).[143] After coming into Manhattan via the new tunnel, the railroad's commuter trains would proceed to the Metropolitan Transportation Center, a new facility to be located in the heart of the midtown business district at Forty-eighth Street and Third Avenue. This would alleviate the congestion and inconvenience caused by the present system, in which trains terminated on the fringe of the west side at Pennsylvania Station. The arrangement reflected an agreement between the city and the state to coordinate transit planning and operations under a new superagency, the Metropolitan Transit Authority (MTA), which would become operational on March 1, 1968.[144]

In October 1969, after a healthy process of competitive bid-

ding, the MTA selected a joint-venture contractor to build the double-decked, 3,140-foot-long tunnel, scheduled for completion in 1975.[145] Construction, however, was delayed as negotiations concerning the park's preservation unfolded. The Transit Authority's plan called for open-cut construction along Sixty-third Street and for two trenches through the park, rather than a more expensive but less destructive tunnel; MTA officials claimed that rock and soil conditions rendered tunneling impractical.[146] In 1970 Community Planning Board 8 began to raise questions about the destruction the cut-and-cover construction process would cause to Central Park, as well as to an attractive, valuable crosstown street. Conservationists objected that the construction would damage an existing bird sanctuary and duck pond in addition to scenic rock outcroppings in the park. On May 27, 1970, August Heckscher, speaking at a meeting of Community Planning Board 8, stated that he would not grant the required permits until he was convinced that "both in design and construction every measure has been taken to protect the park and the park users."[147] The editors of the New York Times, supporting Heckscher's stance, urged greater coordination between the MTA and the Park Department while lamenting that the open cuts would make Central Park look as if it "were a profitable strip mine somewhere in Appalachia."[148]

In June 1970, responding to the growing opposition and Heckscher's contention that a change of route would allow for tunneling, Mayor Lindsay requested that an engineering firm be hired to study trenching alternatives. The firm of Singstad, Kehart, November & Hurka was selected; Ole Singstad had worked on the Holland Tunnel (1927) and was the principal engineer for the Lincoln Tunnel (1937), the Queens-Midtown Tunnel (1940) and the Brooklyn-Battery Tunnel (1950).[149] The firm issued a report which maintained that there was no practical alternative to at least limited trenching. Heckscher would later recall that "the reports from the engineers were favorable to shifting the alignment, but a final set of borings . . . showed the rocks to be too soft a composition to permit the desired tunneling. At least I had the satisfaction in this case of knowing I had been defeated by nature, not by man."[150] Nonetheless, the report said that damage could be lessened by reducing the proposed seventy-five-foot-wide park trench to forty feet and banning trucks from above-ground access. On February 26, 1971, Heckscher agreed "reluctantly" to the revised plan, which reduced by 53.4 percent the amount of parkland that would be disturbed and shortened from three to two years the anticipated time required to complete the park portion of the project.[151] Mayor Lindsay praised the agreement as a "substantial victory" for park supporters.[152]

Elaborate plans for the area's restoration after the completion of the open-cut work included preserving the pieces of a rock outcropping that was in the way, labeling them and storing them for reassembly later.[153] While even the restricted plan necessitated the temporary loss of the playground near Fifth Avenue and Sixty-third Street, the Park Department built an alternate facility directly to the west when subway construction began. Although the commencement of construction elicited protest ranging from, as John C. Devlin reported in the New York Times, "shouting mothers carrying babies" to demonstrators applying graffiti to construction fences, the project went forward.[154] The triple-pronged threat of technological problems, bureaucratic inefficiency and economic recession, however, delayed completion of the project until October 28, 1989.[155]

Bethesda Fountain and Tavern on the Green

August Heckscher announced his resignation as park commissioner and stepped down in November 1972. His replacement, Richard M. Clurman, set an even higher priority on park maintenance.[156] In October 1973 Clurman's department set before the City Planning Commission a request to establish a line in the city's budget for a twelve-year program of park restoration and maintenance.[157] But with the city's budget in disarray, the timing was clearly wrong, and the long overdue, desperately needed work had to be deferred again or funded privately. By 1976, given 23 percent cuts in department personnel as compared to 13 percent in other agencies, private funding began to seem the only possible choice.[158] One such effort was the restoration of the Ladies Pavilion facing the lake near Central Park West and Seventy-fifth Street, undertaken with the support of the Greensward Foundation.[159] The drawings for the restoration were prepared by Adams & Woodbridge.

The city's declining fortunes and the growing problems that plagued inner-city life during the late 1960s and early 1970s were mirrored in Central Park in general, and in the Bethesda Fountain in particular. Although in 1966 the fountain had been the site for a reborn urban sophistication in the form of the Fountain Café (see above), by 1969 it had become a regular hangout for flower children and other countercultural types. At first the scene at "Freak Fountain," as *Newsweek* described it, seemed more or less innocent: "Bethesda Fountain has become a true melting pot of New York and the craziest gathering place in the city. Hippies and hipsters make the fountain their headquarters. They are joined by blacks from Harlem, Puerto Ricans from El Barrio, and East and West Siders for a perpetual Be-In every weekend."[160] But by 1971 drug traffic had become a serious problem at the fountain, and within the next two summers gangs had divided the area into territorial turf. Young Hispanics gathered around the fountain itself while white patrons huddled behind the portable barriers of the café, which had lost its tents and been reduced to simple umbrella tables, chairs and plain food. A year later the café closed, ostensibly to make repairs to the fountain possible, and the fountain terrace became an almost exclusively Hispanic meeting area.[161] Except for the overflow of illegal vendors, drug dealers and gamblers who by this time had invaded the Mall, Bethesda became a wasteland.

In contrast, in 1976 one project pointed to Central Park's resurgence as a middle-class playground: the reopening of the Tavern on the Green.[162] Since the Battle of the Tavern on the Green (see above), the restaurant had continued to function, but with declining style and declining financial success. It continued to falter when it was taken over by Restaurant Associates in the 1960s; it came to be known by its new management as the Tavern in the Red. In 1974 Warner LeRoy, whose east side watering hole, Maxwell's Plum, had established an all-time high in ambient glitz (see chapter 6), negotiated a new lease with the city for the operation of the Tavern. Working with his architect, Paul Chen, LeRoy restored the remaining elements of the original Sheepfold and created a series of spectacular if improbable dining rooms that seemed straight out of a late-nineteenth-century operetta gone mad. This theatricality was completely intentional, for LeRoy saw a restaurant as "a kind of living theater in which diners are the most important members of the cast."[163] The Tavern opened in September 1976, lifting the city's spirits at a most welcome time. Paul Goldberger praised the renovation as a "loving, even innocent creation—exactly the opposite of the cynical environments of hotel ballrooms that represent true bad taste."[164]

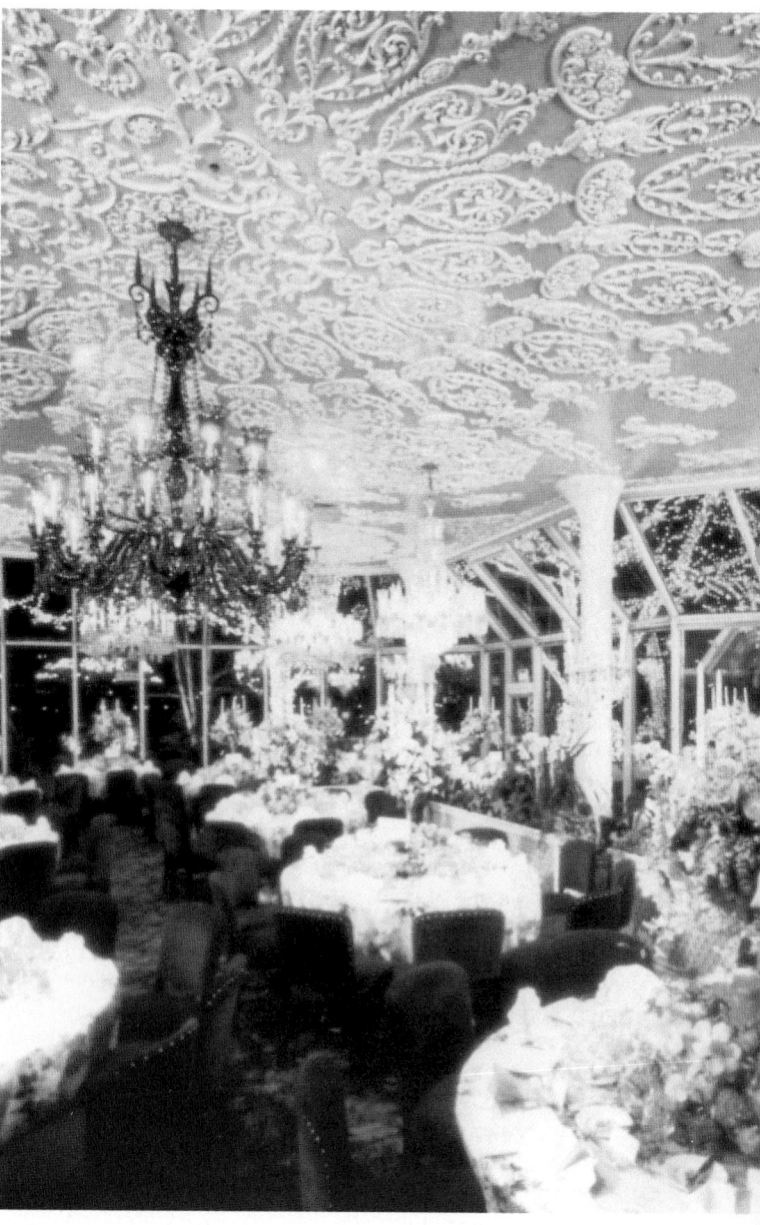

Tavern on the Green, near Central Park West, between West Sixty-sixth and West Sixty-seventh streets. Paul Chen and Warner LeRoy, 1976. Redecorated interior. WL

The focal point of the new Tavern was the glassed-in room created in the courtyard between the building's two wings. With "enough Baccarat and Waterford chandeliers to look like a lighting showroom," as Goldberger put it, the room created "a dazzling array of reflections, with the image of the chandeliers bouncing off the glass walls, gently played off against the lights in the park beyond, visible through the glass."[165] At night, with thousands of lights outlining the trees that enclosed the former Sheepfold and the warm sparkle of colored crystal spilling out into the park, the Tavern was a beacon of renewed pride, a representation of New York's continuing capacity to marry fantasy with bottom-line economics, to turn the everyday realm into high drama.

Metropolitan Museum of Art

Central Park's most notable and in some ways its most incompatible feature, the Metropolitan Museum of Art, embarked on a major expansion plan in 1967, under the direction of former Park Commissioner Thomas P. F. Hoving.[166] The controversy engendered by the Metropolitan's expansion into Central Park was far from unprecedented; indeed, the museum's location had been rigorously debated from the start. Trustees of the museum, which was founded in 1867 by the Art Committee of the Union League Club, were originally uncertain as to whether a Central Park location was ideal, fearing that many people would be reluctant to travel so far north of the city's core to view art. Most of the members of the museum's executive committee preferred a site then known as Reservoir Square, bounded by Fifth and Sixth avenues, Fortieth and Forty-second streets, and ultimately occupied by Bryant Park and the New York Public Library (Carrère & Hastings, 1897–1911). Despite the committee's collective stance, Andrew Haskell Green, the charismatic president of the Central Park Commission, succeeded in persuading the New York State Legislature to pass a bill enabling the commission to build within the park "a meteorological and astronomical observatory, and a museum of natural history and a gallery of art."[167] Further legislation provided for the construction of a building or complex of buildings to house the Metropolitan and the American Museum of Natural History at Metropolitan Square, officially part of Central Park, bounded by Central Park West, Columbus Avenue, Seventy-ninth and Eighty-first streets.

By 1872 the Metropolitan Square site had been designated for the American Museum of Natural History alone and the Metropolitan moved to the so-called Deer Park, the section of Central Park bordered by Fifth Avenue, the East Drive, and the transverse roads at Seventy-ninth and Eighty-fourth streets. The Metropolitan was opened to the public in 1880 in a building designed by Calvert Vaux and Jacob Wrey Mould in a Ruskinian Gothic vocabulary.[168] Theodore Weston added a neo-Grec wing in 1888 and Arthur Tuckerman contributed another wing in 1890–94.[169] Though Frederick Law Olmsted and Calvert Vaux's original "Greensward" plan of 1856 had called for the conversion of the Arsenal (Martin E. Thompson, 1847–51), which stood in the park facing Fifth Avenue at Sixty-fourth Street, into a museum, and the construction of a facility combining a conservatory and a music hall, Olmsted increasingly objected to the intrusion of buildings into his naturalistic landscape. In 1895 he stated bluntly that buildings, as well as monuments and statues, "take much from [Central Park's] value" and "would be worth more to the city if they were elsewhere."[170]

Despite Olmsted's objections, the Metropolitan continued to expand, occupying more and more of its site. Richard Morris Hunt's building, including an entrance pavilion and the Great Hall, with a robust Classical facade that reoriented the museum away from the park and toward Fifth Avenue, was realized between 1894 and 1902.[171] Two wings designed as part of McKim, Mead & White's master plan of 1905 were realized in 1906 and 1926,[172] and Grosvenor Atterbury's American Wing, which incorporated the principal facade of the demolished United States Branch Bank (Martin E. Thompson, 1822–24), was completed in 1924.[173] Following the completion of the second McKim, Mead & White addition, their master plan, which had called for a monumental carriage entrance facing west toward the park, was dropped.[174] The museum did not expand at all throughout the Great Depression.

While no expansion plans were contemplated before World War II, the Metropolitan did establish the Junior Museum within its walls, reflecting a growing national trend toward catering to the educational needs of the young.[175] To provide for the 300,000 schoolchildren who visited the museum annually, the Junior Museum, opened in October 1941, was temporarily installed on the first floor of the South Wing, adjacent to the park entrance, where plaster casts had previously been displayed. The special facilities included exhibits for the children, as well as a checkroom, toilets, an auditorium and a small library.

In 1943 the Metropolitan and the Whitney Museum of American Art entered into an agreement to consolidate their holdings; the Whitney's collections and activities would be housed in a separate wing to be built at the Metropolitan as soon as the war was over.[176] The decision was influenced in part by the death in 1942 of the Whitney's founder, Gertrude Vanderbilt Whitney, and in part by the presence at the Metropolitan of the George Hearn Fund, earmarked for the purchase of American art but virtually untapped in a generation by the Metropolitan's curators, who were not interested in the subject, so that the principal and its unused income had grown to significant proportions. In 1945 plans were announced for a massive expansion and rebuilding of the Metropolitan, to be timed to its Diamond Jubilee year in 1947.[177] According to Francis Henry Taylor, the Metropolitan's director:

> The principle of these plans has been to unite the present disparate and far-flung collections of the museum into an organic whole, a plan destined to make the museum's collections more legible and understandable to the visitor and to eliminate the grave discomforts and inconveniences which he now must suffer. The museum, which has now reached such proportions that no normal human being can be expected to digest the whole in a single visit with any degree of comfort or sanity, will become under the new scheme a complex of museums united under one administration.[178]

The centerpiece of the $10 million Diamond Jubilee building program was the new Whitney Wing, to be located at the south end of the building, extending behind McKim, Mead & White's 1926 pavilion. Working within a new master plan developed by Robert B. O'Connor and Aymar Embury II, Miller & Noel designed the new Whitney Wing. However, plans for the wing were abandoned in 1948, when the two institutions, which had never formally executed their agreement, rejected the plans to merge. This decision came at the instigation of the Whitney's trustees, who felt that the aims of the two museums with respect to contemporary art were divergent and that "grave doubts" had arisen over whether the Whitney's traditions could be preserved

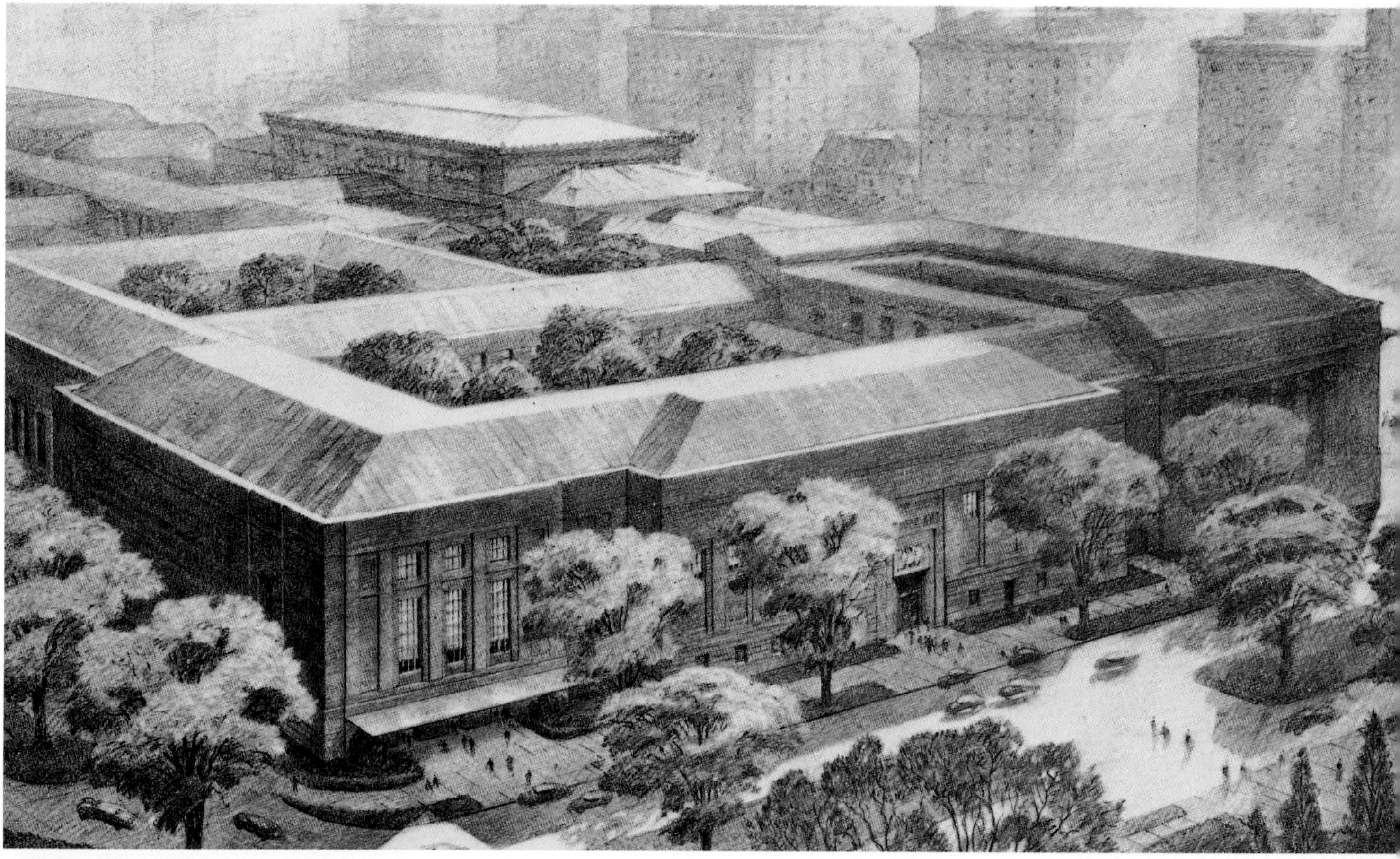

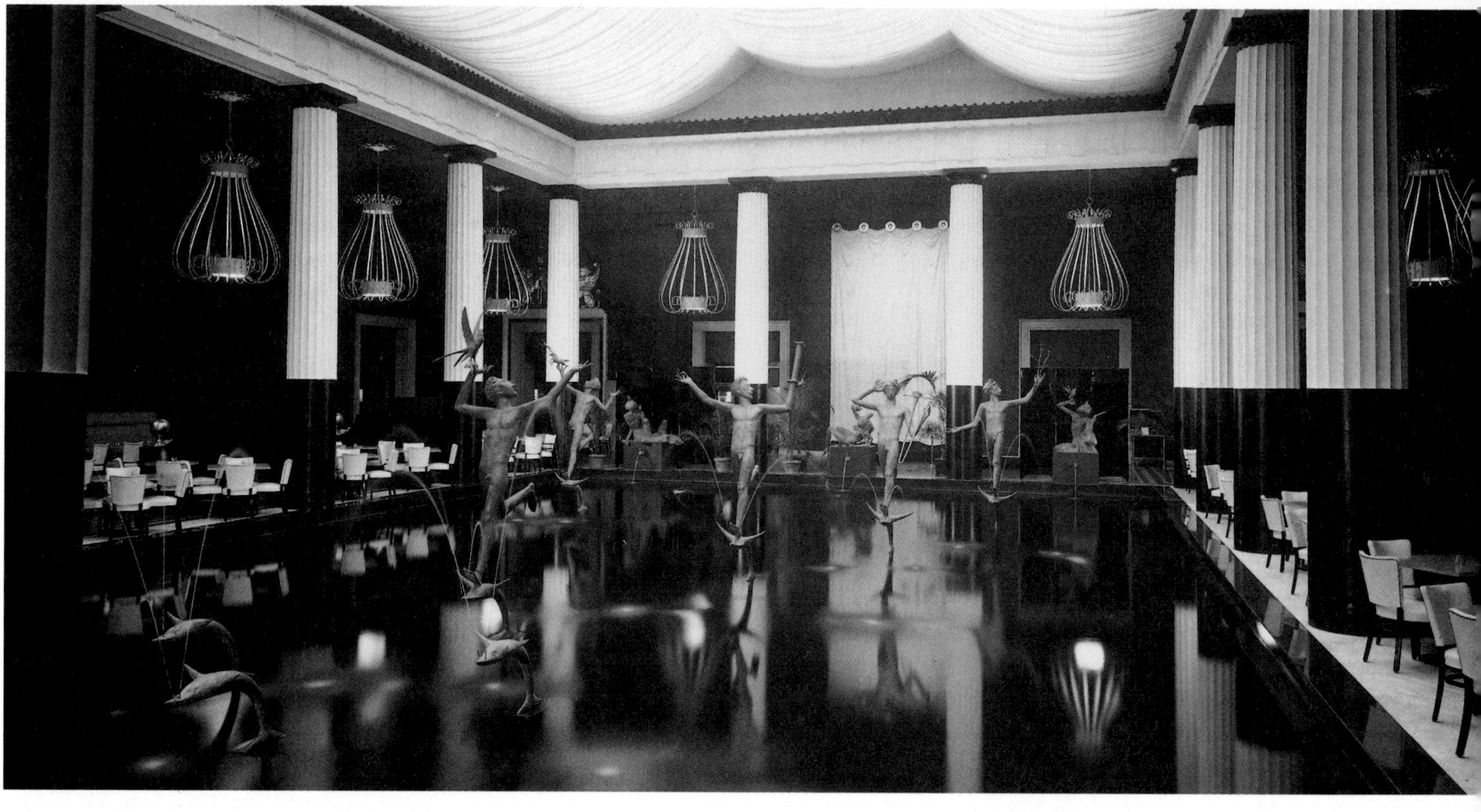

Top: Proposal for Whitney Wing of American Art, Metropolitan Museum of Art, Fifth Avenue at East Eighty-second Street. Miller & Noel, 1945. Rendering by Hugh Ferriss of view to the northeast. MET

Bottom: Restaurant in the former Roman Court, Metropolitan Museum of Art. Dorothy Draper, 1954. View showing sculptures by Carl Milles. MET

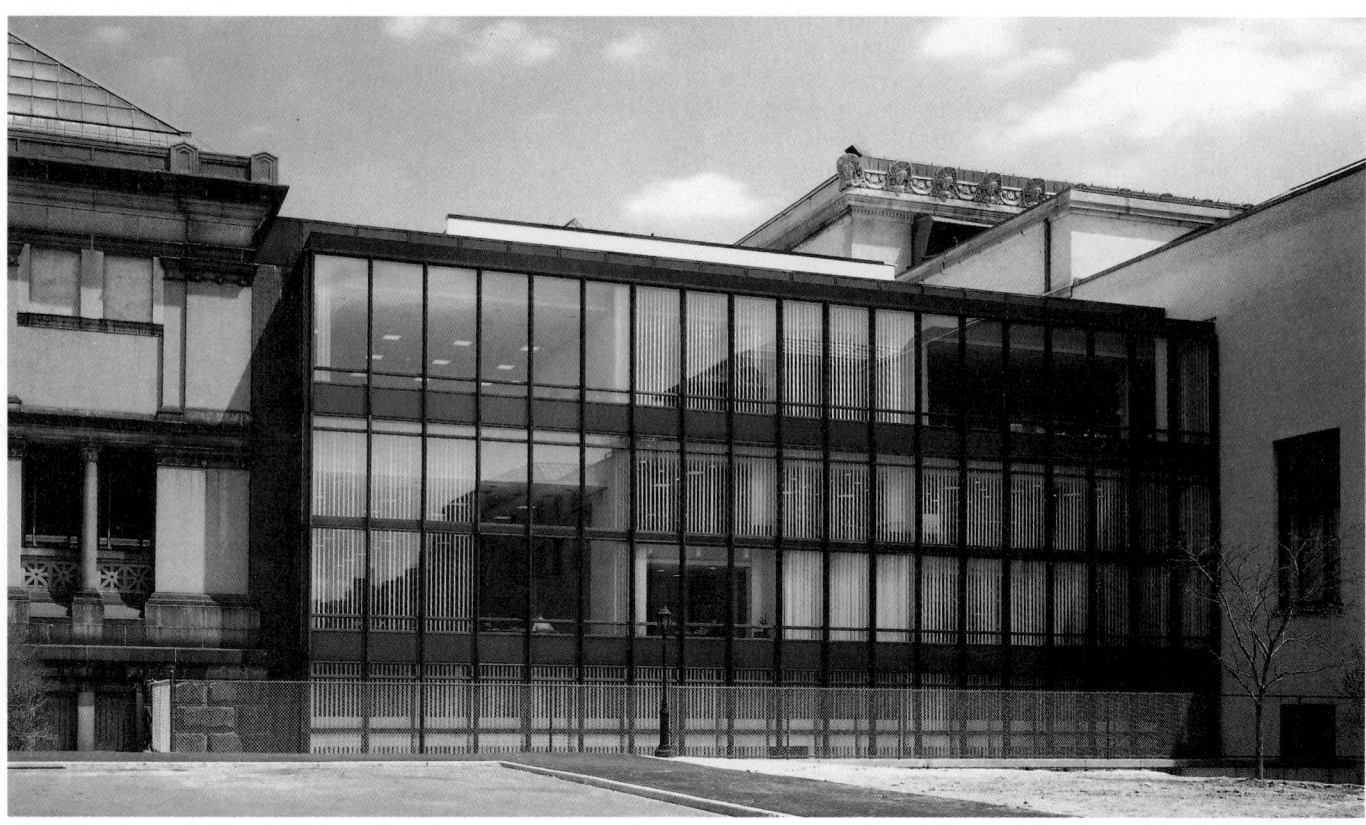

Thomas J. Watson Library, Metropolitan Museum of Art, Fifth Avenue at East Eighty-second Street. Brown, Lawford & Forbes, 1965. View to the north. MET

after the coalition.[179] Moreover, Park Commissioner Robert Moses, who sat on the Metropolitan's board as an ex-officio member, had castigated the proposed Whitney Wing as "another wart" on the landscape of Central Park and refused to approve the preliminary plans.[180] Moses had also informed the museum's trustees that the city would pay for only half the cost of any new building they might propose. Although this did not directly relate to the Whitney Wing, which was to be built with funds provided in Mrs. Whitney's $2.5 million bequest to the museum she had founded, it did create problems for the Metropolitan's Diamond Jubilee plans. The Metropolitan, the Whitney and the Museum of Modern Art then entered into another agreement concerning the distribution of their collections and defining spheres of interest for future collecting; this coalition also proved troublesome and was soon abandoned.[181]

The city did, however, provide funds for the rehabilitation of existing facilities; these funds, together with private contributions, resulted by 1954 in the extensive renovation of ninety-five galleries and six period rooms, the conversion of the Roman Court in the South Wing on Fifth Avenue into a restaurant, and the replacement of the old lecture hall in the North Wing with the 700-seat Grace Rainey Rogers Auditorium.[182] All of these elements were proposed in revisions made in 1950 to the O'Connor and Embury master plan after the Whitney withdrew.

The cost of the gallery renovations as well as the construction of a new unit linking the North Wing on Fifth Avenue with the American Wing was approximately $7 million, of which $3.1 million was borne by the city. The Rogers Auditorium, which cost $1.1 million, was paid for solely with private funds. Most of the renovation took place in the oldest museum buildings, now jointly designated as the West Building. While the bulk of the

money went toward a desperately needed overhaul of the electrical and mechanical ventilating systems, the effect of the renovated galleries was easily visible to the public, who could enjoy familiar works in totally new settings with improved lighting.

To the new generation, the renovation was a revelation, since most of the Metropolitan's collection had been in storage during the war and only a fragment had been on view afterward as the work got under way. Under the supervision of Theodore Rousseau, Jr., curator of paintings, and Benjamin Knotts, display designer, the planning of the new picture galleries was guided by the belief that a museum was "a mixture of a theater and a university; the idea is that we're involved in both show business and education."[183] The new galleries were not only brighter and better ventilated than their predecessors, but they were also more intimately scaled. As John McAndrew noted: "The extensive remodelling of some of the vast old halls into smaller galleries has brought many advantages: the sizes and shapes of the rooms themselves and the variety in their sequence certainly seem more pleasant, and nearly everywhere there is an agreeable sense of spaciousness, increased rather than diminished by the interposition of a few small rooms with low ceilings."[184]

In his assessment of the Rogers Auditorium, which was designed by Voorhees, Walker, Foley & Smith, John Mason Brown, the well-known lecturer, observed that, although the old lecture hall had been a "stately" room, "it so pushed dignity to the point of bleakness that it seemed meant only for a toga or an autopsy." The new auditorium, which was abundantly provided with the cloakrooms and washrooms its predecessor had sorely lacked, could be used after the museum's regular hours and could serve as both lecture and concert hall. With its superior acoustics and its simple, almost bland decor, with walls and ceilings covered in light tan kouna (South African whitewood), the auditorium, said Brown, had "a beauty of its own, the beauty of being right to the point of inevitability."[185] The auditorium's most notable feature was the integration of the stage with the room as a whole (there was no stage loft or proscenium), which encouraged the unity of audience and performer, a particularly valuable quality in the question-and-answer portions of lecture programs. Thin plywood vaulted panels, joined to form a canopy over the stage to help with the acoustics, provided the principal decorative effect.

The new restaurant in the former Roman Court was a strong contrast to both the quiet, period-inspired good taste of the gallery installations and the bland Modernism of the Rogers Auditorium. As "designed and styled" by Dorothy Draper, the much-beloved Roman Court was transformed into a dramatic, 300-seat dining room in a style A. L. Chanin described as "Hollywood-baroque-moderne."[186] Draper's design enhanced the court with a new seventy-five-foot-long decorative pool, which held sculptures of dolphins and nymphs by Carl Milles. The existing skylight over the pool was draped in white nylon. The Doric columns defining the peristyle around the pool were painted black and white to set them off against the outer walls and the ceilings, which the designer had painted in "blackberry," a deep shade of near black. The black-and-white color scheme was carried into most of the furniture, although the banquettes along the walls were upholstered in coral-colored fabric and those in the entrance foyer were covered in sea blue. The most notable new features were the eight-foot-high birdcage chandeliers Draper designed for the peristyle, with vaselike shapes described by ribs of white-painted metal. "The place looked too big," Draper said, "so we painted the walls and ceilings the same color, put in those big lighting fixtures, and made everything in scale."[187]

To many observers the renovation was a sure sign of the museum's vulgarization. The Metropolitan's previous restaurant, opened in October 1941 and located just off the Hall of Armor, had been modest in size and tastefully Adamesque in style—rather like a Schrafft's or a Stouffer's.[188] Draper's room was quite another story. As Calvin Tomkins reported in his centennial history, when Director Taylor greeted the delegates attending the International Council of Museums, who gathered at the Metropolitan for their regular meeting in 1954, he "accepted with good grace the many unkind remarks about [the restaurant's] purple and red decor. . . . Taylor had already started calling it the 'Dorotheum.'"[189]

Though Draper's design had all the drama of the high-class hotels she was famous for, the restaurant was also practical and democratic: the food was served not at the table but from a buffet. Everything, Draper said, was "practical, everything . . . plastic, everything . . . nylon."[190] But it was also sophisticated, with a coffee bar that featured espresso. Carleton Varney, Draper's biographer and head of her successor firm, has written that the designer saw the restaurant as "a monument to herself."[191] But Draper was never completely happy with the design; she felt in particular that Milles's sculptures had not been properly installed and that they looked as if they were jumping out of the pool rather than gliding along its surface.

The extensive renovations and new facilities opened to the public in 1954 were but the first phase of the museum's program for reconstruction and expansion. By 1954 the architects Brown, Lawford & Forbes were already at work designing subsequent elements of the master plan, including the reconfiguration of the South Wing to provide for a new Junior Museum.[192] In 1959 Edward Durell Stone released his plans for the redesigned Costume Institute, which had been founded in 1937 as the

Museum of Costume Art, administratively incorporated into the Metropolitan in 1944 and opened in the museum in 1946.[193] Featuring Stone's signature filigree screen walls and draped bangles, the design of the new institute, although not as lavish as originally planned, nonetheless provided an elegant and sophisticated setting for window-display-like vignettes illustrating the history of fashion.

In 1964 the Metropolitan unveiled the second stage of its comprehensive renovation with the completion of a new seven-story power plant added to the rear; the installation of the Far Eastern gallery; the opening of the Thomas J. Watson Library containing 150,000 books; and the unveiling of the Velez Blanco Patio, which had been bequeathed to the museum in 1941 by George Blumenthal, the Metropolitan's president from 1934 to 1941, whose Park Avenue house it had adorned for more than twenty years.[194]

The Watson Library, a three-story building of glass and bronze-colored aluminum, facing west toward Central Park, was designed by Brown, Lawford & Forbes with room for a collection twice the present size. Though bland as a work of International Style Modernism, the library marked a significant change in the direction of the museum's architectural style; but in its very break with the Roman Classicism of the previous wings, it was a natural part of the stylistic eclecticism that had characterized the evolution of the museum complex as a whole since the first Gothic-style building was opened to the public in 1880. "The Metropolitan is an interesting conglomerate of styles and periods," Ada Louise Huxtable noted in a 1965 article, "a virtual witches brew: [the] new library is a fine and lively gift of modern seasoning." Visitors entered the Watson Library through one of the elaborately carved portals of the Blumenthal patio, a "ploy" based, Huxtable said, on "the esthetics of contrast," which could either "jar or delight." While Huxtable welcomed the museum's decision "to build for today in today's terms," she deplored the skimpiness of the final effect, which she blamed on the fact that not enough funds—coming from both private and city sources—were allocated for the project:

> If the anodized aluminum framing of the exterior had been bronze, instead of bronze-colored, if the budget had permitted more special detailing, tasteful serviceability could have become jewel-like distinction. . . . If the building, like many other new museum structures around the country, had been a private project without any city funds, this kind of quality might well have been attainable. But in New York, the poorest of rich cities, it is not.[195]

The completion of the Watson Library was vastly overshadowed by the installation of the sixteenth-century Velez Blanco Patio from Spain, which had never before been displayed in the museum (see chapter 16).

By 1965, under James J. Rorimer, who first joined the staff in 1930 and succeeded Francis Henry Taylor as director in 1954, the museum was a very different place from the sleepy institution it had been before the war.[196] It was Rorimer's curatorial intelligence that had shaped the Cloisters; he had also been responsible under Taylor for supervising the plans for the museum's renovation and expansion. With boundless energy and a meticulous eye for details of both connoisseurship and housekeeping, he presided over the entire museum operation as its gallery space grew 41 percent and its attendance skyrocketed from 2,830,000 visitors in 1955 to nearly 6,000,000 in 1965.

When Rorimer died suddenly in May 1966, Thomas Hoving was picked to head the museum.[197] He was thirty-five years old, brash and flamboyant. And though he was a serious

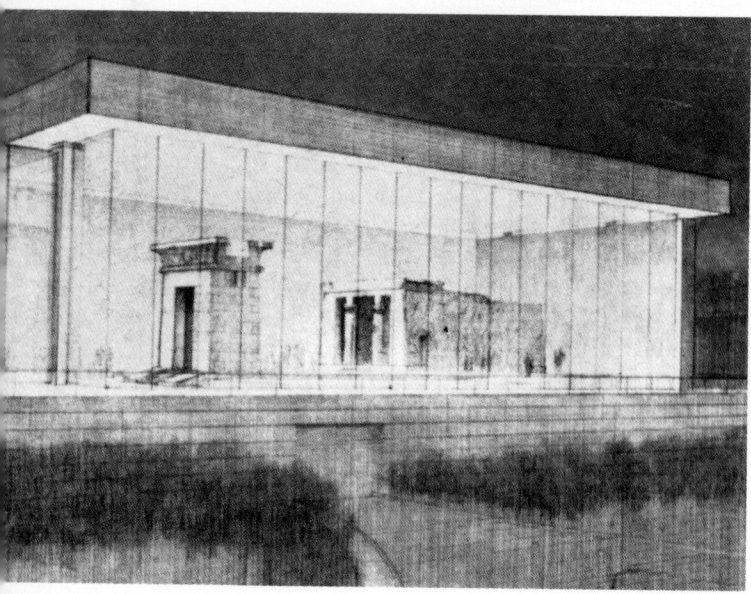

Above: Proposal for Temple of Dendur Pavilion, Metropolitan Museum of Art, Fifth Avenue at East Eighty-second Street. Brown, Lawford & Forbes, 1967. Rendering by Ara Derderian of view to the southwest. MET

Top right: Renovated Fifth Avenue facade, Metropolitan Museum of Art. Kevin Roche and John Dinkeloo, 1970. View to the northwest showing entrance to the Great Hall (Richard Morris Hunt, 1894–1902) in the center and North Wing (McKim, Mead and White, 1906) on the right. MET

Bottom right: Renovated Fifth Avenue facade, Metropolitan Museum of Art. Model. View from above showing entrance to the Great Hall, plaza and fountains. Stoller. ©ESTO

scholar and had been a curator at the Metropolitan's Cloisters, the popular glory he had earned as park commissioner caused him to be regarded with suspicion by many of the museum's trustees. Yet his appointment seemed just right for the times; as Tracy Atkinson, director of the Milwaukee Art Center, said, it reflected the direction museums would begin to take "toward involvement of the public."[198] Hoving welcomed the crowds, extending the Metropolitan's hours to include Tuesday evenings. Not everyone was pleased with such democratizing measures. Richard Randall, of the Walters Art Gallery in Baltimore, felt that the Metropolitan had become a "great big bing-bang show, a buzz bomb," in which it was no longer possible, at least on a Sunday afternoon, to spend a few quiet moments with great works of art.[199] But amid all the razzmatazz, Hoving introduced some profound curatorial changes, the most important being the elevation of contemporary painting to the status of the old masters.

Seizing the fund-raising possibilities of the museum's centennial in 1969–70, Hoving aggressively pushed toward the realization of long-delayed plans for expansion. Save for the power plant and the Watson Library, the Metropolitan's postwar building activities had been little more than small-scale renovations. But in 1965 Rorimer had begun planning for the construction of new facilities to be timed to the centennial; his plans, in some measure inherited from Taylor, focused on a new American Wing. Hoving incorporated this element in the far grander vision he began promoting soon after he took over at the Metropolitan in May 1967.

After only a few weeks as director, Hoving released Ara Derderian's rendering of a glassy pavilion to house the Temple of Dendur, a small Egyptian ruin of the Graeco-Roman era, which had been removed from its site on the Nile 130 miles from Dendur when the High Dam at Aswan was constructed.[200] The temple was dismantled by the Egyptian government in 1962 and was offered to the United States in gratitude for the $16 million the country had contributed toward saving such older and grander temples as Abu Simbel. Twenty American museums contended for the privilege of housing the temple. Secretary of the Interior Udall lobbied to have the temple erected out-of-doors in Washington, D.C., where nine million tourists could visit it annually, but consulting experts from the Metropolitan claimed that such outdoor display would cause it to erode into a pile of sand and stone stumps within thirty years. As part of the museum's own bid for the temple, Hoving, working with the Metropolitan's architects, Brown, Lawford & Forbes, devised a 136-foot-long, north-facing glass-walled display hall—Hoving called it a vitrine—to be built just behind the North Wing. At night the room would be lit to make the temple visible to passersby on Fifth Avenue. The proposal was unanimously endorsed by the commissioners charged with recommending a home for the temple to President Johnson. The Metropolitan's centennial plans were off and running with a new treasure and a new wing.

By September 1967 Hoving had incorporated the Dendur hall into a comprehensive plan for the museum's expansion, devised by Kevin Roche and John Dinkeloo, who were called in to replace Brown, Lawford & Forbes as master planners and architects for the museum's expansion.[201] Their assignment was to provide for the full utilization of the Central Park acreage allotted to the museum by the city and to develop detailed plans for the Dendur hall, the American Wing and Hunt's Great Hall, which was to be restored. Given his background in the Park Department, Hoving was acutely sensitive to the issue of en-

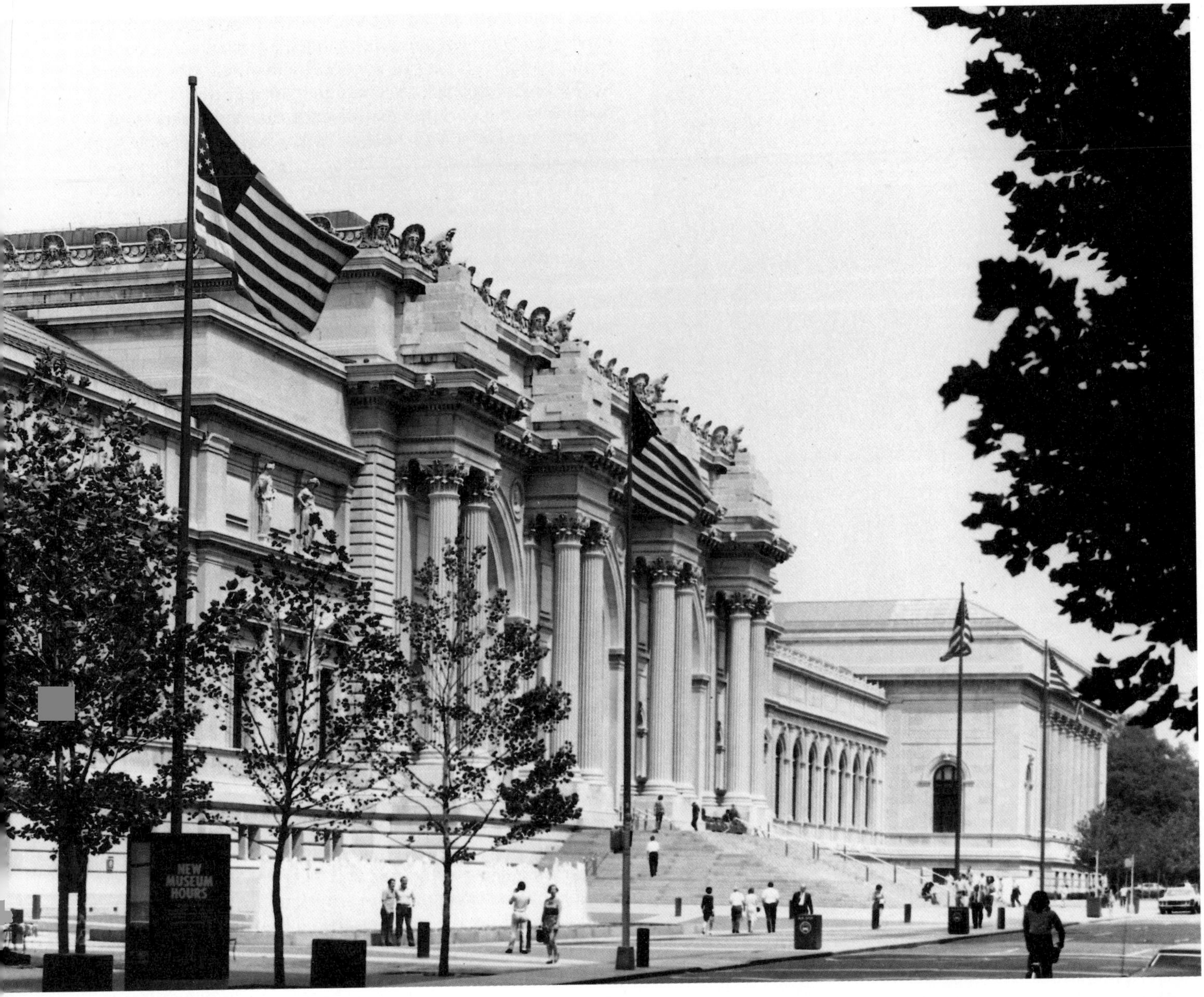

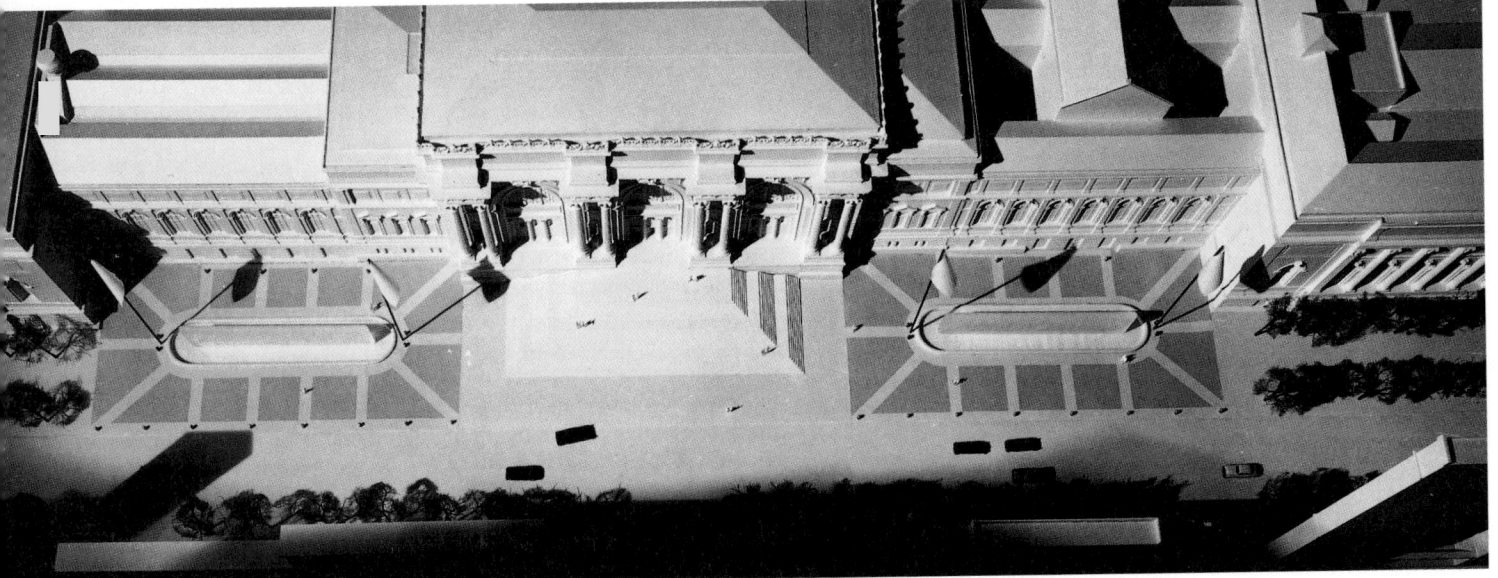

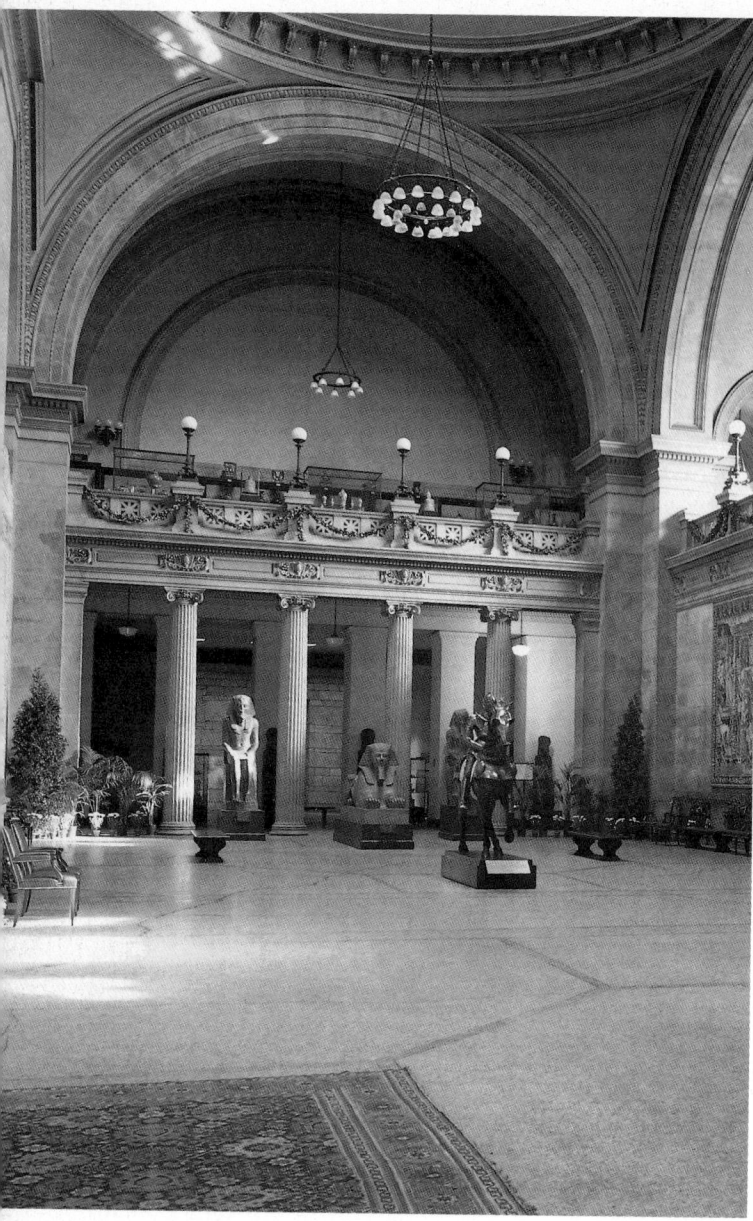

Above: Great Hall, Metropolitan Museum of Art, Fifth Avenue at East Eighty-second Street. Richard Morris Hunt, 1894–1902. View to the north, October 1941. MET

Right: Renovated Great Hall, Metropolitan Museum of Art. Kevin Roche and John Dinkeloo, 1970. View to the north. Ries. SR

croachment in planning for expansion. "Anything we build," Hoving said, "will be, in some manner, a sympathetic extension of the park."[202] It was such concerns that led Hoving to the Roche firm, who had designed the Oakland Museum, which demonstrated a unique blend of landscape and architecture,[203] and the Ford Foundation in New York, which had a lushly landscaped interior atrium (see chapter 5). Hoving would later recall that he had considered Philip Johnson and I. M. Pei but had chosen Roche-Dinkeloo in part because they were a rising young firm and might thus show an extra degree of effort, and in part because their work was highly favored by Ada Louise Huxtable. At the time of the announcement, Roche mused on the direction his firm's work at the Metropolitan might take, outlining a new form of curatorial organization: "You can organize collections so they become more meaningful. There are certain turning points in the history of man that are like tremendous anchors, around which works of art revolve. We want to approach the collections in that sense."[204]

The master plan was expected to take the form of an initial study, to be prepared in a year's time, and a full master plan, due in two or three more years. Simultaneous with the selection of the Roche-Dinkeloo firm, Hoving hired the architect Arthur Rosenblatt, who had served as first deputy administrator of recreation and cultural affairs when Hoving was park commissioner, as administrator for architecture and planning at the Metropolitan Museum.[205]

One year after being retained, Roche-Dinkeloo had prepared plans for what Ada Louise Huxtable described as a "major face-lifting" for the Metropolitan's 1,200-foot-long Fifth Avenue facade.[206] More than a simple restoration, Roche-Dinkeloo's proposal for the facade called for the removal of the "dog house" vestibule that had since 1902 buffered the Great Hall from the exterior chill, the replacement of the narrow front steps and carriage drive with a much broader, three-tiered pyramidal flight of steps, the redesign of the museum's entire "front yard," with new plantings and 100-foot-long basins from which 15-foot-high fountains would rise, and the installation of new exterior lighting and street furniture as well as night lighting for the facade. Roche saw his work on the Fifth Avenue facade as an important part of his assignment, explaining that although it was "really a street facade," it "had to be made more than a street facade."[207] The net result of these changes was to diffuse the impact of Hunt's central pavilion as it commanded the axis of Eighty-first Street and to create in its place what Huxtable described as "an environmental, open space design for a five-block stretch of Fifth Avenue," whereby the entrance would be not the doors to the building so much as the public plaza along its length.[208]

Work on the new facade cost about $2 million; of that sum, $470,000 came from city funds, and $1 million was donated anonymously by Lila Acheson Wallace, co-founder of *Reader's Digest* with her husband, Dewitt. Mrs. Wallace also provided a similar amount to reconstruct the Great Hall. The facelifting of the facade and the hall was almost complete by April 13, 1970, the museum's centennial. Several months later, Ada Louise Huxtable expressed her displeasure with the improvements: "I find myself increasingly distressed by the initial steps of the remodeling that is part of the planning projected for the museum's second century. The distress grows on every return visit. . . . There is something very wrong going on architecturally at the Met that bodes ill for the second century." Huxtable regretted the loss of the "throwaway grandeur, great scale without pomposity, quality with quiet ease" of the Metropolitan of her youth

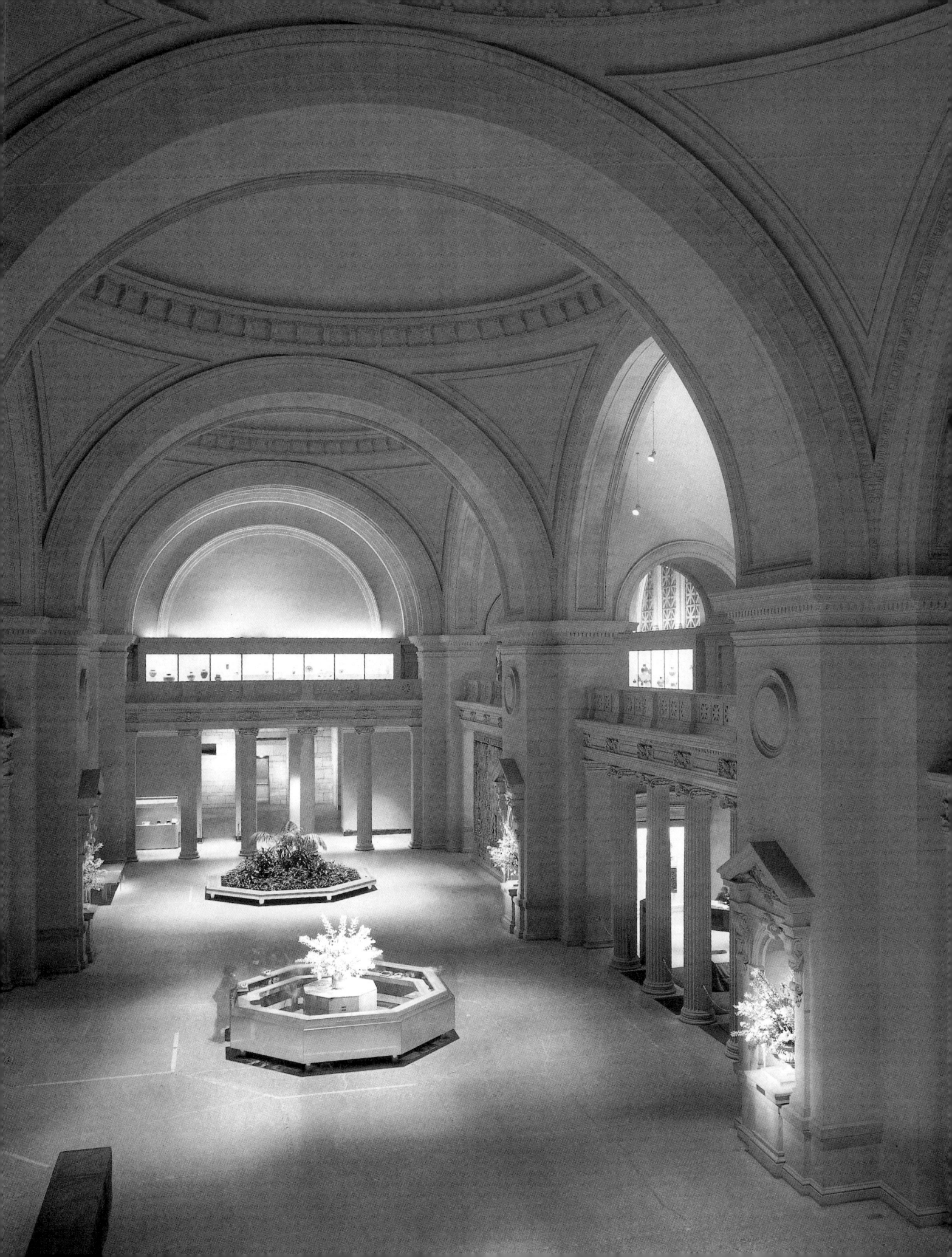

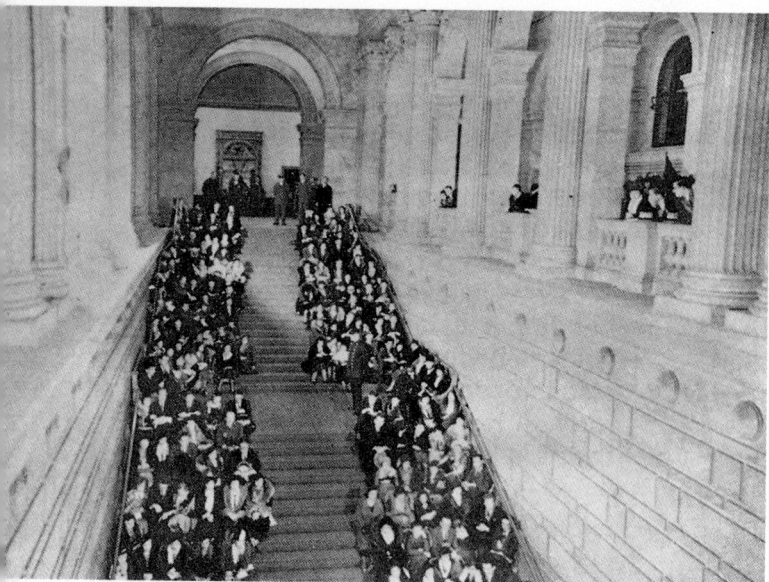

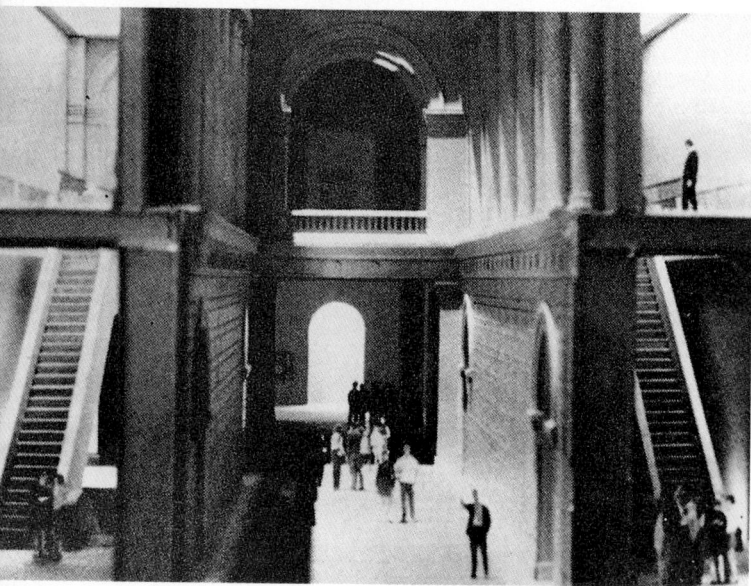

Top: Main staircase, Metropolitan Museum of Art, Fifth Avenue at East Eighty-second Street. Richard Morris Hunt, 1894–1902. View to the west. MET

Bottom: Proposal for the replacement of the main staircase with escalators, Metropolitan Museum of Art. Kevin Roche and John Dinkeloo, 1970. Model. View to the west. MET

Top right: Master plan for the Metropolitan Museum of Art. Kevin Roche and John Dinkeloo, 1970. Photographic montage of model. View to the east. KRJDA

Bottom right: Master plan for the Metropolitan Museum of Art. Plan. KRJDA

and especially of the "cultural potpourri of the Great Hall." She criticized the "overstaired" approach to the hall and the handling of the Fifth Avenue frontage, which now lacked the subtlety of Hunt's and McKim's Classicism: "The building is downgraded, overwhelmed by the overscaled approach, the overlong and sterile fountains (great space fillers, fountains), the overdose of hard-surfaced pavement flanked at the too-far ends by regimented trees."[209] Bernhard Leitner, writing in *Artforum*, also complained that the Hunt building had been diminished: "The new composition makes Hunt's elevation and the later additions equal parts of the superplaza. Hunt's subtle and well-proportioned building is over-run by the obtrusive dictatorship of the new scale."[210]

The Great Hall, said Huxtable, now exuded a "commercial grand luxe that even comes off—whisper it—as a kind of provincial grandeur." Huxtable regretted the substitution of new downlighting for the old chandeliers, which had "enhanced the hall's sense of size and scale. The space is now efficiently and uniformly lit, every surface washed . . . with no shadowed suggestion of awesome height, no mystery, no revelation, or emphasis." She also objected to the whittling away of wall surface to create cloakrooms along the east wall, which she called an act of "mutilation." All of these elements, Huxtable felt, resulted from a misreading of Hunt's intentions:

> The fact is that the concept and function of Hunt's Great Hall have been completely misunderstood. It was a palatial Grand Room. The around the edges messiness has been cleared away, replaced by a new and wrong kind of order—three "things" plunked down right under the domes, a central information desk and two big planters. In spirit, the Grand Room has become a cross between an information concourse and an expensive bank with corporate accessories to match. This is heartbreakingly, totally wrong.[211]

Roche's plan also called for the removal of Hunt's monumental staircase, which led westward from the Great Hall to the principal painting galleries on the second floor. Roche claimed that the staircase was to be removed to alleviate congestion, although the real reason was to meet the stipulations of the Robert Lehman bequest, which required that the Lehman Wing be directly accessible and visible from the museum entrance. Huxtable was also critical of this proposed change:

> This is the last remnant of the knowing use of a monumental hierarchy of forms and spaces that Hunt and his successors (it doesn't matter who did what, it all works together) provided with conspicuous success. The replacement will be an escalator-flanked bowling alley with free traffic flow. The unavoidable question is whether the Lehman collection as now planned, and the removal of the stair as a "barrier" to it, is either correct or justified. It will be the last step in the wrecking of a landmark interior.[212]

The problems raised by the Lehman Wing and its connection to the Great Hall were among the issues addressed in the museum's master plan, first presented to the public on the museum's centennial.[213] The plan provided for a museum more than one-third again as large as the present facility, with 325,000 square feet of new space. It called for expansion behind the North and South wings, the creation of skylit courts flanking the park side of the existing central museum block, an octagonal pavilion housing the Lehman collection and intruding into the park area at the center of the central block, and a new American Wing at the northwest corner of the complex. Also part of the plan was the construction of underground garage

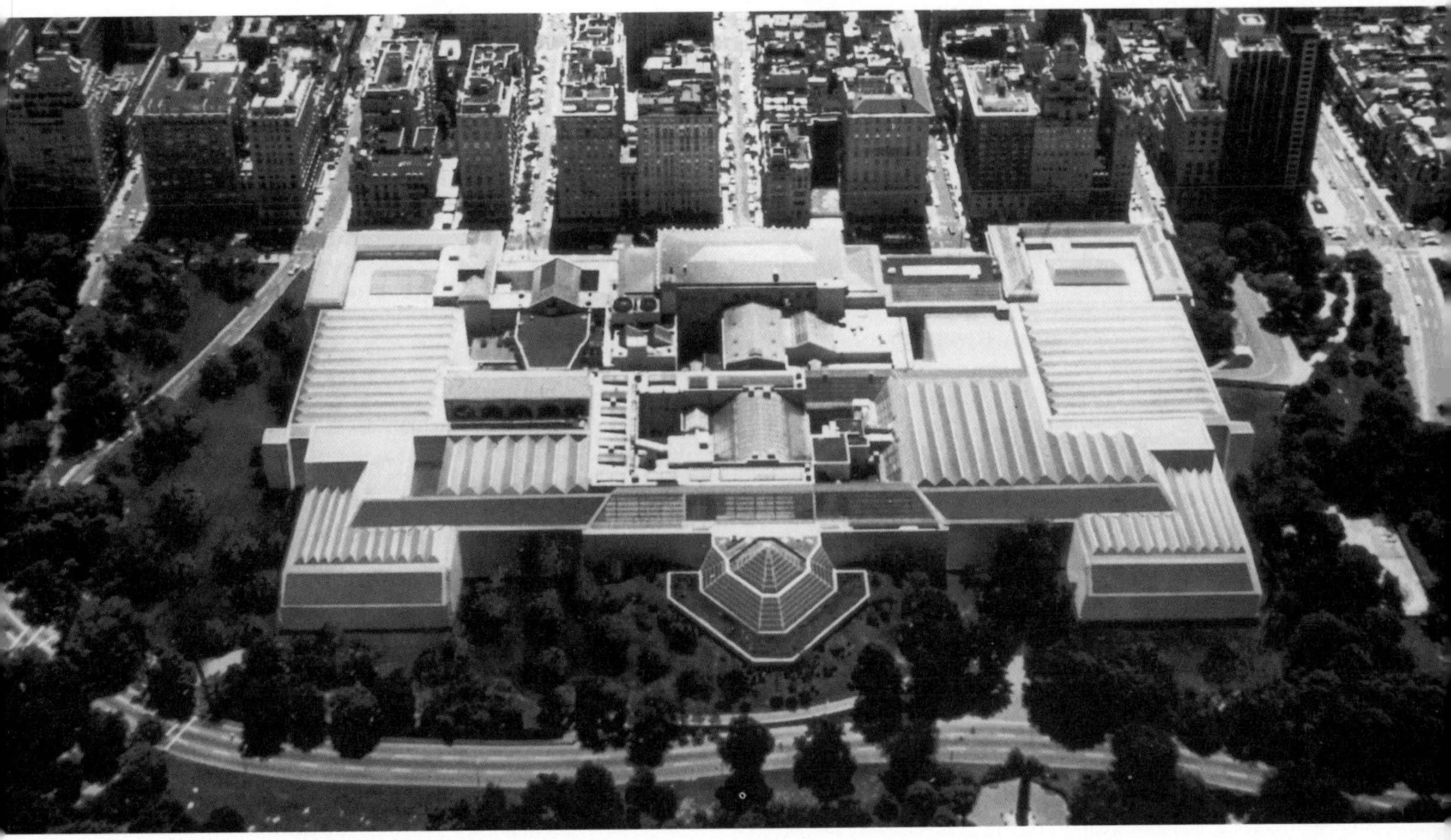

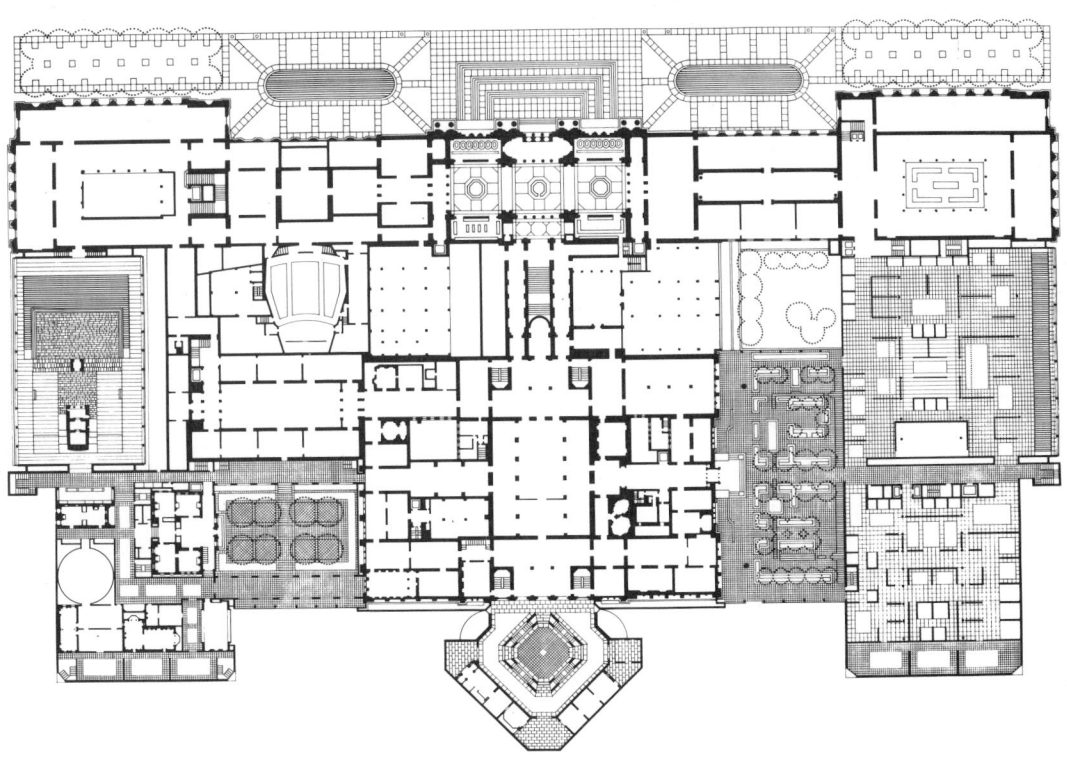

space for 312 cars and 20 buses, which would replace the surface parking space for 200 cars now on the site, a feature that was strongly protested by conservationists when it was built in 1957.

Even before it was officially presented to the public, the proposed expansion had raised a storm of controversy. The objections were exacerbated by the fact that, though the master plan proposed the direction for the museum's growth in the foreseeable future, it was not an abstraction or a wish list: three major components were already funded—the Dendur hall, the Robert Lehman Wing and the Michael Rockefeller Wing, featuring primitive art. "Suddenly it all began to come together," Roche recalled, "almost before we had the plan completed. Robert Lehman came through with his collection. The Temple of Dendur was secured. We started to *build* the master plan almost before the plan was finished. It happened very quickly."[214] A fourth section, the American Wing, seemed a reasonable likelihood as well.

The protest against the museum's plan centered on two issues: encroachment on parkland and the future of the supermuseum. Those who were concerned with encroachment began to campaign against the Metropolitan's plan well in advance of its release to the public; their first picket line was formed on January 30, 1970. No one denied that enabling legislation passed in 1872 gave the Metropolitan the right to use all the parkland east of the East Drive from Seventy-ninth to Eighty-fourth Street; at issue was whether the museum could proceed with plans after receiving permission from the city's Art Commission or whether the Park Department also had the right of review. Hoving felt that the Park Department definitely had the right, but to conservation-minded critics who claimed that vast areas of usable greenery would be swallowed up, he replied that 90 percent of the expansion would take place over existing parking lots. Nonetheless, Hoving was aware that his public image was in a precarious state: "Word spread that I had stopped 'saving' the park, that with my expansion plans I had sold my soul to the director's post and the museum's social glitter. None of this ever appeared in print or on TV, but it was like rust, silently corroding my reputation."[215]

Other critics protested the idea that the Metropolitan was becoming a supermuseum, suggesting that it could serve the widest number of people by opening up satellite museums in the outer boroughs rather than intensifying its activities on Fifth Avenue. In response to such arguments, Hoving emphasized the virtues of size: "We're not a gallery of pictures. We have 18 departments, six million visitors annually, 800 employees. We're an encyclopedic institution, a national museum, a museum of cultural history. We have 18,000 costumes, an exhibit of 39 fantastic beds from Egypt to the 20th century. We have 40,000 works out on loan. Thank God somebody decided to become a comprehensive institution. Our problem right now is we're not big enough."[216] He was not, however, against satellite programs: the Metropolitan was sponsoring a mini-museum on wheels that would bring lesser treasures to the outer boroughs; and, working together with Park Commissioner August Heckscher, Hoving was planning a satellite museum in Queens. Though the museum already ran one successful decentralized facility—the Cloisters—the trustees balked at considering another, despite a request by the City Planning Commission to do so. In discussing the issue of decentralization, Hoving said: "We will provide whatever the communities tell us they want, when they let us know. We have been probing beyond the white middle-class liberals who yell decentralization. Decentralization is mostly a coverup for the rabid park person who doesn't want us to build on our own property."[217]

Although many observers were relieved by the fact that the expansion plan seemed finite rather than open-ended and that little greenery would be disturbed, others objected to the overall architectural character of the proposal, which they saw as unnecessarily austere. *Time* reported that "some critics already feel that the new park facade is blank and featureless; it seems more appropriate to a factory than to one of the world's greatest art museums."[218] In defending the design, Roche argued that the park elevation was deliberately understated—in effect a garden wall punctuated by greenhouses, like those found in Kew Gardens, London, the Bronx Botanical Garden and Golden Gate Park in San Francisco. Roche saw the challenge as "how to put together these two disparate styles, the classic Beaux Arts and the glass-house expression." He cited the example of the National Botanical Garden in Washington, D.C., where the "building has a formal facade facing the Mall and, on the other side, a fairly exuberant glass-house. . . . No effort was made to integrate the two styles; where one stopped, the other just began, as in nature, at a forest line on a mountain." Roche said he was seeking a similar result: "When the building and landscaping are entirely finished, you will begin to see the original intended effect of urban architecture and park architecture forming one building. We were being sympathetic to the park."[219]

On April 12, 1970, the Metropolitan held a black-tie gala to honor its centennial and celebrate its new master plan.[220] As throngs of elegantly attired guests swept up the newly expanded front steps, a group of pro-park protesters, also smartly dressed, paraded along Fifth Avenue carrying placards, forming what one observer described as "the most genteel demonstration of upper-class ire since their parents trekked to the local Trans-Lux to hiss Roosevelt."[221] The celebration itself was spectacular. Each of four spaces was handled by a different interior designer or firm: Sister Parish and Albert Hadley decorated the museum's arms and armor wing to look, as Hoving put it, "like a ballroom of the Tenderloin epoch";[222] McMillen & Company decorated the Velez Blanco patio in Belle Epoque style; Billy Baldwin turned Draper's restaurant into a fin-de-siècle Viennese scene inspired by the work of Gustav Klimt; and, in perhaps the most inventive design, Angelo Donghia transformed the Egyptian sculpture court into a 1930s-style, Egypt-inspired supper club complete with monumentally scaled, faux-turquoise columns.

On June 4 of that year a spectacle of a very different order unfolded. August Heckscher, who had succeeded Hoving as park commissioner, had called a public hearing to review the proposed master plan. Held in the auditorium of the American Museum of Natural History and attended by about 350 people, the meeting opened with words from Heckscher, and from Cultural Affairs Commissioner Dore Schary. Hoving spoke next. After outlining the master plan, he went on to announce that he had received a "communication" from the Lehman Foundation saying that if the collection did not find its home in the Metropolitan as the plan envisioned, it would be moved to another city. The proceedings continued, with pro-expansion speakers alternating with those against the master plan. The former group included Marcel Breuer, Philip Johnson, Tom Beuchner, director of the Brooklyn Museum, and Ken Donahue, director of the Los Angeles County Museum, while the latter group, said Hoving, was "lopsided with conservationists, parks purists, and liberal politicians."[223]

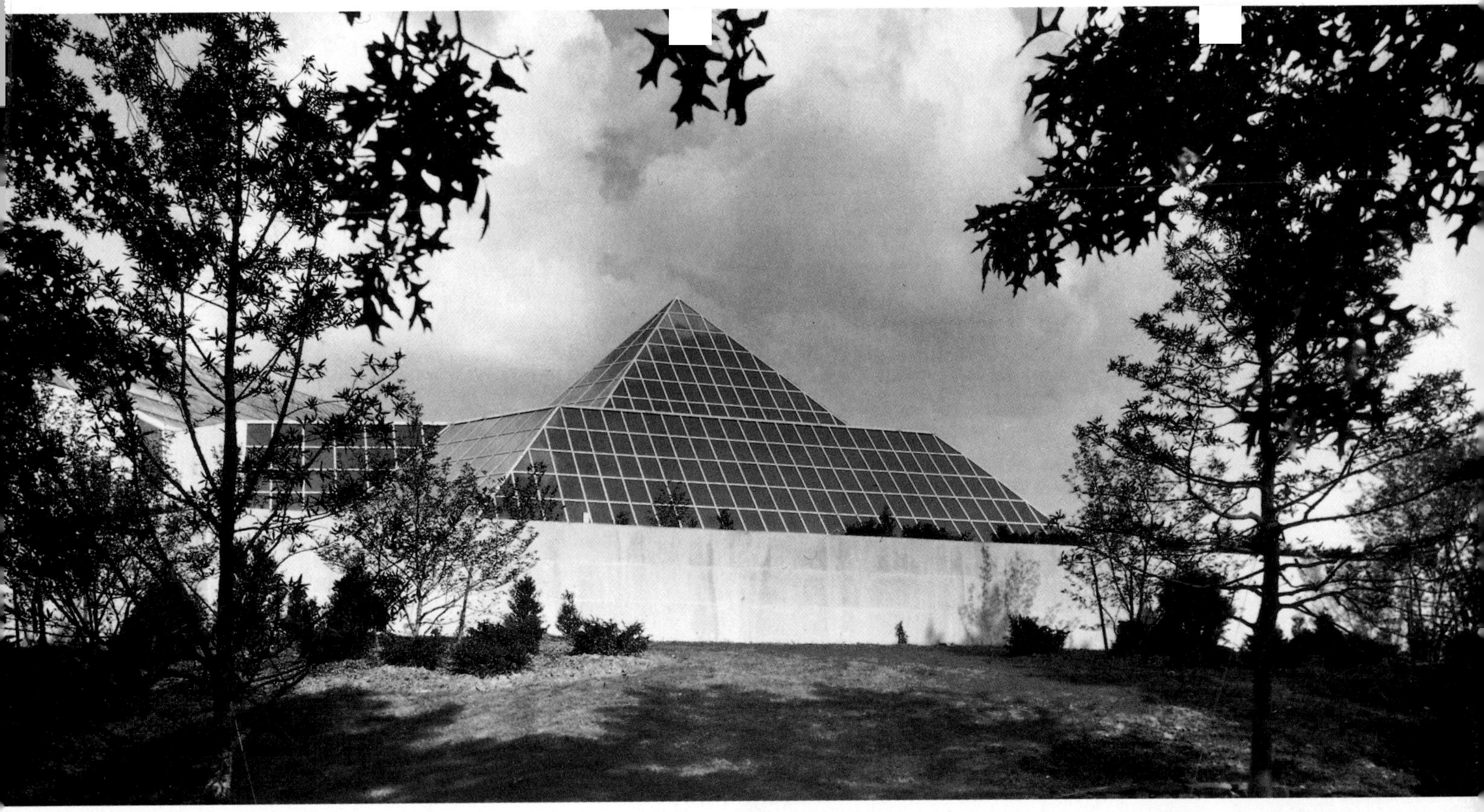

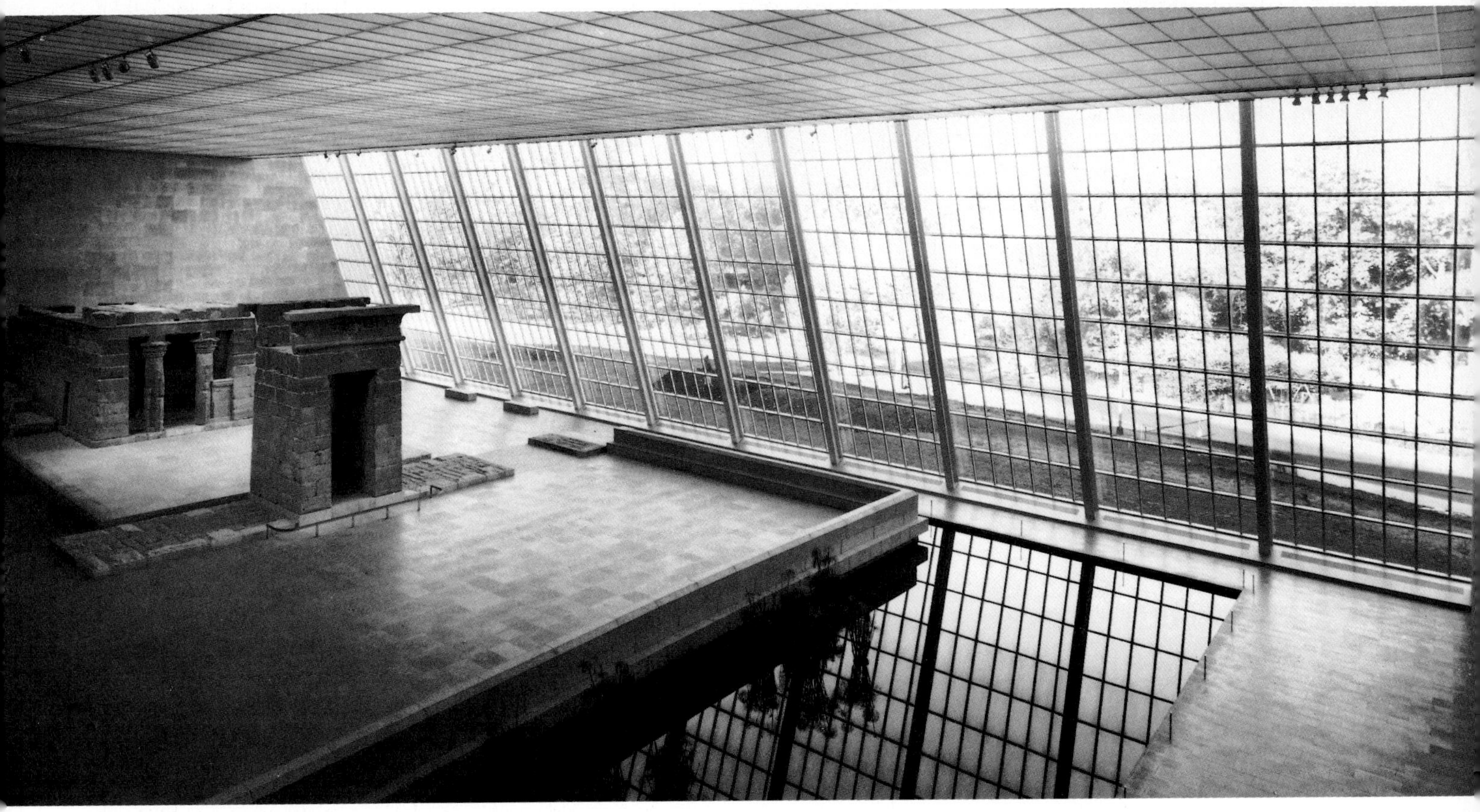

Top: Robert Lehman Wing, Metropolitan Museum of Art, Fifth Avenue at East Eighty-second Street. Kevin Roche and John Dinkeloo, 1975. View to the southeast. ©Norman McGrath. NM

Bottom: Sackler Wing, Metropolitan Museum of Art. Kevin Roche and John Dinkeloo, 1978. Interior view to the northwest showing Temple of Dendur. KRJDA

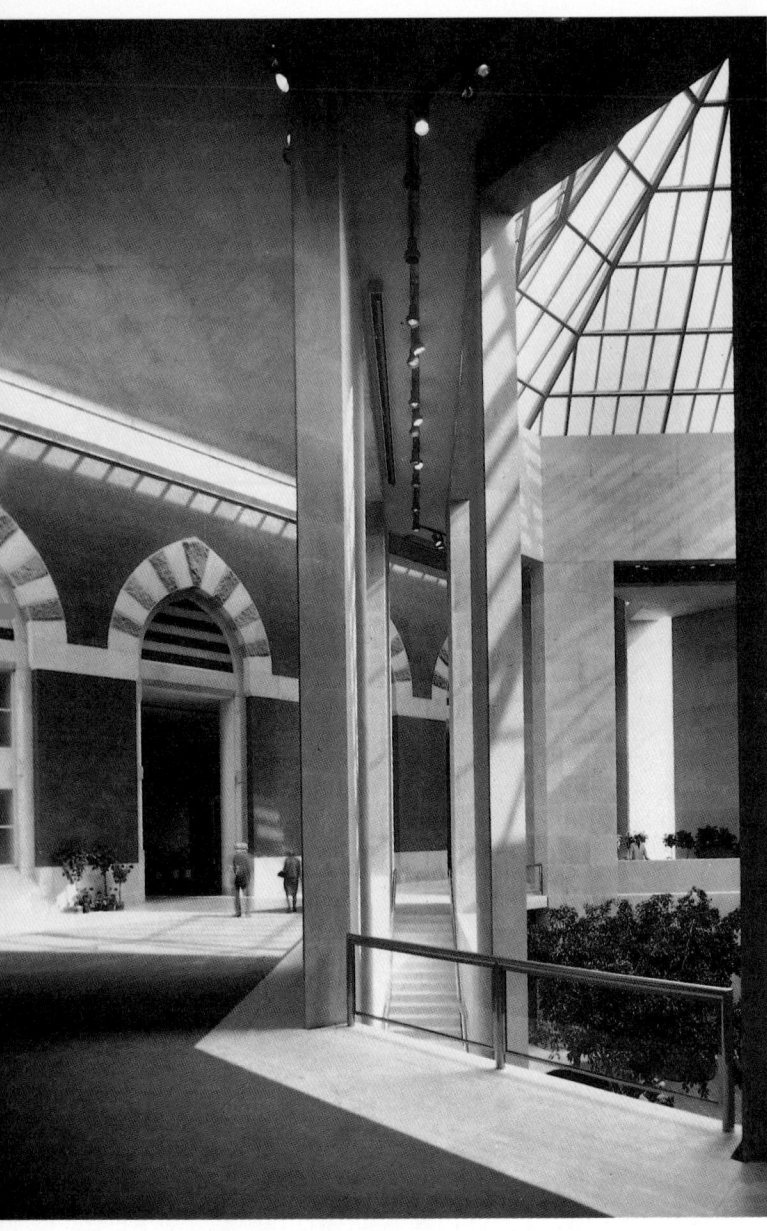

Robert Lehman Wing, Metropolitan Museum of Art, Fifth Avenue at East Eighty-second Street. Kevin Roche and John Dinkeloo, 1975. View to the southeast showing exposed facade of original Metropolitan Museum of Art (Calvert Vaux and J. Wrey Mould, 1880). ©Norman McGrath. NM

The evening reached a watershed when Karl Katz, chief curator of the National Museum of Israel and director of the Jewish Museum, both in Jerusalem, addressed the hearing. Alluding to the National Museum's already completed building, which was three times the size of the Metropolitan's proposed expansion, Katz said, "Who could object to what the Met needs when in Jerusalem they have taken sacred lands and said, 'Build a museum'? I am for the Met's expansion plans."[224] Hoving would recall: "It was as if a prophet had come down from the hills and exposed the whole hearing—the petty controversy—as nonsense, something hardly worth the attention of aware and intelligent human beings. . . . The evening dragged on for a little longer, but the affair was over. And we had won. I just knew it."[225]

While the Park Department's permission for the expansion was by that point pretty much a foregone conclusion, the museum plans still had to be reviewed by the Landmarks Preservation Commission, which heard the case on August 11, 1970, before a crowd of nearly 100 people who turned out to encourage the 27 speakers who opposed the plan.[226] While much of the opposition's testimony was political in tone, William J. Diamond, chairman of Community Planning Board 8, representing the Upper East Side, offered a distinctly architectural assessment: "We are not convinced by arguments that the park appearance will be improved by covering parking lots or changing ugly facades that were imposed upon us by the museum in the first place. We are unimpressed by an institution that creates a monstrous environment over parkland and then expects to take even more parkland to correct the damage. Let the museum improve the facade at the current boundaries."[227] The hearing dealt only with the appropriateness of the proposed additions and related work for the Temple of Dendur and for the Robert Lehman Wing. The commission had previously held that the museum, which had been landmarked in 1967, was a private institution and was therefore bound by the commission's judgments. But in what appeared to be an eleventh-hour decision, Chairman Harmon Goldstone announced at the hearing that, because of the city's $1.3 million gift to the Dendur hall and, presumably, the continuous support the city would provide for its maintenance, the commission would treat the museum as a city institution, thereby making its recommendations merely advisory. In a report kept, as Grace Glueck put it, "more or less under wraps" until it was publicly disclosed by Diamond, the commission found "the competing character and mass of the proposed Lehman wing inappropriate to the existing landmark" and recommended that the proposed design be rejected.[228] But because the report was only advisory, little was done to amend the design, except that a decision was made to preserve and expose a portion of the facade of Vaux and Mould's 1880 building on the inside face of the glazed Lehman pavilion.

Official Park Department approval for the master plan was issued in January 1971, following prior approval by the city's Art Commission, which had as four of its members active museum trustees and advocates. Only one member of the Art Commission, the landscape architect Robert Zion, dissented. But as late as March 1971 the fate of the master plan was still in flux, with the Parks Council and the Municipal Art Society suing to prevent Park Commissioner Heckscher from issuing a building permit until the master plan had been approved by the Board of Estimate. When New York State's Court of Appeals dismissed the suit on November 18, 1971, construction began on the Lehman Wing.

In 1974, when construction was well under way on the Lehman, American and Temple of Dendur wings, Paul Goldberger attempted to analyze the master plan from a purely architectural viewpoint, which had been so obscured by the political debates over park encroachment and decentralization. "If the premise of vastly increased gallery space on the present site is accepted," he wrote, "the Roche-Dinkeloo plan is a superbly thought-out, and at times truly exciting, means toward that end." Goldberger admired the positive attitude the plan took toward the museum's long-neglected park setting and the symmetry of the overall composition, which led to a strong sense of order. He also praised the extensive use of sloped glass proposed for the park facade and "the sharply articulated combination of glass and limestone," which "relates intelligently to the . . . Hunt and McKim wings, making neither false gestures of imitation or defiance."[229]

The first new wing of the Roche-Dinkeloo master plan to be realized was the Lehman Wing, which opened on May 27, 1975.[230] The Robert Lehman Foundation's gift of the Lehman collection, deemed the finest private collection in American hands, had been announced on September 25, 1969, at a dinner launching the museum's centennial. The collection, which contained Italian and Spanish masterpieces of the Renaissance as well as important nineteenth- and twentieth-century European paintings, was begun in 1911 by Robert Lehman's father, Philip; both father and son were prominent financiers. Robert Lehman, a museum trustee, had put his collection on extended loan to the museum in 1954 but had quietly withdrawn it in the early 1960s, reputedly because he was irritated with museum policy and unhappy that he had not been given an important post on its board. In 1967 Lehman was elected to a newly created post, chairman of the board, but he made no firm commitment for the gift. After his death in August 1969, it was discovered that the collection had been left to his family, although Hoving had been conducting negotiations concerning the collection for some time. Ultimately, the Lehman Foundation gave the $100 million collection to the museum, but only on the condition that it be displayed as a unit in a discrete set of rooms that re-created or evoked the surroundings of Lehman's townhouse (John H. Duncan, 1905) at 7 West Fifty-fourth Street.

Five schemes had been presented to the museum before Roche-Dinkeloo's final design was accepted. The first called for relocating the Lehman townhouse to the middle of the parking lot directly south of the museum; the second placed the townhouse farther west, opposite the red-brick facade of Vaux and Mould's original building. In the third proposal the townhouse was located in a generously scaled, glass-roofed court within the museum complex, while the fourth placed it in the American Wing, adjacent to the transplanted facade of the United States Branch Bank. The fifth proposal, a scheme for a boldly geometric new pavilion, was ultimately selected.

The principal feature of Roche-Dinkeloo's design for the Lehman Wing was the 14,000-square-foot glazed octagonal pavilion. This centerpiece was so grand that, despite the decision to retain Hunt's staircase, it acted as a powerful conclusion to the long axis of circulation from Fifth Avenue. Set at forty-five degrees to the Metropolitan's grid, the eight-sided pavilion was not a pure octagon but a near square, a simple shape enriched by glazed chamfered corners. Two layers of limestone walls separated the inner court from the exhibition rooms, defining a continuous picture-lined gallery for promenading. Approached from Fifth Avenue, the space of the court opened up and down to the viewer; at the square's chamfered corners, stairs led between the stone walls to further heighten the drama of vertical space. At the edges, special rooms from Lehman's house were installed, a fulfillment of the donor's wishes. Although these rooms were central to the pavilion's overall impact, they were enclosed in cinder block and designed so that they could be removed easily in case the collection was ever dispersed and the wing used exclusively to house temporary exhibitions. To minimize the impact of the new building on the park, the landscape architects Coffey, Levine & Blumberg provided a landscaped mound of earth up against the Lehman Wing's west wall, leaving only the glass pyramid exposed as a large-scale prismatic sculpture.

In his initial assessment of the design, Paul Goldberger saw the scheme as flawed, and he attributed the problem, "at least in part, to the tendency of Mr. Roche to make his buildings abstract objects as much as anything else." It was difficult, Goldberger said, "not to feel that the over-all concept of this building emerged as much from a desire to create the pyramid of glass as from a desire to create a functional gallery space. This desire to make the glass pyramid the main motif seems to have led to the central court, and the exhibition spaces are simply at its edge."[231] Goldberger was also critical of the installation of the Lehman rooms, which he likened to model rooms at Bloomingdale's department store. He was pleased, however, with the retention of the west wall of Vaux and Mould's building, with its red brick and five-pointed limestone arch, and the way Roche-Dinkeloo picked up some of its details in their own work. In a review accompanying Goldberger's, the art critic Hilton Kramer was also negative, decrying the pavilion's "peculiar and somewhat suffocating character." Here, he said, "we see great paintings tethered to the sumptuous tastes of their former owners, immured forever in an atmosphere of decorative extravagance that—to some eyes, at least—denies these paintings their proper ambiance. . . . In the Lehman wing, we see great art enveloped in a broker's vision of the good life."[232]

Ada Louise Huxtable was even less kind: "If one can, as a start, accept as desirable the reproduction of a 1959 Paris decorator's version of how to turn 1905 rooms designed by the architect of Grant's Tomb into an 'appropriate' background for Renaissance art—the rooms laid end-to-end in the park (buried and blind) instead of top-to-bottom on a city street—then one will have no ambivalent feelings about the building." The Lehman rooms, she said, captured none of the "discovery and nostalgia" offered by museum period rooms. "These are not great rooms; they are just elaborate rooms filled with great things. This is a trip to nowhere." Huxtable did, however, acknowledge the difficulty of acquiescing to the donor's wish to reproduce his house and keep the collection intact, and said she was impressed with the architects' skill in designing "their way out of the trap set by the terms of the gift . . . with taste and expertise." But, she argued, the pavilion "vastly overcelebrates the collection and the donor," overlooking its functions as the central compositional motif of the new west facade and as the conclusion of the east-west axis.[233]

It was not until 1978 that the Metropolitan would open another wing, the Sackler Wing, as the new home of the Temple of Dendur was called. In the meantime, in October 1976, the reinstallation of the Egyptology department in the North Wing was unveiled. Designed by Kevin Roche—in association with the graphic design firm of Rudolph de Harak Associates, the Metropolitan's curator of Egyptology, Christine Lilyquist, Arthur Rosenblatt and Hoving—this project, more than any other since the Blumenthal patio, garnered critical praise. Huxtable felt it created "an exemplary balance between art and information,"[234] while John Russell, the *New York Times* art critic, found the general tone of the installation "conversational."[235]

797

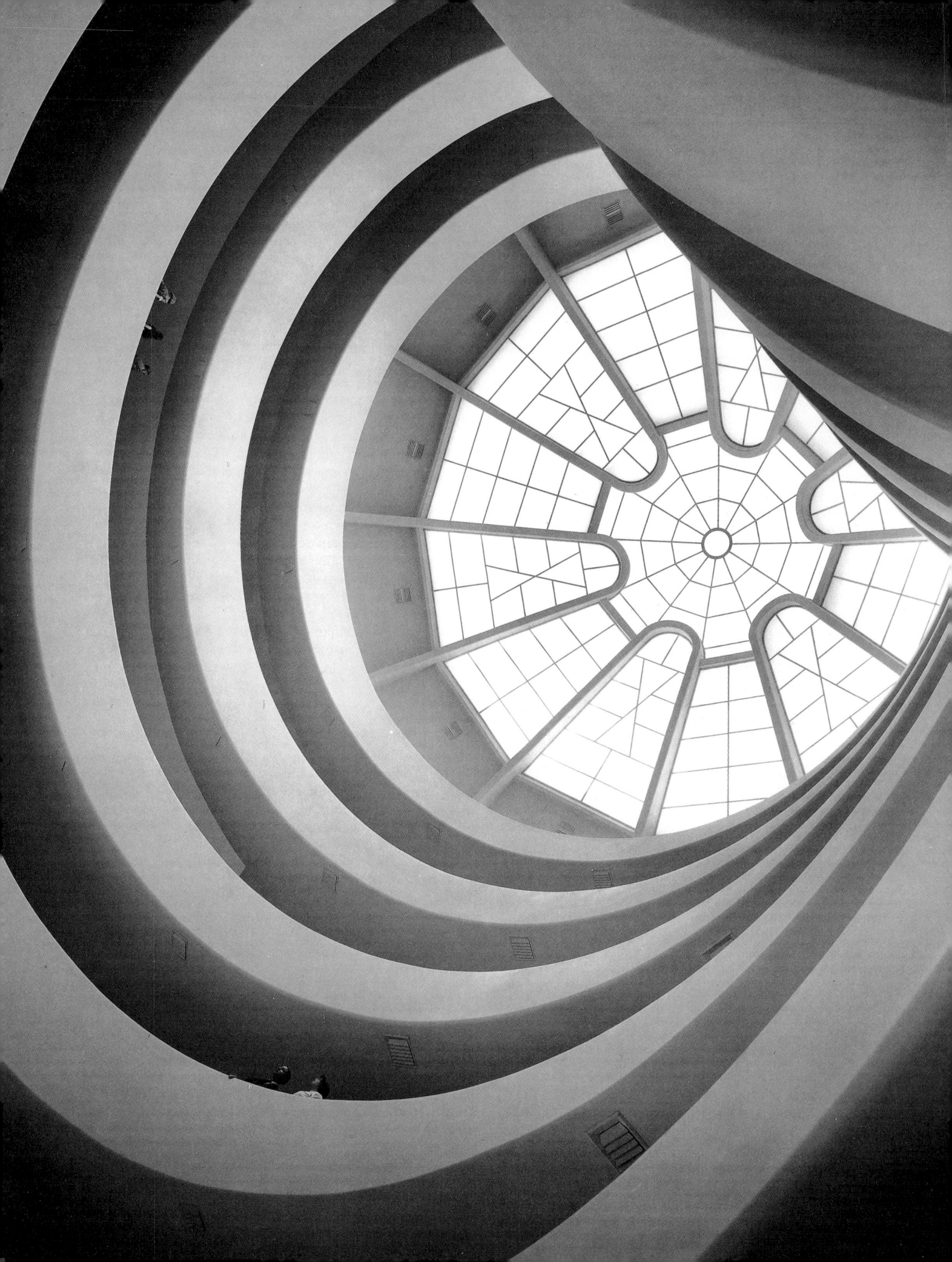

Chapter 11

Upper East Side

On the Upper East Side of Manhattan is the largest concentration of wealth of any residential district in the world. In this narrow grid of streets (Henry James called them pettifogging parallelograms) live the rich of New York, and those who would appear to be.
—Joyce Peterson, 1964[1]

THE PLIGHT OF THE PROSPEROUS

The Upper East Side, between Central Park and the East River, from Sixtieth to Ninety-sixth Street, was the site of extensive rebuilding during the postwar era. Traditionally New York's smartest residential quarter, with the greatest concentration of exemplary townhouses and apartment houses as well as many museums, the area was roughly divided along its length by Lexington Avenue. To the west was a posh, mostly residential area, a continuous "Gold Coast" oriented toward Central Park that included the loosely defined neighborhoods of Lenox Hill and Carnegie Hill, both named after important citizens who made their homes there in the nineteenth century. During the interwar years mansions and townhouses gave way to carefully articulated, grandly proportioned apartment buildings. In the postwar era many of the Upper East Side's finest remaining houses were replaced by apartment buildings that were inferior to their earlier counterparts; nonetheless, the area retained not only a large measure of its prewar urbanism but its unchallenged status as the city's most exclusive residential neighborhood.

East of Lexington Avenue, the Upper East Side had for a long time been home to working-class people, many of whom worked for the industries that lined the East River or for local breweries, including Jacob Ruppert's plant, which stretched along the east side of Third Avenue from Ninetieth to Ninety-fourth Street. While the area was home to many ethnic groups, by the First World War it was dominated by German-speaking immigrants who mostly settled in the Yorkville section, between Eighty-sixth and Ninety-sixth streets. The departure of industry

to suburban locations in the interwar years stimulated the gradual transformation of the East River frontage around Gracie Mansion (1799), which became the official home of the mayor of New York in 1942, into an exclusive residential enclave generally known as Gracie Square. The tenement-lined area between the Gold Coast and the river was peppered with a number of interwar apartment houses, as well as some historic houses that had been restored and attracted a monied crowd—for example, Treadwell Farm, located on the midblocks of Sixty-first and Sixty-second streets between Third and Second avenues.[1] With the removal of the elevated trains that ran along two of the area's avenues—the Second Avenue El was demolished in 1942, the Third Avenue in 1956—this area was extensively rebuilt with luxury apartment houses catering to a middle-aged, upper-middle-class tenantry, many of them former city dwellers returning from the suburbs after raising their children. While all the principal north-south avenues benefited from this postwar redevelopment, Third Avenue was the most completely transformed. Not so the tenement-lined side streets, which remained largely untouched, although their apartments increasingly became home to young professionals as the old-line ethnics moved up the economic ladder and on to the suburbs.

As large parts of the Upper East Side were being rebuilt, some New Yorkers began to express the view that the new construction was of inferior quality. In 1950 Lewis Mumford, commenting on the postwar rebuilding of the Gold Coast that had already commenced and would continue for decades, opened a *New Yorker* essay titled "The Plight of the Prosperous" by writting:

> For a long time I have been wanting to say a word about the apartment buildings that have sprung up since the war in the wealthy and fashionable parts of the city, mainly on and near upper Park Avenue and Fifth Avenue. . . . While all over town the New York City Housing Authority has been erecting, for the low-income group, skyscraper apartments that provide light and air and walks and sometimes even patches of grass and forsythia, the quarters for the prosperous are still being put up with positive contempt for the essentials of good housing. . . . Altogether, a candid assessment of the new apartments for the upper-income groups puts these tenants definitely in the class of the underprivileged.

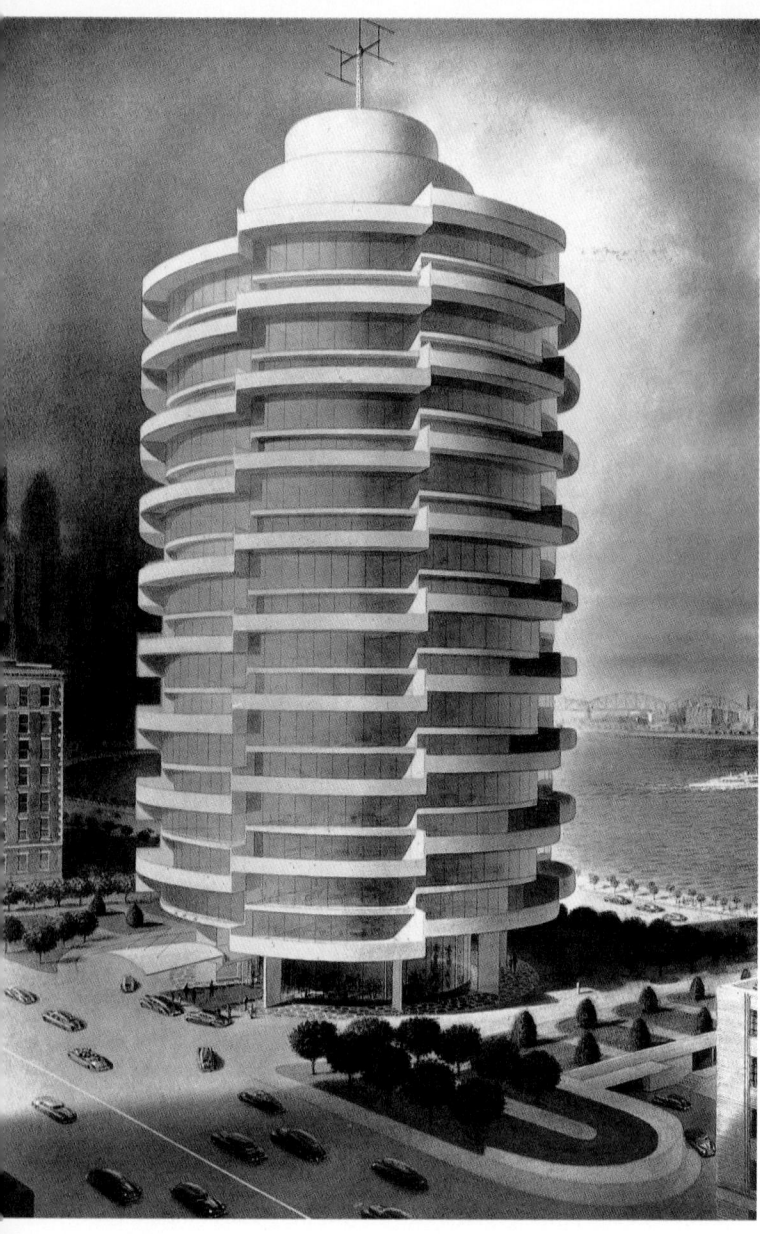

Proposal for Helix apartment building, Sutton Place South. I. M. Pei, 1949. Rendering by A. Leydenfrost of view to the northeast. Wurts. MCNY

Describing one unidentified new building, Mumford said that the interior, "like the interiors of all the neighboring buildings, has been governed by only one consideration, maximum coverage of the land," resulting in a lack of cross ventilation, a comparatively small number of units with southern exposure and oddly proportioned rooms. He concluded: "This is about the best that money can buy in Manhattan today, and the result falls so deplorably short of decent living quarters that it seems obvious to me that something more than money is needed if there is to be a real change for the better in the housing of the upper-income groups."[2]

The developer William Zeckendorf also recognized the inadequacy of the new apartment buildings. In 1949, shortly after putting I. M. Pei on his payroll, Zeckendorf requested that Pei rethink the idea of that building type, using as his model the principle of the tree, with utility and services contained within the trunk. This idea had been advanced by Frank Lloyd Wright in his St. Mark's-in-the-Bouwerie apartment scheme in 1929 and was in the process of being realized for another building type in Wright's S. C. Johnson Research Tower in Racine, Wisconsin of 1950.[3] Within two weeks Pei had turned Zeckendorf's idea into a sketch for a scheme he and Zeckendorf named the Helix, a cylindrical apartment building, ideally twenty-two stories, composed of concentric rings around a core.[4] Inside the core were the elevators and fire stairs; on the innermost ring was a circular corridor for each floor and a mechanical shaft; then came a ring of bathrooms and kitchens, followed by one of living quarters and an outermost ring of balconies. The key to the Helix design was flexibility: tenants could acquire or dispose of the wedge-shaped apartment units according to need. As Zeckendorf observed: "All the big apartments on Park Avenue are obsolete because with present taxes, hardly anyone can afford to live that way—but it costs as much to cut them up into small units as it costs to build a brand new building."[5] Zeckendorf wanted to test the idea on a site facing the East River Drive on Sutton Place South, but he was unable to move forward with the project. Although unsuccessful in developing the East River site, Zeckendorf continued to promote the Helix design, proposing a version of it in the mid-1950s for the Battery Park area in lower Manhattan, but he was never able to realize the scheme.

Writing in 1961, eleven years after Mumford's observations, Thomas H. Creighton, the editor of *Progressive Architecture*, found that the situation had improved little. Lamenting not only the ubiquitous mediocrity of the new buildings but the architectural losses incurred in the rebuilding process, Creighton said: "Looking around . . . I see a very few distinguished buildings that have gone up during the past year, and many to be ashamed of. Twice each day I walk through the devastation of the upper East Side, where block after block of reasonably well-designed buildings is being torn down and replaced with unrelated brick 'luxury' apartments—boxes with air holes in them."[6]

Surveying the eastern reaches of the Upper East Side in 1979, when low standards in upper-income housing were so much the norm as to barely elicit comment, Paul Goldberger found that "There are a few isolated patches of attractiveness here, but for the most part [it] is an uncomfortable mix of tenements gone fancy and new high-rise apartments. Most of the new buildings were quickly and cheaply constructed, with something of the air of Quonset huts thrown up to house military personnel—only, this time there is no war, just a complete surrender of the territory to the upper-middle class." Noting the profound changes in both architecture and ambience that had swept the area during the postwar era, Goldberger concluded, "It is all a jumble, a loud, tense one—cleaner and richer than the jumble of Broadway on the Upper West Side, but also more frenetic, more desperate, less relaxing. It all came very quickly, and you feel it may all disappear tomorrow."[7]

FIFTH AVENUE

By 1940 the future of Fifth Avenue, as both an architectural and a social phenomenon, was cloudy. The diminishing quality in apartment building design that would become a hallmark of the postwar era would be most evident on the stretch of Fifth Avenue facing Central Park, which in palmier days had been the most exclusive section of what Montgomery Schuyler characterized in 1901 as the "Billionaire District."[1] Despite the replacement of most townhouses with apartment blocks during the 1920s and 1930s, its urbanism remained essentially intact. Although radical transformation would eventually threaten the avenue's cohesion, its architectural history had been characterized by change for decades. Fifth Avenue above the park was a comparative wasteland until the 1890s, when it became the preferred location for the mansions of the superrich. A scant twenty years later the avenue entered a second stage of development when these houses were replaced by skillfully designed and luxuriously appointed apartment buildings that set new standards for the type. Collectively the apartment houses formed one of the most cohesive building ensembles the city had ever seen, a grouping that was in fact more consistent than the somewhat individualistic mansions of the previous era.[2] Only the twin palisades of apartment buildings that flanked Park Avenue had a more uniform urbanism. After the Second World War Fifth Avenue entered the final phase of its transformation from an avenue of townhouses to one of apartments. The postwar apartment houses were in no way as commodious or as aesthetically refined as those of the 1920s, but because most of them were built before the zoning change in 1961 the street wall was maintained and the height and density of the new buildings complemented those of the older buildings. Thus, though the effect was diluted it was not destroyed, and the avenue's location, combined with its residue of prewar apartment houses, enabled it to remain one of the city's most prestigious addresses.[3]

During the 1930s Park Avenue replaced Fifth Avenue as *the* highest-status urban address in the nation, and during that decade Fifth Avenue became something of a ghost town. The replacement of the avenue's townhouses by apartments, which had begun in the 1920s, took on a new twist in the Depression, when many of the mansions were simply abandoned and boarded up because, without significant demand for new apartments, there was no point in incurring demolition costs. By the late 1930s the economic situation had changed enough so that some boarded-up mansions were torn down to make way for new apartment houses. In 1938 Irving Margon's 965 Fifth Avenue was completed, replacing Freeman & Thain's residence for Jacob Schiff of 1900–1901.[4] Emery Roth's apartment houses at 930 and 875 Fifth Avenue were completed in 1940. Located on the northeast corner of Fifth Avenue and Seventy-fourth Street, the nineteen-story 930 Fifth replaced four nineteenth-century townhouses: the William Von Antwerp residence (William Cauvet, 1882) at 930, the James D. Layng residence (William C. Mowbray, 1886–87) at 931, the Jacob Schiff residence (1884–86) at 932 and the Leonard F. Beckwith residence (John H. Duncan, 1893–96) at 933.[5] Occupying the southeast

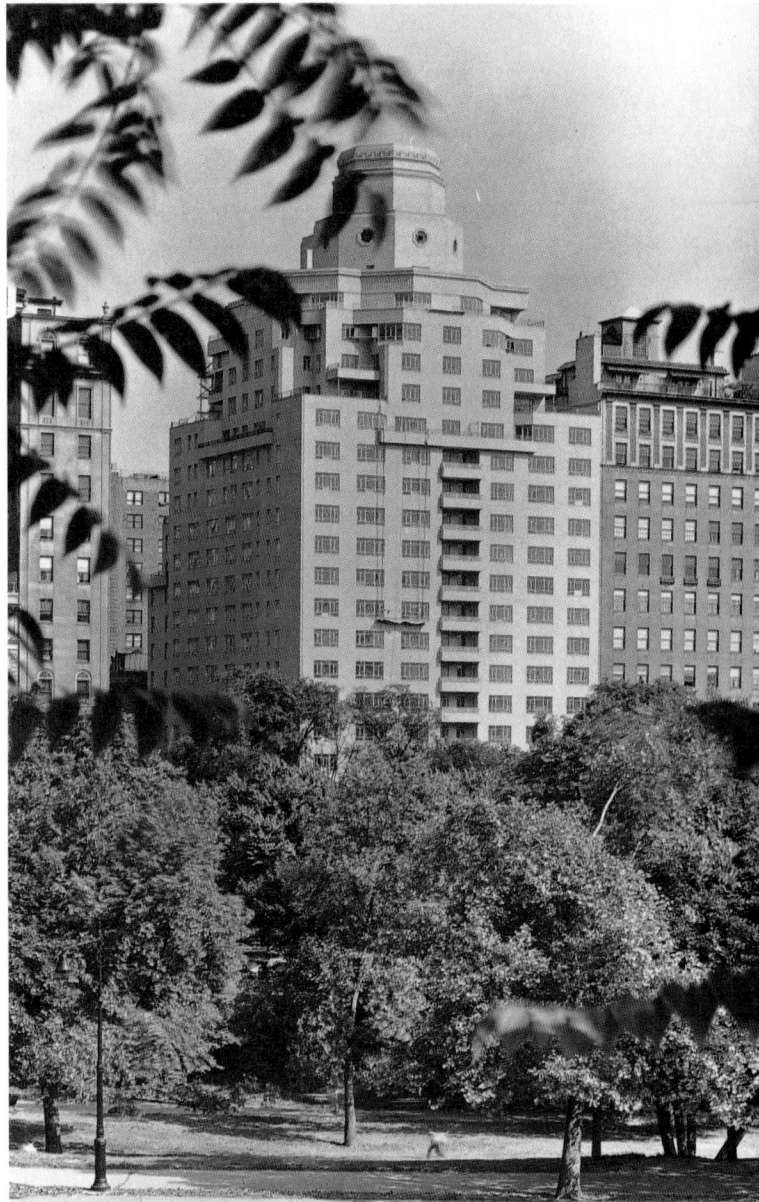

945 Fifth Avenue, southeast corner of East Seventy-sixth Street. Emery Roth & Sons, 1949. View to the southeast. Wurts. MCNY

corner of Sixty-ninth Street, 875 Fifth, also nineteen stories, replaced four townhouses: number 875 (Welch, Smith & Provot, 1900–1901), the Mary Harrison residence (C. P. H. Gilbert, 1900–1901) at 876, the Ogden Mills residence (Richard Morris Hunt, 1885–87) on the corner site and the Maturin Livingston residence (Richard Morris Hunt, 1887–88) at 4 East Sixty-ninth Street.[6]

Roth's new Fifth Avenue buildings, though they lacked some of the visual interest and vitality of his earlier apartment houses on Central Park West and Riverside Drive, were nonetheless more than adequate additions to the avenue, amalgamating the Classicism of the pre-Crash era with a new Modernist-inspired aesthetic.[7] With limestone bases, beige-brick facades, moldings and generously scaled public lobbies, these buildings were considerably better than what was to come. The Seventy-fourth Street facade of 930 was punctuated by a symmetrically placed, recessed principal entrance, surmounted by a frieze, leading to a lobby containing a black-and-white marble floor and a fireplace. The Fifth Avenue facade featured large window surrounds articulated with pilasters, balustrades and broken pediments, further enlivened by depictions of cherubs. Beginning at the sixteenth floor the building incorporated a series of setbacks. A robustly detailed water tower, complete with a broken pediment and framed by dramatically scaled pilasters rising its full height, surmounted the building. By contrast, 875 was smoother and sleeker, without overt historical references. The streamlined aesthetic found expression in curved corner windows, sweeping, cantilevered upper-story terraces and, most dramatically, glass-brick corners on the rooftop water tower. Decorative brickwork on the principal facade's spandrels augmented the overall design. A symmetrically placed Fifth Avenue entrance led to a streamlined lobby featuring red marble walls and a gray tremolite floor; a second, similarly articulated lobby was approached directly from Sixty-ninth Street. Although the building exuded a sense of up-to-date style and the rooms were not large, the layouts reflected the traditional standards of luxury and service that Fifth Avenue residents had come to expect; every unit, even those lacking separate dining rooms or maids' rooms, had a servants' entrance leading from a vestibule connected to the kitchen.

In 1941 plans were announced to demolish the adjacent houses of Edward H. Harriman (Herter Brothers, 1879–81), on the northeast corner of Fifth Avenue and Sixty-ninth Street, and of Adolph E. Lewisohn (C. W. Clinton, 1880–82), at 881 Fifth Avenue, between Sixty-ninth and Seventieth streets. Both houses were vacant and had been purchased previously by a British investor whose plans for their future were interrupted by the war, causing them to be foreclosed. It was not until 1948 that these landmarks were replaced by Emery Roth & Sons' 880 Fifth Avenue, a 162-unit apartment house.[8] The building rose as a mass to a series of setback terraces surmounted by two penthouse elevator towers, which were a scaled-down version of the twin towers of Roth's San Remo (1930) across Central Park.[9] Cantilevered terraces that stretched across the seventeenth and twentieth floors reflected the building's dominant Modernism, but they also visually served as cornices, relating to the forms of the surrounding prewar apartment buildings. Inside, though some apartments contained only two rooms—minuscule when compared to an earlier era's standards for luxury—every living room was equipped with a fireplace and some units contained up to eight rooms, including two maids' rooms.

The Roth firm's 945 Fifth Avenue (1949), on the southeast corner of Seventy-sixth Street, occupied the former site of

Temple Beth-El (Brunner & Tryon, 1891), whose fate was symptomatic of the avenue's shaky status.[10] In 1927 the congregation of Beth-El merged with that of Temple Emanu-El, and two years later the combined group began to worship in the latter's richly ornamented building (Kohn, Butler & Stein with Goodhue Associates, 1929), newly completed on the northeast corner of Fifth Avenue and Sixty-fifth Street.[11] Because there was no demand for Temple Beth-El's grandly domed building or its site, the structure stood unused until it was demolished in 1947, when the economy was at last robust enough to support a new building. The Roths' nineteen-story apartment building, completed two years later, was a straightforward composition rendered in beige brick above a two-story limestone base. Its principal facade was distinguished primarily by a centrally located vertical row of recessed terraces and culminated in a series of upper-story setbacks, some with chamfered corners. At the top, the elevator machinery and the building's water tower were housed in a spectacularly massed octagon.

Rosario Candela and Paul Resnick's nineteen-story apartment house (1949) at 1 East Sixty-sixth Street replaced a brownstone (D. & J. Jardine, 1881–82) and the H. O. Havemeyer residence (Charles Coolidge Haight, 1891–93).[12] Numerous angular bays provided sidewise views to Central Park, and setbacks began above the fifteenth floor. Limestone stringcourses and a principal entrance frame in red marble lent some distinction to the otherwise bland design. To make way for William I. Hohauser's 870 Fifth Avenue (1949), on the northeast corner of Sixty-eighth Street, the houses of M. C. Inman (R. H. Robertson, 1893) and Robert L. Stuart (William Schickel, 1882) were demolished.[13] The Stuart house had been extensively altered by McKim, Mead & White following its purchase in 1897 by the financier and sportsman William C. Whitney. The new building, with nineteen stories and a penthouse, lacked the interest and panache of the Century, the New Yorker, the Cardozo and the other small-scale, shipshape hotels in Miami Beach for which Hohauser had become known.[14] It was not even as interesting as his Depression-era apartment houses on the Bronx's Grand Concourse, such as the Dorhage and the Edna.[15] Still, the beige-brick building, which incorporated a three-story stone-clad base and, beginning at the thirteenth floor, a series of setbacks, contained numerous indentations and rounded bays to create a lively effect. But it also essentially filled its site and zoning envelope, respecting the street's dominant building wall. The building's principal entrance was set into a two-story-high concave recession along the Sixty-eighth Street facade.

In late 1946 construction commenced on the Roths' 3 East Seventy-first Street, just off the avenue.[16] Replacing McKim, Mead & White's H. A. C. Taylor residence, the dignified apartment building marked the beginning of the end for a quintessential townhouse row that included the residence of Mrs. Hamilton McK. Twombly (Warren & Wetmore, 1926), which would be demolished in the late 1950s to make way for Sylvan and Robert Bien's nineteen-story and penthouse apartment building at 900 Fifth Avenue (1958), on the northeast corner of Seventy-first Street.[17] The white-brick facades of 900 Fifth were detail-free except for two massively scaled, crudely detailed polygonal bays beginning at the second story on the Fifth Avenue side and running the structure's full height. Spandrels were clad in dark gray metal and individual windows were framed in aluminum. Inside, generously sized six- and seven-room apartments featured central air conditioning.

Sylvan Bien's banal eighteen-story, white-brick-clad building at 923 Fifth Avenue, on the northeast corner of Seventy-third

Street, was completed in 1951 for Sam Minskoff & Sons.[18] When the project was announced in September 1945, it heralded, as the editors of the *Real Estate Record and Guide* put it, "the beginning of the long-awaited post-war development of New York City's most fashionable residential district."[19] In addition to 1 East Seventy-third Street, the George Q. Palmer residence (Palmer & Hornbostel, 1903), and a townhouse at 3 East Seventy-third Street, the new building was to replace the townhouses of George Quintard (Arthur Gilman, 1880–82) at number 922, Eliza Guggenheimer (Robert Maynicke, 1898–99) at number 923, and George H. Warren (Warren & Wetmore, 1902–3) at number 924. The only distinctive elements of Bien's building were the three-story limestone base, the corner terraces and a lobby decorated with eighteenth-century antiques by Dorothy Draper. The inclusion of a sixty-car subterranean parking garage reflected the changing requirements of wealthy New Yorkers.

To make way for Sylvan Bien's nineteen-story, beige-brick apartment house at 860 Fifth Avenue (1950), on the southeast corner of Sixty-eighth Street, the Renaissance-style Thomas Fortune Ryan house (William Schickel & Company, 1893–95), at 858 Fifth Avenue, as well as the adjoining Italian garden, were demolished.[20] The site had already seen significant change: in order to create the garden in 1912, Ryan had torn down Charles T. Yerkes's house (R. H. Robertson, 1896); when the garden was redesigned by Carrère & Hastings in 1925, it was ornamented by thirty-two white marble columns that had framed the staircase of the Yerkes house. Bien's apartment building was organized around a centrally located shallow entrance court facing Fifth Avenue, overlooked by long balconies that were divided into sections. Upper-level setbacks culminated in a two-story-high water tower.

On the southeast corner of Eighty-seventh Street, 1056 Fifth Avenue (1951), designed by George F. Pelham, Jr., replaced the James Speyer mansion, which had been willed to the Museum of the City of New York, an institution Speyer had helped found.[21] The principal feature of Pelham's generally bland nineteen-story, beige-brick block was the placement of a one-story parking garage adjacent to the building along Eighty-seventh Street, which guaranteed light and air to the rear apartments and fostered the appearance of a freestanding tower, as Raymond Hood had done in his American Radiator (1924) and Daily News (1929) buildings.[22] The arrangement was widely studied by developers and planners, particularly as the City Planning Commission began to consider revisions to the zoning ordinance that would reduce allowable bulk to insure more light and air for surrounding streets. The building's principal facade combined cantilevered and recessed terraces in a syncopated composition that was more visually chaotic than interesting. The editors of *Architectural Forum* observed that in an "effort to assuage the city dweller's hankering for a front porch all his own—space is snipped from the living room to allow for patching in a petite balcony."[23] The lobby was designed by Beryl Austrian to evoke, as the decorator put it, "the spirit and character" of the demolished Speyer mansion.[24] In addition, a bronze plaque on the new building was inscribed with a quotation, attributed to Abraham Lincoln, that was a favorite of Speyer's: "I like to see a man proud of the place in which he lives. I like to see a man live so that his place will be proud of him."[25]

Two new ecclesiastical buildings contributed to the street's evolving character. The first was Harry M. Prince's eleven-story office building for the Union of American Hebrew Congregations (1950), on the southeast corner of Sixty-fifth Street,

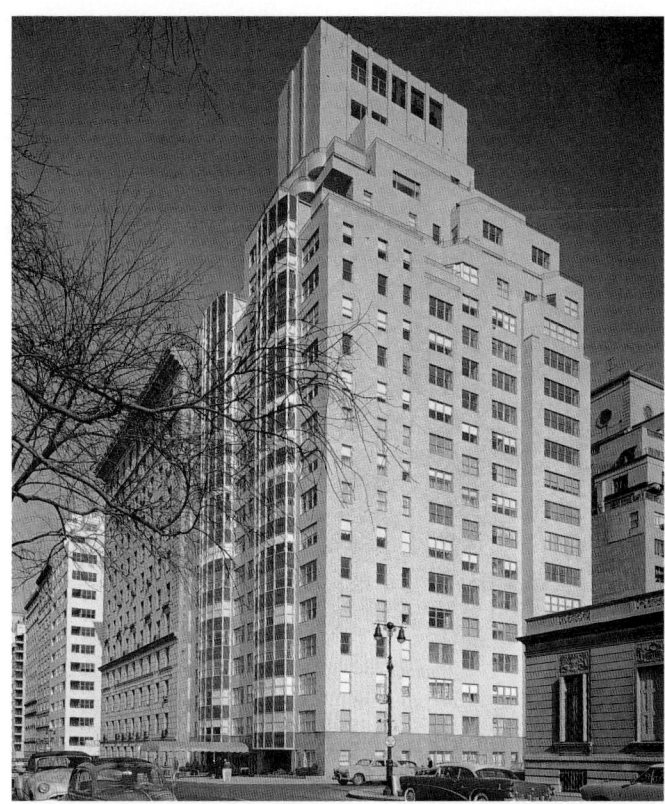

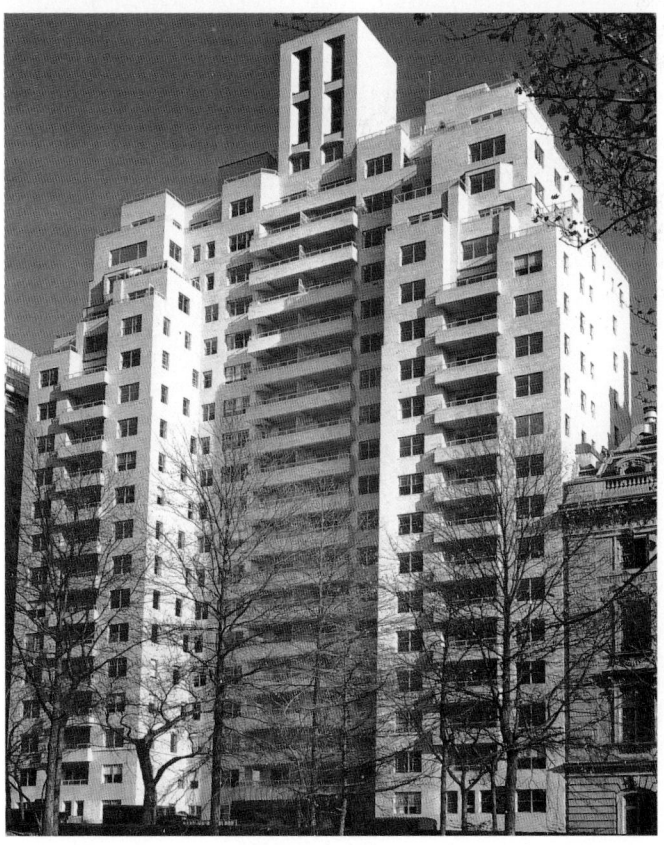

Top: 900 Fifth Avenue, northeast corner of East Seventy-first Street. Sylvan and Robert Bien, 1958. View to the northeast. OMH

Bottom: 860 Fifth Avenue, southeast corner of East Sixty-eighth Street. Sylvan Bien, 1950. View to the northeast. EG

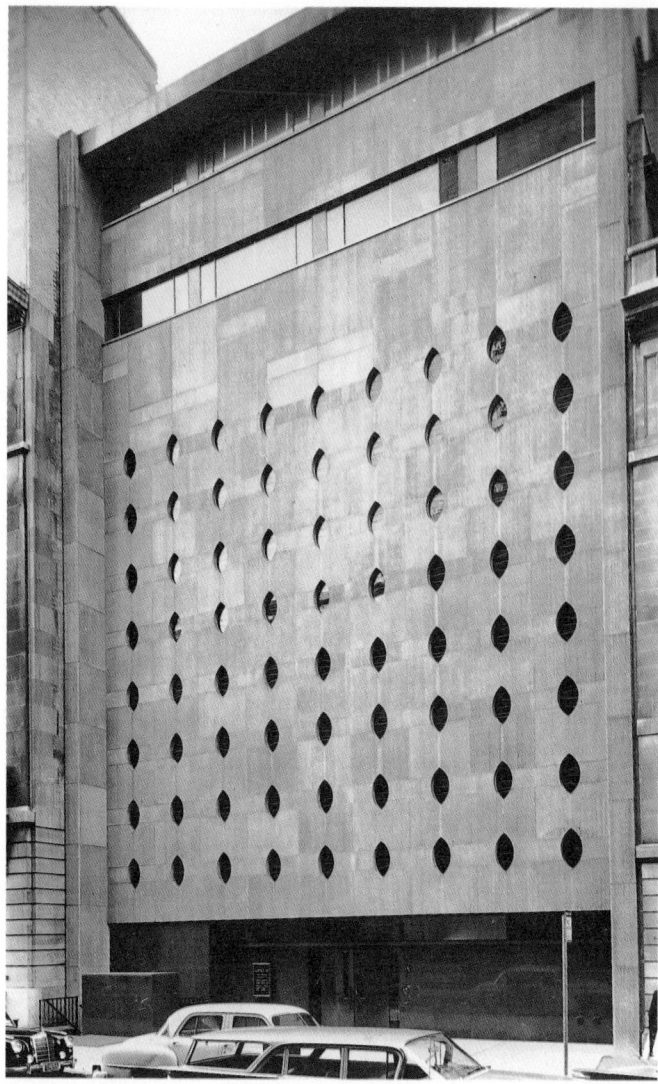

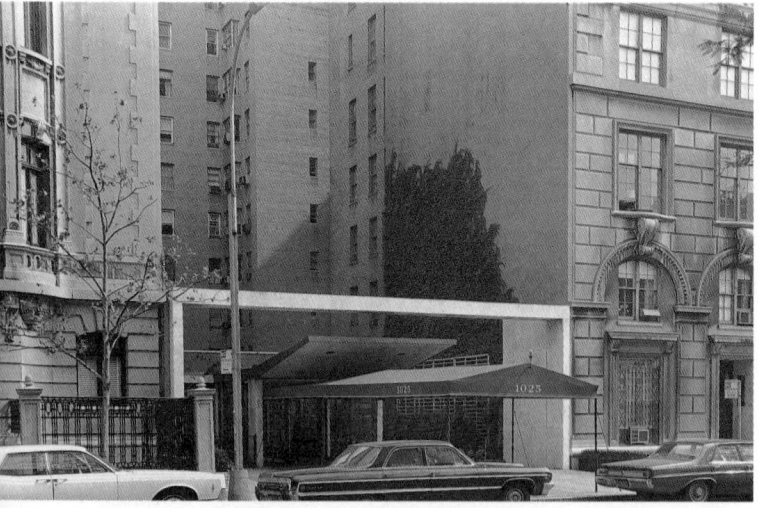

Top: Fifth Avenue Synagogue, 5 East Sixty-second Street, between Fifth and Madison avenues. Percival Goodman, 1956. View to the northwest. CU

Bottom: 1025 Fifth Avenue, between East Eighty-third and East Eighty-fourth streets. H. I. Feldman and Raymond Loewy Associates, 1956. View to the southeast. OMH

which replaced the Sophia A. Sherman residence (William H. Russell, 1892–94).[26] The dignified limestone-clad building was suitably deferential to Temple Emanu-El across the street. Its Fifth Avenue facade, which contained three vertically arranged rows of paired windows with spandrels featuring golden-colored stone insets and decorative panels inscribed in Hebrew with the Ten Commandments, culminated in a gently arched parapet. Romanesque details, such as rope moldings and twisted columns, decorated the principal arched entrance. The Sixty-fifth Street facade, with horizontal strip windows, adopted a more Modernist aesthetic. Although the building's synthesis of utilitarianism and historicism was tepid, given the blandness of most postwar apartment buildings, Prince's contribution to the avenue was notable. Percival Goodman's Fifth Avenue Synagogue (1956), at 5 East Sixty-second Street, was clad in striated limestone, punctuated by a grid of seventy-two hexagonal stained-glass windows designed by Robert Pinart; while in no way traditional, the design was dignified if somewhat stolid.[27]

In 1954 plans were announced for two companion twelve-story buildings to be built on back-to-back midblock sites, between Fifth and Madison avenues, facing Eighty-third and Eighty-fourth streets.[28] The project replaced the frame house at 3 East Eighty-third Street (1853–62), and the adjoining brownstone houses at 7 and 9 East Eighty-third Street and the brick stables at their back, facing Eighty-fourth Street, all dating from the 1880s. The project's developers were also able to obtain one property along Fifth Avenue, the forty-foot-wide Lloyd S. Bryce house (Ogden Codman, 1906). In what was surely one of the more ingenious if urbanistically destructive moves on the avenue, the developers demolished the house and used the site for a 100-foot-long entrance arcade that would connect their midblock buildings to the avenue, collectively providing them with the prestigious address of 1025 Fifth Avenue. H. I. Feldman designed the bland midblock buildings (1956), but Raymond Loewy Associates, the industrial design firm that dabbled in architecture, developed the Fifth Avenue approach.

At Fifth Avenue, Loewy slid a seventeen-foot-long inclined, cantilevered canopy of reinforced concrete through a fifteen-foot-high, forty-foot-wide, one-foot-thick rectilinear marble arch inserted between the flanking buildings. The entrance walk leading east was paved in black and white terrazzo and flanked by gardens, forming a landscaped sliver court that also contained a sculpture by Constantino Nivola set against a brick wall. The enclosed passageway-cum-lobby, with a travertine floor, mirrors and decorative wood panels and screens, was flashy but elegant. According to Herbert Fischbach, president of Herbert Charles & Co., Inc., the sales and management agent for the project, "The combined appeal of the Fifth Avenue address and the Loewy designed lobby has increased apartment sales value by 20% to 25%."[29] Whatever the lobby's effectiveness, or its merit as an isolated piece of design, the absence of a building along Fifth Avenue, despite the gesture of the marble arch, dealt a significant blow to the integrity of the avenue's cohesive urbanism.

In 1953 plans were announced for the demolition of two vacant houses at 935 and 936 Fifth Avenue, on the southeast corner of Seventy-fifth Street, and their replacement by a cooperative apartment, with seventeen stories and a penthouse, designed by Harman Associates.[30] The corner site had been owned by Simon Guggenheim, Otto H. Kahn and then Mrs. Grace Rainey Rogers, who in 1907 built a house designed by Carrère & Hastings. In 1909 the Rogers house, 936 Fifth Avenue, was sold to Edwin Gould, whose family owned it until 1953. The house one site in from the corner, at 935 Fifth Avenue, was built in 1910 by S. Reading Bertron and designed by Warren & Wetmore. Harman Associates' architecturally undistinguished beige-brick building, completed in 1955, became one more addition to the avenue that was more memorable for what it replaced than for what it contributed. Even within the context of what had, by this time, become a hackneyed format for apartment building design, number 935 was a weak exemplar; its upper-level setbacks presented disorganized, asymmetrical profiles to both Seventy-fifth Street and Fifth Avenue.

By 1957, when Irving Brodsky purchased the Rovensky mansion (Guy Lowell, 1916) at 1051 Fifth Avenue, on the northeast corner of Eighty-sixth Street, as well as the adjoining house at 1053 Fifth Avenue (Herts & Tallant, 1904) and two nineteenth-century townhouses at 1 and 3 East Eighty-sixth Street, Fifth Avenue's postwar transformation was virtually complete.[31] The Rovensky mansion, a last vestige of the avenue's gilded era, was still intact and still inhabited by the family that had built it. The house had been designed for the shipping and railroad tycoon Morton F. Plant and his second wife, the former Mae Caldwell Manwaring, who married financier John Rovensky after Plant's death in 1918. The stately houses were demolished to make way for Sylvan Bien's 1050 Fifth Avenue, a nineteen-story buff-brick building with a few upper-level setbacks.

Not only was Fifth Avenue's grand architectural heritage of townhouses almost completely destroyed, but some of the well-designed pre–World War II apartment houses on the avenue also came to be considered "old hat" and, therefore, suitable for "modernization" if not expendable. Such renovation was, of course, a by-product of rent control, but it also reflected the belief that the very rich were abandoning the city as their principal place of residence and would need only small apartments to serve as pieds-à-terre. For example, as palatial apartments—some containing up to twenty-eight rooms—became available in J. E. R. Carpenter's twelve-story building at 907 Fifth Avenue (1916), on the southeast corner of Seventy-second Street, management divided them into smaller units, but the building's elegantly restrained exterior was left untouched.[32] A building directly across the street, 910 Fifth Avenue (Fred F. French, 1919), received far shabbier treatment. Not only were its apartments broken up into smaller units in 1959 but its Classically inspired facades were ripped off and replaced with white-brick cladding in a design by Sylvan and Robert Bien that arguably represented the nadir of the avenue's postwar architecture.[33]

Though the postwar evolution of Fifth Avenue was characterized by the demolition of townhouses, the reckless remodeling of existing apartment buildings and the construction of new apartment houses, one new building located just east of the avenue bucked the trend and attested to the enduring appeal of living in "a house in town." In 1959 the architect Felix Augenfeld, working in association with Jan Pokorny, completed the Joseph Buttinger residence, a combination townhouse and research library located at 10 East Eighty-seventh Street.[34] The five-story building, whose principal facade was clad in travertine on the ground floor and Italian glass mosaic tile above, contained a duplex for the owners as well as a separate, top-floor apartment for the resident librarian, who was responsible for the 50,000-volume collection. Augenfeld's highly reductive Modernist design, with an internal organization reminiscent of William Hamby and George Nelson's stylistically audacious Sherman M. Fairchild house (1941), placed the two-story, U-shaped library toward the back of the lot, behind an entrance vestibule and a

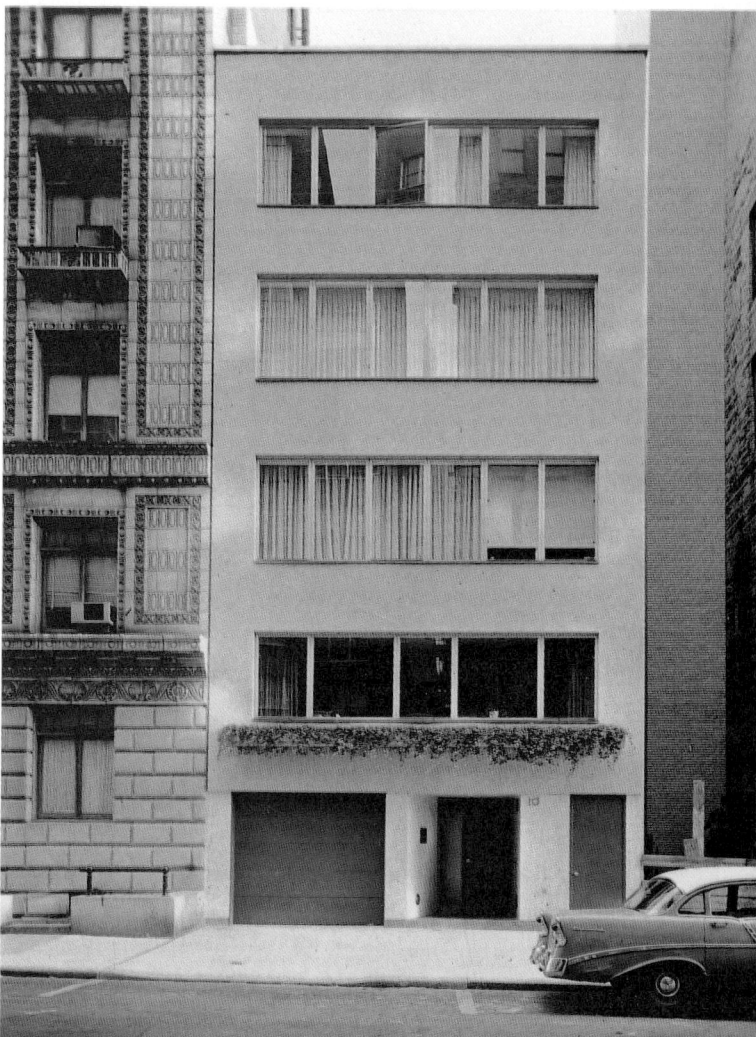

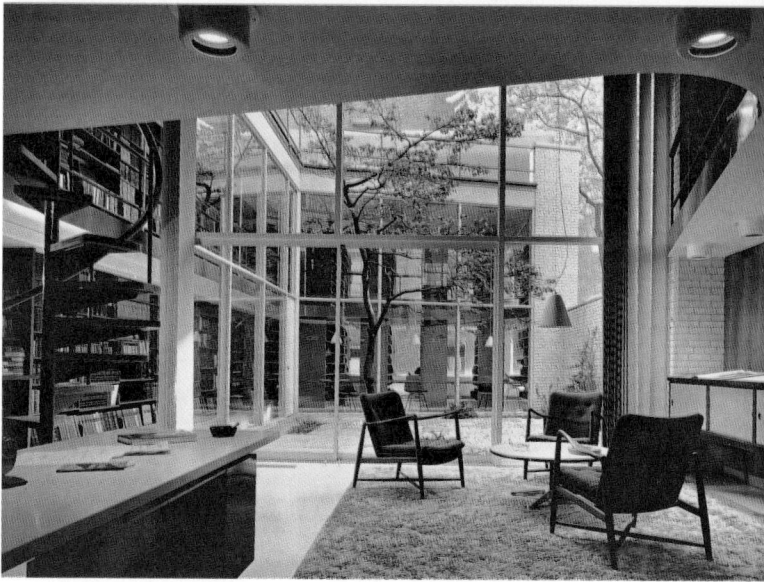

Top: Joseph Buttinger residence, 10 East Eighty-seventh Street, between Fifth and Madison avenues. Felix Augenfeld in association with Jan Pokorny, 1959. View to the south. CU

Bottom: Joseph Buttinger residence. Library and interior courtyard. CU

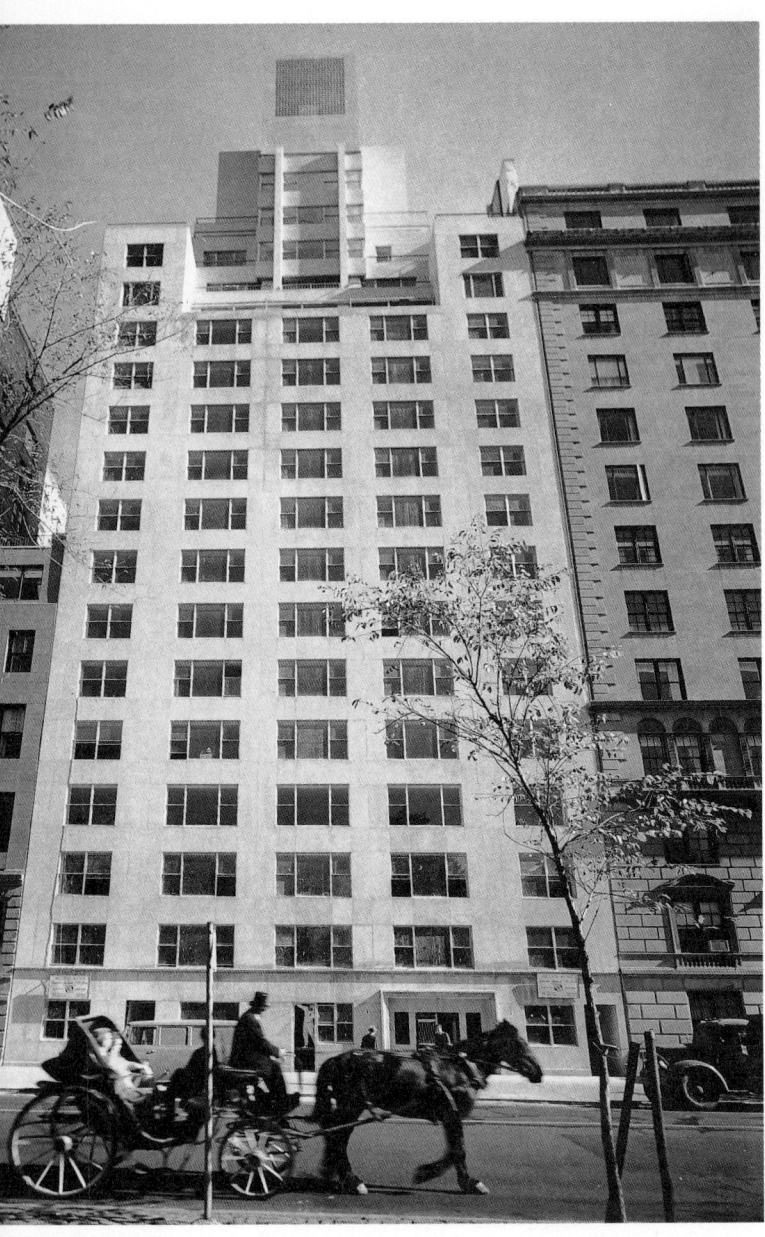

812 Fifth Avenue, between East Sixty-second and East Sixty-third streets. Robert Bien, 1961. View to the east. EG

one-car garage.[35] A glazed passageway linked the library's main reading areas and its book stacks as it skirted a trapezoidal, landscaped courtyard, providing what *Progressive Architecture* rather lyrically described as an "effect of deep transparency throughout the house."[36] The Buttingers' living quarters included a rooftop terrace that overlooked the courtyard.

The year 1959 also saw the completion of the National Academy of Design's School of Fine Arts, just off Fifth Avenue at 5 East Eighty-ninth Street.[37] The school had been planning to build a new facility since 1945. Designed by William and Geoffrey Platt, the three-story building presented a windowless expanse of buff-colored bricks arranged in decorative diamond-shaped patterns above a single-story base punctuated by an asymmetrical composition of five windows and a door. Inside, six studios accommodated a total of 500 students. The building's austere facade, appropriate within the context of Fifth Avenue, was perhaps even more effective as a foil to the school's flamboyant neighbor, the Solomon R. Guggenheim Museum, also completed in 1959 and located just across Eighty-ninth Street (see below).

Robert Bien's eighteen-story apartment building at 812 Fifth Avenue (1961), a midblock site between Sixty-second and Sixty-third streets, replaced three townhouses, at numbers 812 (D. & J. Jardine, 1870–71), 813 (D. & J. Jardine, 1870–71; C. P. H. Gilbert, 1897–98) and 814 (S. A. Warner, 1870–71).[38] The new apartment house was more dignified than most of its contemporaries, presenting a limestone-clad facade to Fifth Avenue. Above the thirteenth floor symmetrically arrayed setbacks created a "tower," partially clad in the glazed white brick that was becoming such a ubiquitous feature of the Upper East Side.

In 1961 yet another venerable Fifth Avenue townhouse, the fifty-room, six-story limestone mansion at 1 East Sixty-seventh Street, was purchased by a builder and slated for demolition.[39] The house had been designed in 1895 by Horace Trumbauer for George Jay Gould. In 1924, a year after Gould's death, it was purchased by Mrs. Cornelius Vanderbilt II. When Mrs. Vanderbilt died in her house in 1934 at the age of eighty-nine, her daughter, the Countess László Szechenyi, sold it to the Institute of International Education. The garish seventeen-story apartment building at 857 Fifth Avenue (1963) that replaced the Gould house was designed by Robert Bien. It was a glaring contrast to its predecessor, whose "aura of old, pre-Revolution Paris," according to *New York Times* reporter Thomas W. Ennis, had helped make it "one of the most imposing of the many costly homes that made Fifth Avenue a world-famous residential thoroughfare."[40] The new building's lower floors flaunted to passersby the aggressive banality of the architect's design: along its Fifth Avenue frontage the building was raised on two-story-high, red-marble-clad columns set upon a landscaped podium that seemed better suited to an outer-borough or suburban location than one on Fifth Avenue. The cladding continued along the Sixty-seventh Street facade, which contained the building's principal entrance. Above the base, a predominantly white-brick exterior included a disarming array of other materials and decorative elements. As the architect Andrew Alpern noted, "The facade is a gauche assemblage . . . that contrasts sharply with its more sedate neighbors."[41] Among the building's tackier details were the black metal railings enclosing the awkwardly recessed terraces that faced Central Park and the Brutalist-inspired, oddly undulating concrete piers on the Sixty-seventh Street facade. Inside, the apartments were quite luxurious by contemporary standards, with one unit to a floor; a triplex penthouse had two shiplike curving bay windows slightly cantilevered out toward Central Park. The generosity of the apartment layouts made the building's facade seem all the more regrettable.

The apartment building at 1045 Fifth Avenue (1965–67), located on a midblock site between Eighty-fifth and Eighty-sixth streets and designed by Horace Ginsbern & Associates, broke with the avenue's typical formula of windows punched into brick or stone walls.[42] Replacing two Beaux-Arts houses designed by Welch, Smith & Provot and completed in 1906, the fourteen-story building offered the avenue a facade composed almost entirely of dark-brown-tinted glass.

Although ignorance and apathy characterized the public attitude toward Fifth Avenue's architectural heritage throughout most of the 1940s and 1950s, by 1964, when the so-called Brokaw houses at the northeast corner of Seventy-ninth Street were bought by developers and slated for demolition, the tide of popular taste had begun to turn (see chapter 16). Though the growing preservation movement, catalyzed by the recent demolition of Pennsylvania Station, failed to save the Brokaw houses, the loss did help to transform an enthusiastic but unorganized group of individuals into a powerful political force. But the short-term results of the demolition were not so positive: the two buildings erected on the site did little to ameliorate the downward spiral of the avenue's architecture. The first of the two, at 980 Fifth Avenue (Paul Resnick and Harry F. Green, 1966), was the first building along the avenue's park frontage designed under the city's new zoning resolution.[43] The twenty-seven-story slab clad in dark brown brick and concrete was set back from the traditional street wall on both its Fifth Avenue and its Seventy-ninth Street frontages. The resultant open space, called a "plaza," was in fact nothing but an automobile drop-off. The second building on the site, a twenty-four-story buff-brick midblock apartment house, 985 Fifth Avenue (Wechsler & Schimenti, 1970), stood just to the north, on the former site of one of the Brokaw houses as well as the site of the Simon H. Stern residence (A. J. Manning, 1899–1901).[44] Incorporating extensive glazing and balconies, 985 Fifth Avenue abounded in crudely handled details such as the metal grilles that covered air-conditioning units recessed below the windows. Like its neighbor, it was set back from the street to form a "plaza." Although this one was even more constricted in size, it contained a circular driveway and a small patch of landscaping that provided the setting for a sculpture by Priscilla Kapel titled *The Castle*, which had far more architectural charm than the building that constituted its backdrop.

Solomon R. Guggenheim Museum

Frank Lloyd Wright's Solomon R. Guggenheim Museum (1943–59) offered the first dramatic challenge to Fifth Avenue's traditional urbanism and became its most memorable monument. On June 1, 1943, the curator of the Solomon R. Guggenheim Foundation, Baroness Hilla von Rebay, initiated discussions with Wright that would result in the construction of the masterpiece of his late maturity. The building was not completed until 1959, and its history over the sixteen intervening years form a remarkable chapter in the history of American architectural practice. The extraordinary and in so many ways improbable collaboration between Wright, Rebay, minerals magnate Solomon R. Guggenheim and Guggenheim's heirs to realize the building in the face of often conflicting ideals and a largely unsympathetic city bureaucracy is documented at length in correspondence.[45] Six separate sets of plans and 749 draw-

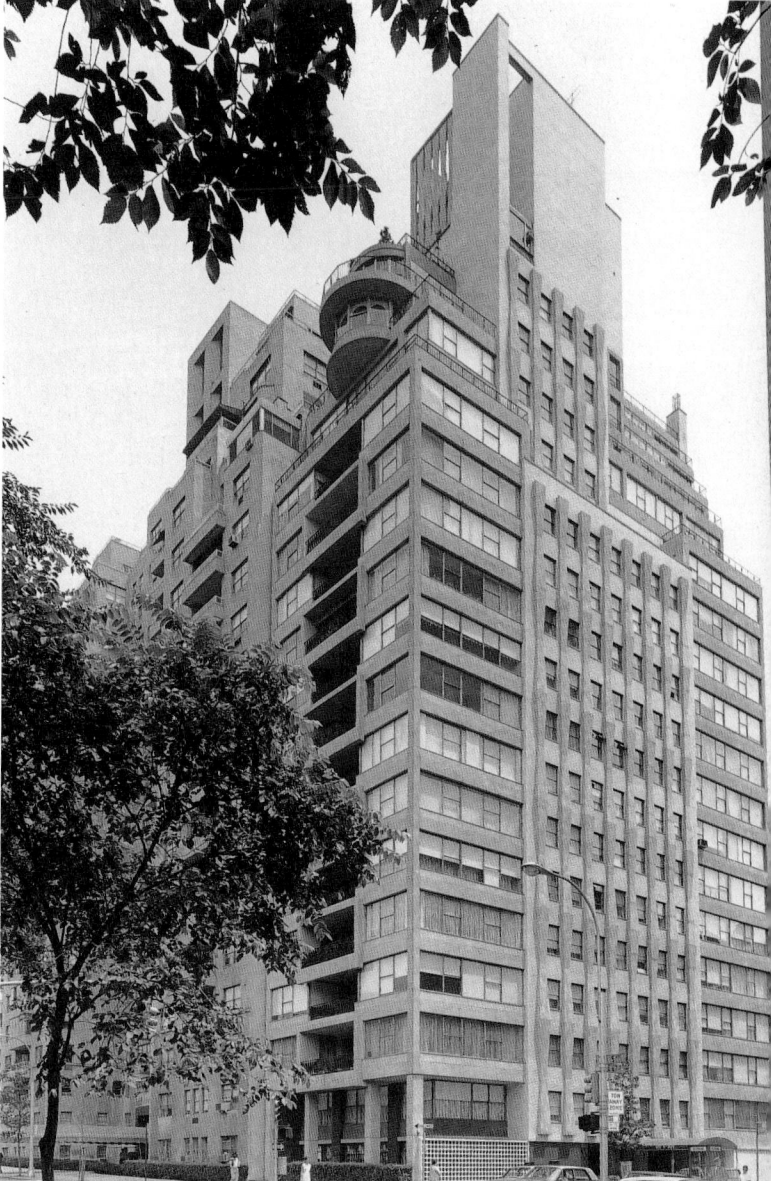

857 Fifth Avenue, northeast corner of East Sixty-seventh Street. Robert Bien, 1963. View to the northeast. OMH

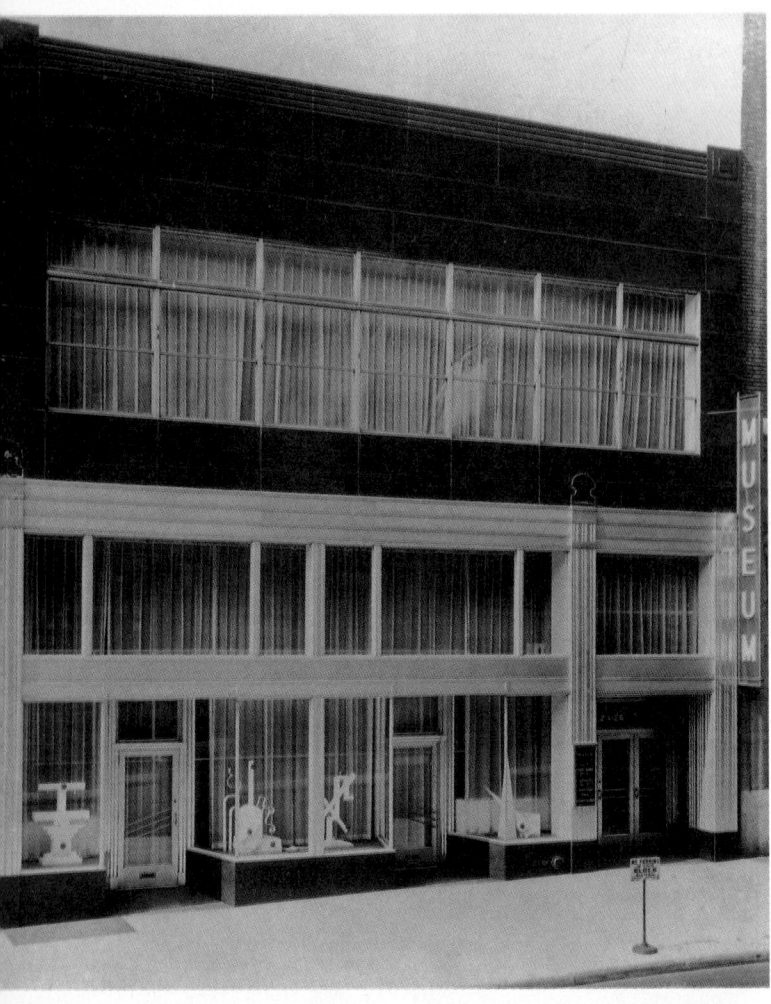

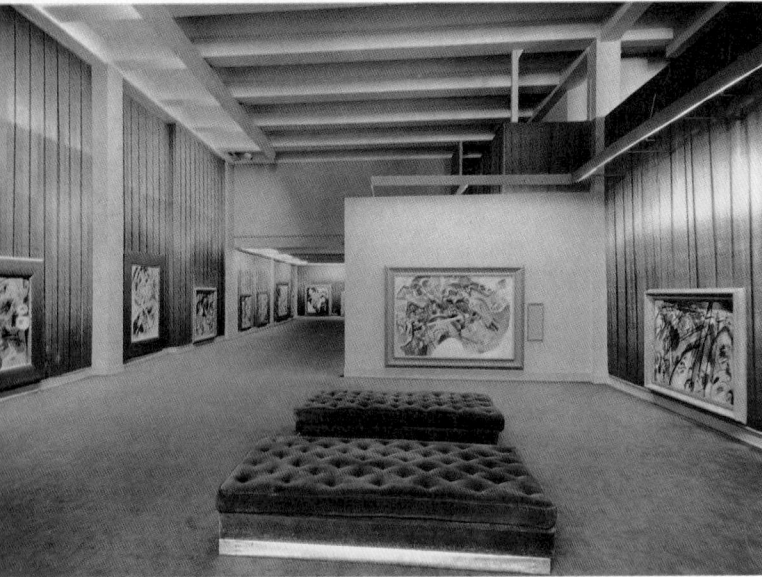

Top: Museum of Non-objective Painting, 24 East Fifty-fourth Street, between Madison and Park avenues. Cross & Cross, 1937. View to the south showing renovation (Hilla von Rebay with William Muschenheim, 1939). Beckman. GM

Bottom: Museum of Non-objective Painting. Hilla von Rebay with William Muschenheim, 1939. Gallery showing Wassily Kandinsky exhibition, 1945. GM

ings were made before ground was broken in 1956 for construction of the building, which occupied the east blockfront of Fifth Avenue between Eighty-eighth and Eighty-ninth streets and replaced a number of buildings, including J. E. R. Carpenter's thirteen-story apartment house at 1070 Fifth Avenue (1929). But when at last the building was realized, the heroic effort to bring it into being seemed unquestionably worthwhile.

The Guggenheim collection had been assembled by Rebay, an abstract painter descended from lesser German nobility who was said to be Solomon Guggenheim's mistress, assisted by another painter, Rudolf Bauer, who had been Rebay's lover in the 1920s. Most of the collecting was done during the late 1920s and early 1930s, and by 1933 there had already been serious discussion of a museum to house the collection, with a possible location in the cultural complex proposed for the northward extension of Rockefeller Plaza.[46] When the Rockefeller Center plan, which was discussed as late as 1936, failed to materialize, Rebay and Guggenheim suggested that the collection be displayed at the forthcoming World's Fair, with Rebay going so far as to prepare sketches for a pavilion to be paid for by Guggenheim.[47] But, on the advice of Bauer, who wrote Rebay that he was "revolted by the thought of erecting a house, especially a good one, and tearing it down afterward," the World's Fair venue was abandoned in favor of a permanent location in Manhattan.[48] This museum was to be the principal philanthropic activity of the Solomon R. Guggenheim Foundation, which was established in 1937. On May 31, 1939, the Museum of Non-objective Painting, as the Guggenheim enterprise came to be called, was opened at 24 East Fifty-fourth Street, a stylish two-story aluminum-clad automobile showroom redesigned by Rebay, who was assisted by William Muschenheim, a young American architect who had studied with Peter Behrens in Vienna in the late 1920s and worked with Joseph Urban upon his return to New York.[49] The environment they created was luxurious yet simple, with walls covered in pleated gray velour interspersed with walls painted white to heighten drama, along with gray carpeted floors and indirect fluorescent lighting; Muschenheim claimed this was the first such installation of fluorescent lighting in New York. The paintings were hung close to the floor in enormous silver frames.

The Fifty-fourth Street gallery was necessarily temporary, and Rebay continued to plot for Guggenheim's commitment to the construction of a permanent home for the collection. By 1943, with Guggenheim now in his eighties, Rebay had come to realize that time was running out and that decisive action needed to be taken. It was then that she opened conversations with Wright. Rebay had not at first considered the seventy-six-year-old architect, whom she thought dead, but it is believed his name was brought to her attention by Solomon's wife, Irene Rothschild Guggenheim. In her first letter to Wright, dated June 1, 1943, Rebay set the tone of their collaboration on "a building for our collection of non-objective paintings":

> I feel that each of these great masterpieces should be organized into space and only you so it seems to me would test the possibilities to do so. . . . I do not think these paintings are easel paintings. They are order creating order and are sensitive (and corrective even) to space. As you feel the ground, the sky and the "in-between" you will perhaps feel them too; and find the way. I need a fighter, a lover of space, an originator, a tester and a wise man. . . . I want a temple of spirit, a monument! And your help to make it possible, specially with our trustees and president.[50]

By June 29 Wright had entered into a contract with Solomon Guggenheim, president of the foundation, to construct for a 10 percent fee a $750,000 building on an undetermined site to cost an additional $250,000. (If the site were to cost less, the difference would be added to the building's budget.) In mid-July Wright toured New York with Robert Moses to inspect possible sites. Although Wright and Moses were distantly related by marriage and sometimes addressed each other as "Cousin," they rarely saw eye to eye on matters of aesthetics.[51] Moses offered eight acres of parkland he was developing along the Henry Hudson Parkway in Riverdale. In a letter to Guggenheim, Wright said that he admired the site and argued that there the new building "would form an individual hill crown, rising up from within and above the new municipal park areas which within a decade will be to Greater New York what Central Park is now to little old New York." Wright went on to imagine a "new Type of Treasury for works of art, one that would be a haven of refuge for city dwellers. . . . Now, in the view of Moses (and it is my own view), this is a break from the old Museum tradition, but it is a desirable one to make now, if we are heading straight into the future as we ought to be." Anticipating Guggenheim's reluctance to construct his memorial in an outlying area, Wright argued that "helicopter and motor travel will become quite universal after the war" and that the museum, set apart "in inspiring surroundings," would provide "a genuine relief from the cinder heap old New York is bound to become."[52]

In the same letter, Wright told of his visit with John D. Rockefeller, Jr., who had rejected the possibility of locating the museum on West Fifty-third Street opposite the Museum of Modern Art, a site that had been part of the earlier cultural center plan and would become home to the Donnell Library in 1955, but held out the possibility of building east of the museum's garden on West Fifty-fourth Street. Wright ranked this 176-by-54-foot site, which would eventually be used by the Modern itself, as his second choice. He was even less enthusiastic about an impressive site occupying the full blockfront on the west side of Park Avenue from Sixty-ninth to Seventieth Street, which would require demolition of the George Blumenthal house (Trowbridge & Livingston, ca. 1910) and the Arthur Curtis James house (Allen & Collens, 1916), the former now owned by the Metropolitan Museum, the latter by the James Foundation.[53] Wright told Guggenheim the building could be squeezed onto either the Fifty-fourth Street or the Park Avenue site, and he acknowledged Moses's estimate of $250,000 to acquire either one. But, he said, "These latter locations are the NOW, more or less. They are not the future and they tie us down to the conventional idea of the Art Museum on hard pavements. Not so much a living memorial as a monument. Not caring so much for monuments and preferring the more lively memorial, you, of course, know where I stand in the whole matter."[54] Other sites were also considered, including that of the J. P. Morgan, Jr., mansion, on the northwest corner of Park Avenue and Thirty-sixth Street, which Wright was attracted to, and the east blockfront of Madison Avenue between Fifty-sixth and Fifty-seventh streets, now occupied by the Parke-Bernet Galleries.[55]

As the search for a site dragged on into late 1943 and Wright began to realize that a mid-Manhattan location was Guggenheim's distinct preference, he reconstructed his mental image of the proposed building: although he had originally thought of it as a horizontal structure, he now began to think of it as vertical. By January 20, 1944, he had committed to paper a design for the spiral form that would be the principal feature of the completed building. The evolution of this feature was as fascinating as the concept was compositionally bold and structurally daring: originally it rose from a wide base to a narrow top, and at one point it was made up of straight sides; ultimately, it became a continuous curve cantilevered upon itself as it rose from a narrow base to a wide crown. One preliminary scheme presented a building internally organized around a continuous ramp but externally rejecting a circular form in favor of a hexagonal one.

To prepare Rebay for the design, Wright wrote to her January 20, 1944: "A museum should be one extended expansion well proportioned floor space from bottom to top—a wheel chair going around and up and down, *throughout*. No stops anywhere and such screened divisions of the space gloriously lit from above as would deal appropriately with every group of paintings or individual paintings as you might want them classified."[56] A site on Fifth Avenue was located on March 13, 1944, and later that month Guggenheim, after considering a plan to create the museum as part of Columbia University, acquired the vacant property, at the southeast corner of Fifth Avenue and Eighty-ninth Street. By midsummer of the same year Guggenheim had approved Wright's sketches and authorized the development of detailed drawings for the building, which Wright preferred to call an "Archeseum," meaning "a building in which to see the highest."[57]

When Wright first visited the site, he instantly grasped its potential. "The new building will be a magnet to draw many people," he reassured Rebay, who presumably had doubts about the museum being so far uptown, "and out of desire to see that wonder numbers of them will discover the new paintings. I doubt if it is the noon-hour lovers you want," Wright continued. "One seeker after significant truth who has the desire to find it is better for us than any amount of merely curious hoi-polloi only seeking sensation. . . . I think all of present New York that is overbuilt already is going down and out—why not step aside and be safe and serene on the border of Central Park which ensures light, fresh air and advantages in every way but one and that is congestion."[58] Wright reported to Rebay that his design, developed before a site had been chosen, "suits the plot even better than the imaginary one."[59]

In July 1945 drawings and models of the museum were released to the public at a press luncheon held at the Plaza Hotel.[60] On September 7 the working drawings for the building were completed. Wright's design proposed a swelling, spiral-lined, glass-domed viewing rotunda located at the corner of Eighty-ninth Street and Fifth Avenue. At the press conference, Wright patted the model of the building as if it were a baby, saying: "This building is built like a spring. You can see how the ramp, which is coiled in the shape of a true logarithmic spiral, is one continuous piece from top to bottom, integral with the outside wall and the inside balcony. When the first atom bomb lands on New York it will not be destroyed. It may be blown a few miles up into the air, *but when it comes down it will bounce!*"[61] The building was to be approached through a ground-level recessed entrance where cars could drop visitors off at the front door. Inside, the main gallery space consisted of a twenty-five-foot-wide ramp rising one and a half inches every twenty feet, spiraling up ninety-two feet, or seven revolutions, to the top; two elevators were also provided, as well as a much steeper spiral ramp system tangent to that of the gallery, which served as a second means of egress. Elevator landings were located at the points of tangency between the two ramps. Wright's preferred route of circulation was from the top down. He told Ben Raeburn, his publisher:

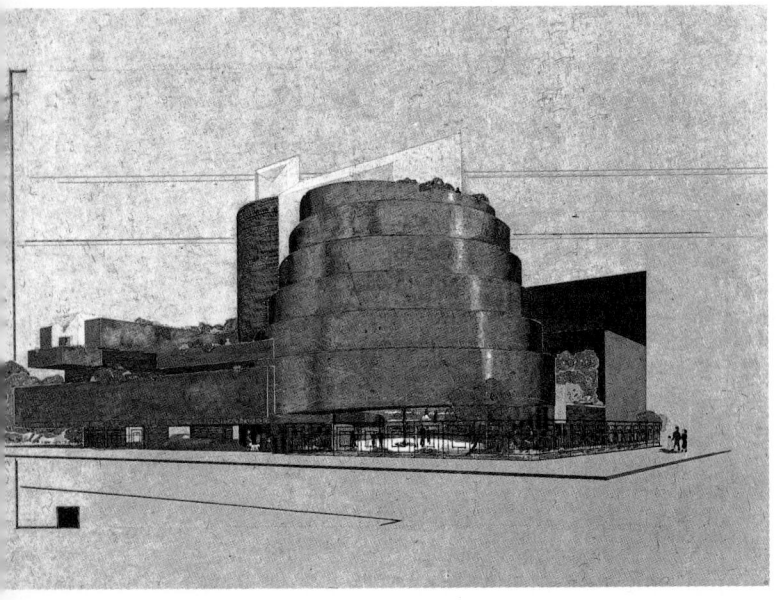

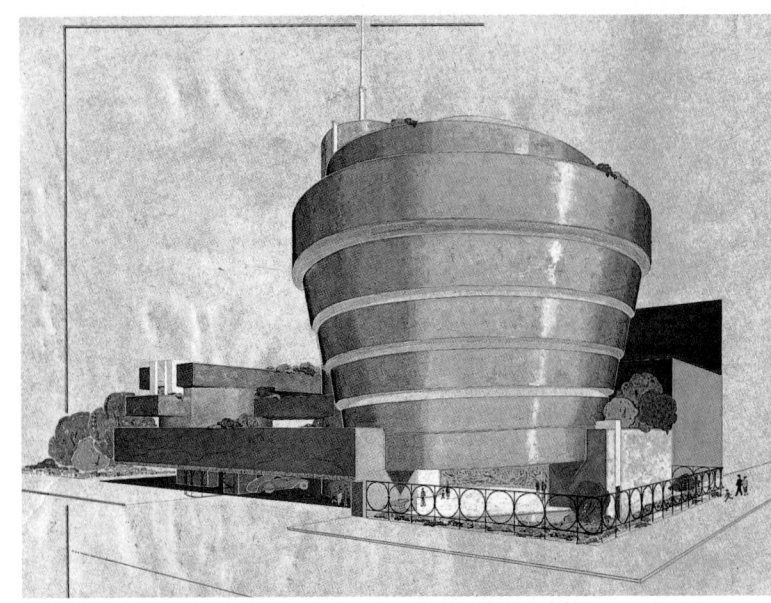

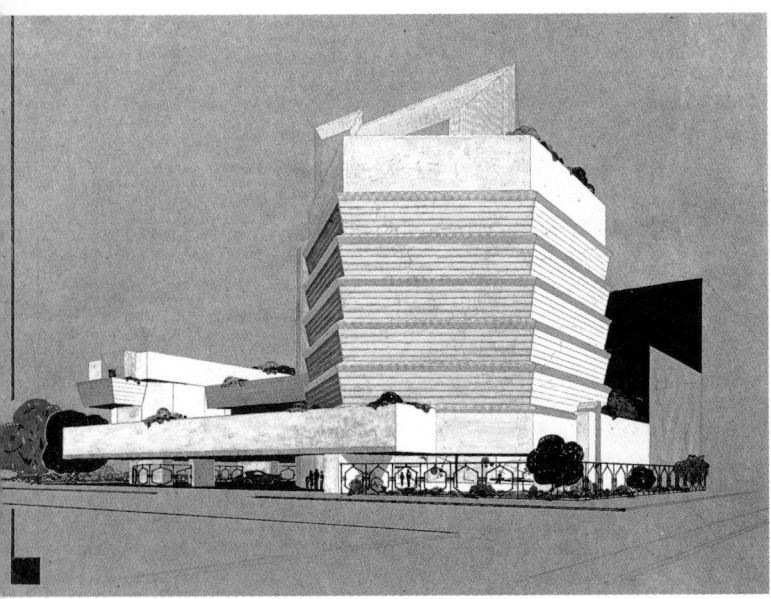

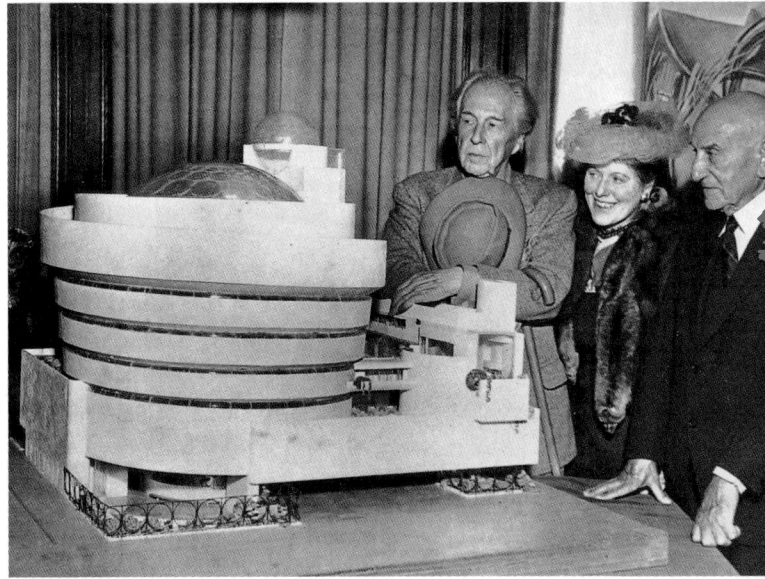

Top left: Proposal for Solomon R. Guggenheim Museum, Fifth Avenue, East Eighty-eighth to East Eighty-ninth Street. Frank Lloyd Wright, 1944. Rendering of view to the northeast. FLWA

Bottom left: Proposal for Solomon R. Guggenheim Museum. Frank Lloyd Wright, 1944. Rendering of view to the northeast. FLWA

Top right: Proposal for Solomon R. Guggenheim Museum. Frank Lloyd Wright, 1944. Rendering of view to the northeast. FLWA

Center right: Proposal for Solomon R. Guggenheim Museum. Frank Lloyd Wright, 1945. Model. Frank Lloyd Wright is on the left, Hilla von Rebay is in the center and Solomon R. Guggenheim is on the right. FLWA

Bottom right: Proposal for the annex of the Solomon R. Guggenheim Museum, Fifth Avenue, between East Eighty-eighth and East Eighty-ninth streets. Frank Lloyd Wright, 1947. Rendering of view to the northeast. FLWA

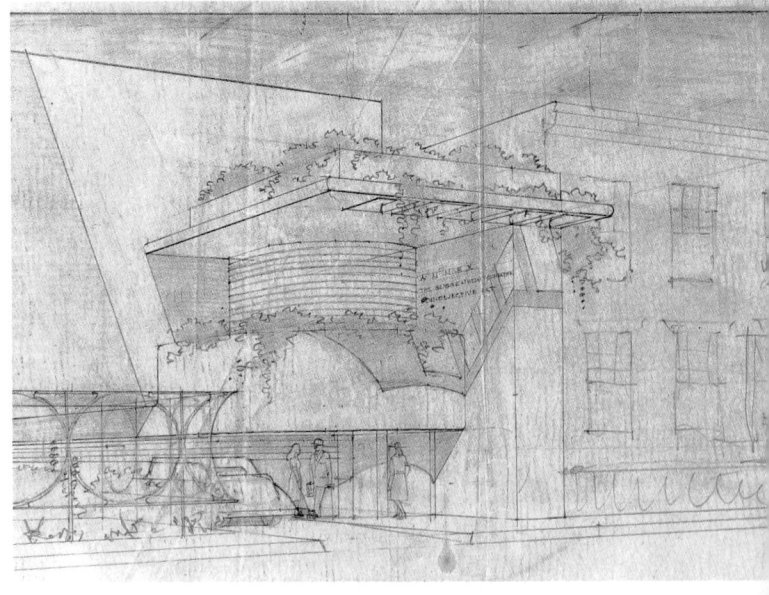

It always seemed to me that when you go to an art museum as they have been designed and built for the last four or five hundred years, you walk and walk and walk looking at the various paintings, sculpture, collections, whatever. And when you have finished, you have to retrace your steps, seeing the whole thing again, just to get back to where you began. Now what I wanted to achieve in this Museum was to once and for all eliminate the to and from, the back and forth, and give a better circulation for viewing paintings. You see, in this building you come in off the main street into a generous open brightly lit court, take an elevator to the top level, and begin your descent on a gradual, comfortable ramp down. At any point in your tour you can look into the courtyard, see where you have been and see where you are going next. If your eye catches a particular painting farther down, you can come around to the elevator shaft, always tangential to the ramp as it makes its revolution. . . . When you are done with the tour, you are right where you began. You can go into the small cafe for coffee or tea, buy some cards or books if you wish, all on the ground level, and eventually you step outside onto Fifth Avenue. There is no retracing your circuit. You have made the tour once, going always forward, and at the end you are right at the entrance![62]

The continuous galleries along the ramps were 9'6" tall, and the outer walls—a surface of about three-quarters of a mile—were tilted to form a ninety-seven degree angle with the floor; paintings were thus exhibited, Wright would claim, as if on an easel. Light would enter through concentric rings of glass tubing as well as through a glass dome, whose mullion pattern suggested the coffering of traditional domes, and through some smaller, bubble-type domed skylights—all devices the architect had used before, mostly at the Johnson Wax Building in Racine, Wisconsin (1939).[63] A grand gallery was located to one side of the skylit rotunda on the main floor, one level above the ground floor. This room, which Wright dubbed "The Holy of Holies," was designed to permit Rebay to install pictures as she had at Fifty-fourth Street: in a letter to Rebay, Wright said that in this room "you have about the same gallery space and height (you like it high) that you have in the 54th St. place. You can have carpets, stuff draping the walls, etc., etc., just as you had it—just for contrast with the main museum."[64] To the south of the rotunda, a lower building was designed to house curatorial work spaces, offices and an apartment for Rebay. Wright also supported Rebay's desire to include a "little restaurant" as a "nice idea" that "made the whole thing gemütlich instead of a Salon in the grand manner only."[65] A theater was located in the basement.

By early 1945 Rebay had begun to have doubts about the building's design, particularly the main gallery's sloping walls and the indirect lighting Wright proposed. In a March 1945 letter, Wright explained to her that "all you have to imagine concerning the lighting of the pictures is the ideal light from above tempered upon a wall slightly tilted backward—artifical light coming from the same place above as daylight—to see that any conceivable degree of light in any quality desired is an actual circumstance in this building. There is about a mile of such surface. And nothing could be more ideal."[66] Rebay's misgivings about the functional suitability of the ramped galleries intensified when, as the project was being launched, Wright stalled on the construction of a full-sized mock-up of the gallery space.[67] Correspondence between the two recorded the tension over this point (Rebay, under wartime law classified as an enemy alien—she became a U.S. citizen in 1947—was unable to travel to Wisconsin to meet with Wright). "About the building being suitable for the particular type of picturizing we are building it to

display," Wright wrote to Rebay on August 2, 1945. "I know no substitute for Imagination, Hilla. Can it be possible that at this late day you have no feeling amounting to knowledge concerning this fundamental point? I find myself stunned, unable to believe you."[68]

Rebay began to suspect that Wright had little respect for painting as compared to architecture, a fear Wright did little to assuage when he wrote to her that architecture is "the Mother-art of which Painting is but as a daughter."[69] Rebay stated her viewpoint clearly: "While I have no doubt that your building will be a great monument to yourself, I cannot visualize how much (or how little) it will do for the paintings. . . . We need a monument to painting also which is our main interest."[70] The argument over this issue never ceased; in 1949, for example, Rebay told Wright that a building in itself could never be a pure work of art since it had to be "used for practical living" and that the architect "has not the spiritual freedom which the painter has."[71]

From the first, Wright had wanted to realize his design in reinforced concrete, but he also considered welded steel and other innovative structural techniques. As he explained to Rebay in June 1945: "The building is a modern problem in air-conditioning and acoustics. The structure itself is novel in New York. A fibrous fabrication like a steel basket shot with gunnite (a high-pressure plastic concrete)—a new process saving several hundred thousand of dollars over standard construction. . . . We cannot possibly use the standard means either of getting all these new materials into effect. We are cultivating the man and the means able to perform as they must."[72] Although the city's Department of Buildings was also beginning to raise doubts about the building, and general contractors were expressing considerable reluctance to take on the project, it was not the building's innovative structural ideas that ultimately delayed construction but its estimated cost, which exceeded the budget.

In July 1945 Solomon Guggenheim purchased additional property that had become available, adding thirty feet to the Fifth Avenue frontage and an outlet to Eighty-eighth Street. While Guggenheim believed that the war's end would bring an economic recession and with it a decline in building costs, the opposite turned out to be true. The building's budget, which had already been increased to $1 million, was still inadequate. The project was in effect "on hold" during 1947 and 1948, but Wright made every effort to keep the project alive. In 1947 the Guggenheim Foundation proposed relocating their present gallery from Fifty-fourth Street to a temporary facility on a narrow lot that had become available on Eighty-eighth Street, east of the apartment building at 1070 Fifth Avenue. Wright thought that the construction of a temporary museum on this lot would be a waste of money and might jeopardize the construction of his design. To meet the needs of the foundation, he instead proposed in a September 1947 letter to Solomon Guggenheim that a low, narrow structure that he called the Annex be designed for the lot, which would initially serve as a temporary museum but would then be attached to the main building and function as office space and a curator's apartment.[73] He hurriedly prepared a design, and by the end of the month he had completed a set of presentation drawings of his proposal, which were approved by Guggenheim and Rebay in a visit to Taliesin, Wright's home and studio in Wisconsin. After Wright had made the designs for the Annex, he realized the advantages of buffering the museum from future developments along its rear (east) elevation and prepared a more elaborate building that rose twelve stories to house studio-apartments.

But the project did not move toward realization. In a January 1948 issue of *Architectural Forum* devoted to Wright's work, no construction date was given for the building.[74] In April of that year a rumor that groundbreaking was imminent concealed quite the opposite situation.[75] With costs constantly escalating, Wright proposed to Guggenheim that the site be sold and that a free site be found in a park.[76] Yet the action taken was precisely what Wright had feared: the existing, stone-fronted, Beaux-Arts-style George H. Penniman house (Babb, Cook & Willard, 1898) at 1071 Fifth Avenue, now being used as the Gardner School, was acquired by the foundation and converted into a temporary museum in 1947–48 by William Muschenheim.[77] Working directly with Rebay, Muschenheim gutted the interior, installed egg-crate fluorescent lighting and carpeting, and painted and draped the rooms in tones of gray.

Despite the lack of progress toward construction, and regardless of the reservations expressed by Rebay as well as some foundation executives and trustees, Guggenheim remained committed to Wright's project. At a luncheon hosted by Guggenheim for Wright and his wife at the Plaza Hotel, Mrs. Wright said: "Mr. Guggenheim, many are in doubt about the museum. It has been delayed for so long now that they think it will never be built." To which he replied: "The House of Guggenheim never goes back on its word—the museum will be built. You should pay no attention to what people say."[78] But when Guggenheim died on November 3, 1949, at age eighty-eight, the future of the project was put seriously in doubt, in part because of the vaguely worded provisions of his will and in part because Rebay, now acting as the sole client, was becoming erratic in her behavior. Some of the trustees and staff members saw this as an opportune time to get rid of Wright and his building as well as the increasingly difficult Rebay. To make matters worse, late in 1950 the Fifth Avenue Association announced that it would object to the construction of Wright's design.

Wright continued to fight for his building, enlisting the support of Solomon Guggenheim's nephew Harry, newly elected as the foundation's president. Wright also rallied Guggenheim's daughter and son-in-law, Lady and Lord Castle-Stewart, to the cause. When he met them in London in the summer of 1950 he asked that the rest of the Fifth Avenue blockfront be acquired; by the summer of 1951 the deed was done.[79] That same year a new perspective for a design using the entire blockfront and showing a twelve-story apartment and office building on the site of the Annex was prepared. The expanded site permitted the rotunda to be relocated to the south, where it would have more impact on visitors arriving from downtown, and the development of a smaller rotunda in the staff wing at the site's north corner. With the support of the younger Guggenheims came a more positive tone in Wright's letters to Rebay; after he was given the go-ahead to develop a building for the entire site, Wright wrote to her with enthusiasm about the additional space and criticized the temporary museum on the site:

As it seems to me, the whole project is greatly improved by the reversal made possible by the acquisition of the new lot. Nothing of the old plans—except the idea—is usable. All has had to be begun anew and the general effect of the idea is greatly improved—leaving out the domestic arrangements of the old has made new facilities available. It would be a great pity now were you to obstruct the realization of the Memorial itself by extending further the obstructions already unwittingly raised by these temporary collaterals.[80]

By July 1951 Wright was at work on a revised set of working drawings, which progressed through 1952. Rebay, who had been in precarious health, resigned in 1952; she was replaced by James Johnson Sweeney. As Wright prepared for the monumental struggle to obtain a building permit, he also struggled to establish a rapport with Sweeney, whom he deemed "a standard museum man with established ideas and friends."[81] Though it is likely that Sweeney did not like Wright's design, he at least brought to the design process a professionalism and a working knowledge of museums that Rebay had lacked. In so doing, he expanded the building program, forcing Wright to struggle to accommodate new elements while holding on to his basic idea.

In late 1953 an exhibition of Wright's work, "60 Years of Living Architecture," which had been touring Europe, returned to the United States and was exhibited in a temporary pavilion Wright designed for the museum's site.[82] Construction on the pavilion began in September 1953, and it opened on October 22. The exhibition remained on view through the end of November. The 145-by-50-foot pavilion covered a vacant lot that was being used for parking and stood adjacent to the temporary museum at 1071 Fifth Avenue. Built of pottery-red concrete block, gray-colored cement asbestos panels and glass, the pavilion presented a nine-foot-high wall to Fifth Avenue. The structure was topped by a roof, made of alternating bands of Cemesto and sandblasted wire glass, that rose to a height of about twenty feet. The large slope of the asymmetrically pitched roof, which was supported on a lightweight steel structure, faced the Fifth Avenue sidewalk, where it created a dramatic and unusual effect. Along the pavilion's northern edge, on Eighty-ninth Street, the scale was more gentle. There the asymmetrical gable of the roof was visible behind the low sheltering walls of the full-size, Wright-designed two-bedroom Usonian house that was part of the exhibition. Entered through an arch cut through the north wall of 1071 Fifth, the pavilion space soared over an exhibition of twenty-five scale models of Wright's work, as well as photos of the buildings, enlarged so that, as Wright put it in an interview, "you will almost feel you are entering the buildings."[83] The Usonian house addressed the same middle-class family targeted by Marcel Breuer's and Gregory Ain's houses installed at the Museum of Modern Art several years earlier (see chapter 5). As Herbert Muschamp has observed, the Usonian house was the first Wright building to be erected in New York City, "and, ironically, it was the last private residence to be built on Fifth Avenue. It was also the shortest lived."[84]

In December 1953, with the success of the exhibition behind him, and with plans for the museum building complete and the machinery of the city's approvals process already in motion, Wright sent Harry Guggenheim a telegram notifying him that he was withdrawing the application for the building permit because he had worked out a new way to construct the building that would result in considerable savings. In addition to changes in detail, the revised design spread the ramp wider and separated the little rotunda from the main rotunda, simplifying their relationship. As redesigned, the building was a totally monolithic work of structural reinforced concrete. Shortly after revealing the revised plans to his client, Wright decided to relieve Arthur C. Holden, who had been his New York–based collaborating architect on the project since its inception, from his responsibilities and establish his own small New York office, which would be staffed by his son-in-law, William Wesley Peters. Once construction was under way, Wright expected to visit the site every few weeks, with Peters providing the day-to-day supervision the project required. In 1954, believing that construction of the project was about to begin, Wright rented an

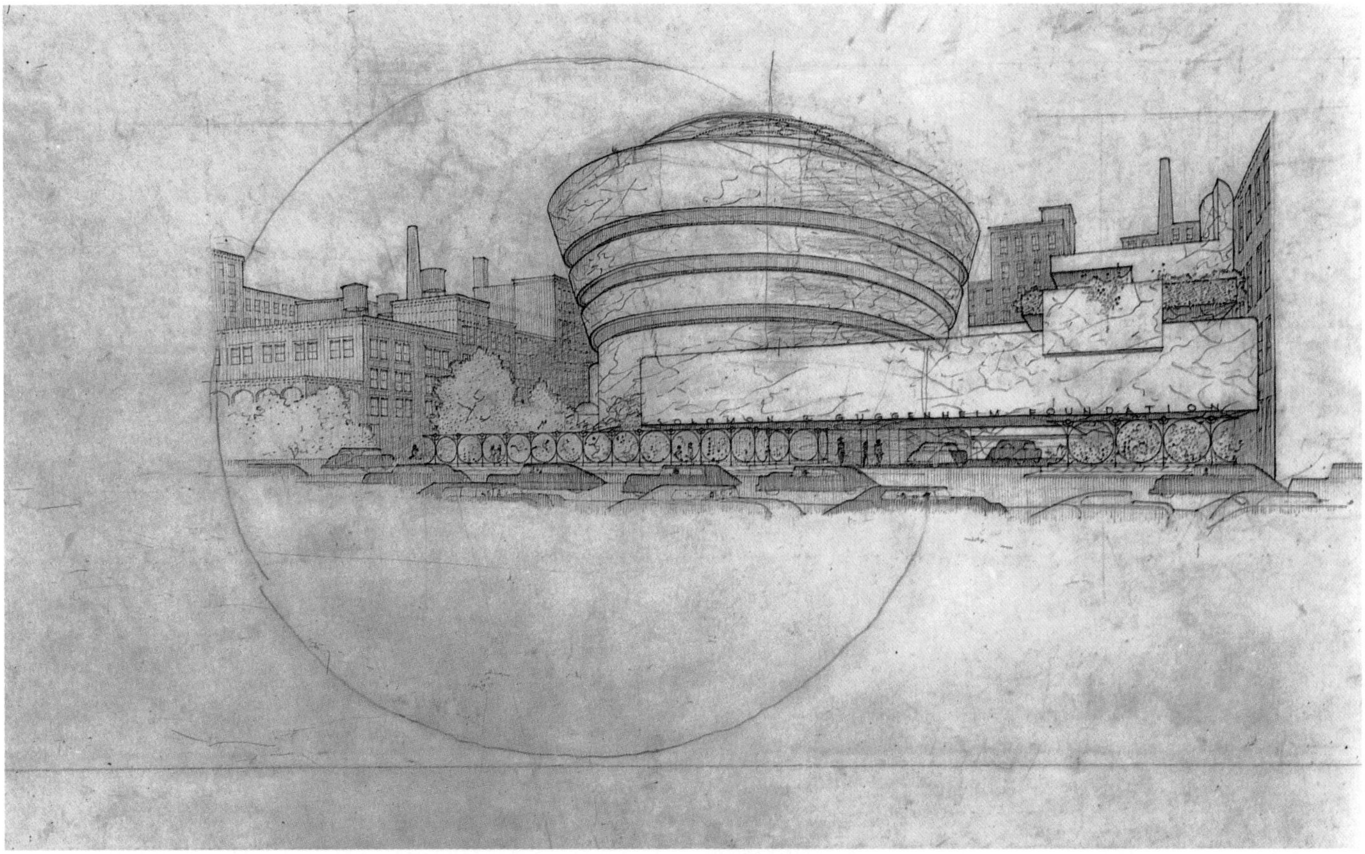

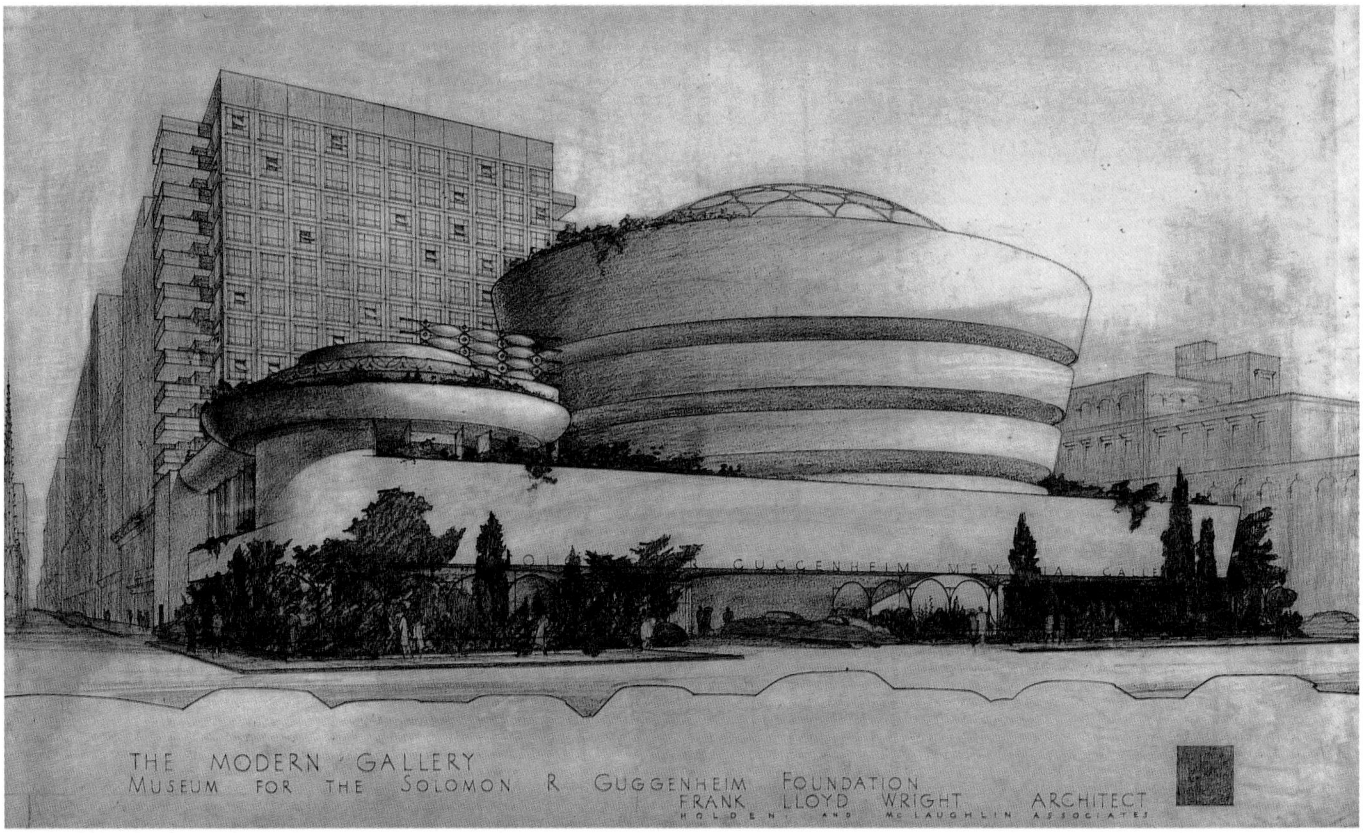

Top: Proposal for Solomon R. Guggenheim Museum, Fifth Avenue, East Eighty-eighth to East Eighty-ninth Street. Frank Lloyd Wright, 1948. Rendering of view to the northeast. FLWA

Bottom: Proposal for Solomon R. Guggenheim Museum. Frank Lloyd Wright, 1951. Rendering of view to the southeast. FLWA

813

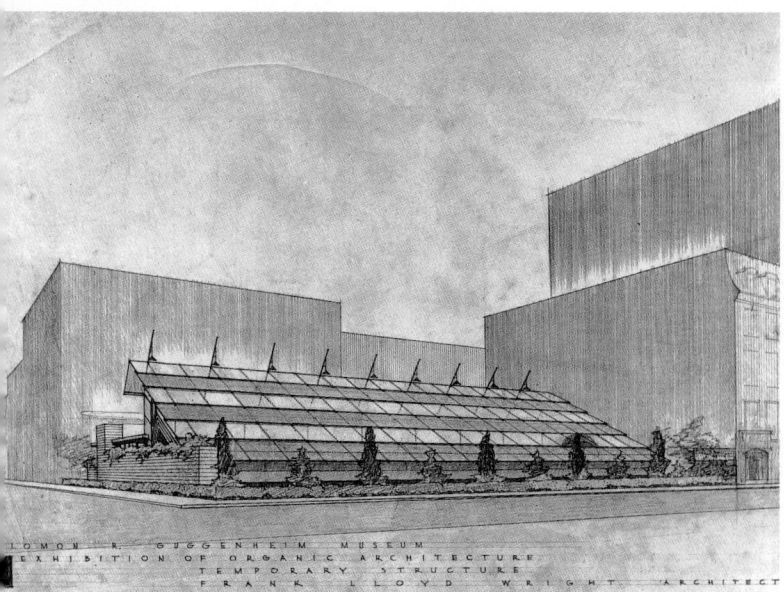

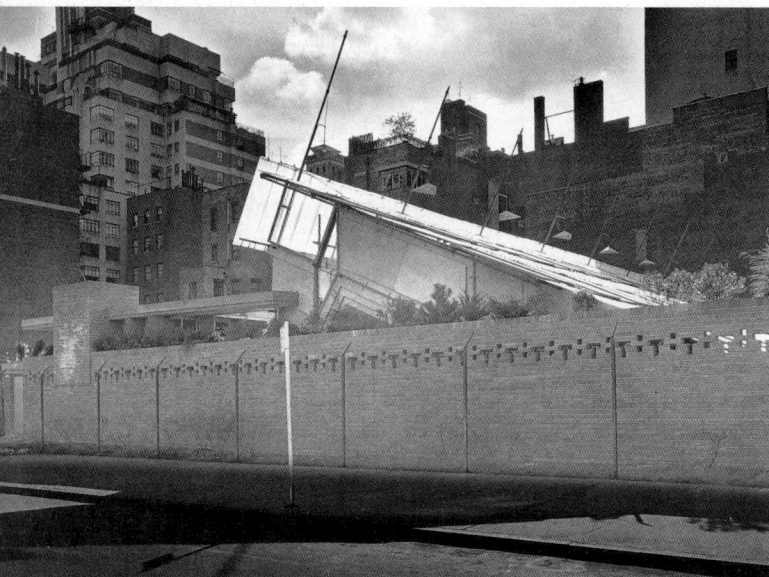

Top: Temporary pavilion for "60 Years of Living Architecture" exhibition, southeast corner of Fifth Avenue and East Eighty-ninth Street. Frank Lloyd Wright, 1953. Rendering of view to the southeast. FLWA

Bottom: Temporary pavilion for "60 Years of Living Architecture" exhibition. View to the southeast. FLWA

apartment in the Plaza Hotel to serve as his New York home and office (see chapter 16). In late September 1954 five bids for the building's construction were received, four of them for almost $4 million, and one for about $3 million. The low bidder, Euclid Construction Company, headed by George Cohen, was selected in 1955. In order to reduce costs, the design was once again revised, mostly by eliminating many of the back-of-the-house curatorial facilities Sweeney had requested. The savings were, however, largely negated by wage increases in the building trades, and the building was finally rebudgeted at $2.5 million.

But cost overruns were not the only problem at this point. Even as final preparations were being made to begin construction, Sweeney continued to argue against Wright's lighting plan. In a letter to Sweeney, Wright rehashed the arguments he had first marshaled to make his points with Rebay:

> The strength of the Guggenheim . . . is as a space in which to view the painter's creation truthfully, that is to say *honestly,* in the varying light as seen by the painter himself and in which it was born to be seen. This plus (in our case) an atmosphere of space and dignity in quiet *human* scale—no exaggeration. The beholders will see it as something they may well live with. . . . That is our Archeseum to supplant the phony museum. A humanist must believe that any picture in a fixed light is only a "fixed" picture![85]

The Department of Buildings also raised numerous issues and objections, ranging from the difficulty of determining occupancy limits to the lack of sufficient fire stairs and, most significant, the building's radical structural system. To quell the department's fears about the structure, Wright, assisted by the New York structural engineer Jacob Feld, added slim, finlike columns to support the coil of concrete. These were given an inverted tapering shape that swelled to thirty-two feet at the top. Wright also widened the rotunda's single fire stair, changed the angle of the flight of steps and introduced an additional fire stair. The building permit was issued on May 23, 1956.

Ground was broken on August 16, 1956, thirteen years after the building commission was initially awarded to Wright.[86] For the duration of construction the museum, located since 1948 in the townhouse at 1071 Fifth Avenue, was relocated to the Oliver Gould Jennings house (Ernest Flagg and Walter B. Chambers, 1899), at 7 East Seventy-second Street.[87] Once construction began, the administrative plan Wright had established several years before did not prove workable. Old and comparatively frail, he made fewer trips to the site than he had expected, and William Wesley Peters remained based at the Taliesins. The day-to-day supervision of the project was left to William Short, who had worked in the firm of Holden, McLaughlin & Associates and had played a role in shepherding the drawings through the Board of Standards and Appeals and in obtaining the building permit.

No sooner had the intention to break ground been announced than criticism of the building began in earnest. In an editorial in *Arts,* Hilton Kramer, the magazine's managing editor, challenged not Wright's genius but his views on painting and sculpture, which he "has relegated . . . to an inferior status in the architectural environment when [he] has not banished them altogether." In Kramer's view, the new building was a "grand architectural statement without special concern for the *esthetic* (as against the merely physical) requirements of the works of art it is intended to house." Although he criticized the sloping gallery walls, Kramer praised Wright for his use of natural light, which he deemed "one of the few admirable features in the building so far as function goes." But his conclusion was that, "far from being 'natural' or even appropriate, the plans for the new Guggenheim Museum strike one as another instance of what Lewis Mumford has described as Wright's 'misplaced creativity.'"[88] The editors of the *New York Times* said they were "aghast" at the design, whose "net effect," they averred, "will be precisely that of an oversized and indigestible hot cross bun."[89]

In December criticism of the building took on an uglier tone when twenty-one artists protested the design of the building's galleries in an open letter to the foundation's trustees and to Sweeney.[90] The artists, who included George L. K. Morris, Milton Avery, Willem de Kooning, Herbert Ferber, Adolph Gottlieb, Philip Guston, Franz Kline, Robert Motherwell and Jack Tworkov, said that they "strongly urge the Trustees of the Guggenheim Museum to reconsider the plans for the new building."[91] Behind their criticism of the building's interior, especially Wright's intended method of display, lay disapproval of the building's overall design; as one of the signatory artists, George Constant, told the *New York Times*, the building Wright deemed "a little temple in a park" was a "Roman Coliseum; it doesn't belong in these surroundings."[92] While Harry Guggenheim's reply was temperate, Wright was characteristically caustic: "I am sufficiently familiar with the incubus of habit that besets your minds to understand that you all know too little of the nature of the mother art—architecture."[93]

In September 1957 the *New York Times* published Aline B. Saarinen's account of a "tour" of the building conducted by Wright. Saarinen began with a description of the building's extraordinary popularity, even in its unfinished state, particularly among "young students, with crew-cuts, blue shirts and khaki pants, [who] aim the Cyclops-eye of a camera upward toward the astonishing structure. Then they turn eagerly toward the workmen's shack, hoping to get a glimpse of Frank Lloyd Wright, the world's best-known living architect." Wright, followed by William Short, led Saarinen through the building, "stepping lightly, surefootedly in his pointed black shoes over little bridge-like planks."[94] The architect extolled the virtues of the building's central rotunda and the structure that encased it, and also praised its relationship to Fifth Avenue: "We're the only concern along Fifth Avenue that sees the park. We've cooperated with it. This will really be a little park with a building in it."[95]

In May 1958, to accompany a portfolio of drawings and progress photos of the museum, Wright issued what was to be his last written statement about the museum, describing once again his basic ideas and paying tribute to Solomon Guggenheim. Finally secure in the knowledge that the building would be realized as he had designed it and as Guggenheim had approved it, Wright concluded:

> What stands there now in his name is envisioned as a unique quiet retreat where the collection of the "non-objective" (so called) art he believed in and made could be greatly extended. He saw his museum as it is built to his will—thanks to his trustees. He did not want an office building or anything like one and left no money to build one. He envisioned a museum pretty much as it stands. Unique, a genuine intelligent experiment in museum-culture where pictures could be better seen with less discomfort in an atmosphere peculiarly belonging to the free forms of art he loved for itself—a true friend of the future.[96]

Construction moved along through 1958 and the museum was topped out by the workers in May.[97] The scaffolding was removed in late August. As construction progressed and the building began to make its presence felt, it became one of the principal features of New York cultural life. In September

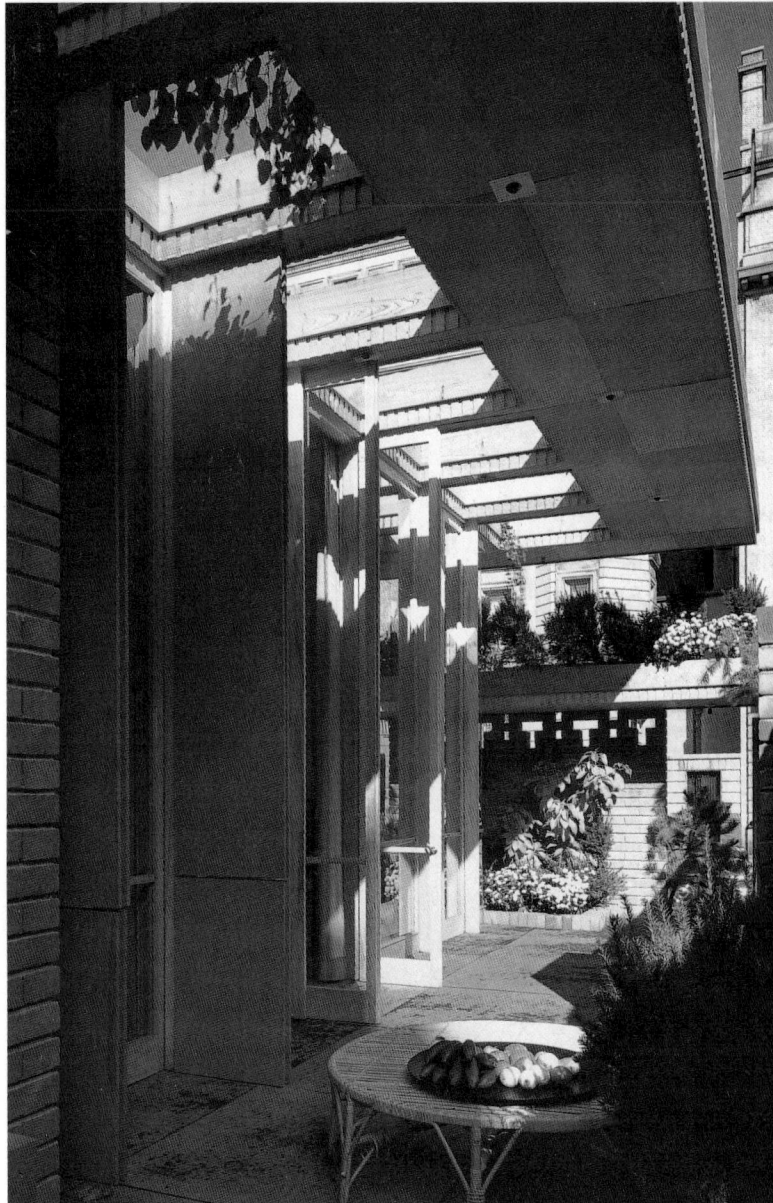

Temporary pavilion for "60 Years of Living Architecture" exhibition. Stoller. ©ESTO

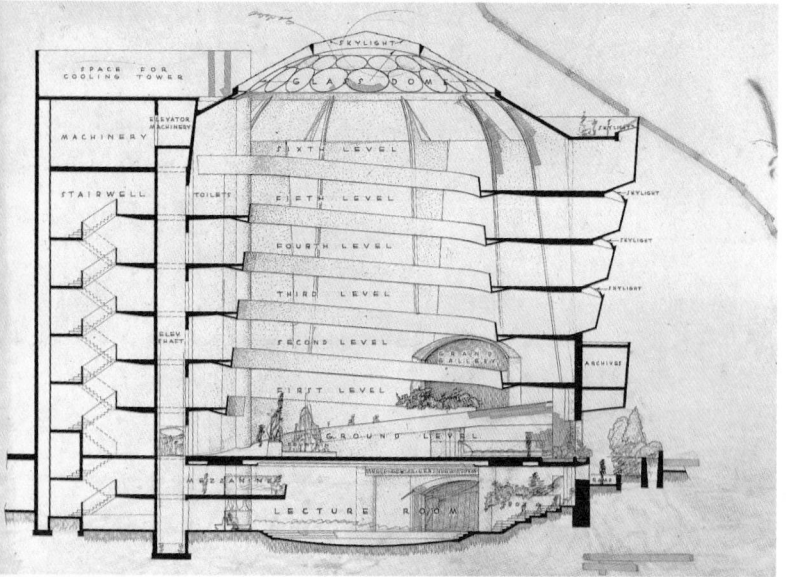

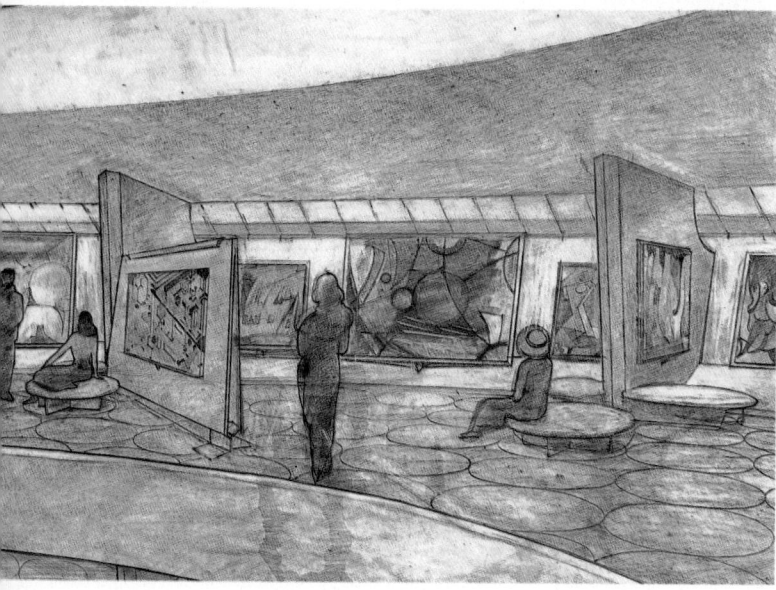

Top: Proposal for Solomon R. Guggenheim Museum, Fifth Avenue, East Eighty-eighth to East Eighty-ninth Street. Frank Lloyd Wright, 1953. Section. FLWA

Bottom: Proposal for Solomon R. Guggenheim Museum. Frank Lloyd Wright, 1958. Rendering of proposed installation method. FLWA

Top right: Solomon R. Guggenheim Museum, 1071 Fifth Avenue, East Eighty-eighth to East Eighty-ninth Street. Frank Lloyd Wright, 1943–59. View to the northeast. Stoller. ©ESTO

Bottom right: Solomon R. Guggenheim Museum. Gallery. Stoller. ©ESTO

1958, in a poll of 500 leading architects who were asked to list the "Seven Wonders of American Architecture," the Guggenheim was among a list of runners-up, finishing as number 18 out of more than 100 buildings selected.[98] (Wright's Robie and Kaufmann houses, as well as his S. C. Johnson office complex, were three of the seven buildings selected.) The still-unfinished building was becoming internationally known through text and photographs; pictures by William Short, for instance, accompanied a sympathetic interpretation by Edgar Kaufmann, Jr., of Wright's design in the winter 1958–59 issue of *Art in America*.[99]

When viewed from the street, the building seemed to be proceeding toward completion with ease. There were comparatively few problems with the construction, and George Cohen, head of Euclid Construction, proved remarkably sympathetic, so much so that his name, along with Wright's, was placed on the building's cornerstone.[100] The problem remained literally and metaphorically internal: Sweeney was staging a last-ditch effort to reconfigure the interiors, in particular to eliminate the sloping outer walls along the ramps and to reduce the natural light. Wright was so uncertain of the ultimate fate of the interiors, and his ability to see his plans through (he was in his nineties), that in 1958 he prepared a set of perspectives illustrating his ideas about the installation of the art and distributed bound copies of the drawings not only to the trustees but to the editors of influential architectural journals throughout the world. His last great struggle with Sweeney was over the color scheme of the interiors. Wright argued for a subtle, soft ivory, while Sweeney preferred the now standard Modernist bright white. In his book of museum sketches, Wright wrote: "White, itself the loudest color of all, is the sum of all colors. If activated by strong light it is to color like a corpse. To use it as a forcing-ground for a delicate painting would be like taking high C in music as a background for orchestral tonality. Easy to see this as ruinous in music—if one is not deaf. If not color blind, whitewashed environment is just as ruinous to the sensitive color-sense of painting. Background becomes foreground!"[101] Relations between Sweeney and Wright had so degenerated that by the spring of 1958 they were no longer on speaking or writing terms; all communication was conveyed through Harry Guggenheim.

On his last trip to New York, in January 1959, Wright reviewed the site with George Cohen and William Short, observing the workmen apply the soft cream gray exterior paint he had specified. He instructed Cohen by letter to paint the interior with two coats of ivory and said that "when the museum is thus seen as an integral whole I doubt much that they will want to daub it with whitewash."[102] To demonstrate once and for all the wisdom of his ideas, Wright also proposed that he and Sweeney undertake two separate installations—Sweeney's near the bottom of the ramp, where there was not much natural light, and Wright's, with nonobjective art from Guggenheim's original collection, shown near the top. Wright did not live to see this happen; he died on April 9, 1959, six months before the museum opened.[103]

The Guggenheim was at last opened in a private party on the evening of October 20, 1959, and to the public at 2:00 P.M. the following day.[104] Sanka Knox, the *New York Times* reporter covering the opening festivities, described the museum as "the most controversial building ever to rise in New York."[105] In its final form, the building sat on a 201-by-120-foot site, and its ramp rose at a 5 percent grade, coiling five times around the central shaft of the rotunda. The ramp itself was still the concrete spring

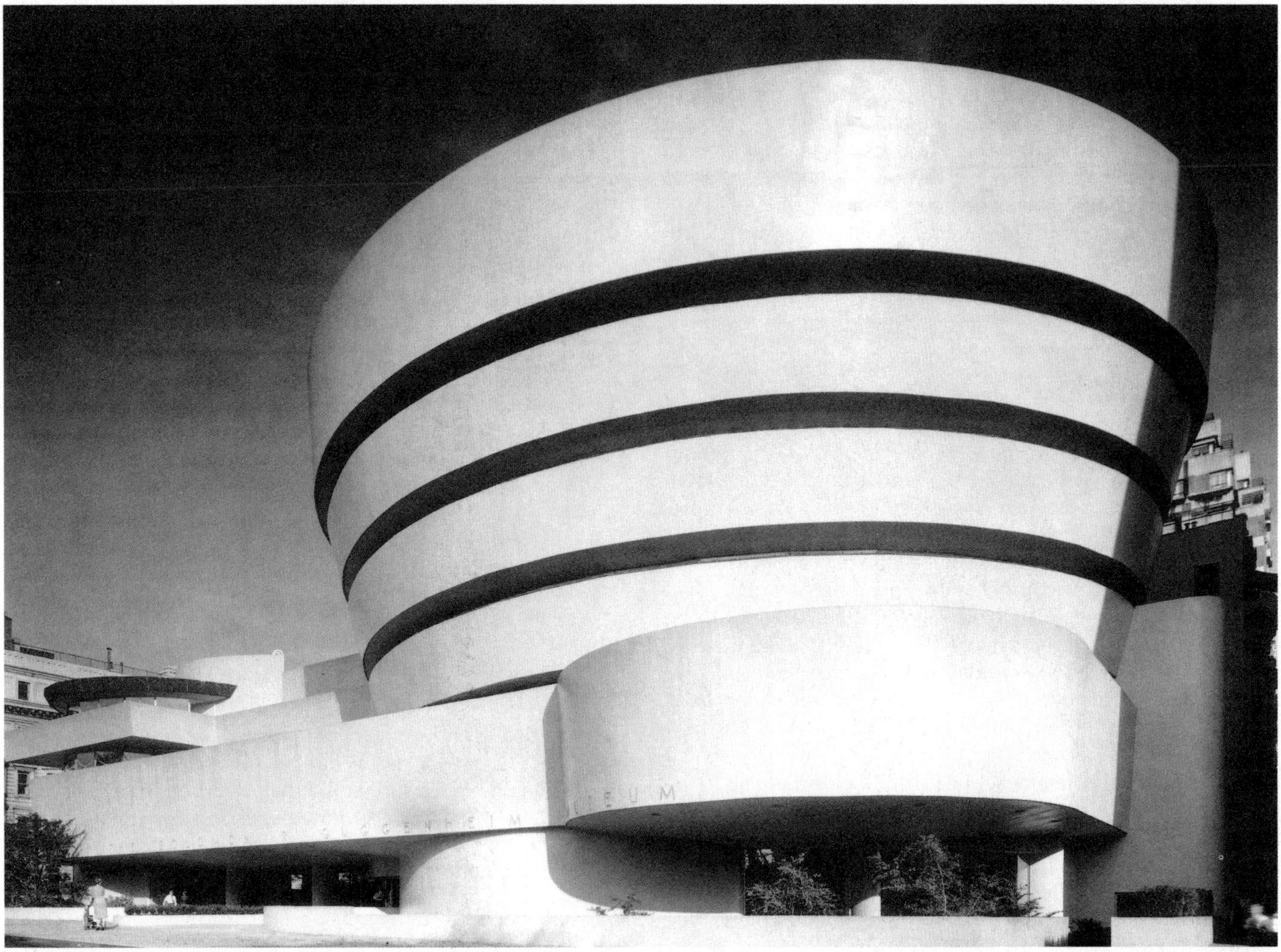

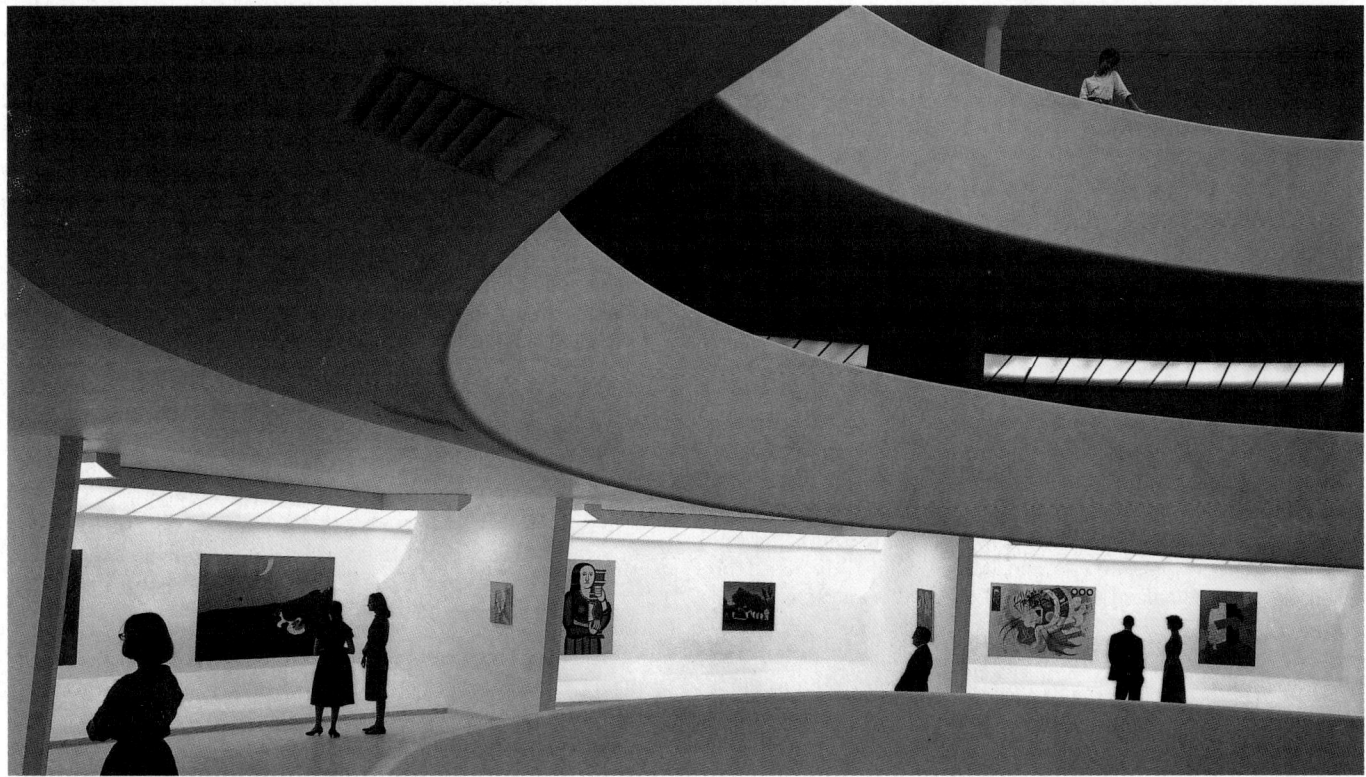

Wright had described, fixed in its inside diameter but increasing at its outer edge as it climbed. But despite the claims of Harry Guggenheim and others connected with the museum that it was not substantially different from the structure Wright had designed, the interior had been compromised by Sweeney: not only was it painted bright white, but the skylights that brought the natural light into the spiraling galleries were largely ignored in favor of bright artificial lighting from a combination of incandescent and fluorescent sources that would overpower all but the brightest rays of a summer day; only the glazed dome functioned as Wright had intended.

In addition, Sweeney refused to hang the paintings against the sloping walls but instead hung them on projecting metal supports so that they floated in front of the walls and were presented vertically in the conventional way. Though this installation technique was adopted to mollify the earlier criticism of artists who had asked that the galleries more closely conform to those of other museums, it proved a serious point of contention from the start. At the preview, one artist told Sanka Knox: "A picture—even an abstraction—is conceived as a window, into the mind or the soul. . . . It needs a wall, a frame. It cannot float like a ghost."[106] John Canaday, the *New York Times* art critic, said that while Sweeney's installation allowed the paintings to be "beautifully revealed," he felt that this occurred "at the expense of the total architectural harmony. They occupy their space so uncomfortably, like intruders, that their clear revelation loses much of its point." The entire design of the museum, Canaday said, was "a war between architecture and painting in which both come out badly maimed. The Pyrrhic victory belongs to the architecture, or to the shade of the architect." He concluded that, although Wright's building might be a masterpiece when "stripped of its pictures, existing solely as a design," as it was, "the pictures disfigure the building and the building disfigures the pictures, and in honesty . . . there is no point in pretending anything else."[107]

In her review of the museum, Ada Louise Huxtable was rather more sympathetic, reporting that the visitor experienced what Wright had promised in his numerous pronouncements: "a luminous, soaring, unified space, the circling ramp leading his eye to the delicately detailed, handsome skylit dome ninety-five feet above the terrazzo floor on which he stands." And Huxtable praised the drama of the architecture itself: "What Mr. Wright has given us is an impressive demonstration of modern construction in reinforced concrete at its most imaginative: the open spans, the daring cantilevers, the unorthodox building shapes that add up to a spectacular new architecture of great visual excitement." But she could not reconcile the design with the building's functional program: "A museum's purpose is primarily to be a background; it is a setting created to serve other forms of art. In spite of Wright's repeated picturesque statements that man and his needs were at the center of all that he did, one has the persistent impression that human and practical considerations were always subordinate to his personal work of art."[108]

Other critics who took up the issue of the aesthetic struggle between the container and the contained saw it somewhat differently. For example, the art critic Frank Getlein, who liked the building, viewed it as an effective antidote to the excesses of the contemporary New York school of Abstract Expressionist painting: "In Wright's great ramp, all the hokum about gesture and size, texture and space simply vanishes, lost in monumental space, obliterated by the gesture of a giant. You are looking at daubs and may like them or not with no reference at all to the rhetoric."[109] Walter McQuade, writing in the *Nation*, found

Sweeney's installation "commercial" in character, which he attributed principally to the artificial lighting scheme, explaining that "Wright's buildings need sunlight and some contact with the real world." The "shadowless" lighting, he said, was "like wall-to-wall carpeting, emblandishing an environment, washing out not only the shadows but the toughness, the fiber, the difficulties of life, of creativity."[110]

Lewis Mumford emphasized the powerful effect that people on the ramps would have on Wright's interior and the tremendous draw the great room would have on the public:

As an object by itself, the Guggenheim Museum interior is, like the exterior, a remarkable example of abstract sculpture; indeed, it is a new kind of mobile sculpture, whose dynamic flow is accentuated by the silhouettes of the spectators, who form a moving frieze against the intermittent spots of paintings on the walls. Thus Wright permitted the requirements of his composition to dominate both the works of art and the freedom of the viewer. They are needed to complete it, but apart from this they do not signify. Those who respond to the interior do proper homage to Wright's genius. If the purpose of the Museum is solely to exhibit Wright, the interior has magnificent justification for its existence. And if the spectator forgets the other works of art it contains, the building is—for him if not for the neglected artists—a compensation and a unique reward. What other monumental interior in America produces such an overwhelming effect?

But he also acknowledged the space's profound drawbacks: "Short of insisting that no pictures at all be shown, Wright could not have gone much further to create a structure sublime in its own right but ridiculous as a museum of art." Mumford continued: "This museum is a Procrustean structure; the art in it must be stretched out or chopped off to fit the bed Wright prepared for it."[111]

William Barrett, the philosopher and former editor of *Partisan Review*, the influential literary magazine, also found the Guggenheim's interiors wanting. In a review of what he called "Frank Lloyd Wright's Pictorama," he related the museum to certain trends in Modernist architecture as a whole: "This absence of rooms, real rooms, in modern architecture, is a strange denial of the human need to be isolated, alone, to shut a door. Is it the case that this architecture has accommodated itself too willingly to the spirit of the machine age, that it thinks always in terms of factories and office buildings?" Barrett likened the flowing crowds moving along the ramp to "a kind of conveyor belt of customers," like those found at world's fairs, "where people must perpetually come for the building and not the paintings." He was particularly critical of the distant view of the pictures that Wright's scheme made possible:

Some people I know have been much impressed by the view you get if you look across the rotunda at the paintings on the opposite wall. The effect, I admit, is very splashy. But it is also one of the most subtly dangerous effects of the building, especially if the museum is considered an institution to educate public taste. The effect of seeing paintings strung out along the wall at a distance of a hundred or more feet is to reduce the individual paintings to rather gay posters ornamental to the building. The pictures sink to a common indifferent level.[112]

In December 1960 John Portman, a little-known young architect from Atlanta, Georgia, who visited New York frequently, wrote a long letter in praise of the Guggenheim's interior. In formulating his assessment, he spelled out the direction his own highly influential work would take in the decades ahead:

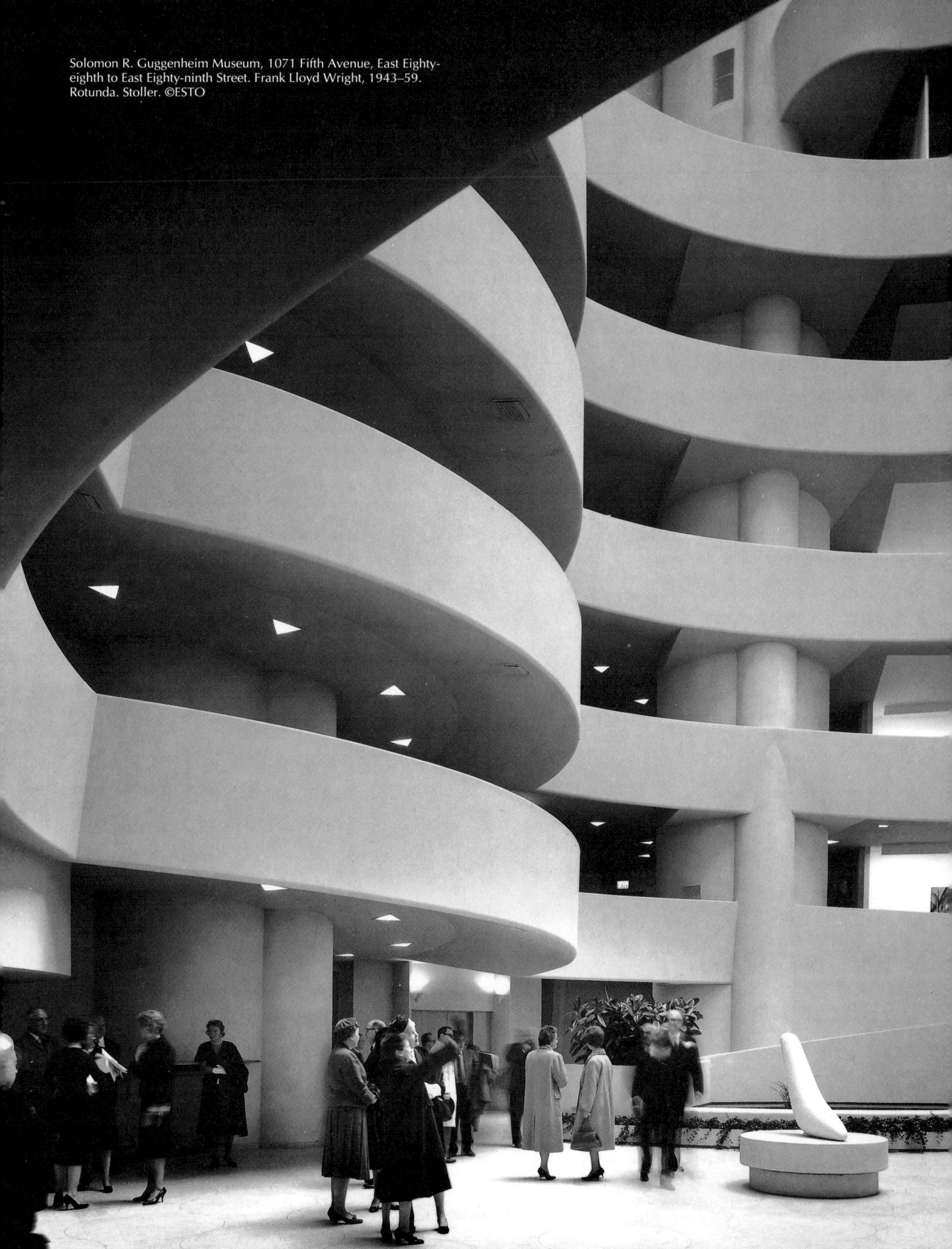

Solomon R. Guggenheim Museum, 1071 Fifth Avenue, East Eighty-eighth to East Eighty-ninth Street. Frank Lloyd Wright, 1943–59. Rotunda. Stoller. ©ESTO

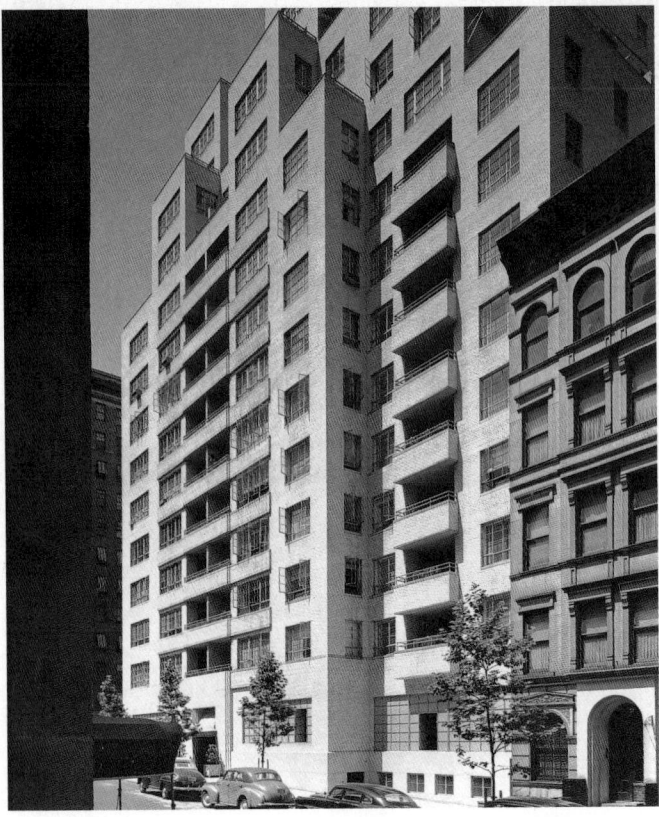

Wright gives people something else to do when they have had their fill of paintings. Whenever I go to the Guggenheim, I first feel again that great sense of elation one gets upon entering. I walk up the ramp, enjoying certain paintings, finding new interest in many that I had seen before. But after a time I find myself leaning on the rail and looking around. A lot of other people are doing the same thing—leaning on the rail and looking around, at the building, at all the other people. People have never looked more interesting. Their movements are graceful, their stops and starts intriguing, the profile of their figures sharp and unique. Some are seen from the waist up, others in full figure, those on the ground floor from a rare vantage point—all appearing abstractly free.[113]

Obviously, Portman was not alone in his enjoyment of the museum. Indeed, despite a fairly steep admission charge, the Guggenheim quickly became a destination point for as many as 3,000 people a day. In explaining the appeal of the museum shortly after its opening, Harry Guggenheim said: "People come initially because of the great controversy, and because they have been Frank Lloyd Wright-educated. They are attracted by the museum's novel forms. But they come back because they are inspired and delighted with what they see. We believe the building is both beautiful and functional, and that the architect has devised a revolutionary method of interest and value for viewing art."[114] In a Gallup poll taken early in 1960, the lure of the building itself was confirmed: nearly four out of every ten visitors (38 percent) interviewed came to see the building; 53 percent came to see the building and the art; and only 5 percent came for the art alone.

MADISON AVENUE

Madison Avenue was once a street of private houses rivaled only by Fifth Avenue, but by the 1920s many of these had been renovated to accommodate ground- and second-level shops with small apartments above, or demolished to make way for prestigious apartment houses, most with entrances on the crosstown streets.[1] In the immediate postwar era, Madison Avenue saw the construction of a number of new apartment houses that were a cut above the typical product, although none were as interesting as the Modernist design of 25 East Eighty-third Street (Frederick L. Ackerman with Charles George Ramsey and Harold Reeve Sleeper, 1938), on the avenue's northwest corner.[2] Despite their comparatively large scale, these buildings had little effect on the avenue's intimate mix of sophisticated shops and neighborhood service stores.

Sylvan Bien's 20 East Seventy-fourth Street (1947), on the southwest corner of Madison Avenue, was a sixteen-story brick block featuring street-facing balconies, piped-in music and conduits for televisions in each apartment.[3] In a gesture toward maintaining the street's commercial character, stores filled the building's one-story, stone-clad base along Madison Avenue. The fifteen-story apartment house at 47 East Eighty-seventh Street (Leonard Schultze & Associates, 1947), on the northeast corner of Madison Avenue, also contained stores on its granite-clad ground floor.[4] The building was distinguished principally by its large recessed terraces, as well as those incorporated into upper-level setbacks. As *Architectural Record* perhaps somewhat hyperbolically put it, the building "advances the balcony motif to a point where [its] closest definition might be: a *hanging* garden apartment."[5] Another brick-clad apartment building, at 15 East Ninety-first Street, on the northwest corner of Madison

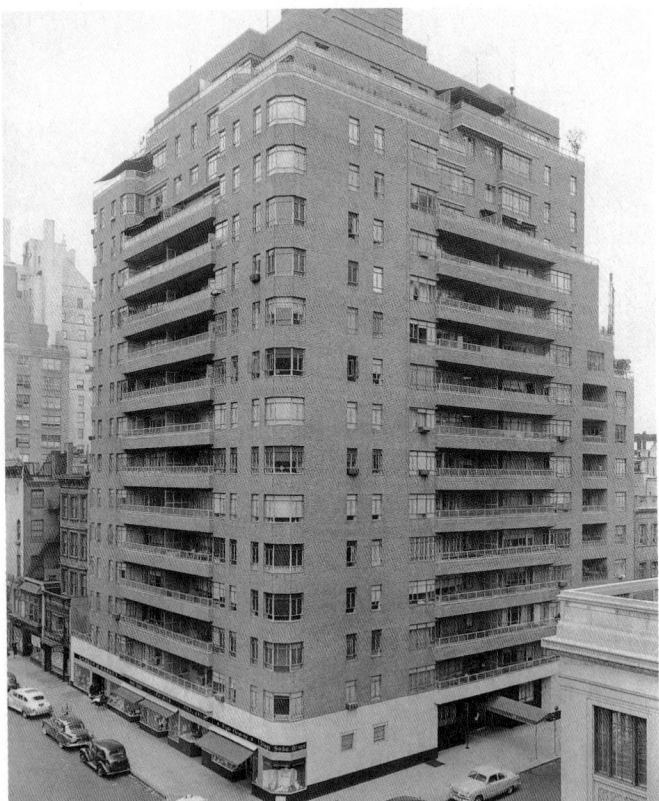

Top: 47 East Eighty-seventh Street, northeast corner of Madison Avenue. Leonard Schultze & Associates, 1947. View to the northwest. Stoller. ©ESTO

Bottom: 20 East Seventy-fourth Street, southwest corner of Madison Avenue. Sylvan Bien, 1947. View to the southwest. EG

Avenue, was completed the following year by the same firm.[6] The fifteen-story building contained ten-by-eleven-foot corner terraces that could easily be glassed in to serve as additional rooms.

In 1949 plans were announced for a twenty-two-story apartment building, designed by George F. Pelham, to occupy the full east blockfront of Madison Avenue between Eighty-first and Eighty-second streets.[7] Pelham's design called for numerous facade indentations, as well as a 215-car, two-story parking garage on the eastern edge of the site. The building's design provided every one of its 317 apartments with a minimum of two exposures and also included 150 terraces and several units equipped with wood-burning fireplaces. The building was never realized, and in 1953 the full-blockfront plot became the site of Public School 6.[8] Designed by Eric Kebbon, the three- and four-story, L-shaped, red-brick building was set back on all street frontages; an asphalt-paved playground was located in the northeast corner of the site, facing Eighty-second Street. The principal entrance was contained in a four-story tower with a vertically arranged, limestone-framed band of windows. Similarly articulated fenestration, which included dark-green stone spandrels, was utilized throughout the school.

Carlton House (Kenneth B. Norton, 1951) occupied the full blockfront of Madison Avenue between Sixty-first and Sixty-second streets.[9] Utilizing staff members of the former Ritz-Carlton Hotel, demolished in 1951, the apartment-hotel maintained a high level of personal services of the type that were rapidly vanishing in residential buildings throughout the city. Despite large casement windows, the architecture of the sixteen-story Regency-style building of red brick and limestone cast a backward glance, particularly in its Classically articulated three-story limestone base, complete with fluted pilasters culminating in garlands, which lent a welcome note of old-fashioned charm and civility to the quickly changing avenue. Completed three years later, 40 East Eighty-first Street (I. L. Crausman), on the southeast corner of Madison Avenue, was a comparatively banal fourteen-story red-brick building with stores and professional suites on its ground floor.[10]

The twenty-story 50 East Seventy-ninth Street (Brown & Guenther, 1958), on the southeast corner of Madison Avenue, had setback terraces beginning at the fifteenth floor; inside, the apartments were distinguished by such features as maids' rooms and separate service entrances.[11] The sixteen-story Montclair (Paul Resnick and Harry F. Green, 1959), at 35 East Seventy-fifth Street, on the northeast corner of Madison Avenue, had oriel-like projections that enclosed extensively glazed, octagonal "sun rooms."[12] Also completed in 1959 were 30 East Sixty-fifth Street, designed by Kokkins & Lyras, on the southeast corner of Madison Avenue, and 27 East Sixty-fifth Street, designed by Anthony M. Pavia, on the northeast corner of the avenue.[13] The rather run-of-the-mill buildings were seventeen and fifteen stories high, respectively, and both incorporated ground-level commercial space on the avenue and setbacks above the eleventh floor. Number 30 was clad in white brick, standard by then, while the brick cladding of number 27 was robin's-egg blue, a feature that distinguished but did not enhance its design. The apartments of 10 East Seventieth Street (Emery Roth & Sons, 1960), another fifteen-story, white-brick banality, were distinguished only by their views of the Frick Museum across the street.[14]

Perhaps the only architecturally significant addition to Madison Avenue's postwar apartment buildings was 45 East Eighty-ninth Street (1969).[15] This thirty-story Brutalist high rise,

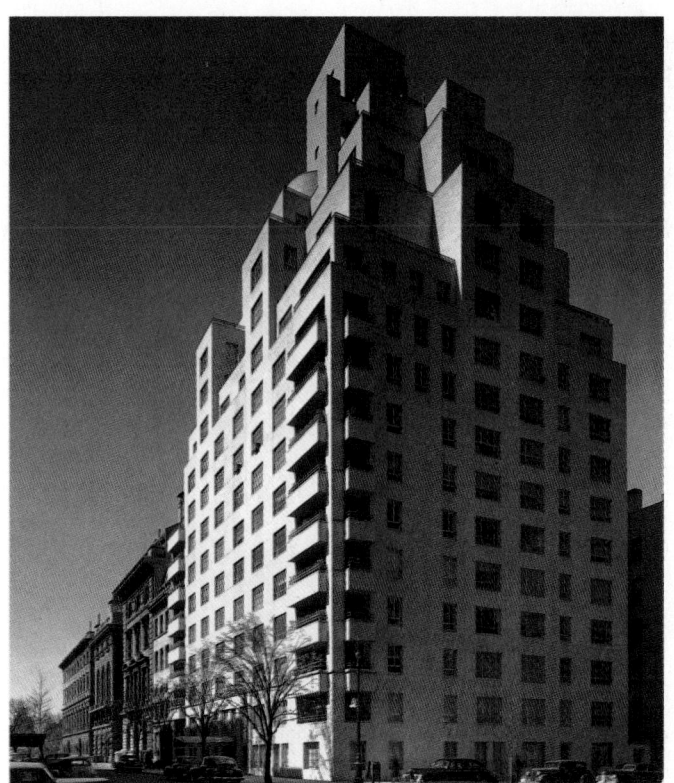

Top: 15 East Ninety-first Street, northwest corner of Madison Avenue. Leonard Schultze & Associates, 1948. View to the northwest. Stoller. ©ESTO

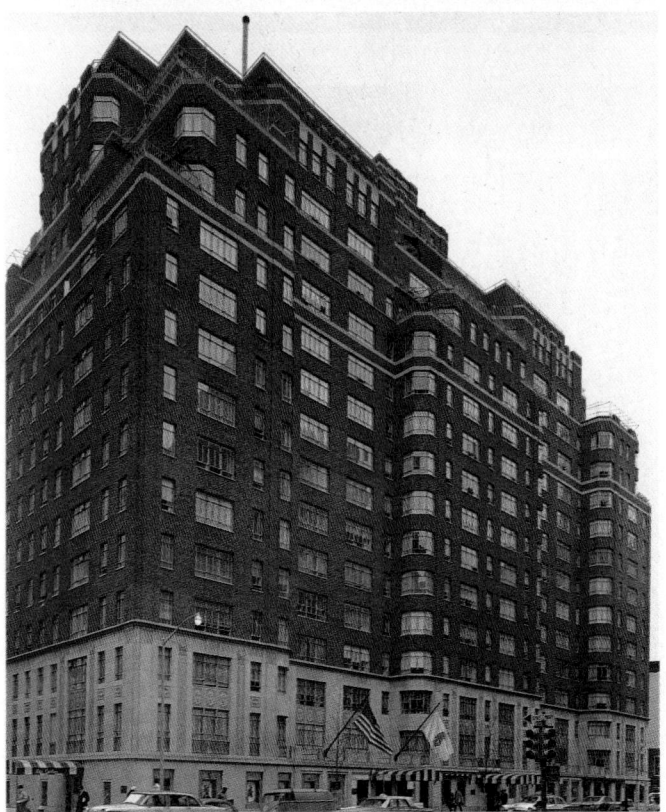

Bottom: Carlton House, 680 Madison Avenue, East Sixty-first to East Sixty-second Street. Kenneth B. Norton, 1951. View to the northwest. OMH

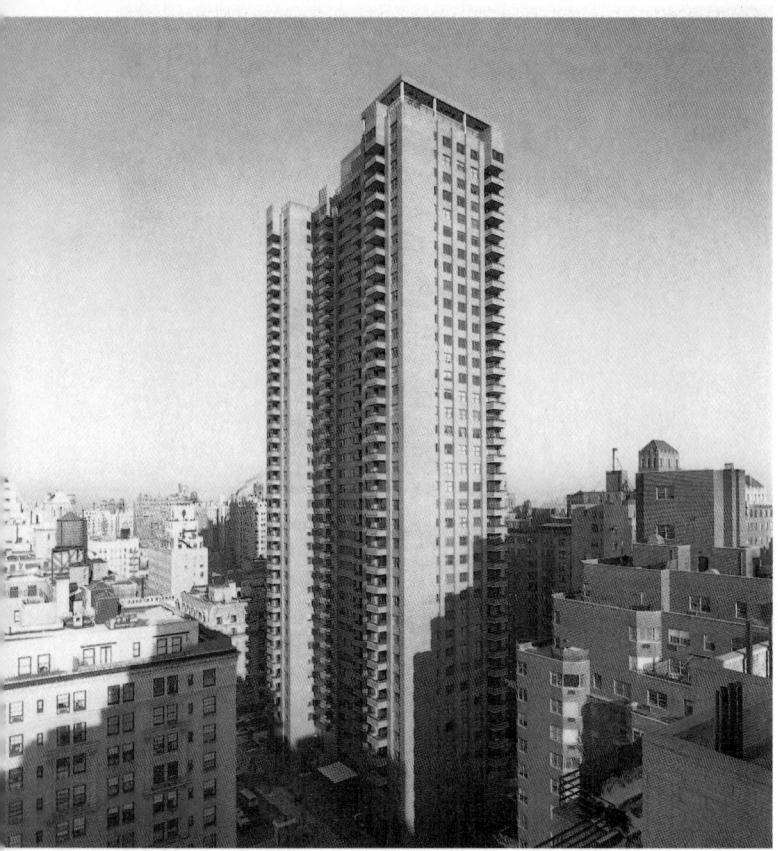

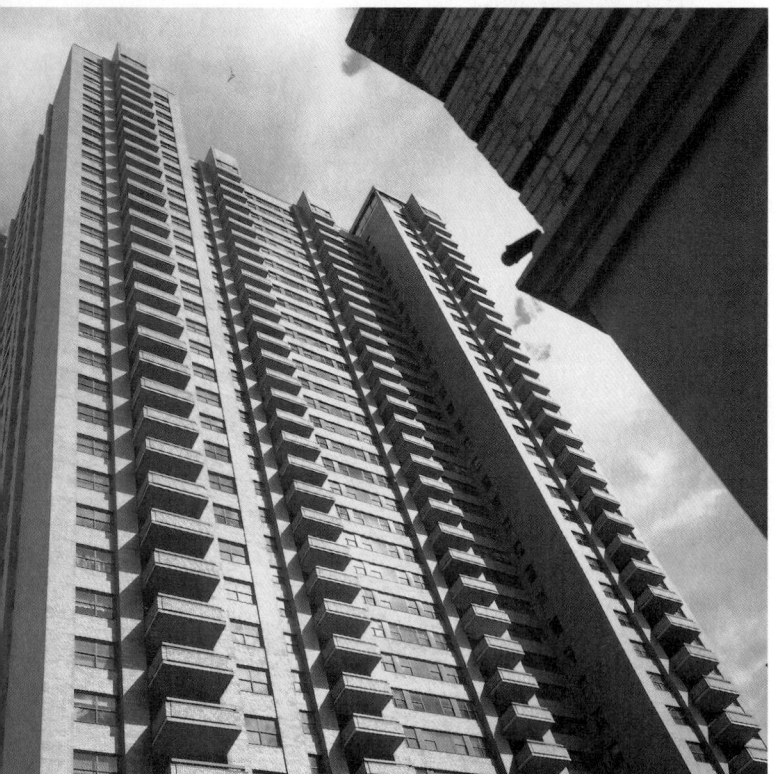

Top: 45 East Eighty-ninth Street, east side of Madison Avenue, East Eighty-ninth to East Ninetieth Street. Oppenheimer, Brady & Lehrecke, 1969. View to the northeast. OMH

Bottom: 45 East Eighty-ninth Street. View to the southeast. Stoller. ©ESTO

occupying the entire east blockfront of Madison Avenue between Eighty-ninth and Ninetieth Streets, was designed by Thomas Lehrecke of Oppenheimer, Brady & Lehrecke from a scheme initially worked out by Philip Birnbaum. Towering above its neighbors, the building reflected the effects of the 1961 zoning resolution, and its overwhelming bulk memorialized the abuse of the zoning's plaza bonus. The building was set back from all three flanking streets by mini-plazas, which were paved in a brick similar to the brown iron-spot brick that clad its facades and were punctuated by truncated pyramidal brick planters. The most generously scaled plaza—the one that made possible the building's tremendous height—was located to the east and protected by a one- and two-story wing extending past the midblock point of Eighty-ninth Street. The hulking mass of Lehrecke's tower was relieved by cantilevered concrete-floored terraces partially walled in with the same brick used for the plazas, and by thin stringcourses defining every floor. All of the apartments contained two or three bedrooms and had nine-foot-high ceilings, a comparative rarity in an era when ceilings six inches or a foot lower were standard. On the roof was a health club featuring a year-round swimming pool and saunas.

Andrew Alpern felt that the building conveyed a "clean-lined and classically contemporary" image and that the plaza paving and planters added "a note of warmth."[16] John Tauranac disagreed: "This is not a warm and gentle building. Its terraces bristle, and its lower floors . . . give the feeling of a Romanesque fortress."[17] The building had the greatest effect not at its base but at its pinnacle; its looming presence created a particularly startling image when viewed from across Central Park. As the journalist Joseph P. Fried observed in the *New York Times*:

> The new tower has displaced another and much smaller landmark—the snail-shaped concrete outline of the Guggenheim Museum . . . as the most striking feature of Central Park's eastern skyline. To those who like their skylines fairly even and orderly, the new structure will no doubt seem a jarring blockbuster. But to those who feel that sudden interruptions and jagged variety lend a sense of excitement to a skyline, the Madison Avenue building will be a welcome addition. Skyline connoiseurs, like devotees of painting, are varied in their tastes and can argue the esthetics of a pleasing skyline with the same gusto as an adherent of the Italian Renaissance confronting a proponent of abstract expressionism.[18]

While Norval White and Elliot Willensky noted that 45 East Eighty-ninth Street was a "notch above its competition," they asserted that its "blockbuster" mass constituted "a state of affairs that can't be condoned, regardless of other virtues."[19]

Two other apartment buildings—one on Madison and one just off the avenue—also exemplified the effects of the new zoning, although both were less brutal and less memorable than 45 East Eighty-ninth Street. Rising sheer and unmodulated by setbacks, the twenty-five-story reinforced-concrete structure of Charel House (Schuman, Lichtenstein & Claman, 1971), at 40 East Eightieth Street, on the southeast corner of Madison Avenue, clad in buff brick with dark-tinted windows, was set back on both street frontings to create an L-shaped, landscaped plaza.[20] Inside, apartments featured marble-floored foyers, solid wood doors, masonry walls and operator-driven elevators. The dark-brown-brick, thirty-one-story tower at 50 East Eighty-ninth Street (Emery Roth & Sons, 1974), between Madison and Park avenues, occupied only 40 percent of its through-block site, which extended south to Eighty-eighth Street.[21] The southern portion of the block contained a private garden. A subterranean driveway linked Eighty-eighth and Eighty-ninth streets and provided access to a parking garage. Four first- and second-floor duplex units were treated as maisonettes, each with its own street entrance and rear second-floor garden; spatially if not stylistically evocative of the area's brownstones, these duplexes reinforced the neighborhood's urbanistic traditions.

The Milton Steinberg House (Kelly & Gruzen, 1955), at 50 East Eighty-seventh Street, between Madison and Park avenues, was an addition to the Park Avenue Synagogue (Walter S. Schneider, 1927) that contained offices and an activities center.[22] In striking contrast to the richly ornamented, rather fussy Romanesque and Moorish synagogue next door, this building offered a Modernist grace note to the area. Above a slightly recessed windowless one-story base, the principal facade of the Steinberg House consisted of a curtain wall of stained-glass panels designed by the noted Abstract Expressionist painter Adolph Gottlieb. The windows, combining transparent and transluscent sections, were particularly striking at night when illuminated from within.

Another addition to the Park Avenue Synagogue was proposed in 1970 for a site on the southeast corner of Madison Avenue and Eighty-seventh Street but was never realized.[23] Conklin & Rossant's proposal, which would have replaced several nineteenth-century rowhouses, called for a complexly modeled six-story building suspended from a steel space frame spanning the sixty-foot-square site. Extensively glazed floors were to be arranged in reverse setbacks, leaving a generously scaled plaza at the corner. In addition to its technical functions, the space frame was to serve a visual purpose, acting as a cornice that maintained the building line along both street frontages. Pipe columns, serving as suspension members, were to be sheathed in bronze, as were all spandrels.

By the early 1960s Madison Avenue had begun to emerge as a major focus of the art world, with important galleries initially attracted to the area by the construction of the Parke-Bernet Building in 1949.[24] Before relocating to 980 Madison Avenue, on the west blockfront from Seventy-sixth to Seventy-seventh Street, facing the Carlyle Hotel, the auctioneers Parke-Bernet had occupied the American Art Association and Gallery Building (J. D. Leland & Company, 1922), twenty blocks south.[25] Parke-Bernet's new site had previously been home to five rowhouses (ca. 1880) facing Seventy-sixth Street, as well as the Seth Milliken house (pre-1867) at the southwest corner of Seventy-seventh Street. Walker & Poor designed the block-long six-story building for the City Investing Company, headed by the prominent realtor Robert W. Dowling, who also controlled the Carlyle Hotel and saw the new building as a physical and social complement to it. Working in association with Walker & Poor, the architect and decorator Eugene Schoen designed the two floors that would be occupied by the auction house, the building's prime tenant: the second floor, to house administrative offices, and the third floor, to house the auction rooms, whose unfenestrated walls became a principal element of the facade.

Although the Parke-Bernet Building was unpopular with Modernists, it seemed pleasingly modern to traditional architects. William A. Delano, for instance, said in a speech at the building's dedication that "it combines all the best of traditional and modern schools of architectural thought."[26] Lewis Mumford also lauded the building, describing it as "one of those structures, still far too rare, on which there was collaboration from the beginning between the owner, the users, and the architects." He praised several of the building's features, such as the elaborate roof gar-

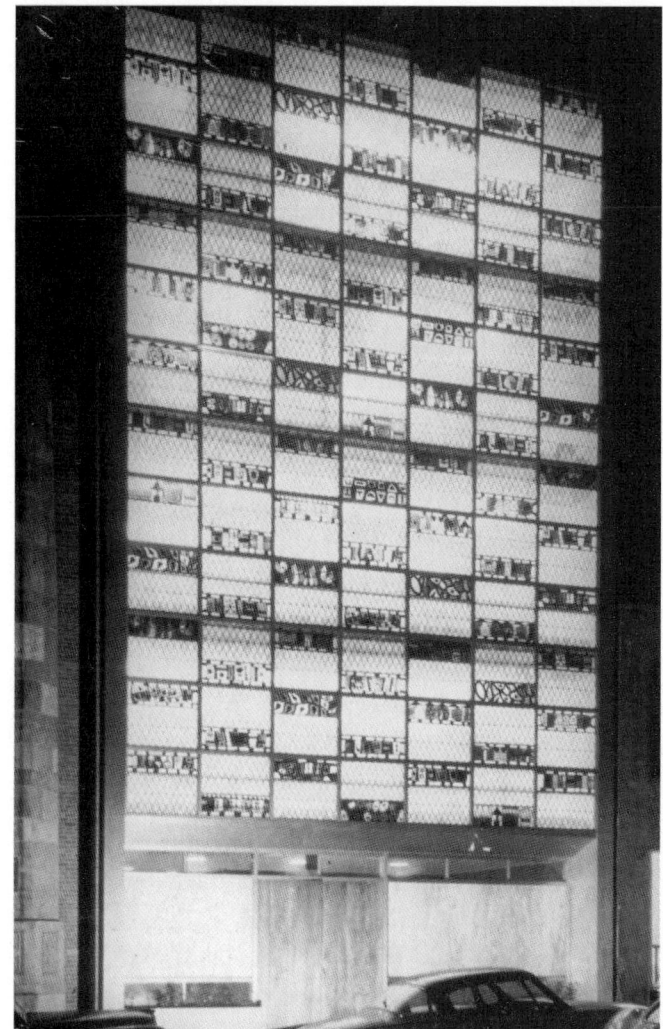

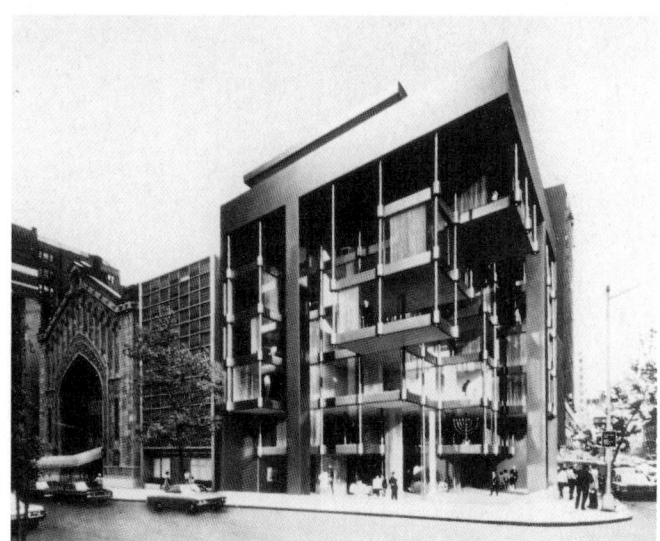

Top: Milton Steinberg House of the Park Avenue Synagogue, 50 East Eighty-seventh Street, between Madison and Park avenues. Kelly & Gruzen, 1955. View to the south. GS

Bottom: Proposal for addition to Park Avenue Synagogue, southeast corner of Madison Avenue and East Eighty-seventh Street. Conklin & Rossant, 1970. Photographic montage showing view to the southeast. CR

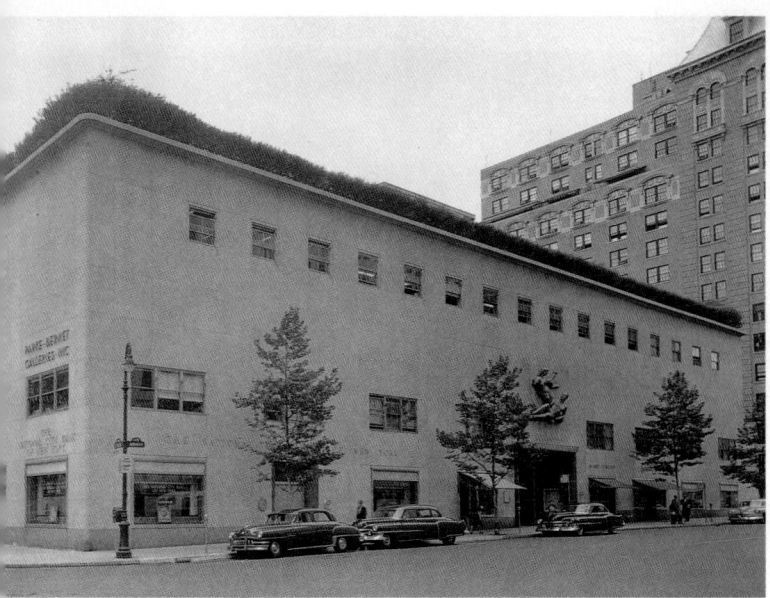

Above: Parke-Bernet Building, 980 Madison Avenue, East Seventy-sixth to East Seventy-seventh Street. Walker & Poor, 1949. View to the northwest. OMH

Top right: Whitney Museum of American Art, 945 Madison Avenue, southeast corner of East Seventy-fifth Street. Marcel Breuer with Hamilton Smith, 1966. View to the southeast. Stoller. ©ESTO

Bottom right: Whitney Museum of American Art. View to the east. Stoller. ©ESTO

Top far right: Whitney Museum of American Art. East-west section. WMAA

Bottom far right: Whitney Museum of American Art. North-south section. WMAA

den, "the existence of which is barely suggested to anyone in the street—whose purpose becomes comprehensible only if one learns something about the reason for the building." He also admired the building's urbanism: "Those who chose the site and conceived the structure exercised a private sense of civic responsibility in exemplary fashion."[27] As Mumford pointed out, the decision to build a low building and to landscape its fifth- and sixth-floor rooftops was made not only to provide an amenity for patrons of the auctions but also to protect the light, air and Central Park views of the residents in the Carlyle.

Mumford observed that the Parke-Bernet Building's elevations were "conceived with such simplicity that the slightest error in taste, the faintest blemish in workmanship, would seem like a rattle of static in the midst of a Mozart quartet," and he praised their "unbroken stone surfaces" and the "simple, clear-cut rectangular cornice." He also noted that the windows were set almost flush with the stone facing "in such elemental composition" that the variation of the windows on the second and fourth floors, contrasted with the blank third floor between, was enough to create "a happy, decorative effect." He appreciated the overall simplicity of the building's facade: "Mies van der Rohe likes to make more of a show of structural details, but the exterior of the Galleries has been conceived by architects with an equal respect for formalized elegance." Mumford also commented on *Venus and Manhattan*, an aluminum sculpture by Wheeler Williams that was mounted on the facade just above the main entrance; he felt that in addition to emphasizing the entrance, it carried out "the theme of the building—the combination of freshness and traditionalism, of the modern and the second-hand, that reflects the enterprise it houses."[28]

Mumford concluded his assessment of the building with qualified praise: "A building so reticent, so chaste, is a welcome contribution to the street picture. . . . One would hesitate to call this a true example of organic architecture, but in the existing metropolis, where Venus is married to Midas instead of Vulcan, it is about as satisfactory as can be expected. Not the least important mission of modern architecture in its transitional phase is to bring back to our confused environment a few modest symbols of order and peace."[29]

Whitney Museum of American Art

Madison Avenue's identity as an art center was solidified in 1966 when the Whitney Museum of American Art opened its headquarters at 945 Madison Avenue, on the southeast corner of Seventy-fifth Street. With the addition of the Whitney, Madison Avenue became more than just a tony shopping destination; it took on a civic dimension similar to that provided by the numerous art museums lining Fifth Avenue. The Whitney Museum had been founded in 1931 by Gertrude Vanderbilt Whitney as an outgrowth of her Whitney Studio (1914) and the subsequent Whitney Studio Club (1918).[30] Its first home was a building at 8–12 West Eighth Street, renovated by G. McCullough Miller and Augustus L. Noel in 1931. Charming though it was, the Eighth Street building was inadequate: its safety and security provisions were primitive, it lacked adequate storage and curatorial space and its downtown location, an advantage when the museum was still close to its origins as the Whitney Studio, was now a drawback in attracting big-money contributors, who felt the neighborhood was out of the way and overly bohemian. When Whitney died in 1942, she bequeathed $2.5 million to the museum. In 1943 a plan was announced by Francis Henry

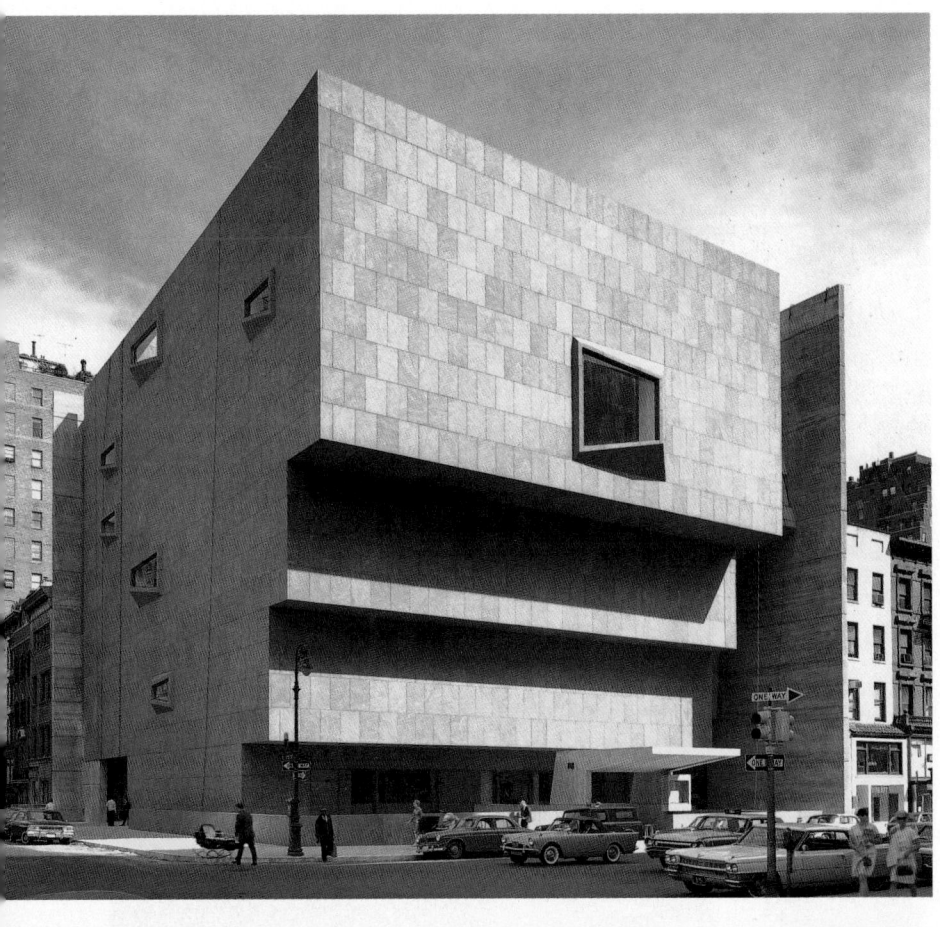
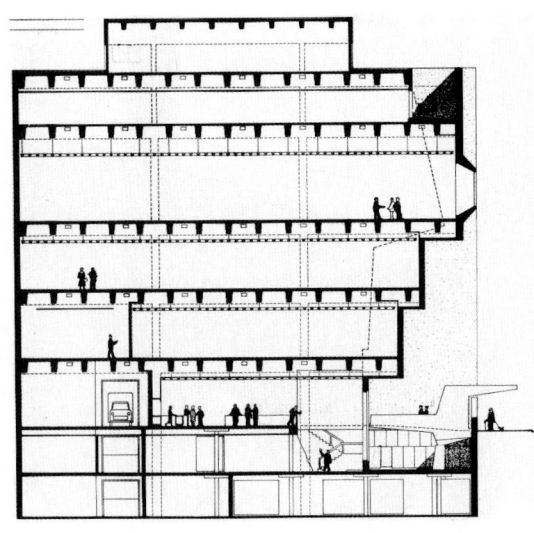
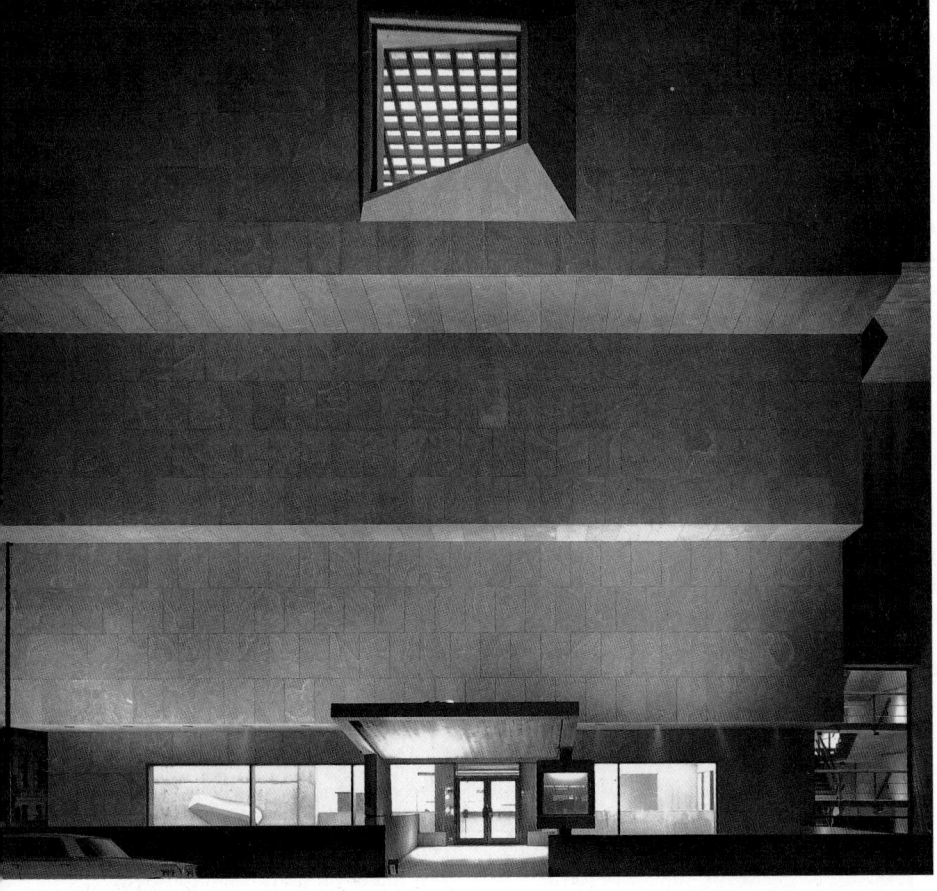
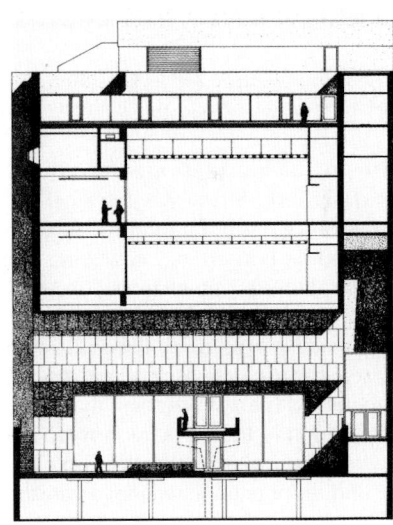

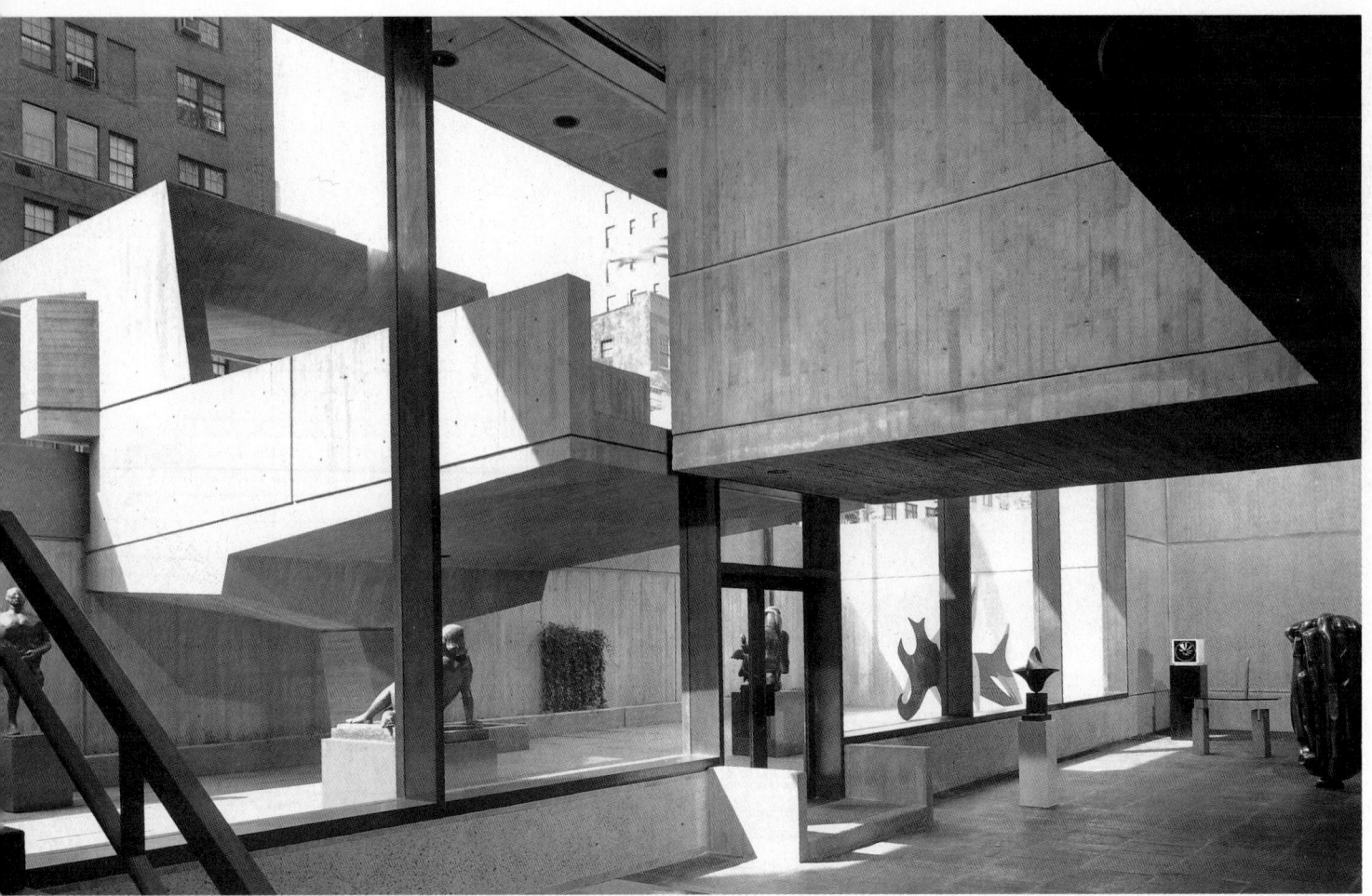

Whitney Museum of American Art. 945 Madison Avenue, southeast corner of East Seventy-fifth Street. Marcel Breuer with Hamilton Smith, 1966. View of sunken sculpture court from basement-level gallery. Stoller. ©ESTO

Taylor, director of the Metropolitan Museum of Art, and Whitney's daughter, Flora Whitney Miller, in which the Whitney Museum would abandon its independent facility on Eighth Street and be housed in a new wing at the Metropolitan to be built after the war (see chapter 10). While the *New York Times* was not against the merger, it did lament the passing of the original Whitney Museum: "Reconstruction of several fine old houses served to create a museum structure quite unique; one impregnated with an atmosphere that seemed warmly reciprocal in its relation to the art there shown. True, the art will be the same when the collection moves uptown. Yet something memorable and unforgettable will have vanished."[31]

The plan for the Whitney Wing was abandoned in 1948, as was a subsequent plan for cooperation between the Whitney, the Metropolitan and the Museum of Modern Art. In 1949 the Whitney entered into an agreement with the Modern to occupy part of its new wing at 22 West Fifty-fourth Street (see chapter 5). Although the Fifty-fourth Street facility marked a significant functional if not aesthetic improvement over the Whitney's former home, the museum's trustees and staff almost immediately recognized that the building was woefully inadequate in size and was little more than a stepchild of the Modern. In 1958 the Whitney staff began to look for a site for a new building that would be three times larger. In early 1963 they found a 13,000-square-foot parcel—104 feet along Madison Avenue and 125 feet along Seventy-fifth Street—that the Jonathan Woodner

Company had already begun excavating for a co-op apartment house but was having difficulty financing. The Whitney's decision to purchase the lot was announced in June 1963, by which time Marcel Breuer had been selected after interviews with several other architects, including Edward Larrabee Barnes and Louis I. Kahn. The new location, in the very heart of the fashionable Upper East Side residential and gallery district, was different in every way from the bohemian setting Gertrude Whitney had established in Greenwich Village.

The new Whitney Museum, designed by Marcel Breuer and executed by him with his partner Hamilton Smith, was perhaps the most talked about and written about new building in New York in the 1960s, and it at last provided the museum with an identifiable image.[32] Breuer's plans, released in December 1963, called for a startlingly sculpted mass, an inverted, granite-clad ziggurat, with the Madison Avenue elevation rising in three cantilevered elements from a moatlike sunken sculpture court. Along Seventy-fifth Street, the building was set back thirty-five feet from the street line and rose eighty-five feet sheer to the top of its roof parapet. This extraordinary shape was framed on the two inner edges of the building plot by sheer walls of exposed, board-formed reinforced concrete that rose the museum's full height. These walls seemed to defend—and certainly isolate—the bold new building from the existing city fabric and were devised, according to Breuer, to "emphasize the completeness of the architectural form." They constituted, he said, "an attempt to

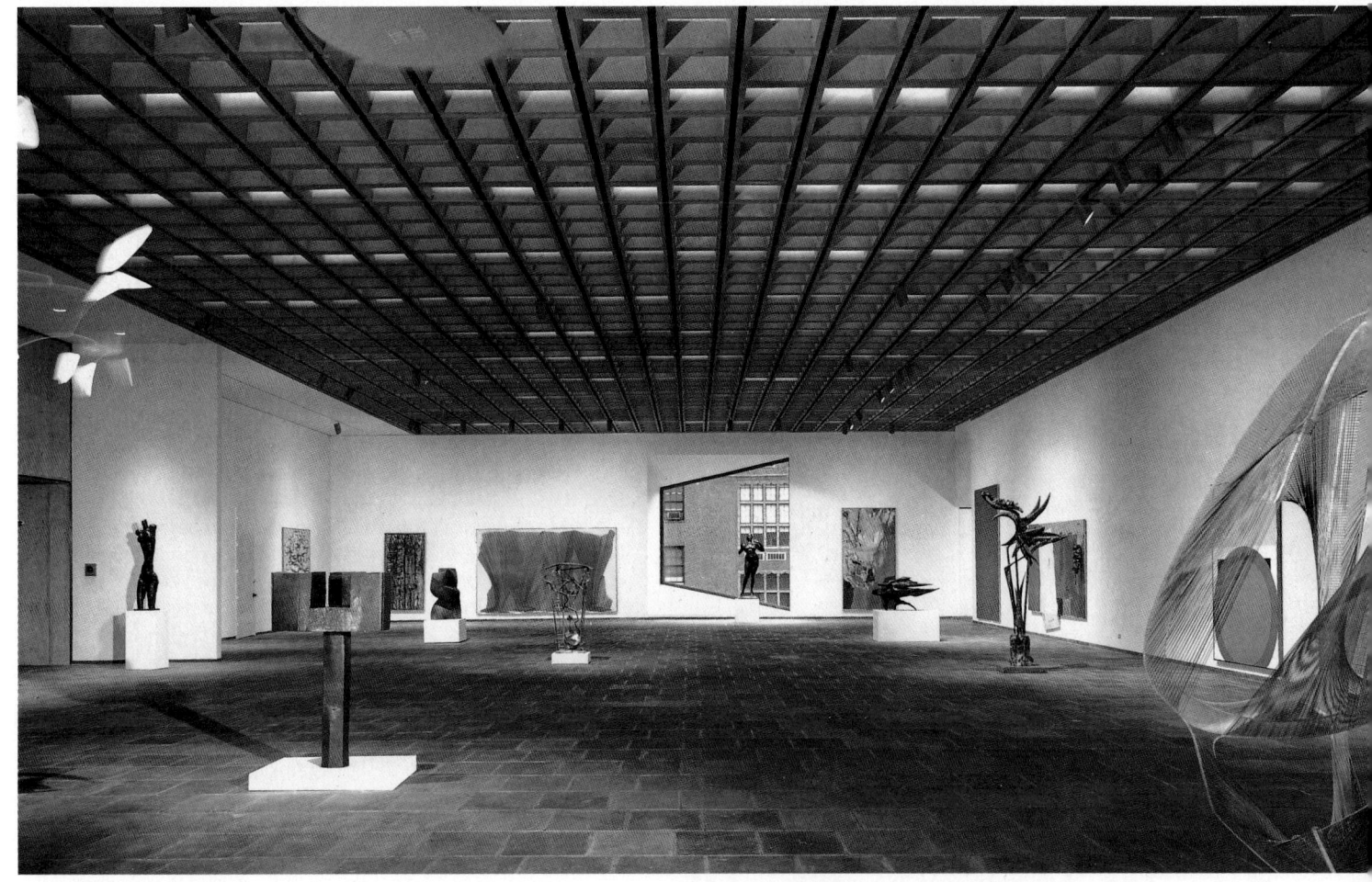

Whitney Museum of American Art. Gallery. Stoller. ©ESTO

solve the inherent problem of a corner building which otherwise could easily look like a quarter part of something." He explained further:

> The project transforms the building into a unit, an element, a nucleus, and lends it a direction towards Madison Avenue. The overall granite facing, homogeneous, extending out and over towards Madison Avenue, reaching down into the sunken garden with openings which grow out of the surface, with the modulation of the Madison Avenue gap between it and the neighboring buildings, with the granite parapet along the sidewalk and with the structural concrete form of the bridge—all this is to form the building as a sculpture.[33]

Breuer was forthright about the building's aggressive anticontextualism: "Maybe I built it to rebel against skyscrapers and brownstones. I didn't try to fit the building to its neighbors because the neighboring buildings aren't any good."[34]

The walls were separated from the main building mass by recessed strips of vertical glazing, which introduced light into the stairwells, one of the building's most widely admired elements. As James R. Mellow wrote:

> It is, oddly enough, in such accessways as the stair landings that one gets a sense of the refinement of the building as compared with the awesomeness of the large gallery spaces. It is almost as if, having designed the large public spaces for flexibility and unobtrusiveness, the architect has confined his per-

sonal taste to the transitional areas like the stairways between floors. . . . With their simple forms and their frank use of materials—stone steps, concrete walls, metal balustrades, teak handrails—these areas have a cloistered or monastic feeling, providing a space in which to collect one's thoughts between the experience of one gallery level and another.[35]

The building was largely unglazed, except for the west walls of the lobby and the basement level and the six angled bay windows that punctuated the north facade, placed in a seemingly random arrangement, as well as the single, similarly articulated cyclopean window facing Madison Avenue. The natural light that entered through the windows was intended to provide what Breuer described as a "psychological" release from museum fatigue.[36]

Access to the building's main entrance, placed just to the right of the principal facade's center, was over a thirty-five-foot-long sculptural bridge across the sunken moat. In the first schemes the bridge was uncovered; later a decorative hood was added to provide a more distinct entrance. Immediately inside the entry was a lobby, with a ticket counter, a small shop and checkrooms; a small gallery was also located on this floor. A double-height space opening down revealed the restaurant and sculpture court below, which could be reached by an open stair. Though an elaborately composed and crafted exposed-concrete fire stair could be used to reach the three floors of galleries above, the preferred circulation was by means of the two eleva-

827

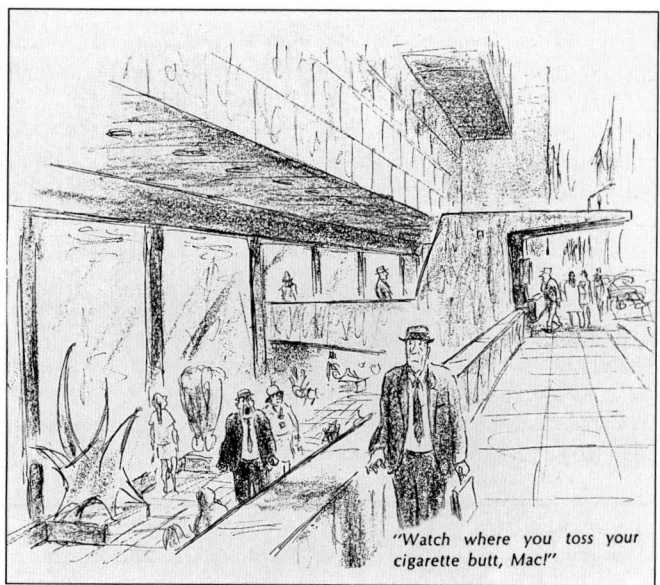

"Watch where you toss your cigarette butt, Mac!"

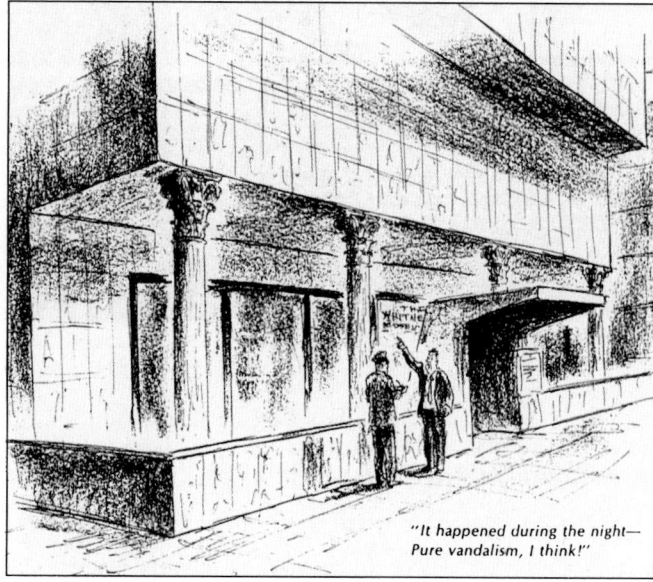

"It happened during the night—
Pure vandalism, I think!"

Top: Cartoon. Alan Dunn, 1967. PDE

Bottom: Cartoon. Alan Dunn, 1966. PDE

tors; one of these, sized to double as a freight elevator for moving large-scale artworks, had colossal proportions—it measured 8'1½" wide, 10'5" deep and 12'5" high—and was a phenomenon in and of itself. The largely column-free galleries included a fourth-floor double-height (17'6") space to accommodate the large paintings and sculptures that were increasingly part of the American art scene. All galleries had a concrete ceiling grid to insure flexibility for the incandescent lighting system and the movable partition system Breuer designed. Staff offices and a library were located on the fifth floor, which was set back from the building's edge to provide an outdoor terrace, concealed from public view by the parapet.

In her assessment of the first drawings, Ada Louise Huxtable said that although the "serious and somber" building would be "sympathetic to its neighbors . . . in scale and surface simplicity," it was also "meant to be both noticeable and distinctive."[37] This was the view that Breuer put forward at the press conference where the plans were first presented, when he characterized the building as a "sculpture" that was meant not only to meet the museum's complex functional requirements but to have a strong identity "in the midst of the dynamic jungle of our colorful city."[38] Emily Genauer, writing in the *New York Herald Tribune*, questioned the building's sheer massiveness, which seemed a throwback to the "blockiness of design that was the hallmark of [the] Bauhaus. . . . It is a heaviness the more regrettable at a moment when structural technology is making possible architectural conceptions of new grace and elegance."[39]

In late December 1963, ten days after her first article, Huxtable defended the design against the "criticism" and "outrage" it had met with:

> It may be too somber and severe for many tastes, but it is still a careful, conscientious search for a creative solution. . . . The almost windowless dark gray granite, the bulky overhangs and the sunken sculpture court that suggests swirling little dust storms among the statues below grade, all promise to be pretty gloomy. . . . The new building may turn out to be impressive in a kind of stygian way, or it may be a kind of miniature Alcatraz on Madison Avenue. But it will not be cheap, thin, tinny, thoughtless, dull, facile, shoddy or routine, and that is more than can be said of most of the city's current construction.[40]

Three weeks before the building's official opening on September 28, 1966, Huxtable offered another appraisal: "At first, second and third glance, the building suggests a mannered tour de force in the current mode of architecture for sculpture's sake. On fourth, fifth and further inspections, matching interior to exterior, it reveals itself as a carefully calculated design that squeezes the most out of a small awkward . . . corner lot with maximum artistry and almost hypnotic skill." She took great pleasure in Breuer's use of materials and his handling of details:

> The building has an extraordinary urbanity, which masquerades as a kind of "back-to-structure" crudeness. . . . It stresses masses of stone, largely unpolished—in this case a truly beautiful gray granite outside and in—raw concrete complete with board marks of forms, rugged, bush-hammered concrete aggregate for interior walls, bluestone and split-slate floors. The trick—and again the hand is quicker than the eye—is the subtly scooped curve of a stone stair riser, the shape of a teak rail, or the juxtaposition of a rough-surfaced concrete wall with the extravagant luxury of the massive, silky bronze doors.

But Huxtable was not without criticism of the design. She found the bay windows "arbitrary" despite the "full battery of irrelevant functional rationalizations" mustered on their behalf. And the court, she said, when viewed from the street, "has a suggestion of the jailyard, not entirely dispelled by the stony severity inside," although "the view from below is impressive."[41]

Huxtable wrote about the building yet again soon after it had opened. "At the moment," she said, "the most disliked building in New York is undoubtedly the Whitney Museum." But, she continued, "like that fine old saying about sin, first the Whitney repulses; then it intrigues; and finally, it is embraced." She said that the building offered "several architectural lessons":

In addition to its virtues of thoughtful planning and sensitive artistry in the use of materials, it is an effective demonstration of the fact that the anonymous, flexible exhibition space most directors want need not be reduced to the lowest barn, warehouse, or factory common denominator. . . . But with all of the Whitney's flexibility and mechanical marvels, a sense of architecture remains. . . . [Breuer] never smothers with the conventional trappings of pseudo-glamor, and he offers convincing evidence that new buildings need not be routinely finished inside with the sleekly monotonous, expensive packaged excellence of the contemporary corporate cliché.

More than any other commentator, Huxtable recognized that the Whitney trustees' decision to build a strong, even eccentric building grew out of a sense that they needed an icon, a monument to put their museum on the map. Breuer's building, she said, successfully fulfilled that mission, but not "at the expense of its pleasantly elegant, if architecturally undistinguished surroundings. One of the Whitney's more significant lessons, this time in urban design, is that the new and different is not necessarily destructive, and the timid and traditional does not necessarily preserve and protect." Huxtable made a critical distinction between the Whitney building and the Guggenheim: "New Yorkers, conditioned by the Guggenheim, will probably accept the Whitney fairly quickly. In doing so, it is to be hoped that they will recognize that the Guggenheim is an *objet d'art*, inside and out, with its staff battling endlessly to make it a workable museum, while the Whitney is a workable museum raised to the level of architectural art."[42]

By the time of the building's completion, Emily Genauer's initial skepticism about the design had grown into downright dislike:

It's one of the most aggressive, arrogant buildings in New York. Already being called the Madison Avenue Monster, even when viewed from across the street it threatens to reach out and strike the hurrying pedestrian. To someone walking along the grim, gray, upside-down-pyramid of granite, the deeply cantilevered sides hang so heavy overhead as to seem waiting momentarily to crush one. Separating the hundred-foot Madison Avenue facade from the sidewalk is another portentous feature, a stone ditch (called a sculpture garden) about thirty feet wide and fifteen deep, which suggests a tomb built to surround this temple-tower so like an inverted Babylonian ziggurat.

Although Genauer found the Whitney building "alive"—"alive as a clenched fist, maybe, but alive"—she said it lacked an "exalting experience" similar to that of the Guggenheim's ramp spiraling up toward the sky. And contrary to Huxtable's opinion, she felt that Breuer's building was more competitive with the art displayed than Wright's was; while the Guggenheim seemed to say, "there's Something bigger than both of us," Genauer contended, the Whitney seemed to say, "to artists, in any case . . . 'You're not as big as you think.'" Genauer was one of the few writers to question the wisdom of the trustees' decision to relo-

cate to so tight a site: "Why a building of such importance and cost ($6,000,000, with land) had to be constructed on a small corner plot, I cannot imagine. . . . The needed floor area . . . had to be from six to seven times greater than the existing site, yet the building could reach no higher than 85 feet. . . . Breuer figured out a vigorous, tough-minded, logical, interesting solution to a problem that shouldn't have existed."[43]

Thomas Hess, the influential editor of *Art News*, discussed the new Whitney in the context of the museum's previous character. "Of all American museums," he wrote, "the Whitney is known as the most warmhearted: generous, considerate, loyal to old flames, highly susceptible to new advances. And it has also wallowed in the defects of its lovable virtues. . . . We are accustomed to finding the Whitney in a homey homely setting, with bad lighting, terrible fixtures and generally unworkable quarters." All that changed, Hess said, with the new building:

At first [it] seemed another mistakenly self-indulgent piece of architectural sculpture, a monument to its maker, like a "Guggenheim with corners," as one painter remarked. Then it was sheathed in black granite, giving it a mineral, prison look, made more menacing by the top-heavy effect of its overhangs. A gate-structure was thrown across the main entrance, like a toll-barrier for some medieval samurai. A "sunken sculpture garden" appeared; it looked like a fortress moat. And eccentric fenestration pierced the walls with mock-monster eyes to glare out at what is, after all, one of the most domesticated urban scenes in the world. What were our dear old friends up to, decreeing a black Crusader Castle among the tearooms and boutiques of Madisonia?[44]

When he entered the building, Hess had an entirely different view. He was particularly impressed by the fourth-floor gallery, which "gives a landscape vista to the whole area, [and] is one of the most handsome interiors in America." From the inside, even the "strange" windows lost their "Dr. Caligari quality" and became "refreshing sources of daylight that softens and varies the even illumination which streams from overhead grids." The facade's "infernal quality," Hess said, was "qualified and explicated by elegant juxtapositions of large masses of wood, stone and bronze on the floors, doors, stairs, etc.—agglomerate concrete walls, for example, echo the fortress motif, but make it warm, human, protecting." Hess could not, however, find any merit in the sculpture garden, arguing that "the strength of the underview of Breuer's entrance ramp . . . so dominates the area that any nearby sculpture is drained of scale and substance."[45]

Olga Gueft, the editor of *Interiors*, provided a succinct summary of the Whitney's building: "Of all the public buildings which have been erected in New York in the past two decades, none is so completely free of concessions to supposed popular taste, and none is so completely invulnerable." She praised not only Breuer's solution to the problems raised by the site's limitations but also the decision to build on this site rather than one in an easier, more remote location: "To dodge the dilemma by choosing another site would have meant giving up an ideal location among Manhattan's major museums and galleries."[46]

Writing in 1979, with the wisdom—or at least the larger perspective—granted by the passage of time, Paul Goldberger offered a measured assessment:

[The Whitney] is an arrogant, utterly abstract form, concerned more with its own shape than with any role it plays in the streetscape of Madison Avenue. . . . Yet . . . the Whitney is almost all right. The gallery spaces are ample and flexible . . . and

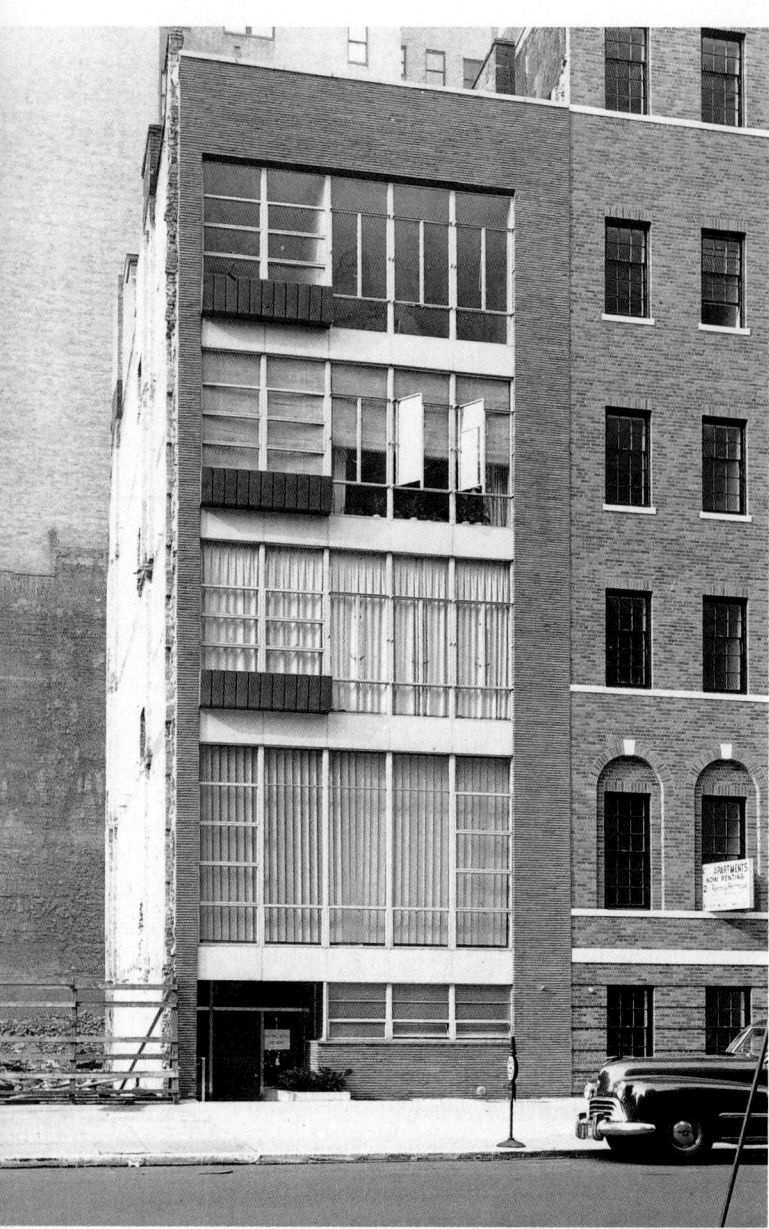

54 East Seventy-second Street, between Madison and Park avenues. Morris Lapidus, 1950. View to the south. Gottscho-Schleisner. LOC

there is a general air of smooth functioning to this building. And even the overbearing, rather brutal form, when you have seen it once or twice, gets less threatening and seems to strike a cautious détente with the rest of Madison Avenue. This will never be the ideal building either for its site or for its program, and it will never fully overcome that sense that all Marcel Breuer buildings give of being objects before they are buildings, but it deserves, after a decade, a grudging respect.[47]

PARK AVENUE

In contrast to the dramatic changes that characterized Fifth Avenue's Gold Coast in the postwar era, the comparable stretch of Park Avenue, from Sixtieth to Ninety-sixth Street, was relatively stable, with most of its 1920s apartment houses remaining intact.[1] A few new buildings, such as 737 Park Avenue (Sylvan Bien) and 785 Park Avenue (George F. Pelham, Jr.), usually with less luxurious appointments than the deluxe buildings of the 1920s, had been built in the late 1930s.[2] That trend continued with the construction in 1941 of 530 Park Avenue, on the southwest corner of Sixty-first Street, which, according to its developer, Anthony Campagna, represented "the latest evolution of the Park Avenue apartment": units with only one or two bedrooms and only one or even no maid's room. As Campagna explained: "New York families who have the means to live as they choose still demand a choice location and spacious rooms, but not so many of them."[3] Designed by George F. Pelham, Jr., the 135-unit apartment building reflected the impact of reductive Modernism in the restrained simplicity of its detailing, but it also maintained the solidity and sense of mass characteristic of New York's traditional urbanism.

The trend of remodeling venerable older buildings by dividing apartments into smaller units began during the Depression; in 1936 Warren & Wetmore's 400 Park Avenue was the avenue's first apartment building to have its units broken up. Initially a response to the devastated economy, the practice continued in the 1940s as a means of circumventing the effects of rent-control legislation. In 1941 Louis S. Weeks, who made something of a specialty of this type of work, having renovated the Alwyn Court on Seventh Avenue in 1938,[4] redesigned Pickering & Walker's 823 Park Avenue (1910), transforming twelve duplex apartments, each with twelve rooms, into thirty-seven smaller suites.[5] The history of 820 Park Avenue was particularly interesting in this light. In 1921 Mrs. Millbank Anderson built a coolly elegant Adam-style townhouse, designed by John Mead Howells, on the site. In 1924 a new owner, the real estate developer and publisher A. J. Kobler, had the house's interiors refitted by Harry Allan Jacobs; the following year, Kobler demolished his house and replaced it with an apartment building, designed by Jacobs, in which he occupied an eighteen-room triplex unit that was subsequently leased to Walter P. Chrysler. In 1941, upon Chrysler's death, the triplex was divided up into six apartments.[6]

For the young architect Minoru Yamasaki, working on the staff of Harrison, Fouilhoux & Abramovitz but already pursuing independent projects, the idea of converting large apartments had a special appeal. In a project published in 1944, Yamasaki proposed not only to break up the apartments of a typical pre-1929 building but also to reclad the structure in a manner consonant with the principles of International Style Modernism.[7] A related trend was the conversion of townhouses and rowhouses into multi-unit apartment buildings, including the 1950 remodeling of a brownstone at 54 East Seventy-second Street by Morris Lapidus, who stripped away the brownstone facade and replaced it with a nearly unbroken wall of elaborately mullioned glass, which despite its modernity succeeded in maintaining the block's existing scale.[8]

In 1946 plans were announced for 715 Park Avenue, on the southeast corner of Seventieth Street, which was completed in 1950.[9] Designed by George F. Pelham, Jr., the building was characterized by a diminution of detail that was becoming typical of postwar apartment house design throughout the city. The nineteen-story red-brick-clad building incorporated projecting balconies and, on its top four floors, terraces recessed into setbacks. Sylvan Bien's 710 Park Avenue, though announced in 1947, after the plans for 715 Park were presented, was completed in 1948, making it the avenue's first postwar building.[10] The twenty-story red-brick building, located on the southwest corner of Seventieth Street, rose from a two-story limestone base trimmed with polished black granite. Recessed terraces were included on the third through the thirteenth floor; upper-story setbacks were also utilized as terraces. The apartments contained as many as seven rooms, and some were duplex units. The building replaced Trowbridge & Livingston's elegant palazzo of 1911 for investment banker George Blumenthal (see chapter 16), which had itself replaced the Union Theological Seminary after that institution moved to Morningside Heights.

In 1951 plans were announced for Horace Ginsbern's 750 Park Avenue, a seventy-two-unit, eighteen-story building to be erected at the southwest corner of Seventy-second Street.[11] The new building marked a radical departure from Park Avenue's traditional aesthetics; even the more reductive recent designs had maintained the mass-positive, punched-window approach of the avenue's older apartment buildings. Ginsbern's design, which may have been based in part on a 1928 proposal of William Lescaze for an apartment house on the same site, employed stressed horizontals in the form of boldly configured, glass-railed balconies.[12] Inside, many rooms contained "picture" windows beginning one foot above the floor and providing, in effect, a glazed wall.

In 1954 Sylvan Bien's 605 Park Avenue, on the southeast corner of Sixty-fifth Street, gained the dubious distinction of being the first white-glazed-brick apartment building on the avenue.[13] The twenty-one-story building, which replaced eight rowhouses—two facing the avenue and six facing the side street—had a one-story polished granite base, corner balconies and setbacks above the fourteenth floor. Three years later 1036 Park Avenue was completed on the southwest corner of Eighty-sixth Street.[14] In an attempt to enliven the facade of this banal nineteen-story red-brick apartment building, the architect, Gustave Wiser, used ceramic blue-green panels, some placed beneath corner windows, but to little effect.

Paul Resnick's 116 East Sixty-sixth Street (1955), occupying a midblock site between Park and Lexington avenues, was discreet if unremarkable.[15] The twelve-story buff-brick building, which replaced three nineteenth-century stables, had a principal facade with baylike projections and various setbacks, yet it managed to hold the street wall. Another tall midblock apartment building of 1955 was 135 East Seventy-first Street (H. I. Feldman).[16] Built on the site of nineteenth-century rowhouses, the seventeen-story building was clad in yellowish brick and featured upper-level setbacks and a rooftop garden. Philip Birnbaum's 45 East Seventy-second Street (1959), an eighteen-story apartment building clad in white glazed brick, replaced four neo-Grec-style rowhouses (Robert E. Lynd, 1882).[17]

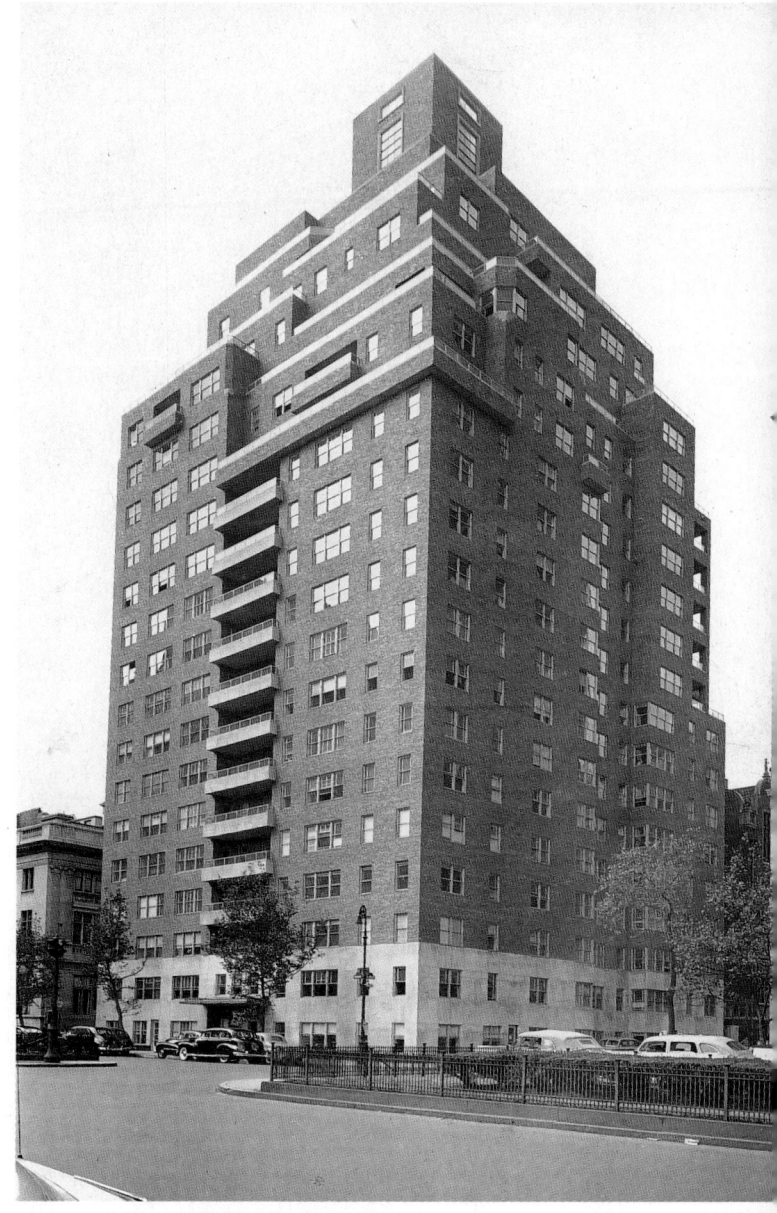

710 Park Avenue, southwest corner of East Seventieth Street. Sylvan Bien, 1948. View to the southwest. EG

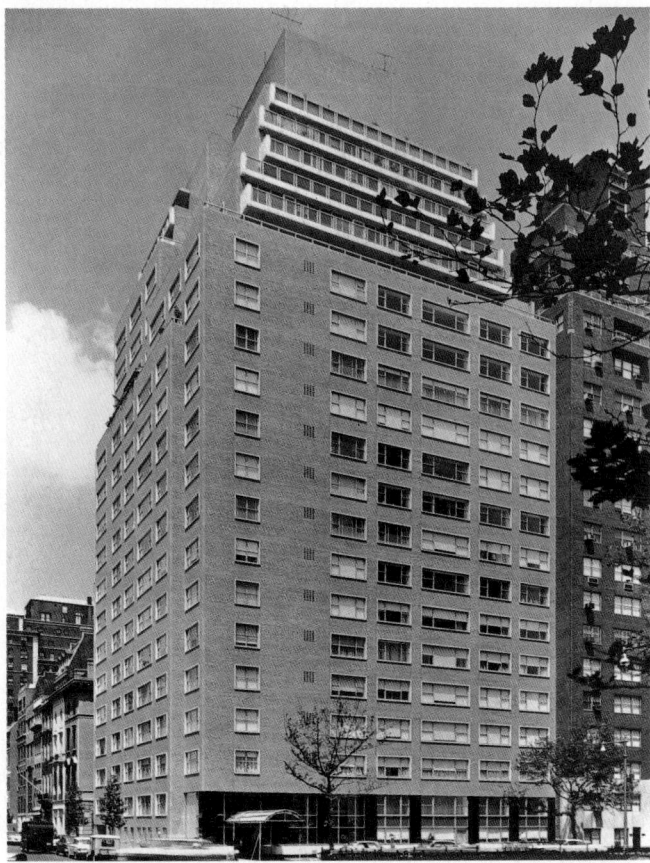

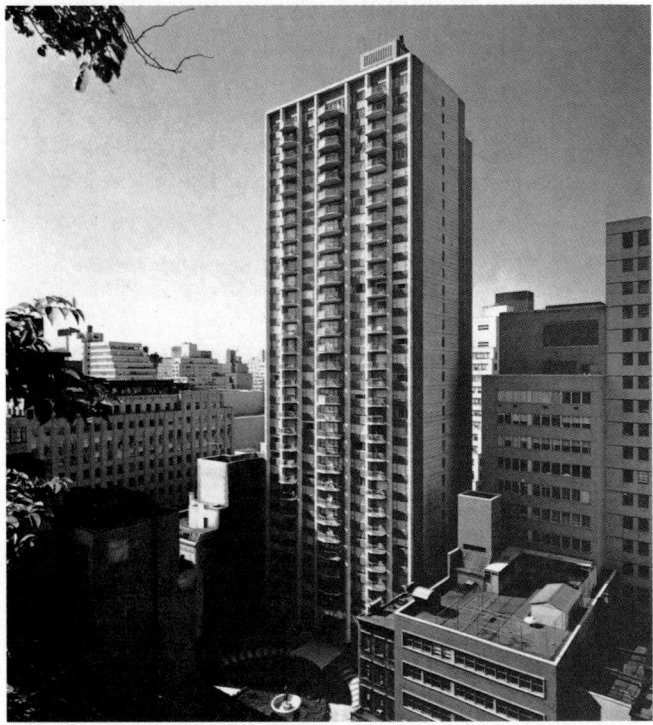

Top: 700 Park Avenue, northwest corner of East Sixty-ninth Street. Kahn & Jacobs and Paul Resnick and Harry F. Green, 1959. View to the northwest. Wurts. MCNY

Bottom: Plaza Tower, 118 East Sixtieth Street, between Park and Lexington avenues. Samuel Paul and Seymour Jarmul, 1965. View to the southeast. SPDP

In 1959 one of the few remaining luxurious townhouses on Park Avenue, the fifty-four-room, gray-marble, loosely English Renaissance–style house Allen & Collens had designed for Arthur Curtiss James in 1916, succumbed to the wrecker's ball.[18] The site, on the northwest corner of Sixty-ninth Street, was redeveloped as 700 Park Avenue (1959). The architects, Kahn & Jacobs and Paul Resnick and Harry F. Green, gave the new nineteen-story building a somewhat traditional character by using gray brick and including a two-story polished granite base.

Robert Bien's 1199 Park Avenue, on the northeast corner of Ninety-fourth Street, an eighteen-story, red-brick building, was completed in 1961.[19] The building's numerous cantilevered balconies, on both street frontages, made it look out of place on the avenue. While the massing of the twenty-one-story, buff-brick building at 1020 Park Avenue (Wechsler & Schimenti, 1962), on the northwest corner of Eighty-fifth Street, with setbacks starting at the sixteenth floor, was more in keeping with that of the traditional Park Avenue apartment house, its crude detailing prevented it from being a strong addition to the avenue.[20]

A twenty-story apartment building (John M. Kokkins, 1963) at 650 Park Avenue, on the southwest corner of Sixty-seventh Street, replaced the Sulgrave Hotel (Rouse & Goldstone, 1925) as well as a two-story restaurant extension added to the hotel in 1956.[21] The exterior of the new building, a bland composition with upper-story setbacks, seemed better suited to a less prestigious location, perhaps one farther east, but inside it maintained Park Avenue standards, featuring numerous duplex units. In 1965 an architecturally undistinguished six-story brick-clad apartment building designed by Schuman & Litchtenstein was completed at 115–117 East Seventy-first Street, between Park and Lexington avenues.[22] The building was noteworthy only for what it replaced, Mott B. Schmidt's imposing, Georgian-style double townhouse for A. A. Fowler (1921).[23]

Plaza Tower (Samuel Paul and Seymour Jarmul, 1965), a thirty-four-story apartment house at 118 East Sixtieth Street, occupying a midblock site between Park and Lexington avenues, introduced a staggering new scale to the area as it provided an early indication of the effects the city's new zoning regulations would have on residential design (see chapter 2).[24] Set back from the street sixty-five feet, the building was approached by a cobblestone-paved circular driveway that passed beneath a porte cochere. The height of the building, which rose sheer without a setback, was particularly jarring given its midblock location. Concrete piers that ran to the building's summit further emphasized its height. Wedge-shaped, glass-railed balconies punctuated the principal facade. Inside, a striking if not exactly refined lobby, designed by Raymond Loewy/William Snaith, mixed such Modernist features as a shallow, bowl-like fountain with reproduction period furniture. In contrast to the large size of traditional Park Avenue apartments, the units at Plaza Tower ranged from studios to five rooms.

The first residential building directly on the avenue to demonstrate the impact of the new zoning was Kahn & Jacobs's 733 Park Avenue (1971), on the southeast corner of Seventy-first Street, a thirty-story tower that replaced the quietly dignified, English Regency–style residence of Senator Elihu Root (Carrère & Hastings, 1903–5).[25] The Landmarks Preservation Commission had tried to save the thirty-room mansion, placed on the market by Mrs. Carll Tucker, who had owned and occupied it since 1915, but the commission was unable to find a buyer who was willing to preserve its exterior. Although the New York Heart Association had considered purchasing the house and using it as office headquarters, the organization determined that the projected cost of interior renovation was prohibitive.

Number 733 was the first building since the 1940 Hunter College building (Shreve, Lamb & Harmon in association with Harrison & Fouilhoux), on the east blockfront between Sixty-eighth and Sixth-ninth streets, to be set back from the avenue's rigorously maintained street wall.[26] Though 733 Park did not carry the polemical weight of Hunter, which had proclaimed the era's ascendant Modernism, it exerted a far more devastating impact on the avenue's hitherto coherent urbanism. Raised above a travertine-clad first floor that was recessed behind stilts clad in brown granite, the dark-brown-brick building was set back on a travertine-paved plaza. The plaza, extending not only along the building's Park Avenue frontage but along its north and south frontages as well, eroded all definition of the corner and visually detached the building from its immediate context. The tower seemed most brutal along its windowless eastern facade.

Regardless of its exterior, historian Andrew Alpern said that the interior of 733 Park embodied "a style of luxuriously exclusive urban living that has all but vanished from the city."[27] The principal Park Avenue entrance, marked by a bronze-toned aluminum canopy, led to a travertine-lined lobby. Despite the building's size, a single walnut-paneled passenger elevator sufficed, since the tower contained only twenty-eight apartments, with twenty-seven identical, full-floor units and a duplex penthouse. The apartments were distinguished primarily by their size: each 3,420-square-foot unit contained nine rooms, including a maid's room, four-and-a-half bathrooms and such auxiliary spaces as a generously proportioned foyer and a butler's pantry. Ceilings were 8'11" high, nearly a foot higher than those of typical postwar apartments, but similar to the ceilings in the handful of new buildings that aspired to the standards of prewar luxury housing. Separate principal and service entrances gave the apartments a sense of formality and privacy that was rare in postwar buildings; the four-inch-thick, plaster-covered masonry interior walls allowed for even greater privacy. The penthouse featured four exposures, three terraces and two working fireplaces. Because the building had been planned during the boom of the late 1960s but was not completed until the recession of the early 1970s, the cooperative apartments were sold, according to the builder, Stephen Muss, at substantially below cost.

Park 900 (Philip Birnbaum, 1973), a twenty-eight-story apartment building on the northwest corner of Seventy-ninth Street, followed the lead of 733 Park.[28] The negative impact of the building, a sheer slab set back from both streets on a landscaped plaza, was exacerbated by the fact that the plaza was recessed below the sloping grade of Park Avenue in a moatlike arrangement, which removed the hulking tower even more from the avenue's largely intact building wall. Park 900, which replaced the elaborate, Tudoresque John Sherman Hoyt residence (I. N. Phelps-Stokes, 1917), was clad in limestone and had dark-tinted windows.[29] The public rooms, including a restaurant reserved for tenants and their guests, were decorated by Jay Spectre, Inc. in a glitzy Modernist style. "The design statement adopted," said the editors of Interior Design, "presents a departure from the fake French furniture/crystal chandelier/antiqued mirror approach often seen in expensive metropolitan apartment buildings. Instead . . . the designers opted for a svelte built-in look suggesting interiors on a luxury ocean liner."[30] The apartments contained from three to six rooms and were quite ordinary, with low ceilings.

In 1974 the building received recognition for a nonarchitectural feature—a seven-foot-long abstract bronze sculpture by Henry Moore titled *Reclining Connected Forms* that temporarily graced the building's plaza, which sported the increasingly cliché cobblestone-paved circular drive. While Mayor Abraham Beame praised Moore's piece as a "priceless addition to the cultural life of the city,"[31] an editorial in the *New York Times* titled "Missing Element" expressed a different view:

> There is a curious mix of esthetic values at the corner of 79th Street and Park Avenue now that a Henry Moore sculpture has been installed, with conspicuous fanfare, in front of a big, new apartment house. It could be called throwing good art after a bad building. . . . There are a few notably handsome and well-handled examples of apartment-house design currently visible in New York, but the trend, particularly in the high-rent category, continues to be to offer corn for class. Since the Moore cost nobody anything—it is apparently "on loan"—it is a free art ride for the neighborhood and free publicity for the builder. One wishes he had put his good intentions where the building is. Plaza dressing does nothing more than disguise a standard speculator product with fancy trim. Architecture is still the missing element. It's a cultural con game.[32]

Paul Goldberger would later lambast the building and its plaza for creating "a sense of void at a crucial intersection."[33]

One year earlier, in 1973, Park Avenue had become permanent home to a piece of Modernist sculpture with aspirations to civic monumentality, Louise Nevelson's *Night Presence IV* (1972), a 22'6"-tall self-weathering Cor-ten steel construction installed on the mall on the north side of Ninety-second Street.[34] The brooding abstract work, based on a small wooden piece the sculptor had made in 1955, consisted of four undulating elements reminiscent of the forms of the French artist Jean (Hans) Arp, more complexly modeled elements based on wooden doorknobs, and an abstract depiction of a bird. Nevelson had donated the sculpture to the city on the occasion of her fiftieth year of working and living in New York, and it had originally been placed in Grand Army Plaza, at the southeast entrance to Central Park. When the Department of Parks, Recreation and Cultural Affairs designated the site an outdoor exhibition space for changing displays of contemporary sculpture, a new location for the Nevelson piece had to be found. A possible location at Lincoln Center was rejected because the Juilliard School already contained an example of the sculptor's work. On the Park Avenue site, which Nevelson had helped select, the sculpture stood near the crest of a hill and could be seen from some distance, but it was visually overwhelmed by the man-made canyon of Park Avenue and its impact was diminished by the near-constant swirl of traffic. Although Norval White and Elliot Willensky would characterize the work as no more than "a forlorn modern loner in . . . neo-Renaissance precincts,"[35] Margot Gayle and Michele Cohen felt the sculpture's forms had "a totemic quality."[36]

Though the great era of townhouse construction was a thing of the past, a number of townhouses were built or extensively reconstructed on the Upper East Side after World War II. In addition to Felix Augenfeld and Jan Pokorny's Joseph Buttinger residence just off Fifth Avenue (see "Fifth Avenue," above), three townhouses, each occupying a midblock site just off Park Avenue, were particularly interesting. In 1958 Edward Durell Stone, then at the peak of his fame as a result of his designs for the United States Embassy in New Delhi and the United States Pavilion at the World's Fair in Brussels, renovated a brownstone at 130 East Sixty-fourth Street (James E. Ware, 1878), between

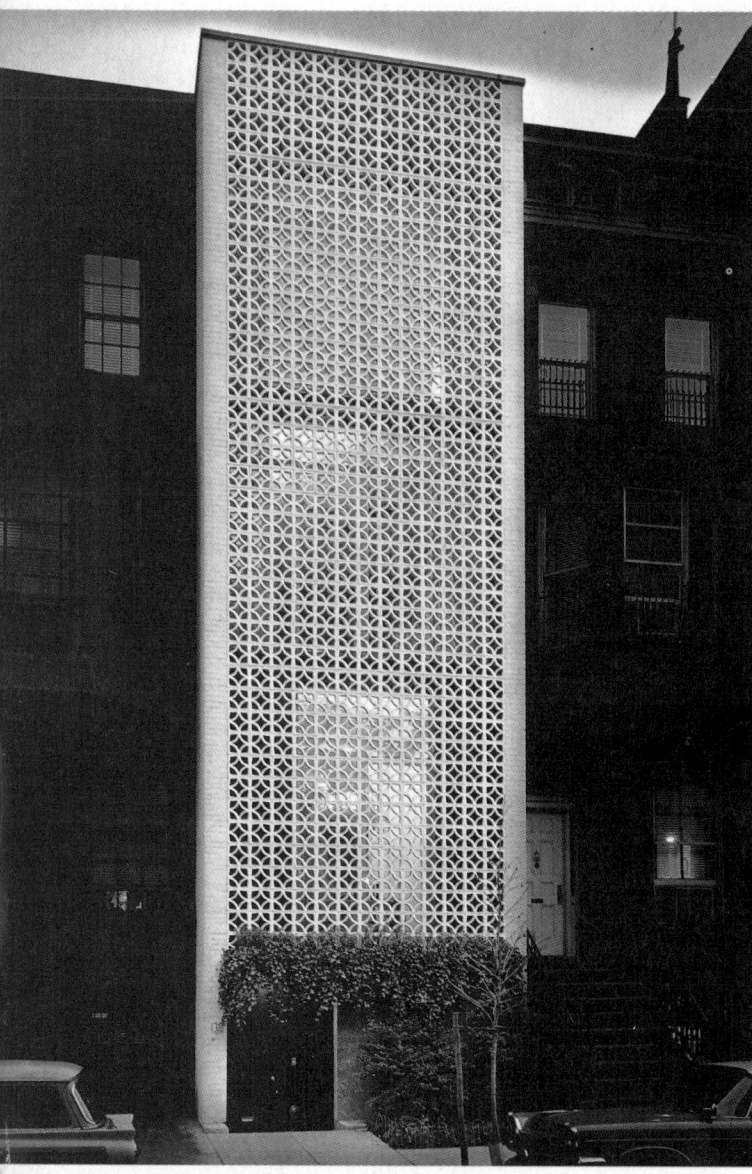

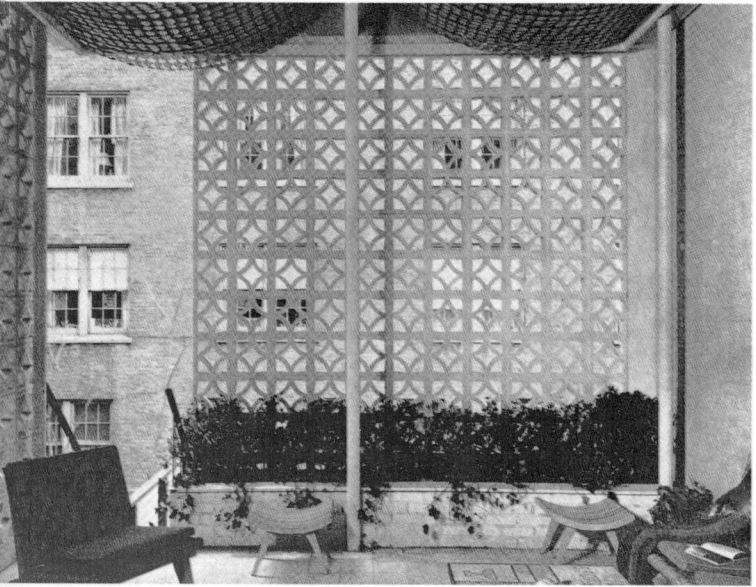

Park and Lexington avenues, for his own use.[37] Stone's sweeping reorganization and opulent decoration of the existing house, which he described as "undistinguished and drab," transformed most of the interior spaces; only the original Eastlake-style paneled parlor was retained. But it was the handling of the facade that was the most significant aspect of the design: Stone stripped away the brownstone and replaced it with a sheer wall of glass; one foot in front of the wall he constructed what had become one of his design signatures, a freestanding concrete grille that acted as a facade-screen for the rooms behind. The grille provided complete privacy during the daytime. The new facade, Stone said, "lights the interior and enables us to see out without being observed by the passers-by. In my opinion, the grille is the perfect solution to the problem of privacy in the lower floors of apartments and town houses."[38] For the south-facing, rear elevation, Stone again employed grilles to screen the windows and to create privacy for a sun porch.

Stone's facade imposed a wholly new and essentially scaleless feature to the block. But at the time of its completion, as the editors of *Vogue* noted, the design made the former brownstone "the most talked-about house in New York," one that captured the public's imagination.[39] According to *Time*, it even attracted the attention of Frank Lloyd Wright, who, after seeing the house, rang Stone's doorbell and said to him, "You know, Ed, we'll have to trade details." He added, "And they say that the old crank never has a kind word to say about anything. But I'm raving."[40] Writing in 1979, Paul Goldberger would comment that "the building is small enough and the grille light enough so that this affectation does no real harm to the block, but it hardly upgrades it, either. It all comes off rather like a parody of Ed Stone done by a clever and malevolent student."[41]

The area's most substantial new townhouse belonged to Paul Mellon, the financier, philanthropist and art collector.[42] Designed by H. Page Cross and completed in 1966, it was built on a double lot at 125 East Seventieth Street, between Park and Lexington avenues, that had previously been occupied by two rowhouses built in the 1860s. In keeping with the block's special covenant, which required an additional ten-foot setback, Cross's French-inspired yellow stucco townhouse with ivory-colored shutters was separated from the street by a high-walled garden. While the principal mass rose four stories to an occupied, dark-tiled mansard, the east wing was set back at the third floor to create a terrace with treillaged walls.

Paul Rudolph's design for the Alexander Hirsch townhouse (1970), at 101 East Sixty-third Street, between Park and Lexington avenues, was far more aesthetically provocative.[43] Rudolph's first building in New York and one of his most successful designs, the townhouse was built on the frame of a 25-foot-wide, 100-foot-deep carriage house that had belonged to Edward J. Berwind. The 100-year-old carriage house facade was replaced with large panes of brown-tinted glass set within a black-painted steel frame whose proportions expressed the principal spaces immediately behind the facade: garage, entry hall, master bedroom and guest bedroom. The planes of glass stepped forward from the recessed garage at street level to the guest bedroom at the top, providing a strong cornicelike termination to the facade.

Rudolph initially proposed working within the existing building's mass and creating an interior arrangement based on interesting curvilinear forms. But he eventually changed his mind, reorganizing most of the interior as a set of levels, like rec-

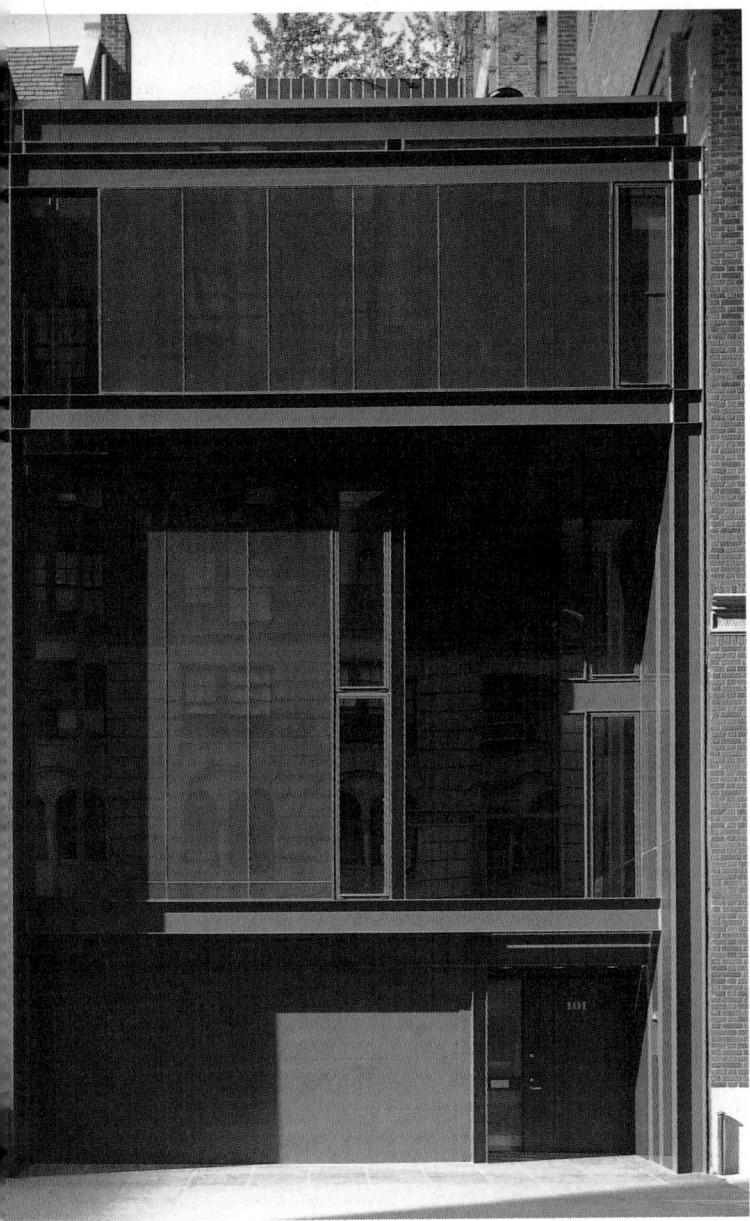

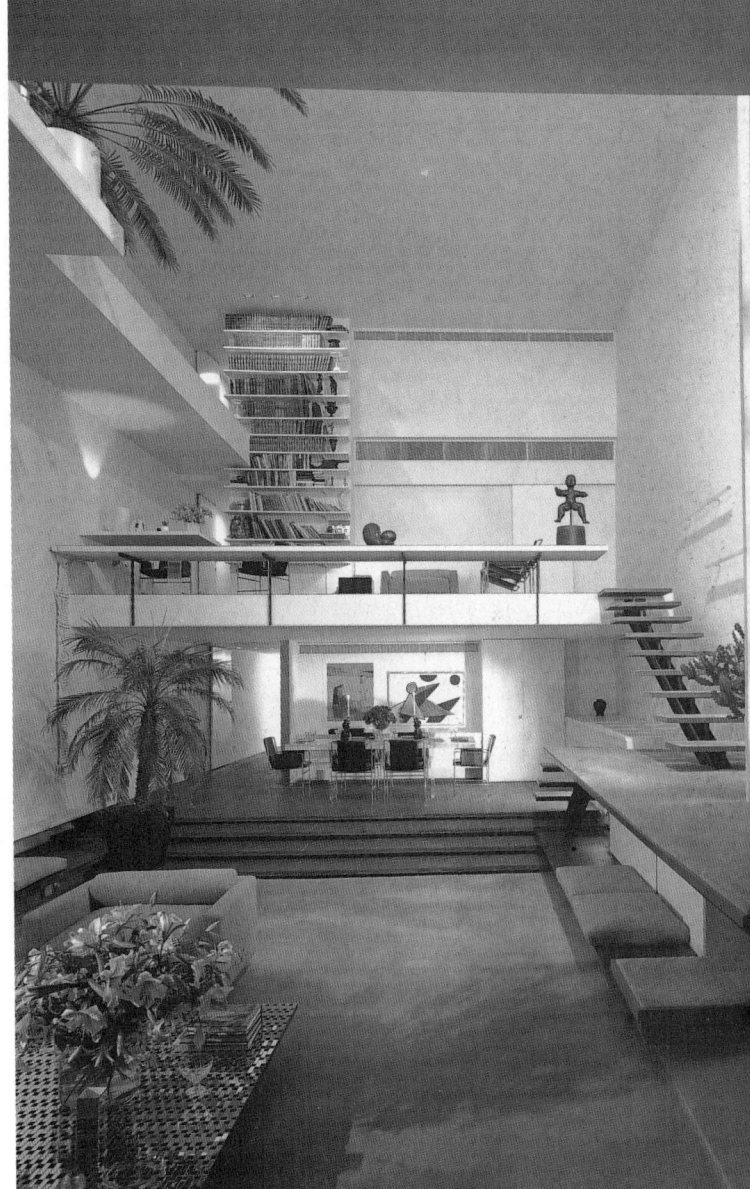

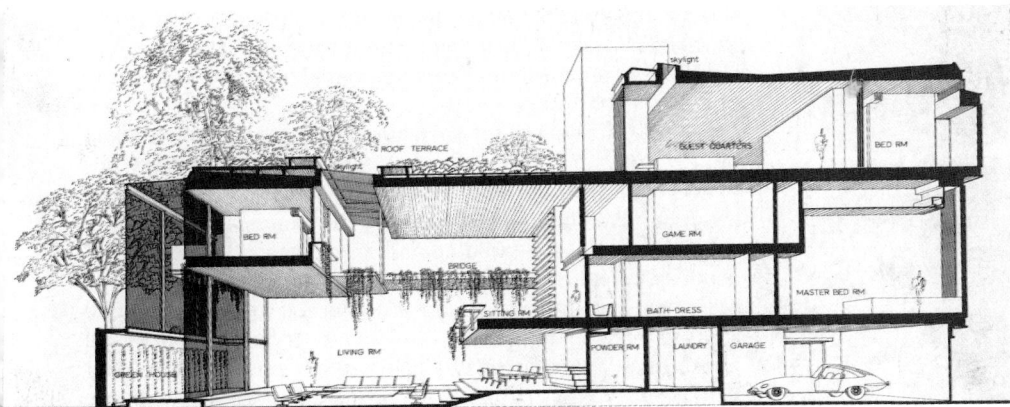

Top far left: Edward Durell Stone residence, 130 East Sixty-fourth Street, between Park and Lexington avenues. Edward Durell Stone, 1958. View to the south. Guerrero. PEGU

Bottom far left: Edward Durell Stone residence. Interior. IN. CU

Top left: Alexander Hirsch residence, 101 East Sixty-third Street, between Park and Lexington avenues. Paul Rudolph, 1970. View to the north. Stoller. ©ESTO

Bottom left: Alexander Hirsch residence. Longitudinal section. PR

Above: Alexander Hirsch residence. Interior. Stoller. ©ESTO

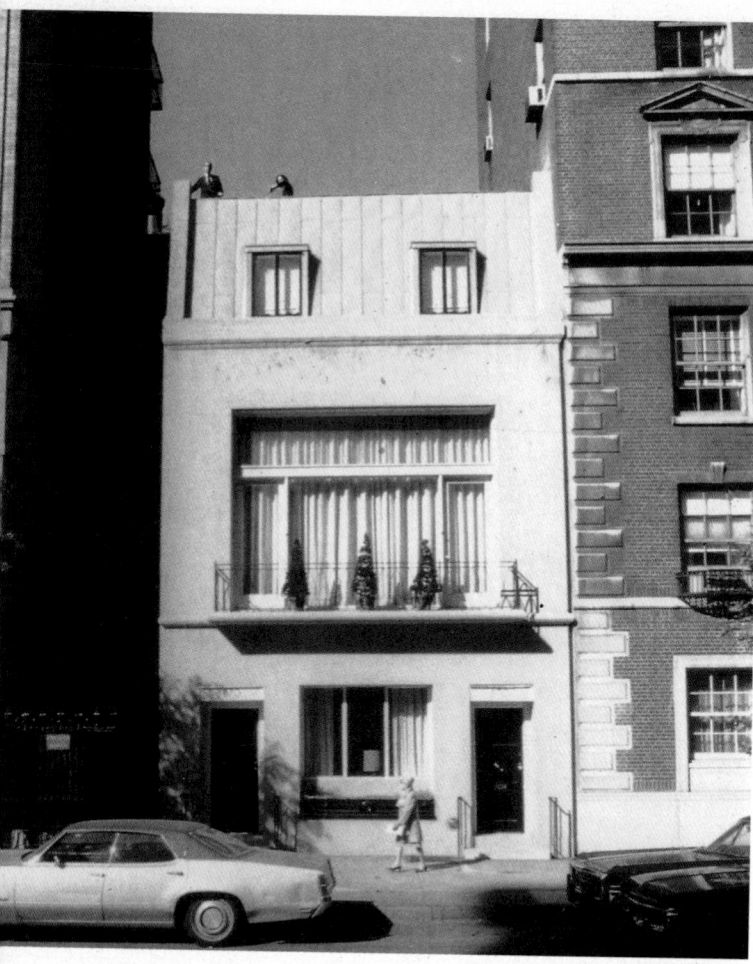

Above: 870 Park Avenue, between East Seventy-seventh and East Seventy-eighth streets. Paul Lester Weiner, 1963. View to the west. RAMSA

Top right: Leonard Stern residence, 870 Park Avenue, between East Seventy-seventh and East Seventy-eighth streets. Robert Stern and John S. Hagmann, 1976. View to the west. Stoecklein. RAMSA

Bottom right: Leonard Stern residence. Living room. Stoecklein. RAMSA

tilinear trays or bridges, crisscrossing a toplit twenty-seven-foot-high atriumlike living room. The scheme essentially built on the earlier Modernist townhouse designs of William Hamby, George Nelson and Felix Augenfeld, but Rudolph internalized the courtyard space and organized the cross section more subtly, so that, instead of requring ramps and narrow passages, the rooms themselves seemed to operate simultaneously as places for circulation and repose.[44] At the back of the living room was a glass-walled greenhouse, mirrored on three sides to visually extend the space and further the illusion of lush greenery. Most surfaces were either carpeted or painted white; eschewing traditional vocabulary and even the fine materials favored by many Modernists, Rudolph let the complex interplay of high and low spaces and the elegantly articulated stairs provide the principal interior decoration.

In 1976 Robert Stern and John S. Hagmann completed the Leonard Stern townhouse at 870 Park Avenue, in the middle of the west blockfront between Seventy-seventh and Seventy-eighth streets.[45] The building had begun as a carriage house and was converted into an apartment above a doctor's office in 1940. It was extensively renovated again in 1963 by the architect Paul Lester Weiner, who, working with his associate Richard Bender and the interior designer Ala Damaz, added a copper-clad mansard.[46] The rooms of the renovated building, some flowing freely into each other, were decorated in an eclectic manner combining modern and traditional elements.

Stern and Hagmann left intact the house's double entry—with one door leading to the doctor's office—and radically redesigned the rest of the facade. A large window, divided into quadrants and articulated with a narrow balcony, dominated the facade's middle portion; pilasterlike elements appeared at the edges. A bay window above extended across the entire facade, visually disconnecting a cornice that incorporated a rectangular cutout and seemed to be dropped from above. The critic Stanley Abercrombie said that the facade, "while unmistakenly new, attempts references to the mildly classical design of its neighbors by its three-part vertical division (recalling base, shaft and capital or the stacked floors of a Renaissance palazzo)."[47] Writing in *Progressive Architecture*, Sharon Lee Ryder interpreted the design differently: "One interesting and deliberate aspect of the facade . . . is a lack of the traditional articulation of various floor levels. There is no indication of the immense volume which it encloses. It all seems far too modest and almost apologetic, the poor cousin to the 20-story apartment buildings on either side."[48] To Paul Goldberger, the facade's allusions to traditional townhouse designs "give this house a strength that allows it to hold its own against the large apartment houses on either side of it."[49]

Inside, the major living and entertaining spaces were linked by a *promenade architecturale* extending from the front entrance hall up to the master bedroom suite at the top. Other means of circulation were provided by a circular stairway toward the rear of the building and an elevator. Because of the depth of the house, a four-story-high atrium was introduced to bring light from monitor windows above and to give an internal focus to the plan and section. Goldberger commented that "the house does as much as Philip Johnson's classic Rockefeller Guest House [see chapter 5] to kill the New York townhouse stigma—it feels neither narrow nor dark."[50]

While Park Avenue and the adjoining blocks between Sixtieth and Ninety-sixth streets remained essentially residential, several new institutional buildings were built during the postwar period. In 1957 Lenox Hill Hospital commenced a multistage renovation and expansion program. The 190-bed Wollman Pavilion, designed by Rogers & Butler and completed in 1959, consisted of a twelve-story slab placed perpendicular to the east side of Park Avenue between Seventy-sixth and Seventy-seventh streets and entered from Seventy-seventh Street.[51] The new building, which replaced the hospital's oldest structure, a four-story brick building (Carl Pfeiffer, 1869), boldly contradicted the avenue's masonry walls with a curtain wall of glass and porcelain-enamel panels finished in tones of pink. Though an advertisement for the Armco Steel Company, which manufactured the panels, asserted that the building had "a fresh look indicative of . . . modernization" and that "its color harmonizes with surrounding brick structures," the addition projected an awkwardly saccharine tone that made it look decidedly undignified and out of place in its setting.[52]

In 1961 and 1964 the hospital demolished its two remaining original buildings, erected in 1880 and 1888, and replaced them with the Charles R. Lachman Community Health Center and William Black Hall.[53] Designed by Rogers & Butler, the banal red-brick buildings extended the hospital complex east along the entire south blockfront of Seventy-seventh Street between Park and Lexington avenues. In 1975 the hospital somewhat redeemed its architectural reputation with the Percy and Harold D. Uris Pavilion, designed by the same firm responsible for the Wollman building, now Rogers, Butler, Burgun & Bradbury.[54] The deeply modeled red-brick building, on the northeast corner of Park Avenue and Seventy-sixth Street, replaced the hospital's six-story, Italian Renaissance–style Ottendorfer Dispensary (Schickel & Ditmars, 1907). Like the earlier Wollman Pavilion, the new twelve-story, 180-bed building, set back ten feet from Seventy-sixth Street, was a narrow slab placed perpendicular to Park Avenue. The arrangement created a deep space along Park Avenue, exposing to view the west facade of the hospital's Classically articulated ten-story principal building (Isaac Ditmars, 1914). The avenue's street wall was maintained, in part, by a one-story-high brick wall. The rather brutal facade of the Uris Pavilion incorporated deeply punched corner windows and a fourth-floor, midblock terrace. The "handsome carved-brick monolith," as Norval White and Elliot Willensky described the building, overpowered the thinness of the adjacent structure's pink curtain walls; it also proved a somewhat aggressive neighbor to the more delicately scaled and articulated apartment houses along the avenue.[55]

In 1976 the Rogers firm replaced the mansarded French Second Empire–style Presbyterian Home (Joseph Esterbrook, 1869) with the rather stolid James Lenox House, which provided housing for the elderly.[56] Set back from the street at 49 East Seventy-third Street, between Madison and Park avenues, the twelve-story building was made up of an exposed-concrete grid filled in with red brick, glass and metal spandrels. White and Willensky said that "social values prevailed" in the creation of this "spare and inelegant" building, "without architecture in concert."[57]

The most architecturally significant institutional building erected in the area after the war was Philip Johnson's Asia House (1959), at 112 East Sixty-fourth Street, between Park and Lexington avenues, occupying the site of two rowhouses (F. S. Barus, 1874–76) and just a few doors west of Edward Stone's house (see above).[58] Johnson's seven-story building, which

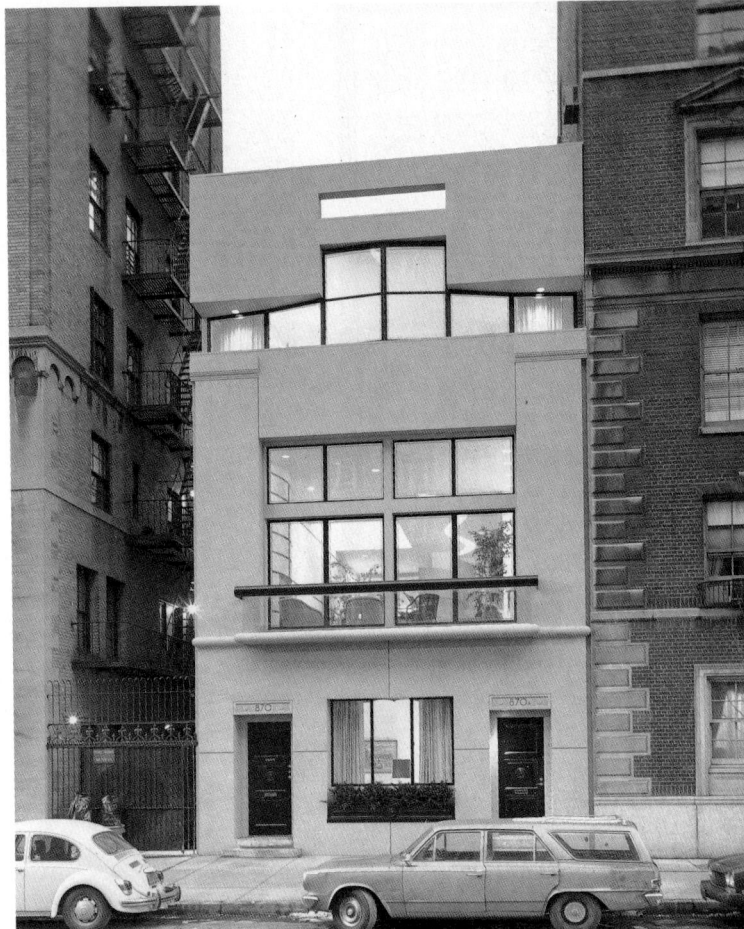

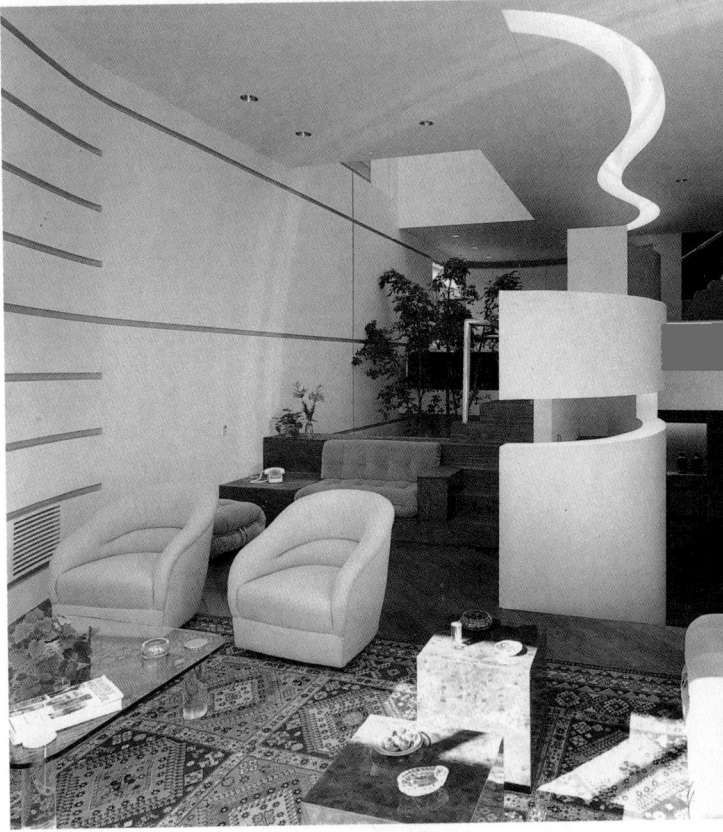

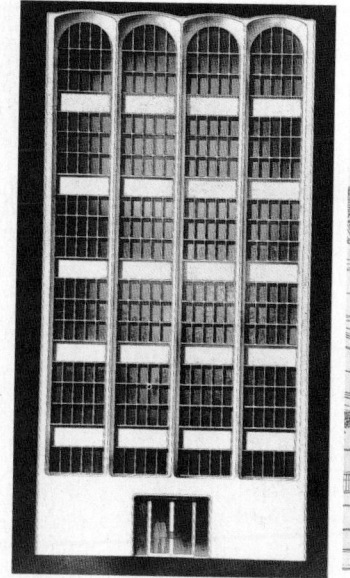

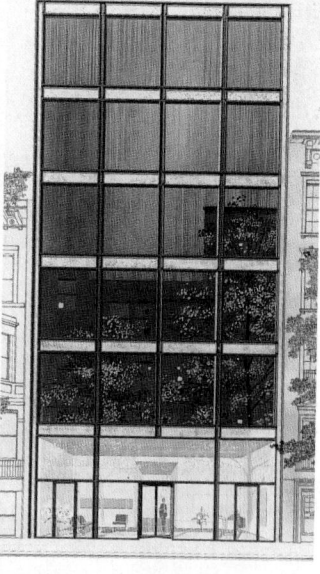

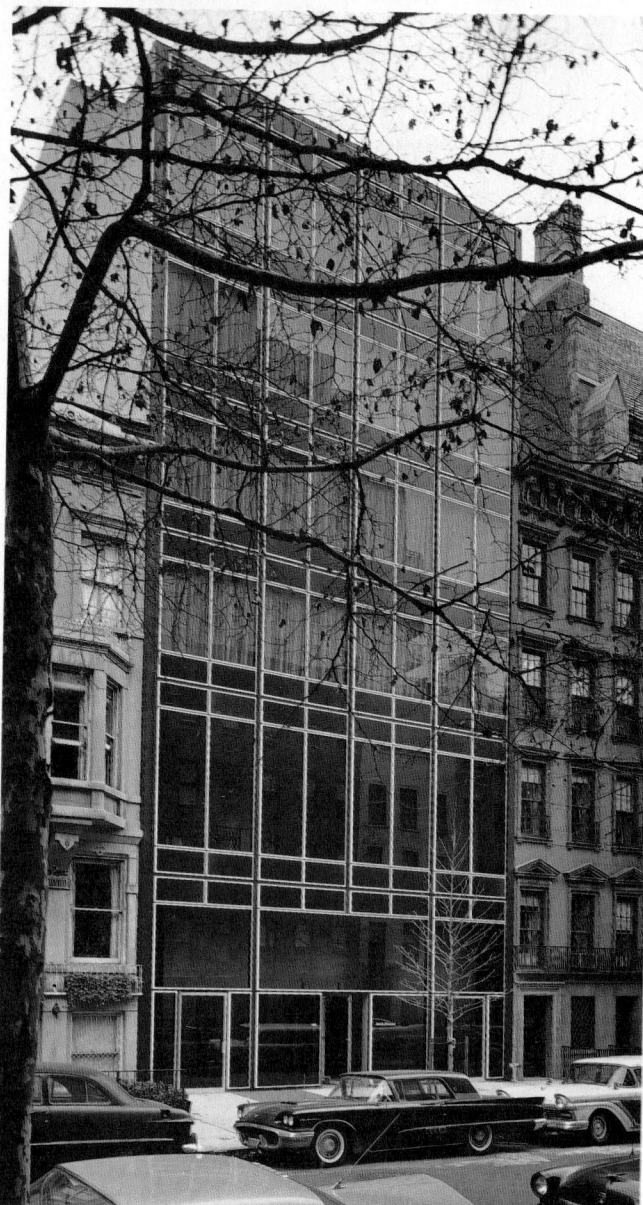

housed the galleries and offices of the Japan Society and the Asia Society, was clad in an impeccably detailed Miesian curtain wall of dark-tinted glass set into a delicate, white-painted steel frame. The design managed to work well with the adjacent brownstones and rowhouses, as well as with the side facade of the Gothic Central Presbyterian Church, originally the Park Avenue Baptist Church (Henry C. Pelton and Allen & Collins, 1922), which exerted a formidable presence two lots to the west.[59]

Johnson's design was the last of three he had proposed. One rejected scheme called for a sculptural facade treatment in which a windowless one-story base was to be surmounted by four vertical rows of windows culminating in arches. The second called for a bronze-and-glass grid based on Johnson and Mies van der Rohe's Seagram Building (see chapter 5). Critic John M. Jacobus, Jr., writing in 1962, noted that "something of the chameleon-like character of recent architectural design in general can be appreciated by studying the . . . range of possibilities for the Asia House facade, and by the realization that each of the three alternatives was of an inherently individual and unique character." The third and realized design was "aristocratic," he said, "with a tendency toward faint decorative mannerism."[60] The art critic Stuart Preston, writing in the *New York Times*, gave the building a mixed review, characterizing it as "a handsome, rather antiseptic specimen of modern architecture."[61] Vincent Scully said that the building "was an exquisite facade, indeed only a facade, but in this it fulfilled very well its primary urban responsibility to the street."[62] Writing in 1972, the critic Charles Noble asserted that the building represented "Johnson's design at its most slavishly Miesian."[63] Seven years later Paul Goldberger would say that "Mies himself would have found too decorative" the building's "sleek grid pattern." Nonetheless, Goldberger argued, the grid "helps make this a comfortably scaled object for this side street," a building that was "most interesting for the suggestion it offers that glass skins can work at . . . this small scale."[64]

In 1962 the Buckley School, a venerable private school for boys, extensively renovated the former Arthur C. Train residence (George B. Post & Sons, 1908), at 113 East Seventy-third Street, between Park and Lexington avenues, into an addition to the Classically articulated brick building it occupied on Seventy-fourth Street (John T. Simpson, 1917).[65] Designed by Brown, Lawford & Forbes, the renovation included a Modernist facade that was a modestly scaled essay in horizontal fenestration. Though the five-story building maintained the street wall, the first floor, a red-brick wall surmounted by a thin band of windows, was elevated slightly above the street and recessed behind a planter. The Hewitt School, a private school for girls, chose a very different architectural expression for its new building on the south side of Seventy-sixth Street between Madison and Park avenues.[66] The five-story building, which replaced two brownstones (1882 and 1884), was designed in 1965 by Evans & Delehanty in a carefully detailed Federalist vocabulary, complete with a principal entrance surmounted by a fanlight, to convey an image of stability and tradition. The addition was also meant to stylistically echo the school's existing townhouse (Cross & Cross, 1924–25), at 45 East Seventy-fifth Street, to which it was connected.

In 1967 another educational facility, Hunter College's School of Social Work, was completed on a midblock site on Seventy-ninth Street between Park and Lexington avenues that had contained the garage and sunken garden of the adjacent

Vincent Astor residence (Mott B. Schmidt, 1926) at 130 East Eightieth Street.[67] Designed by Wank Adams Slavin Associates, the bleakly diagrammatic ten-story building consisted of a gray terra-cotta base, above which extended a white iron-spot brick wall punctuated by narrow, deeply punched vertical windows.

A number of religious institutions were also housed in new buildings on or near Park Avenue. The red-brick-and-limestone Eighth Church of Christ, Scientist (Charles Faulkner, 1951), at 103 East Seventy-seventh Street, between Park and Lexington avenues, presented a windowless street facade that gently bowed at the principal entrance below a steeple formed of two stacked volumes topped by a copper-clad flèche.[68] A flagstone-paved garden east of the church could be glimpsed from the street through a decorative perforated-metal gate. Faulkner's design, which the *New York Times* described as a "modern colonial edifice," seemed perhaps more informed by the work of Eliel Saarinen.[69]

The two-story Chapel of the Reformed Faith (Adams & Woodbridge, 1952), occupying a midblock site on the west side of Park Avenue between Ninety-first and Ninety-second streets, continued the vocabulary of the adjacent Brick Presbyterian Church (York & Sawyer, 1938), a skillful brick-and-limestone essay inspired by the eighteenth-century London churches of John James and James Gibbs.[70] Three years earlier, in 1949, the congregation had completed a parish house at 62 East Ninety-second Street, a four-story building designed by Adams & Woodbridge that eschewed an historicist vocabulary.[71] The parish house's principal facade, an austere, Modernist design clad in limestone, featured polished red-granite walls flanking the slightly recessed main entrance.

The Manhattan Church of Christ (Eggers & Higgins, 1967), occupying a midblock site at 48 East Eightieth Street, between Madison and Park avenues, adopted a Modernist expression that seemed to parody the sculptural forms of Le Corbusier.[72] On the asymmetrically composed, precast-concrete principal facade, a massive curve-cornered pier was contrasted with the slightly recessed main entrance and, above, a large expanse of thick stained glass that represented an abstract crucifix. Above the glass panel was a bulky wedge-shaped form punctuated by a thin horizontal strip window. The building was planned as part of a larger complex, but a second building, intended for the adjacent corner site on Madison Avenue, was never realized.

Temple Israel (Schuman & Lichtenstein, 1967), located on a midblock site on Seventy-fifth Street between Park and Lexington avenues, was an overpowering, 100-foot-wide, seven-story building.[73] A cylindrical structure that rose through the building housed a lower, 459-seat sanctuary and an upper, 500-seat sanctuary, as well as two stories of classrooms. The lower sanctuary was expressed on the principal facade as a sweeping semicircular projection punctuated by thin vertical strips of stained-glass windows; the rainbow theme of the windows, designed by Efraim Weitzman, symbolized God's covenant with Noah. The projection was flanked by deeply recessed entrances, and the resulting irregularly shaped open spaces served as a forecourt. The three stories surmounting this cavernous space presented a windowless facade to Seventy-fifth Street and rigorously held the building line, which was further emphasized by a black- and gold-painted fence incorporating decorative panels that echoed the stained-glass windows behind.

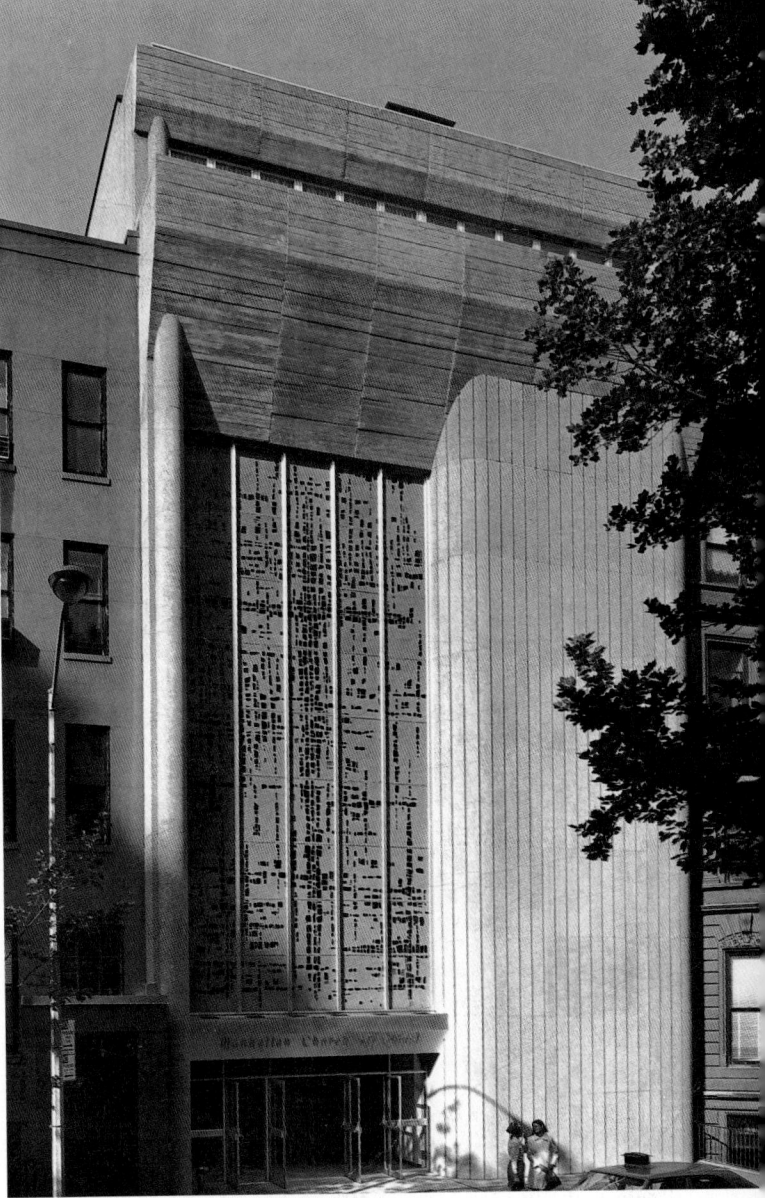

Top far left: First proposal for Asia House, 112 East Sixty-fourth Street, between Park and Lexington avenues. Philip Johnson, 1958. East Sixty-fourth Street elevation. PJA

Top left: Second proposal for Asia House, 112 East Sixty-fourth Street, between Park and Lexington avenues. Philip Johnson, 1958. East Sixty-fourth Street elevation. PJA

Bottom left: Asia House, 112 East Sixty-fourth Street, between Park and Lexington avenues. Philip Johnson, 1959. View to the southwest. Molitor. JWM

Above: Manhattan Church of Christ, 48 East Eightieth Street, between Madison and Park avenues. Eggers & Higgins, 1967. View to the south. EG

The demolition of the Third Avenue El in 1956 had a profound effect on that avenue, including the portion that extended through the Upper East Side. Within fifteen years the rather rag-tag collection of tenements that had lined the avenue from Sixtieth to Eighty-sixth Street for fifty years or more had been replaced with high-rise, so-called luxury apartments. South of Seventy-ninth Street the rebuilding process was particularly swift and virtually complete; above Eighty-sixth Street change came very slowly.

Even before the El was demolished, the New York Life Insurance Company began the reconstruction of Third Avenue when it acquired the two blocks bounded by Second and Third avenues, Sixty-fourth and Sixty-sixth streets.[1] The southern block, which the city had previously condemned, was leased to the insurance company in 1948 for fifty years to create a partially underground parking garage topped by a public park (see chapter 1). The proposed park would form a front lawn to a nineteen-story tower housing 600 families that New York Life was planning to build on the northern block. According to the editors of Architectural Forum, the 1,400-car garage solved "three pressing municipal problems at one whack. . . . 1) slum clearance housing; 2) a public parking garage (only 300 stalls will be reserved for apartment tenants); 3) widening of three cross-town streets. . . . The project is a good example of how public aid in land acquisition can stimulate large-scale urban redevelopment and coordinate it with other city needs."[2]

In 1950 the northern block became home to Manhattan House, which replaced a Third Avenue Transit Corporation carbarn the insurance company had purchased four years earlier for $1.6 million; the elaborate mansard-roofed French Second Empire building of 1896 had been designed by Henry J. Hardenbergh.[3] As conceived by Skidmore, Owings & Merrill and Mayer & Whittlesey, Manhattan House was the most literal manifestation in New York of Le Corbusier's postwar conception of vertical living, which the master himself was not to realize until 1952 in his Unité d'Habitation at Marseilles.[4] As the editors of Architectural Record put it, the architects "boldly" turned "their backs on the usual practice of building along the street lines with open courts in the interior."[5]

By April 1949, when construction began, the scope of the project had been modified, eliminating the southern block with its vast garage. After exploring a scheme calling for three slab-like buildings (two paralleling the avenues and a central slab running east-west), the architects adopted a nineteen-story palisadelike slab that contained 581 apartment units ranging from two to seven rooms. The rents were high, and the emphasis was not on family living; of the original tenant families, only seventy-eight had children. The slab rose from a landscaped podium set atop a 175-car garage; a rooftop solarium was also included. As part of the project negotiations, a forty-foot-wide strip of land on Sixty-sixth Street was given to the city to permit a substantial widening of the street right-of-way and the creation of a secondary road for local traffic. The apartments were entered on the north, and the garage and service entrances were tucked into the parking podium on the Sixty-fifth Street side, taking advantage of the southward slope of the site. The podium also included shops along Second and Third avenues; at the site's southwest corner, a two-level restaurant, originally a branch of the Longchamps chain, incorporated a private outdoor dining terrace.

To counteract its mammoth scale, Manhattan House was divided into separate compartments, with elevators and fire stairs housed in the dark crossings created by the modified H-plan. While many apartments had a southern exposure, allowing tenants to enjoy the sunshine and, from the upper floors, superb views of the midtown skyline, even those on the north side had at least one second exposure to the east or west. Gordon Bunshaft, Skidmore, Owings & Merrill's principal designer on the project, took a high apartment on the south side for himself (see chapter 6).

Manhattan House became known as the city's first white-brick apartment building (although its self-washing glazed brick cladding was in fact light gray), a type that would proliferate in the 1960s. Together with elegantly thin window frames of white-painted metal and carefully detailed balconies, the glazed brick rendered Manhattan House a genteel manifesto for architecture's brave new world, a reassuring statement that Modernist minimalism had more than cost benefits. In addition, the slab offered a distinct contrast with its mundane surroundings—the still-functioning Third Avenue El and its immediate neighbors, mostly old- and new-law tenements. To protect the building's flanks, New York Life acquired the row of tenements on the north side of Sixty-sixth Street, renovated their interiors and painted the facades a tasteful dark gray trimmed in white.[6]

The principal innovations of Manhattan House were the bold scale resulting from its single-slab configuration; the departure from traditional urban space making in the refusal to hold to the street front except at the base; and the blurring of distinctions between exterior and interior space, as well as front and back yards, by the use of large amounts of glazing at the lobby level. In discussing this last point, the editors of Architectural Record, presumably quoting from a New York Life press release, said that "the entire development 'carries out on a large scale, in a big city, an indoor-outdoor synthesis hitherto found mostly in modern country homes.'"[7]

Lewis Mumford offered qualified praise for Manhattan House, declaring that "this White Whale of an apartment house . . . has been conceived and carried through with a sort of crystalline logic, and the good elements in the plan and the design are immediately visible." Mumford also observed, however, that the design "is afflicted with the schizophrenia that undermines almost every current attempt to deal in a building with the problems of life in New York—a conflict between bad old habits and new needs and purposes." While he applauded the inclusion of underground parking as well as the street widening and entrance drives as significant mitigations to traffic congestion, he complained that not enough parking was provided to satisfy the requirements of the tenants. But Mumford maintained that the problem was not that there were too few parking spaces but too many dwelling units. "There can be no relief from traffic problems," he explained, "until a lid has been placed upon density of occupation."[8]

Although Mumford described Manhattan House as "a paragon of economy, elegance and utility," he criticized it for being too large and out of scale with its surroundings. The views afforded by Manhattan House, Mumford pointed out, were possible "only because it has been built in a district whose buildings are mostly four or five stories high," a situation whose passing he saw as inevitable: "Manhattan House cannot count permanently on being an isolated and dominating structure, for eventually other tall apartment houses will begin to crowd around it, and as a pattern for rebuilding the city it sets as bad an example as the New York City Housing Authority's most overcrowded projects." Mumford also questioned the usefulness of the balconies and called attention to the failure to provide air conditioning,

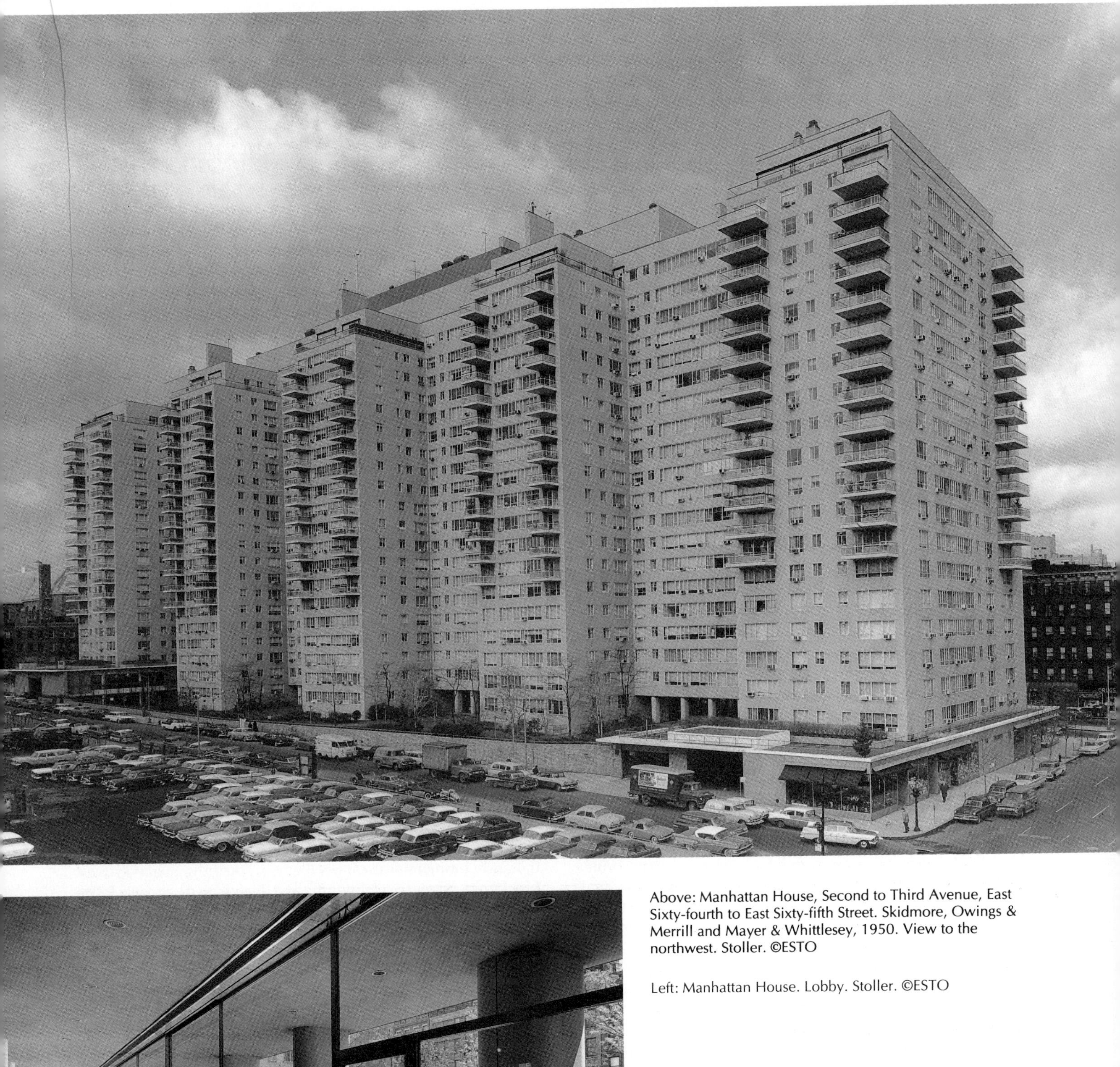

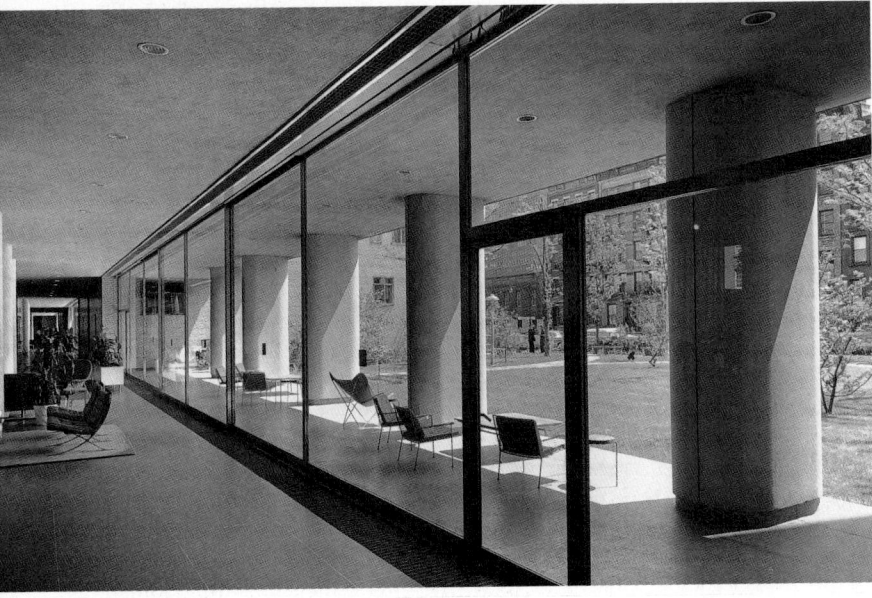

Above: Manhattan House, Second to Third Avenue, East
Sixty-fourth to East Sixty-fifth Street. Skidmore, Owings &
Merrill and Mayer & Whittlesey, 1950. View to the
northwest. Stoller. ©ESTO

Left: Manhattan House. Lobby. Stoller. ©ESTO

which led to the building's facades being almost immediately defaced by the installation of innumerable window units. "Since the aesthetics of this building depend on purity and refinement," Mumford said, "they are literally blots on the composition."[9]

New York Life's plans for Manhattan House also included a two-story commercial structure, built to preserve the views from the apartment building.[10] Designed by Fellheimer & Wagner and completed in 1952, the low-rise building contained a branch of the Corn Exchange Bank on the northeast corner of Sixty-fifth Street and Second Avenue, and the Beekman Theater, at 1254 Second Avenue. The theater, which featured art films and served coffee in the lobby, lent a note of sophistication to the area. The *New York Times* film critic Bosley Crowther applauded the decision to include the theater: "Despite all the dire prognostications of the ruinous competition of TV, not to mention the mischievous rumors that the public is getting tired of films, the big New York Life Insurance Company had the courage to go right ahead and back this new theater construction, to the tune of a million or so." The theater's Modernist design, Crowther said, was a vast improvement over the previous era's vast and ornate picture palaces and an overdue response to public preference. "For a long time it has been apparent," he asserted, "that one of the several things that have caused a decline in movie-going, especially by people of better taste, has been an increasing aversion to the older downtown and neighborhood 'barns'. . . . Clean and respectable though they may be, they are architecturally passé and dull." In contrast, Crowther said, the Beekman was "tastefully planned and decorated in sleek but not ostentatious style, with plenty of room for lounging, having coffee and stretching the legs, as well as for freedom of passage in and out of the widely spaced rows." All in all, he said, the theater had an "air of refinement, elegance and chic that bathes the discriminating patron with a relaxing warmth."[11] The lobby was redesigned in 1962 by Rolf Myller to include a free-form, undulating bank of seating that accommodated up to seventy-five people.[12]

Few developments on the Upper East Side followed the precedent set by Manhattan House, largely because block-size sites were virtually unavailable in the area. Among the exceptions was Emery Roth & Sons' Imperial House, completed in 1960 on a site between Lexington and Third avenues, Sixty-eighth and Sixty-ninth streets, that had been occupied principally by the former New York Foundling Hospital building.[13] Though surely lacking the aesthetic quality of Manhattan House, the building did include a stylish lobby, designed by William Raiser of Raymond Loewy/William Snaith and featuring a marble terrazzo floor and extensively mirrored walls. The Roths' 215 East Sixty-eighth Street (1962), the largest luxury apartment house undertaken up to that time in the city, occupied a two-acre site between Sixty-eighth and Sixty-ninth streets, extending west from Second Avenue to a point just short of Third.[14] This thirty-three-story tower flanked by two nineteen-story wings was an even less successful exemplar of the superblock approach.

In 1959 Thomas W. Ennis reported in the *New York Times* that "so many apartment houses [are] planned for Third Avenue from Fifty-seventh to Eighty-sixth Street that the virtual rebuilding of the area appears certain in the next two or three years."[15] Ennis counted seventeen buildings in the immediate future that would join Manhattan House and three others built since 1955. Still, though the buildings commanded high rents, Third Avenue was not yet considered a desirable street; as Ennis observed, only one of the new buildings would have a Third Avenue address. By 1961, with developers rushing to get as much built un-

der the old zoning laws as possible, the Third Avenue boom was at its peak, with a new apartment house under construction on every intersection from Sixty-fifth to Seventy-fifth Street.[16]

The first apartment house to be constructed on Third Avenue under the new zoning was Tower East (1962), a thirty-four-story cooperative that rose without a setback from a one-story base filling the west blockfront site on the avenue between Seventy-first and Seventy-second streets.[17] Designed by Emery Roth & Sons, the 132-unit building, which replaced the palatial Loew's Seventy-second Street movie theater (Thomas Lamb and John Eberson, 1932), was decisively Modernist, with concrete columns exposed along the two longer sides facing east and west and, on the north and south, an exposed-concrete sheer wall punched with identical square windows.[18] Behind the exposed frame, the Roths set alternating bands of glare-resistant gray-tinted window glass and aluminum spandrels coated with a dark, bronze-colored duranodic finish. Apartments were comparatively spacious, with five to seven rooms and only four units to a floor. The base accommodated shops and a 500-seat movie theater. Next to the building's entrance on Seventy-second Street, the boldly detailed pedimented facade of the Nineteenth Ward Bank (William Emerson, 1906) provided a strong contrast to the dull neutrality of Tower East's commercial base.

The consequences of the new zoning could also be seen at Phoenix House (1969), a thirty-one-story slab on the west blockfront between Sixty-fourth and Sixty-fifth streets.[19] Phoenix House was also designed by the Roths, but it was more refined than Tower East. The slab was broken into three elements: a black-walled core, exposed to view, separating identical tower-like masses, which were extensively glazed behind an exposed grid of structural concrete. M. Paul Friedberg designed a small garden behind the lobby, which opened off Sixty-fifth Street and overlooked the townhouse gardens to the west.

Bayard House (Horace Ginsbern & Associates, 1965), at 200 East Seventy-third Street, was a 117-unit luxury tower built by the New York Bank for Savings and named after its first president, William Bayard.[20] The tower was a bit more elegant than most buildings of its type, and its appearance was enhanced by eighteen lampposts, complete with handblown lanterns, commissioned by the bank to ring the eastern end of the block. Park Lane Plaza (H. I. Feldman, 1967) was a thirty-four-story residential and commercial complex that occupied the avenue's west blockfront between Eighty-fifth and Eighty-sixth streets.[21] The dullness of the basic mass, oriented with its long facades facing east and west, was relieved by rows of finlike trapezoidal balconies as well as curved balconies wrapping around the building's corners. Along its Eighty-sixth Street frontage the complex incorporated 5,500 square feet of commercial space organized around a 25-by-100-foot plaza sunken several feet below street level. Klonsky Associates, landscape architects, collaborated with Feldman on the design of the plaza, which, the *New York Times* contended, resembled what "might be found in any suburban shopping center."[22]

The Jacob Ruppert Brewery, a local landmark and a lingering reflection of the area's gritty, industrial past and its ethnic traditions, closed its doors on December 31, 1965.[23] It had been founded in 1867 by a German immigrant and taken over in 1917 by the founder's eldest son, Jacob Ruppert, Jr.—a Tammany Hall–supported congressman, a noted bon vivant and later owner of the New York Yankees. The brewery eventually occupied thirty-five red-brick buildings that dominated the blocks between Ninetieth and Ninety-fourth streets, Third and Second avenues, but by the 1960s labor problems and obsolete facilities doomed the operation. Four months after the plant's closing, the city designated the twenty-acre four-block parcel a renewal site and commissioned Conklin & Rossant to devise a master plan.[24] Their proposal called for two apartment towers, one forty-eight and one sixty stories tall, and four eight-story buildings organized around courtyards; the complex would contain a total of 2,500 high- and moderate-income units. In addition, the plan included a 4,000-student high school, a 1.5-acre public park, a movie theater, a restaurant and stores. A subsequent plan called for a luxury apartment building, which at seventy-eight stories would have been the world's tallest. Despite initial municipal approval of the mixed-income scheme, strong community opposition to the inclusion of high-end units succeeded in blocking the plan.

The linchpin of a new plan for the site, which was realized in 1975, was three immense towers designed by Davis, Brody & Associates.[25] The buildings were financed with the support of the city, the state's Mitchell-Lama program and the federal government. The stylistically consistent towers occupied three corners of a superblock site between Ninetieth and Ninety-second streets, Third and Second avenues, with Ninety-first Street treated as a cobblestone-paved pedestrian mall; a multilevel park and playground filled the site's southeast corner. Like Waterside, the firm's architecturally distinguished housing complex on the East River (see chapter 5), the three complexly massed brick-clad towers incorporated vertical strips of windows and dark-metal spandrels, numerous chamfered corners and cantilevered elements. Ruppert Towers, occupying the east blockfront of Third Avenue between Ninetieth and Ninety-first streets, contained 549 units and ranged in height from twenty-four to thirty-four stories; Yorkville Towers, located directly across Ninety-first Street, contained 710 units and ranged in height from thirty-two to forty-two stories. Both buildings were set back from Third Avenue on large triangular plazas, flanked by ground-level commercial spaces, that formed a monumental gateway to the pedestrian mall that bisected the complex. Occupying the site's northeast corner, at Second Avenue and Ninety-first Street, was the forty-story Knickerbocker Plaza, which contained 578 units—70 percent reserved for senior citizens, and 20 percent set aside for low-income tenants.

The journalist Alan S. Oser, writing in the *New York Times*, described the development as a "new colossus,"[26] and the critic Andrea O. Dean argued that the complex "has major problems, being too massive and densely populated for its site."[27] Norval White and Elliot Willensky said that although the density of the complex was "immense and overwhelming," the architects had handled the "unfortunate program in a sophisticated manner." They added, however, that "talent can't save us from behemoths."[28] August Heckscher, the former Park Commissioner and a longtime resident of the area, described the development as "sober in aspect and uncomfortably dense," but also characterized it as an asset: "Today, a harmoniously integrated population gives new life to the surrounding streets."[29]

Among the few architecturally significant institutional buildings constructed on Third Avenue and the adjoining blocks during the postwar era was the Buckley School's Hubball Building (Brown, Lawford & Forbes, 1974), at 210 East Seventy-third Street and 209 East Seventy-fourth Street, between Third and Second avenues.[30] A suave Brutalist essay in brick and concrete, the building, which replaced a Consolidated Edison substation, housed the school's indoor athletic facilities.

Despite the amount of large-scale construction on Third Avenue during its post-El boom, the street remained surprisingly vital, lined with shops and restaurants catering to neighborhood

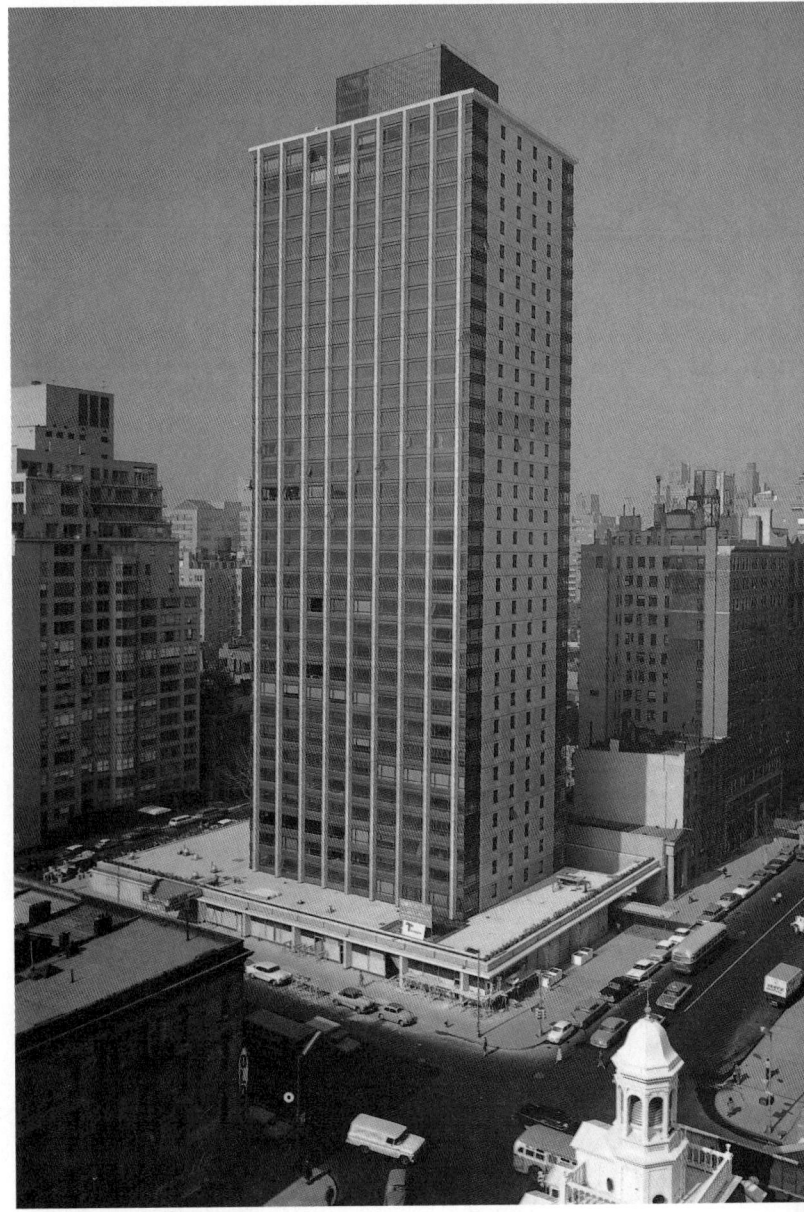

Tower East, west side of Third Avenue, East Seventy-first to East Seventy-second Street. Emery Roth & Sons, 1962. View to the southwest. Reens. LR

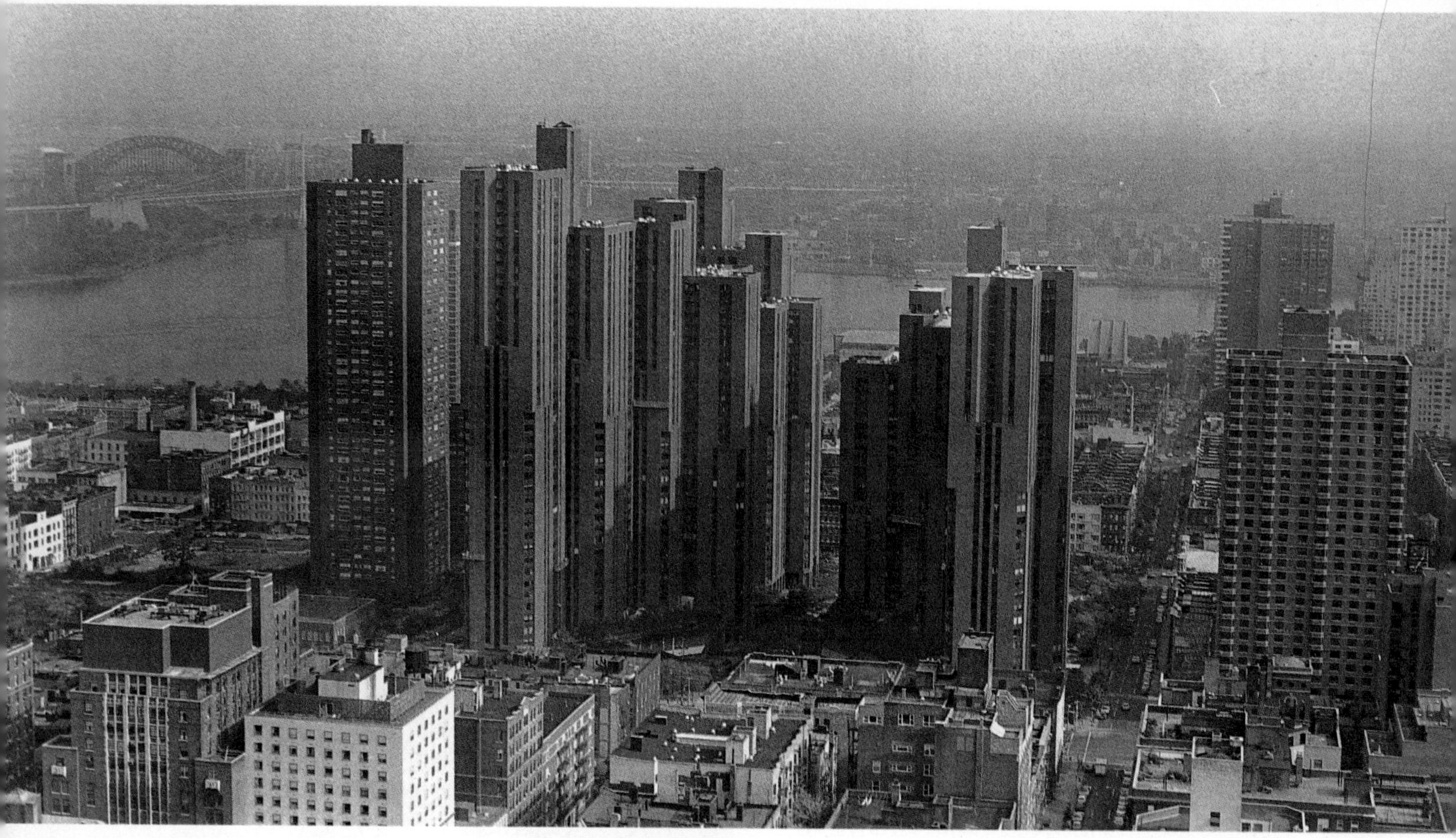

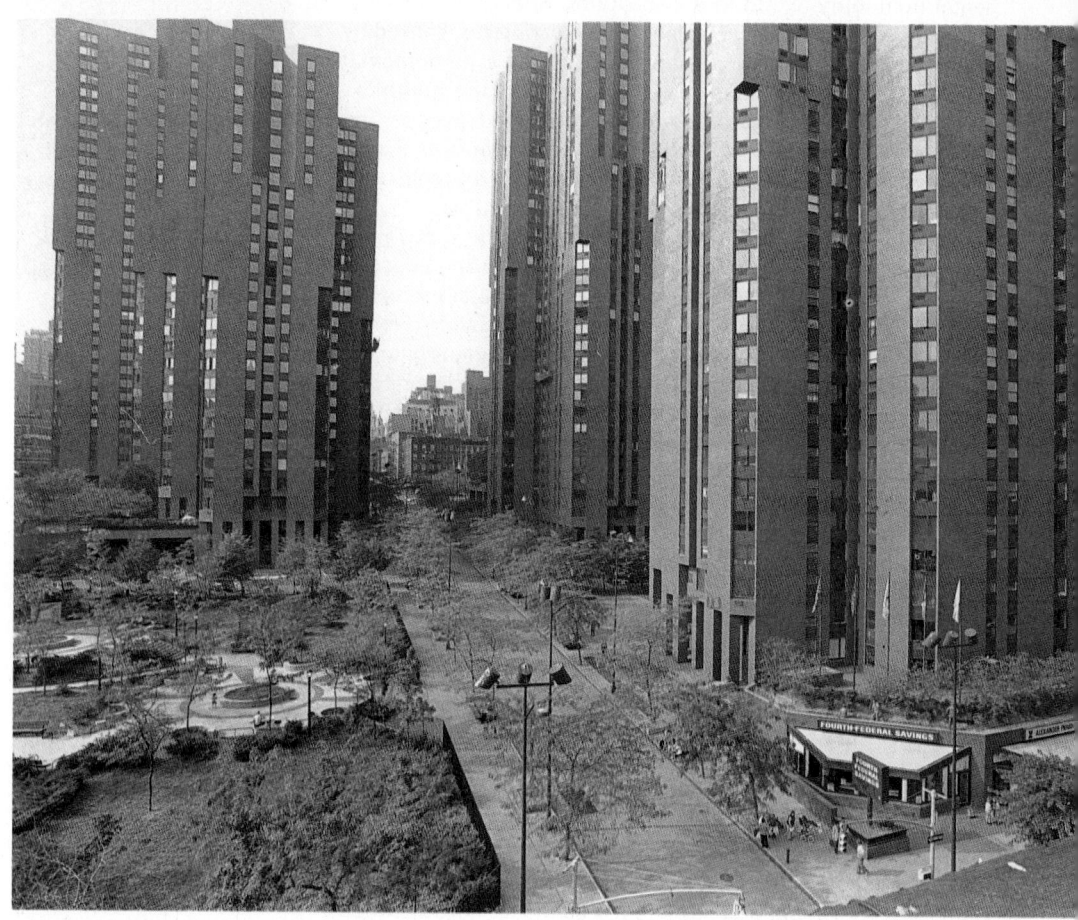

Above: View to the east showing former site of the Jacob Ruppert Brewery, between Second and Third avenues, East Ninety-first to East Ninety-fourth Street. The three towers in the center are, from left to right: Yorkville Towers, Knickerbocker Plaza and Ruppert Towers (all Davis, Brody & Associates, 1975). Zamdmer. DBA

Right: View to the west along East Ninety-first Street showing, from left to right: Ruppert Towers, Yorkville Towers and Knickerbocker Plaza. Zamdmer. DBA

residents as well as attracting visitors in small numbers. According to a survey done in 1967 by the realtors Charles H. Greenthal & Co., there were 395 retail establishments along the avenue between Sixtieth and Eighty-sixth streets.[31] Although almost all of them were from the postwar era, the study claimed that the flavor of the old Third Avenue had been retained. While most of the rundown bars and junk shops had disappeared, long-established antiques shops continued to thrive, along with stylish new bars and restaurants—the single largest category of business along the avenue—and thrift shops run by various charitable organizations. Whatever the avenue's continuity with its past, however, the scene had clearly and unalterably changed. The Uptown Racquet Club (Copelin, Lee & Chen, 1976), a ribbed-concrete block set atop existing street-level shops at 151 East Eighty-sixth Street, between Lexington and Third avenues, may have been a "stylish form," as White and Willensky observed, but its primary importance was as a telling reflection of the area's decidedly upscale new demographics.[32]

FAR EAST SIDE

Although the East River waterfront was almost exclusively devoted to commerce and manufacture through the end of World War I, in the 1920s small enclaves of fashion were established at Sutton Square and soon after at Beekman Place and around Gracie Mansion.[1] In the late 1930s the construction of the East River Drive marked the end of pier-side commerce on the Upper East Side. During the Depression the practice of rehabilitating and, in some cases, gentrifying the area's predominant building type—tenements of four, five and six stories—began to transform the long, relatively characterless blocks between Third and York avenues, Sixtieth and Ninety-sixth streets.[2]

Often these renovations involved two or three tenements, which were combined to provide more flexibility in reconfiguring interior layouts and a greater number of units under one roof so as to offset capital improvements such as elevators and reduce operating costs such as salaries for superintendents and janitors. A few of these conversions achieved a measure of artistic excellence, as in the designer Harold M. Schwartz's 1956 rehabilitation of two walk-up tenements into a single elevator building at 321–325 East Sixty-ninth Street, between Second and First avenues.[3] The converted building, called the Atrium, confronted the street with continuous metal balconies that partially concealed exposed fire escapes and a wall of double-hung sash stripped of the surrounds and cornicelike lintels that had contributed to the character of the original buildings. Inside, the apartments, according to Interiors, had "unusual charm and joie de vivre."[4] The conversion was also highly successful from a financial standpoint. As Thomas W. Ennis, reporting in the New York Times, explained in 1956, Schwartz bought the tenements for $40,000, "a price now regarded as absurdly low. . . . Today the property is worth almost a half-million dollars."[5]

Edward Larrabee Barnes's conversion of a four-story tenement at 347 East Seventy-second Street into the United Lodge of Theosophists (1954) was a little more unusual.[6] Barnes approached the old building with respect, retaining the sash and the flat trim that helped band the windows into horizontal rows but painting the brick light gray. Inside, he created a spare, simply detailed worship room that focused on a shallow, elliptical niche into which he set a small stage for speakers.

With the demolition of the Third Avenue El in 1956 and the simultaneous destruction of the psychological barrier between the Gold Coast and the areas further east, new apartment houses began to be developed, generally along the avenues but occasionally in the midblocks along the side streets. Mayer, Whittlesey & Glass's 333 East Sixty-ninth Street (1963), designed under the direction of William Conklin, a partner in the firm, was one such midblock building.[7] The twelve-story, 118-unit structure occupied a large lot, 200 feet wide and 100 feet deep, but was uncharacteristically sensitive to the comparatively small scale of its setting, including Harold M. Schwartz's Atrium next door. Conklin exposed the concrete structural frame, infilling it with buff brick set behind small gardens. The ground floor contained independent entrances for a series of duplex apartments, an echo of Emery Roth's strategy in his midblock Dorset Hotel a generation before.[8] Most of the balconies were recessed behind the building's street wall, creating deep shadows and functioning as patios surrounded by the rooms of the individual apartments they served. On the top two floors, the balconies cantilevered forward to suggest an articulated cornice. The roof incorporated a glassed-in solarium and a wind-protected sunning deck for tenants, and the mechanical penthouse was given a stylish shape.

During the middle and late 1950s Second Avenue was the site of intense real estate activity and construction.[9] Nearly all of the new buildings, many of which were clad in glazed white brick, were indescribably banal. A rare exception was 245 East Eighty-seventh Street, occupying the entire west blockfront of Second Avenue between Eighty-seventh and Eighty-eighth streets. Completed in 1966 after an initial wave of development on the avenue and designed by Paul & Jarmul, the nineteen-story brick-clad building, which replaced a row of tenements, presented a rather austere but carefully composed facade to the avenue, with balconies partially enclosed by low brick walls. Norval White and Elliot Willensky praised the design: "The same economics, the same materials, the same zoning and building laws as its speculative apartment-house peers, here in the hands of someone who cares: the bold massing of the balconies reads with great richness on the avenue."[10]

David Todd & Associates' 230 East Eighty-eighth Street (1968), between Third and Second avenues, was also a cut above most of the area's high-rise apartment buildings.[11] Instead of the traditional double-loaded corridor, Todd used exterior galleries, regrettably set behind metal grilles, to provide access to the cross-ventilated, floor-through apartments. Also completed in 1968 was the Jewish Board of Guardians Group Residence for Young Adults, at 217 East Eighty-seventh Street, between Third and Second avenues.[12] A strident essay in Brutalist aesthetics rendered in rough-finished concrete, it was designed by Richard Coates of Horace Ginsbern & Associates. Set back from the street, the principal facade of the three-story building incorporated cantilevered elements, including a visually dominant top-floor projection punctuated by a horizontal strip of windows that evoked both Le Corbusier's La Tourette (1960) and Kallman & McKinnell's Boston City Hall (1963–68).[13] A ground-level concrete wall maintained the street's building wall. Despite this gesture, the building's massing and, more important, its aggressive stylistic expression were jarringly at odds with the surrounding context of old tenements and new high-rise apartment buildings. While Paul Goldberger was sympathetic to the building's aesthetics, he admitted that Brutalism was "an odd image for a residence, for it is openly and proudly harsh as a style."[14]

Built for the New York City Housing Authority, Frederick G. Frost, Jr. & Associates' Stanley Isaacs Houses (1966), on the east side of First Avenue between Ninety-third and Ninety-fifth

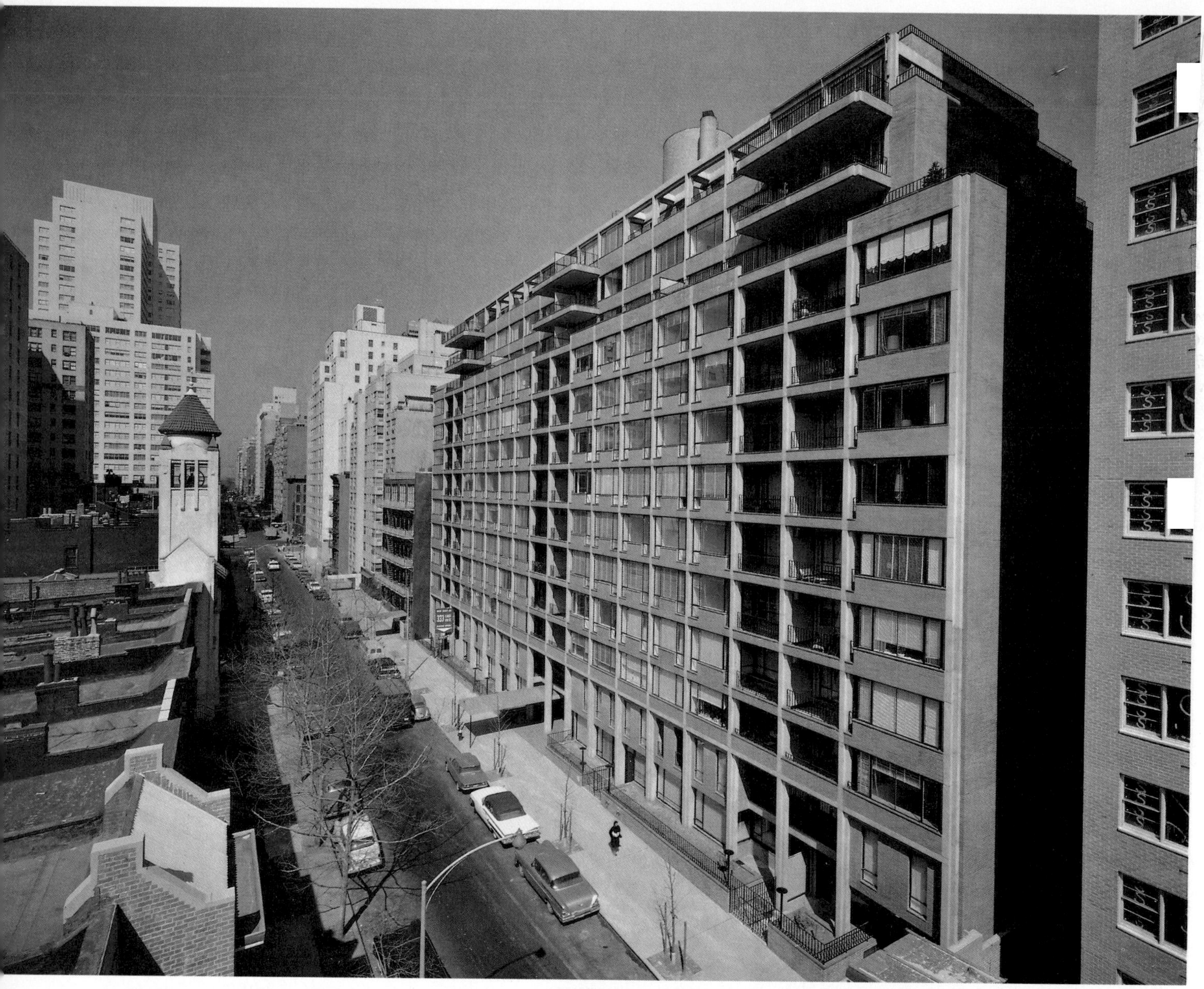

Above: 333 East Sixty-ninth Street, between First and Second avenues. Mayer, Whittlesey & Glass, 1963. View to the northwest. Stoller. ©ESTO

Right: Jewish Board of Guardians Group Residence, 217 East Eighty-seventh Street, between Second and Third avenues. Horace Ginsbern & Associates, 1968. View to the northeast. ©Gil Amiaga. HASU

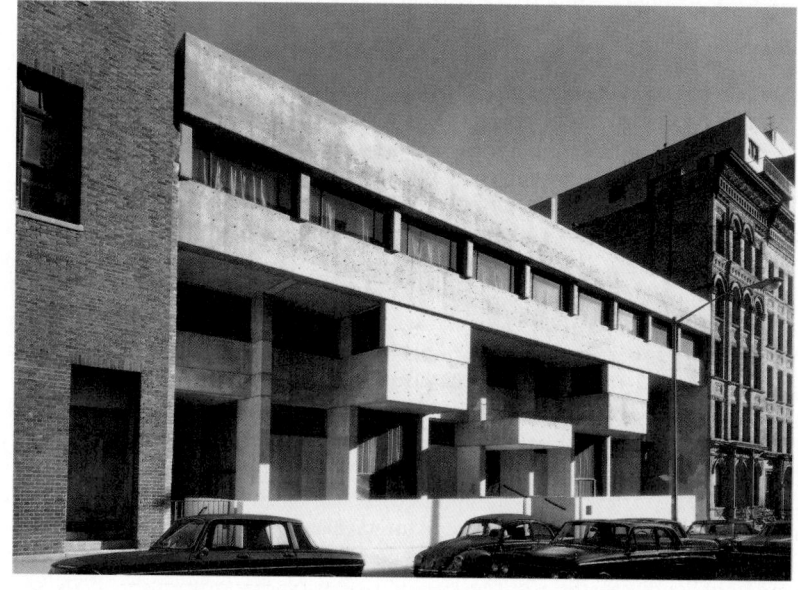

streets, consisted of three twenty-four-story red-brick slabs.[15] Access to the apartments was provided by exterior balconies, and almost every unit had a view to the East River. As White and Willensky put it, "The poor have the best views, and breezes, in New York."[16] The project also included a community center with a barrel-vaulted roof. But even such amenities could not compensate for the numbing banality of the Housing Authority's design formula, which made every project more or less like any other despite the use of different architects, the introduction of occasional special features, the presence of views or even, as in this case, a location at the edge of a desirable neighborhood.

Of the area's principal avenues, York Avenue, the northward extension of Sutton Place, held the most architectural interest. Originally a street of working-class tenements and manufactories, York Avenue began to be rejuvenated around 1900, with the initial construction of the Rockefeller Institute for Medical Research between Sixty-fourth and Sixty-eighth streets and the model tenements built by the City and Suburban Homes Company between Seventy-eighth and Seventy-ninth streets.[17] Intermittent rebuilding occurred during the interwar period, including such notable structures as Andrew J. Thomas's courtyard housing development (1926) between Sixty-fifth and Sixty-sixth streets and the Swedish-inspired Church of the Epiphany (Wyeth & King and Eugene W. Mason, 1939), at 1393–1399 York Avenue, on the northwest corner of Seventy-fourth Street.[18]

H. I. Feldman's 500-unit Sutton Terrace (1950) faced a gardenlike entrance court on the west side of York Avenue between Sixty-second and Sixty-third streets, a site long held by the Consolidated Edison Company.[19] In the early 1940s the land had been sold to the New York Infirmary, which intended to utilize it as the site of a new hospital, but when plans fell through, the land was purchased by the Tishman Realty and Construction Company for residential use. Sutton Terrace consisted of two midblock twelve-story buildings and a thirteen-story building, with ground-level stores, facing York Avenue. Beneath the landscaped courtyard, which was approximately an acre in size, a four-level parking garage accommodated 300 cars. All three buildings were clad in red brick and featured decorative brickwork and limestone trim on their first stories and recessed trapezoidal terraces above.

According to Sutton Terrace's developer, Norman Tishman, "a large part of the renting success of this new apartment group" could be attributed to the courtyard. "Tenants," he said, "were quick to recognize the pleasant contribution such a setting would make to their living pattern and were eager to take advantage of the opportunity to combine the benefits of city facilities with suburban charm, without the inconvenience of commuting."[20] Lewis Mumford was, not surprisingly, more critical in his assessment. While he praised the building's garden, he lambasted the architecture: "In its details, the monotonous rhythm of its windows, the design of its balconies (which are recessed into the outer walls), the uneasy combination of limestone lintels and copings and warm red brick, with just enough whiteness to be disturbing, Sutton Terrace is an indecisive mixture of the old and the new."[21] Greenberg & Ames's Royal York (1955), located directly to the north, was another courtyard apartment building complex, which consisted of twin twelve-story redbrick buildings at 425 East Sixty-third Street and 420 East Sixty-fourth Street.[22] Although, like Sutton Terrace, the Royal York was almost suburban in character, its quality was not as high as its predecessor's.

The new York Avenue buildings sought to capitalize on the cachet of riverfront living that had been established during the interwar period at Sutton Place, farther to the south. As the *New York Times* said of Sutton Terrace, "The atmosphere of gracious living that has marked the fashionable Sutton Place apartment colony is spreading northward, where developers are taking advantage of the East River vista."[23] In 1951 work was completed on 60 Sutton Place South, which occupied a blockfront created by the block-long extension of Sutton Place south to Fifty-third Street.[24] Designed by Arthur Weiser, the apartment complex, originally developed for the site of Schwab House on Riverside Drive, consisted of two twenty-story slabs linked near their midpoints by a low, glass-enclosed lobby. Weiser visually broke up the slabs by canting the walls of the living rooms and master bedrooms to shelter a terrace and to create a diagonal orientation east, toward the river views, for even the rear-most apartments. This feature, probably derived from Loebl, Schlossman & Bennett's Darien Apartments (1948–51) on Lake Shore Drive in Chicago, resulted in five-sided bedrooms and living rooms.[25]

Most of the new construction in the area was related to the expansion of the Rockefeller Institute, the Memorial Sloan-Kettering Cancer Center and the New York Hospital–Cornell Medical Center. In 1957 Harrison & Abramovitz were the architects chosen to help with the expansion of Rockefeller University, as the institute was renamed in 1954, when it established a graduate program. Wallace K. Harrison was not a surprising choice, given his long personal and professional relationship with the Rockefeller family.

Rockefeller University's existing campus was entered through gates at York Avenue and Sixty-sixth Street; a driveway led up the sloping site to the so-called Central Laboratories (Shepley, Rutan & Coolidge, 1906), later renamed Founders Hall, a rather stolid, Classically articulated six-story building clad in buff brick and limestone.[26] Perpendicular to this main axis, Harrison created a north-south tree-lined mall, designed by the landscape architect Dan Kiley. To foster a sense of oasis, Harrison placed two long, narrow four-story buildings running north-south to help isolate the mall from the avenue. The two buildings were similarly articulated, with rough-hewn limestone bases and curved corners that added to the sense of refinement. Rather severe limestone facades were turned toward the avenue; visually lighter glass-and-metal facades were oriented east toward lushly landscaped grounds. The northern building, completed in 1958, was divided into two sections: the southern section, known as Caspary Hall, housed executive offices, while the northern portion, Abby Aldrich Rockefeller Hall, contained visitors' facilities and dining rooms, some of which opened out onto a patio elegantly defined by open limestone framework.[27] Farther north, a large flagstone-paved terrace, ringed by hedges, covered a subterranean parking lot; the two levels were linked by an open suspended staircase. The southern building, which was completed a year later, housed graduate students and visiting scientists.[28]

Harrison's most architecturally daring building for the university was Caspary Auditorium (1958), intended to serve not only as a conventional lecture hall but also as a venue for movies, concerts and scientific meetings.[29] Bolt, Beranek & Newman served as the project's acoustical engineers. Acknowledging the paradigm of the ancient Greek amphitheater as the source of his design, Harrison gave the auditorium a circular form, enclosing it in a sweeping, forty-foot-high, ninety-foot-diameter hemispherical dome. On the outside, the concrete dome was sheathed in Italian tiles, predominantly blue, but white, yellow and green as well; within eight months of the building's completion, however, the tiles began

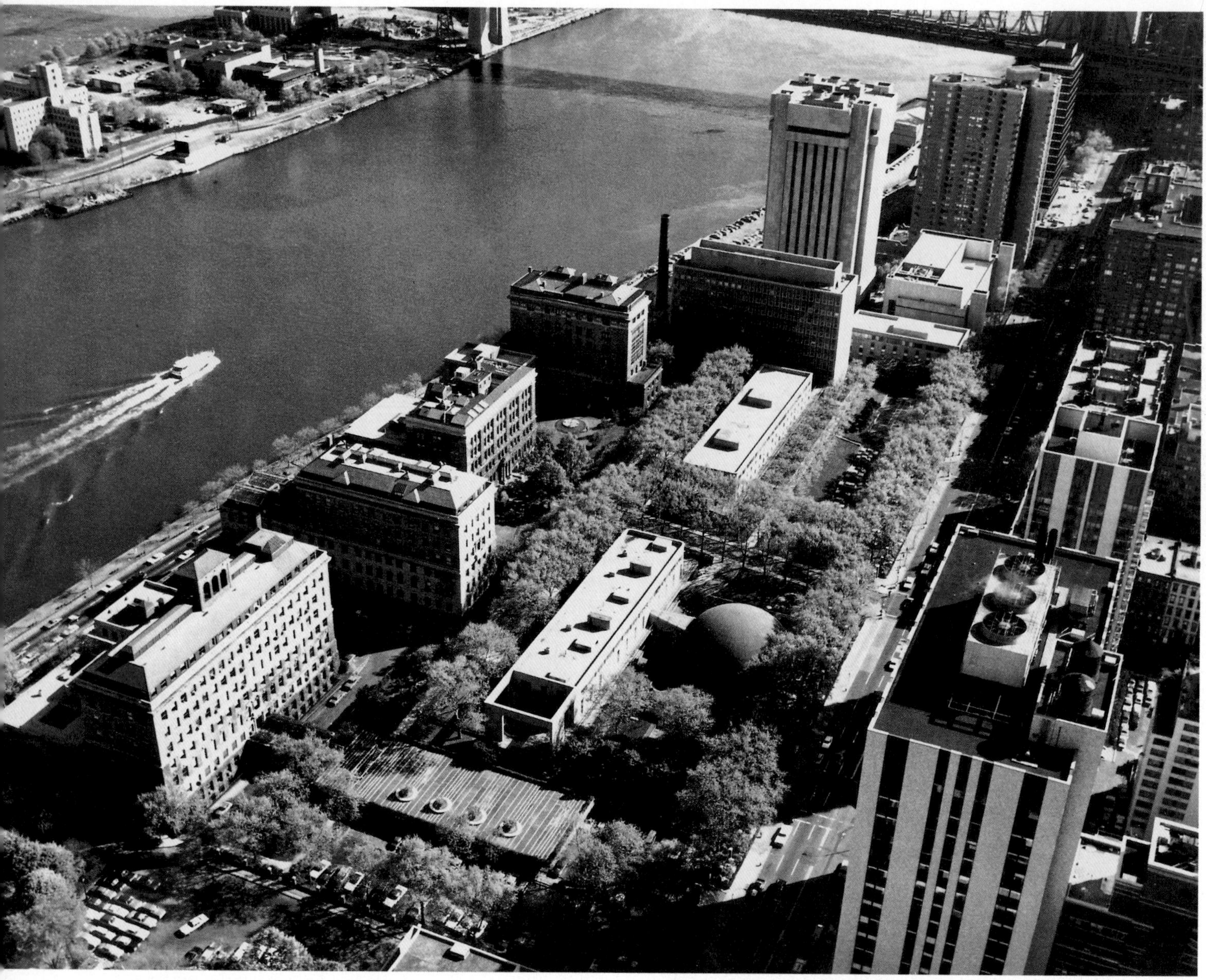

Above: View to the southeast showing Rockefeller University, York Avenue to Franklin Delano Roosevelt Drive, East Sixty-second to East Sixty-eighth Street. Gillette. ROARC

Right: Abby Aldrich Rockefeller Hall, Rockefeller University. Harrison & Abramovitz, 1958. View to the southwest. ROARC

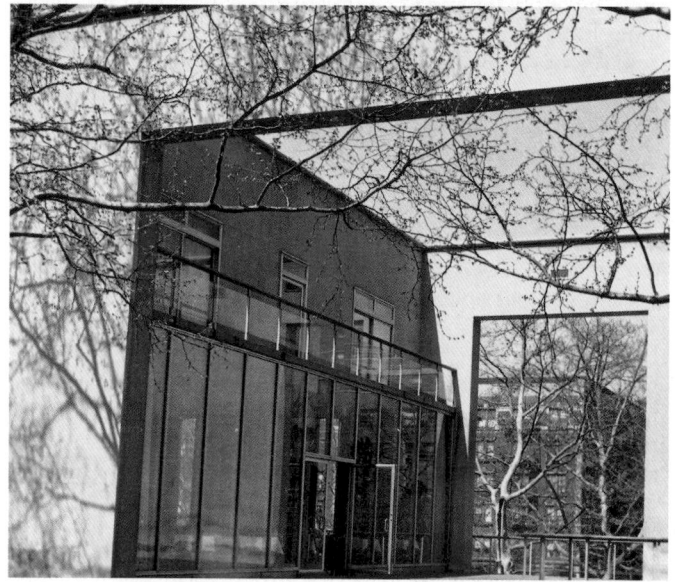

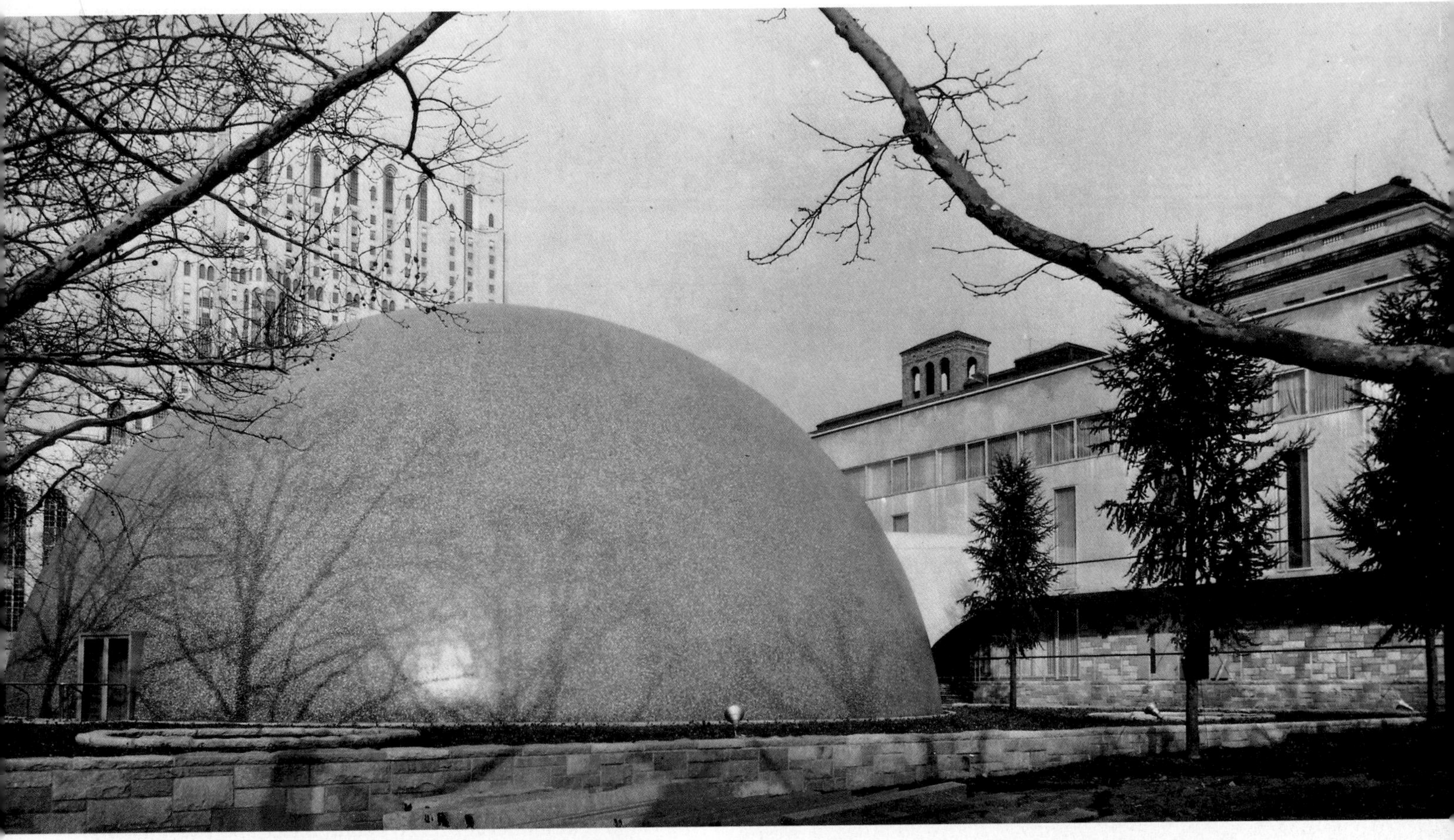

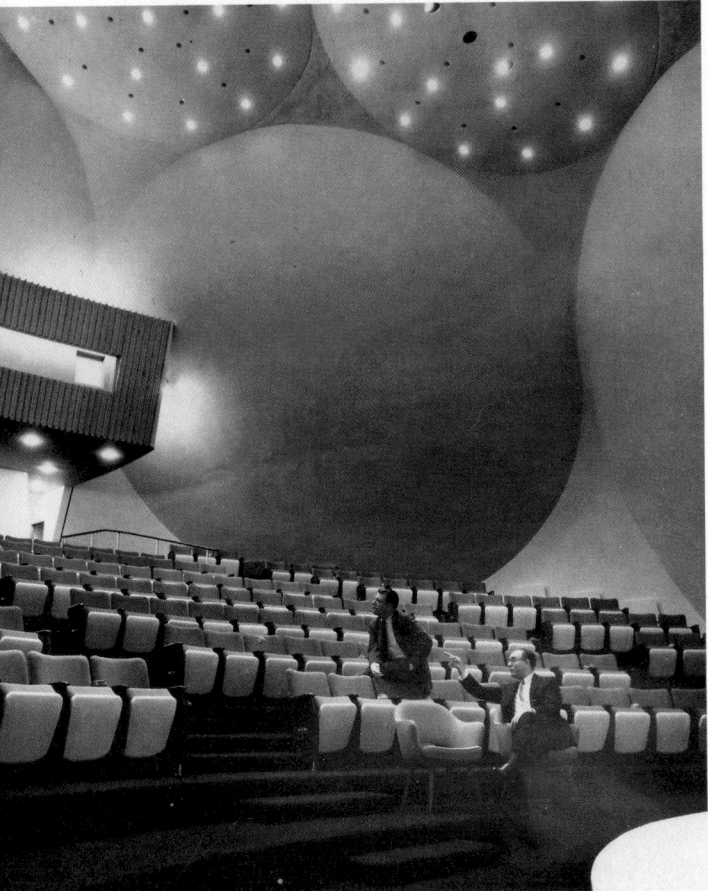

Above: Caspary Auditorium, Rockefeller University. Harrison &
Abramovitz, 1958. View to the northeast. ROARC

Left: Caspary Auditorium. Interior. ROARC

849

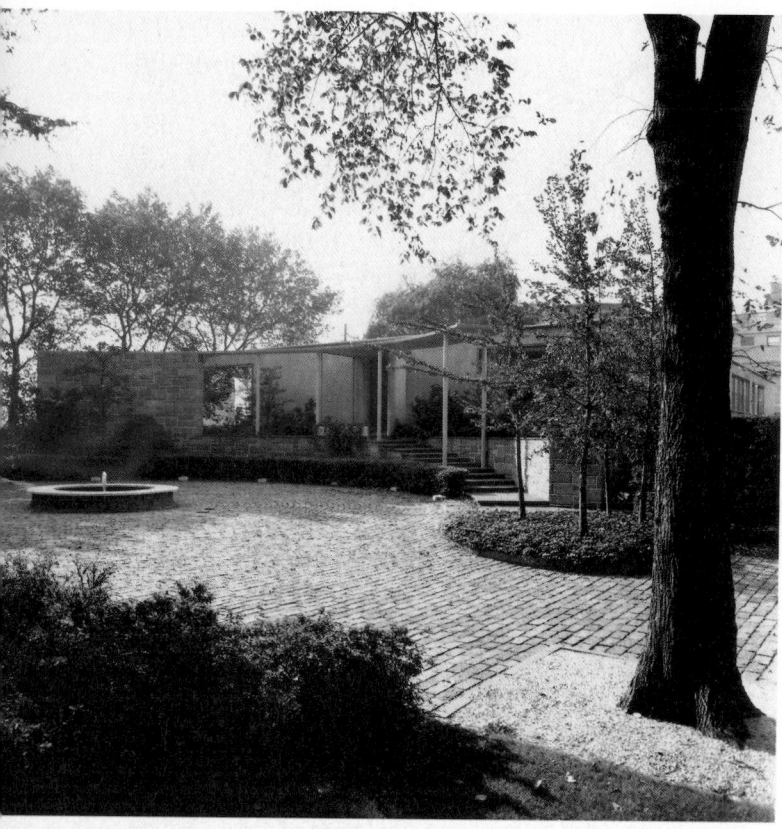

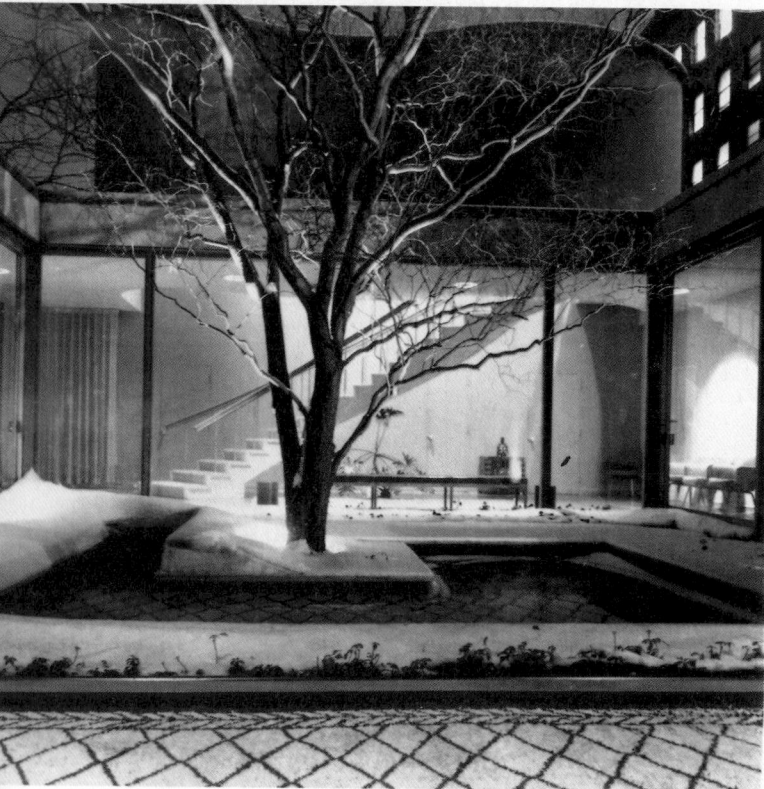

Top: President's House, Rockefeller University, between York Avenue and Franklin Delano Roosevelt Drive, near East Sixty-eighth Street. Harrison & Abramovitz, 1958. View to the southeast. Barnell. ROARC

Bottom: President's House. Courtyard. Barnell. ROARC

to fall off, and the dome's concrete shell was left exposed. The auditorium was linked to Caspary Hall by an enclosed bridge, which also served as the principal entrance. The constricted passageway leading to the open space of the auditorium established a dramatic sense of procession. The auditorium floor was pitched at a sharp angle and supported semicircular rows of seating. Variously sized convex circles articulated the ceiling; a portion of one of the circles, placed behind the proscenium stage, contained an adjustable sound baffle. The effect was spectacular, suggesting the advanced structural forms of Buckminster Fuller while recalling the dramatic Expressionist theater designs of the 1920s.

Harrison's Detlev W. Bronk Laboratory (1958) served as the southern terminus of the new mall.[30] The nine-story slab turned a pristine glass-and-metal curtain wall, with gray opaque glass panels, north to the mall; a limestone-clad facade, punctuated by square punched windows, faced south. Harrison's limestone-clad President's House, also completed in 1958, was an elegant two-story suburban-scaled residence that fully exploited its parklike campus setting and sweeping views of the East River.[31] The house contained floor-to-ceiling sliding glass partitions that opened onto an enclosed landscaped courtyard containing a decorative pool which served as an internal focus. Among the house's thirteen rooms was a dining room large enough to seat fifty people. Victoria Newhouse, Harrison's biographer, felt that the architect took "special pleasure" in executing the design of the house, which "carries to a handsome conclusion the institute's pastoral campus atmosphere."[32]

In 1963 construction of a subway tunnel running beneath the campus at the level of Sixty-fourth Street and extending to Queens threatened to disrupt the university's functioning; negotiations led to the project's relocation one block south (see chapter 10). In the following years the university continued to expand its facilities, announcing in 1968 that it would build a seventeen-story building housing offices and laboratories.[33] Designed by Nelson W. Aldrich, a cousin of the Rockefellers and a partner in Campbell, Aldrich & Nulty, the massive, limestone-clad science tower (1974) was an aesthetically weak addition to Harrison's campus. Located at the campus's southern end and separated from the Bronk Laboratory by a rather lifeless plaza, the building had austere facades punctuated by narrow vertical incisions containing windows and dark metal spandrels. A top-level projection visually served as a cornice. Visible from throughout the campus, the tower—a pale and clumsily detailed version of Philip Johnson's Henry L. Moses Research Institute (1965) at Montefiore Hospital in the Bronx (see chapter 13)—seemed like an uninvited intruder.

Horace Ginsbern & Associates' Faculty House (1975) extended the institute's facilities to a full-block site bounded by Sixty-second and Sixty-third streets, York Avenue and the Franklin Delano Roosevelt (FDR) Drive.[34] The first structure erected in Manhattan as a result of a "design/build" competition conducted by the New York State Dormitory Authority, the building was designed by Harold Sussman of the Ginsbern office to take "advantage of the emotional stimuli of river, university campus, Gothic bridge (59th Street bridge)" as well as provide "shelter from a plethora of automobile traffic to and from the adjoining highway."[35] Set on a podium containing a parking garage, the 250-unit, twenty-six-story balconied slab was bent to exploit river views. However, when viewed from the university, the arrangement created a jarring visual effect because the angled slab was out of alignment with the campus's rigorously maintained gridded plan. Rough-textured, ribbed-concrete facades reminiscent of the work of Paul Rudolph enhanced the building's strong sculptural presence.

The Memorial Sloan-Kettering Cancer Center occupied various buildings on the full block between Sixty-seventh and Sixty-eighth streets, First and York avenues. Its main building (James Gamble Rogers, 1938), at 444 East Sixty-eighth Street, was an architecturally sophisticated twelve-story brick-clad building that incorporated strip windows punctuated by angular bays.[36] In 1950 Skidmore, Owings & Merrill's James Ewing Memorial Hospital was built to function as part of the complex.[37] SOM's sleek brick facades with unbroken horizontal window bands carried to its logical minimalist conclusion the nearly explicit Modernism of Rogers's design.

As new techniques for treating cancer were developed, the hospital's mission grew as well, demanding more space for treatment and research, as well as staff housing. Harrison & Abramovitz's Sloan House (1962), at 1233 York Avenue, between Sixty-sixth and Sixty-seventh streets, was a twenty-story residential tower that provided 150 apartments for nurses.[38] Each apartment had a generously proportioned living room with a balcony. Victoria Newhouse viewed the design as only somewhat successful: "In what appears to be an attempt to relate the building to the nearby [Rockefeller] university, Harrison placed the tower on a planted terrace. . . . The effect is pleasant from the interior, but the landscaped area is too small to affect the building's rather bland presence within the city block."[39]

To meet similar housing needs, the New York Hospital–Cornell Medical Center built the Laurence G. Payson House (Frederick G. Frost, Jr. & Associates, 1966), at 435 East Seventieth Street, on the northwest corner of York Avenue, which consisted of three staggered slabs linked by two service corridors to create a dramatic self-referential form set on a plaza.[40] Nine years later Payson House was joined by Conklin & Rossant's Jacob S. Lasdon House across the street, at 420 East Seventieth Street, which housed apartments for medical students.[41] Occupying a large midblock site, the Brutalist fifteen-story slab was set back from the street atop a one-story buff-brick base that held the building line. Above, the building's exposed-concrete frame was filled in with glazing. The austere composition was slightly softened by the presence of a landscaped second-level terrace.

By the 1970s it was becoming clear that Sloan-Kettering and the New York Hospital–Cornell Medical Center, with no particular plan, had become one of the world's most intensely developed medical campuses but that they were severely hampered in their programs by a lack of space. Working together, they obtained enabling legislation in 1971 authorizing the city to sell the air space over the FDR Drive to owners of adjoining property. In 1972, as the City Planning Commission debated the transaction and the price to be paid, Skidmore, Owings & Merrill prepared a master plan for expansion that called for a forty-five-story cruciform in-patient hospital housing 1,088 beds, a 286,000-square-foot medical services building and other facilities, as well as parking, to be realized over ten years on a continuous platform covering the FDR Drive.[42] An elevated river-facing esplanade extending from Sixty-third to Seventy-second Street was to replace the existing pedestrian footpath. The plan was never realized.

North of Seventy-second Street, York Avenue became home to luxury-type apartment houses, including the Pavilion, at 500 East Seventy-seventh Street, designed by Philip Birnbaum.[43] The building replaced a public bath (Stoughton &

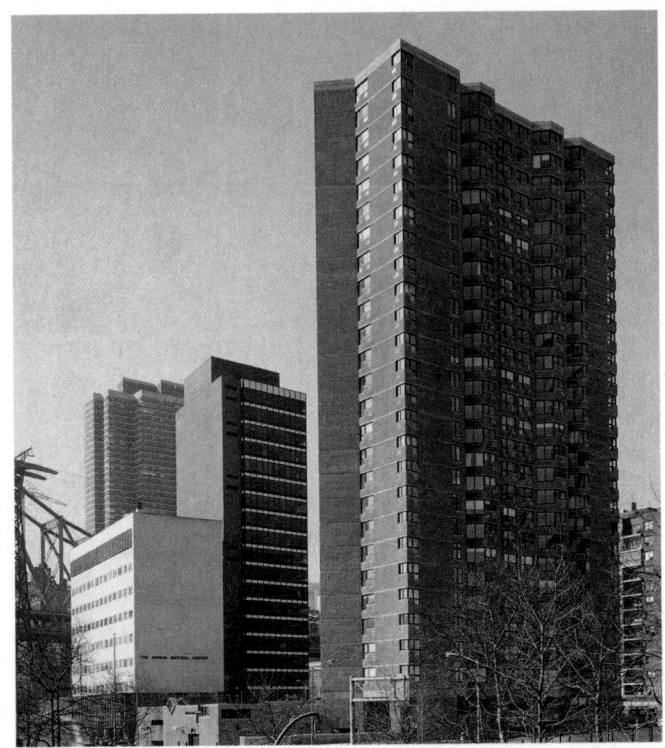

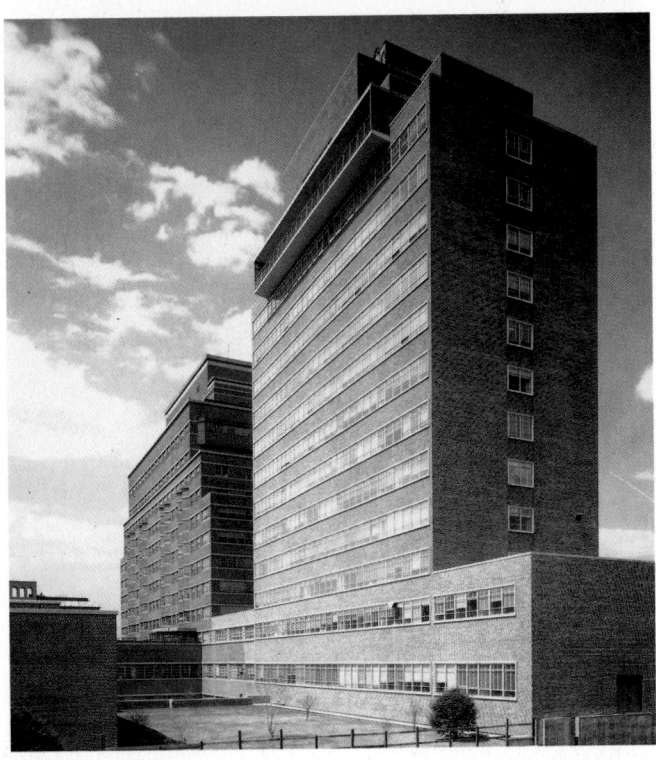

Top: Faculty House, Rockefeller University, York Avenue to Franklin Delano Roosevelt Drive, East Sixty-second to East Sixty-third Street. Horace Ginsbern & Associates, 1975. View to the southwest. Rothschild. HASU

Bottom: James Ewing Memorial Hospital, Memorial Sloan-Kettering Cancer Center, between First and York avenues, East Sixty-seventh and East Sixty-eighth streets. Skidmore, Owings & Merrill, 1950. View to the northeast including Main Building (James Gamble Rogers, 1938) of Memorial Sloan-Kettering Cancer Center on the right. Freedman. LF

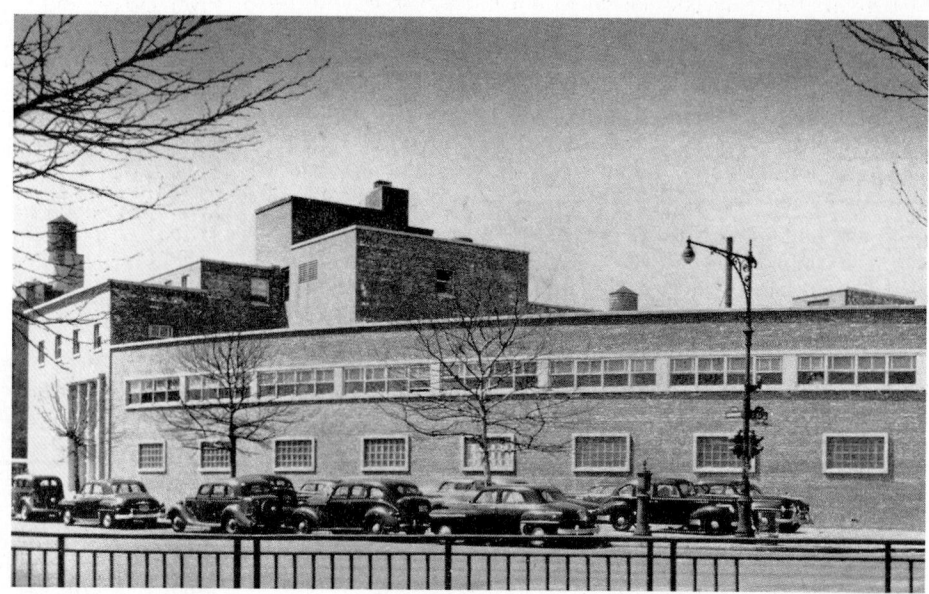

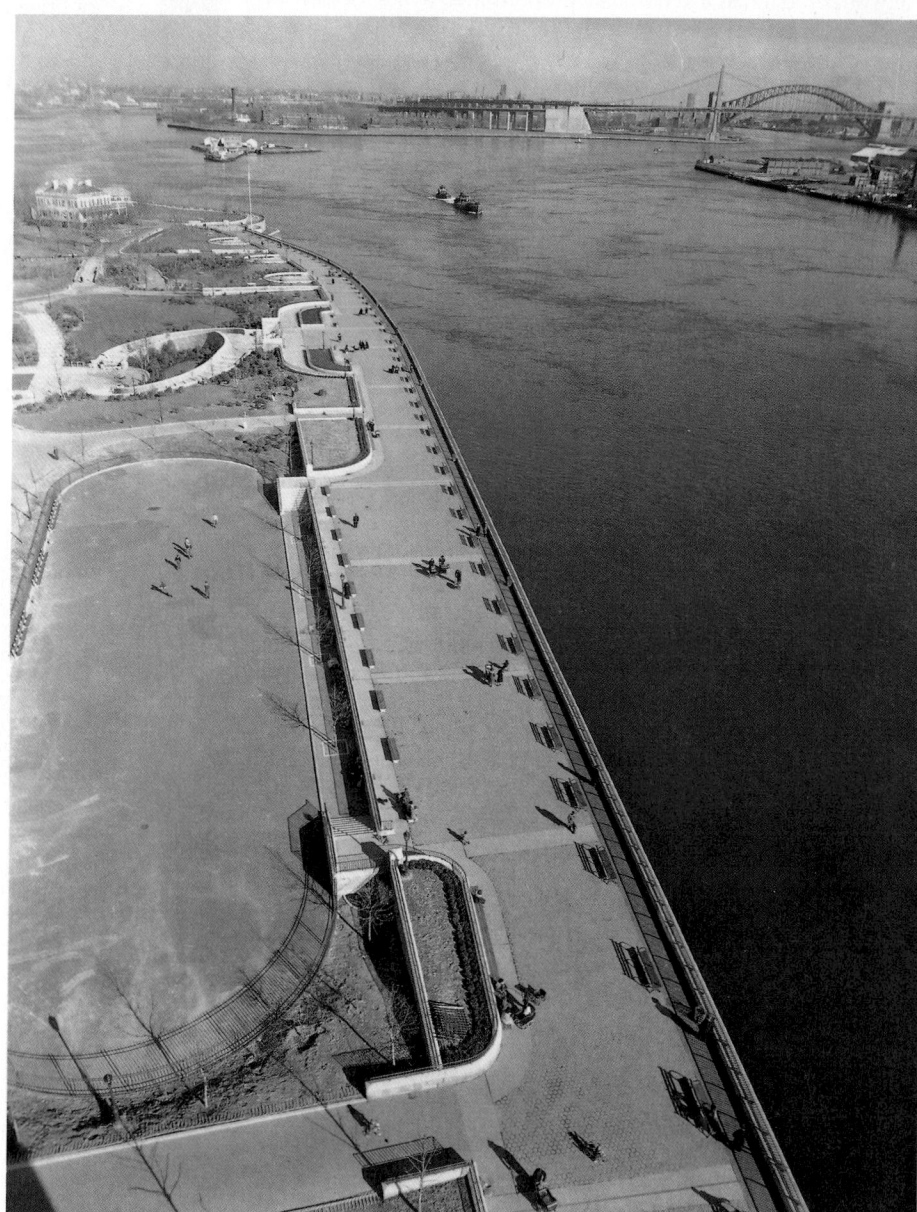

Top: New York chapter of the American Society for the Prevention of Cruelty to Animals, east side of York Avenue, East Ninety-second to East Ninety-third Street. Walker & Poor, 1950. View to the southwest. Gottscho-Schleisner. AR. CU

Bottom: Carl Schurz Park, East End Avenue to the East River, East Eighty-first to East Ninetieth Street. Harvey Stevenson, 1941. View to the north. R. M. Morgan. NYCPPA

Stoughton, 1902), in addition to tenements and shops. At the time of its completion in 1964, the thirty-five-story Pavilion, clad in white glazed brick and housing 852 families, was the largest apartment building in the city. Six rooftop gardens on the two major wings featured approximately 150 evergreens, 100 crab apple trees, 50 weeping willows, 30 Japanese red maples and hundreds of flowering shrubs.

One postwar institutional building added a grace note to the predominantly residential area, the headquarters of the New York chapter of the American Society for the Prevention of Cruelty to Animals.[44] The principal aesthetic feature of Walker & Poor's two- and three-story brick-clad building, completed in 1950, was a sweeping curved wall that reflected the wedge-shaped site, on the east side of York Avenue from Ninety-second to Ninety-third Street. Highly visible to motorists passing by on the FDR Drive, the facade was punctuated by nine rectilinear windows surmounted by a narrow glazed ribbon, all trimmed in limestone. The building's three-story principal facade, along Ninety-second Street, incorporated an asymmetrically placed entrance framed by a portico. Inside, the building contained offices, an animal hospital and kennels; animal exercise runs also extended outdoors.

At Seventy-ninth Street, York Avenue yielded to East End Avenue as Manhattan's easternmost avenue. The blocks of East End Avenue south of Eighty-fourth Street held on to their gritty past, although the apartment house at One East End Avenue (Pennington & Lewis, in association with McKim, Mead & White, 1929) was a top-flight building.[45] The most fashionable stretch of East End was in the immediate environs of Carl Schurz Park, from Eighty-fourth to Ninetieth Street, where the small houses of Henderson Place contributed a bit of nineteenth-century charm and the apartment houses represented the best of the interwar era's large-scale residential designs. Among these were buildings developed by Vincent Astor, including 120 East End Avenue (Charles Platt, 1931), and others, such as 10 Gracie Square (Van Wart & Wein with Pennington & Lewis, 1930).[46] The presence of two exclusive private schools for girls, Brearley (Benjamin W. Morris, 1928) and Chapin (Delano & Aldrich, 1928), also contributed to the neighborhood's prestige.[47] The rebuilding of Carl Schurz Park, and its extension south to Eighty-first Street along the East River via John H. Finley Walk (1941), which formed the top deck of the recently completed East River Drive, were the responsiblity of architect Harvey Stevenson. The cutout identification signs Stevenson produced for Finley Walk with cartoonist Edwin Marcus were a notable feature of the design.

Louis E. Jallade's Welfare Island Dispensary (1940), at 535 East Eightieth Street, on the northwest corner of East End Avenue, was built for the city's Department of Hospitals and served as a branch of the facilities located on Welfare Island, which was connected to Manhattan by a ferry that landed nearby at Seventy-eighth Street.[48] Jallade's Modern Classical design was simple, if not inspiring.

William I. Hohauser's River Edge House (1941), at 33 East End Avenue, occupying the south blockfront of Eighty-first Street between East End Avenue and the East River Drive, initiated the reconstruction of lower East End Avenue.[49] The principal feature of the bland, brick-sheathed building was its river-facing balconies. In 1950 River Edge House was followed by Emery Roth & Sons' 150-unit building at 45 East End Avenue, occupying the north blockfront of Eighty-first Street between East End Avenue and the FDR Drive (formerly the East River Drive) and replacing a parking lot.[50] Like Hohauser's building, the Roths' design retained the firmness of pre-Modernist work, although the large windows gave the building a more cagelike expression. Similarly, H. I. Feldman's 100 East End Avenue (1951), on the southwest corner of Eighty-fifth Street, managed to hold on to some measure of the old sense of scale.[51] This was not true of Sylvan Bien's twenty-story Riverview North (1954), at One Gracie Terrace, which extended a full block between Eighty-second and Eighty-third streets, East End Avenue and the FDR Drive.[52] Along the drive a staggered arrangement of rooms were banded together by continuous projecting balconies to create a composition with a strong sense of visual movement.

The twenty-one-story Gracie Towers (Sylvan and Robert Bien, 1960), at 180 East End Avenue, between Eighty-eighth and Eighty-ninth streets, was a conventional, glazed-white-brick apartment building distinguished by its size and the recreational facilities it contained.[53] Located directly opposite Gracie Mansion and Carl Schurz Park and commanding sweeping river views, the building embraced an entrance court, complete with circular driveway and porte cochere, that led to a glazed two-story lobby which in turn opened onto a midblock garden. A twenty-by-forty-foot rooftop swimming pool and adjoining cabana, dubbed the "Riviera on the River" by the editors of *Interior Design*,[54] constituted, according to *Real Estate Record and Guide*, "the first such facility in the history of apartment house construction."[55]

Since 1927 the former grounds of the House of the Good Shepherd, which was demolished that year to make way for an ultimately unrealized forty-story apartment hotel designed by Emery Roth, had remained vacant. The Good Shepherd block was bordered by East End and York avenues, Eighty-ninth and Ninetieth streets, at a point where the still ethnic Yorkville section intersected with the upper reaches of fashionable East End Avenue. In 1941 Gracie Square Gardens was proposed for the site.[56] As initially conceived, a 575-unit group of six six-story Georgian-style apartment buildings, designed by Sylvan Bien, was to take advantage of river views across Carl Schurz Park and the East River Drive. In keeping with the widespread trend toward suburbanization, the scheme not only called for low buildings but also occupied only 50 percent of the site, with gardens filling up the generously proportioned courtyards. The real estate broker William J. Demorest, of the William A. White agency, emphasized the importance of the open spaces: "The undertaking may be considered significant, not only because of its size and because it is being carried out by private capital, but also because it will provide apartments of a type designed to encourage people to remain in Manhattan. The liberal allotment of space for gardens will enable the tenants to enjoy many of the advantages of suburban life."[57] As built and completed in 1942, still to the designs of Sylvan Bien, the project contained only four seventy-unit buildings at 515 and 525 East Eighty-ninth Street and 520 and 530 East Ninetieth Street.[58] Tennis courts were located at the east and west ends of the site, which were in effect reserved for future high-rise construction, a decision influenced in part by the impending construction of the Municipal Asphalt Plant, which would compromise the site's river views in the midblock.

Located just north of East End's northern endpoint at Ninetieth Street, on a large site bounded to the west by York Avenue and to the east by the East River Drive, the Municipal Asphalt Plant (Kahn & Jacobs, 1941–44) was undoubtedly one

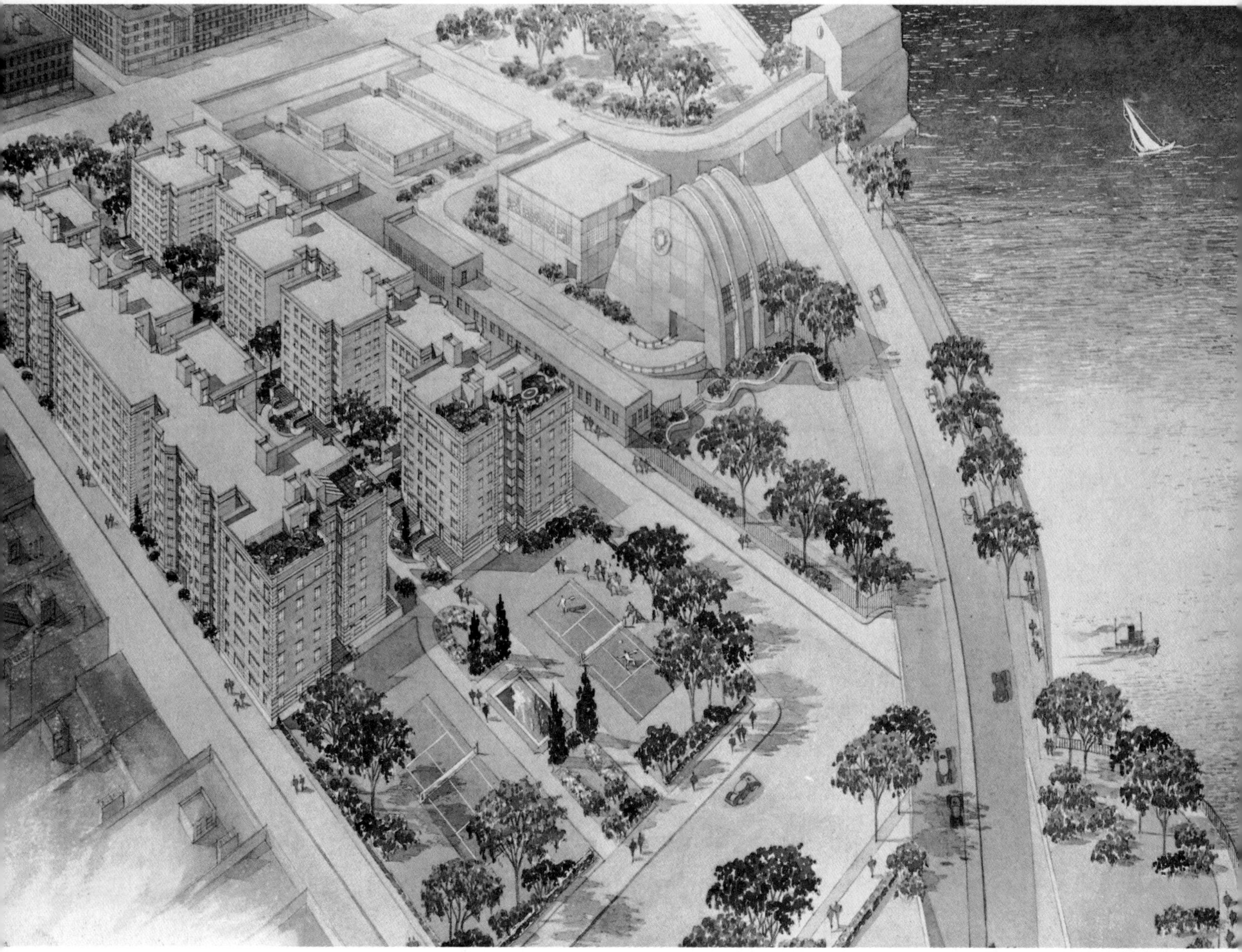

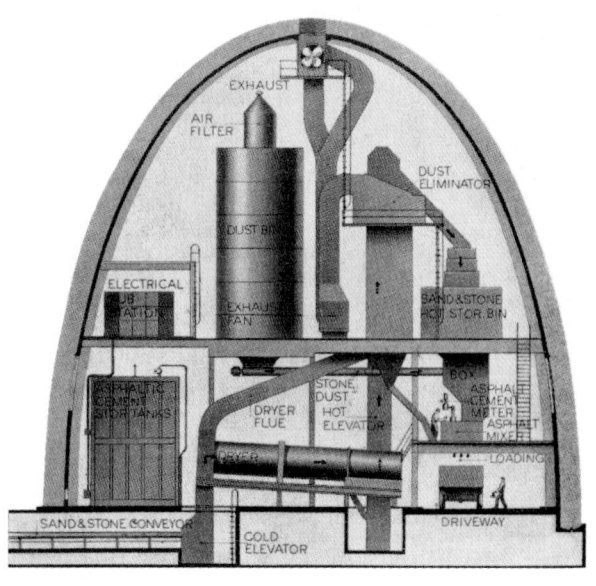

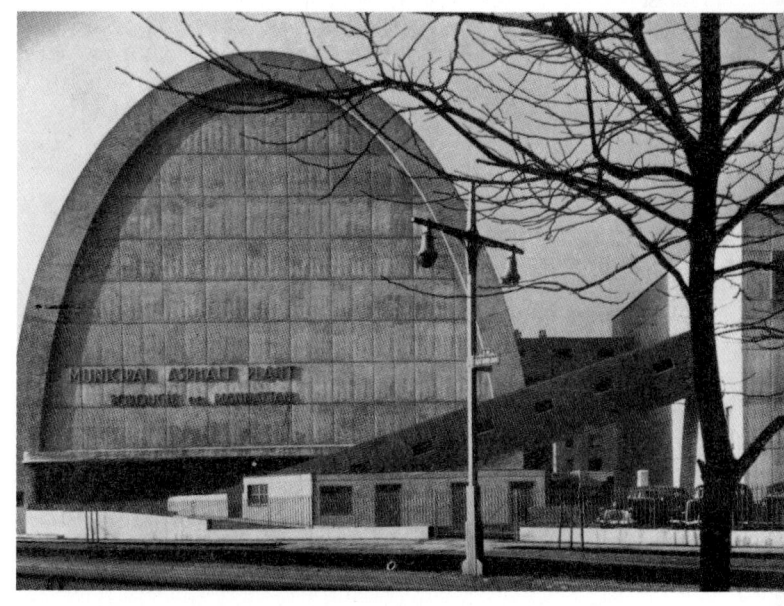

of the city's most important Modernist buildings.[59] Replacing another such facility that was deemed obsolete, Kahn & Jacobs's design, a bold invocation of the work of the French engineer Eugène Freyssinet, consisted of exposed concrete cast over parabolically arched steel frames to form a large single room, which contained equipment for mixing the asphalt to pave the city's streets. Next to the plant was a rectilinear storage building, whose austere exposed-concrete walls were punctuated by upper-level ribbon windows; natural light illuminated the interior's catwalks and conveyor belts, located above immense bins. A conveyor tunnel beneath the East River Drive connected the building to a pier-side hopper, where raw materials were delivered by barge; the building was in turn connected to the plant by both a bridge and a tunnel.

Park Commissioner Robert Moses criticized the aesthetics of the complex, which he described as "a Cathedral of Asphalt with a nearby corrugated shoebox."[60] Moses predicted that the "freakish experiment" represented by the complex would prove to be part of a stylistic trend toward "plenty of horrible modernistic stuff in statuary and architecture."[61] A spokesman for the Museum of Modern Art quickly countered with a positive assessment: "The bold semi-ellipse of the mixing plant is no affectation. These clean curves represent the most efficient structural form which could house the machinery. . . . Here is industrial architecture which is a distinct asset to its residential neighborhood and an exciting experience for motorists on the adjacent super-highway."[62] The editors of *Architectural Forum* also defended the plant: "Probably because arch construction has been used almost exclusively for elongated structures such as hangars, drill halls, auditoriums, etc., the building at first glance appears chopped off and incomplete. This impression undoubtedly stems more from association than from a sense of proportion."[63] The design withstood the changing winds of architectural fashion; twenty-three years after the complex was completed, Norval White and Elliot Willensky would state simply that "this bold work of 'industrial architecture' has not been matched in New York for bald functional and esthetic logic."[64] Paul Goldberger would go even further, writing in 1979 that the plant was "New York's great piece of mid-twentieth century industrial architecture. . . . The only real comparison one can make is with the huge grain elevators that assert themselves across the Middle Western landscape: they are inadvertent but great pieces of monumental architecture, and so is this."[65]

Without question the most aesthetically and technologically daring postwar proposal for the Upper East Side's riverfront was Moshe Safdie's unrealized Habitat I (1968).[66] Like Safdie's similar and also unrealized Habitat II, later proposed for lower Manhattan (see chapter 3), the sprawling development, which included stores, parking and a marina in addition to housing, was to be composed of complexly interlocking lightweight concrete modular units. The project, planned for a platform to be built in the East River, would extend roughly from Ninety-first to Ninety-fourth Street; a portion of the complex was to span the FDR Drive. Each octahedral unit was to be thirty-two feet across; some apartments would feature duplex formats, skylights and landscaped terraces. Pivoting interior walls would allow for the simple redesign of room configurations.

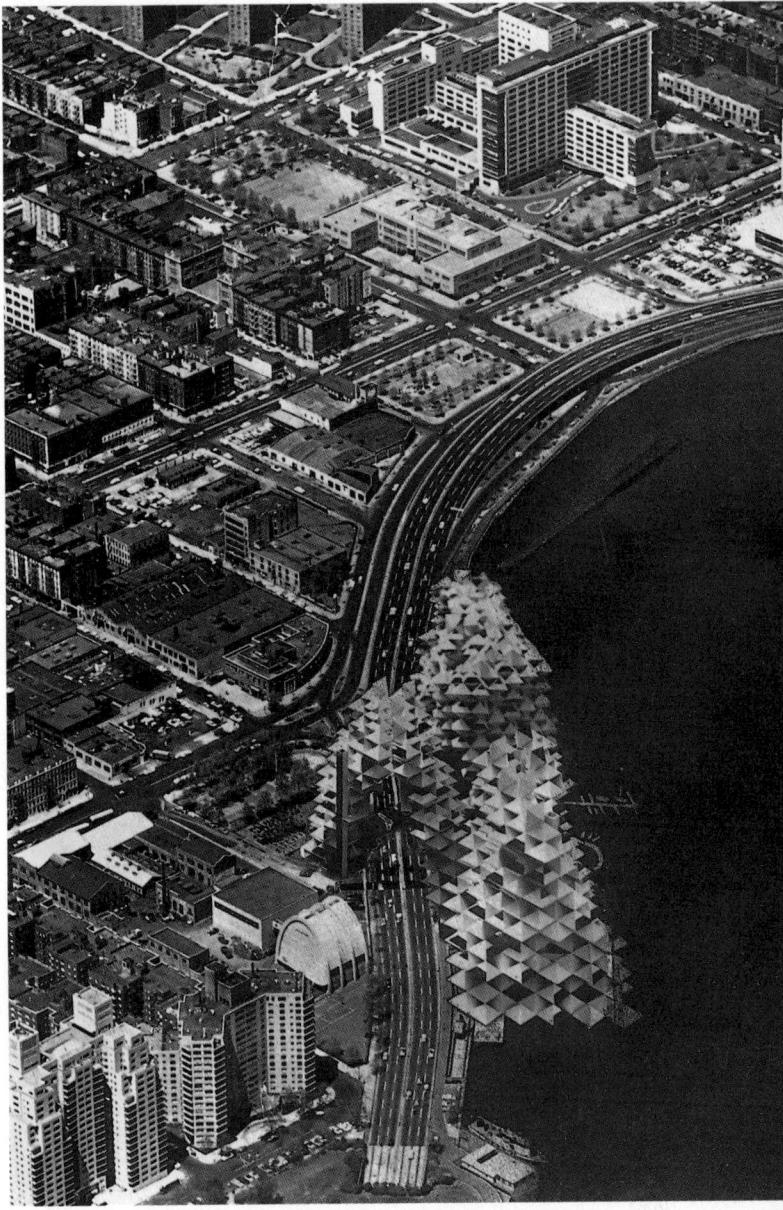

Top left: Gracie Square Gardens, East End to York Avenue, East Eighty-ninth to East Ninetieth Street. Sylvan Bien, 1942. Rendering by R. W. Allen of view to the northwest. EG

Bottom far left: Municipal Asphalt Plant, between York Avenue and East River Drive, north side of East Ninetieth Street. Kahn & Jacobs, 1941–44. Cutaway rendering. AF. CU

Bottom left: Municipal Asphalt Plant. View to the south. AF. CU

Above: Proposal for Habitat I, platform in East River, between East Ninety-first and East Ninety-fourth streets. Moshe Safdie, 1968. Photographic montage. View to the northwest. MSA

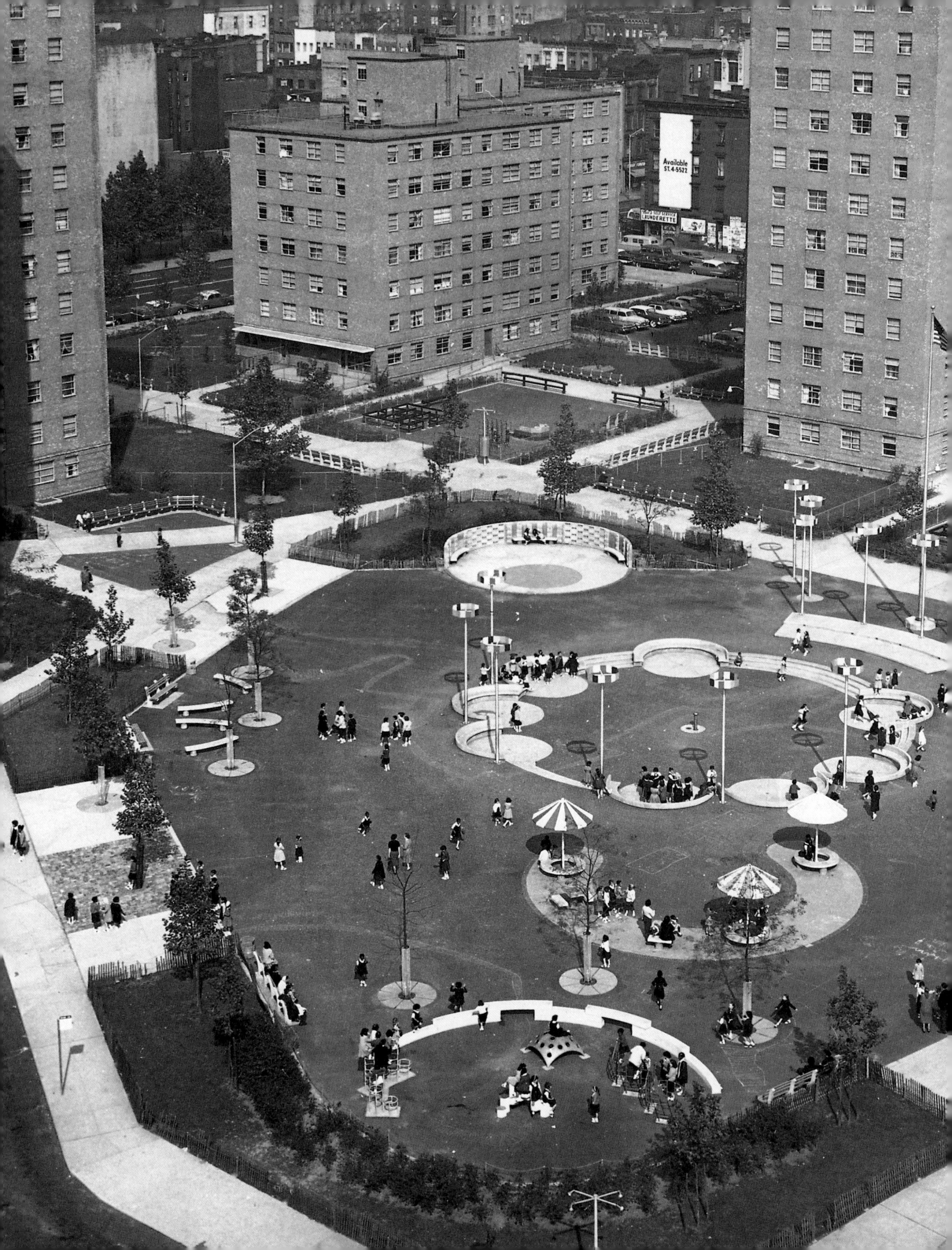

Chapter 12

Harlem and
Upper Manhattan

Harlem . . . is not the solidest or the best organized Negro community (Negro political representation came to Chicago a full decade before New York). It is not the most depressed, even in the New York area—that honor belongs to Bedford-Stuyvesant over in Brooklyn. But Harlem is a Negro capital, much as New York is an unofficial American capital.
—Michael Harrington, 1961[1]

BLACK AMERICA'S CAPITAL CITY

In the interwar years Harlem had shifted from a moderately prosperous neighborhood populated largely by first- and second-generation Irish-, German- and Italian-Americans into an almost entirely African-American ghetto. By the end of World War II Harlem was a distinct city within the city; for most whites, it was now a district as unfamiliar and as full of myth as a foreign country. This point was illustrated by the popular novelist Fannie Hurst, writing in the *New York Times* in 1946:

> Harlem, to the millions of whites who close it in on four sides, is a badlands where the chauffeur or the housemaid goes home to sleep, where the children have rickets, and no man is safe after dark. It is an incubator for vice, a lunatic fringe of savage music, a breeding ground for race riots. All Harlem is musically talented, unreliable, un- or a-moral. . . . The pity of it, indeed, the danger of it, is that the large majority of Harlem, who lead ordered, backbone-of-the-nation lives, are seldom heard of. They form little part, if any, of the public's concept of Harlem.[1]

By the early 1960s, with a new sense of black identity and pride emerging as part of the national civil rights movement, Harlem had taken on new significance. Harlem's accession to the status of black America's capital city was not without its painful aspects. As part of a series documenting current changes in New York and its suburbs, the journalist Layhmond Robinson, Jr., writ-

ing in the *New York Times* in 1955, said that "in the years between the start of World War I and the end of World War II, Harlem changed from a melting pot into the city's boiling pot."[2] That boiling pot had first overflowed when the community rioted in March 1935; riots occurred again in August 1943, leaving five people dead and 500 injured.[3] Though racial tensions in the city clearly ran high, some observers, including District Attorney William Copeland Dodge, attributed the 1935 riots, triggered by a sixteen-year-old stealing a ten-cent knife from a store on West 125th Street, to Communist agitation. And both Mayor La Guardia and representatives of the National Association for the Advancement of Colored People (NAACP) denied that the 1943 disturbances, catalyzed by a white policeman shooting a black soldier accused of assault, were race riots. The editors of the *New York Times* noted, however, that while La Guardia was "correct in the literal meaning of his words when he said that the disturbances which began in Harlem . . . were 'not a race riot' . . . everyone knows that there would have been no trouble in Harlem if race feeling in that district had not been tense."[4]

James Felt, the enlightened real estate developer, observed of the 1943 violence that "nearly every account of the recent Harlem riot underlines housing as a primary cause of racial unrest."[5] One of the principal housing problems in Harlem, according to Felt, was overcrowding. Before 1940, 60 percent of Manhattan's 300,000 blacks were jammed into "Harlemile," the area bounded by Fifth and Eighth avenues, 110th Street and the Harlem River; most of the other 40 percent lived close by along the periphery. A second cause of Harlem's housing crisis, Felt said, was the increasing deterioration of its overall housing stock, which occurred at a faster rate than that of the rest of Manhattan. While Harlem's typical buildings were not significantly older than those of Manhattan as a whole, their rate of replacement with new buildings was significantly slower; between 1930 and 1940 only 2 percent of Harlem's housing stock was new, as opposed to 6 percent downtown. Felt argued, however, that the heart of Harlem's problems lay not in overcrowding or building deterioration but in discrimination:

> Harlem housing, evaluated in a vacuum—bricks, mortar, plumbing and other component parts—is not in itself the major

View of Gala East Harlem Plaza (Mayer, Whittlesey & Glass, 1960) and Jefferson Houses (Brown & Guenther, 1959), First to Second Avenue, East 112th to East 115th Street. NYCHA factor causing the unrest and discontent which may have activated the riot. The main source of Harlem's problems is a combination of adverse economic factors and social ills, stemming from racial discrimination. If Negroes are continually confronted with employment barriers, and exclusion from many aspects of the normal life of citizens, the neighborhoods in which we live are bound to reflect these conditions.[6]

Felt's views were the exception, though; most observers in planning circles believed that Harlem's best hope lay in its physical development. As the *New York Times* editorialized: "What can be done has been shown in Corlears Hook, once a discreditable slum and now a bright spot. The cost of similarly transforming Harlem will be high, but the investment in modern structures . . . is well worth making. No community has done more than this city to keep itself in good health. To neglect Harlem would be a confession of failure."[7]

Despite the appalling living conditions in Harlem, the area prospered along with the rest of the city after the war, and by the mid-1950s it began to witness the beginnings of a massive program of redevelopment that promised better housing as well as new schools and other community facilities. Harlem was in fact the locus of so much public development that the area's traditional physical structure was transformed more rapidly and more extensively than that of any other part of the city. By 1955 Harlem had the greatest concentration of new public housing developments in the city, with 8,701 units occupied and 3,184 under construction, covering 160 acres in all.[8] In addition, ten public schools had been built since the war.

But the improvements in housing did not solve the problem of racial unrest in Harlem. On a hot July weekend in 1964, residents of the neighborhood rioted once again.[9] This time the violence was set off when an off-duty policeman fatally shot a black fifteen-year-old from the Bronx who had allegedly threatened him at knifepoint in front of an apartment building at 215 East Seventy-sixth Street. Despite the fact that the incident did not take place in Harlem and did not involve a Harlemite, the riots broke out in the great black ghetto. According to the political scientist and social activist Michael Harrington, "Everyone knew the Harlem riots were coming. The 'long hot summer' is a way of saying that insane social conditions would goad people to desperate action. Everyone knows they will come again. Yet no one has proposed the only solution: to tear the ghetto down. We could hire the Harlem poor, and the whites in the same position, to destroy the infamy and build decent integrated housing, schools, and hospitals. We could. We won't."[10]

By the mid-1960s most Harlemites, like ghetto residents and the poor all over the city, were disillusioned with physical redevelopment without social change; some had even come to see that redevelopment had resulted in dehumanization, a decline in social values and an institutionalization of the status quo. The renowned writer James Baldwin described one of the postwar projects, the Abraham Lincoln Houses (see "Central Harlem," below), which replaced the house he had grown up in, as looming "over the avenue like a monument to the folly, and the cowardice of good intentions," and went on to castigate others like it:

The projects in Harlem are hated. They are hated almost as much as policemen, and this is saying a great deal. And they are hated for the same reason: both reveal, unbearably, the real attitude of the white world, no matter how many liberal speeches are made, no matter how many lofty editorials are written, no matter how many civil-rights commissions are set

up. The projects are hideous, of course, there being a law, apparently respected throughout the world, that popular housing shall be as cheerless as a prison. They are lumped all over Harlem, colorless, bleak, high and revolting. . . . Even if the administration of the projects were not so insanely humiliating . . . the projects would still be hated because they are an insult to the meanest intelligence.[11]

Some observers argued that if the projects failed, it was because they were not physically or conceptually big enough to completely transform the environment. This was the viewpoint of R. Buckminster Fuller, the engineer and inventor, who in 1965 released his Skyrise proposal for Harlem. In this scheme 250,000 people would be rehoused in megastructures lifted above the ground as high as the elevation of Morningside Heights, leaving the ground plane clear for roads and parks.[12] A supercolossal version of Le Corbusier's cataclysmic plans of the 1920s for rebuilding Paris, the Skyrise called for fifteen widely spaced towers, each consisting of 100 circular living decks suspended by cables from a central mast. Spiral vehicular ramps would connect individual apartments with each other as well as with the ground and elevated expressways. The lowest level of the development would begin at ten stories, so the existing buildings that remained standing as the Skyrise was built would not compromise the new vision. At once too impractical and too simpleminded, Fuller's project was never built.

Foremost among those who sought to effect change in Harlem, both sociological and physical, was the Architects Renewal Committee in Harlem, known as ARCH.[13] The organization was founded in 1964 by Richard Hatch, a young architect who had become acquainted with the Harlem community through his volunteer work for the politically activist Student Non-Violent Coordinating Committee (SNCC). Following a presentation describing Harlem's slum conditions held by the American Institute of Architects' New York Chapter—the chapter's most heavily attended meeting to date—Hatch gained the profession's support to establish ARCH, for which he organized four groups of twelve to sixteen volunteer architects and urban planners. Funded by the Office of Economic Opportunity, as well as by private grants and commissions, ARCH set up an office in Harlem and hired a full-time staff of three. With a mandate to provide planning and urban design services to low-income groups that would not otherwise have access to them, ARCH helped obtain funds for low-cost housing projects, interpret rent and housing laws and develop community-supervised urban renewal plans. Although ARCH struggled to attract white investment, Hatch fought against gentrification and insisted that regardless of the source of funds, control of the new projects be kept within the Harlem community. As he said, the group sought to give Harlemites "some initiatory power to cope with their own problems—to determine what kind of city should be built for them."[14]

J. Max Bond, a Harvard-trained African-American architect who worked with ARCH in 1967 and 1968, understood the extraordinary potential of Harlem, which, unlike the Lower East Side or parts of the Bronx that were built for poor immigrants, started out as a middle-class neighborhood and thus had a rich housing stock, broad boulevards and considerable parkland. Bond also emphasized the value of the neighborhood's street-oriented culture, which shocked so many whites, and even some middle-class blacks:

The elements in the Black community that we would like to maintain as good, that we feel are good, have their origins in the street organization. You can send your children out to play and the neighborhood will take care of them, because the street is the living room. The streets are informal, they're real. They're the place where your friends are, but where the enemy (the police) is, too. Black people enjoy the streets; they like to go for walks. Everyone is at home outdoors.[15]

In 1968 Bond outlined a compelling vision of a revived Harlem, although it was sociologically rather than architecturally based. Full of high ideals and a commitment to dismantling the structures of the white world, it attempted to synthesize third world spontaneity and modern, Western order:

> We are concerned with changing the architect's role. We envision a change from the architect representing the rich patron to the architect representing the poor, representing them as individuals and as an interest group. This implies, we feel, studying cities from a different point of view, . . . finding out what ideas people have about modern technology, about a good kitchen, about a good street, about a desirable way to live. . . . What we are trying to capture is not Brasilia but that shantytown next to Brasilia."[16]

As Priscilla Tucker observed, what ARCH was working toward was not "city building" but "city living." "What they expect to produce," she said, "is not a revolutionary master plan but a city village, reflecting a different balance between local, neighborhood needs and metropolitan priorities."[17]

On January 23, 1967, at a luncheon attended by Mayor Lindsay as well as a host of other notable figures in politics and planning, the Museum of Modern Art opened an exhibition called "The New City: Architecture and Urban Renewal."[18] Cosponsored by the museum and the city, "The New City" was a significant departure from the Modern's normal postwar fare but was in some ways reminiscent of the socially responsive exhibitions on housing and urban planning that had been mounted in the early 1940s. The show represented the first large-scale architectural plan ever prepared for Harlem as a whole, although, in recognition of the area's complexity, the sponsors did commission separate area studies from four different design teams. Though it posed provocative ideas for Harlem's physical redevelopment, the exhibition was distinctly out of step with the prevailing beliefs of planners and political leaders who favored community participation, small-scale, incrementally realized projects and, whenever possible, rehabilitation rather than redevelopment of existing properties.

Richard Hatch castigated the museum and its design teams for failing to undertake a true master plan for redevelopment and for failing to strike a utopian note in their proposals. "It is not clear," he argued, "whether these proposals . . . are intended to crystallize wholly new alternatives for the public or simply to demonstrate the present state of the art of urban design. . . . They do not contain the important elements of utopian plans—a strong idea about the function of a place in the total fabric, and about the way men might live together—or the strength of detail required by practical proposals." Three of the four projects, he said, "tend to treat Harlem as if it were simply an ugly place, a blemish to be repaired by cosmetic surgery"; if these plans were realized, the result would be a gentrification process that would victimize Harlem's citizens: "Harlem occupies a desirable place at the heart of the New York region—it wouldn't take much to bid up prices so that only the well-to-do could be housed there. . . . If the project architects by and large have no feeling for Harlem as a community and an important low-rent housing area, they have less comprehension of its special character: the

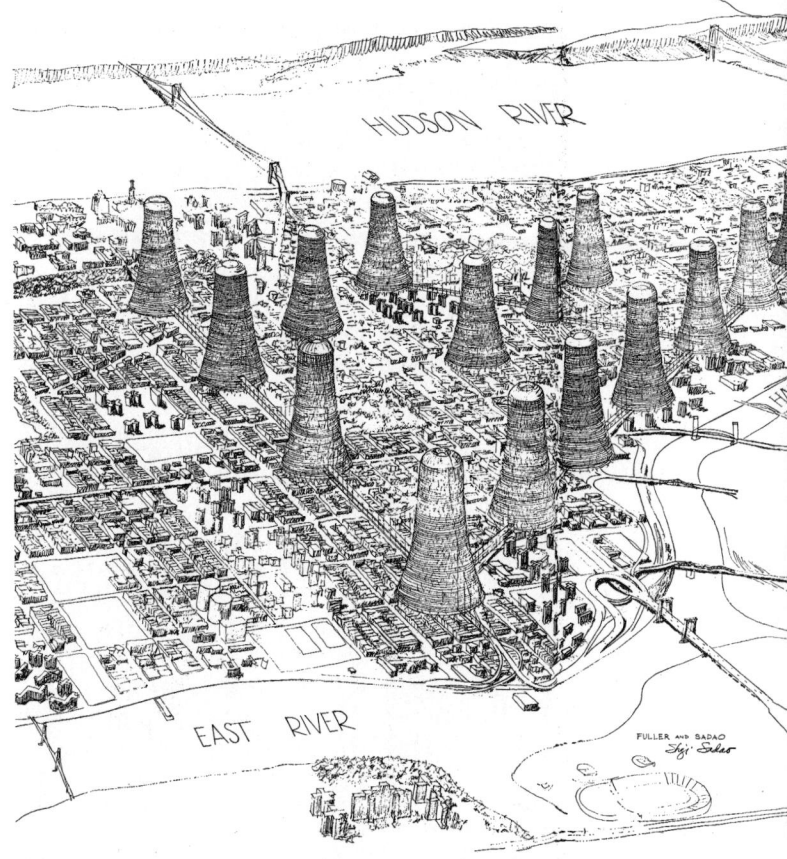

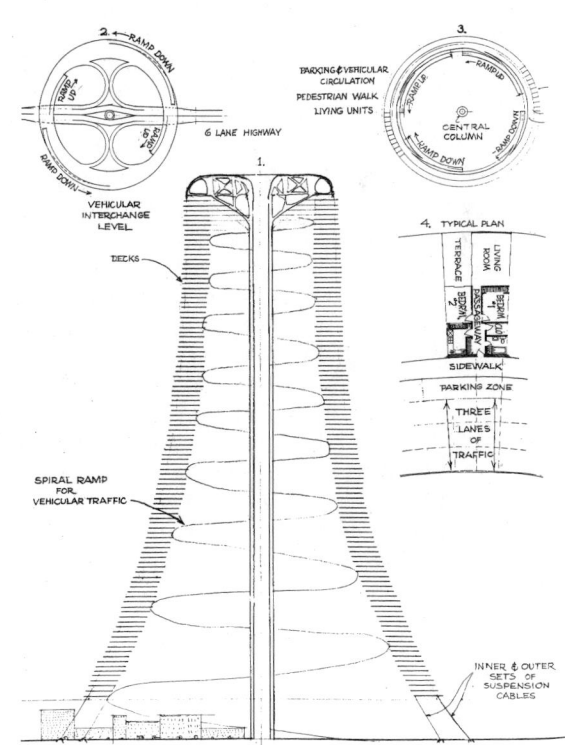

Top: Skyrise proposal for Harlem. Fuller & Sadao, 1965. Rendering by Shoji Sadao of view to the northwest. ©Allegra Fuller Snyder. Courtesy, Buckminster Fuller Institute, Santa Barbara. BFI

Bottom: Skyrise proposal. Plans and section. SS

859

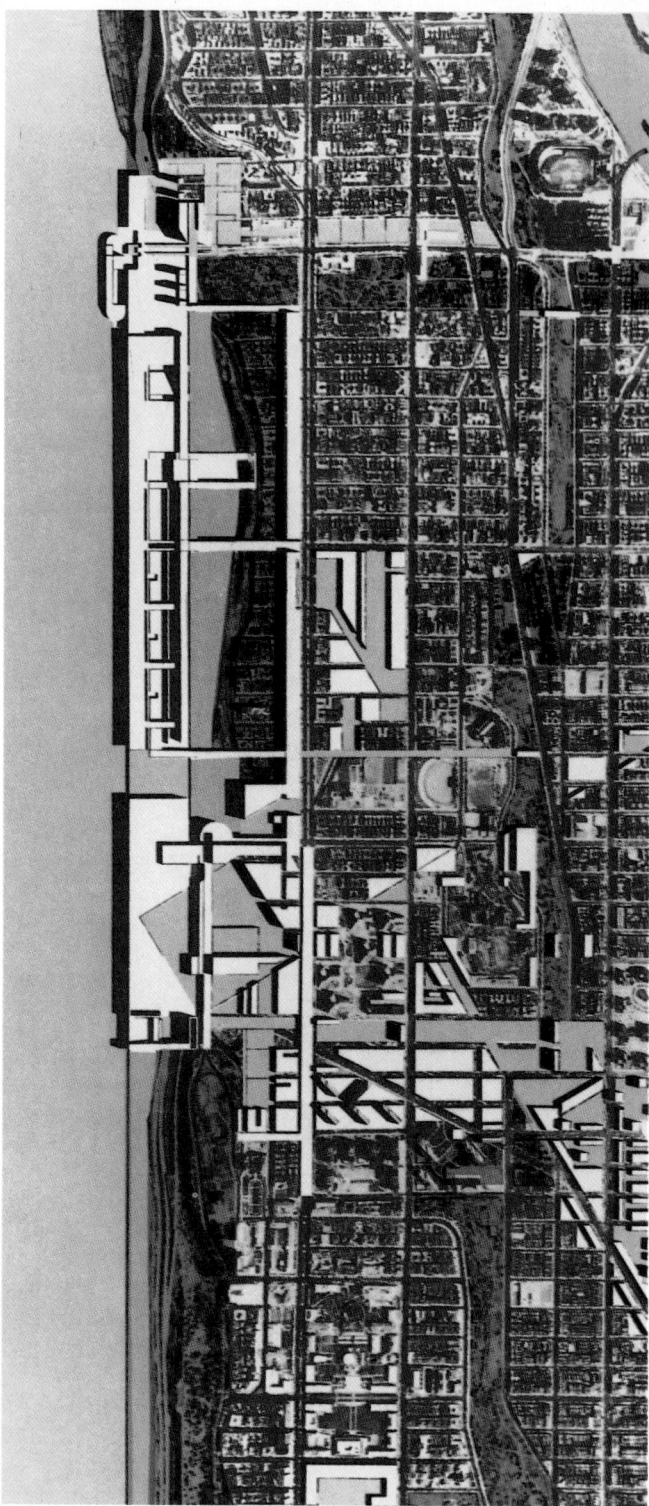

Proposal for West Harlem and Hudson River. Peter Eisenman and Michael Graves, with G. Daniel Perry, Stephen Levine, Jay Turnbull, Thomas C. Pritchard and Russell Swanson, 1967. Photographic montage. MOMA

four proposals would be at home in almost any city, inhabited by any group of mid-1960 middle class families."[19]

The four teams selected by Arthur Drexler, chairman of the museum's Department of Architecture, were each encouraged to focus on a specific approach to urban redevelopment. The Princeton team, led by Peter Eisenman and Michael Graves, and including G. Daniel Perry, Stephen Levine, Jay Turnbull, Thomas C. Pritchard and Russell Swanson, was asked to address Harlem's lack of a civic focus by developing plans for the stretch of the area's underutilized Hudson River waterfront and related uplands extending from Columbia University north to about 155th Street. Capitalizing on the Harlem Valley's role as the area's only water-level pass between the Hudson and the rest of Harlem, the team proposed a major activity center around a square located at the intersection of 125th Street and the river, where its diagonal orientation might foster a confluence of the West Harlem, Central Harlem and Morningside communities. They also proposed a thirty-block-long riverside megastructure containing shops, housing and light industry, which would have the effect of creating a lagoon between the new structure and the existing neighborhood. For Hatch, this proposal demonstrated a "will to form" that had "taken precedence over the necessity to give form to life. It is as if the designers believe there is nothing worth preserving in the local scene."[20]

The Cornell team, led by Colin Rowe and Thomas Schumacher, with Jerry A. Wells and Fred Koetter, assisted by Steven Potters and Michael Schwarting, among others, was asked to explore the area of Central Harlem lying at the foot of Morningside and St. Nicholas parks. Although in some ways this site was the most typical of the four, with block upon block of gridded streets, the natural topography of its parks and the diagonal street pattern along their edges made it decidedly atypical. Examining ideas that would later evolve into Rowe and Koetter's theory of Collage City, the Cornell team modified the grid plan to improve circulation and encourage the development of more parkland, which would give the neighborhood an even more distinct identity based on its dramatic natural terrain.[21] The mixed-use plan featured long building groups containing housing, offices and light industrial facilities. The team also explored the area south of 110th Street in an attempt to link Central Harlem with the Manhattan Valley section of the Upper West Side.

Hatch felt this proposal was a failed attempt to reconcile two theories of city design: the traditional city of solid mass with spaces cut out, and the city of towers in a park. "The attempted reconciliation," he wrote, "seems to have been abandoned for a more easily achieved non-aggression pact." Hatch questioned the provision of so much space for offices and factories "with midtown only ten minutes away by subway." He criticized the near-wholesale abandonment of the area's grid plan, which provided "legibility and accessibility," and was appalled by the team's proposal to close 125th Street to crosstown through traffic. He also found the planned reduction of residential density "morally and politically unacceptable," and felt the project would result in "an upper-middle class semisuburb—a pleasant, high-rent district inhabited by people who are not afraid to walk in sparsely protected parks." But the real failure of the plan, Hatch concluded, "lies in its lack of comprehension of growth in time, and, hence, its inability to guide us in the incremental activities which would produce a loosening of the grid at a socially permissible cost. Any plan that does not include a satisfactory explanation of the intermediate steps in its achievement must, today, be *prima facie* suspect."[22]

The MIT team, consisting of Stanford Anderson, Robert Goodman and Henry A. Millon, was asked to create 270 acres of new land by damming up and filling in the East River between Manhattan, Ward's and Randall's islands, creating a high-density equivalent to the Charles River basin that fronted their academic home in Cambridge, Massachusetts. The proposal would provide housing without requiring tenant relocation and would make Robert Moses's recreation areas under the Triborough Bridge more accessible. While the bold gesture of the MIT proposal was notable, the designers' intentions were only vaguely outlined. Hatch seemed satisfied, however, that their architecture was "meant to allow incremental growth and infinite variation of form in response to use and to time," and he said that theirs was the only proposal among the four to be worthy of "serious attention."[23]

The Columbia team was led by Jaquelin T. Robertson, Richard Weinstein, Giovanni Pasanella, Jonathan Barnett and Myles Weintraub, who were assisted by Benjamin Mendelsund, George Terrien and Paul Wang as well as the structural engineer David Geiger and a number of other technical consultants. Their proposal, to cover the New York Central Railroad's Park Avenue viaduct as it ran along Park Avenue from Ninety-seventh to 134th Street, would provide new housing without forcing Harlem residents into disruptive relocations. Developed by a New York–based team with clear connections to City Hall, this was the scheme with the greatest popular and political appeal. Similar in spirit to the plan simultaneously being considered by Mayor Lindsay for a linear city and expressway to be built over five and a half miles of railroad track in Brooklyn (see chapter 13), the Columbia proposal called for covering the viaduct and the twin roadways of Park Avenue with an eight- to ten-block reinforced-concrete tunnel, a solution to the technical and financial infeasibility of depressing the railroad tracks below grade. Built atop the tunnel would be housing and related open spaces, as well as a high-rise mixed-use structure at 125th Street containing a hotel, an office building, a convention center and a railroad station.

Although Hatch found the possibilities of the Columbia scheme "intriguing," he feared that the continuous development atop the viaduct would be "dull and undifferentiated" and would hinder east-west movement through the area: "New development in this area should serve to bring the two Harlem communities together but this design suggests a fortified wall and emphasizes their separateness." As for the mixed-use building at 125th Street, he said, it was full of "everything architects like but Harlem probably doesn't need."[24] When Jonathan Barnett, one of the project's designers, reassessed the scheme in 1974, he made a similar point:

> The proposal had most of the defects that we now find so laughable in other people's plans. It was a product of "superior wisdom" planning, done without any community consultation, and exhibited at the Museum of Modern Art, the true embodiment of elitism if there ever was one. Further, the project was only feasible if it were done all at once, requiring split-second timing between numerous different agencies, none of which were used to working with each other.[25]

After the members of the Columbia team left teaching to form the Urban Design Group in the City Planning Commission, they revised the scheme, working with the Harlem Model Cities Office under the direction of Lauren Otis and Edwin Woodman, who introduced a dimension of community participation. David Geiger, the structural engineer, working with Woodman, was

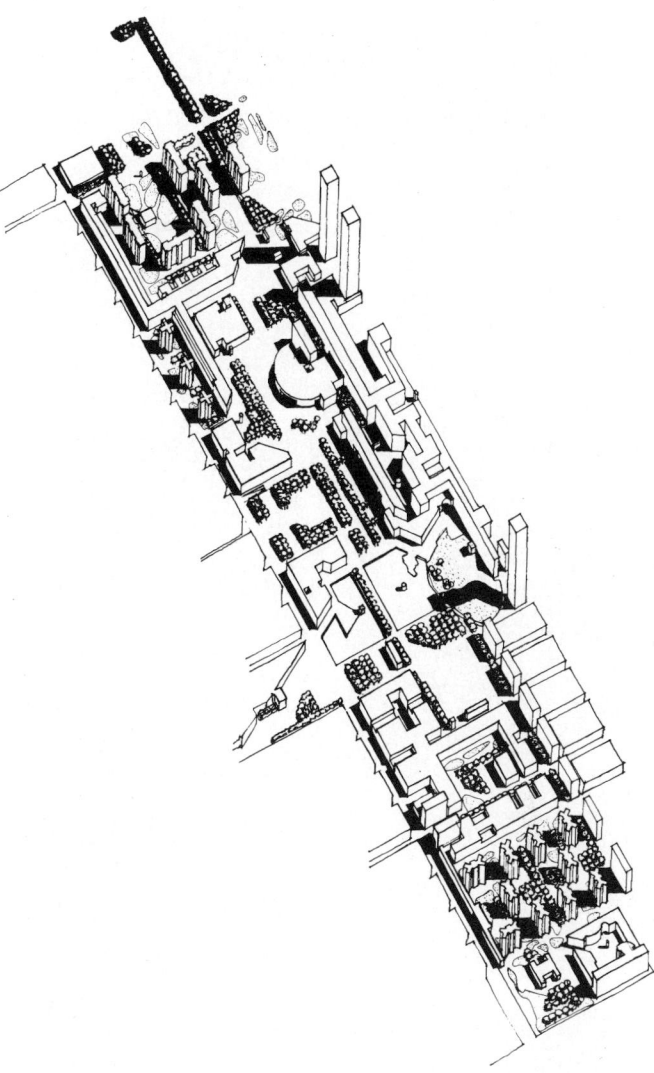

Proposal for Central Harlem. Colin Rowe and Thomas Schumacher, with Jerry A. Wells and Fred Koetter, assisted by Steven Potters and Michael Schwarting, 1967. Isometric. MOMA

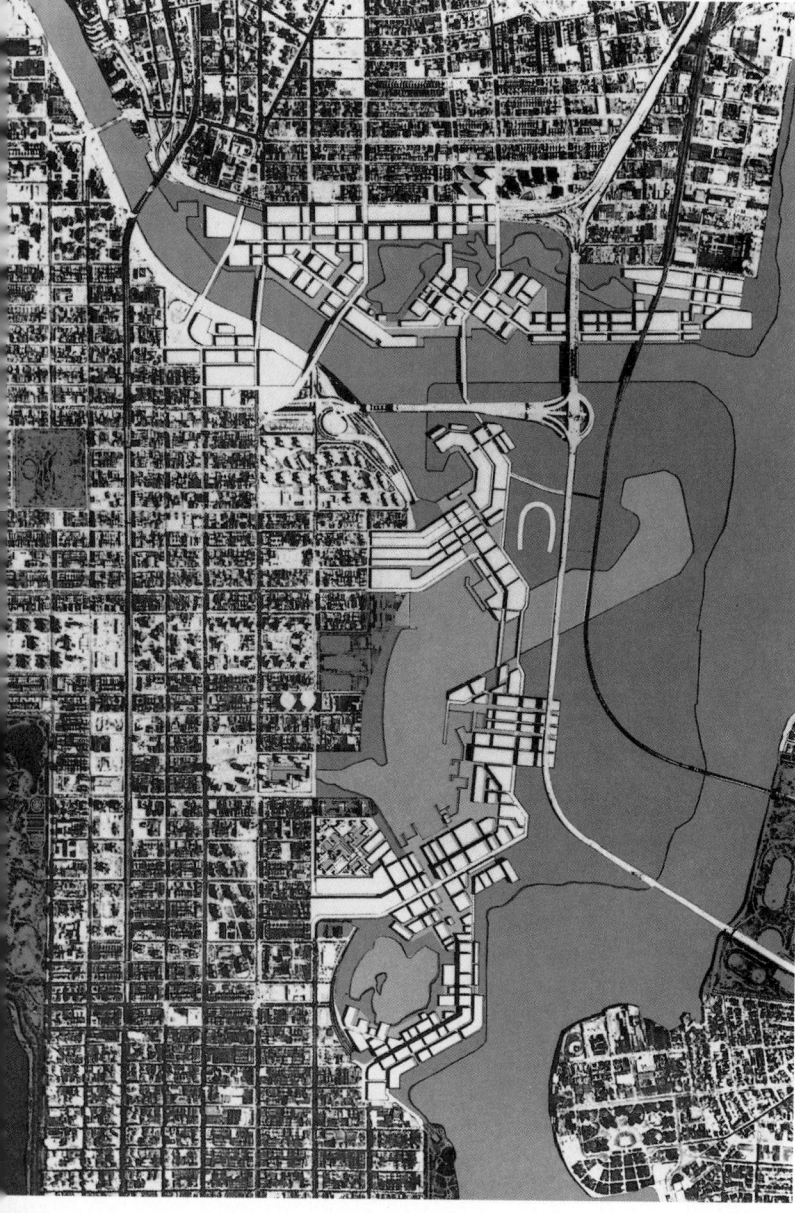

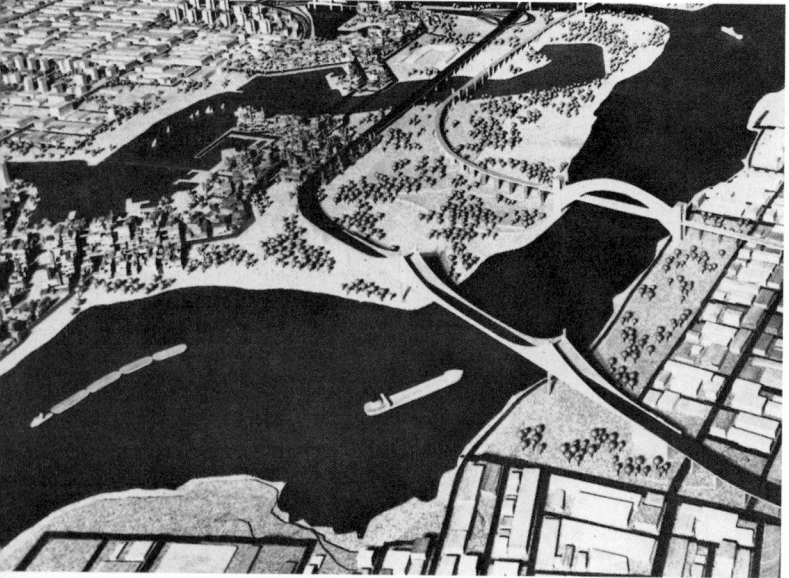

also able to refine his designs for the tunnel so that the project could be realized more incrementally. A new plan was prepared for a pilot segment, extending from 110th to 122nd Street, that would have resulted in smaller buildings and smaller blocks to create greater variety and more intimate scale. But due to a lack of funds, this proposal was never realized.

In addition to documentation of the four schemes, the exhibition catalogue included a proposal, identified as Project for a Community of 150,000 and also known as the Third City, designed by Philip Johnson in 1966.[26] Dramatically turning its back on local building traditions and the surrounding urban fabric, the project epitomized the type of large-scale, idealistic plan that many members of the Harlem community were increasingly coming to loathe and fear. The project constituted a virtual city-within-a-city, occupying a roughly triangular site bounded by Lenox Avenue and the Harlem River, 116th and 135th streets, with south and west borders each approximately a mile long. The plan was based on the notion that predictability rather than flexibility was the most effective foundation of urban planning, squarely rejecting the idea of an ever-expandable "linear city" in favor of a Renaissance-type fortification. Ringed by a continuous line of twenty-story apartment building slabs, the entire development was raised above the existing street grid by means of pedestrian bridges and plazas; minimal motor traffic would be permitted on the newly created street grid above. Inside the community's "walls" would be low-rise structures, most of them seven-story apartment buildings incorporating generously scaled interior courtyards. In contrast to this low-lying cityscape, a twin-towered office complex located near the development's center, above the intersection of Fifth Avenue and 125th Street, was to rise 150 stories. Surrounded by parkland and public buildings, the skyscraper, to be the world's tallest, would provide a dramatic landmark for the community, widely visible beyond the project's clearly demarcated confines. While Mt. Morris Park was to be retained, virtually every other trace of the existing urban fabric was to be erased. The provocative scheme was never realized, which came as no surprise to Johnson. As the architect said in 1976: "The purpose of the Third City exercise was to investigate the effect of super skyscrapers constructed over an existing public transportation node surrounded by low- and medium-rise blocks built on existing street grids. In other words, how to recondition a city in a grand way. It was not a realistic exercise."[27]

By the mid-1970s all of Harlem seemed to be languishing, the militantism of the mid-1960s having collapsed in the face of a seemingly insurmountable, grinding poverty. In 1974, as the New York State Urban Development Corporation prepared to undertake a ten-year plan for Harlem that would have resulted in the construction or rehabilitation of over 50,000 apartments, it commissioned the pollster Louis Harris to survey the area. The result of that poll, "Living in Harlem: A Survey of Residents' Attitudes," confirmed that the prevailing mood was one of hopelessness. According to Harris, most Harlem residents felt their neighborhood's problems were worse than those of the city in general and that that they lived in Harlem because they "had no other real choice."[28] The promised land for generations of ambitious rural blacks had become the dumping ground for the least fortunate, many of whom had been relocated to Harlem from elsewhere to make way for new construction. Clearly, what had once been the cultural capital of the black world was in disarray, demonstrated not only by the area's declining spirit but also by its decreasing population: in 1950, 772,000 people lived in Harlem; in 1970, there were 564,000.

But not all was bleak. By the mid-1970s increased prosperity for at least some blacks, combined with the "brownstone fever" that ran rampant throughout the city, together sparked the middle-class black gentrification of parts of Harlem, particularly Hamilton Heights, with its fine housing stock. As journalist Lena Williams reported in the *New York Times* in 1976: "While many blacks think of Harlem only as a place characterized by overcrowded tenements, garbage-filled streets and a high crime rate, a small but growing number of black middle-class families have been moving into the area in the last three or four years."[29] In addition to comparatively affordable rowhouses, Harlem offered the opportunity to live in the nation's most important black community, a factor that attracted public figures such as Eleanor Holmes Norton, then New York City's Human Rights Commissioner, and numerous professionals. As one Hamilton Heights homeowner, high school principal Benjamin Grant, put it, "We wanted to show people, especially the young kids, that Harlem does have a future; that there are some positive influences here, if only blacks would take advantage of them."[30]

EAST HARLEM

Although East Harlem, bounded by the Harlem and East rivers on the north and east, and by Ninety-sixth Street and Park Avenue on the south and west, began the postwar period as a neighborhood populated primarily by Italian-Americans, it was soon dominated by Hispanics.[1] The area's ethnic transformation, its simultaneous degeneration into one of the city's most deteriorated slums and subsequent efforts to improve the neighborhood, were among the most dramatic episodes in the history of postwar American urbanism. In 1950 the boundaries of Spanish or Puerto Rican Harlem, also known, particularly to area residents, as El Barrio, were generally considered to be Ninety-sixth and 120th streets, and Park and Third avenues. West of Park lay black Harlem; east of Third was Italian Harlem. In 1930 only 15,000 Puerto Ricans lived in East Harlem, but with the growth of economic opportunity spurred by war preparations in the late 1930s and full mobilization in the early 1940s, the rate of immigration swelled dramatically; by 1949 roughly 250,000 Puerto Ricans were said to be living in the area. The rate of immigration from Puerto Rico to New York reached its peak in the late 1940s, when about 1,000 newcomers arrived per week, an influx reported to be second in number only to that of Jews migrating to Israel.[2] The influx of poor, ill-educated Puerto Ricans, many from rural backgrounds, exacerbated the area's decline, but the problems had been there for years. In 1942, when East Harlem was inhabited by a lively—though tense—mix of Puerto Ricans, blacks and Italian-Americans, it was already deemed dangerously rundown and overcrowded, with 20 percent of Manhattan's entire population living within its confines, an area that constituted only 10 percent of the island's acreage.[3] Health and social conditions were worse in Spanish Harlem than anywhere else in New York. According to the editors of *Time*, reporting in 1950, 30 percent of the city's Puerto Ricans received some form of welfare, and fifteen to twenty-five babies in Spanish Harlem were bitten by rats each week.[4]

East Ninety-sixth Street was the area's definitive southern boundary. In one of the city's most dramatic contrasts, the street divided not only whites from nonwhites, but some of the city's richest residents from some of its poorest. On a visit to the city in 1964, the writer V. S. Pritchett captured the significance of the

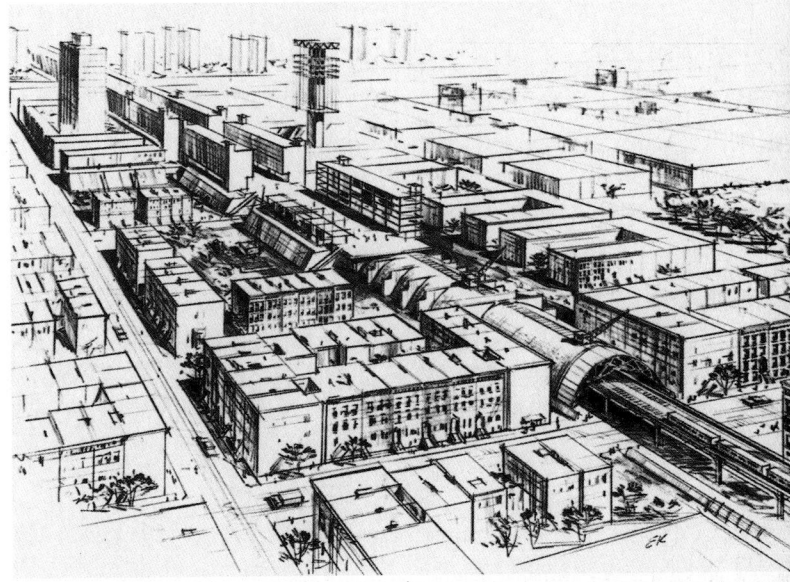

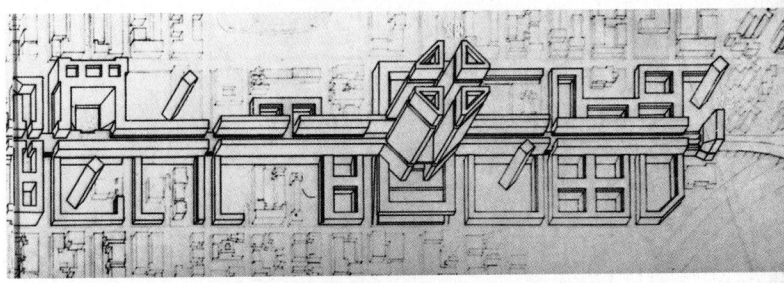

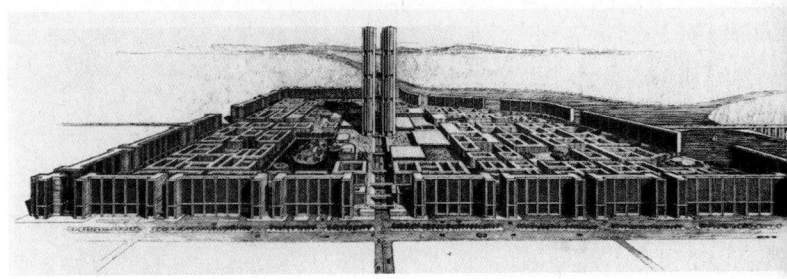

Top left: Proposal for East River, Ward's Island and Randall's Island. Stanford Anderson, Robert Goodman and Henry A. Millon, 1967. Photographic montage. MOMA

Bottom left: Proposal for East River, Ward's Island and Randall's Island. Model. View to the northwest. MOMA

Top: Proposal for elevated Park Avenue viaduct above East Ninety-seventh Street. Jaquelin T. Robertson, Richard Weinstein, Giovanni Pasanella, Jonathan Barnett and Myles Weintraub, assisted by Benjamin Mendelsund, George Terrien and Paul Wang, 1967. Rendering of view to the northeast. MOMA

Center: Proposal for elevated Park Avenue viaduct. Axonometric. MOMA

Bottom: Third City proposal. Philip Johnson, 1966. Rendering of view to the north. PJA

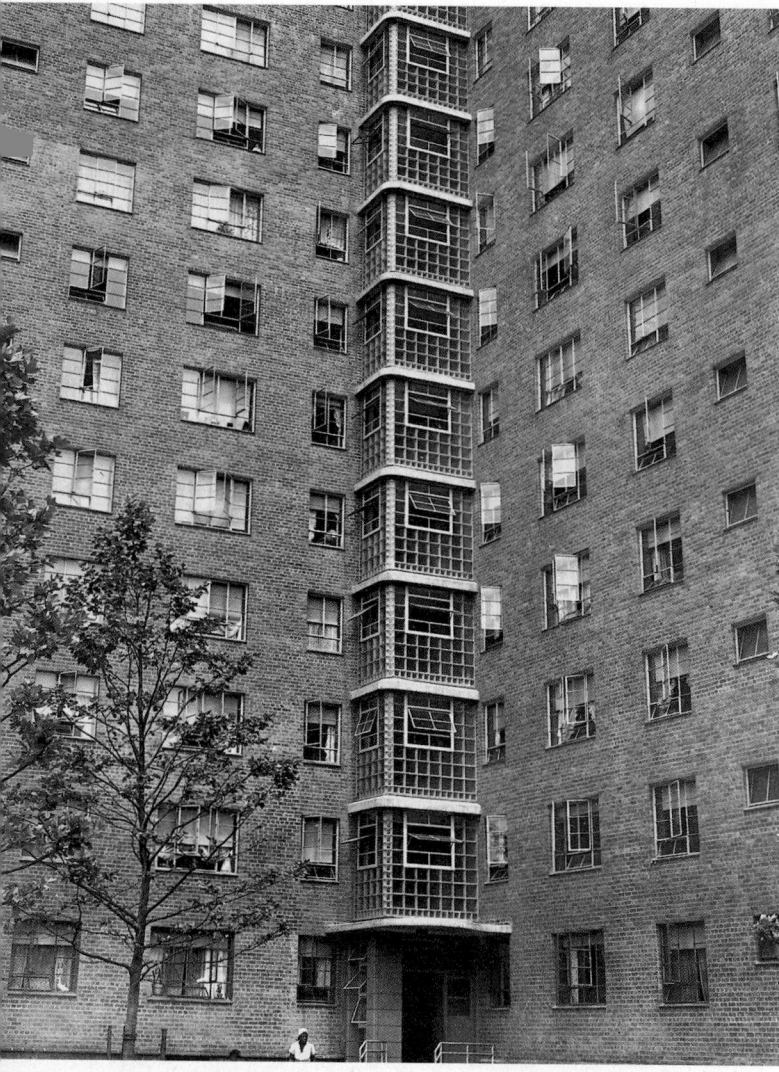

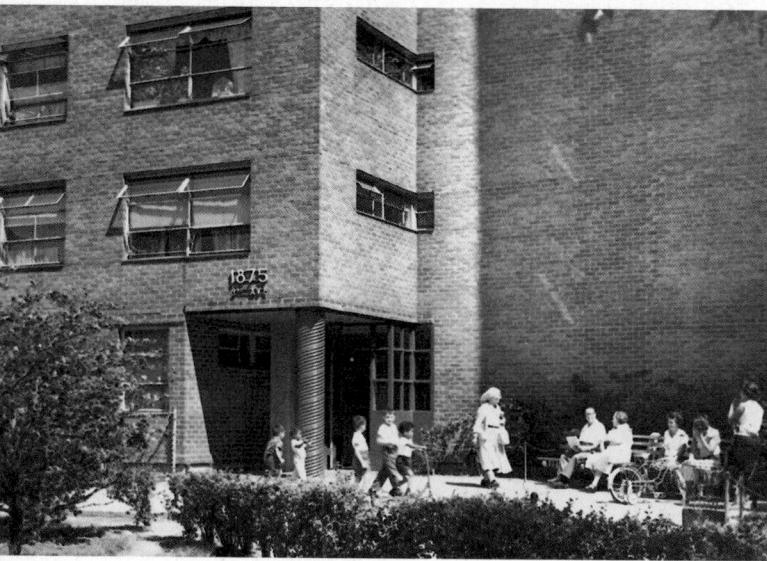

Top: James Weldon Johnson Houses, Park to Third Avenue, East 112th to East 115th Street. Julian Whittlesey, Harry M. Prince and Robert J. Reiley, 1947. NYCHA

Bottom: George Washington Houses, Second to Third Avenue, East Ninety-seventh to East 104th Street. Hopkins & Associates, 1954. NYCHA

boundary: "The street is nothing less . . . than Manhattan's Berlin Wall. You stare across it as you stare over the wire at checkpoint Charlie into East Berlin, into another dispensation. You are staring into the Caribbean and Africa. You stand on wealthy ground staring at poverty; and wealth and poverty have this in common: the first sight of both is frightening."[5] Fifteen years later the situation was little changed. As Paul Goldberger noted:

> There is perhaps no other place in the United States where the necessity of tolerance is made so visible as the intersection of Park Avenue and 96th Street, for there is no other place in which the very rich live in such proximity to the very poor without a hint of the middle-class buffer upon which they both depend. . . . The view from expensive cooperative apartments is one of tenements, and the view from tenements is one of luxury, and the two exist in a cautious state of détente.[6]

Most of the postwar construction in East Harlem addressed the urgent need for decent housing. Unlike other parts of the city, such as Central Harlem, that were now home to the underprivileged, East Harlem had never been a middle-class enclave and had no significant residue of high-quality housing stock. After 1945 the area became a principal target of Robert Moses's slum clearance program. Ground was broken in June 1946 for the James Weldon Johnson Houses, a 1,300-family project located on a 10.5-acre superblock between 112th and 115th streets, Park and Third avenues.[7] First planned in 1943 and completed in 1947, the project was named for the founder of the National Association for the Advancement of Colored People (NAACP). The architects of the project, Julian Whittlesey, Harry M. Prince and Robert J. Reiley, tried to relieve the uniformity of the red-brick complex of six- and fourteen-story irregularly shaped, multiwinged towers by using glass brick to light the emergency staircases and providing setbacks at the ends of the top four floors of the buildings. The site plan, including a landscaped plaza and small courts, was also somewhat more composed than that of the typical public housing project. Lewis Mumford felt, though, that such modifications did not in any way alter the buildings' "grimness," their "inhuman scale" or their "barracks-like air."[8]

In the 1950s vast areas of East Harlem were rebuilt as public housing projects. James Berlinger's Lexington Houses (1950) accommodated approximately 400 families on a site bisected by Lexington Avenue and stretching from Park to Third Avenue and Ninety-eighth to Ninety-ninth Street.[9] Hopkins & Associates' George Washington Houses (1954) divided a site between Second and Third avenues, Ninety-seventh and 104th streets, into three superblocks accommodating 1,515 families.[10] The plan of this complex of fourteen slabs, each twelve or fourteen stories tall, was based on ideal solar orientation. But the results, a phalanx of slabs skewed off the Manhattan grid, constituted one of the most hostile confrontations between traditional city fabric and new development in the postwar era. The individual buildings were predictably bland and uniform, although some visual relief was provided at the entrances. By comparison, the Senator Robert F. Wagner, Sr. Houses (Starrett & Van Vleck in association with Reginald E. Marsh Associates, 1956), bounded by Second Avenue, the Franklin Delano Roosevelt (FDR) Drive, 120th and 124th streets and housing 2,158 families in twenty-two buildings, was quiet, even cozy.[11]

Holden, Egan, Wilson & Corser's 1,250-family Benjamin Franklin Houses (1959), occupying a superblock site bounded by 106th and 108th streets, First and Third avenues, and traversed only by Second Avenue, was built by the Housing Authority as subsidized public housing, but in 1962 community groups transformed the apartment towers, renamed Franklin Plaza, into cooperatives.[12] The use of slender towers rather than the typical slabs managed to create an environment that conveyed the positive values of the open city in a way few postwar projects had. In 1964 Mayer & Whittlesey sensitively redesigned the outdoor public spaces, defining a pedestrian street running between First and Third avenues, as well as creating lushly landscaped recreation areas for both children and adults.[13] Wilson Houses (Pomerance & Breines, 1961), three buildings occupying a site bounded by First Avenue and the FDR Drive, 105th and 106th streets, furthered the transformation of the East River waterfront into a floating world of public housing towers and slabs set in a nearly continuous landscape of trees, walkways and small playgrounds.[14]

Jefferson Houses (Brown & Guenther, 1959), occupying a superblock bounded by First and Second avenues, 112th and 115th streets, a site penetrated by a single cul-de-sac, consisted of eighteen buildings ranging in height from seven to fourteen stories.[15] The project housed 1,495 families, many of them Italian-Americans who had resided in the area before the development was built. In 1960 the central space of Jefferson Houses was redesigned by Mayer, Whittlesey & Glass as the Gala East Harlem Plaza, complete with an open-air bandstand, spray and wading pools and brightly colored beach-type umbrellas in metal. The redesign reflected the belief of many planners that barren plazas were a poor and sometimes dangerous interpretation of the high-minded towers-in-the-park *parti*.

Almost from the beginning of the postwar period, the dramatic physical transformation of East Harlem in accord with the new urban ideal of isolated towers set within near-continuous landscaped open space had raised questions among planners and public interest groups. In 1950 the Citizens' Housing and Planning Council devoted most of its July newsletter to the "challenge" posed by the area. "What will East Harlem be like in 1975?" one article asked. "Will it be an area with wide thoroughfares, parks, adequate schools, health and community services, and housing for various income groups and for people of different races? Will it be an uncoordinated collection of community facilities and of public housing projects tenanted by low-income Negroes and Puerto Ricans?" While the council did not question the value of the new urbanism, the group voiced concern that the area was being redeveloped on a piecemeal basis with no overall plan and no attempt to provide significant parks, public space or community facilities: "By the haphazard placing of improvements . . . a neighborhood picture will be created which will look like pieces of a jigsaw puzzle that just don't fit together."[16] Moreover, the organization feared that the new housing projects only reinforced the area's racial homogeneity, institutionalizing the black and Puerto Rican ghetto on a long-term basis.

In 1957, when the *New York Times* reported on East Harlem's redevelopment, the character of the new work was not brought into question:

The biggest concentration of public housing projects in the city is cutting a swath through Harlem. In a mass attack on one of the worst slum areas in the metropolitan area, the New York City Housing Authority is leveling 137 acres of slums. Hardly a street from Madison Avenue to the East River, between 97th and 115th streets, has been left untouched. Blocks of old, dark buildings have been ripped out, letting in sunlight and air. . . . Twelve projects, providing new homes for 13,500 families—some 53,000 persons—are taking the place of decayed and overcrowded buildings. Most of them take in and consolidate

two to six or seven adjacent city blocks, forming a superblock. The Housing Authority finds the superblock projects make planning, construction and management more economical and efficient. In addition, the buildings can be widely spaced, exposing them to sunshine and air on all sides; and much of the open space can be landscaped and part of it used for playgrounds and off-street parking.[17]

Though the editors of the *New York Times* were slow to realize the limitations of the bulldozer approach, they did begin to take a more critical view of the areas left behind by the renewal process. In this they were stimulated in part by social activists who began to focus public attention on the living conditions in the remaining historical neighborhood fabric, the urbanistic limbo the projects created for the intervening tenement-lined streets. In 1962 East 100th Street between First and Second avenues, a kind of oasis of unredeemed slumdom, was declared "the worst block" in the city by a *Times* reporter.[18] By that time, though, the prevailing planning philosophy had begun to change and the block was designated a "pilot block" for renewal rather than redevelopment. Landlords were enlisted to cooperate with city officals in removing code violations, and only the worst buildings were to be designated for demolition. Serving as a powerful symbol of urban decay, the block was visited by national politicans concerned with the plight of cities, including Governor Mark Hatfield of Oregon (in 1960), Senator Thomas Dodd of Connecticut (in 1962) and Senator Robert F. Kennedy of New York (in 1965), as well as Mayor Wagner and other local officials and politicians. It had been brought to national attention by Woody Klein, a reporter, who went on to write a book about the block in 1964, *Let in the Sun*, which focused on the house at 311 East 100th Street.[19] Forty feet wide, eighty-seven feet deep and sixty-one feet tall, with a crudely ornamented facade laced with iron fire escapes, the building had been broken up into thirty-three minuscule apartments. In December 1961 number 311 was the focal point for an NBC television film documentary prepared for "David Brinkley's Journal" by Ted Yates, assisted by Klein, and in 1964 it was listed by the city's Department of Buildings as one of the ten worst slum buildings in New York, although there were thousands of vastly overcrowded tenements in the city that were not much better.[20]

In April 1964 number 311 was declared dead by its community, its passing marked with a funeral procession on 100th and 101st streets. As a local clergyman put it, number 311 and three equally dilapidated buildings "had been abandoned by their landlords and the buildings themselves are dead as far as services are concerned."[21] Between June 25, 1964, when the city took over the building under its receivership law, and January 1, 1966, over $15,000 in repairs were made. In 1966–67, when Klein was working for the city's Housing and Development Administration, another $12,000 was spent on the building, bringing the cost of repairs to "about half the purchase price for a fashionable, renovated brownstone." Yet despite all efforts, the building remained a largely undesirable property, not, as Klein put it, "the kind of decent home we in city government would like to see for every New Yorker."[22]

By the late 1960s it was becoming clear that community groups in places like East Harlem were no longer willing to accept large-scale redevelopment and were prepared to move in small increments, working with what they had, no matter the cost. A successful attempt at small-scale redevelopment was realized in 1966 when the U.S. Gypsum Company, the world's largest building-materials concern, completed the renovation of six tenements located on 102nd Street between First and Second avenues.[23] U.S. Gypsum purchased the buildings, gutted them and rebuilt the interiors in an aesthetically straightforward style; the facades were left intact. Many of the rehabilitated units were rented to the original tenants at increased but still affordable rates. The project came in on budget, costing half of the $22,500 per unit typical of a new public housing project; to finance the renovation U.S. Gypsum had secured low-interest federal financing and municipal tax abatements. The company eventually sold the renovated buildings to Metro East Housing, a non-profit neighborhood organization. Perhaps the most outstanding feature of the renovation was the very fact of its completion. Zion R. Paige, a longtime resident of one of the buildings, said that when the project manager approached the tenants, "he had three strikes against him. He was white, he was with a big company, and he was telling a story. Everybody around here has heard a story. This neighborhood has been politically exploited. But [he] delivered. Gypsum is now accepted and respected."[24]

In 1963 a new approach to large-scale slum-area redevelopment was clearly manifest when the city's Housing and Redevelopment Board joined with the Ruberoid Company to sponsor a competition for the design of twelve largely uninhabited acres between 107th and 111th streets, stretching from First Avenue to the FDR Drive.[25] The location was one of the few remaining industrial sites along the East River, a vestige of the area's history as a manufacturing and warehousing district. The jury for the competition consisted of Sir Leslie Martin, an influential British architect; New York designer and planner Albert Mayer; Harry Weese, the Chicago-based architect; Herbert Gans, the sociologist; David A. Crane, the director of land planning and design of the Boston Redevelopment Authority; Lewis E. Kitchen, a Kansas City realtor; and Milton Mollen, the chairman of the New York City Housing and Redevelopment Board. B. Sumner Gruzen served as professional adviser. The competition was organized in two classes—one for professionals and one for students—a traditional feature of the Ruberoid competitions, of which this was the fifth in a series. The competition called for 1,500 units of varying size, with approximately 15 square feet of storage space per apartment; approximately 8,000 square feet of community activity space; 30,000 square feet of retail and professional space; children's play areas; and 750 on-site parking spaces. The program also suggested uses for the East River waterfront across the FDR Drive from the housing project site. Two of the student submissions—one by Michael Wurmfeld of Princeton, the other by Philip Shive, Woodrow Wilson Jones, Jr., and Garrard Raymond of North Carolina State College—were notable for their boldly sculptural forms, although both employed a superslab to close the new development off from the troubled East Harlem neighborhood to the west. This approach was also adopted by Hanford Yang and Amiel Vassilovski, the designers of Pedersen & Tilney's submission in the professional category.

The winning professional scheme, designed by Thomas Hodne of Hodne Associates, a Minneapolis firm, offered a significant alternative, inspired by the ideas of Jane Jacobs. Rejecting both the superslabs favored by so many architects and the isolated towers-in-the-park that were stereotypical of New York's public housing, Hodne's proposal devoted most of the site to five- and six-story buildings that would complement the scale of the surrounding neighborhood. To achieve the requisite 125-unit-per-acre density, he called for four twenty-story slender towers to be built along the FDR Drive. Unlike typical superblocking, Hodne's design retained the existing crosstown

streets as shop-lined pedestrian access routes through the site, thereby maintaining the traditional connections of the upland neighborhood to the riverfront. Also interesting was the second-prize scheme by Edvin Stromsten, Ricardo Scofidio and Felix Martorano. The Stromsten team proposed a community of high-density low-rise buildings, with parking integrated within the structures. The jury deemed their scheme the "least like public housing . . . a fresh and most radical approach."[26]

Amazingly, the competition winners were retained by the city and their project was put into the housing "pipeline," although it would not emerge until twelve years later, by which time it had been completely redesigned as 1199 Plaza.[27] The project's progress was bogged down for lack of a sponsor until 1968, when at last the city found one: Local 1199 of the Drug and Hospital Worker's Union, which could take advantage of the Mitchell-Lama low-interest mortgage program as well as tax abatements available for middle-income cooperative housing. In addition, the union could qualify for federal funding that would permit some of the project's units to be further subsidized for moderate-income families. But in the five years since the scheme had been designed, the high ideals of its open site plan had been tainted by the growing psychology of fear, which, as the critic Suzanne Stephens put it, led to the desire for "restricted points of access to the housing: something the penetration of the street grid wouldn't accomplish." In addition, the sponsors and community representatives felt that the apartments in the low-rise buildings would be dark, and they complained that river views would be denied to many families. Objecting, in short, to the very contextuality that was the project's strength, they were seeking, as Stephens pointed out, "image and identifiability, a visible affirmation of the community's sense of pride and upwardly mobile aspirations. High-rise housing was more clearly and positively associated in their minds with the luxury apartment buildings in the rest of Manhattan."[28]

In response, Hodne/Stageberg Partners (as the firm was now called) redesigned the project, housing 1,600 families in four towers that rose to thirty-one stories along the site's western borders but stepped down to form lower east-west wings defining U-shaped private courtyards opening toward the river. One key feature of the original plan was retained in the final complex, which was completed in 1975: the four tower-courtyard buildings were treated as independent "blocks" so that the cross streets extended through the site visually if not actually. In addition, the middle of the three towers placed along First Avenue (the fourth was set midblock behind an existing industrial building) was set back to form a shop-lined entrance plaza. Though the planning and massing of the complex may have been enlightened, the brown-brick exteriors of the buildings were somewhat grim. Nonetheless, a syncopated rhythm of recessed and cantilevered balconies helped relieve the mass, while the complex skyline silhouette, as well as the inflection of the towers toward the southeast to exploit river views, resulted in a surprisingly lively effect.

In 1968 the city, spurred to action by Community Planning Board 11, hired the Moroccan-born, French-educated social activist and architect Roger Katan, assisted by Serge François and Douglas Kourves, to conduct a feasibility study for the redevelopment of 116th Street between Fifth Avenue and the East River.[29] Katan, who had moved to Harlem in 1964, proposed to build a two-level covered shopping arcade along 116th Street between Madison and Third avenues and an elevated industrial strip development above the New York Central's Park Avenue railroad tracks. The section of 116th Street between Third and Pleasant avenues was to be redeveloped as a residential district;

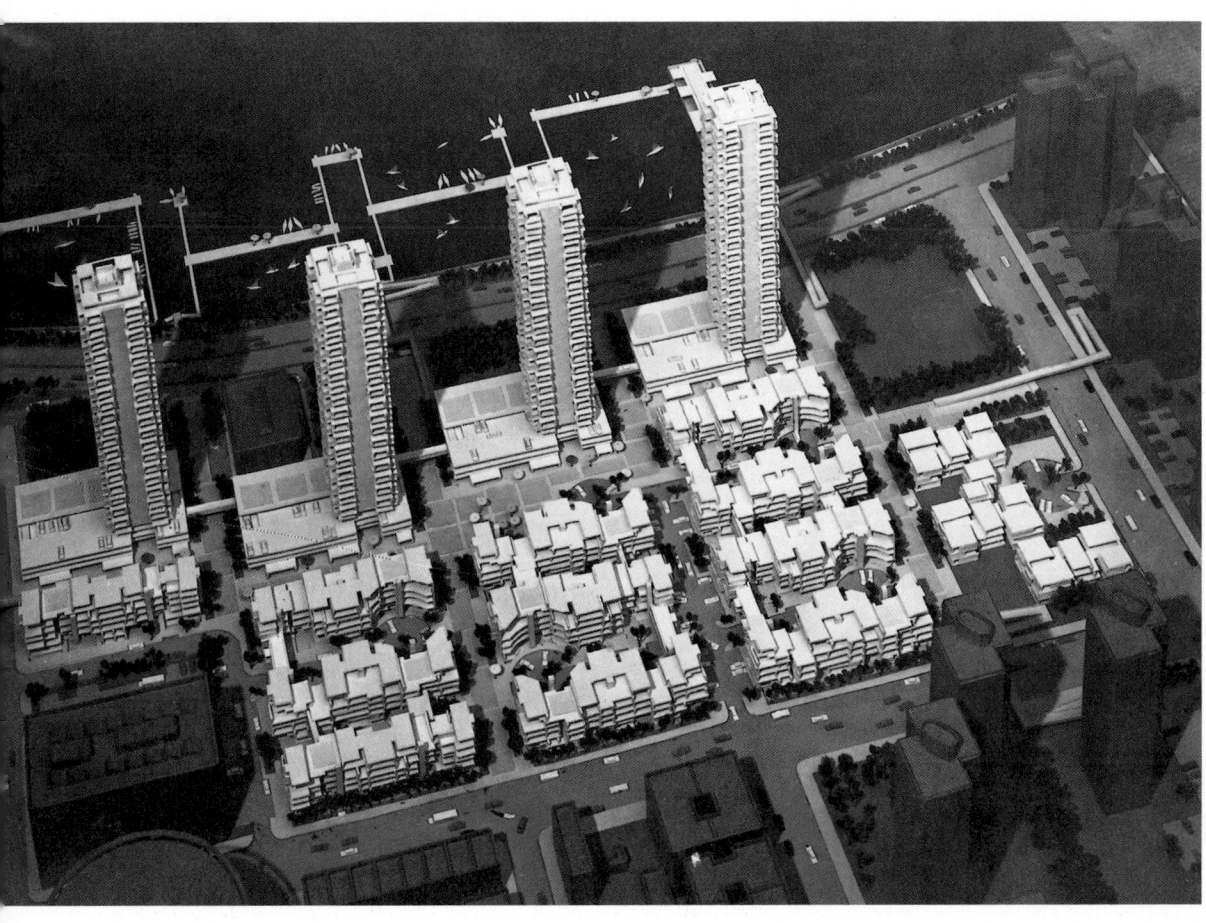

Left: Winning professional entry of Ruberoid competition, First Avenue to Franklin Delano Roosevelt Drive, East 107th to East 111th Street. Thomas Hodne, 1963. View to the southeast. THHO

Below: 1199 Plaza, First Avenue to Franklin Delano Roosevelt Drive, East 107th to East 111th Street. Hodne/Stageberg Partners, 1975. View to the northwest. ©Norman McGrath. NM

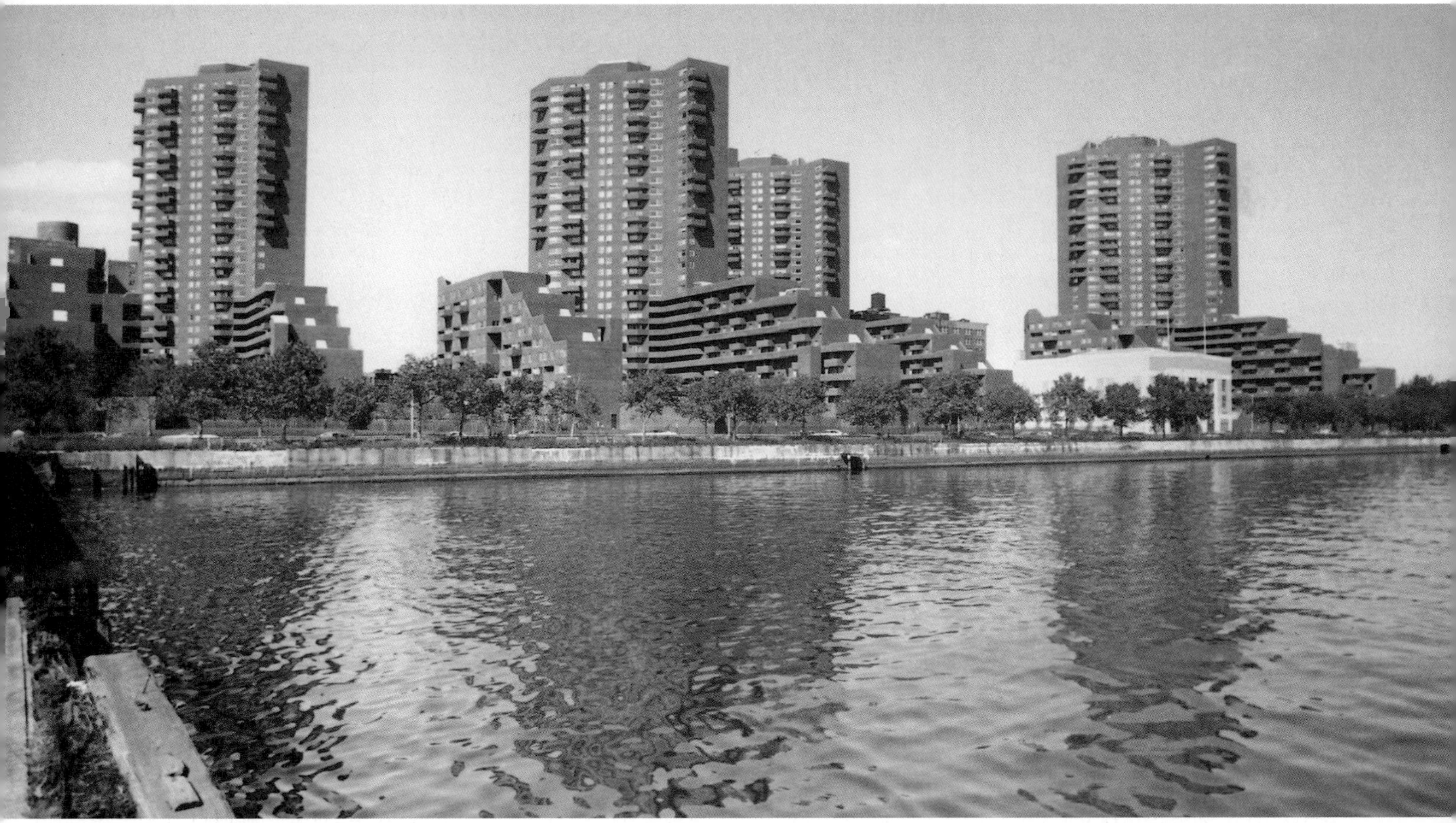

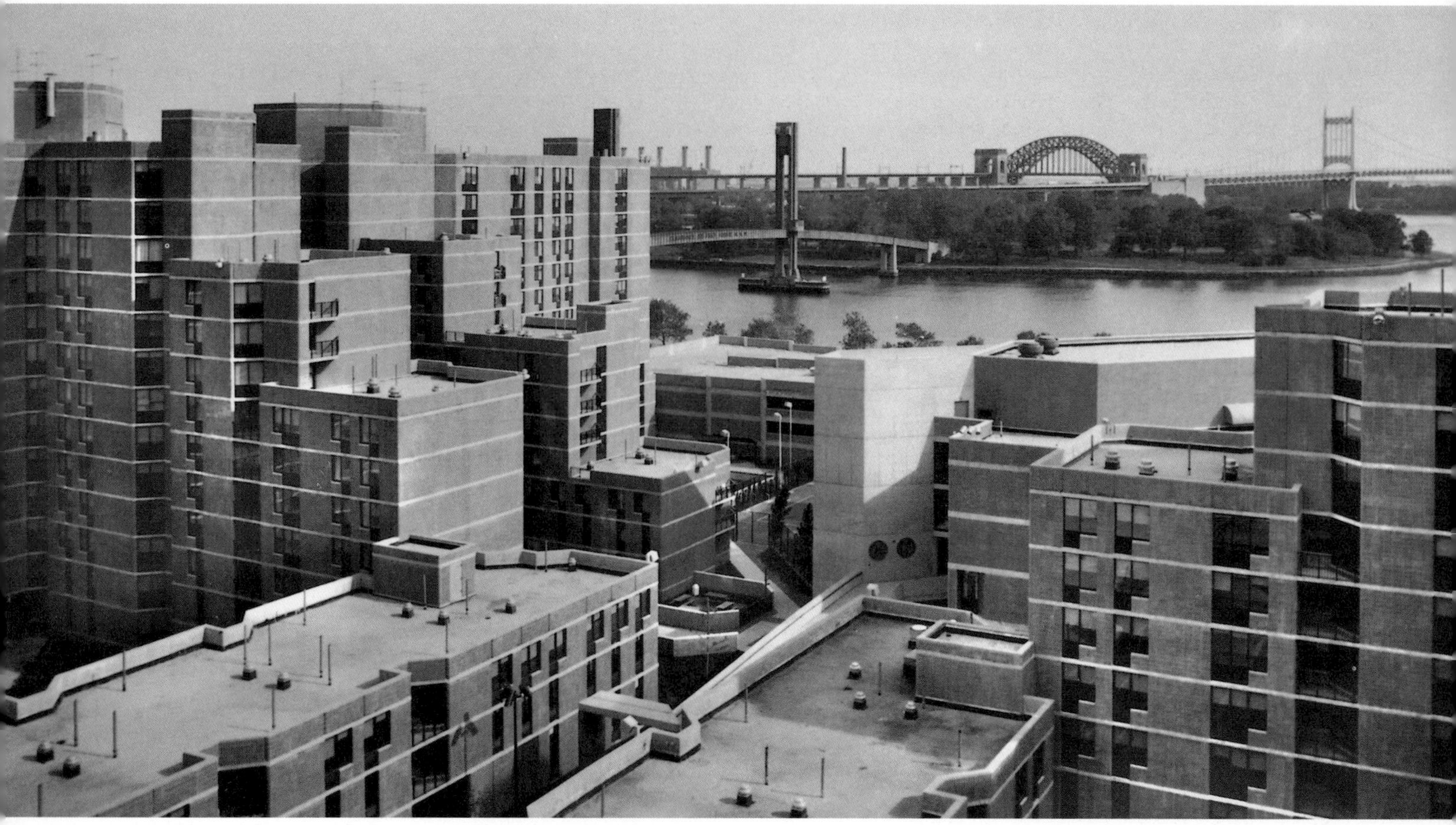

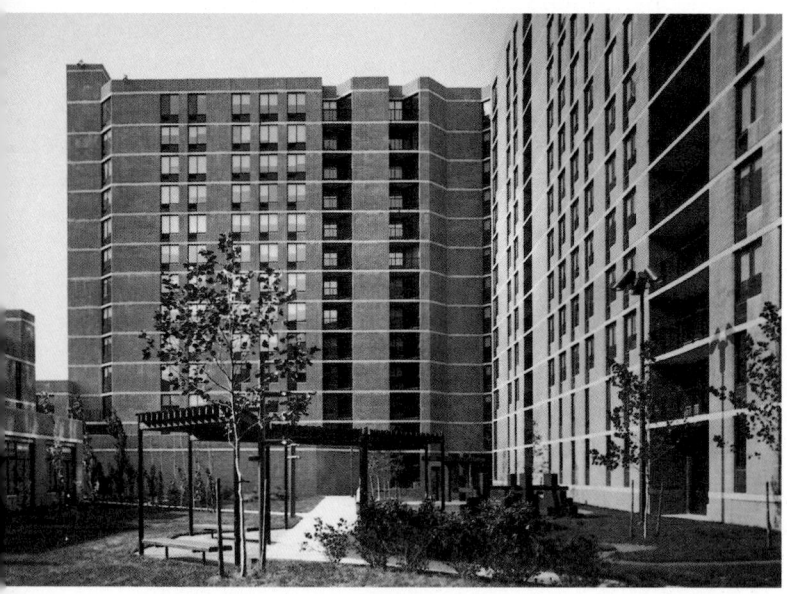

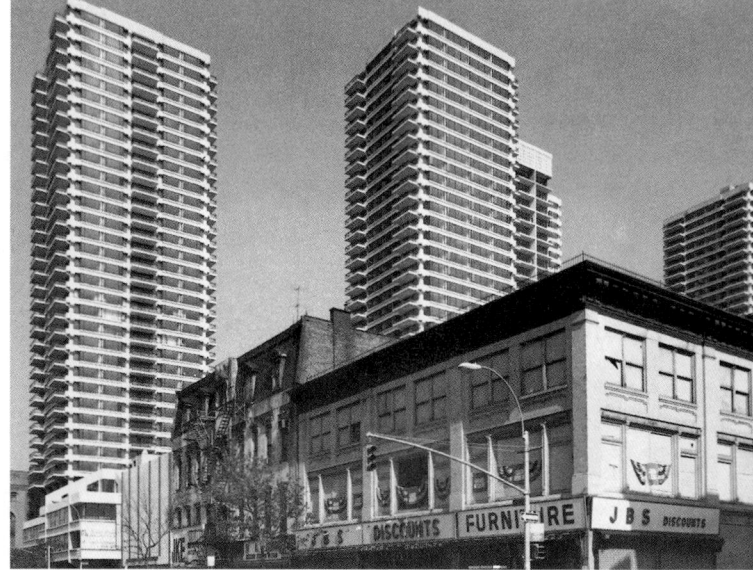

Top: Metro North Plaza/Riverview Apartments, First Avenue to Franklin Delano Roosevelt Drive, East 100th to East 102nd Street. Conklin & Rossant, 1976. View to the northeast. ©Norman McGrath. NM

Bottom left: Metro North Plaza/Riverview Apartments. ©Norman McGrath. NM

Bottom right: Taino Towers, Second to Third Avenue, East 122nd to East 123rd Street. Silverman & Cika, 1979. View to the northeast. Dunlap. DD although a high-rise apartment building housing elderly residents, community facilities, midblock plazas and an open-air café would be added, existing brownstones would also be retained. High- and low-rise new construction were to be mixed throughout the development, with slabs alternating with "pyramiding pueblo constructions," as Dorothy Kalins Wise called them in *New York* magazine.[30] Rising incrementally from street level, as if in ultimate fulfillment of the setback tendencies first encouraged by the pioneering zoning law of 1916, the pyramids utilized prefabricated elements that allowed for a great degree of individualized design on the part of different tenants.

The final element of Katan's proposals was the construction of a four-level stepped platform over the FDR Drive between 114th and 116th streets, from the grounds of the boldly scaled late-Georgian Benjamin Franklin High School (Eric Kebbon, 1941) to the East River.[31] The structure would serve as a riverside recreational complex, supporting shops, a restaurant, an outdoor skating rink, a theater and a playground, and terminating in a marina. Directly north of the proposed facility, fronting the river between 116th and 117th streets, stood the Washburn Wire Company factory, at the time Manhattan's largest industrial complex in terms of both physical size and number of workers. To accommodate the company's desire to expand without relocating out of the neighborhood, Katan proposed to build the enlarged factory out into the river on landfill and surmount the expansion with both low- and middle-income housing, along with recreational facilities. Despite efforts to gain the support of the Housing and Development Administration (HDA) and the New York State Urban Development Corporation (UDC), the ambitious plan was never realized.

The Metro North Plaza/Riverview Apartments (1976), designed by Conklin & Rossant, marked another serious attempt to create high-density housing without resorting to superscale slabs.[32] Jointly sponsored by the UDC and the New York City Educational Construction Fund, the complex occupied a site bounded by First Avenue, the FDR Drive, 100th and 102nd streets. Made of exposed cast-concrete structural frames filled in with ribbed concrete block, the project's five buildings varied in height from three to thirteen stories. A courtyard oriented east-west, and defined by two mirror-image U-shaped buildings and two slabs, terminated in a ramp leading to Public School 50, the Vito Marcantonio School (1975). Designed by the same architects, the school was stylistically consistent with the rest of the complex. Regrettably, the project's parking garage was the principal feature to face the FDR Drive.

Taino Towers, occupying the full-block site bounded by 122nd and 123rd streets, Second and Third avenues, was one of the most striking postwar additions to East Harlem and perhaps the most luxurious federally subsidized low-income housing ever built.[33] In 1965 the firm of Silverman & Cika approached the East Harlem Tenants' Committee about initiating a pilot housing project in an attempt to improve the area's deplorable housing conditions. The tenants' group insisted that the development incorporate extensive community facilities, which the architects agreed to. But even after Silverman & Cika obtained a guaranteed price from a contractor, S. S. Silberblatt, they were unable to get financial backing from city or state sources. The East Harlem Tenants' Committee then created a nonprofit corporation that secured a mortgage guaranteed by the Federal Housing Administration, promising to make the development New York's first low-income housing project to be owned and managed by its tenants. The Department of Housing and Urban Development also provided funds to reduce interest rates from 7 to 2 percent

and to subsidize rents in 40 percent of the apartments; municipal and federal sources, including the nationwide Model Cities progam, provided another $6 million. City land condemnation and tax abatements further stimulated development.

The project, named after a Caribbean Indian tribe, consisted of four thirty-five-story towers rising from six-story bases that helped define landscaped plazas and open spaces. The towers, of precast and poured-in-place white concrete, were wrapped in horizontal bands of floor-to-ceiling glass. Paul Goldberger contended that the buildings had balconies "detailed so well they look as if they could have been done by Skidmore, Owings & Merrill, and concrete corners detailed to look almost like heavy timber. What it all looks like is rich people's housing in Caracas, a vision of sophisticated Latin richness."[34] Suzanne Stephens, writing in *Progressive Architecture*, was somewhat more critical of the buildings' articulation, saying that although "the entire assemblage comes off rather elegantly," the "concrete spandrel bracket and corner elements fit together in a klutzily manneristic way."[35]

Stephens also commented on the importance of the towers' style: "If it borders on Miami Modern perhaps that was the point. That style, usually reserved for luxury condominiums, contains a particular meaning or association. It has become a significant form for large segments of the American public. This is what this community wanted and what they got."[36] While some members of the community may have been satisfied, the design's total repudiation of both the architecture and the urbanism of the surrounding area caused a disjunction that was no less damaging to the urban fabric than many far more conventional red-brick public housing slabs. As Goldberger noted, "the project's utter lack of relation to its context is disturbing—not the least of the reasons for this being that it gives the sense that the project's sponsors (and its architects) were taking as the basis for their design a total rejection of all that now exists in East Harlem."[37]

Even more than their sleek exteriors, Taino Towers were distinguished by their interior layouts and amenities. One tower contained only four apartments per floor, while another was composed of cleverly interlocking duplex units, some with up to six bedrooms and living rooms with eleven-foot-high ceilings. The buildings were equipped with central air conditioning, and most apartments contained a balcony. Public hallways and lobbies were clad in graffiti-resistant Italian tile. Laundry facilities were located on the roof of each building and were flanked by outdoor play areas, where parents could supervise their children while doing household chores. New York's first fully mechanized vacuum disposal equipment provided garbage removal at an annual savings to the city of $50,000.

Clustered in the complex's base was a staggering array of community facilities, occupying a total of 240,000 square feet; these included a health clinic, a day-care center, a job-training center, social centers for teenagers and the elderly, meeting rooms, art workrooms, a theater, an auditorium, an exhibition space and a swimming pool. An additional 30,000 square feet of space was reserved for commercial tenants. The project's sponsors relied on this potential rental revenue to help subsidize the low apartment rents, though many officials in city and state housing agencies questioned the viability of such an approach; in fact, the inclusion of such a large amount of nonresidential space had motivated both the HDA and the UDC to withhold financial support for the project. Overseeing Taino Towers' development was Robert Nichol, a former Presbyterian minister at an East Harlem church, who became the project's full-time head administrator. Nichol fought tenaciously for the project's amenities, aggressively combating those who charged that the project was inappropriate for low-income tenants. "It's a question of whether we have a viable city or go on building slums for the poor," Nichol argued. "I know we have been accused of over-designing for the poor, but we are concerned with changing people's lives, not just creating another future slum."[38] To help foster that change, tenants were required to attend three five-hour-long demonstrations on apartment and building maintenance.

Despite a surplus of good intentions, as well as what Stephens described as "a lot of chutzpah and persistence on the part of the architects and sponsoring group," the project stumbled.[39] After the start of construction in 1972, progress was stymied by bureaucratic entanglements; failure to rent the commercial space, including decisions by the Health Insurance Plan and the Board of Education to renege on prior commitments; and the recession of the mid-1970s. Although the towers were completed in 1979, many of the apartments stood empty until 1985, a costly and embarrassing reminder of the heady and overreaching optimism of the 1960s "war on poverty." By the time of the towers' completion, even the design of their facades seemed anachronistic: in light of the "energy crisis" following the Arab oil embargo of 1973–74, the floor-to-ceiling glazing struck many observers as not only extravagant but, in federally subsidized housing, patently irresponsible. In 1979 Goldberger would question not only the viability of Taino Towers as a paradigm but also its value to the community at all. The project, he said, was "far superior to the wretched boxes being passed off as 'luxury' housing to people downtown," but he noted, "how much good that will do for East Harlem remains doubtful."[40]

While it was the proliferation of large-scale housing developments that most profoundly transformed East Harlem, the area also witnessed the construction of numerous institutional buildings. The opening of the Machine and Metal Trades High School (1941), on the northwest corner of Ninety-sixth Street and First Avenue, reflected the demand for skilled labor to fuel the nation's war effort and the working-class character of the adjacent East Harlem community.[41] The school was housed in a three-story H-shaped facility designed by Eric Kebbon that effectively married Classical composition to Modernist details. Inside the building, which was the most heavily electrified high school in the city, traditional classrooms were largely replaced by factory-like workshops containing a full array of mechanical equipment. The historian and critic Talbot Hamlin was lavish in his praise of the school's design:

> Here is perhaps the most effective, even the most beautiful, of New York City schools built within recent years. The long horizontals of its First Avenue front and the simple patterning of its masses, the attractive studied feeling of all its details are an almost perfect expression of its problem. It is slightly factory-like, yet not at all a factory; it is slightly school-like, yet by no means the ordinary secondary school. The openness and horizontality of the windows of its shops somehow express the big areas within. The clean neatness of its detailing has some of the quality of good machines.[42]

Another notable public school building was Ballard, Todd & Snibbe's Public School 57 (1964), the James Weldon Johnson School, on the southwest corner of Third Avenue and 115th Street.[43] The school was a delicately scaled composition, with an overhanging cornice, small-paned windows and molded bricks, projecting a far more positive attitude toward the neighborhood's tenements and brownstones than that taken by the starkly minimalist Johnson Houses (see above) behind it.

In 1960 four East Harlem Protestant church groups occupying rather cramped, rundown former commercial spaces—examples of the so-called storefront congregations that dotted the area's streets and had become a distinctive symbol of both squalor and hope—banded together to build a new church.[44] The congregations had sought a new home more out of a sense of survival than a need to realize an architectural vision. As the pastor of the new church, the Reverend Charles Farrell, explained: "We weren't particularly unhappy with our storefronts. We considered them appropriate to the community and close to its problems. But already two storefronts were uprooted by renewal, and we knew the other two would get it soon. We were running out of cheap space to rent." The church was also inspired by a desire to demonstrate that the congregation was not likely to leave East Harlem for greener pastures. The congregation, Farrell said, "finally decided that it would be wise to have equity in the community."[45]

The new building, the Church of the Resurrection (1965), at 325 East 101st Street, between First and Second avenues, was a boldly sculptural, minimally embellished mass. The church was designed by Victor Lundy, who accepted the challenge of working within the confines of an 80-by-100-foot midblock site and a minuscule $200,000 budget. Assuming that the deteriorating tenements surrounding the site would eventually be replaced by middle- or high-rise projects, Lundy treated the building "as a piece of sculpture to be looked down upon from above." This verticality also served a practical purpose, fitting the building's requisite space within a tight envelope, as well as an ecclesiastical one, providing a metaphoric representation of spiritual aspiration or, as Lundy said, the quality of reaching "upward, toward the sky." The architect also sought to firmly establish the church's processional aspect, creating a carefully modulated series of interior spaces. With these goals in mind, Lundy said, the design process became "a tug of war between the inside and outside to make a unity."[46]

Lundy's original design called for a virtually windowless two-level building completely clad in brick, including the roof and the surrounding paving. The building's complexly composed, highly angular mass consisted of a square box, out of which emerged a diamond-shaped, steeply pitched roof that rose dramatically to its highest point in back, at the building's northwest corner. Inside, a long, upwardly inclined hallway took a circuitous route, with two 180-degree turns, from the recessed main entrance to the sanctuary. Lundy described the passageway as "an artificial hill or mountain, up which one slowly climbs in enclosed space to burst finally into the glowing, up reaching spaciousness of the sanctuary."[47] The second-level sanctuary was located beneath the "prow" formed by the building's angled walls and roof and was dramatically lighted by a partially concealed skylight. Carried on a concrete slab, the sanctuary was visible from the entrance through a glass partition. Although the building's basic spatial organization and massing were realized as planned, budgetary considerations necessitated several changes in materials. These included the replacement of the brick cladding—the original plan had called for the bricks to be placed vertically and the interstices studded with colored glass—with dark-colored concrete blocks, and the replacement of the brick roof with a far less expensive mineral surfacing material. One rather odd feature of the Church of the Resurrection as realized was the presence of a crack between some of the principal facade's concrete blocks. Although this seemed, as the critic James Bailey reported in *Architectural Forum*, "to be the result of sloppy workmanship," the gap was in fact internally glazed and functioned as a window for the pastor's office.[48]

Bailey praised the building for its role as a catalyst in the neighborhood's physical renaissance as well as "a powerful new symbol of hope." He also noted that the austere building "reflects the circumstances of those who worship in it: materially poor but, in Lundy's words, 'rich in the wealth of their emotions and involvement with life.'"[49] Paul Goldberger observed that although the design of the church could be seen as "poor man's Eero Saarinen—it strives toward drama at the expense of any obvious relationship to its context," it was saved by the fact that the form was not too theatrical. "One passes this church," Goldberger said, "convinced that the sculptural form is a correct choice for this situation. . . . It speaks strongly of the notion that a religious house should stand for a certain irrationality of form—how else to know it from its banal neighbors?"[50] Norval White and Elliot Willensky were far more critical of Lundy's design. While acknowledging that "its starkness was meant as a bold and powerful contrast" to the surrounding tenements, they found the result "contrived," "falling somewhere between a fallout shelter and a Maginot Line fortress."[51]

Several large medical facilities anchored East Harlem's southern boundary. Metropolitan Hospital, initially planned in 1945 as part of the city's postwar building program and completed ten years later on a site bounded by First and Second avenues, Ninety-seventh and Ninety-eighth streets, replaced a former facility on Welfare Island.[52] The new eighteen-story building, designed by Charles B. Meyers, was a moderately stylish Modernist essay clad in white brick; each floor of the minimally detailed building terminated in a glass-enclosed solariumlike room. In 1962 the Metropolitan Hospital complex added a new building, Meyers's Draper Hall, a nurses' residence, located on the west side of First Avenue at Ninety-eighth Street.[53] The fourteen-story building, clad in light gray brick and porcelain enamel, was intended to harmonize with the hospital across the street.

Mount Sinai Hospital's medical complex was concentrated on a superblock site bounded by Fifth and Madison avenues, Ninety-eighth and 101st streets, but the hospital maintained buildings on nearby blocks as well.[54] In the 1950s and 1960s the hospital erected a series of buildings that vastly expanded the complex's facilities and fortified its presence in the neighborhood, although they were rather banal essays in Modernist aesthetics, largely indistinguishable from the most mediocre postwar office and apartment buildings. The best of the new buildings were Kahn & Jacobs's nine-story Klingenstein Pavilion (1952), a maternity facility at 1176 Fifth Avenue,[55] and the firm's adjacent Atran Laboratory and Berg Institute for Research (1954), extending east to Madison Avenue.[56] Less satisfying were Eggers & Higgins's twelve-story Klingenstein Clinical Center (1962), a psychiatric facility at 1450 Madison Avenue;[57] and Brown & Guenther's List Nurses' Residence (1962), a twelve-story red-brick building at 3 East 101st Street.[58] The most distinguished of the lot was Pomerance & Breines's narrow, seventeen-story, balcony-studded Baum-Rothschild Staff Pavilion apartment tower (1967), at 1249 Park Avenue, on the southeast corner of Ninety-seventh Street.[59] The design added a lively if somewhat incongruous note to the avenue, mediating between the dominant uniformity of the stylistically restrained, Classical prewar luxury apartment buildings to the south and the tenements to the north.

In the early 1970s Mount Sinai succeeded in having the city demap Ninety-ninth and 100th streets, thus creating a site for its

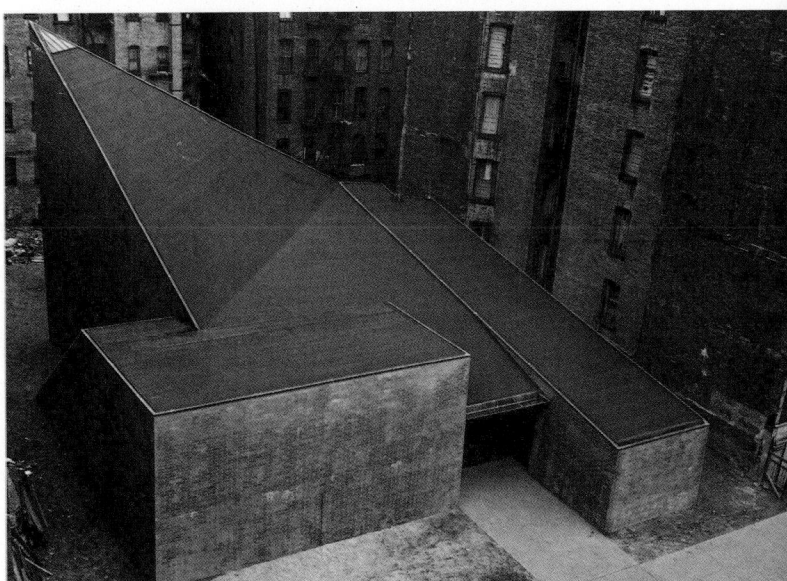

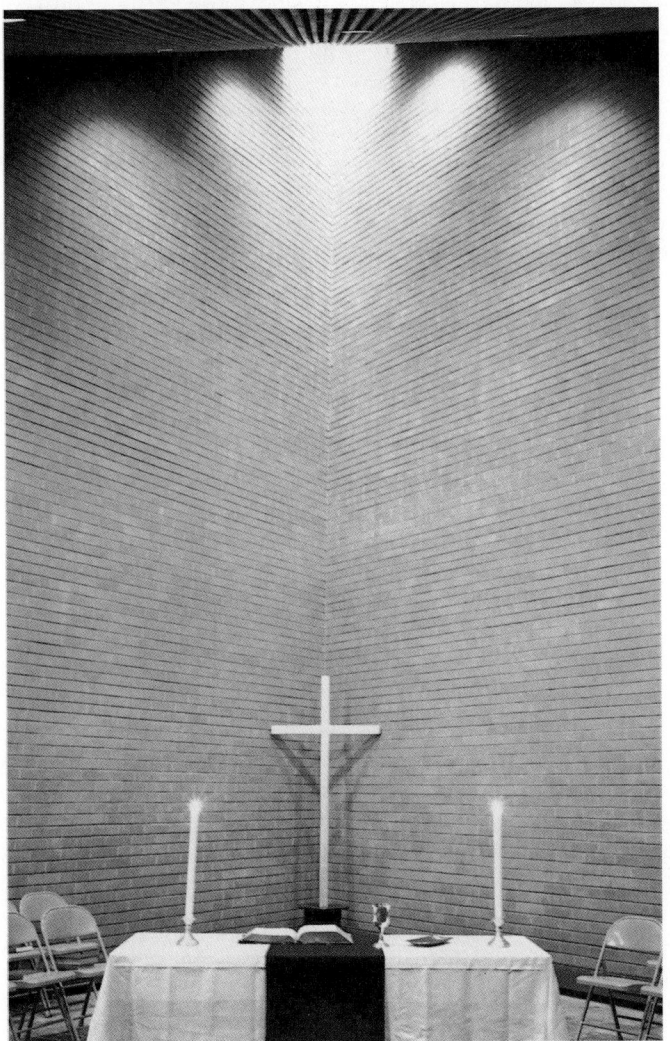

Top: Church of the Resurrection, 325 East 101st Street, between First and Second avenues. Victor Lundy, 1965. View to the northeast. Cserna. GC

Bottom: Church of the Resurrection. Sanctuary. Cserna. GC

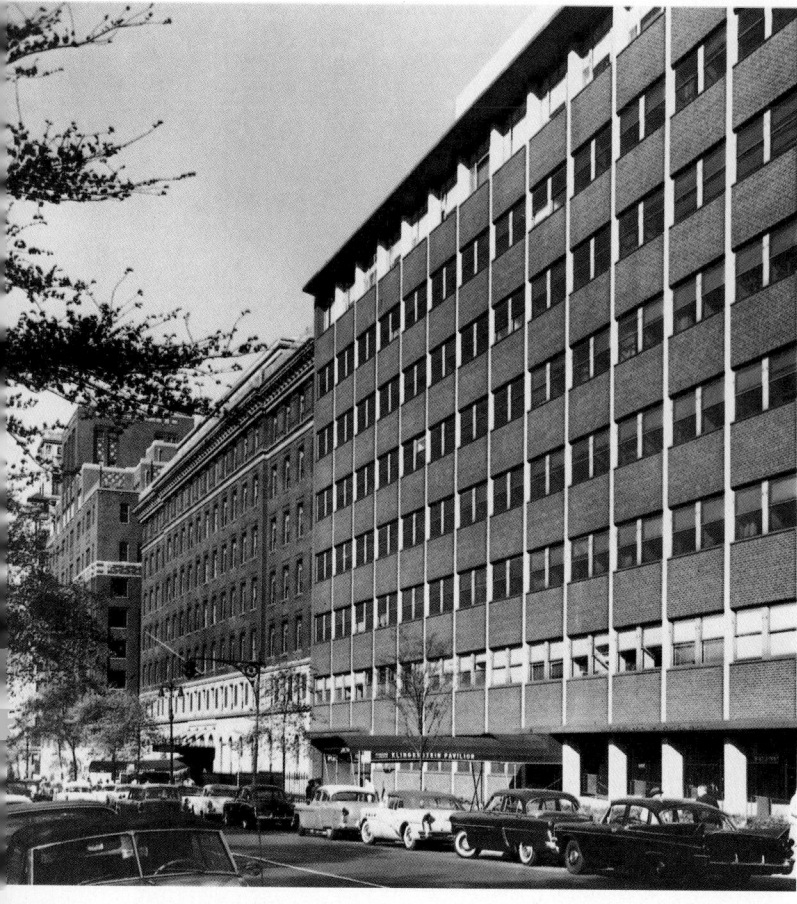

largest postwar addition, the thirty-one-story Annenberg Building (1974), which housed the Mount Sinai School of Medicine, founded in 1968.[60] Designed by Skidmore, Owings & Merrill, with Roy O. Allen serving as partner in charge of design, this behemoth of self-weathering Cor-ten steel and dark-tinted glass towered above its surroundings, a jarring and ominous intruder on the skyline when viewed from either Central Park or East Harlem. At ground level the building was no more benign, rising from a banal plaza relieved only by a sculpture by Arnaldo Pomodoro titled *Large Sphere* (1967).[61] Norval White and Elliot Willensky called the building "cadaverous."[62] Paul Goldberger was equally biting in his criticism:

> This is a mass so huge, so brutal, as to make everything around it seem pitiful and weak. One wonders if this building was in fact commissioned not by the hospital at all, but by the builders of some of the overblown high-rise apartment towers nearby, so as to make their own offenses pale by comparison. . . . In true Skidmore, Owings & Merrill fashion, this is a box, making no concessions whatsoever to anything around it, but bursting into the neighborhood and thrusting itself onto the skyline like the town bully.[63]

Another type of health-care facility, Exodus House (Smotrich & Platt, 1968), a drug treatment center located at 309 East 103rd Street, constituted, at a small scale, one of New York's premiere examples of the Brutalist aesthetic popularized by the English critic Reyner Banham.[64] The building had concrete-block facades sparingly punctuated by horizontal strip windows and expanses of glass, some set at an incline. A high wall pushed out to the lot line partially enclosed a side court. White and Willensky liked the "gutsy" Exodus House, which had "no fancy materials or details" and "no sanctimonious messages in its simple forms."[65] The center's building program also included the renovation of an adjacent tenement to be used as dormitory space. William N. Breger Associates' Florence Nightingale Nursing Home (1974), on the northwest corner of Third Avenue and Ninety-seventh Street, was another prominent addition to the East Harlem streetscape.[66] The boldly sculptural mass of the building, clad in oversized brick, incorporated windowless projecting elements that ran the structure's full height, adding a distinctive though disparate stylistic note to the area.

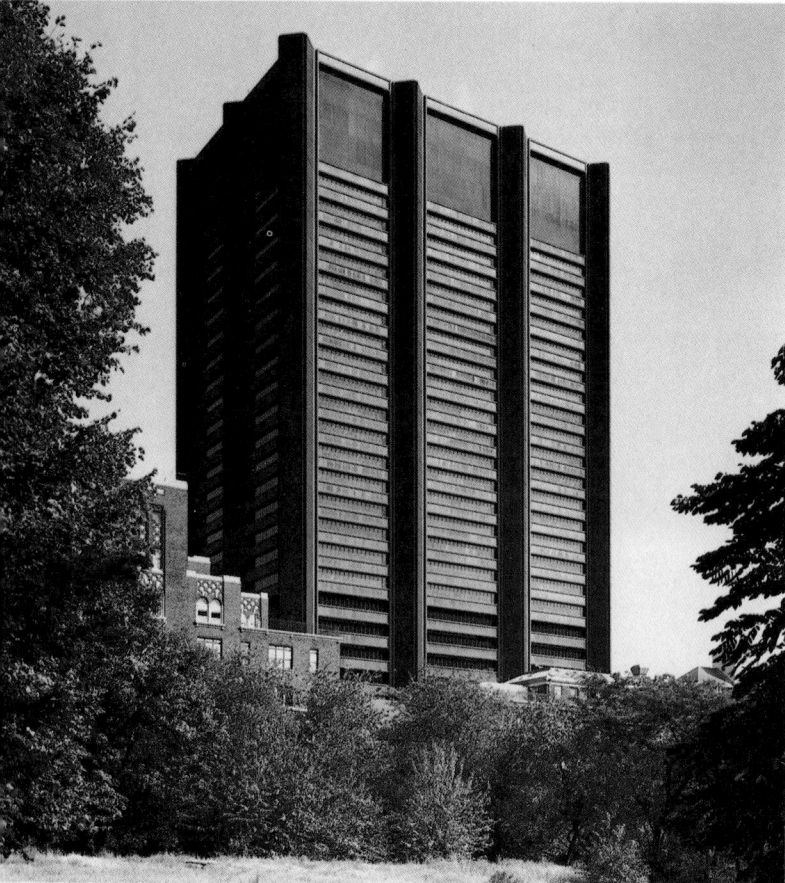

East Harlem's pressing recreational needs were in part alleviated by the opening of the Ward's Island Pedestrian Bridge in 1951, which made readily accessible to neighborhood residents the vast but little-used park that Robert Moses had established in 1936.[67] Described by the editors of the *New Yorker* as "probably the handsomest and costliest footbridge in the world,"[68] the bridge was designed by the master bridge builder Othmar Hermann Ammann, whose previous landmark works included the George Washington Bridge (1926–31), the Bayonne Bridge (1927–31) and, designed with the architect Aymar Embury II, the Triborough Bridge (1936) and the Bronx-Whitestone Bridge (1939).[69] The $2.1 million, 956-foot-long pedestrian bridge incorporated a twelve-foot-wide walkway connecting Manhattan's East River shore at 103rd Street to Ward's Island. To allow large ships to pass under the bridge on the Harlem River, Ammann had originally considered building the bridge 135 feet above the water, the same height as the Triborough Bridge. But this arrangement was rejected because of the anticipated difficulty of keeping pedestrian traffic moving with the elevators that would have been necessary. Instead, Ammann designed a central 350-ton, 312-foot girder lift span—the world's longest—that could be raised eighty feet above its

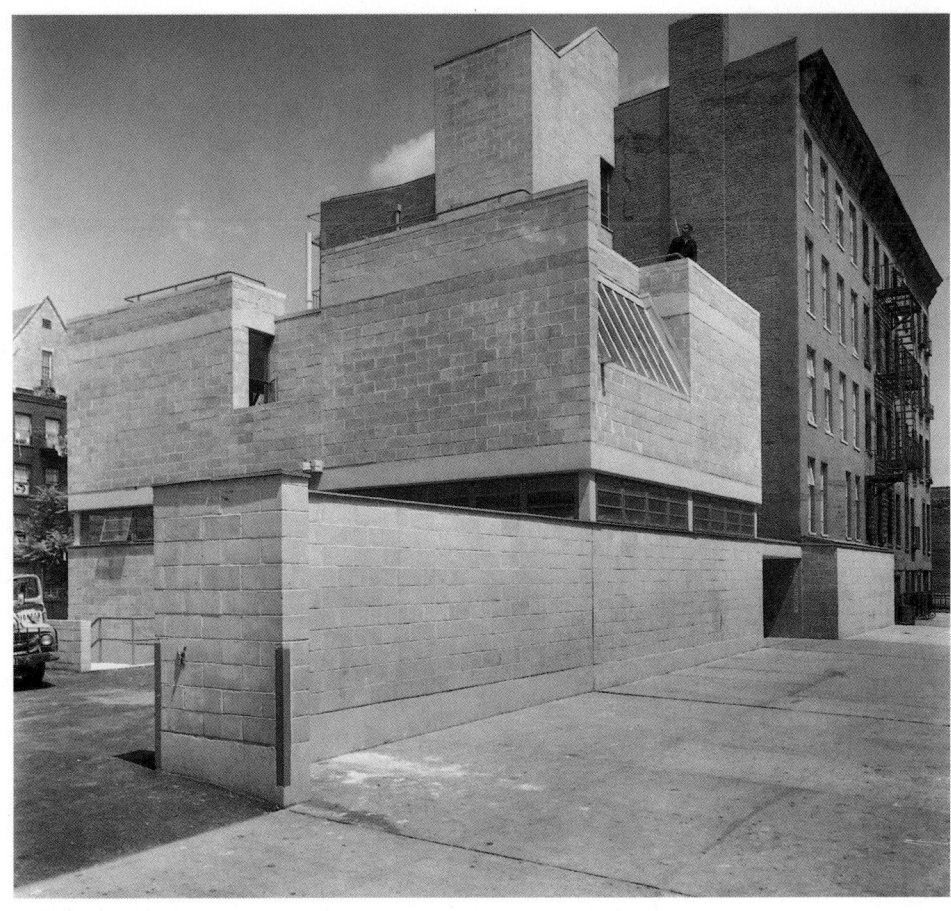

Top far left: Klingenstein Pavilion, Mount Sinai Hospital medical complex, 1176 Fifth Avenue. Kahn & Jacobs, 1952. View to the northeast. MA

Bottom far left: Annenberg Building, Mount Sinai Hospital medical complex, Madison Avenue and East 100th Street. Skidmore, Owings & Merrill, 1974. View to the southeast. Stoller. ©ESTO

Left: Exodus House, 309 East 103rd Street, between First and Second avenues. Smotrich & Platt, 1968. View to the northeast. ©Norman McGrath. NM

Below: Ward's Island Pedestrian Bridge, East River at East 101st Street. Othmar Hermann Ammann, 1951. View to the northeast. TBTA

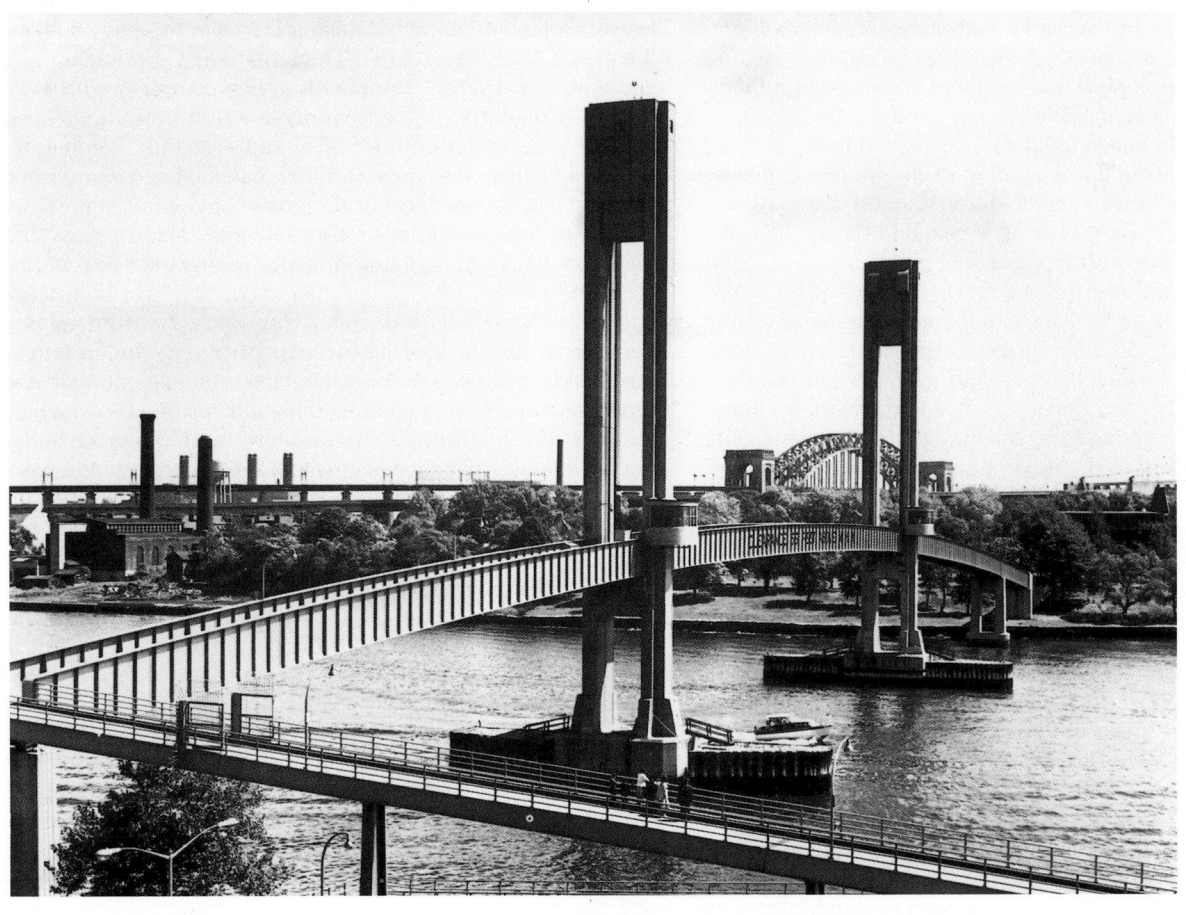

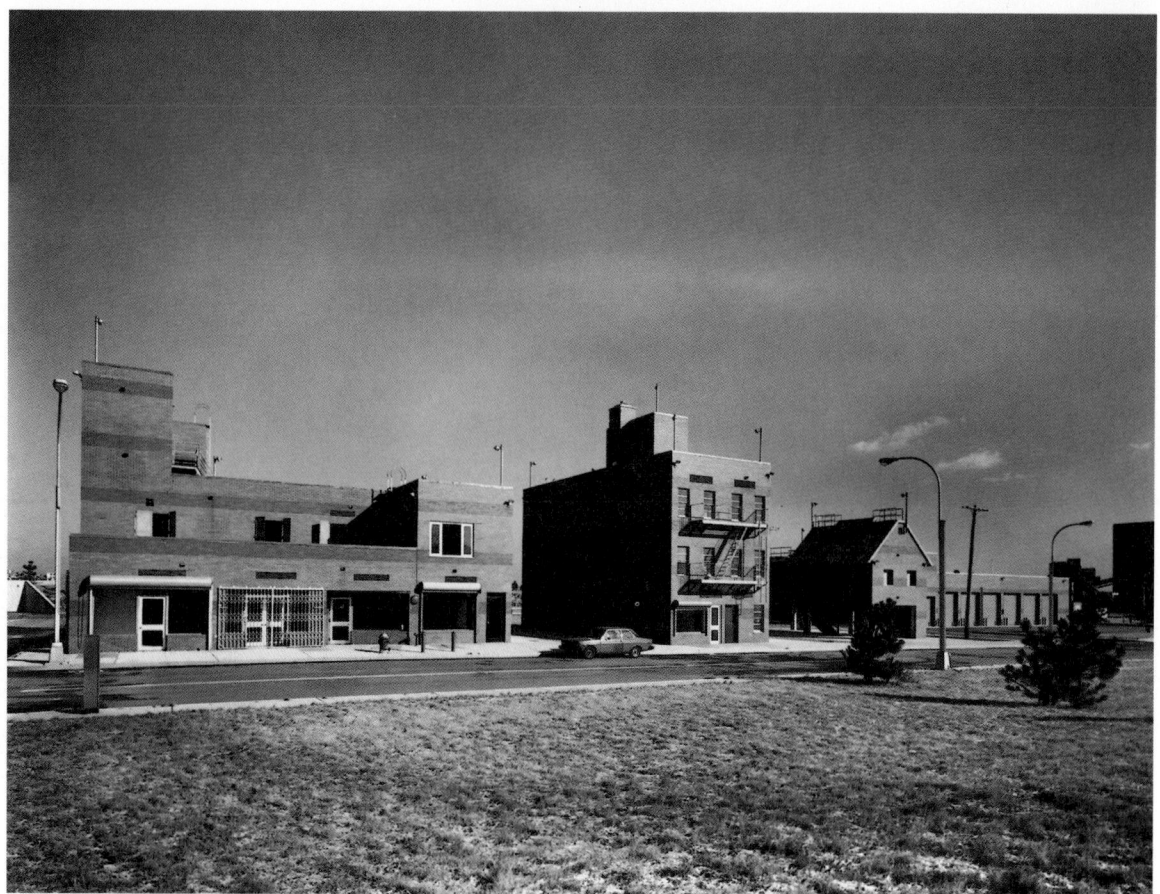

Firemen's
Training Center,
Ward's Island.
Hardy Holzman
Pfeiffer, 1975.
Training
buildings.
©Norman
McGrath. NM

fifty-five-foot height in two and a half minutes. Minimally detailed and clad in steel plates painted gray-green, the structure was of more technological than aesthetic interest, but it maintained a slender, elegant profile.

In 1976 the architects William Conklin and James Rossant were hired to oversee the repainting of the bridge, choosing blue-violet for the towers, cadmium yellow for the walkway and vermilion for the trim. Norval White and Elliot Willensky enthusiastically cheered the color scheme as a "spectacular improvement" that transformed the bridge into "urban sculpture of the finest sort."[70] Paul Goldberger disagreed, saying that while the paint job might "liven up the dreary views along the Franklin D. Roosevelt Drive and give the East Harlem neighborhood a needed boost . . . it doesn't work architecturally. The bright colors force this bridge, once a handsome background element in the urban environment, into the foreground, and they make it shriek and scream. . . . The bridge becomes not a real element of the cityscape but a child's toy, a colorful plaything."[71]

During the 1970s Ward's Island, legislatively a part of Manhattan, became home to several new city- and state-run facilities. The Rehabilitation Building (Caudill Rowlett Scott, 1970) of Manhattan State Hospital, which consisted of one-, two- and three-story wings scattered about a sloping site, was a skillful Modernist essay in exposed concrete and dark-buff brick.[72] The New York State Department of Mental Hygiene's Manhattan Children's Treatment Center (Richard G. Stein & Associates, 1972) was a similarly low-lying, campus-style building group, featuring expanses of tinted glass block, that successfully exploited the parklike setting.[73]

Most interesting from an architectural standpoint was

Hardy Holzman Pfeiffer's Firemen's Training Center, built by the New York State Urban Development Corporation and completed in 1975.[74] The nine-building complex, which occupied a recently created twenty-six-acre landfill site and housed facilities for both physical and academic training, replaced a facility on Roosevelt Island that had been demolished to make way for the large-scale redevelopment of that island. The long, narrow administration building, clad in glass and corrugated aluminum, incorporated a steeply pitched roof that blended into the slope of the man-made site. Five bright-red-painted sewer ducts, unexpectedly used as entranceways, punctuated the massive landscaped berm. On the building's higher side, a water tank contained the principal entrance and served as a vestibule; two other tanks, enclosing offices, poked through the roof. Inside, a 365-foot-long corridor ran the building's full length and gave access to a series of freestanding enclosures, each clad in different materials. Brightly colored surfaces added a further measure of visual excitement to the highly keyed environment. Perhaps even more startling was a series of training buildings designed to repeatedly "burn down" in mock fires; the brick-clad concrete structures re-created quintessential New York building types: a tenement, a frame dwelling, a ground-level storefront, a tower and a loft building. Goldberger observed that "one irony of the project—and one cannot imagine that this did not delight the architects enormously—is that the training buildings, which are not real at all, look real, while the education and administrative building, which has a very real and traditional function, is far more radical in appearance."[75] White and Willensky praised the training center as "a confident work of architecture and a witty one, too."[76]

CENTRAL HARLEM

By the early 1940s, when politicians or planners spoke of Harlem, they were referring to what was, from a strictly geographical point of view, Central Harlem and, from an ethnographic point of view, black Harlem. The boundaries of Central Harlem were strongly defined: Park Avenue (with its railroad viaduct), the twin escarpments of Morningside and St. Nicholas parks, Central Park and the Harlem River. Central Harlem had been built beginning in the 1880s as an area for middle- and upper-middle-class whites. When speculative excess left much of its real estate vacant in the early 1900s, the area was gradually opened up to blacks, although it remained a mixed if not truly integrated community well into the 1920s. With many tenements and middle-class apartment houses without tenants, landlords encouraged blacks to abandon the overcrowded conditions of San Juan Hill on the Upper West Side and move uptown.

While black Harlem seemed to prosper in proportion to the rest of America in the 1920s, it collapsed to even greater depths than did the primarily white areas of Manhattan in the Depression of the 1930s. With families doubling and even tripling up on living accommodations, it was claimed that Central Harlem sheltered more blacks per square mile than any other spot on earth. During World War II, black Harlem's population began to decline as families decamped to the outer boroughs or followed job opportunities in other employment centers. Nonetheless, the area remained seriously overcrowded, as well as undersupplied with municipal services; as the black writer Roi Ottley put it, "the human and prosaic characteristics" of life in Central Harlem became "scorched beyond normal recognition in the crucible of a segregated society," with blacks becoming "slum-shocked," an equivalent to the shell-shocking of actual warfare.[1]

In 1944 the architect William Lescaze, assisted by his staff, including Sidney L. Katz and Read Weber, and the realtor James Felt, developed a master plan for the redevelopment of Central Harlem.[2] Lescaze's study included eighty blocks (356 gross square acres) bounded by Fifth Avenue and Morningside Park, 110th and 126th streets. He found that most of the side streets, as well as Eighth Avenue—until very recently blighted by the elevated railroad—were plagued by an abundance of undesirable old-law tenements. No matter that some of the area's principal avenues were lined with still reasonably desirable new-law tenements, or that many brownstones built for middle-class tenants were still in relatively good shape. Lescaze called for the replacement of all buildings between Fifth and Lenox avenues, 110th and 125th streets, except for Public Schools 120 and 181. In their place, he proposed to create two housing superblocks below Mt. Morris Park, with only 116th Street running between them, and to redevelop the west and north sides of that park, where once solidly middle-class rowhouses abounded, as a cultural center and civic center respectively. One project, adapted from Lescaze's geometrically insistent yet gently scaled Williamsburg Houses (1934–38), called for much taller buildings, eight- and thirteen-story superslabs, with two to four wings each, cranked thirty degrees off the street grid for ideal solar orientation.[3] In all, 3,637 apartments were planned.

Although Lescaze's project was speculative, in 1946 plans were announced by the New York City Housing Authority for the realization of his southern superblock (although it extended only to 115th Street).[4] The Stephen Foster Houses, designed by William I. Hohauser to house 1,320 families, was a group of ten

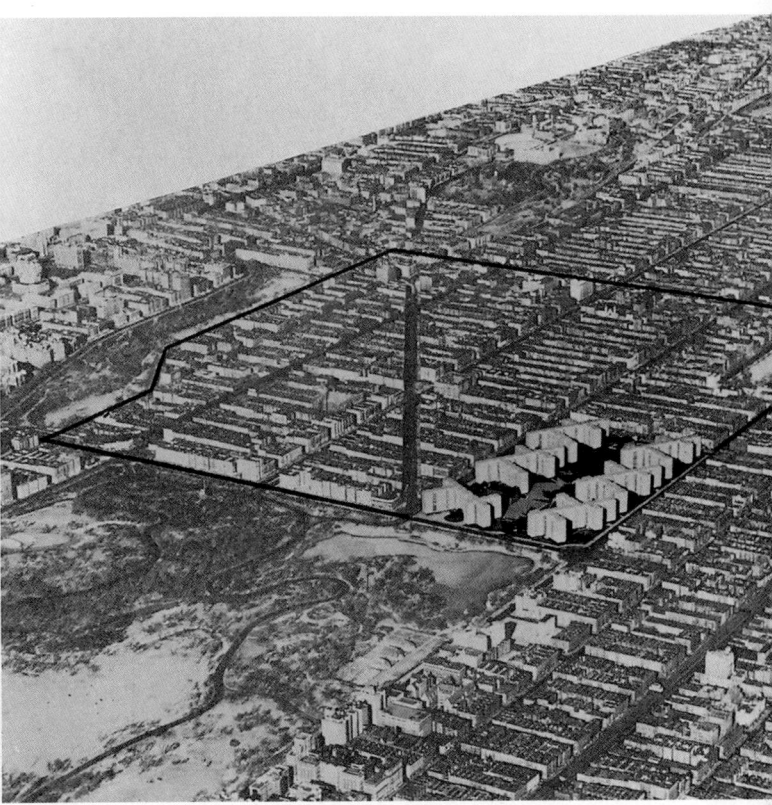

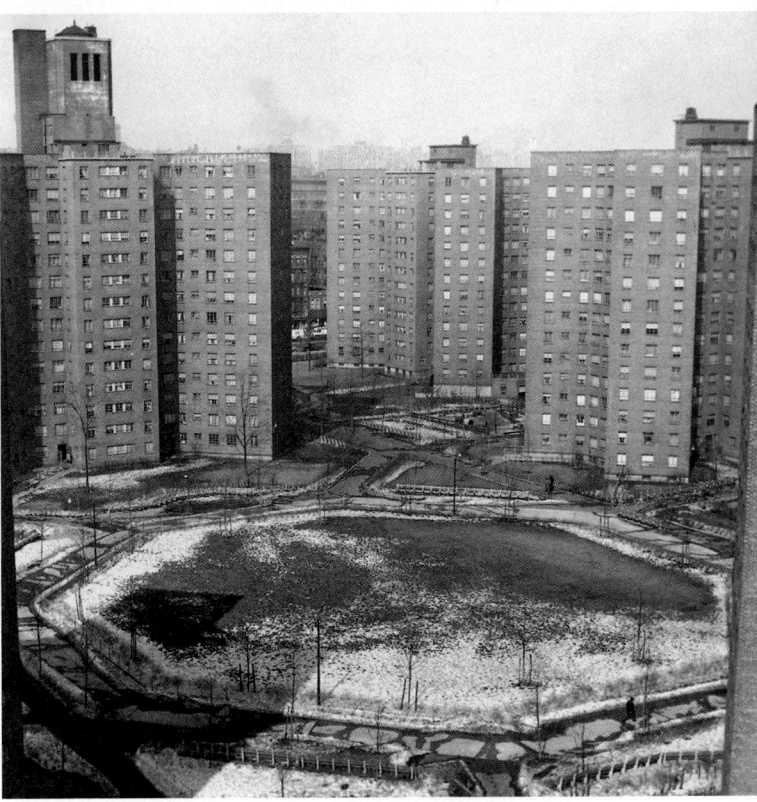

Top: Master plan for redevelopment of Central Harlem. William Lescaze, 1944. Rendering of view to the northwest. AF. CU

Bottom: Stephen Foster Houses (after 1968, Martin Luther King, Jr. Houses), Fifth to Lenox Avenue, East 110th to East 115th Street. William I. Hohauser, 1946. View to the northwest. NYCHA

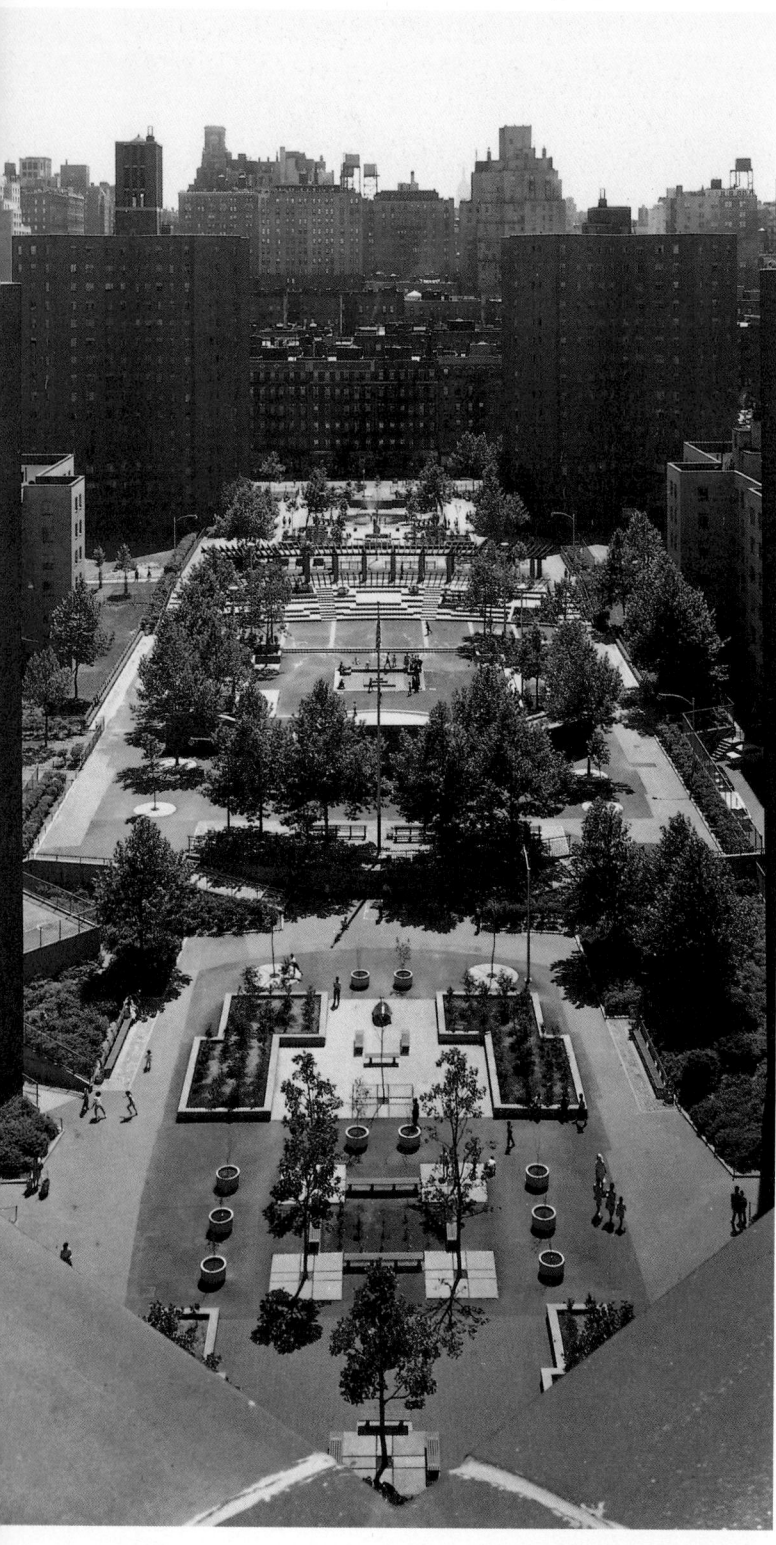

Carver Houses, Madison to Park Avenue, East Ninety-ninth to East 104th Street. Kahn & Jacobs, 1956. View to the south of recreation area (Pomerance & Breines and M. Paul Friedberg, 1964). Hirsch. NYCHA

thirteen- and fourteen-story buildings whose shape was far more complex than what Lescaze had proposed: mirror-image V's, with their apexes joined by a slab that was itself bisected·by a perpendicular slab. In 1968 the project's name was changed to the Martin Luther King, Jr. Houses.

In the 1950s and 1960s the heart of Central Harlem was systematically rebuilt along the diagrammatically logical lines of Lescaze's plan, with most of the strip of land between Fifth and Park avenues, 111th and 115th streets being reconstituted as a public housing ghetto. New projects were announced one after another in quick succession. The James Madison Houses, a complex of four twenty-story buildings designed by Harry M. Prince, were begun in 1961; containing a total of 622 apartments, the project was located between Madison and Park avenues, 107th and 110th streets.[5] Madison Houses was followed by De Young, Moscowitz & Rosenberg's Senator Robert A. Taft Houses (1962), consisting of nine slabs occupying a superblock site bounded by Park and Fifth avenues, 112th and 115th streets.[6]

Taft Houses was distinguished not by its architecture or planning, both of which were banal, but by a bold attempt at community-initiated design undertaken five years after the project was completed: in 1967 the United Residents of Milbank–Frawley Circle–East Harlem presented a proposal, developed with Roger Katan, to socially and physically reconfigure the project.[7] To ameliorate the bleakness of Taft Houses, the Housing and Development Administration (HDA), working with the architectural firm of Fisher-Jackson and community representatives, had proposed a scheme of low-rise infill housing conceived along the urbanistic lines outlined by Lawrence Halprin in his *New York, New York* study.[8] The United Residents, believing that the HDA proposal would hasten the decline of the overall neighborhood, developed instead a plan that would accommodate middle-income as well as low-income families, arguing that as low-income families prospered they could remain in their apartments and simply pay more rent. Katan's design called for a series of three- to eleven-story-high "shelves" that stretched across Taft Houses parkland as well as the surrounding area, using air rights over intervening streets. These shelves were to contain prefabricated houses as well as community facilities—including health centers, cooperatively run stores and offices for both public- and private-sector enterprises—that were to help turn the project into a nearly self-sufficient neighborhood. The ambitious but essentially unrealistic plan, which aroused strong passions and charges of unfairly raising community expectations, was not realized, nor was any other more modestly scaled redevelopment plan.

Like Taft Houses, Kahn & Jacobs's Carver Houses (1956), located on a site between Madison and Park avenues, Ninety-ninth and 104th streets and accommodating over 1,200 apartments in thirteen buildings, was noteworthy not for its original design but for a later proposal, although this one was realized.[9] In 1964 the project's open spaces were the site of a dramatic renovation, financed by the Vincent Astor Foundation. Designed by the architects Pomerance & Breines and the landscape architect M. Paul Friedberg, the newly orchestrated spaces provided active play areas for teenagers and children while also meeting the recreational needs of adults. Taking advantage of the existing planting and the mall-like space that ran north-south through the project, the designers created a series of geometrically clear open spaces defined by low walls, steps and planters, culminating in an amphitheater covering 60,000 square feet near the midpoint, where lower buildings bounded the edges. Large enough to accommodate 1,500 people seated on permanent bleacherlike steps, the amphitheater included a circular stage area backed by U-shaped brick walls. A 1,000-square-foot pool, used for wading by day and serving as a fountain at night, was placed between the stage and the seating; in the winter the pool could be used as a skating rink. The renovation turned relatively useless greenery into open space that invited programmed as well as spontaneous, random activity.

The following year, 1965, saw the completion of another innovative playground, this one on a small, city-owned garbage-strewn site at 52 East 129th Street. The playground was organized by the Harlem Neighborhoods Association, which planned ten other such "vest-pocket" parks. Designed by the architect Pedro Lopez in conjunction with local artists, it included a spray pool featuring a sculpted hippopotamus and a boa constrictor; a basketball hoop; and what Mary Perot Nichols, writing in the *Village Voice*, described as "lusty murals" created by neighborhood children.[10] Another such park, spearheaded by John Emmerling, a copywriter at the advertising agency of Young & Rubicam who helped create a nationwide fund-raising campaign for vest-pocket parks, was completed in 1970 at 121 West 115th Street.[11]

The 1,200-unit Drew-Hamilton Houses (1965), occupying a superblock site bounded by Seventh and Eighth avenues, 141st and 143rd streets, were marginally better than the typical housing project.[12] Designed by Katz, Waisman, Weber, Strauss, the complex adopted the ubiquitous towers-in-the-park format. But here the diagonally oriented towers, which rose from lowrise bases containing stores, were pushed to the lot line, so that at least at ground level some measure of traditional urbanism was maintained.

In 1969 Lescaze's twenty-five-year-old proposal to transform part of Mt. Morris Park into a cultural and civic center came to partial fruition with the completion of Lundquist & Stonehill's Mt. Morris Recreation Center and Amphitheater, opposite West 122nd Street, and Ifill & Johnson's Mt. Morris Park Swimming Pool and Bathhouse, southwest of Madison Avenue and East 124th Street.[13] These two brutal intrusions into an historic green space could just as easily have been built on any number of nearby properties made vacant through abandonment and arson.

Some of the systematic reconfiguration taking place in Central Harlem was undertaken for the benefit of middle-class blacks. In September 1944 the Metropolitan Life Insurance Company announced plans for Riverton (Irwin Clavan), a 1,232-family housing project for blacks that was to be a separate-but-equal response to the all-white Stuyvesant Town project (see chapter 5).[14] Five of the six Riverton tower slabs occupied a superblock created between 135th and 138th streets, Fifth and Madison avenues; the sixth building was set apart at the northeast corner of Madison Avenue and 135th Street. To the east of the site lay the proposed southern extension of the Harlem River Driveway and the river itself; to the west, aging but still desirable brownstones; to the south, the much less desirable tenements slated to become the site of the vast Abraham Lincoln Houses (see below). Though Riverton replaced some aging tenements, most of the site was occupied by industrial buildings; thus, the relocation problems encountered in building Stuyvesant Town were largely avoided.

The plan of Riverton was clear, with the five slabs defining a central mall in a manner recalling, at a much larger and more generous scale, Andrew J. Thomas's 1924 Metropolitan Life apartment houses in Queens, as well as his work for the Queensboro Corporation in Jackson Heights.[15] The slabs were articulate in their massing, and although the ornament-free brick walls were severe, that quality was somewhat ameliorated by extensive planting. The buildings occupied only 25 percent of the

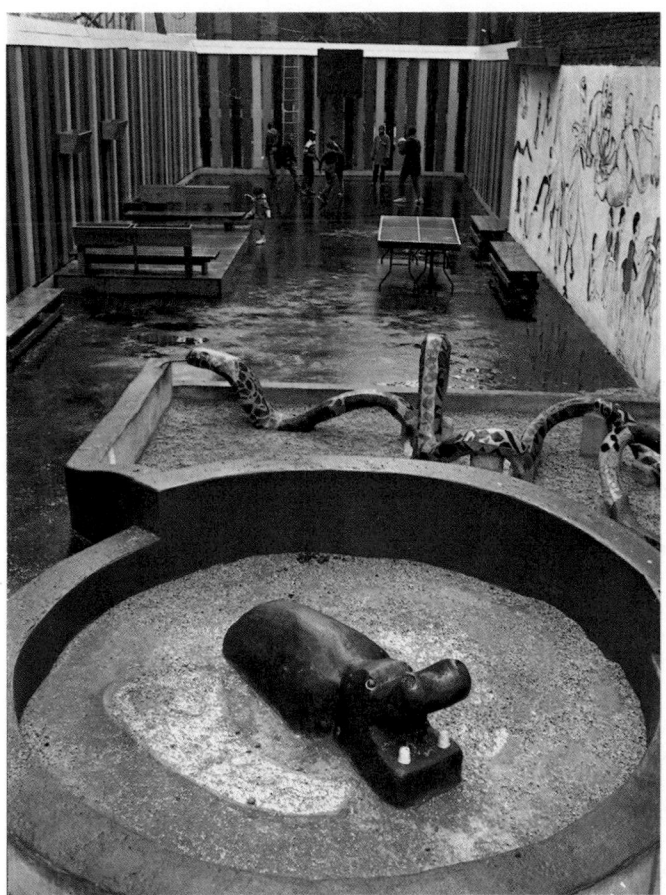

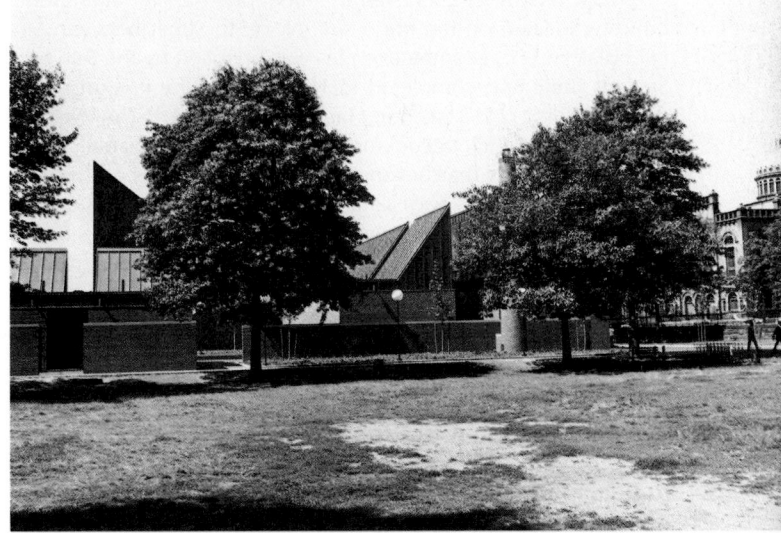

Top: Vest-pocket playground, 52 East 129th Street, between Madison and Park avenues. Pedro Lopez, 1965. View to the south. Fred W. McDarrah. FWM

Bottom: Mt. Morris Recreation Center and Amphitheater, Mt. Morris Park, opposite West 122nd Street. Lundquist & Stonehill, 1969. View to the east. LS

twelve-acre site, with some of the remaining land given over to the by-now-requisite peripheral street widenings, as well as lawns, playgrounds, gardens and extensive tree planting.

The writer James Baldwin saw Riverton not as a middle-class oasis but as a symbol of racism. In his 1960 essay on the Harlem of his youth, "Fifth Avenue, Uptown," Baldwin wrote: "Harlem got its first private project, Riverton . . . because at that time Negroes were not allowed to live in Stuyvesant Town. Harlem watched Riverton go up, therefore, in the most violent bitterness of spirit, and hated it long before the builders arrived. They began hating it at about the time people began moving out of their condemned houses to make room for this additional proof of how thoroughly the white world despised them."[16]

To counterbalance the privately financed Riverton, the Housing Authority moved forward with the Abraham Lincoln Houses (1948), designed by Edwin M. Forbes, the black architect Vertner W. Tandy, and Skidmore, Owings & Merrill.[17] The complex housed 1,289 families in fourteen modified-X-shaped fourteen-story buildings on a superblock bounded by 132nd and 135th streets, Fifth and Park avenues. After finishing Lincoln Houses, the Housing Authority moved right on to the eight four-teen-story buildings of Colonial Park Houses (Julian Whittlesey, Harry M. Prince and Robert J. Reilly, 1951), which occupied a site bounded by the Polo Grounds, the Harlem River Driveway and the Harlem River Drive.[18] Next came St. Nicholas Houses (York & Sawyer, 1952), a 1,526-family development on a 16.4-acre superblock site occupying most of the area bounded by Seventh and Eighth avenues, 127th and 131st streets.[19] Thus, within five or six years an entire mixed-use area dating back fifty or more years had been completely obliterated in favor of a single use (housing) and a single building type (the high-rise tower-slab) and, with the exception of Riverton, for a single class (the very poor).

York & Sawyer's 211-family, moderate-income apartment building located on the north side of 145th Street between St. Nicholas and Edgecombe avenues was financed by the Bowery Savings Bank and completed in 1956; it was the first unsubsidized building undertaken in Harlem since 1938.[20] The twelve-story brick building, occupying the full blockfront, featured two deep open courts that began at the third-floor level and faced the street. Stores, as well as a branch of the Bowery Savings Bank—according to the New York Times, the first savings bank to open in Harlem in forty-eight years—were incorporated into the project. Many observers hailed the project as a hopeful sign for Harlem's future, including James Felt, who wrote: "To be sure, the Bowery project is not a cure-all. . . . But when New York City's largest savings bank has the vision, wisdom and courage to identify itself with Harlem, bring to this district its great facilities and experience in the encouragement of thrift and develop much needed housing in the process, we can look forward hopefully to a better and earlier understanding of the problems generated by the Harlems of America."[21]

In 1957 Riverton was joined by another middle-income project, Maxon, Sells & Ficke's Delano Village, consisting of seven sixteen-story buildings, constructed on 12.5 acres bounded by Fifth and Lenox avenues, 139th, 141st and 142nd streets, and replacing tenements, garages and parking lots.[22] A privately planned project, Delano Village included apartments for 1,785 families, as well as stores and parking facilities. It was the first project ever built under the Title I program in a slum area to receive a federally guaranteed loan.

Lenox Terrace (1957), six sixteen-story red-brick buildings intended for 1,716 families, was another effort to create middle-income housing in Harlem, also financed under the Title I provisions of the Federal Housing Act.[23] Located to the west of Riverton and to the south of Delano Village, Lenox Terrace helped anchor this end of Harlem as a middle-income area, despite the presence of the Abraham Lincoln Houses; at the same time it was but one more element in the almost continuous "slum clearance" project that came to characterize Harlem. Lenox Terrace was designed by S. J. Kessler & Sons and occupied a three-square-block area between Fifth and Lenox avenues, 132nd and 135th streets. Even more than at Riverton, the intention here was to create an upmarket ambience, complete with terraced apartments, driveway entrances and such "luxury" amenities as uniformed doormen. Each building at Lenox Terrace had an individual name: the Americana, the Buckingham, the Continental, the Devonshire, the Eden Roc and the Fontainebleau, the last two recalling popular, glamorous Miami Beach hotels.

The project succeeded in attracting affluent and professionally accomplished tenants, including Manhattan Borough President Percy Sutton. The journalist Ernest Dunbar, writing in the New York Times in 1968, observed that "El Doradoes, Rivieras, Mercedes and Jaguars crouch between concrete separators along the driveways," yet he also noted that the complex had a distinctly heterogeneous if almost entirely black population, a mix that reflected the incongruities and changing nature of the Harlem community as a whole: "Many of the Terrace's inhabitants could, if they wished, live in more expensive lodgings; for others, each month is another round in the constant struggle to make rent money. The affluent and the marginal, celebrities and cliff-hangers, custom-tailored and off-the-rack types, Ph.D.'s and blue-collar workers—all mingle in the elevators of the Terrace in a potpourri of color, class and life style."[24] Despite Lenox Terrace's status as Harlem's most sought-after apartment address, however, its architecture and planning were not as distinguishable from its low-income counterparts as might have been expected. "It would not be surprising," Paul Goldberger noted, "if the physical similarity between New York luxury housing and New York public housing causes more pain here, to these residents, than it does anywhere else."[25]

Yet another middle-income housing development, 1270 Fifth Avenue, occupying the northeast corner of Fifth Avenue and 108th Street, was announced in 1957.[26] But this one was different: not a project but a single cooperative apartment house, it was the first building to be built in Manhattan under a new federal program guaranteeing loans for developers of middle-income cooperatives. Designed by H. Herbert and Clarence Lillien as a dull fourteen-story brick box that resembled innumerable apartment buildings on the Upper East Side, it represented an integrative, assimilationist appproach that because of its blandness was able to reach across social borders in a way that no previous Harlem housing had. Rather than an abstract ideal rendered in stone, steel and glass, 1270 Fifth Avenue was just an apartment house.

One of Harlem's legendary night spots, the Cotton Club, on the east side of Lenox Avenue between 142nd and 143rd streets, was demolished in 1967 to make way for Bethune Tower (1970), a housing project for middle-income families realized under the provisions of the Mitchell-Lama program.[27] The club's destruction marked the end of an era that had reached its peak in the early 1930s, when Harlem was a swank and mildly exotic destination for nocturnal, pleasure-seeking whites, and continued into the 1950s, when it was headquarters to sophisticated blacks. The new housing project, designed by Edgar Tafel, consisted of a thirteen-story residential tower rising above a two-story base containing offices and a recreational center. The rather ordinary balconied brick complex was enlivened by three distinguished public sculptures by black artists Daniel Johnson, Todd Williams and Mel Edwards.

The Polo Grounds Houses, completed in 1968, replaced another Harlem landmark, the Polo Grounds, located beneath the escarpment known as Coogan's Bluff, where Eighth Avenue terminated at the Harlem River.[28] Demolished in 1964, the Polo Grounds had held a hallowed position in baseball history, having served as home to the New York Giants (see chapter 16). Designed by Ballard Todd Associates, the Polo Grounds Houses consisted of four red-brick slabs distinguished only by their thirty-story height, which made them the tallest Housing Authority project to date. The site's former significance was acknowledged only by a plaque at the base of one of the buildings, marking the spot where home plate had once been.

In 1969 the city targeted the St. Nicholas Park neighborhood, bounded by St. Nicholas and Seventh avenues, 127th and 145th streets, as a major urban renewal area, for which a Housing and Development Administration design team consisting of Robert Stern, Edward L. LaMura, Jonathan Stoumen, Romin Koebel and Anthony Thompson developed a comprehensive redevelopment plan.[29] Although influenced by Colin Rowe and Thomas Schumacher's earlier proposal (see "Black America's Capital City," above), the new plan made more serious efforts to preserve the existing structurally sound housing as well as traditional neighborhood scale. Projected over ten years, the plan called for the replacement of a total of 6,000 housing units. Avenue-facing tenements were to give way to similarly scaled six- and eight-story buildings, while the Drew-Hamilton Houses (see above) were to be "infilled" with six-story apartment buildings, helping to create a midblock pedestrian street and provide spatially defined, campuslike open spaces. Highrise apartment buildings were to be built along St. Nicholas Avenue and connected by a pedestrian bridge to an elevated location along the park's rocky precipice. Three towers located along the south side of 135th Street between Seventh and Eighth avenues were to provide additional housing as well as retail, office and community space. The plan was never realized, but in 1974 Bond Ryder Associates' Lionel Hampton Houses, named for the jazz musician who had once lived nearby at 337 West 138th Street, were completed within the proposed renewal district on an irregularly shaped site straddling St. Nicholas Avenue between 130th and 131st streets.[30] The masonry complex consisted of one high-rise and two low-rise apartment buildings, the facades of which were punctuated by L-shaped windows. A two-story building containing stores and office space completed the ensemble.

The most architecturally innovative and distinguished publicly assisted housing project realized in Harlem during the postwar period was Davis, Brody & Associates' Riverbend Houses (1967).[31] Occupying a triangular waterfront site bounded by 138th Street, Fifth Avenue and the Harlem River Driveway and traversed by an access ramp at 139th Street, the Mitchell-Lama complex rejected the prevailing low-density towers-in-the-park planning type in favor of ten interconnected slabs of eleven, sixteen and nineteen stories housing a total of 624 families. Echoing such pioneering working-class apartment projects as William Field & Son's Home Buildings (1877), Tower Buildings (1879) and Workingmen's Cottages (1879), located in the Cobble Hill section of Brooklyn,[32] Davis, Brody utilized open walkways and organized the slabs around courtyards, enclosing

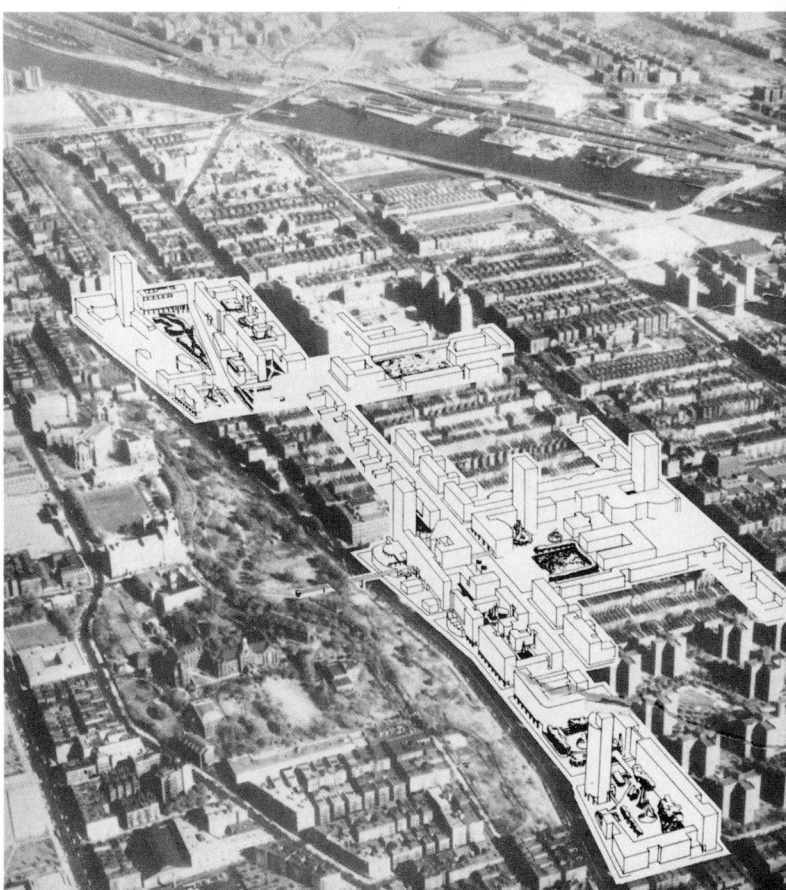

Master plan for St. Nicholas Park neighborhood, St. Nicholas to Seventh Avenue, West 127th to West 145th Street. Robert Stern, Edward L. LaMura, Jonathan Stoumen, Romin Koebel and Anthony Thompson, 1969. Rendering of view to the northeast. AR. CU

second-level plazas above commercial spaces. Riverbend's two-story open passages, which also reflected the influence of contemporaneous European developments, served as private "streets"; off of these passages raised areas not only provided access to the project's houselike duplex dwelling units but also acted as "front yards." This sophisticated organization of external passageways, while expressing an optimistic social vision, was also a cost-saving method of complying with municipal fire codes. Riverbend constituted Davis, Brody's first large-scale urban housing development, a type in which the firm would later specialize. The project also introduced the "jumbo" brick, a construction innovation, designed by the architects in conjunction with labor unions, that was soon widely adopted. Like its standard predecessor, the jumbo brick was eight inches long, but it was five-and-a-half instead of two-and-a-half inches wide. Although perhaps crude, the new brick offered an alternative that saved labor, time and, consequently, money.

In 1969, when a jury headed by the architectural historian and critic Sibyl Moholy-Nagy bestowed on Riverbend a Bard Award for excellence in urban planning and civic architecture, the development was hailed as "the first and only New York housing project that fulfills its responsibility toward the river landscape, and toward each tenant by relating him to the river."[33] Norval White and Elliot Willensky praised the project as a "monumental breakthrough in urban, publicly subsidized housing," noting that "social and aesthetic concerns are here melded into a

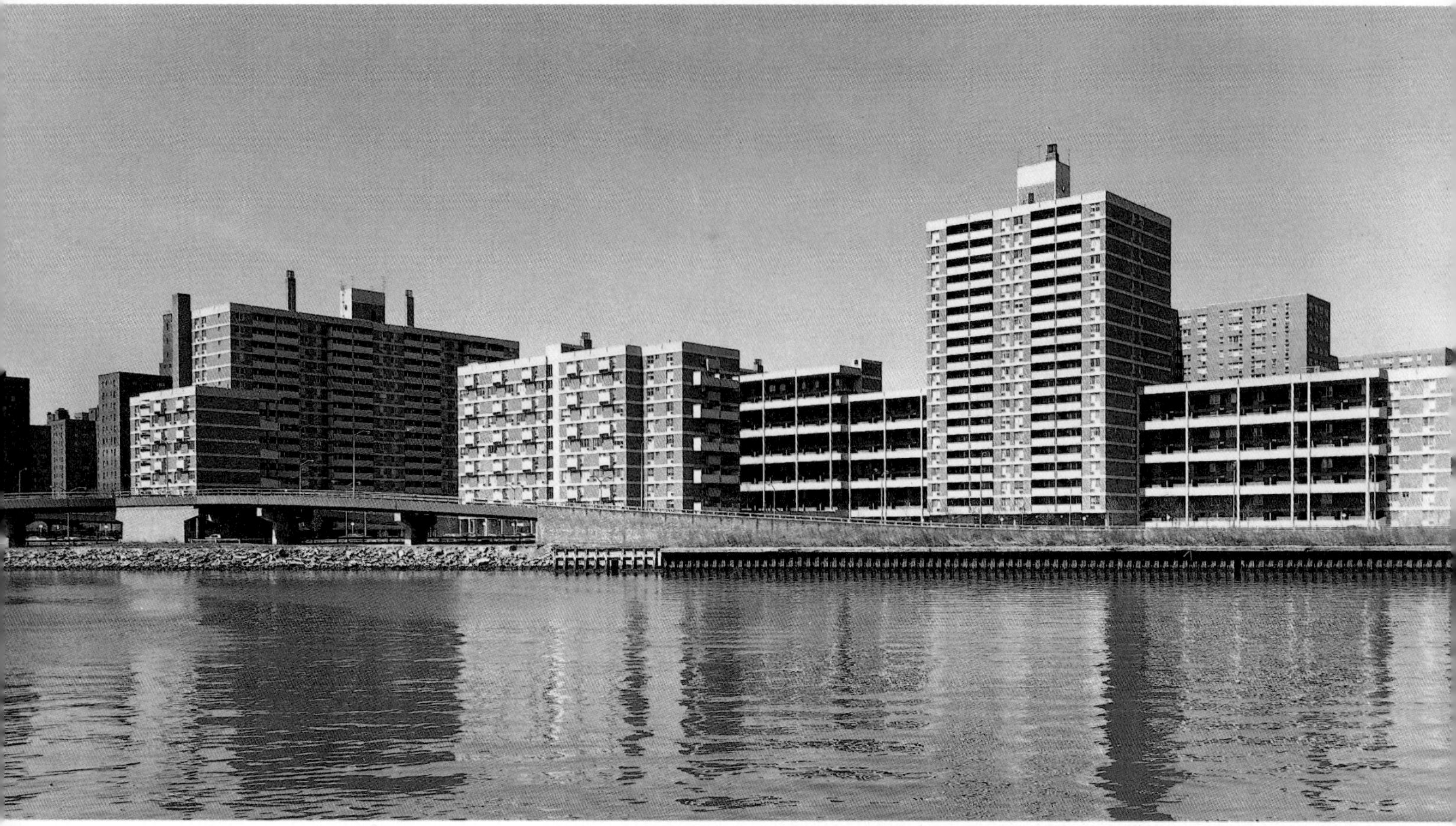

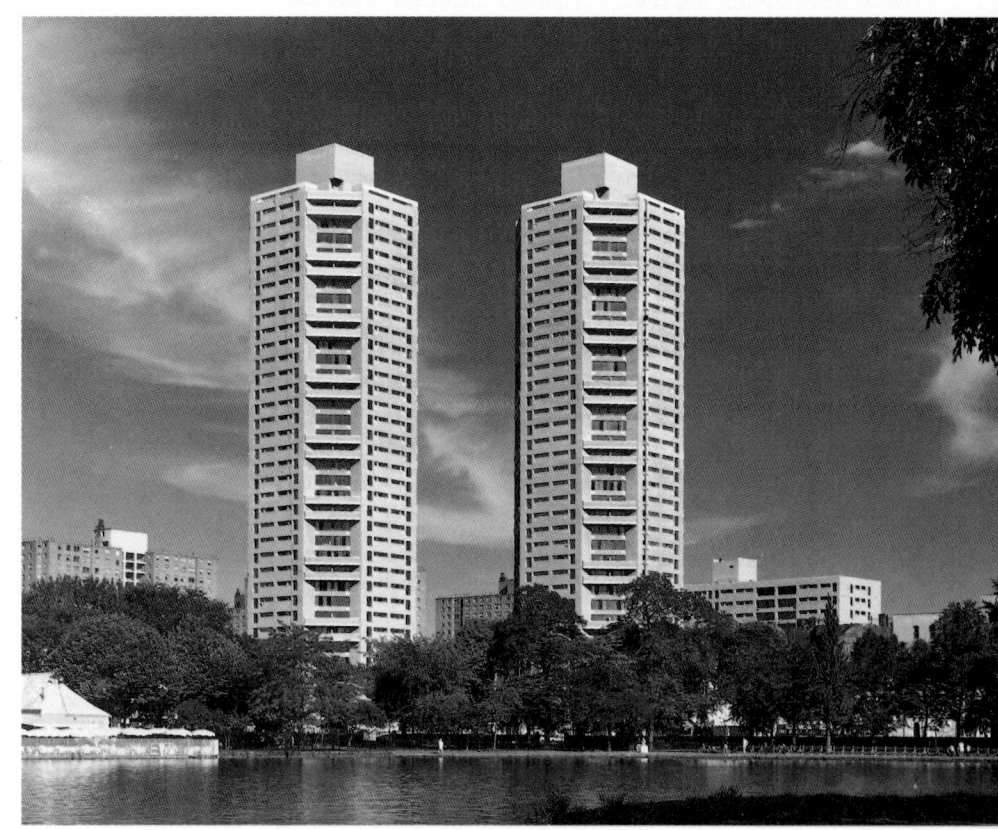

Above: Riverbend Houses, Fifth Avenue to Harlem River Driveway, East 135th to East 139th Street. Davis, Brody & Associates, 1967. View to the southwest. ©Norman McGrath. NM

Right: Arthur A. Schomburg Plaza, Fifth to Madison Avenue, East 110th to East 111th Street. Gruzen & Partners in association with Castro-Blanco, Piscioneri & Feder, 1975. View to the northeast. Hirsch. GS

single, eminently successful apartment development respectful of street lines."[34] Writing in 1969, Peter Blake contended that despite "a couple of minor flaws," Riverbend was "quite clearly, the best housing project built in Harlem to date."[35] Paul Goldberger concurred, saying, "These buildings are *housing*, not institutions, and they feel that way through and through."[36]

In 1965 a proposal was presented for Arthur A. Schomburg Plaza, a mixed-income project designed by Gruzen & Partners in association with Castro-Blanco, Piscioneri & Feder for a site that formed the northeast quadrant of Frawley Circle, bounded by 110th and 111th streets, Fifth and Madison avenues.[37] The design placed twin thirty-five-story reinforced-concrete octagonal towers along the circle and an eleven-story slab along Madison Avenue. Sponsored by a coalition of neighborhood groups and the New York State Urban Development Corporation (UDC), the project was completed in 1975. Like other superscaled housing projects, the towers of Schomburg Plaza loomed above their surroundings, but here they added an arguably appropriate landmark to the city's skyline at a pivotal intersection on a key corner of Central Park. The buildings' facades were well articulated and effectively punctuated by pairs of recessed balconies located with two floors between each pair. The design resolution at street level was less successful, with the buildings failing to coherently define Frawley Circle. In addition to housing, the complex contained commercial space, a day-care center and the Northside Center for Child Development. A multilevel, landscaped outdoor space within the complex provided an inviting public space, punctuated by wooden gazebos, a contrast to the barren plazas that had become a hallmark of so many housing developments.

In 1976 Gruzen & Partners, again working in association with Castro-Blanco, Piscioneri & Feder, completed the Fifth Avenue Lakeview Apartments, another skillfully articulated if less dramatically designed housing project.[38] Sponsored by the UDC, the low- and moderate-income development was located on the block bounded by Fifth and Madison avenues, 106th and 107th streets. The complex, containing a total of 446 units, consisted of two exposed-concrete-block, modified-L-shaped building groups, each composed of interlocking sections that ranged in height from ten to twenty-three stories and incorporated recessed terraces. At the site's southwest corner, a landscaped plaza and children's play area extended beneath the Fifth Avenue–facing portion of the complex, which was raised on columns one story above street level. A second open area, facing 107th Street, was utilized as a parking lot. Ground-level stores faced Madison Avenue. Though the site plan effectively allowed the Fifth Avenue street wall to be maintained while providing a maximum amount of midblock open space, the low-cost materials that were required gave the project an institutional appearance, decisively setting it apart from its grander prewar neighbors.

Though the bulk of Central Harlem's postwar townscape consisted of housing projects, some facilities were built that not only provided the neighborhood with sorely needed services but also reintroduced a small measure of aesthetic variety and intimate scale. Louis Allen Abramson's 135th Street Branch of the New York Public Library, located on the north side of the street between Seventh and Lenox avenues, was completed in 1941.[39] Annexed to an existing facility by McKim, Mead & White (1905), the new wing, which extended through the block north to 136th Street, incorporated reading spaces for high school students and adults as well as room for the famous Arthur A. Schomburg Collection of source material on black American

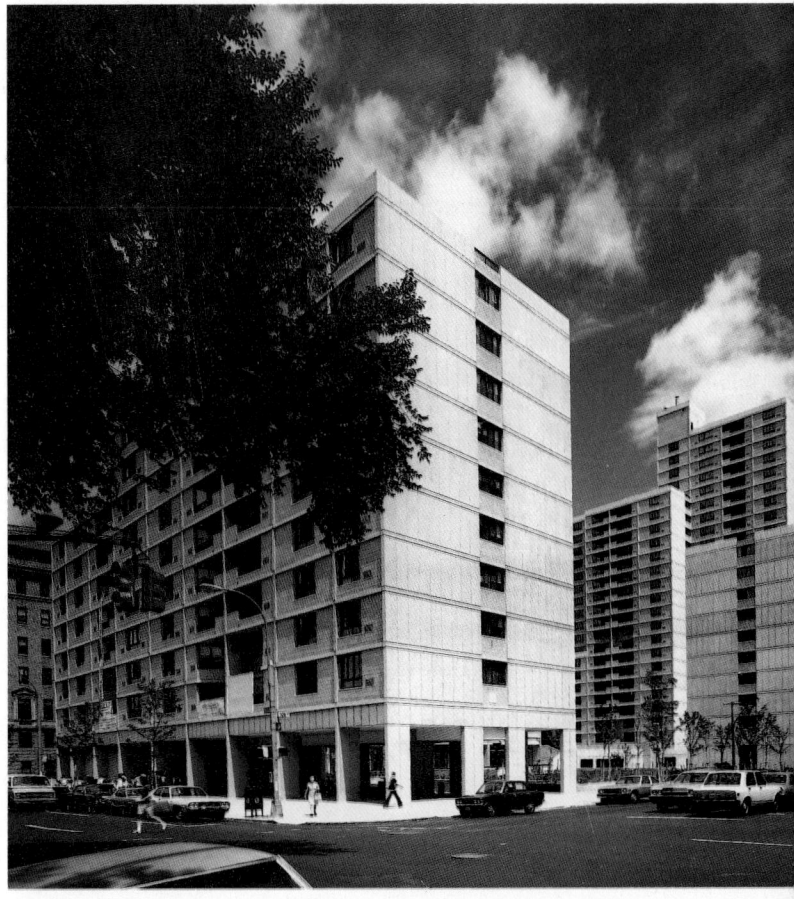

Fifth Avenue Lakeview Apartments, Fifth to Madison Avenue, East 106th to East 107th Street. Gruzen & Partners in association with Castro-Blanco, Piscioneri & Feder, 1976. View to the northeast. ©Gil Amiaga. GA

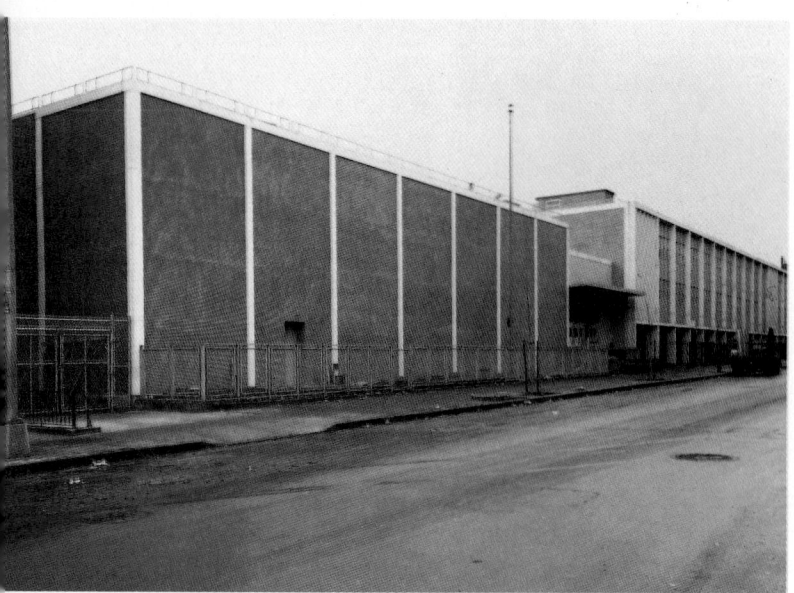

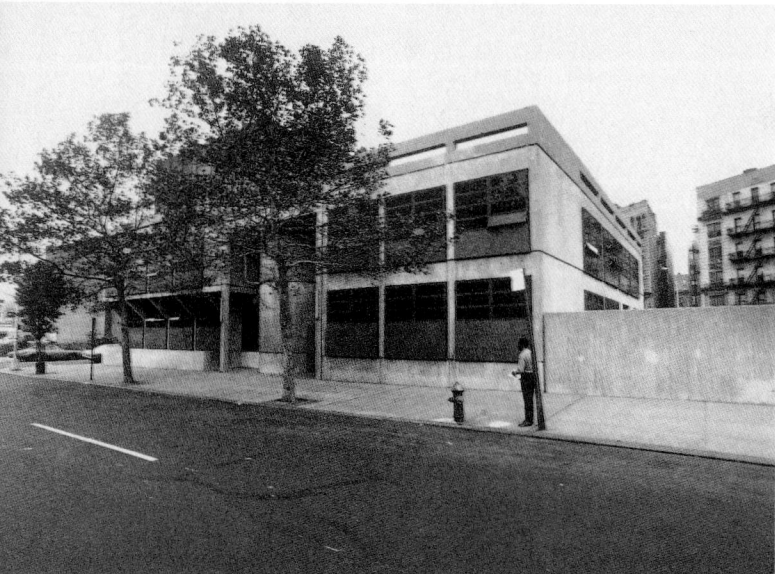

Top: John Hancock School, Public School 154, Seventh to Eighth Avenue, West 126th to West 127th Street. Paul R. Williams, 1961. View to the southwest. NYCBE

Bottom: Twenty-eighth Precinct Headquarters, St. Nicholas to Eighth Avenue, West 122nd to West 123rd Street. Lehrecke & Tonetti, 1974. View to the northeast. TA

history and culture. In addition, the existing building was renovated to include a fireside area for story-telling groups, a service for children left at the library for long periods of time by their working mothers. Abramson's vigorous design, boldly breaking with the brownstones at its flanks, made the most of a simple palette of brick cladding and large metal-framed windows wrapping its concrete structural frame. Spandrels were treated as false balconies to create a lively play of shadows. Inside, the double-height adult reading room, bathed in light, was overlooked by a mezzanine art gallery.

The Harlem Boy's Club (1941), built on a midblock site between Lenox and Fifth avenues, extending from 133rd Street through to 134th Street, reflected the private sector's efforts to provide Harlem with much-needed educational and recreational facilities.[40] Designed by Louis E. Jallade, the building had a highly reductivist but nonetheless lively principal facade: above a granite base, the yellow and orange brick cladding was punctuated by a syncopated pattern of metal casement windows that, despite its overall asymmetry, was divided into three discrete and symmetrically arranged sections. Inside, the well-equipped building housed an auditorium, a gymnasium and a range of workshops for instruction in manual trades including automobile repair.

From the outset of postwar efforts to improve conditions in Harlem, it was widely recognized that after housing, education ranked as perhaps the area's most pressing need. Even as early as 1943, the special investigative commission established by Mayor La Guardia to study the Harlem riots cited the aging and rundown condition of many of the area's public schools as a contributing factor. While the Board of Education acknowledged the existence of poor physical conditions, following World War II it adopted a policy of concentrating new construction in rapidly expanding parts of the city, particularly in Queens and outlying parts of Brooklyn, rather than in older neighborhoods where populations were more stable or even declining in number. Nonetheless, some public school construction, especially at the elementary school level, did occur; and in the context of postwar Harlem, the neighborhood school took on new architectural and urbanistic significance, constituting perhaps the single redeeming antidote to the filing-cabinet-like uniformity of the typical housing project. The Board of Education was by no means a consistently enlightened patron of design, but many of the schools it built in Central Harlem were at the very least decent, and a few were rather more than that.

Eric Kebbon's James Fenimore Cooper Junior High School (1942), occupying the block bounded by Fifth and Madison avenues, 119th and 120th streets, was one of the last public school buildings completed before wartime restrictions shut down virtually all building activity.[41] The three-story red-brick building was trimmed in limestone, with green marble used to enhance the principal entrance. A pleasant entrance court faced north across 120th Street to Mt. Morris Park and a three-story-high row of square columns marked the principal entrance. Though Lewis Mumford thought the building was satisfactory, he observed that the school was "modern" only "by omission rather than by conviction and commission."[42] But it was the simplicity with which Kebbon handled the elements of his composition that gave it strength; he pruned away inessential details to keep to a tight budget and reassure the taxpayers that no frivolous expenditures were being made on nonfunctional features. By the time he designed the three-story Public School 108 (1950), occupying a full block site bounded by Madison and Park avenues, 108th and 109th streets, Kebbon's stripped Classicism had become diluted.[43] Like so many other architects of his generation, he was trying to combine traditional mass with International Style details and not succeeding very well. The rather tepid Classical building was clad in brick with limestone trim and adopted a traditional H-shaped plan. It was pushed to the lot lines at the western end of the site and flanked to the east by a playground.

Holden, McLaughlin Associates' Public School 156 (1952), the Eugene Percy Roberts School, at 2960 Eighth Avenue, was a two- and three-story L-shaped brick building featuring horizontal bands of windows and a principal glass-enclosed entrance surmounted by a gently undulating roof.[44] Public School 154 (1961), the John Hancock School, occupying a full block site bounded by Seventh and Eighth avenues, 126th and 127th streets, was designed by the Los Angeles–based black architect Paul R. Williams, who in the 1930s and 1940s had specialized in luxurious homes for movie stars.[45] None of that glamour was to find its way to P. S. 154, however; it consisted of a three-story concrete-framed building filled in with aluminum sash and glazed ceramic tile and an adjacent gymnasium structure. The principal facade was punctuated by an asymmetrically placed main entrance as well as three secondary entrances, each surmounted by a double-height expanse of glass covered with a decorative, geometrically patterned grille. Percival Goodman's Public School 92 (1965), the Mary McLeod Bethune School, at 22 West 134th Street, between Seventh and Eighth avenues, was a sophisticated Modernist essay that subtly contrasted cast concrete, exposed aggregate and red brick in a complexly massed and aggressively manipulated composition.[46] Katz, Waisman, Weber's Public School 208 (1968), the Alain L. Locke School, at 21 West 111th Street, and Public School 185 (1968), the John Mercer Langston School, at 20 West 112th Street, were set back to back on a midblock site; both schools were modest compositions in brick with trim of exposed aggregate concrete.[47]

By the mid-1960s public school buildings had begun to be transformed from comparatively open-faced structures, bringing a note of accessible civicism to local communities, into fortified strongholds, refuges against the decaying city. None was more hostile in its impact than Curtis & Davis's Intermediate School 201 (1966), the Arthur A. Schomburg School, at 2005 Madison Avenue, between 127th and 128th streets.[48] The school confronted its neighborhood with windowless facades consisting of two floors of brick and concrete carried on pilotis. An open ground-floor space beneath the building was intended for public use as a passageway or recreation area, but the space was so low, especially in relation to its width and length, that it was dark and dreary and proved uninviting. Inside, the lack of windows in the classrooms (there were windows in the corridors) was meant to heighten students' concentration by isolating them from their undesirable surroundings, but the design became a symbol for the status of inner-city blacks as "invisible" members of society.

Other neighborhood facilities reflected the degenerating quality of life in Harlem and in the city as a whole. In 1969, to help with the spiraling drug problem, plans were announced for a so-called halfway house, to be built next to an existing drug-treatment facility on the northwest corner of Mt. Morris Park West and 120th Street, under the auspices of the city's Narcotic Addiction Control Commission.[49] Russo & Sonder's proposed seven-story brick-and-concrete building, though intended to maintain the area's low-rise character, was taller than its brownstone neighbors and featured boldly cantilevered elements. Its entry level was to be depressed several feet below the street and set back on a sunken plaza, which the architects hoped would attract impromptu gatherings much as traditional stoops had. Community opposition to the project arose on the grounds that because the new building was to be situated within the Landmarks Preservation Commission's proposed Mt. Morris Park historic district, the requisite demolition of several brownstones was objectionable. In addition, some community members feared the intrusion of addicts and the expansion of drug-treatment facilities, even if demolition and new construction were not involved. The project was never realized, and in 1971 the area roughly bounded by Mt. Morris Park West, Lenox Avenue, and 119th and 123rd streets was designated the Mt. Morris Park historic district.[50]

Lehrecke & Tonetti's Twenty-eighth Precinct Headquarters (1974) housed the police department on a prominent but difficult triangular site bounded by Eighth and St. Nicholas Avenue and 123rd Street. With perhaps excessive praise, Norval White and Elliot Willensky deemed the "carefully designed" two-story building of exposed concrete and brick a "superb architectural work that observes a subtle and witty respect for materials not unlike that of Louis Kahn's late efforts."[51]

WEST HARLEM

West Harlem, stretching from St. Nicholas Avenue to the Hudson River and from 125th to 155th Street, saw far less building activity than either Central or East Harlem during the postwar period. This was in part a reflection of West Harlem's inherent social stability as a lower-middle-class and working-class neighborhood with a reasonably solid stock of housing that could be retained through preservation rather than replaced through redevelopment.

Among the relatively few privately financed apartment buildings constructed in the area soon after the war was Ivey Terrace, a crisply detailed six-story building adopting a vaguely streamlined Modernist style, complete with round-cornered balconies; located at 21 Hamilton Terrace and completed in 1951, the building was designed by Vertner W. Tandy.[1] Most of West Harlem's housing projects were built in the area near the 125th Street valley, where new development primarily replaced outmoded industrial buildings and old-law tenements. The New York City Housing Authority's Manhattanville Houses (William Lescaze, 1961), a six-building complex housing 1,273 families and occupying a superblock site located between 129th and 133rd streets, Broadway and Amsterdam Avenue, furthered the towers-in-the-park approach to redevelopment adopted by nearby Morningside Gardens and the General Grant Houses (see chapter 9).[2] Built under the Title I program, the project was composed of three-winged red-brick buildings with glass-enclosed public hallways radiating from centrally located elevators. Manhattanville Houses was perhaps more interesting from an economic than an aesthetic standpoint, filling an important niche in the real estate market, with apartments renting at rates between those charged in the middle-income Morningside Gardens and the low-income Grant Houses.

Two limited-profit cooperative apartment buildings announced in 1962, River View Towers and River Terrace, were the first new residential construction projects undertaken on Riverside Drive since Schwab House, which had been completed in 1950. Unlike most of Harlem's postwar housing, these were not "projects," and they were not intended for the poor. Kelly & Gruzen's River View Towers (1963), between 139th and 140th streets, a state-aided, middle-income apartment house

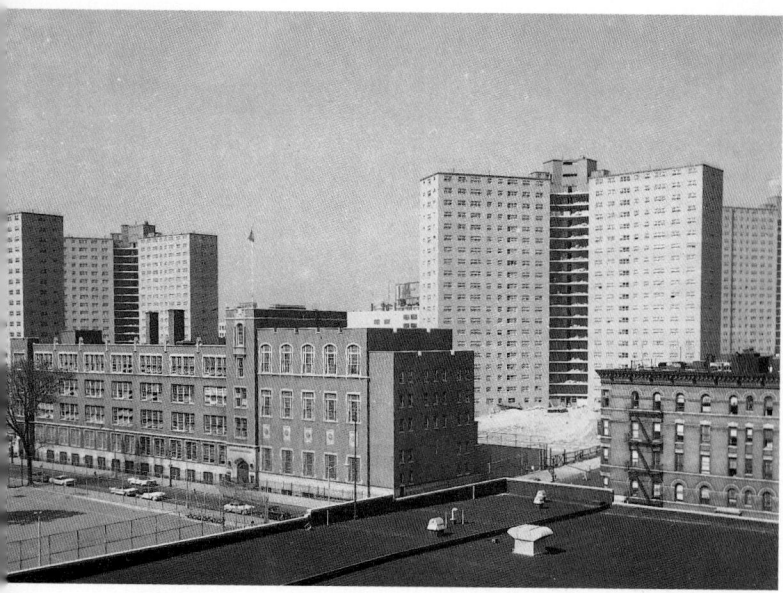

built under the Mitchell-Lama law, was a slender twenty-four-story slab set perpendicular to its Riverside Drive frontage.[3] The site had been occupied by St. Regis Convent (1896) until 1955, when the city appropriated the property to build a hospital for tuberculosis patients. But when advances in treatments for the disease rendered such a facility unnecessary, the site was made available for residential development. The Yeshiva Haichel Hatorah was also located on the site. At a public hearing held by the City Planning Commission, Senator Jacob Javits and several rabbis protested the city's eviction of the private school, but it was demolished nonetheless. River View Towers, which at completion was the tallest building on Riverside Drive, was set back from the cross streets and incorporated landscaped grounds as well as a 150-car parking garage. Though the position of the slab dramatically broke with the continuous wall along the drive, it offered sweeping diagonal views to all 384 apartments. And even though the context-breaking massing allied it with the "projects," most units had balconies, a feature that linked the building to upscale developments in more affluent parts of the city. Paul & Jarmul's sixteen-story River Terrace (1963), which replaced several parking garages on Riverside Drive between 157th and 158th streets, was also built under the Mitchell-Lama program to house middle-income residents; it offered balconies to two-thirds of its tenants.[4]

In 1972 Riverside Park Community, a supersize apartment house that included educational facilities, was announced for a site bounded by Twelfth Avenue and Broadway, 133rd and 135th streets.[5] The project had grown out of an unrealized plan for a vast mixed-use complex, to cover the same site as well as adjacent property, that had been proposed in 1968 by the Negro Labor Committee and designed by Richard Dattner & Associates and Henri A. LeGendre & Associates. As redesigned by the same architects, this time in collaboration with Max Wechsler & Associates, and under the sponsorship of the New York City Educational Construction Fund, the radically reduced complex contained a single massive apartment building, along with Intermediate School 195, the Roberto Clemente School, named after the Dominican-born baseball player who died in a plane crash in 1972. The red-brick-clad apartment house was composed of five connected slabs of progressively greater height forming an incomplete octagon; the slabs defined the edges of an elevated plaza that surmounted a parking garage and contained the public school. The Brobdingnagian complex, Paul Goldberger said, was a "set of far too big red-brick slabs" that looked particularly "dreadful" from Riverside Drive, "where the contrast between its huge size and that of everything around it is, curiously, more disturbing than from close up on local streets."[6]

In addition to residential development, the area was the site of several significant proposals for civic projects, though most were never realized. In 1967 Mayor Lindsay, as part of his administration's citywide effort to commission leading architects for public works, announced that Philip Johnson had been hired to redesign a sewage-treatment plant on concrete piles along the bank of the Hudson River extending from the latitude of 137th Street to that of 145th Street; the mayor had hoped that a new design would quell community opposition to the plant.[7] Johnson's response to the challenge of, as the editors of *Progressive Architecture* put it, "turning a beast into a beauty" was to cover most of the plant's twenty-two-acre roof with reflecting pools and fountains, four of which would shoot up 200-foot-high columns of water.[8] The water garden was to be more than ornamental: sculptures in the four-acre reflecting pool were

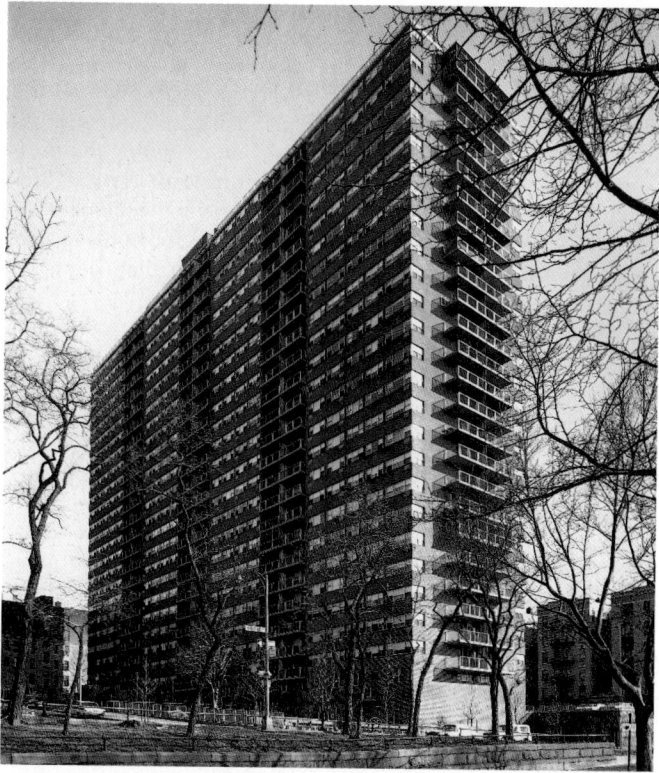

Top: Manhattanville Houses, between Broadway and Amsterdam Avenue, West 129th and West 133rd streets. William Lescaze, 1961. View to the northwest. NYCHA

Bottom: River View Towers, 626 Riverside Drive, West 139th to West 140th Street. Kelly & Gruzen, 1963. View to the southeast. GS

to house mechanical equipment, while an eleven-acre pool would contain a grid of aeration nozzles. These would produce, according to Johnson, "a continuous shimmering haze of droplets of water lighted at night and blown about in the wind during the day."[9] But local residents remained unimpressed, and community representatives demanded that Johnson's proposal be replaced by plans for a children's playground or an adult recreation area. The project dragged on for years and was finally completed by different architects in a very different form in 1993.

In 1969 plans were announced for a coordinated complex of residential, commercial and health facilities centered around the Knickerbocker Hospital (John Oakman, 1921), on the west side of Convent Avenue between 130th and 131st streets, and extending to fill a superblock site bounded by Amsterdam, Convent and Morningside avenues, 125th and 131st streets.[10] The project, initially named the Knickerbocker Health Park and later called the Manhattanville Health Park, was designed by Max O. Urbahn Associates and Lucas & Edwards to include a series of connected housing slabs presenting a·saw-toothed facade along Convent Avenue; a glass-enclosed "medical mall" linking hospital buildings running parallel to Amsterdam Avenue; a commercial mall facing 125th Street; a convent and school affiliated with and located next to St. Joseph's Church (Herter Brothers, 1889), at 401 West 125th Street, on the northwest corner of Morningside Avenue; and a central open green space separating the various components. The plan was never realized.

While most of the superscale projects remained unbuilt, several smaller institutional buildings were realized in the area. The Upper Manhattan Medical Group Building (1954), on the northeast corner of Amsterdam Avenue and 152nd Street, was a small-scale health facility that added an understated grace note to the neighborhood.[11] Designed by Nemeny, Geller & Yurchenko, the two-story building surrounded a central courtyard and featured a gray-painted concrete frame filled in with red brick and an irregular, syncopated window pattern. The critic Frederick Gutheim was particularly impressed with the building. "In this colorful, fresh building," he said, "one is entirely rid of the institutionality of the hospital, the impersonality of medical practice, the idea that design is controlled more by germs than by people, much less any overtone of socialism or collective action. . . . What has been achieved is a friendly building, domestic in scale, intimate in feeling, warm in expression."[12] Abraham W. Geller & Associates' Lower Washington Heights Neighborhood Family Care Center (1975), on the northeast corner of Amsterdam Avenue and 145th Street, was much less distinctive; its massive bulk, exacerbated by overscaled square windows, embraced a large but rather barren entrance court.[13]

Costas Machlouzarides' Church of the Crucifixion (1967), on the northwest corner of Convent Avenue and 149th Street, was typical of the idiosyncratic, sculptural forms common to many of the era's religious buildings. The church's undulating concrete walls were surmounted by an airfoil roof, a composition that Norval White and Elliot Willensky described as an "overdesigned tour de force" and "a kind of hallucinogenic version of Le Corbusier's Ronchamp."[14] Public School 153, also known as the Adam Clayton Powell, Jr. School (1975), on the west side of Amsterdam Avenue between 146th and 147th streets, was a restrained if rather anonymous essay in red brick, designed by the Board of Education's in-house staff.[15]

By far the most important public institution in West Harlem, the City College of New York, which became the City College of

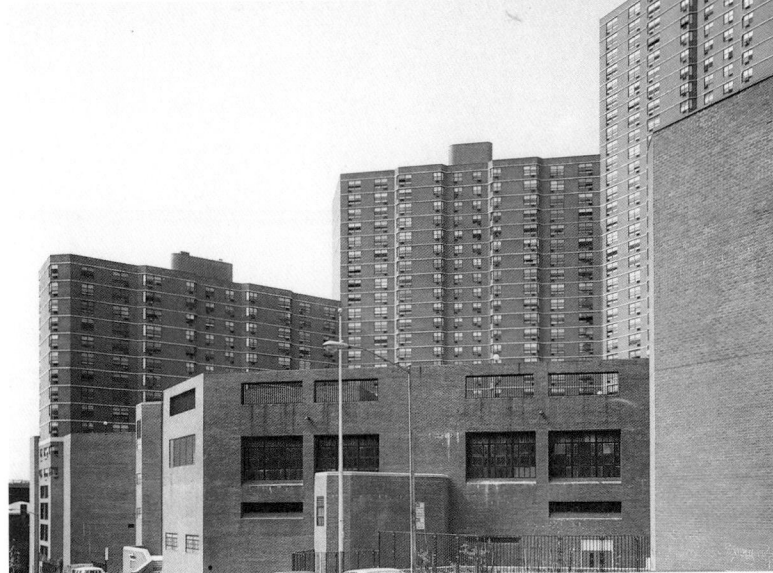

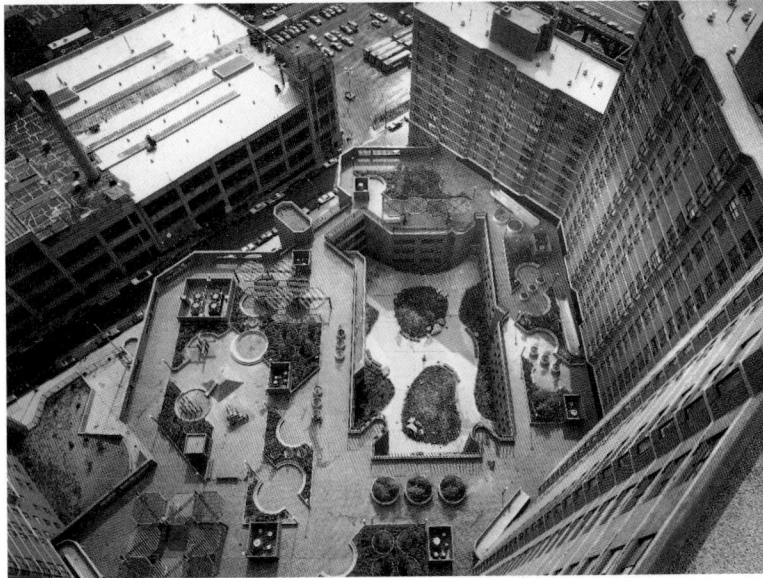

Top: Riverside Park Community, Broadway to Twelfth Avenue, West 133rd to West 135th Street. Richard Dattner & Associates, Henri A. LeGendre & Associates and Max Wechsler & Associates, 1972. View to the northwest. RD

Bottom: Riverside Park Community. Courtyard. RD

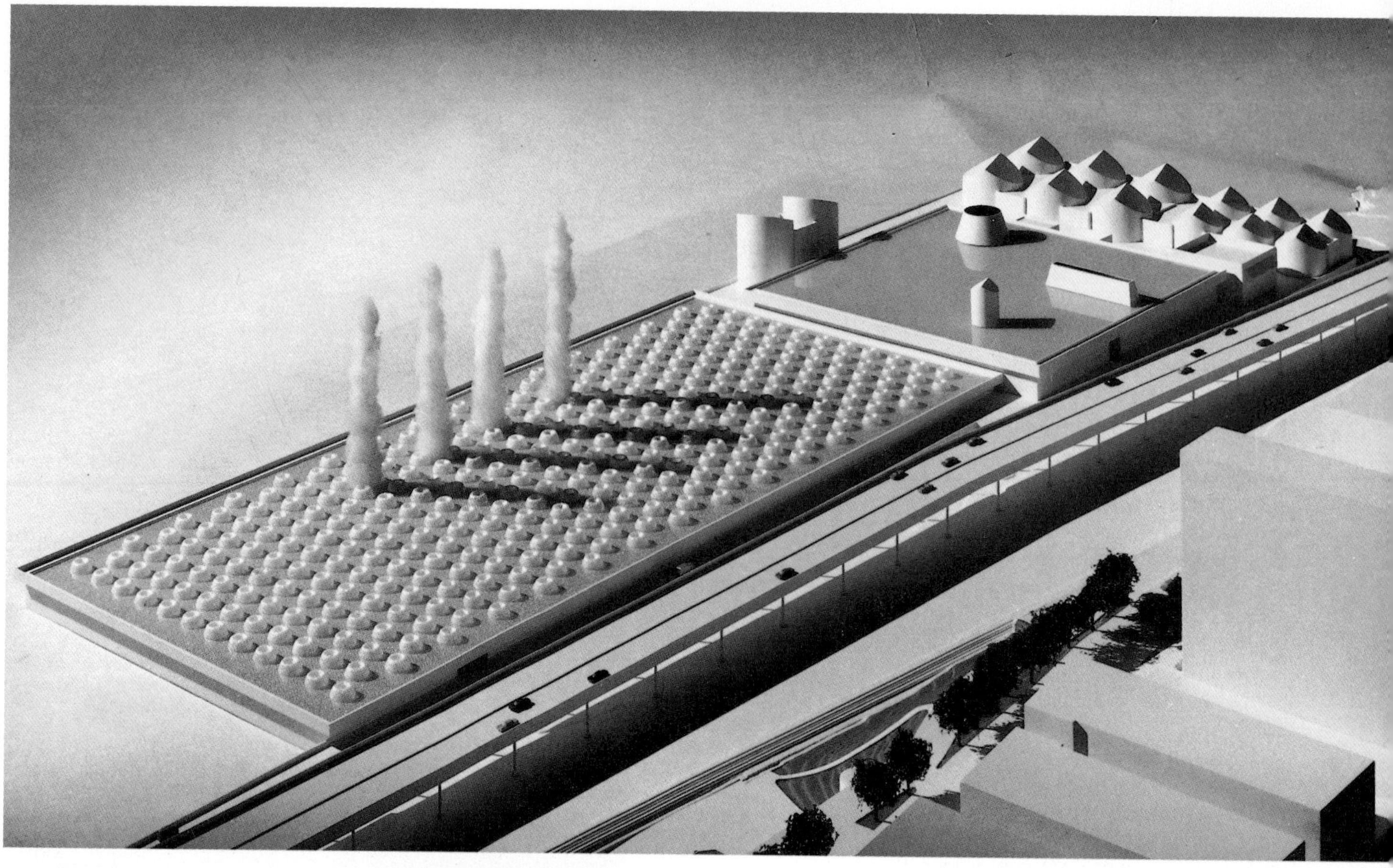

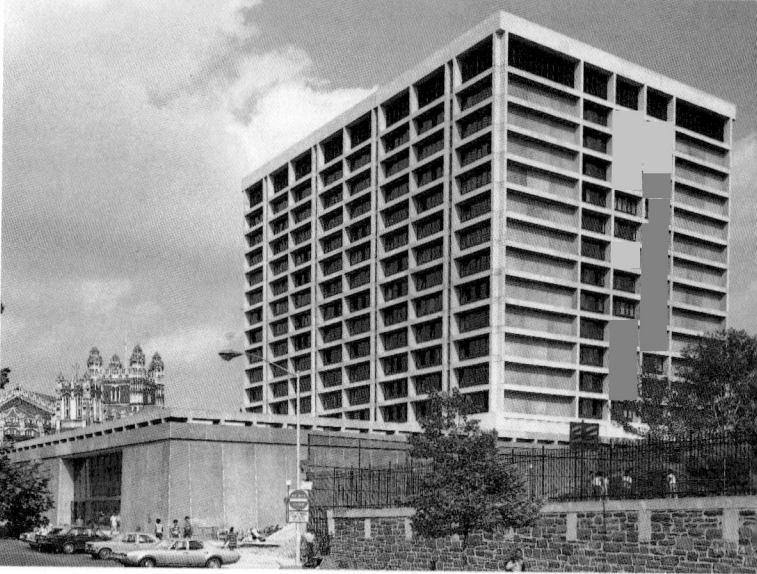

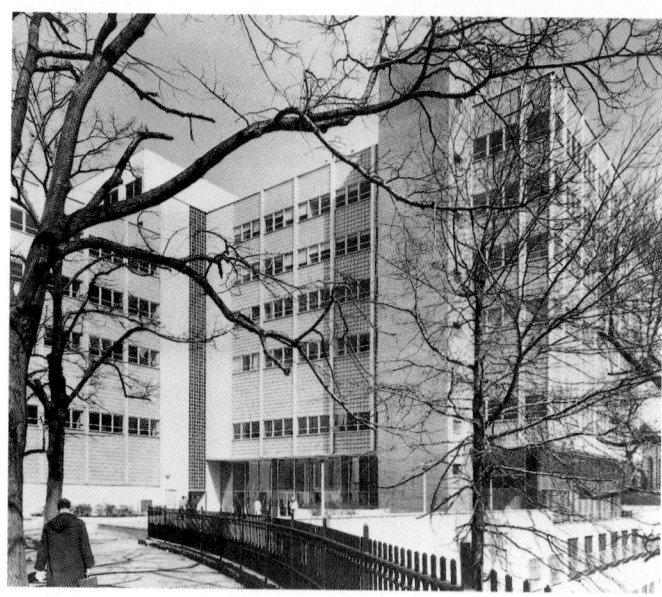

Top: Proposal for sewage-treatment plant, on piles in the Hudson River, West 137th to West 145th Street. Philip Johnson, 1967. Model. View to the northwest. Checkman. LC

Bottom left: Steinman Hall, City College, east side of Convent Avenue, between St. Nicholas Terrace and West 141st Street. Lorimer & Rose, 1962. View to the northwest. CCNYOP

Bottom right: Robert E. Marshak Science Building, City University of New York, between Convent Avenue and St. Nicholas Terrace, West 136th and West 138th streets. Skidmore, Owings & Merrill, 1971. View to the northeast. CCNYOP the City University of New York in 1969, undertook ambitious construction plans in the decades following the war. Lorimer & Rose's Morris Raphael Cohen Library (1957), on the southeast corner of Convent Avenue and 135th Street, occupied a site on the school's South Campus bounded by Convent Avenue, St. Nicholas Terrace, 130th and 135th streets, which City College had acquired from the Manhattanville College of the Sacred Heart when that institution moved to Westchester County in 1952.[16] In sharp contrast to the architecturally and urbanistically cohesive ensemble of Gothic buildings on the college's main campus (George B. Post, 1905), the four-story Cohen Library adopted a Modernist vocabulary, including expanses of glass brick, and featured a virtually windowless principal facade.[17] Lorimer & Rose also designed Steinman Hall (1962), on the east side of Convent Avenue between St. Nicholas Terrace and 141st Street, which housed the college's engineering department.[18] Another essay in Modernist minimalism, this six-story T-shaped building had facades of white glazed brick, marble and glass brick.

In the mid-1960s City College hired Skidmore, Owings & Merrill (SOM) to draw up a new master plan.[19] Projected to cost $40 million and to be realized in three phases over approximately five years, the scheme would allow the college to expand its enrollment by 30 percent. SOM proposed a complex of Modernist buildings to be raised on a podium and linked to each other, as well as to the existing Gothic buildings, by underground passageways, elevated terraces and pedestrian bridges. In reporting on the plan, Ada Louise Huxtable wrote in the New York Times: "City College is about to go from Collegiate Gothic to Collegiate Concrete in a master plan for its uptown campus that is a sample demonstration of some of the most progressive principles of today's architecture and design." She said that the "sprinkling of standard commercial additions" that constituted the campus's existing postwar buildings were a reflection of "the almost universal unsureness in university circles of what to do with modern architecture." In contrast, Huxtable said, the "platforming concept" represented in the SOM plan was not only an effective solution to City College's design problems but "probably the logical and inevitable way that the rebuilding of cities must be carried out in the immediate future."[20]

The first and only building of SOM's master plan to be realized, the Robert E. Marshak Science Building, was completed in 1971.[21] Wrapped in exposed-concrete grilles and perched on a base of rough-hewn precast concrete, the building contained a library, a greenhouse, a planetarium, a gymnasium and a swimming pool, in addition to offices and classrooms. Although SOM's Brutalist approach was no doubt intended as an appropriate Modernist equivalent to the original campus's tough Gothic style, it made for a building that was more menacing than medieval in effect. Although Huxtable had praised preliminary drawings of the building, saying that it "could be a surprisingly harmonious foil for the picturesque Gothic of the old campus," when completed it was widely criticized both within and outside the college community.[22] Goldberger stated that while it "seems to be trying, like so much of Skidmore's work, to evoke an image of corporate suavity," it ends up being "not corporate at all, but pretentiously and arrogantly institutional."[23]

Extensive problems in the construction of the Marshak building, involving both delays and cost overruns, led the college to take legal action against SOM and to replace their master plan with one by John Carl Warnecke & Associates, drawn up in 1969 and revised in 1971.[24] The North Academic Center, a modified-Z-shaped megastructure occupying a site bounded by Convent and Amsterdam avenues, 135th and 138th streets, was the only element of the Warnecke plan to be realized; it was not completed until 1983. The construction of the center necessitated the demolition in 1973 of one of City College's, and indeed the city's, most beloved cultural landmarks, Lewisohn Stadium, designed by Arnold Brunner and completed in 1915. Surrounded by an imposing Doric colonnade and with a seating capacity of nearly 25,000, the stadium was the site of the college's commencements, as well as college and local athletic events. But for most New Yorkers the stadium was best known from 1918 to 1966 as home to a summer concert series organized by Mrs. Charles S. Guggenheimer that over the years had featured such artists as George Gershwin, Marian Anderson and Eugene Ormandy. With tickets costing a mere twenty-five cents for much of the series' duration, the stadium was, as Carter Horsley put it in the New York Times, "an outdoor Carnegie Hall, with the patrons in shirtsleeves and work pants," furthering City College's reputation as the "Harvard of the proletariat."[25]

The replacement of Lewisohn Stadium with high-density university development reflected City College's decision not to expand into surrounding West Harlem but to fully exploit its existing real estate holdings; this decision was based in part on Columbia University's painful conflicts with its surrounding community, a situation that had reached a climax in the late 1960s (see chapter 9). Surprisingly, Ada Louise Huxtable was not sorry to see the passing of the monumental Classical structure, arguing that it was "a cultural, not an esthetic landmark. Built in municipal disposal-plant style embellished with a Rockette-row of squat classic columns and faced with blank walls of less than classic beauty, it gains its charm from moonlight and Mendelssohn. In unorchestrated daylight, it is about as ugly a structure as can be found anywhere."[26] Whatever the stadium's architectural merit, its destruction was a sign of changes in the tastes and patterns of Manhattan's middle class and in the character of West Harlem in particular; postwar prosperity, the massive exodus to the suburbs and the increasingly menacing quality of the City College area had conspired to diminish the crowds who once enjoyed the stadium's offerings.

125TH STREET

Harlem's most important street, from a sociological as well as an economic and a political standpoint, was without question 125th Street. It was at once a lively Main Street, lined by mom-and-pop stores and small-scale buildings, a link between several of the villagelike neighborhoods that constituted Harlem, and a world-renowned symbol of African-American cultural life. It was also a traffic-clogged artery, providing the only unbroken river-to-river commercial connection between midtown and Washington Heights, and a principal approach to the Triborough Bridge. The architectural and urbanistic challenge of 125th Street after World War II was in large part an attempt to cope with the through traffic, which contributed nothing to the local economy, and to define a role for the street that would give it a status comparable to that of Forty-second or Fifty-seventh street.

Early postwar activity concentrated on the street's western end. Buildings housing Columbia University's School of Engineering and faculty apartments provided an institutional presence, while the General Grant and Manhattanville public housing projects offered a strong but not necessarily positive image of urban redevelopment (see chapter 9 and "West Harlem," above). Later,

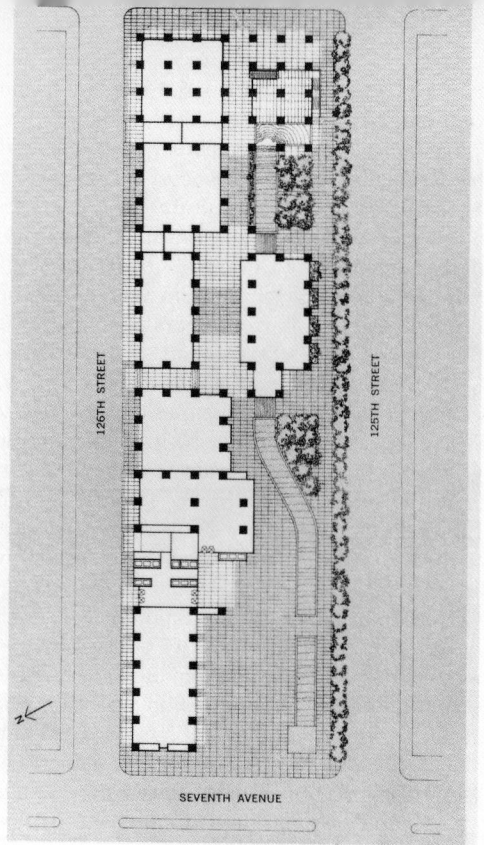

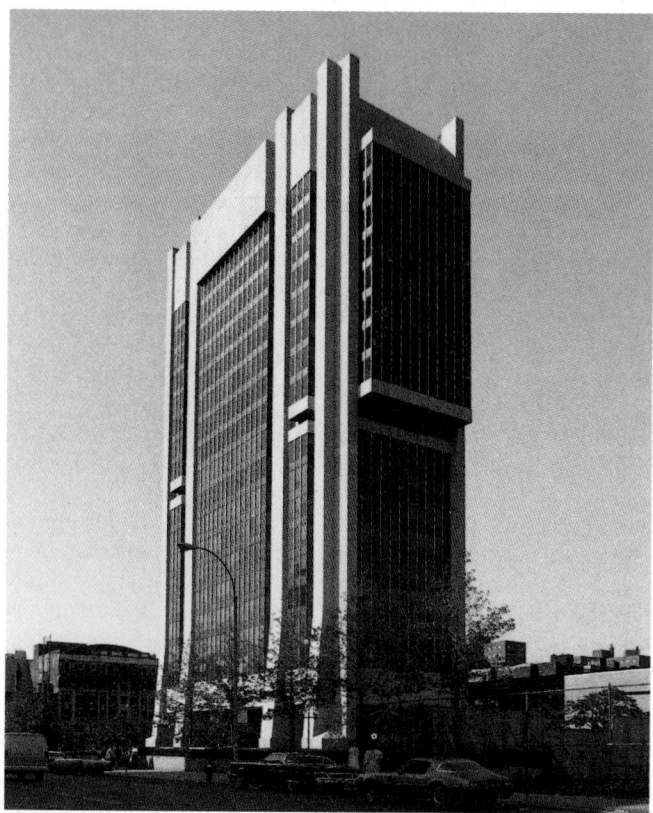

Top: Proposal for Harlem State Office Building, Lenox to Seventh Avenue, West 125th to West 126th Street. Philip Johnson and John Burgee, 1966. Plan. AF. CU

Bottom: Harlem State Office Building, east side of Seventh Avenue, West 125th to West 126th Street. Ifill Johnson Hanchard, 1973. View to the northwest. Dunlap. DD

the Knickerbocker Health Park, announced in 1969 though ultimately unrealized, promised to bring a community-based institution to the street's western end (see "West Harlem," above).

After the 1964 Harlem riots ambitious plans for 125th Street, concentrating on its central portion, began to come forth, most notably the controversial proposal to locate a major office facility for the State of New York on a large site along the east side of Seventh Avenue between 125th and 126th streets.[1] The Harlem State Office Building was first proposed by Governor Rockefeller in 1966. He offered the commission to Philip Johnson and John Burgee, who prepared some drawings outlining a block-long sequence of buildings of various heights defining an interior pedestrian "street." But they ultimately withdrew from the project "for the simple reason," Johnson would say in 1973, "that I was convinced it wasn't very good politics for a white man to do a building up there."[2]

Johnson and Burgee were replaced by Ifill & Johnson, whose principals were black. In 1968 they revealed plans for a twenty-four-story freestanding tower and an adjacent three-story extension, to be set back in a generously proportioned plaza at the northeast corner of 125th Street and Seventh Avenue. The office building was to occupy only the western part of the site, which extended all the way to Lenox Avenue; although the entire block was to be cleared, plans for the eastern end were not announced. (According to Ada Louise Huxtable, writing in February 1968, Philip Johnson was at work designing a cultural center for the site.)[3] Ifill & Johnson proposed a bulky tower of dark glass, black-anodized aluminum and light-colored granite, cantilevered in portions and partially raised above the plaza on splayed piers that ran the full height of the building.

Although there was immediate community opposition to the project, the state proceeded with its plans. But demands for radical changes to the building program and design did not die down, and in the fall of 1969 local protesters started a three-month-long "squat-in" at the site, long cleared of its tenements, brownstones and low-rise commercial buildings. The Architects Renewal Committee in Harlem (ARCH) did not unconditionally oppose construction of the tower, which had become known as the S.O.B. (short for State Office Building, as well as the more colloquial meaning) and as "Rockefeller's Vietnam." But in October 1969 the group set forth three different proposals, which together called for the inclusion of low-income housing, schools and cultural and commercial facilites on the full-block site. Two months later Rockefeller called on Edward Logue, then head of the New York State Urban Development Corporation, to negotiate with the community. Logue presented a compromise plan for a mixed-use complex that included the tower. On December 15, after a fractious two-day "town meeting" at which a wide variety of proposals were suggested, community group representatives voted overwhelmingly to oppose Logue's proposal. Efforts were then made to form a community-controlled housing cooperative to fill the entire site. Despite the seemingly intractable opposition, Rockefeller went ahead with his plans, saying that "no one can realistically expect that Harlem, a community larger than some states in our nation, will speak with a single voice."[4] As the editors of *Architectural Forum* observed: "The Governor seemed to think that Harlem should be grateful for any skyscraper it could get. Ignoring some of the noisy opposition, Rocky seemed ready to negotiate with any black 'silent majority' he could find."[5]

The building was finally completed in 1973, and its design, by Ifill Johnson Hanchard (the new name of the firm), was close to their original proposal, although its height was reduced to nineteen stories. Related in its scale and its confrontational stance to Governor Rockefeller's vast South Mall complex in Albany (Wallace K. Harrison, 1962–77), the Harlem State Office Building seemed more like a celebration of the government's power than of the community's potential, a misguided architectural restatement in rather banal Modernist terms of traditional civic pride and grandeur.[6] Paul Goldberger said that if nothing else the new building "proves that the State of New York is even-handed—it is willing to give Harlem the same mediocre architecture it dishes out everywhere else. . . . In the end, all this looks like is not big architecture but big government."[7]

Despite the rocky road to its completion, the announcement and final realization of the Harlem State Office Building did stimulate construction activity, or at least real estate interest, along the 125th Street corridor. As Ada Louise Huxtable noted a little more than a year after the building was first publicly proposed, "What no one visualized was the speed with which the developers would start wheeling and dealing along 125th Street. The new state building was the match that sparked an explosion of construction proposals."[8] Among these was the 1968 announcement of plans for a privately financed, thirty-three-story tower housing twenty floors of office space, a 200-room hotel, a rooftop restaurant and retail space, perhaps including a department store.[9] The complex, known as Triboro Plaza, was to be located in East Harlem, five blocks east of the Harlem State Office Building, and to occupy the majority of the block bounded by 124th and 125th streets, Lexington and Third avenues. Designed by Ifill Johnson Hanchard, Triboro Plaza was to be clad in masonry, with large expanses of glass. Despite the enthusiastic support of financial backers and several civic leaders, including Manhattan Borough President Percy Sutton, numerous community groups protested the project on the grounds that they had not been asked to participate in its development. The protesters also felt that the project should allow for some measure of community ownership and management, as well as job-training and employment opportunities. Community opposition successfully blocked the project's realization. In 1971 Ifill Johnson Hanchard announced plans for another mixed-use project on the same site, this time calling for two thirty-story towers to house commercial space as well as 400 lower-middle-class apartments, but this plan was also not realized.[10]

According to Ada Louise Huxtable, additional proposals for 125th Street included a Harlem Opera House, to be designed by Edward Larrabee Barnes and sponsored by the Italian impresario and composer Gian-Carlo Menotti as well as, perhaps, by the city itself; and several mixed-use projects utilizing the air rights over the New York Central Railroad's elevated Park Avenue viaduct, including one proposed as part of the Museum of Modern Art's exhibition "The New City: Architecture and Urban Renewal" (see "Black America's Capital City," above). These projects, along with other realized and unrealized proposals for the street, led Huxtable to question the nature of the street's redevelopment. Huxtable wrote:

> As things stand now on 125th Street, we have in hand two office buildings, some institutional construction and an assortment of cultural monuments. Is this really community revitalization? Beyond the fact that it represents the badly needed economic impetus of new construction, what does it do for Harlem? Is it not, perhaps—oh, dreadful thought—a fine collection of those middle-class values that the black community keeps telling the white community not to impose on it. . . . The new buildings are meant to be anchors for a revitalized community. But too many anchors can sink a ship.[11]

In 1967 a group known as the Community Association of the East Harlem Triangle, which subsequently opposed the Triboro Plaza project (see above), became the city's first local organization to receive a federal grant to devise a renewal plan.[12] The group, which represented the area bounded by 125th Street, Park Avenue and the Harlem River, commissioned the Architects Renewal Committee in Harlem (ARCH), with Roger Katan serving as urban design consultant, to devise a plan for the physically and economically devastated neighborhood. The language of ARCH's highly controversial report unabashedly reflected a political as well as an architectural and urbanistic agenda. The report was dedicated, it said, to the "concept of full and participatory partnership between local community organizations and professional technical advisors, sensitive to the needs of the indigenous peoples" and to "exploding the myth that Afro-American and Spanish American people lack the necessary organizational and technical skills to plan their own destinies." The authors of the report went on to say: "For too long now, white people lacking both sympathy and sensitivity to critical issues confronting us, have been allowed to come into our communities to plan for us. The result of these attempts to ameliorate the conditions of our lives makes itself quite evident in any major American city. Such is the nature of racist white America."[13]

ARCH and Katan's plan, exploiting the area's role as a transportation gateway to the city, focused large-scale development near the Triborough, Willis Avenue and Third Avenue bridges, leaving much of the riverfront area between them to be used for parkland and recreational facilities. It constituted an aggressive departure from both Harlem's traditional low-rise urbanism and its postwar towers-in-the-park housing projects. A complex of high-rise buildings connected by a series of multi-level pedestrian bridges was to be built above the network of ramps providing access to the Triborough Bridge; one building adopted an arc shape, conforming to half of the full-spiral ramp below, while others, rising from a base that conformed to the street grid, were set at dramatic angles, and still others adopted stacked pyramidal shapes. The plan also called for 2,400 units of new housing, 1,800 of them for low-income residents and the remainder for middle-income residents. ARCH favored a system of community ownership in conjunction with federally funded rent-supplement programs.

In order to bolster 125th Street's traditional role as the area's commercial hub, Katan suggested closing the street to through traffic, with the exception of buses and taxis, and bisecting the thoroughfare with a landscaped median strip. To relieve congestion in the area and reestablish its viability as a residential district, Katan also advocated closing 127th and 128th streets between Lexington and Second avenues and 129th Street between Park and Lexington avenues, as well as relocating the New York Central Railroad's above-ground 125th Street station from the middle of Park Avenue to the southwest corner of that intersection. The block bounded by Lexington and Third avenues, 126th and 127th streets was to be rebuilt as the Triangle Commons, a low-lying complex of buildings providing community services; these would be placed within landscaped open spaces and linked by enclosed elevated passageways. Stressing the speed with which they sought to realize their proposal, the authors of the report concluded: "For a very long time America has romanticized over the quiet and graceful patience exercised by black people in the face of an American racism which systematically denied them their manhood. Now is the time to transform patience into community development action pro-

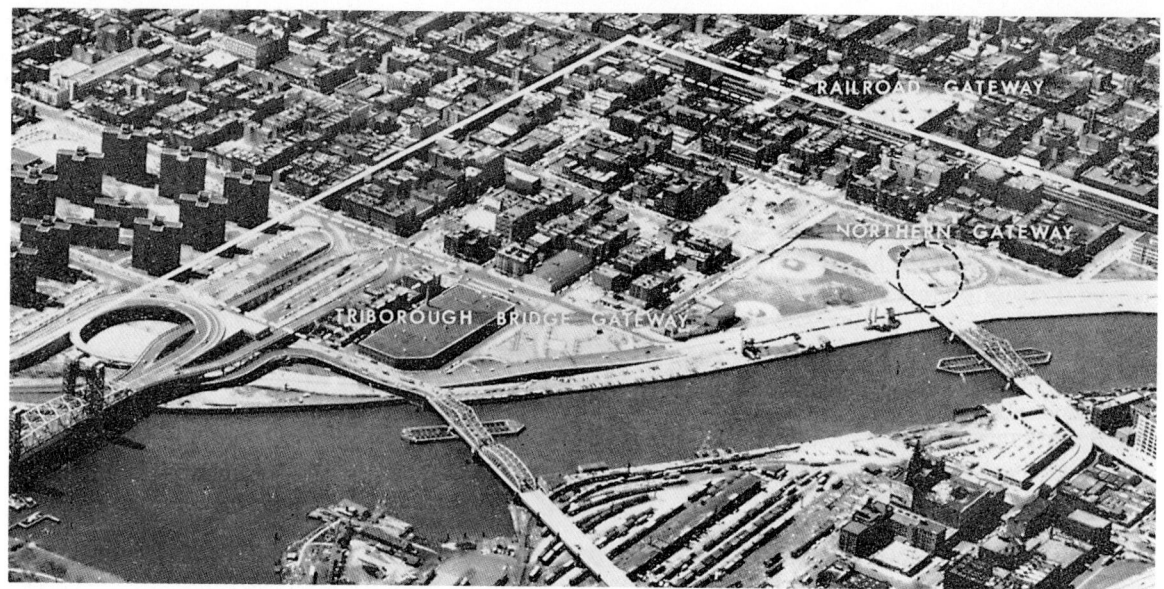

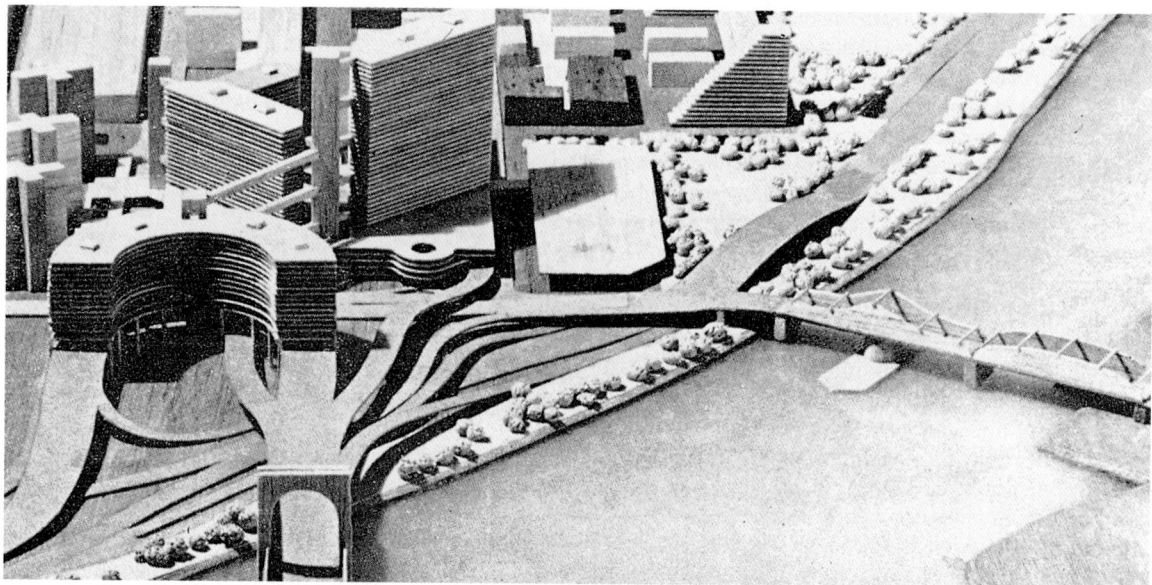

Top: Master plan for East Harlem Triangle, between Park Avenue, the Harlem River and East 125th Street. Architects Renewal Committee in Harlem with Roger Katan, 1967. Aerial view to the southwest showing existing area. ADA. CU

Center: Master plan for East Harlem Triangle. Model. View to the west. ADA. CU

Right: Master plan for East Harlem Triangle. Plan. *East Harlem Triangle Plan.* CU

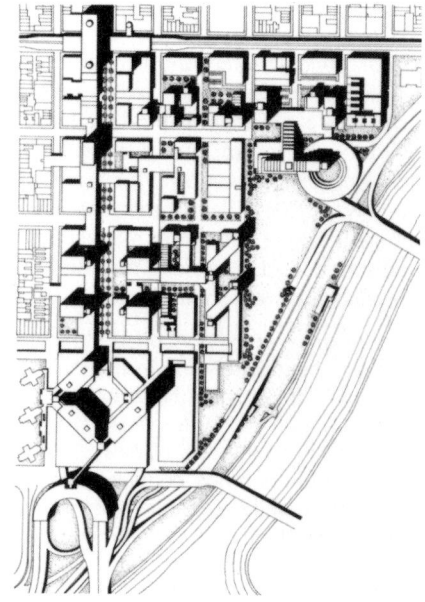

grams. In the present era there is no time for anything but action and the triangle won't have it any other way."[14] ARCH and Katan's plan was not implemented.

In 1967–68 the architect John Johansen also conducted a feasibility study, called "Leapfrog Housing," for the redevelopment of the so-called East Harlem Triangle.[15] In the backyards between existing tenements, Johansen proposed building slender towers that would serve as the structural and mechanical cores of clustered housing units; the housing would be cantilevered from, and stretched between, the towers. This concept of a rebuilt neighborhood that would ultimately incorporate separate levels for vehicular and pedestrian traffic recalled the visionary schemes that Harvey Wiley Corbett and Hugh Ferriss had produced in the 1920s.[16] Yet Johansen's urban vision was also married to a concern for community life that was characteristic of the 1960s: "If areas could be immediately and continually renewed, decaying parts replaced by new construction with no displacement of tenants within but simply moved upstairs, we would be respecting existing living patterns as well as the natural processes of the city as a living organism."[17]

In addition to the Harlem State Office Building, two other large-scale projects for 125th Street were realized in the early 1970s: the Commonwealth Building (Hausman & Rosenberg, 1971) and the CAV Building (Kahn & Jacobs, 1973). The Commonwealth Building, a six-story commercial structure located at 215 West 125th Street, between Seventh and Eighth avenues, was jointly backed by a local community group and a suburban development concern.[18] Above the ground-floor retail space, the building constituted a jazzed-up version of I. M. Pei's Kips Bay Plaza (see chapter 5). The fourteen-story, 188,000-square-foot CAV Building was located on the northwest corner of 125th Street and Lenox Avenue.[19] At the time of its completion, the building, developed by Charles A. Vincent, the principal of CAV Enterprises, Inc., was the nation's largest office building owned and operated by black management. Echoing the sentiments of other observers who saw black entrepreneurship as key to Harlem's redevelopment, Vincent said: "We can walk around with all our dashikis and bones and earrings in our noses. They mean nothing until we get into the mainstream of the economy by controlling some of the green."[20] At the building's dedication, Deputy Mayor–designate David Dinkins commented, "I think an awful lot of the money that used to go downtown will now stay up here. And it should."[21] The building's banal Modernist design was not, however, nearly as noteworthy as its financial underpinnings. In addition to underground parking, the building housed Vincent's Place, Harlem's largest restaurant and banquet facility.

UPPER MANHATTAN

Upper Manhattan, extending north of Harlem, from 155th Street to the northern tip of the island, and encompassing the Washington Heights and Inwood neighborhoods, was an often overlooked part of the city. Nevertheless, during the postwar period, the area was the site of several architecturally significant projects, most of them for institutional clients.

In 1952, twenty-seven years after the architect Donn Barber had designed the Broadway Temple, a brooding, boldly massed forty-six-story mixed-use tower for Dr. Christian F. Reisner's Methodist congregation, to occupy the entire west blockfront of Broadway between 173rd and 174th streets, the church's expansion was finally realized, although in a radically reduced form.[1] Two twelve-story apartment buildings located at the block's endpoints had been completed in 1927; the final articulation and realization of the design of the apartment buildings had been entrusted to McKenzie, Voorhees & Gmelin following Barber's death in 1925. The central portion of the site was to be filled by Barber's tower, which would contain a sanctuary at its base and feature a thirty-foot-high, revolving, illuminated cross at the top. The tower's construction was delayed by cost overruns and decisively halted by the Depression. As finally completed in 1952, the three-story church, designed by Shreve, Lamb & Harmon, was a pale reflection of its spectacular forerunner. Nonetheless, the pitched-roofed sanctuary, flanked by a campanile, was a competent if uninspired design, enhanced by vaguely Romanesque detailing.

The Columbia-Presbyterian Medical Center was the area's dominant institution; in 1928 the medical school and hospital had established a twenty-two-acre Washington Heights campus designed by James Gamble Rogers and bounded by 165th and 168th streets, Broadway and Riverside Drive.[2] By 1964, when it opened the William Black Medical Research Building, a rather conventional twenty-story glass-and-steel structure at 630 West 168th Street, the institution had lost touch with its distinguished architectural past.[3] The new facility, designed by Rogers & Butler, the successor firm to the medical center's original architects, was named after a Columbia University alumnus who was the founder and chairman of the board of the Chock full o' Nuts Corporation.

In 1971 Columbia-Presbyterian completed construction of the Bard-Haven Towers for faculty and married students.[4] The three narrow thirty-story slabs, designed by Brown, Guenther, Battaglia & Galvin, were arranged in a line running north-south on an elongated site atop a bluff between Riverside Drive and Haven Avenue, 169th and 172nd streets. The reinforced-concrete buildings clad in beige brick rose on piers from a four-level corbeled base containing office space and a parking garage built into the site's rocky cliff. Housing 410 apartments in total, the buildings incorporated vertical stacks of bay windows that ran the full height of the building's eastern and western facades, as well as glass-enclosed projections cantilevered from the narrow end facades. The design, though not simple, was commonplace, creating an effect that was far more interesting when viewed from a passing car along the Henry Hudson Parkway below than from close up; furthermore, the style was incompatible with both the site and the vocabulary of the medical center as a whole.

In 1976 Columbia-Presbyterian completed the twenty-story Health Sciences Tower–Augustus Long Library on a pie-shaped site bounded by 169th Street, Fort Washington and Haven avenues.[5] Designed by Warner, Burns, Toan & Lunde, the tower of brick and self-weathering steel, which Norval White and Elliot Willensky characterized as a "somber blockbuster," exerted a massive, brutal presence, comparable to that of Skidmore, Owings & Merrill's Annenberg Building at Mount Sinai Hospital (see "East Harlem," above).[6]

The other large institution in upper Manhattan was Yeshiva University, whose main building (Henry Beaumont Herts and Charles B. Meyers, 1928) adopted a Byzantine style.[7] Close to bankruptcy in the Depression, Yeshiva did not regain its momentum until the 1950s. In the late 1960s the university began to expand its facilities, calling on the services of Armand Bartos, who had worked, in collaboration with Frederick Kiesler, for the university in developing parts of its Albert Einstein College of

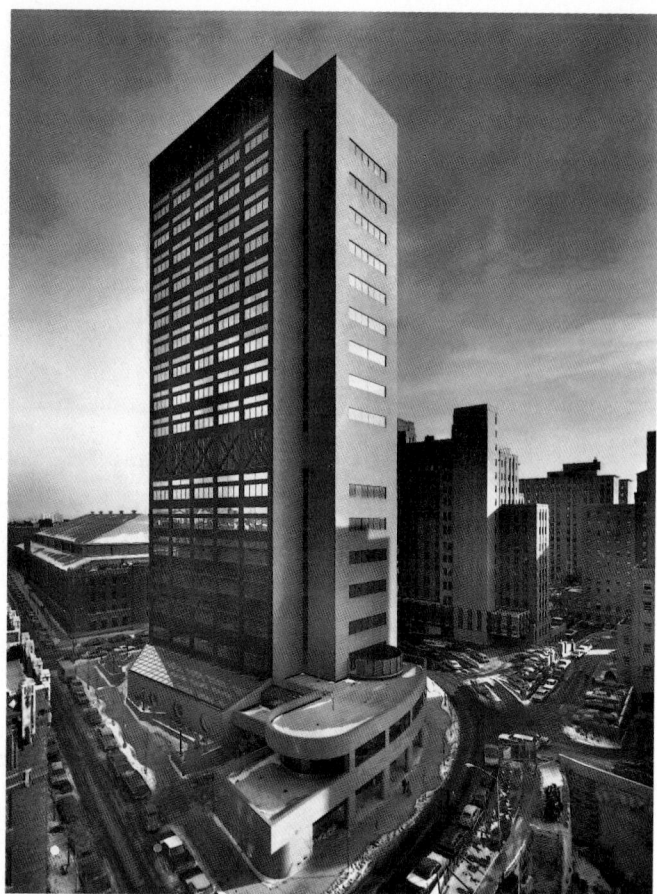

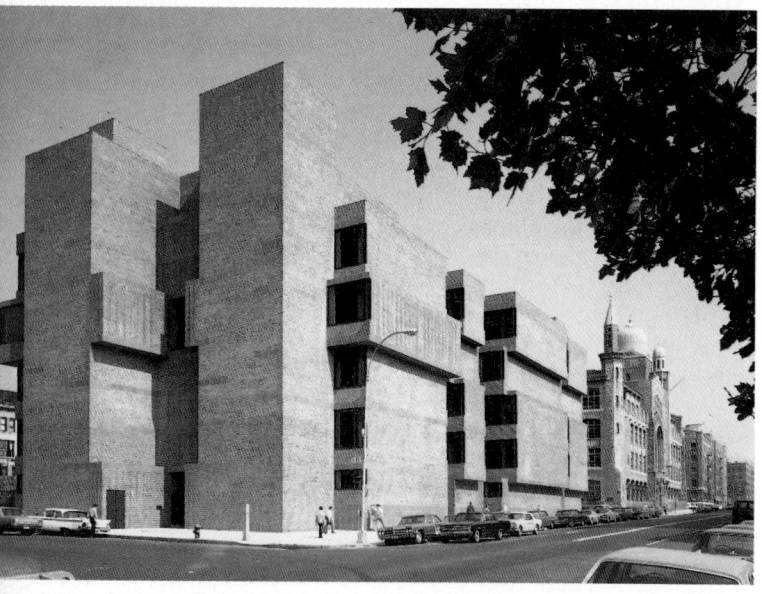

Top: Health Sciences Tower–Augustus Long Library, between Fort Washington Avenue, Haven Avenue and West 169th Street. Warner, Burns, Toan & Lunde, 1976. View to the southeast. ©Norman McGrath. NM

Bottom: Mendel Gottesman Library, northwest corner of Amsterdam Avenue and West 185th Street. Armand Bartos, 1967. View to the northwest. Stoller. ©ESTO

Medicine campus in the Bronx (see chapter 13); Bartos took the institution's design in an aggressively Modernist stylistic direction. Because Yeshiva's Manhattan campus was not a large superblock like Columbia's or City College's, its expansion was done on a piecemeal basis as individual sites and funds became available. The result, as White and Willensky have observed, was "a mixed bag of architectural tricks, more a collection of separate opportunities, successes, and failures than an integrated whole or sum."[8] Nonetheless, as the *New York Times* noted in 1969, more than forty years after establishing itself in upper Manhattan, the school was "finally assuming the proportions of a campus."[9]

In 1967 the university completed Bartos's 600,000-volume-capacity Mendel Gottesman Library, on the west side of Amsterdam Avenue, between 185th and 186th streets, a starkly unornamented composition of articulated brick-clad volumes trimmed in terra cotta that stood in bold contrast to the original university building next door.[10] On the ground floor, the building included a sunken reading room and a museum that were open to the public, above which were book stacks surrounded by individual seminar rooms, classrooms, offices and reading rooms. These elements constituted the building's principal exterior features, forming inverse bays that presented brick walls to the street but were enclosed by glass at each end. Paul Goldberger felt that this play of masses was "an attempt to get arty" and that "the boxy forms set in and out at intervals come off looking rather as if they were Moshe Safdie's Habitat put through a compressor."[11] Bartos's next building for the university, the Belfer Graduate School of Science (1968), on the east side of Amsterdam Avenue and 184th Street, was a hulking vertical composition inspired by Louis I. Kahn's Richards Medical Research Building at the University of Pennsylvania (1957–61), with tall shafts of brick housing ducts and stairwells separated by narrow continuous strips of aluminum-framed windows.[12]

A few postwar additions were made to upper Manhattan's housing stock, most of which was built between the two world wars. While the area's vernacular was simple apartment houses interspersed with some stylishly Modernist designs near Columbia's Baker Field, two notable large-scale projects, Hudson View Gardens (George F. Pelham, 1924) and Castle Village (George F. Pelham, Jr., 1938), were exceptional landmarks.[13] In 1941 the area's last major interwar-period project, Arthur Weiser's seven-story, red-brick, Georgian-inspired Riverside Houses, was completed on a 580-foot-long stretch of Riverside Drive between 158th and 161st streets.[14] A typically banal product of the New York City Housing Authority, the low-income Dyckman Houses, designed by William F. R. Ballard, were begun in 1940 but were interrupted by the war effort and not completed until 1950.[15] Occupying a trapezoidal 14.2-acre site bounded by Nagle and Tenth avenues, Dyckman and 204th streets, the project housed 2,700 families in seven fourteen-story buildings.

Several projects related to the George Washington Bridge were also completed in the 1960s. As part of the double-decking of the bridge in 1962—an element called for in Othmar Hermann Ammann's original design of 1926–31—the limited-access roadway leading across Manhattan was reconstructed as a twelve-lane below-grade expressway.[16] A total of 1,850 families were displaced for the construction of the expressway, which spawned dramatic, spaghettilike interchanges linking it with the Henry Hudson Parkway, the Harlem River Driveway and the Major Deegan and Cross-Bronx expressways via the New York City Department of Public Works' Alexander

Hamilton Bridge (1964), a competently designed but visually unexciting 1,526-foot-long span over the Harlem River.[17] One of the city's most unusual housing projects, Brown & Guenther's Bridge Apartments (1963), was built straddling the new roadway.[18] The project's four thirty-two-story aluminum-clad north-south slabs, housing 960 families, were not only banal but were subject to appalling environmental conditions: noxious fumes from the traffic below rose from the highway that separated the pairs of slabs, rendering the balconies useless and the apartments almost uninhabitable.

In 1963 the Port Authority opened its uptown bus terminal, another structure straddling the new expressway.[19] In a bold move in 1957, the Port Authority had chosen not to use its in-house staff to design the building but called on the sixty-six-year-old Italian architect-engineer Pier Luigi Nervi, whose designs in reinforced concrete approached the sublime poetics of the great engineering of the early Roman empire. In 1962 Ada Louise Huxtable, a Nervi biographer, identified the uptown bus terminal as the latest in a series of buildings that had established Nervi as "one of the significant architectural innovators of the age."[20] Seventeen years later, following Nervi's death, Huxtable eulogized him as "one of that company of giants that included Le Corbusier, Mies van der Rohe, Alvar Aalto and Frank Lloyd Wright; he ranked among the master builders of the modern age."[21] The bus terminal was realized almost simultaneously with the Leverone Field House at Dartmouth College; these were Nervi's first two works in the United States.

The new terminal was a two-story facility located between 175th and 176th streets over the depressed expressway between Fort Washington Avenue and Broadway, with ramps over Broadway leading to a turnaround, parking and storage area between that street and Wadsworth Avenue. It provided New Jersey commuters bound for midtown with a direct connection to the Eighth Avenue subway. The terminal could accommodate 255 buses per hour, a 70 percent increase over the number of buses previously using the bridge. The building's principal glory was the elaborate truss system forming the roof, which Donald Canty described in *Architectural Forum* as "26 giant slices of cast-in-place concrete pie." Fourteen of the ninety-two-foot-wide by sixty-six-foot-high truss slices were raised on angular vents to let fresh air flow through the open-air upper deck area. The trusses were carried on six hefty seventeen-and-a-half-foot-tall central columns, sculpted to express their structural responsibilities: from narrow bases, which maximized platform space, they flared into wide, sheltering capitals. On the north and south sides of the building, the trusses were carried on another triangulated truss that formed the terminal's longitudinal boundary walls. Viewed from the neighborhood, the terminal had a somewhat brutal aspect, like "a bristling warship moored among tugboats," as Canty put it, but given the context of bland brick apartment houses, the sculptural power of the structure made a strong point.[22]

Wherever the hand of the Port Authority designers could be seen in the terminal, the effect was unfortunate, as in the glass-and-metal storefronts created at street level or the baby blue enamel panels placed in some of the structural triangulations to break the velocity of the wind, which proved greater than anticipated (a triumph for Nervi, who had promised that his design would avoid the need to air condition the terminal). The public spaces inside the terminal were unexceptional at best, exuding, as Canty put it, "all the charm of a public restroom in a Miami Beach resort."[23]

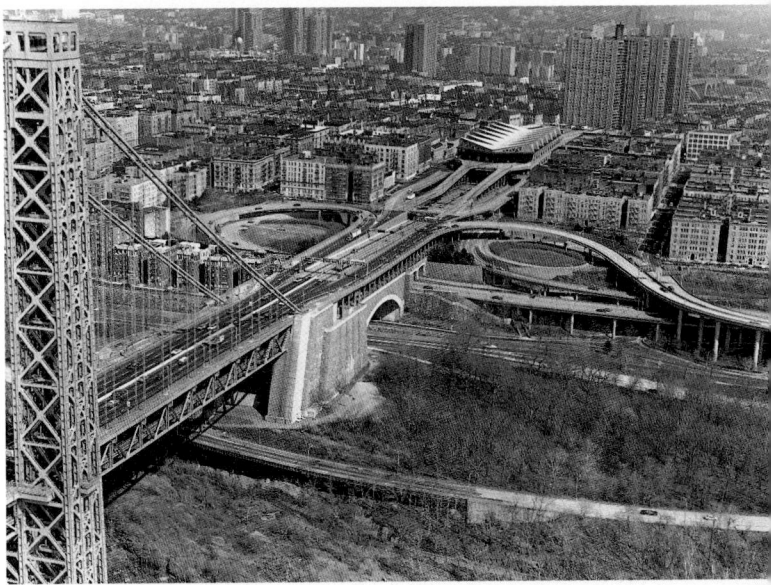

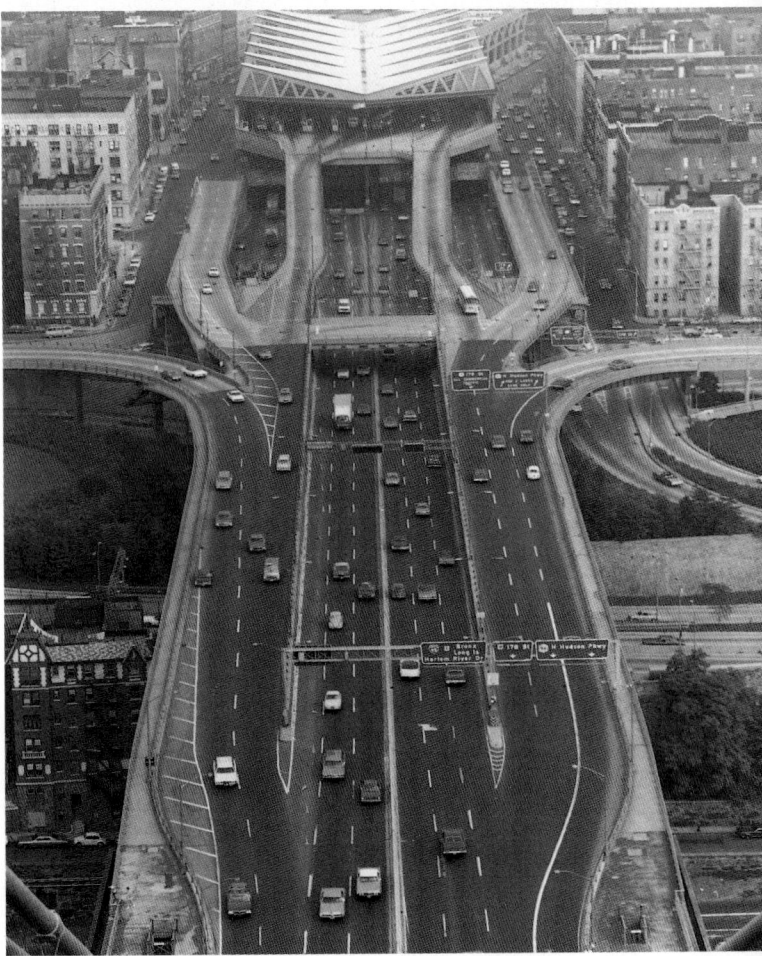

Top: Port Authority uptown bus terminal, Fort Washington Avenue to Broadway, West 175th to West 176th Street. Pier Luigi Nervi, 1963. View to the northeast showing George Washington Bridge (Othmar Hermann Ammann, 1926–31) on the left, the Port Authority uptown bus terminal in the center and the Bridge Apartments (Brown & Guenther, 1963), Broadway to Amsterdam Avenue, between West 175th and West 176th streets, on the upper right. PANY

Bottom: Port Authority uptown bus terminal. View to the east. PANY

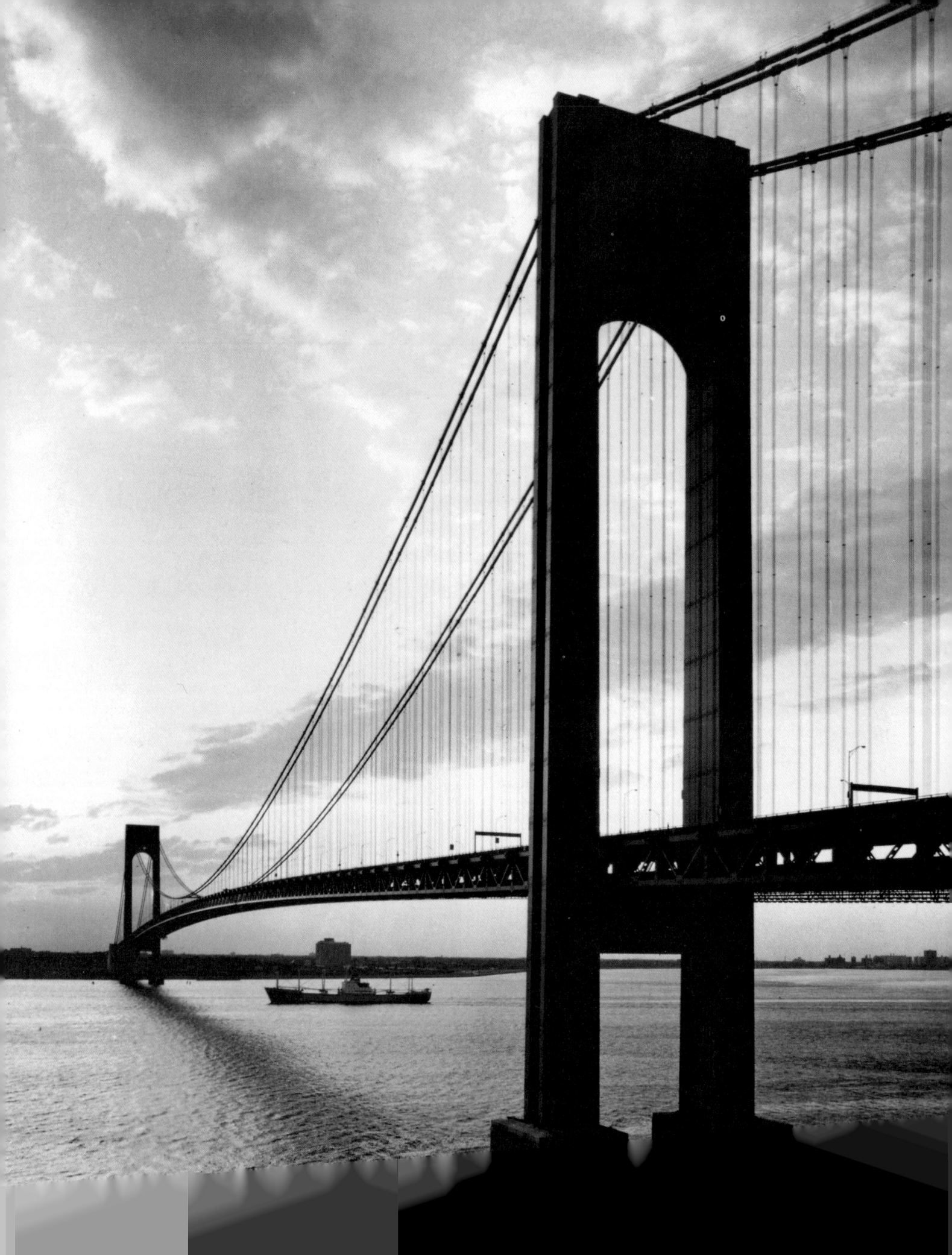

Outer Boroughs

BROOKLYN

Dere's no guy living dat knows Brooklyn troo and troo.
—*Thomas Wolfe, 1935*[1]

A mosaic of twenty-six villages that were gradually joined to their historic focus, the village of Breukelen (established 1657; incorporated as a city in 1834), Brooklyn was a genteel, relatively homogeneous, mostly low-density environment, yet it was populous enough to constitute the fourth largest city in the United States by 1898 (outranked by New York, Chicago and Philadelphia), when it became part of Greater New York. Brooklyn had begun to grow after the Civil War, and with the 1883 opening of the Brooklyn Bridge, which connected its historic center with that of New York, its growth increased rapidly. The opening of the Williamsburg Bridge in 1903 linked the borough directly to the teeming Lower East Side slums, dealing its previously homogeneous character a wrenching blow from which it would never fully recover. As *Business Week* observed fifty years later, the opening of the bridge was "like pulling a cork out of a bottle. The slum dwellers—mostly Jewish—poured into the relatively open, clean areas across the bridge, and the original settlers—mostly German and Irish—retreated before the wave, first into Bushwick, then into Ridgewood, eventually into Queens."[2] This first wave of immigrants also initiated the out-migration of wealthy and upper-middle-class Brooklyn families, many of whom relocated to Manhattan.

A second wave of immigrants came during and after World War I, when the subways, extending deep into the borough, opened up ever more areas to recently arrived immigrants, mostly Italians and Eastern European–born Jews. In the late 1930s and early 1940s a third wave of immigrants, African-Americans, discovered Brooklyn by reversing Billy Strayhorn's song and taking the newly completed "A" train subway line *from* Harlem.[3] The more affluent blacks moved to Bedford-Stuyvestant; the less well-off settled for Brownsville and East

New York, where poor Jews had settled a generation before. In the 1950s, as the aging Jewish population began to die off and their children moved to more fashionable neighborhoods in Manhattan or in the suburbs, vast areas of Brooklyn became centers of nonwhite populations; African-Americans were joined by Hispanics, mostly from Puerto Rico, who settled largely at the edges of the Civic Center.

Although the immigrants brought problems, they also brought new energy. But this quality was not particularly valued in a borough that was inherently prosuburban and antiurban. As Brooklyn became increasingly cosmopolitan, it began to lose its sense of itself. The borough's most historic neighborhoods were particularly hard hit. Brooklyn Heights, once a prosperous suburb of Manhattan, was by the 1930s and 1940s a slum of rooming houses serving dock and Navy Yard workers. But a handful of old-line aristocracy continued to inhabit big houses facing the harbor, and Brooklyn Heights attracted a cadre of literary personalities, including the playwright Arthur Miller and the novelists Norman Mailer and Truman Capote.[4]

The rebirth of Brooklyn Heights, culminating in its establishment as New York's first federally designated historic district and its first municipally designated historic district (see chapter 16), both in 1965, was in many ways exceptional, although it stimulated a revival in other nearby neighborhoods as well. But despite this renaissance, Brooklyn's reputation was on the decline. It wasn't that the place had changed so much but that it had begun to be viewed differently by natives and outsiders alike, who began to focus on issues hitherto neglected, especially the poverty and ghettoization of African-Americans, who had made Brooklyn's vast central area into a larger settlement of blacks than were to be found in Harlem.[5]

To some local observers, Brooklyn's problems could be traced back to its consolidation with New York in 1898, a loss of independent status that many had thought unwise. (In fact the vote on consolidation lost by 1,034 votes in Brooklyn, but was carried in the city as a whole.)[6] It was probably not consolidation, however, but transportation that robbed Brooklyn of its cultural identity. The subways, and later Robert Moses's arterial highways, made it too easy for Brooklynites, many of whom worked in Manhattan, to seek their entertainment and culture in

Verrazano-Narrows Bridge, spanning the Narrows, from Fort Wadsworth, Staten Island, to Bay Ridge, Brooklyn. Othmar Hermann Ammann, 1964. View to the southeast. Link. TBTA what they steadfastly called "the city," returning home afterwards to what was alternately called the Borough of Homes or the Borough of Churches. As Christopher Morley put it in 1917:

> New York is Babylon; Brooklyn is the true holy City. New York is the city of envy, office work, and hustle; Brooklyn is the region of homes and happiness. It is extraordinary: poor, harassed New Yorkers presume to look down on low-lying, home-loving Brooklyn, when as a matter of fact it is the precious jewel their souls are thirsting for and they never know it. . . . There is no hope for New Yorkers, for they glory in their skyscraping sins; but in Brooklyn there is the wisdom of the lowly.[7]

Resentment of Manhattan's hegemony had barely abated forty-five years after consolidation, when Assemblyman Fred G. Moritt of Brooklyn introduced a secession proposal in the New York State Assembly. According to the *New York Times*, Moritt believed that Brooklyn, subject to the whims of Manhattan, had been deprived of the cultural centers, theaters, orchestras and libraries that would have been its patrimony had it remained independent.[8] Although Moritt was not taken seriously, the idea of secession never completely disappeared. In 1971, when Brooklyn's prospects, dimmed by racial tension and a failed war on poverty, seemed bleaker than ever, the columnist Pete Hamill raised the issue again: "The great experiment [of consolidation], after 73 years, has failed . . . the time has come to dismember Greater New York."[9]

Old Brooklyn

The area bounded by the East River on the west and north and by Classon Avenue, Atlantic Avenue, Third Avenue and the Gowanus Canal constituted the heart of Old Brooklyn, incorporating within it the Civic Center and downtown shopping and business districts, the Navy Yard, the East River piers, and the residential neighborhoods of Brooklyn Heights, Cobble Hill, Boerum Hill, Carroll Gardens and Red Hook along the west and Fort Greene and Clinton Hill on the east. While a good deal of Old Brooklyn's building stock dated from before the Civil War, the extensive building boom that accompanied Brooklyn's extraordinary growth in the 1870s to 1890s meant that even into the 1930s the characteristic flavor of the area was that of the late nineteenth century.

By 1940 Old Brooklyn was in decline, its principal streets choked with trolleys and cars headed to and from the Brooklyn and Manhattan bridges. In addition, Fulton Street and Myrtle Avenue were overshadowed by the elevated railroads that since 1888 had carried passengers from Manhattan to Brooklyn neighborhoods as far distant as Bay Ridge and East New York. Amid this decline, Cleveland Rodgers, editor of the borough's leading newspaper, the *Eagle*, initiated a campaign for the area's regeneration. In 1937 Rodgers became a member of the City Planning Commission, from which position he was able to advance his ideas toward a legislated plan of action.[10] In this effort he was supported by Borough President John Cashmore, who recognized that the proposed construction of the Brooklyn-Queens link of the belt system of highways and, especially, the interchanges required to connect it with the Brooklyn and Manhattan bridges, combined with the need to quickly build housing for war workers near the Navy Yard, presented an ideal opportunity to design a coordinated plan for the area and to see a good deal of it quickly realized.

In 1941 the City Planning Commission approved Cashmore's plan for the improvement of the Brooklyn approach to the Brooklyn Bridge and also drew attention to the need for a more general plan that would presumably help correct the area's deficiencies as enumerated by the Mayor's Committee on Property Improvement.[11] The mayor's report revealed that only one-fifth of downtown Brooklyn's land area was covered with structures erected since 1900, that the building stock was in serious disrepair and that the rate of demolition of outmoded structures, frequently to create parking lots, was increasing exponentially. Already 2,000,000 square feet of land was vacant, and an additional 1,600,000 square feet contained abandoned and boarded-up buildings. Although funding was not yet available to undertake a plan, the City Planning Commission did list a number of key projects that would form its backbone: the Brooklyn Bridge improvement, the expansion of the Navy Yard, the construction of Fort Greene Houses, the completion of the Brooklyn-Battery Tunnel and the creation of a Civic Center focused around Borough Hall, with new buildings for the Supreme Court and Hall of Records and a replacement for the Raymond Street jail. These projects did not exactly represent a new vision; rather, as the *New York Times* put it, they were "vital improvements which are mostly the fruits of years of effort by civic groups and public officials."[12]

Central to the plan was the construction of the Brooklyn-Queens Expressway and the interchanges with the two bridges. Construction on the expressway had begun in the 1930s; an elevated section over Newtown Creek as well as surface segments between the Manhattan Bridge and Queens Boulevard had opened in 1939.[13] In Old Brooklyn, construction of the expressway, which ran as a six-lane surface boulevard east for a mile along Tillary Street, had necessitated the demolition of more than 600 houses. In 1940 Robert Moses proposed the construction of the key stretch between the Manhattan Bridge and the Gowanus Parkway.[14] Hearings on the proposed route were held in 1943, and in 1944 drawings were published to reassure the public that the double-decked portion of the highway would be threaded under the Brooklyn Bridge without damaging the historic structure.[15] Construction was delayed by the war and did not begin until 1946.[16]

On its leg from the Gowanus Expressway to Atlantic Avenue, the six-lane expressway cut a destructive swath through South Brooklyn, separating its more middle-class areas—Carroll Gardens and Cobble Hill—from the grittier waterfront. It ran as a depressed roadway just west of Hicks Street, thereby at least sparing Alfred T. White's landmark Tower and Home Buildings and Workingmen's Cottages (William Field & Son, 1877–79), bounded by Hicks, Warren and Baltic streets and Warren Place, and Henry V. Murphy's Catholic Seamen's Institute (1943), at 653 Hicks Street (see below).

At Atlantic Avenue the expressway swung to the west as it emerged from below ground to run along the waterfront above and to the east of Furman Street.[17] This was the most controversial portion of the design. The City Planning Commission's plans of 1942 for this section of the expressway would have cut Brooklyn Heights in two, running in a curved diagonal from Atlantic Avenue and Hicks Street to Tillary and Washington avenues. After local residents objected, a new, equally disastrous plan was proposed, calling for an elevated six-lane highway on top of the embankment east of Furman Street, directly against the west side of Columbia Heights. In 1943 the Brooklyn Heights Association prepared an alternate scheme consisting of two three-lane highways, one on top of the other, with a cover on the

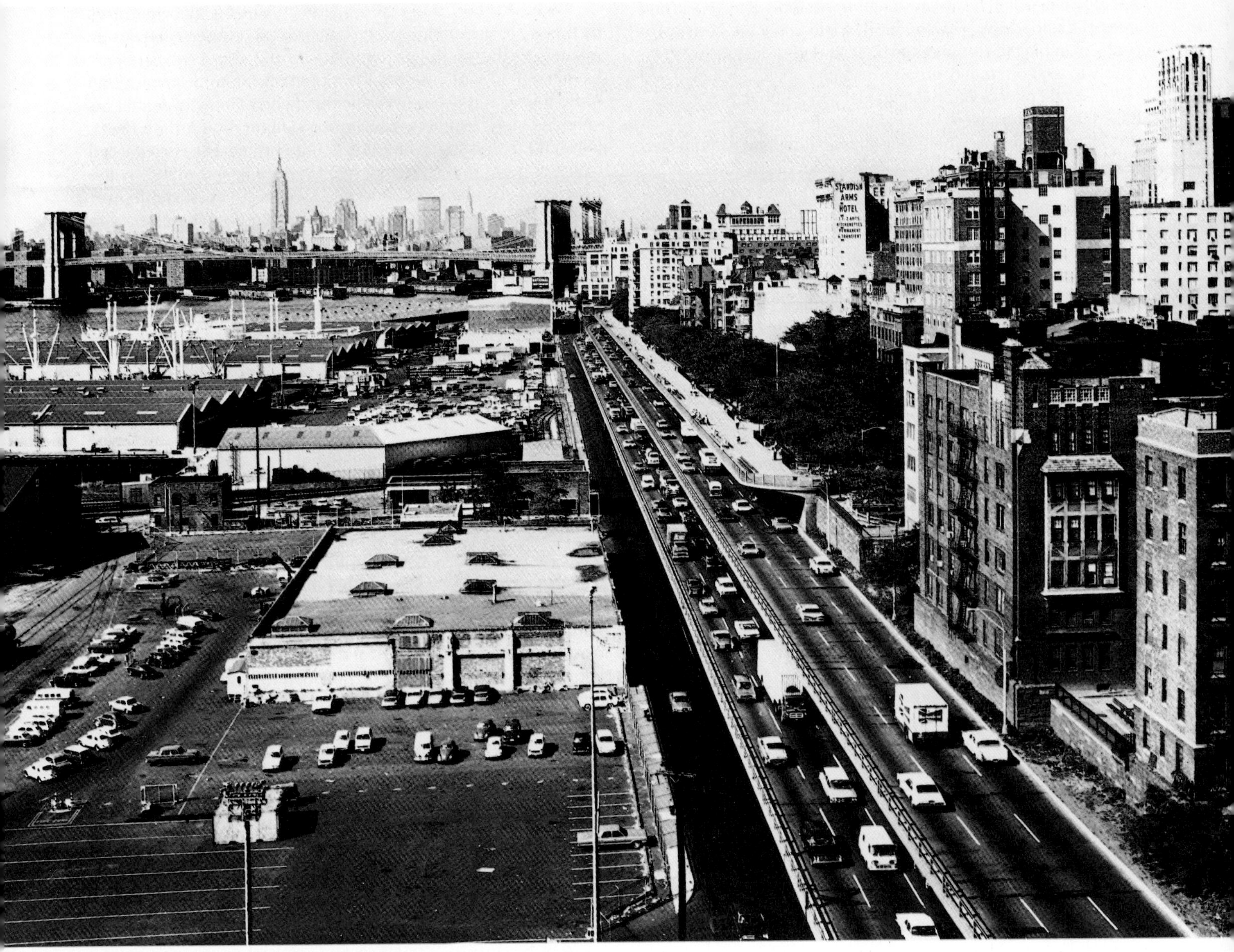

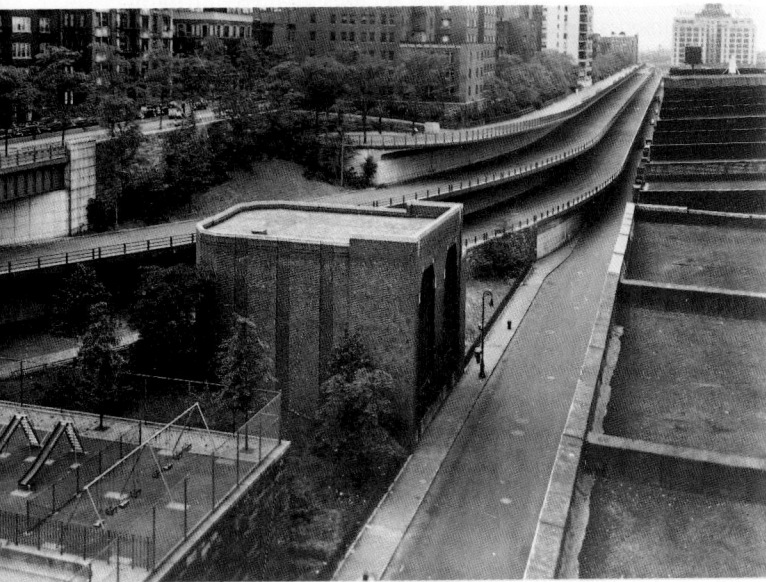

Above: Brooklyn-Queens Expressway, cantilevered portion, between Columbia Heights and Furman Street, Atlantic Avenue and the Brooklyn Bridge. Andrews, Clark & Buckley with Clarke & Rapuano, 1950. View to the north with Brooklyn Bridge (John A. Roebling and Washington Roebling, 1867–83) in the distance. C&R

Left: Brooklyn-Queens Expressway, cantilevered portion. View to the south along Furman Street. TBTA

upper level to shield nearby residents from some of the noise and fumes of the roadway. This top level would allow the homeowners of Columbia Heights to retain their gardens. Moses reacted favorably to the community group's recommendation but changed the top-level cover from private gardens to a public promenade. Still, some buildings were lost, including the three-story house at 106 Columbia Heights where Washington Roebling had directed the construction of the Brooklyn Bridge from his sickbed.

When it was at last opened in 1950 (Andrews, Clark & Buckley, engineers; Clarke & Rapuano, landscape architects), Lewis Mumford regarded the triple-decker highway at the edge of Columbia Heights as "among the most satisfactory accomplishments in contemporary urban design," for both drivers and urban promenaders. The promenade, Mumford said, reached a "breathless architectural climax" at its northern end, where it "terminates in a small circle surrounded by a stone wall. . . . Within the circle, there are benches and trees, all arranged in the same circular pattern, while the stone paving consists of circular bands of texture—broken stone, hexagonal blocks, cobblestones—forming a complicated pattern with which the eye could play for hours at a time if it were tired of looking across the Bay." The embankment leading from the circle to the ramp was planted with rhododendrons. Mumford raved about the overall impression created by this end of the promenade: "The concentrated effect of the complex forms and textures, the dynamic rhythm of the space itself, are almost too good to be true. Here abstract geometry, landscape gardening, and architecture, along with the tactile value of sculpture and painting, unite in a deeply satisfying composition."[18]

North of Orange Street, the four-level arrangement gave way to a double-decked expressway without promenade as the alignment turned east, slipping under the Brooklyn and Manhattan bridges. It assumed a more conventional, single-level format above Tillary Street as it girdled the Navy Yard, creating a far more dank nether world beneath it than had the airy, slatlike structures of the elevated railways being pulled down in the name of progress. Nonetheless, the completion of the expressway linking the Gowanus Parkway with the two bridges had a remarkably beneficial effect, removing the traffic from Hicks and Henry streets that had been so destructive to the Heights and to the neighborhoods south of it, and thereby setting the stage for their rebirth.

Although each of the various elements of the transportation puzzle was under the supervision of a different agency, plans for the interchanges with the two bridges required some degree of coordinated planning; this was especially true in the case of the interchange with the Brooklyn Bridge, which was also in serious need of repair. In February 1941 plans for the improvement of traffic at both ends of the Brooklyn Bridge were submitted to the Board of Estimate and Mayor La Guardia by the presidents of the two boroughs affected.[19] The plans, which formed the heart of a proposal for the Civic Center (see below), called for the elimination of the elevated lines on Park Row from Chatham Square to the Brooklyn Bridge, Manhattan, and the termination at Sands Street, Brooklyn, of the Myrtle Avenue and Lexington Avenue (Brooklyn) elevated lines that since 1898 had used the bridge to take passengers to Manhattan. Trolley service on the bridge was to be maintained. In 1942 permission was granted to implement the first stage of the 1941 master plan, but work was delayed for over a year until the War Production Board received assurances that the removed steel would be used exclusively for scrap.[20] On March 1, 1944, elevated service was discontinued after forty-six years of operation.

In September 1948 David Steinman, an engineer, was hired by the city to undertake a year-long process of survey and design leading to the complete overhaul of the Brooklyn Bridge.[21] Steinman had written a book about the bridge's designer, John A. Roebling, and his son Washington, who completed it after his father's death.[22] Although Steinman's admiration for the Roeblings and their bridge was sincere, he had not always regarded their design as inviolate. In a 1934 proposal, sponsored by the Aluminum Company of America, Steinman had suggested replacing the existing bridge roadway with a double deck of the same weight. According to Stanley Hyman, who profiled Steinman in the New Yorker, he had also wanted "to remove the picturesque but inefficient diagonal stays completely, put in fewer and stronger vertical suspenders, and end up with twelve ten foot traffic lanes."[23] Such changes would have completely altered the appearance of Roebling's venerated structure. But by 1939 Steinman was advocating Moses's Battery-to-Brooklyn bridge as a sensible alternative to renovating the Brooklyn Bridge. According to Hyman, after studying the bridge in 1948, Steinman planned "to convert the present two-lane auto roadway . . . into a six-lane modern concrete highway,"[24] but this time he would not change the bridge's appearance: "To me, Brooklyn Bridge is sacred," Steinman said.[25]

Before renovation the bridge provided two eastbound and two westbound lanes on its outer flanks as well as two inner lanes in each direction reserved for the streetcars that now used the right-of-way of the removed elevated. Between these opposing streams of traffic lay a pedestrian boardwalk. Steinman's new plan called for removal of the trolley line that shared the vehicular roadway, so that three traffic lanes could be provided for each direction. The trusses that ran the length of the bridge between the car tracks and the motor lanes were to be removed, and the two outside trusses were to be strengthened to carry 50 percent of the suspended structure, instead of the 10 percent they currently carried. The pedestrian walk would be left in the center. The improvement also included the construction of new approaches at each end.

The project began in March 1950, when trolley service was discontinued, and involved the work of up to 3,000 men.[26] When the bridge reopened on May 3, 1954, many observers welcomed the new configuration of wide roadways devoted exclusively to automobile traffic.[27] But a handful were troubled by the steel box trusses Steinman had devised to strengthen the bridge for the traffic. The editors of Architectural Forum, for instance, pointed out that although "the main structural expedient used was simple enough to seem like an engineering inspiration," causing "minimal disturbance" to the old bridge lines, the trusses had one very negative effect: they destroyed the sightlines from the elevated pedestrian walkway over the suppressed outer trusses to the water and distant shore, replacing them with a welter of metal and electrical wires that almost completely cut off the walker's view of the water. As Forum reported, walkers returning to their beloved bridge for the first time after reconstruction felt a "vague discomfort, a 'boxed-in' feeling. Everything was there except the old soaring magic. . . . This one crucial sightline had helped open an epoch and shape the building which to all the world spelled America."[28] Public Works Commissioner Frederick H. Zermuhlen dismissed Forum's criticism as "the disjointed mish-mash of balderdash and twaddle" and defended the work on the grounds of public safety.[29] He also sought to demonstrate through photographs that he took—in contrast to those of the Forum's photographers—that the new construction did little damage to the view. The evidence of his photos was not completely convincing.

Another key to Old Brooklyn's future lay in the completion of the Brooklyn-Battery Tunnel.[30] Construction for the tunnel had been authorized in 1940, after Robert Moses's plan for a bridge connecting lower Manhattan with Red Hook had been rejected by Secretary of War Harry Woodring in 1939. In 1941 Moses pushed forward with the twin two-lane tunnels that had originally been conceived as the critical link in the circumferential highway system he had been developing since the mid-1930s. While the tunnel lacked the artistic potential of a bridge, which could have been Moses's most visible monument, its entrance plazas and ventilating structures—especially the midpoint ventilator, to be prominently located at the north end of Governor's Island—offered opportunities to make a statement. In 1941 the New York City Tunnel Authority, reacting to pressure from citizen groups, organized a competition to select the design of the Governor's Island tower, leaving the towers at the tunnel's ends to its own in-house staff. Talbot Hamlin wrote of the potential offered by the competition: "Here was to be built a structure of considerable bulk and height at the very front door of New York . . . [that] would form an important element in the view from Battery Park, from Governor's Island, or from anyone coming down the East River on a boat or passing by the lower end of Manhattan Island. No finer site for an important and exciting piece of architecture could be imagined." The competition's program, which called for an octagonal tower and two separate exhaust-duct structures that were to reach above the main mass, asked the architects to confine their efforts to the building's facades, an aspect that was troubling to Hamlin: "Here is no opportunity for a great three-dimensional imagination to take a need and transform it into significant form. Instead there is merely the opportunity to take basic forms and sizes already determined and drape around them an exterior surface."[31]

The entries prepared for the competition clearly reflected the split among leading architects between traditionalism and Modernism. The two types of solutions proposed were one in which parapets concealed the differences between the elements, and another in which expression of the octagon was suppressed in favor of an emphasis on the towers. The former direction was adopted by the winning firm, McKim, Mead & White, in their suave, Modern Classical design, while the latter approach was adopted by the second-prize winner, Archibald Manning Brown, whose severe, cubic composition had about it an air of straightforward engineering. Among nonpremiated designs, which were exhibited at the Architectural League, the Modernist schemes of William Lescaze, Wallace K. Harrison, Antonin Raymond and Ely Jacques Kahn were notable; William Lawrence Bottomley and Harvey Wiley Corbett offered powerful Classical schemes that called for significant embellishment by sculptors. Edward Durell Stone created the most interesting design of all, treating the ventilator as an abstract solid surrounded by a basin filled with a spectacular array of fountains. Hamlin was not pleased by the choice of McKim, Mead & White's design, whose "false monumentality" he saw as the result of a confusion about the role of monumental structures in the modern world:

> We *should* be building monuments, expending money and effort on structures built for themselves alone, either to satisfy our aesthetic sense, to memorialize great ideas and people, or to express our civic and national pride. Monuments such as these should be solid and sculptural. Yet we rarely have the opportunity to design such buildings, and our frustration in this desire leads us astray again and again into an attempt to contradict essential architectural integrity by trying to make monuments of utilitarian structures.[32]

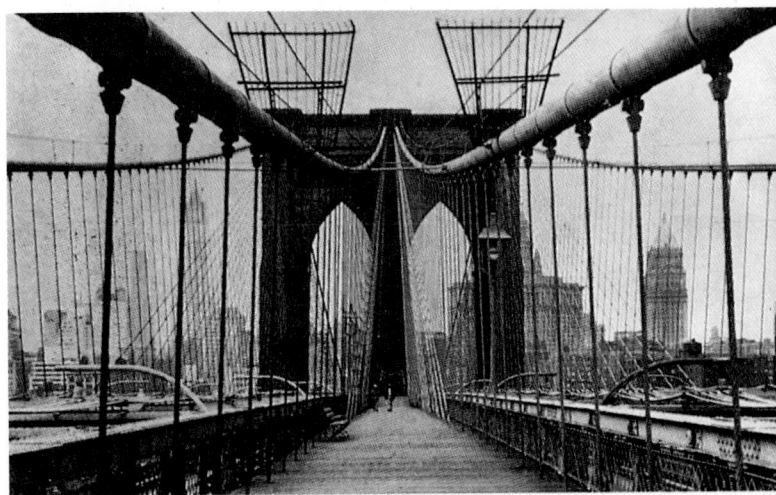

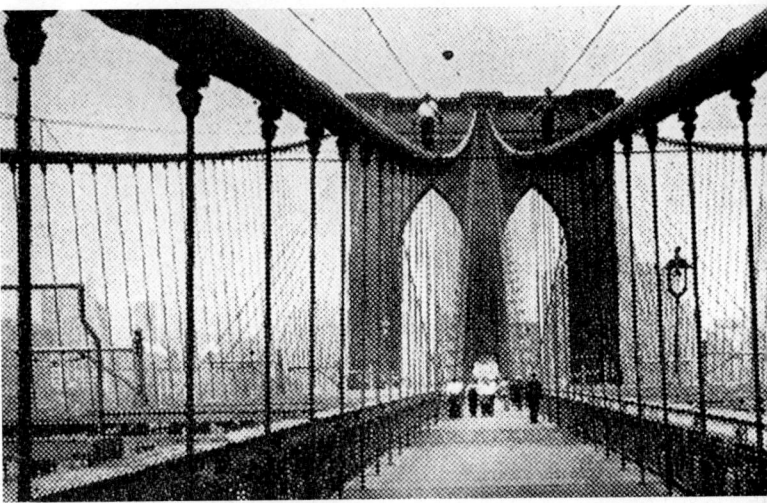

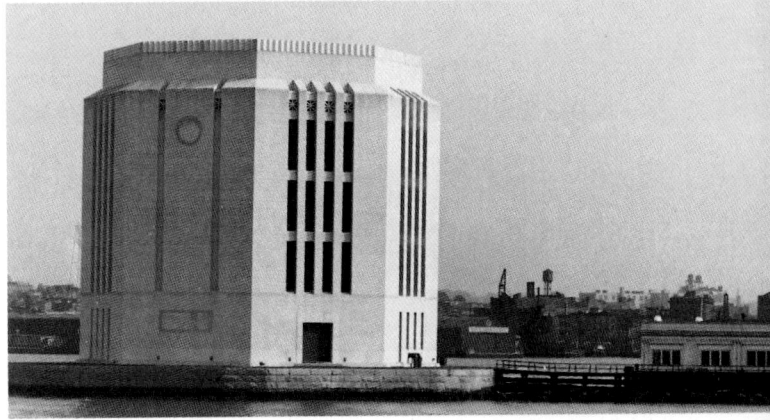

Top: Brooklyn Bridge, spanning the East River, from Civic Center, Manhattan, to Fulton Ferry, Brooklyn. John A. Roebling and Washington Roebling, 1867–83. View to the west showing remodeling (David Steinman, 1954) and steel box trusses on each side of the pedestrian walkway. AF. CU

Center: Brooklyn Bridge. View to the west before remodeling, 1934. AF. CU

Bottom: Brooklyn-Battery Tunnel ventilation tower, Governor's Island. McKim, Mead & White, 1950. View to the southeast. Gottscho-Schleisner. LOC

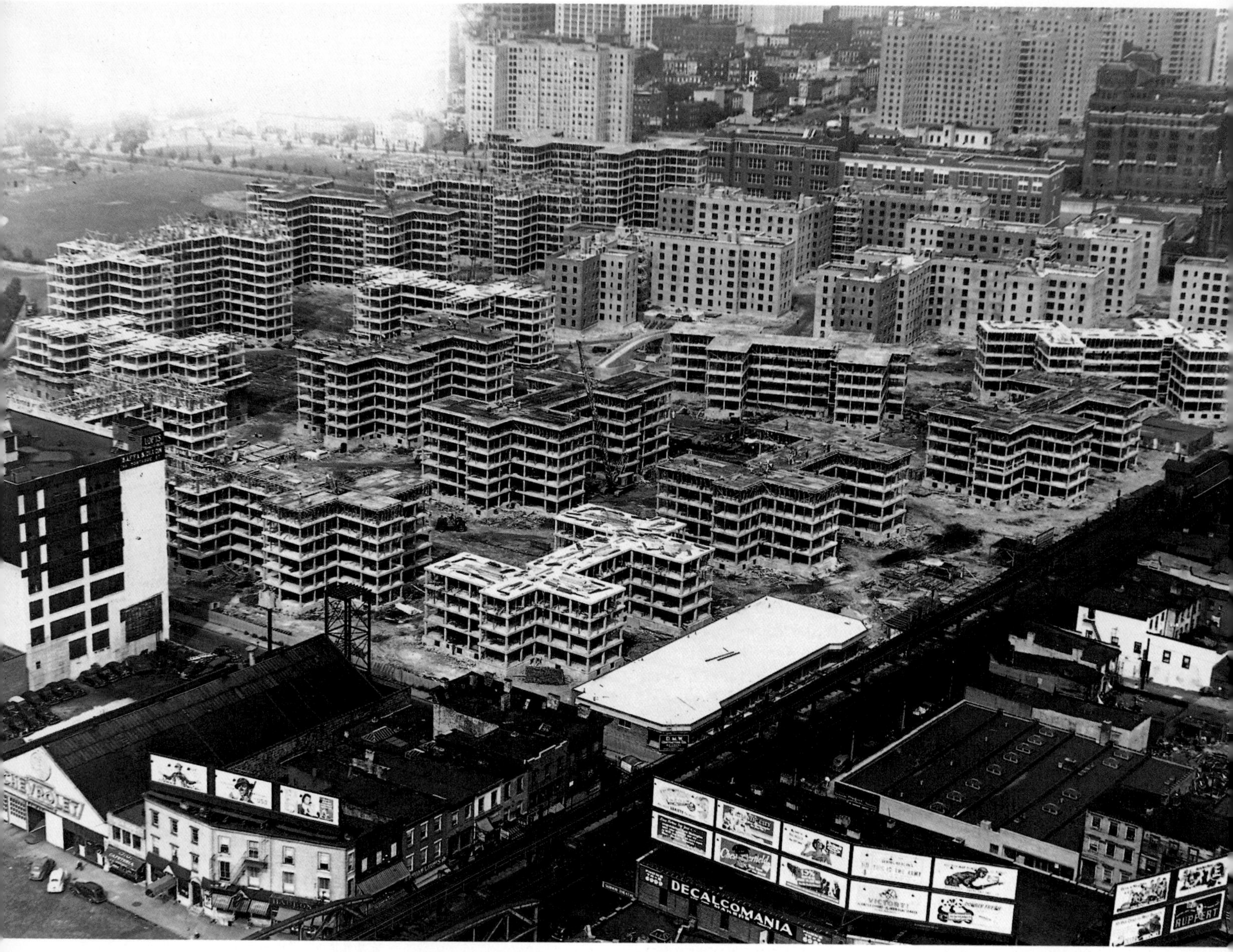

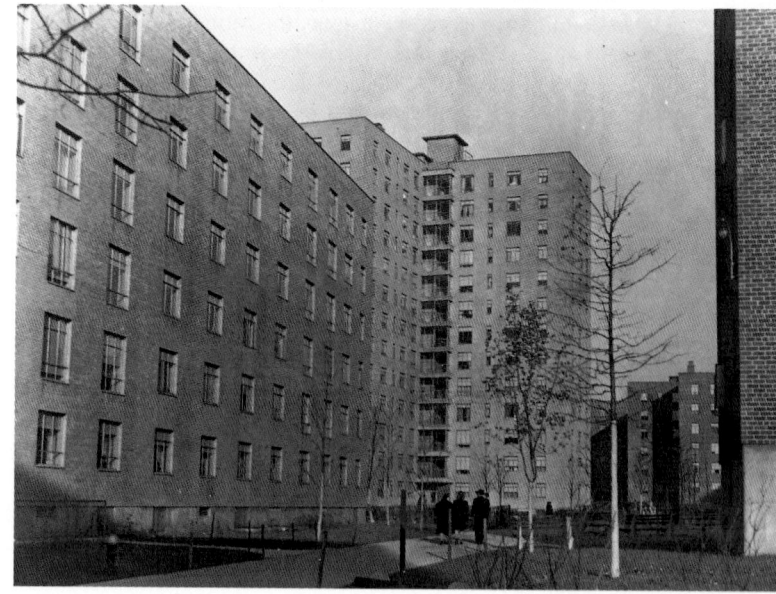

Above: Fort Greene Houses, bounded by Myrtle, Park and Carlton avenues and Prince Street, Fort Greene. Rosario Candela, André Fouilhoux, Wallace K. Harrison, Albert Mayer, Ethan Allen Dennison, William I. Hohauser, Ely Jacques Kahn, Charles Butler, Henry Churchill and Clarence Stein, 1942–44. View to the northeast showing buildings under construction in August 1942. NYCHA

Right: Fort Greene Houses. Interior pathway. NYCHA

Ground was broken for the two-mile-long Brooklyn-Battery Tunnel, designed by Ole Singstad, on October 31, 1940, but construction did not begin until the middle of 1941. Although the tunnel was to have been completed in 1944, work was stopped in October 1942 because of the war and was not resumed until November 1946. Even after the war, progress was slow, largely because of difficulties in obtaining building materials. The two independent thirty-one-foot-diameter tunnels were fourteen feet apart and were each built in two sections, working from the Brooklyn and Manhattan ends. At its lowest point the pavement was 115 feet below mean high water, making it one of the deepest tunnels ever built. It was also the second longest ventilated vehicular tunnel in the world, exceeded only by the Queensway Tunnel under the Mersey River between Birkenhead and Liverpool, England. The tunnel roadways were paved in brick and the walls were sheathed in white ceramic tile, which glistened under the light cast from continuous lines of fluorescent tubing. When the Brooklyn-Battery Tunnel opened on May 25, 1950, it was the largest piece of public construction completed since the war; eight lives had been lost in the course of construction. The tunnel was linked to Manhattan's Franklin Delano Roosevelt Drive and West Side Highway by elevated extensions of these roads and by a tunnel under Battery Park, whose construction was begun early in 1949.[33]

While it took more than a decade to realize the highways that would relieve Old Brooklyn of the through traffic that threatened to destroy its neighborhoods, its most rundown area, within the shadow of the elevated just south of the Brooklyn Bridge and at the periphery of the Navy Yard, was redeveloped much more quickly. The outbreak of World War II turned the Navy Yard into a beehive of activity, requiring new housing for the influx of workers. Furthermore, the Navy Yard area would also be seriously affected by the construction of the Brooklyn-Queens Expressway, which Robert Moses had already begun to build along Park Avenue, where it would cut in two a neighborhood that had stretched south to Fort Greene Park. The proposed extension of the expressway around the Manhattan Bridge would further isolate the area from Brooklyn's Civic Center and downtown.

In a 1941 report, *Vital Arterial Gaps and the Navy Yard Neighborhood*, Moses argued in behalf of a coordinated approach to redevelopment that would address housing problems in the wider context of neighborhood planning, and he cited the changes in the Navy Yard district as an example of "something approaching the right way to replan the rundown areas of the city." Moses accused the Housing Authority of blocking "in every possible way" an effort to create a genuine neighborhood rehabilitation plan for the Navy Yard area, castigating the authority, an operating agency, for failing to do what the City Planning Commission was actually charged to do. According to Moses, the authority "refused at first to provide for the expansion of City Park and of Cumberland Hospital. It did not wish to take care of the park problem or the street problem or the Brooklyn-Queens Connecting Highway or the proper planning of the area so as to preserve the approach to Fort Greene Monument."[34] Moses's report recommended a coordinated approach that would not only include local agencies but also those of the federal government, whose abrupt expansion of the Navy Yard, he claimed, destroyed necessary facilities such as the old Wallabout Market while burdening the city with the responsibility of paying for substitutes out of city funds.

The first housing in the area, rushed to completion for workers involved in national defense, was William I. Hohauser,

Carl A. Vollmer and Walter Wefferling's Wallabout Houses (1941), which accommodated 207 families in two thirteen-story towers that occupied 25 percent of the site, bordered by the Navy Yard (Flushing Avenue), Park Avenue, North Elliot Place and North Portland Avenue.[35] Reserved for families of enlisted Navy personnel, it contained somewhat more generously proportioned apartments than in previous federally sponsored projects. Wallabout was formally dedicated just four days before the Japanese bombing of Pearl Harbor.

In May 1941 Mayor La Guardia and Governor Lehman spoke at the groundbreaking ceremonies for Fort Greene Houses, also to provide accommodation for the ever-swelling ranks of Navy Yard workers.[36] Although construction was delayed because of wartime material shortages, in October 1942 the first 816 units of the 3,501-unit project were opened. When completed in 1944, Fort Greene Houses covered a twenty-three-block, thirty-eight-acre site bounded by Myrtle, Park and Carlton avenues and Prince Street. Left standing within its boundaries were the Cumberland Hospital, St. Edward's Roman Catholic Church (John J. Deery, 1902) and Public School 67. The huge team of architects assembled for the project—Rosario Candela, André Fouilhoux, Wallace Harrison, Albert Mayer, Ethan Allen Dennison, William I. Hohauser, Ely Jacques Kahn, Charles Butler, Henry Churchill and Clarence Stein—managed to create a coherent and even interesting design, consisting of mostly fourteen-story double-cruciform slabs whose arrangement crudely evoked some of the odd geometries of the area's historic plan. Nonetheless, the overall effect was monolithic and institutional.

By the 1950s Fort Greene Houses would be one of the city's most troubled projects, singled out by the editors of *Newsweek* in a July 27, 1959, exposé called "Metropolis in a Mess":

> The public-housing projects . . . have become million-dollar barracks, in which no one develops a sense of responsibility, or of belonging, or wanting to belong. Fort Greene Houses . . . is one of the starkest examples. It cost $20 million and houses 3,400 near-destitute families, and from the outside, at a distance, it has the look of a fine development. Closer inspection reveals windows broken as in an abandoned factory; walls cracking; light fixtures inoperative; doors unhinged; elevators that clearly are used as toilets.[37]

In reply Mayor Wagner stated: "Fort Greene was the first state-aided public-housing project in the nation. It was completed with 'ersatz' war materials, used as a barracks for war workers and too big to begin with."[38] In 1957–58, the project was rebuilt and divided into two separate entities, named after Walt Whitman and Raymond V. Ingersoll.[39]

Just as the first units of Fort Greene Houses were being completed, in January 1942, construction was begun on Clinton Hill Apartments, the second project in the city to take advantage of the new state law permitting life insurance companies to invest resources in low-rent housing.[40] Following the Metropolitan Life Insurance Company's Parkchester development in the Bronx (see "The Bronx," below), Clinton Hill was developed by the Equitable Life Assurance Society and their architects, Harrison, Fouilhoux & Abramovitz, in consultation with Irwin Clavan and the landscape architect Gilmore D. Clarke. The Equitable had hoped to develop a project in lower Manhattan, but because of wartime priorities they were granted permission to build only near the Navy Yard. The plan for the mid-rise garden village consisted of twelve- to fourteen-story buildings, six on a parcel bounded by Myrtle, Willoughby, Vanderbilt and Waverly avenues and intersected by Clinton

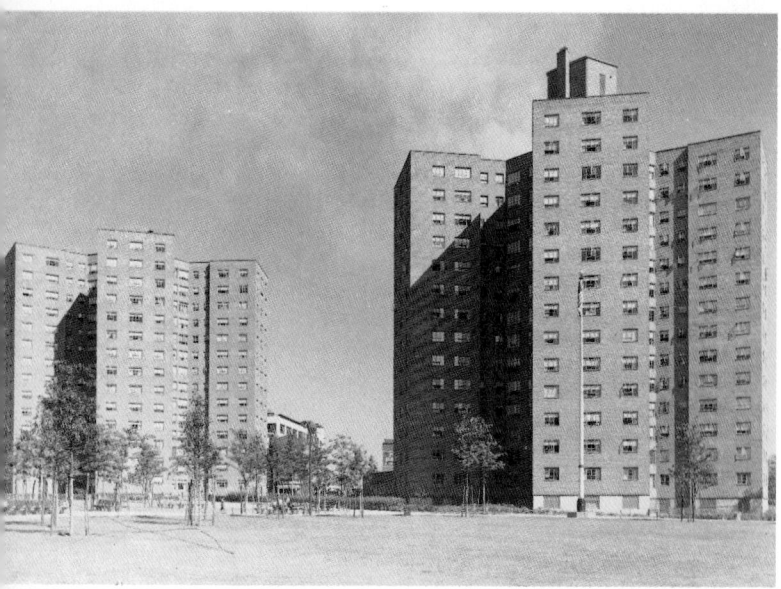

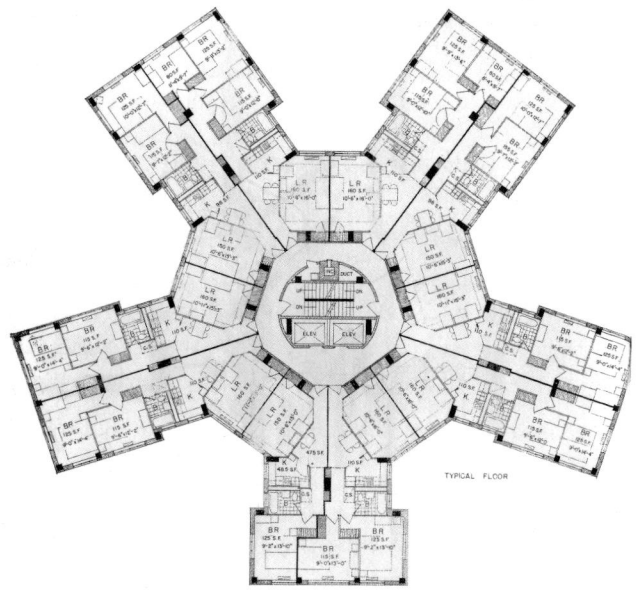

Top: Farragut Houses, bounded by Brooklyn-Queens Expressway, York, Concord, Navy and Bridge streets, Fort Greene. Alfred Fellheimer, Stewart Wagner and Carl A. Vollmer, 1952. View to the northwest. Gottscho-Schleisner. LOC

Bottom: Farragut Houses. Typical floor plan. AF. CU

Top right: Cadman Towers, Clark Street between Henry Street and Cadman Plaza West; Monroe Place and Clinton Street between Clark and Pierrepont streets, Brooklyn Heights. Glass & Glass and Whittlesey & Conklin, 1973. View to the northwest. CR

Bottom right: Edward Blum School, Public School 46, 100 Clermont Avenue, between Park and Myrtle avenues, Fort Greene. Katz, Waisman, Blumenkranz, Stein, Weber, 1958. View to the southwest. Stoller. ©ESTO

Avenue, and another five a block away, on a site bounded by DeKalb, Greene, Waverly and Classon avenues, intersected by Lafayette Avenue. The development's long buildings were placed at the ends of the blocks to clearly define pleasant, open spaces; although the brick exteriors of the buildings were bland, they were enlivened by decorative blue-and-white nautical motifs atop each entranceway. Despite the density of the project, two-thirds of the land was left open. To clear the site, a number of fine but semiderelict mansions were demolished, including some of the houses built by the Bedford, Pouch and Pratt families. Herbert L. Pratt's house (John Brite, 1906), on Willoughby Avenue between Clinton and Waverly avenues, which had stood vacant for most of the years since the Pratts moved to Manhattan in 1914, was a particularly distinguished loss.

Although Talbot Hamlin had a generally favorable opinion of the Clinton Hill project, he questioned its density, which he pointed out was 50 percent greater than that of the East River Houses (Voorhees, Walker, Foley & Smith in association with C. W. Schlusing and Alfred Easton Poor, 1941) and was exceeded only by that of London Terrace (Farrar & Watmaugh, 1929) and Knickerbocker Village (John S. Van Wart and Frederick L. Ackerman, 1934), which were located in the more traditionally dense environment of Manhattan.[41] He found the density particularly objectionable given the neighborhood, "a part of Brooklyn that has long been a dying residential region of large, comfortable houses, some even lavish, set on large lots, so that the population concentration has been very low." Hamlin also raised the issue of the site itself, which he felt was poorly served by public transit and lacking sufficient public schools. But he did applaud Clinton Hill's architects for producing "perhaps the most brilliant, carefully studied, and beautifully integrated unit plans that any middle-income housing development has yet achieved."[42] He especially admired the generously sized rooms and the logical organization of the individual apartments.

In 1947 the Housing Authority advanced plans for another low-income project near the Navy Yard: Farragut Houses, which provided accommodation for 1,400 families in ten buildings on a site bounded by the Brooklyn-Queens Expressway, York, Concord, Navy and Bridge streets.[43] The architects, Alfred Fellheimer, Stewart Wagner and Carl A. Vollmer, established a five-point configuration for the typical floor plan, reducing corridors and fire stairs to an absolute minimum and maximizing solar orientation for each apartment. Farragut Houses marked a step in the evolution of tower plans from the cruciform configuration of East River Houses to the modified-X-shaped configuration of Abraham Lincoln Houses in Harlem (see chapter 12). As Architectural Forum put it, the basically circular floor plan was "like a giant cog wheel," placed on the site to define the edges of a large central mall.[44] The efficiency of the plan permitted site coverage to be reduced to 11 percent, as opposed to the 23 percent achieved in Fort Greene Houses. But the configuration also sacrificed such traditional urban hierarchies as front and back, thereby creating what Richard Plunz has characterized as the "ultimate spatial pathology between a public housing project and the surrounding context."[45] Furthermore, despite the plan's efficiency, the detailing of the exteriors was typically dull, conforming to the Housing Authority's standard, anonymous brick-box mode.

In 1952 plans were advanced to create a Fort Greene redevelopment area under Title I of the Housing Act of 1949, sponsored by the Mayor's Committee on Slum Clearance, which was headed by Robert Moses.[46] The five-block, 11.28-acre area bounded by Flatbush Avenue Extension, Myrtle Avenue, Fort Greene Park and DeKalb Avenue was to be cleared to make way for expanded facilities for Long Island University, housed in the upper floors of the Paramount Building, and Brooklyn Hospital, as well as two cooperative housing projects for a total of 782 families. As part of the area's renewal, the Raymond Street Jail was to be demolished. Ultimately, the renewal area made possible the 1967 alteration and expansion by Rogers, Butler & Burgun of the Brooklyn Hospital (J. M. Hewlett, 1920) and the construction of staff apartments (Walker O. Cain & Associates, 1976).[47]

Less successful was the fifty-acre Clinton Hill renewal area, created in 1954, which consisted of once magnificent but now decrepit houses, some apartment houses and ordinary building stock surrounding Pratt Institute.[48] The site was bounded by St. James Place, Hall Street, Myrtle Avenue, Emerson Place and Willoughby, Classon and Lafayette avenues. Knowing that demolition was planned, property owners ceased to maintain their buildings, and the area became the slum Moses had claimed it to be when he first advanced plans for its renewal. When Clinton Hill's renewal was completed, the only original building standing was a rundown shoe factory at the northern border of the site. In place of the many fine buildings that had once occupied the site stood a dreary towers-in-the-park development, S. J. Kessler's Willoughby Walk Apartments (1957), between Classon, Willoughby and Myrtle avenues and Hall Street, which had a strong visual impact on the neighborhood.[49]

In 1958 one of the Board of Education's more stylistically inventive schools, Public School 46, the Edward Blum School, was opened at 100 Clermont Avenue, between Park and Myrtle avenues.[50] Designed by Katz, Waisman, Blumenkranz, Stein, Weber, the three-story, white-glazed-brick building rose from a blue-banded base. Arriving children may have felt more like hotel guests than students as they entered the school under a porte-cochere-like canopy of thin-shelled concrete turned up at the ends and carried on four posts.

By the 1950s activity was winding down at the Navy Yard. Once the area's principal source of jobs, it remained a powerful symbol of New York's history, not only for its contributions to the nation's military strength but for its role as a great seaport. Perhaps this was what the architect John Barrington Bayley, a Modernist turned Classicist, had in mind in 1957 when he proposed a monumental entrance to the Navy Yard.[51] Despite its past significance, the Navy Yard was officially closed by the federal government on June 25, 1966, resulting in a loss of some 10,000 to 15,000 jobs. After a long period of debate and inaction concerning the Navy Yard's future, the city and the federal government reached an agreement in 1969 on the purchase price of the 292-acre property, which was to be turned into an industrial park operated by a quasi-public agency of the city's newly formed Public Development Corporation.[52] But it would be another three years before the city could take possession.

The Cadman Plaza urban renewal project, which dragged on from 1959 until 1973, was also ill-advised, although not nearly so destructive to its immediate environs as the Clinton Hill renewal project.[53] When the removal of the elevated tracks along Fulton Street fully revealed the existing heritage of nineteenth-century buildings, the immediate reaction was to tear down and rebuild. On the east side of Fulton Street, this process led to the creation of the mall-like park that became S. Parkes Cadman Plaza (see below). On the west side, the blocks be-

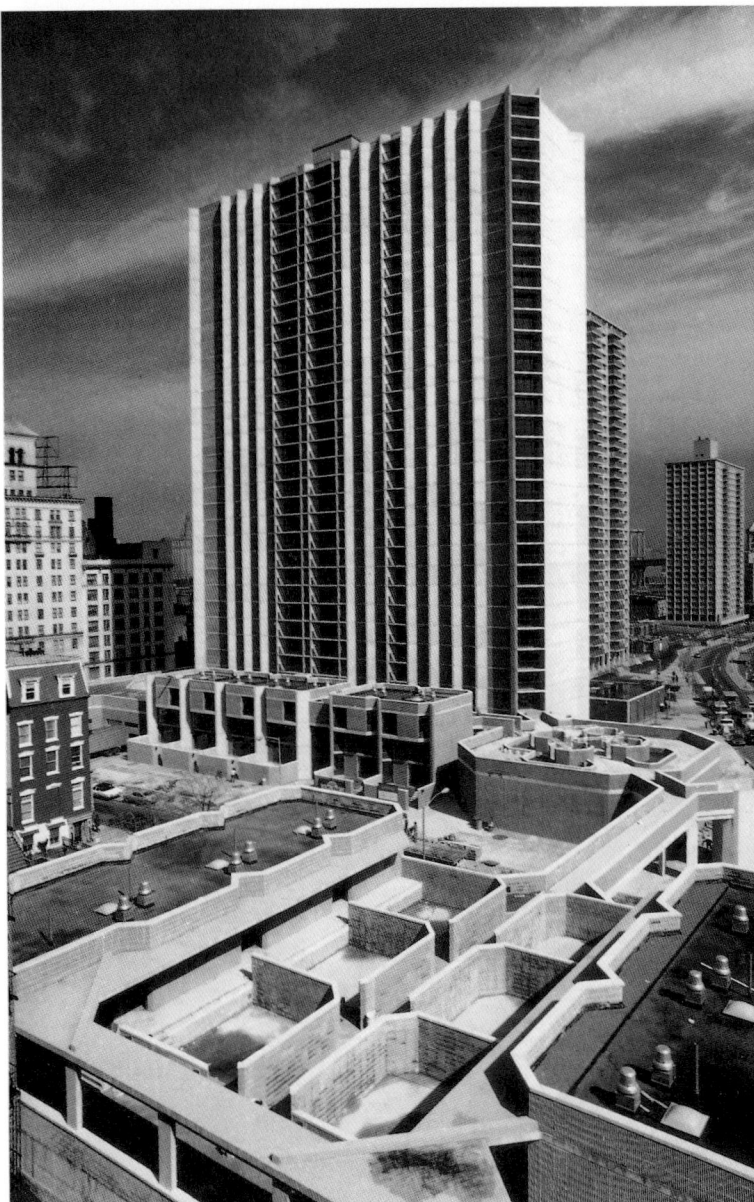

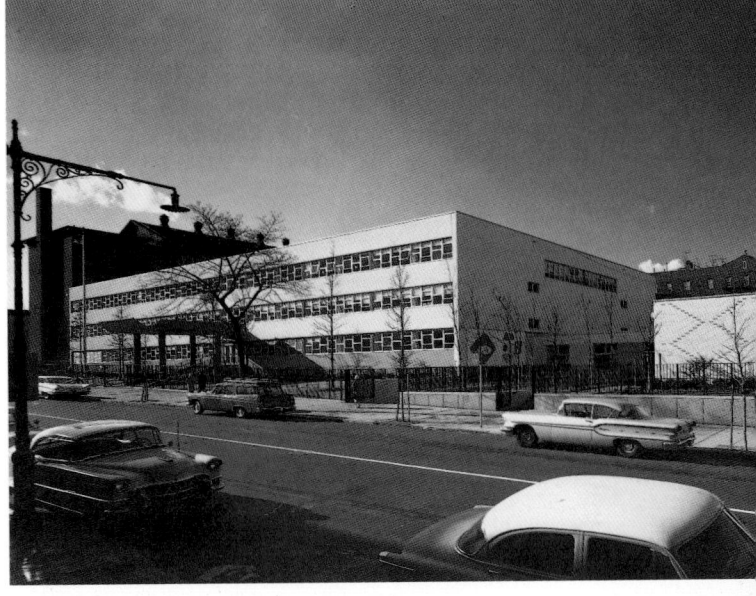

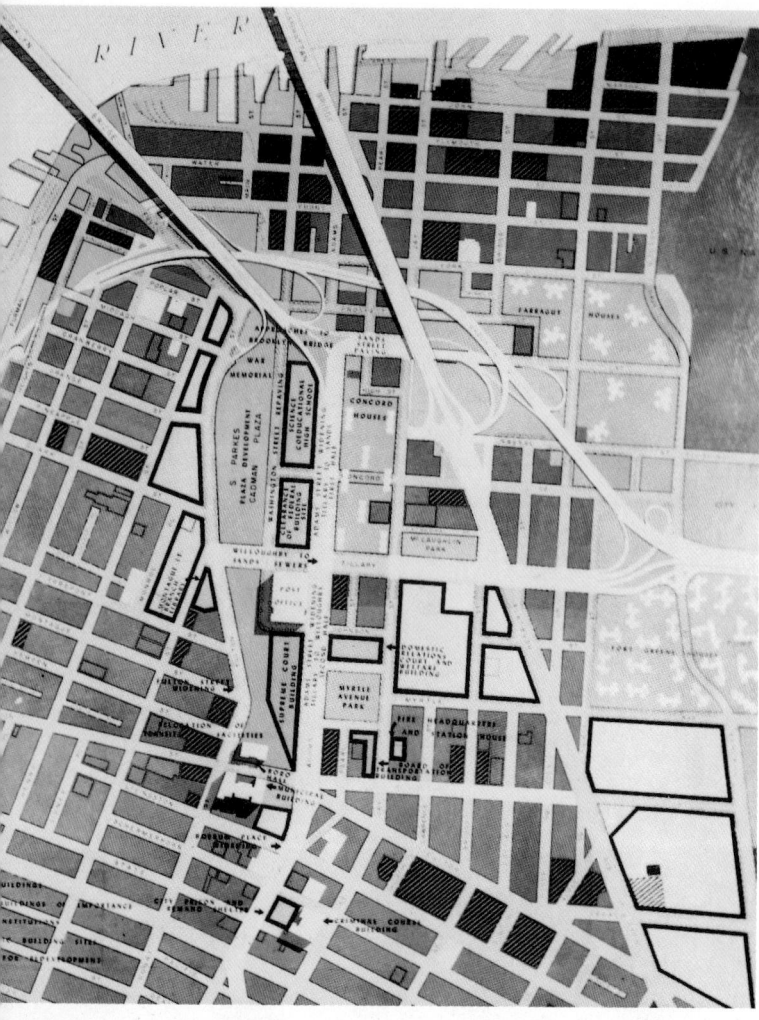

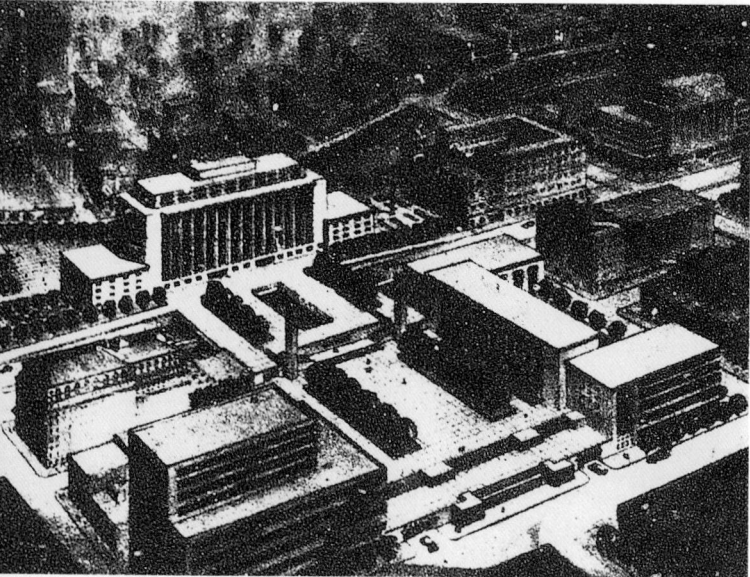

Top: Master plan for Brooklyn Civic Center, between Flatbush Avenue and Henry Street, Atlantic Avenue and York Street. Lorimer Rich, Gilmore D. Clarke and W. Earle Andrews, 1944. Site map. C&R

Bottom: Master plan for Brooklyn Civic Center. Rendering of view to the northwest showing proposed New York State Supreme Court Building on the top left. NYT

tween Monroe Place and Clark Street, extending back to Henry Street, were cleared to form the Cadman Plaza Urban Renewal Area. This development was mired in controversy from the very beginning, when it was proposed by the Mayor's Committee on Slum Clearance. The original developer, S. Pierre Bonan, one of the nation's leading urban redevelopers specializing in Title I projects, working with Harrison & Abramovitz, proposed a luxury rental development with small apartments. In response to the increasing desirability of Brooklyn Heights as a place for family living, the project was then reconfigured to provide larger, fully tax-paying cooperative apartments.

After the slum clearance committee gave way to the Housing and Redevelopment Board in 1960, Bonan continued to press for the project, which at last was designated in 1963 as a mixed-income enclave. Bonan agreed to develop a combination of 250 units of Mitchell-Lama subsidized middle-income apartments and 340 tax-paying cooperatives. Then, as the project dragged on, the growing interest in landmark and community preservation resulted in pressure to save some of the buildings on the site. In 1964 the editors of *Housing and Planning News* wrote of the stalemate the project had been brought to: "The stories of some of the city's renewal projects could have been composed only by very inferior dramatists: they trail on and on before a final resolution, long after all serious interest has evaporated. This is the unhappy fate of Cadman Plaza, which has been prominent on the agenda of those administering Title I for more years than anyone cares to remember."[54] In addition to arguments over the value of the older buildings to be saved, the development was stymied by increasing pressure to provide housing for the less advantaged, as well as calls for a new public school and more play space for children. By this time Bonan had replaced Harrison & Abramovitz with Morris Lapidus, whose design for the buildings did little to make the project more appealing: it consisted of two boxy towers bookending eighteen townhouse units, called Whitman Close in honor of the poet whose house had once occupied a part of the site; little sense of traditional exterior spatial enclosure was provided. When Lapidus's buildings were finally completed in 1967, *Progressive Architecture* was less than kind, describing the towers as "monuments in a vacuous space" and declaring that the ground-level open space was "wasted, because it bears no direct relationship to people who live, not on it, but above it."[55]

Cadman Plaza also included a southern parcel. Here, a second developer, Max Mishken, working with Glass & Glass and Whittlesey & Conklin, had initially proposed Brooklyn Heights Towers—later to be called Cadman Towers—along with street-facing townhouses; the interior of the block would be taken up by covered garage space.[56] Although the program required a high-density residential compound including shops, a movie theater and a school, the architects took their responsibilities to the surrounding context seriously. Raised above fifty duplex townhouses, commercial space and enclosed parking facilities were two twenty-two-story towers set within an elevated landscaped plaza. The saw-toothed composition of the complex, executed in poured concrete and striated block, enhanced corner views for both the townhouses and the apartments while suggesting traditional bay windows. Although the landscaped plaza did serve the apartment and townhouse dwellers, the project's commercial and public amenities failed to engage the community and went largely underutilized. Despite the comparative architectural success of Cadman Towers, by the time of its completion in 1973, the entire undertaking had come to be seen as inappropriate to a neighborhood that was increasingly mindful of its nineteenth-century scale and character.

In 1944, as the war seemed to be nearing an end, Brooklyn politicians began to address the future of their borough's historic core: the Civic Center and downtown business district. It was clear that there were a number of serious problems that needed to be addressed. Government activities were inadequately housed, and despite the superficial vitality of the Fulton Street shopping and entertainment area, the overall impression was one of decay. The assumption was that the new Civic Center would stabilize the area and that developers and merchants would then feel confident enough in the future of Brooklyn's downtown to make the necessary investments in its business district.

In 1944 Joseph D. McGoldrick, the city's comptroller, in trying to advance a master plan for the Civic Center and downtown area, argued for a "test case in rehabilitation": "While we cannot hope to 'rebuild' the city as a whole in one grand rush, we can prepare for a gradual improvement by administering radical treatment to the blighted areas, so common to American cities, and by grasping the relationship of these districts to the whole. It was with this thought in mind that I have endeavored to push the principle of a completely integrated plan covering the Brooklyn Bridge area." The plan was developed by the City Planning Commission, with its consultants, architect Lorimer Rich, landscape architect Gilmore D. Clarke and engineer W. Earle Andrews. In McGoldrick's words, it called "for the purchase of all the dilapidated buildings, for removing the tumble-down structures, and for the rezoning and offering for sale at auction of new super lots, or parts thereof." He contended that the Civic Center would be "an asset to all the Greater City" and that the "program of complete rejuvenation as well as the removal of the blight from this mongrel area . . . would constitute the first continued attack upon the problem of slum clearance and total or integrated civic improvement. . . . The importance of the plan and technique lies not alone in its possibilities for Downtown Brooklyn but in its possibilities for wider application."[57]

The Civic Center plan proposed the wholesale clearance and reconstruction of over forty-five acres, with the newly vacant land rearranged as eight superblocks dedicated to government buildings and parks.[58] It was the largest postwar civic center project in the country, comparable in scale and intention to the City Beautiful civic center projects of the pre–World War I era such as that of Cleveland, Ohio.[59] The plan called for the widening of Adams and Tillary streets to 160 feet, the creation of S. Parkes Cadman Plaza and the construction of new buildings for the Supreme Court, High School of Specialty Trades, Board of Transportation, Brooklyn Fire Department, Department of Public Works Bridge Repair Shop, Welfare Center and Borough Office, Remand Shelter and Adolescents Court, Civil Jail, Domestic Relations Court, City and Municipal Courts and City Prison. Adams Street was to be depressed below a grade-level plaza as it passed in front of the new Supreme Court. According to Robert Moses, commenting in 1955, the Civic Center was to be "to Brooklyn what the great cathedral and opera plazas are to European cities. [It will] be as much the pride of Brooklyn as the Piazza San Marco is the pride of Venice and the Place de la Concorde the cynosure of Paris."[60]

The centerpiece of the Civic Center was S. Parkes Cadman Plaza, an eight-acre, mall-like landscaped open space bounded by Cadman Plaza West, Court, Joralemon and Adams streets and the approaches to the Brooklyn Bridge; it was designed and built between 1950 and 1960 by the staffs of various city and borough agencies. In 1971 A. Ottavino designed the base for Emma Stebbins's statue of Christopher Columbus, which was relocated to the plaza from Central Park; in 1972 Anneta Duveen's sculpture of Robert F. Kennedy was placed to the west of the Supreme Court Building.

The focus of Cadman Plaza was the dignified if dry War Memorial designed by architects Eggers & Higgins and sculptor Charles Keck in 1951.[61] The memorial grew out of a competition initiated at Robert Moses's suggestion by the Brooklyn Eagle in 1944. The first prize in the competition had been awarded to Stuart Constable, chief designer of the Park Department, who collaborated with sculptor Elizabeth Gordon; Aymar Embury II and Gilmore D. Clarke were given second prize for a sculpted and inscribed Wall of Honor in a loggia set in front of a memorial auditorium; and third prize went to Paul Fitzpatrick, vice president of the American Architectural Association, for his Hall of Arbitration. All three schemes were competent essays in the Modern Classical monumentality characteristic of the 1930s, but Constable's emphasized landscape over architecture. In 1947, when public subscriptions for the memorial failed to raise enough money, the Park Department took over and retained Eggers & Higgins, whose stripped Classical design was described by Lewis Mumford as "one of those anomalous structures nearly every American city now boasts, which testifies to pious intentions rather than to understanding of those who have fostered them. . . . The building is not very useful, is not very beautiful, and is not in the least eloquent. In fact, it is principally a warning of what may easily happen to the entire [Civic Center] if the easy and obvious stereotypes of an older day prevail."[62] The writer, art critic and publisher Leslie Katz, in a scathing denunciation of the Civic Center that was published in the Nation in 1962, likened the War Memorial to "a billboard made of stone, with two apathetic stone giants doing a television commercial for grief on either side."[63]

To make way for the Civic Center 304 buildings were demolished, including such notable structures as the Brooklyn Savings Bank and the Jefferson and Arbuckle buildings. In addition, 426 parcels of land were acquired for the project. Like most large-scale planning of the period, the center's renewal was predicated on the creation of superblocks, and peripheral streets were widened to compensate for the elimination of the smaller streets within. The master plan called for the widening of Fulton Street, which bounded Cadman Plaza on the west and Adams Street on the east; it was reconfigured as a six-lane, 160-foot-wide boulevard that served as a principal approach road to the Brooklyn Bridge. As with the significant widening of Tillary Street, the enlargement of Fulton Street made it relatively easy for motorists to get from the bridge to Flatbush Avenue, the principal surface artery leading to Brooklyn's hinterlands.

In April 1953, when the Civic Center site was only partially cleared, Lewis Mumford undertook a preliminary assessment of the project, which he saw as being of comparable importance to the creation of the Jefferson Memorial Park and Gateway on the St. Louis waterfront, the reconstruction of the Golden Triangle in Pittsburgh and the rebuilding of the area west of Center Square in Philadelphia. While he believed that the Civic Center plan as a whole "deserves support,"[64] he was extremely critical of the plaza, which he described as "a long stretch of formal garden with a grass plot in the middle and a big limestone wall, which turns out to be the rear wall of a war memorial, in the middle distance, flanked in the foreground by a comfort station and a park-maintenance building." He was troubled by the design of

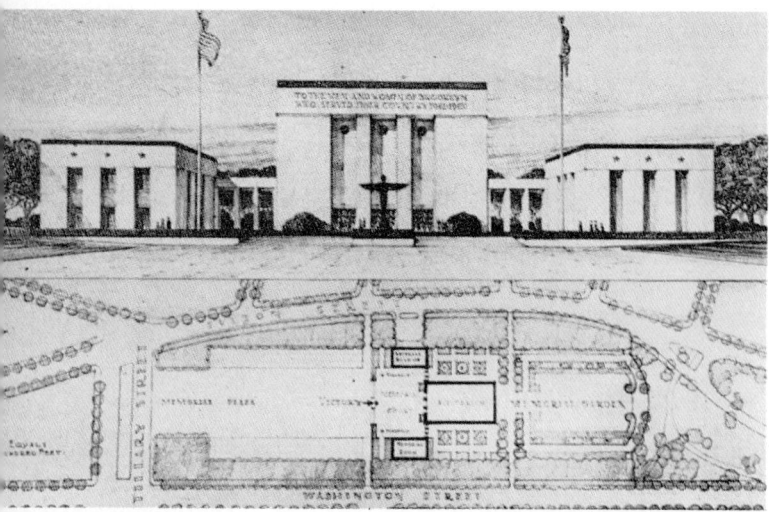

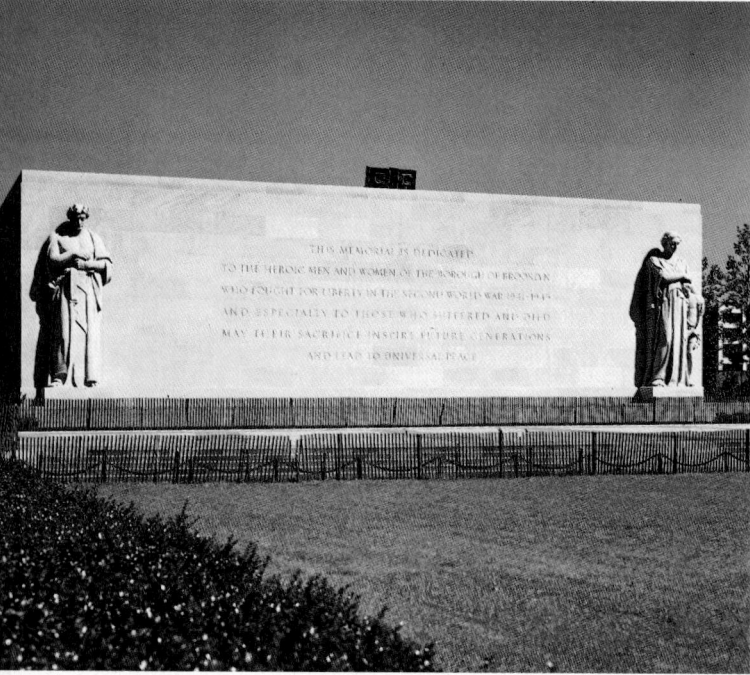

Top: Winning entry for Brooklyn War Memorial competition, S. Parkes Cadman Plaza. Stuart Constable with Elizabeth Gordon, 1944. Rendering of view to the north and site plan. PP. CU

Bottom: Brooklyn War Memorial, S. Parkes Cadman Plaza. Eggers & Higgins with Charles Keck, 1951. View to the north. Morgan. EG

Top right: New York City Board of Transportation Building, 370 Jay Street, northwest corner of Willoughby Street. William E. Haugaard and Andrew J. Thomas, 1951. View to the southwest. Lincoln. PENN

Bottom right: New York City Board of Transportation Building. Open-air concourse. Lincoln. PENN

the open space itself and by the lack of a coordinated vision governing the design of the buildings that would become its frame. But he also questioned the very idea of the plaza: "Do not think I would have the city forfeit a single square foot of ground now dedicated to parks, greens, and plazas. But there is a better treatment than a wholesale concentration of open space."

Mumford would have preferred a parade ground or festival square, a public processional way to be filled on special occasions. Moreover, he would have spread the open space out, articulating it into different kinds of smaller parks and squares planned in relationship to the buildings. "Setting aside one huge slab of open space," he wrote, "and allowing the rest of the area to be built up in the usual monumental manner is no solution." Rather than the continuous open spaces of orthodox Modernism or the grand planning of Beaux-Arts Classicism, Mumford argued for an articulated hierarchy of outdoor rooms: "This civic center should have a number of gathering places, human catchment basins, to bring people together; Cadman Plaza, as it is now conceived, is an area of dispersal whose inviolable green lawns naturally reduce the number of people who can congregate."[65] Mumford's analysis proved correct: as the Civic Center began to take form, the vast greensward of Cadman Plaza revealed itself more a voided center than a focus of civic life.

William E. Haugaard and Andrew J. Thomas's building for the New York City Board of Transportation, at 370 Jay Street, on the northwest corner of Willoughby Street, was the first public building completed in the master plan area, though it was not built on land cleared as part of the Civic Center renewal area.[66] The design of the thirteen-story limestone-clad mass, which extended back to Pearl Street, was initially undertaken by Haugaard before the war and was completed after his death by Thomas in 1951. The facade was distinguished by an austere, deadpan pattern of fenestration consisting of large glazing panels set nearly flush in the wall. Within each panel, a fixed central pane of glass was flanked by operable casements and horizontal units above and below, an arrangement similar to, but even more severe than, the one employed by Cross & Cross in their Aetna Building of 1940.[67] The services were gathered in a powerfully massed tower at the rear that became a notable feature when viewed from the widened Adams Street. The building was also notable for the airy concourse that led passengers via escalators from the street to the Jay Street subway station, and for the below-grade track siding that enabled special cars to deliver money collected from subway stations all over the city to a central vault housed within.

Mumford found the Transportation Building a fine expression of unaffected modernity: "This facade is simplicity itself," he observed. He liked the size of the principal mass, whose dimensions—356 feet long by 82 feet wide—he found "ideal" for a building designed to make maximum use of natural lighting and natural ventilation. The building's size was also ideal, he said, "for a business district that seeks to eliminate the handicaps of congestion." He praised the functional aspect of the building: "This seems to be the very model of an efficient office building. Not a cathedral of commerce, not a temple of advertising, not a palace of municipal power: just a group of offices arranged for the efficient dispatch of administration." Most important, for Mumford, was the fact that the Transportation Building served as a model of successful urbanism: "A business district that consisted mainly of buildings of this type would be far more efficient and far more handsome than anything the rest of the city could show. It would have qualities that, if less striking than those of our cloud-capped towers, would give greater promise of durability. . . . Properly grouped, a half-dozen Transportation Buildings would create a new kind of urban space, distinguished by composure and order."[68]

Concord Village, on Tillary Street between Adams and Jay streets, was a group of seven fifteen-story red-brick-clad slabs erected by a consortium of eighteen Brooklyn savings banks to provide housing for 481 middle-class tenants.[69] Three buildings, designed by Benjamin Braunstein and Alfred H. Ryder, were completed in 1952; four more buildings, designed by W. T. McCarthy and Rosario Candela, were completed six years later. Despite delays in site acquisition, it was the first component of the Civic Center to be completed. Mumford felt the "gawky" buildings of Concord Village sounded "the wrong note for the whole development."[70]

In May 1949 plans were submitted to the Art Commission for Bloch & Hesse's five-story Welfare Center Building, proposed for the southeast corner of Jay and Johnson streets.[71] The limestone-clad building, completed in 1955, was an awkward attempt to balance the mass and symmetry traditional to civic architecture with the new aesthetics of Modernism, in recognition of its role as an office building.

La Pierre, Litchfield & Partners' Brooklyn Men's House of Detention (1956), at 275 Atlantic Avenue, between Smith Street and Boerum Place, marked the southernmost representation of government in the Civic Center.[72] The building replaced the fifty-nine-year-old battlemented Gothic Raymond Street Jail, at 149 Ashland Place, which was torn down as part of the Fort Greene renewal area (see above). The new eleven-story slab, clad in granite, glass and brick, housed 817 inmates and contained a rooftop recreation area as well as medical and dental clinics and a chapel. As the *New York Times* reported, the design quality of the jail, which looked like it "might have been one of the newer Madison Avenue office buildings," was startling, given the building type.[73] This was attributed to the care lavished on the design by Clarence B. Litchfield, who, according to the *Times*, regarded penology as a hobby as well as a principal professional interest.

In February 1949 Shreve, Lamb & Harmon's designs for the new New York State Supreme Court Building, at 360 Adams Street, the largest public building proposed for the Civic Center, were submitted to the Art Commission.[74] Completed in 1958, the new courthouse consisted of three ponderous limestone-clad, granite-trimmed masses: a central eleven-story section housing the Supreme Court and three-story wings on each side accommodating the Surrogate's Court in addition to offices of the County Clerk, Registrar, Public Administrator and Sheriff. All in all, twenty-eight courtrooms and six hearing rooms were included in the new building. Leslie Katz described the Supreme Court as "a breathtaking sight," notable for its unattractiveness: "It may have the distinction, externally, of being the ugliest new building in America. Imagine an old transatlantic liner with the prow and stern and funnels cut off, every line made straight, planted on open land. The building looks curiously incomplete, with ribbons of black stone joining the windows, a gigantic flower planter without flowers."[75]

Carson & Lundin, in association with Lorimer Rich & Associates, designed the Federal Building and Courthouse (1962), at 275 Washington Street, on the northeast corner of Tillary Street, which also faced directly onto Cadman Plaza.[76] A double structure separated by a low entry lobby, it consisted of a six-story courtroom block at Washington Street and a four-story office building facing Tillary Street. The overall effect of the

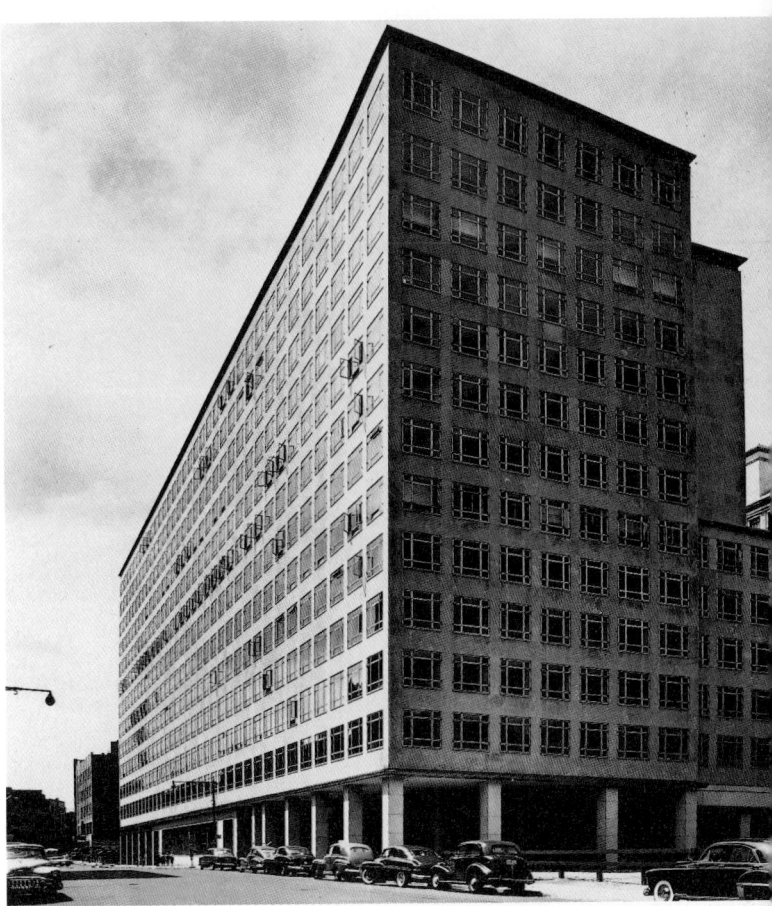

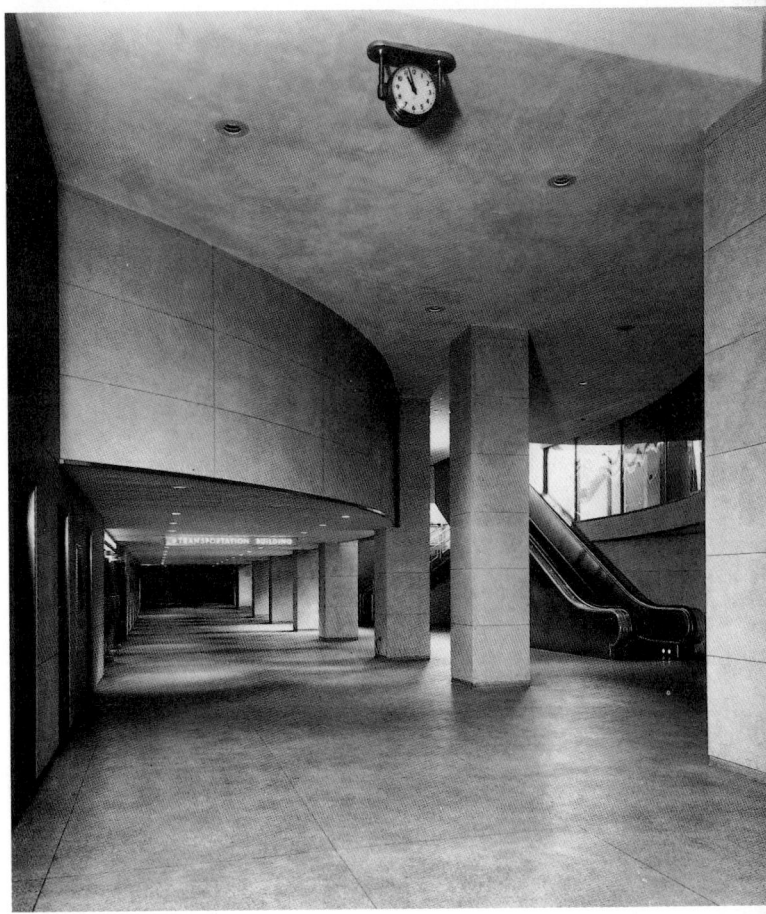

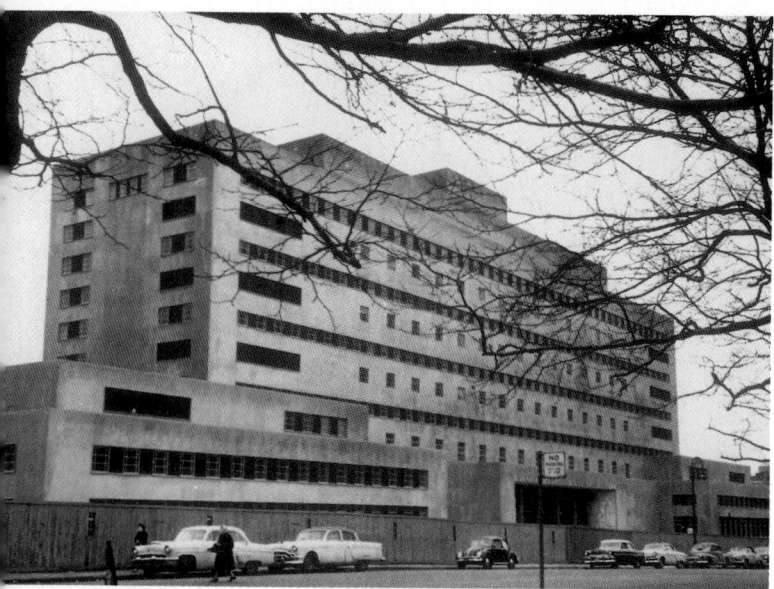

Above: New York State Supreme Court Building, 360 Adams Street, between Johnson and Joralemon streets. Shreve, Lamb & Harmon, 1958. View to the southeast. NYT

Top right: Wallachs, 16 Court Street, between Remsen and Montague streets. Morris Ketchum, Jr., 1942. Entrance and interior at night. Stoller. ©ESTO

Center right: Balch Price, 380 Fulton Street, between Smith Street and Red Hook Lane. José Fernandez, 1944. Fitting rooms. Gottscho-Schleisner. LOC

Bottom right: Martin's, 400 Fulton Street, between Smith Street and Gallatin Place. Morris Lapidus, 1944. Boys' barber shop. ML

design was banal, although an attempt was made to dignify the composition by cladding the repeated verticals of the structural fins in buff-gray marble.

The Civic Center also included an underground parking garage (James R. Frases, 1960), a 702-car facility entered from Jay Street next door to the Transportation Building and tucked under a one-acre park created on the roof of the sloping site.[77] Developed as part of Traffic Commissioner T. T. Wiley's program for creating parking garages under parkland throughout the city (see chapter 1), which had been opposed by Robert Moses and others, this facility occupied a vacant site.

In 1965, at the request of Borough President Abe Stark, the Brooklyn Chapter of the American Institute of Architects sponsored a competition for the design of what was called Borough Hall Square, the 160-foot-long, 35-foot-wide sliver of space at the southeast corner of Borough Hall.[78] A jury that included Max Abramovitz, Harmon Goldstone, Samuel Ratensky, Frederick Woodbridge and Douglas Haskell selected Hanford Yang and Alexander A. Gartner's proposal, which called for a one-story Brutalist information pavilion set on a stone plaza articulated into a number of levels. The proposal was not realized.

One of the principal goals of the Civic Center plan was the stabilization of Brooklyn's downtown business district, where lawyers were the principal tenants of the tall office buildings that clustered to the west around Court Street and where long-established department stores, shops, restaurants and movie theaters stretched eastward along Fulton Street to Flatbush Avenue. The Civic Center stimulated the construction of only one sizable new office building, Morris Lapidus's fifteen-story building (1959) at 141 Livingston Street, with a curtain wall of gray and gold aluminum.[79] But it encouraged the construction of two new school facilities. Francis Keally designed a windowless auditorium and gymnasium building (1962), clad in white- and blue-glazed brick, for Brooklyn Community College, at 285 Jay Street, between Tillary and Johnson streets.[80] Above the entrance was a mural in blue and green ceramic tile by Nat Choate featuring stylized representations of drama, music, arts, recreation, health and competition. The Brooklyn Law School moved to a new home from its previous building (Mayers, Murray & Phillip, 1929), at 375 Pearl Street, north of Fulton Street, an eight-story Romanesque-inspired facility featuring a top-floor loggia; the building was taken over by the Brooklyn Friends School.[81] The new law school building (Praeger-Kavanagh-Waterbury, 1967), at 250 Joralemon Street, which replaced the venerable Kings County Courthouse, was a banal nine-story, white-marble-clad structure set behind a windswept plaza and topped by a prominent mechanical penthouse.

Fulton Street between Boerum Place and Flatbush Avenue was Brooklyn's Main Street. Economically viable department stores and specialty shops, housed mostly in buildings from the 1880s and 1890s, jostled each other in the shadows of the elevated railroad that had run along its length since 1888. The demolition of the elevated in 1941 stimulated proposals for physical improvements to the buildings that became totally visible for the first time in more than fifty years.

In 1940, as part of a large remodeling effort involving eight of its stores, Bloch & Hesse prepared five alternate designs for a new facade to be grafted onto the existing Schrafft's restaurant at 386 Fulton Street.[82] The following year a sleekly moderne new building for the 107-year-old jewelry concern William Wise & Sons (Benjamin Driesler, Jr., 1941), was constructed at 487 Fulton Street.[83] Also in 1941 the Downtown Brooklyn Association sponsored "Fulton Street—1942," an architectural competition and building exhibition.[84] The competition, restricted to students at Pratt Institute, concentrated on the improvement of the triangular block on the north side of the street just east of Borough Hall. In addition, five architects—Slee & Bryson, Githens & Keally, Lorimer Rich, C. C. Briggs, and Koch & Wagner—were assigned existing commercial buildings along Fulton Street and asked to demonstrate how they would redesign the facades. The participating architects removed all traces of the buildings' nineteenth-century origins, designing facades that spoke only of the present.

In 1942 the first of what would become a series of shops designed by Morris Ketchum, Jr., for the Wallachs chain of men's haberdasheries was built.[85] Located as 16 Court Street, close to the Fulton Street shopping district, this new store featured a bold, diagonal glass storefront. Inside, existing columns were sheathed in woven hardwood and given sculpturally forceful round or kidney shapes. The stylistically varied interiors of José Fernandez's Balch Price fur shop (1944), at 380 Fulton Street, occupied a rambling ground-floor space running through several buildings.[86] While the design contained a number of interesting details, its overall effect was episodic, perhaps deliberately so.

In 1944 Morris Lapidus brought his characteristic flair to Fulton Street with the design of the street-level shop that housed the men's clothing department of Martin's, Brooklyn's leading specialty department store.[87] One year later Lapidus converted the fourth floor of Martin's into a "delightful children's world," as the New York Times put it, including individually styled sections ranging from the layette shop with its curvilinear showcases to the boys' barber shop, which featured stools fashioned to look like catchers' mitts placed on top of baseball bats.[88] In 1944 Bond Stores, sellers of clothing for both men and women, announced plans to build a new facility at 400 Fulton Street, replacing a small store nearby at 447 Fulton Street.[89] The new Bond's (1949), designed by Louis Allen Abramson, occupied a 95-by-100-foot parcel at Fulton Street and Gallatin Place. The stylish Modernist vocabulary of the four-story, 55,000-square-foot building clad in granite and limestone included large areas of glass that flooded the double-height main floor with light. In 1954 Mays Department Store vastly expanded its operations at 510 Fulton Street, between Hanover Place and Bond Street, where it had begun in 1924 in an eight-by-twenty-four-foot space.[90] Designed by Leo V. Berger, the new, 300,000-square-foot Mays combined a four-story building along Fulton Street with a seven-story building facing Livingston Street in a blandly Modernist design. At the Civic Center's eastern gateway to Fulton Street was De Young, Moscowitz & Rosenberg's Fulton Savings Bank (1955), which replaced the Star burlesque theater.[91] More successfully than most buildings in the area, the design combined monumental scale with Modernist-inspired flattened planes of granite and glass.

While Brooklyn's largest department store, Abraham & Straus, continued to prosper in the postwar era, other old-line department and specialty stores closed, unable to cope with suburbanization and the demographic changes that gradually robbed Fulton Street of its carriage-trade clientele.[92] The closings of Loeser's and Namm's were symptomatic. In February 1952 Frederick A. Loeser & Co., the chief rival of Abraham & Straus, citing a $600,000 operating loss for the previous twelve months, announced that it was closing its store at 484 Fulton Street, which it had occupied since 1886.[93] Within a month its neighbor, the Namm Store (Robert D. Kohn, 1924–28), purchased Loeser's name; the combined store was called Namm-Loeser's. By April,

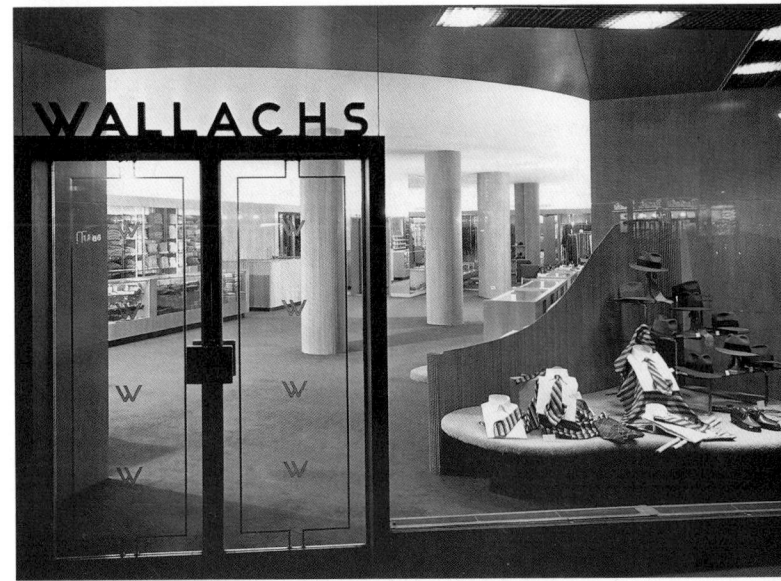

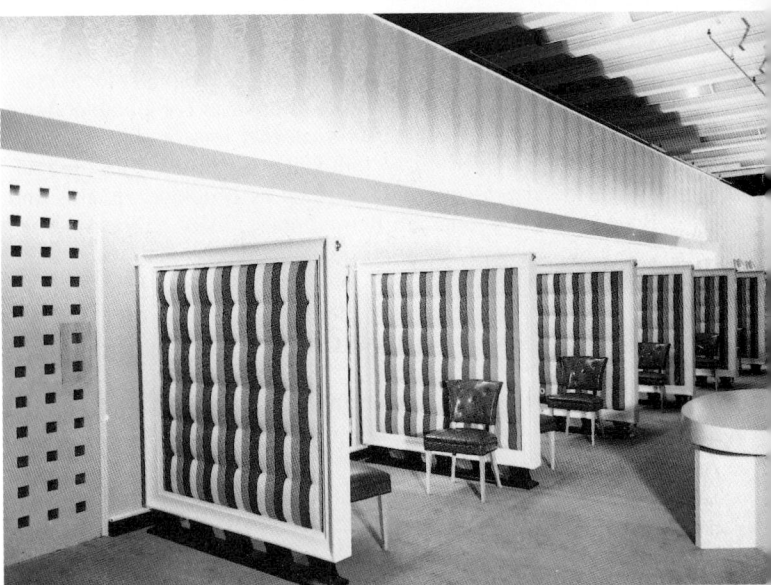

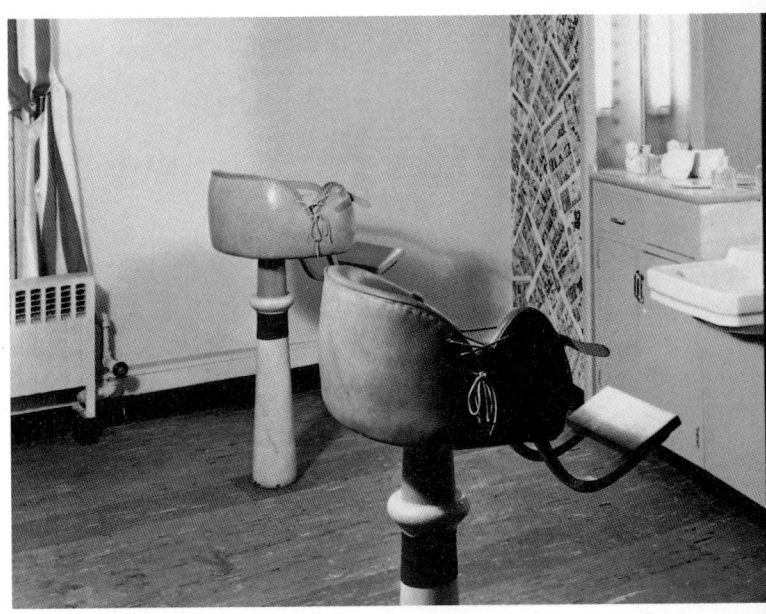

Mays Department Stores had bought Namm-Loeser's Fulton Street building; according to Joe Weinstein, the president of Mays, this was done "to make certain that the Fulton Street area maintains its current prestige as one of the nation's major shopping centers."[94] Only five years later, in February 1957, Namm-Loeser's announced it was closing its Brooklyn store, although it was keeping open its two Long Island branches.[95]

By the mid-1960s it was clear that, though Fulton Street was, in terms of sales, the sixth most active retail district in the nation, its mix of shops had declined disastrously into a redundancy of stores specializing in fast food, wigs and fancy shoes. Of the department stores, only Abraham & Straus, Mays and Martin's held on.[96] The major entertainment palaces had closed down as well. In 1962 the 4,400-seat Brooklyn Paramount (Rapp & Rapp, 1928), on the southeast corner of Flatbush and DeKalb avenues, the borough's leading movie palace, closed and was taken over by Long Island University (see chapter 16). The Brooklyn Fox Theater (C. Howard Crane, 1928), which since 1966 was virtually closed except for a few cultural events, was demolished in 1970–71.[97] The only remaining theater was the 2,000-seat RKO Albee (Thomas W. Lamb, 1925), 1 DeKalb Avenue at Albee Square.

The projected opening of King's Plaza shopping center at Mill Basin in 1970 (see chapter 15) threatened to further erode Fulton Street's traditional appeal to the borough's middle-class whites, who would now be able to drive to comparable shops located nearer to home. Although this loss of shoppers was somewhat mitigated by an influx of new buyers from the revitalized nearby neighborhoods such as Brooklyn Heights and Boerum Hill, as Jonathan Barnett noted, these "'brownstoners' had a tendency to take their buying power to Manhattan."[98] In 1968 Stephen and George Klein, the father-and-son owners of Barton's, a candy company that employed 700 workers in its plant just east of the Fulton Street shopping district, hired Katz, Waisman, Weber, Strauss to design an expansion of its manufacturing operation as well as 600,000 square feet of office and shopping space.[99] The Kleins drew their inspiration from the success of the conversion of an old chocolate factory into Ghirardelli Square (Wurster, Bernardi & Emmons, architects; Lawrence Halprin & Associates, landscape architects, 1962–67), a sophisticated shopping center in San Francisco.[100] The Brooklyn plan, for a superscaled, Paul Rudolph–inspired office tower with a raised plaza and stepped podium, was conceived as the visual conclusion to a proposed pedestrian mall along Fulton Street. The proposal did not go forward, but it did influence a more serious study of the area undertaken with a broader-based sponsorship headed by the Kleins.

In 1967 a number of key downtown merchants and institutions, led by Dennis Durden, Vice President for Urban Affairs of Federated Department Stores, the parent organization of Abraham & Straus, banded together to form the Downtown Brooklyn Development Committee, which retained the city's Urban Design Group to undertake a study of the area.[101] Under the direction of Richard Rosan, the city established an Office of Downtown Brooklyn Development as an outgrowth of the Urban Design Group's initial efforts. A fifteen-year, $500 million development plan for a seventeen-block, forty-acre area bounded by Boerum Place, Myrtle Avenue, Ashland Place, Flatbush and Atlantic avenues was announced in 1969, during Mayor Lindsay's reelection campaign. The plan was adopted and gradually implemented, including the transitway, a modified pedestrian mall along Fulton Street's shopping blocks that permitted limited traffic, particularly buses. The plan also called for the construction of new office buildings at the east end of the

Fulton Street business district on land assembled by the city through urban renewal. There were to be no "write downs" on the cost of this land because it was believed that by 1975, when this portion of the plan would be realized, the new development could easily absorb the office buildings. The designated renewal was needed as a mechanism to assemble large sites from the many small lots that existed under diverse ownerships. While such large sites would enable the construction of big buildings, they would involve considerable sacrifice to diversity, a point that was downplayed by the plan's promoters.

In July 1970 the City Planning Commission approved the Brooklyn Center Project, which was to be developed by the Kleins for a much reduced area, seventeen acres bounded by Ashland Place, DeKalb and Lafayette avenues and Livingston Street, as well as small parts of Nevins Street and Grove Place.[102] For this project, Skidmore, Owings & Merrill (SOM) sketched a futuristic master plan that juxtaposed a circular tower and a slab atop a raised, six-story podium connected via pedestrian skybridges to satellite podiums on the west side of Flatbush Avenue. In 1972 SOM completed the first office building of the Brooklyn Center Project for the Consolidated Edison Company, Brooklyn Division, at 30 Flatbush Avenue, between Nevins and Livingston streets, on the site of the former Fox Theater.[103] The Consolidated Edison building featured windows deeply recessed behind an exposed concrete frame. This design, which recalled the work of I. M. Pei, established a formidable if not very articulate presence for the utility company. SOM created a more restrained design for their second building in the area: the New York Telephone Company Office Building (1975), at 395 Flatbush Avenue Extension, between DeKalb Avenue and Fulton Street, occupying a site that had been cleared as part of the reconstruction of the DeKalb Avenue subway interchange below.[104]

For the Schermerhorn-Pacific Urban Renewal Area, Benjamin Thompson's firm was given the task of designing the housing that was to be built on a five-block-long site stretching along the south side of Schermerhorn Street, where since the 1930s parking lots had sat atop the Hoyt-Schermerhorn subway station.[105] Thompson, an architect based in Cambridge, Massachusetts, who had considerable experience in the design of college dormitories and a growing specialty in urban marketplaces, struggled to breathe life into the inherently cavernous spaces of the subway concourse. Along with the 992 units of new housing, the Office of Downtown Brooklyn Development proposed the Hoyt-Schermerhorn Mezzanine, a three-level, 250,000-square-foot complex devoted to shopping, pedestrian circulation and transportation services.[106] In 1973 the design was given a "first award" by Progressive Architecture in its Design Awards program. But after the Board of Estimate had approved the Schermerhorn-Pacific project in July 1973, it ran into political, legal and economic problems. Among these were charges of racism and, ultimately, a lawsuit brought by Manhattan Borough President Percy Sutton, in response to the decision of the New York State Urban Development Corporation (UDC), which had taken on the project, to separate the 727 middle-income units from the 265 moderate- and low-income units. The economic problems proved even tougher to beat, and rising costs forced the UDC first to scale down the project and then to abandon it altogether when the organization collapsed in 1975. Although the city attempted to regain control of the project, in 1976 it was handed over to private developers, the Caldwell-Wingate Company and Sylvan Lawrence, who proposed a modest 280 rental apartments located in thirty-five four-story buildings.

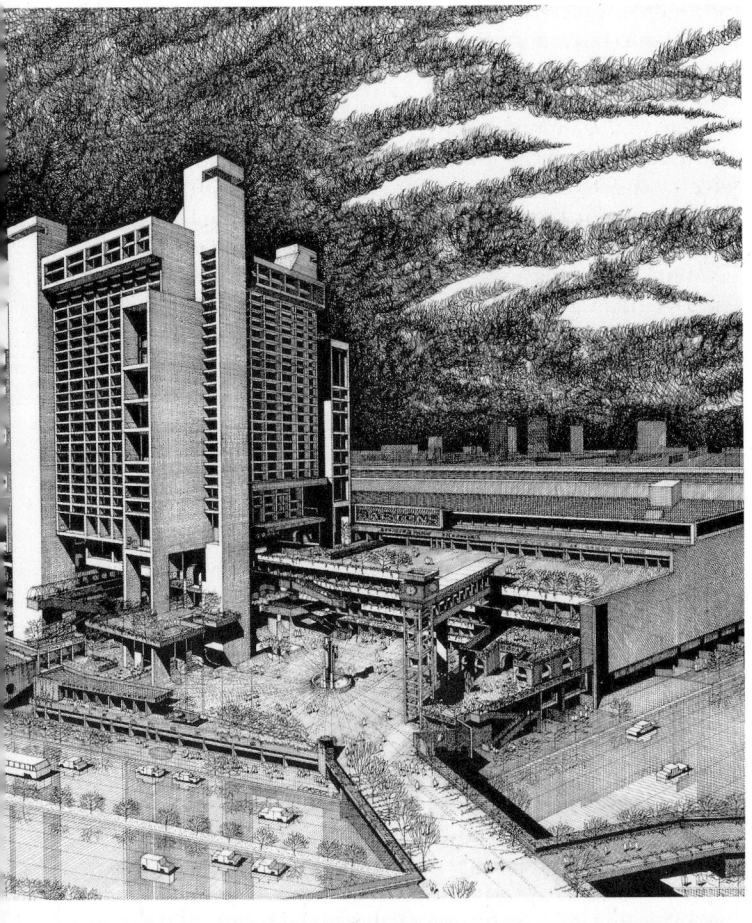

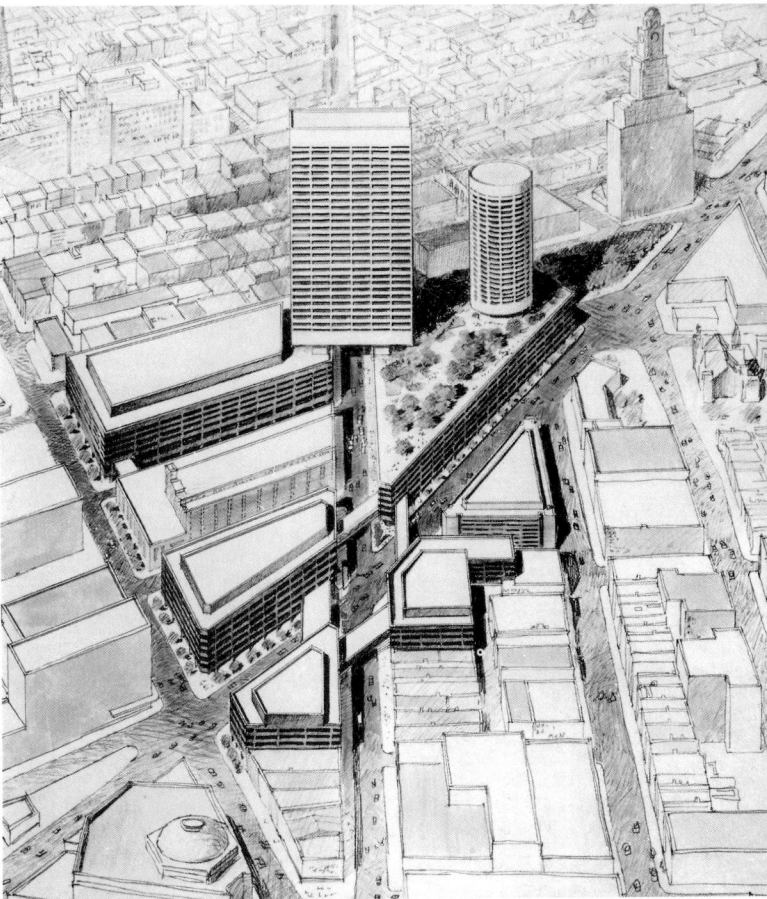

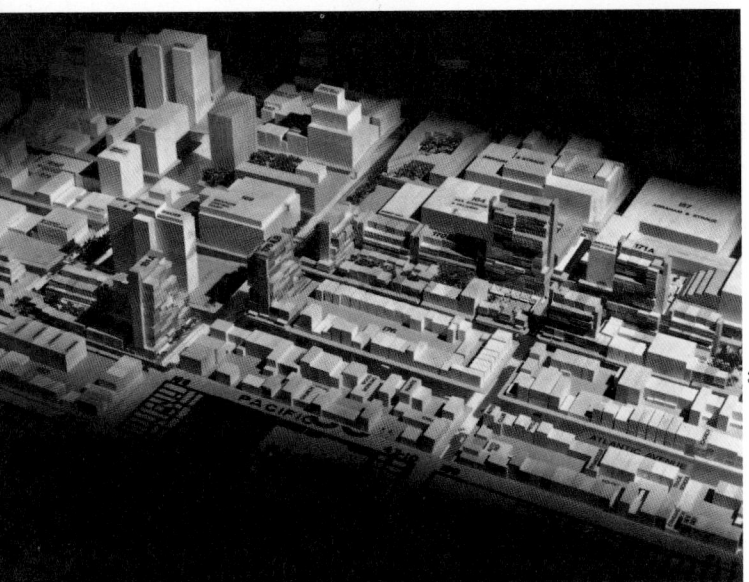

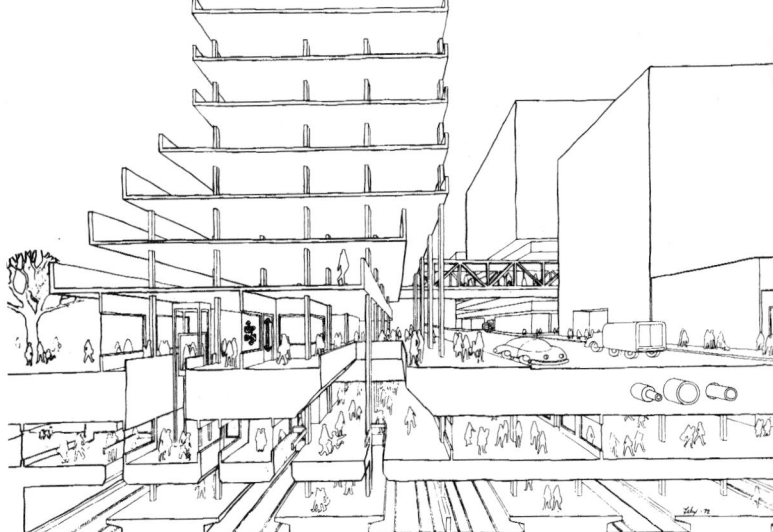

Top left: Proposal for shopping and office complex for Barton's, at Fulton Street and Flatbush Avenue. Katz, Waisman, Weber, Strauss, 1968. Rendering by Lorenz of view to the northeast. ©Gil Amiaga. GA

Bottom left: Master plan for Schermerhorn-Pacific Urban Renewal Area, south side of Schermerhorn Street, between Hoyt and Bond streets. Benjamin Thompson, 1972. Model. View to the northwest. Stoller. ©ESTO

Top right: Brooklyn Center Project, bounded by Ashland Place, DeKalb Avenue, Lafayette Avenue, Livingston Street and adjoining segments of Nevins Street and Grove Place. Skidmore, Owings & Merrill, 1972. Perspective showing view to the southeast. SOM

Bottom right: Hoyt-Schermerhorn Mezzanine, Schermerhorn-Pacific Urban Renewal Area. Office of Downtown Brooklyn Development, 1973. Section perspective. NYC

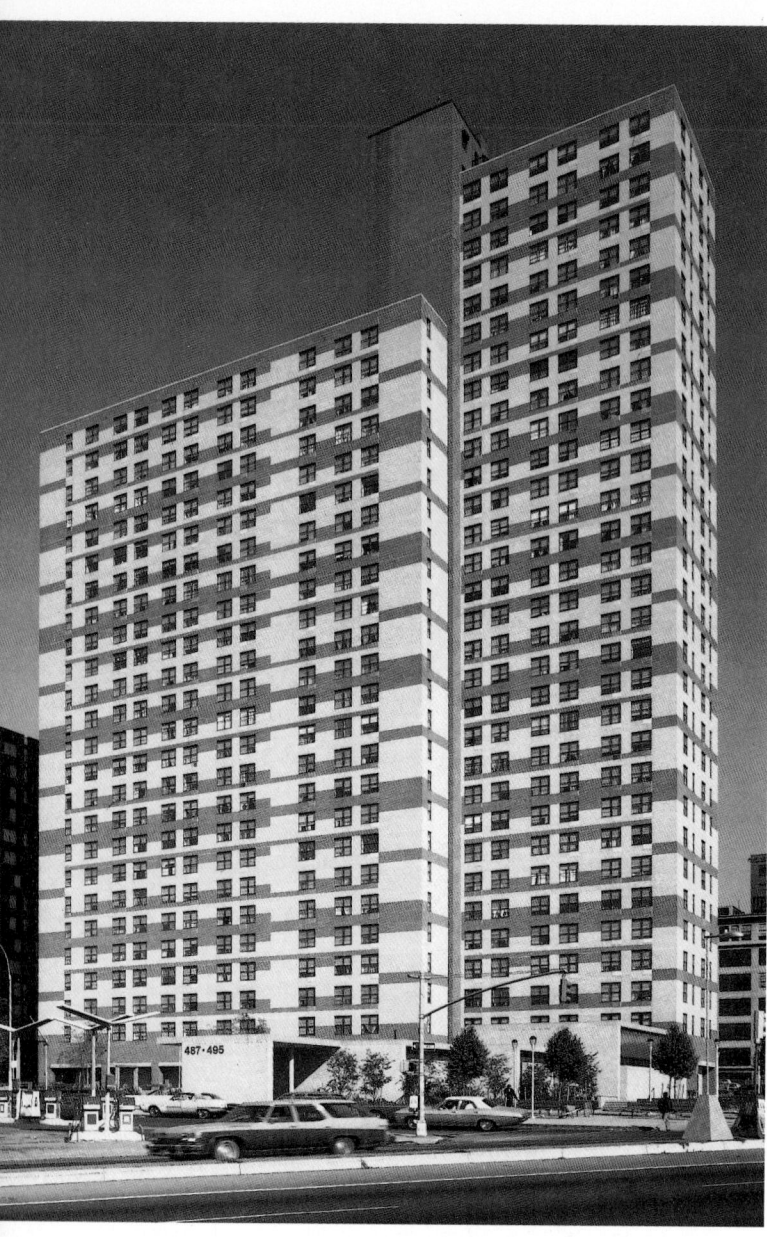

Atlantic Terminal Houses, 487–495 Carlton Avenue, northeast corner of Atlantic Avenue, Fort Greene. James Stewart Polshek & Associates, 1976. View to the northeast. NYCHA

As plans were fitfully progressing for the rehabilitation of Brooklyn's business core, designers in the city's Office of Housing and Development struggled to give form to yet another renewal area, Atlantic Terminal, a 104-acre site roughly bounded by Vanderbilt and Greene avenues, Hanson Place, Lafayette, Flatbush and Third avenues and Pacific Street, most of which consisted of the open-air Fort Greene Meat Market.[107] The site was cut along its eastern axis by Atlantic Avenue, which included open tracks serving the Long Island Railroad's Atlantic Terminal, a heavily used but outmoded facility at its western end. The plan proposed to cover the open cut with buildings and plazas and ingeniously slip through the welter of underground rail and subway lines to create a connected network of new businesses and institutional functions concentrated around the high-intensity intersection of Atlantic and Flatbush avenues. To replace the market, 2,400 units of low- and middle-income housing were proposed on a vast superblock, as well as some light industrial structures, two parks and a fourteen-acre campus for the City University's Baruch College.

The Fort Greene Meat Market was originally planned to be relocated to a thirteen-acre site along the East River between the Brooklyn and Manhattan bridges. But after considerable protest the market was moved to another waterfront site, this one in the Sunset Park section, bounded by Fifty-fourth and Fifty-seventh streets, First Avenue and the pierhead line. Although Baruch College remained in Manhattan, and the megastructural super-scale of the Housing and Development plan was not realized, a different version of the housing in the renewal area was completed in 1976. This included middle-income buildings at 170 South Portland Avenue and 161 South Elliott Place, between Hanson Place and Atlantic Avenue; 455 and 475 Carlton Avenue, between Fulton Street and Atlantic Avenue; and 770 Fulton Street, between Carlton Avenue and Adelphi Street, all the work of Bond Ryder Associates. A low-income project of the Housing Authority, Atlantic Terminal Houses, 320 units designed by James Stewart Polshek & Associates, was also built at 487–495 Carlton Avenue, on the northeast corner of Atlantic Avenue. According to Polshek, his design "depended upon the 'painterly' use of different colored bricks for its iconography"; nonetheless, in its crude use of materials and its bulky massing it very much reflected the new Brutalist tradition of postwar English public housing.[108]

In a 1975 *New York Times* article Ada Louise Huxtable greeted the planning activity in downtown Brooklyn and the beginning of actual construction with enthusiasm. The "lessons in architecture and urbanism" offered in Brooklyn, she said, "largely involve informed efforts to turn around an area decimated by a residential and commercial flight to the suburbs of the 1950's and 1960's." While much of her article rhapsodized about the revival of Brooklyn neighborhoods, and the role of Richard Rosan and his development office, she concluded by turning her attention to one of Old Brooklyn's least known sections, the historic waterfront that lay between the Brooklyn and Manhattan bridges, at the bottom of Fulton Street, where Robert Fulton's ferry service had begun in 1814. Huxtable praised an as yet unreleased plan of the development office for a renewal area at Fulton Ferry, but she concluded by advising her readers not to wait for that redevelopment to explore "the architectural marvels of the dramatic brick Empire Stores with their griffons and eagles and arched gates at the water's edge."[109] One who seemed to anticipate Huxtable's call was David Morton, a young architect who in 1973 converted a former toilet-seat factory, the Berglas Building, at 8 Fulton Street, into housing.[110] The unconventional project, though promising, was a bit ahead of its time and proved difficult to rent. But in 1977 the area began to come into its own when Michael (Buzzy) O'Keefe established the River Café on a barge moored at the end of Fulton Street, becoming New York's only waterside restaurant.[111]

Even before the designation of Brooklyn Heights as a landmark district in 1965, its value as a collection of architecturally significant individual buildings, as well as an increasingly rare example of a cohesive, predominantly low-rise urban environment, was widely recognized by both architects and the general public. Several postwar building projects proposed for the neighborhood reflected the growing emphasis on contextually appropriate design. In 1948–49, Meyer Parodneck commissioned the architect Samuel J. Glaberson to convert a nineteenth-century carriage house, located at 278 Hicks Street, that had once belonged to Alfred T. White.[112] Though Glaberson established a frankly contemporary expression inside, exposing brick walls and creating an intermediate-level sleeping loft, he showed more restraint on the exterior. The former stable's rear wall was opened up with glass, creating an intimate relationship with the backyard, but the principal facade was scrupulously maintained, respecting its neighborhood context by revealing no hint of the changes within.

In 1963 the young architect Lee Harris Pomeroy, in association with Harvey A. Berg, won a *Progressive Architecture* Design Citation with a proposal to convert a six-story warehouse built in 1885—formerly belonging to the Mason Au & Magenheimer Candy Company—at 20 Henry Street, on the northwest corner of Middagh Street, into living and working quarters for artists.[113] Pomeroy's solution was significant not only because it called for the restoration of the existing building fabric but also because it treated the building's formerly blank party walls, now exposed to view, in the same manner as its original facade and not as an exercise in up-to-date, high-style Modernism. As completed in 1975 by Pomeroy, Lebduska Associates, in association with Martyn and Don Weston, the Henry Street Studios had the great merit of both leaving well enough alone—the heavy timber frame was exposed inside, the brick exterior walls left untouched—and enhancing the existing structure: the original sign reading "Peaks Mason Mints" was repainted and served visually as a cornice.

While most of the new householders were attracted to Brooklyn Heights by the nineteenth-century houses, a few empty lots in the less grand fringe areas provided opportunities to build from scratch. Three related townhouses at 40, 44 and 48 Willow Place, begun before the area was designated, turned a frankly Modernist face to the otherwise traditionally articulated surrounding architecture.[114] Designed by Joseph and Mary Merz, the houses might well have faced stiff opposition from preservationists had their construction been proposed later, but they nonetheless made a sophisticated and urbane contribution to the neighborhood. Although the pink-toned brick facades were severe and the openings were of vastly different proportion and scale from the typical windows of the neighboring houses, the overall rhythm of the facades managed to seem sympathetic. The biggest of the three was the Leonard Garment double house, which provided a covered garage and a play area on the ground floor, and a generous sweep of living space stretching across the building's rear on the second floor.[115] Joseph Merz collaborated with Benjamin Baldwin on the spare interior design of the Garment house, which featured a boldly patterned rug against the stark white wall of the double-height living space.

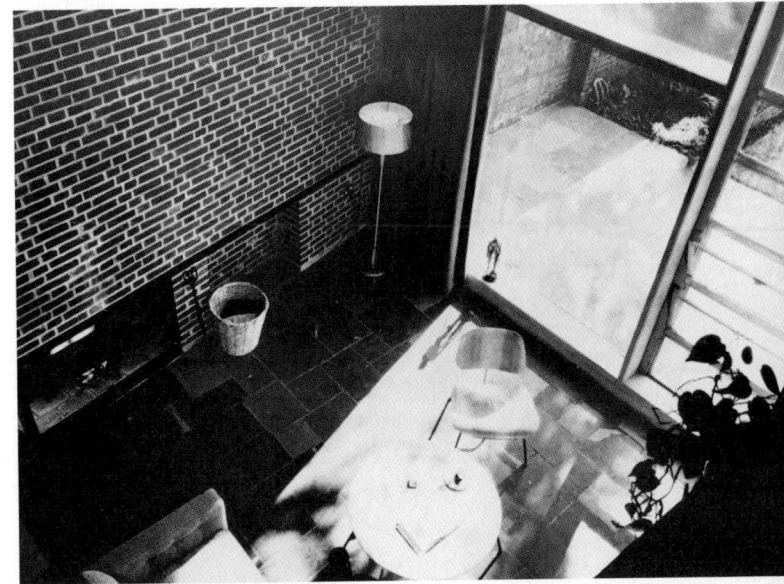

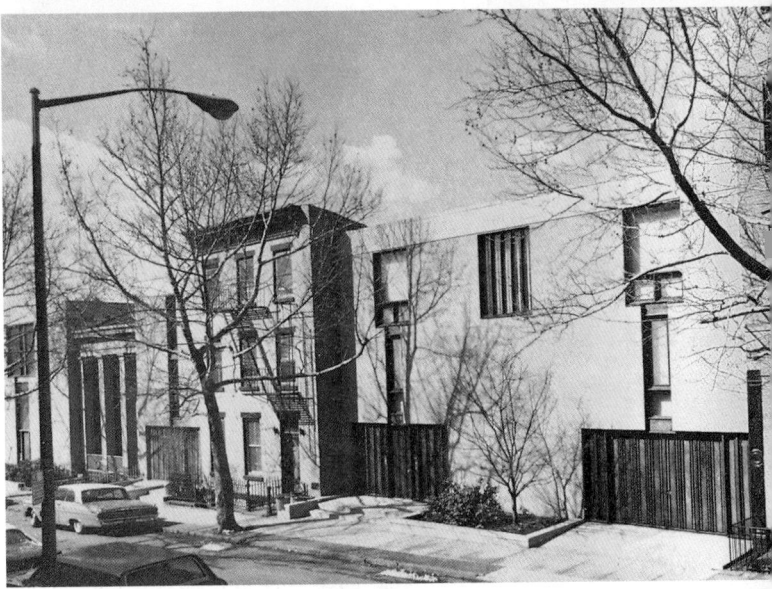

Top: Meyer Parodneck residence, 278 Hicks Street, between Joralemon and State streets, Brooklyn Heights. Samuel J. Glaberson, 1948–49. Interior. Freedman. LF

Bottom: Leonard Garment double house, 40 Willow Place, between State and Joralemon streets, Brooklyn Heights. Joseph and Mary Merz, 1966. View to the southwest. ©Norman McGrath. NM

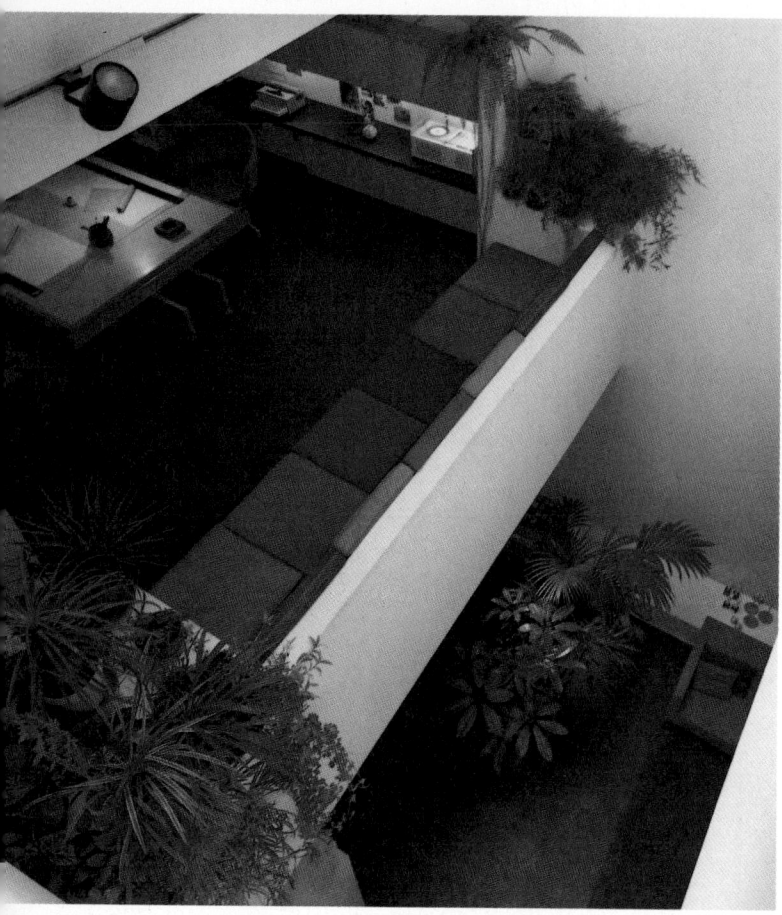

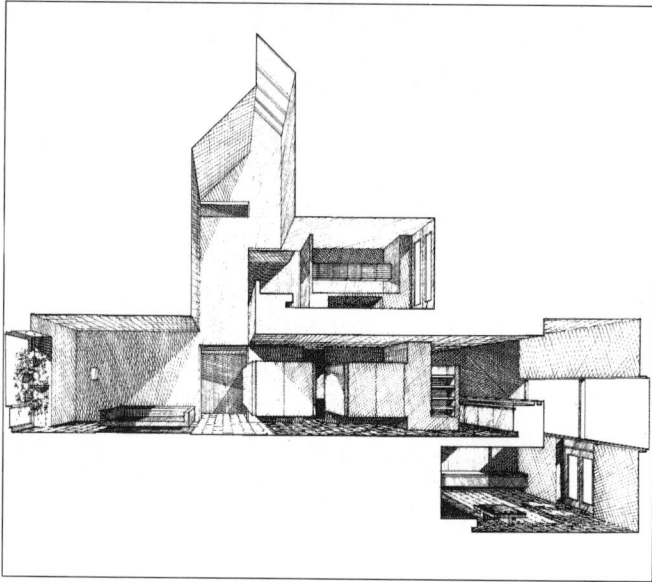

Top: Stanley and Laurie Maurer residence, 172 Amity Street, Cobble Hill. Stanley and Laurie Maurer, 1969. Lightwell. SLM

Bottom: Stanley and Laurie Maurer residence. Section perspective. SLM

The designation of Brooklyn Heights as a historic district marked its reestablishment as a desirable neighborhood and pushed the prices of its real estate beyond the reach of most young buyers. As a result, many of them turned their attention to other Old Brooklyn neighborhoods such as Boerum Hill, Cobble Hill, Carroll Gardens and, a bit farther into the borough's heartland, Park Slope.[116]

Boerum Hill was located southeast of Brooklyn Heights. Its name was not historical but was coined in 1962 by middle-class families moving into the neighborhood, who preferred it over the less euphemistic but more geographically accurate Brooklyn Heights East or the name it had known for over two centuries, North Gowanus.[117] The historic neighborhood, bounded by Court Street on the west, Fourth Avenue on the east, Atlantic Avenue on the north and Wyckoff Street on the south, had reached its peak of development before 1875.[118] It had drifted into decline in the 1930s and 1940s when its buildings began to fall prey to "tin men" who peddled aluminum siding as well as artificial stone to reclad the mostly brick and brownstone houses. In the postwar era the neighborhood's traditional mix of mostly white blue-collar workers and modestly well-to-do professional people changed dramatically; by 1960 Puerto Ricans and African-Americans dominated the neighborhood.

Once a prosperous area, by the early 1960s Boerum Hill had one of the lowest per capita incomes in the nation, with terrible overcrowding. Yet its location and the fundamental value of its housing stock made it a ripe target for gentrification. By the late 1960s young white professionals began to be attracted to the neighborhood, but the area's gentrification was not typical: although the new settlers may have been middle class in outlook, they were not necessarily so in income. As one observer, L. J. Davis, put it in 1969, "If they'd had the money, they would have gone to the Heights, Carroll Gardens or Cobble Hill." They came not from the suburbs but from tough city areas, particularly Manhattan's Lower East Side. But even these urban villagers, sensitive as they were to the impact of gentrification on the local scene, wished to improve the neighborhood, and tensions quickly arose. Some of the minority locals who owned their houses were able to sell them at a profit and move to more suburban areas, fulfilling the dream of rising up the American class ladder. But the renting poor, as Davis wrote, were forced to move on, "across Fourth Avenue and up into Fort Greene—places where renovation movements are also underway—and for them nothing has changed, one way or the other. The rooms are the same size and the streets are just the same, and one day, they will probably move again."[119]

The issue of how much gentrification was appropriate was a complex one. In 1972 George Herzog, past president of the Boerum Hill Association and a landlord, explained: "What is at stake here is our last chance for a mixed community. In the past five years, 500 houses in Boerum Hill have been taken over by middle-class people. Rooming houses which used to house at least 15 poor people have been refurbished for high-income tenants. Houses which used to be occupied by three or four familes are now lived in by one or two."[120]

To the southwest of Boerum Hill lay Cobble Hill, roughly bounded by Atlantic Avenue on the north, Sackett Street on the south, Hicks Street on the west and Court Street on the east. Its name was also recently coined, in this case by a real estate broker in the 1950s who discovered the name Cobleshill on the 1766 Ratzer map of New York and Brooklyn.[121] Cobble Hill was a neighborhood of varied housing ranging from spacious rowhouses to the model low-income Tower and Home complex. It was also home to the Long Island College Hospital, which expanded greatly in the 1970s with the completion of its E. M. Fuller Pavilion (Ferrenz & Taylor, 1974), at 70 Atlantic Avenue, on the southeast corner of Hicks Street, a blocky, red-brick-clad, twelve-story building that loomed over the neighborhood.[122]

Among Cobble Hill's early resettlers were the architects Stanley and Laurie Maurer, who renovated a house for their own use in 1969.[123] The house had an interesting past, having served as a brothel, and it had been condemned by the Department of Buildings before the Maurers took it over. The new interior gathered living, sleeping and working spaces around a tall skylit lightwell that connected the three floors of the Maurers' apartment but did not penetrate into the ground-floor rental apartment.

The sixty-block area of Carroll Gardens, historically considered part of Red Hook, was another South Brooklyn neighborhood that tried to improve its fortunes with a name change in the mid-1960s.[124] Roughly bounded by the Gowanus Canal, the Gowanus Expressway, Columbia and Degraw streets, postwar Carroll Gardens was a solidly white, mostly Italian, working-class neighborhood that had at its core an area distinguished by unusually deep blocks yielding generous front lawns. This was the result of the efforts of land surveyor Richard Butts, who mapped out the area in 1846. The predominantly residential neighborhood featured a rich array of two- and three-story brick and brownstone rowhouses built between the late 1860s and the early 1880s.

Several interesting nonresidential buildings were built in the area. One of these was Henry V. Murphy's Catholic Seamen's Institute (1943), at 653 Hicks Street, on the northeast corner of Rapelye Street, a cultural, recreational and religious center created to promote the welfare of the merchant marine.[125] The severe abstracted colonnade of the building's brick mass was relieved by decorative sandblasted stone spandrels picturing merchant vessels and maps in relief. The principal feature of the design was the lighthouselike corner tower, which housed the principal entrance between twin buttresses that rose to visually support a circular glass-block lantern held in place by flattened Classical moldings. Above the tower, a thirty-foot-tall steel mast carrying code flags and national colors rose to greet shipboard sailors entering the harbor. Inside, in addition to straightforwardly detailed recreation, dining and social rooms, the building included a chaplain's office styled like the cabin of an old sailing vessel, with end walls that approximated the curve of a ship; a paneled, clublike lounge; a library; and an elaborately paneled, flat-ceilinged, Gothic chapel, described by the sponsors as the "climax of an effort to welcome men home from the sea."[126]

A second notable nonresidential building in Carroll Gardens was William I. Hohauser's Clinton Theater (1944), a 1,644-seat movie house.[127] Built next to Electus D. Litchfield's Red Hook Houses (1935–37) at Clinton and Mill streets, the Clinton was a stylish if understated brick box punctuated by a sleek band of windows.[128] It featured a dramatic glass-block corner tower beneath which a dynamically curved marquee sheltered a deep outside vestibule.

In 1968 the Carroll Gardens Association, which included only about 400 of the area's 45,000 residents, commissioned the architect Richard D. Kaplan to prepare a redevelopment plan for the Gowanus Canal.[129] One component of Kaplan's unrealized proposal—the inclusion of public housing to be built along the canal—was controversial and unpopular in the stable, tree-lined neighborhood. But the 1960s and 1970s saw little

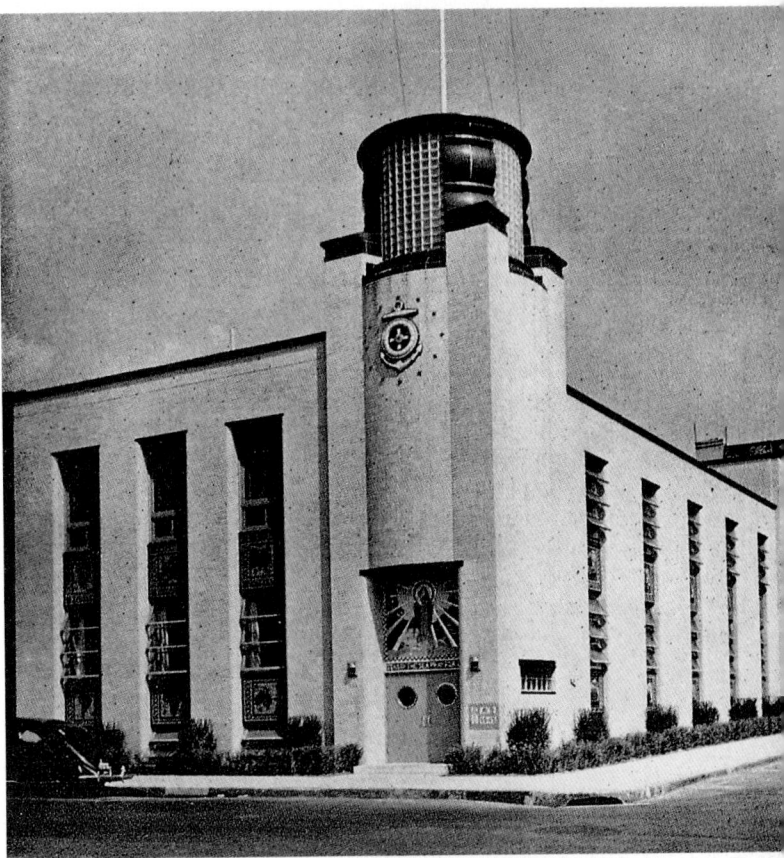

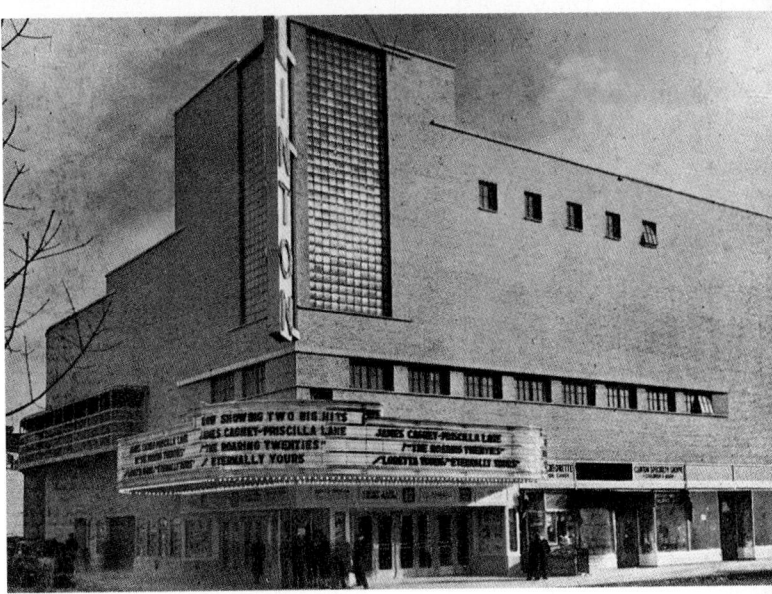

Top: Catholic Seamen's Institute, 653 Hicks Street, northeast corner of Rapelye Street, Carroll Gardens. Henry V. Murphy, 1943. View to the northeast. Molitor. AR. CU

Bottom: Clinton Theater, northeast corner of Clinton and Mill streets, Carroll Gardens. William I. Hohauser, 1944. View to the northeast. IN. CU

building activity in the area and the population of Carroll Gardens declined slightly. After more than a decade of protest over environmental conditions and an uninterrupted flow of noxious effluent in the Gowanus Canal, the waterway was officially declared a health hazard by the Environmental Protection Agency and the Red Hook Water Pollution Control Project was undertaken. In 1975 a serious dredging and cleanup of the canal was begun.[130]

Around Prospect Park

With the completion of Prospect Park in 1874, the area to its west, a long slope of meadowlands leading down to the harbor, began to develop as a fashionable upper-middle-class residential community, Park Slope, bounded by Flatbush Avenue, Prospect Park West, Fifteenth Street and Fourth Avenue, with luxurious homes, clubs and later apartment houses concentrated at the Grand Army Plaza and along Prospect Park West. The park's northern edge was bounded by Frederick Law Olmsted's Eastern Parkway (1870–74), the nation's first parkway, along which stood more modest houses and, after World War I, middle-class apartments, as well as the fifty-acre Brooklyn Botanical Garden (1910), the Brooklyn Museum (McKim, Mead & White, 1897–1924) and the headquarters of the Brooklyn Public Library (Githens & Keally, 1941).[131]

Along Washington Avenue lay what was arguably the area's best-known, best-attended institution, Ebbets Field (C. A. Buskirk), the home of the Brooklyn Dodgers baseball team from 1913 until 1957.[132] In 1955 the Dodgers' management had begun negotiations with the city for the construction of a new stadium, proposed for a site east of the intersection of Flatbush and Atlantic avenues, and in 1956 the team played seven of its home games in Jersey City. At the end of the 1956 season, the Dodgers sold the field to Marvin Kratter, a developer, retaining an option to play there for three more years. The Dodgers ended their 1957 season at Ebbets Field under the threat of a move to Los Angeles, but it was not until the World Series began that the team officially and irrevocably announced its decision to go. The hastily formed Ebbets Field Productions leased the stadium in 1958–59 to stage various sporting events and theatrical, musical and novelty attractions, beginning with stunt car entertainer Jack Kochman and his "helldrivers," who presented the first post-Dodger event over Memorial Day weekend 1958.[133]

Demolition of Ebbets Field began in February 1960 to make way for the construction of what *Housing and Planning News* attacked as a "mastodon among middle-income housing projects."[134] Completed in 1962, Brown & Guenther's Ebbets Field Apartments housed 1,317 families in one twenty-five-story slab connected to seven twenty-story wings that dominated the 5.5-acre site. Inside the building's seven lobbies, murals created by Stuyvesant Van Veer portrayed great moments and personalities in Dodger history.

Meanwhile, plans were advanced for a new stadium, at first intended for the Dodgers and later, after they had decamped, for a new team. One plan advanced in 1955 by Dodgers president Walter F. O'Malley called for a geodesic dome to cover the stadium for year-round, all-weather play. O'Malley commissioned R. Buckminster Fuller to pursue this idea with twenty-five graduate students in the Princeton School of Architecture.[135] In 1956 the New York State Legislature established a Brooklyn Sports Center Authority.[136] At this time, Mayor Wagner reviewed preliminary plans developed by Brooklyn Borough President

Cashmore for the redevelopment of downtown Brooklyn that included a new 50,000-seat sports stadium to be built in an area bounded by Warren Street and Fourth, Flatbush and Fifth avenues.[137] Once the Dodgers left, the need for a new stadium became less urgent and the cost became even more of an obstacle to its realization.[138] In 1973 the idea of a stadium was revived again, this time in the form of a Madison Square Garden–type facility to be located in downtown Brooklyn.[139] Two years earlier New York had lost another of its sports institutions, the New York Giants football team, which had signed a thirty-year lease to play in a stadium to be built in New Jersey's Hackensack Meadows (Giants Stadium was completed in 1976). By the 1970s serious observers were arguing that the desire to keep teams in the city could no longer be justified economically. As *New York Affairs* put it:

> Sports fans and civic boosters obviously get a lot of satisfaction from having "our own" teams; it's nice to be in the big leagues. And there are 2,000 or so people directly employed in commercial sports in New York City, mostly in relatively unskilled jobs that would disappear when and if a team departs or a track closes. But it is not clear that the presence of big-league commercial sports yields any benefits of consequence, aside from civic pride and a few on-site jobs. . . . Attendance at big-time sports is now very auto-dominated. . . . Unlike the situation in earlier generations when the pedestrian route from subway station to ballpark was lined with heavily frequented retail establishments, the new model stadium or arena sits—like Shea Stadium—as an island in a sea of parking fields.[140]

After the war Park Slope, like so many of the city's older residential neighborhoods, went into a slow decline as the middle class drifted away to what they perceived as more desirable suburban areas. But some families chose to remain, and residents of one choice block, Third Street, organized the Park Slope Betterment Committee, persuading banks to give mortgages to newcomers and advising prospective neighbors on buying and renovating houses.[141]

In 1967, as a new generation of "brownstoners" were moving into Park Slope, John H. Beyer of Victor Gruen Associates proposed a broad-scale study of the area for the Park Slope North Improvement Corporation, a nonprofit group headed by Frederick W. Richmond, whose foundation financed the project.[142] Beyer's plan concentrated on the problems of the area's lower-income families, some of whom were threatened by gentrification and others who lived in the traditionally working-class areas at the Slope's bottom and were plagued by the usual gamut of housing and social problems. The study targeted an action area of six blocks just south of Flatbush Avenue, bounded by Fifth and Sixth Avenues, Berkeley Place and St. Marks Place, where the neighborhood was still in a steep decline; many of its brownstones had been converted to single-room occupancy, with most of the residents low-income nonwhite tenants. Beyer called for the transformation of the area into three superblocks housing approximately 2,000 persons on each block, the introduction of midblock walkways in addition to the "play streets" created by the superblocks, and the construction of new low-rise housing near an existing public school. The plan also called for the rehabilitation of brownstones as small, family-oriented apartments rather than single-room occupancy rooming houses. Eventually Beyer, as a partner in the firm of Beyer Blinder Belle, was able to help create a facility that would address some of the social issues that had inspired his plan: the Helen Owen Carey Child Development Center (1974), at 71 Lincoln Place, between Fifth and Sixth avenues, which was a boldly scaled—perhaps overscaled—school and recreational facility jammed into an established street of brownstones.[143]

By the 1940s Frederick Law Olmsted and Calvert Vaux's Prospect Park, whose presence had fostered the neighborhood's early development, was also beginning to show signs of wear. Although regarded by its designers as their masterpiece, the park, like all the city's parks, had begun a slow decline in 1934, when the Park Department cut back its maintenance budget to help pay for Robert Moses's construction programs.[144] That decline accelerated in the 1950s, and the park became run-down, its waterways clogged and its meadows untended. There was one bright note in the 1950s, however: the construction of a new carousel, built to replace the merry-go-round that had burned down in 1935.[145] Completed in 1952, the octagonal structure in bright yellow and red brick was a duplicate of the one built in Central Park the previous year (see chapter 10). Like the Central Park effort, the carousel was a gift of the Michael Friedsam Foundation; its horses came from an old Coney Island merry-go-round.

In 1959 the Park Department announced a five-year rehabilitation program aimed at sprucing up the shabby and overgrown areas of the park.[146] That same year the Wollman Foundation pledged $300,000 to help defray the costs of a proposed $800,000 ice-skating rink.[147] The banal Modernist skating complex (Hopf & Adler, 1961) included the 140-by-203-foot Kate Wollman Skating Rink and a one-story service and concession building.

In 1965, timed to coincide with the park's centennial the following year, the City Planning Commission approved over $900,000 in funds for the restoration of three neglected landmarks: the Vale of Cashmere, Olmsted's once-triumphant example of lush landscape scenography; the disheveled Rose Garden; and Helmle & Huberty's terra-cotta-clad Boathouse (1905), which had become a favorite target of vandalism along the neglected, silted-in lullwater and had narrowly escaped demolition the year before.[148] Park Commissioner Newbold Morris's proposal to demolish the Boathouse was approved in December 1963, and it was a year before anyone voiced concern about the building's fate. Protests began only two days before the contract for demolition was let when Borough President Abe Stark, the Municipal Art Society and other organizations began to take action, led by Henry Hope Reed, Jr., and Clay Lancaster, an architectural historian whose study of Brooklyn Heights was a landmark in the interpretation of historic neighborhoods.[149] Even Morris was amazed that the decision to demolish had gone so long unchallenged.

In 1966 Thomas P. F. Hoving, in one of his first acts as Park Commissioner, appointed curators for New York's principal parks; Clay Lancaster was given responsibility for Prospect Park.[150] Hoving also initiated significant projects including the restoration of A. J. Davis's Italianate Litchfield Villa (1857), which predated the park itself, and McKim, Mead & White's Croquet Shelter (1904).[151] Both projects were completed under the direction of August Heckscher, who succeeded Hoving as Park Commissioner in 1967.

When the restored Rose Garden and Vale of Cashmere were reopened in 1969, they received less than universal praise, with complaints centering around the choice of new plantings and the lack of a maintenance plan.[152] The Boathouse took far longer to restore.[153] Work on the project, which was supervised by Brown, Lawford & Forbes, did not begin until 1971, and the rededication was a year later. But it was not until the summer of 1974 that boats reappeared on the lake. Only a year after its triumphant reopening, the Boathouse was closed again due to delays in a minor repaving job. In addition, six windows were boarded up because they had been damaged by vandalism.

Another project for the park—the Children's Farm, sponsored by Abraham & Straus—was delayed because of the controversy it raised.[154] To be located between the carousel and the zoo, and designed by Edward Coe Embury, architect of the Children's Zoo in Central Park, the three-acre farm was to include a barn, a silolike lookout and a slide built to look like a haystack; it would be stocked with cows, hens, geese, goats and other farm animals. Although Mayor Wagner accepted Abraham & Straus's offer in 1965, opposition grew quickly, based principally on the maintenance costs the city would have to bear and on what many believed to be the commercial nature of the farm. Clay Lancaster, a leading opponent of the project, declared that it would be "the worst effacement" of the park.[155] Nonetheless, in 1971, after years of litigation and protest, the Children's Farm was opened to the squeals of delighted children.

Bedford-Stuyvesant and Crown Heights

The postwar term "Bedford-Stuyvesant" brought together the names of two communities of the old City of Brooklyn: Bedford, on the west, and Stuyvesant Heights, on the east. Both were developed in the post–Civil War era as middle-class neighborhoods. The portion of Bedford south of Atlantic Avenue and north of Empire Boulevard, stretching between Washington and East New York avenues, also incorporated the small village of Weeksville, east of Rochester Avenue, which consisted of four houses occupied between 1830 and 1870 by James Weeks and friends, who were free blacks.[156]

Bedford-Stuyvesant, the area roughly bounded by Flushing Avenue on the north, Broadway on the east, Eastern Parkway and East New York Avenue on the south, and Washington Avenue on the west, was by the early 1940s Brooklyn's principal area of African-American settlement.[157] While predominantly a white community until the 1930s, affluent blacks had settled in the area around 1900, as they had in the Adelphi area around Pratt Institute. The opening of the "A" line of the Independent subway made the area easily accessible to Harlem. At first it attracted the more prosperous members of the Depression-hit black middle class, who managed their mortgages by renting apartments or rooms to boarders.[158] During World War II blacks poured in, settling in the neighborhood because it was the closest housing they could get in the area of the Navy Yard, where many of them were employed. By 1950, 155,000 blacks lived in Bedford-Stuyvesant, 53 percent of the population. By 1968, 95 percent of the population was black.

After the war Bedford-Stuyvesant was used as a dumping ground for families dislocated by massive urban renewal projects in Harlem. As the political writer Jack Newfield, who grew up in the area in the early 1950s, observed in 1968, what had once been a model of middle-class life, first white and then black, had become "the place where people land when they fall out of Harlem; it is where the Wagner Administration used to dump the victims of its urban renewal bulldozers."[159] By the mid-1960s, Bed-Stuy, as it was colloquially referred to, was the country's largest ghetto. If it had been an independent city, it would have been among the nation's thirty most populous. It had the country's highest infant mortality rate (39 per 1,000). Yet, with its handsome tree-lined streets of rowhouses and apartments, the area was physically far from a slum.

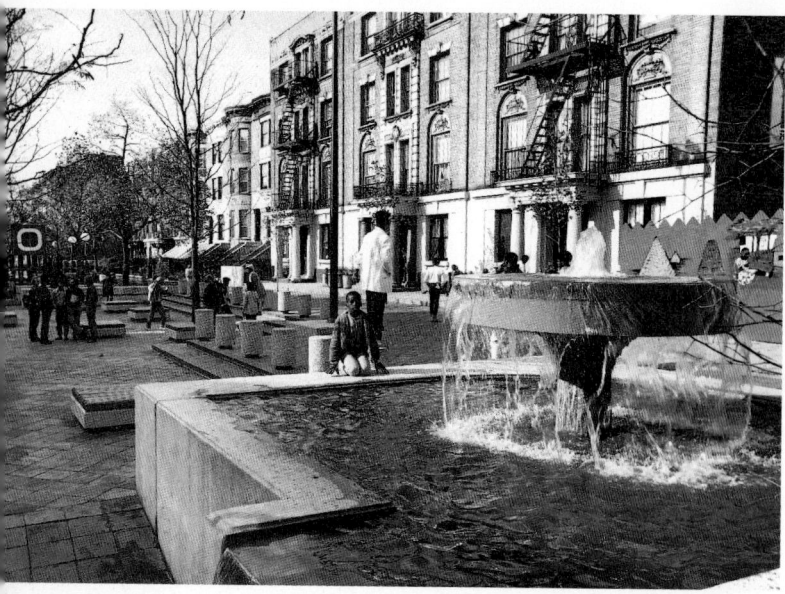

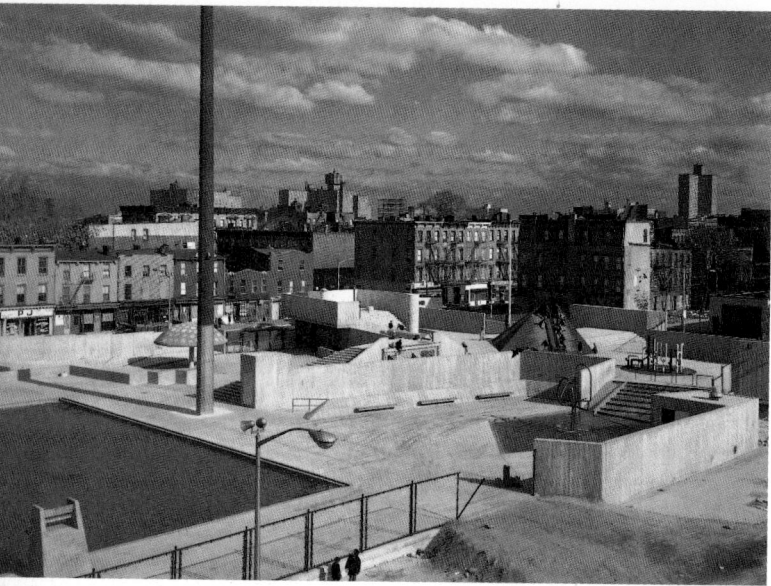

Top: Street park, St. Mark's Avenue, between Kingston and Albany avenues, Bedford-Stuyvesant. I. M. Pei and M. Paul Friedberg & Associates, 1969. View to the northwest. Cserna. PCF

Bottom: Bedford-Stuyvesant Community Pool, west side of Marcy Avenue, between Kosciusko and DeKalb avenues, Bedford-Stuyvesant. Morris Lapidus, 1971. View to the northeast. Stoller. ©ESTO

Until the mid-1960s, outsiders paid little attention to the Bedford-Stuyvesant ghetto. All that changed in the week of July 20, 1964, when during a summer hot spell, the neighborhood broke out in four days of rioting triggered by the fatal shooting of a fifteen-year-old black boy, James Powell, by a white off-duty police lieutenant. As the *New Yorker*'s editors explained, the rioting confirmed what New York police and a few sociologists and housing experts had been saying for a long time: "Bedford-Stuyvesant, spreading its borders every day in Brooklyn, is bigger than Harlem, more densely populated than Harlem, and, in the final accounting, a tougher ghetto than Harlem."[160] Jack Newfield was to write in 1968 that the shooting "signaled the end of the civil rights movement and the beginning of the long hot summers," the race riots and then Vietnam protests that were to plague the nation's ghettos for nearly a decade.[161]

On February 4, 1966, Robert F. Kennedy, United States Senator for New York since 1964, took a walking tour of Bedford-Stuyvesant.[162] At the end of his tour, he met with local leaders, who berated him for what they saw as a pattern of neglect toward the community from city, state and federal governments. Ten months later Kennedy returned with a plan for the physical rehabilitation of Bedford-Stuyvesant's neighborhoods and the development of job skills for its citizens.[163] The plan was supported by a group of businessmen and community leaders whom Kennedy enlisted to the cause, as well as leading local and federal politicians including New York's Republican senator, Jacob Javits. Kennedy's plan put into motion two corporations: the Development and Services Corporation, supported by city and national business leaders, who would help with funds and provide access to managerial expertise, and the Restoration Corporation, later reconstituted as the Bedford-Stuyvesant Restoration Corporation, which was made up of twenty established corporate and community leaders headed by Civil Court Judge Thomas Jones.

The Development and Services Corporation was an attempt to represent community leadership, while the Restoration Corporation was meant to involve the city's business community as a whole. With $7 million in federal funds and some sizable foundation grants, the Development and Services Corporation hired Edward J. Logue as its planning director and commissioned the firms of architect-urban designer David Crane, architect I. M. Pei and planners Raymond & May, who had in 1965 conducted a six-month-long, Pratt Institute–sponsored study of the community's problems, to prepare planning and design studies leading to a coordinated physical plan.[164] While Crane and Raymond & May turned to broad issues of city planning, Pei concentrated on specific design problems, developing a strategy to realize the potential of existing neighborhood streets as recreational assets in a community starved for usable outdoor space.

Pei was invited to participate in the Bed-Stuy project by Robert Kennedy, who asked the architect what he knew about the area. When Pei stated that he "knew nothing," Kennedy suggested that he look the neighborhood over. Pei returned in a week with three proposals, one of which involved closing off several blocks, an approach that Kennedy approved of. As Pei recalled in 1970, "Like most ghettos, Bedford-Stuyvesant had no focus. There are endless streets leading from nowhere to nowhere."[165]

After Robert Kennedy was assassinated in Los Angeles on June 4, 1968, the corporations, spurred by a desire to memorialize him, pushed Pei to develop a tangible project. Working with the landscape architects M. Paul Friedberg & Associates, Pei designed an ingenious "street park," a quarter-acre plaza set across St. Marks Avenue formed by cul-de-sacs that interrupted the flow of traffic between Kingston and Albany avenues. The street park would include adult seating and a children's play area, as well as an "urban stream," a small waterway that ran for 100 feet through a series of concrete troughs and basins. A block away, on Prospect Place, Pei developed two widened sidewalk areas opposite each other and a change in road level to slow the traffic down and provide a small sitting park. The two different designs, both completed in 1969, were a reflection of the two different citizen groups that were Pei's clients: "St. Marks had prostitution, narcotics, welfare families. Prospect had home ownership, what I call lace curtain-and-geranium families. We had thought we could have a standard design for the streets but we soon found out differently. St. Marks wanted no through traffic and a playground. Prospect felt a playground would attract outsiders. They wanted through traffic travelling slower."[166]

According to Pei, two out of three of Bed-Stuy's 653 blocks could have been redeveloped along these lines. But given the unavailability of funds, the likelihood of this happening soon enough to ease the plight of the area's half-million residents was minimal. Furthermore, the city's bureaucracy could not adjust to the novelty of Pei's designs—for example, sanitation truck drivers balked at the inconvenience of the cul-de-sacs. As a result, no further street parks were created.

Other, more grandiose projects of the Kennedy era went unrealized. Edward J. Logue and his team proposed a redevelopment corridor lying between Fulton Street and Atlantic Avenue. High-density "satellite cores" were to anchor each end, at Atlantic Terminal and at Broadway Junction, where Philip Johnson was commissioned to design a shopping center. Pei was to design a combination civic and business center at Nostrand Avenue, and subcores were to be located at key intersections along the route.

The collapse of the Model Cities program (see below) and the city's declining fortunes in the early 1970s left the citizens of Bed-Stuy with lots of dreamy rhetoric but very little in the way of physical change. One exception was the Bedford-Stuyvesant Community Pool, completed in 1971 on Marcy Avenue between Kosciusko and DeKalb avenues.[167] The "People's Pool," as it was called, was the brainchild of Thomas Hoving, who as Park Commissioner in 1966 selected Morris Lapidus as architect, not because of his designs for some of New York's leading hotels but because of his "Miami Beach extravaganzas," as Ada Louise Huxtable noted. Hoving, she said, "wanted an architect who would produce the jazziest pool possible for the grim environs of Bed-Stuy, and he had the Lapidus Fountainebleau fantasies firmly in mind." However, as Huxtable wrote, after five years of bureaucratic foot-shuffling, the pool reflected the design ideas not of Morris Lapidus but of his son Alan and his associates John Bowstead and Marta Enebuske, whose "only fantasy was a giant shade mushroom in concrete."[168] The pool was admirable nonetheless, an Olympic-sized facility with separate diving and wading areas. Executed in reinforced concrete accented with touches of color, it was ingeniously organized on half levels to tuck locker rooms out of the way, maximizing the use of a tight, 2.3-acre site for recreation for the 3,000 people expected to visit it at peak times. In the end this was less a fantasy land than "a serious, sophisticated solution," as Huxtable put it.[169]

Hoberman & Wasserman's Tompkins Park Recreational and Cultural Center (1971) was another imaginative facility.[170] The project began life as a center for the aged, but the community expanded its scope to make it a cultural and recreational fa-

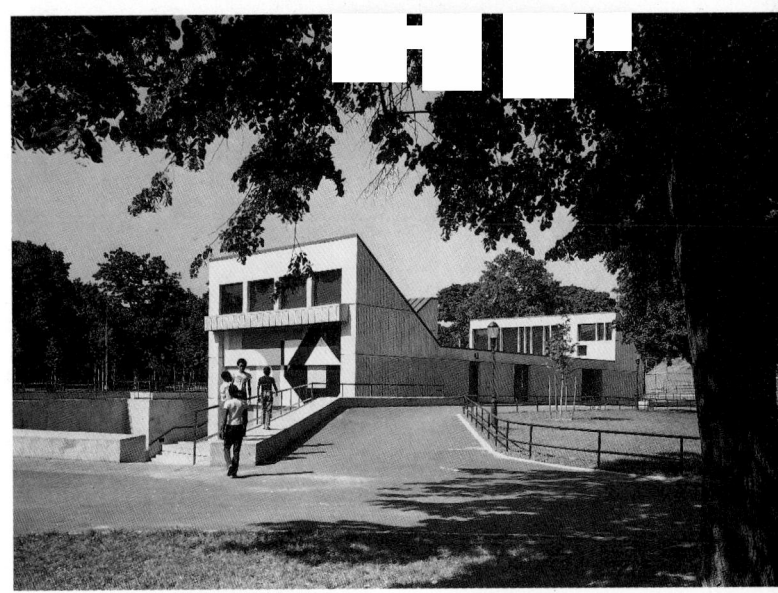

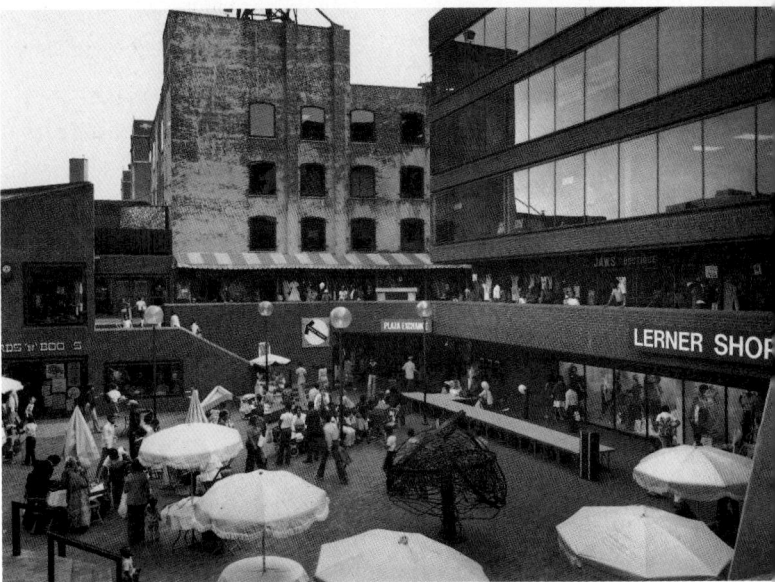

Top: Tompkins Park Recreational and Cultural Center, Tompkins Park, Bedford-Stuyvesant. Hoberman & Wasserman, 1971. View to the southwest. JW

Bottom: Bedford-Stuyvesant Restoration Commercial Center, 1360 Fulton Street, southeast corner of New York Avenue, Bedford-Stuyvesant. Arthur Cotton Moore, 1975. View to the southwest. ©Norman McGrath. ACM

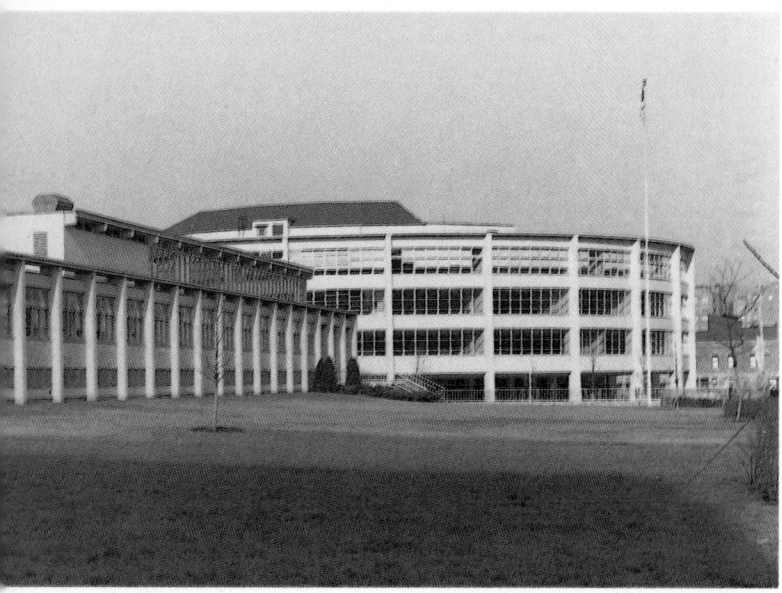

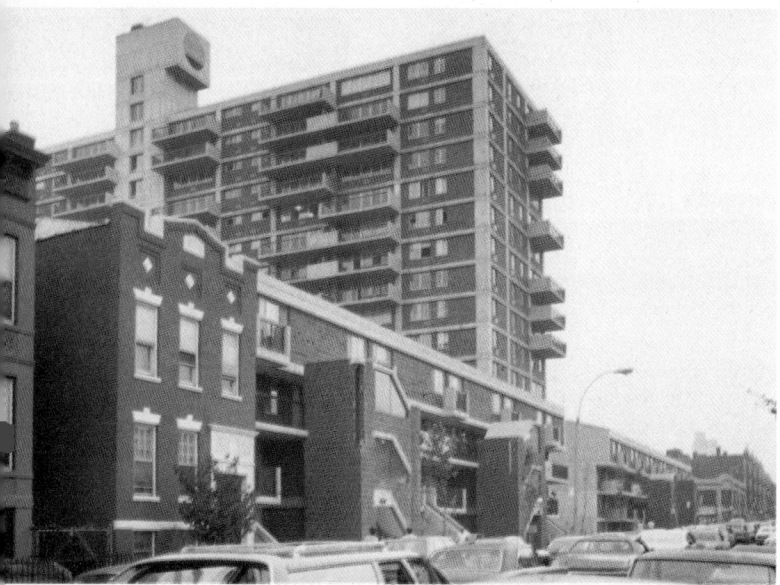

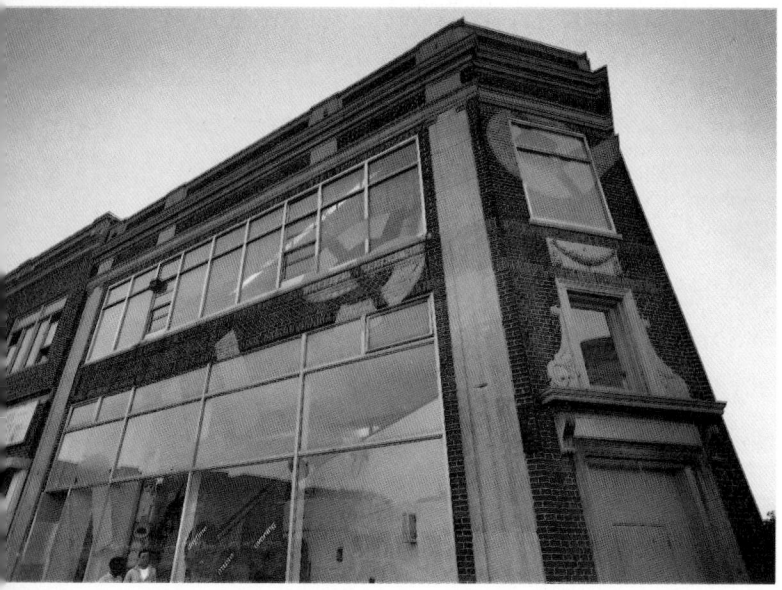

cility for all ages, with a theater and an outdoor amphitheater as well as special rooms for teenagers and senior citizens. To minimize the building's impact on the park, almost half of its programmed space was buried. Less sympathetic to the surroundings were the vertically ribbed, poured-in-place reinforced-concrete walls, which were intended to resist graffiti but were only partially effective; as Norman Hoberman observed: "There is something just too attractive about a concrete wall."[171] Shed-roofed monitors rising above the otherwise flat roof allowed the building to be flooded with light while keeping the glass away from the easy reach of vandals.

There were a number of other notable community projects. Beginning in 1968, renovations were undertaken to create new office space for the Bedford-Stuyvesant Restoration Corporation at 1368–1390 Fulton Street, taking up most of the block bounded by Fulton and Herkimer streets, New York and Brooklyn avenues.[172] Designed by Fisher/Jackson Associates and built inside the shell of a defunct Sheffield Farms milk-bottling plant that had been a glaring symbol of the community's failure to recover its economic health, the 100,000-square-foot facility was opened in 1971 and included a 250-seat auditorium, a cafeteria, recreation facilities and additional leasable office space. Much of the renovation work for the headquarters was done by previously unemployed community residents. In 1972 plans were announced for the Bedford-Stuyvesant Restoration Commercial Center, situated next to the corporation's new offices at 1360 Fulton Street, on the southeast corner of New York Avenue.[173] Designed by the Washington, D.C., architect Arthur Cotton Moore and completed in 1975, the $6 million urban shopping center, also known as Downtown Bedford-Stuyvesant, included thirty-two stores and an 8,500-square-foot outdoor ice-skating rink. James A. Murphy, writing in *Progressive Architecture*, praised the complex as "the brightest thing to happen to the beleaguered community in years."[174] The CABS (Community Action of Bedford-Stuyvesant) Nursing Home (1976), at 270 Nostrand Avenue, between Kosciusko and DeKalb avenues, a 160-bed facility built on a 56,000-square-foot site, was designed by the architect William Breger in association with Leeds Associates and Luis Villa/Lois Sher, landscape architects.[175] The building accommodated 82,000 square feet of usable space on four floors that looked out to the street as well as inward, to a skylit atrium planted with flowers, shrubs and trees, including magnolias and bamboo.

In a neighborhood that was remarkably intact, though in need of repair, new housing was not a significant element in renewal planning. Some housing was built, however, to replace the abandoned tenements that were the principal element of blight in Bed-Stuy. Henri LeGendre's 1660–1670 Fulton Street (1976), opposite Fulton Park, had deepset balconies with masonry parapets; its inexorable composition of advancing and receding masses created an unnecessarily grim impression.[176] Less threatening was Tuckett & Thompson's Remsen Court (1976), between Reid and Stuyvesant avenues, Chauncey and Fulton streets, which featured private courtyards and a lighter handling of the corridor wall.[177]

It was the preservation and restoration of the existing housing stock that distinguished Bedford-Stuyvesant's renewal efforts from those of Harlem, the city's other major ghetto area.[178] A program of exterior renovation begun with a $7 million grant from the Labor Department was initiated in 1967, with the goal of immediately and dramatically demonstrating that physical environment could make a positive difference in people's lives and that the area was not necessarily a slum. It also made visible the fact that the problem of New York's ghettos was neither a simple nor a singular one, and it opened the eyes of many observers to the plight of middle-class blacks as well as that of the poor. Under the program, for $25, regardless of the amount of work involved, a house was painted, stoops, corridors, doors and sidewalks were repaired, and two garbage cans were provided, painted with a large "R" to symbolize the Restoration Corporation. Since 25 to 50 percent of the brownstones in Bed-Stuy were owned by their residents, the program had great appeal.

The benefits of the program were twofold: the improved physical appearance of neighborhoods led to increased community pride and the formation of block and neighborhood associations, and the work itself provided on-the-job vocational training for unemployed Bed-Stuy residents. By 1976, 3,074 house facades had been fixed up under the program and 3,351 residents—including, after 1975, women—had engaged in on-the-job training. The situation had improved so much by 1974 that the *New York Times* could report on the area's gentrification, in which young, middle-class blacks were "coming home to 'Bed-Stuy.'"[179]

To the south of Bed-Stuy lay Crown Heights. Here more stable social conditions prevailed, although the physical condition of the neighborhood—which included luxurious houses, some built as recently as 1930, various types of apartment houses and innumerable tenements—had declined considerably. In 1952 plans were announced for Kelly & Gruzen's George W. Wingate School (1955), at 600 Kingston Avenue, the so-called Banjo School, the first new high school built in the city since the war.[180] The design of the 3,200-student, four-story building, by B. Sumner (Barney) Gruzen and his chief designer, Albert Loecher, was an attempt to reduce the circulation of students between classes. The building consisted of a long rectangular wing containing the administrative offices, the shops and the library, and a squarish wing housing the gymnasium; the two wings were attached to a circular building in which the classrooms were wrapped around a central auditorium.

One significant new housing project, Crown Gardens Apartments (1973), was designed by Richard D. Kaplan, in association with Stevens, Bertin, O'Connell & Harvey.[181] The 239-unit complex was built on a large site that had formerly contained a trolley repair barn. The original plan called for turning the entire block into one Turtle Bay Gardens–like enclave, with the slab lifted on pilotis so that open space could run through from the backyard to the front.[182] In its final form the development, which filled the block along the east side of Nostrand Avenue between President and Carroll streets, consisted of a fifteen-story slab that formed one wall of a courtyard otherwise defined by four-story rows containing stacked townhouses. Although the design's exposed concrete frame, sheer walls and jumbo brick allied the building with the prevailing Brutalist aesthetic, the syncopated placement of balconies and stair towers provided a compensating and welcome lightheartedness.

The year 1977 marked the completion of the long-awaited new home of the Brooklyn Children's Museum in Brower Park. Founded in 1899 as the world's first museum designed for children, the institution had previously been housed in two Victorian mansions, the William Newtown Adams residence (1867) and the L. C. Smith residence (1890). Proposals for a purpose-designed facility had been developed by William Lescaze in the 1930s but never realized.[183] The houses were condemned and demolished in 1967 to make way for a new structure on the

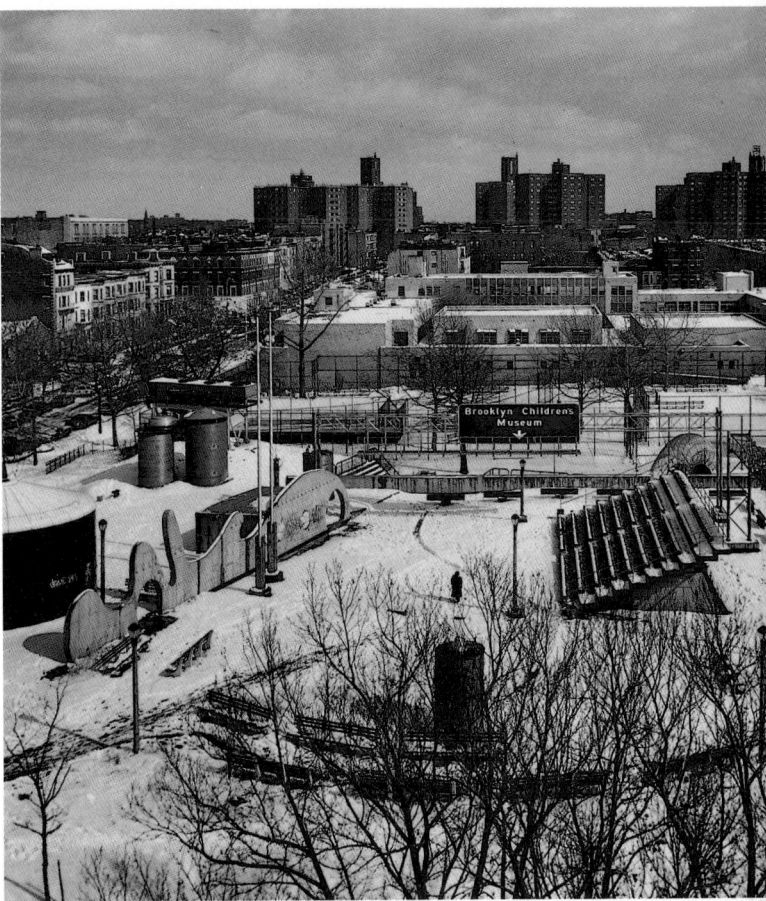

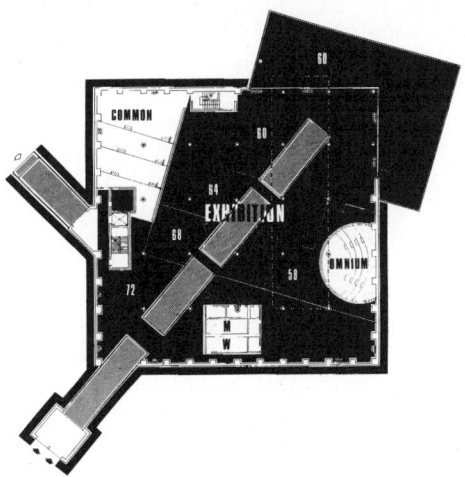

Top left: George W. Wingate School, 600 Kingston Avenue, between Rutland Road and Winthrop Street, Crown Heights. Kelly & Gruzen, 1955. View to the northwest. NYCBE

Center left: Crown Gardens Apartments, east side of Nostrand Avenue, between President and Carroll streets, Crown Heights. Richard D. Kaplan in association with Stevens, Bertin, O'Connell & Harvey, 1973. View to the southwest. Kwartler. MK

Bottom left: MUSE, temporary quarters of the Brooklyn Children's Museum, 1530 Bedford Avenue, northeast corner of Lincoln Place, Crown Heights. Hardy Holzman Pfeiffer, 1967. View to the northeast. ©Norman McGrath. NM

Top: Brooklyn Children's Museum, Brower Park, Crown Heights. Hardy Holzman Pfeiffer, 1975. View to the east. ©Norman McGrath. NM

Bottom: Brooklyn Children's Museum. Plan. HHP

921

site, designed by Hardy Holzman Pfeiffer, who were also commissioned to transform a nearby former automobile showroom and pool hall into temporary headquarters for the museum.[184] The temporary museum, nicknamed MUSE, was located at 1530 Bedford Avenue at Lincoln Place. The facades of the two-story brick and limestone-trimmed building were left largely untouched, except for the addition of bold yellow letters spelling out "MUSE," painted across the building's walls and windows in a dramatic diagonal slash. Inside, a curving entrance hall penetrated to the center of the museum. Diagonally placed walls, mirrors, a large skylight and a mezzanine-level bridge added to the dynamically composed interior.

Though the permanent museum was planned in 1968, construction did not begin until 1972.[185] Even once construction was virtually complete in 1975, the city's fiscal crunch prevented the museum from opening until 1977. Hardy Holzman Pfeiffer's design for the museum was meant to encourage children to explore. Highway signs and a transit kiosk rescued from the Queensboro Bridge marked the entry to the building. A ramp that sliced diagonally through the square plan led into the building's center. Paul Goldberger heralded the children's museum as "a sort of learned funhouse—a collection of educational exhibitions housed in a wildly exuberant structure that is itself the best exhibition of all. The building is a madly active array of tubes big enough to walk through, neon lights, brightly-painted pipes, kiosks, greenhouses and bridges. It is all put together with the skill of a fine composition, but the architecture never gets in the way of the fun."[186]

Brownsville, East New York and Cypress Hills

In 1852 a group of communities broke off from the Town of Flatbush, only to be annexed to the City of Brooklyn in 1886: Highland Park, also known as Cypress Hills, lying north of Atlantic Avenue and east of Pennsylvania Avenue; Brownsville, occupying the roughly triangular area between Remsen and East New York avenues and the right-of-way of the Long Island Railroad; and East New York, extending east from those tracks to the Queens line, between Atlantic Avenue and Jamaica Bay.

For two generations of immigrant Jews from Eastern Europe, Brownsville and East New York had been a step up the ladder from the slums of the Lower East Side of Manhattan. But in the late 1930s the area slowly began to empty out as its more prosperous residents moved on to more attractive parts of Brooklyn, to Queens and to suburbs beyond. After World War II, as the city's housing and urban renewal programs began in earnest, Brownsville and East New York, because of their comparatively high vacancy rates, became ideal places to relocate black and Puerto Rican families displaced from sites cleared for new housing. The Welfare Department flooded the area to capacity and beyond, overtaxing the fragile housing stock until it ceased to function as the foundation of the decent if drab neighborhoods they had once been.

Before the war Brownsville–East New York was the site of two notable large-scale projects. One was the stylish Betsy Head Memorial Playground pool bathhouse (John Matthews Hatton, 1936), one of the most interesting of the similar facilities built throughout the city under Robert Moses's direction.[187] The other was Kingsborough Houses (Bedford-Stuyvesant Associates, 1940–41), a Housing Authority project for 1,166 families on sixteen acres bounded by Pacific and Bergen streets, Rochester and

Ralph avenues.[188] Kingsborough Houses was the first slum clearance project in Brownsville–East New York, replacing 253 dilapidated, mostly wood-frame structures housing 520 low-income families, about 60 percent of whom were black. Its first two units were completed in the summer of 1941; the first families moved in on August 19, after, as the New York Times reported, "their belongings had been fumigated."[189]

In 1944 the Housing Authority announced plans for the redevelopment of an eighteen-acre site bounded by Stone, Sutter, Dumont and Rockaway avenues.[190] Brownsville Houses (1947), designed by Frederick G. Frost and John Ambrose Thompson, consisted of twenty-seven seven-story buildings accommodating 1,338 families. The Housing Committee of the American Institute of Architects' New York Chapter, chaired by Arthur C. Holden, praised the complex as "an outstanding example of the charm and sense of domesticity which can be obtained on an uninteresting, flat site, through the intelligent placing of buildings of varied height, with a plan which is definitely in harmony with human scale."[191]

The literary critic Alfred Kazin, who grew up in Brownsville, was less impressed. In his memoir of 1951, A Walker in the City, Kazin wrote:

> As I walked past those indistinguishable red prisms of city houses, I kept remembering what they had pulled down to make this project—and despite my pleasure in all this space and light in Brownsville, despite even my envious wonder what our own life would have been if we had lived, as soon all of New York's masses will live, just like everybody else, still, I could not quite believe that what I saw before me was real. Brownsville in that model quarter looks like an old crone who has had a plastic operation, and to my amazement I miss her old, sly, and withered face. I miss all those ratty little wooden tenements, born with the smell of damp in them. . . . There is something uncanny now about seeing the old vistas rear up at each end of that housing project. Despite those fresh diagonal walks, with their trees and children's sandboxes and Negro faces calmly at home with the white, so many of the old tenements have been left undisturbed on every side of the project, the streets beyond are so obviously just as they were when I grew up in them, that it is as if they had been ripped out of their original pattern and then pasted back again behind the unbelievable miniatures of the future.[192]

Despite these large-scale projects, for several years after the war Brownsville retained much of its former character. Stable in its own peculiar way, Brownsville's Main Street, Pitkin Avenue, was still lined with busy shops, and on Belmont Avenue pushcarts continued to flourish long after they had all but disappeared on the Lower East Side. Even as the urban decay increased and the demographics changed, the scenario remained much the same; as Murray Schumach, a New York Times reporter, wrote in 1955, the old settlers were giving way to the new, with the African-Americans leaving "Harlem and Negro sections of Brooklyn for the same reason the Jews had left the lower East Side twenty-five years ago."[193] But once the decision was made to renew the area through wholesale demolition and reconstruction, the natural evolution of Brownsville was irrevocably altered. With large-scale housing projects going up one after another, what might have been an orderly process of renewal became a cataclysmic upheaval with disastrous consequences.

In 1950 the Housing Authority commissioned Isadore and Zachary Rosenfield to design a 1,453-unit, low-rent project on a site bounded by Stone, Sutter and Livonia avenues and Powell

Street, adjacent to the site of the relatively low-scale Brownsville Houses.[194] Completed in 1955, Van Dyke Houses consisted of eleven fourteen-story elevator buildings and thirteen three-story walk-ups. The bleak apartment complex also included parking for 220 cars, a playground and a community center. Several other housing projects quickly followed: the 1,441-unit Boulevard Houses (Kelly & Gruzen, 1950), bounded by Linden Boulevard, Ashford Street, Wortman Avenue, Hendrix Street and Stanley and Schenck avenues;[195] the 815-unit Howard Houses (Pomerance & Breines, 1955), bounded by East New York, Stone and Glenmore avenues and Watkins Street;[196] the 1,590-unit Linden Houses (Joseph & Vladeck, 1957), bounded by Vermont Street and Stanley, Schenck and Cozine avenues;[197] and the 998-unit Samuel J. Tilden Houses (H. I. Feldman, 1961), bounded by Dumont, Stone, Livonia and Rockaway avenues.[198]

These new projects, rather than stemming the tide of decay, seemed to accelerate it. When Murray Schumach visited the Brownsville–East New York neighborhood in 1955, he reported that "desperation" characterized the mood of most area residents, who "would, if they could, gladly follow tens of thousands of others who have gone to Nassau County and Queens." Aside from the public housing, little new construction had occurred since the 1920s, and Schumach found that condemned buildings were "not uncommon" and that many tenements seemed "ready to have boards hammered across the windows." True, there were some residents, old people mostly, who were happy to stay in "their neat brick houses fronted with clipped hedges and magnolia," to sit on their porches, "reading *The Jewish Daily Forward* and discussing world affairs and the influx of new peoples." But, as Schumach pointed out, the neighborhood was primarily "for the young and the vigorous." The street, he said, was "the living room of the tenement," and the common language was "the loud, heated style of the city slum."[199]

In 1968 Pomerance & Breines's Glenmore Plaza showed that the large-scale approach could produce something of value, although because of the era's changing political climate and the growing rejection of such major interventions, it was "all but ignored," as *Housing and Planning News* observed.[200] Located between Pitkin and Glenmore avenues, Stone Avenue and Powell Street, Glenmore Plaza rose phoenixlike from the burned-out rubble of Brownsville's decrepit heart. It contained 438 apartments in four buildings that ranged in height from ten to twenty-four stories. Unlike the typical Housing Authority site plans of the 1940s and 1950s, Glenmore Plaza's towers defined a central space. Despite its comparative sophistication, Glenmore Plaza was a last hurrah for the old order of housing projects still advocated by the "housing establishment" as the best way to get the job done. It was also, in its way, a cry in the wilderness. As *Housing and Planning News* observed:

> Around Glenmore Plaza, the old houses of Brownsville, 3 and 4 stories high, festooned with firescapes [sic], charred from fires, blinded with sheet metal windows where they have been abandoned, stand filthy, disreputable, rejected. The city will not build any more Glenmore Plazas on the theory that it is better to develop low-rise housing than to impose fireproof apartment houses on an allegedly unwilling "community." One cannot help pondering the wisdom of this choice.[201]

In the late 1960s, with the notion of wholesale clearance in serious disrepute, Brownsville became one of the target areas of the new, selective clearance and rehabilitation initiatives of the federally funded Model Cities program, which was enacted in 1967. In December 1968 Mayor Lindsay, "wielding a sledge

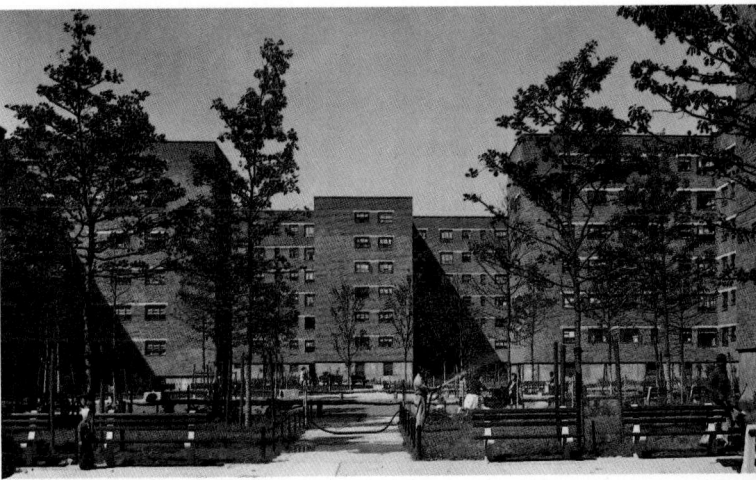

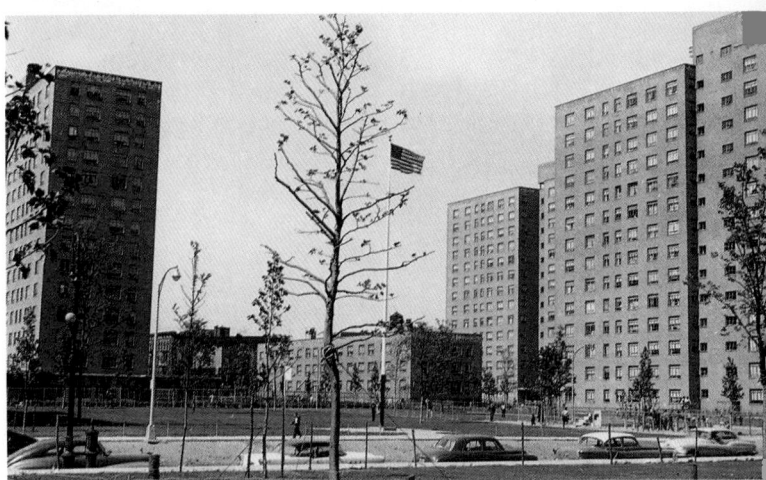

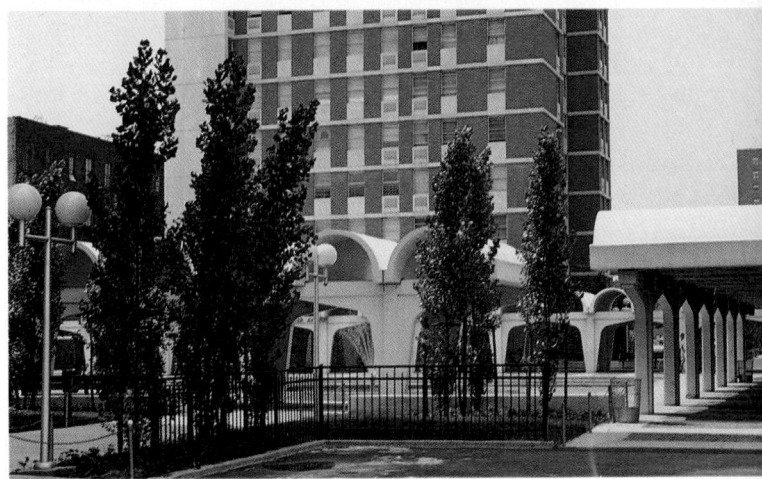

Top: Brownsville Houses, bounded by Stone, Sutter, Dumont and Rockaway avenues, Brownsville. Frederick G. Frost and John Ambrose Thompson, 1947. Interior pathway. NYCHA.

Center: Van Dyke Houses, bounded by Linden Boulevard, Ashford Street, Wortman Avenue, Hendrix Street and Stanley and Schenk avenues, Brownsville. Isadore and Zachary Rosenfield, 1950. View to the southeast. NYCHA

Bottom: Glenmore Plaza, between Pitkin and Glenmore avenues, Stone Avenue and Powell Street, Brownsville. Pomerance & Breines, 1968. Central plaza. NYCHA

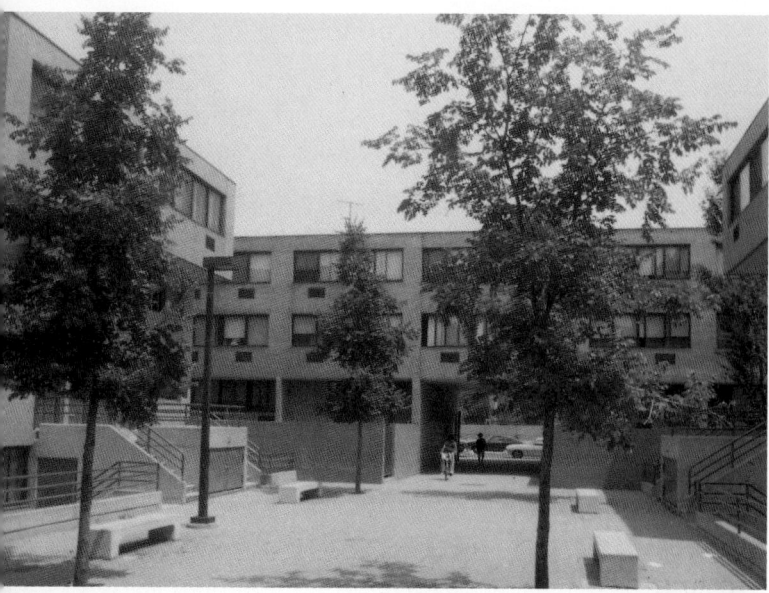

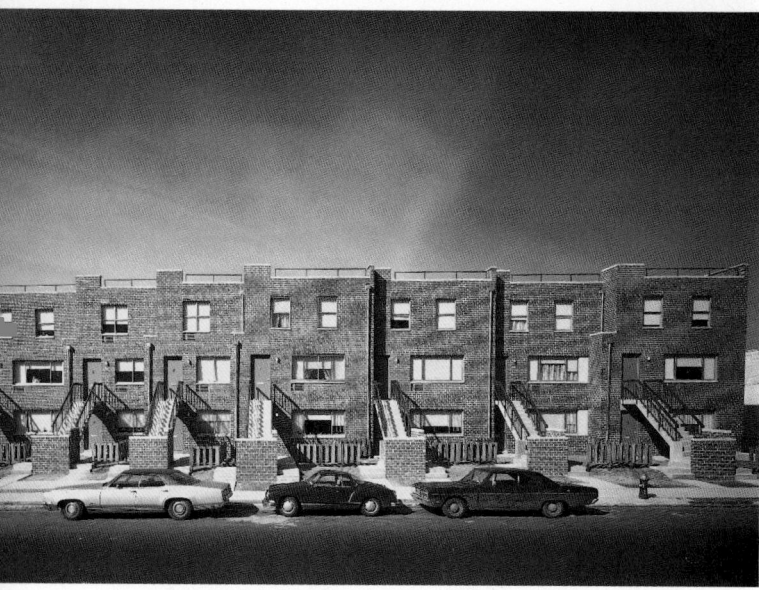

Top: Marcus Garvey Village, between Dumont and Riverdale avenues, Bristol Street and Rockaway Avenue, Brownsville. Kenneth Frampton, Arthur Baker and Peter Wolf; Theodore Liebman, Anthony Pangaro and J. Michael Kirkland; and David Todd & Associates, 1976. View of cul-de-sac. THLI

Bottom: City Line 1 Turnkey Public Housing, 460–470 Fountain Avenue, 1085–1087 Hegeman Avenue, 768–774 Logan Street and 1052–1064 Hegeman Avenue. Ciardullo-Ehmann, 1975. Lieberman. CIAR

hammer tied with a red ribbon, broke down the front door of an apartment house slated for rehabilitation," inaugurating the area's first Model Cities project, which included five sites undertaken by the Baptist Home Mission Society to provide 232 units of new housing and 24 units of rehabilitated housing.[202] Even before the Model Cities initiative, the Baptists had been involved in plans for housing, working with city planner Walter Thabit and black architect Roger D. Glasgow to propose an extensive program of rehabilitation. As Glasgow reported, however, "when we came to implement the plan, the community decided they wanted new units. When we showed them that new units would cost no more than rehabilitation in some of the old houses, they decided they wanted new housing."[203] Community groups also wanted low-density development, partly to help prevent the arrival of more "undesirables" who would come into the neighborhood should an excess number of units be provided. Community members may have been poor, but to them there were other, even less advantaged potential residents—the welfare families who increasingly constituted the tenancy of low-income housing. Although Glasgow's first plans called for new three- and four-story infill units in keeping with the height if not necessarily the scale or character of the prevailing neighborhood building fabric, economics forced him to go to six or seven stories.

Despite the occasional success, the Model Cities program proved unfeasible. According to Elaine Weiss, who worked with the Baptists, "The trouble with the Model Cites program is that it needs the approval of many different groups: the community concerned, the city government, and the Federal Government." Glasgow put it more succinctly: "There is no future in Model Cities. It is completely political."[204]

A promising new approach to redevelopment emerged when the New York State Urban Development Corporation (UDC), working with the Institute for Architecture and Urban Studies (IAUS), undertook a high-density, low-rise housing project on nine blocks of the fifty-seven-block Marcus Garvey Park Village Urban Renewal Area in Brownsville. The IAUS was founded in 1967 as a think tank, but its members were intent on turning ideas into practice. It was not until the Marcus Garvey project, however, that the group would directly translate theory into buildings. The theory in question was very provocative: that one could achieve high-density settlement in low-rise structures that would revive the successful urbanism of the traditional city. On June 12, 1973, the UDC and the IAUS released their findings in a large exhibition, "Another Chance for Housing: Low-Rise Alternatives," held at the Museum of Modern Art, with designs prepared for two sites: Fox Hills, Staten Island (see "Staten Island," below) and Brownsville.[205]

Marcus Garvey Village, completed in 1976, consisted of 625 units on 12.5 acres of land organized in four-story, street-facing townhouselike rows sheltering four-story mews in the block interiors. The project was the work of Kenneth Frampton, Arthur Baker and Peter Wolf of the IAUS, Theodore Liebman, Anthony Pangaro and J. Michael Kirkland of the UDC, and David Todd & Associates. It was intended to provide a density comparable to that of typical high-rise projects, but without the sense of the "vertical ghetto" that characterized most towers-in-the-park schemes, where the buildings' height isolated house-bound mothers from their children playing outside and long corridors as well as elevators served as breeding grounds for crime. In his introduction to the exhibition catalogue, Edward J. Logue, president and chief executive officer of the UDC, carefully outlined the drawbacks of the prevailing approach to inner-city housing:

The family housing now being built in the older cities of the United States seems to be falling behind suburban housing from the point of view of affording some sense of identification between the family and its dwelling. The cost of land and the difficulties of relocation have led to an ever greater emphasis on high rise buildings as the standard urban housing solution for families of low and moderate income. These high rise "projects," as they are usually called, house a great many families on a relatively small amount of land, and they do provide decent living space in quantities which would be difficult to achieve at lower densities. However, their design and landscaping often remain quite sterile. The scale of such projects seems frequently to be way beyond any human dimension, and families, particularly young children, miss the feeling of a familiar, homelike atmosphere. Furthermore, such housing projects often seem not to fit in with the surrounding neighborhood, but rather stand apart from it.[206]

At the conclusion of his catalogue essay, Kenneth Frampton, who was one of the project's principal designers, observed that though "it would be too much to claim that low rise high density housing has begun to resolve the antagonistic split that opened up in the last quarter of the 19th century between town and country . . . at least one may finally acknowledge its pertinence as a mediator in an era when the time honored distinctions between urban and rural are rapidly disappearing."[207] According to Frampton and Anthony Pangaro, perhaps the most important principle affecting the design was the decision to derive criteria "more from the single family terrace house than from the multi-family high rise building." They explained:

At the next scale above the house we sought to achieve a sense of territoriality by striving for outdoor spaces that would clearly differentiate between private, semi-public and public space. . . . In the units themselves we tried to reflect the necessity in the case of a large family for the overall living space to be capable of simultaneous and conflicting use by different family members and for the other spaces, bedrooms in particular, to be capable of being acoustically isolated. In this respect we saw the public porches and stoops as providing an alternative to the private terrace.[208]

The sponsors and designers worked with local community groups and various city agencies to develop, in Logue's words, "a real site and a real program" that could benefit from housing subsidies. "After very careful consideration of various alternatives," Logue said, "we determined that Brownsville would be a very good location for this pilot project. This is a neighborhood that has recently suffered serious deterioration. If it is to be rebuilt successfully, the new low rise prototype, both as a unit and as an aggregate whole, must afford not only a sense of individual identity but also a sense of community."[209]

The vacant site chosen for the demonstration project comprised nine blocks roughly delineated by Rockaway Avenue and Blake, Newport and Hopkinson streets. Down the center, along Livonia Avenue, ran the elevated trains of the IRT, while to the east lay the vast Brownsville, Van Dyke and Tilden housing projects. These contrasted sharply with the area's surrounding blocks of modest but desirable rows of semidetached houses lining quiet and often tree-lined streets, which, despite all manner of social dislocation, still conveyed a sense of family-based civility. Also nearby was the Betsy Head Memorial Playground.

A number of significant modifications to the prototype were made in the actual construction. Small-scale parking lots, originally intended to be placed where they would enhance the complex's public spaces, were instead located next to the ele-

vated tracks, putting to practical use the 100-foot-wide environmental buffer required on each side of its right-of-way. The result, however, was that the tracks and the buffers hopelessly divided the site into northern and southern halves (the southern portion was never built). A second compromise grew out of the decision to retain existing structures on some of the blocks. This meant that the original plan, in which street-facing units enclosed private yards and mews behind them, had to be replaced by a plan of cul-de-sacs perpendicular to the street. Other amendments to the initial idea were made as well: when the original stooplike exterior stairs were deemed illegal, the stairs were turned parallel to the building mass; and the balconies planned for smaller upper-level units were eliminated to save money. The change in the orientation of the stairs seriously curtailed their social role as mediators between the public realm of the street and the private realm of the house, and both compromises resulted in a tighter and less clear organization of buildings, contributing to a sense of overbuilding.

In an assessment of Marcus Garvey Village written in 1979, Suzanne Stephens found it "reassuring to see the housing, now several years old, well maintained, and the residents protective of it." Nonetheless, she criticized "the formal perception of the housing, in terms of what it projects as a place to live and as an architectural artifact to emulate." Although Stephens described the buildings as having "a sturdy simplicity," she felt that formally the project did not "diverge enough from the usual bricks and mortar modified Modern low-rise housing seen elsewhere. And in spite of its density," she continued, "the fact that half of the apartments (the smallest ones at that) lack access to private open space has to be viewed as an unresolved dilemma." Stephens concluded: "The shift from ideal to real proved bumpy. Thus while Marcus Garvey was a worthwhile experiment, it does not offer the ideal promised model for emulation so desired by those who conceived the scheme."[210]

Ciardullo-Ehmann's City Line 1 Turnkey Public Housing (1975), at 460–470 Fountain Avenue, 1085–1087 Hegeman Avenue, 768–774 Logan Street and 1052–1064 Hegeman Avenue, in some ways continued the ideas that informed Marcus Garvey Village.[211] The development stacked duplex apartments over single-floor units to suggest the scale of nearby rowhouses. The buildings, clad in brick, were perhaps overarticulated, but the struggle to make the few functional elements work to maximum effect—the houses can be seen as an essay in the arrangement of downspouts—was commendable.

In 1976 Robert Stern proposed an alternate way of achieving relatively high-density, low-rise housing.[212] In a scheme prepared for the 1976 Biennale held in Venice, Italy, Stern projected a Subway Suburb to occupy much of the undeveloped southern site of Marcus Garvey Village (and, for a bit of ironic effect, the built-up site as well). According to Stern, Subway Suburb was an attempt to define "a new kind of suburb to be built within the legal confines of the city, relatively close to its center, utilizing urban land that has been abandoned and has no apparent higher value." The new development would "utilize existing street and utility grids to offset development costs and take advantage of existing rapid transit services while also accommodating the automobile."[213] Whereas the IAUS design was largely based on European Modernist housing from the 1920s, Stern turned to traditional English and American housing types, including Regency Crescents, planned suburbs such as Forest Hills Gardens and the typical pre–World War I single-family house. An incentive to individual proprietorship of open space would be provided through the reintroduction of identifi-

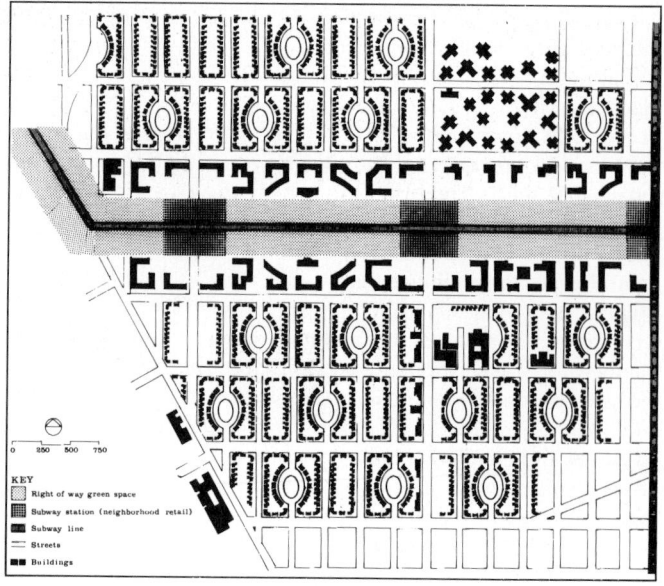

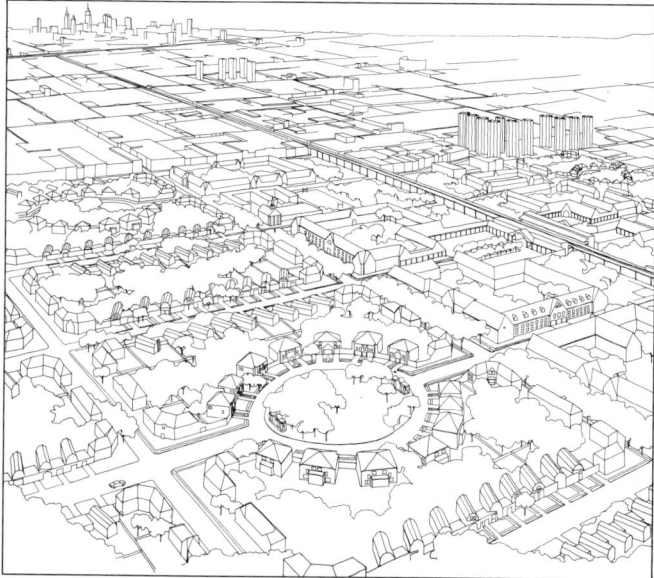

Top: Proposal for Subway Suburb, between Sutter and Hegeman avenues, Junius Street and East Ninety-eighth Street, Brownsville. Robert Stern, 1976. Site plan. RAMSA

Bottom: Proposal for Subway Suburb. Aerial perspective of view to the northwest. RAMSA

Top right: Playground at Cypress Hills Houses, between Fountain and Euclid avenues, Sutter Avenue and Linden Boulevard, Cypress Hills. Charles Forberg, 1967. Seventy-two-foot circle with tower and slide. NYCHA

Bottom right: Rutland Plaza, East New York Avenue to Rutland Road, between East Ninety-second and East Ninety-fourth streets, Brownsville. Donald Stull & Associates, 1976. View to the north. ©Norman McGrath. NM

Bottom far right: United Community Day Care Center, 613 New Lots Avenue, northwest corner of Schenk Avenue, East New York. Robert Mangurian, Les Walker, Craig Hodgetts and Jeff Milstein, 1971. View to the north. LW

able front yards of substantial size. These yards, according to Stern, would "by their very nature . . . mark out a clearly definable turf [to be] maintained by the private citizen for the benefit of the community."[214]

While housing constituted the most visible projects undertaken in the Brownsville–East New York area, public funds were also allocated for the construction of schools. Pedersen & Tilney's Public School 306 (1966), at 970 Vermont Street, on the northwest corner of Cozine Avenue, was a straightforward representation of the diagrammatic Brutalist Modernism virtually institutionalized by the Board of Education in the 1960s.[215] A refreshing departure from type, Perkins & Will's Public School 398 (1976), on the south side of East New York Avenue between East Ninety-third and East Ninety-fourth streets, was a 1,500-student, open-plan elementary school.[216] Conceived as an educational shopping center, the basilicalike school was organized along a streetlike spine. It was built in conjunction with an adjoining 450-unit, stepped-slab apartment house, Donald Stull & Associates' Rutland Plaza (1976), East New York Avenue and Rutland Road, East Ninety-second to East Ninety-fourth Street.

Several other projects oriented toward children were also built in the area. In 1967 two experimental playgrounds, funded by the Housing Authority, the Museum of Modern Art and the Parks Association, were opened on the grounds of the 1,444-unit Cypress Hills Houses (Carson & Lundin, 1954).[217] Designed by Charles Forberg, an exhibition designer, the two round playgrounds, one seventy-two feet, the other thirty-two feet in diameter, featured, as *Progressive Architecture* remarked, "forests of vertical concrete slabs, arranged like a grouping of headstones seen through a fisheye lens." The larger playground included a tower, a slide, a wading pool and a grouping of half-culvert sections supported on concrete stems. Though the project had some attraction as a work of sculpture, said *Progressive Architecture*, "its appeal as a play area seems to be minimal."[218] Parents of younger children felt the concrete forms were dangerous, although older children seemed to enjoy the playground as a setting for rough games of tag.

In 1971 the United Community Day Care Development Fund Company, Inc., a social work organization, announced plans for a day-care facility in East New York to serve more than 180 children.[219] To design the facility, the company commissioned four iconoclastic young architects, Robert Mangurian, Les Walker, Craig Hodgetts and Jeff Milstein, who practiced together as Works (East)—there was a companion group, Works (West) in Los Angeles. The site included a one-story, steel-framed wood building that was extensively renovated as part of the project. The design connected the existing and the new building with a skylit interior streetlike spine, which was furnished with streetlights, fire plugs and walk/don't walk signs, in part to educate the children in street safety and in part to foster a sense of community. With exposed mechanical ducts overhead, the interior street literally hummed with activity. The facade of the existing building, which was used for classrooms, offices and a community room, formed one of the street walls. On the opposite side, the new building was organized as a series of "houses," entered through glazed overhead garage doors, leading to successively more quiet areas. On the second floor of the new building were meeting rooms and a wood shop; the roof of the old building was developed as a playground. Although the exposed concrete-block walls and the exposed ducts and electrical conduit conveyed a sense of toughness, the place seemed warm rather than brutal.

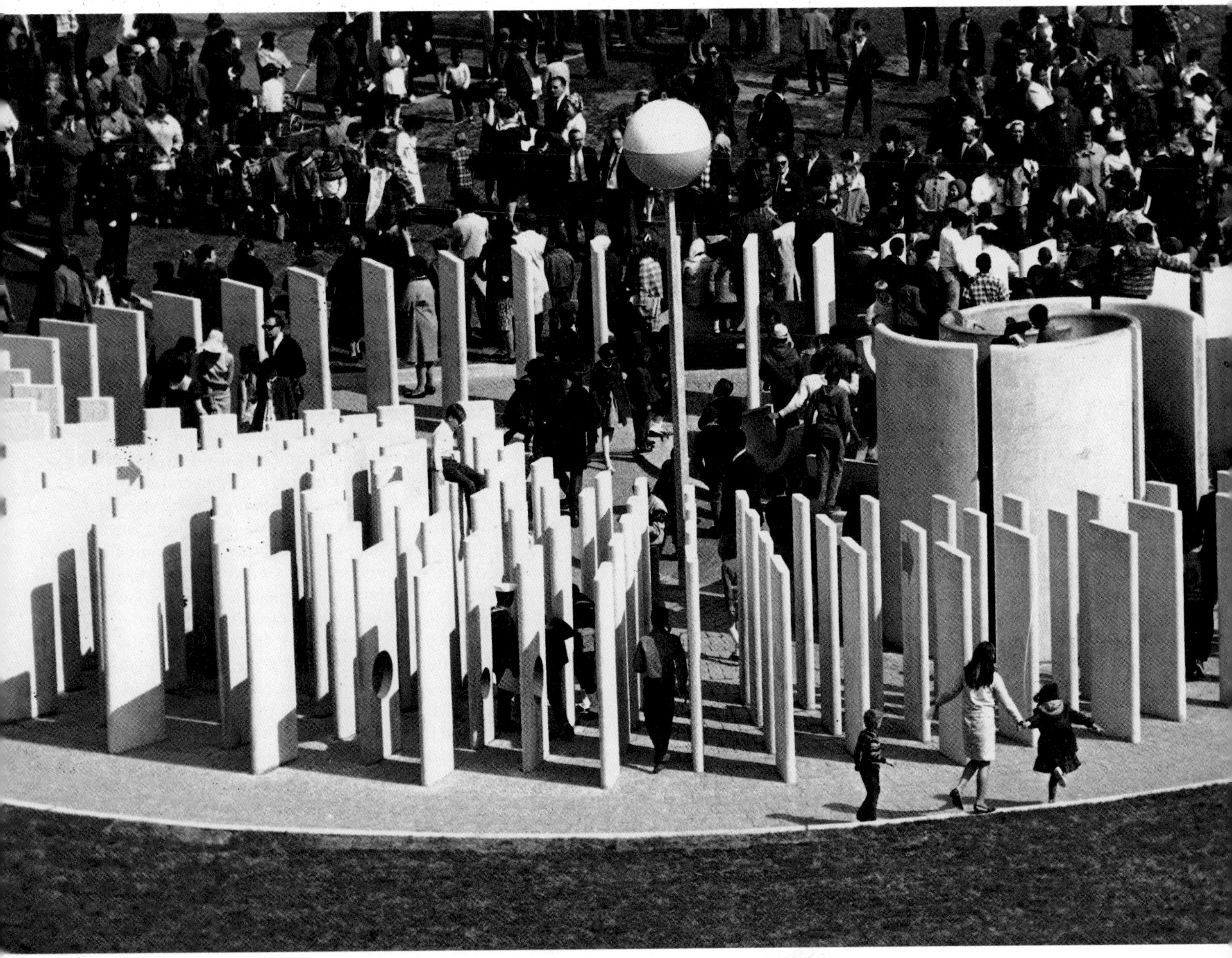

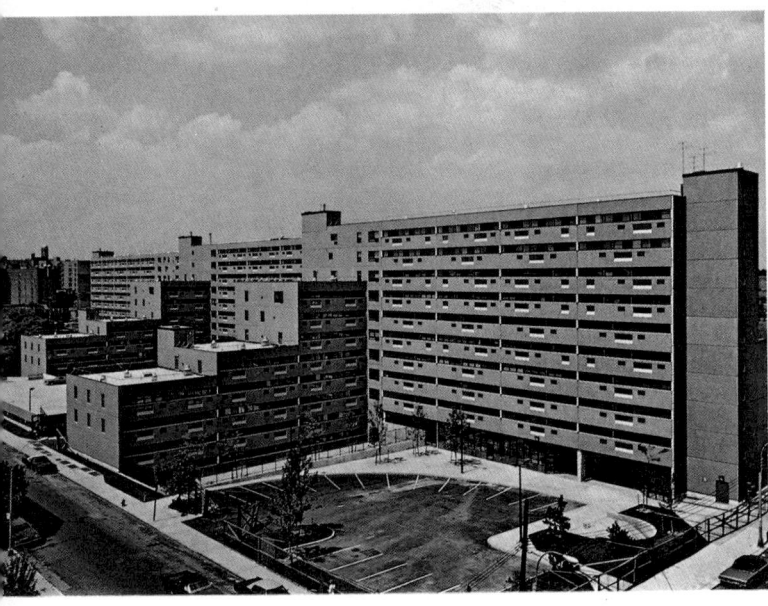

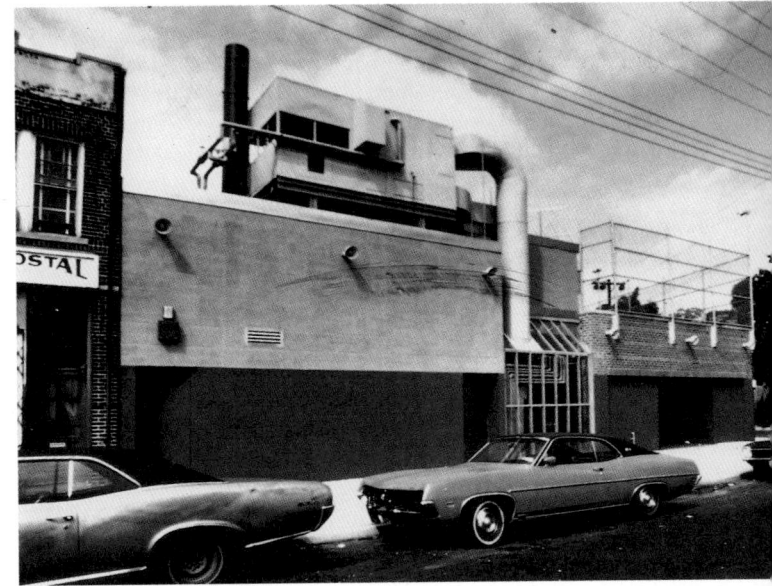

A few other public buildings were built in the 1970s. One notable example was Giovanni Pasanella's Engine Company 238, Squad Company 4, New York City Fire Department (1974), at 885 Howard Avenue, on the southeast corner of Livonia Avenue.[220] Clad in reddish-brown jumbo brick and sparely detailed, the building fit snugly into a tight site bounded on one side by rowhouses and on the other by Livonia Avenue with its elevated tracks. Also of interest was Katz, Waisman, Weber, Strauss's Brooklyn Developmental Center, New York State Department of Mental Hygiene (1974), at 888 Fountain Avenue, south of Flatlands Avenue.[221] The casual grouping of ribbed-concrete-block buildings, although as isolated as its sister institution, the Bronx Developmental Center (see "The Bronx," below), did not inspire the same strong reactions.

One notable work of commercial architecture was also realized in the area: a building for the East New York Savings Bank (1962), at Kings Highway and East Ninety-eighth Street.[222] Designed by Lester C. Tichy, an architect known for shopping centers and for his "improvements" to Pennsylvania Station in the late 1950s (see chapter 16), the building consisted of a circular drum, with glazed Roman arches lighting the banking hall, and a flat, pergolalike element lifted above the roof on columns and cantilevered behind the building wall to suggest a halolike cornice.

Eastern District

To the north of Bedford-Stuyvesant were the towns of Bushwick, established in 1660, and Williamsburg, which broke off from it in 1840. Both merged with the City of Brooklyn in 1855, when the area came to be known as the Eastern District. A prosperous manufacturing neighborhood, especially along the East River and Newtown Creek waterfronts, the Eastern District was largely built up with rowhouses and tenements to house a working-class population, although some of its early real estate was developed as summer houses for wealthy Manhattanites. Dramatic change came with the completion of the Williamsburg Bridge (1903), which provided a direct connection with the overflowing slums of the Lower East Side. The Eastern District saw little new building in the interwar era, and its pre–World War I social character held firm in the largely Polish Greenpoint section in the north; this was not the case, however, in Williamsburg, which shifted from a neighborhood dominated by Irish to one dominated by Eastern European Jews. After World War II, Williamsburg became almost exclusively inhabited by Hasids, as thousands of members of this Orthodox Jewish sect immigrated from Central Europe, especially Poland and Hungary.

The major postwar buildings in the Eastern District were Public School 45 (1966) and Woodhull Hospital (1968–78; opened 1982). Morris Ketchum, Jr. & Associates' Public School 45, at Schaffer Street and Evergreen Avenue in the Bushwick section, brought to Brooklyn the same parti that was introduced in the same year in Curtis & Davis's Intermediate School 201 in Harlem (see chapter 12).[223] Ketchum described P.S. 45 as an "inside-out" urban school, with corridor galleries running along the outer walls and classrooms opening onto interior courts. "By means of a windowless street-side exterior of colorful glazed brick panels with sturdy aluminum grilles, distractions of street noise are warded off, and the school becomes a vandal-proof, breakage-free structure," Ketchum explained. "On the inside,

where the educational process is happening, the three-story school centers on two large, open courts."[224]

P.S. 45, whose budget exceeded that of normal Board of Education projects, served 1,671 students with ten experimental classrooms, thirty-six modified standard classrooms, four kindergartens and rooms for remedial teaching and special education. In addition to the usual recreational and library facilities, there was also an innovative communication center. In Ketchum's ingeniously organized building, the large-span elements of the gymnasium and auditorium were slid under the courtyards, eliminating the visual intrusion of their boxlike masses.

Woodhull Hospital was stupendous, "a superbuilding," as Norval White and Elliot Willensky described it, "a somewhat scary ode to health, dedicated more to efficiency of health economics than to the serenity of its clients."[225] Designed by Kallmann & McKinnell of Boston and Russo & Sonder of New York, the 610-bed, million-square-foot facility, replacing Greenpoint Hospital, occupied a twelve-acre superblock at the southwest corner of Broadway and Flushing Avenue. The site, which was also bounded by Throop and Park avenues, was chosen in part because it was at the boundary of three communities: Williamsburg, Bushwick and Bedford-Stuyvesant. Woodhull was commissioned by the New York State Health and Mental Hygiene Facilities Improvement Corporation, and its program was developed by the New York City Health Services Administration and the city's Health and Hospitals Corporation, which were to run the facility when it was completed.

When construction began in 1971, drawings were still being generated by the architects. Using a construction management procedure not often seen in public works in New York, the architects ordered materials early and constructed portions of the building before detailed designs were complete, hoping to avoid the cost inflation plaguing other projects. Most of the steel frame was in place by July 1972. Although it was planned for occupancy early in 1976, the project was delayed, first by community protests that not enough neighborhood workers were being hired. Even more significant delays were due to the city's fiscal crisis. When the hospital was finally completed in 1978—at a cost of more than $300 million (it was budgeted at $85 million in 1968)—the city, deeming it too expensive to run, tried to interest the Justice Department in taking it over and turning it into a prison. Following this unsuccessful effort, Woodhull was mothballed until the city's fiscal health was restored, and it finally opened in 1982.

The building's vastness was exploited as a positive feature by its designers. The 700-foot-long slab, sheathed in gray-tinted glass with panels of weathering steel, was carried on a grandly scaled exposed framework of the same steel, giving the building the appearance more of a work of engineering than of architecture. Within the slablike volume, patient rooms were arranged between a wide central corridor reserved for medical staff and a corridor for visitors that circled the building's perimeter. The perimeter corridor was extensively glazed, and the patients' rooms were washed with borrowed light admitted through sliding glass doors. Beds were placed at an angle against the outer wall so that patients could look directly into the room or, by turning to one side, out into the corridor and the windows beyond.

Each floor was separated from its neighbors by a deep, interstitial space formed by the eight-foot-deep, sixty-nine-foot-long transverse trusses that allowed for the column-free interior, through which conduit and ventilating equipment could be

Woodhull Hospital, southwest corner of Broadway and Flushing Avenue, between Marcus Garvey Boulevard and Throop Avenue, Flushing and Park avenues. Kallmann & McKinnell, 1978. View to the northwest. KMW

Top: Proposal for Linear City, from Brooklyn College northeast to Linden Boulevard, along the Long Island Railroad right-of-way. McMillan, Griffis & Mileto, 1967–69. Rendering of view to the south. AF. CU

Center: Proposal for Linear City. Section perspective. AF. CU

Bottom: Proposal for Linear City. Site map. AF. CU

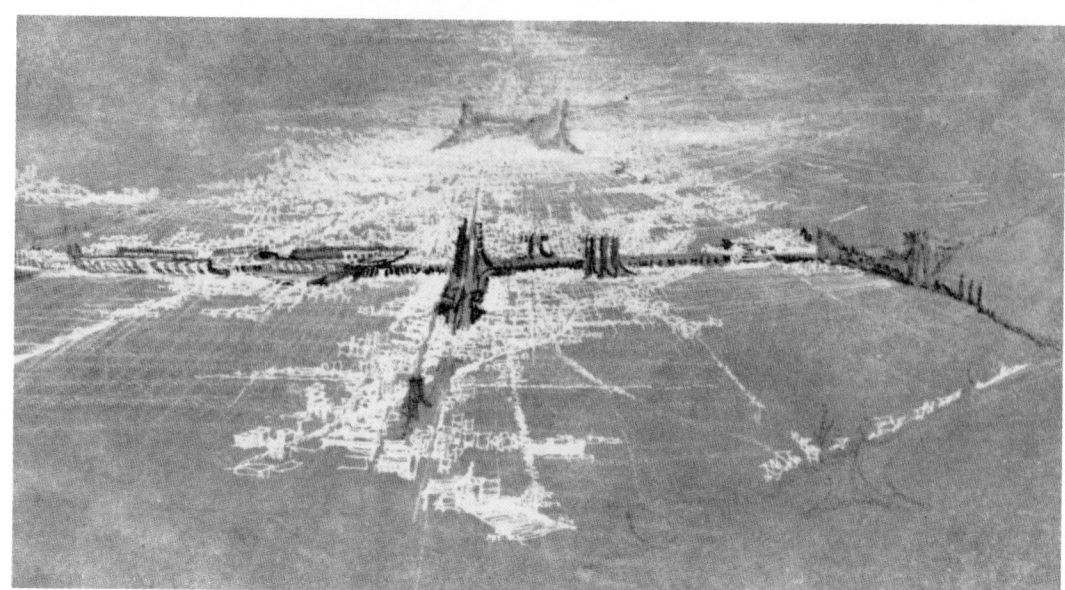

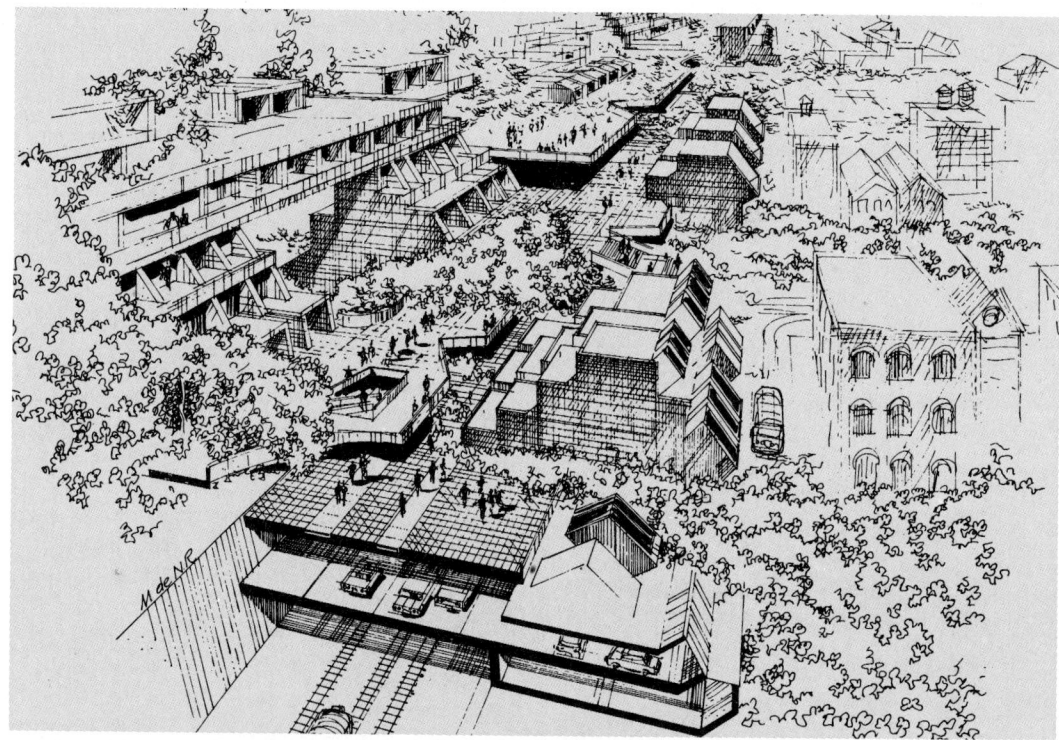

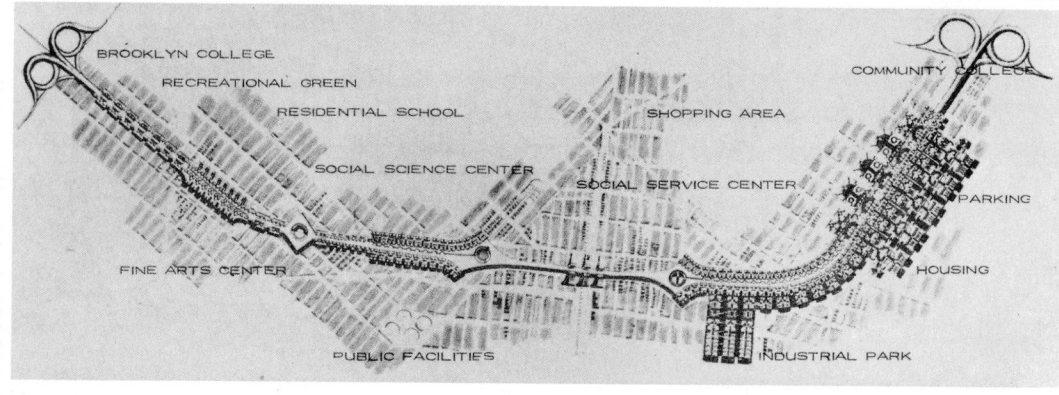

threaded. The interstitial spaces had enough headroom so that service personnel could access equipment without disturbing operations on the floor below. In early schemes, these spaces housed pneumatic chutes through which sealed bags of soiled laundry and trash could be moved, as well as a system of self-propelled electric cars on tracks that would be programmed to carry materials to preset destinations. Although these proposals were not implemented, the nineteen-foot floor-to-floor distance was retained, aggravating the building's gargantuanism.

In his assessment of the hospital in 1982, Paul Goldberger questioned the appropriateness of the design:

> Its 10 stories tower over everything around it. . . . When such vast size is combined with such commitment to the modernist architectural vocabulary, the result is a building that looks something like a cross between a 1920's factory and the Centre Pompidou in Paris. . . . Whether this is the right image for a health-care facility is not the sort of question that was raised very often in the late 1960's, but it is one that it is impossible not to raise now.

Nonetheless, Goldberger described the building as "one of the monuments of modern architecture in New York City," and concluded: "Woodhull is a kind of achievement—certainly a determined attempt to respond seriously to the weaknesses of New York's older hospital buildings. There is even a kind of nobility to this structure, commanding North Brooklyn as it seems to do. If machines for healing were what hospitals were supposed to look like, Woodhull would be ideal."[226]

Linear City

Linear City (1967–69) was a superproject that would have cut a wide swath through Central Brooklyn, affecting communities from Bushwick on the north almost to Bensonhurst on the south.[227] It called for an integrated development of school buildings, housing and parks above the proposed Cross-Brooklyn Expressway that would be routed for five and a half miles above the Long Island Railroad's Bay Ridge division, extending from Brooklyn College northeast to Linden Boulevard. The project grew out of two unrelated community-initiated actions. One was the demapping of Robert Moses's so-called "Bushwick alignment," a Y-shaped highway connecting the Queens-Midtown Tunnel and the Williamsburg Bridge with the Long Island Expressway that would have cut through the heart of Bushwick.[228] The other contributing factor was the efforts of a group of parents in Brownsville–East New York who protested the construction of seven "neighborhood" schools in their area on the grounds that they would be de facto segregated and suggested instead an education park that would draw children from all over Central Brooklyn.

In his efforts to demap Moses's road, State Senator Anthony Travia, whose Bushwick house lay in its path, seized upon the Long Island Railroad right-of-way as a route for the highway that could be built with minimal displacement of families. When Travia convinced Mayor Lindsay of the merits of his case, preliminary planning for the Cross-Brooklyn Expressway began. The expressway was to connect the Verrazano-Narrows Bridge with Brownsville–East New York, where it would proceed north to the Triborough Bridge and east to connect with the Nassau Expressway near Kennedy Airport, comprising 24.5 miles in all.

Meanwhile, the Board of Education had proposed two educational parks, one serving East New York and nearby parts of Queens, the other serving Canarsie, Brownsville, Flatbush, East Flatbush and Midwood, with the goal of racial integration. Some parents supported this plan, but others were in favor of a single educational park and others still approved of the earlier proposal for neighborhood schools. Dr. Cyril Sargent, a professor of education at City College and a member of the Corde Corporation, educational consultants, was called in to examine the situation. In his report, Sargent rejected both the board's proposal and the community's call for a single educational park. Instead, he presented the Long Island Railroad right-of-way as an opportunity to create a linear educational facility connecting many neighborhoods, making it easier to integrate schools at all educational levels. Sargent's report included a schematic section perspective showing dual two-lane roadways reserved for trucking flanking the railroad's single-track freight line, topped by two more two-lane roadways for cars and a fixed rail transit line; atop these, on a platform raised slightly above street level, were planted walkways and plazas, interspersed with school buildings.

Mayor Lindsay and the City Planning Commission seized on this idea, commissioning concept drawings from the firm of McMillan, Griffis & Mileto of New York and Rome, and calling on Rogers, Taliaferro, Kostritsky, Lamb, a Baltimore firm of architects and planners, to develop a modus operandi to bring together the diverse agencies necessary to implement the plan. McMillan, Griffis & Mileto's scheme, which was illustrated with a model as well as drawings, was a dazzling megavision of modular building units strung out along a continuous platform covering the below-level roads. In addition to education and housing facilities, it included a shopping area, a recreational green, social service centers and an industrial park in Flatlands.

In 1968, when the Department of Transportation approved the inclusion of the Cross-Brooklyn Expressway in the interstate highway system, Mayor Lindsay observed: "Linear City will mean that for the first time a highway will become a unifying force in the community—that it will meet social and commercial needs rather than just transportation requirements."[229] But in February 1969, after the state government balked at supporting the project, purportedly because Attorney General Louis J. Lefkowitz felt that there were legal problems in combining financing for schools, housing and highways, Lindsay was forced to withdraw the new schools from Linear City. Three months later, the Cross-Brooklyn Expressway, the base of Linear City, was also dropped by Lindsay.

Flatbush

Flatbush, the heartland of the borough, was founded in 1652 and annexed to the City of Brooklyn in 1894. A rural outpost until the 1880s, by the First World War it was a varied, populous and prosperous suburb, inhabited by middle-income families and some blue- and white-collar wage earners. By virtue of deed restrictions and other controls imposed by developers, the neighborhoods of Flatbush featured houses in a wide variety of styles; most residences were located on either side of the railroad cut of the Brooklyn, Flatbush and Coney Island Railroad, which carried passengers between the ferries to Manhattan and Brighton Beach. In the years between the two world wars, the area remained remarkably stable, but in the late 1930s new six- and seven-story apartment houses began to replace the older houses along the northern end of Ocean Parkway, in Prospect Park South and at other scattered locations. This trend was accelerated after the war, especially after 1954, when the Prospect

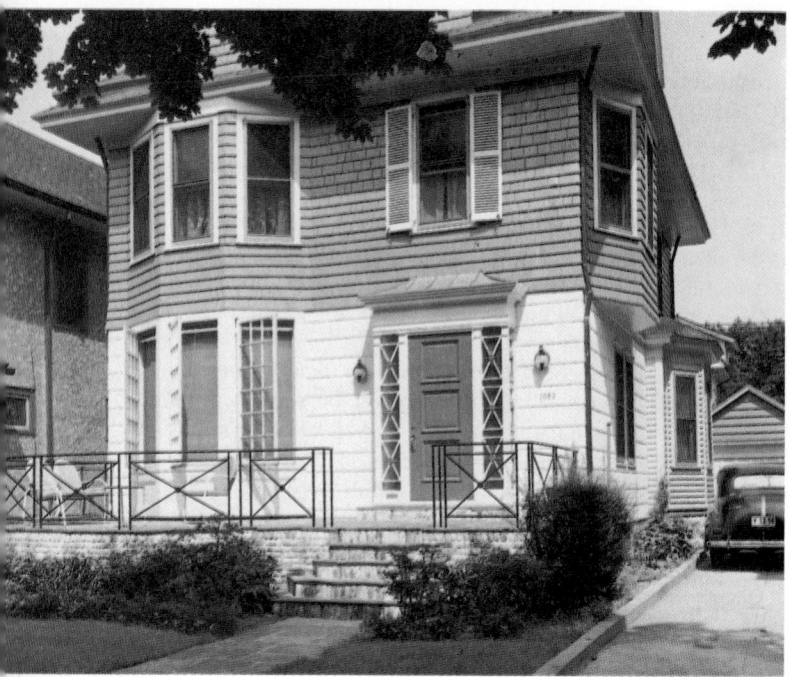

Above: Morris Lapidus Residence, 1059 East Eighth Street, between avenues J and K, Flatbush. Morris Lapidus, 1941. ML

Top right: Shaare Zion synagogue, 2030 Ocean Parkway, between avenues T and U, Flatbush. Morris Lapidus, 1954. View to the southwest. ML

Bottom right: Shaare Zion synagogue. Sanctuary. ML

Top far right: Congregation Beth Torah, 1061 Ocean Parkway, between avenues J and K, Flatbush. Richard Foster, 1969. View to the east. ©Norman McGrath. RF

Bottom far right: Congregation Beth Torah. Sanctuary. ©Norman McGrath. RF

Expressway was driven through the fringes of Park Slope and Windsor Terrace to connect the Belt Parkway with Ocean Parkway at Church Avenue, and Frederick Law Olmsted's tree-lined boulevard (1874–76), replete with separate walking, bicycle and equestrian paths, was insensitively rebuilt by Robert Moses to increase traffic flow.[230]

While the prewar apartment buildings had a certain charm, those built in the 1950s and 1960s were largely characterless, except for a few that featured elaborate lobbies entered under dramatic canopies that evoked the work of Morris Lapidus. Before moving to Miami Beach in the 1950s, Lapidus had been a resident of Flatbush, living at 1059 East Eighth Street, a house he renovated in 1941 to create a "more modern" effect inside and out, ripping off the covered porch to create a terrace and replacing the wood shingles with those of the "composition" type.[231]

In 1954 Lapidus designed the Shaare Zion synagogue at 2030 Ocean Parkway, between avenues T and U, a three-story circular structure featuring a stained-glass dome.[232] New synagogues proliferated from the late 1960s on, particularly nearer to Gravesend, as the neighborhoods on either side of Ocean Parkway became home to a young generation of Orthodox Jews. One of the more notable of the new synagogues was Congregation Beth Torah (1969), at 1061 Ocean Parkway, designed by Richard Foster, in what was one of his first independent commissions after dissolving his partnership with Philip Johnson.[233] Situated on a tight site flanked by a six-story apartment house on one side and two-family houses on the other, the synagogue featured a sanctuary in an iron-spot brick box rounded at the corners and swelled at the rear to accommodate the ark of the covenant. The windowless building was bathed in light from a series of rooftop skylights. To soften the light and aid acoustics, the inside walls, made of the same brick, were broken into a series of turretlike undulations, evoking Louis I. Kahn's unrealized designs for the Mikveh Israel synagogue in Philadelphia as well as some of Johnson and Foster's work for Yale.[234] A velariumlike plaster canopy covering the sanctuary was pierced at two places by large openings, which sent dramatic shafts of light above the ark and the bema.

South Shore

Until about 1900 the various communities that made up the South Shore towns of New Utrecht, which was founded in 1662, and Gravesend, which was founded three years later (both were annexed to the City of Brooklyn in 1894), were largely rural. Of these communities, Bay Ridge, Coney Island, Brighton Beach, Sheepshead Bay and Manhattan Beach had been popular summer resorts for New Yorkers since the nineteenth century. The South Shore became linked to the daily life of the city around World War I, when the various railroad lines that had provided connections with ferries to Manhattan were consolidated as the Brooklyn Manhattan Transit system (BMT) and connected to Manhattan via the Manhattan and Williamsburg bridges and tunnels under the East River.[235] With the completion of the Belt Parkway in 1940, and the use of landfill to create new development areas around Paerdegat Basin and neighboring Marine Park, new communities grew up in Flatlands, better known as Canarsie.

Although many of the nineteenth-century resort communities maintained much of their earlier character until after World

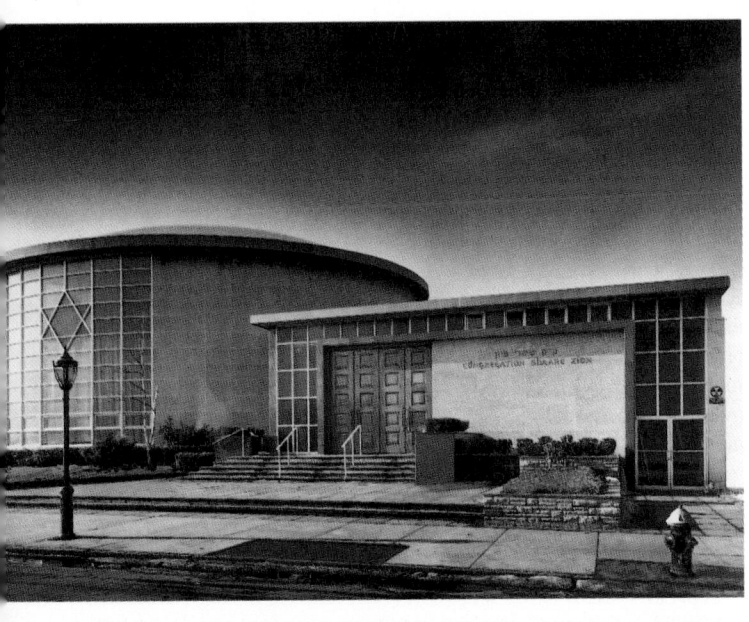

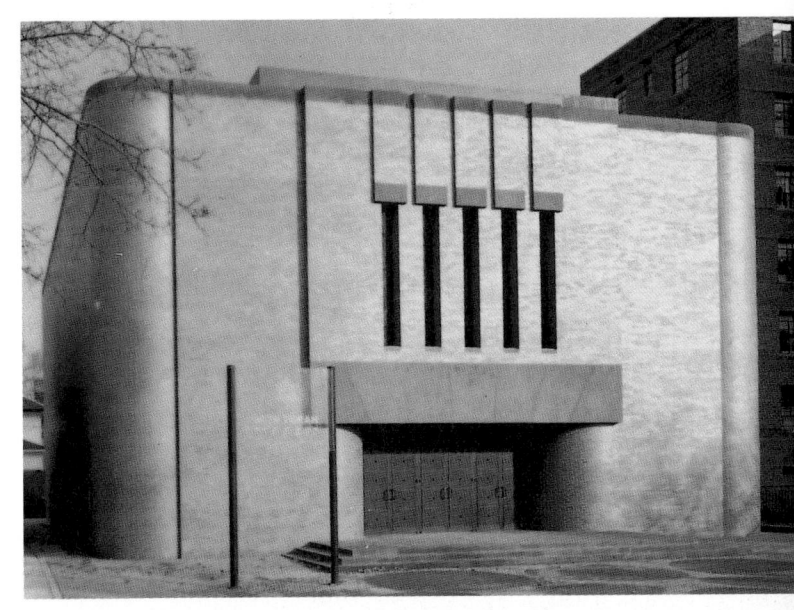

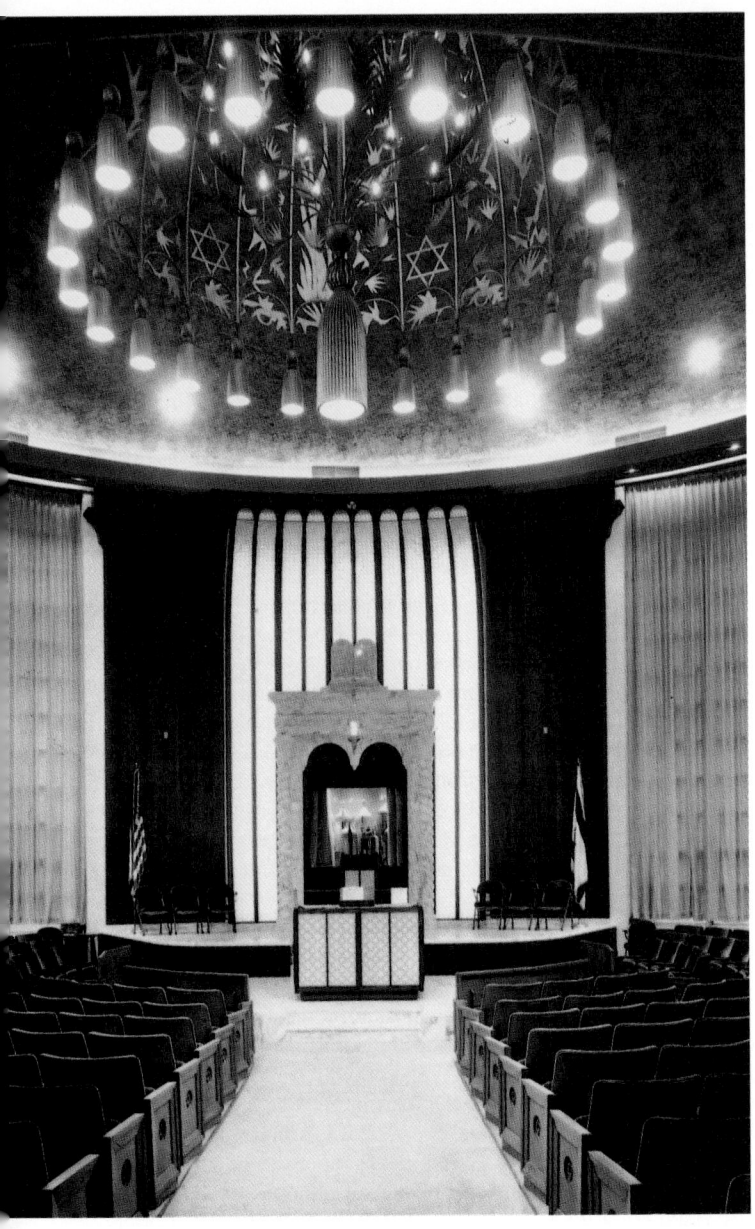

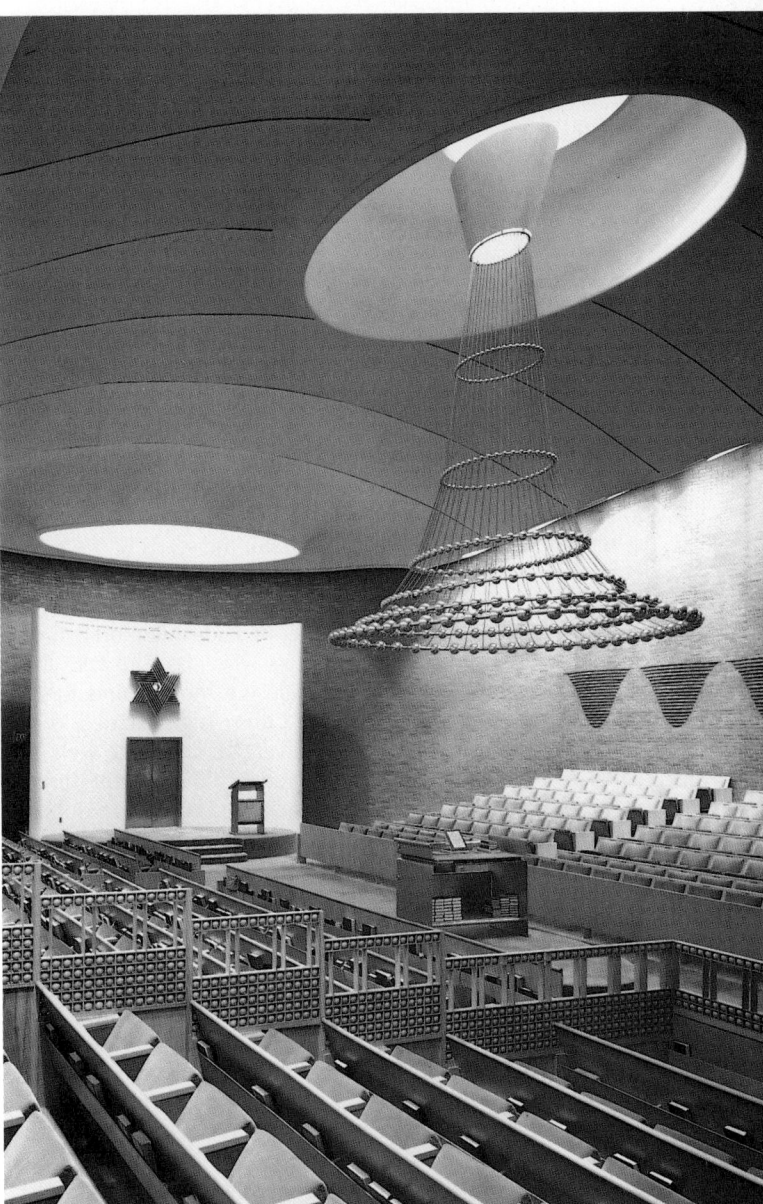

War II, Bay Ridge underwent a definite transformation. In the 1930s its shorefront mansions gave way to apartment houses intended for affluent and middle-class residents. Shore Court, between Colonial Road and Narrows Avenue, and Madeline Court, between Ridge Boulevard and Third Avenue, were among the more interesting of these apartment houses, but none was as impressive as Ernest Flagg's Flagg Court (1933–36).[236] Postwar apartment houses were not as distinguished. Gruzen & Partners' Shore Hill Apartments (1976), at 9000 Shore Road, between Ninetieth and Ninety-first streets, a residence for senior citizens, was too big for its setting and crudely detailed.[237] But the most significant disruption to Bay Ridge's character was the construction of the Verrazano-Narrows Bridge (1964) (see "Staten Island," below), linking the Brooklyn neighborhood with Staten Island.

Of the nonresidential work in the Bay Ridge area, the most distinguished by far was the stylish, Modernist Fort Hamilton Veterans' Hospital (Skidmore, Owings & Merrill, 1950), at 800 Poly Place, between Seventh and Fourteenth avenues.[238] Located on a prominent seventeen-acre site facing the Narrows across Shore Parkway, the complex consisted of a seventeen-story, 1,000-bed, 490-foot-long, south-facing superslab as well as a six-story wing, a nurses' residence and a power plant. Gordon Bunshaft, the designer, used punched rather than ribbon windows in the main building, but to emphasize the horizontal he cantilevered reinforced "eyebrows" whose ostensible function was to serve as sunshades. On the north side, a two-level entrance allowed patients to come in at grade and visitors to enter via a broad curved ramp supported on a single arc of columns.

With the commencement of direct subway service to Manhattan after World War I, Coney Island, a stylish seaside resort in the nineteenth century and a popular one-day destination resort in the first decades of the twentieth, became a year-round home for lower-middle-class straphangers. But the area fully came to life only in the summer, when New Yorkers flocked to its beaches and amusements. The Second World War marked Coney Island's apogee as a popular summertime mecca; with long-distance travel made difficult by severe gasoline rationing, the resort's attractions were packed. But the seeds of the area's decline were already being sown. Luna Park, one of Coney Island's most delightful attractions, burned in 1944 and was not rebuilt.[239] And when postwar prosperity made automobile travel affordable for countless New Yorkers who chose to take their summertime pleasures at more exclusive shore points farther from the city, the once democratic Coney Island started to become a resort of last choice, a haven for the least well off. Increasing problems with water pollution did not help; nor did growing tension between whites, blacks and Hispanics. But perhaps most damaging to Coney Island was the neglect and abuse of the area's delicate physical fabric by landholders who converted ragtag summer cottages into year-round housing to reap large financial gain from the wartime housing shortage.[240] As the shortage abated after the war, those who could get better housing did: according to an analysis by the Community Council of Greater New York, Coney Island's population declined from 81,816 in 1950 to 72,792 in 1960, and by the mid-1960s the dilapidated bungalows were largely inhabited by welfare families.[241]

Coney Island's fate as a problem-plagued neighborhood began to be institutionalized in 1954, when the Housing Authority opened its first project there, Gravesend Houses, accommodating 634 low-income families in fifteen seven-story buildings on West Thirty-third Street between Bayview and Neptune avenues, at the gateway of the still exclusive if no longer fashionable private Sea Gate community.[242] Coney Island Houses (Harry M. Prince), located on a seven-acre site bounded by Surf Avenue, the Boardwalk, West Twenty-ninth and West Thirty-second streets, followed two years later.[243] This Housing Authority project increased the scale—accommodating 534 families in five fourteen-story buildings—and cast a fortresslike pall over the area. With each new low-income blockbuster, Coney Island's lighthearted summertime ambience was further compromised. A crucial blow was dealt to the resort in 1965 when George Tilyou's Steeplechase Park (1897; burned and rebuilt, 1907) was closed, its famous horses sold to an amusement firm in Great Britain and its rides dismantled.[244] The only remnant was the framework of the Parachute Jump, which had been brought to Coney Island in 1940 at the close of the New York World's Fair.

By the 1960s Coney Island was becoming a ghetto for the poor and the aged. In 1961, in order to stem the tide of decline, ironically brought about by large-scale redevelopment, the City Planning Commission designated a thirty-one-acre site, bounded by Gravesend Bay, Bayview Avenue, West Thirty-third Street, Neptune Avenue, West Thirty-seventh Street, Polar Street and Seagate Avenue, as a neighborhood conservation area in which special efforts would be made to retain existing viable housing stock and foster the replacement of deteriorated stock with appropriately scaled housing for the middle class. Despite the devastating combination of exploitive absentee landlordism and a massive infusion of institutionalized low-income housing, Coney Island still held some promise as a balanced and desirable year-round community.

Coney Island's worst area, known as the "Gut," was bordered by Ocean Parkway, West Eighth Street, Surf Avenue and the Belt Parkway. Almost overnight, a new residential quarter sprang up here, dominated by three massive projects: Luna Park Houses, Peter Warbasse Houses and Trump Village. Luna Park Houses (1961), a middle-income cooperative housing project sponsored by the Fund for Urban Improvement, a citizens' group, occupied the twenty-four-acre site of the former amusement park, bounded by Neptune Avenue, West Eighth Street, Surf and Stillwell avenues.[245] Housing 2,576 families in five twenty-story buildings, the project was idealistic in its way: the architects, Kelly & Gruzen, adopted the "sidewalk in the sky" concept they had used in their Chatham Green project in lower Manhattan (see chapter 3), but instead of a serpentine slab, Luna Park was a village of towers. The original proposal was for towers with round plans, which would provide maximum isolation of the individual buildings and thereby create a suburban character. But as realized, the towers had a pinwheel-like configuration, with a central stair and elevator core connected to four comparatively isolated apartment slabs by 20-foot-wide, 100-foot-long shared balcony sidewalks.

Peter Warbasse Houses was originally planned in 1957 as the world's largest middle-income cooperative housing project.[246] Sponsored by Abraham Kazan and the nonprofit United Housing Foundation, the project was to consist of 5,200 apartments in twelve twenty-story buildings on a sixty-five-acre site bounded by Shore Parkway, Ocean Parkway, Seabreeze Avenue, Sheepshead Bay Road, West Fifth and West Eighth streets. Borough President Cashmore opposed the project because, he said, it was unfair to private developers forced to pay full taxes. The developer Fred Trump proposed an alternate plan, a similarly sized complex for the site that would include both cooper-

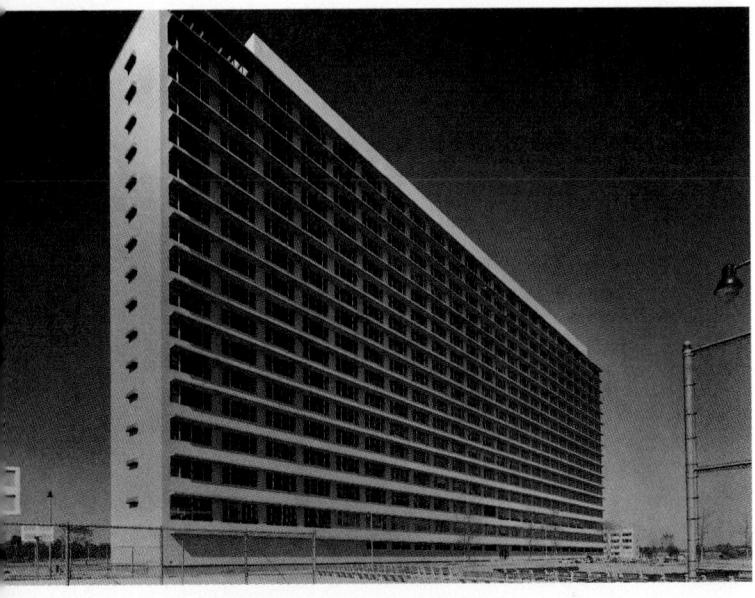

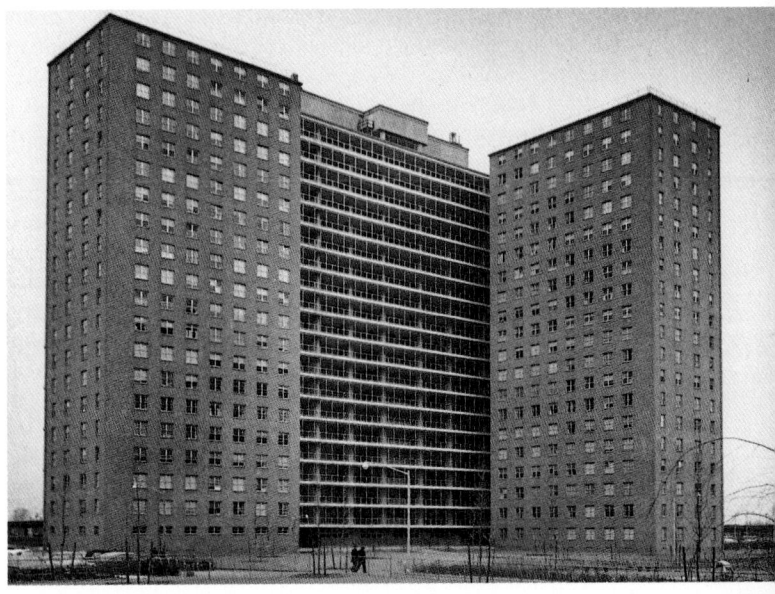

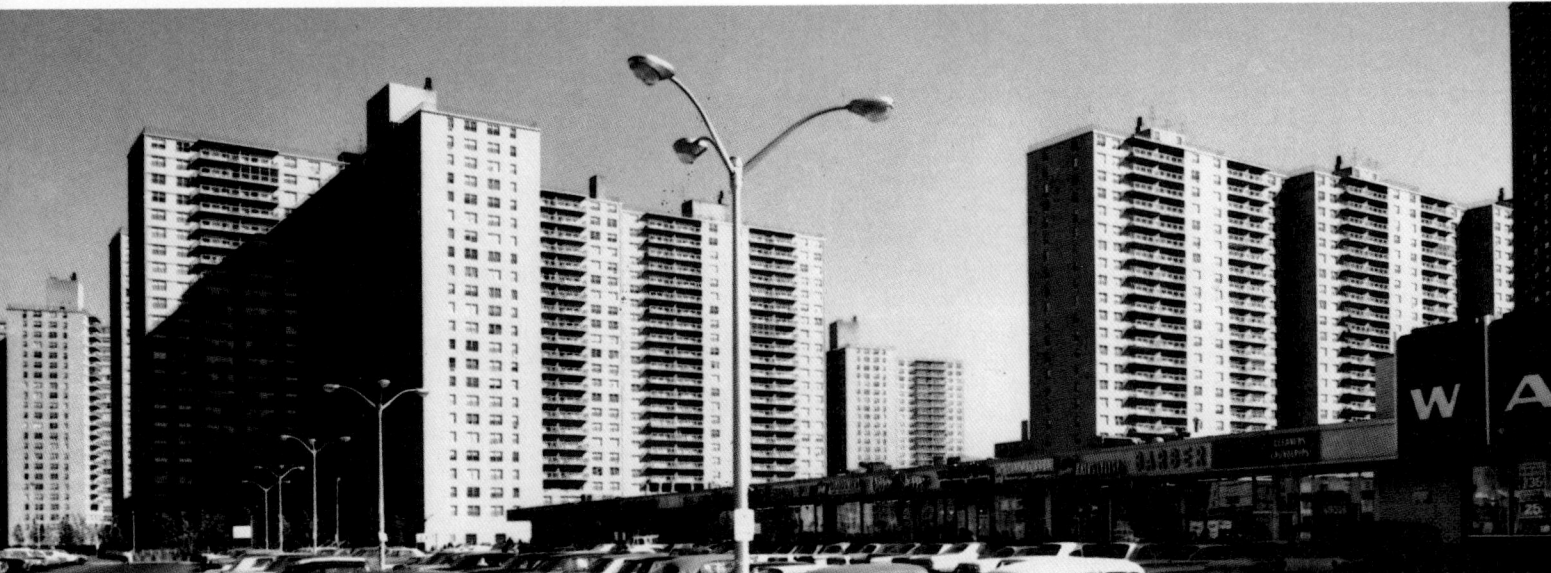

Top left: Fort Hamilton Veterans' Hospital, 800 Poly Place, between Seventh and Fourteenth avenues, Bay Ridge. Skidmore, Owings & Merrill, 1950. View to the northeast. Wurts. MCNY

Top right: Luna Park Village, bounded by Neptune and Surf avenues, West Eighth and West Twelfth streets, Coney Island. Kelly & Gruzen, 1961. Zimbel. GS

Bottom: Trump Village, bounded by Neptune Avenue, Ocean Parkway, Seabreeze Avenue, West Fifth Street, Sheepshead Bay Road, West Eighth Street and Shell Road, Coney Island. Morris Lapidus, Kornblath, Harle & Liebman, 1964. View to the southeast. ML

ative and rental apartments and would provide a greater tax return for the city, although tenants' costs would be substantially higher.

After two years of squabbling over the two proposals, a compromise was reached late in 1959 and the site was divided. The United Housing Foundation was given the twenty-five-acre site north of the newly rerouted Neptune Avenue, which now divided the two parcels. Bounded by Shell Road, Shore Parkway, West Fifth Street, West Avenue, Ocean Parkway and Neptune Avenue, Peter Warbasse Houses (Herman Jessor, 1964) consisted of five twenty-four-story buildings containing 2,585 cooperative apartments. Occupying the southern, forty-acre site, bounded by Neptune Avenue, Ocean Parkway, Seabreeze Avenue, West Fifth Street, Sheepshead Bay Road, West Eighth Street and Shell Road, was Trump Village (Morris Lapidus, Kornblath, Harle & Liebman, 1964), which was built under the state's Mitchell-Lama program.[247] Here 3,800 families were housed in seven twenty-three-story, bland red-brick buildings, two of which were devoted to rentals. Both Warbasse Houses and Trump Village had their own shopping centers.

In 1966 Lapidus, working for Trump, proposed a three-level amusement and parking center to be built between the Boardwalk and Surf Avenue, extending from West Tenth to West Seventeenth Street.[248] The superscaled pleasure dome, with a vaulted 160-foot-high roof of metal-ribbed plastic, was to cover seven acres. The scheme, which also included housing, met with resistance from the local business community and was not realized.

In 1967 the Lindsay administration called for the designation of an urban renewal area in Coney Island, but no real progress was made until 1969, when it was taken over by the New York State Urban Development Corporation as one of its three principal projects in New York City, along with Roosevelt Island (see chapter 8) and Twin Parks (see "The Bronx," below). The UDC's leader, Edward J. Logue, moved swiftly, commissioning a number of "vest-pocket" and medium-sized projects whose goal was to eradicate areas of decay without overwhelming the neighborhood as a whole. Norval White and Elliot Willensky may have been hyperbolic in their assertion that these projects were "risk-taking experiments in quality urban design" that had not been "matched by the New York City Housing Authority since early glories at Williamsburg Houses and Harlem River Houses," but it was true that during the early 1970s Coney Island was in many ways one of the most closely watched areas in the city.[249]

Hoberman & Wasserman were the architects most closely associated with the Coney Island experiments. Their megastructural Sea Rise I (1976), occupying a two-parcel, 3.3-acre site between Neptune and Canal avenues, West Thirty-third and West Thirty-seventh streets, was the best of the developments built in Coney Island.[250] Its stepped silhouette and cranked plan of continuous slabs, clad in precast concrete, offered a lively and refreshing alternative to the monotonous formula of towers-in-the-park public housing. Yet the extreme height of the building and the bold scale of the tower slabs wreaked havoc with the context and raised the usual problems associated with low-income, high-rise living. But because by the 1960s most public housing projects had become so out of touch with their surroundings, this scheme was seen as an important step toward integrating new public construction with the older fabric of Coney Island. As Charles Hoyt observed: "As opposed to the City's earlier projects, the building was brought forward to the street for as much

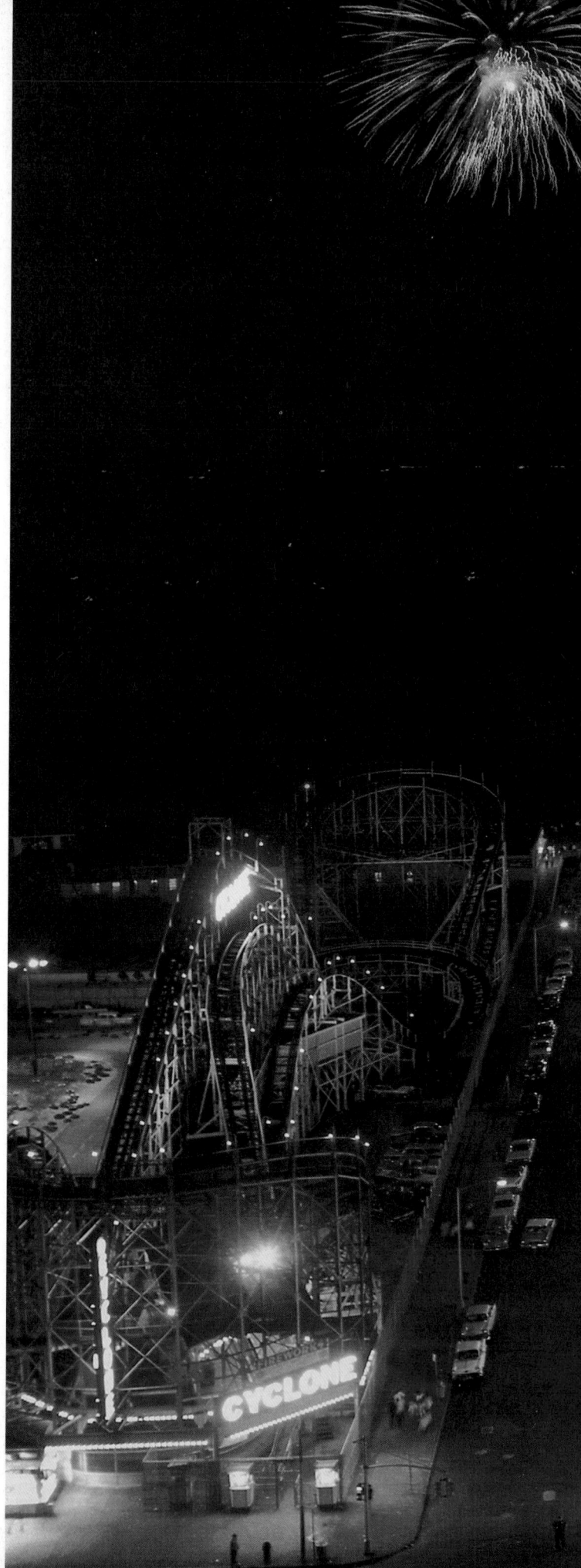

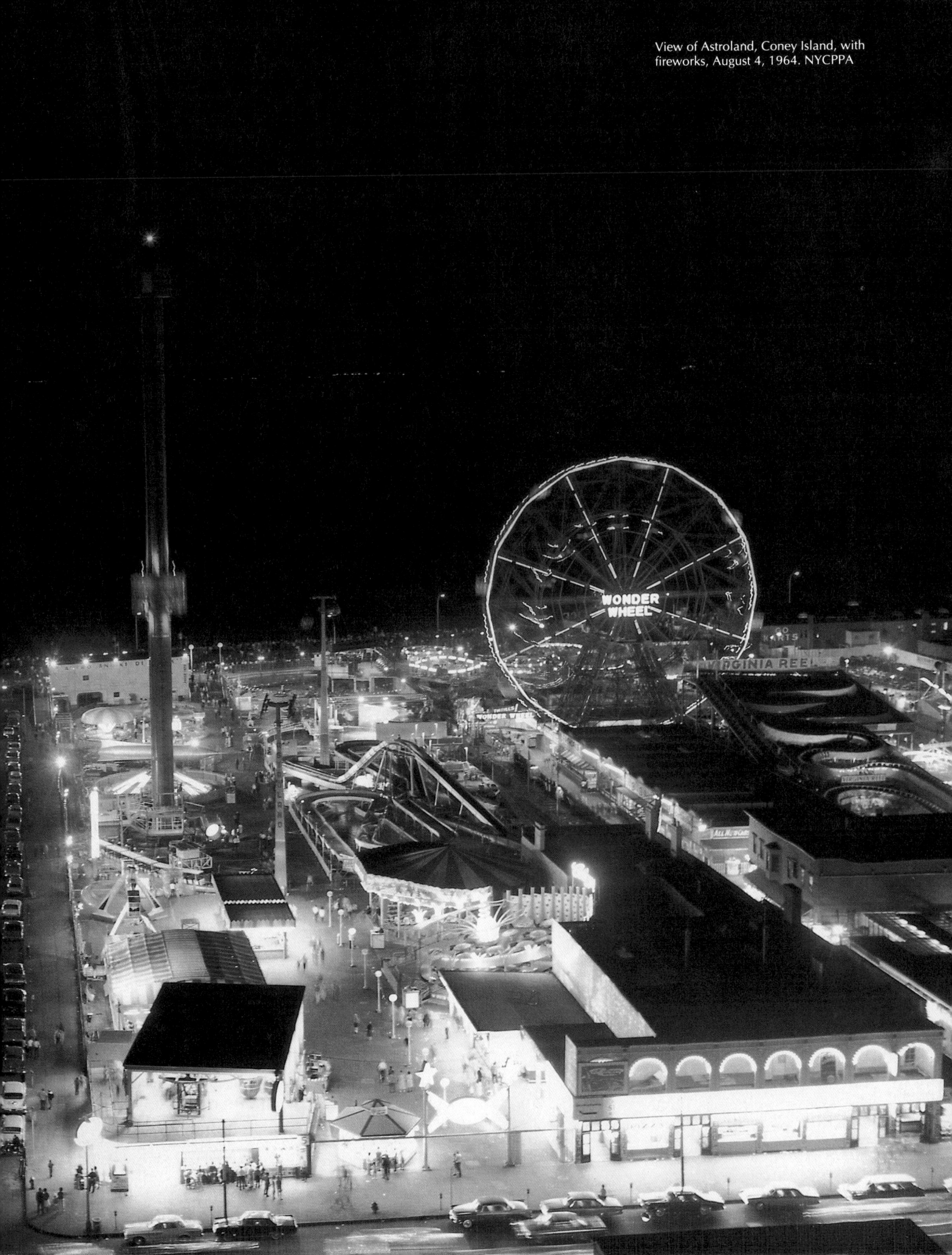

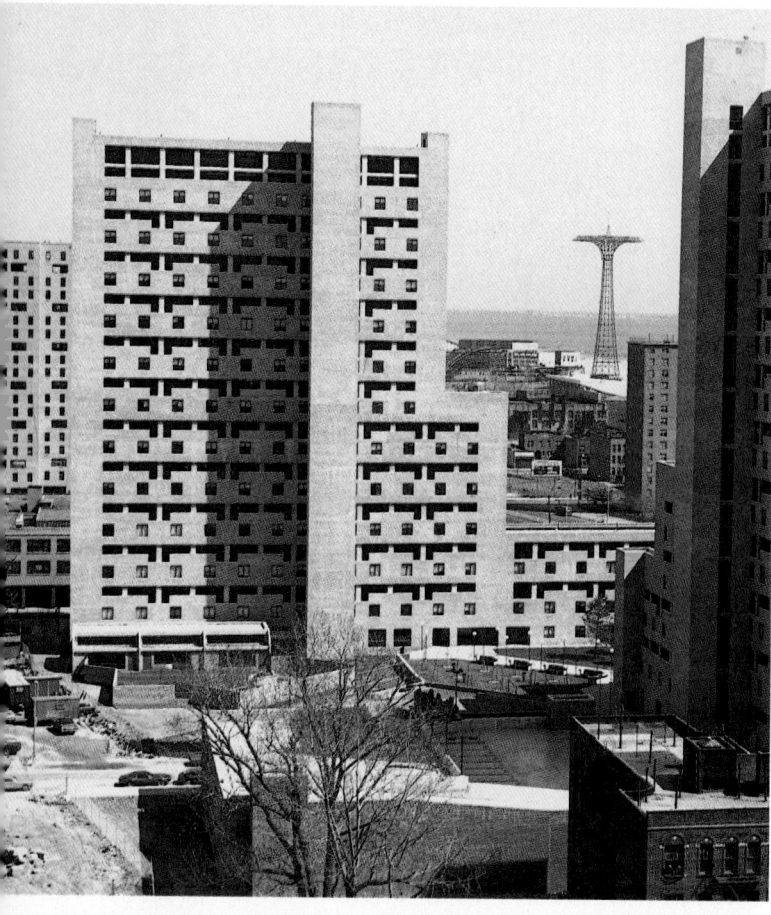

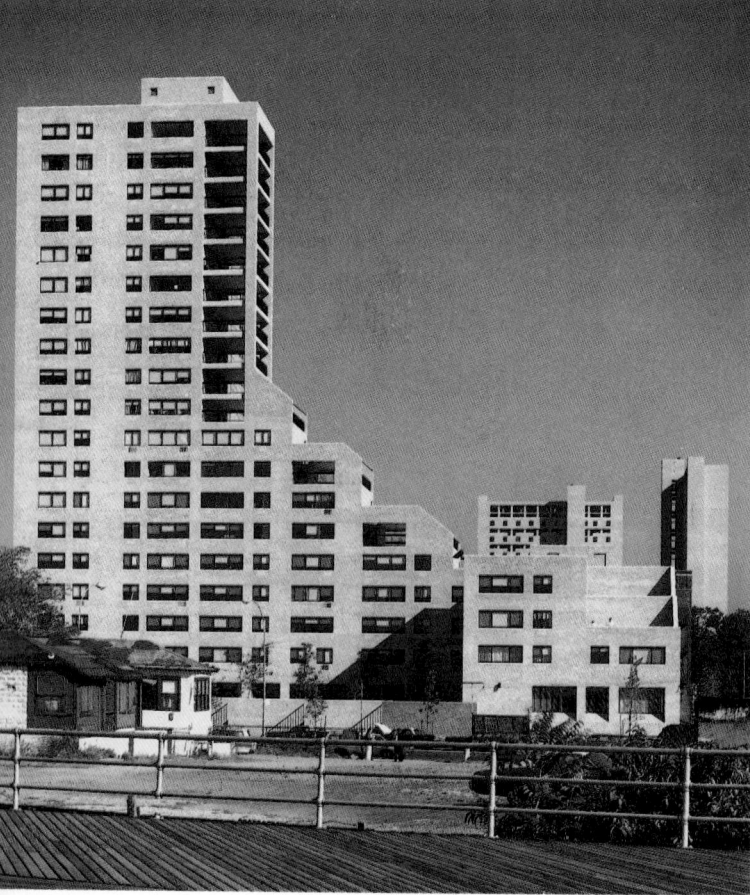

of its length as possible. A sense of 'urban-space' created by compressed human activities and heightened interaction was encouraged on the public sidewalk, while the interior of the site was defined as space for the residents."[251]

Hoberman & Wasserman also undertook two other projects in Coney Island: Site 4A, later called Sea Park East (1975), on the north side of Surf Avenue between West Twenty-seventh and West Twenty-ninth Streets,[252] and Site 9, called Scheuer House (1975), a rent-subsidized apartment house for the elderly on Surf Avenue between West Thirty-sixth and West Thirty-seventh streets, adjacent to Sea Gate.[253] Like the architects' other Coney Island work, Scheuer House was a cranked, continuous slab, stepped in profile, with communal balconies on each floor similar to those in Luna Park Village. It also incorporated extensive community facilities, including a cafeteria, a crafts room, a library and space for the visiting nurses who handled the needs of the elderly living in the building as well as in the surrounding neighborhood. Scheuer House was only a partial success; as Norval White and Elliot Willensky pointed out in 1978, the "stepped terraces are empty: the residents wilfully cluster about the trafficked streets below where the action is, rather than where the architects assigned them space."[254]

Like Hoberman & Wasserman, other architects who tackled projects in Coney Island seemed unwilling or unable to develop a vocabulary of details that related to the small-scale architecture of the surrounding neighborhoods. Skidmore, Owings & Merrill's white concrete apartment towers at 2730 West Thirty-fifth Street (1975), between Bayview and Neptune avenues, had stacks of strongly articulated balconies; White and Willensky characterized the complex as "clever and dull."[255] Skidmore, Owings & Merrill repeated this formula in the high-rise components of two tower and townhouse complexes, one at Sea Park East (1975), a midblock development between West Twenty-eighth and West Twenty-ninth streets, north of Surf Avenue, and another on the south side of Neptune Avenue between West Twenty-fourth and West Twenty-fifth streets (1975).[256] In both cases, Davis, Brody & Associates were responsible for the townhouse sections, which consisted of blocky, coarsely detailed New Brutalist designs in brown brick and exposed concrete.[257] Davis, Brody repeated their formula in a development of townhouses (1975) on the southwest corner of West Thirty-third Street and Bayview Avenue. White and Willensky described the townhouses as "unassuming, understated" and "lovely."[258]

Prentice & Chan, Ohlhausen's Ocean Towers, Surf Avenue between West Twenty-fourth and West Twenty-fifth streets, though less aggressively detailed and visually lighter because it was clad in beige brick, was nevertheless a formidable presence on the Coney Island scene.[259] James Doman & Emil Steo's seven-story buildings at 2920 and 2940 West Twenty-first Street, on the corner of Surf Avenue, were dull but less intrusive.[260]

As a complement to the UDC's housing, the city's Department of Parks, Recreation and Cultural Affairs in 1969 completed Daniel Chait's Abe Stark Center, at West Nineteenth Street and the Boardwalk, a recreational facility that supplemented Coney Island's summertime amenities with an indoor ice-skating rink.[261] Like the UDC's architects, Chait was enamored of hulking scale and brutal details, which made his futuristic design, replete with a saucer dome carried on oversized, Y-shaped buttresses, less than carefree.

Earlier public projects in Coney Island had been more successful. On adjoining sites just north of the Shore Parkway, the city built the Coney Island Hospital and the William E. Grady Vocational High School, both designed by the underappreciated Modernist collaboration of Katz, Waisman, Blumenkranz, Stein, Weber. Grady High School, set on a comparatively spacious site at 25 Brighton Fourth Road, between Brighton Fourth and Brighton Sixth streets, was completed in 1956.[262] The building had a binuclear plan, with a Mies-inspired wing housing classrooms, shops and administration space and a wing accommodating a gym, an auditorium and a cafeteria; a low connector separated the two wings and served as the main entrance. The barrel-vaulted concrete roof spanning the gym provided the building's most memorable feature. Ben Shahn's mosaic mural above the entrance to the gym and the auditorium and Constantino Nivola's cast-concrete bas-relief on the south facade of the gym wing were also important visual contributions to this landmark of cubic Modernism. Coney Island Hospital, designed in association with Andrew J. Thomas, was completed the following year.[263] Located on a ten-acre site at 2601 Ocean Parkway, on the northeast corner of Shore Parkway, it was a 500-bed, 450-foot-long, eleven-story facility. Because the flat, waterlogged site was only a few feet above sea level, preventing the use of cellar areas, the architects placed the utility lines and mechanical equipment below the first-floor slab, where they could be accessed easily for maintenance.

The most notable public institution in Coney Island was the New York Aquarium, located at the Boardwalk, on the northeast corner of West Eighth Street, and occupying two buildings: an exhibition building (Harrison & Abramovitz, 1957),[264] and the Osborn Laboratories of Marine Sciences (Goldstone & Dearborn, 1966).[265] The original aquarium, the first institution of its kind in the United States, had been housed in Castle Clinton in Battery Park and was administered by the New York Zoological Society. According to *Life* magazine, the aquarium had a collection of 12,000 fishes of 450 different species, the largest such collection in the world, and attracted more visitors annually than any other institution in the city.[266] When the aquarium was closed on October 1, 1941, to make way for the construction of the Brooklyn-Battery Tunnel, the exhibition collection was dispersed, although the zoological society kept intact many of the research collections and retained the staff. Although it may have seemed logical to relocate the aquarium to the Bronx, where the zoological society was based, Robert Moses was set on a location on the Coney Island Boardwalk, which the Park Department had taken over in 1938.

Wallace Harrison, whose innovative African Plains installation had opened in 1941 at the zoological society's headquarters, was selected by the society to design the new aquarium.[267] His design for the twelve-acre, oceanfront site Moses had designated was bold and stylish, a long, gently curving single-story building tight against the beach. Nearly five blocks long, the new aquarium was to include a terrace restaurant as well as five dimly lit circular halls. When Harrison, his partner Max Abramovitz and their chief assistant, Harmon Goldstone, were called up for military service, Moses took the opportunity to transfer the project to Aymar Embury II, his favorite architect. But by war's end, the cost of the project had become so high that it was abandoned as unfeasible. In 1954 construction began on a much reduced scheme by Harrison & Abramovitz, and the 216-foot-long, 120-foot-wide New York Aquarium opened to huge crowds three years later. In 1966 the aquarium opened the Osborn Laboratories of Marine Sciences, a research institution. Goldstone & Dearborn's building housed five laboratories in a brick box held in place by a series of folded planes of reinforced concrete.

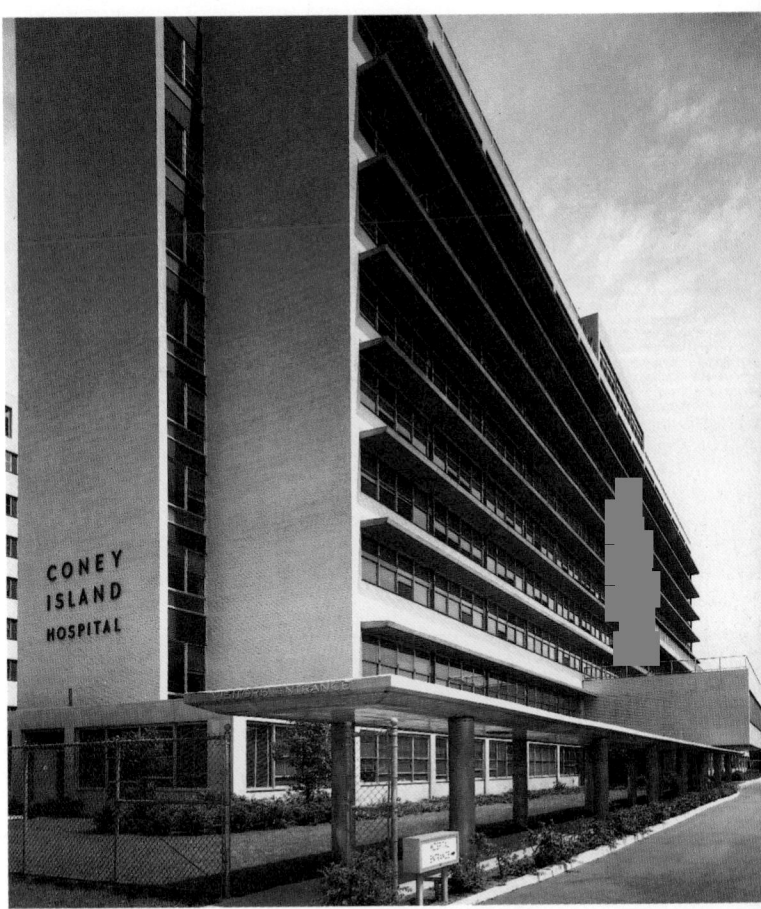

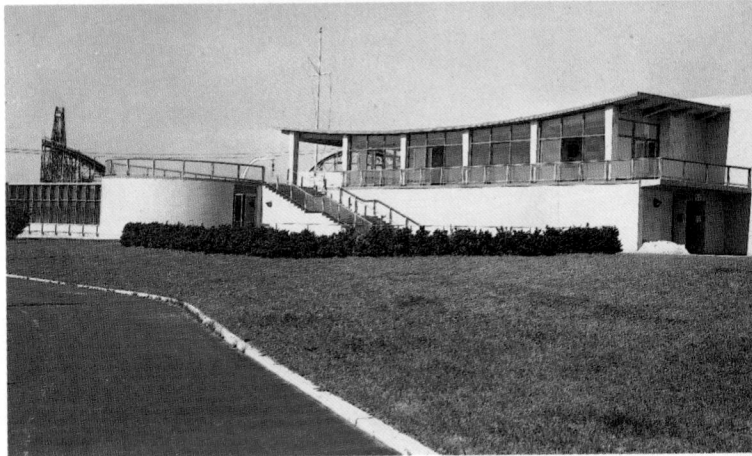

Top left: Sea Park East, north side of Surf Avenue, between West Twenty-seventh and West Twenty-ninth streets, Coney Island. Hoberman & Wasserman, 1975. View to the east. JW

Bottom left: Scheuer House, north side of Surf Avenue, between West Thirty-sixth and West Thirty-seventh streets, Coney Island. Hoberman & Wasserman, 1975. View to the north. JW.

Top: Coney Island Hospital, 2601 Ocean Parkway, northeast corner of Shore Parkway, Coney Island. Katz, Waisman, Blumenkranz, Stein, Weber in association with Andrew J. Thomas, 1957. View to the northeast. Stoller. ©ESTO

Bottom: New York Aquarium, north side of the Boardwalk, northeast corner of West Eighth Street, Coney Island. Harrison & Abramovitz, 1957. View to the northwest. NYZS

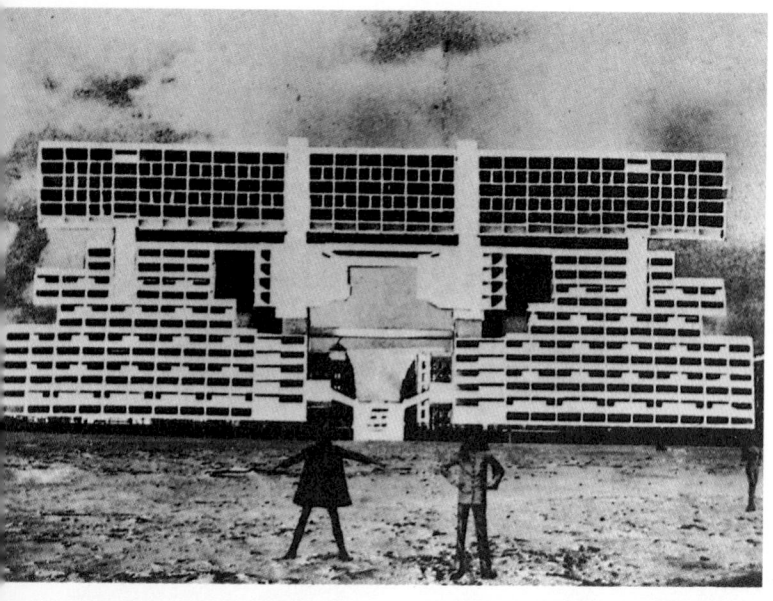

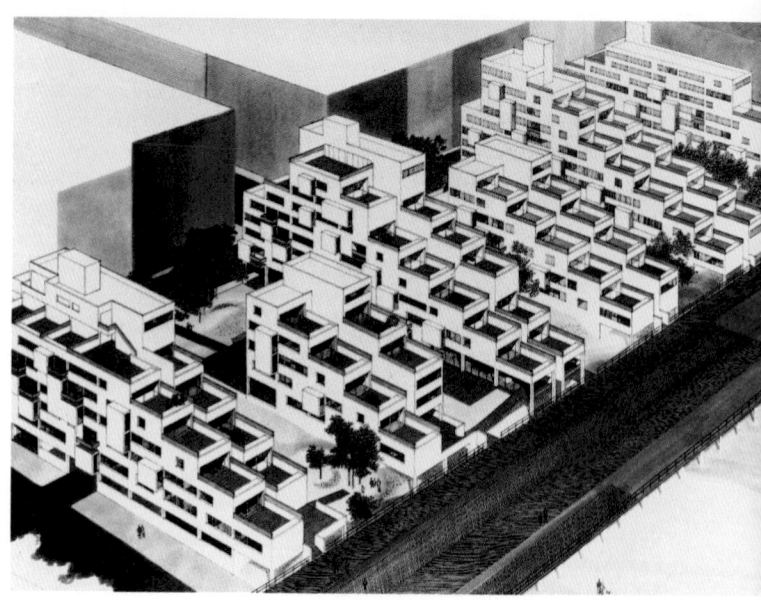

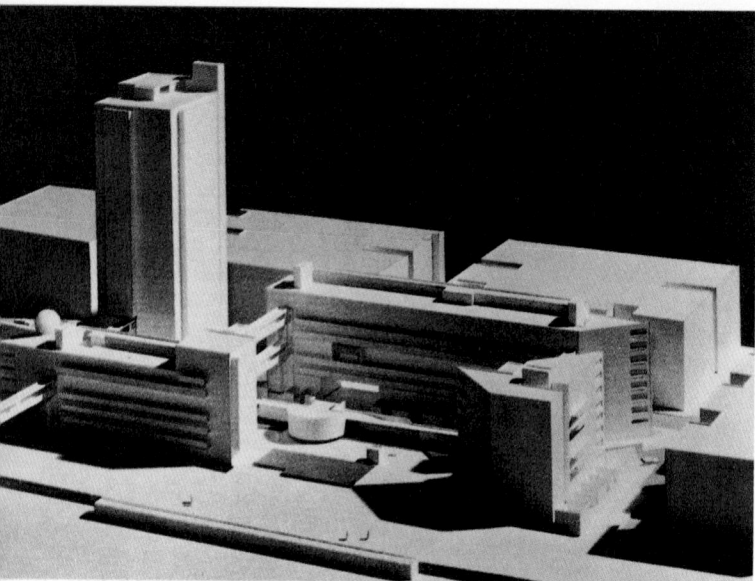

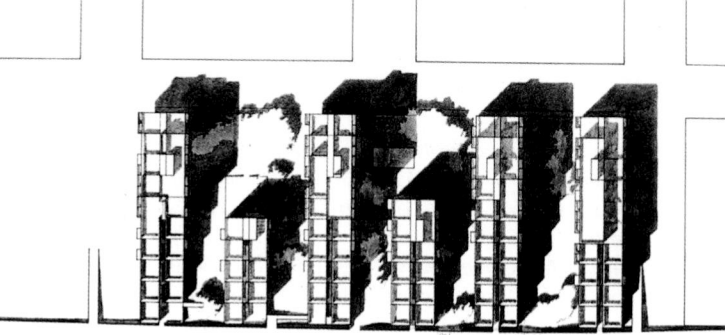

Top left: Entry for Brighton Beach housing competition, bounded by Brighton Second and Brighton Fourth streets, Brightwater Court and the Boardwalk. Abraham W. Geller and Raimond J. Abraham, 1967. Photographic montage showing view to the north. ABGE

Bottom left: Winning entry for Brighton Beach housing competition. Jerry A. Wells and Fred Koetter, 1967. Model. View to the northwest. KKA

Top right: Second-prize entry for Brighton Beach housing competition. Berman, Roberts, Scofidio & Stromsten, 1967. Perspective showing view to the northeast. EKS

Center right: Second-prize entry for Brighton Beach housing competition. Site plan. EKS

Bottom: Third-prize entry for Brighton Beach housing competition. Venturi & Rauch, 1967. Model. View to the northeast. VSBA

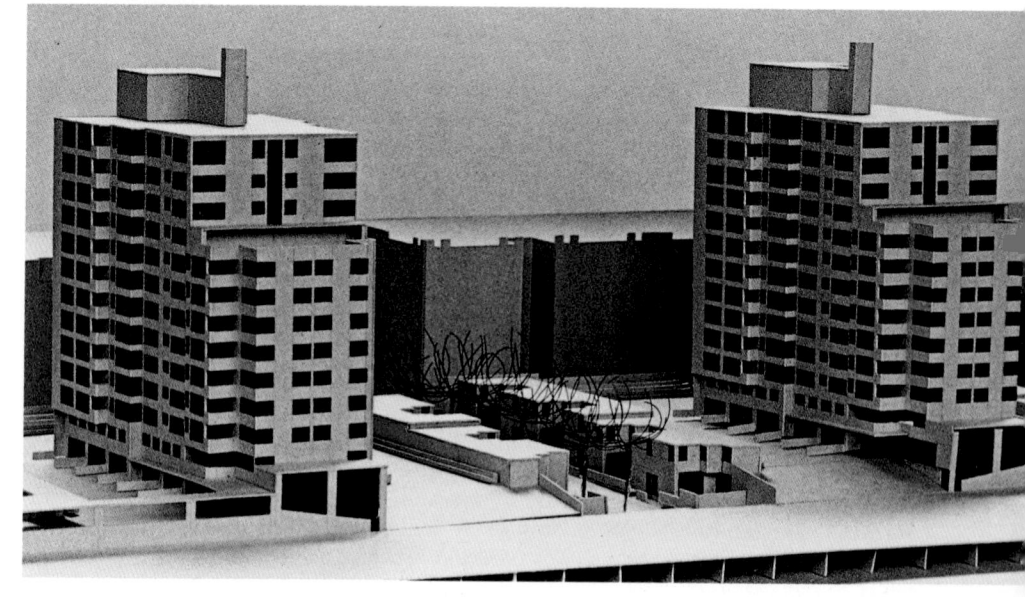

East of Coney Island was Brighton Beach, which, though oriented toward the shore, had no recent associations with amusement parks and honky-tonk; since the First World War it had been a year-round community of modest single and duplex houses and six-story brick-clad apartment houses populated largely by lower-middle-class Jews. In 1967 the city undertook a competition for 300 units of middle-income housing on one of the area's two remaining developable oceanfront sites, bounded by Brighton Second and Brighton Fourth streets, Brightwater Court and the Boardwalk.[268] The competition was spearheaded by Jason R. Nathan, Administrator of the Housing and Development Administration, and shepherded through the bureaucracy by the Assistant for Planning, Design and Research, Samuel Ratensky, a veteran housing and development official who had begun his professional career as one of the first apprentices at Frank Lloyd Wright's Taliesin Fellowship.[269] B. Sumner (Barney) Gruzen, the professional adviser for the competition, assembled a blue-ribbon jury including Ratensky, the planner Charles Abrams, the developer Richard Ravitch and the architects Romaldo Giurgola, Donlyn Lyndon, José Luis Sert and Philip Johnson, who served as its chairman.

The eighty-eight submissions received for the competition offered a fair representation of current thinking: from Miami-for-the-(lower)-middle-class slabs (by architects such as Colasono & Petrides, Butler & Butler and Slater & Salo) to typical towers-in-the-park schemes (Myron Goldfinger, Joshua D. Lowenfish, Danforth W. Toan, Frost Associates and Brown, Guenther, Battaglia & Galvin), from boldly scaled, Corbusian structural grids (Reisner & Loste, Harold Buttrick, Richard D. Kaplan, William Maurer and Neski & Neski) to constructivist assemblages drawing on Paul Rudolph's ideas for using factory-built components in high-rise construction (Poor, Swanke, McKay & Grennan, Patrick Raspante and Sidney Katz, and O'Connor & Kilham). A number of schemes carried this last approach to an extreme of megastructural simplemindedness, including proposals by Sidney M. Shelov, Barry Jackson and Jack P. Coble. Abraham W. Geller, working with Raimond J. Abraham, went the furthest in this direction, proposing twin gridded, sculpturally massed slabs carrying a great Corbusian "egg-crate" to form a triumphal arch at heroic scale. William F. Pedersen, working with Hanford Yang, Fred Bookhardt and Stephen Sanders, reinvigorated the courtyard-apartment type, proposing twin palazzo blocks flanking Brighton Third Street and incorporating circular, interior open spaces. Thomas Killian, working with Michael McCarthy, proposed a single five-story building punctuated by two courtyards, one square and one nearly circular, both opening onto the Boardwalk to increase the number of windows with ocean views.

The winning scheme, by Jerry A. Wells and Fred Koetter, two Cornell professors, called for three six-story slabs, cranked to define two open-sided courtyards, and one twenty-five-story, campanilelike tower. Philip Johnson described the scheme as "a rich and satisfying solution," with a particularly successful urban effect: "The massing of the parks seem especially skillful as against many of the entries whose towers stand up at random from a low grouping." Nonetheless, he felt the grandeur of the scheme, suggesting the spaces at San Marco, might overwhelm the existing apartment buildings, which would also be deprived of their ocean views by the complex; Johnson proposed that when the buildings were realized, the tower "may have to be lowered." In terms of the design itself, Johnson said it had "hardly any innovative features" and "could have been designed at any time in the past 15 years,

but its excellence in the handling of the grammar of our time is praiseworthy."[270]

The second prize went to Berman, Roberts, Scofidio & Stromsten, a loose affiliation of architects created for the competition. Their scheme consisted of six parallel, stepped-back slabs set perpendicular to the ocean, a rationalized version of the hillside vernacular of Italy and Greece as seen through the lens of Le Corbusier. Not surprisingly, this entry was favored by José Luis Sert, whose own work it resembled. He described his impressions in a letter to Jason Nathan: "The second prize winner does not pretend to be monumental, it fits well into the existing neighborhood, and the modest scale of the units is well expressed in the composition. The outdoor spaces are very pleasant, and these together with the private balconies and their view of the sea are appropriate. . . . Of all the projects considered, this one in particular offers the most appropriate and new solution to the conditions of the problem."[271] The *parti* of this scheme would be adopted in Coney Island by Sert's former students Norman Hoberman and Joseph Wasserman (see above), and Sert himself would use it for his buildings on Roosevelt Island (see chapter 8).

Third prize went to the Philadelphia-based firm Venturi & Rauch, who proposed two parallel slabs placed perpendicular to the Boardwalk to ensure maximum ocean views for the new apartments but a minimal blocking of views for tenants in the existing buildings framing the site. Along the former right-of-way, Brighton Third Street, the architects introduced a midblock pedestrian walk lined by two-story townhouses. Johnson reported to Nathan that, along with Abrams, Sert and Ratensky, he felt that the Venturi & Rauch buildings "looked like the most ordinary apartment construction built all over Queens and Brooklyn since the Depression, that the placing of the blocks was ordinary and dull." He continued: "The forms that the buildings took were, in our eyes, deliberately ugly. There were some obvious merits: the town houses set around the cul-de-sac of the street, and the extension of the boardwalk surrounding the base building. But these minor virtues seemed to us overwhelmed by the all pervading ugliness."[272]

The other jury members—Giurgola, Lyndon and Ravitch—felt differently. In a letter to Nathan, written as a response to Johnson's majority report, Giurgola explained his point of view, arguing with the very notion of "'beauty' and 'ugliness,' words which are used extensively in the Chairman's report to establish sides":

Of course everyone is for beauty; who is against it? Only beauty is a relative value, not less nor more than the solution of practical arrangement. Beauty becomes an incomprehensible abstraction when it is separated from the world of life—from the world of everyday life that is. . . . In fact, shouldn't beauty be intended as a coherent development of a way of life? Shouldn't its form fit the human habit and rely on the simple, dignified and clear statement of human purpose rather than any abstract gesture?[273]

Donlyn Lyndon, in his letter to Nathan, said that the Venturi & Rauch proposal had "a modesty that is appropriate to the scale and location of the project." He explained:

The scheme does not detract from or demean the surrounding neighborhood. It respects, but is not bound by the existing order. . . . In our view it offers real benefits for the people who might occupy it rather than polemical satisfaction to those who consider it. . . . The method of building is intrinsically so simple that it could be built well, not meanly. We think this would contribute to the personal dignity of its occupants. . . . Especially we feel that the public spaces have been very well handled—in a way that provides tangible benefits to those people whom you would expect to be there.

In conclusion, Lyndon said: "This scheme seems a well ordered, carefully considered and appropriate response to the conditions of the problem. Nor is the form unrelated to the efforts of many of our contemporaries in the arts to find new relevance in forms to which the public has become accustomed. In short, we think the Venturi and Rauch scheme is relevant, skillful and humane."[274] None of the Brighton Beach competition proposals were built.

East of Brighton Beach, on the peninsula bounded by Sheepshead Bay and the Atlantic Ocean, was Manhattan Beach, an upper-middle-class enclave of spacious single-family houses, mostly built in the 1910s and 1920s. One notable postwar single-family dwelling was the Lustbader house (Breger & Salzman, 1950), at 220 Corbin Place, a one-story wood building located on an imaginatively landscaped 50-by-100-foot corner lot.[275] The Naval Training Station, located at the peninsula's tip, was active during World War II but was abandoned in the 1950s. In 1968 its site became home to Kingsborough Community College of the City University of New York, which commissioned Katz, Waisman, Weber, Strauss to lay out a master plan.[276] But because the plan did not impose a common language on the architects hired to design the various buildings— aside from the Katz firm, these included Lundquist & Stonehill; Warner, Burns, Toan & Lunde; and James Stewart Polshek—the campus lacked coherence. Polshek's Health and Physical Education Building (1969) was by far the boldest structure on the new campus.[277] It was organized along a square that separated in two levels the large spaces of the program (the gymnasium, squash courts and dance studios) from the more secure or private areas (the pool, offices, classrooms and locker rooms). The design, evocative of an ocean liner, employed exposed structural and environmental systems, bold colors and industrial detailing in a way that, as the architect put it, "distinguishes this structure from its neighbors without offending them."[278]

North and east of Manhattan Beach was the town of Flatlands, established in 1666 and annexed to the City of Brooklyn in 1896. Its inland portion was developed early in the century, largely as neighborhoods of one- and two-family houses interspersed with small apartment houses. One building that would have made a notable contribution to the Flatlands area was unfortunately not built. In 1944 a two-story truck garage for the Brooklyn Division of the Department of Sanitation, Districts 47 and 48, was planned for a site on East Forty-ninth Street between Avenue N and Avenue O.[279] The design, by Antonin Raymond, featured extensive glazing with continuous ribbons of industrial sash and promised to be a highly successful exemplar of the straightforward factory aesthetic so important to Modernism. Its precedents were the pre–World War I work of Peter Behrens for the AEG in Berlin, the industrial architecture of the Taut Brothers and Mies van der Rohe in Germany in the 1920s and 1930s and the structures Albert Kahn designed for various automobile companies in and near Detroit in the 1930s and early 1940s. As Pencil Points observed when it published Raymond's drawings for the project, although "efficient storage and servicing of a city department's trucks is an architectural-engineering problem more often handled by rote than with creative imagination," this design "jumps well out of the category of the 'routine' into the realm of progressive architecture."[280]

Thirty years later in his autobiography, Raymond, who could not recall whether it was built or not, did remember that the garage was "not a very inspiring job, but . . . I made a valiant effort for efficiency, simplicity and economy."[281]

Until World War II the shorefront areas of Flatlands, the Carnarsie section, remained in their natural state as tidal wetlands facing Jamaica Bay, but with the designation of Marine Park in 1933 and the completion of the Shore Parkway in 1941, the remote Canarsie shore, which had served as a sewage and sanitation dump, became more easily accessible, better known and, therefore, ripe for development. In 1955 the New York Times reported that "Canarsie, once known only as a lame vaudeville gag," was now the site of "hundreds of one and two-family homes . . . sprouting faster than the tall grass to give middle income groups a new foothold within the subway zone. Some real estate experts call this outbreak of brick and wood the beginning of the biggest building spree in Brooklyn since the Twenties."[282] Along the shore, the Park Department not only developed public beaches but also built the so-called "million dollar pier," a recreational facility at the foot of Rockaway Parkway wide enough to accommodate hundreds of parked cars.

In addition to market-rate houses, some public housing was built, including William I. Hohauser's thirty-building, 1,595-unit Breukelen Houses (1952), Flatlands, Williams and Stanley avenues, East 108th Street, Farragut Road, East 105th Street, Glenwood Road and East 103rd Street.[283] More notable was Katz, Waisman, Blumenkranz, Stein, Weber's Bay View Houses (1955), which consisted of twenty-three well-detailed, eight-story slabs occupying 25 percent of a thirty-acre site facing Shore Parkway.[284] The architects developed a site plan that broke the vast project up into four quadrants, each with a playground and sitting areas, and each with its own identifying color—yellow, blue, brown, green—used on balcony columns, glazed brick patterns, lobby trim and signs. Inside, a screened balcony was located opposite the elevator on each floor, the first use of such a "porch" or terrace in any city housing project. Another project, Fillmore Gardens (Seelig & Finkelstein), Fillmore Avenue between East Fifty-third Street and Avenue T, was an eleven-acre development of seven two-story units housing 346 families, built with a federal subsidy in 1954.[285]

Starrett City (1976) was a megadevelopment designed by Herman Jessor, the architect of Co-op City in the Bronx (see "The Bronx," below).[286] It housed 5,881 families in forty-six tan-brick buildings ranging from eleven to twenty stories, all set on a 153-acre site bounded by Shore Parkway and Miller, Louisiana and Vandalia avenues. The project was originally planned and developed in 1967 by the United Housing Foundation as a middle-income cooperative called Twin Pines Village. But in 1972, after delays made the cost of construction prohibitive, new developers, the Starrett Housing Corporation and the National Kinney Corporation, took over, keeping the basic physical plan but turning the project into a rental development. Built under guidelines set by the state's Mitchell-Lama housing subsidy program, and with an additional federal subsidy, the development was ready for its first tenants in November 1974. The complex included a 100,000-square-foot recreation center, a shopping mall, medical facilities, two schools, plants to supply its own heat and electricity, and parking for 4,500 cars. Due to the proximity of Kennedy Airport, double-glazed windows were provided.

With the neighborhood's development came schools, libraries and religious buildings, but few of them had any architectural distinction. One exception was William Breger's Sea-

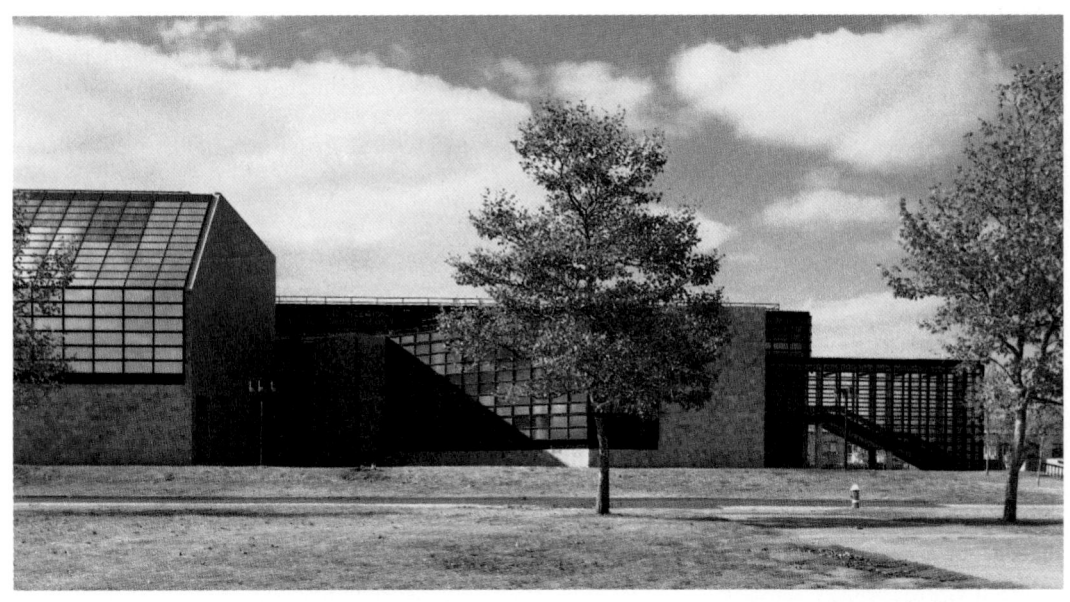

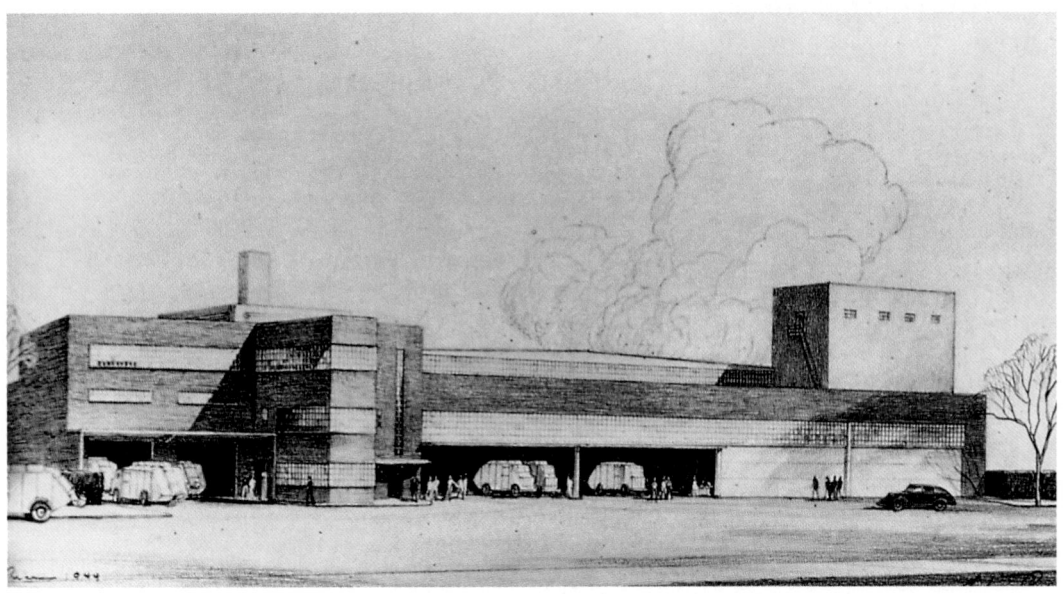

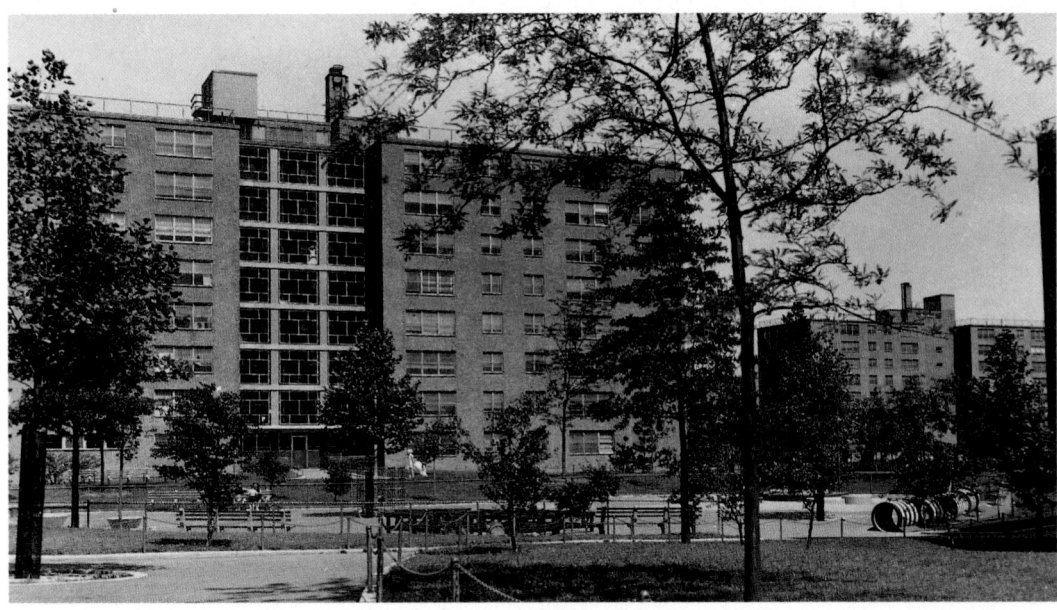

Top: Health and Physical Education Building, Kingsborough Community College of the City University of New York, Manhattan Beach. James Stewart Polshek, 1969. View to the northwest. JSP

Center: Garage for Brooklyn Division of the Department of Sanitation, Districts 47 and 48, East Forty-ninth Street, between avenues N and O, Flatlands. Antonin Raymond, 1944. Rendering. PP. CU

Bottom: Bay View Houses, Rockaway Parkway to East 102nd Street, Seaview Avenue to Canarsie Road, Canarsie. Katz, Waisman, Blumenkranz, Stein, Weber, 1955. NYCHA

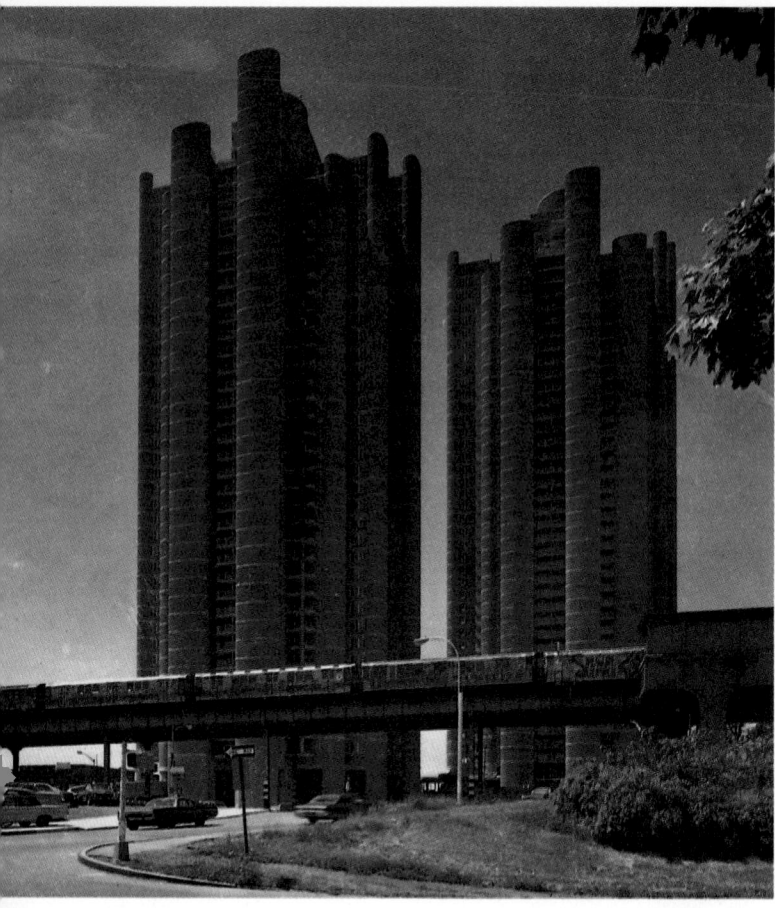

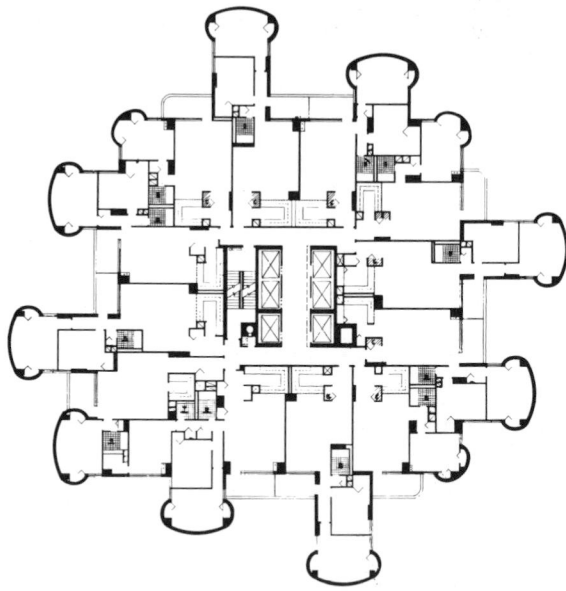

Top: Tracey Towers, 20 and 40 West Mosholu Parkway, southwest corner of Jerome Avenue, Kingsbridge Heights. Paul Rudolph in association with Jerald L. Karlan, 1974. View to the southwest. Cunningham-Werdnigg. PR

Bottom: Tracey Towers. Plan. PR

Right: Master plan for Harlem River Park, between the Harlem River and the Major Deegan Expressway, Washington and University Heights bridges, Morris Heights. M. Paul Friedberg & Associates, 1970. Site plan. DBA

view Jewish Center (1972), an improbably stylish synagogue set amid modest bungalows.[287] The white stucco-covered basilica included a "nave" rising to a continuous barrel vault lighted by an oculus inscribed by a Star of David.

The transformation of Canarsie from a laughing stock into a prosperous area seemed complete in 1970 when the city's first auto-oriented shopping center opened at Mill Basin (see chapter 15).

THE BRONX

The Bronx can go on the way it's going for a long time, probably as long as the city can: superficially modernizing, obviously as dowdy as ever, and secretly sick as the city is sick.
—Peter S. Beagle, 1964[1]

The Bronx was part of Westchester County until 1874, when its western portion—including the villages of Port Morris, Morrisania, West Farms and Kingsbridge, as well as rural areas like Riverdale—was annexed to the City of New York. In 1891 this so-called Annexed District was connected to Manhattan by an extension of the Third Avenue El. The Grand Concourse, completed in 1892, was the Bronx's principal north-south connector, paralleling the New York Central Railroad, which ran along Park Avenue. The railroad had nine stations in what would become the borough of the Bronx in 1898, when the remaining portions of the predominantly undeveloped Westchester peninsula were annexed to the City of New York. By World War I the expansion of the IRT subway system had brought with it a network of connecting elevated lines, fanning out from a hub in the Bronx's southwestern corner, which remained the borough's commercial heart until after World War II. In the postwar era the geography and sociology of the Bronx was radically redefined by the construction of the Cross-Bronx Expressway (1946–63), which divided the south from the north, and the construction of the Bronx River Parkway extension (1951), which divided the east from the west. By the 1970s there were at least two Bronxes: the middle-class, largely white neighborhoods east of the Bronx River Parkway and in the northwestern part of the borough, and the increasingly black and Hispanic lower-class neighborhoods in the lower portion of the former Annexed District, which came to be known as the South Bronx, a collection of neighborhoods lumped together in the public mind as a single troubled area.

West Bronx

In the late 1930s and early 1940s the West Bronx reached its apogee as a setting for respectable lower-middle-class urban life, with densely developed neighborhoods that stretched out north to south between the Harlem River and the eastern slopes below the Grand Concourse. North of Fordham Road many new apartment houses were built in the 1930s; in their stylish streamlined modernity, these buildings were a kind of year-round, northern equivalent of the small winter resort hotels being built at about the same time in Miami Beach, Florida.[2] There was little new construction in the West Bronx in the immediate postwar era, which was not surprising given its density and seeming stability.

One exception was Fordham Hill Village, a 1,118-family middle-class project built on an 8.5-acre site at Sedgwick and Webb avenues that had been home to the Webb Institute of Naval

Architecture.[3] Developed by the Equitable Life Assurance Society and its architects, Leonard Schulze & Associates, Fordham Hill consisted of nine sixteen-story towers grouped around a central landscaped space loosely defined as an oval. Though the buildings were bland, their light yellow brick constituted a positive break with the red brick used throughout the neighborhood. Furthermore, the cluster of towers on the prominent site above the Harlem River gave the neighborhood of low buildings—most of them six stories or less—a visual lift; perhaps because of the towers' floor plans, with their strong corner projections, based in part on upper Manhattan's Castle Village (George F. Pelham, Jr., 1938), they even provided an air of romance.[4]

Aside from Fordham Hill Village and the occasional isolated new apartment house along the Grand Concourse, rent control and changing demographics conspired to push the area into economic decline and physical decay.[5] Efforts to maintain or rehabilitate existing housing stock proved only marginally successful. By the late 1960s it was clear to many observers that bold action was necessary, but problems of tenant relocation, among others, seemed insuperable obstacles to any significant contextual redevelopment. As a result, attention was turned to peripheral sites that could support large-scale projects. One such development was Tracey Towers (Paul Rudolph in association with Jerald L. Karlan, 1974), which partially occupied a platform built over the Jerome Subway Yards at Mosholu Parkway.[6] An exuberant departure from the typical red-brick slabs financed by the Mitchell-Lama program, many of which formed the new landscape of Bruckner Boulevard in the southeast Bronx, Tracey Towers was perhaps New York's ultimate example of futuristic design.

The developer, Frederick De Matteis, suggested the configuration of twin round towers, an idea presumably inspired by Bertrand Goldberg's Marina City (1964) in Chicago.[7] But Rudolph, who designed the project in 1967, balked at the pie-shaped rooms that would result from a round plan and instead devised a cluster of seemingly extruded vertical elements, some of them curved, which would give the illusion of a round tower while permitting essentially rectangular rooms. In a way, the plan was an exaggerated version of Schulze's scheme for Fordham Hill, but to heighten the sense of a round shaft Rudolph emphasized solid walls over glass. The result was individual apartments that were dark, although, unlike units in typical slabs, which had only one wall of windows, most apartments at Tracey Towers had at least two and in some cases three exposures. The towers rose dramatically above their surroundings—one tower was forty-one stories high, the other thirty-eight—offering spectacular views over Mosholu Park and the Jerome Park Reservoir and creating an extraordinary presence when seen from afar. Closer up, however, they were bulky, and the vertical flutes that formed the surface of the concrete-block cladding, which Rudolph was forced to use because of its low cost, lacked the visual intricacy of the striated, poured-concrete walls of his Art and Architecture Building (1963) at Yale University.[8] Tracey Towers was particularly remote from ordinary street life: one of the towers was perched on a platform constructed over the train yards; the other rose directly from Mosholu Parkway, from which it was set apart by elaborately curving ramps designed to lift cars to a raised parking deck.

In 1970 the New York State Urban Development Corporation (UDC) released a master plan, prepared by M. Paul Friedberg & Associates, for the redevelopment of a mile-long stretch along the east bank of the Harlem River between the Washington and University Heights bridges, a site that was bounded on

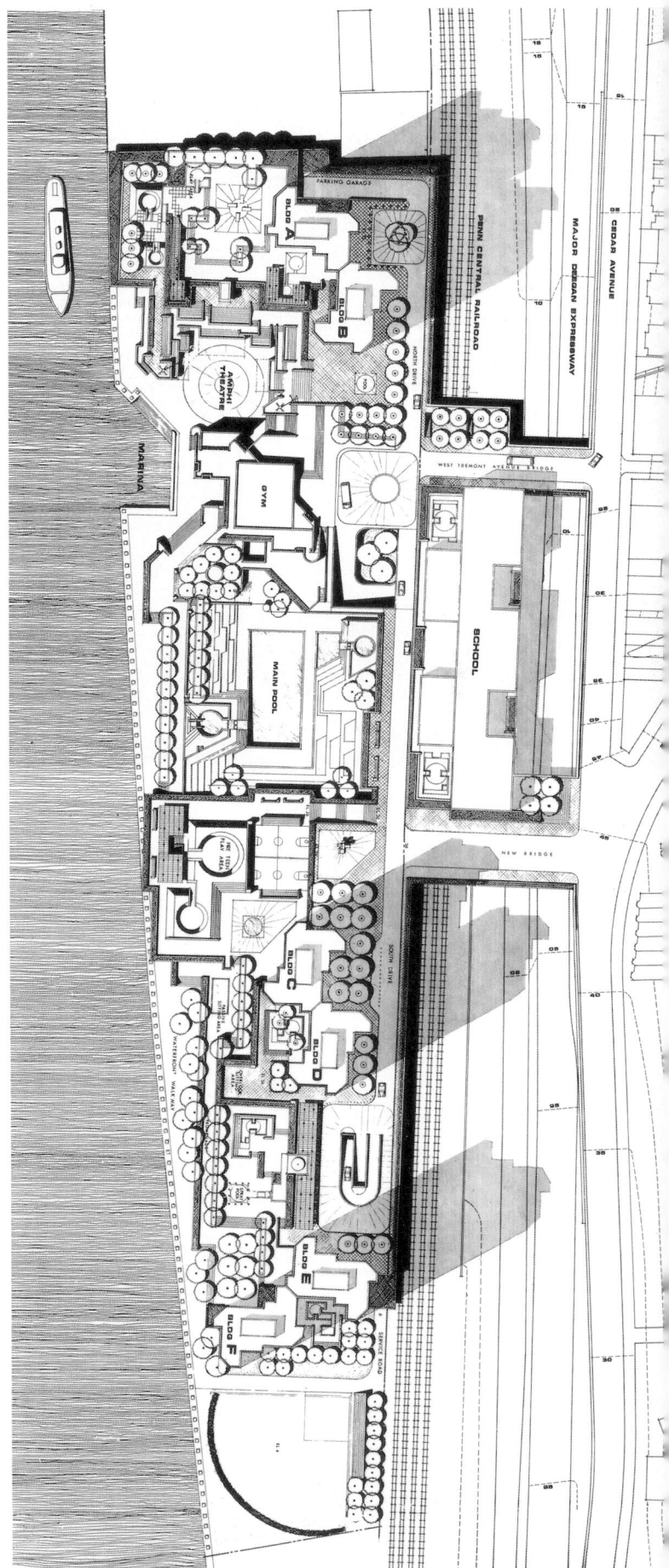

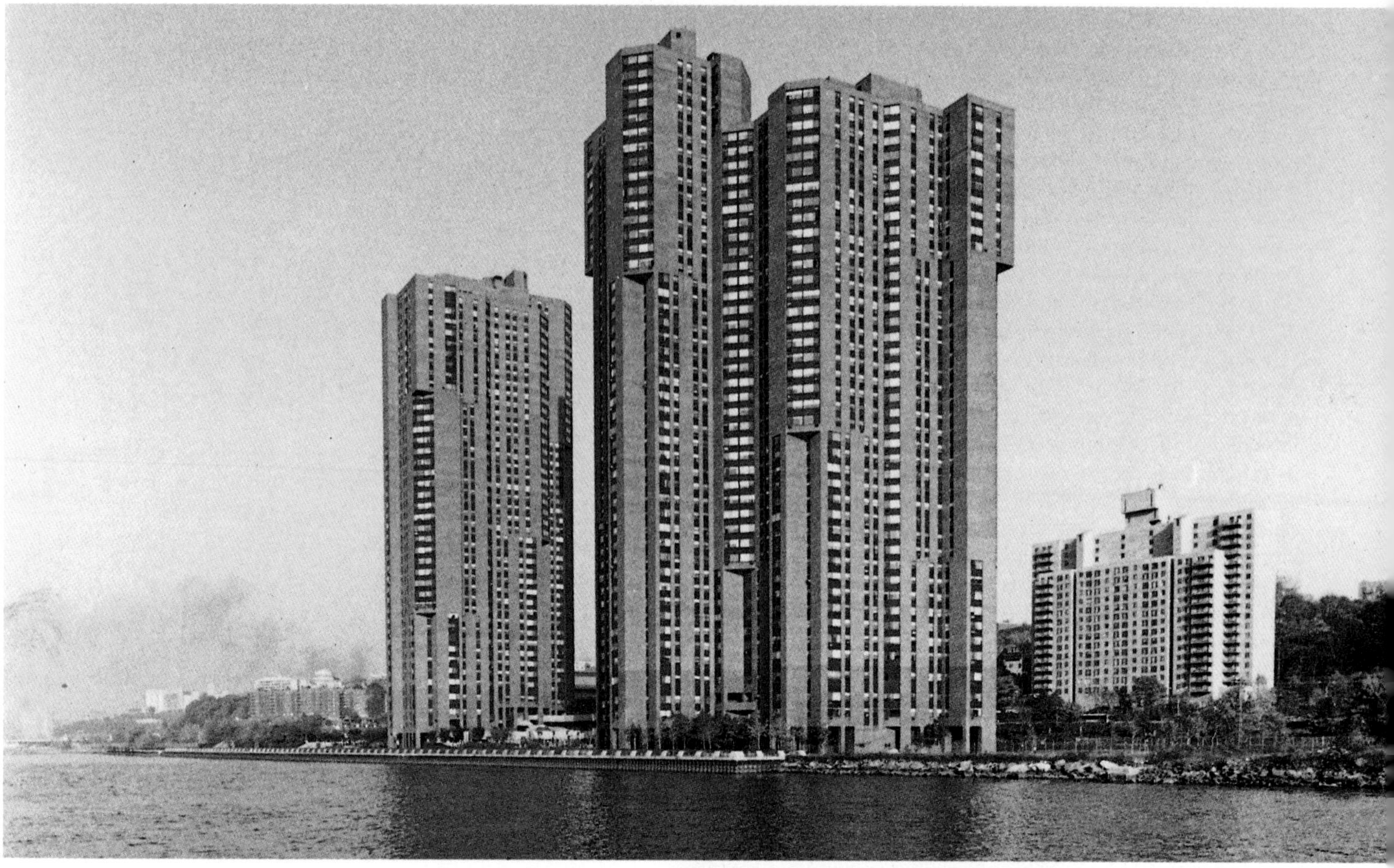

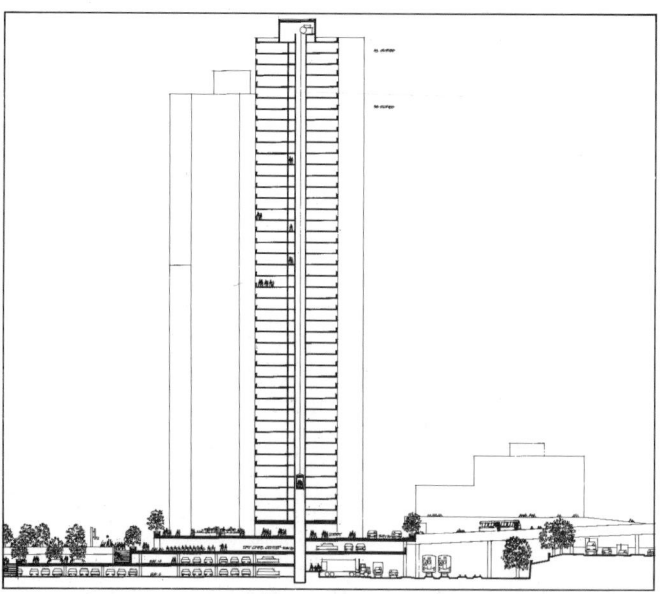

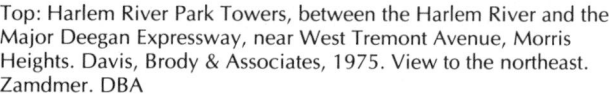

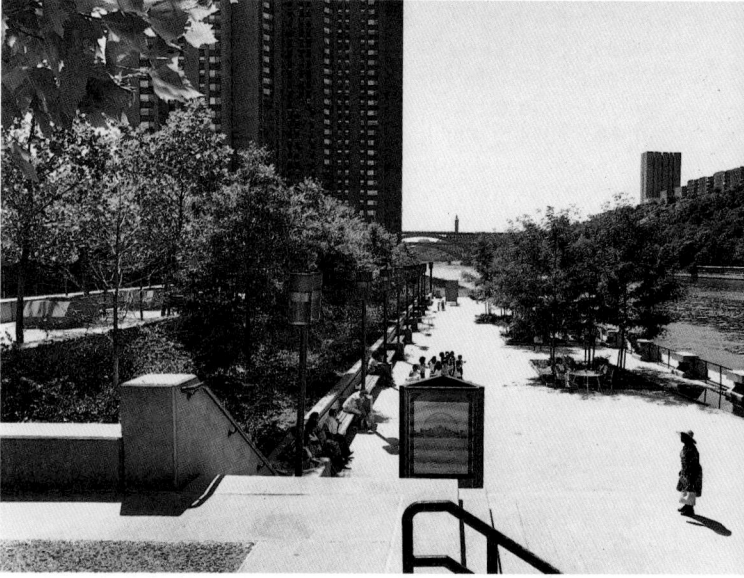

Top: Harlem River Park Towers, between the Harlem River and the Major Deegan Expressway, near West Tremont Avenue, Morris Heights. Davis, Brody & Associates, 1975. View to the northeast. Zamdmer. DBA

Bottom left: Harlem River Park Towers. Section. DBA

Bottom right: Harlem River Bronx State Park (after 1974 Roberto Clemente State Park), between the Harlem River and the Major Deegan Expressway, Washington and University Heights bridges, Morris Heights. M. Paul Friedberg & Associates, 1973. View to the south. MPF

Top far right: Henry L. Moses Research Institute, Montefiore Hospital, 111 East 210th Street, between Kossuth and Bainbridge avenues, Norwood. Philip Johnson, 1965. View to the southwest. Stoller. ©ESTO

Bottom far right: North Central Bronx Hospital, northeast corner of East 210th Street and Kossuth Avenue, Norwood. Carl Pancaldo and Schuman, Lichtenstein & Claman, 1976. View to the south. Rothschild. BR the east by the traffic-clogged Major Deegan Expressway.[9] To develop the plan the UDC worked with the New York State Park Commission for the City of New York, which had recently been formed to provide the city's residents with the kind of state-supported recreational facilities that had hitherto been created only in upstate rural areas. Friedberg's innovative plan would transform a largely derelict waterfront, decked rail yards and highways into an urban park articulated into four principal development areas linked by promenades. The first phase of development—and, as it turned out, the only phase—was a twenty-two-acre site extending from West 176th to West 180th Street, centering on the Tremont Avenue railroad station of the Penn-Central's Putnam line. This park segment, programmed for 3,500 active users plus spectators, was intended to serve the residents of Harlem River Park Towers (see below), as well as citizens drawn from the upland community. Completed in 1973 as the Harlem River Bronx State Park, it featured a recreation building designed by Dean McClure and a waterfront walkway. Regrettably, because of its setting on a platform over the river, the design palette was largely confined to potted planting and the effect was somewhat harsh. The park was later renamed the Roberto Clemente State Park in honor of the Dominican-born baseball star who was killed on New Year's Eve 1972 in an airplane crash.

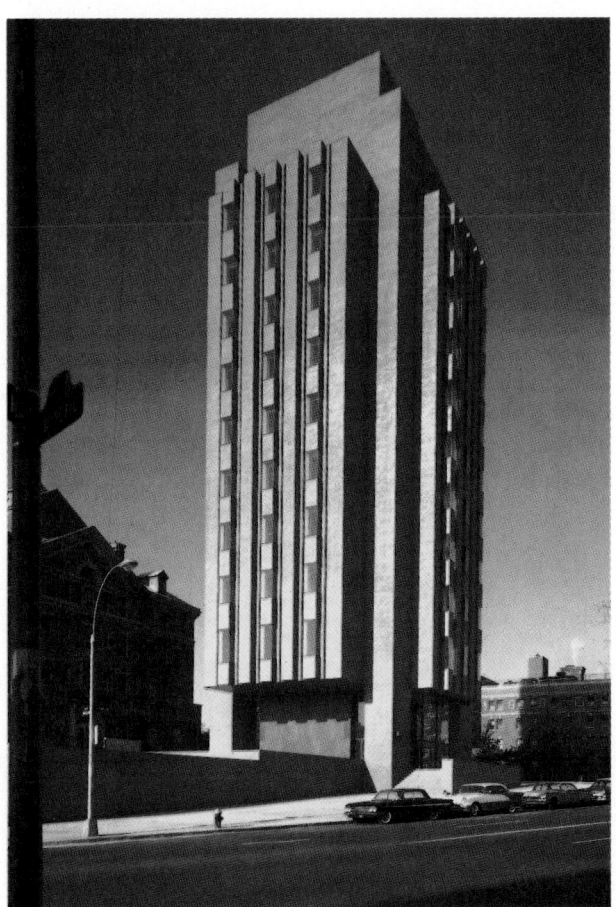

The park was overshadowed by the two superscale, forty-four-story tower-slabs of the UDC-sponsored Harlem River Park Towers (1975), housing 1,650 low- and moderate-income families.[10] The design, by Davis, Brody & Associates, was a variation of the same firm's Waterside (see chapter 5). Linked to the upland by two bridges that extended over the Deegan Expressway to connect with Cedar Avenue, the development included shops and a parking garage, as well as an educational facility. Designed by Caudill Rowlett Scott, the 1977 facility combined Public School 229 and Junior High School 229. The massive, rather anonymous-looking, virtually windowless school sat over the railroad tracks, resembling more a transportation facility than a building devoted to education of the young.

Institutions for health care and education in the West Bronx witnessed considerable expansion in the 1950s and 1960s, with several architecturally impressive buildings. Philip Johnson's building for the Henry L. Moses Research Institute (1965) at Montefiore Hospital, 111 East 210th Street, between Kossuth and Bainbridge avenues, was particularly elegant.[11] The tower, clad in brown brick and articulated with window bays, rose on four shafts that extended the building's full ten-story height. Surrounded by a brick-paved plaza, the building stood free and was highly visible throughout the area. As the historian Henry-Russell Hitchcock noted, the building achieved "urbanistic value" by providing "a bold three-dimensional accent in a thoroughly undistinguished section of the Bronx whose dreary skyline is otherwise broken only by occasional high-rise apartment slabs." In fact, Hitchcock asserted, the building was "intended to be seen from a distance," which justified "the almost brutalist simplicity of the elements of which it is composed."[12]

Just west of Johnson's building, on the northeast corner of East 210st Street and Kossuth Avenue, the team of Carl Pancaldo and Schuman, Lichtenstein & Claman were responsible for the North Central Bronx Hospital (1976), commissioned by the city's Health and Hospitals Corporation.[13] The design, a highly articulated clustering of vertical elements attached to a slab, was notably elegant in its proportions, given the building type, but it was nonetheless brutal in its juxtaposition of brick walls and precast concrete. Although Norval White and Elliot Willensky

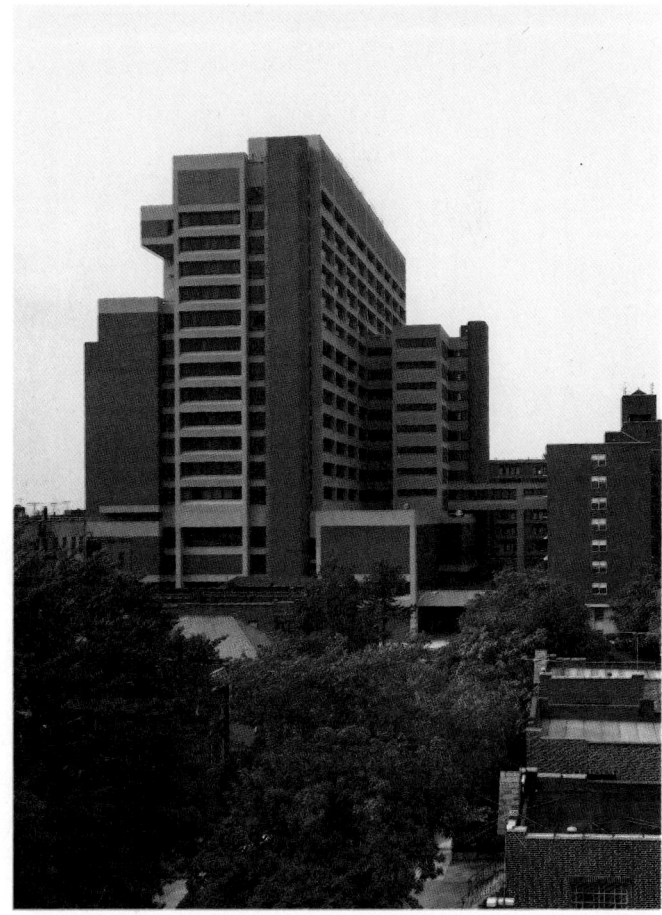

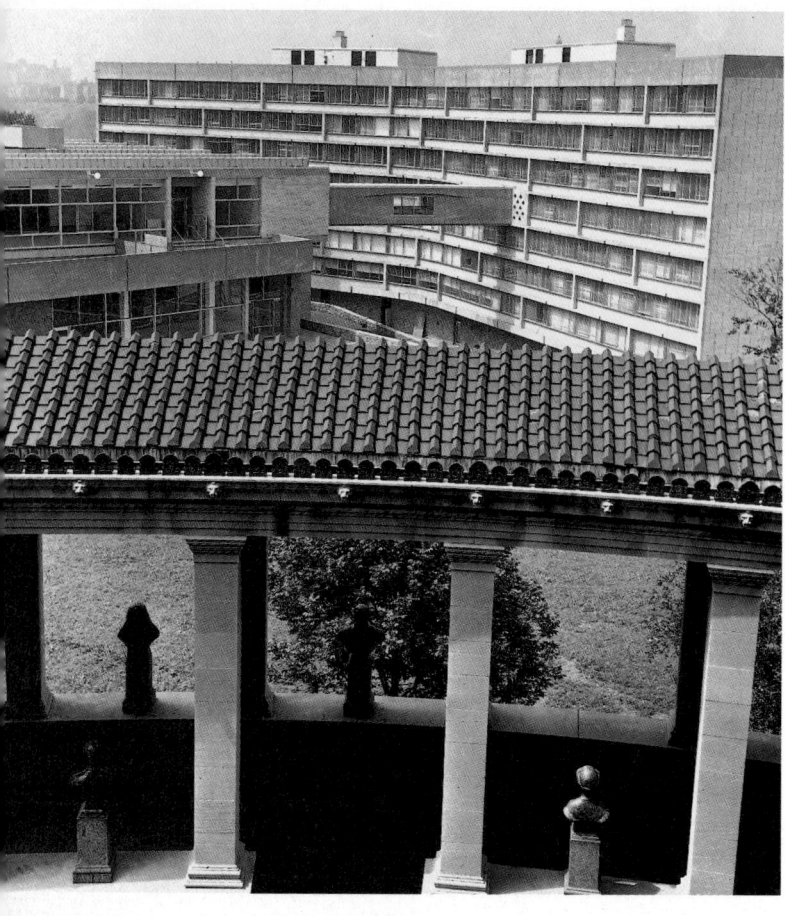

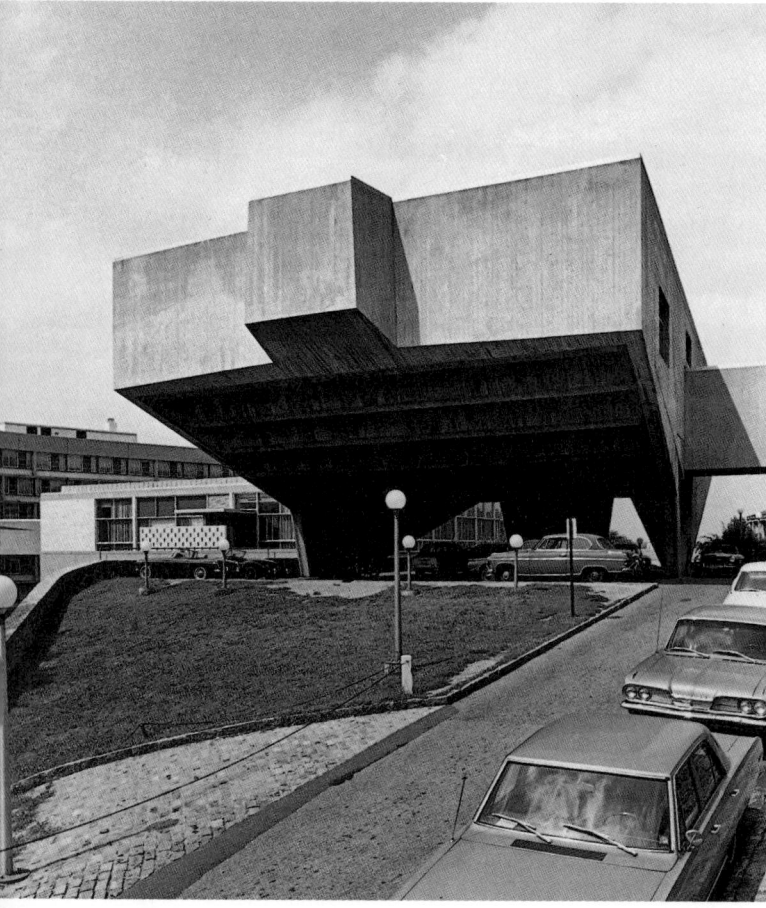

felt it presented "a confident and inviting appearance" and was "spectacularly successful . . . as public architecture," the building virtually overwhelmed its context.[14]

The area's most significant institutional construction was the expansion of New York University's University Heights undergraduate campus—widely known as NYU Uptown—located on a site bounded by Sedgwick and University avenues, West 180th Street and Hall of Fame Terrace; the campus buildings had been erected between 1895 and 1902 in accord with a master plan designed by McKim, Mead & White.[15] In 1956–58 Marcel Breuer, with one of his partners, Hamilton Smith, prepared a new master plan for the campus. Breuer also designed a new complex of interconnected buildings, announced by NYU in 1959, including the Julius Silver Residence Center and Cafeteria, a seven-story coeducational dormitory and dining hall; the Gould Hall of Technology, a laboratory building; and a lecture wing, later Begrisch Lecture Hall, all completed in 1964. Seen from the Harlem River below, the group took a powerful position on the hill. The bent slab of the seven-story, 612-student dormitory, set on piers, commanded the valley with as much confidence as Stanford White's Gould Memorial Library (1900), the principal building of NYU's turn-of-the-century campus, although it lacked the earlier building's subtlety. The lecture wing was raised above the second floor of the laboratory building, creating a dramatic, seemingly airborne concrete monolith that exuded modernity. The complex's bold stylistic stance was further expressed by the thin-shell construction of the saddlelike hyperbolic paraboloid that formed the campus-side entrance to the laboratory wing and the insectile forms of the bridges that connected the dining hall with the dormitory.

This first complex was followed by the Technology Center Two (1972), designed by Breuer as a seven-story building housing laboratories and offices for faculty members and graduate students and a three-story classroom and seminar building. The buildings defined a courtyard and sat atop two underground floors providing 15,500 square feet of library space. In 1973 New York University sold the campus to the City University of New York, which made it home to Bronx Community College.

In 1959 Breuer and his associate Robert F. Gatje completed a new library and a classroom-administration wing, Shuster Hall, for the uptown campus of Hunter College (renamed Herbert H. Lehman College in 1967), on the southeast corner of Goulden Avenue and Bedford Park Boulevard.[16] The complex, the first significant addition to the campus since its completion in 1932, consisted of a one-story library linked, in accordance with the architect's principle of binuclear planning, to a three-story wing that surrounded its own courtyard.[17] Emulating Paul Rudolph's widely published Jewett Arts Center (1955–58) at Wellesley College, though with far less contextual specificity, Breuer wrapped the principal elevations of his buildings in a sunscreen made of orange clay flue tile.[18] The screen was set out four feet from the glass walls to create a contemporary effect that would nonetheless be sympathetic in scale and detail to the original buildings of the Gothic-style campus. The screen was also included to compensate for the fact that the extensively glazed library was not air conditioned. Bookstacks were located in the basement to allow for the building's most distinctive feature, a 120-by-180-foot reading room bathed in light filtered through the sunscreen. The roof of the space consisted of six sixty-foot-square inverted reinforced-concrete umbrellas whose quadrants were hyperbolic paraboloids arching out from their central columns at a point twenty-three feet above the floor. The editors of *Progressive Architecture* felt that Breuer succeeded in

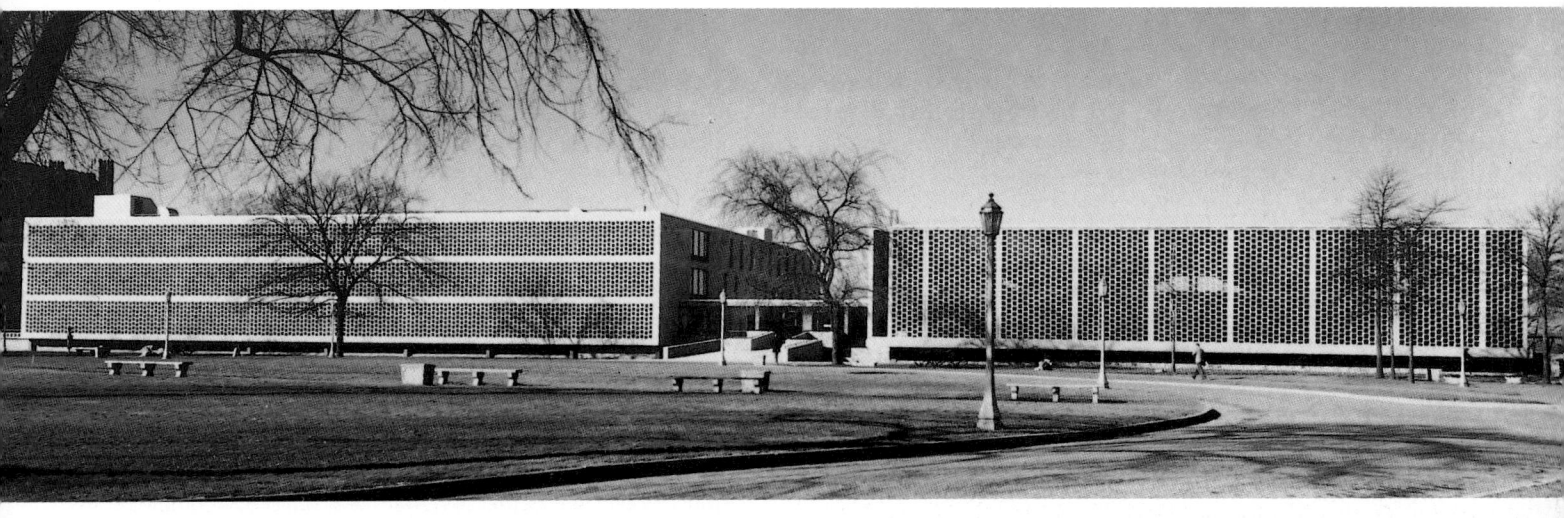

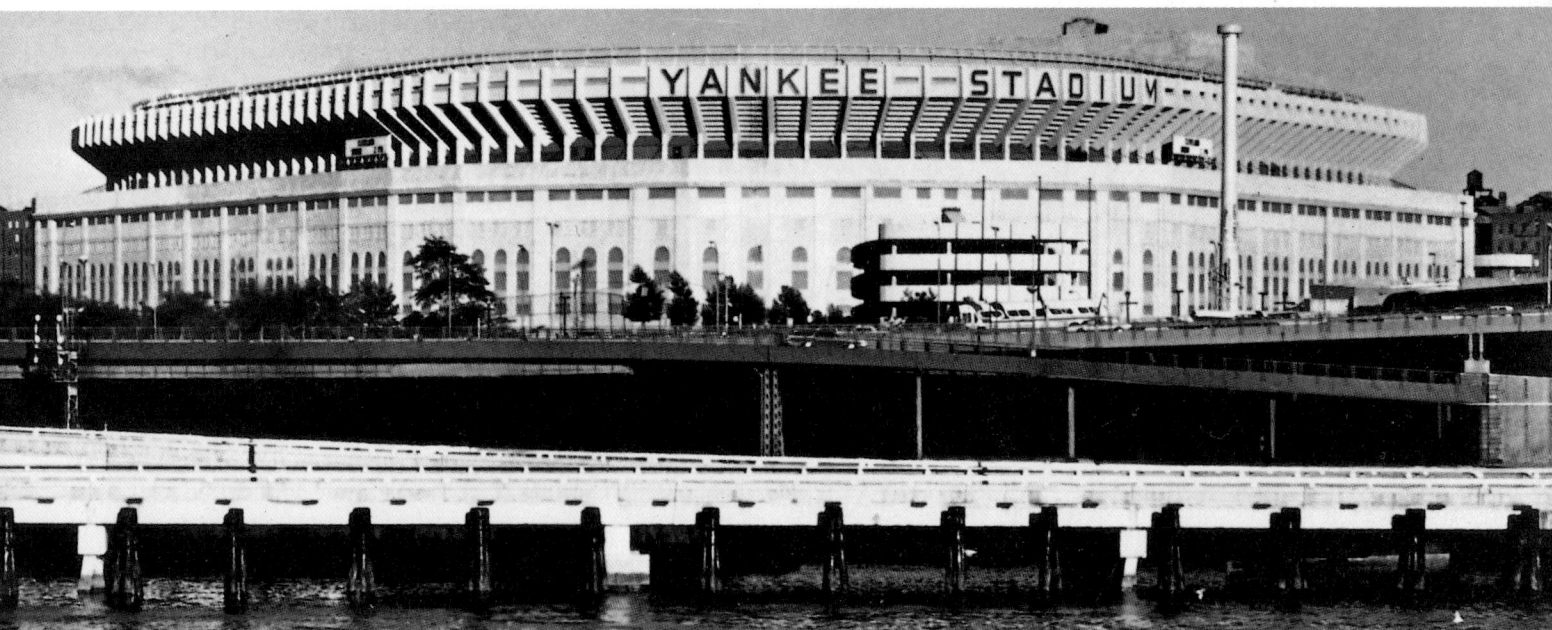

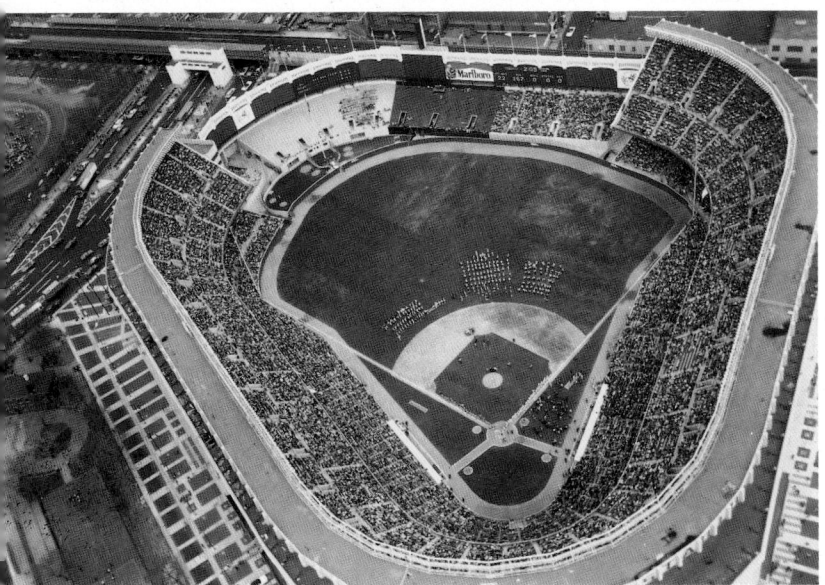

Top far left: Julius Silver Residence Center and Cafeteria, New York University, University Heights undergraduate campus (after 1973 Bronx Community College), bounded by Sedgwick Avenue, West Burnside Avenue, Osborne Place, West 180th Street and University Avenue, University Heights. Marcel Breuer & Associates, 1964. View to the southwest with the Hall of Fame (McKim, Mead & White, 1901) in the foreground. Gooen. NYU

Bottom far left: Begrisch Lecture Hall, New York University, University Heights undergraduate campus. Marcel Breuer & Associates, 1964. NYU

Top: Shuster Hall, uptown campus of Hunter College (after 1967 Herbert H. Lehman College), between Paul and Goulden avenues, Bedford Park Boulevard and West 195th Street, Kingsbridge Heights. Marcel Breuer & Associates, 1959. View to the northwest. MA

Center: Renovated Yankee Stadium, bounded by Ruppert Place, East 157th Street and River Avenue, Melrose. Praeger-Kavanagh-Waterbury, 1976. Aerial view to the east. NYYPD

Bottom: Renovated Yankee Stadium. Aerial view to the east. NYYPD

his goal of integrating the complex with the rest of the campus: "Appropriateness in its (1930's) Gothic setting is achieved by various devices, among them the bold but not overpowering scale of the entire complex, and the small scale of its facade patterning."[19]

In 1959 the prestigious Bronx High School of Science, a renowned public institution established in 1938 in what was originally an elementary school, moved to a purpose-built facility located at 75 West 205th Street, five blocks north of the Hunter campus.[20] Designed by Emery Roth & Sons, the blandly detailed, sprawling, three-story building incorporated strip windows, white brick spandrels and terra-cotta. The school's extensive laboratory facilities, including ground-level and rooftop greenhouses, were exceptional, making the building far more distinguished functionally than it was aesthetically.

In 1971 the West Bronx—and, by extension, the city as a whole—was dealt a potential blow with the announcement that the New York Yankees baseball team intended to depart for points west unless certain conditions were met, not the least of which was the renovation and expansion of historic Yankee Stadium (Osborn Engineering Company, 1922–23).[21] But the city met the team's demands and the Yankees stayed, perhaps a signal, albeit a pricey one, that the "collapsed" city could fight for its survival and win. When the stadium was reopened on April 15, 1976, after two and a half years of reconstruction (during the rebuilding, the Yankees played their home games at Shea Stadium, see "Queens," below), little attention was paid to the expanded bleachers, brighter lighting, improved circulation or to the vast amount of structured parking. Rather, at issue was whether the cost to the city—which had escalated from $24 million in 1971 to $101 million in 1976—had been worth it. A secondary question involved how much of that cost went to construction as opposed to the support of power groups in the construction, parking, canteen and other industries who built the new stadium and contracted for its continued operation. As Nicholas Pileggi put it: "Some New Yorkers might have wished their $101 million had been spent elsewhere. The increasing number of city residents who won't be able to afford the admission price may not care. But to those who promoted it, built it, and insured it, the rebuilding of Yankee Stadium has been the greatest game in town."[22]

Riverdale

Because of its remote location and its suburban qualities, Riverdale, including Fieldston and Spuyten Duyvil, hardly seemed part of the Bronx or, for that matter, even New York City.[23] As established during the 1910s and 1920s, its character was that of an upper-income suburbia, replete with many fine houses designed by leading architects and three country day schools, mostly serving the children of affluent Manhattanites. The area also contained a number of apartment buildings, the earliest of which was the Villa Charlotte Bronte (Robert Gardner, 1926), at 2501 Palisade Avenue, in Spuyten Duyvil, a small and exceptionally charming pair of identical five-story, sixteen-unit villalike buildings perched against a cliff overlooking the Hudson River.[24] Horace Ginsbern's 3875 Waldo Avenue apartments (1928), on the southwest corner of College Parkway, in Fieldston, adopted a Tudor vocabulary that established a similarly romantic tone while also relating to the architectural expression of nearby private houses.[25] These apartment houses were followed in 1940 by the much larger but very dignified Georgian-style Riverdale Park Apartments, on the northwest corner of West 254th Street and Riverdale Avenue, designed by Jardine, Murdock & Wright.[26]

After the war, especially in the 1950s, so many apartment houses were built in Riverdale that the area's traditional character was threatened with extinction. In 1955 the journalist Richard Amper reported in the New York Times on the sweeping changes:

> The upper Bronx is suffering from a split personality. Her desire to be a suburban residential area has clashed with a ceaseless surge of urbanization and new residents. The conflict is nowhere so great or dramatic as in the most un-Bronx part of the borough—the fashionable Riverdale section in the northwest. Here the Bronx wears a lorgnette. From wooded estates and splendid private homes on 1,600 hilly acres dedicated to spacious and gracious living, Riverdale looks down on her less affluent cousins in a welter of apartments and shudders.[27]

Amper noted that of the 201 apartment buildings completed in the Bronx between 1950 and 1955, 46 were in Riverdale; collectively they housed 15,000 people. During that five-year period Riverdale's population increased from 21,000 to 41,000. In large measure because of the construction of new apartment buildings, the assessed value of the area's real estate skyrocketed 100 percent between 1935 and 1955, while that of the Bronx as a whole rose only 30 percent. Spurred by the efforts of area homeowners, the city ratified zoning ordinances in 1955 stipulating that only 40 percent of Riverdale's vacant lots could be made available for apartment houses and that the total number of new apartment dwellers could not exceed 63,000.

When postwar apartment house developers first targeted Riverdale, large-scale developments were proposed for the comparatively big tracts of land that were still available. In 1946 Fort Independence Village, a project calling for 1,000 apartments in eight-story buildings, was proposed for the 500,000-square-foot site bordered by Palisade and Independence avenues and Kappock Street; the project was never built.[28] The next year Anthony Campagna proposed to erect two cooperative apartment buildings at 520 and 530 Spaulding Lane near the Henry Hudson Parkway at West 249th Street.[29] The site was part of Campagna's own estate, which contained a lovely Italian villa designed for him by Dwight James Baum in 1922.[30] Rosario Candela, who had designed many of Campagna's Park and Fifth Avenue apartment buildings before the war, designed the two eleven-story towers, clad in red brick, in a Georgianesque manner. Completed in 1949, the slablike Riverdale Towers exhibited little of the flair of Candela's prewar work and introduced a somewhat brutal, aggressive scale to the residential enclave. In 1952 the Fisher Brothers developed Briar Oaks on an 18.5-acre site that stretched for a half mile west of the Henry Hudson Parkway between West 242nd and West 246th streets.[31] The first phase consisted of two twelve-story buildings housing 150 families each; three buildings housing 750 more families were to be built later. The firm was already at work on a fourteen-story building at Palisade Avenue and Kappock Street, known as the Glen Briar. By 1955 Riverdale had come as close as any American neighborhood to the vision of Le Corbusier's vertical garden city, with isolated towers stretched out along a motorway and surrounded by a sea of greenery dotted with small houses.

In addition to apartment buildings, several institutional buildings were developed in Riverdale in the late 1960s and early 1970s, including expansions of each of the area's long-established private schools—Horace Mann, Riverdale and Fieldston. Horace Mann took on the most ambitious building program, hiring established architects to expand the campus,

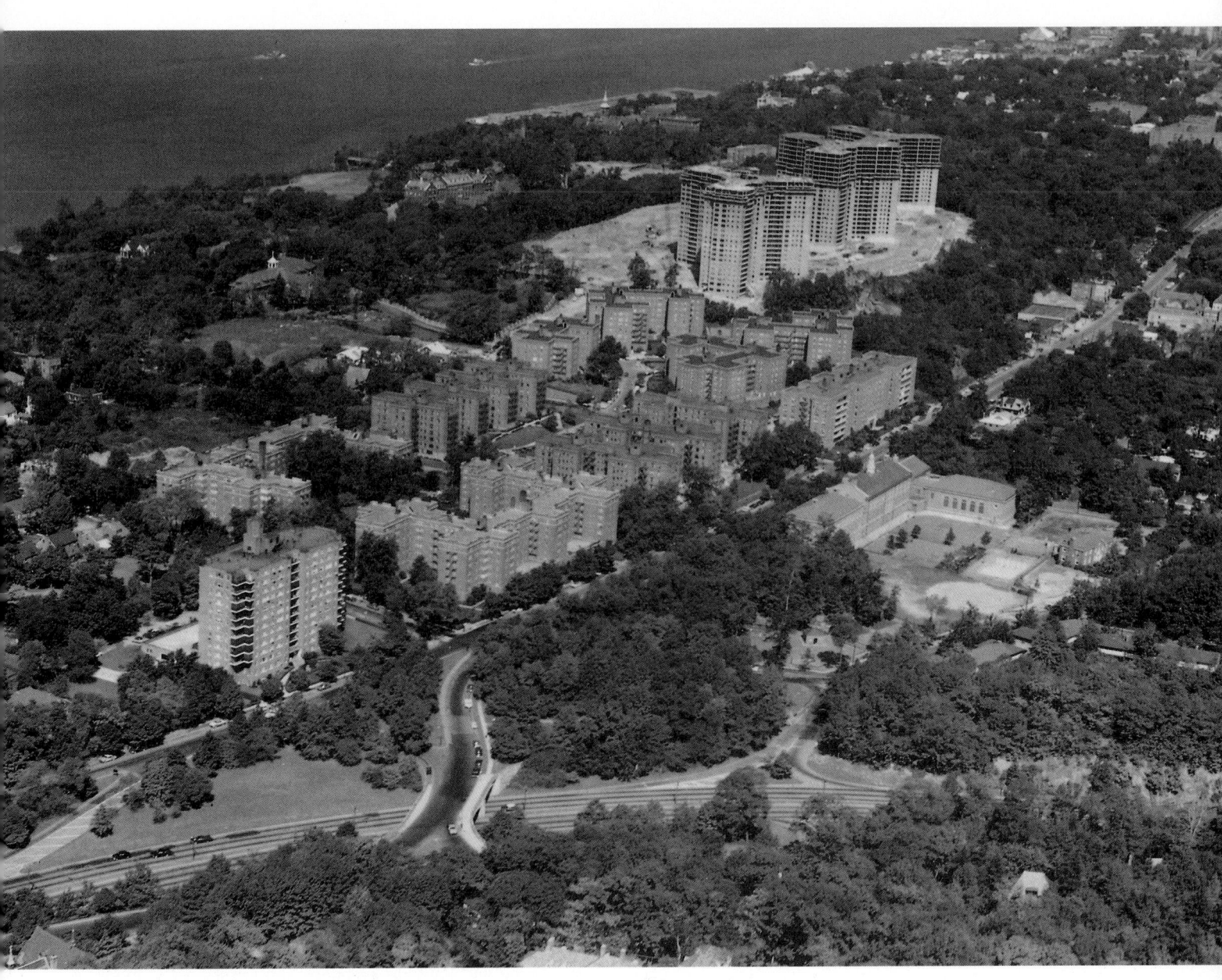

Aerial view to the northwest of Riverdale, with Henry Hudson Parkway
in the foreground, 1961. NYT

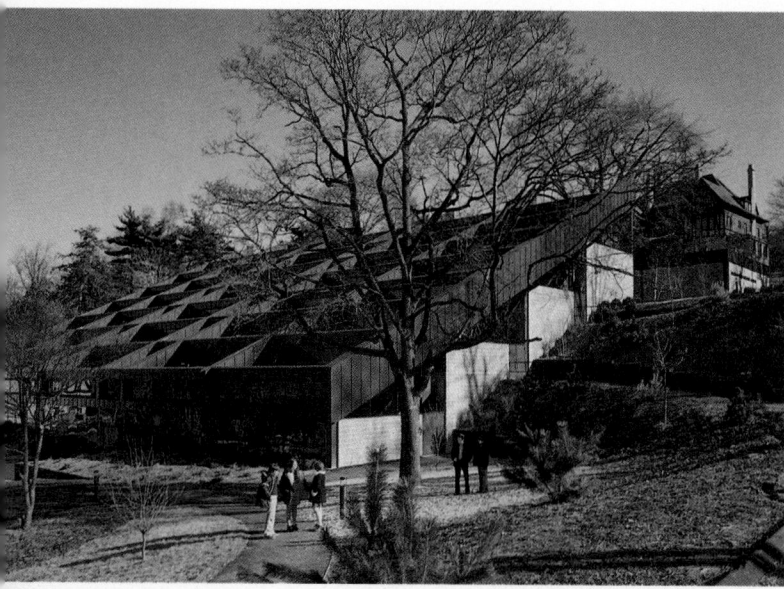

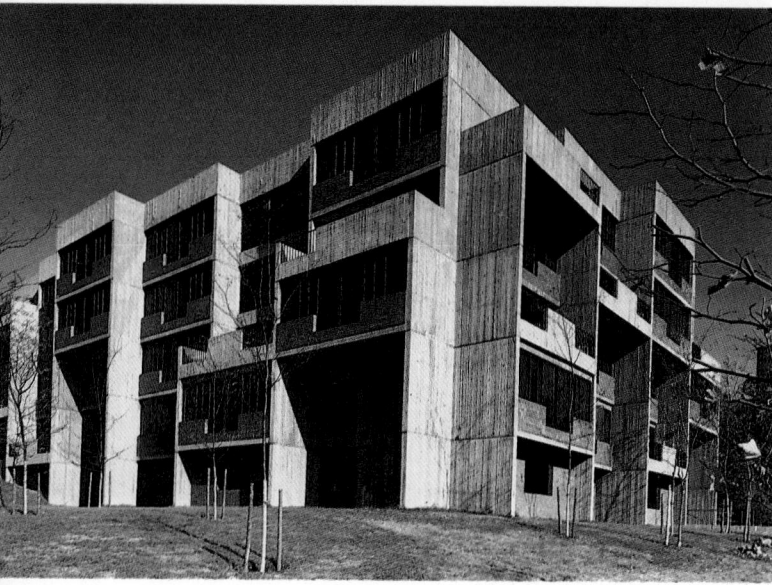

Top: Salanter Akiba Riverdale Academy, 655 West 254th Street, between Independence and Palisade avenues, Riverdale. Caudill Rowlett Scott, 1974. View to the northeast. CRSS

Bottom: Goldfine Pavilion, Hebrew Home for the Aged, 5901 Palisade Avenue, south of West 261st Street, Riverdale. Gruzen & Partners, 1968. View to the northeast. GS

Right: Faraday Wood, diplomatic residence of the United Nations Mission of the Union of Soviet Socialist Republics, 335 West 255th Street, on the northeast corner of Mosholu Avenue, Riverdale. Skidmore, Owings & Merrill, 1975. Diagrams showing structural system. DOM. CU

which consisted of the vaguely English Gothic, rough-stone-clad Tillinghast Hall (Edgar A. Josselyn, 1913), the brick-and-stone gymnasium (Fred F. French Company, 1924) and a single-family residence, the so-called Van Sant Cottage (Edgar A. Josselyn, 1913).[32] The school's expansion included the construction of Pforzheimer Hall (Victor Christ-Janer, 1956), a rectilinear Modernist composition in yellow brick,[33] and Prettyman Gymnasium (Charles E. Hughes III, 1965).[34] In 1970 Frost Associates prepared a master plan for the school.[35] Five years later the firm completed the Gratwick Science Wing, an addition to Pforzheimer Hall, which they also renovated; the new brick-clad wing was distinguished by deep-punched windows and extensive sky-lighting.[36] The Riverdale Country School augmented the two nineteenth-century estate buildings that formed its River Campus, at West 248th Street between Independence and Palisades avenues, with the Perkins Study Center (R. Marshall Christensen, 1967), whose distinctive roof consisted of two concave sides joined at their apex by a building-long skylight.[37] Fieldston built the new Tate Library (Murphy & Mackey, 1971); although its fieldstone cladding related to the original buildings of Clarence Stein and Robert D. Kohn's charming 1929 campus, its extensive glazing and Modernist vocabulary were not so harmonious.[38]

A number of new institutions arrived during the postwar period. Some, like religious centers and libraries, were built to meet the needs of the swelling population; others, like nursing homes, were drawn to Riverdale because its environment was still suburban but also offered easy accessibility by car and rapid transit for patients' families. Percival Goodman's Conservative Synagogue of Riverdale, Congregation Adath Israel (1962), Henry Hudson Parkway East, just north of West 250th Street, was a bold, Brutalist-inspired composition of forms contrasting board-formed concrete with red brick.[39] William Breger's painted-concrete-block building for the Riverdale-Yonkers Ethical Culture Society (1966), at 4550 Fieldston Road, was a gentler though far less interesting example of postwar ecclesiastic architecture.[40] The Riverdale Center of Religious Research's chapel (Brother Cajetan J. B. Baumann, 1967), at 5801 Palisade Avenue, took on a boldly sculptural form.[41]

Caudill Rowlett Scott's 1974 facility for the Salanter Akiba Riverdale Academy, at 655 West 254th Street, between Independence and Palisade avenues, combined three formerly independent schools in a skylit 480-student classroom building that featured a deep, open-coffered steel roof truss.[42] The building stepped down a steep site that was once part of the Wave Hill estate (see chapter 16). The clients had preferred that the academy be built on a flat area of the site, adjacent to an existing building, rather than the steeply sloping bank below. But in response to the requests of environmentalists stationed at Wave Hill that the building not dominate the area, and perhaps inspired by the design of the new Harvard University Graduate School of Design building, Gund Hall (John Andrews, 1969), the architects settled on the final scheme of interior platforms hugging the hillside.[43]

Robert L. Bien's Riverdale Branch of the New York Public Library (1967), at 5540 Mosholu Avenue, was a simple composition of intersecting gables, offering an appropriate image for a community library in a park setting.[44] Giorgio Cavaglieri's Modernist, concrete-and-glass Spuyten Duyvil Branch (1971), at 650 West 235th Street, struggled with a more ragtag setting.[45]

Abraham Geller and Matt Rubenstein's Jewish Board of Guardians' Henry Ittleson Center for Child Research (1967), a facility located at 5050 Iselin Avenue, north of West 250th

Street, and designed for the treatment of disturbed children, was a dramatic composition of beige-colored concrete-block pavilions capped by standing-seam metal roofs.[46] The stylish Modernism of Gruzen & Partners' additions to the Hebrew Home for the Aged at Riverdale (Goldfine Pavilion, 1968; Palisade Nursing Home, 1975), at 5901 Palisade Avenue, south of West 261st Street, reflected changes in architectural taste as well as in the techniques of nursing care. As the architecture writer Betty Raymond put it: "The theme of the game in geriatrics today is 'Don't just sit there Grandma, get with it.' The Hebrew Home for the Aged . . . is very much 'with it.'" The brick-and-exposed-concrete Goldfine Pavilion was built into its sloping site. Despite restless massing and a palette of raw materials, the building managed to convey an appropriately modest scale outside and inside. Bill Bagnall Associates, interior designers, developed furnishings that were distinctly residential in character yet suitable for the institutional care of the elderly. The Goldfine Pavilion, Raymond said, was "a stunning structure that marks a fresh new departure for such institutions."[47] The seven-story, brick-clad Palisade Nursing Home was also noteworthy, although the enthusiasm of Norval White and Elliot Willensky, who described it as "carved from a monumental cube almost as sculptor Gutzon Borglum attacked the Black Hills of South Dakota," may have been a bit exaggerated.[48]

Despite the dramatic change of scale and character brought by the new apartment houses and institutional development, Riverdale not only retained its value as an established single-family residential neighborhood but even attracted newcomers who built houses on the little land that remained. Several architecturally distinguished Modernist houses in the area constituted a rare type in postwar New York because of their suburban-scaled sites. Keith Kroeger Associates' James Strain residence (1970), at 731 Ladd Road, was an elegant composition with extensive glazing set in the thinnest possible frames.[49] The house formed the visual focus of a cluster of houses built after 1957, arranged on a cul-de-sac and sharing a swimming pool. The group included Vincent A. Claps's stained-wood-sheathed house for Eric Schmertz (1971), at 4550 Palisade Avenue, south of West 247th Street, a boldly geometric design with deeply recessed windows,[50] and Hobart Betts & Associates' Edward A. Ames residence (1971), at 709 West 246th Street, west of Independence Avenue, an elegant Modernist essay rendered in cedar and glass.[51]

In 1975 a controversial new apartment house was built in Riverdale: Faraday Wood, the nineteen-story diplomatic residence of the United Nations Mission of the Union of Soviet Socialist Republics, at 335 West 255th Street, on the northeast corner of Mosholu Avenue.[52] Named after its six-acre site, the building, designed by Skidmore, Owings & Merrill, housed 240 units on sixteen floors, as well as, on the three lowest floors, school and community facilities. The articulation of the building, which was clad in metal-laminated panels set in aluminum mullions, was rather banal, but from a technological point of view the structure was quite innovative, with steel-deck floor slabs lifted up on two cast-in-place concrete masts that served as the building's cores.

When the Russians bought the site in 1971, they settled a controversy over its future use that had gone on since 1967, when an eighteen-story apartment house with 340 units, split evenly between middle- and low-income families, was proposed as part of the city's scatter-site housing program. By 1969 the program had become highly controversial, and the mixed-income apartment house was among the most fervently opposed projects. It became such a political hot potato that in his cam-

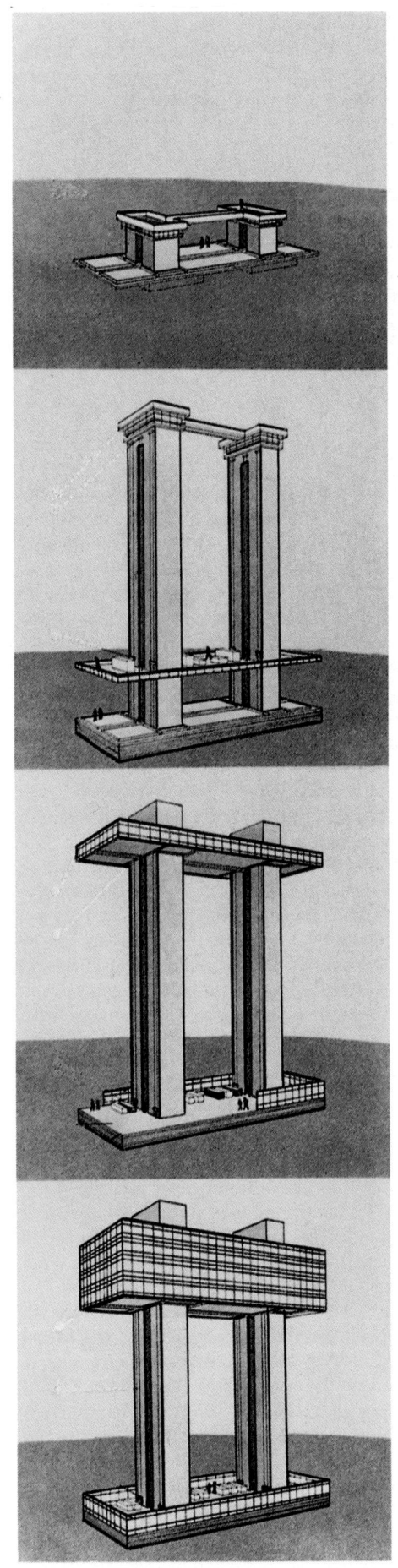

paign for reelection Mayor Lindsay promised to drop it. The project's sponsor, the Association for Middle Income Housing, then brought suit in federal court, charging that the city was bowing to neighborhood pressure to prevent low-income residents from moving in. Before a decision was handed down, the site was sold to the Russians. (Later, in August 1974, Federal Judge Robert J. Ward ruled in favor of the city.) The site was owned by Robert C. Weinberg, an architect and planner who had assembled it over the years. At Weinberg's suggestion the Russians retained Pomerance & Breines; the building they designed was approved by Moscow but proved too expensive to build. In 1972 Soviet officials hired International Environmental Dynamics, a California-based building concern founded in 1968, which held patents on the suspended-street-floor construction system, to realize Skidmore, Owings & Merrill's design.

South Bronx

In contrast to the affluence of Riverdale and the comparative stability of other Bronx neighborhoods, the South Bronx, including the neighborhoods of Mott Haven, Port Morris, Melrose, Longwood, Hunts Point, Morrisania and Crotona Park, fell into a serious state of decline after World War II. There were pockets of substantial housing in this vast area, including the blocks that would later be protected as the Longwood historic district, a landmark neighborhood of masonry rowhouses designed primarily by Warren C. Dickerson between 1897 and 1901.[53] But the majority of the housing stock consisted of old- and new-law tenements. These buildings were occupied by lower-middle-class whites, who, if they were young, were hell-bent on moving up and out, usually to the suburbs, and, if they were older and could afford it, were typically planning on retirement in south Florida. Concerned professional and citizens' groups, including the Bronx Board of Trade, believed that low-cost public housing was a top priority for this area.[54] In 1945 Governor Thomas E. Dewey and New York State Commissioner of Housing Herman T. Stichman, accompanied by a full complement of newspaper photographers, toured the decaying site bounded by Morris and Courtlandt avenues, East 153rd and East 156th streets, which was slated for replacement with the state-financed Melrose Houses (Louis E. Jallade and William T. Koch, 1952). According to *Architectural Forum*, "Governor Dewey spent an hour plodding through alleys, peering up tenement hallways, and exchanging greetings with startled residents" before observing that "most of the buildings are not fit for human habitation."[55]

From the 1950s through the 1970s most of the publicly assisted housing projects built in the borough were built in the South Bronx: Lester Patterson Houses (Morrisania Project Associates, 1950), bounded by Morris and Third avenues and East 145th Street;[56] Forest Houses (Rosario Candela and Paul Resnick, 1956), Trinity and Tinton avenues, East 163rd and East 166th streets;[57] St. Mary's Park Houses (Voorhees, Walker, Smith & Smith, 1959), Cauldwell and Westchester avenues, East 152nd and East 156th streets;[58] Mill Brook Houses (Chapman, Evans & Delehanty, 1959; addition, Lorimer Rich Associates, 1962), Brook and Cypress avenues, East 135th and East 137th streets;[59] William McKinley Houses (Greenberg & Ames, 1962), Trinity and Tinton avenues, East 161st and East 163rd streets;[60] Morrisania Houses (Greenberg & Ames, 1963), Park and Washington avenues, East 168th and East 169th streets;[61] Andrew Jackson Houses (Henry M. Prince, 1963), Park and Courtlandt avenues, East 156th and East 158th streets;[62] Borgia Butler Houses (Joseph

& Vladeck, 1964), Webster and Park avenues, East 169th and East 171st streets;[63] E. Roberts Moore Houses (Edelbaum & Webster, 1964), St. Mary's Park, Jackson Avenue, East 147th and East 149th streets;[64] John Adams Houses (S. J. Kessler & Sons, 1964), Westchester and Union avenues, East 152nd and East 156th streets;[65] Gouverneur Morris Houses (Chapman, Evans & Delehanty, 1965), Washington and Third avenues, East 170th and East 171st streets;[66] Daniel Webster Houses (Seymour R. Joseph, 1965), Webster and Park avenues, East 168th and East 169th streets;[67] Mott Haven Houses (Horace Ginsbern & Associates and Cika & Silverman, 1965), Alexander and Willis avenues, East 141st and East 143rd streets;[68] and Lewis S. Davidson, Sr. Houses (Paul Rudolph, 1973), Union and Prospect avenues, East 167th and Home streets.[69]

While projects located in the more distant areas of the Bronx had the advantages of lower land costs and relatively minor tenant relocation problems, they suffered from the virtual absence of public transportation and other services. Those in the South Bronx, though convenient, required massive relocation of existing residential and business tenants and thus resulted in high development costs and the near-total destruction of existing neighborhood life. By the late 1960s it was clear to most observers that the spreading blight was achieving epidemic proportions and that the proliferation of large-scale housing projects was not only doing virtually nothing to stem the tide but was in fact creating its own culture of social and physical destruction. The South Bronx had become one of the greatest concentrations of financially disadvantaged people in the entire country, a ghetto of color and economics reified in an ill-suited brick-and-mortar landscape.

By 1970, according to the journalist Samuel Kaplan, writing in *New York* magazine, the area had become "New York City's Number One Disaster Area."[70] Half of the borough's 1.5 million people lived in this area, most of them in rundown housing along garbage-strewn streets. In the City Planning Commission's master plan of 1969, the full horror of the area was first officially recognized. In reference to one South Bronx neighborhood—Morrisiana—the commission stated:

> Its streets vibrate to violence and fear; the current arrest rate among its youth is nearly double the city average; the incidence of venereal disease is just short of triple the city-wide figure. Rates of unemployment, juvenile delinquency and infant mortality are among the highest in the City, and nearly half its youth are on some sort of welfare. The community feels abandoned and forgotten; its leadership is understandably frustrated, bitter and hostile.[71]

The City Planning Commission's report placed much of the blame on the physical environment: "In parts of the South Bronx antiquated tenement apartments were subdivided to increase the rent rolls, and many were rented to families with many children. Some buildings now house twice their original population, and most landlords do little or nothing to maintain their property which wasn't very sound to start with."[72] With landlords refusing to take care of their properties, the housing situation was so bad that the Bronx Realty Advisors Board labeled the Bronx "the borough of abandonment."[73] As a result of the South Bronx's decline, despite the construction of the vast Co-op City complex in the Northeast Bronx (see below), the assessed valuation of the borough's real estate declined in 1968, the first time this had occurred in any borough in twenty-five years.

The collapse of the South Bronx's physical structure was accompanied by the dramatic exodus of whites and their re-

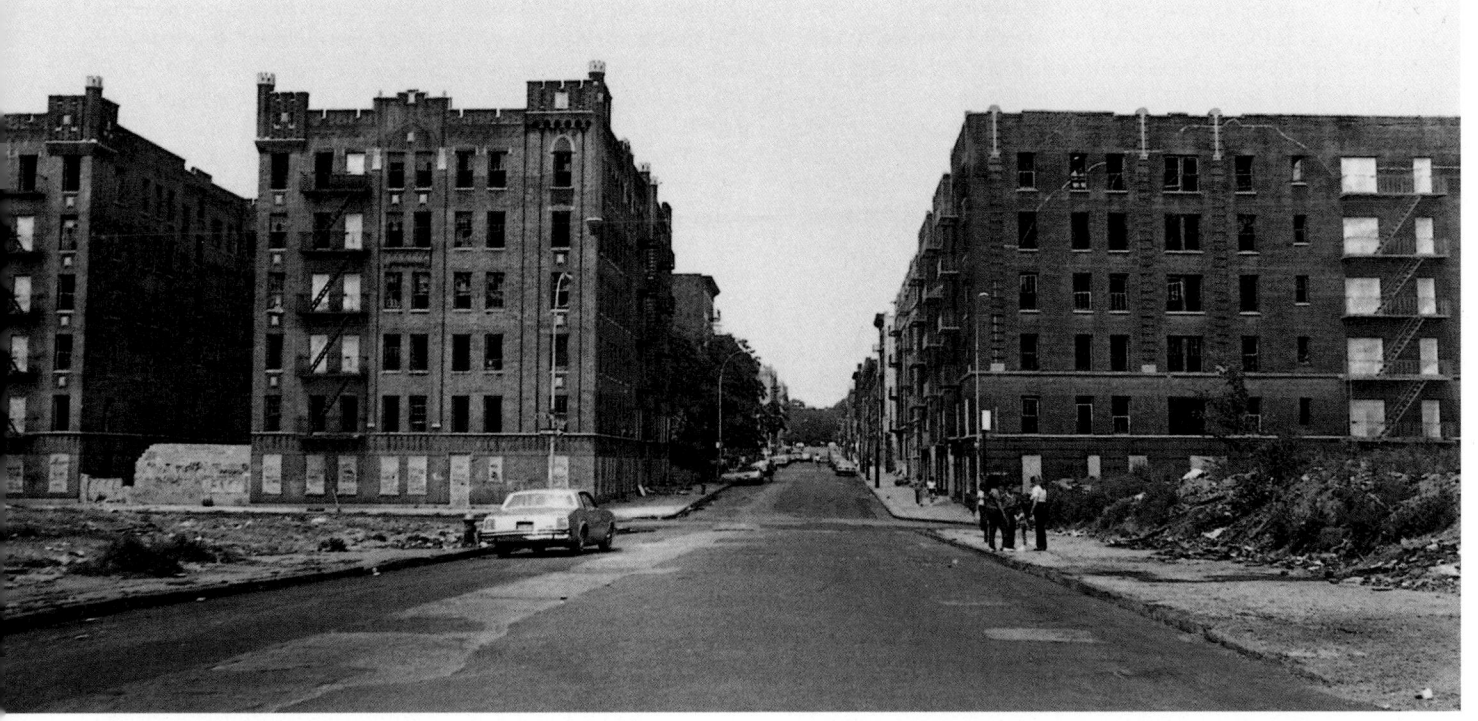

Abandoned buildings in the South Bronx, ca. 1972. Fred W. McDarrah. FWM

placement by blacks and Hispanics.[74] At points of contact between white and black or Hispanic neighborhoods, tension was high. Moreover, as whites fled, municipal services, ranging from street cleaning to park maintenance to medical care, seemed to visibly decline, and many observers believed they were supplied in smaller quantities per capita than in the other boroughs.

Emblematic of the situation was the 148-acre Crotona Park, the area's principal open space. The park was, as Herschel Post put it in 1971, "out of order": bathrooms were either burnt out or tightly locked, row upon row of swing stands had been stripped of their swings, concrete water fountains had been toppled.[75] The boathouse and the lake were permanently empty; one end of the littered picnic grove was used as a dump by the Park Department and virtually everyone else. Only the tennis courts were inexplicably in tiptop shape, but they were used less by neighborhood residents than by people who drove from the borough's farthest reaches or even Queens for their exercise. The situation seemed so hopeless that the City Planning Commission proposed in its master plan that nineteen of the park's acres at the southern end be demapped as parkland and used for housing and that the Board of Education build a high school in the park's northern annex.[76] To the planners' amazement, these proposals were vehemently opposed by residents who valued the park even as it was. The city was slow to realize that in addition to the dramatic racial change in the Crotona Park neighborhood, from 80 percent white in 1960 to 70 percent black and Hispanic in 1970, there was a demographic change, with over half of the 250,000 people living in the neighborhood either children or elderly citizens, both groups who relied on the park. But just as park usage was up and the growth of drug-related crime made surveillance more important than ever before, the city's fiscal situation had forced the Park Department

to drastically cut its staff, including the rest-room attendants who had kept order and the recreation leaders who had organized baseball, basketball and other games that gave the park a social structure.

Another symbol of the South Bronx's plight was Lincoln Hospital, the area's principal medical facility and without a doubt the city's most decrepit one.[77] Located at 320 Concord Avenue, the hospital had been built in 1839 as a nursing home for runaway slaves. It was condemned by the city in 1945, but the long-promised replacement was never included in any of the municipal capital budgets. The situation had become so out of control by the mid-1960s that youth gangs roamed the hospital's hallways threatening doctors. Ground was finally broken in 1970 for a new hospital on a ten-acre site bounded by Park and Morris avenues, East 144th and East 149th streets.[78] Completed in 1976, the eleven-story brick-clad facility, designed by the firm of Max O. Urbahn Associates, offered high-quality health services to a community long in need. More significant in practical and societal terms than in strictly architectural terms, the new hospital, as the journalist David Bird reported in the *New York Times*, "reflects a philosophy that the best health care is everyone's right."[79]

The South Bronx became national news in 1972 when the journalist Stewart Alsop reported on the area, which he said was becoming a "rubble-filled semidesert," for two consecutive weeks in his *Newsweek* column.[80] He pointed out that it was not the blacks and Hispanics who had trashed a place that was until recently tolerably inhabited by whites, but purveyors of the drug trade who had made it intolerable for the blacks and Hispanics. Once these minorities left, there was no one to take their place except the junkies who looted the abandoned buildings. To Martin Tolchin, reporting in the *New York Times*, the South Bronx was a "jungle stalked by fear, seized by rage." He explained: "Even for a native New Yorker, the voyage across the Willis Avenue Bridge is a journey to a foreign country where fear is the overriding emotion in a landscape of despair. The residents, who have long been afraid to go out at night, are now afraid to go out during the day with streets menaced by 20,000 drug addicts and 9,500 gang members."[81] Rage, Tolchin said, was "a condition of life" in the South Bronx: "It permeates the rubble-strewn streets and the unheated tenements. It blazes in the eyes of youth-gang members and smolders in the brooding faces of mothers huddled on predawn lines at welfare centers and stacked in rows of benches in hospital emergency rooms and clinics."[82]

Despite all the gloom, there were a few pockets of hope. Throughout the 1970s publicly assisted community groups attempted small-scale renovation projects, including one in 1972 on a site bounded by Stebbins and Intervale avenues and East 169th Street.[83] These projects, however, remained isolated at best and did little to reverse the dominant downward trend.

Central Bronx

In contrast to the collapsing neighborhoods south of the Cross-Bronx Expressway, two neighborhoods north of the expressway, as well as Bronx Park, which they bordered, had a more positive postwar evolution. One of these neighborhoods, Twin Parks, located between Crotona and Bronx parks, was threatened by change but expressed a fierce will to survive. This fact was emphasized by the New York State Urban Development Corporation (UDC), which undertook a series of projects with the community in the early 1970s.[84] In 1966, when the city had proposed erecting low-income public housing in the area, community leaders had rejected the scheme. Bronx Borough President Herman Badillo subsequently approached Archbishop John Maguire, who had established a diocesan committee on housing and urban renewal, to encourage the area's Catholic clergy to form a nonprofit housing corporation. Among those involved was Father Louis Gigante, a charismatic priest at St. Athanasius Church who later entered city politics.[85] At the same time, the newly established Urban Design Group of the City Planning Commission began to work at a grass-roots level to select acceptable sites for "vest-pocket" renewal scattered throughout the area. According to Jonathan Barnett, one of the founding members of the Urban Design Group, Twin Parks was "typical of many inner city areas in being in the midst of a painful transition from a modest, but satisfactory, neighborhood to a slum." After a long and difficult series of public meetings, the various factions of the larger community agreed on a focused plan that, as Barnett wrote, "grouped the limited housing resources that we had to work with" into two major areas, which came to be called Twin Parks West and Twin Parks East.[86]

Some relatively isolated sites within the area were available that could be used for new housing with minimal tenant relocation. The neighborhood residents, including both the long-established Italian-descended whites and the newly arrived blacks and Puerto Ricans from the South Bronx, wanted to see the area stabilized as a middle-class neighborhood. To this end, the planners, in return for permission to build low-income public housing, were asked to go back to the city authorities and increase the allocations for middle-income units so that equal amounts of each type could be built. New schools were also incorporated in the plan. But the key achievement lay in what the plan did not call for: a disruption of the existing land use patterns or a radical change in the neighborhood's social or architectural complexion. "Instead of enclaves of new construction," Barnett said, "old and new have been re-designed into a single fabric, and schools and other community areas have been designed as an integral part of the new buildings."[87]

The UDC was called in to handle the middle-income housing component of Twin Parks' redevelopment. Under the leadership of Father Mario Ziccarelli, a local cleric, various community organizations united to form the Twin Parks Association, which would sponsor the nonprofit housing.[88] A number of young, talented architects and landscape architects were entrusted with the implementation of the UDC's component. Prentice & Chan, Ohlhausen's apartment buildings at 355–365 East 184th Street and 333 East 181st Street, both completed in 1973, offered aesthetically sophisticated solutions to the problem of providing middle-income housing.[89] Occupying a steeply sloping site, 355–365 East 184th Street was a seven-story, U-shaped building that wrapped a sheltered community park, landscaped by Raymond T. Schnadelbach as a series of terraces. At 333 East 181st Street, an outdoor staircase skillfully negotiated another difficult site. Norval White and Elliot Willensky found the building "an exceptionally satisfying statement—as though [it] was always meant to occupy this site."[90] Syncopated fenestration patterns expressed the intricate combination of simplex and duplex units within 333 East 181st Street; apartments ranging in size from studios to five bedrooms were serviced by skip-stop elevators.

The architect Giovanni Pasanella was assigned responsibility for several sites in Twin Parks West. His buildings at 2000 Valentine Avenue, 1880 Valentine Avenue, 1985 Webster Avenue and 2100 Tiebout Avenue, proved to be, according to White and Willensky, the most controversial in Twin Parks.[91] The exteriors of the buildings, which were completed in 1973, were complexly massed. Inside, they incorporated an ingenious interlacing of simplex and split-level duplex units. The floor-through split-level apartments separated living and sleeping areas by a half-level change, which made it possible for the building's elevators to stop only at every two and a half floors, speeding the trip in the elevator and eliminating 60 percent of public corridor space. This reduction in public hallway space was thought to provide greater security. As the journalist Richard Severo noted in the New York Times, "because so many people in New York's high-crime neighborhoods regard hallways with fear, a Manhattan architect has designed a building that simply eliminates most of them."[92] Pasanella commented: "I didn't start out to design a security system. But when I tried to make the architecture relate to the people who are going to live in these buildings, it came out that way. . . . I wanted these apartments to be a series of interlocking houses—as far as possible from the old-law tenements and even the newer apartment buildings, which in their own way are as sterile as the old."[93]

The southernmost of Pasanella's buildings, 1880 Valentine Avenue, intended for elderly tenants, was a stepped building, rising from a height of four stories at its southern end to eighteen stories on the north. Communal terraces every two floors provided views of adjacent Echo Park. Vincent Scully described the building as "a brilliant exploration of its triangular site," and went on to explain:

> It is a wholly contextual building but as monumental as a temple. Its facade toward Webster Avenue is perfectly flat, while that on the other side responds to the diagonal of Valentine Avenue in a series of wedge-shaped planes. Finally, the enormous steps of the south side are bent back in a sharp crease, so

changing the way the light falls upon each plane that the whole mass seems to come alive and reach forward, eyed by isolated windows near the center and terminating in a tower like a high head. The building thus wraps and enfolds as well as cleaving forward.[94]

White and Willensky were even more lavish in their praise: "On an almost unbuildable narrow triangle commanding the undisciplined open space of a complicated street intersection and a hilly green ether that was once called Echo Park is this brilliant solution to a difficult problem. . . . It's perfect."[95]

But the monumentality and grandeur of the conception—the building's "overall image of one great ship in movement . . . laid like a splendid phantom across the depressed area," as Scully put it—may have been too much for the modest expectations of the program. Furthermore, the handling of the specific elements of the building design—jumbo brick, glass block and exposed concrete—were too bold and brutal on the one hand, and too generic on the other. The building's shape, as Scully said, was "carefully unemphatic and, for all its imagistic power, purposefully inexplicit, so that it only gradually imposes itself on our consciousness, as if emerging as an organism out of some fundamental energy natural to the place."[96]

Seen from the perspective of the surrounding streetscape, and considering the UDC's emphasis on small-scale intervention, Pasanella's Twin Parks West buildings came as a surprise. Visually they seemed to sail, as Scully has written, "like a flotilla of ships along the high spine of the Bronx at Webster Avenue. It is one of the few heartening sights to be seen in that area, and one of the grandest in New York."[97] As for the interiors, Pasanella went a long way toward minimizing the impact of size on both the public spaces and the individual apartments. This was particularly so where he explored skip-stop, split-level planning to create apartments that had the amenities of a split-level house and some of the spatial qualities, even the glamour, of the pre–World War I duplex studio apartments of Manhattan, many of which Pasanella could see from his Carnegie Hall office as he developed the designs with his staff, especially Etel Kramer, whose contribution to the project was decisive. "Gio tried to put Manhattan into the Bronx," said one UDC official, suggesting that the split-level arrangement was too sophisticated for the contractors and for the residents alike.[98] But Pasanella was passionate about this feature: "Something more must be done for people than merely packaging them in an accommodation, stacking them up in units, stringing them out in modules."[99] Scully appreciatively noted that "the freedom and variety of space, light, ventilation, and movement which the apartments offer are . . . far beyond those of any other public housing one can think of, and they compare more than favorably with much more luxurious, private programs."[100] Paul Goldberger similarly praised Pasanella for designing "probably the best apartment layout built for public housing in New York in years."[101]

In addition to the UDC-sponsored housing in Twin Parks West, Pasanella also designed a project for the Housing Authority. Completed in 1974, numbers 353, 355, 360 and 365 Ford Street and 355 and 365 East 183rd Street consisted of one sprawling building that contained 322 low-income units; two projecting wings defined a courtyard, designed by the landscape architect Peter Rolland.[102] Inside, skip-stop elevators provided access to the apartments, half of which contained three or more bedrooms.

Pasanella was also the architect of three other buildings that constituted the so-called Twin Parks East project, all completed in 1975. Keith Plaza, at 2475 Southern Boulevard, on the south-

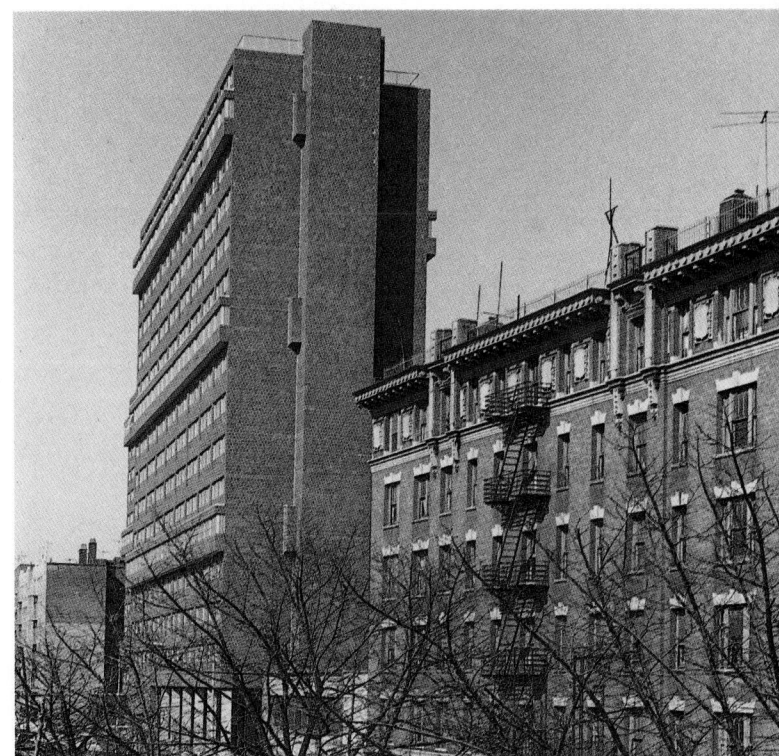

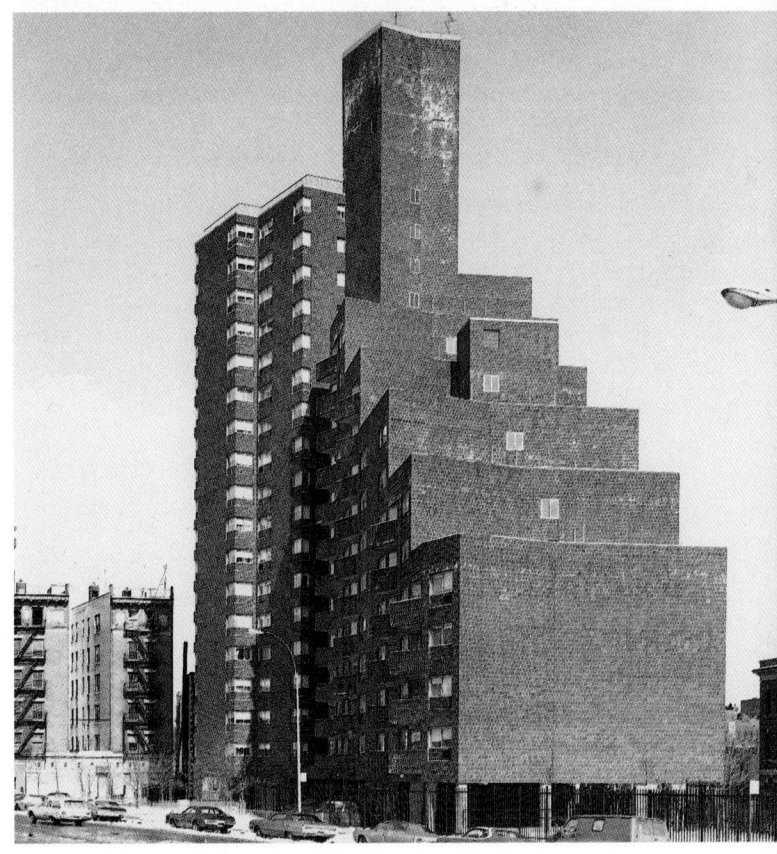

Top: 2000 Valentine Avenue, between East 178th and East 180th streets, Twin Parks West. Giovanni Pasanella, 1973. View to the northeast. PAKL

Bottom: 1880 Valentine Avenue, between Webster Avenue and East 178th Street, Twin Parks West. Giovanni Pasanella, 1973. View to the northeast. PAKL

957

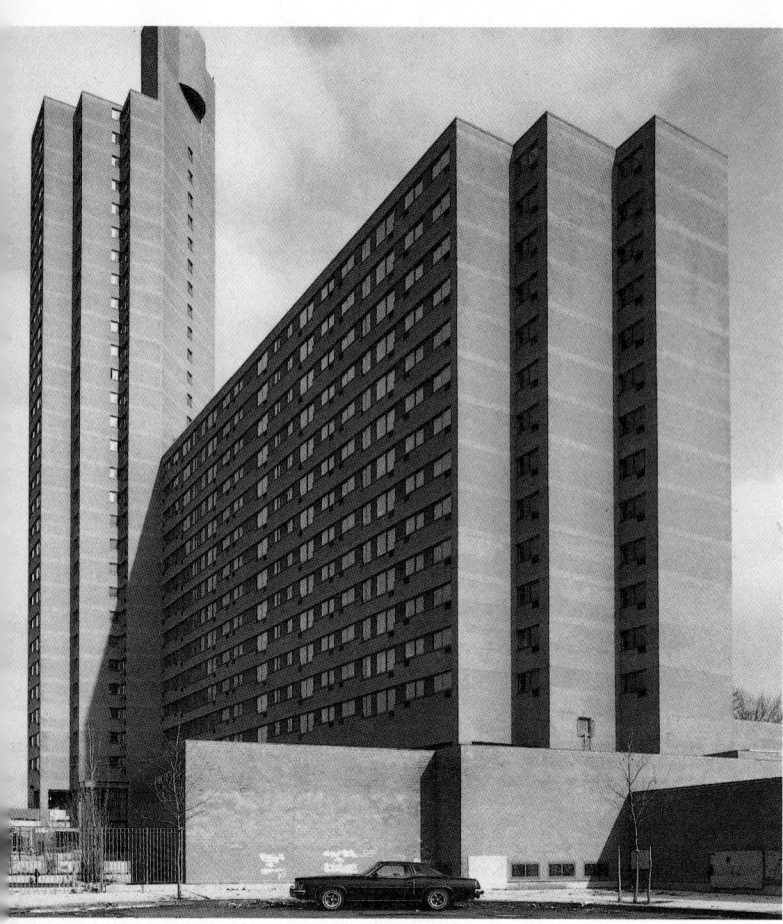

Keith Plaza, 2475 Southern Boulevard, between East Fordham Road and East 187th Street, Twin Parks East. Giovanni Pasanella, 1975. View to the northeast. PAKL

west corner of East Fordham Road, was a thin, thirty-story tower clad in tan brick; at the bottom of the building, and designed in a complementary style, was Bronx Public School 205-A.[103] The tower was dramatically disharmonious with its low-lying context, but it served the neighborhood as a kind of superscale grace note, a secular campanile presiding over the open space of Bronx Park and its New York Zoological Park across Southern Boulevard. Located directly to the south and flanking the intersection of Southern Boulevard and East 187th Street were Kelly Towers North and South, the latter incorporating Bronx Public School 205-B at its base. The sixteen- and eighteen-story buildings were set at mirror-image diagonals, an arrangement that provided most of the apartments with park views and, perhaps more important, established a symbolic gateway to the community from its principal public landmark, Bronx Park. Pasanella had originally intended for the buildings to have complex, interlocking internal plans, but because of the developer's objections he used conventional layouts.

Pasanella's buildings seemed to usurp the role of the area's symbolic gateway played by James Stewart Polshek's previously completed apartment buildings at 2111 Southern Boulevard (1969), on the northwest corner of East 180th Street, and 800–820 East 180th Street (1969), on the southwest corner of Southern Boulevard.[104] Polshek's complex consisted of two boldly striped buildings clad in black and tan brick. The northern building, a rather slender, thirty-one-story tower, conformed to the prevailing street grid, although it was set back from both flanking streets and surrounded by minimally landscaped pedestrian plazas. The southern, nine-story building adopted a modified U shape, with one leg defining a diagonal adjacent to the principal intersection. An enclosed interior courtyard incorporated a sunken amphitheaterlike space. The nine-story building contained duplex units, which were accessible from double-height open-air galleries. These apartments resembled townhouses, complete with stoops and "front yards" (albeit pocket-sized and paved with concrete), a design that seemed to have been influenced by Davis, Brody & Associates' Riverbend Houses (see chapter 12). At ground level, stores were provided to help establish a lively urbanism.

Overall, Polshek's Twin Parks work evidenced a sensitivity to context that reflected a pivotal change in the architect's work, as well as a growing concern for the issue throughout the profession. As the architectural historian Helen Searing would later note: "Working with the archetypal Modernist format of freestanding tower and slab set upon a plaza, Polshek dared to humanize the dwelling units by employing banding in contrasting colors to recall an earlier generation of apartment houses erected in the Bronx during the more ingratiating Art Deco era. At this date, the use of such non-structural polychromy for decorative effects was new, as was the contextual impulse that prompted it."[105]

The Twin Parks project that was most successful at delivering and even enhancing neighborhood scale while providing effective public open space was Richard Meier's Twin Parks Northeast (1967–74).[106] The project was built on portions of three adjacent, irregularly gridded city blocks between Garden and East 183rd streets, Crotona Avenue and Southern Boulevard, with Grote Street and Prospect Avenue dividing it into quadrants. Meier's scheme accommodated 523 families in two towers, one overlooking a new pocket park created by the closing of Grote Street, the other at Southern Boulevard overlooking the zoo. In between, a low

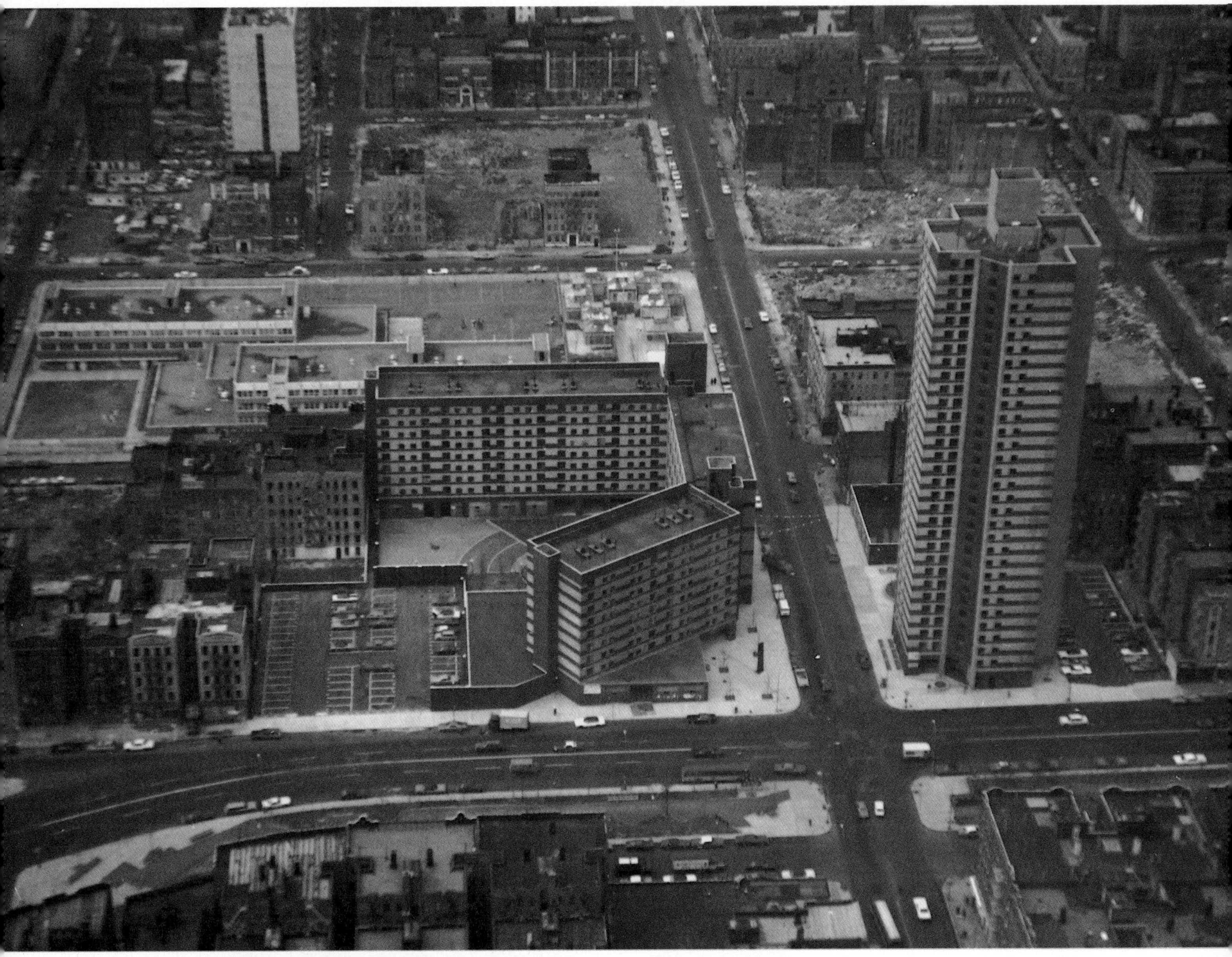

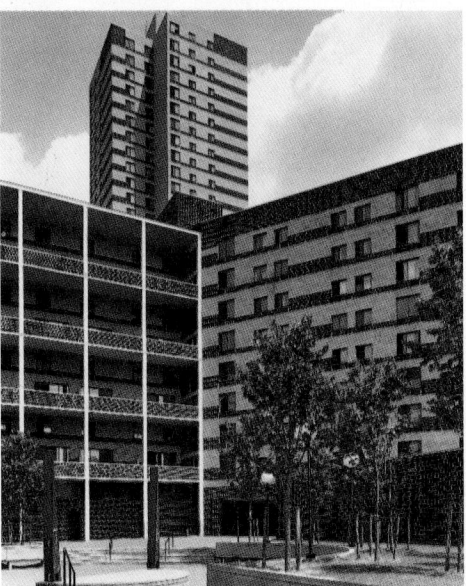

Above: 2111 Southern Boulevard and 800–820 East 180th Street, northwest and southwest corners of East 180th Street and Southern Boulevard, Twin Parks East. James Stewart Polshek, 1969. View to the west. Lieberman. JSP

Left: 800–820 East 180th Street. View to the north showing tower of 2111 Southern Boulevard in the background. Cserna. JSP

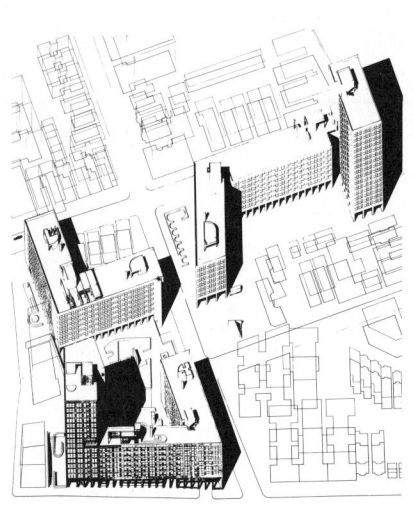

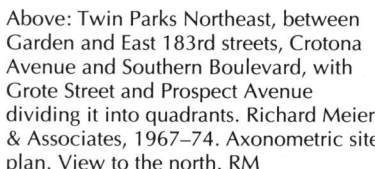

Above: Twin Parks Northeast, between Garden and East 183rd streets, Crotona Avenue and Southern Boulevard, with Grote Street and Prospect Avenue dividing it into quadrants. Richard Meier & Associates, 1967–74. Axonometric site plan. View to the north. RM

Top right: Twin Parks Northeast. View to the southwest. Stoller. ©ESTO

Bottom right: Lambert Houses, east side of Boston Road, between Bronx Park South and East Tremont Avenue, East Tremont. Davis, Brody & Associates, 1973. View to the northeast. DBA

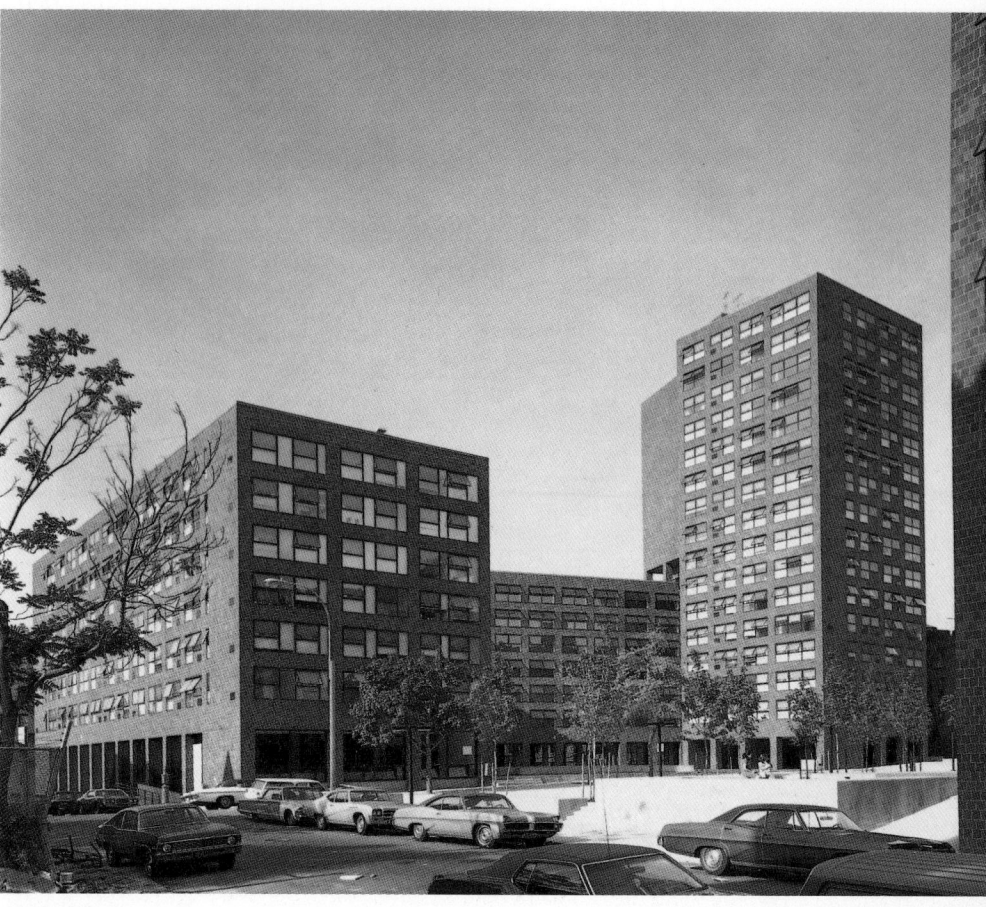

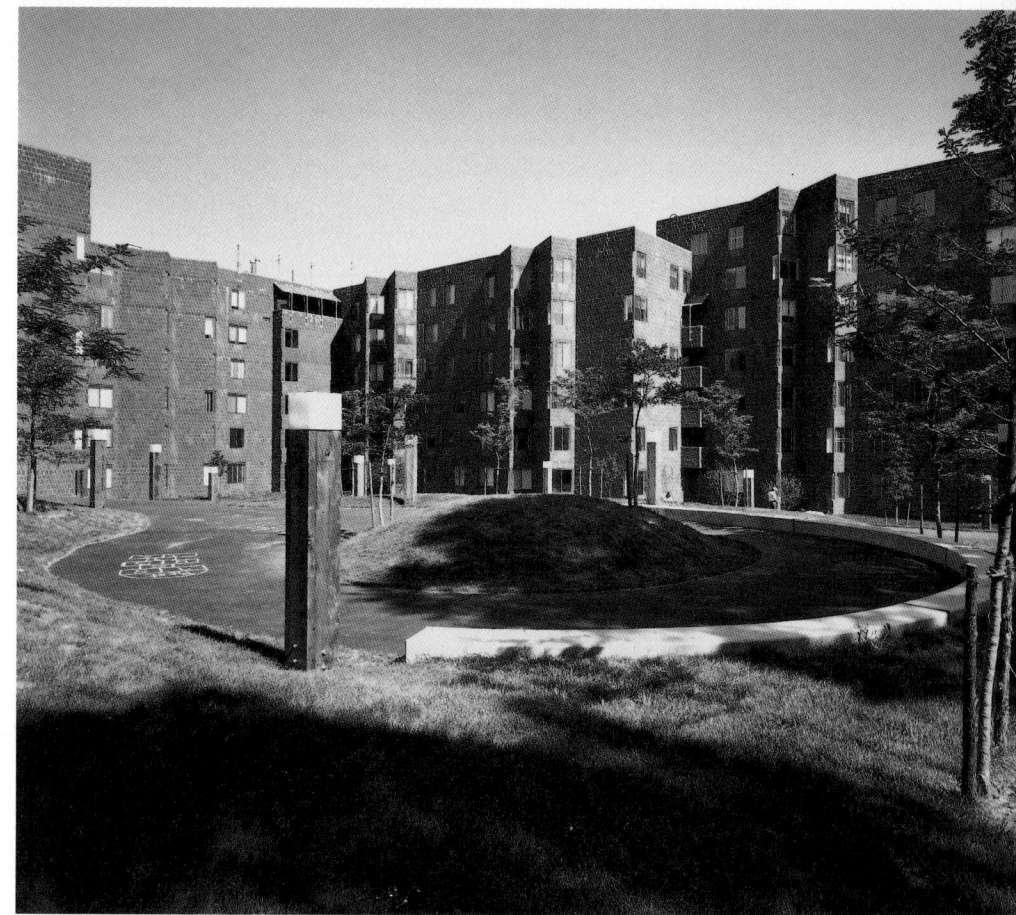

wall of six-story slabs alternately followed and broke with the street wall, simultaneously shaping open space and reinforcing the characteristic texture of the neighborhood, which consisted of tenements and traditional rowhouses. The site was at a critical juncture between the traditional Italian neighborhood and the newly established black community, and the plaza spaces were intended to serve as a mixing place for both groups. To keep within a strict budget, Meier chose to clad his buildings with dark brown jumbo brick, relying for relief on a carefully orchestrated rhythm of very simply detailed large windows, a strategy that wonderfully integrated his design with the surrounding neighborhood.

The principal inspiration for the scheme seems to have been the so-called *à redent* blocks of Le Corbusier's 1920s housing schemes for Paris. Meier's slabs, like Le Corbusier's, were raised on pilotis. But whereas Le Corbusier's ground-level open areas were intended to create a continuous greensward, Meier's were justified as a means to provide ventilation to the garage spaces located beneath them. Though they did enhance visual and functional access to the midblock plazas, they created more of a barrier than a sense of liberated ground space.

Despite the elimination of street closure where it was needed at the ground plane, from the point of view of contextual design, Meier's was the most successful of the Twin Parks projects, avoiding both the visual stridency of Polshek's and the superscale of Pasanella's. Meier himself stressed the urbanism of his complex:

> Twin Parks Northeast is intended not as an architecture of isolated and free-standing buildings in space, but rather as a place of urban continuity. It emphasizes the adaptive capability of the existing city to new structuring, and incorporates some of the quality and texture of traditional building with a humane, modern vocabulary. In both its form and its organization, it expresses the attitude that one of the principal roles of a building in an urban milieu is to make a larger urban statement, to be a generator of social and communal values.[107]

But Meier's scheme was by no means trouble-free. While the architect-critic Kenneth Frampton praised the project's open space "both in relation to its existing urban context and in providing a viable public space for play; a space that seems to have been more than adequately supported by spontaneous use," he had to note that "on occasions, this use had degenerated into violence."[108] Noting that Meier's buildings were raised on stilts, Frampton cautioned:

> The problem posed by pilotis and adjacent public open space . . . is one that is integral to the original model. Even in Le Corbusier's idealized version of a city on piles floating above a continuous park space the problem remains. . . . The designer can never find enough public space in the program to occupy the volume created below the building mass. Thus the undercroft of the Meier scheme sometimes takes on the aura of a wasteland. Even here where the overall provision of public space has been intelligently arranged, excessively large and ill-maintained foyers seem to abound at every corner.[109]

In surveying the collection of buildings that comprised Twin Parks, Paul Goldberger found much to like but ultimately concluded that "design, however compassionate, can mean only so much against the obstacles that make up the housing problem today—budget constraints, bureaucracy, political problems, community pressure, crime." The area, he said, "is undoubtedly a better place than it was," thanks to the new Twin Parks housing, "and better than it would have been had the designs been merely standard examples of banal public housing. But architecture alone, no matter how good, cannot in itself change a neighborhood."[110] In her assessment of Twin Parks, Suzanne Stephens also expressed a belief that the efforts had somehow fallen short:

> The feat of building 1,858 moderate and low-income units . . . on different sites within three years cannot be ignored, no matter how they did it. . . . If social scientists had been involved in the design process, more of the apartments might have fully responded to the users' needs. . . . Yet as the interiors indicate, one still senses that the occupants of the housing are reacting in a very positive way to the apartments. Furnishings give evidence of a response to the architecture, of a strong rooting in the home as an image of self and life style, characteristic of upwardly striving economic groups. But despite Twin Parks' clear successes, it still could be considered as a case where the patient lived while the operation was a failure. In social, urban, and formal terms, none of the architects could produce a complete physical entity applicable as a model for future housing. The lesson for such a utopian goal is still the need for more time, money and research.[111]

Immediately to the southeast of Twin Parks, along the south border of Bronx Park, lay a similar area of rowhouses and tenements, nestled between the park and the elevated subway as it swept in an S-curve to bypass the park on its way to the Northeast Bronx. The demographics here were quite different from those in Twin Parks; this was a predominantly black neighborhood, but many Puerto Ricans lived there as well. The community, led by Barnett Lambert, a local resident, had successfully fought for designation as an urban renewal area. Unable to manage and finance development on their own, the group brought in the Phipps Houses organization, which hired Davis, Brody & Associates to design what came to be called Lambert Houses (1973).[112] The project, for a five-block site spread out along the eastern side of Boston Road between Bronx Park South and East Tremont Avenue, was arguably the era's most contextually responsive high-density, low-rise housing project.

Although Davis, Brody had originally proposed a high-rise scheme, a low-rise approach was ultimately adopted not only because of its inherent values but also to provide tangible recognition that the surrounding low- and mid-rise buildings were worth preserving and rehabilitating. Despite its low height, the scheme increased the site's previous density to contain 731 apartments, 80 percent of the maximum allowed under zoning. Required car parking was handled on an adjacent site, where it was combined with a commercial building. The blocks were filled with six-story, forty-five-unit perimeter buildings that were set back slightly from the street to create grassy buffers and define shared, protected courtyards in the center; although these courtyards were tightly defined, they were not closed off. Davis, Brody's scheme was essentially a return to the garden-type courtyard apartments that had been perfected during the 1920s by Andrew J. Thomas.[113] In addition to the modest height of Lambert Houses, the use of bay windows created an intimate scale that ameliorated the crudity of the buildings' jumbo brick cladding. Inside, a large number of duplex apartments were provided.

Bronx Park, which divided the troubled West and South Bronx areas from healthier regions in the Northeast Bronx, also contained the New York Botanical Garden and Zoological Park. Both institutions survived the upheavals of the neighboring areas in reasonably good shape, and the world-class zoo even added new buildings of considerable architectural distinction. The first buildings of the New York Zoological Park, commonly known as the Bronx Zoo, were designed by Heins & LaFarge and built between 1899 and 1911.[114] Most notable among these was the vast Elephant House (1911), a domed structure that featured late Roman and Byzantine motifs and a basilican interior vaulted with Guastavino tiles. During the interwar period, two architecturally significant additions were made to the zoo complex. In 1934 the architect Charles Platt and the sculptor Paul Manship collaborated on the Paul J. Rainey Memorial Gate, an elegant Modern Classical structure executed in bronze.[115] In 1941 Wallace K. Harrison designed the African Plains, a radical departure from traditional zoo design.[116] The typical bars were replaced with moats to create a more natural environment for the animals, who could roam on the newly created savanna, which was punctuated with native African buildings at full scale. The zoo buildings continued to serve the public effectively throughout the postwar era; in 1972 Ada Louise Huxtable wrote that, in fact, the zoo was a model of architecture in the service of the public, "delivering the best and enriching its resources since 1898."[117]

In 1954 the zoo's renovated reptile house opened, redesigned by Edward C. Embury and Nicholas K. Lucas in association with Aymar Embury II.[118] Inside, Harmon H. Goldstone designed the individually climate-controlled, glass-walled cages to suggest native habitats. James A. Oliver, the zoo's curator of reptiles, said optimistically, "Blue-green tile, tropical plants and a lavish use of color in cage backgrounds create an impression of beauty that will, we hope, lessen the dislike some people have of reptile life."[119]

In 1969 the zoo opened the World of Darkness, a remarkable display habitat for nocturnal creatures housed in an equally remarkable mastaba-inspired pavilion designed by Morris Ketchum, Jr. & Associates and funded equally by the city and the Vincent Astor Foundation.[120] The horseshoe-shaped structure, sited near the Rocking Stone, a large glacial fragment, was based on a radically new approach to displaying nocturnal animals, who in traditional installations would be asleep during normal visiting hours. Researchers at the zoo developed techniques to reverse the animals' cycles, using bright white light during the evening and bright red light—which is invisible to nocturnal animals—during visiting hours, presenting the nocturnal world to zoo goers as it had never been seen before. Ketchum's design dramatically showcased the exhibits in a sculpturally modeled, Modernist-influenced building that was integrated with the environment, in keeping with the philosophy of William G. Conway, director of the New York Zoological Society, who believed that "there ought not to be any visible buildings in the zoo. The zoo should present a strong, pervasive environment, a world of wild creatures. The man-made should be muted with architectural statements [that are] widely dispersed."[121]

At first glance, the building's exterior—inclined walls made of slabs of precast concrete surfaced with black granite chips—seemed unrelated to its surroundings. But closer inspection revealed that it was effectively nestled into its sloping site, and that the black exterior not only helped minimize the structure's size and bulk but also conveyed a sense of the world on display within. To John Margolies, writing in Architectural Forum, the exterior had "a sophisticated theatricality."[122] As Ketchum described it: "Cutting out an entrance court in the circle provided a darkened entry to the almost inky blackness of the visitors' corridor and a similar exit back to daylight. In deference to the

Rocking Stone, part of the entrance court was excavated to untouched glacial rock almost six feet below, thereby creating a geological display for visitors."[123] Despite this somewhat hokey quality, the building was widely admired. In 1969 it received a prestigious Bard Award from the City Club of New York for being "as exciting as a knight's castle, promising endless surprises and discoveries to the young adventurer. This first truly designed exhibition structure in the zoo is a promising indication that recreation has been recognized as an environmental influence that should enhance and relax as much through its architecture as through its contact with nature."[124]

Ketchum followed the World of Darkness with an even larger and in many ways more architecturally distinguished building, the Lila Acheson Wallace World of Birds, whose success, the architect said, could be attributed to "an inspired donor, an imaginative program, and a liberal budget."[125] The donor, who was, with her husband, the founder of Reader's Digest, became immensely philanthropic in her advanced years, concentrating on highly visible projects in New York. Ketchum explained that because of Wallace's great love of birds, "she decided to help fill a sizable gap in the Bronx Zoo's bird presentation . . . a worldwide display of birds that were neither aquatic nor carnivorous. . . . Asked about a budget, Mrs. Wallace said that I should tell her what the budget should be. This was indeed a real and unusual challenge for any conscientious architect."[126] Initially estimated to cost $1.3 million, the completed building cost $4 million.

Ketchum's scheme was a 30,000-square-foot building that consisted of a cluster of skylit concrete cylinders made of vertically striated concrete block rising from a rocky, wooded slope. The design, according to the editors of Progressive Architecture, suggested "so many incipient volcanoes."[127] The critic Carter B. Horsley, writing in the New York Times, said that "from the ground, the building looks like a box for a roller coaster or a forest of tree stumps. From the air, it looks like an exotic honeycomb. It has rakish, soaring exterior ramps that resemble half-extended wings."[128] Each cylinder provided a discrete, enclosed exhibition area, the shape of which was particularly well suited to the display of birds. As Ketchum explained: "Within each display area there are no square corners where birds could break their wings by colliding with the walls." Visitors circulated between cylinders on ramps that lifted them as high as treetop level to afford better views of high-flying species. "Since the majority of bird areas are seen by visitors through vision slots," said Ketchum, "each area is about twenty feet high so that visitors cannot see the top skylight. To bring sunlight down to the earth far below, skylights are sealed with diffusing glass."[129]

After the building opened in June 1972, Ada Louise Huxtable wrote about both of Ketchum's zoo buildings, praising them as demonstrations of "an extremely sophisticated policy of zookeeping and of architectural-ecological environment. . . . Both buildings are impressive as art, science and theater." The two buildings, Huxtable said, were "non buildings, in a calculated sense," in that they had been "carefully inserted in natural settings. The change has been from a museum of living things to a living ecology. The World of Birds, deceptively monumental in photographs, fits the landscape with felicity. . . . Form follows function in a meticulous packaging of the exhibition program. . . . The point . . . is not to create a far-out monument, but an interior of simulated natural environments."[130]

The neighboring New York Botanical Garden, incorporated in 1891, was set up to be both an educational facility and a museum for the public, taking its example from the Royal Botanical Gardens at Kew, England.[131] Calvert Vaux and Samuel Parsons, Jr., chose the site in Bronx Park, and William R. Cobb designed the garden's principal attraction, the Conservatory Range (1902), a group of greenhouses erected by the Lord & Burnham Company. The museum building (1902), which contained classrooms, a domed library and exhibition galleries, was the work of Robert W. Gibson, who won the competition for its design in 1898.

In 1952 plans were announced to convert the three-and-a-half-story fieldstone-and-brick Lorillard Snuff Mill (1840), which had been acquired by the Park Department and used as a carpentry shop and subsequently as a storage shed, into a conference center and restaurant.[132] Opened in 1954, the renovated building included a terrace designed for outdoor dining. Plans for a research laboratory were also announced in 1952. The laboratory, the first such facility at the Botanical Garden, was conceived by the membership, according to *Architectural Record*, "in response to the widespread recognition of the need for basic scientific research in this country, which before World War II had looked to Europe in the botanical field as in other branches of science."[133] The gridded glass building, completed in 1956, was designed by Brown, Lawford & Forbes.

By the late 1960s the Conservatory Range had declined into near dilapidation, a visible sign of the Botanical Garden's overall condition. But by the mid-1970s the garden seemed headed for a rebirth. The Conservatory Range was being restored under the direction of Edward Larrabee Barnes, who also prepared a new master plan that limited automobile and minibus circulation to the perimeter of the grounds and proposed designs for a new entrance.[134] In addition, Barnes, working with his associate Alistair Bevington, was developing designs for a Plants and Man Building, to be constructed out of hexagonal glass modules similar to those developed for the same facility in 1974 as a thesis project by Marcia Seitz Previti of Pratt Institute.[135] According to Barnes, the building would be a totally new kind of glass structure, carried on a system of slender pipe columns, tubular beams and diagonal tension rods and composed of forty-five-foot-wide hexagonal modules that could be grouped together vertically or horizontally to create an environment of any size. As Barnes saw it, these independently climate-controlled modules would be so flexible that they could be expanded vertically as plants grew taller. The building was not constructed.

Northeast Bronx

Extending east of Bronx Park and along the shorelines of Eastchester Bay and the East River, the Northeast Bronx was the borough's least developed section. After a decade of virtual inactivity, it began to come alive with the completion in 1942 of Parkchester, the Metropolitan Life Insurance Company's colossal residential enclave designed by Richmond H. Shreve.[136] Occupying the former site of the New York Catholic Protectory for Boys, bounded by East Tremont Avenue, Purdy Street, McGraw Avenue and White Plains Road, Parkchester's fifty-one red-brick-clad slabs were banal, but they provided not only 12,272 decent, affordable apartments but also an effective urban setting, distinguished by a notable landscaping scheme and a sensitive site plan that reduced automobile through-traffic. Parkchester's town plan recognized some of the special requirements of residents in a dense, highly urban environment peripherally lo-

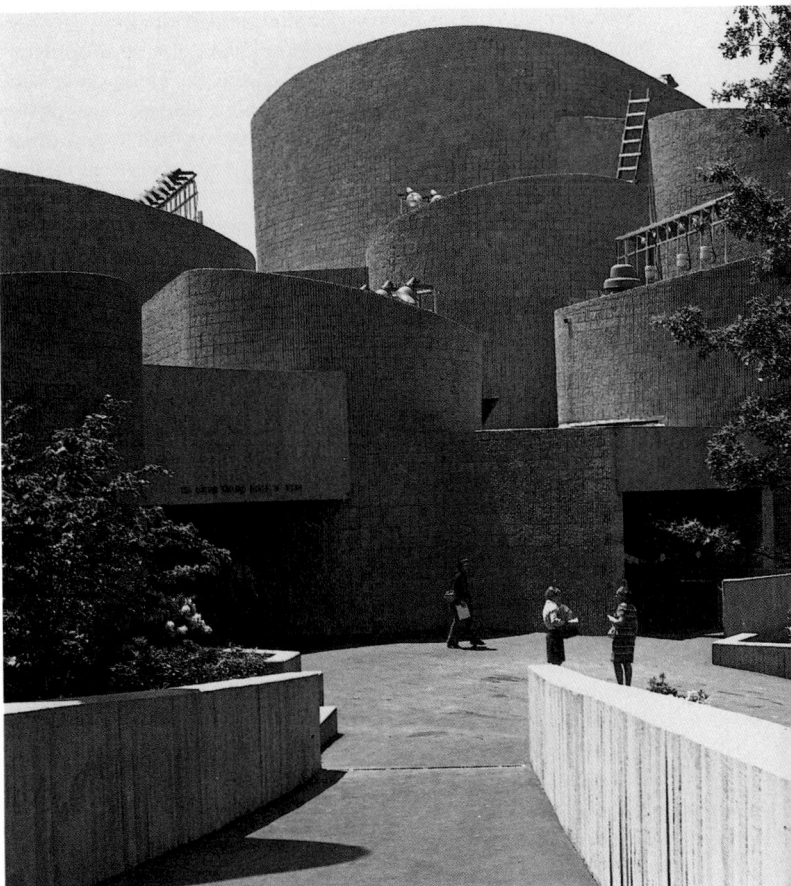

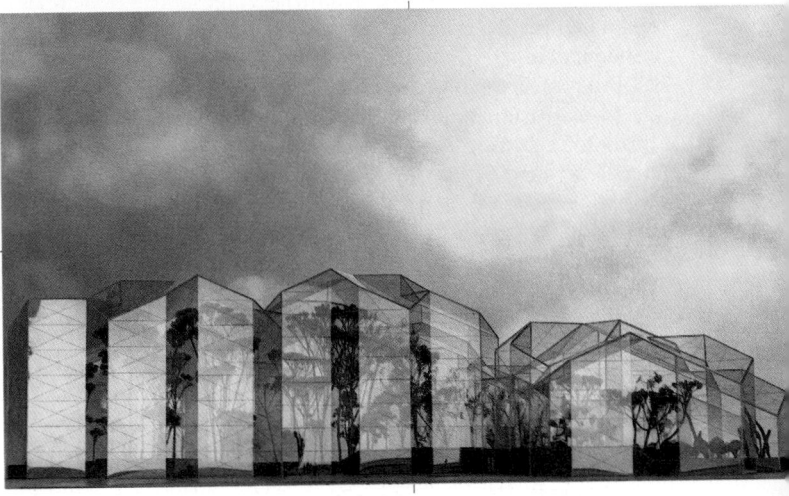

Top: Lila Acheson Wallace World of Birds, Bronx Zoo, Bronx Park. Morris Ketchum, Jr. & Associates, 1972. View to the southeast. NYZS

Bottom: Proposal for Plants and Man Building, New York Botanical Garden, Bronx Park. Edward Larrabee Barnes and Alistair Bevington, 1974. Elevation. Timchula. ELB

cated almost an hour's subway ride from the city's core; for instance, numerous shops were included along the development's
principal streets. Yet its facilities were far from complete:
Metropolitan Life provided no schools, religious buildings or
meeting rooms, so that the 42,000 inhabitants had to go outside
the complex's borders for the normal activities of community life.
Despite its success, Parkchester was the first project to call attention to the limitations of large-scale single-sponsor residential
projects. As Kathryn Close put it in her postwar survey of developments sponsored by insurance companies: "The term 'unified
neighborhood,' so popular with planners, here applies only to
physical appearance. With none of the facilities or stimulation of
a normal neighborhood, a home in Parkchester, while comfortable, becomes just another apartment in a vast maze within the
greater vastness of New York City."[137] Nonetheless, whatever
Parkchester's shortcomings, it provided a far more cohesive environment than the typical outer-edge residential developments
that proliferated in the Northeast Bronx.

One public housing project, Castle Hill Houses (1960), located on three adjacent full-block sites between Havemeyer,
Olmstead, Lacombe and Seward avenues in the Unionport section, made an effort to provide a positive sense of community
through social planning.[138] The development's fourteen slabs,
clad in red brick and ranging in height from twelve to twenty
stories, collectively accommodated 2,025 families. The design,
by Katz, Waisman, Blumenkranz, Stein, Weber, was pretty standard fare, but it did include a two-story community center offering a wider than usual array of services, in an attempt to mitigate
the sense of placelessness and anomie that increasingly plagued
public housing projects. As the editors of Architectural Record
reported: "By planning and coordinating the various age-group
activities (nursery, family health, teenage and aged) in one
building, the architect says, a vital relationship has been established that allows a constant flow of emotions and ideas that establish roots in a community."[139]

New institutional buildings in the Northeast Bronx would
prove to be of much greater architectural interest than its housing
developments. Eventually a vast complex of medical facilities
would be established in the area, a grouping of equal importance
to Manhattan's New York University–Bellevue Medical Center,
Columbia-Presbyterian Medical Center or New York Hospital–
Cornell Medical Center. The first of the area's postwar medical
facilities was Pomerance & Breines's East Bronx Hospital Center
(1955), a two-hospital municipal complex situated on a sixty-
acre tract of land bounded by Pelham Parkway, Eastchester
Road, Morris Park and Seminole avenues.[140] The facility included a seven-story, 500-bed tuberculosis hospital organized
on a Y-shaped plan and a thirteen-story, 898-bed general hospital. The site had been repeatedly passed up because it was hilly,
but working with Clarke & Rapuano, landscape architects,
Pomerance & Breines took advantage of its rough topography by
locating the hospitals on the high ground, where patients could
enjoy the views, and tucking a service building in the hollow.
The Nathan B. Van Etten Tuberculosis Hospital was far and away
the more agreeable of the two hospitals. It featured continuous
balconies opening onto the south side, glazed solaria on the east
and west and a regular pattern of punched openings on the north.
The overall effect was a lively, convincing mix of a health care facility and Modernist design in the tradition of Alvar Aalto's
Tuberculosis Sanitorium at Paimio of 1929–33.[141] The Abraham
Jacobi Hospital, which included extensive facilities for psychiatric medicine, had a cruciform plan extended in one direction to
form a narthexlike outpatient facility.

When it opened in 1955, Jacobi Hospital served as the principal teaching facility for the Albert Einstein College of
Medicine, founded that year as a branch of the Manhattan-
based Yeshiva University.[142] As the East Bronx Hospital Center
was being built, the medical college, intent on establishing a
comprehensive medical center, was beginning to construct its
own physical plant on a triangular campus being developed
according to a master plan prepared by Kelly & Gruzen. The
college campus, immediately to the south of the East Bronx
Hospital Center, was bounded by Morris Park Avenue, Eastchester Road and Newport Avenue. The first Einstein building,
which was sited closest to the municipal hospitals, was the
Forchheimer Medical Science Building (1955), designed by
Kelly & Gruzen.[143] It consisted of a ten-story, slablike hospital
with a continuous aluminum-panel window wall set between
exterior concrete columns and relieved by eyebrow sunshades
on the south side. Running perpendicular to this was a three-
story drumlike administration building, from which a fan-
shaped, 750-seat auditorium dramatically projected toward the
street.

In 1961 Frederick Kiesler and Armand Bartos proposed a
provocative, seven-story hospital with a Y-shaped plan, a departure from Kelly & Gruzen's master plan for Einstein.[144] The
scheme called for eight-sided rooms, which would alleviate the
claustrophobia typical of four-walled, boxy hospital rooms and
offer more flexibility, allowing both patients in double rooms to
have an outside window. The unusual geometry also resulted in
a faceted rather than a straight-line corridor, creating natural
bays where gurneys and wheelchairs could be temporarily
stored without blocking circulation flow. On the exterior,
Kiesler carried out his idea of spatial "continuity" with round-
cornered vertical windows set into precast-concrete wall panels.
Although this scheme was not realized, another, much less daring design by Kiesler and Bartos, for the Ullman Research Center
for Health Sciences, was built in 1962–63.[145] The twelve-story
tower was given an unusual twelve-sided form, designed to provide the advantages of radial planning while retaining straight
windows and walls on the outside band, where the work areas
were located.

In 1957 the State of New York announced the development
of a third medical campus in the area, the Bronx Psychiatric
Center, for a site on 126 acres of reclaimed land bordered by the
Hutchinson River Parkway, the tracks of the Penn-Central
Railroad, the Bronx and Pelham Parkway and Waters Place. The
state proposed to build a 3,000-patient psychiatric hospital, designed by Urbahn, Brayton & Burrows and Hart, Jerman &
Associates, and consisting of four buildings ranging in height
from six to fifteen stories.[146] This project did not go forward, but
in 1969 the Office of Max O. Urbahn redesigned a portion of the
project, the Bronx Children's Psychiatric Hospital, at 1000
Waters Place.[147] Reflecting radically different attitudes toward
health care and social planning than those prevailing a decade
earlier, as well as changing notions of architectural form, the
new hospital was constructed as a collection of eight domestically scaled pavilions with brick bearing walls and shed roofs,
housing 192 five- to sixteen-year-old inpatients. The pavilions
were connected to each other at grade to provide security and
all-weather access to centralized administration, teaching, therapy and recreational facilities. The design was handled with
considerable care to create a humane atmosphere, a quality that
was enhanced by Constantino Nivola's sculpted animals and
cast-relief wall panels. Two years later, in 1971, Gruzen &
Partners added a second well thought-out building to the cam-

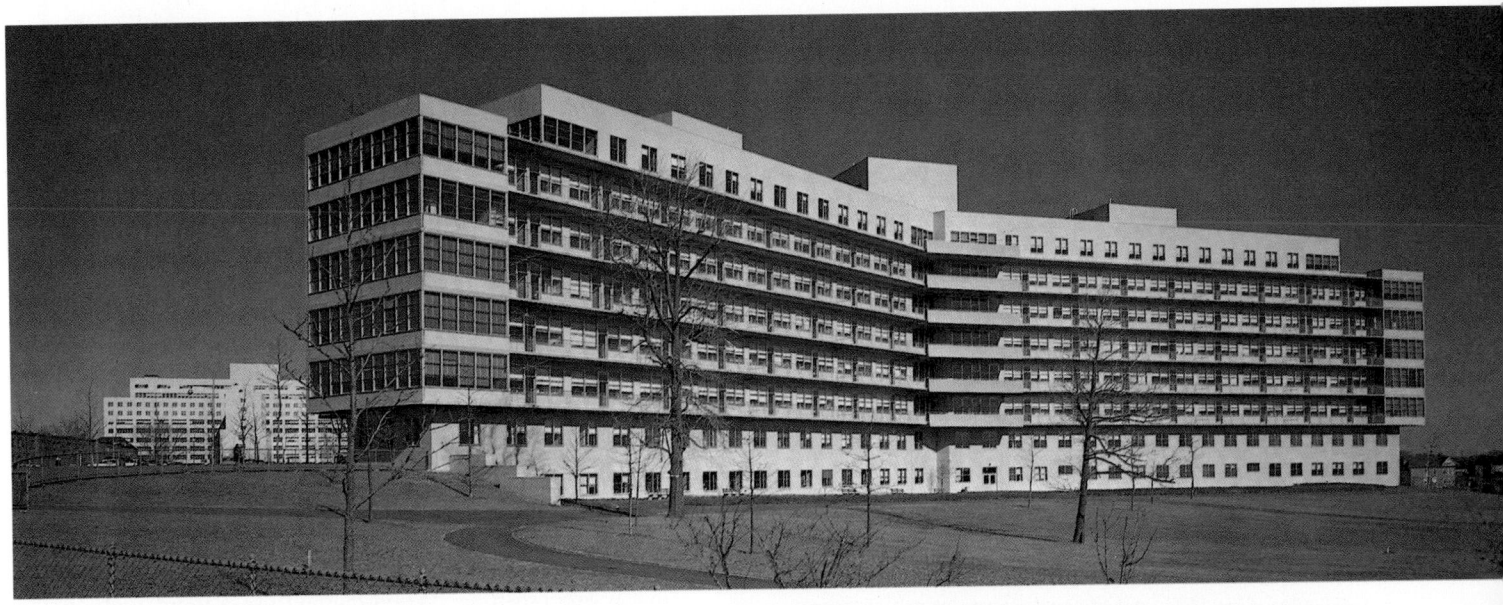

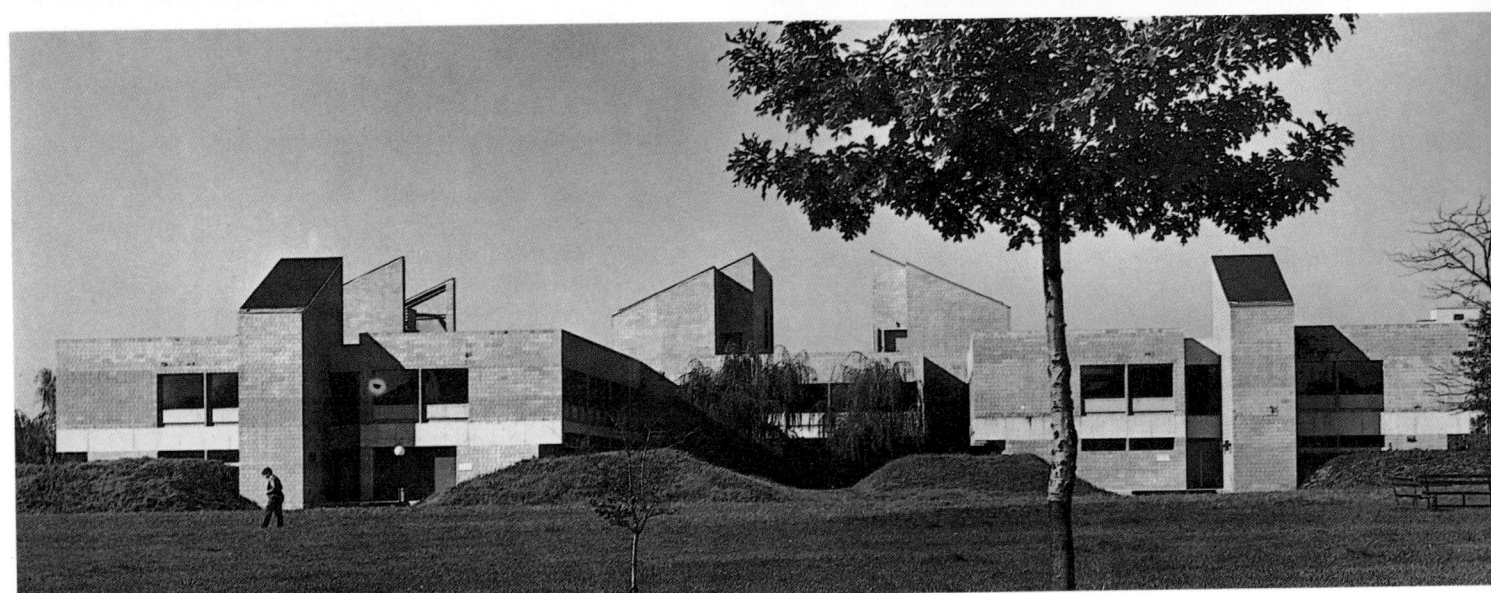

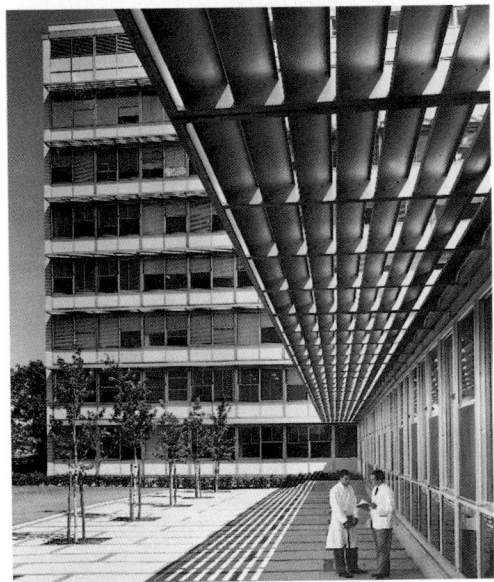

Top: Nathan B. Van Etten Tuberculosis Hospital, East Bronx Hospital Center, bounded by Pelham Parkway and Eastchester Road, Morris Park and Seminole avenues, Westchester Heights. Pomerance & Breines with Clarke & Rapuano, 1955. View to the north. Stoller. ©ESTO

Center: Bronx State Hospital Rehabilitation Center, 1500 Waters Place, between Penn-Central Railroad tracks and Hutchinson River Parkway, Westchester Heights. Gruzen & Partners, 1971. View to the northwest. GS

Left: Forchheimer Medical Science Building, Albert Einstein College of Medicine, bounded by Morris Park Avenue, Eastchester Road and Newport Avenue, Westchester Heights. Kelly & Gruzen, 1955. Schnall. GS

pus: the Bronx State Hospital Rehabilitation Center, at 1500 Waters Place.[148] The building was organized as a series of pavilionlike wings that defined courtyards and established a low, friendly scale; yet it also had very clear circulation patterns, an essential element in accommodating inpatients and outpatients receiving psychological and occupational therapy.

In 1970 Richard Meier was commissioned by the Facilities Division of the New York State Department of Mental Hygiene to add another building to the campus, the Bronx Developmental Center (1977), a total-care residential facility for 750 children with physical and mental disabilities.[149] As built, the facility accommodated 380 resident patients as well as serving outpatients. It occupied a featureless eighteen-acre site squeezed between the Penn-Central Railroad's right-of-way and the Hutchinson River Parkway, directly north of the Bronx Children's Psychiatric Hospital. Meier's design called for three buildings around a courtyard. One building, along the parkway side on the east, consisted of four pavilions connected by a continuous spine. Despite the use of slick, "natural"-finish aluminum panels throughout the complex, the scheme was meant to convey a residential ambience, with each pavilion functioning as a house for inpatients. The appearance of the rectangular service slab that formed the second of the three buildings was intended to establish the complex "as a single unit," but when viewed from the west, the point of arrival for patients and their families, it created an impression of formidable mass and large scale.[150] The third building, on the south, contained areas for physical therapy and a gymnasium.

Meier's complex was rationally planned and utterly logical, but it was also dauntingly abstract in form. As Ada Louise Huxtable observed:

> Immediately upon entry, the glass-walled reception area gives a view of the entire complex that makes its organization clear. The progress from public to private spaces is skillfully controlled, from reception, classrooms, clinics and cafeteria, across the court with its outdoor classroom extension, sculptured steps, walls, slides and amphitheater, by way of a glass roofed corridor or open walk, to the residential quarter. All of these are "coded" visually by the window types, the nature of the exterior skin panels and the articulation of the parts; in this way, the whole building can be "read." The aluminum panels shift from horizontal to vertical, for example, from the classrooms with their elongated windows to a closed, vertical stairwell. The windows themselves are round-cornered, like bus windows . . . and are held rigidly flat with the wall surface in residential and classroom areas. In the more public dining, social or therapy areas (pool, gymnasium) they become larger, slightly inset, mullioned glass expanses. There is a rhythmic fugue of fenestration, allied to a subtly expressive skin.[151]

Even before it was completed, Huxtable observed that the Bronx Developmental Center had become "the cynosure of the architectural world" and "an object of controversy: the building's sleek silvery skin and carefully machined look turn on most professionals and turn off most laymen. It is a landmark before its doors open."[152] The architect John Hejduk, for example, celebrated Meier's design:

> The Developmental Center is a major commentary on just where we are at this three-quarter-mark of our century. It is fashionable to make reference to history and the ancestors of modern architecture, but you know that this Bronx hospital complex is Meier's and Meier's alone. Today, as everything is required to have a message, Meier and his architecture do. It's solid and dense, it's an old message, clear and useful. Most of

all, it's transferable, it's simple and it's devoid of convoluted intellectual musings. The message is that architecture can lift up the spirit and make life a little better.[153]

But the building had many critics as well. Mark Stevens, in his review in Newsweek, went right to the heart of the issue: "Architecture is Art's ambassador to the real world, but some psychologists and parents of retarded people think Meier has forced an unhomelike art upon the lives of his patients."[154] Although Meier claimed that he had tried to create a "microcosm world, a sanctuary with a strong sense of community,"[155] Stevens criticized the design's diagrammatic separation of "public" and "private" space and such features as the window pattern designating the functional components of the building. "Perhaps the design is too powerful," Stevens said. "The architect's hand is too visible—great buildings seem given, not designed." Furthermore, Stevens said, the complex's unrelenting Modernism was off-putting: "However beautifully composed the panels on Meier's building—as the light changes, so does their coloring—they also shoot light back into one's eyes, giving the building a standoffish air. When laymen use a word such as 'unhomelike,' architects feign puzzlement. They should listen harder."[156] The issue of the design's appropriateness, the fit between function and artistic character, an aspect so often ignored in the assessment of important Modernist work during the postwar era, dominated the criticism of Meier's building. For many people, especially the families of patients, the design evoked undesirable associations; as Anthony Pitto, a parent of a mentally disabled child, said, the complex looked like "an architect's nightmare of a submarine."[157]

In her detailed review of the Bronx Developmental Center, Suzanne Stephens found that "in terms of architectural problem-solving," the complex was "clearly a masterpiece . . . of refinement, not invention." But she was critical of its obsessive purism; in Stephens's view, Meier had ignored the context of the medical campus and the site, creating an introverted, "self-contained object." Stephens also pointed out a number of aspects of the design—including open railings, open-tread stairs and an open bridge—that were not particularly well suited to the program. In addition, she touched on the issue of homeyness, noting that in response to the client's request for a "warm homelike atmosphere (home-type finishes)," Meier, known for his pristine cubist-inspired villas, "gave them 47 different colors, wood cabinets, curved windows, natural light. Perhaps the only homes in which one finds interiors like these are ones designed by Richard Meier." Stephens's conclusion raised an issue that other critics had ignored:

> If architecture as an art object inspires guilt, the Bronx Developmental Center compounds one guilt with another: what to do with the mentally retarded? We want them to be made perfect, like the container in which they are contained. And if they can't be perfect, we want them to be hidden, or at least scattered, so we don't have to deal with the fact that three percent of our population is mentally retarded. Bronx Developmental Center lets us know in no uncertain way of their presence.[158]

Whatever its critical reception, the Bronx Developmental Center quickly entered into the realm of popular imagery, briefly enjoying a status comparable to that of the Guggenheim Museum, standing as a symbol of Modernism but also serving as the butt of jokes. It was used in Marshall Brickman's comic film Simon (1980) to portray the fictitious Institute for Advanced Concepts, within whose technologically perfect confines a group of brilliant scientists go mad.[159]

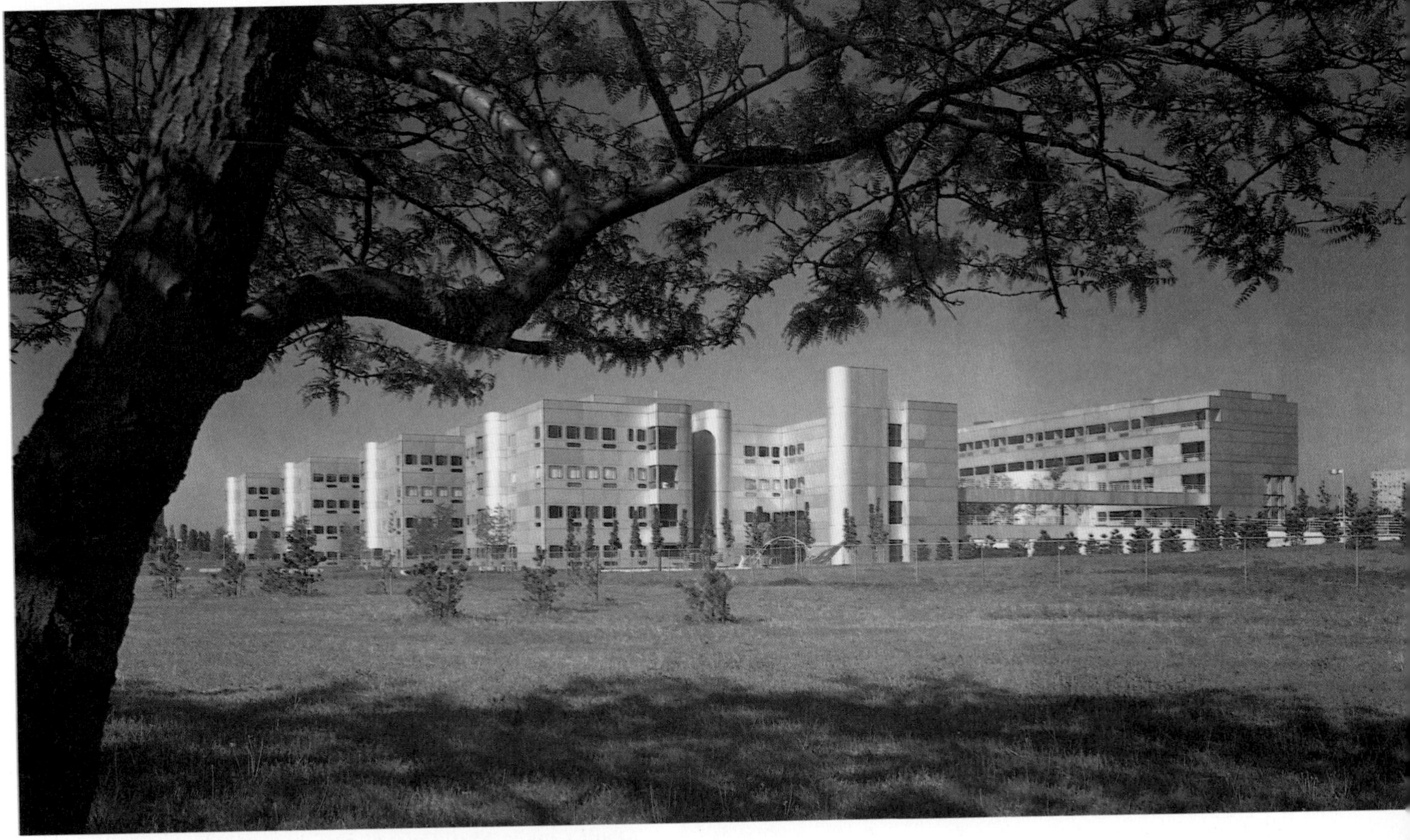

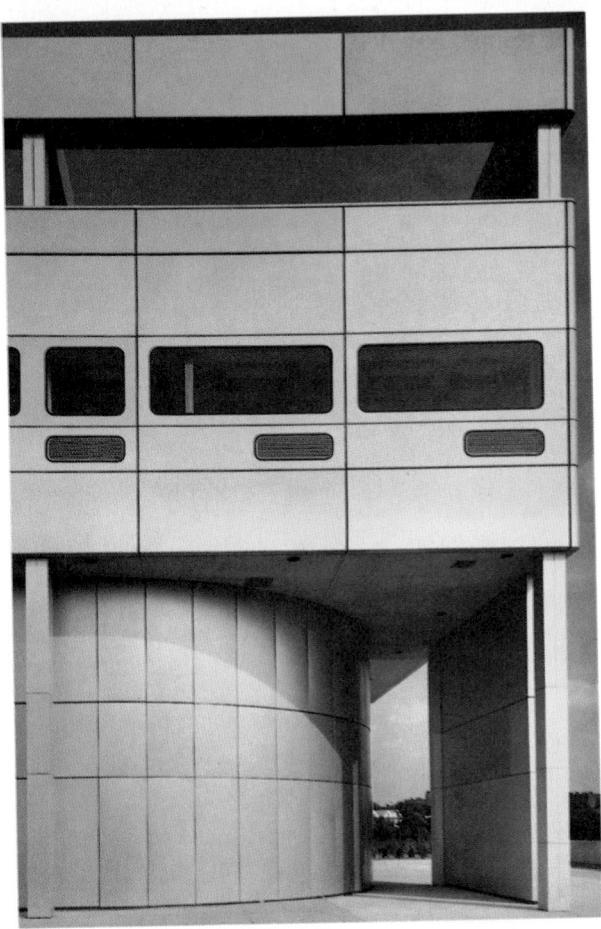

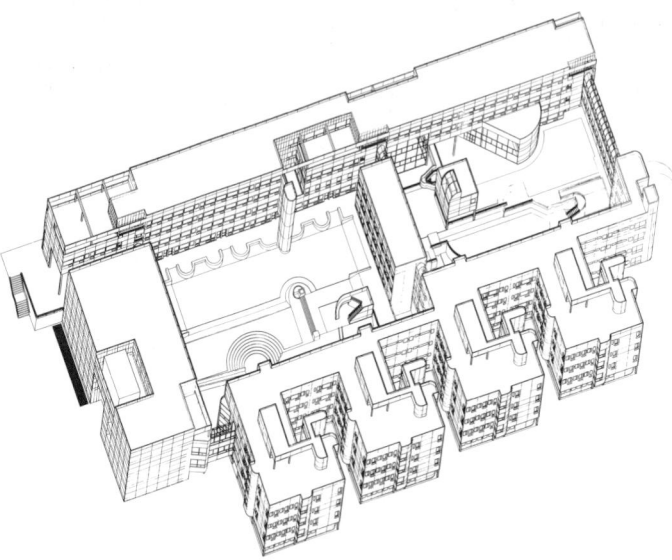

Top: Bronx Developmental Center, Bronx Psychiatric Center, 1200
Waters Place, between Penn-Central Railroad tracks and Hutchinson
River Parkway, Westchester Heights. Richard Meier & Associates,
1977. View to the southwest. Stoller. ©ESTO

Bottom left: Bronx Developmental Center. Stoller. ©ESTO

Bottom right: Bronx Developmental Center. Axonometric showing
view to the northwest. RM

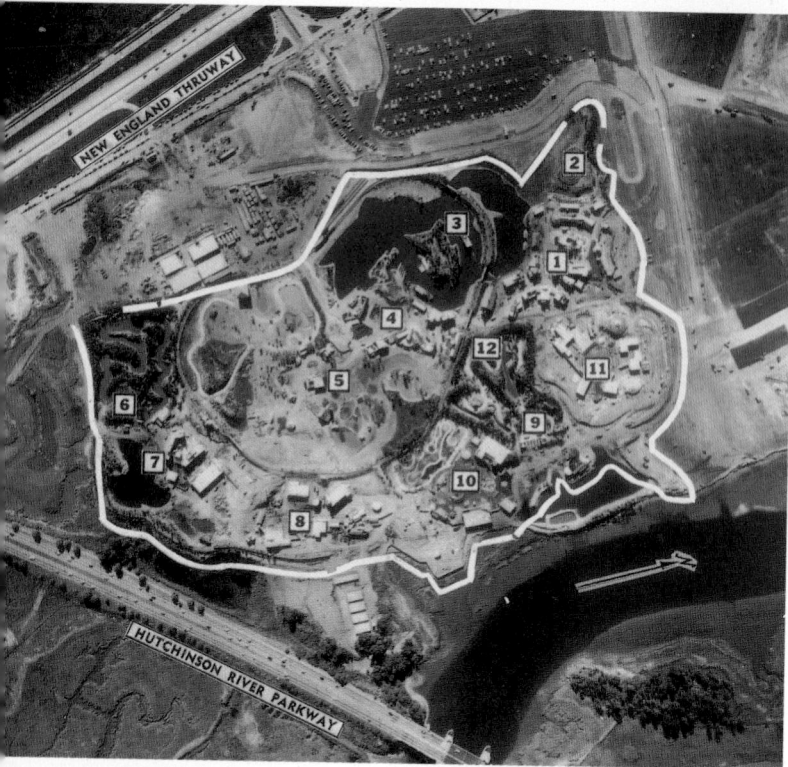

In 1959 C. V. Wood, Jr., who along with Walt Disney had masterminded Disneyland, the pioneering "theme park" opened four years earlier in Anaheim, California, publicly announced the construction of Freedomland.[160] This participatory, live-entertainment amusement park was to be built on a 205-acre, swampy, undeveloped site located between the New England Thruway, the Hutchinson River Parkway and the Hutchinson River in the Northeast Bronx, part of a 400-acre site owned by the real estate concern of Webb & Knapp, which leased the plot to Freedomland. The park, which opened in 1960, contained an eighty-five-acre entertainment area that took the shape of the contiguous United States, and incorporated such features as the Great Lakes, dug seven feet deep, several major cities, and the Rocky Mountains, which rose to a height of approximately fifty feet. Morris Gilbert reported in the *New York Times* that while the park's layout was "perhaps not quite acceptable to the Geodetic Survey because so many dull places have been left out," it did present "a panorama of this nation."[161] The vast majority of visitors were expected to be driving from the outer boroughs and outlying suburban communities. Accordingly, passenger trains were provided to carry visitors from the far reaches of the 120-acre, 9,000-car parking lot to the park's principal entrance, where a re-creation of Little Old New York as it appeared between 1750 and 1850, complete with a fleet of working horsecars, served as an appropriate gateway.

Among the park's forty other attractions were simulations of the landing at Plymouth Rock, the battle of Bunker Hill, Lewis and Clark's expedition, the 1906 San Francisco earthquake, Mardi Gras in New Orleans and the early days of Hollywood. Many of the park's staff of 2,000 full-time employees wore costumes and portrayed a wide variety of roles, including buckskinclad Pony Express riders; firemen putting out the Chicago Fire of 1871, which "ignited" every twenty minutes; Indian tribes; passengers aboard the Sante Fe railroad; and captains and crew members of authentic paddle-wheelers that navigated a re-creation of the Mississippi River. Visitors could board a "Correspondents' Wagon," equipped with a white flag, to safely cross Union and Confederate lines as park staffers in gray and blue enacted a Civil War battle, or they could drive antique cars, some dating back to 1901, through the New England exhibit. In a wink at New York's reputation as a dangerous city, "robbers" regularly held up a bank in Little Old New York. Visitors to the reconstruction of F. & M. Schaefer Brewing Company's first brewery, or to the saloon in the Old Francisco area, would find a clear break with verisimilitude, however: no alcohol was served at the squeaky-clean, family-oriented theme park. Actual business could be conducted within the park in a branch of the Bank of New York, which was housed, according to the *New York Times*, in "a model of a bank of the Eighteen Fifties" and featured employees wearing period costumes "to add the authentic touch."[162] The park's visual evocation of the nation included a million-dollar landscaping program, with magnolia and oleander trees gracing a mock New Orleans, and a cornfield lending a slim measure of credibility to the ersatz Great Plains.

From the first, the developers of Freedomland had thought big. Designed to handle crowds of up to 90,000 people, the park contained rides that could carry 35,000 patrons an hour; Freedomland's restaurants and snack bars were capable of feeding 32,000 people at a time. Given C. V. Wood's background as one of Disneyland's creators, as well as chief super-

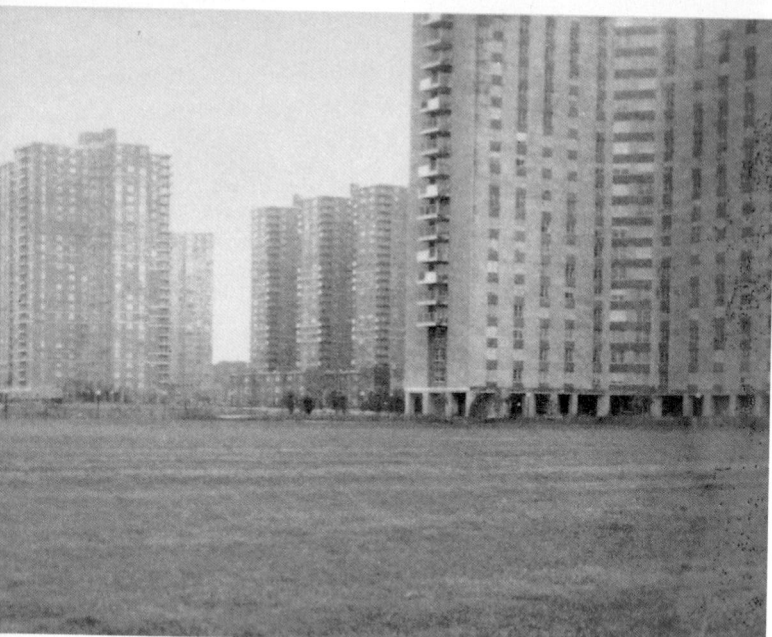

Top: Freedomland, between New England Thruway, Hutchinson River Parkway and Hutchinson River, Baychester. C. V. Wood, Jr., 1960. Aerial view of site showing shape of park. NYT

Bottom: Co-op City, between New England Thruway and Hutchinson River Parkway; and between Hutchinson River Parkway, Boller Avenue and Hutchinson River, Baychester. Herman Jessor, 1965–70. BCHS

visor of its construction and opening year's operation, comparison between the California and New York theme parks was inevitable. Freedomland, run on a day-to-day basis by Frederich V. Schumacher, the former general manager of Disneyland, was clearly intended to outshine its predecessor: it was forty acres larger, contained nineteen more attractions than Disneyland had initially, and had a start-up cost of $65 million, nearly four times that of Disneyland's $17 million. In terms of the individual visitor's experience, the principal difference between the two parks was that while Disneyland presented an array of themes, including the realm of pure fantasy, Freedomland concentrated on significant phases and watershed moments in the country's history. The one exception to Freedomland's unabashedly nostalgic glance backward was an exhibit titled Satellite City, which was meant to present "our nation's city of the future."[163]

At first Freedomland was a big hit. On opening day, crowds began to gather at 7:30 A.M., two and a half hours before visitors were admitted; by 10:00 A.M., bumper-to-bumper traffic on both the Hutchinson River Parkway and the New England Thruway had slowed to three miles per hour. When visitors stayed longer at the park than had been anticipated, others were turned away. But the park's appeal began to fade rather quickly. The big loser in what turned out to be a financial fiasco of the top order was William Zeckendorf, president of Webb & Knapp.

"Rather early in the game," Zeckendorf would later recall, "the project proved to be overpromoted, overexpensive and underfinanced. Too late for us to do much about it, it turned out to be misconceived, grievously mislocated, and utterly mismanaged." At the outset, his company was safe, serving as no more than a landlord, but eventually it became clear that Freedomland's owners couldn't pay their rent. Webb & Knapp accepted stock in the business in lieu of rent, but the situation only got worse, with builders and suppliers "threatening to close things down before the show even started." Nonetheless, as Zeckendorf explained, "Freedomland still seemed like a good promotion: to get our money out, we put more in. . . . The process continued: we ended up owning Freedomland. Show-business productions tend either to make it big or to flop very expensively. Freedomland, with its enormous fixed cost, never got near the break-even point."[164] In September 1964, citing competition from the World's Fair, Freedomland's owners filed in federal court for bankruptcy, under Chapter 11. Management sought to keep Freedomland afloat, considering a move to an adjacent, thirty-acre site, but their efforts failed and the park was replaced by Co-op City.

Co-op City (1965–70) was a phenomenon unto itself, housing approximately 55,000 people in 15,372 apartments.[165] Said to be the largest housing development ever undertaken in the world, exceeding by several thousand units its nearest American rival, Parkchester (see above), Co-op City had the same population as White Plains, New York; had it been an independent city, at the time of its completion it would have been the nation's 110th largest.

The 300-acre site of Co-op City was fairly remote, accessible mostly by car and bus; the two nearest subway stations were both almost a mile away. In addition, it was cut off from the rest of the Bronx on its western flank by the New England Thruway and was bounded on the east by the Hutchinson River; a small part of the site was located across the river and was therefore even more isolated.

The project was organized by the United Housing Foundation (UHF), founded in 1951 by a consortium of labor unions with close ties to the Amalgamated Clothing Workers of America. Since 1959 the UHF had been headed by Abraham Kazan, a pioneer in developing projects for middle-income families, many of whom were unable to obtain adequate housing in the city's nonsubsidized open market and were fleeing to the suburbs. Rents in Co-op City could be held down because the foundation borrowed money at low interest rates from New York State through its Mitchell-Lama program. In addition to housing, Co-op City would include nine parking garages accommodating 10,500 cars, neighborhood shopping centers with community rooms, and a power plant. Ninety acres were set aside for four elementary and two junior high schools, as well as for police and fire-fighting facilities. Of the remaining 210 acres, 85 percent was reserved as open space.

Co-op City was designed by Herman Jessor, who had worked on projects for the UHF from its beginning and had just completed the UHF-sponsored Rochdale Village project in Queens (see "Queens," below). The development consisted of thirty-nine apartment buildings, including twenty-four- and twenty-seven-story articulated slabs and thirty-three-story cruciform reinforced-concrete towers; all the buildings were sheathed in brick and were centrally air conditioned. The design had far more to do with economy than aesthetics, a situation that Jessor lamented: "The moment you depart from standard materials and construction, it is going to cost more. The cheapest wall is still a plain brick wall. We are willing to pay for something practical, but are unwilling to pay for art. And good architecture is an art. Look at Europe. All the arts are subsidized. We are the wealthiest nation on earth; our government should subsidize good architecture, especially on low-income projects."[166] But as the architectural journalist Walter McQuade pointed out, it was not the government but the project's sponsor who should be held accountable:

> We can all be glad that those 15,000 families in Co-op City will be able to live decently. . . . They are getting a pretty good deal for their money. But what is the rest of society getting in return for the immense governmental assistance involved? Not much. It is time for the sponsors of such housing to accept the fact that it is a city they are helping to build, not just so many thousands of indoor rooms. Government is paying most of the ticket on this trip, and government has the right to insist that the destination be pointed not only by economics and engineering, but by sociology and architectural talent as well.[167]

The day after the project was officially announced in February 1965, 1,698 families swamped the UHF's offices with applications for apartments. Several months later, on May 12, the City Planning Commission held a hearing on Co-op City. Maurice W. Kley, speaking on behalf of the New York Chapter of the American Institute of Architects, criticized Jessor's handling of the public spaces and the shopping center: "The unplanned area for an adjoining shopping center, if not integrated into the total scheme, will result in another example of wasteful, piecemeal environmental planning." Kley urged that considerable attention be paid to the overall planning for the project: "Urban amenities and sociological and cultural benefits would result from total planning. There is an opportunity here to bring to the near-in suburbs all the advantages of the city and add them to the recreation and park areas and other amenities of the suburbs."[168]

The subject of the City Planning Commission's hearing was the rezoning of the site necessary to accommodate the project.

The New York Chapter of the American Institute of Architects held that the area should be zoned as a mixed-use development rather than the composition of separate and isolated purposes proposed by Jessor and the UHF. Recognizing the foundation's desire to proceed and its shortage of funds for planning, members of the chapter volunteered their services to provide an alternate plan. Although the City Planning Commission's report stated that they were in agreement "with those who believe that the project should provide an attractive, pleasant, stimulating, and aesthetically satisfying living environment," they granted the zoning changes necessary to allow Jessor's plan to go forward.[169] But the commission did reduce the population density from the originally proposed 17,000 units to 15,372 units, and they requested that a top-flight firm of site planners and landscape architects be retained to help.

Widespread objections to the plan's uniformity, bulk and density continued to be voiced, and several of Jessor's critics advocated the introduction of low-rise elements into the complex. Although Jessor contended that "people just don't want to walk up stairs; that's why we aren't going into garden apartments or town houses," 238 three-story townhouses were eventually included.[170] Even after construction began, Co-op City remained controversial, but the focus of the debate shifted from issues of density and design to concerns about class ghettoization and the project's impact on declining neighborhoods of the Bronx. As Joseph P. Fried, the New York Times housing and real estate reporter, put it: "Critics of the development and of others like it contend that while such projects help to meet the shortage of middle-income housing, they are doing little to meet another drastic need: housing for low-income families. Some critics also assert that the 15,372-family Co-op City will help to create future ghettos by 'siphoning off' middle-class white families from Bronx areas that are in racial transition."[171]

As tenants were about to move into the first completed building, the twenty-four-story unit at 900 Baychester Avenue, on December 10, 1968, the UHF indicated that as many as 4,000 of the 10,000 applicants were white families from the Central Bronx, confirming the dramatic shift that had taken place in the demographics and character of that area. What had once been a major destination for Jewish and Irish New Yorkers, a sign that they were moving up the ladder of economic success, had become for their sons and daughters a place to get away from, either by moving to "the city," that is, Manhattan, or to in-city suburbs such as Riverdale or various parts of Queens, or to the suburbs in Westchester, Long Island and New Jersey.

The causes of the postwar transformation of the Bronx were multiple and complex. According to Roger Starr, the main cause of flight from the Central Bronx was the issue of rent control: "The apartment owners are usually small people who have been badly hurt by rent control. They don't want to invest any more money and they want to get out as soon as possible."[172] But racial tension was an undeniably critical factor in the so-called white flight that accounted for much of Co-op City's appeal. It was thus somewhat surprising that close to 20 percent of the first 6,800 families to move in were nonwhite, a remarkable percentage given that most subsidized middle-income projects had hitherto practiced de facto segregation. There were several reasons for the racial mix. As one black policeman put it: "For a black man, like myself, this was a chance to get in on the ground floor, instead of settling in someplace that the white man had used and left."[173] Nonetheless, to some architects and planners, such as Harry

Schwarz, chairman of the New York Chapter of Planners for Equal Opportunity, a 20 percent nonwhite population was inadequate to the need; he believed that between 33 and 40 percent of the tenants should be nonwhite. This was not possible, however, given the Bronx's social and economic realities.

Despite its success in attracting residents, Co-op City left most architectural critics cold. Ada Louise Huxtable compared it to similarly sized postwar British, Swedish and Finnish towns and found it seriously deficient. Co-op City, she said, was a "singularly American, or New York, product. Its size and scale are monumental; its environmental and social planning is minimal."[174] By the time it was completed, Co-op City had joined the Pruitt-Igoe project in St. Louis, Missouri, as a symbol of what was wrong with the nation's prevailing housing policies. As the editors of Time put it:

> Ringed by highways and anchored in mud, this group of apartment houses stands as both a prediction of huge vertical subdivisions yet to come and a warning of failures that can be avoided . . . . It is relentlessly ugly: its buildings are overbearing bullies of concrete and brick. Its layout is dreary and unimaginative. . . . Even worse, except for some projected excellent landscaping, there is little effort to create neighborhoods at Co-op City or a feeling of community. Instead, residents are treated like clean socks, rolled up and tucked into gigantic bureau drawers.[175]

Amidst all the naysaying, the planner Denise Scott Brown and the architect Robert Venturi argued on behalf of Co-op City. In the late 1960s the writings and buildings of these two young Philadelphia-based practitioner-theorists had become central to the architectural debate over Modernism that swirled about the profession.[176] In an argument that was complicated, subtle and not a little ironic, they proclaimed that Co-op City was not "hideous" or "sterile," as critics had charged, but simply "conventional" and "ordinary," qualities they deemed "good, or potentially good." Countering Jessor's earlier contention, they wrote:

> The city or state should not be asked for extra funds for "urban design." If government has more money, it should go for more housing and we architects and planners are going to have to learn as painters and sculptors have learned before us, to accept the ordinary on its own terms and do it well. If "good design" costs twice as much, then good design is out of step and needs redefinition. . . . Co-op City is not all right: it is almost all right. But we must start from where it is and advocate small and telling changes: when faced with "ordinary" buildings and ordinary budgets, we must learn to rejoice in ordinariness, since . . . this is the way to make necessity good.

Scott Brown and Venturi were not blind to the defects in the design of Co-op City or to the social and environmental problems accompanying any project of such size. But they argued that although many professionals tended "to castigate Co-op City as something we grew out of in the 1930's," the development conveyed an essential humanity: "A 30's air does hang over Co-op City and the central rental offices of the UHF; an air of New-Deal idealism, a little shaken but resolved. It should make us reconsider and augment our aesthetics and philosophies, because Co-op City is more successful than some newer ideas. Perhaps we have seen the past and it works."[177]

In October 1971 Ada Louise Huxtable wrote of the completed Co-op City and praised the landscape architecture of Zion & Breen, who had been retained to ameliorate the impact of the vast buildings on the site, calling it "one of the most successful landscaping jobs that ever turned a lemon into a lemonade."[178] To transform the essentially featureless site, which began as 300 acres of salt sand, the landscape architects planted 22,400 trees and created a gently rolling terrain with hills formed out of sand pumped in from the nearby Pelham Bay and grassy lawns dotted with clumps of willow, Lombardy poplar, London plane and Japanese black pine trees. Play areas were covered with Astroturf, and carefully selected play equipment was placed in sand gardens and lawns. Zion & Breen also helped join four of the five sectors of Co-op City (the fifth was isolated across the river) with a willow-lined greenway that functioned as a traffic-free central park, comparable to those in Clarence Stein and Henry Wright's pioneering development of Radburn, New Jersey (1927).[179]

In her final assessment of the overall project, Huxtable was measured:

> Today, Co-op City is neither the purgatory nor the heaven that its critics and champions predicted. It is a functioning community. Only New York—a city of 8 million snobs, skeptics and desperate survivors—could have swallowed a new town of this size within its limits without a ripple. Anywhere else in the world, there would be a steady stream of visitors to see how a community of 45,000—going on 60,000—takes shape. Co-op City has none of the chic new-town esthetics or life-style cachet of a Reston, Va. It will never be in the fashionable planning spotlight like Welfare Island being built by the New York State Urban Development Corporation. . . . But it has 15,372 well-planned apartments that are no mean achievement in New York's stumbling housing numbers game.[180]

In 1975, in response to enormous rent hikes brought on by cost inflation inspired by the energy crisis, Co-op City's tenants began a thirteen-month rent strike. Creating ill will and leading to a damaging policy of drastically deferred maintenance, the strike eventually drove the UHF out of business. The lack of maintenance had a devastating effect on the buildings, whose quality of construction was not particularly high to begin with, leaving leaky roofs and loose pilings. The problem with the pilings wreaked havoc on the towers they supported, forcing a number of apartments to be vacated for extensive repairs and necessitating the uprooting of large areas of landscaping to get at underground piping that had ruptured as the buildings shifted.

Cross-Bronx Expressway

The construction project that brought the most profound changes to the Bronx during the postwar era was not an individual building or building group but the highly controversial Cross-Bronx Expressway (1946–1963).[181] The expressway made no positive contribution to the economics of the Bronx; in fact, its construction had little to do with the borough's needs at all. It was a road *through* the Bronx but not of it, offering motorists a means of traveling past—or, more precisely, cutting through—the borough on their way between New England and the rest of the United States. The new expressway followed no long-established route: it was neither a shorefront nor a riverfront parkway, nor an updated version of a previously mapped road, as was the Long Island Expressway. As much bludgeoned as built, the Cross-Bronx Expressway was the direct product of a willful engineering decision to link the George Washington Bridge with Long Island and New England by means of a straight line carved through existing neighborhoods, displacing hundreds of busi-

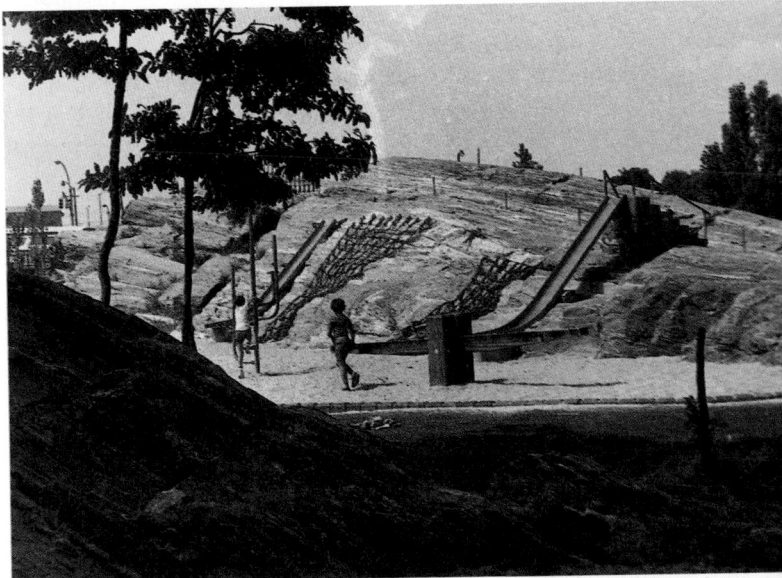

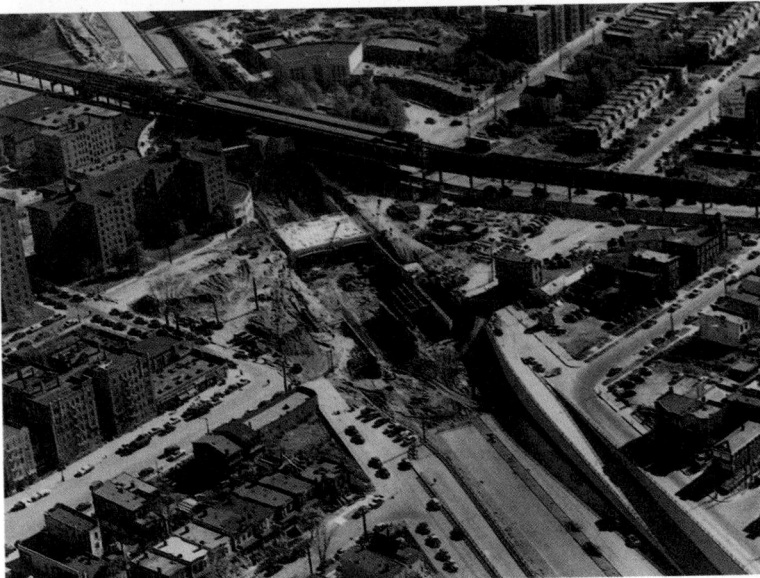

Top: Relandscaped site of Co-op City, between New England Thruway and Hutchinson River Parkway; and between Hutchinson River Parkway, Boller Avenue and Hutchinson River, Baychester. Zion & Breen, 1971. Playground. ZB

Bottom: Cross-Bronx Expressway at Hugh Grant Circle. View to the southeast with East 177th Street IRT station. NYT

nesses and thousands of families. The seven-mile-long, six-lane-wide expressway stretched from the George Washington Bridge, over the Harlem River, to the Throgs Neck Bridge, at the confluence of the East River and the Long Island Sound. Because it was classified as an arterial route, it qualified for federal aid; state and federal funding provided the total cost of construction, initially targeted at $22 million but ultimately exceeding $120 million, and half the cost of land acquisition, with the remaining half paid for by the city.

The expressway's construction was difficult, since much of its route was crisscrossed by a myriad of water mains, gas and sewer lines, electrical and telephone cables, and railroad, subway and elevated railroad lines. Furthermore, the subsurface section of the proposed right-of-way was more than 80 percent rock. No matter how daunting, however, technical considerations would pale in comparison to the problems of tenant relocation. Although the expressway had originally been planned as a major postwar public works project that would provide jobs to compensate for the cessation of wartime industrial production, the anticipated unemployment did not develop. Furthermore, an acute citywide housing shortage soon stymied efforts to relocate the largely lower-middle-class population living in the path of the proposed expressway. Moses alleged that the road's construction would necessitate the demolition of 1,530 apartments and the relocation of 5,000 people, but Robert Caro would later assert in his book *The Power Broker: Robert Moses and the Fall of New York* that Moses's figures were "almost certainly far too low."[182] By 1953 area residents had come to call the project "Heartbreak Highway."[183]

In order to ease the process and minimize the relocation statistics, the project was broken up into short segments. The portion of the expressway that offered the most problems was the .8-mile-long segment between Anthony and Longfellow avenues, traversing the densely populated and lively, if somewhat shabby, neighborhood known as East Tremont. Public officials and community groups, including the vocal East Tremont Neighborhood Association, urged Moses to reroute the expressway to follow a relatively undisruptive route along the northern border of Crotona Park rather than the original route, which cut through the neighborhood's heart just north of East 176th Street. Whereas the alternate route would have necessitated the demolition of only six buildings, Moses's route claimed fifty-four. Despite organized community opposition and the support of several local politicians, Moses steadfastly refused to adopt the alternate route. The reason for his obstinacy in the face of compelling arguments to remap the expressway was not clear. Caro has suggested the possibility of political motivations, including Moses's desire to comply with the wishes of the powerful Third Avenue Transit Company not to move its advantageously located Tremont Depot. But, Caro said, the route Moses selected may have been "based on no more than whim," and his refusal to alter it "due to nothing more than stubbornness."[184] In any case, Moses succeeded in building the highway as he had planned.

In 1963, at the public dedication ceremonies for the final link of the Cross-Bronx Expressway, Moses celebrated the roadway: "The rock outcrop below grade . . . which we made into monolithic landscaping will show no scars and will seem always to have been there. This is no gasoline gully, no elevated eyesore. As it sinks below and soars over the heart of the great city, this is metropolitan architecture in the finest sense." He also defended the methods used to construct the expressway: "This building of public works to meet the challenges of

urban growth is a fascinating and baffling business. . . . Nobody can clear the way for these swaths, which lift and depress expressways . . . without moving people and business, and it can't be done with mirrors, by sleight of hand or by magic."[185]

Five years later, in an interview with Robert Caro, Moses dismissed the expressway's impact on East Tremont: "There's very little real hardship in the thing. There's a little discomfort and even that is greatly exaggerated. The scale was new, that was all that was new about it."[186] Despite Moses's claims to the contrary, the physical and social devastation caused by the expressway was extreme. It unalterably cut the borough in two, with the "haves" to the north and the "have-nots" cordoned off in the ancient tenements and industrial marginalia of the south. Caro viewed the Cross-Bronx Expressway as the principal instrument of decline in the Central Bronx, and the cause of devastation in the East Tremont neighborhood:

> By 1965 the community's "very good, solid housing stock," the apartment buildings that had been so precious to the people who had lived in them, were ravaged hulks. . . . Of the people who had lived in East Tremont, who had found in that neighborhood security, roots, friendship, a community that provided an anchor—friends and synagogue and Y—a place where you knew the people and they knew you, where you could make a stand against the swirling, fearsome tides of the sea of life, only the very old, too poor to move, still lived, almost barricaded in their freezing apartments. As for the rest of the people who had lived there, they were gone.[187]

But the political scientist Marshall Berman has suggested that Caro's view, published in 1974, at the height of the movement against large-scale urban projects, was overstated. Berman felt that Caro's account painted an unrealistically "lovely panorama" of the pre-expressway East Tremont neighborhood, "a sentimental but recognizable blend of [Jane] Jacobs' Hudson Street with *Fiddler on the Roof*." Caro's description of the expressway's impact, said Berman, was "utterly devastating," showing "the blight spreading outward from the Expressway, block by block, year by year, while Moses, like a reincarnated General Sherman running wild in the streets of the North, blazed a path of terror from Harlem to the Sound." But Berman contended that Caro's conclusion that the expressway had been the main cause of the neighborhood's decline may have overlooked key factors. For one thing, said Berman, Caro's assessment was "based on values that are new; they are the values of 1970, and they were nowhere in the picture in 1950, when the neighborhood was still in flower. The ironic fact is that the neighborhood people themselves lacked these ideas when they were most in need of them; they did not even have the vocabulary to defend their neighborhoods because, until the Sixties, that vocabulary simply did not exist."[188] Berman would later articulate a crucial point about the inherent character of the Bronx:

> What if the Bronxites of the 1950s had possessed the conceptual tools, the vocabulary, the widespread public sympathy, the flair for publicity and mass mobilization, that residents of many American neighborhoods would acquire in the 1960s? What if . . . we had managed to keep the dread road from being built? How many of us would still be in the Bronx today, caring for it and fighting for it as our own? Some of us, no doubt, but I suspect not so many. . . . For the Bronx of my youth was possessed, inspired, by the great modern dream of mobility. To live well meant to move out physically; to live one's life close to home was not to be alive at all.[189]

972

Berman saw Moses's expressway in a different light, as a tragic example of the destruction that inevitably accompanied the progress of "modernity":

> I can remember standing above the construction site . . . weeping for my neighborhood whose fate I foresaw with nightmarish precision, vowing remembrance and revenge, but also wrestling with some of the troubling ambiguities and contradictions that Moses' work expressed. The Grand Concourse, from whose heights I watched and thought, was our borough's closest thing to a Parisian boulevard. Among its most striking features were rows of large, splendid 1930s apartment houses. . . . The style of these buildings, known as Art Deco today, was called "modern" in their prime. For my parents, who described our family proudly as a "modern" family, the Concourse buildings represented a pinnacle of modernity. . . . As I saw one of the loveliest of these buildings being wrecked for the road, I felt a grief that, I can see now, is endemic to modern life. So often the price of ongoing and expanding modernity is the destruction not merely of "traditional" and "pre-modern" institutions and environments—and here is the real tragedy—but of everything most vital and beautiful in the modern world itself. Here in the Bronx, thanks to Robert Moses, the modernity of the urban boulevard was being condemned as obsolete, and blown to pieces, by the modernity of the interstate highways. *Sic transit!* To be modern turned out to be far more problematical, and more perilous, than I had been taught.[190]

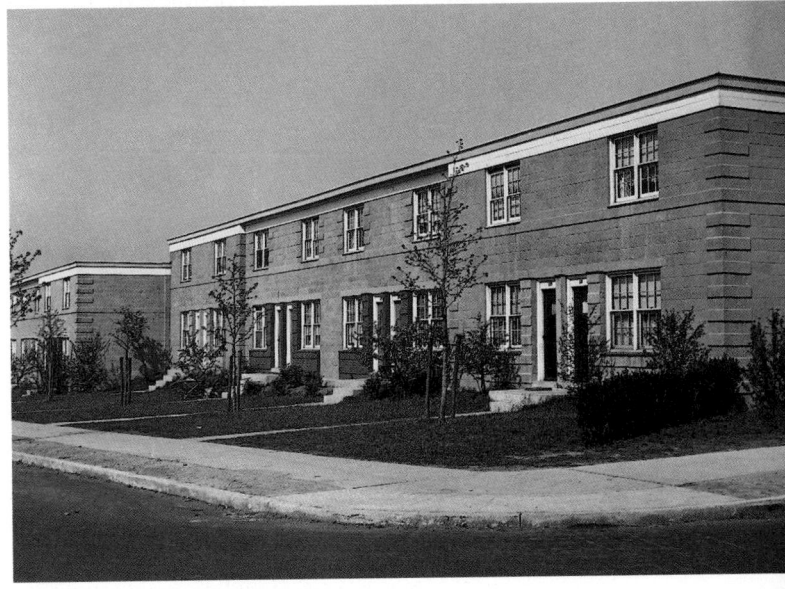

Edwin Markham Houses, bounded by Richmond Terrace, North Burgher Avenue, Wayne Street and Broadway, West New Brighton. De Young & Moscowitz, 1943. NYCHA

STATEN ISLAND

I took the subway to the Battery, got on a ferryboat, and a half-hour later found myself in Staten Island. . . . It was a quiet, peaceful spot, and it was hard to believe you were only forty minutes from the noise of Times Square.
—*Willie Sutton, 1953*[1]

Throughout the 1940s and early 1950s Staten Island remained—to master criminal Willie Sutton as to most others who took the time to visit—what it had always been: the city's sleepy, semi-rural backwater.[2] Affluent Wall Street executives lived on Grymes and Todt hills, while middle-class, clerical and back-office types, many of them employed in the financial enterprises of lower Manhattan or in the civil service, occupied the low-lying villages along the island's northern shore. The southern end of the island, which consisted of sand dunes, flat, open marshy land and forests punctuated by clay pits, was largely unsettled. From 1790 to 1950 Staten Island's population had grown from 3,835 to only 191,555; in contrast, during the same period, the Bronx climbed from 1,781 to 1,451,277, Queens from 6,159 to 1,550,849, and Brooklyn from 4,495 to 2,738,175.[3]

The war effort brought Staten Island closer to the city's mainstream. With important port and ship-building facilities, the island played a significant role in the wartime buildup, and new housing was required to accommodate the rapidly expanding work force. On December 9, 1941, two days after the bombing of Pearl Harbor, plans were announced for the 360-unit Edwin Markham Houses, a twelve-acre village of two-story rowhouses designed by De Young & Moscowitz and Frederick Mathesius.[4] Markham Houses was located on a West New Brighton site bounded by Richmond Terrace, North Burgher Avenue, Wayne Street and Broadway that had held 110 small buildings. While most such projects were delayed until war's end, because of its proximity to shipyards it was rushed to completion and opened early in 1943. With only 100.3 persons per acre, the develop-

973

ment was one of the Housing Authority's least dense projects. The site plan was simple, with parallel rows of units. Access to the buildings was provided by pedestrian walkways that led from perimeter streets and two central parking areas. The Colonial Georgian–inspired design was simply detailed, with cinder-block walls painted yellow, blue, green and red, and the overall impression was surprisingly noninstitutional.

Other public housing on the island included three projects completed in 1949: the 422-unit South Beach Houses (Henry Murphy), bounded by Kramer Street, Lamport Boulevard and McClean, Norway, Reid and Parkinson avenues, which consisted of eight six-story buildings on a 17.8-acre site;[5] the 502-unit Todt Hill Houses (H. I. Feldman), located on a twelve-acre site bounded by Manor Road, Schmidt's Lane, La Guardia and Westwood avenues;[6] and the General Charles W. Berry Houses (Holden, McLaughlin & Associates), between Richmond Road, Dongan Hills Avenue, Jefferson Street and Seaver Avenue, a 506-unit project in the Dongan Hills section.[7] In 1951 plans were announced for Mariner's Harbor Houses, the first project on Staten Island developed under Title I guidelines.[8] Completed three years later and designed by Coffin & Coffin, the complex included twelve three-story and ten six-story buildings housing 607 families on a 20.8-acre site bounded by Lockman Avenue, Continental Place, Grandview Avenue and Roxbury Street. Richmond Terrace Houses (LaPierre, Litchfield & Partners, 1961) was a 489-unit complex located on a 10.5-acre site bounded by Richmond Terrace, Westervelt and Crescent avenues and Cleveland and Jersey streets, in the northeast corner of the borough in the New Brighton area.[9] The largest public housing project on Staten Island was the 693-unit Stapleton Houses (Ballard, Todd & Snibbe, 1962), between Broad Street, Tompkins Avenue and Hill, Warren and Gordon streets, in a neighborhood of wooden rowhouses that, though run-down, were not without charm.[10] The six eight-story superlong slabs bounded two courtyards and incorporated exterior circulation balconies, the first to be approved by the Housing Authority. Another notable effort of the Housing Authority was Cassidy-Lafayette Houses (Difiore & Giacobbe, 1971), a small-scale and relatively noncontroversial example of the scatter-site program that generated so much anger in other parts of the city, most notably Forest Hills, Queens (see "Queens," below).[11] Designed for the elderly, the 380-unit project consisted of four six-story buildings occupying a 5.15-acre site in New Brighton bounded by Cassidy Place, Fillmore Street and Lafayette and Clinton avenues.

Although most of Staten Island's distinguished residential architecture predated World War I, in the prime hilltop areas a few notable houses were built in the 1950s and 1960s. Among these was the relaxed International Style Jack Friedland house (1961), designed by Harold E. Diamond for a 2.5-acre site overlooking the Narrows.[12] Even more interesting was the construction in 1959 of Crimson Beech, Frank Lloyd Wright's third building in New York City, built for William and Catherine Cass, a young Queens couple; Mr. Cass had developed a fascination with Wright after he saw him interviewed on television.[13] Unlike the Usonian house erected by the Guggenheim Museum (see chapter 11), this exceptionally low-slung, prefabricated ranch-type house, built at 48 Manor Court, west of Lighthouse Avenue, was not site specific. Sheathed in masonite boards and wood battens and roofed with terne, Crimson Beech had been designed by Wright for the Marshall Erdman Company of Madison, Wisconsin, which successfully adapted the L-shaped plan to the Casses' cliff-edge site, where it commanded superb views of the ocean. Wright died before the house was completed under the

supervision of Morton Nelson, one of his former students who represented him in New York. Not everyone admired the house; in the first edition of their guide to New York architecture, published in 1967, Norval White and Elliot Willensky castigated it as a "cream colored masonite building with tacky metal roof, totally lacking dignity or style."[14]

On June 25, 1946, the St. George Ferry Terminal (Carrère & Hastings, 1908) burned to the ground, on the very day that plans and a model for a proposed new terminal were presented to the city.[15] Madigan-Hyland, engineers, had already been at work for over a year on the elaborate though stiffly monumental design for the new terminal, to replace the outmoded facility.[16] The final design incorporated the principal functional features of the original proposal, although it lacked its civic grandeur.[17] The new ferry terminal, not completed until 1951, was dominated by a 161-by-98-foot main waiting room, which was 25 percent larger than the one that had burned. Designed to accommodate 45,000 commuters per hour, the red-brick terminal also included extensive ramp facilites for passengers arriving by bus, train or automobile.

Verrazano-Narrows Bridge

Discussion of a crossing at the Narrows had begun forty years before the realization of the Verrazano-Narrows Bridge in 1964. In 1923 Mayor John Hylan had authorized the start of construction on an auto and rail tunnel under the Narrows, and shafts were dug on both shores before rising costs brought the work to a halt. In 1940 Ernest Flagg proposed that rather than connecting Staten Island with Brooklyn, it should be connected to Manhattan by means of a tunnel and a floating bridge similar to the one being built across Lake Washington, east of Seattle, or a causeway like the one leading to Key West, Florida.[18] According to Flagg's plan, a half-mile-long tunnel would lead from St. George, Staten Island, to Robbins Reef; a three-and-a-half-mile-long causeway or bridge would run from there to Ellis Island; and a mile-long tunnel would run from Ellis Island to the Battery. Flagg's suggestion was not adopted.

The idea of a crossing at the Narrows was not seriously revived until July 1948, when Robert Moses's Triborough Bridge and Tunnel Authority applied to the War Department for permission to construct the world's longest suspension bridge.[19] The decision to build a bridge instead of a tunnel, based on relative cost, angered residents of Bay Ridge, Brooklyn, who felt that destruction of their neighborhood was an inevitable by-product of construction, but it delighted real estate speculators, who began to buy up land on both sides of the water.[20] The Army approved the bridge in January 1949.[21] Designed by Othmar Hermann Ammann, the proposed structure was part of a sprawling network of new and existing high-speed roads that would bind the city's five boroughs more tightly with each other and with nearby New Jersey.[22] The project was then delayed as Moses sought approval from various city and state government agencies.

In 1959, as construction on the Narrows bridge was about to begin, a dispute arose over its name. The Italian Historical Society lobbied for a memorial to Giovanni da Verrazano, who explored the area in 1524, while the Staten Island Chamber of Commerce wanted it to be named after their borough, not after "a foreigner who made a navigational mistake." They asked: "Why should there be a Brooklyn, Bronx, Queensboro and Manhattan Bridge and not a Staten Island Bridge?"[23] A compro-

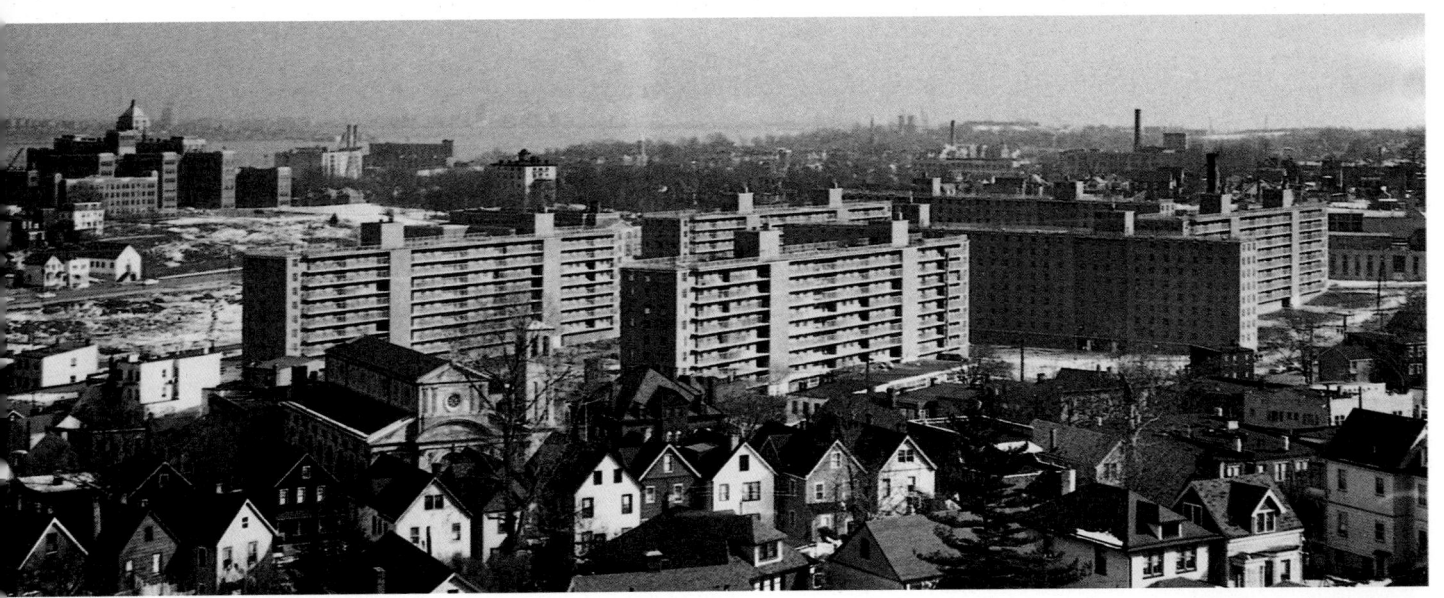

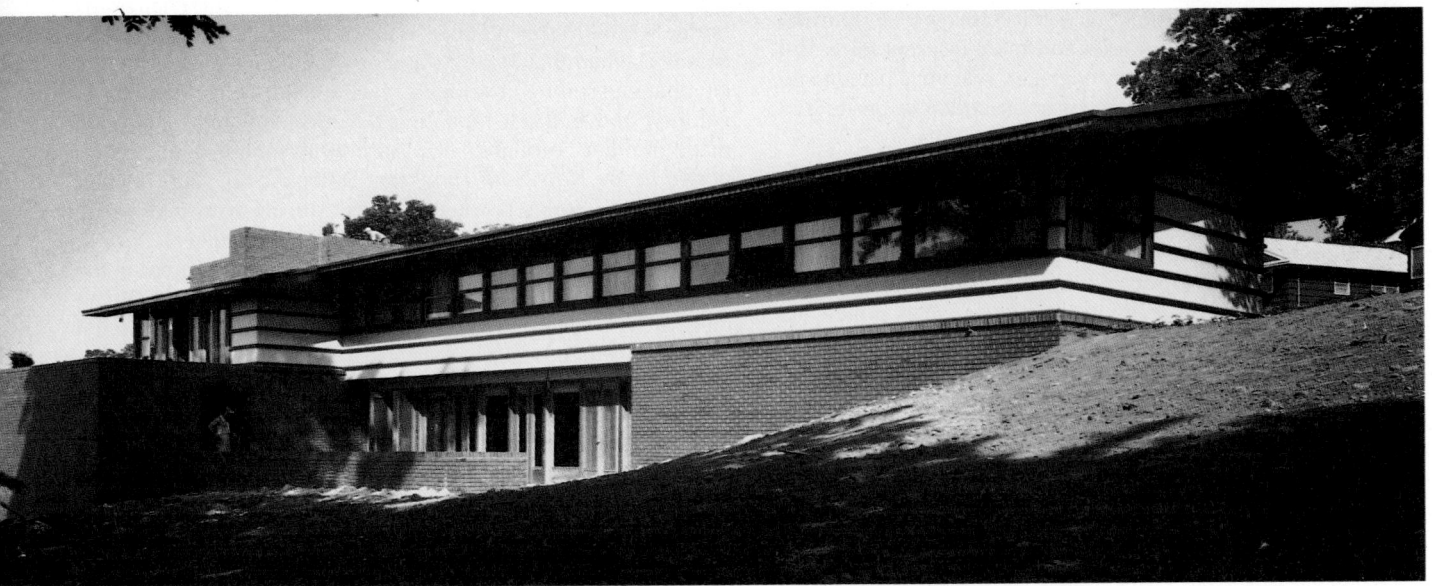

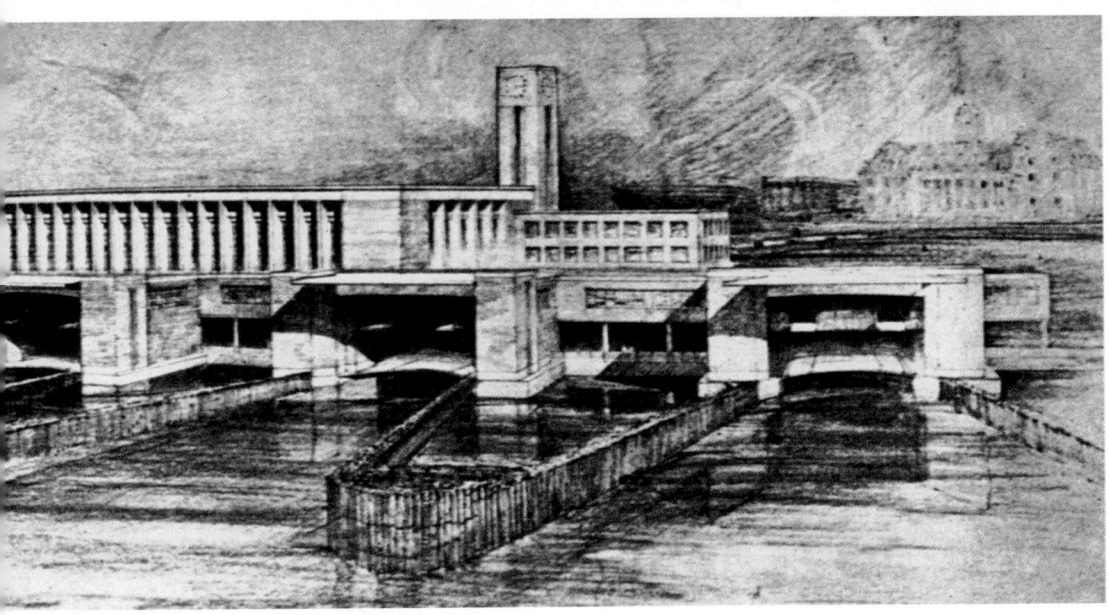

Top: Stapleton Houses, bounded by Broad Street, Tompkins Avenue and Hill, Warren and Gordon streets, Stapleton. Ballard, Todd & Snibbe, 1962. View to the northeast. NYCHA

Center: Crimson Beech, 48 Manor Court, west of Lighthouse Avenue, Richmondtown. Frank Lloyd Wright, 1959. View to the northwest. Guerrero. PEGU

Bottom: Proposed St. George Ferry Terminal, St. George. Madigan-Hyland, 1946. Rendering of view to the southeast. AR. CU

mise was eventually reached: it would be called the Verrazano-Narrows Bridge.

Lewis Mumford voiced more serious reservations about the bridge in late 1959, calling it a "destructive" proposal that came not from the city planners he had learned to distrust "but from highway engineers, though, to their shame, many city planners have accepted it as if it were unchallengeable." Mumford saw the bridge as a major and disastrous step toward the destruction of the remaining countryside on Long Island and the suburbanization of vast areas at the edges of the New York region as a whole. He also lamented the loss of neighborhoods at the bridge's Brooklyn terminus. The design of the bridge and its approaches, Mumford said, was based on an "oversolicitude for motor traffic" and "sheer indifference to the comfort of urban living." To accommodate the twelve-lane-wide elevated approaches, Mumford reported, nearly 8,000 Bay Ridge residents would be displaced. "This says nothing of the many other people whose lives or properties will be unfavorably affected by the elevated highway through their neighborhood," he continued. "At the very moment . . . that we have torn down our elevated railways, because of their spoilage of urban space, our highway engineers are using vast sums of public money to restore the same nuisance in an even noisier and more insistent form. But what is Brooklyn to the highway engineer—except a place to go through quickly, at whatever necessary sacrifice of peace and amenity by its inhabitants?"[24]

Mumford also saw the Narrows bridge in a broader context, as "part of a larger and even more disastrous program for expanding our federal highways, a project that is working similar havoc in every part of the country—slashing through old neighborhoods, stealing land from public parks, dumping traffic on urban centers that are already overcrowded." This policy, he warned, would have disastrous urban effects:

> At a time when our cities can be made livable again only by isolating their residential neighborhoods from through traffic and rebuilding our decaying systems of mass transportation, our public authorities are busily breaking down the structure of neighborhoods and parks and devoting public funds to private transportation and private speculative building at random. As a formula for defacing the natural landscape and ruining what is left of our great cities, nothing could be more effective.[25]

The construction of the bridge, which began in January 1960, was the biggest project ever for bridge builders.[26] This engineering "dream," as David Steinman, consulting engineer in the reconstruction of the Brooklyn Bridge (see "Brooklyn," above), put it, could be described only in dimensional superlatives.[27] Its 690-foot-tall towers dwarfed all but a few of Manhattan's skyscrapers; its 4,260 feet of clear span, 235 feet above the water, was 60 feet longer than its nearest rival, San Francisco's Golden Gate Bridge.

The bridge was so long that the two towers, built perpendicular to the earth's surface, were 1⅝ inches farther apart at their tops than at their bases to compensate for the curvature of the earth. The towers' steel-plate construction rendered them far more massive and yet more visually serene than the towers of earlier bridges, like the George Washington Bridge (1926–31), also designed by Ammann, which consisted of openwork lattice.[28] But as *Engineering News-Record* noted: "The mass of the structure, no matter how impressive, is insignificant when compared with its complexity. Its individual components are numbered in tens of millions, each with its own place and its own sequence for placement."[29] But the Verrazano-Narrows Bridge was more than an amazing feat of engineering; it was also art. As

Ammann explained, the bridge was conceived "as an enormous object drawn as faintly as possible."[30]

When the bridge opened for traffic on November 21, 1964, even Brooklyn's Bay Ridge section got caught up in the spirit of the celebrations.[31] Only a picket line of teenagers protesting the bridge's lack of pedestrian walkways marred the scene. As if to climax the ceremonies, the liner *United States*, passing under the bridge on her way back to New York from her annual dry-docking in Newport News, Virginia, gave a mighty blast. In June 1969 a lower six-lane deck was added, doubling the capacity of the bridge.[32] Although the second deck was originally planned to be opened in 1980, the tremendous increase in traffic necessitated its early completion.

After the Bridge

Although Staten Island had remained a backwater after World War II, its character changed almost overnight as the construction of the Verrazano-Narrows Bridge became a reality.[33] Real estate developers were quick to sense the dramatic change the bridge would make in Staten Island's fortunes. In 1957 Robert Moses claimed that Staten Island was "the only borough in the city that can still be developed as we would all like it to be developed and without repeating the mistakes that have been made in other boroughs."[34] In April 1959 John P. Callahan reported in the *New York Times* that Staten Island, "the 'sleeper' among New York's boroughs," was "stirring with dreams."[35] With only 20,000 of the island's 38,600 acres developed—a street system had been mapped for the undeveloped areas in the 1920s but never built, nor had sewer lines been installed in these areas—major growth was seen as some years ahead in the future. Nonetheless, business leaders were projecting a population of half a million people by 1975, a gain of 288,000 over the 1959 population of 212,000. Others predicted a population of 350,000, which turned out to be the island's population in 1980. By the late 1950s speculation had already pushed land prices to four times what they had been before the bridge was announced, encouraged not only by the promised bridge but by a proposal to crisscross the island with a series of parkways and expressways that would ease connections with Brooklyn, and thus Manhattan, and also with New Jersey via the three existing bridges. Student and faculty teams at the architecture schools of Cooper Union and Pratt Institute prepared studies of the island's future, helping to fill what appeared to be a vacuum in official planning efforts.[36]

The boom came far more quickly than had been anticipated, producing acres of ill-planned, ill-designed, but distinctly affordable, one-, two- and three-family houses. In 1963, with the bridge's completion more than a year away, Bernard Stengren reported in the *New York Times* about the changes that were affecting the borough:

> Staten Island's image as the city's last vestige of open country, "suburban" pace and eccentric isolation is rapidly disappearing. . . . Evidence of change meets the eye continually—in the panorama of deep red where hillsides have been slashed away for the arterial roads leading to and from the big bridge; in thousands of new homes and apartments recently occupied or under construction; in double sessions in the schools; [in] crowded buses making their way through rush hours near the ferry terminal at St. George and in the way "island-born" has lost its connotation of preference in business and politics there.[37]

For typical Staten Islanders, the bridge marked the end of a small-town, almost Midwestern way of life. As one islander put it: "I used to take my mother for a drive on Sunday, but now the roads are crowded with people from Brooklyn looking at houses."[38]

So mediocre was most of the bridge-inspired housing and so execrable the accompanying town planning that the normally Manhattan-bound Ada Louise Huxtable was moved to make the journey across the bay to see for herself. In 1965 Huxtable reported: "Nine months after the Verrazano-Narrows Bridge to Staten Island opened with the promise of a last chance for a new, improved suburbia in the greater metropolitan area, the dreams of beauty and better living are mired in mud. The mud has been created by bulldozers ruthlessly leveling wooded hills, rolling sites and unspoiled farmland for what critics call some of the most inadequately designed and planned housing in the country." These "ugly" houses, Huxtable said—"ordinary, minimum builders' modules on scant 40-by-100-foot lots"—were being "scattered throughout Staten Island's . . . open, undeveloped land with a haphazard abandon that could not be better calculated to destroy the countryside if it had been planned by enemy action."[39] The boom in small-lot development was in part due to builders rushing to complete construction within the two-year grace period following approval of the new zoning law of 1961, after which such narrow lots would be outlawed.

Huxtable reported that, according to Staten Island Borough President Albert V. Maniscalco, some planning for better land use was being done but only "through the back door," which to Huxtable meant "a defensive battle to hold token parcels of city land for future community use and, at the same time, to pursue an uncompromising policy of selling vast amounts of other city-owned property." One delay in development resulted from the fact that street and drainage maps of newly surveyed land were being kept on the shelves of the understaffed City Planning Commission's offices, thereby preventing the sale of the land— much of which had been acquired by the city over the years in lieu of back taxes. In addition, parkland was being acquired wherever possible, but it was to be used to border high-speed roadways rather than as "integral parts of growing communities." Huxtable decried the city's failure to develop a positive planning approach for the island's physical growth:

> Back-door planning relies on a single inadequate tool—the zoning law—to control the tide of jerry-built, rubber-stamp row houses that are springing up in the sylvan wilderness like August weeds. Regulation by zoning is limited to the enlargement of lots and reduction of densities and does nothing to promote the creative design of planned new communities. All this is piecemeal, catch-as-catch-can control, comparable to fighting a forest fire with an eyedropper.[40]

There were two elements on Staten Island that did receive more considered planning: a 1,080-acre tract in the Annadale-Huguenot section that was declared an urban renewal area, and the so-called greenbelt running along the island's center across the lush vegetation of its principal hills (see below). The City Planning Commission's Annadale-Huguenot plan was released in the fall of 1962.[41] The site, in the southeastern area of the island, was roughly bounded by Amboy Road, Arden Avenue, Wolf's Pond Park and Raritan Bay. Hyland Boulevard, one of the island's major arteries, ran through the area near the waterfront. Sixty percent of the site was owned by the city. The plan, developed by Bernard J. Albin, called for the replacement of the typical gridiron plan with a hybrid scheme that gathered the north-south streets into a series of loops and cul-de-sacs running off

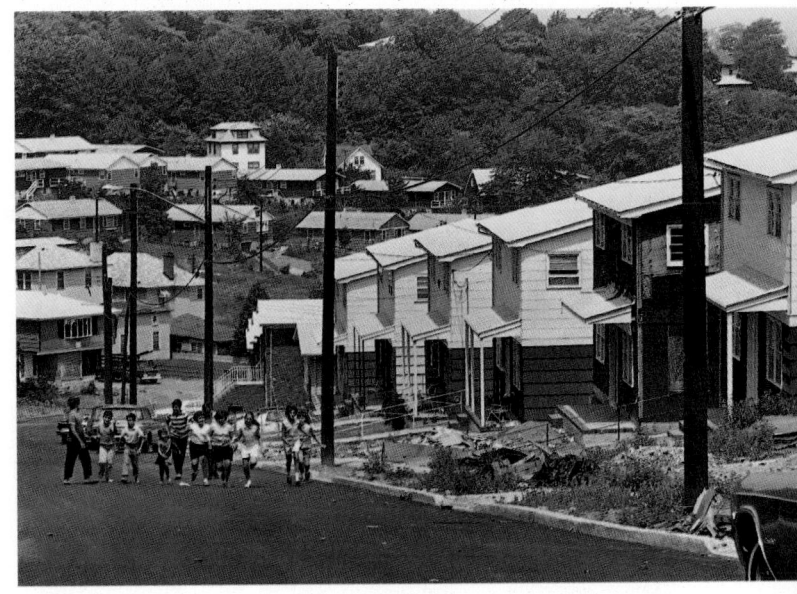

View of new suburban houses on Staten Island, 1965. NYT

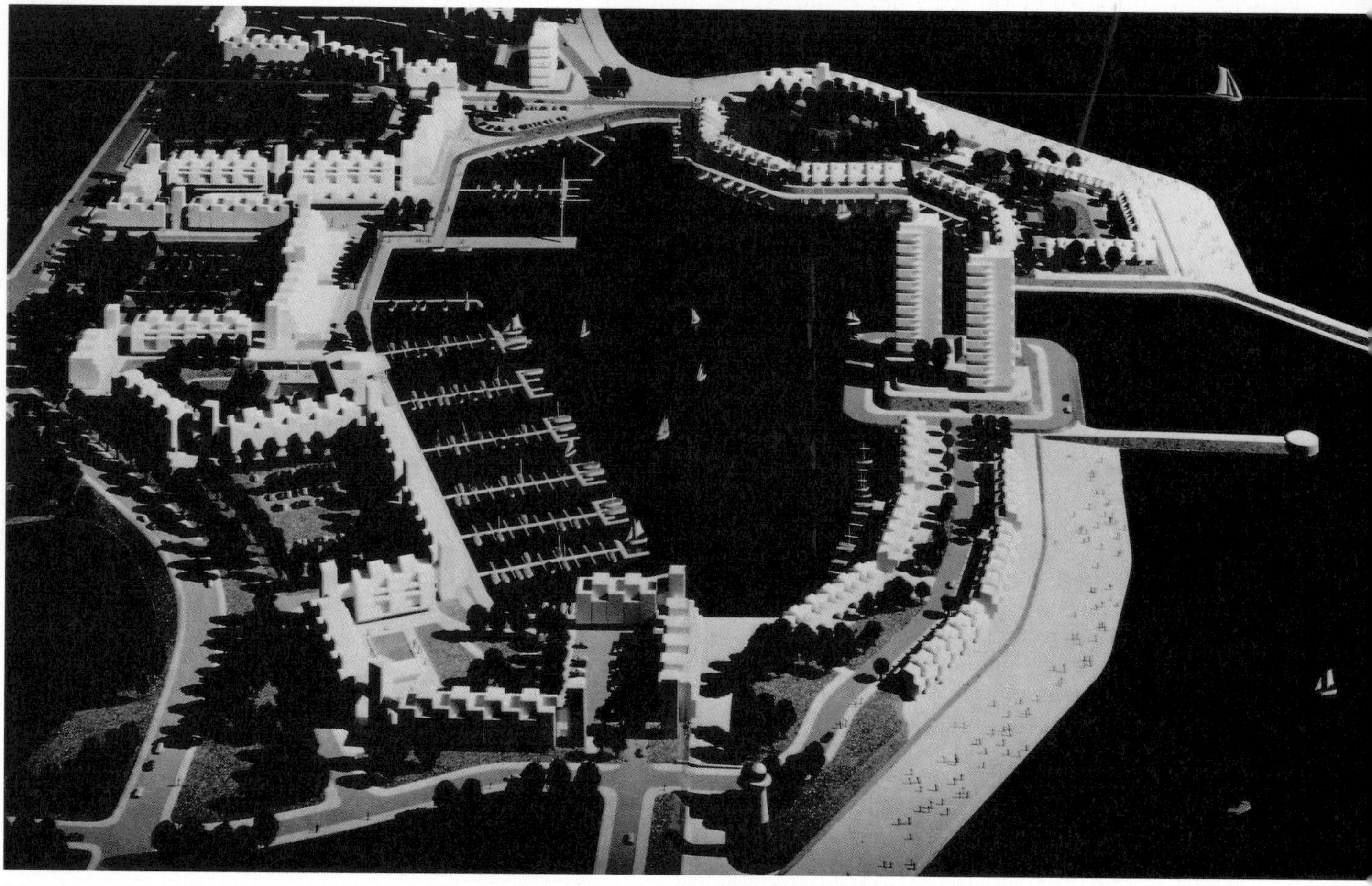

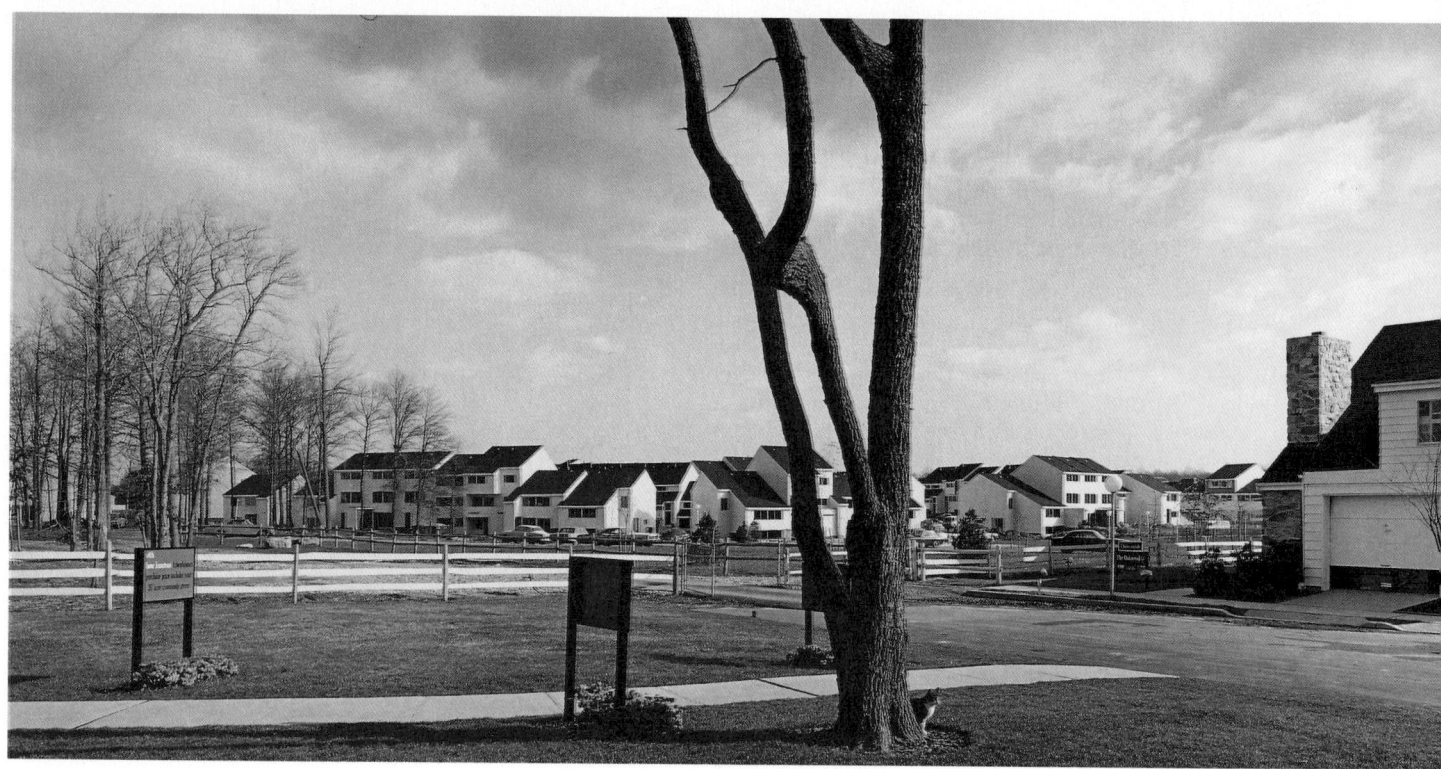

Top: Third proposal for Annadale-Huguenot residential community.
Raymond & May Associates, in collaboration with Shankland, Cox &
Associates, M. Paul Friedberg, and Eberlin & Eberlin, 1967. Model.
View to the northeast. *Annadale-Huguenot.* CU

Bottom: Village Greens, Arden Avenue, between Arthur Kill Road and
Bunnell Street, Arden Heights. Norman Jaffe, 1969–74. NJ

the major east-west avenues. These not only broke down the relentless grid into neighborhood sectors but also permitted the development of fingerlike greenbelts recalling those at Radburn, New Jersey, and Greenbelt, Maryland.[42] The plan used much of the existing mapped street system and could be realized, as Albin put it, "without the usual clearance associated with urban-renewal projects."[43]

Although the initial reaction to the plan was mildly negative, opposition grew strong in April 1963, when the area was designated an open-lands project under a provision in the federal Urban Renewal Act for model communities. Hearing the words "urban renewal," local residents feared massive public housing projects and an influx of minorities, while real estate developers opposed the idea that the quantity and quality of what they could build would be regulated. But there was some support for the proposal on Staten Island as well as widespread support from civic organizations and individuals from other parts of the city. In 1965, after Borough President Maniscalco and Mayor Wagner asked the City Planning Commission to abandon the renewal plan, the *New York Times* enthusiastically supported it:

> There is still time for Mr. Wagner and Mr. Maniscalco to exercise leadership for once, to support their city planners and to help dispel the utterly groundless fears over urban renewal. There is still time, too, for Annadale-Huguenot residents to re-examine a plan that would prevent blight and would give them a model community with "village greens" in a pattern that other still-unspoiled sections of Staten Island could emulate to the benefit of the city and the people who live in it.[44]

The City Planning Commission refused to rescind the plan and urged the Housing and Redevelopment Board to implement it.

In 1966, under the new administration of John V. Lindsay, the project was temporarily dropped due to a lack of federal funds.[45] To get the project back on track, in February 1967 Lindsay released city funds to pay for the development of a more complete plan by Raymond & May Associates, in collaboration with Shankland, Cox & Associates of London, M. Paul Friedberg, landscape architect, and Eberlin & Eberlin, consulting engineers.[46] At this point, the city was in a race with developers who owned land in the Annadale-Huguenot tract and who had recently won court decisions allowing them to build. In October 1967 Raymond & May Associates presented four different plans. The first consisted entirely of single-family homes to be placed within the traditional street grid but occupying sixty-foot-wide lots, twenty feet wider than the previous minimum. The second proposal was also for single-family homes on sixty-foot-wide lots, but the lots were clustered to create larger open areas. The estimated population for both proposals was 12,000. The fourth proposal consisted primarily of apartment houses (76 percent) and accommodated a population of 35,000.

But it was the third proposal that Raymond & May Associates recommended and developed in the greatest detail. Designed to accommodate a population of 23,000, and consisting of a mix of townhouses (61 percent), single-family houses (16 percent) and apartments (23 percent), it featured cluster zoning that grouped the buildings into ten "neighborhoods," connected by a network of parks that often bordered natural streams and fenways. This plan also included a man-made lagoon on Raritan Bay. A watered-down version of this proposal, one that featured more single-family housing, became the recommended proposal, which the *New York Times* urged the city to implement: "This is to be New York's alternative to the economically wasteful and aesthetically dreadful urban-suburban develop-

ments now proliferating in Staten Island and elsewhere. It must now move rapidly from the stage of gorgeous brochure to physical reality; it ought not die through failure or delay in funding."[47] The Annadale-Huguenot Urban Renewal Plan did not go forward.

In 1969 the city hired the Rouse Company, developers of the new town of Columbia, Maryland, to undertake an economic feasibility study for the 7,300 acres adjacent to the Annadale-Huguenot Urban Renewal Area, a good portion of which the city still owned.[48] Rouse's proposal called for the creation of a new town housing between 300,000 and 450,000 people, to be called South Richmond, which would use the 7,300 acres as well as an additional 3,300 acres that would be created by filling in the coast along Raritan Bay. The town would contain a large industrial zone, a downtown and a dozen villages of 35,000 to 40,000 people each. The villages would in turn be broken down into neighborhoods of 5,000 inhabitants. Public open space, comprising 20 percent of the entire site, would separate the neighborhoods. James W. Rouse, the firm's principal, believed that South Richmond could be realized in twenty-two years with no cost to the city, and that it would turn over a billion dollars of tax revenues to the city by century's end. The project foundered, however, because of issues of political control, the typical islander's innate conservatism and the deep-seated antagonism toward the use of eminent domain, which would be required to acquire the property. After efforts to push enabling legislation through the New York State Legislature failed in 1973, the City Planning Commission established a task force to produce a development plan. Their plan, adopted late in 1973, preserved the best of the area's natural features, capped building heights at four stories and mapped a network of open space linked to parkland.

Norman Jaffe's Village Greens residential development (1969–74), on Arden Avenue between Arthur Kill Road and Bunnell Street, was the only large-scale, "planned" project to go forward in the South Richmond area, and it constituted less than a third of the 2,000-family development initially planned for the 160-acre site in Arden Heights.[49] Though the City Planning Commission endorsed the attempt to create cluster housing and maximize open space, and though Jaffe and his landscape consultant, Courtland Paul, paid close attention to the site's topography and vegetation, the results were disappointing. While the model houses were imaginatively designed, with highly articulated rooflines, the built units were less subtly shaped and quite densely massed. The houses "appear to be very busy visually," said Norval White and Elliot Willensky, "thus intensifying the cheek-by-jowl feeling."[50] But it was poor management, not aesthetic matters, that caused the Loew's Corporation and J. H. Snyder of Los Angeles, the developers of Village Greens, to back away from the project after only a portion of it was completed. Absentee management resulted in chaotic site conditions, with an extraordinarily high rate of pilfering, and an inability to deliver the product quickly enough to the consumer. Furthermore, the decision to build two of the world's largest natural-gas storage tanks and a 600-inmate prison nearby confounded efforts to establish an image of country living. The decline of the city's fortunes, as well as rising interest rates, also had a negative effect. As the *New York Times* editorialized: "There is no dream that cannot be defeated by inflation and bureaucracy. But nothing is more vulnerable to rising costs and red tape than the dream of a better place to live."[51]

The building of the Verrazano-Narrows Bridge also focused attention on Staten Island's increasingly underutilized industrial

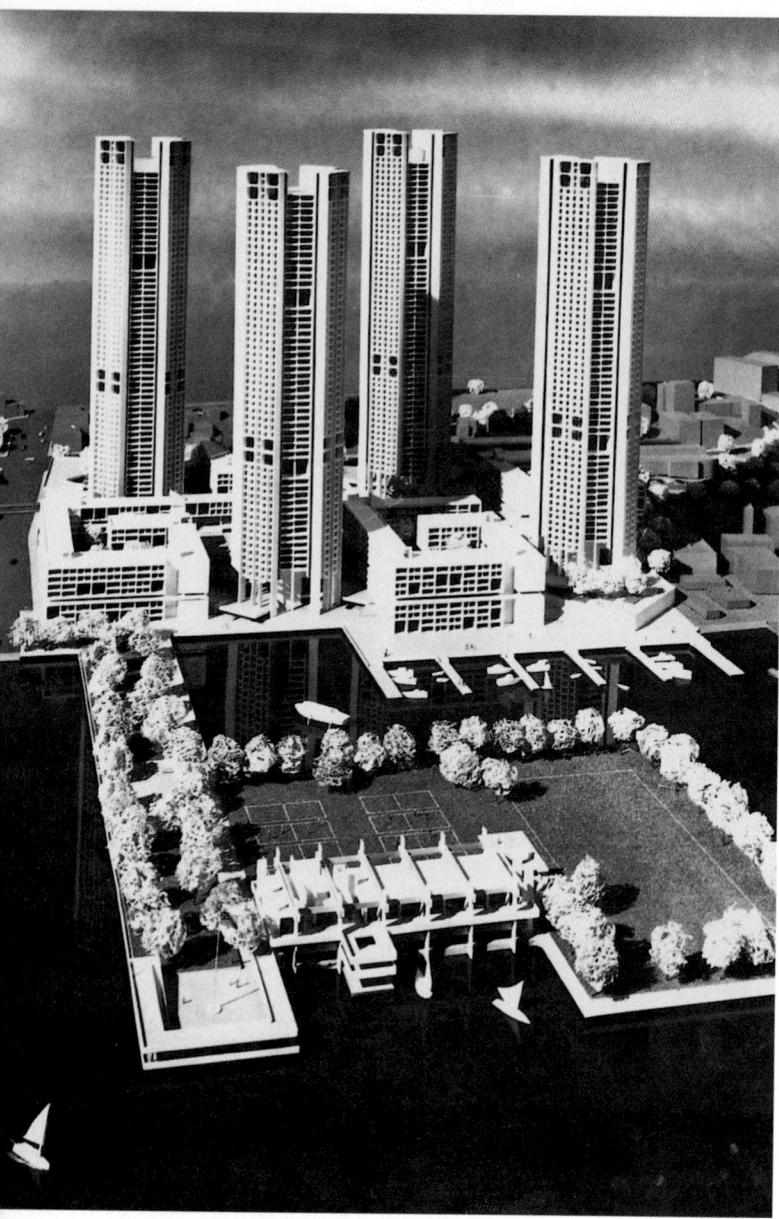

Above: Proposal for Harbour House, near St. George Ferry Terminal, St. George. Kelly & Gruzen, 1962. Model. GS

Top right: Proposal for St. George Place, near St. George Ferry Terminal, St. George. I. M. Pei & Partners, 1972. Model. PCF

Bottom right: Proposal for Fox Hills. Arthur Baker, Kenneth Frampton and Peter Wolf in consultation with David Todd & Associates, 1973. Perspective by Ellen Cheng of stepped row units. EC

waterfront, which ferry service rendered so convenient to lower Manhattan. In 1962 the entrepreneurial William Zeckendorf and his Webb & Knapp company purchased a thirty-six-acre parcel of deteriorated waterfront property just to the southeast of the ferry terminal.[52] He retained Kelly & Gruzen to create a master plan for Harbour House, including 4,000 dwelling units, 80,000 square feet of commercial space, parking for 2,800 cars, 10.2 acres of park and recreation space and 10 acres of marina-related facilities. Designed under Jordan Gruzen's direction by Peter Samton and a team including Robert Genchek and Edward Kelbisch, the complex consisted of four boldly articulated, octagonal concrete apartment towers averaging fifty-four floors and four low-rise *à redent* blocks varying in height from three to nine stories. The towers had a strong silhouette, creating a sculptural presence that would have read well against the hill that climbed up behind, especially when seen from ferryboats in the harbor. Because Webb & Knapp declared bankruptcy in 1965, Zeckendorf was unable to go forward with his plan, but he did retain control of the property. In 1975 the architects, now known as Gruzen & Partners, realized certain aspects of the design in their Arthur A. Schomberg Plaza apartments in Harlem (see chapter 12).

In 1972 the idea of developing large-scale housing on the site reemerged as a project to be partially subsidized by the government and sponsored by the General Property Corporation, headed by Zeckendorf's son, William Zeckendorf, Jr., and Westinghouse.[53] Plans for St. George Place, a "waterfront city" for 3,500 households, were prepared by I. M. Pei's office, under the direction of design partner James Ingo Freed, and with a team including Rosaria Piomelli and Kellogg Wong. Their plan built on the earlier Kelly & Gruzen proposal, taking advantage of the site's fifty-three-foot-high slope to create a multilevel platform housing parking, community facilities and commercial spaces, as well as a looping internal street system, to free the waterfront and the landscaped deck of all vehicular traffic. Similar in some ways to Paul Rudolph's Tracey Towers in the Bronx (see "The Bronx," above) and to Pei's own Harbor Tower Apartments in Boston,[54] St. George Place called for nine towers, rising from sixteen to thirty-five stories high, with pinwheel-like plans; some towers were on their own, while others were joined in pairs. The architects described the towers as being clustered like molecules, with each molecule having its own elevator and lobby and floors with only eight or nine apartments per corridor. St. George Place was also not built.

In 1973 the New York State Urban Development Corporation proposed a project called Fox Hills, which would be developed along the same lines as Marcus Garvey Village in Brooklyn (see "Brooklyn," above), a project the UDC had also undertaken with the Institute for Architecture and Urban Studies.[55] Unlike the worn-out setting of Marcus Garvey Village, Fox Hills was to be built amid greenery on a portion of what had once been the sixty-one-acre estate of banker Lewis Henry Meyer. The 9.8-acre parcel had served as an army encampment during both world wars and had escaped postwar development. The plan, designed by a team led by Arthur Baker, Kenneth Frampton and Peter Wolf in consultation with David Todd & Associates, called for four-story row- and cluster-type units arranged among public greens and off-street parking areas; anonymous and unassigned space were kept to an absolute minimum. Ada Louise Huxtable described the unrealized Fox Hills proposal as "handsomer" than Marcus Garvey Village, "with a very sophisticated use of simple elements for considerable richness and surface interest."[56]

One of Staten Island's last hopes of maintaining a semblance of its pre-bridge character was the preservation of its

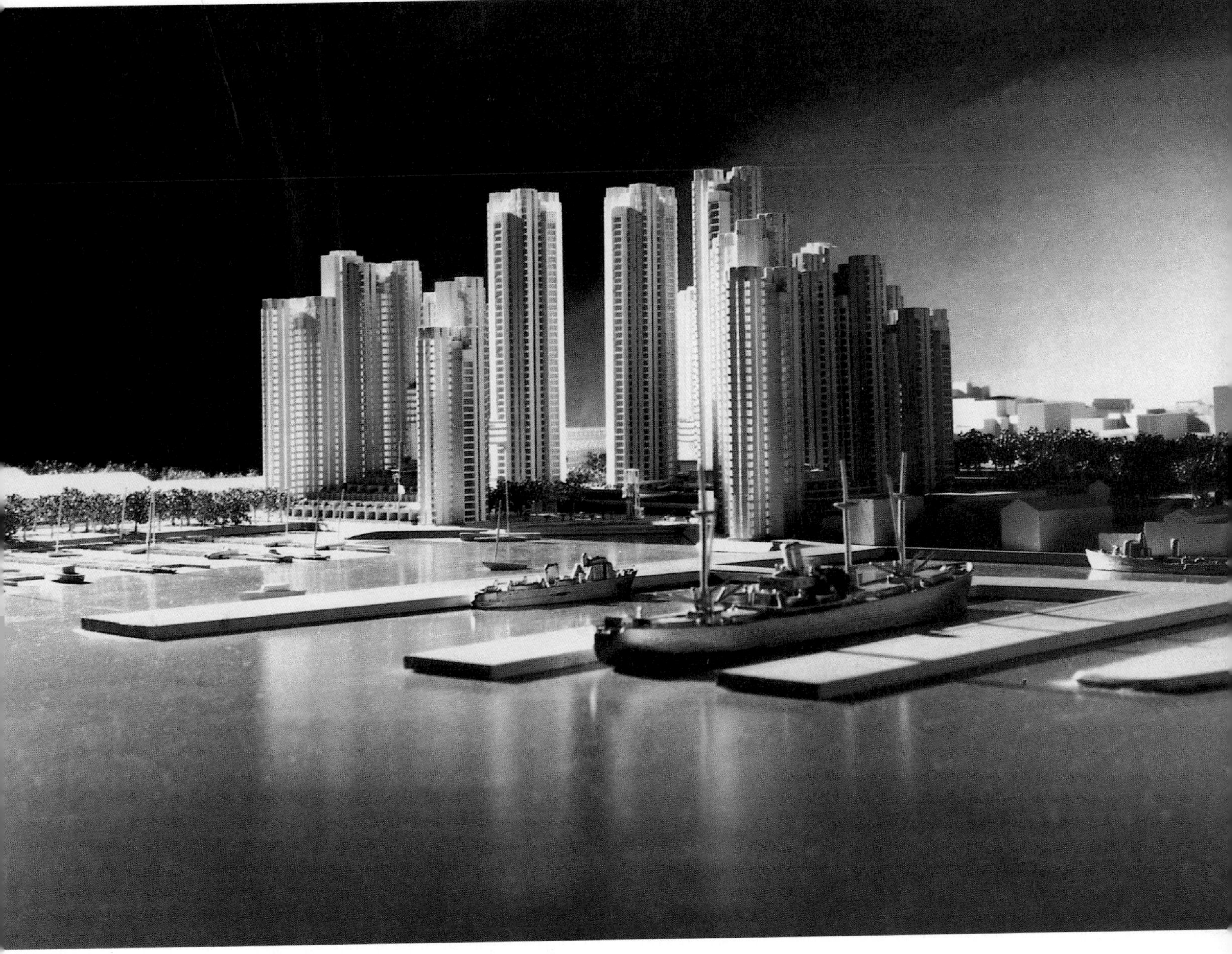

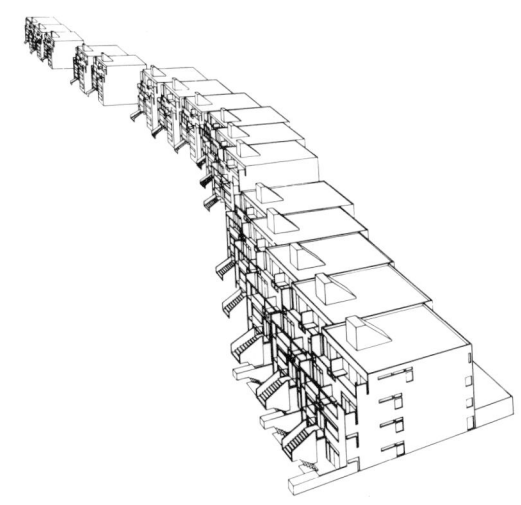

greenbelt, a chain of parks, private camps, a country club and low-density residential areas that ran roughly north-south along the island's central wooded ridge. In December 1964 the City Planning Commission, fearing the kind of large-scale development that was bringing blight to other parts of the island, instituted a stopgap measure by rezoning the area to allow only the construction of private homes on large lots.[57] Included in the southern portion of the rezoned area was the Girl Scouts' Camp High Rock. In February 1965 the Girl Scouts, explaining that the fifty-six-acre camp was run-down and too expensive to maintain, sold the property, reportedly for $1 million, to New Dorp Gardens, Inc., a private real estate development concern. Foundation work was begun before the city stepped in and purchased the tract from the developer, utilizing unused state bond funds provided by Governor Rockefeller to pay for 75 percent of the cost. The area was remapped for parkland, and in July 1965 the city opened the High Rock Nature Conservation Center on the former campsite.

Robert Moses's Richmond Parkway presented a more serious challenge to the greenbelt. First proposed in 1947 (Andrews, Clark & Buckley, engineers), Richmond Parkway was not revived until 1964, when plans were announced for a four-year, three-part construction schedule to begin the following spring.[58] The first two sections of the 9.5-mile-long roadway were to be the most destructive. The six-lane parkway would begin at the Sunnyside interchange of the Staten Island Expressway, cross Todt Hill and cut through the heavily wooded area to the west of the Richmond County Country Club and the Moravian Cemetery. The second part would continue along the eastern border of LaTourette Park, cross Richmond Creek and stop at the intersection of Arthur Kill Road, Richmond Avenue and Drumgoole Boulevard. The final part would continue south and west until it linked up with the Outerbridge Crossing.

Surprisingly, the initial response to the highway was favorable. An editorial titled "Best Yet to Come" in the *Staten Island Advance* praised the roadway, especially the fact that, as a parkway, it would exclude commercial traffic. "It will be the main route along the axis of the borough," the editors wrote, "a road that is sure to be more welcome each year as the cars multiply and our local roads become ever more clogged."[59] But within a year organized opposition had grown, headed on the island by the Staten Island Citizens Planning Committee. They focused their attention on the two northern sections of the parkway, which were now consolidated into a single 4.7-mile-long segment.[60] The citizen group recommended that the Outerbridge Crossing connection be built and that the section affecting the greenbelt area be restudied. They also proposed an alternate route, west of and roughly parallel to the original route, which Moses rejected as "impractical and visionary."[61]

In February 1966 the City Planning Commission released their own plans for an alternate route.[62] In addition to expanding its use to include commercial traffic, the roadway was shifted to the west, so that it disturbed only about a mile of the greenbelt area. William F. R. Ballard, chairman of the City Planning Commission, contended that the new route had four major advantages over the old one: it had less impact on parklands; provided new access to the growing commercial center off Richmond Avenue; created a direct connection to the Willowbrook Expressway leading to the Bayonne Bridge; and eliminated the steep grades required by the original plan. Moses insisted on his route, however, and he was supported by Borough President Robert T. Connor and State Senator John Marchi. Opposing them were the newly elected mayor, John

Lindsay, and his park commissioner, Thomas P. F. Hoving. Although Mayor Wagner had approved Moses's plan in the last two days of his administration, Lindsay's right to rescind the project was recognized by the State Department of Public Works. After a delay in the start of construction was granted, the Lindsay administration came forward with five more proposals, all located to the west of the original proposal, either sparing the greenbelt area altogether or disturbing a much smaller portion than Moses's route.

The controversy over the highway route was one element in the ongoing power struggle between Lindsay and Moses, in which Lindsay attempted to remove Moses as head of the Triborough Bridge and Tunnel Authority. On April 27, 1966, the two men exchanged icy smiles and polite greetings at groundbreaking ceremonies for Richmond Parkway's southern section.[63] In August 1966 Hoving upped the confrontational ante by proposing a park along Moses's highway route.[64] Called the Olmsted Trailway in honor of Frederick Law Olmsted, who lived on the island and ran a model farm there between 1848 and 1854, the 300-foot-wide linear park would include hiking and bicycle trails, bridle paths, boating and fishing facilities and an arboretum. At the end of 1966 Lindsay presented his choice for the northern Richmond Parkway route, a 3.9-mile-long stretch that started three miles to the west of the already built Sunnyside interchange.[65] This plan generally followed a path adjacent to the Willowbrook State School and Willowbrook Park and crossed the Richmond Creek Marshlands at its southern end.

For the next two years, while the southern portion of the highway was being built, controversy raged over the merits of Moses's and Lindsay's routes for the northern portion.[66] In 1968 Lindsay released a report supporting his plan, *The Least Social Cost Corridor for Richmond Parkway*, prepared by Wallace, McHarg, Roberts and Todd, who were commissioned by August Heckscher, head of the Department of Parks, Recreation and Cultural Affairs.[67] In 1970 Governor Rockefeller rejected the Lindsay route, offering a compromise that ran along the western edge of the greenbelt and connected with the Sunnyside interchange.[68] Lindsay reluctantly accepted Rockefeller's four-lane route, which avoided most of the greenbelt but did cut into it at two points. Conservationists quickly filed suit against the city and state to block Rockefeller's proposal, and the project languished, with Moses's original route remaining on official maps. In 1974 Lee Dembart of the *New York Times* observed that the "Richmond Parkway is rivaled only by the Second Avenue Subway as the longest-talked-about city project yet to be built."[69] The parkway's northern extension was never built, and in 1984 nearly 1,800 acres in the greenbelt were officially designated parkland.[70]

Though neither the public nor the private sector accomplished anything of distinction in residential architecture after the bridge was completed, some fine school and health-care facilities were built on the island. With more land at its disposal than usual, the Board of Education attempted to develop new prototypes for its Staten Island schools. In 1945 the board commissioned William Lescaze to prepare plans for Public School 14, to be located on Tompkins Avenue and Hill Street in the Stapleton section of the borough.[71] Lescaze, whose Ansonia High School (1936) in Connecticut was one of the earliest schools in the International Style, designed a loosely arranged group of reinforced-concrete pavilions set askew from the site's geometry at an angle to maximize sunlight.[72] When only one contractor bid on the project, the Board of Education decided

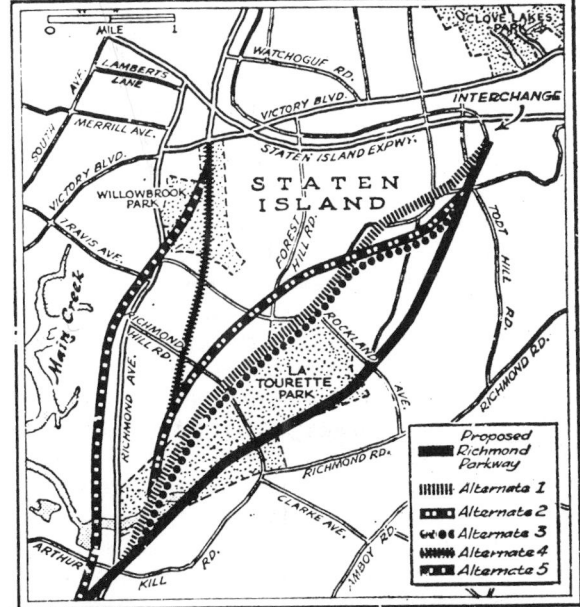

Top: Proposals for Richmond Parkway, April 1966. NYT

Center left: Proposal for Public School 14, northwest corner of Tompkins Avenue and Hill Street, Stapleton. William Lescaze, 1945. Model. SU

Center right: Public School 14, northwest corner of Tompkins Avenue and Hill Street, Stapleton. Eric Kebbon, 1948. View to the southwest. NYCBE

Bottom: Tottenville High School, 100 Luten Avenue, between Eylandt and Chisolm streets, Huguenot. Daniel Schwartzman & Associates, 1972. Stoller. ©ESTO

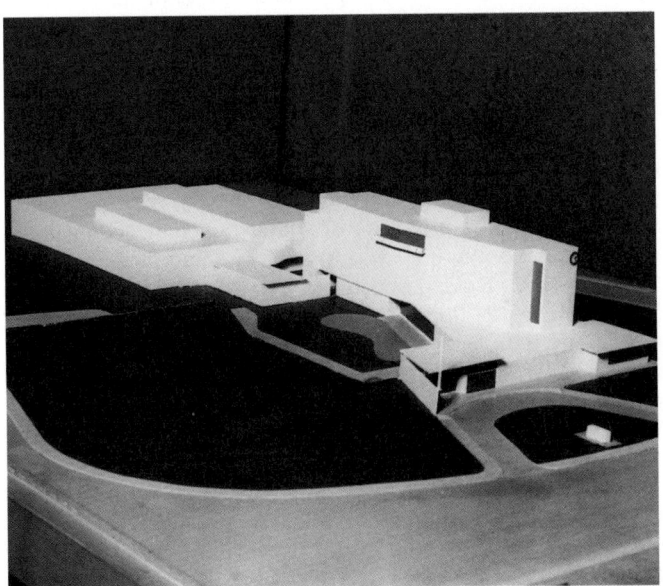

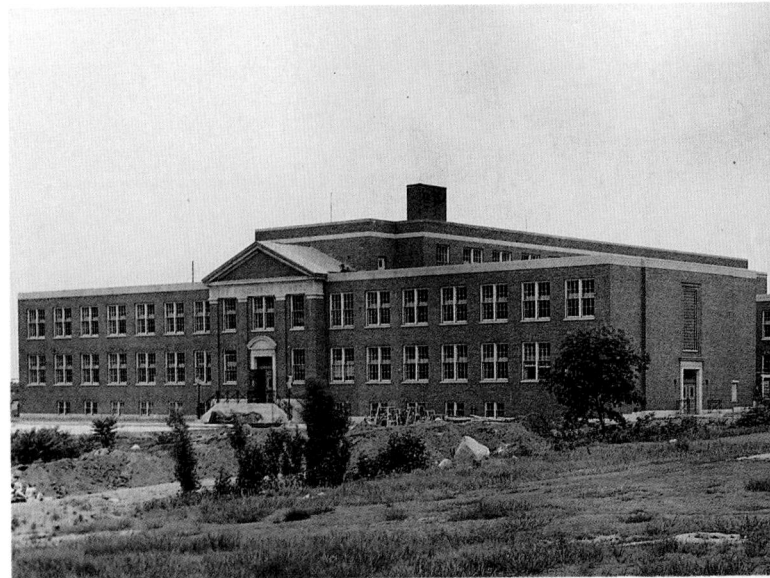

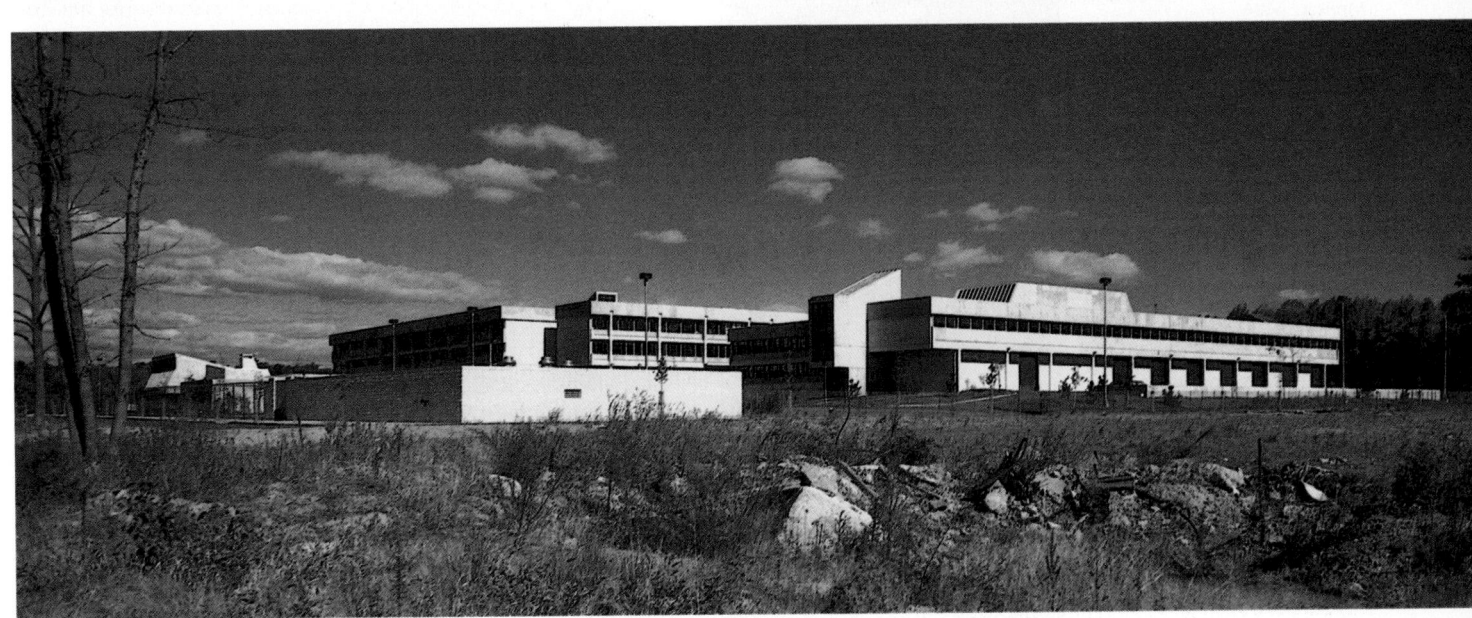

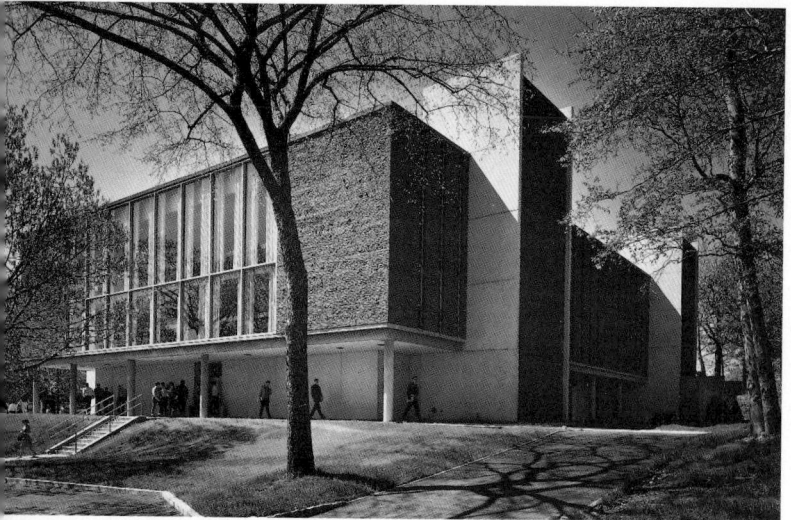

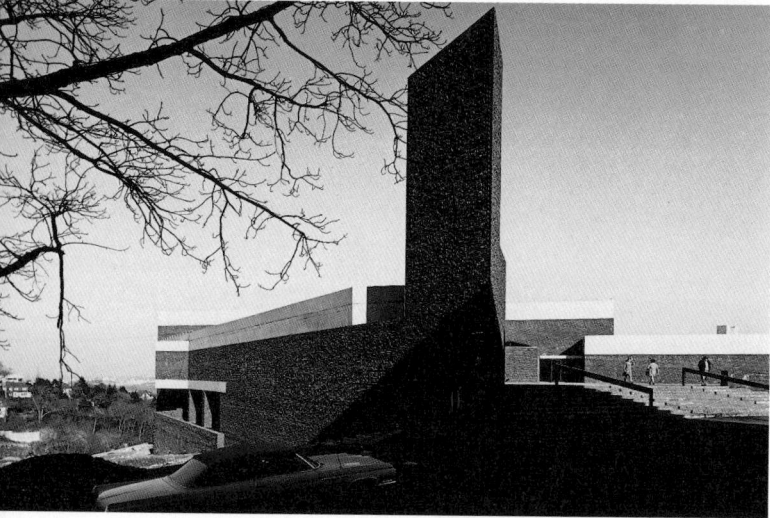

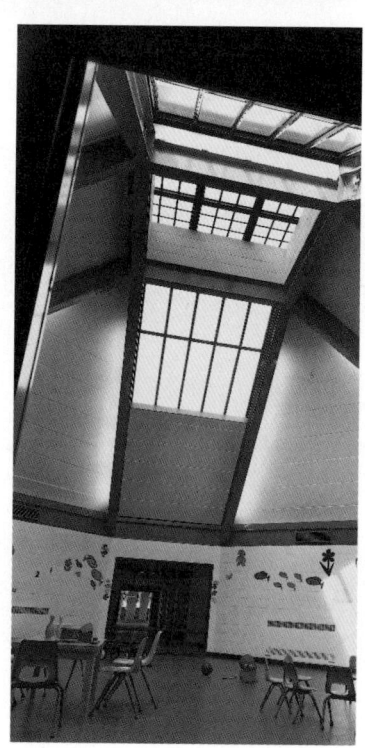

Top: August Horrmann Library, Wagner College, Grymes Hill. Perkins & Will, 1961. View to the northwest. Molitor. JWM

Center: Student Union, Wagner College, Grymes Hill. Perkins & Will, 1970. View to the southwest. Rothschild. PW

Bottom: Intensive Therapy Center, Willowbrook State School, bounded by Willowbrook Park, Willowbrook Park Road and Forest Hill Road. Merz & Pasanella, 1965. Interior of corridor intersection. Hirsch. PAKL

Far right: South Beach Psychiatric Center, 777 Seaview Avenue, South Beach. John Carl Warnecke & Associates, 1973. View to the north with Verrazano-Narrows Bridge (Othmar Hermann Ammann, 1964), on the upper right. JCW

not to revise the plans but to substitute a more conventional Colonial Georgian–inspired design (Eric Kebbon, 1948). "Thus," *Architectural Forum* commented, "New York City will invest in a structure already obsolete."[73]

Charles Luckman Associates' Monsignor Farrell High School (Roman Catholic) (1962), at 2900 Amboy Road, on the southwest corner of Tysen's Lane, was a boldly scaled, sophisticated essay in postwar Corbusian aesthetics that could easily be mistaken for a corporate office building.[74] Richard Stein's P.S. 55 (1965), at 54 Osborne Street, on the southeast corner of Woods of Arden Road, and the playground he completed two years later, with an abstract sculpture by Constantino Nivola, reflected an aesthetic Brutalism combined with a far more gentle, people-oriented sense of planning.[75] Tottenville High School (Daniel Schwartzman & Associates, 1972), at 100 Luten Avenue, on the northwest corner of Deisius Street, was one of the newly programmed comprehensive high schools that called for close integration of vocational and academic programs.[76] Despite its twenty-acre site, the 4,000-student school projected an image of imposing institutionality, rather like a suburban corporate headquarters. Belfatto & Pavarini's schools, I.S. 72 (1975), the Rocco Laurie School, at 33 Ferndale Avenue, between Travis and Saxon avenues, and P.S. 69 (1976), the Daniel D. Tompkins School, at 144 Keating Place, between Rockland and Travis avenues, managed to convey a modicum of dignity and urbanism within the banal suburbia of the so-called Heartland Village.[77]

In 1975 the Eggers Partnership's design for New Dorp High School, at 465 New Dorp Lane, a 4,000-student facility, was released.[78] The new school was to be located on 26 acres of the 213-acre Miller Field, a deactivated Army air base. A vast facility containing 421,000 square feet of space, it was divided into four nearly self-contained sub-schools, each occupying the upper two floors of the three-story wings; on the first floors were the common facilities such as the library, cafeteria and laboratories. Clad in iron-spot brick and dark-finished aluminum-framed windows, and with a ceremonial flight of entrance stairs, the design conveyed a sense of traditional dignity typical of the city's older public schools. The release of the design coincided with the city's fiscal crisis, and the school was not completed until 1982.

Wagner College, a private Lutheran institution located on the former Cunard estate 370 feet above sea level on the brow of Grymes Hill, built a number of admirable academic buildings, following the master plan prepared in 1960 by Perkins & Will.[79] For the college's August Horrmann Library (1961), Perkins & Will selected a prime spot with sweeping views of the Narrows, Brooklyn and Governor's Island.[80] Although the detailing of the building was minimal and its mass was boxy, the use of clinker brick for the walls and exposed concrete for the stair towers helped integrate the new facility with the adjacent Tudor-style Administration Building (Smith, Conable & Powley, 1930). Later buildings included the Towers Dormitory (Sherwood, Mills & Smith, 1964), the Mergerle Science and Communications Center (Perkins & Will, 1968) and the more daring Student Union (Perkins & Will, 1970).[81] The three buildings preserved the open character of the site, and because they were all clad in unglazed red-face brick and exposed concrete, they managed to create a kind of unity. Sherwood, Mills & Smith's prismatic, red-brick-clad Harbor View Dormitory (1968) was an elegantly proportioned fourteen-story tower that commanded sweeping views, although because of its size it was less sympathetic to the site.[82]

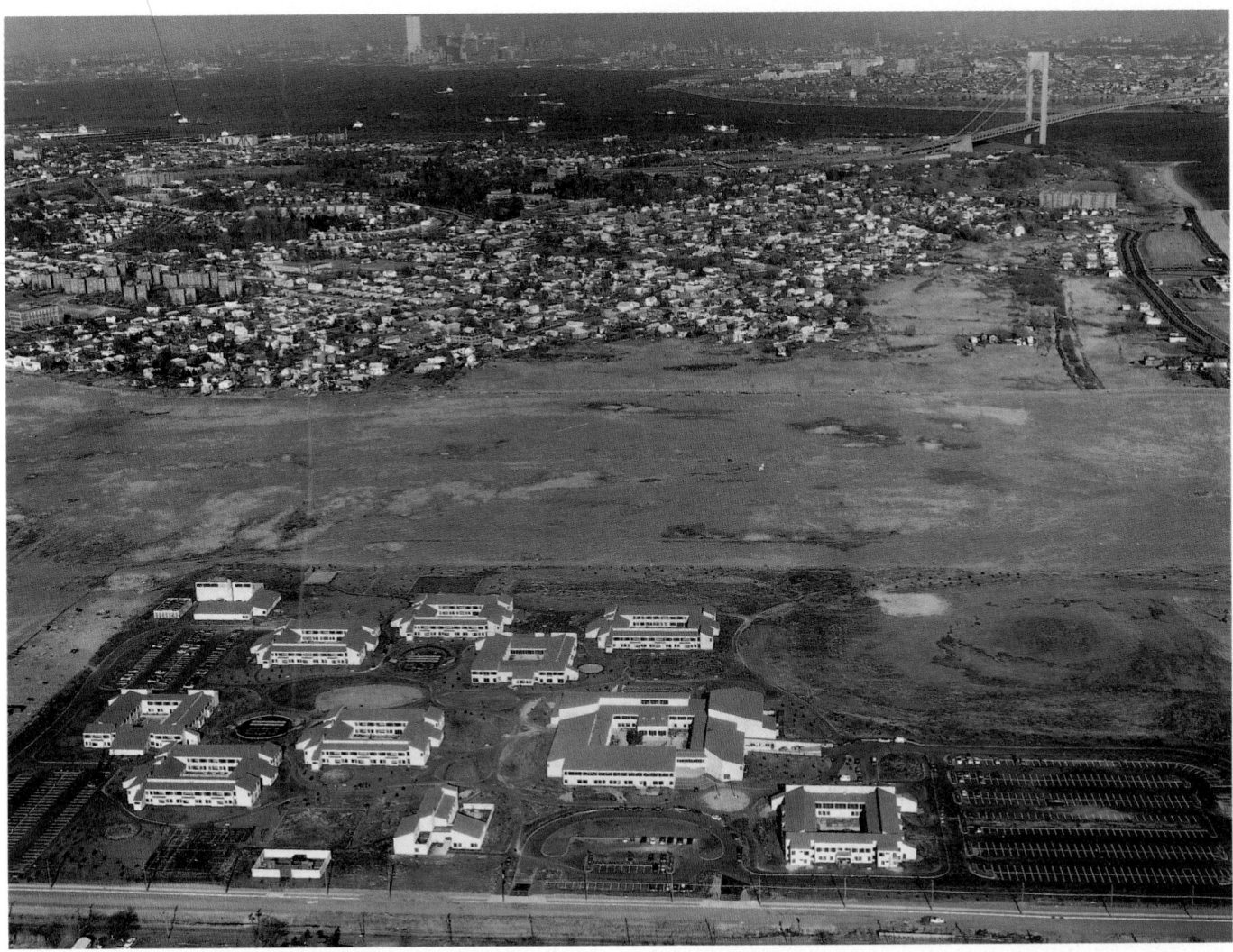

Before the opening of the Verrazano-Narrows Bridge, Staten Island's comparative isolation made it an ideal place to house facilities dealing with certain things society often prefers to ignore, such as death (it was home to many cemeteries) and problems of mental health. A major hospital campus operated by the state at Willowbrook, in the highlands near the island's center, catered to the mentally disabled. The oldest building on the campus, Willowbrook State School (1941), designed by William E. Haugaard in an institutional version of streamlined Classicism, was built for mentally disabled children.[83] It functioned as an army hospital during the war, when a one-story surgery wing (William Gehron, 1943) was added. Merz & Pasanella's Intensive Therapy Center (1965) at Willowbrook was a logically planned one-story facility that organized classrooms around courtyards and along streetlike, toplit corridors whose intersections were marked by high, glazed, truncated pyramids.[84] In 1967 another facility for Willowbrook, the New York State Research Institute for Mental Retardation, was designed by Fordyce & Hamby.[85] The pioneering facility was perhaps the first in the world to have programs in eight to ten disciplines in the basic sciences focused entirely on mental disabilities. It featured single-story wings for administration, for animal experimentation and for a forty-patient ward, in addition to a five-story research tower. By the time of the building's completion, the Willowbrook operation was the subject of a major controversy over care for the mentally disabled, and the institution was severely downsized in 1975 after a three-year-long court case.[86]

Closer to the ferry terminal, in the Hamilton Park subdivision that had its flowering in the 1850s to 1870s, were two buildings used by the Children's Aid Society. The first was the Goodhue Children's Center Recreation Building, housed in Woodbrook (ca. 1845), the former Jonathan Goodhue residence, at 304 Prospect Avenue at Clinton Avenue. The second was Davis, Brody & Associates' William H. Wheelock Residence Facility (1971), at 290 Prospect Avenue, the first building realized as part of a master plan for the society developed by the firm.[87] The suavely composed one-story building, designed for experimental group living for eight teenagers, was surfaced in jumbo brick, and its appearance was not so different from that of the Brutalist-inspired, high-style beach and country houses popular at the time.

Located on the eastern shore of the island was a much larger facility, John Carl Warnecke & Associates' South Beach Psychiatric Center (1973), at 777 Seaview Avenue.[88] Designed to accommodate 740 inpatients, as well as day patients attending on a regular basis and outpatients, the ten-building complex totaled approximately 330,000 square feet of space. In order to avoid an institutional look, the rather bleak site was treated as a campus of domestically scaled buildings grouped in quadrangle and courtyard spaces, but without creating a sense of confinement. To ease problems of orientation, a building identification system based on lettering and color coding was adopted.

QUEENS

The Moslem may long for Mecca, but middle-class families long for Queens as they swelter in the stony places of Manhattan, Brooklyn and the Bronx. It is, in fine, the place where you can exchange a lease for a mortgage, an apartment for a house, and a strip of sidewalk for a lawn.
—Hal Burton, 1952[1]

Even more than Brooklyn, Queens was an amalgam of villages and neighborhoods—over sixty in all. Until the 1930s outer Queens was largely undeveloped, its semirural character established by a combination of summer resorts, golf courses and small farms. The atmosphere throughout the rest of the borough, where modest, freestanding houses sat behind small front lawns, was close to that of small-town America, even more so than on Staten Island, which seemed a true backwater by comparison. In the minds of the borough's residents, Queens was not a single political entity but a collection of distinct communities. Loyalties belonged to the historical villages (Astoria, Corona, Jamaica, Flushing) and to the defined neighborhoods (Sunnyside, Bayside, Jackson Heights, St. Albans), not to the borough.

But by the early 1930s the small-town feeling was under siege. The new subway lines were bringing rapid change, and the open land that was once the main source of the borough's strength was disappearing.[2] In the 1930s and 1940s the borough's population burgeoned, with more people moving into Queens in the 1940s than into all the other boroughs combined.[3] Almost all the new immigrants were middle-class, white and proudly "white collar"; in 1952 more than half of the city's 18,000 policemen lived there, and the population of civil service employees was estimated at 50,000.

Unlike Brooklyn, which had been an independent city with a rich culture of its own before the consolidation of New York in 1898, Queens was not united until it became a borough that year. (When Greater New York was formed, Queens County was split in two and its eastern half became Nassau, then an area of farming and estates for the wealthy.) Queens had no museums, no tradition of theater or music or art, no great gardens, not even a baseball team. But it did have two fine racetracks which remained open long after those in the Bronx and Brooklyn had succumbed to development. One of these, Jamaica, closed in 1958 and was replaced by a housing project, Rochdale Village (see below).[4] The other, Aqueduct, was rebuilt in 1959 (see below).

The postwar history of Queens was marked by the typical problems of modern city planning: overdevelopment and decay. By 1970, when the City Planning Commission released its master plan for the borough, Queens was riddled not only with problems similar to those of the other boroughs but also with several of its own: inadequate sewers, overcrowded public transit and, worst of all, two airports that congested its highways and polluted its air space with noise.[5]

Long Island City

Long Island City, incorporating several villages and hamlets, principally Hallet's Cove, Astoria, Steinway, Ravenswood and Hunter's Point, existed as an independent entity for only twenty-eight years before it was consolidated into Greater New York in 1898.[6] Astoria, to the north along the East River shorefront, near Hell Gate, was originally a summer retreat for Manhattanites. Later, in the 1870s, it became the site of housing for employees of the Steinway piano company, which until 1910 had its factory in Manhattan, on the east side of Park Avenue between Fifty-second and Fifty-third streets.[7] Long Island City also included a wealth of solid one- and two-family houses interspersed with small apartment houses and commercial and community facilities.

In 1944 the Housing Authority, following up on its Queensbridge Houses (William F. R. Ballard, 1939),[8] embarked on its second major project in Long Island City, Astoria Houses, to be built on a thirty-one-acre site bounded by Twenty-seventh Avenue on the north, Hallet's Cove and Astoria Boulevard on the south, the East River and First Street on the west, and Vernon Boulevard and Eighth Street on the east.[9] Astoria Houses was designed by Harrison & Abramovitz to include twenty-two identical seven-story brick cruciform buildings containing 1,104 apartments. To ameliorate the problem of tenant relocation, the project was built in two stages: ten buildings were completed in 1948–49 on the vacant southern portion of the site, and the remainder were finished in 1951 on land that had previously held 190 families, 140 of whom were accommodated in the new buildings and other Housing Authority projects.

Another large-scale, low-rent Housing Authority project completed in 1951 was Frederick G. Frost's Ravenswood Houses.[10] Located south of Astoria Houses on a forty-eight-acre site bounded by Thirty-fourth Avenue, Twenty-fourth Street, Thirty-sixth Avenue and Twelfth Street, Ravenswood consisted of fourteen six- and seven-story buildings housing 2,650 families.

At the same time that the city condemned the twelve blocks of light industrial buildings, vacant land and some houses needed for the Ravenswood site, it also acquired an additional four-block, ten-acre parcel immediately to its north, which it sold to the Queensview Housing Cooperative, a group of civic-minded businessmen led by Gerard Swope and the veteran houser Louis Pink. Queensview (1951), their nonprofit, middle-income, cooperative housing development, was made possible by a loan from the Mutual Life Insurance Co. of New York, which had a provisory clause in their contract that a low-income housing project (which became Ravenswood) be built on an adjoining site.[11] The complex housed 728 families in fourteen elegantly detailed rectangular towers, each fourteen stories high and raised on pilotis, occupying only 13 percent of a superblock bounded by Thirty-third Road, Crescent Street, Thirty-fourth Avenue and Twenty-first Street. Queensview was designed by George Brown and Bernard Guenther, whose partnership would never again achieve so high an aesthetic level. Generous, fifteen-by-eighteen-foot living rooms, eat-in kitchens, large foyers and ample closet space were matched by crisply detailed windows and stylish, sheltered ground-floor entrances that adapted high-style Modernist pilotis to the requirements of urban apartment living. Construction costs were kept low by using precast concrete blocks. Queensview was so successful that a year after its completion plans were announced for an expansion. Queensview West (Brown-Guenther-Booss, 1958) consisted of seven fourteen-story buildings containing 364 apartments on an adjacent five-acre site bounded by Thirty-third Avenue, Twenty-first Street, Thirty-fourth Avenue and Fourteenth Street.[12]

North of Queensview was one more large-scale project of note, Samuel Paul and William M. Dowling's Marine Terrace Garden Apartments (1948), between Shore Boulevard, Twenty-ninth Street, and Twentieth and Twenty-first avenues, a private rental development for 1,388 families.[13] Marine Terrace's twenty-six buildings occupied 30 percent of the forty-acre site, which was once part of the historic Rapelje Farm, and were sited to take advantage of East River views.

One notable ecclesiastical building was built in the area, Henry V. Murphy's Church of the Immaculate Conception (Roman Catholic) (1950), at 29-01 Ditmars Boulevard, on the northeast corner of Twenty-ninth Street, Astoria.[14] It was one of a handful of churches built in the city in the late 1940s and early 1950s that exhibited the firmness and confidence of the best traditional work. The church's Lombardy Romanesque style was perfectly suited to its broad, largely unornamented brick walls, which were probably as much a by-product of a modest budget as a reflection of the impact of Modernist minimalism on the tastes of traditional architects. The elegantly proportioned tower with its corbeled arches made a strong symbolic statement in an area of almost exclusively one- and two-story buildings.

South of Astoria, the area traditionally called Long Island City, as well as the areas of Hunter's Point and Ravenswood, were almost solid with factories and warehouses. The neighborhoods were visually dominated by the superstructure of the Queensboro Bridge (Henry Hornbostel and Gustav Lindenthal, 1901–9) and, after 1961, by the Ravenswood Plant of the Consolidated Edison Company, at Vernon Boulevard and the East River, in which "Big Allis," the enormous electrical generator manufactured by Allis-Chalmers, was housed.[15] While most of the factories and warehouses built between 1910 and 1930 were multilevel loft buildings—like those built for Brewster & Company (Stephenson & Wheeler, 1911) at Queens Plaza and for the American Chicle Company (Ballinger & Perot, 1919) on Thomson Avenue—postwar buildings were seldom more than three stories tall and some had only one story.[16] By far the most elegant of these was Ulrich Franzen's factory for Barkin, Levin & Company (1958), manufacturers of ladies' coats, at 12-12 Thirty-third Avenue, on the southwest corner of Thirteenth Street.[17] More residential than industrial in character, Franzen's highly refined design combined a brick-walled one-story manufacturing plant with a glassy pavilion, the roof of which consisted of nine steel "umbrellas." Set on a two-acre landscaped plot, the building contained 50,000 square feet of work space in which, for the first time in New York, every element necessary in the manufacture of a coat was contained, thus streamlining production by eliminating the need to move the garment from one plant to another at different stages of assembly. Harrison, Fouilhoux & Abramovitz's one-story bottling plant for Pepsi-Cola (1943), at 46-00 Fifth Street, was less precious but almost as elegant, with continuous glazing set flush with the brick facing and a thin plane of reinforced concrete forming a canopy over the loading platform.[18]

Three radically different large-scale, mixed-use proposals, all unrealized, were advanced for the Long Island City area in the decades after the war. In 1946 the architects Pomerance & Breines, Andrew J. Thomas and Percival Goodman chose a large area encompassing Queensbridge Houses that was bounded by Hallet's Cove, Forty-eighth Avenue, the East River and the Sunnyside railroad yards as the site of a three-part effort to rebuild some of the blighted industrial section, which was so close to midtown Manhattan and well served by public transportation.[19] A broad riverfront park would run along the site's entire length. Approximately 114 acres, or 25 percent of the site, were reserved for Riverview Housing, a project intended to house 50,000 persons in both high-rise and low-rise buildings; new schools, libraries and a shopping center were also included. North of Thirty-fifth Street would be a less dense housing area, an almost suburban scattering of buildings arrayed to complement the irregular shoreline.

About ten years after this failed proposal, Henry Hope

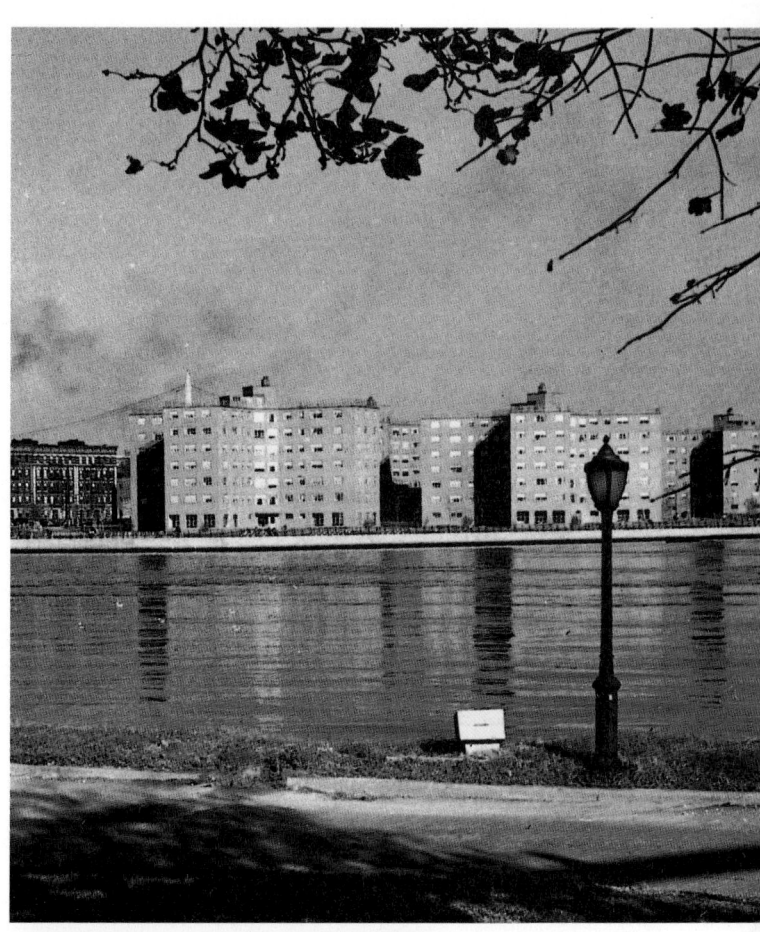

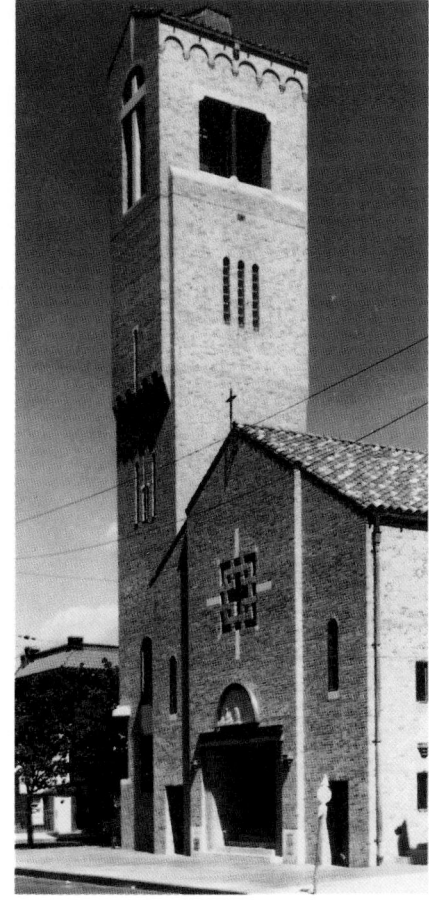

Top: Astoria Houses, bounded by Twenty-seventh Avenue, Eighth Street, Vernon Boulevard, Hallet's Cove, Astoria Boulevard, First Street and East River, Astoria. Harrison & Abramovitz, 1948–51. View to the northeast. NYCHA

Left: Church of the Immaculate Conception, 29-01 Ditmars Boulevard, northeast corner of Twenty-ninth Street, Astoria. Henry V. Murphy, 1950. View to the northwest. THTA

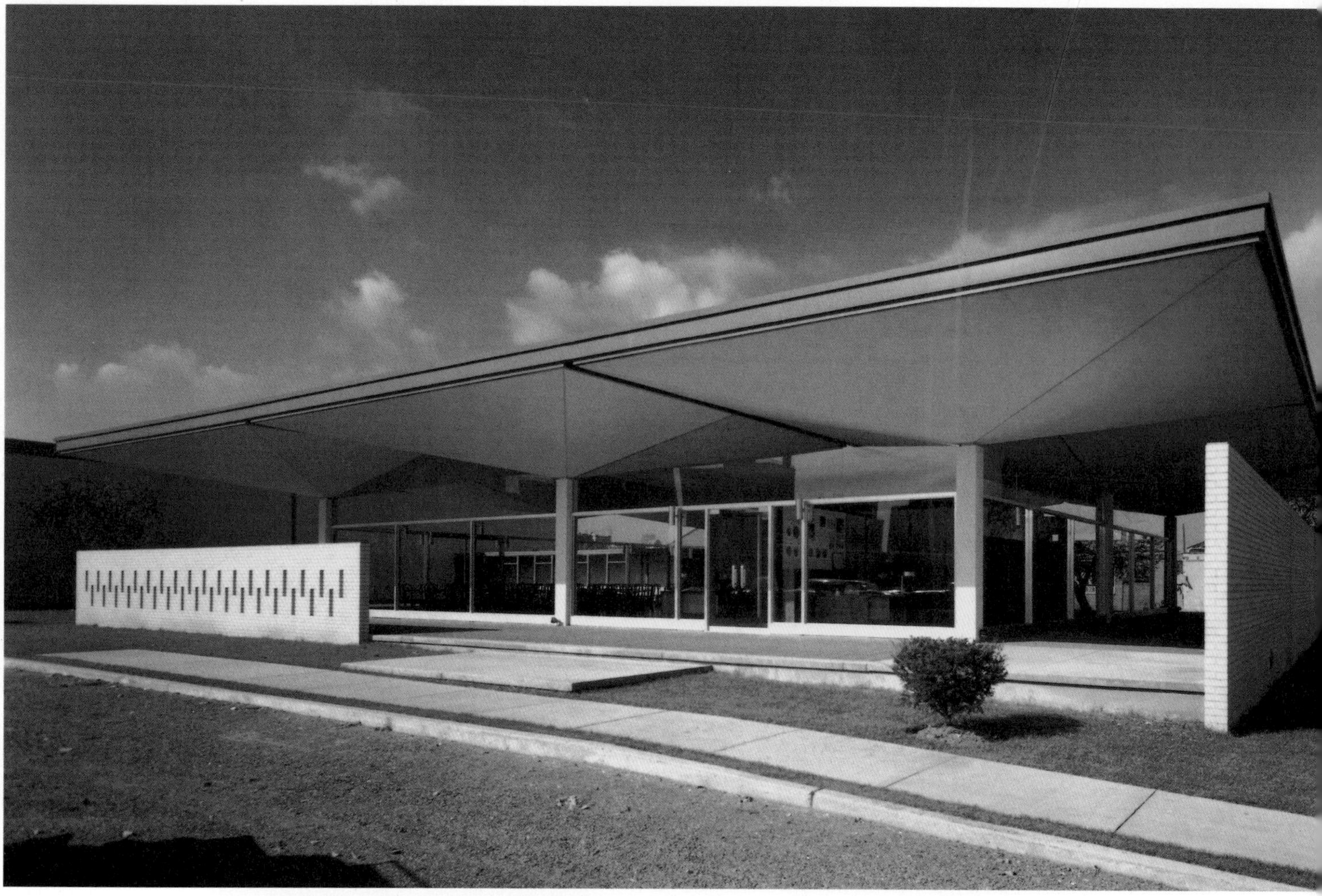

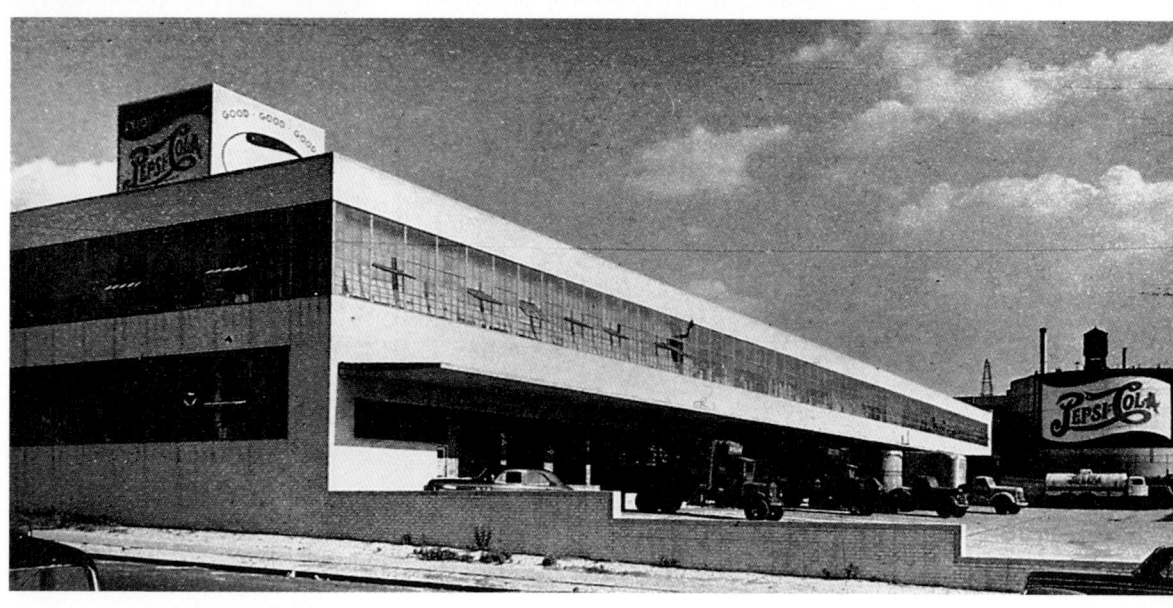

Reed, Jr., picked the Hunter's Point area as the ideal spot for a new arts center and residential quarter.[20] Reed's proposal, presented in an article accompanied by drawings by the architect John Barrington Bayley, called for palatial Classical buildings facing a giant elliptical basin, all on axis with the United Nations headquarters across the East River. "There would be sites for arches, rostral columns, plain columns and obelisks, and the buildings would be decorated both inside and out with painting and sculpture," Reed explained. This arts center would have an important function: "Here the nation could boast of its arts, the *visual* along with the musical and the dramatic. Here the American people could bid a superb welcome to the United Nations, offer an artistic expression of their faith in world government and confirm, as if to say 'This is our mark,' their longing for world peace."[21]

In 1970 the New York State Urban Development Corporation presented a plan for decking over the below-street-level Sunnyside railroad yards, which had opened in 1910 as part of the electrification and integration of the Pennsylvania and Long Island railroads.[22] The 300-acre site was roughly bounded by Northern Boulevard, Skillman and Thomson avenues and Forty-third Street. Gruzen & Partners' multilevel, multiuse project would have allowed the rail yards to continue operating during the construction above the tracks of high-density housing for 60,000 persons, office space for 35,000 persons, schools, industrial loft space, parking, a pedestrian promenade and a shopping mall. Even though the plan, developed with the help of the Lefrak Organization, had the advantage of requiring no tenant relocation, it went unrealized because of the depressed market for office space. By 1973 it had been replaced by a proposal for an immense sports center, sponsored by the New York State Racing and Wagering Board.[23] Planned in part as a response to New Jersey's proposed athletic center in the Hackensack Meadows, and also as an alternative to a sports center projected for downtown Brooklyn, the Sunnyside facility would be platformed over the rail yard and include two race tracks, an 80,000-seat football stadium and a 1,000-room resort and convention hotel. But after the negative results of a feasibility study undertaken by the state were released in March 1975, the project was dropped.

La Guardia Field

When La Guardia Field (Delano & Aldrich, 1940) opened, it was lauded as the "world's largest and finest" airport.[24] But La Guardia's limitations soon became obvious. First of all, the site was constantly being eroded by the sea; built on marshland, the runway area sank three inches a year and had to be kept "afloat" with a system of sand drains and a dike to prevent water from rising onto the field. Furthermore, the airport's system for moving passengers between the planes and ground transportation was wholly inadequate, and passengers were forced to traverse the tarmac, which was crowded with service vehicles. And although preticketed passengers could go directly to the boarding concourse, the rest had to make their way through the crowded, undersized terminal building, notable for its elegant but narrow curving stairs that to one critic seemed "to have been designed for a residence."[25]

In 1947 the Port of New York Authority took over the operation of La Guardia. One of the first improvements was the construction in 1948 of a temporary streamlined metal-and-glass snack bar, designed by Lester Tichy and located to the

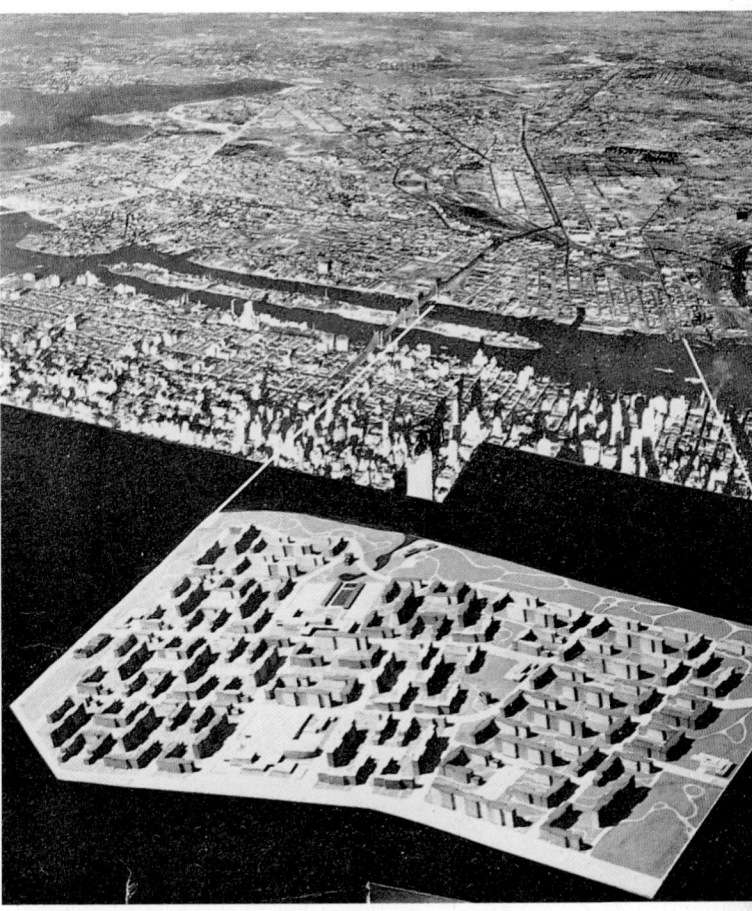

Top left: Barkin, Levin & Company, 12-12 Thirty-third Avenue, southwest corner of Thirteenth Street. Ulrich Franzen, 1958. View to the southwest. Stoller. ©ESTO

Bottom left: Pepsi-Cola bottling plant, 46-00 Fifth Street, between Forty-sixth Road and Forty-seventh Avenue, Long Island City. Harrison, Fouilhoux & Abramovitz, 1943. View to the northeast. AF. CU

Above: Proposal for Long Island City redevelopment, bounded by Hallet's Cove, Forty-eighth Avenue, East River and Sunnyside railroad yards. Pomerance & Breines, Andrew J. Thomas and Percival Goodman, 1946. Photographic montage of view to the northeast. AF. CU

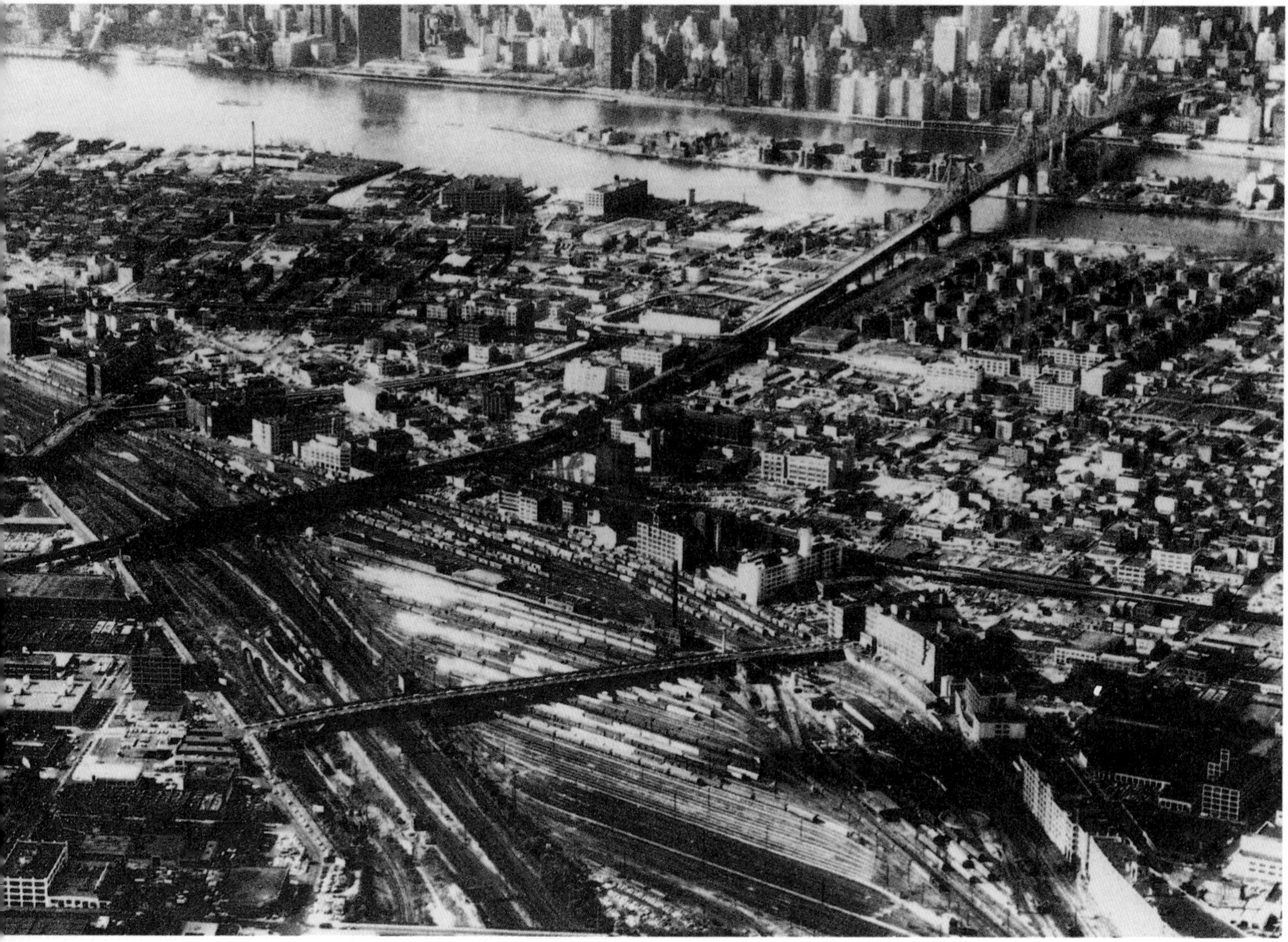

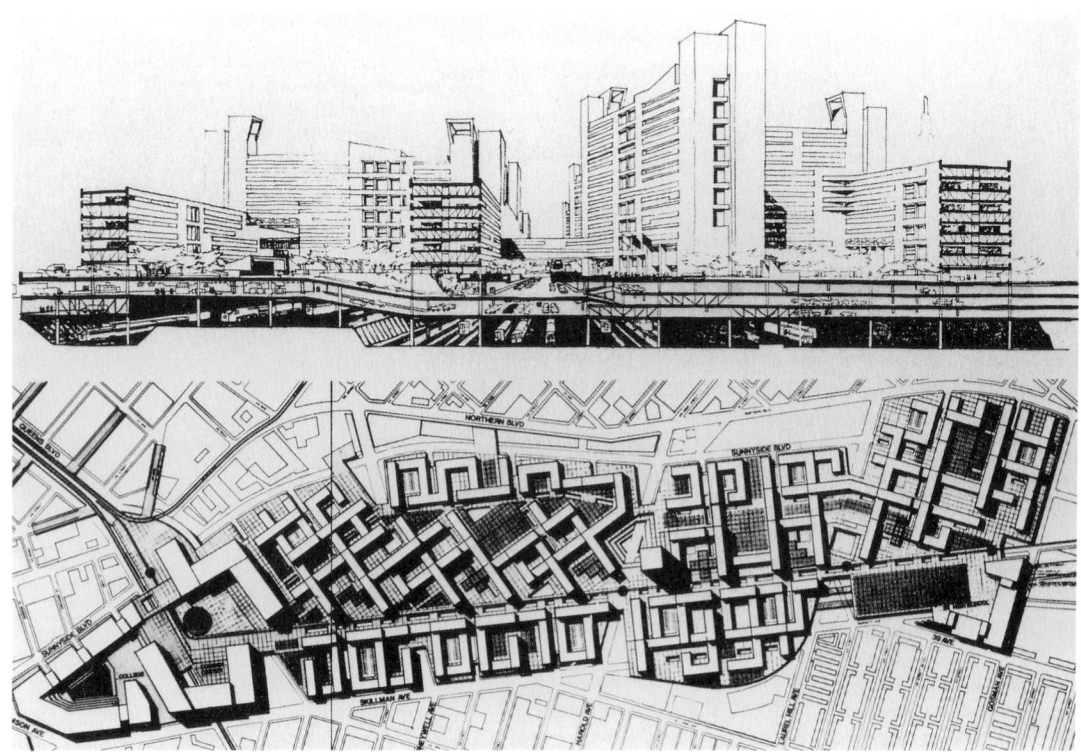

Top: View to the southwest of Sunnyside railroad yards, 1970. GS

Bottom: Proposal for redevelopment of Sunnyside railroad yards, bounded by Northern Boulevard, Skillman and Thomson avenues and Forty-third Street, Long Island City. Gruzen & Partners, 1970. Elevation and site plan. GS

side of the Marine Terminal, which now served international aircraft passengers. Tichy's flashy, aluminum-finished, Modernist-inspired composition of pipes, corrugated wall planes and up-turned metal roof stood in stark contrast to Delano & Aldrich's facility, admired only a few years before for its modernity but now dismissed as an exemplar of a "rather sterile formalism."[26]

In June 1957, nine years after international and transcontinental traffic was shifted to Idlewild (see below), the Port Authority announced a five-year plan for La Guardia's complete reconstruction.[27] Developed over two years' time, the plan called for an expansion of the facilities to comfortably accommodate the seven million short- and medium-haul passengers expected by 1965. The plan proposed the construction of two new wings flanking the existing terminal and, once they were completed, the replacement of the existing building with a new one. The new terminal was to form a semicircular, two-level, 1,100-foot-long, 100-foot-deep, 380,000-square-foot structure, three times the size of the current facility. In addition, the long, drafty passageway that led to the existing boarding gates would be replaced with four two-story fingers ranging from 475 to 720 feet in length, extending at right angles from the terminal onto the field to provide berthing places for thirty-six planes, only eight more than the airport's present capacity. A new 150-foot-tall control tower would be incorporated at the end of the western finger. In presenting the plan to the public, Mayor Wagner observed that in 1956 La Guardia Field, the nation's second busiest airport (exceeded only by Chicago's Midway Field), handled five million passengers and 229,714 aircraft movements in a facility designed for far less activity.

The Port Authority's design for the arc-shaped facility revealed a utilitarian metal- and glass-walled structure lined on the entrance side with arcaded sidewalks and access ramps. Cupped within the arc was a parking area for 3,200 cars, created by draining the unused boat basin that had provided a picturesque forecourt to the original terminal. An ungainly three-story element broke the roof's horizontal sweep at the center and projected over the upper-level access drive. Two years later, when Harrison & Abramovitz were called in to redesign the project, this element was eliminated and the building was lengthened to 1,250 feet, increasing its size to 500,000 square feet.[28] In 1963 the control tower was the first element of the revised scheme to be completed. Punctuated with a grid of circular glass "portholes," the twelve-story, circular rubbed-concrete tower flared toward the top, evoking an Egyptian palm column. The remaining elements of the proposal were completed the following year, and the new terminal was dedicated on April 16, 1964.[29]

Progressive Architecture praised Harrison & Abramovitz's design as "a straightforward, no-hokum curtain-walled structure whose arc shape reflects the bi-level roadway system serving it."[30] As a counterpoint to the slick, elegant curtain wall, the design incorporated a number of interesting features, including the slanted parasol roof, which focused the view to the field from the building's open-air observation deck, and the creaturelike open staircases that provided outside connections between the two roadway levels. In addition to the area of surface parking embraced by the terminal's arclike mass, the front of the airport featured a garden, almond-shaped in plan, designed by the Port Authority's in-house staff.

Inside, Harrison & Abramovitz's work was largely confined to areas devoted to circulation and public convenience, since the various airlines retained independent designers to configure their sales and gate area facilities. On the fourth floor of the

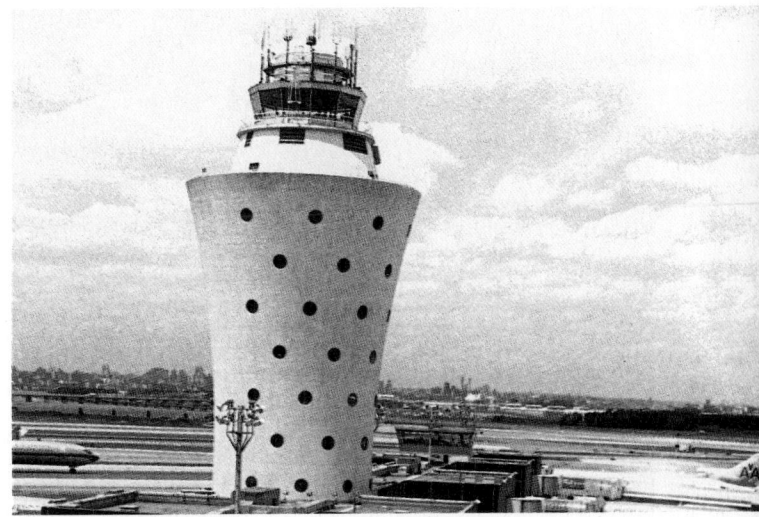

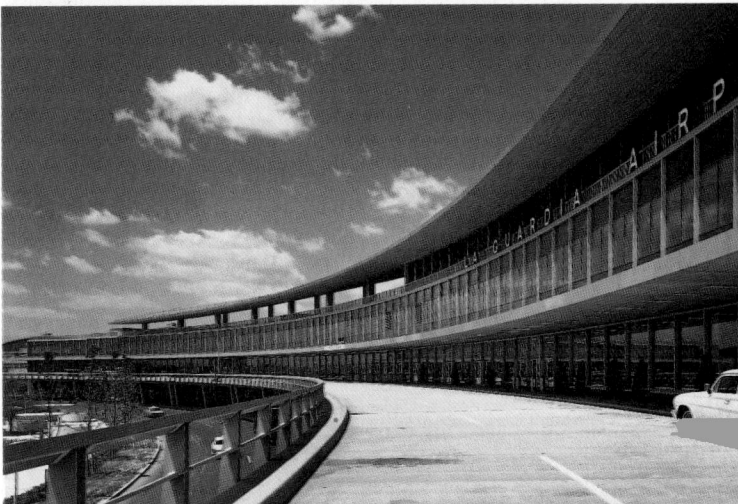

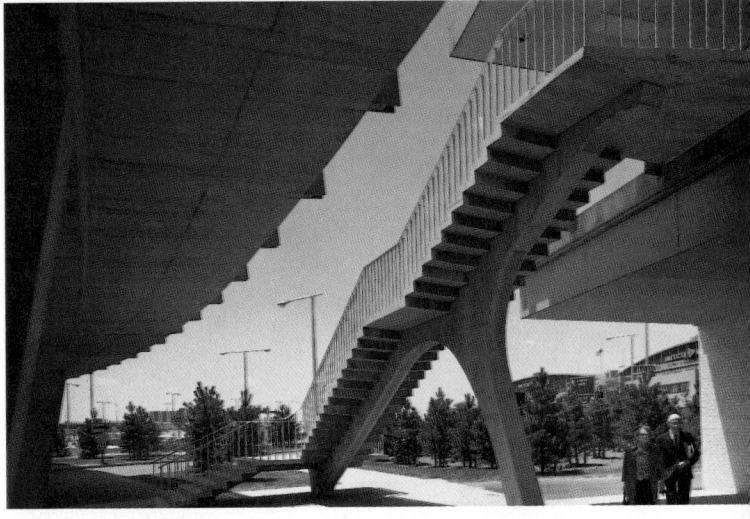

Top: Control tower, La Guardia Airport. Harrison & Abramovitz, 1963. View to the north. PANY

Center: Terminal, La Guardia Airport. Harrison & Abramovitz, 1964. View to the northwest. Maris. ©ESTO

Bottom: Terminal, La Guardia Airport. Exterior staircase. Stoller. ©ESTO

991

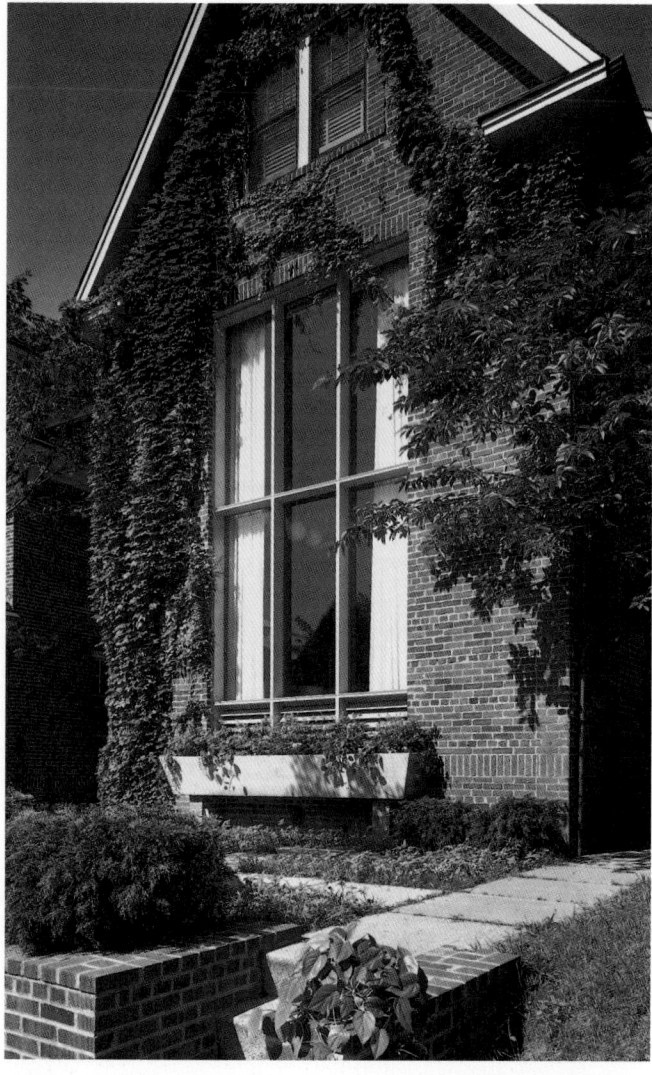

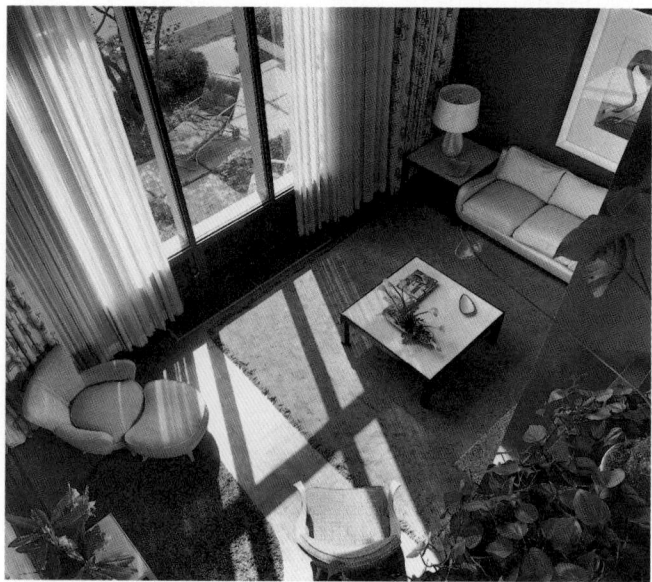

Top: Frank Yerby residence, 33-28 Eighty-sixth Street, between Northern Boulevard and Thirty-fourth Avenue, Jackson Heights. Jedd Reisner and Max Urbahn, 1949. View to the west. Stoller. ©ESTO

Bottom: Frank Yerby residence. Living room. Stoller. ©ESTO

building's central section was an upscale restaurant, operated by Restaurant Associates and designed by Warner, Burns, Toan & Lunde, whose efforts to transform a cavernous volume into an intimate dining room resulted in a rather hokey semblance of a garden court.[31]

In order to bypass the headaches and delays associated with the trip to La Guardia from Manhattan, a novel form of transportation was attempted in 1964.[32] In August of that year, American Hydrofoil Lines began service to the airport from marinas at East Twenty-fifth Street and South Street, with travel times of twenty-five and thirty-five minutes respectively. Although American Hydrofoil's thirty-three-foot, twenty-two-passenger crafts were averaging close to 1,000 passengers per day in their service to the World's Fair from the same Manhattan docks, the company ran into financial difficulties and service to La Guardia was soon discontinued. Not everyone was displeased, as many travelers admitted to preferring the congestion of the roadways to the possible nausea of the rough waters.

A number of new hotels were built around La Guardia for passengers who needed to remain overnight in New York but wanted to avoid the expense and inconvenience of a trip to Manhattan. In 1953 plans were announced for the 40-room, two-story La Guardia Hotel, located on a five-acre site just south of the Grand Central Parkway at 100th Street and Ditmars Boulevard, only a quarter mile from the airport's passenger terminal.[33] A. N. Sirof, the architect, in stressing that soundproofing was the most crucial aspect of his otherwise unremarkable design, confidently predicted that "an airplane engine thirty feet from the outside wall of the building will sound, inside the bedrooms, no louder than the rustle of leaves in an autumn breeze."[34] Sirof's plans to dampen the noise, which added 20 percent to the construction costs, featured ceilings made of pyrobar, a precast gypsum block with large holes running through the middle, often used for partitions that held electrical wiring or tubing. With the blocks mounted so that the flat side would serve as the ceiling's surface, the interior holes would then be able to trap sound waves, where they would be free to reverberate and weaken. Sirof also included nonstructural walls suspended from flexible spring steel clips in order to put some give in the flat surfaces, allowing sound waves to "kick around" and further dissipate. Double-thick permanently sealed windows blocked off even more sound.

The hotel's interiors were decorated by Ellen Lehman McCluskey. The 156-room Travelers Hotel (Arnold Arbeit), located on a 100,000-square-foot triangular plot bounded by Ditmars Boulevard, Ninety-fourth and Ninety-fifth streets and Twenty-third Avenue, was completed in 1956.[35] William Eli Kohn's three-story, fifty-five-room Skyway Hotel (1957), at 102-10 Ditmars Boulevard, overlooking Flushing Bay, featured balconies off every room.[36] And in 1962, opposite the airport at Twenty-third Avenue and Ditmars Boulevard, the eight-story, 138-room Crossway Motor Inn (Brodsky, Hopf & Adler) was opened.[37]

Newtown

The town of Newtown, first settled in 1642, incorporated most of central Queens, including the neighborhoods of Jackson Heights, Corona, Elmhurst, Rego Park, Forest Hills and Kew Gardens. Jackson Heights, the brainchild of E. A. MacDougall, a high-minded real estate man who headed the Queensboro Corporation, was a residential development begun before World War I. Construction was drastically curtailed by the Depression, although some new apartment houses were built in the area, damaging the balance between buildings and open space that had been so critical to the area's pre-Crash success. Among these were Philip Birnbaum's Berkeley Gardens (1938), at 35-26 Seventy-eighth Street, Andrew J. Thomas's Dunnolly Gardens (1939), at Thirty-fourth Avenue between Seventy-eighth and Seventy-ninth streets, and Joshua Tabatchnik's Arlington Apartments (1939), at 79-05 Thirty-fifth Avenue. During the war more land was sold to outside developers, so that what had begun as an experiment in high-density suburban-style living within the city's borders seemed destined to decline into just another overbuilt neighborhood of apartment houses.

Although the Jackson Heights neighborhood was dominated by apartment houses, it also contained rowhouses and some single-family houses, many of which had been built by MacDougall before the Crash. One of these belonged to Frank Yerby, a successful novelist.[38] The house was renovated by Jedd Reisner and Max Urbahn to accommodate Yerby and his family. The architects opened up the front to two stories to create a grand living room and screened off a dining room with wood slats that perfectly complemented the chairs and table designed by George Nakashima.

In 1947 Andrew J. Thomas designed a new headquarters for the Queensboro Corporation, a two-story Georgian-style building located at the northwest corner of Seventy-ninth Street and Thirty-seventh Avenue.[39] It was Thomas's last commission for the real estate firm, ending a twenty-eight-year association; E. A. MacDougall had died in 1944, and his son A. E., who had been serving as vice president, took control of the company.

Carlton House, the first postwar cooperative in Jackson Heights, was completed in 1947.[40] Designed by Philip Birnbaum, who had become known as a specialist in apartment house architecture for his work in Forest Hills,[41] Carlton House was located on the east side of Eighty-fifth Street between Thirty-fourth and Thirty-fifth avenues. When the public proved to be uncomfortable with cooperative housing, whose value had collapsed along with the stock market in 1929, the developers were forced to offer the apartments as rental units. Two years later, in 1949, Queensboro successfully marketed a cooperative, Boris Dorfman's three-story, Georgianesque Greenbrier, on Eighty-fourth Street between Thirty-fifth and Thirty-seventh avenues.[42]

In 1950 thirty-eight new apartment buildings were built in Jackson Heights, a record boom. Many were designed by Birnbaum, whose increasingly diagrammatic Georgian styling on the whole did little more than highlight the quality of Thomas's prewar work.[43] By the late 1950s Jackson Heights was almost completely built out, having been transformed from an idealistic real estate development into just another neighborhood. The open-space amenities had disappeared; gone were the golf course and the tennis courts, replaced by block upon block of mediocre apartment buildings and rowhouses.

At the intersection of Astoria Boulevard, Grand Central Parkway and Boody Street, just east of St. Michael's Cemetery in Jackson Heights, the Bulova Watch Company erected a 400,000-square-foot defense plant (Alexander D. Crosett & Associates, 1953), specializing in precision instruments and research on transistors.[44] The site had once been home to the long-abandoned Holmes Airport and in more recent years had accommodated 154 veterans in temporary wooden houses. The design, although out-of-date, was stylish, reflecting the stripped monumental Classicism of the 1930s; it was similar to Paul Cret's Federal Reserve Board Building (1935–37) in Washington, D.C.[45] The three-story, 450-by-350-foot plant included lab-oratories, executive and administrative offices, a 500-car parking lot for employees and a five-acre recreational field open to the public. Local residents had been opposed to the project, and the City Planning Commission agreed to the zoning change required for light industry only after Bulova submitted an extensive landscaping plan for the twenty-five-acre plot and agreed to relocate the veterans who were living on the site.

To the east of Jackson Heights were the long-established residential communities of Corona and Elmhurst, and beyond them Flushing Meadows–Corona Park, site of the World's Fair in both 1939–40 and 1964–65 (see chapter 14). One permanent building, Aymar Embury II's City Building, was left behind from the earlier fair, and several buildings remained from the later fair: the Singer Bowl (Architectural Enterprises), the Hall of Science (Harrison & Abramovitz), the United States Pavilion (Charles Luckman Associates), the New York State Pavilion (Philip Johnson and Richard Foster) and the fair's theme structure, the Unisphere (Gilmore D. Clarke and Peter Müller-Munk Associates). North of the park and across the tracks of the Port Washington Branch of the Long Island Railroad was Shea Stadium (Praeger-Kavanagh-Waterbury, 1964), built to house the New York Mets baseball team and the New York Jets football team.[46] Shea seated 55,000 for baseball and could be reconfigured to seat an additional 5,000 for football. Located on a site bounded by Northern Boulevard, Roosevelt Avenue, Grand Central Parkway and 126th Street, the stadium sat in the midst of a vast parking lot for 8,000 cars. One year after it opened, Shea was the scene of another kind of spectacle, the first American concert of the Beatles.[47]

Queens Boulevard, running southeast from Bridge Plaza to 138th Place and Hillside Avenue, was the borough's principal traffic artery and, beginning in the late 1950s, its principal shopping street. The most intense development on the street was concentrated near its intersection with Woodhaven Boulevard and the Long Island Expressway; with the completion of the expressway's Queens section in 1958, it became the first direct east-west arterial connection between Manhattan and Nassau County.[48] The thirteen-mile, six-lane Queens segment, first approved by the City Planning Commission in 1951, consisted of the Queens-Midtown Expressway and Horace Harding Boulevard, both vastly expanded from their previous size (the latter was widened from 160 to 260 feet), and a new link between the two roadways. The link was constructed west of Queens Boulevard, joining the Queens-Midtown Expressway at the Meeker Avenue cloverleaf near Calvary Cemetery, where the Brooklyn-Queens Expressway also crossed.

The importance of Queens Boulevard was guaranteed not only by its direct access to Manhattan but also by the routing of the city's Independent subway line under the road, beginning with service as far as Jackson Heights in 1933 and extending to Kew Gardens three years later.[49] The opening of the subway, combined with the glamour of the 1939–40 World's Fair so nearby, stimulated the construction of apartment houses, some of which faced the boulevard and had ground-level retail space. A large concentration of six-story Georgianesque apartment houses were built in the area called Thorneycroft, straddling Queens Boulevard between the Long Island Railroad (Austin Street), Yellowstone Boulevard, Sixty-third Road and Sixty-seventh Avenue. The Thorneycroft development, some forty blocks situated in a large, practically vacant area in Rego Park, was interrupted by the war. In 1943 the architects Albert Mayer and Julian Whittlesey, hoping to influence the area's future pattern, encouraged the larger property owners of adjoining open land to join together and provide the neighborhood with open space

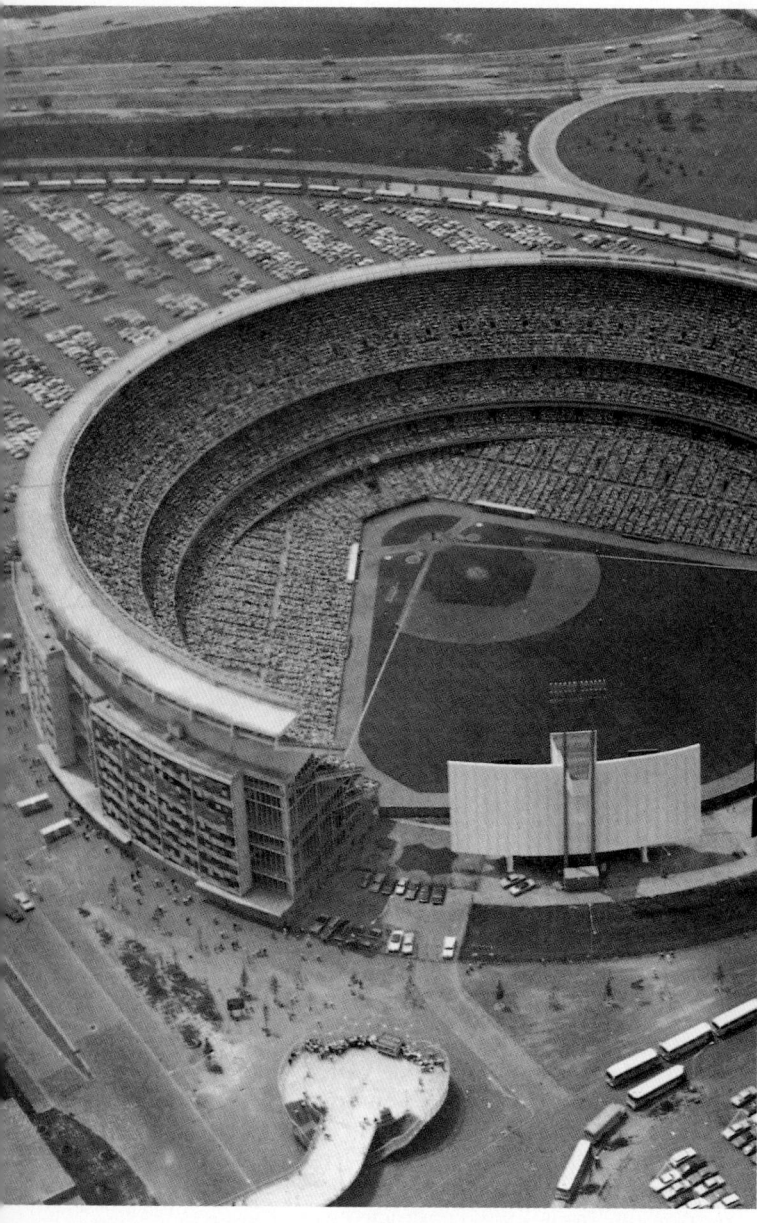

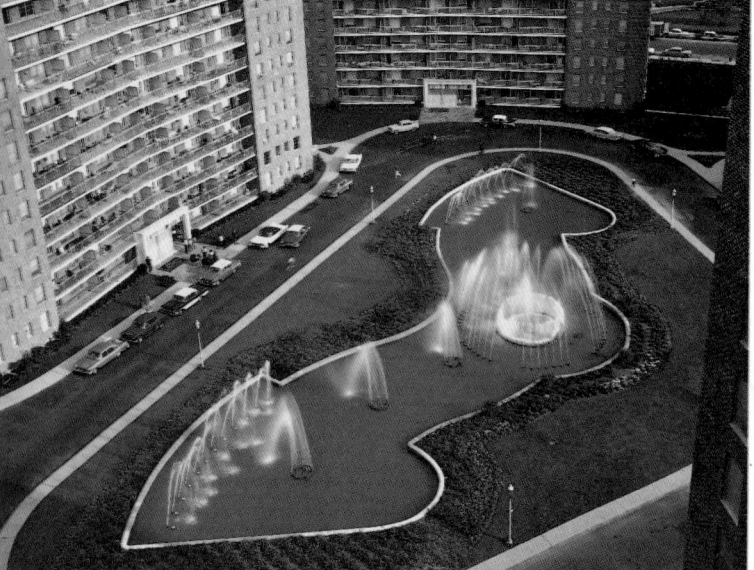

and community facilities on a triangular block bounded by Queens Boulevard.[50] Their plan was not adopted.

More apartment houses were built in the Rego Park area after the war, and they were much larger than their earlier counterparts. Among these was Leo Stillman's Walden Terrace (1948), Ninety-eighth to Ninety-ninth Street, Sixty-third Drive to Sixty-fourth Road, two full blocks of eight-story superslabs defining landscaped courtyards which abandoned the genteel Georgianism of prewar work for a modern vocabulary that relied on exposed concrete frames to articulate the elevations.[51] The scale of development was transformed even more dramatically in 1960 when Philip Birnbaum completed Saxon Hall, at 62-60 Ninety-ninth Street, a sixteen-story bent slab with continuous balconies ringing each floor that conveyed the feeling of a Miami Beach hotel.[52] Birnbaum's Park City Estates (1959), between Sixty-second Drive, Ninety-eighth and Ninety-ninth streets, and the Long Island Expressway, housed 4,000 families in three fourteen-story extensively balconied apartment towers; the complex overlooked a free-form 2.5-acre lagoon aerated by fountains and illuminated at night with colored lights, again looking as though a Miami Beach hotel had come north.[53]

These apartment projects were soon dwarfed by Lefrak City, a massive, forty-acre development stretching along the Long Island Expressway and bounded by Junction Boulevard, Fifty-seventh Avenue and Ninety-ninth Street in Elmhurst.[54] The Lefrak Organization was headed by Samuel J. Lefrak, whose Russian immigrant father had started out in the construction business in 1905 and had gone on to build up a portfolio of almost 500 buildings inhabited by close to 250,000 tenants. By 1960 the firm was landlord to one out of every thirty-two New Yorkers, an even greater number than those living in Housing Authority projects. Samuel Lefrak had begun acquiring property and planning for the city that would later bear his family's name in 1955, when he undertook the construction of the first six buildings of what he called Forest Hills Park, a development intended to ultimately consist of twenty-two seven-story buildings housing 1,200 families. George G. Miller, Shulman & Solloway and Kavey & Kavowitt were the architects for these conventional, stripped-down, red-brick "Colonial" buildings. By 1960 the Lefrak Organization had expanded and consolidated its holdings in the area and announced what Lefrak described as the largest apartment house development in the world to be built without government assistance.

Designed by Jack Brown, the Lefrak Organization's in-house architect, this new project, which was called Lefrak City, was far bigger and denser than any previous development in Queens. It consisted of twenty sixteen-story apartment slabs as well as an office building and two theaters. Extensive recreational facilities, including tennis courts and swimming pools, were provided, as were garages for parking. The buildings were little more than balconied brick boxes, but the site plan was somewhat more imaginative, featuring groups of four towers built at right angles to each other linked together by circular gardens with fountains. To give the new city a cosmopolitan air, each building was named after a city, such as Rome or Sydney, or an exotic location like Shalimar or Mandalay.

By 1963 enough of the project had been completed for it to be known by most New Yorkers. Recognition of Lefrak City was helped by its exceptionally prominent location along the Long Island Expressway. Taking advantage of the tens of thousands of motorists who inched by the development in commuter traffic jams on their way to and from Manhattan, Lefrak mounted billboards facing outbound traffic saying: "If we lived here, Daddy,

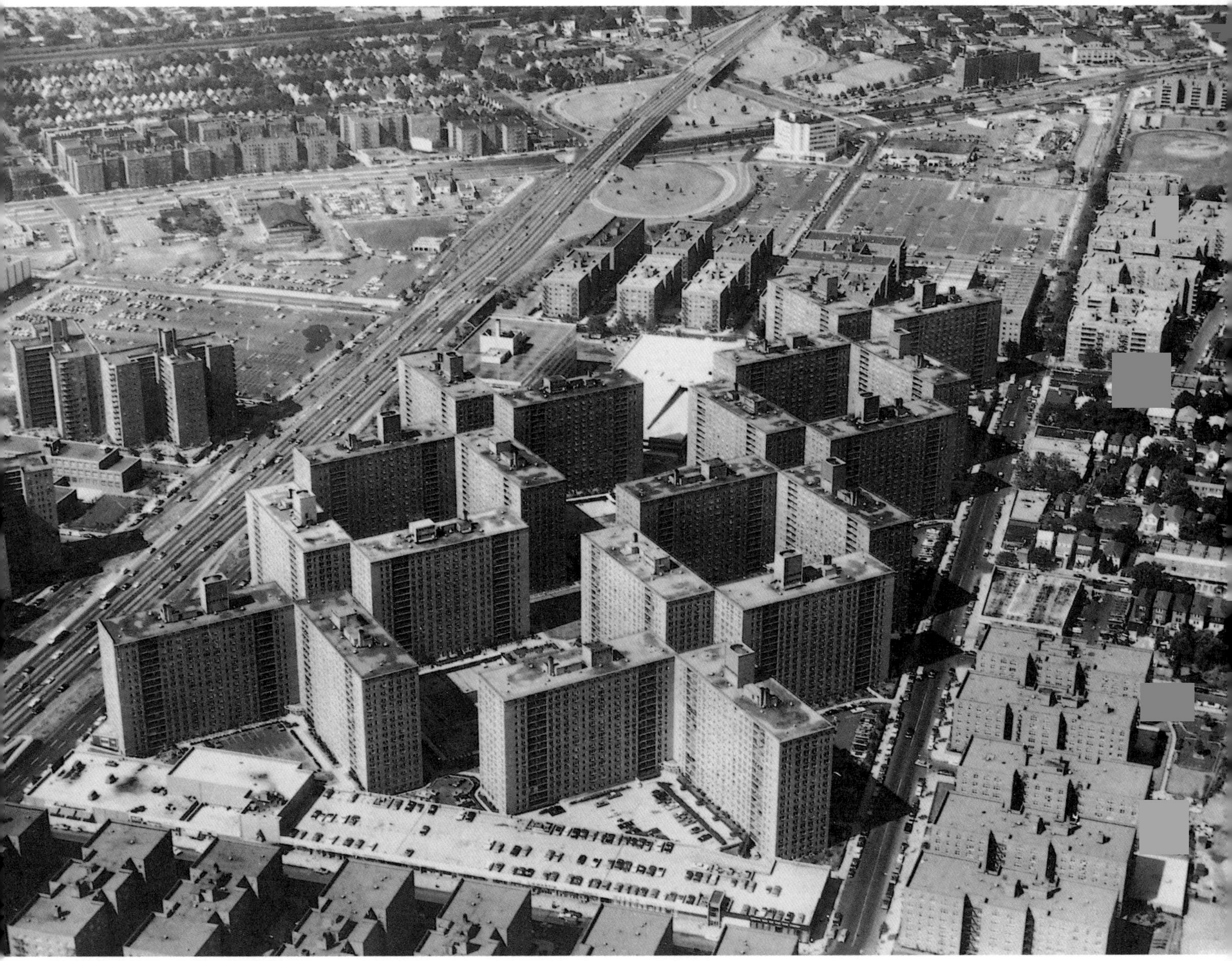

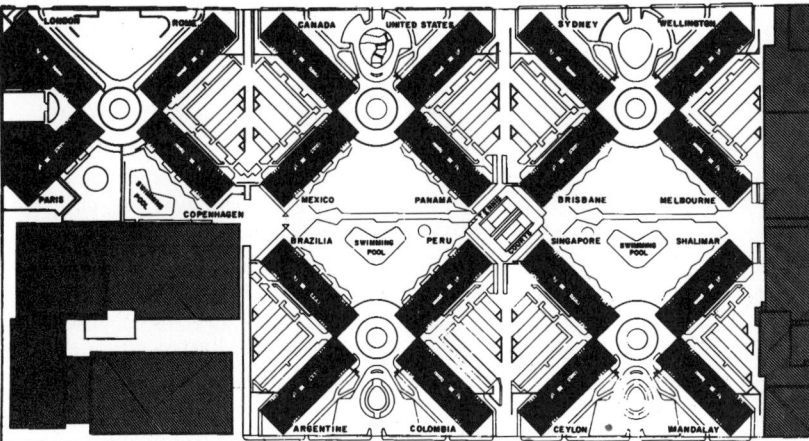

Top far left: Shea Stadium, bounded by Northern Boulevard, Roosevelt Avenue, Grand Central Parkway and 126th Street, Flushing Meadows. Praeger-Kavanagh-Waterbury, 1964. Aerial view to the northwest. NYM

Bottom far left: Park City Estates, between Sixty-second Drive and Long Island Expressway, Ninety-eighth and Ninety-ninth streets, Rego Park. Philip Birnbaum, 1959. Stoller. ©ESTO

Above: Lefrak City, between Junction Boulevard and Ninety-ninth Street, Long Island Expressway and Fifty-seventh Avenue, Elmhurst. Jack Brown, 1960–67. View to the southwest. LO

Left: Lefrak City. Site plan. *A History of Housing.* RP

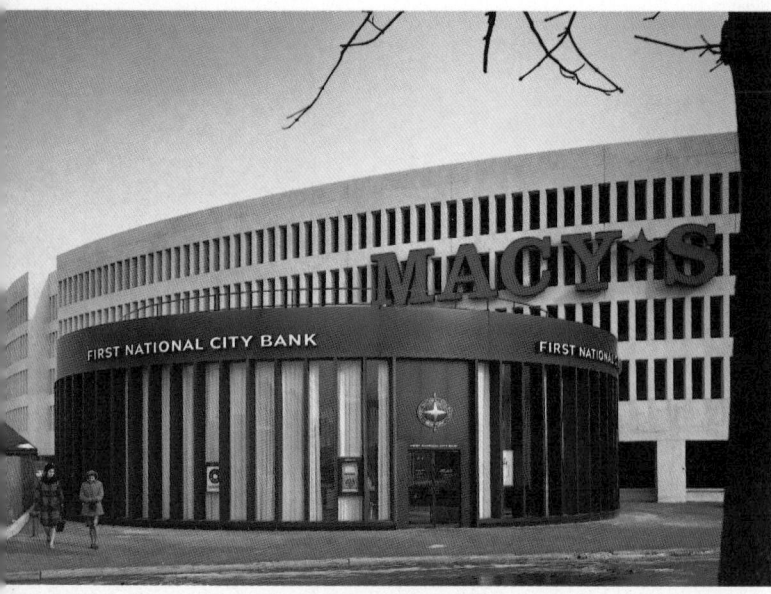

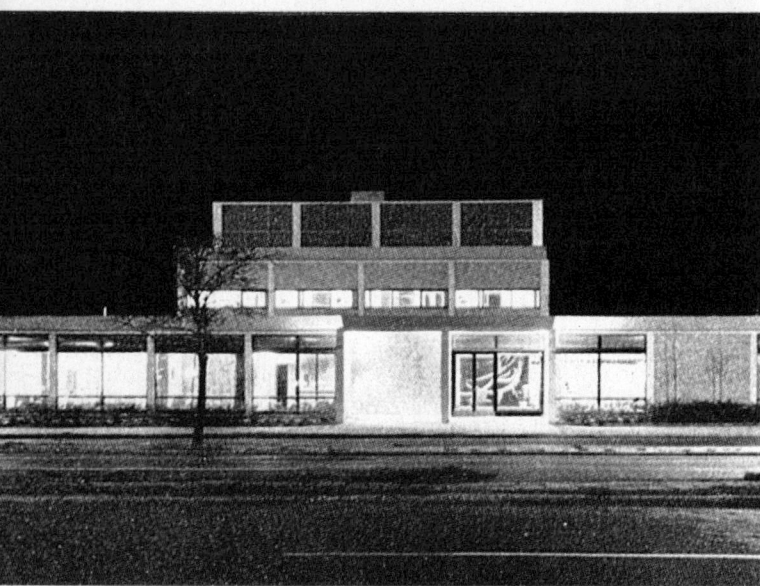

Top: First National City Bank, Elmhurst branch, 87-11 Queens Boulevard, between Fifty-fifth and Fifty-sixth avenues, Elmhurst. Skidmore, Owings & Merrill, 1966. View to the northeast. Stoller. ©ESTO

Bottom: Queens Boulevard Medical Building, 86-15 Queens Boulevard, between Broadway and Fifty-fifth Avenue, Elmhurst. Abraham Geller & Associates, 1957. View to the northeast. PA. CU

you'd be home now." In the 1963 *Look* magazine survey called "The New New York," Lefrak City was given as a principal example of the city's "instant neighborhoods," where "the host of home-hungry, middle-income families live, those who cannot afford Manhattan's luxury housing and scorn the suburban alternative." But, as *Look*'s editors explained, these "tight, bright, functional monoliths," like so many other postwar projects, were "socially . . . not a part of the city at all, but a vest-pocket suburb, a fact which was reflected in Lefrak's promotion of the project as 'a self-contained apartment community.'"[55]

Despite decent apartment plans and reasonably high construction standards as well as glitzy lobbies and some useful amenities, Lefrak City was a drab environment. To those who criticized the complex, however, Lefrak responded: "We're not trying to build great landmarks. We're trying to build a way of life."[56] And, in fact, Lefrak City was more than just a large development of apartment houses. "My aim in Lefrak City," the developer said in 1968, "was not only to create housing and recreational facilities for 5,000 families, but also to create employment opportunities while furthering the 'walk-to-work' concept and providing a great labor market for major corporations expected to move into the area."[57] Lefrak's vision fostered the development of Queens Boulevard as a regional center: "Queens Boulevard should be lined with office buildings," he said in a *New York Times* interview in 1970. "We have a population of 2.2 million in Queens, and a big labor force. And there's a confluence of highways here. Each borough should be a microcosm, with residences and jobs for the people living there."[58] In 1961 Lefrak completed his first office building at Lefrak City, Lefrak Tower, at 97-45 Queens Boulevard, a thirteen-story, glass-sheathed bent slab designed by Jack Brown.[59] It was followed in 1968 by a six-story office building, including a 22,000-square-foot post office, facing the Long Island Expressway, and in 1970 by a 500,000-square-foot, twenty-story, glass-walled blockbuster—the largest office building in Queens—which also loomed over the expressway.[60] Both were designed by Jack Brown.

Insofar as Queens had a downtown in the postwar era, the intersection of Queens Boulevard and the Long Island Expressway in Rego Park was that place.[61] The original Rego Park was a neighborhood of one- and two-family houses built in the 1920s—the word "Rego" came from the Rego (Real Good) Construction Company, the name of the firm that began the area's development—on land south of Queens Boulevard and east of Woodhaven Boulevard. Large-scale retailing with a suburban flavor had come to Rego Park in the wake of Lefrak City with the opening of branches for Macy's and Alexander's, as well as Queens Center, an enclosed shopping mall (see chapter 15). Two notable bank branches also contributed to the area's development: First National City Bank's Elmhurst branch (1966), at 87-11 Queens Boulevard, a small cylinder designed by Skidmore, Owings & Merrill to emulate the bigger cylinder of Macy's, designed the year before by the same firm;[62] and William Cann's Jamaica Savings Bank (1967), at 89-01 Queens Boulevard, a daring if improbable design in which a hyperbolic paraboloid–shaped roof sheltered a modest banking hall.[63]

Another notable building in the area, Abraham Geller & Associates' Queens Boulevard Medical Building (1957), at 86-15 Queens Boulevard, between Broadway and Fifty-fifth Avenue, offered an important service for a new type of medical practice, a partnership of physicians who worked with 30,000 health-insurance-plan members, providing comprehensive, coordinated services and complete diagnostic and treatment facilities on an outpatient basis.[64] The crisply detailed building, a model of clarity in its motley setting, took its principal expression from the regular bays of its reinforced-concrete frame, infilled on the exterior with gray ceramic-brushed brick. Boulders, a stream and subway tracks under one-third of the lot made foundation work difficult, as did the topography of the site, which rose dramatically to the rear, where it abutted a residential neighborhood. To minimize the problems, parking was held away from the back of the building with a retaining wall, which formed a garden court on the ground floor that illuminated all five waiting rooms and a sunken garden that brought light and a view into the basement-level doctors' lounge. Inside, Marion Geller of Integra skillfully combined Scandinavian-inspired wood furniture and neutral fabrics with specially commissioned art.

In 1974, despite the city's declining fortunes, the area bustled with new projects. These included a banal, eleven-story, 200,000-square-foot office building clad in bronze solar glass and anodized aluminum, built on Queens Boulevard between Junction Boulevard and Sixty-second Drive, and the Rego Park Communications Center, New York Telephone Company (1976), designed by Kahn & Jacobs as a somewhat fortresslike brick mass set on a battered granite podium that filled the site bounded by Queens Boulevard, Sixty-second Avenue and Sixty-second Drive.[65]

Forest Hills

Just to the east of Rego Park was the large and ambiguously defined area called Forest Hills. It included the planned enclave of Forest Hills Gardens, which by 1940 was largely built up but was the site for one new apartment house, the six-story Tudoresque Leslie Apartments (Fellheimer & Wagner, 1943), built on an irregularly shaped site across from P.S. 101 (William H. Gompert, 1929), bounded by Slocum Crescent and Greenway Circle.[66] While Forest Hills was not graced with any really distinguished postwar architecture, Ulrich Franzen's Forest Hills Tower (1981) was many notches above Jack Brown's typical product.[67] A sixteen-story office building at 118-35 Queens Boulevard, on the northwest corner of Seventy-eighth Crescent, Forest Hills Tower provided a highly visible marker at the edge of Flushing Meadows–Corona Park.

The progress of planning and architecture in postwar Forest Hills might have been of virtually no further consequence had it not been for a single public housing project. On November 30, 1966, the first official act of Donald Elliott, Mayor Lindsay's first appointee to the City Planning Commission (he eventually became its chairman), was to approve a controversial proposal for developing a low-rent public housing development in a predominantly white, Jewish, middle-class neighborhood in Forest Hills. Mario Cuomo, who in 1982 was to become governor of New York, played a pivotal role in resolving the controversy that grew up over this housing project. As he explained in 1974:

> Although the area immediately affected was relatively confined—perhaps a few sparse miles—the bitter cries of Forest Hills were heard across the nation. The issues touched a number of sensitive nerves that quickly transmitted the pain to various areas of the body politic. It was interpreted by many as a fight between whites and blacks, and more specifically between the Jew and the black. Planners and sociologists saw it as a critical commentary on this nation's crippled low-income housing policy. Urbanologists read it as a test of city govern-

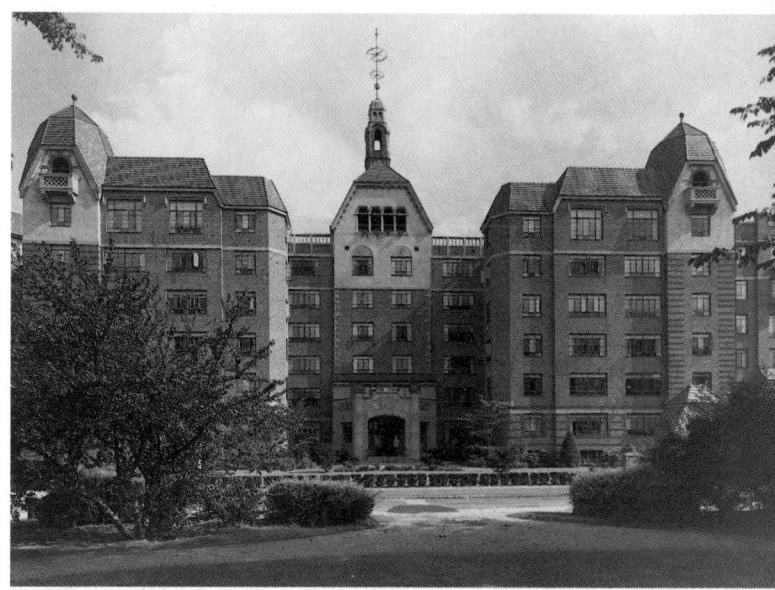

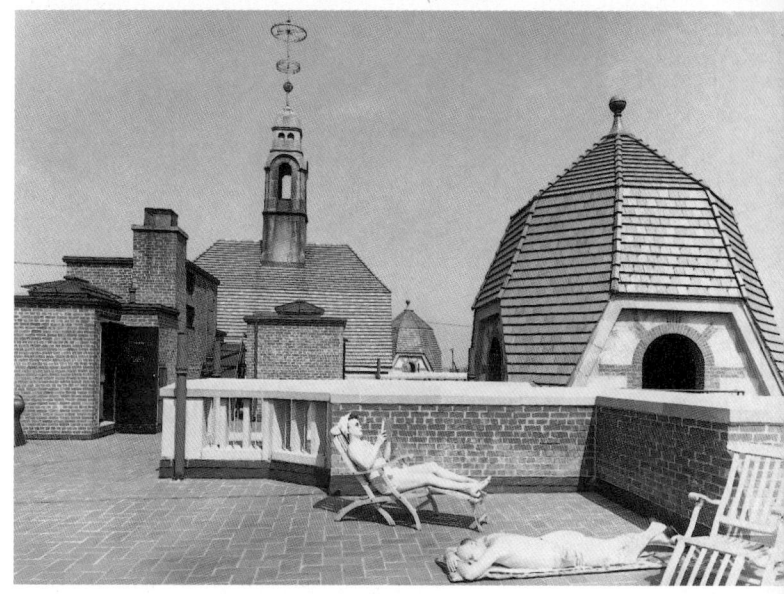

Top: Leslie Apartments, bounded by Slocum Crescent and Greenway Circle, Forest Hills. Fellheimer & Wagner, 1943. View to the south. Gottscho-Schleisner. LOC

Bottom: Leslie Apartments. Roof terrace. Gottscho-Schleisner. LOC

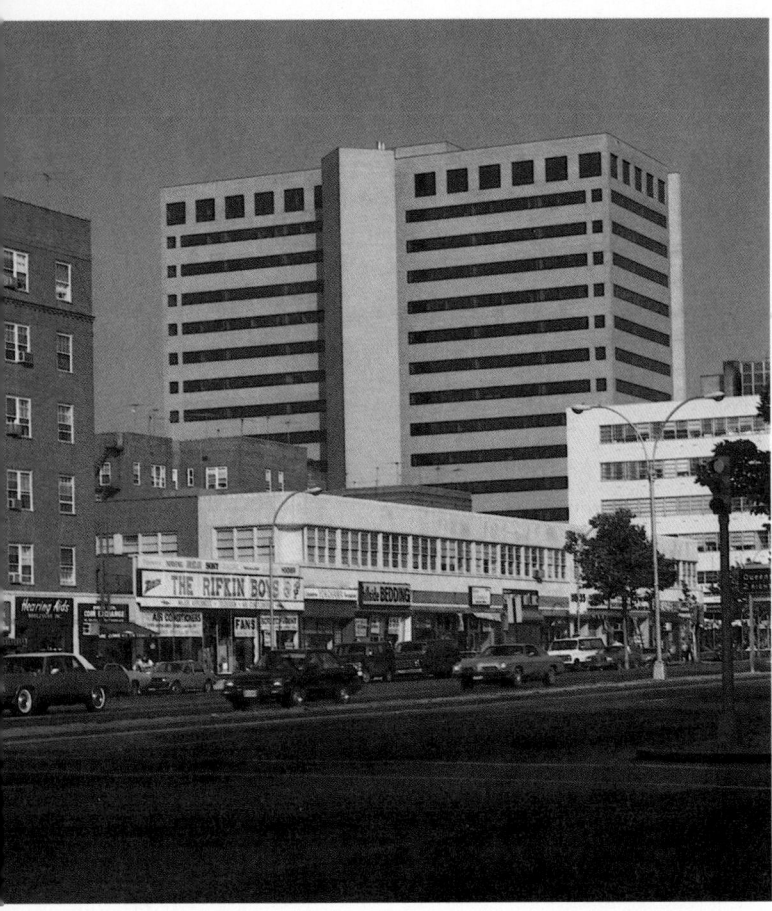

Above: Forest Hills Tower, 118-35 Queens Boulevard, northwest corner of Seventy-eighth Crescent, Forest Hills. Ulrich Franzen, 1981. View to the northeast. UF

Top right: Proposal for Forest Hills scatter-site housing, bounded by Long Island Expressway, Colonial Avenue, Sixty-second Drive and 108th Street, Forest Hills. Ulrich Franzen, 1969. Model. View to the north. UF

Bottom right: Forest Hills Cooperative, bounded by Long Island Expressway, Colonial Avenue, Sixty-second Drive and 108th Street, Forest Hills. Samuel Paul, 1975. View to the northeast. NYCHA

ment's ability to deal with what have become commonplace traumas in urban life. Still others interpreted it as the defiant voice of an aroused middle class which, frustrated by its own growing problems, could no longer tolerate the demands being made upon it by the so-called disadvantaged.[68]

The housing project was originally slated for a 4.5-acre plot in Corona, a largely white, middle-class neighborhood north of Forest Hills.[69] Although the Corona site was mostly vacant, containing four houses, only one of which was owner-occupied, massive opposition to the location was expressed at the Board of Estimate's hearing on October 27, 1966. "It is not clear exactly who orchestrated the opposition," Cuomo wrote, "or at whose insistence the opponents were there, but it is clear who did not make up the opposition. It was not the people of Corona . . . but busloads of people from the Lefrak City area appeared and argued furiously that there was a much greater need for a high school than there was for a low-income housing project."[70] The protests had the desired effect, and the Corona site was withdrawn from consideration as the location for the housing project but was slated for development instead as a high school and athletic fields.

The Forest Hills site was proposed as an alternative site for the housing project, which city housing and planning officials felt a commitment to realize. But, as Cuomo observed, the choice of site was not "preceded by the kind of investigation, study, and deliberate judgment that the complexities of the situation deserved. The school for Corona was a product of the sudden decision to replace the housing project. That, in turn, required a second precipitous determination to compensate for the initial switch by finding a new site for the project." As Cuomo explained, "the planning for the school was particularly egregious," with the city expanding the original 4.5-acre site for the project into a 12.5-acre site to accommodate the school and fields, which "would have required the obliteration of sixty-nine homes in Corona and five of its business establishments. With one stroke it would have destroyed the heart of Corona."[71]

Despite the ill-considered choice of the Forest Hills site, and the stormy testimony it evoked at the City Planning Commission's hearing, the location was approved. As the *New York Times* reported, the City Planning Commission used unusually blunt language in announcing its decision after five and a half hours of debate: "Certain of the fears and anxieties expressed by residents of the community are based on a desire for security, tranquility and a better life. These goals are not unique for one class, but are shared by all citizens. We believe they are achievable, but only if we respond to the needs of the less fortunate."[72] The decision was ratified, with almost no protest, by the Board of Estimate on December 7, 1966. While the Forest Hills housing project appeared to lay dormant, the Corona community, finally aroused to its potential fate, halted the school plan for three years. In December 1970 Mayor Lindsay announced that a compromise plan for the high school had been reached.[73] It called for the construction of the school on only part of the 12.5-acre site at 101st Street and Lewis Avenue, and the inclusion of the athletic fields in nearby Flushing Meadows–Corona Park; this plan would save all but fourteen of the sixty-nine houses initially slated for demolition. After another eighteen-month fight, the plan was approved by Governor Rockefeller on June 8, 1972. But by the time the Board of Education was ready to begin letting bids for foundation work in September 1974, the city's fiscal crisis had intervened. The high school and athletic facilities were never built, although several homes had been demolished.

The Forest Hills housing project was to be built on an 8.46-acre plot bounded by the Long Island Expressway, Colonial Avenue, Sixty-second Drive and 108th Street. The proposal was one of thirteen "scatter-site" projects planned by the Housing Authority to house 7,500 families as part of a policy of deghettoizing the poor and deinstitutionalizing public housing by building smaller projects on "vest-pocket" sites in stable—that is to say white—neighborhoods. Of the thirteen projects, only one was completed by 1971—Cassidy-Lafayette Houses in Staten Island, reserved for the elderly (see "Staten Island," above). Community opposition blocked most of the other proposals for scatter-site housing.

The switch from Corona to Forest Hills made no planning sense. It seemed, however, politically astute, as city officials believed that the Jewish apartment dwellers of Forest Hills would accept the housing more willingly than the Italian homeowners of Corona. The simple fact, as it turned out, was that neither Paul nor Saul wanted the housing project. At first glance the Forest Hills site seemed the better suited of the two. The new buildings would hardly be noticed among the gloomy forest of residential towers that defined its edges. But, on second glance, the site revealed several inherent problems, not the least of which was a stream known as Horse Brook that ran beneath the site, making for poor subsoil conditions that necessitated expensive pilings. In fact, the site had been passed by as recently as the early 1960s when probable foundation costs caused a developer to abandon plans for two twenty-three-story apartment buildings. Roger Starr, executive director of the Citizens' Housing and Planning Council, immediately recognized the site's shortcomings, and urged in his testimony at the Board of Estimate that the location be more carefully considered before going on with the project. "Certainly," he said, "there is no need for haste so pressing at this moment that the Board of Estimate should be asked to approve one project when a wholly different project may emerge under the pressure of Federal cost limitations and construction problems."[74]

Starr proved correct: the original design, by Ulrich Franzen & Associates (1969), which called for 828 apartments in seven buildings ranging from ten to twenty-two stories in height, proved too expensive. Franzen's scheme, which Ada Louise Huxtable called an "innovative, environmentally conscious plan," also included rows of two-story community facilities clustered to form a pedestrian street running through the site. Huxtable contended that this proposal was rejected not only on the basis of cost but also because of "a change in policy among the city's housing agencies away from progressive design and back to 'cookie cutter' formulas, and what observers call an intractable city housing bureaucracy."[75]

In 1969 Franzen was replaced by the veteran apartment house architect Samuel Paul, who reconfigured the project as three twenty-four-story buildings housing 840 families, as well as a community center and a parking lot. The new complex was the largest and tallest scatter-site project undertaken by the city, with about twice as many apartments as its closest competitor in the program.[76] Between 1967 and 1969 the plans were developed, without community consultation and at a rather slow pace; some hinted that this was a conscious strategy to keep the hostile Forest Hills community from getting upset and casting their votes against Lindsay in the 1969 mayoral race. The plans continued to be developed in private until early 1971, when they had to be revealed if construction was to commence in the summer, as had been promised.

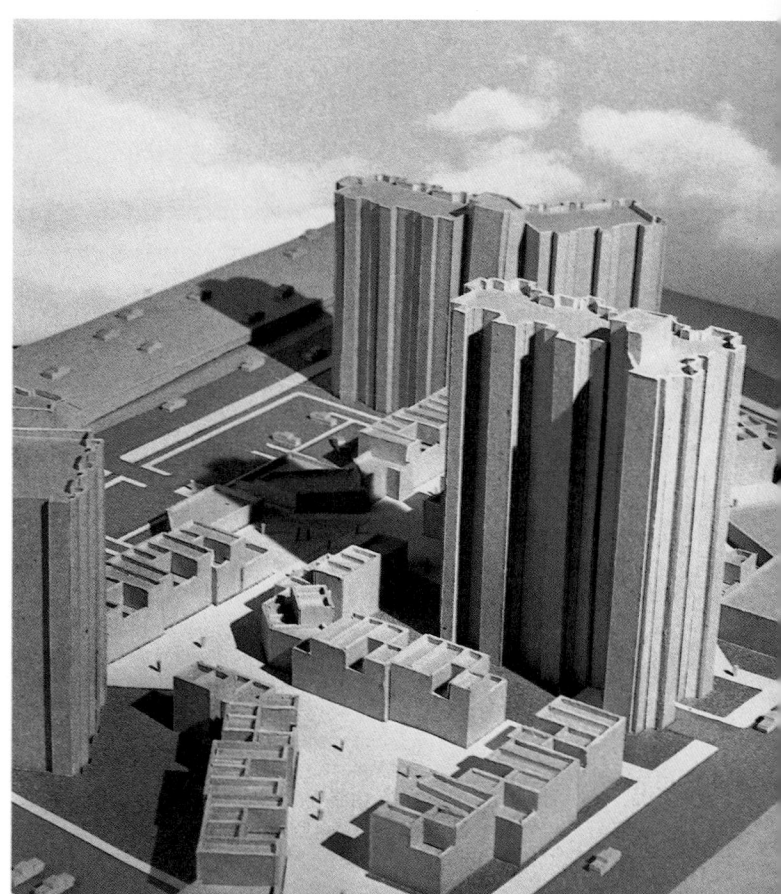

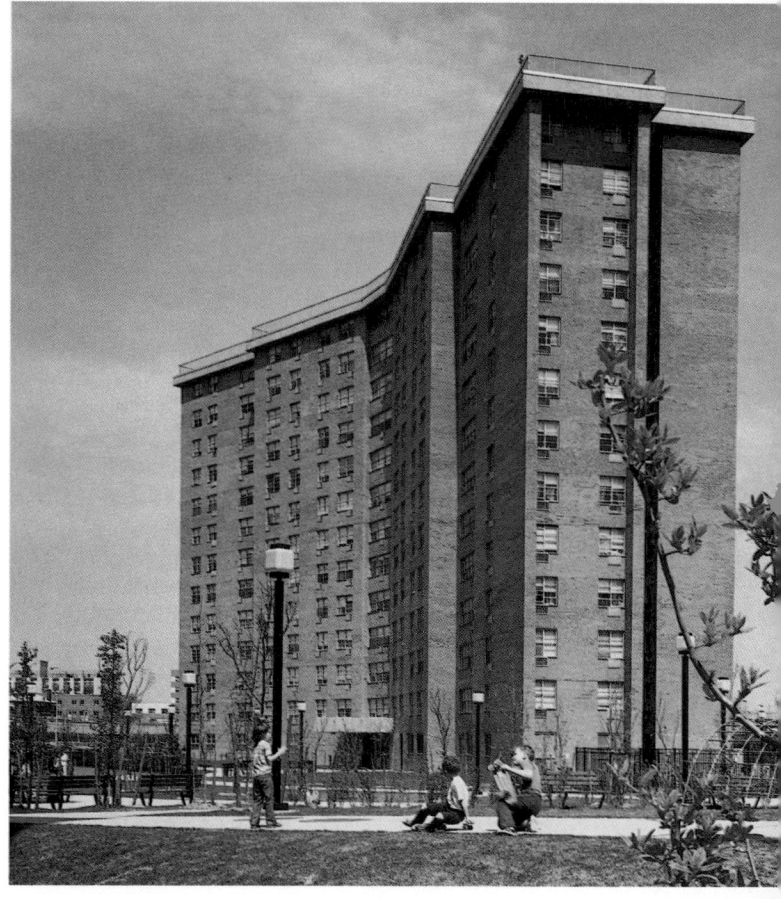

The plans met with intense opposition, and progress was delayed during the summer as the State Supreme Court heard arguments over a suit brought by the Forest Hills Residential Association to prevent construction. But after the court ruled in favor of the Housing Authority, groundbreaking was scheduled for November 1971.[77] As construction began, community opposition grew stronger every day, and on November 18, an overflow meeting ended in a torchlight parade that quickly got out of hand.[78] Mayor Lindsay stood by the project, however, calling the protests "deplorable" and obtaining a restraining order from the courts to prevent the community's further interference.[79]

News of the controversy spread beyond the pages of the New York Times and other local newspapers, becoming the focus of a debate televised on November 21, 1971. The debate pitted Jerry Birbach, leader of the Forest Hills Residents Association, against Simeon Golar, head of the Housing Authority, and Herbert Kahn, president of the Council for Better Housing, who had previously urged reconciliation between the two groups.[80] By this time the dispute had grown well beyond the particulars of this project to encompass not only issues of class and race but also a consideration of the federal and city policies of scatter housing. Enlisting the support of Senator James Buckley, Birbach suggested that the federal government intervene to stop the project, but George Romney, secretary of Housing and Urban Development, said that he could see no "basis in which I can reverse prior firm contractual commitments."[81]

On November 24, the New York Times reported that discussions were being held among top city officials to scale down the project, and thus eliminate one of the principal objections.[82] Around this time, the situation in Forest Hills began to attract national attention, with an article in Time headlined "Fear in Forest Hills" and one in Newsweek titled "Rage in Forest Hills," both emphasizing the racial fears of the neighborhood's Jewish residents.[83] Clark Whelton, a writer for the Village Voice, presented the controversy in near-incendiary terms, describing it as one in which "the middle class fights back."[84] Congressman Herman Badillo, a politician of Puerto Rican descent, replied that "Forest Hills is not the bucolic community of small homes that so many imply. It houses tens of thousands of families, many of whom live in high-rises just a few blocks away from the . . . site, so at best 840 units are hardly enough to tip it."[85] Congressman Edward I. Koch, who would later become the city's mayor (1977–89), also got into the act, criticizing Badillo for "aligning himself with the Lindsay administration, which continues to ignore middle-class needs and belittles middle-class fears. If the middle class continues to leave this city, we will have gained nothing even if we build 10 Forest Hills. And, unfortunately, the poor will suffer most."[86] The New York Times editorialized in favor of the scatter-site approach while skirting the underlying human and social issues that were obvious to all.[87]

Angry crowds booed the bulldozers breaking ground in December. Romney again refused to halt the project, and the White House stated that it would not intervene in the controversy.[88] Meanwhile, the racial tension escalated. On December 17 Mayor Lindsay, after meeting with the project's supporters and opponents together at City Hall, said that a compromise was impossible and that a smaller project would be economically unfeasible.[89]

On February 16, 1972, New York State Supreme Court Justice Irving H. Saypol ordered a halt to the project, ruling that it was so different from the one originally approved by the Board of Estimate in 1966 that new hearings and new approvals were required.[90] Meanwhile, Lindsay's former deputy mayor, Richard

R. Aurelio, now managing the mayor's race for the presidency, was said to have worked out a compromise plan in private discussions with black and Jewish leaders that would scale down the Forest Hills project by about a third and, in compensation, would revive a smaller version of a project for the Underwood section of Queens that had recently been killed by the Board of Estimate. Taken together, the two projects would provide almost the same amount of housing as the controversial Forest Hills plan. The court order provided all the combatants with a much-needed opportunity to cool off.

On May 4 the Appellate Court reversed Judge Saypol's decision and ruled that the project could "be carried to completion."[91] That same month the State Assembly passed a bill requiring a county referendum on every public housing project, and the State Senate passed a bill requiring new approval for a project if a specified amount of construction had not been completed within five years.[92] On May 13 Governor Rockefeller, calling on Mayor Lindsay and other interested parties to work out a compromise, vetoed the Assembly's bill.[93] (The Senate bill was later vetoed as well.) On May 17 Mario Cuomo, a lawyer and Queens resident, was requested by the mayor "to make an independent exploration of possible revisions in the Forest Hills housing project and the overall planning for low-income housing in Queens and to make recommendations to the Mayor, the City Council and the Board of Estimate for any changes."[94]

On July 14 Cuomo, who had met almost nightly with community leaders, issued a preliminary report, which called for a 50 percent cut in the number of units. Claiming to be heartened by what he called "a spirit of compromise," he said that the community realized "that if there is no compromise, the original project will be built."[95] Cuomo's official report to Lindsay, dated July 25, 1972, called for a reduction in the number of dwellings to 430 in three twelve-story buildings, similar in height to the adjoining Fairview Avenue Apartments and more in keeping with the immediate context. The proposal also called for a tenant mix that reserved 40 percent of the units for the elderly and 60 percent of the units for low-income families. In the "concluding note" to his report, Cuomo wrote: "As a matter of plain legal and moral obligation to thousands of low-income families, housing must be provided and it must be provided on an integrated basis. The only devices available to do this are at best imperfect, but they must be utilized for what they are worth. These devices should be re-studied and improved, but we cannot afford the luxury of doing nothing while we are waiting to find a way of doing everything."[96]

Cuomo's compromise plan was immediately rejected as "outrageous" and "manifestly absurd" by Simeon Golar and "totally unacceptable" by Jerry Birbach.[97] But the New York Times, in a July 29 editorial, supported the compromise.[98] On August 12 Golar, foreseeing a year's delay in Cuomo's proposal as well as substantial additional costs, proposed continuing the construction of all three twenty-four-story buildings but then selling one to house middle-income families.[99] According to Golar's plan, which was similar to one advanced by the Citizens' Housing and Planning Council, the 280 lost low-income units would be replaced with an equal or larger number of comparable units on smaller sites elsewhere in Queens.

On August 20 Mayor Lindsay accepted "the basic guideline" of Cuomo's proposal; he also hinted that he might accept a recommendation of Queens Borough President Donald Manes that the project not be limited to low-income families.[100] But Lindsay went on to suggest that if there were to be an income mix, the taller buildings should be built so as not to reduce the actual number of low-income units supplied. Civil rights activists found fault with the Cuomo proposal. Vernon E. Jordan, Jr., executive director of the National Urban League, saw it as "a failure of leadership and a failure of reasoning," and he was particularly critical of the efforts of local politicians:

> The Federal Government's housing policies have often been criticized, but in this instance Federal officials stood by the project while local politicians hacked it to death. Lost in the charade over Forest Hills is the basic question: Where do poor people who need decent housing go? That's a question that has to be answered on a national scale. New York's answer seems to be: "Let them stay in the slums." That answer, like the compromise that threatens to kill the project, is totally unacceptable.[101]

On September 5 Borough President Manes offered yet another plan, calling for the conversion of Cuomo's proposal into a low-income cooperative, which, he argued, would give the new residents "a stake in the community" as owners.[102] Manes proposed a tenant mix of 65 percent elderly residents and 35 percent war veterans. This idea found favor in many quarters, including the Housing Authority; Simeon Golar pointed out that such a scheme "has never been done in the country with respect to high-rise multiple dwellings."[103]

On October 4 the City Planning Commission voted 4 to 2 to accept the Cuomo plan of 430 units, leaving the ultimate fate of the project to the Board of Estimate. In his remarks, City Planning Commission Chairman Donald Elliott said of the compromise: "If it can move us from the tactics of confrontation and the excesses of emotionalism toward a more reasonable and humane society, it will be worth it."[104] On October 26, at the end of an exceptionally acrimonious daylong hearing, the compromise plan was approved by the Board of Estimate by a vote of 20 to 2, with Manhattan Borough President Percy Sutton casting the dissenting votes.[105] Mayor Lindsay was heavily criticized for not attending the meeting. The vote left the economic and age mix of the building's occupants undecided, although the board urged the Housing Authority to support Manes's cooperative plan. Restrained by law from accepting the Board of Estimate's recommendations, the Housing Authority retained the proposed mix of 40 percent of the units for the elderly, 60 percent for low-income families. In 1974 Manes's proposal to make the project a low-income cooperative was approved.[106]

When the Forest Hills Cooperative was finally opened in 1975, after all the rancor and protest, its impact on the community was far from disastrous. In their 1988 biography of Edward Koch, *City for Sale: Ed Koch and the Betrayal of New York*, Jack Newfield and Wayne Barrett described the final outcome of the Forest Hills story, which they called "a watershed in New York's tortured recent history of race relations":

> The neighborhood thrived with greater diversity. Crime did not increase. Real estate values went up, not down. About a thousand residents did move out but were replaced mostly by immigrant Soviet Jews and younger orthodox Jews, making Forest Hills "feel" even more Jewish than before. The population of the project is now 750 whites, 175 blacks, 100 Hispanics, and 135 "others," mostly Asian and South American. Two percent of the tenants are welfare recipients.[107]

Barry Jacobs, a Queens resident, described the completed project in a 1984 article in the *Village Voice*: "The place is well-tended, peaceful. It's a Saturday and old men sit in the playgrounds reading Russian newspapers. White, black, and Hispanic kids play stickball against a building wall. Black-suited Orthodox Jewish men chat in clusters. It's heartening to see how wrong the anti-project people were in thinking that these 'poor' people would bring drugs and crime into their neighborhood. It's also maddening."[108]

Flushing

The northeastern section of Queens was originally the town of Flushing, first settled in 1642. Until the end of the Second World War the historic village of Flushing was a neighborhood of wooden houses from the 1880s and 1890s interspersed with apartment houses that had been built between 1920 and 1940. The inevitable explosion that was to transform Flushing into a busy "market town" was delayed by the war; but the area's future was seen clearly by William Zeckendorf, even though he was unable to realize his bold plan for a massive shopping center (see chapter 15).

There were a few churches of note built in the area, including Henry V. Murphy's St. Andrew of Avellino (Roman Catholic) (1940), at 157-01 Northern Boulevard, on the northeast corner of 157th Street, a Moderne version of the Romanesque, with intricately designed and beautifully crafted carving in stone and superb metalwork.[109] At 34-21 Union Street, on the southeast corner of Thirty-fourth Avenue, stood Bentel & Bentel's St. John Vianney Church (Roman Catholic) (1974), a dignified dark-brick box modified to feature a curved garden wall.[110] Raymond & Rado's St. Nicholas Greek Orthodox Church (1974), at 196-10 Northern Boulevard, on the southeast corner of 196th Street, a brick and concrete essay in elemental geometry, was deliberately crude but also interesting in its way.[111]

Gruzen & Partners' Kissena II Apartments (1970), at 137-47 Forty-fifth Avenue, off Kissena Boulevard between Forty-fifth and Geranium avenues, was one new apartment building worth noting.[112] Its facades were remarkably refined, given the use of an exposed concrete grid inset with brick and glass.

North of historic Flushing, along the East River shore, lay the communities of College Point, Malba, Whitestone, Beechhurst and Bayside, for the most part developed before World War I as summer resorts and still characterized by a substantial stock of houses from that period. In Beechhurst, Alfred Levitt, an amateur architect and the brother of William, the developer of Levittown, worked closely with George G. Miller on the design of Levitt House (1958), bounded by 162nd and Totten streets, Powell's Cove Boulevard and Twelfth Avenue.[113] This collection of thirty eight-story apartment buildings was built on a thirty-acre site on Cryder's Point overlooking the Long Island Sound that had been purchased from five owners of small estates. Included among these properties was the two-and-a-half-story house of Arthur Hammerstein (Dwight James Baum, 1924), which Levitt retained as a clubhouse for the residents.[114]

Levitt had designed the houses his brother marketed to create Levittown, but he had left the firm of Levitt & Sons to set up on his own as Levitt, Inc., with the idea of building affordable apartment houses utilizing cost-cutting techniques similar to those developed for suburban tract housing. "Once the Levittown house was standardized," Levitt told *Architectural Forum*, "I had designed myself right out of a job and, frankly, I got bored with the standardized house." Levitt believed that between the poles of high-rise luxury housing and public housing projects, there were only "six-story, red-brick monsters" that "look like institutions, not dwellings. You live in a filing cabinet."[115] He proposed a new apartment house type, which consisted of identical units with four apartments per floor, raised on pilotis, with the ground floor housing only the lobby. The facades were organized in horizontal bands of windows. Two of the four facades had corner balconies and continuous glazing, creating a reasonable representation of the International Style Modernism that was frequently proposed for housing in the 1930s but rarely realized. The buildings were framed in steel and the spandrels built of a specially coated concrete block painted in a combination of brown, yellow and blue to establish a lively yet delicate appearance.

In Bayside, the Oakland Golf Course and Club, bounded by Fifty-sixth Avenue, Cloverdale Boulevard, Garland and Kenilworth drives and Alley Pond Park, became the site in 1960 for Queensborough Community College, for which a master plan was prepared in 1962–67 by Frederick Wiedersum & Associates and Holden, Egan, Wilson & Corser.[116] The two firms also designed the library, the gymnasium and the science, humanities and Campus Center buildings. The last of these was the most interesting; square in plan but complex in section, it had a strong central element that rose to a monopitched roof, which was designed to compositionally relate to the golf course clubhouse, retained as a faculty center and connected to the new building by a glassy enclosed bridge.

On the far side of Little Neck Bay, the communities of Douglaston Manor, Little Neck, Douglaston and Glen Oaks, developed as summer resorts, seemed more intimately tied to the town of Great Neck, in Nassau County, with which they shared a peninsula, than to Flushing or "the city." Nonetheless, with the postwar boom, these communities were confronted with dramatic new realities and pressures.

Glen Oaks Village (Benjamin Braunstein, 1948) was a 576-family garden apartment development with twenty-four two-story buildings, supplemented by 197 garages clustered stable-yard fashion in the center of the blocks; the buildings occupied only 20 percent of the twenty-seven-acre site.[117] A second section, housing 2,342 additional families, followed a year later on a larger lot to the east. The west parcel was bounded by 249th Street, Union Turnpike, Commonwealth Boulevard and extended just north of Seventy-sixth Avenue. Its site plan reorganized the mapped city grid, which consisted of ten separate blocks, into a plan of four blocks, allowing for a sophisticated arrangement of buildings reminiscent of college quadrangles. The main entrance, along the axis of 247th Street, led to the development's only unique building, a manor-house-like unit whose apartments were set behind a double-height colonnade of paired columns. In the center of the composition were a pediment and a rooftop cupola, in keeping with the development's Georgianesque vocabulary of red-brick walls and shuttered casement windows. The rooms of the apartments throughout the complex were small, but the rents were affordable. Shops were provided as part of the development, while schools and golf courses were also nearby—in short, all the suburban amenities for those who could not yet afford a suburban house of their own. The 140-acre eastern parcel, bounded by Union Turnpike, 263rd Street, Seventy-third Avenue, Langston Avenue, 260th Street and Little Neck Parkway, consisted of 111 similarly sited and detailed two-story red-brick buildings and featured a new public school, a three-acre park and a fifteen-acre shopping center designed by Leo V. Berger.

In 1975 North Shore Towers (A. H. Salkowitz), three virtually identical thirty-three-story apartment buildings housing 1,700 families in all, were built on the site of the former Glen Oaks Country Club, at 269-10, 270-10, 271-10 Grand Central

Parkway, located at the Nassau County line.[118] Sigmund Sommer, the developer, at first planned to fill the 126-acre plot with six-story apartment houses, but after meeting with planning and building officials he decided to retain the golf course and erect buildings that occupied less than 2 percent of the site. Rising from the lush greenery of their parklike site and with major highways intersecting at their doorsteps, these apartment buildings looked uncannily like a vision out of Le Corbusier's 1920s urbanist schemes.

Louis Allen Abramson's Long Island Jewish Hospital (1954), built to crown a wooded 8.5-acre site adjacent to the much larger site of Hillside Hospital, almost at the Queens-Nassau boundary, was a stolid slab characterized by an almost clinical modernity.[119] However, the interiors by Designs for Business, Inc. revealed an unexpected delicacy of color and style. Particularly noteworthy was the one-and-a-half-story lobby, located in a block projecting from the main building; its comfortable scale and wood paneling were as worthy of a suburban hotel as of a hospital. With the merger and subsequent growth of the Long Island Jewish and Hillside hospitals, the sylvan setting gave way to an ill-organized collection of buildings. One exception was the Jewish Institute of Geriatric Care (1972), at 271-11 Seventy-sixth Avenue, opposite 271st Street, in which Katz, Waisman & Blumenkranz displayed the same skill at adapting Modernism to the problem of hospital design that they first showed at Coney Island Hospital (see "Brooklyn," above).[120]

The large area bounded by Kissena Park Corridor, Cunningham Park, Union Turnpike and Flushing Meadows–Corona Park included a fifty-acre tract that had been planned in 1905 as a development called Utopia, a "Jewish colony" intended for relocated residents of Manhattan's Lower East Side.[121] The streets of Utopia, which lay between what became 164th Street and Fresh Meadow Lane, Horace Harding Boulevard and Jewell Avenue, were intended to be named after streets on the Lower East Side, like Ludlow, Hester and Division. (Utopia Parkway, running north-south from the Cross Island Parkway to the Grand Central Parkway, recalls the area's origins.) The scheme failed, however, and the land was sold in 1911. The area began to take on an affluent character at that time, and a country club was established to its east, at Fresh Meadows. In 1946 the club sold the land to the New York Life Insurance Company, which built an innovative housing project there over the next three years, designed by Voorhees, Walker, Foley & Smith.[122] Fresh Meadows, located on a 170-acre site roughly bounded by 186th and 197th streets, Horace Harding Boulevard and Seventy-third Avenue, was New York Life's response to the high-density, high-rise projects in Manhattan and the Bronx sponsored by its rival, Metropolitan Life. Unlike Metropolitan Life's Stuyvesant Town (see chapter 5), Fresh Meadows was built without public aid. And whereas Stuyvesant Town was superurban in density, Fresh Meadows was distinctly suburban in scale and density: if it had been built at the density of Stuyvesant Town, Fresh Meadows would have housed 75,000 people.

The principal feature of the design was the spacious site plan, in which buildings covered less than 15 percent of the site. As Otto L. Nelson, New York Life's vice president, explained, the development was intended to function "not merely as 'housing' but as a complete residential community for a healthful and pleasant life for the whole family—particularly the family with children."[123] The development's site plan carried forward the organizing ideas of Forest Hills Gardens (Grosvenor Atterbury and the Olmsted Brothers, 1909–12);[124] the postwar, automobile-age equivalent of the Gardens' Station Square was a village green

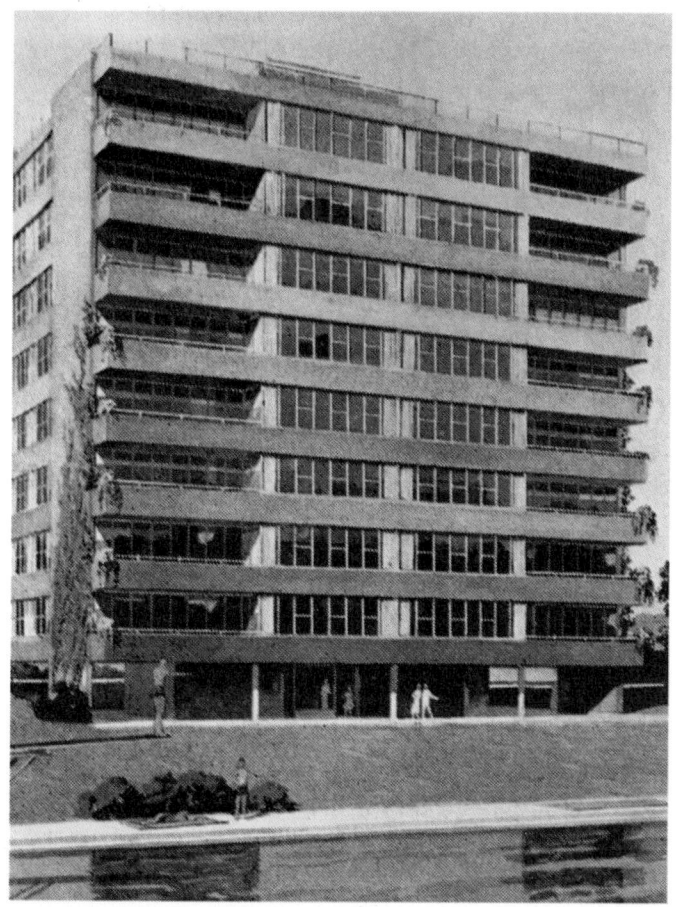

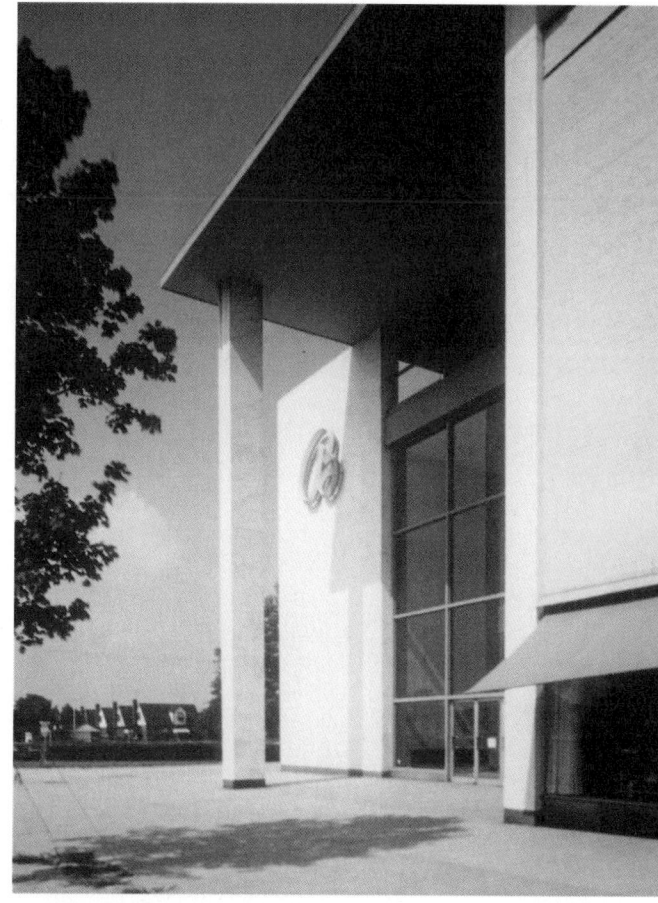

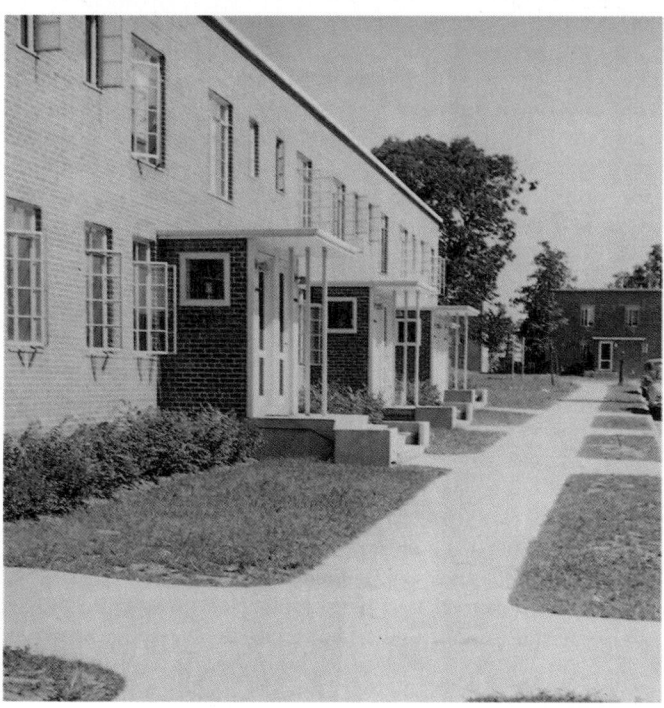

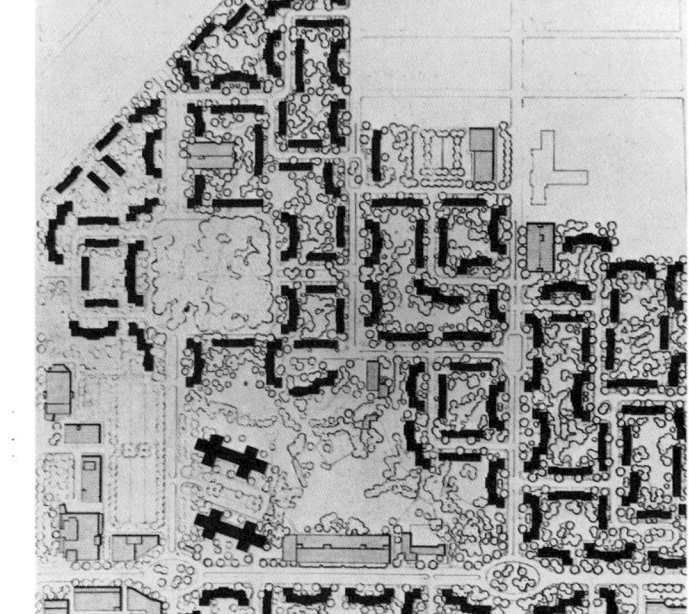

Top left: Levitt House, bounded by 162nd and Totten streets, Powell's Cove Boulevard and Twelfth Avenue, Beechhurst. Alfred Levitt with George G. Miller, 1958. AF. CU

Top right: Bloomingdale's, southeast corner of Horace Harding Boulevard and 188th Street, Fresh Meadows. Voorhees, Walker, Foley & Smith, 1949. View to the southwest. HLW

Bottom left: Fresh Meadows, between 186th and 197th streets, Horace Harding Boulevard and Seventy-third Avenue. Voorhees, Walker, Foley & Smith, 1949. HLW

Bottom right: Fresh Meadows. Site plan. ADA. CU

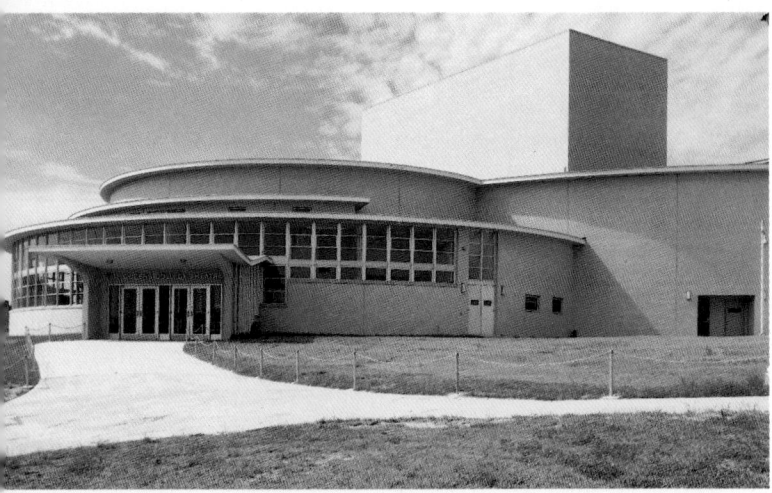

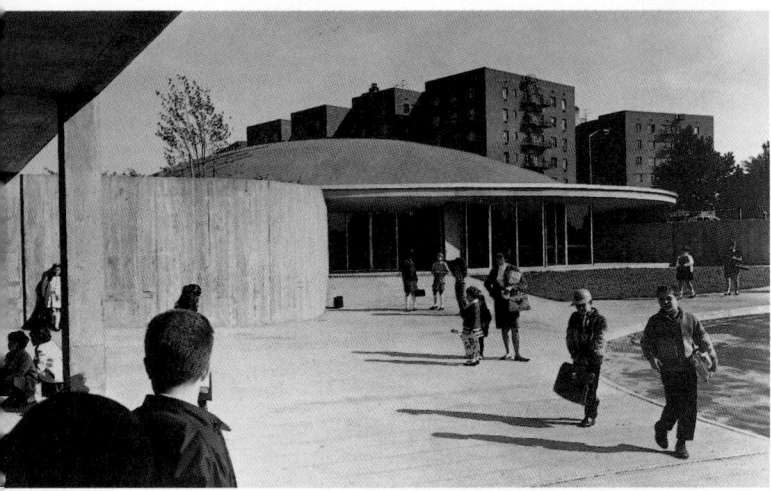

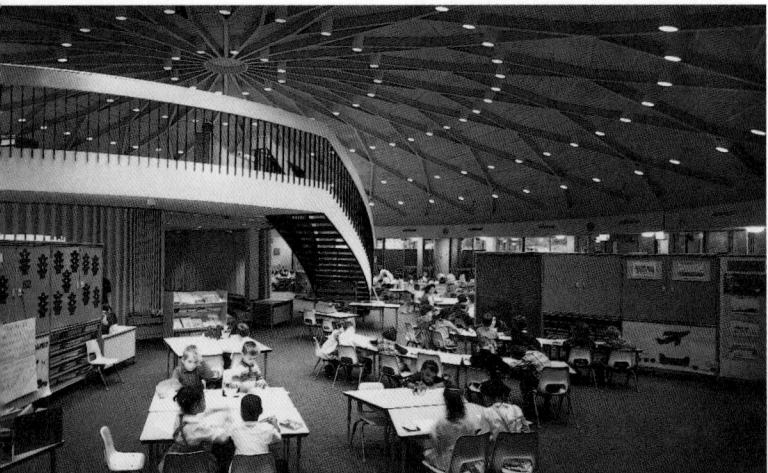

Top: Charles S. Colden Center, Queens College, bounded by Reeves Avenue, Kissena Boulevard, Melbourne Avenue and Main Street, Flushing. Fellheimer & Wagner, 1960. View to the southwest. Gottscho-Schleisner. LOC

Center: Paul Klapper School, Public School 219, 144-39 Gravett Road, east of Main Street, Flushing. Caudill Rowlett Scott, 1966. View to the southeast. CRSS

Bottom: Paul Klapper School. CRSS

marking the development's principal entrance at Horace Harding Boulevard, a main thoroughfare targeted for rebuilding as an expressway. In place of Station Square's arcades, shops and hotel, the green at Fresh Meadows was surrounded by shops, a movie theater and Bloomingdale's first branch department store (Voorhees, Walker, Foley & Smith, 1949). Just beyond the green, along 188th Street, which was the project's principal north-south spine, stood two apartment towers, vertical elements equivalent to the hotel at Forest Hills Gardens, except that here they were isolated in a sea of green instead of linking up to lower buildings to form a cloister.

While an echo of the Gardens' strongly articulated streetscape could be felt in the occasional ovals and miniparks that interrupted the flow of the principal streets in Fresh Meadows, there was none of the earlier development's hierarchy of street patterns or its sense of a sequence of movement through the project area. Fresh Meadows also lacked the diagrammatic clarity of Radburn, New Jersey (Clarence Stein and Henry Wright, 1927);[125] in fact, the site plan avoided the cul-de-sacs that, since Radburn, had been a feature of sophisticated suburban planning, in the belief that they overstressed the residents' need to protect themselves from the automobile. At Fresh Meadows, the intention was to bring the car to the door but to maintain private open space by grouping the units in quadrangles. Where the streets of Forest Hills Gardens constituted a metaphor for the journey from city to country, leading from the train station to Forest Park, the plan of Fresh Meadows was intended to suggest a landscaped park with buildings scattered in it. The principal landscape feature was the twenty-acre central open area, which had been the immediate setting for the clubhouse of the golf course. The apartment towers, the nursery and, oddly, a garage, were the only buildings permitted to encroach on this space.

The contracts for construction of the 3,200-unit housing estate were let in 1946, before the architects, assisted by New York Life's own architect, G. Harmon Gurney, had completed the plans. The design called for two thirteen-story towers housing a total of 600 families, and a mixture of seventy-two two-story and sixty-eight three-story buildings housing the remainder of the residents. In addition to the village center, two neighborhood shopping centers as well as a community center were provided to meet the needs of the 11,000 people who would live in the development. Off-street spaces for 1,000 cars were provided in central garages.

Although Fresh Meadows was well planned and formed an impressive ensemble, the red-brick, flat-roofed, lightly detailed buildings did not hold up to close scrutiny on an individual basis. As Architectural Record put it: "The buildings do not assert their smartness in the current vocabulary; neither do they hum softly in the sweetness of yesterday. They do not impress one with the gadgetry of sun control or factory assembly. Their effect, aesthetically, is a great, timeless unobtrusiveness."[126]

Lewis Mumford had high praise for the development, whose design he said was pervaded by "order and comeliness and charm." He explained: "The community as a whole is probably the best-looking piece of architecture in the metropolitan area, for it presents a series of architectural compositions, executed with a varied play of light and shade, of masses and volumes, and of color, that have all but disappeared from the urban architect's repertoire." He also extolled the project's low density—seventeen units to the acre—and its extraordinary amount of open space: "Apart from those two dominating thirteen-story apartment houses, the human scale (one- to three-story buildings) has everywhere been maintained, and the aesthetic qualities are balanced by human qualities."[127] Mumford saw Fresh Meadows as the culmination of a sequence of projects that began with Sunnyside Gardens, Queens (Clarence Stein, Henry Wright, Frederick L. Ackerman, Marjorie Sewell Cautley, 1924–28), and continued outside of New York with Radburn and with the Greenbelt towns.[128] According to Mumford, Fresh Meadows was "not just more housing" but "a slice of the City of Tomorrow—not the futuramic city of Hugh Ferriss's theatrical (and moonstruck) charcoal architectural sketches but a place that will stand up under the closest critical inspection."[129]

To the west of Fresh Meadows, along Horace Harding Boulevard, was Queens College, roughly bounded by Reeves Avenue, Kissena Boulevard, Melbourne Avenue and Main Street.[130] Founded in 1937, the college occupied nine Spanish Mission–style buildings built in 1908 for use as the New York Parental School, an institution devoted to the education of troubled children and truants. The new college quickly added acreage and buildings to the complex, gradually replacing the original structures but retaining the grassy mall as a focus for the expanded campus. The overall development was stylistically incoherent, with the architect of each building seemingly in competition with the others. Fellheimer & Wagner's Charles S. Colden Center (1960) was the college's most important new building, a mixed-use facility for music and the arts that incorporated a 2,200-seat concert hall, a 500-seat theater and two classroom wings.[131] The elements were arranged in a kind of butterfly plan radiating from a voided center that was intended to be used for outdoor concerts but was rendered virtually useless by the noise of airplanes headed to La Guardia and of traffic on nearby busy roads, including the Long Island Expressway.

On a corner of the campus, at 144-39 Gravett Road, east of Main Street, was P.S. 219, the Paul Klapper School (1966), named for Queens College's first president.[132] The architects, the Texas firm of Caudill Rowlett Scott, known for their innovative school design, grouped the classrooms together as one 7,850-square-foot room under a steel lamella dome, which was set atop three brick-clad hollow piers that were big enough to house small officelike spaces devoted to "observation" and remedial work. The school was intended as a laboratory to introduce new ideas in education to Queens College students learning to be teachers. An adjacent rectangular building of more conventional design, planned to accommodate 892 elementary students in regular classrooms, was built at the same time.

Jamaica

The town of Jamaica, founded in 1656 and called Rustdorp by the Dutch, stretched south from Union Turnpike to Jamaica Bay and included an array of diverse communities within its boundaries, ranging from the relatively well-to-do, stable residential neighborhoods of Ozone Park, Richmond Hill and Woodhaven to the bustling commercial district in Jamaica itself to the poor slums of South Jamaica.[133] Jamaica Estates, an affluent suburban enclave of 1,700 single-family homes dating from 1910, was bounded by Union Turnpike, 188th Street, Hillside Avenue, Home Lawn Street and Utopia Parkway.[134] As with other parts of the city, the continuation of the subway—in 1937 the Independent line extended service from Kew Gardens to Jamaica—had an enormous impact on southern Queens.

In 1946 city officials, working with Trygve Lie, Secretary General of the United Nations, selected a forty-acre tract in Jamaica to serve as the site of an apartment complex open exclusively to U.N. employees for its first five years (although a few veterans were allowed to live in the project).[135] The site was roughly halfway between the U.N.'s temporary headquarters at the New York City Building on the grounds of the World's Fair and at the Sperry Gyroscope Company in Lake Success, Nassau County. Completed two years later, Leonard Schultze & Associates' Parkway Village, bounded by Union Turnpike, Parsons Boulevard, Grand Central Parkway and Main Street, housed 685 families in 110 two-story buildings.

In 1955 St. John's University, which had been located near Borough Hall, Brooklyn, relocated to the 100-acre site of the former Hillcrest Golf Club, lying between Union Turnpike, Utopia Parkway, Grand Central Parkway and 168th Street.[136] Henry V. Murphy was selected to draft a master plan in 1946, seven years before St. John's took over the site, and he designed some of the structures, including the liberal arts (1955) and science (1958) buildings. Carson, Lundin & Shaw's seven-story-high law school building, Frumkes Hall (1972), marked an effort on the university's part to achieve architectural distinction, though the articulated brick-clad box, with dark-tinted glazing arranged in horizontal bands, was somewhat heavy-handed.[137] Other buildings on the campus were bland to excess, with the exception of Sun Yat-sen Hall, Center of Asian Studies (Herman C. Knebel, 1973), which had a certain thematic charm.[138]

South and slightly east of St. John's was a massive housing project, Rochdale Village (Herman Jessor, 1963), built on the site of the Jamaica racetrack, which was closed in 1958.[139] Developed by Abraham Kazan's United Housing Foundation, which would soon complete another huge housing project designed by Jessor, Co-op City in the Bronx (see "The Bronx," above), Rochdale Village consisted of twenty fourteen-story buildings housing 5,860 families in middle-income cooperatives. The 170-acre site was bounded by Baisley Boulevard, Bedell Street, 137th Avenue and New York Boulevard. Ten acres were set aside for shopping, and three public schools were also built. Eight years after the completion of Rochdale Village, an innovative ten-acre park was designed within the development by Richard G. Stein & Associates, who relieved the relentlessly flat racetrack site by creating huge pyramidal berms, some as tall as thirty feet, inadvertently tempting pranksters and vandals to throw rocks through nearby third-story apartment windows.[140]

In 1959, one year after the Jamaica track closed, Queens's other racetrack, Aqueduct, was rebuilt by Arthur Froehlich & Associates.[141] The 203-acre complex in Ozone Park, roughly bounded by Rockaway Boulevard, 114th Street, North Conduit Avenue and Centerville Street, featured a 110-foot-tall, 350-foot-deep, 1,050-foot-long grandstand-clubhouse framed in steel and clad in precast-concrete panel; it was designed to seat 23,000 and accommodate a total crowd of 80,000. It also included 738 pari-mutuel windows, numerous restaurants, extensive stable and paddock facilities, eighty acres of parking and its own stop on the Independent subway's Rockaway line. Inured to the inadequacies of the old Aqueduct and Jamaica tracks, Arthur Daley, a sportswriter for the New York Times, rhapsodized about the new facility: "It has the same air of unreality as something from the Arabian Nights. A genie might have emerged from the magic lamp and created a dream castle of such breathtaking vastness and opulence, one that should be approached only on a magic carpet. But the new Aqueduct race track was built by mortals and can be reached by conveyance as prosaic as the subway."[142]

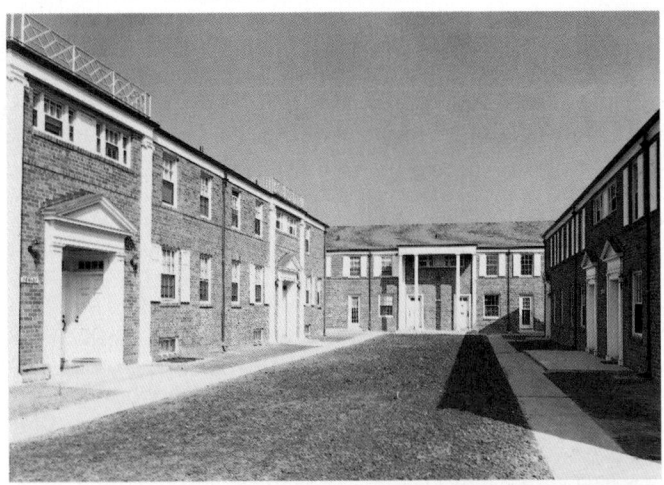

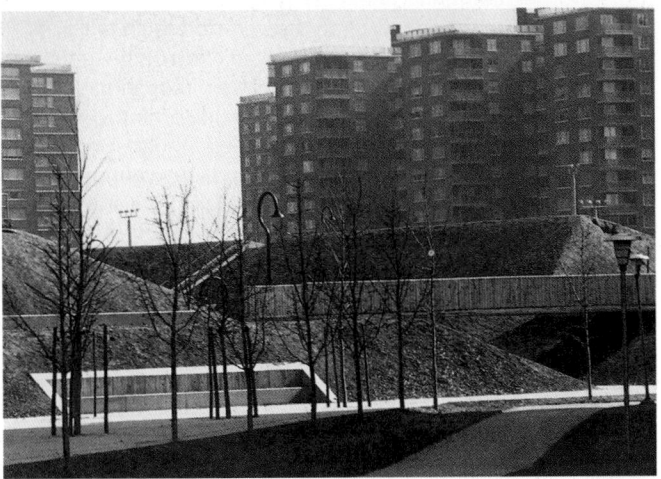

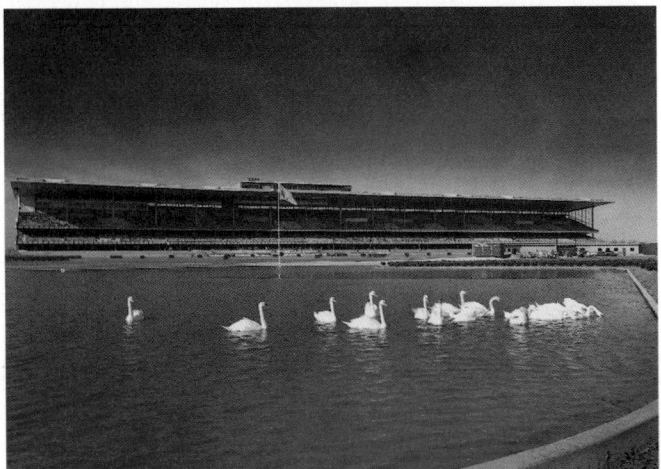

Top: Parkway Village, bounded by Union Turnpike, Parsons Boulevard, Grand Central Parkway and Main Street, Jamaica. Leonard Schultze & Associates, 1948. Courtyard. Gottscho-Schleisner. LOC

Center: Rochdale Village, bounded by Baisley Boulevard, Bedell Street, 137th Avenue and New York Boulevard, Jamaica. Herman Jessor, 1963. View of park (Richard G. Stein & Associates, 1971) with apartments behind. STPA

Bottom: Aqueduct, bounded by Rockaway Boulevard, 114th Street, North Conduit Avenue and Centerville Street, Ozone Park. Arthur Froehlich & Associates, 1959. View to the northwest. Laxer. FKG

By the mid-1960s Jamaica, although still the city's third busiest shopping center and a major transportation hub, was in need of repair.[143] In 1965 the Regional Plan Association suggested the area around the intersection of Jamaica Avenue and Parsons Boulevard as the perfect spot for one of the new regional subcenters they believed essential to the metropolitan area's continued growth. Plans for a new Jamaica Center, first released by the city in 1968, called for the construction of office buildings, new housing, hotels, educational facilities and a medical center and the destruction of the BMT elevated running above Jamaica Avenue. Armed with the motto "Change at Jamaica," taken from the cry of conductors on the Long Island Railroad, the project was vigorously supported by Mayor Lindsay, local residents and the Greater Jamaica Development Corporation, headed by F. Carlisle Towery, an architect and urban designer who had helped prepare the Regional Plan Association's studies of midtown Manhattan. In 1972 the National Municipal League awarded Jamaica the title of "All-America City," the first time in the history of the twenty-three-year-old award that a community which was part of a larger city was so honored. Unfortunately, the optimism generated by all the planning activity was halted by the city's fiscal crisis.

On the whole, Jamaica was not an architectural showcase. But in nearby Hollis there was one notable postwar building, Peter Blake and Julian Neski's hyperminimal, Mies-inspired Hollis Unitarian Church (1961), at 195-39 Hillside Avenue.[144] Cut into a steep hillside, the boxlike church sat on a partially buried podium. A recessed ground floor containing the lobby and classrooms was set behind a colonnade of steel structural columns infilled above with brick to enclose a 180-seat meeting hall. The hall's principal decoration was provided by the exposed steel roof trusses and the natural light that washed the concrete-block walls from concealed peripheral ribbon skylights.

To the south of Jamaica, along the bay, stretched the marshlands that also characterized Brooklyn's shorefront. In Brooklyn some of the marshlands were preserved as part of the public open space of Marine Park. In Queens they were turned to a different public purpose, to become the site of Idlewild Airport, New York's international airport and the world's busiest.

Idlewild Airport

In 1941, with La Guardia Field open only one year and already working at near capacity, 1,100 acres along Jamaica Bay at Idlewild, Queens, were designated for the site of a new airport, Municipal Airport No. 2, to meet the city's needs in the postwar era.[145] The key parcel of the marshy site, located thirteen miles east and a few miles south of Manhattan on the south shore of Long Island, was the Idlewild golf course, which was acquired in 1942. In April of the same year, the city began to prepare Idlewild's sand flats for what was conceived from the first to be the world's largest airport. By the war's end the site had been expanded to over 3,000 acres—six times the area of La Guardia. The new field would handle both transcontinental and international flights, leaving La Guardia free for short-haul travel.

The decision to go forward with an airport of this magnitude was made by Mayor La Guardia, a flying enthusiast who was determined that New York retain its position as the nation's principal port of entry in the age of flight.[146] Idlewild was the greatest construction project ever undertaken in the city, in both size and the scope of its ambitions. And the city's reclamation of the site would constitute the largest land reclamation project ever realized in the nation. By the time of Idlewild's completion, the low areas in the marshlands were pumped with 68,000,000 cubic yards of sand—enough to cover every street in Manhattan to the depth of eight feet. The most extensive well-point system ever made was installed to control the water.

By early 1946 Idlewild Airport was ready to open for service on a limited basis.[147] The initial stage of construction consisted of three of twelve proposed runways, essential taxiways and a temporary terminal building as well as hangars and other service facilities for individual airlines. The early site preparation was financed by the proceeds from the sale of Floyd Bennett Field in Brooklyn to the U.S. Navy, but it soon became clear that the city's Airport Authority, established by the state in April 1946, was not able to raise enough capital to handle the project and to fund the construction necessary to counteract the erosion at La Guardia Field.[148] After months of complex negotiations and public hearings, and a bitter power struggle between Robert Moses and the Port Authority, the city's Airport Authority was taken over by the Port Authority on June 1, 1947. In return for an annual rent to the city, the Port Authority agreed to take over La Guardia and the as yet incomplete Idlewild for fifty years.[149] Soon after, Newark Airport would be included in the Port Authority's system (see below).

The city's original proposal for the airport was prepared by the architects of La Guardia Field, Delano & Aldrich, and a team of engineers.[150] It called for a dramatically sculpted, 1,700-foot-long central administration building spanning an inner oval, around which were strung eighty-six plane-loading stations. The plan was innovative: rather than the customary arrangement such as that at La Guardia Field, where the administration building and hangars were located on one side of the complex, at Idlewild the administration area and apron formed the hub of the runway system. The building was to be four stories in height and about 500 feet in diameter, covering a ground area of 205,000 square feet. The ground floor would accommodate airlines, customs facilities and air express; the lobby, one floor above, would contain information, concessions and reservation desks in a central rotunda; the second floor, wrapped by observation terraces, would house general offices; restaurants and hotel rooms would be on the third floor, and more offices would be on the fourth floor; the building would be capped by a control tower. A two-level arcade extending from the terminal would follow an irregular but symmetrical path around the central hub to provide access to the planes. The lower level of the arcade would accommodate baggage and crew, and the upper level would be for passengers. The Port Authority proposal, prepared by staff architect Walter McQuade, offered a far less elegant solution to the problem of the administration building, calling for two separate terminals—one at each end of the oval—as well as a 250,000-square-foot office building and a hotel. Their plan did not come to terms with the vast number of airplane gates that would be needed.

The plan for Idlewild was vast in every respect: not only was it physically enormous, it required enormous resources to be operated. Early estimates suggested that when the airport was completed, 40,000 to 50,000 people would be employed there and 30,000 to 100,000 passengers and visitors would use it each day, requiring 30,000 parking spaces. By 1965 these projections would become reality.

After delays caused by sandstorms, among other things, Idlewild opened as a full-fledged facility on October 1, 1947.[151] Although workmen had been planting beach grass (*Ammophilia*

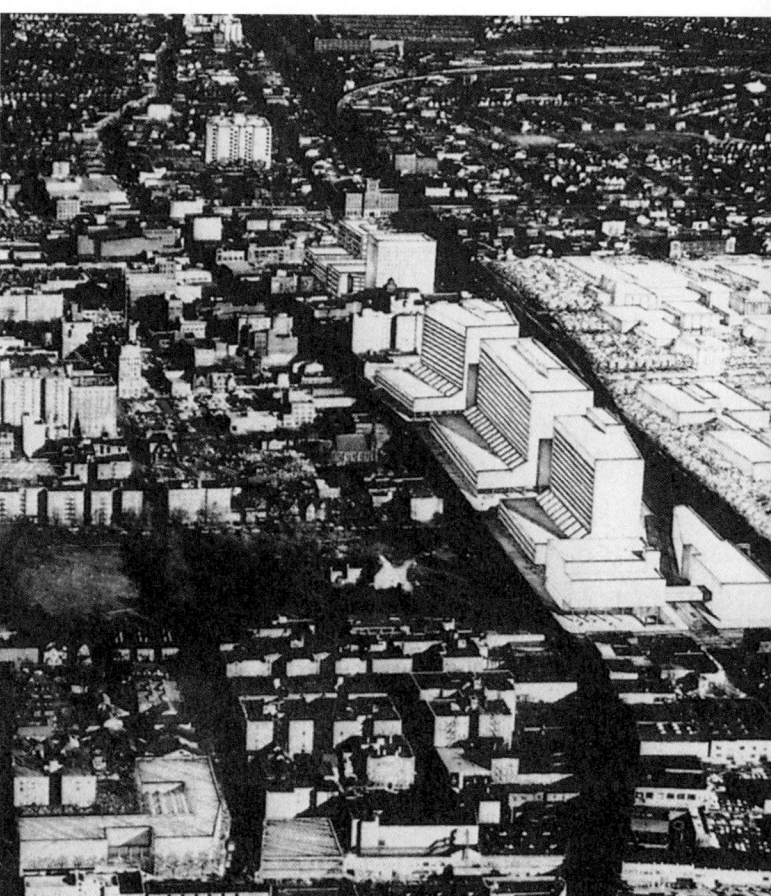

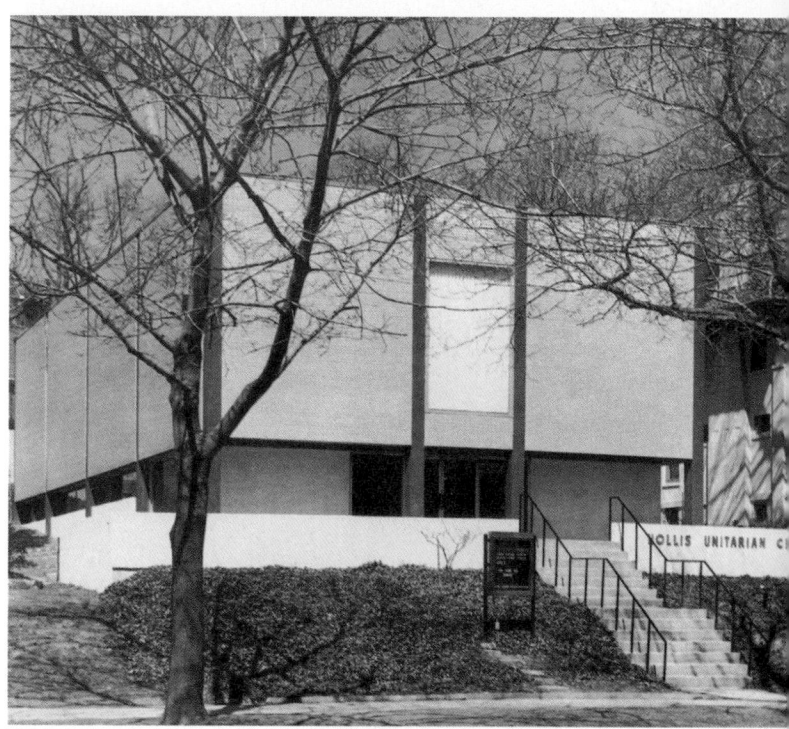

Top: Proposal for Jamaica Center. Office of Jamaica Planning and Development, 1968. Photographic montage. View to the east. JB and NYC

Bottom: Hollis Unitarian Church, 195-39 Hillside Avenue, opposite 195th Place, Hollis. Peter Blake and Julian Neski, 1961. View to the north. Cserna. PEBL

1007

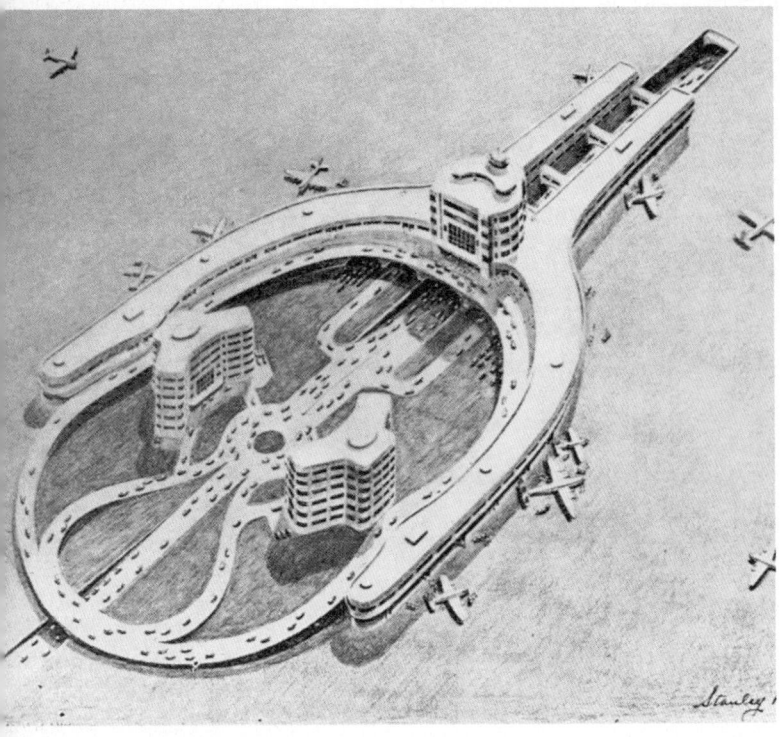

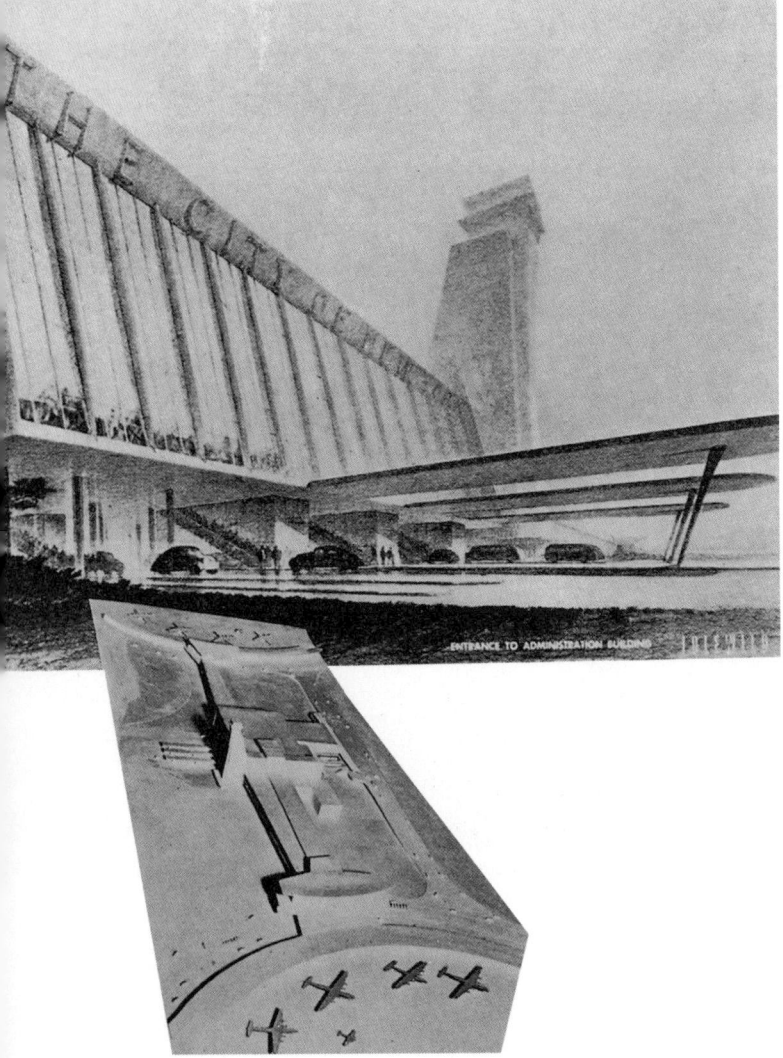

areharia) since 1943 to prevent erosion, only 65 percent of the site had been covered by the opening; the source of the beach grass, in Montauk, had been exhausted, and it was now being imported from Cape Cod. The airport began serving foreign-flag carriers on July 1, 1948, with facilities limited to two hangars and a small temporary administration building that was little more than a modified quonset hut. By the time Idlewild was officially dedicated on July 31 at a ceremony attended by President Harry S. Truman and his election rival, Governor Thomas E. Dewey, it had grown to 4,900 acres, or 7.1 square miles—roughly the size of Manhattan Island from the Battery to Forty-second Street.

Construction continued steadily as the Port Authority pushed forward with its commitment to create a permanent facility adequate for the requirements of burgeoning air traffic. Modern approach roads were developed, the highlight of which was a dramatic overpass designed by Clarke, Rapuano & Holleran that carried an airport taxiway over a depressed stretch of divided highway.[152] The world's largest steel-arched hangars (1950) were built to the designs of Lorimer & Rose, working in association with Roberts & Schaefer, structural engineers.[153] In 1954 the Port Authority's own engineers designed a hangar to house eight of the new giant-sized Lockheed Constellation airplanes, creating extraordinary cantilevers in steel to provide two enormous 133-by-400-foot covered areas.[154] Reinhard, Hofmeister & Walquist's Federal Building (1950), the first permanent building at Idlewild built by the Port Authority, was a conservative design that recalled government work of the New Deal era.[155] It was followed in 1952 by an eleven-story, 150-foot-high control tower, the world's tallest.[156] Though the tower was fitted out with the latest technology, no thought was given to its architectural design; it was seen as little more than a routine problem of engineering. The airport's passenger facilities remained makeshift.[157]

In February 1955 the Port Authority unveiled a five-year, $60 million plan to transform Idlewild, now swelled to 5,070 acres, into a proper gateway.[158] Because the 140 planes to be accommodated would have required a two-mile-long depot, the dispersed plan of gates that had been prefigured in the city-sponsored Delano & Aldrich scheme was adopted. The idea of a centralized terminal was dropped, however, in favor of an innovative plan, perhaps an outgrowth of McQuade's twin-terminal idea, calling for decentralized facilities with individual terminals for each important carrier. The decision to adopt this approach was based not only on the enormous rise in air traffic and projections that the trend would continue but on the realization that Idlewild's complex operations, combining domestic and international travel, did not lend themselves to a single-terminal facility. Furthermore, as *Business Week* reported, at least three major air carriers "spoke out to the Port Authority for terminals of their own." The airlines' desire for separate facilities was based at least partly on the idea that the terminal buildings could become a "competitive service weapon"—in effect, a three-dimensional advertisement—in a business where strict governmental regulations tended to standardize all aspects of air travel.[159] In addition to allowing 140 planes to load and unload at the same time—a vast gain over the available slots at La Guardia or Newark—the new plan would mean that passengers would never have to walk more than 400 feet between the gate and ground transportation.

The new master plan, intended to make Idlewild the "most beautiful, efficient and functional" air terminal in the world, was drawn up by Wallace K. Harrison, who between 1954 and 1960 was retained as the Port Authority's Coordinator of Exterior Architecture.[160] Harrison had worked on the airport's design once before, in 1946. Expanding on his early studies, Harrison's new plan broke completely with the single-terminal model to establish a 655-acre core development called Terminal City, a collection of seven independent airline terminals for American-flag carriers as well as an international arrivals building combined with departure facilities for foreign-flag carriers, all grouped around a 160-acre open space containing a landscaped mall and surface car parking. The recently completed control tower would become part of the international arrivals building. *Architectural Forum* extolled the new master plan, calling it "a design revolution in reverse—a deliberate giant step in the 'backward' direction of *fragmentation*, whereas all up-to-date airport design theory favors more *consolidation*. It was a step dictated, in the end—after a prolonged flirtation with consolidation—by the sheer statistics of the case."[161] Every aspect of Terminal City was designed with an eye toward being the most advanced. The night lighting, for example, was designed by Abe Feder, working with General Electric, to provide higher levels of illumination than ever before and to create "the illusion of never ending daylight" without interfering with pilots' visibility during take-offs and landings.[162]

In 1955 a period of tremendous activity began at Idlewild: work on the Terminal City core began, three hangars were completed, and the construction of three more hangars and four large buildings was under way.[163] By 1957 the airport was a hive of construction activity, as the Port Authority rushed to complete the road system as well as the terminals.[164] The new Terminal City and the reorganized airport as a whole was beginning to take form. As the *New Yorker* reported in September 1957:

> If you haven't been out to Idlewild Airport for a year or so, the chances are you'd scarcely recognize the place. Trees, grass, reflecting pools, and a lagoon have appeared, lights mounted on stylish, lyre-shaped struts now line the roads . . . [an] International Hotel has been started and a huge International Arrivals Building almost finished, and, in general, the whole compound has begun to take on a sleek, futuristic look, replacing the familiar bareness, which always suggested to us a landscape on the moon.[165]

"Already," *Business Week* reported in the same month, "the dazzling control tower and illuminated fountains give the area a futuristic look of a world's fair."[166]

On December 5, 1957, the first building in Terminal City, the International Arrivals Building and its adjoining foreign-flag airline wings, was opened, accommodating all arriving international travelers as well as international passengers departing on foreign-owned airlines.[167] The sleek 2,300-foot-long International Arrivals Building was designed by Charles Evan Hughes III and J. Walter Severinghaus of Skidmore, Owings & Merrill (SOM), in collaboration with Thomas S. Sullivan, head of the Port Authority's aviation planning division. The showplace of the Terminal City complex, the steel-framed, glass-walled building contained 362,000 square feet of floor space on three floors; the two wings, also three stories tall, contained an additional 225,000 square feet. The eleven-story control tower, located at its main entrance although not technically a part of the building, was dramatically altered: its bottom six floors, which had once been little more than an openwork of steel, were framed in to provide additional office space, and the entire structure was sheathed in the same curtain wall as that of the arrivals building.

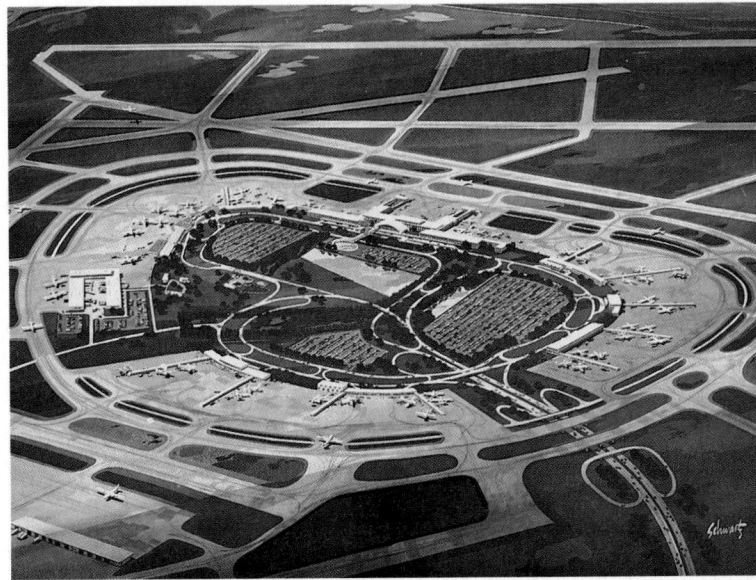

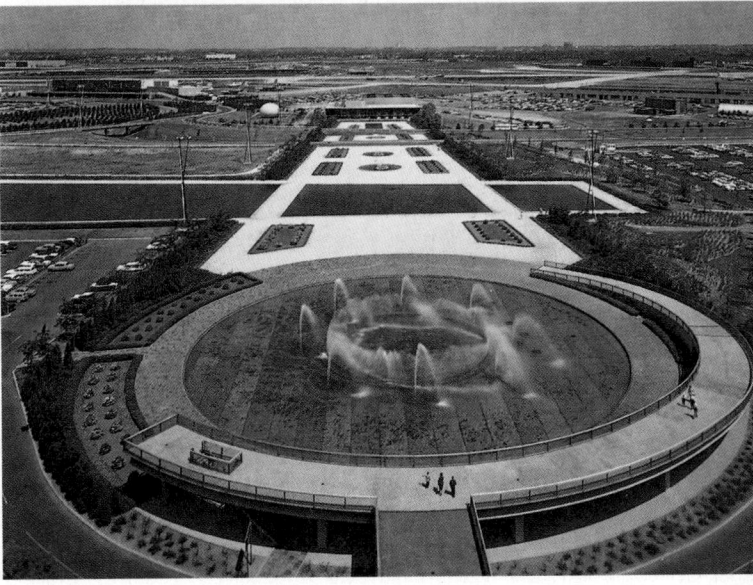

Top left: Port Authority proposal for Idlewild Airport. Walter McQuade, 1947. Rendering by Stanley Bate showing air terminal, with office building and hotel in the center. AR. CU

Bottom left: Airport Authority proposal for Idlewild Airport. Delano & Aldrich, 1947. Rendering by Hugh Ferriss showing entrance to administration building, with photograph of model below. CU

Top: Proposal for Terminal City, Idlewild Airport. Wallace K. Harrison, 1955. Rendering by Robert Schwartz of aerial view to the southeast. PANY

Bottom: Liberty Fountain, Idlewild Airport. Skidmore, Owings & Merrill, 1957. View to the northwest. Molitor. JWM

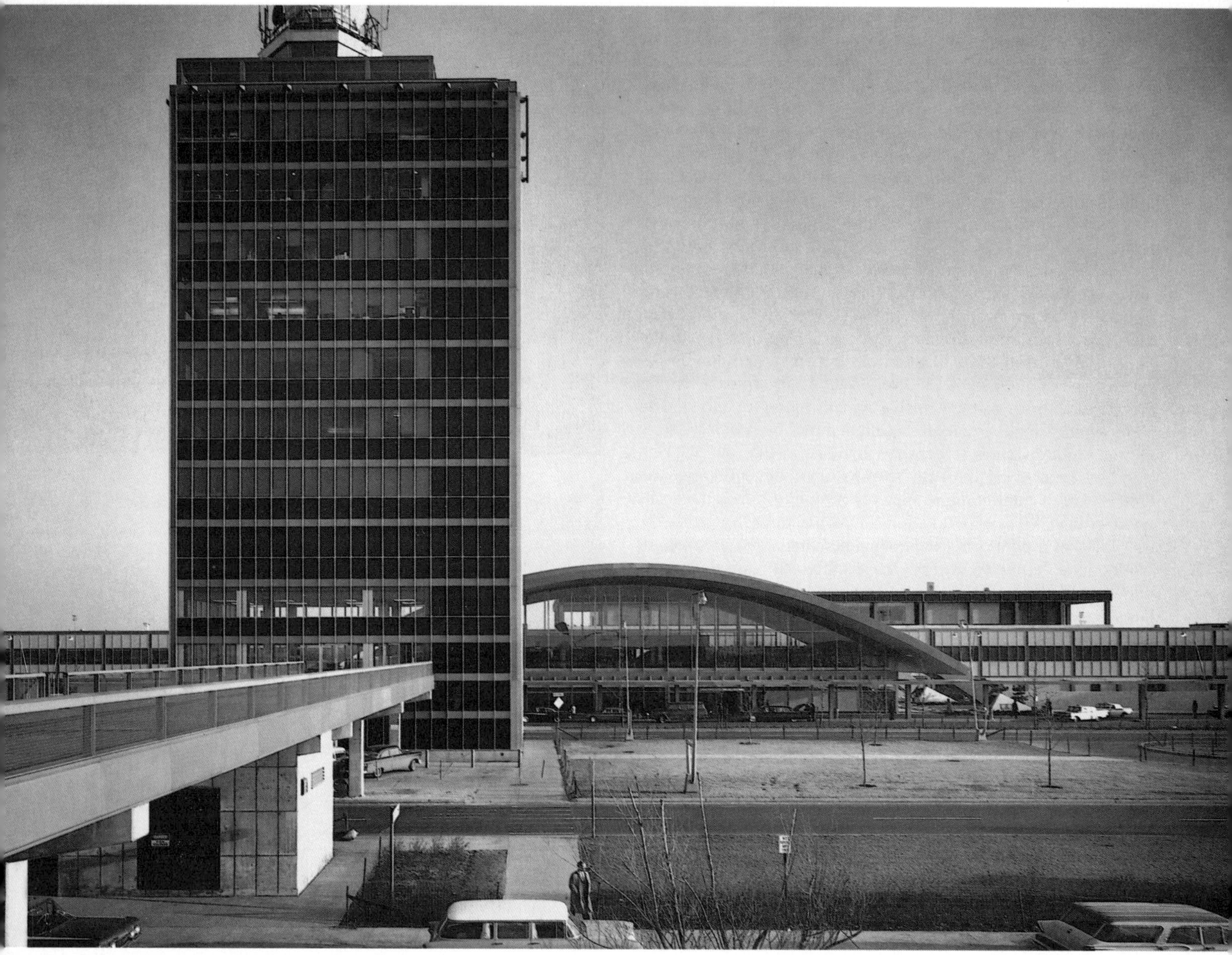

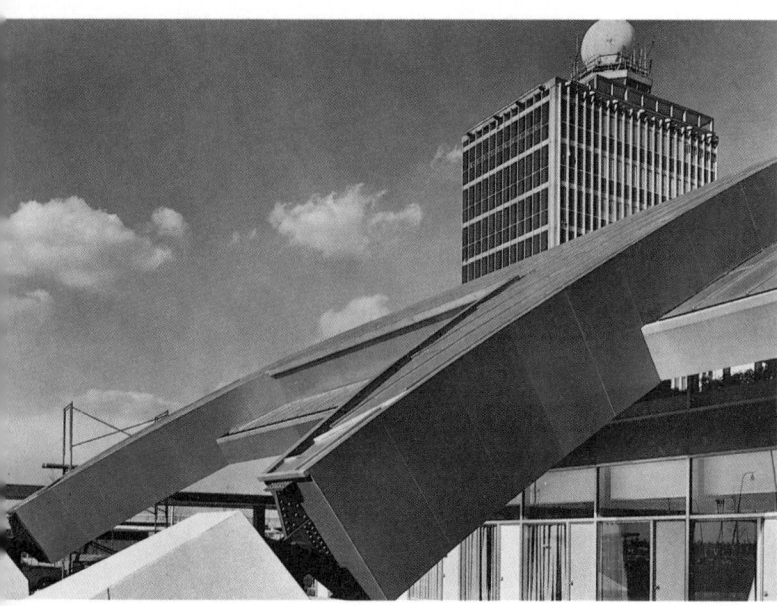
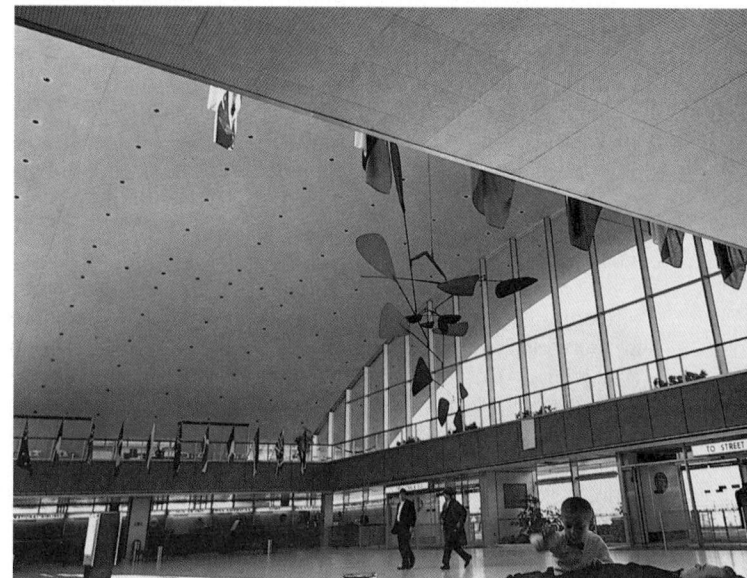

On axis with the International Arrivals Building, at the opposite end of the mall, was the airport's Central Heating and Cooling Plant (1957), which SOM encased in a simple box with a black-painted exposed-steel frame, infill walls of gray-glazed brick on three sides and a wall of fixed glass facing south toward the arrivals building. Inside the plant, the various feed lines were each painted a different color—blue, green, orange and red—so that at night, when the facility was illuminated from within, it looked like a stage set for a machine-age ballet from the 1920s.

The mall extending between the International Arrivals Building and the Central Heating and Cooling Plant was also dramatically planned. To tie the entire complex together, an elevated walkway led over the vehicular drop-offs and through the tower's base from the second level of the International Arrivals Building's main waiting room to a pair of curved ramps that swept down to the mall. There they embraced the circular Liberty Fountain, which sent water sixty feet up into the air in various patterns; at night, the colors of the fountain's lights were also varied. The baroque exuberance of this bit of design, the most tangible example of Harrison's contribution to Terminal City, best embodied the world's fair spirit that characterized its overall planning and design.

For the arriving passenger, the new International Arrivals Building was a revelation of efficiency. Clear paths of circulation led to a double-height customs hall, above which, behind glass, observers could monitor the progress of arriving passengers. The inspection stations were designed to resemble supermarket checkout counters, giving a witty, distinctly American flavor to a normally dehumanizing process. Once cleared of customs, arriving passengers entered the main arrivals hall, whose stainless-steel-framed parabolic vault, together with the control tower, formed the principal focus of the building's exterior composition. A forty-foot-wide mobile by Alexander Calder hung above the hall, and along the edges of the room continuous counters accommodated various services, ranging from ground transportation to baggage claim.

Passengers departing on foreign-flag carriers were handled in the east and west wings. From the street-level arcade passengers would proceed inside for ticketing and then up an escalator to the second-floor concourse. where they would await boarding. On the third floor, the various carriers had their offices as well as specially designed lounges for their preferred customers. The design of these interiors was left to the airlines themselves, many of whom commissioned New York–based architects and designers rather than turning over the projects to firms in their own countries. The office facility of KLM Royal Dutch Airlines was designed by Raymond & Rado, who also designed their Fifth Avenue offices (see chapter 5); Sabena-Belgian World Airlines worked with Lawrence Lerner, chief designer of Michael Saphier Associates;[168] Air France employed Itkin-Affrime-Becker,[169] as did LAV (the airline of Argentina and Venezuela);[170] British Overseas Airways Corporation, which was soon to build its own terminal (see below), commissioned the architects LaFarge, Knox & Murphy;[171] Swiss Air employed the Swiss architects Haefeli, Moser, Steiger and a New Yorker, John Weber, who had worked on the Swiss Pavilion for the 1939 World's Fair;[172] El Al (Israel) worked with Kelly & Gruzen in association with Israeli architects Axelrod & Goldner;[173] Varig (Brazil) hired Charles J. Lane; and Kemper & Schwartz designed a combined departure station for Icelandic and Iberia airlines.[174] On the building's roof level, the Knoll Planning Unit, under the design direction of Florence Knoll, created what *Progressive Architecture* described as "an atmosphere of welcome and luxury"

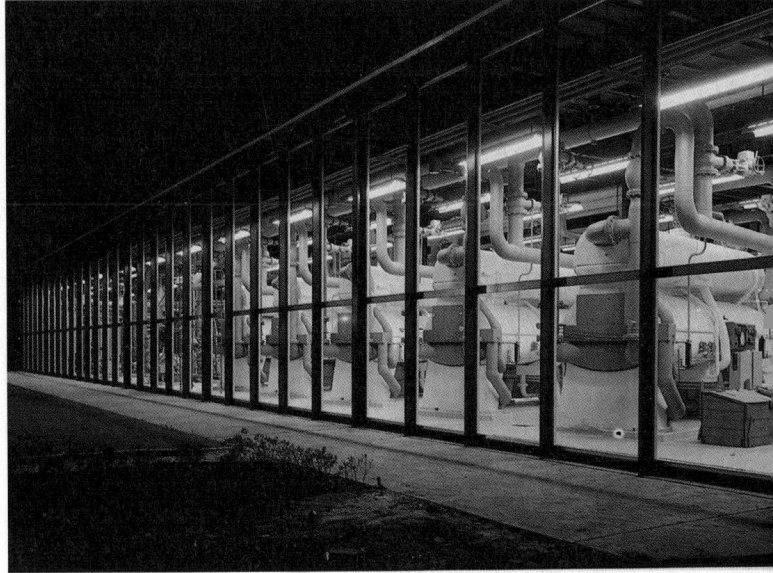

Top left: International Arrivals Building, Idlewild Airport. Skidmore, Owings & Merrill, 1957. View to the southeast. Stoller. ©ESTO

Bottom far left: International Arrivals Building. View to the north. Wurts. MCNY

Bottom left: International Arrivals Building. Main arrivals hall with mobile by Alexander Calder. Stoller. ©ESTO

Above: Central Heating and Cooling Plant, Idlewild Airport. Skidmore, Owings & Merrill, 1957. View to the southwest. Gottscho-Schleisner. SOM

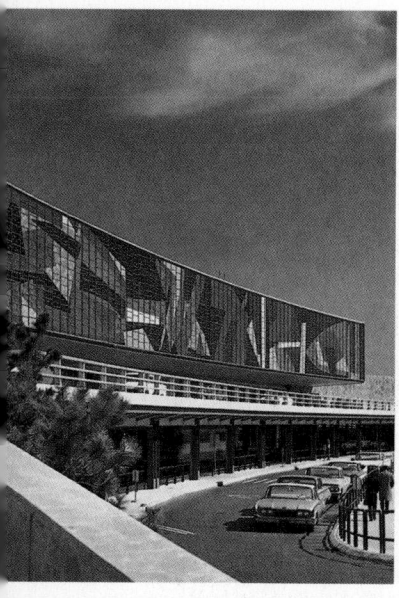
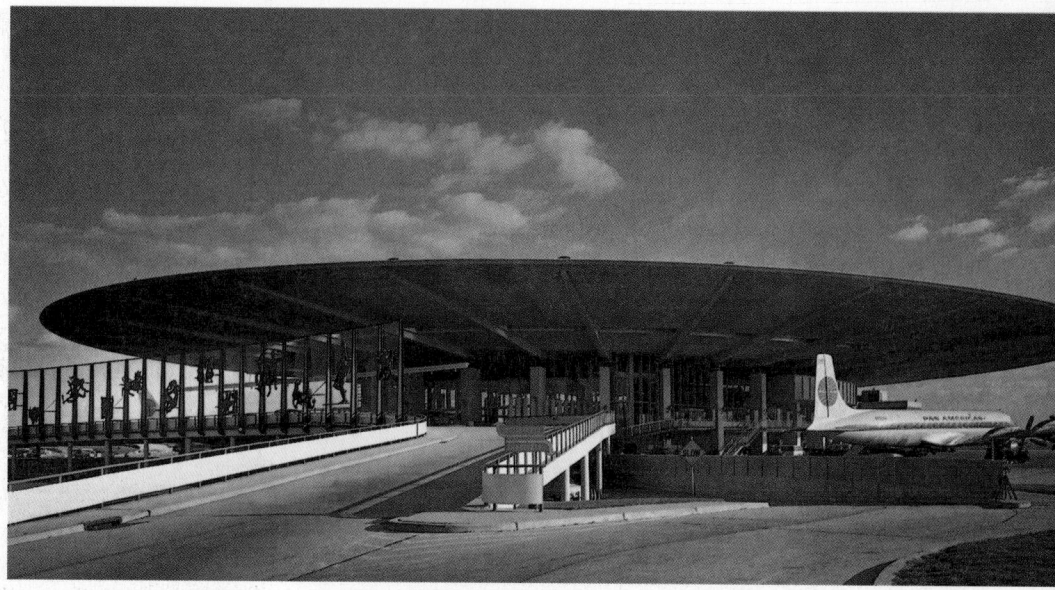

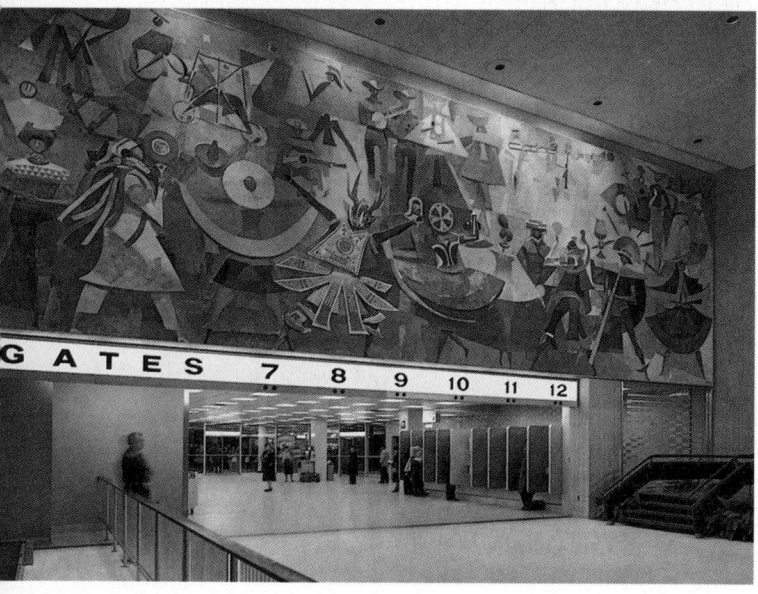
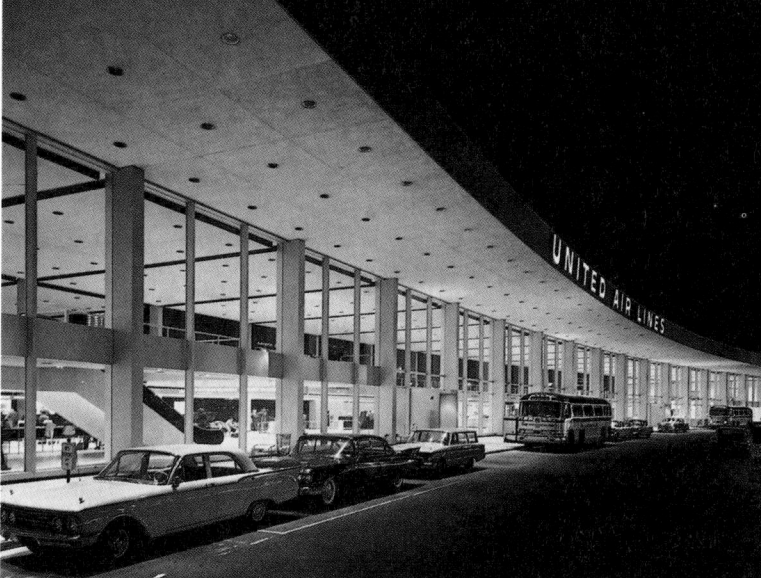

Top: American Airlines terminal, Idlewild Airport. Kahn & Jacobs, 1960. View to the northeast. Stoller. ©ESTO

Bottom: American Airlines terminal. Main concourse with mural by Carybé (Hector Bernabó). Stoller. ©ESTO

Top: Pan American terminal, Idlewild Airport. Tippetts-Abbett-McCarthy-Stratton in association with Ives, Turano & Gardner, 1960. View to the southeast. Stoller. ©ESTO

Bottom: United Airlines terminal, Idlewild Airport. Skidmore, Owings & Merrill, 1961. View to the north. Stoller. ©ESTO

by organizing the 20,000-square-foot, 400-seat Golden Door Restaurant into eight dining sections defined by subtle changes in lighting and color as well as low screen walls, sofas and planters.[175]

In December 1957 American Airlines unveiled plans for its terminal (1960), designed by Kahn & Jacobs and consisting of a central facility with two fingerlike extensions where planes were docked.[176] The main building featured a double-level roadway system to help separate arriving and departing passengers. Though basically an unmemorable, bland design, the terminal was distinguished by the gentle curve of its principal facade, which consisted mostly of a 317-foot-long, 22'6"-high stained-glass window, said to be the world's largest, designed and executed by Robert Sowers in three types of glass. Inside the American terminal, in the privileged recesses of the airline's Admiral's Club, special patrons were bathed in the colored light coming through Sowers's mural. In the main concourse were two representational murals by a Peruvian artist, Carybé (Hector Bernabó), depictions of a dancing girl holding a fish and a masked man spinning about like a whirling dervish.

Pan American's terminal (1960) was more daring, at least structurally, but far more problematic from a functional point of view.[177] In a departure from the norm, Tippetts-Abbett-McCarthy-Stratton (TAMS), a large firm of architects and engineers, working in association with Ives, Turano & Gardner, created a 100,000-square-foot, freestanding oval building from which a great four-acre elliptical umbrellalike canopy of concrete and steel was cantilevered. This plan permitted the airplanes to dock virtually all around the building, reducing the distance passengers needed to traverse between ground and air transportation. Aside from the bold engineering of the cable-supported roof, the design held little interest; particularly egregious was the ungainly windscreen at the entrance, which featured Milton Hebald's trite sculptures representing the signs of the zodiac.

Although the building's plan was ingenious, it was not an "unmixed blessing," as *Architectural Record* explained a year after it opened: "By placing the aircraft around the terminal and nosed into it, the maximum number of aircraft that could be handled at a given time has been exactly fixed. There is no apparent way to expand the present design concept."[178] This observation proved correct, and the terminal's functional limitations became painfully evident almost immediately. In 1968 the airline began construction on an addition that was over seven times the size of the original facility.[179] In designing the addition, completed in 1976, TAMS abandoned the centralized plan of their original building. Faced with a site that had very narrow frontage on the access road, they devised a fan-shaped plan behind the original terminal, which was retained to serve as a reception area for the vastly expanded facility.

SOM's design for the United Airlines terminal (1961) was slick but not memorable.[180] Chester L. Churchill's Eastern Airlines building (1959), with its huge 28,600-square-foot lobby, was well planned but unattractive: "Never have so many exotic marbles been used for so bleak an effect," Ada Louise Huxtable said. "An arched ceiling, cut ruthlessly by partitions, curves to nowhere, its indecision revealed awkwardly on the exterior. Enormous, confused, heavy handed and dull, it is a vast monument to pretentious mediocrity."[181] BOAC, British Overseas Airways Corporation, was the only foreign carrier to erect its own terminal (1970), the first in the United States to be built by a foreign carrier.[182] Designed by the English firm of Gollins, Melvin, Ward & Partners, the battered-walled pavilion awkwardly combined Miesian openness with Brutalist mass. According to the

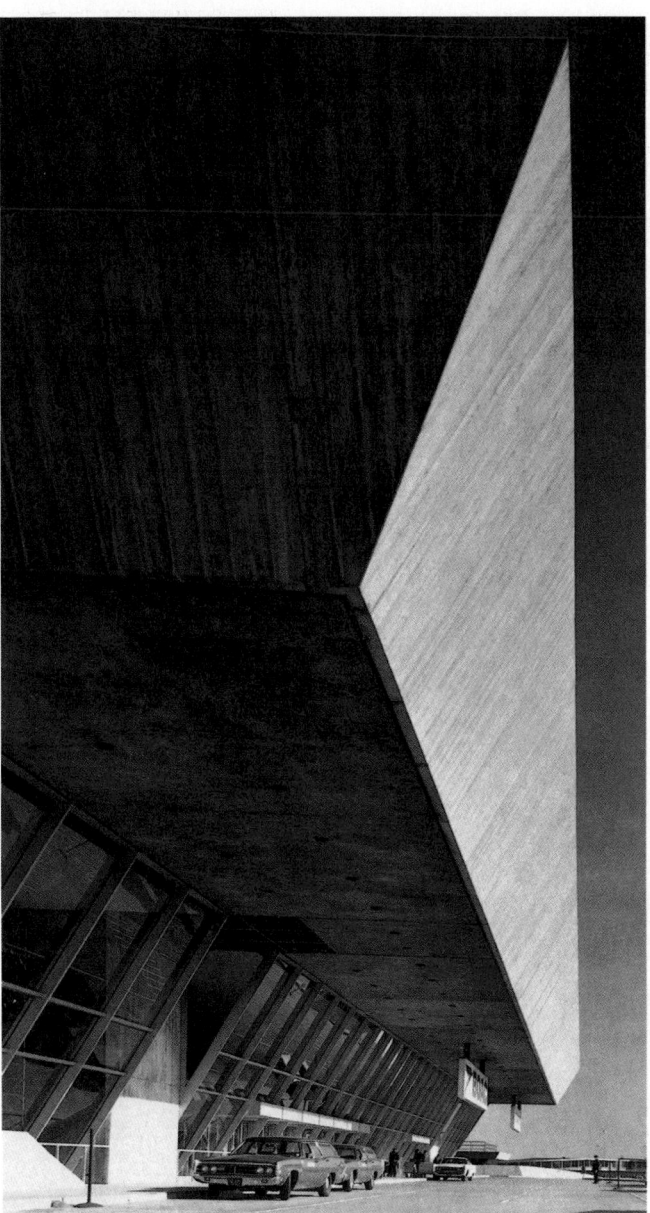

British Overseas Airways Corporation terminal, Idlewild Airport. Gollins, Melvin, Ward & Partners, 1970. View to the southwest. GMWP

1013

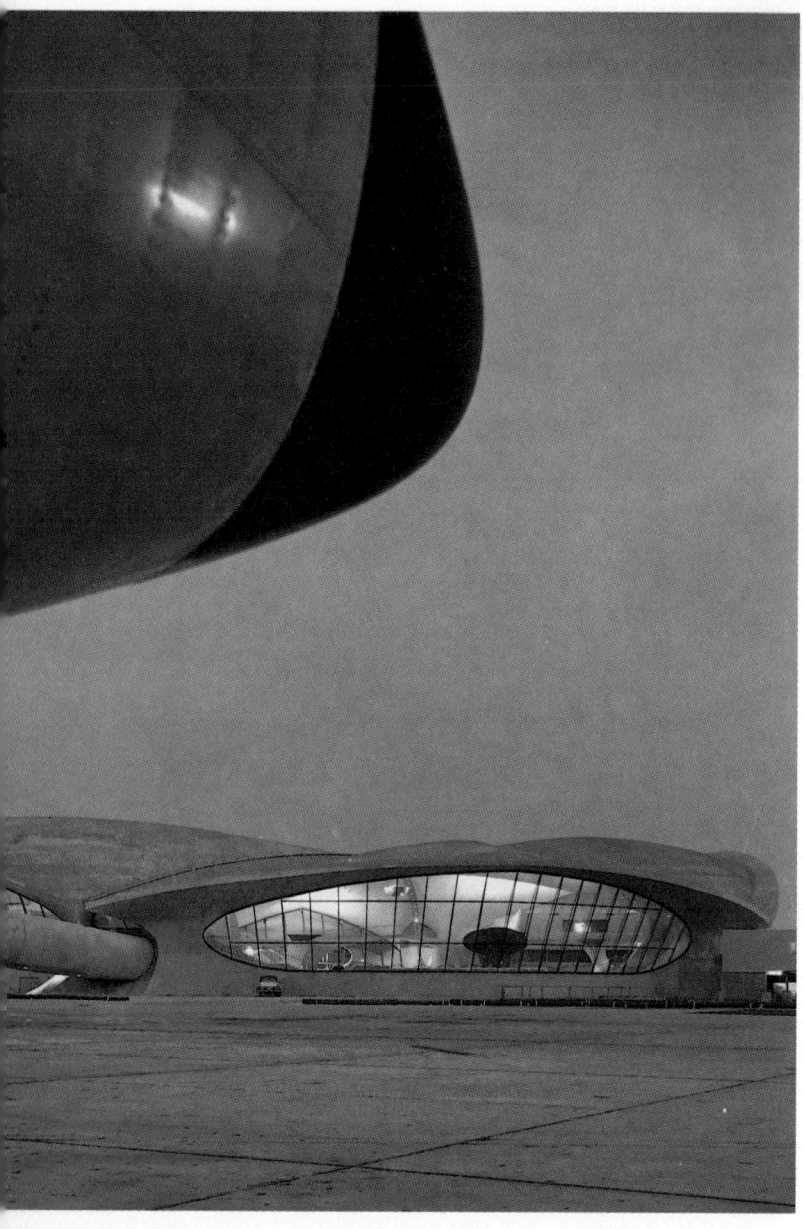

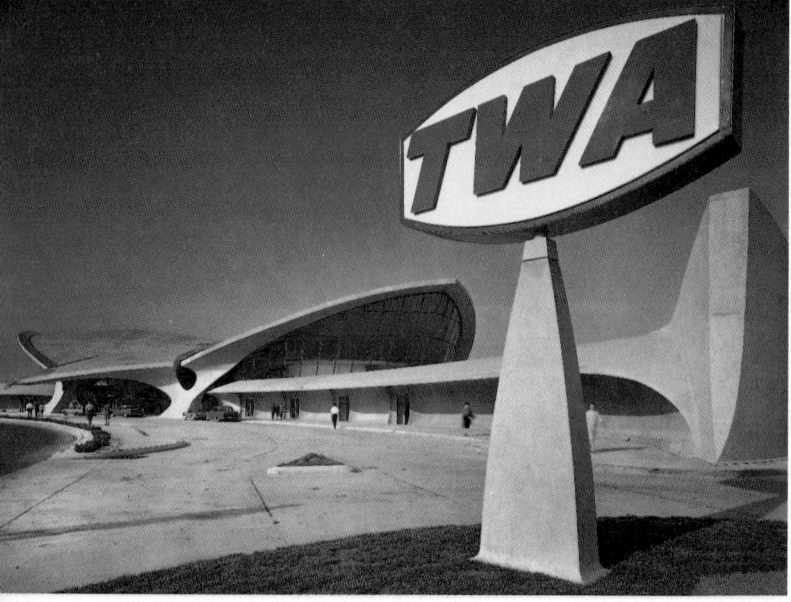

architects, it was intended to express flight: "We tried to make the building look as if it were floating . . . to give it an airlike quality," explained Edward F. Ward, one of the partners. "There is a relationship between the form of the building and the form of aircraft."[183]

Eero Saarinen & Associates' TWA terminal (1962) was unquestionably the most talked about building at Idlewild.[184] The commission came to Saarinen in 1956. Located on a corner site, the building terminated the axis of Terminal City's principal inbound access road, and its sculptural bravura served as a brilliant counterpoint to the geometrical regularity of the International Arrivals Building. Though in photographs it appeared vast in size and scale, in reality TWA's central building was relatively small, measuring 322 feet by 222 feet at its extremities, with vaults that rose only 51 feet above the ground. The design of the terminal, which Saarinen developed with his associate Kevin Roche, consisted of a strikingly modeled and vaulted reinforced-concrete central structure containing waiting rooms and restaurants. Working with Ammann & Whitney, structural engineers, Saarinen designed four intersecting vaults of thin-shell concrete rising from four massive piers to create a canopy over the spaces of the central building. Extending in opposite directions from the central building on the in-board side were two single-story projecting arms, one for check-in facilities, the other for baggage claim. On the out-board side, two 125-foot-long passageways led from the central structure to remote boarding lounges, increasing the perimeter area of the tight corner site and permitting a total of fourteen jet planes to dock at one time. In the original plans the two boarding arms were skylighted, the connections between the terminal and the boarding lounges included moving sidewalks, and the boarding lounges were concentrically placed around a central atrium garden. But these features were dropped in the course of design as cost-saving measures for the financially troubled airline.

The terminal was laid out not only to provide passengers with a smooth flow of travel between arriving at the building and boarding their planes but to dramatically elevate that journey to a rite of passage; travelers would become part of the drama of flight itself. As John Jacobus pointed out, "What the architect sought was an updated *architecture parlante*, not a style but, in a curious return to eighteenth-century methodologies, a literary architecture that would arouse emotions and affect sentiments."[185] Saarinen explained his goals for the terminal:

> The challenge of TWA was twofold. One, to create within the complex of Idlewild a building which would be distinctive and memorable . . . one which could relate to the surrounding buildings in mass but still assert itself as a dramatic accent. Two, to design a building in which the architecture itself would express the excitement of air travel . . . in which the architecture would reveal the terminal, not as a static enclosed place, but as a place of movement and transition.[186]

To shape the sequence of spaces, and to give the building a memorable image, Saarinen continued the theme of structurally determined form that he had pursued in earlier projects for the Massachusetts Institute of Technology and Yale University. "As the passenger walked through the sequence of the building," Saarinen explained, "we wanted him to be in a total environment where each part was the consequence of another and all belonged to the same form-world."[187] Unlike earlier projects, however, here Saarinen added a greater geometrical complexity and a more literal expressiveness of silhouette bordering on the picturesque. Some observers saw the Guggenheim Museum as Saarinen's inspiration for the design, while others mentioned

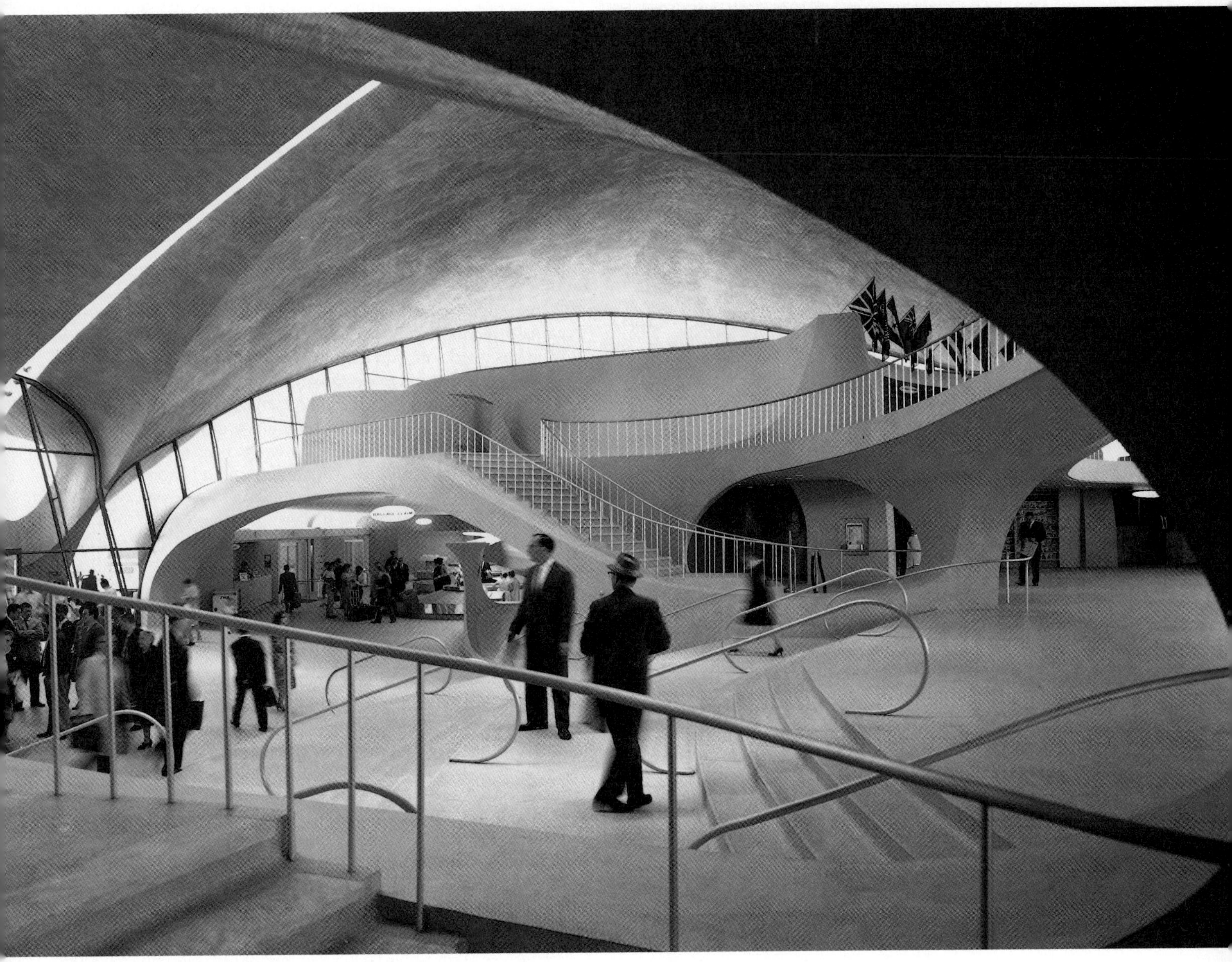

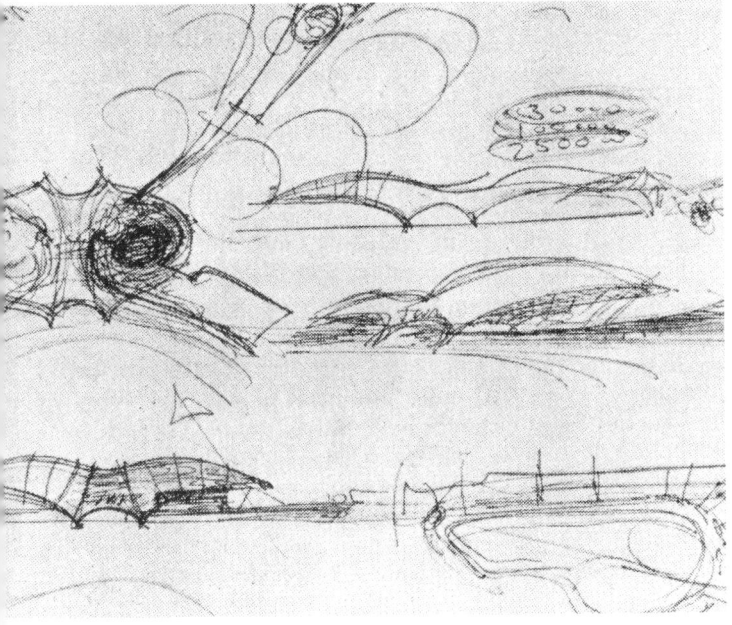

Top far left: TWA terminal, Idlewild Airport. Eero Saarinen & Associates, 1962. View to the east. Stoller. ©ESTO

Bottom far left: TWA terminal. View to the northeast. Stoller. ©ESTO

Above: TWA terminal. Lobby. Stoller. ©ESTO

Left: TWA terminal. Preliminary sketches. WE. CU

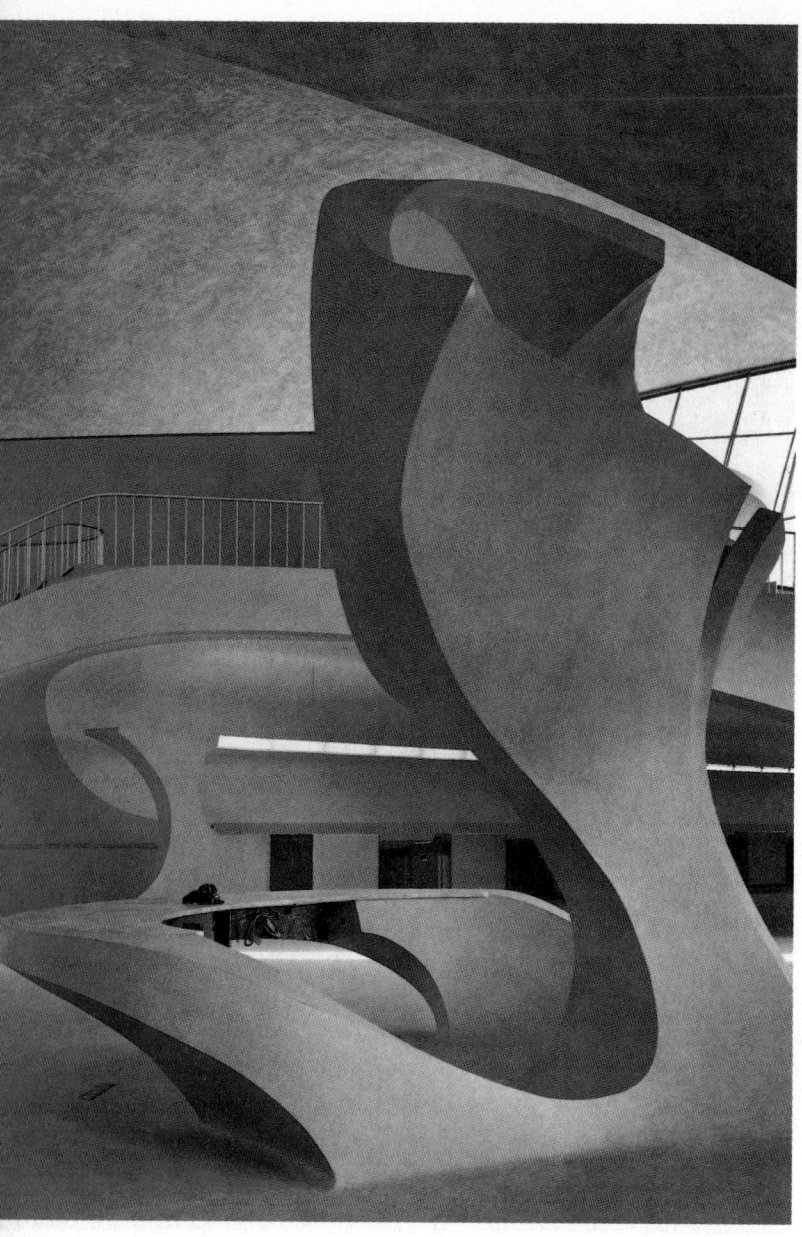

TWA terminal, Idlewild Airport. Eero Saarinen & Associates, 1962.
Lobby with information desk and flight board. Stoller. ©ESTO

Naum Gabo's unrealized proposal for the Palace of the Soviets (1930), the sketches of Erich Mendelsohn and Jørn Utzon's early drawings for the Sydney (Australia) Opera House, which Saarinen had studied carefully when, as a member of the competition jury, he helped select the scheme in 1957. The building received as much attention for its strong representational form as for its structural daring. In the first of three significant presentations of the building that *Architectural Forum* was to publish, the editors described it as "looking like a giant bird in flight," an "eye-stopping design" that was "appropriate as a symbol of an airline."[188]

While *Forum* and other observers at the time were uncomfortable with the direction toward expressive form that Saarinen seemed to be taking, the tight bonding of architecture with advanced technology in the TWA design offset such criticism. "The best evidence that the building is not just a shallow stunt," *Forum* said, was in the process of the building's design, which was "more akin to plane design than to conventional methods of building design. Instead of using the age-old techniques of the architect and making complex drawings from which structures would be derived, Saarinen first made *models* from which the drawings were then made."[189] Eventually the design was crystallized: "One of the happiest days," Saarinen said, "was after we had worked out the supports in model form. Finally we were able to make drawings of what we actually had. In these drawings, we found that the support plans were marvelous looking things, showing forms that could never have been arrived at on paper."[190]

Realizing Saarinen's design in three dimensions proved difficult. "How does a contractor actually build a 'free-form' building, shaped like a big bird?" asked *Architectural Forum* in August 1960. The problem of constructing a building with a shape "like a huge piece of sculpture," *Forum* said, was "unprecedented."[191] Plotting the structure's lines of force, shaping it in detail, and engineering the structure as well as the scaffolding needed to hold the formwork for the poured-in-place concrete required the collaboration of the architects, the engineers and the contractor, Grove, Shepherd, Wilson & Kruge. The terminal's vaults would not have been affordable were it not for the ingenious system of formwork they designed, whereby the curved shapes were all built out of straight sectioned boards. The last of TWA's four roof shells was poured in early October 1960, and it was at this point—with no glass infill walls to compromise the sense of voided closure and no casework to compromise the sculpted terraces of the interior—that the building reached its most enthralling state. Visiting the site in April 1961, the last time before his death, Saarinen averred: "TWA is beginning to look marvelous. If anything happened and they had to stop work right now and just leave it in this state, I think it would make a beautiful ruin, like the Baths of Caracalla."[192]

The terminal was opened to the public on May 29, 1962, eight months after Saarinen's death at age fifty-one on September 1, 1961. The impression of the completed building was disappointing, not just because the glazing compromised the expressive form, but also because the shape itself seemed awkward. *Architectural Forum* was more favorably disposed to the building when it was viewed from ground level than from above; from grade, the editors said, it was "a stirring object, its structure swooping in high-speed curves all around, like an oversize Gaudi sculpture of the jet age." But overall, *Forum* said, the terminal looked "more like a giant horseshoe crab than a bird in flight."[193] In a letter to *Forum*, architect Remmert Huygens argued that despite its promised representation of flight,

TWA "sits low, flat and heavy on the ground. But why," he asked, "should a building try to fly at all?" Huygens argued that the building "attempts to be significant, so loudly that it is impossible to ignore."[194] Vincent Scully was also outspoken in his criticism of the terminal's self-conscious design, placing it in the context of Saarinen's corporate work as a whole: "The ingredients are always obvious, and they have remained the clients' delight: (a) one whammo shape, justified by (b) one whammo functional innovation . . . and by (c) one whammo structural exhibition, which is always threatening, visually at least, to come apart at the seams."[195]

Although the exterior may have been disappointing, the interior spaces were a fresh revelation of corporate Modernism's potential. Edgar Kaufmann, Jr., described the TWA terminal as "one of the few major works of American architecture in recent years that reaches its full stature *as an interior*." The exterior, he said, should be viewed in terms of its relationship to the interior:

> The strong shape outside, rhythmically modeled in receptive, cup-like sequences, prepares one partly for the serene shock of the interior. Space is defined by a full orchestration of curved forms, unfamiliar, but immediately comprehensible thanks to their bilateral correspondence around an open, unmistakable center. Light permeates this space from every direction and is reflected from the off-white and pale-gray concave surfaces; a light that is nowhere sharp, issuing from innumerable alternations of openings, reflections, and backlightings. Space, form, and light emerge into one effect.[196]

Visitors entered the building at principal portals that were swept around an extraordinarily modeled information desk and flight board. A white-tiled floor led up via exceptionally wide, shallow steps under a bridge to an enormous conversation-pit-like lounge carpeted in red. In this sequence, Kaufmann wrote, "the ordinary complex of travel facilities" was transmuted "into a festival of ordered movements and exhilarating vistas."[197] This was in keeping with Saarinen's goal, to create an interior experience in which "the human being felt uplifted, important and full of anticipation."[198] Off to either side, the low wings accommodated ticketing and baggage claim.

Saarinen's plan for the TWA interiors provided for five eating and drinking areas, but his firm was commissioned to design only the posh second-level Ambassador Club. They outfitted this rambling space with molded seating and pedestal tables, placing the furniture wherever possible in alcoves of the architectural shell, creating what Olga Gueft praised as "an appropriately organic space-age amalgam."[199] The office of Raymond Loewy/William Snaith designed the other four restaurants. While the Loewy/Snaith designs were sophisticated and some of the specially designed furniture was quite elegant, the thematic approach they were forced to adopt for the Lisbon Lounge, the London Club, and the Paris Café necessarily compromised the unity of Saarinen's space. The fourth eating spot designed by the firm was a snack bar.

In the late 1960s, as the volume of air traffic soared, TWA's interiors were renovated, but the fundamental character of the space remained. In 1973 John Morris Dixon wrote in *Progressive Architecture* that "TWA remains, despite unimaginable changes in airline procedures and passenger volumes over the past decade, an interior superbly attuned to the state of mind of the user; it remains the only air terminal I know where the threat of a delay is offset by the prospect of watching the movement of aircraft passengers and ground traffic form a variety of comfortable vantage points."[200]

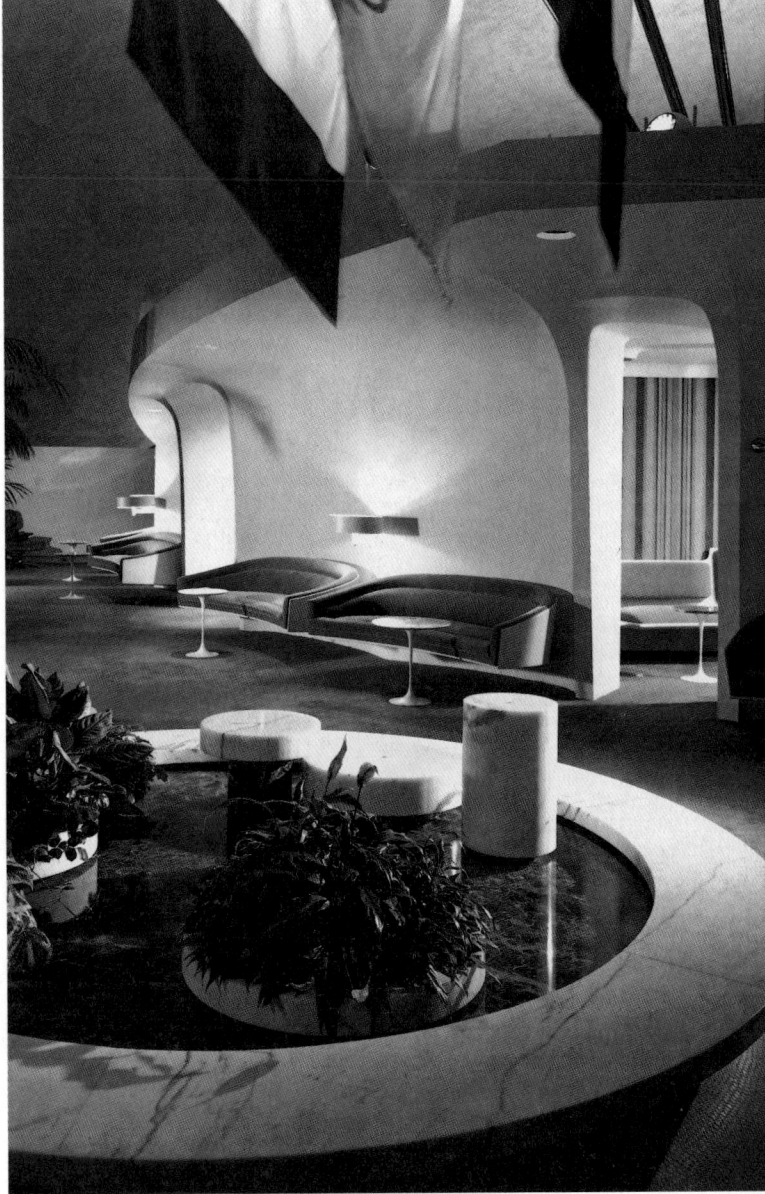

Ambassador Club, TWA terminal, Idlewild Airport. Eero Saarinen & Associates, 1962. Stoller. ©ESTO

Top left: National Airlines terminal, Idlewild Airport. I. M. Pei & Partners, 1971. View to the east. Naar. PCF

Top right: National Airlines terminal. View to the northeast from interior. Cserna. PCF

Bottom: Tri-Faith Chapels Plaza, Idlewild Airport. View to the northeast showing, from left to right: Jewish chapel (Bloch & Hesse, 1966), Protestant chapel (Edgar Tafel & Associates, 1966) and Catholic chapel (George J. Sole, 1966). PANY

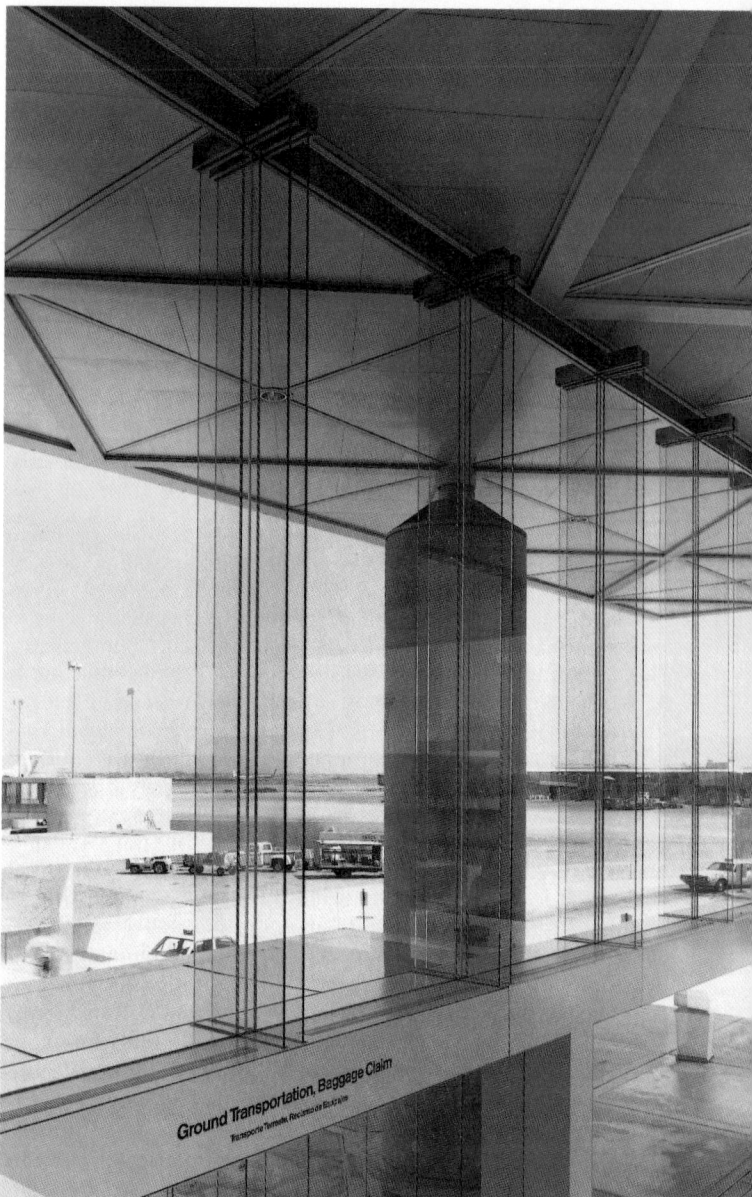

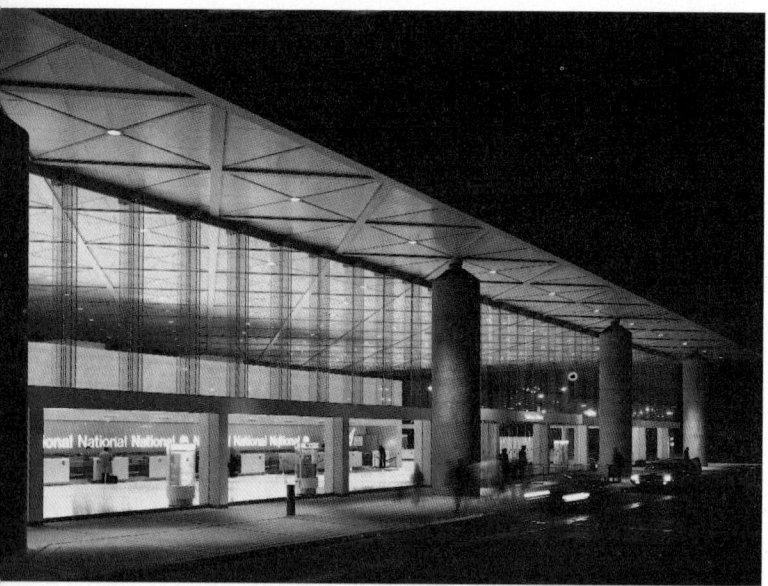

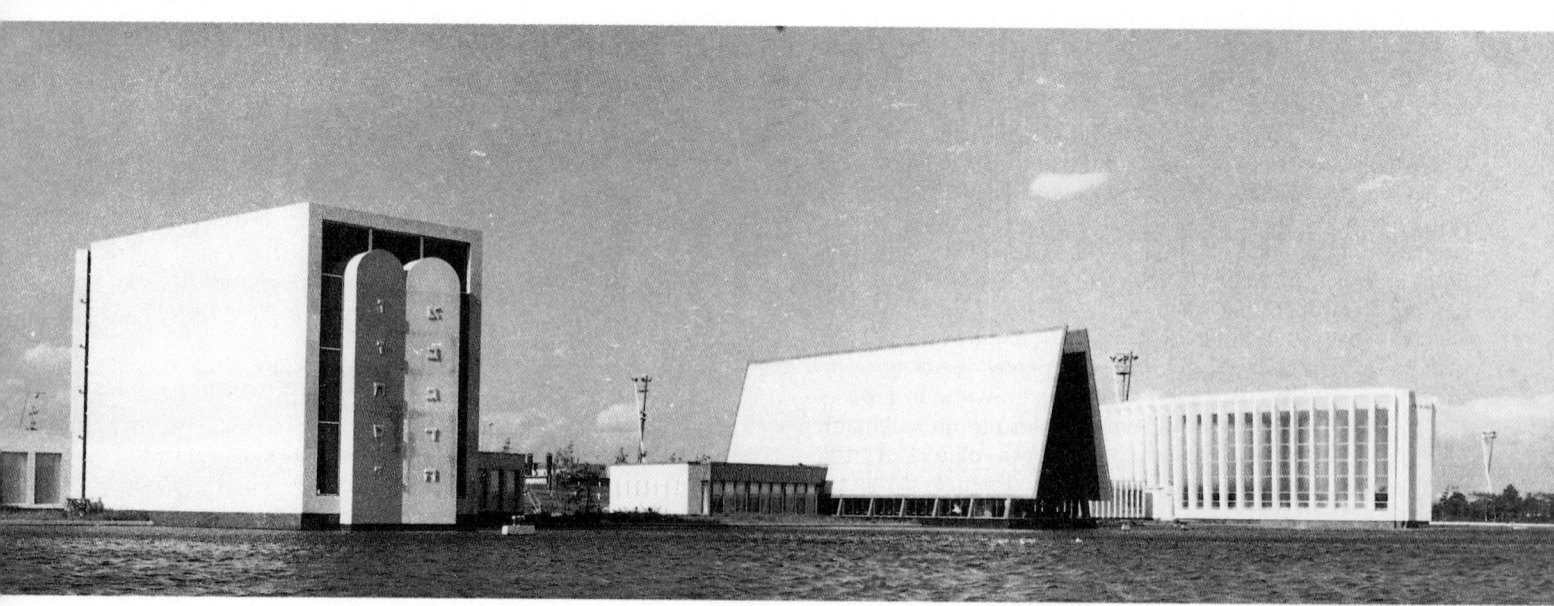

In 1961 a combined ten-gate terminal for Braniff, Northeast and Northwest Orient, designed by John Jamieson White of White & Mariani, was completed.[201] With a concrete canopy of three rows of thirty-six-foot octagonal slabs carried on central columns, the terminal was welcomed by Ada Louise Huxtable as "a simple, clean, direct, unpretentious structure of basically sound intentions, with an interior refreshingly free of overbearing materials or details. The result verges on distinction, but falls sharply short of it."[202]

In 1959 the Port Authority held a limited competition for a new multi-airline terminal, which would be the tenth terminal completed at the airport.[203] The competitors were I. M. Pei, B. Sumner Gruzen of Kelly & Gruzen, Arvin Shaw III of Carson, Lundin & Shaw, Morris Ketchum, Jr., of Ketchum & Sharp, and Philip Johnson. Gruzen's entry called for a free-form curved roof carried on a web of steel; Shaw proposed a series of saddle-shaped panel vaults that framed a two-story concourse; Ketchum advanced a strict rectilinear structure articulated by seven hollow brick piers, with concrete columns supporting a radiating exposed-concrete roof structure; and Johnson's design laced together an undulating concrete-plank roof with a grid of steel pipes resting on column clusters.

The jury, consisting of Wallace Harrison, Pietro Belluschi and Bancel LaFarge, selected I. M. Pei's scheme, which, they said, provided "good flexibility and has great clarity."[204] In contrast to the structural acrobatics of several of the other proposals, Pei's design, developed with his associates Henry N. Cobb, Leonard Jacobson and Kellogg Wong, and the engineers Ammann & Whitney, was for a large-span structure that defined a Classically inspired, 328-foot-long, 30-foot-high rectangular pavilion. Glazed on all four sides, it was roofed by a space frame made up of steel-pipe tetrahedrons arranged on a 12'6" grid, tied together at the top by a reinforced-concrete slab and at the bottom by tension cables. The composite roof structure was to be carried by gracefully tapered freestanding reinforced-concrete pylons located outside the glass walls. As the project dragged on, however, the roof was modified to a more conventional steel truss. More important, to handle far greater crowds than had originally been anticipated, the original scheme, which proposed two fingers leading directly to the terminal, was revised to provide a second vehicular drive behind the terminal for arriving passengers, and beyond that a two-level facility, connected to the terminal by bridges, containing departure lounges on the second level and luggage claim areas below.

By the time the new terminal opened in 1971, it was home to National Airlines. Through a decade of volatile changes, Pei's concept of a neutral pavilion had remained, although the terminal was repeatedly replanned. As built, the bold, 430-foot-long volume, with six columns supporting a white-painted fascia, looked serene and almost deferential. Pei's use of glass mullions, the first such use in America of a technique developed in Europe, provided structural clarity: as Pei explained, "When the mullions [at TWA] were strong enough to take the wind, they looked strong enough to support the building. . . . If the mullions are glass, there is no doubt about what is holding up the roof."[205]

Terminal City also included three freestanding chapels, sited in a row at the edge of the central landscaped mall and in front of the lagoon.[206] A temporary Roman Catholic chapel, Our Lady of the Skies, designed by George J. Sole, had already been built on a nearby site in 1955, but it was demolished in 1966 to make way for the BOAC terminal (see above).[207] Before the announcement of a coordinated site plan, Edgar Tafel had developed plans for a Protestant chapel whose thirty-five-foot-high nave was formed out of sloped coffered slabs.[208] In 1960–61 Tafel wrangled over the design with Wallace Harrison, who acted on the Port Authority's behalf. Tafel ultimately modified the chapel's shape, used stone instead of exposed concrete to clad the exterior and lowered the height to bring it in line with George Sole's new Catholic chapel and Walter Hesse's Jewish chapel, which would be built on either side of the Protestant one.[209] With the Protestant chapel reconfigured, the new ensemble consisted of three rectangular masses, each about 110 feet long, which seemed to cantilever out over the lagoon. Ground was broken for the three chapels in June 1963, and they were completed in 1965–66.[210] Despite the repetition of the massing, the so-called Tri-Faith Chapels Plaza failed to create a strong impact on the chaotic airport scene. The flattened hexagon of the Jewish chapel (International Synagogue), which included a museum and information center, faced the lagoon with two forty-foot-high tablets of the Ten Commandments; its 150-seat interior was said to be modeled after the old Touro Synagogue in Newport, Rhode Island. The forty-two-foot-high, oval-shaped Catholic chapel featured an aluminum statue of Our Lady of the Skies above the altar.

The 1955 master plan for Idlewild also called for a 240-room hotel to be erected near the airport's perimeter. Designed by William Tabler, with public rooms decorated by Dorothy Draper, the International Hotel (1958) was a blandly Modernist 320-room facility, described by Architectural Forum as "efficient but architecturally unexciting."[211] As air traffic grew, other hotels would be built by private developers just outside the airport, though none had architectural distinction. Leo Kornblath's 1962 design for a Guggenheim-inspired hotel with 420 rooms spiraling around a glass-domed atrium would have been a spectacular exception, but it was not realized.[212]

One last building rounded out Terminal City's facilities: a gas station. Designed by Edward Durell Stone for the Gulf Oil Corporation (1959), it was a miniaturization—and a trivialization—of Stone's notable United States Embassy Building (1954) in New Delhi, India.[213] Ada Louise Huxtable dismissed it is as "an unpardonable reductio ad absurdum" of Stone's earlier triumph, "its screen walls one more discordant personal mannerism in the general turmoil."[214]

Just beyond Terminal City, along the access road, SOM designed a far more convincing commercial facility, for First National City Bank (1959), a minimally detailed, nine-bay, square pavilion, with the piano nobile of the banking hall lifted on pilotis and the drive-in services tucked under the resultant ground-level arcade.[215]

Most observers agreed that, while the individual buildings at Idlewild were of varying quality, the airport as a whole was an urbanistic failure. Rather than viewing it as the cohesive urban place implied by the name Terminal City, many critics referred to it as an "architectural zoo," a phrase first used in the late 1950s. Huxtable regarded it as "a curious exercise in architectural anarchy" in which "nothing focuses; everything fights. The terminal buildings wage incessant war on one another through their aggressively individualistic and unrelated design."[216]

In December 1963 Idlewild was renamed John F. Kennedy International Airport (JFK) to honor the assassinated president.[217] By this time the growth of air travel, which dangerously crowded the skies over all major airports, also slowed the roadways leading to and through airports. And in the case of JFK, there was no rapid transit to ease the congestion. The airport's original planners, who could not foresee the tremendous postwar growth of

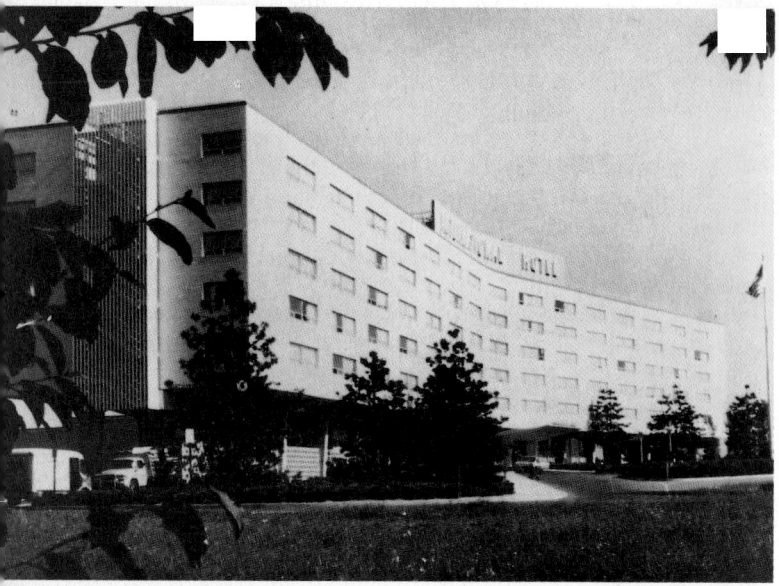

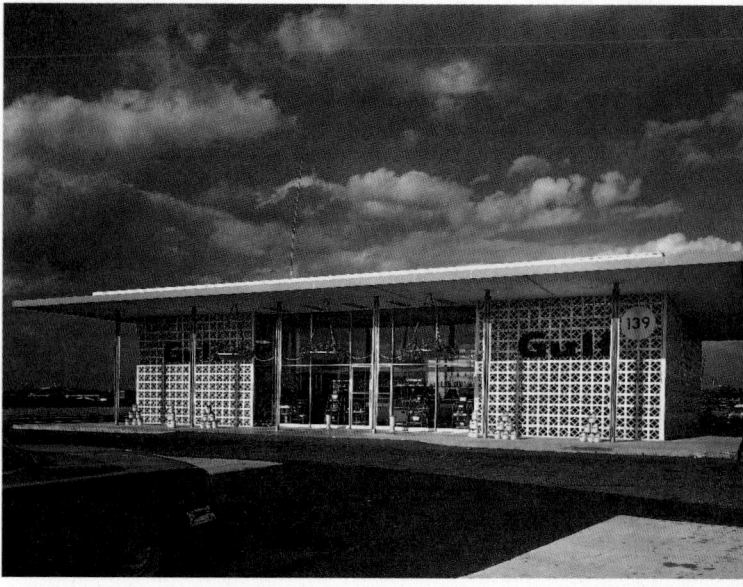

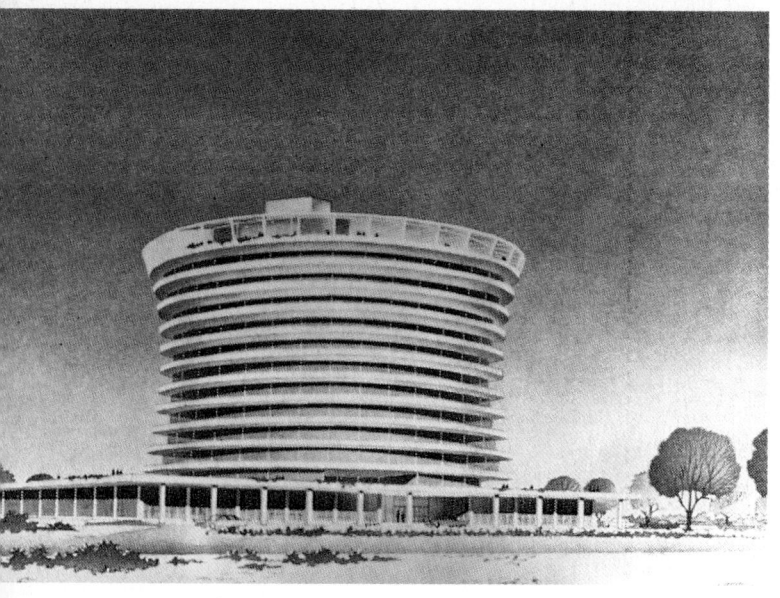

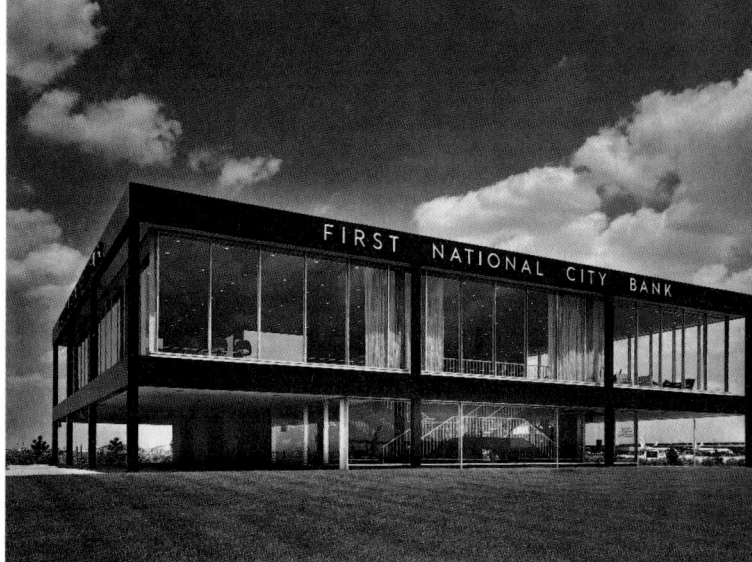

Top: International Hotel, Idlewild Airport. William Tabler, 1958. View to the northwest. WBT

Bottom: Proposal for hotel, Idlewild Airport. Leo Kornblath, 1962. AF. CU

Top: Gulf Oil Corporation gas station, Idlewild Airport. Edward Durell Stone, 1959. View to the northwest. Molitor. JWM

Bottom: First National City Bank, Idlewild Airport. Skidmore, Owings & Merrill, 1959. View to the east. Molitor. JWM

both automobile and air traffic, had argued that the trip to the airport from Manhattan would take only twenty-six minutes via the projected Van Wyck Expressway. In fact, however, at peak hours, ground traffic to and from the airport seemed almost perpetually halted. Other aspects of the airport also functioned less and less well as air traffic increased. When, on a weekend in February 1969, seventeen inches of snow trapped 6,000 people at the airport and the city failed to respond quickly enough with snow-removal equipment to clear the access highways, the story of the airport's inadequate facilities and services became international news, embarassing both the city and the Port Authority.[218]

To meet the requirements of the so-called second jet revolution, marked by the introduction of large-capacity, long-range "jumbo" passenger jet aircraft in 1969, the Port Authority and various airlines sought to expand and upgrade their terminal facilities.[219] In 1970 TWA added the second wing originally called for in the Saarinen design, retaining Saarinen's successors, Kevin Roche and John Dinkeloo, for the job.[220] Pan American, whose terminal could not easily be expanded, completely rebuilt its facility (see above). No substantial expansion of the international arrivals complex was possible because it was sited between the loop roadway system and a principal runway, but passenger volume was reduced by locating customs halls in the terminals of America-based carriers so that only foreign-flag carriers used the facility.

Most architects and planners believed that the real answer to the airport's problems lay in the expansion of the airfield itself. In 1960 architect E. N. Turano proposed the creation of a new system of precast-concrete runways carried on piles over Jamaica Bay.[221] Other, similarly "futuristic" schemes, which were both expensive and ecologically problematic, were offered throughout the decade.[222] In the late 1960s, when the Port Authority began to consider expanding the airport, it too explored the possibility of extending runways into the bay, where it was conceivable that in the future a completely new terminal complex would be constructed and connections made to a new complex at Floyd Bennett Field.

Toward the end of the 1960s, however, the area's air traffic began to decrease, in part because of the city's economic decline, in part because for the first time long-range aircraft made it possible to handle nonstop European traffic out of American cities other than New York.[223] Furthermore, the Port Authority began to recognize the ecological problems that expansion would create. Spurred on by environmentalists raising questions about the ecological impact of expansion, the Port Authority called on the Environmental Studies Board, a joint board of the National Academy of Sciences and the National Academy of Engineering, to examine the problem. Their report, *Jamaica Bay and Kennedy Airport: A Multidisciplinary Environmental Study*, concluded that any runway construction would not only cause irreversible ecological danger to the natural environment but would also be detrimental to existing neighborhoods exposed to aircraft noise.[224]

With the possibility of expanding JFK remote, some planners, arguing that increasing population dispersion made the airport's location less and less central, called for a totally new facility or a site distant from the metropolitan area. The airport would be reached by most travelers via STOL-craft (short take-off and landing, commuter-type planes) from the Port Authority's existing airports as well as from smaller facilities, such as those at White Plains and Islip.

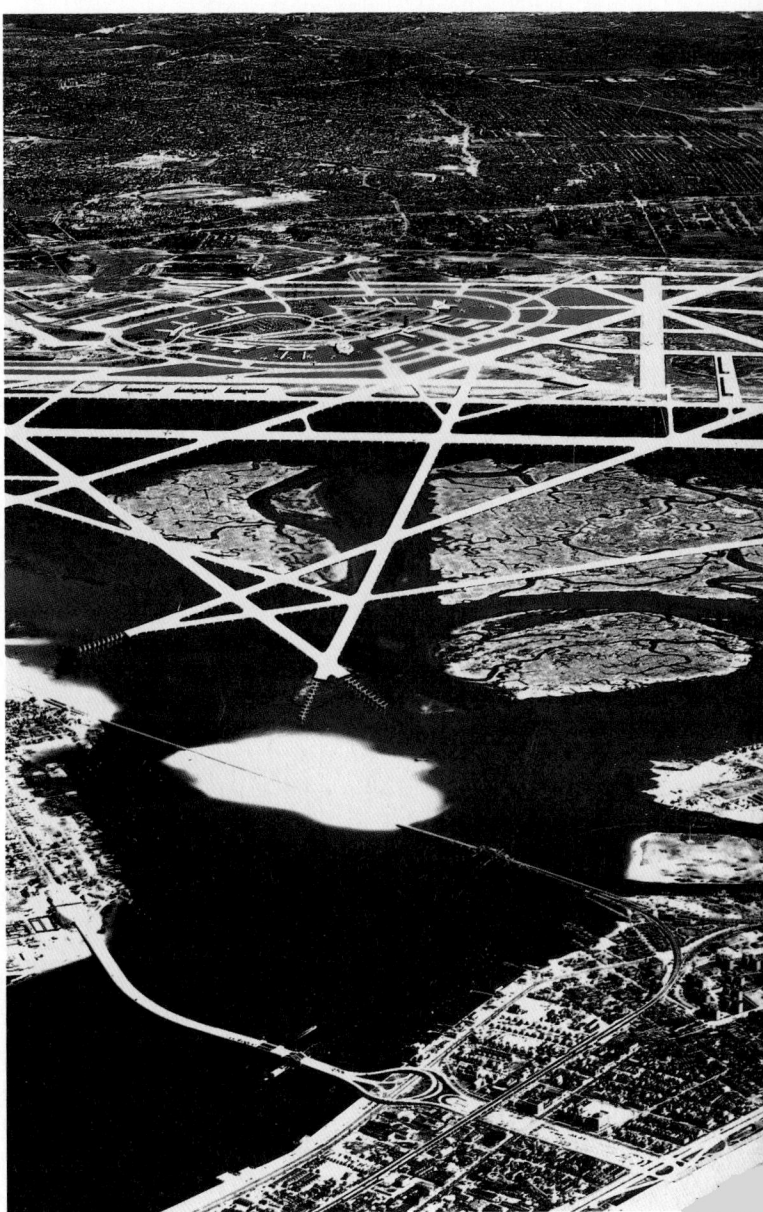

Proposal for runway system on piles over Jamaica Bay, Idlewild Airport. E. N. Turano, 1960. Photographic montage showing aerial view to the northeast. ENT

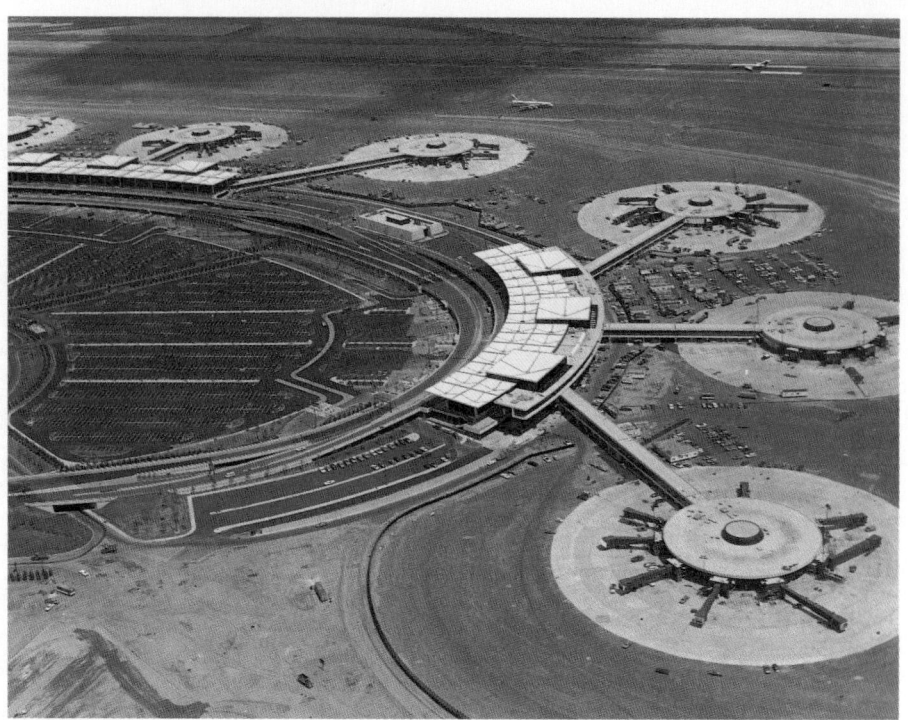

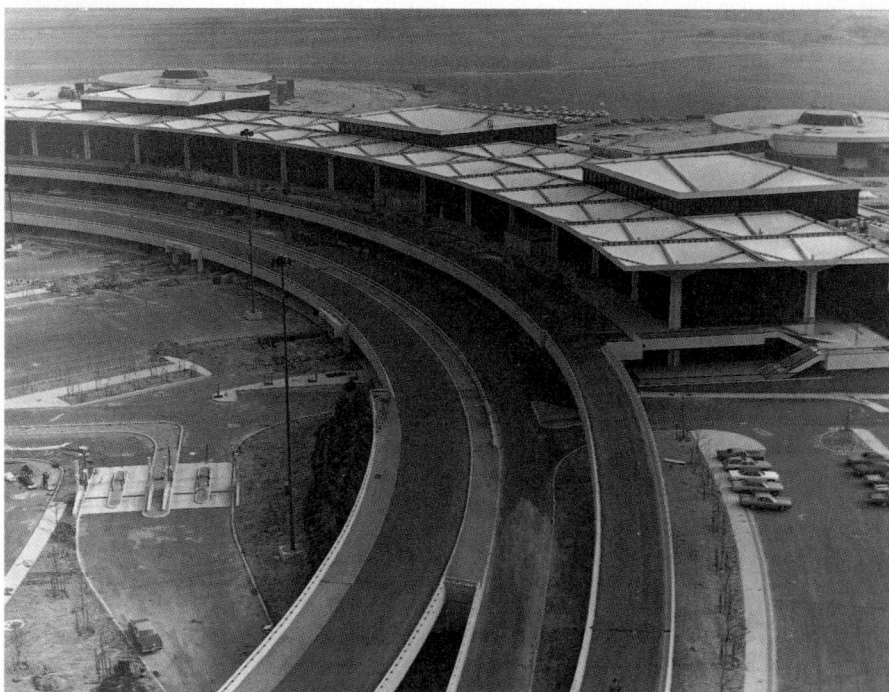

Top: Newark Airport, Newark, New Jersey
John P. Veerling, Sheldon D. Wander and
George E. Ralph, 1974. View to the east.
PANY

Bottom: Newark Airport. View to the
southeast. PANY

The Port Authority had steadfastly argued for a fourth jet-port since 1959, when they proposed a site in Morris County, New Jersey.[225] That site was opposed not only by the airlines but also by environmentalists, who eventually secured protection for the area as a National Wildlife Refuge. The Port Authority's second choice was Solberg, Hunterdon County, New Jersey, a site that was finally quashed by Governor William Cahill, who in his 1969 election bid campaigned against it or any other new jetport in New Jersey. The Port Authority then focused on Calverton Air Force Base on the eastern end of Long Island, Pine Island in Orange County, New York, and later on Stewart Air Force Base in Newburgh, Orange County, a sixty-five-mile drive from Columbus Circle in Manhattan.[226] New York State ac-

quired Stewart in 1970; in 1971 it acquired an additional 8,657 adjoining acres to bring the total size of the proposed field to 10,209 acres, twice that of JFK. A report prepared for the state called for the conversion of Stewart into a major jetport by 1990 to handle 36,000,000 passengers per year.

In 1971 the Federal Aviation Agency sponsored a study that considered the feasibility of constructing an airport off Long Island's shores to ultimately replace JFK and perhaps even La Guardia as well. But the Regional Plan Association raised doubts about this plan, and the Environmental Studies Board's *Jamaica Bay and Kennedy Airport* report recommended that the offshore plan be abandoned. The report also strongly suggested that the Port Authority solve its problems at JFK by building a new airport, intensifying the hunt for a site. One thing was certain by the early 1970s: no expansion of existing facilities or any new airport construction would be permitted without the support of an ecologically sensitized electorate. But by the mid-1970s, as air traffic began to rise again, no decisions about a fourth jetport had been made.

In addition to La Guardia and JFK, the other major airport in the metropolitan area was New Jersey's Newark Airport, located about sixteen miles west of midtown Manhattan. Newark, which opened in 1929, was also taken over by the Port Authority in 1947.[227] It was to function as a companion to La Guardia by providing short-haul service for Jerseyites, leaving Idlewild to supply the transcontinental and international service for the entire New York region. In 1950 the Port Authority announced the construction of a new terminal, which was completed in 1953.[228] Designed by the Port Authority's staff architects, in consultation with A. Gordon Lorimer, the terminal was a 150,000-square-foot building resembling the Port Authority's bus terminal in Manhattan. The sole focus of the exterior, which had horizontal strip windows, was an enormous projecting entrance. Inside, the plan was simple and clear: the high-ceilinged, 500-foot-long, 166-foot-wide concourse was spacious and almost grandly monumental. The Newarker restaurant, located on the upper level at the west end of the terminal, quickly became known for a standard of cuisine and service unusual for an airport. The new terminal's completion coincided with the airport's reopening after public concern over three crashes, which killed a total of ten residents in the abutting town of Elizabeth, New Jersey, had forced the airport authorities to close down the entire operation in February 1952.[229]

Though a new, 150-foot-tall control tower was completed in 1960, little else was done to develop the facility, which continued to be regarded by most New Yorkers as a provincial outpost.[230] This all changed in 1965, when the Port Authority undertook a $150 million expansion program intended to double the airport's capacity.[231] The basic concept, heavily influenced by the work of Minoru Yamasaki, who was serving as a consultant to the Port Authority as well as the architect for the agency's World Trade Center (see chapter 3), was developed by a team of Port Authority architects, including John P. Veerling, Sheldon D. Wander and George E. Ralph. The Grad Partnership executed the interiors of Terminal A, and Abbott, Merkt & Company handled those in Terminal B (both completed in 1974); Terminal C was deferred for a future date. Wald & Zigas took a strong hand in developing the dramatic indirect lighting that flooded the underside of the reinforced-concrete hyperbolic paraboloids on tapered columns—the structural parasols that were the principal agents of closure in the terminals.

Each terminal was arc-shaped to fit the plan of the vast oval described by the access roadways. The oval contained surface parking, while covered parking was accommodated in the terminals. The terminals were designed with a split-level cross section; grade-level parking was placed below two levels of roadway, the first for arrival and the second for departure. These were all interconnected with stairs, elevators and escalators to the midlevel concourse, which led, via 600-foot-long arcades, to remote boarding lounges. The scheme combined the best aspects of the rebuilt La Guardia—the arc-shaped building plan and the uniform architectural expression—with the decentralization of Idlewild, resulting in what was, from the passenger's point of view, the New York area's most easily comprehended airport.

On the far side of Jamaica Bay and to its east, in what had been the town of Hempstead before the creation of the consolidated city, were the Rockaways, including Arverne and other small communities that had functioned as oceanfront resorts for almost a hundred years.[232] Accessible from Manhattan by the Long Island Railroad since 1892, and after 1925 by a series of causeways that carried Woodhaven Boulevard south across Broad Channel, supplemented in 1937 by the Marine Parkway Bridge (David Steinman), the Rockaways that were within the city limits were far from fashionable, although Neponsit and Belle Harbor had a certain middle-class status.[233] In 1953 the city's Transit Authority took over the operation of the Rockaway line from the virtually bankrupt Long Island Railroad, which had petitioned to abandon Rockaway service after a particularly bad fire ruined nearly 1,800 feet of trestle on May 7, 1950.[234] After massive rebuilding efforts, on June 28, 1956, the city opened the Rockaway branch of the Independent line and created its first two-fare zone. In order to complete the line, the Transit Authority had built two small islands in Jamaica Bay to provide a roadbed for the subway trestle.

With the Rockaways cheaply, if not swiftly, connected to the central city (the ride from Columbus Circle to Far Rockaway took sixty-seven minutes), the shorefront seemed poised for development. Certainly the subway made it a lot easier to get to the area's beaches, the most notable of which was Jacob Riis Park (1933–37).[235] But it also attracted far more people to the area not just for a day's outing but to take up residence in the hundreds of marginal wood bungalows that, like those in Coney Island, had been built in the 1920s as cheap seasonal accommodation. Like postwar Coney Island, Arverne and Far Rockaway quickly became blighted slums, thereby provoking massive renewal efforts, including the construction of several housing projects by the Housing Authority. The first of these, Arverne Houses (Simeon Heller, 1950), located on an 8.5-acre site on Beach Channel Drive between Beach Fifty-fourth and Beach Fifty-sixth streets, consisted of fourteen six-story buildings housing 400 families.[236] Two years later, in Far Rockaway, the sixteen-building, six-story, 450-unit Redfern Houses, designed by the redoubtable Andrew J. Thomas, was opened on a twenty-acre site bounded by Redfern Avenue, Beach Channel Drive, Hassock Street and the Queens-Nassau border.[237] Also in Far Rockaway, the privately financed Wavecrest Gardens (Maxon-Sells, 1952) consisted of fourteen six-story red-brick buildings that occupied only 20 percent of a thirty-four-acre site bounded by Fernside Place, Plainview Avenue, Beach Twentieth Street and the Boardwalk that had previously been the location of a convalescent home.[238] A private pedestrian walk leading from the apartment buildings to the Boardwalk and beach set the complex apart from typical government-sponsored work. Six underground garages, accommodating 721 cars, were built between the buildings and featured landscaped sitting areas on their roofs, which extended just above ground level. A two-acre, one-story shopping center, also designed by Maxon-Sells, served Wavecrest Gardens' 1,656 families.

Several interesting housing projects were built in the area during the 1970s. Gruzen & Partners' Roy Reuther Houses (1971), at 711 Seagirt Avenue, between Beach Sixth and Beach Eighth streets, faced out to sea and consisted of four staggered superslabs of varying heights between thirteen and twenty-five stories.[239] A 915-unit, middle-income complex, it was built for the elderly by the United Automobile Workers. In Arverne, Carl Koch & Associates' Ocean Village (1975), Rockaway Beach

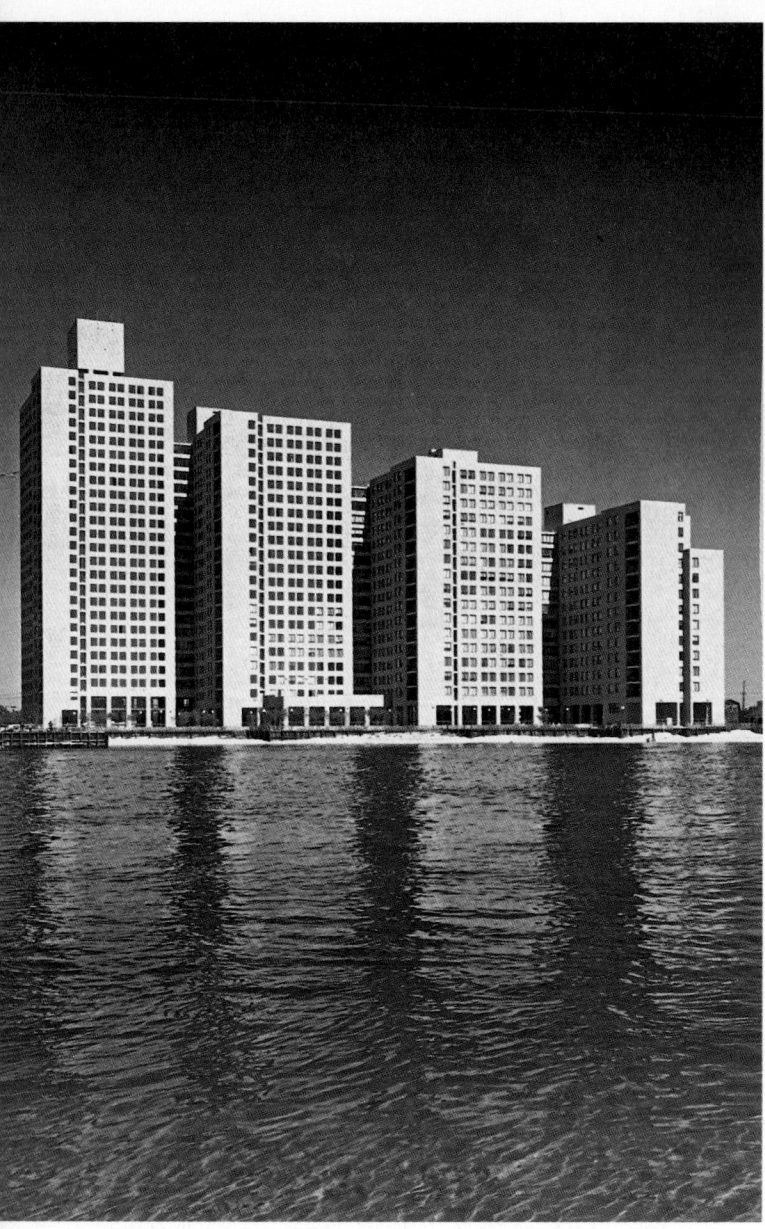

Roy Reuther Houses, 711 Seagirt Avenue, between Beach Sixth and Beach Eighth streets, Far Rockaway. Gruzen & Partners, 1971. View to the north. GS

Boulevard to the Boardwalk, between Beach Fifty-sixth and Beach Fifty-ninth streets, with precast-concrete and brick slabs and towers wrapping around a courtyard, was one of the city's few realized experiments in prefabrication.[240] Built by the New York State Urban Development Corporation, it consisted of eleven buildings containing 1,100 units.

One distinctive school facility was also built in the area, Victor Lundy's Intermediate School 53 (1972), the Brian Piccolo School, named for the football star who died of cancer in 1970.[241] Located at 1045 Nameoke Street, between Cornaga and Mott avenues, Beach Eighteenth Street and Foam Place, just south of Redfern Houses, the structure was far and away the most inventive of the inward-looking schools being designed at the time. To get away from the typically monolithic configuration of city schools, Lundy organized the brick-clad building into three connected four-story elements enclosing a courtyard, which was entered from the street under a bridge connecting the classrooms with the gymnasium. Taking advantage of an oddly shaped, multiangled site, the bridge paralleled the angle of Nameoke Street and served as the school's main approach. Each floor of the otherwise windowless building was stepped back from the one below, creating slots of windows that washed the classroom walls with light.

At the western end of the Rockaway barrier beach, where it formed a peninsula, lay Breezy Point. Here a community of privately owned bungalows and year-round homes, locally known as the Irish Riviera, had existed since 1910 on 400 acres leased from private developers. In 1960 the homeowners purchased the land from Breezy Point Ventures and created a gated cooperative of 2,650 houses, similar in spirit to Sea Gate, the private, turn-of-the-century enclave on Coney Island's western tip.[242] Breezy Point Ventures, which had acquired the property from the Rockaway Point Development Corporation only a year before, retained ownership of the 3.5-mile-long tract running on either side of the cooperative from Rockaway Point to Fort Tilden. When the developers announced plans to build a "city within a city" consisting of high-rise apartment houses, shopping centers, private clubs, schools and other community facilities, opposition quickly materialized. The Regional Plan Association proposed that the entire area be turned into a vast waterfront park, a plan that was supported by most civic groups but opposed by local government officials, the new cooperative's homeowners and the developers, now known as the Atlantic Improvement Corporation.[243]

Amid the swirling debate, construction began on the project, designed by Tippetts-Abbett-McCarthy-Stratton, which was to include 6,900 units of middle-income housing on a 217-acre site bounded by Beach 183rd Street above Fort Tilden, Beach 201st Street, Rockaway Inlet and the ocean. In 1963, as structural work on two fifteen-story apartment towers reached the eleventh floor, the city announced that it was going ahead with the park proposal and began condemnation proceedings on Atlantic Improvement's holdings. In 1969, after six years of debate and litigation, the federal government stepped in and proposed to include Breezy Point in a massive, 26,000-acre national park that would also include Fort Tilden, Jacob Riis Park, Jamaica Bay, Floyd Bennett Field, Great Kills Park, and Sandy Hook in New Jersey.[244] The owners of the Breezy Point Cooperative would be permitted to keep their homes but had to forfeit their mile-long ocean frontage to allow for an uninterrupted stretch of beach from Jacob Riis Park to Rockaway Point. Three years later, on October 28, 1972, President Nixon signed legislation creating the Gateway National Recreation Area.[245]

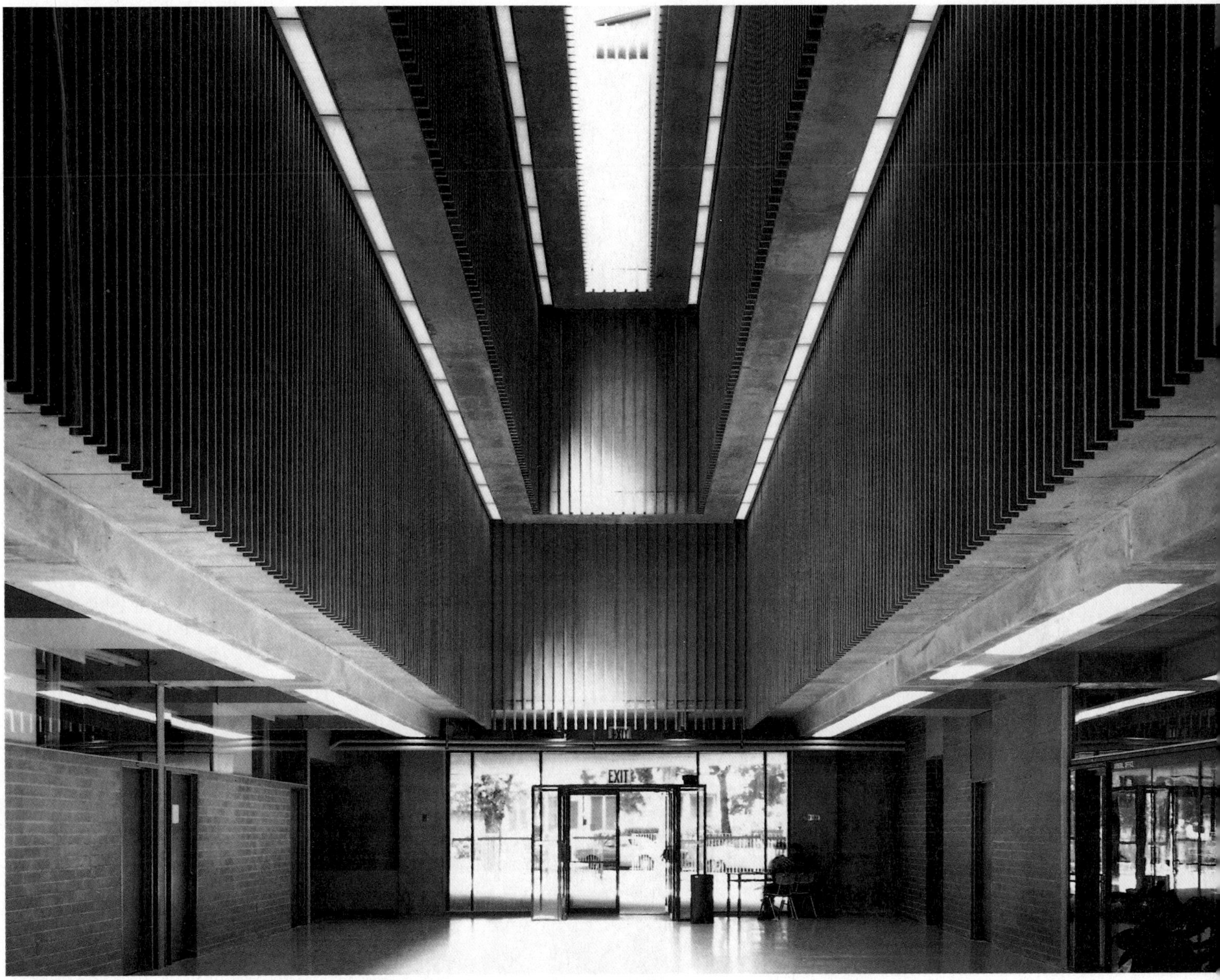

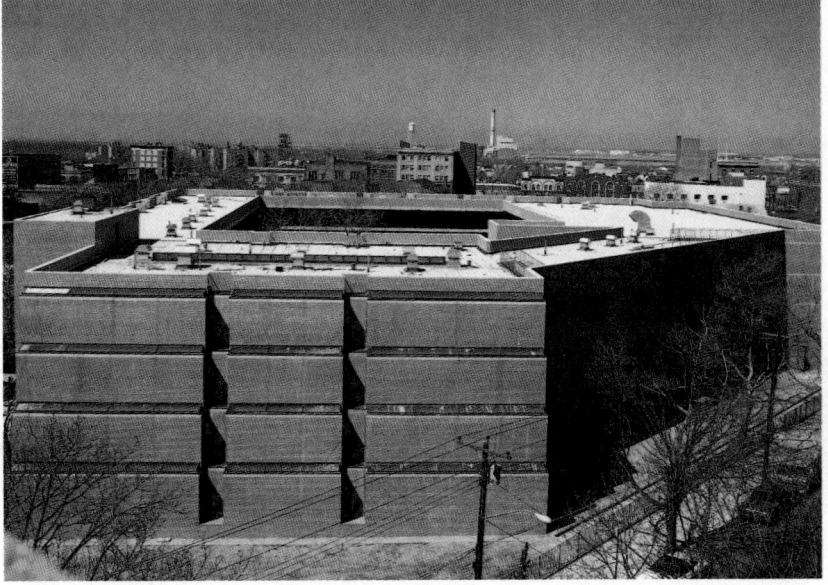

Above: Brian Piccolo School, Intermediate School 53, 1045 Nameoke Street, between Cornaga and Mott avenues, Beach Eighteenth Street and Foam Place, Far Rockaway. Victor Lundy, 1972. Interior. Cserna. GC

Left: Brian Piccolo School, Intermediate School 53. View to the south. Cserna. GC

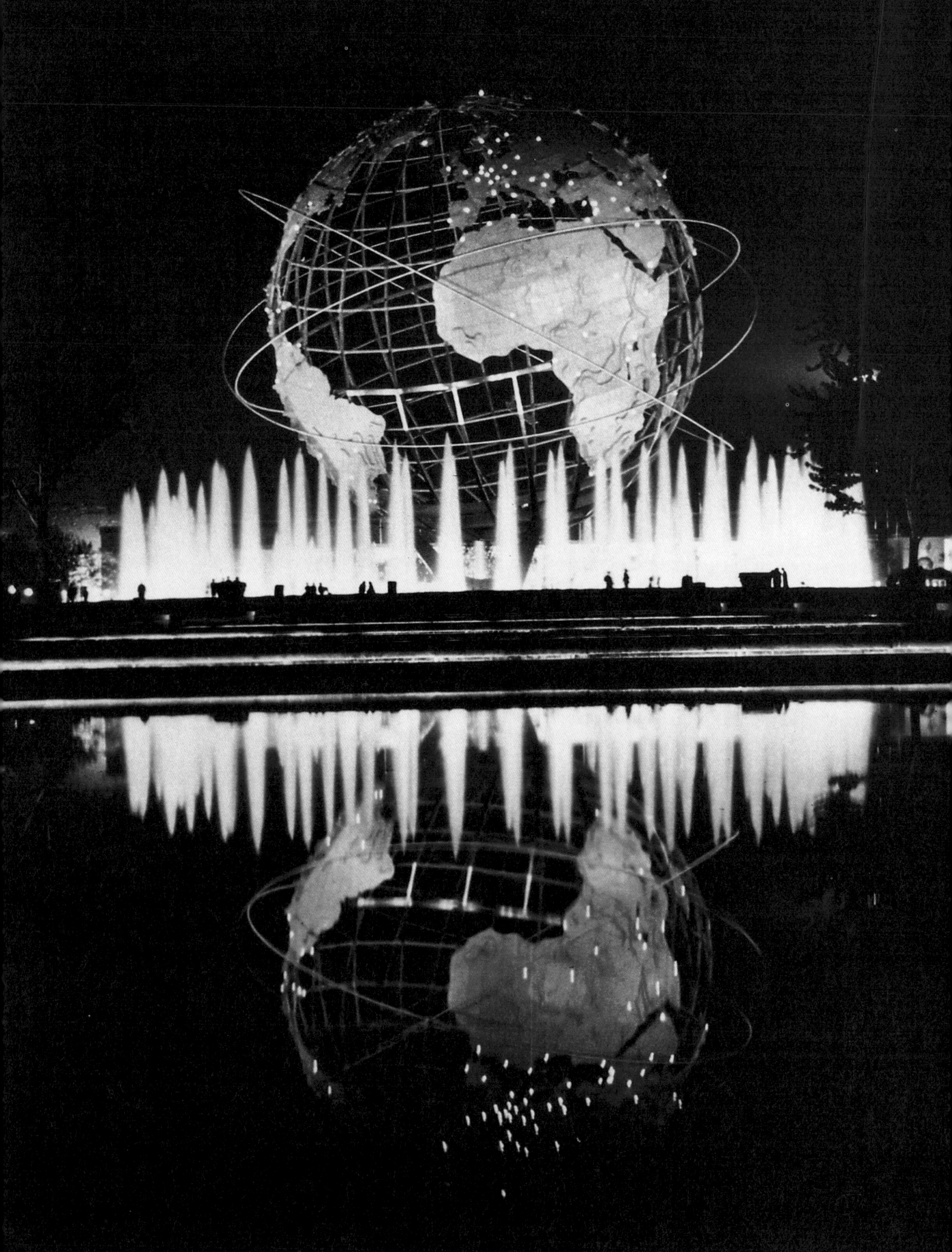

Chapter 14

1964-65 New York World's Fair

Nobody departs, until it closes,
From the Promised Land of Mr. Moses.
—Ogden Nash, 1964[1]

In 1959, twenty years after the "World of Tomorrow" took shape on reclaimed dumping grounds at the edge of Flushing Bay in Queens, another New York World's Fair was proposed.[2] Organized by Thomas J. Deegan, Jr., a public relations executive who served as chairman of the fair's planning committee, the fair was projected to open in 1964 and to be the largest exposition ever held.[3] As with its predecessor, whose ostensible purpose was to commemorate the 150th anniversary of George Washington's inauguration as president, a dubious official reason was provided for the 1964–65 fair: it would celebrate the 300th anniversary of the name "New York."

In contrast to the joyful and liberating futurism of the 1939–40 fair's "World of Tomorrow" theme, the 1964–65 fair took a more sober view of the human condition, with the theme of "Peace Through Understanding." From an architectural point of view the two fairs were quite different as well. The 1939–40 fair showcased a pivotal moment in the course of world architecture, presenting shifting styles and ideologies in European and American work and marking the emergence of American aesthetic hegemony. The 1964–65 fair came at a time of relative calm within the profession, complacency even, in which the conventions of Modernism were widely accepted and its American interpretation was the virtually unchallenged world standard. Although the 1964–65 fair was widely criticized by many intellectuals and artists as self-serving, cynical boosterism, it did offer an opportunity, as Edmund Bacon, the Philadelphia city planner, pointed out in a letter to the editors of *Progressive Architecture*, for architects to study it "as a means of taking stock of where we are going."[4]

According to the journalist Martin Mayer, the 1964–65 fair was originally the brainchild of Robert Kopple, "a bony, nervous, oddly idealist lawyer," who, early in 1958, reminiscing about the 1939–40 World's Fair of his youth, proposed the idea of another international exposition to help educate the younger generation.[5] Kopple gained the support of several influential friends and acquaintances, but he required federal authorization of the fair since private citizens could not solicit foreign governments to build pavilions. New York's bid faced opposition from an international exposition proposed for Washington, D.C., that was supported by Senator J. William Fulbright, among others.[6] Because the Bureau of International Expositions in Paris limited a nation to one major fair per decade, President Eisenhower appointed an ad hoc advisory group to decide which city should receive federal approval.[7] The New York delegation that went to Washington included Mayor Robert F. Wagner, Governor Nelson A. Rockefeller and Robert Moses, who saw the proposed fair as an opportunity to further his vision for Flushing Meadows, the site for the 1939–40 fair he had created but never fully realized on the former Corona dump. Although New York was chosen over the nation's capital, bitter political fighting left a feeling of animosity between the two metropolises, and two years later Senator Fulbright temporarily obstructed the appropriation of funds for the fair's United States Pavilion.[8]

With federal approval granted, the New York World's Fair 1964–1965 Corporation, established in 1959, began to look for a president.[9] Among the numerous people considered was Robert Moses, whom Kopple opposed, arguing that the seventy-year-old Moses was too old, that he lacked aesthetic judgment and that his aggressive personal style would not be effective in persuading major corporations and foreign countries to participate. Nonetheless, Moses was offered the job and accepted it.[10] There was cynical political logic in the choice of Moses, as Mary Perot Nichols suggested in the *Village Voice*. Mayor Wagner and his administration were eager to see him leave his post in the city's slum clearance program following the Title I scandals. Nichols wrote:

> One might have thought that after the monumental mess Robert Moses and his associates made of New York City's slum clearance program, our City Fathers would have been more than content to present him with a solid gold erector set and the assurance that parting is a sweet but necessary sorrow. . . . But no, Mayor Robert F. Wagner . . . decided to give Mr. Moses and almost the whole cast of characters from the Slum Clearance Committee fiasco a great public park free of charge,

Unisphere, New York World's Fair, Flushing Meadows, Queens. Gilmore D. Clarke and Peter Müller-Munk Associates, 1964. Night view to the west. NYPL back it up with city treasury, and allow them to set up a kind of real estate corporation, now popularly known as the New York World's Fair of 1964–65.[11]

Nichols went on to quote Douglas Haskell, the architectural critic and editor of *Architectural Forum*, as saying, "They had to sacrifice the World's Fair in order to save New York City."[12] The editors of *Progressive Architecture* similarly noted that some observers were "torn between sorrow that Moses would be in charge of such an international showplace for architecture, and joy that, at last, he would no longer be powerful in city jobs. One architect said, 'It's a hell of an expensive way to get rid of him!'"[13]

Moses accepted the job on one condition: that Kopple be removed from the committee; Kopple soon resigned. Upon assuming his post, Moses took charge with customary vigor, making three decisions that would prove critical in determining the fair's character. First, he decided not to cooperate with the Bureau of International Expositions, dismissing it as "three people living obscurely in a dumpy apartment in Paris," and to appeal directly to foreign governments; the bureau promptly issued an official disapproval of the fair and requested that member nations not participate.[14] Second, remembering the 1939–40 fair's dismal financial record, in which bondholders were returned only thirty-nine cents on every dollar invested, Moses decided to charge high rents and take a high percentage of all concession earnings. Even taking inflationary trends into consideration, the decision to rent space at ten times the rate charged in 1939–40 represented a significant increase that in large measure would determine who could afford to participate in the fair. In 1939 businesses could afford to exhibit on a whim; in 1964 they could exhibit only if the probability of meeting their expenses was high. Moses's third significant decision was that the fair corporation itself would build as few pavilions as possible, a move that prevented any coordinated palnning by, in effect, surrendering architectural control to outside forces. In contrast, nearly one third of the pavilions at the 1939–40 fair, including the instantly recognizable and highly memorable Theme Center, consisting of the Trylon and Perisphere, had been built by the fair corporation. The tone of stylistic moderation established by the organizers of the earlier fair had provided both an overall sense of visual harmony and a quiet foil to the more exuberant designs of individual exhibitions. Moses's vision, however, was based on bottom-line, not aesthetic, considerations; despite inflation, Moses would build the 1964–65 fair for little more than the cost of the 1939–40 fair.

Moses's approach dashed the hopes of those who sought to create an overall plan that would be both innovative and cohesive, including a five-member design committee, appointed by the fair corporation and organized by Wallace K. Harrison, that had proposed a comprehensive plan.[15] The committee, which included Edward Durell Stone, Gordon Bunshaft, the industrial designer Henry Dreyfuss and the engineer Emil H. Praeger, had proposed a variety of site configurations, ultimately advocating a "doughnut plan" calling for a single unified composition focused around the lake. This plan, which relied heavily on construction sponsored by the fair itself, was rejected in October 1960 in favor of reusing a pattern of individual pavilions sited similarly to those in the 1939–40 fair, which would yield a heterogenous landscape of shapes anchored to a stiffly Classical, twenty-five-year-old plan.[16] The fair corporation argued that, in addition to cutting costs, using the existing structure of sidewalks, water and sewage pipes and underground wiring would allow for easier reconversion of the site to a park.

When the fair corporation rejected the design committee's plan, Bunshaft resigned. Several weeks later, once they realized, as the editors of *Time* would later write, "that no one was going to mastermind more than grass seed," the other members resigned as well, although Harrison retained his position as the only architect on the fair's 100-member executive committee.[17] Although Moses issued a statement in November declaring that the design committee had completed its work and retired, the members refused to bow out gracefully, publicly stating that they had resigned for ideological reasons. "I quit because I didn't want to participate in something I didn't believe in," Bunshaft said. "We were trying to design a plan that would be an expression for our times. Mr. Moses and board wanted a repeat of the old World's Fair plan of 1939. Why should architects hang around four years beating an old cat?"[18]

Criticism of the fair corporation's decision to use the old plan was immediate. The December 1960 issue of *Architectural Forum* said: "The New York World's Fair for 1964 seems to be going forward now on the quaint theory that world's fairs are the one kind of amusement that requires no artistry in the planning. . . . It is the first fair to depend entirely on what it can get cheaply out of a shabby old ground plan that was already obsolete in 1939 when it was first put into operation." The journal lamented the wider implications of the fair's conventional plan: "The New York World's Fair threatens to convey an impression of immaturity and arrested cultural development that many foreign observers will ascribe to the U.S. as a whole."[19] The architect and industrial designer George Nelson observed that "the old plan is being repeated a quarter-century later because—in the immortal words of Sir Edmund Hillary—it was there."[20]

Moses had become so unpopular among architects that the editors of *Progressive Architecture* characterized him as the "Fair Fuehrer."[21] And Moses gave architects every reason to be concerned. In a speech delivered at Brandeis University on March 23, 1961, he stated, with no irony intended, that the fair would have "no predominating architectural concept."[22] In another context he proclaimed:

> The Fair administration belongs to no architectural clique, subscribes to no aesthetic creed, favors no period or school, and worships at no artistic shrine. . . . I get a little weary of the avant garde critics who see in a World's Fair only an opportunity to advance their latest ideas, to establish a new school of American planning, architecture and art, and place their individual seal on one grand, unified, integrated concept which will astonish the visitors from the hinterlands and rock the outer world.[23]

Confirming the worst fears of those who worried that he had no aesthetic discernment, Moses said, "Greek and Barbarian, traditionalist and modernist, conservative and iconoclast, right wing and left all look alike to us."[24] Moses felt that many of his critics were forgetting the economic realities of what was essentially a trade show. "Those who demand that the Fair vindicate their ideas of our national culture," he said, "ignore the fact that . . . it is dependent on exhibitors and concessionaires for money. As Damon Runyon would say, 'Leave us, my fine friends, not to be too noble.'"[25]

The final product seemed to fulfill the direst predictions of the architects and planners. Reviewing the fair for *Life*, architectural historian Vincent Scully wrote: "World's Fairs give architects a chance to do two things: to put up more advanced buildings than can be easily constructed elsewhere, and to suggest new solutions to the problems of city planning as a whole. . . . In 1964, we badly need some fresh ideas in both departments. But

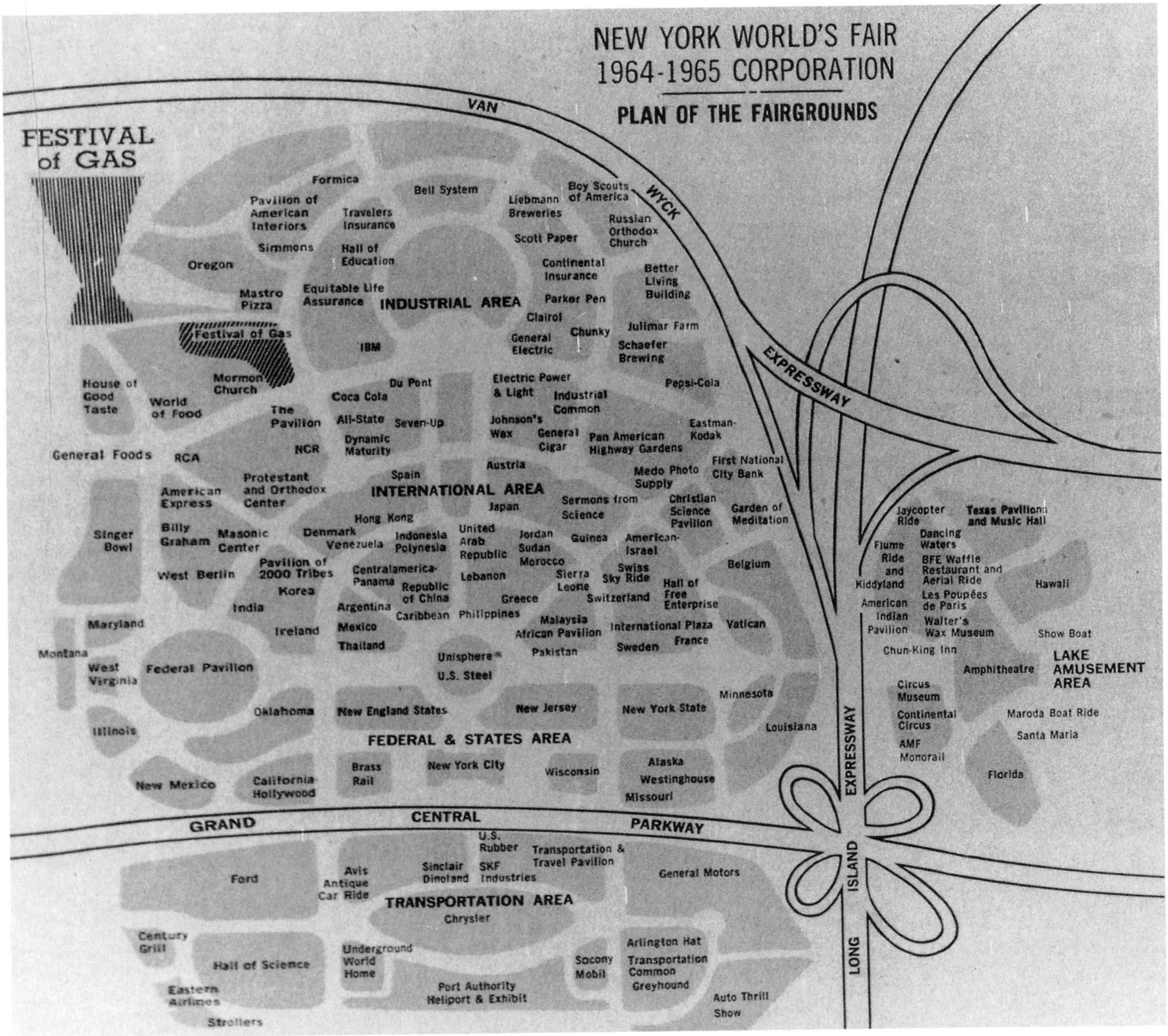

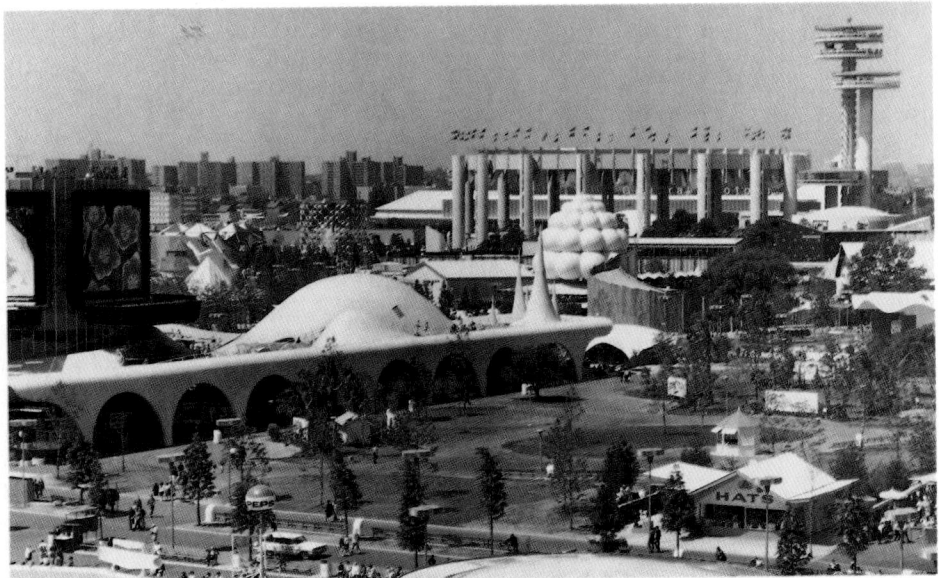

NEW YORK WORLD'S FAIR 1964-1965 CORPORATION

PLAN OF THE FAIRGROUNDS

VAN
WYCK

FESTIVAL of GAS

Formica
Bell System
Boy Scouts of America
Pavilion of American Interiors
Travelers Insurance
Liebmann Breweries
Russian Orthodox Church
Simmons
Hall of Education
Scott Paper
Oregon
Continental Insurance
Better Living Building
Mastro Pizza
Equitable Life Assurance
INDUSTRIAL AREA
Parker Pen
Clairol
Chunky
Julimar Farm
Festival of Gas
IBM
General Electric
Schaefer Brewing
EXPRESSWAY
House of Good Taste
Mormon Church
Du Pont
Electric Power & Light
Industrial Common
Pepsi-Cola
World of Food
Coca Cola
The Pavilion
All-State
Seven-Up
Johnson's Wax
General Cigar
Pan American Highway Gardens
Eastman-Kodak
General Foods
RCA
NCR
Dynamic Maturity
Austria
Medo Photo Supply
First National City Bank
American Express
Protestant and Orthodox Center
Spain
INTERNATIONAL AREA
Sermons from Science
Christian Science Pavilion
Garden of Meditation
Singer Bowl
Billy Graham
Masonic Center
Denmark
Hong Kong
Japan
Jaycopter Ride
Texas Pavilion and Music Hall
West Berlin
Pavilion of 2000 Tribes
Venezuela
Indonesia Polynesia
United Arab Republic
Jordan Sudan Morocco
Guinea
American-Israel
Belgium
Dancing Waters
Flume Ride and Kiddyland
BFE Waffle Restaurant and Aerial Ride
Korea
Centralamerica-Panama
Lebanon
Sierra Leone
Swiss Sky Ride
Hall of Free Enterprise
Hawaii
India
Argentina
Republic of China
Greece
Switzerland
American Indian Pavilion
Les Poupées de Paris
Walter's Wax Museum
Maryland
Ireland
Mexico
Caribbean
Philippines
Malaysia African Pavilion
International Plaza
Vatican
Show Boat
Montana
Thailand
Unisphere
Pakistan
Sweden
France
Chun-King Inn
LAKE AMUSEMENT AREA
West Virginia
Federal Pavilion
U.S. Steel
Circus Museum
Amphitheatre
Oklahoma
New England States
New Jersey
New York State
Minnesota
Continental Circus
Maroda Boat Ride
Illinois
FEDERAL & STATES AREA
Louisiana
AMF
Santa Maria
New Mexico
California-Hollywood
Brass Rail
New York City
Wisconsin
Alaska Westinghouse
Monorail
Florida
Missouri
GRAND CENTRAL PARKWAY
U.S. Rubber
Transportation & Travel Pavilion
EXPRESSWAY
Ford
Avis Antique Car Ride
Sinclair Dinoland
SKF Industries
General Motors
LONG ISLAND
Century Grill
TRANSPORTATION AREA
Chrysler
Hall of Science
Underground World Home
Socony Mobil
Arlington Hat
Transportation Common Greyhound
Eastern Airlines
Port Authority Heliport & Exhibit
Auto Thrill Show
Strollers

Above: Site plan for 1964–65 New York World's Fair. New York World's Fair 1964–1965 Corporation, 1960. NYP

Left: View to the northwest of New York World's Fair showing Eastman Kodak Pavilion (Will Burtin, Inc. and Kahn & Jacobs, 1964) in the center and New York State Pavilion (Philip Johnson and Richard Foster with Lev Zetlin, 1964) in the upper right. Golby. QM

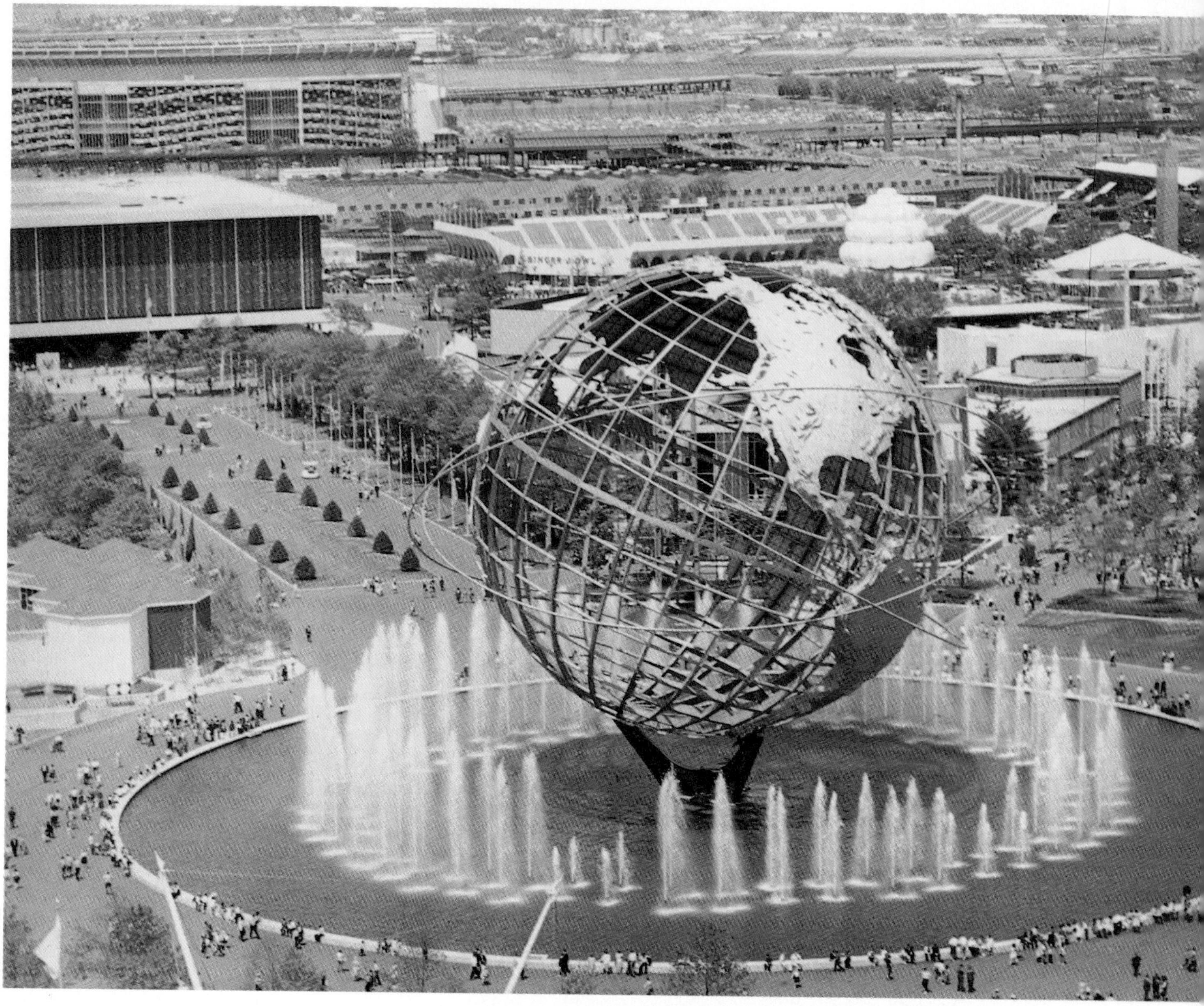

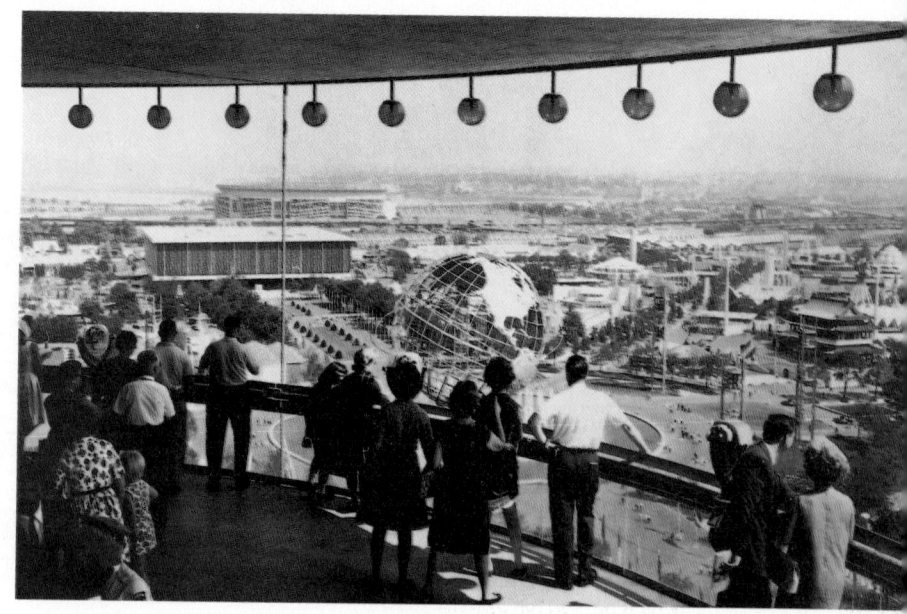

Above: Unisphere, New York World's Fair. Gilmore D. Clarke and Peter Müller-Munk Associates, 1964. View to the northeast. Golby. QM

Right: View to the northeast of New York World's Fair from New York State Pavilion (Philip Johnson and Richard Foster with Lev Zetlin, 1964) showing United States Pavilion (Charles Luckman Associates, 1964) on the left, and Unisphere (Gilmore D. Clarke and Peter Müller-Munk Associates, 1964) in the center. Shea Stadium (Praeger-Kavanagh-Waterbury, 1964) is in the background. B. Cohen. NYCPPA

if the current extravaganza in Flushing is the best we can do, then God help us all. I doubt whether any fair was ever so crassly, even brutally conceived as this one."[26]

The lack of architectural innovation and focus reflected the deeper problem of an overall lack of purpose to the fair. The journalist Martin Mayer addressed this issue:

> At least in retrospect, Fairs seem to have some reason behind them. New York's 1939–40 Fair marked the successful assertion of a new world capital, and the coming elaboration of the Automobile Age. Seattle's Century 21 celebrated the emergence of the Pacific Northwest to national importance . . . [and] Brussels' 1958 Fair symbolized the return of Europe to international prominence with the coming of the Common Market. "In these terms," says Judge Sam Rosenman, a Director of the Fair and attorney for Moses' New York State Power Authority, "I guess there isn't any reason for this Fair."[27]

The fair was repeatedly lambasted as a business boondoggle. Architectural critic Wolf Von Eckardt, in an article titled "As the Hucksters See Us," wrote that the fair "only reflects, in a billion-dollar surrealist distortion mirror, what huckster greed and hard-sell free enterprise does to us all over the land."[28] The art critic Robert Hughes similarly charged: "From the moment you enter Flushing Meadow, you become a fetus in the bulging womb of commerce, suspended in an amniotic fluid of ballyhoo and gimmickry. You are disoriented and cushioned, and thus made porous to the seepage of advertising copy which is the sole reason for the fair."[29] George Nelson lamented the passing of "the old-fashioned way to do a World's Fair," which was "to have a Dream, a Plan or an Idea which was given expression in the buildings put up by the Fair Commission. The new way," he said, "is the way of the speculative housing development or shopping center: provide enough parking and sales will take care of themselves. The new way is to avoid the Dream (too authoritarian), and the Idea (too subversive) and to create a Vacuum. . . . The idea is simply Total Amortization of Investment."[30]

Nonetheless, based on the city's previous experience, and on the success of other American and European fairs, the 1964–65 event promised to be a big draw. Not only did it provide, as the author Bruce Bliven put it, "a shiny new objective for the next vacation trip," it also offered an opportunity for participatory public celebration in an era when entertainment had become increasingly passive and privatized, a development due particularly to the pervasive influence of television.[31] As Martin Stone, a lawyer and television producer who was hired as the exclusive licensing agent of the fair's name and symbol, said, "We are now a nation of spectators. We've been driven into the home for our entertainment. We have a yen to *share* experiences, to participate—and that's what a Fair gives us."[32]

The fair opened as scheduled on April 22, 1964.[33] Cold, rainy weather discouraged would-be fairgoers, as did the possibility of a "stall-in" advocated by civil rights activists who threatened to block traffic on the highways and parkways leading to the fairgrounds. A modest crowd of approximately 93,000, less than half the number expected, showed up to hear President Johnson's opening address. Though the "stall-in" did not materialize, members of the Congress on Racial Equality demonstrated to bring attention to what the organization's national director, James Farmer, called "the melancholy contrast between the idealized, fantasy world of the fair and the real world of brutality, prejudice, and violence in which the American Negro is forced to live."[34] Johnson was heckled and 300 demonstrators were arrested.

The fair was rushed to completion for the opening and probably would not have come to fruition without Moses's superior organizing skills.[35] While the editors of *Business Week* noted that "critics liken his techniques to a steam roller aimed downhill,"[36] Moses did have a genius for dealing with public officials, whom he dismissed as "idiotic and inefficient."[37] Around the time of the fair's opening, Moses surveyed the grounds from the top of one of the taller structures and concluded, "Well, I guess they'll have to say that the old s.o.b. has done it again."[38]

Although he was famous for getting his own way, Moses ran into stiff opposition when he refused to grant reduced group-rate admission prices to New York City schoolchildren. The decision quickly gained the public's attention and was transformed from a practical consideration into an emotion-charged issue. As Mary Perot Nichols reported in the *Village Voice*, "The question of whether the school kiddies will get into the New York World's Fair for 25 cents is beginning to take on a soap opera aura. Will poor little Nell be able to enjoy all those marvelous educational benefits to be offered by the Fair?"[39] Finding himself on the unpopular side of the fence, Moses eventually gave in.

Moses also had to wage battle with the Great Atlantic & Pacific Tea Company, the supermarket chain widely known as A&P. The company had erected a 265-foot-long illuminated sign promoting its Jane Parker baked goods on its property near the fairgrounds. Moses castigated the advertisement as a "baleful neon eye" that would "contaminate" fairgoers, and he asked A&P to voluntarily remove the sign, but the company refused.[40] Moses proposed hiding the sign behind an enormous smoke screen, but engineers advised against it, noting the unpredictable wind patterns of Flushing Meadows. He then suggested building a mammoth screen of artificial shrubbery and ten-foot-diameter balloons advertising the Jones Beach State Park pavilion and its theatrical presentation, *80 Days Around the World*. The matter was complicated by the fact that Huntington Hartford, an heir to the A&P fortune and one of the company's principal stockholders, was also on the fair's board of directors. After a major court battle was threatened, Moses eventually backed down, leaving one observer, John Skow, wondering "what the fuss was about—the sign, in modest 10-foot-high red letters, blends unobtrusively with the *decor* that is genuine Moses."[41]

While the architects and the critics could see almost nothing good in the fair, its opening was greeted with some enthusiasm by the public and the general press. Peter Lyon, writing in *Holiday*, labeled it "a glorious nightmare."[42] The editors of *Time* wrote that "much of it, to be sure, has a tacky, plastic, here-to-day-blown-tomorrow look, as if it were a city made of credit cards. But most of it has grace and substance." They concluded that although "the crammed buildings are engaged in a mad struggle for attention . . . somehow, in its jostling, heedless, undisciplined energy, it makes a person happy to be alive in the 20th century."[43] Ada Louise Huxtable said it was "everything the critics predicted it would be—disconnected, grotesque, lacking any unity of concept or style." But, she added, "it is just those accidental juxtapositions and cockeyed contrasts built into the fair that gave it its particular attraction and charm."[44] The public, at least initially, seemed to be enthusiastic about the fair. Approximately 30,000 people visited the Flushing Meadows site to sneak a view before the fair opened, and more than six million people visited within the fair's first six weeks. Emerson Goble, the editor of *Architectural Record*, said that while "early efforts of New York architects to establish the principle of design discipline were a quick and total failure . . . attendance figures are amazingly high, and great queues form at many of the ex-

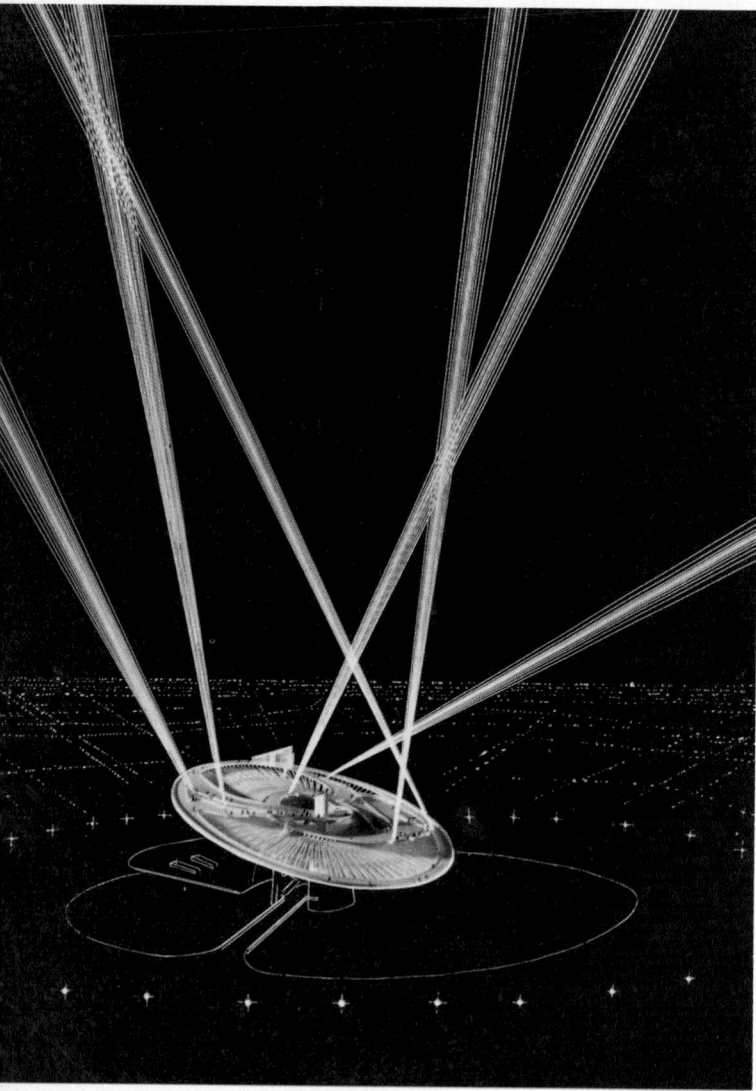

Unisphere

The fair occupied a full square mile of parkland and contained 156 pavilions, and was the world's first exposition to claim a worth of one billion dollars. It was divided into five thematically defined areas: federal and state, international, industrial, transportation and amusement, with the last two occupying the same sites they had during the 1939–40 fair. Located at the heart of the fairgrounds, between the federal and state area and the international area, was the Unisphere, the dominant visual symbol of the fair.[46] Unlike the 1939–40 fair's memorable Trylon and Perisphere, the Unisphere, which stood on the same site and used the earlier structure's wood pilings for its foundation, was neither a functioning pavilion nor a construction sponsored by the fair itself. Paid for by the U.S. Steel Corporation, it was designed by Gilmore D. Clarke, a landscape architect who frequently worked with Moses, and by Peter Müller-Munk Associates. The monumentally scaled sculpture served to illustrate the fair's theme, but it also hyped the sponsor's principal products.

In 1960, prior to the design of the Unisphere, Moses had asked the industrial designer Walter Dorwin Teague to devise a Theme Center.[47] Teague proposed a 170-foot-high aluminum-and-steel structure rising from a circular reflecting pool. The tower, to be known as Journey to the Stars, was to take the shape of an inverted cone and be encircled by a continuous spiral form; star-shaped, helium-filled balloons were to float above. In one version, the tower, illuminated by roving searchlights, incorporated an unspecified mode of transportation providing access to a top-level observation deck. Moses rejected the proposal, explaining: "At the risk of being put down as a barbarian, I think it is a cross between a part of a brake engine and a bed spring, or should I say between a Malayan Tapir and a window shutter."[48]

In 1961 the Portland Cement Association commissioned Paul Rudolph to design a Theme Center that would also house exhibits on man's exploration of outer space and showcase innovative uses of concrete.[49] The so-called Galaxon called for a 300-foot-diameter saucer-shaped platform elevated above an amphitheater and a circular moat on two curved concrete walls. The platform was to be constructed of a series of concentrically arranged prestressed, precast-concrete elements cantilevered from a centrally located cast-in-place ring. Tilted at an eighteen-degree angle, the platform's perimeter was to rise 160 feet above the ground at its highest point and 70 feet at its lowest. Visitors would reach the platform via elevators or escalators and proceed on curved ramps to a moving sidewalk located at the perimeter, leading to exhibition spaces, planetary viewing spots and a restaurant. The spectacular proposal was rejected by Moses.

As publicly announced in 1961, the Unisphere design was to be a 120-foot-diameter globe set within a 250-foot-wide reflecting pool containing fountains and steel statues of the zodiac signs that would be floodlit at night in a variety of colors. The stainless-steel frames forming the spherical cage represented lines of longitude. Continents and large islands were to be raised in steel mesh; national and state capitals were to be indicated by blinking colored lights. The globe was to be accurately tilted at an angle of 23.5 degrees. Three elliptical bands were to represent the orbits of satellites. On unveiling the initial design,

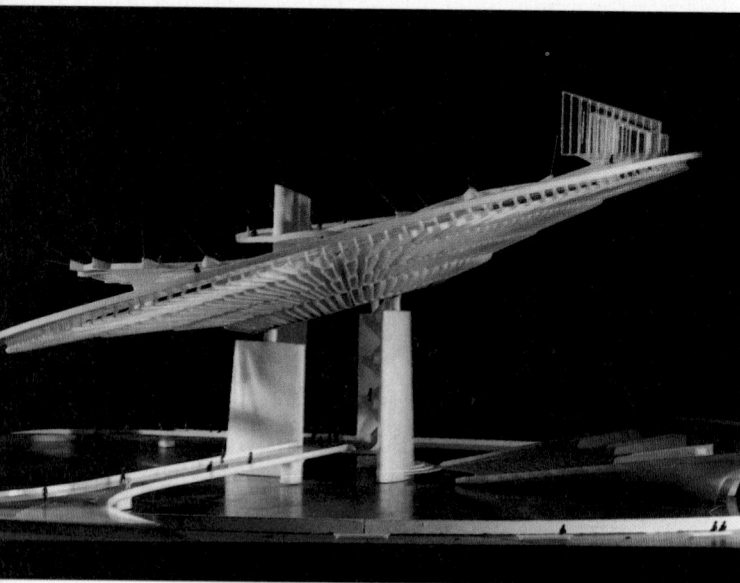

Top: Proposal for the Galaxon, New York World's Fair. Paul Rudolph, 1961. Rendering of night view. PR

Bottom: Proposal for the Galaxon. Model. Watson. PR

Moses proclaimed that the structure "illustrates, symbolizes and embodies man's achievements on a shrinking globe in an expanding universe."[50]

When the press proved less enthusiastic about the design, questioning whether the Unisphere's meanings would be clear to fairgoers, Moses retorted: "Frankly, I never understood the Trylon and Perisphere."[51] The critic Ralph Caplan, writing in *Industrial Design*, said that when the fair corporation unveiled the symbol, they absolved "the designer from the deed by acknowledging that he 'was simply the one to put down on paper what was in the mind of Mr. Moses and the Executive Committee.' . . . Mr. Moses' defense of the symbol is that he understands it (it is a globe, and stands for the world) and that for 20 years, he resented the mysteries of the Trylon and Perisphere."[52] The editors of *Progressive Architecture* described the structure as looking "like the set for the 'spectacular' finale of a 1930's Warner Brothers musical."[53] Walter McQuade, writing in the *Nation*, said that if this "enormous piece of hardware . . . this bit of roadside inspirational decoration, a trite cartoon in iron, is a symbol of the fair, may the Lord save us from the physical reality of the rest of it."[54]

Caplan urged the architectural community to actively oppose the design: "In the past few years, on issues relating to public welfare, Mr. Moses has been defeated by concerned groups . . . that had nothing in common but a passionate objection to being badly used. The lesson of history is that when Robert Moses is blatantly wrong, he can be beaten by anyone who cares enough about what is right. Do designers and architects care enough?"[55] Bruno Zevi, writing in the Italian journal *L'Architettura cronache e storia*, made a similar call to action: "The silly idea of the Unisphere is a cause for concern. The prestige of the Kennedy Administration, of the United States, of the western world in general are at stake. . . . If President Kennedy truly believes in a New Frontier, in a broader horizon for the release of the repressed ethical potential of the American society, he cannot miss this opportunity. His immediate intervention is necessary."[56]

Despite the massive amount of criticism, the Unisphere was built, although its design deviated from the initial proposal in one principal aspect: the land masses were represented by solid steel forms. As a result, the Unisphere contained 900,000 pounds of stainless steel, presenting staggering technological problems for the American Bridge division of the U.S. Steel Corporation, which was responsible for its construction. According to Austin J. Paddock, an administrative vice president of U.S. Steel, the task of designing an open steel frame that would be resistant to wind load and meet the program's aesthetic requirements necessitated the solution of 670 simultaneous mathematical equations and was "not too unlike fastening a beach ball to a golf tee."[57] It was estimated that without the aid of computers the mathematics involved would have taken ten years.

The National Arts Club described the Unisphere as "one of the outstanding achievements in structural sculpture of this decade."[58] But they were virtually alone in their opinion; no major critic or publication publicly praised the structure. And despite its size, the Unisphere's shape and material seemed to imply a quality of impermanence that undercut its monumentality. In a letter to the editor a reader of *Progressive Architecture* wrote: "The Eiffel Tower has long been a landmark and symbol of Paris; the Space Needle of Seattle will soon join it; but what will happen to . . . the Unisphere, that stainless-steel ball? Its shape suggests that, at the fair's end, it will be rolled away by the highest-bidding scrap dealer."[59] Although the critics hated it, the Unisphere was popular with visitors, and at the fair's end it was preserved as a permanent memorial of the event.

Federal and State Area

The federal and state section, located just north of Grand Central Parkway, was dominated by the United States Pavilion, the design of which sparked controversy from the first.[60] In 1961 the fair had unsuccessfully proposed to the federal government that the U.S. exhibit be housed in a permanent building, to be called the Franklin National Center for Science and Education. A preliminary scheme, designed by Wallace Harrison, called for a semispherical structure encircled by a series of arc-shaped glass expanses and flanked by two low-lying, rectilinear projections. In August 1962 the Kennedy administration announced that Charles Luckman Associates had been selected to design the pavilion. According to *Architectural Forum*, however, the firm had begun work on the pavilion, whose theme was "Challenge to Greatness," considerably before they were formally appointed, and the design was "officially considered more or less 'frozen.'" *Forum* questioned why an open competition for the design of "this important symbol of our democracy" had not been held, and criticized the selection of Luckman: "Charles Luckman is an enormously successful architect, and no decent person begrudges him the size of his success. But there is a difference between 'bigness' and 'greatness,' and it is most apparent in the arts."[61]

Descriptions of Luckman's initial design, which apparently called for three spherical forms that seemed to be suspended from a central structure, were widely circulated. The editors of *Architectural Forum* said the design looked "like the familiar pawnshop sign known to every inhabitant of every skid row," and further commented: "We can see the headline in *Pravda* now: 'America—Pawnbroker of the World.' Is that the image the Administration wishes to project?"[62] The urban planner Edmund Bacon and the architect Percival Goodman, in letters to the editor, strongly supported the journal's opinion, as did Arthur Drexler, the director of the Museum of Modern Art's Department of Architecture and Design, who wrote: "The New York World's Fair has become a far more significant symbol of American life than its promoters ever meant it to be. *Forum* deserves congratulations for stating publicly, and politely, what we have all regretted in private."[63]

In response to this early criticism, Luckman presented the government with twenty-eight alternate proposals. In the fall of 1962 the final scheme for the pavilion, for which Leon Deller of the Luckman office received design credit, was released. It consisted of an elevated, two-story, reinforced-concrete structure with exterior walls of translucent blue and green plastic, cantilevered seventy-five feet beyond four massive pylons.[64] Surrounding the building was a circular moat, punctuated by fountains and crossed by four bridges. The pavilion was focused around a central courtyard reached by elevator or by four broad pyramids of steps that tapered to four feet at the top. Eighteen monumental sculptures by American artists, including Alexander Calder, John Chamberlain, Herbert Ferber, Raoul Hague, Reuben Nakian, Louise Nevelson, Isamu Noguchi and George Sugarman, were installed around the base or beneath the overhang of the pavilion. While the effect of a monumental building that seemed to be delicately balanced on a pyramid of stairs was striking, the lack of a clear entrance was problematic.

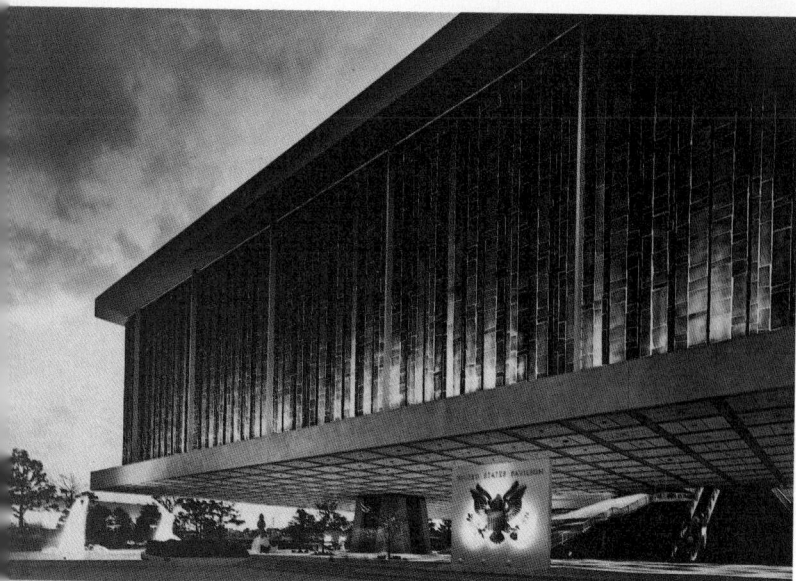

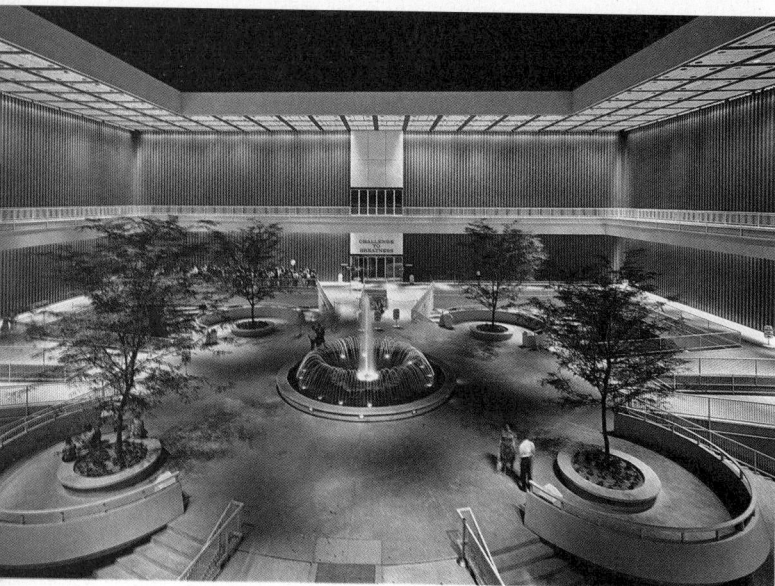

Top: United States Pavilion, New York World's Fair. Charles Luckman Associates, 1964. View to the northwest. CLA

Bottom: United States Pavilion. Interior courtyard. Georges. CLA

Critical reactions to the design were mixed. When the model was unveiled, Ada Louise Huxtable cheerfully reported in the *New York Times*: "The Stormy Saga of the United States Pavilion . . . which has had rough going through government agencies, Presidential advisers and sharp professional criticism, reached a happy ending this week in New York . . . and the story might well be called 'All's Well that Ends Well.'"[65] *Time* said that while "some of U.S. architecture's proudest names are represented at the fair . . . none come off with any particular distinction, except perhaps Charles Luckman with his severely simple United States Pavilion."[66] Ellen Perry and James T. Burns, Jr., editors of *Progressive Architecture*, said that the building was "rather better than we feared, but still a bit heavy on pomposity," and described it as "a gigantic ice-cream sandwich above [a] ceremonial entrance mound, blue and green plastic where the vanilla would be."[67] Vincent Scully, however, was adamantly negative about the pavilion, calling it "the world's worst building . . . [a] pompous pile of absolutely nothing."[68]

Inside, the United States Pavilion featured what Ralph Caplan described as a "film and buggy trip through American history."[69] Fairgoers boarded a fifty-five-seat grandstand "wagon" to ride through a 1,200-foot tunnel lined with more than 100 movie screens of various shapes and sizes on which they could view a film presentation, produced by Jeremy Lepard of Cinerama, depicting watersheds in American history. The film was accompanied by a recorded second-person narrative that *Time* said was "straight from *This is Your Life* . . . telling each and every American that *you* tamed the wilderness, then *you* invented the electric light, and *you* are now assaulting the universe."[70] The author George W. S. Trow, Jr., who in his twenties had worked for Robert Moses at the fair, would later recall that the exhibit's narration had a "booming" quality. "The syntax was that of Walt Whitman, within a public-relations framework," he said. "*America* was made personal in a way that made her sound like a smug bully. . . . Emerging from the ride, one wanted never to hear another word about America or any event associated with America, and one wanted never to hear again any sentence cast in the historical present."[71]

Visually dominating the area of the federal and state section farthest from the United States Pavilion was the New York State Pavilion, designed by Philip Johnson and Richard Foster, with Lev Zetlin serving as structural engineer.[72] Johnson's pavilion captured the ebullient spirit of a fair more potently and directly than any other structure; it was also a virtuosic illustration of the engineer's art. Occupying nearly all of its 129,392-square-foot site—the largest devoted to a state-sponsored exhibit—the pavilion consisted of an elliptical structure called the Tent of Tomorrow, a circular theater and a grouping of three towers. Each tower consisted of a slender column supporting exterior, glass-walled elevators and surmounted by broad circular platforms. The lower tower rose 60 feet, the middle tower rose 150 feet, and the highest soared to 226 feet, dominating the fair's "skyline" as its tallest structure. The lower tower housed restaurants, and the other towers contained open observation decks.

The 250-by-350-foot Tent of Tomorrow, the pavilion's principal feature, was a superscaled big top, with the world's largest suspension roof—50,000 square feet—made of multicolored, translucent plastic panels and supported at its perimeter by a series of 100-foot-high concrete columns. The roof was constructed on the ground and then hoisted into place. The tent contained exhibition space on a two-level promenade and mezzanine encircling the central floor, which featured an immense plastic map of the state.

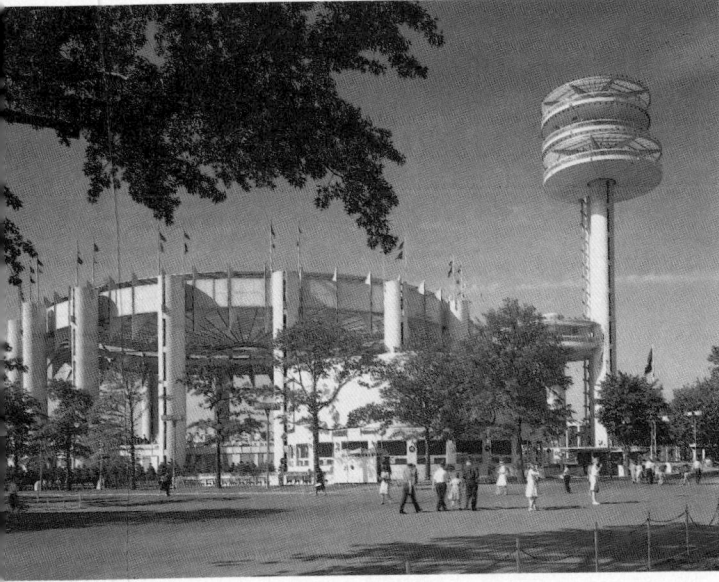

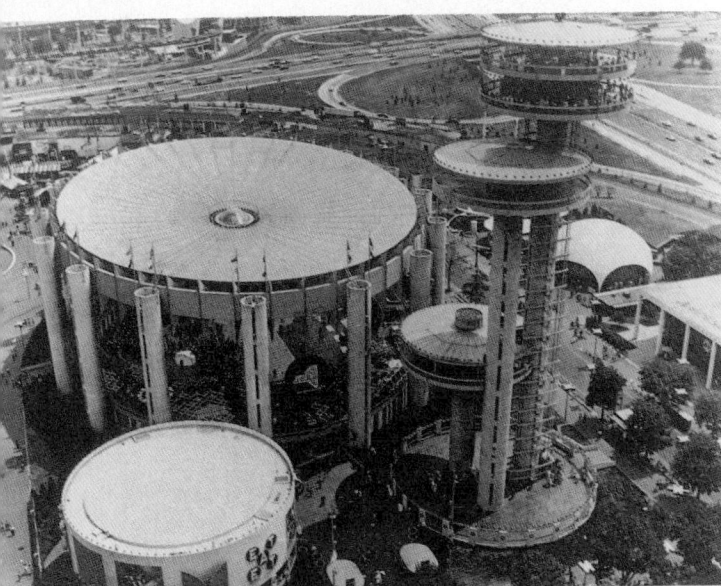

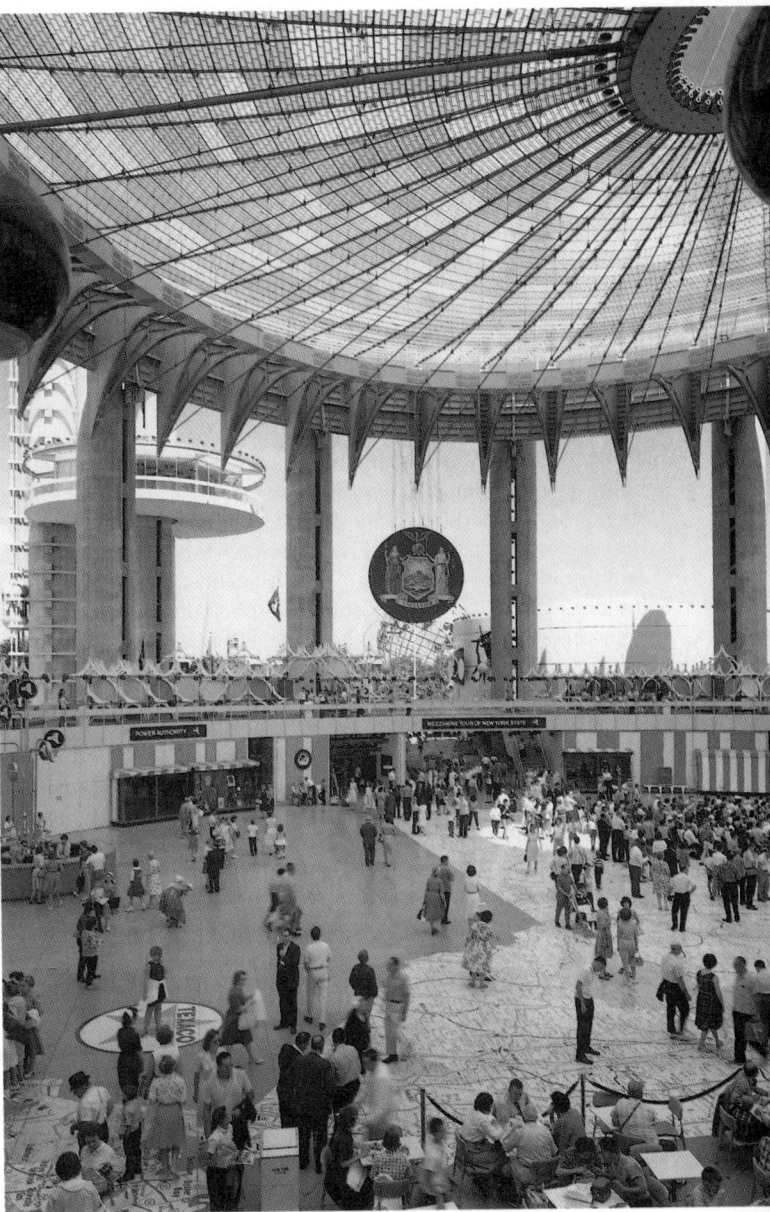

Top: New York State Pavilion, New York World's Fair. Philip Johnson and Richard Foster with Lev Zetlin, 1964. View to the west. Stoller. ©ESTO

Bottom: New York State Pavilion. Aerial view to the southwest. NYP

New York State Pavilion. View showing interior of Tent of Tomorrow. Stoller. ©ESTO

The pavilion was so seductively garish that only hard-core purists could resist its fun-loving spirit. The art critic Max Kozloff grudgingly complimented the pavilion's architect: "Doubtless the man of the hour here is Philip Johnson, whose garrulous control-observation tower with the gaudy plastic canopy, at the New York State Pavilion, is far more uninhibitedly and agreeably *kitsch* than his new theater at Lincoln Center."[73] Perry and Burns described the pavilion as a "three-ring circus" that was "great, good fun."[74] Scully said that Johnson's grand gesture of towers and a canopy was "almost great,"[75] while Huxtable said that it was the fair's "runaway success, day or night . . . a sophisticated frivolity . . . seriously and beautifully constructed. This is 'carnival' with class."[76]

The exterior of the pavilion's 100-foot-diameter circular theater was given an avant-garde look when it was decorated with ten works of contemporary American art commissioned by Johnson, who argued that "American art is at a lively stage, at such a very American lively stage, so varied, so to the point in time and in space, we should all be happy as kings."[77] The artists represented were Roy Lichtenstein, Alexander Liberman, Robert Indiana, James Rosenquist, John Chamberlain, Robert Mallary, Peter Agostini, Robert Rauschenberg, Ellsworth Kelly and Andy Warhol.

Warhol's contribution proved to be the most controversial. It consisted of a twenty-five-unit grid of silkscreened photographic images of men on the New York City Police Department's most wanted list. Because Warhol used photographs that were only an inch wide, the images when enlarged to forty by forty-eight inches were grainy and distorted. Three blank panels were left in the grid's lower-right-hand corner; according to Warhol's biographer, David Bourdon, this "might have implied that some of the men had been captured or that there was room for more faces." State officials feared that lawsuits might result from Warhol's work and asked that the mural be removed. Warhol retaliated by silkscreening twenty-five portraits of a menacingly smiling Robert Moses, which he proposed to substitute, but, according to Bourdon, "Johnson balked, thinking it would be in extremely bad taste to offend the head of the fair."[78] The final decision was to leave the existing panels in place but to cover them with a coat of silver paint. As the art historian Robert Rosenblum would later write, the mural had perhaps proven "too disturbingly real to survive the Fair's glut of superannuated American dreams."[79]

Among the pavilion's other outstanding artworks were Indiana's black-and-white painting spelling out the word "Eat," with each letter outlined in lights; Rauschenberg's "combine," which included three repeated images of the late President Kennedy; Lichtenstein's comic-strip-inspired representation of a young woman at a window; and Rosenquist's densely composed painting that included cropped images of a car, a woman's crossed legs and a top hat decorated with the stars and stripes, among other things. While Max Kozloff characterized Johnson's selections as "sophisticated," he asked whether the architect had anticipated the effect these works would have when "blown up to epic proportions, and clarioned outdoors for all to see." He described the result: "Deprived of their intimate gallery atmosphere, the silk-screen-transformed color photographic and billboard montages of [Rauschenberg and Rosenquist] are returned to their appropriate point of origin, and the displacement which once gave them so much pungency is minimized. These works of art cease to be creative expressions intruding into the world of manufacture, and become instead equivocal flora of that world."[80] Other critics were just plain negative: Wolf Von

New York State Pavilion, New York World's Fair. Philip Johnson and Richard Foster with Lev Zetlin, 1964. Night view to the southeast. NYPL

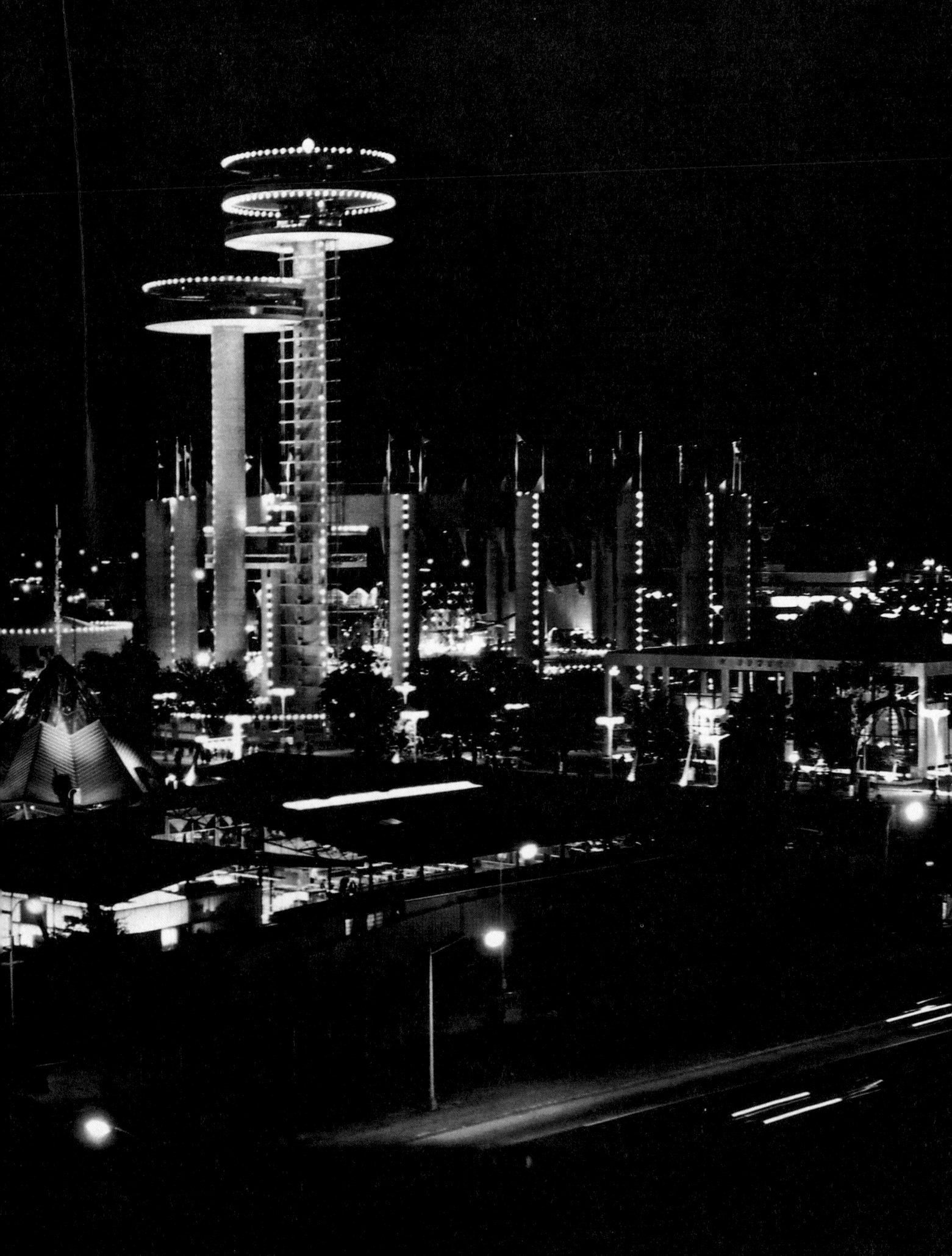

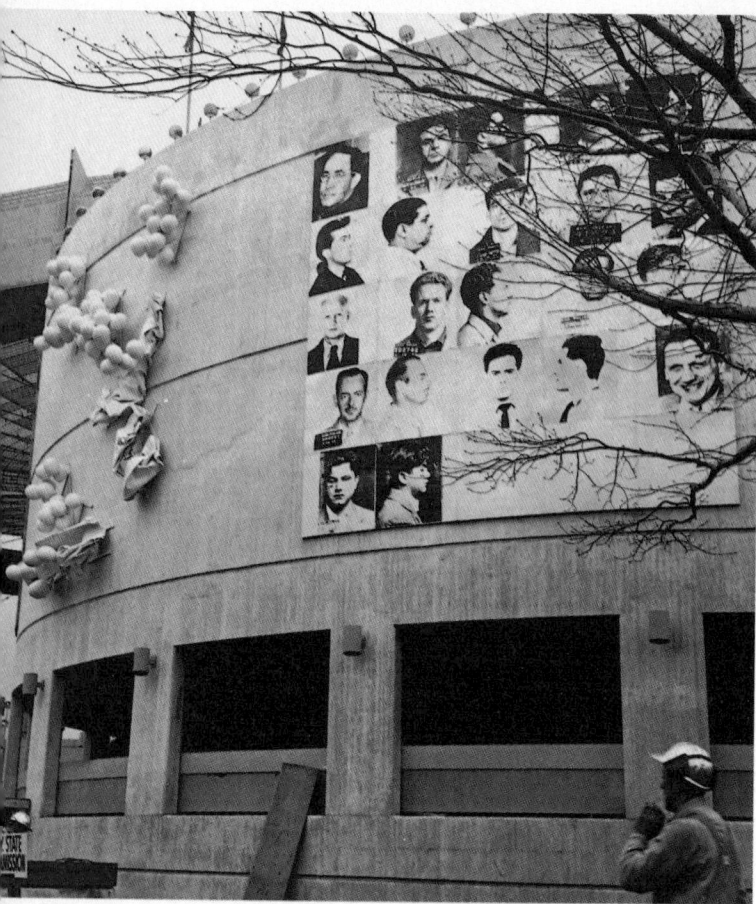

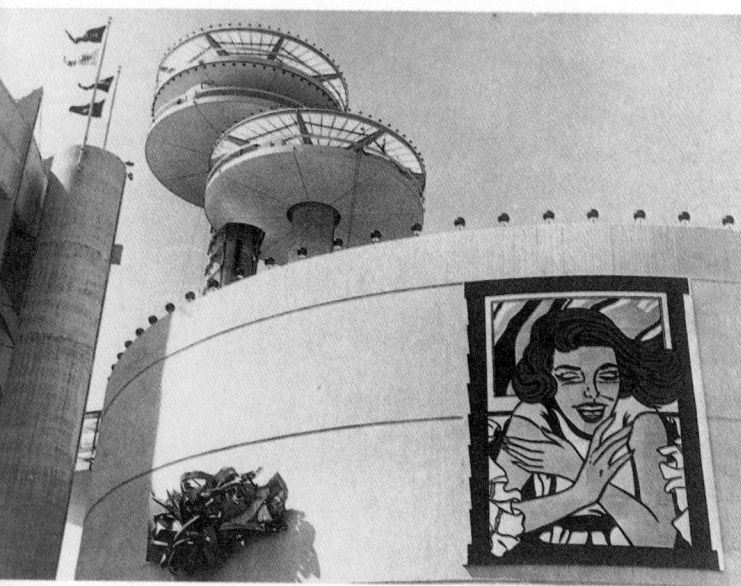

Top: New York State Pavilion, New York World's Fair. Philip Johnson and Richard Foster with Lev Zetlin, 1964. Exterior of circular theater with mural by Andy Warhol (1964). UPIB

Bottom: New York State Pavilion. Exterior of circular theater with mural by Roy Lichtenstein (1964). NYP

Eckardt dismissed the entire pavilion and its art as "a pretentious piece of pop architecture, adorned by, of all things, still more pop art."[81]

New Jersey's was the next most engaging of the state-sponsored pavilions at the fair.[82] Celebrating its tercentenary in 1964, New Jersey held a statewide design competition for the pavilion. The winning scheme, out of a field of 115 entries, was submitted by a thirty-two-year-old Princeton architect, Philip Sheridan Collins. The pavilion's design, which was ultimately credited to the firms of Collins, Uhl & Hoisington and Peter Quay Yang Associates, incorporated twenty-one small pavilions, one for each county in the Garden State, elevated on platforms above a continuous reflecting pool and clustered around a central theater. Each pavilion was roofed by a steel space frame and a tent-like vinyl covering, and the entire complex was supported by a network of cables and booms suspended from sixteen-foot-high masts arranged in groups of four.

The Illinois Pavilion, designed by Skidmore, Owings & Merrill, was an understated brick building distinguished by two curvilinear walls, one containing the main entrance and the other enclosing a landscaped courtyard.[83] The pavilion's outstanding feature was not its architecture, however, but an exhibit designed by Walt Disney featuring a life-size mechanized model of native son Abraham Lincoln. The model was technologically remarkable, capable of 250,000 combinations of gestures and expressions. During the model's construction, the New Yorker noted: "Mr. Disney, we heard, took particular pains with the Lincoln figure which can walk, talk, turn, gesture and even get out of a chair 'like a human being and not like a robot'. . . . When he talks his tongue moves about inside his mouth and he furrows his brow."[84] Just after the fair's opening, Time reported: "Audio-animatronic Abe Lincoln, who had been suffering from electronic migraines until engineers fiddled with the circuitry that make his eyes blink, his voice rasp and his hands gesture, began to work. Abe rose to greet 500 people at a time, pushed back his coattails and gave them a ten-minute talk on liberty."[85]

Not all observers appreciated Disney's version of American history. George Trow characterized the display as "almost sadistic in its absurdity," arguing that while automated figures in other fair exhibits "gestured and smiled and moved and did this and did that just the way a certain sort of person would . . . the Lincoln automaton was less ambitious." Trow described the scene: "He sat there, just the way he does at his great memorial in Washington—in that pose—and then he stood up, and talked and talked, putting forward a pastiche of his great words, and then, at a certain moment, he moved a finger of his right hand in a kind of twitch. Then, at the end, at a time when people in the audience were beginning to retch with boredom, he sat down." Trow said that "the important moment of the show" was when Lincoln stood up: "He did it in two movements. He pushed himself forward, head down, and propelled himself out of his chair. Then he raised the top half of his body. He stood. It was poignant that he could stand. After I saw this spectacle a few times, I realized Lincoln was being portrayed as a cripple."[86] Vincent Scully also vehemently criticized the Lincoln model: "Disney caters to the kind of phony reality—most horribly exemplified by the moving-and-talking figure of Lincoln . . . that we all too readily accept in place of the true. Mr. Disney, I'm afraid, has our number."[87] Regardless of the critical reception of the Lincoln figure, it proved immensely popular, and Disney emerged as the dominant artistic voice of the fair.

The allure of the nation's past, presented in a sanitized,

theme-park fashion, was strong at the World's Fair. Many state-sponsored pavilions, like some of their national counterparts, built fully articulated versions of authentic regional building types. Montana's pavilion, designed by Oswald Berg & Associates, simulated a frontier town;[88] New Mexico's pavilion, designed by William Leftwich, looked like an adobe pueblo;[89] Wisconsin's pavilion, designed by John W. Steinmann, took the form of a tepee (the pavilion was reassembled after the fair in Neillsville, Wisconsin);[90] West Virginia's pavilion, designed by the pioneering Modernist firm of Irving Bowman & Associates, in association with Frederick Wiedersum & Associates, resembled a mountain lodge;[91] and Louisiana's pavilion, designed by Albert C. Ledner, Saputo & Rowe and Furman & Furman, was an edited version of Bourbon Street in New Orleans.[92]

The New York City Pavilion was housed in the New York City Building, which Aymar Embury II had designed for the 1939–40 World's Fair.[93] The building was redesigned by the architect Daniel Chait and the design firm of Lester Associates, whose principal alteration was to place a grille across the rather staid Modern Classical colonnades, giving them a decidedly more trendy and quite tacky appearance. While the celebration of the city's 300th birthday was all but lost amid the fair's aesthetic free-for-all, the New York City Pavilion was noteworthy for its "Panorama Around New York" exhibit, a 100-by-180-foot model of the city, rendered at 1"=100' scale and representing all of the 835,000 buildings in the city's five boroughs. The panorama attracted 10,000 spectators daily who took a six-minute ride in seats that moved around its perimeter.

The only other American city to have a pavilion at the fair was Hollywood, which, politically speaking, was not really a city at all.[94] As orchestrated by the former actor George Murphy and designed by Randall Duell, Inc., Donald Schwenn, and Oppenheimer, Brady & Lehrecke, the pavilion was a re-creation of Meyer & Holler's grandly iconic Grauman's Chinese Theater of 1926–27, itself an inspired if half-mad interpretation of Oriental architecture.[95] Inside, the pavilion contained sets or reconstructions of sets from the movies *Cleopatra* and *Irma la Douce*, as well as life-size photographic cutouts of stars next to which visitors could have their pictures taken.

International Area

The park's international area was, as John Brooks said in the *New Yorker*, "as conspicuous for national absences as national presences."[96] The only Western European countries to be represented by government-sponsored pavilions were Ireland and Spain, although Austria, France, Greece, Italy, Switzerland and Sweden were represented by exhibits organized by nongovernmental sponsors. Most of the British Commonwealth countries, including Great Britain, Canada and Australia, were absent. Perhaps most significant in terms of belittling the fair's theme, "Peace Through Understanding," was the absence of every Communist nation, including the Soviet Union, which failed to participate after complex negotiations fell through.

In the 1939–40 fair the national pavilions had been the foot soldiers of the stylistic battle between Modern Classicism and International Style Modernism. In 1964 the stylistic war was clearly over, and many of the national pavilions struggled to synthesize a technologically based Modernist vocabulary with traditional and vernacular influences in order to reflect a particular national identity. Some countries simply rejected Modernism completely, building convincing if not always historically

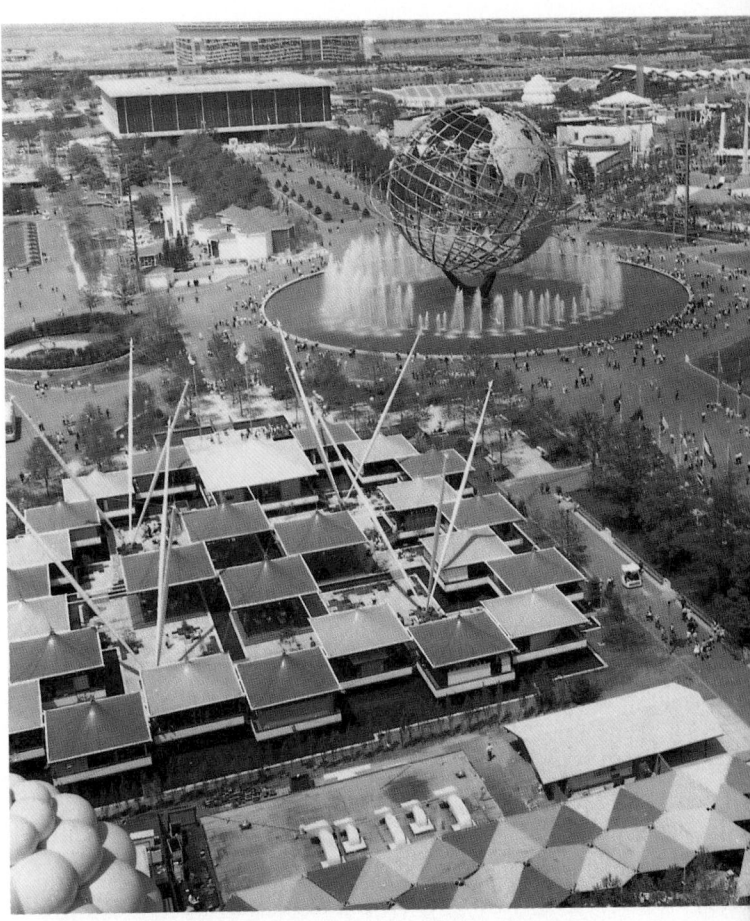

View to the northeast of central court of New York World's Fair showing New Jersey State Pavilion (Collins, Uhl & Hoisington, 1964) in the lower left, Unisphere (Gilmore D. Clarke and Peter Müller-Munk Associates, 1964) in the center and United States Pavilion (Charles Luckman Associates, 1964) in the upper left. Golby. QM

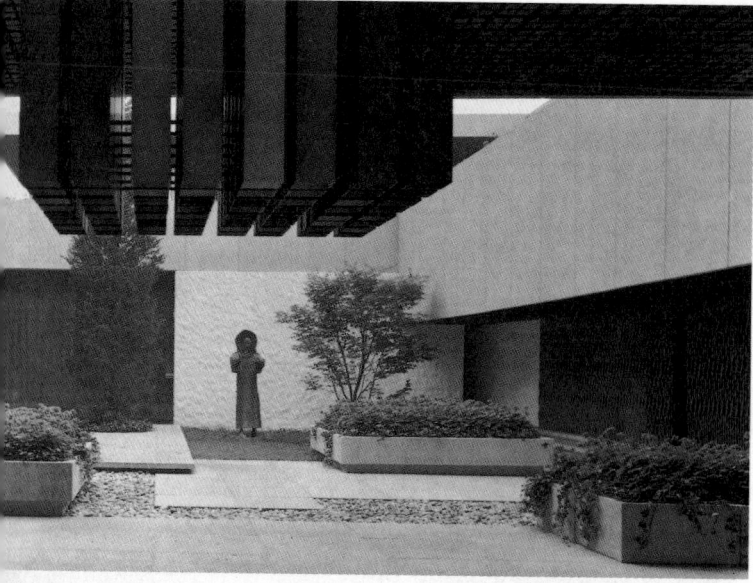

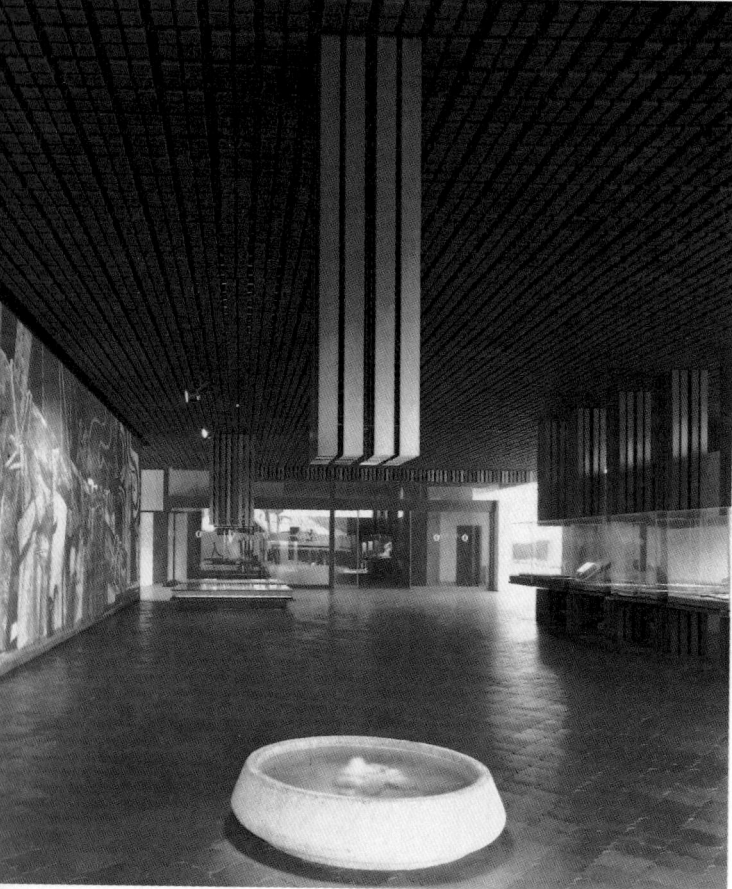

Top: Spanish Pavilion, New York World's Fair. Javier Carvajal in association with Kelly & Gruzen, 1964. Interior courtyard. Reens. LR

Bottom: Spanish Pavilion. Gallery. Reens. LR

correct renditions of indigenous architectural styles. But a few countries presented pavilions in a contemporary idiom. Most notable among these was Spain, whose pavilion, designed by Javier Carvajal, working in association with Lloyd Siegel and Rolland Thompson of the New York firm Kelly & Gruzen, was widely considered to be one of the fair's most architecturally distinguished buildings.[97] It was also the fair's most heavily staffed government-sponsored foreign pavilion, employing 600 people to operate restaurants and present a broad array of activities, which *Progressive Architecture* described as "comparable to those of a resort hotel."[98]

The building was a remarkable marriage of International Style Modernist forms and vernacular Spanish space-making. Like a typical Spanish house, it turned a virtually windowless exterior to the public street and focused inward on a series of lushly landscaped patios and courtyards. The street facades were divided horizontally into two components: above a base of white-painted, rough-stuccoed concrete were walls composed of rectangular precast-concrete panels arranged in a grid pattern. The design clearly succeeded on both formal and narrative grounds, at once constituting a sophisticated, understated composition and an immediately identifiable Spanish presence. *Progressive Architecture* noted that the pavilion, "surrounded by the frivolous honky-tonk of the Fair, stands with handsome refinement and unfestive serenity, aptly exemplifying Spanish pride and dignity."[99]

The pavilion was entered by way of a monumental wrought-iron gate designed in a contemporary manner by Spanish artist Amadeo Gabino. Inside, Carvajal's design brilliantly evoked the surprising spatial sequences—alternating between light and dark, constricted and expansive, inside and outside—that characterize traditional Spanish architecture. Floors were laid with Moorish terra-cotta tiles, and ceilings were constructed of suspended wood blocks, between which aluminum tubes shot beams of light to exhibits raised on tubelike bases. At some points, ceiling modules extended to the floor, forming columns and supports for partitions. White plaster walls were separated from the dark floor and ceiling by continuous recessed coves containing floodlights. Contemporary Spanish art—some of it commissioned for the pavilion, such as Antonio Cumella's ceramic relief sculpture *Homage to Gaudí*—complemented Old Master paintings on loan from the Prado, including works by El Greco, Velázquez and Goya's famous *Clothed Maja* and *Naked Maja*, which were protected by uniformed members of the Guardia Civil. The pavilion also displayed paintings by Salvador Dalí and Joan Miró, and three works by Pablo Picasso.

In striking contrast to the exhibition spaces, where there was, according to *Life*, an "almost religious hush," the patios pulsated with the rhythms of the Corsos y Danzas flamenco troupe and the sounds of the lively Taberna Marisqueria café. Some of the pavilion's upper-level interior spaces were separated from the courtyards by José Marca de Labra's delicately perforated, wood "celosia" jalousies. Throughout the pavilion, specially built furniture, in both traditional and Modernist styles, as well as graphic displays, all of which were designed by Carvajal, contributed to the total effect.

The Spanish Pavilion was widely praised in both the architectural and the general press. Olga Gueft, editor-in-chief of *Interiors*, selected it as one of the four best buildings at the fair,[100] while Ellen Perry and James Burns of *Progressive Architecture* said it was "unquestionably the best architecture at the Fair, further enhanced by impeccably presented exhibits, fine (if somewhat expensive) cuisine, and excellent Spanish entertainment."[101] Ralph Caplan lavished praise on the building, describing it as "an eloquent statement of what display can be, of what lighting can be and, for that matter, of what a national contribution to a World Fair can be."[102] Ada Louise Huxtable summed up the pavilion's quality, writing that "Spain has put together a superbly integrated, beautifully selected, absolutely topnotch show."[103]

Spain's pavilion was so popular that a movement to preserve it quickly emerged. The editors of *Time* observed that the "incredibly beautiful pavilion could probably ride the meadow for a thousand years if it were permitted to, and it should at least be moved somewhere in 1965."[104] C. J. McNapsy, writing in *America*, similarly advocated its conversion into a permanent institution: "What a waste if this jewel of a building were to be torn down after the fair. We need something to remind America, even North America, of its immense Iberian heritage and links. . . . New York especially, with as many Spanish-speaking inhabitants as Seville, needs a worthy symbol of this part of its inheritance. Why can't the Park Commission, the Spanish-American Chamber of Commerce and the Hispanic Society work together to save the pavilion?"[105] The building was saved, but not for New York: after the closing of the fair's second season, it was moved to St. Louis, where it was refitted to function as part of a hotel.

The Irish Pavilion was also an architecturally distinguished building.[106] Designed by the Irish architect Andrew Devane, principal of the firm of Robinson, Keef & Devane and a onetime apprentice of Frank Lloyd Wright, the two-story building was built of irregularly shaped stones set in concrete and organized around a courtyard partially covered by a low wood trellis.[107] George Nelson and Robert Fymat designed the interiors and exhibits of the pavilion, which Caplan described as "a lusty, light-hearted grey stone affair."[108] Patrons at an open-air café featuring Irish coffee were cooled by Indian fans that lent the courtyard an exotic and curiously British imperialist touch. In the center of the pavilion, a truncated, conical tower that recalled Irish coastal watchtowers housed an exhibit of Gaelic artifacts and products. Other exhibits included audio recordings of Irish actors reciting great works of Irish literature, and a film of the country's landscape projected on a screen embedded in the floor, giving the illusion that the observer was in a hot-air balloon.

Denmark's pavilion, designed by Erik Moeller, was notable as an elegant example of Scandinavian Modernism.[109] Distinguished by facades incorporating delicate wooden lattice-work and large expanses of glass, the pavilion was, according to Mildred Schmertz, "beautifully detailed," but it was also a bit cloying.[110] Its miniature Tivoli Garden, where for a fee of fifty cents parents could leave their children under the supervision of young Danish women for two hours, gave it a bit of much-needed energy.[111]

The Belgian Village, designed by Alfons De Dijdt and the firm of Hooks & Wax and occupying the longest site in the international area, consisted of 134 buildings organized to resemble a Flemish town.[112] Plagued with problems during its construction, it was not completely open until near the end of the fair's first season. To some extent the Belgian Village echoed the strategies of José Puig y Cadafalch's Pueblo Español, built for Barcelona's International Expo in 1929.[113] But whereas the Pueblo Español was comprehensive, presenting vignettes of architecture and urbanism from virtually every important Spanish city and town, the Belgian Village transported visitors to a single medieval environment that resembled Bruges, but without the

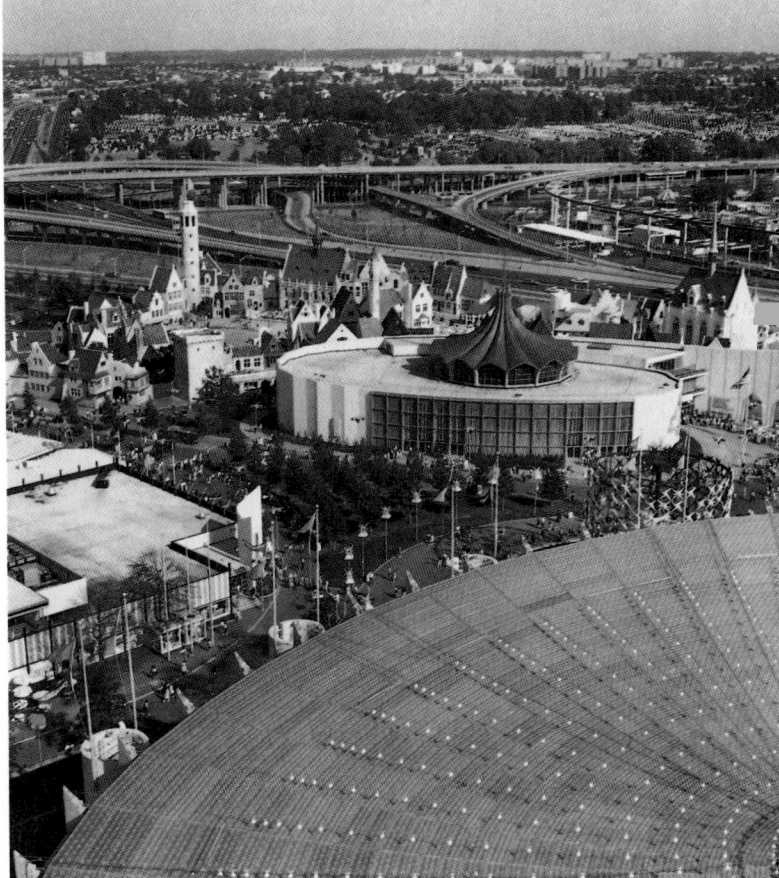

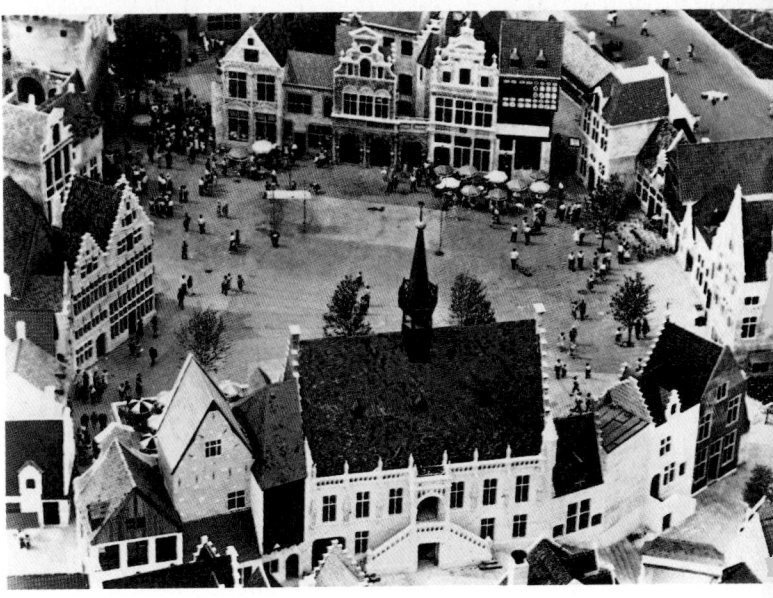

Top: View to the southeast of New York World's Fair from New York State Pavilion (Philip Johnson and Richard Foster with Lev Zetlin, 1964), showing International Plaza (Ira Kessler & Associates, 1964) on the lower left, Vatican Pavilion (York & Sawyer, Hurley & Hughes and Lunders & Associates, 1964) on the right, and Belgian Village (Alfons De Dijdt, 1964) in the background. Golby. QM

Bottom: Belgian Village, New York World's Fair. Alfons De Dijdt, 1964. Aerial view to the northwest. NYPL

1041

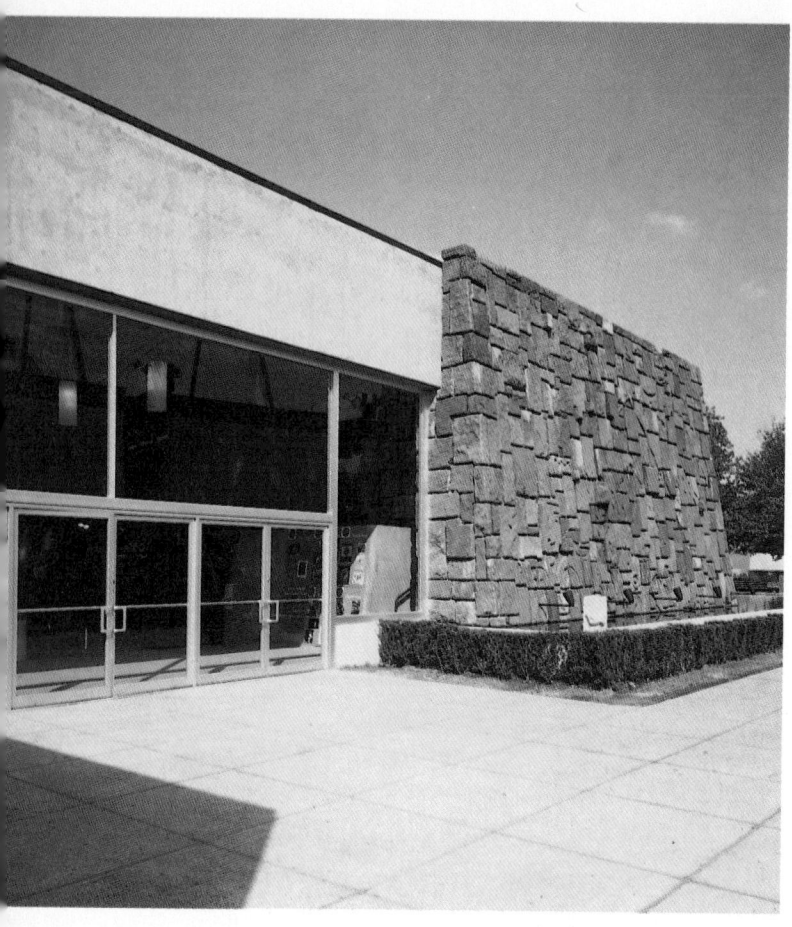

Japanese Pavilion, New York World's Fair. Kunio Mayekawa with Kiyoshi Seike and Kyoritsu Sekkei Jimusho; Oppenheimer, Brady & Lehrecke; and Chapman, Evans & Delehanty, 1964. View to the northwest showing lava-rock wall fountain by Masayuki Nagara. OBV

canals. Buildings with steeply pitched, step-gable roofs lined a spacious town square and crooked cobblestone streets. (The paving stones, so evocative of the Low Countries, were actually taken from a New Jersey highway.) The overall image was compromised by a restaurant, inexplicably serving Hungarian cuisine, and a discotheque. One of the main attractions of the Belgian Village was the strawberry-covered waffles served there; known as Bel-Gem Waffles, they became so popular that they were served not only throughout the pavilion but throughout the fairgrounds. In addition to its culinary allure, the pavilion also demonstrated the powerful appeal of traditional urban forms for a society surrounded by superhighways and high rises. While Von Eckardt dismissed the Belgian Village as "unspeakable *kitsch,*" other critics saw the implicit message of the pavilion's popularity more clearly.[114] To Perry and Burns, for instance, it was "a lesson that pleasant urban spaces solely for pedestrians are still possible and desirable."[115]

Israel proposed to build a complexly massed six-sided structure consisting of a tubular space frame covered with plastic panels; the plan was based on a series of interlocking triangles and hexagons.[116] The scheme, designed by A. Mansfield, assisted by A. Edelman and D. Yanai, was granted a *Progressive Architecture* design award. After much vacillation, however, the Israeli government decided not to participate in the fair, in part because it felt that the $2 million required to build and run the pavilion could be put to better use. Jewish organizations in the United States offered to make substantial contributions to help finance the pavilion, but the Israeli government remained firm in its decision. Subsequently, a private organization, the American-Israel World's Fair Corporation, was founded and sponsored a pavilion. Designed by Ira Kessler & Associates, the curvilinear, mahogany-clad form rose in a sweeping spiral to enclose a space that housed what *Art News* described as a "spooky pitch-dark-tunnel-with-shadowbox presentation of historical scenes, [that] incorporates some minor archeological relics."[117] The pavilion also included a shopping mall and a snack bar serving the fair's only kosher food.

Jordan's pavilion, which featured an undulating concrete canopy studded with multicolored glass insets, was designed by James A. Evans and Jerusalem-born Victor Bisharat, who would later gain notoriety for the highly sculptural office buildings he would design for Stamford, Connecticut (see chapter 15).[118] Inside, a mural depicting an Arab mother and child, with accompanying text documenting their displacement from the region formerly known as Palestine, proved highly controversial; in June 1964 a group of Jewish community leaders were arrested for picketing at the pavilion.

The Indian Pavilion, designed by Mansinh Rana and Stonorov & Haws, was a rather understated composition with a glass-enclosed ground floor surmounted by a windowless block of ruddy, rough-hewn composition stone.[119] The principal building was awkwardly connected across a courtyard to a circular restaurant that served traditional Indian cuisine. Exhibition designer Ratna Mathur Fabri presented an impressive array of ancient and modern objects in glass cases and suspended textile-covered panels from a ceiling trellis built of Shisham wood, leaving the glass walls virtually unblocked. In the center of the pavilion, traditionally decorated doors, arches and columns defined more intimate exhibition spaces. Although the exterior of the pavilion was not particularly distinguished by day, at night it took on an almost otherworldly dimension as the interior displays were revealed through an illuminated veil of water that fell outside the glass walls.

The African Pavilion, sponsored by a private investment group called African Pavilion, Inc., housed exhibits by twenty-four independent nations.[120] The scenic and exhibit designer Tom John had originally proposed a series of rondavels, or traditional round houses, raised up on wooden stilts. But the executing architects, Kahn & Jacobs, rejected a scholarly, archaeological approach to traditional form in favor of a stylized Modernism. The pavilion's most notable feature was Paolo D'Anna's second-story Tree House restaurant and bar, which featured wood-plank floors, bright yellow and red walls covered with plastic vines, and large glassless windows equipped with wooden shutters. D'Anna decorated the rooms with items he purchased on a nine-week trip through Africa: musical instruments, embroidered tapestries, fetishes and carvings. Colorful appointments at the pandamis-covered rattan tables were intentionally mismatched, as were the waiters' Nigerian batik uniforms. From the restaurant, diners could view the Burundi drummers and the Ivory Coast and Zulu dancers who performed outside, as well as watch a caged giraffe named Suzie. Mary Simons, writing in *Interiors*, described the restaurant as "an unpretentious fantasy of Africa."[121] Perry and Burns were decidedly less impressed with the entire pavilion, criticizing it as a demonstration of outmoded imperialism: "A 'white hunter' shills the public into the interior court where 'colorful natives' perform for the nice people. The whole thing is embarrassingly patronizing."[122]

The Japanese Pavilion, designed by the architect Kunio Mayekawa, working with Kiyoshi Seike, Kyoritsu Sekkei Jimusho, and the firms of Oppenheimer, Brady & Lehrecke and Chapman, Evans & Delehanty, consisted of a main building, whose design was a synthesis of modern and traditional Japanese architecture, and a fully traditional auxiliary building.[123] The main building looked like a Japanese castle; it was surrounded by a moat and clad in sculpured, lava-rock panels designed by the Japanese sculptor Masayuki Nagara. Six hundred tons of stone were imported from Japan for the walls, which also incorporated pipes that spewed water into the moat. While *Art News* said merely that "Japan's dark, rough-textured rock looks good in juxtaposition to the shoddiness of many of its neighbors,"[124] Von Eckardt characterized the building as "almost self-effacingly handsome,"[125] and *Time* noted that some observers found Nagara's work the best art created for the fair.[126] Exhibits in the main building stressed the superiority of Japanese industry; in the auxiliary building were samisen and koto concerts, demonstrations of flower arranging and the tea ceremony, and, according to *Newsweek*, "a geisha house offering cut rates for group reservations."[127]

The Swiss Pavilion was conventional, made up of a group of chalets, but the country also sponsored the spectacular Swiss Sky Ride, a string of brightly colored gondolas that took passengers on a breathtaking four-and-a-half-minute ride 115 feet above the fair.[128] The pavilions of Korea (Chung Up Kim and Walter Dorwin Teague), the Republic of China (C. C. Yang and Paul K. Y. Chen & Associates), Hong Kong (Eldridge Snyder) and Thailand (Gasehm Suwongsa) each represented their nation's traditional architecture.[129] The Hong Kong Pavilion, surrounded by a moat containing sampans, was, according to Perry and Burns, "just as commercial as the place itself," with pretzels being sold from one of the boats and made-to-measure clothing, ready in two hours, available for purchase at supposedly bargain prices.[130] Thailand's pavilion was a plywood replica of the Mondop of Saraburi, an eighteenth-century Buddhist shrine; the intricately decorated roof of the replica was built in Thailand and reconstructed at the fair.

Unlike the corporation-sponsored pavilions of the 1939–40 World's Fair, which set the pace for daring, innovative, streamlined design, almost none of the corporate buildings that constituted the industrial area of the 1964–65 fair were stylistically distinguished. While the best of the 1939–40 fair's corporate-sponsored pavilions presented a consumer-accessible future, their 1964–65 counterparts emphasized the beneficial power of sophisticated technology, which the buildings themselves embodied through hyperbolic displays of engineering and constructionally exhibitionist architecture.

Prominently located in front of the Fountain of the Planets and closing the fair's principal axis down the 600-yard-long central mall was the Bell Telephone System Pavilion, designed by Harrison & Abramovitz with Henry Dreyfuss serving as design consultant and Paul Weidlinger serving as structural engineer.[131] The 400-foot-long winglike structure was elevated on twenty-four-foot pillars that permitted bold, 108-foot cantilevers. A 180,000-square-foot skin composed of forty-by-twelve-foot fiberglass panels was wrapped around the steel structure, creating an overall effect that looked, to the editors of *Industrial Design*, "somewhat like a grounded flying saucer,"[132] and to the editors of *Time* like "a big hunk of sedimentary rock."[133] Next to the building stood a 130-foot tower used for radio and television transmission. Inside the pavilion, visitors could take a twelve-minute ride seated on a conveyor belt to view an animated exhibit staged by the Broadway theatrical designer Jo Mielziner.

The Travelers Insurance Pavilion, designed by Kahn & Jacobs with Donald Deskey, was shaped like the company's logo—two opposing umbrellas, one of which was bright red.[134] The umbrella forms, engineered by Lev Zetlin, were supported by cables as well as by boomerang-shaped ribs emanating from a tension hub on top. The innovative scheme rendered a traditional compression ring unnecessary and radically reduced the amount of steel required; it also provided a column-free interior space.

Adopting a similarly sculptural design, the General Electric Pavilion, designed by Welton Becket & Associates, consisted of a large dome suspended from pipes that spiraled around the outside.[135] More interesting from a structural perspective was the Schaefer Center, designed by Eggers & Higgins and Walter Dorwin Teague and engineered by Seelye, Stevenson, Value & Knecht. The pavilion, which housed historical exhibits documenting the production of beer, as well as a bar and several restaurants, was composed of a cluster of interlocking curvilinear areas covered, in part, by three inflated, pillowlike nylon-and-fiberglass roofs. The circular "balloon" roofs rested on plastic-coated steel columns that were tapered at opposite ends. Beneath the largest roof, which was eighty-eight feet in diameter and twelve feet deep, the space was enclosed by transparent plastic walls embossed with a grid pattern of semicircular forms; the intended effect was, according to *Progressive Architecture*, to simulate the appearance of beer bubbles.[136]

The Eastman Kodak Pavilion, designed by Will Burtin, Inc., and executed by Kahn & Jacobs, was visually dominated by its reinforced-concrete roof, known as the "Kodak magic carpet."[137] The undulating, warped and molded surface of the roof, covered in synthetic rubber and reached by means of escalators, included an eighty-foot-high tower supporting five photographs, each thirty by thirty-six feet, that the sponsor claimed were the world's largest photographic prints. The rooftop also featured a

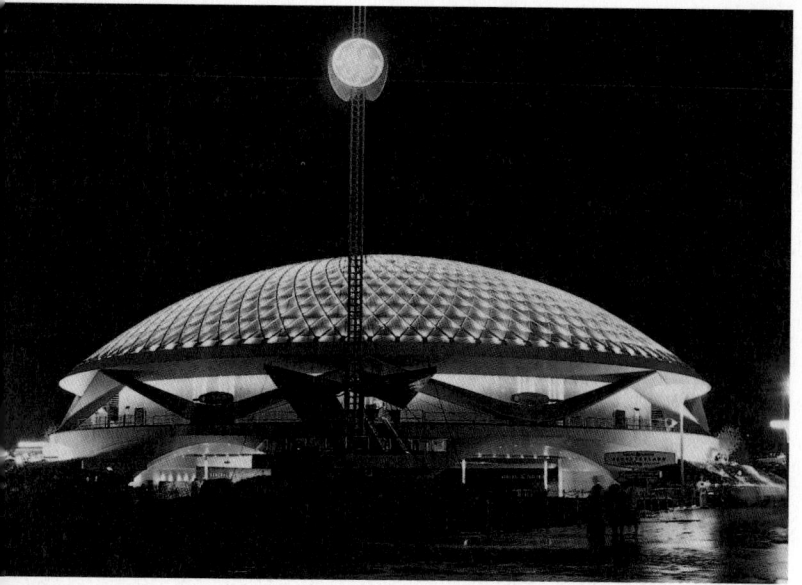

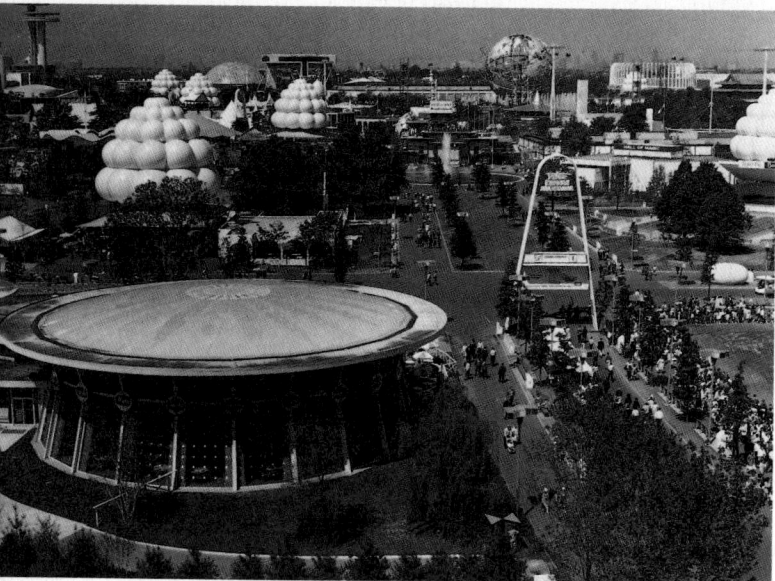

Top: General Electric Pavilion, New York World's Fair. Welton Becket & Associates, 1964. Night view to the southeast. NYPL

Bottom: View to the southwest of New York World's Fair showing Schaefer Center (Eggers & Higgins and Walter Dorwin Teague, 1964) in the lower left, and four Brass Rail food concession stands (Vollmer Associates and Victor Lundy, 1964) behind. Golby. QM

children's play area, including a monumentally scaled photograph of the circus clown Emmett Kelly, but it was principally a highly abstract, lunarlike landscape that the sponsor hyped as an ideal setting for taking photographs.

The Pepsi-Cola Pavilion, called "It's a Small World," was designed by WED Enterprises, the Disney-owned corporation responsible for the design of Disneyland (WED stood for Walter Elias Disney).[138] The pavilion was announced by the Tower of the Four Winds, a 120-foot-high openwork structure made up of a collection of fancifully shaped aluminum parts that moved in the wind. Edward Carpenter, writing in *Industrial Design*, noted that it looked "like a windmill from Oz . . . what an over-enthusiastic press agent might describe as a symphony of color and motion."[139] Within the banal, containerlike building, which would have looked at home on any suburban commercial strip, visitors rode in boats through a tunnel simulating an around-the-world trip as hundreds of animated models of children and animals sang a spirited song titled "It's a Small World After All." The anthem, according to *Time*, was "an original tune about the cohesion of the peoples of the world that might have been composed by Wendell Willkie."[140] The exhibit proved particularly popular with young fairgoers, but Ralph Caplan was less than entranced: "I must admit that a little of Disney's best goes a long way with me, and the fair is loaded with his second best. For Pepsi Cola, he plugs one world by presenting all the world's children as identical simpering dolls."[141]

Welton Becket & Associates, designers of the Coca-Cola Pavilion, eschewed dazzling technological feats and animated wonders, joining many of the foreign pavilions in presenting convincing if far from scholarly re-creations of other places—in this case, five exotic locations in countries where the soft drink was sold: the Taj Mahal, the temple of Angkor Wat, Hong Kong, the Alps and a cruise ship anchored in Rio de Janiero (which allegedly provided week-long shelter for a runaway local boy).[142]

The humorously titled Festival of Gas, financed by companies representing the gas industry and designed by Walter Dorwin Teague, consisted of two massive columns supporting gypsum-covered steel trusses that cantilevered out over 30,000 square feet of space.[143] The exhibitions featured futuristic appliances, including a dry-cleaning machine designed for home use and a machine that produced disposable plastic dishes. The pavilion's indoor-outdoor restaurant, called Festival '64 and operated by Restaurant Associates, furthered the theme by utilizing futuristic portable tableside cooking and serving carts designed by the operators in cooperation with Corning Glass Works and Teague. Restaurant Associates took the futurist theme close to the level of absurdity in their "U.S. menu of tomorrow," which included, according to *Newsweek*, such curiously inventive dishes as green-corn pie with shrimp and black walnut fried pike.[144]

More architecturally striking than the Festival of Gas was the Tower of Light, sponsored by investor-owned electric utility companies.[145] Designed by Synergetics, Inc., and based on an initial design concept by Robinson-Capsis-Stern Associates, the pavilion consisted of 600 glistening aluminum-surfaced prisms, a construction Von Eckardt dismissed as "an oddly squashed mass of cubes."[146] But the building's unusual shape was not its most outstanding feature. Above the principal entrance, which boasted "The Brightest Show on Earth" and was crowned by a visually delicate-looking, spirelike suspended sculpture by Kenneth Snelson, the pavilion emanated skyward a 12-billion-candlepower search beam, equivalent to the light projected by 340,000 automobile headlights.

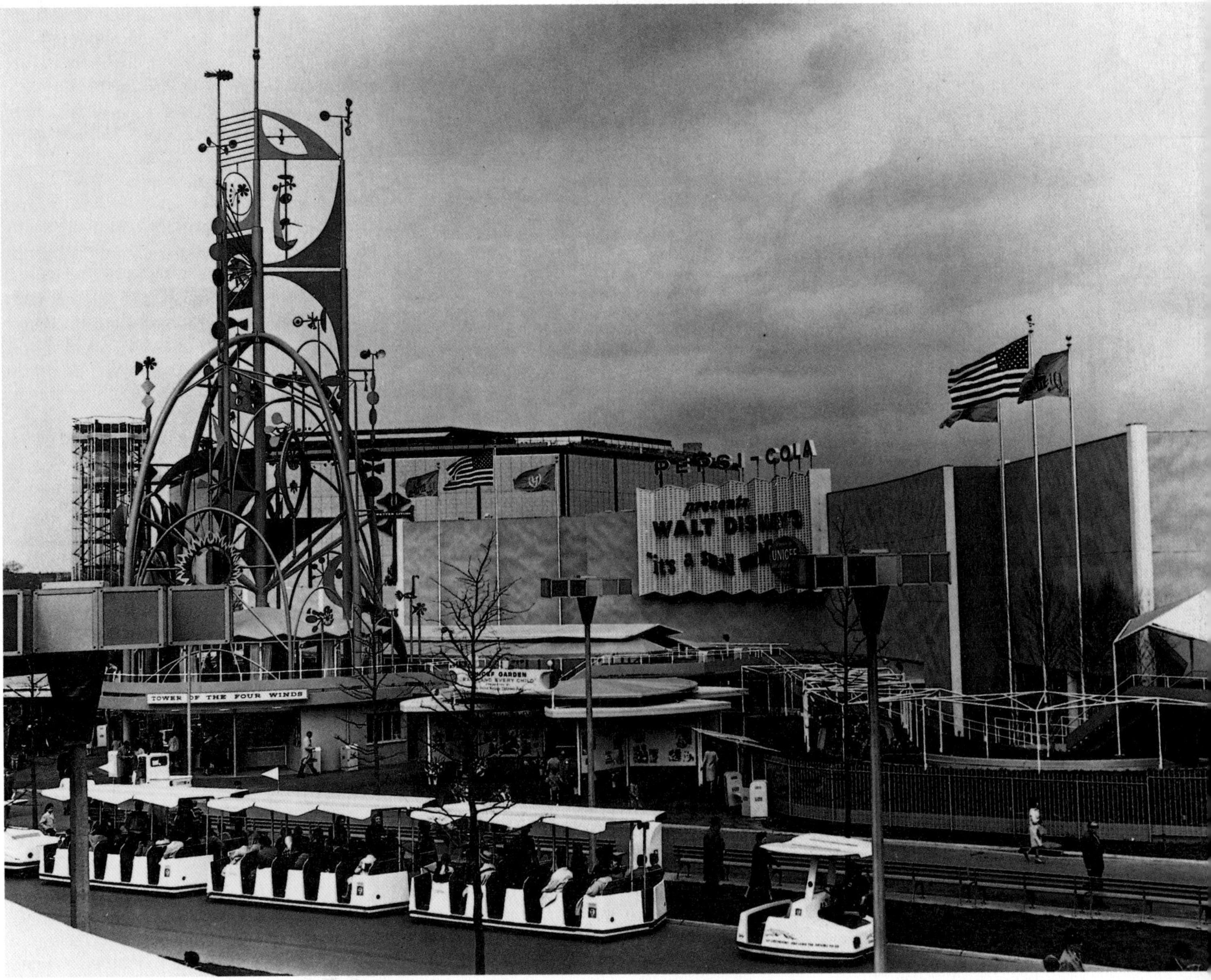

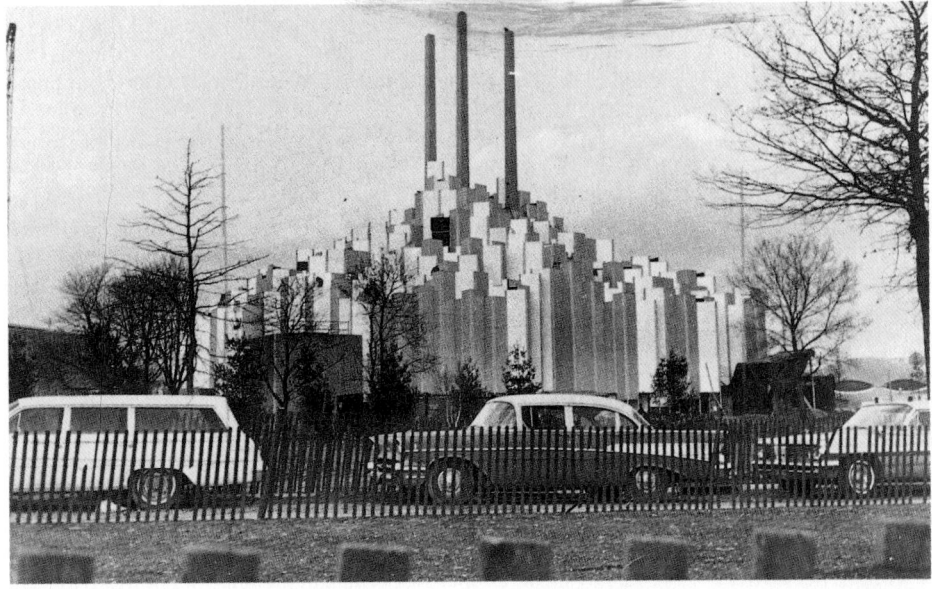

Above: Pepsi-Cola Pavilion, New York World's Fair. WED Enterprises, 1964. View to the northeast. NYPL

Left: Tower of Light, New York World's Fair. Synergetics, Inc. and Robinson-Capsis-Stern Associates, 1964. View to the north. Liotta. NYP

The Johnson's Wax Pavilion, designed by the architectural firm of Lippincott & Margulies, with Severud-Elstad-Krueger serving as engineers, consisted of the Golden Rondelle Theater, raised above the ground and supported by six columns that curved to meet above its gold-colored, steel-ribbed dome.[147] Inside, a highly praised film, *To Be Alive*, was shown on a three-part screen. Following the fair's closing, the theater was transported to the company's headquarters in Racine, Wisconsin, Frank Lloyd Wright's landmark corporate complex of 1939.[148]

Of the more than forty corporation-sponsored pavilions located in the industrial area, none more effectively integrated architecture and exhibition design than the structurally daring IBM Pavilion, designed by Eero Saarinen & Associates and Charles Eames.[149] The vast, steel-framed ovoid form, whose white, gunite-sprayed surface was embossed with a pattern of the company's initials, rested on a canopy of 14,000 gray and green plexiglass panels supported by forty-five intertwined, thirty-two-foot-high steel "trees" allowed to rust to give them a naturalistic color. Inside the one-acre "garden," a multitude of exhibits and puppet shows dramatized the history and workings of computers. Entertained by an accordian player, visitors walked along catwalks suspended above a shallow pool of water before seating themselves in a 500-person-capacity grandstand that the sponsor called the "people wall." After a master of ceremonies dressed in white tie and tails descended from near the ceiling, the grandstand was hydraulically lifted fifty-three feet up into the "egg" form, which was 115 feet long, 89 feet wide and 58 feet high. There visitors were treated to a slide and film presentation, created by Charles Eames and his wife Ray, a fast-paced, kaleidoscopic show, simultaneously projected on fourteen screens, that sought to explain the complexities of computers.

Vincent Scully gave a vivid description of the fairgoer's experience of the IBM Pavilion:

> You take your place, part of a vast shelf of humanity, and are lifted backward up into the egg where a delightful multi-screen movie by Eames is shown. The film is more or less about computers. Then all opens and down you slide again, cheered on by a splendid fellow who began the whole business by appearing before you high in space on a platform let down from the egg—like a jolly young god, triumphant over gravity. At his appearance the children of every performance scream for joy. In this punctual *deus ex machina* the designers have hit a Dionysian button calling up emotions of awe, terror, recognition and joy.[150]

The pavilion was widely praised. Ralph Caplan found it to be "the most inviting at the Fair,"[151] while Perry and Burns succinctly stated that it was "one of the few that didn't lay an egg. See it, THINK, and marvel at the mind of man and his machines."[152] Huxtable said that the pavilion was "an imaginative fun fair of information [and] proves that the corporate message can be put across as an integrated architectural-design concept."[153] The editors of *Newsweek* described the film presentation as "wonderfully imaginative" and the other exhibits as consistently "tasteful" and "non-commercialized."[154] In a generally negative article about the fair published prior to its opening, Martin Mayer said that the presence of the IBM Pavilion meant that "there will be at least one genuinely distinguished exhibit."[155] The pavilion's attempt to tell the story of computers in "one structural extravaganza" demonstrated, according to *Esquire*, that "the IBM show is bidding to make World's Fair history (just as cast iron and steam power had their monument in London's 1851 Crystal Palace, steel in Paris' 1880 Eiffel Tower,

internal combustion engines in the 1939–40 Futurama exhibition of the earlier New York Fair)."[156] The pavilion did have its detractors, however. Von Eckardt was harsh in his criticism, writing that the pavilion "doesn't come off as anything but another bit of architectural acrobatics. . . . Saarinen's architecture, I'm sorry to report, doesn't help but hinders IBM's efforts to communicate its story."[157]

Scattered throughout the fair's industrial area were several pavilions featuring exhibits on domestic architecture and interior decoration. Though they presented a full range of stylistic vocabularies, the emphasis was not so much on style, nor were futuristic themes important. What counted in these icons of consumerism were the familiar manifestations of the good life in America. The fair's third largest pavilion, the Better Living Center, designed by John Lo Pinto & Associates, was characterized by *Interior Design* as "probably the shoddiest exhibit hall at the fair and certainly the crassest in its blatant commercialism."[158]

Other pavilions related to interiors were a bit more successful. The four-story glass-and-steel Pavilion of American Interiors was designed by Thomas H. Yardley and John Vassos and consisted of three intersecting circular structures containing fourteen rooms, each designed by members of the American Institute of Interior Designers to reflect the traditions of a different state or region.[159] One room, sponsored by the International Silver Company and designed by Ellen Lehman McCluskey, went far beyond regional or even national boundaries: her so-called Moon Room incorporated a clear lucite table and chairs that were meant to provide "gracious dining, even in outer space."[160]

The House of Good Taste, named by Thomas Deegan, of the fair's original organizing committee, was in fact made up of three houses and a separate structure.[161] Located near the fair's main entrance, the exhibit occupied a two-acre site landscaped by Clarke & Rapuano. The pavilion was the brainchild of Lady Malcolm Douglas Hamilton, a socialite who was not professionally trained as a designer. Working with the American Institute of Approval, a group of socially prominent "non-professional women deeply interested in good taste" whom Lady Hamilton selected, she asked three architects to each design a house, costing between $30,000 and $40,000, that represented "a different American architectural philosophy."[162] The houses, labeled Modern, Contemporary and Traditional, were intended, according to Lady Hamilton, "to present a national concept of the attractive living which is within reach of all Americans as the result of the combined creativity and industry of American business and labor."[163]

The Modern House was designed by Edward Durell Stone, by far the best known of the three architects participating in the project.[164] It was built out close to the edge of its hypothetical lot line and had a square plan organized around an atrium containing a glass dome twenty-two feet in diameter and a sunken reflecting pool paved with fieldstone. According to the editors of *Interiors*, Stone's goal in this internally focused design was to provide "an antidote to the growing sprawl of tract homes on patch lawns,"[165] what the architect derided as "Mount Vernons and Monticellos on 50-by-100-foot lots."[166] The editors asserted that Stone's design constituted "a return to the Greek and Roman concept of town houses."[167] The house's interiors, decorated by Sarah Hunter Kelly and Esther Wilcox, featured contemporary paintings and sculpture lent by the Whitney Museum. The Contemporary House, designed by Jack Pickens Coble, with interiors by Dede Draper working in association with Arturo Pini di

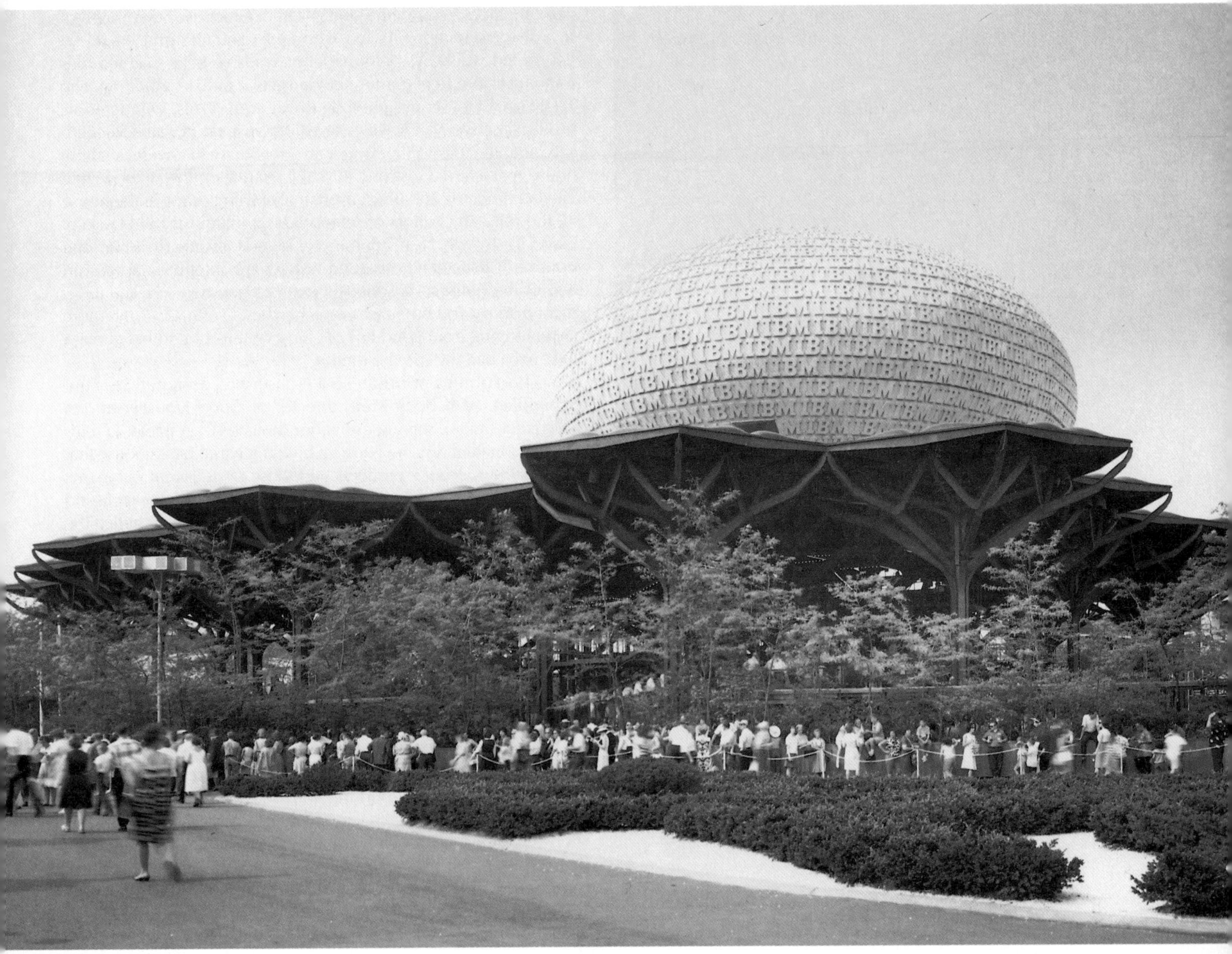

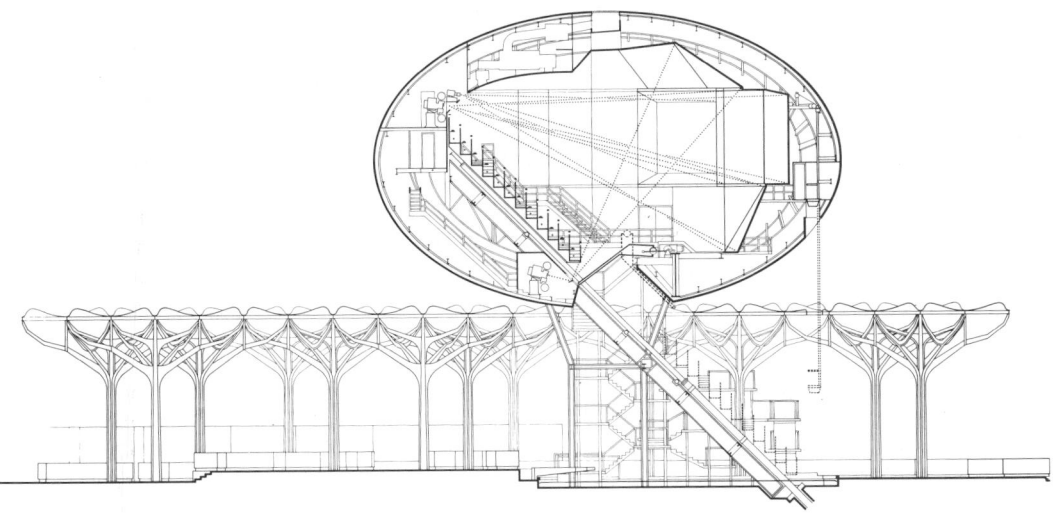

Above: IBM Pavilion, New York
World's Fair. Eero Saarinen &
Associates and Charles Eames,
1964. View to the northeast.
KRJDA

Left: IBM Pavilion. Section.
KRJDA

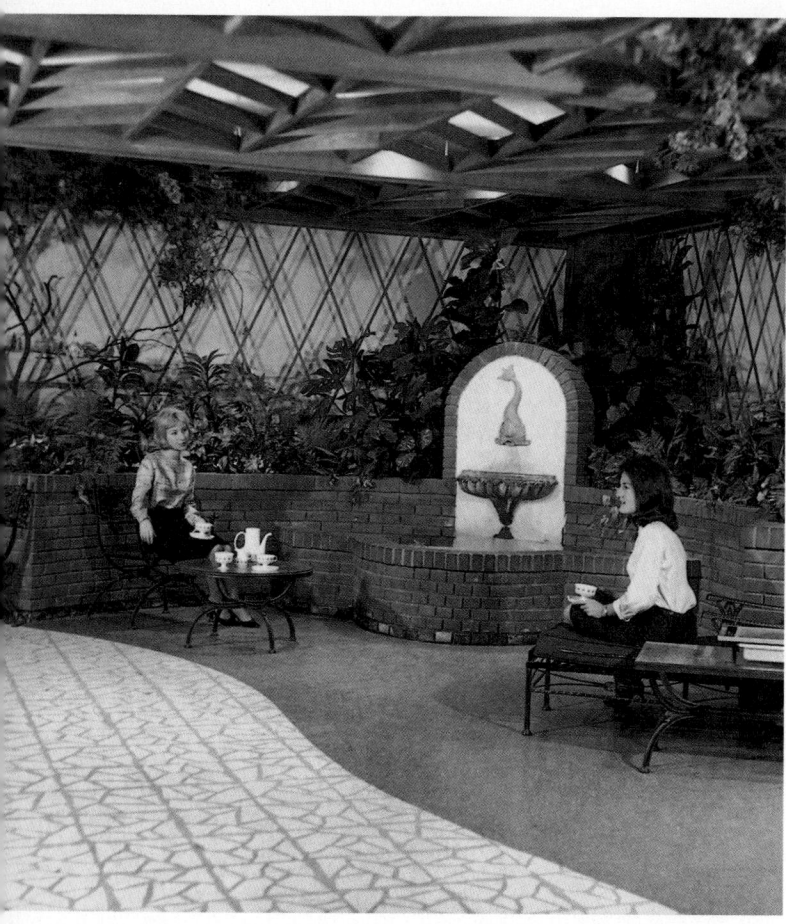

Underground Home, New York World's Fair. Jay H. Swayze with
Marilyn Motto, 1964. Patio. PF

San Miniato, Dora Brahms and Michael Greer, was composed of
five discrete sections roofed with cedar shingles and linked by
flat-roofed walkways. With exterior walls of beige-painted aluminum set into steel frames, the house was rather forbidding. The
Traditional House, designed by Royal Barry Wills, with interiors
by Ellen Lehman McCluskey, Everett Brown and C. Eugene Stephenson, adapted a Colonial American vocabulary to a wide, shallow
house that exerted a strong formal presence on the street. White
vinyl clapboards and black asphalt roof shingles made the house
all too real. The editors of *Interior Design* said that the House of
Good Taste was "a misnomer on several counts. It is not one
house but three, and the good taste of the interiors—at least in
two of the houses—is seriously open to question."[168] The judgment of Perry and Burns was even harsher: "Taste, taste and more
taste, ranging from good to bad, most of it just middling enough
to leave a bad taste in the mouth."[169]

The Formica World's Fair House was designed by Emil
Schmidlen, with Betty Kraft, director of *Good Housekeeping's*
Decorator Studio, serving as interior designer.[170] A paean to middle-class mediocrity, the Formica building was a ranch house that
hustled the sponsor's products and those of its parent company,
American Cyanamid. One mildly futuristic touch was the inclusion
of a push-button telephone in every room. Intended to entice the
consumer and influence the market, the Formica house was one of
six models designed by Schmidlen in a variety of styles, including
Cape Cod and Regency, that were to be franchised nationwide.

The Underground Home was developed to save the American landscape from the onslaught of both high-rise and tract-
house construction.[171] Improbably located in the transportation
area, it was sponsored by a former carpenter, builder and
teacher of chemical warfare techniques, Jay H. Swayze, who
had prospered as the owner of a large building supply company
in Texas. Swayze had built himself a ten-room underground
house in Texas which, like the subsequent house at the fair, was
equipped with a wood-burning fireplace and rheostats for mod-
ulating the light in the space between the exterior wall of the
house and the surrounding concrete retaining walls to simulate
various weather conditions and times of day. The retaining walls
around the exhibition house featured "dial-a-view," a selection
of landscape murals that furthered the illusion of above-ground
space and light. Swayze argued that the radical concept of the
house, which he hoped would serve as a prototype for future development, needed to be tempered by a conventional interior
treatment, in this case a watered-down Mediterranean scheme
devised by Marilyn Motto. Despite the reassuringly familiar
decor, the house was disquietingly macabre, as if William Levitt
had teamed up with Charles Addams.

Swayze claimed that in addition to preserving the natural environment, underground living also provided numerous health and
economic advantages. Many visitors saw it more as a kind of insurance plan in the face of an apocalyptic future. Perry and Burns
designated the house "winner of P/A's Dr. Strangelove Award."[172]
After an initial visit to the underground house, the editors of the
New Yorker said that it had "come to haunt our dreams." In a subsequent visit, they observed: "It is buried, like a qualifying footnote,
under an archway that proclaims the theme of the fair to be 'Peace
Through Understanding.' On the whole, it is an anomalous piece
of domestic architecture, combining the small, familiar pleasures
of the hearth with the headier excitements of Doomsday. It will not
suit every temperament. It did not suit ours."[173]

Located in both the international and industrial areas were
several pavilions sponsored by religious groups. While their
presence implied the potential of the world's religions to facili-

tate "peace through understanding," their architecture was less than inspirational. The Mormon Church Pavilion, designed by Fordyce & Hamby, grafted a replica of the principal facade of the Tabernacle in Salt Lake City, Utah, onto a rather undistinguished Modernist building.[174] This was the closest most people would come to walking through the doors of the imposing temple, as the original was open only to Mormons. Perry and Burns ridiculed the false-front structure as "surely the world's largest (perhaps its only) free-standing facade. . . . The stonework is of a material strangely resembling divinity fudge."[175] Von Eckardt was characteristically scathing in his criticism of "the giant papier-mâché replica of the Ulysses S. Grant Gothic Mormon Temple in Utah," which he characterized as one of the fair's "hideous transgressions of architectural decency."[176] At the fair's close, the pavilion was dismantled and transported to the town of Plainview, Nassau County, where it was to be used as a Mormon chapel.

Edward Durell Stone designed two linked, seven-sided buildings for the Christian Science Pavilion (an earlier, unrealized scheme had called for a building in the shape of a six-pointed star).[177] He also designed an octagonal building for the Billy Graham Evangelistic Association in which a film, Man in the Fifth Dimension, featuring the famous evangelist, was presented and translated simultaneously into six languages.[178]

By far the most popular religious pavilion, and in fact the second most heavily visited pavilion at the fair, was that sponsored by the Vatican.[179] It was also, for what it was worth, the fair's cultural highlight. Designed by the firms of York & Sawyer, Hurley & Hughes and Lunders & Associates, the elliptical building was surmounted by a circular, tentlike cupola topped by a crucifix—a composition that was, as Perry and Burns rather charitably put it, "no threat to St. Peter's architecturally."[180] Among the pavilion's exhibits were slides of the Sistine Chapel, Cardinal Spellman's personal coin and stamp collection, a replica of Peter's tomb and a variety of historical artifacts. But what made the pavilion extraordinary was its display of Michelangelo's Pietà.

When Pope John XXIII agreed in 1962 to exhibit the Pietà at the fair, art lovers were alarmed that damage might occur during the cross-Atlantic shipping. Alfred Frankfurter, editor of Art News, went so far as to state that transporting the two-ton marble sculpture, which had been moved only twice, both times within Rome, since it was completed around 1499, constituted a "drastic and gratuitous act of vandalism."[181] Despite such fears, the Pietà made the trip safely. Among the millions who visited it at the fair were Pope Paul VI, who went to the pavilion following a trip to the United Nations on October 4, 1965.

In a setting designed by Jo Mielziner, the Pietà was displayed against blue drapery and illuminated by hundreds of flickering colored electric lights, meant to evoke votive candles; recorded Gregorian chants were played. The Pietà was placed behind thick bulletproof plastic, sixteen feet away from the spectators, who traversed the pavilion on three moving sidewalks and were given less than a minute to gaze at the work of art. Vincent Scully described the setting as "shameful."[182] Robert Hughes felt that in showing the Pietà "the Vatican managed to imply that the Catholic Church had been specially invented for the World's Fair by an impresario from Las Vegas," and he criticized the display techniques: "The warm old marble is drained by lights to a dead fish-belly white: is it really the Pietà, this ghost behind its bullet-proof glass, or is it a wax effigy from Madame Tussaud's?"[183] John Leo, writing in the Catholic journal Commonweal, criticized the entire pavilion, which he said was

"awash in flickering slides, banners, posters, photos, medieval knickknacks and fatuous slogans—an ecclesiastical Automat to tempt the taste of any tourist."[184]

Transportation Area

As in the 1939–40 fair, the transportation industry earned an area of its own, and once again it was dominated by pavilions sponsored by the nation's three largest automobile companies: Chrysler, Ford and General Motors. Chrysler's presentation, designed by George Nelson, consisted of numerous pavilions and outdoor exhibits located on five islands linked by bridges and placed within an almond-shaped reflecting pool.[185] One building was shaped like an enormous car; among the exhibits were a model of an automobile engine large enough to walk through, and a replica of an assembly line along which visitors could ride in an open car frame. Punctuating the parklike setting were "bucket seats" that served as benches. Scully found the entire Chrysler exhibit to be "the surprise of the fair," and he praised it as "pop-art at its best," presenting "Detroit with welcome wit and irony."[186]

Ford's enormous pavilion, designed by Welton Becket & Associates, was distinguished by a 235-foot-diameter glass rotunda encircled by sixty-four soaring pylons that rose above the building and curved inward to the top, as well as by two spiraling glass-enclosed roadways.[187] Perry and Burns commented on the menacing appearance of the towering, tentacular pylons of the pavilion, which they pronounced "winner of [the] Venus Flytrap Award."[188] But it was the pavilion's principal exhibit that stole the show. Seated in 1964 Ford convertibles, visitors were electronically moved along tracks in the roadways and through WED Enterprises' "Magic Skyway" exhibit, a "time tunnel" that presented Walt Disney's version of history from the Mesozoic era through the present and into the future. Along the twelve-minute journey, fairgoers looked at lavishly detailed animated dioramas while they listened to a narration available in four languages on their push-button car radios. Prior to the exhibit's opening, the editors of Newsweek noted that "prehistoric beasts with intestines of transistors, magnetic tape, and air pumps will fight, feed, and slog through primeval swamps; cavemen will move about, grunt, wave, hunt animals, paint cave figures, and in the words of a Ford Pavilion official, one of Henry Ford's forebears will invent the wheel."[189] The ride ended with a glimpse of a "Space City" of the future.

Robert Malone, editor of Industrial Design, described the "future" portion of the ride, "which looked like nothing so much as the inside view of the '49 Wurlitzer. . . . All kinds of what must be flying roadways twisted between pre-Bel Geddes building shapes, and stars whirled over head in configurations and revolutions really out of this world or any other."[190] Newsweek noted the emphasis on automobiles in Ford's view of the future: "Space City is clogged with cars. But where are the people?"[191] Scully once again scathingly criticized the exhibit's principal creator, Walt Disney, stating that he "so vulgarizes everything he touches that the facts lose all force, living things their stature, and the 'history of the world' its meaning."[192] But the exhibit proved immensely popular with the fairgoers. As Time observed: "Ford's Magic Skyway is worth a wait of perhaps 30 minutes, on a cool day. But lines mass there as if the company were giving away Fords. The superb showmanship of putting people in new automobiles and driving them past an assemblage of plastic reptiles and plastic cavemen by Walt Disney is more than the contemporary world is able to resist."[193]

1049

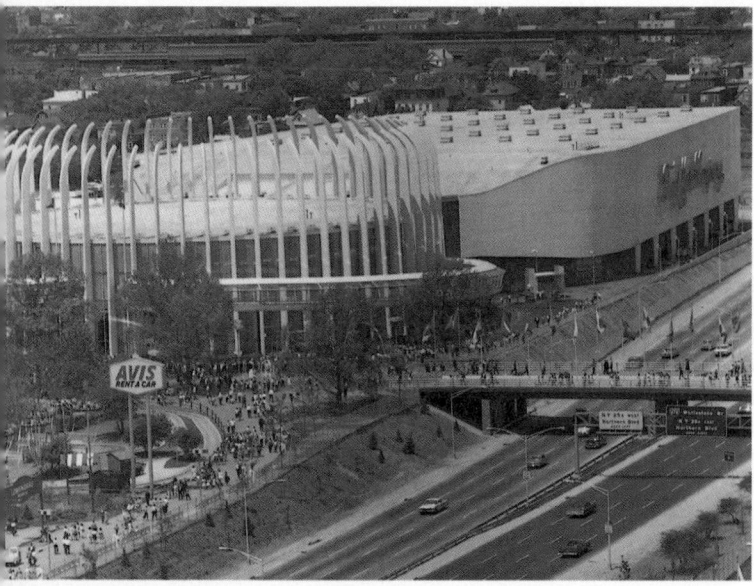

The star of the transportation area, and the most heavily attended attraction of the fair, was the General Motors Pavilion.[194] The building was designed by Sol King and the firm of Albert Kahn Associated Architects & Engineers; Kahn, who had died in 1942, designed General Motors' entry at the 1939–40 World's Fair.[195] The pavilion was a crisper but less inventive version of the streamlined Modernism celebrated at the earlier fair. In 1960, when General Motors first considered participating in the fair, it commissioned a design from Louis I. Kahn, who proposed several schemes, all of which called for a series of pavilions arranged, with varying degrees of geometric rigor, in an arc shape.[196] One scheme incorporated an arrangement of 100-foot-wide, 20-foot-high octagonal pavilions that were connected by trapezoidal and pentagonal linkages and rose to a height of 250 feet. Kahn's final proposal consisted of seven inflated dome-shaped structures, each composed of an outer layer of cloth and an inner layer of plastic, all held up by a middle layer of helium balloons. Two large structures, approximately 250 feet in diameter, flanked five others, about 150 feet in diameter. The pavilions' inner domes served as curved projecting screens.

As built, the General Motors Pavilion was a rectilinear building punctuated at one end by a domed, circular structure where cars and other General Motors products were displayed and at the other end by a curved, ten-story-high, aluminum-clad facade that jutted forward at an acute angle and contained the principal entrance. Resembling the tail fin of a late model car, the facade was an attempt, not altogether successful, to keep consumer-oriented, streamlined Modernist architecture as up-to-date as automobile design. In fact, Ralph Caplan said, rather than evoking mobility, the building looked as if it was "about to fall on its face."[197] Whereas much of the architecture at the 1939–40 World's Fair had effectively synthesized architecture and advertising, the 1964–65 General Motors Pavilion seemed to sacrifice the former in service to the latter; as the editors of *Time* put it, the building's "gigantic tail fin . . . may be good as advertising but is ridiculous as architecture."[198]

Inside, General Motors safely echoed the techniques it had used so successfully at the 1939–40 fair. Once again the Futurama ride proved to be the fair's most heavily attended attraction, outstripping even the *Pietà* in popularity, testimony to the extraordinary affection and esteem the 1939–40 exhibition had earned in the American psyche. Its popularity also demonstrated the extent to which the country's largest corporation had come to embody national values and aspirations. Large crowds waited for hours to see the exhibit, which was designed to accommodate 70,000 visitors daily. Designed by General Motors' own design staff, the exhibit presented a ride on moving, contoured armchairs, past an animated model of the future, complete with an underwater hotel, a jungle cleared by lasers and a desert made verdant by desalinated water. Except for their moving sidewalks, cities of the future seemed largely the same as cities of the present, dominated by skyscrapers and highways. Although the designers sought to avoid what many observers considered to be the major pitfall of the earlier Futurama—that it was outdated too soon—the future as envisioned by General Motors was neither very brave nor very new. "GM's future," said Caplan, "is only the technological present stretched to cover more territory."[199] Perry and Burns found the exhibit "an overbearing and somewhat frightening view of traffic eventually determining the shape of man's life (present-day harbingers can be seen right outside in the coils of expressways which snake around the fairgrounds)."[200] Scully flatly stated that the exhibit

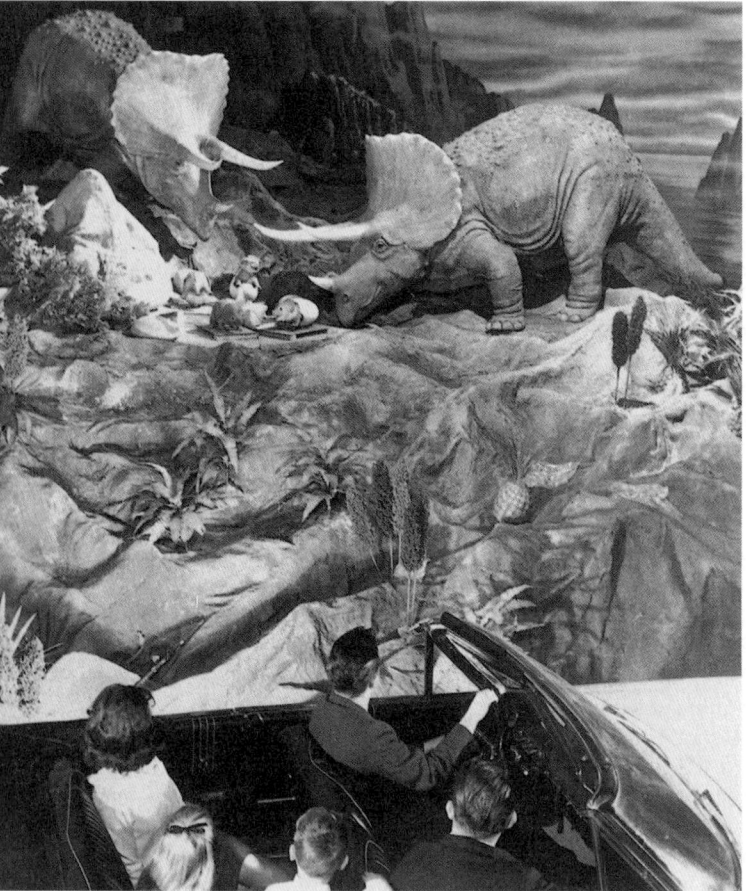

Top: Ford Motor Company Pavilion, New York World's Fair. Welton Becket & Associates, 1964. View to the northwest. Golby. QM

Bottom: Ford Motor Company Pavilion. Magic Skyway exhibit. NYP

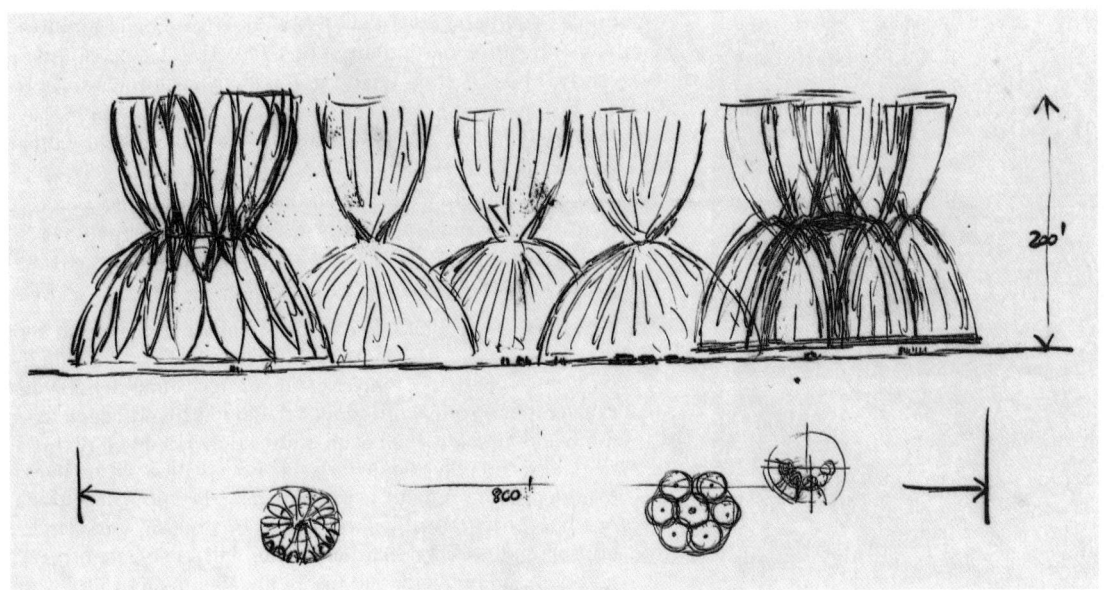

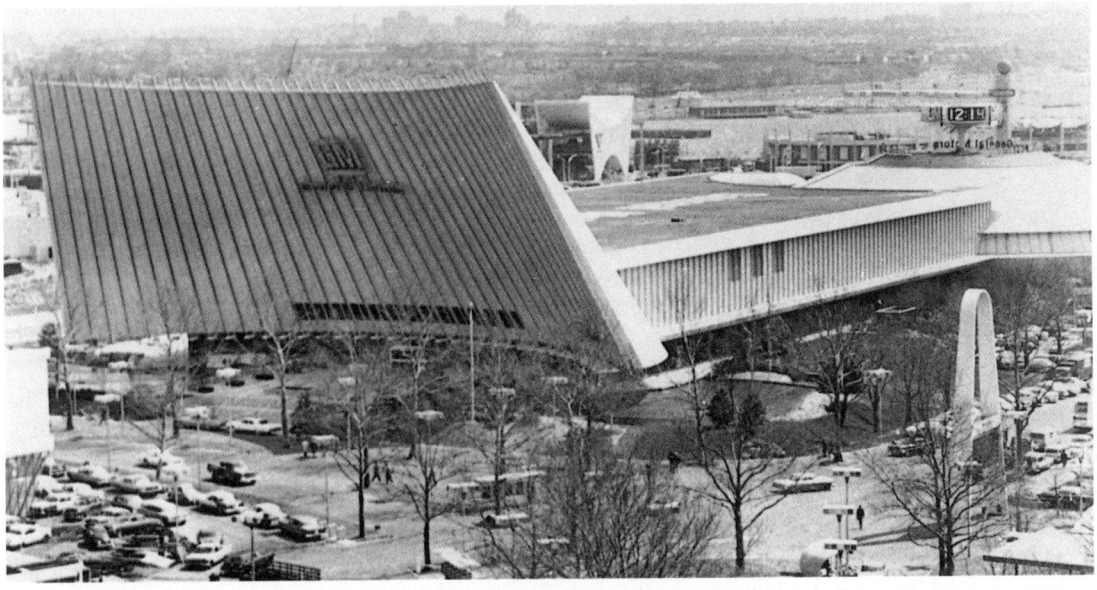

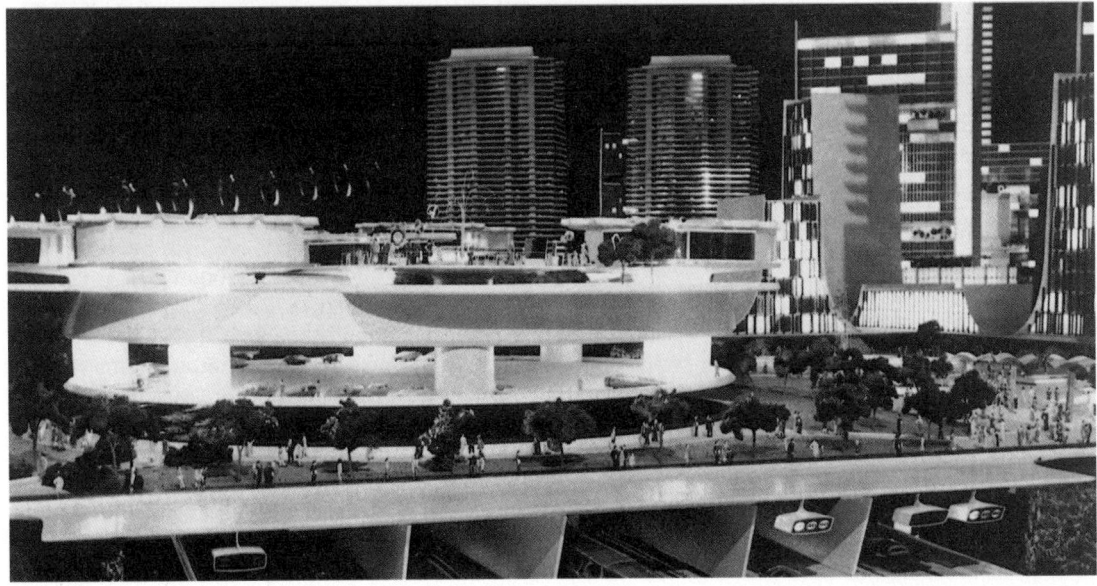

Top: Proposal for General Motors Pavilion, New York World's Fair. Louis I. Kahn, 1961. Preliminary sketch of plan and elevation. MOMA

Center: General Motors Pavilion, New York World's Fair. Sol King and Albert Kahn Associated Architects & Engineers, 1964. View to the southeast. Jacobellis. NYP

Bottom: General Motors Pavilion. Futurama exhibit. General Motors design staff, 1964. Scale model of city of the future. NYP

1051

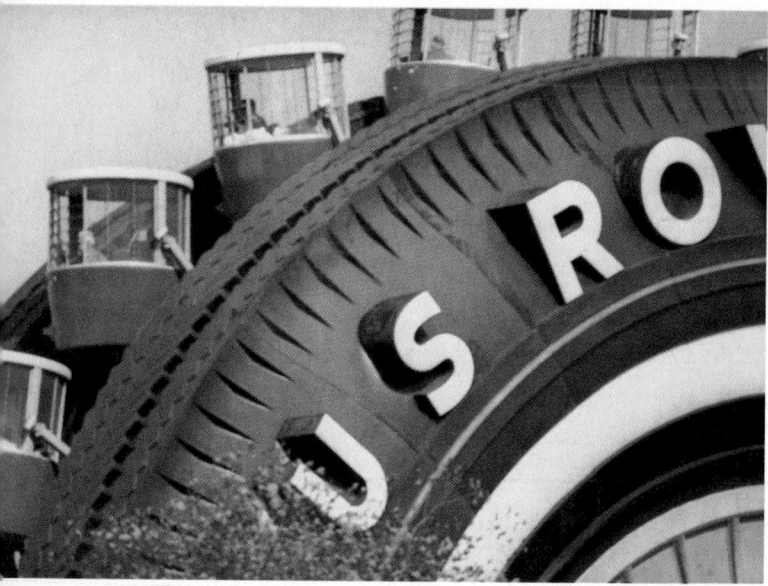

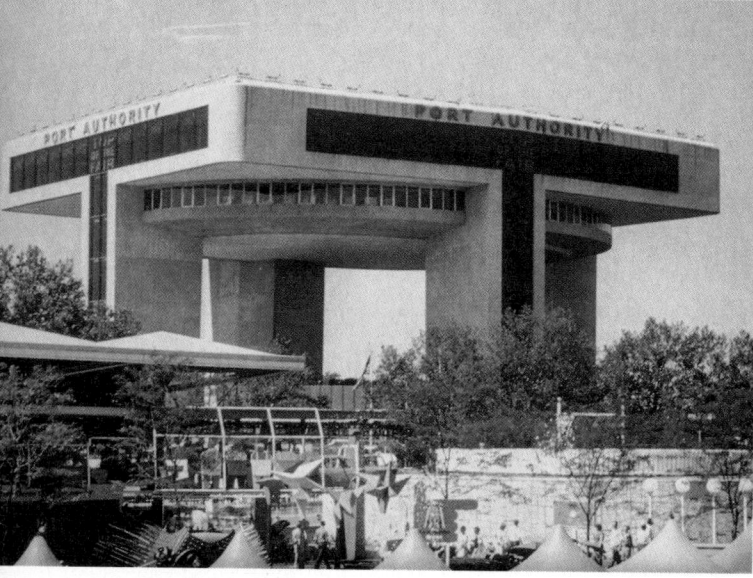

Top: U.S. Rubber Company exhibit, New York World's Fair. Shreve, Lamb & Harmon Associates, 1964. Golby. QM

Bottom: Port Authority Building, New York World's Fair. A. Gordon Lorimer, John Pile, Ray Monte and E. Donald Mills, 1964. View to the southwest. Golby. QM

Top right: Hall of Science, New York World's Fair. Harrison & Abramovitz, 1964. View to the northeast. Stoller. ©ESTO

Bottom right: Hall of Science. Interior. Stoller. ©ESTO

"embodies no ideas newer than those developed by Norman Bel Geddes in his original Futurama of 1939. The 'vision of the future' shown here is stale where not actively revolting, and provides a strong argument against letting auto manufacturers have a say in city planning. All those roads!—the American archetype of movement commercially woven to strangle us all."[201]

While the exhibit was an impeccably produced piece of showmanship, its singlemindedly optimistic attitude rendered it a virtually useless, didactic and rather banal model. Robert Malone described the exhibit's impact:

Traveling through GM's new super-duper Futurama, we kept asking ourselves exactly whose future GM was depicting—ours, theirs, or that of a mythical race. Let's admit right off that GM has put on a real pro show. . . . But if the world depicted is the world to come, then each of us should get down on his or her knees and pray that in our next reincarnation we arrive as a machine. . . . Fanciful or nightmarish? Never! This is what nearly is or darn well will be, but as in a mirror, and cleaned up, spit and polished, hard edges and interactions removed—no bomb, no homicide, no lust of the kind that is either interesting or forbidden, no peace or war marches, and at a scale where discount houses and green stamps cannot be identified.[202]

In addition to the three major automobile manufacturers, smaller companies in related industries also sponsored exhibits in the transportation area. Sinclair Oil's Dinoland, designed by J. Gordon Carr, exploited the company's symbol, a dinosaur, which represented the geologic age when oil was formed.[203] The principal exhibit consisted of nine life-size animated replicas of prehistoric animals created by the sculptor Louis Paul Jonas. Located adjacent to Dinoland was the U.S. Rubber exhibit, an eighty-foot-high ferris wheel designed to resemble a tire, complete with whitewalls, which Perry and Burns declared "winner of the P/A Pop Art Award."[204]

Two of the fair's permanent structures were located in the transportation area. The Port of New York Authority Building, designed by the agency's chief architect, A. Gordon Lorimer, engineers John Pile and Ray Monte and planning chief E. Donald Mills, consisted of four massive, 120-foot-high stilts holding a two-story structure atop which was a 175-by-200-foot helicopter landing platform.[205] Horizontal strip windows on the two-story portion of the building combined with vertical strips on the support columns to make each of the building's elevations resemble an enormous T (for transportation). Located on the upper floor was the Top of the Fair, a 1,100-seat restaurant. Designed by Lorimer, in collaboration with the architectural firm of Berger & Hennessey, the interior design firm of Chandler Cudlipp Associates, and the art director and design consultant Arturo Pini di San Miniato, the restaurant's dining room was terraced to exploit the far-ranging views. The lower, oval-shaped floor, which housed the restaurant's kitchens, was ringed around its circumference by a bar called Drinks Around the World. The Port Authority grandly identified their building as the "aerial gateway" to the fair.[206] Although the arrival and departure of tourists via helicopter did lend the fair a vaguely romantic, futuristic air, the structure itself was decidedly uninspired.

The Hall of Science, designed by Wallace Harrison as a permanent museum, was one of the fair's most architecturally distinctive and functionally problematic structures.[207] One of the few buildings sponsored by the fair corporation, the pavilion was controversial from the start. In December 1962 New York State's Board of Regents chartered the New York Museum of Science and Technology, which was planned to rival the famous science

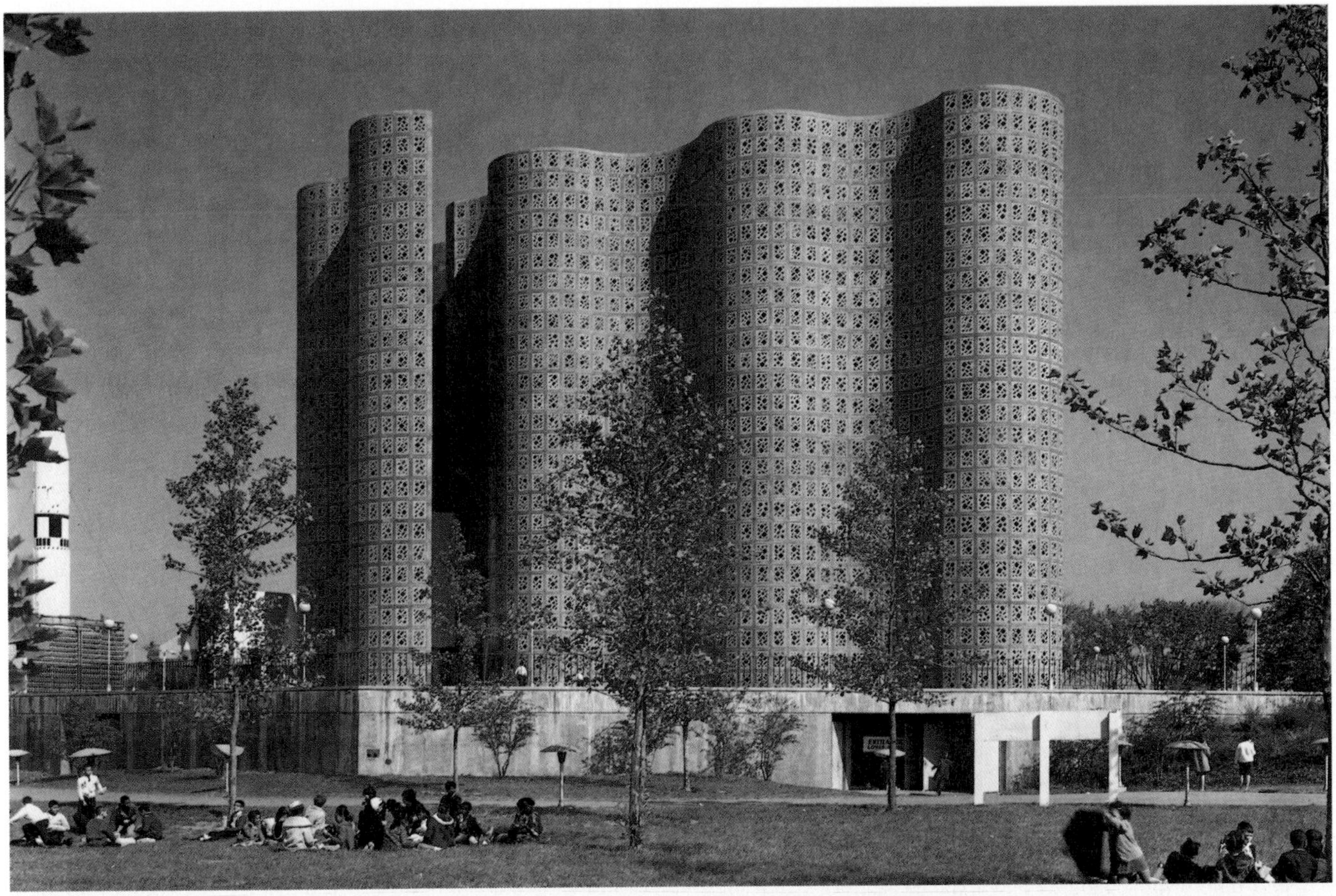

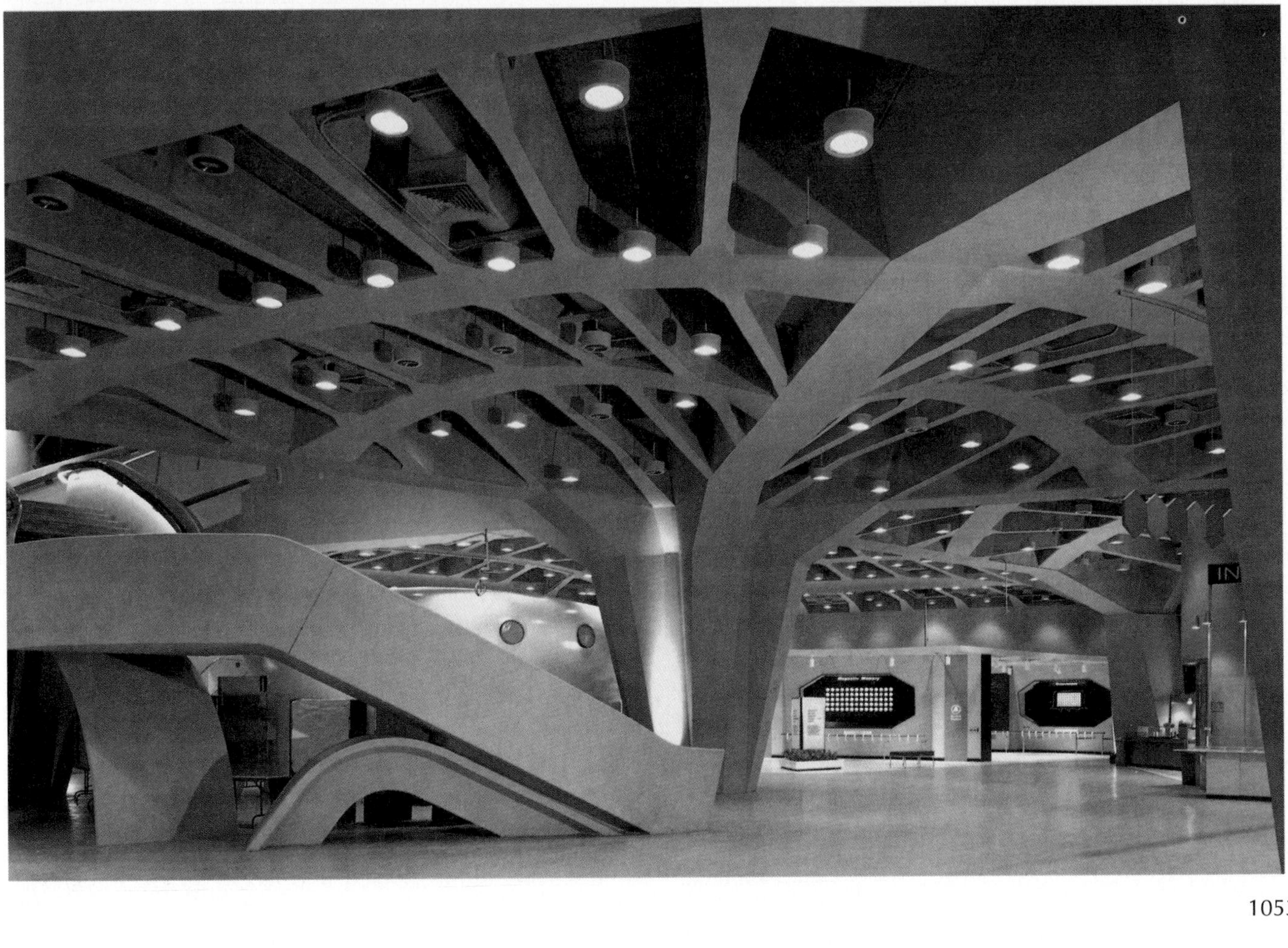

museums of Chicago and Munich, and designated a board of trustees who were charged with the task of finding a site. The following year Robert Moses, Mayor Wagner and Paul E. Screvane, president of the City Council, reputedly in an effort to fill some of the space left vacant by foreign nations that declined to participate, bypassed the museum's board and proposed to build a Hall of Science at the fair which would later serve as a permanent museum. Despite the vigorous opposition of the new museum's board, the fair proposal won Board of Estimate approval.

Harrison's design consisted of a six-sided windowless structure surmounted by a reflecting pool and, rising out of the water and its gushing fountains, a honeycombed, eighteen-inch-thick undulating wall made of concrete containing pieces of bright blue glass. The wall spiraled in on itself to enclose an eighty-foot-high free-form interior space; additional exhibition space was provided below. A long ramp led to the entrance court located on top of the platform. The effect was spectacular, combining a timeless sense of drama with technological modernity. Ada Louise Huxtable enthusiastically endorsed the design of "the extraordinary new building," which she called "an exotically handsome, highly romantic structure of great dramatic impact and considerable aesthetic allure." She continued:

> [The building] has a somber, surrealistic intricacy worthy of the cabinet of Dr. Caligari. This may be modern technology in the service of science, but it is a frankly visual and sensuous way of using it that pulls out all the emotional stops that architecture can command. . . . Here one thinks immediately of the 13th century rather than the 20th; of Sainte-Chapelle; of the drama of soaring heights stained with colored light. For this is a Cathedral of Science, rather than a Hall of Science, its luminous blue walls suggesting limitless extensions of space. At a time when science vies with religion in explaining the mysteries of the universe, this is an oddly significant architectural twist.[208]

Huxtable asserted that the building's program had been so broadly stated as to give the architect "virtual carte blanche," and she raised the issue of its suitability as a museum: "The obvious fact is that Mr. Harrison, like any architect worth his salt, wanted to build a beautiful building. He might not have designed this particular building if his assignment had been for, say, a pretzel factory, but it would surely have evolved in similar form for any amenable purpose that presented itself. It may be architectural heresy to say so, but if it works, it's all right."[209] But when Harrison's building was evaluated in 1966 in conjunction with plans to build an extensive nuclear science center nearby, along with an adjacent education and exhibit building, both designed by Max O. Urbahn & Associates, the museum was found severely lacking. The following year the City Planning Commission determined that the Hall of Science possessed "only limited salvage value" and that the city had been "saddled with a totally inadequate building which had a poorly designed exhibition space, which was an acoustical nightmare and which had a long, unattractive ramp entry."[210] The plan for new construction, which also called for extensive changes to the existing structure, was never realized.

Amusements

Like virtually every other major international fair, the 1964–65 fair exploited the timeless appeal of thrilling rides and dazzling spectacles; at the same time, like the 1939–40 fair, it maintained an official stance advocating entertainment that educated rather than entertainment that merely amused. The earlier fair had sought to establish an overall tone of highmindedness but also included a popular amusement section presenting such attractions as the highly publicized Parachute Jump and Salvador Dalí's Dreams of Venus, as well as theatrical stars such as Eleanor Holm, Johnny Weismuller and Gypsy Rose Lee.[211] In contrast, the 1964–65 fair delivered little in the way of either sophisticated or lowbrow live entertainment.

In this regard, Robert Moses revealed himself a patronizing bluenose. Robert Fontaine, an author and playwright, commented in the *Atlantic Monthly* in 1960: "I am given to understand that the dignified characters in charge of the forthcoming World's Fair . . . have loudly proclaimed that the fair will have no honky-tonk, no strip-teasers, no razzle-dazzle and no whoop-dee-do. . . . What the directors of the fair intend to do, apparently, is . . . to substitute tractors for mirth and electronic machines for good humor."[212] Fair officials may have been motivated by more than puritanical attitudes. As the editors of *Time* noted: "Girlie shows at the recent Seattle fair were a financial disaster, and efforts by operators to stimulate business by stimulating the customers brought the paddy wagon for the peelers."[213] While former Judge Samuel I. Rosenman, who served as the fair's concession consultant, insisted that there was no problem with "artistic" shows such as Paris's Folies-Bergère or Lido revues, he said that "we want entertainment, all right, but something the police won't raid."[214]

The closest the fair got to traditional Midway-style entertainment was a slightly risqué puppet show called *Les Poupées de Paris* and a lavish stage and water show, "Wonder World," staged by Leon Leonidoff and held at the amphitheater that had formerly featured Billy Rose's Aquacade.[215] In addition to these attractions, there was a replica of Christopher Columbus's Santa Maria, docked in Meadow Lake, and one memorable ride: a monorail sponsored by the American Machine and Foundry Company.[216] The amusement area, described by the editors of *Time* as a "monorail-belted ghetto for fun and games," was a financial disaster.[217] "Wonder World" alone lost an estimated $5 million before closing prematurely.

Twenty-five Brass Rail food concessions were scattered throughout the fairgrounds; the basic tentlike stands, consisting of 60-by-100-foot canopies, were designed by Vollmer Associates.[218] Ten of the stands were distinguished by towering beehivelike translucent white fiberglass "air flowers," inflated structures supported by central masts that rose above canopies. These joyously voluptuous structures, designed by Victor Lundy, perfectly defined a carefree, carnival atmosphere, and because they were instantly identifiable, they were particularly welcome as one of the few consistent visual themes amid the fair's general chaos. Huxtable described them as "repeated grace notes, cloud-like in daylight, glowing at night,"[219] and Perry and Burns argued that there were not enough of them: "If the Brass Rail people had been brave enough to use the balloons on *all* of their eateries, they would really have taken over the Fair."[220]

When the fair closed its first season on October 18, 1964, 200,000 people turned out.[221] In excess of twenty-seven million people had visited the fair, and while this was well below the goal of forty million, it was more than any fair held in the United States had ever drawn during a comparable period of time. The winner of the attendance sweepstakes was the General Motors Pavilion, topping the charts with more than fourteen million visitors; the Vatican finished a close second with thirteen million. The New York State and Ford pavilions both attracted more than six million visitors.

At first the fair seemed a financial success as well, paying off a quarter of its $30 million worth of promissory notes by August 1, 1964. But by January of the following year, things did not look so rosy. Giving only a few hours' notice, five of the nine bankers who formed the fair's financial committee resigned, charging that they had not been properly informed about the fair's financial problems. Robert Moses attacked the bankers, proclaiming that the fair needed "boosters not knockers," and accused George Moore, president of the First National City Bank and former chairman of the financial committee, of "sabotaging" the fair.[222] But whatever the sharpness of Moses's verbal counterattack, more than words were needed to balance the books. Moses laid off 3,000 fair workers, reduced the publicity budget by more than half, and raised the price of admission from $2.00 to $2.50.

When the fair opened its second season on April 21, 1965, there were few changes in the attractions.[223] An exhibit that documented the life and work of Winston Churchill, who had recently died, included thirty of his paintings and occupied a geodesic dome, designed by Eggers & Higgins, that during the previous season had housed an exhibit on the fair sponsored by the fair corporation itself. A free show, "The Florida Citrus Water Ski and Boat Thrill Show," replaced "Wonder World." In addition to these changes, the major difference from the previous season was the emphasis on adult nightlife: as Newsweek said, the fair now had "nine—count 'em—nine discothèques."[224]

Even with these changes, the fair's second season failed to meet expectations, and investors received only 19.2 cents on the dollar.[225] Halfway through the second season it became clear that the fair would not attain its financial goals. Although Moses had predicted attendance would increase by 37 percent over the previous season, it decreased by 30 percent. And while only 13,000 visitors attended the fair over the Fourth of July weekend, more than 90,000 went to the Palisades Amusement Park in New Jersey. Part of the problem seemed to lie outside the fairgrounds, with the city itself. The heavily publicized riots in Harlem in July 1964, as well as inflated reports of hotel-room shortages and crime, caused many out-of-towners to stay home. Furthermore, New Yorkers themselves tended to be highly critical. As Moses put it: "Most criticism is homegrown; it does not come from abroad, or from the hinterlands. . . . New York is a highly vocal, articulate town where the critics don't hesitate to foul their own nest."[226] One exhibitor at the fair plainly stated that "New Yorkers murdered us. It became very fashionable around town to make fun of the fair, even if you really enjoyed it. In any other city we would have been boffo."[227]

Despite the second season's disappointing turnout, there was a final surge in attendance, with a record crowd of 446,953 gathering for the fair's closing. The closing day, October 17, 1965, was a bizarre event: well-dressed ladies tore up newly planted beds of chrysanthemums and put the flowers in their purses or on their hats, while other fairgoers destroyed or stole everything from a statue of King Tut outside the Egyptian Pavilion to silverware and salt shakers. The editors of Time described the scene as "frightening [and] straight out of a Federico Fellini film fantasy."[228]

The last-minute crowds at the fair were due in part to the widespread feeling that lavish international fairs were outmoded and that the New York fair offered a last chance to attend such a superscale exposition. Although Moses boasted that the fair "cannot be covered in a leisurely, appreciative way in less than a week," to many visitors, the fair's enormous size was a liability, helping to render it obsolete.[229] High prices were an addi-

tional problem. But perhaps the fair's greatest deficit was that the "World of Tomorrow" promised by the 1939–40 fair had, in reality, outpaced anything that a new fair could document or imagine. As Time noted, "fairs are no longer the futuristic fairylands they used to be, mostly because magazines, increased travel, movies and TV have made virtually all the offerings of science, architecture and foreign culture déjà vu."[230] Russell Lynes, writing in Harper's, voiced a similar opinion: "The failure of the fair was in its concept. It was an idea that has no place in an age when a mighty ocean is only six man-hours wide and when ideas are exchanged between continents with the speed of light."[231]

Yet it was the very fact that it was out of place amid the realities of life in the nuclear age that paradoxically made the fair compelling. The Great Depression and the threat of war had made the 1939–40 fair a stage set on which to act out fantasies of a better life. The 1964–65 fair provided visitors a different kind of escape, a voyage into clichés about the American future, clichés already being overturned on college campuses, on the battlefields of Vietnam and in the laboratories of NASA. Whether or not the fair offered great architecture, great social commentary or even great fun, it was an escapist environment of unprecedented size and complexity.

But few architectural critics could see the merits of this escapist spirit. Wolf Von Eckardt, one of the fair's most acerbic observers, summed up his impressions after it had closed:

> The New York World's Fair of 1964-1965 probably sprouted more of this kind of cheaply ingratiating architecture in one place than we have ever seen this century. It dazzled the eye with a chaotic accumulation of architectural stunts and colossal banalities, much as it dumbfounded the ear with a relentless din of sweet Muzak and electronic hawking of all kinds. Sure, there was fun. There were even bright flashes of beauty. But the fun was the fun of the thrill, souped up by the Benzedrine charges of artificial stimulation. It was not the fun of an elation that you only get when your senses respond because you are in happy empathy with a happy environment. The beauty was in the flowers and some girls which no planner could plan and no designer design. . . . The monumental razzle-dazzle of the corporate pavilions and stunt shows of organized religion have been mercifully dismantled. Michelangelo's Pietà is safely home in St. Peter's. The one really good building in the whole sorry show, the gracefully disciplined Spanish Pavilion, has been shipped to St. Louis. Instead, we are left with Charles M. Luckman's banal U.S. Pavilion. . . . This American surreality, circa 1964, characteristially slashed by a monstrous freeway and full of messy alleys, showed us a frightening image of ourselves.[232]

Flushing Meadows–Corona Park

Even before the World's Fair was open, plans were being considered for the ultimate use of Flushing Meadows, which had never come into its own as a recreational asset. In the Park Department's budget for 1963–64, a proposed $8 million item was included to cover the cost of repairing the park after the fair; should the fair corporation be able to return funds to the city, the $8 million would not be needed.[233] By late 1964, however, such an event seemed unlikely. Also unlikely was the realization of Moses's vision, outlined in a January 1964 fair corporation pamphlet titled Flushing Meadows and Beyond, of a string of parks in which Kissena, Cunningham and Alley Pond parks would connect Flushing Meadows with the Nassau County line.[234]

In October 1966 newly elected Mayor John V. Lindsay and his park commissioner, Thomas P. F. Hoving, set out to plan for Flushing Meadows' future, capitalizing on its developing role as an exhibition sports center with the completion of Shea Stadium (see chapter 13) and the Singer Bowl. An architecturally undistinguished 18,000-seat stadium designed by the firm of Architectural Enterprises, the Singer Bowl had been built as part of the World's Fair and was located near the fairground's main entrance gate; it was to be maintained as a permanent facility after the exposition's closing.[235] Hoving announced that he had asked the architect Marcel Breuer, who had just completed the Whitney Museum of American Art (see chapter 11), and the Japanese architect Kenzo Tange, famous for two enclosed stadiums he had designed for the 1964 Olympics in Tokyo, to prepare plans for a 620-acre sports park on the former site of the fair.[236] Soon afterward Lawrence Halprin, the landscape architect, was asked to join the team. At a lunch sponsored by the Women's Auxiliary of the New York Chapter of the American Institute of Architects, where he announced the commission, Hoving denounced city-sponsored construction over the preceding thirty years as "hideous" and "disgraceful" and declared that it was time to bring to the parks "the excitement and creativity of modern design."[237]

By April 1967 the master plan began to take shape, calling for a vast sports park that was to include a 5,000-seat indoor basketball arena; a 2,200-person recreational and competitive swimming facility with seating for 2,500 people, as well as a restaurant with a glass wall where diners could view scuba-diving exhibitions; a purified Meadow Lake for summertime swimming; a ski-toboggan run with artifical snow; and a drag-racing track, enclosed to keep the noise down and to provide second-level space for a half dozen indoor tennis courts. In addition there would be outdoor spaces for football, soccer, volleyball, archery and model plane flying as well as broad terraces for spectators. An arts section was to include art studios, dance rehearsal rooms, a 1,000-seat theater and a "mixed media sensorium," described as a dance hall where films and other events geared to young people could be presented. It was estimated by city officials that the project would take eight to ten years to complete and cost $120 million.

All of the proposed park's facilities were distilled into what Tange would later describe as "a spatial structuring scheme . . . which included linear pedestrian and bus movement systems starting at the mass-transit station and leading to the lakeshore area. . . . Linear structure was useful as a tool in coordinating the different kinds of architectural complexes."[238] Surrounded by open playing fields, the built portion of the complex consisted of three parts: two building clusters separated by a centrally located mall, which was itself flanked by two low buildings housing public dressing rooms, stores and restaurants. Designed by Breuer and his partner Herbert Beckhard, the low buildings were surmounted by rooftop terraces articulated with pergolas. At the mall's southern end, Breuer and Beckhard proposed two large enclosed arenas, one devoted to track and basketball, the other to swimming. The aquatic arena, containing three indoor swimming pools, was flanked by three outdoor pools. Both arenas were visually dominated by a precast-concrete roof suspended on cables from a central concrete frame. In one version of the design the frames were complexly modeled, "folded" forms; in another, they adopted graceful parabolic shapes evocative of Le Corbusier's 1931 design for the Palace of the Soviets.[239] Tange designed the plan's northern building group, organizing it into two parts, one for indoor recreation, the other

for the arts; the arts complex was focused around a central observation and restaurant tower. To give form to the arts complex, Tange employed the superscaled hollow structural elements that he first developed as part of his Metabolist project for Tokyo Bay. Glass-enclosed hallways provided horizontal circulation, while elevators housed in cylindral forms provided vertical access.

In describing the plan Ada Louise Huxtable said, "Planners who have seen the design for the old World's Fair site call it a breakthrough. They believe it is as important for New York in the 20th century as Olmsted's Central Park was in the 19th century."[240] Nonetheless, the hugely ambitious project was soon bogged down by bureaucratic tangles. The Park Department, eager to realize the scheme, had hired the architectural team without the required approval of the City Controller's office, which was responsible for allocating payment. In August 1967 the city refused to pay the architects for the first phase of work, pending the requisite contractual investigations. In addition, the city argued that it could not legally contract for services from either Tange or Halprin, who were not registered architects in the State of New York. Municipal officials claimed that payments were being delayed because, as Huxtable put it, "the city cannot determine whether Mr. Halprin's work in site design, which includes the location of roads and bridges, is architecture or landscape architecture. Since he is a landscape architect . . . his contract would be illegal if he is practicing architecture."[241] The plan for the sports park was eventually dropped.

The United States Pavilion, which had remained in Flushing Meadows after the fair, was the focus of other unrealized plans.[242] In 1966 Mayor Lindsay proposed that the pavilion be retained as an educational center. Five years later, despite Robert Moses's disapproval of what he called the "extremely dubious business" of trying to maintain the pavilion, preservation efforts continued, now spearheaded by Wallace M. West.[243] The president of the Queens Arts Council, West sought to transform the building into a multipurpose arts center that would show both world-class traveling exhibitions and work by Queens-based artists. Other proposals also surfaced, including plans to use the building as a health-education center and as an "international festival," complete with cultural displays, an outdoor café and duty-free shops. None of the plans were realized, however. In 1976 the dismissal of a suit brought in United States District Court against the federal government's General Services Administration by an ad hoc citizens' group paved the way for the building's demolition by the end of the year.

Although few of the buildings from the 1964–65 fair were retained, the fairgrounds were transformed into a park, albeit a rather minimally equipped one, and the city thus gained a valuable bit of rus in urbe. As Charles Grutzner reported in the New York Times, "The pheasants have found their way back to the Flushing Meadow. So have the rabbits."[244] On June 3, 1967, Moses officially gave the converted fairgrounds to the city; together with existing public parkland, the newly created 1,258-acre Flushing Meadows–Corona Park was the city's second largest park, surpassed only by the 1,454-acre Great Kills Park on Staten Island.[245] In February of the following year, on a 3.6-acre site in the former transportation area of the fair, Moses opened the Queens Zoo's Children's Farm, complete with a white clapboard farmhouse.[246] The rest of the zoo, which was the borough's first, was opened eight months later. The zoo featured North American animals, housed not in traditional cages but in natural habitats separated by dry moats or low walls. The geodesic-domed building that contained the Winston Churchill exhibit at the fair became a lushly landscaped aviary.[247]

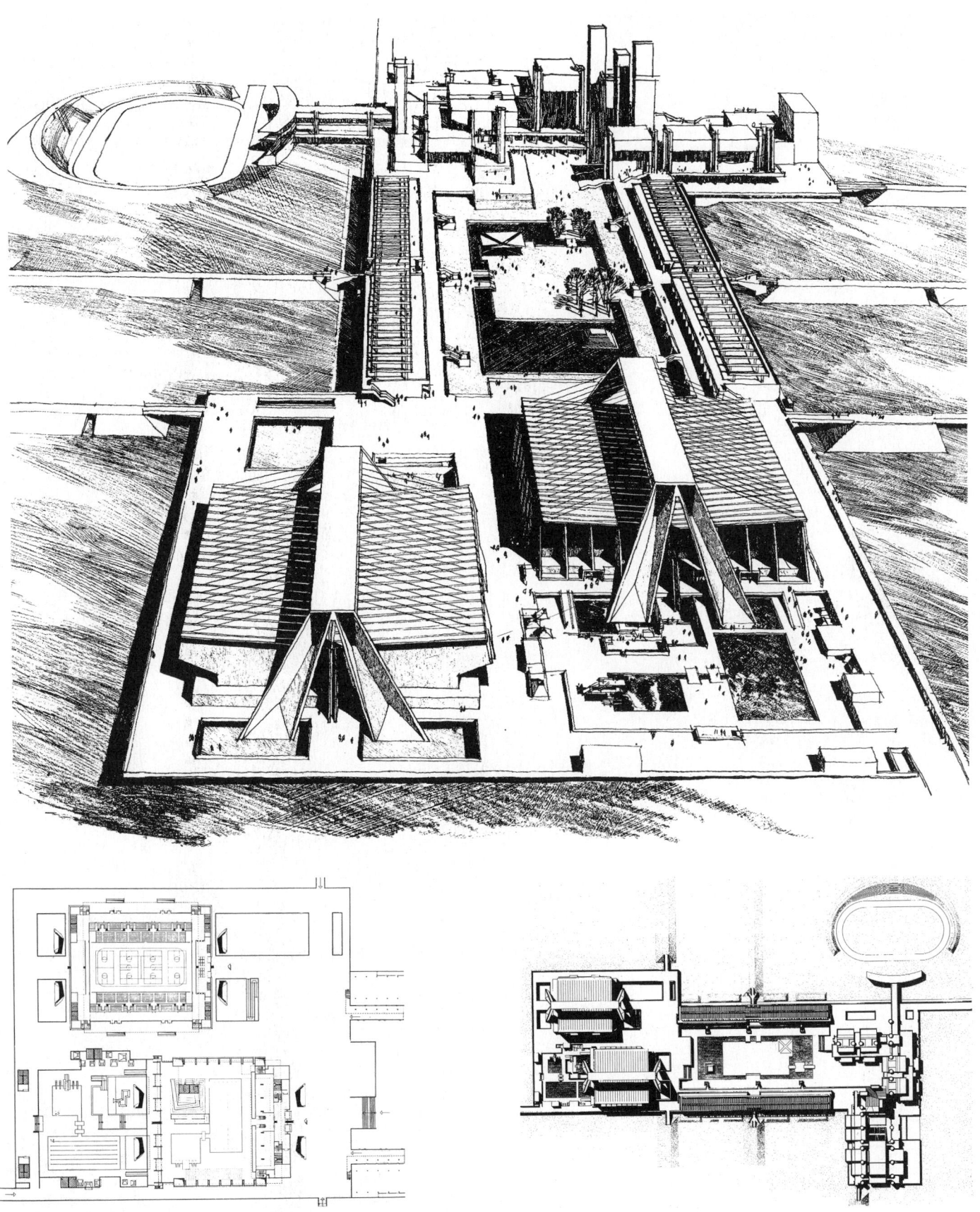

Top: Proposal for sports park, Flushing Meadows, Queens. Marcel Breuer and Herbert Beckhard; Kenzo Tange; and Lawrence Halprin, 1967. Perspective drawing of view to the north. HB

Bottom left: Proposal for sports park. Plan. HB

Bottom right: Proposal for sports park. Plan of swimming arena and indoor arena. HB

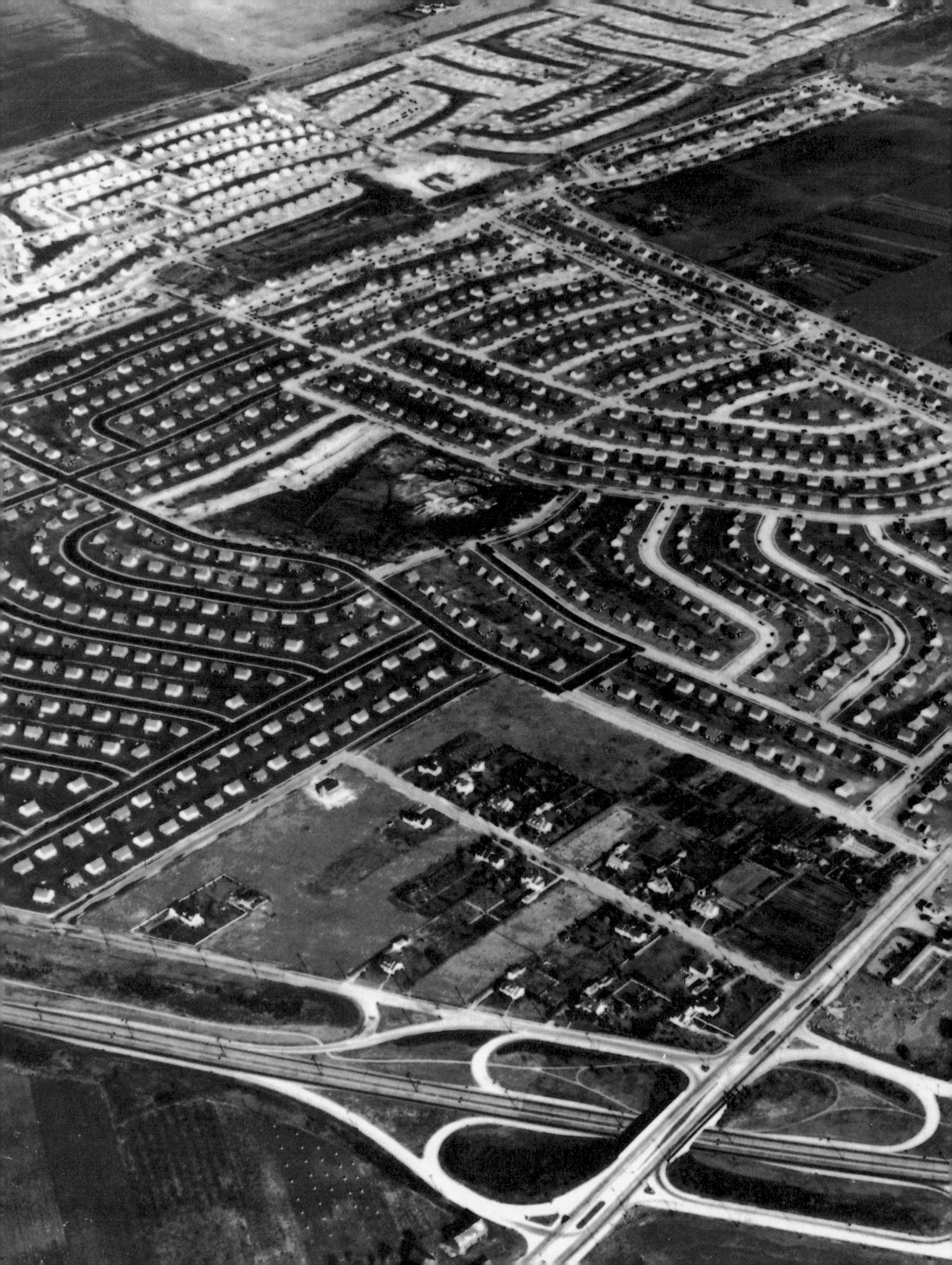

Chapter 15

Beyond the Boroughs

Every graceful multilane ribbon of asphalt that skirts a small town and winds through farmland is like the touch of Midas, transforming old pastures and woods into precious real estate ripe for the developer who wants land for an office building, a shopping mall, a tract of houses. . . . As the region grows . . . the highway network virtually guarantees that the growth will lead away from urban areas.
—David K. Shipler, 1971[1]

While the endless sprawl of a characterless suburbia became a hallmark of post–World War II development and a decisive factor in the city's transformation from a coherently defined metropolis to a node, albeit the biggest node, within Megalopolis, suburbs were hardly a new feature of New York. It is arguable that the city's suburbanization was set in motion in 1814 when Robert Fulton began his ferry service across the East River, making it possible to live in "suburban" Brooklyn and work on Manhattan Island. Modern—that is, ruralesque—suburbia came to New York in 1853 when the entrepreneur Llewellyn Haskell and the architect Alexander Jackson Davis laid out Llewellyn Park, New Jersey, located twelve miles west of Fifth Avenue and intended as an enclave of "country homes for city people."[2] As the city's decentralization continued, distinct developments were produced at Douglaston (1866),[3] Garden City, Nassau County (1869),[4] Bronxville, Westchester County (1892),[5] Prospect Park South (1899),[6] Kensington, Nassau County (1909),[7] Forest Hills Gardens (1912),[8] and Riverdale and Fieldston (1913),[9] to name some of the best planned and most aesthetically notable examples. In the interwar period the suburban ideal of *rus in urbe* was made accessible to middle-class New Yorkers living close to the city's core in developments such as Sunnyside Gardens (1924),[10] Radburn, New Jersey (1927),[11] and Green Acres, Nassau County (1936),[12] while Munsey Park, Nassau County (1927),[13] continued the tradition of well-designed suburbs for more affluent citizens.

What distinguished post–World War II suburban development was not only a widespread degeneration of architectural and urbanistic standards, but a fundamental shift in the nature of the suburb as a planning type. No longer a villagelike community offering a daily arcadian respite from the city's relentless and anarchic energy, in the postwar era the suburb evolved into two types. One was a kind of satellite city, increasingly independent of the core city and usually focused on a preexisting town such as White Plains, Westchester County; Hicksville, Nassau County; or Stamford, Fairfield County, Connecticut. The other type was a vast, inherently arbitrary, commuter-oriented subdivision unconnected to a traditional town or even to the central city except via highways; Levittown, on Long Island, was the quintessential example of the subdivision type.

Nowhere could the impact of the postwar regional transformation be seen more clearly than in the development of suburban corporate office complexes and in the migration of many of New York's leading department stores to the suburbs. Each corporate and commercial relocation made suburban citizens less dependent on the central city. The development of office parks also generated new patterns of commutation; those who lived in one suburb often traveled to another suburb to work, while many of those who chose to live in the city now traveled to workplaces in the suburbs, a reversal of the usual pattern.

These new patterns were in large part fostered by the ever-increasing number of car owners, as well as the staggering number of highways completed in the New York area in the 1940s and 1950s. During the interwar period the New York metropolitan region's parkway system had been masterminded by Robert Moses to open up suburban Westchester County and Long Island to middle-class, car-owning inner-city residents who might visit for purposes of recreation but would just as likely choose to settle there. While the pioneering generation of middle-class New Yorkers who resettled in suburban areas continued to rely on the city not only for employment but also for shopping and entertainment, by the end of World War II a new spirit of self-sufficiency had begun to evolve in many suburban communities. It is reasonable to assume that Moses, who often pooh-poohed arguments in behalf of decentralization, did not anticipate such a trend.[14] At first, the tendency toward decentralization was viewed positively: suburbanization was not perceived as a threat—even a potential one—to the viability of

Levittown, Hicksville, New York. Levitt & Sons, 1947–51. Aerial view showing first 2,000 houses, 1947. CP

New York as a distinct metropolitan entity. In his book *The Building of the City*, published as part of the *Regional Plan of New York and Its Environs* in 1931, Thomas Adams favored balanced patterns of growth: "The five-cent fare, coupled with increasing commuting fares outside of the city, still operates to hold the population within the city. It is remarkable that in spite of this the parts of the Region outside the city added to their population but 141,902 less than the city. This decentralization movement is good both for the city and the environs, but there is need of more control of the building developments that respond to it."[15]

Adams advocated that New York be encircled with "a great metropolitan highway loop parallel with a circumferential rapid transit and freight distribution line."[16] According to a proposal drawn up by the Regional Plan Association, within this bimodal loop, to be located at approximately a fourteen-mile radius from New York's City Hall in lower Manhattan, a loose grid of highways would provide both east-west and north-south access. Twenty radial highways would extend past the loop and be linked by other circumferential highways located approximately five and ten miles farther out. Part of the second ring would function as a "metropolitan bypass," serving long-distance traffic. The route would extend north from Morristown, New Jersey, to Peekskill, New York, and east from there to Bridgeport, Connecticut. In 1933 the Regional Plan Association surveyed the progressive realization of its proposals, noting that while a considerable amount of radial highway construction had been completed, the construction of circumferential routes had lagged, a situation that had aggravated traffic problems.[17] Five years later the Regional Plan Association would note that while highway construction continued at a fast clip, with radial routes receiving the most attention, efforts at completing a comprehensive trunk-line railroad system had been devastatingly unsuccessful. Failing to grasp the impending hegemony of the automobile and its ramifications not only for industrial development but for metropolitan growth in general, the association offered the rather weak explanation that "the nature of rail improvements is such that advancement is necessarily slow even in times of prosperity."[18]

Although the immense importance of the automobile and its dominance over other modes of transportation may have eluded the Regional Plan Association, it was not lost on Robert Moses, who after 1940 inaugurated a differentiated road network, with parkways for pleasure vehicles and expressways for mixed traffic. In 1942 the journalist O'Brien Boldt, writing in the *New York Times*, praised the expressway type as "a striking departure from earlier treatment of city roadways," and explained:

> The design regards motor travel as a dominant transport medium. The scheme is being superimposed on the sprawling urban structure which grew around the harborsides and railroads of New York Port. Here, as elsewhere, piers and rails first dictated the physical order of the city and arranged streets and highways to suit the pattern. The traffic light, an indignity to which ships and trains are rarely subjected, is symbolic of makeshift adaption of a hand-me-down street design.[19]

Whereas previous efforts had concentrated on radial roads, Moses focused on what he called "loops" or "belt" roads, urging a public plagued with war jitters in the early 1940s to build belt highways as an important part of the city's efforts to protect itself in case of war.[20] In 1941 he proposed the Brooklyn-Queens Expressway and the Harlem River Driveway as "defense highways," alleging that while German and Italian delegations had already traveled to the United States to study both proposed and realized roadways before building their own extensive arterial highway system, New Yorkers had yet to complete their own.[21] Whatever the importance of such highways to the national defense, military considerations proved a compelling spur to their completion. The Harlem River Driveway, together with the previously completed Henry Hudson Parkway, Westside Highway and East River Drive, directed express traffic around the circumference of Manhattan. The Brooklyn-Queens Expressway, Belt Parkway, Laurelton Parkway, Cross Island Parkway, Whitestone Expressway and portions of the Grand Central Parkway encircled the boroughs of Brooklyn and Queens, while the Cross-Bronx Expressway was the realization of a northern portion of the "metropolitan loop" first envisioned by the Regional Plan Association.

Though the Cross-Bronx Expressway proved to be, as John E. Booth, writing in the *New York Times*, predicted, "a boon to both Bronx and Queens motorists heading for New Jersey, upper New York and New England resorts," it did not radically alter development or commuting patterns in the metropolitan region.[22] The first postwar highway to gain that distinction was the 10.3-mile-long Cross Westchester Expressway, connecting the New York State Thruway at Elmsford to the New England Thruway at Rye.[23] Completed in 1960, the much-debated project had been opposed vehemently by some Westchester officials on the grounds that the requisite acquisition of land would cut into the county's tax base. In 1954 Joseph C. Ingraham wrote in the *New York Times*: "Because the program is so highly controversial, many residents of Central Westchester have been saying that the project would be fallow for at least ten years. They concede it is necessary now, but in any place except their own area."[24] Despite the opposition, the project proceeded. By the time the expressway was opened, the completion of the New York State Thruway had shown that the subsequent rise in development more than compensated for the loss in taxable property. Officially named Interstate Route 287, the Cross Westchester Expressway was the first toll-free expressway completed in New York State under the auspices of the federal government's National System of Interstate and Defense Highways. Ninety percent of the funds for the expressway came from the federal government, 10 percent from New York State. The Cross Westchester Expressway's role as the region's first "metropolitan bypass"—an idea originally outlined by the Regional Plan Association in 1931—was a significant factor in the region's evolving urbanism.

As Ingraham noted, the expressway constituted "the first real advance in the move to overcome the metropolitan area's multi-faceted problem," connecting with fourteen highways along its right-of-way and serving the needs of long-distance travelers, for whom circumventing the city would be convenient.[25] But the highway was also heavily utilized by suburbanites and exurbanites, who had increasingly little contact with the city itself, delivering a decisive blow to New York's traditional role as the region's linchpin. In 1963 the Port of New York Authority issued a report documenting a sharp rise in the number of suburban jobs and an accompanying increase in "suburb-to-suburb" travel.[26] Though the Regional Plan Association's proposed circumferential loop provided for both automobile and railroad access, intersuburban travel in the early postwar era would be almost exclusively restricted to cars. The Port Authority noted that "non-Manhattan bound" traffic rose from 40 percent of the region's total before the Second World War to 51 percent in 1963; the authority predicted that by 1980, it would account for 55 percent of the total on weekdays and 70 percent on weekends.

The ease of intersuburban travel would have been facilitated further had the so-called Long Island Sound Crossing been built.[27] This six-mile-long bridge between Rye in Westchester County and Oyster Bay in Nassau County, first officially proposed in 1964, would have formed a pivotal link in a monumentally scaled metropolitan bypass bookended by the Cross Westchester and the Wantagh–Oyster Bay expressways. Robert Moses, whose parkways and expressways had done so much to affect the region's decentralization, sought to oversee the bridge's construction. For many years Moses had discussed the possibility of instituting a ferry service between the Port Chester vicinity and Oyster Bay. But he later advocated a bridge as the most efficient means of providing Westchester County residents more direct access to Jones Beach and his other recreational facilities on Long Island, and by 1965 he was calling the bridge's construction "inevitable."[28] A preliminary proposal, sponsored by the Triborough Bridge and Tunnel Authority and designed by the engineering firm of Madigan-Hyland, called for a sleek, minimally detailed structure incorporating a 1,200-foot central span punctuated by a single pylon at either end.

At first the bridge was routed to cross near or directly over Manursing Island, which contained some of Westchester's most opulent shoreline estates, but after strong opposition to the plan, it was rerouted to connect Bayville, Long Island, with Rye. The bridge would have traversed portions of Oyster Bay and Mill Neck Creek, which were protected as the Oyster Bay National Wildlife Refuge. On March 22, 1967, Governor Nelson A. Rockefeller endorsed the proposal, also recommending a second, 14.6-mile-long bridge to cross the Long Island Sound, connecting Port Jefferson, Suffolk County, to Bridgeport, Connecticut. On March 31 the New York State Assembly approved Rockefeller's transportation plan, but growing opposition to the Bayville-Rye span was mounted not only by property owners but by yachtsmen and conservationists, who, fearing damage to the sound, proposed a tunnel crossing instead.

Moses, who never lost an opportunity to take a swipe at the very rich, countered: "We find these aristocratic sportsmen oblivious of world ferment . . . actually demanding a hearing on their crazy tunnel. It would have to be served by electric flat cars or be ventilated. In a hard-pressed economy, with so many other demands, such a scheme is ludicrous, and only people living in another social world and devoid of humor would advocate it."[29] Despite Moses's continued support of the long-debated project, on March 16, 1969, the United States Department of the Interior denied permission for the bridge to cross the wildlife refuge, thus killing the proposal.

In 1971 the journalist David K. Shipler reported in the New York Times on the powerful role that highways had played in the region's transformation:

> In five weeks of travel through the suburbs, a team of New York Times reporters found that the power of the highways to determine how land developed, and thus how millions of people will live and where they will work, is surer than all the careful reasoning of government planners or the defensive rhetoric of small town politicians. Every day in outer counties, planners who try to fight sprawl and revive mass transportation by encouraging new development in downtown centers are being defeated by the growth that spreads along the highways, that clusters around the new interchanges. The highways' influence has been enhanced by the resistance of many suburbanites to growth in their own towns.[30]

Although highways were the prime determinant of development patterns, they were rarely planned with consideration of the ur-

banistic implications. As Keith Rosser, the planning director of the New Jersey State Department of Transportation, bluntly stated in Shipler's article: "Our planning has been one to date of reaction. The money is not there to plan intelligently. We construct highways, very frankly, where we're permitted to construct highways."[31]

The diffuse, characterless urbanism that resulted from uncontrolled growth—what would become widely known as "slurbia" or, as William B. Shore, a Regional Plan Association vice president, more euphemistically labeled it, "spread city"—was especially prevalent on Long Island.[32] Extensions to Moses's pioneering Northern and Southern State parkways were completed in 1949; new highway construction continued throughout the 1950s and early 1960s with the completion of the Sagtikos Captree, Sunken Meadow and Heckscher State parkways.[33] Moses's landscaped parkways were originally designed to provide access to recreational facilities and to constitute scenic greenwards enjoyed by motorists on leisurely "Sunday drives." But by 1963, as Joseph Ingraham noted, the Southern State Parkway had become the most heavily traveled parkway in the world, carrying thirty-three million cars a year. "Under these conditions," Ingraham said, "the term 'parkway' today is merely a formal designation."[34]

In 1954, in an effort to ameliorate what had already become an overburdened parkway system, Governor Thomas E. Dewey announced a plan to build an expressway extending nearly seventy miles from the Long Island entrance of the Queens-Midtown Tunnel to the town of Riverhead in eastern Suffolk County.[35] The impact of the Long Island Expressway (LIE), which Moses refused to coordinate with mass-transit systems, was enormous, opening up large tracts of land to development. The LIE soon became so successful that it was unable to handle the volume of commuters it attracted. Originally designed to accommodate a maximum of 80,000 vehicles a day, by 1963 the Queens section of the LIE was carrying 132,000 vehicles a day and in excess of fifty million a year; in 1967 that same portion carried more than 160,000 vehicles a day and sixty million a year. During rush hours cars traveled at an average speed of five miles per hour, motivating one observer to characterize the LIE as the "perfect example of a road where motorists can drive to work and read the daily paper simultaneously."[36] As Ingraham noted in 1963, "a road prescribed less than 10 years ago as a specific remedy for the post-war traffic ills that were beginning to plague the eastern metropolitan area now has become part and parcel of the ailment." In fact, he said, the road qualified as an "emergency case" and had been "declared inadequate by virtually every highway expert in the city. Angry motorists use much stronger language to describe its shortcomings."[37]

The "slurbia" that would come to dominate so much of Long Island was both initiated and epitomized by Levittown—the paradigmatic post–World War II automobile suburb.[38] In 1947, capitalizing on the surge of house-seeking GIs, the forty-one-year-old lawyer and developer William Levitt built his first large-scale development of low-cost houses on the site of a 4,000-acre former potato farm near Hicksville, New York, just twenty-nine miles from Manhattan. By the time Levitt began to build his community, initially to be called Island Trees but by 1948 officially named Levittown, he was already a successful suburban developer. Working with his brother Alfred, who handled design issues, and his father Abraham, who oversaw landscaping details, Levitt served as president of Levitt & Sons, based in a modestly scaled Colonial-style building in Manhasset. In the

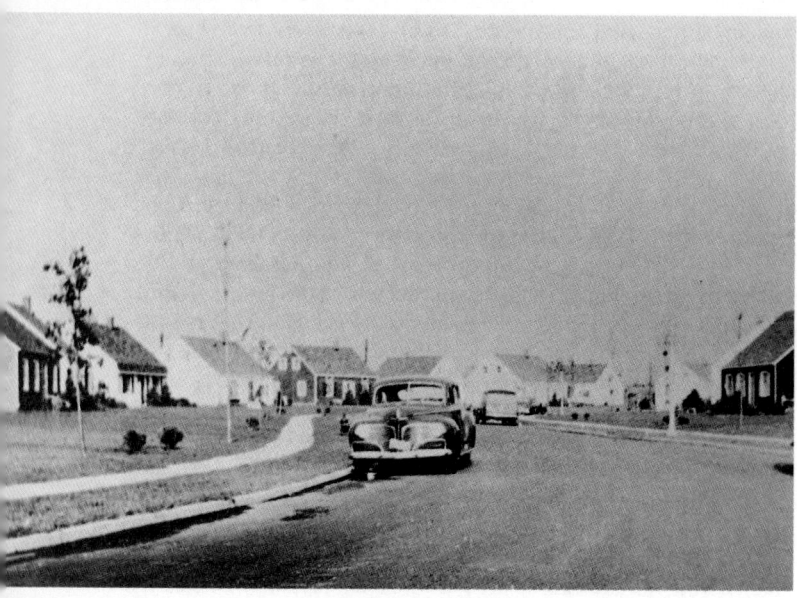

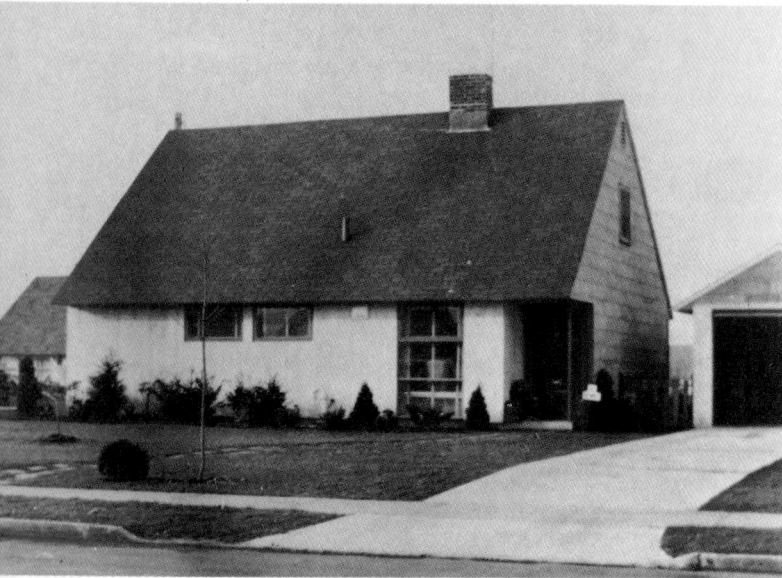

Top: Levittown, Hicksville, New York. Levitt & Sons, 1947–51. Cape Cod houses. LPL

Bottom: Levittown. Ranch house. LPL

1930s Levitt & Sons had built two upscale enclaves, both known as Strathmore, located in Manhasset and Great Neck. Following the wartime construction of 2,350 houses he developed for the United States Navy in Norfolk, Virginia, Levitt became committed to mass-producing low-cost houses. He faced the challenge with ingenuity and verve, learning from the automobile industry; according to *Time*, he described his company as the "General Motors of the housing industry."[39] In essense Levitt reversed the assembly line process: teams of workers moved from one 60-by-100-foot house site to the next, with each individual worker, or small group of workers, performing one of the approximately 100 tasks required to complete a house—ranging from pouring the 25-by-30-foot concrete-slab foundation to caulking windows and installing Venetian blinds. Adopting these methods, Levitt was able to put up houses with remarkable speed and in great quantity, which in turn enabled him to buy building materials in bulk as well as produce and cut his own lumber supply, eliminating the distributor's markup. As the editors of *Life* put it, "Levitt is best characterized not as a builder but as a manufacturer of houses."[40]

"Everything that is wrong with U.S. housing—high prices, slow production, labor troubles, archaic building codes—can be licked by size," Levitt contended, and indeed, Levittown was the largest development ever erected by a single builder. In explaining why neither his own organization nor the subcontractors it worked with were unionized, Levitt had a pragmatic justification: "I'm not against unions. I just think we can build faster without them."[41] In order to hold costs down, Levitt's houses were standardized; although there were five exterior designs, all variations of the Cape Cod type, they differed only in their fenestration. Every basement-less house had the same foundation, which included radiant heat coils. They all featured a twelve-by-sixteen-foot living room, two bedrooms, one bathroom and a kitchen that came complete with a refrigerator, an electric range, a Bendix washer and a Colonial-style corner hutch. The attics were unfinished, and could be remodeled to contain two bedrooms and an additional bath. Like Frank Lloyd Wright's Usonian houses, Levitt's houses had an open arrangement of spaces and a symbolically important core at the center—a built-in fireplace.[42] Beginning in 1950 Levitt also sold every house with its own built-in television set. Though only on-street parking was available at first, in 1950 carports were added as a standard feature. Again taking a cue from Wright, Levitt moved the parking area, which in earlier suburban houses had replaced the stable at the back of the house, to the front, acknowledging the car's importance by placing it next to the front door.

Levittown's first 1,800 houses were rented exclusively to veterans for sixty-five dollars a month, with an option to buy after one or two years. The first houses sold for $6,990. Prices were quickly raised to $7,990, but terms were so favorable, especially for veterans, that buying was still less expensive than renting, and nearly everyone purchased. Beginning in 1949, houses were only available for sale. For many residents Levittown fulfilled a lifelong dream of home ownership. Yet the emphasis on the individual home owner seemed to lead to a diminution of community spirit. Indeed, though it did contain some recreational facilities and stores, Levittown was far less a town in the traditional sense than a pragmatic land subdivision. As the editors of *Time* observed: "The community has an almost antiseptic air. Levittown streets, which have such fanciful names as Satellite, Horizon, and Haymaker, are bare and flat as hospital corridors."[43] The Levitt organization required that the development's shipshape appearance be maintained; if home owners failed to mow their lawns at least once a week, Levitt had it done for them and billed them for the service.

Levittown was immensely popular from the very beginning. Within months of the project's announcement, Levitt had received 50,000 applications, though only 6,000 houses would be completed in the first year. Lines of prospective buyers started to form three days before the development's first houses went on sale; the day before sales began, police were brought in to manage the crowd. Levitt couldn't build the houses fast enough, although his company was churning out a house every sixteen minutes in 1948, with up to 600 being built at the same time. On a single day in 1949, 1,400 contracts were negotiated. Levittown eventually grew to contain 17,400 houses and a population of 82,000.

While Levitt's ability to understand the public's tastes and requirements was nothing short of brilliant, many critics were not impressed with his achievement. Lewis Mumford took a particularly harsh view of Levittown, describing the development in 1961 without specifically citing it:

> In the mass movement into suburban areas a new kind of community was produced, which caricatured both the historic city and the archetypal suburban refuge: a multitude of uniform, unidentifiable houses, lined up inflexibly, at uniform distances, on uniform roads, in a treeless communal waste, inhabited by people of the same class, the same income, the same age group, witnessing the same television performances, eating the same tasteless pre-fabricated foods, from the same freezers, conforming in every outward and inward respect to a common mold, manufactured in the central metropolis. Thus, the ultimate effect of the suburban landscape in our own time is, ironically, a low-grade uniform environment from which escape is impossible.[44]

Although, as the editors of *Time* remarked in 1950, Levittown was viewed by some observers as the "slum of the future," this turned out not to be the case.[45] In fact, the development became a stable, prosperous community and a paradigm for Levittowns built across the nation, as well as in France, Spain and Germany. In 1972, on the twenty-fifth anniversary of the first Levittown, Angela Taylor, writing in the *New York Times*, surveyed the development's history:

> From the air, the ticky tacky boxes looked like the houses in a Monopoly game. They sat there, depressingly alike, on barren ground. . . . To many New Yorkers, it seemed that Abraham Levitt and his sons . . . had created a joke. . . . Today, trees have grown to shade the houses and families have striven for individuality with paint and landscaping. . . . Those who have stuck it out have turned their homes into attractive, spacious places and say they have no plans to move. . . . And they have had the last laugh on the sophisticated city dwellers who used to think of them as automated toys in their little boxes.[46]

Looking back on Levittown, Paul Goldberger, writing in 1981, praised the original house design for its provision of affordable accommodation: "No one could look at a Levittown Cape Cod and be inspired to wax eloquently about Palladio. But these houses were practical and well-designed and they possessed a degree of common sense that was frequently lacking in their counterparts of the 1960's and 1970's. . . . Their point was not to stir the imagination, but to provide reasonable and decent housing." Goldberger found considerably less to admire in the development's urbanism: "The economies that made the house itself so fine made Levittown an urban planning disaster—a sea of virtually identical cottages, the intelligent planning of the individual house obscured by the banality of their total effect."[47]

In 1951 Levitt proposed to build a model suburb to be located on 675 hilly acres situated between the Jericho Turnpike and the Northern State Parkway in the town of Jericho.[48] The most significant planning feature of the development, to be known as Landia, was the inclusion of a thirty-acre industrial zone shielded by a greenbelt. The presence of an industrial area directly addressed a principal problem of postwar bedroom suburbs: how to increase the community's tax base without increasing the density of residential development. Landia was to include a single through street, a sixty-foot-wide thoroughfare with a twenty-foot-wide landscaped central mall, lined by all of the community's public and commercial buildings. The development's 1,750 two-story houses were to be located on sites of approximately one-third acre distributed in seven distinct neighborhoods, each defined by a circumferential road. Though the houses promised to be standard Levitt fare, the development's overall plan ensured a level of urbanistic interest and coherence that would elevate Landia above the level of the increasingly ubiquitous sprawling subdivision. Landia's realization, however, was delayed, and ultimately blocked, by the advent of the Korean War.

Shopping Centers

Beginning in the 1930s, department stores searching for upscale markets and low-priced real estate followed their middle- and upper-middle-class patrons to the burgeoning suburbs. The suburban branch department store, geared overwhelmingly to the needs of customers arriving by car, was initially developed as a distinct building type, markedly different from its inner-city counterpart. Soon the presence of such stores triggered the development of shopping centers near or around them; by the late 1950s the typical shopping center included one or more department stores as "anchors." Although the shopping center was a new development, it did have precedents: its roots were in the traditional urbanism of small-town Main Streets, rather than dynamic Manhattan crossroads such as Herald Square or the intersections of Fifth Avenue and Thirty-fourth or Fifty-seventh streets. With the exception of the freestanding single-family house, the suburban shopping center became the most powerful architectural reflection of the tastes and requirements of automobiling suburbanites.

New York's department stores had begun to operate suburban branches as early as 1929, when Best & Company opened a small facility in Garden City, Nassau County, in November, just a month after the stock market crash. Best & Company's sagacious president, Philip Le Boutillier, would continue to pioneer the suburban market, opening other small branch stores in Mamaroneck, Westchester County, and East Orange, New Jersey, in 1930, and other department stores would also establish branches—B. Altman's opened a small facility on Mamaroneck Avenue in White Plains in 1934 and Arnold Constable opened one in New Rochelle in 1937.[49] But the Depression largely delayed the widespread suburban expansion of department stores, which would quickly follow economic recovery and fully flower after World War II.

In 1941 Macy's edged toward suburbia with a branch in the planned housing development of Parkchester, in the northeastern Bronx.[50] Located on the community's main thoroughfare, Metropolitan Avenue, Macy's Parkchester was designed as part of the apartment-block complex by its team of architects, headed by Richmond H. Shreve, who was assisted by Raymond

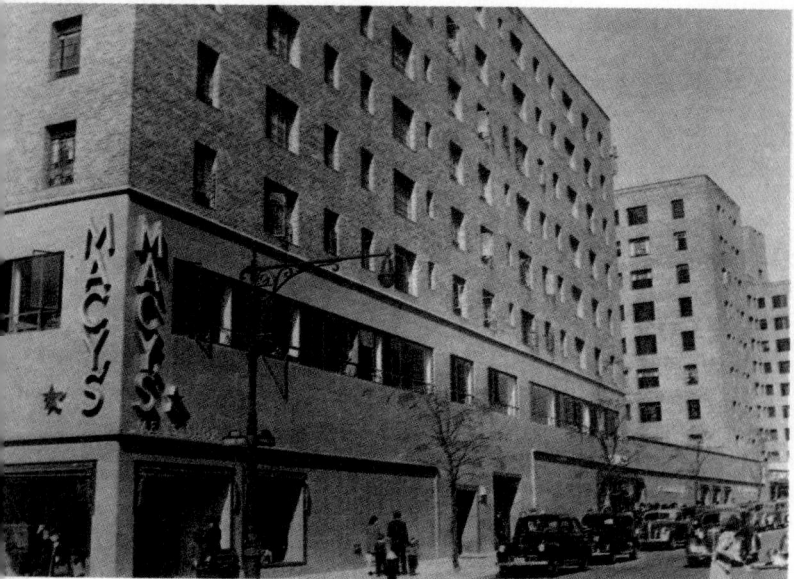

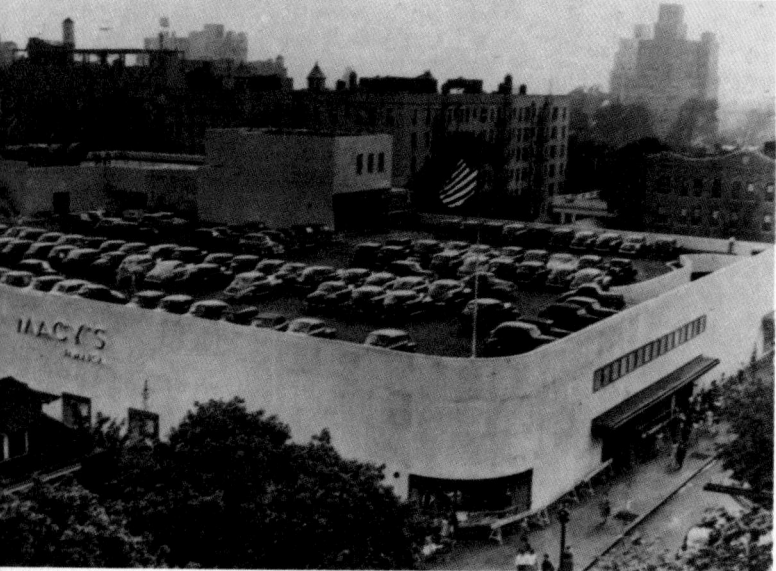

Top: Macy's, 1441 Metropolitan Avenue, between Wood Road and Wood Avenue, Parkchester, the Bronx. Richmond H. Shreve and Raymond Loewy, 1941. View to the northwest. NYP

Bottom: Macy's, 89-22 165th Street, Jamaica, Queens. Robert D. Kohn and John J. Knight in consultation with Richard C. Belcher, 1947. Courtesy R. H. Macy & Co., Inc. RHM

Top right: Bonwit Teller, 42 South Broadway, between Martine Avenue and Main Street, White Plains, New York. Kahn & Jacobs, 1947. PP. CU

Center right: Lord & Taylor, 1440 Northern Boulevard, Manhasset, New York. Raymond Loewy with Starrett & Van Vleck, 1941. View to the south. LT

Bottom right: Lord & Taylor. Beauty salon. IN. CU

Loewy. The store spread through the lower two stories of two buildings and filled in the gap between them. Although the terra-cotta panels of the exterior were bland, the streetscape was nonetheless lively because of the show windows and the numerous entranceways to the long narrow space that paralleled the street.

In 1947, building on the success of its Parkchester branch, Macy's completed the first phase of a three-part "peripheral expansion" plan, opening a 157,500-square-foot store in Jamaica, Queens.[51] Macy's shaped its overall merchandising program for the postwar era so that the main store at Herald Square would continue to handle all buying, advertising and administrative functions and the suburban branches would be "mainly a glorified retail sales room," as the editors of *Architectural Forum* noted.[52] Designed by Robert D. Kohn and John J. Knight, with Richard C. Belcher serving as consulting architect, the gray-limestone-clad Jamaica branch exerted a respectful if undistinguished presence in an outer-borough neighborhood containing both commercial and residential development. The editors of the *New York Times* viewed the store's opening in the context of the neighborhood's evolution: "Macy's is, of course, a youngster compared with Jamaica. That settlement dates from about 1650 and some of the houses still standing were built before the Revolutionary War. It has a long and honorable history as one of the most important centers in Queens and undoubtedly feels it was high time that Macy's came to it instead of it to Macy's."[53]

The most outstanding exterior feature of Macy's Jamaica branch was the provision of rooftop parking space for approximately 150 cars. While the parking lot indicated the increasing influence of driving customers, even in relatively high-density areas close to the central city, the authors Geoffrey Baker and Bruno Funaro dismissed it as only "a token amount of parking."[54] Architects Daniel Schwartzman and Kenneth C. Welch designed and planned the interiors, devising a free-flow plan of individually configured, curved sales counters and areas that departed from the standard gridiron arrangement of uniform, rectilinear sales islands. The innovative plan offered shoppers a welcome change, but the architect Morris Ketchum, Jr., found the layout too extreme: "Its chief fault lies in a sort of strained restlessness, a lack of dignity and comfort, and a different type of monotonous uniformity."[55]

In 1952 Macy's completed its outer-borough expansion plan with a branch store on the corner of Flatbush and Tilden avenues in Brooklyn.[56] Designed by Voorhees, Walker, Foley & Smith, the four-story building was a dramatically massed, monumental essay in the transitional Modern Classicism that was the firm's specialty. The long facade along Tilden Avenue featured a double-height glass window incorporating ground-level display space as well as a small showcase window located near the corner; the short facade, which contained the principal entrances, was composed entirely of a recessed glass curtain wall. Tiers of awnings partially shielded the large glass expanses and established a festive note.

Three years earlier, in 1949, Macy's had extended its program beyond the city's borders with a branch store housing approximately 323,000 square feet in the heart of the shopping district in White Plains.[57] Designed by Lathrop Douglass, working in association with Voorhees, Walker, Foley & Smith, the building's four-story, curving brick facade turned away from the street to reveal a full-height expanse of glass that contained the store's main entrance. According to Baker and Funaro, the store seemed to be "invading a suburban Main Street" with its high-profile, sculptural architecture.[58]

In contrast to Macy's, which began its postwar expansion in middle-class outer-borough neighborhoods, Bonwit Teller moved directly into the suburban counties in 1947, opening a branch in White Plains, where the store could tap into the immense concentration of affluent suburbanites in central Westchester.[59] An elegant if highly reductivist essay in Modern Classicism designed by Ely Jacques Kahn and Robert Allan Jacobs, with Harry Leonard Miller serving as associate architect, Bonwit's was quite urban in character. Built almost out to the property line, with just a narrow landscaped strip separating it from the sidewalk, the building maintained a strong relationship to the street. Its symmetrically composed, two-story limestone streetfront made no gesture toward domesticity despite its location at the edge of a neighborhood of modest houses. Although most customers arrived by car, the six bronze-trimmed display windows that flanked the main entrance were scaled to be seen by passing pedestrians. Despite its orientation to the street, the ample parking lot in the rear acknowledged the realities of the store's suburban location. Inside the store, the architects more firmly established a suburban tone with wide aisles, mirror-clad columns, numerous plants and, on the second floor, abundant natural light that created a spacious, airy feeling. Display cases, service counters and wall paneling made of bleached rift-sawn oak furthered the sense of relaxation. In the third-floor "penthouse" an employee lounge, also used for receptions and fashion shows, opened onto a landscaped roof terrace.

Even before Macy's and Bonwit's expanded their operations into the suburbs, Lord & Taylor opened a branch in 1941 on Northern Boulevard in Manhasset, Long Island.[60] Designed by the industrial designer Raymond Loewy, working with the architectural firm of Starrett & Van Vleck, the branch went a long way toward establishing a distinctly suburban look for the department store type. According to Loewy, the basic concept behind the design preceded and in fact inspired the Lord & Taylor commission. In 1937 Loewy and his partners discussed the fact that American department store architecture, which had remained largely unchanged since the introduction of technological innovations such as electric lighting, elevators and escalators in the 1890s and early 1900s, needed to be redesigned to reflect the concept of the store "as a type of selling machine" and not merely "a building raised around a series of pushcarts."[61] Loewy discussed the subject with his friend Dorothy Shaver, the dynamic president of Lord & Taylor, who shared her ideas with Loewy as he planned a prototypical suburban store to be built within approximately twenty miles of New York. For the site of their first suburban branch, Lord & Taylor chose Manhasset, which was, as the editors of *Interiors* proclaimed, "15 miles from the Queensboro Bridge and yet within cannon shot of most of the well-to-do homes and country clubs in Nassau County."[62] To suit the typical Lord & Taylor customer, who was accustomed to genteel, personal service, Loewy's ideal suburban selling machine included "Little Shops—gay as country fairs and as cozy as possible—wandering around the peripheries of informally shaped areas that remove from the layout all traces of stiffness and formality. Counters are gracefully curved, lights are designed to flatter the sandiest Canasta complexion, and the suburban store itself becomes American Suburbia's favorite village green."[63]

Recognizing that the vast majority of customers would be motorists, Loewy discarded the conventional street-oriented design that emphasized display windows in favor of one in which the entire building functioned as a three-dimensional roadside advertisement. Located at the southeast corner of Northern

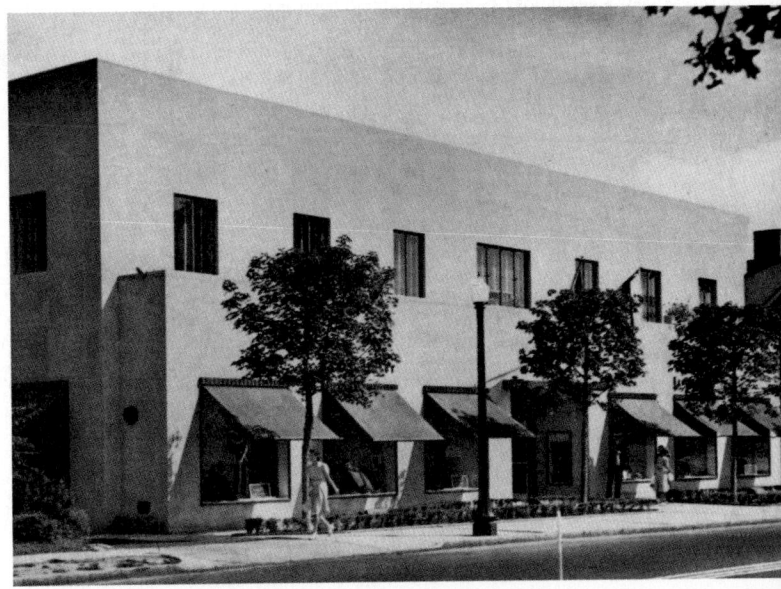

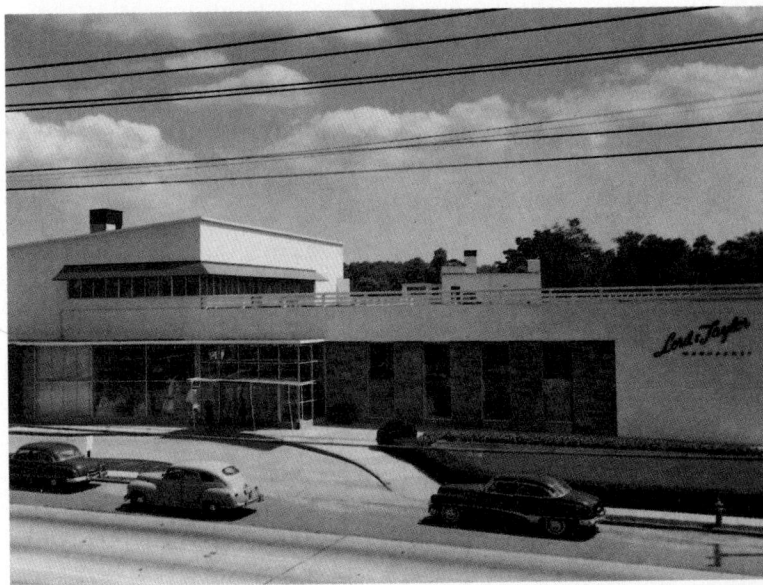

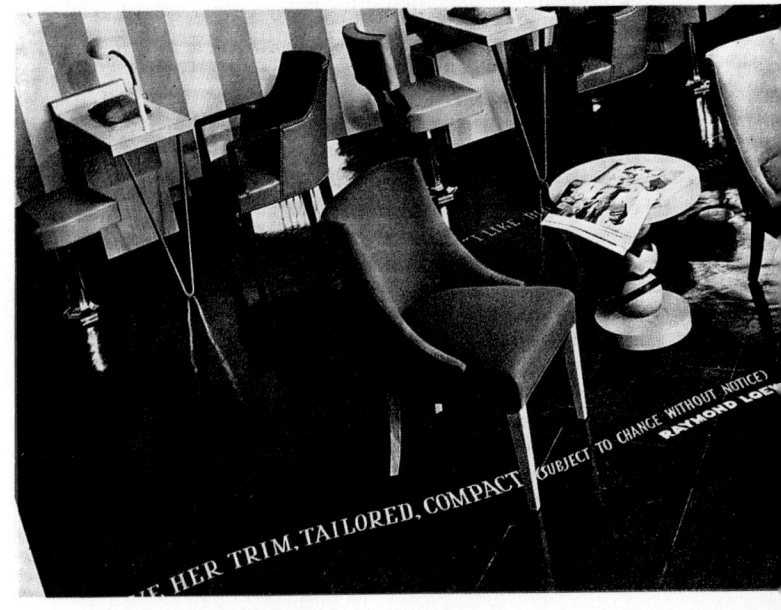

Boulevard and Shelter Rock Road, the store was set back from the street amid lushly planted lawns, terraces, flower-bordered walkways and a landscaped parking lot that occupied one third of the site. Loewy synthesized a Modernist approach to composition—asymmetrical massing and an extensive use of plate glass—with a Colonial Georgian–inspired domesticity that reflected the surrounding neighborhood's residential architecture as well as what *Interiors* described as the "instinctively conservative" tastes of most Lord & Taylor customers.[64] He clad the facades in imported fieldstone and whitewashed brick to create what *Interior Design and Decoration* labeled a "Country-Modern" style.[65]

A curved driveway led from Northern Boulevard to the store's principal entrance, placed within a glass-enclosed projection that blurred the distinction between indoors and outdoors, a feature that would become a hallmark of suburban domestic architecture. To the left of the entrance, the curved glass wall enclosed a display area through which a large portion of the main selling floor could be seen clearly from the driveway as well as from passing cars. Exploiting a sloping site, the store's lower level, which contained a children's clothing department and a beauty salon, could be entered directly from the parking lot. Indeed, in this way the department store came to resemble the typical suburban house, in which the back door replaced the one in front as the principal entrance.

Inside, the main floor combined elements of an open plan with a series of independent departments defined only by low partitions but given individual character with different decorative schemes. According to the editors of *Interiors*, because Loewy and Calvin McDonald, who designed most of the furniture, "felt that the life of the suburban wife is often pretty grim," they "determined to make this store a place where shopping should be Fun. They have tried, successfully, to get a little humor into modern interior design."[66] The semicircular wall of the sports department was decorated with a trompe l'oeil mural that seemed to place display racks within striped tents at a country fair and transform a three-part mirror into a ticket booth. In the Young New Yorker Shop, clothes racks were placed within picture frames hung from enormous taffeta bows, and upholstered seats were shaped like park benches. White clouds seemed to float up the walls and onto the ceiling of the pink and blue Infant's Shop; countertops were covered in blue rubber decorated with white stars, combining practicality with wit. For the Intimate Apparel Shop Loewy adopted an almost surreal tone, continuing a trend established by Ladislas Medgyes and Martine Kane's extravagant interiors of 1937 for the Helena Rubinstein Salon and Salvador Dalí's infamous "Day" and "Night" display window designs of 1939 for Bonwit Teller.[67] The walls of the department were lined with valentines and dance programs, and the doors leading to the stock room contained windows outlined by red velvet lips. In the Beauty Salon, Loewy took the surreal even further, painting the walls with his own murals, juxtaposing a hot-air balloon, a column surmounted by a sculpted bust and an easel holding the image of a disembodied eye.

Further mining the rich market of Nassau County's affluent North Shore, real estate developer Sol G. Atlas built a "strip" shopping center adjacent to Lord & Taylor's department store, lining both sides of Northern Boulevard with one- and two-story commercial buildings in the "Country-Modern" style that Loewy had established.[68] Dubbing the development the "Miracle Mile," a term he may have picked up from the arcaded street of shops built in the 1920s in Coral Gables, Florida, by George Merrick,[69] or from the commercial development along Wilshire

Boulevard in Los Angeles built by A. W. Ross, also in the 1920s,[70] Atlas leased space to such well-known retailers as Lane Bryant, James McCutcheon, Peck & Peck, Black, Starr & Gorham, Best & Company, W. & J. Sloane and the restaurant chain Louis Sherry. (He also provided a five-story medical center and hospital.) The development was not so much a shopping center as a glamorous Fifth Avenue–type shopping promenade adapted to motorists rather than pedestrians. It surrounded Munsey Park's neighborhood commercial center (Frederick L. Ackerman, 1931), which had been set back from the street with a small parking lot in front of crescent-shaped, Georgian Colonial buildings designed in accordance with the planned community's building code.[71] In contrast to the typical Modernist-influenced buildings of the Miracle Mile, Munsey Park's center, with its bay windows and slate hipped roofs punctuated by dormers and a cupola, looked decidedly quaint.

Although clearly geared toward customers who arrived by car, the Miracle Mile provided only limited parking space. Most stores were placed close to the highway with parking lots in back. The division of parking space into separate lots and the lack of pedestrian passageways leading to the street meant that shoppers often had to park and repark several times during a single trip. Although, from the merchants' point of view, the scarcity of parking space helped to prevent the intrusion of inferior enterprises that would take advantage of the superior businesses' drawing power and parking facilities to attract customers, for consumers it was simply an inconvenience. Morris Ketchum, Jr., assailed the Miracle Mile as "a haphazard collection of stores placed on either side of a main highway" where "shoppers on foot take their lives in their hands." "The highway itself is choked with traffic on every busy shopping day," he continued. "The miracle of the 'Miracle Mile' is that it does not die in its own traffic snarl. That it has not is due to its rich market area, its top-flight store tenants, and the complete absence of competition from any nearby shopping centers worthy of the name."[72]

The eastern end of the Miracle Mile was anchored in 1947 by a B. Altman's branch store designed by the architectural firm of Alfred Hopkins & Associates and the design firm of Amos Parrish & Company.[73] In a design marked by an overall lack of imagination, the architects shaped an essentially flat site to provide principal entrances on both floors of the two-story building, thus creating two "ground-floor" selling areas. The use of rough-hewn stone on the exterior, though it related somewhat to the materials of the nearby houses, gave the building a rather massive, brutal appearance.

In 1947 Lord & Taylor opened a branch store at the intersection of White Plains and Wilmot roads in Eastchester, Westchester County.[74] Construction of the building in the formerly residential area required a zoning change and provoked considerable community opposition, despite the store's promise to establish an appropriate tone. Designed by William T. Snaith of Raymond Loewy Associates and the firm of Starrett & Van Vleck, with interiors designed by Edgar Tallman, the head of Lord & Taylor's interior display department, the store followed the lead of the Manhasset branch. The White Plains store combined asymmetrical massing with Colonial-inspired, whitewashed brick and rough-hewn fieldstone. Inside, Tallman continued the whimsical tone previously set by Loewy. Although Tallman's overall design was somewhat toned down, the decor of the lingerie department was strictly tongue in cheek: pink chairs with hourglass-shaped backs sported brown "corsets" that were laced up in back and incorporated what Ketchum described as "appropriately upholstered fronts."[75]

No matter how elegant the commercial tenant, the isolated department store and the "strip" development could not fully meet the demands of driving shoppers. The solution was the pedestrian-oriented shopping environment, in which parking lots were separated from internal walkways. The nation's first such mall, the Northgate Regional Shopping Center in Seattle, Washington, was opened in 1950 and designed by John Graham, Jr.[76] Morris Ketchum, Jr., who, with the architect Victor Gruen, had pioneered the use of a recessed outdoor display area in the Lederer's shop (1939) on Fifth Avenue, claimed that he had been the first to imagine the shopping mall.[77] In his autobiography, *Blazing a Trail*, Ketchum recalled, "The Lederer de Paris lobby was popular because it gave window shoppers an escape from sidewalk pedestrian traffic. . . . Why, I thought, couldn't suburban centers use a grander shopping lobby—in fact, a centralized outdoor pedestrian mall—to escape from being hemmed in by auto traffic and parking areas. Wouldn't this solution be better than the strip centers plastered on streets and highways?"[78] The idea was also considered by Kelly & Gruzen, who in 1949 proposed an innovative plan for the Maybrook Shopping Center, to be located on a triangular site in Maywood, New Jersey.[79] The unrealized plan called for a circle of stores, including a department store and a supermarket, to occupy the wide base of the triangular site and enclose a circular, landscaped pedestrian mall containing small concession stands. Five arcades were to penetrate the circle, leading from the surrounding parking lots to the mall. A theater and restaurant separated from the main complex would have occupied the apex of the triangular site.

In 1949 plans were also announced for the construction of the Cross County Shopping Center in Yonkers, another center with a mall *parti*.[80] Occupying sixty acres at the intersection of the Cross County Parkway and Central Park Avenue, the complex was to be located just where the city met the suburbs, a point easily reached by bus from the Bronx and downtown Yonkers and by car from Westchester County's inner suburban villages such as Scarsdale, Bronxville, Larchmont and Mount Vernon. The center was also planned in anticipation of the New York State Thruway's construction along Central Park Avenue, which would make the site exceptionally accessible. Thus, unlike the basically local orientation of the Miracle Mile, the Cross County Shopping Center was intended to serve both local and regional markets. The center was to include supermarkets, restaurants, filling stations, chain clothing stores, branch department stores and a movie theater. An unrealized scheme by Harris & Brown called for a U-shaped complex of buildings, flanked by adjoining wings, with parking lots on three sides and a broad, landscaped pedestrian mall in the center. In the middle of the proposal was a dominant five-story office building, which pushed the center even more in the direction of a traditional mixed-use downtown. A John Wanamaker's department store, to be located on a separately owned adjacent site, was also proposed.

But the Cross County Shopping Center remained dormant until Sol Atlas stepped in with a plan designed by Lathrop Douglass.[81] By the time the center opened in 1954, the New York State Thruway was a reality and the location was among the most desirable in any eastern city. Douglass replaced the original plan for the center, which now covered seventy acres and contained parking space for 5,140 cars, with a more casual arrangement. The Wanamaker's store, designed by Copeland, Novak Associates, working in cooperation with Douglass, had a three-level parking area that allowed direct entry to each of the store's three floors. Recalling Wanamaker's New York headquarters on Tenth Street between Broadway and Fourth Avenue, the mall entrance to the suburban store was flanked by two large stone lions. The store's interiors, designed by William Pahlmann, were full of references to the surrounding Hudson River Valley, including scene paintings, murals and, in the shoe department, brass and red-glass riverboat lanterns, captain's chairs and a steering wheel from an old packet. Continuing in the store's civic-minded tradition, Wanamaker's Westchester store also featured a community meeting room. The Cross County Shopping Center contained another branch department store, the first suburban satellite of Gimbel's. Designed by Douglass, with interiors by Raymond Loewy, the architecturally undistinguished store contained 212,000 square feet of floor space divided into 124 departments. The low, sprawling silhouette of the shopping center was interrupted by the centrally located, eight-story Cross County Medical Center, also designed by Douglass. A banal rectangular slab with horizontal strip windows on its long facades and stark, windowless end facades, relieved on one end only by the center's logo, the building was clad in blue glazed brick.

By the mid-1950s the automobile-oriented shopping center was a major retailing venue and a familiar sight in the suburban landscape. Retail sales in Manhattan rose by only 4 percent in 1955, as compared to 27 percent in the surrounding suburbs.[82] In 1957 Ketchum wrote that for retail businesses, "the race to the suburbs is still going full tilt."[83] The same year, the Urban Land Institute stated without qualification that "the Shopping Center is today's extraordinary retail business evolvement. . . . The automobile accounts for suburbia, and suburbia accounts for the shopping center."[84]

All of New York's suburban shopping developments paled in comparison with Roosevelt Field Shopping Center, located in Garden City on Long Island.[85] Designed by I. M. Pei, with Robert Zion serving as landscape architect and Abe Feder in charge of special lighting, Roosevelt Field, with 1,387,000 square feet of retail selling space, was the world's largest shopping center when it opened in 1956. It was only one part of an integrated commercial, office and industrial development, masterminded by real estate wizard William Zeckendorf, that included fifty acres of office space and one million square feet of industrial space leased to Pepsi-Cola Bottling, Sperry Rand Marine Division, Graybar Electric and others. Rather than merely a place to visit between major shopping trips to Manhattan, Roosevelt Field, with its office and industrial components, was a substitute for the city, not just for housewives, but for the entire community. (Furthering the sense that it was a world unto itself, Roosevelt Field Shopping Center became an enclosed, climate-controlled mall in 1967.) The Roosevelt Field development occupied the former site of the airfield identified as the nation's "cradle of aviation"; it was there, in 1927, that Charles Lindbergh took off for Paris.[86] By the late 1940s, with worldwide flights commonplace and housing developments springing up like weeds around the once-isolated airstrip, Roosevelt Field seemed outmoded; in 1951 it was closed.

The explosive suburban growth that doomed the airstrip gave birth to the dreams of Zeckendorf, who sought to harness the county's commercial possibilities. Nassau's population increased 140 percent between 1940 and 1954, and by 1956 it was estimated that there was a potential market of 1.3 million customers within a ten-mile radius of the shopping center. In 1950 Webb & Knapp, Zeckendorf's realty firm, bought a 60 percent interest in Roosevelt Field, Inc., paying an average of nine

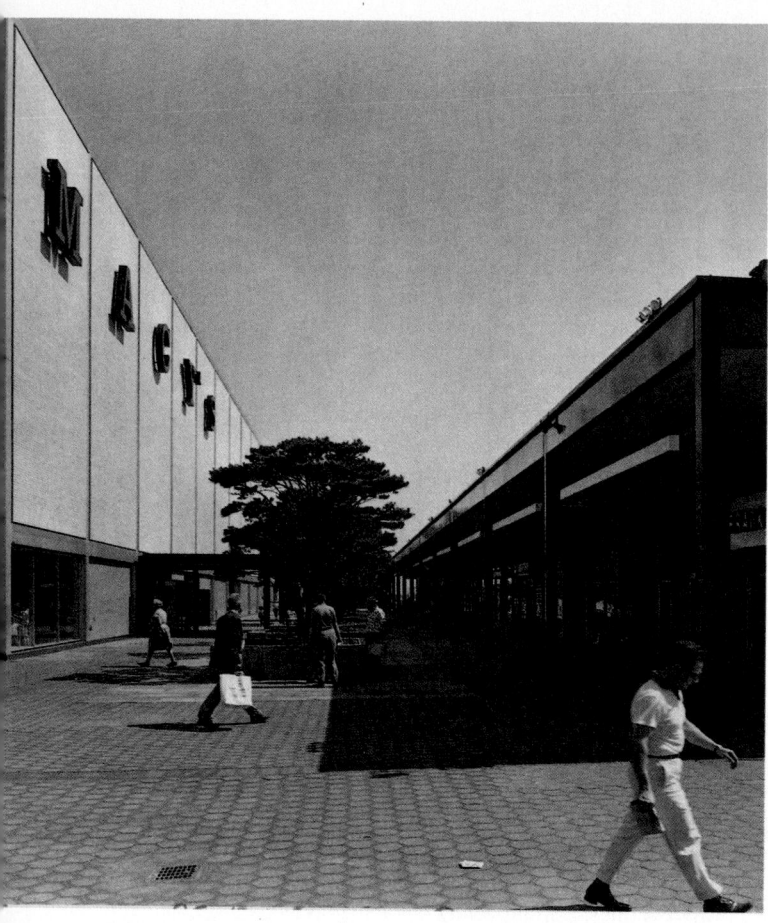

Roosevelt Field Shopping Center, Old Country Road, Garden City, New York. I. M. Pei, 1956. Interior walkway with Macy's (Skidmore, Owings & Merrill, 1956) on the left. OMH

dollars a share, for a total of $1.5 million. Five years later, shares were listed on the American Stock Exchange at forty-five dollars and had split three for one.

Roosevelt Field was reached by way of two cloverleaf interchanges from the extension of Meadowbrook Parkway, which was opened concurrently with the shopping center. The complex consisted of a cluster of buildings linked by walkways and malls and surrounded by an 11,000-car-capacity parking lot. It was anchored at its southern end by a two-story building housing the largest suburban branch of Macy's; the northern end was occupied by two supermarkets, which in 1960 were joined by a Gimbel's branch store. Between the anchors, three rows of one-story buildings housed approximately 100 stores, divided into three categories: variety and lower-priced clothing stores, specialty shops, and upmarket stores, primarily specializing in clothing. Separating the rows of stores were the Fountain Mall, featuring low- and high-spouting fountains illuminated at night by underwater lights, and the International Flight Mall, dedicated at the center's opening ceremonies by 200 aviation cadets. All the buildings were designed by Pei, with the exception of Macy's, which was designed by Skidmore, Owings & Merrill. Pei adopted a Mies-inspired, modular dark brown steel frame, filled in with rough-faced, off-white brick and glass. A bus terminal located at the center's edge was elegantly defined by a steel framework covered by corrugated plastic panels. The Macy's department store harmonized with the rest of the center, incorporating glazed-brick facades.

While the architecture was strictly ordered and somewhat bland, it consistently maintained a human scale, effectively keeping the huge complex from overwhelming its patrons. As James S. Hornbeck, senior editor of Architectural Record, noted, the center's planning provided an "easy-to-learn traffic flow for pedestrian and driver."[87] The pedestrian circulation malls were intentionally narrow to encourage cross shopping but were kept visually stimulating by distinctive landscaping. Courtyards, including the highly decorative, granite-paved Continental Court, provided additional public space and visual interest. Beneath the shopping center, an underground concourse housed twenty-five more stores, as well as administrative offices, a radio studio, a 400-seat community meeting room, an exhibition area for the display of home-building products and an art center. An outdoor skating rink was located at the northern terminus of the Fountain Mall. An unrealized pavilion, meant to provide both shelter and a dramatic visual focal point, was to consist of a 40-foot-high steel column supporting a circular space frame, 150 feet in diameter, covered with glass or plastic elements set at different angles. The most significant feature of the center, however, was not its architecture or planning per se but its enormous size, the wide variety of concerns housed, the generous provision of public amenities and the meticulous attention to detail, which created an overall sense of both variety and harmony.

Pei's design control also extended to a comprehensive graphics program, supervised by the head of his graphics department, Don Page. The program included display letters and street signs that helped to establish a dignified but upbeat atmosphere. At the entrance, the center's name was announced by forty-inch plastic globes, raised high on vine-covered aluminum tubes, and each internally lighted and painted with a letter. Additional globes sported the center's logo, a stylized drawing of a balloon inscribed with the center's name, a symbol also used on paper shopping bags. Flags decorated with colorful, abstract motifs by Kenneth Resen adorned the International Flight Mall. Boldly designed signs identified sections of the immense parking area. Scattered throughout the center, ten kiosks used as signboards and vending stands enhanced the sense of "street life" and added what Hornbeck described as a "delightful continental touch."[88] To visually tie together the buildings and public areas, the malls and walkways were paved with hexagonal asphalt blocks and divided by a grid of stone blocks that aligned with the buildings' modular pattern.

Two other large centers opened on Long Island in 1956, Lathrop Douglass's Mid-Island Plaza in Hicksville and the Green Acres Shopping Center in Valley Stream.[89] The Green Acres Shopping Center, which rivaled Roosevelt Field in size if not aesthetics, was designed by Irwin S. Chanin and developed by the Chanin Organization as the final phase of an 800-house subdivision begun in 1936 and originally envisioned to grow to 1,800 houses.[90] Chanin had proposed a ribbon park system that was to provide Green Acres residents with seven miles of continuous walking and biking trails, as well as playgrounds for each group of fifty to seventy-five houses. In the middle of the development a broad boulevard was to be lined with apartments and shops and lead to a civic center, a feature that Chanin developed after the war as the Green Acres Shopping Center. The shopping center conformed to the by then conventional pattern: a cluster of buildings linked by pedestrian malls and surrounded by parking lots. Gimbel's and J. C. Penney's, represented by its largest suburban store, were among the tenants of Green Acres.

Victor Gruen's design of 1958 for the Westchester Terminal Plaza was a mixed-use project proposed for New Rochelle but never realized.[91] Despite the success of his pioneering Southdale Center (1956) in Minneapolis, which was widely recognized as the prototype for the enclosed suburban shopping mall, Gruen radically departed from the typical low-lying arrangement surrounded by parking lots. He proposed instead a twenty-four-level complex, which included a fifteen-story office building wrapped in a gold-anodized-aluminum grille, to be built over the tracks of the New York, New Haven & Hartford Railroad; the railroad would sell its land and air rights and lease a new station to provide direct access to the complex. Parking and shopping areas were to be integrated to a degree unprecedented in a suburban shopping center: two levels of shops were slipped between three floors of basement parking and two floors of roof parking, which together occupied two-thirds of the total space. Macy's was to share the center with seventy smaller shops. Enclosed, climate-controlled malls were to be landscaped with semitropical plants, and live birds would add an exotic touch. The complex was also to include a 100-room motel equipped with a swimming pool. Although the innovative design was never realized, an alternate scheme, named the New Rochelle Mall, was completed in 1967 across the street from the original site on a parcel of land slated by the city for urban renewal.[92] Designed by Copeland, Novak & Israel, the mall contained stores and restaurants located on two levels, as well as a 1,200-seat theater and an ice-skating rink. The mall's principal commercial tenant was a branch store of Macy's, designed by the firm of Abbott, Merkt & Company.

The Mall at Short Hills, New Jersey, designed by Skidmore, Owings & Merrill (SOM) in 1962, effectively brought the firm's brand of coolly elegant Miesian Modernism to the design of a high-end shopping center whose tenant list—according to Hornbeck, "a miniature Fifth Avenue Association"—included Bonwit Teller, Peck & Peck and Stouffer's.[93] Adopting a uniform pattern of column spacing, SOM wrapped large spaces in glass and aluminum skins; other facades were built of light beige-gray

brick. Broad roof overhangs created sheltered walkways in some areas; in others, a similar effect was established by a cantilevered second story. Entrance porticoes and double-level covered walkways were supported by thin columns. Throughout the complex, SOM controlled the design of storefronts and exterior graphics. Eschewing the casual atmosphere of most other shopping centers, the Mall at Short Hills adopted a relentlessly reductivist aesthetic, making it the suburban equivalent of the Modernist high rises that were reshaping Manhattan.

The rapid growth of affluent suburbs throughout northeastern New Jersey fueled the development of superscale shopping centers. By the mid-1960s Paramus had become a paradigmatic example of postwar placelessness, a suburban area that had attracted an enormous number of urban facilities, but with little or no urban planning.[94] The first large shopping center in Paramus was Garden State Plaza (1957), designed by Abbott, Merkt & Company as a watery version of I. M. Pei's Mies-inspired Roosevelt Field.[95] One of the nation's largest shopping centers at the time, Garden State Plaza followed the conventional pedestrian mall organization. An underground truck road handled all deliveries and service activities, aiding the separation of automobile and pedestrian traffic. Branch stores of Bamberger's (the Newark, New Jersey, affiliate of Macy's) and Gimbel's were among the principal tenants. One interesting local tenant was the Arcadian Gardens, which sold plants and gardening books in supermarket fashion. Like Roosevelt Field, Garden State Plaza was built on a large site that would eventually include offices and medical facilities.

In 1960 the opening of the vast Bergen Mall, designed by John Graham, Jr., gave Paramus the distinction of having the largest concentration of suburban department stores in the New York metropolitan region.[96] Although the Garden State Plaza and the Bergen Mall were located within a mile of each other, little commercial development existed between them and they did nothing to create a unifying urbanism. The Regional Plan Association, in a supplement to its *Second Regional Plan*, advocated that the two malls be integrated as part of a metropolitan center that would serve the surrounding area.[97] The association called for the construction of office buildings, a university and perhaps an affiliated medical center connecting the two shopping centers, which would also be linked by automated buses or some other rapid-transport system. The proposal was never implemented.

The suburban department store type and shopping center became such central features of American life that they began to make inroads into more heavily urbanized areas. In 1957 Alexander's opened a branch, designed by Francis X. Giná & Associates, on the corner of Queens Boulevard and Sixty-third Road in Rego Park.[98] The department store proved so successful that in 1967 the same firm was hired to expand the facility, wrapping it in vermilion glazed brick.

In 1965 Macy's opened a 326,500-square-foot branch in the Elmhurst section of Queens—by then the fifty-first store in its nationwide chain—that in both size and emphasis on the automobile was clearly intended to compete with nearby suburban shopping centers.[99] At the same time, it occupied a constricted site in a relatively high-density area near the Lefrak City development, where Macy's estimated that 725,000 potential customers lived within a three-mile radius. To most effectively exploit the irregularly shaped, five-acre site, bounded by Queens Boulevard, Justice Avenue, Fifty-fifth and Fifty-sixth avenues, the architects, Skidmore, Owings & Merrill, with William S. Brown serving as partner in charge, ingeniously combined store and

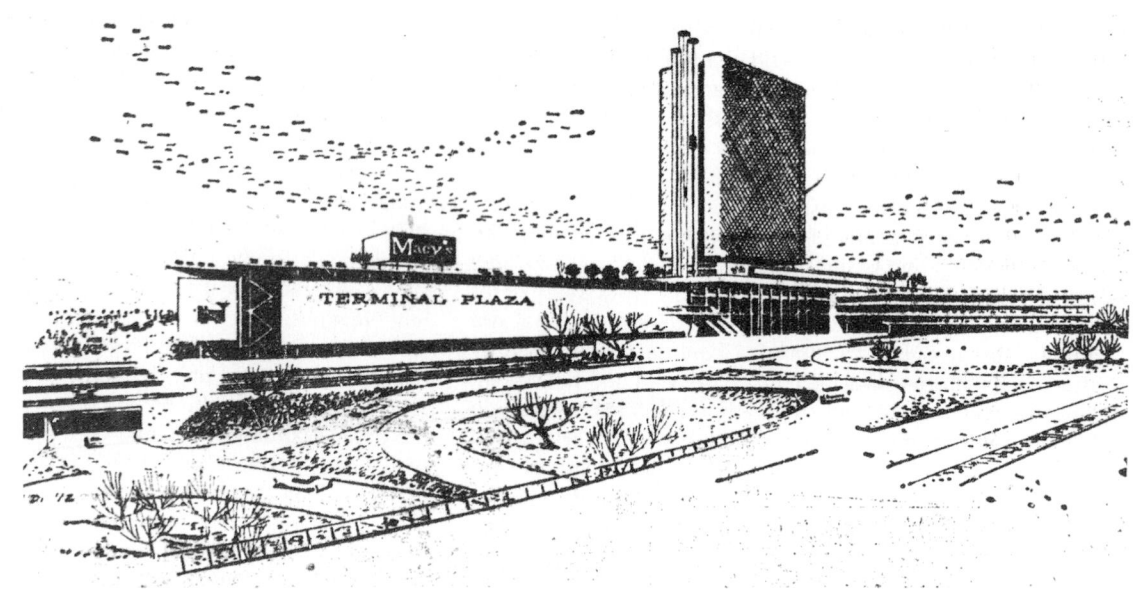

Top: Proposal for
Westchester
Terminal Plaza,
New Rochelle, New
York. Victor Gruen,
1958. Perspective.
NYT

Center: The Mall at
Short Hills, 1200
Morris Turnpike,
Short Hills, New
Jersey. Skidmore,
Owings & Merrill,
1962. Interior
walkway. Molitor.
SOM

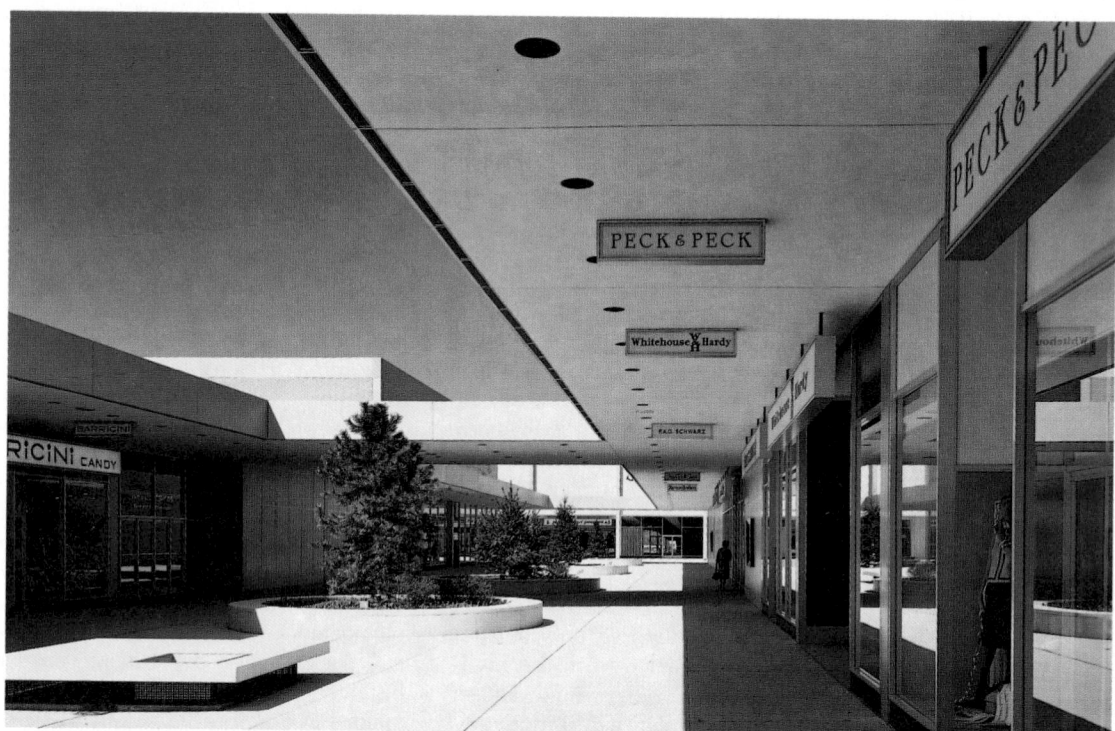

Bottom: Macy's,
88-01 Queens
Boulevard, between
Fifty-fifth and Fifty-
sixth avenues,
Elmhurst, Queens.
Skidmore, Owings &
Merrill, 1965. View
to the northeast.
Stoller. ©ESTO

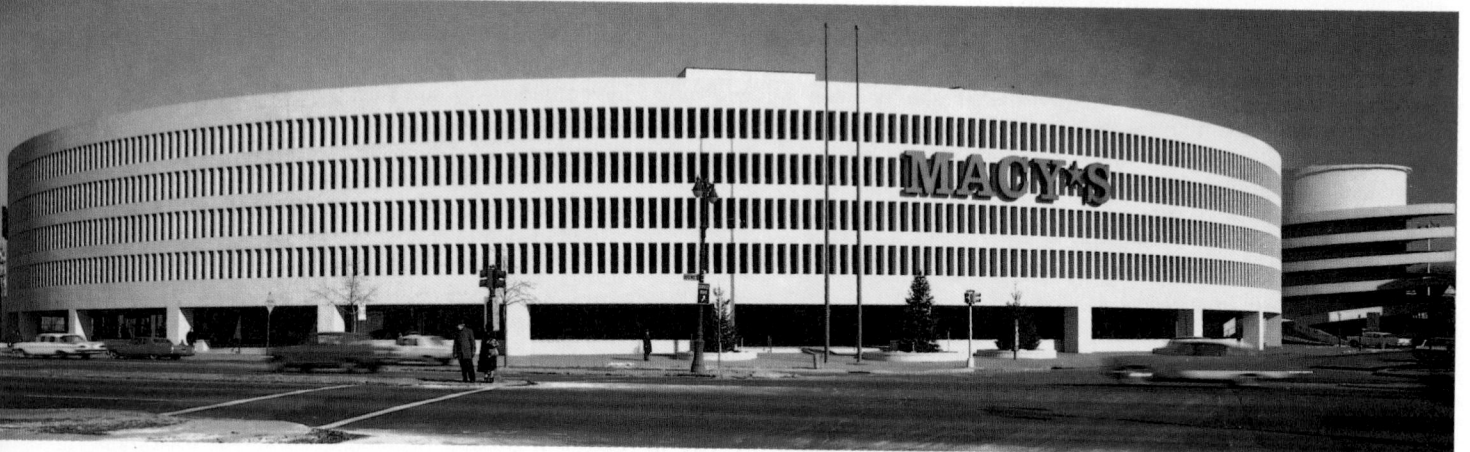

parking facilities in a single, 426-foot-diameter cylindrical structure—what *Progressive Architecture* called "a unique department store-cum-parking garage."[100] To the journalist William Robbins, writing in the *New York Times*, the structure looked "from the air like a stack of giant silver dollars and from the ground like a football stadium."[101]

Skidmore, Owings & Merrill had presented the store's management with five schemes. Because the site's high water table had prevented the obvious alternative of burrowing a garage below grade, four of the proposals consisted of buildings with attached parking garages. The fifth scheme proposed a single cylindrical building with the first floor dramatically cantilevered from a central core. The client preferred one of the conventional, rectangular plans, but SOM was in favor of the more innovative design; ultimately the cantilevered floor was eliminated but the cylindrical shape was retained. While the original plans called for a perfectly circular building, Macy's was unable to acquire all of the necessary property for the design: the owner of a 169-foot-deep residential lot at the corner of Queens Boulevard and Fifty-fifth Avenue, which was occupied by an architecturally undistinguished 20-by-30-foot house, refused to sell, despite offers amounting to five times the property's market value. The architects had no choice but to revise their building plans, cutting a small notch into the building. More significant was the loss of an imposing entrance plaza.

In its final form, the building's three selling floors were wrapped in five rings of parking, each fifty-six feet wide and providing a total of 1,250 spaces; the parking rings were in turn wrapped in a poured-in-place, reinforced-concrete grille that simultaneously provided a sense of enclosure and allowed exhaust fumes to escape without a mechanical ventilation system. The exterior of the building was finished in sandblasted, white quartz aggregate concrete. In addition to saving valuable land, the design eliminated the sometimes long walk from car to store across the sea of parking space in a typical suburban shopping center. With every car located within seventy-five feet of the store, SOM's design approximated the convenience of "curb-side parking"; in addition, a computerized signal system indicated the location of available parking spaces. Separate entrance and exit automobile ramps were placed within back-to-back double helices on the site's eastern edge. At peak traffic periods, such as closing time, both helices could channel cars one way. The store was constructed to support an additional floor and two more levels of parking, but these were not built.

Pedestrians entered through five entrances distributed around the building's circumference and set within a thirty-five-foot-wide covered arcade. Facing the arcade, the store's ground-level exterior wall was clad with colored mosaic tile and punctuated by eight display windows. Inside, the store's ground-level selling space was shaped like a Greek cross and upper-floor selling areas took the shape of modified rectangles, curved at opposite ends; the remaining spaces were occupied by inventory. As designed by Copeland, Novak & Israel, the vast selling areas were ringed by a series of small shops, which reduced the amount of undifferentiated open space and introduced a sense of intimacy. A basement level housing storage and truck service facilities was accessible by a ramp beneath the helices.

While Macy's Elmhurst store clearly reflected the influence of its suburban counterparts, the accommodations made to its small site offered lessons to a rapidly urbanizing suburbia: the generous amount of gross rentable space it housed would not have been possible on a suburban site of the same size because of the outlying areas' low-density residential development and dependence on surface parking. The store's consolidation allowed it to effectively meet its patrons' shopping needs; in addition, the distinctive, well-articulated design exerted a strong architectural presence that surpassed its commercial function to contribute to the surrounding community's civic identity. The store's enveloping concrete grille was particularly impressive at night, when, as *Progressive Architecture* noted, "the store will function as a civic monument, with light shining through the slits of the facade—a Queens Coliseum of sorts, sitting amidst the ruins."[102]

Kings Plaza (1970), located on a twenty-three-acre site at the intersection of Flatbush Avenue and Avenue U in Brooklyn and designed by Emery Roth & Sons, brought the conveniences of a complete suburban shopping mall into the city limits.[103] While the complex's rather undistinguished, stripped-down architecture and enclosed mall organization were consistent with many of its suburban counterparts, its constrained site was not. Approximately one third of Kings Plaza's site was originally part of Mill Basin, a narrow inlet of Jamaica Bay; the additional land was created by the straightforward if costly process of landfill. A riprap dike was built in Mill Basin along the property line and the area between the existing shoreline and the dike filled in with compacted hydraulic fill. Fully exploiting the site, the center contained 1.1 million square feet of gross rentable space, approximately seven times the amount possible on a typical suburban site with surface parking. To achieve this density, the main building complex was located on the northern portion of the site, near the principal roads, and a 4,000-car, five-level enclosed parking garage was located on the landfill. Each level of the garage covered an area of almost seven acres. Although the capacity of the garage was small by suburban standards, it worked reasonably well for Kings Plaza, given that nearly half of the patrons used public transportation. In addition to parking, the structure housed administrative offices, community meeting rooms and facilities serving the adjacent 150-boat marina. Stores and mall areas were double-decked and anchored by three-story branches of Alexander's and Macy's. The desire to maximize available ground-level retail space, as well as the proximity of groundwater, necessitated the placement of loading facilities on the roof, where direct access was provided to the stores' top floors.

Queens Center (1973), located not far from Macy's on the northeast corner of Queens Boulevard and Fifty-ninth Avenue, was a 1.4-million-square-foot enclosed shopping mall housing numerous smaller shops as well as branches of Ohrbach's and Abraham & Straus. Designed by Gruen Associates, the mall was sheathed in metal panels and glazed brick and was adjoined by a concrete parking garage. Norval White and Elliot Willensky described the mall as a "modernistic reprise to the 1930s" and the enclosed three-story-high interior space as "sparkling."[104]

In 1973 the 1.8-million-square-foot Staten Island Mall, designed by Welton Becket & Associates and located at 2655 Richmond Avenue in New Springville, introduced a climate-controlled shopping environment to the least urban of the city's boroughs.[105] The mall was anchored by a branch of Macy's, with interiors designed by Copeland, Novak & Israel, and a branch of Sears, designed by Abbott, Merkt & Company. The complexly massed but rather undistinguished two- and three-story complex, surrounded by parking for 10,000 cars, was originally intended to be linked to a tall office building, but this was never realized.

In 1974 the completion of Rentar Plaza brought a vast shopping complex to Metropolitan Avenue and Sixty-fifth Lane in the Middle Village section of Queens.[106] The immense three-story building, which contained as much floor space as one of the World Trade Center's twin towers, was designed by Robert E. Levien Partners and clad in brown-glazed brick. It incorporated exterior roadways leading to a 1,200-car-capacity rooftop parking lot. White and Willensky ridiculed the shopping center as "an aircraft carrier gone astray."[107]

The Suburbanization of Work

The phenomenon of corporations building headquarters in the suburbs of New York rather than in the city itself had a profound effect on the urbanistic character of the postwar metropolitan region, transforming the traditional hierarchy in which the city served as the "front office" and the suburbs functioned as "bedroom communities." The pivotal change was presaged by the outward movement of manufactories. Printing and publishing concerns were among the first to move their plants, sometimes accompanied by office facilities, out of Manhattan and often out of the city altogether. As early as 1910, Doubleday & Company moved its operations from New York City to Garden City,[108] and in 1922 Condé Nast moved his publications' operating plant from the city to Greenwich, Connecticut.[109]

After the Second World War the number of companies building suburban facilities increased dramatically. In 1945 the technologically innovative Johns-Manville building materials company began to build a research center on a ninety-three-acre site in Manville, New Jersey.[110] Though the two- and four-story U-shaped complex (Shreve, Lamb & Harmon, 1949) contained state-of-the-art laboratories based on a standardized eleven-by-twenty-six-foot module separated by movable interior walls, it eschewed a typical industrial appearance (see chapter 1). According to Clifford F. Rassweiler, a Johns-Manville executive, both the stripped-down Modern Classical buildings and the complex's bucolic site, bordered by the Raritan River and landscaped by the firm of Clarke, Rapuano & Holleran, were designed so that "the ensemble would resemble a modern college campus," providing aesthetically satisfying surroundings that he felt would have practical benefits. Whereas during the interwar years the business community recognized the advertising potential of good architecture, seizing upon the skyscraper as the preeminent symbol of corporate power and pride, in the postwar years many businesses would utilize design as a kind of employee benefit that would in turn aid management through increased worker stability and productivity. As Rassweiler explained: "The architects were instructed to pay special attention to making the center as attractive as possible, both inside and out. . . . The company has been amply rewarded for its concern. . . . In the past two years, turnover of technical personnel has been less than four per cent per year from all causes—an unusually low figure which is a source of pride."[111]

Johns-Manville was not alone in advocating the suburbanization of plants and attendant facilities. In 1952 the Regional Plan Association publicly released the findings of a twelve-month study surveying industrial development patterns in the New York area between 1946 and 1951.[112] The study showed that more than 80 percent of the 2,658 manufacturing plants opened during the period were located outside the principal industrial districts as they had been defined at the war's end. Five counties in New Jersey—Bergen, Essex, Hudson, Middlesex and Union—accounted for half of the total. The association attrib-

uted the exodus to five factors: the greater availability of land in outlying areas more easily accommodated such amenities as employee cafeterias, recreational facilities and parking, as well as future expansions; the lack of space limitations often allowed for one-story structures, which were more economically efficient, particularly for assembly-line production; suburban locations provided for greater efficiency in the delivery of materials and the distribution of products; taxes, though not necessarily lower, were, in the words of the report, "steadier and more predictable"; and, finally, the suburbs were seen as less vulnerable to air attack, a lingering concern in the Cold War era.[113]

Corporate office headquarters soon followed manufacturing plants out of the city; like the blue-collar exodus, the white-collar migration had begun before the war. In 1922 the *Reader's Digest*, which had published its first issue earlier that year from cramped quarters at One Minetta Lane in Greenwich Village, where its founders, DeWitt and Lila Acheson Wallace, lived and worked, moved to more spacious headquarters in the town of Pleasantville, Westchester County, which they again used for both business and domestic life.[114] By the late 1930s the magazine had once again outgrown its facilities. For their new headquarters the Wallaces decided to build on a sprawling, 156-acre site, formerly part of a subdivision, Lawrence Farms, in Chappaqua, Westchester. The Wallaces wanted their offices housed not in a typical office building but in a structure that resembled the manor house on an estate. Citing the architecture of the restored Colonial town of Williamsburg, Virginia, which they admired, the Wallaces instructed William McKenzie, their architect, to take inspiration from the Capitol and Governor's Palace there, as well as from the Wren Building at William and Mary College. He designed a red-brick Georgian building surmounted by an imposing cupola, complete with an anthemion-decorated cornice. McKenzie had intended for the cupola to incorporate four sculpted, spread-winged eagles, but Mrs. Wallace, who designed the building's traditionally articulated interiors, as well as the complex's extensive landscaped grounds, requested that the copper sculptures depict the company's symbol, the mythical winged horse Pegasus.

In 1951 the Standard Oil Corporation opened regional headquarters in Pelham, New York, designed by Eppel Seaman.[115] The horizontality of the low-lying, two-story building was emphasized by the strips of industrial sash that punctuated its brick facades. The high point of the design, an understated interpretation of 1930s streamlined Modernism, was the building's corner entrance, where a double-height L-shaped canopy was supported by flanking finlike walls. In 1953 the company completed an administrative facility in Linden, New Jersey.[116] Designed by Lathrop Douglass, the six-story building was distinguished by its pioneering use of modular office furniture. In order to accommodate the greatest layout flexibility for desk units attached to six-foot-high partitions, large interior spaces were left undifferentiated and windows were located seven feet above the floor.

In 1953 General Foods, the nation's largest manufacturer of packaged food, broke ground for its new national headquarters on a forty-six-acre site in White Plains, New York.[117] The editors of *Business Week* noted the significance of the company's move: "Manufacturing facilities, large and small, have been trickling into the suburbs for years. So have laboratories. But so far there has been no mass flight of companies that employ large forces of office workers." With General Foods' decision to relocate, the editors said, "a giant corporation" was choosing to "grab its hat out of the New York City ring":

Not all types of businesses would agree with General Foods that executive elbow-rubbing in the heart of midtown isn't essential. Advertising agencies like to be near the media. . . . Bankers want to be where the big accounts and the big borrowers are. . . . But what about the general offices of a manufacturer? . . . In General Foods' case, the answer obviously was that the company simply wasn't dependent upon being at the very hub of business activity—but that it is still dependent upon being out on the rim.[118]

General Foods had begun relocation studies as early as 1937, sixteen years after the company had moved to New York from Battle Creek, Michigan. In 1944, having outgrown the Postum Building (Cross & Cross and Phelps Barnum, 1924) at 250 Park Avenue, which had served as its headquarters since 1926, the company took additional space in the Knapp Building at 383–385 Madison Avenue (Cross & Cross, 1922–23); several years later the company expanded again, taking over more space in the Knapp Building. But the company remained pressed for space. In 1950, to eliminate the inefficiences inherent in running corporate offices distributed among fifteen floors in two buildings, the company purchased the expansive White Plains site, located away from the suburban community's central business district but within the city limits.

The immense four-story building (1954), designed by Voorhees, Walker, Smith & Smith, was clad in red brick with limestone trim and took a modified U shape, enclosing a grandly scaled, multilevel landscaped courtyard. An unrelieved grid of punched windows punctuated the minimally detailed facades. The rather austere design was given some visual interest by the principal entrance, where, above a canopied entryway, a limestone expanse incorporated deeply recessed, vertical slit windows. Above the building's tile-covered pitched roof, a pavilionlike structure contained a similar window treatment and a flat roof with generous overhangs. Richard F. Crandell described the building as "the 'Shangri-La' of Big Business"; commenting on the courtyard, where curved, brick-enclosed stairwells connected different levels, he said: "Sunshine, fresh air and a relaxed atmosphere stimulate the executives to creative thinking. . . . The ordinary city office building, in contrast, is grim and formal."[119] Inside, amenities included a central air-conditioning system and an employee cafeteria, features lacking in many Manhattan corporate headquarters. The completion in 1962 of an extension enclosing the building's open space gave the complex a more urban presence, but the wing's gently arc-shaped form went a long way toward diminishing the overall sense of bulk.

The General Foods headquarters was an important early step in corporate suburbanization. The attention paid by the general press to the details of the company's move was in itself telling, indicating the pioneering nature of the move and the degree to which it served as a paradigm. Both the *New York Times* and *Business Week* reported that the move was accomplished over the course of three consecutive weekends and involved 1,000 employees and 18,000 pieces of office equipment and furniture. The company went to considerable lengths to entice employees to make the move, providing assistance in finding suburban homes; paying for moving expenses and such costs as lease-cancellation fees; and granting a paid day off. The incentives seemed to work: 85 percent of the New York headquarters staff made the move; over two-thirds of those who chose to relocate also moved their homes to the suburbs, while the remaining percentage continued to live in the city, pioneering the "reverse commute," a new phenomenon facilitated by the New

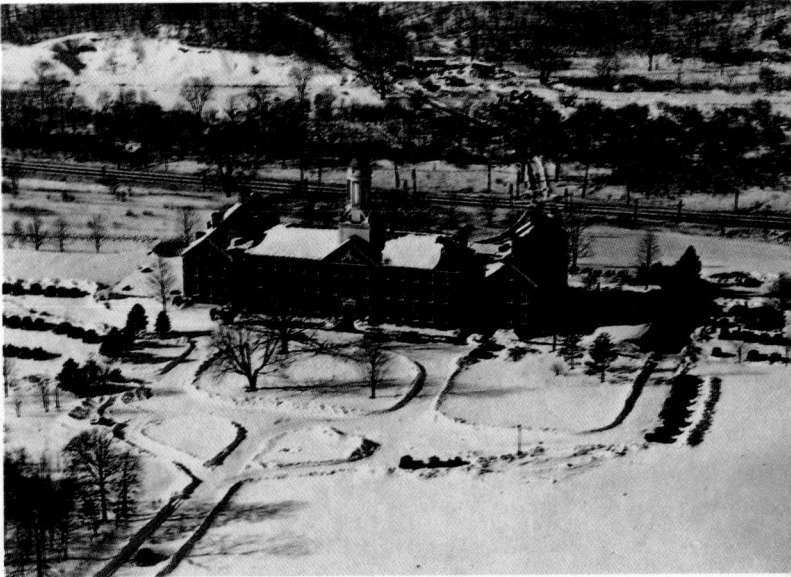

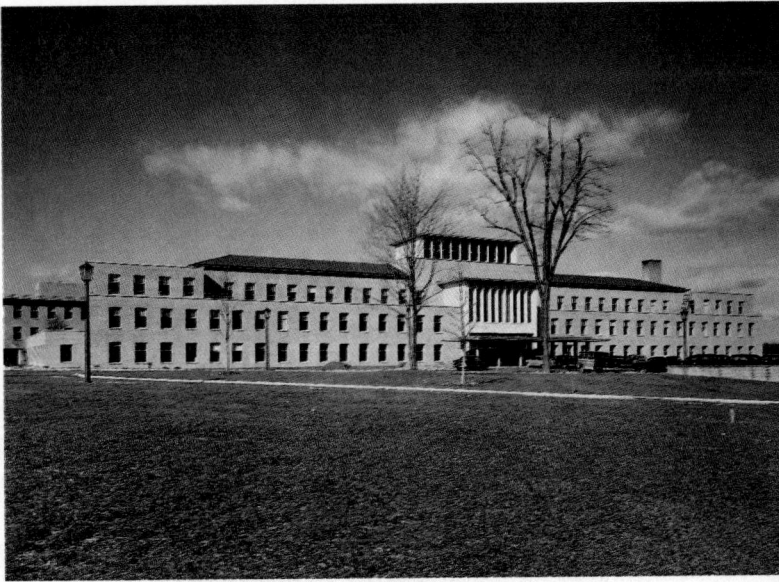

Top: Reader's Digest, Reader's Digest Road, Chappaqua, New York. William McKenzie, 1939. REDI

Bottom: General Foods, 250 North Street, White Plains, New York. Voorhees, Walker, Smith & Smith, 1954. Morgan. GF

York Central Railroad's addition of a Grand Central–White Plains express train leaving New York daily at 8:02 A.M. An official company statement proclaimed that the new facility offered "a hushed change from the turbulence and tempo of New York" and that "a window for every two employees" would provide views unimpeded by "other people's skyscrapers." The on-site cafeteria would obviate the need "to rush out Manhattan fashion to try to find a seat or table at lunch time."[120]

The editors of Architectural Forum were quick to discern a trend, noting that between 1950, when General Foods acquired its Westchester site, and the beginning of 1953, fifty companies had purchased land in the affluent suburban county with the intention of moving some or all of their Manhattan office operations there. "Reasons behind corporate moves varied," the editors pointed out:

Many a big Manhattan company scattered inefficiently throughout several buildings cannot readily find more space except in new buildings at, say, $6 a sq. ft.—two or three times what companies pay for similar space under long-term leases in old buildings nearby. Although executives do not like to talk about it, fear of atom bombing probably influences decisions as does the noise and crush of city traffic and congestion, and the fact that many top brass already live in Westchester County or adjacent Connecticut.[121]

Although the suburbanization of office headquarters promised convenience for top-level personnel as it engendered another new commutation pattern—suburb-to-suburb travel—it also threatened to diminish the quality of suburban life. As the editors of Architectural Forum presciently warned:

Whatever else it brings, the transition in Westchester promised a crop of problems that other suburbs could do well to watch. Some officials feared the advantages which drew firms to Westchester—good schools, parks, parkways, rail transportation and country-like scenery—would be submerged. Worst of all, they feared zooming taxes such as have confronted many a suburban community whose postwar housing boom has swamped its school system and municipal services.[122]

Community officials in favor of what Forum called "selective surrender" argued that corporate headquarters would benefit the county by increasing tax assessments while also paying for their own police and fire protection as well as access roads and sewer systems.[123] The scarcity of affordable housing for clerical workers loomed as a major problem, however. This was exacerbated by local zoning laws that required generous minimum lot sizes in an effort to maintain the county's tony status; the town of Bedford, for example, enforced a minimum of four acres.

To many urbanists, the suburbanization of the corporate world was cause for alarm. The realtor and city planner James Felt, who from 1956 to 1964 served on the New York City Planning Commission, warned that "the movement of middle-income population out of the city and the heightening interest on the part of large organizations in locating their offices and plants beyond city limits should not be accepted with complacency."[124] Herman T. Stichman, the New York State Housing Commissioner, shared this point of view: "Now is the final opportunity for New York City to try to turn the tide and keep middle-income families and large employers from moving out. That can only be done if its officials give the people what they seek when they move to the country, namely, neighborhood living."[125] But the city's ability to deal with the problem was seriously open to question, as the editors of the New York Times suggested: "Is New York City too large, too secure in its su-

premacy as a center of population, business and industry or possibly too lethargic in its governmental leadership to be anxious about the increasing drift of substantial residents to the suburbs, and the tremendous exodus of business activity to outlying areas?" They stated the issue succinctly: "One need not be an alarmist to be somewhat concerned about the city's future and to raise questions about what steps are practicable and desirable to better it. . . . The question . . . is whether there is some way, or a variety of ways, to cope with what the automobile is doing to the city."[126]

In 1956 the editors of Business Week analyzed some of the problems associated with corporate relocation to the suburbs and confidently proclaimed the trend over:

The singing of birds turned out to be a poor substitute for the dedicated roar of the city. Executives felt isolated, away from where things were happening. They missed the lunch clubs, the secluded nooks, the glamorous receptionists, the sidewalks crowded with men on fiercely purposeful missions. Women employees missed the big city stores, and as a result good secretaries were hard to attract. It was also discovered that in the Metropolitan Area, where all roads lead to Manhattan, it is virtually impossible in many cases to commute by public transit from one suburb to another. Sorrowfully eyeing the distant Manhattan skyline, many a self-exiled company realized that New York's bigness, while attended by many evils, nevertheless is the soil in which management thrives best.[127]

Though the media would continue to document the city's continuing strength as a business capital throughout the postwar era, the editors of Business Week had prematurely pronounced as dead a trend that had only just begun.

No company would more vividly reflect the expansive suburban presence of corporate America during the 1960s than the International Business Machines Corporation. IBM would become not only the area's most prolific suburban corporate builder, constructing six buildings in the New York area during the decade, but its stylistic leader. IBM's buildings, designed by eminent architects, were part of a comprehensive design program that made the company, as John Morris Dixon would write in Architectural Forum, "a symbol of enlightened corporate patronage."[128] The program was initiated in 1956 by Thomas J. Watson, Jr., who four years earlier had become president of the company that his father had transformed, over the course of forty-two years at its helm, from the Computing-Tabulating-Recording Company into a multinational corporate giant specializing in technically advanced information and communication systems. The younger Watson chose the architect and industrial designer Eliot Noyes to serve as the company's "consultant director of design"; at the time, Noyes was working in the office of Norman Bel Geddes on the redesign of an IBM typewriter. Noyes continued to revamp the product line and hired the graphic artist Paul Rand to redesign the company's logo. He then tackled the problem of giving the company an appropriate architectural expression, remodeling its Manhattan showroom (see chapter 6) and designing two interconnected laboratory buildings for its production facility in Poughkeepsie, New York. The sleek Poughkeepsie facility, incorporating curtain walls of gray porcelain enamel and corregated aluminum, established a high level of design sophistication that would become the company's standard.[129] Noyes did not, however, intend the building to serve as a prototype; instead, he advocated the hiring of a variety of topflight architects to design in a wide range of styles.

The first building completed under this program in the New York City area, and arguably the first architecturally dis-

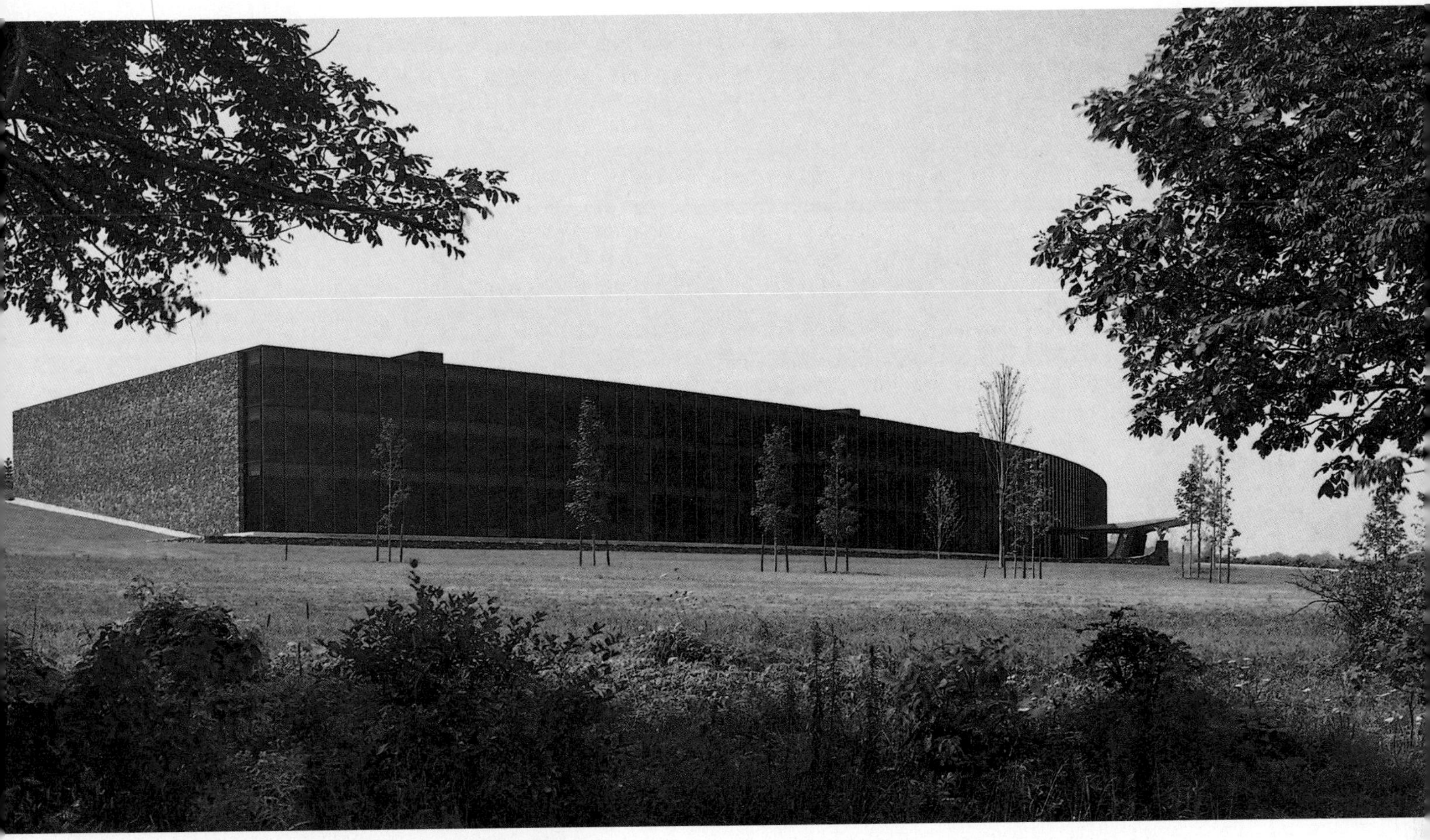

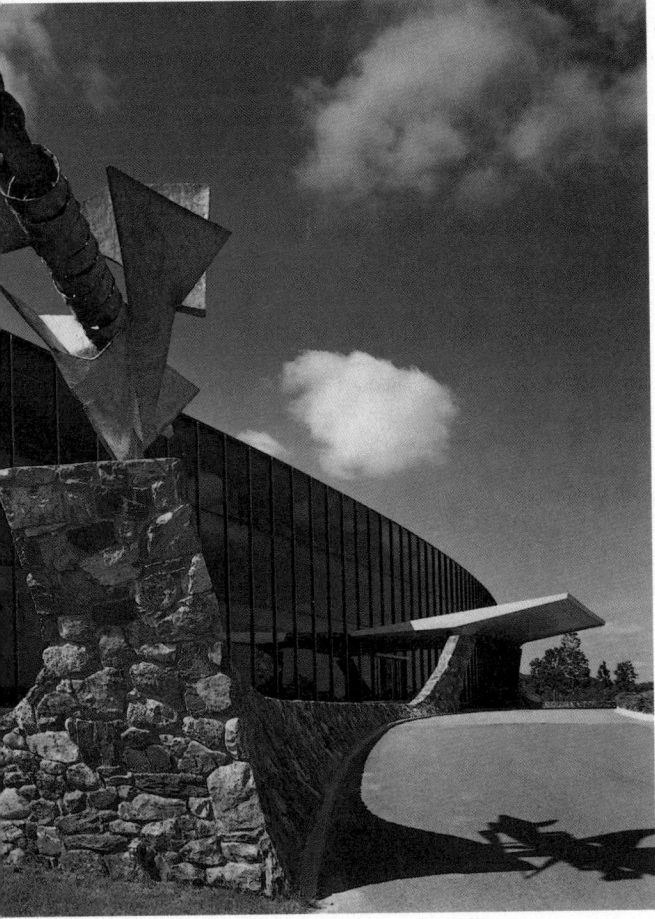

Above: IBM, Thomas J. Watson Research Center, Route 134 at Kitchawan Road, Yorktown Heights, New York. Eero Saarinen & Associates, 1960. Stoller. ©ESTO

Left: IBM, Thomas J. Watson Research Center. Stoller. ©ESTO

tinguished suburban office building, was the Thomas J. Watson Research Center in Yorktown Heights, New York, forty miles from Manhattan.[130] The building was designed by Eero Saarinen, who had received national attention when he was the subject of a *Time* magazine cover story in 1956.[131] Completed in 1960, the building, which combined high-wire aesthetics and provocative functional organization, set the standard by which all subsequent corporate campuses and suburban corporate office buildings would be measured. A preliminary design by Saarinen had called for a complexly massed series of interlocking buildings pierced by small open spaces and focused on a centrally located courtyard. As built, the research center consisted of a three-story, 1,090-foot-long, 146-foot-wide curving mass that was at once understated and an architectural tour de force. The building commanded a hillcrest set within 240 acres of wooded countryside and was approached by a sweeping, curvilinear road that passed a man-made lake; it was revealed in stages as part of a dramatic, orchestrated procession. The critic Allán Temko described the experience of arrival: "As it is approached on the winding road, which Saarinen thoughtfully led through the hollow in which he created a little lake, the building vanishes momentarily—as do European hilltop monuments such as Vézelay—only to reappear with a sudden statement of scale, unexpectedly large and even formidable, as detail after eloquent detail comes into sight across the lifting terrain, to contribute to the sweeping grandeur of the facade."[132]

The building's convex, north-facing wall, which Temko characterized as "one of the majestic facades of modern times," incorporated the principal entrance and was comprised of floor-to-ceiling panels of highly reflective, dark-gray-tinted glass framed by off-black porcelain-enameled aluminum mullions. The opposite long wall, facing a parking lot and directly exposed to the sun, was more shielded, containing alternating expanses of glass and fieldstone. The latter material, also used for the unbroken short end walls, was collected, Temko said, from the site's "Frostian pasture barriers."[133]

In place of the conventional double-loaded interior corridor scheme, wide hallways flanked the outside walls and ran the building's full length. Between the hallways, short passageways spanned the building's width, giving access to offices on one side and laboratories on the other. The labs were placed back-to-back and separated by four-foot-wide spaces that economically housed the extensive utilities. The short passageways, in addition to being quieter than longer ones, facilitated frequent meetings between coworkers, fostering the exchange of ideas considered essential to effective research. While the principal corridors were continuously glazed—providing a view that *Architectural Forum* claimed was "about as spectacular as a Cinerama travelogue"—the offices and laboratories were windowless, with artificial ventilation and light.[134] In an effort to establish a sense of human scale within the 1,090-foot-long corridors, Saarinen ingeniously curved the entire building, reducing the vista discernible at any given point in the hallways to between 80 and 100 feet. The building's arc, which encompassed seventy-four degrees, or close to one fifth of a circle, was particularly well suited to the site's topograpy; it was also meant to easily accommodate future expansion.

The building's main entrance, perhaps the weakest feature of the design, was marked by a futuristic canopy, a low stone wall rising to form two posts that supported a concrete slab. The wall also supported two abstract metal sculptures by Seymour Lipton, *Argonaut I* and *Argonaut II*, which, according to *Architec-*

tural *Forum*'s editors, were intended to "symbolize man's search into the unknown."[135] Temko criticized the placement of the "badly overwhelmed sculpture," which he said "belongs indoors in some museum."[136] Located between the building's northern facade and the parking lot was a sunken garden designed by the landscape architects Sasaki, Walker & Associates. More than an acre in size, the Japanese-influenced garden featured a ground cover of white limestone pebbles punctuated by elliptical grassy "islands" sprouting willow and crab apple trees. Three pedestrian bridges, as well as a loading dock, crossed over the garden, connecting the building's third floor directly to the parking lot. Saarinen continued the building's understated tone in the interiors, incorporating black slate flooring and gray-painted walls. The main lobby, which contained a sweeping, curved mezzanine utilized as an exhibition space, also housed a bust of Thomas J. Watson, Sr., by Jacques Lipchitz.

In Saarinen's hands, the suburban corporate complex looked for inspiration to the American college campus, not only in terms of its siting but its architecture and ambience as well. Despite the minimalist aesthetics of the design, Saarinen stated that he had intentionally avoided a "high-tech" appearance in favor of an environment that evoked and fostered a traditional sense of collegiality. "It has always seemed to me," Saarinen said, "that many scientists in the research field are like university professors—tweedy, pipe-smoking men. We wanted to provide them with a relaxed, 'tweedy,' outdoor environment in contrast to the efficient, precise laboratories and offices. The beautifully hilly site and the landscape with its characteristic fieldstone walls encouraged this aim."[137] Frank Sanchis, a historian of Westchester County architecture, contended that "corporate building design really began to hit its stride" with the building's completion.[138]

IBM followed the Yorktown Heights research facility with new corporate headquarters located on 405 acres in Armonk, New York, thirty-five miles from New York City.[139] Most of the company's office operations were moved to the new facility, but the former headquarters building, on the southwest corner of Madison Avenue and Fifty-seventh Street, was retained as a Manhattan base. The new corporate headquarters (1964), designed by Skidmore, Owings & Merrill, with Gordon Bunshaft serving as chief designer, was not as dramatic as Saarinen's building, but it was a sophisticated design nonetheless. It was also, after the relocation of General Foods to White Plains, the most significant corporate move to the suburbs to date.

Like IBM's Yorktown Heights building, the Armonk headquarters commanded a hilltop, but in contrast to Saarinen's curvilinear composition, which seemed to gently crown its site, SOM's massive, acid-etched white quartz aggregate concrete structure adopted a more Classical, templelike stance, standing squarely on a fieldstone platform. Along its 575-foot-long east- and west-facing facades, the four-story building incorporated a grid of X-shaped exposed-concrete columns set at twenty-five-foot modules, with continuous glass curtain walls recessed six feet behind them. On the building's 260-foot-wide north and south sides, floor slabs were cantilevered out six feet past the glass walls. In the early stages, when the building was planned as a regional facility, Bunshaft had proposed an H-shaped plan embracing open courts. But after the structural frame had been erected, Watson decided that the building would serve as IBM's principal headquarters, and the building's open courts were closed off with additional offices to provide more space. The building's two enclosed courtyards, each 70 by 165 feet and separated by a three-level, glass-enclosed passageway housing banks of escalators, were landscaped in an elegantly minimalist, Japanese-inspired manner by the sculptor Isamu Noguchi. According to Noguchi, the south garden symbolized the past and the north garden symbolized the future.[140] The stark south garden consisted exclusively of natural elements, while the north garden contained several bold sculptural forms—a red dishlike fountain; a low black dome inscribed with scientific equations; a symmetrical pyramid symbolizing atomic energy; and an abstract bronze sculpture whose intertwining cantilevered forms represented genetic structures.

In 1965 IBM completed its Garden State Branch Office in Cranford, New Jersey, sixteen miles from New York City.[141] The project was assigned to a promising young architect, Victor Lundy, who struggled to elevate the program, which was comparatively inconsequential in the corporate hierarchy, and the banal site, adjacent to the Garden State Parkway, by turning to an improbable source for visual inspiration: the architecture of the pre-Columbian Mayan city of Uxmal. Lundy's one-story building consisted of a series of pavilionlike sections defined by windowless, sculpted concrete walls and joined by narrow bronzed glazing strips. The architect evoked the complex surface textures of Uxmal's stone-mosaic-covered buildings with geometrically patterned, pink-toned concrete block; in addition, the symmetrically composed building reflected the severity, frontality and geometric rigor characteristic of Mayan architecture. Behind the concrete-block walls, a network of treelike concrete columns swept upward to form a coved ceiling; the highly theatrical interiors, which were punctuated by freestanding partitions, recalled Lundy's shoe store for I. Miller on Fifth Avenue (see chapter 6).

Though functionally problematic, Lundy's design was certainly impressive. The network of "trees" could be glimpsed from the outside only through the principal entrance, where an opening in the fortresslike exterior walls led to a fifteen-foot-high central space. Lundy had originally intended for the building to be covered by a zigguratlike stepped pyramidal roof, separated from the main structure by a glazed clerestory. By the time of the building's completion, however, IBM had instituted a severe austerity program, largely turning its back on its innovative architectural program and sometimes hiring "package builders" instead of architects. As John Morris Dixon wrote in Architectural Forum in 1966, "Overnight, it seems, IBM has become less a patron than a hard-nosed client out to build cheap and fast."[142] In the case of Lundy's building, cost-cutting measures resulted in a radically less sculptural roof design that significantly diminished the building's architectural interest. Despite this change, the design of the building was still highly innovative—perhaps too innovative. Claiming that IBM's Garden State Branch Office "may be the world's most complicated one-story office building," Dixon argued that "Lundy's apparent fascination with surface textures, however interesting the textures may be, gives the building a somewhat overwrought look, a feeling that nothing (except the gypsum board partitions) has been left alone." Dixon acknowledged that, "as a place to work, the building is bound to be exciting, even by the standards of past IBM buildings," but he wondered whether "such a small building—of such unexceptional purpose—[is] worth the expenditure of so much ingenuity, so many textures, so many complicated details?"[143]

Economic considerations would compromise another IBM building project, Paul Rudolph's combined laboratory, factory and office building, completed in 1966 in East Fishkill, New York, about fifty miles north of New York City.[144] The rambling,

four-story concrete building was an elegant if not particularly distinctive version of Rudolph's signature synthesis of Wright- and Le Corbusier-inspired Modernism, complete with glass-enclosed hallways and sections raised on pilotis. To cut costs without changing one of the building's most expensive features—the placement of mechanical equipment between two occupied floors, which IBM insisted on retaining—the company eliminated the proposed top-story brise-soleil, thereby destroying much of the building's grace.

In 1967 IBM completed a small branch office in Garden City, New York.[145] Although the modestly scaled, three-story building, designed by Eliot Noyes, clearly reflected the company's new austerity, it still managed to maintain the high level of design that Noyes had been instrumental in establishing. The building was clad in six-by-twelve-foot precast-concrete panels, finished on the exterior in a rough-textured brown aggregate and prepared on the interior for painting. At a cost similar to that of a conventional curtain wall, Noyes was able, as the editors of Architectural Record noted, "to provide attractive interiors of architectural character."[146]

IBM may have been the postwar era's most prominent corporate builder in New York's suburbs, but other corporations would also make their mark. The Endo Laboratories complex in Garden City, New York, designed by Paul Rudolph and completed in 1964, was a boldly modeled composition that dominated its eight-acre site just west of the Roosevelt Raceway. Sitting atop a bluff overlooking a sweeping curve in the Meadowbrook Parkway, the highly controversial building was broadly visible to passing motorists and quickly became, as John Morris Dixon reported in Progressive Architecture, "a landmark for multitudes of commuters and beach-goers."[147] The building's principal material, on both the exterior and interior, was cast-in-place concrete, finished with the same ribbed, exposed-aggregate treatment as Rudolph's Art and Architecture Building at Yale University, completed in 1963.[148] Numerous turretlike cylindrical forms of different sizes punctuated the irregularly massed structure, giving it a highly distinctive, fortresslike appearance. In addition to serving an expressive function, the turrets housed stairwells, air-circulation ducts and desk alcoves for executives. Large windowless expanses were compensated for by extensive skylights. The three-story, 160,000-square-foot building contained production facilities on its ground floor, and research labs and administrative offices stacked on the floors above; the third floor was arranged around two large roof gardens incorporating planting beds in serpentine patterns that harmonized with the building's curvilinear forms.

Employees entered the building at ground level through a rear entrance directly accessible from the parking lot, but guests were treated to a far grander approach, with a monumentally scaled, gradually ascending double staircase that swept up to the building's second story. The exaggeratedly wide and low steps in effect rendered the staircase a ramp, forcing visitors to adopt a slower than normal pace. The architect acknowledged this goal: "I want people to have to think about going up those stairs; in 100 years buildings won't have stairs, but this building will be here, and so will its stairs."[149] Ada Louise Huxtable felt that the entire composition was "bound together stylishly" by this "Fountainebleau-like stairway,"[150] while the editors of the English journal Architectural Review hypothesized that the "broad Baroque stairway," the building's "final pièce de résistance," was perhaps inspired by Le Corbusier's design for the Carpenter Center for Visual Arts at Harvard University.[151] Inside, a glass-enclosed reception area looked out onto a roof terrace.

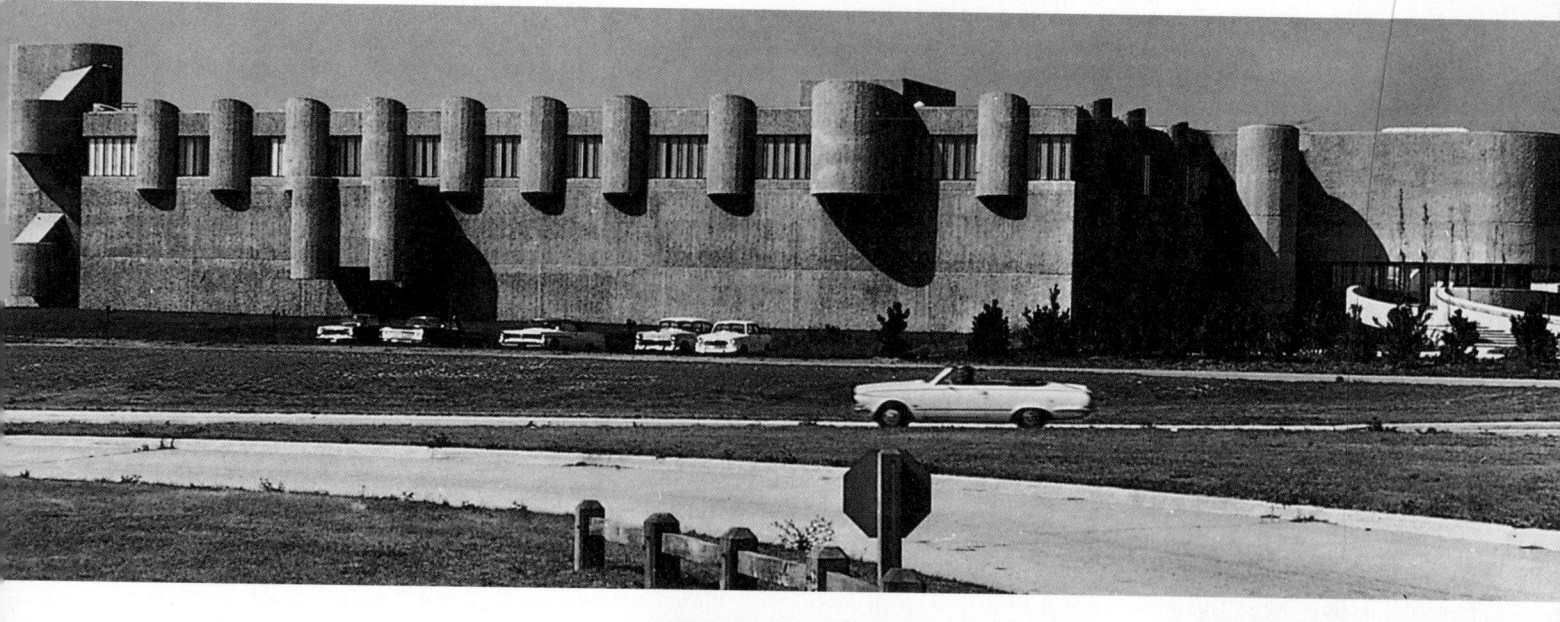

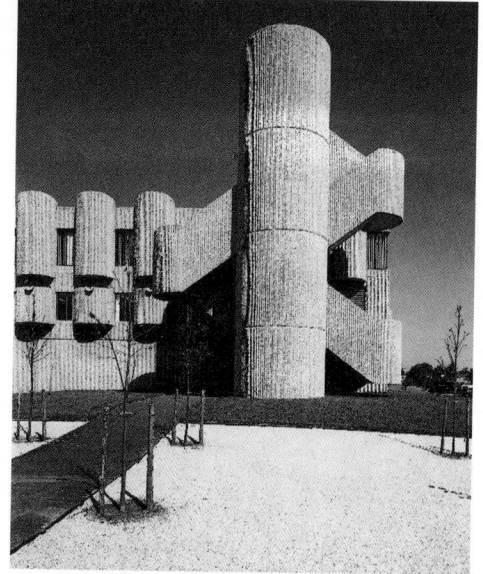

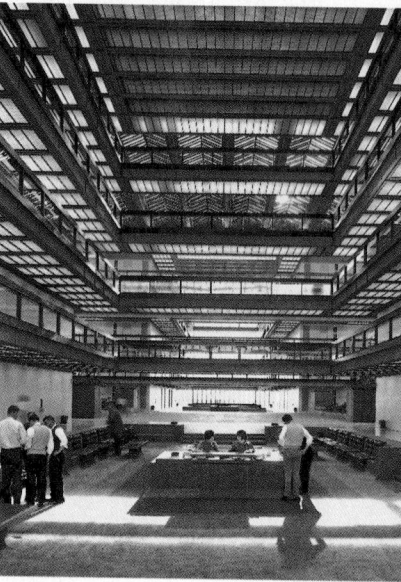

Top: Endo Laboratories, 1000 Stewart Avenue, Garden City, New York. Paul Rudolph, 1964. View to the west from Meadowbrook Parkway. Cunningham-Werdnigg. PR

Center left: Endo Laboratories. Stair tower. Perron. PR

Center right: Bell Telephone Laboratories, 101 Crawford Corner Road, Holmdel, New Jersey. Eero Saarinen & Associates, 1962–67. Reception area. Robinson. CERO

Bottom: Bell Telephone Laboratories. Robinson. CERO

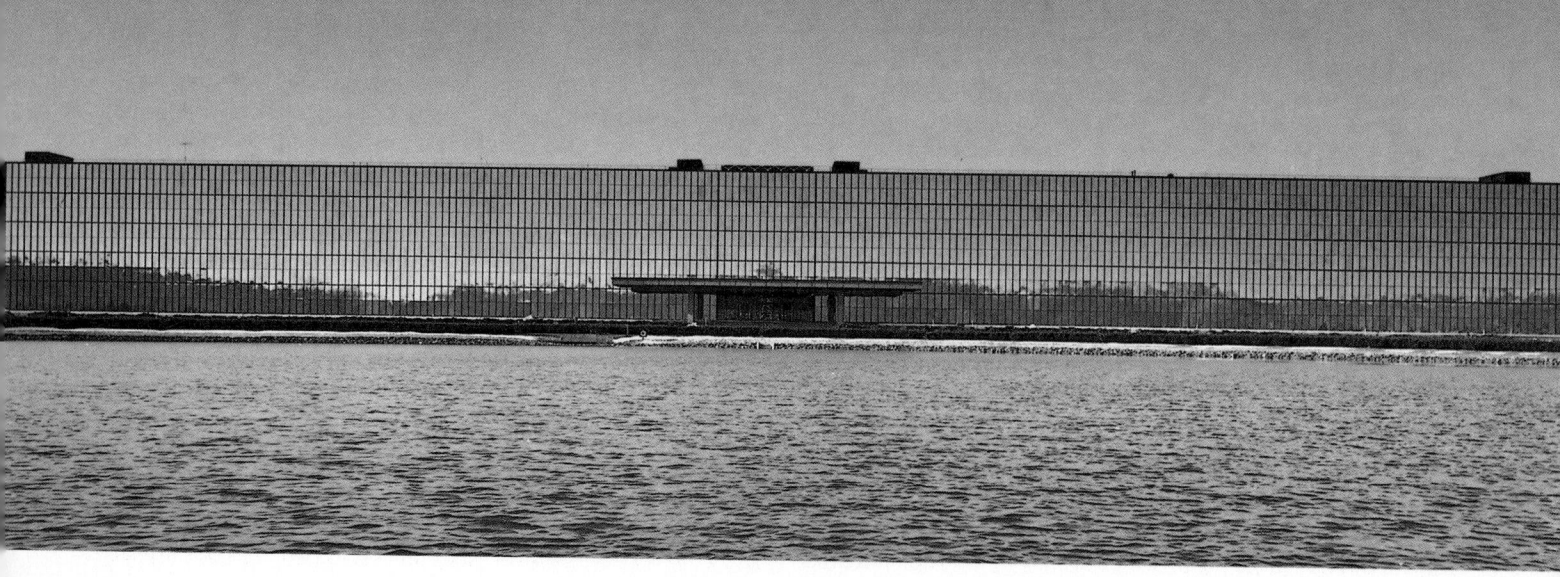

An elevator, isolated in a cylindrical tower at the end of a short, narrow hallway, led to the third floor, while glazed passageways led to concrete-enclosed rooms that Huxtable described as "cave-like."[152] Floors covered in either black slate or bright orange carpet contrasted with the neutrally colored exposed-concrete walls.

The Endo building was widely covered by the architectural press, particularly British and European journals, which were perhaps more sympathetic to, or at least more compelled by, Rudolph's interpretation of Corbusian Modernism than were American observers. To the critic Rupert Spade, the building constituted "the nearest approach Rudolph has yet made to the kind of latter-day château building for U.S. Corporations at which Eero Saarinen became so successful."[153] But unlike IBM's typical office buildings, the Endo complex was highly visible from the public road, so much so that in April 1964, six months before the building's official dedication, the Long Island State Park Commission planted nine twenty-foot-tall evergreen trees to minimize the view of the building for passing motorists. The journalist Ronald Maiorana reported in the New York Times that Park Commission workers characterized the building as "an eyesore" and explained that "We're trying to hide this thing from people on the parkway."[154] Though the commission's executive secretary, Chester R. Blakelock, denied that an effort was being made to obscure the building, Joseph Ushkow, Endo's president, was outraged; Rudolph was somewhat more measured, observing that "anything that is good is bound to arouse controversy," but adding that he too was "somewhat taken aback."[155]

In writing about the "embattled building that looks like a battlemented fortress," Ada Louise Huxtable pointed out the contradictory reactions to the Endo facility: "It has already been awarded the dubious distinction of having a short row of tall trees planted in front of it by the Long Island State Park Commission . . . as well as the more conventional honor of being named the 'Concrete Building of the Year' by the Concrete Industries Board." It was the building's strong character that elicited such a range of reactions: "In the muddled mediocrity of Long Island's architectural junkyard, Endo's boldly unconventional research, manufacturing and administrative headquarters is an electrifying sight. Strongly sculptured shapes and roughly striated reinforced concrete walls admit no ambivalent feelings; it inspires either love or hate." Huxtable was clear as to which side of the critical fence she stood on, describing Endo's facility as "one of the best buildings in the New York area" and "a conspicuous triumph for enlightened business patronage of the arts." She went on to explain:

> There is a heady effect of rugged exotic beauty. . . . It is also efficient and economical, and the exhilarating result is a definitive argument for art and excellence in the practice of construction. Buildings like this one are the real legacy of Frank Lloyd Wright and Le Corbusier. . . . The style of the new Endo building is a dynamic, evolutionary synthesis of the innovations of the masters. It may be unfamiliar to local eyes, accustomed to bowling alley modern, but it is representative of the best and most vital construction being done today.[156]

In 1957 Eero Saarinen began to design a six-story, 5,000-employee laboratory facility for Bell Telephone, to be relocated from West Street in Greenwich Village to a site about fifty miles from Manhattan, in Holmdel, New Jersey.[157] The first phase of construction was completed in 1962, one year after Saarinen died; the rest was completed by 1967. It was clear from the first, as Allan Temko observed in 1962, that the building would be "even finer than I.B.M., Yorktown, and perhaps will be one of the influential buildings of the age. . . . Bell is a work of fully matured genius, and suggests how far Saarinen might have gone in this objective idiom."[158] In contrast to the naturalistic landscaping that dominated other suburban corporate complexes, Saarinen orchestrated Bell's Holmdel campus with a rigorous formality—according to Rupert Spade, a "grandiloquent indulgence in the landscape world of Louis XIV."[159] The entrance to the 460-acre parklike setting was dramatically marked by a 300,000-gallon water tower. From there a winding road led to a 3,000-foot-diameter looped road that crossed a six-acre pond studded with hundreds of fountains arranged in an arc. The laboratory building faced the pond, which, in addition to serving a decorative purpose, functioned as part of the air-conditioning system and as an auxiliary source of water in case of fire. Also contained within the loop were two smaller ponds, a network of service roads and a 4,500-car parking lot. "It would be difficult," Temko asserted, "to surpass the splendor of Bell's palatial baroque park which, in this country at least, is unrivaled as a formal setting for a technological building."[160]

The Bell labs consisted of four separate and identical blocks containing back-to-back rows of windowless labs and offices, all enclosed by glazed corridors. "The logical rectilinear order of the internal laboratory blocks," Temko observed, "makes them rigorously consistent with the discipline of machine-made materials and modular utilities."[161] The blocks, built two at a time, were arranged in a tight rectangle. Ultimately, the spaces between the blocks were roofed over, forming a spectacular indoor garden, 100 feet wide, 70 feet high and 700 feet long. The first such space to be included in a corporate building, the atrium evoked great public spaces such as the Galleria Vittorio Emanuele II (Carlo Amati, 1865–67) in Milan. It would in turn influence the design of the Ford Foundation Building (see chapter 5) by Kevin Roche, who worked with Saarinen on the Bell labs and helped finish them after his death. Flanking the open spine were a large entrance lobby and an employee lounge. All of these spaces were traversed by pedestrian bridges at each level and surmounted by a heat-absorbing, glass-enclosed space frame made of self-oxidizing steel.

Saarinen had originally proposed that the buildings be clad in mirrored glass, which appealed to the client because it reflected between 70 and 80 percent of the sun's heat, resulting in substantial savings. By the time the first phase was completed, however, only enough mirrored glass—which Temko claimed was invented for this project—had been produced to cover the building's south wall, and the other walls were covered in conventional glass.[162] As Architectural Forum put it, Saarinen's "ideas were running ahead of technology." When the reflective glass eventually became available, the conventional glass cladding of the completed portions of the complex was replaced. According to Forum, the mirrored facades had "the eerie effect of turning a 12-million-cu.-ft. structure into an ephemeral pattern of rolling hills, shifting clouds, or of parking lots—depending on one's point of view."[163] Temko felt that "like most technological advances, this one carries with it the possibility of an advance in esthetic expression which Saarinen unerringly seized. These softly gleaming laboratories, everywhere organized with quiet perfection, will be a civilized beacon of human knowledge."[164]

In the beginning of 1967 two large corporations dealt a blow to Manhattan's status as the undisputed center of worldwide corporate activity.[165] On February 10, Pepsico announced that it would abandon its architecturally distinguished Park

Avenue building (see chapter 5), completed only seven years earlier, for new headquarters, to be built on a 112-acre site that had contained the polo fields of the Blind Brook Club in Purchase, New York, about thirty miles north of New York City. Less than a week later, on February 15, after lengthy negotiations, Greenwich, Connecticut, officials granted preliminary approval for the American Can Company's plan to move its offices from 100 Park Avenue to new headquarters on a 141-acre site within a premiere estate section of the community. The two announcements were reported in the national press, including *Time*, which noted that although New York "is beefing up its effort to attract new industries, it drives old ones away by reason of costs and congestion, smog and stickups, traffic and taxes that rise in a wry ratio with strikes and relief rolls."[166]

In 1968 the realty firm of Sulzberger-Rolfe surveyed twenty-seven businesses that had left New York during the previous year and found that one motivating factor was the perceived public relations value of erecting and solely occupying a new building, which for many companies was economically viable only in the suburbs.[167] In explaining their decision to relocate, Pepsico officials had specifically cited the lack of high-quality clerical help in New York City. Merrill Folsom noted in the *New York Times* that companies were leaving New York "to escape city income and sales taxes, to benefit from available pools of white-collar workers including young housewives with college degrees and to minimize the companies' contacts with unions."[168]

While the corporate exodus was clearly bad news for the city from the start, its negative effects on the suburbs were more slowly discerned. Whereas in 1963 Folsom had reported in the *New York Times* that "the continuing march of corporate office headquarters into Westchester County has converted more and more apple orchards, cow pastures and wooded hillsides into big real-estate taxables with job opportunities," several years later popular attitudes had changed.[169] Well-established affluent communities that had once welcomed corporate development were growing wary of it. Although the communities' tax bases had expanded, this was often offset by an increased demand for services. In addition, traffic problems were aggravated, and the increasingly rare undeveloped land that had once given suburban and exurban areas much of their character was becoming environmentally endangered. Perhaps most objectionable was the mere visibility of large-scale buildings that overwhelmed both the landscape and the prevailing domestic scale. Although suburban communities did not manage to significantly slow the rate of corporate growth, they did effect development patterns and, to some extent, design programs through zoning laws and building ordinances.

Pepsico opened its new world headquarters in Purchase in 1970.[170] While General Foods had justified its move to White Plains at least in part on operational efficiency, Pepsico had only recently built its own headquarters in town, and the move thus seemed a real slap in the city's face. Pepsico's move also represented a triumph of negotiating. IBM had previously tried to secure the rezoning of the Blind Brook Club site and had failed; in order to get the zoning, Pepsico went out of its way to ensure that the new complex, designed by Edward Durell Stone, with landscaping by Edward Durell Stone, Jr., would be an idealized form of both corporate power and nature.

Pepsico's offices far surpassed their routine practical functions to define a rural retreat of unabashed yet understated privilege and prestige. The complex consisted of seven equally sized, square buildings ordered in a staggered arrangement around a central cruciform courtyard; the buildings were kept to four stories to conform to the forty-foot-height established by local building law. The buildings were shaped like inverted stepped pyramids; successive floors, defined by panels of white, gently patterned precast concrete and deep-recessed, brown-tinted glass, were cantilevered out beyond the floor below. The buildings were connected to each other by means of corner elevators and stair towers. Planting beds encircled every floor; ivy freely cascaded over the fascias in a contemporary corporate interpretation of the hanging gardens of Babylon. In addition to 3,000 specimens of thirty-eight varieties of trees and a 4.5-acre man-made lake with a towering *jet d'eau*, the manorlike grounds contained an impressive collection of twentieth-century sculpture including works by Alexander Calder, Alberto Giacometti, Jacques Lipchitz, Henry Moore and David Smith.

The American Can Company, headed by William F. May, a Greenwich resident, also went to great lengths to build a headquarters that would please not only its own management and employees but community officials and residents as well.[171] After interviewing Charles Luckman, Philip Johnson and Gordon Bunshaft of Skidmore, Owings & Merrill, among others, May hired SOM with the stipulation that Bunshaft serve as chief designer. Local authorities specified five requirements aimed at minimizing the building's negative impact on its surroundings: the building was not to rise more than forty feet above grade; parking was to be as concealed from view as possible; company employees were not to use an existing two-lane road on the property for daily commutation; interior lighting was not to be highly visible at night; and as few trees as possible were to be felled. Community officials suggested four separate buildings arranged in a campus plan, presumably believing it was most appropriate to the rural site, whose quality Ada Louise Huxtable described as nothing short of "idyllic splendor."[172] But because the site included a deep ravine, a conventional campus plan would have necessitated covering the available flat land with parking lots and clustering the buildings around the natural recession; the sprawling plan would also have required the loss of many trees and to a large extent diminished the site's visual appeal. Rejecting a campus plan, Bunshaft came up with an ingenious scheme that placed a three-story building atop a six-story podium slipped relatively inconspicuously into the ravine; the podium was to contain a 1,700-car parking garage and simultaneously act as a dam, creating a small lake adjacent to the building that served to regulate the flow of water to a nearby swamp, which was protected as a bird sanctuary. Bunshaft would later explain: "I always took great pride in solving the environment, solving the workings of the company, and creating the beautiful lake."[173]

As built, the complex consisted of two buildings set on top of the podium. The main building incorporated a framework of poured-on-site grayish reinforced concrete sandblasted to show an aggregate, with white precast twin girders supporting double-web precast-concrete ceiling beams. The framework's coloration harmonized with the building's recessed curtain walls of gray-tinted solar glass. The building enclosed a landscaped central courtyard, adopting the "square doughnut" plan that had become a Bunshaft signature. East of the main building stood a similarly articulated though more luxuriously appointed one-story executive building. Beneath the buildings, on the podium's top level, a cafeteria opened onto a terrace cantilevered out over the man-made lake. The rest of the space within the podium was dedicated to parking. The company's private, four-lane highway split into four separate roadways as it led into the garage, each

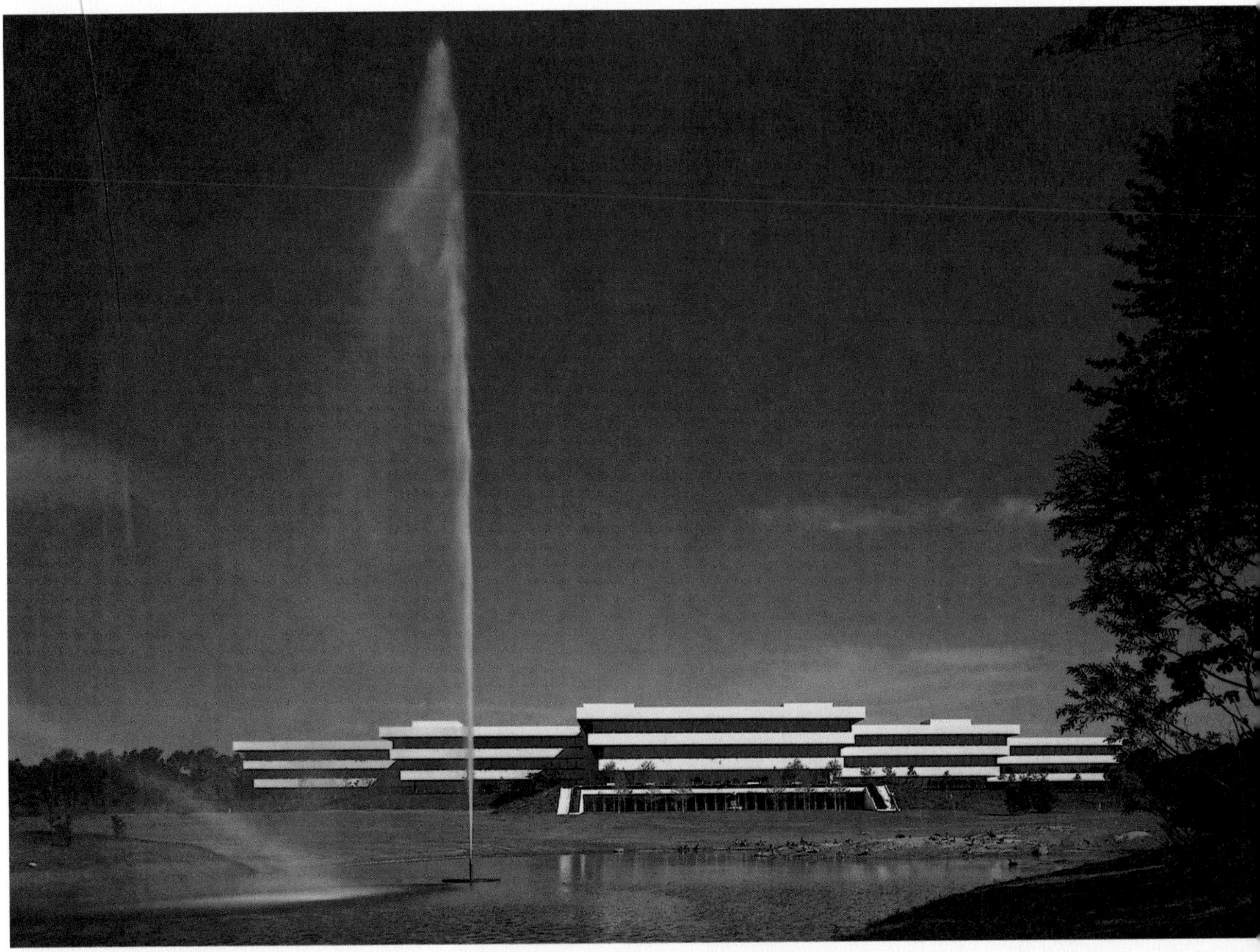

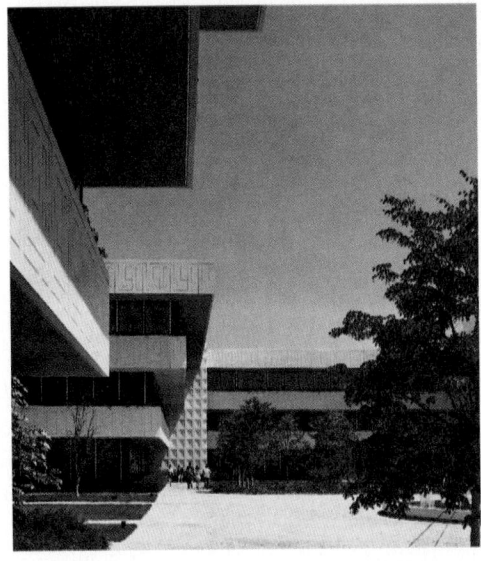

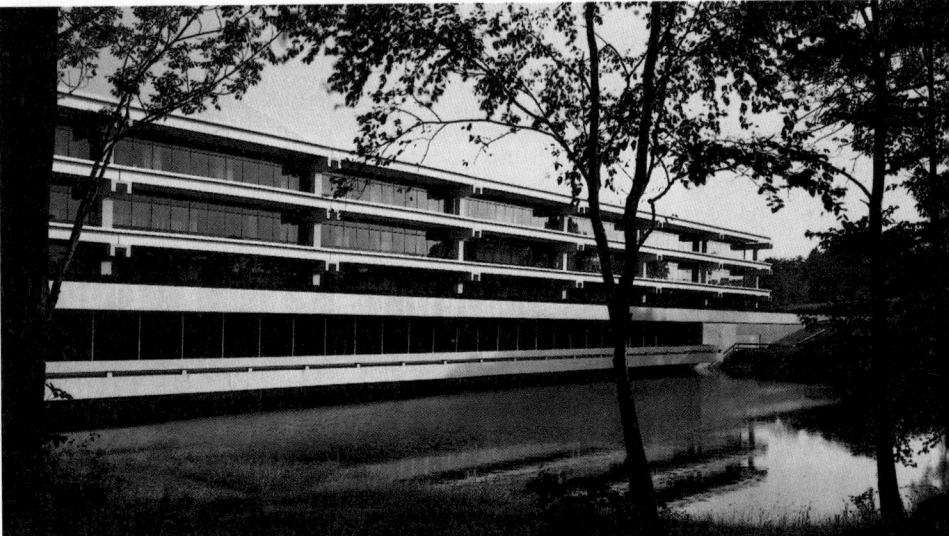

Top: Pepsico, 700 Anderson Hill Road, Purchase, New York. Edward
Durell Stone, 1970. Stoller. ©ESTO

Bottom left: Pepsico. Courtyard. Stoller. ©ESTO

Bottom right: American Can Company, American Lane, Greenwich,
Connecticut. Skidmore, Owings & Merrill, 1970. Stoller. ©ESTO

connecting directly to a different level. Though the parking itself was carefully concealed, the system for directing traffic seemed disproportionate to the task. Nonetheless, Bunshaft's design for American Can represented a notable exception to the widespread failure of architects to produce creative design solutions to the problem of automobile access and parking in the suburban office complex.

Ada Louise Huxtable was lavish in her praise for the entire complex: "It offers comfort, efficiency and structural grand luxe, tastefully controlled. And it is a triumph of environmental consideration." Both buildings, she said, demonstrated "structural bravado" in their "use of unprecedented modern structural techniques for a rational combination of functional purpose and dramatic architectonic effect." Huxtable was not, however, without her criticisms, especially of the main building's interiors. She described the ubiquitous red carpeting as "high intensity," and offered a recommendation: "If you like insistent red carpet, fine. If it gives you a headache, stay away. It must be said here that S.O.M. furnishings sink deeper and deeper into a familiar, formalistic rut. At American Can, it is no less deadly because it is red, white and blue." And however distinguished Huxtable may have found Bunshaft's design, she questioned the entire notion of corporations leaving the city for the suburbs, challenging it on societal, urbanistic and aesthetic grounds:

> What part of a work force does a commuter's country-club plant set in Greenwich's restrictive zoning serve? What does it do for larger considerations of regional planning? After how much captive pastoral beauty does one crave the lively, bad vibes in town? Defectors are few, according to American Can's low turnover figure. After all, you can get out of your car or leave the cafeteria with its lovely lake views and humdrum food for a scenic walk to the carefully preserved swamp or the sewage plant. And you can breathe the air, which is fully conditioned and artificially controlled in a sealed building all year round.[174]

General Electric's headquarters, also designed by SOM, but with Roy Allen serving as partner in charge, was similarly placed on a podium housing a parking garage.[175] Located in Fairfield, Connecticut, and completed in 1974, the headquarters consisted of two buildings containing 6'6"-deep, white-painted steel trusses spanning columns set eighty feet apart. Offices were wrapped in recessed, dark-tinted windows. The rough texture and warm color of the aggregate-finished concrete podium contrasted with the sleek glass-and-steel buildings. Landscaped interior courtyards and a wide array of amenities, including three restaurants and a store featuring General Electric products, added a small measure of distinction to the rather banal if skillfully articulated corporate complex.

In the 1960s and early 1970s Tarrytown, New York, located about fifteen miles north of New York City, became home to three new corporate buildings. The first of these was an educational facility (1969) built by the Olivetti Corporation, whose sleekly fashioned office equipment and dramatically designed Fifth Avenue showroom (see chapter 5) had established it as a leader in corporate design.[176] Designed by Rotwein & Blake, the one- and two-story building was small but highly visible, occupying an eight-acre site adjacent to the New York State Thruway. A framework of self-weathering Cor-ten steel, filled in with dark-brown-tinted glass, contrasted with expanses of fieldstone to create a whole that seemed an appropriate expression of both Olivetti's high-tech products and the surrounding rural setting. Kahn & Jacobs's 400,000-square-foot Technicon International Science Center, on ninety-six-acres on the edge of Tarrytown, was also completed in 1969.[177] The glass-and-aluminum curtain-

wall facade, marked by prominent vertical mullions, read as a single story while enclosing two, thus disguising the building's bulk. Fieldstone walls, reflecting pools and extensive landscaping enhanced the suburban ambience.

The Union Carbide Technical Center (1970), designed by Vincent G. Kling & Associates, was Tarrytown's most architecturally distinguished corporate complex.[178] Containing more than 700,000 square feet of space, the facility occupied a 300-acre tract that had formerly comprised the James Butler estate and, at one time, the village of Eastview, which John D. Rockefeller had demolished in the early 1900s because it cluttered the view from his estate in nearby Pocantico Hills. In order to make efficient use of the site, which was bisected by the Old Saw Mill River Road, the architects devised a linear configuration that encompassed the Spline Building, which housed offices and public spaces, and the Linde Laboratories. A three-level, bridgelike segment of the 1,200-foot-long, poured-concrete Spline Building crossed the highway; two floors of offices as well as a 20-foot-wide glass corridor were suspended between concrete piers set 180 feet apart on either side of the highway. Inside the building, a continuation of the highway-spanning hallway traversed the soaring, triple-height main lobby. An employee cafeteria was distinguished by six dining alcoves, three of which were externally expressed as prominent bays. The Linde Laboratories, located at the Spline Building's southern end, was a straightforward rectangular mass wrapped in anodized aluminum and glass. The building's interior included two skylit triple-height galleries overlooked by offices and labs.

In 1976 Edward Larrabee Barnes completed a headquarters building for the IBM World Trade Americas/Far East Corporation in Mount Pleasant, New York, that effectively restored IBM's reputation as a leader in corporate design.[179] The new building stood on a seventy-nine-acre site that had been owned by the Rockefellers, who sold the land to IBM with the proviso that any new building not be visible from their estate in nearby Pocantico Hills. In order to make it as unobtrusive as possible, the three-story building was built into the slope of a low-lying meadow surrounded by deep woods of hickory, oak, silver maple and sycamore trees. The site's drainage problem was ameliorated by the creation of a moat on one side of the building that, along with a connected stream and duck pond, did double duty as water sources in case of fire. The moat was electrically heated to prevent freezing in winter. In order to visually reduce the building's bulk, Barnes gave it a W-shaped plan. The building was wrapped in alternating bands of butt-joined, mullion-free windows and dark green, anodic-coated aluminum spandrels. The main entrance, which because of the site's slope was located on the building's second floor and directly accessible from the facility's parking lot, was surrounded by clear glass and surmounted by a pyramidal skylight. Inside, the building's 383,000 square feet of space was dominated by open areas, and a circulation space was located along one exterior wall. Together, these features provided 95 percent of the company's 1,000 employees with views of the outdoors; it was estimated that only 5 percent would have had exterior views had the building adopted a conventional interior layout. *Architectural Record* editor Mildred F. Schmertz had high praise for the building: "Barnes has created an elegant building that gives an esthetic pleasure which is almost Japanese in its refinement. Although it is doubtful that IBM's employees have the time or inclination for Zen-like contemplation during the work day, the building's quiet spirit would seem to invite it, because for this suburban office, as for the Katsura Palace, the landscape is everything."[180]

As many of the urban problems that had motivated corporations to leave New York City came to plague suburbia—with crime, costs and labor problems all increasing—the suburbs proved to be something less than a corporate nirvana. Nonetheless, by the mid-1970s suburban corporate headquarters seemed a permanent aspect of New York's regional profile. Despite the call in 1973 of civic booster Lewis Rudin, chairman of the Association for a Better New York, for corporations to get "back where the action is in New York City," the best New York could hope for was that corporations remaining in the city would expand their operations there; among those that had done so by 1976 were American Express, Avon Products, Bristol-Myers, Equitable Life Assurance, McGraw-Hill, Pfizer, Philip Morris, Seagram's and Simon & Schuster.[181] Curiously, as William H. Whyte, the urban planner and author of the pioneering corporate study *The Organization Man*, noted in 1976, some of these corporations "have made studies, too; using the same data as the move-outs, looking at the same city, they have come to an opposite conclusion."[182] Edgar Bronfman, chairman of Seagram's, argued that the city could best provide for the personal contact essential to conducting business. "It's eyeball to eyeball here," he said, "and that's what it's all about."[183] Whyte compellingly argued the city's case:

> The standard pitch concentrates on exactly the things enemies concede: theaters, restaurants, quaint ethnic neighborhoods, skylines, glamour, and so on. This helps bring in tourists but it does nothing about the basic image of bad New York. What we ought to be talking about is New York as a *work* place, and how subtly, intricately, and superbly it functions. This is the unknown New York and it is a fascinating place to discover. . . . It is the agora at its liveliest and we have it right here, right now.[184]

Satellite Towns

The proliferation of corporate campuses not only affected the character of developing suburban areas and the outer reaches of the city itself but also drained the strength of outlying towns. This trend had begun to manifest itself first in the late 1930s in the borough of Queens, which was then still more or less a collection of independent villages. Until the 1930s the town of Flushing was, as the *New York Times* put it, "a city within a city."[185] By the time of the Second World War, its commercial district, centered around Main Street, had become congested and outmoded. In 1941 the real estate firm of Webb & Knapp began to buy land in the area that contained small-scale commercial buildings and houses. The first and single largest purchase was made from Vincent Astor, one of the firm's principal clients. William Zeckendorf, head of Webb & Knapp, working with the architect Lester Tichy, began to outline the development of a mixed-use commercial center that was to be financed by the Metropolitan Life Insurance Company.[186] Encouraged by Tichy, Zeckendorf continued to buy land, largely from individual home owners; by 1946 he had assembled 90 percent of a projected twenty-acre, T-shaped site roughly bounded by Main Street, Kissena Boulevard, Thirty-eighth Avenue and Barclay Avenue. The site was ideally located with respect to subway and bus lines, the Long Island Railroad and a network of highways and bridges, providing easy access to both city and suburban dwellers. As part of the project, the developers proposed to rebuild and enlarge the North Shore Bus Company's terminal and

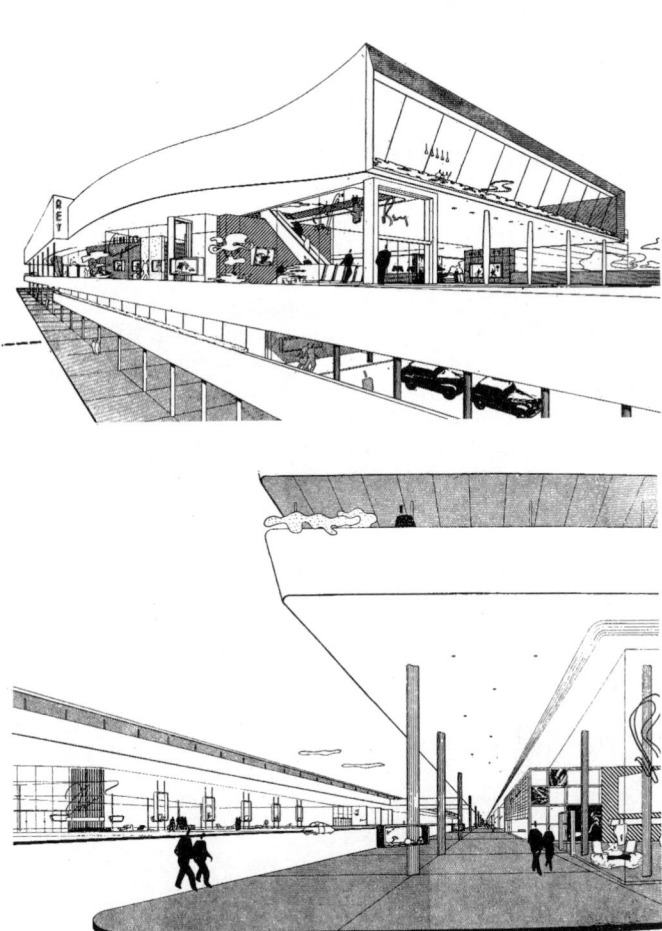

Top: Proposal for suburban retail center, bounded by Main Street, Kissena Boulevard and Thirty-eighth and Barclay avenues, Flushing, Queens. Lester Tichy, 1946. Developed by William Zeckendorf. Perspective. AF. CU

Bottom: Proposal for suburban retail center, Flushing, Queens. Rendering of interior walkway. AF. CU

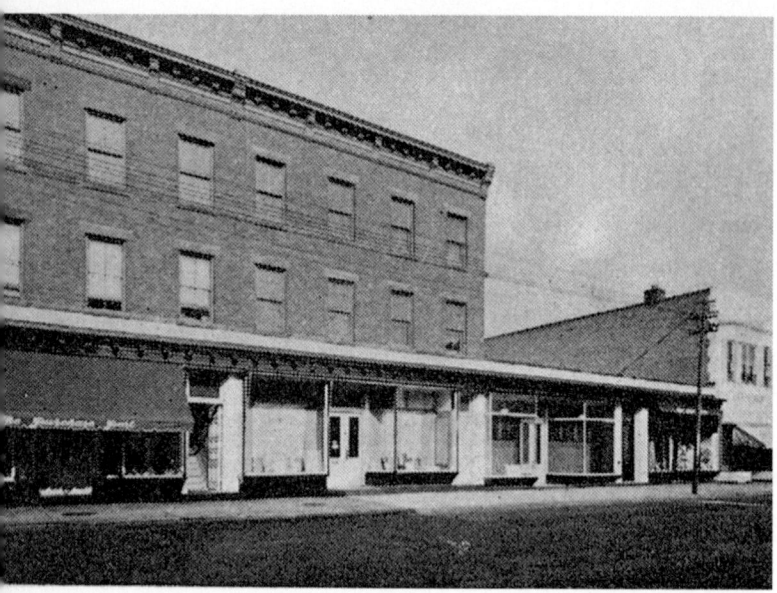

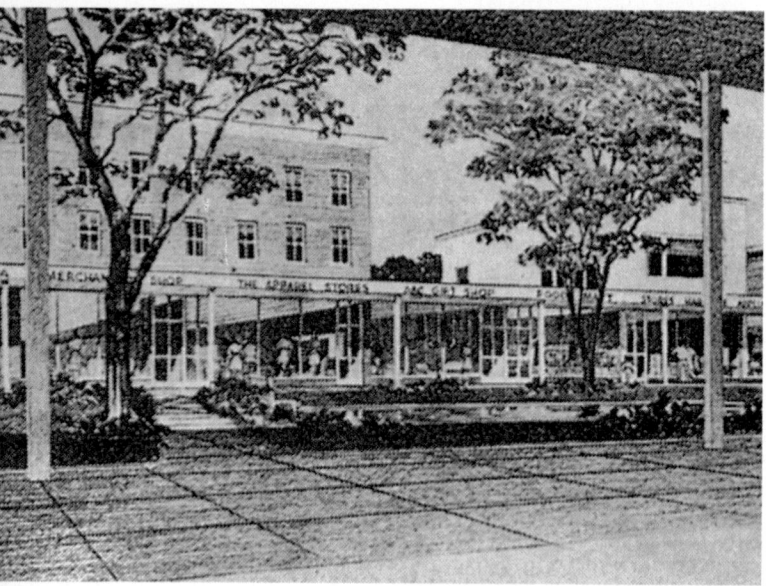

Top: View of shopping street in Rye, New York. 1946. AF. CU

Bottom: Proposal for pedestrian mall, Rye, New York. Ketchum, Giná & Sharp, 1946. Rendering of street converted into pedestrian mall. AF. CU

to rebuild the Long Island Railroad's Flushing station, which would become part of the proposed development. The area's abundant public transportation facilities helped to create heavy pedestrian traffic; in 1946 it was estimated that an average of 46,000 pedestrians per hour walked on Roosevelt Avenue between 8 A.M. and 10 P.M., nearly as large a volume, when measured per square foot of sidewalk, as at the intersection of Fifth Avenue and Forty-second Street. To help relieve street-level congestion, Tichy proposed placing loading docks beneath the bus station and equipping the center with a subterranean railroad siding.

When Zeckendorf's Flushing project was announced in 1946, it was to contain a department store, approximately sixty shops, a cooperative farmers' market selling Long Island produce and a commercial plant nursery that would double as a park. Zeckendorf also conceived of a renewed entertainment center, with restaurants, a movie theater, a dance hall, a skating rink and a children's play area supervised by nurses. Jack Raymond reported in the *New York Times* that the project was "a dream center for shopping, offices and amusements, to be the largest in the world, where the streets will be warm in winter and cool in summer, where pedestrians will not walk but will be moved along on sliding sidewalks."[187] And, as *Architectural Forum* noted, it was intended to "transform the heart of Flushing into a shopping center for a good part of suburban New York."[188] The grandly scaled, futuristic development, a superexuberant essay in International Modernism, Latin American style, vividly reflected the aspirations of a public finally liberated from the deprivations of the Depression and wartime rationing. Located close to the site of the 1939–40 World's Fair, it promised not only to realize the consumerist fantasies implicit in the fair's "World of Tomorrow" theme but to realize in the United States the Modernist architecture that had developed in Latin America during the war years when construction at home was at a virtual standstill.

Tichy's design control was planned to extend to all buildings, storefronts, exterior signs and even, perhaps, the stores' interior displays. He designed the complex as a loosely organized composition set within the existing street pattern. Most of the individual buildings were three stories high and made extensive use of glass, sleek curvilinear forms, irregular massing and open plans. Rising above the low-lying buildings were to be three eight-story slabs housing professional offices and a private hospital, general offices and a hotel. The buildings were to be placed within a parklike setting and arranged on a diagonal, parallel to each other, eschewing a traditional urban relationship to the street. A serpentine pedestrian bridge over Forty-first Avenue was to link a major parking area with a restaurant and adjoining 5,000-seat movie theater whose free-flowing shapes epitomized the center's architecture. The theater was to contain a stage large enough, its developers boasted, for shows "to rival Radio City Music Hall type productions."[189]

The complex was to contain a mile of arcaded, air-cooled pedestrian walkways and be surmounted by covered rooftop parking for 5,000 cars. The columns of the pedestrian arcades were to support eye-level display cases. According to the editors of *Architectural Forum*, the cases "relieve the monotony of the regularly spaced supports and create the illusion that the sidewalks are actually part of the shops," an illusion, they said, that "is heightened by the provision of flush lighting fixtures on the sidewalk canopies."[190] Four thousand feet of underground moving sidewalks would connect directly with subway and bus terminals, moving slowly enough to allow riders to step on and off to visit basement-level shops. More than a convenience, the moving sidewalks promised to be a compelling attraction, adding to the center's lightheartedly futuristic atmosphere. In its emphasis on diverting activities, the center was to be an updated version of the original nineteenth-century department stores where visitors, particularly women, could not only shop but spend an entire day socializing and being entertained.

Construction of the project would have required the city's granting of zoning changes and the condemnation of a few properties. At first Mayor William O'Dwyer expressed his support for the plan, but four months later, in December 1946, the Board of Estimate unanimously adopted the City Planning Commission's unfavorable report. James A. Burke, Borough President of Queens, sharply criticized the decision, charging that it was based not on an analysis of the project itself but rather on "personal animosities."[191] Burke pointed out that soon after rejecting the Flushing project the board had approved a New York Life Insurance proposal to build a parking garage on Sixty-fourth Street between Second and Third avenues in Manhattan, which also required marginal land acquisition through condemnation. Whatever the validity of Burke's charges, Zeckendorf and Tichy's version of the "World of Tomorrow" was never realized. The opening of a Gertz branch department store (Abbott, Merkt & Company, 1951) on Roosevelt Avenue between Main and Union streets brought to Flushing only a very modest slice of what might have been a model for suburban-style commercial development.[192]

Although the rate of postwar suburban growth did not become explosive until the 1950s, by the late 1940s it was clear that formerly discrete outlying towns were rapidly being transformed into commuter suburbs. The increase in the number of both residents and cars threatened once quaint communities with paralyzing congestion. Traffic not only affected the ambience of the towns, it weakened their economic viability, rendering their commercial Main Streets less competitive with new large-scale shopping centers; located on major highways and equipped with vast parking lots, these new centers were efficiently designed to attract and accommodate driving shoppers.

In 1944 the Westchester town of Rye found that a third of the $9 million in retail purchases made annually by its residents was spent outside the town; congestion along the town's principal shopping thoroughfare, five-block-long Purchase Street, was found to be the main reason shoppers went elsewhere. In addition to shoppers' cars, the street was choked with through traffic moving to and from nearby Route 1, the former Boston Post Road. On-street parking served both shoppers and commuters who used the railroad station located at one end of Purchase Street. The town commissioned Ketchum, Giná & Sharp to devise an urban plan that would prevent Rye from "drowning in a traffic snarl," as Morris Ketchum, Jr., put it.[193] The architects proposed rerouting traffic on a circumferential road and converting the shopping street into a landscaped, arcade-lined pedestrian mall; parking lots were to be placed between the stores and the ring road, in effect transforming the street into a suburban-style shopping center. An additional parking lot was to be built at the railroad station. The Rye plan, which may have been the first to transform a small-town street into a pedestrian mall, was only partially realized—parking lots were built behind the stores—but it was very influential nonetheless, establishing a pattern for the renewal of small-town downtowns that swept across the country in the 1950s.

In 1956 the 106-year-old town of Mount Kisco, also in Westchester, hired the firm of Raymond & May Associates to supervise its growth.[194] Following two years of study, the firm presented its suggestions, which focused on ways of handling automobile traffic. Recognizing the increasing importance of inter-suburban travel, the firm advocated the construction of an east-west highway linking Ossining to Bedford Village and South Salem through Mount Kisco, and a north-south highway linking Mount Kisco to Chappaqua. Following the lead of Rye's planners, Raymond & May also suggested that to ameliorate in-town congestion, South Moger Avenue, located in the middle of Mount Kisco's downtown, be closed to motor vehicles and transformed into an open-air mall. The proposal was never realized, in part due to the bureaucratic complexities of town and country government, and growth continued in an uncontrolled fashion. The journalist Doris Faber, writing in the New York Times in 1970, described Mount Kisco's traffic problems in down-to-earth terms: "Everyone who lives or works in this northern Westchester village, which may or may not be on the verge of becoming a city, has trouble turning left."[195]

Until the 1950s White Plains, the Westchester county seat, was a small city with a village atmosphere. But it had excellent rail and road connections to the city, a nearby airport that was ideal for private craft, and a strategic location as the nexus of a number of the nation's most prosperous suburban residential towns—including Scarsdale, Bronxville, Purchase and Briarcliff Manor. All of these factors made it attractive not only to corporations seeking suburban locations convenient to the city but also to department stores, especially those catering to the affluent. By the mid-1950s downtown White Plains had begun to change dramatically from a small city to a new hybrid—more shopping center than town center. Altman's had opened in White Plains in 1934 and Bonwit's and Macy's followed in 1947 and 1949 respectively, but all of these were comparatively small facilities. Raymond Loewy Associates and Starrett & Van Vleck collaborated on the design of a branch of Lord & Taylor in White Plains that opened in 1948; the store was similar to the same firms' earlier work for Lord & Taylor in Manhasset (see above).[196] It was only in 1952, however, when Altman's opened a much larger branch on the outskirts of the downtown commercial district, that the urban character of White Plains was decisively transformed.

The new Altman's, designed by Kahn & Jacobs, was a box-like design whose austerity was only slightly relieved by an ample amount of greenery; flanked by parking lots, the store had no sense of traditional, street-oriented urbanism.[197] Two years later Saks Fifth Avenue opened a White Plains branch on a five-acre site nearby on Bloomingdale Road.[198] Also designed by Kahn & Jacobs, with the firm of Clarke & Rapuano serving as landscape architects, this store was surrounded by parking lots as well. Clad in various shades of gray-glazed brick and trimmed in white Vermont marble and stainless steel, the building gained a small measure of grace from the way its L-shaped mass was built into the slope of a hilly site. Originally the store's executives had proposed a less expensive rectangular, Colonial-Georgian style building located at the low corner of the site, but test borings uncovered a small underground lake. Given the site constraints, Kahn & Jacobs developed a tasteful if not inspired design, which Architectural Forum described as "every bit as dignified as a colonial imitation, and a lot more interesting to look at."[199]

While Altman's and Saks prospered, smaller stores in the central business district of White Plains began to suffer in the late 1950s.[200] Though few stores actually stood vacant, a trend toward disinvestment led to the development of a large blighted area, and White Plains became one of the first suburban cities to

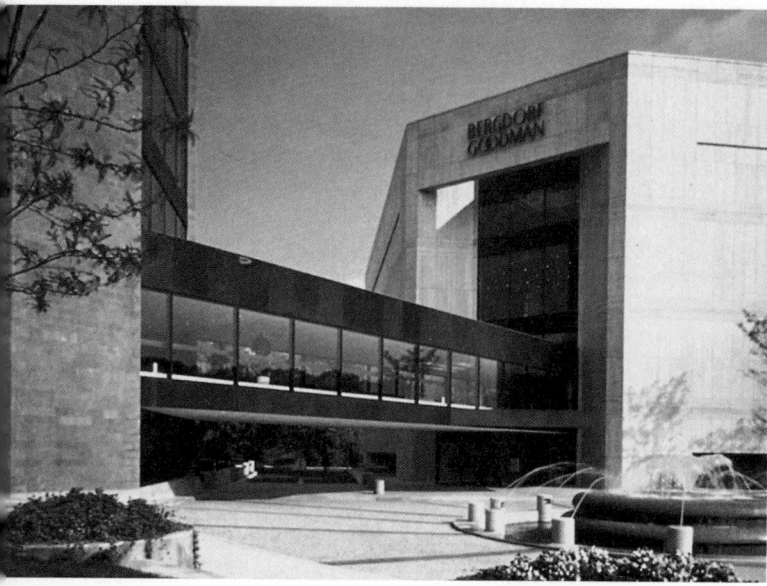

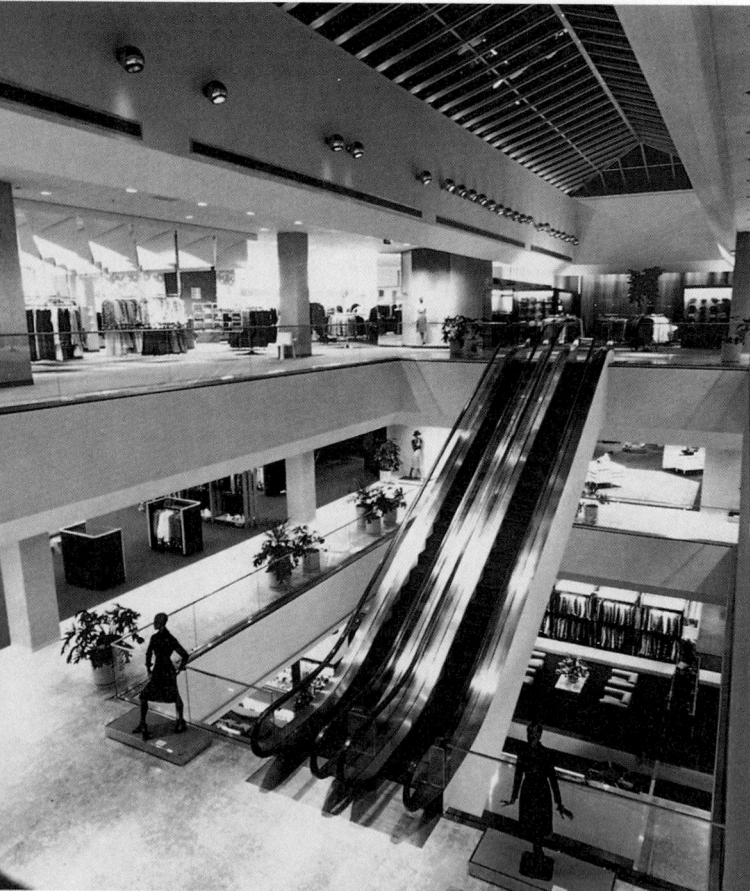

Top: Bergdorf Goodman, corner of Maple and Paulding avenues, White Plains, New York. John Carl Warnecke & Associates, 1975. Hilfer. JCW

Bottom: Bergdorf Goodman. Interior. Hilfer. JCW

undertake the kind of urban renewal characteristic of the oldest, largest inner-city areas. In 1957 the town slated 130 acres, constituting almost one third of the downtown area, for redevelopment.[201] The federally assisted purchase, demolition and clearance of nearly every building in the district was under way by 1966. A plan for the area, which was adjacent to the town's railroad station and included the county courthouse, the public library and an office building, was devised by the White Plains Urban Renewal Authority and called for the construction of a department store, a new courthouse and library, two or three hotels, several apartment buildings to house those displaced by renewal, "luxury" condominiums and numerous office buildings. By 1974 the project had garnered the largest amount of federal capital grants in the nation. By the end of the decade, with much of the project completed or under way, including the fifteen-store White Plains Mall, designed by Welton Becket & Associates and completed in 1972, and the mammoth, 150-store Galleria, designed by Copeland, Novak, Israel & Simmons and completed in 1980, White Plains had been revitalized.[202] However, the community had lost most of its former charm as a small-town county seat at the edge of a vast metropolis and had become instead a node in Megalopolis.

Two new department stores were also built outside the urban renewal district. Bloomingdale's White Plains branch (Hamby, Kennerly, Slomanson & Smith, 1975), on Bloomingdale Road just off Westchester Avenue, was a mirror-glass box set on a virtually windowless masonry base and surrounded by parking lots.[203] The building's slick glass skin, embellished only by the store's logo, perfectly expressed Bloomingdale's reputation as a premier purveyor of trendy goods. The extensive use of glass provided a twist on previous suburban department store design: whereas the early branch stores had used traditional display windows to attract pedestrians and those of the 1950s had used large expanses of glass to attract motorists, Bloomingale's White Plains used glass principally to reflect back a shimmering version of the outside world.

The first branch of Bergdorf Goodman, the quintessential upper-class specialty department store, opened at the intersection of Maple and Paulding avenues in White Plains in 1975.[204] Designed by John Carl Warnecke & Associates, with A. Eugene Kohn serving as partner in charge and the firm's subsidiary, Eleanor Lemaire Associates, handling the interior design, the building was one of the era's most architecturally ambitious suburban department stores. Subtly echoing the urban amenities of the flagship store, which occupied New York's most dramatic department store location on Fifth Avenue between Fifty-seventh and Fifty-eighth streets, opposite Grand Army Plaza and Central Park, the White Plains store was also located across the street from a park and was approached from a plaza incorporating a fountain.[205] The four-story, travertine-clad building was square, with chamfered corners. Instead of traditional display windows or large glass expanses, the architects used only a rather grand flight of stairs leading to the principal entrance, recessed into one of the corners, to lure shoppers inside. Bergdorf's elegantly understated exterior, bordering on anonymity, seemed to be the architectural equivalent of high-style product packaging; discerning consumers did not need to see the contents inside because the product's quality was taken for granted.

Inside, the selling floors were wrapped around a full-height atrium, set on a diagonal axis and enclosed by a 200-foot-long, mirror-glass skylight that during the day permitted light to flood in and at night provided a kaleidoscopic reflection of the merchandise and shoppers below. The store's escalators, rather than adopting the usual zigzag arrangement, were placed in a row, establishing a smooth traffic flow horizontally as well as vertically through the store. In addition to providing visual interest and giving customers access to the series of boutiquelike departments that lined its perimeter, the generously scaled atrium allowed the entire store to be seen at a glance, constantly orienting the shopper. As the editors of *Architectural Record* put it, the "open space functions much as a street would—Fifth Avenue, for instance."[206]

The circular Plaza Gowns department was appointed with traditional furniture and surmounted by a dramatic, 13'6"-high mirrored dome. A series of men's departments that shared a separate entrance were decorated in natural woods and leathers. Throughout the interior, beige Lioz marble imported from Portugal was used to pave central areas, and all custom metalwork was bronze. Despite the lavish materials, the design had none of the intimate scale or elegance of the New York store. Bergdorf's failed to attract enough customers, and after several years it closed its operations in White Plains. The store was renovated in 1980 to accommodate Neiman-Marcus, another member of Bergdorf's parent company, the Carter Hawley Hale group.

The transformation of an outlying town was nowhere more dramatic than in Stamford, Connecticut, where the emergence of Megalopolis, which turned farmland into housing subdivisions and traditional towns into satellite cities, was thoroughly and devastatingly complete.[207] Founded in 1642 by a group of zealous Calvinists, Stamford remained a rather isolated and homogeneous New England town until 1848, when the New Haven Railroad connected it to New York. The railroad's completion coincided with the last of three successive waves of immigration from Ireland, in 1845, 1846 and 1848; many Irish immigrants arriving at Ellis Island settled in Stamford. In 1869 the town's first large-scale factory opened, the Yale & Towne Manufacturing Company, which produced locks and keys. In the 1890s a flurry of factory building was fueled by new waves of immigrants, principally from Italy and Eastern Europe. By 1910 approximately one third of Stamford's citizens were foreign-born. Though the city continued to prosper throughout the 1920s, sensitive observers noted its gradually disintegrating status as an independent urban entity. In 1929 the city of Stamford hired the New York City–based urban planner Herbert S. Swan to conduct a planning study. In his report, published as *Plan of a Metropolitan Suburb*, Swan argued that while "Stamford has an identity altogether its own," it "is in a real sense a part of the New York metropolitan area."[208] The tendency toward suburbanization and toward the development of Megalopolis was greatly amplified by the completion of the Merritt Parkway in 1938; with the construction in 1950–58 of the Connecticut Turnpike, which paralleled the New Haven's tracks and cut through downtown Stamford, the transformation was vastly escalated.

By the mid-1950s Stamford had experienced a significant downturn in its industrial fortunes and, simultaneously, a widening economic gulf between its working-class population, living in increasingly deteriorated conditions downtown, near the dwindling number of factories, and its wealthy citizens, living in the suburban and semirural settings of its "back country" and Long Island Sound shoreline. During the late 1940s and 1950s a number of manufacturers moved out of Stamford, including, most significantly, Yale & Towne. During the same period, celebrities like jazz musician Benny Goodman, baseball player

Jackie Robinson and conductor Leopold Stokowski and his wife, Gloria Vanderbilt, bought homes in Stamford's outlying areas. As Stamford's industrial base evaporated, its once vibrant ethnic neighborhoods suffered; accompanying the industrial decline was a change in the area's racial mix, with an influx of Hispanics and African-Americans, who found it increasingly difficult to enter the economic mainstream. In the late 1950s Stamford began to wake up to its plight, stimulated to action by the construction of the Connecticut Turnpike, which replaced a significant section of the town's historic business core as well as some run-down housing and a model housing project called Grasmere.

Stamford's half-decayed downtown had already begun to change course in 1954, when Bloomingdale's opened its third and largest branch store at the corner of Broad Street and Washington Boulevard, which was designed to meet the needs of the affluent among Stamford's population as well as residents in other nearby Fairfield County towns.[209] The architect, William T. Snaith of Raymond Loewy Associates, continued the synthesis of Modernist and Colonial vocabularies that the firm had previously pursued for Lord & Taylor (see above). The building turned its back on the town's ailing downtown, setting itself apart behind a white-painted, split-rail fence that bounded a generously planted front lawn. Snaith's highly eclectic design included references to the work of Le Corbusier and of his Brazilian disciple, Oscar Niemeyer; the teakwood awnings and alternating panels of warm-toned, salmon-colored brick and white-painted common brick also brought a measure of 1940s-style Scandinavian Modernism.

In 1960 the city of Stamford signed an agreement with two private sponsors, S. Pierre Bonan, a New York developer, and the F. D. Rich Company, a Stamford-based contractor, for a renewal project to occupy a sixty-six-acre site adjacent to the elevated turnpike.[210] Victor Gruen, the project's urban planner and architect, prepared a plan calling for the construction of shops, apartment buildings, multilevel parking garages and some light industrial facilities; new streets, sewers and storm drains; and the conversion of Main Street, from Atlantic Square to City Hall, into a pedestrian mall. Five years later the city, still trying to begin implementation of its plan, rejected a proposal by Lord & Taylor to build a branch store on the city's outskirts, arguing that it would pull business away from downtown and jeopardize redevelopment.[211] Yet inner-city renewal was stymied by two lawsuits, one initiated by parties seeking to hold the city responsible for relocating all people displaced by the project, and the other brought by the United Oil Company in an effort to block the acquisition of a plot on Broad Street. The first suit was ultimately resolved by a plan revision that resulted in a threefold increase in the number of housing units provided, and the second was settled out of court.

In 1966 construction finally began with the building of St. John's Towers, three moderate-income, seventeen-story oval-shaped buildings sponsored by St. John's Roman Catholic Church and the Diocese of Bridgeport, as well as by the federal government.[212] The project was developed by the F. D. Rich Company and designed by Victor Bisharat, a Jerusalem-born local architect who was to become the most powerful design force in the city's redevelopment. The sculptural, glass-sheathed towers were encircled by continuous balconies, divided into separate units by finlike vertical sprayed-on-concrete forms. The futuristic towers sat on a sixteen-foot-high, sprayed-on-concrete podium incorporating retail space, professional offices and parking beneath its landscaped roof, which curved upward at its perimeter

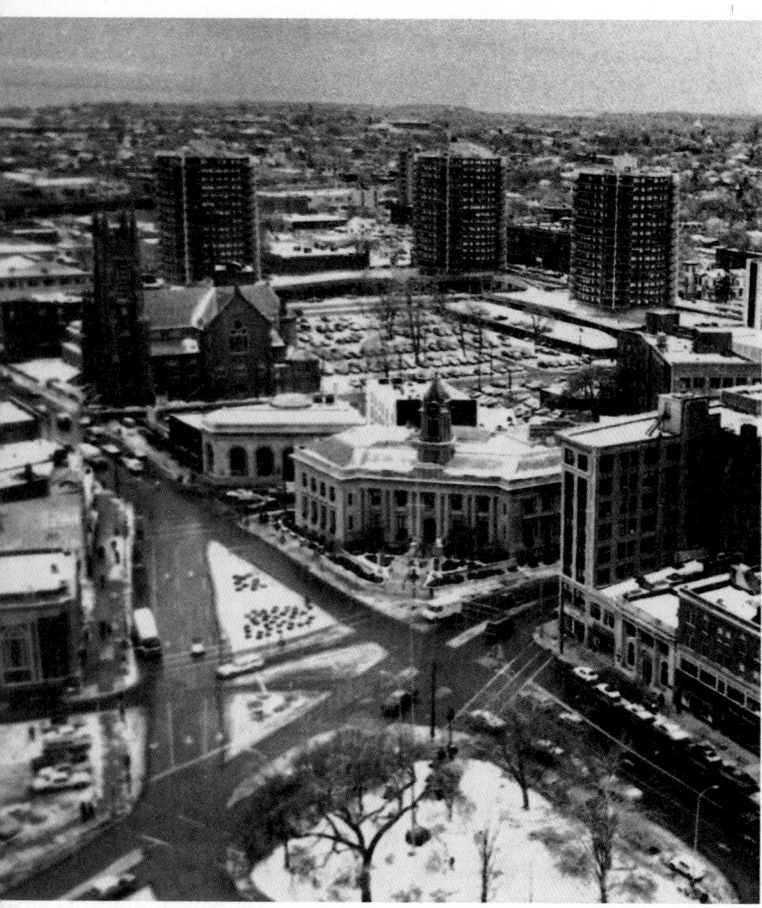

Above: St. John's Towers, between Washington Boulevard and Atlantic Street, Tresser Boulevard and Bell Street, Stamford, Connecticut. Victor Bisharat, 1971. View to the southwest. Best. SHS

Top right: General Telephone and Electronics Building, 201 Tresser Boulevard, Stamford, Connecticut. Victor Bisharat, 1973. View to the north. Best. SHS

Bottom right: Landmark Tower, 101 Broad Street, Stamford, Connecticut. Victor Bisharat, 1973. View to the northwest. Best. SHS

to form a solid parapet. The towers were criticized from the beginning by groups who maintained that isolated high-rise housing projects would create "concrete ghettos" and that building commercial space without previous tenant commitments would create "white elephants" which would burden the city.

Despite the criticism, progress continued on the downtown redevelopment project. In 1967 Gimbel's and J. C. Penney's announced plans to open branches facing the pedestrian mall. Nearby, a twenty-one-story speculative office building, Landmark Tower, at 101 Broad Street, and a thirteen-story headquarters for General Telephone and Electronics, built just to the north of the turnpike, both designed by Bisharat, were completed in 1973.[213] Landmark Tower, which incorporated a sunken skating rink and a top-floor restaurant, was, at the time of its completion, the tallest building between New York and New Haven. The building consisted of a boldly modeled mass—sloping walls set between sculptured concrete walls to create an obelisklike profile—with four scallop-shaped entrances opening onto a landscaped plaza; its futuristic style complemented the adjacent St. John's Towers. The General Telephone and Electronics Building, a striking inverted, stepped pyramid wrapped in mirror glass, stood above a three-story parking garage and was planned as part of the Stamford Forum, which was to encompass several office buildings on an eighteen-acre platform. The building marked a watershed in the history of American urban renewal: it was, according to Robert Rich, president of the F. D. Rich Company, the first time that a major corporation chose to relocate from New York to a downtown area, rather than to a suburban setting.

By the mid-1970s much of Stamford's urban renewal project, which had expanded to cover a 130-acre area that included most of downtown, was completed or under way.[214] Glass-enclosed walkways connecting Landmark Tower to nearby movie theaters, opened in 1976, were the first links in a network of proposed walkways that promised to transform downtown into what Michael Knight, writing in the New York Times, called a "Disney-like 'megastructure.'"[215]

Spurred by the renewal project, a host of major corporations, including American Thread, Champion International, Continental Oil, General Electric, Marx Toys, Olin, Schweppes, Shell Chemical Company and Xerox, moved to Stamford during the 1960s and early 1970s. In 1974 Michael Knight reported on the town's new status: "Once a sleepy little city in the heart of Connecticut's affluent Gold Coast, Stamford is now hard at work recreating the urban dream. And Stamford, close enough to New York to reap its big-city benefits and far enough away to escape its big-city problems, is reveling in its newly found position of eminence."[216] By this time, Stamford had earned the name of "The Corporate City," a title it had been optimistically given in 1958 as it searched for a new economic identity.

But Stamford's renewal project, ultimately realized with city, state, federal and private funds, was not without its problems. In the face of impending redevelopment, most of the lower-income whites who lived in the renewal area left, giving way to low-income Hispanic and nonwhite minorities who moved there because they were unable to afford housing in other areas or were kept from other neighborhoods by racism. As landlords stopped maintaining properties that were soon to be purchased as part of the urban renewal process, the area deteriorated to a level associated with the worst inner-city slums. Stamford's Urban Redevelopment Commission became the area's dominant landlord, but its failure to relocate tenants led to a nearly year-long freeze on most federal funds allocated to the project, further delaying renewal and, in the process, sacrificing significant revenue due to the city. Salem Shapiro, director of the commission, observed: "This whole relocation mess could have been avoided if there was a possibility of housing these people in other parts of the city. But everybody was shouting, 'Not in my neighborhood!'"[217] While it was estimated in 1972 that the completed project would bring the city $5 million annually in taxes, redevelopment virtually wiped out the city's downtown commercial tax base. "This project cannot help but succeed when it is finally completed," said Mayor Julius M. Willensky, "but how do you measure what we have lost in dollars and divisiveness in the community?"[218]

Even the architectural aspect of Stamford's redevelopment came under attack, not only from critics but from the project's principal architect, Victor Bisharat. According to an October 1980 article by Andree Brooks in the New York Times, Bisharat had deep regrets about the project: "I hate how it all looks," he said. "I try to block it all out of my mind. I even look the other way when I go by on the highway. I had the greatest opportunity in the world and I failed." Bisharat felt that he had lacked clout with his clients and that his own reticence, combined with economic considerations and a desire to get the job done, had contributed to the project's shortcomings. "If I had to do it all over again," he said, "I would have insisted on certain changes."[219]

By the early 1980s Bisharat's futuristic Modernism seemed distinctly out-of-date to other observers as well. Ada Louise Huxtable dismissed the Stamford buildings as "gymnastics" and "a kind of venture architecture." Referring to Bisharat's comment that he didn't like to look at his buildings when he drove by on the Connecticut Turnpike, Huxtable said, "Funny, that's the way I felt a decade and a half ago."[220] In response to Huxtable's criticism, Bisharat claimed that he had been misquoted and misrepresented by Brooks (a claim she denied) and that although he had tried "to create a total environment of architectural integrity in the city of Stamford . . . those buildings constructed subsequent to my work have failed to achieve this end."[221]

Whatever the merits of Bisharat's work, Stamford's renewal was largely successful. By 1974 Stamford was a major destination point, with three times as many people commuting daily to the town as from it. What helped transform Stamford from little more than a service town for commuters, economically dependent in large measure on New York, into a vital city was the fact that it had for so long been overlooked. Typically, overcrowded cities surrounded by comparatively inexpensive open land had suffered when the middle class, and the businesses that catered to it, fled to the suburbs. But in a process that was consistent with prevailing planning philosophy, the city of Stamford, already closed in by affluent suburbs, practiced the wholesale destruction of slums to create new land at the core.

In Stamford, the middle class, which had once rejected urban shopping districts in favor of suburban shopping centers, rediscovered the pleasures of a downtown, albeit a downtown mall. When finally completed in 1982, the mall was not only pedestrianized but also enclosed, connecting J. C. Penney's, Macy's, Saks Fifth Avenue, Brooks Brothers, Abercrombie & Fitch, F.A.O. Schwartz and 125 other stores.[222] Though named the Stamford Town Center, the mall provided none of the around-the-clock public street life characteristic of a traditional town, nor the variety of use and social class that such a name implied. Nonetheless, Stamford's urban renewal project did succeed in creating a sanitized, corporate dreamworld with a distinctly small-town feel to it, and it immeasurably enriched the city's coffers.

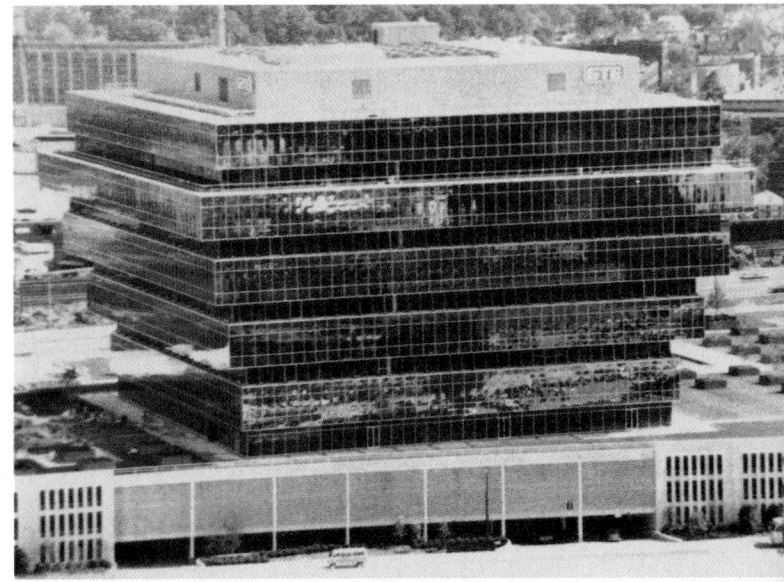

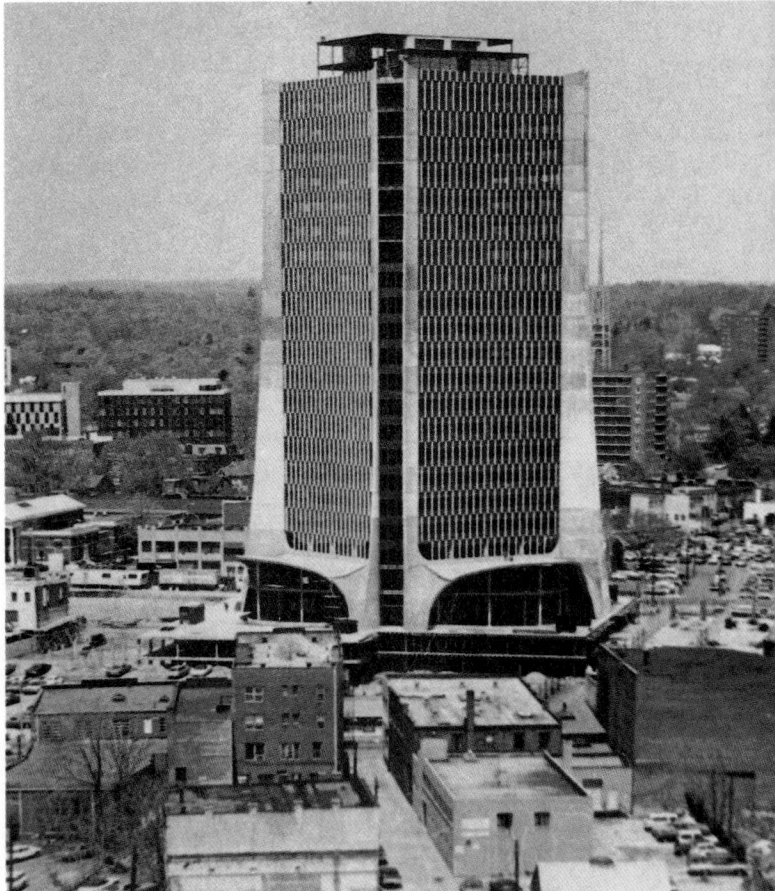

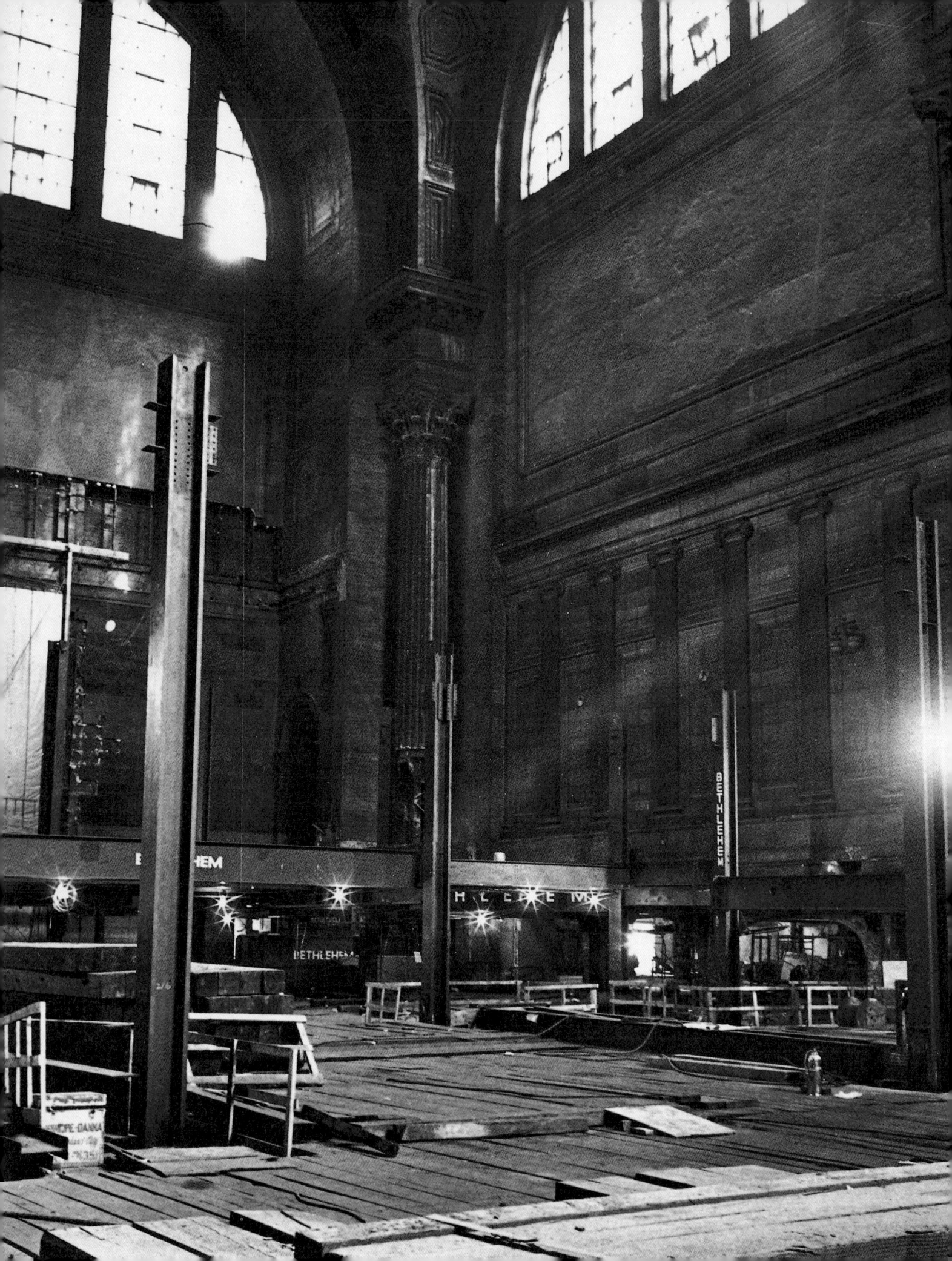

Chapter 16

Historic Preservation

Out for a walk, after a week in bed,
I find them tearing up part of my block
And, chilled through, dazed and lonely, join the dozen
In meek attitudes, watching a huge crane
Fumble luxuriously in the filth of years.
Her jaws dribble rubble. . . .
As usual in New York, everything is torn down
Before you have had time to care for it.
Head bowed, at the shrine of noise, let me try to recall
What building stood here. . . .
—James Merrill, 1962[1]

The emergence of the historic preservation movement as a powerful force in the evolution of New York's architecture and urbanism began not with an act of conservation but with an act of destruction: the demolition in 1963 of McKim, Mead & White's Pennsylvania Station. The loss of the station was deeply shocking to New Yorkers and provoked the establishment of a mechanism for the legal protection of the city's architectural heritage. The rapid development of the historic preservation movement into a major political as well as cultural force in New York was one of the principal "success stories" in the city's evolution from the mid-1960s on. The establishment of the New York City Landmarks Preservation Commission in 1965 was as decisive for the physical and social history of the city as the passage of the new zoning law four years before. In many ways it was, in fact, the antidote to that ordinance and, as such, a powerful planning tool in its own right.

Although it was not until the 1960s that the city would wake to the need for action, the issue of preserving the city's architectural heritage was hardly new to New Yorkers.[2] As early as 1831 the editors of the *New-York Mirror* decried the destruction of a seventeenth-century Dutch house at 76 Pearl Street, writing that its loss was "in compliance with that irreverence for antiquity which so grievously afflicts the people of this city, many of whom, we are credibly informed, demolish one house just for the pleasure of building another in its place."[3] In 1845 Mayor

Philip Hone even more pointedly wrote in his diary: "Overturn, overturn, overturn! is the maxim of New York. The very bones of our ancestors are not permitted to be quiet a quarter of a century, and one generation of men seem studious to remove all relics of those which preceded them."[4] In 1869 the editors of *Harper's Weekly* noted that in "a city where new construction is constantly in progress, demolition of the old and the excavation of the site are a commonplace to which New Yorkers have long been accustomed."[5]

Despite the occasional outbreak of sentiment on behalf of the old, until World War II the prevailing attitude toward preservation was at best apathetic and at times even hostile. This was vividly demonstrated in the loss of the General Post Office (Alfred Mullet, 1870), which stood at the southern tip of City Hall Park.[6] In 1938 the city purchased the building, which had been unused for a year, for one dollar and proceeded to demolish it, at a cost of $63,000, to make way for the enlargement of the park. The exuberant, robustly articulated Second Empire building, surmounted by a fifty-five-foot-high dome that had powerfully formed the apex of the triangular park, was roundly dismissed by the editors of the *New York Times* as a "hideous pile" whose demolition would provide "little occasion for sorrow over the disappearance of another historic landmark." Noting that when the structure was built it had been critically well received, the editors, tenuously grasping at art-historical straws, went on to explain: "It was perhaps the perfect architectural example of that early General Grant period when the classical was dying of its bleak attempt to appear cozy." The editors' failure to place the building within the broad context of the changing winds of architectural fashion, to see its inherent value as a "perfect architectural example," was symptomatic of New Yorkers' myopic view toward the physical growth of their own city.[7]

Well into the 1950s, the loss of architecturally significant buildings seemed an inevitable if mildly regrettable feature of the city's evolution. Even when a sense of loss was acknowledged, it was generally as a quaint exercise in nostalgia rather than a serious call for preservation. The widespread belief that architectural losses were in essence inconsequential was bolstered by the assumption that any building, regardless of its importance, would give way to one that was not only bigger but also better.

Pennsylvania Station, Seventh to Eighth Avenue, West Thirty-first to West Thirty-third Street. McKim, Mead & White, 1904–10. Waiting room during demolition, February 9, 1965. Fred W. McDarrah. FWM

By the advent of the Second World War, a formidable number of exceptional buildings had been lost. Such masterpieces as McKim, Mead & White's Madison Square Presbyterian Church, demolished in 1913, only seven years after its completion, and the same firm's Madison Square Garden of 1890, demolished in 1925, fell without a whimper of protest.[8] The imminent loss of St. John's Chapel (1803), the masterpiece of John McComb, Jr., who was also coarchitect of City Hall, was perhaps the first instance of destruction to elicit widespread concern.[9] The church's demolition in 1918 to permit the widening of Varick Street was preceded by years of organized efforts to save the building. In 1904 St. John's, widely considered by architects, historians and the general public to be, as the editors of the *New York Times* stated, "one of the finest specimens of church architecture not only in this city but in America," was closed by the Trinity Corporation, which argued that it was neither good business nor good religion to continue conducting services when attendance was so minimal.[10] During the next fourteen years a variety of plans for the reuse of St. John's were proposed: it was suggested that the building be used as a hospital or a recruiting center to help with the war effort, as a local civic center or as headquarters for the American Scenic and Historic Preservation Society. Preservationists eventually waged a legal battle, seeking a permanent injunction barring the closing of the church.

The building's demolition was opposed not only because of its quality but because, by the advent of World War I, the Georgian architecture of Colonial and Early Republican America had become so highly appreciated as to be nearly sacred. The deification of the Georgian style reflected a confluence of cultural values, ranging from general concern for the preservation of beautiful and historically significant buildings to xenophobia on the part of many descendants of Colonial families, a fear inspired by recent mass immigration from southern and eastern Europe. Despite the preservation efforts, however, St. John's was demolished. By 1957 Marshall B. Davidson, writing in *Art in America*, could accurately say, "There is far less standing of colonial New York than there is of Periclean Athens."[11]

The desire to honor the city's early architectural history did have some success, however, especially in the preservation of Colonial houses as museums.[12] The first of these Colonial house-museums, the Van Cortlandt Mansion (1748)[13] and the Morris-Jumel Mansion (John Edward Pryor, 1765),[14] were established in Manhattan in 1897 and 1903 respectively; the Poe Cottage (ca. 1812), in the Bronx, followed in 1913;[15] and the Dyckman House (ca. 1783), in Manhattan, in 1915.[16] The Christopher Billopp House (1680–88), on Staten Island, also known as the Conference House, was established as a house-museum in 1929,[17] as was the Abigail Adams Smith House (1799), in Manhattan, in 1939.[18] During the 1930s efforts to preserve Staten Island's Colonial architecture also focused on the protection of numerous buildings erected in the hamlet formerly known as Richmondtown.[19] Beginning in 1958, the Richmondtown Restoration, as the Williamsburg-like preserve was called, was maintained by the Staten Island Historical Society under the auspices of the Park Department, and in 1969 it was designated a landmark.

The Seabury Treadwell House (1831–32), at 29 East Fourth Street, was unique among the city's old houses in that it had been owned and occupied by the original family for ninety-eight years and retained virtually all of its furnishings.[20] In 1936, three years after the death of the last Treadwell daughter, Gertrude, at the age of ninety-three, the house, known as the Old Merchant's House, was purchased and operated as a museum by the private, nonprofit Historic Landmark Society, founded by her nephew, George Chapman. In 1945 it was rumored that, due to a lack of funds for maintaining the property, the house was to be demolished, but Chapman was able to pay off the mortgage on the house and ensure its survival. Despite its designation as a New York City landmark in 1965, however, the house-museum remained poorly funded and it stood, as Ada Louise Huxtable observed in 1972, "slowly disintegrating on a casually grubby street . . . its original furnishings, unspoiled by later decorating vanities, ready to crumble at a touch."[21] Funds raised from a variety of public and private sources were used to conduct a much-needed structural renovation in 1972, supervised by New York University architect Joseph Roberto, who worked in close cooperation with the Landmarks Preservation Commission. The inside of the house, which had survived in its original if somewhat tattered state, was designated a landmark in 1974 and underwent a restoration, also supervised by Roberto and completed in 1979.

The earliest and perhaps most significant example of the successful preservation of a historic house was that of Gracie Mansion, a Federal-style country house built in 1799 for Archibald Gracie, a Scottish immigrant who became a successful merchant and a founder of the *New York Evening Post*.[22] Gracie Mansion was acquired by the Park Department in 1886, and the grounds, together with the adjacent East River Park, were renamed Carl Schurz Park (1911). In 1927 the long-neglected house finally underwent some restoration. Further restoration was undertaken in 1942, when the house became the city's official mayoral residence after Mayor Fiorello La Guardia chose it over the lavish, French Renaissance–style Charles Schwab mansion. The restored Gracie Mansion was furnished in part with period pieces lent by the Metropolitan Museum of Art, the Museum of the City of New York and the Brooklyn Museum, as well as private donors. The mansion quickly became the best-known house of its era in New York, and during the Wagner administration it was increasingly used for official receptions, conferences and civic meetings, and was also open to public tours that attracted around 2,000 visitors annually. This situation did not please preservationists, who feared that the house was being subjected to too much use, nor did it please the mayor's wife, Susan, who felt the family's privacy was being unduly impinged upon.

Mrs. Wagner initiated a plan to add a reception wing that would enable the original building to be used exclusively as a private house. Ada Louise Huxtable lambasted a preliminary scheme for the wing, presented on October 17, 1964, saying it possessed "all the charm and suitability of a suburban garage."[23] In May 1965, following Mrs. Wagner's death, the Committee for Gracie Mansion, chaired by the real estate developer Peter Grimm and the lawyer Harold Riegelman, was established to raise money for and oversee the construction of a reception wing. A committee was formed to ensure that the wing would be not only stylish but also carefully designed to fit seamlessly with the existing building. The committee, headed by the first executive director of the newly established Landmarks Preservation Commission, James Grote Van Derpool, hired Mott B. Schmidt as the architect, to be assisted by the architects Edward Coe Embury, F. Burrall Hoffman and John Barrington Bayley, and the interior designers Francis Henry Lenygon, chairman of the American Institute of Interior Designers' National Committee on Historic Preservation, Ellen Lehman McCluskey and Stephen J. Jussel. The Susan Wagner wing, as the new addition was called, was completed in 1966, the same year that Gracie Mansion was protected as a designated landmark. Historically correct in its details and inventive in its composition, the new wing incorporated fragments from demolished eighteenth-century houses in an original design. Huxtable praised the results as "an object lesson in excellence."[24]

Though support was strong for the preservation of Colonial houses, other building types and styles were often neglected. During the La Guardia administration, the Park Department had assumed responsibility for all municipally owned sculpture, monuments and historic buildings, and Park Commissioner Robert Moses had instituted a massive program of restoration. Yet official attitudes toward preservation remained mixed during the 1940s. Moses himself was ambivalent at best; "We have inherited from past Administrations some God-awful monstrosities," he said in 1941, but he added, "We are also the legatees of some very fine things."[25]

On February 6, 1941, following the defeat of his highly controversial Brooklyn-Battery Bridge proposal and the adoption of alternate plans for a tunnel, Moses declared his intention to demolish Castle Clinton (John McComb, Jr., 1807) as part of a concomitant redesign of Battery Park.[26] The building, which had been erected by the federal government as a fort, was ceded to New York City in 1823 and converted to Castle Garden, which served as the venue for numerous spectacular social and cultural events, including the American debut in 1850 of soprano Jenny Lind. Beginning in 1855 it served as an immigrant landing depot where a total of 7.5 million people were processed; and in 1896 the building was expanded and converted into the New York Aquarium. Despite its colorful past, Moses dismissed the building as "a large red wart" that "has no history worth writing about." He argued for demolition on practical grounds as well, claiming that construction of the Brooklyn-Battery Tunnel would "undermine" the building's structural integrity.[27]

Numerous observers disputed Moses's claim, including Ole Singstad, the engineer in charge of the tunnel's construction, and Walter Binger, the engineer in charge of the West Side Highway approach, both of whom noted that no construction would be conducted within 170 feet of the fort. Robert Caro, who wrote a debunking biography of Moses, would later argue that Moses's motivation in advocating demolition was to get revenge on those who had worked to defeat the Brooklyn-Battery Bridge plan.[28] At first Moses thought only a few do-gooders would oppose his plan, and after announcing that Castle Clinton would be demolished, he gloated that "there was not a dry eye at the Knickerbocker Club, all the shades were drawn at the Century Association and heart-rending sobs issued from the dusty diggings of the American Scenic and Historic Preservation Society . . . but somehow the great popular uprising against the razing of the structure hasn't materialized."[29]

By October 1941 Moses had succeeded in closing the aquarium (which was reopened sixteen years later in a new building at Coney Island; see chapter 13) and demolishing the addition; he had also received the Board of Estimate's approval to tear down the rest of the fort. The following year, just as demolition of Castle Clinton had begun, opposition began to gather force, leading the Fine Arts Federation of New York to organize an open competition for the redesign of Battery Park that stipulated the preservation of the building. Moses fought back, ridiculing the opposition as "stuffed shirts";[30] the editors of the *New York Herald Tribune* wrote that "with the unleashing of [Moses's] dread artillery, it is clear that Castle Clinton, along with the traditionalists . . . are done for."[31] But the nation's entrance into

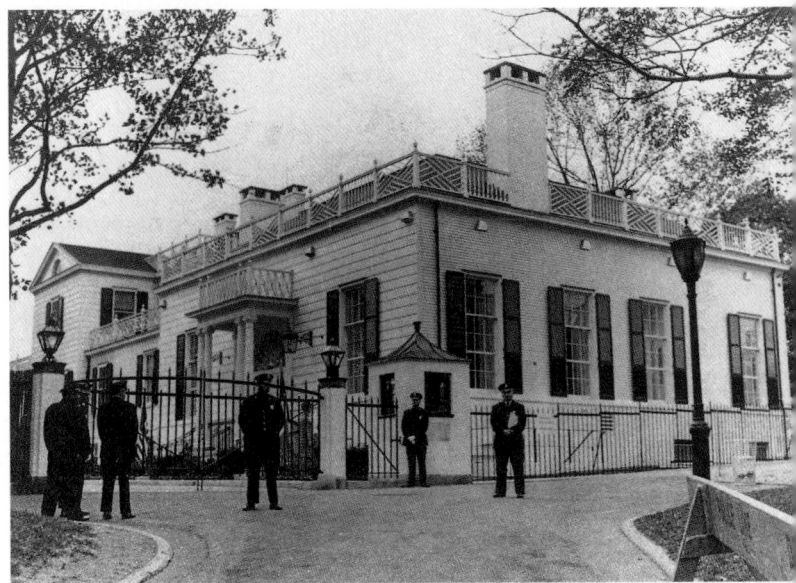

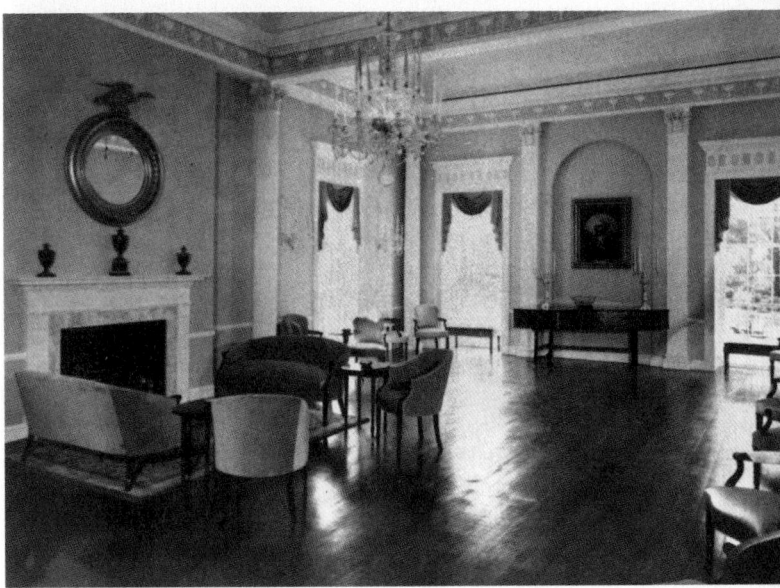

Top: Susan Wagner wing, Gracie Mansion, Carl Schurz Park, between East Eighty-eighth and East Eighty-ninth streets. Mott B. Schmidt, 1966. View to the northeast. DeLucia. NYP

Bottom: Susan Wagner wing. Ballroom. NYP

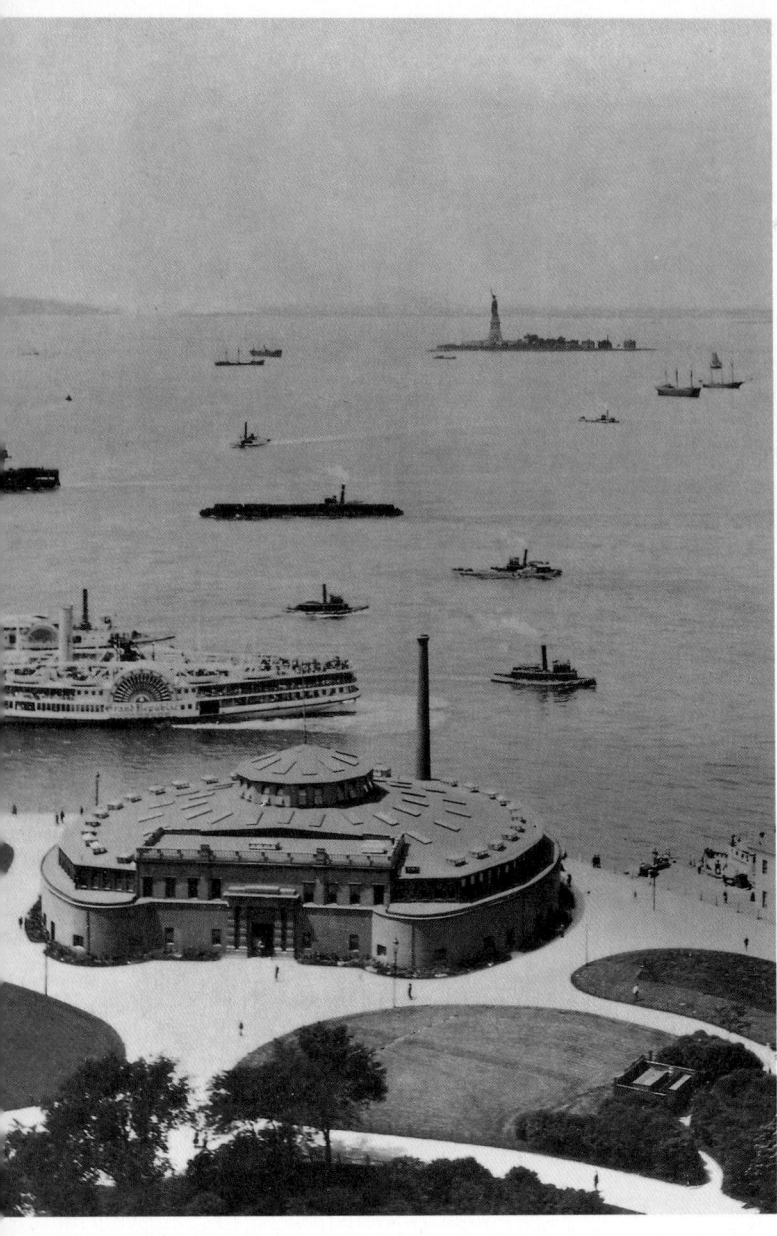

New York Aquarium (formerly Castle Clinton), Battery Park. John McComb, Jr., 1807; renovation, McKim, Mead & White, 1896. View to the south, ca. 1902. Wurts. MCNY

World War II halted Moses's progress, providing an opportunity for the opposition to regroup. With the help of former Manhattan Borough President George McAneny, they convinced the city's congressmen to lobby for the fort's protection as a national monument. In the bitter feud that ensued, several lawsuits were filed and Moses claimed that, during the five years Battery Park had been closed and fenced off, the fort had already been substantially demolished. This proved untrue.

In 1948 an anonymous letter to the editor of the *New York Times* called attention to Castle Clinton's still uncertain fate and stated that "action now, before it is too late, might preserve the city's priceless heritage in what few links remain with its colorful past."[32] In his own letter to the *Times* in response, Moses said that the "dreary warning opens up a dismal vista of stealthy official removal of priceless hydrocephalic bronze heads from public places and sale of ancient landmarks to junk yards. Ignorance of historic landmarks is to be expected and condoned in a busy metropolis, but worrying and croaking over wraiths and figments marks the transition from history to hysteria."[33] In 1950, after ten years of sometimes vicious battle, Congress approved the fort's status as a National Historic Monument and appropriated funds for its restoration and maintenance as a museum.

Support for the preservation of New York's architectural past continued to grow among both the architectural community and the general public throughout the 1950s, and New Yorkers took a growing interest in their architectural heritage. Andreas Feininger and Susan Lyman's 1954 book, *The Face of New York*, which contrasted period and contemporary views of the city, was an especially powerful tool,[34] as was John Kouwenhoven's *Columbia Historical Portrait of New York*, also published in 1954, on the occasion of Columbia University's 200th anniversary, which reminded New Yorkers of their physical past, much of which was lost.[35] In 1952 the architectural historian and critic Talbot Hamlin, discussing the tension between "historical heritage" and "the march of 'progress,'" advocated legally mandated preservation, basing his recommendation on the notion "that the facts of architectural excellence, community harmony, and historical association create social values of the first importance, and civic and national pride, and hence create better citizens with richer lives, give a sense of community continuance, and make the city and the country both more lovable and more livable."[36]

That same year, the Municipal Art Society and the New York Chapter of the Society of Architectural Historians, two organizations that, according to the *Journal of the American Institute of Architects*, were "becoming worried at the increasingly rapid demolition of well-known landmarks" in the city, embarked on a six-year study of architecturally significant buildings built before World War I.[37] The study was supervised by an architectural historian, Mrs. John M. Gilchrist, who included on the list of approximately 200 buildings the Quaker Meeting House (1694–95) in Flushing, Queens; the original Erasmus Hall school building (1786) in Brooklyn; and City Hall (1803–12), the University Club (1899) and the Woolworth Building (1913) in Manhattan. In addition, the buildings of Greenwich Village, Gramercy Park and Brooklyn Heights were noted "because of their community contribution rather than intrinsic value."[38] Five years after the completion of the study, the Municipal Art Society sponsored the publication of an illustrated version, edited by Alan Burnham.[39]

The proposed destruction in the early 1950s of George B. Post's robust, Romanesque-style Produce Exchange Building to make way for Emery Roth & Sons' Two Broadway office building signaled the emerging conflict between the forces of economic development and a new sense of both the value and the fragility of the city's architectural heritage.[40] Rather than lamenting the potential loss of one of New York's most significant buildings, the editors of *Architectural Forum* commented that with the announcement of the building's replacement, "the shipping-financial-commercial district got its best news in years," since the "concentration of new, modern space in the midtown Grand Central–Rockefeller Center area has made it difficult for owners in the aging downtown district to rebut reports that the area was doomed to succumb soon to galloping obsolescence."[41] But Talbot Hamlin described Post's building as "one of the distinguished landmarks of our crowded island" and said:

> There [is] something particularly unfortunate in the proposed unnecessary destruction of this building, so striking in its color, so powerful in its design, so expressive of its time. Historically, too, it is important for its court wall is the earliest example of metal-framed construction in New York and one of the earliest in the country. Is the city and are its inhabitants such slaves to economic pressures that they can have no say in what they see, no power to preserve what they love?[42]

Once the undistinguished Two Broadway office building was built, it became all too clear, as the architect Nathan Silver bluntly stated, that "the Produce Exchange, one of the best buildings in New York, was replaced . . . by one of the worst."[43]

Number Two Broadway realized the worst fears of a public that was becoming increasingly skeptical of contemporary architecture. In a decisive break with the sentiments of pre–World War II observers, the view was becoming more widespread that "progress" was a material but not necessarily an aesthetic fact—that the new building going up might be bigger and more technologically advanced than the one coming down, but it was probably not as artistically well considered. Throughout the 1950s, while architects and journalists advocated a "less is more" approach, public concern over the fate of New York's rich architectural heritage was in direct proportion to their disenchantment with the prevailing reductivist aesthetics of postwar Modernism.[44]

In the spring of 1956 Henry Hope Reed, Jr., an architectural historian, began to conduct walking tours of New York, sponsored by the Municipal Art Society and the local chapter of the Society of Architectural Historians and concentrating on the city's architectural past. Reed had been actively crusading on behalf of American Classicism in general and New York's great "Beaux-Arts" monuments in particular since 1952, when he participated in the Civic Art Conference at Yale University; the conference, which focused on Classical art and architecture, was accompanied by an exhibit curated by Lamont Moore and Christopher Tunnard.[45] Subsequently Reed and Tunnard, a Modernist landscape architect and city planner turned historian, organized "Planning Your Town," an exhibition designed by students in Yale's Department of Architecture and Graduate School of Planning and circulated by the Virginia Museum of Fine Arts.[46] They followed this with an influential book, *American Skyline* (1955), one of the first books in its field to be published in a paperback edition.[47] In it they presented a positive case for Academic Classicism, especially as practiced during the 1890s and early 1900s. Reed was not only an advocate of Classicism but also an active opponent of Modernism, a position he argued in his essay "For the 'Superfluous' in Buildings," published in the *New York Times Magazine* in 1956,[48] and in his book *The Golden City* (1959), in which he juxtaposed photographs of functionally similar buildings in the two styles.[49]

Reed's walking tours proved to be very popular, even "celebrated," as the editors of the *New Yorker* put it.[50] The editors described an incident that occurred on one of the tours:

> Approaching the Battery, Mr. Reed asked us to admire two monumental groups of stone horses prancing on the battlements atop the nineteenth floor of the Cunard Building. Someone in the group made bold to ask Mr. Reed what possible excuse there could be for stone horses at that strange height. Mr. Reed whirled with relish on his questioner. "Why do you wear a hat?" he demanded. "Ornament is to a building what clothes are to a man. . . . All the stone horses, griffons, serpents, masks, and lions' heads in this city exist for a single reason—to give us delight. We city dwellers need these riches. Let those who like plain buildings move to the country and live in barns."[51]

Also significant, though less widely recognized at the time, was a campaign waged by the architect John Barrington Bayley to positively reevaluate the Classical architecture of the late nineteenth and early twentieth centuries. Bayley had studied at Harvard under the arch-Modernists Walter Gropius and Marcel Breuer but was never comfortable with their point of view, and a tour of duty in Paris during World War II, followed by a four-year stay in Rome, turned him into a committed Classicist. In 1959 some of Bayley's grand Classical proposals for New York were published in Reed's *The Golden City*.[52]

In 1957 public perception of New York's historic architectural treasures was further enhanced when the New York Community Trust initiated a program of identifying notable buildings with plaques outlining their historical and artistic importance and providing the buildings' dates, the names of the original owners and the architects.[53] While most of the buildings identified were built before World War I, the program also included Howells & Hood's Daily News Building of 1929.[54]

Some preservationists, keenly aware of the carefully designed and crafted ornamental details that defined New York's traditional architecture and helped give the city's older buildings human scale, visual interest and individual character, argued that if whole buildings could not be saved, at least fragments could be salvaged. In the late 1950s Ivan Karp, who later became the director of the highly influential Leo Castelli art gallery and subsequently of his own enterprise, the O.K. Harris gallery, founded the Anonymous Arts Recovery Society, a group that scoured the city to save architectural ornaments from doomed buildings.[55] By 1965 the group, with around 100 dues-paying members, had "managed to cart off for posterity more than 100 tons of chips off notable old blocks," according to the editors of *Time*, and had given approximately 500 objects to the Brooklyn Museum to serve as the core collection of the Frieda Schiff Warburg Sculpture Garden.[56] Although the group had been granted tax-exempt, nonprofit institutional status and could thus offer tax deductions to building owners who donated objects, obtaining items was not always easy. "Demolition is such a desperately competitive business," Karp explained, "that the people involved in it are apt to be cynical and devious. If you succeed in striking the right note with them, it's generally by offering cash. My usual procedure is to negotiate directly with the foreman on a unit basis, but even that is getting alarmingly expensive. Things that used to go for between five and twenty-five dollars now often cost three times as much."[57]

The group concentrated its efforts, as Karp stated, "on the period from 1875 to 1910—a moment in American architecture and decorative arts that has been completely uncelebrated. The stones we save are both art objects and a historical record of one

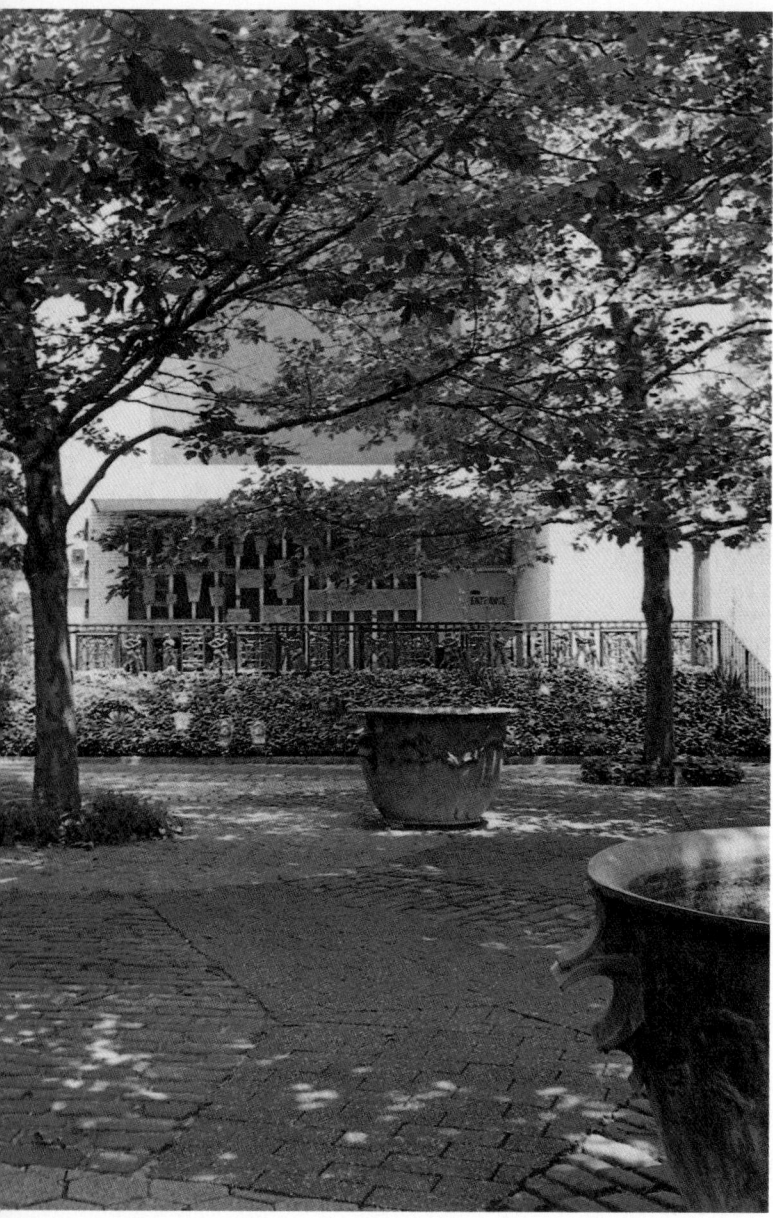

of the greatest building booms New York has ever known—a tumultuous and exciting time. They also represent the end of artisanship—individual stone-carving—and the last applications of ornament to classically oriented buildings."[58] The sculpture garden at the Brooklyn Museum represented a major achievement for preservationists and a significant contribution to the city's cultural assets. Designed by Ian M. White, assistant director of the museum, the garden contained pathways lined by architectural ornaments and fragments, as well as by antique lampposts and park benches. But, as the museum's director, Thomas S. Beuchner, noted, "Sadly, the continuing accumulation of such delightful fragments depends on continuing destruction of handsome buildings."[59]

The Wrecker's Ball

The destruction of the city's pre–World War I architecture seemed to reflect not only economic factors—the increased pressures of a booming real estate market—but also a moralistic embrace of a brave new world liberated from unabashed hedonism. This self-righteous and self-imposed austerity—an odd phenomenon, given the era's exceptional prosperity—was aimed first and foremost at the most obvious symbol of wealth, the mansions and townhouses of the super-rich, the city's private palaces. The loss of the houses of the rich was justified by many observers as an inevitable and desirable by-product of increasing democratization, a visible symbol of the collapse of a pretentious, monied pseudo-aristocracy. This view eventually widened to embrace not only private palaces but also public palaces of pleasure and production, ranging from theaters to department stores. By extension, virtually all building types of New York's Metropolitan era, both monumental and vernacular, came to be seen as impediments to the rebuilding of the city along efficient lines. The rejection of the past was also, of course, based on a shift in aesthetics: for the first time ever, architects and designers not only were contemptuous of styles that differed from their own preferences but also rejected any use of the past as a source for the present.

Fine buildings fell to the wrecker's ball all over the city, but the area that suffered the greatest architectural losses was Manhattan's east side, where, beginning in the 1870s, the super-rich had fashioned a "Gold Coast," principally along Fifth and Park avenues and the adjacent side streets. Many of this area's most important specimens were torn down in the 1920s to make way for high-class, often architecturally distinguished apartment houses. Many more were demolished between the beginning of World War II and the passage of the Landmarks Preservation Commission Law in 1965, as the southern end of the area gave way to midtown office development and the northern end to superscale apartment buildings.

In 1942 the Harry Payne Whitney house at 871 Fifth Avenue, on the northeast corner of Sixty-eight Street, fell to the wrecker's ball; it was originally designed for the sugar magnate Robert L. Stewart in 1884 by William Schickel and renovated for William C. Whitney in 1896–1904 by McKim, Mead & White to include what was claimed to be New York's largest private ballroom.[60] In 1945 the house of George Blumenthal (Trowbridge & Livingston, 1911), a financier and onetime president of the Metropolitan Museum of Art, became the first of many important Upper East Side townhouses to be demolished after World War II.[61] The destruction of the house, located on the southwest corner of Park Avenue and Seventieth Street, oc-

Above: Frieda Schiff Warburg Sculpture Garden, Brooklyn Museum, 200 Eastern Parkway, Institute Park, Brooklyn. Ian M. White, 1966. View to the east. BMA

Top right: George Blumenthal residence, southwest corner of Park Avenue and East Seventieth Street. Trowbridge & Livingston, 1911. View to the southwest. Wurts. MET

Center right: Velez Blanco Patio, George Blumenthal residence. Installation by Trowbridge & Livingston, 1911. MET

Bottom right: Velez Blanco Patio, Metropolitan Museum of Art, Fifth Avenue at East Eighty-second Street. Installation by Brown, Lawford & Forbes, 1964. View to the southeast. Stoller. ©ESTO

curred in a more complex manner than that of other houses which were simply reduced to rubble. In 1941 Blumenthal, who had decided to relinquish his mansion, rejected the idea of turning the house into a museum and bequeathed it and the land it occupied to the Metropolitan Museum of Art, stipulating that the gift was "for the purpose of (a) having my house dismantled, (b) having such structural parts of my house as can be advantageously installed in the present buildings of its Museum or in the buildings hereafter to be erected by it transferred to and installed in such buildings, (c) having the rest of the structural parts of my house disposed of in such manner as it may see fit."[62] Francis Henry Taylor, writing in the *Metropolitan Museum of Art Bulletin*, compared the collection to that of Isabella Stewart Gardner's celebrated Fenway Court in Boston and characterized Blumenthal's gift as "certainly the largest, richest, and most catholic group of works of art to be received in many years [and] a worthy complement to its predecessors." Taylor added that "the value of the collection rests not alone in the objects themselves; it is in the liberality and vision of the testator, who, after years of practical experience as President of the Museum, placed no restrictions upon his gift."[63]

Among Blumenthal's gifts were major portions of an early-sixteenth-century Spanish patio built as part of a castle by the Marquis of Velez between 1506 and 1515 on the foundations of a Moorish fortress. By the nineteenth century the castle had been virtually abandoned and left to fall into ruins. In 1904 a French interior decorator and art dealer purchased the patio, which incorporated delicate carvings by Italian sculptors specially brought in to do the work, and transported it to Paris, where he sought an American buyer; sparked by the work of such architects as Charles McKim and Stanford White, the American market for Renaissance objects and architectural elements was strong. Blumenthal purchased the patio and installed it as part of his house.

When the Blumenthal house was sold, the so-called Velez Blanco Patio was dismantled and its 2,000 marble blocks catalogued and put into storage. In 1964, after more than five years of intensive study, including site research in Spain, the patio was reassembled in a manner as close as possible to its original condition. The two-story patio, crudely glazed over to provide environmental control, was turned into an exhibition area as well as the entrance to the museum's Renaissance galleries and the new Thomas J. Watson Library. "To the moony-minded it may appeal as a bit of picturesque old Spain transported to Fifth Avenue," the critic John Canaday said of the patio. "Avant-gardists may feel safer in rationalizing it as a prototype of the experiments in walk-in art called 'environments.'"[64]

Although the Velez Blanco Patio was saved, the loss of the rest of the Blumenthal house and its replacement by 710 Park Avenue, an apartment building designed by Sylvan Bien and completed in 1948, had a profoundly negative effect on the surrounding stretch of Park Avenue, where the mansion, along with other imposing houses, a few churches and clubs and the Seventh Regiment Armory, had given the area a low, almost intimate scale.

Many other landmark-quality east side townhouses would be demolished in the postwar years. In 1947 the destroyed houses included 640 Fifth Avenue (John B. Snook and Charles Atwood, 1879–82), on the northwest corner of Fifth Avenue and Fifty-second street, which William Henry Vanderbilt built for his two daughters, Margaret Vanderbilt Shepard and Emily Vanderbilt Sloane, and their families;[65] and, to make way for Best & Company's new department store, the mansionlike for-

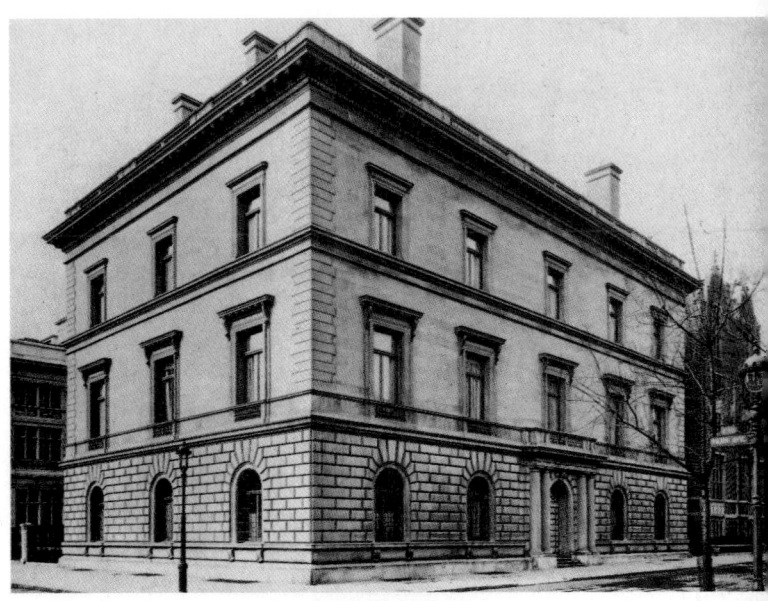

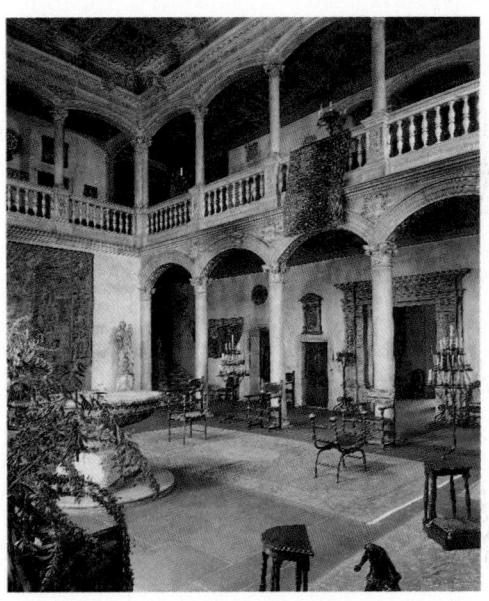

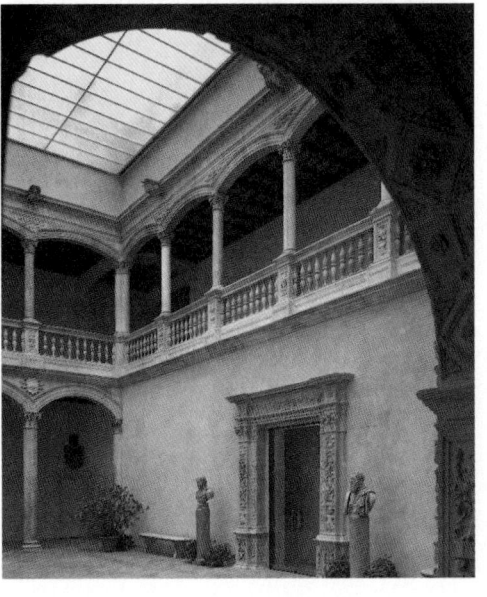

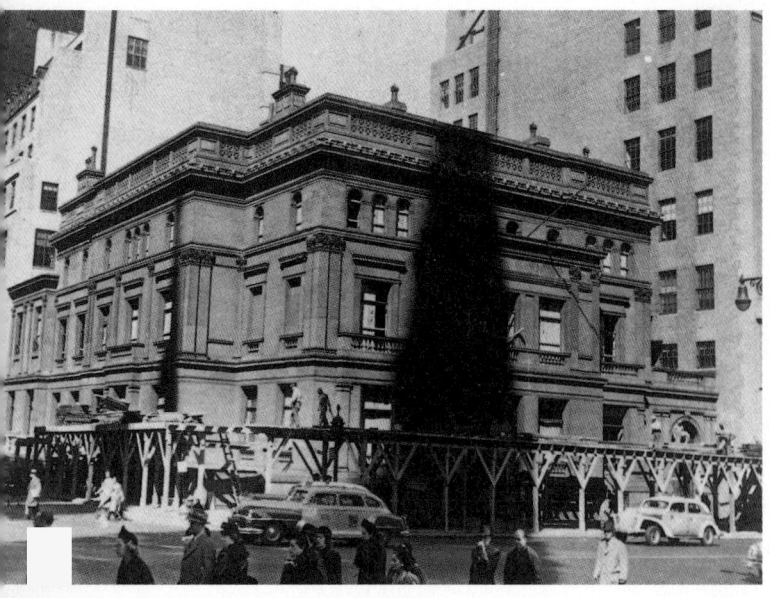

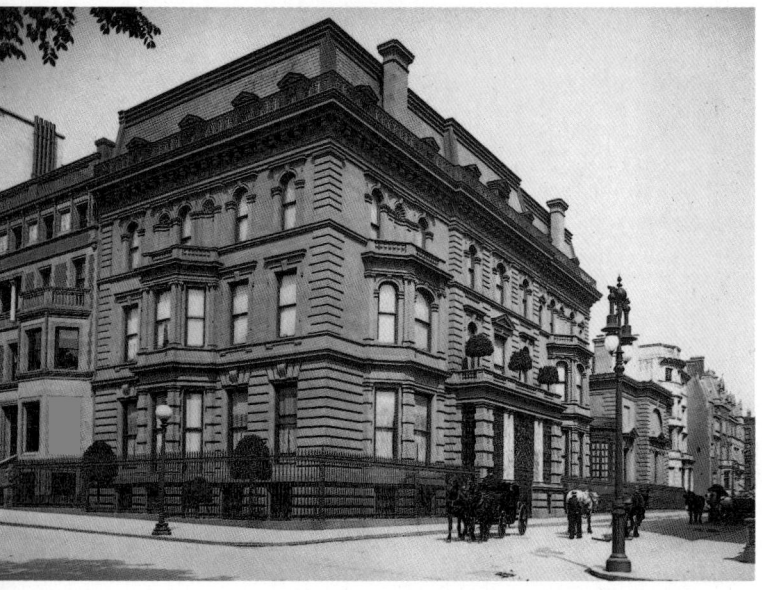

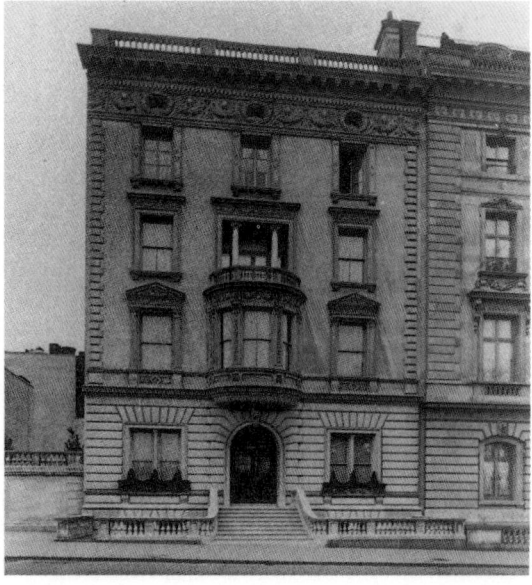

mer home of the Union Club (Cass Gilbert and John DuFais, 1902), on the northeast corner of Fifth Avenue and Fifty-first Street.[66] These were followed in the next four years by the Robert L. Stuart house (William Schickel, 1884; altered for William C. Whitney by McKim, Mead & White, 1897)[67] and the M. C. Inman house (R. H. Robertson, 1882),[68] both located on Fifth Avenue between Sixty-eighth and Sixty-ninth streets, which gave way to W. I. Hohauser's 870 Fifth Avenue (1949); the Thomas Fortune Ryan house (William Schickel & Company, 1893–95)[69] and the Charles Tyson Yerkes house (R. H. Robertson, 1893–96),[70] which were replaced by Sylvan Bien's 860 Fifth Avenue (1950); the George H. Warren house (Warren & Wetmore, 1902–3), at 924 Fifth Avenue, between Seventy-third and Seventy-fourth streets, replaced by Sylvan Bien's 923 Fifth Avenue (1951);[71] a group of brownstones and studio buildings at 571–591 Madison Avenue that had been renovated by J. D. Leland & Company in 1922 to serve the needs of the American Art Association and Gallery and were replaced by 575 Madison Avenue, a twenty-six-story office building (Emery Roth & Sons, 1961);[72] and the Sophie A. Sherman house (William H. Russell, 1892–94), on Fifth Avenue between Sixty-fourth and Sixty-fifth streets, to make way for Harry M. Prince's office building for the Union of American Hebrew Congregations (1950).[73]

In 1953 the Lloyd S. Bryce house (Ogden Codman, 1906), on the east blockfront of Fifth Avenue between Eighty-third and Eighty-fourth streets, was replaced by a new apartment building known as 1025 Fifth Avenue; to make way for the new building, a modest frame house at 3 East Eighty-third Street (1853–62), one of the area's few remaining such buildings, was also torn down.[74] That same year, the mansionlike Duveen Gallery (Rene Sargent in association with Horace Trumbauer, 1911), on the northwest corner of Fifth Avenue and Fifty-sixth Street, was demolished and replaced by an office building designed by Emery Roth & Sons. Henry Hope Reed, Jr.'s juxtaposition of the house and the office building in his book *The Golden City* was particularly telling.[75] In 1954 the Jonathan and Frederick Sturges houses (Gambrill & Richardson, 1869–70), at 38 Park Avenue and 40 East Thirty-sixth Street, were demolished and replaced by an apartment house.[76] The Florence Vanderbilt Twombly house (Warren & Wetmore, 1926), located on Fifth Avenue between Seventy-first and Seventy-second streets, was demolished in 1958 to make way for a twenty-story apartment building by Sylvan and Robert Bien.[77] In 1959 an apartment building, 1070 Fifth Avenue (J. E. R. Carpenter, 1929),[78] fell along with a former townhouse next door at number 1071 (Babb, Cook & Willard, 1898) to make way for the Solomon R. Guggenheim Museum. That same year the Arthur Curtiss James house (Allen & Collens, 1916), located on the northwest corner of Park Avenue and Sixty-ninth Street, was torn down and replaced by an apartment building, 700 Park Avenue, designed by Kahn & Jacobs and Paul Resnick and Harry F. Green.[79] In 1961 the George J. Gould house (Horace Trumbauer, 1907–9), on the northeast corner of Fifth Avenue and Sixty-seventh Street, was replaced by Robert Bien's 857 Fifth Avenue (1963).[80] In 1962 the Arthur C. Train house (George B. Post & Sons, 1906–8), at 113 East Seventy-fourth Street, between Park and Lexington avenues, was rebuilt by Brown, Lawford & Forbes for the Buckley School.[81] In 1963 the Princeton Club (a large townhouse remodeled by Aymar Embury II in 1923), on the northwest corner of Park Avenue and Thirty-ninth Street, was replaced by Emery Roth & Sons' 90 Park Avenue office building.[82]

With the destruction of the Isaac Vail Brokaw family houses—1 East Seventy-ninth Street (Rose & Stone, 1887–90),

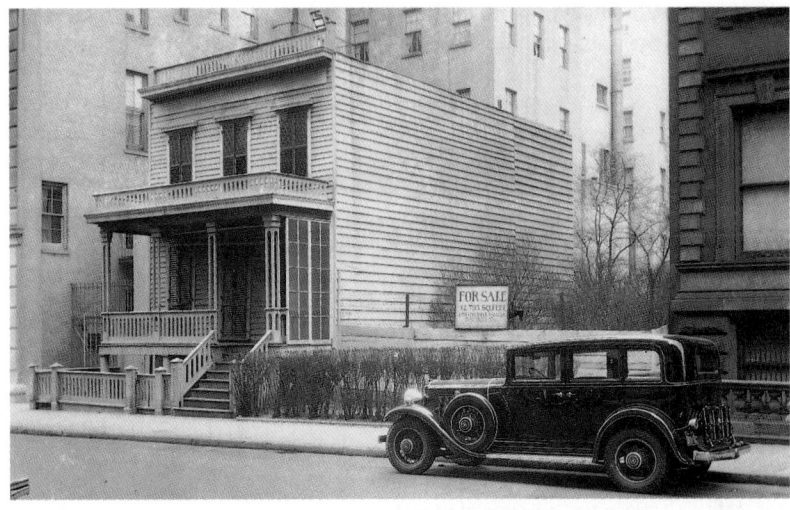

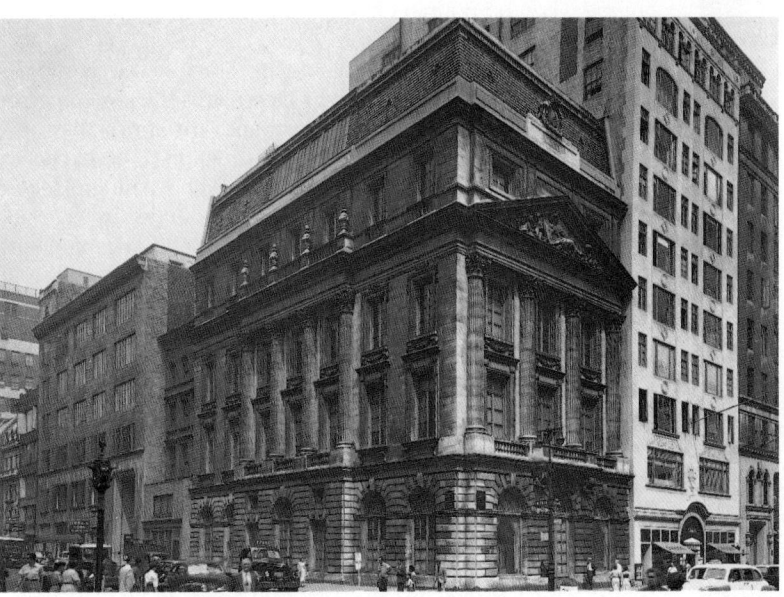

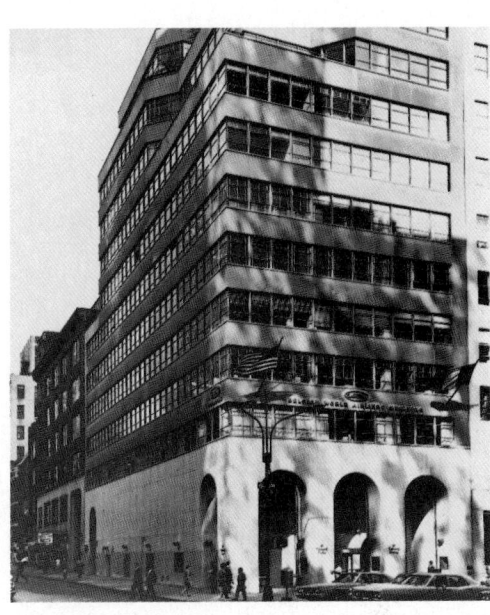

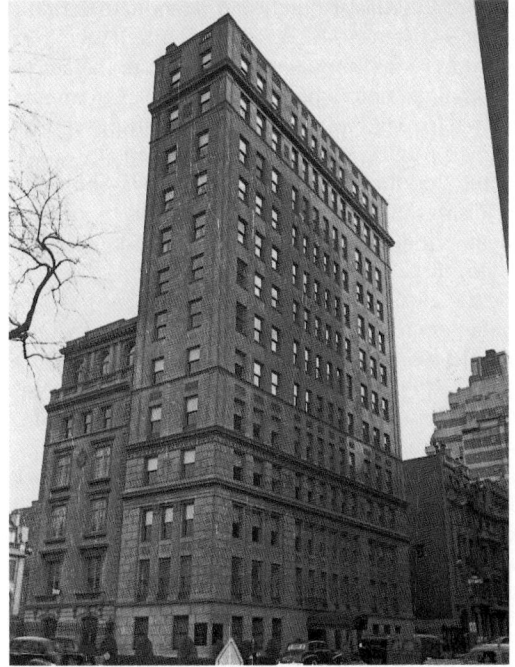

Top far left: Elliot F. Shepard and William D. Sloane residence, 640 Fifth Avenue, northwest corner of West Fifty-first Street. John B. Snook and Charles Atwood, 1879–82. View to the northwest during demolition in 1947, showing shadow of St. Patrick's Cathedral (James Renwick, Jr., 1878). Wide World. NYP

Center far left: Robert L. Stuart residence (later William C. Whitney residence), 871 Fifth Avenue, northeast corner of East Sixty-eighth Street. William Schickel, 1884; altered for William C. Whitney by McKim, Mead & White, 1897. View to the northeast also showing M. C. Inman residence (R. H. Robertson, 1882) on the left, ca. 1900. Byron. MCNY

Bottom far left: Thomas Fortune Ryan residence, 858 Fifth Avenue, between East Sixty-seventh and East Sixty-eighth streets. William Schickel & Company, 1893–95. View to the east. Levick. NYP

Top: 3 East Eighty-third Street, between Fifth and Madison avenues. 1853–62. View to the northwest, 1932. MCNY

Center left: Duveen Gallery, 720 Fifth Avenue, northwest corner of West Fifty-sixth Street. Rene Sargent in association with Horace Trumbauer, 1911. View to the northwest, ca. 1950. OMH

Center right: 720 Fifth Avenue, northwest corner of West Fifty-sixth Street. Emery Roth & Sons, 1954. View to the northwest showing Hallmark Card store (Edward Durell Stone, 1965). HHR

Bottom: View to the northeast showing George H. Penniman residence (Babb, Cook & Willard, 1898), 1071 Fifth Avenue, between East Eighty-eighth and East Eighty-ninth streets, on the left, and 1070 Fifth Avenue (J. E. R. Carpenter, 1929), northeast corner of East Eighty-eighth Street, in the center, 1940. MA

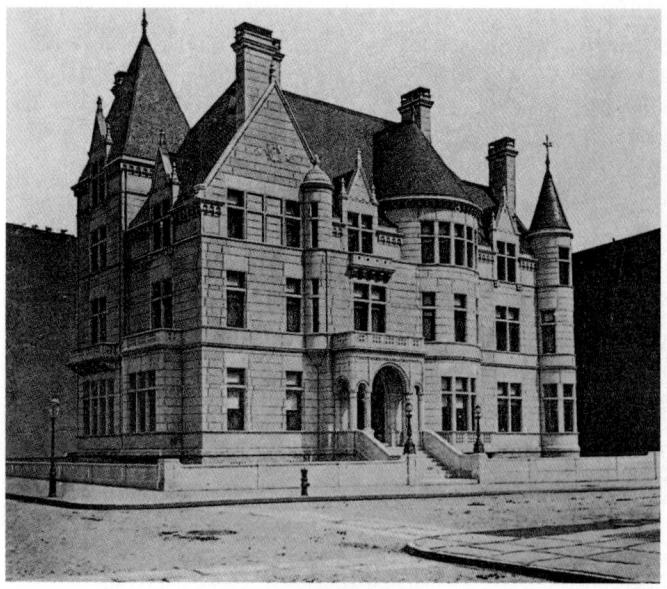

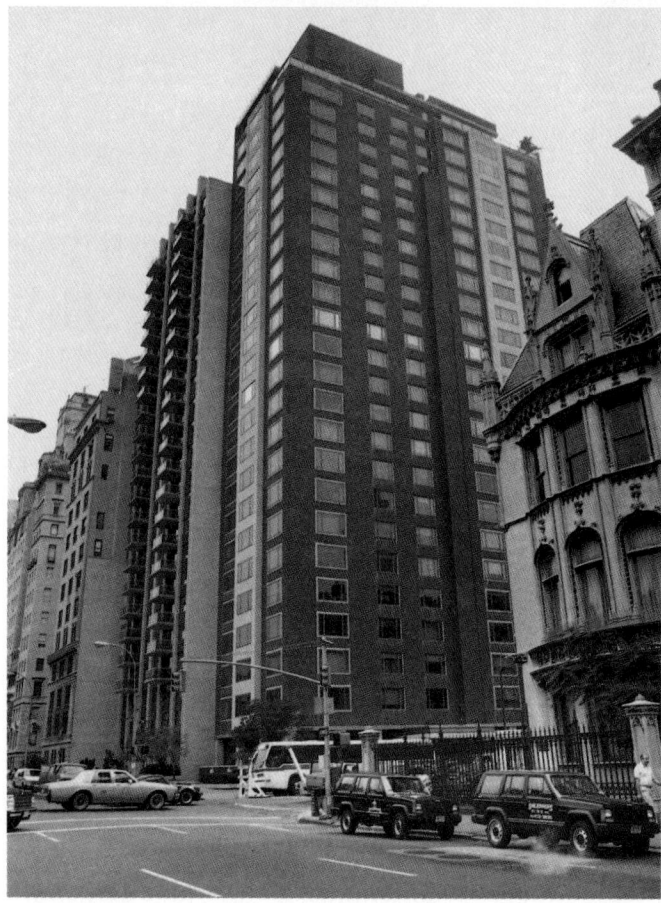

Top: Isaac Vail Brokaw residence, 1 East Seventy-ninth Street, northeast corner of Fifth Avenue. Rose & Stone, 1887–90. View to the northeast, 1893. AABN. CU

Bottom: View to the northeast of 980 Fifth Avenue (Paul Resnick and Harry F. Green, 1966), northeast corner of East Seventy-ninth Street, in the center, and 985 Fifth Avenue (Wechsler & Schimenti, 1970), between East Seventy-ninth and East Eightieth streets, on the left. NYP

984 Fifth Avenue (Charles Frederic Rose, 1905) and 7 East Seventy-ninth Street (H. Van Buren Magonigle, 1911)—to make way for two undistinguished high-rise apartment towers, the public began to lose its temper. Strong opposition to the demolition emerged when it was first announced in September 1964.[83] "The devastation of New York City's gracious older structures to make way for speculative make-a-buck buildings continued to read like a serial episode of 'Perils of Pauline,'" wrote the editors of *Progressive Architecture*, "with the difference that in each perilous incident in Manhattan the threat is actually carried through: Pauline really falls off the cliff, is rent asunder by the buzz saw, or perishes in the flooded cellar."[84] The demolition was begun rather surreptitiously on a Saturday in February 1965. As Ada Louise Huxtable noted, Saturday was "not a normal building trades working day," and she explained: "The Campagna Construction Corporation, the owners and builders of a new apartment house on the site, were taking no chances. It was a dandy way to do enough massive damage at a time when no normal channels are functioning, to assure the building's doom."[85]

Across town, on the west side, declining real estate values brought at least one bright note: as townhouses were converted to apartments and single-room-occupancy dwellings, there was much mutilation but little outright destruction. One exception was the loss in 1948 of the Schwab mansion (Maurice Hébert, 1901–7), which occupied the entire block bounded by Riverside Drive and West End Avenue, Seventy-third and Seventy-fourth streets.[86] Three years later the building that had once housed Columbia University's College of Physicians and Surgeons (W. Wheeler Smith, 1886), on the north side of Fifty-ninth Street between Ninth and Tenth avenues, was replaced by a parking lot.[87] A large-scale fire ravaged St. Andrew's Methodist Episcopal Church (J. C. Cady, 1889), at 120 West Seventy-sixth Street; when it was rebuilt to serve the needs of the West Side Institutional Synagogue in 1958, the building's original roof and steeple were not replaced, robbing it of much visual interest.[88] Another victim of fire, the Church of St. Matthew and St. Timothy (William Halsey Wood, 1893), at 26 West Eighty-fourth Street, which burned in 1965, was torn down and replaced.[89] In 1963 two adjoining townhouses at 331–332 Riverside Drive became the New York Buddhist Church and American Buddhist Academy. Number 331 (Janes & Leo, 1902), formerly occupied by William Randolph Hearst's longtime companion, the actress Marion Davies, remained untouched on its exterior, but number 332 was demolished to make way for an Oriental-inspired structure whose entrance portico sheltered a monumentally scaled bronze statue of the Buddhist sect's founder, Shinran-Shonin.[90]

The theater district was particularly devastated by demolition, with the theaters that clustered around Times Square giving way sometimes to office buildings but more often to parking lots. One by one the glorious monuments to high times in New York's Metropolitan era fell to a new, far less ebullient image of urban life. In the 1940s the demolished theaters included the Forty-ninth Street Theater (Herbert J. Krapp, 1921), at 235 West Forty-ninth Street;[91] the Comedy Theater (D. G. Malcolm, 1909), at 108 West Forty-first Street;[92] and the Forty-fourth Street Theater (William A. Swasey, 1913), at 216 West Forty-fourth Street.[93] In 1951 the Belmont Theater (De Rosa & Pereira, 1918), at 123 West Forty-eighth Street, was demolished;[94] in 1953 the Empire Theater (John B. McElfatrick & Son, 1893), at 1430 Broadway, gave way to an office building designed by Emery Roth & Sons;[95] and in 1954 the Avon Theater (Eugene De Rosa, 1921), at 251 West Forty-fifth Street, was torn down.[96] That

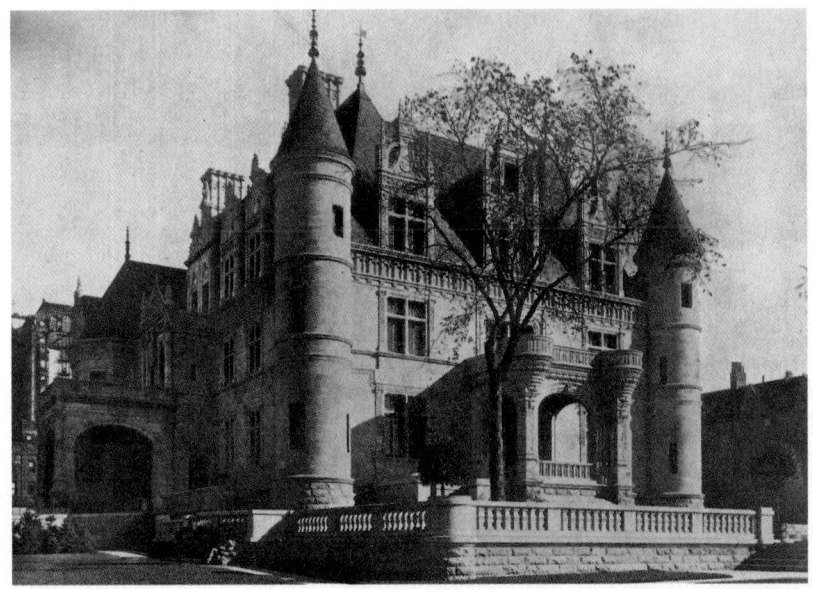

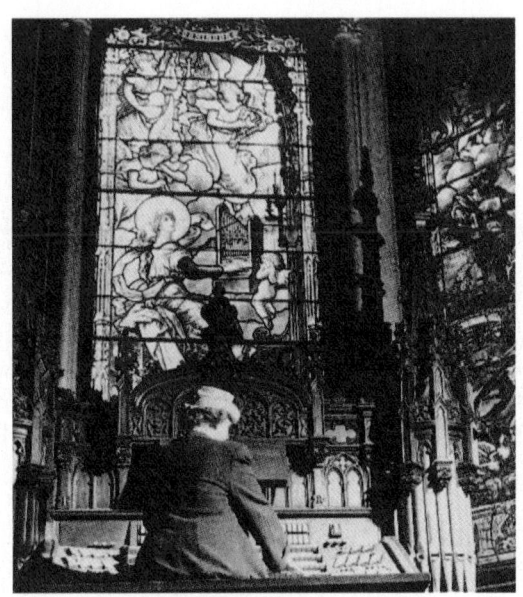

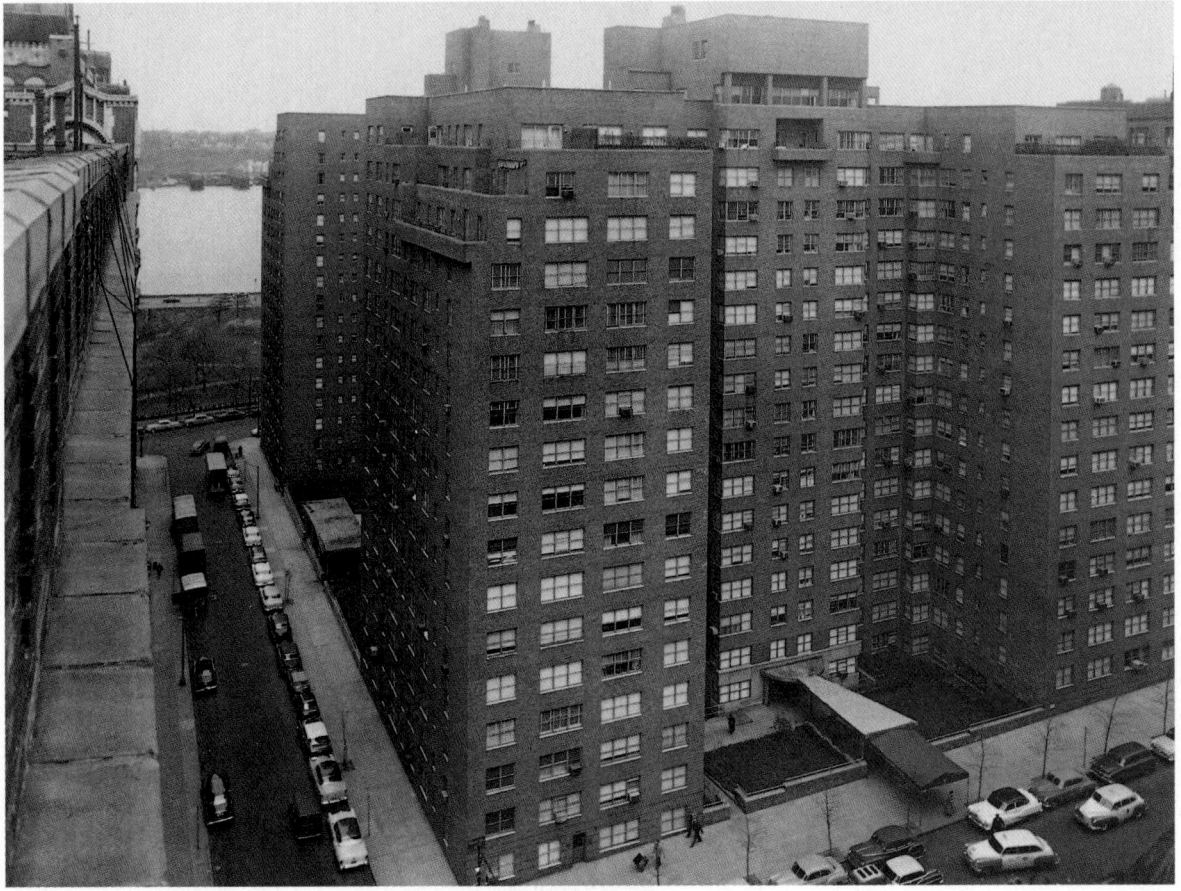

Top left: Schwab residence, Riverside Drive to West End Avenue, West
Seventy-third to West Seventy-fourth Street. Maurice Hébert, 1901–7.
View to the northeast, 1905. AABN. CU

Top right: Schwab residence. View of chapel, 1947. NYP

Bottom: Schwab House, 11 Riverside Drive, Riverside Drive to West
End Avenue, West Seventy-third to West Seventy-fourth Street. Sylvan
Bien, 1950. View to the northwest. OMH

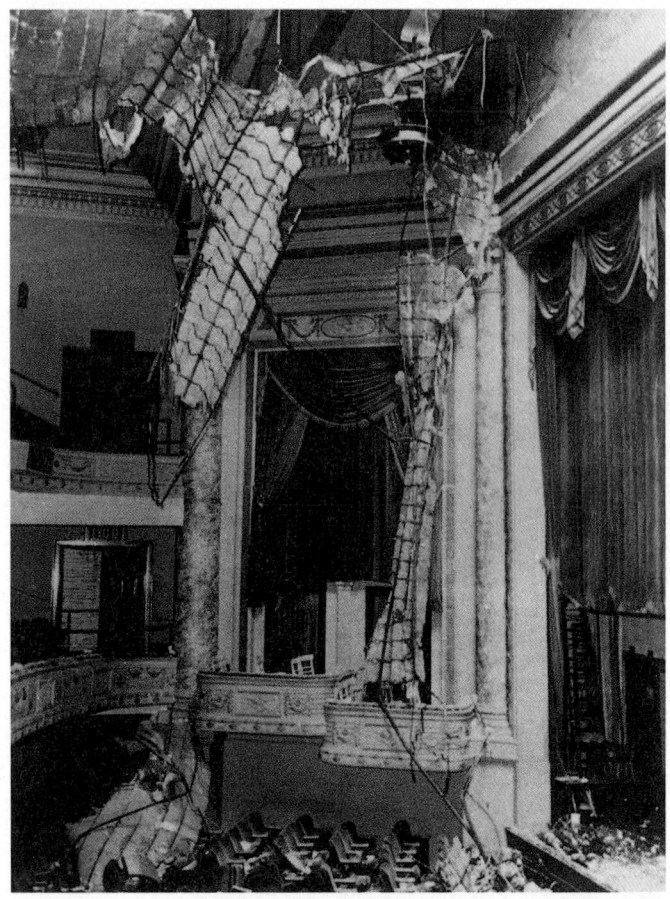

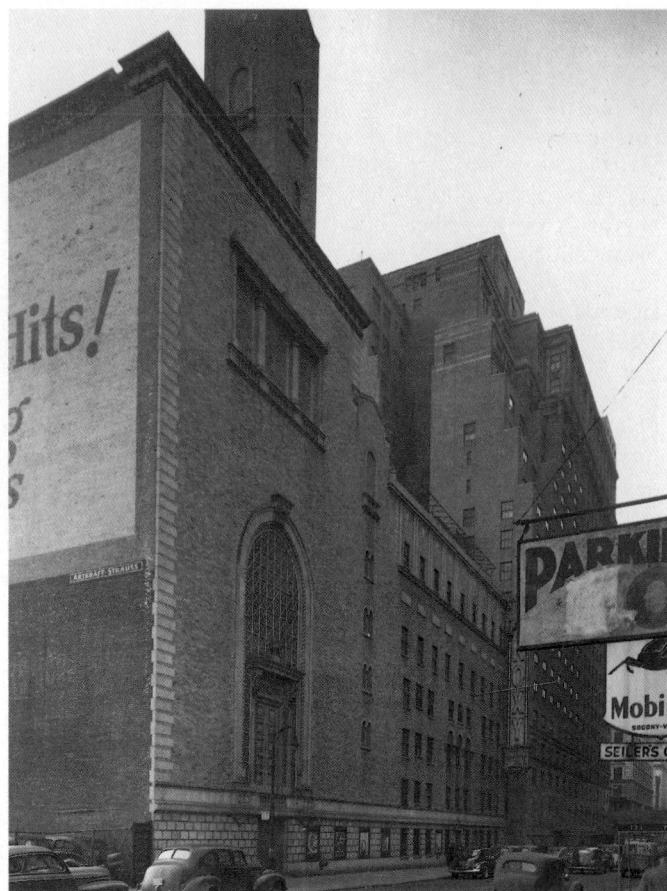

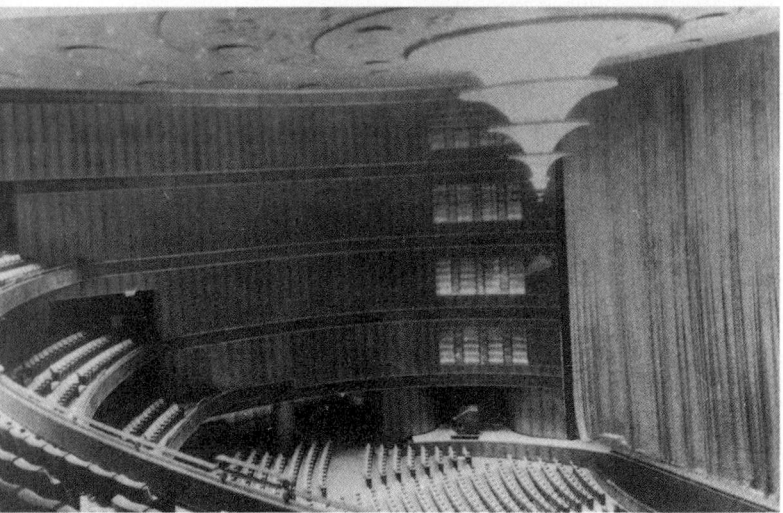

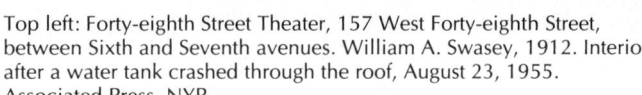

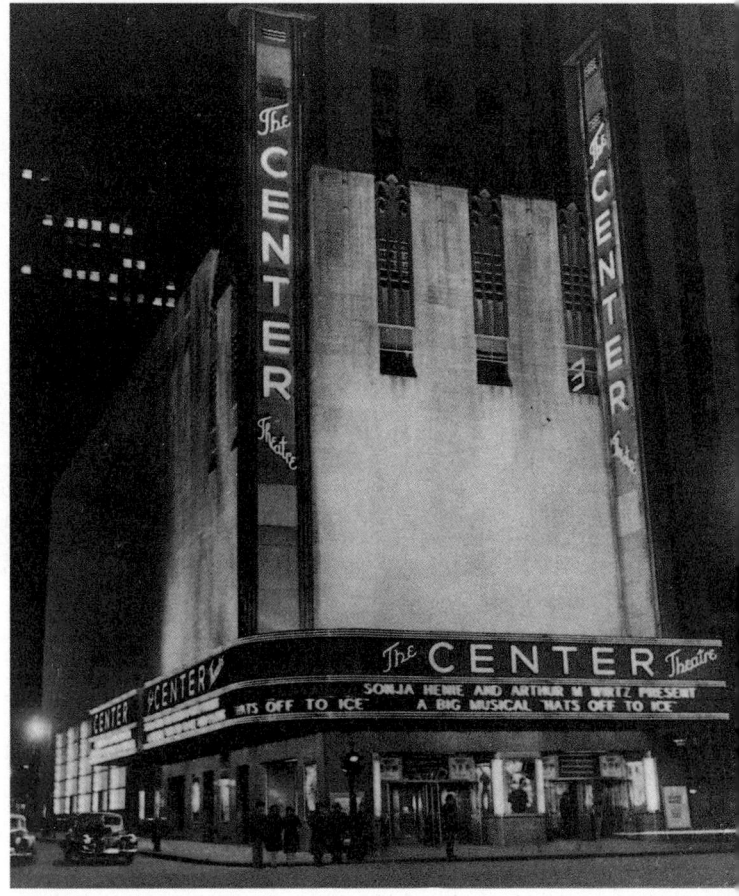

Top left: Forty-eighth Street Theater, 157 West Forty-eighth Street, between Sixth and Seventh avenues. William A. Swasey, 1912. Interior after a water tank crashed through the roof, August 23, 1955. Associated Press. NYP

Top right: Roxy Theater, West Fiftieth to West Fifty-first Street, between Sixth and Seventh avenues. Walter Ahlschlager, 1927. View to the southwest along West Fifty-first street, ca. 1940. OMH

Bottom left: Center Theater, southeast corner of Sixth Avenue and West Forty-ninth Street. Associated Architects and Eugene Schoen, 1932. Interior. NYP

Bottom right: Center Theater. View to the southeast, 1946. Associated Press. NYP same year the city also lost Rockefeller Center's 3,500-seat Center Theater, originally called the RKO Roxy (Associated Architects; interior design by Eugene Schoen, 1932), located on a midblock site east of Sixth Avenue between Forty-eighth and Forty-ninth streets; the theater was converted into offices.[97] Also in 1954 the International Theater, formerly the Cosmopolitan Theater and originally the Park Theater (John H. Duncan, 1904), at Five Columbus Circle, was torn down to make way for the monumentally banal New York Coliseum.[98] The theater had been inventively redesigned in 1923 by Joseph Urban and was later restored with funds provided by the Marquis de Cuevas before ultimately falling to the wrecker's ball.[99] In 1955 the Forty-eighth Street Theater (William A. Swasey, 1912), at 157 West Forty-eighth Street, and the Princess Theater (William A. Swasey, 1913), at 104 West Thirty-ninth Street, fell;[100] in 1959 Maxine Elliott's Theater (1908), at 109 West Thirty-ninth Street, designed by the Chicago firm of Marshall & Fox, was also lost.[101] The Roxy Theater (Walter Ahlschlager, 1927), located on a midblock site extending from Fiftieth to Fifty-first Street between Sixth and Seventh avenues, was demolished in 1960 for the construction of the Time & Life Building and a restaurant and parking garage serving the Hotel Taft.[102] The demolition of the legendary theater was later lamented by the theater historian Ben M. Hall, who said that the Roxy "vanished in a pile of rubble and dust and some shards of gold-leafed plaster of Paris. Fallow ground where only an office building could grow marked the realm where romance and adventure flourished, where magic and charm united us all to worship at beauty's throne."[103] The sense of loss inspired by the Roxy's demolition was brilliantly captured in a photograph by Eliot Elisofon, first published in *Life* magazine, portraying the aging actress Gloria Swanson, her arms plaintively outstretched, cloaked in a black evening dress and feather boa, standing amid the ruins of the theater.[104]

Perhaps the greatest architectural loss to the Times Square area was that of the twenty-six-story Times Tower (Cyrus L. W. Eidlitz, 1904).[105] Preservation of the building was virtually assured by changes in the city's zoning laws that made maintaining the building's structure more profitable than demolishing it—a new building on the site could not have been as big—and in 1963 the Allied Chemical Corporation purchased the building from the *New York Times*. In 1965, however, the building's Giottoesque facades were lost when the corporation hired Eidlitz's successor firm, Smith, Smith, Haines, Lundberg & Waehler, to renovate the building. The architects reclad the structure in five-inch-thick concrete panels faced with less than an inch of Imperial Danby marble quarried in Vermont, a treatment that the editors of *Progressive Architecture* called "a face-lifting job of thorough-going blandness."[106] The new Allied Chemical Tower, which looked at once too self-consciously pristine and too shoddy for its surroundings, was strikingly out of place within the vibrant if vulgar environment of Times Square; only the famous moving sign that flashed the day's major headlines, an element that was retained from the old tower, related effectively to the context. A 1975 proposal, designed by Gwathmey Siegel, to reclad the building with reflective glass and add a sharply sloping clear glass roof was never realized.[107] A multicolored, forty-by-twenty-foot electrical sign was added in 1976.[108]

The loss of the city's great theaters was not confined to the Times Square area. In 1962 the "atmospheric" Loew's Seventy-second Street Theater (Thomas Lamb and John Eberson, 1932), on the southwest corner of Third Avenue, was demolished to

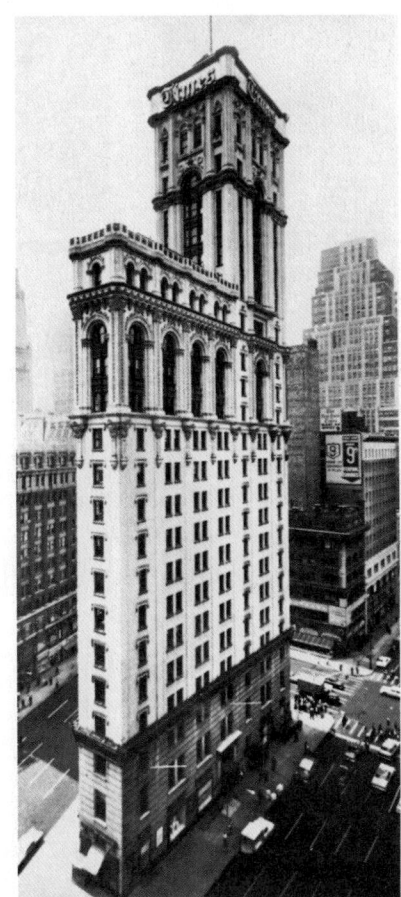

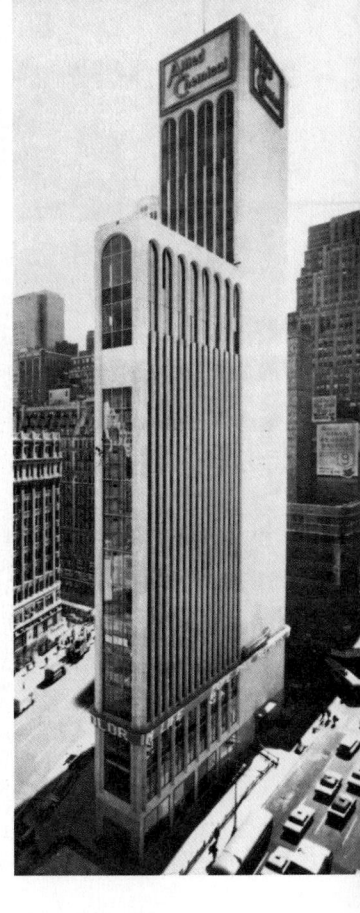

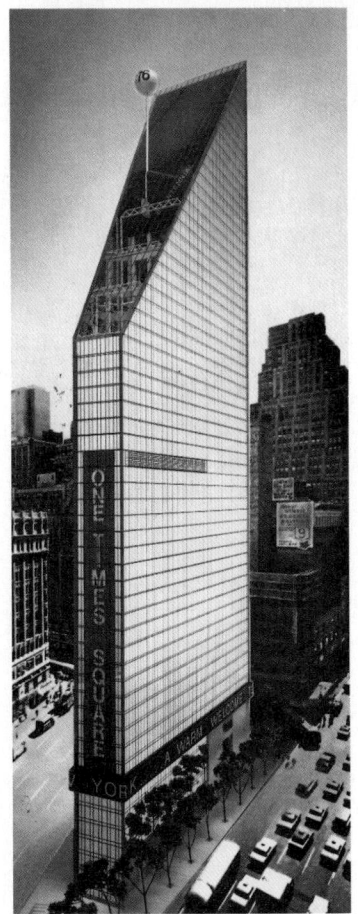

Top left: Times Tower, bounded by Broadway, Seventh Avenue and West Forty-second Street. Cyrus L. W. Eidlitz, 1904. View to the southeast, ca. 1960. GSA

Top right: Allied Chemical Tower (formerly Times Tower), bounded by Broadway, Seventh Avenue and West Forty-second Street. Cyrus L. W. Eidlitz, 1904; renovation, Smith, Smith, Haines, Lundberg & Waehler, 1965. View to the southeast. GSA

Bottom: Proposal for renovation of Allied Chemical Tower (formerly Times Tower). Gwathmey Siegel, 1975. Photographic montage. View to the southeast. GSA

1103

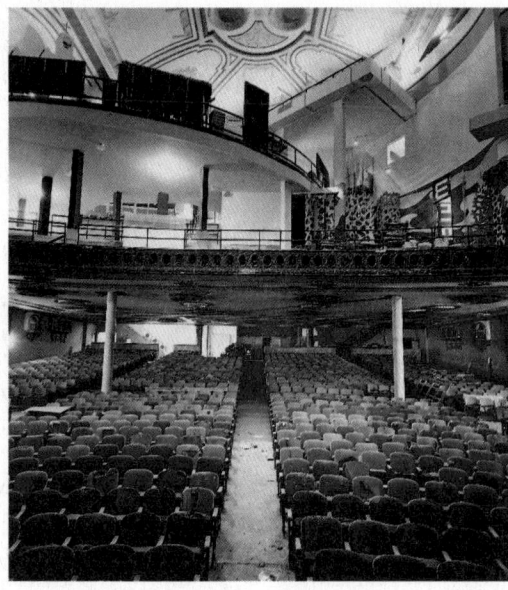

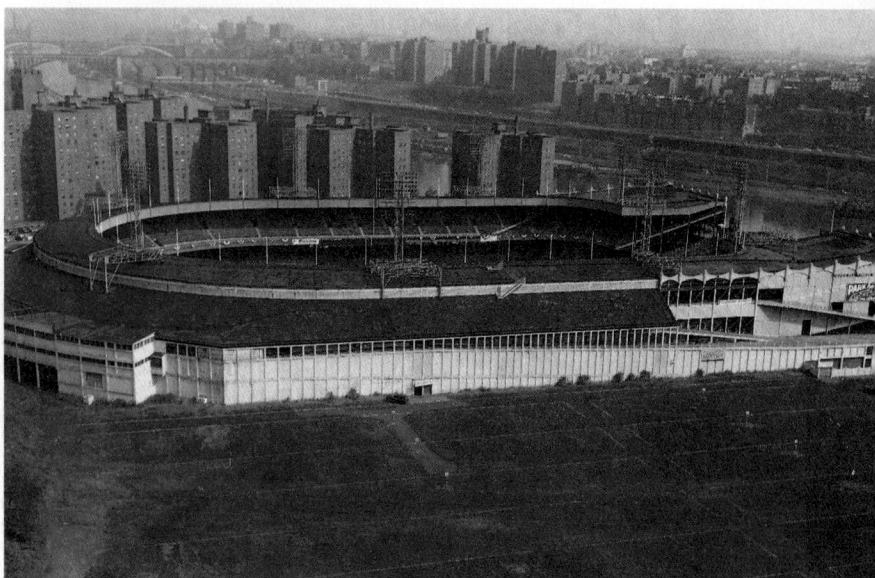

Above: Bronx Cultural Ethnic Center (formerly Fairmount Theater), 708 East Tremont Avenue, East Tremont, the Bronx. Joseph Orlando, 1928; renovation, Hardy Holzman Pfeiffer, 1972. Interior. ©Norman McGrath. NM

Top right: Polo Grounds, bounded by Eighth Avenue, West 155th Street and Edgecombe Avenue, Highbridge Park and the East River. Henry B. Herts, 1912. View to the northeast, 1959. NYCHA

Center right: Polo Grounds. Demolition with construction workers on left, 1964. NYCHA

Bottom right: Polo Grounds Houses, bounded by Harlem River Drive, West 155th Street and Harlem River Driveway. Ballard Todd Associates, 1968. View to the west. NYCHA

Top far right: Murray Hill Hotel, west blockfront of Park Avenue, East Fortieth to East Forty-first Street. Stephen D. Hatch, 1883. View to the southwest, ca. 1940. OMH

Center far right: Ritz-Carlton Hotel, west blockfront of Madison Avenue, East Forty-sixth to East Forty-seventh Street. Warren & Wetmore, 1910. View to the southwest, 1949. Wide World. NYP

Bottom far right: Ritz-Carlton Hotel. Japanese tea garden. OMH

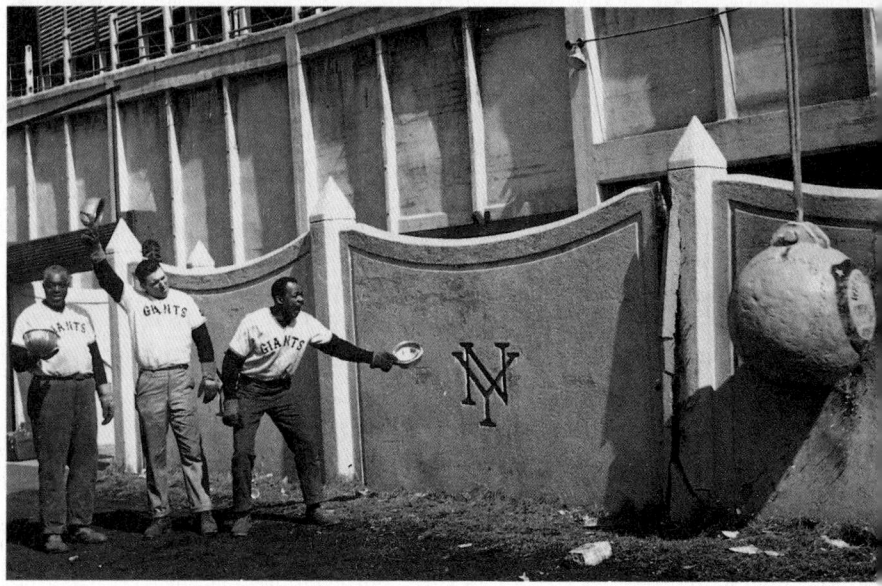

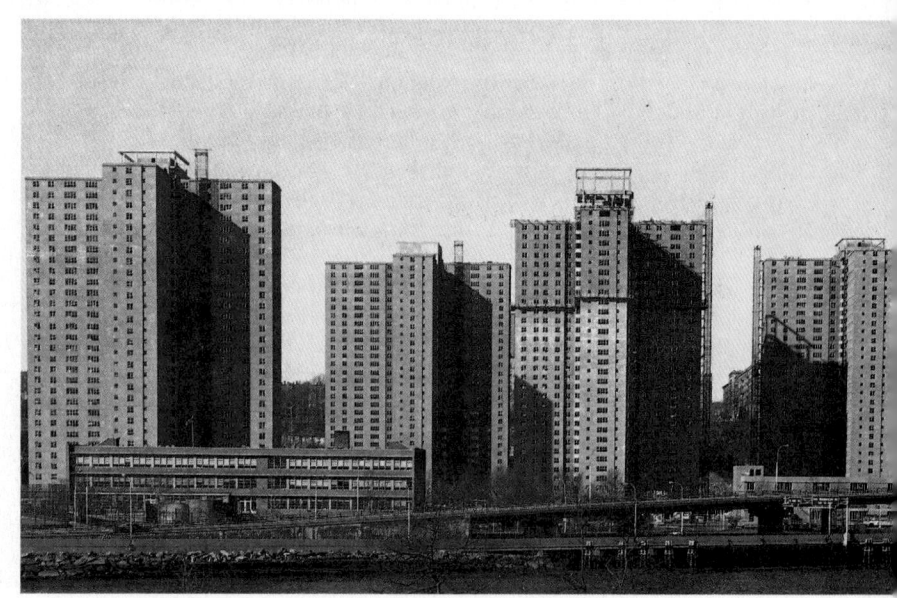

make way for the Tower East apartment house;[109] Proctor's New Fifty-eighth Street Theater (Thomas Lamb, 1928), located on Lexington Avenue, gave way to Alexander's department store in 1965;[110] and Loew's Sheridan Theater (P. C. Reilly and Douglas P. Hall, 1920), located on a triangular site bounded by West Twelfth Street, Seventh and Greenwich avenues, was demolished in 1970 to be replaced first by a garden, known as the Village Garden, and eventually by the Materials Handling Center of St. Vincent's Hospital (Ferrenz, Taylor, Clark & Associates, 1987).[111]

In 1963 Harlem's Casino, on the northeast corner of 124th Street and Seventh Avenue, built in the 1890s and converted to a movie theater in 1910 by the architect S. S. Sugar, became home to the Church of Our Lord Jesus Christ of the Apostolic Faith.[112] Renovated by Costas Machlouzarides, the theater interior was gutted and the second balcony and boxes removed. Reemerging as the Greater Refuge Temple, the grand space culminated in a fifty-foot-high, onion-shaped dome. In 1969, after a fire destroyed the four-month-old home of Harlem's New Lafayette Theater, at 137th Street and Seventh Avenue, Hardy Holzman Pfeiffer converted the interior of the former Renaissance Theater without severely compromising the original outline.[113] In addition, an art gallery that could also serve as a community meeting hall was carved out of the existing space. In 1972 an ornately decorated, cavernous movie palace, the Fairmount Theater (Joseph Orlando, 1928), located at 708 East Tremont Avenue in the Bronx, was also preserved by Hardy Holzman Pfeiffer, who reconfigured the interior to serve as the Bronx Cultural Ethnic Center, housing an auditorium, offices, classrooms and exhibition space.[114] The Brooklyn Paramount (Rapp & Rapp, 1928) was adapted in 1962 by the architect Lionel K. Levy to serve as the Arnold and Marie Schwartz Athletic Center of Long Island University.[115] (An adjacent office tower had been converted into Founder's Hall and Tristam W. Metcalf Hall in 1950.)

Several of the city's most popular sports facilities succumbed to the wrecker's ball as well. Brooklyn's pride received a shocking blow with the loss of an internationally celebrated symbol of New York life, Ebbets Field (C. A. Buskirk, 1913), home of the Brooklyn Dodgers baseball team until 1957; it was torn down three years later to make way for a huge apartment house.[116] In 1964 demolition began on another cherished symbol, Manhattan's Polo Grounds (Henry B. Herts, 1912), home of the New York Giants, who had relocated to San Francisco in 1958, and of the New York Mets for two years before they took up quarters in Shea Stadium in Queens; located at Eighth Avenue and 155th Street, the Polo Grounds were replaced by an undistinguished public housing project in 1968.[117] Yankee Stadium (Osborn Engineering Company, 1922–23), in the Bronx, remained intact, although it was renovated in 1976.

The toppling of some of New York's most elegant hotels—buildings that had symbolized the city's vitality, wealth and glamour—stunned residents and visitors alike. One after another, these world-famous hotels were demolished with no more than a fleeting and nostalgic public notice. The Murray Hill Hotel (Stephen D. Hatch, 1883), on the west side of Park Avenue between Fortieth and Forty-first streets, was torn down in 1947 to make way for 100 Park Avenue;[118] the Ritz-Carlton Hotel (Warren & Wetmore, 1910), on the west side of Madison Avenue between Forty-sixth and Forty-seventh streets, which had once housed an exotic Japanese tea garden, was sacrificed in 1951 to an office building;[119] the Hotel Renaissance (Clarence Luce, 1894; Howard & Cauldwell, 1898), on the

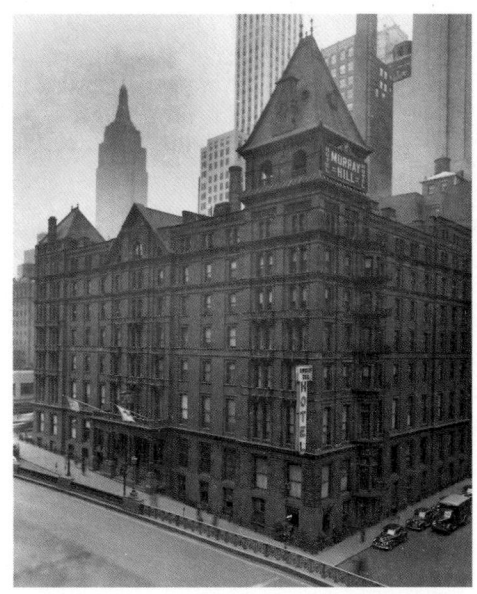

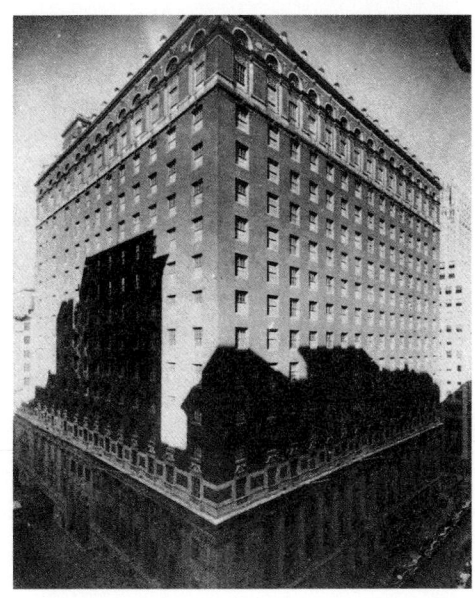

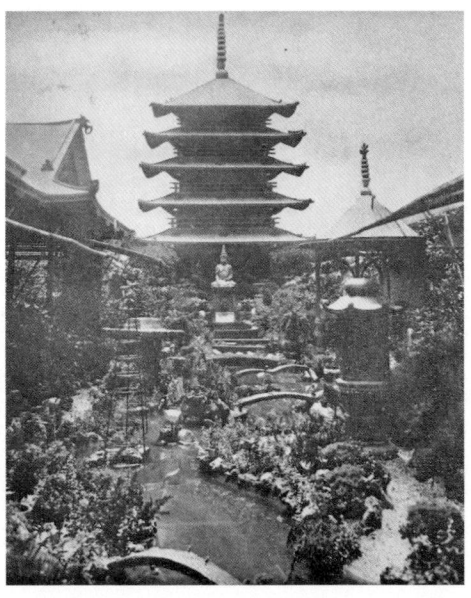

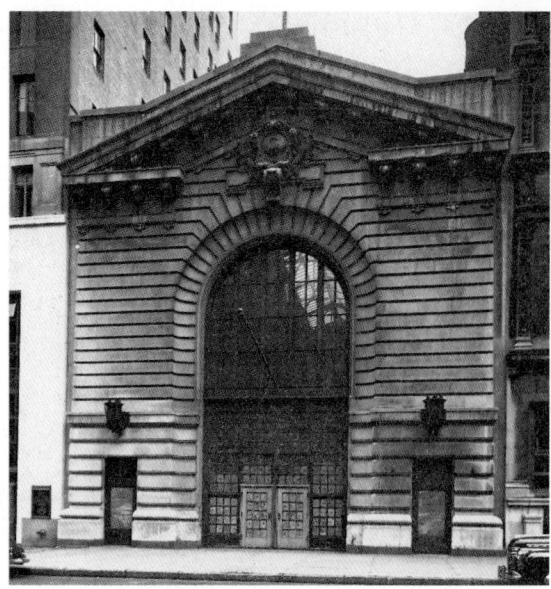

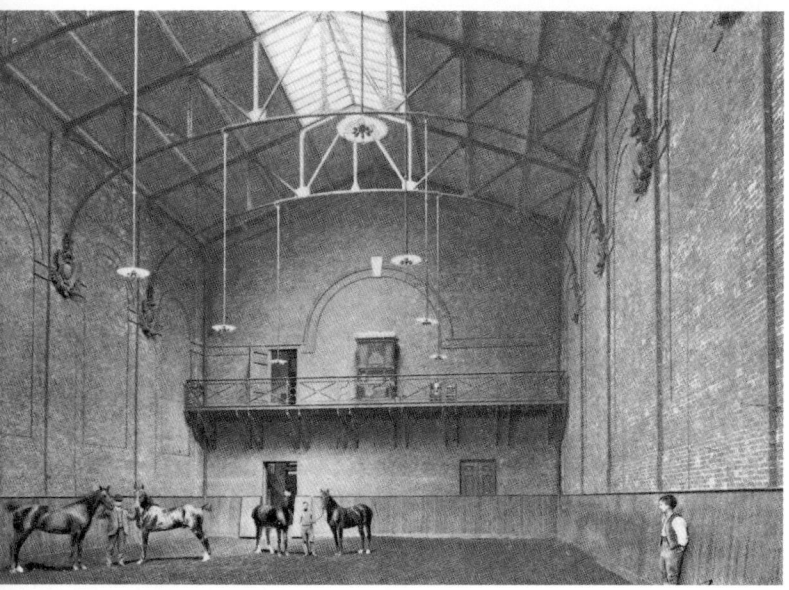

Top: Gould riding ring, 219 West Fifty-seventh Street, between Seventh and Eighth avenues. York & Sawyer, 1902. View to the north, ca. 1940. OMH

Bottom: Gould riding ring. Interior. CU

southwest corner of Forty-third Street and Fifth Avenue, was demolished in 1952 to make way for a Manufacturers Hanover Trust branch;[120] the Hotel Brevoort (converted from existing townhouses in 1854 by George Provot), on the northeast corner of Fifth Avenue and Eighth Street, gave way to an apartment house in 1954.[121] The Manhattan Hotel (Henry J. Hardenbergh, 1897; renovated for office use, McKim, Mead & White, 1922), on the northwest corner of Forty-second Street and Madison Avenue, was demolished in 1961 to make way for 330 Madison Avenue, a forty-one-story office building designed by Kahn & Jacobs.[122] The Marie Antoinette Hotel (Julius Munckowitz, 1895) and an annex (C. P. H. Gilbert, 1903), located on the west side of Broadway between Sixty-sixth and Sixty-seventh streets, which eventually became the Dauphin Hotel, were demolished in 1961 and 1962, respectively, and jointly replaced by a glass-and-metal office building.[123]

High-quality buildings of all types were destroyed, often to be replaced by less distinguished buildings.[124] McKim, Mead & White's terra-cotta-clad Herald Building (1893), occupying the full block bounded by Broadway, Sixth Avenue, Thirty-fifth and Thirty-sixth streets, was replaced in 1940 by a nondescript four-story commercial building designed by H. Craig Severance.[125] Several of the original building's decorative features, including two bronze bell ringers, were preserved and incorporated into a clock tower, designed by Aymar Embury II, that ornamented the small triangular sliver of parkland in Herald Square. The Cosmopolitan Productions Building, on the east side of Second Avenue between 127th and 128th streets, where studio head William Randolph Hearst had shot movies starring Marion Davies, was torn down in 1941 to make way for a bus garage.[126] Prior to demolition the building had served as a factory where the General Motors Futurama ride, exhibited at the 1939–40 World's Fair, was manufactured. In 1945 York & Sawyer's grandly Classical enclosed riding ring built for Frank Gould at 219 West Fifty-seventh Street, and used briefly as an automobile showroom, was demolished.[127] Even parks and park structures were destroyed. In 1946 Carrère & Hastings's elegantly articulated stone terraces and pavilion at Hudson Park, on the east side of Hudson Street between Clarkson Street and St. Luke's Place, were replaced by a softball field.[128]

In 1949 the St. Nicholas Collegiate Reformed Protestant Dutch Church (W. Wheeler Smith, 1872), on the northwest corner of Fifth Avenue and Forty-eighth Street, was demolished after considerable public debate to make way for the Sinclair Oil Building.[129] Three years before, the governing body of Reformed Protestant Dutch Churches of New York had announced it was considering the sale of the Gothic-style brownstone church, whose design was distinguished by an elegantly tapered spire that, according to John A. Bradley in the New York Times, "many declare . . . the most beautiful in this country."[130] The church's congregation, which was the oldest in Manhattan, dating back to 1628, immediately protested the proposed sale and demolition. The church's pastor, the Rev. Dr. Joseph R. Sizoo, argued that selling the building was tantamount to "putting the dollar sign before the cross. . . . This is not another church. It is a shrine."[131] Although the initial proposal ultimately fell through, Sizoo resigned his position and a majority of the congregation withdrew from the church over the issue. A second, similar proposal was presented and approved, and the building was torn down.

In 1951 the former Tiffany & Company Building (McKim, Mead & White, 1906), on the southeast corner of Fifth Avenue and Thirty-seventh Street, which had been used as a Red Cross training center since the jeweler's move to Fifty-seventh Street in 1940, was significantly "modernized" by Charles and Selig Whinston.[132] Large display windows were cut into the ground-floor masonry facades; the opulent, high-ceilinged lobby was divided into two floors; and the main entrance was moved to the side street. Lewis Mumford bemoaned the proposed changes. "There should be a Society for the Prevention of Cruelty to Buildings," he said, "to insist that the owners of the Tiffany store either entirely rebuild the facade or make do with the present one."[133]

In 1951 the top floor of the Claremont Inn (reputedly built by George Pollock in 1783), located on Riverside Drive directly north of Grant's Tomb, was lost when a fire of questionable origin occurred shortly after city-funded demolition had been initiated to make the site available for a public playground.[134] The building had been built as a private house and was briefly owned by Napoleon Bonaparte's brother, Joseph, a former King of Spain; sometime before the Civil War it began serving as a fashionable inn. After its purchase by the city in 1872, the facility was maintained as a popular restaurant. In 1949, when much of the wooden structure was found to be rotting, the city closed the restaurant and decided not to appropriate the funds required for its restoration, thus allowing an historic house and a colorful part of the city's social scene to be lost.

The so-called Mark Twain house (James Renwick, ca. 1842), at 21 Fifth Avenue, was demolished in 1953 to make way for an apartment building.[135] Three years later Renwick's Rhinelander Gardens (ca. 1850), a row of houses at 110–124 West Eleventh Street, made way for Public School 41.[136] In 1954 the Studio Building (Richard Morris Hunt, 1858), at 15 West Tenth Street, was replaced by the architecturally undistinguished Peter Warren apartment building.[137] Hunt's building had been home to such artists as William Merritt Chase, Frederick Church, John F. Kensett, Albert Bierstadt and Winslow Homer and was once the site of Hunt's own atelier, where a generation of American architects, including Frank Furness, received their training. The Pulitzer Building, also known as the *New York World-Telegram* Building (George B. Post, 1890), a landmark of the New York skyline, was sacrificed to a new approach to the Brooklyn Bridge in 1955.[138] Also in 1955 the United Lutheran Church, which ten years before had purchased the J. P. Morgan mansion (Isaac Newtown Phelps, 1852), on the southeast corner of Thirty-seventh Street and Madison Avenue, and would later overturn the building's official landmark designation, demolished the building's eight chimneys when their brownstone facing was found to be in disrepair.[139]

Two adjoining brownstones that in 1890 had been internally connected and remodeled by the financiers Martin Marble and Albert C. Mowry to serve as the Fifth Avenue Bank of New York, gave way in 1956 to the twenty-six-story Bank of New York Building, at 530 Fifth Avenue; an adjacent carriage house, which had been remodeled by the bank in 1910 to serve, in part, as a drawing room for female patrons, was also demolished.[140] That same year another bank, Alfred H. Taylor's Union Dime Savings Bank (1910), on the northwest corner of Sixth Avenue and Fortieth Street, was demolished to make way for an office building.[141]

In 1957 a key work of Richard Morris Hunt's, the pioneering Stuyvesant apartment building (1869), at 142 East Eighteenth Street, said to be the city's first apartment building and certainly one of its most architecturally significant, was demolished to make way for an utterly banal fourteen-story apartment house called Gramercy Green (1961).[142] That same year a five-story

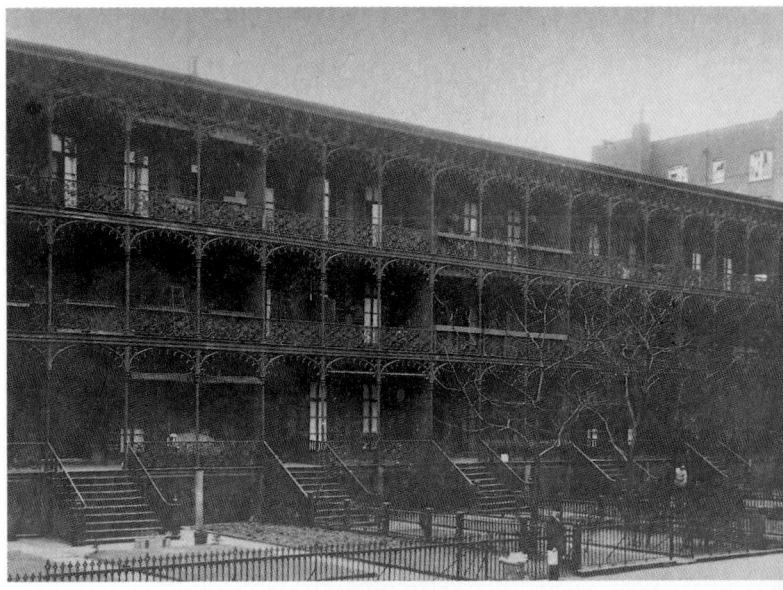

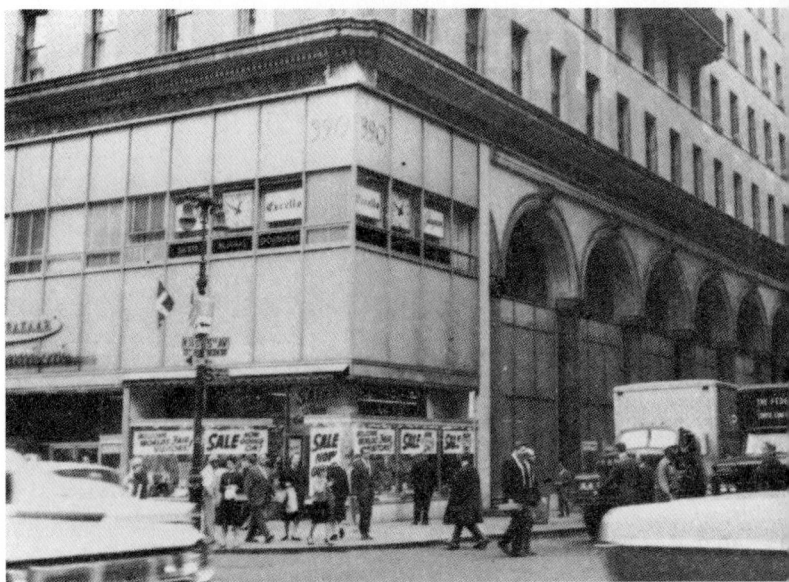

Top: Rhinelander Gardens, 110–124 West Eleventh Street. James Renwick, ca. 1850. View to the southwest, ca. 1920. NYHS

Bottom: Gorham Company Building, 390 Fifth Avenue, southwest corner of West Thirty-sixth Street. McKim, Mead & White, 1905; renovation, Herbert Tannenbaum, 1960. View to the southwest. AIA. CU

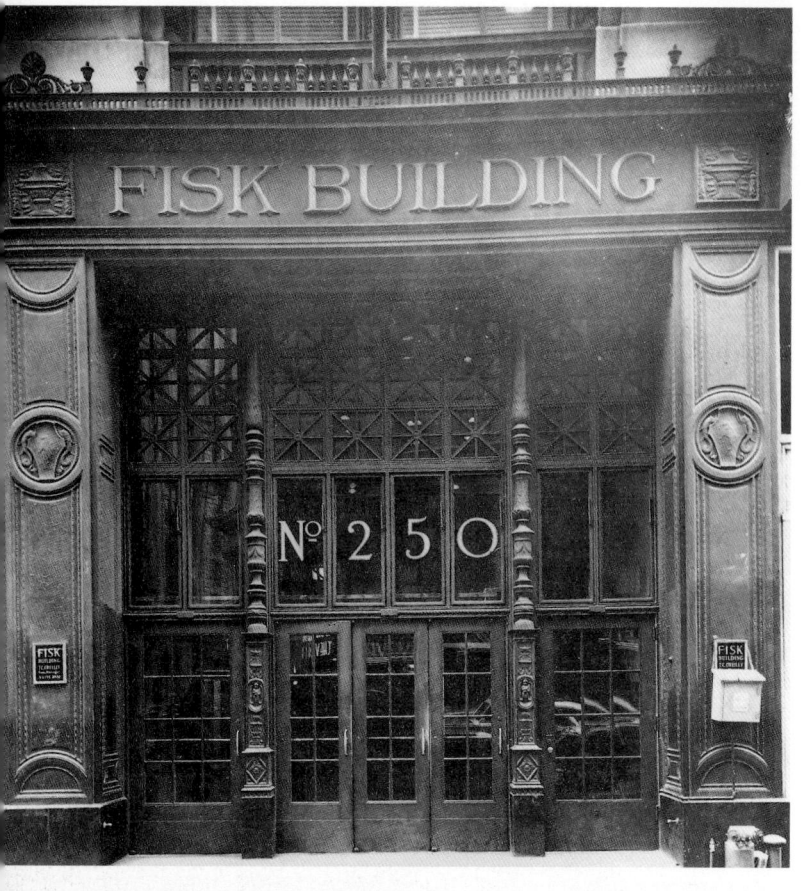

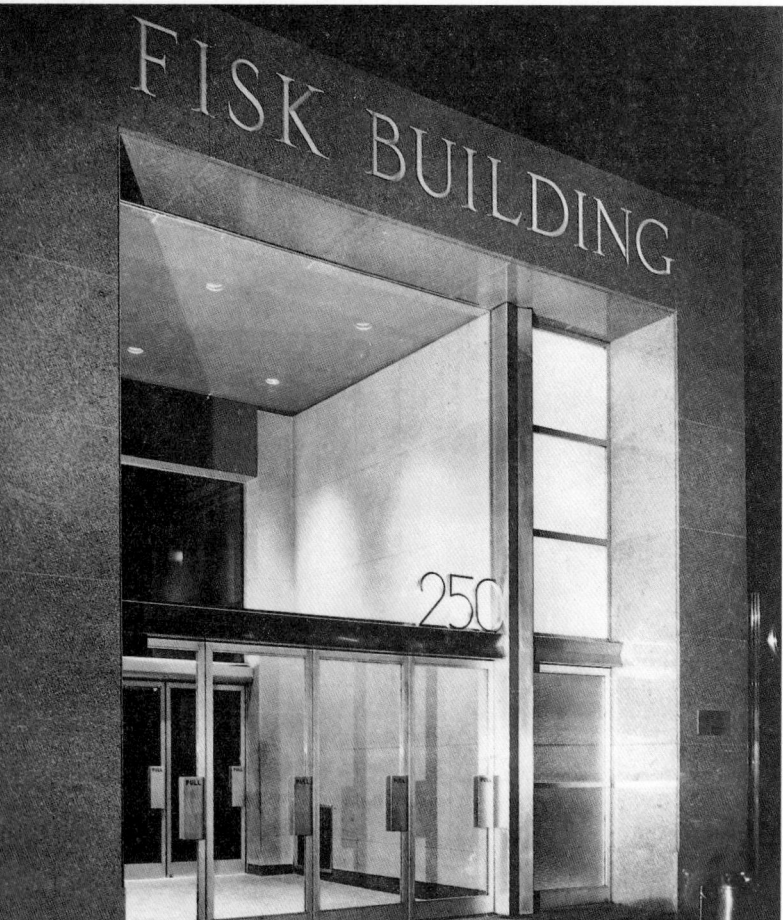

commercial building on the northwest corner of Fifth Avenue and Fifty-second Street, designed by Springsteen & Goldhammer in 1927, was pulled down to make way for 666 Fifth Avenue, an office building. The 1927 building had replaced the William K. Vanderbilt house (Richard Morris Hunt, 1882)[143] and the Mrs. William K. Vanderbilt, Jr., house (McKim, Mead & White, 1905–6).[144] In 1959 the stylishly modern Foltis-Fischer Building (Hector Hamilton, 1932), on the southeast corner of Third Avenue and Forty-second Street, was replaced by an office building designed by Emery Roth & Sons.[145]

In 1960 the Gorham Company Building (McKim, Mead & White, 1905), at 390 Fifth Avenue, was radically altered to serve as an office building, losing its striking, eight-foot-deep cornice and its three-bay avenue-facing arcade, which was replaced by the most ordinary curtain wall.[146] The National Park Bank (Donn Barber, 1904), at 214 Broadway, a key exemplar of fin-de-siècle Modern French Classicism,[147] and the twenty-five-story St. Paul Building (George B. Post, 1897–99), at 220 Broadway,[148] were razed in 1961 to make way for Shreve, Lamb & Harmon's exceptionally banal Western Electric Building.

In 1963 the Hospital for Ruptured and Crippled Children (York & Sawyer, 1911) sold its facility on the north side of Forty-second Street between First and Second avenues; the five-story building soon made way for Kevin Roche and John Dinkeloo's Ford Foundation Building.[149] The next year, the nine-story Main Building (Napoleon Le Brun, 1892) of the Metropolitan Life Insurance Company complex on Twenty-third Street between Madison and Park avenues was replaced by a twelve-story building designed by Lloyd Morgan; in addition, much of the ornament of Le Brun's iconic Metropolitan Life Tower (1909) was removed to give the building a more "modern" look.[150]

In 1964 Hausman & Rosenberg renovated the Black, Starr & Frost Building (Carrère & Hastings, 1912), at 592 Fifth Avenue, on the southwest corner of Forty-eighth Street.[151] Although the new owners called the project a "remodeling" and the editors of the *New York Times* said that the architects "tried to preserve the classical feeling of the original structure," all notable aspects of the building were lost; not only was the elegantly detailed main-floor shop gutted, but the finely articulated Classical facade was entirely reclad in white marble punctuated by elongated, portholelike windows.[152] Ada Louise Huxtable described the original building as "one of Carrère and Hastings's best small classical confections" and decried its redesign. "The facade was destroyed for a slotted marble slipcover of pompous vacuity," she wrote. "Art and delight were demolished for a lesser contemporary cliche. This is the kind of before and after that could make one cry."[153]

Even some comparatively new buildings of quality were lost or significantly compromised in the postwar years. In 1949 the twenty-four-story Fisk Building (Carrère & Hastings and Shreve, Lamb & Blake, 1921) underwent à "modernization" designed by Giorgio Cavaglieri, who replaced the Renaissance-inspired entrance and lobby with a sleekly glazed modern design. The editors of *Architectural Forum* praised Cavaglieri's design, which retained many of the lobby's original decorative features. "The new glazing," they said, "makes much of the nice detail of the old ceiling, retaining grace, removing grime."[154] Lewis Mumford was even more laudatory in his praise of the new entrance, which, he said, had "a simplicity, a freshness, an elegance altogether lacking in the first effort." He went on to compare the two designs: "The interesting thing about these designs, the old and the new, is how different their effect is. The original scheme was an attempt to apply the conventions of

Renaissance design to a new problem; the new design sweeps away the irrelevant historic forms and achieves clarity and composure without posturing of any kind."[155]

In 1952 Gladys Miller renovated the lobbies and corridors of Irwin Chanin, Jacques Delamarre and Sloan & Robertson's streamlined masterpiece, the Majestic Apartments (1930), at 115 Central Park West.[156] As the editors of *Interiors* explained, Miller removed "depression era ornament and stuffiness in general" and established "a unity . . . achieved by well-timed repetitions of wall-covering patterns and textured zonolite ceilings." Furniture was kept "to propriety's absolute minimum" and upholstered in "vinyl plastic, which can be wiped clean after child residents have been around."[157]

In 1959 the U.S. Rubber Company Building (Carrère & Hastings, 1912), at 1540 Broadway, was renovated by its new owners, the West Side Federal Savings and Loan Association, who, according to architect Herbert Tannenbaum, wanted a design with "more punch." "I gave them several alternatives," Tannenbaum later recalled, "but urged them not to destroy the beauty of the building. But landmark buildings were not in vogue then." The base of the building was given a completely new facade, with the lower-level floors reconfigured in polished gray marble and stainless steel trim, a solution that Tannenbaum believed was "a good design, but in the wrong building."[158] Going quite the opposite way, in the same year, the Corning Glass Building (Platt & Platt, 1937), at 718 Fifth Avenue, on the southwest corner of Fifty-sixth Street, was drastically remodeled by the Parisian architect Jacques Regnault to serve the needs of the jewelry concern Harry Winston.[159] In striking contrast to the Modernist original, with its dramatic glass-block exterior walls, the new store was a travertine-clad evocation of eighteenth-century France.

"Progress" not only demanded the destruction or severe alteration of significant works of architecture, but also of engineering. The Sixth Avenue El, which incorporated stations designed by the artist and architect Jasper Cropsey, discontinued service in 1938 and was demolished the following year;[160] demolished in 1940 was the Ninth Avenue El, and with it went the spectacular high-curving structure that swept trains over Cathedral Parkway as the right-of-way shifted from Ninth to Eighth avenues;[161] the Second Avenue El was torn down by 1942;[162] and demolition of Manhattan's last remaining elevated train line, the Third Avenue El, was completed on February 16, 1956.[163] In Brooklyn the Fulton Street El was torn down in 1941; its sister, the Myrtle Avenue El, popularly known as "Old Myrt," was not demolished until 1969.[164] Though long considered a nuisance, bringing dark shadows, noise and grime into neighborhoods throughout the city, the elevated lines nonetheless represented a remarkable technological achievement that had played a central role in New York's urbanistic evolution, and their demolition further taxed an already overburdened subway system.

The Third Avenue Transit Corporation's French Second Empire–style carbarns (Henry J. Hardenbergh, 1896), located between Second and Third avenues, Sixty-fifth and Sixty-sixth streets, were demolished in 1949 to make way for Manhattan House.[165] In 1953 an imposing yellow-brick trolley line power station (1898) distinguished by soaring arched windows, which had been built by the Metropolitan Street Railway Company and occupied the block bounded by First Avenue, the Franklin Delano Roosevelt Drive, Ninety-fifth and Ninety-sixth streets, was demolished to make way for an approach to the Triborough Bridge.[166] Even the Brooklyn Bridge, the city's most widely rec-

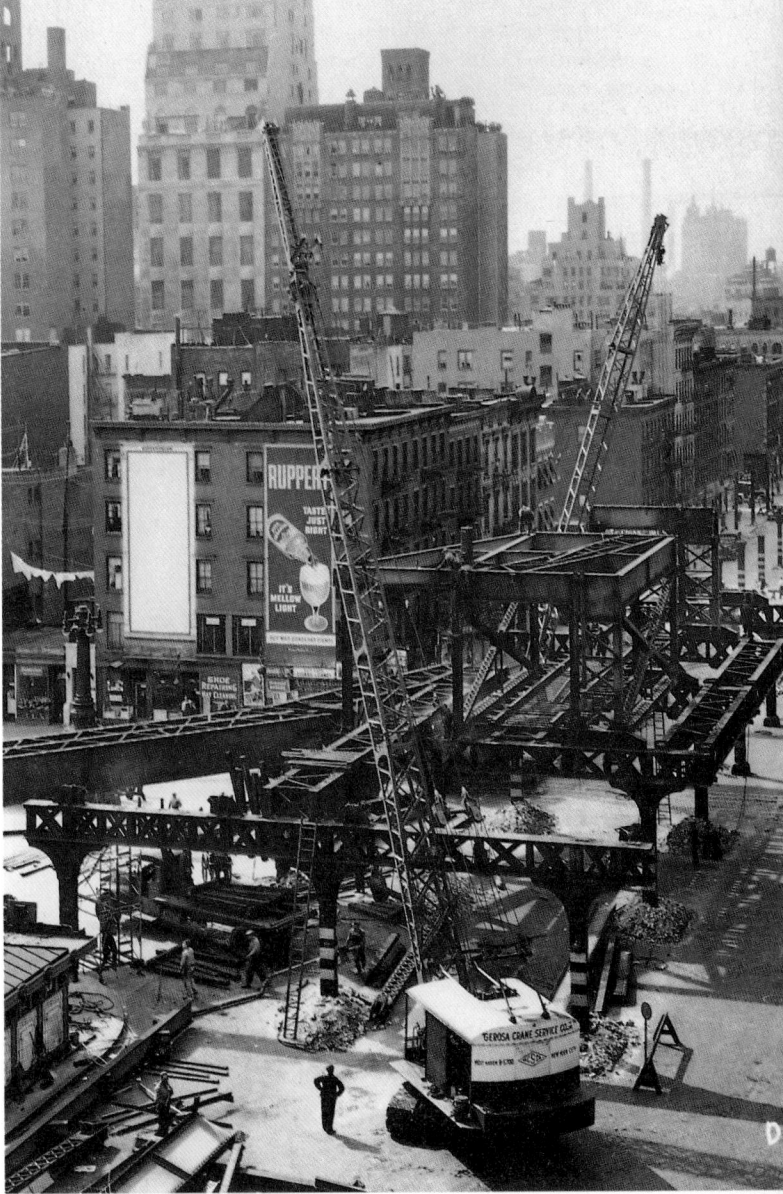

Top left: Fisk Building, 250 West Fifty-seventh Street, between Broadway and Eighth Avenue. Carrère & Hastings and Shreve, Lamb & Blake, 1921. View to the south. GICA

Bottom left: Fisk Building. Renovation, Giorgio Cavaglieri, 1949. View to the southwest. Adelberg. GICA

Above: View to the south from East Sixtieth Street showing demolition of the Second Avenue El, 1942. MA

1109

ognized and revered gateway, suffered alteration in 1950–54 when the bridge's design was rather thoughtlessly changed as part of a renovation to accommodate more automobile traffic (see chapter 13).

Preservation Victories before 1965

Before 1965 the task of preserving the past fell largely to individuals, working on their own or in groups. Given that the imperialistic monuments of the Metropolitan era were the principal victims of postwar development, it was not surprising that among the first to rally on behalf of the city's turn-of-the-century architecture were members of "old families" who had frequented the world these houses and places once represented. Though these individual efforts were commendable, they may have slowed the development of a popular preservation movement, because they fostered a belief that preservation was inextricably linked with an elitist social order. Nonetheless, some of the most important preservation victories involved single-family houses in Manhattan's toniest neighborhoods, where the future of treasured artifacts was secured by rededicating the house to an institutional purpose. In 1941, four years after the death of Felix Warburg, his widow, Frieda Schiff Warburg, had reluctantly sold the family's mansion, designed by C. P. H. Gilbert in 1908 and located on the northeast corner of Fifth Avenue and Ninety-second Street, to the developer Henry Kaufman and the architect Emery Roth, who intended to replace it with an eighteen-story apartment building.[167] Mrs. Warburg had tried to donate the house to a cultural institution, but her efforts had failed. After Kaufman and Roth's plans fell through, however, Mrs. Warburg, whose family had long supported Jewish causes, gave the mansion to the Jewish Theological Seminary, which moved its Jewish Museum there from the school's Morningside Heights campus.

In 1946, following the death of Andrew Carnegie's widow, Louise, the buccaneer capitalist's imposing but rather dour Scottish-Georgian mansion (Babb, Cook & Willard, 1901), on the east blockfront of Fifth Avenue from Ninetieth to Ninety-first Street, was given to Columbia University, which used it to house its School of Social Work.[168] In 1972 the building came under the auspices of the Smithsonian Institution, and it was granted landmark status two years later. In 1976 it was opened to the public as the Cooper-Hewitt Museum, administered by the Smithsonian and containing the extensive decorative arts collection formerly housed in the Cooper Union building, which was undergoing extensive renovation (see below). Hardy Holzman Pfeiffer's sensitive 1977 renovation for the Cooper-Hewitt, developed in close collaboration with Lisa Taylor, the museum's director, retained and restored many of the building's features. Although the renovation reflected the era's pro-preservationist sentiments, it flew in the face of prevailing curatorial tastes for featureless white galleries to display art. Ada Louise Huxtable noted that in the building's domestically scaled rooms, a contrast to the cavernous spaces typical of contemporary museums, the Cooper-Hewitt's "fine, small-scale possessions will not have to compete with overwhelming grandeur."[169] The critic Thomas B. Hess found the building somewhat less successful, describing it as "skillfully, tactfully, if coolly renovated to something of its old grandeur."[170]

In the late 1950s another of Fifth Avenue's great mansions, designed in 1909–12 for the tobacco tycoon James Buchanan Duke by the noted Philadelphia-based architect Horace Trum-

bauer, was saved from probable demolition when Duke's daughter Doris, who was also instrumental in preserving the historic architecture of Newport, Rhode Island, donated the house to New York University's Institute of Fine Arts.[171] Doris Duke had lived in the mansion, on the northeast corner of Seventy-eighth street, with her mother, Nanaline, since her father's death in 1925. The institute hired the architects Venturi, Cope & Lippincott to design the interior renovation, which drew a sharp contrast between old and new elements. The architects explained their aims:

> To create harmony through contrast rather than similarity; to employ the principal of juxtaposition rather than integration; to visually separate the old and new; to change by adding rather than modifying the existing elements; to consider furniture rather than structural architecture as the new element, to use furnishings which, if they were not 18th century in form, were not of modern design in the fine arts sense but rather contemporary objects often industrially produced and designed . . . not primarily for esthetic effect.[172]

Two prominent Park Avenue townhouses, numbers 680 and 684, threatened with demolition in 1965, were rescued by the efforts of a single wealthy individual who had no direct connection with the buildings.[173] The houses, designed by McKim, Mead & White for the financier and philanthropist Percy R. Pyne and his son-in-law, Oliver D. Filley, were completed in 1911 and 1926 respectively. Together with the adjacent townhouses at 686 Park Avenue, completed for William Sloane by Delano & Aldrich in 1919, and 690 Park Avenue, designed for Henry P. Davidson by Walker & Gillette and completed in 1917, they constituted the so-called Pyne block, on the west side of Park Avenue between Sixty-eighth and Sixty-ninth streets, a remarkably cohesive ensemble in the Georgian style. In 1965 the Institute of Public Administration, which owned 684 Park Avenue, put the house up for sale. Despite the fact that the developer Sigmund Sommer, who intended to assemble the block for an apartment house, bid $8,000 more than the real estate agent Peter Grimm, who was working on behalf of an anonymous client, the building's owner accepted the lower bid in exchange for Grimm's assurance that his client would not tear down the building. The new owner subsequently ensured the building's preservation as the home of the Spanish Institute.[174] Ada Louise Huxtable reported that a presentation by James Grote Van Derpool, a professor of architecture history at the Columbia University School of Architecture and a member of the mayor's temporary committee on landmarks, was influential in the Institute of Public Administration's decision to try to preserve the building and that the transaction was "probably the first sale of a New York building in which the judgment of the city's Landmarks Commission has played a part."[175]

The fate of 680 Park Avenue was even more interesting. After World World II the Pyne family had sold the house to the Chinese delegation to the United Nations, and later it served as the Soviet Consulate and the Soviet Mission to the United States. The house became world famous in 1960 when Soviet Premier Nikita Khrushchev held an unscheduled news conference from its Park Avenue balcony. Despite the house's colorful history, it seemed doomed in 1965 when Sommer purchased it, installed scaffolding around it, and authorized wreckers to begin removing parts of the floors and chimneypieces. But 680 Park was given a reprieve when an anonymous individual came to the rescue, buying it from Sommer for a reputed $2 million and guaranteeing its preservation.[176] Following the presentation of a citation by the New York Chapter of the American Institute of Architects to the anonymous preservationist, the *New York Times* revealed that the buyer of both 680 and 684 Park Avenue was the Marquesa de Cuevas, a granddaughter of John D. Rockefeller. "The new is not enough," the Marquesa explained, "a city should be old too."[177] She subsequently gave number 680 to the Center for Inter-American Relations, an independent, nonprofit organizaton founded by David Rockefeller and others to promote economic and cultural ties between the United States and Latin America, with the stipulations that the building's exterior not be altered and that any alterations undertaken on the interior retain the original decorative architectural features, including an Adam ceiling panel by the eighteenth-century painter Angelica Kauffmann.

The Marquesa de Cuevas also saved the Mrs. J. William Clark house (Trowbridge & Livingston, 1914), a Colonial Revival townhouse at 49 East Sixty-eighth Street that complemented the Pyne block. Unlike the houses facing Park Avenue, the Clark house was drastically remodeled in 1970 by Lehrecke & Tonetti to serve as Automation House, headquarters for the nonprofit American Foundation on Automation and Employment.[178] It also housed the Institute of Collective Bargaining and Group Relations, the Center for Job Training Information, and Experiments in Art and Technology, Inc., also known as E.A.T., for which the physicist J. William Klüver served as president and the artist Robert Rauschenberg served as vice president. Although the Landmarks Preservation Commission had landmarked the building, they approved the radical alteration of the entrance within the ground-level loggia and the installation of bronze double-glazed sliding windows. Inside, the building was also dramatically changed: all the rooms were replaced by nearly full-floor spaces incorporating ceiling grids that anchored movable partitions and incorporated track lighting, projection screens and hanging frames for slide projectors, televisions and exhibition material.

In 1960 the principal house of one of the city's few remaining country estates—and certainly one of its most extensive and architecturally distinguished—was saved when Wave Hill House, at 675 West 252nd Street in the Riverdale section of the Bronx, was given to the Park Department by Mr. and Mrs. Edward U. Freeman, son-in-law and daughter of the financier George W. Perkins, who had owned the property since 1903.[179] The fieldstone house, built in 1843, incorporated a Gothic-inspired armor hall, designed in 1928 by Dwight James Baum.[180] It had served as a residence for several important figures, including Theodore Roosevelt, Samuel Clemens, Arturo Toscanini and the publisher Thomas H. Appleton; it had also served as the official residence of the United Kingdom's chief delegate to the United Nations. Following the property's transfer to the city, it became the Wave Hill Center for Environmental Studies, a cultural and educational institution.

Some nonprofit organizations took the initiative and purchased landmark-quality structures to serve as their headquarters. Often these sales came about because a preservation-minded owner, who could doubtless have received a higher price from a private developer, looked to a nonprofit owner as a reasonably secure way to protect the property. In 1952 Mrs. Harrison Williams, one of the city's most celebrated hostesses, sold the former Willard D. Straight house (Delano & Aldrich, 1913–15), at 1130 Fifth Avenue, which she had lived in for more than two decades and established as a stylish "salon," to the National Audubon Society; in this case preservation was guaranteed since the deed to the Straight house prevented its de-

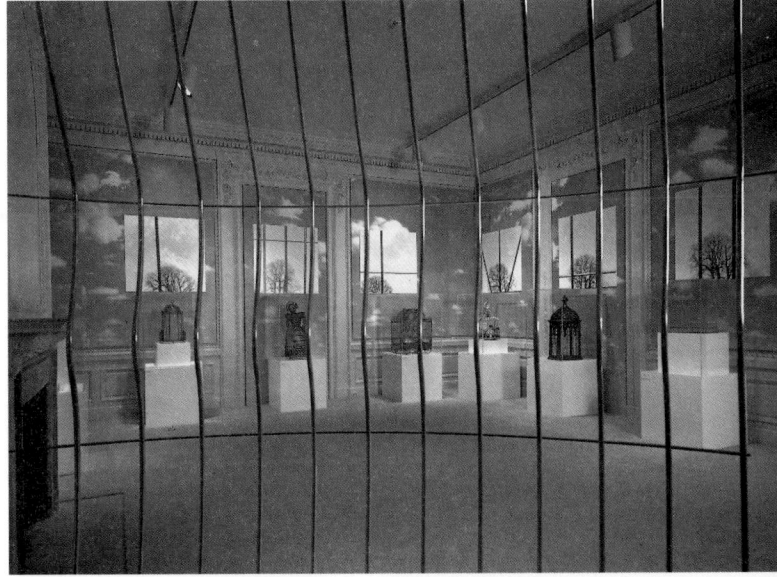

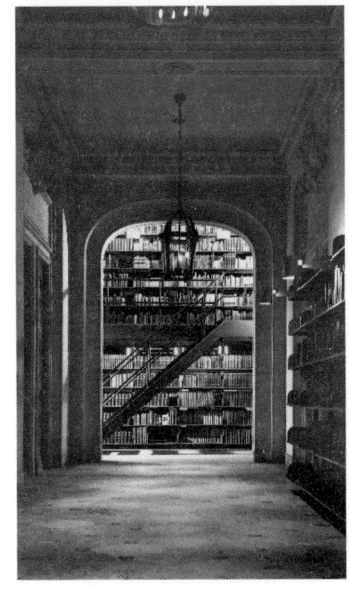

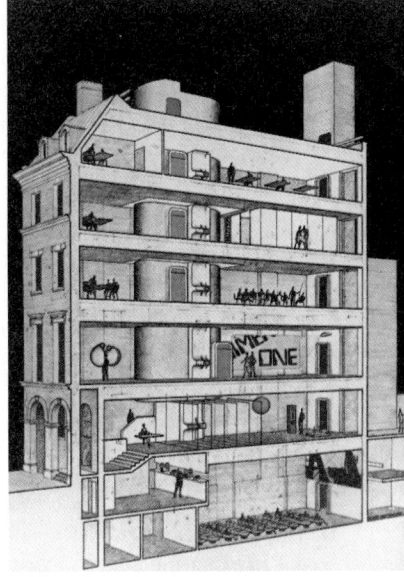

Top: Cooper-Hewitt Museum (formerly Andrew Carnegie residence), east blockfront of Fifth Avenue, East Ninetieth to East Ninety-first Street. Babb, Cook & Willard, 1901; renovation, Hardy Holzman Pfeiffer, 1977. Interior showing display of birdcages. ©Norman McGrath. NM

Bottom left: New York University Institute of Fine Arts (formerly James Buchanan Duke residence), 1 East Seventy-eighth Street, northeast corner of Fifth Avenue. Horace Trumbauer, 1909–12; renovation, Venturi, Cope & Lippincott, 1958. Library. Iselin. VSBA

Bottom right: Automation House (formerly Mrs. J. William Clark residence), 49 East Sixty-eighth Street, between Fifth and Park avenues. Trowbridge & Livingston, 1914; renovation, Lehrecke & Tonetti, 1970. Section perspective. TA

molition.[181] In 1974, six years after the house became a designated landmark, it was purchased by the recently founded International Center of Photography.

Another Upper East Side townhouse converted into institutional office space was 41 East Seventieth Street, designed by Aymar Embury II and built during the 1920s for the financier Walter Rothschild. Edward Larrabee Barnes remodeled the house for the 20th Century Fund, retaining some of the original room divisions and decorative elements while using, according to the editors of *Architectural Forum*, "neat details, good taste and gallons of white paint to transform the rich and darkly paneled parlors into spare, well-scrubbed offices."[182]

In 1965 the domestically scaled, Colonial-style Colony Club (McKim, Mead & White, 1908), at 120 Madison Avenue, between Thirtieth and Thirty-first streets, was transformed into headquarters for the American Academy of Dramatic Arts.[183] In his renovation Giorgio Cavaglieri maintained the facade, although an original portico had been removed several years earlier and replaced by pilasters set directly against the wall in a renovation designed by the architect W. Whitehill to make way for a widened roadway. Inside, in rooms originally designed by Stanford White and Elsie de Wolfe and subsequently renovated by the gymnast Vic Tanny, Cavaglieri inserted a sparsely detailed auditorium with amphitheater-style seating.

Although the city's most architecturally distinguished apartment buildings were not particularly susceptible to demolition, since they were generally built to a greater density than present-day zoning would permit, neither their facades nor their interiors were secure from renovation. Many large apartments were broken up in the 1930s, and interior detail was sacrificed in the process. In the case of 910 Fifth Avenue (Fred F. French, 1919), on the northeast corner of Seventy-second Street, not only were the building's interiors completely gutted to create smaller apartments but the limestone-clad, Classically inspired facade was stripped off.[184]

On the Upper West Side, the Dakota apartment building (Henry J. Hardenbergh, 1882), with a large site (including an open lot along its western side) and spacious apartments whose bearing-wall construction made subdivision difficult, was highly vulnerable to demolition.[185] The editors of *Progressive Architecture* said in 1961 that the "atmospheric" building's location on a prominent site at the northwest corner of Central Park West and Seventy-second Street "fuels the heat of the real estate tycoon."[186] Spurred by rumors that William Zeckendorf was interested in buying and demolishing the building, the tenants—who in 1961 included such celebrities as the actresses Judy Holliday and Lauren Bacall and who, as *Progressive Architecture* put it, "could, if they wished, move to the East Side into more modern, less charming surroundings"—successfully saved their building.[187] Two residents, C. D. Jackson, the publisher of *Time*, and Ernest Gross, an international lawyer and United States delegate to the United Nations, approached developer Louis J. Glickman, whose reputation among New York's artistic community had been badly tarnished during the battle over Carnegie Hall (see below) and who was, consequently, eager to restore his image as a friend of the city. They asked him to purchase the Dakota and then sell it back to the tenants at a minimal profit; Glickman would retain the building's parking lot, located directly to the west, which had once contained rose gardens, tennis courts and a lawn for playing croquet. The tenants and Glickman agreed to the deal, and after the purchase he sold the adjacent land to the Mayfair Corporation, which erected a twenty-seven-story apartment building that dwarfed the Dakota and blocked most of its western light.

The unique construction of the Dakota posed serious preservation problems. Even before the building was declared a legally protected New York City landmark in 1970, its board of directors had taken a hard line over the installation of through-the-wall air-conditioning units that would mar the building's appearance and compromise the integrity of its bearing-wall construction. When Frederick Victoria, an antiques dealer who lived in the building, petitioned for permission to install a through-the-wall unit, his request was denied by the board and, later, by the Landmarks Preservation Commission. Victoria then petitioned the commission to allow him to install double-layered insulating glass but again was denied permission. A fellow resident of Victoria's, Lauren Bacall, who also wanted to install through-the-wall air-conditioning in her apartment, found the commission's stance "absolutely asinine."[188] Victoria approached one of the members of the commission on the actress's behalf; the commissioner's response was, reputedly, "Will I get to meet Miss Bacall?"[189] Following drinks at Bacall's apartment, for which she appeared, as the social historian Stephen Birmingham put it, not as "the earthy, salty, sardonic and self-mocking woman—New York housewife and mother of three who usually tossed an old sweater over her blouse and slacks when she went out to walk her dog in the park—that Dakotans knew as neighbor," but rather as "her sultry, sexy, movie-star best . . . the Hollywood Legend,"[190] Bacall was granted permission to install a through-the-wall air-conditioner. The commission demanded, however, that she catalogue and store all the bricks and stone that were removed and promise to either restore the facade when she moved or have the next owner take on the responsibility.

The "white shoe" character of the preservation movement began to change dramatically in 1955, with the proposed demolition of a building of major civic significance: Carnegie Hall.[191] Designed by William B. Tuthill, with Dankmar Adler and Richard Morris Hunt as consultants, Carnegie Hall had occupied an important place on the international roster of great musical showcases since its completion in 1891. Although the building was somewhat awkwardly massed and rather stolid, the auditorium was distinguished by superb acoustics. And unlike the Metropolitan Opera House, which was deemed a palace of the rich, Carnegie Hall was a popular landmark that in some way or other had touched almost every New Yorker. As the editors of *Life* observed:

> [The building] is as much an archive as an auditorium, for within its walls Carnegie Hall holds almost all the rich and resonant history of music in the U.S. Since the Russian composer Peter Ilyich Tchaikovsky dedicated it in 1891, every artist of importance in the world has played there, seasoning it with magnificent performances until the hall with its uncanny acoustics has taken on the qualities of a massive instrument, a superb Stradivarius responding to master musicians.[192]

In 1955, when the hall's principal occupant, the New York Philharmonic orchestra, contemplated moving to its own auditorium in the proposed Lincoln Square cultural complex, the building was threatened with demolition.

When the Glickman Corporation, a real estate firm, purchased the building in 1956 and announced plans to replace Carnegie Hall with a forty-four-story office building, no strong public reaction was initially registered. New Yorkers seemed to greet the loss of yet another historic building as inevitable. The building that would replace it, designed by Pomerance & Breines, promised to become one of the city's most noticeable structures. Set back from the street and rising from a sunken plaza designed to serve as an outdoor exhibition space, the building was to be sheathed in a checkerboard pattern of gold-tinted windows, trimmed in low-luster, gold-anodized aluminum, alternating with vermilion porcelain spandrels. The building's developer, Louis J. Glickman, cited Raymond Hood's McGraw-Hill Building (1931) as precedent,[193] but boasted that his new building would be "the city's first truly 'colorful' color building." "We believe that American cities should not remain drab, gray and colorless," he said. "Therefore we gave the architects a blank check to use their imagination to create a building which set a colorful pattern for the future."[194] In what the editors of the *Real Estate Record and Guide* called "a gesture of his interest in the continuation of the famed Philharmonic Orchestra," Glickman offered to sell individual bricks of the original building on its behalf, and a mezzanine-level gallery overlooking the sunken plaza was planned to feature exhibits on musicians who had performed at Carnegie Hall.[195]

Glickman's plans languished, however, when funds for the building, which was reported to have a budget of $22 million, did not materialize. In the meantime Robert Simon, Jr., whose father had formed and headed the Carnegie Hall Corporation, which had purchased the hall from Andrew Carnegie's estate in 1925, joined with the tenants who occupied the building's apartments and studios to plot the building's preservation. The violinist Isaac Stern approached his friends Alice and Jacob M. Kaplan, the philanthropists, who in turn asked Raymond S. Rubinow, the administrator of the J. M. Kaplan Fund, to explore alternate means for saving the hall. Stern, the Kaplans and Rubinow recruited other supporters, and together they decided that the most effective approach was to seek aid from the city government. On February 7, 1960, the Citizens Committee for Carnegie Hall was formed, a group that subsequently proposed that the city take possession of the building and lease it to the tax-exempt Carnegie Hall Corporation. The committee also proposed that the city issue bonds to pay for the hall's purchase and renovation and that the Carnegie Hall Corporation pay off the bond indebtedness, which would result in the corporation becoming the building's owner. After the enactment of the necessary state laws, the city purchased Carnegie Hall and leased it to the corporation. When news that the legislation had been passed was relayed to Leopold Stokowksi, who had worked to save the building, he called for a fanfare to be played during the televised children's concert he was conducting in the hall at the time.

The Destruction of Pennsylvania Station

The loss of McKim, Mead & White's masterpiece, Pennsylvania Station (1904–10), in 1963 made clear to even the most casual observer that virtually no building in New York was sacred.[196] This was more than just an architectural loss; it was a trenchant example of a real estate market gone out of control, and a reflection of a municipality's helplessness to protect its own heritage and, in large measure, control its own destiny. No act of demolition would more effectively serve to alter the process of saving the city's architectural heritage, transforming it from, as the preservationists Harmon Goldstone and Martha Dalrymple put it, "a series of hysterical skirmishes among aroused citizens into an integral part of city government."[197]

The destruction of Pennsylvania Station was considered nearly inconceivable to many observers until the moment the

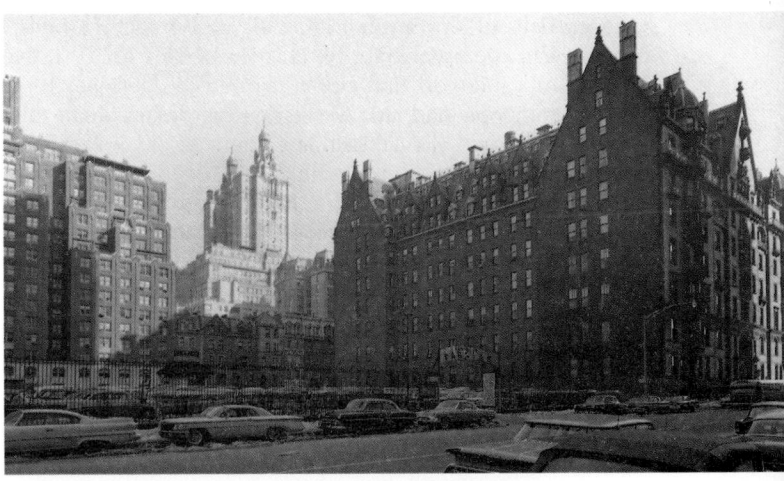

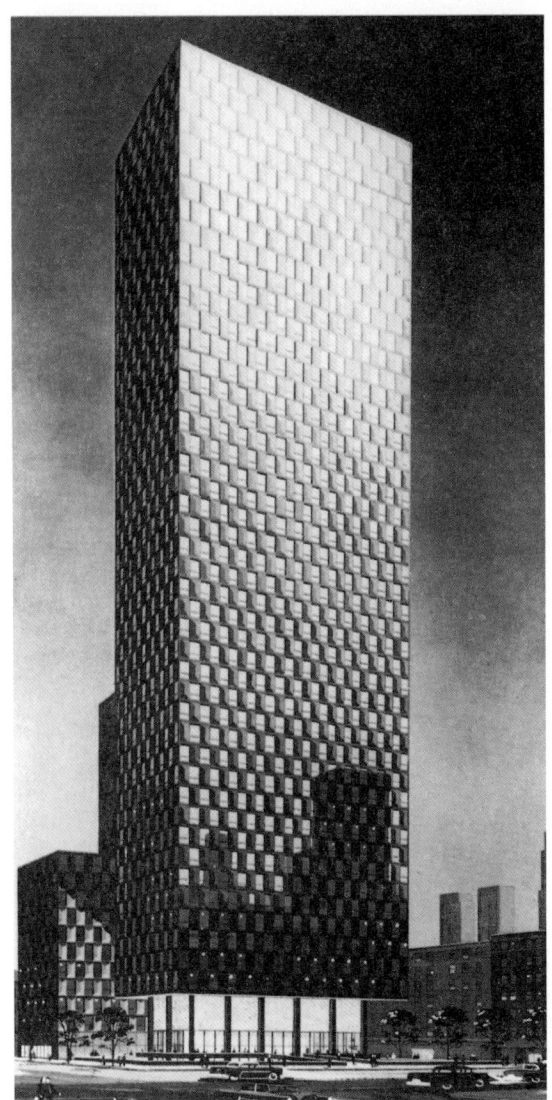

Top: Dakota, 1 West Seventy-second Street, between Central Park West and Columbus Avenue. Henry J. Hardenbergh, 1882. View to the northeast showing the Dakota on the right and the parking lot, formerly gardens and tennis courts, on the left, ca. 1960. OMH

Bottom: Proposal for tower on the site of Carnegie Hall, southeast corner of Seventh Avenue and West Fifty-seventh Street. Pomerance & Breines, 1956. Rendering of view to the southeast. PB

wrecking balls hit on October 28, 1963, but in fact the building's fate had been sealed for some time. As early as 1942, the Pennsylvania Railroad had commissioned the designer Raymond Loewy, who had also worked on the design of the railroad's locomotives, to "modernize" the station's lower concourse.[198] The series of compact, streamlined shops Loewy created were stylistically inconsistent with their grand surroundings, but their small scale and location kept them from constituting a major disruption. After World War II the fortunes of the station were affected by the vast increase in automobile traffic and, more important, commercial aviation, which had benefited from wartime developments in technology. By 1951 the Pennsylvania Railroad was in serious financial trouble; with a deficit of $72 million, the company considered selling the air rights to the yards it owned between Ninth and Tenth avenues near the station, but no deal was developed.

In March 1954 even the ardent Modernist Lewis Mumford criticized the insensitive way the grandly Classical building was being maintained in an attempt to cut costs. Mumford observed that although the station "has been singled out by the Municipal Art Society as a public monument worthy of preservation, the managers of the Pennsylvania Railroad take a dimmer view of this noble possession." He discussed the most egregious examples of poor maintenance:

> For one thing, they have practiced economy in cleaning this structure to the extent of allowing even the great maps in the main concourse to be obliterated by grime. . . . As if this dirt were not bad enough, the superb effect of the steelwork in the Pennsylvania train shed has been marred by spraying the lower half of the metal columns with aluminum paint—which is the aesthetic equivalent of replacing a healthy leg by a wooden one, so completely does it demolish the strength and unity of the black steelwork. Why should an architect be concerned to produce a masterpiece if, only forty years later, it will be subject to vandalism? Fortunately, the remedy is simple: black paint for the steel, soap and water for the murals.[199]

Several months later, however, other alterations that were not so easily remedied were set into motion. In December 1954 the editors of *Business Week* announced that the financially ailing railroad had granted the developer William Zeckendorf's firm, Webb & Knapp, an option on the station's air rights.[200] Zeckendorf proposed to demolish the above-ground portion of the station and build a merchandise mart called the Palace of Progress, to be designed by I. M. Pei and Lester Tichy. The mart was to be the world's largest and most expensive building, a $100 million, thirty-two-story-high behemoth containing approximately 154 million cubic feet of space—nearly twice that of the Pentagon and 6 million cubic feet more than the Pyramid of Cheops. According to *Architectural Forum*, the railroad would "modernize its station below ground [and] end up with virtually a new terminal, $17 million in pocket, and a huge new building overhead that would surely boost its rail traffic."[201] In 1956 Zeckendorf abandoned the plan for the mart, but, according to the historian Lorraine Diehl, unbeknownst to the press or the public, in 1955 he had entered into an agreement with James Symes, the railroad's president, to purchase the air rights above the station and build a new station below grade.[202]

In 1958 the railroad completed a significant and controversial renovation of the station's interior, designed by Tichy.[203] The most striking feature of the renovation was the installation of an illuminated, plastic-clad, crescent-shaped canopy that projected into the main waiting room and was suspended above new ticket-selling booths arranged in a sawtooth pattern; designed in association with the structural engineer Paul Weidlinger, the canopy was hung by wires from the room's Corinthian columns. In a letter to the editors of *Architectural Forum* published before the plan's realization, Walter Kidney, an enthusiast for the traditionalist architecture of the recent past, described the proposed canopy as "a fluttery fatuous kiosk" that was "as appropriate as an installation of juke boxes in Westminster Abbey." Kidney argued that "a man must be found who will consent to abandon the thought of making [Pennsylvania Station] slick or bright and chirpy . . . a man who is capable of using travertine and soft warm light, who can devise an ornament that will lighten and articulate a structure so large [and] give us an even greater work of architecture."[204]

The *Forum*'s editors disagreed: "With all that travertine around, why more? The canopy is airy and gracious, and acknowledges the formidable pomp around it with a friendly smile."[205] Once the renovation was completed, the editors commented further: "The station room affords a curious study in scale, in which the element which declares to the viewer that it is simple and light—in this case the canopy—dwarfs the elements which declare they are heavy and grand, in this case the colonnaded ends of the waiting room. It's an Alice-in-Wonderland feeling. But there's a sweep in that canopy which has a brilliance all its own."[206]

In a polemic titled "The Disappearance of Pennsylvania Station," Mumford described the current state of the "superb" building: "Even the fifty-year accumulation of grime on the travertine walls of the interior," he wrote, "has not robbed this building of its essential grandeur, which now suggests what one is aware of in the misty subterranean passages of a Roman bath." Mumford viewed the interior renovation as nothing short of tragic:

> No one now entering Pennsylvania Station for the first time could, without clairvoyance, imagine how good it used to be, in comparison to the almost indescribable botch that has been made of it. . . . The spaciousness of the corridor, with its long view, has been diminished by a series of centrally placed advertisements. . . . Happily, these obstacles serve an esthetic function; they soften the shock that one encounters at the head of the stairs to the main floor. There one discovers that almost the whole interior arrangement has been swept away.

As for Tichy's plastic canopy, which Mumford described as "a masterpiece of architectural and visual incongruity," the critic said that "if the planners had cut the height of the main level in two by inserting another floor above it, they could not have debased the original design more effectively than they have by introducing that mask of light, suspended by wires." Mumford's "only consolation," he said, was that "nothing more that can be done to the station will do any further harm to it. As in nuclear war, after complete destruction has been achieved, one cannot increase the damage by doubling the destructive forces."[207]

But Mumford was wrong; plans to effect worse damage would materialize only too soon. In 1960 the Graham-Paige Corporation, which owned Madison Square Garden, then located on the west side of Eighth Avenue between Forty-ninth and Fiftieth streets, announced plans to demolish their facility and erect a $38 million sports and entertainment complex as "a counterpoint to Lincoln Center."[208] The complex, for an unspecified location in midtown Manhattan, was designed by Charles Luckman Associates, who proposed an oval, bowl-shaped, enclosed arena that could seat 25,000 spectators and could also be converted into the world's largest convention hall; restaurants, a bowling alley, an indoor swimming pool, an out-

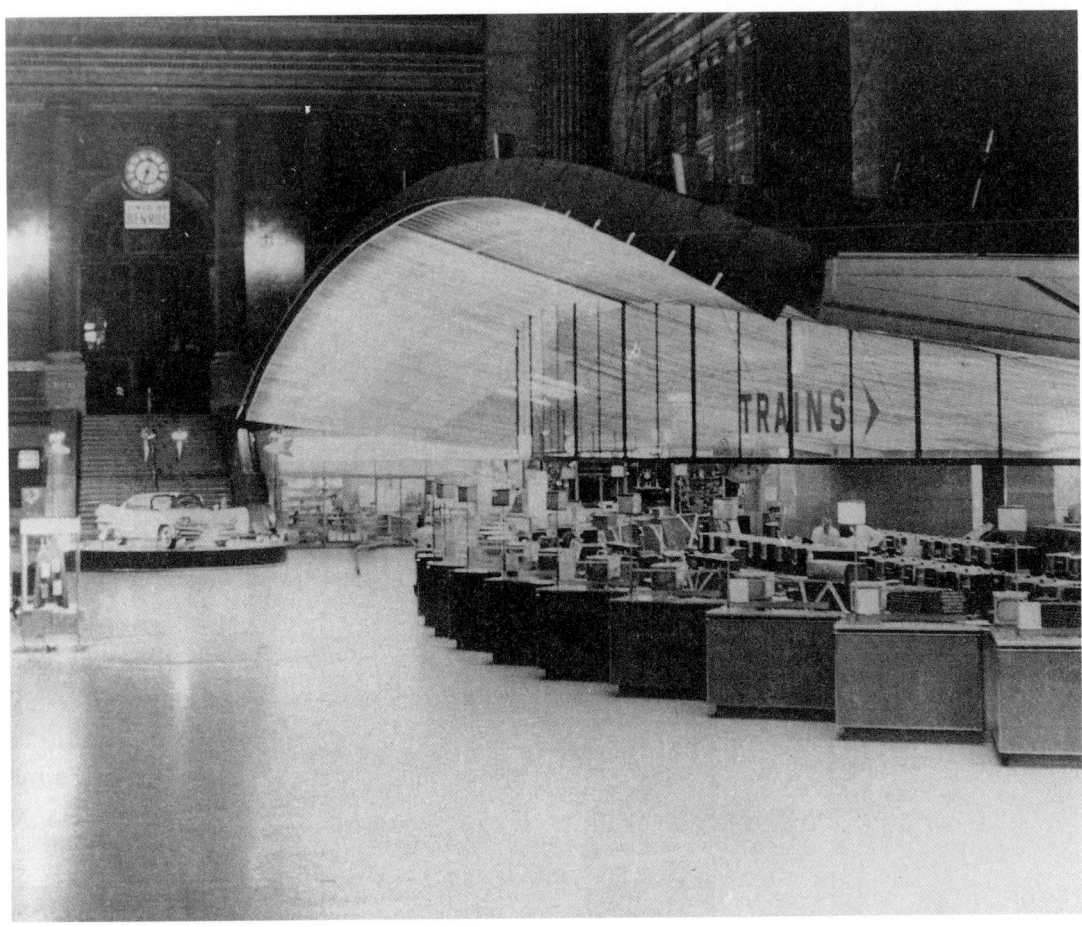

New ticket booths, Pennsylvania Station (McKim, Mead & White, 1904–10), Seventh to Eighth Avenue, West Thirty-first to West Thirty-third Street. Lester C. Tichy with Paul Weidlinger, 1958. Jacobellis. NYP

door swimming pool and skating rink, enclosed parking for 3,000 cars and two circular buildings housing additional theaters and exhibition space were also included. In 1961 it was announced that the complex, modified to include a thirty-four-story office building and a twenty-eight-story hotel but fewer entertainment facilities, was planned for the site of Pennsylvania Station. An alternate scheme called for the oval-shaped arena to be flanked by three circular buildings housing additional arenas, theaters and restaurants. "With progress aforethought," the editors of *Architectural Forum* noted, the station that had "haunted New York's West Side . . . with visions of the Baths of Caracalla" would be replaced, although the main waiting room would be preserved.[209]

Negative reactions to the station's proposed demolition were widespread and vehement. "The fact that the passenger handling section is based on the Grandeur of Rome, and the train departure and arrival section frankly expresses its construction, is a significant and illuminating example of the thinking of the age," wrote the architectural critic Aline B. Saarinen. "Although the interior has been almost entirely ruined, its great space and nobility are still visible. . . . I would do everything possible to urge its restoration and imaginative re-thinking in order to make it again functional."[210] The pioneering Dutch Modernist architect J. J. P. Oud stated: "It is one of the few examples of building in a classical style that has been executed in a living and refined manner, giving the surroundings the impressive scale which it itself possesses. . . . I would regret it very much if the building were to be demolished: it should, if at all possible, be preserved."[211]

Attesting to the fact that the station's demolition was an issue of international concern, the editors of the Italian journal

Casabella commented on the proposed replacement, calling it "awkward and rather unhappy."[212] The architect Percival Goodman wrote: "First Tichy ruined the main space, now Luckman & Associates will complete the wreck. *Sic transit.*" He added, "I have a good idea: If we can get the wreckers to leave the old room at the right moment stripped of its plaster decoration, etc., we might have a Piranesi right in the heart of New York—a real tourist attraction."[213] The author Norman Mailer took a historical view of the building's status: "The architectural face of the enemy has shifted. Twenty years ago Pennsylvania Station . . . seemed a monstrosity, forbidding, old, dingy, unfunctional, wasteful of space, depressing in its passages and waiting rooms. The gloomy exploitative echoes of the industrial revolution sounded in its grey stone. And yet today the plan to demolish it is a small disaster."[214] The preservation of Pennsylvania Station even received a federal endorsement, from August Heckscher, a consultant on the arts to President Kennedy: "Pennsylvania Station is a noble space," he said, "a fitting entrance to a great city. Our determination to build in a style worthy of today must be matched by a determination to preserve and make use of the grand efforts of the past. Only thus can New York and our other cities keep a rich and varied environment."[215]

The architectural community's opposition to the station's demolition took a political form when six young architects established the Action Group for Better Architecture in New York (AGBANY), whose goal was to advocate high architectural and planning standards in general and the preservation of Pennsylvania Station in particular. The group, whose founding members were Jordan Gruzen, Norman Jaffe, Diana Kirsch, Peter Samton, Norval White and Elliot Willensky, attracted other

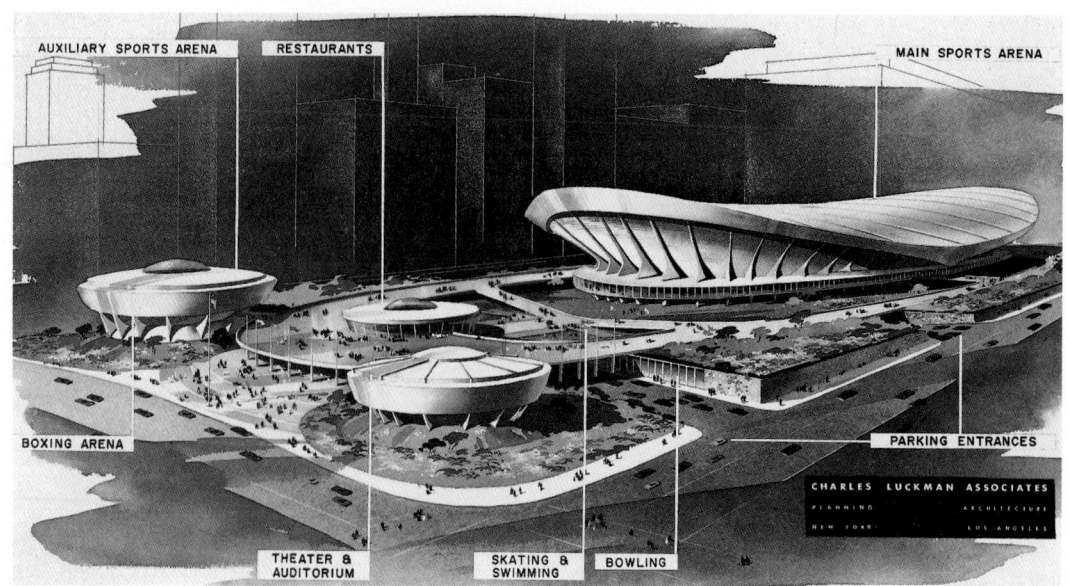

Top: Proposal for New York Sports and
Entertainment Center. Charles Luckman
Associates, 1960. Rendering showing proposal on
an unspecified site. CLA

Center: Proposal for New York Sports and
Entertainment Center. Site plan. CLA

Bottom: Proposal for Madison Square Garden
Center, Seventh to Eighth Avenue, West Thirty-
first to West Thirty-third Street. Charles Luckman
Associates, 1961. View to the southeast of
proposal with office towers. CLA

Top far right: Pennsylvania Station, Seventh to
Eighth Avenue, West Thirty-first to West Thirty-third
Street. McKim, Mead & White, 1904–10. Carved
eagle being removed during demolition. Stein. NYP

Bottom far right: View of Action Group for Better
Architecture in New York (AGBANY)
demonstration in front of Pennsylvania Station's
Seventh Avenue colonnade, August 2, 1962. NYP

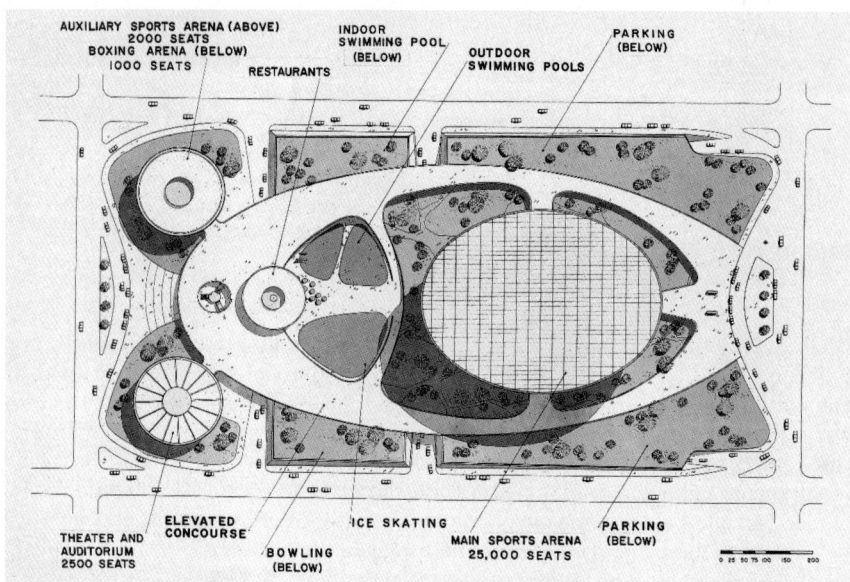

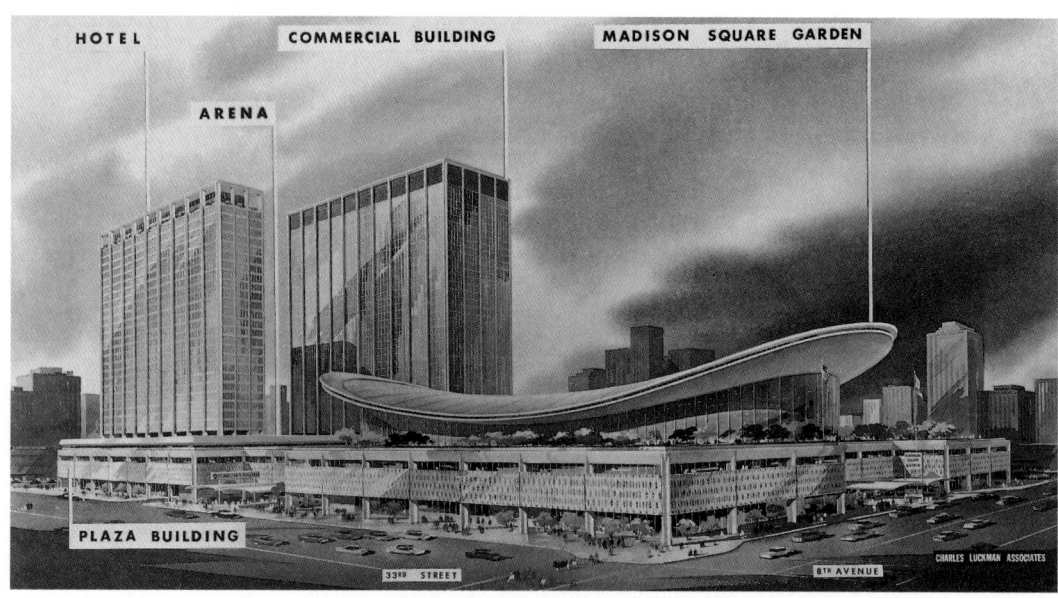

architects, as well as architectural writers and concerned citizens. It soon included among its members Norman Mailer, August Heckscher, Lewis Mumford, Henry Hope Reed, Jr., the planner Charles Abrams, the architectural historian Wayne Andrews, and the architects Max Bond, Jr., Giorgio Cavaglieri, James Marston Fitch, Ulrich Franzen, Romaldo Giurgola, John Johansen, J. J. P. Oud, Giovanni Pasanella, Paul Rudolph and Edgar Tafel.

On August 2, 1962, AGBANY staged a peaceful demonstration in front of the station's Seventh Avenue colonnade. The group of approximately fifty protesters, carrying placards bearing such slogans as "Save Face—Keep Penn in Place," "Don't Amputate: Renovate," "Don't Demolish It! Polish It!" and "Ban the Wreckers," included AGBANY's six original members as well as Franzen, Heckscher, Mumford, Jonathan Barnett, Peter Blake, Arthur Drexler, Jane Jacobs, Mrs. Bliss Parkinson, Aline Saarinen and, most notably, Philip Johnson, who had been a leading proponent of International Style Modernism but was now an advocate of an architecture grounded in history. In an article reporting on the demonstration, Norval White called the station "the foremost example of neoclassic architecture of our time,"[216] and Arthur Drexler, the director of the Museum of Modern Art's Department of Architecture and Design, noted that "the great rooms of the station are not the kind of public spaces New York can afford to lose."[217] Philip Johnson argued that New Yorkers "deserve these bits of grandeur in their lives"[218] and that inside the station "you realize that man can build nobly."[219] After the demonstration, *Time* quoted Irving Felt, the promoter of the new complex and brother of James Felt, who then served as City Planning Commissioner, as saying, "Fifty years from now, when it's time for our Center to be torn down, there will be a new group of architects who will protest."[220]

The *New York Times* called the demonstration "one of the city's strangest and most heartening picket lines,"[221] while the editors of *Architectural Record* acknowledged the phenomenal outpouring of professional support but wondered if an equal amount of public support would develop: "For all the distinguished support, and for all the poignant bravura of the demonstration, it seemed possible that AGBANY's first cause would be a lost cause. . . . Only extraordinary political action could save Penn Station now and only extraordinary evidence of extraordinary public interest could spur such action. What does the *public* interest require?"[222]

Norval White tried to convince the Port of New York Authority to purchase and administer the building, but his attempt was unsuccessful. Late in 1962 two other members of AGBANY, the architects Jean Pierre Le Gouis and Norman Jaffe, put forth a compromise in which the station would be preserved but the site would be developed. They proposed that towers be constructed in the station's two massive air wells, a solution that would save the building from demolition while generating revenue for the railroad. Their essentially wrongheaded idea was not seriously considered, however.

Preservation efforts continued throughout the fall of 1962. In November the architectural critic Walter McQuade, writing in the *Nation*, reiterated the importance of the building as an exemplary civic structure: "It is a public object, in the realest sense. Little pieces of thousands of lives can be recalled there— a function of civic architecture at its most effective, standing as a set of milestones in time. . . . I'm sentimental about the astounding old building . . . thousands of people are and should be. That is the point: there *should* be a lot of memories among the soot." He advocated a continued protest, voicing hope that

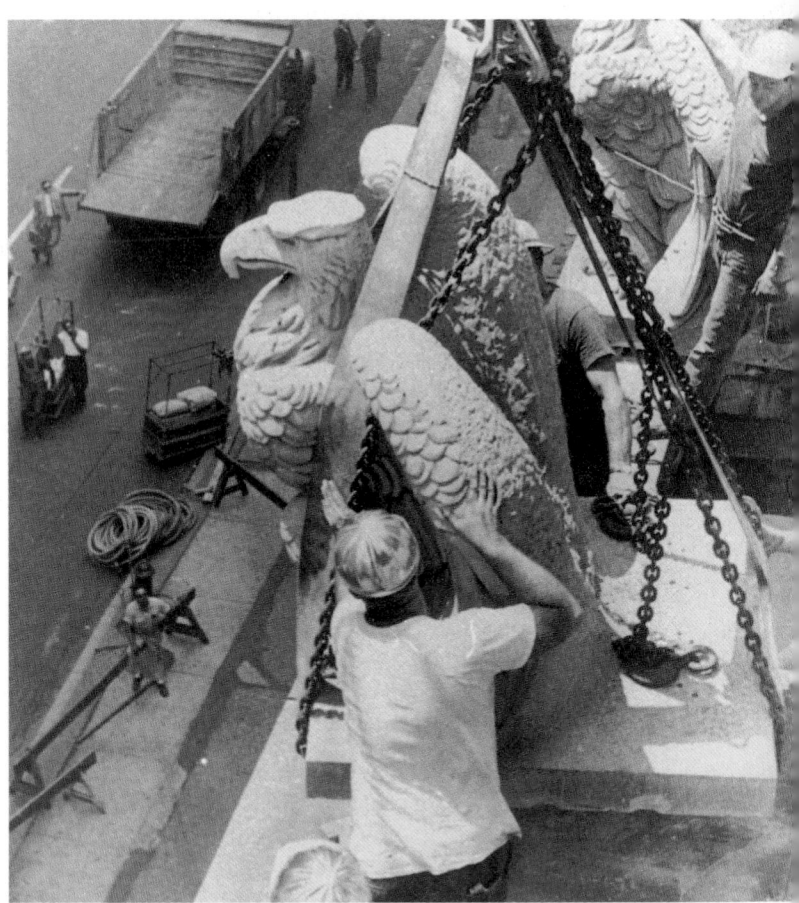

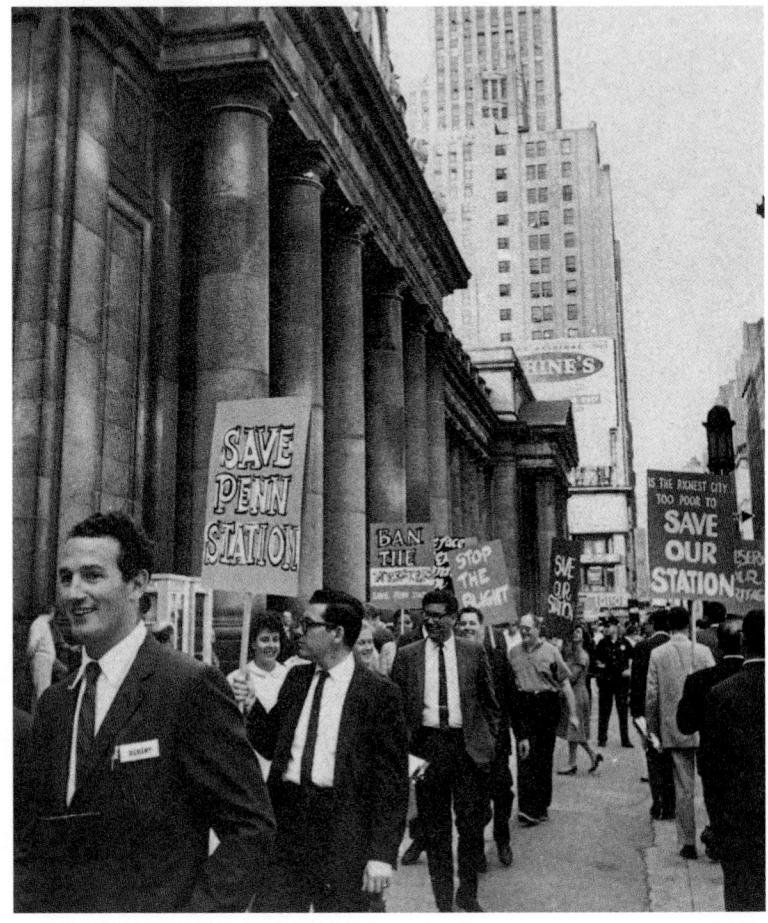

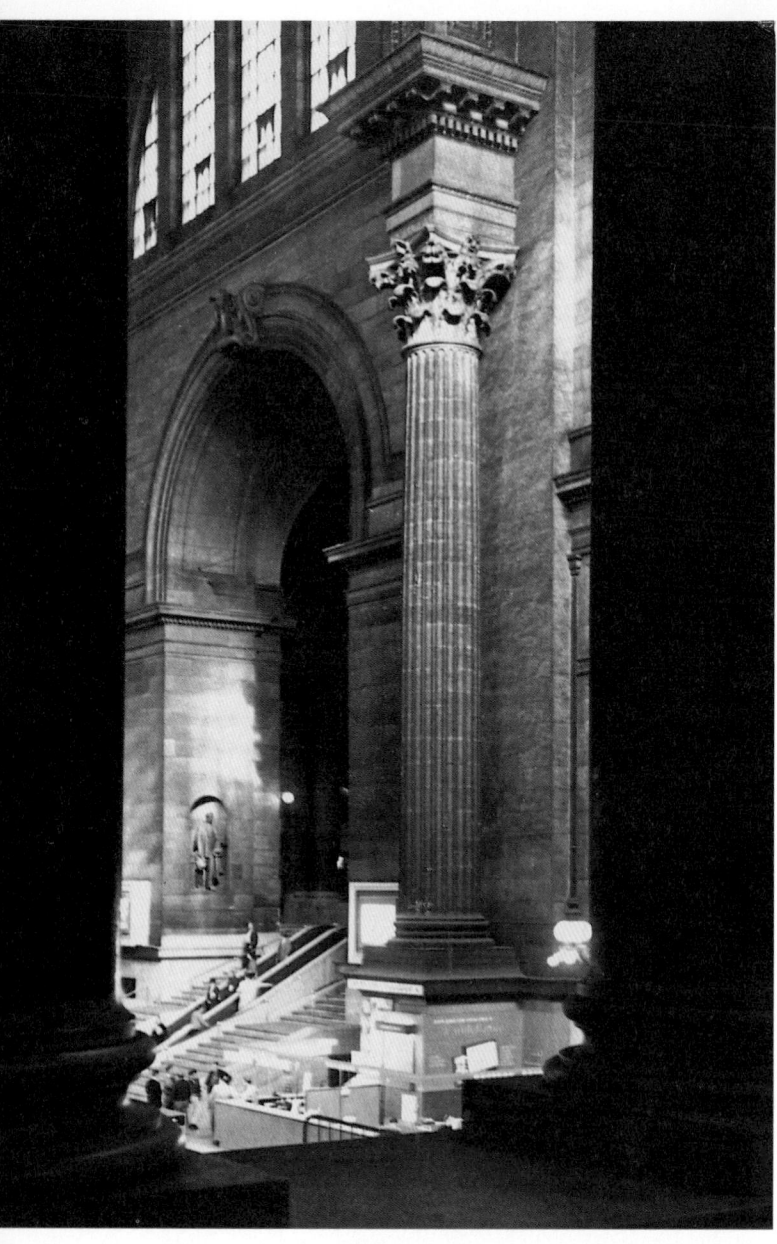

Pennsylvania Station, Seventh to Eighth Avenue, West Thirty-first to West Thirty-third Street. McKim, Mead & White, 1904–10. Waiting room, October 18, 1963. Fred W. McDarrah. FWM

public opinion might succeed in provoking governmental action: "The promoters are treading on the public toes in their assumption that they can destroy this place for a few men's personal gain—even in commercial old New York. The public resentment should be continued, for it can work. . . . Perhaps the time has come for a wing of government to buy [the building] from the railroad, with some of that railroad subsidy money."[223]

In response to the growing protest, A. J. Greenough, then president of the Pennsylvania Railroad, asked in a letter to the editor of the *New York Times*, "Does it make any sense to preserve a building merely as a 'monument' when it no longer serves the utilitarian needs for which it was erected?"[224] Some architects apparently agreed with Greenough; Jonathan Barnett would later recall that Max Abramovitz, lecturing at the Architectural League after the station's demolition, said that "he could not understand the sentiment for saving Pennsylvania Station" and that "as a young man . . . he would have been picketing to have it torn down."[225]

In January 1963 the station's fate was determined when the City Planning Commission, chaired by Francis Blaustein, acting chairperson from December 1962 to September 1963, following James Felt's resignation (in order to avoid the appearance of a conflict of interest because of his brother's involvement), granted the permission necessary to erect the new complex. The editors of *Progressive Architecture* wrote: "The great hall will go, the great concourse will fall, the traveler will be mashed into subterranean passageways like ancient Christians while the wrestler and the fight promoter will be elevated to the vast arena. The Decline and Fall of the American Empire—*sic transit gloria mundi*."[226] As Nathan Silver pointed out, the building was ultimately "sacrificed through the application of the real estate logic that often dictates the demolition of the very building that makes an area desirable."[227]

The editors of *Life* argued that the building's destruction was the inevitable result of years of neglect:

> In recent years the sweep of [the station's] majestic spaces has been invaded by ticket booths and other facilities which, though essential, are poorly designed and improperly integrated into the halls. There was no attempt at an over-all adaption of the station to changed needs, so the impression was created that it was obsolete. Thus the climate was right when real estate developers turned up before the City Planning Commission with a jackpot scheme to replace the single-purpose monument with a multipurpose pile. While admitting that "the protection of our cultural heritage is a matter of legitimate public interest," the commission ignored historical and esthetic considerations, concentrating on whether the new building would be justified in terms of revenue, housing and traffic problems.[228]

But, as Ada Louise Huxtable explained, that was all the commission could do: "However much the commission might be moved in the area of its civic conscience by such arguments it was totally without power to act on them. As it pointed out in its report, it is permitted only to pass on the *proposed* use of land, not on its *existing* use, and therefore cannot rule on the value of a building that is already on the site, but only on the nature of its replacement."[229]

Demolition of Pennsylvania Station began on October 28, 1963, and ended in the summer of 1966. Morris Lipsett, who with his brother Julius owned the wrecking company that demolished the station, was cynical about the building's loss: "If anybody seriously considered it art," he said, "they would have put up some money to save it."[230] The editors of *Architectural*

Forum noted that Morris Lipsett looked "confidently to the future: 'These new curtain wall buildings will be much easier to wreck than the old ones.'"[231] Huxtable commented that the last wall of the station "went not with a bang or a whimper, but to the rustle of real estate stock shares," and she saw in the building's demise a reflection of widespread moral bankruptcy.[232] "It's time we stopped talking about our affluent society," she said. "We are an impoverished society. It is a poor society indeed that . . . has no money for anything except expressways to rush people out of our dull and deteriorating cities and that treats land values as the highest morality."[233] The editors of the *New York Times* also saw the station's destruction as a symbol of skewed values: "Monumental problems almost as big as the building itself stood in the way of preservation; but it is the shame of New York, of its financial and cultural communities, its politicians, philanthropists, and planners, and of the public as well that no serious effort was made. A rich and powerful city, noted for its resources of brains, imagination and money, could not rise to the occasion. The final indictment is the values of our society." The *Times* concluded: "Any city gets what it admires, will pay for, and, ultimately, deserves. Even when we had Penn Station, we couldn't afford to keep it clean. We want and deserve tin-can architecture in a tin-horn culture. And we will probably be judged not by the monuments we build but by those we have destroyed."[234]

In the spring of 1962, before demolition had begun, the city had made an attempt to save a fragment of the building when Park Commissioner Newbold Morris proposed using the station's eighty-four Doric columns to create a monumentally scaled folly in Flushing Meadows, Queens.[235] Together with the New York Chapter of the American Institute of Architects, Morris later suggested placing eighteen of the columns, each surmounted by a stone eagle, in a double row in Battery Park. In the fall of 1963 the editors of the *New Yorker* expressed their opinion of the idea, which lingered even after demolition began: "People are still talking seriously about a plan to move the stone pillars . . . and we regard this as a dirty trick on future archeologists. When an archeologist finds an enormous stone ruin, he should be able to assume it is in its proper place; he should not have to consider the possibility that the Colosseum of Rome was actually constructed at Ostia and its ruins moved to make way for shipping piers."[236] Other ideas for saving the columns continued to pour forth. The architect Sal Grillo proposed placing them along the Mall in Central Park.[237] Edward Durell Stone suggested putting them around Columbus Circle, an idea that Paul Goldberger later said "made tremendous sense; for it would have given [the circle] some sense of definition and order."[238]

Ultimately, one column base and capital, as well as a carved Classical figure that had adorned a clock, made their way to the Brooklyn Museum's sculpture garden. Two of the station's twenty-two original carved eagles, created by the sculptor Adolph A. Weinman, were installed permanently near the Seventh Avenue entrance to the new Pennsylvania Station; four others found their way to Philadelphia, where they adorned a bridge close to the Pennsylvania Railroad's Thirtieth Street Station; and still others wound up in suburban railroad stations. Most of the wreckage, however, was discarded. "Tossed into the Secaucus graveyard are about 25 centuries of classical culture and the standards of style, elegance and grandeur that it gave to the dreams and constructions of Western man," wrote Ada Louise Huxtable. "That turns the Jersey wasteland into a pretty classy dump."[239]

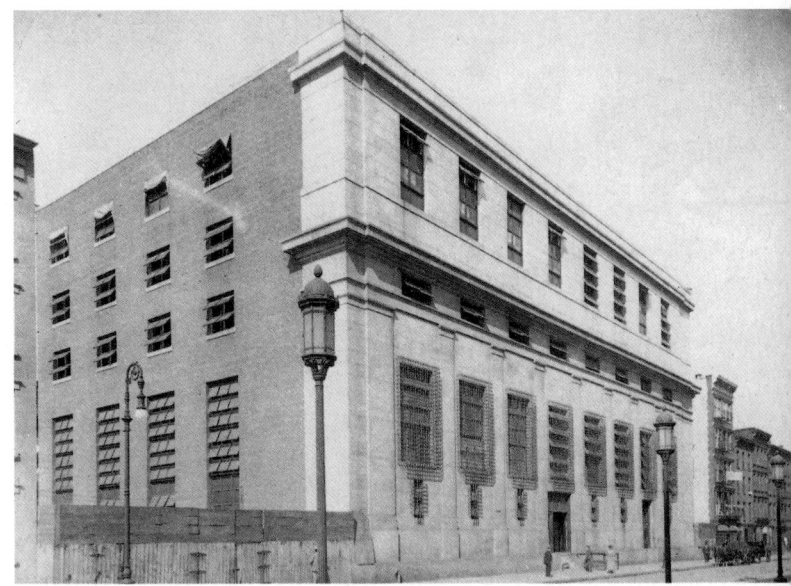

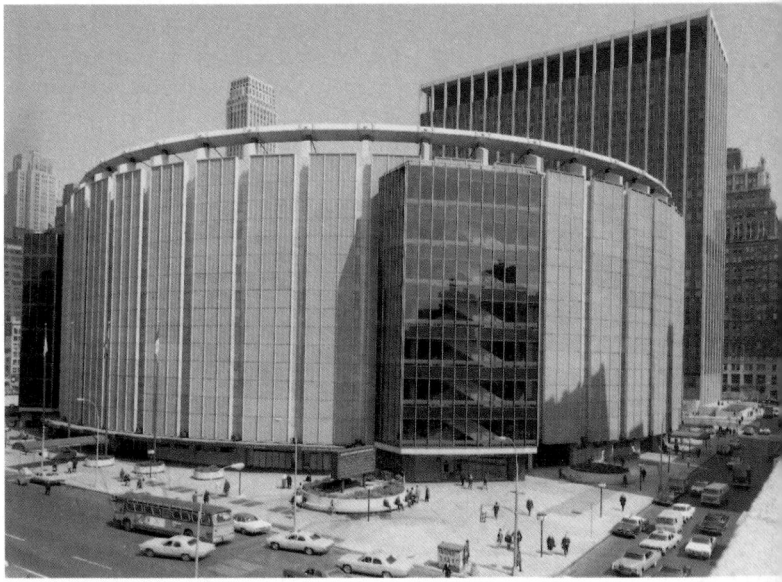

Top: Pennsylvania Station Service Building, 242 West Thirty-first Street, between Seventh and Eighth avenues. McKim, Mead & White, 1908. View to the southwest, ca. 1910. CU

Bottom: Madison Square Garden and Two Penn Plaza, Seventh to Eighth Avenue, West Thirty-first to West Thirty-third Street. Charles Luckman Associates, 1968. View to the northeast. OMH

One separate component of the station complex did successfully escape the wrecker's ball, the Pennsylvania Station Service Building (1908), at 242 West Thirty-first Street.[240] Designed by McKim, Mead & White, and in particular by McKim and his partner William Symmes Richardson, the building was set behind a strikingly unornamented facade incorporating a row of Roman Doric pilasters. The austere Classical building, which supplied the energy used for heating, lighting, elevator hydraulics, refrigeration and incineration in the station, as well as for arriving and departing engines, at once related and stood in sharp contrast to its monumental neighbor.

The complex that replaced Pennsylvania Station, Charles Luckman Associates' Madison Square Garden Center, consisted of a banal twenty-nine-story glass-and-precast-concrete office building, Two Penn Plaza, and an equally uninspired if somewhat more curious precast-concrete-clad circular building housing the third Madison Square Garden.[241] (Although Luckman had designed a monumentally scaled, twin-towered film center to replace Thomas W. Lamb's second Madison Square Garden of 1927, on the west side of Eighth Avenue between Forty-ninth and Fiftieth streets, the site was cleared in 1967 to make way for a parking lot.)[242] An elliptical, fifty-two-story office building designed by Kahn & Jacobs as part of the complex was never realized.[243] The new thirteen-story-high, 425-foot-diameter Garden, containing a remarkable array of facilities, including the 20,500-seat arena, the 4,600-seat Felt Forum and a forty-eight-lane bowling alley, was spanned by a cable-suspended roof, the largest of its kind in the country, which allowed for clear space without view-obstructing columns.[244] The editors of *Architectural Forum* described preliminary plans for the complex as looking "rather like a giant mambo palace,"[245] and the playwright John Guare later described it as "the dump that replaced the masterpiece."[246] Huxtable suggested that the complex's style was "not Roman Imperial but Investment Modern,"[247] and Goldberger flatly concluded, "For this there is no excuse."[248]

Pennsylvania Station's main concourse was pushed completely below grade and redesigned to resemble, as Goldberger put it, "a subway station with terrazzo floors and slightly cleaner shops than in the real subway," allowing "train riders to enjoy all of the vulgarity and oppressiveness of airports right in the middle of town."[249] Writing in 1963 before the new terminal's completion, Norman Mailer voiced a similar opinion: "It will waste no space for high vaulted ceilings and monumental columns, it will look doubtless like the inside of a large airport. And one will feel the same subtle nausea coming into the city or waiting to depart from it that one now feels in such plastic catacombs as O'Hare's reception center in Chicago, at United or American Airlines in Idlewild."[250]

In his book *American Architecture and Urbanism*, published in 1969, Vincent Scully recalled the old station as being "all public grandeur, embodying a quality too rare in America." In assessing the destruction of the station, Scully viewed it in the context of changing architectural fashion:

A later generation was to deride its formal dependence upon the Baths of Caracalla. One is less sure than one used to be that such was a very relevant criticism at all. Much more memorable now that it is gone is the rhythmic clarity of the generous big spaces of the station and the majestic firmness with which the great piers and columns and the coffered vault defined them. It was academic building at its best, rational and ordered according to a pattern of use and a blessed sense of civic ex-

cess. It seems odd that we could ever have been persuaded that it was no good and, finally, permitted its destruction. Through it one entered the city like a god. Perhaps it was really too much. One scuttles in now like a rat.[251]

The Landmarks Preservation Commission Law

On April 19, 1965, the city finally acted to protect its architectural heritage when Mayor Robert F. Wagner signed the New York City Landmarks Preservation Commission Law.[252] Four years earlier an advisory committee on preservation appointed by Mayor Wagner had recommended that legislation be drafted and an inventory of worthy buildings be taken; the following year a second committee, headed by the architect Geoffrey Platt, who had also headed the first committee, embarked on these tasks. Platt became chairman of the new commission, which was charged with the identification, designation and regulation of landmark properties.[253] As defined by the law, a landmark was required to be at least thirty years old. The law described the protection of the city's architectural and urbanistic heritage as "a public necessity . . . required in the interest of the health, prosperity, safety and welfare of the people" and identified the aims of preservation as including the stabilization and improvement of property values, the enhancement of civic pride and the stimulation of the city's tourist trade.[254]

The new law specified that the commission would consist of eleven members, to be selected by the mayor for three-year terms, during which the commissioners would work on a part-time, unpaid basis. The commission was required to include at least one member from each borough, three architects, one historian, one realtor and one landscape architect or city planner. The additional five commissioners could be either professionals or laymen; usually at least one commissioner was an attorney or someone well versed in the operation of city government. The fact that none of the commissioners, except for the chairman, were compensated tended to reinforce if not foster the impression that their job was somehow less serious than that of paid members of the City Planning Commission. The landmarks commission also included a paid, full-time staff composed of architects, architectural historians, restoration experts, legal advisers, researchers and administrators. In addition, it was aided by volunteers and students paid by the federal government.

Nominations for landmark designation were accepted from concerned citizens, property owners, commissioners, staff members of the commission and members of city government; a survey of properties became the commission's principal source of information leading to designation. The survey was conducted by the commission staff, who researched nominated sites and presented their findings to the commissioners; at a public executive session, the commissioners then decided which buildings should be further researched. Commissioners made site visits to buildings under consideration whenever possible. At a subsequent public executive meeting, the commission selected which buildings would be discussed in a public hearing held at the Board of Estimate Room in City Hall. Hearings were advertised and all property owners notified so that any interested party could testify either for or against the proposed designation. The new commission was to hold public hearings during its initial eighteen months, after which hearings would be held during six-month periods separated by three-year-long hiatuses. In 1973 the commission's procedures were amended to allow for hearings to be held whenever they were deemed necessary; in addi-

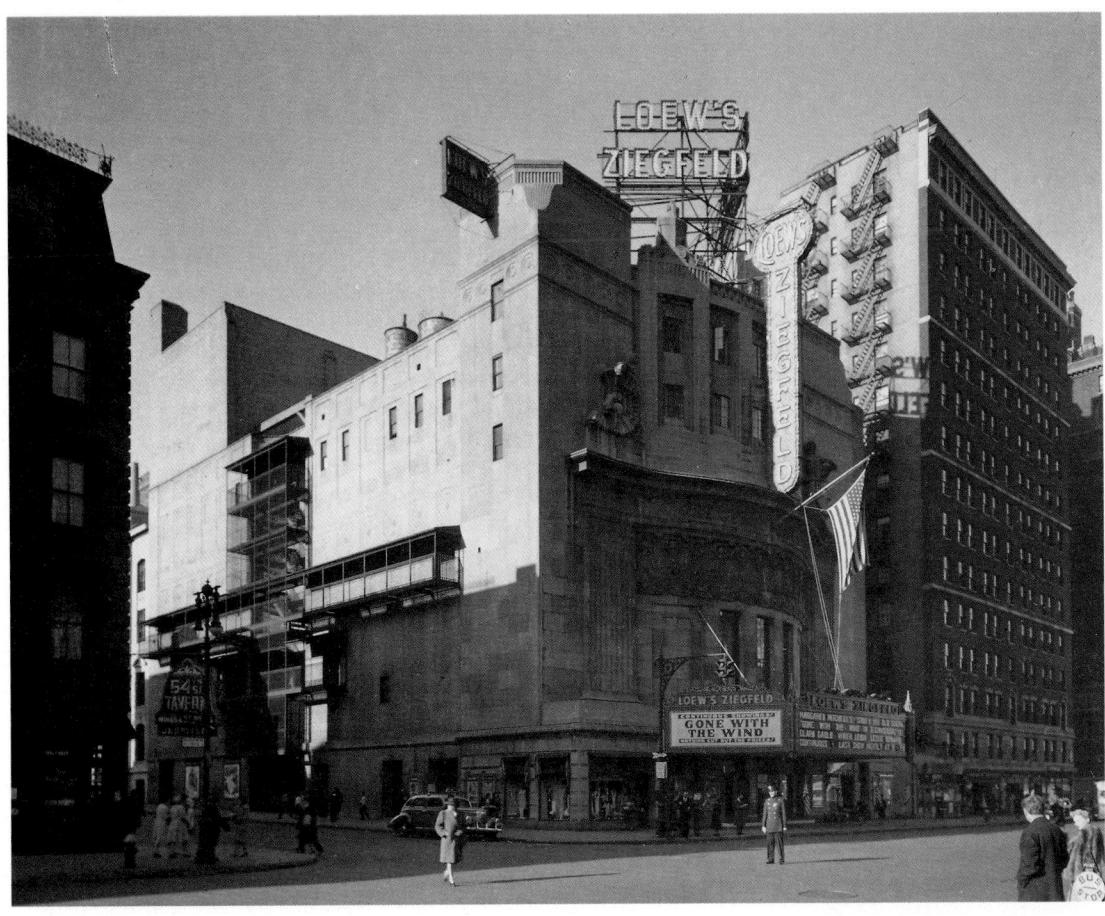

tion, the commission's jurisdiction was broadened to include interior and scenic landmarks.[255] Final selections were determined after a preliminary designation report was prepared by the commission's research department. Six affirmative votes were required to declare a proposed site a landmark, regardless of how many commission members were present. Within a ninety-day period, the Board of Estimate, having received a mandatory report from the City Planning Commission, as well as optional reports from the Board of Standards and Appeals and the Buildings, Fire and Health departments, was entitled to modify or veto the approved designation.

A designated landmark was legally protected against any and all changes without public review. An owner seeking to make changes to a building was required to submit a proposal to the commission, which would grant a "certificate of appropriateness" if the changes were acceptable. While landmark designation provided legally binding protection, it did not ensure a building's survival if the owner could successfully argue economic hardship, which was defined as the inability to garner a 6 percent return on the investment. Legal provisions granted the commission specific steps through which to save such a building, including finding a buyer who would preserve the threatened building and purchase it at a fair price; granting the owner a tax abatement or remission; and, after 1968, when an amendment to the New York City Zoning Resolution was passed, permitting the owner to sell his property's unused development rights, provided that the new building was contextually appropriate to its landmark neighbor. If an arrangement satisfactory to the owner had not been reached, and the city chose not to buy the property or acquire it through condemnation proceedings, the owner was permitted to demolish the building.

In its first year of existence, the commission designated thirty-seven individual landmarks and one historic district; the decisions were based primarily on aesthetic grounds, with a limited number of designations awarded on the basis of a building's or site's historical or cultural significance. While the commission demonstrated a certain breadth of vision, designating a stylistically and programmatically eclectic mélange of buildings from all periods of the city's history, it nonetheless concentrated on obvious and uncontroversial choices, leaning toward buildings that were already safe in the hands of preservation groups, well-established institutions or the city itself and thus avoiding potential conflicts with real estate interests. In several cases, including those of Castle Clinton (see above) and Federal Hall National Memorial (formerly the United States Custom House; Ithiel Town, Alexander Jackson Davis, Samuel Thompson and John Frazee, 1834–42),[256] the buildings were already legally protected by the federal government.

Landmarks Lost after 1965

Although the passage of the landmarks preservation law began to establish a context for saving the city's architectural heritage, during the early years of the landmarks commission quite a few significant buildings were lost. Much of the demolition occurred with no public outcry; some notice was taken by the press, however, which was becoming increasingly attentive to preservation issues. In 1966 Richard Morris Hunt's New York Tribune Building (1876), on the northeast corner of Nassau and Spruce streets, once the city's second tallest building (the first being Trinity Church), fell to make way for Eggers & Higgins's massive

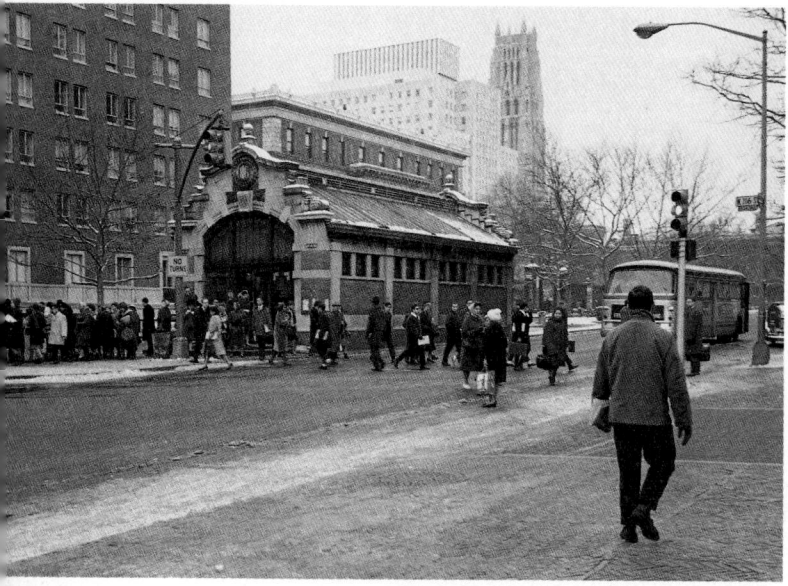

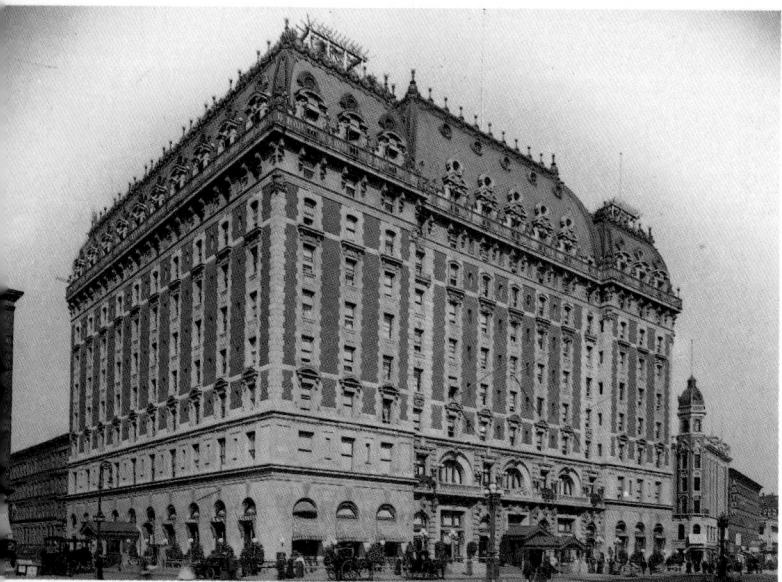

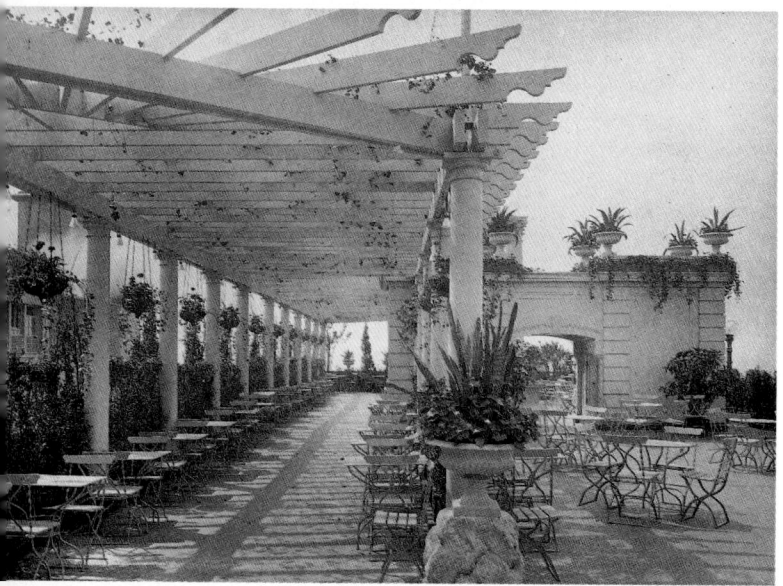

complex for Pace University.[257] In the following year the Guaranty Trust Company Building (York & Sawyer, 1913), at 140 Broadway, was torn down to make way for the Marine Midland Bank Building,[258] and the Ziegfeld Theater (Joseph Urban, 1927), on the northwest corner of Sixth Avenue and Fifty-fourth Street, fell to permit construction of Burlington House, a huge office tower.[259] The loss of the Paramount Theater (Rapp & Rapp, 1926), located in the Paramount Building, on the west side of Broadway between Forty-third and Forty-fourth streets, which was gutted and converted into additional newsrooms for the *New York Times* in 1967, was widely mourned.[260] Reporting in the *New York Times* on the theater's destruction, Thomas W. Ennis said, "For months, the interior of the auditorium—the temple where bobbysoxers of the nineteen-forties worshipped their idol Frank Sinatra—has looked like a murky corner of Hell."[261] Sanka Knox, also reporting for the *Times*, noted the irony apparent in the sale of the theater's fixtures: "Out of fashion for years, a good many of the Paramount's elaborate and sometimes dazzling ornaments chalked up dazzling prices, showing the full circle popular taste has undergone."[262] Also lost in 1967 were the garage and garden adjacent to the Vincent Astor residence (Mott B. Schmidt, 1926), located on the north side of Seventy-ninth Street between Park and Lexington avenues; they were replaced by the Hunter College School of Social Work.[263]

In 1968 the 116th Street control house of the IRT subway (Heins & LaFarge, 1904), a grace note in the middle of the Broadway mall and, for generations of commuting students, the front door to Columbia University, was demolished and replaced by nothing more than concrete pavement.[264] Also in 1968 the 5,300-seat Capitol Theater (Thomas Lamb, 1919) was replaced by the Uris-developed office building at 1633 Broadway, designed by Emery Roth & Sons;[265] and the Broadway Tabernacle (Barney & Chapman, 1904) fell to make way for another office tower, 888 Seventh Avenue, also by the Roth firm.[266] In 1969 two prominent hotels, the Astor (Clinton & Russell, 1909),[267] on Broadway between Forty-fourth and Forty-fifth streets, and the Ambassador (Warren & Wetmore, 1921),[268] on Park Avenue between Fifty-first and Fifty-second Streets, were demolished for new office buildings. Another hotel, McKim, Mead & White's Hotel Imperial (1890), which had fallen on hard times, was replaced that same year by Shreve, Lamb & Harmon's undistinguished thirty-eight-story office building at 1250 Broadway.[269] Also in 1969 Carrère & Hastings's English Regency–style house of 1903–5 for Senator Elihu Root, on the southeast corner of Park Avenue and Seventy-first Street, was replaced by 733 Park Avenue, an apartment building designed by Kahn & Jacobs.[270] In 1973 the George D. Widener house (Warren & Wetmore, 1911), at 5 East Seventieth Street, gave way, eventually to be replaced by an extension of the Frick Museum.[271] In 1974 three architecturally distinguished buildings in lower Manhattan were torn down to allow for street widenings: the seven-story W. R. Grace Building (James W. O'Connor, 1913), at 7 Hanover Square;[272] the twenty-story building at 1 Liberty Street (Hill & Stout, 1907);[273] and the thirteen-story John Wolfe Building (Henry J. Hardenbergh, 1895), at 80 William Street.[274] The same year, the Wurlitzer Building (Maynicke & Franke, 1919) was replaced by a rather lifeless plaza adjacent to the New York Telephone Company's headquarters on the west side of Sixth Avenue between Forty-first and Forty-second streets.[275]

Not all buildings disappeared so quietly. Many people were shocked to learn in autumn 1964 that the Savoy-Plaza Hotel

(McKim, Mead & White, 1927), located on the east side of Fifth Avenue between Fifty-eighth and Fifty-ninth streets, where it was part of one of the world's best-known ensembles, would be torn down to make way for an office building for the General Motors Corporation.[276] In January 1965 a group of women including the novelist Fannie Hurst and Mrs. John A. Warner, the daughter of Alfred E. Smith, formed a preservationist committee called Save Our Landmarks!—Save the Plaza Square. Glenn Fowler later reported in the *New York Times* that "socially prominent women and financially potent women stockholders threatened the $17-billion-a-year giant of American industry with instant destruction unless it abandoned its plan to erect what they called a tombstone in the Savoy Plaza's stead."[277] Here, as the social commentator Roger Starr put it, "was a group of ladies not generally considered to be revolutionary" threatening to "abstain from the purchase of Cadillacs" until a beloved landmark was saved.[278] Nonetheless, the following year the grand hotel gave way to the wrecker's ball.

Loss of the hotel provoked a legitimate fear that there would be more demolition in the area. In August 1968 the City Planning Commission announced that it would rezone a three-block area around Grand Army Plaza to prohibit office development.[279] In December 1969 the Landmarks Preservation Commission designated the Plaza Hotel (Henry J. Hardenbergh, 1907) a landmark,[280] and five years later, in July 1974, it designated Carrère & Hastings's Grand Army Plaza (1916).[281]

Though both the planning and landmark commissions were slow to recognize the depth and sincerity of the public's concern over the increasing depletion of the city's architectural treasury, the management of the Plaza Hotel was not. In the 1950s they embarked on a program of restoring portions of the building to their turn-of-the-century appearance. When the hotel was opened, the State Suite, on the first floor, overlooking Central Park and Fifth Avenue, had been reserved for dignitaries, but it later became part of Solomon R. Guggenheim's private apartment. In 1954 James S. Graham, Jr., a decorator with Marshall Field & Company, restored the room to its 1907 state so that it could be used for private functions.[282] But not all of the hotel's renovations were so carefully considered. In 1955 the Palm Court's Tiffany stained-glass ceiling, through which light had filtered from an open courtyard above, was replaced by a vaguely Dorothy Draperesque dropped ceiling.[283] In 1965, anticipating the replacement of the Savoy-Plaza across Fifth Avenue, the Plaza's management played on the public's growing sense of dismay by running advertisements describing "the day New York almost vanished." Although the unabashedly self-serving copy was no doubt intended to be amusing, it raised issues that were all too real for many New Yorkers:

> It didn't happen all at once. They did it very gradually. "We can't alarm the people!" they said. So they removed a little house here. And a great hotel there. And then a few limestone banks and all the cast-iron store fronts they could find. And very quietly one night they stole a railroad station and buried it in New Jersey. A few people grumbled. . . . But most people were complacent. Until they discovered that their city had been entirely replaced with glass. . . . Soon after this, on one ghastly glittering morning, an observant executive walking to work paused on Fifth Avenue at Fifty-ninth Street to clean his heavy dark goggles. Squinting, he looked around. And gasped! There was The Plaza where he had always remembered it. "It can't be!" he said and rubbed his eyes. He looked again. "It *is* there!" he said. And ran to work. He called his wife. "We'll go there tonight, before it's too late. Don't tell anyone!" he hissed.

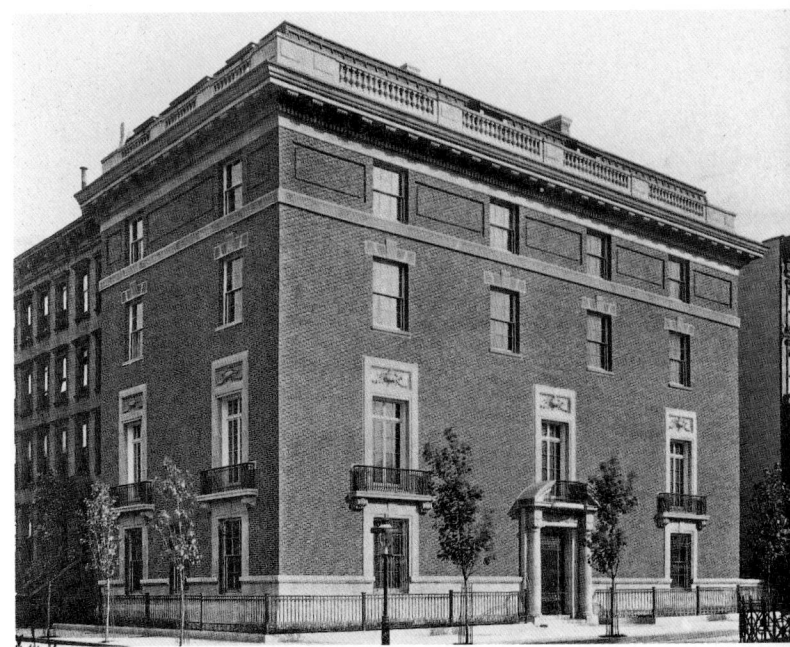

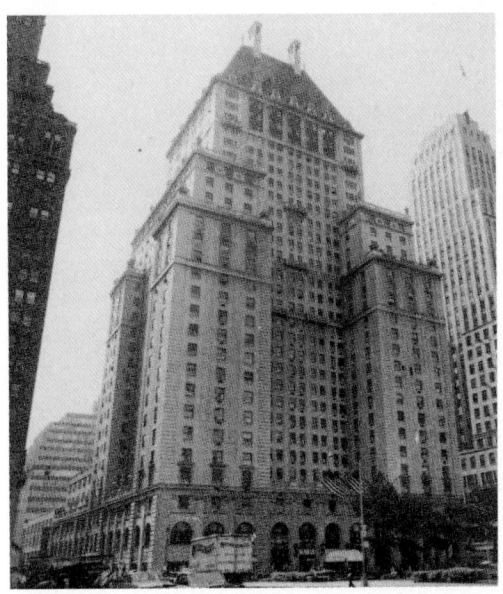

Top left: West 116th Street control house of the IRT subway, Broadway mall at West 116th Street. Heins & LaFarge, 1904. View to the northwest, ca. 1965. CCT

Center left: Hotel Astor, west side of Broadway, West Forty-fourth to West Forty-fifth Street. Clinton & Russell, 1909. View to the northwest also showing Astor Theater (George Keister, 1906), ca. 1910. Ingalls. NYHS

Bottom left: Hotel Astor. Roof garden. Byron. MCNY

Top: Elihu Root residence, 733 Park Avenue, southeast corner of East Seventy-first Street. Carrère & Hastings, 1903–5. View to the southeast. ARCH. CU

Bottom: Savoy-Plaza Hotel, east side of Fifth Avenue, East Fifty-eighth to East Fifty-ninth Street. McKim, Mead & White, 1927. View to the southeast, ca. 1964. NYP

1123

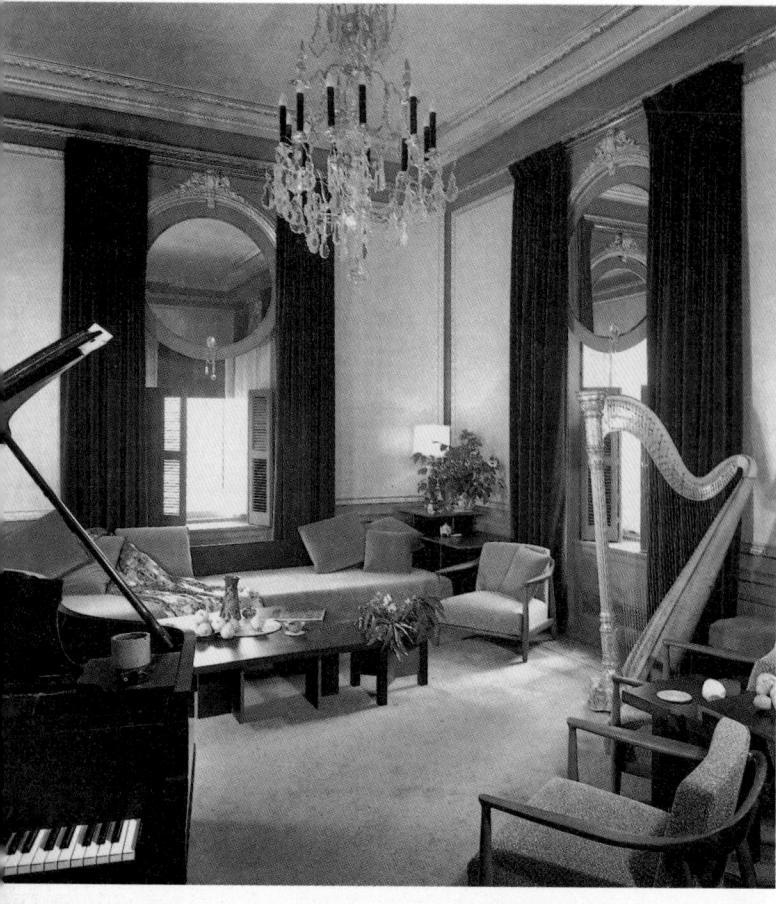

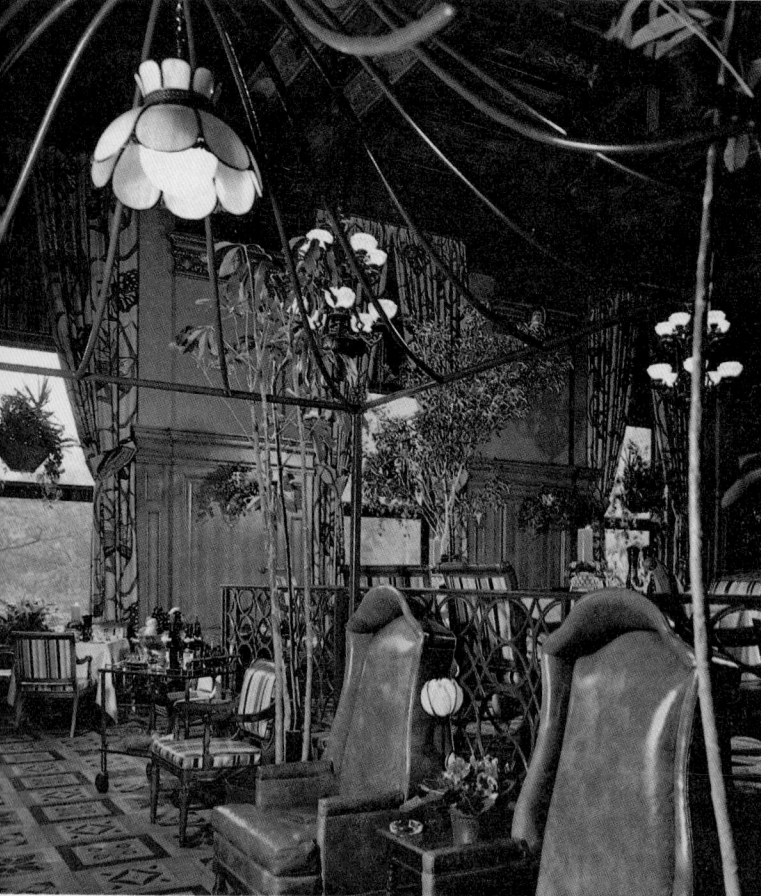

So she only told her very best friend. Soon everyone knew. Crowds gathered. They wandered in the lobbies. They caressed the marble, admired the gilded cherubs. And the caryatids in the Palm Court where palms still swayed. They feasted in the baronial splendor of the Edwardian Room.[284]

The Plaza had a surprising advocate in Frank Lloyd Wright, one of its most illustrious residents. Despite the fact that Wright was widely known for his anti-urban proselytizing and his dislike of New York in particular, his trips to the city had become so regular by 1953 that he and his wife, Olgivanna, rented suite 223, located in the northeast corner of the second floor, an apartment they retained until Wright's death in 1959.[285] As his wife would later recall, Wright appreciated the Plaza's architecture and atmosphere: "He had high esteem for Henry Hardenbergh . . . and thought his work had style."[286] In an interview conducted by Brendan Gill for a 1953 *New Yorker* "Talk of the Town" piece, Wright not only praised the hotel but took credit for the preservation of some of the hotel's interiors. "I've stayed here for forty years," Wright stated. "They started to remodel it downstairs a few years back, but thank God I got here in time to stop them. . . . I saved the Oak Room and the dining room."[287]

Wright designed his three-room suite, where he stayed while overseeing several New York projects, most notably the Guggenheim Museum, to do double duty as an apartment and an office, complete with drafting stations. In contrast to the hotel's guest rooms, which were packed full of period furniture by the professionals Wright ridiculed as "inferior desecrators," his apartment featured simple red- and black-lacquered wooden furniture.[288] Wright's design also included walls covered in panels of gold-colored Japanese paper bordered in rose-colored outlines. Arched window frames housed circular mirrors that concealed light fixtures. Dark red velvet drapes extended nearly the full height of the rooms and were equipped with pull cords terminating in crystal spheres. Although Wright's stylistic vocabulary was radically different from that used elsewhere in the hotel, Olgivanna Wright felt he had "interpreted the old style of the building in new terms which were sympathetic to the past."[289] To the critic Herbert Muschamp, the suite celebrated both the architect's achievements and the city itself. "More than a grand-luxe foreman's hut," Muschamp wrote, the suite "was a handsomely appointed symbol of Wright's hugely successful rejuvenation. His passage from the 'worm's eye view' of New York in the twenties to a treetop-view suite at the Plaza in the fifties was just the kind of success story for which Manhattan has always provided a thrillingly dramatic background."[290]

In 1971, in a demonstration of corporate amnesia, new management reneged on the hotel's commitment to preservation and started to pick away at more of its beautiful interior. Though the Edwardian Room was never directly threatened with demolition, it was treated with something less than reverence when it was rechristened the Green Tulip Room and redesigned by interior designer Sally Dryden.[291] The new design was meant to visually link the room to Central Park through the use of potted trees, hanging plants and metal gazebos called "sangria trees" that served as wine-serving stations. Dryden also painted the dark woodwork a lighter pecan color, re-covered its chairs with boldly striped fabric, and lifted diners on an eighteen-inch-high platform to give them a better view of the park. To add insult to injury, she flanked the room's entrance with contemporary, Tiffany-inspired stained-glass panels, while the genuine articles presumably moldered in the hotel's attic.

Ada Louise Huxtable was appalled by the redesign: "The

changes do not involve demolition, just the slow erosion of its traditional style and grace. . . . What is real, now looks fake. Class is out. Confusion is in. . . . The dignity, scale and period authenticity of the Oak Room make the Green Tulip look like something out of a shopping center department store."[292] The editors of *Interior Design* disagreed, arguing that while the design "may score negatively with those who associate the landmark hotel . . . with enduring and untouchable elegance . . . the fact remains that 'today' and 'tomorrow' are key words in contemporary commercial design, and sentimentality alone is out of place in the highly competitive hotel business."[293] Whatever the critical reactions to the Green Tulip, the public made its negative feelings known quite clearly, and the restaurant was a financial failure. In 1974 the hotel's management restored much of its former decor, and Huxtable rejoiced: "When the Plaza returned its conventionally schlocked-up Green Tulip restaurant to something resembling its original Edwardian Room authenticity, business shot up."[294] Two years later the hotel hired the Rambusch Company to carefully restore the Oak Room and Oak Bar.[295]

In one early case that occurred soon after the landmarks law was passed, the landmarks commission made an unsuccessful effort to halt a building's destruction. The French Second Empire–style Leonard Jerome house (T. R. Jackson, 1859), on the southeast corner of Madison Avenue and Twenty-sixth Street, was designated a landmark in November 1965, seven months after the property had been sold to a development group that sought to assemble a site for a thirty-three-story office tower.[296] The house had been built by Winston Churchill's maternal grandfather and later served as home to the Manhattan Club. In February 1966 the buyers, headed by Jackson A. Edwards, sued the Landmarks Preservation Commission over the right to demolish the building; the New York State Supreme Court denied the request and the designation was upheld.[297] Even after the purchasers had made full payment in cash, the commission continued to look for a buyer who would preserve the building, but to no avail. Arguing their case on the basis of economic hardship, the building's new owners applied to the commission for permission to demolish the building, which was granted in September 1967. Emery Roth & Sons' banal, black-glass-clad forty-two-story tower for the New York Merchandise Mart was completed on the site in 1973.[298]

Perhaps as a result of the failed attempt to preserve the Manhattan Club, the commission shied away from fully exercising its legal rights, fearful that its credibility would be further tarnished or its very existence successfully challenged. Often the commission seemed to lack the courage to protect worthy buildings if it meant opposing determined real estate interests and thus stirring publicity and controversy. Resting on its successes rather than squarely facing its failures, the commission tended to stay within the shadow of politicians and developers, and even of critics and journalists, who closely monitored and sharply criticized its activities, treating it like a favored but mercurial and spoiled child. Regrettably, the commission often displayed indecisiveness over difficult cases, sometimes failing to take any action at all.

In 1967, following the relocation of the Metropolitan Opera Company to new headquarters in Lincoln Center, the original Metropolitan Opera House (J. C. Cady, 1883; interior renovation, Carrère & Hastings, 1903), on the block bounded by Broadway, Seventh Avenue, Thirty-ninth and Fortieth streets, was demolished despite strong opposition.[299] The Old Met Opera House Corporation, which counted among its trustees the soprano Lucia Albanese and United States Senator Jacob K.

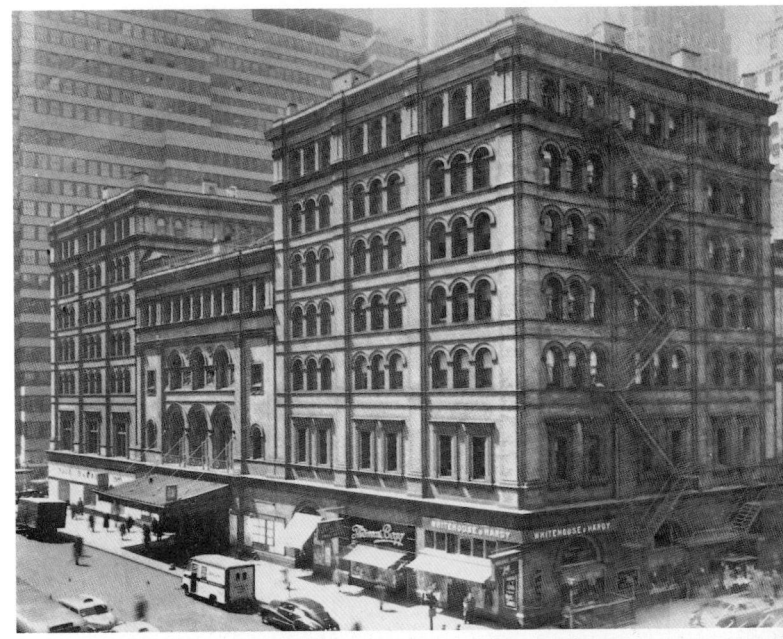

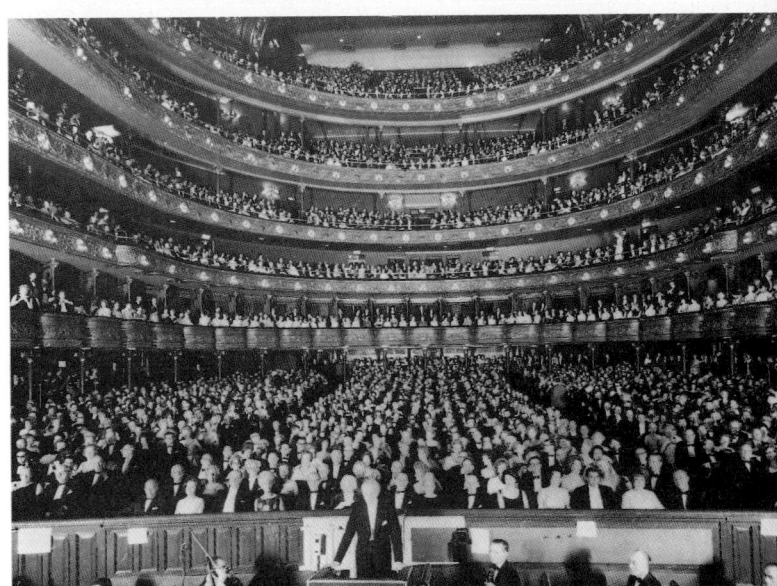

Top left: Suite 223, Plaza Hotel, west side of Grand Army Plaza, West Fifty-eighth to West Fifty-ninth Street. Henry J. Hardenbergh, 1905–7; renovation, Frank Lloyd Wright, 1953. Living room. Stoller. ©ESTO

Bottom left: Green Tulip Room (formerly Edwardian Room), Plaza Hotel. Henry J. Hardenbergh, 1905–7; renovation, Sally Dryden, 1971. ID. CU

Top: Metropolitan Opera House, Broadway to Seventh Avenue, West Thirty-ninth to West Fortieth Street. J. C. Cady, 1883; interior renovation, Carrère & Hastings, 1903. View to the southwest, ca. 1950. MOA

Bottom: Metropolitan Opera House. Closing night, Leopold Stokowski conducting, April 16, 1966. MOA

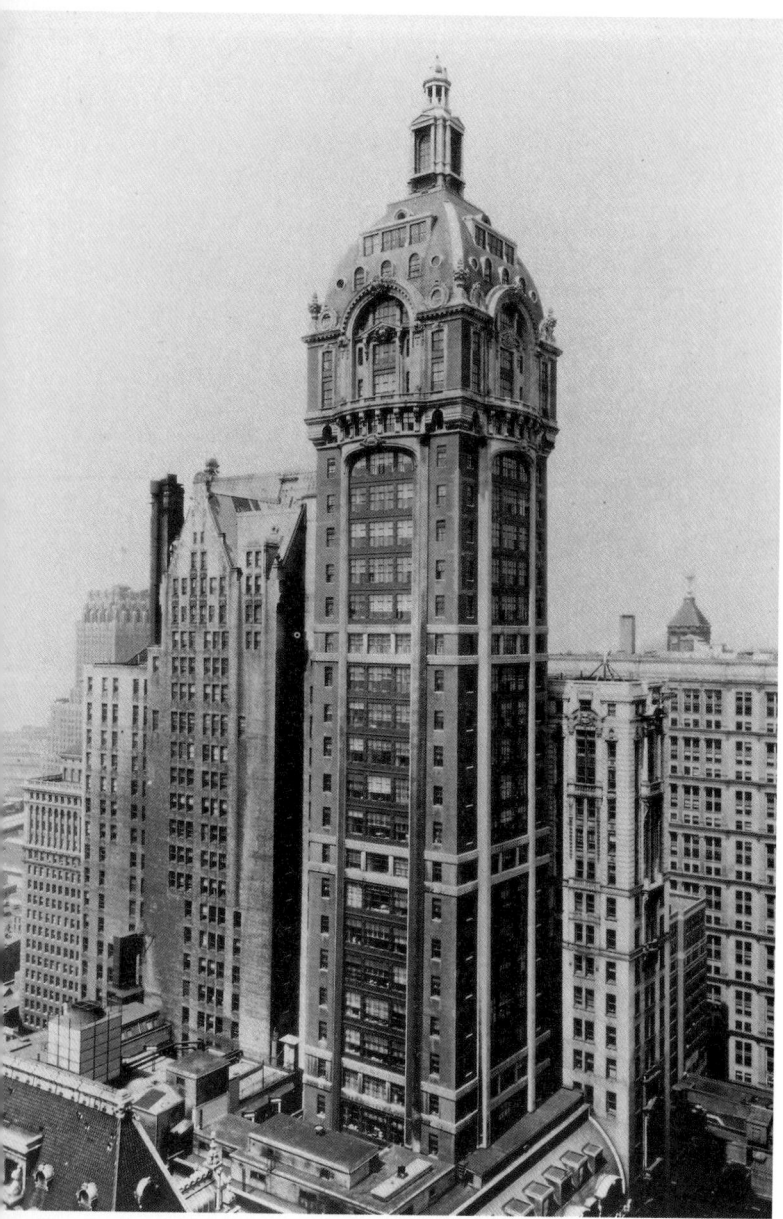

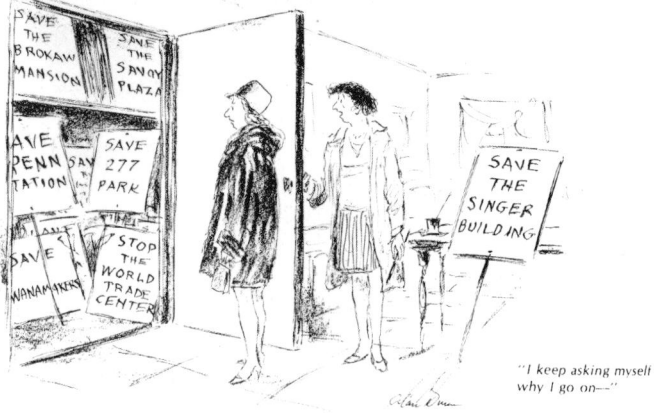

"I keep asking myself
why I go on—"

Top: Singer Tower, northwest corner of Broadway and Liberty Street. Ernest Flagg, 1908. View to the northwest. OMH

Bottom: Cartoon. Alan Dunn, 1968. PDE

Javits, was unable to raise the money required to purchase and preserve the building. The local chapter of the American Institute of Architects also failed in its effort to have the building, or at least the auditorium, incorporated into the office building erected on the site. All that was saved was an elegantly detailed bar, which was transported to St. Louis, where it was installed in a palatial 1925 movie theater that had been transformed into a symphony hall.

On January 18, 1967, the day demolition began, a crowd gathered outside the opera house; among the demonstrators was Huntington Hartford, the arts patron and heir to the A&P fortune, who said, "This is going to give America a black eye for years to come."[300] Reporting for the *New York Times*, Theodore Strongin wrote of the demolition: "Inside the 84-year-old house dust hung ominously in the air. All was silent except for an occasional thunder provided by the wreckers on the roof. The atmosphere was that of the Death of Gods scene in Götterdämmerung."[301] But not all observers were saddened by the demise of the old opera house; the editors of the *New York Times*, notoriously prodevelopment, supported the building's demolition on the grounds that its preservation might be a financial threat to the opera company. Furthermore, they said, "the exterior of the building . . . is uncommonly ugly. Even by the standards of a storage warehouse, it is an eyesore."[302]

The loss of other significant buildings reflected the commission's tendency to overlook the achievements of the recent past, particularly commercial buildings. In 1967 Ernest Flagg's Singer Tower of 1908, once the world's tallest and still one of its most distinguished skyscrapers, gained the dubious distinction of being the tallest building ever torn down.[303] Flagg had designed the tower to rise above the ten-story, mansard-roofed Singer headquarters he had completed in 1899. A brilliant marriage of Beaux-Arts compositional rationalism, Modern French style and state-of-the-art technology, the slender tower was only sixty-five feet square and rose thirty-seven stories to climax in a nobly proportioned lantern. The steel-frame building had a seven-to-one height-to-width ratio, establishing a record that, just prior to its demolition, the editors of *Architectural Forum* hypothesized might still be unsurpassed.[304] The building was also distinguished by its opulent double-height, marble-clad lobby, which had served several generations as a favorite meeting place.

In 1954, when the Wall Street real estate market was languishing, William Zeckendorf purchased the Singer Tower and adjacent properties to make way for a new building for the New York Stock Exchange. Zeckendorf's plan fell through, however, when the Stock Exchange elected simply to expand to one side of its temple-fronted building on Broad and Wall streets (George B. Post, 1903; addition, Trowbridge & Livingston, 1923).[305] The Exchange constructed an undistinguished twenty-two-story office building on the site, replacing two landmark-quality office buildings, the Blair Building (Carrère & Hastings, 1902–3) and the adjacent Commercial Cable Building (Harding & Gooch, 1897).[306] But the Singer Tower's reprieve was short-lived, its fate sealed when the nearby construction of the World Trade Center in the 1960s sent property values soaring. Despite the objections of Ada Louise Huxtable and others, as well as the suggestion made by the editors of *Architectural Forum* that at least the tower's lobby be preserved and incorporated into the new building proposed for the site, the city approved demolition.[307] The two-year-old Landmarks Preservation Commission proved inadequate to the task of saving the tower; as Alan Burnham, executive director of the commission, explained: "If the building were made a landmark, we would have to find a buyer for it or the city would have to acquire it. The city is not wealthy and the commission doesn't have a big enough staff to be a real-estate broker for a skyscraper."[308]

Huxtable commented on the scene of the building's destruction:

> Piranesi, anyone? The master never produced a more impressive ruin than the Singer Building under demolition. Curious New Yorkers who risk a piece of Pavonazza marble on the head by looking beyond the boarding that surrounds the . . . tower . . . will find a scene of rich, surrealist desolation. Domed vaults supported by bronze-trimmed marble columns wait inside in half-light and plaster dust for the sledgehammer. . . . The distinctive tower, a triumph of "modern" steel construction that added its Beaux Arts silhouette to the picturesque bouquet of early skyscraper spires, will probably be replaced by one more "flat-top," diminishing the character of the downtown skyline.[309]

Along with the Singer Tower, several other buildings, including the imposing thirty-two-story City Investing Building (Francis H. Kimball, 1908),[310] were torn down to clear the two-block site bounded by Church, Cedar and Cortlandt streets and Broadway for U.S. Steel's new headquarters. Designed by Skidmore, Owings & Merrill, the fifty-four-story building was a particularly graceless steel-and-glass superslab that rose sheer from an austere plaza, whose inclusion allowed for the construction of such an immense building in the first place. What was lost in the demolition of the Singer Tower was not only a vital part of the city's architectural past but a telling lesson in the humanistic urbanism of the tower-base skyscraper type. Chandeliers from the building's boardroom, a pathetically small reminder of the Singer Tower's grandeur, were salvaged and installed in Pratt Institute's East Building.

Even after the loss of the Singer Tower, the need to protect the city's iconic skyscrapers was not fully perceived or heeded. Despite a growing interest throughout the 1960s and 1970s in the design of the interwar period, reflected in the buying habits of such collectors as the Pop artist Andy Warhol[311] as well as the publication of such books as Cervin Robinson and Rosemarie Haag Bletter's *Skyscraper Style: Art Deco New York* (1975),[312] virtually all of the city's Modern Classical architectural treasures stood unprotected for years after the passage of the landmarks law. The Chrysler Building (William Van Alen, 1930) was not designated a landmark until 1978.[313] The integrity of the Empire State Building (Shreve, Lamb & Harmon, 1931) was threatened until it was designated in 1981.[314] Though it had been enhanced with the construction of a 222-foot-tall television mast in 1951[315] and, on the occasion of its twenty-fifth anniversary in 1956, with the installation of two sweeping light beacons,[316] the Empire State Building was eclipsed as the world's tallest building in the mid-1970s by the twin towers of the World Trade Center and by Chicago's Sears Tower. To meet these challenges, two proposals were advanced by Robert W. Jones, a principal in the firm of Shreve, Lamb & Harmon, for an extension that would increase the building's height from 1,250 feet to 1,494 feet.[317] Both of Jones's proposed designs eliminated the tower's distinctive, stepped-back crown; one called for an elongated but truncated pyramid beginning on the eighty-first floor, and the other called for a flat-topped rectilinear mass slightly cantilevered out over the existing building's eighty-sixth floor to rise sheer, with the exception of a single minor setback near its 113th-story top. Both designs called for the building to be surmounted by a mast. Neither of these proposals went beyond the drafting board.

Because most skyscrapers were built to higher densities than current zoning would permit, only a few actually fell to make way for new buildings. Quite the opposite was true for low-rise buildings, and theaters—many of which were located in midtown at the edge of the burgeoning office building district—were particularly vulnerable to destruction. Even the internationally famous Radio City Music Hall was threatened.[318] Despite its distinction as the city's only movie theater to still present stage shows, Radio City experienced a steady loss of clientele beginning in the late 1960s; between 1967 and 1977 annual attendance plummeted from five million to two million. In 1972 Harrison & Abramovitz began to design a skyscraper office building for the site that would require demolition of the theater. Changes in the municipal building code, however, made it possible to combine theater and office uses, and later schemes retained the Music Hall in a renovated form. The dwindling market for office space in the early 1970s offered the Music Hall a reprieve, although the theater's box office continued to decline. On January 5, 1978, Alton G. Marshall, president of Rockefeller Center, Inc., announced that the theater, which had sustained a $2.3 million loss in 1977, would be permanently closed. For once strong public opposition was matched by decisive municipal action: on March 28, 1978, the Landmarks Preservation Commission designated the theater's interior a landmark.[319] The subsequent financial restructuring of the theater and its abandonment of first-run movies in favor of live entertainment rendered the theater economically viable and ensured its survival. The potential loss of Radio City Music Hall heightened concern for the preservation of all of Rockefeller Center; it was not until 1985, however, that the exterior of the complex (as completed in 1947) was designated a landmark.[320]

In the mid-1960s the coordinated group of Italian Renaissance–style houses that McKim, Mead & White had designed for Henry Villard (1882–86), on the east side of Madison Avenue between Fiftieth and Fifty-first streets, was threatened with demolition to make way for a skyscraper.[321] Prior to World War II, the north and south wings of the complex had been vacated and closed by their owners; during the war the wings were used by the Women's Military Service Club and the Friends of Free France respectively. After the war, a proposal to use part of the complex as a temporary headquarters for the United Nations was put forward, but this did not come to pass. In 1946 the publishers Random House purchased the northern Madison Avenue portion of the complex from Joseph P. Kennedy, who had bought it as an investment. Three years later the Archdiocese of New York acquired the rest of the building group, renting the only one of the houses not entered from the forecourt (24 East Fifty-first Street) to the Capital Cities Broadcasting Corporation and using the remainder of the complex for its own offices and as a residence for some of its clergy. Little substantial damage was done to the interiors; although in the early 1950s the firm of Voorhees, Walker, Foley & Smith was hired to convert the Archdiocese's portion into modern office space, the plan was never realized.

In 1967 the founder and president of Random House, Bennett Cerf, who had professed devotion to the Villard Houses, announced that the publishing company was moving its offices to a new building on the northeast corner of Fiftieth Street and Third Avenue. A year later Cerf said, "We will probably sell. It's too valuable to keep."[322] Cardinal Terence J. Cooke's secretary, Monsignor James Rigney, expressed the church's desire to maintain ownership of its property but added that "with all our schools and responsibilities, at some point we would have to wonder whether we are justified in keeping property as valuable

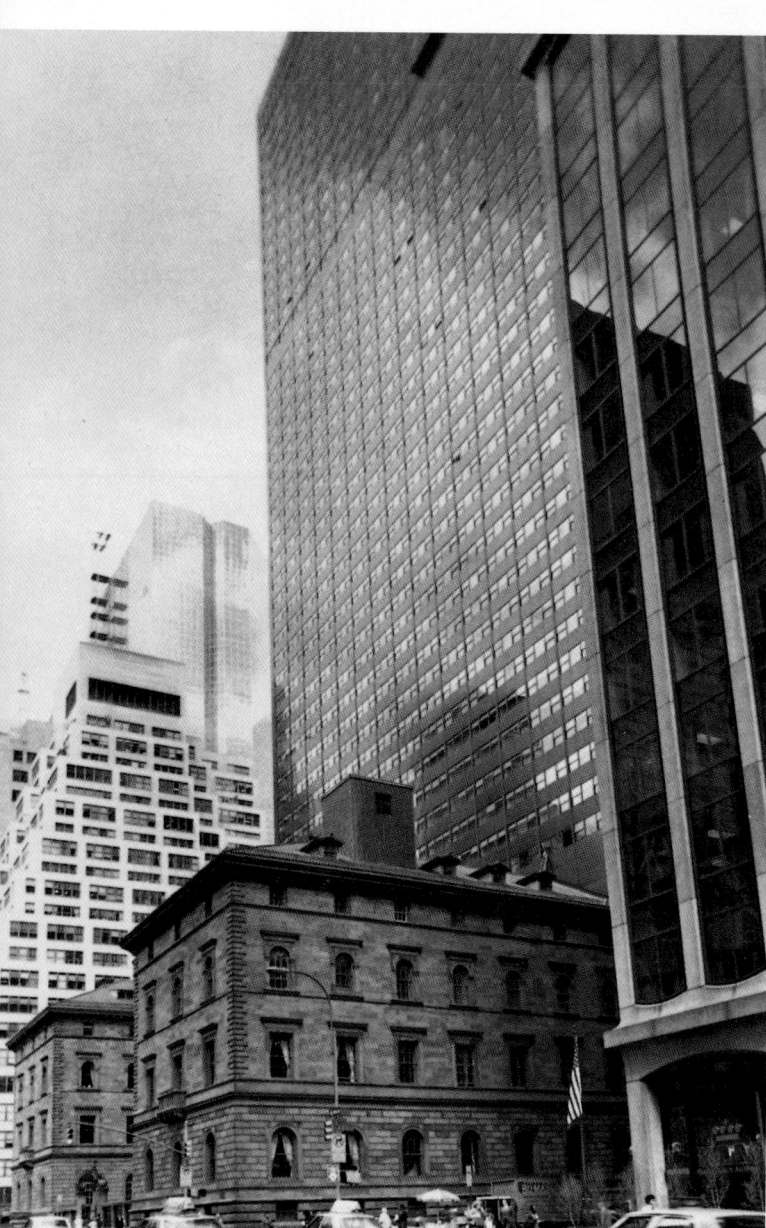

Helmsley Palace Hotel and Urban Center (formerly Villard Houses), 455 Madison Avenue, East Fiftieth to East Fifty-first Street. McKim, Mead & White, 1882–86; renovation and addition, Emery Roth & Sons, 1980. View to the northeast showing hotel addition in the background. ERS

as this."[323] Ada Louise Huxtable lamented the situation:

> No savvy New Yorker would give any odds on the demolition of this landmark for another Madison Avenue office building. . . . No one denies that the quality of the city is eroded and ultimately lost by the destruction of such buildings. . . . The bankers and real estate men who have conventionally written off any construction approaching the century mark as outmoded and uneconomic have learned to say "Too bad." That somehow makes it worse. To destroy out of ignorance is one thing; to destroy out of understanding of the meaning and consequences of the act is a sordid commentary on the values and morality of men.

On September 30, 1968, in an effort to save the buildings, and perhaps to ensure awareness of their architectural significance, the Landmarks Preservation Commission designated them a landmark. The Villard Houses posed different questions, however, than most other landmark properties that were subject to strong real estate market pressures; because the principal owner was the Archdiocese of New York, the issue of what constituted appropriate behavior carried special weight. "There are several questions to be raised now before the sellers weep all the way to the bank," Huxtable noted. "They concern the church position as leader, upholder and protector of community standards and of those values that have traditionally been called spiritual, beyond Mammon. . . . With its tax-exempt status it can even be argued that the church has an obligation to resist Mammon in the interest of the city's irreplaceable public heritage, or public good."[324] Although the Archdiocese was using only a little of its space, it was keenly aware of the civic value of the Villard Houses and chose to maintain ownership of the near-vacant buildings for the time being, despite the fact that church property which is not utilized for religious, educational or charitable functions is subject to taxation. As a result, the Archdiocese paid annual taxes of more than $700,000 on the buildings while behind-the-scenes negotiations over their future proceeded.

In 1974, in what amounted to a compromise between publicly supported preservation and still-likely demolition, the developer Harry Helmsley expressed interest in purchasing the houses and their air rights and building a fifty-two-story building combining hotel facilities and office space adjacent to them. As designed by Emery Roth & Sons, the plan called for a slab resembling Helmsley and the Roths' Park Lane Hotel on Central Park South, with travertine piers culminating in arches running the building's height. The plan entailed the demolition of part of the eastern portion of the complex and the gutting of the central section's interior to accommodate the hotel's lobby. Huxtable characterized the plan as "a death-dealing rather than life-giving 'solution,'" explaining: "The superb Belle Epoque interiors—virtually all that are left in New York of the Vanderbilt-Astor era—are written off as so many square feet of 'hard to use' space. . . . If the architect and developer had set out to kick the landmark in the pants, they could not have done a better job." While acknowledging that the Roth office had conducted numerous reuse studies, Huxtable found that the plan left the Villard Houses underutilized and did not sufficiently provide for the buildings' survival, the ostensible reason for permitting the construction of the adjacent skyscraper. "The threat still remains," she said, "that if no tenants materialize and the building continues to be a financial burden to owner and lessee, application for demolition can be made under the landmarks law. In spite of the economic benefits that would accrue to owner and developer in this dubious scheme, the Villard Houses aren't home safe yet."[325]

In January 1975 the Landmarks Preservation Commission approved the plan in principle but requested specific design revisions. Speaking on behalf of the commission, Chairman Beverly Moss Spatt advocated the use of a less obtrusive glass curtain wall than the original proposal had called for, as well as the preservation of the existing buildings' interiors. At the same time, perhaps sensing the increasingly controversial nature of the project, Helmsley commissioned the architectural firm of Kahn & Jacobs to work simultaneously with Emery Roth & Sons on an alternate design for the project; Paul Goldberger noted that this "use of two architectural firms working separately on what are, in effect, competing designs for the same building is considered highly unorthodox in architectural circles."[326] The Roth office was ultimately retained as the project's architect. Although the revised design was for a more understated tower, the overscaled arches, in a material resembling brownstone, were retained along the north and south facades and the interiors were still to be demolished. Huxtable was unimpressed with the design, saying that "by any measure except computerized investment design, the results are a wretched failure."[327] A third design, calling for the construction of a fifty-seven-story tower of bronze-anodized aluminum and dark-tinted glass and the incorporation of the Gold Room and other existing interiors into the hotel's public spaces, was then proposed. But because of the depressed state of the city's economy, the sponsoring banks and insurance companies requested the elimination of office space and a reduction in the building's height. As finally completed in 1980, the Roths' Helmsley Palace Hotel had fifty-one stories, still enough for it to qualify as the city's tallest hotel.

The interiors of the two townhouses on the east side of the courtyard were destroyed and only their principal facades and a bit of their roofs were retained. The north and south wings were treated with more reverence: the south wing, which contained the grandest interiors of all, including the Gold Room, was incorporated into the hotel; most of the north wing was renovated by James Stewart Polshek to serve as the Urban Center, an umbrella organization created to bring together under one roof the Municipal Art Society, the Parks Council, the Architectural League and the New York Chapter of the American Institute of Architects.[328]

While the overall preservation of the Villard Houses was without question positive, the design of the Helmsley Palace Hotel significantly compromised the integrity of the original complex. Ostentatious new gates to the courtyard immediately signaled that the refined luxury of McKim, Mead & White's design was not enough to suit the taste of the new owners. Parts of the combined restoration and renovation project were inspired: the replacement of the city's standard street lights, which had been designed by Donald Deskey in 1960, with more contextually appropriate "bishop's crook" style lampposts, modeled after Richard Rodgers Bowker's design of 1892, struck a positive note. Other elements were not so successful: the new fenestration and doorways on the eastern houses, for instance, were blowsy and overstated. Still other areas, such as the lobby, where a restaurant, cocktail lounge and ballroom were linked to the street-level, block-through passage by means of a new, monumentally scaled marble staircase, were just plain garish. While most preservationists were perhaps not entirely satisfied, they generally considered the outcome of the struggle for the Villard Houses a victory. As Huxtable wrote, "To Mr. Helmsley, for [his] extra efforts, we raise a glass."[329] Nonetheless, the inescapable presence of the fifty-one-story slab trivialized the historic ensemble, rendering it little more than a decorative doormat to a banal behemoth.

The Villard Houses complex was not the only landmark that was as much violated as preserved in the interests of progress. A case in point was the Squadron A Armory (John R. Thomas, 1895), which occupied the full-block site between Madison and Park avenues, Ninety-fourth and Ninety-fifth streets.[330] The monumentally scaled brick building, which resembled a fourteenth-century French fortress, complete with square towers, round turrets and a crenellated parapet, had originally been used by a volunteer unit called the First New York Hussars or the First Dragoons and later by a National Guard unit; after being used during World War I by the 105th Machine Gun Battalion, it served as one of New York's most unusual recreational facilities: indoor polo grounds. In the early 1960s the building was targeted as the site of a school and subsidized housing. Although the mixed-use project was subsequently abandoned as economically unviable, the armory building was given to the Board of Education for use as the site of Intermediate School 29. The board concluded that the building could not be structurally transformed to suit the school's functional requirements and rejected proposals by the Municipal Art Society and the New York Chapter of the American Institute of Architects that it be used as a sports center or that a new school building be built within its shell. Late in 1968, after significant portions of the armory had already been torn down to make way for a new building to be designed by Morris Ketchum, Jr. & Associates, public protest succeeded in halting the demolition and drawing the attention of the Landmarks Preservation Commission, which designated the remaining western facade, facing Madison Avenue, a landmark on October 19, 1966.

Ketchum, who would later serve as a member of the Landmarks Preservation Commission (1972–79), designed a fortresslike building for Intermediate School 29, with castellated brick facades. He retained the one remaining facade of the former armory as a dramatic backdrop for the school's playground. The Citizens' Housing and Planning Council, which had not favored the designation of the armory facade, dismissed it as looking "like a sand castle built partly beyond the reach of the biggest waves."[331] As for the decision to incorporate the facade into the new building design, the council said, it was the result of "a moment of bemused sentimentality"[332] and was based on questionable motives:

> Is anyone suggesting that the wall will improve the school's utilization of the playground space? Is anyone suggesting that the $200,000 estimated cost of the adaptation could not be spent on improving this school's usefulness or enhancing its beauty? . . . How sound is the assumption that preservation of the wall is devoutly desired by nearby residents and that its retention will help to reconcile them to the disappearance of polo ponies and their replacement by an interracial school population?

Furthermore, the group argued, retention of the facade damaged the cause of preservation in general: "The Armory wall seems . . . unworthy, not only because it is a trifle foolish and somewhat extravagant with money and space, but also because, by opening landmark standards to question, it may help to undermine other, more significant older structures elsewhere."[333] Although most preservationists welcomed the commission's shift in emphasis toward less obvious designations, the transformation of the building into what amounted to a monumental sculpture took the concept of adaptive reuse to an almost absurd extreme.

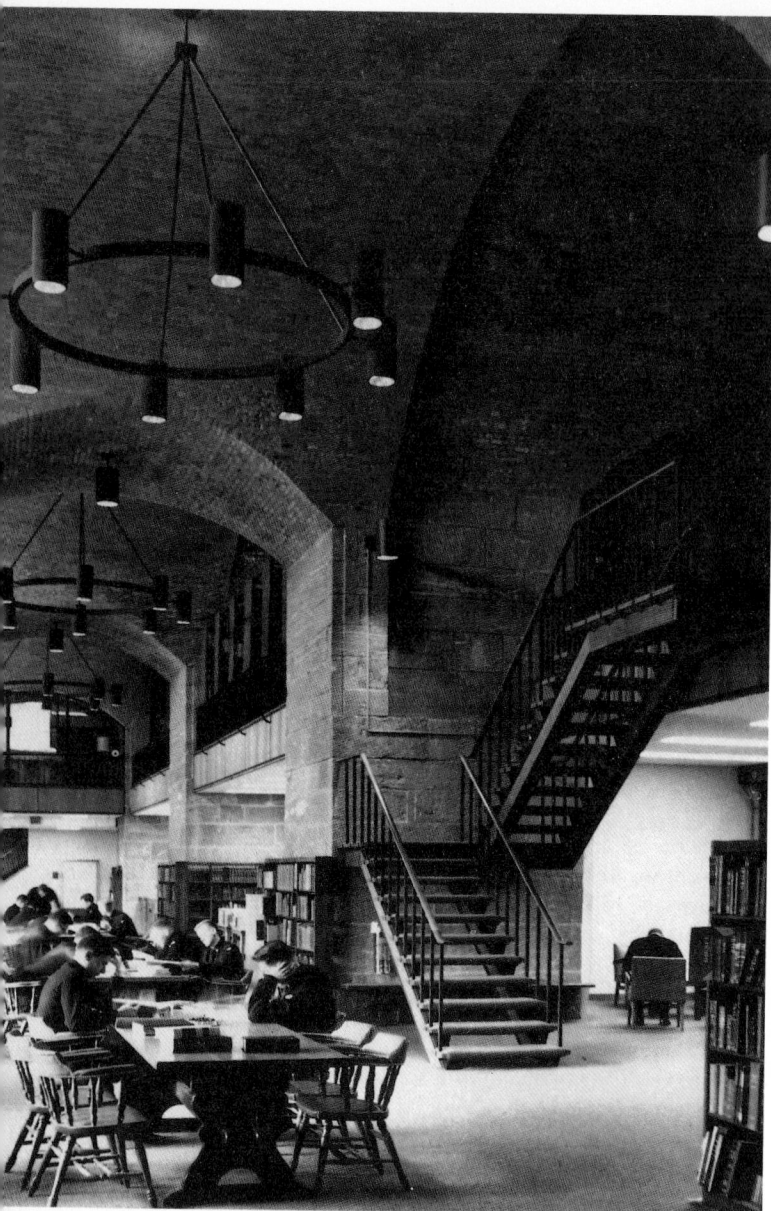

In 1976 another picturesquely medieval-style armory, the 71st Regiment Armory (Clinton & Russell, 1905), on the southeast corner of Park Avenue and Thirty-fourth Street, gave way to Shreve, Lamb & Harmon Associates' Three Park Avenue, a thirty-four-story brick tower that housed office space above an eleven-story facility for the Norman Thomas High School.[334] Other military structures in the city, however, were recognized as the architectural landmarks they were. The imposing Fort Schuyler (1834–38), built of rough-hewn granite ashlar and located on the Throgs Neck peninsula in the Bronx, had been converted into facilities for the State University of New York Maritime College in 1934–38 by Captain I. L. Smith with the use of WPA funds; in 1964 the architect William A. Hall converted the college's dining hall into the Admiral Stephen Bleecker Luce Library.[335] Ballard, Todd & Associates further transformed sections of the former fort into dormitory and educational facilities in 1963–64.[336] Fort Schuyler was designated a landmark in 1966. The Seventh Regiment Armory (Charles W. Clinton, 1878–80; additions, 1909, 1930), at 634 Park Avenue, complete with interior embellishments by Louis Comfort Tiffany,[337] and the Kingsbridge Armory (Pilcher & Tachau, 1912–17), at 29 West Kingsbridge Road in the Bronx,[338] were protected as designated landmarks on June 9, 1967, and September 24, 1974, respectively. Several architecturally significant armories in Brooklyn survived, although they were not protected as landmarks: the 17th Corps Artillery, formerly the 47th Regiment Armory and originally the Union Grounds (1883), located between Marcy and Harrison avenues, Heyward and Lynch streets;[339] the 13th Regiment Armory (Rudolph L. Daus, 1894; Parfitt Brothers, 1906), at 357 Sumner Avenue;[340] and the 14th Regiment Armory (William A. Mundell, 1895), at 1402 Eighth Avenue.[341] Armories landmarked after 1976 were the 23rd Regiment Armory (Fowler & Hough, 1891–95), at 1322 Bedford Avenue in Brooklyn;[342] the 69th Regiment Armory (Hunt & Hunt, 1904–6), at 68 Lexington Avenue;[343] and the 369th Regiment Armory Drill Shed (Tachau & Vought, 1921–24) and Administration Building (Van Wart & Wein, 1930–33), at 2360 Fifth Avenue.[344]

Above: Admiral Stephen Bleecker Luce Library (formerly Fort Schuyler), State University of New York Maritime College, Throgs Neck, the Bronx. 1833–56; renovation for maritime college, Captain I. L. Smith, 1934–38; renovation for library, William A. Hall, 1964. Interior. WAH

Top right: Public Theater (formerly Astor Library), 425 Lafayette Street, between East Fourth Street and Astor Place. South wing, Alexander Saeltzer, 1853; center section, Griffith Thomas, 1859; north wing, Thomas Stent, 1881; renovation, Giorgio Cavaglieri, 1967. Florence Sutro Anspacher Theater. Cserna. GICA

Bottom right: Jefferson Market Library (formerly Jefferson Market Courthouse), bounded by Sixth and Greenwich avenues and West Tenth Street. Calvert Vaux and Frederick Clarke Withers, 1877; renovation, Giorgio Cavaglieri, 1967. Interior. Neuhof. GICA

Adaptive Reuse: Some Success Stories

Unlike such cases as the Villard Houses and the Squadron A Armory where only partial preservation was achieved, several landmark buildings were not only preserved or restored but also imaginatively adapted to new uses. The idea that fire stations could become houses, or factory buildings could be made to serve as community centers, posed a serious challenge to real estate interests who fought preservation efforts by arguing that specific types of functions required specific types of space. Reuse also flew in the face of architectural Modernism, whose proponents insisted that the new language of form had been created in large measure to meet the challenges of specific new functional programs and of new building technologies, suggesting that as functions changed and newer technologies came along, "obsolete" buildings should be discarded and replaced, like cars or appliances.

The city's first structure to be saved from imminent destruction and adapted for a new use under the landmarks preservation law was the Astor Library, located at 425 Lafayette Street, between East Fourth Street and Astor Place. The brick-and-brownstone Romanesque Revival building was built in three stages between 1853 and 1881 and designed by Alexander Saeltzer, Griffith Thomas and Thomas Stent, respectively.[345] In 1911 its collection was absorbed into the newly established New York Public Library, and from 1920 to 1965 the building served as the headquarters of the Hebrew Immigrant Aid Society. In 1965, after the library had been designated a landmark, the society decided to move and to sell the building to a developer. This was prevented, however, when, with the Landmarks Preservation Commission functioning as intermediary, Joseph Papp acquired the library as the winter headquarters of his New York Shakespeare Festival productions, which were staged in the open-air Delacorte Theater in Central Park during the summer months.[346]

Papp hired Giorgio Cavaglieri to remodel the building and renamed it the Public Theater. Cavaglieri preserved many of the original elements of the lobby and approach areas, including the massive cast-iron columns, and imaginatively reorganized the loftlike interiors to create seven individual theaters. Within the largest of these, the Florence Sutro Anspacher Theater, on which Cavaglieri collaborated with the theater designer Ming Cho Lee, the space's existing double-tiered rows of columns, complete with gold-leaf-covered capitals, and a finely decorated, curved, skylit ceiling were contrasted with exposed mechanical equipment. Two of the columns were stripped to their iron cores and used to support light and sound equipment, as well as a catwalk. Papp's first production in his new headquarters, the self-proclaimed "American tribal love-rock musical" *Hair* (1967), made theater history and, before moving uptown to Broadway, served to publicize the space. Reviewing the musical, *Newsweek*'s theater critic Jack Kroll wrote: "The whole idea of Joseph Papp's new Public Theater is wonderful . . . and the first of his working arenas immediately becomes the most delightful show-space in New York, jumping into life with a young company positively pop-eyed with conviction and energy."[347] Ada Louise Huxtable also praised the remodeled building, stating that "the new theater is a heart-warming hit."[348]

Cavaglieri's 1967 transformation of the Jefferson Market Courthouse in Greenwich Village, an area of the city that became a focus of preservation efforts (see below), into a branch of the New York Public Library was a pioneering example of adaptive reuse undertaken by government in the postwar years.[349] Designed by Calvert Vaux and Frederick Clarke Withers, the Jefferson Market Courthouse, officially designated the Third Judicial District Courthouse (1877), originally shared the triangular block bounded by Sixth and Greenwich avenues and West Tenth Street with the Jefferson Market Prison (1877), also designed by Vaux & Withers;[350] in 1931 a third building, Sloan & Robertson's Women's House of Detention, was built on the block (see below). All three buildings were architecturally distinguished in their own way. The courthouse building, which the editors of *Progressive Architecture* described as "more English than American," incorporated steeply pitched roofs, gables and leaded windows, as well as a picturesque clock tower that made it a highly visible feature of the neighborhood.[351] In 1885 a nationwide survey of architects and builders proclaimed it one of the country's ten most beautiful buildings. After ceasing to function as a courthouse in 1945, the building was the local headquarters of civil defense organizations and was rumored to be a training ground for riot control forces.

By the mid-1950s the building's fate had become uncertain. In 1956 the editors of the *New Yorker* praised the "exuberant, if somewhat addleheaded" style of the building, which they considered to be "easily the most conspicuous architectural or-

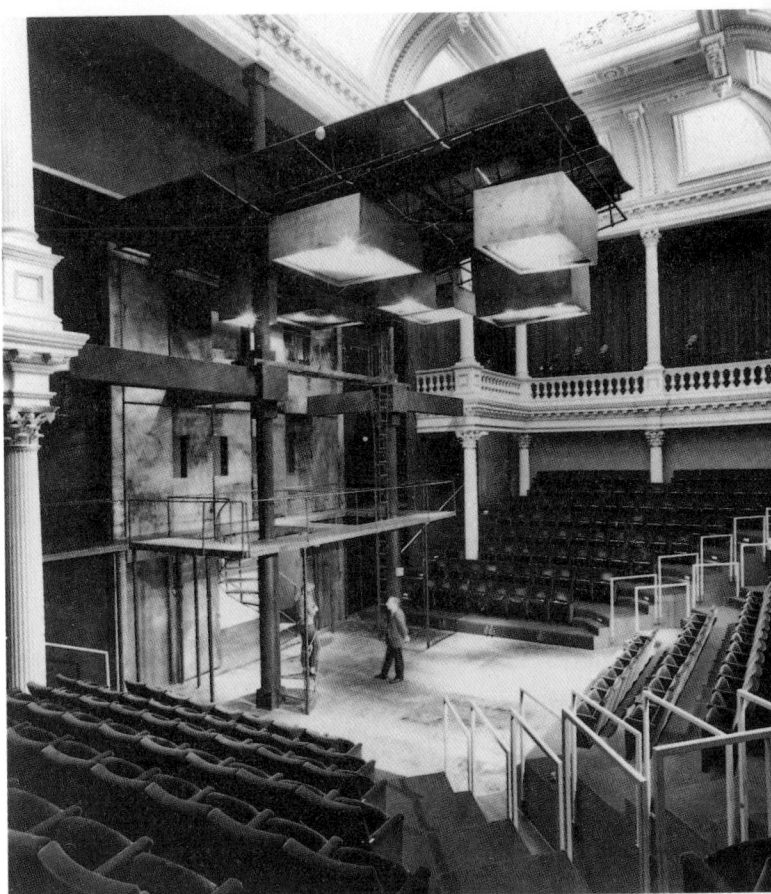

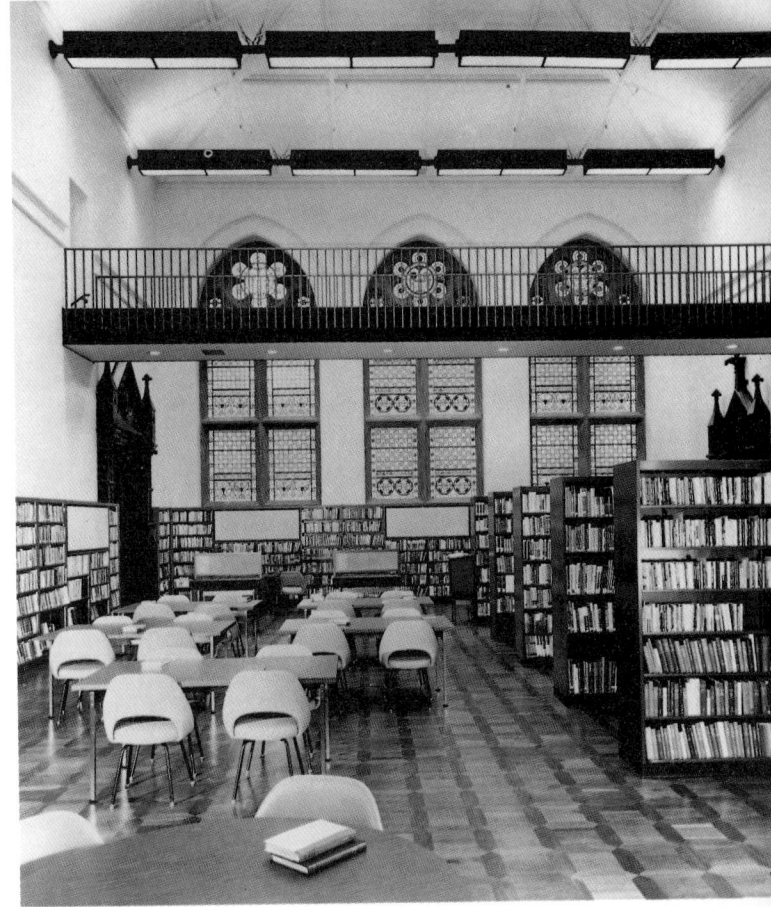

1131

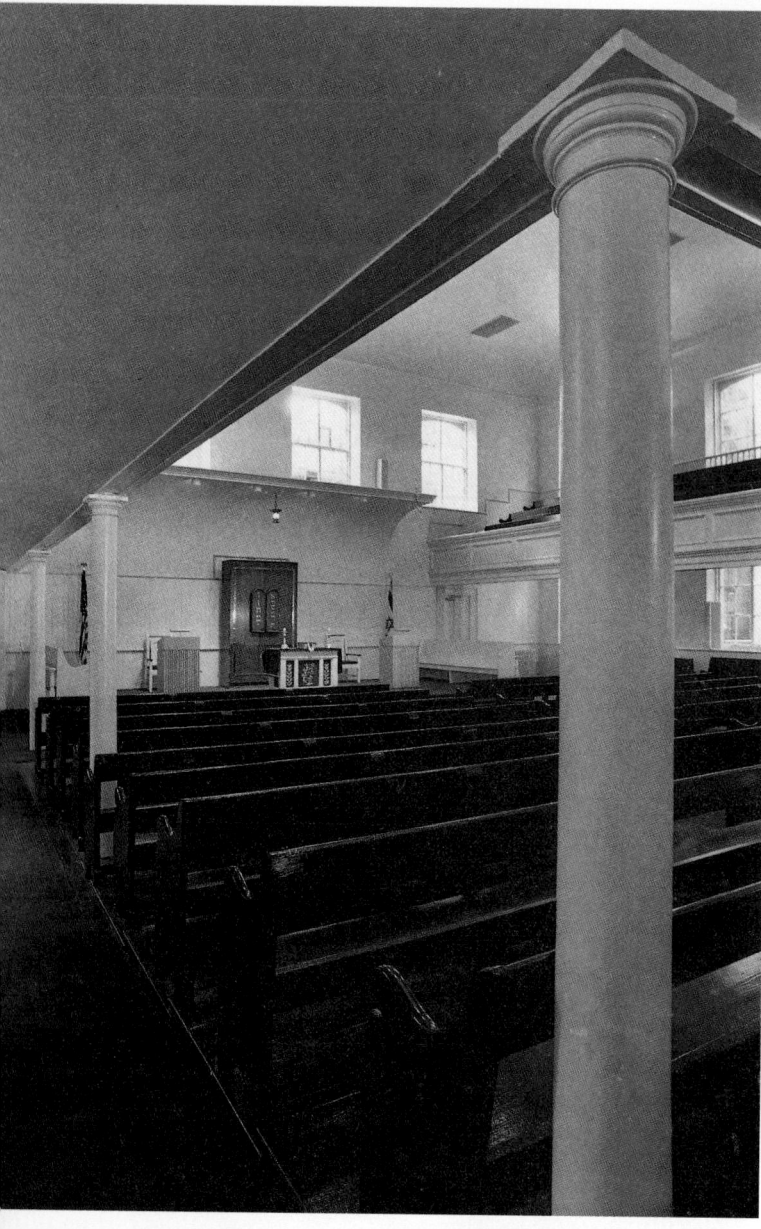

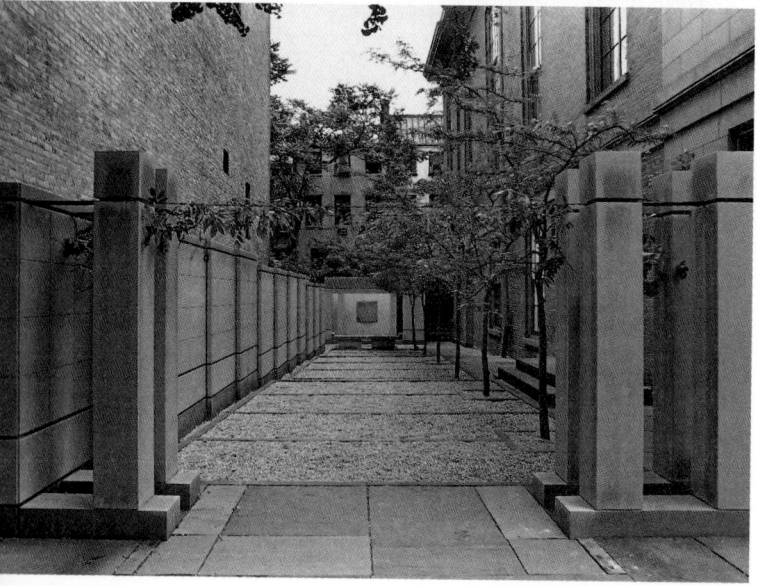

nament of Greenwich Village." Not everyone found the building pleasing; as the editors said, "There are many who see it as one of those cosmic blunders our ancestors were forever making on their way up the ladder of taste from the bustling horrors of the mid-nineteenth century to the glossy refinement of the mid-twentieth." Yet, they argued, "to the more sympathetic eye of the historian and lover of the past, for whom the ladder of taste may be said to be lying on the ground, no rung higher than any other rung, the Court House, far from being a blunder, is a delightful experiment."[352]

In 1959 the Bureau of Real Estate took over the property and began to arrange for its sale to a bank that planned to construct a large apartment house on the site. This inspired local political leader and architecture writer Margot Gayle, working with Judge Harold Birns, city commissioner for Housing and Buildings, to fight for repair of the building's defunct clock and to stimulate general interest in preserving the building by organizing the Village Committee for the Clock on the Jefferson Market Courthouse. Two years later, after efforts by Grove Press to purchase the building had fallen through, Gayle, working with lawyer Philip Wittenberg, the brother-in-law of Lewis Mumford, went a step further and formed the Committee for a Library in the Jefferson Courthouse. Through the efforts of the group, which included Mumford, the actor Maurice Evans and the poet e. e. cummings among its members and had the support of Mayor Wagner and other city officials, the New York Public Library was persuaded to adapt the existing building. Cavaglieri was hired to supervise the exterior restoration and design the interior renovation, both of which were completed in 1967. Though it included the installation of unsympathetic fluorescent lighting and played up the contrast between old and new elements with features such as doors framed in travertine, the renovation was executed, as the editors of *Interiors* put it, "in such a way as not to do violence to the building's romantic Gothicisms, but rather to enhance them."[353] Ada Louise Huxtable marveled at the preservationists' success, stating that it constituted "a study in organized public interest, dogged persistence, practical sentimentality and civic savvy—or how to make a determined group of citizens an effective force for the achievement of an objective generally considered hopeless."[354]

James Stewart Polshek's handling of the Friends' Meeting House (King & Kellum, 1859), located on East Twentieth Street at the southeast corner of Gramercy Park, was also a notable example of a preservation project that accommodated a programmatic change.[355] In 1958, when the Society of Friends moved some of their activities to their meeting house on Stuyvesant Square, they began to neglect the maintenance of the elegantly chaste Italianate Gramercy Park building. Seven years later the Friends gave an option to a developer who wanted to replace the building with a thirty-story apartment house. Neighborhood protest stimulated the landmark designation of the building and the establishment of a foundation dedicated to buying it and transforming it into a performing arts center. That plan was not realized, however, and the Friends sold the building to the United Federation of Teachers. When the federation's intention to use the building for office and meeting space went unfulfilled, the structure was purchased in 1975 by the Brotherhood Synagogue. Both Polshek and the contractor, Lawrence Held and Son, worked without fees to restore the building, sacrificing design innovation for good clinical practice—as Polshek put it, "stone 'pathology,' paint 'dermatology,' and various 'intrasclerotic' probes (the medical terminology is particularly apt in such preservation projects)."[356] The architect's only changes to the existing interior were the installation of a central light fixture and a bema. In 1977 the architect completed a sparsely detailed and austerely landscaped memorial garden on a narrow site directly to the east of the synagogue, incorporating a stepped wall to create a forced perspective and focus attention on the minimally detailed altarlike structure that culminated the vista. The Landmarks Preservation Commission had initially judged the garden "inappropriate," but once it was moved a foot farther back from the street, approval was granted.

The changing attitudes among architects, preservationists and the public at large toward what constituted the proper adaptive reuse of a landmark building could be clearly seen in the fate of Cass Gilbert's United States Custom House (1907), which Norval White and Elliot Willensky described in 1978 as "the *grandest* Beaux Arts building of New York, now re-loved by modernists searching for renewed meaning in architecture."[357] Designated a landmark in 1965, the building was abandoned by the Customs Service eight years later in favor of larger quarters in the World Trade Center. In 1974 I. M. Pei proposed a radical renovation of the building to house stores and theaters, as well as a hotel or office space. The plan called for the insertion of fifty-five-foot-high arcades surrounding the building's existing rotunda; the removal of masonry cladding from the central court's walls and the subsequent glazing of the exposed structural bays; and the replacement of the seventh-floor-level copper cornice and slate mansard with glazing. Four years later the federal government's General Services Administration sponsored a design competition for the building's restoration and adaptive reuse to serve several federal agencies and an unnamed public institution, possibly the Museum of the American Indian. James Stewart Polshek, working in association with Marcel Breuer & Associates, won the competition with a scheme that sensitively modified the interior, which was landmarked in 1979, to suit its new functions.

In 1975 the American Surety Building (Bruce Price, 1894–96), at 100 Broadway, a building of landmark quality that did not enjoy landmark designation, was at least temporarily protected against future development by its new owner, the Bank of Tokyo, which built a dramatic new banking hall.[358] The design was executed by the staff architects of the bank's construction firm, Kajima International, Inc., under the supervision of Nobutaka Ashihara, who had worked in Kevin Roche's office and who credited Roche with advising him to respect the original building in his new design. The remodeled ground-floor space was visually opened up to the street by setting a wall of frameless glazing behind the existing row of two-story Ionic columns. Inside, the building's former lobby was converted into a sleek, white marble banking room enlivened by the existing brownish gray marble Corinthian columns that rose to the thirty-two-foot-high intricately coffered ceiling. An encircling mezzanine and second floor were barely visible behind dark glass partitions. The most striking new element in the room was a massive, sharply rectilinear brushed-aluminum sculpture by Isamu Noguchi; hung from the ceiling, it pointed downward like a suspended knife. Huxtable praised the sculpture as "a stunning and studied transition from 19th to 20th century" and said that the overall effect of the renovation was of "a dramatically successful counterpoint of new and old." Although she recognized that "strict preservationists will probably cavil at the loss of all but selected parts of the original ground floor interior and their calculated combination with starkly contrasting surfaces," Huxtable found the result "a model of a sensitive, sophisticated, rational solution for contemporary use and the bank's particular

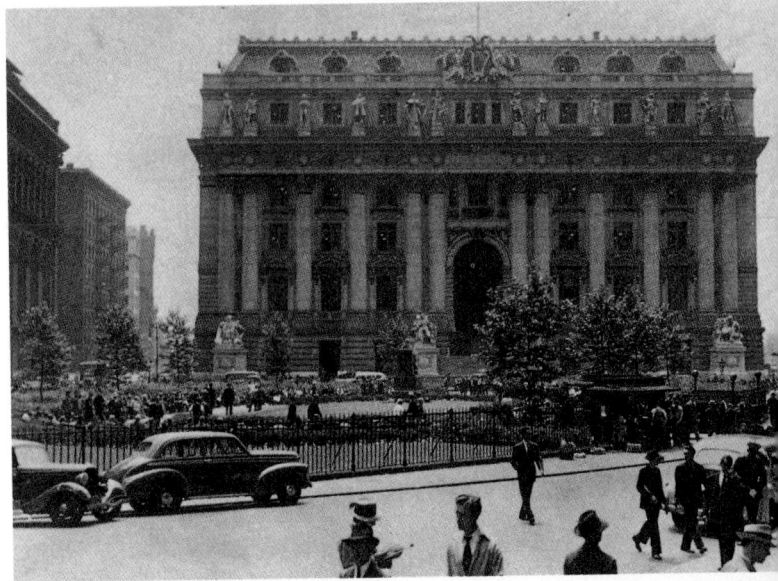

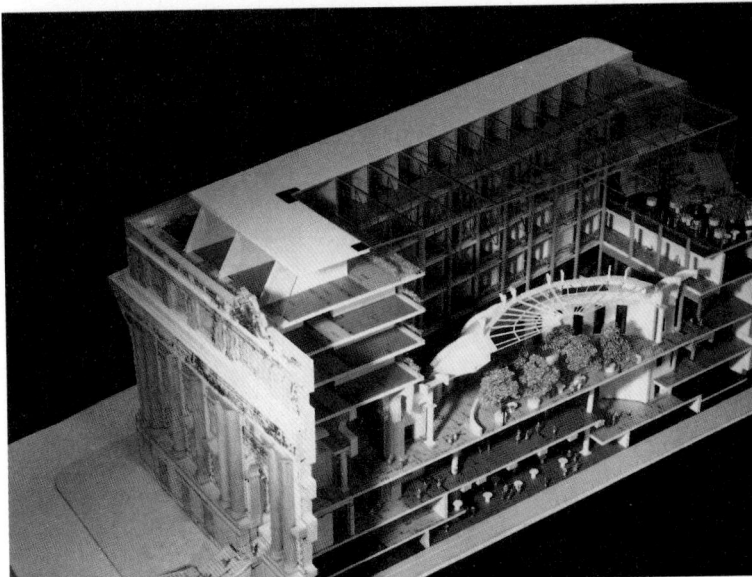

Top left: Brotherhood Synagogue (formerly Friends' Meeting House), 28 Gramercy Park South, between Irving Place and Third Avenue. King & Kellum, 1859; restoration, James Stewart Polshek, 1975. Sanctuary. Beckhard. JSP

Bottom left: Garden of Remembrance, Brotherhood Synagogue. James Stewart Polshek, 1977. View to the south. Rosen. LARO

Top: United States Custom House, bounded by Bowling Green Park and State, Whitehall and Bridge streets. Cass Gilbert, 1907. View to the southeast, 1941. NYP

Bottom: Proposal for renovation of the United States Custom House. I. M. Pei & Partners, 1974. Model. Cutaway view. PCF

1133

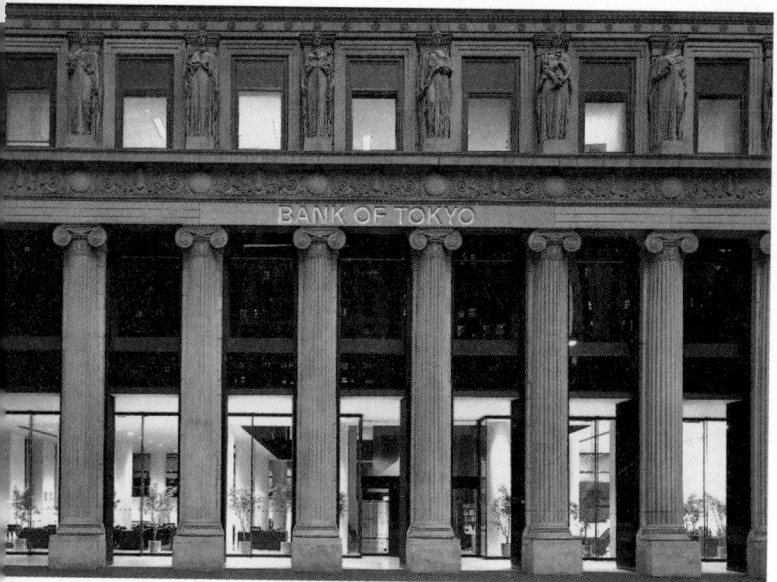

needs, with maximum architectural and cultural impact and a heightened sense of past and present."[359]

In 1976 MacFadyen/De Vido renovated the ground floor of the former American Fine Arts Society Building (Henry J. Hardenbergh in association with John C. Jacobson and Walter C. Hunting, 1892), at 212 West Fifty-seventh Street, to serve as an art supply store.[360] Their design presented new casework and steel-pipe scaffolding, from which light fixtures, signs and decorative banners were hung, startlingly juxtaposed with the interior's original vaulted ceiling and ornamental plasterwork. In addition, the use of floor-to-ceiling display windows, framed on top by three boldly colored pipes, stood in sharp but effective contrast to the Gothic detailing of the building's facade. One innovative adaptive reuse proposal that was unfortunately not realized was I. M. Pei's 1973 scheme to transform part of the space beneath the Manhattan approach of the Queensboro Bridge (Henry Hornbostel and Gustav Lindenthal, 1901–9) into a film center modeled on the Cinémathèque in Paris.[361]

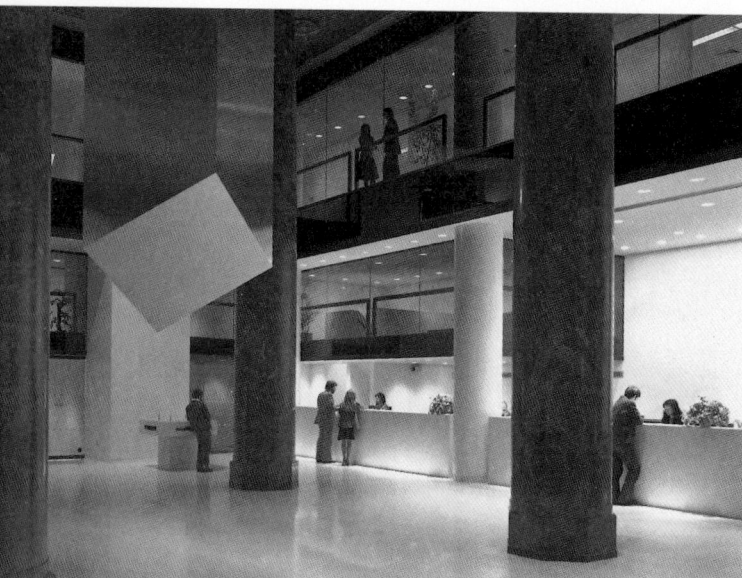

Top: Bank of Tokyo (formerly American Surety Building), 100 Broadway, between Wall and Pine streets. Bruce Price, 1894–96; renovation, staff architects of Kajima International under the supervision of Nobutaka Ashihara, 1975. View to the east. Stoller. ©ESTO

Bottom: Bank of Tokyo. Lobby with hanging sculpture by Isamu Noguchi. Stoller. ©ESTO

Ellis Island

One of the postwar era's most complex and controversial attempts to effectively reuse historically significant buildings focused on Ellis Island, which had functioned as the country's main port of entry for immigrants since 1892. On November 12, 1954, the island was closed, a victim as much to air travel as to the legislated decline in immigration and procedural changes in which processing was no longer done in the United States but abroad or on board ship prior to an immigrant's arrival.[362] The three-acre island, located in Upper New York Bay and at various times known as Oyster, Buching and Gibbert island, was originally utilized by Dutch colonists as a scenic spot for recreational outings. In 1875 its owner, Samuel Ellis, put the island up for sale along with "a few barrels of excellent shad . . . and a few thousands of red herring of his own curing."[363] The largely neglected island was acquired by New York State, which in turn sold it to the federal government for $10,000. By 1900 the island had increased in size, gaining 24.5 acres through landfill, and had taken on a new importance, replacing the overburdened immigration processing facilities at Castle Garden in lower Manhattan to become a powerful symbol of the national "melting pot."

In 1956, less than two years after its closing as a gateway, New Jersey state officials proposed that the island be turned into a park with an "ethnic museum" that would highlight the contributions of foreign-born Americans.[364] The federal government, however, showed no interest in turning the property over to New Jersey, and in May 1956 it proposed to trade the island to the city in exchange for a site near Foley Square where it could build a consolidated facility for the United States Court of Claims, the Tax Court and many other government agencies.[365] By September government officials had changed their minds and were prepared to sell the island, an action that would most likely prevent its preservation as a museum or recreation area.[366] According to a government spokesman, neither New York nor New Jersey had come forward with a proposal for the island, although New York City had considered it as the site of a prison.

In February 1958 a high bid of $201,000 for the island was received from Sol G. Atlas, a developer who proposed to build a resort and cultural center.[367] Working with the architects Bruce Campbell Graham, Herbert A. Tessler and Romero Corbelletti, Atlas proposed to tear down the existing complex of buildings (Boring & Tilton, 1898) and replace them with a language school,

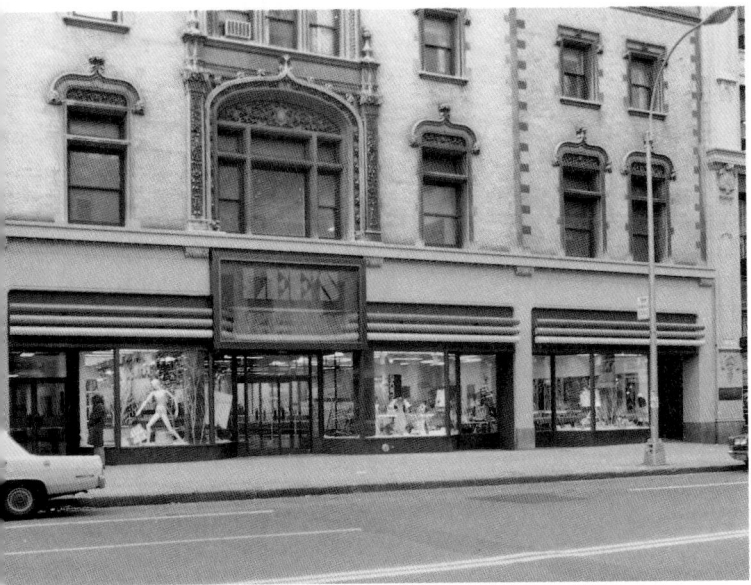

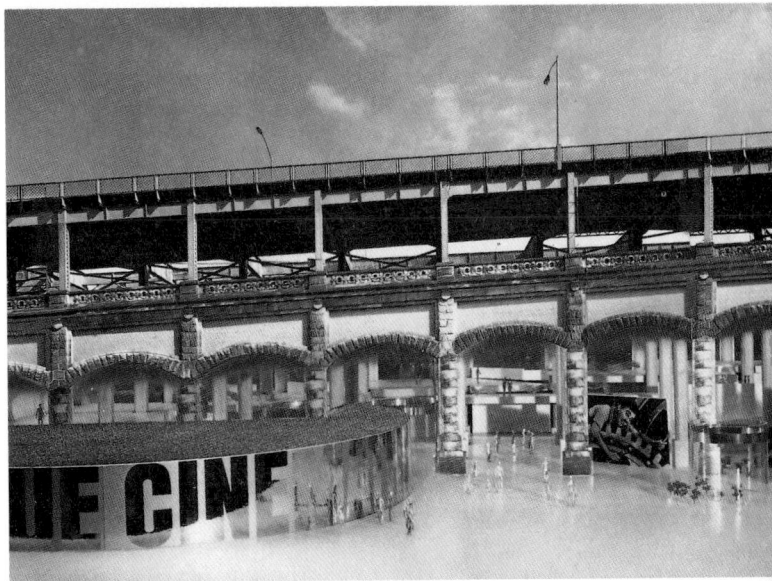

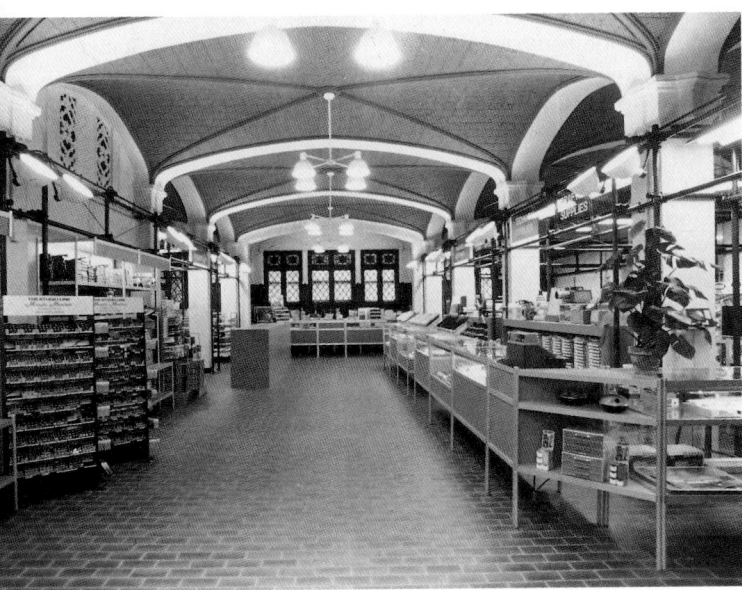

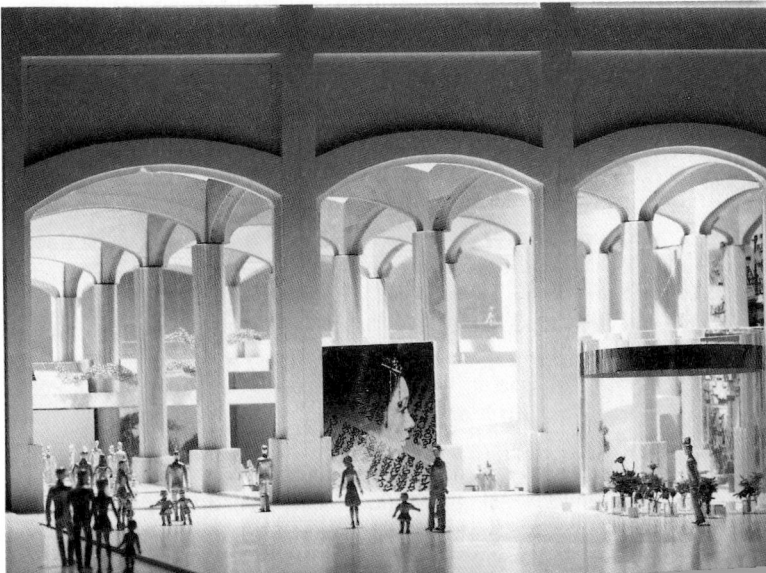

Top: Lee's Art Shop, American Fine Arts Society Building, 212 West Fifty-seventh Street, between Broadway and Seventh Avenue. Henry J. Hardenbergh in association with John C. Jacobson and Walter C. Hunting, 1892; renovation, MacFadyen/De Vido, 1976. View to the south. Stoecklein. ADV

Bottom: Lee's Art Shop. Interior. Stoecklein. ADV

Top: Proposal for film center beneath and adjacent to the Manhattan approach to the Queensboro Bridge (Henry Hornbostel and Gustave Lindenthal, 1901–9). I. M. Pei & Partners, 1973. Model. View to the north. Lieberman. PCF

Bottom: Proposal for film center. Model. Entrance lobby from plaza. Gabriel. PCF

a band shell dedicated to the memory of Arturo Toscanini, a convention hall, tennis courts, helicopter landing pads and a control tower, and a marina complete with an outdoor, 500-capacity "boat-in" movie theater. Atlas rejected suggestions by senators Irving M. Ives and Jacob K. Javits to turn the buildings into a hospital operated by the United States Public Health Service for narcotic addicts, arguing that it would turn the site into a "Devil's Island." "I am sure," he said, "that I can prove to the supporters of such an idea that it would be more costly to renovate its vermin-infested, rat-overrun buildings, than to build a suitable hospital."[368] Nonetheless, the government rejected Atlas's offer, a move that met with the approval of the New York Chapter of the American Institute of Architects, which called for the preservation of the island for use by the public.[369]

Four years later, in May 1962, the Damon Doudt Corporation, headed by two radio and television executives, Jerry Damon and Elwood Doudt, offered the government ten times Sol Atlas's price to build a futuristic city on the island using an unrealized sketch prepared by Frank Lloyd Wright. Wright's visionary project, called The Key "because for 20 million immigrants it was the key to a land of freedom and opportunity," as the developers put it, was the last project the architect worked on before his death in 1959.[370] According to William Wesley Peters, Wright's son-in-law and collaborator, Damon and Doudt had contacted Wright in 1959. The architect had met the two promoters in Washington and New York and, with his assistants, had developed a series of drawings that called for apartments and hotels accommodated in towers set atop a semicircular deck in part supported by structural masts. At the water's edge, a series of domed theaters and shops were to be set in a park overhung by cables suspended from the masts. The scheme was never built.

In 1964 Paul Douglas Roller, a student of theology and architecture, proposed that an ecumenical center for the Eastern Orthodox, Roman Catholic, Protestant and Anglican churches be built on Ellis Island.[371] The most distinctive feature of the center designed by Roller was to be a parabola-shaped sanctuary supported by streamlined flying buttresses and surmounted by a finial incorporating a monumentally scaled cross and orb. The proposal, which included a suggestion that the site be renamed Unity Island, was never realized.

In 1963 plans for the island's future began to take a positive turn when Mayor Wagner, flatly opposed to the island's sale to developers, proposed that all planned immigration museums and shrines be shifted to Ellis Island and developed in an outdoor setting by the National Park Service.[372] Though the agency objected to this idea on the grounds that such a park would be too small and too difficult to reach, Wagner pushed for his plan, and in 1965 Philip Johnson was chosen by Secretary of the Interior Stewart L. Udall to turn the island into a National Immigration Museum and Park.[373] The plan was projected to take between eight and ten years to realize and cost approximately $12 million. While previously most of the buildings on the island had seemed doomed to destruction, Johnson was committed to utilizing at least some of them in his design. According to the editors of Time, Johnson had decided that "the existing turn-of-the-century architecture was scarcely worth preserving, but the nostalgia certainly was."[374] "I know the old immigration building," Johnson said, "and we will take its flavor and use it, with its associations, to make the place into something interesting and attractive so people will want to go there."[375] A causeway would link the new park to New Jersey, 1,300 feet away, where another

400 or so acres of greenery would be carved from the derelict docks and industrial buildings along the shore.

On February 25, 1966, Secretary Udall and other officials broke ground on the New Jersey acres, which would become Liberty State Park, and Johnson unveiled his design at a news conference held in the Federal Hall Memorial in Manhattan. Johnson proposed to "stabilize the ruins" of the island—that is, its two largest buildings, the immigration station and the hospital complex that flanked the ferry slip—and to build walkways through the gutted, vine-covered buildings. "The point is to let the spectator himself re-create the feeling of those hard times," Johnson explained.[376] At the south side of the island, he proposed to build a spiraling monument dedicated to the sixteen million people who had passed through Ellis Island on their way to becoming American citizens. The truncated hollow cone was to be 300 feet in diameter at the base and incorporate eight-foot-wide ramps spiraling up and down, held in place by prestressed reinforced-concrete ribs, along which would be a wall inscribed with as many names of immigrants as could be culled from ships' passenger lists. A pool of water 100 feet in diameter was to be placed in the center of the structure. A fortresslike restaurant with slit windows would provide diners with a view of the harbor and the Manhattan skyline. In order to respect the Statue of Liberty, which was only 1,700 feet away on Bedloe's Island, Johnson designed his "Wall of the Sixteen Million" to be only 180 feet high, about 20 feet lower than Richard Morris Hunt's base for Frédéric Auguste Bartholdi's colossal statue (1886).

Udall was enthusiastic about the design: "Here we see what art and architecture and history can do when we bring them all together," he said.[377] The editors of the British journal Architectural Review noted, however, that "the emotions of frustration and despair with which the place was filled half a century ago still linger in the ruined prison-like buildings" and that the new park and museum would "bring back memories—often uncomfortable memories—to thousands of first-generation Americans."[378] Ada Louise Huxtable was favorably disposed to Johnson's design. As a "romantic ruin," she said, Ellis Island had "excellent precedents—the war-damaged churches carefully preserved as half-ruins at the heart of rebuilt German cities; the shell of historic Canterbury Cathedral maintained as a forecourt to the new church. The romantic ruin can evoke a more immediate and emotional sense of the past than the most accurate reconstruction." Leaving Boring & Tilton's buildings in their dilapidated state was appropriate, said Huxtable, since "the most charitable judgement . . . must rate their historical implications higher than their architectural quality. The prohibitive cost of extensive restoration of the sprawling complex would not be justified by what would be, at best, dubious esthetics." Nonetheless, Huxtable was troubled by the "schizoid split" between new and old that Johnson's overall strategy for the island represented.[379]

In contrast, the editors of the New York Times were completely unimpressed with Johnson's plan. "Of all the symbols to use in the projected national shrine at Ellis Island," they argued, "a wall would seem to be the least appropriate. Walls are built to exclude, as Berlin's Wall of Shame reminds us. Ellis Island was America's gateway for six decades: erecting 'The Wall of the Sixteen Million' is a poor way to convey that idea, even if millions of names are inscribed on the monument." The editors also criticized the proposal on strictly aesthetic grounds, charging that it looked "more like a rheostat cast in concrete than a wall." They concluded that "both the design and the concept could stand reconsideration."[380] Other observers were also negative: Inez

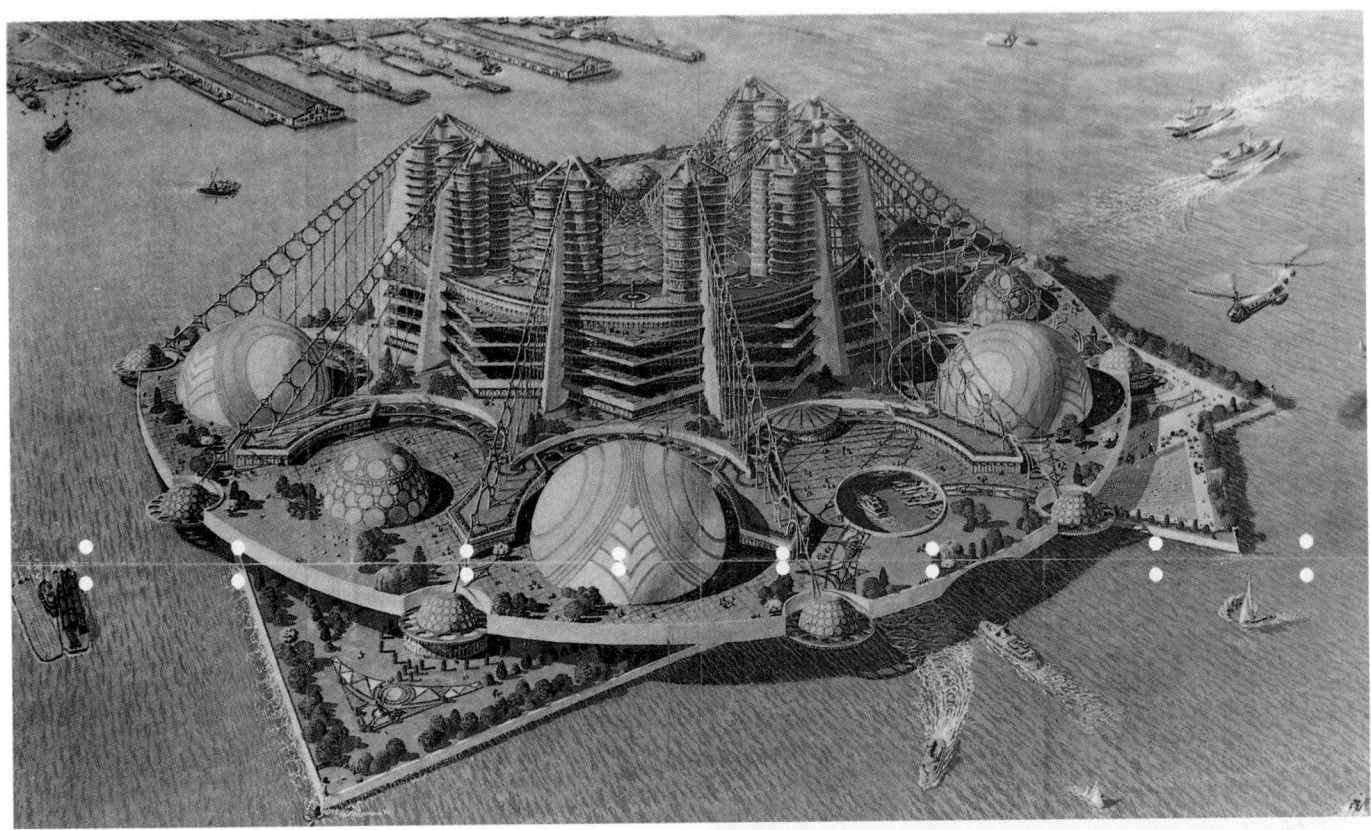

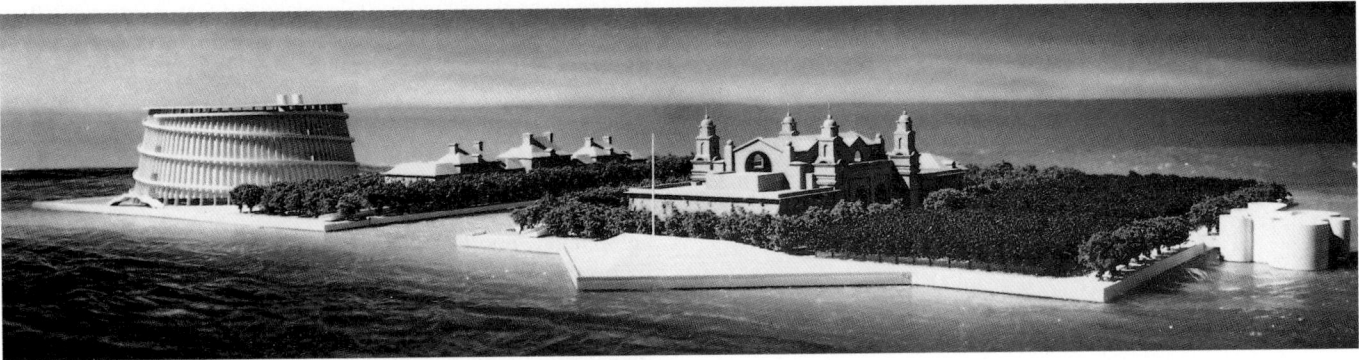

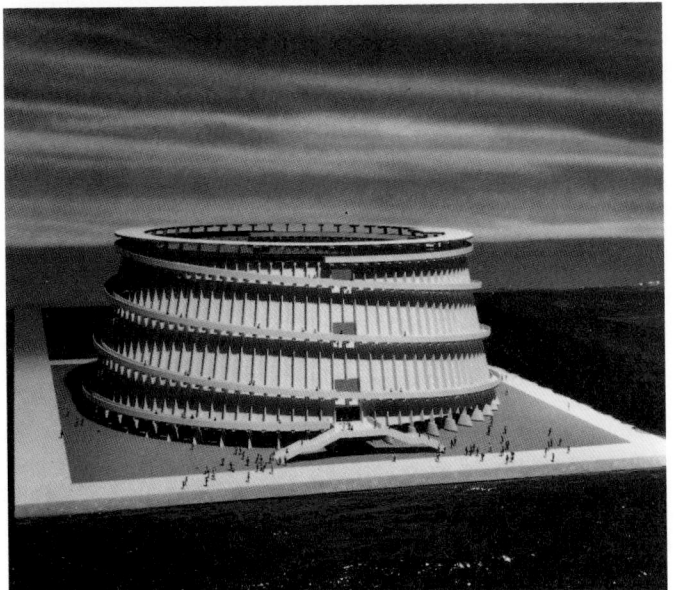

Top: Proposal for The Key, Ellis Island. Frank Lloyd Wright, 1959. Rendering of view to the northwest. FLWA

Center: Proposal for National Immigration Museum and Park, Ellis Island. Philip Johnson, 1966. Model. View to the southwest showing monument dedicated to immigrants. Checkman. PJA

Left: Proposal for National Immigration Museum and Park. Model. Monument dedicated to immigrants. Checkman. PJA

Robb, a columnist for the Scripps-Howard chain, called Johnson's design a "'concrete whatzits' that resembled an athletic stadium built by alumni too stingy to put in an elevator."[381]

Conrad L. Wirth, a former director of the National Park Service, questioned the need for any architectural memorial on Ellis Island, given its proximity to the Statue of Liberty, which "to America's immigrants . . . has always symbolized the American dream." He argued that the museum of immigration already being planned for a site in the Statue of Liberty's base would be sufficient, and proposed that the buildings on Ellis Island be destroyed and the land returned to nature. Wirth also challenged the particulars of Johnson's design: "I visualize hordes of people looking for the name of some long-dead relative, and upon finding it attempting to scratch their own name alongside."[382] The editors of the Jesuit publication *America*, who dismissed Johnson's memorial as "an absurd ziggurat," also endorsed the idea of an island park, which they claimed would be "more useful to a metropolitan population starved for air and greenery, and make us look less foolish to forthcoming generations."[383]

The realization of Johnson's plan was stalled by the lack of available federal funds during the Vietnam War, and the island and its buildings became increasingly decayed. "Right now, Ellis Island is pretty much at its low point in history," Lester McClanahan, the National Park Service officer placed in charge of it, told a *New York Times* reporter in March 1968.[384] Things got even worse during the summer of 1970 when squatters, members of a group called National Economic Growth and Reconstruction Organization (NEGRO), moved in for thirteen days. As a result of this demonstration, they were given a permit to remain on the island for five years and turn it into a rehabilitation center for 2,500 narcotics addicts, former convicts and their families.[385] NEGRO was headed by Dr. Thomas W. Matthew, a neurosurgeon who had recently been released from prison after serving time for income tax evasion. Matthew's plan to restore the buildings did not materialize and he was convicted for fraud in connection with misuse of Medicaid money. In 1974 the *New York Times*, in a follow-up on the island's development, reported that no plans were under way.[386] A few months later the editors of *Architectural Record* reported that the buildings were near ruin.[387] Ellis Island would continue to languish for close to two decades before historic preservation efforts would ultimately succeed.

The Battle for Grand Central Terminal

Many of the era's key preservation issues—the validity of traditional architectural styles, the appropriateness of alterations to landmark buildings, the feasibility of adaptive reuse proposals and the use of air rights as a way of allowing both the preservation of old buildings and the construction of new ones—came together in the efforts to preserve Grand Central Terminal (Reed & Stem and Warren & Wetmore, 1903–13).[388] The battle over Grand Central spanned more than two decades and provoked a wide range of emotions that sometimes bordered on hysteria; this was perhaps not surprising given the quality of the building's architecture and its pivotal urbanistic role. After 1963, it also reopened for many New Yorkers the wound of losing Pennsylvania Station, the city's other great, monumental gateway.

The proposed demolition or radical alteration of Grand Central, which was first announced in September 1954, was not without warning signs. In 1950 the financially troubled New York Central Railroad made an attempt to squeeze revenue out

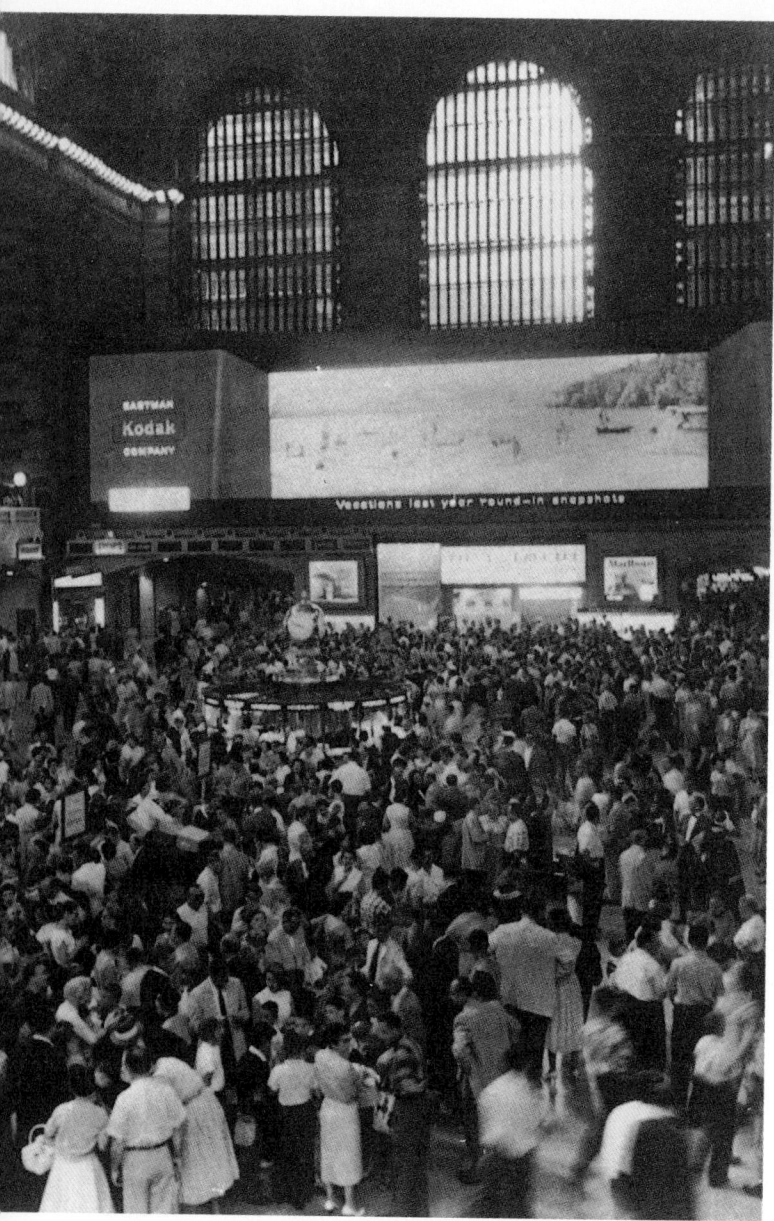

Grand Central Terminal, East Forty-second Street at Park Avenue. Reed & Stem, Warren & Wetmore, 1903–13. View to the east showing Eastman Kodak's Colorama (1950). Associated Press. NYP

of its stately building by leasing a large portion of the main concourse's east balcony to the Eastman Kodak corporation, which installed an information center, a model darkroom, an exhibition space and, most notably, an eighteen-foot-high, sixty-foot-wide, backlit color transparency—the world's largest—called the Colorama.[389] Adolph Stuber, the Kodak executive who first conceived of what he called the "colossal as well as beautiful" Colorama, informed the editors of the *New Yorker* that "We've had our eyes on this balcony for some time. . . . The pictures will harmonize with the Terminal architecturally and esthetically. . . . Most of the pictures will probably show somebody taking a photograph with a Kodak, but there'll be nothing high pressure about them." The first image, taken by photographer Valentino Sarra, depicted a mother photographing her two children. Stuber commented, "We want men who have had a hard day at the office to look up at it on their way to catch the 5:28 and like their wives and children the better for it when they get home."[390] Whatever its contribution to domestic bliss, the Colorama detracted from the dignity of the concourse, overwhelming its nearly sublime, dim luminosity with an inappropriate brightness. But its success as a marketing tool initiated a series of disastrous physical assaults on the space, including additional commercial signage, a Merrill Lynch information booth and an enormous Westclox clock known as "Big Ben." Combined with the railroad's increasingly careless housekeeping, these new elements would all but obscure the room's great qualities of light, volume and convenience that had inspired so many observers in the past.

When the New York Central announced in 1954 that it was considering demolition of the terminal, two proposals for the site's future were on the table: one prepared by I. M. Pei for the developers Webb & Knapp; the other by Fellheimer & Wagner, successors to the station's codesigners, Reed & Stem. As the *New York Times* noted, the land occupied by the terminal gained much of its value from the connection to the suburbs that the railroad provided; ironically, this very convenience threatened the future of the railroad's architectural monument because it made the site that much more attractive for an office building. "We sometimes hear the phrase 'free as the air,'" the editors wrote. "Yet in the Grand Central area of New York at least, nothing is so costly as to hold land and not fully use the air above. Demand for office space thereabouts seems insatiable."[391]

Pei's scheme was rumored to consist of approximately five million square feet of office space packaged in an eighty-story building surmounted by an observation tower that would make it the world's tallest building. But before any drawings were released publicly, Webb & Knapp declared that its proposal was being reworked (see below). Fellheimer & Wagner's rather heavy-handed proposal called for six connected low-rise structures surmounted by roof gardens, as well as an H-plan tower with the narrow bar extended to the north and south for about two-thirds of its height, thus creating the impression of comparatively slender towerlike masses on axis with Park Avenue. At the tower's base were to be stores and restaurants adjoining the elevated, landscaped spaces, while at the building's summit was to be a heliport. The severed portions of Forty-third and Forty-fourth streets were to be connected through the building at street level, and the serpentine Park Avenue viaduct, which wound itself around the existing terminal building, would be tunneled straight through the new structure. The building would also include garage space for 2,400 cars.

Fellheimer & Wagner's proposal elicited strong protest almost immediately. The editors of *Architectural Forum* spoke out in support of preserving the concourse, suggesting that an international design competition be held for a new scheme incorporating the great room. *Forum*'s editors also wrote a letter to the two railroads using Grand Central Terminal—the New York Central and the New Haven railroads—urging that the concourse be preserved; the letter was circulated to architectural and planning professionals with a call for their support:

> The concourse may not be the most efficient railroad station conceivable for 1955, but—*the Grand Central Concourse is probably the finest big room in New York.* It belongs in fact to the nation. People admire it as travel carries them through from all parts of the world. It is actually one of those very few building achievements that in many minds has come to stand for our country. . . . Its appeal recognizes no top limit of sophistication, no bottom limit. The most exacting critic agrees in essentials with the newsboy at the door. . . . Gentlemen, we plead that you do not tear it down, that you not trust yourselves to replace it.[392]

Of the 428 people who received the letter, 235 responded, 220 of them voicing support of the concourse's preservation. There were, however, several well-known architects who wrote in favor of replacing the concourse, including, of course, Alfred Fellheimer. He said in his own defense:

> We carefully weighed our own pride in the present building, and its emotional and esthetic significance to people all over the world. Our reluctant but firm conclusion is that neither pride nor reverence should be permitted to clot the vitality of a great metropolis. In turn, that very vitality may guarantee that if one expression of human aspirations must be destroyed in the process of growth, it will be replaced by an even greater one.[393]

Marcel Breuer, who had been involved in the redesign of existing stations in his capacity as a design consultant to the New Haven Railroad and would soon become a major figure in the controversy, argued that contemporary architecture should not be dismissed outright: "We should not put obstacles in the way of a new project which may create a still better architecture. . . . I believe in the vitality of our time. Good contemporary architecture stands up against the great creations of the past. Any 'cultural' or 'local patriotic' hampering of free development of contemporary architecture is dangerous. Let us wait until a new project crystallizes and decide then."[394]

Minoru Yamasaki, who also served as a consultant to the New Haven,[395] directly attacked the existing building's architecture: "Though it is a marvelously beautiful room, Grand Central is in an archaic style [and] does not particularly express the exciting materials or exciting methods of construction we have today."[396] George Howe, a leading architecture educator and spokesman for the Modernist cause, argued against preservation:

> I will admit that I have had much pleasure in the past years, from entering and circulating in the Grand Central because of its fascinating complexity of passages and levels woven about a great space, but once these are removed I see no great architectural virtue in the great space itself. The exterior to the south and the office tower to the north are in any case deplorable. So putting aside sentiment, I say let the nature of taxation of aerial rights take its course.

At the conclusion of his remarks, Howe added "Sorry!"[397] Douglas Haskell, *Forum*'s editor, wrote a separate editorial urging careful consideration: "There are places and occasions . . . where the past can be acknowledged and preserved to our advantage: not as a tourist curiosity but as part of our continuing

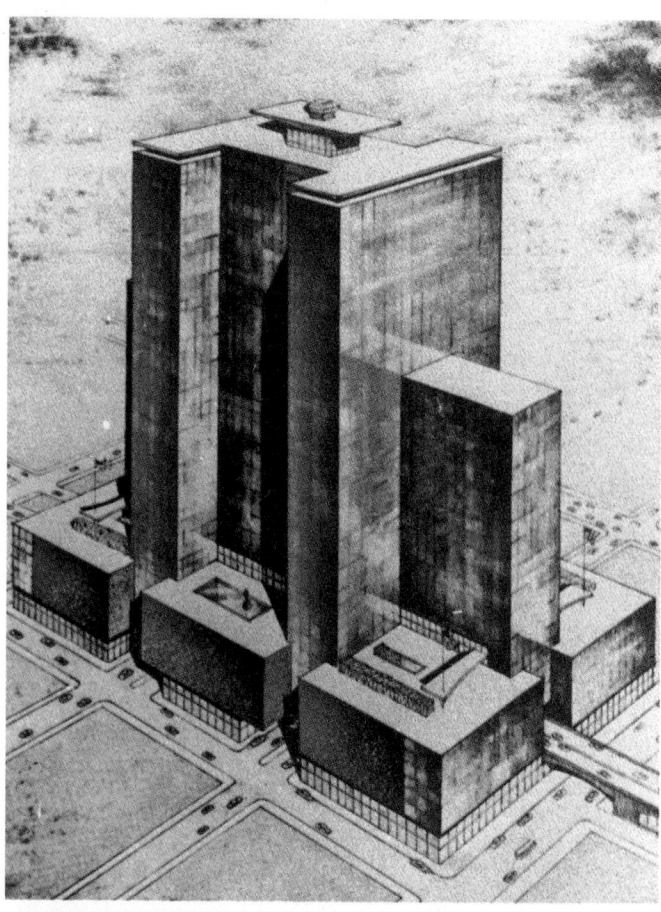

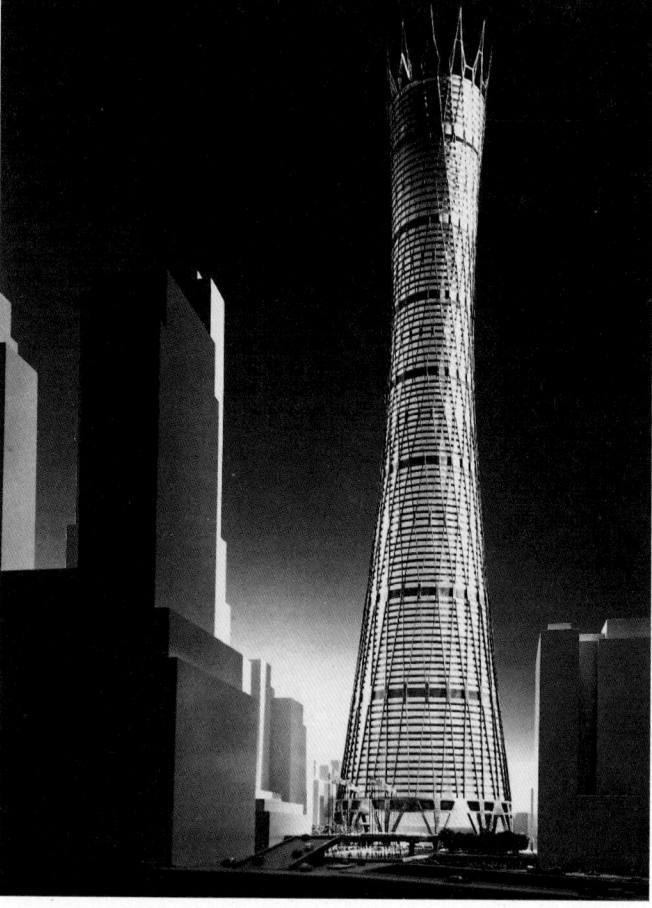

daily business life. That is why *Forum* asks the most careful scrutiny when the chance comes to retain such past achievements as the Grand Central concourse in New York."[398]

I. M. Pei's proposal, released in 1956, also boldly flew in the face of rising preservationist sentiment, replacing the terminal's Beaux-Art facades with an unabashedly futuristic scheme known as the Hyperboloid.[399] Above a rectilinear base surmounted by the elevated extension of the Park Avenue viaduct, a slender eighty-story tower, circular in plan and approximately 200 hundred feet in diameter at its base, would rise from a flagpole-studded plaza. The building tapered as it rose, narrowing to a width of approximately 100 feet at around its fiftieth floor, before flaring outwards toward its top. The tower was to be encircled by an exposed network of twelve wedge-shaped supports, crisscrossing to form a diamond grid pattern; extending beyond the tower's roofline, pairs of girders met to form a crownlike pattern that gave the building a distinctive and instantly identifiable silhouette. The design as a whole was undeniably spectacular and, if realized, would have in effect substituted one landmark for another. Two years after Pei's scheme was released, plans were announced for another project, Emery Roth & Sons' Grand Central City, which preserved the terminal's facade and main concourse; although not built to the Roths' original designs, this project was ultimately realized as the Pan Am Building in 1963 (see chapter 5).

In 1961 Jesse Weingart and Irving Fagenson proposed building a three-level, forty-four-lane bowling alley inside the terminal's south waiting room, reducing the height of the lofty vaulted space from fifty-eight to fifteen feet. The editors of *Progressive Architecture* protested: "A new activity called 'Let's See What We Can Do Next to Louse Up Grand Central Station' is New York's current favorite indoor sport." Noting that the proposed bowling alley had been devised by two little-known designers, the architect Lino G. Ferrari and the industrial designer Vito J. Tricario, the editors quipped, "It's a living, we guess."[400] But New York's Board of Standards and Appeals refused to grant the variance required by zoning laws that prohibited the construction of bowling alleys in the Grand Central area. Olga Gueft, the editor of *Interiors*, applauded the board's action but observed that the "ruling that stopped the proposed desecration was only a brief reprieve based on the wrong pretext—on the *purpose for which* the noble historic landmark was to be ruined rather than the fact of the ruin itself."[401] Although most New York architects had opposed the plan, one group had hedged their bets: the Architectural Bowling League, including individuals who had protested the project, had requested reservations in the bowling alley upon its completion.

On September 21, 1967, the Landmarks Preservation Commission designated the exterior of Grand Central Terminal a landmark. The railroad opposed designation but did not appeal the decision. The same day landmark status was granted, vehement opposition to the notion of building a skyscraper above the terminal resurfaced. While no specific proposals had been issued, Philip Johnson labeled the very idea an "outrage,"[402] and later reported that he turned down an opportunity to design a skyscraper on the site: "I didn't want to be responsible for ruining a landmark that I had worked so hard to defend," he said.[403] Richard Roth, one of the principal architects of the Pan Am Building, along with Walter Gropius and Pietro Belluschi, said: "We put the Pan Am Building way back from the main part of the terminal, replacing an ugly structure over the train shed. It formed a gracious backdrop for the terminal itself. But now they want to do violence to the terminal. Half a dozen builders have asked me to make studies to help them in bidding on the Central's invitation. I won't do it."[404]

In April 1968 it was announced that the English developer Morris Saady had commissioned Marcel Breuer, the Hungarian-born, Bauhaus-trained Modernist architect who had taught at Harvard between 1937 and 1946, to design a building above the terminal, eighty feet south of the Pan Am Building. Under the city's zoning laws, the new tower could be as tall as fifty-five stories. Although the terminal's interior was not legally protected, Breuer stated that he intended to preserve much of it; however, construction of a new building would require, according to the editors of *Progressive Architecture*, the placement of trusses and elevator shafts in the waiting room. Despite this aspect of the plan, the editors argued that Breuer's appointment "may be a boon to those who love the grand spaces and old (1913) facade of Grand Central." The editors speculated on Breuer's motives for accepting the commission:

> Breuer's concern, and indeed his reasons for taking the job, may go back to his years at the Bauhaus. It was part of the Bauhaus teaching that an architect or designer should take a distasteful commission and do his best with it, lest someone else botch it. . . . And now two mammoth skyscrapers—one by the Bauhaus' founder and one by a former pupil—will stand facing one another in the middle of Manhattan, defiantly guarding the air space above Grand Central. Breuer has the more difficult task. How will he produce a Charybdis to go with Gropius' Scylla?[405]

Russell Lynes took a much more cynical view of Breuer's acceptance of the project:

> It would be unreasonable to expect architects to turn down good clients just because the clients happened to want to build where there were already too many buildings for the good of the community. It is, after all, the architect's function to produce an aesthetically satisfactory and efficient structure where his client wants to put it; the architect is essentially just a hired hand, a man with a special skill for surrounding air with construction materials to make several enclosed layers of air and thus make a parcel of land into a layer cake of parcels.[406]

Breuer himself explained that he was simply seizing a valuable opportunity: "Without doubt, this project is controversial. I knew there would be objections. Because I wanted to weigh the pros and cons, I didn't accept the job right away. After a week, I came to the conclusion—somewhat to my surprise—that the project offers an opportunity, though an unconventional one, for a great urban building."[407]

On June 19, 1968, Breuer presented his plans for a thin, fifty-five-story concrete-and-granite slab to be positioned parallel to the Pan Am Building and "floated" above Grand Central. The building, to be called 175 Park Avenue, would rise 150 feet higher than the neighboring Pan Am Building because its "ground" floor would be located over the terminal, 188 feet above the street. A core containing service equipment and fifty-two elevators would be anchored in bedrock and rise up through the roof of the main waiting room, where four enormous cantilevered trusses would support the office tower above. Breuer's plan also called for the renovation of Grand Central's concourse, including the removal of advertisements and photographic displays. The waiting room was to be transformed into a vaulted lobby leading to both the office building and the station.

Donald Elliott, chairman of the City Planning Commission, who could not object to the building's construction on legal grounds because it conformed to the city's zoning ordinances,

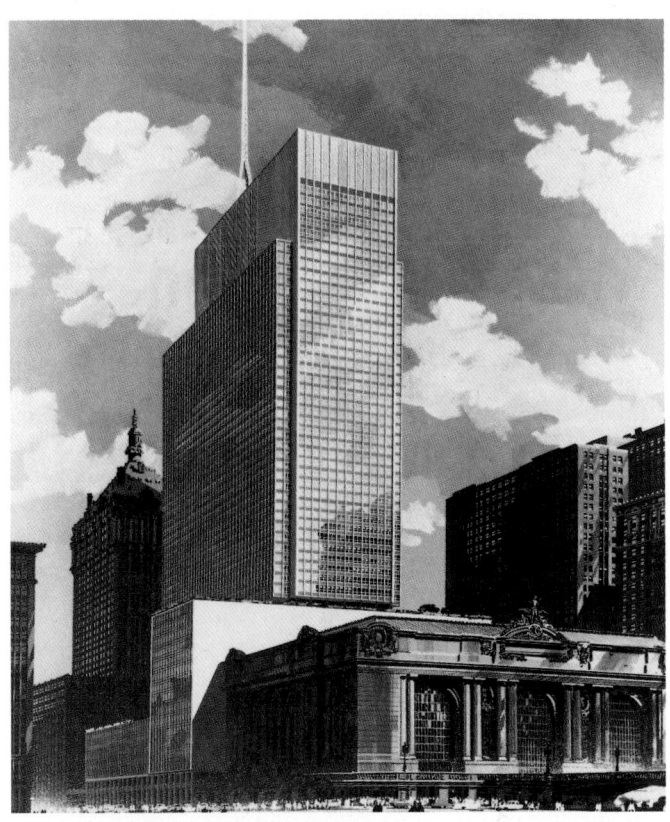

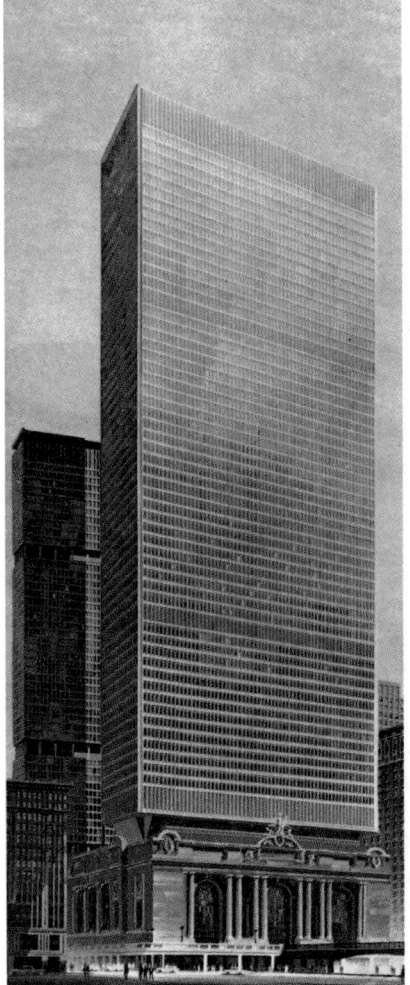

Top far left: Proposal for office tower to replace Grand Central Terminal, East Forty-second Street at Park Avenue. Fellheimer & Wagner, 1954. Rendering of view to the northeast. NYP

Bottom far left: Proposal for Hyperboloid to replace Grand Central Terminal, East Forty-second Street at Park Avenue. I. M. Pei, 1956. Model. View to the northeast. PCF

Above: Proposal for Grand Central City, north of Grand Central Terminal, East Forty-second Street at Park Avenue. Emery Roth & Sons, 1958. Rendering by Robert Schwartz of view to the northeast. ERS

Left: Proposal for 175 Park Avenue, above Grand Central Terminal, East Forty-second Street at Park Avenue. Marcel Breuer, 1968. Rendering of view to the north. AF. CU

called it "the wrong building in the wrong place at the wrong time."[408] The editors of the New York Times acknowledged Breuer's skill but criticized his design:

> As architecture, the new tower soaring from the classical Beaux Arts terminal like a skyscraper on a base of French pastry has the bizarre quality of a nightmare. The job defies the architect's notable taste and talent. Even he has said of the result, "It must be the dada in me." As a distinguished artist who has been through dada, surrealism, Bauhaus, brutalism, and other twentieth century styles, he should know. Fun City into Dada City now? There must be a better way to plan a city—and to stop it from being choked to death.[409]

Ada Louise Huxtable said that although Breuer's solution had "striking technical élan and much more suaveness" than the Pan Am Building, the basic concept was a "grotesquerie." "Give a grotesquerie to a good architect," she said, "and you are going to get a better grotesquerie, like a better mousetrap. Mr. Breuer has done an excellent job with a dubious undertaking, which is like saying it would be great if it weren't awful."[410]

But Breuer's design was not without its supporters in the profession. Walter F. Wagner, Jr., the editor of Architectural Record, said that the building would "make a positive contribution to the overcrowded hub of New York City's transportation systems." He added that much of the criticism leveled against the building was misdirected: "If you think its a bad idea to put still another dense concentration of space and people on 42nd Street . . . that's your right. But don't act surprised and/or outraged when it happens. Don't go on wishing that our free-enterprise, profit-oriented society would only build things that you like on sites of your choosing. Instead, do something about it. Start with your mayor and your planning commission."[411] Peter Blake, a biographer of Breuer, said in New York magazine that the project had "a lot of merit" but was still "at best, an esthetic shotgun wedding." However, Blake blamed not the architect or the developer but rather "our sacrosanct Free Enterprise System, with its equally sacrosanct faith in private ownership of land. It is this system that makes most intelligent planning and urban design virtually unattainable."[412]

The most humorous public response to Breuer's design was a series of proposals made by Howard Smith in the Village Voice. Illustrated with photomontages, the proposals suggested various Modernist "piggyback" buildings utilizing the air rights of landmark properties. One proposal called for a new high-rise building to be punctuated at its midpoint by the Washington Square Arch;[413] another called for the New York Public Library to be tipped on its side and sandwiched between two skyscrapers;[414] a third placed City Hall high atop two skyscrapers, neatly straddling the void between them.[415] Perhaps the wittiest montage presented Breuer's proposed tower placed not above Grand Central but above his own Whitney Museum of 1966.[416]

Although most critics were satisfied that at least the terminal's concourse would be protected, Douglas Haskell noted that the room's southern side-aisle would be removed and that the light passing through the large arched windows would be blocked out. "The whole effect," Haskell said, "is to be squeezed, lopsided."[417] But the fate of the interior lay outside the jurisdiction of the Landmarks Preservation Commission, and thus many observers considered the completion of Breuer's building a fait accompli. As the editors of the New Yorker put it in June 1968, "The thing is to be done, and the only wonder is our own lack of wonderment, our acceptance of the fact that any well-financed irrationality, any guarantee of total urban inconvenience, is almost surely irreversible."[418]

But the battle was not over. On September 20, 1969, the Landmarks Preservation Commission denied the developer a certificate of "no exterior effort."[419] Breuer then redesigned the building, offering a new proposal that called for demolishing the terminal's facade and surmounting its fully preserved and refurbished concourse with a fifty-nine-story building supported by a central core as well as by a peripheral system of support; on the principal facade, four huge inclined columns would carry the weight, while at the rear, existing terminal columns would be used. In defending his scheme, Breuer claimed that the question of whether or not the terminal's facade should be preserved was not an issue of social responsibility but merely of "individual taste and one's personal attachment to something old." The architect charged that "landmarks may have a strait-jacketing effect on an alive and dynamic city such as ours" and that Grand Central Terminal in particular "has outlived its usefulness." Breuer argued that "there will be a large building on that spot, whether in two years or five, whether built by this developer or by somebody else," and that other developers might not be as willing to combine "planning with similar public minded considerations." He concluded that his building, "with its play of sun and deep shadows," would "compensate for the loss of a rather tired landmark which appears doomed anyway."[420]

The developer sought a "certificate of appropriateness" for Breuer's revised proposal from the Landmarks Preservation Commission. The City Planning Commission suggested transferring the terminal's air rights to adjacent blocks where office buildings could be built on as many as four different sites; Jaquelin T. Robertson, an architect who headed the commission's Urban Design Group, argued that this solution would minimize congestion as well as preserve the terminal's facade and the "air park" above it, which, he said, "is in fact the area's only window to the sun."[421] Nonetheless, Saady insisted on going forward with his plans for the Grand Central site, and on August 26, 1969, the Landmarks Preservation Commission denied a "certificate of appropriateness" to the revised building proposal. On October 7 Saady and the railroad filed a suit against the city, asserting that the commission's refusal to allow the construction of the proposed tower was in violation of the Fifth and Fourteenth amendments of the United States Constitution. Asking for $8 million in damages for every year the project was delayed, they argued their case on two principal grounds: first, that denial of the building permit constituted an uncompensated usurpation of private property rights; and second, that the landmark designation placed discriminatory burdens on the railroad not borne by nearby property owners who benefited from the effects of the landmarking process.

Rumors of negotiations abounded prior to the long-awaited decision from the New York State Supreme Court, presided over by Justice Irving H. Saypol. In anticipation of a decision unfavorable to the city, Ada Louise Huxtable reported that the "Corporation Counsel's office would apparently like to have the Landmarks Commission retract designation before the decision actually comes down. This 'settlement' would supposedly avoid the damage suit and the expense of an appeal." Huxtable described the ramifications of such an action:

> Most lawyers like a "climate of settlement," but not at the total sacrifice of the principle of the law. For this is a matter of principle that not even the most negotiable legal conscience can avoid. . . . Both the Landmarks Commission and the City Planning Commission are horrified at the prospect of such a "solution," although Landmarks is understandably running scared. . . . The spectacle of the city withdrawing a designation under threat is ap-

palling; it is an act that would invalidate its own legislation and invite a flood of litigation to undo other designations. It would ultimately undo the law and everything it stands for.[422]

On February 4, 1975, Justice Saypol ruled in favor of Saady and the railroad, granting them the right to erect a building on the site of the terminal, a building the judge said "leaves no reaction here other than that of a long-neglected, faded beauty."[423] Saypol did not question the constitutionality of the law itself but found that designation of Grand Central Terminal had placed an economic hardship on the railroad that "constitutes a taking of property."[424] By the time of Saypol's ruling, however, the economic recession rendered any large-scale construction project unlikely; nonetheless, the city appealed the decision, and efforts to legally protect the terminal continued. Philip Johnson and Jacqueline Kennedy Onassis announced the creation of the Committee to Save Grand Central Station, whose members included Louis Auchincloss, Thomas P. F. Hoving, Edward I. Koch and Paul Rudolph. "Europe has its cathedrals," Johnson proclaimed, "and we have Grand Central Station. Europe wouldn't put a tower on a cathedral."[425]

On December 16, 1975, the Appellate Division of the New York State Supreme Court, with two justices dissenting, reversed the previous decision; in the opinion, Justice Francis T. Murphy stated that economic considerations "must be subordinated to the public weal" and that "the line separating valid regulation from confiscation had not been crossed."[426] On June 23, 1977, the court's decision was unanimously upheld on appeal to New York's highest court, the Court of Appeals.[427] The struggle was finally resolved in 1978 when the case reached the United States Supreme Court, becoming the first historic preservation case to do so. On June 26, 1978, the court, in a vote of 6 to 3, ruled in favor of the Landmarks Preservation Commission, upholding the constitutionality of the landmarks law. The decision was not, however, uncontroversial. The majority opinion, written by Justice William J. Brennan, argued that the commission's denial of permission to build represented the local government's constitutional exercise of its police power and was similar to the enactment of a zoning ordinance; the case thus established aesthetically motivated historic preservation as a valid form of land-use regulation.

But Justice William Rehnquist, joined by Chief Justice Warren Burger and Justice John Paul Stevens, strongly disagreed, stating in his dissent that equating zoning and landmarking "represents the ultimate in treating as alike things that are different."[428] Rehnquist argued that whereas zoning restricted all property owners within a specified area and created benefits enjoyed collectively, landmarking created amenities that were enjoyed by the public at large but paid for only by the individual owner of the designated property. The court had ruled that the city was not "forcing some people alone to bear public burdens which, in all fairness and justice, should be borne by the public as a whole."[429] But Rehnquist asserted that the railroad's sacrifice of approximately $3 million annually in rent from the proposed skyscraper stood in violation of the principle of "an average reciprocity of advantage" as articulated by Justice Oliver Wendell Holmes in the Supreme Court's 1922 decision of *Pennsylvania Coal v. Mahon*.[430]

Rehnquist's criticism notwithstanding, the majority decision prevailed. The court did not rule, however, that the terminal could never be demolished or that the effect of the landmarks law on the building could never be declared unconstitutional, but rather held the law valid and applicable only in respect to the facts as presented in the case, thus leaving open

the possibility of the railroad trying again to prove its case. Nonetheless, the court's decision saved the terminal, at least for the short term, and further served to validate the thirteen-year-old Landmarks Preservation Commission as well as to catalyze the commission to significantly broaden the concept of what constituted a landmark.

Historic Landmark Districts

From its inception in 1965, the Landmarks Preservation Commission designated not only individual landmarks but whole portions of the city. Although they sometimes contained important buildings, these historic districts were more often defined by "everyday masterpieces"—modestly scaled, utilitarian structures, some designed by accomplished architects, some the work of anonymous builders. Vital to rounding out a full picture of the city's past, these neighborhoods and enclaves often constituted remarkably cohesive urban ensembles or richly heterogeneous collections of buildings; in addition to their aesthetic and historical significance, landmark districts were often quite simply desirable places in which to live and work. While zoning could control use and size, only landmarking, being in part an aesthetic program, could protect physical character and detail.

The Landmarks Preservation Commission landmarked twenty-seven historic districts between 1965 and 1975, including parts or all of Brooklyn Heights (see below); Sniffen Court;[431] Turtle Bay Gardens;[432] the Charlton-King-Vandam district on the southwestern border of Greenwich Village;[433] Gramercy Park;[434] the St. Nicholas district, encompassing West 138th and West 139th streets between Seventh and Eighth avenues;[435] MacDougal-Sullivan Gardens;[436] the so-called Treadwell Farm district, located between East Sixty-second and East Sixty-third streets, Second and Third avenues;[437] Hunter's Point, Queens;[438] the area surrounding St. Mark's-in-the-Bowery;[439] Henderson Place;[440] Greenwich Village (see below); Mott Haven, the Bronx;[441] Cobble Hill, Brooklyn;[442] Jumel Terrace;[443] Chelsea;[444] Stuyvesant Heights, Brooklyn;[445] the area west of Mount Morris Park;[446] Riverside–West 105th Street;[447] Central Park West–West Seventy-sixth Street;[448] Park Slope, Brooklyn;[449] SoHo;[450] Carroll Gardens, Brooklyn;[451] Boerum Hill, Brooklyn;[452] Carnegie Hill;[453] Hamilton Heights;[454] and Stuyvesant Square.[455]

The districts went a long way toward furthering the cause of preservation, but the process of designation was not without its shortcomings. First of all, many of the landmarked areas were small, constituting enclaves more nearly than districts. Furthermore, despite the commission's initial choice of Brooklyn Heights for district designation, it concentrated too heavily on Manhattan, neglecting lesser-known areas in the outer boroughs. Most important, many preservationists felt that the restrictions imposed by sweeping district designations were not as likely to be strictly adhered to or enforced as those mandated by individual building designations. The ramifications of district designation were nonetheless often profound. Even though most of the districts were already affluent or at least economically and socially stable areas, designation usually proved a boon to real estate values and in some cases stimulated the "brownstone fever" that was encouraging young urbanites and increasing numbers of returning mature suburbanites to buy and renovate townhouses.[456] As rising prices in Manhattan and Brooklyn Heights discouraged many would-be buyers, the brownstone movement spread to other parts of Brooklyn that also had a rich and varied housing stock. A chain of rejuvenated neighborhoods, including Cobble Hill, Boerum Hill and Park Slope, stretched out from Brooklyn Heights; also prime areas for homeowners and preservationists were Fort Greene[457] and, adjacent to it, the so-called Brooklyn Academy of Music district,[458] as well as Prospect Park South,[459] Prospect Lefferts Gardens,[460] Ditmas Park,[461] Clinton Hill[462] and Greenpoint,[463] which would all be landmarked by the early 1980s.

Brooklyn Heights Historic District

The first historic district, established in November 1965, was Brooklyn Heights, which seven months earlier had been designated a National Registered Historic Landmark by the United States Department of the Interior.[464] Brooklyn Heights was one of the city's best known and best preserved architecturally distinguished neighborhoods, and it also enjoyed the distinction of being America's first suburb. In the 1940s the Heights had been threatened by the construction of the Brooklyn-Queens Expressway, whose original route would have bisected the area, but the road was rerouted to the water's edge, where it skirted the neighborhood and was ingeniously slipped beneath a landscaped pedestrian walkway (see chapter 13). In the process, however, a portion of the Riverside Buildings (William L. Field & Son, 1890), the pioneering courtyard apartment complex built by Alfred T. White, was sacrificed.[465] Also lost was the picturesque Penny Bridge (Minard Lafever, ca. 1853), which crossed Montague Street to connect Pierrepont Place and Montague Terrace.[466]

By the 1960s numerous buildings in downtown Brooklyn—most significantly, the Kings County Courthouse (Gamaliel King and Herman Teckritz, 1862–65)[467] and the Brooklyn Savings Bank (Frank Freeman, 1894)[468]—had been demolished to make way for the long-considered Civic Center development. In discussing the bank's demolition, Olindo Grossi, dean of the Pratt Institute School of Architecture, stated that "though rich in architectural embellishments of the turn of the century [it] is characterized by a grandeur no longer in demand."[469] The architectural significance of several other buildings in the area was recognized, however; the Brooklyn Borough Hall (Gamaliel King, 1846–51),[470] the General Post Office (William A. Freret, after plans by Mifflin E. Bell, 1885–91)[471] and the Brooklyn Fire Headquarters (Frank Freeman, 1892)[472] were all designated as landmarks in 1966.

The Brooklyn Heights historic district contained approximately 1,300 buildings and was roughly bounded by Atlantic Avenue and Fulton, Henry, Clinton and Court streets. The area was distinguished by buildings in a wide variety of nineteenth-century architectural styles, including Federal, Greek Revival, Gothic Revival and Anglo-Italianate. Unlike other areas that would later be suggested by the commission for historic district designation, the designation of Brooklyn Heights had been virtually uncontested.

One of the few property owners to seek exemption from the controls imposed by designation was the Jehovah's Witnesses' Watchtower Bible & Tract Society, which since 1908 had its national headquarters at 122–124 Columbia Heights, and since 1946 produced its numerous publications in an industrial complex at 117 Adams Street, part of which had earlier been occupied by the pharmaceuticals company E. R. Squibb.[473] In 1966, with the historic district already established, the Witnesses sought to build a twelve-story dormitory and library on the southeast corner of Columbia Heights and Pineapple Street. Because the proposed building's site, which included three ad-

joining lots occupied by townhouses, lay within the historic district, both demolition and new construction required the commission's approval. Prior to Brooklyn Heights' designation as a landmark district, the Witnesses, who were large landowners in the area, had erected several banal dormitories, including a high-rise residence at 107 Columbia Heights (Frederick G. Frost, 1960), on the southeast corner of Orange Street.

Zoning restrictions necessitated that the project, to be designed by Frost, be reduced to six stories, and the commission called for the preservation of at least the facades of the townhouses. The architect A. L. Seiden was commissioned to design the building within the new programmatic constraints. His rather tepid Georgian-inspired scheme for the new dormitory and library included a pitched roof surrounded by a balustrade and incorporating dormer windows. The proposal was rejected by the commission; according to Chairman Harmon Goldstone, Commissioner Bancel LaFarge requested "something less pretentious."[474] Seiden submitted four other schemes. The first, a less stylistically specific design, was dismissed by the commission as "bleak and bland." Goldstone described the second scheme, which included projecting triangular bays, as "a cross between Federal and Grand Concourse styles"; the third, which featured a dominant entrance arch, as "a marriage joining Berlage with a lot of Richardsonian elements"; and the fourth, with heavily gridded facades, as "Times Square variations on the New Brutalism."[475]

Following the rejection of these designs by the Landmarks Preservation Commission, the Brooklyn Heights Association urged Seiden to retain a consulting architect and suggested Philip Johnson, Marcel Breuer, Edward Larrabee Barnes or Ulrich Franzen; the firm of Ulrich Franzen & Associates was hired. Franzen's proposal, which gained the commission's approval, was, according to Goldstone, "totally contemporary in character but harmonizing in color, scale and mass with the adjacent houses."[476] Completed in 1970, the new building was a powerfully muscular essay in iron-spot brick that sought to relate to the surrounding buildings not only in materials used but also in the incorporation of three street-level projections resembling traditional bay windows and the alignment of the building's parapets.[477] On the corner, a projection rising above the roofline housed a fire stair and also served as a symbolic watchtower. Despite the commission's approval of the design, not everyone found the building to be an architecturally sympathetic neighbor. The critic Brent Brolin said that when he first saw Franzen's design published, "I assumed it had been offered as an example of what not to do. . . . I was surprised to find it was considered an excellent example of fitting new with old." Brolin went on to charge that the architect's efforts to relate the new building to the surrounding architecture were "superficial" and "obvious" and concluded that "the designer's formula-happy efforts to build a correspondence . . . are just not enough to convince the unconscious wisdom of the eye."[478]

Greenwich Village Historic District

Greenwich Village, the neighborhood that was the site of the era's most prolonged and heated battles over preservation, was long recognized as a mecca for artists, writers and political activists but seldom celebrated for its architecture.[479] This was largely because the buildings in the neighborhood were stylistically heterogeneous and therefore difficult to categorize. Thus, the focus of those who sought to "save the Village" throughout

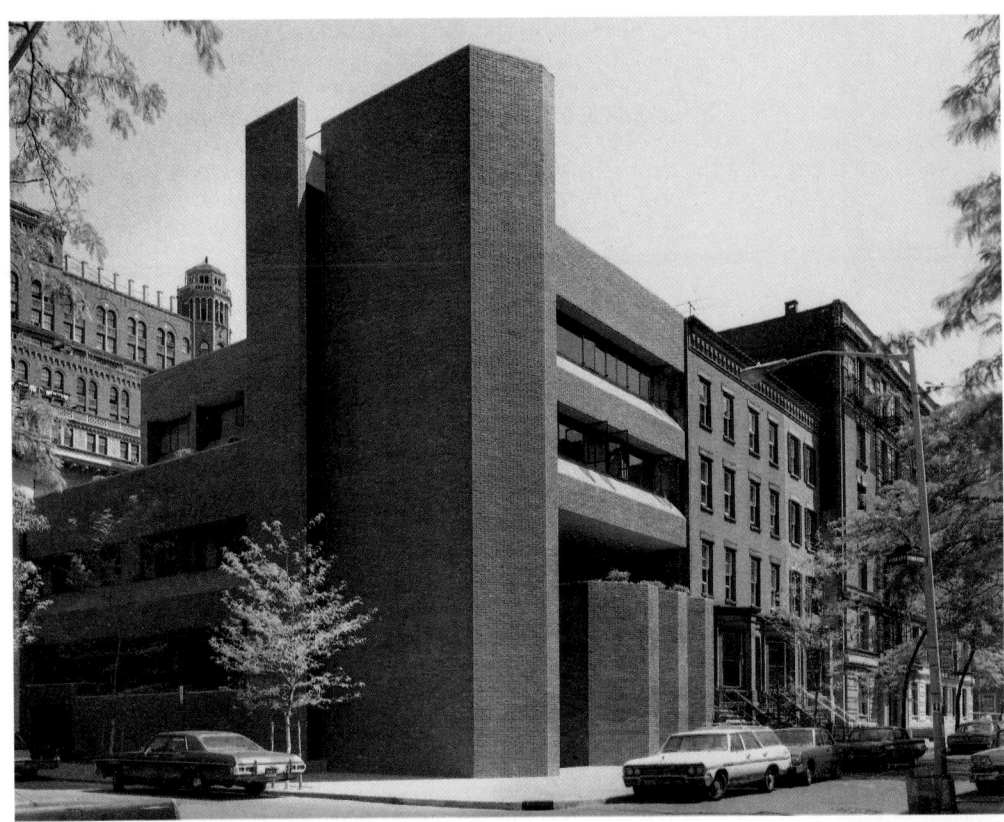

Jehovah's Witnesses' Watchtower Bible & Tract Society dormitory and library, southeast corner of Columbia Heights and Pineapple Street, Brooklyn Heights, Brooklyn. Ulrich Franzen & Associates, 1970. View to the southeast. Cserna. UF

the 1950s and 1960s was not exclusively architectural; they were also trying to protect its history, livability, social heterogeneity and artistic ambience. The widely publicized debates and conflicts that marked Greenwich Village's evolution during the postwar years served not only to delineate a host of pivotal architectural and urbanistic issues but also to lay the groundwork for the transformation of historic preservation from a rather esoteric pursuit to a political force in the city's development.

Some of the Village's most distinctive architecture had already been lost to redevelopment during the interwar period. An enclave of irregularly arranged narrow streets, collectively known as the Minettas, lined with small-scale, dormer-windowed houses dating from between 1825 and 1830, had been severely compromised by the extension and widening of Sixth Avenue in 1927.[480] The demolition in 1940 of eleven houses on Minetta Lane and Minetta Street and their replacement with two six-story apartment buildings designed by H. I. Feldman completed the obliteration of the enclave's identity. A decade and a half later, much of Greenwich Village seemed likely to meet a similar fate. In 1956 the architecture critic Walter McQuade noted that "Greenwich Village and environs still have a number of flavorful, significant old buildings, but it is a sad truth that visiting architects are walking around photographing them these days, sensing that they are not long for this culture."[481]

In the spring of 1959 the local planning board called on the city to protect Greenwich Village's architecture and urbanism by establishing a special "historic" zone.[482] The following year an important step in that direction was made when the City Planning Commission designated the area for R-6 zoning, encouraging low-density development in which buildings would maintain an average height of six stories.[483]

It was not until 1969, however, that Greenwich Village received the full protection that many had sought for it. Initially the creation of eighteen separate historic districts had been proposed, but when community leaders argued that such a plan could compromise the entire area, the Landmarks Preservation Commission designated a single, extensive area bounded roughly by Thirteenth Street, University Place, West Fourth and Washington streets. It was the city's largest historic district, containing approximately 2,000 buildings.

Designation did not, however, save all of Greenwich Village's architecturally significant buildings. Sloan & Robertson's Women's House of Detention (1931), at 10 Greenwich Avenue, between Christopher and West Tenth streets, was a stylish mélange of Dutch and German Expressionist details and included decorative brickwork on its facades ranging in color from deep brown to yellow.[484] In 1955 the city announced that the jail might be abandoned for more spacious facilities on North Brother Island in the East River. Over the next ten years, various proposals were presented to recycle or replace the building with a civic center, an extension of St. Vincent's Hospital and housing of virtually every type, including a project designed by Jane Jacobs and Perkins & Will. One proposal suggested that the building be replaced by a sixteen-story apartment building and adjacent 500-seat theater.[485] The Village Independent Democrats proposed an arts center and published a scheme in the *Village Voice* that called for a six-story rectilinear building and twin hexagonal buildings placed within landscaped grounds.[486] The New School for Social Research expressed an interest in using the site as its Center for New York City Affairs, proposing a building to be designed by Edgar Tafel.[487]

Almost no one came to the defense of the House of Detention itself, whose status as a public nuisance blinded most observers to its value as architecture. David Bourdon, a journalist and Greenwich Village resident who lived across the street, described the typical scene at the jail:

On balmy nights there was often a carnival atmosphere about

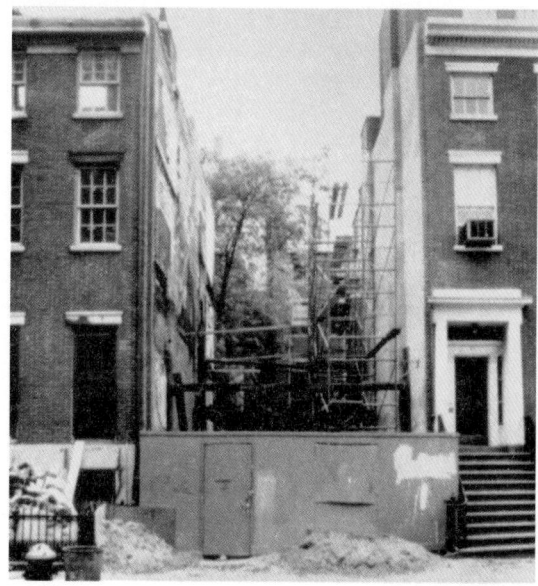

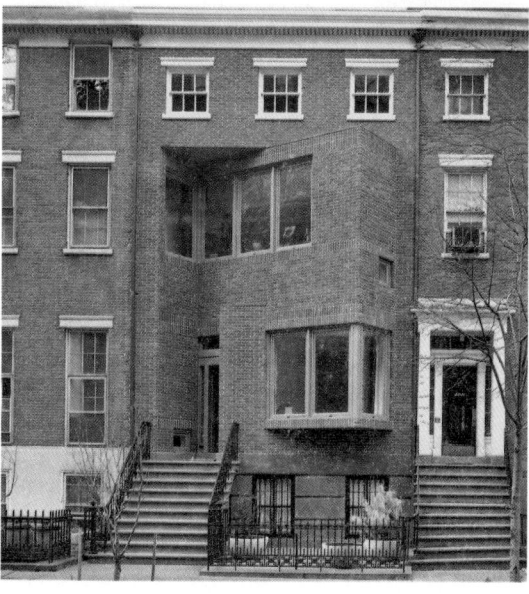

Top: 18 West Eleventh Street, between Fifth and Sixth avenues. Built for Henry Brevoort, Jr., 1844–45. View to the south after explosion, 1970. HHP

Bottom: 18 West Eleventh Street, between Fifth and Sixth avenues. Hugh Hardy, 1979. View to the south. Robinson. CERO

the House of Detention, which attracted visitors from all over the city. Although the Village is a fairly heterogeneous community, the prison visitors—the friends and relatives of the inmates—clearly did not belong in the neighborhood. The majority of these "outsiders"—like those inside—were poor blacks and Puerto Ricans. The visitors usually stood on the opposite side of Greenwich Avenue, where they could be seen from the prison windows, and shouted messages to those within.

Bourdon noted that the local planning board and the Association of Village Homeowners were "hellbent" on demolishing the building. "With a shrillness bordering on paranoia," he said, "they argued that the building, if not immediately demolished, would be used to house male prisoners—and possibly turn Greenwich Village into another Attica."[488] After the prison was closed in 1971, local citizens clamored for its demolition, despite the fact that it stood within the landmark district. Even Mary Perot Nichols, normally a staunch preservation advocate, favored demolition, calling the building "hideous and bulky" and "a monstrosity."[489]

In 1973 the Landmarks Preservation Commission approved demolition of Sloan & Robertson's minor masterpiece. In its report the commission stated, "whatever architectural interest the former Women's House of Detention may have in itself its location is highly detrimental to its neighbor, the Jefferson Market Court House. . . . If a Landmarks Preservation Commission had been in existence . . . when the Women's House was built . . . it would never have approved the erection of a structure that so crowds and overshadows the Jefferson Market Court House."[490] Following the commission's report, the Board of Estimate voted unanimously in favor of destroying the building. In 1974 the prison was replaced by a fenced-in, formal garden maintained by a local group, the Village Community for the Jefferson Market Area. However welcome the garden was, it unfortunately left the courthouse as inappropriately isolated as it previously had been cramped.

On Friday, March 6, 1970, a bomb exploded in a townhouse at 18 West Eleventh Street, a house that belonged to James P. Wilkerson, a former executive vice president of the advertising agency Young & Rubicam and the owner of a chain of Midwestern radio stations.[491] Wilkerson's twenty-five-year-old daughter Cathlyn was a member of the Weathermen, a militant faction of the radical Students for a Democratic Society (SDS).[492] The group, established in 1969, was strongly opposed to the war in Vietnam; among their many slogans was "bring the war home." This Cathlyn Wilkerson and four other Weathermen did, turning the Wilkerson house into what the police termed a "bomb factory" in which the group manufactured explosives presumably to carry out their political program, including the bombing of Columbia University buildings. The accidental explosion occurred when Mr. and Mrs. Wilkerson were on vacation in the Caribbean. It left Theodore Gold, a leader in the 1968 student strike at Columbia University, and two others dead, and made fugitives of Cathlyn Wilkerson and Katherine Boudin, daughter of Leonard Boudin, a prominent Greenwich Village lawyer who had defended the pediatrician Benjamin Spock against charges of conspiracy to support draft evasion. The event sent shock waves across the nation and was later viewed as a watershed, a telling sign that the high ideals of the youth movement of the 1960s had taken an ugly turn leading to senseless violence and tragic self-destruction.

The explosion ripped twenty-foot holes through the house's nearly two-foot-thick walls, collapsed the roof and all four floors and significantly damaged the adjacent house to the east, owned and occupied by the actor Dustin Hoffman. When the remnants of the Wilkerson house were destroyed on the instruction of the insurance company, which wanted to clear the site of debris and the possibility of lingering explosives, a gaping hole was left in the otherwise strikingly cohesive designated landmark row of Greek Revival houses built for Henry Brevoort, Jr., between 1844 and 1845. The hole itself became a kind of landmark, which Ada Louise Huxtable saw as a "fiercely tragic" symbol: "More than words, that gap in the serene Greek Revival row spoke eloquently of the ills of our society and the fragility and vulnerability of history and beauty and the obscene waste of violence."[493]

In 1971 two young families, the Francis Masons and the Hugh Hardys, purchased the empty lot for $70,000, planning to build a two-family house. Designed by Hugh Hardy, the house was to relate to its neighbors in its four-story height, its brick exterior and its inclusion of a stoop. It was not in any way, however, a replica of the house it replaced; as the architect explained: "It is condescending and unpractical to assume we understand another time well enough to recreate it. The past is not a costume rack that we loot to suit our fancy."[494] Although Hardy used some traditional details in the house, he arranged the plan on a diagonal, an orientation that was reflected in the bold angle of the principal facade between the basement and the attic story, which was recessed three feet on the side containing the main entrance and cantilevered out two feet beyond the street wall on the other side. The critic C. Ray Smith wrote that the design at once "recalled the nineteenth-century tradition of bay and bow windows" and presented "a clear and polite, if oblique, expression of the decade of the diagonal."[495]

The design immediately sparked controversy, but Hardy would later recall that this had not been his intention:

> I at first believed that we should go ahead and just do something about a new facade that would not call any attention to itself in any way; just put up some bricks and put some windows in the wall. However, optimistic people advised us, "This is one of the greatest opportunities to do something original and show that it is possible to have a good contemporary solution in historic districts." I gulped and thought "Oh, my God," because I really had not wanted to get into all that, knowing how difficult it would be. I didn't want to get involved personally in a crusade. I simply wanted a house.[496]

Nonetheless, Hardy pursued his innovative design. At a public hearing held by the Landmarks Preservation Commission, many Greenwich Village residents opposed the design, preferring instead a reconstruction of the former house. "I cannot accept the thought of badly reproducing a house of 1844," Hardy argued. "I have tried to knit the wall of the street back together, but with a structure suitable to ourselves."[497] He noted that although he had tried to match certain details of the neighboring houses, such as the cornice, he had not attempted to do so with other features, such as the hand-carved moldings around the entrance doors. In fact, Hardy said, these elements should not be duplicated "because these houses were built by and expressed a society totally dissimilar to ours, one in fact that had slaves. . . . I felt no concern for borrowing a few historic details in order to knit the wall together, but I had no wish to pretend that the 1970's did not exist."[498]

Huxtable explained that Hardy was "not willing to pretend that there was no bomb. Or that history of another kind is not now part of West 11th Street. Architecture is not a stageset: it is the continuing evidence of a city's reality. Nothing can bring number 18 to life again. The house is dead; long live the house."

Huxtable supported Hardy's design, which she called "a brilliant attempt at synthesis of new and old," and agreed with his contention that the architect had a responsibility to express the zeitgeist: "The commission can safely settle for . . . an 'archeological' approach, and run no risks other than those of historical and esthetic hypocrisy. . . . Or it can . . . judge appropriateness in terms of relationships of scale, surface, texture, color, material, general effect and use. . . . Done sensitively, without fakery, this is true historical continuity, and the genuine culture of cities."[499]

The commission ultimately accepted Hardy's design, although by a narrow margin. The approval of the Department of Buildings, however, was slow in coming. By the time it was granted, the cost of construction had escalated from $125,000 to between $175,000 and $200,000, thus increasing the difficulty of getting a mortgage, which was already problematic because of the bankers' stylistic conservatism and cynicism regarding the city's economic future. Hardy explained: "One banker suggested that by making a few changes in the design it would become 'more Villagey' and he thought that then he might be able to do something. But I had already had enough aesthetic arbitration."[500] By the time a mortgage seemed attainable, the Masons and Hardys had lost interest in the project and put the lot up for sale. Although Hardy said he had no regrets about the experience, he was disappointed by the community's response to his proposed design:

> I was . . . amazed to discover people telling me in public hearings that the trouble with my design wasn't really anything about aesthetics or architecture or the history of anything. It was that it looked different. It would be better if my house were anonymous. "Let's don't disturb the neighborhood," they said. "It is a nice neighborhood and you are changing things and we don't want that." It is the kind of suburban conformist mentality that I did not expect to find in the Village.[501]

But ultimately the property was sold to the Langworthy family, who realized Hardy's design in 1979 after being forced to have its appropriateness recertified by the landmarks commission.

East of the landmark district the Foundation Building of the Cooper Union for the Advancement of Science and Art (Frederick A. Peterson, 1859), which had been placed on the National Register of Historic Places in 1962 and designated a city landmark in 1966, was imaginatively renovated in 1975–76 by two alumni, the architect John Hejduk, who was also dean of Cooper Union's School of Architecture, and the engineer Peter Bruder, who was a Cooper Union professor.[502] The goals of the project were threefold: to help the building meet contemporary building and fire codes; to restore the building's imposing if somewhat stolid Anglo-Italianate exterior as fully as possible to its original state; and to completely reorganize the interior spaces to better serve the school's demands and requirements. The building, which occupied the full block bounded by Astor Place, Seventh Street, Third and Fourth avenues, had played an important role in the city's cultural and architectural history. It was built by Peter Cooper, an industrialist who manufactured the Tom Thumb locomotive and was active in the installation of the first transatlantic cable, to house the nation's first privately supported, tuition-free institution of higher learning. The building contained the city's first public library, as well as the basement-level Great Hall, which was New York's largest auditorium at the time and the site of lectures by Susan B. Anthony, Ulysses S. Grant, Theodore Roosevelt, Mark Twain and, most memorably, an address delivered by Abraham Lincoln in 1860 that became known as the "right is might" speech. The six-story,

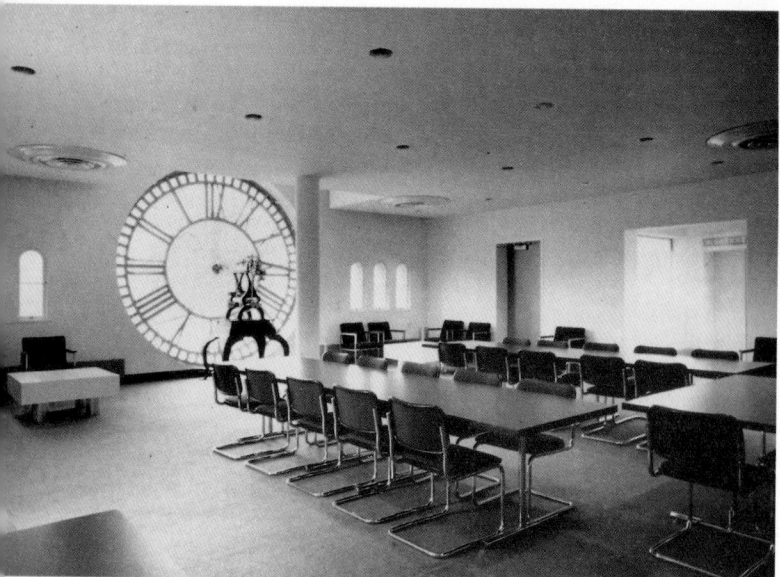

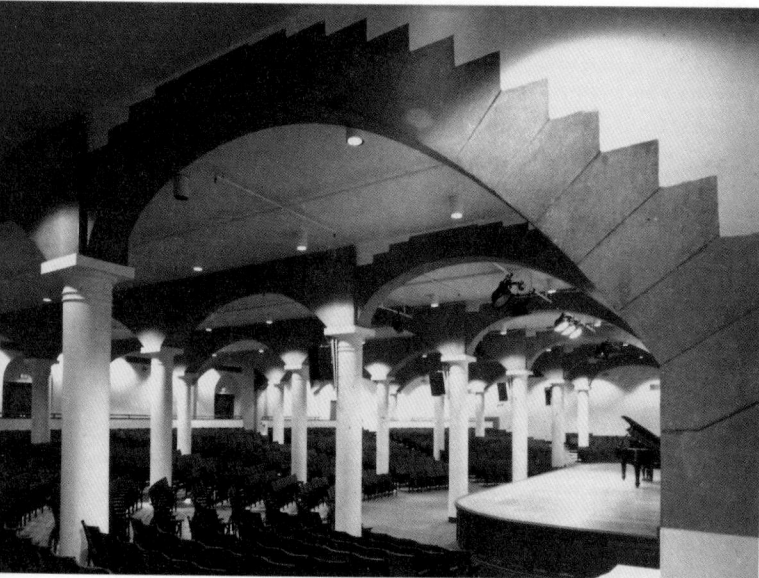

Top: Foundation Building of the Cooper Union for the Advancement of Science and Art, bounded by Astor Place, East Seventh Street and Third and Fourth avenues. Frederick A. Peterson, 1859; renovation, John Hejduk and Peter Bruder, 1975–76. Trustees' room. Ries. SR

Bottom: Foundation Building of the Cooper Union for the Advancement of Science and Art. Great Hall. Ries. SR

brown-sandstone-clad structure was the nation's first building to be framed with steel beams that were rolled as opposed to cast, a technique that would later enable the development of the skyscraper. Cooper also provided a round shaft for the eventual insertion of a passenger elevator, a device whose widespread use he anticipated.

The only visually significant changes to the building's exterior in the 1975–76 renovation were the glazing-in of the ground-floor arcades facing Third and Fourth avenues, the installation of globe light fixtures, which approximated those of the original building, the addition of rooftop terraces and the extension of the round elevator shaft through the roof. The portion of Seventh Street adjacent to the building was permanently closed to traffic and became a plaza connected to Peter Cooper Park. Inside, most of the spaces were gutted, with the notable exception of the Great Hall; in addition, the elevator shaft finally fulfilled its destiny when the existing square cab was replaced with a round one. A new trustees' room, located on the top floor, was dominated by the reverse side of the translucent-faced clock that surmounted the building's facade. Each major discipline within the schools of art and architecture was assigned its own floor, and a library dominated the ground-floor space. The spaces were articulated in a refined, highly reductivist Modernist vocabulary that stood in sharp contrast to the building's exterior.

Critical responses to Hejduk's design were highly favorable. Paul Goldberger said that "the results are superb," and he compared it to McKim, Mead & White's Century Club, which Russell Sturgis had described as "a box with a pretty inside put inside a box with a pretty outside." Goldberger wrote:

> The success with which Hejduk has managed to make his Corbusian vocabulary feel like a box with a pretty inside, and the extent to which he has managed to make that vocabulary meld comfortably with the box with the pretty outside, offer pause for thought: it reminds us that the Corbusian vocabulary need not be an entity unto itself, but in the right hands can be joined gracefully to that very larger stylistic whole which—ironically—it tried so firmly to reject.[503]

David Morton, writing in *Progressive Architecture*, characterized the renovation as a "considerable achievement," and explained that "while the building appears to be completely new inside, it is not, and what it really represents, more than anything else, is the 'purification' of what basically was already there."[504] Huxtable felt that the building's renovation went to the heart of key preservation issues:

> The . . . renovation is an outstanding example of the real meaning of preservation at a time when the "recycling" of older buildings of architectural merit is becoming increasingly common. . . . A good old building should develop layers of esthetic meaning like the rings of a tree, continually enriched, rather than violated, by contemporary functions. . . . Cooper Union is now the best of both worlds. Its "Renaissance" shell is intact. And the clarity and detail of the consciously sophisticated modernism of the interiors speaks of the creative continuity of history and art.[505]

Grace Church, at 800–804 Broadway, on the northeast corner of East Tenth Street, was part of a remarkably cohesive ensemble of Gothic Revival buildings built over a span of more than sixty years between 1843 and 1907.[506] Although the church and rectory, both designed by James Renwick, Jr., in 1843–47, had been noted in the Municipal Art Society study of 1952–58 and were designated as official city landmarks in 1966, the Grace

Church School Memorial House (1882–83), Clergy House (1902) and Neighborhood House (1907), designed by James Renwick, Jr., Heins & LaFarge, and Renwick, Aspinwall & Tucker, respectively, had been largely overlooked. In the mid-1960s the congregation, whose existence increasingly depended on the financial success of its school, announced that it was considering replacing the latter two buildings with a new school and gymnasium addition, which would also serve the needs of a community "outreach" program. The church commissioned Moore & Hutchins (later Hutchins, Evans & Lefferts) to design the addition, but when members of the congregation voiced their desire to have the existing buildings renovated, Oppenheimer & Brady was hired, with the consent of Moore & Hutchins, to explore the possibilities. After a disappointing fund-raising campaign in 1968, the church abandoned plans for a renovation and returned to the original architects for a less expensive new building.

In 1974, with the situation still unresolved, the church again proposed demolition, claiming that it was forced to sacrifice the buildings to protect its very survival. Strong public opposition was reflected in the formation of the Joint Emergency Committee to Save the Grace Church Houses, chaired by the preservationist Selma Rattner, as well as by a demonstration held outside the church by approximately thirty protesters, including members of the Architectural League. "A particular tragedy," Huxtable commented, "in the light of Grace Church's good neighbor intentions, is that its image is taking a beating, in a kind of cultural and community backlash. Even sadder, the church is risking its finances and its future on the plan. It should not have to happen this way, but perhaps it is a measure of our society that we destroy our values while trying to maintain them."[507] Ultimately, the church and the community were able to raise the money necessary to undertake an extensive interior renovation, executed by Hutchins, Evans & Lefferts. Landmark designation for the remodeled Clergy and Neighborhood houses, as well as for Memorial House, was granted in 1977.[508]

Preservation as an Instrument of Urban Renewal

In the spring of 1968, with the construction of the Lower Manhattan Expressway still threatening a significant portion of lower Manhattan's rich architectural legacy (see chapter 4), the City Planning Commission designated an eleven-block, thirty-eight-acre renewal area surrounding the Fulton Fish Market and roughly bounded by the East River, John, Pearl and Dover streets.[509] In contrast to the typical renewal program, the commission sought not to raze and rebuild the district but, as Charles G. Bennett reported in the New York Times, to transform it "into an 'Old New York' neighborhood of restored historic buildings, museums, stores and apartments."[510] The area had first attracted the attention of real estate developers, urban planners and preservationists when, in the early 1960s, the city advocated the relocation of its scattered markets as well as those along Washington Street to a massive new food distribution center in the Hunts Point section of the Bronx.

The project marked the first time in New York's history that large-scale urban renewal focused on the preservation and restoration of existing buildings. Working with the South Street Seaport Museum, a private, nonprofit corporation established in 1967 to create a living maritime museum conceived as an urban version of Mystic Seaport in Connecticut, the City Planning Commission proposed to choose a "representative" date in the nineteenth century and reconstruct the area to reflect that moment, complete with a version of the Fulton Street market. Ada Louise Huxtable praised the project as "the first really promising preservation venture that the city has undertaken in environmental terms" but warned that it was "teetering on the brink of falling into the popular preservation bag." She was particularly critical of the attempt to turn back the architectural clock: "With the best talent in the world, the most imaginative architects, the sophisticated sensibility to bridge old and new . . . why make false copies of the past? The challenge is to make the city's heritage a working part of the dynamic vitality and brutal beauty of this strange and wonderful town. And above all, to make it New York."[511]

By 1969 the South Street Seaport Museum had acquired a number of historic buildings and ships, but the full development of the project, incumbent on the sale and transfer of the museum's unused air rights to allow the construction of adjacent skyscrapers, was stalled by the collapsing office market. Three years later the project was subsumed into a larger redevelopment program when the City Planning Commission approved zoning changes that allowed for the construction of Manhattan Landing, a $1.2 billion city-within-the-city (see chapter 3). At the same time, the commission carved out a six-block South Street Seaport district that was to contain buildings no more than five stories high, be closed to all motor traffic except emergency vehicles and have unobstructed views of the river. Jonathan Barnett served as the district's master planner and Edward Larrabee Barnes served as its architect. The recession of the mid-1970s doomed the megascale project and delayed further development of the living museum. In 1979 the city approved a plan that merged the museum and large-scale commercial interests. As ultimately realized in two phases by the Rouse Company in the mid-1980s (Phase I, 1983; Phase II, 1985), the South Street Seaport justified many of the fears Huxtable had voiced a decade and a half earlier. Shorn of its gritty realities, the district lost its unique sense of place; by the time of its completion, the project had become a prime example of the "Rouseification" that combined a sanitized mix of urban architectural history and suburban shopping mall ambience. For the first time in more than a century, New York seemed a pale reflection of Boston, where Rouse's Faneuil Hall Markets had opened in 1976.

Across lower Manhattan, near the Hudson River, a less extensive preservation project was pursued concurrent with the development of the South Street Seaport. As part of the relocation of wholesale markets to Hunts Point, much of the former Washington Market, an area similar to Covent Garden in London or Les Halles in Paris, had been demolished to create a thirty-eight-acre renewal project adjacent to the site of the World Trade Center.[512] In 1968 the Landmarks Preservation Commission strongly recommended that a group of early-nineteenth-century Federal-style townhouses be renovated for residential use; they had served as warehouses and now stood in a dilapidated state ready for demolition to make way for a key component in the renewal plan, the vast Independence Plaza development (Oppenheimer, Brady & Vogelstein in association with John Pruyn).[513]

Working with the Housing and Development Administration, the commission negotiated to have the restoration of the houses funded and executed as part of the renewal program. Nine two-and-a-half- and three-story houses were brought together along Harrison and Washington streets to form an L-shaped enclave, renovated in 1973 by Oppenheimer, Brady &

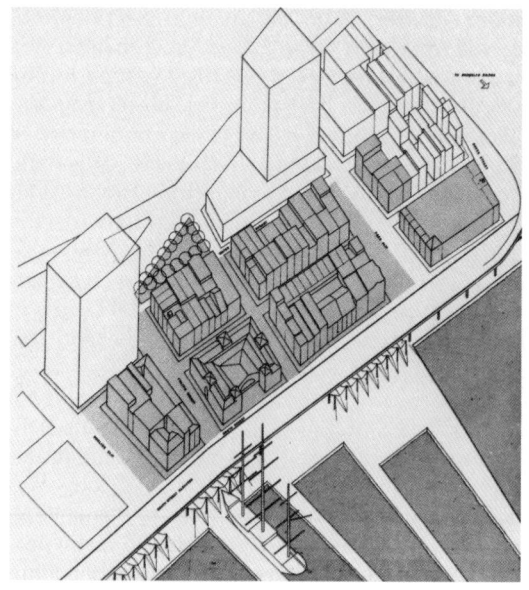

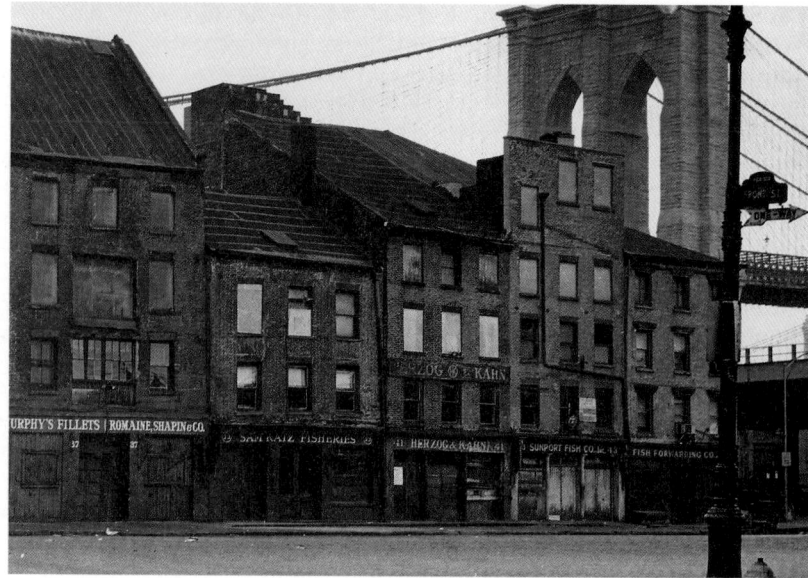

Top left: South Street Seaport district plan, bounded by East River and John, Pearl and Dover streets. Jonathan Barnett and Edward Larrabee Barnes, 1972. Axonometric site plan. JB and SSSM

Top right: Peck Slip, between Front and South streets. View to the northeast, 1959. Fred W. McDarrah. FWM

Center: South Street Seaport district plan. Perspective renderings by John M. Y. Lee. JB and SSSM

Bottom: Fulton Market Building, 11 Fulton Street, Front to South Street. Benjamin Thompson & Associates, 1983. View to the northeast showing Fulton Market Building in the center. On the lower left is 15–19 Fulton Street (Beyer Blinder Belle, 1983). NYP

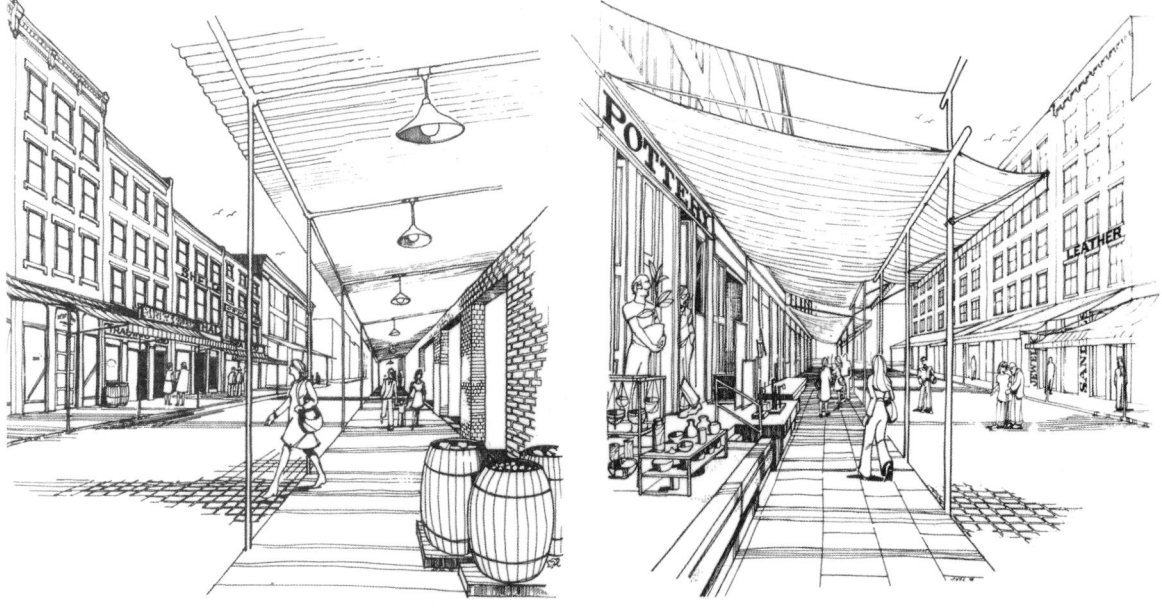

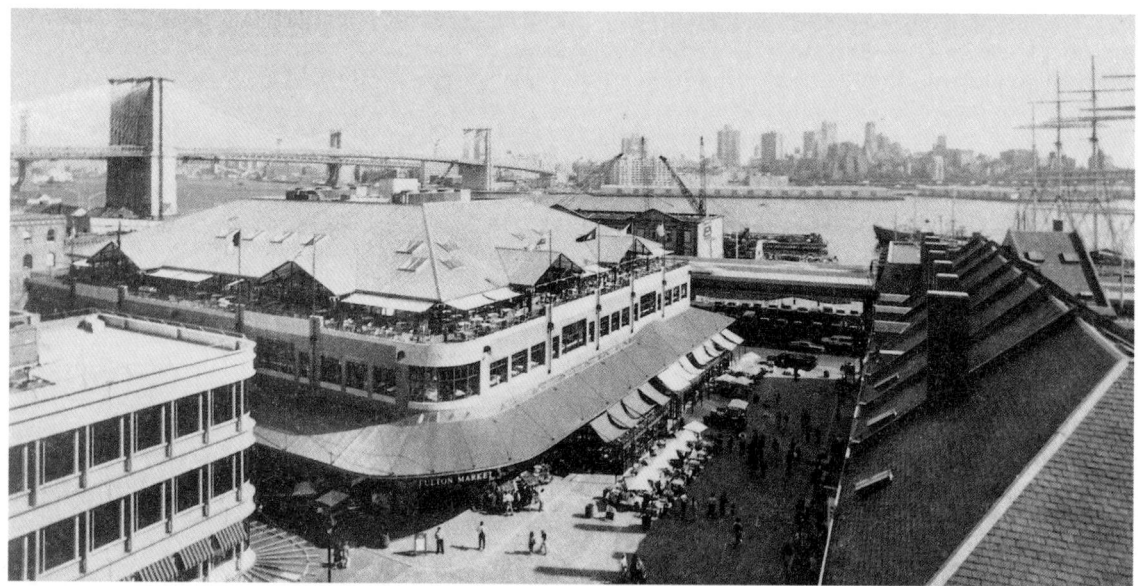

Vogelstein to include newly created cobblestone streets and flagstone sidewalks, as well as a rear courtyard they shared with low-rise apartments. The houses, which had been altered to flat-roofed, three-story structures, were restored to approximate their original appearance. The seven dormered, two-and-a-half-story houses—the Sarah R. Lambert house (1827), the Jacob Ruckle house (1827) and the Ebenezer Miller house (1827), located at 29, 31 and 33 Harrison Street, respectively; the Wilson Hunt house (1828), the Joseph Randolph house (1828) and the William B. Nichols house (1828), at 327, 329 and 331 Washington Street; and the Jonas Wood house (1804), at 314 Washington Street, all designed by unidentified architects—were thought to be among the last remaining examples of their type in Manhattan. The two other houses in the grouping, 315 and 317 Washington Street, were built in 1819 and 1797 respectively and were both designed by John McComb, Jr., New York's first native-born architect and the codesigner of City Hall; McComb himself had lived at number 317. In order to provide room for the Independence Plaza buildings and create a cohesive townhouse ensemble, the two McComb houses were moved from their original sites several blocks south; one collapsed during relocation and had to be significantly rebuilt. The Jonas Wood house was also moved from a site at the southeast corner of Harrison and Greenwich streets. Paul Goldberger found the restoration grotesquely ersatz, "an earnest, well-meaning idea that has turned out disastrously—the houses huddle beneath the towers, looking like children cowering in the presence of stern adults. There are facades at Disneyland that look more real, and all that the houses make you want to do is run back again across Greenwich Street where the old buildings are still real and not kept alive by artificial respirator."[514]

Five connected four-story buildings on the northwest corner of Washington and Murray streets, designed in 1848–49 by James Bogardus, met an even unkinder fate.[515] Collectively known as the Bogardus Building, the structures were the first completely modular glass and cast-iron buildings ever built and had been granted landmark status in 1970. The following year, when much of the Washington Market area was being razed in the name of urban renewal, the Landmarks Preservation Commission and other preservation groups succeeded in acquiring $450,000 in federal funds to disassemble, store and reerect the buildings' facades as part of a new Manhattan Community College campus, to be built just north of where the buildings originally stood.

As directed by the historian and professor James Marston Fitch, Columbia University architecture students produced seventeen sheets of measured drawings and thousands of photographs, all of which were deposited in the Library of Congress. Some of the facades were given to the Smithsonian Institution while the rest were carefully stenciled with serial numbers to ensure proper reassembly and then stored by the Housing and Development Administration. Although rumor had it that the four-ton facades were placed under one of the approaches to the Brooklyn Bridge, they were in fact stored in an empty lot in the renewal area, protected only by a chain-link fence and an unlocked gate. In June 1974 a contractor working in the area witnessed some of the facades being loaded into a truck by three men who intended to sell them by the pound as scrap metal. Following their arrest, the police found a few damaged fragments in a junkyard in the Bronx; most of the panels had been sold, reputedly for $63, and presumably melted down. Upon learning of the heists, Peter Blake, who described the buildings as "the great-grandfathers of the Seagram Building, in almost every detail," wrote: "I had been under the impression that the Bogardus buildings were safely stashed away [but] the city's screwer-uppers had dumped the whole shebang on some vacant lot. . . . Three scavengers will be brought up on some charges while the real culprits, the city's screwer-uppers, will go scot-free, as they always do."[516] Three years later the few remaining panels were also stolen, leaving only those held by the Smithsonian Institution.

Like many observers, Huxtable lamented the loss of the buildings, but she deplored the idea of the proposed reconstruction:

> By tradition and simple definition, a landmark has meant something that marks the land; it creates a distinct character, style and sense of place by being where it is. It puts the stamp of architectural quality or associative history on a particular location, giving it special environmental and cultural values. The point is that when you remove the building you lose those values. . . . Before the [Bogardus] building was stolen for the second time, there was a plan afoot to cast reproductions of its missing panels, to erect a "landmark" that would be one-third old and two-thirds new, and to put this hybrid in the South Street Seaport, where the original never was. The result, too commonly demonstrated elsewhere, would be a kind of Disney historicism or scholarly sideshow. Pious gestures are an empty substitute for preservation. No one needs architectural keepsakes. Better the scrapheap than sanctimonious games. Scrap was probably the best end for the Bogardus Building, after so many ludicrous indignities.[517]

Huxtable's arguments notwithstanding, the Bogardus Building was ultimately "reconstructed" at the South Street Seaport, although as realized in 1983 by Beyer Blinder Belle, with Fitch as consultant, the new building's sleek, sparsely detailed ferrous facades did not attempt to replicate the old buildings' facades but merely to evoke them.

In 1974 the so-called Fraunces Tavern block, bounded by Water, Pearl and Broad streets and Coenties Slip, was threatened with demolition. While Fraunces Tavern (1719; renovation by William Mesereau, 1907) had been an officially designated landmark since 1965, the rest of the block, one of the city's few completely intact early-nineteenth-century blocks, stood unprotected.[518] When the Uris Brothers began tearing down the warehouse buildings at the block's eastern end to make way for a parking lot, Ada Louise Huxtable expressed shock. Identifying the block as "a fragile miracle," she wrote: "Contrary to popular opinion, it can never be rebuilt. And also contrary to popular opinion, such a group is often more significant than the isolated building singled out as a 'landmark.' Knocking down a piece of [it] for a parking lot is about the most banal and vulgar and weary of all demolition cliches."[519]

Demolition was temporarily halted by public protest, spearheaded by a private, nonprofit action group, the New York Landmarks Conservancy, an offshoot of the Municipal Art Society formed in 1973 and chaired by the author and drama critic Brendan Gill. The organization's name had been inspired by the Nature Conservancy, which had pioneered an interventional, aggressively entrepreneurial approach to preserving wilderness areas. The Landmarks Conservancy went beyond the standards established by traditional "do-gooder" civic organizations to become a shrewd though often third-party player in real estate deals to effect the preservation of specific buildings. The group's efforts to preserve the buildings of the Fraunces Tavern block were enhanced by the dubious manner in which their demolition was planned. "The owners tried to tear them down without permits," noted the conservancy's director, Laurie

Beckelman. "That gave us leverage."[520] In 1977, with the properties under new ownership, the conservancy purchased them for only $550,000. "As mendicants," Gill said, "we can get deals that developers can't."[521] A complex arrangement was then established in which Mrs. Vincent Astor donated $250,000 as a down payment and a consortium of investors and developers took over a $300,000 mortgage, with fifty years to pay back the conservancy $250,000 without interest. A second mortgage was used to cover the $4.5 million cost of exterior restoration and interior transformation of the former warehouse spaces into apartments and stores. Largely through the efforts of the conservancy, the block's future seemed bright, and on November 14, 1978, the Landmarks Preservation Commission finally ensured its preservation, designating the entire block an historic district.[522]

Preservation in the 1970s: Checking the Balance Sheet

By the 1970s the preservation movement in New York had come to exert a profound influence on the city. A number of exhibitions on the city's architectural heritage and on efforts to save it reflected the widespread public support for preservation.[523] Nonetheless, many observers criticized the Landmarks Preservation Commission and its designation process for letting significant buildings slip through the cracks. Important—or at least highly interesting—buildings continued to be torn down. In 1970 a former townhouse and connected carriage house at 113 and 115 East Fortieth Street, renovated in 1927 to serve as the clubhouse of the Architectural League of New York (Allen & Ewing) and also occupied by the New York Chapter of the American Institute of Architects, was lost.[524] Nine years later two other buildings on the block, the Architects Building (Ewing & Chappell and LaFarge & Morris, 1912) and the red-brick and white-marble townhouse at 109 East Fortieth Street that the architect Ernest Flagg had designed for himself in 1905, were demolished.[525] Flagg's house contained an internalized porte cochere leading to an elevator that could lower an automobile to the basement-level garage, the first purpose-built car garage in a New York house. This interesting and important row was replaced by the black-glass-clad behemoth 101 Park Avenue (Eli Attia, 1985).[526]

The fate of the former New York County Courthouse (Thomas Little, John Kellum and Leopold Eidlitz, 1861–81), an imposing Classical building situated directly behind City Hall, was another striking example of the commission's timidity; as Ada Louise Huxtable said, the courthouse was "too hot a political potato for the Landmarks Commission to handle."[527] Popularly known as the Tweed Courthouse, after the notoriously corrupt political boss William M. Tweed, who illegally amassed a fortune while serving as a member of the Courthouse Commission, the building remained a potent symbol of cronyism and graft in 1974, nearly a century after its completion, The administration of Mayor Abraham D. Beame advocated replacing the courthouse with a Colonial-style office building free of negative associations. Huxtable lambasted the proposal: "Honest graft is to be preferred to pseudo-historical hypocrisy. Next to that Early Howard Johnson vision, the Tweed Courthouse looks like a rose." Many scholars and preservationists also pointed out that apart from the significant role the courthouse had played in the city's past, it was also a rare example of the

Anglo-Italianate style in New York and a finely crafted, lavishly detailed building worthy of preservation. As Huxtable put it, "Its marble, carved wood, massive construction and profligate space could not be bought today for any rational figure."[528] But the building's survival in the 1970s was due not to any strong commitment from the Landmarks Preservation Commission but to municipal impotence; New York's fiscal crisis rendered virtually all city-funded building projects impossible. The building was finally designated a landmark in 1984.[529]

In 1975 the commission failed to save the grandly Classical Franklin Savings Bank (York & Sawyer, 1899), on the southeast corner of Forty-second Street and Eighth Avenue, which was torn down by its owners, as Huxtable put it, "for parking and taxes."[530] Some of the bank's bronze interior fixtures were salvaged and became part of the permanent collection of the Brooklyn Museum. Edward Rollins, the executive vice president of the bank, dismissed the monumental building as a "dump the city would be better off without." He added: "A building like that is an eyesore if it isn't being used for its legitimate purpose. We don't want to contribute to the Times Square neighborhood going downhill any further."[531] The building's demolition, however, succeeded in doing precisely that; the resultant parking lot became a hangout for some of the area's shadier denizens.

Even more damning than the criticism that the commission failed to designate certain worthy buildings was the charge that it was elitist in its outlook, concentrating its efforts on buildings designed by the most famous architects for the richest clients. Writing in the *New York Times* in 1975, the sociologist Herbert Gans claimed that the commission "mainly preserves the elite portion of the architectural past," allowing "popular architecture to disappear, notably the homes of ordinary New Yorkers, and structures designed by anonymous builders without architectural training." Gans advocated preserving a wide variety of buildings of different types, including "a 19th-century vaudeville theater, a public bathhouse, and some taverns," as well as tenement buildings, some restored and others left "in their dilapidated stinking state." Gans argued that "aside from their historical value, these slums provide those of us lucky enough not to have to live in them visible evidence of how many people still have to call them home in 1975—which might help to get rid of such buildings."[532] Although Huxtable asserted that in its individual and historic district designations the commission had successfully protected a broad range of both monumental and vernacular buildings,[533] Gans countered that she had "presented some highly selective evidence."[534] Whatever the validity of the specific examples cited, it was clear that while the commission had designated a variety of buildings, the net of legally binding protection could be cast wider, particularly when it came to twentieth-century architecture.

Other criticisms were leveled against the commission, principally that landmark designation placed too heavy a burden on the property owner.[535] The law stipulated that the owner of a designated property was accountable for keeping the property in "good repair" and could not demolish or change the property, including such minor alterations as painting, or installing an air conditioner, new door or commercial sign, without the commission's approval; failure to meet these requirements was, in some cases, punishable by imprisonment. Denial of an alteration or demolition permit could be appealed on the grounds of economic hardship if the owner was unable to garner a return of 6 percent on the property's assessed value. Critics charged that the commission, which intentionally rejected financial considerations in conducting the landmarking process, placed owners of designated properties in an economically disadvantageous position, not only because they had to cover potentially increased maintenance costs but also because they were forced to forfeit lucrative development opportunities without compensation. The commission's ability to impose economic restrictions without compensation was supported by the Supreme Court's 1978 decision upholding Grand Central Terminal's landmark status; however, some observers, such as John J. Costonis, a New York University professor of property law, subsequently alleged that the decision applied principally to Grand Central's situation and was inappropriately read as granting license to designate. Critics also charged that the municipal costs of landmarking were high because the process potentially constricted the municipal tax base by preventing development.

As early as 1952, the scholar and critic Talbot Hamlin had pointed out that preservation and free-market economics were to some degree inherently in conflict. He argued that giving market conditions full reign in the determination of landmark properties was unworkable:

> At the present time, preservation of architecturally important monuments or structures with historical associations is totally dependent on two conditions: Either they are making enough money to render it undesirable to change them, or, conversely, they are in financially blighted areas where it will not be profitable to replace them. This in the long run and in terms of the total worthiness of community life, is manifestly absurd.[536]

As the editors of the New Yorker pointed out in 1957, in an article on a walking tour of the East Village led by Henry Hope Reed, Jr.:

> The district has survived as a sort of museum of various architectural styles simply because there has been so little economic inducement to destroy it. "Prosperity is a blessing to architects but a curse to architectural historians," Mr. Reed said. "From my point of view, the ideal city would be just rich enough to keep adding new buildings and just poor enough to insist on saving all the old ones."[537]

But clearly this ideal bore little relationship to the realities of New York real estate, and the potential sacrifice of revenue borne by both individual owners and the municipality as a whole would continue to serve as a compelling argument against preservation. Furthermore, while designation often led to an increase in property values, in some cases owners who successfully argued in court that restriction on development significantly reduced value were granted lower assessments, resulting in a smaller tax base.

Some critics charged that the landmarking procedure was simply too easy and that the lack of legislative checks and balances led to insufficiently considered designations. With a majority vote of the Landmarks Preservation Commission, a designation became effective immediately and could be overturned only if the Board of Estimate voted to do so within ninety days. In contrast, approval of a proposal set before the City Planning Commission required a three-fourths majority vote of the commission, and then a three-fourths majority vote of the Board of Estimate, which was difficult to obtain because it used a weighted voting system. Critics argued that the granting of sweeping powers to the Landmarks Preservation Commission in 1965 may have been correct, or at least understandable, in light of the tragic destruction of Pennsylvania Station, but that the subsequent exploitation of that power was questionable.

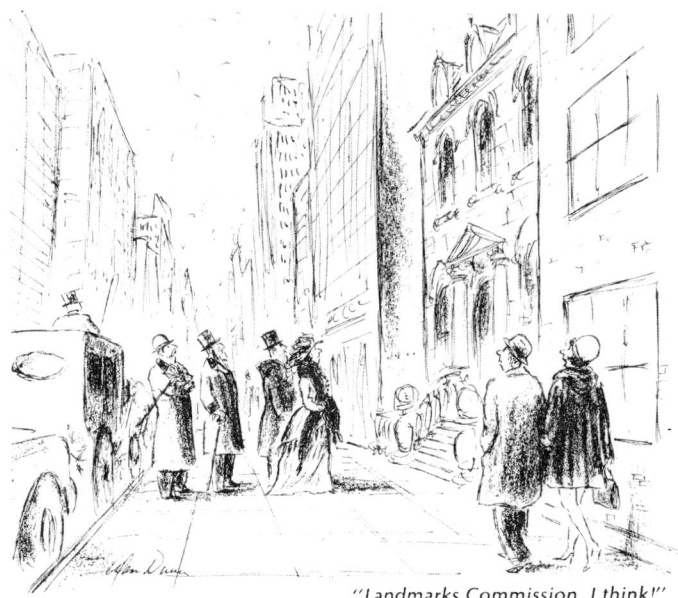

"Landmarks Commission, I think!"

Cartoon. Alan Dunn, 1967. PDE

In addition to the legally binding process of landmark designation, other forces that were perhaps more consistent with free-market practices were also highly successful in promoting the revitalization of whole areas of the city. New York's so-called J-51 legislation, initially enacted in 1955 to eradicate unsafe tenement conditions, was later amended to stimulate the conversion of commercial loft buildings to residential use.[538] Throughout the 1960s and 1970s large numbers of brownstones and loft buildings were preserved and renovated through the J-51 program, whose impact went far beyond what was originally intended or anticipated. Although the legislation proved a tremendous boon to preservation, it was not, due to its lack of stylistic controls, a viable alternative to the aesthetically rooted landmarks law.

Whatever the possible shortcomings or destructive effects of the landmarking process, it was clear that the growth of the historic preservation movement in New York during the postwar years was dramatic and swift. In 1974 Ada Louise Huxtable noted:

> In one decade the cause of preservation has undergone a remarkable transformation from an odd and harmless hobby of little old ladies in floppy hats who liked old houses to an integral, administrative part of city government dealing with an essential part of the city's fabric. From a cultural nicety it has developed into an environmental necessity of important sociological impact—a remarkable consequence no one foresaw.[539]

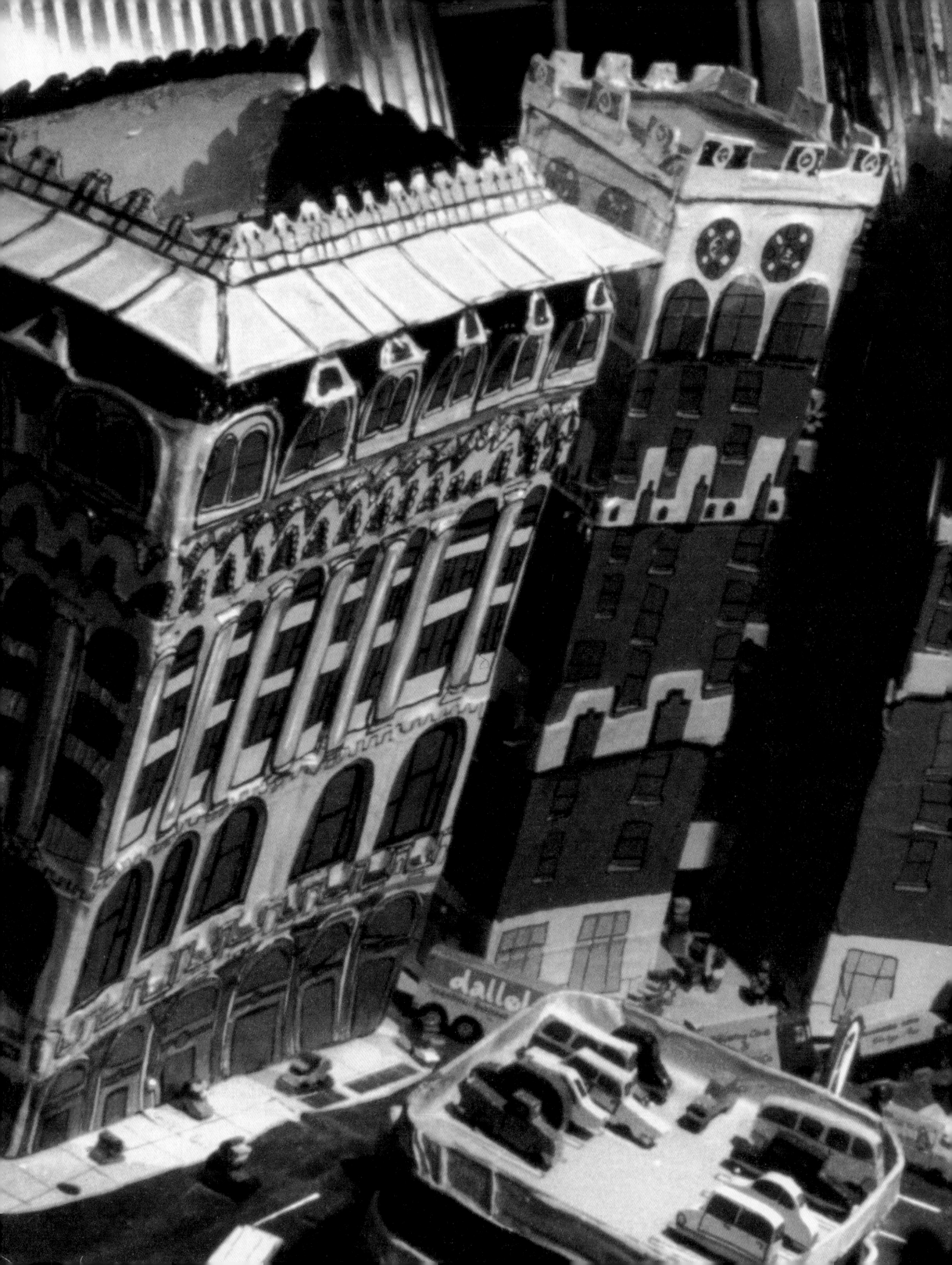

Chapter 17

New York and the Arts

By 1960, when Pop Art just came out in New York, the art scene
here had so much going for it that even the stiff European types
had to finally admit we were part of world culture.
—Andy Warhol, 1980[1]

NEW YORK IN PAINTING AND SCULPTURE

During the postwar period, as the unprecedented office-building boom reflected New York's new status as the world's economic capital and the United Nations complex established the city as the center of international affairs, the arrival of important European artists and the subsequent colonization of the city by American artists, as well as the development of a large and sophisticated art audience, rendered New York the world's undisputed art capital. Artists between the world wars had taken New York as their subject almost as much as late-nineteenth-century artists had embraced Paris. Postwar artists, on the other hand, typically chose highly idiosyncratic themes or pure abstraction. The city's newly legitimized artists shunned the exterior landscape of nature and buildings in favor of the interior landscape of the mind.

Notwithstanding the general trend, some artists chose not to become obsessed with the psyche, preferring instead to chronicle the city. Usually these were older artists such as Louis Lozowick, who came to Modernism through Cubism.[1] Lozowick's lithograph *Winter Fun* (1940) depicts children sledding in Central Park with some of the city's most familiar buildings, including the Sherry-Netherland Hotel (Schultze & Weaver and Buchman & Kahn, 1927), the Plaza Hotel (Henry J. Hardenbergh, 1907) and the RCA Building at Rockefeller Center (Associated Architects, 1931–40), clearly visible in the background.[2] In Lozowick's art, a benign skyscraper city embraces nature and humanity as easily as monumental architecture. In 1943 Lozowick portrayed himself working outdoors in Central Park, an arcadian landscape that overpowers the schematically rendered skyscrapers.

George Ault, who during the 1920s and 1930s had been associated with the Precisionist painters, created a surprising, surreal portrait of city life in *New York Rooftop* (1940), in which a solitary nude woman, seen from behind, contemplates the cityscape from a nondescript rooftop.[3] In the 1950s the more accomplished Precisionist Charles Sheeler, who like Ault had reached artistic maturity between the wars, increasingly reduced his formal vocabulary, composing architectural scenes with unadorned planes.[4] *New York #2* (1951) depicts light-colored skyscrapers pushing up from the dark, brownstone nineteenth-century city. Sheeler's buildings, with their punched windows and setback masses, belong more to the 1920s and 1930s than to the postwar world of the United Nations and Lever House structures, which the artist captured in brilliant photographs in 1951 and 1953. Sheeler's flat, graphic *Skyline* (1950) reflects the Constructivist-inspired minimalism of Dutch-born Piet Mondrian, who lived the last years of his life in New York (see below), and his disciples such as Fritz Glarner.

Charles G. Shaw, who had previously employed a strict Cubist vocabulary, also began to move toward simpler forms.[5] His *New York Skyline* (1942) depicts a moonlit city in which a neat row of buildings occupies a single plane. Shaw abandoned naturalism, depicting the buildings in a variety of colors, including teal blue and olive green, with pink and lavender windows forming spirited geometric patterns.

Edward Hopper continued to document the city's architecture as the setting for loneliness.[6] *Nighthawks* (1942) depicts late-night stragglers in a diner seen through a large plate-glass window. The dark, deserted street, the harsh diner lights and the lack of engagement among the patrons convey the alienation that was increasingly seen as a hallmark of urban life. Hopper's *New York Office* (1962) shows a woman standing at a desk in a prewar office building. Oddly, the woman wears a sleeveless dress more suited to a night on the town than a day at work.

If Hopper painted lives of quiet desperation, the painter, editor and art dealer David Burliuk depicted a more explicit angst.[7] In *Dreams About Travel* (1943), Burliuk, who was born in Ukraine and had been associated with the Russian Futurists as well as with the Blaue Reiter and Sturm groups in Germany before emigrating to the United States in 1922, used a crude but

---

Ruckus Manhattan. Red Grooms, 1975. Mixed media. Detail of
sculpture showing view of lower Manhattan. ©1994 Red
Grooms/Artists Rights Society, New York. MAG

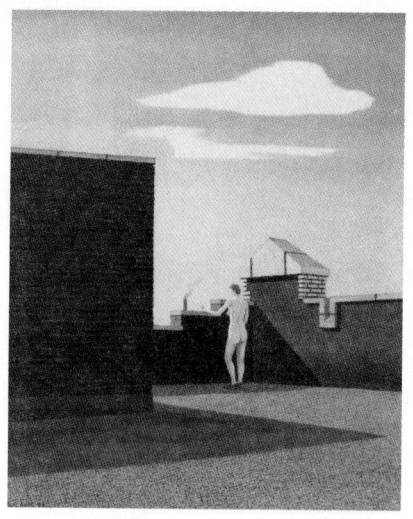

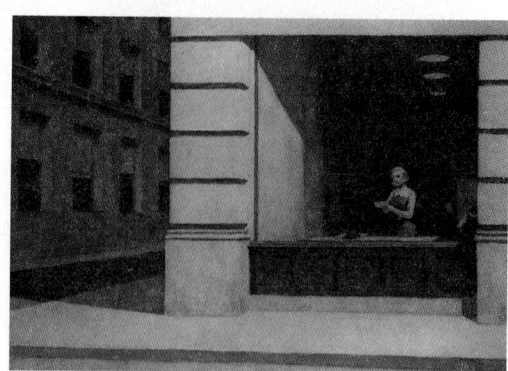

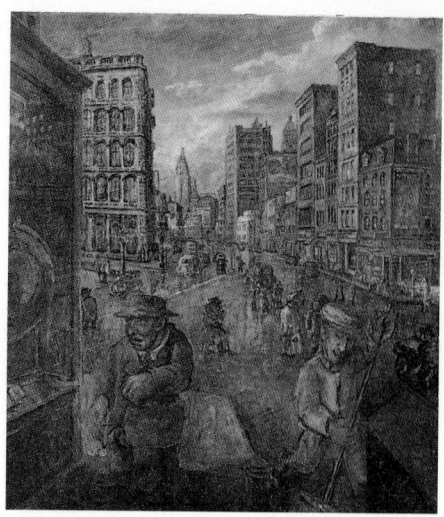

New York Rooftop. George C. Ault, 1940. Oil on canvas. Private collection. HAG

New York Office. Edward Hopper, 1962. Oil on canvas. MMFA

Dreams About Travel. David Burliuk, 1943. Oil on canvas. HMSGA

detailed realism to depict the view looking north from Fourth Avenue just above Cooper Square. Burliuk rendered the tower of the Consolidated Gas Company Building (Henry J. Hardenbergh, 1915; tower, Warren & Wetmore, 1926), the Metropolitan Life Tower (Napoleon Le Brun & Sons, 1909) and the Empire State Building (Shreve, Lamb & Harmon, 1931), which serves as the distant focal point, under a sunny sky.[8] Cars and pedestrians traverse the streets as a smiling street sweeper goes about his job. Burliuk altered the contented, lively and livable city, however, by inserting in the foreground a man who peers into a store window containing a large globe and books (presumably travel guides). The man's tense, weary expression suggests that whatever the city's opportunities and conveniences, for many inhabitants it remains a disquieting environment from which they yearn to escape.

Florine Stettheimer, whose artistic career first flourished in the 1920s, used the Great Hall of the Metropolitan Museum of Art as a setting for *Cathedrals of Art* (dated 1942, the work remained unfinished at the time of her death in 1944).[9] The iconographically complex painting, which incorporates a self-portrait of the artist, articulates Stettheimer's musings on the history and future of art. The Museum of Modern Art, a nexus of cultural life, appears as a fanciful stage set. Dancing female figures from a Picasso painting and the lion from Henri Rousseau's *The Sleeping Gypsy* (1897) come to life in front of the building.

Port of Refuge: Arrival of the Modernists

The collapse of Europe in the late 1930s and early 1940s and the consequent arrival in New York of many leading members of the European artistic community triggered the transfer of artistic leadership from Paris to New York. Beyond the visual propaganda generated under Communism and Nazism, most European artists were committed to nonrepresentational Modernism. As William Seitz later observed, "The Nazi-Soviet nonaggression pact, signed in August 1939, turned out to be the Magna Carta of the American abstract artist."[10] As early as 1935, the Spanish Surrealist Salvador Dalí, one of the first important European Modernists to spend time in New York, inspired a num-

ber of Americans such as the Egyptian-born, New York–bred O. Louis Guglielmi. Guglielmi described the city as "a veritable jungle that delighted and frightened me. . . . For me a city landscape is an exercise in the abstract construction of forms, shapes of patterns, and the rhythm of the angular."[11] East Harlem, once Guglielmi's home, formed the subject matter of many paintings, but the artist roamed the city in search of backgrounds. *Terror in Brooklyn* (1941) depicts three widows in black dresses held captive under a bell jar in a desolate street. *Mental Geography* (1938), painted during the Spanish Civil War, depicts the Brooklyn Bridge partially destroyed by an air raid. In explaining his intentions, Guglielmi commented that he "meant to say that an era had ended and that the rivers of Spain flowed to the Atlantic and mixed with our waters as well."[12]

Of the European Modernists who emigrated to New York, the Surrealists had perhaps the most profound effect on the local art scene and the city's cultural life.[13] Dalí returned to New York in 1939 to startle the locals with his window displays for the Bonwit Teller department store and his Dream of Venus pavilion at the World's Fair.[14] The Surrealists' leader, André Breton, followed, as did Yves Tanguy, André Masson, Marcel Duchamp, Roberto Sebastiano, Matta Echaurren and Ossip Zadkine. The German Max Ernst escaped Gestapo internment with the help of Peggy Guggenheim, to whom he was briefly married, and arrived in New York in 1941. Guggenheim solidified the Surrealist influence over experimental American painting when she opened her Art of This Century gallery (see chapter 6) in 1942.

The painter Lyonel Feininger, who had exhibited with the Blaue Reiter group in 1913 and later served as one of the first teachers at the Bauhaus in Weimar, fled Germany to settle in New York in 1937. Feininger remained in the city until his death in 1956.[15] Feininger, who struck many American colleagues as quintessentially German and quintessentially Modernist, had in fact been born to German parents in New York, where he lived until he was sixteen. Feininger found readjusting to his native city difficult and for two years produced very little work, but in 1940 he embarked on a series of paintings of Manhattan that brought a heightened lyricism to his Cubist-inspired geometric work. Manhattan's monumental skyscrapers and insistent grid suited Feininger's sensibility; more surprising is how the city's

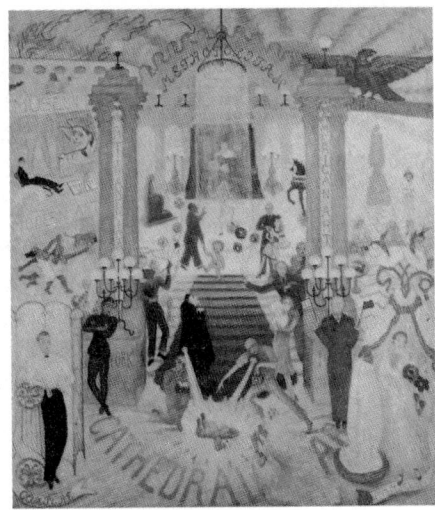

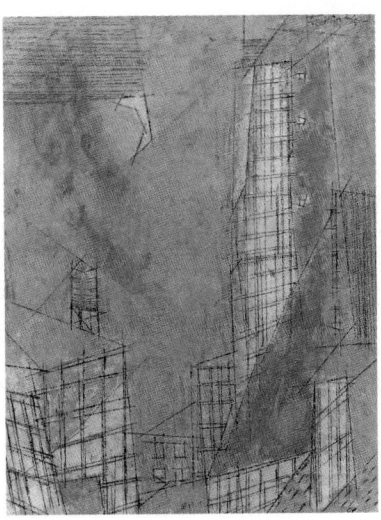

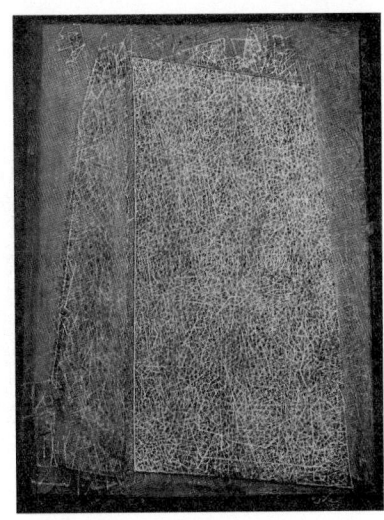

Cathedrals of Art. Florine Stettheimer, 1942. Oil on canvas. MET

City Moon. Lyonel Feininger, 1945. Oil on canvas. NAAC

New York Tablet. Mark Tobey, 1946. Opaque watercolor and chalk on paper on wood panel. MWPI

fragile light captured his imagination. In a letter of February 3, 1942, to the curator Alois Schardt, Feininger wrote: "I am working just now on a series of architectural 'visions.' . . . New York is the most astonishing city in the world for atmosphere, color, and contrast. . . . I use a new approach in some of my works, with graphic elements, lines, in fields of strong color. I had to come to America to free myself of the severe constraint of the straight and rigid line."[16]

In *Manhattan, from the Earle* (1944), based on a sketch Feininger made seven years earlier of the view from a hotel overlooking Washington Square, linear elements form a loose grid that impressionistically traces the cityscape. Patches of ivory, pink, lavender and brown only roughly correspond to the hard-edged subject matter. Feininger consistently portrayed New York as a skyscraper city in which the compelling technological bravura of the buildings perfectly complements nature. In *City Moon* (1945), an angular white crescent floats in a green and terra-cotta sky, a counterpoint to the gleaming white skyscraper that towers even higher. Feininger's portrayals of New York rarely include people. An exception is *Manna-Hata* (1952), in which an angular, abstracted, faceless male figure wearing a bow tie and top hat harmonizes with the surrounding buildings and a stylized, black and white moon: man, nature and artifice form a cohesive whole.

In 1940 the Dutch minimalist Piet Mondrian arrived in New York. Mondrian spent the last and (according to the artist) happiest three and a half years of his life there, living first at 353 East Fifty-sixth Street and then in a larger studio at 15 East Fifty-ninth Street.[17] Ironically, given his lifelong quest for a reductive and, arguably, nonrepresentational art, Mondrian was one of few European-born artists to find New York a stimulating subject. His *Broadway Boogie-Woogie* (1942–43) celebrates Manhattan's grid and the steel openwork that frames its buildings, as well as the signs of Times Square—of which he reputedly remarked, "How beautiful! If only I couldn't read English."[18] Mondrian superimposed a syncopated pattern of brightly colored squares and rectangles of color over the grid. With this painting, Mondrian changed the course of his art. Leaving the white paradise of his earlier work behind, as the younger painter Robert Motherwell observed, Mondrian "entered the world."[19]

Mondrian's Fifty-ninth Street studio became his last work, a three-dimensional exploration of the spatial ideals of his paintings. Against the off-white studio walls he hung rectangular blue and gray. The carefully calculated arrangements constituted what the artist and writer Harry Holtzman described as Mondrian's "only compositions in environmental scale."[20] A desk, stool and shelves, fabricated by the artist from packing crates, were his only three-dimensional constructions. *Victory-Boogie-Woogie* (1943), incomplete at the time of Mondrian's death, was the only painting on display.

The war and long reconstruction period in Europe provided, as the historian Thomas Bender has observed, "both an opportunity and, as many of New York's intellectuals saw it, a responsibility for international and cultural leadership."[21] At the forefront was art critic Clement Greenberg, who said in 1948 that "the main premises of Western art have at last migrated to the United States, along with the center of gravity of industrial production and political power."[22] Three years later the critic Thomas B. Hess similarly claimed that just as Paris had become "an accepting center of cosmopolitans" in the nineteenth century, "polyglot New York" could create a fertile breeding ground for art and welcome the international spirit "with enthusiasm."[23]

The presence of European artists in New York catalyzed native American creativity. American-born artists saw that their European rivals "acted as though art were a distinguished profession."[24] Challenged by the influx of so much self-possessed talent, many American artists turned away from prewar representational American Modernism to create passionately self-referential painting which came to be known as Abstract Expressionism. Though the European influence was undeniable, the foundation of this new artistic community, later identified as the New York School, lay in the Federal Arts Project of the Works Progress Administration. During the late 1930s the program had brought artists from all over the United States to New York to work, united by a single patronage that cultivated a distinctly American artistic expression. Most New York School artists established relationships with each other under the WPA.[25]

By the mid-1950s Manhattan had become, as the editors of *Time* proclaimed, "art's avid new capital." Though the editors cited the "slow westward drift of Western art" as an historical inevitability, they seemed amazed by New York's new prominence. Not yet in their view a center of artistic creativity or a city beautiful enough to inspire artists (though it had done so for at least two generations of painters and sculptors), New York was for *Time*'s editors a principal art marketplace. But they were sharp enough to observe that the leading lights of the "School of Paris" were old and that a "New York School" seemed to be emerging, nurtured "in an artistic climate similar to that of Paris in the 1900s." Moreover, New York had ingredients to support a creative scene: it was full of young artists, most of whom, eschewing schools of art, "find their instruction and inspiration in a vast weekly banquet of important and exciting art shows."[26] Its museums were so popular with artists and the general public that annual attendance reached 3.5 million, exceeding the combined attendance of the city's two baseball stadiums.

The New York School

The New York School sought a transcendent modern American art out of a primordial pictorialism that was to be as unself-conscious and direct as nature itself, although the physical environment that fostered the movement was hardly natural. New York was in many ways quite antithetical to the hermetic, introspective, abstract art that emerged. Although members of the New York School enlivened bars such as the Cedar Tavern (82 University Place) with endless discussions about art and life and contributed to the prestige of an American culture with New York at its center, their art offered little appreciation, explanation or criticism of the city itself. Nonetheless, the city showed its influence. Working outside the rather closed, male-dominated inner circle of the Abstract Expressionists, Louise Nevelson produced abstract art nearly unimaginable outside New York's physical setting.[27] Born in Kiev, Russia, and raised in Rockland, Maine, Nevelson first produced figurative drawings, paintings and sculptures, but she found her voice in the 1950s with a series of monumental steel and wood sculptures that typically incorporated found architectural elements. Nevelson later reflected on her relationship with her adopted home: "I've lived in New York 60 years—my whole adult life. . . . I have fulfilled much of my life here. . . . New York as I feel it permitted me a fuller scope—my world is New York City."[28] In describing the effect of the city, Nevelson recalled seeing primitive sculpture while in Paris in 1931:

> Someone took me to the Musée de l'Homme and they had an exhibition of African sculpture. There were masks and full figures, and I took one look and saw their power. . . . I didn't have to study African sculpture, I immediately identified with the power. When I returned to New York, I would go in the subways and see the black supporting columns and recognize their power and strength standing there. They did something to me. . . . It was as if they were feeding me energy like the primitive sculpture did.[29]

Franz Kline stands out among the Abstract Expressionists for consistently engaging the city. *Wanamaker Block* (1955) and *Crosstown* (1955), each with broad black bands slashing across a raw canvas, suggest a nonmimetic search for the essence of New York's form.[30] Kline, born in Wilkes-Barre, Pennsylvania, first settled in New York in 1938 and never abandoned it. He accepted the city for what it was. "If you've been here more than a year," he said, "it's beyond your liking or not."[31]

The Polish-born painter Jack Tworkov, who divided his time between New York and Provincetown, Massachusetts, also abandoned figurative subject matter for an entirely abstract vocabulary.[32] Yet some of Tworkov's abstract work reflects the influence of the city. In *West 23rd* (1963) slashes of red, white and blue rise from a yellow ocher band extending across the bottom of the canvas. Perhaps abstracted from the rapid movement of pedestrians above a yellow-painted curb, the painting distills the city's vivacity.

To the mystical painter Mark Tobey, a member of the Baha'i faith and a practitioner of Zen meditation, New York was a pulsating concentration of light and energy.[33] Tobey's *Broadway Boogie* (1942) is covered with dancing figures and abstracted neon lights. In *New York* (1944), figures have disappeared, leaving a web of dark and light lines. A similar web appears in *New York Tablet* (1946), this time contained within a parallelogram, outside of which the "white writing" for which Tobey had become well known appears in varying densities.

Barnett Newman, a rare native New Yorker among the postwar artists, was, according to his wife Annalee, "romantic about New York: this was his city."[34] Newman was committed to enhancing New York's role as an international art center. Moreover, his devotion to the city's old neighborhoods, especially those in lower Manhattan, where he worked during the 1940s and where he painted from 1950 until his death, set him apart. Beginning in the mid-1950s younger artists congregated on and around nearby Coenties Slip (see chapter 3). In a posthumously published essay on New York, Newman commented, "The world knows New York by its new landmarks. Every city has its label, and since modernity is the label of New York, the city is seen in its terms. . . . To the world New York is an exercise in modern construction. Yet there is a part of New York where one gets . . . the sense of history, the charm of age and tradition."[35]

The work of the Abstract Expressionists was an intensely private act, an art of self-dramatization. For that very reason the media found it fascinating and turned many of its proponents into public figures. Thus while the city made almost no direct, visible impact on their art, these painters became intimately associated with New York in the public's mind. Franz Kline, Willem de Kooning, Barnett Newman, Robert Motherwell and Mark Rothko were little known outside the art world, but Jackson Pollock became New York's first art superstar. Breaking the ice of the nativist provincialism of the WPA era, Pollock became in the late 1940s, as the critic Thomas B. Hess put it, "by an act of will The Greatest Artist in the World."[36] Nonetheless, Americans, even sophisticated New Yorkers, were slow to realize that local artists were the leading exemplars of the postwar sensibility. New York School artists still had to affirm themselves not only against contemporary European masters like Picasso but against younger Europeans like Nicholas de Staël, Pierre Soulages and Hans Hartung. Even the mediocre artist Bernard Buffet, because he was French and seen as a descendant of Impressionism and Post-Impressionism, was in some quarters taken quite seriously. Buffet's 1958 visit to New York resulted in a series of paintings of familiar local landmarks that the critic Alexander Watt, writing in *The Studio*, described as "totally devoid of any plastic quality. The harsh outline of the cold steel-and-cement skyscrapers, the empty facades and the blatant, almost monochromatic, coloring of the buildings, and background, reflect, truly enough, the tough, non-romantic 'look' of New York. Buffet's scenes of the capital of America convey an admirably suitable impression of take-it-or-leave-it."[37]

Pop Goes the Art World

The New York School's power was short-lived, losing its center soon after Pollock's death in a car accident in 1956. By the time Kline died of natural causes six years later, de Kooning had turned to representation focusing on the human figure. Perhaps more decisively, a new generation had thrown down a challenge with a wide variety of postabstract stylistic vocabularies soon lumped together under the rubric "Pop art." Marcel Duchamp, a cofounder of the Dada group, virtually ceased creating art in 1923, yet during intermittent visits to New York between 1915 and 1942 and later, when he became a permanent resident, he exerted a tremendous influence on the city's art world.[38]

Duchamp's "ready-mades," commonplace manufactured objects selected by the artist and exhibited as art, compelled Robert Rauschenberg to ask de Kooning for a drawing, which he proceeded to erase and exhibit as *Erased de Kooning* (1959).[39] Rauschenberg worked closely with the physical realities of his adopted city in his so-called dirt paintings of 1953, in which the artist stuffed urban muck into crates. As the critic Peter Conrad has pointed out, "The city's first gift to Rauchenberg was its indeterminacy."[40] Rauschenberg himself said: "New York is a maze of unorganized experiences peopled by the unexpected—change is unavoidable."[41] His influential "combine" paintings collage together a wide variety of visual images, many drawn from art history, with the pedestrian's random view of New York reflected in prosaic photographs of the city taken from the windows of the artist's Fulton Street studio. The ordinariness evokes the daily experience of the city and subordinates specific architectural references to a dynamic visual whole. Rauschenberg's "snapshot" photographs support Pop art's celebration of the commonplace and banal. *Estate* (1963) incorporates images mostly drawn from the architecture of lower Manhattan, functioning as a visual record of a flaneur's journey through the city streets.

Rauschenberg's reverence for collage mirrored his view of the city as so multifaceted and contradictory that it cannot cohere naturally. For Rauschenberg, the two-dimensional format seemed too confining; even incorporating three-dimensional objects was not enough. During the 1950s and early 1960s Rauschenberg was increasingly drawn to avant-garde dance and particularly to the work of Merce Cunningham, who together with the musician John Cage advocated an art that embraced what they considered to be the aleatory nature of existence. The critic Calvin Tomkins has described Cunningham's influence:

> Cunningham's ideas have always had much in common with those of his contemporaries in the visual arts, and for this reason some of his most loyal admirers and supporters have been painters and sculptors. His dances have been compared to the canvases of Jackson Pollock, in which there is no fixed center but, rather, an all-over relatedness of shifting movement. His feeling that any movement can be a part of dance has its echo in the assemblages and combines of Robert Rauschenberg, among others.[42]

From 1954 to 1964 Rauschenberg designed costumes and sets for Cunningham and accompanied the group on tour as lighting designer and stage manager.

Other visual artists pushed the limits of plastic art toward theater, creating striking tableaux that often relied on audience participation and blurred the boundaries between artist and viewer. Allan Kaprow pioneered the tendency toward "live" art, using the term "happening" to describe the new form, which was "something spontaneous, something that just happens to happen."[43] To Kaprow, such work grew directly out of his predecessors' obsession with art as act—Abstract Expressionism was often called Action painting. Kaprow explained: "Pollock, as I see him, left us at the point where we must become preoccupied and even dazzled by the space and objects of everyday life, either our bodies, clothes, rooms, or, if need be, the vastness of Forty-second Street. Not satisfied with the *suggestion* through paint of our other senses, we shall utilize the specific substances of sight, sound, movements, people, odors, touch."[44]

In the fall of 1959 Kaprow presented his ninety-minute *18 Happenings in 6 Parts* at the Reuben Gallery, 61 Fourth Avenue, for which he sent invitations stating, "you will become a part of the happenings; you will simultaneously experience them."[45] Kaprow used clear plastic sheets to divide the gallery's loft space into three rooms. Spectators seated in chairs arranged in circles and rectangles watched performers, including Kaprow, the sculptor George Segal and the painters Sam Francis and Alfred Leslie, march, recite, bounce balls. play musical instruments and play cards. Although it seemed spontaneous, *18 Happenings in 6 Parts* was rehearsed for two weeks prior to opening and throughout its week-long run. Kaprow's *Courtyard* (1962), staged in the courtyard of the rather seedy Mills Hotel (Ernest Flagg, 1897), at 160 Bleecker Street, involved a twenty-five-foot-high pyramid made of paper and a woman in a nightgown representing Mother Nature and Aphrodite.[46]

Red Grooms, who moved to New York from Nashville, Tennessee, in 1957, used the happening to create witty visual send-ups of his adopted city.[47] In *The Burning Building* (1959), Grooms pushed the nascent art form closer to theater as he spoofed melodramas. Performed in Grooms's Lower East Side loft, which he dubbed the Delancey Street Museum, the ten-minute piece featured the protagonist, played by Grooms, somersaulting out the window of a blazing building. According to Thomas B. Hess, the piece "succeeded in transferring some of the visual expression of Abstract Expressionist painting off the canvas . . . to the streets, and it bounced around the lofts and metaphysical barricades of downtown New York."[48]

When in 1975 Grooms took over the lobby of 88 Pine Street with a zany sculptural display of models of New York buildings titled *Ruckus Manhattan*, he reached his stride as the city's most inspired visual chronicler. The monumentally scaled artwork was the highlight of "Immovable Objects," a free-form, interactive event in the tradition of happenings, sponsored by the Cooper-Hewitt Museum. The event was directed by Dorothy Twining Globus and designed by Robert Mangurian and the architecture and design firm Works.[49] On opening day of this outdoor exhibition involving the buildings, streets and parks of lower Manhattan, held from June 18 to August 8, 1975, people costumed as buildings marched and danced from City Hall to Chase Manhattan Plaza. Perhaps inspired by the costumed architects at the 1931 Beaux-Arts Ball (recently rediscovered by the Dutch architect Rem Koolhaas), the parade was organized by Karen Bacon and led by the Muskrat Banjo Band.[50] A spokesman for the exhibit said, "We thought that since it was an immovable objects show, it would be fun to have the buildings moving. The aim is to humanize the buildings. *They* are the characters of our city."[51] The costumes were created by architectural firms and artists. Skidmore, Owings & Merrill fashioned versions of the firm's Chase Manhattan Bank, Dubuffet trees and all, the Marine Midland Building with its Noguchi red cube and One Liberty Plaza. The artist Rolando Vega created a papier-

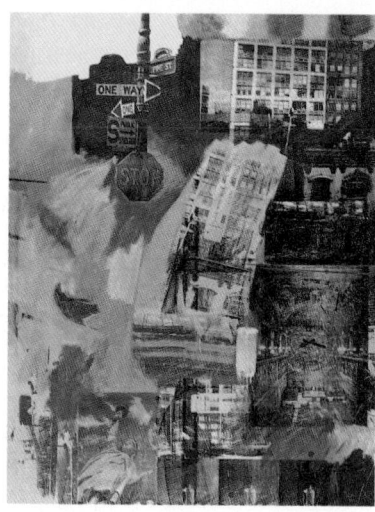

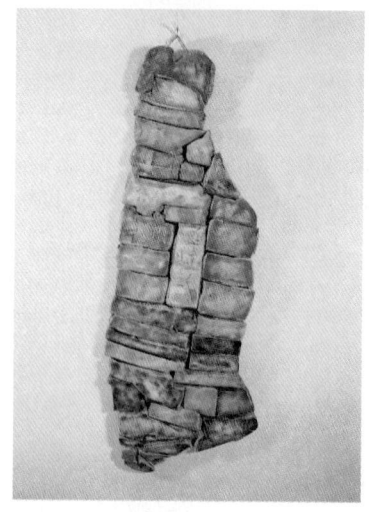

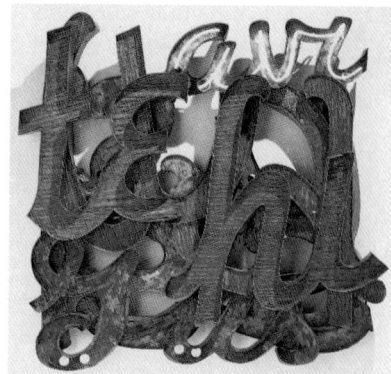

Estate. Robert Rauschenberg, 1963. Oil and printer's ink. ©1994 Robert Rauschenberg/VAGA, New York. PMA

Soft Manhattan #1 (Postal Zones). Claes Oldenburg, 1966. Canvas filled with kapok. AKAG

Times Square Sky. Chryssa, 1962. Neon, aluminum and steel. WACA

maché version of the Brooklyn Bridge to be worn by two people. Grooms himself re-created Cass Gilbert's U.S. Custom House in painted canvas and styrofoam.

The 6,400-square-foot *Ruckus Manhattan* sculpture was created by Grooms with the assistance of his wife, Mimi Gross Grooms (the daughter of the sculptor Chaim Gross), and twenty-one helpers called the Ruckus Construction Company. A walk-through show of small-scale buildings and full-scale figures, it featured a model of the Woolworth Building that "bent forward jauntily," as Ada Louise Huxtable put it, "held firmly in the protective embrace of a dragon . . . [rising] with a cheerful and total disregard for gravity and the plumb line." Grooms's thirty-foot-high models of the twin World Trade Center towers were, according to Huxtable, "a cockeyed triumph, a lighthearted critique of the skyscraper ego. One shaft narrows in fake perspective with a canvas cloud pinned at its top and the other widens in reverse perspective, with an easy disrespect for architecture overreaching. . . . The Ruckus artists have achieved the ultimate putdown. They have simply turned the ribbon-thin mullions into looped and tangled spaghetti."[52] *Ruckus Manhattan* proved immensely popular; approximately 50,000 people saw it in its downtown incarnation, and another 10,000 visited it when it was reinstalled in 1976 in the Marlborough-Gerson Gallery on Fifty-seventh Street (see chapter 6). Not every critic, however, was convinced of its significance. Richard Lorber, writing in *Arts*, described it as "a realization worthy of Cecil B. DeMille," and explained:

> Unabashedly anecdotal, [the installation] has many stories to tell which are communicated equally through the faces of [Grooms's] characters as through the facades of his buildings. Far from a distinctively personal vision, Grooms has sought the lowest common denominators of distortion and compulsion in his crafting to render a mass-media archetype of the Big Apple in all its sordid glory. . . . This homunculus city bespeaks a primitivism and infantilism in Grooms' aesthetic ambition to engorge all of reality. Only time will tell whether the eccentricity of *Ruckus Manhattan* wears better as autobiography or art.[53]

Some critics also had misgivings about the tone of Grooms's social satire. Thomas B. Hess asserted that "Grooms leans hard on ethnic stereotypes. No one will object, of course, because

creeps, greasers, weirdos, nudists, and other cretins aren't on the 57th Street circuit, and, also, there's that general air of good clean American fun that captivates so many of Grooms's assistants, promoters and fans all over the world."[54]

Claes Oldenburg, who arrived in New York from Chicago in 1956, fixated on the architecture of New York in both painted sculpture and happenings. Living in decrepit buildings in marginal Manhattan neighborhoods, Oldenburg searched for what he called the "damaged life forces of the city street."[55] Using the city's garbage in his art, he argued that "a refuse lot in the city is but all the art stores in the world."[56] Oldenburg's *The Street* (1960), an exhibition at the Judson Gallery made of garbage pickings, illustrated his point. The environmental sculpture became the site for a happening titled *Snapshots from the City.* Intended, according to a press release, as a "painting in the shape of a theater," the event incorporated elaborately costumed performers portraying stereotypical characters.[57] Fellow performance artist Al Hansen recalled: "In the basement gallery were Oldenburg and his wife, Pat, covered in bandages and paint, charging about, dying. It was like a Shinbone Alley aftermath of Hiroshima in Manhattan. There were shreds of buildings—objects made of cardboard and blackened edges—and Claes moved about like a modern mummy waving a bottle and being a cross between a Bowery bum and an accident victim."[58] Oldenburg emphasized that "the place in which the piece occurs, this large object, is part of the effect, and usually the first and most important factor determining the events (materials at hand being the second and players the third)." As the site for his 1965 performance *Washes,* Oldenburg chose the swimming pool at Al Roon's Health Club in the Ansonia Hotel (Graves & Duboy, 1899–1904), although he contended that the place could be "any extent, a room or a nation."[59] Oldenburg, who embraced, as he put it, "the city filth, the evils of advertising, the disease of success, popular culture," was the most articulate of the street-oriented perpetrators of happenings:

> The city is a landscape well worth enjoying—damn necessary if you live in the city. . . . Dirt has depth and beauty. I love soot and scorching. . . . I am for an art that is political-erotical-mystical, that does something other than sit on its ass in a museum. I am for an art that embroils itself with the everyday crap

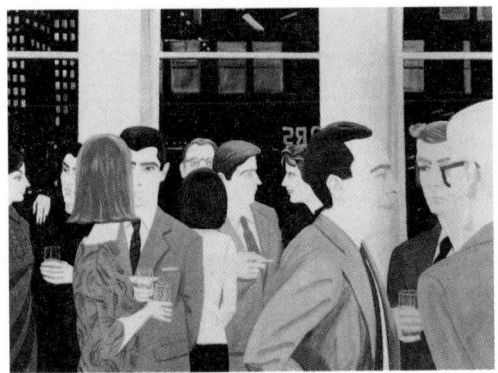

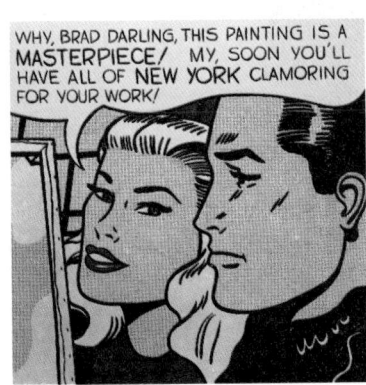

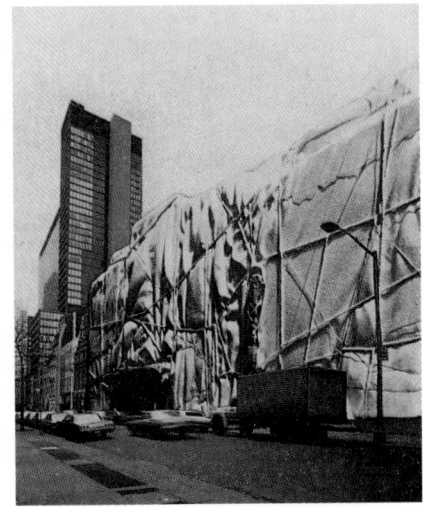

The Cocktail Party. Alex Katz, 1965. Oil on canvas. ©1994 Alex Katz/VAGA, New York. Courtesy Marlborough Gallery. MAG

Masterpiece. Roy Lichtenstein, 1962. Oil on canvas. ©Roy Lichtenstein. LCG

"The Museum of Modern Art Packed" Project. Christo, 1968. Photomontage and drawing with oil, pencil, pastel, colored pencil, cut-and-pasted tracing paper and scotch tape, mounted on cardboard. MOMA

and comes out on top. I am for an art that tells you the time of day, or where such and such a street is. I am for an art that helps old ladies across the street.[60]

Although happenings perfectly reflected Oldenburg's commitment to art that embraces the circumstances of everyday life, he concentrated on sculpture. In *The Store* (1962), he created his own version of an old Lower East Side dry goods shop, at once happy and hapless.[61] *Upside Down City* (1962) consisted of five skyscraperlike forms made out of old socks, painted to suggest windows and shaped in the dramatic silhouettes of the buildings of the 1920s and 1930s, but hung upside down from a clothesline to spoof the optimistic, Cubist-inspired formalism that such structures had inspired in artists like John Marin and Georgia O'Keeffe a generation before.[62]

Between 1965 and 1969 Oldenburg offered a series of monumental projects for New York sites, *Proposals for Monuments and Buildings*.[63] In Oldenburg's hands, as Peter Conrad has written, the city appeared to be "an infantile paradise, a Disneyfied Arcady with cuddly, consumable toys as its monuments—a teddy bear in Central Park, a Good Humor bar gooily obstructing Park Avenue—[but] it's also a wrecked place, an apocalyptic dump, a bombed big store tough and serious."[64] Oldenburg's proposed collapsed vacuum cleaner, intended to lie on its side in Battery Park (1965), was downright sinister, suggesting a deflated, even ravaged city. For Oldenburg, New York and his studio became one, with the city serving as, in the artist's words, his "favorite 'room.'"[65] Perhaps his most charming images of the city are his maps, such as *Soft Manhattan #1 (Postal Zones)* (1966), and a monumental electric fan for Staten Island designed to dispense with the city's odors. Also notable are the grand hot dog surmounted by a tomato and impaled by a toothpick proposed for Ellis Island, the blatantly phallic peeled banana for Times Square and the Good Humor bar for Park Avenue that permitted cars to travel through the gap formed by a missing bite (see chapter 5). Oldenburg's *War Memorial (Proposed Monument for the Intersection of Canal Street and Broadway, NYC: Block of Concrete Inscribed with the Names of War Heroes)* (1965) was less benign. As the artist stated:

Many of my monuments reintroduce the idea of the monument as obstacle or disruption in the city. Many monuments, of course, are exactly that: the Arc de Triomphe, for one, is an aggressive obstacle in that traffic must be rerouted around it. So is my War Memorial. I wanted it to be like a wound in the city. Studies have indicated, in fact, that the intersection of Canal and Broadway, where the memorial would be, is the perfect spot to drop the H-bomb in order to create maximum damage and fallout throughout the New York area.[66]

Some observers have viewed Oldenburg's proposals as truly subversive. In 1968 the political philosopher Herbert Marcuse, considering the actual realization of Oldenburg's proposals, asserted, "If you could ever imagine a situation in which this could be done, you would have the Revolution. If you could envisage a situation where at the end of Park Avenue there would be a huge Good Humor ice cream bar and in the middle of Times Square a huge banana I would say—and I think safely say—this society has come to an end."[67]

The Belgian-born artist Jean Tinguely shared Oldenburg's darkly comic view of New York's apocalyptic fate. To Tinguely the city seemed destined to fall apart, or perhaps more precisely to self-destruct under the weight of its own dynamism. On the evening of March 17, 1960, Tinguely displayed his thirty-foot-long, twenty-foot-high construction *Hommage à New York* in the Museum of Modern Art's sculpture garden. The Rube Goldbergesque contraption destroyed itself during its single presentation, which Walter Thabit writing in the *Village Voice* described as "the most unusual artistic event of the year."[68] The motorized machine incorporated wildly disparate components: bicycle wheels, bottles, pulleys, rolls of paper, oil cans, a piano, an orange weather balloon, an answering machine and a chamber pot. Tinguely found many of these objects along Canal Street, near his studio. The machine made manic movements and generated clouds of smoke. Peter Conrad later asserted that Tinguely had acted as a kind of "mad scientist, unleashing the energy which in the city is harnessed to human uses. What would happen if that electric motivation were allowed to riot out of control? The city would destroy itself. Tinguely's invention burned through a short happy life, smoking, blazing, exploding, and stinking until it left a rusting corpse in the museum's trash cans."[69]

To the Athens-born sculptor Chryssa, New York was at once vulgar and profound.[70] When the artist moved to New York in 1954, she was immediately struck by the visual power of Times Square, which embodied the "boldness of America." There, she said, "the sky is like the gold background of Byzantine mosaics of icons."[71] The artist attributed her appreciation of the area's anarchic visual display to her status as a foreigner and particularly to her Greek heritage, which allowed her to see Times Square's "wisdom" as "Homeric—even if the signmakers did not realize that."[72] Chryssa's *Homage to Times Square* (1958) is a square, white-painted aluminum relief sculpture in which raised rectangular elements form an arrow evocative of those seen on neon signs. In a series of paintings produced between 1959 and 1962 the artist used a rubber stamp made from fragments of the *New York Times* to explore the expressive potential of ordinary urban signs and symbols. Chryssa also made sculptures out of sign fragments. *Times Square Sky* (1962) was her first work to exploit neon, the medium that became Chryssa's artistic signature and most directly reflected the city's influence on her work. The wall sculpture consisted of overlapping layers of sign fragments; on top, a neon sign spelled out the word "air." *The Gates to Times Square* (1964–66) was a walk-through environment made of welded stainless steel, cast aluminum, acrylic plastic and neon. Unable to find a fabricator who could meet her qualifications, Chryssa established her own workshop, producing most of the piece's 130 elements. Preliminary studies gave rise to numerous independent works including *Cent Sign Travelling from Broadway to Africa via Guadaloupe* (1968), a comment on money as the common denominator between the city's frivolity, symbolized by a Times Square penny arcade, and its power.

Richard Artschwager, who was raised in Washington, D.C., and New Mexico before he moved to New York in 1948 at the age of twenty-five, exploited the tabloids as a source for his art.[73] In the early 1960s the artist began to use a grid system to manually transpose photographic images to canvas. He soon learned that his friend Franz Kline was painting on celotex, a paper composite. Artschwager found celotex particularly suited to his work, as its surface accentuated blurry edges, evoking the black-and-white snapshots that he sought to re-create, including the grainy images of newly built apartment houses from the *New York Post*'s real estate section. *Lefrak City* (1962), a large, black-and-white painting, depicts the architecturally banal complex. *High-Rise Apartment* (1964) depicts postwar "luxury" housing, with the building's crudely rendered edges set against a stark white background, as if the image had been clipped from the newspaper.

The Art Scene

Unlike Paris in the 1920s and 1930s, where the art world operated independently of other professional and social spheres, in the New York milieu a highly eclectic, heterogeneous mixture of artists, critics, dealers, collectors and a broad cross-section of high society came to constitute what was called "the art scene."[74] The painter Alex Katz brilliantly captured this in his painting *The Cocktail Party* (1965), a larger-than-life-scale rendering of an "in-crowd" gathering at the artist's studio, with Katz himself in the foreground.[75] The partygoers, seemingly caught unaware as if in a freeze-frame of a home movie, exude the prevailing "cool" of the art world.

With the rebuilt cities of Tokyo and Düsseldorf joining Paris and London as leading artistic subcenters, New York remained

the art capital, reflecting American financial power as much as the vitality of the city's artistic community. In the 1960s the boundaries between contemporary art and commerce began to blur, first for members of the New York School and then for Pop artists, who turned the new scene to their advantage. While the New York School and the various earlier Modernisms had constituted hermetic mini-scenes enlisting critics and dealers as apostles to the holy works of the artists themselves, the Pop artists were open to all comers. They were intimate with the dealers, in particular Leo Castelli. The Pop artists established themselves with art-world critics and collectors in part so that they could sell paintings. The ironically titled *Masterpiece* (1962), by Roy Lichtenstein, offers a prophetic comment on this self-congratulatory art scene. A balloon of text typical of comic strip art shows an elegant blond woman telling her artist companion: "Why, Brad darling, this painting is a MASTERPIECE! My, soon you'll have all of NEW YORK clamoring for your work!"

In the mid-1960s, partially in response to what some artists considered the New York art world's obsession with financial gain, conceptual art emerged. The new genre eschewed traditional art objects, which could be bought and sold, in favor of neo-Dadaist proposals and happenings-inspired events known as performance art. In 1958, while living in Paris, the Bulgarian-born conceptual artist Christo Javacheff, known professionally by his first name, began to wrap common objects, imbuing them with a sense of mystery while updating the Dadaist *objet trouvé*.[76] Six years later the artist and his French wife and collaborator, Marie-Claude, proposed their first work for the city, *Two Wrapped Buildings in Lower Manhattan, Project for New York* (1964–66), which targeted the abysmal Two Broadway (Emery Roth & Sons, 1959) and the far more engaging City Bank Farmers Trust Company Building (Cross & Cross, 1931), at 22 William Street.[77] Temporarily robbed of their facades, the buildings entered into a dialogue; but this was not a traditional architectural discourse conducted in stylistic terms across time. Rather, Christo highlighted the basic formal characteristics—one building was squat and one slender—and the element of unpredictability: what lay under the wrapping was, at least to the uninformed, completely a matter of conjecture. The plan was documented with an elegantly rendered drawing incorporating photomontage. In time, Christo would use the proceeds from the sale of such drawings to finance his large-scale projects.

In 1968 Christo proposed wrapping the Allied Chemical Tower, formerly the Times Tower (Cyrus L. W. Eidlitz, 1904),[78] with dark fabric, giving the wedge-shaped landmark a brooding presence in contrast to its celebratory environment. Christo also made proposals for two New York museums: the Whitney Museum of American Art and the Museum of Modern Art. He suggested that MOMA and its sculpture garden be wrapped and that a wall of oil barrels barricade West Fifty-third Street, with more barrels in the museum's lobby. None of Christo's New York projects were ever realized.

The poet and conceptual artist Vito Acconci saw the entire city as a theatrical stage.[79] In *Following Piece* (1969), part of a series of performances titled *Street Works IV*, Acconci followed individuals on the street until they entered buildings. In *Telling Secrets* (1971), he stood on a deserted Hudson River pier between 1:00 and 2:00 A.M., whispering to any visitors secrets that he later stated, "could have been totally detrimental to me if publicly revealed."[80] Acconci explored similar themes in his notorious performance *Seedbed* (1971), which also served as a scathingly sarcastic comment on the art world. In the piece, performed at the Sonnabend Gallery, 420 West Broadway, the artist lay masturbating out of view under a large wooden ramp, which visitors walked on as they moved through the gallery.

Realist Painters in New York

Despite the dominance of the New York School, Pop art and, increasingly, conceptual art during the 1950s and 1960s, the postwar period also witnessed artists working in a "realistic" manner. Many of these artists, stylistically out of step with the reigning powers of the art world, or more precisely of the art marketplace, worked in obscurity. While depicting the city's architecture with varying degrees of verisimilitude, they shared an emphasis on mood, defining the city alternately as a place of unbridled energy, haunting melancholy and lyrical quietude.

Ralph Fasanella celebrated the city's architecture and vitality in a style firmly rooted in American folk art. Earning his livelihood at his brother's gas station, Fasanella remained largely unrecognized until the age of fifty-eight, when folk art expert Fred Freed introduced the artist to agent/promoter Jay Hoffman. Exhibition offers, interviews, a one-man show at Automation House and a *New York* magazine cover story that included an unprecedented seven-page spread of color reproductions followed.[81] Fasanella depicted the everyday world of the city's poor, filling every inch of the canvas with detail. *Pie-in-the-Sky* (1947) transforms a tenement, seen in cross-section, into a cathedral. The crucifix lifts the viewer's eye to the top, where heaven is a suburban house set in a garden. In *Sunday Afternoon* (1953), Fasanella captures urban street life, conveying the community of New York's ghettos, as neighbors linger outside storefronts and children play in the street. The highly ambitious *New York City* (1957) depicts the entire city. Throwing geographic accuracy to the wind, Fasanella's densely woven jumble of tenements, skyscrapers, streets, rivers, bridges and even a colony of suburban houses protected by a greensward captures the spirit of the city.

Paul Cadmus developed an immaculate drawing style to portray a New York defined by alienation and eroticism.[82] Cadmus's *Playground* (1948) is a cement-paved refuge bordered by a chain-link fence and overlooked by burned-out but still inhabited tenements. Lincoln Kirstein, Cadmus's brother-in-law, vividly described the scene:

> A quartet of adolescent, amateur hoodlums, idle, unfocused, and still at-large, lounge in lackluster joblessness. Nubile sex fondles its meager consolation. . . . Rough comradeship, a picked nose, the empty disarray of an unwanted, superfluous generation declare the steady defeat of our urban disinherited. . . . The only "play" possible on such a patch of ground is strained expectancy or vague fantasies that may fill or even revive lives as hard and void as this cement plot, less playground than prisonyard.[83]

Twenty-eight years later, in 1976, when Cadmus had been largely forgotten by the art establishment, he completed *Subway Symphony*, a joyfully satiric work that presented the city's transportation system as a real-life, contemporary version of Dante's Inferno. The Union Square subway platform is littered with unsavory types and skid row flotsam. Acknowledging that he had "chosen the worst in every bit of the painting," Cadmus joked, "I have always thought that if no one else would buy it, the Moscow subway might like to expose it in their pristine subway."[84]

In 1950, long before the subway system had descended into a morass of inefficiency, danger and filth, George Tooker saw it as a symbol of deracinated urban life.[85] *The Subway* chill-ingly portrays distraught travelers moving through a claustrophobic subterranean world, rendered more disorienting by the use of three perspective vanishing points. Tooker said: "I was thinking of the large modern city as a kind of limbo. The subway seemed a good place to represent a denial of the senses and a negation of life itself. Its being underground with great weight overhead was important."[86]

Isabel Bishop found the subway a hospitable place to observe unself-conscious men and women.[87] Beginning in 1934, Bishop daily commuted via subway from her home in the Riverdale section of the Bronx to her studio at 857 Broadway, overlooking Union Square. For her, the subway encapsulated a city defined by movement and anonymity. In *Subway Scene* (1957–58), a subway station's utilitarian architecture takes on a highly refined, almost religious quality. Like much of Bishop's work, the painting's warm colors evoke Renaissance art, in this case a luminous ocher. A loose pattern of horizontal lines recalls a technique used by Rubens to impart structure. Over this, Bishop layered alternating passages of translucent and opaque paint, employing scumbling and graining to create a shimmering effect.

From the late 1940s to the mid-1970s Herman Rose, a largely neglected native Brooklyn painter, sensitively recorded New York architecture, including that of its outer boroughs. Thomas B. Hess compared Rose's cityscapes to those of the eighteenth-century Venetian painter Canaletto and said that they reflected "a similar ironic distance between the artist and his view."[88] Laurence Campbell claimed that Rose was "not only the best living painter of the cityscape, but also the only one to present New York as a kind of Venice of blight, of dead walls, of live windows, of vacant, junk-filled lots, of overpasses and glass roofs, of steeples, all of it stretching on and on without any thought of social conscience or self-pity, until it crashes against the rocks of distant skyscrapers."[89] In *East New York* (1948), the Brooklyn neighborhood seems far removed from the bustling metropolis. Low-lying buildings stand next to empty lots crisscrossed by ramshackle wood fences more suited to a rural landscape than to the industrial outskirts of a great city. Many New York artists depicted the view seen from the windows of their homes or studios; Rose took to the roof of his tenement on East Nineteenth Street and Third Avenue for *Chimney & Skyscraper* (1948), depicting a brick chimney and unornamented secondary facades as a stack of abstract forms except for the signature lantern of the Consolidated Gas Building. "I was stunned by this scene," the artist said. "I was awed, and proud of man's achievement . . . and it was with this feeling that I painted the picture. I set about chimney by chimney, brick by brick—plastering even the sky."[90] In *Manhattan from Hoboken* (1968), the distant city of towers rises above a low-lying, tree-spotted residential area. Unmodulated patches of colors create a brilliant effect; the dreamlike skyline, though immediately identifiable as New York, seems to fade into the sky itself.

In 1966, on a visit to New York, the Viennese painter Oskar Kokoschka portrayed the southern end of Manhattan as seen from the thirty-third floor of a building on East Fortieth Street.[91] *View of Downtown Manhattan with Empire State* captures the city's dynamic spirit but takes license with geography. The Empire State Building appears at the far edge of the composition, not near the middle, where its Fifth Avenue location would rightfully place it.

Alice Neel, born in 1900 to an old Pennsylvania family, came to New York at the age of twenty-seven and lived the remainder of her life in Manhattan, much of the time in modest circumstances

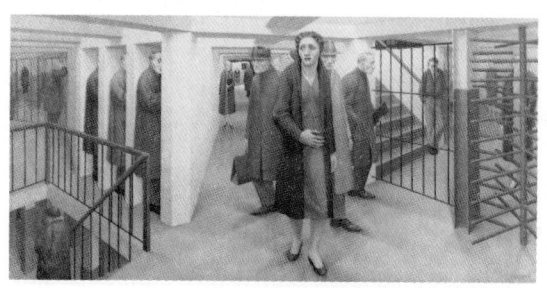

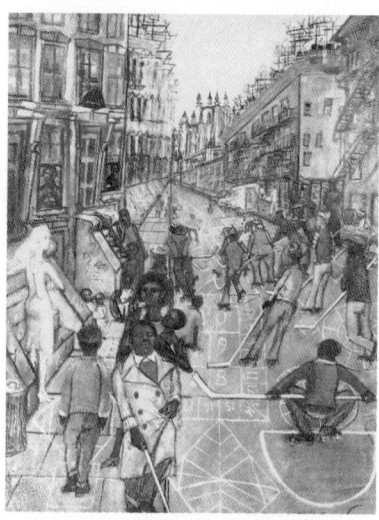

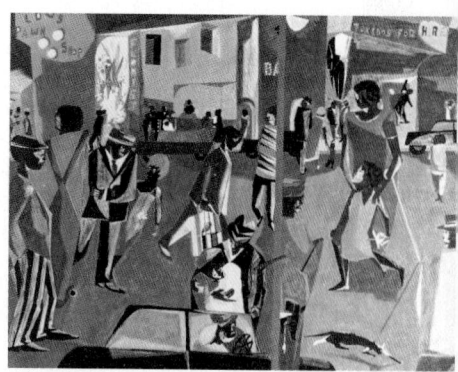

The Subway. George Tooker, 1950. Egg tempera on composition board. Collection of Whitney Museum of American Art, New York. Purchase, with funds from the Juliana Force Purchase Award. WMAA

Sunny Side of the Street. Philip Evergood, 1950. Egg-oil varnish emulsion with marble dust and glass on canvas. Collection of Corcoran Gallery of Art. Museum purchase, Anna E. Clark Fund. CGA

Fulton and Nostrand. Jacob Lawrence, 1958. Oil on canvas. Private collection. Courtesy of Terry Dintenfass, Inc. TDG

on the Upper West Side and in East Harlem.[92] Known primarily for her portraits of both "ordinary" people and celebrities, painted in a direct, deliberately unacademic manner, Neel also painted several memorable images of her East Harlem neighborhood. *Fire Escape* (1946) focuses on a tenement as an interplay of repetitive shapes and patterns. *Harlem Nocturne* (1952) depicts two buildings isolated amid empty lots. Despite their bulk, the buildings, internally illuminated under the glow of the moon, take on a romantic air.

Philip Evergood used a simplified drawing style to pack an emotional punch, delivering trenchant social commentary.[93] Though as an artist he identified with the underclass, Evergood had grown up in a world of privilege. Born in New York to an American father and an English mother, he was raised primarily in England, where he graduated from the Eton School, studied at Trinity Hall College, Cambridge University, and later graduated from the Slade School in London. Evergood returned to the United States in 1926 and between 1934 and 1937 painted murals for the WPA. During the winter of 1949 he lived on Pacific Street in Brooklyn, close to the predominantly black ghetto of Bedford-Stuyvesant. Evergood's *Sunny Side of the Street* depicts the area's street life; the title was borrowed from Jimmy McHugh and Dorothy Field's popular song.[94] Like the song, the painting describes the triumph of attitude over circumstance. A blind black man, a blond woman and children playing roller-skate hockey in the street suggest that human dignity prevails. In the background, above the rowhouse- and tenement-lined street, the finials of the Manhattan Bridge (Carrère & Hastings and Leon Moisieff, 1904–9) loom like a castle over a peasant village.[95] Evergood later observed of a particular ghetto street:

> There, sick people, maimed people and sad people abounded. On one side of the street there was generally a patch of sunlight. A crippled woman always sat at the window in that patch and a blind man generally fumbled his way out a dank, odious hallway, scratched and marked by kids, to the world of noise, aggression, sunlight and danger. . . . Within this framework— people existed, smiled, laughed, and were mostly kind to one another. I made two or three little pictorial notes on envelopes and scraps of paper. Out of these, and the very sharp impression of the whole, which was burned into my memory like a brand sears flesh, came my picture.[96]

In *Dowager in a Wheelchair* (1952), Evergood documented a very different kind of street life. The painting's distorted, primitivist-inspired perspective is dominated by a formidable old woman. She clearly surveys and judges every activity of the busy street, full of taxicabs and well-dressed pedestrians and lined by red-brick apartment buildings, the first-floor windows of which are cheerfully decorated with window boxes.

The postwar period brought an increasingly democratic culture, yet only a handful of African-Americans found a place in the art world. Those who did tended to embrace societal concerns in their work, reviving the social realism that had been the preferred mode of expression for artists from other disenfranchised groups during the 1930s. In the 1960s Romare Bearden produced numerous works documenting New York, including *The Street* (1964), which employed photographic montage to fill a small canvas with a rich depiction of street life.[97] *Childhood Memories* (1965) indicates that overwhelming societal problems were nothing new for New York's black community; the collage presents a street filled with flashy cars, slickly dressed black men and one white man, apparently buying or selling drugs, set against a cityscape in which Gaetano Russo's sculpture *Columbus* (1892) is overwhelmed by the glaring signs on shops dispensing burgers and loans. Jacob Lawrence powerfully documented Harlem, where he grew up, and Bedford-Stuyvesant in Brooklyn, where he lived during the 1950s and 1960s.[98] *Fulton and Nostrand* (1958) is a freewheeling Cubist narrative that takes the viewer to the heart of the Brooklyn ghetto on a summer night. Beauford Delaney depicted Greenwich Village, where he lived from 1930 to 1953, in numerous Fauvist-inspired compositions, including *Untitled (Washington Square)* of 1951.[99]

The Iowa-born Jane Wilson brought a rural sensibility to a series of paintings of Tompkins Square Park, located across the street from her home of ten years.[100] Depicting the often crowded East Village oasis devoid of people, she emphasized the stillness that can sometimes be found in the city. *January: Tompkins Square* (1963), painted in muted colors, captures the quiet, snow-covered park encircled by low-rise buildings.

56th Street (1968–71), by Fairfield Porter, who usually worked in Maine and on Long Island, was intended as a "portrait

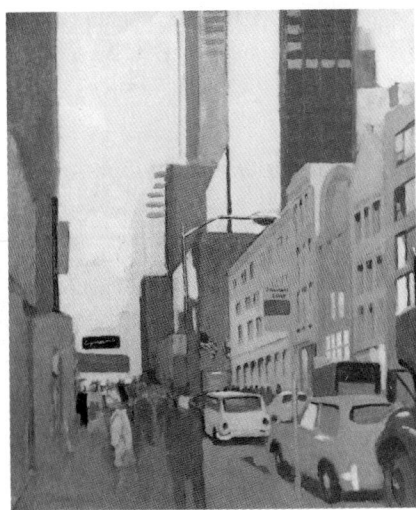

56th Street. Fairfield Porter, 1968–71. Oil on canvas. Zindman/Fremont. HAM

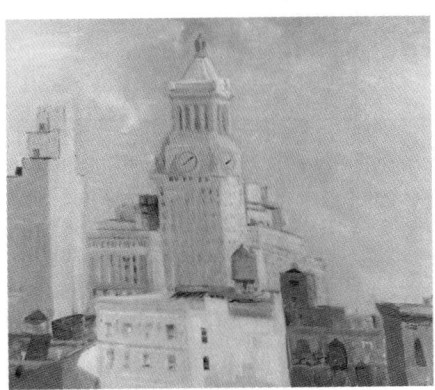

Con Edison. Jane Freilicher, 1970. Oil on canvas. FG

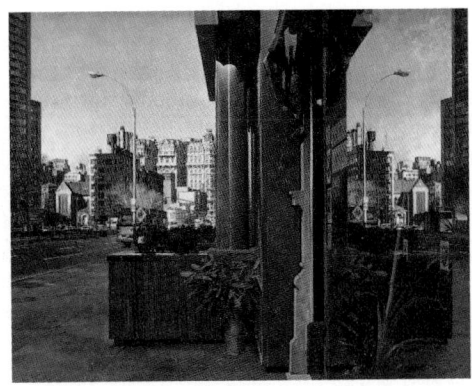

Ansonia. Richard Estes, 1977. Oil on canvas. Collection of Whitney Museum of American Art, New York. Purchase, with funds from Frances and Sydney Lewis. ©1994 Richard Estes/VAGA, New York. Courtesy of Marlborough Gallery. WMAA

of a New York street."[101] The scene, densely packed with pedestrians and cars, conveys an overall calm, in part through the warm, late-afternoon light. The painting's consistent coloration unifies the street's architectural cacophony, which ranges from four-story townhouses to skyscrapers.

In 1967 the painter Nell Blaine, who had served as the first graphic designer of the *Village Voice*, produced city views from the windows of her apartment at 210 Riverside Drive (Schwartz & Gross, 1909). Blaine's paintings, though quite detailed, are loosely rendered. Unrealistically bright color suggests the city as an upbeat but seemingly uninhabited place. *Rooftops I* and *II* were painted from a neighbor's north-facing apartment. The poet and art critic James Schuyler described the paintings: "Tarred roofs, bricks, wells, unexpected lumps, buildings faced with stone that rise above their neighbors with the weary, round-shouldered apathy their designers must have felt: meretricious, shoddy, shabby, speckled all over with windows. And how extraordinarily beautiful [the view] is, painted like this, an inextricable delight of interlocking shapes."[102]

Jane Freilicher also depicted the view from her windows.[103] *Con Edison* (1970) contrasts the tower of the Con Edison Building with the lower buildings around it, as well as with a large, gesturally painted blue sky. The appearance in so many postwar paintings of the building, formerly the Consolidated Gas Company Building, not among the city's most memorable skyscrapers, can be explained by its proximity to Greenwich Village, where many artists lived and worked. The luminosity and overall carefree mood of Freilicher's *Con Edison* link it to the artist's well-known landscape paintings of eastern Long Island. Despite Freilicher's widely divergent subject matter, the art critic Peter Schjeldahl saw continuities in her work, stating that her "cityscapes, quite as much as her landscapes, gloriously exemplify [a] sort of, as it were, objective romanticism. They are about New York, but not the way one sees New York when one is merely looking. Rather, they are about the way one sees the city when one is simultaneously *noticing* and *remembering*."[104]

John Koch specialized in apartment interiors and the view from his apartment on Central Park West. The impressionistic *Across the Park* (1954) shows the park through metal casement windows framed by diaphonous curtains. The artist returned to the same subject over and over, but also turned inward to depict the spacious, high-ceilinged rooms of his own apartment, typical of prewar buildings along the park. In these paintings, and in others such as *Movers* (1954), *Cocktail Party* (1956) and *The Lesson* (1970), depicting his own and similarly gracious apartments, Koch portrayed not only a prized slice of New York's real estate pie, but a certain social milieu: the privileged but self-consciously dressed-down intelligentsia of the Upper West Side. In 1973 the curator Mario Amaya noted, "There is hardly ever a dramatic or immediate impact in a Koch interior but rather one must search things out in these paintings, the way you do when you visit someone's house for the first time. . . . All around you, in understated terms, is a world that is comfortable, rich in objects of the past, old friends, music, and a certain kind of ease that we are told once existed in New York."[105]

By the late 1960s a heightened taste for reality took over for many artists who looked not to traditional painting for inspiration but, like the Pop artists before them, to the photographic image. "Photorealism" was championed by Richard Estes, who after 1970 became New York's leading urban landscapist.[106] Estes's bright views of the city manage to be both superbly realistic and idealistic: although free of grime and foreboding, his images are absolutely faithful portraits of buildings and streets. Estes's style, according to Peter Conrad, is that of an "idyllic consumerism. . . . Newly cleansed and emptied, New York has attained that mood which, in Warhol's meditation on the Empire State [Building], is the sanctity of pop—a beatific blandness."[107] Estes's subjects are not the city's beautiful set pieces but its ordinary streets: Broadway in the sixties, West Thirty-fourth Street, Seventh Avenue, common shops, cheap eateries and supermarkets. But he rarely included the garbage that had become ubiquitous by the 1960s. "I only eliminate garbage because I can't really get it to look right," the artist explained. "It's really a technical deficiency on my part. I really try to make things look dirty, but it's interesting because even in a photograph it doesn't look as dirty as it really is."[108]

Estes's *Central Park* (1965) introduced New York as a principal subject, though the painting showed little of the park itself, concentrating on figures, mostly seen from the waist down. *Flatiron Building Reflected in Car with Figure in Bus* (1966) es-

1165

tablished two main currents in Estes's oeuvre: architecture and reflected images. *Hot Foods* (1967)—in which the glazed front of a luncheonette reflects the Empire State Building, marrying the city's vernacular and monumental architecture in a seamless whole—established a third hallmark: the storefront or restaurant window. *Ansonia* (1977) meticulously depicts a New York City landmark, visible in the background.[109] Estes's paintings struck some observers as revelatory. As the art critic John Canaday wrote: "Never before have there been cityscapes exactly like these, where the haphazard conjunctions of commonplace details are transformed into a matrix that would be violated if any of its multitudinous bits and pieces were excised from the mass."[110] Not every critic was so impressed. Barbara Rose described the work as being "crammed with an incredible number of nostalgia-evoking details" and said it was "like a visual soap opera."[111]

Other Photorealists also documented New York. In 1964 and 1965, Lowell Nesbitt, who later turned his attention to flowers, painted the *New York Facade Series*, depicting the cast-iron facades of SoHo loft buildings.[112] Though not as detailed as Estes's paintings, Nesbitt's cool canvases stood apart, in both technique and tone, from traditional realism. "What I was after was reportage," Nesbitt said. "The theme of the 'Facade' oils was the almost musical repetition of the windows, doors and columns."[113] To the editors of *Arts*, the series portrayed "New York's monuments to its own energy . . . stripped of meaning. The Manhattan Bridge becomes a solitary, displaced curio of a bygone era, like a plaster prop to be drawn in an academy studio."[114]

Throughout the postwar period the architecturally trained cartoonist Saul Steinberg, whose work often appeared in the *New Yorker*, wryly commented on the city's architecture and urbanism.[115] While Steinberg did not create his most memorable and widely reproduced image of New York, *View of the World from Ninth Avenue* (see Afterword), until 1975, throughout the preceding decades his urban caricatures were increasingly enjoyed by a broad audience that unofficially elevated the rather humble genre of captionless mass-market cartoons to the level of fine art. Melvin M. Webber, writing in the *Journal of the American Institute of Planners* in 1961, equated Steinberg with Thorstein Veblen, David Riesman and H. L. Mencken, claiming that the four men were "of a breed . . . who have challenged our most cherished doctrines while holding out the promise of a better world built of reason and of an untarnished ethic. Iconoclasts offering better icons, they have been the biographers of our failures and of our hopes."[116]

Steinberg's *Third Avenue* (1951) has a critical edge; the collage incorporates a fragment of a metal garbage can transformed into a streetfront. The media reflect the work's subject, a street dominated by junk shops, seedy bars and run-down tenements. The buildings dwarf the stick figures and cars, giving the scene a menacing aspect. In an untitled work of 1961, Steinberg literally peeled away part of a brownstone facade to reveal the numerous apartments within. A multiplicity of life-styles and decorative schemes appear, but each embodies domestic contentment (despite a few cockroaches and mice burrowed into the walls). *New York Totems* (1966) pays tribute to three of the city's architectural symbols: the Statue of Liberty, the Chrysler Building and the Solomon R. Guggenheim Museum. Accompanying the carefully selected triumvirate, which stands for civic pride, commerce and culture, a cannon alludes to the city's colonial past and a soaring rocket suggests its future. *Bleecker Street* (1971) gently pokes fun at the self-conscious bohemianism of Greenwich Village with a parade of odd creatures, some part-animal, part-human. A police car in full chase and cars blasting heavy exhaust recall the sad realities of urban life, yet Steinberg implies that an authentic New York experience is not complete without at least oblique contact with its dark side.

Taking It to the Streets: Public Art

As vital as New York's art scene was in the 1960s, with galleries and museums clamoring to present new talent, some artists were not content with the existing opportunities to exhibit their work. Instead, they literally took to the streets. In June 1967 the artist Allan D'Arcangelo began painting the first mural to be executed on one of the city's many unadorned party walls, sites that he deemed an eyesore. The untitled work, on the exposed wall of a tenement at 340 East Ninth Street, was commissioned by David Bromberg, a thirty-four-year-old planner, described by the art critic Grace Glueck as a "practical civic dreamer," who hoped to brighten up the rather dreary East Village block.[117] The fifty-by-sixty-foot mural, painted with acrylics, was a flat, colorful, Pop-inspired landscape of tall grass rising to the sky. Cutting across the scene, a yellow-and-black-striped barrier of the type used to indicate emergency construction along highways disrupted the neighborhood's fabric. Bromberg went on to organize other mural projects. Indeed, Harold C. Schonberg reported in the *New York Times*, "If [Bromberg] had his way, New York would be a gigantic mural, with wall after wall coalescing into the one Wall, the Platonic Wall, the absolute essence of Wall, the World as Wall and Idea. Picasso could do one side of the Empire State Building, and sign it. Siqueiros could complement it with a mural covering all of Stuyvesant Town."[118]

By 1970 D'Arcangelo had joined forces with Robert Wiegand and the Polish-born artist Tania, as well as Jason Crum, who had previously lived near Los Angeles and studied with the distinguished Mexican muralist José Clemente Orozco in Guadalajara, to form City Walls, Inc., an artist-controlled, nonprofit organization.[119] Initially guided by Annie Damaz, whose managerial style was blissfully casual—"Just find a good wall and approach the owner"[120]—City Walls, Inc. was principally funded by the J. M. Kaplan Fund; additional funding was provided by the Merrill, Noble and Buttenweiser foundations, as well as by the city and the individual philanthropists William Bernhard and David Rockefeller.

City Walls ultimately fell under the auspices of the Public Art Fund, Inc., presided over by Doris Freedman, who had previously served as the director of the city's Department of Cultural Affairs and who from the first had enthusiastically supported the efforts of publicly minded mural artists. In 1981 Freedman emphasized the program's urban dimension, recalling D'Arcangelo's first mural: "The visual and psychological effects on the community were startling. The drab dismal atmosphere of the block was suddenly transformed by a bright illusionary landscape. . . . For artists concerned with halting urban decay, this wall demonstrated new possibilities of eliciting community pride by providing areas throughout the city with colorful focal points."[121] Freedman said that the artists, who were supported by the Public Art Fund, "wish to establish direct lines of communication with the community and to end their traditional isolation from the mainstream of civic activity."[122]

By 1970 fifteen murals had been painted, thirteen of them by D'Arcangelo, Crum and Wiegand. The murals tended to be boldly colored, geometric abstractions and were executed by professional sign painters. Mel Pekarsky's untitled mural at Mulberry and Lafayette streets, painted in 1970, occupied a narrow, seven-story-high wall above a gas station and subway entrance. Black outlines, as well as deep browns, purples, yellows and solid white, created a Pop art–inspired landscape with Art Nouveau overtones, which art critic Lawrence Alloway described as "a topical pastoral image."[123] Wiegand's *At the Astor Bar*, a geometric mural at 441 Lafayette Street, formed a seventy-by-ninety-foot backdrop to the parking lot facing Astor Square where the Cooper Union planned to build a new building.[124]

Jason Crum was the program's most prolific muralist. His forty-by-forty-foot mural consisting of a grid of squares overlaid by diagonal bands formed the backdrop to the vest-pocket park at the southwest corner of East Twenty-ninth Street and Second Avenue (see chapter 5).[125] At 187 Third Avenue, Crum skewed his geometry to echo the slope of the building's roof, so that, as Alloway put it, "the red, yellow, green and blue rectangles seem to skip across the wall." Alloway felt that Crum's best pieces were those that "get away from the grid and into stacks of rippling forms," as at the playground at 198 East Seventh Street and in a two-part mural, titled *Peace*, which confronted an empty lot on the southeast corner of Houston Street and West Broadway with superscaled, diagonal, ropelike bands of color.[126]

A 163-foot-high mural, by Tania, at Mercer and East Third streets was, according to Alloway, "a climax of wall painting's modular form, with its combination of regularity and spatial kinks." In what Alloway called a "decisive departure" from the "monotonous cheer" of the early murals, Tania's work was a "subtle but absolutely clear succession of black, white and grays, with subordinate slices of yellow, red, blue and green, each appearing only once."[127]

City Walls' murals were not confined to tenement walls. Nassos Daphnis's sixty-square-foot mural, clearly visible from Madison Square Park, projected black, white and yellow arcs on a red background to decorate the top of an office tower on the north side of East Twenty-sixth Street between Madison and Park avenues.[128] Helen DeWitt's mural at 509 Amsterdam Avenue used arcs and circles to reveal a playful side.[129] City Walls also sponsored murals in the outer boroughs. Jay Rosenblum's wall painting incorporating stacked triangles, at 89-54 163rd Street, and Pierre Clerk's mural featuring vertical stripes, at 90-14 161st Street, both contributed bold geometry to the Jamaica section of Queens. A mural by Tania, which formed a backdrop to a Bedford-Stuyvesant playground, was, according to the artist, "nobody's property and . . . everybody's property, the way art should be."[130]

In a 1970 assessment of the City Walls program, Alloway raised questions about the murals' success and, more generally, about the function of public art, contrasting Daphnis's East Twenty-sixth Street mural and nearby nineteenth-century public sculpture, including Augustus Saint-Gaudens's statue of Admiral Farragut (1880), which stood in Madison Square Park on a base designed by Stanford White. Alloway argued that while the sculpture achieved "a strong public presence by drawing on a common knowledge of symbols," the murals had little such effect:

> Successive bands of color or modular patterns, which echo systems of architectural construction in terms of a decorative overlay, do not have a public content. They embellish "ugly" points in the city, but that merely reduces their content to being a symbol of sensitivity and control in a squalid or untidy environment. This aestheticizing function needs to be coordinated with a public content, if the ambitions of a social art are to be fully satisfied. There is a risk that public art without a public iconography, and in the absence of a strong sense of the artist's identity and his work's internal logic, will resemble Basic Design rather than art.[131]

Jason Crum, defending City Walls' interpretation of public art, stated that it "established beauty and a sense of one person reaching out to touch another, as part of the experience of city life."[132]

A 1971 mural by the abstract painter Knox Martin triggered *New York Times* art critic John Canaday to enter the lively debate. Canaday described the site as a "spot where 19th Street comes to a messy death under the West Side Highway" and "a decayed and ruptured bit of cityscape that can use a lot of brightening." Though he conceded that "Mr. Martin's is easily the best of all of the City Wall projects that I have seen," he argued that the mural was "the only one exhibiting a degree of professionalism much beyond what could be expected of a well-supervised school child equipped with a ruler, a compass, and a paint box." Canaday went on to challenge the very premise of the murals project:

> Whether [Martin's] painting as painting is good or bad is not the first question, or even the second. The first is whether it or any other painting should occupy the spot it does, and the second is whether, given the right to be there, it exhibits a sense of responsibility to the city environment it is supposed to serve. I say no on both counts, and I wish City Walls, Inc., would go soak its head. . . . Whether I am listening to music or looking at painting, I want to be able to decide where, when, and what. These paintings, including Mr. Martin's . . . don't allow the choice. Their way of improving the environment is simply to annihilate it.[133]

Not surprisingly, Doris Freedman offered a populist rebuttal: "For every truck driver who feels it brightens the place up, and for every citizen who looks out of his window on a brightly painted wall instead of the filthy gray brick . . . I say let the artists paint the town! And perhaps if there is any 'head soaking' to be done, we should let the public tell us whose head it should be."[134]

In 1972 City Walls completed two more murals. An untitled mural by Richard Anuszkiewicz on the side of the YWCA's Westside branch, on the southeast corner of West Fiftieth Street and Eighth Avenue, was a highly colorful, geometrically obsessive design, a mural big enough, Alloway said, "to be competitive against the cluttered townscape."[135] The other new mural was by Mel Pekarsky, who stacked four horizons' worth of stylized mountains, one above the other, at the corner of Houston and Crosby streets.[136]

City Walls sparked other groups to explore outdoor public mural art, which was made increasingly durable and inexpensive as acrylic paints improved. In contrast to the highly aestheticized City Walls, CityArts Workshop, Inc., formed in 1970 and supported by state and national arts funds as well as the Park Department, was inherently political, taking as its mandate the development of a public art that would include community participation.[137] As the group's founder and first director, the ceramicist Susan Shapiro-Kiok, explained, the goal of CityArts Workshop was to express the concerns and aspirations of the Lower East Side's low-income residents, who were "discovering their unique ethnic identity and power."[138] The first mural was executed in 1970 by teenagers living near the Alfred E. Smith Recreational Center at Cherry and Caroline streets. Stylized figures depicted a cop taking a bribe, people shooting drugs, a mugging incident, and a group with upraised Black Power fists. According to C. Ray Smith, the black teenagers intended the work, titled *Anti-Drug Abuse Mural*, to be "the saga of a black drug addict turning his back on drugs." Smith described how the work was created: "With the direction of the Community Arts Workshop . . . the teenagers staged and photographed various

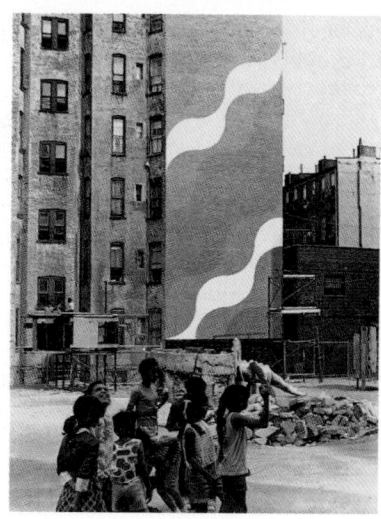

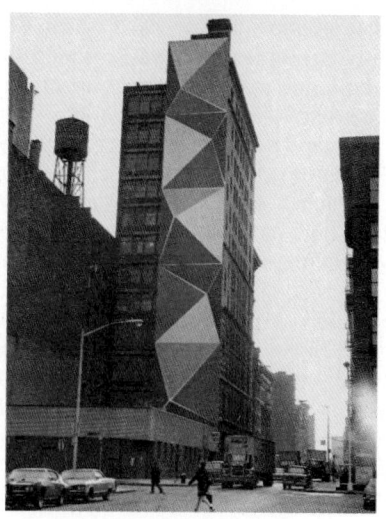

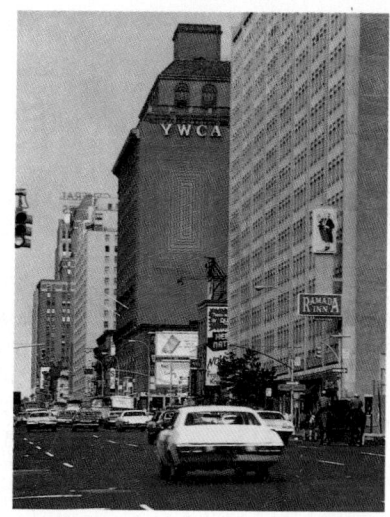

Untitled mural, vest-pocket park, between Avenue B and Avenue C, East Sixth and East Seventh streets. Jason Crum, 1969. Fred W. McDarrah. FWM

Untitled mural, northeast corner of Mercer and East Third streets. Tania, 1970. NYU

Untitled mural, southeast corner of West Fiftieth Street and Eighth Avenue. Richard Anuszkiewicz, 1972. ©Richard Anuszkiewicz/VAGA. City Walls/Public Art Fund. PAFI

scenes in drug life as the young artists saw it. . . . The artists projected their slides of the scenes on panels [and] painted blue and red silhouettes of them."[139] The following year the community once again employed projection to create a mural, titled *Black Women of America Today*.[140]

Nearby, at Bowery and Chatham Square, the heart of Chinatown, a mural by Alan Okada, titled *History of Chinese Immigration to the United States* (1971), was painted with the assistance of community teenagers. Executed in a style similar to that of a movie poster, the mural, according to Alloway, visually eased into its environment "rather than resisting the competing sign systems all around it."[141] *Arise from Oppression* (1972) was painted on the side wall of the Henry Street Settlement Playhouse at Pitt and Grand streets, where neighborhood youths worked under the direction of two artists from the workshop, Susan Caruso-Green and James Januzzi.[142] The mural depicted figures, as if seen in an X-ray image, overcoming drug addiction, poverty and other societal ills. CityArts also sponsored the realization on the Lower East Side of the murals *Chi Lai—Arriba—Rise Up!* (1974) and *Work, Education, and Struggle: Seeds for Progressive Change* (1975), under the direction of Alan Okada; both reflected the Latin American and Asian cultures that constituted two strains of the area's rich if sometimes uneasy ethnic mix.[143]

CityArts sponsored two projects at Curtis Park, on West Forty-sixth Street between Ninth and Tenth avenues. A modular wall in cast cement was built with the labor of approximately 150 community residents who, under the direction of Philip Danzig, impressed ceramic chips and fragments into curving concrete slabs. A nearby mural, *Against Domestic Colonialism* (1972), painted by the Mexican painter and muralist Arnold Belkin, recalled his country's rich tradition of socially conscious art.[144] It also expressed a topical theme: the potential displacement of the area's lower-middle-class, racially and ethnically mixed population for the anticipated construction of high-rise, high-income apartment buildings.

Studio in the Streets was another public art effort. Organized by the Harlem Studio Museum to distribute art to public sites, the group helped four artists to create a mural on Seventh Avenue and West 126th Street, permitting each to work

in his own way; Alloway presumed that the mural's "jumps in style" were meant to be "symbols of autonomy (doing your own thing without interference)."[145] Throughout the 1970s politically charged murals sprang up in many poorer neighborhoods. Lucy Mahler, the director of an artists' group named the Freedom and Peace Mural Project, executed a 27-by-116-foot mural on a facade of the Wright Brothers High School in Washington Heights. Painted with student assistance, *Let a People, Loving Freedom, Come to Growth* incorporated portraits of neighborhood adults encouraging young people in a variety of activities including reading and playing basketball.[146]

In 1974 City Walls took a different direction when it sponsored Richard Haas to paint a trompe l'oeil mural, completed the following year. With breathtaking realism and technique, Haas created a new facade for the exposed brick side wall of 114 Prince Street in SoHo.[147] The architect-critic Peter Blake noted that Haas created "an illusory, five-story-tall, cast-iron style facade . . . complete with two real windows and one phony cat . . . demonstrating that it takes only genius and a few gallons of the right colors to enhance our gloomy environment."[148] Paul Goldberger later said of Haas's work:

> [The mural] pays homage to the real cast-iron facade, and by implication to all the cast-iron fronts of SoHo, but it is also about completion—about the filling in of a missing part, the making of a totality. Haas is attempting to make the neighborhood whole. But he does so with a certain hint of irony—we know that that wall is not real, and we realize that it is all something of a game that the artist is playing with us. But Haas takes the ideas behind the game very seriously—it is hard not to think that he really wants to make over the city here.[149]

Haas followed this mural with a painting depicting a new group of shops on Mulberry Street, where the Little Italy Restaurant Association wanted to convey at least the appearance of a lively streetfront despite the presence of 160 feet of bricked-up bays set between the cast-iron columns of a warehouse. Haas saw his work as "a form of urban surgery that takes care of uncalled-for or undesired gaps. . . . It's binding up the wounded areas."[150]

In October 1967 the city's Office of Cultural Affairs mounted an open-air exhibition, "Sculpture in the Environ-

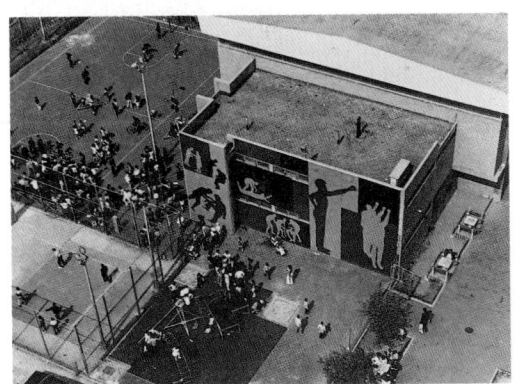

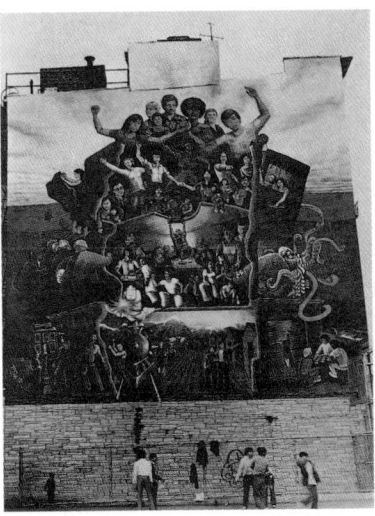

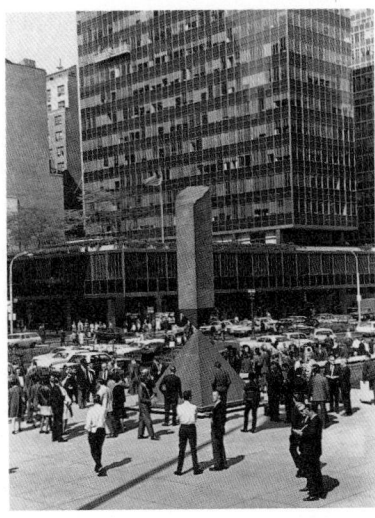

Anti-Drug Abuse Mural, Alfred E. Smith Houses. Susan Shapiro-Kiok with CityArts Workshop, 1970. Cortijo. CI

Chi Lai—Arriba—Rise Up!, Madison Avenue and Pike Street. Alan Okada with CityArts Workshop, 1974. CI

The Broken Obelisk, Seagram Building plaza, east side of Park Avenue, between East Fifty-second and East Fifty-third streets. Barnett Newman, 1967. Cor-ten steel. Fred W. McDarrah. FWM

ment," which, according to the critic Hilton Kramer, was the largest temporary display of new sculpture ever mounted by a municipality.[151] Privately funded, the exhibition, curated by Samuel Adams Green, former director of the Philadelphia Institute of Contemporary Art, consisted of twenty-six sculptures placed on sites ranging from the Battery to Harlem and including works by such artists as Alexander Calder, Mark diSuvero, Marisol, Robert Morris, Louise Nevelson, Barnett Newman, Claes Oldenburg, George Rickey, Bernard (Tony) Rosenthal, David Smith, Tony Smith and Richard Stankiewicz. Among the most noteworthy works was Newman's twenty-five-foot-high, Cor-ten steel *Broken Obelisk* (1961–63), placed prominently on the plaza in front of the Seagram Building. While the building provided an elegant backdrop for the austere but poetic sculpture, the work was soon covered with graffiti. When the sculpture was permanently installed in Houston, a surrounding reflecting pool was added to discourage graffiti artists.

Reviewing the exhibition, Kramer questioned the nature of public art:

> Works of art designed for public sites and executed on a monumental scale are . . . obliged to speak not only the language of the studio but also, as it were, the language of the street. And the latter may be even more important than the former. . . . What is striking about so much of the work in the . . . display is the way it violates rather than adorns the urban environment in which it has been placed. To most of these sculptors, the language of the street is as alien as Sanskrit. They are simply—all too simply—speaking the language of the studio on a public platform, and their voices either do not carry or only add to the general noise.

Although Kramer found *Boss Linco*, a brightly colored arch by Lyman Kipp that was placed on the Mall in Central Park, "rather handsome," he said that, given the location, "almost anything of a certain size and color would." That particular site, Kramer said, was "an easy environment for sculpture," but the city at large was not. What the program demonstrated, he concluded, was that "our sculptors have nothing useful to tell us at the moment about how this unhappy situation might be changed for the better."[152]

Late in 1971 the Association for a Better New York (ABNY), a group of approximately one hundred prominent businessmen, announced that they would mount a Christmastime exhibition of six large-scale sculptures at various public sites.[153] One of the works, a thirteen-foot-high, orange-painted sculpture by Buky Schwarz titled *Number Three*, was ridiculed by Robert Moses, who said: "This futile steel caterpillar reminds one of the Laocoon family in Virgil, squeezed to death by a huge serpent. When the Romans sculptured a snake, it was a real honest-to-God sinuous serpent with muscle and oomph, not an amorphous red crawler with no beginning or end."[154] In a letter to the editor published in the *New York Times*, Doris Freedman responded that "Robert Moses' opinions on contemporary sculpture are embarrassing."[155]

In October 1975, as part of a one-man show at the Whitney Museum, the sculptor Mark diSuvero installed fourteen large-scale abstract pieces made primarily of steel in public parks throughout the city, including *For Lady Day* (1968–69), located in Battery Park, and *Victor's Lament* (1970), in Astoria Park in Queens.[156] According to the editors of the *New Yorker*, "The people in [Astoria] park said that the sculpture looked like many things: a bird; a giant jack; an insect; very weird; unfinished; a woman with her legs crossed; I don't know; a large toy; and something that probably belonged in Manhattan."[157] Despite its ambiguous visual references, the art critic John Russell felt diSuvero's work had qualities that rendered it particularly appealing to New Yorkers: "At a time when New York City could hardly have more problems, Mark diSuvero sets us an example of problem solving at its most elegant and definitive. In a mysterious way, people wanted this work at this time in this place. They've got it, all over the town, and it's well worth seeking out."[158]

NEW YORK IN PHOTOGRAPHY

Great architectural photography rises above its principal purpose—the accurate documentation of buildings and their settings—to become art. Joseph and Percy Byron and Norman and Lionel Wurts brilliantly captured the fin-de-siècle city; between the two world wars Samuel H. Gottscho and his son-in-law,

William H. Schleisner, were the undisputed masters of New York portraiture, and they continued to take beautiful pictures of the city into the 1970s.[1] Modernism, a revolution in aesthetics, and vast improvements in photographic technology accompanied a new approach to the subject. With fast film, photographers no longer needed to shoot buildings early in the morning on weekends, when traffic was light, and the urban setting, with its diversity, vitality and clutter, became part of the story. On the other hand, Modernists saw each building as a pristine object. The photographs that best express the postwar International Style are highly polished and often intensely focused on the individual building at the expense of its relationship to the context; gone is the soft focus of earlier photographs. Although high-speed color film was available, the high cost of reproduction for books and magazines confined most architectural photography to black-and-white film.

Ezra Stoller dominated postwar architectural photography.[2] Before becoming a professional photographer, Stoller had received undergraduate architectural training at New York University and, during the late 1930s, made numerous trips to Harvard University, where he visited friends studying with Walter Gropius and Marcel Breuer. Modeling his business on groups like Magnum, Stoller created an archive as well as a stable of photographers, who would continue to dominate the scene into the 1970s and after, as the master withdrew from active practice. Stoller photographs are informative and unsentimental; seemingly objective, they are in fact as minimalist and abstract as the buildings they document and celebrate. The critic William S. Saunders has succinctly stated that Stoller's photographs reflect a "phenomenal technique apparent in unerring sharpness of focus at all distances at once, in the capturing of extraordinary detail, and in a simple, balanced, classical composition of unquestionable good taste."[3] Stoller's influence was so profound that Philip Johnson considered his buildings incomplete until they had been "Stollerized."

Stoller's mature photographic style perfectly matched the highly refined International Style Modernism of the late 1950s and 1960s. Centered, frontal compositions stress the building as an abstract composition. Cloudless, nearly white background skies sacrifice naturalism to emphasize stark formal geometries. Elsewhere Stoller would wait for the environmental conditions that most effectively complemented the building. Stoller also compensated for and underscored Modernism's reductive aesthetics. As the critic Michael Sorkin has noted, Stoller "waits a week for the right cloud, the right shadow, the right reflection to occur, creating the single moment in which the building performs beautifully in its setting." Indeed, Sorkin contended that Stoller had a "capacity for rendering certain architectural conditions beautiful by artistic falsification."[4] Paul Goldberger charged that the seemingly objective images in fact present a skewed vision; writing in 1980, he said that "Stoller photographs make buildings into objects and frequently rather precious objects, too." Goldberger conceded, however, that "it is only fair to remember that that was precisely what most of the architects of the buildings Mr. Stoller has photographed over the years wanted."[5]

Strong pictorial depth is a hallmark of Stoller's work, as is the transformation of three-dimensional spaces, experienced through movement and over time, into quickly "readable" two-dimensional images. Many Stoller photographs, particularly of interiors, are organized around single-point perspectives and feature views down long hallways or rooms or along side walls. Backlighting also emphasizes depth; distant objects and spaces

jump forward. Stoller sometimes introduced people as a comical, playful element, as with the two rotund men who complement the full sculptural forms in a photograph of Eero Saarinen's TWA terminal (1962). In a shot of the entrance plaza of Skidmore, Owings & Merrill's Union Carbide Building (1960) Stoller somewhat waggishly juxtaposed the colonnade of square columns with a sidewalk "colonnade" of businessmen dressed in near-identical suits. In the photographer's image of a typical Union Carbide Building interior, amid a sea of identical, relentlessly minimalist International Style offices and work stations designed for equally anonymous workers, a secretary stares blankly into space.

Stoller had a keen ability to portray buildings within their architectural contexts, if only to emphasize how few gestures they made to their surroundings. This aspect of Stoller's work has often been overlooked or belittled, reflecting the anticontextualism of the 1950s and 1960s; to remain true to his objective of accurately reflecting the architect's intent, Stoller treated many subjects as self-referential objects. Nonetheless, his iconic photograph of Ludwig Mies van der Rohe's Seagram Building (1958), taken from an elevated vantage point, delivers a clear narrative: Mies's masterwork is the new king of Park Avenue. The building, seen in its entirety, stands beside understated masonry buildings and the flamboyant Waldorf-Astoria Hotel (Schultze & Weaver, 1931),[6] which provides a stylistic foil. Barely visible along the right edge is SOM's pioneering, Modernist Lever House (1952), which paved the way for the avenue's postwar transformation but which, Stoller implies, was to be relegated to the sidelines by Mies's more Classical, refined and enduring design. Stoller later recalled the experience of working with Mies:

> I have always wished I had photographed more of Mies's work but he seemed uninterested in photography. When I was to photograph the Seagram Building and Phyllis Lambert arranged a meeting between me and Mies, we sat in uncomfortable silence with each other for several minutes. When Phyllis returned to the room he said, "Mr. Stoller will take many pictures and we will select a few," reversing his *less is more* dictum. This statement distanced me from Mies as a thinker. Good architectural photography is best done, I think, with a great deal of care and forethought, with pre-editing. Editing after taking a large number of relatively thoughtless pictures is less likely to turn up much of value.[7]

Regardless of Stoller's differences with Mies, the photographer produced a memorable suite of photographs that constituted the definitive portrait of the landmark.

A photograph of SOM's Pepsi-Cola Building (1960) points out that some Modernist buildings respect the existing setting. The sleek glass-and-steel curtain-wall facade, in striking contrast to its masonry neighbors, is underscored by a brilliant spot of reflected light. Yet, because it is photographed as the northern endpoint of a cohesive street wall of buildings, terminating at the southern end in the freestanding tower of the New York Central Building (Warren & Wetmore, 1929),[8] the Pepsi-Cola Building takes its place in the larger urban scheme, though in a very standoffish way. Stoller subsequently clarified his editorial intentions: "This perfectly proportioned building, photographed at a time when Park Avenue had a dignity and presence into which this building fit well, supports Lewis Mumford's contention that buildings should be no more than eleven stories high."[9]

By 1980 Arthur Drexler could accurately say that "Ezra Stoller's photographs are now a part of the history of modern ar-

1170

chitecture in the United States."[10] Despite the undeniable importance of Stoller's work, however, William Saunders has argued that the degree to which Stoller expressed the architect's intentions limited the photographs. Saunders charged that Stoller's "record is not for historians, anthropologists, or sociologists. It may even not be inclusive enough for architecture historians. Stoller was not hired to tell the whole story and he does not do so. But he does tell one true story wholly: the real ideal of the building."[11] Whatever the long-range usefulness of Stoller's photographic record, it influenced an entire generation of architects. As Drexler concisely said, "If [Stoller] made some buildings look a little better than they were, the improvement provided an image for aspiring architects. For better or worse, his photographs have been more real to architectural students, and more intensely experienced, than most of the buildings they memorialized."[12]

Traditional, "fine art" photographers also continued to mine the city's architecture and urbanism for imagery. The hungarian-born photographer André Kertész began taking lyrical pictures of New York when he arrived in the city in 1936 and did so until his death in 1985.[13] *Lost Cloud* (1937), which shows a cloud hovering beside the RCA Building (Associated Architects, 1932–33),[14] reflects a wry sense of humor. In 1948, while under contract with *House and Garden*, Kertész shot the arresting *River Walk of Carl Schurz Park*. Snow-covered and sparsely populated, yet showing numerous footprints of earlier visitors, the park symbolizes urban solitude. At the same time, the distorted perspective, with the pathway seeming to end in midair, as if at the edge of a precipice, gives a disquieting feeling to the otherwise melancholy scene. *Rooftop Water Tanks, New York* (1951) was photographed through a telephoto lens from the third-floor apartment at 31 East Twelfth Street where Kertész and his wife lived from 1944 to 1952. The close-cropped composition, which focuses on two wood-clad water tanks separated by a sliver of sky, treats the city in purely formal terms.

In 1952 the Kertészes moved to a twelfth-floor apartment in a recently completed apartment building at Two Fifth Avenue (Emery Roth & Sons, 1952). The apartment proved a boon to Kertész's work, providing many photographic opportunities from the west-facing bedroom windows, the south-facing living room terrace and the rooftop, the latter two commanding sweeping views of Washington Square Park. *Greenwich Village Rooftops, Day* (ca. 1952) and *Greenwich Village Rooftops, Evening* (1954) emphasize complex geometric patterns while portraying an unpopulated New York in quiet, tranquil terms. *Washington Square, Winter* (1954) depicts two strollers almost lost amid snow-covered curvilinear paths and gnarled branches. The critic Peter Conrad asserted that Kertész lived in Washington Square "because the rooftops there remind him of Paris. In midair, an amiable or sensual or relaxed life can be enjoyed, which the streets forbid. . . . But such beauty can be sustained only by keeping a distance. The rooftop, after all, is a retreat."[15] *Landing Pigeon, New York City* (1960) shows a bird against the backdrop of the exposed interior wall of a tenement being demolished. The building communicates a romantic aura more commonly associated with European cities than with New York. Kertész would recall that the original idea for the photograph, taken on Fifty-ninth Street, dated back to his days in Paris, when he "saw some run-down houses and wanted to photograph them with a pigeon. But the pigeon never came." Then, he said, one day in New York, "the moment was there. I had waited maybe thirty years for that instant."[16] *Puddle, Empire State Building, New York* (1967) attests to the building's enduring status as the iconic New York skyscraper, but its inverted reflection on wet pavement turns traditional hierarchies on their head.

In 1946 Todd Webb, a returning GI who had studied photography with Ansel Adams, devoted a year to documenting the city, concentrating on daily activities with architecture as background. Beaumont Newhall, writing in *Art News*, said that Webb's "respect for the optical image gives a maximum feeling of authenticity, and makes the prints historical records of obvious documentary value. More than this: they are personal interpretations, through which he has imparted to us warmth of appreciation and the excitement of visual discovery."[17]

Many postwar photographers documenting New York's inhabitants concentrated on people who had become marginal members of society because of poverty, disease or behavior widely regarded as deviant. Helen Levitt, who also made documentary films, focused on the street life, particularly of children, in the city's poorer precincts. Between 1938 and 1948 Levitt took a haunting series of photographs of children's chalk drawings scrawled on sidewalks and the sides of buildings, a contemporary, urban hieroglyphics, alternately reflective, angry and inspired.[18] Through the lenses of such photographers as Usher (later Arthur) H. Fellig,[19] known as Weegee, and Diane Arbus,[20] the city appears as a hellish collection of grotesques. Weegee's *Coney Island, 4:00 in the Afternoon, July 28, 1940*, suggests the bovine obedience of an endless crowd, exposing their corpulent bodies as they wave to the elevated camera. Arbus's startling portaits describe New York's darker side; she found the people who frequented Washington Square Park particularly compelling subjects. Arbus recalled taking photographs there during the summer of 1966:

> The park was divided. It has these walks, sort of like a sunburst, and there were these territories staked out. There were young hippie junkies down one row. There were lesbians down another, really tough amazingly hard-core lesbians. And in the middle were winos. They were like the first echelon and the girls who came from the Bronx to become hippies would have to sleep with the winos to get to sit on the other part with the junkie hippies. It was really remarkable. . . . [The people] were a lot like sculptures in a funny way.[21]

Garry Winogrand exposed the city's cultural elite in brutally candid photographs of museum openings.[22] His most devastating series was taken at the Metropolitan Museum of Art's Centennial Ball in 1969. Ten years earlier Winogrand had exposed the macabre dimension of New York life in *Park Avenue, New York* (1959). The photograph depicts a rather ordinary scene—a couple in a convertible looks back toward the camera with the New York Central Building (Warren & Wetmore, 1929) looming in the background—except for the pet monkey in the back seat. Monkeys also disturb an otherwise familiar scene in Winogrand's *Central Park Zoo, New York City* (1967): two monkeys dressed in children's clothing rest in the arms of a smartly dressed interracial couple. In *Peace Demonstration, Central Park, New York* (1970), Manhattan appears as a city of love, with its signature skyline, as seen along the park's southern and western boundaries, unexpectedly overshadowed by a sea of humanity sprawled across the Sheep Meadow and a balloon-covered sky.

In 1951 California-born photographer Ruth Orkin moved to New York and began taking pictures from the bay window of her brownstone apartment on West Eighty-second Street.[23] Though the photographs reveal Orkin's artistic competence and

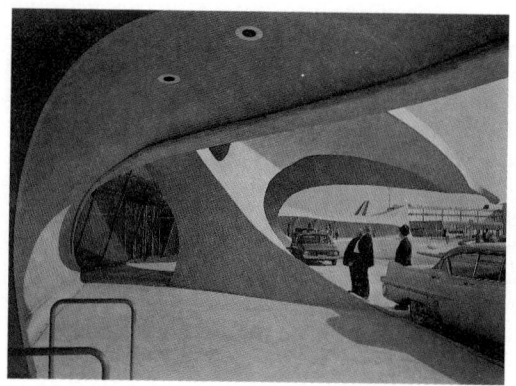

TWA terminal. Ezra Stoller, 1962. ©ESTO

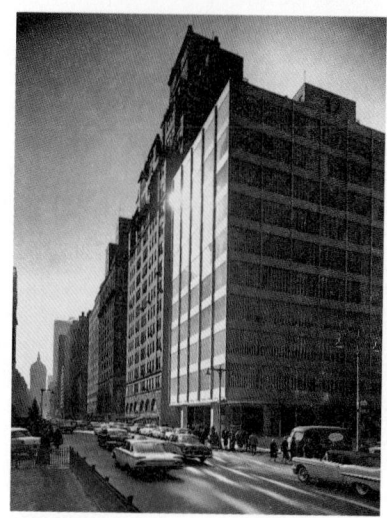

Pepsi-Cola Building. Ezra Stoller, 1960.
©ESTO

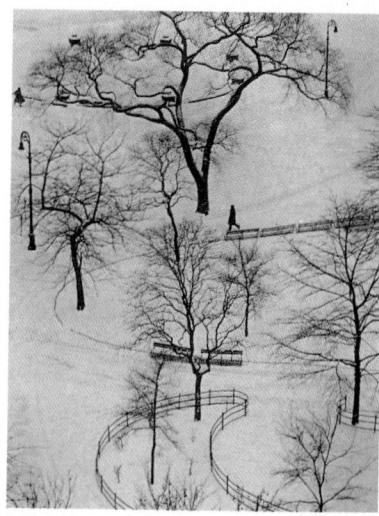

Washington Square, Winter. André
Kertész, 1954. AK

sensitivity to her urban surroundings, it was not until she moved to an apartment on the fifteenth floor of 65 Central Park West that her work fully blossomed. Orkin explained the fortuitous quality of her new location:

Contrary to what could be assumed, I didn't choose this apartment [on Central Park West] because I wanted to photograph the view. . . . In fact, I wasn't crazy about the immediate view at all. Rather than face the backyard of Tavern-on-the-Green, I would have preferred something prettier like the Lake around Seventy-third Street. Little did I realize then, that *this* was where the action was. Sheep Meadow, during the sixties and seventies, had supplanted Times Square as the place for happenings big and small.[24]

In the late 1950s Orkin photographed two nighttime events in the park that defined the political climate of the times: the helicopter arrival of Vice President Richard Nixon and the preparation of the Naumburg Bandshell (William G. Tachau, 1923) for a speech by Fidel Castro. In both cases the meadow is brightly illuminated, not an arcadian oasis but a locus of activity framed by a stream of passing cars, recorded in long-exposure photographs as ribbons of light.

Orkin's Central Park West photographs, taken over the course of more than thirty years, constitute an invaluable record of architectural change. To many observers the changes were negative, particularly in midtown, where distinctively profiled, masonry-clad buildings were replaced or overwhelmed by glass-and-steel boxes and open sky was obliterated. Orkin had a much more optimistic view. "As every new building went up below Fifty-ninth Street," she said, "I would envision it throwing the composition, from my angle, out of balance. Instead, each one has settled into the spaces between the older buildings, creating a new composition as aesthetically pleasing as the old one."[25]

Harry Callahan was similarly optimistic about the city's changing architecture, and he found the Modernist high rises along Park Avenue and in lower Manhattan visually compelling.[26] In a number of untitled photographs taken between 1969 and 1974, Callahan portrayed the postwar skyscrapers as monumental sculptures, imbued with a surprising degree of

grace, despite the crude detailing. In one photograph, taken at a sharp upward angle, the tops of the buildings along the east side of Park Avenue between East Fiftieth and East Fifty-third streets appear to form a single mass penetrated by a slender shaft of light. The rooflines form a dramatic zigzag, Manhattan as a manmade mountain range. Elsewhere Callahan zoomed in on facades, capturing, for instance, the World Trade Center's twin towers, whose dark vertical strips of glass and light stainless steel filled the frame. Callahan dramatically rendered the towers by emphasizing the patterns of their curtain-walled facades and the light falling across them; the buildings look like Op art paintings.

In 1969 Duane Michals, who specializes in sequential photographs, often accompanied by a title or text handwritten in wobbly print or cursive, created the six-part piece called *The Human Condition.*[27] The first three photographs were shot on a Fourteenth Street subway station platform. Here the subway appears not merely as a part of daily urban experience but as a place of mystical potential. In the first photograph, a casually dressed young man faces the camera with a stationary train behind him; the photograph is dark and the man is not clearly visible. In the second photograph, the man stands in the same location, but he is now bathed in a spot of light; the train is in motion, reflecting the passage of time. In the third photograph, the light grows brighter; in the fourth, the man is completely obscured by the light, which now floats in the star-filled universe. The last two photographs depict the cosmos. Michals seems to suggest that even in the most mundane New York locations, it is possible to imagine, and perhaps even experience, transcendence.

Beginning in the 1930s and continuing after the war, photographers known primarily for journalistic work also vividly documented the city. Outstanding among these was Andreas Feininger, son of the painter Lyonel Feininger.[28] The younger Feininger produced four books of New York photographs, many originally commissioned by *Life* magazine. His first book, *New York*, recorded the city in 1940.[29] Feininger emphasized not the energy of city life but the juxtaposition of tradition and modernity. His best photographs contrast the nineteenth-century port with Wall Street's early-twentieth-century skyscrapers. In a photograph of Peck Slip, Feininger showed the grinding poverty of the unemployed, their "faces empty of hope," lighting fires in

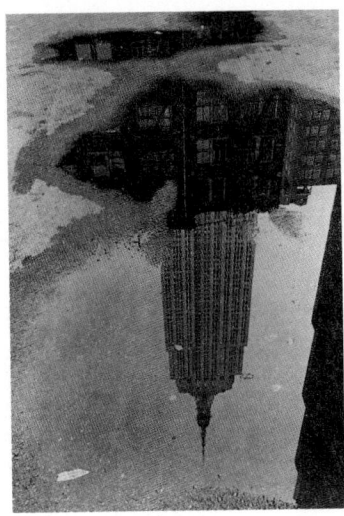

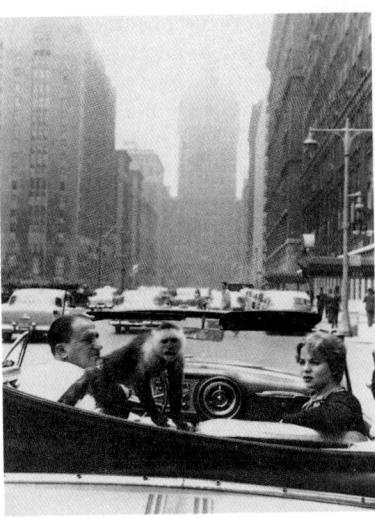

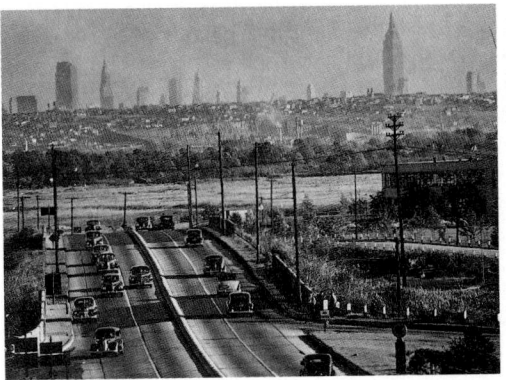

Puddle, Empire State Building, New York. André Kertész, 1967. AK

Park Avenue, New York. Garry Winogrand, 1959. Gelatin-silver print. FRGA

New York Skyline Seen from Route 3, New Jersey. Andreas Feininger, 1947. BBG

empty ruins to keep the cold away, while the "distant structures of the financial district loom in ironic contrast."[30]

Feininger's record of the city has a particularly strong architectural focus because, as the photographer himself put it, "I started my career as an architect; and maybe I became an architect because I have always been fascinated by structures and buildings of all kinds." New York provided the Cubist-inspired photographer with "the basic material for that special way in which I like to do photography—right angles and straight lines, repetition of formal elements (windows!), three-dimensionality in its most pronounced form, and spatial order."[31] Feininger's pioneering use of telephotography produced startling views of the skyline, especially taken from across the cemeteries of Queens, from Brooklyn and from the Meadowlands of New Jersey. In *Lunch Hour on Fifth Avenue* (1949), Feininger captures the overwhelming density of streets teeming with people, taxis, trucks and buses. Through the anonymous multitude of faces charging down the avenue, Feininger defines New York. To Peter Conrad, the photograph revealed Feininger's belief in the city's viability:

> The crowds . . . don't recede into depth but pile up the height of the photograph, and because the lens has narrowed the space occupied by the cross streets, the cars seem to be plowing across the sidewalk through the pedestrians. . . . The cars and the pedestrians don't collide because the city sees to it that they proceed at right angles to each other. . . . The more his lens, in its condensing of Fifth Avenue, creates muddle, the more surely does the city sort out the mess.[32]

In 1954 Feininger contrasted his own photographs focusing on Manhattan and its harbors with historical views of the city in *The Face of New York: The City as It Was and as It Is*, which included a text written by Susan E. Lyman.[33] Ten years later he collaborated with the travel writer Kate Simon on yet another book on New York, significant for its introduction of color photography.[34] The orientation is toward a new New York, a city of three-dimensional grids, of glass and reflections, of innumerable buildings under construction and of incredible vitality. The city seems reborn, more diverse than ever, in no way genteel. Gone are the stark contrasts between old and new; in their place is a mixture of the two, appearing in the buildings as well as in the faces of the people who crowd the streets—a blend of young and old, rich and poor, white and black and Asian.

In 1978 Feininger revised *New York*, now accompanied by a text by John von Hartz and published as *New York in the Forties*.[35] In the introduction, von Hartz favorably praised the 1940s as a golden, pre-Megalopolitan era for the city, a time when "New York still grew up, not out."[36] While much of the material was familiar, new views rounded out the portrait. For example, Feininger's early view of the Ninth Avenue El from Twentieth Street, which in 1954 he had contrasted with a photograph of the street after the structure was torn down, is here juxtaposed with a shot taken in 1940 as it was being demolished, its structural piers forming a heroic colonnade down the avenue.

Alfred Eisenstaedt, one of *Life*'s original in-house photographers, portrayed Manhattan's Grand Army Plaza in 1947 as the ultimate embodiment of urban elegance and sophistication.[37] Shot from within the Max Schling florist shop, located on the ground floor of the Savoy-Plaza Hotel, the photograph shows a chic woman walking two French poodles, with the Plaza Hotel and the Pulitzer Fountain visible in the background. Framed by foreground floral arrangements and the shop's name seen in reverse on the plate-glass window, the densely layered photograph illustrates a spontaneous moment when daily routine is elevated to the level of high drama—or at least to that of a fashion shoot—and the city's architecture provides a setting more wonderful than any Broadway stage or Hollywood back lot.

In 1951 the groundbreaking photojournalist Margaret Bourke-White, whose work had been featured on the premier cover of *Life*, pioneered a new method of aerially recording the city: the helicopter.[38] The helicopter provided a unique vantage point, higher than that of a skyscraper and lower than that of an airplane. *The Face of Liberty* (1951) zeroes in on the head of the famous statue, its crown full of curious sightseers straining for a view of the nearby aircraft. *Beach Accident, Coney Island* (1951) was taken moments after Bourke-White happened on the unanticipated event. Amid a scattering of beachgoers at the water's edge, a dense human swarm encircles those trying to resuscitate a swimmer.

The German photographer Ingrid Molchin documented New York in color in 1957.[39] Though her collection of photographs depicts a predictable array of locations, one reflects an attitude toward New York's industrial architecture presented two decades earlier in the polemical photographs of the Modernist architect Erich Mendelsohn.[40] In Molchin's photograph, which contrasts a typical step-back, interwar loft building with five-story tenements, she employed a technique previously used by Mendelsohn, restricting the view to the building's unadorned secondary facade.

William Klein's photographic essay *New York,* published in London in 1956, pioneered a casual visual style in which the city was captured in images resembling snapshots.[41] While the majority of Klein's informal but artfully composed photographs focus on the city's inhabitants, others document its architecture, sometimes as part of a spontaneously observed blend of people and buildings, other times as a subject in itself. Pages containing a series of dramatically cropped photographs arranged in an asymmetrical pattern vividly evoke the random observations made by someone on a leisurely stroll through New York.

In 1959 Dimitri Kessel, a *Life* staff photographer, took a memorable photograph of a lone surviving townhouse in the East Sixties standing amid rubble-strewn empty lots.[42] Jagged bits of brick wall, once belonging to adjoining townhouses, sprout forth from either side, a particularly poignant indication that the city's fabric was being ruthlessly torn apart at the seams. In the foreground, three passersby seem indifferent, or at least inured, to the change.

In 1962 Lee Lockwood took a decidedly more positive stance toward the city's architectural evolution in a color photograph of the New York Hilton under construction.[43] The image recalls the work of Lewis Hine, whose book *Men at Work* (1932), documenting the Empire State Building's construction, featured dizzying photographs of workers in midair.[44] The workers in Lockwood's composition seem less precarious, standing on a scaffolding grid that fills the frame. The city below expands under the steel grid; above, blue sky fills the modules. The ubiquitous grid has an ominous edge, however, as the observer knows that with the building's completion the view will disappear.

NEW YORK ON FILM

Almost from their inception, motion pictures focused on New York life as a principal subject. Before the film industry migrated to Hollywood, the city provided the pictorial backdrop for such realistic early films as D. W. Griffith's *The New York Hat* (1912) and his *Musketeers of Pig Alley* (1912).[1] By the 1920s and especially during the economically depressed 1930s, the typical "New York film" dealt very little with the reality of city life, offering instead a mythology of glamorous urbanity more "modern" and more visually breathtaking than the real thing could ever be. Most interwar films about New York were made on Hollywood sound stages and back lots with an occasional process shot of the real city, but a few films took to the streets. Among silent films with significant on-location sequences were Alan Dwan's *Big Brother* (1923), *Manhandled* (1924) and *A Society Scandal* (1924), as well as Sydney Olcott's *Salomé of the Tenements* (1924). Among the early "talkies" to incorporate on-location shooting were Rouben Mamoulian's *Applause* (1929) and Hobart Henley's *The Big Pond* (1930). Typically during the interwar period, diagrammatic sound-stage re-creations of New York provided a general urban sense rather than a specific architectural presence. In some cases, however, particularly in

lavish movie musicals such as *Swing Time* (1936), starring Fred Astaire and Ginger Rogers, the detailed sets helped to establish New York's signature visual style.[2]

After the war, along with technological advances—including the development of color photography and negative film for wide-screen projection—high-speed film and the increasing miniaturization of photographic and sound equipment made on-location shooting (which the introduction of sound in 1927 had rendered prohibitively expensive and technically near impossible) once again affordable and practical. The resurgence of on-location shooting affected both the appearance and the content of films. In contrast to 1930s escapist depictions of New York, postwar movies portrayed the main currents of urban life in an effort to expose and elucidate, not gloss over, its true nature. When cameramen hit the streets, the city became a place where real people did real things at specific locations: streets, buildings and rooms, many identifiable, were carefully chosen. The city became not only the stage but a leading player. New York, the quintessential twentieth-century metropolis, now photographed directly, was no longer just a symbol but a representative character.

Hollywood was wary of New York as a film location because of the myriad independent and frequently squabbling city agencies that controlled the permit process. Vexatious too were a tax on filmmaking and censorship by individual city departments. In the immediate postwar period, bureaucratic obstacles combined with the still strong Hollywood "studio system" to discourage filmmaking in New York. To justify the added expense, directors had to incorporate the city in ways that could not be duplicated by a sound-stage or back-lot set. Thus, while some movies shot in New York before the mid-1960s could have been filmed elsewhere, if perhaps less effectively and dramatically, many more could have been made *only* in New York. Such films helped to define the city itself. If New Yorkers often found their city larger than life, it was in part because projected on the silver screen, it was.

While more films were at least partially shot in New York during the 1940s and 1950s, it was not until the late 1960s that New York became a truly important film center, largely through the encouragement of Mayor John V. Lindsay, a show-business enthusiast. Lindsay encouraged Hollywood to make films in the city's buildings and streets as well as on its sound stages, the largely idle but once significant facilities that had been an important part of the film industry in the late 1920s and early 1930s. In courting Hollywood, Lindsay took advantage of a dramatic change in how feature films were made and financed: the breakup of Hollywood's "studio system" in the late 1950s and early 1960s resulted in greater independence for film producers. The demands of increasingly sophisticated young moviegoers, who dominated the audience and who had been raised on live television coverage of major events, gave New York a competitive edge over studio locations that had made many feature films seem little more than elaborate stage plays. And while downtown Los Angeles had once provided effective backdrops for the movies—including early silent films such as Fred Newmeyer and Sam Taylor's *Safety Last* (1923), starring Harold Lloyd—the precipitous postwar decline of L.A.'s core rendered it virtually useless as a location for the kind of urban dramas postwar audiences demanded.[3]

Lindsay's campaign to have films made in New York was so successful that *Newsweek* reported in 1967 on "New York—The Big Set."[4] According to the magazine's editors, while Julie Andrews was filming parts of *Star!* in the theater district, Richard Widmark was holding up traffic in front of the Sherry-Netherland Hotel as he appeared in a sequence from *Madigan*, Sidney Lumet was shooting *Bye Bye Braverman* in Brooklyn and, back in Manhattan, George Peppard and Mary Tyler Moore were rushing up and down City Hall's marble stairs as part of George Seaton's *What's So Bad About Feeling Good?* Twenty-five feature films were made wholly or in part in the city in the first six months of 1967.

Occasionally, Lindsay used his personal influence to get noncity institutions and private corporations to cooperate. He persuaded the trustees of the New York Public Library to allow parts of the main library on Fifth Avenue to be used in the farce *You're a Big Boy Now* (1967). He exerted influence over the Board of Education, which had turned down the producers of *Up the Down Staircase* (1967), an unflattering portrait of the city's school system written by a former New York school teacher. "I told them it meant three to four million dollars worth of jobs to the city," Lindsay said. "The day before the company was ready to leave for Chicago, the board finally cooperated."[5] Film director Sidney Lumet, raised in Brooklyn's Brownsville section, became a principal proponent of New York as a movie set and arguably the city's most eloquent cinematographic interpreter. "The history of art is the history of great cities," Lumet commented. "There is a hysteria about New York, its very ugliness makes it beautiful. It has the highest energy of any city in the world. When you shoot here, it's like sitting on a big lid ready to blow up. This energy reaches the screen."[6] Mel Brooks put the case for filming in the city succinctly: "New York is live, not on tape."[7]

Yet the city did not have enough sound stages and backup facilities to seriously rival Hollywood. A proposal put forth by Irving M. Felt, president of the Madison Square Garden Corporation, to partially replace the famous entertainment complex with a $50 million Cinema City was never realized. Finally, in 1975 the derelict Astoria Studio in Queens, designed and engineered by the Fleishman Construction Company in 1920 for the Famous Players–Lasky Company, officially reopened for feature film production.[8] During the Second World War the facility had been used by the United States Army to produce training films and entertainment features for troops such as *Sing Along with the Stars*. The army later used the facility to make educational films aimed at returning servicemen. During the Korean War the studio was once again used to make training films, and until 1970 the army used the studio for radio and television production, introducing many broadcasting techniques that were subsequently adopted by commercial networks. Richard C. Sarafian's political thriller *The Next Man* (1976), starring Sean Connery as a Saudi Arabian minister of state, constituted the first major commercial venture undertaken at the Astoria Studio in decades.[9]

During Lindsay's administration 366 movies were shot in New York, an average of more than 45 per year. Lindsay's personal interest in the entertainment business and his charisma played a significant role in stimulating the city's film industry. Even in the early 1970s, despite the decline in the city's fortunes and the bad press it was receiving nationwide, New York remained a desirable location for many directors. According to Steven Kesten, first assistant director on John Schlesinger's *Marathon Man*, the city's well-defined architectural settings and the sense of ever-present danger that its multiethnic population conveyed to the average filmgoer made New York "the greatest back lot in the world. . . . Eight million people live in New York, 180 million people read about New York. It's always in the headlines, whether it's the muggings or the arts."[10] Kesten un-

knowingly echoed the anonymous author of the chapter on motion pictures in *New York Panorama*, the 1938 companion guide to *The WPA Guide to New York City*, who wrote that "the most crowded cage in the zoo attracts the greatest number of spectators. If the essence of all drama lies in a conflict of forces, then New York must necessarily continue to be one of the screen's principal sources of material."[11]

New York as a Period Piece: Lights, Camera, Nostalgia

In the 1940s, in an effort to distract filmgoers from tumultuous events in Europe and Asia, Hollywood turned its attention backwards in time. New York was a particularly popular setting for historical films depicting an urban life that seemed simpler, gentler and more romantic, at least through the rose-colored lens of nostalgia. These included Robert Stevenson's *Back Street* (1941),[12] William A. Seiter's *Broadway* (1942),[13] Walter Lang's *Coney Island* (1943),[14] Vincent Sherman's *Mr. Skeffington* (1944),[15] Walter Lang's *Greenwich Village* (1944),[16] Tay Garnett's *Mrs. Parkington* (1944),[17] William A. Seiter's *Up in Central Park* (1948)[18] and William Wyler's *The Heiress* (1949), the last based on Henry James's novel *Washington Square*.[19] Though Orson Welles's *Citizen Kane* (1941) revealed the seamier side of New York's politics, the city nonetheless seemed a simpler place as he portrayed it—ironically simple, like the film hero's black-and-white view of his relationship to the world.[20] In 1942 Alexander Hall brought to the screen the Broadway play *My Sister Eileen* (1940), based on Ruth McKenna's semiautobiographical *New Yorker* short stories about bohemian Greenwich Village during the 1930s. The movie starred Rosalind Russell and Janet Blair.[21] In 1953 McKenna's stories were reinterpreted as a Broadway musical, *Wonderful Town*, which in turn became a movie musical, once again titled *My Sister Eileen* (1955), starring Betty Garrett and Janet Leigh.[22] After the 1940s the appeal of historical movies set in New York waned, but such films nonetheless continued to be made: in 1952 Charles Walters directed *The Belle of New York*, set in the 1910s;[23] in 1968 William Friedkin's *The Night They Raided Minsky's*,[24] set in the 1920s, was released, as was the movie version of the Broadway musical *Funny Girl*,[25] which also focuses on early-twentieth-century New York; 1969 saw the release of the film version of the immensely popular Broadway musical *Hello, Dolly!*, set in the 1890s;[26] and in 1975 Joan Micklin Silver's *Hester Street*, a bittersweet look at Lower East Side immigrant life at the turn of the century, was released.[27]

Broadway Melodies: The Beat Goes On

No part of New York's cultural life fascinated the general public more than Broadway, where the whole city seemed to be a stage. In the early 1940s, to an economically recovering nation still obsessed with the availability of jobs, the Great White Way was not only a glamorous workplace but a world unto itself. *Broadway Melody of 1940*, directed by Norman Taurog, stars Fred Astaire and the athletic Eleanor Powell, Astaire's first dancing partner after his breakup with Ginger Rogers.[28] Though *New York Times* movie reviewer B. R. Crisler found the film "much more convincingly Broadway" than its predecessors and "much more than usually melodious," the backstage saga about mounting a Broadway show, in which a down-on-his-luck dancer triumphs despite a predictable mistaken identity mix-up, is hack-

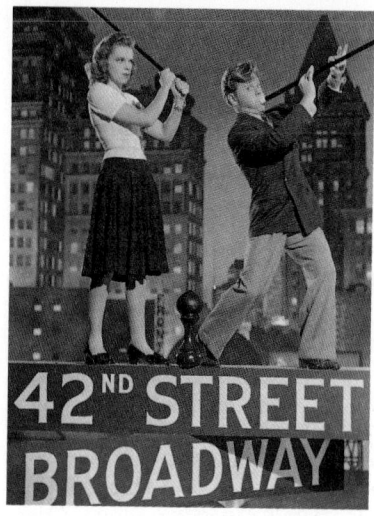

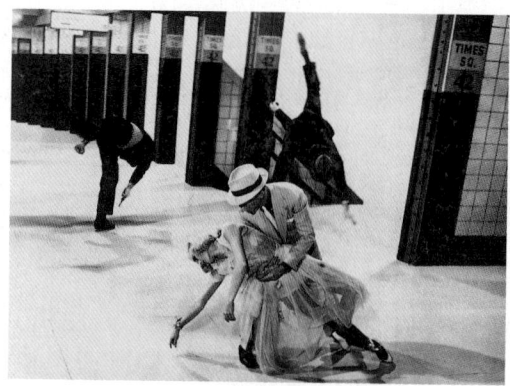

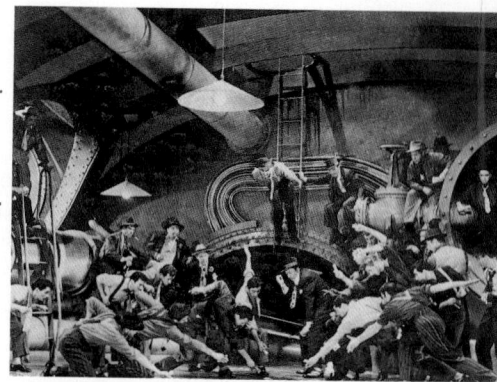

Babes on Broadway, 1941. Film still. Director, Busby Berkeley. ©1941 Turner Entertainment Co. All Rights Reserved. TEC

The Band Wagon, 1953. Film still. Art director, Cedric Gibbons; director, Vincente Minnelli. MOMA

Guys and Dolls, 1955. Film still. Art director, Joseph Wright; director, Joseph L. Mankiewicz. MOMA

neyed and clichéd.[29] The film signaled the beginning of the end of a genre and, arguably, of the widespread belief that talent always triumphs on Broadway. This myth, however, died a slow death. It cropped up again in Busby Berkeley's *Babes on Broadway* (1941), the story of young, ambitious actors who, as movie critic Thomas M. Pryor wrote in the *New York Times*, "You can observe, any day in the week . . . congregating on the corners of Forty-fourth and Forty-fifth Streets swapping tales of their experiences."[30] The film's diminutive stars, Judy Garland and Mickey Rooney, perched on an oversized replica of a Broadway street sign with the skyline visible in the background, created a lasting image of New York.

Angels over Broadway (1940), written, directed and produced by Ben Hecht, features Broadway not as the heart of New York's theater world but as a colorful, dramatic backdrop for the life of everyman.[31] A "melodramatic fantasy" starring Douglas Fairbanks, Jr., the film develops from "a haphazard conjunction of a small handful of lonely and widely separated characters on a single rainy night in New York."[32] Alfred E. Green's *Copacabana* (1947) stars Groucho Marx and Carmen Miranda. Just as nightclubs were beginning to seem old hat after the war, so too were movies about them. As Crowther put it, "If you've seen one nightclub picture, you have pretty well seen them all."[33] In keeping with New York's changing film image, even musical films about Broadway became more realistic. *Lullaby of Broadway* (1951), a musical directed by Earl Baldwin, stars Doris Day as a rising young singer who returns from a tour of England to find her mother, a former Broadway star, an alcoholic singing in a seedy nightclub; the film provides a seemingly unintentional comment on the decline of New York's show world.[34] The previous year, Day had starred, along with Kirk Douglas and Lauren Bacall, in Michael Curtiz's *Young Man with a Horn*.[35] This predictable account of a troubled musician's turbulent life is distinguished by a soundtrack featuring Harry James and on-location photography of lower Manhattan, including shots taken from an elevated train and footage of Coenties Slip.

The Band Wagon (1953), one of the great Hollywood musicals, provides a brilliant commentary on Broadway's changing fortunes.[36] It was directed by Vincente Minnelli, written by Betty Comden and Adolph Green and filmed on Metro-Goldwyn-Mayer's lot in Culver City, with highly effective sets designed by Oliver Smith under the supervision of Cedric Gibbons. Loosely based on a successful 1931 Broadway revue starring Fred and Adele Astaire, the movie features Fred Astaire in the role of Tony Hunter, a has-been movie star who returns to Broadway after a long absence. Hunter travels to New York on the Twentieth Century Limited, which is first seen speeding past the Hudson and then diving into the Park Avenue tunnel before arriving at Grand Central Terminal. When Hunter walks along West Forty-second Street to Times Square he is shocked to find that what he remembers as the city's greatest theater street, catering to the "carriage trade" only, is now a democratic public place full of discount shops and honky-tonk amusements. He is sad to find that the once grand Eltinge Theater (Thomas W. Lamb, 1912) houses a cheap eatery and a penny arcade.[37] Some of the city's old romance is still intact in the film, however: Central Park, re-created on a sound stage, is the pristine backdrop for "Dancing in the Dark," a dance number for Astaire and Cyd Charisse. Yet the sinister aspects of postwar urban life is represented in the climactic dance number, "Girl Hunt," danced by Astaire and Charisse. Stylized sets of city streets evoke the Surrealist-inspired loneliness of Edward Hopper's New York paintings, with a measure of the photographer Weegee's macabre sensibility thrown in. The sequence takes the dancers into the Times Square subway station, in a set evocative of George Tooker's haunting painting *The Subway* (1950).

In 1955 Hollywood once again mined the enduring if flagging Broadway mythology in *Guys and Dolls*, based on the musical play of 1950 by Jo Swerling and Abe Burrows, which in turn derived from a short story by Damon Runyon.[38] Directed by Joseph L. Mankiewicz and starring Marlon Brando, Jean Simmons, Vivian Blaine and Frank Sinatra, the film lacks the fast pace and energy of Broadway musicals and Broadway itself. However, Oliver Smith's dreamily evocative and visually compelling, cartoonish sets are superb send-ups of the real Times Square. Best, perhaps, is the sewer set for the key musical number, "Luck Be a Lady," sung by Brando. Smith's sewer is a witty commentary on Constructivist architecture, with brightly colored tiles and cables, as well as a hardwood floor. The film ends with an upbeat musical number which is set, like the opening

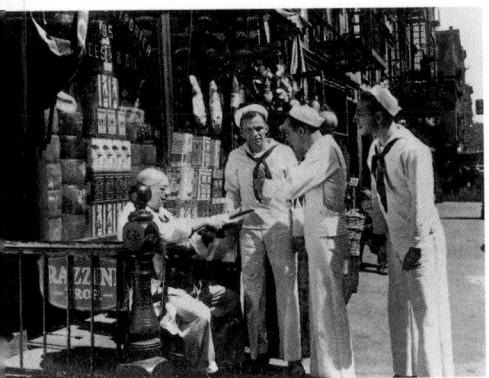

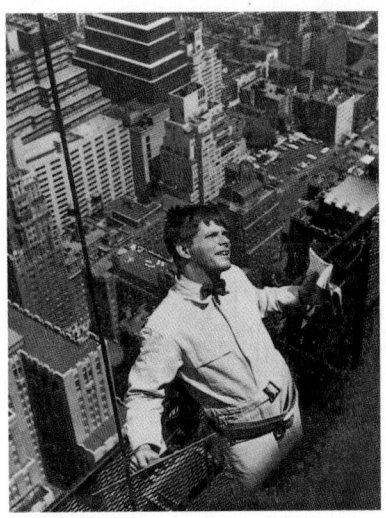

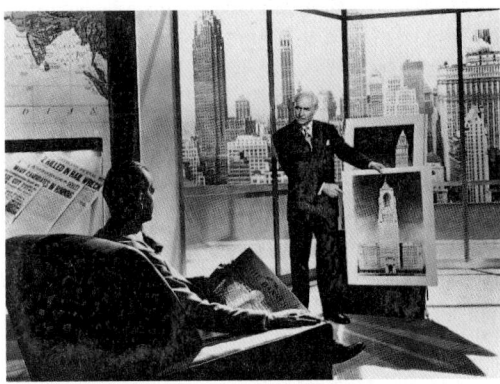

On the Town, 1949. Film still. Art director, Cedric Gibbons; director, Gene Kelly. ©1949 Turner Entertainment Co. All Rights Reserved. TEC

How to Succeed in Business without Really Trying, 1967. Film still. Art director, Robert Boyle; director, David Swift. MOMA

The Fountainhead, 1949. Film still. Art director, Edward Carrere; director, King Vidor. MOMA

sequence, in Times Square, providing the audience with a snapshot souvenir to take home.

George Cukor was the first important Hollywood director to combine the new, darker view of theater life with on-location filming in New York. Cukor's *A Double Life* (1947), an intriguing film about the psychology of actors, written by the husband-and-wife team of Garson Kanin and Ruth Gordon and starring Ronald Coleman and Signe Hasso, makes memorable on-location use of the lobby of the Lyceum Theater (Herts & Tallant, 1903) and the Empire Theater (John B. McElfatrick & Son, 1893; demolished in 1953).[39] Joseph L. Mankiewicz's hard-boiled *All About Eve* (1950), starring Bette Davis and Anne Baxter in an acid-tongued tale of backstage Broadway maneuvers, uses exterior shots of the Golden Theater (Herbert J. Krapp, 1927).[40] Alexander Mackendrick's *Sweet Smell of Success* (1957) offers another tough look at Broadway.[41] Focusing on a publicist, played by Tony Curtis, and a gossip columnist whose quest for power knows no bounds, played by Burt Lancaster, the film features on-location cinematography by James Wong Howe. For *New York Times* critic A. H. Weiler, the film captured "the sights and sounds of Manhattan's Bistro Belt" and a "fair portion of our town's fast tempo, its night spots and its sleazy aspects."[42] In 1991 the historian and author Michael Pye described the film as a "sardonic nightmare which turns a Broadway press agent into Faust," noting that its director "had to walk the streets with a camera to work out how little the eye really needs to be sure we are in Manhattan."[43] Sidney Lumet's *Stage Struck* (1958), a backstage romance starring Henry Fonda and Susan Strasberg, presents a kinder, more complicated vision of Broadway. According to Weiler,

> [Lumet] searched out and photographed in vivid and lovely color nearly every nook and cranny connected with the theater—from poetry-filled Greenwich Village bistros to swank penthouses, from rehearsal calls on bare stages to glamorous, tense first nights, from the fascinating mechanics of backstage operations to the hysteria indigenous to producers' offices and dressing rooms. . . . In shooting the film here in its entirety he and his cinematographers have captured the singular beauties of a veritable Bagdad-on-the-Hudson.[44]

In 1968 New York's theater world was given a first-class send-up by Mel Brooks, author and director of *The Producers*.[45]

The film features Zero Mostel as a down-and-out Broadway producer who cons his mousy accountant, played by Gene Wilder, into participating in a mad get-rich-quick scheme: they plan to sell backers 25,000 percent of a truly tasteless Broadway musical, *Springtime for Hitler*, which they expect to be a flop, and then make off with the money. The duo's shenanigans take them all over town. Perhaps the most memorable scene occurs on the central plaza of Lincoln Center, which becomes a player in the story: the moment Wilder agrees to Mostel's proposal, Philip Johnson's Revson Fountain explodes in a tower of water, Wallace Harrison's Metropolitan Opera House lights up and fireworks explode overhead.

New York, Hollywood and World War II: From Prewar Angst to Postwar Anomie

During World War II Hollywood alternately portrayed New York as a dangerous place vulnerable to enemy war efforts, a place of refuge and a backdrop for romance. Alfred Hitchcock's *Saboteur* (1942), starring Robert Cummings and Norman Lloyd, is a complex, fast-paced thriller in which a Nazi is chased from Los Angeles to New York and ultimately stopped, but only after he has set ablaze a battleship docked in the harbor.[46] The picaresque chase ends in Radio City Music Hall, in one of filmmaking's most memorable shoot-outs. As a movie is being shown at the music hall (a Hollywood sound-stage re-creation), the villain, chased by police, runs onto the stage. While the music hall audience howls with laughter at the corny film-within-the-film—a melodrama in which a jealous husband shoots his rival—real shots are fired. *Saboteur's* climax occurs at another famous location, the Statue of Liberty. In a quintessentially Hitchcockian twist, the Statue of Liberty (also a re-creation) is at once the logical destination of an American odyssey and the ironic setting for a dangerous duel in which, presumably, the nation's freedom hangs in the balance. The Nazi arsonist falls to his death from Miss Liberty's torch, and the city prevails as the embodiment of American values. In a wartime version of a similar story, Alan Ladd stars in the title role of Frank Tuttle's *Lucky Jordan* (1943), a suspense film about a soldier who has gone AWOL in New

York.[47] A protracted chase scene incorporates on-location shots of Fifth Avenue and a Long Island estate. Vincent Sherman's *All through the Night* (1942), a lively melodrama tinged with unexpected comic touches, tells of efforts to stamp out Fifth Columnist activity in Manhattan's Yorkville section.[48] The film, which pits the hero, played by Humphrey Bogart, against Nazis played by Conrad Veidt, Peter Lorre and Judith Anderson, includes a chase scene shot on location in Central Park.

As directed by Henry Hathaway, *The House on Ninety-second Street* (1945), produced by Twentieth Century–Fox with the cooperation of the Federal Bureau of Investigation, uses both documentary and feature-film techniques to tell the fact-based story of a Nazi spy's efforts to uncover the "Manhattan project" in wartime New York.[49] The film's producer, Louis de Rochement, is best known for his dramatic documentary film series, *The March of Time. The House on Ninety-second Street* was shot at many locations throughout the city and Long Island where real Nazi agents had operated, but some liberties were taken: the titular house occupied by Elsa Gowns, a dress shop serving as a front for Fifth Columnists, was actually at 53 East Ninety-third Street.

Wartime New York became the ideal setting for romance in Vincente Minnelli's sentimental film *The Clock* (1945), the story of a chance encounter between a boy from Indiana, on a forty-eight-hour leave in New York before being shipped off to England, and a New York girl.[50] The two travel about the city, losing and finding each other several times, falling in love in the process. The *New Yorker* critic Wolcott Gibbs noted that "the hero and heroine have a way of meeting under the clock at the Astor, never exactly associated in my mind with romance." Re-creating New York locations on a Hollywood back lot, the art director William Ferrari, working under the supervision of Cedric Gibbons, invented a hybrid railroad terminal for the city by having Grand Central's lofty concourse lead to Pennsylvania Station's glazed train room. There the soldier is, as Gibbs put it, "entranced by his first ride on an escalator. He ventures out of the station, is terrified by the skyscrapers (which *do* seem to be closing in on him), and bolts back into the station."[51] Other New York locations were re-created in Hollywood, including the seal tank in Central Park's zoo and the Metropolitan Museum of Art's Egyptian galleries, but actual footage of the museum's exterior is used as a backdrop for process shots showing the stars on the famous Fifth Avenue steps. Minnelli later recalled that he had decided "to make New York one of the characters—the third character."[52] *New York Times* critic Thomas Pryor said that the film recorded "the pulse beats of Manhattan—the roaring elevators, the screeching police sirens, the basso whistling of big boats in the Hudson, the crashing of garbage cans on the midnight pavements and all the other voices of cosmopolitan life—with electrifying effect. The sound track of this film is a composition in itself, not just a mechanical device."[53]

Though not completed until 1949, *On the Town*, directed by Gene Kelly and Stanley Donen, with a screenplay that Adolph Green and Betty Comden adapted from their own successful Broadway musical of 1944 (itself based on Jerome Robbins's 1943 ballet *Fancy Free*), was the definitive wartime New York musical.[54] With a score by Leonard Bernstein and additional music by Roger Edens, the film is a joyous romp with nutty dialogue and imaginative music and dancing, recounting the story of three sailors who land in New York on a twenty-four-hour leave with two goals: to see the sights and to meet a girl. Art director Cedric Gibbons used many on-location sequences that perfectly complement the sailors' antic pursuit of urban sophistication. The opening number, "It's a Wonderful Town," includes shots of the Brooklyn Bridge, Federal Hall, Chinatown, Little Italy, the Statue of Liberty, Washington Square, Grant's Tomb, a horse-drawn carriage in Central Park, a double-decker bus on Fifth Avenue and the Prometheus Fountain at Rockefeller Center, among other views. On-location live-action-photography was virtually unprecedented in a musical, but Donen and Kelly insisted on it, and the film documents the look and feel of the city before the dramatic transformation of postwar development. The city is clean, safe and stylish. It is also easily comprehensible—"The Bronx is up and the Battery's down"—and the distance "from Yonkers to the Bay" can be swiftly traversed by subway and taxi. New York is, for the sailors, the nation's capital; it is, in fact, the greatest city in the world.

In 1955 many of the same people who had put *On the Town* together made *It's Always Fair Weather*, an attempt to update the earlier film. The story is of three World War II soldiers (Gene Kelly, Dan Dailey and Michael Kidd), who, while celebrating the war's end and their return to New York, decide they will reconvene in the same spot exactly ten years later.[55] Their meeting place is Tim's Bar on Third Avenue, a friendly neighborhood joint cozily nestled in the dappled shadows of the Third Avenue El. In 1955, when the three vets meet again, Tim's is about the same, but they have changed drastically and so has the city, beginning with Third Avenue. The friends' downbeat mood reflects a fundamentally negative vision of the city. Dan Dailey's character, a hard-drinking Madison Avenue ad man, epitomizes the 1950s "man in the gray flannel suit" and New York's emerging role as the quintessential "executive city." Dolores Gray, playing the shrill hostess of a crass audience-participation television program called "The Throb of Manhattan," furthers this bleak portrait when she claims that the program proves that "the big, cold canyon that we call New York really has a heart."

The City at Work

By the 1950s many New Yorkers who were eager to reap the benefits of postwar prosperity struggled to make it in what was widely perceived as an increasingly harsh job market. Keeping pace with changing issues and trends, Hollywood turned to New York not as a theater world but as a real-world workplace. Michael Gordon's *I Can Get It for You Wholesale* (1951) focused on the garment industry, which had long embodied New York as a place of economic opportunity and cut-throat competition.[56] Based on Jerome Weidman's 1937 novel of the same name, the film included a memorable performance by Susan Hayward as a ruthless designer willing to do anything to get ahead. Six years later Hollywood tackled the garment industry's rougher aspects in Vincent Sherman's *The Garment Jungle*.[57]

David Swift's 1967 film version of the 1961 Broadway musical *How to Succeed in Business without Really Trying*, a send-up of the corporate rat race, is a rags-to-riches fable set in the offices of the Worldwide Widget Company, the quintessential manufacturer of useless objects. The gently satiric film follows the escapades of an ambitious young man who starts his climb up the corporate ladder washing the windows of a gleaming, glass-and-steel midtown office building. Swift exploited on-location shots of the city, using, as Crowther put it, "New York as his color-drenched setting—the hustle and bustle in the streets, the views from tops of skyscrapers and shots of the skyline at dawn."[58]

Stanley Donen's visually inventive musical *Funny Face* (1957) is set amid the high-style world of fashion magazines. Incorporating a charming thirty-year-old score by George and Ira Gershwin, which includes "He Loves and She Loves" and "'S Wonderful," as well as the title song, *Funny Face* tells the story, as Crowther put it, "of a drab little Greenwich Village salesgirl [Audrey Hepburn] who is grabbed up by a pertinacious troupe of style-magazine super-worldlings . . . and turned into a dazzling super-dress model, with whom the blasé photographer [Fred Astaire] falls in love."[59] The story is reputedly based on the real-life romance between the model-turned-actress Suzy Parker, who appears briefly in the film as a dancer, and the fashion photographer Richard Avedon, who served as the film's visual consultant. Contrasting bohemian Greenwich Village's quaint bookstores and cafés with corporate midtown's editorial offices, where New York's role as a national tastemaker is parodied in the musical number "Think Pink" (one of several new songs written for the film by Leonard Gershe and Roger Edens), the city is above all stylish.

Where the New York of *Funny Face* was largely crafted on sound stages, Jean Negulesco's *The Best of Everything* (1959), starring Suzy Parker along with Hope Lange, Joan Crawford and Louis Jourdan, adapts Rona Jaffe's 1958 novel about Manhattan "working girls."[60] The film features splendid on-location photography, including a memorable sequence showing the coolly sophisticated Parker striding across the plaza of the Seagram Building, an ideal match to Mies van der Rohe's elegant design.

Budd Schulberg and Elia Kazan's *A Face in the Crowd* (1957)[61] offered the toughest look at the New York media since John Conway's 1947 exposé of the city's radio industry, *The Hucksters*, starring Clark Gable and Deborah Kerr.[62] *A Face in the Crowd* chronicles the rise and fall of the duplicitous Lonesome Rhodes (Andy Griffith), a struggling guitar player who becomes a power-wielding television personality. *Network* (1976), Paddy Chayefsky's brutal, surreal dissection of the broadcasting business, is also an indictment of the corporate rat race.[63] Directed by Sidney Lumet and starring Peter Finch, Faye Dunaway, William Holden and Robert Duvall, the film depicts the brutally competitive world of television news, where even a man's imminent suicide serves the ratings. Filmed at various Manhattan locations and in East Hampton, Long Island, *Network* portrays New York as a city populated by amoral workaholics; its citizens seethe with not-so-quiet desperation. When Finch's character opens his office window and shouts, "I'm mad as hell, and I'm not going to take it anymore," he sets off a chain reaction throughout the city. To *New Yorker* critic Pauline Kael, the film was an expression of Chayefsky's overall vision of the city: "He's got the New York City hatreds, and ranting makes him feel alive."[64]

The business that most compelled Hollywood's attention and symbolized postwar corporate New York was advertising. Nunnally Johnson's *The Man in the Gray Flannel Suit* (1956), an early film critique of the advertising business based on Sloan Wilson's 1955 novel of the same name, sympathetically casts Gregory Peck as an advertising executive who struggles to keep his Westport, Connecticut, domestic life intact amid the rigorous demands of his Manhattan career.[65] The book and film were largely responsible for stereotyping the gray flannel suit as corporate America's uniform, a perfect complement to the steel-and-glass office buildings that concealed elitism behind a veil of architectural anonymity. In 1969, when youth counterculture was taking hold, Robert Downey's biting satire *Putney Swope* offered a devastating spoof of the advertising world, chronicling the transformation of a lily-white ad agency taken over by new, black management.[66]

Blue-collar New York is explored in Gregory Ratoff's decidedly sunny if not entirely realistic *Taxi* (1953), starring Dan Dailey as a gregarious cabbie. Following the driver's daily rounds, Ratoff, as Crowther put it, "photographed his picture pretty much in the streets of New York, not to mention Queens and Brooklyn, which makes for both scenic detail and a lively and plausible presentation of a hack driver's battleground."[67]

Budd Schulberg's screenplay for *On the Waterfront* (1954) is based on the muckraking journalist Malcolm Johnson's Pulitzer Prize–winning series of newspaper articles on corruption within the longshoremen's union.[68] As directed by Elia Kazan, with incidental music by Leonard Bernstein and memorable performances by Marlon Brando, Eva Marie Saint, Karl Malden, Lee J. Cobb and Rod Steiger, the grittily realistic black-and-white movie was shot entirely in Hoboken, New Jersey, still an important port. Three years later Martin Ritt's *Edge of the City*, a stark account of shipping industry brutalities, in some ways rehashed *On the Waterfront*. Nonetheless, the film, which Robert Alan Arthur adapted from his previously aired television play, packed a punch, in part through on-location shots of freight terminals near the West Side Highway.[69]

King Vidor's *The Fountainhead* (1949), in which one of the protagonists rises from blue-collar poverty to white-collar riches only to be confounded by his inability to control his architect's talent, is unrealistic and stagy yet completely riveting.[70] Ayn Rand adapted the screenplay from her own novel of 1943, which she had begun to write six years earlier while working as a secretary in the architectural firm of Ely Jacques Kahn. Although the story was said to be inspired by the career of Frank Lloyd Wright, the action takes place in New York, where the architect had only one significant chance to build. Vidor asked Wright to design the film sets, but the job went to Edward Carrere when Warner Brothers balked at the $250,000 fee Wright supposedly demanded.

Presaging changes that would soon transform the city, Carrere's sets depict historicist prewar architecture being replaced by International Style Modernism, including one skyscraper office where an exceptionally thin-mullioned glass wall looks out on Ernest Flagg's Singer Tower and a sweeping skyline. Carrere located Enright House, a Fifth Avenue luxury skyscraper apartment building designed by Howard Roark, the film's architect protagonist (played by Gary Cooper), on the site of Henry Hardenbergh's Fifth Avenue Estates Building (1903), between the Hotel Pierre (Schultze & Weaver, 1928) and the Sherry-Netherland Hotel (Schultze & Weaver with Buchman & Kahn, 1927).[71] In contrast to its classically inspired neighbors, Enright House, a stack of horizontal slabs presumably enclosed by an envelope of glass so as to seem invisible, recalls the work of William Lescaze more than Wright. Bosley Crowther described the fictitious design as "trash,"[72] while John McCarten noted that the "hero designs buildings so free from classical taint that they resemble waffle irons or upended tombstones."[73] The architect and designer George Nelson similarly dismissed the movie's sets as "the silliest travesty of modern architecture that has yet hit the films."[74] In the movie, Roark himself, dissatisfied by alterations imposed on his design, agrees to have credit bestowed on a colleague but, ultimately unable to live with the situation, blows up Enright House. Brought to trial, he argues for the rights of the individual in society and is acquitted.

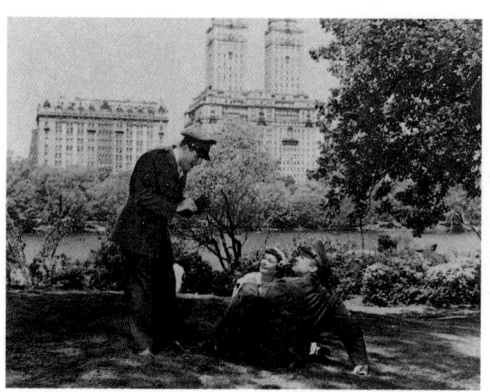

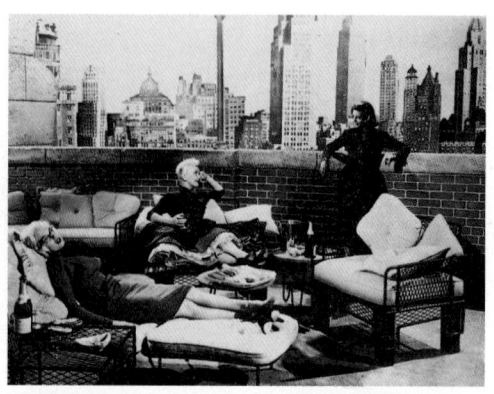

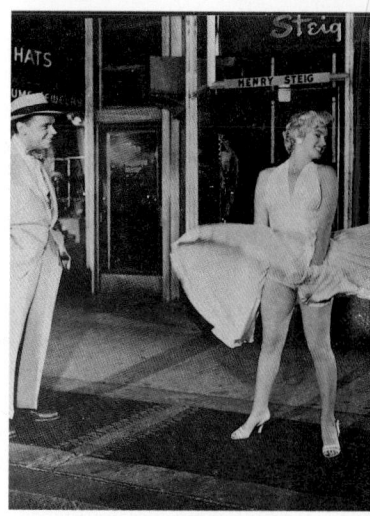

Miracle in the Rain, 1956. Film still. Art director, Leo K. Kuter; director, Rudolph Maté. MOMA

How to Marry a Millionaire, 1953. Film still. Art directors, Lyle Wheeler and Leland Fuller; director, Jean Negulesco. MOMA

The Seven Year Itch, 1955. Film still. Art director, Lyle Wheeler; director, Billy Wilder. MOMA

The City of Love

In the postwar era, as before, nothing held the attention of the movie audience as much as a good love story, and New York provided a powerfully glamorous if sometimes jaded backdrop for romance. In 1941 Alfred Hitchcock temporarily abandoned the mystery genre to try his hand at screwball comedy-romance in *Mr. and Mrs. Smith.*[75] Starring Carole Lombard and Robert Montgomery, the film tells of a husband and wife who suddenly find that their marriage is legally void. The film uses one New York location to memorable effect: seeking a romantic good time, the protagonists visit the Parachute Jump amusement at the New York World's Fair, only to get stuck in midair.[76] The scene recalls the real-life misadventures of Mr. and Mrs. J. Cornelius Rathborne, whose five-hour ordeal had been immortalized by the photographer Jerome Zerbe. In Julien Duvivier's *Tales of Manhattan* (1942), with a screenplay by ten different authors, including Ben Hecht, four loosely connected independent stories are set in New York, which appears as a place of professional disappointment, upward mobility and, of course, romance.[77]

The real star of Robert Z. Leonard's *Weekend at the Waldorf* (1944), despite a stellar cast that includes Lana Turner, Van Johnson, Ginger Rogers, Walter Pidgeon and Xavier Cugat, is the grand Waldorf-Astoria Hotel (Schultze & Weaver, 1931) itself.[78] Supplementing on-location cinematography, Hollywood sets meticulously duplicate parts of the hotel, including the Starlight Roof, to which some changes were made: the film's art director, Daniel B. Cathcart, working under the direction of Cedric Gibbons, altered its interior to yield a more contemporary feeling, moving away from the Art Décoratif–inspired original to something more reminiscent of the work of Dorothy Draper.

George Cukor's *Adam's Rib* (1949) is a quintessential New York drama by Garson Kanin and Ruth Gordon. A husband and wife who are rival lawyers—Spencer Tracy is the district attorney and Katharine Hepburn is in private practice—oppose each other in court over a shooting that has shattered a lower-middle-class love triangle.[79] Location shots make vivid the class distinction between the crime suspects and the attorneys. The shooting takes place in a small east side apartment. The spurned wife,

played by the comedienne Judy Holliday, reaches the apartment via a crowded subway. The lawyers travel to work from their luxurious Sutton Place apartment in an open convertible that passes effortlessly south along an almost car-free Franklin Delano Roosevelt Drive, photographed before the reconstruction required to make way for the United Nations. Three years later Cukor again directed Holliday in a New York–based romantic comedy written by Gordon and Kanin, *The Marrying Kind,* which documents the typical domestic problems of a newly married couple in the city.[80] The female protagonist, a secretary played by Holliday, meets her future husband, a post office worker played by Aldo Ray, in Central Park; soon they are newlyweds living in Peter Cooper Village. In *Let's Make Love* (1960), starring Yves Montand and Marilyn Monroe, Cukor once more used actual New York locations but to much less effect; as the film historian Gary Carey said, Cukor's Greenwich Village shots "suggest certain parts of London more than they do New York."[81]

Peter Godfrey's *The Girl from Jones Beach* (1949) is a slight romance that uses New York's most architecturally significant seaside recreational facility as a setting for a story in which a recent Czech immigrant (Ronald Reagan) follows his night-school American history teacher (Virginia Mayo) to the beach.[82] Mervyn LeRoy's *East Side, West Side* (1949), starring Barbara Stanwyck, James Mason and Ava Gardner, is a conventional story of amorous intrigue enlivened by colorful New York location shots. According to Crowther, the film poses the urgent question of whether "a rich and charming lady should endure the infidelity of her spouse. Should she wait at home on the terrace of their East River duplex while he stays out to all hours of the night with a charmer who has a little shack off Washington Square?"[83]

William Dieterle's *Portrait of Jennie* (1949), based on Robert Nathan's popular 1940 novel of the same name, is an unabashedly romantic yet unconventional drama, telling of a painter who falls in love with the beautiful ghost of a long-dead woman.[84] Starring Joseph Cotten and Jennifer Jones, the film incorporates shots of several New York locations but focuses on Central Park as a nearly fantastical setting for the supernatural. Central Park also serves as the setting for otherworldly romance

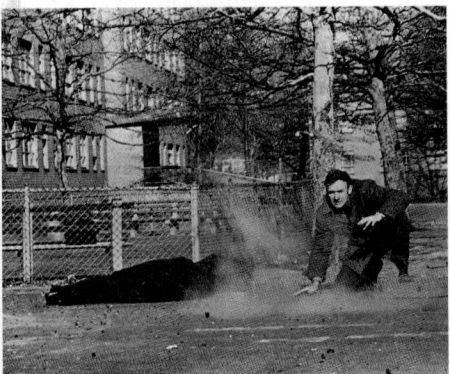

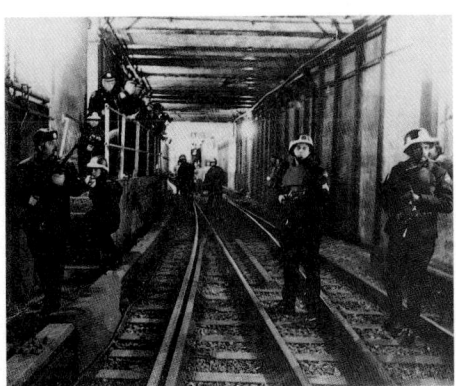

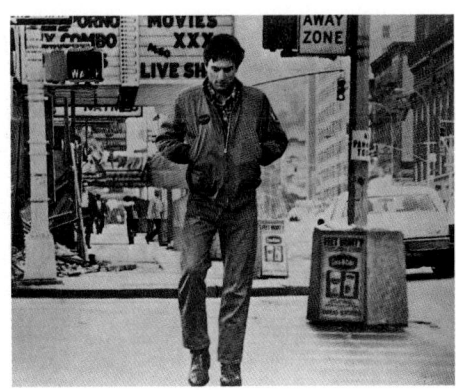

The French Connection, 1971. Film still. Art director, Ben Kazaskow; director, William Friedkin. MOMA

The Taking of Pelham One Two Three, 1974. Film still. Art director, Gene Rudolf; director, Joseph Sargent. MOMA

Taxi Driver, 1976. Film still. Art director, Charles Rosen; director, Martin Scorsese. MOMA

in Rudolph Maté's *Miracle in the Rain* (1956), a sentimental tale of love triumphing over death, in which a secretary (Jane Wyman) and a soldier (Van Johnson) meet and fall in love in Central Park.[85] Several days later the soldier is shipped off to fight in World War II, where he is killed in action. The twist comes when the two "meet" again, this time in St. Patrick's Cathedral (James Renwick, Jr., 1878). A. H. Weiler noted in the *New York Times*: "In filming on location here last spring, the producer illustrated that our town can be lovely and exciting. The sylvan vistas of Central Park; its lake and skyline; St. Patrick's Cathedral (including shots of the vast, vaulted interior) . . . prove that Gotham is photogenic and that authentic locales are an attribute."[86]

The supernatural features again in Richard Quine's romantic comedy *Bell, Book, and Candle* (1958), based on John Van Druten's Broadway play of 1950, in which a young woman (Kim Novak) employs witchcraft to win a naive fellow (James Stewart). Crowther, who praised the film's color photography, stated that "from the atelier of the heroine, who is a dealer in primitive art, to a smoky nightclub in Greenwich Village, where the local sorceresses and their apprentices play, it is vividly visual and suggestive. . . . And what they have done with New York street scenes at dusk and twilight is necromancy for fair."[87] The film also includes a sequence shot at the Flatiron Building (D. H. Burnham & Company, 1903),[88] where the protagonists have a romantic liaison on the roof.

In Jean Negulesco's *How to Marry a Millionaire* (1953),[89] Lauren Bacall, Betty Grable and Marilyn Monroe portray three classic gold diggers who lease a $1,000-per-month penthouse on Sutton Place South from which they hope to snare rich husbands. While the apartment's interior is a set, the exterior is the real thing, as are some of the views seen out the windows and from the terrace and a spectacular view of lower Manhattan from the Staten Island ferry.

In Billy Wilder's *The Seven Year Itch* (1955), the city serves as the alluring, mildly dangerous setting for the fantasies of a married man (Tom Ewell) whose wife and children go out of town for the summer.[90] Ewell catches a severe case of wandering eye, brought on by the proximity of a sexy new neighbor (Marilyn Monroe). In one scene, the seductively dressed Monroe demonstrates to Ewell one way to beat the heat: when the two hit the sidewalk after a movie at the Trans-Lux Theater on

Lexington Avenue, she stands above a subway grating as the rush of air caused by trains passing below sends her skirt above her shoulders. The scene was shot on location at 2:00 A.M.; despite the hour, thousands of spectators gathered to watch.

Charles Walters's *The Tender Trap* (1955) also portrays the city as a place of tantalizing romantic possibility. A very single, thirty-five-year-old theater agent, played by Frank Sinatra, maintains a busy bachelor pad on Sutton Place until he is snagged by the pert Debbie Reynolds.[91] The Empire State Building provides the setting for the climax of Leo McCarey's *An Affair to Remember* (1957),[92] a sentimental tale of star-crossed lovers based on McCarey's own popular film of 1939, *Love Affair*. Columbia University, seen in on-location opening shots, serves as the setting for George Seaton's *Teacher's Pet* (1958), in which Doris Day plays a journalism professor who dumps her bookworm boyfriend (Gig Young) for a hard-boiled newspaperman (Clark Gable) who is a guest lecturer in the night class she teaches.[93] Day stars in another New York–based romantic comedy, *Pillow Talk* (1959), directed by Michael Gordon. Here she portrays a chic interior designer who first encounters a songwriter (Rock Hudson) when the two unintentionally share a telephone party line. After a series of antics and deceptions, they fall in love, while various locations throughout New York collectively function as a backdrop.[94]

The mechanics of romance in New York take a darker turn in Daniel Mann's *Butterfield 8* (1960), with a screenplay that Charles Schnee adapted from John O'Hara's novel of 1935. Starring Elizabeth Taylor as a prostitute who hopes to find happiness with a rich man caught in an unsatisfying marriage, the stylishly produced film, as Crowther stated, "offers admission to such an assortment of apartments, high-class bars [and] Fifth Avenue shops . . . that it should make the most moral status seeker feel a little disposed toward a life of sin."[95] In contrast to the hooker's childhood boyfriend, who lives in a tiny Greenwich Village apartment, the object of her adult desire lives in a ten-room Fifth Avenue suite.

Billy Wilder's sharp-edged comedy-drama *The Apartment* (1960), starring Shirley MacLaine, Jack Lemmon and Fred MacMurray, with a script cowritten by Wilder and I. A. L. Diamond, tells the story of an ordinary insurance company clerk, played by Lemmon, who gets an extraordinary idea for advancing his career: he will lend the keys to his brownstone apartment to a philandering executive.[96] The scheme leads to better treatment at the office, for which exterior footage of the Seagram Building is used. Inside, the office is chillingly portrayed as an anonymous, dehumanized, fluorescent-lit, International Style Modernist environment—a veritable sea of desks where Lemmon feels adrift.

Peter Tewksbury's *Sunday in New York* (1964) uses the city as the sophisticated and mildly menacing setting for the soul-searching deliberations of a young woman from Albany concerned with maintaining her "virtue."[97] The protagonist, played by Jane Fonda, spends a single rainy afternoon in New York, where, as fate would have it, she runs into the object of her affection—and temptation—on a Fifth Avenue bus.

Gene Saks's 1967 film adaptation of Neil Simon's popular play *Barefoot in the Park*, which had opened on Broadway three years earlier, uses New York locations as the backdrop for the story of Corie and Paul Bratter, a zany housewife and her staid lawyer husband, portrayed by Robert Redford and Jane Fonda.[98] The film includes views of the newlywed couple's Greenwich Village apartment (the interiors of which were created on a Hollywood sound stage) at 111 Waverly Place. Shots of Village haunts abound, including Washington Square Park.

The movie musical *Sweet Charity* (1969), directed by Bob Fosse, uses New York as the setting for a pessimistic if somewhat sentimental story of a romance that doesn't work out.[99] Based on Fosse's own successful Broadway musical, which had incorporated a Neil Simon book loosely derived from Federico Fellini's film *Nights of Cabiria* (1957), the film stars Shirley Maclaine as a taxi dancer who dreams of being an upstanding member of society. Though one dance number on a tenement rooftop is visually engaging, some location shots seem at odds with Fosse's surreal, sexually charged choreography. The problem had been anticipated from the first by the film's screenwriter, Peter Stone, who told Fosse, "The realism of a movie is overwhelming. You can't have real people standing in the middle of a real street in New York singing and dancing. That's over."[100] As film critic Vincent Canby noted, the number called "I'm a Brass Band," in which Charity celebrates a triumphant moment, becomes "a production number the size of 'War and Peace,' filmed against the real dwarfing backgrounds of Lincoln Center, Brooklyn Bridge and Wall Street."[101]

Herbert Ross's *The Owl and the Pussycat* (1970) is a tale of an improbable romance between a pure-hearted New York prostitute (Barbra Streisand) and a nebbishy aspiring writer (George Segal).[102] The movie was partially shot on location, including a scene in a Doubleday bookstore, where Segal's character works. Another exuberant New York prostitute is the focus of Nicholas Sgarro's *The Happy Hooker* (1975), starring Lynn Redgrave in the title role. The critic Vincent Canby praised the movie, which includes on-location sequences filmed throughout Manhattan, as "a cheerily amoral New York comedy about greed and lust in the land of opportunity."[103]

Stuart Rosenberg's *The April Fools* (1969) involves a Wall Street stockbroker (Jack Lemmon) who, having lived for years in the suburbs with his shrewish wife, meets and falls in love with a beautiful married woman (Catherine Deneuve) at a fashionable cocktail party in the United Nations Plaza apartment building.[104] Standing outside the apartment house, which in the three years since its completion had become a symbol of cool elegance, one character says, "If there is a God . . . this is where he lives."[105] Arthur Hiller's *Plaza Suite* (1971), adapted from Neil Simon's successful stage play of 1968, consists of three vignettes each focusing on a couple who, at different times, occupy the same suite in the Plaza Hotel (Henry Hardenbergh, 1907).[106]

While tales of romance, told with varying degrees of cynicism, would continue to hold movie audiences in thrall throughout the postwar period, filmmakers increasingly turned to the broad range of societal problems that more and more came to define daily life in New York. Laslo Benedek's *Port of New York* (1950) tells of drug smuggling and efforts to eradicate it. The critic A. H. Weiler asserted that the film's producer "obviously told his director to load this film . . . with New York atmosphere" and that the director "followed those instructions carefully," amassing "reel after reel of honest local scenery" that added "a certain amount of authority."[107] George Sherman's *The Sleeping City* (1950),[108] starring Richard Conte, also took on the city's illegal drug trade. The film treated audiences to a near-two-hour-long tour of Bellevue Hospital, from patients' rooms and wards to kitchens, corridors, recreational areas and the rooftop. Crowther noted that despite the "pictorial asset" of the hospital itself, the film "is not the fine cosmopolitan drama of medical practice and human life that it had every chance to be."[109] Mayor William O'Dwyer requested that Conte return to the hospital to film a prologue informing viewers that the story was fictitious and showing drawings for new buildings that would replace McKim, Mead & White's vast original complex (1908–39), which by 1950 seemed not only functionally obsolete but actively malevolent.[110] The film also made use of the Horn & Hardart Automat at 200 East Forty-second Street (formerly the Foltis-Fischer Building; Hector Hamilton, 1932), and the Williamsburg Bridge (Leffert L. Buck, 1896–1903).[111] In 1971 Arthur Hiller's film *Hospital*, written by Paddy Chayefsky and starring George C. Scott, offered audiences another close look at a New York medical center, Metropolitan Hospital.[112] Long corridors and small rooms frame a scathingly dark comedy that realized the audience's worst nightmares about what really goes on in big-city hospitals. To New Yorkers, it constituted a comment on health care and on the Kafkaesque state to which the municipal bureaucracy had descended.

Based on an article by Milton Lehman that appeared in *Cosmopolitan*, Earl McEvoy's *The Killer that Stalked New York* (1951) tackles two threatening social problems, crime and disease, as it tells of a fugitive diamond thief infected with smallpox.[113] Like *The Sleeping City*, this film includes on-location hospital scenes, though here they are less extensive and the identity of the hospital is never revealed. Still, Crowther noted that the hospital sequences, including scenes of mass vaccinations, vividly re-created the mass anxiety that had accompanied an actual smallpox outbreak in New York several years earlier.

Richard Brooks's *Blackboard Jungle* (1955), starring Glenn Ford as an earnest teacher in the fictitious North Manual Trades High School and a young Sidney Poitier as a heroic student among hoodlums, depicts the hellish world of inner-city education.[114] The controversial film derives from Evan Hunter's 1954 novel, which he based on his seventeen years' experience as a substitute teacher at the Bronx Vocational High School. A year after the publication of the book, which "shocked" New York Senator Herbert H. Lehman, Hunter's teaching license was revoked.[115] The film, Crowther said, was "no temperate or restrained report on a state of affairs that is disturbing to educators and social workers today. It is a full-throated, all-out testimonial to the lurid headlines that appear from time to time, reporting acts of terrorism and violence by uncontrolled urban youths. It gives a blood-curdling, nightmarish picture of monstrous disorder in a public school."[116] Eleven years later, Robert Mulligan's *Up the Down Staircase* (1966), starring Sandy Dennis, presented a more poignant view of life in a New York City public school but nonetheless depicted the turmoil besetting its largely under-privileged students.[117] The dramatization of Bel Kaufman's novel, which detailed her experience as a teacher in the New York City school system, was filmed largely at the somewhat de-crepit but grandly Dutch Gothic–style Haaren High School, for-merly De Witt Clinton High School,[118] on Amsterdam Avenue between West Fifty-ninth and West Sixtieth streets.

Hy Averback's *Where Were You When the Lights Went Out?* (1968), starring Doris Day, is a humorous look at the city as it coped with the electrical blackout that darkened much of the northeastern United States on November 9, 1965.[119] The film's up-beat tone, like its star, seemed to belong to an earlier, breezier era. Three years later *Panic in Needle Park* (1971), directed by Jerry Schatzberg with a screenplay by Joan Didion and John Gregory Dunne, offered a relentlessly grim study of the city's junkies, who by the time of the film's release had become a widely recognized feature of the cityscape. The nickname for Verdi Square in the film's title refers to the hypodermic needles used by drug addicts who inhabited the small green triangle bounded by Broadway, Amsterdam Avenue and West Seventy-third Street.[120]

The French Connection (1971), William Friedkin's thriller, involves the efforts of Popeye Doyle, a tough narcotics division detective, played by Gene Hackman, to nail cocaine dealers.[121] Filmed on location throughout the city, the movie includes a scene in which the police try to stop a hijacked train on an ele-vated portion of the B line running along Eighty-sixth Street in Brooklyn. Greenspun claimed that "the potential for failure . . . of all action in the great doomed city" was the film's real subject and that Doyle "exists neither to rise nor to fall, to excite neither pity nor terror—but to function. To function in New York City is its own heroism, and the film recognizes that."[122]

In Frank D. Gilroy's *Desperate Characters* (1971), the malaise that engulfs the protagonists, Sophie and Otto Bent-wood (Shirley MacLaine and Kenneth Mars), seems a direct re-flection if not result of the city's devastation.[123] Sophie, a house-wife and translator, and Otto, a successful lawyer, live together at the edge of Brooklyn Heights in a refurbished rowhouse com-plete with a complex burglar alarm system, the kind of place, said feminist Betty Friedan, "we would all love to live in if we hadn't moved to the suburbs because we can't afford to send our kids to private school."[124] Contending that the film was "full of the details of urban desperation, painfully and accurately ob-served at eye level," Canby wrote:

> [The Bentwoods'] emotional lives are scarred as their reno-vated brownstone is handsome and spruce. They are childless, middle-class city dwellers, coming apart in a world whose problems have grown beyond the liberal's capacity to compre-hend, much less solve. . . . The subways they ride are inhabited by two kinds of people, those who talk to themselves and those who pretend not to notice. The streets are boobytrapped with garbage and dog excrement and drunks who might be stiffs.[125]

In Arthur Hiller's *The Out of Towners* (1970), an Ohio ex-ecutive (Jack Lemmon), accompanied by his wife (Sandy Dennis), comes to New York for a job interview.[126] "Expecting a provincial dream of mid-Manhattan luxury," as Roger Green-spun wrote, "the couple instead endure airport stacking pat-terns, diversion to Boston, lost luggage, a train ride to New York, a transit strike, a taxi strike, a sanitation strike, canceled hotel reservations, robbery, kidnapping, a rainy night in Central Park, a New York City dog, a New York City bus ride, and many other local pleasures."[127]

Melvin Frank's *The Prisoner of Second Avenue* (1975), with a screenplay by Neil Simon that he adapted from his own Broadway play of 1971, stars Jack Lemmon and Anne Bancroft as Mel and Edna Edison, a couple who live in an enormous apartment building located at 245 East Eighty-seventh Street (Paul & Jarmul, 1966).[128] Pauline Kael discussed the film's mes-sage in her review in the *New Yorker*:

> Implicit here, as in much of Simon's other work, is the familiar idea that New York is a battleground; either you put on your brass knuckles and become a power broker or a mugger, or you're buried. There are jokey news dispatches dropped in from time to time—by a narrator—as if from the frontlines. And at the end, when Mel announces that he and Edna won't leave the city, it's like a wartime-movie speech about fighting on—and the audience responds with cheers. Is Simon saying that things are so awful in New York City that you're kind of a hero if you live here and a coward if you escape?[129]

The Taking of Pelham One Two Three (1974), directed by Joseph Sargent, presents a city defined by disaster.[130] Four crimi-nals hijack an IRT subway and take eighteen passengers hostage, threatening to kill the passengers unless they receive over a million dollars. Sargent shot much of the film in actual subway cars and on the IND-line tracks at the Hoyt-Schermerhorn station in Brooklyn, giving moviegoers a tour of the city's ravaged public transportation system. The film critic Nora Sayre commented on the absurdly en-tertaining aspect of watching the city subsumed by alternating states of paranoia and rage. "It's been a while," Sayre wrote, "since we've had a movie that really catches the mood of New York and New Yorkers. The crisis mentality of what Henry James called the 'vast hot pot' . . . is reflected in 'The Taking of Pelham One Two Three.'" The film's criminals, she said, "one glazed with a sleazy regret, the other endowed with a calm brutality—are all too likely as your typical rush-hour hijackers." Sayre concluded that "the hi-jacking seems like a perfectly probable event for this town" and that "perhaps the only element of fantasy is the implication that the city's departments could function so smoothly together."[131]

In 1974 Vincent Canby assessed some main currents run-ning through New York movies of the period, especially those that portrayed the metropolis as a disaster area. "New York City has become a metaphor for what looks like the last days of American civilization," Canby wrote. "New York is a mess, though most filmmakers tend to overdramatize the effects while oversimplifying the causes." He noted that this negative view of the city seemed to attract a big audience. "I'm not as worried about the city's bad notices," he said, "as I am curious as to why the matter has suddenly become of interest to filmmakers. Is be-ing a mess box office?" He traced the beginning of the current view of New York to the late 1960s, when Mayor Lindsay had encouraged filmmakers to shoot in the city:

> When filmmakers arrived to work here in quantity, they began to make movies that weren't simply set in New York but were also about New York. . . . The image of New York in contem-porary movies . . . has to do with the decline of the Hollywood studios—physically and psychologically, with the conviction of an increasing number of filmmakers that movies should be made on location as often as possible (one result of the influ-ence of foreign films of the fifties), and with the emergence of what might be called the regional or environmental American film, the film in which the locale may be as important as plot. . . . In this fashion the *availability* of New York City, for better or worse, is having a direct influence on the content of what we're seeing in movie theaters.[132]

The City as Psychosis: New York Unhinged

Postwar filmmakers also focused on how New York's identity influenced, and was reflected in, the individual. In some films, New York seems like an appropriate, indeed a nearly inevitable, setting for individual neurosis; in other cases, filmmakers went a step further, portraying the city as the cause or catalyst of individual psychosis. Billy Wilder's classic film *The Lost Weekend* (1945), which established the director as a major talent, uses both studio and on-location photography to recount the story of a five-day binge in the life of an alcoholic writer, played by Ray Milland.[133] A terrifying sequence documenting the realities of delirium tremens was shot in the detoxification ward of Bellevue Hospital. Wilder had to scrap footage shot in P. J. Clarke's pub, on the northeast corner of Third Avenue and East Fifty-third Street, because the noise from the Third Avenue El was too intrusive. Instead, the bar was duplicated on a sound stage at Paramount Studios in Hollywood. Nonetheless, Wilder persisted in his search for authenticity, fighting with studio executives for on-location shots. The harrowing footage of the protagonist's desperate search, on Yom Kippur, to find an open pawnshop where he could raise cash for liquor by hocking his typewriter, was filmed on Third Avenue. Wilder and his cameraman, John Sertz, hid cameras in empty storefronts and laundry trucks to record portions of the sequence, which tracks Milland for fifty blocks.

Twelve years later addiction to narcotics provided the subject for another gripping New York–based film, Fred Zinnemann's *A Hatful of Rain* (1957).[134] Based on Michael Vincente Gazzo's stage play of 1955, the film, starring Eva Marie Saint and Don Murray, uses on-location shooting to telling effect. Crowther noted that "in the hard black-and-white pictorial pattern Mr. Zinnemann has employed," the actors "loom honestly against a background of a low-cost housing project in New York and swirl in the cold, impersonal eddies of the windy streets of the East Side."[135]

Alfred Hitchcock's melodrama *Rope* (1948), starring James Stewart, John Dall and Farley Granger, goes beyond a conventional murder story to provide a psychological portrait of two New Yorkers who decide to test the Nietzschean concept of the *Übermensch* by killing a friend just for the excitement of it.[136] The single, continuous scene was filmed on a set depicting a posh Manhattan penthouse with a greenhouselike enclosure providing expansive views of the city's skyline, seen primarily at night. The ingeniously designed set allowed the camera to glide smoothly from room to room, with dividing walls moving into studio flies. The penthouse apartment takes on an eerie and claustrophobic presence, as if it were the dark heart of the glittering city seen spreading out below. Technically, the re-creation of the nighttime city is the set's most spectacular feature. As the sky gradually darkens, the city's lights go on; each miniature building in the mock city was wired individually, with lights ranging from 25 to 150 watts, and 26,000 feet of wiring was used to conduct 126,000 watts of electrical current.

Equally taut is John Frankenheimer's thriller *The Manchurian Candidate* (1962), in which a patriotic Korean War veteran, who lives in an apartment at 67 Riverside Drive (George F. Pelham, 1907), on the southeast corner of West Seventy-ninth Street, is transformed into a political assassin.[137] Political assassination is treated again in Edward Dmytryk's *Mirage* (1965), in which Gregory Peck stars as a scientist who invents a method for eliminating nuclear fallout only to end up a potential victim.[138] The rather routine thriller includes on-location scenes filmed in Central and Battery parks.

In Frank Perry's *Diary of a Mad Housewife* (1970), a completely sane individual is viewed through the distorting lens of an insane city, or at least of a particular social milieu within that city.[139] With a screenplay by the director's wife, Eleanor Perry, adapted from the 1968 novel by Sue Kaufman, the film traces the unravelings and marital vicissitudes of Tina Balser (Carrie Snodgress) and her lawyer husband Jonathan (Richard Benjamin). The film, shot entirely on location in New York, focuses predominantly on Central Park West and the East Fifties, though it includes scenes filmed in a downtown loft, the Richard Feigen Gallery and the fashionable Upper East Side restaurant Elaine's. The art critic Grace Glueck noted in the *New York Times*:

> The Perrys . . . have had the wit to make the city a protagonist of the film, lapping away at the Balsers' marriage like an erosive tide. But nothing conveys the milieu so well as the art-adorned flat on Central Park West into which the ménage is shoehorned. A claustrophobic trapful of high-class consumer goods, it rocks in one inspired scene with a barrage of noise and movement—buzzers, telephone bells, a washing machine, a barking dog, the comings and goings of sullen help—that symbolically project both Tina's confusion and that of the maddening city.[140]

Penelope Gilliatt described the importance of the film's setting:

> The characters seem almost literally to take their sense of the shape of the world from the shape of the floor plan of their apartments. This is their only substantive order. No rival outer system is palpable, no policies intrude, no foreigners, no history, no possibility of change; the rims of the apartment embody rules that can be touched, and that are made verbal in this sort of comedy by the foolish, luxuriant argot of group therapy. Manhattan has reflected a tiny, sterile new vein of entertainment that is a sort of psychoanalytical slapstick.[141]

Sidney Lumet's *Dog Day Afternoon* (1975), based on an actual bungled robbery attempt, documents not only individual madness but a collective lunacy engulfing New York that turns criminal acts into political circuses and media spectacles.[142] On August 22, 1972, in ninety-seven-degree heat, an attempt was made to rob the Chase Manhattan Bank branch at 285 Avenue P in Brooklyn. In the film account, the inept robbers, identified as Sonny and Sal and played respectively by Al Pacino and John Cazale, find that the bank is immediately surrounded by police and FBI agents; they confront other unexpected complications as well, including the fact that the bank contains only $1,100 in cash and that its air-conditioning system is on the fritz. Panicked, the two take several bank employees hostage. During fourteen hours of negotiations with the police, the charismatic but clearly unstable and deluded Sonny, who is bisexual and is seeking money to pay for his boyfriend's sex-change operation, addresses the crowds that have gathered outside, turning the event into a street festival with political overtones. Lumet filmed on location, keeping the action almost exclusively in the bank and the surrounding neighborhood. To Jack Kroll, writing in *Newsweek*, the film "at least glancingly captures the increasingly garish pathologies of our urban life."[143] Canby wrote that "Mr. Lumet's New York movies are as much aspects of the city's life as they are stories of the city's life" and characterized the film as "a gaudy street-carnival of a movie that rudely invites laughs at inappropriate moments, which is in keeping with the city's concrete sensibility."[144] He further commented:

> The movie's concentration of time and place adds terrific intensity to the melodrama, though it limits the psychological territory that can be covered. This, however, is a perfectly honor-

able artistic decision to have made and, indeed, it's a part of the content and style of this quintessential New York film. More than any other city I know, New York is a present-tense town, a place where the moment is everything, yesterday is prehistory and the future, when and if it comes, will be suddenly transformed into the now.[145]

Karel Reisz's *The Gambler* (1974) tells of Axel, an erudite English professor (James Caan) who is a compulsive gambler.[146] The film, mostly shot in New York, contrasts the quiet, refined atmosphere of the walled-in Riverdale estate where Axel's grandfather lives with the tawdry, violent, Harlem betting parlor where the wildly self-destructive Axel winds up.

Martin Scorsese's *Taxi Driver* (1976), which stars Robert DeNiro as Travis Bickle, an emotionally remote Vietnam War veteran who drives a cab in New York, is perhaps the most powerful postwar film to explore the devastating effect the city has on some of its inhabitants.[147] Obsessed with what he characterizes as the city's human wreckage, Bickle ultimately suffers a psychotic episode that manifests itself in a murderous rampage. Canby described Bickle as "more than a character who is certifiably insane":

> He is a projection of all our nightmares of urban alienation . . . [and] every paranoid taxi driver you've ever met on your wildest nightmare ride. Unable to connect with anyone . . . he comes to loathe the inhabitants of the city to which he has been drawn, and in the way of those obsessed, he sees only his obsessions: the hookers, the hustlers, pimps, freaks—the "garbage"—people who are successfully making out in a city that barely tolerates him.[148]

Filmed on location throughout the city, the movie focuses on the sleazy Times Square area, home to a variety of characters including a teenage prostitute (Jodie Foster) and her pimp (Harvey Keitel). Scorsese's city is relentlessy dark and hopeless. Even its minor details have an explicitly satanic edge. As Canby noted, "The steam billowing up around the manhole cover in the street is a dead giveaway. Manhattan is a thin cement lid over the entrance to hell."[149] For Pauline Kael, Scorsese's city also gave off "the stench of Hell":

> As Scorsese has designed the film, the city never lets you off the hook. There's no grace, no compassion in the artificially lighted atmosphere. The neon reds, the vapors that shoot up from the streets, the dilapidation all get to you the way they get to Travis. . . . The cinematographer, Michael Chapman, gives the street life a seamy pulpiness. . . . Scorsese's New York is a voluptuous enemy. The street vapors become ghostly . . . the porno theaters are like mortuaries; the congested traffic is macabre. And this Hell is always in movement.[150]

After the film's violent climax, Kael said, Travis looked pacified, but this was not a hopeful sign: "He's got the rage out of his system—for the moment, at least—and he's back at work, picking up passengers in front of the St. Regis. It's not that he's cured but that the city is crazier than he is."[151]

Lonely Town: The City without a Heart

If the city's potentially oppressive energy, at once relentless and anarchic, pushes some New Yorkers beyond reason, it leaves others plagued by anomie. George Cukor's *It Should Happen to You* (1953) tells the story of an ordinary young woman, Gladys Glover (Judy Holliday), who is determined to rise above the depressing anonymity of big-city life; she hits upon the idea of having her name painted on an empty billboard overlooking Columbus Circle.[152] Filming on location in New York, Cukor and his assistants carefully combed Columbus Circle, blocking shots. They also visited advertising agencies and the editorial offices of *Look* magazine to learn how the burgeoning fields of public relations and marketing worked. After her publicity stunt, Glover finds herself overwhelmed by her instant celebrity status. Surviving a series of disastrous romantic entanglements that reveal a city full of scoundrels and phonies, she marries an earnest documentary filmmaker, played by Jack Lemmon, who has recorded the vicissitudes of their courtship on film in what becomes their good-bye note to the city. The couple abandons the metropolitan rat race at the film's end, which features a spectacular view of the Manhattan skyline shot from a car descending into the Lincoln Tunnel.

Perhaps no movie personage more fully captured the spirit of the lonely New Yorker than the title character of *Marty* (1955), written by Paddy Chayefsky and directed by Delbert Mann. Portrayed by Ernest Borgnine, Marty is an unmarried thirty-four-year-old Italian-American butcher born, raised and still living in the Bronx who ultimately finds happiness when he meets a schoolteacher, played by Betsy Blair. To Bosley Crowther, Mann's "excellent staging" captured "the feel and the flavor of the Bronx."[153]

In contrast to this essentially optimistic and heartwarming story of urban loneliness, Sidney Lumet's searing drama *The Pawnbroker* (1965) centers on Sol Nazerman, a Holocaust survivor (Rod Steiger) who shuns virtually all human contact.[154] Nazerman runs a Harlem pawnshop that is a front for mob activity. Working with cameraman Boris Kaufman, Lumet focused on Harlem, depicting an urban nightmare of litter-strewn empty lots, aging tenements and street violence. Shots of Nazerman's New York life are interspersed with flashbacks of his concentration-camp imprisonment. In a particularly chilling scene, a crowded subway car triggers the memory of a train bound for the concentration camp.[155] In scenes featuring Marilyn Birchfield (Geraldine Page), a sad, well-meaning social worker who tries to befriend Nazerman, Lumet captures the fearful respectability of life in the recently completed Lincoln Towers complex. The immense urban renewal project offers a bold if visually uninspiring contrast to Harlem's squalor, yet its painfully anonymous and monotonous design, rendered at enormous scale, embodies the impersonality of city life.

John Schlesinger's *Midnight Cowboy* (1969) offers a brutal portrait of a city whose emotional parameters are disappointment and alienation.[156] The film documents the adventures of Joe Buck (Jon Voight), a twenty-eight-year-old dishwasher from Texas who comes to New York with priapic fantasies of getting rich as a for-hire lover to the city's well-heeled and oversexed women. Buck is befriended by Ratzo Rizzo, a sleazy, Bronx-born swindler who becomes his pimp; the part was brilliantly played by Dustin Hoffman. Filmed mostly on location in New York, the movie captures the city's seedy side, concentrating on Forty-second Street and Times Square, where Buck eventually ends up hustling. Canby noted that when the film's "focus is on this world of cafeterias and abandoned tenements, of desperate conjunctions in movie balconies and doorways, of catchup and beans and canned heat . . . [it] is so rough and vivid that it's almost unbearable. You won't ever again feel detached as you walk down West 42nd Street, avoiding the eyes of the drifters, stepping around the little islands of hustlers and closing your nostrils to the smell of rancid griddles."[157]

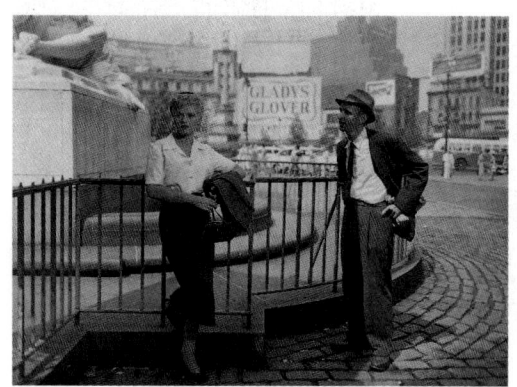

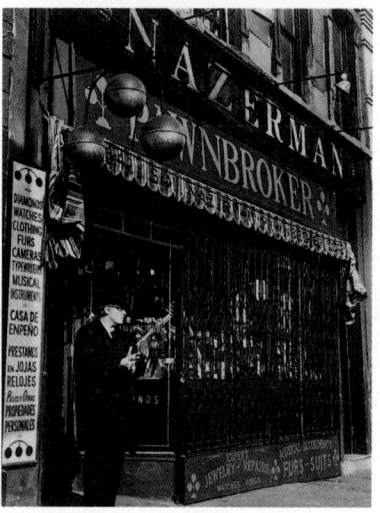

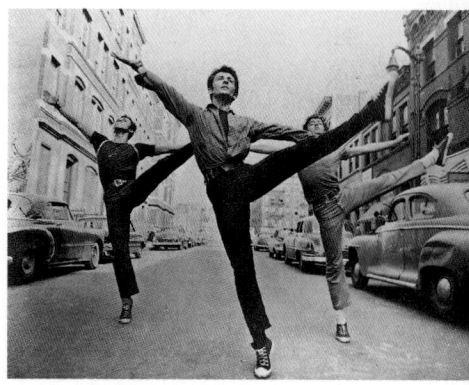

It Should Happen to You. 1953. Film still. Art director, John Meehan; director, George Cukor. MOMA

The Pawnbroker, 1965. Film still. Art director, Richard Sylbert; director, Sidney Lumet. MOMA

West Side Story, 1961. Film still. Production designer, Boris Leven; director, Robert Wise. MOMA

Out of the Melting Pot and into the Fire: Ethnic New York

During the postwar years, directors turned to an aspect of New York that had long been a hallmark of the city: its varied and often intensely colorful blend of ethnic groups. While some of these had been pictured in a folkloric way before, postwar filmmakers hit on the problems of assimilation, homogenization and prejudice. Director Elia Kazan's first film, *Gentleman's Agreement* (1947), squarely confronts anti-Semitism in America.[158] The film is set in New York but shot on Hollywood sound stages. Gregory Peck portrays the journalist Phil Green, who, as part of his research for an article on anti-Semitism, assumes a Jewish identity. The film depicts various swank locations, including the home of Green's well-heeled non-Jewish girlfriend, played by Jane Wyatt, who lives in an apartment with a terrace overlooking the East River. She also owns a spacious house in a Connecticut town where "restrictions" are commonplace.

Joseph L. Mankiewicz's *House of Strangers* (1949) offers a vivid portrait of a nouveau-riche Italian-American family. As an aggressive usurer who has raised himself out of the depths of the Lower East Side, "Papa" Gino Monetti (Edward G. Robinson) reigns over his family from an apartment in the Dakota (Henry J. Hardenbergh, 1882), a parvenu setting that Bosley Crowther described as "a horrendously vulgar uptown home."[159]

Sidney Lumet's *A View from the Bridge* (1962), which screenwriter Norman Rosten adapted from Arthur Miller's 1955 play, involves suppressed incestuous lust and ultimate betrayal within a working-class Italian-American family in Brooklyn.[160] Crowther lavishly praised the director's work, stating that he had done "all that was technically possible . . . to make a compelling motion picture" from the original play:

> [Lumet's] exteriors shot on-location on the Brooklyn waterfront and his interiors filmed in the harsh confinement of conspicuously realistic sets drenches the drama in a proletarian atmosphere so absolute and authentic that actuality seems to pulsate on the screen. The rambling and gritty quality of the Brooklyn waterfront, the lofty and mercantile authority of the freight ships tied up at the docks, the cluttered and crowded oppressiveness of the living rooms of the dockside slums are caught in

his camera's comprehension, to pound it into the viewer's head that this is an honest presentation of the sort of personal involvement that one might watch—might spy upon—through a telescope set on Brooklyn Bridge.[161]

In 1949 Jerome Robbins, Arthur Laurents and Leonard Bernstein began to toss around the idea of collaborating on a musical updating of Shakespeare's *Romeo and Juliet*.[162] The musical was to tell the story of an Italian boy and a Jewish girl living on Delancey Street on the Lower East Side. By the time the project got off the ground, the new story seemed not so new: the Italians and the Jews had moved on. In 1955 Laurents recast the idea in more contemporary terms: the proposed *East Side Story* became the *West Side Story* of a Polish-American boy and a Puerto Rican girl. The show, which opened on Broadway on September 26, 1957, was quickly hailed as an American classic; four years later Robert Wise and Jerome Robbins's film starring Natalie Wood, Richard Beymer and Rita Moreno was similarly deemed a landmark.[163] Only the film's opening shots were filmed on location, but sound-stage sets created the look and feel of the tenement-lined streets of the west side. Though the movie's story was as current as a newspaper headline, the actual film location—West Sixty-eighth Street between Amsterdam and West End avenues—would soon be history, not merely "renewed" but obliterated to make way for the superblock setting of the Lincoln Towers complex.

Arthur Hiller's *Popi* (1969), starring Alan Arkin and Rita Moreno, takes a more lighthearted look at the lives of the city's Puerto Rican population.[164] Arkin plays a poor widower who is trying to get his two young sons out of East Harlem. Howard Thompson, reviewing the film for the *New York Times*, praised "the pungent authenticity" of the scenes shot on location in Brooklyn and East Harlem: "The teaming tenement area . . . graphically conveyed in the swarming streets, the miserable apartments and the confining atmosphere, all have immediacy in the muted color photography."[165] Vincent Canby, however, contended that although the film seemed to be "the story of a desperate man in a desperate world," the settings "look about as desperate as Sophia Loren's Naples." Canby concluded that "the movie thus superimposes a perfectly respectable, though not very interesting, middle-class comedy form—a sort of 'Bringing

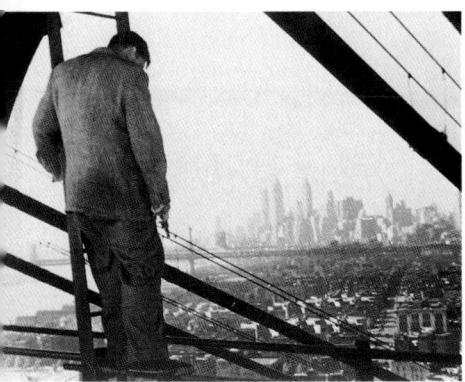

The Naked City, 1948. Film still. Art director, John F. DeCuir; director, Jules Dassin. MOMA

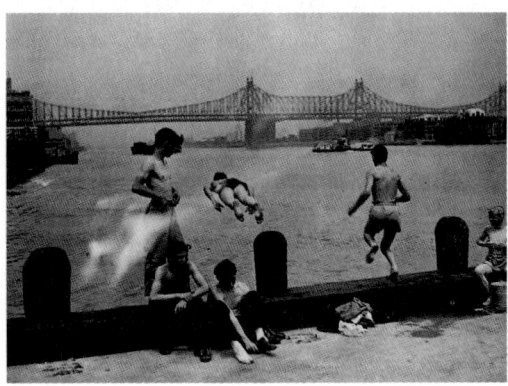

The Naked City. Film still. MOMA

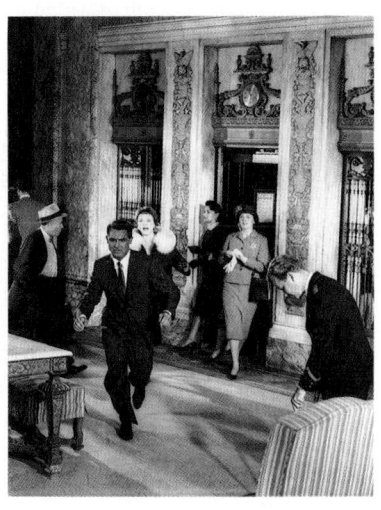

North by Northwest, 1959. Film still. Art director, William A. Horning; director, Alfred Hitchcock. ©1959 Turner Entertainment Co. All Rights Reserved. TEC

Up Father' ethic—on characters and situations trying to survive in the lower depths."[166]

In the late 1960s filmmakers focused on New York's Jewish community, adopting a biting or at least ironic tone. Sidney Lumet's *Bye Bye Braverman* (1968), based on Wallace Markfield's 1964 novel, *To an Early Grave*, satirically explores the lives of four middle-aged, second-generation American intellectuals and their responses to the premature death of a common friend.[167] Filmed entirely on location, the movie includes scenes shot in Brooklyn on Eastern and Ocean parkways, as well as in Williamsburg and in cemeteries in Queens. As film critic Renata Adler put it, Lumet "gets a chance to explore some Brooklyn neighborhoods and to show some Orthodox Jews in their relative Old Testament purity." Adler contended that "the photography, through some early shots of the city and some later shots of the rows of highwayside cemeteries on Long Island, certainly establishes the mortuary aspect of the New York skyline."[168]

In 1969 director Larry Peerce adapted Philip Roth's 1959 novella, *Goodbye Columbus*, about a romance between an earnest young Jewish man from a lower-middle-class neighborhood in Newark, New Jersey, and a spoiled young Jewish woman from the affluent suburban community of Short Hills, located nearby. The principal locations were changed so that Neil (Richard Benjamin) lives in an apartment house in the Bronx and his girlfriend, Brenda (Ali McGraw), lives in a large brick house in the Westchester County community of Larchmont. Three years later another work by Philip Roth would make it to the big screen. As directed by Ernest Lehman, the film adaptation of Roth's 1970 comic novel, *Portnoy's Complaint*, was widely dismissed as an unfunny, even offensive, Jewish joke. Canby further criticized the film for distorting the look and feel of New York, charging that scenes of the protagonist, played by Richard Benjamin, and his girlfriend, played by Karen Black, cavorting around the Upper East Side were so "dumbly romantic looking" that they resembled perfume ads.[169]

In the early 1970s filmmakers working in New York began to create mainstream films that dealt with black themes and used predominantly black casts. During the 1920s and 1930s a black film industry had arisen, but it had died out as black actors secured parts in mainstream films.[170] The one-hour "documen-

tary drama" *The Quiet One* (1949), directed by Sidney Meyers with a screenplay cowritten by Meyers, Helen Levitt and Janice Loeb with additional commentary by James Agee, was a film about black life in the city.[171] Narrated by Gary Merrill and using pickup actors and an untrained child in the title role, the movie documents the experiences of a ten-year-old black boy living in Harlem who is labeled a juvenile delinquent and sent to the Wiltwyck School for Boys in Esopus, New York. The gritty, unpretentious film was shot entirely on location, including, as Bosley Crowther put it, "the concrete streets of New York" and "sleazy Harlem apartments."[172] John McCarten stated that the protagonist's "surroundings are photographed with ruthless realism, and the various types he comes across while strolling along Harlem streets make an interesting aggregation for the camera. This sort of documentary walk has, of course, been taken by a good many cameras before, but never in a more interesting neighborhood."[173]

Dutchman (1967) features a screenplay that LeRoi Jones adapted from his own one-act play of 1964.[174] Directed by Anthony Harvey and filmed on a New York subway car, the movie consists of a dialogue between a psychotic white woman, played by Shirley Knight, and a credulous black man, played by Al Freeman, Jr. The woman's tone fluctuates between friendly, seductive and abusive. When the man eventually expresses his rage, verbally attacking his provocateur, she responds by stabbing him. The crime is witnessed by several other passengers, all of whom remain silent. Jones clearly intended the piece to read as a comment on race relations in America, as epitomized by the situation in New York.

Brian DePalma's *Hi, Mom!* (1970), filmed entirely in Greenwich Village, savagely lampoons the "radical chic" of upper-middle-class liberals amid the dismal state of race relations in New York.[175] The film's protagonist, Jon Rubin (Robert DeNiro), is a failed pornographic filmmaker turned insurance salesman who so thoroughly identifies with society's outcasts that he becomes a member of a radical, all-black theater group whose actors mingle among the politically liberal white audience members and then proceed to rob, assault and rape them. The penultimate scene shows Rubin packing dynamite into a washing machine in the basement laundry room of the apartment building in Washington Square Village where he and his wife live. The building is destroyed and its occupants, including Rubin's wife, are killed; the violence was a curious parallel of the real-life explosion of a townhouse at 18 West Eleventh Street, which was bombed by student radicals seven weeks before the film's release (see chapter 16).

Hal Ashby's *The Landlord* (1970) provides another hard-hitting image.[176] The film tells of a rich young white man (Beau Bridges) who asserts his independence from his family by purchasing an occupied tenement building on Prospect Place, Brooklyn, which the black film critic Clayton Riley waggishly described as·an "urban plantation."[177] Filmed on location, the movie reveals the contradictions and ironies inherent in the protagonist's efforts to reconcile two worlds.

In 1970 the black author and actor Ossie Davis broke ground in his directorial debut by creating a film with black protagonists that appealed to white audiences as entertainment. *Cotton Comes to Harlem* is based on a comic mystery novel by Chester Himes featuring the detectives Coffin Ed Johnson and Grave Digger Jones, played in the film by Raymond St. Jacques and Godfrey Cambridge.[178] Despite being filmed entirely on location in Harlem, Vincent Canby felt that, "aside from its honest black idioms and actors, 'Cotton Comes to Harlem' is a conventional white movie that employs terrible white stereotypes of black life. Its soul looks very much like rhythm."[179]

Shaft (1971), directed by the well-known black *Life* photographer Gordon Parks, introduced a tough-talking, pistol-packing sexually athletic black New York private eye, played by Richard Roundtree, to a broad audience.[180] The hugely popular movie also established a film genre that capitalized on the stereotypical view of black men as more virile than their white counterparts; this led to the denunciation of *Shaft* and other films like it as "Blaxploitation."[181] Despite pressure from studio executives to shoot the film in Hollywood, Parks insisted on filming in New York; he later explained that "Hollywood wasn't Harlem with its hard, gritty atmosphere. Shooting beneath palm trees wasn't shooting beneath the tired tenements around 116th Street."[182] The film's main character, John Shaft, maintains a threadbare office near Times Square and, as Canby put it, a "book-lined, stereo-equipped Village duplex [where he] keeps his extra gun (the one with the pearl handle) in the fridge,"[183] but much of the film's action takes place in Harlem. Roger Greenspun noted how the protagonist's color serves his role as a risk-taking New York hero: "For who better than a black man . . . to have that freedom of the city that is the point of the detective film and that, at least where many of us live, is no longer a right freely granted to anyone named Marlowe or Harper or even Madigan." Greenspun added that Parks "showed a grace in putting the horror of the city to the purposes of entertainment that seems especially welcome considering the options."[184] The black critic Clayton Riley, however, found the movie "a disaster" that promulgated lies about black life in New York. As an example, Riley cited a scene near the film's end:

> As Shaft prepares to pull off a heavy rescue caper, he calls the Harlem vice king who hired him and asks him to have four cabs waiting on a rainy Greenwich Village street at a certain hour. These are to be the all-important getaway cars. . . . Gordon Parks, come on. What Black man would be naive enough to think one taxi, let alone four, will stop to take some Negroes back to Harlem in the middle of the night? Think about it.[185]

Among the "son-of-Shaft" films shot in New York is Parks's *Shaft's Big Score* (1972), distinguished only by a climactic chase scene—by car, speedboat and helicopter—commencing in a Long Island cemetery and winding up on the shores of Brooklyn.[186] Filmed on location in Brooklyn's Bedford-Stuyvesant section, Parks's *The Super Cops* (1974) is based on the real-life experiences of two unconventional policemen—one black, one white—who called themselves Batman and Robin and, while off-duty, foiled a drug syndicate.[187] The film critic A. H. Weiler discredited the simplistic *Black Caesar* (1973), directed by Larry Cohen and starring Fred Williamson in the title role, stating that the movie "may have been shot in fine colors in Harlem and elsewhere but its bullet-filled contents are unbelievably black and white."[188] Greenspun found that Barry Shear's violent drug-war tale, *Across 110th Street* (1972), starring Anthony Quinn and Yaphet·Kotto and shot on location in Harlem, "really does exploit its situations and its actors and even its violence, in a desperate rip-off of the latest news about the death of our cities."[189] To Howard Thompson, Ossie Davis's *Gordon's War* (1973), which tells the story of four black Vietnam veterans attempting to stop New York drug lords, managed to capture "the argot, the flavor and sinister ambiance" of "the crime-ridden underbelly of Harlem," but achieved little else as either art or political statement.[190] Michael Campus's *The Education of Sonny Carson* (1974) depicts a young black gang leader in Brooklyn who becomes a political activist.[191] Starring Rony Clanton, Don Gordon and Joyce Walker, the film was shot entirely on location in Bedford-Stuyvesant. Lawrence Van Gelder, writing in the *New York Times*, characterized the movie as a "howling brute of a film [that] possesses very real beauty and power."[192]

New York: Crime Central

Postwar life in the city was increasingly defined by one phenomenon above all: crime. In the 1940s filmmakers used New York as a suitable but largely coincidental locale for murder stories. By the 1960s filmmakers were exploring crime not as a series of isolated events but as the obsessive reality of daily life in the city. The city was depicted more and more not merely as the setting for criminal activity but as its cause.

S. Sylvan Simon's mystery-comedy *Grand Central Murder* (1942) treats its subject with a light touch. So unthreatening is the fictitious event that Bosley Crowther could recommend it "as a pleasant diversion—say, between trains."[193] Lew Landers's *Murder in Times Square* (1943) is similarly light entertainment that Lewis B. Funke described as "neither too troublesome nor overdepressing."[194] Otto Preminger's *Laura* (1944), based on Vera Caspary's novel, stars Gene Tierney, Dana Andrews, Clifton Webb and Vincent Price in a tale of seduction, betrayal and murder set in New York but filmed in Hollywood.[195] The action unfolds in the middle of a hot summer when the heat, combined with wartime blackouts and air-raid drills, gives the city a decidedly infernolike quality. As directed by Henry Hathaway, *Kiss of Death* (1947), with a screenplay by Ben Hecht and Charles Lederer, offers a better-than-average crime story shot exclusively on location in New York, principally in Manhattan.[196]

The Naked City (1948) was the most compelling of the New York crime films made immediately after World War II.[197] This brilliant film noir, produced by Mark Hellinger, who for many years had written about the city for the *New York Daily Mirror*, was directed by Jules Dassin. Shot at 107 locations throughout the city by the superb cinematographer William Daniels, the film includes a narration spoken by Hellinger, who died in December 1947 while the film was in post-production. Because it includes footage shot through one-way glass by cameras hidden in a moving van, and features non-Hollywood actors and nonprofessional extras, *The Naked City* is characterized by a realism comparable to that of Roberto Rossellini's *Open City* (1945), which documents Rome as it emerged from Fascism. But *The Naked City* is not a political tract. It depicts an everyday world torn apart by the madness of murder. In the opening sequence, while a night-shift cleaning lady vacuums the lobby of the Roxy Theater (Walter Ahlschlager, 1927),[198] Hellinger informs the audience that "there are eight million stories in the Naked City." Inspector Dan Muldoon, played by Barry Fitzgerald, supervises a team of detectives trying to solve the murder of a woman living in an apartment building at 52 West Eighty-third Street. Muldoon works in the Tenth Precinct station house at 230 West Twentieth Street, which Hellinger described as "a rather shabby building on a rather shabby street."[199] The climatic chase scene through the Lower East Side ends in a dramatically shot sequence on the Williamsburg Bridge. *The Naked City* is a poison-pen valentine to the city itself, a penetrating look at its seamy side and an homage to its heroic scale and complexity. As Crowther stated in his *New York Times* review: "Hellinger's personal romance with the City of New York was one of the most ecstatic love affairs of the modern day. . . . 'The Naked City' . . . is a rambling, romantic picture-story based on a composite New York episode. . . . And it is also a fancifully selective observation of life in New York's streets, police stations, apartments, tenements, playgrounds, decks, bridges and flashy resorts."[200]

While John McCarten acknowledged that "a good many realistic views of Manhattan, pinned down by a competent camera, distinguish 'The Naked City,'" he complained that "Mr. Hellinger's remarks are about as penetrating as the spiel of a guide on a sightseeing bus, and the film resorts to all kinds of flummery to force the real complexities of New York to conform to the simple and sentimental concept of the city so often set forth in Broadway columns."[201] Seeing the film for the first time some thirty years after its completion, the literary critic Morris Dickstein felt like "Proust munching on the madeleine," as he explained:

> These crowded streets of the Lower East Side, with their grimy tenements and narrow sidewalks, their tiny candy stores, push-cart peddlers, and slope-backed cars, gave me back some vivid images from my childhood. Here was Columbia Street, where my father grew up and his brothers lived; wide Delancey Street, with its grand movie palace and innumerable lanes of traffic leading onto the Williamsburg Bridge on which the film's brilliant climactic chase takes place. Here was the city itself as it appeared in the 1940s, the real protagonist of the movie.[202]

The memorable film served as the inspiration for a popular television series produced from 1958 to 1963.[203]

Abraham Polonsky's *Force of Evil* (1948) is a tough film about a lawyer's efforts to legalize gambling in New York as his numbers-runner brother descends into a world of crime and ultimately murder.[204] According to Crowther, the film, which stars John Garfield as the lawyer, commented on "lust for the dangerous and unknown . . . in startling situations and in graphic dialogue, in shattering cinematic glimpses and in great, dramatic sweeps of New York background."[205] Among the memorable

on-location shots is the final, devastating image of the lawyer finding his brother's dead body floating in the Hudson River beneath the soaring towers of the George Washington Bridge (Othmar Herman Ammann, 1926–31).[206] Anatole Litvak's *Sorry, Wrong Number* (1948), with a screenplay that Lucille Fletcher based on her own radio drama, involves a plot to murder a wealthy, bedridden woman, played by Barbara Stanwyck. Through a series of telephone mix-ups the victim learns that the crime will coincide with a train's crossing the Queensboro Bridge.[207] The helpless woman watches for the train from the window of her Sutton Place townhouse; here the city's constant movement takes on a ghoulish cast.

Anthony Mann's *Side Street* (1950) is a documentary-style account of attempted robbery that includes a chase scene shot on location in lower Manhattan; Crowther found the film "played for considerable realism against the actuality background of New York."[208] Otto Preminger's *Where the Sidewalk Ends* (1950) tells of a sadistically inclined detective who accidentally commits a murder and subsequently tries to pin it on a mobster. Howard Thompson felt that the film's "expert photography . . . resulted in a most vivid blend of action and New York City backgrounds."[209] William Wyler's *Detective Story* (1951), with a screenplay adapted from Sidney Kingsley's 1949 play by Phillip Yordan and Robert Wyler and starring Kirk Douglas, is a gripping film noir that is, as Crowther put it, "long on graphic demonstration of the sort of raffish traffic that flows through a squad-room of plainclothes detectives in a New York police station-house."[210] Samuel Fuller's *Pickup on South Street* (1953), starring Richard Widmark as a grifter who physically abuses his girlfriend, offers, according to Crowther, a "highly embroidered presentation of a slice of life in the New York underworld."[211]

Alfred Hitchcock's gripping *Rear Window* (1954) functions as both a taut murder mystery and a brilliant psychological study of New Yorkers.[212] Jimmy Stewart plays Jeff, a globe-trotting photojournalist whose broken leg confines him to his Greenwich Village apartment. To pass the time, he watches his neighbors in the buildings across the courtyard, first through a camera equipped with a telephoto lens and later through binoculars, and eventually he becomes fixated on one neighbor, a brutish man who he comes to believe has murdered his wife. Although the film was shot exclusively in Hollywood, the set is nonetheless a carefully detailed, credible re-creation of a typical Greenwich Village scene. Crowther saw the film as a middle-class version of Elmer Rice's play *Street Scene* (1929; film version, directed by King Vidor, 1931), but "viewed from the back instead of the front."[213]

Hitchcock followed his claustrophobic *Rear Window* with the chillingly realistic *The Wrong Man* (1956), filmed largely in New York and based on a true story.[214] In the spring of 1953 a Stork Club musician named Christopher Emanuel was arrested in his Jackson Heights home and charged with having committed a series of armed robberies in the area. Despite numerous positive identifications, Emanuel (Henry Fonda) maintained that he was innocent, a claim that was ultimately proven true when the real criminal confessed. According to A. H. Weiler, the film had a "quasi-documentary style," incorporating a great deal of on-location photography, including sequences at the Stork Club and in the IND subway line's Fifth Avenue and Roosevelt Avenue stations, as well as throughout Jackson Heights. Shots of actual residential interiors vividly document daily life in that largely working-class neighborhood.

Twelve Angry Men (1957), which screenwriter Reginald Rose adapted from his own television play of 1954, was Sidney

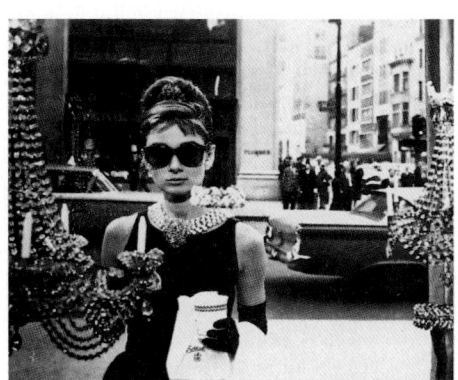

Breakfast at Tiffany's, 1961. Film still. Director, Blake Edwards. MOMA

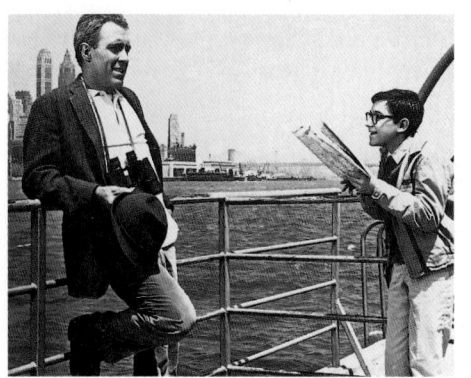

A Thousand Clowns, 1965. Film still. Set designers, Herbert Mulligan and George DeTitta; director, Fred Coe. MOMA

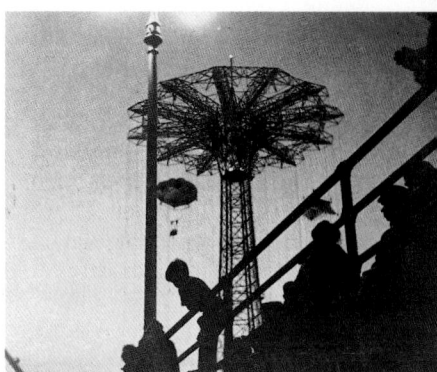

Little Fugitive, 1953. Film still. Directors, Ray Ashley, Morris Engel and Ruth Orkin. MOMA

Lumet's first directorial effort in film.[215] A gripping tale of murder seen from the various viewpoints of the members of a jury, the film was photographed primarily on location in New York, including scenes at the New York County Courthouse (Guy Lowell, 1926),[216] by the cameraman Boris Kaufman.

In Alfred Hitchcock's *North by Northwest* (1959), a picaresque, quintessentially Hitchcockian tour of the United States begins in New York, where the film's unlikely hero, an impeccably tailored, totally conventional advertising executive played by Cary Grant, is mistaken for an FBI agent by foreign spies.[217] The movie's opening sequence shows Grant leaving his office in the CIT Building, walking north on Madison Avenue, and getting into a cab that travels west, immediately establishing the direction of the cross-country action indicated by the film's title. When he arrives at the Plaza Hotel, he inadvertently becomes involved in the web of espionage. The Plaza sequence and subsequent on-location footage shot at Grand Central Terminal and the United Nations headquarters portray New York as a glamorous, bustling city.

Terence Young's taut thriller *Wait until Dark* (1967) tells of a group of thugs who terrorize a blind woman (Audrey Hepburn) while searching for a stash of heroin.[218] The movie, based on Frederick Knott's successful play of the same name, which opened on Broadway in 1966, incorporates on-location shots of Greenwich Village, including an apartment at 4 St. Luke's Place. Against the quiet domesticity of the West Village, the gang's evildoings take on an even more sinister tone.

Don Siegel's *Blindfold* (1966) is a film about a New York psychologist (Rock Hudson) who gets tangled up in a suspense caper.[219] The film, partially shot on location, includes one visually interesting scene in which Hudson gets yanked from a cantering horse during a spirited ride through Central Park. Siegel's *Madigan* (1968), starring Richard Widmark in the title role of a hard-boiled detective, is a skillfully executed if not particularly distinctive crime-beat yarn. Howard Thompson, reviewing the film for the *New York Times*, noted that "the color photography continually stamps the incidents with the authentic familiarity of various facades and corners of New York."[220] Also released in 1968 was another crime film directed by Siegel, *Coogan's Bluff*, starring Clint Eastwood as a tough Arizona sheriff named Coogan who goes to New York to extradite an alleged criminal for trial in Arizona.[221] The film was shot at numerous locations, including Tavern on the Green and the Cloisters.[222] To Vincent Canby, the movie's "mythic hero . . . looks as out of place in Manhattan as Tarzan might, since he is constantly being upstaged by more colorful minor characters and the restless scenery of the big city."[223]

Sidney Lumet's *Serpico* (1973) is based on the real experiences of Frank Serpico, an unconventional detective with the New York Police Department who investigated and ultimately exposed widespread corruption. Serpico, played by Al Pacino, lives on the western fringes of bohemian Greenwich Village but works in the South Bronx, a location Lumet exploits as the quintessential urban battleground. The film was shot exclusively on location in New York, "a city," Canby noted, "that Lumet knows better than any other director working today."[224]

Martin Scorsese's *Mean Streets* (1973), starring Robert DeNiro and Harvey Keitel, presents an uncompromising look at Mafiosi activity in Little Italy, where the director grew up.[225] Shot principally on location (some New York scenes were actually shot in Los Angeles), in part during the annual San Gennaro festival, the film portrays the area and its social milieu as at once gritty and poetic. The New York Mafiosi's world of money, power, loyalty and retribution was given another powerful treatment in Francis Ford Coppola's *The Godfather* (1972)[226] and its sequel, also directed by Coppola, *The Godfather, Part II* (1975).[227] Both were partially shot on location in New York. For the first film, an enclave of Tudor-style houses in the Todt Hill area of Staten Island is used to portray the Long Island home of the fictitious Corleone family. The second film includes historical scenes, treated as flashbacks, that take place in lower Manhattan.

By the mid-1970s the tone of many New York crime films had changed dramatically to reflect broad trends in entertainment standards and audience tastes and the realities of daily life in the city. In these films, violent crime is viewed neither as a deliberate act of one person on another nor as the by-product of war between organized groups of gangsters but as a societal illness, a malevolent virus as likely to affect one innocent person as another. Michael Winner's sensationally violent *Death Wish*

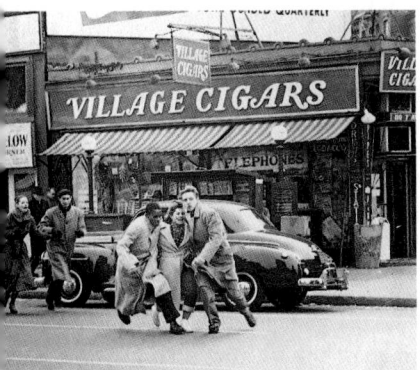

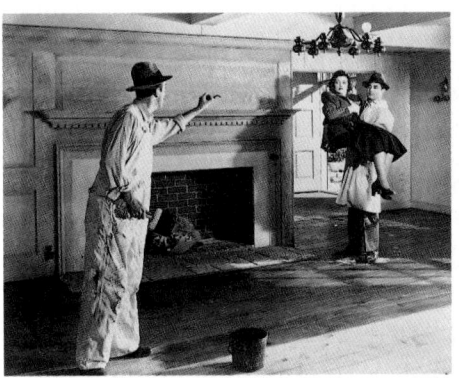

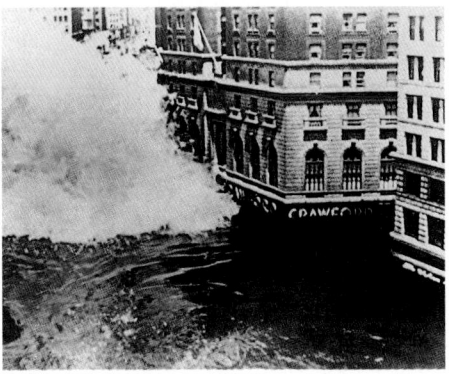

Next Stop, Greenwich Village, 1976. Film still. Production designer, Phil Rosenberg; director, Paul Mazursky. MOMA

Mr. Blandings Builds His Dream House, 1948. Film still. Art director, Albert S. D'Agostino; director, H. C. Potter. MOMA

When Worlds Collide, 1951. Film still. Art director, Hal Pereira; director, Rudolph Maté. MOMA

(1974) depicts a New York, as Vincent Canby put it, "so filled with vandals, would-be muggers, rapists and the like" that the film "seems to have been made for no reason except to exploit its audience's urban paranoia and vestigial fascination with violence for its own sake."[228] The film tells of a successful, politically liberal architect, played by Charles Bronson, who, after his wife is murdered and his daughter traumatized by a group of muggers, becomes a highly skillful vigilante. Although it effectively uses location shots of numerous Upper West Side venues, including the cavernous hall of the Central Savings Bank (York & Sawyer, 1928),[229] the Eighty-first Street station of the IND Eighth Avenue subway line, and the architect's apartment at 33 Riverside Drive (George F. Pelham, 1927), as well as the TWA Terminal at Kennedy Airport, 2 Park Avenue (Buchman & Kahn, 1926–27)[230] and the Oyster Bar in Grand Central Terminal, the film offers a wildly distorted view of the city. As Canby put it, the movie shows a New York so crime-ridden that "Charlie never goes home without scoring. On streets, in parks, in subway cars. It's like shooting ducks in a bird sanctuary." Characterizing the film as "despicable," Canby concluded, "I have no doubt that muggers, especially, will find it a great deal of fun."[231] *New Yorker* critic Penelope Gilliatt also commented on the film's negative impact:

[The] film is given over to characters who voice every bigotry about New York that runs rampant in the rest of the world, which seems to believe that New York's upper middle classes had better move posthaste to the suburbs before their wives are raped or their children learn Spanish, and that the bums who make up the rest of the city are just "freeloading off welfare" with a switchblade in every pocket. . . . One is hardly likely to forget this film's blasphemous dislike of New York. Evacuate the streets, it says, in effect; decimate the population by killing it off to bring down the crime rate; give every law-abiding citizen a gun to show the police how to do their work. "Death Wish" is full of fallacies.[232]

Law and Disorder (1974), the second American film by Czechoslovakian director Ivan Passer, takes a humanist and humorous look at the efforts of individual citizens to cope with the city's sometimes daunting crime problem.[233] The lyrical film traces the adventures of two aging residents of the Lower East Side's Corlears Hook Houses (Carroll O'Connor and Ernest Borgnine) who form a citizen's security unit to police their housing project. Canby, who found the film to be "a poet's appreciation of lives lived on the edge of the precipice by people whose finger-holds are giving out," argued that it constituted a new type of New York movie.[234] He explained:

Passer starts his film with a long, leisurely, horizontal pan shot along the New York skyline, then cuts to a series of uproariously outrageous crimes taking place within that city. The old-time movie about New York might open with a stockshot of Manhattan seen from the air, followed by a slow pan down the side of a tall building (sometimes the Empire State Building), ending with a quick dissolve to a California studio and a familiar, much-used, city street set. Passer eases directly into a real New York in his film, which is less about individual character than about coping nowhere else but in New York City. . . . "Law and Disorder," which attempts to capture the desperation, humor, squalor, confusion and frustration of living in New York, could not have been conceived as a studio film.[235]

Sydney Pollack's *Three Days of the Condor* (1975), a suspenseful, fictional story of corruption within the Central Intelligence Agency, uses numerous on-locations sequences, including some scenes filmed at the World Trade Center, the Guggenheim Museum, the Promenade in Brooklyn Heights, the Ansonia Hotel and Central Park, to create a striking urban backdrop.[236] John Schlesinger used New York as a battleground for a to-the-death struggle between an ex-Nazi (Laurence Olivier) and a Columbia University graduate student (Dustin Hoffman) in *Marathon Man* (1976).[237] On-location photography features Columbia, the Andrew Carnegie house (Babb, Cook & Willard, 1899–1902),[238] the diamond district on Forty-seventh Street, the Brooklyn Bridge and the Central Park reservoir, as well as the interior of one of the reservoir's pump houses. In discussing the film, Canby asked: "Are the audiences . . . who cheer and laugh during some of the rougher moments of 'Marathon Man,' reacting to a metaphor or to violence as style? . . . The latter, I suspect. After all, violence . . . may be defined as nothing more than the extreme form of rudeness, and rudeness is more or less how New Yorkers live."[239]

While many films depicting crime in New York adopted a cynical and sometimes even nihilistic point of view, other postwar movies used the serious subject as a source of comedy. Jack Smight's *No Way to Treat a Lady* (1968) is pure slapstick. A Broadway producer, played by Rod Steiger, dons a wide variety of disguises to gain access to the apartments of single women in order to murder them. "Luckily," Canby wrote, "despite the fact that [the film] was beautifully photographed in color entirely in New York, it has absolutely no reality."[240] Alan Arkin's *Little Murders* (1971), about a New York woman murdered on her wedding night, could be seen as an extended metaphor for life in the city.[241] Using a screenplay that the author and cartoonist Jules Feiffer based on his own 1967 stage play, the dark comedy, shot principally on location in New York, documents daily life in claustrophobic apartments and on menacing streets. Canby wrote that the film, "instead of miniaturizing a world . . . magnifies the geography of the human soul, presenting it, in macrocosm, as New York City, a territory of treacherous labyrinths, of dangers suspected but never seen, of sudden, unreasonable explosions, of dimouts, brownouts and blackouts, a place enslaved in frustration and finally freed in rage."[242] Pauline Kael also saw the film as reflecting the nightmarish quality of New York life:

> We do, increasingly, view the day as an obstacle course, and when we hear ourselves describing the madwoman who jabbed at us with an umbrella, or the screams in Central Park, or the muggers on both sides of the street on warm nights divvying up the passersby, we know that we probably sound paranoid. Normal life does seem to have gone mad. . . . Our lives have become a psychopathic comedy, so we are prepared to laugh at Feiffer's jokes—perhaps even overprepared.[243]

Filmed at various locations in Brooklyn, including DeGraw Street in Red Hook, and Kennedy Airport in Queens, James Goldstone's *The Gang that Couldn't Shoot Straight* (1971), with a screenplay by Waldo Salt based on Jimmy Breslin's 1969 comic novel of the same name, spoofs the activities of small-time Mafiosi. Although he found little to like about the film, *New York Times* movie critic Howard Thompson said that "Brooklyn, there in the background, looks real enough."[244] Peter Yates's *The Hot Rock* (1972) is a high-spirited crime caper that in an odd way boosted Brooklyn's status by focusing on an attempted gem heist at the Brooklyn Museum (McKim, Mead & White, 1895–1915), where much of the film was shot.[245]

Aram Avakian's comic film *Cops and Robbers* (1973) chronicles the illegal activities of two policemen who, as Greenspun put it, "though tied to pregnant wives, the Long Island Expressway and plastic swimming pools in the backyard . . . dream of better, or at least richer things." Greenspun asserted that the film was "the first movie in a long time to understand, rather than merely exploit, its New York City locales."[246]

"You'd Have to Be Crazy to Live There": Offbeat New York

Among the many types of New Yorkers portrayed in postwar films were those who simply marched to the beat of a different drummer, unconventional individuals who did not merely add to the city's complexity but internalized it, reveled in it and were nurtured by it. In the late 1950s New York's identity as a haven for benign misfits achieved its full cinematic destiny. The title character of Morton DaCosta's *Auntie Mame* (1958) is an eccentric par excellence. Starring Rosalind Russell, the film, with a screenplay by Betty Comden and Adolph Green, is based on Patrick Dennis's semiautobiographical novel, which had also inspired a stage play starring Russell.[247] The dramatic flair and the flighty nature of the wealthy, sophisticated protagonist, whom Crowther described as a "Beekman Place maharanee," are apparent in her Hollywood-set apartment, whose "lavish decor," Crowther noted "is changed almost as frequently as are her flashy costumes."[248] Predictably, Mame's taste in interior decoration runs to the exotic and ultra-modern.

In the 1961 film *Breakfast at Tiffany's*, based on Truman Capote's novella of 1958, Blake Edwards depicts the city as an enchanted place inhabited by gloriously offbeat if amoral characters: the perfect home, indeed the only viable home, for lovable misfits.[249] Capote's protagonist, Lulamae Barnes (Audrey Hepburn), may have been born in Tulip, Texas, but only in Manhattan could she have remade herself as the unforgettable Holly Golightly. She lives in a brownstone apartment at 171 East Seventy-first Street, between Lexington and Third avenues, which A. H. Weiler described in the *New York Times* as "amazingly half-furnished . . . complete with a bath-tub-like sofa and a striped alley cat."[250] Living in the same charmingly down-at-the-heels brownstone is Holly's neighbor, a young writer (George Peppard) with whom she falls in love. Location shots of the Upper East Side, as well as of the exterior and main selling floor of Tiffany & Company (Cross & Cross, 1940), add a measure of reality to this urban fairy tale.

New York is similarly though less scintillatingly portrayed as a bohemian haven in Robert Wise's film adaptation of William Gibson's two-character comic play, *Two for the Seesaw* (1962), starring Robert Mitchum and Shirley MacLaine.[251] Though the film effectively uses a split screen in several sequences, its on-location shots are relatively uninspired, causing Crowther to complain that Wise "has photographed his action (and inaction) in a naturalistic type, viewing New York and its bohemians in arid black-and-white."[252]

Written, produced and directed by Jack O'Connell, the cinema verité *Greenwich Village Story* (1965), starring Robert Hogan and Melinda Plank, tells of a struggling young writer's life and romantic entanglements.[253] The rather hackneyed treatment is given a degree of verisimilitude by on-location photography. A. H. Weiler noted:

> With the aid of the principals and the unwitting citizens of Manhattan's Bohemia who never previously faced cameras professionally, and with the excellent assistance of his photographer, Baird Bryant, Mr. O'Connell has roamed the bars and beatnik caverns, the dingy pads and lofts and the colorful, clangorous confines of Washington Square Park and Bleecker Street to come up with a Cook's Tour that is both picturesque and germane to his tale of young love and desire for a place in the arts in Gotham.[254]

Stefan Shariff's *Across the River* (1965) is a leisurely, lyrical portrayal of the forgotten industrial fringes of Queens, where an elderly vagrant, Obadiah (Lou Gilbert), lives in a lumberyard on the bank of the East River. Obadiah survives by tending a goat and selling its milk to the custodian of a posh riverside apartment building in Manhattan, and by collecting scraps of cloth that he peddles to Lower East Side merchants. Crowther noted that Obadiah is "simply one of New York's countless oddballs, a happy and harmless old man. This is all quite graphic and guileless, a pretty scanning of the East River scene, with a standard intermingling of seagulls, wistful water-watchers and lounging bums."[255]

A Thousand Clowns (1965), directed by Fred Coe, depicts efforts by the Child Welfare Bureau to put into foster care a ten-year-old boy who lives with his irresponsible but lovable and loving uncle (Jason Robards).[256] Crowther felt the film's panoramic, traveloguelike on-location sequences added little to the story: "Somehow these cinematic splashes of action and atmosphere, which are bright in themselves, seem extraneous and unharmonious with the long and stagy scenes of kooky but constructed conversation that take place mainly in one room. It is as though the interludes are but filling to suggest the look and the frenzy of New York that are already well enough suggested in the deliciously erratic dialogue."[257] Brendan Gill, reviewing the film for the *New Yorker*, had a different take, praising the film's depiction of "the streets and docks and rivers and parks and skyscrapers of our incomparable Manhattan, marvellously photographed by Arthur J. Ornitz and Joe Coffee; on film, as in life, it is a fine place to be."[258]

A peculiar pair of roommates is the focus of Gene Saks's 1968 film adaptation of Neil Simon's 1965 Broadway hit, *The Odd Couple*, which tells of two men, Oscar Madison (Walter Matthau) and Felix Unger (Jack Lemmon), both estranged from their wives, who decide to share a Riverside Drive apartment. Though the movie incorporates on-location photography, including shots of a seedy hotel on West Forty-seventh Street where Unger finds refuge before moving in with Madison, the action takes place largely on a set designed by Robert Benton and Ray Moyer, depicting a prototypical prewar Upper West Side apartment, which the critic Renata Adler found "very convincing."[259] Two years later, when the play was transformed into a highly successful television situation comedy that ran for five years, Madison and Unger, played by Jack Klugman and Tony Randall, respectively, shared an apartment at 1049 Park Avenue.[260]

In *Rosemary's Baby* (1968), starring Mia Farrow and based on Ira Levin's best-selling novel of 1967, Roman Polanski raised the level of New York eccentricity to new heights.[261] It is the story of a young, demure, pregnant newlywed, Rosemary Woodhouse, who, with her actor husband, moves into an old Upper West Side apartment building and befriends an elderly couple who, it turns out, are not merely kooky but are a bona fide witch and warlock. The imposing, almost brooding forms of the chateaulike apartment building, called the Bramford in the film but actually the Dakota, powerfully mirror the story's darkness. In fact, Polanski later said his intention was that "the real star of the picture would be the New York apartment where Rosemary and Guy go to live."[262] Two weeks of location shooting augmented extensive filming on a superbly crafted set that re-created a Dakota apartment, supervised by the production designer Dick Sylbert and built on the Paramount Studio back lot in Hollywood.

City Kids

Tales of children and coming of age have long fascinated movie audiences. In New York City these rites of passage are bound to be especially complex and intriguing. Maxwell Shane's *City Across the River* (1949) presents the tough Brooklyn neighborhood of Brownsville as a breeding ground for juvenile delinquency.[263] Shot on location, the film, which stars Tony Curtis, focuses on teenage gang members who kill a high school teacher. By filming on Brooklyn streets, Crowther noted, "Mr. Shane has caught the atmosphere . . . of a teeming city."[264]

Little Fugitive (1953), a low-budget film written, directed and produced by three photojournalists, Ray Ashley, Morris Engel and Ruth Orkin, uses the colorful background of Coney Island and Bensonhurst to document the adventures of a charming and resourceful seven-year-old boy who takes off on his own after mistakenly believing he has killed his older brother.[265] The film presents the city as a playland for an imaginative child. George Roy Hill's 1964 film *The World of Henry Orient* takes a similarly buoyant look at the city and its youth.[266] With a screenplay based on Nora Johnson's 1958 novel and cowritten by Nora and her father, Nunnally Johnson, the film tells of two affluent teenage girls who become gleefully obsessed with a pretentious pianist who calls himself Henry Orient (Peter Sellers). Much of the film was shot on location in Manhattan, including sequences filmed in Central Park and Carnegie Hall. In discussing the film, Brendan Gill said that "the directors of photography, Boris Kaufman and Arthur J. Ornitz, deserve our thanks for portraying the island as the beautiful impossibility that, on its best days, it manifestly is."[267]

In 1967 twenty-seven-year-old Francis Ford Coppola directed *You're a Big Boy Now*, for which he also wrote the screenplay, based on a novel by David Benedictus.[268] Filmed exclusively on location in New York, the old-fashioned tale involves a young man's attempts to grow up and free himself of his parents. Howard Thompson commented in his *New York Times* review that "Mr. Coppola figure skates his picture all over town, which has never looked more radiantly scenic—the gleeming cavern of the reading-room in the main Public Library, the lustrously carpeted Central Park, the spangled night facade of 42nd Street and quaint Greenwich Village byways. No wonder the credits salute Mayor Lindsay's helping hand."[269] In 1968 the twenty-eight-year-old director Brian DePalma released *Greetings*, a film that Thompson characterized as a "comic-strip movie romp," following three young men as they wander around Manhattan and parts of New Jersey encountering young women and satirizing a wide variety of contemporary topics, from the Warren Commission to draft dodging.[270]

Fred Coe's *Me, Natalie* (1969) is a downbeat movie about the trials of a girl (Patty Duke) whose hackneyed search for a more meaningful life begins at her parents' outer-borough nest and ends in a Greenwich Village apartment. Vincent Canby was particularly critical of the film's on-location photography:

> In New York-made movies there is a tendency toward the overuse of the "in-transit" scene. To take advantage of geography, characters spend an inordinate amount of time simply getting from one spot to another. In a studio movie, it would be a fast cut. Also, characters don't face crises or reach understandings in kitchens or bedrooms or even bathrooms. Like pigeons, they fly off to Central Park. When Natalie decides to drown herself . . . she goes all the way to Long Island City, where, of course, she has the towers of Manhattan as a backdrop. What is meant to be a funny-sad scene becomes, instead, scenic.[271]

Despite being filmed entirely in New York and largely on the Columbia University campus, Leonard Horn's *The Magic Garden of Stanley Sweetheart* (1970), which stars Don Johnson in the title role of an amorous Columbia College junior, has little sense of reality. The screenplay, which Robert T. Westbrook based on his own 1969 novel, makes no reference to Columbia's widely publicized and ongoing student unrest, nor to the pervasive issues of the Vietnam War and the draft.[272] In contrast, Stanley Hagmann's *The Strawberry Statement* (1970), with a screenplay by playwright Israel Horowitz, was based on

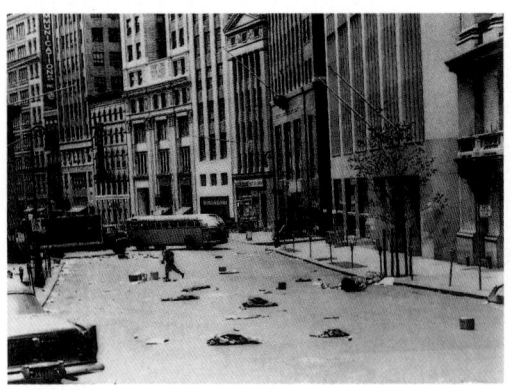

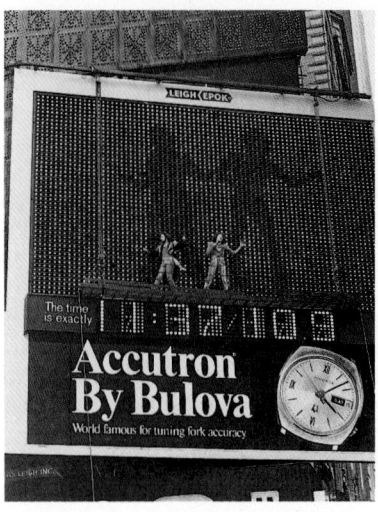

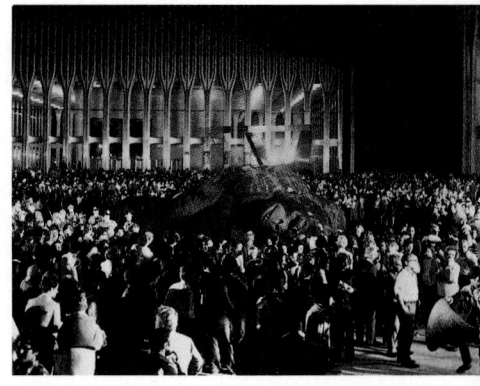

The World, the Flesh and the Devil, 1959. Film still. Art director, William A. Horning; director, Ranald MacDougall. ©1958 Turner Entertainment Co. All Rights Reserved. TEC

Godspell, 1973. Film still. Art director, Ben Kasazkow; director, David Greene. MOMA

King Kong, 1976. Film still. Art directors, Archie J. Bacon, David A. Constable and Robert Grundlach; director, John Guillermin. MOMA

a diary kept by a twenty-year-old, self-proclaimed "college revolutionary," James Simon Kunen, during and after the violent demonstrations that rocked Columbia University and the Morningside Heights community in 1968 (see chapters 1 and 9).[273] Despite the inherently confrontational subject, the film fails to convincingly reflect campus realities. Because Columbia denied MGM permission to film on campus, the movie was shot instead in and around San Francisco. Columbia became "Pacific Western University" and James Simon Kunen became Simon James, a blond Californian.[274] These changes cut out the heart of the story, robbing it of the opportunity to explore coherently the roots of the Columbia insurrection, and sacrificing an accurate portrayal of the era's radical politics.

Arthur Barron's *Jeremy* (1973), a tale of first love between two students at the High School of Music and Art, is unabashedly escapist entertainment reflecting the nation's disenchantment with the media focus on angry, politicized youth.[275] Shot on location in New York, the film struck Greenspun as "a movie of rather heavy calculation, indulging in almost every cliché available to young love in Manhattan—the city at night, rainy afternoons, the camera floating over Park Avenue, or looking up through the sun-dappled leaves of Central Park."[276]

The Lords of Flatbush (1974), codirected by Stephen F. Verona and Martin Davidson, is a decidedly nostalgic look at the lives of several teenagers—"the leather jacket-bobby soxer Brooklyn high school set," as A. H. Weiler put it—during the year 1957.[277] The movie, filmed on location in Flatbush, conveys the realities of the 1950s as well as the mid-1970s rejection of 1960s-style radicalism. It also reflects the fond memories of Brooklynites (and ex-Brooklynites) whose native borough had fallen on hard times.

Fielder Cook's *From the Mixed-Up Files of Mrs. Basil E. Frankweiler* (1973) is a children's movie about a brother and sister, ages ten and twelve, who run away from their suburban New Jersey home and hide in the Metropolitan Museum of Art.[278] Filmed largely within the museum, the movie implies that while the suburbs are boring and the city at large is menacing, the Metropolitan's grand marble confines are user-friendly, at least for precocious children.

Next Stop, Greenwich Village (1976) offers perhaps the era's most significant cinematic account of growing up in New York.[279] Written, directed and produced by Paul Mazursky, the semiautobiographical film presents a vivid, highly selective memoir of leaving his parents' Brownsville apartment and starting out in the theater in Greenwich Village in the 1950s. The film includes numerous on-location sequences, including one at Brooklyn's Newkirk Avenue station and another at the Village's famous Café Reggio. Mazursky portrays Manhattan as a place full of promise and opportunity for an ambitious young man from Brooklyn. This image was particularly compelling in 1976, a low point in the city's self-esteem. Pauline Kael felt that the film provided "the best portrait of Village life ever put on the screen; the casualness, the camaraderie, and the sexual freedom are balanced by glimpses of the lives of those who are in the Village because they don't fit in anywhere else."[280]

Out of It: Suburban New York

Released in 1945, at a time when New Yorkers, finally relieved of the constraints of war and economic depression, began to move to the suburbs in record numbers, Peter Godfrey's *Christmas in Connecticut* presented an ideal image of the suburban house as family temple: a quaint converted farmhouse miles from any neighbor in the picturesque Connecticut countryside.[281] An inspired plot twist, however, adds complexity and irony to the picture-perfect image and antic humor to the film. A New York–based journalist (Barbara Stanwyck) who writes a food and home column is asked to entertain a war hero at the antique-filled house she supposedly shares with her husband and eight-month-old child. The problem is that the journalist is neither married nor particularly domestic, and she lives in New York. In order not to disappoint her publisher, she tries, within the span of a few hours, to acquire all of the elements of suburban bliss. Though she expresses some ambivalence about her single life in the city and her fabricated, familial one in Connecticut, Stanwyck's character and her archetypal house reassured moviegoers that their dreams of the arcadian good life could indeed become real.

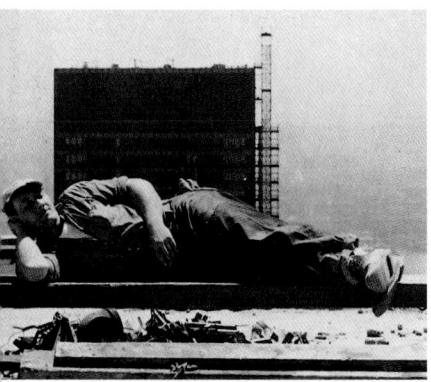

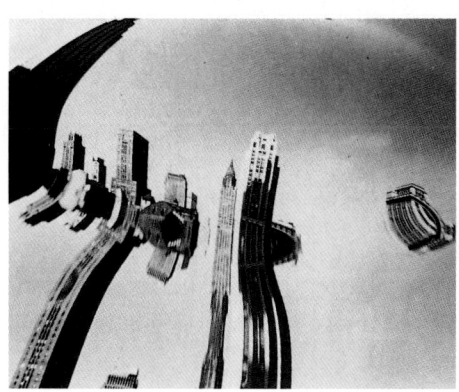

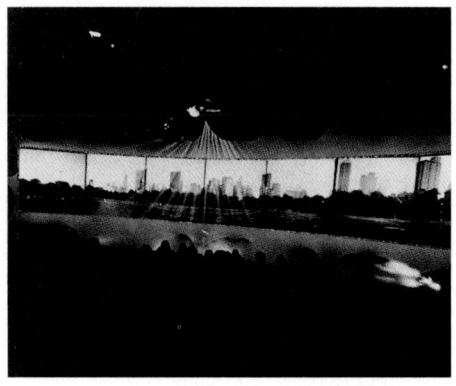

Skyscraper, 1959. Film still. Director, Shirley Clarke in collaboration with Willard van Dyke, Irving Jacoby, D. A. Pennebaker and Wheaton Galentine. MOMA

N.Y., N.Y., 1957. Film still. Director, Francis Thompson. MOMA

The New York Experience, 1973. Director, Rusty Russell. Multiscreen film presentation. NYP

H. C. Potter's *Mr. Blandings Builds His Dream House* (1948) is based on the popular, witty novel by Eric Hodgens.[282] The film tells of Jim Blandings, a successful advertising copywriter (Cary Grant), and his wife (Myrna Loy), who together with their two children escape the bustle of the city for the calm of the country. The film's opening sequence depicts the city's harrowing daily grind, as experienced in midtown in the shadow of the New York Central Building (Warren & Wetmore, 1929) at 230 Park Avenue.[283] Fed up with New York, the Blandingses leave their rental apartment in an eighteen-story building on the Upper East Side for a charming if dilapidated farmhouse in Connecticut. After experiencing a series of disasters in trying to renovate their old house, they hire an architect to design a completely new one; many headaches and many overspent dollars later, the Blandingses complete their dream house.

By 1960, when Charles Walters's *Please Don't Eat the Daisies*, based on a novel by Jean Kerr, wife of the drama critic Walter Kerr, was released, the moviegoing public was no longer quite so intoxicated by suburbia.[284] The film told the story of a family—a drama-critic husband (David Niven), a homemaker wife (Doris Day), three hell-raising kids, a baby and a particularly photogenic English sheepdog—who moved from a cramped Manhattan apartment to a sprawling house in the suburbs. Though not without its charms, the semiautobiographical film seemed a bit old hat.

By 1968, when Frank Perry's *The Swimmer* was released, a darker view of suburbia prevailed.[285] Adapted by Eleanor Perry from John Cheever's short story and starring Burt Lancaster, the film lyrically dissects the overwhelming sense of quiet desperation that, by the late 1960s, had for many people tainted a once idealized vision of life in New York's rich bedroom communities. Cheever's ingenious story tells of Neddy Merrill, an aging bon vivant of the country club scene, who sets out to swim across Westchester County, moving from one friend's backyard pool to another. In the process, Merrill reviews his life, gradually descending into madness. Though the Perrys' film was shot largely in and near Westport, Connecticut, rather than in Westchester, it nonetheless effectively captures the story. As Canby put it, the film has "the look and smell of authentic suburbia—of burnt lawns and chlorinated water."[286]

New York of the Mind

New York is an ideal setting for film fantasies. *Tarzan's New York Adventure* (1942) brings the beloved jungle hero, played by Johnny Weissmuller, to the Big Apple in search of his son, Boy, who has been kidnapped by a circus owner.[287] Theodore Strauss, writing in the *New York Times*, noted that "Tarzan continues to behave as if he still wore nothing more substantial than a breech clout. He swings across the dizzy canyons of Manhattan via flagpole riggings, leaps from Brooklyn Bridge and even walks into a shower fully clothed and exclaims 'Rain, rain feel good!' Tarzan is still Tarzan."[288]

George Seaton's *Miracle on 34th Street* (1947), a Christmastime fable, was filmed largely on a Hollywood sound stage, although, as Bosley Crowther noted, the "scenes shot in actual New York settings add credibility."[289] New York also serves as an effective backdrop for Norman Z. McLeod's *The Secret Life of Walter Mitty* (1947), with a screenplay adapted by Ken Englund and Everett Freeman from James Thurber's short story, which delineates the grandiose daydreams of a beleaguered Milquetoast, played in the film by Danny Kaye.[290]

Rudolph Maté's *When Worlds Collide* (1951) is rather standard science fiction—scientists preparing for the apocalypse—but the film is distinguished by highly theatrical special effects, including a scene in which Manhattan is submerged by a tidal wave.[291] Ranald MacDougall's *The World, the Flesh and the Devil* (1959) presents a terrifying though not very realistic vision of New York after an unexplained nuclear catastrophe has wrought worldwide devastation.[292] Three survivors, played by Harry Belafonte, Inger Stevens and Mel Ferrer, encounter each other in the deserted city. Belafonte, the first to arrive, crosses the George Washington Bridge, which is littered with abandoned automobiles. He is later seen on Wall Street, shouting his name and announcing the mere fact of his existence, his lonely cry reverberating down the man-made canyon. Crowther commented that the depiction of the empty city, "the buildings and apartments houses stark and still, stabs the imagination and gives the viewer the creeps."[293]

Charlie Chaplin's *A King in New York* is a comic fantasy that takes a serious look at McCarthyism. Due to its topicality, and Chaplin's own problems with American immigration laws, the film, completed in 1957, was not widely released in the United States until 1973.[294] The film tells the fictional story of a deposed Estrovian king, Igor Shahdov, played by Chaplin, who travels to New York in an effort to promote world peace but winds up caught in the city's publicity and monetary whirl. Shot entirely on sound stages in London, the film received poor reviews upon its initial release, in particular because of its low production quality.

In Jack Arnold's satiric *The Mouse that Roared* (1959), an English film, New York became the setting for nuclear-era political fantasy about the imaginary country of Grand Fenwick, with several roles being played by Peter Sellers.[295] Grand Fenwick's army, which consists of twenty soldiers in chain mail equipped with bows and arrows, crosses the Atlantic in a tugboat, only to arrive in New York during an air-raid drill. The city is deserted, with all of its inhabitants seeking shelter in the subway tunnels. When the first group of New Yorkers returns to the street, they mistake the Grand Fenwickians for invaders from another planet. On-location shots of the Grand Fenwickians in New York provide a comment on the city's global power: it is, after all, in New York, and not Washington, D.C., that they gain superpower status.

George Seaton's psychedelic-era romantic comedy *What's So Bad About Feeling Good?* (1968) presents a benign fantasy image of New York. A magical South American toucan flies to New York and spreads a virus, the symptoms of which are a sense of calm, personal freedom and unbounded optimism. The principal victims include an ex–Madison Avenue executive, played by George Peppard, his hip live-in girlfriend, played by Mary Tyler Moore, and several of their East Village friends. Though the entire film was shot on location, Vincent Canby felt the movie had "the point of view of an insular, slightly out-of-date Hollywood." Nonetheless, the critic acknowledged that "there are some nice things . . . such as the opening shots of Manhattan as if observed by an astronaut coming in low over Staten Island."[296]

Dreadful science fiction images of a future New York returned to the screen in Richard Fleischer's *Soylent Green* (1973), a portrait of the city in the twenty-first century, when the earth's resources are so depleted that people consume synthesized plankton. A. H. Weiler, reviewing the film for the *New York Times*, wryly stated that "New Yorkers certainly have problems these days—graffiti, income tax, the Yankees—but nothing like the horrors due in 2022," when the city would be full of "a bewildering succession of hungry citizens, overcrowded streets, fancy pads and the resident luscious lasses (called 'furniture' here) of the rich few."[297]

David Greene's *Godspell* (1973) uses New York as the unlikely but highly effective setting for a contemporary retelling of the Gospel according to St. Matthew. Based on a successful off-Broadway rock-musical that consists of a series of non-site-specific scenes, the film, shot exclusively on location in the city, provides the ancient story with a measure of youth-oriented "relevance." With high-spirited actors dressed as clowns, complete with white face makeup, the film transforms New York into a lyrical, almost otherworldly environment. Canby noted that *Godspell* was "less a celebration of the life and teachings of Christ than it is a celebration of theater, music, youthful high spirits, New York City locations and the zoom lens. . . . I can't remember another film that seems to have caught the way New York appears on a lot of hot summer days, when its jagged outlines are softened by a golden smog.

The atmosphere may be lethal, but it's also incomparably romantic."[298] Perhaps the most memorable scene depicts the characters of Jesus (Victor Garber) and John the Baptist (David Haskell) doing a soft-shoe dance routine in front of a massive electric sign in Times Square, their amplified, moving reflections silhouetted in blinking light.

Ralph Bakshi's *Heavy Traffic* (1973) is a full-length animated cartoon for adults set in a decaying New York full of fringe characters who embody the city's dissolute character and its tenacious vitality. Roger Greenspun found the movie "a cruel, funny, heartbreaking love note to a city kept alive by its freaks, and always, always dying." Bakshi's dense, colorful, animated drawings, with their biting, exaggerated depictions bordering on the grotesque, seem indebted to a wide variety of sources, from George Grosz to Red Grooms, with an odd measure of the urban malaise so brilliantly captured by Edward Hopper thrown in. Greenspun noted that despite the kaleidoscopic array of colorful personages, "Bakshi's subject is really the city, New York City, the sum of his many characters' lives, and yet desolate, depopulated. Generally it looks as if news of some impending disaster had reached everybody in time to leave New York deserted—except for the creatures in the movie, who live together in the shadow of a doom they don't understand but somehow express."[299]

Woody Allen's *Sleeper* (1973) presents a howlingly funny look at America in the year 2173; it also constitutes an extended inside joke for New Yorkers.[300] Allen, playing the hyper-health-conscious Miles Monroe, a co-owner of a health food restaurant in Greenwich Village, is admitted to St. Vincent's Hospital for treatment of an ulcer. Though the surgery is minor, an unidentified mishap results in Monroe being frozen for 200 years. He thaws out to find that the United States has fallen under the rule of an evil dictator who has transformed it into a police state. Apparently this tragedy occurred when a nuclear bomb fell into the hands of Albert Shanker, a real-life character widely known to the New York audience as the sometimes intransigent head of the teachers' union. Offering an inside joke to New York's architectural community, an institute staffed by mad scientists was filmed in Richard Meier's elaborately Modernist Weinstein house (1969–71) in Old Westbury, Long Island.[301]

In 1976 the producer Dino De Laurentiis's extravagant remake of Ernest B. Schoedash and Merian C. Cooper's classic *King Kong* (1933) provides a perhaps unintended comment on the city's declining fortunes. In this version, directed by John Guillerman and starring Jessica Lange, Beau Bridges and Charles Grodin, the gorilla chooses the monumentally banal World Trade Center over the masterful Empire State Building.[302] Vincent Canby complained about the change of venue, charging that the World Trade Center "is a very boring piece of architecture. The Empire State Building is not. Though Kong's last fight with Army helicopters is beautifully (and bloodily) done, the setting trivializes it."[303] Indeed, the Empire State Building management was so miffed that the skyscraper was not used for the remake that it hired men dressed as apes and equipped with picket signs to demonstrate on the observation deck. While the first *King Kong* had been filmed exclusively in Hollywood, with location photography confined to process shots, the new version made extensive use of the city's streets. On the nights of June 21–23, 1976, crowds were assembled on the World Trade Center Plaza to serve as extras. Though less than shining, the film proved that for the paradigmatic twentieth-century metropolis, no other city would do.

Documentary New York: The City as Objet Trouvé

During the postwar era, documentary filmmakers, like their feature-film counterparts, turned to New York as both a shooting location and a principal subject; in many ways, however, documentaries, usually high on visual creativity and low in budget, shared more with contemporaneous painting than with the standard, big-budget Hollywood product. Eschewing the traditional narrative structure of newsreel-style documentaries about New York—the paradigmatic interwar examples being Paul Strand's poetic *Manahatta* (1920) and Ralph Steiner and Willard Van Dyke's didactic *The City* (1939)—postwar filmmakers orchestrated the city's imagery to emphasize its visual patterns. The result was a New York less "real" even than that of fictional feature films in which the photography was more straightforward.[304] Surprisingly, in contrast to postwar feature films that grappled with compelling urban problems, many documentaries overlooked the city's social realities, or treated them lyrically, focusing on New York as an art object, the ultimate *objet trouvé*.

In 1949 the Swiss-born photographer and documentary filmmaker Rudy Burckhardt, who would emerge as perhaps the most elegiac postwar cinematographer to focus on New York, released the twenty-minute silent film *The Climate of New York*, incorporating subtitles excerpted from poems written by the poet and dance critic Edwin Denby.[305] The film juxtaposes leisurely family outings shot on a Sunday in Astoria, Queens, with footage of subway trains and Manhattan skyscrapers, the latter photographed at dusk. Burckhardt's fifteen-minute *Under Brooklyn Bridge* (1955) contrasts images of naked boys diving and swimming from an abandoned pier beneath the monumental span with images of the demolition of a decrepit warehouse. Here the city is portrayed as at once enduring and ever changing, imposing and playful, a vast metropolis seemingly created by giants but enlivened by high-spirited youths who transform it into their own humanly scaled playground.[306] Though unsentimental, the film is infused with a sense of nostalgia, recalling the interwar paintings of Reginald Marsh, particularly *Naked Over New York* (1938), as well as earlier Ash Can School works by such artists as Robert Henri.[307] The editors of the *Village Voice* praised Burckhardt's "photographic detail [and] his unpretentiousness. There are sequences—and the children swimming under the Brooklyn Bridge is one—which belong to the best footage on New York by anybody."[308] Burckhardt's *Eastside Summer* (1958) focuses on what the *Village Voice* called "the gray poetry of the Lower East Side."[309] Providing, as A. H. Weiler put it, "unadorned portraiture" of the predominantly Hispanic community clustered around avenues A, B and C, the film continues the understated sympathy of *The Climate of New York*, once again focusing on one of the city's less affluent but vital ethnic neighborhoods.[310] Burckhardt's *Square Times* (1967) reflects the sordid dimension of Times Square's nighttime entertainments.[311]

In the Street (1951), directed and filmed by Helen Levitt, Janice Loeb and James Agee, is both a casually structured montage and a surprisingly intimate and revealing portrait of one of the city's poorest, transitional areas, East Harlem.[312] Not originally intended for public release, the short film resulted from the collaborators' efforts to familiarize themselves with the medium. Agee, a film critic for *Time* and other magazines, had long been interested in still photography and was particularly fascinated by Levitt's shots of children in Harlem; Levitt's psychologically penetrating but seemingly impromptu photographs recall the work of Henri Cartier-Bresson. In the early 1940s Agee and Levitt agreed to collaborate on a book that would document Harlem street life and function as a kind of urban equivalent to Agee and Walker Evans's landmark study of rural American poverty, *Let Us Now Praise Famous Men* (1941),[313] but the project languished. (Ultimately titled *A Way of Seeing*, it was published in 1965, long after Agee's death.)[314] Still compelled by the Harlem subject matter, Agee and Levitt acquired financial backing from the independently wealthy painter Janice Loeb and took to the streets with a borrowed sixteen-millimeter camera equipped with an angle-viewer. The filmmakers thus concealed their activity from the objects of their attention, thereby creating remarkably natural and unself-conscious portraits of city dwellers. In the preface to the film, Agee says: "The streets of the poor quarters of great cities are, above all, a theater and a battleground. There, unaware and unnoticed, every human being is a poet, a masker, a warrior and, in his innocent artistry, projects against the turmoil of the street an image of existence."[315] In its informality and candor the frankly unambitious film became a forerunner of the "hand-held camera" technique characteristic of far more pretentious "art films" made in the 1960s.

While *In the Street* synthesized aesthetic and sociological concerns, John Arvonio's *Abstract in Concrete* (1952), as its title indicates, eschews societal comment in favor of purely visual composition.[316] Over the course of several years, Arvonio haunted the Times Square area on rainy nights, recording with color film the signature neon signs reflected on wet streets and sidewalks. After assembling the footage into a short silent film, he showed the work at a friend's party. There the composer Frank Gaskin Fields recalled a piece he had written twenty-two years earlier, that he felt would provide an effective musical complement to Arvonio's poetic images. Arvonio and Fields were surprised by how well the film and music worked together. The result is an engagingly fresh look at one of the city's most familiar and most photographed locations.

N.Y., N.Y. (1957), directed by Francis Thompson, was the most daring and satisfying of the postwar era's celebrations of the city.[317] Only fifteen minutes long, the film was ten years in the making, with an initial release in 1951 and a final one six years later. Edited down from thousands of feet of film, it offers an object lesson in film craft as well as a bold example of what Thompson wittily called "optic nerve."[318] An innovative effort to move away from traditional cinematic forms, *N.Y., N.Y.* presents the city's buildings and bridges in a series of images bent into impossible shapes and configurations through distorting, short-focal-length lenses and prisms of Thompson's own manufacture. Multiple images blend into each other and rotate to create a particularly dense and kinetic effect. Extreme close-up shots also render familiar images strange. The journalist Flora Rheta Schreiber found that "the New York of this film, angular and surrealistic, was not the New York one sees with normal vision. This film . . . made [the city] look, on seeing it again, as if it were a dream configuration."[319] Film historian Elodie Osborn wrote of the film:

> [It] was the most ambitious and successful of cinematic presentations of the city . . . [a] most startling and bizarre fantasy. . . . Visions which remind one of a rhythmic repetition of analytical cubist pictures glide into the fluid distortions of quicksilver shapes. A lively musical accompaniment unifies this work into a fine visual and aural symphony of the spirit and structure of today's complex urban life. With such films as this, cinema breaks away from the mere presentation of reality; qualities of fantasy, poetry and magic are introduced in film terms completely liberated from the story form.[320]

Hilary Harris vividly exploited a sense of movement as a metaphor for the city's relentless dynamism in his short film *Highway* (1958), photographed behind the wheel of a car moving along highways surrounding the city. The movie, which incorporates a pulsing rock 'n' roll soundtrack, focuses on what Osborn described as "exhilaration conveyed through its kinetic expressions of driving along an urban road."[321] D. A. Pennebaker's sixteen-millimeter film *Daybreak Express* (1964) similarly uses speed as a metaphor for urban life.[322] Shooting throughout the city from old elevated train lines, Pennebaker enhanced the visual impact by manipulating the film. According to Osborn, the filmmaker "created his own palette of color by exposing the film to enrich its color values and, by shooting at a speed which accelerates the visual impression, he has arrived at an imagery which only the motion picture camera can reveal."[323]

Shirley Clarke's four-minute *Bridges-Go-Round* (1958) is a poetic montage depicting some of the city's bridges.[324] More journalistic but nonetheless lyrical is the twenty-minute *Skyscraper* (1959), documenting the construction of 666 Fifth Avenue, which Clarke directed in collaboration with Willard van Dyke, Irving Jacoby, D. A. Pennebaker and Wheaton Galentine.[325] Kevin Smith served as cameraman. John White wrote the film's humorous narration and Teo Macero composed the upbeat, jazz-inspired music. An undercurrent of belligerent Modernism shades the narration spoken by Gene Mumford and John Sylvester and the opening song, the counterpoint to a cinematic montage of glass-and-steel curtain-wall facades. Boasting of the "shadowless" city of the future, the narrators chant: "Magic city climbing high, charming walls reflect the sky. Magic city in the sun, has the darkness on the run. It's growing bright the city, light the city, right the city now. We're going to chase the shadows, erase the shadows, from our city now." Against images of the Bayard Building (Louis Sullivan and L. P. Smith, 1897) and the Little Singer Building (Ernest Flagg, 1902–4),[326] carefully chosen representatives of the city's increasingly threatened architectural heritage, the song proclaims: "Old facades must pass away, like the horse they've had their day. Old walls tumbling into dust, signs proclaiming dig we must." Chronicling the building's creation from preliminary models through the installation of interiors and the activation of mechanical systems, the film concentrates on the construction of the building's steel skeleton, featuring impressive if nerve-wracking shots of construction workers nonchalantly napping on girders high above the pavement. Film historian Lewis Jacobs grouped *Skyscraper* with *N.Y., N.Y., Highway* and *Bridges-Go-Round* as "impressionistic, semi-abstract profiles of the metropolitan scene" and explained their similarities:

> For the most part, the films in this group were conceived and executed by one person for the purpose of self-expression. The main thrust was not journalism or polemics, but "pure cinema." It was a commitment to a plastic order that often called upon distortion lenses, prisms, special mirrors, multiple images, and rhythmic cutting syncopated to jazz or rock-and-roll scores, for a minimum of meaning and a maximum of effect. Nearly all of the films contained sequences that were dazzling, witty and engaging. Animated by a drive toward cinematic virtuosity and the belief that film was the true art of the time, these filmmakers aimed at personal statements, not about their subjects, but about their medium.[327]

Similar to these films in appearance and tone, if not intention, is Wheaton Galentine's *Big City* (1958), which telescopes twelve hours of life from dawn to dusk into two and a half minutes of hyperactivity.[328] Traffic patterns, pedestrian circulation and the movement of sun and shadow across building facades represent the passage of time, as Osborn put it, "in terms of a day barely captured before it is gone."[329] The film, intended to illustrate the nature of American life, had been commissioned by the United States Department of State for presentation at the 1958 Brussels World Exposition, where a number of two-and-a-half-minute "loops" made by independent filmmakers in New York were run continuously.

On the Bowery (1956) is a distinctly different type of documentary film, one that self-consciously abandons artistic considerations in favor of a penetratingly "real" look at the life of an alcoholic living on New York's skid row.[330] As written by Mark Sufrin, produced by Lionel Rogosin, codirected by Sufrin and Richard Bagley and photographed by Bagley, the film chronicles two days in the life of Ray Sayler, an itinerant railroad laborer. Rogosin, a thirty-three-year-old former executive in a New York–based textile concern, embarked on his film project after six months of observing life on the Bowery. Shot with a concealed camera and tape recorder, *On the Bowery* was the most biting American film to tackle the problem of alcoholism since Billy Wilder's 1945 feature film, *The Lost Weekend* (see above). Widely praised in Europe, where it premiered, it was the first American film to receive the grand prize at the Venice Film Festival. American observers seemed less impressed. Reviewing the film for the *New York Times*, Bosley Crowther wrote:

> Not to be churlish about it but simply to state the case as it appears to a cheerful film reviewer and ex-reporter in the byways of New York, this is a dismal exposition to be charging money to see. You can see the same thing in many places in this city without going too far from where you live. Indeed [the film] is merely a good montage of good photographs of drunks and bums, scrutinized and listened to ad nauseam. And we mean ad nauseam.[331]

Crowther felt that though the filmmakers were "realistic observers" and "unrelenting reporters" who knew "how to use a camera," they didn't understand "the art of films. At least, in this well-intended effort, they have failed to display a skill in the creative treatment of actuality." Thus, although Crowther said that "the clear-eyed photography is withering" and that "the unappetizing scene of missions, flophouses and gin-mills are viewed and reported to a T," the film left him cold.[332]

Throughout the 1960s Andy Warhol, the Pop art icon-maker par excellence, shot many so-called underground films in New York. Two of these use the city as their principal subject. His eight-hour silent film *Empire* (1965) was shot from an office on the forty-fourth floor of the Time & Life Building, with a single stationary camera aimed at the Empire State Building (Shreve, Lamb & Harmon, 1931) from 8:00 P.M. to 4:00 A.M. the following morning.[333] *Empire* pushed documentary filmmaking toward pure art—or intolerable boredom, depending on one's point of view. According to poet and longtime Warhol collaborator Gerard Malanga, the idea for *Empire* came from John Palmer, who codirected the film. Warhol was delighted with the results, which seem at once totally devoid of content and assertive of the building as phallic symbol. "The Empire State Building is a star," Warhol said. "It's an eight-hour hard-on. It's so beautiful. The lights come on and the stars come out and it sways. It's like Flash Gordon riding into space."[334] Malanga described the movie as one "where nothing happened except the audience's reaction."[335] Among the critics who found meaning in *Empire* was Peter Gidal, who stated that the movie's "emphasis is on the nature of film reality, the gradation of shades from black to white on film, the nature of time's (forward) movement past a nonentity (which the Empire State Building certainly is; so nothing that it attains neutrality), and the emotive connotations thereof through the description of nothingness (a traditional art concern by now)."[336]

In comparison with *Empire*, Warhol's three-and-a-half-hour *Chelsea Girls* (1966) is almost traditional. The film documents the daily activities and preoccupations—including sex, drugs and chitchat—of a collection of people living in the Chelsea Hotel (Hubert, Pirsson & Co., 1884), at 222 West Twenty-third Street.[337] The cinema verité film, which stars numerous members of Warhol's "Factory"—including Nico, Edie Sedgwick, Ingrid Superstar and International Velvet—firmly established the hotel, long a home to artists and writers, as a symbol of the radically decadent turn bohemian life was taking in New York during the mid-1960s. When *Chelsea Girls* originally came in at close to seven hours, Warhol decided that rather than cut it down, he would use a split screen, showing two reels at once, one in color and the other in black and white. Only one side of the screen "talked" at any given moment. The film, premiered downtown by the Film-Makers' Cinemathèque, proved an immediate popular success and quickly moved to a "legitimate" theater uptown. Before the move, however, all of the film's references to specific room numbers were taken out, following the hotel management's threat of a lawsuit. *Chelsea Girls* was Warhol's greatest commercial success up to that time and arguably the first underground film to find a mainstream audience; as Jack Kroll put it, the film was "the *Iliad* of the Underground."[338] The art critic Brian O'Doherty found the film to be "a strange near-amalgam, somewhat as if *Last Exit to Brooklyn* had been crossed with *Grand Hotel*. The whole ambience tends, through a very carefully handled effect of boredom, to dissociate mind and body, and thus to become metaphysical."[339] Dan Sullivan, writing in the *New York Times*, gave perhaps the most even-handed assessment: "Andy Warhol has produced a film that is half Bosch and half bosh. At its best 'The Chelsea Girls' is a travelogue of hell—a grotesque menagerie of lost souls whimpering in a psychedelic moonscape of neon red and fluorescent blue. At its worst it is a bunch of home movies in which Mr. Warhol's friends, asked to do something for the camera, can think of nothing much to do."[340]

If Warhol's film portrays the Chelsea Hotel as a hip hell, Chantal Akerman's sixty-five-minute silent movie *Hotel Monterey* (1972), uses the lower Manhattan hostelry as the setting for an obsessive search for beauty amid tawdry surroundings. The Belgian director, working with cinematographer Babette Mangolte, lingered on such architectural details as the porthole windows of elevator doors and dim lights viewed down long, narrow corridors. Here such features, easily overlooked, become, as the reviewer Stephen Holden put it in the *New York Times*, "spiritual beacons in an environment glowing with arcane romantic secrets."[341] Akerman's ninety-minute *News from Home* (1976) even more intensely scrutinizes New York as a cityscape laden with lyrical despair. Shot throughout the city, on streets and in the subway, the film juxtaposes New York's sights and sounds with a soundtrack that includes long passages (spoken in a near-monotone) from letters written to the filmmaker by her mother in Brussels, who aimlessly recounts domestic banalities. "A paradox of Miss Akerman's film," Holden

pointed out, "is that almost everywhere she sets her camera, she finds a stark beauty. In the camera eye of her cinematographer . . . the girders of the Times Square subway station form majestic abstract compositions. Scenes of pizzerias and diners have the same desolate, elegiac beauty as Edward Hopper's cityscapes."[342]

Street Scenes 1970, directed by Martin Scorsese for the New York Cinetracts Collective, the cinematic branch of a political activist group called the National Student Strike, depicts the city as something close to a battleground. The film documents the demonstrations held on Wall Street on May 20, 1970, in which anti–Vietnam War protesters clashed violently with war supporters, many of them construction workers. Howard Thompson, reviewing the film for the *New York Times*, noted that "the eeriest sight of all is a group of hard-hat workers carrying huge flags through a milling throng in the canyon streets. Most of the violence is shown in the distant background."[343]

The New York Experience (1973), produced by Bing Crosby and the Trans-Lux Corporation, is an elaborately constructed and visually dazzling multiscreen film presentation that unapologetically advertises the city.[344] The film's technological bravura was touted more heavily than that of any film since *This Is Cinerama!* (1952), a lavishly filmed travelogue that included brief shots of the New York skyline. Written, designed and directed by Rusty Russell, *The New York Experience* was intended for exclusive showing at the custom-designed Trans-Lux Experience Theater in the McGraw-Hill Building on Sixth Avenue. Created in anticipation of the celebration of the nation's bicentennial in 1976, the fifty-eight-minute film, which was simultaneously projected on sixteen screens arranged in a semicircle and viewed from swivel chairs, features interviews with ordinary citizens and quotations from famous observers ranging from Mark Twain and Mrs. Trollope to Jacob Riis, Thomas Wolfe and Le Corbusier. These complement a kaleidoscopic array of archival photographs and new footage chronicling the city's history and defining its character. Dramatic scenes depict fog rolling down the East River beneath the Brooklyn Bridge, the former Third Avenue El rumbling overhead, an electrical storm above the Empire State Building and the dedication of the Statue of Liberty.

The film proved popular with the public but received less than raves from the press. Paul Gardner, writing in the *New York Times*, noted, "The show does not take any point of view or try to make a complex city comprehensible."[345] Burt Supree, writing in the *Village Voice*, asserted that "it tries to cover everything and always with very hopped-up energy. But one effect of all this excitement is that one feels rather *absent* . . . which seems fine while it's going on but disagreeable as soon as you pick your regular body out of the seat at the end and face exciting Sixth Avenue and the exciting subway."[346] Patricia O'Haire commented in the *New York Daily News* on the film's lack of realism: "It's a rather nice place that the film depicts—where no rain or snow is seen and where buildings stand majestically against the sky, unobscured by dirt, fog, clouds or pollution. It's a place where everyone interviewed says the city is, among other things, a 'challenging' place to live. No doubt that is true. But judging from this film, the proper words to describe New York would be clean, delightful and charming."[347] The film's Pollyanna outlook was surely a deliberate attempt on the part of its sponsors and creators to reduce tourists' anxieties and apprehensions. As Rusty Russell himself joked, "It's a good way to see the city without getting mugged."[348]

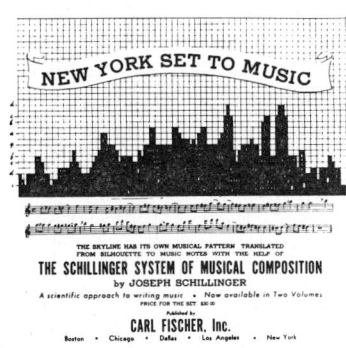

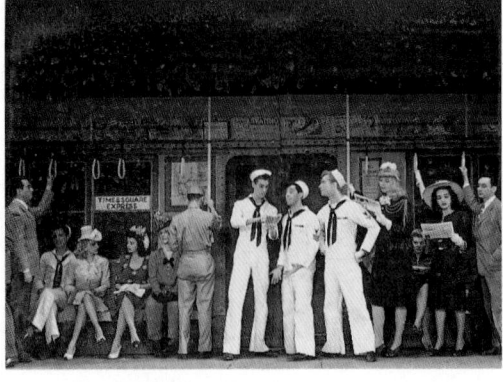

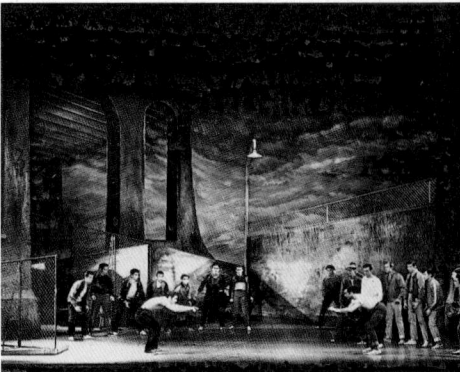

"New York Set to Music," 1946. Joseph Schillinger, based on melody by Heitor Villa-Lobos. RN

On the Town, 1945. Set designer, Oliver Smith. NYPL

West Side Story, 1957. Production associate, Sylvia Drulie. NYPL

NEW YORK IN MUSIC AND DANCE

The City on the Stage

Just as Los Angeles is "Hollywood," New York is "Broadway." Throughout the post–World War II years, composers and choreographers, working in a remarkably diverse range of styles, explored New York's physical and psychological character, creating some of the era's most viscerally emotional portraits of the evolving city. Perhaps the city's most representative product, the Broadway musical, provided a rich source of "song and dance" routines about New York. Though seen by a much smaller audience than that for a Hollywood film, the Broadway show was not insular; many plays and most successful musicals were taken on the road to the American hinterlands and some were even showcased on foreign stages. Many were later memorialized as movies with even wider circulation. Popular songs from musicals were played over and over again on the radio and later heard on television broadcasts.

Beginning with *Show Boat* (1927), Broadway musicals became less a series of unrelated set pieces in the manner of a review and more a coherent story-telling form akin to European operetta. However, Broadway musicals were often topical in theme; their components were less integrated than those of operettas and their spoken and musical diction relied more on the vernacular. A principal theme of the post–*Show Boat* musical was the history of New York City, and a kind of "New York cycle" was initiated with *Knickerbocker Holiday* (1938).[1] Featuring music by Kurt Weill and a book and words by Maxwell Anderson, the show, which ranges backward in time from New York in 1809 to New Amsterdam in 1647, interprets some of the satiric tales that Washington Irving wrote under the pseudonym Diedrich Knickerbocker. This show was followed by *Up in Central Park* (1945)—directed by John Kennedy, with a book by Dorothy and Herbert Fields, music by Sigmund Romberg and words by Dorothy Fields—which advances the city's story along in time to the 1870s. The musical is conventionally romantic in most ways, but its realistic edge documents the efforts of Tammany Hall political boss William Marcy Tweed and his cronies to line their pockets with money designated for Central Park's construction.[2] *Miss Liberty* (1949), di-

rected by Moss Hart, with a book by Robert E. Sherwood and words and music by Irving Berlin, takes place in 1885, the time of the Statue of Liberty's completion.[3] *Hello, Dolly!* (1964), directed by Gower Champion, with a book by Michael Stewart and words and music by Jerry Herman, is based on Thornton Wilder's play *The Matchmaker* (1954) and set in fin-de-siècle New York, bringing to life the past glories of now forlorn Fourteenth Street.[4] *Funny Girl* (1964), directed by Garson Kanin, with a book by Isobel Lennart, words by Bob Merrill and music by Jule Styne, traces the career of comedienne Fanny Brice and vividly depicts tenement life and Broadway glamour in early-twentieth-century New York.[5]

Fiorello! (1959), directed by George Abbott, with a book by Jerome Weidman and George Abbott, words by Sheldon Harnick and music by Jerry Bock, takes New York's history well into the twentieth century, chronicling the political career of the city's beloved Mayor LaGuardia.[6] *Wonderful Town* (1953), with a book by Jerome Chodorov and Joseph Fields, words by Betty Comden and music by Leonard Bernstein, sentimentalizes bohemian life in Greenwich Village in the 1930s.[7] The show is based on Ruth McKenna's short stories, which previously had been transformed into the stage play *My Sister Eileen* (1940)[8] and were twice interpreted on the silver screen. *Guys and Dolls* (1950), based on Damon Runyon's short story "The Idyll of Miss Sarah Brown," portrays oddball New Yorkers as "just folks."[9] With a book by Jo Swerling and Abe Burrows and words and music by Frank Loesser, the musical looks back at Times Square lowlife during the 1930s. *On the Town* (1945) captures the spirit of wartime New York while celebrating the contemporary city.[10] Based on the ballet *Fancy Free* (see below), *On the Town* features a memorable score by Leonard Bernstein and a witty book and lyrics, both by Betty Comden and Adolph Green. Its most famous song, "New York, New York," became a virtual anthem for the city: "The Bronx is up but the Battery's down,/And people ride in a hole in the ground." The show presents New York as a "helluva town," the ideal place for adventure and romance, where minds are stretched and spirits soar.

In 1957, twelve years after the opening of *On the Town*, Bernstein, together with writer Arthur Laurents and lyricist Stephen Sondheim, brought New York City's story right up to the present, concluding the "New York cycle" with another tri-

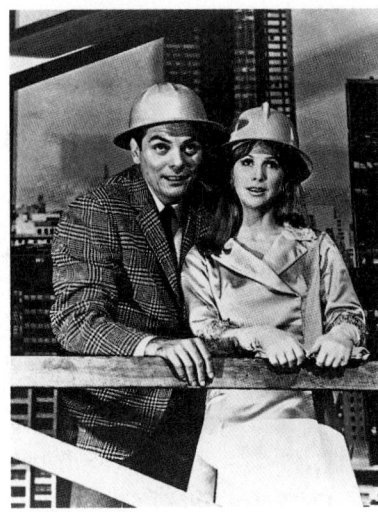

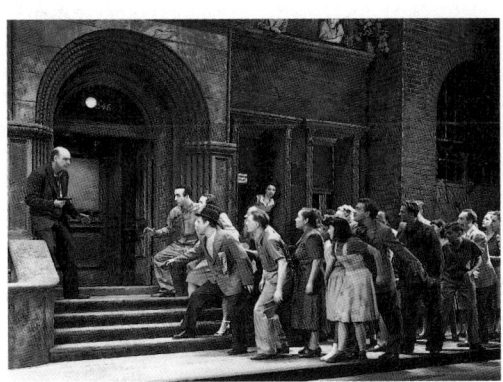

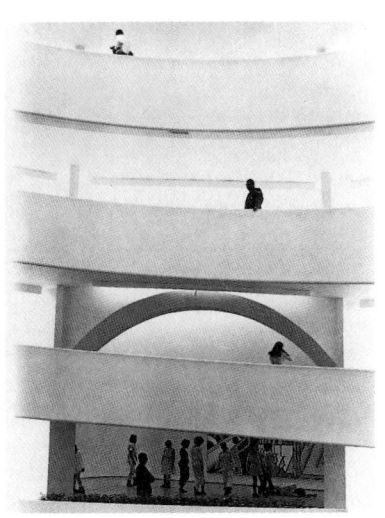

Skyscraper, 1965. Set designer, Robert Randolph. NYPL

Street Scene, 1947. Set designer, Jo Mielziner. NYPL

Juice, 1969. Choreographer, Meredith Monk. Moseley. NYPL

umph, *West Side Story*,[11] which was made into a movie in 1961. A contemporary version of Shakespeare's *Romeo and Juliet*, *West Side Story* involves two young lovers—Tony, a Polish-American boy and Maria, a Puerto Rican girl—and presents a vivid portrait of working-class life in the inner city. In the high-spirited song "America," key distinctions between life in New York and in Puerto Rico are frankly enunciated. When a character named Rosalia imagines moving back to San Juan, she says, "Everyone there will give big cheer!" Her friend Anita taunts her in her response: "Ev'ryone there will have moved here!" The song concludes on a bitter note with the observation that "Everything's right in America,/If you are white in America."[12] Reviewing *West Side Story*, the *New York Times* theater critic Brooks Atkinson commented that "Bernstein has composed another one of his nervous, flaring scores that capture the shrill beat of life in the streets."[13]

Other musicals also looked at the city through the eyes of ordinary individuals. *Hazel Flagg* (1953),[14] with a book by Ben Hecht, is a musical version of William Wellman's 1937 film *Nothing Sacred*,[15] which Hecht also wrote. The story, about some Vermont "hicks" outsmarting sophisticated New York journalists, takes a sardonic look at the Fourth Estate. The score of *Hazel Flagg*, with words by Bob Hilliard and music by Jule Styne, includes the clichéd but tuneful "Ev'ry Street's a Boulevard (in Old New York)."[16] *How to Succeed in Business without Really Trying* (1961), with a book by Willie Gilbert, Jack Weinstock and Abe Burrows and words and music by Frank Loesser, offers a brilliant send-up of corporate culture.[17] A darker side of New York life is documented in the underappreciated musical *Subways Are for Sleeping* (1961), based on a 1957 novel by Edmund G. Love, with words by Comden and Green and music by Jule Styne.[18] The musical offers a remarkably frank view of New York as a harsh and indifferent place—though also one where, despite all odds, love can prevail in unlikely settings. The song "Ride through the Night" sees the subway as the metropolitan equivalent of an amusement park's tunnel of love.[19]

Golden Boy (1964) presents an even darker view of city life.[20] Written by Clifford Odets and William Gibson and based on Odets's 1937 play about a boxer struggling to escape the confines of the ghetto, the show explores the complexities of an interracial romance. Life in Harlem is bitingly portrayed in Lee

Adams's lyrics for Charles Strouse's song, "Don't Forget 127th Street": "Don't Forget one hundred and twenty-seventh street!/ No siree, there's no slum like your own!/I remember winter evenings at the window,/Watching those evictions in the snow."[21]

Sweet Charity (1966) offers a grim view of Manhattan nightlife. With a book by Neil Simon, words by Dorothy Fields and music by Cy Coleman, the musical was adapted from an Italian film, Federico Fellini's *Nights of Cabiria* (1957), and would itself be interpreted on film.[22] In a reversal of the standard show-business sequence, Billy Wilder's New York–based film *The Apartment* inspired the Broadway musical *Promises, Promises* (1968), with a book by Neil Simon, words by Hal David and music by Burt Bacharach.[23]

Although the musical *Skyscraper* (1965) contributes no memorable songs about the city, its book, which Peter Stone loosely based on Elmer Rice's play *Dream Girl* (1945), has a powerful architectural agenda.[24] Updating Rice's rather simple story about Georgina Allerton, who is given to elaborate day-dreams, the musical's protagonist owns a mid-Manhattan brownstone where she lives and operates a ground-floor antiques shop called the Litterbug. A real-estate development concern has hired the Bushman Construction Company to build a skyscraper on the adjoining lots and makes a bid on her house. Georgina's steadfast refusal to sell out and make way for "progress" is based, as the critic John McCarten put it in his *New Yorker* review, on "her intense conviction that too many high-rise horrors are going up in Manhattan and too many landmark buildings are coming down."[25] Georgina's resolve weakens when she falls in love with the skyscraper's architect, who dreams of building literally to the stars. Though *Newsweek*'s editors contended that "it's grisly to think that anyone could take satisfaction in the thought of thousand-story apartment buildings, to say nothing of ones that touch Betelgeuse or Andromeda," the heroine feels otherwise. "Stepping swiftly aside, she falls into [the architect's] arms and the monstrosity is allowed to make its way starward."[26] Though public and critical response to the show tended to be negative, Howard Taubman, reviewing it for the *New York Times*, praised choreographer Michael Kidd for "volatile dances that pay their respects to . . . dynamic aspects of New York. . . . His dance of construction workers going about their business of rearing a skyscraper has vivacity and humor and his choreography for an auction is full of spirited comment." Taubman also felt that Robert Randolph's sets, including one in which a monumentally scaled photographic mural of Manhattan serves as the backdrop for an on-stage skyscraper skeleton, caught "the mood of New York."[27]

In 1967 *Hair*, described as "the American tribal love-rock musical," featuring a book and lyrics by Gerome Ragni and James Rado and music by Galt MacDermot, burst on the scene, inaugurating a new era in popular entertainment and opening Joseph Papp's Public Theater. The song "Frank Mills," chronicling an unrealized romance, portrays New York's Greenwich Village in its new incarnation as a hippie meeting ground, a less druggy version of San Francisco's Haight-Ashbury district.[28]

New York's theater world, long a staple of Hollywood films, was movingly captured in two stage musicals of the 1970s: *Follies* (1971) and *A Chorus Line* (1975). Stephen Sondheim wrote the words and music for *Follies*, an impassioned tribute to a seemingly lost era of New York theater. Produced by Harold Prince and directed by Prince and Michael Bennett, the show, with a book by James Goldman, conclusively demonstrated that despite the city's declining fortunes, Broadway's ability to raise daily reality to the level of myth remained undiminished. Sondheim's score examines the complex motivations behind our capacity to sustain the mythology of Broadway itself. In the song "Broadway Baby," Hattie Walker, an aging Ziegfeld Follies star first played by Ethel Shutta, herself a semiretired former vaudevillian and musical comedy star, sings:

> I'm just a Broadway Baby,
> Walking off my tired feet,
> Pounding Forty-Second Street to be in a show.
> Broadway Baby,
> Learning how to sing and dance,
> Waiting for that one big chance to be in a show.
> Gee, I'd like to be on some marquee,
> All twinkling lights, a spark to pierce the dark
> From Battery Park to Washington Heights.
> All my dreams will be repaid.
> Hell, I'd even play the maid to be in a show.[29]

In retelling the age-old story of young actors trying to make their way on the Broadway stage, Michael Bennett's *A Chorus Line* forever altered the traditional "book musical" format by bringing the unsung heroes and heroines of the Broadway musical, the chorus "boys" and "girls," to center stage.[30] The show reflects not only many of the harsh realities of the New York theater world but the self-absorbed aspect of New York's collective personality. Asserting that the musical "takes a close hard squint at Broadway babies on parade—here and now," the dance and theater critic Clive Barnes identified the series of monologues that make up its script as a "psychological striptease."[31] *A Chorus Line* struck a nerve with New Yorkers and the nation as a whole, becoming the longest-running musical ever on Broadway.

Company (1970) was an earlier effort to express New York's enduring vitality, its élan, even in the face of increasingly grim social and economic realities. Produced and directed by Harold Prince, with a book by George Furth and music and lyrics by Stephen Sondheim, *Company* examines the relationship of the very eligible bachelor Robert to five very married couples and to various single women. One of the latter sings "Another Hundred People," a song that powerfully describes the city's frenetic pace and the inhabitants' sense of alienation:

> Another hundred people just got off of the train
> And came up through the ground
> While another hundred people just got off of the bus
> And are looking around
> At another hundred people who just got off of the plane
> And are looking at us
> Who got off of the train
> And the plane and the bus
> Maybe yesterday.
> It's a city of strangers—
> Some come to work, some to play—
> A city of strangers—
> Some come to stare, some to stay,
> And every day
> Some go away.[32]

On Stage but Off Broadway

Several operas also attempted to portray aspects of life in New York. *Street Scene* (1947)—with a book that Elmer Rice adapted from his own Pulitzer Prize–winning play of 1929, music by Kurt Weill and lyrics by Langston Hughes—was a scorching tale of love and murder in New York's poorest precincts.[33] The completely scored opera includes the song "Wouldn't You Like to Be on Broadway?" in which the conniving Harry Easter tries to lure the innocent Rose Maurrant into an adulterous affair that promises fame, fortune and, perhaps most tantalizing, escape from the crowded tenements. The opera *The Saint of Bleecker Street* (1954), with words and music by Gian-Carlo Menotti, involves the conflicts between a saintly young woman, her cynical brother and his earthy mistress.[34] Menotti's opera was commissioned by the City Center for Music and Drama and produced with funds provided by the Rockefeller Foundation. The production's harshly stylized sets were designed by Robert Randolph under the supervision of Lincoln Kirstein. Situated entirely in Greenwich Village, the opera includes scenes that take place in a cold-water tenement apartment on Bleecker Street; amid the buildings and empty lots of Mulberry Street; in a dimly lit, basement-level Italian restaurant; and in a near-deserted subway station, the design of which was suggested by George Tooker's haunting painting *The Subway*. Kirstein wrote of the set:

> The extraordinary sensitivity and secure technique of Robert Randolph has transformed Tooker's tempera panels into a workable geography for Menotti's people. An atmosphere of pregnant emptiness, the focusing on a site where incident is about to take place, similar to the clear, blankly imposing backgrounds of the predella panels of Sassetta and Botticelli, but painted as if Botticelli and Sassetta were living in New York today: that was what Menotti had hoped for, and it is what he has been given.[35]

While opera successfully turned its attention to the contemporary city, ballet tended to eschew the subject in favor of either traditional themes or non-narrative treatments of psychological conflict. A notable exception is *Fancy Free* (1944).[36] Choreographed by Jerome Robbins to a score by Leonard Bernstein, the ballet documents the exploits of three sailors on leave in New York prior to setting sail for battle in Europe, powerfully celebrating the vibrant skyscraper city as a setting for romance. The work brilliantly invigorates classical steps with the Latin-inspired jazz rhythms that had become synonymous with New York's sophisticated nightlife. The ballet's folksy story was soon reinterpreted on the Broadway stage and subsequently on film as *On the Town.*

Throughout the 1950s and early 1960s most dance treating New York as a principal subject was restricted to the Broadway stage. In the late 1960s, however, several young modern dance choreographers, taking their cues from the Pop art–inspired "happenings" that had first emerged on the art scene a decade earlier, engaged the city as both a venue for and a subject of their work. These performances implicitly invited audience members to reevaluate their urban surroundings, daily observed but rarely fully appreciated. In his book *All That Is Solid Melts into Air* (1982), Marshall Berman provocatively linked key arguments offered by Jane Jacobs in her *Death and Life of Great American Cities* with a renewed interest in dance during the 1960s. Jacobs had pointed out that street life is "the art form of the city," evocative of an intricate ballet in which the individual dancers all have distinctive parts that miraculously reinforce each other and compose an orderly whole.[37] Although Berman qualified Jacobs's claim by pointing out that dance, with its precise structure and intricate choreography, is "worlds away from the spontaneity, openness and democratic feeling of the Jacobean street," he went on to observe that "as Jacobs assimilated the life of the street to the dance, the life of modern dance was striving to assimilate the street."[38]

In 1969 Meredith Monk presented the first segment of *Juice,* a "three-part theater cantata," as she described it, in the Guggenheim Museum; the second part was staged in a theater and the third in a loft.[39] At the Guggenheim, the audience, seated on the ground floor of the rotunda, watched eighty-five dancers create moving tableaux on the fourth, fifth and sixth levels of the spiraling ramp. In *Man Walking Down the Side of a Building* (1969), Trisha Brown turned the city on its head, or at least its side. A man, equipped with a mountaineering harness and ropes, walked down the side of a seven-story building in lower Manhattan.[40] Brown invited spectators to take a fresh look at the familiar and portrayed the city as an inherently disorienting environment where seemingly simple acts are burdened with a large measure of risk. The following year Brown's similar *Walking on the Wall* was performed inside the Whitney Museum.[41] In 1972 Marilyn Wood used the Seagram Building and its plaza as the site, and to a large extent the subject, of a celebratory multimedia performance (see chapter 5).

In 1973 Twyla Tharp choreographed what is perhaps the most accessible and exhilarating tribute to city life in postwar dance. *Deuce Coupe* (which was revised in 1975 as *Deuce Coupe II*) was set to music by the Beach Boys and originally performed by Tharp, five members of her company, and the Joffrey Ballet (see chapter 2).[42] Near the beginning of the piece, six members of the United Graffiti Artists entered downstage and, wielding spray cans, proceeded to paint three rolling paper panels. By the end of each performance, the artists had completed murals that looked, as the dance critic Deborah Jowitt put it, "something like the outside of a Seventh Avenue express train. Only more."[43] *New York Times* dance critic Anna Kisselgoff saw a dark message in the piece: "Perhaps unintentionally," she said, "'Deuce Coupe' is about co-optation. Without being romantic about the frenzy of graffiti that burst upon the city, it is illuminating to find that their creators are now apt to perform onstage for others rather than just for themselves."[44] The employment of the graffiti artists offered compelling proof that despite the city's troubles, its energy was still second to none.

From the song "The Sidewalks of New York" (1894)[45] through "Autumn in New York" (1934),[46] some of the most enduring "standards" of the pre–World War II era celebrate the city. In 1941 Ralph Freed and Burton Lane's "How About You" furthered a romantic image of New York, posing the questions: "I like New York in June,/How about you? . . . /I like to window shop on Fifth Avenue,/I like banana splits,/late supper at the Ritz./How about you?"[47]

During the immediate postwar years, New York continued to be portrayed in a positive light in such songs as Gordon Jenkins's "New York's My Home," part of his suite *Manhattan Tower: A Musical Narrative for Piano, Voice and Mixed Chorus* (1946). The song's lyrics unapologetically celebrated New York, responding to "a rumor goin' 'round,/That some of you good people want to leave this town," by saying that "You'd better consult with me before you go,/'Cause I've been to all those places and I know." The song goes on to describe the elements that set New York apart:

> Well, Chicago's all right. . . .
> But it hasn't got the hansoms in the park.
> It hasn't got the skyline after dark. . . .
> San Francisco's a lovely place. . . .
> But it hasn't got the Bow'ry or the Bronx,
> It hasn't got the Harlem honky tonks. . . .
> Lots of people here like St. Louis. . . .
> But it hasn't got the op'ra in the "Met,"
> It hasn't got a famous string quartet. . . .
> Hollywood's got movie stars and movie czars. . . .
> But it hasn't got the handy subway. . . .
> Save your railroad fare,
> Save your time and trouble. . . .
> 'Cause when you leave New York,
> You don't go anywhere.[48]

But by the late 1960s, New York had taken on an unwelcoming, even menacing face in popular song. Jim Croce's "New York's Not My Home" (1971) spins a yarn of alienation, internal chaos and hard luck, for which a change of venue seems to be the only cure. Croce laments:

> Don't you know that I gotta get out of here,
> 'Cause New York's not my home.
> Though all the streets are crowded,
> There's something strange about it,
> I lived there 'bout a year and I never once felt at home.
> I thought I'd make the big time,
> I learned a lot of lessons awful quick
> And now I'm telling you that they were not the nice kind;
> And it's been so long since I have felt fine.[49]

Jenkins's and Croce's songs were separated by a generation, during which time a dramatic change in attitude and musical style had occurred. This shift even affected songs written about Brooklyn, regarded by writers as the folksiest of the city's boroughs. In "The Brooklyn Bridge" (1947), written by Sammy Cahn and Jule Styne for the rather forgettable movie *It Happened in Brooklyn* (1947), the lyrics openly express the pride many Brooklynites showed in their borough and their competitiveness toward Manhattanites: "Folks in Manhattan are sad/ 'Cause they look at her and wish they had/ The good old Brooklyn Bridge. . . . / We forever claimed her/ When we proudly named her/ The Brooklyn Bridge."[50] The songwriter and comedian Abe Burrows paid tribute to Brooklyn and its local argot in his song "Brooklyn, U.S.A." (1955), proudly proclaiming: "Yes, I've seen the Taj Mahal, Shmaj Mahal,/Flatbush it ain't,/ Take me back to Brooklyn U.S.A."[51] Thirteen years later, that pride in a thriving culture had turned into nostalgia for a lost world in "Brooklyn Roads" (1968), Neil Diamond's tribute to the cozy domestic setting of his youth:

> Two floors above the butcher, first door on the right,
> Life filled to the brim as I stood by my window and looked
>   out on those Brooklyn Roads. . . .
> Thought of going back, but all I'd see are strangers' faces, and
>   all the scars that love erases.
> But as my mind walks through these places, I'm wonderin'
> Does some other young boy come home to my room?
> Does he dream what I did as I stood by my window and
>   looked out on those Brooklyn Roads?[52]

As in the past, the lyrics of popular songs in the 1940s and afterwards continued to focus on well-known places in New York, particularly Harlem and Broadway. "Harlem Nocturne" (1940), with words by Dick Rogers and music by Earle Hagen, depicts Harlem as a stark emotional landscape, a place defined by the blues: "Deep music fills the night, deep in the heart of Harlem./And tho' the stars are bright, the darkness is taunting me./Oh! what a sad refrain."[53] In contrast, Phil Spector and Jerry Leiber's "Spanish Harlem" (1960), first recorded and popularized by Ben E. King, portrays that section of Harlem as a magical place:

> There is a rose in Spanish Harlem
> A rare rose up in Spanish Harlem
> It is a special one
> It's never seen in the sun
> It only comes up when the moon is on the run
> And all the stars are gleaming
> It's growing in the street
> Right up through the concrete
> But soft and sweet and dreaming.[54]

Barry Mann, Cynthia Weil, Mike Stoller and Jerry Leiber's "On Broadway" (1962) updates a classic song theme, Broadway as a street of broken but enduring dreams:

> They say the neon lights are bright on Broadway;
> They say there's always magic in the air;
> But when you're walkin' down the street
> And you ain't had enough to eat
> The glitter rubs right off and you're nowhere. . . .
> They say I won't last long on Broadway;
> I'll catch a Greyhound bus for home, they say;
> But they're dead wrong, I know they are
> 'Cause I can play this here guitar
> And I won't quit till I'm a star on Broadway.[55]

"Funky Broadway" (1967), with words and music by Arlester Christian, describes the street as the embodiment of an attitude, with the song's title representing both a night club and a dance:

> Down on Broadway, (yeah!) there's a dance,
> Name of the dance
> Funky, Funky Broadway.
> Wiggle your legs now baby,
> Shake your head, Do a shing-a-ling, now, baby. . . .
> Doin' the Funky Broadway.
> Dirty, filthy Broadway.[56]

The singer-songwriter Laura Nyro, described by the music critic John Rockwell as "New York City's very own pop composer, singer and flower child"[57] and by Maggie Paley as the "funky Madonna of New York soul," wrote several songs that took the city as their subject.[58] "Mercy on Broadway" (1969) warns about life in the sometimes heartless city:

> There ain't no mercy now
> on Broadway . . .
> Baby on Broadway
> Is she mild
> like mother and child?
> does she obey? . . .
> don't you believe it
> you'd better know what I say
> she'll make you pay.[59]

Recalling the upbeat song "Spanish Harlem," Nyro wrote in "Map to Treasure" (1971): "Where is your woman?/gone to Spanish Harlem/gone to buy you pastels . . . /gone to buy you books and bells."[60] In Nyro's highly personal "New York Tendaberry" (1969), the city's physical aspect takes on redemptive power: "I ran away in the morning/now I'm back/unpacked/Sidewalks/and pigeon/you look like a city/but you feel like religion/to me."[61]

Bruce Springsteen, a singer and songwriter from New Jersey who powerfully documented working-class life, turned his attention to New York in such songs as "Does This Bus Stop at 82nd Street" (1972),[62] "Incident on 57th Street" (1973),[63] "New York City Serenade" (1973)[64] and "Tenth Avenue Freeze-Out" (1975).[65] The latter portrays the Clinton neighborhood—with its walk-up apartment buildings and industrial marginalia, including former warehouses transformed into music studios where hopefuls await their first break—as alternately vibrant and desolate:

> The night is dark, but sidewalk's bright and lined with
>   the living.
> From a tenement window a transistor blasts.
> Turn around the corner, things got real quiet real fast.
> I walked into a Tenth Avenue Freeze-Out!
> And I'm all alone,
> I'm all alone,
> And I'm on my own,
> I'm on my own,
> And I can't go home.

Although lyrics provide the most direct form of narrative, a number of composers tried to capture the spirit of New York in instrumental music. The Brazilian composer Heitor Villa-Lobos's "New York Set to Music" (1946) uses the Joseph Schillinger System of Musical Composition to transpose a pictorial image of the Manhattan skyline into a musical score.[66] *Manhattan Sketches: New Yorkaise Suite* (1956) is a sentimental set of piano pieces composed by Avenir de Monfred, who during the 1950s gave Sunday morning organ concerts televised on NBC and also composed jingles for radio and television commercials.[67] Duke Ellington's jazz piece "New York City Blues" (1952) pays a sophisticated, sexy musical tribute to the city, incorporating lilting trumpet solos and rhythmically staccato passages, elaborating the compositionally innovative music he had begun to develop in New York between the two world wars.[68] In 1964 the jazz musician Dave Brubeck was commissioned to write the theme and incidental music for *Mr. Broadway*, a short-lived CBS comedy-drama television series about the head of a public relations firm and his efforts to promote and protect his clients' reputations. Brubeck described his goal as "basically . . . to capture the rhythm and atmosphere of New York City." In addition to the requisite background music and a short theme,

Brubeck produced enough material to fill several record albums. He recorded twelve songs, collectively titled "Jazz Impressions of New York."[69]

During the city's near collapse in 1975, several songwriters came to its defense. Singer and songwriter Billy Joel, in "New York State of Mind," recalled his transcontinental travels and asserted, "It was so easy livin' day by day, out of touch with the rhythm and the blues./But now I need some give and take, /The New York Times and the Daily News."[70] In "New York City Rhythm," Barry Manilow and Marty Panzer expressed the feelings of many who still believed in the city:

> Ya know the movement seems to soothe me, and the tempo
> takes control, and I lose my blues when the New York City
> rhythm fills my soul. . . .
> In the funky dives on the old west side there's always
> something going down.
> Oh yes, I live my life with strangers, and the dangers
> always there, but when I hit Broadway and it's time to play,
> ya know that I don't care;
> it's the New York City rhythm runnin' thru' my life.[71]

ARCHITECTURAL CULTURE: DISCOURSE

During the postwar period, New York was the nation's architectural capital. About 50 percent of the country's registered architects practiced on Manhattan Island. It was the arrival point for visiting and emigrating European and South American architects, who added a cosmopolitan luster to the local scene. As early as 1935, Le Corbusier's visit to New York, followed by his book *Quand les cathédrals étaient blanches* (1937; published in 1947 as *When the Cathedrals Were White*),[1] had established the city as the benchmark against which all modern urbanism and urban architecture was to be measured. Many observers, especially Modernists, argued that New York was not the nation's most architecturally distinguished city—citing Chicago, with its consistent tradition of "no-nonsense" commercial architecture—but no one seriously challenged New York's status as the focus of postwar architectural culture. The nation's principal architecture journals were based there. The *New York Times*, the only American paper that had an international readership, began to take architecture seriously in the mid-1950s, leading to the appointment in 1963 of Ada Louise Huxtable as the first full-time staff architecture critic on any American newspaper. The *New Yorker* magazine also included a regular architecture column, "The Sky Line," which was written by Lewis Mumford from 1931 until 1963.

New York's central role in national and even international architectural culture was further solidified by the Museum of Modern Art's commitment to architectural discourse. Beginning with its landmark "International Exhibition of Modern Architecture" in 1932,[2] the museum mounted a series of provocative and increasingly scholarly exhibitions highlighting twentieth-century architecture. The museum pioneered a Department of Architecture in the same year, with Philip Johnson serving as its first director; Johnson's departure two years later for a career in politics left the department somewhat rudderless. In 1937 the department was expanded as the watery Department of Architecture and Industrial Art; with the renaming, John McAndrew replaced Ernestine Fantl as curator of architecture. From 1940 to 1945 the museum had separate departments of architecture and industrial design; Elizabeth

Mock, formerly an apprentice to Frank Lloyd Wright at Taliesin and McAndrew's assistant at the museum, headed the former, while Eliot Noyes oversaw the latter. For the most part, beginning in the mid-1930s and extending through the 1940s, the emphasis was not on architecture but on product design. The museum became a leader in exhibiting new trends in decorative and industrial arts, usurping the role the Metropolitan Museum of Art had established after World War II under the curatorship of Richard Franz Bach.[3] In 1938 McAndrew curated "Useful Household Objects Under $5.00", initiating a seven-part series produced sporadically until 1948, by which time inflation had pumped the show up to "100 Useful Objects of Fine Design, Available Under $100."[4] In 1941 the Museum of Modern Art featured an international mix of contemporary furniture in its exhibition "Organic Design."[5] The furniture, designed in the United States, was mass-produced and sold in twelve participating department stores nationwide, including Bloomingdale's in New York.

René d'Harnoncourt and Robert Goldwater's exhibition "Modern Art in Your Life" (1949) struck some viewers as naive.[6] Far more successful was "Good Design" (1950), for which Edgar Kaufmann, Jr., who as an unpaid member of the museum's staff exerted a powerful influence within the Department of Architecture and Design, enlisted the joint sponsorship of the Merchandise Mart of Chicago.[7] The exhibition was curated by the California-based husband-and-wife designers Charles and Ray Eames. Kaufmann encouraged the Merchandising Mart to hold similar exhibitions twice a year from which a single Museum of Modern Art exhibition could be culled. "Good Design 1952" incorporated an extremely stylish installation by Paul Rudolph.[8] Three years later Rudolph installed Edward Steichen's somewhat saccharine but immensely popular photographic exhibition, "The Family of Man," which touched on building as a universal activity.[9]

Two notable exceptions to the museum's concentration on design during the early years of the postwar period were "Built in USA: 1932–1944" (1944)[10] and "Built in USA: Post-war Architecture" (1952),[11] the latter assembled under the direction of Philip Johnson. Now a graduate of Harvard's architecture school and a former GI, Johnson had returned to the museum in 1946 as director of the Department of Architecture. From 1949 to 1954 he served as director of the newly unified Department of Architecture and Design.

The first "Built in USA" exhibition, curated by an executive committee consisting of Alfred Barr, Philip Goodwin and Elizabeth Mock, included four examples from New York: Rockefeller Center (Associated Architects, 1932–40),[12] the Museum of Modern Art (Philip Goodwin and Edward Durell Stone, 1939),[13] the Belt Parkway Footbridge (Clarence C. Combs, 1939)[14] and the Edward A. Norman House (William Lescaze, 1941).[15] The second exhibition, curated by Henry-Russell Hitchcock, was accompanied by a catalogue with a preface by Philip Johnson, who succinctly noted that the show's aim differed from that of previous architecture survey shows held at the museum. "The battle of modern architecture," he stated, "has long been won. Twenty years ago the Museum was in the thick of the fight, but now our exhibitions and catalogues take part in that unending campaign described by Alfred Barr as 'simply the continuous, conscientious, resolute distinction of quality from mediocrity—the discovery and proclamation of excellence." Johnson noted that every featured building "would look different if it had not been for the International Style, yet few buildings today recall the rigorous patterns of those days—the cubic boxes with asym-

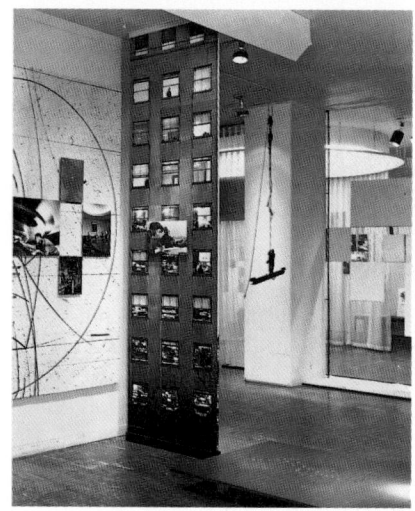

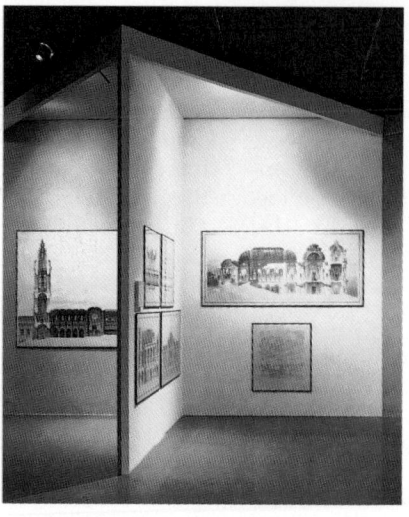

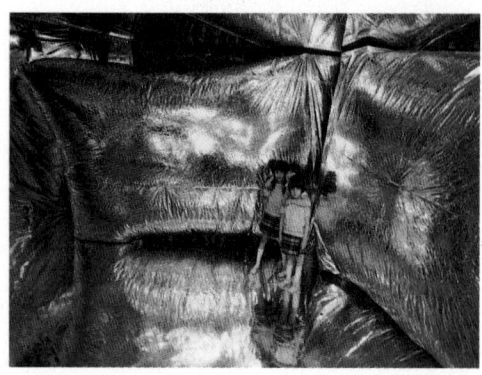

"The Family of Man," January 24–May 8, 1955, Museum of Modern Art, 11 West Fifty-third Street. Photography by Edward Steichen. Installation by Paul Rudolph. MOMA

"The Architecture of the Ecole des Beaux-Arts," October 28, 1975–January 4, 1976, Museum of Modern Art, 11 West Fifty-third Street. Installation by Arthur Drexler. MOMA

Slipcover. Les Levine, 1967. Architectural League of New York, 41 East Sixty-fifth Street. Levine. LL

metric window arrangements so characteristic of the twenties."[16] The exhibition included two New York buildings: the United Nations Secretariat Building and Lever House.

In 1956 Arthur Drexler succeeded Philip Johnson as director of the museum's Department of Architecture and Design; Drexler would remain in the post until his death in 1987. Under his direction, the department's exhibitions became increasingly scholarly. Drexler discontinued the "Good Design" exhibitions, later stating that "the material was running pretty thin, and they were big shows that took a lot of time and got on everybody's nerves here, and besides, it had become a sort of shoppers' service."[17] While Drexler deemphasized the museum's role as a tastemaker in the realm of mass-produced objects, he did not completely abandon the commitment to showcasing quality product design. In 1958, for the first time, the museum exhibited a major portion of its design collection; six years later the museum's expanded physical plant allowed Drexler to put at least a small part of the collection on permanent view.

With Drexler at the helm, the department mounted superb historical shows, many of which featured architects who were hardly connected with the canonic Modernism that had inspired Alfred Barr and Philip Johnson a generation before. Among the outstanding curatorial achievements were "Antonio Gaudí" (1957–58),[18] "The Drawings of Frank Lloyd Wright" (1962),[19] "Hector Guimard" (1970),[20] "Visionary Architecture" (1960),[21] "Twentieth Century Engineering" (1964)[22] and "Architecture without Architects" (1964).[23] Such exhibitions offered a subversive polemic against the antihistory of canonic Modernism. Drexler also sought to broaden the museum's still rather restricted vision of what Modernist architecture could or should be, occasionally mounting provocative one-person and thematic exhibitions such as "Louis I. Kahn, Architect, Richards Medical Research Building" (1961).[24] Mostly Drexler tried to downplay individual architect-artists—and, some argued, the very nature of architecture itself—with thematic exhibitions such as "The New City: Architecture and Urban Renewal" (1967), which elevated urban design over building design (see chapter 12),[25] and "Architectural Fantasies" (1967), which presented the visionary work of three young Viennese architects, Raimond J. Abraham, Hans Hollein and Walter Pichler, which

suggested that buildings were not as important as drawings.[26] Drexler tried to shatter the primacy of traditional tectonics in such shows as "Two Models of an Unimaginable City" (1969), featuring the work of the architect Theodore Waddell,[27] "Will Insley: Ceremonial Space" (1971)[28] and "The Work of Frei Otto" (1972).[29] From 1969 to 1976, with Emilio Ambasz serving as curator of design, the department advanced a view of architecture as a fine art. The exhibition "Architectural Studies and Projects" (1975) included visionary projects such as Raimond Abraham's "House with Flower Walls," Peter Eisenman's "House Six: Transformations #14," Friedrich St. Florian's "Himmelblett, Penthouse Version (with Holographic Heaven)" and Ettore Sottsass's "Rafts for Listening to Chamber Music" and "Temple for Erotic Dances."[30] Drexler and Ambasz succeeded in putting the museum back at the center of debate, though their focus on architecture increasingly separated theory from practice.

One exception to this trend toward the margins of architectural practice was "The Architecture of the Ecole des Beaux-Arts," perhaps Drexler's most influential show, or at least his most sensational and widely discussed. This exhibition was held from October 1975 to January 1976, just as Post-Modernism, with its interest in ornament and lush coloration, was emerging as the dominant trend in architecture.[31] Drexler was explicit in his goals; in the preface to the exhibition's copiously illustrated, ambitiously scholarly catalogue, he wrote: "Some Beaux-Arts problems, among them the question of how to use the past, may perhaps be seen now as possibilities that are liberating rather than constraining. . . . Now that modern experience so often contradicts modern faith, we would be well to reexamine our architectural pieties."[32]

Drexler's reexamination of the very nature of modernity powerfully captured the imagination of the architectural community and the public at large. Assessing the exhibition within its historical context, *Progressive Architecture*'s editor, John Morris Dixon, said: "Though unlikely to redirect the course of architecture, the exhibition is nevertheless a milestone: the citadel of the Modern Movement celebrating the system those Modern pioneers had to overthrow. At the least, the event marks a reconciliation, an expression of respect for the vanquished."

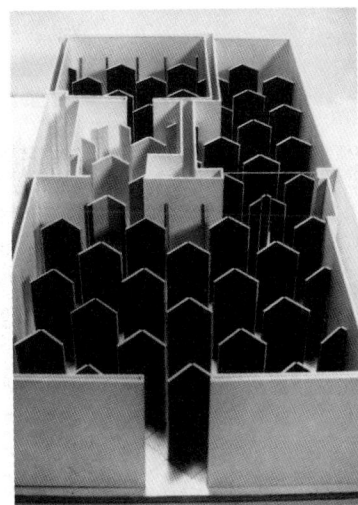

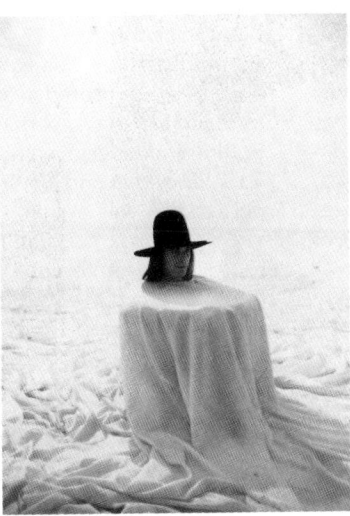

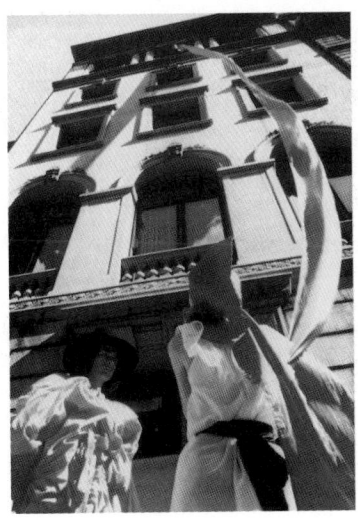

Corridors. John Lobell, 1967. Architectural League of New York, 41 East Sixty-fifth Street. Model. Veltri. JL

Fly. James Lee Byars, 1968. Architectural League of New York, 41 East Sixty-fifth Street. Propper. JL

Do. James Lee Byars, 1968. Procession beginning at the Architectural League of New York, 41 East Sixty-fifth Street. Propper. JL

Dixon put his finger on Drexler's signature brand of polemical historiography, noting that the curator "has chosen to stimulate [a] re-examination" of Modernism "not by singling out any promising current directions; instead, he is recalling the virtues of a previously rejected alternative."[33]

Though those who followed trends in the fine arts continued to look to the Museum of Modern Art as a judge of taste in architecture and design, architectural professionals began to turn to other venues as they challenged the now established Modernism and forged new directions. Many were put off by the increasing marginality of the museum's shows, which were seen as elitist and just plain irrelevant. By the late 1960s Ada Louise Huxtable, who had herself served as an assistant curator at the museum from 1946 to 1950, could characterize it as "arbiter of blue-chip selections, and status-insured activities."[34] To fill the void, two institutions became the twin foci of debates: the Architectural League of New York, much older than the Museum of Modern Art but virtually moribund since the 1940s as a result of the museum's hegemony, and an offshoot of the museum, the Institute for Architecture and Urban Studies.

In 1958 the architect Morris Ketchum, Jr., became the Architectural League's president and began to wake the sleeping organization.[35] Ketchum revived the league's once prestigious National Gold Medal of the Building Arts Exhibition in 1960, emphasizing the collaboration of architects with engineers, artists and craftsmen.[36] In 1961 the league joined *Architectural Forum* in sponsoring a five-part series titled "The New Forces in Architecture," which began with Vincent Scully's plea for architecture as environmental action. Subsequently, Philip Johnson and the English critic Reyner Banham debated over the future of the International Style; the art collector Ralph F. Colin moderated a panel on the current art market, with participants including the architect-critic Peter Blake, the president of Parke-Bernet, Leslie Hyam, the art dealer Samuel M. Kootz, and the painter Jack Levine. Marcel Breuer and Paul Rudolph tackled the issue of individual expression versus order; and Louis I. Kahn shared a platform with Catherine Bauer Wurster, José Luis Sert and the psychiatrist Ernest Van den Haag to discuss the new art of urban design.[37]

In 1965 the league's board, anxious to do more, invited Philip Johnson to become president. In a speech, Johnson graciously refused and instead proposed that funds from a new bequest be used to hire Robert Stern, then completing his architectural training at Yale, as program director, working under a committee consisting of Johnson, Robert Cutler and Robert Allan Jacobs.[38] Under Stern, the league mounted a series of informal shows, "Making the Scene: The New Talent," that introduced an emerging generation of architects to the New York public, including Mitchell Giurgola Associates, Venturi & Rauch, and Moore, Lyndon, Turnbull & Whitaker. An exhibition of photographs by Tony Woolner illustrating the plight of Staten Island after the building of the Verrazano-Narrows Bridge provided impetus for Ada Louise Huxtable to travel across the bay to see the haphazard development that would become the focus of her Pulitzer Prize–winning analysis.[39] Stern concluded his term at the league with the synoptic "40 under 40: An Exhibition of Young Talent in Architecture," which revived a league exhibition format from the early 1940s.[40] The show opened in the gallery of the American Federation of Arts in April 1966 before traveling nationally.[41]

In the fall of 1966, under the new president, Ulrich Franzen, the league vacated its historic premises on East Fortieth Street, later to be replaced by an office building,[42] and reconstituted itself as a membership organization devoted to lectures and exhibitions dealing with architecture and its associated arts. In 1967 the league undertook a series of "Environment" exhibitions in the townhouse galleries it shared with its new landlord, the American Federation of Arts, at 41 East Sixty-fifth Street. The series, one of the era's most important demonstrations of new artistic trends, including site-specific installations, performance and participatory art, got off to what the *Architectural Forum* editors described as a "slow start" with "a random collection of artifacts (or possibly facts) randomly and somewhat depressingly displayed," including wrapped-up objects by the Bulgarian-born artist Christo and a photoelectric pinball machine by the sculptor Castro-Cid.[43] *Environment II*, designed by Charles Ross and held in January 1967, took light as its theme. The room was lined with polyethylene sheets dripping with yellow water and illuminated by a stroboscopic ceiling light that flashed on and off at irregular but rapid intervals, transforming viewers into actors in a kinetic performance. The editors of *Architectural Forum* praised the exhibition as "the greatest show in town."[44] In May the league mounted an even bolder environmental display, Les Levine's *Slipcover*.[45] Levine covered the walls, floors and ceilings of three rooms with highly reflective, silver-colored mylar, shining colored lights against the surfaces and throwing images of New York architecture, the lights of Broadway and portraits of himself from six carousel slide projectors. To further the environmental dynamics, the mylar along the walls was loosely mounted on wood frames, with fans set behind to create billowing forms, "like giant air-filled Baggies," as Levine put it.[46] Ann Tabachnick, writing in *Art News*, described the forms as "organlike."[47] The critic William Gordy noted, "From time to time a glittering shape deflates and lies quietly for a while, then suddenly becomes turgid again, nudging the unwary in a faintly sexy way."[48]

In June the league presented *Subways*, in which Barbara Stauffacher emblazoned the walls, floors and ceilings of its galleries with "supergraphics," a new approach to environmental signage that the San Francisco–based artist had devised in collaboration with Charles Moore and William Turnbull, who served as architectural consultants to the show. Using numbers, arrows, signs, maps, stripes and symbols to clarify passenger movement, Stauffacher, Moore, Turnbull and Hugh Hardy, who acted as lighting consultant, proposed to transform the subway environment, which Stauffacher described as "in some measure the very image of New York to New Yorkers."[49]

In the fall of 1967 the young architect John Lobell, working under Franzen, pushed the league to even further extremes, collaborating with the sculptor Michael Steiner on *Corridors*, described by the designers as a "musical instrument of architectural scale," in which the viewer, entering the diagonal corridors, activated special lighting and a recording of electronic sound.[50] In reviewing the work the art critic Dore Ashton argued:

> Where Lobell might have miscalculated, according to my experience in this environment, is in believing that he could produce a musical instrument as an architectural structure. The music recedes, as it must in the face of the powerful experience of moving through physically shaped spaces. It is really incidental music. The human physique is the fly in the ointment. We have flat feet and stand on a baseline, and are—at least for the moment—gravity bound. Newtonian physics may have been bypassed intellectually, but it still pertains to the human plant.

Still, Ashton praised the league's series for serving "as a laboratory for fresh ideas about how to make environments reflect the new artistic and philosophic preoccupations of both artists and architects."[51]

In December 1967 *Environment V: Vibrations* transformed the gallery into a kinetic light environment designed by "artists-in-light" Jackie Cassen and Rudi Stern.[52] Describing the scene, the critic N. J. Loftis stated, "To my left, a geodesic sphere is dancing, wearing the smell of orange, blue and green perfume. Before it, careful not to touch each other, a sculptural shape revolves like a trained bear, in a glittering robe of lights. While on the far wall, as across a screen, a window . . . flashes red, now purple, now green." While noting that "young people recline on the floor enraptured" and that "one is dazzled by the display," Lewis concluded that "one is never wholly absorbed. The lights shine on me, not in me."[53]

On September 12, 1968, the thirty-six-year-old Detroit-born artist James Lee Byars startled New York with the first of six league-sponsored avant-garde performances, which he preferred to call plays, perhaps punning on the word's meanings as both drama and juvenile activity.[54] The plays—*Do, Fly, Can't, Talk, Breathe* and *Try*—were presented over a three-week period. *Do* was arguably the most arresting. Guests were invited to don a "communal garment," a ten-foot-wide, mile-long, red acetate strip punctured every five feet by holes through which the participants put their heads. The parading crowd proceeded from the league's headquarters at 41 East Sixty-fifth Street around the block, walking to the accompaniment of a tuba ensemble playing Bach. Byars later stated, "I would like to put the whole world in the same dress. . . . Why do women have to wear dresses and men pants anyway?"[55] When the marchers completed their route, Byars's friends cut apart the garment, releasing the participants in groups of five. At the post-event reception, the garment was further divided into one- and two-person segments. Grace Glueck reported on the event for the *New York Times*: "Was it a protest? A love-in? A graduation procession? Or maybe—heaven forbid—a Shriners' convention? Those were some of the questions blasé Upper East Siders asked last evening as they watched some 130 people . . . joined together in a communal garment of red acetate." She continued:

> "I thought it was very beautiful, very successful," said Mr. Byars, fingering the black Navejo [sic] hat that covered his shoulder-length hair. . . . One of the aims of the series, he noted, was "to get people to describe and discuss their perceptions, to become aware of their life styles—and what they eat, their behavioral cycles, everything involved with the way they live." Some questions posed in his "plays," he noted, are "What is the speed of an idea? Are all people interchangeable at some level? What does pretend mean?"[56]

Whatever Byars's intentions, the event succeeded as a joyful embodiment of the era's preoccupation with participatory performance art.

Byars followed *Do* with similarly offbeat events. Glueck, who asserted that the series "gives the phrase 'far-out' an entirely new dimension," reported:

> One play . . . is "Four in a Hat," a marathon session in which Byars and drop-ins from the street don a quartet of Liberty caps, joined to each other by scarlet streamers, and sit on the floor discussing the contents of their heads. "It feels fabulous to have your head hooked up to others," says Byars. Also in the series are "100 in an Airplane," offering participants a chance to poke their heads through 100 holes in a giant pink silk plane and pretend to fly it; and "Twelve in a Pink Pants," a discussion event similar to "Hat" except that discussers do their thing in a dozen inter-connected pants suits of pink silk.[57]

Labeling Byars's work "psychosculpture," the editors of *Time* noted the "eerie visual unity" of *Four in a Hat*.[58]

In February 1972 the league's environmentalism reached its zenith when the conceptual artist Alan Sonfist presented *Army Ants: Patterns and Structures,* in which three million ants marched around a four-hundred-square-foot sandbox constructed in the galleries of Automation House. Sonfist believed that by studying the ants' habits and their system of creating nests, "we might become aware of our integration with and dependence upon those systems and thereby learn to perpetuate our own."[59] However, as the editors of *Architectural Forum* put it, the three million ants "had a better idea" just prior to the exhibition's opening: "Like every first-time visitor to Manhattan, they wanted to have a night on the town and, discovering a tiny aperture in the plastic-covered sides of the sandbox, they proceeded to march through it and out into the darkened galleries of Automation House."[60] An observant night watchman brought out the bug spray, and killed all but fifteen thousand of the ants. Undaunted, Sonfist had a batch of two million ants sent from Panama; they arrived in time for the official opening and a televised press conference. After performing brilliantly for the cameras, the ants began to show signs of weakness; most of them died before week's end, marking a sad but timely end to the league's most experimental series.

From time to time, the league also focused on more conventional architectural manifestations, but viewed in unusual and provocative ways. In November 1967 the league presented, in an exhibition more in line with Ambasz's efforts at the Museum of Modern Art, a collaboration between architect John Hejduk and painter Robert Slutzky. The two used models, drawings and canvases to illustrate the dynamism inherent in the diamond shape.[61] In January 1970 the league used the conventional monographic approach to document the work of the idiosyncratic, counterestablishment architect Bruce Goff.[62] The Goff show was followed by "Morris Lapidus: Architecture of Joy," which cut even closer to the establishment bone.[63] Organized by John Margolies, a sometime architectural journalist then serving as the league's director of exhibitions, in association with Billy Adler and Robert Jensen, the show opened in October 1970. It was designed by Lapidus's son Alan, also an architect, and John Bowstead, a designer on staff at Morris Lapidus Associates, and included photographs and film footage of some of the sixty-eight hotels and 18,000 hotel rooms Lapidus had designed, as well as documentation of his other projects and examples of Lapidus-designed furniture, architectural elements and bellhop uniforms draped on mannequins. Two curving walls of photographic panels and a dramatically processional curved staircase leading to nowhere in particular echoed the architect's signature use of such forms. Emphasizing the work's unabashedly democratic aspect, Muzak was played throughout the exhibition. Even before the show opened, it was caught up in controversy. Some members of the league's board questioned the wisdom of the enterprise; others, including new board member Peter Eisenman, as well as John Johansen and Les Levine, wrote in support of the show to the league's president, Arthur Rosenblatt. One of the exhibition's principal critics was Ulrich Franzen, under whose leadership the league had embarked on its adventure into the avant-garde; he deemed Lapidus "the Lawrence Welk of hotel architecture."[64] In an overwhelmingly negative review of the show, Ada Louise Huxtable said flatly, "one man's joy [is] . . . another man's hell."[65]

During the early 1970s the Architectural League was challenged in its role as the city's most vital forum for architectural experiment and discourse by a newcomer, the Institute for Architecture and Urban Studies. Founded in 1967 as both an outgrowth of the Museum of Modern Art's provocative exhibition "The New City: Architecture and Urban Renewal" and a response to Cornell University's ill-fated attempt to establish a portion of its architecture program in New York City, the institute was a joint venture of the museum and the university.[66] In an effort "to bridge the chasm between the 'ivory tower' of the institutional professor and the urgent problems of the nation's cities," as Steven V. Roberts reported in the New York Times, the

institute, supported by private foundations, was to function as a think tank working with graduate students to take on practical urban problems.[67] According to Peter Eisenman, its founding director:

> Architects have abrogated their responsibility to deal with social problems. They have left it to the nuts-and-bolts boys; they haven't really been in the fight. On the other hand, politicians have never seen the organization of space as crucial to social problems. There has to be blame on both sides. But the result has been that architects have never participated in the basic decisions about cities. They've just been called in to put the icing on the cake.[68]

From the beginning Eisenman, who was trained at Columbia, Cornell and Cambridge, saw the institute as a way of correcting the course of Modernist architecture. As the architect put it: "People who taught me modern architecture didn't see the social implications of European theory. They saw only the forms. Thus American architecture became style rather than an idea, or a way of life."[69] The institute began in a loft at 5 East Forty-seventh Street, with five students from Cornell working with Eisenman and Colin Rowe, a Cornell professor of architecture. By the early 1970s the institute had evolved into a hothouse of theoretical speculation, masterminded by Eisenman, who proved a brilliant polemicist and showman. In 1972 the book Five Architects, featuring the independent work of Eisenman, Michael Graves, Charles Gwathmey, John Hejduk and Richard Meier, was published; containing essays by Arthur Drexler, Kenneth Frampton and Colin Rowe, the book was to some degree the product of the Conference of Architects for the Study of the Environment, held in 1969 at the Museum of Modern Art. It met with a rebuttal in five essays by historicist and contextualist Post-Modernists Robert Stern, Allan Greenberg, Jaquelin Robertson, Romaldo Giurgola and Charles Moore, collectively titled "Five on Five" and published in Architectural Forum. Together the two documents established a new level of discourse that would have wide ramifications.[70] According to Paul Goldberger, writing in the New York Times, "the two approaches have created in New York today a period of deep architectural thought that was not seen throughout the nineteen-sixties."[71]

In 1973, intent on translating theory into actual building practice, the institute, represented by Kenneth Frampton, Arthur Baker and Peter Wolf, collaborated with the New York State Urban Development Corporation and the architectural firm of David Todd & Associates on the design of Marcus Garvey Village in the Brownsville section of Brooklyn (see chapter 13). By the mid-1970s, however, the institute was close to becoming, for better or worse, Eisenman's personal fief—the Eisenman Institute, as loyal supporter Philip Johnson dubbed it. In 1974, in an effort to broaden the institute's appeal and extend its educational mission, Eisenman devised an elaborate education program incorporating lectures, seminars and courses intended for the public at large as well as for architecture students.[72] The following year he introduced an active exhibition program including "Goodbye Five: Work by Young Architects."[73] Most importantly, Eisenman launched Oppositions, a journal published under the auspices of the institute from 1973 until 1984.[74]

By 1974 Goldberger could report that the institute, now located in the penthouse space at 8 West Fortieth Street (originally the offices of Starrett & Van Vleck Architects), had become "the closest thing New York has to an ongoing architectural forum. It is where most overseas visitors, both scholars and practicing architects, seem to congregate when they arrive in New York, and it is the only center of architectural education anywhere where the student body ranges from ninth grade through postdoctoral scholars."[75]

Critical Voices

During the postwar period architectural criticism garnered the attention of an unprecedentedly large general audience. Previously, architectural criticism had been read mainly by members of the field's professional and academic communities. Two outstanding critics of the interwar period, Talbot Faulkner Hamlin and Douglas Haskell, continued to write about architecture in the 1940s and 1950s, with their audiences remaining largely unchanged. One important exception to the prevailing insularity of architectural criticism was Lewis Mumford, whose "Sky Line" column for the *New Yorker* influenced professionals and the public alike between the wars.[76]

Mumford continued to be a decisive critical voice after the war, writing the "Sky Line" column until December 7, 1963. In 1942 Mumford had terminated the column, but Harold Ross, the editor of the *New Yorker*, persuaded him to resume it in 1947 on a less regular basis. When Ross offered Mumford the job back, he said, "There is no one else. The new generation is a collapse. It has produced no talent of any kind."[77] In addition to the praise, Ross offered Mumford twice his previous salary and stated flatly that if he didn't take the job, the column would be dropped completely. Throughout the postwar period Mumford's criticism continued, as it had in the 1930s, to emphasize the social dimension of architecture, reflecting his belief that the primary criterion for judging a building was its ability to improve users' lives. His postwar "Sky Line" took on public housing, inner-city highways and neighborhood planning. Before turning to technology, philosophy and the vicissitudes of his own life, the subjects that dominated his last years, Mumford also wrote important essays on such postwar monuments as the United Nations, Lever House, the Manufacturers Trust Company's Forty-third Street branch and the Seagram Building.[78]

Aline Bernstein Louchheim Saarinen provided another significant critical perspective on postwar architecture in New York. From 1947 to 1959 Louchheim, who had been educated at Vassar College and New York University's Institute of Fine Arts and had been the managing editor of *Art News*, served as an associate art editor and associate art critic at the *New York Times*.[79] Though concentrating on art criticism, Louchheim wrote occasionally on architecture, including, in 1953, an article on Eero Saarinen published in the *New York Times Magazine*.[80] In 1954 she married Saarinen. While Louchheim, now Aline B. Saarinen, continued to write on architecture, the potential conflict of interest arising from her marriage resulted in her focusing on historical subjects, including the increasingly pressing issue of preservation. Saarinen's 1955 *Vogue* essay "Four Architects Helping to Change the Look of America," which profiled her husband along with Mies van der Rohe, Philip Johnson and Gordon Bunshaft, was accompanied by an editor's note specifying that the selection of the architects had been made prior to commissioning the author.[81] In 1962 Saarinen edited the writings of her husband, who had died the previous year at the age of fifty-one.[82] Saarinen's 1962 appearance on a CBS television program about Lincoln Center so impressed an NBC producer that he hired her as a regular contributor to the *Today* show, where she served as on-screen commentator, researcher, writer, producer and director. Both Saarinen's writing and television criticism were widely praised for lucidly conveying the complexities of architectural theory and practice to a broad audience. Her sharp pronouncements on aesthetic quality, delivered with utter self-confidence, were also famous. The editors of *Time* described her as "a one-woman cultural explosion."[83] Saarinen died in 1972 at the age of fifty-eight. A memorial service was held at Lincoln Center's Vivian Beaumont Theater, which her late husband had designed.

While Saarinen had covered architectural subjects for the *New York Times* until 1959, it was not until four years later (when, perhaps not coincidentally, Mumford stopped writing his "Sky Line" column for the *New Yorker*) that the *Times* appointed Ada Louise Huxtable as its full-time architecture critic.[84] Huxtable became the first person ever to hold such a job on an American newspaper. A graduate of Hunter College, Huxtable had done advanced work in architectural history at New York University's Institute of Fine Arts. She went on to become an assistant curator of architecture at the Museum of Modern Art between 1946 and 1950, when Philip Johnson was the department's director. She left the museum to spend two years studying contemporary Italian architecture and design in Milan as a Fulbright scholar. Upon returning to the United States in 1952, Huxtable rejoined the Museum of Modern Art to organize a circulating exhibition on the work of Pier Luigi Nervi, the Italian engineer-architect; this led to her first book, *Pier Luigi Nervi* (1960).[85] From 1956 to 1958 she published a twenty-article series in *Progressive Architecture* discussing significant historical American buildings from an aesthetic and structural point of view. Four of the articles focused on New York, featuring Grand Central Terminal, two cast-iron buildings built for Harper and Brothers and E. V. Haughwout and Company, and the Brooklyn Bridge.[86] In 1958 Huxtable was awarded a Guggenheim Fellowship. By the early 1960s she was a contributing editor of *Progressive Architecture* and *Art in America* and an occasional contributor to other publications, most notably the *New York Times*. She also collaborated with her husband, the industrial designer L. Garth Huxtable, on various projects, including the design of the tabletop items used in the Four Seasons restaurant.

Huxtable wrote *Four Walking Tours of Modern Architecture in New York City*, copublished by the Museum of Modern Art and the Municipal Art Society in 1961, which discussed fifty-eight Manhattan buildings.[87] Surprisingly, it was only the second guidebook ever published on New York's architecture. The first, Huson Jackson's *A Guide to New York Architecture 1650–1952* (1952), is more comprehensive but less detailed.[88] Huxtable's second book, *Classic New York: Georgian Gentility to Greek Elegance* (1964), is a scholarly guide to Manhattan's surviving early-nineteenth-century buildings. (The book was originally intended as one of a series of six that would bring New York's architectural history up to the present, but the project was abandoned when the pressures of writing for a daily newspaper placed too great a demand on Huxtable's time.) *Classic New York* was published on the heels of Alan Burnham's *New York Landmarks: A Study and Index of Architecturally Notable Structures in Greater New York* (1963), and together the two books hastened an increasingly alarmed public to fight for legislative protection of the city's architectural heritage.[89] Huxtable proved an important advocate of the historic preservation movement, and in article after article she pushed for the establishment of the New York City Landmarks Preservation Commission.

In 1958, in an article in the *New York Times Magazine*, Huxtable made the case for architectural criticism as a regular feature of newspaper journalism:

> The press, which regularly reviews art, literature, theater, movies, music and dance, ignores architecture, except for building news on the real estate page. Architectural criticism as a standard feature is virtually unknown, in spite of the direct and inescapable impact of architectural production. Superblocks are built, the physiognomy and services of the city are changed, without discussion except in a few of the more sophisticated or specialized journals. Unless a story reaches the proportions of a scandal, architecture is the stepchild of the popular press.[90]

Huxtable garnered the grudging support of the *Times*'s editorial staff. Managing editor Clifton Daniel understatedly told *Newsweek* that her "commentary is needed. In New York there's a lot to be criticized."[91] After 1963 Huxtable's regular writing in the *New York Times* focused public opinion on the city's built environment as never before. In 1965 her devastating critique of Staten Island's post–Verrazano-Narrows Bridge building boom,[92] perhaps her most outspoken piece, helped win her a Pulitzer Prize, the first ever awarded to a critic in any field.[93] By then she had become a major force on the New York scene, having transformed, as the editors of *Newsweek* reported, "the puffery of back-page real estate news into a new architecture beat and gotten page-one play time after time."[94]

Feared by the architectural profession and real estate interests, Huxtable was a darling of the public. In 1968 the noted architectural cartoonist Alan Dunn captured the extent of her renown and influence in the pages of the *New Yorker*. Amid a bustling construction site, one hard hat says to another: "Ada Louise Huxtable already doesn't like it!"[95] Three years later another *New Yorker* cartoon, this one by Donald Reilly, would also pay tribute to the critic. Two men stand in a real estate developer's office viewing a model of a futuristic skyscraper; the caption reads: "I'd give anything to be there when Ada Louise Huxtable gets a load of this."[96] In an article that appeared on the front page of the *Wall Street Journal* on November 7, 1972, Stephen Grover chronicled Huxtable's achievements, contending that she was "perhaps the most powerful individual on the *Times*'s roster of critics—including the newspaper's mighty reviewers of drama."[97]

Huxtable became known not only for the critical content of her essays but for her prose style. She could also be witty to devastating effect. She dismissed the Gallery of Modern Art that Edward Durell Stone designed for Huntington Hartford as a "die-cut Venetian palazzo on lollypops."[98] Huxtable's punchy style seemed appropriate to the task at hand; in contrast to Lewis Mumford, who had been able to luxuriate in seemingly limitless *New Yorker* pages, Huxtable had to get the reader's attention and make her points quickly. In 1972 Mumford said that "it wasn't until the *Times* got Huxtable that people really began to pay attention to architecture criticism."[99]

Despite Huxtable's success, not everyone was impressed. The architectural historian and critic Vincent Scully, responding to Huxtable's negative review of his book *American Architecture and Urbanism* (1969) in a letter to the editors of the *New York Times*, charged, "It has never been possible to value Mrs. Huxtable's writing for her critical acumen or command of history. Its most positive quality has seemed to be a kind of hectic candor, but that, too, must be called into question now."[100]

Huxtable's forthright sting was undeniable. In 1963 she took on the firm of Emery Roth & Sons, then at the peak of its success, stating: "This is a Roth city. The Roth firm has lined Manhattan streets and avenues with the Roth style of financial expediency."[101] She often drew the ire of the real estate establishment. Huxtable had written of the immensely successful Uris Building Corporation, which frequently patronized the Roth firm, that such a large firm "owes the city something. . . . There must be some kind of conscience that can be pricked."[102] Harold Uris, one of the two brothers who ran the corporation, complained that she "always describes the outside of a building, never the inside. Somebody should go in and take a look and ask the people are they happy in them."[103] Richard Roth, Sr., echoed a frequently voiced complaint when he told the editors of *Newsweek* that "if she likes the architect then she likes what he does."[104]

On September 25, 1973, almost ten years to the day after becoming the *New York Times*'s first architecture critic, Huxtable was named to the newspaper's editorial board.[105] The appointment provided the already powerful critic with immense influence. She surrendered her writing in the daily paper, except editorials, and wrote only a regular Sunday column.

In 1973 the *New York Times* appointed Paul Goldberger as its full-time architecture critic. The twenty-three-year-old Yale graduate had begun his career in architectural journalism while still in college, publishing an extensive article on the work of Robert Venturi and Denise Scott Brown in the *New York Times Magazine* in 1971.[106] Goldberger joined the magazine's editorial staff the following year. As a critic Goldberger spoke in a milder tone and reflected broader tastes than his predecessor had. While championing the emerging Post-Modernist aesthetic, Goldberger offered carefully modulated reviews, considered prudent by some, noncommital by others. Nonetheless, Goldberger's influence would increase steadily. By the late 1970s his word was as powerful as Huxtable's had once been.

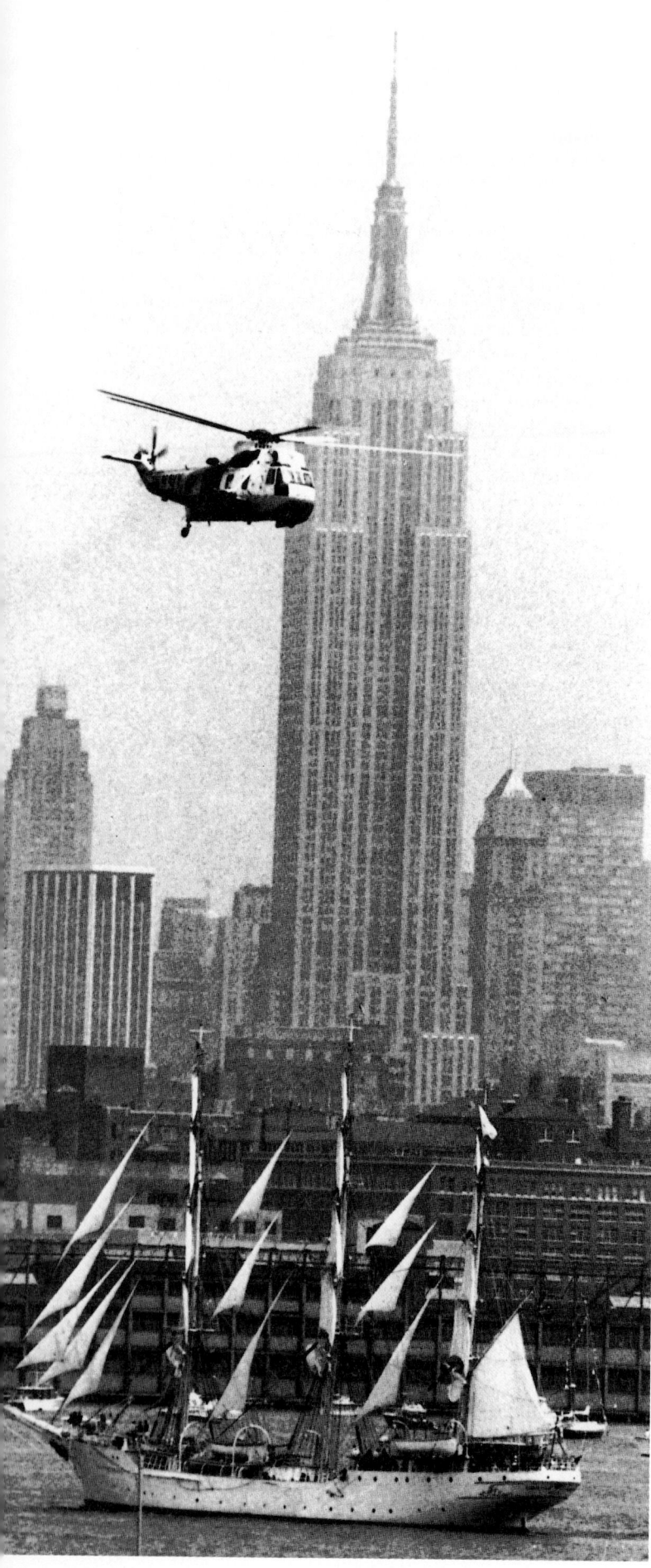

View to the northeast of midtown Manhattan during Operation Sail, July 4, 1976, showing the Norwegian tall ship *Christian Radich* in the foreground and the Empire State Building (Shreve, Lamb & Harmon, 1931) in the background. UPIB

In 1975, some thirty years after it had been crowned the world's capital, New York teetered on the brink of collapse. It had lost its economic clout; worse still, most Americans seemed to regard the city, once the nation's standard of quality and sophistication, as the embodiment of all that was wrong with modern life. Even many New Yorkers agreed, and New York's self-esteem was at an all-time low.

Not everyone, however, had given up on the city. In 1975 the cartoonist Saul Steinberg, who had long used New York as a subject, created *View of the World from 9th Avenue,* his most memorable depiction of the city. The cartoon, which appeared on the cover of the *New Yorker*'s March 29, 1976, issue, was such a powerful image of the city that it soon would become a virtual badge of New York's status as a vital and fiercely proud, if self-obsessed, city. Rendered from an elevated vantage point, the drawing presents Ninth Avenue in the foreground and, in a radically telescoped perspective, Tenth Avenue, the Hudson River and the entire contiguous United States beyond; in the distance are China, Japan and, ultimately, Siberia. The drawing lampoons the typical New Yorker's myopia while at the same time suggesting that the city's self-confidence and even its boastfulness are entirely justified; if you have the misfortune of venturing across the Hudson, Steinberg suggests, you might as well be in Siberia. New Yorkers' long-standing belief that the nation's real center of power was located in their city, not in Washington, is reflected by the capital's marginal location near the edge of the drawing, next to Mexico.

Other observers not only touted the city's strengths but also expressed faith in New York's economic revitalization. James B. Lindheim, a vice president of Yankelovich, Skelly and White, a marketing and research firm, detected the emergence of a new group of urban dwellers who would replace the industrial and blue-collar workers who had long been the staple of the city's economy. This group, which Lindheim called "the hippoisie" but would soon come to be known as "yuppies" (young urban professionals), comprised the maturing postwar baby-boom generation. Lindheim described this new group, which would replenish much of the city's "flair, magnetism, and power":

> The hippoisie is not characterized—as were previous social classes in the dialectic march to utopia—by particular occupations or income levels. It helps, of course, to be "in the arts," although the arts can include New York's enormous advertising

Afterword

industry, as well as starving poet-waitresses and Geraldo Rivera. It also helps to have money. It always has. But this class defies standard socioeconomic categorization, because it is defined by its consumption patterns, not by its production role. What the hippoisie makes is less important than what it popularizes.

While the hippoisie was emerging in every important American city, Lindheim argued that New York's hippoisie would set the tone: "The hippoisies are the city's arrogant, smart children, and their frantic pursuit of a personal identity in the midst of the crowd—only an exaggerated version of everyone's dilemma—pushes forward the culture of the city and twentieth century America."[1]

But the yuppie revolution would take time. A more immediate boon to the city came in the summer of 1976 when a confluence of events gave New York an opportunity to feel good about itself while putting its best foot forward to the world at large. On July 4 the city hosted the most spectacular event to mark the occasion of the nation's bicentennial—Operation Sail, the international parade of tall sailing ships in New York harbor. A few weeks later the Democratic party gathered in the city to nominate Jimmy Carter as its candidate.

The weather on the Fourth of July was breathtakingly clear. The city, its harbor and the Hudson River sparkled as 212 sailing ships from thirty-four nations, including 169 of the world's largest windjammers, glided past an honor guard of warships including the U.S.S. *Forrestal*, as well as an estimated 30,000 small boats.[2] Approximately two million people participated in the festivities south of Fifty-ninth Street in Manhattan—almost as many people as the total number of Americans two hundred years before. There were twenty-one ethnic mini-festivals. The president, the vice president and the secretary of state all came to view the proceedings. And in the evening, Macy's paid for spectacular fireworks that were computer-orchestrated by experts from Walt Disney World.

The columnist Pete Hamill wrote that the sailing vessels "might not have symbolized anything great about America, but they reminded us of how spectacular an accident is the city of New York."[3] In his August editorial, the *Architectural Record*'s editor, Walter F. Wagner, Jr., described the positive impact of Operation Sail:

There were almost no cars on the city streets, and people walked towards the river laughing and swinging their picnic baskets. New York's ubiquitous hot dog vendors slapped on the sauerkraut and mustard with uncommon style and élan; people were polite even at the most crowded of ports, and the policemen seemed to be looking, at least this day, not for trouble but for ways to help. New York City hasn't had an awful lot to be festive about lately—but the City (if you can personalize eight million residents and five or more million visitors) had a wonderful time on the Fourth of July—and the word seems to be sticking. It's as though everybody had such a good time swinging through the streets being pleasant to each other that they decided to keep it up even though the celebration was over and the ships have slid down the river and headed off for other cities or for home.[4]

Two weeks later 5,000 delegates and alternates as well as 15,000 party workers, family members, journalists and others gathered at Madison Square Garden to hold the Democratic National Convention. The city was on its best behavior, aware that, as *Time* put it, there "are lovelier places in the U.S. to hold a political convention than Eighth Avenue and 33rd Street."[5] *Daily News* columnist William Reel cautioned New Yorkers to maintain the good manners they had shown during the bicentennial celebrations: "Don't blow this opportunity, New York. The Democrats are coming. Let's give them a good impression. If you see a guy wearing a ten-gallon hat and a cowboy shirt and talking too loud, bite your tongue. Remember, the guy probably owns Texas. Maybe he can do us a favor, maybe co-sign a note for us. So swallow all comments about hayseeds and huckleberries. Kill the guy with courtesy."[6] Every effort was made to help the conventioneers enjoy themselves, and the favorable coverage on television and in the press went a long way toward repairing New York's image in the hinterlands.

Pete Hamill captured the city's euphoria during that period: "This is the best summer New York has had since the '50s. Something extraordinary is in the air. Part of it is a sense of relief. The feds have done their worst. . . . We are dirtier, less charitable, less grand, and less just. But we are here. We have survived."[7] But the political scientist Andrew Hacker offered a cautionary note: "New York has perhaps one more generation during which it can command preeminence. But not much more. Those who enjoy its life should make the most of it, for it can't last."[8]

PHOTOGRAPHERS

Aaron: Peter Aaron
Abbott: Berenice Abbott
Acs: Sandor Acs
Adelberg: Peter Adelberg
Alden: Florence Alden
Arnold Newman: Arnold Newman
Associated Press: Associated Press Photo
B. Cohen: Ben Cohen
Barnell: J. D. Barnell
Beckhard: Robert Beckhard
Beckman: Hannes Beckman
Berinsky: Burton Berinsky
Best: Elaine Best
Budnick: Dan Budnick
Byron: Joseph Byron, Percy Byron, the Byron family
Cabrera: Robert Cabrera
Chalfant: Henry Chalfant
Checkman: Louis Checkman
Cohen: Marc Cohen
Cortijo: Nester Cortijo
Crane: Tom Crane
Cserna: George Cserna
Cunningham-Werdnigg: Bruce Cunningham-Werdnigg
DeLucia: Vic DeLucia
DeMarsico: Dick DeMarsico
Dunlap: David W. Dunlap
Finkelman: Allan Finkelman
Fred W. McDarrah: Fred W. McDarrah
Freedman: Lionel Freedman
Fullerton: Henry S. Fullerton
Gabriel: George Gabriel
Garber: Maurey Garber
Georges: Alexandre Georges
Gil Amiaga: Gil Amiaga
Gillette: Guy Gillette
Golby: Bob Golby
Gooen: Irwin Gooen
Gottscho-Schleisner: Samuel H. Gottscho, William H. Schleisner
Graham: Kathryn Graham
Guerrero: Pedro E. Guerrero
Hans Namuth: ©Estate of Hans Namuth
Hedrich-Blessing: Hedrich-Blessing
Hicks: Mason Hicks
Hilfer: Martin Hilfer
Hill: John T. Hill
Hirsch: David Hirsch
Hopkins: John E. Hopkins
Hoyt: Wolfgang Hoyt
Hubmann: Franz Hubmann
Hujar: Peter Hujar
Ingalls: Frank M. Ingalls
Iselin: Leni Iselin
Jacobellis: William Jacobellis
Jones: Christopher E. Jones
Kaha: Arthur Kaha
Kwartler: Michael Kwartler
Langley: J. Alex Langley

Lavine: Arthur Lavine
Laxer: Jack Laxer
Leeser: Paulus Leeser
Levick: Edwin Levick
Levine: Les Levine
Lieberman: Thorney Lieberman
Liebman: Bernard Liebman
Lincoln: Fay S. Lincoln
Link: O. Winston Link
Liotta: Louis Liotta
Maris: Bill Maris
Maris/Semel: Bill Maris/Julie Semel
Mazza: Joseph Mazza
Mélançon: Louis Mélançon
Menard: Normand Menard
Merit: Merit
Migdoll: Herbert Migdoll
Molitor: Joseph W. Molitor
Moore: Peter Moore
Morgan: Don Morgan
Moseley: Monica Moseley
Naar: Jon Naar
Neuhof: Marc Neuhof
Norman McGrath: Norman McGrath
Oakley: William P. Oakley
Parker: Bo Parker
Perron: Robert Perron
Petrilli: Robert Petrilli
Plowden: David Plowden
Pohl: George Pohl
Propper: Robert A. Propper
R. M. Morgan: Rodney McCay Morgan
Ratcliffe: Edward Ratcliffe
Reens: Louis Reens
Ries: Stan Ries
Robinson: ©Cervin Robinson
Rodriguez: Robert F. Rodriguez
Rogers: Hugh Rogers
Rosen: Laura Rosen
Rosenthal: Steve Rosenthal
Rothschild: Bill Rothschild
Schnall: Ben Schnall
Severin: Michael Severin
Silva: Ernest Silva
Stein: Barney Stein
Steiner: Christian Steiner
Stern: Bert Stern
Stoecklein: Edmund Stoecklein
Stoller: Ezra Stoller
Studly: Adolph Studly
Sunami: Soichi Sunami
Suttle: William Suttle
Timchula: Alex Timchula
Underhill: Irving Underhill
Veltri: John Veltri Studio
Watson: Joe A. Watson
Webb: Todd Webb
Wide World: Wide World Photos
Wood: Robert Wood

Wurts: Wurts Brothers
Zamdmer: Mona Zamdmer
Zimbel: George Zimbel
Zindman/Fremont: Zindman/Fremont

COLLECTIONS

AB: Estate of Alan Buchsbaum
ABGE: Abraham W. Geller & Associates, New York, New York
ACL: Albert C. Ledner, Architect, Metairie, Louisiana
ACM: Arthur Cotton Moore/Associates, Washington, D.C.
ADV: Alfredo De Vido Associates, New York, New York
AGP: Archivio Gio Ponti, Milan, Italy
AHH: Atelier Hans Hollein, Vienna, Austria
AK: ©Estate of André Kertész
AKAG: Albright-Knox Art Gallery, Buffalo, New York, Gift of Seymour H. Knox, 1966
AKS: Abramovitz Kingsland Schiff, New York, New York
ALC: Archives of Lincoln Center for the Performing Arts, Inc., New York, New York
AMNH: Courtesy Department of Library Services, American Museum of Natural History, New York, New York
AN: Arnold Newman Studios, New York, New York
ARS: Artists Rights Society, New York, New York
ASB: Andrew S. Blackman Associates, New York, New York
BBB: Beyer Blinder Belle, New York, New York
BBG: Bonni Benrubi Gallery, Inc., New York, New York
BCHS: Courtesy of the Bronx County Historical Society Collection, Bronx, New York
BDW: Barbara D'Arcy White, Bloomingdale's, New York, New York
BFI: Buckminster Fuller Institute, Santa Barbara, California
BJ: Buffie Johnson, New York, New York
BMA: The Brooklyn Museum, Brooklyn, New York
BR: Bill Rothschild, Wesley Hills, New York
BS: Bernard Spitzer, New York, New York
BST: Bert Stern, New York, New York
BT&A: Benjamin Thompson & Associates, Cambridge, Massachusetts
BTA: Breger Terjesen Associates, New York, New York
C&R: Clarke & Rapuano, Inc., New York, New York
CCNYOP: City College of New York, Office of Public Relations, New York, New York
CCP: Center for Creative Photography, The University of Arizona, Tucson, Arizona
CCT: Columbia College Today, New York, New York
CERO: Cervin Robinson, New York, New York
CG: Chermayeff & Geismar, Inc., New York, New York
CGA: In the Collection of the Corcoran Gallery of Art, Washington, D.C., Museum Purchase, Anna E. Clarke Fund
CH: Cooper-Hewitt Museum, the Smithsonian Institution's National Museum of Design, New York, New York (Donald Deskey Archive)

Photographic Sources

CHS: Hedrich-Blessing photograph, courtesy Chicago Historical Society, Chicago, Illinois
CI: CityArts, Inc., New York, New York
CIAR: Ciardullo Associates, New York, New York
CJP: Carl J. Petrilli, Flushing, New York
CLA: The Luckman Partnership, Inc., Los Angeles, California
CMA: Courtesy of the Chase Manhattan Archives, New York, New York
CNY: Community Church of New York, New York
COGR: Commerce Graphics, East Rutherford, New Jersey
CP: Culver Pictures Inc., New York, New York
CR: Conklin Rossant Architects, New York, New York
CRSS: CRSS Architects, Houston, Texas
CU: Columbia University, New York, New York (Collection of the Avery Architectural and Fine Arts Library, including the Drawings Collection)
CUOPI: Columbia University Office of Public Information, New York, New York
CW: Craig Whitaker, New York, New York
DBA: Davis, Brody & Associates, New York, New York
DCJ: Collection Donna and Carroll Janis
DD: David W. Dunlap, New York, New York
DDC: Dorothy Draper & Company, New York, New York
DSA: Der Scutt Architect, New York, New York
DT: David F. M. Todd, New York, New York
EC: Ellen Cheng, New York, New York
EDS: Edward Durell Stone Associates, New York, New York
EG: The Eggers Group, New York, New York
EKS: Edvin Karl Stromsten, Architect, New York, New York
ELB: Edward Larrabee Barnes/John M. Y. Lee, New York, New York
ELC: Elaine Lustig Cohen, New York, New York
EMC: Ellen McCluskey Associates Inc., New York, New York
ENT: E. N. Turano, Boca Raton, Florida
ERS: Emery Roth & Sons, New York, New York
ESTO: Esto, Mamaroneck, New York
FE: Ford & Earl Associates, Inc., Troy, Michigan
FG: Courtesy Fischbach Gallery, New York, New York
FIT: Fashion Institute of Technology, New York, New York
FKG: Froehlich, Kow & Gong Architects, Los Angeles, California
FLWA: Courtesy of The Frank Lloyd Wright Archives of The Frank Lloyd Wright Foundation, Scottsdale, Arizona (all images Copyright ©The Frank Lloyd Wright Foundation)
FRGA: Courtesy Fraenkel Gallery, San Francisco, California, ©The Estate of Garry Winogrand
FUA: Fordham University Archives, Bronx, New York
FWM: Fred W. McDarrah, New York, New York
GA: Gil Amiaga, New York, New York
GC: George Cserna
GEZ: Gamal El-Zoghby, New York, New York

GF: General Foods USA, White Plains, New York
GICA: Giorgio Cavaglieri Architect, New York, New York
GM: Courtesy, Solomon R. Guggenheim Museum, New York, New York
GMWP: GMW Partnership, London, England
GS: Gruzen Samton, New York, New York
GSA: Gwathmey Siegel & Associates Architects, New York, New York
HAG: Courtesy Hirschl & Adler Galleries, New York, New York
HAM: Courtesy Hirschl & Adler Modern, New York, New York
HASU: Harold Sussman, New York, New York
HB: Herbert Beckhard, New York, New York
HC: Henry Chalfant, New York, New York
HFDA: Hodgetts & Fung Design Associates, Santa Monica, California
HHP: Hardy Holzman Pfeiffer Associates, New York, New York
HHR: Henry Hope Reed, Jr., New York, New York
HLW: Haines, Lundberg & Waehler, New York, New York
HMSG: Hirshhorn Museum and Sculpture Garden, Smithsonian Institution, Washington, D.C., Gift of the Joseph H. Hirshhorn Foundation, 1966
HMSGA: Hirshhorn Museum and Sculpture Garden, Smithsonian Institution, Washington, D.C., Gift of Joseph H. Hirshhorn, 1966
HS: Hugh Stubbins, Cambridge, Massachusetts
HY: Hanford Yang, New York, New York
IBM: Courtesy of International Business Machines Corporation, Hawthorne, New York
IIE: Institute of International Education, New York, New York
ILGWU: ILGWU "Justice," New York, New York
INF: Isamu Noguchi Foundation, Inc., Long Island City, New York
JA: Japan Airlines, New York, New York
JB: Jonathan Barnett, Washington, D.C.
JCW: John Carl Warnecke & Associates, San Francisco, California
JDA: James Doman & Associates, New York, New York
JES: Courtesy of Joseph E. Seagram & Sons, Inc., New York, New York
JH: James Hadley, Greenwich, Connecticut
JL: John Lobell, New York, New York
JOF: The Joffrey Ballet, New York, New York
JP: John Portman & Associates, Atlanta, Georgia
JSP: James Stewart Polshek and Partners, New York, New York
JW: Joseph Wasserman, Southfield, Massachusetts
JWM: Joseph W. Molitor, Valhalla, New York
KGA: Courtesy the Knoll Group Archives, New York, New York
KKA: Koetter, Kim & Associates, Boston, Massachusetts
KMW: Kallmann McKinnell & Wood, Boston, Massachusetts
KP: Kouzmanoff Partnership, New York, New York

KRJDA: Kevin Roche John Dinkeloo and Associates, Hamden, Connecticut
KSW: Kyu Sung Woo, Cambridge, Massachusetts
LARO: Laura Rosen, Brooklyn, New York
LC: Louis Checkman, Jersey City, New Jersey
LCG: Leo Castelli Photo Archives, New York, New York
LF: Lionel Freedman, Ardsley, New York
LIK: Louis I. Kahn Collection, Archives of the University of Pennsylvania and Pennsylvania Historical and Museum Commission, Philadelphia, Pennsylvania
LL: Les Levine, New York, New York
LO: Lefrak Organization, Rego Park, New York
LOC: Library of Congress, Washington, D.C. (including New York World-Telegram & Sun Collection; Gottscho-Schleisner Collection, courtesy of Mrs. William H. Schleisner)
LPL: Levittown Public Library, Levittown, New York
LR: Louis Reens, Dallas, Texas
LS: Lundquist & Stonehill, New York, New York
LT: Lord & Taylor, New York, New York
LW: Les Walker, Woodstock, New York
M&S: Mayers & Schiff Associates, New York, New York
MA: Municipal Archives of the City of New York, New York
MAG: Courtesy, Marlborough Gallery, New York, New York
MCNY: Museum of the City of New York, New York (including Byron Collection; Changing New York Collection, photographed by Berenice Abbott; Wurts Collection)
MD: Mancini Duffy, New York, New York
MET: Metropolitan Museum of Art, New York, New York
MF: Mitchell Fontana Associates, Inc., New York, New York
MG: Mitchell/Giurgola Associates, New York, New York
MK: Michael Kwartler, New York, New York
ML: Morris Lapidus, Miami Beach, Florida
MLI: Metropolitan Life Insurance Company, New York, New York
MMFA: Collection of The Montgomery Museum of Fine Arts, Montgomery, Alabama, the Blount Collection
MOA: Metropolitan Opera Archives, New York, New York
MOMA: Photographs courtesy The Museum of Modern Art, New York, New York (including the Film Stills Archive). Proposal for West Harlem and Hudson River: PRINCETON UNIVERSITY TEAM: Peter D. Eisenman, Michael Graves; G. Daniel Perry, Stephen Levine, Jay Turnbull, Thomas C. Pritchard, Russell Swanson. *Project 3. Building the Waterfront.* Drawing for the exhibition "The New City: Architecture and Urban Renewal," The Museum of Modern Art, New York. January 24–March 13, 1967. Proposal for Central Harlem: CORNELL UNIVERSITY TEAM: Colin Rowe, Thomas Schumacher; Jerry A. Wells, Alfred H. Koetter. *Project 1.*

Opening the Grid Plan. Drawing for the exhibition "The New City: Architecture and Urban Renewal," The Museum of Modern Art, New York. January 24–March 13, 1967.

Proposal for East River, Ward's Island and Randall's Island: MASSACHUSETTS INSTITUTE OF TECHNOLOGY TEAM: Stanford Anderson, Robert Goodman, Henry A. Millon. *Project 4. Designing New Land*. Site plan showing modification of North Channel and damming of East River at two points to join Randall's and Ward's Islands to Manhattan and detail looking northwest. Drawing for the exhibition "The New City: Architecture and Urban Renewal," The Museum of Modern Art, New York. January 24–March 13, 1967.

Proposal for elevated Park Avenue viaduct above East Ninety-seventh Street: COLUMBIA UNIVERSITY TEAM: Jaquelin T. Robertson, Richard Weinstein, Giovanni Pasanella; Jonathan Barnett, Myles Weintraub, Benjamin Mendelsund, George Terrien, Paul Wang. *Project 2. Housing Without Relocation*. Aerial view and axonometric drawing. Drawing for the exhibition "The New City: Architecture and Urban Renewal," The Museum of Modern Art, New York. January 24–March 13, 1967.

Proposal for General Motors Pavilion, New York World's Fair: KAHN, Louis I. *General Motors Exhibition, 1964 World's Fair, New York City*. Project. Elevation and plans. 1961. Ink on white tracing paper, 12 x 21¼". The Museum of Modern Art, New York. Gift of the architect.

"The Museum of Modern Art Packed" (photomontage): CHRISTO (Christo Javacheff). *"The Museum of Modern Art Packed" Project*. 1968. Photomontage and drawing with oil, pencil, pastel, colored pencil, cut-and-pasted tracing paper and scotch-tape mounted on cardboard; overall, 21¾ x 15⅝". The Museum of Modern Art, New York. Gift of D. and J. de Menil. (Matthews 1886)

The Family of Man: Installation view from the exhibition "The Family of Man." January 24–May 8, 1955. The Museum of Modern Art, New York. (R. P. 6474)

The Architecture of the Ecole des Beaux-Arts: Installation view from the exhibition "The Architecture of the Ecole des Beaux-Arts." October 28, 1975–January 4, 1976. The Museum of Modern Art, New York. (Keller A1840)

MPF: M. Paul Friedberg & Partners, New York, New York

MS: Michael Schwarting, New York, New York

MSA: Moshe Safdie and Associates, Inc., Sommerville, Massachusetts

MWPI: Munson-Williams-Proctor Institute, Museum of Art, Utica, New York, Edward W. Root Bequest

NAAC: Nebraska Art Association Collection, Sheldon Memorial Art Gallery, University of Nebraska–Lincoln

NG: Naomi Goodman, New York, New York

NJ: Norman Jaffe, F.A.I.A., Bridgehampton, New York

NM: Norman McGrath, New York, New York

NYC: Used by permission of the New York City Department of City Planning, New York, New York

NYCBE: New York City Board of Education Archives, Milbank Memorial Library, Teachers College, Columbia University, New York, New York

NYCHA: New York City Housing Authority, New York, New York

NYCPPA: New York City Parks Photo Archive, New York, New York

NYHS: Collection of The New-York Historical Society, New York, New York

NYM: New York Mets, Flushing, New York

NYP: New York Post, New York, New York

NYPL: New York Public Library, New York, New York (including Public Relations; Rare Books and Manuscript Division, New York Public Libary, Astor, Lenox and Tilden Foundations; Dance Collection and Billy Rose Theater Collection, New York Public Library for the Performing Arts, Astor, Lenox and Tilden Foundations)

NYT: New York Times, New York, New York

NYU: University Archives, New York University, New York, New York

NYYPD: New York Yankees Publicity Department, New York, New York

NYZS: ©NYZS/The Wildlife Conservation Society, Bronx, New York

OBV: Oppenheimer, Brady & Vogelstein, New York, New York

OMA: Office for Metropolitan Architecture, Rotterdam, Netherlands

OMH: Office for Metropolitan History, New York, New York

OTA: Olympic Tower Associates, New York, New York

PAFI: Public Art Fund Inc., New York, New York

PAKL: Pasanella + Klein, Architects, New York, New York

PANY: Photos courtesy of The Port Authority of New York and New Jersey, New York, New York

PB: Pomerance & Breines, New York, New York

PCF: Pei Cobb Freed & Partners, New York, New York

PCO: Prentice & Chan, Ohlhausen, New York, New York

PDE: Pamela D. Ellis, Alan Dunn Estate

PEBL: Peter Blake, Branford, Connecticut

PEG: Perls Galleries, New York, New York

PEGU: Pedro E. Guerrero, New Canaan, Connecticut

PENN: Historical Collections and Labor Archives, The Pennsylvania State University Libraries, University Park, Pennsylvania (Fay S. Lincoln Collection)

PF: Photofest, New York, New York

PG: Photographs courtesy of The Pace Gallery, New York, New York

PHAI: Parish Hadley Associates, Inc., New York, New York

PJA: Philip Johnson Architects, New York, New York

PM: Peter Moore, New York, New York

PMA: Philadelphia Museum of Art: Given by the Friends of the Philadelphia Museum of Art, Philadelphia, Pennsylvania

PR: Paul Rudolph, New York, New York

PW: Perkins & Will, New York, New York

QM: Queens Museum, Flushing, New York

RAC: Roger A. Cumming, Architect, New York, New York

RAMSA: Robert A. M. Stern Architects, New York, New York

RD: Richard Dattner, Architect, New York, New York

REDI: The Reader's Digest Association, Inc., Pleasantville, New York

RF: Richard Foster Associates, Greenwich, Connecticut

RHM: R. H. Macy & Co., Inc., New York, New York

RKG: Robert Koch Gallery, San Francisco, California

RLA: Robert L. Amico, South Bend, Indiana

RM: Richard Meier & Partners, New York, New York

RN: Regeen Najar, New York, New York

ROARC: Courtesy of the Rockefeller Archive Center, North Tarrytown, New York

RP: Richard Plunz, New York, New York

RPA: Regional Plan Association, New York, New York

RWS: Richard W. Snibbe, New York, New York

SA: Sandor Acs, New York, New York

SD: Courtesy of Sam Davis, Berkeley, California

SDG: Space Design Group, New York, New York

SHS: The Stamford Historical Society Inc., Stamford, Connecticut

SJA: Sert, Jackson & Associates, Lexington, Massachusetts

SLM: Maurer & Maurer Architects, Brooklyn, New York

SOM: Skidmore, Owings & Merrill, New York, New York

SPDP: Samuel Paul and David J. Paul, Architects, Woodmere, New York

SR: Stan Ries, New York, New York

SS: Shoji Sadao, Long Island City, New York

SSSM: South Street Seaport Museum, New York, New York

ST: Susana Torre, New York, New York

STPA: The Stein Partnership, New York, New York

SU: Syracuse University, Syracuse, New York (The George Arents Research Library, Lescaze Collection)

TA: Tonetti Associates, New York, New York

TBTA: Triborough Bridge and Tunnel Authority, New York, New York

TC: Teachers College, Columbia University, New York, New York

TCF: Reprinted with permission from the Twentieth Century Fund, New York, New York

TDG: Terry Dintenfass Gallery, New York, New York

TEC: Turner Entertainment Co., Los Angeles, California

THHO: Thomas Hodne Architects, Inc., Minneapolis, Minnesota

THLI: Theodore Liebman, Architect, New York, New York

THTA: The Tablet, Brooklyn, New York

TL: Thorney Lieberman, Boulder, Colorado

TMM: Times Mirror Magazines, Inc., Los Angeles, California

TT: Thornton-Tomasetti Engineers, New York, New York

UDC: New York State Urban Development Corporation, New York, New York

UF: Ulrich Franzen, New York, New York

UN: United Nations, New York, New York

UPIB: UPI/Bettmann Newsphotos, New York, New York

UPV: Reprinted by permission of the University Press of Virginia, Charlottesville, Virginia

VDSS: Vidal Sassoon Salons and Schools, London, England

VSBA: Venturi, Scott Brown and Associates, Philadelphia, Pennsylvania

WACA: Collection Walker Art Center, Minneapolis, Minnesota, Gift of the T. B. Walker Foundation, 1964

WAH: William A. Hall & Associates, New York, New York

WB: Ward Bennett, New York, New York

WBT: William B. Tabler Architects, New York, New York

WFC: W. F. Chun, New York, New York

WG: Wilder Green, New York, New York

WK: Wallace Kaminsky Architects, New York, New York

WL: Warner LeRoy, New York, New York

WM: William Maurer, St. Simon's Island, Georgia

WMAA: Whitney Museum of American Art, New York, New York

WPA: Warren Platner Associates Architects, New Haven, Connecticut

WZ: William Zeckendorf, Jr., New York, New York

ZB: Zion & Breen Associates, Imlaystown, New Jersey

PERIODICALS

AABN: *American Architect and Building News*

AC: *American City*

AD: *Architectural Design*

ADA: *L'Architecture d'Aujourd'hui*

AF: *Architectural Forum*

AIA: *Journal of the American Institute of Architects*

AR: *Architectural Record*

ARCH: *Architecture*

CA: *Casabella*

CHCHN: *Citizens' Housing Council Housing News*

DOM: *Domus*

ID: *Interior Design*

IN: *Interiors*

PA: *Progressive Architecture*

PP: *Pencil Points*

PS: *Popular Science*

RERG: *Real Estate Record and Guide*

TDT: *Theater Design and Technology*

WE: *Werk*

BOOKS

A History of Housing: Richard Plunz, *A History of Housing in New York City* (New York: Columbia University Press, 1990)

Annadale-Huguenot: Raymond & May Associates, in association with Shankland, Cox & Associates, *Annadale-Huguenot: Planning for a New Residential Community on Staten Island* (New York, October 1967)

East Harlem Triangle Plan: Architects Renewal Committee in Harlem, *East Harlem Triangle Plan* (New York: Community Association of the East Harlem Triangle and the New York City Housing and Development Administration, August 1968)

East Island: Victor Gruen, *East Island: A Proposal for the Conversion of Welfare Island* (New York: East Island Development Corporation, 1961)

Final Report: New York Chapter, American Institute of Architects, *Final Report on the Voorhees, Walker, Smith & Smith Proposal for a Zoning Resolution for the City of New York* (New York: New York Chapter, American Institute of Architects, December 11, 1959)

Le Corbusier: Oeuvre complète: W. Boesiger, ed., *Le Corbusier: Oeuvre complète 1946–1952*, vol. 5 (Zurich: Editions Girsberger, 1955)

Linear City: Rogers, Taliaferro, Kostritsky, Lamb, *Linear City and Cross Brooklyn Expressway* (Baltimore, Md., September 1967)

Roosevelt Island Housing Competition: *Roosevelt Island Housing Competition* (New York: New York State Urban Development Corporation, 1974)

The Island Nobody Knows: Philip Johnson and John Burgee, *The Island Nobody Knows* (New York: New York State Urban Development Corporation, 1969)

The Port of New York: Ebasco Services, Inc; Moran, Proctor, Mueser & Ruttledge; and Eggers and Higgins, *The Port of New York. Comprehensive Economic Study: Manhattan North River Development Plan, 1962 to 2000* (New York: Department of Marine and Aviation, 1962)

World Trade Center: Downtown–Lower Manhattan Association, *World Trade Center: A Proposal for the Port of New York* (New York, 1960)

Notes

Preface

1. Jean Gottmann, *Megalopolis: The Urbanized Northeastern Seaboard of the United States* (Cambridge, Mass.: MIT Press, 1961).
2. Le Corbusier, *The City of Tomorrow and Its Planning*, trans. Frederick Etchells (New York: Payson & Clarke, 1929), 280–81. The text was translated from the eighth French edition of *Urbanisme*, originally published in 1925.
3. Jane Jacobs, *The Death and Life of Great American Cities* (New York: Random House, 1961).
4. James Lardner, "Profiles: The Whistle-Blower—Part I," *New Yorker* 69 (July 5, 1993): 52–56, 58–64, 66–70.
5. William Zeckendorf quoted in Gilbert Burck, "Headquarters Town," *Fortune* 61 (February 1960): 93–96, 258, 263–64, 266.
6. Charles Abrams, "Downtown Decay and Revival," *Journal of the American Institute of Planners* 27 (February 1961): 3–9.

Chapter 1
Introduction

1. John Steinbeck, "Autobiography: Making of a New Yorker," *New York Times* (February 1, 1953), VI: 26–27, 66–67.
2. "Skyline Drops," editorial, *New York Times* (December 11, 1940): 26.
3. Robert H. Armstrong, "The Extent of New York Decentralization," *Real Estate Record and Guide* 147 (May 10, 1941): 3–4; Charles M. Chuckrow, "Urban Development Act as Blight Cure," *Real Estate Record and Guide* 147 (May 10, 1941): 6; Edgar Ellinger, "Program to Curb the Manhattan Exodus," *Real Estate Record and Guide* 147 (May 10, 1941): 5–6; Joseph D. McGoldrick, "Private Enterprise and Decentralization," *Real Estate Record and Guide* 147 (May 10, 1941): 4.
4. "Regional Plan's Analysis of New York Population," *Real Estate Record and Guide* 148 (July 1941): 5, 21.
5. Regional Plan of New York, *Regional Survey of New York and Its Environs*, vols. 1, 1A, 1B, 2–8 (New York, 1928–31). For an extensive discussion of the Regional Plan Association and its publications, see Robert A. M. Stern, Gregory Gilmartin and Thomas Mellins, assisted by David Fishman and Raymond W. Gastil, *New York 1930: Architecture and Urbanism Between the Two World Wars* (New York: Rizzoli International Publications, 1987), 41–45.
6. Clair Price, "An Older and Wiser New York," *New York Times* (January 19, 1941), VII: 10, 22.
7. Price, "An Older and Wiser New York": 10, 22.
8. "New York City Gets a Flood of War Visitors; Service Men and Families See the Sights," *New York Times* (April 14, 1942): 23.
9. Tania Loring, "Home—After London," *New York Times* (October 31, 1943), II: 13.
10. Bayrd Still, *Mirror for Gotham: New York as Seen by Contemporaries from Dutch Days to the Present* (New York: New York University Press, 1956), 324. Also see Carlos P. Romulo, *My Brother Americans* (Garden City, N.Y.: Doubleday, 1945).
11. Sergeant Milton Lehman, "Home from the War to a Friendly Town," *New York Times* (July 8, 1945), VI: 7, 45–46.
12. Charles Grutzner, "V-E-V-J Days in Our Block," *New York Times* (October 7, 1945), VI: 18–19.
13. "N.Y. Hunts Work," *Business Week* (July 18, 1942): 35–37.
14. John Joslin, "Our Incredible City—Capital of the World," *New York Times* (December 22, 1946), VI: 10–11, 51.
15. Joslin, "Our Incredible City—Capital of the World": 11.
16. George Horne, "Mayor Orders Virtually Entire City Closed as Tugboat Strike Emergency Continues; Transit Service Cut, Food Places Excepted," *New York Times* (February 12, 1946): 1, 18; Ernest L. Stebbins, "City Shutdown Order," *New York Times* (February 12, 1946): 1; "City Fuel Supplies at Critical Stage," *New York Times* (February 12, 1946): 1, 18.

17. "The Talk of the Town: Notes and Comment," *New Yorker* 22 (February 23, 1946): 21–22.
18. Marya Mannes, *The New York I Know*, with photographs by Herb Snitzer (Philadelphia and New York: J. B. Lippincott, 1961), 9–10.
19. "Official Survey: Now Race Problem Is Changing Nation's Biggest City," *U.S. News & World Report* 43 (November 29, 1957): 42–45.
20. Will Lisner, "18 Branches Set Up by City's Big Shops," *New York Times* (June 11, 1949): 15.
21. Richard H. Parke, "Trend of Industry to Suburbs Found; Jersey Is Favored," *New York Times* (August 11, 1952): 1, 22.
22. Jean Gottmann, "The Skyscraper amid the Sprawl," in Jean Gottmann and Robert A. Harper, eds., *Metropolis on the Move: Geographers Look at Urban Sprawl* (New York: John Wiley & Sons, 1967), 125–50.
23. "City Losing Trade at Alarming Rate, State Study Warns," *New York Times* (April 12, 1943): 1, 16.
24. *Herald Tribune*'s assessment quoted in Clarence S. Stein, "The Future of New York," *Post War Planning News Digest* 1 (July 10, 1943): 1–7.
25. Richard H. Rovere, "The Decline of New York City," *American Mercury* 58 (May 1944): 526–32.
26. Robert Moses, "It's Going to Be Quite a Town," *New York Times* (February 16, 1947), VI: 7, 57–59.
27. Moses, "It's Going to Be Quite a Town": 58–59.
28. John Allen Krout and Allan Nevins, eds., *The Greater City: New York, 1898–1948* (New York: Columbia University Press, 1948); "All Americans Get Bids to City's Fete," *New York Times* (January 27, 1948): 27; "Exhibit to Display City's Government," *New York Times* (March 22, 1948): 25; Paul Crowell, "New York at 50," *New York Times* (May 2, 1948), X: 11; "New York City: 1898–1948," editorial, *New York Times* (June 12, 1948): 14; "Jubilee Exhibition Will Open Aug. 23," *New York Times* (August 11, 1948): 23; Walter Sullivan, "City's Exposition for Jubilee Opens in Blaze of Lights," *New York Times* (August 22, 1948): 1, 21; "Wonders of City Graphically Told," *New York Times* (August 22, 1948): 23; "Jubilee to Live in Exhibit Form," *New York Times* (September 20, 1948): 27. Also see Editors of *Look*, in collaboration with Frederick Lewis Allen, *Look at America: New York City* (Boston: Houghton Mifflin, 1948).
29. "America's Leading Tourist Resort," *Travel* 91 (December 1948): 33.
30. "Trucks Take Tube Mail," *New York Times* (December 10, 1953): 37; "Post Office Ends Tube Mail Service," *New York Times* (December 30, 1953): 26; "Mail Tube System Grew Up with City," *New York Times* (January 3, 1954): 41.
31. Saul Bellow, *Seize the Day* (New York: Viking Press, 1956), 33.
32. "Garages Warned on Price Gouging," *New York Times* (August 1, 1950): 25; "Fair Garage Fees," editorial, *New York Times* (August 11, 1950): 18.
33. "Snapshots of the Interstate Metropolis," *Reporter* 13 (September 8, 1955): 18–23.
34. Bert Pierce, "Traffic Held Peril to City's Business," *New York Times* (July 24, 1948): 17; Bill Davidson, "New York Fights the World's Worst Traffic Jam," *Colliers* 125 (April 8, 1950): 20–21, 50–52.
35. Joseph C. Ingraham, "Traffic Director Post Is Offered by O'Dwyer to Detroit Engineer," *New York Times* (February 1, 1949): 1, 28.
36. Kenneth Campbell, "New Traffic Board to Weigh Use Here of Parking Meters," *New York Times* (February 2, 1949): 1, 30; H. H. Estes, "All Manhattan's Traffic Signals Are Now Timed Automatically," *American City* 64 (August 1949): 125–26; T. T. Wiley, "Making Better Time at the Same Speed," *American City* 65 (March 1950): 141; "The Talk of the Town: Modified Progressive," *New Yorker* 26 (March 25, 1950): 22–23; "The Talk of the Town: Commissioner," *New Yorker* 26 (July 1, 1950): 16; "The Talk of the Town: Traffic," *New Yorker* 26 (November 18, 1950): 40–41.
37. Joseph C. Ingraham, "1st and 2d Aves. Go One-Way on June 4," *New York Times* (May 22, 1951): 1, 36; "Headway on Traffic," editorial, *New York Times* (May 23, 1951): 34.
38. Joseph C. Ingraham, "7th and 8th Aves. Will Be One-Way, Probably in May," *New York Times* (February 19, 1954): 1, 19; "A Year's Test of One-Way," editorial, *New York Times*

Times (May 1, 1954): 14; Joseph C. Ingraham, "7th and 8th Aves. Shift to One-Way," *New York Times* (June 7, 1954): 1, 17.

39. "5th Avenue—One Way!" *Village Voice* 4 (January 7, 1959): 1; Peter Kihss, "5th and Madison Avenues Become One-Way Friday," *New York Times* (January 12, 1966): 1, 16; Martin Arnold, "Traffic Is Speeded as 5th and Madison Change to One-Way," *New York Times* (January 15, 1966): 1, 11.

40. Grover A. Whalen, "What the Abuse of the Parking Privilege Costs New York," *American City* 56 (November 1941): 87.

41. Stern, Gilmartin and Mellins, *New York 1930*, 664–65, 671, 700–701.

42. "Parking Jam," *Architectural Forum* 85 (September 1946): 8–10.

43. Jacob Moscowitz, "City Planning Commission's Recommendation on Traffic Congestion," *Citizens' Housing Council Housing News* 5 (November–December 1946): 3, 6.

44. "Park-Garage Plan Upheld by Rogers," *New York Times* (July 14, 1947): 23–24; "Park Garage Plan Draws Moses' Fire," *New York Times* (July 21, 1947): 19; "Underground Garages in New York," *Landscape Architecture* 38 (October 1947): 34-35.

45. "Tishman Hails Planning Commission's New Residential Proposal as Logical Step Toward Relieving Street Congestion," *Real Estate Record and Guide* 167 (May 12, 1951): 3.

46. "Adequate Parking Space for Tenants of New Apartments Gaining Importance," *Real Estate Record and Guide* 169 (April 26, 1952): 3.

47. Robert H. Arnow quoted in "Endorses Proposed Zoning Amendment Requiring Garage Facilities in New Commercial Structures," *Real Estate Record and Guide* 173 (February 20, 1954): 3–4.

48. T. T. Wiley quoted in "The Talk of the Town: Insoluble," *New Yorker* 30 (April 3, 1954): 19–20.

49. "New York's First City-Owned Shoppers' Lot," *American City* 69 (June 1954): 149, 151.

50. Christopher Gray, "Neighborhood: Nifties from the Fifties," *Avenue* 14 (January 1990): 117–23.

51. "'Rotary' Garages Provide Maximum Parking Space on a Small City Plot," *Architectural Record* 118 (October 1955): 247.

52. Huntington Hartford quoted in "Automatic Garage to Rise in Manhattan," *Real Estate Record and Guide* 58 (February 15, 1958): 4. Also see "Automatic Parking Garage Here Will Be Run by the Cashier's Key," *New York Times* (January 6, 1958): 30; "New City Garage to Be Automated," *New York Times* (June 15, 1960): 22; "8-Story Garage Will Run Itself," *New York Times* (October 3, 1960): 51; "Automated Parking Demonstrated Here," *New York Times* (December 14, 1961): 24; Stacy V. Jones, "Inventor of Automated Garage Patents a Better Elevator for It," *New York Times* (November 17, 1962): 29. For other midtown garages, see "A 320-Car Garage Set for 8th Ave.," *New York Times* (January 17, 1958): 46; "Housing Projects to Cost 82 Million," *New York Times* (October 16, 1958): 26; "320-Car Garage Is Scheduled for 8th Ave. and 42d St.," *New York Times* (January 2, 1959): 27; Charles G. Bennett, "Downtown Plan Approved by City," *New York Times* (January 23, 1959): 27; "New Garage on 43d St.," *New York Times* (August 6, 1959): 43; "Midtown Garage Approved," *New York Times* (October 1, 1959): 69.

53. Joseph C. Ingraham, "Mid-City Garages for 10,000 Autos Urged by Wiley," *New York Times* (January 18, 1960): 1, 23; "Parking to Help Business," editorial, *New York Times* (January 18, 1960): 26; Victor Gruen, "City Garages: A Boost to Retail Sales or to Traffic Jams?" *Progressive Architecture* 41 (March 1960): 35, 40, 46, 234, 236, 242. Also see Victor Gruen and Herbert Askwith, "Plan to End Our Traffic Jam," *New York Times* (January 10, 1960), VI: 90.

54. T. T. Wiley quoted in Victor Gruen, *The Heart of Our Cities* (New York: Simon & Schuster, 1964), 118. For a detailed analysis of Wiley's proposal, see pages 118–23.

55. Gruen, "City Garages: A Boost to Retail Sales or to Traffic Jams?": 234.

56. See Gruen, *The Heart of Our Cities*, 118.

57. Gruen, "City Garages: A Boost to Retail Sales or to Traffic Jams?": 242.

58. "Private Group Offers Parking Garage Plan," *Real Estate Record and Guide* (February 6, 1960): 4; Bernard Stengren, "First City Garage in Midtown Is Opened by Wagner and Aides," *New York Times* (September 16, 1960): 28; Gray, "Neighborhood: Nifties from the Fifties": 121.

59. "Planning Commission Raps New Garages," *Housing and Planning News* 19 (March–April 1961): 4.

60. Edward T. Chase, "New York Could Die," *Dissent* 8 (summer 1961): 297–303.

61. Quoted in Chase, "New York Could Die": 298.

62. "City Walkers Asked to Balk Garage," *Village Voice* 8 (September 5, 1963): 3; Carol Greitzer, "For Madison Square Park," letter to the editor, *Village Voice* 8 (September 19, 1963): 4.

63. Nan Robertson, "Throngs of Youngsters in Holiday Mood Jam Midtown," *New York Times* (December 28, 1961): 1, 28; Paul Crowell, "Mayor Dismisses Chief of Markets," *New York Times* (December 29, 1961): 1, 8; Bernard Stengren, "Wiley Replaced as Traffic Head," *New York Times* (December 31, 1961): 1, 36; "A Decade of Service," editorial, *New York Times* (January 5, 1962): 28; "Traffic Switch," *Architectural Forum* 116 (February 1962): 11.

64. Chase, "New York Could Die": 298.

65. Percival and Paul Goodman, "Banning Cars from Manhattan," *Dissent* 8 (summer 1961): 304–11, also published in *Program: The Journal of the School of Architecture, Columbia University* (spring 1961): 35–42.

66. "Traffic Chief, Expert on Selling, Is Pragmatic and Unorthodox," *New York Times* (December 31, 1961): 36; "Barnes and Snarls," *Architectural Forum* 116 (June 1962): 15; Paul O'Neill, "Keep 'em Rolling—To the Final Jam," *Life* 57 (November 13, 1964): 98–100, 102, 104, 107–8, 110–12, 114.

67. "Mad Square Is Traffic's Next Target," *Village Voice* 9 (October 1, 1964): 9.

68. Mary Perot Nichols, "Opponents Charge Secrecy Over Madison Square Garage," *Village Voice* 10 (March 11, 1965): 18.

69. Jean Gottmann, *Megalopolis: The Urbanized Northeastern Seaboard of the United States* (Cambridge, Mass.: MIT Press, 1961). Also see Martin Arnold, "Northeast Cited as World Center," *New York Times* (November 27, 1961): 31; "The Biggest City," editorial, *New York Times* (December 4, 1961): 36; Jean Gottmann, *Economics, Esthetics, and Ethics in Modern Urbanization* (New York: Twentieth Century Fund, 1962); Richard A. Miller, "Megalopolis: The Urbanized Northeastern Seaboard of the United States," book review, *Architectural Forum* 116 (March 1962): 163; Wolf Von Eckardt, *The Challenge of Megalopolis* (New York: Macmillan, 1964); Claiborne Pell, *Megalopolis Unbound* (New York: Frederick A. Praeger, 1966); Anthony Bailey, *Through the Great City* (New York: Macmillan, 1967), 126; Robert McNee, "The Challenge of the New Urbanization to Education," in Gottmann and Harper, eds., *Metropolis On the Move*, 179–91.

70. "In New York, Planners Look Into Biggest City's Future: Middle-Age Spread," *Architectural Forum* 115 (December 1961): 5, 9.

71. Gottmann, *Megalopolis: The Urbanized Northeastern Seaboard of the United States*, 19.

72. Andrew Sinclair, "Mid-Twentieth-Century New York," in Arnold J. Toynbee, ed., *Cities of Destiny* (New York: McGraw-Hill, 1967), 332.

73. Edgar M. Hoover and Raymond Vernon, *Anatomy of the Metropolis: The Changing Distribution of People and Jobs Within the New York Metropolitan Region*, vol. 1 (Cambridge, Mass.: Harvard University Press, 1959). Also see Clayton Knowles, "Decline of Cities in 3-State Area Feared in Study," *New York Times* (June 1, 1959): 1, 16; "Regional Fact-Finder," *New York Times* (June 1, 1959): 16; "Text of Harvard Study of the Metropolitan Area," *New York Times* (June 1, 1959): 16; Clayton Knowles, "Area Study Links Decline of Cities to Suburbs' Rise," *New York Times* (October 19, 1959): 1, 24; David A. Grossman, "Urban Structure," book review, *Progressive Architecture* 41 (June 1960): 228, 230, 236.

74. Knowles, "Area Study Links Decline of Cities to Suburbs' Rise": 24.

75. "Metropolis in a Mess," *Newsweek* 54 (July 27, 1959): 29–31.

76. "The Big Town—The Big Mess," *Newsweek* 54 (September 14, 1959): 55.

77. Fred J. Cook and Gene Gleason, "The Shame of New York," *Nation*, special issue (October 31, 1959): 284–300. Also see Lincoln Steffens, *The Shame of the Cities* (New York: McClure, Phillips, 1904).

78. Roy B. Helfgott, W. Eric Gustavson and James M. Hund, *Made in New York*, vol. 2 (Cambridge, Mass.: Harvard University Press, 1959); Oscar Handlin, *The Newcomers: Negroes and Puerto Ricans in a Changing Metropolis*, vol. 3 (Cambridge, Mass.: Harvard University Press, 1959); Martin Segal, *Wages in the Metropolis: Their Influence on the Location of Industries in the New York Region*, vol. 4 (Cambridge, Mass.: Harvard University Press, 1960); Sidney Robbins and Nestor E. Terleckyj, *Money Metropolis: A Locational Study of Financial Activities in the New York Region*, vol. 5 (Cambridge, Mass.: Harvard University Press, 1960); Benjamin Chinitz, *Freight and the Metropolis: The Impact of America's Transport Revolution on the New York Region*, vol. 6 (Cambridge, Mass.: Harvard University Press, 1960); Robert M. Lichtenberg, *One-Tenth of a Nation: National Forces in the Economic Growth of the New York Region*, vol. 7 (Cambridge, Mass.: Harvard University Press, 1960); Robert C. Wood with Vladimar V. Almendinger, *1,400 Governments: The Political Economy of the New York Metropolitan Region*, vol. 8 (Cambridge, Mass.: Harvard University Press, 1961); Raymond Vernon, *Metropolis 1985: An Interpretation of the Findings of the New York Metropolitan Region Study*, vol. 9 (Cambridge, Mass.: Harvard University Press, 1960). Wood and Almendinger's book, though the eighth volume in the series, was published after Vernon's concluding volume. Also see Hans Blumenfeld, "New York Metropolitan Region Study," *Journal of the American Institute of Planners* 27 (February 1961): 91–93.

79. "New York 1985: Still the Leader," *Business Week* (October 8, 1966): 118–25, 127.

80. Robert W. Dowling quoted in Glenn Fowler, "Building in City Put at 7.7 Billion for All Projects," *New York Times* (May 16, 1960): 1, 31.

81. Ralph Caplan and Ursula McHugh, "New York," *Industrial Design* 7 (October 1960): 47–53.

82. William Zeckendorf quoted in Gilbert Burck, "Headquarters Town," *Fortune* 61 (February 1960): 93–96, 258, 263–64, 266.

83. Charles E. Silberman, "The Home of the Middle Class," *Fortune* 61 (February 1960): 269, 272.

84. Silberman, "The Home of the Middle Class": 269, 272.

85. William Zeckendorf quoted in "Zeckendorf Hails Transition of City," *New York Times* (March 23, 1956): 29.

86. Sinclair, "Mid-Twentieth-Century New York," in Toynbee, ed., *Cities of Destiny*, 331.

87. "A Walking Tour," *Journal of the American Institute of Architects* 34 (September 1960): 26; "50 Guided Around Wall Street Area in Historical Tour," *New York Times* (June 12, 1961): 31; Philip Benjamin, "Suspicious 'Villagers' Mistake Walking Tour for City Planners," *New York Times* (July 10, 1961): 14.

88. Andreas Feininger, *The Face of New York: The City As It Was and As It Is*, with a text by Susan E. Lyman (New York: Crown Publishers, 1954).

89. Gilbert Millstein, *New York: True North* (Garden City, N.Y.: Doubleday & Co., 1964).

90. Louis B. Schlivek, *Man in Metropolis: A Book about the People and Prospects of a Metropolitan Region* (New York: Doubleday & Co., 1965). Also see Christopher Tunnard, "The Places We Call Home," book review, *New York Times* (December 19, 1965), VII: 3, 13.

91. Arthur Cort Holden, *Sonnets for My City: An Essay on the Kinship of Art and Finance* (New York: Schulte, 1965). Also see "Books," *Journal of the American Institute of Architects* 45 (January 1966): 76, 80; Robert C. Weinberg, book review, *Journal of the American Institute of Planners* 32 (January 1966): 56–57; Harmon H. Goldstone, "Pecuniary Poetry," book review, *Progressive Architecture* 47 (May 1966): 236, 240, 248, 256.

92. Mannes, *The New York I Know*, 148. Also see Allen Churchill, "Around the Island," book review, *New York Times* (September 10, 1961), VII: 40; Mary Perot Nichols, "The New York I Know," book review, *Village Voice* 7 (December 14, 1961): 5.

93. "Citizen Group Calls for Further Cafes on City Sidewalks," *New York Times* (May 18, 1964): 32; Frank J. Landers, "Against Sidewalk Cafes," letter to the editor, *New York Times* (June 1, 1964): 28; "The Talk of the Town: Notes and Comment," *New Yorker* 40 (June 13, 1964): 30–32; Elaine Kendall, "Need for a Sidewalk Cafe Society," *New York Times* (July 5, 1964), VI: 12–13, 16; Jeanette E. Lambert, "Floating Cafes," letter to the editor, *New York Times* (July 19, 1964), VI: 4; Guy D'Ambry, "Not for Us," letter to the editor, *New York Times* (July 19, 1964), VI: 4.

94. Gay Talese, "Now New Yorkers, Too, Can Sit and Sip and Sit at Sidewalk Cafes," *New York Times* (June 28, 1965): 31.

95. "Sidewalk Cafes to Increase Here," *New York Times* (May 16, 1967): 29; "Mayor Approves 2 New Agencies," *New York Times* (April 23, 1968): 49; Seth S. King, "New Bill Assists Sidewalk Cafes," *New York Times* (May 5, 1968): 41; David K. Shipler, "Sidewalk Cafes Bloom Here Despite Soot and Noise," *New York Times* (June 17, 1968): 41.

96. John Darnton, "Enclosed Sidewalk Cafes Facing Closer Regulation," *New York Times* (July 6, 1974): 1, 22.

97. "Sidewalk Cafes Get Hearing at City Hall," *New York Times* (June 25, 1976), B: 1.

98. "Plight of the Cyclists," *Newsweek* 69 (March 27, 1967): 88.

99. Nancy Moran, "Cycling Lane Likely for a Major City Street," *New York Times* (September 17, 1970): 1, 40; Clark Whelton, "Cyclists in the City: Ride On!" *Village Voice* 15

(September 25, 1970): 1, 3; "The Talk of the Town: Bike to Work," *New Yorker* 46 (September 26, 1970): 28–29.
100. Stephen Zoll, "Superville: New York—Aspects of Very High Bulk," *Massachusetts Review* 14 (summer 1973): 447–538.
101. Quoted in Geoffrey Moorhouse, *Imperial City: New York* (New York: Henry Holt, 1989), 243.
102. Robert F. Wagner quoted in Moorhouse, *Imperial City: New York*, 254.
103. "The Lure of the City," *House Beautiful* 107 (August 1965): 71.
104. August Heckscher, "I Happen to Be a City Man," *House Beautiful* 107 (August 1965): 74, 123–24; Andy Logan, "We Never Left," *House Beautiful* 107 (August 1965): 119, 132, 134; Mary Scott Welch, "We Moved Back to the City," *House Beautiful* 107 (August 1965): 118, 125–26.
105. "The Voters' Own Urban Renewal," *Fortune* 72 (December 1965): 134, 136.
106. Martin G. Berck, "From High in the Sky Lindsay Cites City Ills," *New York Herald Tribune* (July 24, 1965): 5; Ada Louise Huxtable, "Lindsay Surveys City from Copter," *New York Times* (July 24, 1965): 8.
107. "Can New York Find a Cure for Urban Ills?" *Business Week* (December 25, 1965): 34–38.
108. "Sick in New York," *Architectural Forum* 124 (January–February 1966): 30; Walter McQuade, "And It Came Unto New York City," *Architectural Forum* 124 (January–February 1966): 96; "Fresh Style at City Hall," *Time* 87 (January 14, 1966): 27–28; Richard J. Whalen, "'This Lindsay' Takes On That City," *Fortune* 73 (June 1966): 126–29, 226.
109. Roger Starr, *The Rise and Fall of New York City* (New York: Basic Books, 1985), 12.
110. John V. Lindsay quoted in Lael Scott and Maurice Carroll, "Mayor Takes a Lofty View of His Troubles," *New York Post* (January 4, 1966): 1.
111. William V. Shannon, "Lindsay—The First Six Months," *New Republic* 155 (July 16, 1966): 16–19.
112. "The Jungle and the City," *Time* 88 (July 29, 1966): 11–12.
113. "Is New York's New Mayor Solving the City's Problems?" *U.S. News & World Report* 61 (August 15, 1966): 66–68; William V. Shannon, "Crisis of the Cities," *Commonweal* 83 (December 3, 1966): 264–65.
114. Peter Blake, "A Timely Compliment," *New York* 2 (October 20, 1969): 42. For Wagner's anti-architectural stance, see "'No Architect,'" editorial, *New York Times* (November 6, 1962): 32.
115. "Judge Rules Dancers Can Keep On Go-Going," *New York Times* (July 13, 1967): 32.
116. Andrew Hacker, *The New Yorkers: A Profile of an American Metropolis* (New York: Mason/Charter, 1975), 16–17.
117. Saul Bellow, *Mr. Sammler's Planet* (New York: Viking Press, 1970), 304.
118. Phil Berger, *Miracle on 33rd Street: The New York Knickerbockers' Championship Season* (New York: Simon & Schuster, 1970); Marv Albert, *Krazy About the Knicks* (New York: Hawthorn Books, 1971).
119. Larry Borstein, *Super Joe: The Joe Namath Story* (New York: Grosset & Dunlap, 1969); Joe Willie Namath with Dick Schaap, *I Can't Wait Until Tomorrow. . . 'Cause I Get Better-Looking Every Day* (New York: Random House, 1969).
120. For the Ansonia, see Robert A. M. Stern, Gregory Gilmartin and John Montague Massengale, *New York 1900: Metropolitan Architecture and Urbanism 1890–1915* (New York: Rizzoli International Publications, 1983), 384–86.
121. Joseph Durso, *Amazing: The Miracle of the Mets* (Boston: Houghton Mifflin, 1970); Larry Fox, *Last to First: The Story of the Mets* (New York: Harper & Row, 1970). Also see Nat Hentoff, *A Political Life: The Education of John V. Lindsay* (New York: Alfred A. Knopf, 1969); Joe Flaherty, *Managing Mailer* (New York: Coward-McCann, 1970).
122. Nathan Glazer, "The New New Yorkers," in Peter D. Salins, ed., *New York Unbound: The City and the Politics of the Future* (New York: Basil Blackwell, 1988), 54–72.
123. "New York City Goes Out in a Rowboat," *Time* 97 (June 21, 1971): 13–15.
124. Fernando Wood quoted in "Should New York City Be the 51st State?" *Time* 97 (June 21, 1971): 14–15. Also see Jerome Mushkat, *Fernando Wood: A Political Biography* (Kent, Ohio: Kent State University Press, 1990), 111–15.
125. "New York, N.Y.: Citizens of New York, Arise! Throw Off Albany's Shackles and Assume Statehood," *Look* 17 (May 1953): 17.
126. "A Stand-by Emergency Tax," editorial, *New York Times* (November 23, 1965): 44; David Lopez, "Tax on Nonresidents Using City's Services," letter to the editor, *New York Times* (November 24, 1965): 38; Clayton Knowles, "City Income Tax of 2% Proposed by Wagner Panel," *New York Times* (November 29, 1965): 1, 44; Richard L. Madden, "Lindsay Sees Tax as a 'Last Resort,'" *New York Times* (November 29, 1965): 1, 44; "A City Income Tax Next?" editorial, *New York Times* (November 29, 1965): 34; Robert Alden, "Council Votes Income Tax after Albany's Approval; Medicaid's Scope Reduced," *New York Times* (July 2, 1966): 1, 8; Richard L. Madden, "Legislators End Stalemate but Put Off Adjournment," *New York Times* (July 2, 1966): 1, 8; Steven V. Roberts, "City Withholding Will Begin Sept. 1," *New York Times* (July 2, 1966): 1, 8; Richard L. Madden, "Governor Repeats Pledge to Aid City in Tax Deficiencies," *New York Times* (December 22, 1966): 1, 27; "The City Needs More Revenue," editorial, *New York Times* (December 22, 1966): 32; "Commuter Group to Test New York's Income Taxes," *New York Times* (April 2, 1967): 96; "Commuters Seek U.S. Ruling to End Nonresident Taxes," *New York Times* (October 5, 1967): 80; "Suit Fails to Halt Nonresident Tax," *New York Times* (December 21, 1967): 41.
127. "Should New York City Be the 51st State?": 14.
128. Norman Mailer, "Why Are We in New York?" *New York Times* (May 18, 1969), VI: 30–31, 96, 98, 101, 103, 106, 108–9, 111, 113.
129. Mailer, "Why Are We in New York?": 98.
130. Mailer, "Why Are We in New York?": 103.
131. Robert T. Connor quoted in "Should New York City Be the 51st State?": 14.
132. Pete Hamill, "Notes of a New York Nationalist," *New York* 5 (June 5, 1972): 48–52; Pete Hamill, "Don't Tread on Us: New York Should Secede from the Union," *Village Voice* 20 (June 23, 1975): 13–15.
133. Phil Tracy, "It's Now or Never for the 51st State," *Village Voice* 16 (August 19, 1971): 1, 8, 10.
134. "A Massive Majority for Statehood. . . ," *New York* 4 (August 23, 1971): 26–27.
135. Michael Harrington, ". . . But Is Statehood for New York City Really the Answer?" *New York* 4 (August 23, 1971): 28–33.
136. B. Bruce-Briggs, "Abolish New York," *New York Affairs* 5, no. 3 (1979): 5–9.
137. Martin Arnold, "Knocking City Draws No Smiles," *New York Times* (February 2, 1972): 45; Paul J. C. Friedlander, "Salesmanship Shines New York's Image," *New York Times* (October 14, 1973), X: 33.
138. Gerald Leonard Cohen, *Origin of New York City's Nickname "The Big Apple"* (Frankfurt am Main: Forum Anglicum Series, Peter Lang, 1991). Also see Rex Roberts, "Apple Turnovers," book review, *Columbia* (winter 1992): 40.
139. William Safire, "The Big Apple in a Big Pickle," *New York Times* (May 19, 1975): 29.
140. "Business Feels Better about New York City," *Business Week* (April 7, 1973): 92, 94.
141. Eli Ginzberg, ed., *New York Is Very Much Alive* (New York: McGraw-Hill, 1973), see especially Richard Knight, "Growth Pole": 3–19; Thomas M. Stanback, Jr., "Suburbanization": 42–67; Eli Ginzberg, "Precipitations": 273–84; Eli Ginzberg, "Priorities": 285–96. Also see Annmarie Walsh, "Tale of Two Cities," book review, *New York* 6 (May 7, 1973): 71–74.
142. Felix Rohatyn, "On the Brink," *New York* 21 (April 11, 1988): 81.
143. "A Moral Issue," *Time* 105 (March 10, 1975): 40.
144. "The Big Apple On the Brink," *Time* 105 (April 7, 1975): 50.
145. Martin Mayer, "Plunging into Bankruptcy; Or How to Get New York Back into the Swim," *New York Times* (May 19, 1975): 29.
146. "Big Mac for the Big Apple," *Newsweek* 89 (June 23, 1975): 29.
147. "The Banks Rebuff New York Again," *Business Week* (September 8, 1975): 58–59; Jack Newfield, "Who Broke New York and How to Rebuild It," *Village Voice* 20 (September 15, 1975): 9–11; "The Talk of the Town: Notes and Comment," *New Yorker* 51 (October 27, 1975): 31–32; "Congress Goes Slow on Saving New York," *Business Week* (November 3, 1975): 31–32; Richard Reeves, "Will Congress Save New York? Don't Bet on It," *New York* 8 (November 3, 1975): 45–48.
148. "Ford, Castigating City, Asserts He'd Veto Fund Guarantee; Offers Bankruptcy Bill," *New York Times* (October 30, 1975): 1. Also see Francis X. Clines, "Beame and Carey Decry Ford Plan," *New York Times* (October 30, 1975): 1, 48; Fred Ferretti, "Pension Funds Near Pact on Backing Loans to City," *New York Times* (October 30, 1975): 1, 48; Martin Tolchin, "'Bailout' Barred," *New York Times* (October 30, 1975): 1, 46; "Transcript of President's Talk on City Crisis, Questions Asked and His Responses," *New York Times* (October 30, 1975): 46; R. W. Apple, Jr., "City a '76 Issue for Ford; Democrats Doubt Its Value," *New York Times* (October 31, 1975): 1, 12; Francis X. Clines, "Carey Mobilizing Response to Ford," *New York Times* (October 31, 1975): 1, 13; Ernest Holsendolph, "Mayors Dispute Ford on Aid for New York," *New York Times* (October 31, 1975): 12; James M. Naughton, "President, on Coast, Makes New York's Crisis Focus of His Political Campaigning," *New York Times* (October 31, 1975): 12; Martin Tolchin, "Senate Unit, 8 to 5, Backs Loan Guarantee for City Despite Threatened Veto," *New York Times* (October 31, 1975): 1, 12; "The Birth of an Issue," *Newsweek* 86 (November 10, 1975): 18–22, 25, 28, 31.
149. "Ford to City: Drop Dead," *Daily News* (October 30, 1975): 1.
150. Gerald R. Ford quoted in "Transcript of President's Talk on City Crisis, Questions Asked and His Responses": 46.
151. "The City Gears for D-Day," *Time* 106 (November 10, 1975): 8–9; "The Talk of the Town: Notes and Comment," *New Yorker* 51 (November 17, 1975): 35.
152. Ken Auletta, "Finally, the Harsh Truth: The Buck Stops with Us," *New York* 8 (November 17, 1975): 50–53; "We've Got to Help Ourselves," editorial, *New York* 8 (November 17, 1975): 48–49.
153. Gerald R. Ford quoted in "Last-Minute Bailout of a City on the Brink," *Time* 106 (December 8, 1975): 8–9. Also see "The Talk of the Town: Notes and Comment," *New Yorker* 51 (December 1, 1975): 41; "Back and Free," *Newsweek* 86 (December 8, 1975): 23; Roger E. Alcaly and David Mermelstein, *The Fiscal Crisis of American Cities: Essays on the Political Economy of America with Special Reference to New York* (New York: Vintage Books, 1976); Fred Ferretti, *The Year the Big Apple Went Bust* (New York: Putnam, 1976); James Ring Adams, "Why New York Went Broke," *Commentary* 61 (May 1976): 31–37; "NYC: Who's to Blame," exchange between Esther Goldberg and James Ring Adams, *Commentary* 62 (September 1976): 14, 16, 18.
154. Michael Ruby with Pamela Ellis Simons, "The Diminished Apple," *Newsweek* 86 (December 15, 1975): 78. Also see William A. Emerson, Jr., "Make Mine Manhattan," *Newsweek* 86 (December 29, 1975): 9; Richard Poirier, "In the Middle of a Muddle," *Atlantic Monthly* 237 (March 1976): 12, 14, 18.
155. Richard Wade, "The End of the Self-Sufficient City," *New York Affairs* 3, no. 4 (1976): 3–8.
156. Starr, *The Rise and Fall of New York City*, 227.
157. Lou Winnick quoted in Jerome Charyn, *Metropolis: New York as Myth, Marketplace, and Magical Island* (New York: G. P. Putnam's Sons, 1986), 86.
158. Thomas Bender, *New York Intellect* (New York: Alfred A. Knopf, 1987), xviii.
159. Samuel J. Lefrak, "Of Planners, Head-Bopping and Mountain Goats," *New York Times* (January 18, 1974): 33.
160. Hacker, *The New Yorkers: A Profile of an American Metropolis*, 140.
161. Kurt Vonnegut, Jr., "New York: Who Needs It?" *Harper's* 251 (August 1975): 3.
162. Roger Starr, "Play It Again, Mies," *Harper's* 251 (August 1975): 5.
163. Lee Levitt, "Is New York as Bad as People Say?" *New York Affairs* 2 (November 1, 1974): 4–15.
164. Marshall Berman, "Ruins and Reforms: New York Yesterday and Today," *Dissent* 34 (fall 1987): 421–24.
165. Lewis Lapham, "City Lights: A Defense of New York," *Harper's* 252 (June 1976): 8, 13–14.
166. Hacker, *The New Yorkers: A Profile of an American Metropolis*, 2.
167. Hacker, *The New Yorkers: A Profile of an American Metropolis*, 5.
168. Felix Rohatyn quoted in Peter Hellman, "The Wizard of Lazard," *New York Times* (March 21, 1976), VI: 19, 24, 26, 28, 30, 32, 34, 37.
169. Eugene Lewis, *Public Entrepreneurship* (Bloomington, Ind.: Indiana University Press, 1980), 218.
170. Stern, Gilmartin and Mellins, *New York 1930*, 691, 694.
171. Nathan Glazer and Daniel Patrick Moynihan, *Beyond the Melting Pot* (Cambridge, Mass.: MIT Press, 1963), 3–4.
172. Robert A. Caro, *The Power Broker: Robert Moses and the Fall of New York* (New York: Alfred A. Knopf, 1974), with excerpts published in the *New Yorker* 50 (July 22, 1974): 32–38, 40, 44–46, 48–50, 52–64; (July 29, 1974): 37–56, 58–65; (August 12, 1974): 40–44, 47–49, 52–75; (August 19, 1974): 42–52, 54, 56–74, 77. Also see Paul Goldberger, "Book on Robert Moses a 7-Year Job," *New York Times* (August 21, 1974): 30; Michael T. Kaufman, "Moses Rips Into 'Venomous' Biography," *New York Times* (August 27, 1974): 25; Christopher Lehmann-Haupt, "Books of The Times: You Couldn't

Fight Bob Moses," book review, *New York Times* (September 9, 1974): 33; Richard C. Wade, "The Power Broker," book review, *New York Times* (September 15, 1974), VII: 1–3; Peter S. Prescott, "Master Builder," book review, *Newsweek* 84 (September 16, 1974): 80–82; Philip Herrera, "The Book of Moses," book review, *Time* 104 (September 16, 1974): 100, 107; Jane Holtz Kay, "The Master Builder and His Works," book review, *Nation* 219 (September 28, 1974): 277–78; Dick Netzer, "The Man and the City," book review, *New Republic* 177 (September 28, 1974): 18–19; J. S. Fuerst, "Moses' New York," book review, *Progressive Architecture* 55 (December 1974): 110, 112, 114; C. Richard Hatch, "Destroying New York in Order to Save It," book review, *Harper's* 250 (January 1975): 86–88, 90; Charles W. Froessel, "In Defense of Robert Moses," letter to the editor, *New York Times* (January 25, 1975): 26; Charles S. Ascher, "Ascher on Moses," *New York Planning Review* 17 (spring 1975), A: 11–13; Arthur C. Holden, "Holden on Moses," *New York Planning Review* 17 (spring 1975), A: 14–15. For an in-depth discussion of Moses's role in the post–World War II redevelopment of New York, see Joel Schwartz, *The New York Approach: Robert Moses, Urban Liberals, and Redevelopment of the Inner City* (Columbus, Ohio: Ohio State University Press, 1993).

173. Marshall Berman, *All That Is Solid Melts Into Air* (New York: Simon & Schuster, 1982), 308.

174. Marshall Berman, "Buildings Are Judgement," *Ramparts* 13 (March 1975): 33–39, 50–57.

175. Rodgers, *New York Plans for the Future*, 261–62. Also see Douglas Haskell, "Review," *New Pencil Points* 24 (April 1943): 92.

176. Frances Perkins quoted in Berman, *All That Is Solid Melts Into Air*, 304.

177. Charles G. Bennett, "Council to Query Moses on Policies," *New York Times* (June 13, 1956): 39; Alexander Feinberg, "City Is Defended on Tenant Shifts," *New York Times* (September 23, 1956): 1, 76; Harris L. Present, "For Housing Study," letter to the editor, *New York Times* (May 30, 1957): 18; "Civic Groups Here Fight U.S. Grants," *New York Times* (April 30, 1958): 26; Philip Benjamin, "Housing Tangles Face New Board," *New York Times* (May 4, 1958): 1, 80; Joseph Kahn and William Haddad, "City Admits Shifts from Slums to Slums," *New York Post* (April 1, 1959): 4, 36; "Judgment Day for Slumlords?" editorial, *New York Post* (April 1, 1959): 45; Joseph Kahn and William Haddad, "Slum Clearance Official's Bank Linked to Million $ Title I Deal," *New York Post* (June 16, 1959): 5, 23; Joseph Kahn and William Haddad, "2d Slum Clearance Aid Linked to Title I Banks," *New York Post* (June 18, 1959): 3, 81; "Lost Voices," editorial, *New York Post* (June 18, 1959): 57; "Mr. Moses and His Legend," editorial, *Village Voice* 14 (June 24, 1959): 4; Joseph Kahn and William Haddad, "The Press Agents on the Inside," *New York Post* (June 26, 1959): 5, 22; "Mayor, Moses Meeting on Title I," *New York Post* (June 26, 1959): 5; Wayne Phillips, "Title I and Slum Clearance: A Decade of Controversy," *New York Times* (June 29, 1959): 1, 24; Wayne Phillips, "Unorthodox Title I Procedures Used by Moses Create Disputes," *New York Times* (June 30, 1959): 1, 34; Emmanuel Perlmutter, "Inquiry Ordered on Title I Award," *New York Times* (July 1, 1959): 1, 23; Wayne Phillips, "Scandal Charges Buffet Title I Projects in City," *New York Times* (July 1, 1959): 23; Charles Grutzner, "Mayor Chides Title I Body; Bars Architect in Scandal," *New York Times* (July 2, 1959): 1, 12; Wayne Phillips, "Title I Slum Clearance Proves Spur to Cooperative Housing in City," *New York Times* (July 2, 1959): 13; Charles Grutzner, "Moses Says Title I Is a 'Dead Duck'; Decries Charges," *New York Times* (July 4, 1959): 1, 30; "Statement and Letter by Moses on Title I Slum Clearance," *New York Times* (July 4, 1959): 30; "Code Asks Ban on Shanahan Title I Loans," *New York Post* (July 22, 1959): 47; Joseph Kahn and William Haddad, "U.S. Tightening Title I Rules Here," *New York Post* (July 26, 1959): 10; William Haddad, "Shanahan Reported Losing Authority to Clear Sponsors of Title I Projects," *New York Post* (July 28, 1959): 5, 59; "New York's Title I Controversy Spotlights Architect Kessler—A Combination of Know-How and Know-Who," *Architectural Forum* 111 (August 1959): 13–14, 16; William Haddad, "Moses Paid Spargo $243,000 Fees, Also Bares Funds in Shanahan Bank," *New York Post* (August 24, 1959): 2; Joseph Kahn, "'Windfall' Figure Gets New Title I Project," *New York Post* (August 24, 1959): 4, 54; "The Title I Mess (cont.)," editorial, *New York Post* (August 24, 1959): 23; Stephen G. Thompson, "The Future of Title I," *Architectural Forum* 111 (September 1959): 107–9, 194, 198; John Sibley, "New Title I Plan Outlined for City by Housing Board," *New York Times* (June 5, 1960): 1, 78; Robert Moses, *Public Works: A Dangerous Trade* (New York: McGraw-Hill, 1970), 458–62; Caro, *The Power Broker*, 979–83, 1005–13.

178. Lewis, *Public Entrepreneurship*, 219.

179. Fred J. Cook, "Robert Moses, Glutton for Power," *Dissent* 8 (summer 1961): 312–20.

180. Cook, "Robert Moses, Glutton for Power": 320.

181. Martin Gansberg, "Moses Cautions New Authority," *New York Times* (February 19, 1968): 31; Edith Evans Asbury, "Another Opening, Another Closing for Moses," *New York Times* (February 29, 1968): 39; Sylvan Fox, "A Peppery Moses Recalls His 50 Years of Public Life," *New York Times* (August 2, 1968): 35, 66; Moses, *Public Works: A Dangerous Trade*, 303–9, 899–904.

182. Wade, "The Power Broker": 3.

183. Moses, *Public Works: A Dangerous Trade*, 897. Also see Caro, *The Power Broker*, 1117–44.

184. E. F. Schumacher, *Small Is Beautiful: A Study of Economics as if People Mattered* (London: Blond and Briggs, 1973).

185. Robert Moses quoted in Kaufman, "Moses Rips Into 'Venomous' Biography": 25.

186. Wade, "The Power Broker": 2.

187. Netzer, "The Man and the City": 18.

188. Berman, "Buildings Are Judgement": 55. Also see "Buildings Are Judgement II," *Ramparts* 13 (May 1975): 45–55.

189. Jane Jacobs, *The Death and Life of Great American Cities* (New York: Random House, 1961), with excerpts published in *Architectural Forum* 115 (September 1961): 122–25 and *Vogue* 139 (January 1, 1962): 73, 130. Also see Emerson Goble, "The Death and Life of the Housing Project," editorial, *Architectural Record* 130 (November 1961): 9; Marya Mannes, "A Fresh Look at Cities. . . ," book review, *Architectural Forum* 115 (December 1961): 149; "This Is an Attack on Current City Planning," editorial, *Architectural Forum* 116 (January 1962): 69; Herbert Gans, "City Planning and Urban Realities," book review, *Commentary* 33 (February 1962): 170–75; Edward T. Chase, "A New Standard for Cities," *Architectural Forum* 116 (March 1962): 90–91; Edward J. Logue, "The View from the Village," *Architectural Forum* 116 (March 1962): 89–90; Sibyl Moholy-Nagy, "In Defense of Architecture," letter to the editor, *Architectural Forum* 116 (April 1962): 19; Hatch, "Destroying New York in Order to Save It": 86–88, 90; Francis Morrone, "Citizen Jane Jacobs," *New Criterion* 12 (May 1994): 24–28.

190. Suzanne Stephens, "Voices of Consequence: Four Architectural Critics," in Susana Torre, ed., *Women in Architecture: A Historic and Contemporary Perspective* (New York: Whitney Library of Design, 1977), 136–43.

191. Jane Jacobs, "New York's Office Boom," *Architectural Forum* 106 (March 1957): 104–13.

192. Jane Jacobs, "Metropolitan Government," *Architectural Forum* 107 (August 1957): 124–27.

193. Jane Jacobs, "Downtown Is for People," *Fortune* 57 (April 1958): 133–40, 236, 238, 240–42, reprinted in *The Exploding Metropolis*, with an intro. by William H. Whyte, Jr. (Garden City, N.Y.: Doubleday, 1958), 140–68.

194. Jacobs, *The Death and Life of Great American Cities*, 373.

195. Jacobs, *The Death and Life of Great American Cities*, 371.

196. Landmarks Preservation Commission of the City of New York, *Greenwich Village Historic District Designation Report* (New York, 1969), 399–400.

197. Jacobs, *The Death and Life of Great American Cities*, 50.

198. Jacobs, *The Death and Life of Great American Cities*, 15.

199. Charyn, *Metropolis: New York as Myth, Marketplace, and Magical Island*, 41.

200. Jacobs, *The Death and Life of Great American Cities*, 50.

201. Jacobs, *The Death and Life of Great American Cities*, 215.

202. Jacobs, *The Death and Life of Great American Cities*, 218.

203. Jacobs, *The Death and Life of Great American Cities*, 270–71.

204. Jacobs, *The Death and Life of Great American Cities*, 392.

205. Jacobs, *The Death and Life of Great American Cities*, 394–95.

206. Jacobs, *The Death and Life of Great American Cities*, 399.

207. Jacobs, *The Death and Life of Great American Cities*, 400–401.

208. Jacobs, *The Death and Life of Great American Cities*, 439.

209. Mannes, "A Fresh Look at Cities. . . ": 149.

210. Gans, "City Planning and Urban Realities": 172.

211. Gans, "City Planning and Urban Realities": 173–74.

212. Gans, "City Planning and Urban Realities": 175.

213. Walter McQuade, "Architecture," *Nation* 194 (March 17, 1962): 241–42. Also see "The Laws of the Asphalt Jungle," press release, no. 8, February 2, 1962, Museum of Modern Art.

214. McQuade, "Architecture": 241.

215. McQuade, "Architecture": 241.

216. Logue, "The View from the Village": 89.

217. Chase, "A New Standard for Cities": 90–91.

218. Chase, "A New Standard for Cities": 91.

219. Lewis Mumford, "The Sky Line: Mother Jacobs' Home Remedies," *New Yorker* 38 (December 1, 1962): 148, 150, 152, 154, 157–58, 160, 162–64, 167–68, 170–74, 177–79, reprinted as "Home Remedies for Urban Cancer," in Lewis Mumford, *The Urban Prospect* (New York: Harcourt, Brace & World, 1968), 182–207 and, with the same title, in Donald L. Miller, ed., *The Lewis Mumford Reader* (New York: Pantheon, 1986), 184–200.

220. Mumford, "The Sky Line: Mother Jacobs' Home Remedies": 154, 158, 160.

221. Mumford, "The Sky Line: Mother Jacobs' Home Remedies": 167–68.

222. Mumford, "The Sky Line: Mother Jacobs' Home Remedies": 179.

223. Wolf Von Eckardt, *A Place to Live: The Crisis of the Cities* (New York: Delacorte, 1967), 48.

224. Moholy-Nagy, "In Defense of Architecture": 19.

225. Roger Starr, *The Living End: The City and Its Critics* (New York: Coward McCann, 1966), 164.

226. Charyn, *Metropolis: New York as Myth, Marketplace, and Magical Island*, 39.

227. Jane Jacobs, *The Economy of Cities* (New York: Random House, 1969), 3–4. Also see Leticia Kent, "Jane Jacobs: Against Urban Renewal, for Urban Life," *New York Times* (May 25, 1969), VI: 34–35, 67, 70, 92, 95, 97–98; Charles Abrams, "The Economy of Cities," book review, *New York Times* (June 1, 1969), VII: 3; James Marston Fitch, "The Economy of Cities," book review, *Architectural Forum* 131 (July–August 1969): 98–99; Gerald Hodge, "The Economy of Cities," book review, *Journal of the American Institute of Planners* 36 (March 1970): 133–34; Stephens, "Voices of Consequence: Four Architectural Critics," in Torre, ed., *Women in Architecture: A Historic and Contemporary Perspective*, 138.

228. For the McGraw-Hill Building, see Stern, Gilmartin and Mellins, *New York 1930*, 574–75, 579–80, 584–85.

229. Stern, Gilmartin and Mellins, *New York 1930*, 355.

230. *Buildings for Business and Government*, exhibition catalogue (New York: Museum of Modern Art, 1957).

231. S. Giedion, "The Experiment of S.O.M.," *Bauen und Wohnen* 12 (April 1957): 113–14; William E. Hartmann, "S.O.M. Organization," *Bauen und Wohnen* 12 (April 1957): 116; Mario José Buschiazzo, *Skidmore, Owings & Merrill* (Buenos Aires: Instituto de Arte Americano e Investigaciones, 1958); "The Architects from Skid's Row," *Fortune* 57 (January 1958): 137–40, 210, 212, 215; "Designers for a Busy World," *Newsweek* 53 (May 4, 1959): 97–100; Ernst Danz, *Architecture of Skidmore, Owings & Merrill, 1950–1962*, with an intro. by Henry-Russell Hitchcock (New York: Frederick A. Praeger, 1963); Christopher Woodward and Yukio Futagawa, *Skidmore, Owings & Merrill* (New York: Simon & Schuster, 1970); Nathaniel Alexander Owings, *The Spaces in Between: An Architect's Journey* (Boston: Houghton Mifflin, 1973); Axel Menges, *Architecture of Skidmore, Owings & Merrill, 1963–1973*, with an intro. by Arthur Drexler (New York: Architectural Book Publishing Co., 1974); "Skidmore, Owings & Merrill," *A + U*, special issue (January 1974); Bernard Michael Boyle, "Architectural Practice in America, 1865–1965—Ideal and Reality," in Spiro Kostof, ed., *The Architect: Chapters in the History of the Profession* (New York: Oxford University Press, 1977), 324–31; "Recent Works of Skidmore, Owings & Merrill," *Space Design* (May 1979): 3–84; "SOM's Computer Approach," *Architectural Record* 168 (mid-August 1980): 84–91; Suzanne Stephens, "SOM at Midlife," *Progressive Architecture* 62 (May 1981): 138–49; *Skidmore, Owings & Merrill: Architecture and Urbanism, 1973–1983*, with an intro. by Albert Bush-Brown (New York: Van Nostrand Reinhold, 1983); "Skidmore, Owings & Merrill," *A + U* (March 1983): 24–58; *Bruce Graham of SOM*, with an intro. by Stanley Tigerman (New York: Rizzoli International Publications, 1989).

232. Quoted in John Winter, "Skidmore, Owings & Merrill," in Anne Lee Morgan and Colin Naylor, eds., *Contemporary Architects* (Chicago: St. James, 1987), 848.

233. David Jacobs, "The Establishment's Architect—Plus," *New York Times* (July 23, 1972), VI: 12–14, 16–19, 21, 23; Paul Spreiregen, "Gordon Bunshaft," in Morgan and

Naylor, eds., *Contemporary Architects*, 136; Carol Herselle Krinsky, *Gordon Bunshaft of Skidmore, Owings & Merrill* (New York: Architectural History Foundation; Cambridge, Mass.: MIT Press, 1988). For Skidmore and Owings's work at the New York World's Fair of 1939–40, see Stern, Gilmartin and Mellins, *New York 1930*, 746–47.
234. Krinsky, *Gordon Bunshaft of Skidmore, Owings & Merrill*, xi, 1.
235. Hitchcock, "Introduction," in Danz, *Architecture of Skidmore, Owings & Merrill, 1950–1962*, 13.
236. Steven Ruttenbaum, *Mansions in the Clouds: The Skyscraper Palazzi of Emery Roth* (New York: Balsam Press, 1986), 41–44. Also see "Emery Roth Dies; Noted Architect," *New York Times* (August 21, 1948): 16; Dennis Duggan, "The 'Belly' School of Architecture," *New York Sunday Herald Tribune Magazine* (December 15, 1963): 7–10.
237. Stern, Gilmartin and Massengale, *New York 1900*, 385, 388; Ruttenbaum, *Mansions in the Clouds: The Skyscraper Palazzi of Emery Roth*, 40–41, 44–46.
238. For the Ritz Tower, see Stern, Gilmartin and Mellins, *New York 1930*, 212–15. For the Oliver Cromwell, the San Remo and the Eldorado, see Stern, Gilmartin and Mellins, *New York 1930*, 403, 406–9.
239. Ada Louise Huxtable quoted in "The Skyline Factory," *Newsweek* 70 (September 18, 1967): 98.
240. Richard Roth quoted in Duggan, "The 'Belly' School of Architecture": 9.
241. Richard Roth, "High-Rise Down to Earth," *Progressive Architecture* 38 (June 1957): 196–98.
242. Richard Roth quoted in Duggan, "The 'Belly' School of Architecture": 10.
243. Stern, Gilmartin and Mellins, *New York 1930*, 603–10.
244. Wolf Von Eckardt, *Eric Mendelsohn* (New York: George Braziller, 1960), 21–23, plates 19–20, 32–34.
245. For the unrealized CBS building in New York, see Stern, Gilmartin and Mellins, *New York 1930*, 267–69. For the CBS Building in Hollywood and the Longfellow Building, see Christian Hubert and Lindsay Stamm Shapiro, *William Lescaze* (New York: Institute for Architecture and Urban Studies; New York: Rizzoli International Publications, 1982), 63, 98–100, 108, 112.
246. W. Boesiger, ed., *Le Corbusier and Pierre Jeanneret: Oeuvre complète 1929–1934*, vol. 2 (Zurich: Editions Girsberger, 1935), 97–109.
247. For Mies's unrealized projects, see Arthur Drexler, *Ludwig Mies van der Rohe* (New York: George Braziller, 1960), 14–15, plates 1–4. For the Hallidie Building, see "An All-Glass Front: Some Day-lighting Features of the Hallidie Building, San Francisco, California," *American Architect* 113 (March 27, 1918): 393–94; "Hallidie Building, San Francisco," *Architectural Record* 69 (February 1931): 131; William H. Jordy, *American Buildings and Their Architects: Progressive and Academic Ideals at the Turn of the Twentieth Century*, vol. 3 (Garden City, N.Y.: Doubleday & Co., 1972), 67, 69–70; Richard Longstreth, *On the Edge of the World: Four Architects in San Francisco at the Turn of the Century* (New York: Architectural History Foundation; Cambridge, Mass.: MIT Press, 1983), 302–4.
248. Stern, Gilmartin and Massengale, *New York 1900*, 153.
249. Philip Johnson quoted in John W. Cook and Heinrich Klotz, *Conversations with Architects* (New York: Praeger, 1973), 32–33.
250. Philip Johnson, "Informal Talk," delivered at the Architectural Association, School of Architecture, London, November 28, 1960, published in Peter Eisenman and Robert A. M. Stern, eds., *Philip Johnson: Writings* (New York: Oxford University Press, 1979), 106–16.
251. Olga Gueft, "Non-Conformity on Columbus Circle," *Interiors* 123 (June 1964): 92–96.
252. "Yamasaki's Serene Campus Center," *Architectural Forum* 109 (August 1958): 78–83; "Minoru Yamasaki: Projets et Réalisations Récents," *L'Architecture d'Aujourd'hui* 31 (April–May 1960): 49–63; "Six New Projects by Yamasaki," *Architectural Record* 130 (July 1961): 124–40; "Yamasaki's Concrete 'Trees,'" *Architectural Record* 131 (April 1962): 146–48; "College of Education Building, Wayne State University, Detroit, Michigan," *Michigan Society of Architects Monthly Bulletin* 36 (May 1962): 32–35.
253. Norman Mailer, "The Big Bite," *Esquire* 59 (May 1963): 37, 40.
254. Norman Mailer quoted in "Mailer vs. Scully," *Architectural Forum* 120 (April 1964): 96–97. Also see "Is Architecture Totalitarian?" *Village Voice* 9 (April 16, 1964): 1.
255. Mary Nichols, "Mailer's Castle: Far Out, Way Up, and Swinging," *Village Voice* 10 (February 18, 1965): 1, 7.
256. Vincent Scully quoted in "Mailer vs. Scully": 96–97.
257. Robert Venturi, *Complexity and Contradiction in Architecture* (New York: Museum of Modern Art, 1966), 102.

Chapter 2
Death by Development

1. Horace Sutton, "You Can't Live in New York," *Saturday Evening Post* 234 (March 11, 1961): 32–33, 93–94.
2. *Herald Tribune*'s assessment discussed in Clarence S. Stein, "The Future of New York," *Post War Planning News Digest* 1 (July 10, 1943): 1–7.
3. "The Great Manhattan Boom," *Time* 62 (December 21, 1953): 43–46.
4. William Zeckendorf quoted in "City's Future Is Bright in Zeckendorf's Opinion," *New York Times* (January 19, 1954): 22.
5. Quoted in "City Claims Title of Office Capital," *New York Times* (November 7, 1956): 39.
6. Charles Luckman quoted in Wesley W. Stout, "Why New York?" *Saturday Evening Post* 222 (February 11, 1950): 27, 106–8.
7. Stout, "Why New York?": 108.
8. Daniel Bell, "The Three Faces of New York," *Dissent* 8 (summer 1961): 222–32.
9. "The Corporate Image Concept Nourishes N.Y. Office Construction," *Real Estate Record and Guide* 188 (September 23, 1961): 3.
10. "New York: The Executive City," *Business Week* (October 20, 1956): 140–52.
11. "The City Whose Business Is Bigness," *Business Week* (October 13, 1956): 125–41.
12. Gilbert Burck, "Headquarters Town," *Fortune* 61 (February 1960): 93–96, 258, 263–64, 266.
13. John McDonald, "The $2-Billion Building Boom," *Fortune* 61 (February 1960): 48–122, 232, 234, 236, 238, 243–44, 246. Also see Maurice Mogulescu, *Profit through Design* (New York: American Management Association, 1970), 9–15.
14. Stern, Gilmartin and Massengale, *New York 1900*, 165, 175–77.
15. Stern, Gilmartin and Mellins, *New York 1930*, 603–10.
16. Louis Sill quoted in "The Corporate Image Concept Nourishes N.Y. Office Construction": 3.
17. Bell, "The Three Faces of New York": 227.
18. "Office Building Spree in New York Loses Some of Its Pep," *Business Week* (November 9, 1957): 88–89.
19. "Comment and Reports to Record and Guide," *Real Estate Record and Guide* 170 (October 25, 1952): 3; "Office Building Revival Gets Bolder; Will Set a Record," *Architectural Forum* 98 (January 1953): 39, 41.
20. "New New York," *Newsweek* 48 (July 9, 1956): 87–92.
21. "City Claims Title of Office Capital": 39.
22. "Demand Slows for New York Office Space," *Architectural Forum* 108 (May 1958): 47–48.
23. Norman Tishman quoted in "Strong Demand for Office Space Continues," *Real Estate Record and Guide* 182 (August 30, 1958): 3–4.
24. Thomas W. Ennis, "Boom in Offices Continued in '60," *New York Times* (January 1, 1961), VIII: 1, 3; "Occupancy Rate in Manhattan Office Buildings at 97.2%," *Real Estate Record and Guide* 188 (July 22, 1961): 2–3; "Real Estate Board of N.Y. Survey Reveals Occupancy Rate in Manhattan Office Buildings at 97.1%," *Real Estate Record and Guide* 190 (August 18, 1962): 2–3.
25. Daniel Seligman, "The Future of the Office-Building Boom," *Fortune* 67 (March 1963): 84–88, 214, 216, 220, 222–23.
26. "Big Cities Report on Building Prospect," *Architectural Forum* 120 (February 1964): 7. Also see Daniel M. Friedenberg, "The Coming Bust in the Real Estate Boom," *Harper's* 222 (June 1962): 29–40; "Decline Forecast in Office Building," *New York Times* (December 2, 1962), VIII: 1, 7.
27. "Studley Sees Need for Construction Speed-Up in Manhattan," *Real Estate Record and Guide* 192 (November 9, 1963): 2–3.
28. "Fuse Is Lit for Another Office Building Boom," *Business Week* (July 24, 1965): 28, 30.
29. "Acute Shortage of New Manhattan Offices with Heavy Demand for Space Seen in 1966," *Real Estate Record and Guide* 196 (December 18, 1965): 2. Also see Thomas W. Ennis, "New Office Space Still Not Enough," *New York Times* (January 2, 1966), VIII: 1–2.
30. "Record Office Construction in Manhattan," *Real Estate Record and Guide* 200 (September 23, 1967): 4.
31. "Office Boom Changes the Scene," *Business Week* (October 7, 1967): 167–68, 172.
32. "What Keeps the Office Boom Going? Survey Provides Answers," *Real Estate Record and Guide* 201 (April 6, 1968): 2–3; "Manhattan Surges Skyward," *Engineering News-Record* 181 (November 28, 1968): 72–75, 78, 82, 84–85.
33. "Annual Production of Office Space Will More than Double in '68," *Real Estate Record and Guide* 201 (January 13, 1968): 2.
34. S. Dudley Nostrand, "Office Boom Will Accelerate," *Real Estate Record and Guide* 203 (January 11, 1969): 2.
35. Eleanore Carruth, "Manhattan's Office Building Binge," *Fortune* 80 (October 1969): 114–17, 176, 178, 183–84, 186.
36. "Vast Office Space Output to Bring Problems, Says Studley," *Real Estate Record and Guide* 204 (October 4, 1969): 2–3. Also see Alan S. Oser, "Boom in Office Space Demand Slows a Bit," *New York Times* (January 18, 1970), VIII: 1, 6; "Office Building Developers Are Cautioned to 'Go Slow' Right Now," *Real Estate Record and Guide* 205 (March 7, 1970): 2.
37. H. D. Harvey, Sr., quoted in "Why Offices Stay Unrented," *Business Week* (December 5, 1970): 83, 86.
38. Eleanore Carruth, "New York Hangs Out the For-Rent Sign," *Fortune* 83 (February 1971): 86–90, 114–15, 118. Also see "Office Space Goes Begging in New York," *U.S. News & World Report* 70 (February 1, 1971): 50–51.
39. Charles Urstadt quoted in Carruth, "New York Hangs Out the For-Rent Sign": 118.
40. "Are Big Cities Worth Saving?" interview with George Sternleib, *U.S. News & World Report* 71 (July 26, 1971): 42–46, 49.
41. Carruth, "New York Hangs Out the For-Rent Sign": 118.
42. Quoted in Carruth, "New York Hangs Out the For-Rent Sign": 118.
43. Regina Belz Armstrong, *The Office Industry: Patterns of Growth and Location* (Cambridge, Mass.: MIT Press, 1972). Also see "The Office Boom Jolts the Planners," *Business Week* (January 23, 1971): 59, 62.
44. William Shore quoted in "The Office Boom Jolts the Planners": 62.
45. Marya Mannes, *The New York I Know*, with photographs by Herb Snitzer (Philadelphia and New York: J. B. Lippincott, 1961), 152, 154.
46. For First Houses, see Stern, Gilmartin and Mellins, *New York 1930*, 444–45.
47. Cleveland Rodgers and Rebecca B. Ranken, *New York: The World's Capital City* (New York: Harper & Brothers, 1948), 307.
48. "Significant News of the Week in Review," *Real Estate Record and Guide* 147 (March 8, 1941): 2–3.
49. "50,000 Here Have Low-Cost Housing," *New York Times* (October 18, 1941): 34.
50. "More City Housing Set for After War," *New York Times* (June 24, 1942): 35; "The Architects of Six Postwar Public Housing Projects Were Announced Recently by the New York City Housing Authority," *New Pencil Points* 24 (July 1943): 14; "New York's 13 Housing Projects," *Interiors* 104 (September 1944): 10.
51. Edmond Borgia Butler, "The Social Justification for Public Housing in New York City," *Real Estate Record and Guide* 151 (January 1943): 7–8, 18.
52. "'Housing Week' Is Set to Open Here May 21," *New York Times* (April 30, 1944): 34; "Meeting and Exhibits Feature 'Housing Week' Starting Today," *New York Times* (May 21, 1944), VIII: 1; "Housing Comes Home to All," editorial, *New York Times* (May 24, 1944): 18; "Everybody's Business," *Architectural Forum* 80 (June 1944): 60–62.
53. Stanley M. Isaacs quoted in "Everybody's Business": 60.
54. "Architects Urge Wider City Plan," *New York Times* (October 25, 1943): 26.
55. Eugene Henry Klaber, "Walled Towns or Neighborhoods?" *Journal of the American Institute of Planners* 12 (spring 1946): 26–29.
56. "Housing Authority's Clearance Schedule Running According to Plan," *Real Estate Record and Guide* 156 (December 15, 1945): 3.
57. "New York in Trouble," *Architectural Forum* 84 (June 1946): 10.
58. Robert Moses quoted in "New York in Trouble": 10.

59. "Self-Aid Is Urged in Slum Clearance," *New York Times* (May 7, 1948): 3; "Architect to Offer Plan to O'Dwyer, Dewey for Self-Help to 'De-Blight' Slums Here," *New York Times* (December 8, 1948): 37.
60. Thomas H. Creighton, "There Are Other Approaches to This Problem," editorial, *Progressive Architecture* 29 (July 1948): 136.
61. "Urges City Grant Tax Exemption on Cost of New Apartment Construction as Step toward Alleviating Housing Shortage," *Real Estate Record and Guide* 159 (May 17, 1947): 3–4.
62. George Fred Pelham II, letter to the editor, *Progressive Architecture* 28 (April 1947): 8.
63. "Statement Issued by CHC Appraises Housing Authority Report on Decade of Public Housing in New York City," *Citizens' Housing Council Housing News* 4 (September 1945): 1, 4.
64. "Building Stalls," *Architectural Forum* 83 (December 1945): 7; "Portent?" *Architectural Forum* 83 (December 1945): 7.
65. "4-Year Project to House 1,268,400 Offered by Moses," *New York Times* (June 2, 1946): 1, 8.
66. "New York's Housing Prospects—CHC Reports," *Citizens' Housing Council Housing News* 4 (June–July 1946): 1, 5.
67. "Housing Bogs Down," editorial, *New York Times* (June 28, 1946): 20.
68. "No Apartments Finished in 1946," *New York Times* (December 14, 1946): 17.
69. "Housing Shortage Easing, Moses Says," *New York Times* (December 24, 1947): 34; "32,808 Apartments Planned by City," *New York Times* (February 1, 1948): 15; William M. Farrell, "Trend Is Reversed, City Gains Housing," *New York Times* (February 27, 1948): 23.
70. William M. Farrell, "City to Spend $200,000,000 for Housing 17,000 Families," *New York Times* (March 13, 1948): 1, 10; "For 17,000 New Apartments," editorial, *New York Times* (March 19, 1948): 22; "Housing Program Expanded by 150%," *New York Times* (July 4, 1948): 26; William M. Farrell, "Housing Shortage to Ease in Year, Survey Indicates," *New York Times* (July 27, 1948): 1, 44; "Crisis in Housing Seen Easing Soon," *New York Times* (August 1, 1948): 49; "New Veterans' Housing," editorial, *New York Times* (September 30, 1948): 26.
71. "Housing in New York," *Architectural Record* 104 (October 1948): 176.
72. Robert Moses quoted in "Moses Voices Hope O'Dwyer Stays On," *New York Times* (May 4, 1949): 35.
73. *The Significance of the Work of the New York City Housing Authority, Large-Scale Housing in New York* (New York: New York Chapter, American Institute of Architects, May 1949). Also see Charles Ascher, "Under the Microscope," *Citizens' Housing Council Housing News* 8 (October 1949): 1, 4.
74. Quoted in Ascher, "Under the Microscope": 1, 4.
75. Lewis Mumford, "The Sky Line: The Red-Brick Beehives," *New Yorker* 26 (May 6, 1950): 92, 94–98.
76. Mumford, "The Sky Line: The Red-Brick Beehives": 92, 94.
77. Lewis Mumford, "The Sky Line: The Gentle Art of Overcrowding," *New Yorker* 26 (May 20, 1950): 79–83.
78. Mumford, "The Sky Line: The Gentle Art of Overcrowding": 82.
79. Mumford, "The Sky Line: The Red-Brick Beehives": 94–95.
80. Mumford, "The Sky Line: The Red-Brick Beehives": 96–97.
81. Mumford, "The Sky Line: The Red-Brick Beehives": 97–98.
82. Mumford, "The Sky Line: The Gentle Art of Overcrowding": 82–83.
83. "New York City to Scatter Public Housing Units," *American City* 71 (April 1956): 178.
84. "Public Housing: New York Probes Charges Reds Turn Projects into Slums," *House & Home* 11 (April 1957): 65, 77.
85. Joseph Martin, Dominick Peluso and Sydney Mirkin, "Reds Peril N.Y. City Housing," *Daily News* (February 18, 1957): 1, 3, 26. Also see Martin, Peluso and Mirkin, "The Housing that Your Jack Built Is Now Tobacco Road," *Daily News* (February 19, 1957): 3, 26; Martin, Peluso and Mirkin, "Housing Bungle Piped Afar, Even to Kitchen Sink," *Daily News* (February 20, 1957): 3, 32; Martin, Peluso and Mirkin, "Housing Execs Admit Red Role," *Daily News* (February 21, 1957): 3, 48; Martin, Peluso and Mirkin, "Bronx Housing a Sick Baby, All Run Down," *Daily News* (February 22, 1957): 3, 24; Martin, Peluso and Mirkin, "Slums Built Into City's Housing," *Daily News* (February 23, 1957): 3, 12; Martin, Peluso and Mirkin, "Repair Charges Harass Tenants," *Daily News* (February 25, 1957): 3, 24; Martin, Peluso and Mirkin, "Tag 5 Project Mgrs. as Red," *Daily News* (February 26, 1957): 3, 20; Kitty Hanson, "The Project Tenants Sound Off," *Daily News* (February 27, 1957): 3, 34; Martin, Peluso and Mirkin, "Project Half Built—And Shot," *Daily News* (February 28, 1957): 3, 34; Martin, Peluso and Mirkin, "Red Hook—Pearl of a Project," *Daily News* (March 1, 1957): 3, 30; Martin, Peluso and Mirkin, "Thick on Brass, Thin on Project Coppers," *Daily News* (March 4, 1957): 3, 28; Martin, Peluso and Mirkin, "Crime Does Not Seem to Bother Project Biggies," *Daily News* (March 5, 1957): 22; Martin, Peluso and Mirkin, "Failure of Project Policing Creates a Juvenile Jungle," *Daily News* (March 6, 1957): 36; Martin, Peluso and Mirkin, "Housing Managers Shut Eyes," *Daily News* (March 7, 1957): 34.
86. Catherine Bauer, "The Dreary Deadlock of Public Housing," *Architectural Forum* 106 (May 1957): 140–42, 219, 221. Also see Jane Jacobs, "'The Dreary Deadlock of Public Housing' Experts Stress Need for New Approach," *Housing and Planning News* 15 (May–June 1957): 1, 4.
87. Charles Abrams and Stanley Tankel quoted in "The Dreary Deadlock of Public Housing—How to Break It," *Architectural Forum* 106 (June 1957): 139–41, 218, 222, 224, 226, 228, 230, 232.
88. Harrison E. Salisbury, *The Shook-Up Generation* (New York: Harper, 1958); Harrison E. Salisbury, "Youth: On the Streets, in the Schools," *New York Times* (March 24, 1958): 1, 17; Salisbury, "Youth Gang Members Tell of Lives, Hates and Fears," *New York Times* (March 25, 1958): 1, 26; Salisbury, "'Shook' Youngsters Spring from the Housing Jungle," *New York Times* (March 26, 1958): 1, 32; Salisbury, "Youth Outbreaks Traced to Turbulence in Family," *New York Times* (March 27, 1958): 1, 28; Salisbury, "School Violence Reflects Instability in Adult World," *New York Times* (March 28, 1958): 1, 22; Salisbury, "Well-Run Schools Solving Problems in City 'Jungles,'" *New York Times* (March 29, 1958): 1, 20; Salisbury, "Lethargy of Public Found at Root of Youth Problem," *New York Times* (March 30, 1958): 1, 72. Also see "One Out of 18 New Yorkers a Public Housing Tenant," *Architectural Forum* 114 (April 1961): 7, 9.
89. Salisbury, "'Shook' Youngsters Spring from the Housing Jungle": 1, 32.
90. Percival Goodman quoted in "What's Wrong with Public Housing?" *Architectural Record* 124 (July 1958): 182–86. Also see John P. Callahan, "Experts Critical of Public Housing," *New York Times* (July 20, 1958): 1, 6; Mike Miller and Carl Werthman, "Public Housing: Tenants and Troubles," *Dissent* 8 (summer 1961): 282–86.
91. William H. Whyte quoted in "'Projects' Assailed as 'Dull Utopias' at Packed Meeting," *Village Voice* 3 (July 2, 1958): 1, 3.
92. "Public and/or Housing," *Housing and Planning News* 17 (February–March 1959): 2.
93. David B. Carlson, "The New Urbanites: Nature and Dimensions," *Architectural Forum* 112 (June 1960): 116–17, 190–91, 194.
94. David Carlson, "The New Urbanites and the City Housing Crisis," *Architectural Forum* 113 (July 1960): 118–19, 190–92.
95. "Committee Organized by CHPC Urges Changes in City Renewal," *Housing and Planning News* 18 (January–February 1960): 1, 4. Also see Seymour Posner, letter to the editor, *Architectural Forum* 113 (August 1960): 178.
96. John Crosby, "Who Says What Is a Slum?" *New York Herald Tribune* (March 13, 1961): 19, quoted in "Two Fellows Named John," editorial, *Housing and Planning News* 19 (March–April 1961): 2.
97. Mary Perot Nichols, "Humanizing Process: No More '1984' in Housing Projects," *Village Voice* 6 (September 28, 1961): 1, 8.
98. Elizabeth Wood, *Housing Design: A Social Theory* (New York: Citizens' Housing and Planning Council of New York, 1961).
99. Elizabeth Wood quoted in "Former Housing Director Hits Bleak Public Housing," *Architectural Forum* 115 (September 1961): 8–9.
100. Jane Jacobs, *The Death and Life of Great American Cities* (New York: Random House, 1961), 3.
101. Charles Abrams, "Criteria for Urban Renewal," *Architectural Record* 13 (May 1962): 155–58.
102. Charles Abrams, *The City Is the Frontier* (New York: Harper Colophon, 1965).
103. Lewis Mumford, "The Sky Line: Mother Jacobs' Home Remedies," *New Yorker* 38 (December 1, 1962): 148, 150, 152, 154, 157–58, 160, 162–64, 167–68, 170–74, 177–79.
104. Norman Mailer, "The Big Bite," *Esquire* 59 (May 1963): 37, 40.
105. Woody Klein, "Housing the Poor," *Commonweal* 82 (June 11, 1965): 377–79.
106. John V. Lindsay, "Foreword," in Woody Klein, *Let In the Sun* (New York: Macmillan, 1964), viii.
107. Thomas C. Wheeler, "New York Tries a New Approach," *Reporter* 23 (June 17, 1965): 18–20.
108. Samuel Kaplan, "City Told to Shift Its Aim in Housing Toward the Poor," *New York Times* (December 15, 1965): 1, 51. Also see Samuel Kaplan, "City Slum Drive to Seek U.S. Aid," *New York Times* (December 16, 1965): 41.
109. Frank S. Kristof, "Housing Policy Goals and the Turnover of Housing," *Journal of the American Institute of Planners* 31 (August 1965): 232–45.
110. Study Group of the Institute of Public Administration to Mayor John V. Lindsay, *Let There Be Commitment: A Housing, Planning and Development Program for New York City* (September 1966). Also see "Logue Group Issues Report," *Housing and Planning News* 25 (September–October 1966): 1, 3.
111. Study Group of the Institute of Public Administration to Mayor John V. Lindsay, *Let There Be Commitment: A Housing, Planning and Development Program for New York City*, vii.
112. David A. Crane, *Planning and Design in New York: A Study of Problems and Processes of Its Physical Environment* (New York: Institute of Public Administration, September 1966), 9, reprinted in *Zodiac* 17 (1967): 176–95.
113. Stephanie Harrington, "Planner Logue: Is There a New Moses in the Wings? Maybe," *Village Voice* 11 (February 3, 1966): 1, 27.
114. Edward J. Logue quoted in Allan R. Tallot, "The Easy Chair: Boston's Bristly Mr. Logue," *Harper's* 233 (November 1966): 18, 23–24, 26, 28, 30, 33–34.
115. Tallot, "The Easy Chair: Boston's Bristly Mr. Logue": 18, 23–24, 26, 28, 30, 33–34.
116. Steven V. Roberts, "Lindsay Creates Agency to Direct Fight on Slums," *New York Times* (November 23, 1966): 1, 27; Ada Louise Huxtable, "SOS to Washington: Save Our City!" *New York Times* (October 3, 1966): 46; "New York City's Housing Program 1967," *Housing and Planning News* 25 (March–April 1967): 1–5.
117. David K. Shipler, "The Changing City: Housing Paralysis," *New York Times* (June 5, 1969): 1, 40.
118. Shipler, "The Changing City: Housing Paralysis": 1, 40. Also see "When Landlords Walk Away," *Time* 95 (March 16, 1970): 88, 90.
119. Ira S. Lowry, "How to Rescue New York's Vanishing Housing Stock," *New York Affairs* 1 (1973): 20–45.
120. "Swift Slum Clearance," *Scientific American* 214 (May 1966): 56, 61. Also see "Rehabilitation Goes Through the Roof," *Progressive Architecture* 47 (May 1966): 62.
121. "Instant Rehab Not So Instant," *Architectural Record* 141 (January 1967): 175–76.
122. Steven V. Roberts, "A Lower East Side Story: In 48 Hours, a Decaying Tenement Becomes a Modern Apartment House," *New York Times* (April 14, 1967): 41; "Instant Rehab Transforms Slum," *Engineering News-Record* 178 (April 20, 1967): 32–33; "Dropping In, Speeding Up," *Time* 89 (April 21, 1967): 60; "Slums: Instant Renewal," *Newsweek* 69 (April 24, 1967): 84; "Instant Rehab," *Architectural Forum* 126 (May 1967): 90; "Out of Slums into Instant Homes in 48 Hours," *Life* 62 (May 12, 1967): 57–58; "48-Hour Rehabilitation: What Next?" *Progressive Architecture* 48 (July 1967): 46.
123. See Alan Dunn, "It's Marvelous—You Come Back in 48 Hours and Find the Rent Has Doubled!" cartoon, *Architectural Record* 142 (August 1967): 10.
124. Robert Weaver quoted in "Slums: Instant Renewal," *Newsweek*: 84.
125. Jason Epstein, "Stranded in the Future," review of V. S. Pritchett's *New York Proclaimed*, *Commentary* 39 (May 1965): 80–82, 84.
126. Edward L. Friedman, "Search," *Progressive Architecture* 41 (October 1960): 160–65.
127. Mannes, *The New York I Know*, 156–57.
128. Roger Starr, *The Living End: The City and Its Critics* (New York: Coward-McCann, 1966), 161.
129. Quoted in Dennis Duggan, "City Apartments Draw Criticism," *New York Times* (April 1, 1962), VIII: 1, 10.

130. Duggan, "City Apartments Draw Criticism": 1.
131. Quoted in "The Upper Depths," *Time* 80 (November 23, 1962): 40.
132. John Berendt, "Patterns of Decay," *Esquire* 59 (June 1963): 96–99.
133. Sam Blume, "Ode to the Great 5'x9' Outdoors," *New York Times* (April 26, 1964), VI: 21, 39–40, 44, 46, 49.
134. For 240 Central Park South, see Stern, Gilmartin and Mellins, *New York 1930*, 424–25.
135. Richard Roth quoted in Blume, "Ode to the Great 5'x9' Outdoors": 44.
136. *Housing Quality: A Program for Zoning Reform* (New York: City Planning Commission, 1973). Also see Joseph P. Fried, "Lindsay Proposes a Limit on High-Rise Apartments," *New York Times* (July 13, 1973): 39; Carter B. Horsley, "Le Corbusier Vision of a City Rejected in Zoning Plan," *New York Times* (July 22, 1973), VIII: 1, 8; Alexander Cooper, "Zoning with the User in Mind," *Journal of the American Institute of Architects* 60 (December 1973): 42–46; Carter B. Horsley, "Top Planner Hints a Zoning Overhaul," *New York Times* (May 19, 1974), VIII: 1, 14.
137. Oscar Newman, *Defensible Space: Crime Prevention Through Urban Design* (New York: Macmillan, 1972). Also see Samuel Kaplan, "Defensible Space," book review, *New York Times* (April 29, 1973), VII: 16.
138. Philip Birnbaum and Simon Breines quoted in Horsley, "Le Corbusier Vision of a City Rejected in Zoning Plan": 8.
139. New York City Planning Commission, *Zoning for Housing Quality* (New York, 1975); New York City Planning Commission, *Plazas for People: Streetscape and Residential Plazas* (New York, 1976); "New York Adopts Zoning Amendment to Encourage Better Housing Quality," *Practicing Planner* 6 (September 1976): 11; "Opening City Space," editorial, *New York Times* (September 22, 1976): 40.
140. Quoted in Alexander Burnham, "City Held Failure in Architecture," *New York Times* (May 14, 1963): 28. Also see Ada Louise Huxtable, "Architectural Dynamite," *New York Times* (May 14, 1963): 28; "The Quality of Architecture," editorial, *New York Times* (May 16, 1963): 34; "No Bard Award," *Progressive Architecture* 44 (June 1963): 70; Mary Perot Nichols, "Private Opinion: Face of a City: New York Is an Architectural Disaster," *Village Voice* 8 (June 6, 1963): 1, 7; "New York: 'Fruitless Search?'" *Journal of the American Institute of Architects* 40 (July 1963): 138, 140; Thomas Devine, "Architectural Jollities," letter to the editor, *Village Voice* 8 (July 4, 1963): 4; Mary Perot Nichols, "Private Opinion: In Civic Architecture, It Pays to Be an Ugly," *Village Voice* 8 (July 4, 1963): 4–5; Jan C. Rowan, "Editorial," *Progressive Architecture* 44 (August 1963): 85; Starr, *The Living End: The City and Its Critics*, 151–52.
141. Huxtable, "Architectural Dynamite": 28.
142. "The Quality of Architecture": 34.
143. Starr, *The Living End: The City and Its Critics*, 151–52.
144. Quoted in "New York: 'Fruitless Search?'": 138.
145. Simon Breines quoted in "New York: 'Fruitless Search?'": 138.
146. Quoted in "New York: 'Fruitless Search?'": 140.
147. "New York City's Ten-Year Plan," *American City* 62 (June 1947): 125, 127, 129.
148. "Park Avenue's New Lighting Hailed," *American City* 63 (November 1948): 135, 159.
149. Lewis Mumford, "The Sky Line: Big Buildings and Tremendous Trifles," *New Yorker* 27 (December 22, 1951): 63–65.
150. Henry Hope Reed, *The Golden City* (New York: Doubleday, 1959), 16–17.
151. Malcolm J. Brookes, "Street Lighting and People," *Industrial Design* 10 (June 1963): 48–55; "The Talk of the Town: Shedding Light," *New Yorker* 41 (July 10, 1965): 16–18; David A. Hanks with Jennifer Toher, *Donald Deskey: Decorative Designs and Interiors* (New York: E. P. Dutton, 1987), 150, figs. 169–71.
152. *Signs in the Street*, exhibition catalogue (New York: Museum of Modern Art, 1954); "Street Scene," *Time* 63 (April 5, 1954): 53.
153. Gaylord J. Hoftiezer, "Combating the Crime of the Streets," *Industrial Design* 16 (January 1969): 44–47; "Signs Projects," *Casabella* 339/340 (August–September 1969): 56–69.
154. Lacey Fosburgh, "City Will Build 1,000 See-Through Bus Stop Shelters," *New York Times* (February 12, 1970): 1, 25; "Helter-Shelter," *Industrial Design* 17 (May 1970): 10, 15.
155. C. Sidamon-Eristoff, "The Shelters Are Coming," letter to the editor, *New York Times* (December 3, 1973): 38; James Stewart Polshek, "Notes on My Life and Work," in *James Stewart Polshek: Context and Responsibility* (New York: Rizzoli International Publications, 1988), 35–36.
156. Glenn Fowler, "Bus-Shelter Plan Approved by City," *New York Times* (May 9, 1975): 39; Philip H. Dougherty, "Advertising: Bus Shelters," *New York Times* (May 15, 1975): 73; Edward C. Burks, "Bus Shelters Here Lauded," *New York Times* (December 6, 1975): 31; Glenn Fowler, "Bus Shelters," *New York Times* (April 9, 1976): 20; Philip H. Dougherty, "Advertising: Bus-Stop Bonanza Is Under Way," *New York Times* (July 28, 1976): 49; "600 Additional Safety-Glass Bus Shelters Planned for New York City in Next Year," *New York Times* (September 16, 1976): 43.
157. Berck, "From High in the Sky Lindsay Cites City Ills": 5; Huxtable, "Lindsay Surveys City from Copter": 8.
158. "Lindsay Picks Paley to Head City Beautification Project," *New York Times* (April 15, 1966): 44.
159. Mayor's Task Force on Urban Design, *The Threatened City* (New York, 1967). Also see "The Design of the City," editorial, *New York Times* (February 13, 1967): 32.
160. Mayor's Task Force on Urban Design, *The Threatened City*, 3.
161. Stern, Gilmartin and Massengale, *New York 1900*, 48–49.
162. Mayor's Task Force on Urban Design, *The Threatened City*, 12.
163. Mayor's Task Force on Urban Design, *The Threatened City*, 15–16.
164. Mayor's Task Force on Urban Design, *The Threatened City*, 47–48.
165. "The Design of the City": 32.
166. Philip C. Johnson, I. M. Pei, Jaquelin Robertson and Robert A. M. Stern, "Report on City's Design," letter to the editor, *New York Times* (February 17, 1967): 36.
167. Stephen Zoll, "Superville: New York—Aspects of Very High Bulk," *Massachusetts Review* 14 (summer 1973): 447–538.
168. Mayor's Task Force on Urban Design, *The Threatened City*, 39.
169. Zoll, "Superville: New York—Aspects of Very High Bulk": 513–15.
170. "Architects and Mayors: Advice and Authority," *Architectural Record* 142 (December 1967): 10.
171. Steven H. Rosenfeld, "Architects and New York City," *Journal of the American Institute of Architects* 58 (September 1972): 40–44.
172. "Mayor Promises Quality Buildings," *New York Times* (May 18, 1967): 47; John V. Lindsay, "A Public Servant Looks at Design," *Journal of the American Institute of Architects* 48 (August 1967): 49–51.
173. Donald H. Elliott, "The Role of Design in the Governmental Process," *Architectural Record* 143 (January 1968): 141–44.
174. "Advocacy Planning: What It Is, How It Works," *Progressive Architecture* 49 (September 1968): 102–4; Albert Melniker and Harry Keifetz, "Replies to Urban Design Group's Claims," letters to the editor, *Progressive Architecture* 49 (November 1968): 6; Urban Design Group, "UDG Responds to Critics," *Progressive Architecture* 50 (January 1969): 6; "Young Architects Tackling City Design Problems," *New York Times* (January 26, 1969), VIII: 1, 6.
175. *Urban Design in New York*, exhibition catalogue (New York, 1969); Walter McQuade, "Foreword," in *Urban Design in New York*, reprinted as "A Tip from M. T. Cicero," *Architectural Forum* 130 (June 1969): 96, and "Urban Design in New York," *Casabella* 339/40 (August 1969): 52–55; "'Urban Design' in Display," *New York Times* (May 23, 1969): 45; Ada Louise Huxtable, "The City, Dear Brutus," *New York Times* (July 6, 1969), II: 20. Also see Jonathan Barnett, "Urban Design as Part of the Government Process," *Architectural Record* 147 (January 1970): 131–35.
176. Zoll, "Superville: New York—Aspects of Very High Bulk": 491–92.
177. "Appointments," *Progressive Architecture* 54 (April 1973): 73.
178. "People," *Architecture Plus* 2 (January–February 1974): 114–15. Also see Ada Louise Huxtable, "'Nothing Is the Way It Was,'" *New York Times* (February 11, 1973), II: 25, 27.
179. Norman Mailer, "The Faith of Graffiti," in Mervyn Kurlansky, Jon Naar and Norman Mailer, *The Faith of Graffiti* (New York: Praeger, 1974), unpaginated.
180. E. B. White, "Here Is New York," *Holiday* 5 (April 1949): 34–41.
181. "Museum of Modern Art Takes a Wartime Precaution," *New York Times* (December 11, 1941): 23; "Raid Precautions Taken by Utilities," *New York Times* (December 11, 1941): 23; "Two 'Raid Alarms' Clear Times Sq.," *New York Times* (December 16, 1941): 24; "Practical Air Raid Precautions Make a New York Office Building as Safe as Most Shelters and Much More Convenient," *Architectural Forum* 76 (March 1942): 147–49.
182. "Asserts Our Cities Invite Bombers," *New York Times* (August 7, 1941): 9.
183. "Bomb Proof City," *New York Times* (November 11, 1940): 17.
184. "New York Dim-out," *Life* 14 (February 1, 1943): 73–77.
185. "Skylight a Source of Danger in Raid," *New York Times* (March 16, 1941): 24.
186. "Blackout Material on Every One's List," *New York Times* (December 16, 1941): 39. Also see Carleton Varney, *The Draper Touch: The High Life & High Style of Dorothy Draper* (New York: Prentice Hall Press, 1988), 146–47.
187. "Cites Bomb Safety in Tall Buildings," *New York Times* (July 6, 1941), XI: 2.
188. "Caves for New York," *Architectural Forum* 78 (February 1943): 2; Hugh Ferriss, *Power in Buildings* (New York: Columbia University Press, 1953), figs. 46–47.
189. Frank Adams, "Bomber Hits Empire State Building, Setting It Afire at 79th Floor; 13 Dead, 12 Hurt; Wide Area Rocked," *New York Times* (July 29, 1945): 1, 25; Alexander Feinberg, "Survivor Likens Crash to a Quake," *New York Times* (July 29, 1945): 1, 28; George Horne, "Crash Described by Eyewitnesses," *New York Times* (July 29, 1945): 29; "La Guardia Field Cleared Bomber," *New York Times* (July 29, 1945): 31; "Mayor Lays Crash to Bomber Pilot; 8 Dead Identified," *New York Times* (July 30, 1945): 1, 7; "Empire State Held 'Safe' After Crash," *New York Times* (July 31, 1945): 21; "Army Sifts Crash into Empire State," *New York Times* (August 17, 1945): 19; Thomas Gallagher, "Nightmare on the 79th Floor," *Reader's Digest* 70 (March 1957): 49–53. For a discussion of the Empire State Building, see Stern, Gilmartin and Mellins, *New York 1930*, 612–15.
190. Quoted in "La Guardia Field Cleared Bomber": 31.
191. White, "Here is New York": 40.
192. "Skyscraper Reaches the Top," *Life* 28 (August 28, 1950): 30–31.
193. Jerry Finkelstein quoted in "They Say," *Journal of the American Institute of Architects* 14 (October 1950): 183–84.
194. "The City Under the Bomb," *Time* 56 (October 2, 1950): cover, 12–14. Also see John Lear, "Hiroshima, U.S.A.," *Collier's* 126 (August 5, 1950): 11–17; Richard Plunz, *A History of Housing in New York City* (New York: Columbia University Press, 1990), 279.
195. "Sheltering 135,000 from Bombs," *Business Week* (February 3, 1951): 22–23.
196. "Defenses Drafted at Grand Central," *New York Times* (January 1, 1951): 6; "Empire State Set for Aerial Attack," *New York Times* (January 14, 1951): 35; Thomas P. Ronan, "City Civil Defense Mobilized in Drill for 'Atom Bombing,'" *New York Times* (November 15, 1951): 1, 16; "Harbor Vessels Test Evacuation," *New York Times* (November 15, 1951): 16.
197. "Silence Descends on the City," *Life* 31 (December 10, 1951): 40–43. Also see "Civilian Defense: New York Shows the World . . . ," *Newsweek* 38 (December 10, 1951): 22–23.
198. Milton Bracker, "54 Cities 'Raided' in U.S. Bomb Drill," *New York Times* (June 15, 1954): 1, 32; Russell Porter, "City at Standstill in U.S.-Wide Atom Raid Test: 5 Bombs 'Wipe-Out' New York—Drill Called Best Yet," *New York Times* (July 21, 1956): 1, 6.
199. "Air Raid, Old Style," editorial, *New York Times* (June 15, 1954): 28.
200. "The Pros and Cons for Civil Defense," *Progressive Architecture* 32 (September 1951): 67.
201. "Architects, Engineers Collaborate on Civil Defense Plan," *Progressive Architecture* 40 (March 1959): 151.
202. Nan Robertson, "Bomb Defense Widely Doubted; Rockefeller Calls Shelter Parley," *New York Times* (September 2, 1961): 1, 4.
203. Charles G. Bennett, "City Council Votes New Smoke Agency; 'Ripper' Step Seen," *New York Times* (July 3, 1952): 1, 26; "Smoke Control Department Voted by Board of Estimate," *New York Times* (August 22, 1952): 1, 8; "Smoke Is Costly," editorial, *New York Times* (August 23, 1952): 12; "Mayor Signs Bill on Smoke Control," *New York Times* (September 25, 1952): 32; "First Chief Named for Air Pollution," *New York Times* (November 16, 1952): 1, 33.
204. Edith Iglauer, "A Reporter at Large: Fifteen Thousand Quarts of Air," *New Yorker* 40 (March 7, 1964): 54–55, 58, 61–62, 64, 66, 68, 71–72, 74, 76, 78, 83–84, 86, 88, 90, 95–96, 98, 100–102, 107–8, 110, 112–14, 117.
205. Charles Grutzner, "City's Dirty Air Called a Factor in Rising Deaths," *New York Times* (June 23, 1965): 1, 30; "Sewer in the Sky," *Newsweek* 66 (July 5, 1965): 59; "The Aerial Sewer," *Progressive Architecture* 46 (September 1965): 47–48.

206. James Ridgeway, "Stench from New Jersey," *New Republic* 155 (July 16, 1966): 13–15. Also see "Most Poisonous Air," *Newsweek* 67 (May 23, 1966): 104, 108.
207. "Increase in Pollution Caused by 'Lid' of Air," *New York Times* (November 24, 1966): 79; "Lethal Canopy," editorial, *New York Times* (November 25, 1966): 36; Homer Bigart, "Smog Emergency Called for City; Relief Expected," *New York Times* (November 26, 1966): 1, 28; Jane E. Brody, "Millions Plagued by Air Irritants," *New York Times* (November 26, 1966): 1, 28; Richard Reeves, "Emergency Antipollution Techniques Used in Alert," *New York Times* (November 26, 1966): 28.
208. "Tough Act," *Architectural Forum* 126 (March 1967): 28.
209. Roger Minkoff quoted in "The Talk of the Town: The Powdery Element," *New Yorker* 43 (July 15, 1967): 21–23.
210. "News Reports," *Architectural Record* 147 (April 1970): 40.
211. "Forum," *Architectural Forum* 132 (May 1970): 27.
212. "The Talk of the Town: Commissioner Rickles," *New Yorker* 61 (May 9, 1970): 33–34.
213. "Misery in New York," *Time* 96 (August 10, 1970): 37–39.
214. Edward Ranzal, "5th Ave. to Be Shut to Vehicles in Test," *New York Times* (July 1, 1970): 1, 32; Murray Schumach, "Crowds Stroll in Fifth Avenue," *New York Times* (July 12, 1970): 1, 52; "Reactions to Experiment Are Mixed on 5th Avenue," *New York Times* (July 12, 1970): 52.
215. Peter Kihss, "Mayor Urged to Ban Cars Below 59th St. During Day," *New York Times* (August 23, 1970): 1, 63.
216. David Gurin, "The Poisons in the Air: Toward a Carless City," *Village Voice* 16 (December 23, 1971): 17–18, 60.
217. David Bird, "U.S. Accepts Traffic Plan to Cut Air Pollution Here," *New York Times* (June 16, 1973): 1, 56; "Fast Traffic, Clean Air," editorial, *New York Times* (July 4, 1973): 14.
218. "New York City: Disaster Area?" *U.S. News & World Report* 65 (November 4, 1968): 49–51.
219. "Power Cut Off for 500,000 in Manhattan: Failure in Heat Hits Travel, Hospitals, Extra Police Patrol in Dark; Park Shut," articles by George F. Barrett, Homer Bigart, James Feron, John Osmundsen, Gay Talese, *New York Times* (August 18, 1959): 1, 20–21; "The Lights that Failed—Over Uptown Manhattan," *Business Week* (August 22, 1959): 34; Sam Pope Brewer, "City Puts Blame Upon Con Edison in Power Failure," *New York Times* (August 25, 1959): 1, 26; "Text of City Report on Power Failure and Con Edison," *New York Times* (August 25, 1959): 26; "The City's Electricity," editorial, *New York Times* (August 25, 1959): 30; "The Friendly Night," *Newsweek* 54 (August 31, 1959): 26–27; Robert S. Strothers, "Power Failure!" *Reader's Digest* 77 (September 1960): 235–38.
220. "Power Failure Snarls Northeast; 800,000 Are Caught in Subways Here; Autos Tied Up, City Gropes in Dark," articles by Samuel Kaplan, Peter Kihss, John D. Pomfret, Fred Powledge, *New York Times* (November 10, 1965): 1–3; "How City Met the Emergency: Off-Duty Men Are Mobilized," *New York Times* (November 10, 1965): 1–2; Michael T. Kaufman, "Trouble Spot Big Mystery," *New York Times* (November 10, 1965): 2; Gene Smith, "A Nationwide Grid Termed Solution," *New York Times* (November 10, 1965): 2; "A Lesson of the Blackout," editorial, *New York Times* (November 14, 1965), IV: 10; Loudon Wainwright, "The View from Here: A Dark Night to Remember," *Life* 59 (November 19, 1965): 35; "The Big City Lived by the Light of the Moon," *Life* 59 (November 19, 1965): 36–47; Theodore H. White, "What Went Wrong? Something Called 345 KV," *Life* 59 (November 19, 1965): 47, 51–52; "The Disaster That Wasn't," *Time* 86 (November 19, 1965): cover, 36–41, 41A, 41B, 42–43; "The Talk of the Town: Notes and Comment," *New Yorker* 41 (November 20, 1965): 43–47; "The Longest Night," *Newsweek* 66 (November 22, 1965): 27–33; "Lighting Up the Blackout," *Newsweek* 66 (November 22, 1965): 92; "And Then the Lights Went Out," *Progressive Architecture* 46 (December 1965): 37, 39; Eileen Shanahan, "F.P.C. Criticizes Power Systems in Nov. 9 Failure," *New York Times* (December 7, 1965): 1, 40–41; "Behind the Blackout," editorial, *New York Times* (December 7, 1965): 46.
221. "City Transit Unit Is Now a Reality," *New York Times* (June 13, 1940): 25–26. Also see Stern, Gilmartin and Mellins, *New York 1930*, 702. For a description of the evolution of the subway system, see Stern, Gilmartin and Massengale, *New York 1900*, 45–49.
222. Ben Grauer quoted in "New Subway Line on 6th Ave. Opens at Midnight Fete," *New York Times* (December 15, 1940): 1, 56.
223. John D. Rockefeller, Jr., quoted in "New Subway Line on 6th Ave. Opens at Midnight Fete": 1.
224. William R. Conklin, "Fares Rise Tonight; Mayor to Be Here by Cutting His Trip," *New York Times* (June 30, 1948): 1, 20; Stan Fischler, *Uptown, Downtown: A Trip Through Time on New York's Subways* (New York: Hawthorn Books, 1976), 259. Also see "City's Subway, Now 45 Years Old, Has Grown to 241 Miles Yielding 6,500,000 Dimes a Day," *New York Times* (October 27, 1949): 29.
225. "The Talk of the Town: Notes and Comment," *New Yorker* 23 (July 19, 1947): 17–18.
226. Lewis Mumford, "The Sky Line: The Genteel and the Genuine," *New Yorker* 25 (July 9, 1949): 42–46.
227. Joel Rogers, "Buck Rogers' Subway Cars," letter to the editor, *Interiors* 108 (January 1949): 8.
228. "Streamlining for the Underground," *Interiors* 109 (November 1949): 14, 16; Wesley S. Griswold, "The Great Subway Maze Is Still Growing," *Popular Science* 161 (June 1952): 60–63, 214, 216.
229. Paul Crowell, "$500,000,000 Voted for 2d Ave. Subway by Estimate Board," *New York Times* (September 14, 1951): 1, 18.
230. Stern, Gilmartin and Mellins, *New York 1930*, 702.
231. "Endless Train to End New York Subway Jam," *Popular Science* 158 (May 1951): 100–101; "'Moving Sidewalk' Shown," *New York Times* (July 27, 1952), V: 8; "Fund for a Moving Platform Asked to Replace Grand Central Shuttle," *New York Times* (August 8, 1952): 1, 31; "Crosstown by Conveyor Belt," editorial, *New York Times* (August 8, 1952): 16; "Conveyer Belt May Replace Subway Shuttle," *Architectural Record* 112 (September 1952): 14; "Conveyor Belt Shown as Replacement for Shuttle," *New York Times* (April 22, 1953): 31; "Conveyor Belt Tested on Passenger Traffic," *Architectural Record* 114 (September 1953): 352; Arthur W. Baker, "Urban Transportation," *Britannica Book of the Year* (Chicago: Encyclopaedia Britannica, 1954): 727; "Subway of the Future," *Time* 64 (November 15, 1954): 104.
232. For Norman Bel Geddes's Futurama, see Stern, Gilmartin and Mellins, *New York 1930*, 744–45, 748–49, 751.
233. Paul Crowell, "Fare Rise Held Likely on Private Bus Lines," *New York Times* (June 15, 1953): 1, 16; Brian J. Cudahy, *Under the Sidewalks of New York*, rev. ed. (Lexington, Mass.: Stephen Greene Press, 1979, 1988), 128.
234. "Freight Line Proposed for New York's Second Avenue Subway," *American City* 69 (September 1954): 171.
235. Ralph Katz, "Addition Planned for 6th Ave. Line," *New York Times* (January 31, 1962): 1, 62.
236. Sigurd Grava, "The Express Bus Says," *New York Affairs* 5, no. 3 (1979): 111–23.
237. "Subway Cars," *Industrial Design* 16 (September 1969): 14.
238. Douglas Robinson, "Queens IND Crash Kills 2, Injures 71," *New York Times* (May 21, 1970): 1, 38; Paul L. Montgomery, "37 Hurt in Crash of Two IND Trains," *New York Times* (July 18, 1970): 1, 15; Paul L. Montgomery, "Fire in IRT Tunnel Leads to a Death; Smoke Fells 50," *New York Times* (August 2, 1970): 1, 50; "A Little Sand," *Nation* 211 (August 3, 1970): 69; Francis X. Clines, "500 Flee IRT Accident; Fire Delays Penn Central," *New York Times* (August 4, 1970): 1, 19; "New York's Sick Subways," *Newsweek* 76 (August 31, 1970): 79.
239. "New York's Sick Subways": 79.
240. "'Taki 183' Spawns Pen Pals," *New York Times* (July 21, 1971): 37; Donald Janson, "Spray Paint Adds to Graffiti's Damage," *New York Times* (July 25, 1971): 31; Frank J. Prial, "Subway Graffiti Here Called Epidemic," *New York Times* (February 11, 1972): 39; "An Identity Thing," *Time* 99 (March 13, 1972): 44; "Up Against the Wall," *Newsweek* 79 (May 8, 1972): 81; "Nuisance in Technicolor," *New York Times* (May 21, 1972): 66; "The Graffiti 'Hit' Parade," *New York* 6 (March 26, 1973): 32–34; Richard Goldstein, "This Thing Has Gotten Completely Out of Hand," *New York* 6 (March 26, 1973): 35–39; Mitzi Cunliffe, "The Writing on the Wall," *New York Times* (July 29, 1973), IV: 13; Peter Schjeldhal, "Graffiti Goes Legit—But the 'Show-Off Ebullience' Remains," *New York Times* (September 16, 1973), II: 25; "Underground Artists," *Newsweek* 82 (October 1, 1973): 69–70; David Bird, "Noise, Graffiti and Air Grate on Riders of City Subways," *New York Times* (October 11, 1973): 47, 90; Alfred E. Clark, "Persistent Graffiti Anger Lindsay on Subway Tour," *New York Times* (October 11, 1973): 47; Mailer, "The Faith of Graffiti," in Kurlansky, Naar and Mailer, *The Faith of Graffiti*, unpaginated; Anatole Broyard, "The Handwriting on the Wall," book review, *New York Times* (May 1, 1974): 43; Corinne Robins, "The Faith of Graffiti," book review, *New York Times* (May 5, 1974), VII: 51; Barbara Rose, "Dubuffet: Seeing New York His Way," *Vogue* 164 (September 1974): 172; Nathan Glazer, "On Subway Graffiti in New York," *The Public Interest* 54 (winter 1979): 3–11, reprinted in Nathan Glazer and Mark Lilla, eds., *The Public Face of Architecture: Civic Culture and Public Spaces* (New York: Macmillan, 1987), 371–78; Carol Stern and Robert Stock, "Graffiti: The Plague Years," *New York Times* (October 19, 1980), VI: 44, 48, 50, 54, 58, 60; Craig Castleman, *Getting Up: Subway Graffiti in New York* (Cambridge, Mass.: MIT Press, 1982); Nathan Glazer and Mark Lilla, "Introduction," in Glazer and Lilla, eds., *The Public Face of Architecture*, 331.
241. Gary Winkel quoted in "The Graffiti 'Hit' Parade": 33.
242. Fredric Wertham quoted in "The Graffiti 'Hit' Parade": 33.
243. Saul Steinberg quoted in "The Graffiti 'Hit' Parade": 33.
244. Claes Oldenburg quoted in "The Graffiti 'Hit' Parade": 33.
245. "The Graffiti 'Hit' Parade": 32–34.
246. Emanuel Perlmutter, "Fines and Jail for Graffiti Will Be Asked by Lindsay," *New York Times* (June 26, 1972): 66; "Action on Dog Litter and Graffiti Put Off for Months by Council," *New York Times* (July 6, 1972): 75; "Lindsay Assails Graffiti Vandals," *New York Times* (August 25, 1972): 30; Edward Ranzal, "Ronan Backs Lindsay Anti-graffiti Plan: Including Cleanup Duty," *New York Times* (August 29, 1972): 66; "Officials Testify in Favor of Mayor's Graffiti Bill," *New York Times* (September 1, 1972): 25; "Stiff Antigraffiti Measure Passes Council Committee," *New York Times* (September 15, 1972): 41; "Scratch the Graffiti," editorial, *New York Times* (September 16, 1972): 28; Edward Ranzal, "Antigraffiti Bill Is One of Four Gaining Council Approval," *New York Times* (October 11, 1972): 47; "Fight Against Subway Graffiti Progresses from Frying Pan to Fire," *New York Times* (January 26, 1973): 39; Michael T. Kaufman, "Boy Scouts Scrub Graffiti Off Walls of Subway Cars," *New York Times* (February 26, 1973): 35; Murray Schumach, "At $10 Million, City Calls It a Losing Graffiti Fight," *New York Times* (March 28, 1973): 46; Edward C. Burks, "MTA to Use Dogs in Its Battle on Graffiti," *New York Times* (July 30, 1974): 35; "Going to the Dogs," editorial, *New York Times* (August 5, 1974): 22; "Subway Graffiti Campaign Given Lower Priority," *New York Times* (August 7, 1975): 29; Ralph Blumenthal, "Subways Are Rated by Experts," *New York Times* (March 18, 1976): 45; "Subway Graffiti," *New York Times* (March 20, 1977): 45.
247. Mailer, "The Faith of Graffiti," in Kurlansky, Naar and Mailer, *The Faith of Graffiti*, unpaginated.
248. "Razing of 'El' Approved," *New York Times* (May 15, 1942): 17; Frank W. Crane, "Razing of 2d Ave. 'El' Structure Stimulates East Side Activity," *New York Times* (July 5, 1942), IX: 1, 4; "Mayor Starts Demolition of 2d Ave. 'El'; 25,000 Tons of Scrap Metal to Aid War," *New York Times* (July 8, 1942): 25; Fischler, *Uptown, Downtown: A Trip Through Time on New York's Subways*, 252, 259.
249. Edward C. Burks, "Lower East Side Loop Offered for 2d Ave. Subway by M.T.A.," *New York Times* (January 31, 1970): 1, 42; Richard Reeves, "Ronan Pledges Public Hearings on 2d Ave. Subway Station Sites," *New York Times* (September 2, 1970): 1, 74; Richard Cohen, "Second Avenue Subway: Bumpy Road Ahead," *New York* 4 (February 8, 1971): 36–39; Irving Spiegel, "M.T.A. Agrees to Station at 96th St. on 2d Ave. Line," *New York Times* (October 4, 1971): 1; "Rockefeller and Lindsay Break Ground for 2d Avenue Subway," *New York Times* (October 28, 1972): 35; Boris Pushkarev, "The Future of Subways," *New York Affairs* 1, no. 2 (1973): 72–91; "Zoning Goes Underground in New York," *Journal of the American Institute of Architects* 61 (April 1974): 21; "First Stop," *Architecture Plus* 2 (May–June 1974): 41; William H. Quirk, "Tunnels," *Americana Annual for 1974* (New York: Grolier, 1975): 232; Sigurd Grava, "Is the Second Avenue Subway Dead in Its Tracks?" *New York Affairs* 6, no. 3 (1980): 32–41.
250. "Downtown-Lower Manhattan Group Propose an Additional Subway," *Real Estate Record and Guide* 198 (September 10, 1966): 2–3.
251. Quoted in Cohen, "Second Avenue Subway: Bumpy Road Ahead": 38.
252. Jonathan Barnett, *Urban Design as Public Policy* (New York: Architectural Record Books, 1974), 148–56; "Zoning Goes Underground in New York": 21.
253. Raquel Ramati quoted in "Zoning Goes Underground in New York": 21.
254. "First Stop": 41.

255. Edward C. Burks, "Subways Lose Riders but Are on Time More," *New York Times* (October 8, 1973): 1, 46; Victor K. McElheny, "Subway Maintenance Is Better Than It Was," *New York Times* (October 9, 1973): 1, 92; Deirdre Carmody, "Subway Crime Rises 26% and Patterns Are Changing," *New York Times* (October 10, 1973): 49, 93; Bird, "Noise, Graffiti and Air Grate on Riders of City Subways": 47, 90; Robert Lindsey, "The Subway Prospect: Better Service, Fewer Riders and Clamor for Subsidy," *New York Times* (October 12, 1973): 45, 86.
256. Abraham Beame quoted in Grava, "Is the Second Avenue Subway Dead in Its Tracks?": 40.
257. Grava, "Is the Second Avenue Subway Dead in Its Tracks?": 32, 41.
258. "The Talk of the Town: Twist," *New Yorker* 29 (May 2, 1953): 21–22; Edward Edelsberg and Philip Cane, "First Aid for an Ailing Bridge," *Popular Mechanics* 105 (February 1956): 126–30, 278, 280, 282. For the Manhattan Bridge, see Stern, Gilmartin and Massengale, *New York 1900*, 51–53.
259. "Madison Ave. Bridge Closing for Repair," *New York Times* (February 20, 1959): 50; "Harlem Bridge Closed," *New York Times* (February 25, 1959): 20. For the Madison Avenue Bridge, see Sharon Reier, *The Bridges of New York* (New York: Quadrant Press, 1977), 85, 88.
260. "Water Main Break Blocks Sixth Ave. IND as Flood Spills Through Midtown Streets," *New York Times* (July 2, 1957): 29; "Broken Water Mains and Fires Snarl Midtown Area," *New York Times* (July 3, 1957): 1, 24; Milton Bracker, "Main Break Jams Midtown Traffic," *New York Times* (July 16, 1957): 1, 54; "Breaks in Big Water Mains Here Are Laid to Settling of Ground," *New York Times* (July 17, 1957): 29; "Midtown Flooded as Main Breaks; Subways Slowed," *New York Times* (November 8, 1957): 1, 14; Homer Bigart, "Breaks in Mains Flood 2 Subways; 300,000 Delayed," *New York Times* (November 9, 1957): 1, 16; Murray Illson, "Broken Mains Set One-Night Record," *New York Times* (November 9, 1957): 16.
261. "950,000 Potholes Filled by City in '63," *New York Times* (January 3, 1964): 24.
262. "Annual Drive to Repair Potholes Starts Today," *New York Times* (March 16, 1964): 16; "264,124 Potholes Filled This Spring," *New York Times* (April 27, 1964): 33.
263. Murray Schumach, "Highway Repairs to Start in Fall," *New York Times* (August 19, 1973): 51; Edward C. Burks, "West Side Highway Work Expected to Cause Tie-Ups," *New York Times* (September 26, 1973): 81.
264. "Truck and Car Fall as West Side Highway Collapses," *New York Times* (December 16, 1973): 76; Emanuel Perlmutter, "Indefinite Closing Is Set for West Side Highway," *New York Times* (December 17, 1973): 41.
265. Edward C. Burks, "City Accused of Lagging on West Side Road Job," *New York Times* (June 14, 1974): 1, 65.
266. Edward C. Burks, "Mayor Acts to Speed Emergency Repairs on West Side Road," *New York Times* (June 21, 1974): 1, 32.
267. Edward C. Burks, "Demolition of Part of West Side Highway May Start in September," *New York Times* (May 25, 1976): 39; John K. Evans, "West Side Promenade," letter to the editor, *New York Times* (September 25, 1976): 18; Francis X. Clines, "About New York: The View from the West Side Highway," *New York Times* (October 29, 1977): 25; Robert Nersesian, "Quick, Before It Crumbles: Running on the West Side Highway," *New York Times* (February 8, 1981), V: 2; "New Demolition Set for Westway," *New York Times* (August 31, 1981), B: 3.
268. New York State Urban Development Corporation, *Wateredge Development Study: Hudson River Edge Development Proposal* (New York, May 1971). Also see Joel Mandelbaum, "West Side Highway: Hopes vs. Fears," *Housing and Planning News* 29 (summer 1971): 1–3; Peter Blake, "The City Politic: Ratensky's Raiders," *New York* 4 (July 5, 1971): 8–9; Robert Alden, "New West Side Highway Above River Proposed," *New York Times* (August 29, 1971), VIII: 1, 7; "West Side Story," *Industrial Design* 18 (September 1971): 16; Thomas G. Morgansen, "West Side Highway," letter to the editor, *New York Times* (September 5, 1971), VIII: 4; Otis Kidwell Burger and Jerry M. Schwartz, "West Side Highway Plan Causes Chagrin," letters to the editor, *New York Times* (September 12, 1971), VIII: 4; Joel Mandelbaum, "Highway in the Hudson: Why They're Edgy About Wateredge," *Village Voice* 16 (December 9, 1971): 1, 93–94; Mildred F. Schmertz, "Open Space for People," *Architectural Record* 152 (July 1972): 131–40; David Gurin, "New Highway in Town: What, *More* Cars?" *Village Voice* 17 (November 30, 1972): 17–20, 38, 40; Frederic Morton, "Let a Highway Rot Instead of a School," *Village Voice* 17 (November 30, 1972): 5, 18; Mary Perot Nichols, "Private Opinion: Sound the Alarum, a New Highway Is Coming," *Village Voice* 18 (March 15, 1973): 3, 10; Frank J. Prial, "West Side Studies 6 Highway Plans," *New York Times* (March 30, 1973): 41, 61; David Rothman, "The Monster Builders (cont.) They're Killing the West Side: Last Exit from the Superhighway," *Village Voice* 18 (May 24, 1973): 5–8, 11; Edward C. Burks, "One Plan, Put at $1-Billion, Would Place Road Under a Land Fill," *New York Times* (August 20, 1973): 33, 36; John Darnton, "State-City Design Team at Work Since April, '72," *New York Times* (August 20, 1973): 36; Murray Schumach, "Project Brings New Cooperation by State, City and Community," *New York Times* (August 20, 1973): 33; "Planners Weigh 7 Routes to a Better West Side Highway," *New York Times* (August 20, 1973): 33; "West Side Vision," editorial, *New York Times* (August 22, 1973): 36; Jesse Bryant, "Open Hudson Shoreline," letter to the editor, *New York Times* (August 25, 1973): 22; David Y. Allen, "West Side Highway Project: Blueprint for a Fossil Monster," letter to the editor, *New York Times* (September 3, 1973): 14; "Plans for Highway Scored in 'Village,'" *New York Times* (September 21, 1973): 82; Barnett, *Urban Design as Public Policy*, 144–49; "Side Streets: Can the West Side Highway End World Hunger?" *New York Affairs* 2, no. 2 (1974): 118–19; "Island Sculpting," *Progressive Architecture* 55 (April 1974): 46, 48; Edward C. Burks, "Five Proposals Analyzed for West Side Highway," *New York Times* (April 8, 1974): 39; Terry Pristin, "'Deciding the Future of New York.' West Side Highway Meetings," *Village Voice* 19 (May 2, 1974): 36–37; Charlie McCollum, "'Deciding the Future of New York.' Federal Pollution Standards," *Village Voice* 19 (May 2, 1974): 26–27; Terry Pristin, "West Side Highway Proposals: Highway Opponents Gain Time," *Village Voice* 19 (May 23, 1974): 3, 14; Otis Kidwell Burger, "Everything You Want to Know About the West Side Highway," *Village Voice* 19 (June 20, 1974): 3, 29, 32; "Conflict of Disinterest: West Side Highway," editorial, *Housing and Planning News* 32 (September 1974): 1, 4; Emanuel Perlmutter, "Moses Has West Side Highway Plan," *New York Times* (November 25, 1974): 60; Steven R. Weisman, "City Plans a Tunnel for West Side Road South of 42d Street," *New York Times* (November 27, 1974): 1, 49; Steven R. Weisman, "City's West Side Highway Plan Criticized by Community Boards," *New York Times* (November 28, 1974): 42; "West Side Highway," editorial, *New York Times* (December 3, 1974): 40; Edward C. Burks, "The West Side Highway Project," *New York Times* (February 3, 1975): 29; "Carey Task Force, 3 to 2, Urges Interstate Plan for the West Side," *New York Times* (February 12, 1975): 74; Edward C. Burks, "Interstate Highway Backed for West Side," *New York Times* (March 8, 1975): 1, 52; "West Siders Protest Interstate Plan," *New York Times* (March 9, 1975): 50; Carolyn S. Konheim, "The Case Against Westway," letter to the editor, *New York Times* (March 21, 1975): 36; "Westway Debate," editorial, *New York Times* (April 7, 1975): 30; "West Siders Protest Park-Cut Plan," *New York Times* (April 7, 1975): 35; Edward C. Burks, "West Side Road Stirs New Fears," *New York Times* (November 12, 1975): 45, 75; Ralph Blumenthal, "West Side Highway Foes Find a Target," *New York Times* (March 13, 1976): 29; Katie Kelly, "Westway Ho! Here's the Answer to the West Side Highway," *Village Voice* 21 (April 5, 1976): 5, 20; Carter B. Horsley, "Park Extension Sought by Trump," *New York Times* (May 9, 1976): 43; "Time to Go Westway," editorial, *New York Times* (October 2, 1976): 24; Bunny Gabel, "Why the Westway 'Must Be Scrapped,'" *New York Times* (October 13, 1976): 42; Edward C. Burks, "Prospects Brighten for Westway," *New York Times* (October 14, 1976): 30; "Westway Is Opposed by City Club in Call for 'More Modest' Plan," *New York Times* (November 5, 1976), B: 3; Edward C. Burks, "New Campaign Is Begun by the Opponents of Westway as Decision Time Nears," *New York Times* (November 7, 1976): 62; "Fighting Westway. . . ," editorial, *New York Times* (November 27, 1976): 22; Paul Goldberger, "Uncertainty Clouds Westway's Amenities," *New York Times* (January 13, 1977): 37, 48; Steven R. Weisman, "Koch Calls Westway a 'Disaster' and Vows It 'Will Never Be Built,'" *New York Times* (October 28, 1977): 1, 16; Richard J. Meislin, "The Westway Loses First Round as State Questions Pollution," *New York Times* (December 17, 1977): 1, 41.
269. Regional Plan Association, *Regional Plan Bulletin* 104 (December 1966): 54–57, 61–67, 74, 78; F. Carlisle Towery and Philip Israel, *The Lower Hudson* (New York: Regional Plan Association, December 1966); "Gateway to a Commitment," *Architectural Forum* 126 (January–February 1967): 111; "Regional Plan Warns: $3 Billion 'Opportunity of the Century' on Lower Hudson Soon to Be Lost," *Real Estate Record and Guide* 199 (January 7, 1967): 2–3.
270. Lowell K. Bridwell quoted in Gurin, "New Highway in Town: What, *More* Cars?": 17–20, 38, 40.
271. "Planners Weigh 7 Routes to a Better West Side Highway": 33.
272. "Side Streets: Can the West Side Highway End World Hunger?": 118–19.
273. "Side Streets: Can the West Side Highway End World Hunger?": 118–19.
274. "Conflict of Disinterest: West Side Highway": 1, 4.
275. "Conflict of Disinterest: West Side Highway": 1.
276. Quoted in Goldberger, "Uncertainty Clouds Westway's Amenities": 37.
277. Edward I. Koch quoted in Weisman, "Koch Calls Westway a 'Disaster' and Vows It 'Will Never Be Built'": 1.
278. Sam Roberts, "Battle of the Westway: Bitter 10-Year Saga of a Vision on Hold," *New York Times* (June 4, 1984), B: 1, 4; Sam Roberts, "For Stalled Westway, a Time of Decision," *New York Times* (June 5, 1984), B: 1, 4; George Haikalis, "Westway II: Shaping an 'Inboard' Alternative to Westway," *New York Affairs* 9, no. 2 (1985): 89–94; Craig Whitaker, "Design Arguments for an Urban Highway," *Urbanismo Revista* 3 (September 1985): 39–48; Michael Oreskes, "New York Leaders Give Up Westway and Seek Trade-In," *New York Times* (September 20, 1985), A: 1, B: 2; Sam Roberts, "Westway Alternatives Raising New Questions," *New York Times* (September 20, 1985), B: 2; "The Next-Best Way," editorial, *New York Times* (September 20, 1985): 30; Carter Wiseman, "Where Westway Went: A Case Study in Changing Urban Priorities," *Architectural Record* 174 (February 1986): 81, 83; Patrick Phillips, "Whither Westway? Highway Controversy Leaves an Uncertain Future," *Urban Land* 45 (February 1986): 36–37.
279. Peter Kihss, "2 Million in Contracts Let for Park Atop Westway," *New York Times* (July 2, 1980), B: 4; "Westway Wonderland," *Progressive Architecture* 65 (February 1984): 34; Paul Goldberger, "3 Design Plans Being Considered for Proposed Park Over the Westway," *New York Times* (March 28, 1984), B: 1, 4; "Westway Park," *Princeton Journal* 2 (1985): 196–99; Grace Anderson, "Big Park for the Big Apple," *Architectural Record* 173 (January 1985): 124–31; A. Sanmartín, ed., *Venturi, Rauch & Scott Brown* (London: Academy Editions, 1986), 132–35; Vincent Scully, "Robert Venturi's Gentle Architecture," in Christopher Mead, ed., *The Architecture of Robert Venturi* (Albuquerque, N. M.: University of New Mexico Press, 1989), 28.
280. Jacobs, *The Death and Life of Great American Cities*, 183.
281. "Moses Refuses to Head City Planning Board; 'I'd Rather Do What I'm Doing,' He Says," *New York Times* (December 10, 1937): 10; "Planning Board to Meet," *New York Times* (January 1, 1938): 17. Also see Cleveland Rodgers, *New York Plans for the Future* (New York and London: Harper & Brothers, 1943), Chapter IX.
282. "Common Sense City Planning," editorial, *New York Times* (April 11, 1939): 22. Also see Michael V. Namorato, *Rexford G. Tugwell* (New York: Praeger, 1989), 130–35.
283. "Common Sense City Planning": 22.
284. "Homes Near Work Envisaged in Plan for City of Future," *New York Times* (April 10, 1939): 1, 18.
285. Quoted in "Homes Near Work Envisaged in Plan for City of Future": 18.
286. "Topics of The Times: Famous Exodus Halted," *New York Times* (November 23, 1940): 16; "Master City Plan Put Before Public; Guides All Zoning," *New York Times* (December 6, 1940): 1, 26; Charles G. Bennett, "To Draw Families of 'Middle' Income Back to the City," *New York Times* (December 15, 1940), XII: 1, 3.
287. Bennett, "To Draw Families of 'Middle' Income Back to the City": 1.
288. Robert Moses quoted in "Master Plan Ideas 'Silly,' Says Moses," *New York Times* (December 12, 1940): 56. Also see "City Master Plans Denounced as 'Time Bomb' with Threat of Inestimable Damage to Realty," *New York Times* (February 22, 1941): 32; Robert M. Hallett, "The City They Plan," *New York Times* (September 13, 1941), II: 89; Namorato, *Rexford G. Tugwell*, 138–39. For Saarinen's view, see Eliel Saarinen, *The City: Its Growth, Its Decay, Its Future* (New York: Reinhold Publishing Corp., 1943), 217–40.
289. Robert Moses quoted in "Master Plan Ideas 'Silly,' Says Moses": 56.
290. "Plan Modification Sought," *Real Estate Record and Guide* 149 (January 10, 1942): 2–3. Also see "City's Master Plan Held Too Radical," *New York Times* (January 5, 1942): 19.
291. "Tugwell Resigns City Planning Job," *New York Times* (July 26, 1941): 13.
292. "Mayor Names Moses to Planning Body," *New York Times* (November 28, 1941): 47.
293. "Huie Sworn in New Job," *New York Times* (June 19, 1942): 26.
294. Fiorello La Guardia quoted in "Mayor Names Moses to Planning Body": 47.
295. Quoted in "Sues to Oust Moses from Plan Board," *New York Times* (July 8, 1942): 25.

296. "Court Backs Mayor on Planning Posts," *New York Times* (May 28, 1943): 35.
297. Robert Moses, "The Changing City," *Architectural Forum* 72 (March 1940): 142–56. Also see "Robert Moses," editorial, *Architectural Forum* 72 (March 1940): 141.
298. Robert Moses, "Parks, Parkways, Express Arteries and Related Plans for New York City After the War," *American City* 58 (December 1943): 53–58.
299. Robert Moses, "Mr. Moses Dissects the 'Long-Haired Planners,'" *New York Times* (June 25, 1944), VI: 16–17, 38–39. Also see Frank Lloyd Wright, *The Disappearing City* (New York: Farquhar Payson, 1932).
300. Moses, "Mr. Moses Dissects the 'Long-Haired Planners'": 39.
301. "Moses—Or the Bull Rushes," *Time* 44 (July 24, 1944): 82, 84. Also see Kenneth Reid, "More Planning Is Wanted—Not Less," editorial, *Pencil Points* 25 (September 1944): 43.
302. Joseph Hudnut, "A 'Long-Haired' Reply to Moses," *New York Times* (July 23, 1944), VI: 16, 36–37, excerpted as "Hudnut v. Moses," *Time* 44 (July 31, 1944): 38. Also see Hermann Herrey and Lloyd Morgan, "On Moses Manifesto," letters to the editor, *Architectural Forum* 81 (August 1944): 34, 120.
303. Robert Moses, "Moses v. Hudnut," letter to the editor, *Time* 44 (August 14, 1944): 6. Also see Robert Moses, "Mr. Moses Does Not Agree," letter to the editor, *New York Times* (July 24, 1944): 14.
304. Fiorello La Guardia quoted in "New York Opens Its Post-War Exhibit," *American City* 59 (May 1944): 5. Also see "New York Gapes at Its Future," *Architectural Forum* 80 (May 1944): 57; "Planning with You: New York's Billion Dollar Postwar Program Makes Its Bow to Public Plaudits and Planners' Protests," *Architectural Forum* 80 (June 1944): 87–89; "New York's Postwar Exhibition," *Architectural Record* 95 (June 1944): 16; Talbot F. Hamlin, "Postwar Question Mark," *Pencil Points* 25 (July 1944): 73–78.
305. Quoted in "New York Gapes at Its Future": 57.
306. "Planning with You: New York's Billion Dollar Postwar Program Makes Its Bow to Public Plaudits and Planners' Protests": 87.
307. Hamlin, "Postwar Question Mark": 73–74.
308. Hamlin, "Postwar Question Mark": 77–78.
309. "Plan Group Is Asked Its Basic Objectives," *New York Times* (June 28, 1943): 34; Thomas S. Holden, "More Information Desired," letter to the editor, *New York Times* (July 3, 1943): 12.
310. Stein, "The Future of New York": 1–7. Also see Lee E. Cooper, "Post-War Plans Stress the Need to Rebuild Cities," *New York Times* (July 25, 1943), VIII: 1–2.
311. "Architects Urge Wider City Plan," *New York Times* (October 25, 1943): 26.
312. Percival Goodman and Paul Goodman, "A Master Plan for New York," *New Republic* 111 (November 20, 1944): 656–59, reprinted in *Journal of the American Institute of Architects* 3 (February 1945): 69–75.
313. Percival and Paul Goodman, *Communitas: Means of Livelihood and Ways of Life* (Chicago: University of Chicago Press, 1947). Also see James Marston Fitch, "Review," *Architectural Forum* 86 (June 1947): 140, 142, 144; "Philosophic Planning," book review, *Interiors* 107 (August 1947): 18.
314. See Stern, Gilmartin and Massengale, *New York 1900*, 29–30.
315. Rem Koolhaas, *Delirious New York: A Retroactive Manifesto for Manhattan* (New York: Oxford University Press, 1978).
316. Goodman and Goodman, "A Master Plan for New York": 659.
317. "New York in 1999—Five Predictions," *New York Times* (February 6, 1949), VI: 18–20, 51, 53. Also see "Prophets See It at Century's End as a Vastly Different City," *Architectural Forum* 90 (March 1949): 26–28.
318. Harvey Wiley Corbett, "A Sort of Modern Venice," in "New York in 1999—Five Predictions": 19.
319. Robert Moses, "Not So Different," in "New York in 1999—Five Predictions": 19.
320. Eliel Saarinen, "Decentralized City," in "New York in 1999—Five Predictions": 51.
321. Wallace K. Harrison, "Limited Objectives," in "New York in 1999—Five Predictions": 53.
322. Hugh Ferriss, caption accompanying drawing, in "New York in 1999—Five Predictions": 19–20.
323. "A Notable Anniversary," editorial, *New York Times* (June 2, 1941): 16; "Peril in War Seen in Flaws of Zoning," *New York Times* (June 3, 1941): 29. Also see Stern, Gilmartin and Massengale, *New York 1900*, 24, 176.
324. For the Seabury inquiry, see Samuel Seabury, "In the Matter of the Investigation of the Departments of the Government of the City of New York, etc., Pursuant to Joint Resolution Adopted by the Legislature of the State of New York, March 21, 1931," *Intermediate Report to Hon. Samuel H. Hofstadter, Chairman of the Committee, Appointed Pursuant to Said Joint Resolution* (New York, January 25, 1932); Seymour I. Toll, *Zoned American* (New York: Grossman Publishers, 1969), 208–10.
325. Lawrence Orton, "Letter to the Review Editors," *Journal of the American Institute of Planners* 33 (March 1967): 142–43.
326. Committee on Civic Design and Development, New York Chapter, American Institute of Architects, *Some Basic Redevelopment Problems. Second Public Report. Zoning and Master Plan* (New York, May 25, 1944), excerpts published in "The Making of a City," *Journal of the American Institute of Architects* 2 (September 1944): 107–13.
327. "Public and City Regime Are Urged to Support Rezoning Proposal," *New York Times* (June 23, 1944): 21; "New Master Plan and Zoning Law Urged to Guide New York Growth," *New York Times* (July 9, 1944), VIII: 1; Lee E. Cooper, "Fear Proposed Zoning Changes Would Retard Post-War Growth," *New York Times* (July 16, 1944), VIII: 1; "Commissioner Sampson," *Architectural Forum* 81 (August 1944): 63; "Building: Second Installment," *Interiors* 104 (August 1944): 13; "Skyscraper Spree," *Architectural Forum* 81 (September 1944): 79–80; "New York's Zoning Tangle," *Architectural Record* 96 (September 1944): 10, 13; "Improve Zoning Now!" *Citizens' Housing Council Housing News* 3 (September 1944): 2; Arthur C. Holden, "Reduction of Bulk through Zoning Should Be Followed by More Comprehensive Revision," *Citizens' Housing Council Housing News* 3 (September 1944): 3; "Re-zoning N.Y.," *Interiors* 104 (September 1944): 10; Cleveland Rodgers, *Robert Moses: Builder for Democracy* (New York: Henry Holt & Co., 1952), 162–63.
328. "City Plan Report to Be Ready November 1," *New York Times* (September 14, 1944): 23; "Fight Is Organized on Zoning Changes," *New York Times* (October 3, 1944): 25; "Meet to Protest City Zoning Plan," *New York Times* (October 15, 1944), VIII: 1; "Rezoning New York," *Interiors* 104 (November 1944): 12, 98; "Moses Zoning Plan Is Voted for City," *New York Times* (November 21, 1944): 21; "Zoning, Last Chapter?" *Interiors* 104 (December 1944): 10; "New Zoning Laws Voted by Council," *New York Times* (December 1, 1944): 16; "No Brake on Over-Building," *Architectural Forum* 82 (January 1945): 9–10.
329. Orton, "Letter to the Review Editors": 142–43. Also see "Dowling Wins Round Two," *Architectural Forum* 84 (February 1946): 28, 32; "Moses Zoning Plan Loses Last Appeal," *New York Times* (July 24, 1946): 1, 34; "Decision on Zoning," editorial, *New York Times* (July 25, 1946): 20; "New York Set-Back," *Architectural Forum* 85 (September 1946): 14.
330. "New York to Rezone After 32 Years," *American City* 63 (June 1948): 5; Rodgers, *Robert Moses: Builder for Democracy*, 167–68.
331. Guy Greer, "Zoning in New York—Today and Tomorrow," *Citizens' Housing Council Housing News* 8 (September 1949): 1, 4.
332. Robert Moses quoted in Thomas Creighton, "P.S.," editorial, *Progressive Architecture* 30 (August 1949): 140.
333. Harrison, Ballard & Allen, *Plan for Rezoning the City of New York* (New York: City Planning Commission, October 1950). Also see Harold R. Sleeper, "Architects Advise on City Planning," *Journal of the American Institute of Architects* 13 (January 1950): 31–34; "Plan for Rezoning Outlined by Mayor," *New York Times* (August 24, 1950): 29; "Rezoning the City," editorial, *New York Times* (August 25, 1950): 20; "New York Rethinks Its City Plan," *Architectural Forum* 93 (September 1950): 122–27; Charles G. Bennett, "Family Shrinkage to Expand Housing," *New York Times* (September 11, 1950): 25; "City's Growth Tied to More Factories," *New York Times* (September 14, 1950): 33; "Preface to the Plan for Rezoning New York City," *Citizens' Housing Council Housing News* 9 (October–November 1950): 1, 4; "That Zoning Report," editorial, *New York Times* (October 17, 1950): 30; "Realty Men Back Plan for Rezoning," *New York Times* (November 23, 1950): 51; Bruno Funaro in association with Geoffrey Baker, *A Review of the Proposals for Rezoning New York City* (New York: New York Chapter, American Institute of Architects, 1951); Sylvia W. Stark and Allan Turchell, "New York Prepares to Pioneer Again in Zoning," *Citizens' Housing Council Housing News* 9 (April 1951): 1–4; Charles G. Bennett, "New Zoning Draft to Aid City Growth Offered for Study," *New York Times* (April 30, 1951): 1, 26; "N.Y.C. Planning Commission Proposes a Radical Change in Zoning Regulations," *Engineering News-Record* 146 (May 3, 1951): 26–27; "P/A Reviews," *Progressive Architecture* 32 (June 1951): 144, 146, 148, 150; Frank B. Williams, "Review," *Journal of the American Institute of Planners* 17 (summer 1951): 153–56; Henry S. Churchill, "New York Rezoned," *Magazine of Art* 44 (December 1951): 326–31, reprinted in *Journal of the American Institute of Architects* 17 (May 1952): 202–9; Carol Aronovici, "New York City Attempts Rezoning," *Journal of the American Institute of Planners* 18 (spring 1952): 84–89; Arthur C. Holden, "New York's Proposed Zoning Ordinance," *Journal of the American Institute of Planners* 18 (winter 1952): 4–13; Stanislaw J. Makielski, Jr., *The Politics of Zoning: The New York Experience* (New York: Columbia University Press, 1966), 71–81.
334. W. Boesiger and O. Stonorov, eds., *Le Corbusier et Pierre Jeanneret: Oeuvre complète 1910–1929*, vol. 1 (Zurich: Editions Girsberger, 1929), 108–19.
335. Richard A. Miller, "A Key to Open Cities," *Architectural Forum* 108 (February 1958): 94–97.
336. Aline B. Louchheim quoted in "Still the Ziggurat," *Architectural Forum* 99 (November 1953): 47.
337. Churchill, "New York Rezoned": 327–28.
338. James Felt quoted in Makielski, *The Politics of Zoning: The New York Experience*, 84. Also see Roger Feinstein, book review, *Journal of the American Institute of Planners* 33 (March 1967): 126–28; Orton, "Letter to the Review Editors": 142–43; Peter Collison, "Review," *Town Planning Review* 38 (April 1967): 74–75.
339. Voorhees, Walker, Smith & Smith, *Zoning New York City* (New York, August 1958); "Planning Commission Presents Zoning Plan," *Housing and Planning News* 17 (February 1959): 1; Sam Pope Brewer, "Planners Sketch Tomorrow's City," *New York Times* (February 16, 1959): 23; Charles Grutzner, "New Zoning Plan Offered to Guide Growth of City," *New York Times* (February 16, 1959): 1, 23; Joseph G. Herzberg, "Zoning for Living," *New York Times* (February 16, 1959): 23; "Main Points of New Zoning Plan for a More Orderly, Less Cramped City of the Future," *New York Times* (February 16, 1959): 22; "Man in the News: City's Master Planner, James Felt," *New York Times* (February 16, 1959): 23; "Parking Lots Proposed, except in Busy Areas," *New York Times* (February 16, 1959): 22; Voorhees, Walker, Smith & Smith, *Rezoning New York City* (New York, February 16, 1959); "Keep 'Em Out," *Time* 73 (March 2, 1959): 14; "Proposals for Revised New York Zoning Would Affect Design," *Architectural Record* 125 (April 1959): 32, 36; New York City Planning Commission, *Rezoning New York City: A Guide to the Proposed Comprehensive Amendment of the Zoning Resolution of the City of New York* (New York, December 1959); New York Chapter, American Institute of Architects, *Final Report on the Voorhees, Walker, Smith & Smith Proposal for a Zoning Resolution for the City of New York* (New York: New York Chapter, American Institute of Architects, December 11, 1959); Voorhees, Walker, Smith, Smith & Haines, *75th Anniversary* (New York, May 1960), 58; Makielski, *The Politics of Zoning: The New York Experience*, 83–106; Michael Kwartler, "Legislating Aesthetics: The Role of Zoning in Designing Cities," in Charles M. Haar and Jerold S. Kayden, eds., *Zoning and the American Dream: Promises Still to Keep* (Chicago: Planners Press, American Planning Association in association with Lincoln Institute of Land Policy, 1989), 200–203, 207–9; Roy Strickland, "The 1961 Zoning Revision and the Template of the Ideal City," in Todd W. Bressi, ed., *Planning and Zoning New York City: Yesterday, Today and Tomorrow* (New Brunswick, N.J.: Center for Urban Policy Research, 1993), 48–60; Norman Marcus, "Zoning from 1961 to 1991: Turning Back the Clock—But with an Up-to-the-Minute Social Agenda," in Bressi, ed., *Planning and Zoning New York City: Yesterday, Today and Tomorrow*, 61–102.
340. James Felt, "Preface," in "Main Points of New Zoning Plan for a More Orderly, Less Cramped City of the Future": 22.
341. "Parking Lots Proposed, except in Busy Areas": 22.
342. "Architects Back Rezoning Plans," *New York Times* (February 17, 1959): 33.
343. "Builder Asks for Realistic Criticism of New Zoning Law," *Real Estate Record and Guide* 183 (April 11, 1959): 2; "Zoning Proposal Meets Opposition," *New York Times* (April 12, 1959), VIII: 1, 8; "Planning Commission Listens: Public Discusses Zoning Maps," *Housing and Planning News* 17 (May 1959): 1.
344. See Committee for Modern Zoning, *A City Speaks* (Englewood Cliffs, N.J.: Prentice Hall Press, 1960).
345. Victor Gruen, "No More Off-Street Parking in Congested Areas," *American City* 74 (September 1959): 161, 163.

346. Voorhees, Walker, Smith & Smith, *Zoning New York City*, x.

347. Glenn Fowler, "New Zoning Code for the City Seen Enacted by Next Summer," *New York Times* (December 13, 1959), VIII: 1, 6.

348. New York Chapter, American Institute of Architects, *Final Report on the Voorhees, Walker, Smith & Smith Proposal for a Zoning Resolution for the City of New York*; "More Air Space, Less Car Space," *Engineering News-Record* 163 (December 17, 1959): 45.

349. James Felt quoted in Charles Grutzner, "Zoning Plan Resubmitted by City After 300 Changes," *New York Times* (December 21, 1959): 1, 22.

350. "Architects, Realtors Split Over N.Y. Zoning Plan," *Architectural Forum* 112 (February 1960): 9, 11; "Communiqué on the Zoning War," *Housing and Planning News* 18 (March–April 1960): 2–3.

351. Robert Moses quoted in Makielski, *The Politics of Zoning: The New York Experience*, 102. Also see "Moses Belabors City Zoning Plan," *New York Times* (June 7, 1960): 37; "Mayor Criticizes Moses on Zoning," *New York Times* (June 8, 1960): 41.

352. Charles G. Bennett, "Revised Zoning Plan Is Submitted to City," *New York Times* (August 18, 1960): 1, 17; "Zoning Divides Land in City Into 3 Major Use Categories," *New York Times* (August 18, 1960): 17; "'Mandate' for a Better City," editorial, *New York Times* (August 18, 1960): 26; "Final City Action Looms: Commission Prints Zoning Plan," *Housing and Planning News* 18 (summer 1960): 1; "Rezoning's Final Victory," editorial, *New York Times* (December 16, 1960): 32; Walter H. Stern, "The New Zoning Code," *New York Times* (December 25, 1960), VIII: 1–2; "New Zoning for New York Will Control City's Destiny," *Architectural Forum* 114 (January 1961): 9.

353. New York City Planning Commission, *Rezoning New York City: A Guide to the Proposed Comprehensive Amendment of the Zoning Resolution of the City of New York*, 4.

354. Thomas W. Ennis, "Skyscraper Owners Give Up Floor Area for Open Plazas," *New York Times* (July 3, 1960), VIII: 1, 4.

355. James Felt quoted in "Personalities," *Progressive Architecture* 41 (August 1960): 59.

356. Zoll, "Superville: New York—Aspects of Very High Bulk": 447–538. Also see Jane Holtz Kay, "Architecture," *Nation* 219 (August 3, 1974): 93–94.

357. "A Zone-Law Deadline Brings Flood of Plans," *New York Times* (October 14, 1961): 34; "Briefs," *Architectural Forum* 115 (December 1961): 11.

358. Daniel Seligman, "The Future of the Office-Building Boom: The Real Estate Markets, I," *Fortune* 67 (March 1963): 84–88, 214, 216, 218, 220, 222–23.

359. "New Zoning Presents Major Economic Problems to Builder of Luxury Rentals," *Real Estate Record and Guide* 189 (March 17, 1962): 2.

360. Arthur K. Beman, "The Effect on Land Value of the New Zoning Law," *Real Estate Record and Guide* 190 (December 15, 1962): 2–3; "Upzoning Is Key to Increased Private Construction in New York," *Real Estate Record and Guide* 201 (June 22, 1968): 2–3.

361. "Can Laws Beautify a Skyline?" *Business Week* (October 13, 1962): 160–61.

362. "Plazas, Nice for Strollers, Give Builders Problems," *New York Times* (August 24, 1969), VIII: 1, 8.

363. William H. Whyte, *City: Rediscovering the Center* (New York: Doubleday, 1988), 233.

364. *New Life for Plazas* (New York: New York City Planning Commission, Doc NYC DCP 75-08, 1975); "New Zoning Improves Plaza Amenities," *Progressive Architecture* 56 (December 1975): 27; Whyte, *City: Rediscovering the Center*, 234–35, Appendix A.

365. Edward Sulzberger quoted in "Plazas, Nice for Strollers, Give Builders Problems": 8.

366. Charles G. Bennett, "Zoners Propose Odder Buildings," *New York Times* (April 15, 1965): 35. Also see "Zoning Law Aids Original Designs," *New York Times* (July 18, 1965), VIII: 1, 10.

367. "Felt, Top Planner, to Quit Post He Held Since 1956," *Village Voice* 8 (December 20, 1962): 2, 28; "City Planning Commission to Be Headed by Ballard," *New York Times* (September 13, 1963): 1, 34; "New Top City Planner," editorial, *New York Times* (September 14, 1963): 24.

368. Ada Louise Huxtable, "Planner Defends Cars in Midtown," *New York Times* (October 16, 1963): 47.

369. See Daniel M. Friedenberg, "Speaking Out: Slum Clearance Is a Hoax," *Saturday Evening Post* 238 (August 28, 1965): 12, 14.

370. Martin Anderson, *The Federal Bulldozer* (Cambridge, Mass.: MIT Press, 1964).

371. New York Chapter, American Institute of Architects, *The State of the City* (New York, July 1964), unpaginated. Also see R. W. Apple, "Architects Ask City to Establish Order in Frantic Growth," *New York Times* (July 13, 1964): 1, 24; "New York Chapter American Institute of Architects Issues Report on City," *Real Estate Record and Guide* 194 (July 18, 1964): 2–3; "Ill Planned and Ugly," *Newsweek* 64 (July 27, 1964): 75.

372. "Ballard Presses for Master Plan," *Harvard Planning News* 22 (February–March 1964): 3; "New York Needs a Master Plan," editorial, *New York Times* (July 14, 1964): 32.

373. Ada Louise Huxtable, "Realistic View of City," *New York Times* (October 17, 1964): 58. Also see Joseph Watterson, "The Editor's Page," *Journal of the American Institute of Architects* 42 (December 1964): 20, 88; Bernard J. Albin, "Can Anybody Save New York City?" *Landscape Architecture* 55 (January 1965): 88, 91; Mary Perot Nichols, "Plotting New York's Future," *Progressive Architecture* 46 (February 1965): 10, 62; James Rosgood and Robert C. Weinberg, "The Wonders of New York," letters to the editor, *Journal of the American Institute of Architects* 43 (April 1965): 80, 84, 86.

374. Henry Fagin quoted in Huxtable, "Realistic View of City": 58.

375. Martin Cherkasky quoted in Huxtable, "Realistic View of City": 58.

376. Allan Temko quoted in Nichols, "Plotting New York's Future": 10.

377. Richard J. Whalen, *A City Destroying Itself: An Angry View of New York* (New York: William Morrow, 1965), 38, 43.

378. Barry Gottehrer, "Urban Conditions: New York City," *Annals of the American Academy* 371 (May 1967): 141–58.

379. Walter McQuade, "Notes on the Margin of a Master Plan," *Architectural Forum* 131 (December 1969): 80.

380. New York City Planning Commission, *Plan for New York City, vol. 1: Critical Issues* (New York, 1969); New York City Planning Commission, *Plan for New York City, vol. 2: The Bronx* (New York, 1969); New York City Planning Commission, *Plan for New York City, vol. 3: Brooklyn* (New York, 1969); New York City Planning Commission, *Plan for New York City, vol. 4: Manhattan* (New York, 1969); New York City Planning Commission, *Plan for New York City, vol. 5: Queens* (New York, 1969); New York City Planning Commission, *Plan for New York City, vol. 6: Staten Island* (New York, 1969).

381. New York City Planning Commission, *Plan for New York City, vol. 1: Critical Issues*, 5, 21.

382. Michael Stern, "6th and Last Part of the Master Plan on City Released," *New York Times* (December 8, 1970): 1, 52.

383. Ada Louise Huxtable, "Plan Is Regarded as Break with Tradition," *New York Times* (November 16, 1969): 84, reprinted in *Journal of the American Institute of Planners* 36 (November 1970): 436–37; "New York Plan: The Battle Begins," *Business Week* (November 22, 1969): 134, 136; "New Master Plan Proposed in New York City," *Engineering News-Record* 183 (November 27, 1969): 16–17; "New York City Gets Its First Comprehensive Plan," *Architectural Record* 146 (December 1969): 36; Robert C. Weinberg, "New York's Master Plan," letter to the editor, *Architectural Forum* 132 (March 1970): 76, 78; Beverly Moss Spatt, "A Report on the New York Plan," *Journal of the American Institute of Planners* 36 (November 1970): 438–44; Sigurd Grava, "New York City Master Plan and Service Systems," *Journal of the American Institute of Planners* 36 (November 1970): 444–47; Paul L. Nubanck and Marcia Marker Feld, "Review Forum," *Journal of the American Institute of Planners* 36 (November 1970): 448–49; Beverly Moss Spatt, *A Proposal to Arrange the Structure of City Planning: Case Study of New York City* (New York: Praeger, 1971); Louis K. Lowenstein, "Review Comment," *Journal of the American Institute of Planners* 37 (September 1971): 354–56; Richard May, Jr., "New York City Plan," *Town and Country Planning* 39 (October 1971): 446–49; David K. Shipler, book review, *Architectural Forum* 136 (March 1972): 15.

384. Huxtable, "Plan Is Regarded as Break with Tradition": 84.

385. Huxtable, "Plan Is Regarded as Break with Tradition": 84.

386. Beverly Moss Spatt quoted in Huxtable, "Plan Is Regarded as Break with Tradition": 84.

387. Brian J. O'Connell, "Concentration—The Genius of the City: A Critique of the Plan for New York City," *Journal of the American Institute of Planners* 42 (January 1976): 64–65.

388. Spatt, "A Report on the New York Plan": 438–44.

389. Thomas P. Ronan, "Local Planners Held 'Toothless,'" *New York Times* (February 2, 1969): 40; Ralph Blumenthal, "Local Boards Are Gaining in Power After 2 Years," *New York Times* (December 20, 1971): 12.

390. John Zuccotti quoted in O'Connell, "Concentration—The Genius of the City: A Critique of the Plan for New York City": 65.

391. John Zuccotti quoted in Paul Goldberger, "Why City Is Switching from Master Plan to Miniplan," *New York Times* (June 27, 1974): 47. Also see Glenn Fowler, "Planning Unit Introduces Neighborhood Miniplans," *New York Times* (June 26, 1974): 1, 70.

392. John Zuccotti quoted in Goldberger, "Why City Is Switching from Master Plan to Miniplan": 47.

393. Goldberger, "Why City Is Switching from Master Plan to Miniplan": 47.

Chapter 3
Lower Manhattan

1. Paul Goldberger, *The City Observed: New York* (New York: Random House, 1979), 3.

LOWER EAST SIDE

1. Federal Writers' Project, *The WPA Guide to New York City* (New York: Random House, 1939; New York: Pantheon Books, 1982), 108. For a general social history of the Lower East Side, see Diana Cavallo, *The Lower East Side: A Portrait in Time* (New York: Crowell-Collier Press, 1971). Also see Milton Hindus, *The Old East Side, An Anthology* (Philadelphia: Jewish Publication Society of America, 1969); Ronald Sanders, *The Downtown Jews: Portrait of an Immigrant Generation* (New York: Harper & Row, 1969).

2. For discussion of the Tenement House Act of 1901, see Stern, Gilmartin and Massengale, *New York 1900*, 287; Richard Plunz, *A History of Housing in New York City* (New York: Columbia University Press, 1990), 85–86.

3. Joseph Platzker, "20 Year Campaign for Better Housing on the Lower East Side," *East Side Chamber News* 20 (March 1947): 47–56; Milton Levenson, "New Wave of 'Immigrants' Reverses Exodus from Lower East Side," *New York Times* (January 15, 1949): 19, reprinted in *East Side Chamber News* 22 (May 1949): 6–7.

4. Murray Schumach, "The East River Shore Regains Its Glory," *New York Times* (January 19, 1947), VI: 8.

5. For an in-depth discussion of the area's synagogues, see Jo Renee Fine and Gerard R. Wolfe, *The Synagogues of the Lower East Side* (New York: Washington Mews Books, 1978). Also see Paul Goldberger, "Design Notebook," *New York Times* (September 15, 1977), C: 10.

6. Milton Glaser and Jerome Snyder, "Yonah Shimmel Vs. the Mock Knish," *New York World Journal Tribune* (April 16, 1967): 4, 6–7.

7. Richard F. Shepard, "Orchard St.—A Bargain at Any Price," *New York Times* (December 17, 1976), C: 23.

8. Stern, Gilmartin and Mellins, *New York 1930*, 716.

9. "Architects Picked for Housing Jobs," *New York Times* (July 6, 1943): 30; "Plans Are Filed for Wald Houses," *New York Times* (November 14, 1944): 35; Lee E. Cooper, "City Housing Plans Go to $260,000,000; 16 Projects Added," *New York Times* (December 17, 1944): 1, 16; "Housing Project," *Architectural Record* 97 (April 1945): 10; "Housing Aid Set Up," *New York Times* (December 13, 1945): 41; "Low Rent Apartments," *Architectural Record* 99 (January 1946): 68–80; Jack Raymond, "$1,200,000,000 Plan for State Housing Offered by Butler," *New York Times* (June 25, 1946): 1, 16; Louis Justement, "Housing Study: A Thesis by Ilse Meissner," *Progressive Architecture* 28 (February 1947): 42–49; "Housing Project Gets 1st Tenants," *New York Times* (April 19, 1949): 33; Mary Roche, "Pratt Students Include Fixed-Up Cast-Offs in Furnishings for a Lillian Wald Apartment," *New York Times* (May 19, 1949): 33; Lewis Mumford, "The Sky Line: The Red-Brick Beehives," *New Yorker* 26 (May 6, 1950): 92, 94–98; New York City Housing Authority, *Project Statistics* (New York, December 31, 1960), 6; Thomas E. Norton and Jerry E. Patterson, *Living It Up: A Guide to the Named Apartment Houses of New York* (New York: Atheneum, 1984), 352.

10. For discussions of Lillian Wald's life and work, see Sally Rogow, *Lillian Wald: The Nurse in Blue* (Philadelphia: Jewish Publication Society of America, 1966); Doris

Daniels, *Always a Sister: The Feminism of Lillian D. Wald* (New York: Feminist Press at the City University of New York, 1989).

11. "Riis Houses Financing," *New York Times* (August 11, 1944): 25; Lee E. Cooper, "East Side Housing Plans Extending to Cover 25 Waterfront Blocks," *New York Times* (December 3, 1944): 1, 48; Cooper, "City Housing Plans Go to $260,000,000; 16 Projects Added": 1, 16; "The New York City Public Housing Program," *Architectural Forum* 85 (October 1946): 74; Justement, "Housing Study: A Thesis by Ilse Meissner": 42–49; William I. Hohauser, "Honor for Riis Housing Project," *East Side Chamber News* 22 (May 1949): 1; "Towards Better Standards of City Living," *Progressive Architecture* 30 (October 1949): 14, 16, 18; Mumford, "The Sky Line: The Red-Brick Beehives": 92, 94–98; New York City Housing Authority, *Project Statistics*, 3, 10; Norton and Patterson, *Living It Up*, 283.

12. For discussions of Jacob A. Riis's life and work, see Jacob A. Riis, *How the Other Half Lives: Studies Among the Tenements of New York* (New York: Scribner's, 1890); Jacob A. Riis, *The Making of an American* (New York: Macmillan, 1901); Louise Wane, *Jacob A. Riis, Police Reporter, Reformer, Useful Citizen* (New York: D. Appleton-Century, 1938); Alexander Alland, Sr., *Jacob A. Riis: Photographer and Citizen* (Millerton, N.Y.: Aperture, 1974); James B. Lane, *Jacob A. Riis and the American City* (Port Washington, N.Y.: Kennikat Press, 1974); Edith Patterson Meyer, *"Not Charity, but Justice": The Story of Jacob A. Riis* (New York: Vanguard, 1974).

13. Mumford, "The Sky Line: The Red-Brick Beehives": 94.

14. Mumford, "The Sky Line: The Red-Brick Beehives": 98.

15. Ada Louise Huxtable, "Grass at Riis Houses Giving Way to a Plaza," *New York Times* (July 14, 1965): 39; "Once More, with Feeling," *Progressive Architecture* 46 (October 1965): 68; "'The Path Is Dead' in Manhattan," *Landscape Architecture* 56 (April 1966): 231; "Outdoorsman of the Big City," *Life* 60 (April 29, 1966): 39–41; "Objects in the Open Air," *Interiors* 125 (May 1966): 12, 14; "The Talk of the Town: Beauty and Horror," *New Yorker* 41 (May 28, 1966): 28–31; "New York's Most Spectacular Playground," *Village Voice* 11 (June 2, 1966): 1, 26; "Outdoor Rooms," *Time* 87 (June 3, 1966): 52; Mildred F. Schmertz, "Shaping the Community in an Era of Dynamic Social Change," *Architectural Record* 140 (July 1966): 189–205; "Frog into Prince," *Progressive Architecture* 47 (July 1966): 170–72; Walter F. Wagner, Jr., "Riis Plaza: Design with 'Keen Understanding of Human Needs,'" *Architecture* 140 (December 1966): 134–35; "A Place to Play: Riis Plaza Makes the Most of the Least Space," *Horizon* 9 (spring 1967): 42–49; "AIA Honor Awards," *Architectural Forum* 126 (June 1967): 28; "Bard Awards," *Architectural Forum* 126 (June 1967): 83; "Four New York Projects Receive 1967 Bard Awards," *Interiors* 126 (June 1967): 10; "AIA Honor Awards to 14 Firms, 20 Projects," *Progressive Architecture* 48 (June 1967): 59; William H. Whyte, "Fun and Games. . . but Where?" *New York* 1 (September 23, 1968): 32–34; M. Paul Friedberg, "Sharing the Spaces, Sharing the Yields," *Journal of the American Institute of Architects* 51 (March 1969): 51–53; "Projects for Urban Spaces," *Design Quarterly* 77 (1970): 1–30; Charles E. Thomsen, "Open Spaces: Their Shape and Scale," *Journal of the American Institute of Architects* 54 (December 1970): 30–34; Cavallo, *The Lower East Side: A Portrait in Time*, 106–7, 109; Norval White and Elliot Willensky, *AIA Guide to New York City*, rev. ed. (New York: Macmillan, 1978), 103.

16. Thomas P. F. Hoving quoted in "The Talk of the Town: Beauty and Horror": 29.

17. "Once More, with Feeling": 68.

18. M. Paul Friedberg quoted in "'The Path Is Dead' in Manhattan": 231.

19. Simon Breines quoted in Huxtable, "Grass at Riis Houses Giving Way to a Plaza": 39.

20. "The Talk of the Town: Beauty and Horror": 29.

21. Whyte, "Fun and Games. . . but Where?": 33.

22. "New York's Most Spectacular Playground": 1.

23. Schmertz, "Shaping the Community in an Era of Dynamic Social Change": 197.

24. "Frog into Prince": 170.

25. M. Paul Friedberg quoted in "A Place to Play: Riis Plaza Makes the Most of the Least Space": 49.

26. "Tenants Build 'Back-Pocket' Park," *New York Times* (November 13, 1967): 50.

27. For both projects, see Stern, Gilmartin and Mellins, *New York 1930*, 427–29.

28. Stanislaus von Moos, *Venturi, Rauch & Scott Brown* (New York: Rizzoli International Publications, 1987), 330; Rebecca Read Shanor, *The City that Never Was* (New York: Viking, 1988), xv–xvi.

29. "New York Postwar Housing," *Architectural Forum* 79 (July 1943): 94, 96; "East Side to Get Statue of Smith," *New York Times* (December 30, 1944): 13; *Governor Smith Memorial* (New York: Governor Smith Memorial Fund, 1945); "Delay Asked on Housing," *New York Times* (May 23, 1946): 11; "Move? Certainly, but Where to and How? East Side Dealers Facing Ousters Ask," *New York Times* (November 16, 1946): 9; Murray Schumach, "The East River Shore Regains Its Glory," *New York Times* (January 19, 1947), VI: 30, 38–39; Joseph Platzker, "Gov. Dewey Starts Ground-Breaking for Gov. Alfred E. Smith Houses," *East Side Chamber News* 21 (October 1948): 7, 10; Robert Weisberger, "1,140 Tenants Begin Moving into New Gov. Alfred E. Smith Houses This Month," *East Side Chamber News* 22 (October 1949): 1–2; "The Governor Smith Houses," *New York Times* (October 20, 1949): 28; "First Tenants Gay in Smith Houses," *New York Times* (October 25, 1949): 32; *Governor Smith Memorial Dedication, June 11, 1950* (New York: Governor Smith Memorial Fund, 1950); "Gov. Smith Houses Opens New Section," *New York Times* (November 11, 1952): 27; "Smith Houses II Open in New York City," *New York Times* (November 27, 1952): 44–45; New York City Housing Authority, *Project Statistics*, 7; Norval White and Elliot Willensky, *AIA Guide to New York City* (New York: Macmillan, 1967), 32; Paul Goldberger, *The City Observed: New York* (New York: Random House, 1979), 44–46; Norton and Patterson, *Living It Up*, 315; Margot Gayle and Michele Cohen, *The Art Commission and the Municipal Art Society Guide to Manhattan's Outdoor Sculpture* (New York: Prentice Hall Press, 1988), 65–66. For discussions of Alfred E. Smith, see Emily Smith Warner, *The Happy Warrior: A Biography of My Father* (Garden City, N.Y.: Doubleday, 1956); Oscar Handlin, *Al Smith and His America* (Boston: Little, Brown, 1958); Richard O'Connor, *The First Hurrah: A Biography of Alfred E. Smith* (New York: Putnam, 1970); Paula Eldot, *Governor Alfred E. Smith: The Politician as Reformer* (New York: Garland Publishing, 1983); Donn C. Neal, *The World Beyond the Hudson: Alfred E. Smith and National Politics, 1918–1928* (New York: Garland Publishing, 1983).

30. Goldberger, *The City Observed*, 45–46.

31. Norval White and Elliot Willensky, *AIA Guide to New York City*, 3rd ed. (New York: Macmillan, 1988), 74.

32. "Baruch, at 79, Looks Ahead to 100th Year; City Housing to Bear His Father's Name," *New York Times* (August 19, 1949): 28; Meyer Berger, "Old Folks Quit Tenements Sadly to Make Way for Baruch Housing," *New York Times* (February 22, 1952): 23; "$31,410,000 Housing Project to Be Erected Here," *New York Times* (April 7, 1952): 27; New York City Housing Authority, *Baruch Houses and Playground* (New York, 1953); Charles Grutzner, "President Defends Housing Fund Cuts; Day Here Crowded," *New York Times* (August 8, 1953): 1, 17; "Vandals Attack Housing," *New York Times* (September 19, 1953): 17; Richard Roth, "Baruch Houses: $30,000,000 Worth of Slum Clearance for New York City," *Empire State Architect* 14 (July–August 1954): 9–11; "Visiting Polish Housing Experts Impressed by U.S. Techniques," *New York Times* (November 24, 1956): 14; New York City Housing Authority, *Project Statistics*, 3; Norton and Patterson, *Living It Up*, 57; Plunz, *A History of Housing in New York City*, 268, 270–71.

33. For a discussion of the life and work of Simon Baruch, see Frances Anna Hellebrandt, *Simon Baruch: Introduction to the Man and His Work* (Richmond, Va.: Baruch Center of Physical Medicine and Rehabilitation of the Medical College of Virginia, 1950).

34. Plunz, *A History of Housing in New York City*, 268, 270.

35. Helen Hall, *Unfinished Business* (New York: Macmillan, 1971), 237.

36. Berger, "Old Folks Quit Tenements Sadly to Make Way for Baruch Housing": 23.

37. "Architect Edgar Tafel's Plan for the DeWitt Church within the Baruch Housing Project," *Village Voice* 1 (May 9, 1955): 1; "Housing Project Gets New Church," *New York Times* (January 6, 1958): 34; White and Willensky, *AIA Guide* (1967), 41.

38. Edgar Tafel quoted in "Architect Edgar Tafel's Plan for the DeWitt Church within the Baruch Housing Project": 1.

39. Norman Vincent Peale quoted in "Housing Project Gets New Church": 34.

40. White and Willensky, *AIA Guide* (1967), 41.

41. "Board Approves Plan for 4 Housing Sites," *New York Times* (December 28, 1951): 19; "Garment Union Lends $7,500,000 for Big East Side Housing Project," *New York Times* (May 8, 1952): 1, 28; "Union Housing," editorial, *New York Times* (May 12, 1952): 20; "Four Redevelopment Projects Under Way," *Citizens' Housing News* 11 (September 1952): 3; "Cooperative for Redevelopment," *Journal of Housing* 9 (October 1952): 345–47; "Big Housing Plan Filed," *New York Times* (July 22, 1953): 43; "Another Slum Cleared," editorial, *New York Times* (November 27, 1953): 26; "Tallest Crane Boom," *Architectural Forum* 102 (June 1955): 159; Joseph C. Ingraham, "Our Changing City: Old Lower Manhattan Area," *New York Times* (June 24, 1955): 23; Ralph Katz, "Garment Union Housing Project on the Lower East Side Is Dedicated," *New York Times* (October 23, 1955): 1, 67; "The Garment Workers Build," editorial, *New York Times* (October 24, 1955): 26; "I.L.G.W.U. Cooperative Village," *Citizens' Housing News* 14 (November 1955): 1, 4; "A Garment Union Turns to Bricks and Stone," *Fortune* 52 (November 1955): 67; "Goulart Visits Housing," *New York Times* (May 17, 1956): 14; Robert Moses, "Thoughts of a City Builder," *Journal of the American Institute of Architects* 26 (December 1956): 241–47; Charles Grutzner, "Cities and Suburbs in Race Against Spreading Slums," *New York Times* (January 31, 1957): 1, 16; White and Willensky, *AIA Guide* (1978), 58; Norton and Patterson, *Living It Up*, 129.

42. Grutzner, "Cities and Suburbs in Race Against Spreading Slums": 1.

43. Stern, Gilmartin and Mellins, *New York 1930*, 453.

44. Morris Kaplan, "New Look Coming to Old East Side," *New York Times* (May 16, 1957): 31.

45. New York City Housing Authority, *Project Statistics*, 19; Fund for Urban Improvement, Inc., press release (1963); "East Side Project Converted to Co-op," *New York Times* (June 13, 1967): 40. For discussions of Mary K. Simkhovitch's work, see Mary Kingsburg Simkhovitch, *The City Worker's World in America* (New York: Macmillan, 1917); Mary Simkhovitch and Elizabeth Ogg, *Quicksand: The Way of Life in the Slums* (Evanston, Ill.: Row, Peterson, 1942).

46. William J. Conklin, "Apartments—For Urban Redevelopment High- and Low-Rise Combined," *Architectural Record* 131 (January 1962): 97–112; Housing and Redevelopment Board of the City of New York, *Profile and Proposed Redevelopment of the Two Bridges Urban Renewal Area* (New York, 1964); Housing and Redevelopment Board of the City of New York, press release (April 12, 1967); Virginia Lee Warren, "Bulldozer Can Upset Best-Laid Plan," *New York Times* (July 25, 1967): 26; "'2 Bridges' Approved for Housing," *New York Times* (March 7, 1972): 41.

47. Conklin, "Apartments—For Urban Redevelopment High- and Low-Rise Combined": 97–112.

48. Abeles, Schwartz and Associates, *Forging a Future for the Lower East Side* (New York: City of New York Housing and Development Administration and City Planning Commission, 1972). Also see Steven R. Weisman, "A New Lower East Side Envisioned in City Report," *New York Times* (May 23, 1971): 1, 55; Ralph Blumenthal, "Residents Challenge East Side Redevelopment Plan," *New York Times* (November 29, 1971): 52; Harry Schwartz assisted by Peter Abeles, *Planning for the Lower East Side* (New York: Praeger, 1973).

49. Quoted in Weisman, "A New Lower East Side Envisioned in City Report": 1.

50. For a description of Howe & Lescaze's proposal for the Chrystie-Forsyth Street site, as well as more conventional plans presented by Holden, McLaughlin & Associates, John J. Klaber, Sloan & Robertson and Andrew J. Thomas, see Stern, Gilmartin and Mellins, *New York 1930*, 438–42.

51. "To Bear La Guardia Name," *New York Times* (June 1, 1950): 29; "Plans Made Public for More Housing," *New York Times* (October 23, 1950): 20; John Sibley, "City Seeking Art for Its Housing," *New York Times* (February 16, 1960): 29; New York City Housing Authority, *Project Statistics*, 4; Norton and Patterson, *Living It Up*, 198.

52. Ira S. Robbins quoted in Sibley, "City Seeking Art for Its Housing": 29.

53. New York City Housing Authority, *Project Statistics*, 19; Norton and Patterson, *Living It Up*, 293.

54. Philip J. Cruise, "Housing Authority Plans Samuel Gompers Houses for Hamilton Fish Area," *East Side Chamber News* 26 (February–March 1953): 5; "U.S. and City Join on New Housing," *New York Times* (October 22, 1959): 21; New York City Housing Authority, *Project Statistics*, 18; Norton and Patterson, *Living It Up*, 154. For a discussion of Samuel Gompers's life and work, see Harold C. Livesay, *Samuel Gompers and Organized Labor in America* (Boston: Little, Brown, 1978).

55. "4 Projects Voted for 1,700 Families," *New York Times* (August 18, 1955): 34; "U.S. and City Join on New Housing": 21; New York City Housing Authority, *Project Statistics*, 19.

56. William Reid quoted in "U.S. and City Join on New Housing": 21.

57. White and Willensky, *AIA Guide* (1978), 54. For a discussion of the so-called turnkey method of financing, see Harold K. Bell and Granville H. Sewell, *Turnkey in New York: Evaluation of an Experiment* (New York: Columbia University School of Architecture, 1969).

58. "Masaryk Towers Co-op Set for Opening on East Side," *New York Times* (September 18, 1966), VIII: 10; "Masaryk Towers Is Dedicated," *Real Estate Record and Guide* 198 (October 29, 1966): 4; Kalev Pehme, "More of the Mitchell-Lama Morass: Masaryk Residents Fight for Interest Decrease," *Our Town* (September 3, 1976): 1, 19; Norton and Patterson, *Living It Up*, 238.
59. "Education: Award Citation," *Progressive Architecture* 38 (January 1957): 94–95; White and Willensky, *AIA Guide* (1967), 41.
60. "Theater Is Planned on Lower East Side," *New York Times* (March 25, 1961): 17.
61. New York City Committee on Slum Clearance, *Seward Park Project Preliminary Report* (New York, 1956); New York City Committee on Slum Clearance, *Seward Park Slum Clearance Plan under Title I of the Housing Act of 1949 as Amended* (New York, 1956); Housing and Redevelopment Board of the City of New York, *Seward Park Extension* (New York, 1962).
62. White and Willensky, *AIA Guide* (1967), 42; Landmarks Preservation Commission of the City of New York, LP-0637 (February 28, 1967); Barbaralee Diamonstein, *The Landmarks of New York* (New York: Harry N. Abrams, 1988), 109.
63. White and Willensky, *AIA Guide* (1967), 56.
64. White and Willensky, *AIA Guide* (1967), 56; Landmarks Preservation Commission of the City of New York, LP-0181 (April 19, 1966); Diamonstein, *The Landmarks of New York*, 64.
65. "Seward Park Extension: An Enclave Away from Urban Din," *Architectural Record* 145 (January 1969): 108–9. Also see Robert A. M. Stern, *New Directions in American Architecture*, rev. ed. (New York: George Braziller, 1969, 1977), 102, fig. 106.
66. White and Willensky, *AIA Guide* (1978), 54, 56.
67. "Seward Park Extension: An Enclave Away from Urban Din": 109.
68. "Seward Park Police Station and Fire House," *Progressive Architecture* 51 (February 1970): 31; White and Willensky, *AIA Guide* (1978), 56.
69. Laurie Johnston, "Housing Complex Slated for Seward Park in '73," *New York Times* (August 31, 1971): 35.
70. Kenneth Frampton, "The Generic Street as a Continuous Built Form," in Stanford Anderson, ed., *On Streets* (Cambridge, Mass.: MIT Press, 1978), 309–37; Plunz, *A History of Housing in New York City*, 306–8.
71. For discussion of Andrew J. Thomas's apartment house developments in Jackson Heights and elsewhere, see Stern, Gilmartin and Mellins, *New York 1930*, 478–86; Daniel Karatzas, *Jackson Heights: A Garden in the City*, with an intro. by Robert A. M. Stern (New York: J. M. Kaplan Fund and Jackson Heights Beautification Group, 1990), xiii–xv, 53–113.
72. George Gent, "Henry St. Settlement to Build Arts Center," *New York Times* (April 15, 1970): 52; "Arts-for-Living Center," *Progressive Architecture* 51 (June 1970): 54; "Arena for the Arts," *Architectural Forum* 133 (September 1970): 11; Ada Louise Huxtable, "Henry Street's New Building—An Urban Triumph," *New York Times* (August 10, 1975), II: 25; Suzanne Stephens, "Street Smarts," *Progressive Architecture* 56 (November 1975): 64–70; White and Willensky, *AIA Guide* (1978), 56; Goldberger, *The City Observed*, 54; Brent C. Brolin, *Architecture in Context: Fitting New Buildings with Old* (New York: Van Nostrand Reinhold, 1980), 48. Also see Alice Lewisohn Crowley, *The Neighborhood Playhouse: Leaves from a Theater Scrapbook* (New York: Theater Arts Books, 1959).
73. Stephens, "Street Smarts": 64, 66.
74. Huxtable, "Henry Street's New Building—An Urban Triumph": 25.
75. White and Willensky, *AIA Guide* (1978), 56.
76. For general descriptions of Chinatown in the postwar era, see Carl Glick, *Shake Hands with the Dragon* (New York: Whittlesey House, 1971); Chester Rapkin, "The Current Status of Two of America's Chinatowns," paper presented at the Chinatown Urban Renewal Workshop, Honolulu, September 28, 1971; Chia-ling Kuo, *Social and Political Change in New York's Chinatown* (New York: Praeger, 1977).
77. "Chinatown Housing Study Begun for State by Locality Volunteers," *New York Times* (June 15, 1950): 33.
78. Milton M. Levenson, "Plans to Rebuild Chinatown and 2 Other Slums Started," *New York Times* (May 25, 1950): 1, 24; "Moses Ridicules Chinatown Plan," *New York Times* (June 4, 1950): 56; "Stichman Retorts to Gibes by Moses," *New York Times* (June 7, 1950): 41; "New Chinatown Gains Momentum," *New York Times* (June 10, 1950): 32; "Source of Chinatown Plan," *New York Times* (June 26, 1950): 14; "Commissioner Stichman Asks President's Aid in Getting $7½ Million Aid for Chinatown Project," *New York Times* (July 11, 1950): 22; "Chinatown Plan Moves Forward," *New York Times* (December 30, 1954): 19.
79. "Commissioner Stichman Asks President's Aid in Getting $7½ Million Aid for Chinatown Project": 22.
80. Levenson, "Plans to Rebuild Chinatown and 2 Other Slums Started": 1.
81. Robert Moses quoted in "Moses Ridicules Chinatown Plan": 56.
82. Herman T. Stichman quoted in "Stichman Retorts to Gibes by Moses": 41.
83. "Chinatown Plan Moves Forward": 19.
84. Charles G. Bennett, "Housing Project Set for City Hall Area," *New York Times* (January 3, 1956): 1, 37; Charles Grutzner, "Mayor and Moses Huddle in Public," *New York Times* (September 22, 1959): 36; Thomas W. Ennis, "Downtown Co-ops Are Taking Shape," *New York Times* (February 28, 1960), VIII: 1, 6; "Co-op at Chinatown Is Dedicated by City," *New York Times* (March 20, 1962): 22; "Doing Over the Town," *Time* 80 (September 28, 1962): 56–69; White and Willensky, *AIA Guide* (1967), 31–32; John W. Cook and Heinrich Klotz, *Conversations with Architects* (New York: Praeger, 1973), 155; Goldberger, *The City Observed*, 33; Christopher Gray, "Schlock of Ages," *Avenue* 17 (December 1992): 31–32, 34, 36, 38.
85. Hulan Jack quoted in Bennett, "Housing Project Set for City Hall Area": 1.
86. For Le Corbusier's Obus Plan, see Manfredo Tafuri and Francesco Dal Co, *Modern Architecture*, trans. Robert Eric Wolf (New York: Harry N. Abrams, 1974), 143, 145. For Affonso Eduardo Reidy's Pedregulho housing project, see John Jacobus, *Twentieth-Century Architecture: The Middle Years 1940–65* (New York: Frederick A. Praeger, 1966), 55–57.
87. Goldberger, *The City Observed*, 33.
88. "New York City Middle-Income Cooperatives," *Architectural Forum* 112 (May 1960): 63; "O'Rourke Saloon Doomed by Co-op," *New York Times* (May 2, 1962): 39; Charles Friedman, "Gypsum Gets Manhattan Test in the Chatham Towers Project," *New York Times* (January 17, 1965), VIII: 1, 7; "Awards of Merit by New York State Association of Architects: Chatham Towers—Kelly & Gruzen, Architects," *Empire State Architect* 25 (March–April 1965): 27–28; Ellen Perry, "Middle Income Project in Lower Manhattan," *Progressive Architecture* 47 (February 1966):130, 132–39; Robert F. Kennedy, S. F. Boden and Percival Goodman, "Chatham Towers: Imagination and Innovation," letters to the editor, *Progressive Architecture* 47 (May 1966): 6, 10; "Tours d'Habitation à New York," *L'architecture d'Aujourd'hui* 36 (June 1966): 94–95; "Chatham Towers, New York," *Deutsche Bauzeitung* 100 (October 1966): 837–40; White and Willensky, *AIA Guide* (1967), 31–32; "1967 Bard Awards Announced," *Empire State Architect* 27 (May–June 1967): 6–10; "Bard Awards," *Architectural Forum* 126 (June 1967): 83; Goldberger, *The City Observed*, 33; John Tauranac, *Essential New York* (New York: Holt, Rinehart and Winston, 1979), 217–18.
89. "O'Rourke Saloon Doomed by Co-op": 39.
90. White and Willensky, *AIA Guide* (1967), 31–32. For the Dakota and 131–135 East 66th Street, see Stern, Gilmartin and Massengale, *New York 1900*, 283–85, 298–99. For Williamsburg Houses, see Stern, Gilmartin and Mellins, *New York 1930*, 495, 497–98.
91. Goldberger, *The City Observed*, 33.
92. Tauranac, *Essential New York*, 217.
93. M. Paul Friedberg quoted in Perry, "Middle Income Project in Lower Manhattan": 136.
94. Perry, "Middle Income Project in Lower Manhattan": 139.
95. "Project Unites Living and Learning," *New York Times* (March 2, 1969), VIII: 4.
96. "Construction Has Begun in Confucius Plaza," *New York Times* (October 7, 1973), VIII: 15; "Confucius Plaza in New York City Combines School, Housing," *Journal of the American Institute of Architects* 60 (December 1973): 60; "Buildings on the Way Up: Chinatown," *Progressive Architecture* 55 (January 1974): 24; Suzanne Stephens, "High-Rise Housing, New York, N.Y. The Last Gasp: New York City," *Progressive Architecture* 57 (March 1976): 61–63; White and Willensky, *AIA Guide* (1978), 35, 37.
97. White and Willensky, *AIA Guide* (1978), 35.
98. Stephens, "High-Rise Housing, New York, N.Y. The Last Gasp: New York City": 63.

CIVIC CENTER

1. For discussions of civic buildings in lower Manhattan from the 1890s through the interwar period, see Stern, Gilmartin and Massengale, *New York 1900*, 60–78; Stern, Gilmartin and Mellins, *New York 1930*, 92–101.
2. New York City Planning Commission, *Manhattan Civic Center and Related Improvements* (New York, 1948); "Manhattan Civic Center," *Interiors* 107 (July 1948): 14, 16; "Leaders Discuss Civic Center Plan," *New York Times* (January 15, 1949): 30; "Plan Is Adopted for Civic Center," *New York Times* (May 19, 1949): 31; "Civic Center Plan," *New York Times* (May 25, 1949): 28; "Manhattan May," *Interiors* 108 (July 1949): 18; "City Planning Unit Maps a New Street," *New York Times* (August 10, 1950): 27.
3. New York City Planning Commission, *Manhattan Civic Center and Related Improvements*, 14.
4. "Leaders Discuss Civic Center Plan": 30.
5. "Manhattan May": 18.
6. "Decade Brings Important Revisions in Map of Lower Manhattan Section," *New York Times* (January 8, 1956), VIII: 1; Paul Goldberger, *The City Observed: New York* (New York: Random House, 1979), 39; White and Willensky, *AIA Guide* (1988), 70; Christopher Gray, "Neighborhood: Nifties from the Fifties," *Avenue* 14 (January 1990): 117–23.
7. Goldberger, *The City Observed*, 39.
8. "Proposed City and Municipal Courts Building," *Architectural Record* 118 (November 1955): 188–91; "Historic Site," *Architectural Forum* 106 (April 1957): 39; "City to Dedicate Courts Building," *New York Times* (April 23, 1961): 73; "Botein Sees Threat of 'Anarchy' if Court Reform Is Not Speeded," *New York Times* (April 26, 1961): 41; "Art and Politics Skirmish in City," *New York Times* (April 30, 1961): 82; "Architecture and the Arts," editorial, *New York Times* (May 1, 1961): 28; A. Raymond Katz, "Architect and Artist," letter to the editor, *New York Times* (May 8, 1961): 34; William N. Breger, "Planning City Structures," letter to the editor, *New York Times* (May 9, 1961): 38; Philip Benjamin, "Architects Seek Voice in City Art," *New York Times* (May 28, 1961): 31; "Inside Courtrooms, Divided Circulation," *Architectural Record* 130 (August 1961): 107–10; White and Willensky, *AIA Guide* (1967), 31; Goldberger, *The City Observed*, 36–37; Christian Hubert, "The Late Work: 1939–1969," in Christian Hubert and Lindsay Stamm Shapiro, *William Lescaze* (New York: Institute for Architecture and Urban Studies; New York: Rizzoli International Publications, 1982), 109, 116; Lorraine Welling Lanmon, *William Lescaze, Architect* (Philadelphia: Art Alliance Press; London and Toronto: Associated University Presses, 1987), 129, 132. For the Criminal Courts Building (1894), see Stern, Gilmartin and Massengale, *New York 1900*, 67.
9. "Architectural Aberrations No. 10, the New Criminal Court Building, New York," *Architectural Record* 3 (April–June 1894): 429–32. For Withers & Dick's Tombs, see Stern, Gilmartin and Massengale, *New York 1900*, 67.
10. "Moses Urges Park on Site of Tombs," *New York Times* (August 13, 1940): 21.
11. Robert Moses quoted in "Moses Urges Park on Site of Tombs": 21.
12. Stern, Gilmartin and Mellins, *New York 1930*, 98–100.
13. "Old Tombs Will Become a Fire 'College'; Prison Bars to Be Torn Out as War Scrap," *New York Times* (February 5, 1942): 23.
14. "Tombs Site Leased at $83,500 a Year," *New York Times* (June 16, 1949): 34.
15. White and Willensky, *AIA Guide* (1978), 34.
16. Goldberger, *The City Observed*, 36.
17. Margot Gayle and Michele Cohen, *The Art Commission and the Municipal Art Society Guide to Manhattan's Outdoor Sculpture* (New York: Prentice Hall Press, 1988), 54.
18. Gayle and Cohen, *The Art Commission and the Municipal Art Society Guide to Manhattan's Outdoor Sculpture*, 55.
19. William Lescaze quoted in Benjamin, "Architects Seek Voice in City Art": 31.
20. Quoted in "Art and Politics Skirmish in City": 82.
21. Harold Weston quoted in "Art and Politics Skirmish in City": 82.
22. Wallace K. Harrison quoted in "Art and Politics Skirmish in City": 82.
23. "Architecture and the Arts": 28.
24. Charles G. Bennett, "City to Increase Its Office Space," *New York Times* (June 12, 1959): 29. For McKim, Mead & White's Municipal Building, see Stern, Gilmartin and Massengale, *New York 1900*, 60, 64–67, 164–65.
25. Nathan Ginsburg quoted in "New York Crusader," *Architectural Forum* 113 (November 1960): 14. Also see "New York Architect Proposes Civic Plaza Plan," *Progressive Architecture* 41 (August 1960): 57; "New York Crusader," *Architectural Forum* 117 (October 1962): 13.
26. "New York Crusader": 14.
27. Max Abramovitz, Simon Breines and Robert Cutler, *New York Civic Center* (New York, 1962); Martin Arnold, "Civic Center to Cost $165 Million Planned for City Hall

Area," *New York Times* (December 8, 1962): 1, 56; "New York Asks for Civic Center," *Engineering News-Record* 169 (December 20, 1962): 54–55; "Architects Plan Civic Center for New York City," *Architectural Record* 133 (January 1963): 12–15; "New York Announces Plan for Civic Center for New York City," *Progressive Architecture* 44 (January 1963): 41; Mary Perot Nichols, "Architects Urge New Look at Mammoth Civic Project," *Village Voice* 9 (February 13, 1964): 1, 9; "Civic Center Plan Attacked in Manhattan," *Architectural Forum* 120 (March 1964): 5; "Esthetics/Lower Manhattan," *Journal of the American Institute of Architects* 41 (April 1964): 106.

28. David W. Dunlap, *On Broadway: A Journey Uptown Over Time* (New York: Rizzoli International Publications, 1990), 52–53.

29. Stern, Gilmartin and Massengale, *New York 1900*, 62–63.

30. Stern, Gilmartin and Massengale, *New York 1900*, 153, 165.

31. James Felt quoted in Arnold, "Civic Center to Cost $165 Million Planned for City Hall Area": 56.

32. Nathan R. Ginsburg quoted in Nichols, "Architects Urge New Look at Mammoth Civic Project": 1.

33. Norval White quoted in Nichols, "Architects Urge New Look at Mammoth Civic Project": 1.

34. Quoted in Nichols, "Architects Urge New Look at Mammoth Civic Project": 1.

35. Sir William Holford quoted in Nichols, "Architects Urge New Look at Mammoth Civic Project": 1.

36. Lewis Mumford quoted in Nichols, "Architects Urge New Look at Mammoth Civic Project": 1.

37. Le Corbusier quoted in Nichols, "Architects Urge New Look at Mammoth Civic Project": 1.

38. Jan Rowan quoted in Nichols, "Architects Urge New Look at Mammoth Civic Project": 1. Also see Alexander Burnham, "Doom Is Feared for Civic Center," *New York Times* (February 5, 1964): 37.

39. Roger Starr quoted in Nichols, "Architects Urge New Look at Mammoth Civic Project": 1.

40. Ada Louise Huxtable, "54 Story Building Planned for Civic Center," *New York Times* (April 21, 1964): 39; "New Civic Center Design Improvements Noted," *Progressive Architecture* 45 (July 1964): 84; Charles G. Bennett, "City Authorized to Buy Land for a Civic Center," *New York Times* (November 17, 1964): 1, 31; "Civic Center Plan Revised in New York," *Architectural Record* 136 (December 1964): 10; "New York's Civic Center Takes Form," *Progressive Architecture* 46 (January 1965): 180–83; Nathan Ginsburg, "The New York Civic Center," letter to the editor, *Progressive Architecture* 46 (March 1965): 30, 258, 260; Charles Thomsen, "Where Are Some Signs of Progress?" *Journal of the American Institute of Architects* 44 (September 1965): 38–40; Edward Durell Stone, *Recent & Future Architecture* (New York: Horizon Press, 1967), 16–19.

41. Stone, *Recent & Future Architecture*, 17.

42. Huxtable, "54 Story Building Planned for Civic Center": 39.

43. Quoted in "New York's Civic Center Takes Form": 180–81.

44. "New York's Civic Center Takes Form": 180, 182.

45. Ada Louise Huxtable, "How to Build a Civic Center," *New York Times* (November 18, 1973), II: 28, reprinted in Ada Louise Huxtable, *Kicked a Building Lately?* (New York: Quadrangle/New York Times Book Co., 1976), 107–11.

46. Ada Louise Huxtable, "Architecture: How Not to Build a City," *New York Times* (November 22, 1970), II: 25. Also see "New York City Federal Building," *Architectural Forum* 113 (November 1960): 63; Ada Louise Huxtable, "Architecture Stumbles On," *New York Times* (April 14, 1963), II: 23; Thomas P. Ronan, "Digging Shifts Foley Square Land, 10 Buildings Will Be Evacuated," *New York Times* (May 1, 1964): 1, 72; Natalie Jaffe, "U.S. Prevails on Foley Sq. Site," *New York Times* (August 9, 1964), VIII: 1, 10; McCandlish Phillips, "Foley Sq. Critics Called 'Gadflies,'" *New York Times* (March 9, 1965): 41; Emanuel Perlmutter, "U.S. Plans 3d Office Building for Foley Square," *New York Times* (July 7, 1965): 1, 34; "New York, N.Y.," *Progressive Architecture* 46 (September 1965): 49; Ada Louise Huxtable, "Architecture: Fun and Games," *New York Times* (June 19, 1966), II: 21; "The Architects Come into Their Own," *Newsweek* 69 (March 20, 1967): 90–92; Ada Louise Huxtable, "King of Checkerboards: Towering New Blockbuster Is Impossible to Miss in Matter-of-Fact Sort of Way," *New York Times* (December 9, 1967): 49, 64, reprinted as "The Federal Government Lays a Colossal Architectural Egg," in Ada Louise Huxtable, *Will They Ever Finish Bruckner Boulevard?* (New York: Macmillan, 1970), 105–7; Huxtable, "How to Build a Civic Center": 28; White and Willensky, *AIA Guide* (1978), 34.

47. Huxtable, "King of Checkerboards: Towering New Blockbuster Is Impossible to Miss in Matter-of-Fact Sort of Way": 64.

48. David L. Eggers quoted in Jaffe, "U.S. Prevails on Foley Sq. Site": 10.

49. Huxtable, "King of Checkerboards: Towering New Blockbuster Is Impossible to Miss in Matter-of-Fact Sort of Way": 64.

50. Huxtable, "King of Checkerboards: Towering New Blockbuster Is Impossible to Miss in Matter-of-Fact Sort of Way": 49.

51. Huxtable, "How to Build a Civic Center": 28.

52. White and Willensky, *AIA Guide* (1978), 34.

53. Goldberger, *The City Observed*, 35.

54. Glenn Fowler, "A.T.& T. to Put Up 550-Foot Building," *New York Times* (November 21, 1967): 50; Glenn Fowler, "Century-Old Cast-Iron Building Facades to Be Saved Downtown," *New York Times* (November 26, 1967), VIII: 1, 4; "Cast-Iron Face-Lift," *Architectural Forum* 128 (January 1968): 46; "The New York Telephone Company Building," *Architectural Record* 143 (January 1968): 40–43; "Telephone Tower for Lower Manhattan," *Progressive Architecture* 49 (January 1968): 28; "Designed for Machines but Mindful of People," *Architectural Record* 146 (July 1969): 123–30; "New York Telephone Company Will Occupy Most of 1095 Sixth Avenue," *Real Estate Record and Guide* 205 (February 21, 1970): 2; Jonathan Hale, "Clients in the 1970s: New Realities, More Management," *Architectural Record* 148 (October 1970): 138–47; "Telephones on High," *Architectural Forum* 136 (April 1972): 7; Pranay Gupte, "Telephone Building Now Windowless," *New York Times* (June 11, 1972), VIII: 8; Paul Goldberger, "When Building for Future Means a Step Backward," *New York Times* (December 6, 1975): 33; White and Willensky, *AIA Guide* (1978), 42–43; Goldberger, *The City Observed*, 39.

55. Vincent Scully, Jr., *Louis I. Kahn* (New York: George Braziller, 1962), 11, 27–30, figs. 64–74.

56. "Designed for Machines but Mindful of People": 126.

57. White and Willensky, *AIA Guide* (1978), 43.

58. Goldberger, *The City Observed*, 39.

59. Ada Louise Huxtable, "Beating the System," *New York Times* (November 9, 1969): 31; "Major Buildings Open in New York, Texas," *Architectural Record* 154 (November 1973): 34; "New York City Opens Police Headquarters," *Architectural Record* 154 (November 1973): 37; Huxtable, "How to Build a Civic Center": 28; James D. Morgan, "Gruzen's Corners," *Architecture Plus* 1 (December 1973): 14; Barclay F. Gordon, "A Firm, New Edge for New York's Chaotic Civic District," *Architectural Record* 156 (November 1974): cover, 107–12; Peter Blake, "The Seventh Annual Cityscape Awards," *New York* 8 (January 13, 1975): 50–51; Frederick Fried and Edmund V. Gillon, Jr., *New York Civic Sculpture* (New York: Dover, 1976), 15; White and Willensky, *AIA Guide* (1978), 33; Goldberger, *The City Observed*, 32–33; Gayle and Cohen, *The Art Commission and the Municipal Art Society Guide to Manhattan's Outdoor Sculpture*, 60.

60. Stern, Gilmartin and Massengale, *New York 1900*, 73.

61. For Kallmann, McKinnell & Knowles's Boston City Hall, see Robert A. M. Stern, *New Directions in American Architecture*, rev. ed. (New York: George Braziller, 1977), 35, fig. 69; Alex Krieger, ed., *The Architecture of Kallmann, McKinnell & Wood* (Cambridge, Mass.: Harvard University Graduate School of Design; New York: Rizzoli International Publications, 1988), 21–37.

62. Gordon, "A Firm, New Edge for New York's Chaotic Civic District": 109.

63. Huxtable, "Beating the System": 31.

64. Huxtable, "How to Build a Civic Center": 28.

65. Gordon, "A Firm, New Edge for New York's Chaotic Civic District": 107.

66. Morgan, "Gruzen's Corners": 14.

67. Gordon, "A Firm, New Edge for New York's Chaotic Civic District": 109.

68. Bernard (Tony) Rosenthal quoted in Fried and Gillon, *New York Civic Sculpture*, 15.

69. Morgan, "Gruzen's Corners": 14.

70. Huxtable, "How to Build a Civic Center": 28.

71. Paul Goldberger, "New Detention Center at Foley Sq. Is Hailed as Advance in Jail Design," *New York Times* (July 26, 1975): 25, 49; Ada Louise Huxtable, "A Happy Turn for Urban Design," *New York Times* (September 14, 1975), II: 31; Suzanne Stephens, "A Higher Level of Concern," *Progressive Architecture* 57 (July 1976): 60–65; Peter Samton, "Federal Meat and Potatoes," letter to the editor, *Progressive Architecture* 57 (September 1976): 10; White and Willensky, *AIA Guide* (1978), 33; Goldberger, *The City Observed*, 33. For Cass Gilbert's United States Courthouse, see Stern, Gilmartin and Mellins, *New York 1930*, 92, 98–99.

72. Goldberger, "New Detention Center at Foley Sq. Is Hailed as Advance in Jail Design": 25.

73. Goldberger, *The City Observed*, 33.

74. "Downtown Manhattan High School," *Architectural Record* 153 (April 1973): 42; "Murray Bergtraum High School," *Progressive Architecture* 55 (September 1974): 45; White and Willensky, *AIA Guide* (1978), 34; Goldberger, *The City Observed*, 33.

75. Stern, Gilmartin and Mellins, *New York 1930*, 92–93, 97–98.

76. Goldberger, *The City Observed*, 33; White and Willensky, *AIA Guide* (1988), 64.

77. White and Willensky, *AIA Guide* (1988), 64.

78. Goldberger, *The City Observed*, 33.

79. "Family Court Building," *Architectural Record* 148 (October 1970): 43; "The New York Family Court Building Sculpture Competition," *Architectural Record* 152 (November 1972): 45; Paul Goldberger, "Architectural Aim of New Court Building Is Admirable, but Falls Short in Execution," *New York Times* (September 28, 1976): 45; White and Willensky, *AIA Guide* (1978), 34–35; Goldberger, *The City Observed*, 36–37; Gayle and Cohen, *The Art Commission and the Municipal Art Society Guide to Manhattan's Outdoor Sculpture*, 53.

80. Goldberger, "Architectural Aim of New Court Building Is Admirable, but Falls Short in Execution": 45.

81. Goldberger, *The City Observed*, 36.

82. Goldberger, "Architectural Aim of New Court Building Is Admirable, but Falls Short in Execution": 45.

DOWNTOWN

1. "Plans Filed for 4 New Skyscrapers in Manhattan at $20,000,000 Cost," *New York Times* (August 3, 1944): 21.

2. "Midtown Offices Grow at Expense of Older Centers," *New York Times* (May 8, 1949), VIII: 1, 6.

3. "Comment and Reports to Record and Guide," *Real Estate Record and Guide* 167 (June 30, 1951): 3; Robert F. R. Ballard, *Directory of Manhattan Office Buildings* (New York: McGraw-Hill, 1978), 134.

4. "New William Street Insurance Building 93 Per Cent Rented," *Real Estate Record and Guide* 168 (December 15, 1951): 3; Ballard, *Directory of Manhattan Office Buildings*, 131.

5. Cited in "Wall Street's Other Boom," *Fortune* 54 (October 1956): 163, 178, 182.

6. "Wall Street's Other Boom": 163, 178, 182; Ballard, *Directory of Manhattan Office Buildings*, 113; Stern, Gilmartin and Mellins, *New York 1930*, 767 (n. 2).

7. "Skyscraper to Be Erected in Financial District First in a Quarter Century," *Real Estate Record and Guide* 176 (November 19, 1955): 3–4; "20 Broad Street 100% Rented at Early Construction Stage," *Real Estate Record and Guide* 177 (June 9, 1956): 3; "Steel Topped Out at 20 Broad St.," *Real Estate Record and Guide* 178 (August 4, 1956): 4; Ballard, *Directory of Manhattan Office Buildings*, 81.

8. Ballard, *Directory of Manhattan Office Buildings*, 130.

9. "Downtown Insurance District as $20,000,000 Construction Program," *Real Estate Record and Guide* 176 (October 22, 1955): 3; "Fabulous New York Office Boom Keeps Growing; Rental Market Still Firm," *Architectural Forum* 104 (January 1956): 12; "Insurance Group Leases Eight Floors in 123 William St.," *Real Estate Record and Guide* 179 (May 4, 1957): 3; Richard Roth, "High-Rise Down to Earth," *Progressive Architecture* 38 (June 1957): 196–200; Ballard, *Directory of Manhattan Office Buildings*, 129.

10. "Wall St. Area Cheered by Plans for New Skyscraper," *Architectural Forum* 99 (October 1953): 74; "The Record Reports," *Architectural Record* 114 (November 1953): 16; "N.Y. Produce Exchange First to Sign Lease for Space in New Skyscraper," *Real Estate Record and Guide* 172 (November 28, 1953): 3; "The Impact of Mechanical Equipment on Design," *Architectural Record* 115 (April 1954): 195–96, 198, 201, 203, 206, 208; "New Building for Produce Exchange at 2 Broadway," *Real Estate Record and Guide* 177 (June 9, 1956): 3; "Plans Revised for 2 Broadway," *Real Estate Record and Guide* 178 (August 11, 1956): 3; Roth, "High-Rise Down to Earth": 198, 200; John P. Callahan, "New Construction Is Changing the Face of Financial District," *New York Times* (July 7, 1957), VIII: 1–2; "Large Leases Highlight Renting in 2 Broadway," *Real Estate Record and*

Guide 180 (October 5, 1957): 3; Henry Hope Reed, *The Golden City* (New York: Doubleday, 1959), 82; Douglas Haskell, "Off-Tune on Broadway," *Architectural Forum* 110 (February 1959): 102–5; "Doing Over the Town," *Time* 80 (September 28, 1962): 56, 58–61, 68–69; White and Willensky, *AIA Guide* (1967), 15; Brent C. Brolin, *The Failure of Modern Architecture* (New York: Van Nostrand Reinhold, 1976), 29; Ballard, *Directory of Manhattan Office Buildings*, 86; Ada Louise Huxtable, *The Tall Building Artistically Reconsidered: The Search for a Skyscraper Style* (New York: Pantheon Books, 1982), 27–28; Barbara Rose, *Lee Krasner: A Retrospective* (Houston: Museum of Fine Arts; New York: Museum of Modern Art, 1983), 117–19; Lorraine Welling Lanmon, *William Lescaze, Architect* (Philadelphia: Art Alliance Press; London and Toronto: Associated University Presses, 1987), 129, 152–53; David W. Dunlap, *On Broadway: A Journey Uptown Over Time* (New York: Rizzoli International Publications, 1990), 15.

11. For Lescaze's Longfellow Building, see Christian Hubert, "The Late Work: 1939–1969," in Christian Hubert and Lindsay Stamm Shapiro, *William Lescaze* (New York: Institute for Architecture and Urban Studies; New York: Rizzoli International Publications, 1982), 108, 112, 122.

12. Haskell, "Off-Tune on Broadway": 104–5.

13. "Chase Manhattan Bank Planning a Downtown 'Rockefeller Center,'" *New York Times* (November 8, 1955): 1, 43; Charles G. Bennett, "City Joins Bank to Assure a New Downtown Center," *New York Times* (December 7, 1955): 1, 41; "Fabulous New York Office Boom Keeps Growing; Rental Market Still Firm": 12; "Buildings in the News," *Architectural Record* 119 (January 1956): 10; "News Bulletins," *Progressive Architecture* 37 (January 1956): 70; "Towering Chase Manhattan Building Will Let Light into Wall St. Canyon Area," *Architectural Forum* 104 (May 1956): 12–13; "Record Reports: Perspectives," *Architectural Record* 119 (May 1956): 9; "Space for People: Superblock Scheme for Office Project Creates a Public Plaza," *Architectural Record* 119 (May 1956): 10; "Towering HQ for N.Y.'s Chase Manhattan Bank to Leave 70% of Site Open," *Progressive Architecture* 37 (May 1956): 86–87; "Downtown Dream," *Newsweek* 48 (July 9, 1956): 92; "Wall Street's Other Boom," *Fortune* 54 (October 1956): 163, 178, 182; *Buildings for Business and Government*, exhibition catalogue (New York: Museum of Modern Art, 1957), 26–29; "Chase Manhattan Bank," *Architectural Record* 121 (March 1957): cover, 248–49; "Modern Architecture Is Finding a New Kind of Patronage," *New York Times* (March 3, 1957), VIII: 1–2; "Tower with a Front Yard," *Architectural Forum* 106 (April 1957): 110–15; Callahan, "New Construction Is Changing the Face of Financial District": 1; "The Architects from 'Skid's Row,'" *Fortune* 57 (January 1958): 137–40, 210, 212, 215; "Changing New York," *Newsweek* 52 (July 14, 1958): 75–77; Earle Shultz and Walter Simmons, *Offices in the Sky* (Indianapolis, Ind.: Bobbs-Merrill, 1959), 246, 253; Haskell, "Off-Tune on Broadway": 102–5; "The War with the Bedrock," *Fortune* 59 (February 1959): 117–19; "Designers for a Busy World: Mood for Working," *Newsweek* 53 (May 4, 1959): 97–100; John P. Callahan, "60-Story Skyscraper Is 'Topped Out' via TV," *New York Times* (September 10, 1959): 37; "Buildings in the News," *Architectural Record* 126 (October 1959): 15; Carter Clarke Osterbind, "Building and Construction Industry," *Britannica Book of the Year* (Chicago: Encyclopaedia Britannica, 1960): 126; Richard E. Paret, "Stainless Steel Flashing," *Progressive Architecture* 41 (May 1960): 182–85; "The Talk of the Town: David Rockefeller," *New Yorker* 36 (July 23, 1960): 15–17; "New Profile in Lower Manhattan," *Architectural Forum* 113 (October 1960): 5; Ada Louise Huxtable, "The Significance of Our Skyscrapers," *New York Times* (October 30, 1960), II: 13; Ada Louise Huxtable, *Four Walking Tours of Modern Architecture in New York City* (New York: Museum of Modern Art and Municipal Art Society of New York, 1961), 68; Cranston Jones, *Architecture Today and Tomorrow* (New York: McGraw-Hill, 1961), 131–32, 134; Ogden Tanner in collaboration with David Allison, Peter Blake and Walter McQuade, "The Chase—Portrait of a Giant," *Architectural Forum* 115 (July 1961): cover, 63, 65–95; "New York's Old Financial District Gets New Skyscraper," *Architectural Record* 130 (July 1961): 141–50; "New Escarpment Among Cliffs of Lower Manhattan," *Progressive Architecture* 42 (July 1961): 50; "1 Chase Manhattan Plaza," *Interiors* 32 (August 1961): 78–87; W. A. Obers, letter to the editor, *Architectural Forum* 115 (September 1961): 153; Nathaniel A. Owings, letter to the editor, *Architectural Forum* 115 (September 1961): 153; Adolf De Roy Mark, letter to the editor, *Architectural Forum* 115 (September 1961): 153; John C. Parkin, letter to the editor, *Architectural Forum* 115 (September 1961): 153; Walter C. Kidney, letter to the editor, *Architectural Forum* 115 (September 1961): 153; Raymond T. O'Keefe, letter to the editor, *Architectural Forum* 115 (September 1961): 153; Walker O. Cain, letter to the editor, *Architectural Forum* 115 (September 1961): 153; Bruce M. Walker, letter to the editor, *Architectural Forum* 115 (September 1961): 153; John Anderson, "Chase Manhattan's New Home," *Interiors* 121 (September 1961): 112–17; "The Talk of the Town: Harmonies," *New Yorker* 37 (September 23, 1961): 33–34; Glay Sperling, letter to the editor, *Architectural Forum* 115 (October 1961): 179; H. C. Turner, Jr., letter to the editor, *Architectural Forum* 115 (October 1961): 179; M. Russell Turley, letter to the editor, *Architectural Forum* 115 (October 1961): 179; Joseph C. Hazen, Jr., "Publisher's Note," *Architectural Forum* 115 (December 1961): 1; Jürgen Joedicke, *Office Buildings*, trans. C. V. Amerongen (New York: Frederick A. Praeger, 1962), 176–78; Ada Louise Huxtable, "Our New Buildings: Hits and Misses," *New York Times* (April 29, 1962), VI: 16–17, 105–6; Marilyn Bender, "Company Executives Often Called Upon to Act as Decorators," *New York Times* (April 30, 1962): 22; Wolf Von Eckardt, "Pan Am's Glass House," *New Republic* 147 (August 13, 1962): 24–26; "Doing Over the Town": 56, 58, 69; Ernst Danz, *Architecture of Skidmore, Owings & Merrill, 1950–1962*, with an intro. by Henry-Russell Hitchcock (New York: Frederick A. Praeger, 1963), 158–69; Martin Meyerson, *Face of the Metropolis* (New York: Random House, 1963), 52–54; "Chase Manhattan Wins Friends and Influences People," *Newsweek* 61 (April 8, 1963): 74–77; John Gruen, "Japanese Garden for Wall St.," *New York Herald Tribune* (September 13, 1963): 13; "A Friend at the Chase," *Business Week* (December 21, 1963): 24–25; James T. Burns, Jr., "A Lung for New York's Financial District," *Progressive Architecture* 45 (September 1964): 214–15; E. J. Kahn, Jr., "Profiles: Resources and Responsibilities—Part 1," *New Yorker* 40 (January 9, 1965): 37–38, 40, 42, 46–47, 50, 52, 54–56, 62, 64, 66, 68, 72, 75–76, 78, 80–83; James Marston Fitch, *American Building, 1: The Historical Forces that Shaped It*, 2nd rev. ed. (Boston: Houghton Mifflin, 1966), 284, fig. 226; John Jacobus, *Twentieth-Century Architecture: The Middle Years 1940–65* (New York: Frederick A. Praeger, 1966), 110–11; "The Talk of the Town: Fountains," *New Yorker* 42 (July 9, 1966): 17–19; "I grandi organismi di progettazione negli Stati uniti," *Casabella* 309 (September 1966): 42–45; Paul Heyer, *Architects on Architecture* (London: Penguin, 1967), 290–91, 365–66; White and Willensky, *AIA Guide* (1967), 22–23; Alden Whitman, "Mumford Finds City Strangled by Excess of Cars and People," *New York Times* (March 22, 1967): 49, 95; Vincent Scully, Jr., *American Architecture and Urbanism* (New York:

Frederick A. Praeger, 1969), 144–45; Robert A. M. Stern, *New Directions in American Architecture* (New York: George Braziller, 1969), 99; William Zeckendorf with Edward McCreary, *The Autobiography of William Zeckendorf* (New York: Holt, Rinehart and Winston, 1970), 264–74; Leonardo Benevolo, *History of Modern Architecture, vol. 2: The Modern Movement*, trans. H. J. Landry (Cambridge, Mass.: MIT Press, 1971), 803, 805, 807; "40-Foot Dubuffet Sculpture Will Complete Chase Plaza in New York," *Architectural Record* 149 (February 1971): 36; "Chase,[sic] Manhattan Will Enhance Bank Plaza with Sculpture by France's Dubuffet," *Journal of the American Institute of Architects* 55 (May 1971): 8; William H. Jordy, *American Buildings and Their Architects: The Impact of European Modernism in the Mid-Twentieth Century*, vol. 4 (Garden City, N.Y.: Doubleday & Co., 1972), 6–7, 254–55; David Jacobs, "The Establishment's Architect-Plus," *New York Times* (July 23, 1972), VI: 12–14, 16–17, 19, 21, 23; "Dubuffet Sculpture Unveiled on Chase Manhattan Plaza," *Architectural Record* 152 (November 1972): 36; "The Talk of the Town: New Sculpture in Town," *New Yorker* 48 (November 11, 1972): 37–38; Thomas B. Hess, "Under the Spreading Plastic Tree," *New York* 6 (January 15, 1973): 70–71; Alan Dunn, "Good God—It Seeds Itself," cartoon, *Architectural Record* 153 (April 1973): 10; Frederick Fried and Edmund V. Gillon, Jr., *New York Civic Sculpture* (New York: Dover, 1976), 14–15; Ballard, *Directory of Manhattan Office Buildings*, 91; Sam Hunter, *Isamu Noguchi* (New York: Abbeville Press, 1978), 145–49; Pamela Jones, *Under the City Streets* (New York: Holt, Rinehart and Winston, 1978), 242–43; Paul Goldberger, *The City Observed: New York* (New York: Random House, 1979), 23–24; Manfredo Tafuri and Francesco Dal Co, *Modern Architecture*, trans. Robert Erich Wolf (New York: Harry N. Abrams, 1979), 308; John Tauranac, *Essential New York* (New York: Holt, Rinehart and Winston, 1979), 208–9; Andreas Franzke, *Dubuffet*, trans. Robert Erich Wolf (New York: Harry N. Abrams, 1981), 183, 193, 204–7; Margot Gayle and Michele Cohen, *The Art Commission and the Municipal Art Society Guide to Manhattan's Outdoor Sculpture* (New York: Prentice Hall Press, 1988), 22–24; Carol Herselle Krinsky, *Gordon Bunshaft of Skidmore, Owings & Merrill* (New York: Architectural History Foundation; Cambridge, Mass.: MIT Press, 1988), 72–77, 122–27, 336, 344–45; Carol Herselle Krinsky, "Architecture in New York City," in Leonard Wallock, ed., *New York: Culture Capital of the World, 1940–1965* (New York: Rizzoli International Publications, 1988), 104–6.

14. "The Architects from 'Skid's Row'": 137–40, 210, 212, 215.

15. "'Downtown': A Last Look Backward," *Fortune* 54 (October 1956): 157–62.

16. For the Mutual Life Insurance Building, see W. Parker Chase, *New York: The Wonder City* (New York: Wonder City Publishing Co., 1932; New York: New York Bound, 1983), 180.

17. For 18 Pine Street (Chase National Bank Building), see Stern, Gilmartin and Mellins, *New York 1930*, 534.

18. See Robert A. M. Stern, *George Howe: Toward a Modern American Architecture* (New Haven, Conn.: Yale University Press, 1975), 108–30, figs. 83–97.

19. Tanner, "The Chase—Portrait of a Giant": 66.

20. For the Federal Reserve Bank, see Stern, Gilmartin and Mellins, *New York 1930*, 174–75.

21. Huxtable, "The Significance of Our Skyscrapers": 13.

22. For the Bank of the Manhattan Company Building, see Stern, Gilmartin and Mellins, *New York 1930*, 602–3, 605.

23. Tanner, "The Chase—Portrait of a Giant": 94.

24. Tanner, "The Chase—Portrait of a Giant": 94.

25. *Hans Hollein*, exhibition catalogue (Vienna: Ministry of Education and Art, 1972), no pagination.

26. Mark, letter to the editor, *Architectural Forum* (September 1961): 153.

27. Kidney, letter to the editor, *Architectural Forum* (September 1961): 153.

28. Edmond J. Bartnett, "New Techniques Used in Building," *New York Times* (March 30, 1958), VIII: 10; "Unusual Methods Used in Downtown Building," *Real Estate Record and Guide* 181 (April 5, 1958): 3–4; "Unfinished Building Opened for Occupancy," *Real Estate Record and Guide* 182 (July 19, 1958): 4; "New Office Bldg. Cited by Downtown-Lower Manhattan Association," *Real Estate Record and Guide* 183 (April 25, 1959): 3; Ballard, *Directory of Manhattan Office Buildings*, 129.

29. Callahan, "New Construction Is Changing the Face of Financial District": 1; "Lower Manhattan Shaft," *Architectural Forum* 107 (October 1957): 39; "Work Started on New Downtown Skyscraper," *Real Estate Record and Guide* 181 (May 31, 1958): 5; "First Steel Set for Skyscraper at 80 Pine," *Real Estate Record and Guide* 183 (April 11, 1959): 3; Ballard, *Directory of Manhattan Office Buildings*, 94.

30. "$28,000,000 Office Building to Be Erected in Downtown Financial District," *Real Estate Record and Guide* 179 (March 9, 1957): 3; "Largest Post-War Office Building Completed," *Real Estate Record and Guide* 182 (August 23, 1958): 4; Ballard, *Directory of Manhattan Office Buildings*, 121.

31. "Four Deals Result in New Office Structure," *Real Estate Record and Guide* 181 (May 31, 1958): 3; "New Office Building for Downtown Manhattan," *Architectural Record* 124 (July 1958): 12; "Contracts Awarded for Downtown Office Building," *Real Estate Record and Guide* 182 (December 13, 1958): 3; Hubert, "The Late Work: 1939–1969," in Hubert and Shapiro, *William Lescaze*, 112–13; Lanmon, *William Lescaze, Architect*, 128, 153.

32. Richard A. Miller, "A.T.&T.'s Architectural Quest," *Architectural Forum* 112 (April 1960): 120–22, 218, 225, 228; Dunlap, *On Broadway*, 38, 40.

33. For Bosworth's building, see Stern, Gilmartin and Massengale, *New York 1900*, 162.

34. "Block to Be Sold in Financial Area," *New York Times* (August 3, 1961): 37; "Buildings in the News," *Architectural Record* 130 (September 1961): 15; "New Buildings in New York Follow New Codes," *Progressive Architecture* 42 (September 1961): 70; "Projects . . . and Downtown," *Architectural Forum* 115 (October 1961): 65; "Wall Street Tower by SOM," *Progressive Architecture* 44 (October 1963): 95; "Marine Midland Grace Picks Home," *New York Times* (October 16, 1965): 30; Byron Porterfield, "A Quiet Tower Downtown Nears Topping-Out Stage," *New York Times* (May 29, 1966), VIII: 1, 12; White and Willensky, *AIA Guide* (1967), 21; "The Sculptural World of Isamu Noguchi," *Interiors* 127 (May 1967): 6; "New Star on Broadway," *Interiors* 127 (June 1967): 90–97; Ada Louise Huxtable, "Sometimes We Do It Right," *New York Times* (March 31, 1968), II: 33, reprinted in Ada Louise Huxtable, *Will They Ever Finish Bruckner Boulevard?* (New York: Macmillan, 1970), 14–18; John M. Dixon, "Down-to-Earth Tower," *Architectural Forum* 128 (April 1968): 36–45; "Buildings in the News," *Architectural Record* 143 (April 1968): 43; "Investimento in forma," *L'architettura cronache e storia* 14 (October 1968): 462–63; "The Once and Future Capital of World Finance," *Fortune* 80 (October 1969): 118–25; Jordy, *American Buildings and Their Architects: The*

Impact of European Modernism in the Mid-Twentieth Century, vol. 4, 6–7; Jacobs, "The Establishment's Architect-Plus": 12–14, 16–17, 19, 21, 23; Axel Menges, *Architecture of Skidmore, Owings & Merrill, 1963–1973*, trans. E. Rockwell (New York: Architectural Book Publishing Co., 1974), 144–49; Arthur Drexler, "Introduction," in Menges, *Architecture of Skidmore, Owings & Merrill, 1963–1973*, 10, 20–21; Ada Louise Huxtable, "Ada Louise, the Mad Bomber," letter to the editor, *New York* 7 (December 9, 1974): 11; Fried and Gillon, *New York Civic Sculpture*, 15; Andrea O. Dean, "Bunshaft and Noguchi: An Uneasy but Highly Productive Architect-Artist Collaboration," *Journal of the American Institute of Architects* 65 (October 1976): 54; Ballard, *Directory of Manhattan Office Buildings*, 91; Hunter, *Isamu Noguchi*, 160, 282–83; Goldberger, *The City Observed*, 8–9; Tauranac, *Essential New York*, 225–26; Paul Goldberger, *The Skyscraper* (New York: Alfred A. Knopf, 1981), 136; Huxtable, *The Tall Building Artistically Reconsidered*, 40–41; Donald Martin Reynolds, *The Architecture of New York City* (New York: Macmillan, 1984), 153–54; Gayle and Cohen, *The Art Commission and the Municipal Art Society Guide to Manhattan's Outdoor Sculpture*, 27; Krinsky, *Gordon Bunshaft of Skidmore, Owings & Merrill*, 161–65, 228–33, 337, 347; Dunlap, *On Broadway*, 26–27, 38.

35. Gordon Bunshaft quoted in Krinsky, *Gordon Bunshaft of Skidmore, Owings & Merrill*, 161.

36. Krinsky, *Gordon Bunshaft of Skidmore, Owings & Merrill*, 163.

37. "The Once and Future Capital of World Finance": 120.

38. Huxtable, "Sometimes We Do It Right": 33.

39. Huxtable, "Ada Louise, the Mad Bomber": 11.

40. Drexler, "Introduction," in Menges, *Architecture of Skidmore, Owings & Merrill, 1963–1973*, 10, 20.

41. Joseph P. Fried, "End Near for Singer Building, a Forerunner of Skyscrapers," *New York Times* (August 22, 1967): 41; "Buildings in the News," *Architectural Record* 143 (May 1968): 42; "Steel Showcase," *Progressive Architecture* 49 (May 1968): 58; "Manhattan Surges Skyward," *Engineering News-Record* 181 (November 28, 1968): 72–75, 78, 82, 84–85; Walter McQuade, "Life in Boxes," *Architectural Forum* 130 (March 1969): 90; "The Once and Future Capital of World Finance": 118–25; Zeckendorf with McCreary, *The Autobiography of William Zeckendorf*, 279–83; Ada Louise Huxtable, "Innovative Design and Planning Take Shape in Lower Manhattan," *New York Times* (June 8, 1973): 41, 48; "Research Leads to a Bolder Expression of the Steel Frame," *Architectural Record* 154 (July 1973): 133–38; Menges, *Architecture of Skidmore, Owings & Merrill, 1963–1973*, 150–57; Drexler, "Introduction," in Menges, *Architecture of Skidmore, Owings & Merrill, 1963–1973*, 10, 18–20; White and Willensky, *AIA Guide* (1978), 21; Goldberger, *The City Observed*, 9; Tauranac, *Essential New York*, 232–33; Andrew Alpern and Seymour Durst, *Holdouts!* (New York: McGraw-Hill, 1984), 33–34; Dunlap, *On Broadway*, 27, 38.

42. For the Civic Center in Chicago, see Carl W. Condit, *Chicago, 1930–70: Building, Planning, and Urban Technology* (Chicago and London: University of Chicago Press, 1974), 134–41.

43. Drexler, "Introduction," in Menges, *Architecture of Skidmore, Owings & Merrill, 1963–1973*, 18, 20.

44. Glenn Fowler, "News of the Realty Trade: Pei Building Starts," *New York Times* (February 15, 1970), VIII: 6; "Chinese Shipping Group to Erect Office Tower in Wall Street Area," *Real Estate Record and Guide* 205 (February 28, 1970): 2; "Buildings in the News," *Architectural Record* 150 (October 1971): 41; Peter Blake, "I. M. Pei & Partners," *Architecture Plus* 1 (February 1973): 52–59; "Urban Centers: New York City," *Architecture Plus* 1 (March 1973): 36–37; "The Reynolds Memorial Award Goes to an Atypical 'Spec' Office Building," *Journal of the American Institute of Architects* 61 (June 1974): 44–45; "Reynolds Award," *Architecture Plus* 2 (July–August 1974): 35; Betty Raymond, "Saving the View at 88 Pine," *Interiors* 134 (August 1974): 74–77; "Pei's Precise Cladding Enriches a Spec Office Building," *Architectural Record* 157 (April 1975): 123–28; Paul Goldberger, "Mostly B's, Some A's," *New York Times* (May 18, 1975), VI: 68–70; Ada Louise Huxtable, "Grooms's Zany 'Manhattan' Puts the City in Focus," *New York Times* (December 21, 1975), II: 1, 41, reprinted as "The Near Past: Through the Artist's Eye," in Ada Louise Huxtable, *Kicked a Building Lately?* (New York: Quadrangle/New York Times Book Co., 1976), 285–87; Fried and Gillon, *New York Civic Sculpture*, 21; Ballard, *Directory of Manhattan Office Buildings*, 94; White and Willensky, *AIA Guide* (1978), 12–13; Goldberger, *The City Observed*, 17–18; Gayle and Cohen, *The Art Commission and the Municipal Art Society Guide to Manhattan's Outdoor Sculpture*, 19; Carter Wiseman, *I. M. Pei: A Profile in American Architecture* (New York: Harry N. Abrams, 1990), 210, 308–9.

45. "29-Story Tower to Rise on Wall at Water Street," *Real Estate Record and Guide* 200 (December 16, 1967): 4; Ada Louise Huxtable, "A New City Is Emerging Downtown," *New York Times* (March 29, 1970), VIII: 1, 4; Ballard, *Directory of Manhattan Office Buildings*, 102.

46. "Urban Centers: New York City," *Architecture Plus*: 37.

47. "The Record Reports," *Architectural Record* 141 (April 1967): 42; Alan S. Oser, "Boom in Office Space Demand Slows a Bit," *New York Times* (January 18, 1970), VIII: 1, 6; Huxtable, "A New City Is Emerging Downtown": 1, 4; "Skyscraper Fire Raises Questions," *Architectural Record* 148 (September 1970): 36; "The New York Plaza Club," *Interior Design* 43 (March 1972): 134–35; Ballard, *Directory of Manhattan Office Buildings*, 103; White and Willensky, *AIA Guide* (1978), 10–11; Goldberger, *The City Observed*, 19; Lanmon, *William Lescaze, Architect*, 131, 158–60; David W. Dunlap, "Primping Up at a Time When the Best Goes Begging," *New York Times* (June 23, 1991), VIII: 15.

48. Huxtable, "Innovative Design and Planning Take Shape in Lower Manhattan": 48.

49. Ada Louise Huxtable, "Downtown New York Begins to Undergo Radical Transformation," *New York Times* (March 21, 1967): 35, 37.

50. Ada Louise Huxtable, "Down Town Blues," *New York Times* (April 16, 1967), II: 29–30, reprinted as "Singing the Downtown Blues," in Huxtable, *Will They Ever Finish Bruckner Boulevard?*, 56–60.

51. Huxtable, "A New City Is Emerging Downtown": 4.

52. Goldberger, *The City Observed*, 19.

53. White and Willensky, *AIA Guide* (1978), 11.

54. "40-Story Skyscraper to Round Out Financial District Complex," *Real Estate Record and Guide* 202 (September 21, 1968): 2; Huxtable, "A New City Is Emerging Downtown": 1, 4; Eleanore Carruth, "New York Hangs Out the For-Rent Sign," *Fortune* 83 (February 1971): 86–90, 114–15, 118; "Buildings in the News," *Architectural Record* 151 (February 1972): 43; Goldberger, *The City Observed*, 19; White and Willensky, *AIA Guide* (1988), 25.

55. Huxtable, "A New City Is Emerging Downtown": 4.

56. Goldberger, *The City Observed*, 19.

57. Carruth, "New York Hangs Out the For-Rent Sign": 86.

58. Huxtable, "Down Town Blues": 29–30.

59. "Uris to Build 3.5 Million Square Foot Office Building on South Street," *Real Estate Record and Guide* 202 (November 2, 1968): 2–3; Ada Louise Huxtable, "A Breakthrough in Planning," *New York Times* (February 7, 1969): 39; Ada Louise Huxtable, "How to Love the Boom," *New York Times* (February 16, 1969), II: 34; Robert Jensen, "Tall Office Buildings: The Process of Development," *Architectural Record* 145 (April 1969): 181–85; Huxtable, "A New City Is Emerging Downtown": 1, 4; Steven Weisman, "Building Will Rise in a Big 'Bathtub,'" *New York Times* (September 6, 1970), VIII: 4; Huxtable, "Innovative Design and Planning Take Shape in Lower Manhattan": 41, 48; Ballard, *Directory of Manhattan Office Buildings*, 104; White and Willensky, *AIA Guide* (1978), 12–13; Goldberger, *The City Observed*, 8; Tauranac, *Essential New York*, 235–36.

60. White and Willensky, *AIA Guide* (1978), 10, 562.

61. Huxtable, "Downtown New York Begins to Undergo Radical Transformation": 35, 37.

62. Huxtable, "How to Love the Boom": 34.

63. Donlyn Lyndon, "Concrete Cascade in Portland," *Architectural Forum* 125 (July–August 1966): 74–79; Lawrence Halprin, *Cities*, rev. ed. (Cambridge, Mass.: MIT Press, 1972), 230–36.

64. Huxtable, "Innovative Design and Planning Take Shape in Lower Manhattan": 48.

65. Grace Glueck, "Museum Planned for Wall St. Area," *New York Times* (July 20, 1971): 22; "Whitney Branch to Open Sept. 18," *New York Times* (June 16, 1973): 14; Murray Schumach, "Lindsay Extols Virtues of Downtown Manhattan," *New York Times* (August 8, 1973): 41; Laurie Johnston, "Whitney Museum Opens Downtown Branch," *New York Times* (September 19, 1973): 49; Hilton Kramer, "Decentralized Art: Great," *New York Times* (September 19, 1973): 49; Piri Halasz, "The Downtown Whitney," *Art News* 72 (November 1973): 58; Lawrence Alloway, "Art," *Nation* 217 (November 26, 1973): 573; "Spreading the Wealth," *New York* 7 (December 31, 1973): 63.

66. Percy Uris quoted in Glueck, "Museum Planned for Wall St. Area": 22.

67. "Swedish Message," *Progressive Architecture* 40 (August 1967): 52; John Morris Dixon, "Bulwark in Lower Manhattan," *Architectural Forum* 132 (January–February 1970): 62–67; Huxtable, "A New City Is Emerging Downtown": 1, 4; Gabriel Hauge, "Trust from Manny Hanny," letter to the editor, *Architectural Forum* 132 (May 1970): 18; White and Willensky, *AIA Guide* (1978), 12; Goldberger, *The City Observed*, 19; Tauranac, *Essential New York*, 226–27.

68. Huxtable, "A New City Is Emerging Downtown": 4.

69. Huxtable, "A New City Is Emerging Downtown": 4. Also see ". . . New York Pop," *Architectural Forum* 132 (March 1970): 70; "There's a Sopwith Camel on the Roof," *Progressive Architecture* 52 (March 1971): cover, 66–67, 70–71; Forrest Wilson, "Curse You Red Baron," editorial, *Progressive Architecture* 52 (March 1971): 65; Melvyn Kaufman, "We Owe Something to the People," *Progressive Architecture* 52 (March 1971): 68–69; A. E. Bye, "A Place to Tarry," *Progressive Architecture* 52 (March 1971): 72–73; "The Interior Designer as Tenant," *Progressive Architecture* 52 (March 1971): 74–76; Huxtable, "Innovative Design and Planning Take Shape in Lower Manhattan": 41, 48; Fried and Gillon, *New York Civic Sculpture*, 18–19; Ballard, *Directory of Manhattan Office Buildings*, 104; White and Willensky, *AIA Guide* (1978), 12; Tauranac, *Essential New York*, 229–30; Gayle and Cohen, *The Art Commission and the Municipal Art Society Guide to Manhattan's Outdoor Sculpture*, 16–17.

70. Kaufman, "We Owe Something to the People": 69.

71. Sharon Lee Ryder, "Looking Up Downtown," *Progressive Architecture* 53 (April 1972): cover, 78–83; Huxtable, "Innovative Design and Planning Take Shape in Lower Manhattan": 41, 48; Andrea O. Dean, "Graphics in the Environment," *Journal of the American Institute of Architects* 64 (October 1975): 19–25, 28–29; Fried and Gillon, *New York Civic Sculpture*, 20–21; Ballard, *Directory of Manhattan Office Buildings*, 125; White and Willensky, *AIA Guide* (1978), 13; Goldberger, *The City Observed*, 16–17; Alpern and Durst, *Holdouts!*, 142–43; Gayle and Cohen, *The Art Commission and the Municipal Art Society Guide to Manhattan's Outdoor Sculpture*, 20.

72. Lobby plaque quoted in Goldberger, *The City Observed*, 17.

73. "The Evolving Urban Architecture of Davis, Brody & Associates," *Architectural Record* 152 (August 1972): 104–5; Huxtable, "Innovative Design and Planning Take Shape in Lower Manhattan": 41, 48; Ada Louise Huxtable, "Adding Up the Score," *New York Times* (January 20, 1974), II: 29; Gerald Allen, "High-Rise Office Buildings—The Public Spaces They Make," *Architectural Record* 155 (March 1974): 138–42; Edward K. Carpenter, "Galleria," *Architecture Plus* 2 (September–October 1974): 108–13; Ballard, *Directory of Manhattan Office Buildings*, 128; White and Willensky, *AIA Guide* (1978), 22; Goldberger, *The City Observed*, 25.

74. "Lehman May Leave a Famous Address," *New York Times* (November 30, 1967): 77; Huxtable, "A New City Is Emerging Downtown": 1; Franklin Whitehouse, "Investors Shelve Plan for Tower in Rental Slump," *New York Times* (August 16, 1970), VIII: 1, 8; Ada Louise Huxtable, "Creations of 3 Top Architects Shown," *New York Times* (September 30, 1970): 38; "Current Works of Roche, Rudolph and Johnson on View," *Progressive Architecture* 51 (October 1970): 27; "Forum: Work in Retrospect," *Architectural Forum* 133 (November 1970): 63; "Work in Progress by Three Top Architects at New York's MOMA," *Interiors* 130 (November 1970): 6, 8; Paul Goldberger, "Form and Procession," *Architectural Forum* 138 (January–February 1973): 32–53; Goldberger, *The Skyscraper*, 124.

75. Quoted in Whitehouse, "Investors Shelve Plan for Tower in Rental Slump": 1.

76. Huxtable, "A New City Is Emerging Downtown": 1; Wolf Von Eckardt, "You Can't See the Foyer for the Trees," *Horizon* 13 (summer 1971): 40–47; Robert D. McFadden, "A New Tower Due in Financial Area," *New York Times* (September 1, 1972): 21; "Building 55 Stories High Will Have 42 Floors," *Engineering News-Record* 189 (September 14, 1972): 21; "Builder Is Allowed 3 Excess Stories in a Deal on Rent," *New York Times* (October 12, 1973): 37; Vincent Scully, "Thruway and Crystal Palace," *Architectural Forum* 140 (March 1974): 18–25; *Kevin Roche, John Dinkeloo and Associates, vol. 1: 1962–1975*, with an intro. by Henry-Russell Hitchcock (Tokyo: A.D.A. Edita, 1975), 186–91; Robert E. Tomasson, "Reserve Bank Abandons Plan to Build Tower," *New York Times* (November 13, 1976): 27; White and Willensky, *AIA Guide* (1978), 22; Francesco Dal Co, *Kevin Roche* (New York: Rizzoli International Publications, 1985), 10, 12, 27, 32, 34, 168–69. For York & Sawyer's Federal Reserve Bank, see Stern, Gilmartin and Mellins, *New York 1930*, 174–75.

77. Kevin Roche quoted in Von Eckardt, "You Can't See the Foyer for the Trees": 42.

78. "Church of Our Lady of Victory," *Architectural Record* 98 (September 1945): 108–9.

79. "Interval in a Street," *Architectural Forum* 127 (October 1967): 64–69; "Civic Center Synagogue," *Architectural Record* 143 (June 1968): 40–43; "William N. Breger, AIA, Civic Center Synagogue, New York, New York," *Journal of the American Institute of Architects* 49 (June 1968): 108; Irving Spiegel, "Procaccino Says Money Won't Win," *New York Times* (September 8, 1969): 36; White and Willensky, *AIA Guide* (1978), 40–41; Christopher Gray, "Streetscapes: The Civic Center Synagogue," *New York Times* (December 24, 1989), X: 2, reprinted in Christopher Gray, *Changing New York: The Architectural Scene* (New York: Dover, 1992), 110; Christopher Gray, "Schlock of Ages," *Avenue* 17 (December 1992): 31–32, 34, 36, 38.
80. "Interval in a Street": 67.
81. "Ten-Story Business School," *Architectural Forum* 105 (December 1956): 24; "Three New Campus Units Announced," *Progressive Architecture* 37 (December 1956): 82; "Cornerstone Is Set for N.Y.U. Building," *New York Times* (May 13, 1959): 34; "Nation's Largest University Constructing Seven Buildings," *Architectural Record* 126 (September 1959): 186–90; "N.Y.U. Unit Dedicated," *New York Times* (January 28, 1960): 22; White and Willensky, *AIA Guide* (1978), 19–20.
82. White and Willensky, *AIA Guide* (1978), 19.
83. "Downtown Manhattan Is Experiencing Tremendous Construction Boom," *Real Estate Record and Guide* 202 (October 19, 1968): 2–3; "Pace Dedicates Campus; 3 Given Honorary Degrees," *New York Times* (September 15, 1970): 41; Gene I. Maeroff, "Pace Opens Fund Drive; Seeks University Status," *New York Times* (October 10, 1971): 84; Betty Raymond, "City Sights without a Sound," *Interiors* 131 (December 1971): 116; White and Willensky, *AIA Guide* (1978), 31–32; Gayle and Cohen, *The Art Commission and the Municipal Art Society Guide to Manhattan's Outdoor Sculpture*, 46.
84. Lawrence O'Kane, "City Hall-Brooklyn Area to Get Middle-Income Housing," *New York Times* (January 10, 1964): 1, 86; "South of Brooklyn Bridge," editorial, *New York Times* (February 10, 1964): 26.
85. White and Willensky, *AIA Guide* (1978), 32.
86. White and Willensky, *AIA Guide* (1978), 31.
87. Iver Peterson, "Pace Graduates to a University," *New York Times* (March 29, 1973): 51.
88. Donald-David Logan, "Opposite of Ivory Tower: The Community College," *Architectural Record* 147 (June 1970): 143–56; "Interior to Come: In New York," *Interiors* 133 (July 1974): 8; "Ground Broken for Borough of Manhattan College," *Architectural Record* 156 (September 1974): 38; Jill Jones, "A Campus in Prospect," *New York Times* (June 29, 1980), VIII: 6; Stephen Kinzer, "Manhattan Community College Gets a Home at Last," *New York Times* (January 11, 1981), B: 3; Gayle and Cohen, *The Art Commission and Municipal Art Society Guide to Manhattan's Outdoor Sculpture*, 40; White and Willensky, *AIA Guide* (1988), 51.
89. Kinzer, "Manhattan Community College Gets a Home at Last": 3.
90. Quoted in Kinzer, "Manhattan Community College Gets a Home at Last": 3.
91. Logan, "Opposite of Ivory Tower: The Community College": 148.
92. "1951 Design Survey: Health," *Progressive Architecture* 31 (January 1950): 57–63; Howard S. Cullman, "The New Beekman-Downtown Hospital," *East Side Chamber News* 26 (April 1953): 7; "Hospital Construction: Metropolitan," *Progressive Architecture* 34 (November 1953): 79–87.
93. "Downtown Manhattan Is Experiencing Tremendous Construction Boom": 3; White and Willensky, *AIA Guide* (1978), 33.
94. Olga Gueft, "Exciting Response to Urban Need," *Interiors* 130 (January 1971): 82–83, 125; "Lower Manhattan Cultural Center," *Architectural Record* 149 (February 1971): 41: "Cultural Center Will Be NYC's Largest Space," *Progressive Architecture* 52 (March 1971): 38, 43.
95. Gueft, "Exciting Response to an Urban Need": 82–83, 125.
96. Stern, Gilmartin and Mellins, *New York 1930*, 689–90.
97. "Face-Lifting Near for Battery Park," *New York Times* (July 15, 1950): 15; "City Will Dedicate New Battery Park," *New York Times* (July 14, 1952): 19; "New Battery Park Is Opened by City," *New York Times* (July 16, 1952): 27; "Battery Park Restored," editorial, *New York Times* (July 17, 1952): 22.
98. John McCandlish, "Fifty Years, Five Cents," *New York Times* (October 23, 1955), VI: 44, 47; George Horne, "New Ferry Depot Is Opened by City," *New York Times* (July 25, 1956): 31; "South Ferry," editorial, *New York Times* (July 27, 1956): 20; White and Willensky, *AIA Guide* (1978), 7.
99. Stern, Gilmartin and Massengale, *New York 1900*, 48–49.
100. "South Ferry": 20.
101. White and Willensky, *AIA Guide* (1978), 7.
102. Ada Louise Huxtable, "Plan for Jewish Martyrs' Monument Here Unveiled," *New York Times* (October 17, 1968): 47, reprinted as "Of Art and Genocide," in Huxtable, *Will They Ever Finish Bruckner Boulevard?*, 108–10; "Expressing the Unspeakable," *Time* 92 (October 25, 1968): 78; "Louis Kahn Designs a Memorial to Six Million Jews," *Architectural Record* 144 (November 1968): 36; "Lest We Forget," *Architectural Forum* 129 (December 1968): 89; "Louis Kahn Monument," *Interiors* 128 (December 1968): 18; "Monuments to Ponder," *Progressive Architecture* 49 (December 1968): 44; Heinz Ronner and Sharad Jhaveri, *Louis I. Kahn: Complete Work 1935–1974* (Basel: Birkhäuser Verlag, 1974), 336–39; Romaldo Giurgola and Jaimini Mehta, eds., *Louis I. Kahn* (Zurich: Artemis, 1975), 158–59; *Louis I. Kahn* (Tokyo: Architecture and Urbanism, 1975), 219; Rebecca Read Shanor, *The City that Never Was* (New York: Viking, 1988), 219–25; David B. Brownlee and David G. DeLong, *Louis I. Kahn: In the Realm of Architecture*, with an intro. by Vincent Scully (New York: Rizzoli International Publications, 1992), 136–37, 139.
103. Louis Kahn quoted in Shanor, *The City that Never Was*, 222.
104. Louis Kahn quoted in "Expressing the Unspeakable": 78.
105. Huxtable, "Plan for Jewish Martyrs' Monument Here Unveiled": 47.
106. Huxtable, "Plan for Jewish Martyrs' Monument Here Unveiled": 47.
107. See Stern, Gilmartin and Mellins, *New York 1930*, 713.

ON THE WATERFRONT

1. Downtown–Lower Manhattan Association, *World Trade Center: A Proposal for the Port of New York* (New York, 1960); Charles Grutzner, "A World Center of Trade Mapped Off Wall Street," *New York Times* (January 27, 1960): 1, 16; "International Trade Mart Proposed for New York," *Progressive Architecture* 41 (March 1960): 61; "The Talk of the Town: David Rockefeller," *New Yorker* 36 (July 23, 1960): 15–17.
2. Port of New York Authority, *A World Trade Center in the Port of New York* (New York, 1961); "New York's World Trade Center Forges Ahead," *Progressive Architecture* 42 (April 1961): 49, 51; "World Trade Center for Lower Manhattan," *Architectural Forum* 114 (May 1961): 49; "Proposed World Trade Center in Manhattan," *Architectural Record* 129 (May 1961): 15; "World Trade Center in Lower West Side Will Be Great Stimulus to City Business," *Real Estate Record and Guide* 189 (March 24, 1962): 2–3; "Yamasaki and Roth for N.Y. World Trade Center," *Progressive Architecture* 43 (October 1962): 92; "Yamasaki in Manhattan," *Architectural Forum* 117 (November 1962): 13; Ada Louise Huxtable, "Pools, Domes, Yamasaki—Debate," *New York Times* (November 25, 1962), VI: 36, 150, 152, 158; "Court Upholds Trade Center Job," *Engineering News-Record* 170 (April 11, 1963): 77; "World Trade Center Plan Has Stimulated R.E. Activity," *Real Estate Record and Guide* 191 (June 29, 1963): 2–3; "The World Trade Center," *Village Voice* 9 (December 5, 1963): 1; Port of New York Authority, *The World Trade Center in the Port of New York* (New York: Port of New York Authority, 1964); "Twin Towers to Go 110 Stories," *Engineering News-Record* 172 (January 23, 1964): 33–34; "Onward & Upward," *Time* 83 (January 24, 1964): 46; "Towers that Top Them All," *Business Week* (January 25, 1964): 29; Ada Louise Huxtable, "Biggest Buildings Herald New Era," *New York Times* (January 26, 1964), VIII: 1, 4; "New World Trade Center for Manhattan," *Architectural Forum* 120 (February 1964): 5; "Yama Designs 110-Story World Trade Center," *Architectural Record* 135 (February 1964): 14–15; "World's Largest Buildings Proposed for Manhattan," *Progressive Architecture* 45 (February 1964): 55, 57–59; "The Talk of the Town: Skyscrapers," *New Yorker* 39 (February 1, 1964): 21–22; "Towers Rise—Records Fall," *Newsweek* 63 (February 3, 1964): 59; "Durst Comments on World Trade Center," *Real Estate Record and Guide* 193 (February 8, 1964): 2; "World's Biggest Skyscrapers Have New York Up in the Air," *Architectural Forum* 120 (March 1964): 118–21; "A Great Port City Planned for New York's Lower West Side," *Architectural Record* 135 (March 1964): 188–89; "Richard Roth Characterizes World Trade Center," *Real Estate Record and Guide* 193 (March 14, 1964): 2–3; Walter McQuade, "Architecture," *Nation* 198 (March 23, 1964): 306; Daniel B. Klein, letter to the editor, *Architectural Forum* 120 (April 1964): 73; The Class of Architectural Design 112X, The City College of New York, "Students Decry Yama's Twin Towers," letter to the editor, *Progressive Architecture* 45 (April 1964): 8; "Structures Can Be Beautiful," *Engineering News-Record* 172 (April 2, 1964): 124–25, 128; Robert J. Piper, "Urbanisms: Contemporary Client," *Journal of the American Institute of Architects* 41 (May 1964): 18; "Trade Center 'Failures,'" *Progressive Architecture* 45 (June 1964): 100; "Yamasaki and the Roths: At Two Ends of the Same Drafting Table," *Engineering News-Record* 173 (July 9, 1964): 46–50; "More on World Trade Center," *Progressive Architecture* 45 (October 1964): 47; E. J. Kahn, Jr., "Profiles: Resources and Responsibilities—Part 1," *New Yorker* 40 (January 9, 1965): 37–38, 40, 42, 46–47, 50, 52, 54–56, 62, 64, 66, 68, 72, 75–76, 78, 80–83; "Realty Group Fighting World Trade Call It a Renting Bust," *Real Estate Record and Guide* 195 (January 23, 1965): 2; "Trade Center Cost: $525 Million," *Engineering News-Record* 175 (September 23, 1965): 29; Charles Thomsen, "Where Are Some Signs of Progress?" *Journal of the American Institute of Architects* 44 (September 1965): 38–40; Alan Dunn, "I Bet Yama Never Had to Clean a Ceiling—," cartoon, *Architectural Record* 138 (October 1965): 10; "World Trade Center Stirs," *Progressive Architecture* 45 (November 1965): 43–44; James Marston Fitch, *American Building, 1: The Historical Forces that Shaped It*, 2nd rev. ed. (Boston: Houghton Mifflin, 1966), 297; Desmond Smith, "World Trade Center: Manhattan's Tower of Babel," *Nation* 202 (February 28, 1966): 235–38; "Trade Center Comes into Focus," *Engineering News-Record* 176 (March 24, 1966): 17; "Gargantua-by-the-Sea," *Architectural Forum* 124 (April 1966): 81–82; "Buildings in the News," *Architectural Record* 139 (April 1966): 42; Wolf Von Eckardt, "New York's Trade Center: World's Tallest Fiasco," *Harper's* 232 (May 1966): 94–98, 100, reprinted in *Bauwelt* 57 (August 8, 1966): 909–12; Ada Louise Huxtable, "Who's Afraid of the Big, Bad Buildings?" *New York Times* (May 29, 1966), II: 13–14, reprinted in Ada Louise Huxtable, *Will They Ever Finish Bruckner Boulevard?* (New York: Macmillan, 1970), 27–32; Ada Louise Huxtable, "City of Hope, Despair," *New York Times* (June 26, 1966), II: 22; "Eavesdroppings," *Progressive Architecture* 47 (July 1966): 52–53; "Pact Clears the Way for $525-Million Project," *Engineering News-Record* 177 (August 11, 1966): 64–65; "Changing the Skyline," *Time* 88 (August 12, 1966): 46; "The Blueprint Parade in Lower Manhattan," *Business Week* (August 13, 1966): 36; "World Trade Center Will Start Construction," *Architectural Record* 140 (September 1966): 36; "World Trade Center NYET?" *Progressive Architecture* 47 (September 1966): 57; Paul Heyer, *Architects on Architecture* (London: Penguin, 1967), 184–85, 194–95; Wolf Von Eckardt, *A Place to Live: The Crisis of the Cities* (New York: Delacorte Press, 1967), 219; White and Willensky, *AIA Guide* (1967), 27; "World Trade Center Price Tag Inches Up," *Progressive Architecture* 48 (February 1967): 31; "Fancy Footwork for the World Trade Center," *Progressive Architecture* 48 (March 1967): 59, 62; "Reviewing the Trade Center," editorial, *New York Times* (April 12, 1967): 46; "Problems Plague Construction of New York World Trade Center," *Engineering News-Record* 178 (April 13, 1967): 62–63, 67; "The Juggernaut," *Architectural Forum* 126 (May 1967): 91; "The Sound of Hearings," *Architectural Forum* 127 (September 1967): 89–90; "Wind, Sun, Rain and the Exterior Wall," *Architectural Record* 142 (September 1967): 213–16; "The Superagency that Moves a Metropolis," *Business Week* (May 11, 1968): 72–76, 78; Alden P. Armagnac, "Twin Towers to Be the Tallest Buildings on Earth," *Popular Science* 193 (October 1968): 98–99; "Foundation for Tallest Towers: Water Out, Trains In," *Engineering News-Record* 181 (October 31, 1968): 30–32; "Manhattan's Financial District Dresses Up," *Business Week* (November 23, 1968): 82–86; Vincent Scully, *American Architecture and Urbanism* (New York: Frederick A. Praeger, 1969), 144, 146, fig. 298; "Trade Center Builds Upward Fast," *Engineering News-Record* 182 (March 13, 1969): 21; "World's Tallest Buildings to Be World's 'Smartest,'" *Real Estate Record and Guide* 203 (May 17, 1969): 2–3; "The Once and Future Capital of World Finance," *Fortune* 80 (October 1969): 118–25; Glenn Fowler, "Trade Center Still a Target," *New York Times* (December 7, 1969), VIII: 1, 4; "World's Tallest Towers Begin to Show Themselves on New York City Skyline," *Engineering News-Record* 184 (January 1, 1970): 26–27; "Part of the Skyline," *Architectural Forum* 132 (May 1970): 6; Richard Blodgett, "Is the World Trade Center Worth All the Problems It's Causing New York?" *New York* 3 (September 7, 1970): 30–33; "Cleaning Army in Training for World Trade Center," *Real Estate Record and Guide* 206 (November 7, 1970): 2; Ada Louise Huxtable, "Concept Points to 'City of Future,'" *New York Times* (December 6, 1970), VIII: 1, 7; "White Elephant Herd," *Newsweek* 77 (February 8, 1971): 76, 80; "Construction's Man of the Year: World Trade Center's Ray Monti," *Engineering News-Record* 186 (February 11, 1971): 24–25, 27–28; Richard Oliver, "The City Politic: A Modest Housing Proposal," *New York* 4 (March 1, 1971): 8–9; "The Port Authority Battles Its Critics," *Business Week* (April 3, 1971): 48–51; Ada Louise Huxtable, "Anyone Dig the Art of Building," *New York Times* (April 11, 1971), II: 26, reprinted as "Art and Theory: Architecture in the 1970s," in Ada Louise Huxtable, *Kicked a Building Lately?* (New York: Quadrangle/New York Times Book Co., 1976), 42–44; Robert Gannon, "Topping Out the World's Tallest Building," *Popular Science* 198 (May 1971): 82–83, 117; William H. Jordy, *American Buildings and*

Their Architects: The Impact of European Modernism in the Mid-Twentieth Century, vol. 4 (Garden City, N.Y.: Doubleday & Co., 1972), 6–7; "Two Tall Towers for World Trade," *Life* 72 (March 31, 1972): 58–61; Edith Iglauer, "Our Local Correspondents: The Biggest Foundation," *New Yorker* 48 (November 4, 1972): 130, 132, 136–40, 142–51; Leslie E. Robertson, "Heights We Can Reach," *Journal of the American Institute of Architects* 59 (January 1973): 25–30; Suzanne Stephens, "W.T.C. 2023," *Architectural Forum* 138 (April 1973): 56–61; Ada Louise Huxtable, "Big but Not So Bold: Trade Center Towers Are Tallest, but Architecture Is Smaller in Scale," *New York Times* (April 5, 1973): 34, reprinted in Huxtable, *Kicked a Building Lately?*, 122–23; Sally Helgesen, "The World Trade Center," *Village Voice* 18 (April 19, 1973): 9–10; "World Trade Center Dedicated in New York City," *Architectural Record* 153 (May 1973): 36; Ada Louise Huxtable, "Innovative Design and Planning Take Shape in Lower Manhattan," *New York Times* (June 8, 1973): 41, 48; "Il World Trade Center a New York," *Domus* 524 (July 1973): 1–3; Douglas Davis, "Towers of Mammon," *Newsweek* 82 (July 2, 1973): 56; Ada Louise Huxtable, "New Custom House: Modern, Functional, No Match for the Old," *New York Times* (October 4, 1973): 47, 90, reprinted as "Dilemmas: An Exercise in Cultural Shock," in Huxtable, *Kicked a Building Lately?*, 262–66; *Minoru Yamasaki: A Retrospective*, exhibition catalogue (Rochester, Mich.: Meadow Brook Art Gallery, 1974), cover, 2, 18; Jean-Michel Folon, "Footnote," cartoon, *Architecture Plus* 1 (January–February 1974): 116; Olga Gueft, "The Port Authority's 20 Acres," *Interiors* 133 (February 1974): 88–93; Gerald Allen, "The World Trade Center," *Architectural Record* 155 (March 1974): 140–42; "Proposal for Manhattan Skyline: World Trade Center," *Architectural Design* 44 (August 1974): 465–66; Grace Lichtenstein, "Stuntman, Eluding Guards, Walks a Tightrope between Trade Center Towers," *New York Times* (August 8, 1974): 20; "High Wire Artist Chooses World Trade Center," *Architectural Record* 157 (September 1974): 35; Peter Blake, "News +," *Architecture Plus* 2 (September–October 1974): 37; Carter C. Osterbind, "Engineering Projects," *Britannica Book of the Year* (Chicago: Encyclopaedia Britannica, 1975): 279; "Vertical Transport Systems Get TLC at WTC," *Buildings* 69 (February 1975): 60–63; "World Trade Center to Get Sprinklers," *Engineering News-Record* 193 (February 27, 1975): 11; C. Ray Smith, "Fast Construction for Fast Food Site," *Interiors* 134 (March 1975): 74–76; "World Trade Center, New York," *L'Architecture d'Aujourd'hui* 178 (March 1975): 7–16; Olga Gueft, "Acre in the Sky," *Interiors* 135 (July 1975): 60–61; "Trade-Offs," *New York* 8 (July 21, 1975): 56–57; "The Talk of the Town: Unfinished Business," *New Yorker* 51 (December 22, 1975): 31; Alison Sky and Michelle Stone, *Unbuilt America* (New York: McGraw-Hill, 1976), 123; Peter Blake, "The Eighth Annual Cityscape Awards," *New York* 9 (January 12, 1976): 55–58; Ada Louise Huxtable, "A Skyscraper Fit for a King (Kong)?" *New York Times* (February 1, 1976), II: 31, reprinted as "The Near Past: Reflections on the Near Past," in Huxtable, *Kicked a Building Lately?*, 278–80; Gael Greene, "The Most Spectacular Restaurant in the World," *New York* 9 (May 31, 1976): 43–53; Paul Goldberger, "Its Lush Interior Is Stylish," *New York Times* (June 24, 1976): 28; "Windows on the World at World Trade Center," *Progressive Architecture* 57 (September 1976): 32, 42; Michael Ruby with Pamela Lynn Abraham, "Windows on the World," *Newsweek* 88 (September 6, 1976): 47; Thomas Meehan, "The World Trade Center: Does Mega-Architecture Work?" *Horizon* 18 (autumn 1976): 4–15; Dorothy Seiberling, "Calder City," *New York* 9 (October 18, 1976): 82; "Manufacturers Go Ape Over 'Kong,'" *New York* 9 (October 18, 1976): 87; Sherman R. Emery, "The Power of Design," editorial, *Interior Design* 47 (December 1976): 101; "Windows on the World," *Interior Design* 47 (December 1976): 102–27; John Simon, "Ape Rape," *New York* 9 (December 27, 1976): 79–82; Leonard I. Ruchelman, *The World Trade Center: Politics and Policies of Skyscraper Development* (Syracuse, N.Y.: Syracuse University Press, 1977); C. Ray Smith, *Supermannerism: New Attitudes in Post-Modern Architecture* (New York: E. P. Dutton, 1977), 69; "New York: A Star Is Born," *Architecture Intérieure* 162 (October–November 1977): 62–67; Robert F. R. Ballard, *Directory of Manhattan Office Buildings* (New York: McGraw-Hill, 1978), 118–19; Pamela Jones, *Under the City Streets* (New York: Holt, Rinehart and Winston, 1978), 243–47; White and Willensky, *AIA Guide* (1978), 24–25; Leonard I. Ruchelman, "The New York World Trade Center in Perspective," *Urbanism Past and Present* 6 (summer 1978): 29–30, 33–38; Paul Goldberger, *The City Observed: New York* (New York: Random House, 1979), 10–11; Manfredo Tafuri and Francesco Dal Co, *Modern Architecture*, trans. Robert Erich Wolf (New York: Harry N. Abrams, 1979), 308–10; John Tauranac, *Essential New York* (New York: Holt, Rinehart and Winston, 1979), 237–39; Minoru Yamasaki, *A Life in Architecture* (New York: Weatherhill, 1979), 32–33, 112–28; Paul Goldberger, *The Skyscraper* (New York: Alfred A. Knopf, 1981), 126–29; Ada Louise Huxtable, *The Tall Building Artistically Reconsidered: The Search for a Skyscraper Style* (New York: Pantheon Books, 1982), 117; Donald Martin Reynolds, *The Architecture of New York City* (New York: Macmillan, 1984), 158–59; Steven Ruttenbaum, *Mansions in the Clouds: The Skyscraper Palazzi of Emery Roth* (New York: Balsam Press, 1986), 196–97, 205, 207–8; Alessandro Anselmi, *Vertical Architecture*, trans. Alessandra Latour (New York: New York Chapter, American Institute of Architects, 1987); Anthony Robins, *The World Trade Center* (Englewood, Fla.: Pineapple Press; Fort Lauderdale, Fla.: Omnigraphics, 1987); Richard David Story, "The Buildings New Yorkers Love to Hate," *New York* 20 (June 15, 1987): 33; Margot Gayle and Michele Cohen, *The Art Commission and the Municipal Art Society Guide to Manhattan's Outdoor Sculpture* (New York: Prentice Hall Press, 1988), 29–33; "The World Trade Center at 20," *Real Estate Forum* 46 (January 1991): 95–96.

3. David Rockefeller quoted in "The Talk of the Town: David Rockefeller": 15–17.

4. For Clinton & Russell's 1908 Hudson Terminal, see Stern, Gilmartin and Massengale, *New York 1900*, 45.

5. Minoru Yamasaki quoted in "Yamasaki in Manhattan": 13.

6. Minoru Yamasaki quoted in Huxtable, "Pools, Domes, Yamasaki—Debate": 158.

7. Minoru Yamasaki quoted in "World's Biggest Skyscrapers Have New York Up in the Air": 118–21.

8. Huxtable, "Pools, Domes, Yamasaki—Debate": 36, 158.

9. For Walker & Gillette's 1935 branch for the East River Savings Bank, see Stern, Gilmartin and Mellins, *New York 1930*, 184–85. For Saks Fifth Avenue, see Stern, Gilmartin and Mellins, *New York 1930*, 317–18.

10. "Onward & Upward": 46.

11. Gueft, "The Port Authority's 20 Acres": 88.

12. Minoru Yamasaki quoted in "Towers Rise—Records Fall": 59.

13. Quoted in "Towers Rise—Records Fall": 59.

14. The Class of Architectural Design 112X, The City College of New York, "Students Decry Yama's Twin Towers": 8.

15. For Cass Gilbert's Custom House, see Stern, Gilmartin and Massengale, *New York 1900*, 74–77.

16. Huxtable, "Who's Afraid of the Big, Bad Buildings?": 13–14.

17. Yamasaki, *A Life in Architecture*, 118.

18. "Reviewing the Trade Center": 46.

19. Huxtable, "Big but Not So Bold: Trade Center Towers Are Tallest, but Architecture Is Smaller in Scale": 34.

20. Philippe Petit quoted in "High Wire Artist Chooses World Trade Center": 35. Also see Lichtenstein, "Stuntman, Eluding Guards, Walks a Tightrope between Trade Center Towers": 20.

21. "The Talk of the Town: Unfinished Business": 31.

22. Greene, "The Most Spectacular Restaurant in the World": 43–44.

23. Meehan, "The World Trade Center: Does Mega-Architecture Work?": 11.

24. Glenn Collins quoted in Meehan, "The World Trade Center: Does Mega-Architecture Work?": 11.

25. See Iglauer, "Our Local Correspondents: The Biggest Foundation": 130, 132, 136–40, 142–51.

26. Harold A. Caparn, "Battery Park Plan Proposed," letter to the editor, *New York Times* (April 1, 1941): 22. Also see Charles Platt, "Battery Plan Held Impracticable," letter to the editor, *New York Times* (April 19, 1941): 14.

27. "Group Will Guide Downtown Plans," *New York Times* (June 25, 1956): 25.

28. Downtown–Lower Manhattan Association, *Lower Manhattan: Recommended Land Use, Redevelopment Areas, Traffic Improvements* (New York, 1958); Charles Grutzner, "Plan to Rebuild Downtown Area Outlined to City," *New York Times* (October 15, 1958): 1, 42; "A New Downtown Manhattan," editorial, *New York Times* (October 15, 1958): 38; "Billion-Dollar Planner: David Rockefeller," *New York Times* (October 15, 1958): 42; "Text of Recommendations for Rebuilding 564-Acre District of Lower Manhattan," *New York Times* (October 15, 1958): 42; "New Life for Lower Manhattan," *Business Week* (October 18, 1958): 32, 34; "New Face for Lower New York," *Engineering News-Record* 161 (October 23, 1958): 77; "City Hall Favors Bay Ridge Route," *New York Times* (October 24, 1958): 35; "News Bulletins," *Progressive Architecture* 39 (November 1958): 38; Paul Crowell, "Downtown Renewal Gets City's Backing," *New York Times* (January 22, 1959): 1, 18; Charles G. Bennett, "Downtown Plan Approved by City," *New York Times* (January 23, 1959): 27; Charles G. Bennett, "Planners Revise Downtown Aims," *New York Times* (April 23, 1959): 1, 14; Charles G. Bennett, "Fulton St. Change Leads to Clash," *New York Times* (May 7, 1959): 35; "Downtown Plan Gains," *New York Times* (October 9, 1959): 31; "East River Waterfront," editorial, *New York Times* (November 17, 1959): 34; David Rockefeller, "Development of City's Piers," letter to the editor, *New York Times* (November 23, 1959): 30.

29. Wylie F. L. Tuttle quoted in "Wylie Tuttle Warns of Strangulation in Financial District," *Real Estate Record and Guide* 184 (October 10, 1959): 2–3.

30. Jim Stratton, *Pioneering in the Urban Wilderness* (New York: Urizen, 1977), 23–24; Paul Taylor, "Love Story," *Connoisseur* 221 (August 1991): 46–51, 94–97; Holland Cotter, "Where City History Was Made, a 50's Group Made Art History," *New York Times* (January 5, 1993), C: 11, 16.

31. Jack Youngerman quoted in Stratton, *Pioneering in the Urban Wilderness*, 24.

32. John Cage quoted in Taylor, "Love Story": 94.

33. Ada Louise Huxtable, *Classic New York: Georgian Gentility to Greek Elegance* (New York: Doubleday, 1964).

34. Charles Grutzner, "City Plans to Sell Downtown Land," *New York Times* (October 22, 1958): 37; Charles Grutzner, "Tishman Realty Named Sponsor of Downtown Title I Housing," *New York Times* (August 18, 1959): 18; "Moses' Slum Plan May Evict Brother from Apartment," *New York Times* (April 7, 1960): 37; Charles G. Bennett, "Renewal Mapped in City Hall Area," *New York Times* (September 29, 1960): 1, 28; "2 Huge Projects Win U.S. Approval," *New York Times* (November 8, 1960): 31; Martin Arnold, "Luxury Housing Limited by City," *New York Times* (March 8, 1962): 1, 24.

35. "Greenwald Getting Nod for N.Y. Title I Job," *Architectural Forum* 106 (March 1957): 7.

36. "Greenwald Getting Nod for N.Y. Title I Job": 7.

37. "Moses to Submit Battery Slum Clearance and Housing Program Today," *New York Times* (January 19, 1959): 1, 18.

38. "Slabs in New York; Slabs in Chicago," *Progressive Architecture* 43 (February 1962): 46–47; *Ludwig Mies van der Rohe*, exhibition catalogue (Berlin: Akademie der Kunste, 1968), 122–23; Philip C. Johnson, *Mies van der Rohe*, 3rd rev. ed. (New York: Museum of Modern Art, 1978), 216; David Spaeth, *Mies van der Rohe* (New York: Rizzoli International Publications, 1985), 134.

39. Ebasco Services, Inc.; Moran, Proctor, Mueser & Ruttledge; and Eggers and Higgins, *The Port of New York. Comprehensive Economic Study: Manhattan North River Development Plan, 1962 to 2000* (New York: Department of Marine and Aviation, 1962); George Horne, "670-Million, 40-Year Waterfront Plan to Alter West Side Is Urged by Mayor," *New York Times* (April 26, 1963): 1, 18; "A Dream Maybe, but a Good One," editorial, *New York Times* (April 26, 1963): 34; "40-Year Plan for New York Riverfront," *Progressive Architecture* 44 (June 1963): 63; "Hudson River Waterfront Development," *Architectural Record* 134 (August 1963): 12; Ann L. Buttenweiser, *Manhattan Water-Bound: Planning and Developing Manhattan's Waterfront from the Seventeenth Century to the Present* (New York: New York University Press, 1987), 219.

40. *"Battery Park City": New Living Space for New York* (New York, 1966); Steven V. Roberts, "Governor Urges 'City' at Battery," *New York Times* (May 13, 1966): 1, 30; "Battery Park City," editorial, *New York Times* (May 13, 1966): 40; "Rock for the Hudson," *Progressive Architecture* 47 (June 1966): 54, 58; Herbert L. Smith, Jr., "The Changing Job to Be Done," *Architectural Record* 140 (July 1966): 230; "Back to the Waterfront: Chaos or Control?" *Progressive Architecture* 47 (August 1966): 128–39; "Political Planning," *Architectural Forum* 125 (October 1966): 31; Peter Blake, "New York: Towards a New Venice," *New York* 4 (July 10, 1971): 24–33; *The New York City Waterfront: Comprehensive Planning Workshop* (New York: New York City Planning Commission, 1974), 22–31, 91, 94; Richard Baiter, *Lower Manhattan Waterfront* (New York: Office of Lower Manhattan Development, 1975), 9–11, 39–61, 90–113; Alexander Cooper Associates, *Battery Park City: Draft Summary Report and 1979 Master Plan* (New York: Battery Park City Authority, 1979); Samuel E. Bleecker, *The Politics of Architecture: A Perspective on Nelson A. Rockefeller* (New York: Rutledge Press, 1981), 115–21; Timothy Gregory Quigley, "Battery Park City: World Financial Center" (Master's thesis, University of Minnesota, 1983); Victoria Newhouse, *Wallace K. Harrison, Architect* (New York: Rizzoli International Publications, 1989), 163–65.

41. Steven V. Roberts, "Battery Will Get Housing and Offices," *New York Times* (April 26, 1968): 1, 60.

42. Ada Louise Huxtable, "Battery Park City, in 3d Plan, Hovers between Dream and a Disaster," *New York Times* (July 14, 1973): 27, 37, reprinted as "Battery Park City: Dream or Disaster?" in Huxtable, *Kicked a Building Lately?*, 118–22.
43. John V. Lindsay quoted in Roberts, "Governor Urges 'City' at Battery": 30.
44. Wallace, McHarg, Roberts, and Todd; Whittlesey, Conklin and Rossant; and Alan M. Voorhees & Associates, *The Lower Manhattan Plan* (New York: New York City Planning Commission, 1966); Ada Louise Huxtable, "City Gets a Sweeping Plan for Rejuvenating Lower Manhattan," *New York Times* (June 22, 1966): 1, 30; "Study Outlines Manhattan Renewal," *Engineering News-Record* 176 (June 30, 1966): 13; "Lower Manhattan Report Provides 'Organizing Concept' for Present and Future Growth," *Architectural Record* 14 (July 1966): 35; "The Future of Lower Manhattan," *Progressive Architecture* 47 (July 1966): 49; Donald Canty, "Framework for Lower Manhattan," *Architectural Forum* 125 (July–August 1966): 48–53; "Back to the Waterfront: Chaos or Control?": 128–39; Wallace Berger, "Plan Review," *Journal of the American Institute of Planners* 33 (July 1967): 284–86; Ian L. McHarg, "Manhattan Credits," letter to the editor, *Architectural Forum* 129 (July–August 1968): 15; Jonathan Barnett, *Urban Design as Public Policy* (New York: Architectural Record Books, 1974), 58–67; Baiter, *Lower Manhattan Waterfront*, 6–8.
45. Edith Evans Asbury, "Landfill Urged at Manhattan Tip," *New York Times* (December 30, 1965): 1, 24.
46. Berger, "Plan Review": 285.
47. Steven V. Roberts, "Conflicts Stall Landfill Plans," *New York Times* (January 17, 1967): 42; Charles G. Bennett, "Downtown Plan Chosen by Mayor," *New York Times* (January 18, 1967): 1, 51; Franklin Whitehouse, "A 'Space Needle' Proposed Here," *New York Times* (June 6, 1967): 54; "A Half-Mile-High Needle Proposed in Battery Park," *New York Times* (June 11, 1967), VIII: 12; Steven V. Roberts, "Downtown Plans Reach an Impasse," *New York Times* (October 6, 1967): 21; Steven V. Roberts, "City Wrings Gains from Developers," *New York Times* (October 15, 1967), VIII: 1, 4; Roberts, "Battery Will Get Housing and Offices": 1, 60; "Landfill Compact," *Architectural Forum* 128 (June 1968): 29–30; "Urstadt Is Elected Head of Battery Park Authority," *New York Times* (August 5, 1968): 30; "Realty News: Loan for Battery Project," *New York Times* (September 13, 1968): 78; "Real Estate Notes," *New York Times* (September 23, 1968): 56; "Mayor and Governor View Battery Park Renewal Site," *New York Times* (October 23, 1968): 94; Huxtable, "How to Love the Boom": 34; "Battery Park: Price Vs. Place," *Housing and Planning News* 27 (April–May 1969): 1, 3–4; Ada Louise Huxtable, "Plan's Total Concept Is Hailed," *New York Times* (April 17, 1969): 49; "New City at the Battery," editorial, *New York Times* (April 21, 1969): 46; "City Within a City," *Newsweek* 73 (April 28, 1969): 62; "Making Manhattan Bigger," *Architectural Forum* 130 (June 1969): 102–3; "Will You Be Living Here in 1974?" advertisement, *New York Times* (June 5, 1969): 38; "Planners' Busiest Day," *Housing and Planning News* 27 (summer 1969): 1, 4; David K. Shipler, "Battery Park City Plans Scored and Praised at Public Hearing," *New York Times* (July 17, 1969): 50; Glenn Fowler, "Lower Manhattan Plan Is a Sometime Thing," *New York Times* (August 10, 1969), VIII: 1, 7; "Manhattan Battery Park City," *AD* 39 (December 1969): 673–76; "Battery Park City Authority Selects Two Consultants," *New York Times* (November 1, 1970): 44; Ada Louise Huxtable, "Architecture: How Not to Build a City," *New York Times* (November 22, 1970), II: 25; "A 'People Mover' Being Considered to Link Subways," *New York Times* (March 24, 1971): 33.
48. Huxtable, "Battery Park City, in 3d Plan, Hovers between Dream and a Disaster": 27, 37.
49. Quoted in "City Within a City": 62.
50. Huxtable, "Plan's Total Concept Is Hailed": 49.
51. Huxtable, "Battery Park City, in 3d Plan, Hovers between Dream and a Disaster": 27, 37.
52. Alan S. Oser, "Battery Park City Presses On without Office Lessee," *New York Times* (February 21, 1971), VIII: 1; "Office Slow but Developments Go," *Housing and Planning News* 29 (summer 1971): 3–4; Blake, "New York: Towards a New Venice": 24–33; Edith Evans Asbury, "Housing Progress Called a Record," *New York Times* (July 16, 1971): 63; "A New Town in Town," *Newsweek* 78 (July 19, 1971): 40–41; Alan S. Oser, "Developer Named for Battery City," *New York Times* (February 2, 1972): 1, 48; "Battery Park City," editorial, *New York Times* (February 25, 1972): 38; Francis X. Clines, "Sponsors of Battery Park City Seek to Cut Number of Low-Income Units," *New York Times* (June 29, 1972): 30; "Battery City Move Assailed by Sutton," *New York Times* (June 30, 1972): 24; Max H. Seigel, "Planners Cut Low-Income Units in Battery Park City Proposal," *New York Times* (July 13, 1972): 38.
53. Huxtable, "Battery Park City, in 3d Plan, Hovers between Dream and a Disaster": 27, 37.
54. Robert E. Tomasson, "Battery Park City to Begin Building, but Cautiously," *New York Times* (July 15, 1973), VIII: 1, 10; John Darnton, "Yet Another Plan for Battery City," *New York Times* (August 8, 1973): 39.
55. Huxtable, "Battery Park City, in 3d Plan, Hovers between Dream and a Disaster": 27, 37.
56. "Enhancement of the Cityscape," *Design & Environment* 6 (summer 1975): 15–16.
57. Joseph P. Fried, "Building of Battery Park City Finally Starts," *New York Times* (September 21, 1974): 1, 26; Paul Goldberger, "Dispute Over Battery Park City Project Pits Architects Vs. Planners Vs. Developers," *New York Times* (November 26, 1974): 41, 52; "6-Hour Shift Asked on Battery Project," *New York Times* (March 13, 1975): 49; Maurice Carroll, "Authority Delays Action on Battery Park Housing," *New York Times* (April 16, 1975): 45; Glenn Fowler, "Battery Park City Asks F.H.A. to Provide Mortgage Insurance," *New York Times* (September 24, 1975): 48; "Battery Park City in Poll Finds 8,500 Are Still Interested," *New York Times* (December 1, 1975): 33; Ada Louise Huxtable, "Splendor Overcomes Snafu in Battery Park City," *New York Times* (July 25, 1976), II: 24.
58. Goldberger, "Dispute Over Battery Park City Project Pits Architects Vs. Planners Vs. Developers": 41, 52.
59. Huxtable, "Splendor Overcomes Snafu in Battery Park City": 24.
60. "Évolution des modes de construction: Moshe Safdie," *L'Architecture d'Aujourd'hui* 39 (September 1968): 46–52; "New York Habitat Scheme II," *Zodiac* 19 (1969): 182–89; Moshe Safdie, *Beyond Habitat* (Cambridge, Mass.: MIT Press, 1970), 187–91; Moshe Safdie, *For Everyone a Garden* (Cambridge, Mass.: MIT Press, 1974), 100–111.
61. Safdie, *Beyond Habitat*, 189–91.
62. Safdie, *Beyond Habitat*, 190–91.
63. John Corry, "Origin of Downtown Project Tied to Variety of Sources," *New York Times* (April 13, 1972): 48; Ada Louise Huxtable, "Environment Key to Downtown Plan," *New York Times* (April 13, 1972): 48; David K. Shipler, "Massive Complex Planned for Platform in East River," *New York Times* (April 13, 1972): 1, 48; "$1.2 Billion Privately Financed Development for Lower Manhattan," *Architectural Record* 151 (May 1972): 38; "River Housing Proposed," *Citizens' Housing and Planning News* 30 (June 1972): 1, 4; "New York's Manhattan Landing Project Gets First Okay," *Progressive Architecture* 53 (August 1972): 29; Tomasson, "Battery Park City to Begin Building, but Cautiously": 1, 10; Baiter, *Lower Manhattan Waterfront*, 10–11, 38–61.
64. "$1.2 Billion Privately Financed Development for Lower Manhattan": 38.
65. John V. Lindsay quoted in "$1.2 Billion Privately Financed Development for Lower Manhattan": 38.
66. Huxtable, "Environment Key to Downtown Plan": 48.
67. Huxtable, "Environment Key to Downtown Plan": 48.
68. "River Housing Proposed": 4.
69. "Big Board Studying New Sites Outside Proposed Trade Center," *New York Times* (October 20, 1961): 43.
70. "Stock Exchange Spurs New Home," *New York Times* (April 2, 1963): 30; "The New Stock Exchange," editorial, *New York Times* (April 9, 1963): 30; Ada Louise Huxtable, "Architecture Stumbles On," *New York Times* (April 14, 1963), II: 23; "Preliminary Proposal for N.Y. Stock Exchange," *Progressive Architecture* 44 (May 1963): 71.
71. "Preliminary Proposal for N.Y. Stock Exchange": 71.
72. For John Quincy Adams Ward and Paul Bartlett's pediment, see Stern, Gilmartin and Massengale, *New York 1900*, 144, 187, 189; Gayle and Cohen, *The Art Commission and the Municipal Art Society Guide to Manhattan's Outdoor Sculpture*, 26.
73. "The New Stock Exchange," *New York Times*: 30.
74. "New Plan Rejected for Stock Exchange," *New York Times* (July 31, 1963): 34; William Zeckendorf with Edward McCreary, *The Autobiography of William Zeckendorf* (New York: Holt, Rinehart and Winston, 1970), 276–79.
75. Zeckendorf with McCreary, *The Autobiography of William Zeckendorf*, 276.
76. Zeckendorf with McCreary, *The Autobiography of William Zeckendorf*, 276.
77. Zeckendorf with McCreary, *The Autobiography of William Zeckendorf*, 276–77. Also see "Technology: Will Hanging Tower Attract Exchange?" *Architectural Forum* 118 (March 1963): 116.
78. William Zeckendorf quoted in Elizabeth M. Fowler, "Zeckendorf Dream Now 'A Lost Cause,'" *New York Times* (September 24, 1963): 51, 53. Also see Dudley Dalton, "Exchange Move Causes a Flurry," *New York Times* (June 16, 1965), VIII: 1, 10.
79. Ada Louise Huxtable, "Upheaval at Battery," *New York Times* (October 10, 1963): 53.
80. "The New Stock Exchange," *New York Times*: 30.
81. Huxtable, "Upheaval at Battery": 53.
82. D. Jeanne Graham, "Cry for Quality Sounded in Manhattan," *Progressive Architecture* 44 (November 1963): 82.
83. Huxtable, "Upheaval in Battery": 53.
84. Quoted in Robert E. Tomasson, "Suit Attacks City on Exchange Site," *New York Times* (June 4, 1964): 39.
85. Raymond Schaffer quoted in Robert E. Tomasson, "City Is Accused of Battery Deal," *New York Times* (July 16, 1965): 28. Also see "John P. McGrath, Sol G. Atlas & New York Stock Exchange Named as Defendants in Land Suit," *Real Estate Record and Guide* 196 (July 24, 1965): 2–3; Steven V. Roberts, "City Moves Alter Plan for Battery," *New York Times* (June 12, 1966), VIII: 1, 16.
86. "SOM Named to Design New York Stock Exchange," *Architectural Record* 138 (October 1965): 36.
87. Robert Alden, "Lindsay Offers Income Tax Plan, Asks 50% Increase in Stock Levy; Exchange Threatens to Quit City," *New York Times* (March 4, 1966): 1, 18. Also see "Stock Exchange on Rollers," *New York Times* (March 5, 1966): 26.
88. Vartanig G. Vartan, "Exchange Drops Plan to Build Here in Dispute Over Stock Tax," *New York Times* (March 18, 1966): 1, 55; Vartanig G. Vartan, "2 States Send Governors Here to Try to Lure Stock Exchange," *New York Times* (March 26, 1966): 13.
89. Russell Baker, "Observer: No Nirvana in Hoboken," *New York Times* (March 13, 1966), IV: 10.
90. Richard Mooney, "Big Board Agrees to Remain in City," *New York Times* (July 21, 1966): 1, 48; Terence Smith, "Moses Urges Hudson Fill as a Stock Exchange Site," *New York Times* (December 7, 1966): 1, 63; Terry Robards, "Big Board Approves a Move to East River," *New York Times* (March 21, 1969): 65, 71; "New Stock Exchange Building to Rise from East River Landfill," *Progressive Architecture* 50 (May 1969): 47.
91. "Big Board Is Offered Trade Center Space," *New York Times* (February 17, 1977): 58.

Chapter 4
Greenwich Village and SoHo

GREENWICH VILLAGE

1. Kenneth Tynan, *Tynan Right and Left* (New York: Atheneum, 1967), 391.
2. For general discussions of Greenwich Village during the postwar period, see Clementene Wheeler, ed. , *Greenwich Village Guide* (New York: Bryan, 1947); Berenice Abbott and Henry Wysham Lanier, *Greenwich Village: Today & Yesterday* (New York: Harper, 1949); Ned Polsky, "The Village Beat Scene: Summer 1960," *Dissent* 8 (summer 1961): 339–59; Marc D. Schleifer, "The Village," *Dissent* 8 (summer 1961): 360–65; Anthony J. Camisa, "Greenwich Village: The Anatomy of a Community" (Master's thesis, Columbia University Graduate School of Architecture and Planning, 1967); Edmund T. Delaney, *New York's Greenwich Village* (Barre, Mass. : Barre, 1968); R. David Corwin, Jerome Krase and Paula Hudis, *Greenwich Village: Statistical Trends and Observations* (New York: New York University Press, 1969); Edmund T. Delaney and Charles Lockwood, *Greenwich Village: A Photographic Guide* (New York: Dover, 1976); Terry Miller, *Greenwich Village and How It Got That Way* (New York: Crown, 1990); Rick Beard and Leslie Cohen Berlowitz, eds., *Greenwich Village: Culture and Counterculture* (New York: Museum of the City of New York, 1993).
3. William Barrett, "The Village: Bohemia Gone Bourgeois," *New York Times* (April 4, 1954), VI: 19–20, 22.
4. Frank W. Crane, "Rhinelanders Will Stay in Realty Despite Sale of Old Home Site," *New York Times* (December 24, 1944), VIII: 1. For MacDougal Alley, see Stern, Gilmartin and Mellins, *New York 1930*, 426–27.
5. For One Fifth Avenue, see Stern, Gilmartin and Mellins, *New York 1930*, 400, 402.
6. "The Talk of the Town: Siegel's Dream," *New Yorker* 20 (January 13, 1945): 15–16.
7. "Against the Rootless," *Architectural Forum* 82 (April 1945): 12, 16.

8. "Against the Rootless": 12.

9. Morris L. Ernst quoted in "Against the Rootless": 12.

10. Joseph Siegel quoted in "The Talk of the Town: Siegel's Dream": 15.

11. Robert Moses quoted in "Against the Rootless": 16.

12. Joseph Siegel quoted in "Against the Rootless": 16. Also see "Oppose Park Re-Zoning," *New York Times* (May 9, 1945): 35.

13. "Wreckers Start Razing Rhinelander Buildings," *New York Times* (November 1, 1945): 34.

14. Lee E. Cooper, "Apartment Project to Replace Historic Washington Sq. Homes," *New York Times* (January 4, 1950): 1, 28; "Cribbage on Washington Square," *Interiors* 109 (February 1950): 10.

15. Samuel Rudin quoted in Cooper, "Apartment Project to Replace Historic Washington Sq. Homes": 28. Also see R. B. Cutler, "Styles in Architecture," letter to the editor, *New York Times* (January 30, 1956): 16.

16. "6-Story Top Sought Around All Parks," *New York Times* (April 7, 1950): 27; "Limit on Buildings Backed by Moses," *New York Times* (April 12, 1950). The amendments were intended to limit the height of buildings around all city parks of fifteen acres or less.

17. "Square Rezoning Opposed," *New York Times* (April 24, 1950): 27. Subsequent resolutions for preservation were introduced in the U. S. Congress by Senator Herbert H. Lehman and Representative Frederic R. Coudert, Jr. See John A. Bradley, "New 19-Story Village Apartment to Have Old-Style Front on Square," *New York Times* (March 4, 1951): 1, 72.

18. "Compromise Ends Row Over Square," *New York Times* (May 11, 1950): 31; Bradley, "New 19-Story Village Apartment to Have Old-Style Front on Square": 1, 72; "Final Plan of Washington Square Block to Provide Suites for 346 Families," *New York Times* (October 14, 1951), VIII: 1, 8. Also see Nathan Silver, *Lost New York* (Boston: Houghton Mifflin, 1967), 42–43; Landmarks Preservation Commission of the City of New York, *Greenwich Village Historic District Designation Report* (New York, 1969), 118, 142–45; White and Willensky, *AIA Guide* (1978), 66; Paul Goldberger, *The City Observed: New York* (New York: Random House, 1979), 74–75; Steven Ruttenbaum, *Mansions in the Clouds: The Skyscraper Palazzi of Emery Roth* (New York: Balsam Press, 1986), 199.

19. Harvey Wiley Corbett quoted in Bradley, "New 19-Story Village Apartment to Have Old-Style Front on Square": 72.

20. Richard Roth quoted in Bradley, "New 19-Story Village Apartment to Have Old-Style Front on Square": 72.

21. Lee E. Cooper, "Big Apartment with Stores, Offices Planned for Broadway in Village," *New York Times* (September 6, 1950): 1, 36; Maurice Foley, "Apartment Boom Brings Rebirth of Area Near Washington Square," *New York Times* (October 24, 1954), VIII: 1, 8; White and Willensky, *AIA Guide* (1978), 63; Donald Martin Reynolds, *The Architecture of New York City* (New York: Macmillan, 1984), 88–89. For Sailors' Snug Harbor, see Barnett Shepherd, *Sailors' Snug Harbor, 1801–1976* (New York: Snug Harbor Cultural Center in association with the Staten Island Institute of Arts and Sciences, 1979).

22. Cooper, "Big Apartment with Stores, Offices Planned for Broadway in Village": 1, 36.

23. "'Snug Harbor' Plot Taken for Housing," *New York Times* (June 2, 1950): 40; Foley, "Apartment Boom Brings Rebirth of Area Near Washington Square": 1; William Robbins, "Suites Closing In in 'Village' Area," *New York Times* (July 24, 1966): 1, 10.

24. Lee E. Cooper, "Block of Apartments with Stores Leads Plans for 'Village' Changes," *New York Times* (September 24, 1950), VIII: 1, 4; "Ceremonies on Site of Big Apartments," *New York Times* (December 18, 1952): 53.

25. Foley, "Apartment Boom Brings Rebirth of Area Near Washington Square": 8.

26. Foley, "Apartment Boom Brings Rebirth of Area Near Washington Square": 1.

27. Lee E. Cooper, "Apartments to Rise on Brevoort's Site," *New York Times* (January 11, 1952): 23; "Hotel Brevoort to Be Demolished for Tall De Luxe Apartment Building," *Real Estate Record and Guide* 169 (January 19, 1952): 3. For the Hotel Brevoort, see Silver, *Lost New York*, 42; *Greenwich Village Historic District*, 46–47.

28. "Two-Level Garage in the Brevoort Leased for a Ten-Year Term," *Real Estate Record and Guide* 174 (December 4, 1954): 3; "Work Is Speeded on the Brevoort," *New York Times* (July 10, 1955), VIII: 1–2; "Artist Supervises," *Village Voice* 1 (November 23, 1955): 1. Also see *Greenwich Village Historic District*, 46; Thomas E. Norton and Jerry E. Patterson, *Living It Up: A Guide to the Named Apartment Houses of New York* (New York: Atheneum, 1984), 72.

29. "Old Restaurant to Be Revived on Former Brevoort Hotel Site," *New York Times* (January 23, 1955), VIII: 1; "Brevoort Restaurant to Re-open on Old Site at 5th Av. and 8th St.," *Real Estate Record and Guide* 176 (September 17, 1955): 3.

30. Maurice Foley, "Builders Acquire Wanamaker Site," *New York Times* (March 18, 1956), VIII: 1; Garden Housing to Go Up on Old Wanamaker Site," *Village Voice* 1 (March 21, 1956): 1.

31. Huson Jackson, *A Guide to New York Architecture 1650–1952* (New York: Reinhold Publishing Corp., 1952), 13; Alan Burnham, "Last Look at a Structural Landmark," *Architectural Record* 120 (September 1956): 273–79; Silver, *Lost New York*, 168; Margot Gayle and Edmund V. Gillon, Jr., *Cast-Iron Architecture in New York* (New York: Dover, 1974), 160–61. For John Kellum, see Deborah S. Gardner, "John Kellum and the Development of New York, 1840–1875" (Ph.D. diss., Columbia University, 1979). For A. T. Stewart, see P. B. Wight, "A Millionaire's Architectural Investment," *American Architect and Building News* 1 (May 6, 1876): 147–49; Jay E. Cantor, *A Monument of Trade: A. T. Stewart and the Rise of the Millionaire's Mansion in New York* (Charlottesville, Va.: University Press of Virginia, 1975).

32. See Stern, Gilmartin and Massengale, *New York 1900*, 192.

33. Meyer Berger, "About New York," *New York Times* (July 16, 1956): 14. Also see Gene Boyo, "Wanamaker to Close Main Store After 58 Years on Broadway Site," *New York Times* (October 26, 1954): 1, 24; "Store Doomed," *Business Week* (October 30, 1954): 34; "Too Far Downtown," *Newsweek* 44 (November 8, 1954): 72; Milton Bracker, "Bell Tolls Closing of Wanamaker's as Saddened Staff Toils to the End," *New York Times* (December 19, 1954): 1, 71; David W. Dunlap, *On Broadway: A Journey Uptown Over Time* (New York: Rizzoli International Publications, 1990), 106–7.

34. Maurice Foley, "3 Properties Sold by Wanamaker's," *New York Times* (January 27, 1955): 16; "Huge Hard Goods Merchandise Mart to Occupy Former Wanamaker Store Properties in Manhattan," *Real Estate Record and Guide* 175 (May 14, 1955): 3–4; "Former Wanamaker Store Being Modernized," *Real Estate Record and Guide* 175 (June 25, 1955): 3; Maurice Foley, "Store Converted to Office Space," *New York Times* (July 7, 1958): 40.

35. Arthur Weiser quoted in Foley, "Garden Housing to Go Up on Old Wanamaker Site": 1.

36. "Wanamaker Fire Imperils IRT Line; 77 Hurt at Scene," *New York Times* (July 15, 1956): 1, 34; Peter Kihss, "East Side IRT and BMT Knocked Out by Water in Fire at Wanamaker's; 187 Firemen Hurt in 25-Hour Fight," *New York Times* (July 16, 1956): 1, 13; Peter Kihss, "BMT Tie-Up Near Fire Is Over; Full IRT Service on East Side May Take 3 Weeks," *New York Times* (July 17, 1956): 1, 12.

37. Burnham, "Last Look at a Structural Landmark": 273.

38. "20-Story Co-op Is Planned for Old Wanamaker Site," *New York Times* (September 21, 1958), VIII: 11; Thomas W. Ennis, "'Village' in Midst of Building Boom," *New York Times* (April 12, 1959), VIII: 1, 10; White and Willensky, *AIA Guide* (1978), 99.

39. Arthur C. Holden, "Plan for Wanamaker Block," letter to the editor, *New York Times* (January 7, 1959): 32; "Wanamaker Site Wanted for Park," *Village Voice* 4 (January 28, 1959): 2.

40. "Apartment Boom Invades 'Village,'" *New York Times* (November 22, 1959), VIII: 1, 4. Also see Ennis, "'Village' in Midst of Building Boom": 1, 10; "'Village' Facing Apartment Boom," *New York Times* (August 2, 1959), VIII: 1–2.

41. "Buildings in the News," *Architectural Record* 128 (July 1960): 14; Stephen G. Thompson, "Fiscal Designs for Two Apartments," *Architectural Forum* 113 (December 1960): 84–89; *Greenwich Village Historic District*, 100; Andrew Alpern, *Apartments for the Affluent* (New York: McGraw-Hill, 1975), 136–37; White and Willensky, *AIA Guide* (1978), 76–77; Goldberger, *The City Observed*, 78–79; John Tauranac, *Essential New York* (New York: Holt, Rinehart and Winston, 1979), 210–12; Brent C. Brolin, *Architecture in Context* (New York: Van Nostrand Reinhold, 1980), 76; Barbaralee Diamonstein, *American Architecture Now II* (New York: Rizzoli International Publications, 1985), 46.

42. *Greenwich Village Historic District*, 100.

43. Robbins, "Suites Closing In in 'Village' Area": 10; *Greenwich Village Historic District*, 35, 37.

44. Robbins, "Suites Closing In in 'Village' Area": 1, 10.

45. Robbins, "Suites Closing In in 'Village' Area": 1.

46. New York City Committee on Slum Clearance, *South Village. Slum Clearance Plan Under Title I of the Housing Act of 1949* (New York, 1951); New York City Committee on Slum Clearance, *Washington Square South. Slum Clearance Plan Under Title I of the Housing Act of 1949* (New York, 1951); "Private Financing Sought to Replace 7 City Slum Areas," *New York Times* (January 22, 1951): 1, 26; "New York City Sets the Pace," *American City* 66 (March 1951): 96–97; Robert Moses, *Public Works: A Dangerous Trade* (New York: McGraw-Hill, 1970), 442–43.

47. For the Sullivan-MacDougal Gardens, see Stern, Gilmartin and Mellins, *New York 1930*, 427–28.

48. "Topics of The Times: New Face for the Village," *New York Times* (March 13, 1951): 30.

49. "Another Look at New York City's Redevelopment Plans," *American City* 66 (March 1951): 7.

50. "Housing and Building: Whither the Village?" *Interiors* 111 (August 1951): 10, 12.

51. Edgar Tafel quoted in "Housing and Building: Whither the Village?": 12.

52. Robert Moses quoted in Cleveland Rodgers, *Robert Moses: Builder for Democracy* (New York: Henry Holt & Co., 1952), 275.

53. "Rebuilding the 'Village,'" editorial, *New York Times* (August 26, 1953): 26.

54. New York City Committee on Slum Clearance, *Washington Square Southeast. Slum Clearance Plan Under Title I of the Housing Act of 1949* (New York, 1953).

55. "Two Housing Projects Slated South of Washington Square," *New York Times* (August 24, 1953): 1, 25.

56. "Villagers Attack Proposed Housing," *New York Times* (October 15, 1953): 35.

57. Hortense Gabel quoted in Robert A. Caro, *The Power Broker: Robert Moses and the Fall of New York* (New York: Alfred A. Knopf, 1974), 978.

58. Caro, *The Power Broker*, 978.

59. "'Village' Project to Start in April," *New York Times* (January 28, 1954): 29; "Slum Project Ok'd," *Engineering News-Record* 152 (February 18, 1954): 192, 195–96.

60. "Battle to Block 'South of Square' Project to Go On," *Village Voice* 1 (March 7, 1956): 1, 12.

61. "Berates Sponsors: Moses Attacks Delays in South Village Project," *Village Voice* 1 (June 6, 1956): 1, 3.

62. "New Sponsors Demanded," *Village Voice* 1 (June 6, 1956): 13.

63. "Changing New York—New Vista in 'The Village,'" *Architectural Forum* 107 (September 1957): 42; "News Bulletins," *Progressive Architecture* 38 (September 1957): 101; Ira Henry Freeman, "New Projects Will Change the Face—And the Character—Of the Washington Square Area," *New York Times* (December 8, 1957), VIII: 1, 4; "Officials Laud Washington Square Village at Dedication," *Village Voice* 3 (December 18, 1957): 1–2; "Officials Dedicate Washington Square Village," *Real Estate Record and Guide* 180 (December 21, 1957): 3–4; "Under Construction: Modern Village for Manhattan," *Interiors* 117 (February 1958): 16; "Village Housing Has Unique Features," *Real Estate Record and Guide* 181 (February 15, 1958): 4; "Demolition Continues at Village Housing Site," *Real Estate Record and Guide* 181 (February 22, 1958): 3; "'Village' Apts. to Use Porcelain Facing," *Real Estate Record and Guide* 181 (March 22, 1958): 3; "Bridge Tresses [sic] Span Street in Project's Construction," *Village Voice* 3 (March 26, 1958): 7; "Washington Square Village: A Special Supplement," *Village Voice* 3 (March 26, 1958): 5–6; "Five Decorators Chosen For Washington Sq. Apts.," *Real Estate Record and Guide* 182 (July 19, 1958): 3; "Washington 'Village' Posts Impressive Rental Record," *Real Estate Record and Guide* 182 (August 2, 1958): 5; "High Fashion Apts. on View in S. Village," *Village Voice* 3 (August 13, 1958): 8; "Washington Sq. Village Opens Five Model Apts.," *Real Estate Record and Guide* 182 (August 16, 1958): 4; Olga Gueft, "Washington Square Village Apartments by Five A.I.D. Members," *Interiors* 118 (September 1958): 106–11; "Model Apartments," *Interior Design* 29 (October 1958): 206–9; "Washington Sq. 'Village' Upgrades Pk. South Area," *Real Estate Record and Guide* 182 (October 11, 1958): 4; Olga Gueft, "Avant-Garde Moods in Washington Square Village," *Interiors* 118 (January 1959): 120–23; Pat McDonald, "Washington Square Village Revisited," letter to the editor, *Interiors* 118 (March 1959): 8; "Big City Two-and-a-Half," *Architectural Record* 125 (June 1959): 204–5; "Washington Square Village: Act II," *Interiors* 119 (September 1959): 10, 12; "Washington Square Village, New York," *L'Architecture d'Aujourd'hui* 31 (April 1960): 68–75 (includes statements by Sigfried Giedion and José Luis Sert on "L'Importance du Washington Square Village pour New-York"); "Cities: The Best of Everything," *Time* 75 (June 6, 1960): 20; Ada Louise Huxtable, *Four Walking Tours of Modern Architecture in New York City* (New York: Museum of Modern Art and Municipal Art Society of New York, 1961), 68; "The City: The Upper Depths," *Time* 80 (November 23, 1962): 40;

White and Willensky, *AIA Guide* (1978), 70; Goldberger, *The City Observed*, 77; Michael Sorkin, "Corb in New York," *Village Voice* 32 (October 27, 1987): 109.

64. For Le Corbusier's urban housing proposals see Le Corbusier, *Urbanisme* (Paris: Editions Crés, 1924), published in English as *The City of Tomorrow*, trans. by Frederick Etchells (Cambridge, Mass. : MIT Press, 1971), 232–40. For l'Unité d'Habitation at Marseilles, see W. Boesiger, ed. , *Le Corbusier: Oeuvre complète 1946–1952*, vol. 5 (Zurich: Editions Girsberger, 1955), 193–227.

65. For Josef Hoffmann, see Eduard F. Sekler, *Josef Hoffmann*, trans. by the author (Princeton, N.J.: Princeton University Press, 1985). Also see Stern, Gilmartin and Mellins, *New York 1930*, 469, 473.

66. Gueft, "Avant-Garde Moods in Washington Square Village": 122.

67. McDonald, "Washington Square Village Revisited": 8.

68. Paul Tishman quoted in "Washington Sq. 'Village' Upgrades Pk. South Area": 4.

69. Sigfried Giedion quoted in "Washington Square Village, New York," *L'Architecture d'Aujourd'hui*, trans. Michelle Huot: 68.

70. Moses, *Public Works: A Dangerous Trade*, 454.

71. Mary Perot Nichols, "Washington Square Village: Project Drops Expansion as Renting Slows Down," *Village Voice* 5 (January 6, 1960): 1–2; "Fight Brews Over NYU Bid to Expand Title I Area," *Village Voice* 5 (January 27, 1960): 1, 16; "Lindsay Hits Plan to Switch Title I Property to NYU," *Village Voice* 5 (February 3, 1960): 1; "Washington Sq. Village Didn't Want It. Mayor's Compromise Gives NYU Lion's Share of Title I Property," *Village Voice* 5 (September 22, 1960): 1, 7. In addition, New York University acquired Washington Square Village in 1963, giving it control of the entire Title I project site. See Mary Perot Nichols, "In Greenwich Village, NYU Is Top Landowner, Buys Washington Sq. Village," *Village Voice* 9 (December 26, 1963): 1, 6, 17.

72. "Cities: The Best of Everything": 20.

73. Edith Evans Asbury, "Village Tenants Sue N.Y.U. On Land," *New York Times* (June 24, 1962): 49.

74. Asbury, "Village Tenants Sue N.Y.U. on Land": 49.

75. "The Shopping Center that Failed," *Village Voice* 7 (May 10, 1962): 1.

76. For a brief general history of New York University, see John F. Ohles and Shirley M. Ohles, *Private Colleges and Universities*, vol. II (Westport, Conn.: Greenwood, 1982), 867–70.

77. Ellen Perry, "An Urban Problem: The People Object," *Progressive Architecture* 47 (June 1966): 180–93.

78. "Block in Washington Square South Chosen for N.Y.U. Law School Site," *New York Times* (February 11, 1948): 1, 56; "Town vs. Gown," *Newsweek* 34 (August 15, 1949): 74; Morris Kaplan, "Occupied Building Faces Collapse Next to N.Y.U. Village Demolition," *New York Times* (August 17, 1949): 1, 21; Robert C. Dott, "N.Y.U. Gets Million for Student Hall," *New York Times* (September 16, 1951): 1, 76; "Alice in Wonderland," *Village Voice* 9 (June 25, 1964): 1; White and Willensky, *AIA Guide* (1967), 67–68.

79. White and Willensky, *AIA Guide* (1967), 68.

80. Perry, "An Urban Problem: The People Object": 183.

81. "Almost a Century and a Half Old," *Village Voice* 1 (September 12, 1956): 3; "NYU Expands on 'Square,'" *Village Voice* 2 (March 27, 1957): 1; "Alice in Wonderland": 1.

82. Dott, "N.Y.U. Gets Million for Student Hall": 1, 76; "NYU Expands on 'Square'": 1.

83. "NYU to Build Residence Halls," *Real Estate Record and Guide* 185 (April 2, 1960): 4; "Campus of the Future," *Village Voice* 5 (September 8, 1960): 3; "Alice in Wonderland": 1.

84. "NYU to Build Big Center, So the Tenants of No. 238 Must Move," *Village Voice* 1 (March 28, 1956): 1; Freeman, "New Projects Will Change the Face—And the Character—Of the Washington Square Area": 1, 4; "NYU Plans $35,000,000 Building Program," *Real Estate Record and Guide* 183 (April 25, 1959): 5; "Shape of Things to Come," *Village Voice* 4 (May 6, 1959): 1; "Nation's Largest University Constructing Seven Buildings," *Architectural Record* 126 (September 1959): 186–90; Thomas W. Ennis, "N.Y.U., New School and Cooper Union Are Expanding," *New York Times* (September 20, 1959), VIII: 1, 14; "New Look on Washington Square South," *Village Voice* 5 (November 11, 1959): 1; "Student Center for Big City University," *Architectural Record* 127 (May 1960): 157–62; "N.Y.U.'s Loeb Student Center," *Interiors* 119 (May 1960): 120–25; "Top Designers Choose Plastics: Interior Design Data," *Progressive Architecture* 41 (June 1960): 196–201; Huxtable, *Four Walking Tours of Modern Architecture in New York City*, 68; "Alice in Wonderland": 1; White and Willensky, *AIA Guide* (1967), 67; White and Willensky, *AIA Guide* (1978), 67; Goldberger, *The City Observed*, 76–77; Miller, *Greenwich Village and How It Got That Way*, 70.

85. Thomas B. Hess, "Today's Artists: Nakian," *Portfolio & Art News Annual* 4 (1961): 84–99, 168–72; "'Fledgling Students,'" *Village Voice* 6 (July 6, 1961): 1; Emily Genauer, "Birds Grounded by a Sculptor," *New York Herald Tribune* (July 16, 1961), IV: 6; Dorothy Adlow, "Our Daring Sculptors," *Christian Science Monitor* (September 2, 1961): 10; Howard Conant, "New York University Collection: Nakian," *Art Journal* 21 (fall 1961): cover, 1, 22; Frank O'Hara, *Nakian*, exhibition catalogue (New York: Doubleday, 1966), 44–45; Margot Gayle and Michele Cohen, *The Art Commission and the Municipal Art Society Guide to Manhattan's Outdoor Sculpture* (New York: Prentice Hall Press, 1988), 77.

86. Reuben Nakian quoted in Gayle and Cohen, *The Art Commission and the Municipal Art Society Guide to Manhattan's Outdoor Sculpture*, 77.

87. Ennis, "N.Y.U., New School and Cooper Union Are Expanding": 1.

88. "New Look on Washington Square South": 1.

89. "N.Y.U.'s Loeb Student Center": 120.

90. White and Willensky, *AIA Guide* (1967), 67; White and Willensky, *AIA Guide* (1978), 67; Goldberger, *The City Observed*, 77; Christopher Gray, "Schlock of Ages," *Avenue* 17 (December 1992): 31–32, 34, 36, 38.

91. White and Willensky, *AIA Guide* (1967), 67.

92. White and Willensky, *AIA Guide* (1978), 67.

93. Goldberger, *The City Observed*, 77.

94. "Leading Architect to Design NYU Housing Project," *Village Voice* 6 (December 22, 1960): 1; "NYU Co-op Ups Number of Family-Size Units in Project," *Village Voice* 6 (July 20, 1961): 1; Susan Goodman, "Two 30-Story Buildings Scheduled for NYU Site," *Village Voice* 9 (October 31, 1963): 1; "N.Y.U. Is Preparing Project in 'Village,'" *New York Times* (March 29, 1964), VIII: 1–2; "Ground Broken for NYU Co-op," *Village Voice* 9 (August 20, 1964): 2; "Pei Buildings for N.Y.U. ," *Progressive Architecture* 45 (October 1964): 93; Douglas Haskell, "Ten Buildings that Climax an Era," *Fortune* 74 (December 1966): 156–62; Stephen A. Kurtz, "And Now a Word from the Users. . . . ," *Design & Environment* 2 (spring 1971): 40–49, 64; Stephen A. Kurtz, *Wasteland: Building the American Dream* (New York: Praeger, 1973), 73; Marguerite Villecco, "Housing," *Architecture*

Plus 1 (March 1973): 68–77; White and Willensky, *AIA Guide* (1978), 70; Goldberger, *The City Observed*, 77; Tauranac, *Essential New York*, 221–22; Carter Wiseman, *I. M. Pei: A Profile in American Architecture* (New York: Harry N. Abrams, 1990), 68–69, 307.

95. "New York Picasso," *Architectural Forum* 127 (December 1967): 24–25; "Picasso in New York," *Journal of the American Institute of Architects* 49 (January 1968): 101; "Observing the Arts: Manhattan, '67," *Progressive Architecture* 49 (January 1968): 34, 36; "Larger than Life," *Architectural Forum* 129 (September 1968): 36, 91; "Of Busts and Buildings: Monumental Picasso Comes to Manhattan," *Interiors* 128 (March 1969): 8; Stanley Abercrombie, "Art and Building," *Architecture Plus* 1 (March 1973): 56–57; Frederick Fried and Edmund V. Gillon, Jr., *New York Civic Sculpture* (New York: Dover, 1976), 24; Gayle and Cohen, *The Art Commission and the Municipal Art Society Guide to Manhattan's Outdoor Sculpture*, 79–80.

96. "Alice in Wonderland": 1; "Gigantic Job for Johnson," *Progressive Architecture* 45 (August 1964): 65–66; Terry Ferrer, "Washington Square: 100 Million Drive for New Complex," *New York Herald Tribune* (November 16, 1964): 23; "NYU to Give New Look to East Side of Square," *Village Voice* 10 (November 19, 1964): 3; "Design Unity for N.Y.U. at Washington Square," *Architectural Record* 137 (January 1965): 15; "Johnson, Breuer Build for NYU," *Progressive Architecture* 46 (January 1965): 52, 54; Mary Perot Nichols, "Local Ire Grows Over NYU Library on Square," *Village Voice* 11 (November 18, 1965): 1; Perry, "An Urban Problem: The People Object": 180–93; "June Issue: One Man's Ugliness Is Another Man's Poison," letters to the editor, *Progressive Architecture* 47 (August 1966): 6, 16, 20; "More Reactions to P/A Ugliness Issue," letters to the editor, *Progressive Architecture* 47 (September 1966): 14.

97. "Alice in Wonderland": 1.

98. "Gigantic Job for Johnson": 65–66.

99. Philip Johnson quoted in "Johnson, Breuer Build for NYU": 52.

100. Philip Johnson quoted in Perry, "An Urban Problem: The People Object": 184.

101. Philip Johnson quoted in Perry, "An Urban Problem: The People Object": 184.

102. Philip Johnson quoted in Nichols, "Local Ire Grows Over NYU Library on Square": 1.

103. James M. Hester quoted in Perry, "An Urban Problem: The People Object": 184.

104. Perry, "An Urban Problem: The People Object": 182, 184.

105. "NYU Library Includes Bit of W. Broadway," *Village Voice* 10 (October 14, 1965): 15; "Library Site: NYU's Request for Slice of Street to Be Aired," *Village Voice* 11 (November 4, 1965): 3; Nichols, "Local Ire Grows Over NYU Library on Square": 1; "NYU Library Model Unveiled," *Progressive Architecture* 46 (December 1965): 41; James Lynn, "Mapping the Trouble in the Square," *New York Herald Tribune* (December 5, 1965): 23; Fred Ferretti, "The Fight for NYU Cubic Library," *New York Herald Tribune* (December 8, 1965): 20; Terry Ferrer, "Elmer Bobst, a Self-Taught Man, Gives NYU $6 Million for Library," *New York Herald Tribune* (March 29, 1966): 25; "Universities: Toward Urban Excellence," *Time* 87 (April 1, 1966): 94; Perry, "An Urban Problem: The People Object": 184–88; "City to Hear Pro & Con of NYU Library," *Village Voice* 11 (June 9, 1966): 3; Marlene Nadel, "NYU Attacked: 'Fraud,' Says Mrs. Jacobs, Library Is Not Library," *Village Voice* 11 (June 23, 1966): 3; Marlene Nadel, "NYU Shows Plans to Prove Library Is Really Library," *Village Voice* 11 (June 30, 1966): 3; "June Issue: One Man's Ugliness Is Another Man's Poison": 6; Ellen Perry Berkeley, "NYU and the Naked Emperor," *Progressive Architecture* 47 (October 1966): 248–50; Robert E. Tomasson, "Judge Dismisses Suit to Bar an N.Y.U. Library," *New York Times* (December 30, 1966): 30; "NYU Library Wins Round," *Village Voice* 12 (January 5, 1967): 3; Paul Goldberger, "Form and Procession," *Architectural Forum* 138 (January–February 1973): 32–53; "The Talk of the Town: Background," *New Yorker* 49 (April 14, 1973): 31–33; "The Talk of the Town: Library's Bobst," *New Yorker* 49 (January 21, 1974): 23; C. Ray Smith, *Supermannerism: New Attitudes in Post-Modern Architecture* (New York: E. P. Dutton, 1977), 267–68; White and Willensky, *AIA Guide* (1978), 67; Goldberger, *The City Observed*, 76; Tauranac, *Essential New York*, 233–35; Miller, *Greenwich Village and How It Got That Way*, 75.

106. Jane Jacobs quoted in Perry, "An Urban Problem: The People Object": 184.

107. Philip Johnson quoted in Nichols, "Local Ire Grows Over NYU Library on Square": 1.

108. Berkeley, "NYU and the Naked Emperor": 248.

109. Berkeley, "NYU and the Naked Emperor": 248.

110. "The Talk of the Town: Background": 31.

111. "The Talk of the Town: Background": 31.

112. James M. Hester quoted in Perry, "An Urban Problem: The People Object": 185.

113. Smith, *Supermannerism*, 267–68.

114. Tauranac, *Essential New York*, 234.

115. Goldberger, *The City Observed*, 76.

116. Tauranac, *Essential New York*, 234.

117. For Low Library, see Stern, Gilmartin and Massengale, *New York 1900*, 405–7, 409.

118. Philip Johnson quoted in Goldberger, "Form and Procession": 45.

119. White and Willensky, *AIA Guide* (1978), 67.

120. White and Willensky, *AIA Guide* (1978), 67.

121. White and Willensky, *AIA Guide* (1978), 67.

122. Goldberger, "Form and Procession": 45, 49; White and Willensky, *AIA Guide* (1978), 68.

123. Goldberger, "Form and Procession": 45.

124. "Bard Awards Honor Five Projects," *Architectural Record* 137 (April 1965): 14, 16; "New York's Bard Awards," *Progressive Architecture* 46 (April 1965): 63–64; James T. Burns, Jr., "Notable Design in Greenwich Village," *Progressive Architecture* 46 (April 1965): 216–21; "New Elegance off Washington Square," *Village Voice* 10 (April 1, 1965): 1; "Selected Detail: Warren Weaver Hall," *Progressive Architecture* 46 (September 1965): 174; White and Willensky, *AIA Guide* (1978), 67.

125. Burns, "Notable Design in Greenwich Village": 221.

126. "In the Heart of the City, Room for a Campus," *Architectural Record* 118 (July 1955): 16; "The Architect, the City, and the Nature of Function," *Architectural Record* 128 (July 1960): 15; "Campus in a City Back Yard," *Architectural Forum* 113 (September 1960): 106–9. For Joseph Urban's building, see Stern, Gilmartin and Mellins, *New York 1930*, 108, 115–19.

127. Jerry Tallmer, "Isamu Noguchi: Abstract Sculptor Has Concrete Objective," *Village Voice* 4 (August 5, 1950): 3, 12.

128. John Anderson, "Women's Store into Graduate School," *Interiors* 129 (March 1970): 118–23.

129. Lewis Mumford, "The Sky Line: Fifth Avenue, for Better or Worse," *New Yorker* 28 (August 16, 1952): 56, 58–63.

130. Anderson, "Women's Store into Graduate School": 118–19.

131. Anderson, "Women's Store into Graduate School": 119.

132. "P.S. 41 Unveiled: Modern Building with an Old Touch," *Village Voice* 1 (November 2, 1955): 3; Fred Rosenberg, "Intra-Regional Failures in School Planning," *Planners' Journal* 23 (winter 1957): 49–56; Silver, *Lost New York*, 135.

133. "St. Barnabas House: New Pattern for a Charity Mission," *Architectural Forum* 86 (March 1947): 15; "Mission Shelter Gets Modern Ideas," *Interiors* 106 (April 1947): 12, 14; "Progress Report," *Progressive Architecture* 28 (April 1947): 20; "Welfare Offices and Shelter: New York, N.Y.," *Progressive Architecture* 31 (April 1950): 49–56; "Selected Details. Institution: Exterior Stairs," *Progressive Architecture* 31 (September 1950): 109; "Selected Details. Institution: Entrance Doorway," *Progressive Architecture* 31 (October 1950): 105; Talbot F. Hamlin, ed., *Forms and Functions of Twentieth-Century Architecture*, vol. 4 (New York: Columbia University Press, 1952), 679–80; White and Willensky, *AIA Guide* (1967), 72.

134. "Avant-Garde Playground," *Village Voice* 9 (August 27, 1964): 3.

135. "Toward a New Continuity," *Architectural Forum* 112 (January 1960): 143–50; "Six Structures Win 5th Ave. Awards," *New York Times* (May 22, 1960), VIII: 1, 16; "Wins Awards," *Village Voice* 5 (May 25, 1960): 1; Nicholas Taylor, "Seeking Roots in New York," *Architectural Review* 137 (March 1965): 236–37; White and Willensky, *AIA Guide* (1967), 61; Goldberger, *The City Observed*, 78.

136. Taylor, "Seeking Roots in New York": 236–37.

137. "$4-Million Union Hq. for Village," *Village Voice* 6 (September 14, 1961): 3; "Headquarters Is Made Ready for N.M.U.," *New York Times* (October 13, 1963), VIII: 1; Mary Perot Nichols, "There Are No Angles on the NMU Building," *Village Voice* 9 (May 7, 1964): 1, 19; White and Willensky, *AIA Guide* (1967), 63; White and Willensky, *AIA Guide* (1978), 76–77; Goldberger, *The City Observed*, 81–82; Miller, *Greenwich Village and How It Got That Way*, 146–47.

138. Nichols, "There Are No Angles on the NMU Building": 1.

139. White and Willensky, *AIA Guide* (1967), 63.

140. Goldberger, *The City Observed*, 81–82.

141. "Veterans Memorial Planned for Union Square Park," *New York Times* (June 21, 1962): 33; "Atrocity at Union Square," editorial, *New York Times* (June 29, 1962): 26; Irving N. Fisher, "Veterans' Building Opposed," letter to the editor, *New York Times* (June 30, 1962): 18; "'Monster' for Union Square?" *Progressive Architecture* 43 (August 1962): 58; "It Is Rather for Us the Living. . . ," *Architectural Forum* 117 (September 1962): 9.

142. "'Monster' for Union Square?": 58.

143. "Atrocity at Union Square": 26.

144. "Union Square, Long-Neglected in New York City, Redesigned by Students," *Architectural Record* 154 (September 1973): 35.

145. "Manhattan's Union Square Gets a Much-Needed Face Lifting," *Architectural Record* 159 (May 1976): 35.

146. John Sibley, "Two Blighted Downtown Areas Are Chosen for Urban Renewal," *New York Times* (February 21, 1961): 37; "14-Block Rehabilitation: Huge Renewal Project Planned for West Village," *Village Voice* 6 (February 23, 1961): 1, 6; "CHPC Okays Planning for Renewal, Housing, in West Village Area," *Housing and Planning News* 19 (March–April 1961): 1, 3.

147. Stern, Gilmartin and Mellins, *New York 1930*, 696–98.

148. "Central to Expand Yard," *New York Times* (December 4, 1959): 62; "Freight Yard to Shut," *New York Times* (January 30, 1960): 9; "N. Y. Central Sells West Street Terminal," *New York Times* (April 8, 1960): 52.

149. Sam Pope Brewer, "Architect Tells of 'Village' Plan," *New York Times* (March 5, 1961): 52.

150. Victor Gruen quoted in Brewer, "Architect Tells of 'Village' Plan": 52.

151. See Sam Pope Brewer, "City Reassures 'Village' Group," *New York Times* (March 8, 1961): 28.

152. "W. Villagers Hit 'Renewal' Plan," *Village Voice* 6 (March 2, 1961): 1.

153. Jane Jacobs quoted in Priscilla Chapman, "City Critic in Favor of Old Neighborhoods," *New York Herald Tribune* 120 (March 7, 1961): 16–17.

154. J. R. Goddard, "Villagers Hoot Down Plea for Renewal Plan," *Village Voice* 6 (March 9, 1961): 1–2; "'Village' Group Protests Survey," *New York Times* (March 13, 1961): 31; Mary Perot Nichols, "Local Groups Mobilize Against West Village Renewal Plan," *Village Voice* 6 (March 16, 1961): 1–2; John Sibley, "'Village' Housing a Complex Issue," *New York Times* (March 23, 1961): 35, 39; "City's West Village Project Hit by More Local Groups," *Village Voice* 6 (March 23, 1961): 3.

155. Jane Jacobs quoted in Sam Pope Brewer, "Project Foe Hits 'Village' Group," *New York Times* (March 14, 1961): 26.

156. Charlotte Schwab quoted in "Project Foe Hits 'Village' Group": 26.

157. "CHPC Okays Planning for Renewal, Housing, in West Village Area": 3. Also see Sam Pope Brewer, "Citizens Housing Group Backs 'Village' Urban Renewal Study," *New York Times* (March 27, 1961): 33, 38.

158. Susan Goodman, "Villagers Develop Own Plan for Area," *Village Voice* 29 (May 9, 1963): 1, 7.

159. Richard J. H. Johnston, "'Village' Group Wins Court Stay," *New York Times* (April 28, 1961): 34; "Fight Against Renewal Plan: Mayor Served with Papers, but City Still Eyeing W. Village," *Village Voice* 6 (May 4, 1961): 1, 12.

160. Jane Jacobs quoted in "Fight Against Renewal Plan: Mayor Served Papers, but City Still Eyeing W. Village": 12.

161. Quoted in "City Planners Back Village Renewal," *Village Voice* 6 (May 4, 1961): 1, 7.

162. Charles Grutzner, "New Housing and Industry Suggested on 18 City Sites," *New York Times* (May 1, 1961): 1, 32.

163. "Housing Study and Action," editorial, *New York Times* (May 3, 1961): 36. Also see "Felt Sees Change in Renewal View," *New York Times* (May 9, 1961): 36.

164. Mary Perot Nichols, "Speaks in Village: Felt Pushes 'Renewal,' Gets Hostile Reception," *Village Voice* 6 (May 18, 1961): 1, 6.

165. Rachele Wall, "Housing Policies Assailed," letter to the editor, *New York Times* (May 12, 1961): 28.

166. Mel Most, "Down with Housing, Up with Houses," *Village Voice* 6 (July 6, 1961): 1, 12.

167. Robert F. Wagner quoted in "Wagner Opposes 'Village' Change," *New York Times* (August 18, 1961): 23.

168. Arthur Levitt quoted in J. R. Goddard, "Levitt Outbids Mayor Wagner on 'No Renewal' for W. Village," *Village Voice* 6 (August 24, 1961): 1–2.

169. Carmine DeSapio quoted in "Lefkowitz Vows Fiscal Integrity, Indicating Pay-as-You-Go Policy," *New York Times* (August 20, 1961): 64.

170. Robert F. Wagner quoted in Charles G. Bennett, "Mayor Abandons 'Village' Project," *New York Times* (September 7, 1961): 31, also quoted in "Wagner Dumps W. Village Project on Primary Eve," *Village Voice* 6 (September 14, 1961): 3, 17.

171. Quoted in Edith Evans Asbury, "Plan Board Votes 'Village' Project; Crowd in Uproar," *New York Times* (October 19, 1961): 1, 30.

172. Asbury, "Plan Board Votes 'Village' Project; Crowd in Uproar": 1.

173. Louis DeSalvio quoted in Asbury, "Plan Board Votes 'Village' Project; Crowd in Uproar": 30.

174. Quoted in Edith Evans Asbury, "Deceit Charged in 'Village' Plan," *New York Times* (October 20, 1961): 68. Also see Walter D. Littell, "West Villagers Still on Warpath," *New York Herald Tribune* (October 20, 1961): 8.

175. David Rose quoted in Asbury, "Deceit Charged in 'Village' Plan": 68.

176. Edith Evans Asbury, "Charge of a Deal in Renewal Plan for 'Village' Denied by Architect," *New York Times* (October 22, 1961): 80.

177. Suzanne Stephens, "Low-Rise Lemon," *Progressive Architecture* 57 (March 1976): 54–57.

178. James Kirk quoted in Edith Evans Asbury, "'Village' Project Backed in Fight," *New York Times* (October 21, 1961): 24.

179. James Kirk quoted in Mary Perot Nichols, "West Village Renewal Fight Arouses Ire on Both Sides," *Village Voice* 7 (October 26, 1961): 1, 9.

180. Jane Jacobs quoted in Edith Evans Asbury, "Board Ends Plan for West Village," *New York Times* (October 25, 1961): 39. Also see Edith Evans Asbury, "I.L.A. Aide Scores 'Village' Project," *New York Times* (November 26, 1961): 87.

181. Ira S. Robbins quoted in Mary Perot Nichols, "City Official Blasts West Village Groups," *Village Voice* 7 (November 23, 1961): 1–2.

182. "Felt Cheers, Then Chills W. Village Renewal Project," *Village Voice* 7 (January 4, 1962): 3.

183. James Felt quoted in "West Village Off Slum Map," *Village Voice* 7 (January 18, 1962): 1. Also see "N.Y.C. Housing Official Resigns," *Architectural Forum* 116 (March 1962): 15.

184. Quoted in "Not a Single Sparrow. . . ," *Progressive Architecture* 44 (June 1963): 61. Also see Alexander Burnham, "'Village' Group Designs Housing to Preserve Character of Area," *New York Times* (May 6, 1963): 1, 42; Goodman, "Villagers Develop Own Plan for Area": 1, 7; James J. Kirk, "A New Jane Jacobs?" letter to the editor, *Village Voice* 9 (November 28, 1963): 4; "The West Village Plan for Housing," *Journal of the American Institute of Architects* 43 (May 1965): 66; Leticia Kent, "City Disavows Mr. Z., Affirms Community Plan," *Village Voice* 13 (February 1, 1968): 3; Mary Perot Nichols, "Six Years Later. Village Housing Plan: Unslumming without Tears," *Village Voice* 14 (January 30, 1969): 3, 23–24; "Planner's Busiest Day," *Housing and Planning News* 27 (summer 1969): 4; "The Village Is Saved," *Architectural Forum* 132 (January–February 1970): 92; Stephens, "Low-Rise Lemon": 54–57; White and Willensky, *AIA Guide* (1978), 88; Goldberger, *The City Observed*, 85–86; Richard Plunz, *A History of Housing in New York City* (New York: Columbia University Press, 1990), 308–12.

185. Jane Jacobs quoted in Goodman, "Villagers Develop Own Plan for Area": 7.

186. "Not a Single Sparrow. . . ": 61.

187. Kirk, "A New Jane Jacobs?": 4.

188. Kent, "City Disavows Mr. Z., Affirms Community Plan": 3.

189. William Zeckendorf quoted in Kent, "City Disavows Mr. Z., Affirms Community Plan": 3.

190. *Richard Meier Architect: 1964/1984* (New York: Rizzoli International Publications, 1984), 388–89.

191. Richard Meier quoted in *Richard Meier Architect: 1964/1984*, 389.

192. Woody Klein quoted in Kent, "City Disavows Mr. Z., Affirms Community Plan": 3.

193. "The Village Is Saved": 92.

194. Nichols, "Six Years Later. Village Housing Plan: Unslumming without Tears": 3.

195. "Not a Single Sparrow. . . ": 61.

196. For Howe & Lescaze's Chrystie-Forsyth Street project, see Stern, Gilmartin and Mellins, *New York 1930*, 438–42.

197. Ray Matz quoted in Kent, "Six Years Later. Village Housing Plan: Unslumming without Tears": 3.

198. Quoted in "Planner's Busiest Day": 4.

199. "Planner's Busiest Day": 4.

200. "Housing Plan Faces Test," *Village Voice* 14 (October 2, 1969): 1; "W. Village Plan Is Set Back," *Village Voice* 14 (October 16, 1969): 14.

201. Judith C. Lack, "Dispute Still Rages as West Village Houses Meets Its Sales Test," *New York Times* (August 18, 1974), VIII: 1, 6.

202. Joseph P. Fried, "A 'Village' Housing Project Becomes Fiscal Nightmare," *New York Times* (August 8, 1975): 29–30.

203. Glenn Fowler, "Unsuccessful Cooperative Will Now Offer Rentals," *New York Times* (March 22, 1976): 29.

204. Alan S. Oser, "Upturn for West Village Houses," *New York Times* (August 20, 1976): 18.

205. Stephens, "Low-Rise Lemon": 57.

206. "West Village Renaissance: 500 Artists' Apartments," *Village Voice* 12 (August 10, 1967): 3; "Art City," *Newsweek* 70 (August 21, 1967): 63; "Homes for Artists on New York's Lower West Side," *Interiors* 127 (September 1967): 14; "Bell Lab: Building to Be Sold," *Real Estate Record and Guide* 200 (November 4, 1967): 2–3; "The Talk of the Town: Westbeth," *New Yorker* 44 (June 8, 1968): 26–28; Ron Rosenbaum, "Westbeth Project: Artists Want Space, Not Gracious Living," *Village Voice* 14 (November 13, 1969): 11–12, 62; William Zeckendorf with Edward McCreary, *The Autobiography of William Zeckendorf* (New York: Holt, Rinehart and Winston, 1970), 9–10; "Westbeth's Rehabilitation Project: A Clue to Improving Our Cities," *Architectural Record* 147 (March 1970): 103–6; Ada Louise Huxtable, "Bending the Rules," *New York Times* (May 10, 1970), II: 23; "One of a Kind," *Architectural Forum* 132 (June 1970): 71–72; Peter Blake, "Downtown Dakota," *New York* 3 (August 3, 1970): 54–57; Ellen Perry Berkeley, "Westbeth: Artists in Residence," *Architectural Forum* 133 (October 1970): 44–49; "Westbeth Artists Housing Rehabilitation Project," *Architectural Record* 149 (January 1971): 42; "The 1971 Honor Awards: Westbeth Artists Housing," *Journal of the American Institute of Architects* 55 (June 1971): 50; Annette Kuhn, "Westbeth's in Trouble," *Village Voice* 16 (November 18, 1971): 1, 30–31, 33; "Künstlerhaus 'Westbeth' in New York," *Baumeister* 69 (January 1972): 24–27; Sally Helgesen, "Hard Times at Westbeth: A Mortgage Falls Due," *Village Voice* 17 (June 8, 1972): 3; Sally Helgesen, "Wasting of Westbeth, Strangling of SoHo," *Village Voice* 17 (June 22, 1972): 3, 28; Barbara Rose, "West-

beth: A Great Idea Whose Time May Be Up," *New York* 5 (July 24, 1972): 60; *Richard Meier Architect: Buildings and Projects 1966–1976* (New York: Oxford University Press, 1976), 112–17; Barbaralee Diamonstein, *Buildings Reborn: New Uses, Old Places* (New York: Harper & Row, 1978), 162–63; White and Willensky, *AIA Guide* (1978), 89; Michael Winkelman, "The New Frontier: Housing for the Artist-Industrialist," *New York Affairs* 4, no. 4 (1978): 49–57; Goldberger, *The City Observed*, 86; Norton and Patterson, *Living It Up*, 361; *Richard Meier Architect: 1964/1984*, 106–9; Eve M. Kahn, "Westbeth at 20: Artists' Utopia Still A-Borning," *New York Times* (February 2, 1989), C: 10; Plunz, *A History of Housing in New York City*, 316.

207. Goldberger, *The City Observed*, 86.

208. Rose, "Westbeth: A Great Idea Whose Time May Be Up": 60.

209. Goldberger, *The City Observed*, 86.

210. Eli Waldron, "The New American Capital of Bohemia," *Saturday Evening Post* 237 (May 23, 1964): 98–102. Also see Edmond J. Bartnett, "'Village' Spills Across 3d Ave.," *New York Times* (February 7, 1960), VIII: 1, 5; "'Village' Scene Spreading East," *New York Times* (December 31, 1961): 1–2; Bernard Weinraub,"Renovations on Lower East Side Creating New Quarters," *New York Times* (May 6, 1963), VIII: 1, 3.

211. Bartnett, "'Village' Spills Across 3d Ave.": 1, 5.

212. Weinraub, "Renovations on Lower East Side Creating New Quarters": 3.

213. Sylvan Fox, "The 2 Worlds of the East Village," *New York Times* (June 5, 1967): 31; Paul Hofmann, "Hippies' Hangout Draws Tourists," *New York Times* (June 5, 1967): 31; John Kifner, "The East Village: A Changing Scene for Hippies," *New York Times* (October 11, 1967): 34; "Ukrainians Yield Slowly but Surely to East Village Hippies," *New York Times* (April 28, 1969): 43.

214. "Hoover to Sponsor Cooper Union Plan for Expansion," *Village Voice* 1 (August 1, 1956): 3; "Cooper Union School of Engineering," *Architectural Forum* 105 (November 1956): 25; "Cooper Union for Advancement of Science and Art," *Progressive Architecture* 37 (November 1956): 96; "Cooper Union's Projected Engineering Building," *Village Voice* 1 (December 19, 1956): 2; "From 1859 to 1961," *Village Voice* 4 (February 18, 1959): 3; Ennis, "N.Y.U., New School and Cooper Union Are Expanding": 1; Voorhees, Walker, Smith, Smith & Haines, *75th Anniversary* (New York, May 1960), 59; "Cooper Union's Mid-20th Century Cubed Response," *Village Voice* 6 (September 21, 1961): 3; "Map Shows Future Plans: Cooper Union Expansion Arouses School's Neighbors," *Village Voice* 8 (September 19, 1963): 3, 8.

215. For McSorley's Old Ale House, see Joseph Mitchell, *McSorley's Wonderful Saloon* (New York: Grosset & Dunlap, 1943).

216. "A New Education Building for The Cooper Union, New York City," *Architectural Record* 142 (December 1967): 43; "Cooper Union Addition Gives Plaza as Bonus," *Architectural Record* 145 (February 1969): 114–16.

217. For Augustus Saint-Gaudens's monument to Peter Cooper, see Gayle and Cohen, *The Art Commission and the Municipal Art Society Guide to Manhattan's Outdoor Sculpture*, 83.

218. Sam Hunter, *Rosenthal: Sculptures*, exhibition catalogue (New York: M. Knoedler & Co., 1968), 7–11; "Sculpture on the Streets," *Architectural Review* 143 (March 1968): 209–12; Gregory Battcock, "Monuments to Technology," *Art and Artist* 5 (May 1970): 52–55; Fried and Gillon, *New York Civic Sculpture*, 30–31; Gayle and Cohen, *The Art Commission and the Municipal Art Society Guide to Manhattan's Outdoor Sculpture*, 82.

219. Hunter, *Rosenthal: Sculptures*, 7.

220. "Stark Urges Revamping Bowery in Industrial-Residential Plan," *New York Times* (April 10, 1956): 33; Miller, *Greenwich Village and How It Got That Way*, 258–59.

221. "Cooper Sq. Project Is Adding 8½ Acres," *New York Times* (November 30, 1956): 25.

222. "Village Planners View Community; Protest Slum Sign," *Village Voice* 4 (January 21, 1959): 3.

223. Thomas W. Ennis, "Residents Urging Cooper Project," *New York Times* (April 23, 1961), VIII: 1, 6.

224. Walter Thabit, *An Alternate Plan for Cooper Square* (New York: Cooper Square Community Development Committee and Businessmen's Association, 1961).

225. Eggers & Higgins, "The Astor-Cooper Square Area Urban Renewal Study," *Journal of the American Institute of Architects* 37 (April 1962): 21–27.

226. Stern, Gilmartin and Mellins, *New York 1930*, 427–28.

227. Mary Perot Nichols, "33–Block Area on E. Side Picked for Urban Renewal," *Village Voice* 9 (January 2, 1964): 2, 11. Also see City of New York, Department of City Planning, *Rehabilitation Report* (New York, August 14, 1963).

228. Thomas W. Ennis, "Cooper Square Plan Set for Decision," *New York Times* (August 8, 1969), VIII: 1–2.

229. David K. Shipler, "City Panel Backs Renewal Project," *New York Times* (January 8, 1970): 25; Iver Peterson, "Project in Bowery Is Approved Following 10-Year Controversy," *New York Times* (February 14, 1970): 15.

230. J. Kirk Sale and Ben Apfelbaum, "Report from Teeny-Boppersville," *New York Times* (May 28, 1967), VI: 1, 24–25, 77, 80–81, 83–84.

231. John Kifner, "The East Village: A Changing Scene for Hippies," *New York Times* (October 11, 1967): 32.

232. "Block Party Held to Create Mall," *New York Times* (October 25, 1967): 23.

233. Tom Prideaux, "Babes in a Turned-On Toyland," *Life* 62 (April 14, 1967): 17; Jack Newfield, "Electric Circus Opens: Hippies & New Frontier on 'Desolation Row,'" *Village Voice* 12 (July 6, 1967): 1, 12; John Leo, "Swinging in the East Village Has Its Ups and Downs," *New York Times* (July 15, 1967): 27, 54; "It's a Circus!" *Progressive Architecture* 48 (September 1967): 58; Judy Klemesrud, "Sideshow at Electric Circus," *New York Times* (October 4, 1967): 50; Dore Ashton, "New York," *Studio* 174 (November 1967): 215–17; "Electric Circus," *L'Architecture d'Aujourd'hui* 39 (December 1967–January 1968): lvii; Smith, *Supermannerism*, 301–2; Miller, *Greenwich Village and How It Got That Way*, 261–62.

234. "It's a Circus!": 58.

235. Leo, "Swinging in the East Village Has Its Ups and Downs": 54.

236. Leo, "Swinging in the East Village Has Its Ups and Downs": 54.

237. "Fish-Eye Architecture," *Progressive Architecture* 50 (June 1969): 34; Michael Knight, "15 at the Electric Circus Injured in Bomb Explosion," *New York Times* (March 23, 1970): 39; Martin Ginsberg, "Electric Circus Turns Off Lights for the Last Time," *New York Times* (August 8, 1971): 51; Smith, *Supermannerism*, 301–2. Also see the advertisement—"The New Electric Circus Is Coming"—that featured the following quotation from Gwathmey: "This job is KILLING me. It's a MOTHER. You've just got to stop making changes!" *Village Voice* 14 (March 20, 1969): 28.

238. "Fish-Eye Architecture": 34.

SOHO

1. John Ashbery, "Under the Archness," editorial, *Art News* 70 (November 1971): 29.

2. "Manhattan Express Highway Proposed by Borough President Nathan," *American City* 59 (July 1944): 11; "City Expressway Plans Hint End of Moses Feud with Village on Traffic in Square," *Village Voice* 4 (December 3, 1958): 3; Stephanie Gervis, "Artists, Politicians, People Join Fight for Little Italy," *Village Voice* 7 (August 30, 1962): 1, 6; Richard L. Madden, "Expressway Decision Put Off," *New York Herald Tribune* (December 7, 1962): 13; Stephanie Gervis, "Political Powerhouse Kills Broome St. Expressway," *Village Voice* 8 (December 13, 1962): 1, 8; "Highwaymen Push Project as Area Goes Downhill," *Village Voice* 9 (June 11, 1964): 3; Ada Louise Huxtable, "Lindsay Surveys City from Copter: Views Problems in Company with Two Architects," *New York Times* (July 24, 1965): 8; Susan Goodman, "Moses Offers Housing Plan for Broome St. Expressway," *Village Voice* 9 (August 6, 1964): 1, 9; "Expressway Battlers Ready for New Round," *Village Voice* 10 (December 10, 1964): 1; "Expressway Means Jobs for Unions," *Village Voice* 10 (December 31, 1964): 1; "A Hard Choice," editorial, *Housing and Planning News* 23 (January 1965): 2–3; David Gurin, "Last Exit to Manhattan," *Village Voice* 10 (January 28, 1965): 4, 6, 8; Mary Perot Nichols, "Expressway: The Case of the Confused Figures," *Village Voice* 10 (February 11, 1965): 3, 6; Mary Perot Nichols, "Moses' Relocation Plan: Five Years & You're Out," *Village Voice* 10 (April 1, 1965): 1, 6; Russell Kirk, "Destroying the Past by 'Development,'" *National Review* 17 (April 6, 1965): 285; "Lindsay Causes Wagner Stall on Expressway," *Village Voice* 10 (May 20, 1965): 3; "Expressway Will Cross Manhattan," *Engineering News-Record* 174 (June 3, 1965): 19; Mary Perot Nichols, "Will Gas Fumes Knockout LBJ's Great Society?" *Village Voice* 10 (June 10, 1965): 1, 6–7; Mary Perot Nichols, "Expressway Has No Part in Lindsay Plan for City," *Village Voice* 10 (July 29, 1965): 9; "Not Good Enough," *Housing and Planning News* 24 (winter 1966): 6; "Expressway Is Out, Price Says," *Village Voice* 11 (March 10, 1966): 1; "Express Is Out," *Progressive Architecture* 47 (April 1966): 74; "Roadway Plan Would Split the Village," *Village Voice* 12 (March 23, 1967): 3; "Expressway Plan Is Now Official," *Village Voice* 12 (March 30, 1967): 3; Leticia Kent, "New Plan Arouses Anger, Want Lindsay's Old Loop," *Village Voice* 12 (April 6, 1967): 40, 42; "Lower Manhattan Expressway," *Architectural Forum* 127 (September 1967): 66–69; Peter Blake, "About Mayor Lindsay, Jane Jacobs and James Bogardus," *New York* 5 (May 6, 1968): 42–45; Leticia Kent, "Lindsay's Green Light Opens Way to Chaos," *Village Voice* 13 (October 31, 1968): 3, 58; Mary Perot Nichols, "City Highway Plan a Low Road for Poor," *Village Voice* 13 (November 7, 1968): 3; "Release of Jane Jacobs," *Architectural Forum* 129 (December 1968): 28; "Lindsay Warned of Expressway Air Pollution," *Village Voice* 14 (December 19, 1968): 1; "Pollution Study Could Doom Expressway," *Village Voice* 14 (January 9, 1969): 1; Ada Louise Huxtable, "Where It Goes Nobody Knows," *New York Times* (February 2, 1969), II: 29, reprinted in Ada Louise Huxtable, *Will They Ever Finish Bruckner Boulevard?* (New York: Macmillan, 1970), 18–24; Peter Blake, "Somebody Up There Likes This City," *New York* 2 (February 3, 1969): 48–49; ". . . And More to Come," *Architectural Forum* 130 (March 1969): 29; Ada Louise Huxtable, "Politics of Expressways: Putting Highways Through City's Core Is Regarded as Poison to a Candidate," *New York Times* (July 17, 1969): 51; Vicki Hodgetts, "The City Politic. LOMEX: Off Again," *New York* 2 (July 28, 1969): 8–9; "Goodbye, Expressway," *Village Voice* 16 (August 28, 1969): 1, 15; "Three Urban Expressways Do Not Slash Through Cities," *Architectural Record* 146 (September 1969): 36; Woody Klein, *Lindsay's Promise: The Dream that Failed* (New York: Macmillan, 1970), 112–13, 134–35; Robert Moses, *Public Works: A Dangerous Trade* (New York: McGraw-Hill, 1970), 305–9; Paul Rudolph, *Drawings* (Tokyo: A.D.A. Edita, 1972), 82–87; Jonathan Barnett, *Urban Design as Public Policy* (New York: Architectural Record Books, 1974), 144; Robert A. Caro, *The Power Broker: Robert Moses and the Fall of New York* (New York: Alfred A. Knopf, 1974), 769–70; Peter Wolf, *New Forms of the Evolving City: Urban Design Proposals by Ulrich Franzen and Paul Rudolph* (New York: Whitney Library of Design, 1974), 48–87; Peter Wolf, *The Future of the City: New Directions in Urban Planning* (New York: Watson-Guptill, 1974), 47, 54, 56–57, 103; Raymond Gindroz and David Lewis, "Urban Design: Contact Sport or Ivory Tower?" book review, *Architectural Record* 157 (February 1975): 45, 47; Marshall Berman, "Buildings Are Judgement," *Ramparts* 13 (March 1975): 33–39, 50–57; Carol Herselle Krinsky, "Architecture in New York City," in Leonard Wallock, ed., *New York: Culture Capital of the World, 1940–1965* (New York: Rizzoli International Publications, 1988), 120; Rebecca Read Shanor, *The City that Never Was* (New York: Viking, 1988), 24–31.

3. Hodgetts, "The City Politic. LOMEX: Off Again": 8.

4. See Hodgetts, "The City Politic. LOMEX: Off Again": 8.

5. "Lower Manhattan Expressway," *Architectural Forum*: 68.

6. Jim Stratton, *Pioneering in the Urban Wilderness* (New York: Urizen, 1977), 32.

7. Gervis, "Artists, Politicians, People Join Fight for Little Italy": 1. For further discussion of subsequent efforts to restore the area known as Little Italy, see Ada Louise Huxtable, "A Recession-Proof Plan to Rescue Little Italy," *New York Times* (May 4, 1975), II: 29.

8. Krinsky, "Architecture in New York City," in Wallock, ed., *New York: Culture Capital of the World*, 120.

9. Robert Price quoted in "Expressway Is Out," *Progressive Architecture*: 74.

10. Jane Jacobs quoted in Gervis, "Artists, Politicians, People Join Fight for Little Italy": 6.

11. Edward I. Koch quoted in "Release of Jane Jacobs": 28.

12. Blake, "About Mayor Lindsay, Jane Jacobs and James Bogardus": 42.

13. Huxtable, "Where It Goes Nobody Knows": 29.

14. Rudolph, *Drawings*, 82–87; Wolf, *New Forms of the Evolving City: Urban Design Proposals by Ulrich Franzen and Paul Rudolph*, 48–87.

15. Wolf, *New Forms of the Evolving City: Urban Design Proposals by Ulrich Franzen and Paul Rudolph*, 56.

16. Wolf, *New Forms of the Evolving City: Urban Design Proposals by Ulrich Franzen and Paul Rudolph*, 60.

17. Gindroz and Lewis, "Urban Design: Contact Sport or Ivory Tower?": 45.

18. See Hodgetts, "The City Politic. LOMEX: Off Again": 8–9.

19. See W. Boesiger and O. Stonorov, eds., *Le Corbusier et Pierre Jeanneret: Oeuvre complète de 1910–1929*, vol. 1 (Zurich: Editions Girsberger, 1929), 34–39, 109–17.

20. Berman, "Buildings Are Judgement": 56.

21. Landmarks Preservation Commission of the City of New York, *SoHo—Cast-Iron Historic District Designation Report* (New York, 1973). Also see Louis Calta, "SoHo to Be Made a Landmark Area," *New York Times* (March 23, 1973): 52; "Artists Cast an Iron," *Architectural Forum* 139 (November 1973): 20; "Cast Iron Reclaimed," *Architectural Forum* 139 (December 1973): 10; Margot Gayle and Edmund V. Gillon, Jr., *Cast-Iron Architecture in New York* (New York: Dover, 1974); Barbaralee Diamonstein, *The Landmarks of New York* (New York: Harry N. Abrams, 1988), 393.

22. "Cast Iron's Advocate: Saving the Past," *New York Times* (October 20, 1991), X: 1.
23. Ada Louise Huxtable, "Exploring New York," *Art in America* 47 (fall 1959): 49, 54–55; Ada Louise Huxtable, "Must Urban Renewal Be Urban Devastation?" *New York Times* (December 24, 1961), II: 14; Ada Louise Huxtable, "Noted Buildings in Path of Road: Cast Iron Structures on Broome St. Seem Slated for Expressway," *New York Times* (July 22, 1965): 33, 62; Ada Louise Huxtable, "Good Buildings Have Friends," *New York Times* (May 24, 1970), II: 26.
24. Huxtable, "Must Urban Renewal Be Urban Devastation?": 14. Also see W. Knight Sturges, "Cast Iron in New York," *Architectural Review* 114 (October 1953): 232–37.
25. Blake, "About Mayor Lindsay, Jane Jacobs and James Bogardus": 42. Also see Henry Hope Reed, *The Golden City* (New York: Doubleday & Co, 1959), 32; "Mies van der Rohe's Forebear," *Village Voice* 10 (January 28, 1965): 1; "Haughwout Wins Out," *Progressive Architecture* 47 (March 1966): 62; Cervin Robinson, "Architectural Iron Works," *Architectural Forum* 126 (May 1967): 63–70; Regional Plan Association, *Urban Design Manhattan* (New York: Viking, 1969), 112; "Doomed Palaces of Style," *Life* 69 (August 14, 1970): 56–61; "The Talk of the Town: The Cast-Iron World," *New Yorker* 50 (June 3, 1974): 30–31; "Honorable Mention Went to Twelve New York State Buildings," *Architectural Record* 156 (November 1974): 39; Barbaralee Diamonstein, *Buildings Reborn: New Uses, Old Places* (New York: Harper & Row, 1978), 158–59.
26. Emmanuel Tobier, "Setting the Record Straight on Loft Conversions," *New York Affairs* 6, no. 4 (1981): 33–44. Also see James R. Hudson, *The Unanticipated City* (Amherst, Mass. : University of Massachusetts Press, 1987), 20–35.
27. Steven Koch, "Reflections on SoHo," in Alexandra Anderson and B. J. Archer, *SoHo: The Essential Guide to Art and Life in Lower Manhattan* (New York: Simon & Schuster, 1979), 9–17.
28. Stratton, *Pioneering in the Urban Wilderness*, 7.
29. "The Angry Dwellers," *Newsweek* 57 (May 29, 1961): 102–3.
30. Michel Duplaix, "The Loft Generation," *Vogue* 55 (June 1961): 108–11. Also see Patrick Chavez, "Evictions Rise: Loft Colony Holds Out as City Lays Siege," *Village Voice* 6 (March 16, 1961): 1, 12; Peter Hellman, "SoHo: Artists' Bohemia Imperilled," *New York* 3 (August 24, 1970): 46–49.
31. Stratton, *Pioneering in the Urban Wilderness*, 7.
32. Edward F. Cavanagh quoted in "The Angry Dwellers": 102.
33. "City May Move to Legalize Artists' Lofts, Stop Strike," *Village Voice* 6 (August 24, 1961): 3.
34. "City Relaxes Pressure on Loft Studios," *Village Voice* 7 (December 4, 1961): 1.
35. "City Cooperates but Artists Face New Problem: Demolition of Loft Area," *Village Voice* 7 (December 21, 1961): 3, 8.
36. Stephanie Gervis, "Loftless Leonardos Picket as Mona Merely Smiles," *Village Voice* 8 (February 14, 1963): 1, 7.
37. Susan Goodman, "City Still Cool to Artists on Loft-Housing Issue," *Village Voice* 9 (November 14, 1963): 1, 17; Tom Bassford, letter to the editor, *Village Voice* 9 (December 12, 1963): 4; Susan Goodman, "State May Allow Artists to Make Wide Use of Lofts," *Village Voice* 9 (February 13, 1964): 1, 8; Susan Goodman, "Picket City Hall: State Softens on Artists, but City Will Not Relent," *Village Voice* 9 (March 19, 1964): 1, 7; Susan Goodman, "1,000 Artists at City Hall Picket for Their Lofts," *Village Voice* 9 (April 9, 1964): 1, 18.
38. "Rockefeller Signs Loft Bill, Artists Await City Action," *Village Voice* 9 (April 30, 1964): 3.
39. Ron Rosenbaum, "Artists' Housing. Soho in New York: A Fight for Survival," *Village Voice* 14 (November 6, 1969): 1, 22–23, 25, 27. Also see "SoHo: Artists Move into New York's Cast Iron District," *Architectural Record* 147 (June 1970): 36.
40. Edward Doremus quoted in "Libs Would Use S. Village Loft Area for Housing," *Village Voice* 6 (December 1, 1960): 1.
41. Thomas W. Ennis, "'Village' Housewife Leads Drive to Build Middle-Income Co-Op," *New York Times* (March 20, 1960), VIII: 1, 7; Thomas W. Ennis, "Housewife Spurs 38 Million Co-op," *New York Times* (August 12, 1960): 28; "South Village Site Picked for Huge Mid-Income Co-op," *Village Voice* 5 (August 18, 1960): 1–2; "A New Housing Project," editorial, *New York Times* (September 2, 1960): 22; A. E. Kazan, "Role of Cooperative Housing," letter to the editor, *New York Times* (September 10, 1960): 20.
42. "A New Housing Project": 22.
43. Jane Eccles, "West Village, cont.," letter to the editor, *Village Voice* (April 6, 1961): 4. Also see Ann Rosenhaft, "West Village, cont.," letter to the editor, *Village Voice* (April 6, 1961): 4.
44. "Renewal Proposed in Downtown Area," *New York Times* (December 1, 1961): 18.
45. Mary Perot Nichols, "Bone of Contention: Huge S. Village Project Gets Boost, Then Blast," *Village Voice* 7 (December 17, 1961): 1, 8. Also see "S. Village Pastor Backs Huge Mi-Cove Project," *Village Voice* 7 (December 21, 1961): 3.
46. Jane Jacobs quoted in Nichols, "Bone of Contention: Huge S. Village Project Gets Boost, Then Blast": 8.
47. Robert Abel, "Fact and Theory," letter to the editor, *Village Voice* 7 (March 15, 1962): 4.
48. Chester Rapkin, *The South Houston Industrial Area* (New York: New York City Planning Commission, 1963).
49. I. D. Robbins quoted in Susan Goodman, "Incubator, Industrial Slum: Which Is the Loft Area?" *Village Voice* 9 (April 2, 1964): 12. Also see City Club of New York, *The Wastelands of New York City* (New York: City Club of New York, 1962).
50. "Instructive Disaster," *Architectural Forum* 124 (March 1966): 26.
51. *SoHo–Cast-Iron Historic District*, 167.
52. Hary Ruhé, *Fluxus: The Most Radical and Experimental Art Movement of the Sixties* (Amsterdam: "A," 1979); John Hendricks, comp., *Fluxus Codex* (Detroit: Gilbert and Lila Silverman Fluxus Collection, in association with Harry N. Abrams, 1988). For further discussion of George Maciunas's real estate activities, see Christopher Gray, "Streetscapes: 80 Wooster Street," *New York Times* (March 15, 1992), X: 7.
53. *SoHo–Cast-Iron Historic District*, 82–83.
54. *SoHo–Cast-Iron Historic District*, 92.
55. *SoHo–Cast-Iron Historic District*, 140.
56. *SoHo–Cast-Iron Historic District*, 159.
57. *SoHo–Cast-Iron Historic District*, 16.
58. Stratton, *Pioneering in the Urban Wilderness*, 31–32.
59. Grace Glueck, "Neighborhoods: SoHo Is Artists' Last Resort Here," *New York Times* (May 11, 1970): 37, 71.
60. Ivan Karp quoted in Glueck, "Neighborhoods: SoHo Is Artists' Last Resort Here": 71.
61. For useful general discussions of SoHo as the city's premier artists' quarter, see Dorothy Seiberling, "SoHo: The Most Exciting Place to Live in the City," *New York* 8 (May 1974): 52–53; Ulrich Eckhardt and Werner Duttman, eds., *New York—Downtown Manhattan: SoHo* (Berlin: Akademie der Kunste–Berliner Festwochen, 1976); Helene Zucker Seeman and Alanna Siegfried, *SoHo* (New York: Neal-Schuman, 1978); Anderson and Archer, *SoHo: The Essential Guide to Art and Life in Lower Manhattan*; C. L. Byrd, *SoHo* (New York: Doubleday, 1981); Charles R. Simpson, *SoHo: The Artist in the City* (Chicago and London: University of Chicago Press, 1981); Kaisa Broner, *New York face à son Patrimoine* (Brussels: Pierre Mardaga, 1986); Hudson, *The Unanticipated City*.
62. Rosenbaum, "Artists' Housing. Soho in New York: A Fight for Survival": 22.
63. Michael T. Kaufman, "SoHo Seeks to Preserve a Life-Style," *New York Times* (January 25, 1972): 37.
64. Rosenbaum, "Artists' Housing. Soho in New York: A Fight for Survival": 1, 22.
65. Koch, "Reflections on Soho," in Anderson and Archer, *SoHo: The Essential Guide to Art and Life in Lower Manhattan*, 11, 13.
66. Ron Rosenbaum, "City Won't Make Loft Living Legal," *Village Voice* 14 (December 4, 1969): 1, 3.
67. "Artists District Plans a Weekend of Shows," *New York Times* (May 8, 1970): 34; Glueck, "Neighborhoods: SoHo Is Artists' Last Resort Here": 37; "Bohemia's Last Frontier," *Time* 95 (May 25, 1970): 82; Stratton, *Pioneering in the Urban Wilderness*, 34–35.
68. Yvonne Rainer quoted in Glueck, "Neighborhoods: SoHo Is Artists' Last Resort Here": 37.
69. "Bohemia's Last Frontier": 82.
70. Mike Leff quoted in Hellman, "SoHo: Artists' Bohemia Imperilled": 48.
71. David Diao quoted in Glueck, "Neighborhoods: SoHo Is Artists' Last Resort Here": 71.
72. Rita Reif, "Dodging Trucks Was a Part of the $125 Tour," *New York Times* (January 26, 1971): 38.
73. Ashbery, "Underneath the Archness": 29.
74. Grace Glueck, "4 Uptown Art Dealers Set Up in SoHo," *New York Times* (September 27, 1971): 40. Also see Paul Gardner, "SoHo: Brave New Bohemia," *Art News* 73 (April 1974): 56–57; Roberta Smith, "Gilbert and George 20 Years Later," *New York Times* (September 27, 1991), C: 28.
75. John Corry, "About New York: Sights and Sites in SoHo," *New York Times* (March 18, 1974): 25.
76. Ashbery, "Underneath the Archness": 29.
77. "City Drafts Plan for Lofts in Soho," *New York Times* (January 11, 1971): 14; Edward C. Burks, "City Planning Board Backs Use of Lofts as Artists' Residences," *New York Times* (January 21, 1971): 22; Ron Rosenbaum, "Legal Lofts Nearing OK," *Village Voice* 16 (January 28, 1971): 1, 3; Edward C. Burks, "Estimate Board Votes Zoning for Artists in the SoHo Area," *New York Times* (January 29, 1971): 41; "SoHo Saved," *Village Voice* 16 (February 4, 1971): 1.
78. Stephen Koch, "Where the Avant-Gardest Work the Hardest," *Esquire* 83 (April 1975): 113–17, 168–70.
79. Ron Rosenbaum, "City May OK Some SoHo Loft Living," *Village Voice* 15 (June 18, 1970): 1, 22–24.
80. Max H. Seigel, "SoHo Residents Split on Sports Center," *New York Times* (September 13, 1972): 29; Grace Glueck, "Pinks and Pastels and Parabolas," *New York Times* (December 10, 1972), II: 29; Stratton, *Pioneering in the Urban Wilderness*, 37.
81. For informative general discussions of residential lofts, see Kingsley C. Fairbridge and Harvey-Jane Kowal, *Loft Living: Recycling Warehouse Space for Residential Use* (New York: Saturday Review/E. P. Dutton, 1976); Jeffrey Weiss, *Lofts* (New York: W. W. Norton, 1979); Suzanne Slesin, Stafford Cliff and Daniel Rozensztroch, *The International Book of Lofts* (New York: Clarkson N. Potter, 1986).
82. "Five Famous Artists in Their Personal Backgrounds: Louise Nevelson," *House and Garden* 128 (December 1965): 180.
83. Elizabeth Sverbeyeff and Sue Nirenberg, "Robert Indiana," *House Beautiful* 112 (February 1970): 52–55, 166; "Four Letter Word," *Architectural Forum* 132 (March 1970): 19.
84. Barbara Plumb, *Young Designs in Living* (New York: Viking Press, 1969), 30–31; *Richard Meier Architect: Buildings and Projects 1966–1976* (New York: Oxford University Press, 1976), 19; *Richard Meier Architect: 1964/1984* (New York: Rizzoli International Publications, 1984), 384–85.
85. Joan Kron, "Lofty Living," *New York* 7 (May 20, 1974): 54–59, 66–69.
86. Larry Rivers quoted in Mary Simons, "Larry Rivers' Living Room," *Look* 31 (March 21, 1967), M: 20, 22–23.
87. Simons, "Larry Rivers' Living Room": 20.
88. Annette Michelson, "An Art Scholar's Loft," *Vogue* 149 (March 15, 1967): 136–43, 154–55; *Richard Meier Architect: Buildings and Projects 1966–1976*, 19; *Richard Meier Architect: 1964/1984*, 386–87. For a profile of William Rubin, see Grace Glueck, "Museum Chooses Head for Division," *New York Times* (July 11, 1967): 34.
89. Michelson, "An Art Scholar's Loft": 136, 142.
90. "Clean-Sweep Space for Living Now: Everything in One Enormous Room," *House and Garden* 140 (October 1971): 102–3; Sharon Lee Ryder, "A Very Lofty Realm," *Progressive Architecture* 55 (October 1974): 92–97.
91. Norma Skurka, "A Landmark Loft in SoHo," *New York Times* (November 24, 1974), VI: 70–71; "Restoring a Landmark Building with a Cast Iron Front," *Architectural Record* 158 (August 1975): 72–73; "A Live-In Gallery," *Interior Design* 46 (October 1975): 118–23; Barbara Plumb, *Houses Architects Live In* (New York: Penguin Books, 1978), 104–7; White and Willensky, *AIA Guide* (1978), 46.
92. Ryder, "A Very Lofty Realm": 95.
93. "The Last Studios": 52.
94. Kaufman, "SoHo Seeks to Preserve a Life-Style": 37.
95. See Anna Mayo, "The Aristoids of SoHo," *Village Voice* 19 (May 16, 1974): 14–15.
96. Tobier, "Getting the Record Straight on Loft Conversions": 37.
97. Walter Karp, "Bohemia Reborn," *Horizon* 16 (spring 1974): 64–77.
98. Julian Weissman, "Standoff in SoHo," *Art News* 73 (September 1974): 92–94.
99. Jason Epstein quoted in Peter Blake, *Form Follows Fiasco: Why Modern Architecture Hasn't Worked* (Boston: Little, Brown and Co., 1977), 120.

Chapter 5
Midtown

1. James Baldwin, *Another Country* (New York: Dial Press, 1962), 230.

EAST SIDE: FROM STUYVESANT TOWN TO TURTLE BAY

1. For a general discussion of east midtown's postwar transformation, see Murray Schumach, "The East River Shore Regains Its Glory," *New York Times* (January 19, 1947), VI: 8–9, 38–39.
2. Stern, Gilmartin and Mellins, *New York 1930*, 428–33.
3. Stern, Gilmartin and Mellins, *New York 1930*, 437–38.
4. "Parkchester 2 for 194X," *Architectural Forum* 78 (May 1943): 66, 160. For Parkchester, see Stern, Gilmartin and Mellins, *New York 1930*, 496–97, 499–500.
5. "Albany Bill Bares Housing Project," *New York Times* (March 11, 1943): 34; "Proposed Postwar Housing Project," *Architectural Record* 92 (June 1943): 16; Arthur C. Holden, "Earnest, Indignant, Vague," letter to the editor, with editor's reply, *Architectural Forum* 79 (August 1943): 38.
6. John Tauranac, *Essential New York* (New York: Holt, Rinehart and Winston, 1979), 190–92.
7. "Stuyvesant Town—Must a Challenging Opportunity Be Lost?" *Citizens' Housing Council Housing News* 1 (June–July 1943): 1–3, 5. Also see "Metropolitan Project to House 30,000," *Pencil Points* 24 (May 1943): 19, 23; "'Stuyvesant Town' Railroaded Through," *Pencil Points* 24 (June 1943): 24; Arthur C. Holden, "Stuyvesant Town Proceedings Demonstrate Need for Coordinated City Planning," *Citizens' Housing Council Housing News* 1 (June–July 1943): 3–4; "Stuyvesant Saga," *Architectural Forum* 79 (July 1943): 40–41; Kenneth Reid, "More Planning Is Wanted—Not Less," editorial, *Pencil Points* 25 (September 1944): 43.
8. Editorial reply to Arthur C. Holden's letter to the editor, *Architectural Forum* 79 (August 1943): 38.
9. "'Stuyvesant Town,'" editorial, *New York Times* (June 2, 1943): 24.
10. Loula D. Lasker, "Housing Plans Disapproved," letter to the editor, *New York Times* (June 1, 1943): 22.
11. Robert Moses, "Stuyvesant Town Defended," letter to the editor, *New York Times* (June 3, 1943): 20.
12. "Editor's Note," following Henry S. Churchill, "Met Gits the Mostest," letter to the editor, *Architectural Forum* 78 (June 1943): 34, 128.
13. Quoted in "Required Reading: Stuyvesant Town," *Architectural Record* 94 (September 1943): 28.
14. Tracy B. Augur, "An Analysis of the Plan of Stuyvesant Town," *Journal of the American Institute of Planners* 10 (autumn 1944): 8–13.
15. Marcel Breuer, "Stuyvesant Six: A Redevelopment Study," *Pencil Points* 25 (June 1944): 66–70, 102, 116. Also see Peter Blake, *Marcel Breuer: Architect and Designer* (New York: Architectural Record Books, in collaboration with the Museum of Modern Art, New York, 1949), 82, 84; Peter Blake, ed., *Marcel Breuer: Sun and Shadow* (New York: Dodd, Mead, 1955), 52–53.
16. Breuer, "Stuyvesant Six: A Redevelopment Study": 69.
17. Edwin S. Burdell, "Rehousing Needs of the Families on the Stuyvesant Town Site," *Journal of the American Institute of Planners* 11 (autumn 1945): 15–19.
18. "Rehousing Families in Stuyvesant Town Area," *Citizens' Housing Council Housing News* 3 (February–March 1945): 1–2; "Stuyvesant Town Site to Be Cleared," *Citizens' Housing Council Housing News* 3 (April 1945): 4.
19. "Work Is Speeded on Housing Projects in City to Meet Heavy Demand," *New York Times* (March 16, 1947), VIII: 1; "Stuyvesant Town," *Architectural Forum* 86 (May 1947): cover, 3; Kathryn Close, "New Homes with Insurance Dollars," *Survey Graphic* 37 (November 1948): 450–54, 487–88; "New York: New Nightmares for Old?" *Time* 52 (December 13, 1948): 27; White and Willensky, *AIA Guide* (1967), 99–100; Robert Moses, *Public Works: A Dangerous Trade* (New York: McGraw-Hill, 1970), 431–33; Paul Goldberger, *The City Observed: New York* (New York: Random House, 1979), 104; Tauranac, *Essential New York*, 190–92; Thomas E. Norton and Jerry E. Patterson, *Living It Up: A Guide to the Named Apartment Houses of New York* (New York: Atheneum, 1984), 324; Carol Herselle Krinsky, "Architecture in New York City," in Leonard Wallock, ed., *New York: Culture Capital of the World, 1940–1965* (New York: Rizzoli International Publications, 1988), 94–95; Richard Plunz, *A History of Housing in New York City* (New York: Columbia University Press, 1990), 255–59.
20. "They Live in Stuyvesant Town," *House and Garden* 94 (September 1948): 118–21, 163. For discussion of another Stuyvesant Town interior, see "Hoffmann and Heidrich," *Interiors* 109 (August 1949): 86.
21. Lewis Mumford, "The Sky Line: Prefabricated Blight," *New Yorker* 24 (October 30, 1948): 49–50, 52, 54–55. Also see "New York: Mumford, Moses Slug It Out over Density of Metropolitan's Project," *Architectural Forum* 90 (January 1949): 22, 24.
22. Lewis Mumford, "The Sky Line: Stuyvesant Town Revisited," *New Yorker* 24 (November 27, 1948): 65–72.
23. Mumford, "The Sky Line: Stuyvesant Town Revisited": 68.
24. Mumford, "The Sky Line: Prefabricated Blight": 49–50, 54.
25. Mumford, "The Sky Line: Prefabricated Blight": 50, 54–55.
26. "Stuyvesant Town Wins Again," *Citizens' Housing and Planning Council Housing News* 7 (January 1949): 5. Also see "White Stuyvesant," *Survey* 85 (January 1949): 56–57; "Discrimination Upheld for Stuyvesant Town," *Survey* 85 (August 1949): 442.
27. Close, "New Homes with Insurance Dollars": 450–54, 487–88.
28. Quoted in Algernon D. Black, "Negro Families in Stuyvesant Town," *Survey* 86 (November 1950): 502–3.
29. Charles Abrams, "Slum Clearance Boomerangs," *Nation* 170 (July 29, 1950): 106–7.
30. "Metropolitan Life Is Accused of Bias," *New York Times* (January 11, 1951): 26; "Council Passes Bill Barring Bias in All City-Aided Private Housing," *New York Times* (February 17, 1951): 1, 8; "Bill Barring Housing Bias Is Signed by Impellitteri," *New York Times* (March 15, 1951): 6; Joseph B. Robison, "The Story of Stuyvesant Town," *Nation* 172 (June 2, 1951): 514–16. Also see Arthur Simon, *Stuyvesant Town, USA: Pattern for Two Americas* (New York: New York University Press, 1970).
31. "Two Up, Three to Go," *Architectural Forum* 82 (February 1945): 7–8; "New Metropolitan Housing Project," *Architectural Record* 97 (February 1945): 116–18; "Architect Files Plans for Cooper Village Houses," *New York Times* (January 10, 1946): 36; "Flowering," *Architectural Forum* 86 (February 1947): 10; White and Willensky, *AIA Guide* (1967), 99; Norton and Patterson, *Living It Up*, 264; Krinsky, "Architecture in New York City," in Wallock, ed., *New York: Culture Capital of the World, 1940–1965*, 95; Plunz, *A History of Housing in New York City*, 253, 255.
32. Mumford, "The Sky Line: Prefabricated Blight": 55.
33. "Bellevue Nurses to Get New School," *New York Times* (March 16, 1944): 30; "Residence and School of Nurses," *Pencil Points* 25 (April 1944): 69–72; "School and Residence at Bellevue Hospital Designed to Attract Nurses," *New York Times* (July 29, 1956), VIII: 1, 6.
34. "Medical Center Planned by N.Y.U.," *New York Times* (October 27, 1944): 25; "Third Medical Center," *Newsweek* 33 (January 31, 1949): 43.
35. "New Center Seen as City Health Aid," *New York Times* (October 2, 1945): 42; "Medical College," *Architectural Forum* 83 (November 1945): 99–103; "Residence Hall," *Architectural Record* 98 (December 1945): 144; "Salmon Predicts East Side Revival," *New York Times* (May 22, 1946): 23; Lee Cooper, "N.Y.U. Acquires Site of Medical Center," *New York Times* (November 3, 1946): 1, 48; "Few Parcels Yet to Be Acquired for Proposed East Side New York University—Bellevue Medical Center," *Real Estate Record and Guide* 158 (November 9, 1946): 3; "1948 Start Slated on Medical Center," *New York Times* (February 24, 1948): 18.
36. "New Medical Units to Shut 4 Streets," *New York Times* (July 24, 1947): 23; Richard H. Parke, "N.Y.U.-Bellevue Plan Grows, with Cost at $32,744,000," *New York Times* (January 17, 1949): 1, 12; "New Medical Center for Manhattan," *Architectural Forum* 90 (February 1949): 13; "Construction of Medical Center to Start Soon," *Architectural Record* 105 (March 1949): 10; "World's Biggest Project," *Interiors* 108 (March 1949): 10; "N.Y. University—Bellevue Medical Center, New York, N.Y.," *Progressive Architecture* 30 (May 1949): 57–69; "City Gives Streets to Medical Center," *New York Times* (January 9, 1950): 27; "New Hospital Aids Civilian Disabled," *New York Times* (January 22, 1951): 19, 23; "Second Unit Begun at N.Y.U.-Bellevue," *New York Times* (February 29, 1952): 24; "Hospitals by Skidmore, Owings & Merrill," *Architectural Forum* 96 (April 1952): 120–29; "Medical Science Building Is 2d Building Added to New N.Y.U. Center," *New York Times* (June 3, 1955): 12; "N.Y.U. Hospital Is Planned, with Research Chief Goal," *New York Times* (April 26, 1957): 1, 18; "Research Hospital," *Architectural Forum* 106 (June 1957): 38; "The Hospital in the City: N.Y.U.'s Giant Medical Center," *Architectural Forum* 120 (April 1964): 92–95; "University Hospital, New York Medical Center," *Interiors* 125 (August 1965): 72–76; White and Willensky, *AIA Guide* (1978), 126.
37. Stern, Gilmartin and Mellins, *New York 1930*, 28–29, 74, 112–13.
38. Stern, Gilmartin and Mellins, *New York 1930*, 113–14, 345.
39. "East Side Chosen for U.S. Hospital," *New York Times* (March 25, 1947): 30; "Proposed Veterans Hospital to Be Constructed Here," *New York Times* (March 28, 1947): 27; Charles G. Bennett, "Bellevue Housing Approved by City," *New York Times* (February 26, 1954): 1, 13; "New V.A. Hospital Opens Here Today," *New York Times* (September 26, 1954): 76.
40. "Bellevue Begins Reconstruction," *New York Times* (June 23, 1963): 68; "Big-City Complex in a Flexible Cube," *Architectural Record* 134 (April 1964): 194–97; Deirdre Carmody, "Ancient Bellevue Is about to Open New Building," *New York Times* (October 3, 1973): 47; White and Willensky, *AIA Guide* (1978), 126.
41. Bernard M. Weinstein quoted in Carmody, "Ancient Bellevue Is about to Open New Building": 47.
42. "Bellevue Begins Reconstruction": 68; "Low-Cost Garage Structure Shows Design Finesse," *Architectural Record* 135 (January 1964): 164–66.
43. "Variety and Open Space for New York," *Architectural Record* 124 (July 1958): 175; "Kips Bay Plaza," *Housing and Planning News* 17 (April 1959): 1; "Cast-in-Place Technique Restudied," *Progressive Architecture* 41 (October 1960): cover, 158–59, 166–69; Edward L. Friedman, "Search," *Progressive Architecture* 41 (October 1960): 160–65; Ada Louise Huxtable, *Four Walking Tours of Modern Architecture in New York City* (New York: Museum of Modern Art and Municipal Art Society of New York, 1961), 68; "I. M. Pei Wins Brunner Award for 1961," *Architectural Record* 129 (May 1961): 12; Philip Johnson, "The International Style—Death or Metamorphosis," speech delivered at the Architectural League Forum, Metropolitan Museum of Art, March 30, 1961, excerpted in *Architectural Forum* 114 (June 1961): 87, and reprinted in Peter Eisenman and Robert A. M. Stern, eds., *Philip Johnson: Writings* (New York: Oxford University Press, 1979), 118–22; Walter McQuade, "Pei's Apartments Around the Corner," *Architectural Forum* 115 (August 1961): 106–14; Ada Louise Huxtable, "Our New Buildings: Hits and Misses," *New York Times* (April 29, 1962), VI: 16–17, 105–6; "Apartment Roundtable Asks: What Price Urban Living?" *Architectural Forum* 120 (March 1964): 84–91; "Ten Buildings that Point to the Future," *Fortune* 70 (October 1964): 134–39; "HHFA Honor Awards 1964," *Architectural Record* 136 (November 1964): 165, 168, 171; Arthur Herzog, "He Loves Things to Be Beautiful," *New York Times* (March 14, 1965), VI: 34–35, 98–99, 101; "New York's Bard Awards," *Progressive Architecture* 46 (April 1965): 63–64; White and Willensky, *AIA Guide* (1967), 98; William Zeckendorf with Edward McCreary, *The Autobiography of William Zeckendorf* (New York: Holt, Rinehart and Winston, 1970), 237–38; Marguerite Villecco, "Housing," *Architecture Plus* 1 (March 1973): 68–77; Goldberger, *The City Observed*, 122; Tauranac, *Essential New York*, 209–10; Norton and Patterson, *Living It Up*, 197; Krinsky, "Architecture in New York City," in Wallock, ed., *New York: Culture Capital of the World, 1940–1965*, 107, 109–10; Plunz, *A History of Housing in New York City*, 288; Carter Wiseman, *I. M. Pei: A Profile in American Architecture* (New York: Harry N. Abrams, 1990), 62–64, 210, 306.
44. I. M. Pei quoted in Wiseman, *I. M. Pei: A Profile in American Architecture*, 62–63.
45. For the Promontory Apartments, see David Spaeth, *Mies Van Der Rohe* (New York: Rizzoli International Publications, 1985), 129.
46. Friedman, "Search": 160.
47. McQuade, "Pei's Apartments Around the Corner": 107.
48. I. M. Pei quoted in "Apartment Roundtable Asks: What Price Urban Living?": 89.
49. "Alcoa Buys into Big Renewal Projects," *Architectural Forum* 117 (December 1962): 10. Also see "The Wheeling and Dealing of William Zeckendorf," *Architectural Forum* 112 (June 1960): 130–31, 198, 202, 210, 216.
50. Zeckendorf with McCreary, *The Autobiography of William Zeckendorf*, 237–38.
51. Carter B. Horsley, "Uris Drops Project; East Side Tract Sold," *New York Times* (April 30, 1972), VIII: 6; "33 Story Apartment Rises at 34th & 2nd," *Real Estate Record and Guide* 211 (June 30, 1973): 2–3; "3 Illegal Stories Added to Building; City Orders a Halt," *New York Times* (September 10, 1973): 18; "Penalty for Builder Who Exceeded Limit on Height Is Urged," *New York Times* (September 16, 1973): 38; "Builder Fined $1,000 for 3 Extra Floors," *New York Times* (October 2, 1973): 36; "Builder Is Allowed 3 Excess Stories in a Deal on Rent," *New York Times* (October 12, 1973): 37.
52. Henry Kibel quoted in "3 Illegal Stories Added to Building; City Orders a Halt": 18.

53. Theodore Karagheuzoff quoted in "3 Illegal Stories Added to Building; City Orders a Halt": 18.
54. "Only a Few Families on Slum Site Can Afford Gramercy Title I Rent," *New York Post* (February 8, 1959): 19; "Slum-Razing Set on the East Side," *New York Times* (February 16, 1959): 19; Robert A. Caro, *The Power Broker: Robert Moses and the Fall of New York* (New York: Alfred A. Knopf, 1974), 1017.
55. Davis, Brody & Associates, *Bellevue Environs* (New York: Davis, Brody & Associates, 1968); Walter F. Wagner, Jr., "Urban Housing: New Approaches and New Standards," *Architectural Record* 143 (June 1968): 147–66; Robert A. M. Stern, *New Directions in American Architecture* (New York: George Braziller, 1969), 97, fig. 102; Don Raney, "East Midtown Plaza: A Meeting Ground for the Community," *Architectural Record* 145 (January 1969): 107; "The Evolving Urban Architecture of Davis, Brody & Associates," *Architectural Record* 152 (August 1972): 97–106; Stanley Abercrombie, "New York Housing Breaks the Mold," *Architecture Plus* 1 (November 1973): 62–75; Ada Louise Huxtable, "Breaking the Mold," *New York Times* (February 10, 1974), II: 22; White and Willensky, *AIA Guide* (1978), 124–25; Goldberger, *The City Observed*, 102–3; Norton and Patterson, *Living It Up*, 128; Plunz, *A History of Housing in New York City*, 301.
56. Davis, Brody & Associates, *Bellevue Environs*, 5, 18–20.
57. Davis, Brody & Associates, *Bellevue Environs*, 15.
58. White and Willensky, *AIA Guide* (1978), 124.
59. Goldberger, *The City Observed*, 102.
60. Susana Torre, "Women in Architecture and the New Feminism," in Susana Torre, ed., *Women in Architecture: A Historic and Contemporary Perspective* (New York: Whitney Library of Design, 1977), 148–61; White and Willensky, *AIA Guide* (1978), 124; Goldberger, *The City Observed*, 102; Norton and Patterson, *Living It Up*, 266.
61. Janet Bloom, "Rock 'n' Roll School," *Architectural Forum* 137 (November 1972): 56–61.
62. White and Willensky, *AIA Guide* (1967), 93; "The Church That Turned a Corner," *Architectural Forum* 127 (November 1967): 82–87; White and Willensky, *AIA Guide* (1978), 124–25.
63. "The Church That Turned a Corner": 86.
64. White and Willensky, *AIA Guide* (1978), 124.
65. White and Willensky, *AIA Guide* (1978), 120–21.
66. White and Willensky, *AIA Guide* (1978), 127; Margot Gayle and Michele Cohen, *The Art Commission and the Municipal Art Society Guide to Manhattan's Outdoor Sculpture* (New York: Prentice Hall Press, 1988), 113.
67. Richard Ravitch quoted in David K. Shipler, "The Long Struggle for Waterside: A Case History," *New York Times* (February 7, 1971), VIII: 1–2.
68. William F. R. Ballard quoted in "Windows on the Waterfront," *Fortune* 72 (December 1965): 72.
69. "Windows Over the Water in Manhattan," *Fortune* 72 (December 1965): 194; Steven V. Roberts, "Housing on East River Platform Is Proposed," *New York Times* (December 21, 1966): 1, 28; Ada Louise Huxtable, "Creative Plan for River," *New York Times* (December 21, 1966): 28; "The City: Extending Manhattan," *Time* 88 (December 30, 1966): 24; "Life on the Waterfront," *Architectural Forum* 126 (January–February 1967): 118–19; "Waterside—Tough Choices," *Housing and Planning News* 25 (January–February 1967): 3; James T. Burns, Jr., "Breakthrough on the River," *Progressive Architecture* 48 (February 1967): 146–49; Davis, Brody & Associates, *Bellevue Environs*, 47–67; Wagner, "Urban Housing: New Approaches and New Standards": 147, 164–66; Stern, *New Directions in American Architecture*, 40–41, fig. 35; "Housing on River Backed on Funds," *New York Times* (June 25, 1970): 23; Shipler, "The Long Struggle for Waterside: A Case History": 1–2; Peter Blake, "New York: Towards a New Venice," *New York* 4 (July 10, 1971): 24–33; "The Evolving Urban Architecture of Davis, Brody & Associates": 97–106; Abercrombie, "New York Housing Breaks the Mold": 62–75; "Waterside Officially Opened," *Progressive Architecture* 54 (November 1973): 32; Joseph Blumenkranz, "New York Housing," letter to the editor, *Architecture Plus* 2 (January–February 1974): 6; Lewis Davis and Samuel Brody, "New York Housing," letter to the editor, *Architecture Plus* 2 (January–February 1974): 6; Huxtable, "Breaking the Mold": 22; Suzanne Stephens, "Manhattan Is Growing, as Always, Horizontally," *New York Times* (June 30, 1974), IV: 5; "The Talk of the Town: Wednesday, December 11, 1974," *New Yorker* 50 (December 30, 1974): 20–23; Peter Blake, "The Seventh Annual Cityscape Awards," *New York* 8 (January 13, 1975): 51; Paul Goldberger, "Waterside Design Builds Reputation," *New York Times* (March 12, 1975): 41, 44; Suzanne Stephens, "Architects in Residence. Design: Two Solutions at the Waterside," *New York Times* (July 13, 1975), VI: 38–40; Charles King Hoyt, "Waterside," *Architectural Record* 139 (March 1976): 119–24; Andrea O. Dean, "Waterside, N.Y. City. Architects: Davis, Brody & Associates," *Journal of the American Institute of Architects* 65 (April 1976): 46–47; White and Willensky, *AIA Guide* (1978), 126; Goldberger, *The City Observed*, 103–4; Tauranac, *Essential New York*, 236–37; Alan Hoglund, "Waterside's Good Intentions Gone Awry," *New York Observer* 2 (May 30, 1988): 10.
70. Samuel Brody quoted in "The City: Extending Manhattan": 24.
71. "UN School Plans Modified," *Progressive Architecture* 47 (March 1966): 55; Kathleen Teltsch, "U.N. School's Site to Be at 25th St.," *New York Times* (May 18, 1969): 37; White and Willensky, *AIA Guide* (1978), 126.
72. Huxtable, "Creative Plan for River": 28.
73. Shipler, "The Long Struggle for Waterside: A Case History": 1–2.
74. Richard Ravitch quoted in Shipler, "The Long Struggle for Waterside: A Case History": 1.
75. Quoted in Shipler, "The Long Struggle for Waterside: A Case History": 2.
76. Goldberger, "Waterside Design Builds Reputation": 41, 44. For discussion of the way two architects, Geoffrey Freeman and Hugh Hardy, furnished their own apartments at Waterside, see Stephens, "Architects in Residence. Design: Two Solutions at the Waterside": 38–40.
77. Goldberger, *The City Observed*, 103.
78. Thomas Adams, *The Building of the City* (New York: Regional Plan Association, 1931), 383, 416.
79. Stern, Gilmartin and Mellins, *New York 1930*, 691.
80. "Crosstown Tubes for Autos Planned," *New York Times* (October 28, 1944): 17.
81. "Plan Urged for Midtown Traffic," *American City* 62 (June 1947): 113.
82. Robert Moses quoted in Cleveland Rodgers, *Robert Moses: Builder for Democracy* (New York: Henry Holt & Co., 1952), 174.
83. "N.Y. Traffic Answer," *Architectural Forum* 85 (December 1946): 9–10; Moses, *Public Works: A Dangerous Trade*, 305–6; Caro, *The Power Broker*, 769–70, 782–85.
84. Quoted in Caro, *The Power Broker*, 784.

85. "Citizens' Housing Opposes 30th Street Expressway," *Citizens' Housing and Planning News* 16 (November–December 1957): 1.
86. Charles S. Ascher, "Opposition Mounting to 30th Street Expressway," *Citizens' Housing and Planning News* 16 (January–February 1958): 4.
87. Ralph Blumenthal, "Paley Is Donating a Vest-Pocket Park to the City on Stork Club Site," *New York Times* (February 2, 1966): 37, 42; Ada Louise Huxtable, "Experiment in Parks," *New York Times* (February 2, 1966): 37, 42.
88. Stern, Gilmartin and Mellins, *New York 1930*, 429.
89. Stern, Gilmartin and Massengale, *New York 1900*, 102–3.
90. Stern, Gilmartin and Mellins, *New York 1930*, 137.
91. Stern, Gilmartin and Massengale, *New York 1900*, 196, 198.
92. Stern, Gilmartin and Massengale, *New York 1900*, 195–96.
93. Thomas W. Ennis, "New Look Is Set for Murray Hill," *New York Times* (January 22, 1956), VIII: 1–2. Also see Lee E. Cooper, "Old Houses in Murray Hill Area Being Razed for New Apartments," *New York Times* (November 29, 1953), VIII: 1, 6; "New Apartments Fail to Disturb the Sedate Character of Murray Hill," *New York Times* (March 5, 1961), VIII: 1; "Contrasts Sharp on Murray Hill," *New York Times* (March 5, 1961), VIII: 1, 9; Thomas W. Ennis, "3d Avenue Is Now High-Rent Area," *New York Times* (August 19, 1962), VIII: 1, 10; "Change Resisted in a Changing City," *New York Times* (March 13, 1969): 49.
94. Maurice Foley, "Builder Acquires Murray Hill Site; 2d Ave. Block Sold," *New York Times* (November 11, 1945), VIII: 1.
95. Maurice Foley, "Razing Old Homes on Park Ave. Site for New Housing," *New York Times* (June 26, 1949), VIII: 1.
96. "Reports New Murray Hill Apartment House Over 85 Per Cent Rented," *Real Estate Record and Guide* 167 (March 3, 1951): 3.
97. James Trager, *Park Avenue: Street of Dreams* (New York: Atheneum, 1990), 208.
98. Trager, *Park Avenue*, 150–51.
99. Trager, *Park Avenue*, 208.
100. "Luxury Apartment Nearing Completion at 80 Park Avenue," *Real Estate Record and Guide* 176 (December 17, 1955): 3; Trager, *Park Avenue*, 208.
101. "Community Church, New York City," *Architectural Record* 102 (September 1947): 110; "Holmes Preaches in New Building," *New York Times* (September 27, 1948): 19; "Holmes Dedicates New Church Here," *New York Times* (October 18, 1948): 19; "Simplified Religious Buildings," *Interiors* 108 (December 1948): 10, 12.
102. Stern, Gilmartin and Mellins, *New York 1930*, 718, 720–22.
103. Quoted in "Community Church, New York City": 110.
104. "Simplified Religious Buildings": 10.
105. John Haynes Holmes quoted in "Holmes Preaches in New Building": 19.
106. "Air-Conditioned Church to Be Dedicated on Thursday," *New York Times* (June 25, 1957): 31; Meyer Berger, "About New York: Stone Carver Comes Out of Retirement at 71 to Do Pointing on Church Edifice," *New York Times* (November 11, 1957): 34; "6-Ton Pillars Delivered to Church," *New York Times* (October 24, 1958): 35; White and Willensky, *AIA Guide* (1967), 106; White and Willensky, *AIA Guide* (1978), 133.
107. Berger, "About New York: Stone Carver Comes Out of Retirement at 71 to Do Pointing on Church Edifice": 34. For St. Bartholomew's Church, see Stern, Gilmartin and Massengale, *New York 1900*, 113, 116, 120–21; Stern, Gilmartin and Mellins, *New York 1930*, 153, 158.
108. White and Willensky, *AIA Guide* (1967), 106. Also see White and Willensky, *AIA Guide* (1978), 133.
109. Stern, Gilmartin and Mellins, *New York 1930*, 526–28.
110. White and Willensky, *AIA Guide* (1967), 108.
111. "Erection of 36-Story, $20,000,000, Office Building on Site of Former Murray Hill Hotel, Further Evidence of Confidence in Future of City and Its Stability of Real Estate Values," *Real Estate Record and Guide* 162 (December 25, 1948): 3–4; "New York Office Building Reverts to Vertical Style," *Architectural Forum* 90 (January 1949): 15; "New York's Skyline Gets a Facelifting," *Business Week* (May 21, 1949): 21–22; "Lobby Ceiling Is Started," *New York Times* (November 13, 1949), VIII: 12; "New York Skyscrapers Are Changing Manhattan's Profile," *Architectural Forum* 91 (December 1949): 10; "New York City's New Skyscraper," *Architectural Forum* 91 (December 1949): 88; "Reports Eighty Per Cent of Space in 100 Park Avenue Leased from Plans," *Real Estate Record and Guide* 165 (February 4, 1950): 3–4; "New 36-Story Office Building at 100 Park Ave. 90 Per Cent Rented," *Real Estate Record and Guide* 165 (June 3, 1950): 3; Lewis Mumford, "The Sky Line: More Pelion, More Ossa," *New Yorker* 26 (February 3, 1951): 76, 79–82; Thomas H. Creighton, "100 Park Avenue: New York, N.Y.," *Progressive Architecture* 32 (May 1951): 53–66; "Notable Post-War Buildings Figuring in Architectural Awards of the Fifth Avenue Association," *New York Times* (April 27, 1952), VIII: 1, 8; Jane Jacobs, "New York's Office Boom," *Architectural Forum* 106 (March 1957): 104–13; Earle Shultz and Walter Simmons, *Offices in the Sky* (Indianapolis, Ind.: Bobbs-Merrill, 1959), 247–48; Robert F. R. Ballard, *Directory of Manhattan Office Buildings* (New York: McGraw-Hill, 1978), 34.
112. Mumford, "The Sky Line: More Pelion, More Ossa": 80–81.
113. "Life Begins at Ten," *Architectural Forum* 114 (May 1961): 130–33.
114. "News: More Park Ave. Offices," *Architectural Forum* 97 (August 1952): 63; "Erection of Tishman Realty & Construction Company's New Skyscraper in Grand Central Zone Gets Underway," *Real Estate Record and Guide* 170 (September 20, 1952): 3; "Tishman Building to Be of Aluminum," *New York Times* (December 18, 1952): 53; "Building: Aluminum Skyscraper in New York," *Interiors* 112 (January 1953): 14; "Covering a Skyscraper in 6½ Days," *Business Week* (August 8, 1953): 28–29; "New Thinking on the Effect of Office Windows on Design," *Architectural Forum* 99 (September 1953): 118–23; "The Record Reports: 26 Stories Enclosed in 6½ Working Days," *Architectural Record* 114 (October 1953): 336, 338; "Tishman Realty & Construction Company Adapts Stage Lighting Effects in 99 Park Avenue Building Lobby," *Real Estate Record and Guide* 174 (July 31, 1954): 3; Lewis Mumford, "The Sky Line: Skin Treatment and New Wrinkles," *New Yorker* 30 (October 23, 1954): 132–38; Jacobs, "New York's Office Boom": 107; Richard Roth, "High-Rise Down to Earth," *Progressive Architecture* 38 (June 1957): 196–200; Jürgen Joedicke, *Office Buildings*, trans. C. V. Amerongen (New York: Frederick A. Praeger, 1962), 92–93; Ballard, *Directory of Manhattan Office Buildings*, 33; Krinsky, "Architecture in New York City," in Wallock, ed., *New York: Culture Capital of the World, 1940–1965*, 100; Trager, *Park Avenue*, 201.
115. Stern, Gilmartin and Mellins, *New York 1930*, 348, 354.
116. Victoria Newhouse, *Wallace K. Harrison, Architect* (New York: Rizzoli International Publications, 1989), 145–47, figs. 125–27.
117. Mumford, "The Sky Line: Skin Treatment and New Wrinkles": 137.

118. White and Willensky, *AIA Guide* (1967), 108; Ballard, *Directory of Manhattan Office Buildings*, 33.
119. Stern, Gilmartin and Mellins, *New York 1930*, 191.
120. "Office Tower atop High School to Rise on Armory Site," *Real Estate Record and Guide* 209 (April 1, 1972): 2; "Demolition," *Progressive Architecture* 53 (May 1972): 33; "Mixed Use Building Replaces Old Armory, School and Offices to Share One Unit," *Journal of the American Institute of Architects* 57 (June 1972): 12; "Central Manhattan High School," *Architectural Record* 152 (July 1972): 43; "Combined Usage Places High School with Offices," *Architectural Record* 156 (September 1974): 37; Blake, "The Seventh Annual Cityscape Awards": 50; White and Willensky, *AIA Guide* (1978), 131–32; Goldberger, *The City Observed*, 120–21; Trager, *Park Avenue*, 202. In 1943 a proposal was announced to replace the armory with a transportation terminal to be designed by Starrett & Van Vleck. See "'Honest' Burton," *Architectural Forum* 78 (March 1943): 104.
121. Goldberger, *The City Observed*, 121.
122. Blake, "The Seventh Annual Cityscape Awards": 50.
123. "New York's $5,500,000 East Side Airlines Terminal," *Architectural Record* 110 (August 1951): 13; Lewis Mumford, "The Sky Line: Terminals and Monuments," *New Yorker* 30 (March 20, 1954): 99–100, 104–7.
124. For Peterkin's 1940 Airlines Terminal, see Stern, Gilmartin and Mellins, *New York 1930*, 704–5.
125. Mumford, "The Sky Line: Terminals and Monuments": 104.
126. Mumford, "The Sky Line: Terminals and Monuments": 99, 105.
127. "Zoning Law Aids Original Designs," *New York Times* (July 18, 1965), VIII: 1; "Telephone Company Puts Up Another Pole," *Progressive Architecture* 47 (February 1966): 57; "New York Telephone Company Will Occupy Most of 1095 Sixth Ave.," *Real Estate Record and Guide* 205 (February 21, 1970): 2; Paul Goldberger, "When Building for the Future Means a Step Backward," *New York Times* (December 6, 1975): 33.
128. "In the Heart of New York, the Atmosphere of a House in the Country," *Architectural Forum* 85 (August 1946): 63–68; "Amster Yard," *House and Garden* 90 (August 1946): 53–57, 93; Olga Gueft, "At Home in Amster Yard at Last," *Interiors* 115 (November 1955): 90–93; Marion Gough, "In the Midst of Manhattan: The Sylvan Urbanity of Amster Yard," *House Beautiful* 107 (August 1965): 102–5, 124; Landmarks Preservation Commission of the City of New York, LP-0277 (June 21, 1966); Ada Louise Huxtable, "City Landmark Gets a Chance for Survival," *New York Times* (August 2, 1970), VIII: 1, 7; White and Willensky, *AIA Guide* (1978), 160–61; Goldberger, *The City Observed*, 130; Barbaralee Diamonstein, *The Landmarks of New York* (New York: Harry N. Abrams, 1988), 152; Mitchell Owens, "One Man's Court," *House and Garden* 164 (October 1992): 72, 74, 76. For an example of James Amster's design work, the D'Orsay Perfumes showroom, see "New York—A 57th Street Salon," *Interior Design and Decoration* 19 (April 1949): 27–29.
129. "In the Heart of New York, the Atmosphere of a House in the Country": 65.
130. Stern, Gilmartin and Mellins, *New York 1930*, 428–29.
131. "Idyll on 48th Street: The Russel Wright Homestead," *Interiors* 109 (September 1949): 88–95.
132. For the Wrights' 1931 apartment, see Stern, Gilmartin and Mellins, *New York 1930*, 460–61.
133. Quoted in "Idyll on 48th Street: The Russel Wright Homestead": 89.
134. "Their Fine Italian Hands," *Interiors* 106 (July 1947): 80–83.
135. Betty Pepis, "A Setting for Art," *New York Times* (January 7, 1951), VI: 36–37; Ian McCallum, *Architecture USA* (London: Architectural Press, 1959), 117; Henry Hope Reed, *The Golden City* (New York: Doubleday, 1959), 10; Huxtable, *Four Walking Tours of Modern Architecture in New York City*, 44, 46; John M. Jacobus, Jr., *Philip Johnson* (New York: George Braziller, 1962), 27–28, plates 18–20; *Philip Johnson: Architecture, 1949–1965*, with an intro. by Henry-Russell Hitchcock (New York: Holt, Rinehart and Winston, 1966), 13, 46–47; White and Willensky, *AIA Guide* (1967), 125–26; Rita Reif, "To Johnson, It Feels Like Home," *New York Times* (January 16, 1974): 44; Goldberger, *The City Observed*, 150–51; Tauranac, *Essential New York*, 195–96; Christopher Gray, "Designs for Living," *Avenue* 11 (November 1987): 158–65; Krinsky, "Architecture in New York City," in Wallock, ed., *New York: Culture Capital of the World, 1940–1965*, 102; Rita Reif, "Manhattan Town House by Johnson Being Sold," *New York Times* (March 27, 1989), C: 14; Christopher Gray, "Neighborhood: Nifties from the Fifties," *Avenue* 14 (January 1990): 117–23.
136. Stern, Gilmartin and Mellins, *New York 1930*, 379–80, 383.
137. Jacobus, *Philip Johnson*, 28.
138. Reif, "To Johnson, It Feels Like Home": 44.
139. "Lapidus to Design Two New York Hotels," *Interiors* 120 (August 1960): 22; "Americana Architect Skyline Changer," press release issued by Americana West of New York, August 10, 1960, in New York Herald Tribune Clipping File, Queens Borough Public Library; "Huge Buildings Planned on Former Zeckendorf Sites," *Architectural Forum* 113 (September 1960): 9; "Hotels and Motels," *Interior Design* 32 (April 1961): 130–45; "Manhattan Greets New Hotel," *Business Week* (July 22, 1961): 32; "First Since Waldorf," *Time* 78 (August 4, 1961): 49; "Tower of Babel," *Newsweek* 58 (July 31, 1961): 76–78; "The Talk of the Town: Playful," *New Yorker* 37 (August 5, 1961): 20–21; "$25 Million Tingle," *Architectural Forum* 115 (September 1961): 7; Olga Gueft, "What Do You Think of the Summit?" *Interiors* 121 (October 1961): 132–39; R. Gary Allen, "Glittering Nightmare," *Architectural Forum* 115 (November 1961): 181; Walter McQuade, "Architecture," *Nation* 193 (December 2, 1961): 457; "Letters to the Editors," *Interiors* 121 (December 1961): 8; "Hotels and Motels," *Interior Design* 32 (October 1961): 142–53; Huxtable, "Our New Buildings: Hits and Misses": 16–17, 105–6; Joseph Wershba, "Americana's Designer," *New York Post* (September 25, 1962): 37; Russell Lynes, "New York Hotels (with Reservations)," *Art in America* 51 (April 1963): 58–61; John W. Cook and Heinrich Klotz, eds., *Conversations with Architects* (New York: Praeger, 1973), 148, 150, 155; Morris Lapidus, *An Architecture of Joy* (Miami, Fla.: E. A. Seemann, 1979), 193–95, 197; Christopher Gray, "Schlock of Ages," *Avenue* 17 (December 1992): 31–32, 34, 36, 38.
140. "Manhattan Greets New Hotel": 34.
141. Lapidus, *An Architecture of Joy*, 129.
142. "Hotels and Motels," (April 1961): 144.
143. Lapidus, *An Architecture of Joy*, 193.
144. Morris Lapidus quoted in Gueft, "What Do You Think of the Summit?": 134.
145. Lapidus, *An Architecture of Joy*, 193.
146. Morris Lapidus quoted in "The Talk of the Town: Playful": 21.
147. Morris Lapidus quoted in "Hotel and Motels" (October 1961): 146.
148. Morris Lapidus quoted in "Hotels and Motels" (October 1961): 150.
149. Lapidus, *An Architecture of Joy*, 193.
150. Gueft, "What Do You Think of the Summit?": 136, 138.
151. McQuade, "Architecture": 457.
152. Lynes, "New York Hotels (with Reservations)": 60.
153. "First Since the Waldorf": 49.
154. "First Since the Waldorf": 49.
155. McQuade, "Architecture": 457.
156. "The Talk of the Town: Playful": 20–21.
157. Huxtable, "Our New Buildings: Hits and Misses": 106.
158. Lynes, "New York Hotels (with Reservations)": 60.
159. Lapidus, *An Architecture of Joy*, 193–95.
160. McQuade, "Architecture": 457.
161. Morris Lapidus quoted in Wershba, "Americana's Designer": 37.
162. Morris Lapidus quoted in Cook and Klotz, eds., *Conversations with Architects*, 174.

WEST SIDE: FROM CHELSEA TO CLINTON

1. White and Willensky, *AIA Guide* (1978), 174; Paul Goldberger, *The City Observed: New York* (New York: Random House, 1979), 107.
2. John A. Kouwenhoven, *The Columbia Historical Portrait of New York* (Garden City, N.Y.: Doubleday & Co., 1953), 406–7; Stern, Gilmartin and Massengale, *New York 1900*, 191–92, 194; M. Christine Boyer, *Manhattan Manners: Architecture and Style 1850–1900* (New York: Rizzoli International Publications, 1985), 43–129; Landmarks Preservation Commission of the City of New York, *Ladies' Mile Historic District Designation Report*, 2 vols. (New York, 1989).
3. For Macy's, Gimbel's and Altman's, see Stern, Gilmartin and Massengale, *New York 1900*, 192–95.
4. Stern, Gilmartin and Mellins, *New York 1930*, 417–18. For the original London Terrace houses, see Nathan Silver, *Lost New York* (Boston: Houghton Mifflin, 1967), 134.
5. Stern, Gilmartin and Mellins, *New York 1930*, 520–22.
6. "'El' Razing Contract Let," *New York Times* (September 13, 1940): 25; "Weather Man Controls Speed of 'El' Demolition," *New York Times* (December 31, 1940): 18; Stan Fischler, *Uptown, Downtown: A Trip Through Time on New York's Subways* (New York: Hawthorn Books, 1976), 12, 259.
7. "Post-War Public Housing and Large Homes Sold in Suburban Neighborhoods," *New York Times* (October 4, 1942), IX: 1; "New York State and City Public Housing," *Interiors* 104 (November 1944): 58–63, 86; "16 Veterans Get New Homes Today," *New York Times* (December 31, 1946): 10; Lewis Mumford, "The Sky Line: Schools for Human Beings, Part I," *New Yorker* 28 (April 19, 1952): 65–66, 68–72; Lewis Mumford, "The Sky Line: Schools for Human Beings, Part II," *New Yorker* 28 (April 26, 1952): 68–74; Christian Hubert, "The Late Work, 1939–1969," in Christian Hubert and Lindsay Stamm Shapiro, *William Lescaze* (New York: Institute for Architecture and Urban Studies; New York: Rizzoli International Publications, 1982), 108, 111; Thomas E. Norton and Jerry E. Patterson, *Living It Up: A Guide to the Named Apartment Houses of New York* (New York: Atheneum, 1984), 133; Richard Plunz, *A History of Housing in New York City* (New York: Columbia University Press, 1990), 261–62.
8. Mumford, "The Sky Line: Schools for Human Beings, Part I": 66.
9. Thomas W. Ennis, "Chelsea Clean-Up Drive Grows into Broad Rebuilding Program," *New York Times* (May 29, 1960), VIII: 1, 8; Robert Conley, "New City Housing to Cost 83 Million," *New York Times* (April 26, 1961): 1, 31; Robet Conley, "New City Housing Reshapes Lives," *New York Times* (April 30, 1961): 81; Norton and Patterson, *Living It Up*, 97.
10. "New School Started," *New York Times* (June 29, 1949): 29; Mumford, "The Sky Line: Schools for Human Beings, Part I": 65–66, 68.
11. Mumford, "The Sky Line: Schools for Human Beings, Part I": 68, 70.
12. Mumford, "The Sky Line: Schools for Human Beings, Part II": 72.
13. Ennis, "Chelsea Clean-Up Drive Grows into Broad Rebuilding Program": 1, 8; "Fulton Houses Dedicated at 9th Ave. near 19th St.," *New York Times* (October 16, 1962): 78; Norton and Patterson, *Living It Up*, 288.
14. Ennis, "Chelsea Clean-Up Grows into Broad Rebuilding Program": 1, 8; Martin Arnold, "Kennedy to Speak at I.L.G.W.U. Co-op," *New York Times* (May 19, 1962): 13; Richard P. Hunt, "President Urges Union to Widen Their Social Aims," *New York Times* (May 20, 1962): 1, 62; "Housing," *Americana Annual for 1962* (New York and Chicago: Encyclopedia Americana Corp., 1963): 309–11; White and Willensky, *AIA Guide* (1967), 87; Goldberger, *The City Observed*, 110–11; Lawrence Halprin, *New York, New York* (New York: Lawrence Halprin & Associates, 1968), 15–21; Ellen Perry Berkeley, "Inquiry into Open Space," *Architectural Forum* 29 (July–August 1968): 96–101; Robert A. M. Stern, *New Directions in American Architecture* (New York: George Braziller, 1969), 100–102; Plunz, *A History of Housing in New York City*, 282, 292–93.
15. For the Church of Holy Apostles, see Landmarks Preservation Commission of the City of New York, LP-0231 (October 19, 1966); Barbaralee Diamonstein, *The Landmarks of New York* (New York: Harry N. Abrams, 1988), 105.
16. John F. Kennedy quoted in Hunt, "President Urges Unions to Widen Their Social Aims": 62.
17. Halprin, *New York, New York*, 103.
18. Goldberger, *The City Observed*, 111.
19. "Seminary Is Razing Library in Chelsea," *New York Times* (April 5, 1959): 86; "Ground Is Broken on Seminary Site," *New York Times* (July 16, 1959): 24; Goldberger, *The City Observed*, 107.
20. Goldberger, *The City Observed*, 107.
21. "Fashion College to Be Built Here," *New York Times* (January 28, 1956): 19; Benjamin Fine, "Fashion College Here to Have 2-Tone Building," *New York Times* (February 8, 1956): 1, 36; "Fashion College Planned for New York Garment Area," *Architectural Record* 120 (October 1956): 402; Herbert Koshetz, "Apparel College Plans Expansion," *New York Times* (May 9, 1957): 45, 51; "P/A News Bulletins," *Progressive Architecture* 39 (June 1958): 40; "Dormitory for Manhattan Fashion Institute," *Architectural Forum* 113 (October 1960): 55; White and Willensky, *AIA Guide* (1967), 87; "Urban Institute of Fashion," *Progressive Architecture* 48 (September 1967): 68; "Buildings in the News," *Architectural Record* 143 (February 1968): 40–43; "Buildings in the News," *Architectural Record* 144 (September 1968): 41; "Fashion Institute Starts Expansion," *New York Times* (April 22, 1969): 93; White and Willensky, *AIA Guide* (1978), 109–10; Goldberger, *The City Observed*, 111–12.
22. Goldberger, *The City Observed*, 111.
23. Goldberger, *The City Observed*, 111–12.

24. White and Willensky, *AIA Guide* (1978), 110.
25. Landmarks Preservation Commission of the City of New York, LP-0666 (September 15, 1970); Diamonstein, *The Landmarks of New York*, 390. The district was extended in 1981 to include adjacent properties to the north. See Landmarks Preservation Commission of the City of New York, LP-1088 (February 3, 1981); Diamonstein, *The Landmarks of New York*, 390.
26. Landmarks Preservation Commission of the City of New York, LP-0679, LP-0680 (September 15, 1970); Diamonstein, *The Landmarks of New York*, 108.
27. Landmarks Preservation Commission of the City of New York, LP-0215 (March 15, 1966); Diamonstein, *The Landmarks of New York*, 182–83. Also see Marshall Smith, "A Room with Ghost $4 and Up," *Life* 57 (September 18, 1964): 134–38, 140.
28. Landmarks Preservation Commission of the City of New York, LP-1295 (October 7, 1986); Diamonstein, *The Landmarks of New York*, 366.
29. David Morton, "Ostrow House: Turning on Chelsea," *Progressive Architecture* 52 (May 1971): 76–79; White and Willensky, *AIA Guide* (1978), 108.
30. For Pennsylvania Station and the General Post Office, see Stern, Gilmartin and Massengale, *New York 1900*, 40–43.
31. Martin Arnold, "Complex over the Pennsylvania Rails Planned to House 1,600 Families," *New York Times* (September 29, 1967): 49; "Johnson Designs Apartments for Site over Pennsylvania Railroad Tracks," *Progressive Architecture* 47 (November 1967): 59; Franklin Whitehouse, "Tight Money Imperils Giant Chelsea Project," *New York Times* (June 2, 1968), VIII: 1, 4; Philip Johnson, "Beyond Monuments," *Progressive Architecture* 138 (January–February 1973): 54–69.
32. "Distribution Center Planned in Midtown," *New York Times* (February 5, 1966): 1, 34; "Monument," *Architectural Forum* 124 (May 1966): 90; "A Building Tailored for the Garment Industry," *Fortune* 74 (September 1966): 166; "Westyard Office—Warehouse: New Lease on Life for Urban Industry," *Architectural Record* 143 (May 1968): 194–95; "A Warehouse Too Handsome to Remain One," *Architectural Record* 147 (May 1970): 113–18; White and Willensky, *AIA Guide* (1978), 129.
33. For further discussion of the Philadelphia School, see Jan C. Rowan, "Wanting to Be the Philadelphia School," *Progressive Architecture* 42 (April 1961): 130–63; Stern, *New Directions in American Architecture*, 11–21, 50–59.
34. "Monument": 90.
35. "Shipshape Sailor's Snug Harbor," *Progressive Architecture* 46 (February 1965): 58; "Leaning Backward to Comply with Setback Law," *Journal of the American Institute of Architects* 45 (March 1966): 10; White and Willensky, *AIA Guide* (1978), 112; Carol Herselle Krinsky, "Architecture in New York City," in Leonard Wallock, ed., *New York: Culture Capital of the World, 1940–1965* (New York: Rizzoli International Publications, 1988), 108; Christopher Gray, "Schlock of Ages," *Avenue* 17 (December 1992): 31–32, 34, 36, 38.
36. "Shipshape Sailor's Snug Harbor": 58.
37. Stern, Gilmartin and Mellins, *New York 1930*, 312, 317.
38. "The Editor's Asides," *Journal of the American Institute of Architects* 8 (August 1947): 93–94.
39. Stern, Gilmartin and Mellins, *New York 1930*, 317.
40. "Keeping the Sales in View," *Interiors* 102 (December 1942): 40–45, 62; John Matthews Hatton, "Mechanical Equipment and Store Design," *Pencil Points* 25 (August 1944): 72–77.
41. "McCreery's Furniture Floor-Full," *Interiors* 106 (June 1947): 100–101; "New Furniture Floor," *Architectural Forum* 87 (July 1947): 114–16.
42. "McCreery's Ending 116 Years as Store," *New York Times* (October 8, 1953): 31.
43. "McCreery's Ending 116 Years as Store": 31; "Ohrbach's Takes McCreery Store," *New York Times* (February 2, 1954): 34; "Move by Ohrbach Set for Thursday," *New York Times* (August 22, 1954), II: 1, 7; "50,000 in 6 Hours Crowd New Ohrbach's; Some Items Sold Out at 34th St. Opening," *New York Times* (August 27, 1954): 11.
44. "Does Macy's Tell Gimbel's?" *Newsweek* 70 (September 25, 1967): 82.
45. Lynn Langway with Pamela Ellis Simons, "Does Bloomie's Tell Macy's?" *Newsweek* 88 (December 13, 1976): 83–84, 86. Also see Paul Goldberger, "Design Notebook: Department Store Face Lifts Succeed, but Not Entirely," *New York Times* (July 28, 1977), C: 12.
46. For DeWitt Clinton High School, see Stern, Gilmartin and Massengale, *New York 1900*, 80–83.
47. Stern, Gilmartin and Massengale, *New York 1900*, 287.
48. "The Growing West Side," *New York Times* (April 17, 1881): 14.
49. Stern, Gilmartin and Mellins, *New York 1930*, 417–18.
50. "Brisk Market for West Side Suites," *Real Estate Record and Guide* 147 (January 25, 1941): 8–9.
51. Frank Chouteau Brown, "Tendencies in Apartment House Design, Part II," *Architectural Record* 150 (July 1921): 44–63.
52. Stern, Gilmartin and Massengale, *New York 1900*, 138–39.
53. Stern, Gilmartin and Massengale, *New York 1900*, 48.
54. "Designed for the Handling of Milk," *Real Estate Record and Guide* 82 (September 12, 1908): 509–10.
55. Christopher Gray, "'Gas Station' Style: An Overlooked Gem of the 1930's," *New York Times* (March 27, 1988), VIII: 14.
56. "United Parcel Service Buys West Side Block," *New York Times* (August 12, 1959): 45; Gray, "Schlock of Ages": 36.
57. "Schools and Colleges," *Architectural Forum* 100 (January 1954): 45; "The Big City School," *Architectural Forum* 102 (April 1955): 139; A. H. Roskin, "New $7,000,000 Printing School to Spur Training of Apprentices," *New York Times* (January 14, 1957): 25; "News Bulletins," *Progressive Architecture* 38 (February 1957): 98; "Printing School Dedicated Here," *New York Times* (January 16, 1959): 56; "Buildings in the News," *Architectural Record* 125 (April 1959): 12; "Tokens of Art in City Schools," *Progressive Architecture* 40 (April 1959): 146–51; *Hans Hofmann* (New York: Harry N. Abrams, 1964), 224; "Architectural Bulletins," *Progressive Architecture* 40 (March 1959): 159; "Buildings in the News," *Architectural Record* 125 (April 1959): 12; Christopher Gray, "Neighborhood: Nifties from the Fifties," *Avenue* 14 (January 1990): 117–23.
58. "Tokens of Art in City Schools": 147.
59. White and Willensky, *AIA Guide* (1978), 145.
60. White and Willensky, *AIA Guide* (1988), 223.
61. "Criminal Prevention Instead of Detention," *Progressive Architecture* 51 (September 1970): 38; Robert Jensen, "Clinton Youth and Family Center," *Architectural Record* 149 (June 1971): 107–10; "Centre de rencontres pour jeunes," *L'Architecture d'Aujourd'hui* 157 (August 1971): 37; C. Ray Smith, *Supermannerism: New Attitudes in Post-Modern Architecture* (New York: E. P. Dutton, 1977), 255–56; White and Willensky, *AIA Guide* (1978), 142–43; *James Stewart Polshek: Context and Responsibility* (New York: Rizzoli International Publications, 1988), 30, 78–79.
62. Jensen, "Clinton Youth and Family Center": 107.
63. Smith, *Supermannerism*, 256.
64. "Windowless Phone Building," *Progressive Architecture* 43 (August 1962): 56, 58; "Windowless Skyscraper," *Architectural Forum* 117 (December 1962): 17; "Bell Builds 'Cellar' in the Sky," *Business Week* (February 9, 1963): 30–31; "New York Telephone Company Will Occupy Most of 1095 Sixth Ave.," *Real Estate Record and Guide* 205 (February 21, 1970): 2; Paul Goldberger, "When Building for Future Means a Step Backward," *New York Times* (December 6, 1975): 33; White and Willensky, *AIA Guide* (1978), 145.
65. For the New York Telephone Company's earlier buildings, see Stern, Gilmartin and Mellins, *New York 1930*, 565–67, 570–71.
66. White and Willensky, *AIA Guide* (1978), 145.
67. William Marlin, "Homing in on Housing," *Architectural Forum* 137 (November 1972): 48–49; Jonathan Barnett, *Urban Design as Public Policy* (New York: Architectural Record Books, 1974), 110–12; Paul Goldberger, "The New Clinton Towers Is Step in Right Direction," *New York Times* (January 23, 1975): 37; "Clinton Towers Dedicated," *New York Times* (January 24, 1975): 35.
68. Goldberger, "The New Clinton Towers Is Step in Right Direction": 37.
69. Glenn Fowler, "City Is Limiting Clinton Building," *New York Times* (November 22, 1974): 43. Also see Laurie Johnston, "Convention Backers Call Zone for Clinton Peril to West Side," *New York Times* (September 24, 1974): 37; "The Clinton Community," editorial, *New York Times* (September 24, 1974): 40.
70. "Redevelopment Promotion: Zeckendorf in New York," *Architectural Record* 119 (February 1956): 48.
71. William Zeckendorf quoted in "Redevelopment Promotion": 48.
72. Port of New York Authority, *A Plan for a New Consolidated Passenger Ship Terminal in the Port of New York* (New York: Port of New York Authority, 1967); George Horne, "6-Liner Super Pier on Hudson Urged," *New York Times* (April 26, 1967): 1, 35; "New Ship Terminal," editorial, *New York Times* (April 27, 1967): 44; "Comfort for Ocean Voyagers?" *Progressive Architecture* 48 (June 1967): 66.
73. Horne, "6-Liner Super Pier on Hudson Urged": 1.
74. Barnett, *Urban Design as Public Policy*, 161.
75. Seth S. King, "Architect Hired for Pier Project: Briton to Plan a Revamping of West Side Area," *New York Times* (November 19, 1967): 40; James Stirling and Arthur Baker, *Midtown Manhattan West* (New York: City of New York, Department of City Planning, 1968); "Manhattan: A Report by James Stirling," *Architectural Design* 39 (December 1969): 663–72; "Outline Renewal Plan for Midtown Manhattan West," *Lotus* 6 (December 1969): 109–15; Peter Arnell and Ted Bickford, eds., *James Stirling: Buildings and Projects* (London: Architectural Association, 1984), 163.
76. John V. Lindsay quoted in King, "Architect Hired for Pier Project": 40.
77. Quoted in "Manhattan: A Report by James Stirling": 670.
78. Barnett, *Urban Design as Public Policy*, 160–71, 196.
79. Edward C. Burks, "New Exhibit Hall Planned Here," *New York Times* (March 25, 1970): 49; Edward C. Burks, "City Planning Convention Center," *New York Times* (February 24, 1971): 1, 81; "New York City Aims to Increase Benefits and Beat Chicago at Convention Game," *Journal of the American Institute of Architects* 56 (November 1971): 18; "Thirty Teams Are for Largest Convention Center," *Engineering News-Record* 188 (February 24, 1972): 15; "SOM Chosen to Design $100-Million Convention Center," *Engineering News-Record* 188 (April 13, 1972): 12; "Big Plans," *Architectural Forum* 136 (May 1972): 19; "Big Doings in New York City," *Progressive Architecture* 53 (June 1972): 35, 41; "New York's Convention Center," *Architectural Record* 153 (March 1973): 40; "New York City Convention and Exhibition Center," *Architecture Plus* 1 (March 1973): 95; Alan V. Tishman, "To Enhance Waterfront Vistas," letter to the editor, *New York Times* (April 23, 1973): 32; Theodore W. Kheel, "The Convention Center: Building First, Planning Later," *Village Voice* 18 (April 26, 1973): 21–22; Theodore W. Kheel, "Convention Center: The Missing Link," letter to the editor, *New York Times* (May 12, 1973): 32; Jack Newfield, "New York's Monster Builders. Tisch Gang: The City's Permanent Government," *Village Voice* 18 (May 17, 1973): 1, 103–5; Murray Schumach, "Convention Center Gains Estimate Board Approval," *New York Times* (May 25, 1973): 1, 14; Jack Newfield, "Why Kheel Opposes the Center," *Village Voice* 18 (August 17, 1973): 104; "Convention Center Up for Vote," *Village Voice* 18 (May 24, 1973): 10; Ada Louise Huxtable, "Anti-Street, Anti-People," *New York Times* (June 10, 1973), II: 24; Jack Newfield, "Seven Reasons Not to Build the West Side Convention Center," *Village Voice* 18 (September 13, 1973): 5–6; John Darnton, "Convention Center Approved by Board," *New York Times* (November 16, 1973): 1, 44; "Good News: Strictly Conventional," *New York* 7 (December 31, 1973–January 7, 1974): 64; Barnett, *Urban Design as Public Policy*, 162–63, 166, 168–71; "A $200-Million Building Revived by Money," *Engineering News-Record* 192 (May 2, 1974): 13; Suzanne Stephens, "Manhattan Is Growing, as Always, Horizontally," *New York Times* (June 30, 1974), IV: 5; Jack Newfield, "City Blights: A West Side Story," *Village Voice* 19 (December 16, 1974): 42–43.
80. White and Willensky, *AIA Guide* (1978), 145.
81. "Buildings in the News," *Architectural Record* 149 (May 1971): 42; "Buildings on the Way Up," *Progressive Architecture* 52 (May 1971): 30–31.
82. Gordon Bunshaft quoted in "New York City's Convention Center": 40.
83. Huxtable, "Anti-Street, Anti-People": 24.
84. Kheel, "Building First, Planning Later": 22. Also see Anthony Downs, *Urban Problems and Prospects* (Chicago: Markham, 1970).
85. Newfield, "New York's Monster Builders": 1, 103–5.
86. Robert Rickles quoted in Newfield, "New York's Monster Builders": 1.
87. Robert Abrams quoted in Schumack, "Convention Center Gains Estimate Board Approval": 14.
88. "A $200-Million Building Revived by Money": 192.
89. Newfield, "City Blights: A West Side Story": 43.
90. "New York City Studies Two Sites for a New Convention Center in Manhattan," *Architectural Record* 159 (February 1975): 35; Glenn Fowler, "Convention Hall Is Weighed Again," *New York Times* (December 13, 1975): 1, 19; "Beame Stands by Battery Center Site," *New York Times* (December 19, 1975): 43.
91. Joseph P. Fried, "2 West Side Rail Yards Are Sought for Housing," *New York Times* (July 30, 1974): 1, 40.
92. Donald Trump quoted in "New York City Studies Two Sites for a New Convention Center in Manhattan": 35. Also see "N. Y. Convention Center—Miracle on 34th Street?"

Interiors 135 (February 1975): 10; "Developer Proposes a Convention Center in Midtown," *New York Times* (December 18, 1975): 49; "Miracle Convention Center," *Domus* 556 (March 1976): 38; Donald J. Trump with Tony Schwartz, *Trump: The Art of the Deal* (New York: Random House, 1987), 35–36, 69–79.

93. Victor Palmieri quoted in Lawrence J. Tell, "Holding All Their Cards: How Donald Trump Cuts Such Wonderful Deals," *Barron's* 64 (August 6, 1984): 6–7, 23–25, also quoted in Trump with Schwartz, *Trump: The Art of the Deal*, 73.

94. Theodore Kheel quoted in "Developer Proposes a Convention Center": 49, also quoted in Trump with Schwartz, *Trump: The Art of the Deal*, 75–76.

95. Trump with Schwartz, *Trump: The Art of the Deal*, 76.

96. Der Scutt quoted in "N. Y. Convention Center—Miracle on 34th St?": 10.

97. "Convention Center," editorial, *New York Times* (January 19, 1976): 28.

98. Steven R. Weisman, "44th Street Leading as Convention Site," *New York Times* (May 1, 1977): 42.

99. Lee Dembart, "Convention Center at 34th Street Site Pressed by Beame," *New York Times* (December 11, 1977), II: 11.

100. Charles Kaiser, "Convention Site at West Thirty-fourth Street Chosen by Koch," *New York Times* (April 29, 1978): 1, 12. Also see Dena Kleiman, "Mayor's Representative on Convention Center: Thomas Heinrich Baer," *New York Times* (April 29, 1978): 12; Pamela G. Hollie, "Clinton Residents Deplore Choice of 34th St. Convention Center," *New York Times* (April 29, 1978): 12; Michael Goodwin, "Builders Say Center Will Revivify Area," *New York Times* (April 29, 1978): 12.

101. Kaiser, "Convention Site at West Thirty-fourth Street Chosen by Koch": 12.

102. Donald Trump quoted in Kaiser, "Convention Site at West Thirty-fourth Street Chosen by Koch": 12.

ROCKEFELLER CENTER

1. See *The Last Rivet: The Story of Rockefeller Center, a City Within a City, as Told at the Ceremony in which John D. Rockefeller, Jr., Drove the Last Rivet of the Last Building, November 1, 1939* (New York: Columbia University Press, 1940). For a detailed account of Rockefeller Center's history and first buildings, see Stern, Gilmartin and Mellins, *New York 1930*, 616–71.

2. Sigfried Giedion, *Space, Time and Architecture*, 3rd ed. (Cambridge, Mass.: Harvard University Press, 1959), 744, 747.

3. Joe Alex Morris, "The City Where Nobody Lives," *Saturday Evening Post* 222 (September 17, 1949): 32, 140, 142, 144, 146. Also see John Chapman, "Enchanted City," *American Magazine* 151 (April 1951): 28–29, 100–104; Laurance S. Rockefeller, "Rockefeller Center," *Coronet* 38 (June 1955): 77–92; Frank Fogarty, "The Earning Power of Plazas," *Architectural Forum* 108 (January 1958): 106–9, 168; Joe Alex Morris, "New York City's Multimillion-Dollar 'Village Green,'" *Reader's Digest* 91 (October 1967): 193–97, 199.

4. Morris, "The City Where Nobody Lives": 146.

5. "Not So Bright This Year," *New York Times* (November 27, 1973): 45; "Rockefeller Plaza Tree to Have Fewer Lights," *New York Times* (November 29, 1973): 45.

6. Vincent Scully, *American Architecture and Urbanism* (New York: Frederick A. Praeger, 1969), 154.

7. Meyer Berger, "Eighth Wonder of the World," *Holiday* 15 (April 1954): 52–55, 57–59, 153–56.

8. "Seven 'Wonders of Architecture' Named in Special Survey," *Architectural Record* 124 (October 1958): 15. Also see "Want to Be Rockefeller?" editorial, *Architectural Forum* 115 (July 1961): 63.

9. "Back to Skyscraping," *Interiors* 105 (August 1945): 14, 104; "News," *Architectural Forum* 83 (September 1945): 7; "Postwar Skyscraper," *Architectural Forum* 84 (May 1946): 91–93; "Esso Building Is Part of Rockefeller Center," *New York Times* (February 5, 1947): 40; "Old Glory 'Tops Out' a New Structure," *New York Times* (March 13, 1947): 48; "New Vistas in Steel," *New York Times* (April 27, 1947), VI: 6–7; "Esso Building," *Architectural Forum* 87 (August 1947): cover, 3; "Moving Stairs Speeded," *New York Times* (March 26, 1948): 23; "Esso Building," *Architectural Forum* 89 (August 1948): cover, 84–89; Ada Louise Huxtable, *Four Walking Tours of Modern Architecture in New York City* (New York: Museum of Modern Art and Municipal Art Society of New York, 1961), 36–38; Allan Balfour, *Rockefeller Center: Architecture as Theater* (New York: McGraw-Hill, 1978), 229–32; Robert F. R. Ballard, *Directory of Manhattan Office Buildings* (New York: McGraw-Hill, 1978), 168; Carol Herselle Krinsky, *Rockefeller Center* (New York: Oxford University Press, 1978), 104–6, 130–31; Walter Karp, *The Center: A History and Guide to Rockefeller Center* (New York: American Heritage, 1982), 32–33.

10. Quoted in "Restaurant in Rockefeller Center," *Architectural Forum* 90 (February 1949): 110–14.

11. "Restaurant in Rockefeller Center": 113. Hokinson's cartoons, published in the *New Yorker*, frequently featured ladies lunching at Schrafft's. See Helen Elna Hokinson, *The Ladies, God Bless 'Em!* (New York: E. P. Dutton, 1950).

12. "Dynamics in the Center," *Architectural Forum* 114 (March 1961): 132–35.

13. Krinsky, *Rockefeller Center*, 107–8.

14. "Rockefeller Center Plans RCA Building Addition," *Architectural Record* 155 (February 1974): 40; "RCA in Manhattan Pioneers Project in Solar Heating," *Interiors* 133 (March 1974): 8; "RCA's Greenhouse," *Architectural Forum* 140 (March–April 1974): 114; "RCA Scientist Predicts Home Use of Solar Energy in Five Years," *Architectural Record* 156 (July 1974): 35; Glenn Fowler, "Center in RCA Building to Draw on Sun for Heating and Cooling," *New York Times* (September 4, 1975): 33; Gene Smith, "Sarnoff Project Scrapped by RCA," *New York Times* (December 5, 1975): 57.

15. "A. M. Van Den Hoek, Floral Expert, 65," *New York Times* (January 5, 1950): 26. For Rockefeller Center's gardens at their best, see "Rockefeller Center Gardens," *Life* 30 (January 8, 1951): 51–55.

16. "Hagemeister, 54, Horticulturist," *New York Times* (April 26, 1959): 86.

17. Stern, Gilmartin and Mellins, *New York 1930*, 23.

18. Paul Goldberger, "Style Moderne—Kitsch or Serious—Is in Vogue," *New York Times* (January 31, 1974): 35, 65; Rita Reif, "Fans of Era Flock to Music Hall," *New York Times* (January 31, 1974): 35; Rita Reif, "Antiques: The Mysteries of Art Deco," *New York Times* (February 2, 1974): 26.

19. Stern, Gilmartin and Mellins, *New York 1930*, 650.

20. Stern, Gilmartin and Mellins, *New York 1930*, 186–87.

21. "Chemical Bank and Trust, New York," *Architectural Record* 97 (January 1945): 100–101.

22. "Double Size for Selling Service," *Architectural Record* 97 (March 1945): 91–98. For Walker & Gillette's 1937 design, see Stern, Gilmartin and Mellins, *New York 1930*, 182, 185–86.

23. "Savings and Loans: 'First Federal,' New York," *Architectural Record* 97 (January 1945): 94–95.

24. "Branch Bank in Rockefeller Center," *Architectural Record* 100 (November 1946): 80–83.

25. "Streamlined Bank," *Architectural Forum* 96 (March 1952): 130–32.

26. "Documentary and Analytical," *Progressive Architecture* 37 (May 1956): 114–20.

27. "Banking Under a Big Top," *Interiors* 123 (September 1963): 96–100.

PARK AVENUE

1. Richard Roth, "The Forces that Shaped Park Avenue," *Perspecta* 8 (1963): 97–102.

2. "Board to Hear Plea on Park Av. Stores," *New York Times* (October 4, 1929): 49; "Retail Zone Extended in Park Av. to 57th St.; $12,000,000 Rise in Property Value Expected," *New York Times* (November 22, 1929): 1; "Theater Ban Sustained," *Real Estate Record and Guide* 138 (August 8, 1936): 5; "Movie for Park Av. Upheld by Court," *New York Times* (October 31, 1936): 21; James Trager, *Park Avenue: Street of Dreams* (New York: Atheneum, 1990), 152.

3. "Developers Mean Business as They Transform Traditionally Residential Park Ave.," *New York Times* (October 7, 1956), VIII: 1, 3.

4. Lee E. Cooper, "Office Skyscraper to Rise on Marguery Hotel Block," *New York Times* (July 22, 1945): 1, 36; "New Apartment and Business Buildings for Fifth Avenue and East Side," *New York Times* (January 12, 1947), VIII: 1–2. For the Marguery Hotel (270 Park Avenue), see Stern, Gilmartin and Massengale, *New York 1900*, 358; Stern, Gilmartin and Mellins, *New York 1930*, 417.

5. "Trend?" *Architectural Forum* 83 (August 1945): 9.

6. Elliman's views are reported in John A. Bradley, "Change Is Cited on Park Avenue," *New York Times* (October 16, 1955), VIII: 1, 9. For Warren & Wetmore's Sherry's (300 Park Avenue), see Stern, Gilmartin and Mellins, *New York 1930*, 390, 392.

7. Lewis Mumford, "The Sky Line: Skin Treatment and New Wrinkles," *New Yorker* 30 (October 23, 1954): 132–38.

8. Ada Louise Huxtable, "Park Avenue School of Architecture," *New York Times* (December 15, 1957), VI: 30–31, 54–56.

9. Huxtable, "Park Avenue School of Architecture": 54.

10. Huxtable, "Park Avenue School of Architecture": 56.

11. Jane Jacobs, "Downtown Is for People," *Fortune* 57 (April 1958): 133–40, 236.

12. Vincent Scully, "The Death of the Street," *Perspecta* 8 (1963): 91–96. Also see Emerson Goble, "New City Image Needed," editorial, *Architectural Record* 131 (January 1962): 9.

13. "The Talk of the Town: Notes and Comment," *New Yorker* 38 (October 13, 1962): 41–42.

14. "New Office Building for Park Avenue Blockfront," *New York Times* (January 27, 1946), VIII: 1; "New York Set-Back," *Architectural Forum* 85 (September 1946): 14; "New Apartment and Business Buildings for Fifth Avenue and East Side": 1, 2; "Office Building, New York, Kahn & Jacobs, Architects," *Architectural Forum* 86 (April 1947): 94–98; "Tishman Realty & Construction Company Move Offices to Its New Building," *Real Estate Record and Guide* 160 (November 29, 1947): 3; "City's First Post-War Office Building Reported 100 Per Cent Rented," *Real Estate Record and Guide* 160 (December 13, 1947): 3; Lewis Mumford, "The Sky Line: The Mud Wasps of Manhattan," *New Yorker* 26 (March 25, 1950): 64, 66, 69–72; Lewis Mumford, "The Sky Line: More Pelion, More Ossa," *New Yorker* 26 (February 3, 1951): 76–82; "Office Space: Still *Not* Enough to End the Squeeze," *Business Week* (December 6, 1952): 86–87; Jane Jacobs, "New York's Office Boom," *Architectural Forum* 106 (March 1957): 104–13; Earle Shultz and Walter Simmons, *Offices in the Sky* (Indianapolis, Ind.: Bobbs-Merrill, 1959), 246; Ada Louise Huxtable, *Four Walking Tours of Modern Architecture in New York City* (New York: Museum of Modern Art and Municipal Art Society of New York, 1961), 25; White and Willensky, *AIA Guide* (1967), 119; Robert F. R. Ballard, *Directory of Manhattan Office Buildings* (New York: McGraw-Hill, 1978), 166; Paul Goldberger, *The City Observed: New York* (New York: Random House, 1979), 155–56; Carol Herselle Krinsky, "Architecture in New York City," in Leonard Wallock, ed., *New York: Culture Capital of the World, 1940–1965* (New York: Rizzoli International Publications, 1988), 98; Trager, *Park Avenue*, 189–90.

15. Philip C. Johnson, *Mies van der Rohe*, 3rd rev. ed. (New York: Museum of Modern Art, 1978), 26, 30–31.

16. Wolf Von Eckardt, *Eric Mendelsohn* (New York: George Braziller, 1960), 13–14, 22–23, plates 32–34.

17. "Office Building, New York, Kahn & Jacobs, Architects," *Architectural Forum*: 98.

18. "Post-War Builders Go for Purchased Steam," advertisement, *Real Estate Record and Guide* 162 (August 7, 1948): 5; "Additions to City Skyline—Products of Latest Real Estate Boom," *New York Times* (August 23, 1954): 19; Ballard, *Directory of Manhattan Office Buildings*, 180; Trager, *Park Avenue*, 190.

19. "New 20-Story Office Structure Planned for Northwest Corner of Park Ave.—57th St.; To Be Erected By Davies Building, Inc.," *Real Estate Record and Guide* 170 (November 8, 1952): 3; "Plans Filed for 20-Story Davies Building, Park Ave.—57th St.," *Real Estate Record and Guide* 170 (November 22, 1952): 3; "Second Aluminum-Faced Office Building to Rise Shortly at 460 Park Avenue," *Real Estate Record and Guide* 172 (November 7, 1953): 3; "The Record Reports: Meetings and Miscellany," *Architectural Record* 114 (December 1953): 15; "Tishman Starts Steelwork for New Skyscraper at 460 Park Avenue," *Real Estate Record and Guide* 173 (February 20, 1954): 3; "Aluminum Panels Will Enclose Park Ave. Building in Single Day," *New York Times* (June 20, 1954), VIII: 1, 8; "Walling a Building While-U-Wait," *Life* 37 (July 5, 1954): 16-17; "Additions to City Skyline—Products of Latest Real Estate Boom": 19; "Texas Lode Claim on Park Avenue," *Interiors* 115 (March 1956): 100–103; Jacobs, "New York's Office Boom": 108; Huxtable, *Four Walking Tours of Modern Architecture in New York City*, 25–26; Ballard, *Directory of Manhattan Office Buildings*, 167; Trager, *Park Avenue*, 192.

20. "Total Reconditioning: 430 Park Avenue," *Progressive Architecture* 35 (May 1953): 106–9; Lee E. Cooper, "New Methods Used to Erect Offices," *New York Times* (August 9, 1953), VIII: 1–2; "New York Transformation: Old Bones to Get New Flesh," *Architectural Forum* 99 (September 1953): 39; "Old Apartment Building Is Undressed to Frame and Floors and Reclothed as New Office Tower," *Architectural Forum* 100 (May 1954): 122–23; Mumford, "The Sky Line: Skin Treatment and New Wrinkles": 135–38; Jacobs, "New York's Office Boom": 108; "Many of City's 'New' Buildings Are Just Old Ones Redressed," *New York Times* (November 21, 1965), VIII: 1, 10; Ballard, *Directory of Manhattan Office Buildings*, 166; Trager, *Park Avenue*, 192.

21. "2nd Apartment on Park Ave. to Be Rebuilt into Office," *Architectural Forum* 100 (March 1954): 62; Jacobs, "New York's Office Boom": 111; Ballard, *Directory of Manhattan Office Buildings*, 164; Trager, *Park Avenue*, 152, 192.
22. "Demonstration in Aluminum," *Architectural Forum* 105 (November 1956): 146–47; Jacobs, "New York's Office Boom": 109; "Colgate-Palmolive Building," *Progressive Architecture* 38 (June 1957): 163; Richard Roth, "High-Rise Down to Earth," *Progressive Architecture* 38 (June 1957): 196–202; Huxtable, *Four Walking Tours of Modern Architecture in New York City*, 18–19; Ballard, *Directory of Manhattan Office Buildings*, 39; Steven Ruttenbaum, *Mansions in the Clouds: The Skyscraper Palazzi of Emery Roth* (New York: Balsam Press, 1986), 202–3; Trager, *Park Avenue*, 90–91, 189, 192.
23. "21-Story Skyscraper to Be Erected at Park Ave. and 54th St.," *Real Estate Record and Guide* 176 (October 15, 1955): 3; "Buildings in the News," *Architectural Record* 118 (December 1955): 10; "21-Story Office Building to Go Up at 400 Park Av.," *Real Estate Record and Guide* 177 (February 25, 1956): 5; Jacobs, "New York's Office Boom": 111; Roth, "High-Rise Down to Earth": 198–99; Ballard, *Directory of Manhattan Office Buildings*, 164; Trager, *Park Avenue*, 152, 192.
24. Stern, Gilmartin and Mellins, *New York 1930*, 395, 400. New York's first new apartment house to be designed with full air-conditioning was Frederick L. Ackerman's, in association with Charles George Ramsey and Harold Reeve Sleeper, 25 East Eighty-third Street (1938). See Stern, Gilmartin and Mellins, *New York 1930*, 400–401.
25. Roth, "High-Rise Down to Earth": 198; Lois Wagner Green, ed., *Interiors Books of Offices* (New York: Whitney Library of Design, 1959), 109; "New Chase Branch Changes the Face of Banking," *New York Times* (October 14, 1959): 61; Stuart Preston, "Art: Bank Shows Interest in Design," *New York Times* (October 24, 1959): 18; "Designing Artistry Blends with Avant-Garde Art in Chase Manhattan's Newest Branch," *Interiors* 119 (December 1959): 100–105; "Christmas in the Modern Manner," *Interiors* 119 (January 1960): 18; White and Willensky, *AIA Guide* (1967), 119; illustrated in *New York* 9 (October 18, 1976): 83; Ballard, *Directory of Manhattan Office Buildings*, 165; Trager, *Park Avenue*, 88–89, 195–96. For Harder's apartment house, see Andrew Alpern, *Apartments for the Affluent* (New York: McGraw-Hill, 1975), 88–89.
26. "New $15,000,000 Building to Be Erected on Park Avenue Blockfront, 55th-56th Streets," *Real Estate Record and Guide* 174 (December 11, 1954): 3; "National Biscuit Co. Leases Six Floors in New Office Building at 425 Park Ave.," *Real Estate Record and Guide* 175 (February 19, 1955): 3; "Big Wave of Office Construction Renews Overbuilding Question," *Architectural Forum* 102 (June 1955): 9; "Demolition of 84-Year-Old Park Ave. Blockfront to Clear Way for New Office Structure," *Real Estate Record and Guide* 175 (June 4, 1955): 3; Jacobs, "New York's Office Boom": 109, 111; "Erratum," *Architectural Forum* 106 (May 1957): 94; "425 Park Avenue, New York, New York," *Progressive Architecture* 38 (June 1957): 162; "Air-Conditioning: Office Buildings," *Progressive Architecture* 39 (March 1958): 116; Ballard, *Directory of Manhattan Office Buildings*, 165; Trager, *Park Avenue*, 192.
27. For Casale & Witt's renovation, see Stern, Gilmartin and Mellins, *New York 1930*, 380.
28. For Raymond Hood's Daily News Building, see Stern, Gilmartin and Mellins, *New York 1930*, 575–79, 583–84.
29. "New Office Structure to Cover Park Ave. Site," *Real Estate Record and Guide* 181 (March 8, 1958): 4; "Adjacent Skyscrapers Planned for Park Avenue," *New York Times* (February 15, 1959), VIII: 7; Ballard, *Directory of Manhattan Office Buildings*, 163; Goldberger, *The City Observed*, 156; Trager, *Park Avenue*, 196.
30. "Adjacent Skyscrapers Planned for Park Avenue": 7; Ballard, *Directory of Manhattan Office Buildings*, 162; Goldberger, *The City Observed*, 156; Trager, *Park Avenue*, 152, 196.
31. "Bankers Trust Building to Rise on Park Avenue," *Real Estate Record and Guide* 186 (November 5, 1960): 2–3; "Union Carbide's Park Ave. Neighbor," *Architectural Forum* 113 (December 1960): 5; "Concrete on Park Avenue," *Progressive Architecture* 41 (December 1960): 54; "3-Way Effort Produces Design for Bankers Trust Skyscraper," *New York Times* (January 28, 1962), VIII: 1, 13; "Industrial Designer's Building," *Industrial Design* 9 (October 1962): 12; "Splendor in the Skies," *Life* 53 (November 9, 1962): 87; "Industrial Design for Park Avenue," *Architectural Record* 133 (January 1963): 14; "Unique Team Creates Bank," *Progressive Architecture* 44 (January 1963): 44; Maud Dorr, "Bankers Trust, Park Avenue: A Designer's Experiment in Architecture," *Industrial Design* 10 (March 1963): 52–55; Priscilla Ginsberg, "Bankers Trust: New Neighbor on Pyrex Row," *Interiors* 122 (April 1963): 90–97; Ada Louise Huxtable, "Architecture Stumbles On," *New York Times* (April 14, 1963), II: 23; Henry Dreyfuss, "Behind the Ratty Cacti," letter to the editor, *Interiors* 122 (June 1963): 8; Richard Kelly, "Lighting Bankers Trust," letter to the editor, *Interiors* 122 (June 1963): 8; White and Willensky, *AIA Guide* (1967), 117; Ballard, *Directory of Manhattan Office Buildings*, 37; Trager, *Park Avenue*, 129, 169, 197.
32. For Warren & Wetmore's apartment house, 290 Park Avenue, see Stern, Gilmartin and Mellins, *New York 1930*, 390, 392, 417.
33. For the Hotel Chatham, see Stern, Gilmartin and Mellins, *New York 1930*, 202.
34. Huxtable, "Architecture Stumbles On": 23.
35. "In 1956," *Interiors* 116 (August 1956): 14; John A. Conway, "Success Story of a Street," *Newsweek* 48 (October 1956): 71–74; "Christmas in the Modern Manner": 18; "Pepsi's Palace," *Architectural Forum* 112 (March 1960): 102–8; "Pepsi-Cola's Curtain-Wall Face Glows by Day and Gleams by Night," *New York Times* (April 10, 1960), VIII: 10; Huxtable, *Four Walking Tours of Modern Architecture in New York City*, 26; Jürgen Joedicke, *Office Buildings*, trans. C. V. Amerongen (New York: Frederick A. Praeger, 1962), 179–81; illustrated in *Architectural Forum* 116 (January 1962): 168; Ernst Danz, *Architecture of Skidmore, Owings & Merrill, 1950–1962*, with an intro. by Henry-Russell Hitchcock (New York: Frederick A. Praeger, 1963), 11, 118–21; Ada Louise Huxtable, "Civic Club Honors Private Building: Pepsi-Cola Structure Cited—City's Architectural Hit," *New York Times* (March 17, 1964): 32; John Jacobus, *Twentieth-Century Architecture: The Middle Years 1940–65* (New York: Frederick A. Praeger, 1966), 108; Paul Heyer, *Architects on Architecture* (London: Penguin Press, 1967), 366–67; White and Willensky, *AIA Guide* (1967), 120; "Pepsi Generation?" *Architectural Forum* 126 (May 1967): 89; Judith Paine, "Natalie de Blois," in Susana Torre, ed., *Women in American Architecture: A Historic and Contemporary Perspective* (New York: Whitney Library of Design, 1977), 112–14; Goldberger, *The City Observed*, 154–55; Paul Goldberger, *The Skyscraper* (New York: Alfred A. Knopf, 1981), 28, 110–11; Ada Louise Huxtable, "500 Park—A Skillful Solution," *New York Times* (May 3, 1981), II: 27; Carol Herselle Krinsky, *Gordon Bunshaft of Skidmore, Owings & Merrill* (New York: Architectural History Foundation; Cambridge, Mass.: MIT Press, 1988), 65–67, 110–13, 336; Krinsky, "Architecture in New York City," in Wallock, ed., *New York: Culture Capital of the World, 1940–1965*, 100; Trager, *Park Avenue*, 195.
36. See Bob Thomas, *Joan Crawford* (New York: Simon & Schuster, 1978), Chapters 20, 21, 24 passim; Richard Alleman, *The Movie Lover's Guide to New York* (New York: Harper & Row, 1988), 132–34.
37. Huxtable, "500 Park—A Skillful Solution": 27.
38. "Lever Bros. Home Features Arcade," *New York Times* (April 30, 1950), VIII: 1; "Miniature Skyscraper of Blue Glass and Metal Challenges Postwar Craze for Over-Building City Lots," *Architectural Forum* 92 (June 1950): cover, 84–90; "19 Stories Held to One Fourth of Site to Achieve Light and Air for 280,000 SQ Ft without Setbacks," *Architectural Record* 107 (June 1950): 12; "Lux Hits Park Avenue," *Interiors* 109 (June 1950): 8; "Skidmore, Owings & Merrill," *Bulletin of the Museum of Modern Art* 18 (fall 1950): 4–5, 10–11; Aline B. Louchheim, "Architecture of and for Our Day," *New York Times* (September 24, 1950), II: 9; "1951 Design Survey: Commerce," *Progressive Architecture* 32 (January 1951): 79; "The Talk of the Town: Solution," *New Yorker* 27 (May 26, 1951): 20–21; Arthur Drexler, "Post-War Architecture," in Henry-Russell Hitchcock and Arthur Drexler, eds., *Built in USA: Post-War Architecture* (New York: Museum of Modern Art, 1952), 24–25, 102–3; Henry S. Churchill, "New York Rezoned," *Magazine of Art* 44 (December 1951): 326–31, reprinted in *Journal of the American Institute of Architects* 17 (May 1952): 202–9; "New Design in Office Skyscraper," *New York Times* (February 10, 1952), VIII: 1; "On the Frontier," *Fortune* 46 (March 1952): 78–79; "Lever House Window Washing Solved by Mobile Elevator," *Architectural Forum* 96 (April 1952): 43; "Window Washers in Gondola Car Speed Cleaning of Glass Building," *New York Times* (April 1, 1952): 31; "The Talk of the Town: Clean," *New Yorker* 28 (April 26, 1952): 27–28; Aline B. Louchheim, "Newest Building in the New Style," *New York Times* (April 27, 1952), II: 9; "Ready to Soar," *Time* 59 (April 28, 1952): 74–75; "Park Avenue Opening," editorial, *New York Times* (April 29, 1952): 26; "They Say: Edward P. Morgan," *Journal of the American Institute of Architects* 17 (May 1952): 239; "Lever House: Spacious, Efficient, and Washable," *Business Week* (May 3, 1952): 76–77; "Glass House . . . on Park Ave.," *Newsweek* 39 (May 5, 1952): 82–83; "Lever House," *Architectural Forum* 96 (June 1952): cover, 101–11; "Lever House, New York: Glass and Steel Walls," *Architectural Record* 111 (June 1952): 130–35; "Shiny New Sight," *Life* 32 (June 2, 1952): 44–47; "New York's Blue Glass Tower: An Insider's View," *Interiors* 112 (August 1952): 58–65, 153–54; Lewis Mumford, "The Sky Line: House of Glass," *New Yorker* 28 (August 9, 1952): 48–50; "Employee Facilities," *Progressive Architecture* 33 (October 1952): 126–27; "Office Space: Still *Not* Enough to End the Squeeze": 86–87; Hugh Ferriss, *Power in Buildings* (New York: Columbia University Press, 1953), plates 24–25; John McAndrew, "Our Architecture Is Our Portrait," *New York Times* (January 18, 1953), VI: 12–14; "Our New Crystal Towers," *Architectural Forum* 98 (February 1953): 142–45; "Perspectives," *Architectural Record* 114 (July 1953): 9; Frederick J. Woodbridge, "Beauty and the Urban Beast," *Royal Architecture Institute of Canada Journal* 30 (July 1953): 206–7; Lenore Hailparn, "Your Future Office," *Independent Woman* 32 (November 1953): 404–6, 423; Jacobs, "New York's Office Boom": 106; Huxtable, "Park Avenue School of Architecture": 30, 54–56; Henry-Russell Hitchcock, *Architecture: Nineteenth and Twentieth Centuries* (Baltimore: Penguin Books, 1958), 415, plate 191; "The Architects from 'Skids Row,'" *Fortune* 57 (January 1958): 137–40, 210–15; Lewis Mumford, "The Sky Line: The Lesson of the Master," *New Yorker* 34 (September 13, 1958): 141–48, 150, 152, reprinted in *Journal of the American Institute of Architects* 31 (January 1959): 9–23; "Seven 'Wonders of Architecture' Named in Special Survey," *Architectural Record* 124 (October 1958): 15; Green, ed., *Interiors Books of Offices*, 58, 108, 119; Ian McCallum, *Architecture USA* (London: Architectural Press, 1959), 133–36; Henry Hope Reed, *The Golden City* (New York: Doubleday & Co., 1959), 25, 53, 57–58; Shultz and Simmons, *Offices in the Sky*, 250–51; Kenneth Tynan, "A Memoir of Manhattan," *Holiday* 28 (December 1960): 96–97, 170–71; Huxtable, *Four Walking Tours of Modern Architecture in New York City*, 14, 21–23; Vincent Scully, Jr., *Modern Architecture* (New York: George Braziller, 1961), 34, fig. 99; *Office Buildings: An Architectural Record Book* (New York: F. W. Dodge Corp., 1961), 7; Reyner Banham, *Age of the Masters: A Personal View of Modern Architecture* (New York: Harper & Row, 1962), 113–15; Joedicke, *Office Buildings*, 35, 94–95, 146–48; Danz, *Architecture of Skidmore, Owings & Merrill, 1950–1962*, 22–27; Hitchcock, "Introduction," in Danz, *Architecture of Skidmore, Owings & Merrill, 1950–1962*, 7–10, 12; Martin Meyerson, *Face of the Metropolis* (New York: Random House, 1963), 55; Scully, "The Death of the Street": 91–96; Arnold H. Lubasch, "Skyscraper Setbacks Serve as Play Areas," *New York Times* (January 28, 1963), VII: 1, 4; John M. Jacobus, Jr., "Skidmore, Owings & Merrill," in Gerd Hatje, ed., *Encyclopedia of Modern Architecture* (New York: Harry N. Abrams, 1964), 23, 60–61; Jacobus, *Twentieth-Century Architecture: The Middle Years 1940–65*, 107, 109; Heyer, *Architects on Architecture*, 364–65; Wolf Von Eckardt, *A Place to Live: The Crisis of the Cities* (New York: Delacorte Press, 1967), 127–30, 132; White and Willensky, *AIA Guide* (1967), 118–19; Vincent Scully, *American Architecture and Urbanism* (New York: Frederick A. Praeger, 1969), 186, fig. 39; John Winter, *Great Buildings of the World: Modern Architecture* (London: Paul Hamlyn, 1969), 24–25; "Wall Painting at Lever Brothers," *Progressive Architecture* 51 (December 1970): 26; William H. Jordy, *American Buildings and Their Architects: The Impact of European Modernism in the Mid-Twentieth Century*, vol. 4 (Garden City, N. Y.: Doubleday & Co., 1972), 236–37, 255–56, 259–63, 265, 268, 276; David Jacobs, "The Establishment's Architect—Plus," *New York Times* (July 23, 1972), VI: 12–14, 16–17, 19, 21, 23; Charles Jencks, *Modern Movements in Architecture* (Garden City, N. Y.: Anchor Press/Doubleday, 1973), 41; Nathaniel Owings, *The Spaces in Between: An Architect's Journey* (Boston: Houghton Mifflin, 1973), 104–10; August Heckscher with Phyllis Robinson, *Open Spaces: The Life of American Cities* (New York: Harper & Row, 1977), 303–4; Paul Goldberger, "Design Notebook: Lever House Has a Birthday," *New York Times* (April 28, 1977), C: 21; White and Willensky, *AIA Guide* (1978), 152; Goldberger, *The City Observed*, 156–57; Leland M. Roth, *A Concise History of American Architecture* (New York: Harper & Row, 1979), 278–79; Manfredo Tafuri and Francesco Dal Co, *Modern Architecture*, trans. Robert Erich Wolf (New York: Harry N. Abrams, 1979), 366–67; John Tauranac, *Essential New York* (New York: Holt, Rinehart and Winston, 1979), 198–99; Stanley Abercrombie, "25-Year Award Goes to Lever House," *Journal of the American Institute of Architects* 69 (March 1980): 76–79; Goldberger, *The Skyscraper*, 106–7; Ada Louise Huxtable, *The Tall Building Artistically Reconsidered: The Search for a Skyscraper Style* (New York: Pantheon Books, 1982), 18; Landmarks Preservation Commission of the City of New York, LP-1277 (November 9, 1982); "Lever Becomes a Landmark, Demolition Threats Continue," *Journal of the American Institute of Architects* 72 (January 1983): 30, 92; Charles K. Hoyt, "Chapter Statement to the Landmarks Preservation Commission," *Oculus* 44 (February 1983): 3; Swanke Hayden Connell, "White Paper on Lever House," *Oculus* 44 (February 1983): 3–6; "Lever House Received AIA Twenty-five Year Award in 1980," *Oculus* 44 (February

1983): 4; "Lever House Designated a Landmark," *Oculus* 44 (February 1983): 4; "Lever's Landmark Status Upheld; Demolition Threats Defeated," *Journal of the American Institute of Architects* 72 (April 1983): 17–18; Donald Martin Reynolds, *The Architecture of New York City* (New York: Macmillan, 1984), 151–53; Richard Sennett, "The Public Domain," in Nathan Glazer and Mark Lilla, eds., *The Public Face of Architecture: Civic Culture and Public Spaces* (New York: Macmillan, 1987), 29–32; Barbaralee Diamonstein, *The Landmarks of New York* (New York: Harry N. Abrams, 1988), 380; Krinsky, *Gordon Bunshaft of Skidmore, Owings & Merrill*, 18–25, 40–45, 57–58, 335; Krinsky, "Architecture in New York City," in Wallock, ed., *New York: Culture Capital of the World, 1940–1965*, 98–99; White and Willensky, *AIA Guide* (1988), 249; Trager, *Park Avenue*, 190–91; Christopher Gray, "Neighborhood: Nifties from the Fifties," *Avenue* 14 (January 1990): 117–23; Andrew S. Dolkart, *Guide to New York City Landmarks* (Washington, D. C.: Preservation Press, 1992), 81–82.

39. Quoted in Owings, *The Spaces in Between*, 108, and in Krinsky, *Gordon Bunshaft of Skidmore, Owings & Merrill*, 19.

40. See Louchheim, "Newest Building in the New Style": 9.

41. "Skidmore, Owings & Merrill," *Bulletin of the Museum of Modern Art*: 11.

42. "Miniature Skyscraper of Blue Glass and Metal Challenges Postwar Craze for Over-Building City Lots": 85–86.

43. "Alcoa Outlines Plan for Tower on Park Avenue," *New York Herald Tribune* (April 14, 1946): 8; "Plans for Building of Aluminum Final," *New York Times* (April 14, 1946): 34; "Aluminum on Park Avenue," *Architectural Forum* 84 (May 1946): 10; "A New Aluminum Tower," *Interiors* 105 (May 1946): 10; "New Offices," *Architectural Record* 99 (June 1946): 16, 18; Victoria Newhouse, *Wallace K. Harrison, Architect* (New York: Rizzoli International Publications, 1989), 146. For Buckham's apartment building, see Stern, Gilmartin and Massengale, *New York 1900*, 479 (n. 262).

44. Trager, *Park Avenue*, 135, 209.

45. For Howe & Lescaze's Philadelphia Saving Fund Society Building, see Robert A. M. Stern, *George Howe: Toward a Modern American Architecture* (New Haven, Conn.: Yale University Press, 1975), 108–30, figures 83–97. Also see Jordy, *American Buildings and Their Architects: The Impact of European Modernism in the Mid-Twentieth Century*, vol. 4, 87–164.

46. Quoted in "The Talk of the Town: Clean": 27–28.

47. Mumford, "The Sky Line: House of Glass": 48–50.

48. Quoted in "The Talk of the Town: Clean": 27–28.

49. Louchheim, "Newest Building in the New Style": 9.

50. "Lever House: Spacious, Efficient, and Washable": 76–77.

51. Mumford, "The Sky Line: The Lesson of the Master": 151.

52. Frank Lloyd Wright quoted in "Frank Lloyd Wright Ridicules Architectural Schools as Waste," *New York Times* (June 26, 1952): 47.

53. "On the Frontier": 78–79.

54. "They Say: Edward P. Morgan": 239.

55. Louchheim, "Newest Building in the New Style": 9.

56. "19 Stories Held to One Fourth of Site to Achieve Light and Air for 280,000 SQ Ft without Setbacks": 12.

57. Louchheim, "Newest Building in the New Style": 9.

58. Woodbridge, "Beauty and the Urban Beast": 206–7.

59. Scully, "The Death of the Street": 91–93. Also see "Architectural League Bewails Boom," *Interiors* 121 (December 1961): 53, 69, 149.

60. Banham, *Age of the Masters*, 114.

61. "Park Avenue to Get New Skyscraper," *New York Times* (July 13, 1954): 25; "Seagram Plans a Monument," *Architectural Forum* 101 (August 1954): 52.

62. For the Montana, see Stern, Gilmartin and Massengale, *New York 1900*, 304–5.

63. Charles Luckman quoted in "The Talk of the Town: Repeat Performance," *New Yorker* 30 (August 28, 1954): 15–17.

64. "Seagram Plans a Monument": 52.

65. Phyllis Lambert quoted in "Monument in Bronze," *Time* 71 (March 3, 1958): 52–53, 55.

66. Olga Gueft, "The Race to Design," *Interiors* 114 (January 1955): 51.

67. Phyllis Lambert quoted in Peter Blake, *The Master Builders: Le Corbusier, Mies van der Rohe, Frank Lloyd Wright* (New York: Alfred A. Knopf, 1960), 250.

68. Aline B. Saarinen, "Pioneer to Design Skyscraper Here," *New York Times* (November 25, 1954): 31; "Wright and Mies Open New York Offices; Mies to Do Modern Park Avenue Tower," *Architectural Forum* 101 (December 1954): 41; Gueft, "The Race to Design": 51; "Seagram's Plans Glass Skyscraper," *New York Herald Tribune* (March 30, 1955): 6; "Seagram's Plans Plaza Tower in New York," *Architectural Forum* 102 (April 1955): 9; Philip Johnson, "Style and the International Style," speech, Barnard College, April 30, 1955, published in Peter Eisenman and Robert A. M. Stern, eds., *Philip Johnson: Writings* (New York: Oxford University Press, 1979), 72–79; "Bronze and Glass," *Architectural Record* 117 (May 1955): 11; "Progress Review," *Progressive Architecture* 36 (June 1955): 12; Bradley, "Change Is Cited on Park Avenue": 1, 9; "38-Story Skyscraper Being Constructed at Park Ave.," *Real Estate Record and Guide* 176 (November 5, 1955): 3; "New Skyscraper on Park Avenue to Be First Sheathed in Bronze," *New York Times* (March 2, 1956): 25; "Gold-Aluminum Tower for NY; Bronze on Seagram Building," *Architectural Forum* 104 (June 1956): 12; "The Talk of the Town: Casa Seagram," *New Yorker* 32 (June 2, 1956): 23–24; "News Bulletins," *Progressive Architecture* 37 (July 1956): 75; "In 1956," *Interiors* 116 (August 1956): 14; "The Editor's Asides," *Journal of the American Institute of Architects* 26 (August 1956): 90; "Success Story of a Street," *Newsweek* 48 (October 1, 1956): 71–74; "Developers Mean Business as They Transform Traditionally Residential Park Ave. ": 1, 3; *Buildings for Business and Government*, exhibition catalogue (New York: Museum of Modern Art, 1957), 16–21; "A New Patina on Park Avenue," *Architectural Forum* 106 (February 1957): 115; "Oasis for Seagram's New Home," *New York Times* (February 24, 1957), VIII: 5; Jacobs, "New York's Office Boom": 111; "The House of Seagram," *Architectural Record* 121 (March 1957): 230–31; "A Special Report on 375 Park Avenue. An International Address of Distinction. The World's First Bronze Skyscraper," special advertising supplement, *New York Times* (April 7, 1957), X; "375 Park Avenue," *Progressive Architecture* 38 (June 1957): 167; Thomas W. Ennis, "Building Is Designer's Testament," *New York Times* (November 10, 1957), VIII: 1, 8; Hitchcock, *Architecture: Nineteenth and Twentieth Centuries*, 389; "The Record Reports: Meetings and Miscellany," *Architectural Record* 123 (February 1958): 24; "Air Conditioning: Office Buildings," *Progressive Architecture* 39 (March 1958): 116–17; "Monument in Bronze": 52–53, 55; Peter Blake, "The Difficult Art of Simplicity," *Architectural Forum* 108 (May 1958): 126–31; Arthur Drexler, "Seagram Building," *Architectural Record* 124 (July 1958): cover, 139–47; "Seagram House Finally Opened," *Progressive Architecture* 39 (July 1958): 39–41; "3 Buildings in Midtown Cited for Architecture," *New York Times* (July 1, 1958): 53; "Footsore Here Find Oasis at Seagram Building Plaza," *New York Times* (July 26, 1958): 12; "Strong Sign of Recovery," *Life* 45 (August 1958): 13; Alan Dunn, "Oh Mr. Mies!" cartoon, *Architectural Record* 124 (September 1958): 25; "Siège de la Société 'Seagram' New-York 1958," *L'Architecture d'Aujourd'hui* 29 (September 1958): 90–95; Mumford, "The Sky Line: The Lesson of the Master": 141–48, 150, 152; William H. Jordy, "Seagram Assessed," *Architectural Review* 124 (December 1958): 374–82; John Anderson, "Seagram Building," *Interiors* 118 (December 1958): 76–81; John Anderson, "Versatile Ad Agency in Seagram Building," *Interiors* 118 (December 1958): 82–85; Green, ed., *Interiors Book of Offices*, 59, 86, 119; McCallum, *Architecture USA*, 58–61; Reed, *The Golden City*, 39; Shultz and Simmons, *Offices in the Sky*, 192, 247, 251; "Un Monumento a New York: Il 'Seagram Building,'" *Casabella* 223 (January 1959): 3–11; Winthrop Sargeant, "Profiles: From Sassafras Branches," *New Yorker* 34 (January 3, 1959): 32–34, 36, 38–49; "Seagram's Lauds New Duct System," *New York Times* (January 18, 1959), VIII: 5; "Seagram's Terrace Gardens Sport Ivy Planted in a Light Mix," *Architectural Record* 125 (February 1959): 338; Phyllis B. Lambert, "How a Building Gets Built," *Vassar Alumnae Magazine* (February 1959): 13–19; Philip Johnson, "Whither Away—Non-Miesian Directions," speech, Yale University, February 5, 1959, published in Eisenman and Stern, eds., *Philip Johnson: Writings*, 226–40; Thomas H. Creighton, "Seagram House Re-Reassessed," *Progressive Architecture* 40 (June 1959): 140–45; J. Artchess, "Setbacks and Sunglasses," letter to the editor, *Interiors* 119 (August 1959): 8; Victor Gruen, letter to the editor, *Progressive Architecture* 40 (August 1959): 58; Eugene Henry Klaber, letter to the editor, *Progressive Architecture* 40 (August 1959): 58; William Lyman, letter to the editor, *Progressive Architecture* 40 (August 1959): 58; William H. Jordy, letter to the editor, *Progressive Architecture* 40 (August 1959): 58, 64, 192, 196; William H. Jordy, "The Mies-Less Johnson," *Architectural Forum* 111 (September 1959): 114–23; "Utah in Manhattan," *Architectural Forum* 111 (September 1959): 174; H. Mathew Lippincott, Jr., "More than Esthetics," letter to the editor, *Progressive Architecture* 40 (September 1959): 62, 66; "Ginkoes in Gotham," *Architectural Record* 126 (December 1959): 9; Blake, *The Master Builders: Le Corbusier, Mies van der Rohe, Frank Lloyd Wright*, 249–56; Arthur Drexler, *Ludwig Mies van der Rohe* (New York: George Braziller, 1960), 27–28, plates 87–91; Douglas Haskell, "Jazz in Architecture," *Architectural Forum* 113 (September 1960): 110–15; Tynan, "A Memoir of Manhattan": 96–97, 170–71; James Marston Fitch, *Architecture and the Esthetics of Plenty* (New York: Columbia University Press, 1961), 151, 197, 199, 267–68; Henry Russell Hitchcock, "The Current Work of Philip Johnson," *Zodiac* 8 (1961): 64–81; Huxtable, *Four Walking Tours of Modern Architecture in New York City*, 15, 19–21; William H. Jordy, "The Place of Mies in American Architecture," *Zodiac* 8 (1961): 29–33; Scully, *Modern Architecture*, 34, figs. 100–101; Banham, *Age of the Masters*, 112–15; Joedicke, *Office Buildings*, 101–3, 158–61; Vincent Scully, Jr., *Louis I. Kahn* (New York: George Braziller, 1962), 27; Philip Johnson, "Schinkel and Mies," speech, Congress Hall, Berlin, March 12, 1961, published in German in *Schriftenreihe des Architekten—und Ingeneurs—Vereins zu Berlin*, XIII, 24, English text published in *Program* (spring 1962): 14–34, reprinted in Eisenman and Stern, eds., *Philip Johnson: Writings*, 164–73; Meyerson, *Face of the Metropolis*, 50–51; Henry S. Churchill, "The Social Implications of the Skyscraper," in *Four Great Makers of Modern Architecture: Gropius, Le Corbusier, Mies van der Rohe, Wright* (New York: Columbia University, 1963), 44–54; Philip Johnson, "A Personal Testament," in *Four Great Makers of Modern Architecture: Gropius, Le Corbusier, Mies van der Rohe, Wright*, 109–12; Sybil Moholy-Nagy, "Has 'Less Is More' Become 'Less Is Nothing?'" in *Four Great Makers of Modern Architecture: Gropius, Le Corbusier, Mies van der Rohe, Wright*, 118–23; Scully, "The Death of the Street": 91–96; Ada Louise Huxtable, "Another Chapter in 'How to Kill a City,'" *New York Times* (May 26, 1963), II: 11, reprinted as "Legislating Against Quality," in Ada Louise Huxtable, *Will They Ever Finish Bruckner Boulevard?* (New York: Macmillan, 1970), 46–51; William H. Jordy, "Ludwig Mies van der Rohe," in Hatje, ed., *Encyclopedia of Modern Architecture*, 189–99; "A Blow for Architecture," editorial, *New York Times* (June 13, 1964): 22; "A Blow to Beauty Seen in Tax Ruling on Seagram Tower," *New York Times* (June 13, 1964): 25; "Seagram Building, 375 Park Avenue, in New York, 1954–1958," *Werke* 51 (November 1964): 408–11; Charles Abrams, *The City Is the Frontier* (New York: Harper Colophon, 1965), 290; Werner Blaser, *Mies van der Rohe: The Art of Structure* (New York: Frederick A. Praeger, 1965), 144–57; Philip Johnson, "Whence and Whither: The Processional Element in Architecture," *Perspecta* 9/10 (1965): 167–78, reprinted in Eisenman and Stern, eds., *Philip Johnson: Writings*, 150–55; "Philip Johnson's New York," *Interior Design* 36 (March 1965): 152–55; James Marston Fitch, *American Building, I: The Historical Forces That Shaped It*, 2nd rev. ed. (Boston: Houghton Mifflin, 1966), 281, 284; Henry-Russell Hitchcock, "Introduction," in *Philip Johnson: Architecture, 1949–1965* (New York: Holt, Rinehart and Winston, 1966), 12–13; Jacobus, *Twentieth-Century Architecture: The Middle Years 1940–65*, 79, 110–11; Ada Louise Huxtable, "Mies: Lessons from the Master," *New York Times* (February 6, 1966), II: 24–25, reprinted in Huxtable, *Will They Ever Finish Bruckner Boulevard?*, 204–9; Heyer, *Architects on Architecture*, 34–35, 185; Von Eckardt, *A Place to Live: The Crisis of the Cities*, 127; White and Willensky, *AIA Guide* (1967), 118; Scully, *American Architecture and Urbanism*, 186–87; Winter, *Great Buildings of the World: Modern Architecture*, 50–63; Leonardo Benevolo, *History of Modern Architecture: The Modern Movement*, vol. 2, trans. H. J. Landry (Cambridge, Mass.: MIT Press, 1971), 669–71, 804–5, 807; Jordy, *American Buildings and Their Architects: The Impact of European Modernism in the Mid-Twentieth Century*, vol. 4, 251–77; Jencks, *Modern Movements in Architecture*, 97, 100–103; Peter Carter, *Mies van der Rohe at Work* (New York: Praeger, 1974), 60–63, 126–29; Heckscher with Robinson, *Open Spaces: The Life of American Cities*, 303–4; Ballard, *Directory of Manhattan Office Buildings*, 163; *The Seagram Plaza: Its Design and Use*, exhibition catalogue (New York: Joseph E. Seagram and Sons, 1978), unpaginated; White and Willensky, *AIA Guide* (1978), 150–51; Goldberger, *The City Observed*, 160–61; Roth, *A Concise History of American Architecture*, 284–86; Tafuri and Dal Co, *Modern Architecture*, 338–40; Tauranac, *Essential New York*, 202–3; Brent C. Brolin, *Architecture in Context: Fitting New Buildings with Old* (New York: Van Nostrand Reinhold, 1980), 144; Goldberger, *The Skyscraper*, 110, 112–13; "6 from 125," *Journal of the American Institute of Architects* 71 (April 1982): 78–79; Huxtable, *The Tall Building Artistically Reconsidered*, 40; Reynolds, *The Architecture of New York City*, 155; "The Seagram Building Wins AIA's 25-Year Award," *Journal of the American Institute of Architects* 74 (April 1984): 25; Franz Schulze, *Mies van der Rohe: A Critical Biography* (Chicago and London: University of Chicago Press, 1985), 272–83; David Spaeth, *Mies van der Rohe* (New York: Rizzoli International Publications, 1985), 162–68; David Spaeth, "Ludwig Mies van der Rohe: A Biographical Essay," in *Mies Reconsidered*, exhibition catalogue (Chicago: Art Institute of Chicago; New York: Rizzoli International Publications, 1986), 30–34; Robert A. M. Stern with Thomas Mellins and Raymond Gastil, *Pride of Place: Building the American Dream* (Boston: Houghton Mifflin; New York: American Heritage, 1986), 287–89; Ezra Stoller, "The Architectural Landscape," *Art News* 62 (November 1987): 162; Krinsky, "Architecture in New York City," in Wallock, ed., *New York: Culture Capital of the World, 1940–1965*, 103–4; "Landmark Designation Sought for Seagram Building," *Oculus* 50 (May 1988): cover, 13; Landmarks Preservation Commission of the City of New York, LP-1664 (October 3, 1989); Landmarks Preservation Commission of the City of New York, LP-1665 (October 3, 1989); Trager, *Park Avenue*, 83, 189, 192–94; Gray, "Neighborhood: Nifties from the Fifties": 117–18, 121; Dolkart, *Guide to New York City Landmarks*, 92–93.

69. Saarinen, "Pioneer to Design Skyscraper Here": 31.

70. Ludwig Mies van der Rohe quoted in Carter, *Mies van der Rohe at Work*, 61–62.

71. Phyllis Lambert, letter to Eve Borsook, December 1, 1954, quoted in Lambert, "How a Building Gets Built": 13–19, and Schulze, *Mies van der Rohe: A Critical Biography*, 273.

72. Phyllis Lambert, letter to Eve Borsook, December 1, 1954, quoted in Lambert, "How a Building Gets Built": 13–19, and Spaeth, *Mies van der Rohe*, 166.

73. "Seagram's Plans Plaza Tower in New York," *Architectural Forum*: 9.

74. For Raymond Hood's RCA Building, see Stern, Gilmartin and Mellins, *New York 1930*, 616, 646–53.

75. Phyllis Lambert, letter dated April 30, 1969, quoted in *The Seagram Plaza: Its Design and Use*, unpaginated.

76. For Donn Barber's YWCA building, see Stern, Gilmartin and Massengale, *New York 1900*, 243, 245.

77. Louis Kahn quoted in Scully, *Louis I. Kahn*, 27.

78. Ludwig Mies van der Rohe quoted in "Monument in Bronze": 55.

79. Jordy, *American Buildings and Their Architects: The Impact of European Modernism in the Mid-Twentieth Century*, vol. 4, 262.

80. Henry-Russell Hitchcock quoted in "Monument in Bronze": 55.

81. Phyllis Lambert quoted in "Monument in Bronze": 55.

82. Mumford, "The Sky Line: The Lesson of the Master": 141–43.

83. Mumford, "The Sky Line: The Lesson of the Master": 143.

84. Mumford, "The Sky Line: The Lesson of the Master": 143–44.

85. Mumford, "The Sky Line: The Lesson of the Master": 145, 147–48.

86. Mumford, "The Sky Line: The Lesson of the Master": 150.

87. Sir Hugh Casson, interview with Jeffrey Ellis Aronin, August 1, 1957, WNYC (NY) radio, transcript in Seagram Building Archive.

88. Artchess, "Setbacks and Sunglasses": 8.

89. Scully, "The Death of the Street": 94–95.

90. Tafuri and Dal Co, *Modern Architecture*, 340.

91. Phyllis Lambert, letter dated April 30, 1969, quoted in *The Seagram Plaza: Its Design and Use*, unpaginated.

92. Olga Gueft, "The Ballplayer on the Plaza," editorial, *Interiors* 124 (July 1965): 59; "The Great Stone Face," *Progressive Architecture* 46 (September 1965): cover, 50, 52.

93. Gueft, "The Ballplayer on the Plaza": 59.

94. "Tune In, Turn On, Put On: Art 1968," *Progressive Architecture* 49 (December 1968): 43.

95. Thomas B. Hess, "New Man in Town," editorial, *Art News* 66 (November 1967): 27; Harold Rosenberg, *Barnett Newman* (New York: Harry N. Abrams, 1978), 72–77, 249–50.

96. Hess, "New Man in Town": 27.

97. George Walco quoted in Nathaniel Sheppard, Jr., "Dubuffet Raises Eyebrows Here," *New York Times* (November 15, 1974): 1.

98. "Going Out Guide: Play Street," *New York Times* (September 29, 1972): 34. Also see Carter, *Mies van der Rohe at Work*, figs. 298, 300.

99. William H. Whyte, conversation with Phyllis Lambert, quoted in *The Seagram Plaza: Its Design and Use*, unpaginated. Also see William H. Whyte, "The Best Street Life in the World," *New York* 7 (July 15, 1974): 26–33.

100. "$4. 5 Million Restaurant to Open Here," *New York Times* (July 16, 1959): 33; "Food Is Also Served," *Time* 74 (July 27, 1959): 61–62, 65; "The Talk of the Town: Creative," *New Yorker* 35 (August 1, 1959): 18–19; Jordy, "The Mies–Less Johnson": 114–23; "Lavish New York Restaurant Ready for Gourmet Palates," *Progressive Architecture* 40 (September 1959): 101; "Restaurants," *Interior Design* 30 (October 1959): 198–201; Craig Claiborne, "Food News: Dining in Elegant Manner," *New York Times* (October 2, 1959): 22; "New York's New 4½ Million Dollar Restaurant," *Look* 23 (October 13, 1959): 58–60; "More Elegance at the House of Seagram," *Architectural Record* 126 (November 1959): 201–4; "The Most Expensive Restaurant Ever Built," *Evergreen Review* 3 (November–December 1959): 108–16; Olga Gueft, "Two Masterpieces: The Guggenheim and The Four Seasons," editorial, *Interiors* 119 (December 1959): 79; "The Four Seasons," *Interiors* 119 (December 1959): 80–87, 166; Karl Linn, Richard Lippold, Garth and Ada Louise Huxtable, "The Four Seasons: Collaboration for Elegance," *Progressive Architecture* 40 (December 1959): 142–47; Alfred John Haddad, "Not Enough Four Seasons," letter to the editor, *Interiors* 119 (January 1960): 8; Robert Sheehan, "Four Seasons: A Flourish of Food," *Fortune* 61 (February 1960): 213–14, 219–20; Edison Price, "Price Fixtures at Four Seasons," letter to the editor, *Interiors* 119 (May 1960): 8; William J. McGuiness, "The Four Seasons Multipurpose Ceiling," *Progressive Architecture* 41 (May 1960): 196, 198; "Un Ristorante di Philip Johnson a New York," *Domus* 367 (June 1960): 9–10; "Return to the Past," *Time* 76 (September 5, 1960): 52–55; Hitchcock, "The Current Work of Philip Johnson": 70–72; "William Pahlmann, F.A.I.D.," *Interior Design* 35 (March 1964): 158–63; "Awards/Citing Collaboration," *Journal of the American Institute of Architects* 41 (April 1964): 10; "Philip Johnson's New York," *Interior Design* 36 (March 1965): 152–55; *Philip Johnson: Architecture, 1949–1965*, 70–71; Heyer, *Architects on Architecture*, 282, 288–89; "Shimmering Chain Curtains," *House Beautiful* 111 (October 1969): 43; Paul Goldberger, "Design for Dining: Feasts for the Eye, Too," *New York Times* (July 30, 1976), III: 13; Maeve Slavin, "The Four Seasons at 25," *Interiors* 143 (July 1984): 128–29; Barbaralee Diamonstein, *American Architecture Now II* (New York: Rizzoli International Publications, 1985), 153; Schulze, *Mies van der Rohe: A Critical Biography*, 283; Christopher Gray, "Streetscapes: The Four Seasons," *New York Times* (July 30, 1989), X: 10, reprinted in Christopher Gray, *Changing New York: The Architectural Scene* (New York: Dover, 1992), 94; Landmarks Preservation Commission of the City of New York, LP-1666 (October 3, 1989); Dolkart, *Guide to New York City Landmarks*, 75.

101. "The Brasserie, in the Seagram Building, New York," *Interiors* 120 (December 1960): 94–95.

102. Mark Rothko quoted in John Fischer, "Mark Rothko: Portrait of an Artist as an Angry Man," *Harper's* 241 (July 1970): 16–23. Also see Sophy Burnham, *The Art Crowd* (New York: David McKay Co., 1973), 14; Lee Seldes, *The Legacy of Mark Rothko* (New York: Holt, Rinehart and Winston, 1978), 43–44; Dore Ashton, *About Rothko* (New York: Oxford University Press, 1983), 146, 153–57, 169; Bonnie Clearwater, *Mark Rothko: Works on Paper* (New York: Hudson Hills Press, 1984), 44–48, 137, figs. 43–44; James E. B. Breslin, *Mark Rothko* (Chicago: University of Chicago Press, 1993), 372–410.

103. Goldberger, "Design for Dining: Feasts for the Eye, Too": 13.

104. Philip Johnson quoted in Goldberger, "Design for Dining: Feasts for the Eye, Too": 13.

105. "More Elegance at the House of Seagram": 201–4.

106. "The Talk of the Town: Creative": 18–19.

107. "The Four Seasons," *Interiors*: 82, 86.

108. Anthony Bailey, "Seagram Besieged: The Ugly Tax on Beauty," *New York Herald Tribune Sunday Magazine* (December 20, 1964): 6–9. Also see Edith Evans Asbury, "Seagram Tower to Appeal on Tax," *New York Times* (May 17, 1963): 35; "A Penalty on Quality," editorial, *New York Times* (May 21, 1963): 36; Russell Lynes, "Space No Land Waste," letter to the editor, *New York Times* (May 21, 1963): 36; Huxtable, "Another Chapter in 'How to Kill a City'": 11; Richard H. Heindel, "Seagram Building Tax," letter to the editor, *New York Times* (June 8, 1963): 24; "It's the Law," *Progressive Architecture* 44 (November 1963): 188; Harry E. Rodman, "The Seagram Building and Our Tax Laws," letter to the editor, *Progressive Architecture* 44 (December 1963): 7; Gerson T. Hirsch, letter to the editor, *Progressive Architecture* 45 (March 1964): 10; Charles D. Bonsted, "The Seagram Decision and Distinctive Design," *Progressive Architecture* 45 (May 1964): 16; "Seagram Building Denied Tax Credit by Appeals Court," *New York Times* (June 11, 1964): 35; "A Blow to Beauty Seen in Tax Ruling on Seagram Tower," *New York Times* (June 13, 1964): 25; Spaeth, *Mies van der Rohe*, 168.

109. "A Blow for Architecture": 22.

110. Huxtable, "Another Chapter in 'How to Kill a City'": 11.

111. "The Rent Was Too High," *Architectural Forum* 136 (April 1972): 22.

112. Edgar Bronfman quoted in Paul Goldberger, "Seagram Building Owners Plan to Seek Landmark Designation," *New York Times* (November 8, 1976): 35. Also see "The Seagram Company Has Asked New York City to Designate Its Mies-Designed Headquarters Building a Landmark," *Architectural Record* 160 (December 1976): 33.

113. Goldberger, "Seagram Building Owners Plan to Seek Landmark Designation": 35.

114. Beverly Moss Spatt quoted in Goldberger, "Seagram Building Owners Plan to Seek Landmark Designation": 35.

115. Robert McG. Thomas, Jr., "Seagram Tower Offered for Sale at $75 Million," *New York Times* (February 26, 1979), B: 3; "Selling a Vintage Building," editorial, *New York Times* (March 16, 1979): 30; Robert McG. Thomas, Jr., "Seagram to Sell Building for $85. 5 Million to Fund," *New York Times* (June 1, 1979), B: 1, 3.

116. "Still Another Office Tower for New York's Park Ave.," *Architectural Forum* 103 (September 1955): 25; "News Bulletins," *Progressive Architecture* 36 (September 1955): 86; "Union Carbon and Carbide's Executive Headquarters . . . ," *Architectural Record* 118 (October 1955): 11; "News Bulletins," *Progressive Architecture* 38 (April 1957): 99; "New Metal Coloring Process Perfected," *Progressive Architecture* 39 (May 1958): 85; "Designers for a Busy World: Mood for Working," *Newsweek* 53 (May 4, 1959): 97–100; "Union Carbide Tops Park Avenue," *Architectural Forum* 112 (February 1960): 9; "Toward Greater Ceiling Flexibility," *Architectural Record* 127 (February 1960): 220–25; "Strip Act on Park Avenue," *Progressive Architecture* 41 (August 1960): 64; "New Design in Sidewalks," *Real Estate Record and Guide* 186 (August 13, 1960): 4; "Carbide Unwrapped," *Architectural Forum* 113 (September 1960): 92–93; "Union Carbide's Shaft of Steel," *Architectural Forum* 113 (November 1960): 114–21; "The Current Pacesetter," *Architectural Record* 128 (November 1960): 156–62; Huxtable, *Four Walking Tours of Modern Architecture in New York City*, 14, 17–18; *Office Buildings: An Architectural Record Book*, 25–37; Robert C. Weinberg, "Carbide Criticized," letter to the editor, *Architectural Forum* 114 (January 1961): 148; Joedicke, *Office Buildings*, 171–73; "Siège de l'Union Carbide, New York, États-Unis," *L'Architecture d'Aujourd'hui* 33 (February 1962): 12–17; "The Talk of the Town: Notes and Comment," *New Yorker* 38 (October 13, 1962): 41–42; "Union Carbide Building Wins Fifth Avenue Association Prize," *Real Estate Record and Guide* 190 (November 24, 1962): 4–5; Danz, *Architecture of Skidmore, Owings & Merrill, 1950–1962*, 142–51; Ada Louise Huxtable, "Does Good Architecture Pay?" *New York Times* (January 11, 1965): 125–26; Barbara Goldsmith, "The Agile Eye of I. M. Pei," *Town and Country* 119 (August 1965): 62, 101–3, 165; Jacobus, *Twentieth-Century Architecture: The Middle Years 1940–65*, 110; White and Willensky, *AIA Guide* (1967), 116–17; Jordy, *American Buildings and Their Architects: The Impact of European Modernism in the Mid-Twentieth Century*, vol. 4, 276; Lila Shoshkes, *Space Planning: Designing the Office Environment* (New York: Architectural Record Books, 1976), 4–6; Paine, "Natalie de Blois," in Torre, ed., *Women in American Architecture: A Historic and Contemporary Perspective*, 112–14; Ballard, *Directory of Manhattan Office Buildings*, 36; Goldberger, *The City Observed*, 127; Roth, *A Concise History of American Architecture*, 286–87; Tauranac, *Essential New York*, 206–7; Judith Graf Klein, *The Office Book* (New York: Facts On File, 1982), 26–27; Huxtable, *The Tall Building Artistically Reconsidered: The Search for a Skyscraper Style*, 51; Krinsky, *Gordon Bunshaft of Skidmore, Owings & Merrill*, 67–70, 114–17, 334, 336; Krinsky, "Architecture in New York City," in Wallock, ed., *New York: Culture Capital of the World, 1940–1965*, 100; Trager, *Park Avenue*, 89, 127, 129, 196.

117. "Developers Mean Business as They Transform Traditionally Residential Park Ave.": 1, 3.

118. For a discussion of Union Carbide's proposed suburban building, see "Flight to the Suburbs," *Architectural Forum* 97 (July 1952): 55.

119. "Union Carbide's Shaft of Steel": 120.

120. Jordy, *American Buildings and Their Architects: The Impact of European Modernism in the Mid-Twentieth Century*, vol. 4, 276.

121. "New Skyscraper Will Rise Opposite Lever House on Park Avenue," *Real Estate Record and Guide* 175 (April 23, 1955): 3; "New York, New York," *Newsweek* 48 (July 9, 1956): 87; John F. Callahan, "Vincent Astor Plans Skyscraper on Park Ave. to Cost 75 Millions," *New York Times* (September 19, 1956): 1, 31; "Astor Plans New Business Center for Park Avenue," *Real Estate Record and Guide* 178 (September 29, 1956): 3; "Astor Building to Face Seagram, Lever Houses," *Architectural Forum* 105 (October 1956): 24; "Astor to Build Park Avenue Skyscraper," *Progressive Architecture* 37 (October 1956):

93; "Success Story of a Street," *Newsweek* 48 (October 1, 1956): 71–74; "Astor Plaza Building," *Architectural Record* 121 (March 1957): 233; "Uptown to Park Avenue," *Newsweek* 49 (April 8, 1957): 81; "New York City's Office Building Boom Is Still Robust, Astor Plaza Postponement Misinterpreted," *Architectural Forum* 108 (January 1958): 11; Glenn Fowler, "Bank Replaces Astor as Park Ave. Builder," *New York Times* (March 27, 1958): 1, 25; "Astor Plaza Loses an Astor and a Plaza," *Architectural Forum* 108 (May 1958): 13–14; "News Bulletins," *Progressive Architecture* 39 (October 1958): 30; "Buildings in the News," *Architectural Record* 124 (November 1958): 20; "First National City Has 'After-Thought' on a Shift Uptown," *New York Times* (January 6, 1959): 39; "1st National City Schedules Move," *New York Times* (March 18, 1959): 53; Huxtable, *Four Walking Tours of Modern Architecture in New York City*, 21; "First National City Bank," *Interiors* 121 (September 1961): 124–27; Andrew Alpern and Seymour Durst, *Holdouts!* (New York: McGraw-Hill, 1984), 58–59; Trager, *Park Avenue*, 193, 195.

122. Jordy, "Seagram Assessed": 374–82.

123. "Park Ave. Skyscraper Explained by Builder," *Real Estate Record and Guide* 182 (September 13, 1958): 3; "New Skyscraper for Park Avenue," *New York Times* (October 22, 1958): 58; "Stahl Equities Plans Park Ave. Skyscraper," *Real Estate Record and Guide* 184 (August 15, 1959): 2–3; "Bulletins," *Progressive Architecture* 40 (September 1959): 99; Thomas W. Ennis, "277 Park Loses Its Last Tenants," *New York Times* (January 16, 1962): 26; "Park Avenue Gets Different Luster," *New York Times* (May 27, 1962), VIII: 1, 10; Dudley Dalton, "Glass Is Gaining for Skyscrapers," *New York Times* (January 26, 1964), VIII: 1, 9; White and Willensky, *AIA Guide* (1967), 117; Lubasch, "Skyscraper Setbacks Serve as Play Areas": 1, 4; Ballard, *Directory of Manhattan Office Buildings*, 37; Goldberger, *The Skyscraper*, 139; Trager, *Park Avenue*, 92–93, 197–98. For McKim, Mead & White's apartment house, see Stern, Gilmartin and Mellins, *New York 1930*, 417.

124. "Skyscraper to Rise on Park Lane Site," *New York Times* (May 25, 1965): 67; "Park Avenue Parade," *Progressive Architecture* 46 (October 1965): 62; Ballard, *Directory of Manhattan Office Buildings*, 38; Trager, *Park Avenue*, 199. For the Park Lane, see Stern, Gilmartin and Mellins, *New York 1930*, 207, 224–25; Trager, *Park Avenue*, 130.

125. For the Barclay, see Stern, Gilmartin and Mellins, *New York 1930*, 207; Trager, *Park Avenue*, 130–31.

126. "Another Plaza to Enhance the Park Avenue View," *New York Times* (September 17, 1967), VIII: 1, 6; "Builder Sacrifices Valuable Space to Create Park Avenue Plaza," *Real Estate Record and Guide* 200 (October 28, 1967): 2; "An Office Building at 345 Park Avenue," *Architectural Record* 142 (November 1967): 41; Ballard, *Directory of Manhattan Office Buildings*, 162; Trager, *Park Avenue*, 129–30, 199. For the Hotel Ambassador, see Stern, Gilmartin and Mellins, *New York 1930*, 201–3.

127. "Seagram's Plans Plaza Tower in New York," *Architectural Forum*: 9.

128. For the Grand Central Palace, see Stern, Gilmartin and Mellins, *New York 1930*, 271, 329–32, 343, 417, 577.

129. "New Buildings in New York Follow New Codes," *Progressive Architecture* 42 (September 1961): 70; "Buildings in the News," *Architectural Record* 131 (February 1962): 13.

130. "Meanwhile, Next Door . . . ," *Progressive Architecture* 44 (May 1963): 82–83; Ada Louise Huxtable, "More on How to Kill a City," *New York Times* (March 21, 1965), II: 17; Ballard, *Directory of Manhattan Office Buildings*, 35; Trager, *Park Avenue*, 186, 197–99.

131. For Emery Roth & Sons' 450 Park Avenue, see Ballard, *Directory of Manhattan Office Buildings*, 167; Goldberger, *The City Observed*, 155–56; Trager, *Park Avenue*, 199.

132. For the New York Central Building, see Stern, Gilmartin and Mellins, *New York 1930*, 590–95.

133. "Central Studies New Terminal Plan," *New York Times* (September 26, 1954): 55; "Perspectives: Zeckendorfitis," *Architectural Record* 120 (November 1956): 9; "Grand Central Site for Largest Office Building," *Architectural Forum* 108 (June 1958): 13.

134. "Central Studies New Terminal Plan," *New York Times*: 55.

135. Alfred Fellheimer quoted in "Is Grand Central Terminal 'Outmoded?' Owners Consider Replacement Schemes," *Architectural Record* 116 (November 1954): 20.

136. Glenn Fowler, "Grand Central 'City' Is Planned," *New York Times* (May 8, 1958): 1, 21; "Grand Central Site for Largest Office Building," *Architectural Forum*: 13; "Complex Construction Techniques in Erecting Grand Central City," *Real Estate Record and Guide* 182 (June 28, 1958): 4; "Grand Central City," *Architectural Record* 124 (July 1958): 13; "Grand Central City Will Use Unusual Leasing Program," *Real Estate Record and Guide* 182 (July 5, 1958): 4; Ruttenbaum, *Mansions in the Clouds: The Skyscraper Palazzi of Emery Roth*, 204.

137. "3 Architects to Plan Grand Central Building," *New York Herald Tribune* (July 31, 1958): 8;"2 Noted Architects to Help Map Center," *New York Times* (July 31, 1958): 14; "Designers Named for Grand Central City," *Real Estate Record and Guide* 182 (August 16, 1958): 3–4; "New Building Will Use Timetable Technique," *Real Estate Record and Guide* 182 (August 16, 1958): 4; "News Bulletins," *Progressive Architecture* 39 (September 1958): 43.

138. See James Marston Fitch, *Walter Gropius* (New York: George Braziller, 1960), plates 114–17.

139. For Belluschi's Equitable Life Assurance Building, see Jordy, *American Buildings and Their Architects: The Impact of European Modernism in the Mid-Twentieth Century*, vol. 4, 229, 233–35.

140. Erwin Wolfson quoted in "3 Architects to Plan Grand Central Building," *New York Herald Tribune*: 8.

141. Thomas W. Ennis, "55-Story Building Set in East Side," *New York Times* (February 18, 1959): 35; William G. Wing, "55-Story Office Building: New 'Grand Central City' Now Slated to Be 8 Sides," *New York Herald Tribune* (February 18, 1959): 3; "Plans Announced for Grand Central City," *Real Estate Record and Guide* 183 (February 28, 1959): 2; "Gropius-Belluschi-Roth Design for Grand Central City," *Architectural Record* 125 (March 1959): 10; "Design of 'Grand Central City' Accepted," *Progressive Architecture* 40 (March 1959): 157; Sybil Moholy-Nagy, "Quantity Vs. Quality," letter to the editor, *Progressive Architecture* 40 (May 1959): 59, 61–62; Natalie Parry, "In Defense of Grand Central City Building Design," letter to the editor, *Progressive Architecture* 40 (August 1959): 49, 54; "Skyscraper Here to Rise Like Vine," *New York Times* (September 20, 1959), VIII: 1, 12; "'First Things First': Not So in Unique Grand Central City Construction Plan," *Real Estate Record and Guide* 184 (October 10, 1959): 4; Martin Pinchis, "Gropius probabilmente erra a New York," *L'Architettura cronache e storia* 5 (November 1959): 435; "Skyscraper Is Begun," *New York Times* (November 27, 1959): 50; Fitch, *Walter Gropius*, plates 136–38; "Britain's Energetic Investor," *Architectural Forum* 112 (January 1960): 14, 16; Ada Louise Huxtable, "Marvel or Monster?" *New York Times* (January 24, 1960), II: 13; Walter McQuade, "Architecture," *Nation* 190 (January 30, 1960): 104–6; "Good Design and Planning in New York Draws Strong Comments at New York School Symposium," *Real Estate Record and Guide* 185 (January 30, 1960): 2–3; Thomas H. Creighton, "P.S.: Who Would Say NO?" *Progressive Architecture* 41 (February 1960): 266; Martin Pinchis, "A Propos du 'Grand Central City,'" *L'Architecture d'Aujourd'hui* 31 (February 1960): xix; "Builder of Skylines: Erwin S. Wolfson," *Time* 75 (February 22, 1960): 92; "Gropius and Garroway," *Architectural Forum* 112 (April 1960): 177, 179; "Una precisazione di Walter Gropius," *L'Architettura cronache e storia* 5 (April 1960): 795; "Problems for Piccadilly; Money for Grand Central," *Progressive Architecture* 41 (April 1960): 86; Edgar Kaufmann, Jr., "The Biggest Office Building Yet . . . Worse Luck," *Harper's* 220 (May 1960): 64–70; Joseph M. Heckoff, "Pie in the Sky?" letter to the editor, *Progressive Architecture* 41 (May 1960): 204, 206; Martin Pinchis, "Tower Can Open or Block Axis," *Progressive Architecture* 41 (June 1960): 210, 212; "Demolition Started at Grand Central City Site," *Progressive Architecture* 41 (August 1960): 64; "More Mosts for Pan Am," *Progressive Architecture* 41 (December 1960): 60; "Big Cork Gets Big Sign," *Progressive Architecture* 41 (December 1960): 61; Gillo Dorfles, "Walter Gropius Today," *Zodiac* 8 (1961): 34–47; Huxtable, *Four Walking Tours of Modern Architecture in New York City*, 14, 17; Richard Witkin, "Heliport Slated atop Skyscraper," *New York Times* (March 24, 1961): 33; Christopher Adams, "Park Avenue Billboards," letter to the editor, *Architectural Forum* 114 (May 1961): 188; "The Largest Construction Loan Ever," *Architectural Forum* 115 (July 1961): 11; Wayne Andrews, "Something Less than Chartres," book review, *Reporter* 25 (July 1961): 49–50; "Textured Masonry Sheathes New Office Buildings," *New York Times* (October 29, 1961), VIII: 1, 6; "Manhattan's Skyline . . . ," *Newsweek* 58 (December 25, 1961): 66–67; Richard Lippold, "Projects for Pan Am and Philharmonic," *Art in America* 50, no. 2 (1962): 50–55; "Concrete Curtain," *Architectural Forum* 116 (January 1962): 10; "Topping-out Tops," *Architectural Forum* 116 (February 1962): 11; David B. Carlson, "Foreign Money Boosts U. S. Building," *Architectural Forum* 116 (February 1962): 83–85; "Lippold Sculpture Planned for Pan Am Building," *Architectural Record* 131 (February 1962): 240; Ada Louise Huxtable, "Our New Buildings: Hits and Misses," *New York Times* (April 29, 1962), VI: 16–17, 105–6; Charles Abrams, "Pan Am Building Defended," *Architectural Record* 131 (May 1962): 197; Emerson Goble, "In Defense of the Pan Am Building," *Architectural Record* 131 (May 1962): 195–200; "The Vertical City: More Efficient for the Business Community," *Real Estate Record and Guide* 189 (June 16, 1962): 2; Raymond Ericson, "Music World: No Sound at All," *New York Times* (August 12, 1962), II: 95; Wolf Von Eckardt, "Pan Am's Glass House," *New Republic* 147 (August 13, 1962): 24–26; "Un Dibattio A New York Sur Pan Am Building," *Casabella* 267 (September 1962): 53–55; Alden P. Armagnac, "The Most Complicated Building Ever Built," *Popular Science* 181 (September 1962): 67–72, 216; "Doing Over the Town," *Time* 80 (September 28, 1962): 56–69; "New York Nears Completion—Almost," *Architectural Forum* 117 (October 1962): 16; "Splendor in the Skies," *Life* 53 (November 9, 1962): 84; Roth, "The Forces that Shaped Park Avenue": 97–102; Scully, "The Death of the Street": 91–96; "The Largest Office Building," editorial, *New York Times* (March 11, 1963): 8; "Extra Grand Central," *Time* 81 (March 15, 1963): 71–72; James T. Burns, Jr., "The Pan Am Building: A Behemoth Is Born," *Progressive Architecture* 44 (April 1963): 59–62; "Pan Am Building, Center of a Storm of Controversy, Nears Completion," *New York Times* (April 7, 1963), VIII: 1, 12; Ada Louise Huxtable, "Architecture Stumbles On," *New York Times* (April 14, 1963), II: 23; Harry Gilroy, "Sculptor Becomes a High-Wire Artist in Pan Am Lobby," *New York Times* (April 25, 1963): 35; Mildred F. Schmertz, "The Problem of Pan Am," *Architectural Record* 133 (May 1963): 151–58; Gunnar Berherts, letter to the editor, *Progressive Architecture* 44 (July 1963): 156; Raniero Corbelletti, letter to the editor, *Progressive Architecture* 44 (July 1963): 156; Lawrence Halprin, letter to the editor, *Progressive Architecture* 44 (July 1963): 156; Leonard K. Eaton, letter to the editor, *Progressive Architecture* 44 (July 1963): 156; Richard W. Snibbe, letter to the editor, *Progressive Architecture* 44 (July 1963): 156; Jim Lamantia, letter to the editor, *Progressive Architecture* 44 (July 1963): 156; Meyer Katzman, letter to the editor, *Progressive Architecture* 44 (July 1963): 156, 158; "Pan Am Lobby Gets Look of Art Gallery," *New York Times* (July 7, 1963), VIII: 1, 4; "World's Largest Executive Suite," *Business Week* (July 20, 1963): 70–72; "Elevators to Run 1,700 ft. a Minute," *New York Times* (July 21, 1963), VIII: 3; Clive Entwhistle, letter to the editor, *Progressive Architecture* 44 (August 1963): 150; Carl A. Bystrom, letter to the editor, *Progressive Architecture* 44 (August 1963): 150; "Lippold Piece Viewed," *Progressive Architecture* 44 (September 1963): 74; Peter Flint, "Escalators in Pan Am Building Create a New Rush-Hour Route," *New York Times* (October 8, 1963): 45; Douglas Haskell, "The Lost New York of the Pan American Airways Building," *Architectural Forum* 119 (November 1963): 106–11; Dennis Duggan, "The 'Belly' School of Architecture," *New York Sunday Herald Tribune Magazine* (December 15, 1963): 7–10; Peter Blake, *God's Own Junkyard* (New York: Holt, Rinehart and Winston, 1964), 25–26; V. S. Pritchett, *New York Proclaimed* (New York: Harcourt, Brace & World, 1964), 10, 14; Kenneth C. Welch, letter to the editor, *Architectural Forum* 120 (January 1964): 43; "Six Offices from New York's Pan Am Building," *Architectural Forum* 120 (January 1964): 102–9; "Three in Pan Am," *Progressive Architecture* 45 (February 1964): 98–107; "New York Is an Architectural Disaster," editorial, *Architectural Forum* 120 (March 1964): 69; Walter Gropius, letter to the editor, *Atlas*, reprinted in *L'Architettura cronache e storia* 9 (April 1964): 866–67; Bruno Zevi, "Il Pan Am Building di Gropius," *L'Espresso*, reprinted in *L'Architettura cronache e storia* 9 (April 1964): 866; Bruno Zevi, "La Protesta di Gropius," *L'Architettura cronache e storia* 9 (April 1964): 877; Betty Raymond, "International Dining in Pan Am's Concourse," *Interiors* 123 (July 1964): 78–84; "Building Skylines Is His Business," *Business Week* (July 11, 1964): 33–34; "Curtain Wall Progression in the Work of Walter Gropius," *Architectural Record* 137 (February 1965): 140–41; Fitch, *American Building, I: The Historical Forces That Shaped It*, 284; Herbert L. Smith, "The Changing Job to Be Done/Building Types and Land Use," *Architectural Record* 140 (July 1966): 228–29; Heyer, *Architects on Architecture*, 206–7; Von Eckardt, *A Place to Live: The Crisis of the Cities*, 10; White and Willensky, *AIA Guide* (1967), 116; Eugen Gomringer, *Josef Albers* (New York: George Wittenborn, 1968), 156, 158, 167; Scully, *American Architecture and Urbanism*, 144, 180, 196–97; Jordy, *American Buildings and Their Architects: The Impact of European Modernism in the Mid-Twentieth Century*, vol. 4, 9–10; Jencks, *Modern Movements in Architecture*, 120; Ballard, *Directory of Manhattan Office Buildings*, 34; Goldberger, *The City Observed*, 127; Tauranac, *Essential New York*, 214–15; Goldberger, *The Skyscraper*, 141; Neal David Benezra, *The Murals and Sculpture of Josef Albers* (New York: Garland Publishing, 1985), 85–94, figs. 56–57; Ruttenbaum, *Mansions in the Clouds: The Skyscraper Palazzi of Emery Roth*, 204–5, 207; Richard David Story, "The Buildings New Yorkers Love to Hate," *New York* 20 (June 15, 1987): cover, 30–32; Krinsky, "Architecture in New York City," in Wallock, ed., *New York: Culture Capital of the World, 1940–1965,* 108–9; Trager, *Park Avenue,* 169, 221–27; Christopher Gray, "Schlock of Ages," *Avenue* 17 (December 1992): 31–32, 34, 36, 38.

142. Richard Roth quoted in Wing, "55-Story Office Building: New 'Grand Central City' Now Slated to Be 8 Sides": 3.

143. W. Boesiger, ed., *Le Corbusier: Oeuvre complète 1938–1946,* vol. 4 (Zurich: Les Editions d'Architecture, 1946, 1966), 44–65.

144. For the Pirelli Building, see Ada Louise Huxtable, *Pier Luigi Nervi* (New York: George Braziller, 1960), 28, figs. 98–101.

145. McQuade, "Architecture": 104.

146. Moholy-Nagy, "Quantity Vs. Quality": 61.

147. Parry, "In Defense of Grand Central City Building Design": 49, 54.

148. Dorfles, "Walter Gropius To-day": 36.

149. Pinchis, "Tower Can Open or Block Axis": 210, 212.

150. Walter Gropius quoted in "Una precisazione di Walter Gropius": 795.

151. Paul Zucker quoted in Gropius, letter to the editor, *Atlas,* reprinted in *L'Architettura cronache e storia*: 866–67.

152. Thomas H. Creighton quoted in "Good Design and Planning in New York Draws Strong Comments at New York School Symposium": 2–3.

153. Pietro Belluschi quoted in McQuade, "Architecture": 106.

154. Abrams, "Pan Am Building Defended": 197.

155. Goble, "In Defense of the Pan Am Building": 195, 197, 200.

156. Roth, "The Forces that Shaped Park Avenue": 101. For a discussion of the "cult of congestion," see Stern, Gilmartin and Mellins, *New York 1930,* 35–39.

157. Huxtable, "Marvel or Monster?": 13.

158. Kaufmann, "The Biggest Office Building Yet . . . Worse Luck": 65, 70.

159. "By Air to the Airports," editorial, *New York Times* (July 9, 1963): 30; Robert D. McFadden, "5 Killed as Copter on Pan Am Building Throws Rotor Blade," *New York Times* (May 16, 1977): 1, 20; Wolfgang Saxon, "Copter Pad Born in Controversy," *New York Times* (May 16, 1977): 20; "Hundreds of Commuters Throng Barriers at Grim Accident Scene," *New York Times* (May 16, 1977): 20; "Helicopter Accident Laid to Landing Gear," *New York Times* (October 14, 1977): 25.

160. Huxtable, "Architecture Stumbles On": 23.

161. "Erwin S. Wolfson Is Dead at 60; Leading Builder of Skyscrapers," *New York Times* (June 27, 1962): 35.

162. Burns, "The Pan Am Building: A Behemoth Is Born": 62.

163. Huxtable, "Architecture Stumbles On": 23.

164. Olga Gueft, "Pan Am's Ticket Office in the Pan Am Building," *Interiors* 124 (November 1964): 90–93.

165. Von Eckardt, "Pan Am's Glass House": 24–26.

166. Walter Gropius quoted in Schmertz, "The Problem of Pan Am": 157.

167. Scully, "The Death of the Street": 95. Also see Jencks, *Modern Movements in Architecture,* 41–42.

168. *Claes Oldenburg, Proposals for Monuments and Buildings 1965–69* (Chicago: Big Table, 1969), 64, 156, plate 13. Also see Scully, *American Architecture and Urbanism,* 196–97.

169. Huxtable, "Architecture Stumbles On": 23.

170. "The Largest Office Building," *New York Times*: 8.

171. For an illustration, see Schmertz, "The Problem of Pan Am": 152.

172. See Story, "The Buildings New Yorkers Love to Hate": cover, 30–32.

FIFTH AVENUE

1. For the interwar evolution of the midtown stretch of Fifth Avenue, see Stern, Gilmartin and Mellins, *New York 1930,* 307–12. Also see "Manhattan Avenues Ranked by Corporation Preferences," *Real Estate Record and Guide* 187 (April 8, 1961): 4.

2. Howard Myers, "A Letter from the Publisher," *Architectural Forum* 86 (May 1947): 50.

3. See "Freedom of Design," letters to the editor by Antonin Raymond, George Fred Keck, Albert Mayer, Marcel Breuer, Ernest Born, Otis Winn, Walter F. Bogner, Bertrand Goldberg, W. L. Pereira, Walter Baermann, Max Abramovitz, John Matthews Hatton, James F. Eppenstein, Kenneth Kassler, Samuel E. Homsey and Robert B. Frantz, *Architectural Forum* 86 (June 1947): 22, 24, 26, 30, 34–35; "Censorship Debate," letters to the editor by William W. Wurster, John Normile, Roi L. Morin (who supported design review), Gardiner A. Dailey, J. Gordon Carr, Eric Mendelsohn, John Hancock Callender, Alvin Lustig, John Gaw Meem, Douglas Orr, Schweikker & Elting, Richard M. Bennet and Talbot Hamlin, *Architectural Forum* 87 (July 1947): 22, 24, 26, 30, 34, 38; "More on Architectural Censorship," letters to the editor by Buford L. Pickens, B. Kenneth Johnstone, C. H. Cowgill, A. S. Langsdorf and Wells Bennett, *Architectural Forum* 87 (August 1947): 30, 34, 38; "More on Censorship," letters to the editor by Elizabeth Wood, L. Morgan Yost, Otto Teegen, Harwell Hamilton Harris, Henry L. Kamphoefner, Edward R. Tauch, Jr., and Mario B. Lanculli, *Architectural Forum* 87 (September 1947): 32, 36, 40; "More on Control," letters to the editor by Hubert H. Humphrey (Mayor of Minneapolis, Minn.), T. R. Letts (Office of the Mayor, San Francisco, Calif.), Earl J. Gladd (Mayor of Salt Lake City, Utah), de Lesseps S. Morrison (Mayor of New Orleans, La.), Dr. Oskar Wlach, Richard J. Neutra, E. W. Blum and John Ekin Dinwiddie, *Architectural Forum* 87 (October 1947): 30, 34, 38, 42, 46.

4. "Review," *Architectural Forum* 81 (May 1944): 55; "Best and Co. to Build New 5th Ave. Store," *New York Times* (December 22, 1944): 21; "'Blitz' in New York," *Architectural Forum* 82 (February 1945): 6; "St. Patrick's Is Damaged," *New York Times* (July 12, 1945): 13; "News: Big Slice," *Architectural Forum* 83 (September 1945): 7; "Best & Co. Moving to Its New Store," *New York Times* (April 14, 1947): 33; "Specialty Store in New Quarters," *New York Times* (April 15, 1947): 30; "Fifth Avenue Opening," editorial, *New York Times* (April 17, 1947): 26; "The First Customer Receives Her Award," *New York Times* (April 21, 1947): 31.

5. For Townsend, Steinle & Hackell's 1910 Best's, see "New Fifth Avenue Store," *New York Times* (October 16, 1910), VIII: 3.

6. For Saks, see Stern, Gilmartin and Mellins, *New York 1930,* 311–12, 317–18. For Cass Gilbert's Union Club, see Stern, Gilmartin and Massengale, *New York 1900,* 233, 236–37.

7. "New York Set-Back," *Architectural Forum* 85 (September 1946): 14; "Fifth Avenue Is Preparing for a New Era of Growth," *New York Times* (January 12, 1947), VIII: 1–2; "New York's Skyline Gets a Facelifting," *Business Week* (May 21, 1949): 22–23; "New York Skyscrapers Are Changing Manhattan's Profile," *Architectural Forum* 91 (December 1949): 10; "Faceless Warrens," *Time* 55 (January 23, 1950): 13; Lewis Mumford, "The Sky Line: The Mud Wasps of Manhattan," *New Yorker* 26 (March 25, 1950): 64, 66, 69–72; Robert F. R. Ballard, *Directory of Manhattan Office Buildings* (New York: McGraw-Hill, 1978), 148. For John B. Snook and Charles Atwood's William Henry Vanderbilt house, see Stern, Gilmartin and Massengale, *New York 1900,* 309; John Foreman and Robbie Pierce Stimson, *The Vanderbilts and the Gilded Age* (New York: St. Martin's Press, 1991), 311–13.

8. "Skyscraper Spree," *Architectural Forum* 81 (September 1944): 79–80.

9. Mumford, "The Sky Line: The Mud Wasps of Manhattan": 69–70.

10. "Insurance Building Squares Off Rockefeller Center," *Architectural Forum* 90 (May 1949): 62, 66; "New York Skyscrapers Are Changing Manhattan's Profile": 10; "Skyscraper's Start," *Life* 28 (June 12, 1950): 136–38, 141–42; "Sinclair Is Moving to Skyscraper on Site of Old St. Nicholas Church," *New York Times* (August 4, 1950): 23; "Sinclair Oil Corporation Leases Eight Floors in New Fifth Avenue Building," *Real Estate Record and Guide* 166 (August 12, 1950): 3; "Skyscraper Reaches the Top," *Life* 28 (August 28, 1950): 30–31; Lewis Mumford, "The Sky Line: Big Buildings and Tremendous Trifles," *New Yorker* 27 (December 22, 1951): 60–65; "New Skyscraper Profits by Rockefeller Center's Experience to Improve Ground Floor Design, Uses Modern Lighting and Air Conditioning to Make Deep Space Rentable," *Architectural Forum* 96 (January 1952): 121–25, 192; Jane Jacobs, "New York's Office Boom," *Architectural Forum* 106 (March 1957): 104–13; Ballard, *Directory of Manhattan Office Buildings,* 21; Landmarks Preservation Commission of the City of New York, *Rockefeller Center Designation Report* (New York, 1985), 10, 193; Landmarks Preservation Commission of the City of New York, LP-1447 (April 23, 1985); Barbaralee Diamonstein, *The Landmarks of New York* (New York: Harry N. Abrams, 1988), 379.

11. For the Goelet Building, see Stern, Gilmartin and Mellins, *New York 1930,* 530–31.

12. "New Skyscraper Profits by Rockefeller Center's Experience to Improve Ground Floor Design, Uses Modern Lighting and Air Conditioning to Make Deep Space Rentable": 121.

13. John Anderson, "Stately Shades of English Gentility in a Practically Provided Manhattan Men's Store," *Interiors* 113 (September 1953): 70–75.

14. "18-Story Offices Set for Fifth Ave.," *New York Times* (August 19, 1952): 40; "Modern 18-Story Office Building to Be Erected on Fifth Avenue at 46th St.," *Real Estate Record and Guide* 170 (August 23, 1952): 3–4; "Fifth Avenue Corners in Midtown Manhattan to Be Improved with Large Office Structures," *Real Estate Record and Guide* 170 (December 20, 1952): 3; Ballard, *Directory of Manhattan Office Buildings,* 20.

15. For Richard Haviland Smythe's John Ward shop at 555 Fifth Avenue, see Stern, Gilmartin and Mellins, *New York 1930,* 300–301.

16. "Fifth Ave. Corner Will Be Improved," *New York Times* (December 14, 1952), VIII: 1; "Fifth Avenue Corners in Midtown Manhattan to Be Improved with Large Office Structures": 3; "Fifth Avenue Office Building Projects Reach Steel Erection Stage," *Real Estate Record and Guide* 172 (August 22, 1953): 3–4; Richard Roth, "High-Rise Down to Earth," *Progressive Architecture* 38 (June 1957): 196–200; Henry Hope Reed, *The Golden City* (New York: Doubleday & Co., 1959), 40–41; Ballard, *Directory of Manhattan Office Buildings,* 178.

17. Ballard, *Directory of Manhattan Office Buildings,* 63.

18. "New Bank Building to Rise on 5th Ave.," *New York Times* (July 2, 1952): 43; Lee E. Cooper, "New Design Used for Bank Edifice," *New York Times* (August 16, 1953), VIII: 1; "Banking Behind Glass," *Business Week* (August 29, 1953): 80; "Something to See," *Time* 62 (August 31, 1953): 78; "Big Banking and Modern Architecture Finally Connect," *Architectural Forum* 99 (September 1953): 134–37; "Record Reports," *Architectural Record* 114 (October 1953): 10–11; R. J. Tuttle, "Glass-Walled Bank Will Glow with Light from Luminous Ceilings," *Lighting* 53 (January 1954): 17–19, 28; "Design Award Program: Commerce," *Progressive Architecture* 35 (January 1954): 88–89; "Glass Walls Will Show Off Bank's Interior," *Engineering News-Record* 152 (January 14, 1954): 24; W. H. Weiskopf and J. W. Pickworth, "Concrete and Steel Framing Combined in Wide-Open Bank Building," *Civil Engineering* 24 (April 1954): 64–65; Aline B. Saarinen, "Art as Architectural Decoration," *Architectural Forum* 100 (June 1954): 132–35; "A Single Pane of Glass—$1,500—Goes into Bank Branch Building," *New York Times* (July 23, 1954): 34; "Putting Bankers in a Gold Fish Bowl," *Business Week* (July 31, 1954): 31; "Topics of The Times," *New York Times* (September 20, 1954): 22; "'Showcase' Bank Holds a Preview," *New York Times* (September 23, 1954): 51; "Glass-Walled Bank," *Architectural Forum* 101 (October 1954): 47; Eleanor Lemaire, "Banks," *Interior Design* 25 (October 1954): 100–101; "The Talk of the Town: Showcase," *New Yorker* 30 (October 2, 1954): 24–25; Richard Amper, "Fortune Is Moved across Fifth Ave.," *New York Times* (October 2, 1954): 6; "15,000 Ooh and Ah at Opening of Dazzling, 'Newfangled' Bank," *New York Times* (October 5, 1954): 29; "40,000 Visit All-Glass Bank," *New York Times* (October 9, 1954): 9; "Bank Counts Its Money in a Glass Showcase," *Business Week* (October 16, 1954): 48–50, 52; "Money Changing in a House of Glass," *Life* 37 (October 25, 1954): 62; "Crowd-Puller on Fifth Ave.," *Architectural Forum* 101 (November 1954): 34; "Manufacturers Trust Company Builds Conversation Piece on Fifth Avenue," *Architectural Record* 116 (November 1954): 149–56; Lewis Mumford, "The Sky Line: Crystal Lantern," *New Yorker* 30 (November 13, 1954): 197–204; "Modern Architecture Breaks through the Glass Barrier," *Architectural Forum* 101 (December 1954): cover, 104–11; Mr. Harper, "After Hours," *Harper's* 209 (December 1954): 73–75; Ada Louise Huxtable, "Bankers' Showcase," *Arts Digest* 29 (December 1, 1954): 12–13; "Metal Sculpture—Harry Bertoia," *Arts and Architecture* 72 (January 1955): 18–19; John Anderson, "The Manufacturers Trust Company," *Interiors* 114 (January 1955): 52–59, 132–33; Gerald B. Ewing, "Lighting Expert's Comment," letter to the editor, *Interiors* 114 (February 1955): 8, 145; Eugene Clute, "Abstractions in Metal," *Progressive Architecture* 36 (February 1955): 104–5; "The Modern Art of Business," *Fortune* 51 (March 1955): 99–103; "États-Unis Banque 'Manufacturers Trust Company' à New York," *Techniques et Architecture* 14 (March 1955): 42–45; Herman H. Glasser, "Glass Records," letter to the editor, *Architectural Forum* 102 (April 1955): 74; "The Shiny New Look," *Newsweek* 46 (July 4, 1955): 75; Aline B. Saarinen, "Four Architects Helping to Change the Look of America," *Vogue* 126 (August 1, 1955): 118–21, 149–50, 152; "Lifting Lobbies," *Architectural Forum* 104 (January 1956): 128; "Manufacturers' Trust Company," *Office Management* 16 (January 1956): 74–76, 80; "Neubau der Manufacturers Trust Company, New York," *Bauen + Wohnen* 10 (February 1956): 49–52; "Parentheses," *Architectural Forum* 104 (March 1956): 48–49, 54, 58; "Bank and Modernized Offices Get Top Architectural Awards," *New York Times* (April 29, 1956), VIII: 1; "Perspectives," *Architectural Record* 119 (May 1956): 9; Olga Gueft, "The Indispensable Splurge," editorial, *Interiors* 115 (June 1956): 91; "The Talk of the Town: In Scale," *New Yorker* 32 (July 7, 1956): 13–14; "New New York," *Newsweek* 48 (July 9, 1956): 90–91; Fifth Avenue Association, *Fifty Years on Fifth,*

1907–1957 (New York: Fifth Avenue Association, 1957), 138; Thomas H. Creighton, "Regionalism," editorial, *Progressive Architecture* 38 (September 1957): 266; Jack Alexander, "The Bank that Has No Secrets," *Saturday Evening Post* 230 (November 30, 1957): 36–37, 105–6; Ian McCallum, *Architecture USA* (London: Architectural Press, 1959), 136–38; Reed, *The Golden City*, 22–23; Ada Louise Huxtable, *Four Walking Tours of Modern Architecture in New York City* (New York: Museum of Modern Art and Municipal Art Society of New York, 1961), 32–33; Ernst Danz, *Architecture of Skidmore, Owings & Merrill, 1950–1962*, with an intro. by Henry-Russell Hitchcock (New York: Frederick A. Praeger, 1963), 42–47; White and Willensky, *AIA Guide* (1967), 110; June Kompass Nelson, *Harry Bertoia, Sculptor* (Detroit, Mich.: Wayne State University Press, 1970), 24, 32–33, figs. 22–23; William H. Jordy, *American Buildings and Their Architects: The Impact of European Modernism in the Mid-Twentieth Century*, vol. 4 (Garden City, N. Y.: Doubleday & Co., 1972), 115, 254, 276; Nathaniel Owings, *The Spaces in Between* (Boston: Houghton Mifflin, 1973), 103–4; John Dixon, "Lantern on Fifth Avenue," *Progressive Architecture* 54 (June 1973): 108–9; Paul Goldberger, *The City Observed: New York* (New York: Random House, 1979), 140–42; Leland Roth, *A Concise History of American Architecture* (New York: Harper & Row, 1979), 286–88; John Tauranac, *Essential New York* (New York: Holt, Rinehart and Winston, 1979), 199–200; Donald Martin Reynolds, *The Architecture of New York City* (New York: Macmillan, 1984), 151–52; Carol Herselle Krinsky, *Gordon Bunshaft of Skidmore, Owings & Merrill* (New York: Architectural History Foundation; Cambridge, Mass.: MIT Press, 1988), 49–52, 82–87, 335; Carol Herselle Krinsky, "Architecture in New York City," in Leonard Wallock, ed., *New York: Culture Capital of the World, 1940–1965* (New York: Rizzoli International Publications, 1988), 102–3; Christopher Gray, "Streetscapes: Manufacturers Hanover Trust at Fifth and 43d," *New York Times* (June 19, 1988), X: 12, reprinted in Christopher Gray, *Changing New York: The Architectural Scene* (New York: Dover, 1992), 54; Christopher Gray, "Neighborhood: Nifties from the Fifties," *Avenue* 14 (January 1990): 117–23.

19. For the Hotel Renaissance, see Stern, Gilmartin and Massengale, *New York 1900*, 264, 267.

20. Louis Skidmore quoted in "Something to See": 78.

21. "Big Banking and Modern Architecture Finally Connect": 135.

22. Gordon Bunshaft quoted in "Big Banking and Modern Architecture Finally Connect": 135. Bunshaft's client said just about the same thing in "Record Reports": 10.

23. Huxtable, "Bankers' Showcase": 13.

24. Quoted in "Bank Counts Its Money in a Glass Showcase": 52.

25. Huxtable, "Bankers' Showcase": 13.

26. Mumford, "The Sky Line: Crystal Lantern": 197.

27. See Lewis Mumford, "The Sky Line: Portholes on the Avenue—Bankers and Goldfish," *New Yorker* 9 (November 4, 1933): 40, 42, 46. Also see Stern, Gilmartin and Mellins, *New York 1930*, 181–82.

28. Mumford, "The Sky Line: Crystal Lantern": 198.

29. "Modern Architecture Breaks through the Glass Barrier": 104.

30. Anderson, "The Manufacturers Trust Company": 58.

31. Goldberger, *The City Observed*, 141–42.

32. "The Talk of the Town: Natural," *New Yorker* 30 (June 5, 1954): 21–22; "The Talk of the Town: Free Speech," *New Yorker* 30 (June 19, 1954): 20; "The Talk of the Town: Too Perfect," *New Yorker* 30 (July 10, 1954): 18–19; "Typewriter Palazzo in New York," *Architectural Forum* 101 (August 1954): cover, 98–103; Olga Gueft, "Olivetti, New York," *Interiors* 114 (November 1954): 124–31; Page Beauchamp, "Showrooms," *Progressive Architecture* 35 (November 1954): 125–31; Lewis Mumford, "The Sky Line: Charivari and Confetti," *New Yorker* 30 (December 18, 1954): 114–19; Olga Gueft, "Selling Typewriters and Writing for the Magazines," editorial, *Interiors* 114 (February 1955): 61; "Noveau magasin Olivetti à New-York," *L'Architecture d'Aujourd'hui* 26 (February 1955): 58–59; "The Modern Art of Business," *Fortune* 51 (March 1955): 99–103; "The Talk of the Town: Personal Note," *New Yorker* 31 (November 19, 1955): 42; Constantino Nivola and Frederick Gutheim, "Le Corbusier and Nivola," letters to the editor, *Architectural Record* 119 (January 1956): 16; Huxtable, *Four Walking Tours of Modern Architecture in New York City*, 30, 33–34; Olga Gueft, "The Flooded Cathedral," editorial, *Interiors* 121 (April 1961): 89; Ezio Bonfanti and Marco Porta, *Città, museo e architettura: Il Gruppo BBPR nella cultura architettonica italiana 1932–1970* (Florence: Vallecchi, 1973), A: 68–69.

33. "The Recent Work of the BBPR Studio," *Architectural Record* 128 (September 1960): 187–96; Bonfanti and Porta, *Città, museo e architettura: Il Gruppo BBPR nella cultura architettonica italiana 1932–1970*, A: 84–86; Arthur Drexler, *Transformations in Modern Architecture* (New York: Museum of Modern Art, 1979), 160–61.

34. Frank O'Hara, *Lunch Poems* (San Francisco: City Lights, 1964). Also see Brad Gooch, *City Poet: The Life and Times of Frank O'Hara* (New York: Alfred A. Knopf, 1993), 440.

35. Natalie Hoyt quoted in "The Talk of the Town: Natural": 21.

36. Enrico Peressutti quoted in "The Talk of the Town: Natural": 21.

37. "Typewriter Palazzo in New York": 99.

38. Gueft, "Olivetti, New York": 124.

39. Gueft, "The Flooded Cathedral": 89.

40. Mumford, "The Sky Line: Charivari and Confetti": 114–16.

41. Mumford, "The Sky Line: Charivari and Confetti": 116–17.

42. "Fifth Ave. to Get New Skyscraper," *New York Times* (June 24, 1956), VIII: 1, 21. For a discussion of W. & J. Sloane's history, see Fifth Avenue Association, *Fifty Years on Fifth, 1907–1957*, 74–76.

43. Myron Kandel, "Sloane's to Occupy Franklin Simon Site," *New York Times* (December 6, 1961): 1, 78; "Sloane's 50 Years at 575 Fifth Ends," *New York Times* (January 7, 1962): 64; "Sloane's Reopens at Its New Store," *New York Times* (January 17, 1962): 41.

44. Myron Kandel, "Oppenheim Collins Is Merging into the Franklin Simon Chain," *New York Times* (December 20, 1961): 47, 51; Myron Kandel, "Franklin Simon Opens on 34th St.," *New York Times* (March 13, 1962): 29.

45. "Korvette to Open Store on 5th Ave.," *New York Times* (June 15, 1961): 45; "Changing Fifth Avenue—1: Discount House Puts on Airs," *Business Week* (February 10, 1962): 72–74; "Discount House on Old Fifth Avenue," *Architectural Forum* 117 (November 1962): 136.

46. "Big Window Area for New Offices," *New York Times* (February 13, 1955), VIII: 1, 4; "N. Y. Building Design Aims at Interior Space Economy," *Engineering News-Record* 154 (February 24, 1955): 25; "Arcades, Windowless Base, Dual Occupancy, Distinguish Newest Metropolitan Buildings," *Architectural Forum* 102 (March 1955): 13; "New Building for Tishman," *Architectural Record* 117 (April 1955): 210; "Office Space Must Be Evaluated as a Business Instrument Realtor Tells Businessmen," *Real Estate Record and Guide* 175 (April 23, 1955): 3–4; "Plans Revealed for New 38-Story Office Building on Fifth Avenue," *Real Estate Record and Guide* 175 (May 14, 1955): 3; "Buildings in the News," *Architectural Record* 118 (December 1955): 10; "Tishman Awards Bethlehem Steel Contract for Largest Rivetless Skyscraper," *Real Estate Record and Guide* 177 (February 25, 1956): 3; "Lobby Decor Set for Skyscraper," *New York Times* (March 4, 1956), VIII: 6; "Manhattan's Temporary Architecture," *Interiors* 116 (August 1956): 14; "Variations on a Theme," *Architectural Record* 120 (September 1956): 11; "Wrecking Can Be Hard As Building," *New York Times* (September 30, 1956), VIII: 1, 14; "666 5th Avenue," *Empire State Architect* 16 (September–October 1956): 61, 85; Jacobs, "New York's Office Boom": 111; "666 Fifth Ave. Building," *Architectural Record* 121 (March 1957): 237; "Bolted Frame Set in New Structure," *New York Times* (April 21, 1957), VIII: 6; "Bossed-Aluminum Curtain Wall to Surface 8 Acres," *Progressive Architecture* 38 (July 1957): 92; "Electronic Elevations in 666 Fifth Avenue," *Real Estate Record and Guide* 180 (July 20, 1957): 3; "666 Fifth Avenue Opens Tomorrow," *New York Times* (November 24, 1957), VIII: 1, 6; "Biggest Aluminum-Faced Skyscraper Opens Here," *New York Times* (November 26, 1957): 37; "The Talk of the Town: Notes and Comment," *New Yorker* 33 (November 30, 1957): 41; "'Tower of Light' Glows on Fifth Avenue," *Real Estate Record and Guide* 181 (June 28, 1958): 3; "Two by Loewy & Stouffer's, and a Suburban Shopper's Oasis," *Interiors* 117 (July 1958): 83; "The Tishman Building," advertisement, *Progressive Architecture* 39 (July 1958): 33–35; "3 Buildings in Midtown Cited for Architecture," *New York Times* (July 1, 1958): 53; Glenn Fowler, "Works of Noted Artists Grace Office Buildings," *New York Times* (August 17, 1958), VIII: 1; "Lighting Is Architecture," *Progressive Architecture* 39 (September 1958): 145–49; Glenn Fowler, "New Skyscrapers Are Reviving Classical Street Arcade," *New York Times* (September 7, 1958), VIII: 1; "The Talk of the Town: Stouffer's Soars," *New Yorker* 34 (November 8, 1958): 33–34; Earle Schultz and Walter Simmons, *Offices in the Sky* (Indianapolis, Ind.: Bobbs-Merrill, 1959), 252; "Tishman Building Dims Floodlight to Aid Birds," *New York Times* (September 18, 1959): 50; "Film Depicts Construction of Office Building," *Real Estate Record and Guide* 185 (June 18, 1960): 2; "New Design in Sidewalks," *Real Estate Record and Guide* 186 (August 13, 1960): 4; Huxtable, *Four Walking Tours of Modern Architecture in New York City*, 36–38; "Christmas Lights On at Tishman Building," *Real Estate Record and Guide* 190 (December 1, 1962): 4; Byron Porterfield, "Aluminum Sheathes Tall Buildings Here with Tones of Black, Silver and Gold," *New York Times* (March 13, 1966), VIII: 1, 18; White and Willensky, *AIA Guide* (1967), 128; Isamu Noguchi, *A Sculptor's World* (New York: Harper & Row, 1968), 165, figs. 215–27; Ballard, *Directory of Manhattan Office Buildings*, 149; Sam Hunter, *Isamu Noguchi* (New York: Abbeville Press, 1978), 246; Goldberger, *The City Observed*, 172; Nancy Grove, *Isamu Noguchi: A Study of the Sculpture* (New York: Garland Publishing, 1985), 138, fig. 152; Krinsky, "Architecture in New York City," in Wallock, ed., *New York: Culture Capital of the World, 1940–1965*, 101; Gray, "Neighborhood: Nifties from the Fifties": 120–21.

47. For Richard Morris Hunt's William K. Vanderbilt house, see Paul Baker, *Richard Morris Hunt* (Cambridge, Mass.: MIT Press, 1980), 274–88, 544; Foreman and Stimson, *The Vanderbilts and the Gilded Age*, 28–39. For McKim, Mead & White's Mrs. William K. Vanderbilt, Jr., mansion, see Stern, Gilmartin and Massengale, *New York 1900*, 320–21; Foreman and Stimson, *The Vanderbilts and the Gilded Age*, 42. For the Lord & Taylor proposal, see "Big Slice," *Architectural Forum* 83 (September 1945): 7.

48. Noguchi, *A Sculptor's World*, 165.

49. "'Tower of Light' Glows on Fifth Avenue": 3.

50. For the Rainbow Room, see Stern, Gilmartin and Mellins, *New York 1930*, 284–85, 291.

51. "5th Ave. Tower to Rise for Canadian Groups in New York," *Architectural Forum* 103 (December 1955): 17; "Buildings in the News," (December 1955): 10; "Canada House Skyscraper," *Interiors* 115 (February 1956): 12; "'Canada House,' New Office Building, Will Go Up at 680 5th Avenue," *Real Estate Record and Guide* 177 (March 3, 1956): 3; "Interest Bought in Canada House," *New York Times* (February 20, 1957): 55; Jacobs, "New York's Office Boom": 112; "Canada House Decorated with Sculptural Stone-Carving," *Real Estate Record and Guide* 180 (November 16, 1957): 3–4; "Canada Boycotts Skyscraper Here," *New York Times* (December 13, 1957): 1, 20; Thomas W. Ennis, "Webb & Knapp Offers to Sell Interest in Canada House Here," *New York Times* (December 14, 1957): 23; "Canada and the U. S.: Retreat from 5th Ave.," *Newsweek* 50 (December 23, 1957): 43; "Stained-Glass Mural Installed as Rear Wall of Lobby in Canada House," *New York Times* (March 27, 1958): 35; "Canada House Features Stained Glass Window," *Real Estate Record and Guide* 181 (April 5, 1958): 3; "Canada House Set for Dedication," *New York Times* (September 28, 1958), VIII: 1, 12; "Flags of Two Nations Raised at New Canada House," *New York Times* (October 2, 1958): 33; "Buildings in the News," *Architectural Record* 124 (November 1958): 20; "Unity Is Achieved by Canada House," *New York Times* (November 9, 1958), VIII: 1, 9; White and Willensky, *AIA Guide* (1967), 130; Ballard, *Directory of Manhattan Office Buildings*, 150.

52. For John B. Snook's Lila Vanderbilt Webb house, see John Tauranac, *Elegant New York* (New York: Abbeville Press, 1985), 114, 117, 141; Foreman and Stimson, *The Vanderbilts and the Gilded Age*, 313.

53. For John B. Snook's Florence Vanderbilt Twombly house, see Tauranac, *Elegant New York*, 114, 117, 141; Foreman and Stimson, *The Vanderbilts and the Gilded Age*, 313.

54. For the RCA Victor Building, see Stern, Gilmartin and Mellins, *New York 1930*, 152–53, 599. For St. Bartholomew's Church, see Stern, Gilmartin and Massengale, *New York 1900*, 113, 116, 120–21; Stern Gilmartin and Mellins, *New York 1930*, 152–53, 158.

55. "Webb & Knapp Announce Signing of Contract to Purchase Easterly Fifth Ave. Blockfront, 55th and 56th Streets," *Real Estate Record and Guide* 175 (January 8, 1955): 3; "Corning to Build a 'Glass Tower,'" *New York Times* (October 10, 1956): 41; "Tower of Glass to Rise on Fifth Avenue," *Real Estate Record and Guide* 178 (October 20, 1956): 3–4; "28-Story Glass Showcase for Fifth Avenue," *Architectural Forum* 105 (November 1956): 24; "Office Buildings Here and There," *Architectural Record* 120 (November 1956): 10–11; "Corning to Erect Glass Tower on Fifth Avenue," *Progressive Architecture* 37 (November 1956): 94; Jacobs, "New York's Office Boom": 112; "Corning 'Tower of Glass,'" *Architectural Record* 121 (March 1957): 240; "Construction Begins on Fifth Ave. Tower of Glass," *Real Estate Record and Guide* 180 (October 19, 1957): 3; "Corning Constructs Fifth Avenue Tower and Plaza," *Progressive Architecture* 38 (December 1957): 71; Lois Wagner Green, ed., *Interiors Book of Offices* (New York: Whitney Library of Design, 1959), 35–37; "Glass Skyscraper Nears Completion," *Real Estate Record and Guide* 182 (March 21, 1959): 5; "Corning's Building Gets Glass Decor," *New York Times* (April 26, 1959): 1, 11; "Buildings in the News," *Architectural Record* 125 (May 1959): 14; "Blithe Showcase," *Interiors* 118 (June 1959): 104–5; "Phantom Setting for Glass," *Interiors* 118 (June 1959): 106–7; "Glass Works Moves into Glass Tower," *Progressive Architecture* 40 (June 1959): 78; John Anderson, "Inside 717 Fifth Avenue," *Interiors* 118 (July 1959): 66–79; "The Talk of the Town: Good Luck," *New Yorker* 35 (July 18, 1959): 16; Jürgen Joedicke, *Office Buildings*, trans. C. V. Amerongen (New York: Frederick A. Praeger, 1962), 152–53; White and Willensky, *AIA Guide* (1967), 132; Charles Thomsen, "The Making of an Architect," *Journal of the American Institute of Architects* 48 (August 1967): 73–78; Ballard, *Directory of Manhattan Office Buildings*, 151; Goldberger, *The City Observed*, 165; Krinsky, "Architecture in New York City," in Wallock, ed., *New York: Culture Capital of the World, 1940–1965*, 103; Victoria Newhouse, *Wallace K. Harrison, Architect* (New York: Rizzoli International Publications, 1989), 152–55; Gray, "Neighborhood: Nifties from the Fifties": 120.

56. Anderson, "Inside 717 Fifth Avenue": 67.

57. For Platt & Platt's Corning Glass Building, see Stern, Gilmartin and Mellins, *New York 1930*, 306–7.

58. "Japanese Dept. Store Will Open on Fifth Ave.," *Real Estate Record and Guide* 181 (May 10, 1958): 5; "Tokyo Opens Fifth Avenue Shop," *Business Week* (October 25, 1958): 50, 54, 56; "News Bulletins," *Progressive Architecture* 39 (December 1958): 34; "Takashimaya's New York Branch," *Japan Architect* 34 (January–February 1959): 110–12; "Japanese Retailers Invade Fifth Avenue," *Architectural Record* 125 (April 1959): 208–9, reprinted in James S. Hornbeck, ed., *Stores and Shopping Centers* (New York: McGraw-Hill, 1962), 62–63; "Tokonoma on Fifth Avenue: Takashimaya's American Branch," *Interiors* 118 (June 1959): 88–91; Glenn Fowler, "Architecture in City Influenced by Influx of Japanese Concerns," *New York Times* (March 22, 1964), VIII: 1, 10.

59. "Tokyo Opens Fifth Avenue Shop": 52.

60. "Japanese Retailers Invade Fifth Avenue": 208.

61. Sanka Knox, "5th Ave. Bookshop Says Buon Giorno," *New York Times* (October 23, 1964): 36; "The Talk of the Town: Molto, Molto, Molto," *New Yorker* 41 (May 1, 1965): 37–39; Goldberger, *The City Observed*, 176; Landmarks Preservation Commission of the City of New York, LP–1533 (January 29, 1985); Diamonstein, *The Landmarks of New York*, 290.

62. For Charles Scribner's Sons, see Stern, Gilmartin and Massengale, *New York 1900*, 200–201. For Brentano's, see Stern, Gilmartin and Mellins, *New York 1930*, 296.

63. For Cartier's, see Stern, Gilmartin and Massengale, *New York 1900*, 200, 312, 314.

64. Goldberger, *The City Observed*, 176.

65. Farnsworth Fowle, "Crowell-Collier Buys Brentano's and Will Run It as Subsidiary," *New York Times* (April 5, 1962): 35; "Brentano's to Add a 48th Street Wing," *New York Times* (February 22, 1965): 19; Harry Gilroy, "Brentano's Bookshop Becoming a Cultural Department Store," *New York Times* (October 28, 1965): 40. For a brief discussion of Brentano's history, see Fifth Avenue Association, *Fifty Years on Fifth, 1907–1957*, 92–93.

66. Leonard Schwartz quoted in Gilroy, "Brentano's Bookshop Becoming a Cultural Department Store": 40.

67. Arnold H. Lubasch, "Doubleday Shops Joining the Fifth Avenue Crowd," *New York Times* (October 1, 1967), VIII: 1, 6. For a brief discussion of Doubleday's history, see Fifth Avenue Association, *Fifty Years on Fifth, 1907–1957*, 93–94.

68. Lubasch, "Doubleday Shops Joining the Fifth Avenue Crowd": 1, 6.

69. Eugene K. Denton quoted in Leonard Sloane, "Tailored Woman to Quit Business," *New York Times* (November 13, 1967): 50.

70. For John B. Peterkin's Airlines Terminal, see Stern, Gilmartin and Mellins, *New York 1930*, 704–5.

71. "KLM," *Interiors* 107 (March 1948): 94–97.

72. Foster Hailey, "Another Airline Shifts to 5th Ave.," *New York Times* (November 8, 1959): 130. For La Maison Française, see Stern, Gilmartin and Mellins, *New York 1930*, 646–47, 650, 656, 666, 668–69.

73. Stern, Gilmartin and Mellins, *New York 1930*, 296.

74. "French National Airline Gets Office Building on Fifth Ave. in a $2,000,000 Leasing Deal," *New York Times* (May 2, 1947): 39; Diana Rice, "News and Notes from the Field of Travel," *New York Times* (March 14, 1948), II: 13.

75. Morris Ketchum, Jr., *Shops & Stores* (New York: Reinhold Publishing Corp., 1948), 112–13; Lewis Mumford, "The Sky Line: Outside Looking In," *New Yorker* 23 (February 14, 1948): 58, 60–62; "KLM," *Interiors*: 94–97; "Royal Dutch Airline Offices," *Architectural Record* 103 (March 1948): 97–101.

76. Mumford, "The Sky Line: Outside Looking In": 60.

77. Mumford, "The Sky Line: Outside Looking In": 58, 60; "Britain Circles the Globe," *Architectural Record* 103 (March 1948): 102–3.

78. Mumford, "The Sky Line: Outside Looking In": 58, 60.

79. "Argentine Airlines Offices," *Interiors* 108 (April 1949): 112–17.

80. "Daytime Ticket Office—Nighttime Display," *Architectural Record* 113 (March 1953): 152–53.

81. "Three Airline Offices," *Architectural Forum* 83 (July 1945): 80–85.

82. "Ticket Office Dramatizes Destination, Wafts a Subtle Echo of Japanese Architecture into New York's Fifth Avenue," *Architectural Forum* 101 (September 1954): 114–17; Morris Ketchum, Jr., *Shops & Stores*, rev. ed. (New York: Reinhold Publishing Corp., 1957), 138.

83. "Office Here Has Oriental Style," *New York Times* (September 9, 1956), VIII: 1, 8; Betsy Darrach, "Footnote of Flight and Destination: Junzo Yoshimura's Ticket Office for Japan Airlines," *Interiors* 116 (June 1957): 106–8; Louise Sloane, "Ticket Offices," *Progressive Architecture* 39 (February 1958): 157–59.

84. Darrach, "Footnote of Flight and Destination: Junzo Yoshimura's Ticket Office for Japan Airlines": 106.

85. Sloane, "Ticket Offices": 157.

86. Betsy Darrach, "Showcase for Travel and Tourism," *Interiors* 116 (June 1957): 102–3.

87. "Travel Rise Seen by London Mayor," *New York Times* (July 2, 1957): 54.

88. Betsy Darrach, "Aeronaves de Mexico," *Interiors* 117 (September 1958): 97.

89. "KLM to Consolidate Local Offices," *New York Times* (May 11, 1958), VIII: 8; "KLM Plans Renovation of 609 Fifth Avenue," *Real Estate Record and Guide* 181 (May 31, 1958): 4; "News of Art and Architecture," *Architectural Record* 126 (November 1959): 32; Edmond J. Barnett, "Extensive Building Alterations Bring Constant Change to 5th Avenue," *New York Times* (November 25, 1962), VIII: 1, 6; "An Office Building Reborn," *Architectural Forum* 112 (January 1960): 119–21, 190; Huxtable, *Four Walking Tours of Modern*

Architecture in New York City, 34; Massachusetts Institute of Technology, Center for Advanced Visual Studies, *The MIT Years, 1945–1977*, exhibition catalogue (Cambridge, Mass.: MIT Press, 1978), 87.

90. Gyorgy Kepes quoted in "News of Art and Architecture": 32.

91. "Bulletins," *Progressive Architecture* 40 (January 1959): 70; Gio Ponti, "La nuova sede dell'Alitalia a New York," *Domus* 354 (May 1959): 7–11; Lisa Licitra Ponti, *Gio Ponti: The Complete Work 1923–1978*, foreword by Germano Celant (London: Thames and Hudson, 1990), 178.

92. Ponti, "La nuova sede dell'Alitalia a New York": 7.

93. Hailey, "Another Airline Shifts to 5th Ave. ": 130.

94. Quoted in Hailey, "Another Airline Shifts to 5th Ave. ": 130.

95. "Air India: A Soupçon of Indian New York," *Interiors* 120 (September 1960): 153.

96. "A Symmetry of Angles and Curves," *Interiors* 122 (November 1962): 120–23.

97. "Showmanship with Light," *Architectural Forum* 115 (August 1961): 122–23; "Air France's New York Ticket Office: A Vivid Fifth Avenue Traffic Stopper," *Interiors* 121 (November 1961): 114–21.

98. Dudley Dalton, "Midtown 5th Ave. an Airline Mecca," *New York Times* (January 31, 1965), VIII: 1, 8.

99. John Anderson, "New Accent on Fifth Avenue," *Interiors* 128 (October 1968): 130–35.

100. "News Report," *Progressive Architecture* 51 (September 1970): 32.

101. "Teamwork by Telex and Telepathy," *Interior Design* 42 (February 1971): 98–103.

102. Lewis Mumford, "The Sky Line: Fifth Avenue, for Better or Worse," *New Yorker* 28 (August 16, 1952): 56, 58–63.

103. Mumford, "The Sky Line: Fifth Avenue, for Better or Worse": 56.

104. "The Seamen's Bank Expands Fifth Avenue Office," *Real Estate Record and Guide* 177 (June 30, 1956): 3.

105. "Builders to Employ Unusual Method in New Bank Building," *Real Estate Record and Guide* 181 (January 18, 1958): 3–4; Ballard, *Directory of Manhattan Office Buildings*, 18.

106. "The Talk of the Town: No Return," *New Yorker* 27 (November 3, 1951): 28–29; "The Talk of the Town: Homesick," *New Yorker* 31 (March 12, 1955): 25–26; "Landmarks Fall on 5th Ave. Block," *New York Times* (April 17, 1955), VIII: 1; "Big Wave of Office Construction Renews Overbuilding Question," *Architectural Forum* 102 (June 1955): 9; "The Talk of the Town: Notes and Comment," *New Yorker* 33 (June 8, 1957): 23–24; "The Bank of New York," *Interiors* 116 (July 1957): 94–97; Voorhees, Walker, Smith, Smith & Haines, *75th Anniversary* (New York, May 1960), 71; Ballard, *Directory of Manhattan Office Buildings*, 19.

107. "The Talk of the Town: Homesick": 25–26.

108. Edmond J. Bartnett, "Building Is Rising on an 1896 Frame," *New York Times* (May 29, 1960), VIII: 1, 8; "One-Block Move Made by Morgan Guaranty," *New York Times* (November 20, 1961): 47; Ballard, *Directory of Manhattan Office Buildings*, 18.

109. For McKim, Mead & White's Sherry's, see Stern, Gilmartin and Massengale, *New York 1900*, 223–25.

110. Marian Page, "A Contemporary Design with Japanese Overtones," *Interiors* 122 (January 1963): 94–97; Fowler, "Architecture in City Influenced by Influx of Japanese Concerns": 1.

111. Page, "A Contemporary Design with Japanese Overtones": 95.

112. "Eyes Right," *Architectural Forum* 129 (November 1968): 64; "Banco do Brasil: Secluded Prestige for a Semi-Private Bank," *Architectural Record* 146 (August 1969): 113–17; "Banque du Brésil à New York," *L'Architecture d'Aujourd'hui* 156 (June 1970): xxxiv-xxxv.

113. For an in-depth discussion of Latin American architecture in the postwar period, see Henry-Russell Hitchcock, *Latin American Architecture Since 1945* (New York: Museum of Modern Art, 1955).

114. "First Israel Bank & Trust Company, New York City," *Architectural Record* 151 (January 1972): 91.

115. "First Israel Bank & Trust Company, New York City": 91.

116. Isadore Barmash, "Best & Co. Is Expected to Close, Speeding Evolution of 5th Ave.: Owners to Meet Today," *New York Times* (October 3, 1970): 1, 10; Michael Stern, "Best & Co. Is Expected to Close, Speeding Evolution of 5th Ave.: Offices Taking Over," *New York Times* (October 3, 1970): 1, 11; Isadore Barmash, "Best & Co. Announces Its Decision to Terminate Business; All 15 Stores Will Close in About 4 Weeks," *New York Times* (October 4, 1970): 49; "Retailing: Naked on Fifth," *Newsweek* 76 (October 19, 1970): 86.

117. Samuel Neaman quoted in Barmash, "Best & Co. Is Expected to Close, Speeding Evolution of 5th Ave.: Owners to Meet Today": 10.

118. For Hunt & Hunt's George W. Vanderbilt house (the northern half of the "Marble Twins"), see Stern, Gilmartin and Massengale, *New York 1900*, 332–33; Diamonstein, *The Landmarks of New York*, 278.

119. For the Morton F. Plant house, see Stern, Gilmartin and Massengale, *New York 1900*, 312, 314; Diamonstein, *The Landmarks of New York*, 269.

120. Glenn Fowler, "Arcade Lined with Shops Set for Building on Site of Best's," *New York Times* (October 7, 1970): 57; "Lapidus to Design Onassis Building," *Progressive Architecture* 51 (December 1970): 22; Morris Lapidus, *An Architecture of Joy* (Miami, Fla.: E. A. Seemann, 1979), 222–28.

121. Lapidus, *An Architecture of Joy*, 222.

122. Lapidus, *An Architecture of Joy*, 223.

123. "Good-by to Fifth Avenue?" editorial, *New York Times* (October 15, 1970): 46.

124. Peter Blake, "The New Fifth Avenue," *New York* 4 (April 12, 1971): 29–34; Jonathan Barnett, *Urban Design as Public Policy* (New York: Architectural Record Books, 1974), 52–57.

125. Merwin Bayer quoted in Isadore Barmash, "Change Stirring on 5th Ave.," *New York Times* (October 30, 1966), III: 1, 12.

126. Harry G. Huberth quoted in "Special City Aid Is Asked for Retail Developers," *Real Estate Record and Guide* 204 (December 20, 1969): 2.

127. Franklin Whitehouse, "City and American Airlines at Odds Over Ticket Office in Old Georg Jensen Building on Fifth Avenue," *New York Times* (April 4, 1971): 53; Carter B. Horsley, "News of the Realty Trade: Airline Forgoing Fifth Ave. Space," *New York Times* (March 31, 1974), VIII: 8; Ballard, *Directory of Manhattan Office Buildings*, 177.

128. Richard Lempert quoted in Whitehouse, "City and American Airlines at Odds Over Ticket Office in Old Georg Jensen Building on Fifth Avenue": 53.

129. "Combined-Use Building Implements Fifth Avenue Plan," *Architectural Record* 150 (October 1971): 36; "5th Avenue's Changing Face," *Interiors* 131 (November 1971): 24;

Carter B. Horsley, "A New Neighbor Is Dwarfing St. Patrick's," *New York Times* (June 24, 1973), VIII: 1–2; "Olympic Tower Lease," *New York Times* (October 21, 1973), VIII: 10; Barnett, *Urban Design as Public Policy*, 52–57; "Olympic Tower Prospectus Issued," *New York Times* (May 5, 1974), VIII: 12; Carter B. Horsley, "Olympic Tower Dedicated Here," *New York Times* (September 6, 1974): 36; "The New Olympians," *Time* 104 (September 23, 1974): 77; "Zoning Innovation Marries Steel Frame to a Concrete Frame," *Engineering News-Record* 192 (November 28, 1974): 18–19; Andrew Alpern, *Apartments for the Affluent* (New York: McGraw-Hill, 1975), 158–59; Ellen Stock, "Best Bet: Taking the Fifth," *New York* 8 (March 17, 1975): 69; Paul Goldberger, "Exclusive New Buildings Here Combine Mixed-Use Facilities," *New York Times* (July 21, 1975): 23, 34; Daniel Delano, "The Towering Unfairness," *Village Voice* 20 (July 21, 1975): 12–13; Suzanne Stephens, "Microcosms of Urbanity," *Progressive Architecture* 56 (December 1975): 37–51; "People Are Talking about . . . . Rich Kids' Compound: Olympic Tower Provides . . . the Best of Everything on Fifth Avenue," *Vogue* 166 (January 1976): 96–97; Norma Skurka, "Being in the Swim in Your Own Home," *New York Times* (November 10, 1976), III: 18; Ada Louise Huxtable, "The Trashing of Fifth Avenue," *New York Times* (December 5, 1976), II: 33–34; Ballard, *Directory of Manhattan Office Buildings*, 148; White and Willensky, *AIA Guide* (1978), 164; Ada Louise Huxtable, "The Sabotaging of Public Space," *New York Times* (January 26, 1978), C: 1, 8; Goldberger, *The City Observed*, 164; Tauranac, *Essential New York*, 239–40; Paul Goldberger, *The Skyscraper* (New York: Alfred A. Knopf, 1981), 144; Thomas E. Norton and Jerry E. Patterson, *Living It Up: A Guide to the Named Apartment Houses of New York* (New York: Atheneum, 1984), 250–51.

130. Whitson Overcash quoted in "People Are Talking about . . . . Rich Kids' Compound: Olympic Tower Provides . . . the Best of Everything on Fifth Avenue": 97.

131. Goldberger, "Exclusive New Buildings Here Combine Mixed-Use Facilities": 34.

132. Stanley Thea quoted in "People Are Talking about . . . . Rich Kids' Compound: Olympic Tower Provides . . . the Best of Everything on Fifth Avenue": 97.

133. Jaquelin Robertson quoted in "People Are Talking about . . . . Rich Kids' Compound: Olympic Tower Provides . . . the Best of Everything on Fifth Avenue": 96.

134. Goldberger, "Exclusive New Buildings Here Combine Mixed-Use Facilities": 34.

135. Huxtable, "The Trashing of Fifth Avenue": 34.

136. Huxtable, "The Sabotaging of Public Space": 8.

137. Stephens, "Microcosms of Urbanity": 47.

138. Leonard Sloane, "DePinna to Close Its Three Stores," *New York Times* (April 4, 1969): 1, 47.

139. For the Margaret Vanderbilt Shepard and Emily Vanderbilt Sloane house, see Stern, Gilmartin and Massengale, *New York 1900*, 309; Foreman and Stimson, *The Vanderbilts and the Gilded Age*, 313.

140. "In Progress," *Progressive Architecture* 57 (February 1976): 36–37; Alan S. Oser, "Iran Is Building a Presence on Fifth Ave.," *New York Times* (February 4, 1976): 54; Ann Crittenden, "The Shah in New York: What Is His Foundation's Aim?" *New York Times* (September 26, 1976), III: 1–2; Ballard, *Directory of Manhattan Office Buildings*, 149; White and Willensky, *AIA Guide* (1978), 165; Goldberger, *The City Observed*, 172; Paul Goldberger, "Architecture: Building that Fits In on 5th Ave.," *New York Times* (May 20, 1979): 54; Carter B. Horsley, "Pahlavi Building 80 Percent Rented," *New York Times* (May 20, 1979), VIII: 4; Alan S. Oser, "Leasing Pahlavi Building," *New York Times* (December 19, 1979), D: 18; "The Ayatollah's Tenants," *New York Times* (December 30, 1979), III: 13.

141. Goldberger, "Architecture: Building that Fits In on 5th Ave. ": 54.

SIXTH AVENUE

1. "6th Ave. 'L' to Shut Down at Midnight Tomorrow," *New York Times* (December 3, 1938): 1, 3; "Romance Marked Elevated's Career," *New York Times* (December 3, 1938): 3; "Gay Crowds on Last Ride as Sixth Ave. Elevated Ends 60-Year Existence," *New York Times* (December 5, 1938): 1, 3; Meyer Berger, "Bedlam Is Raised on the Last Runs," *New York Times* (December 5, 1938): 3; "Farewell to the El," editorial, *New York Times* (December 5, 1938): 22; George M. Mathieu, "'New' Street Takes Form," *New York Times* (March 12, 1939), XII: 4; Ernest La France, "Rebirth of an Avenue," *New York Times* (March 19, 1939), VIII: 11, 19; Lee E. Cooper, "Subway to Foster Growth of Stores along Sixth Ave.," *New York Times* (December 1, 1940), XII: 1–2. Before its complete removal, a portion of the Sixth Avenue El running from Fifty-third to Fifty-eighth Street had been demolished in 1928. See Stern, Gilmartin and Mellins, *New York 1930*, 702–3.

2. La France, "Rebirth of an Avenue": 11.

3. La France, "Rebirth of an Avenue": 11.

4. Edward D. Stone, "Study for an Avenue of the Americas," advertisement, *Architectural Forum* 75 (August 1941): 1–5.

5. Stone, "Study for an Avenue of the Americas": 2.

6. Stone, "Study for an Avenue of the Americas": 2.

7. Ely Jacques Kahn, "Commercial Centers, Prewar Vs. Postwar," *Architectural Record* 93 (April 1943): 74–77.

8. Claim attributed to Jenkins in Stone, "Study for an Avenue of the Americas": 1. Also see "Name of 6th Ave. to Be Changed to the Avenue of the Americas," *New York Times* (September 21, 1945): 23; "Merchants Divide on 6th Ave. Name," *New York Times* (September 23, 1945): 48; Frank W. Crane, "Future Holds Big Possibilities for the Growth of Sixth Avenue," *New York Times* (September 30, 1945), VIII: 1; "6th Avenue's Name Gone with the Wind," *New York Times* (October 3, 1945): 21; "As to Re-naming Streets," editorial, *New York Times* (October 4, 1945): 22; "Navy Steals Show at Dedication of Avenue of Americas by Rios," *New York Times* (October 21, 1945): 1, 5; Sidney Feldman, "For Poetic Street Names," letter to the editor, *New York Times* (March 24, 1950): 24.

9. "New Avenue—New Building," *Interiors* 105 (November 1945): 16.

10. "Proposed for the Avenue of the Americas," *New York Times* (February 20, 1946): 1; "Another 'Good Neighbor' Building," *Interiors* 106 (March 1946): 10.

11. "Out of Schools: Training for Architects," *Interiors* 107 (November 1947): 10; "The Record Reports," *Architectural Record* 102 (December 1947): 132.

12. "Plans Filed for 4 New Skyscrapers in Manhattan at $20,000,000 Cost," *New York Times* (August 3, 1944): 21. For the Hippodrome, see Stern, Gilmartin and Massengale, *New York 1900*, 208–9.

13. "Garage and Office Building to Be Erected on Site of Old Hippodrome," *Real Estate Record and Guide* 163 (February 19, 1949): 3–4; "Combination Office-Garage Planned for Old Hipprodrome Site," *Architectural Forum* 90 (March 1949): 15; Edward J. Matthews, letter to the editor, *Architectural Forum* 90 (June 1949): 36, 40.

14. "Hippodrome Site Gets New Design," *New York Times* (October 14, 1951), VIII: 1, 8.

15. "Eastern Air Lines Leases Space on Sixth Avenue," *Real Estate Record and Guide* 178 (October 6, 1956): 3; Thomas W. Ennis, "6th Ave. Altered by Building Boom," *New York Times* (September 10, 1961), VIII: 1, 6; "6th Avenue Area between Rockefeller Center and Bryant Park Springing to Life as Office Boom Moves Southward," *Real Estate Record and Guide* 189 (April 21, 1962): 2–3; Robert F. R. Ballard, *Directory of Manhattan Office Buildings* (New York: McGraw-Hill, 1978), 6.

16. "Wreckers Knock the Bottom Out of New York Skyscraper," *Architectural Forum* 101 (November 1954): 37; "Exit Center Theater," *Time* 62 (November 2, 1954): 100; Victoria Newhouse, *Wallace K. Harrison, Architect* (New York: Rizzoli International Publications, 1989), 152. For the Center Theater (RKO Roxy), see Stern, Gilmartin and Mellins, *New York 1930*, 656, 658–63.

17. "New Skyscraper to Be Built at Sixth Avenue–40th Street," *Real Estate Record and Guide* 175 (February 12, 1955): 3; "News Bulletins," *Progressive Architecture* 37 (March 1956): 37; John P. Callahan, "New Machine Puts Terra Cotta Back on the New York Skyline," *New York Times* (December 8, 1957), VIII: 1, 6; Ballard, *Directory of Manhattan Office Buildings*, 201. For Taylor's Union Dime Savings Bank Building, see Stern, Gilmartin and Massengale, *New York 1900*, 459 (n. 160).

18. Stern, Gilmartin and Mellins, *New York 1930*, 574–75, 579–80, 584–85.

19. Peter V. Beckley, "New 60-Story Neighbor for Rockefeller Center," *New York Herald Tribune* (November 29, 1955): 1, 16; Thomas W. Ennis, "60-Story Offices to Rise on 6th Ave.," *New York Times* (November 29, 1956): 1, 37; "Beauty Treatment," *Time* 68 (December 10, 1956): 98; "Two Newest N. Y. Towers," *Architectural Forum* 106 (January 1957): 37; "One 'Easy Way' to Get a Loan—Just Once," *Architectural Forum* 106 (January 1957): 46, 50; "More Towers for New York: Major Projects Announced," *Architectural Record* 121 (January 1957): 12; Jane Jacobs, "New York's Office Boom," *Architectural Forum* 106 (March 1957): 104–13; "33 West 51st St. Building," *Architectural Record* 121 (March 1957): 244; "P/A News Survey," *Progressive Architecture* 38 (June 1957): 59.

20. Lee E. Cooper, "Offices to Usurp 'Swing Row' Sites," *New York Times* (August 2, 1953), VIII: 1, 3; "Avenue of the Americas," editorial, *New York Times* (August 7, 1953): 18.

21. Andrew Alpern and Seymour Durst, *Holdouts!* (New York: McGraw-Hill, 1984), 66–67. For a colorful description of Toots Shor, see Earl Wilson, *Sinatra: An Unauthorized Biography* (New York: Macmillan, 1976), 59–61.

22. For the RCA Building, see Stern, Gilmartin and Mellins, *New York 1930*, 616, 646–53.

23. "Textile Company Building Sparkling Home Office Here," *New York Times* (February 22, 1957): 27; "Marble Walls for Manhattan's Textile District," *Architectural Forum* 106 (March 1957): 38; "Design for New Textile Headquarters Deftly Handles Several Problems," *Architectural Record* 124 (December 1958): 119–24, reprinted in *Office Buildings: An Architectural Record Book* (New York: F. W. Dodge Corp., 1961), 103–8; Thomas W. Ennis, "Marble Clad Buildings Brighten Midtown Manhattan," *New York Times* (January 31, 1965), VIII: 1, 4.

24. Ballard, *Directory of Manhattan Office Buildings*, 201; Newhouse, *Wallace K. Harrison, Architect*, 321.

25. Thomas W. Ennis, Jr., "Rockefeller Center to Add Skyscraper," *New York Times* (December 14, 1956): 1, 33; "Two Newest N. Y. Towers": 37; "More Towers for New York: Major Projects Announced": 12; Jacobs, "New York's Office Boom": 113; "Time and Life Building," *Architectural Record* 121 (March 1957): 232; "P/A News Survey" (June 1957): 59; "The Pleasures of Ponti," *Time* 70 (September 1957): 92; "Two Notable New Office Buildings for Manhattan, 2: A Tall Tower for Time Inc.," *Architectural Forum* 108 (January 1958): 94–99; Olga Gueft, "Time-Life into . . . ," *Interiors* 117 (January 1958): 74–109; "P/A News Bulletins," *Progressive Architecture* 39 (January 1958): 74; Glenn Fowler, "Aerial View Confirms Pedestrian's Belief: Construction Here Never Stops," *New York Times* (June 15, 1958), VIII: 1, 13; Peter Kihss, "City Undergoing Vast Face Lifting," *New York Times* (October 18, 1958): 23, 27; Lois Wagner Green, ed., *Interiors Book of Offices* (New York: Whitney Library of Design, 1959), 114–18; Gerald Luss, "The Time-Life Project," in Green, ed., *Interiors Book of Offices*, 88–92, plates i-xii; "Manhattan's Time & Life Building," *Architectural Forum* 111 (August 1959): 11; "Toward a New Continuity," *Architectural Forum* 112 (January 1960): 143–50; Olga Gueft, "What Makes the Boss the Boss," editorial, *Interiors* 119 (January 1960): 71; Olga Gueft, "Third Design Firm Case Study: Designs for Business, Inc.," *Interiors* 119 (January 1960): 72–99, 141; "A New Home for 'Life': Rockefeller Center Moves toward West," *Life* 48 (April 4, 1960): 17–23; Richard E. Paret, "Stainless Steel Flashing," *Progressive Architecture* 41 (May 1960): 182–85; "Two-Purpose Tower," *Architectural Forum* 113 (August 1960): 74–81; "Data Processing Made Available to All," *Architectural Record* 128 (September 1960): 224–25; Harold G. Buttrick, "Model Tower," letter to the editor, *Architectural Forum* 113 (October 1960): 206; Ada Louise Huxtable, "The Significance of Our Skyscrapers," *New York Times* (October 30, 1960), II: 13; Ada Louise Huxtable, *Four Walking Tours of Modern Architecture in New York City* (New York: Museum of Modern Art and Municipal Art Society of New York, 1961), 68; Olga Gueft, "A Style for the Inner Circle," *Interiors* 120 (March 1961): 126–35; "Clubs," *Interior Design* 32 (April 1961): 207–9; "Tower Suite—Hemisphere Club," *Interiors* 120 (May 1961): 122–27; Robert Sowers, "Art in Architecture: Recent Work in New York," *Craft Horizons* 21 (November 1961): 24–25; "The Talk of the Town: Notes and Comment," *New Yorker* 37 (November 4, 1961): 43–44; "Doing Over the Town," *Time* 80 (September 28, 1962): 56–69; Thomas W. Ennis, "14 Major Postwar Buildings Rise from 46th to 57th Street," *New York Times* (October 6, 1963), VIII: 1, 12; White and Willensky, *AIA Guide* (1967), 133; Maurice Mogulescu, *Profit through Design* (New York: American Management Association, 1970), 79, plates III: 7–9, 16; Fred B. Shrallow, "Five Restaurant Interiors," *Interior Design* 44 (October 1973): 176–77; Frederick Fried and Edmund N. Gillon, Jr., *New York Civic Sculpture* (New York: Dover, 1976), 62–63; Alan Balfour, *Rockefeller Center: Architecture as Theater* (New York: McGraw-Hill, 1978), 230–32; Ballard, *Directory of Manhattan Office Buildings*, 188; Carol Herselle Krinsky, *Rockefeller Center* (New York: Oxford University Press, 1978), 111–15, 157–60, 163; White and Willensky, *AIA Guide* (1978), 169–70; Paul Goldberger, *The City Observed: New York* (New York: Random House, 1979), 171–72; John Tauranac, *Essential New York* (New York: Holt, Rinehart and Winston, 1979), 205–6; Walter Karp, *The Center: A History and Guide to Rockefeller Center* (New York: American Heritage, 1982), 32–35, 76–77; Carol Herselle Krinsky, "Architecture in New York City," in Leonard Wallock, ed., *New York: Culture Capital of the World, 1940–1965* (New York: Rizzoli International Publications, 1988), 103–4; Newhouse, *Wallace K. Harrison, Architect*, 106, 154.

26. "Two-Purpose Tower": 75.

27. Wallace K. Harrison quoted in Newhouse, *Wallace K. Harrison, Architect*, 156.

28. For a comprehensive discussion of Ponti's career, see Lisa Licitra Ponti, *Gio Ponti: The Complete Work 1923–1978*, foreword by Germano Celant (London: Thames and Hudson, 1990). For an early work of Ponti's in New York, his model room for Macy's 1928 Exposition of Art in Industry, see Stern, Gilmartin and Mellins, *New York 1930*, 337.

29. Olga Gueft, "The Inn of the Sun," *Interiors* 120 (February 1961): 88–89; "Interior Designed by Alexander Girard for The Inn of the Sun," *Architectural Record* 129 (June 1961): 157–61; "'Fonda del Sol,' Ristorante a New York," *Domus* 380 (July 1961): 20–27; White and Willensky, *AIA Guide* (1967), 133–34; Charles W. Morton, "Any Number Can Eat," *Harper's* 219 (January 1967): 105–6; Catherine C. Crane, "Tabletops," *Interiors* 129 (June 1970): 133–34; Krinsky, "Architecture in New York City," in Wallock, ed., *New York: Culture Capital of the World, 1940–1965*, 119.

30. Alexander Girard quoted in "Interior Designed by Alexander Girard for The Inn of the Sun": 157.

31. See Emilio Ambasz, *The Architecture of Luis Barragán*, exhibition catalogue (New York: Museum of Modern Art, 1976).

32. Gueft, "The Inn of the Sun": 88–89.

33. "A Bank that Lures New Customers," *Architectural Forum* 136 (summer 1972): 60–61.

34. For the Rainbow Room, see Stern, Gilmartin and Mellins, *New York 1930*, 284–85, 291.

35. Shrallow, "Five Restaurant Interiors": 177.

36. "Two Notable New Office Buildings for Manhattan, 2: A Tall Tower for Time Inc.": 96. Also see Walter H. Stern, "Construction Lag on 6th Ave. Cited," *New York Times* (January 11, 1959), VIII: 1, 4.

37. "Equitable Life Plans New Midtown Skyscraper," *Real Estate Record and Guide* 182 (August 23, 1958): 3–4; "Designers for a Busy World: Mood for Working," *Newsweek* 53 (May 4, 1959): 97–100; "Equitable's 42-Story Tower Rises in New York," *Architectural Record* 126 (December 1959): 25; "Trial-and-Error Aids Skyscraper," *New York Times* (October 16, 1960), VIII: 1, 18; "New Equitable Building Offers West Side Contrast to Park Avenue's Union Carbide Tower," *Architectural Forum* 115 (October 1961): 7; "Two New Towers in New York City," *Architectural Record* 130 (November 1961): 14; Ada Louise Huxtable, "Our New Buildings: Hits and Misses," *New York Times* (April 29, 1962), VI: 16–17, 105–6; "Home Office Building for Equitable Life," *Architectural Record* 131 (May 1962): 177–84; "Drop from the 19th Floor," *Architectural Forum* 117 (July 1962): 11; "Up Goes Manhattan! Splendor in the Skies," *Life* 53 (November 9, 1962): 74–75; Ennis, "14 Major Postwar Buildings Rise from 46th to 57th Street": 1, 12; White and Willensky, *AIA Guide* (1967), 134; Peter Blake, *Form Follows Fiasco* (Boston: Little, Brown & Co., 1977), figs. 96–97; Krinsky, *Rockefeller Center*, 114, 148; Newhouse, *Wallace K. Harrison, Architect*, 160.

38. Huxtable, "Our New Buildings: Hits and Misses": 105.

39. "New Equitable Building Offers West Side Contrast to Park Avenue's Union Carbide Tower": 7.

40. William Zeckendorf with Edward McCreary, *The Autobiography of William Zeckendorf* (New York: Holt, Rinehart and Winston, 1970), 286–89. Also see Eugene Rachlis and John E. Marquesee, *The Land Lords* (New York: Random House, 1963), 282–86.

41. "Buildings in the News," *Architectural Record* 125 (March 1959): 12; "P/A News Reports," *Progressive Architecture* 40 (March 1959): 160.

42. Percy Uris quoted in "The Big Hole Finds New Team to Fill It," *Business Week* (November 19, 1960): 198–99, 201–2.

43. "Huge Buildings Planned on Former Zeckendorf Sites," *Architectural Forum* 113 (September 1960): 9; "Design Altered for New Skyscraper," *New York Times* (October 23, 1960), VIII: 13; "The Big Hole Finds New Team to Fill It": 198–99, 201–2; "Rockefeller Center Office Building," *Architectural Forum* 113 (December 1960): 41; "New Neighbor for Rockefeller Center," *Progressive Architecture* 41 (December 1960): 59; "Sixth Avenue Skyscraper Will Be Named Sperry Rand Building," *Real Estate Record and Guide* 187 (March 25, 1961): 3; "New Buildings in New York Follow New Codes," *Progressive Architecture* 42 (September 1961): 70; Thomas W. Ennis, "6th Ave. Altered by Building Boom," *New York Times* (September 10, 1961), VIII: 1, 6; "Designs for New Skyscraper Show Zoning Impact," *New York Times* (September 17, 1961), VIII: 1, 11; "New York Nears Completion—Almost," *Architectural Forum* 117 (October 1962): 12–17; Ennis, "14 Major Postwar Buildings Rise from 46th to 57th Street": 1, 12; White and Willensky, *AIA Guide* (1967), 134; Balfour, *Rockefeller Center*, 230–31; Ballard, *Directory of Manhattan Office Buildings*, 144; Krinsky, *Rockefeller Center*, 114; Karp, *The Center*, 121.

44. "Huge Buildings Planned on Former Zeckendorf Sites": 9; "12,000 Sq. Ft. Added to Uris Hotel Site," *Real Estate Record and Guide* 186 (October 1, 1960): 2; "Rockefeller Center Hotel," *Architectural Forum* 113 (December 1960): 41; "Buildings in the News," *Architectural Record* 128 (December 1960): 13; "Hilton Hotel near Rockefeller Center," *Progressive Architecture* 41 (December 1960): 59; "The Solid Chintz Skyscraper," *Architectural Forum* 115 (August 1961): 67; Ennis, "6th Ave. Altered by Building Boom": 1, 6; "Doing Over the Town": 56; "New York Nears Completion—Almost": 16; "Splendor in the Skies," *Life* 53 (November 9, 1962): 74–88; "Nouvelle Hotel Hilton au Centre Rockefeller à New York," *L'Architecture d'Aujourd'hui* 33 (December 1962): 52–53; Aaron Sabghir, "Building and Construction," *Americana Annual (1963)* (New York and Chicago: Encyclopedia Americana Corporation, 1963): 105; Clive Gray, "A New Venture—The Hilton Hotel Collection," *Art in America* 51 (April 1963): 124–25; Russell Lynes, "New York Hotels (with Reservations)," *Art in America* 51 (April 1963): 58–61; Ada Louise Huxtable, "Architecture Stumbles On," *New York Times* (April 14, 1963), II: 23; Ada Louise Huxtable, "The New York Hilton's Two Faces," *New York Times* (June 30, 1963), II: 13, reprinted as "Schizophrenia at the New York Hilton," in Ada Louise Huxtable, *Will They Ever Finish Bruckner Boulevard?* (New York: Macmillan, 1970), 102–5; B. H. Friedman, "Art for the New York Hilton," *Craft Horizons* 23 (July 1963): 8–15; Walter McQuade, "Architecture," *Nation* 197 (July 6, 1963): 20; "The Talk of the Town: Hilton Opening," *New Yorker* 39 (July 6, 1963): 20–21; "Kismet in New York," *Newsweek* 62 (July 8, 1963): 54–55; Olga Gueft, "Architects Versus Interior Designers," editorial, *Interiors* 123 (August 1963): 45; Olga Gueft, "After 2 Years and 75 Millions, the Colossus Opens: The New York Hilton at Rockefeller Center," *Interiors* 123 (August 1963): 68–85; "Appropriate Hotel for New York," *Progressive Architecture* 44 (August 1963): 49; "The New York Hilton," letters to the editor, *Interiors* 123 (September 1963): 8; "The Hilton Controversy," letters to the editor, *Interiors* 123 (October 1963): 8; Olga Gueft, "The Relevance of Clients," *Interiors* 123 (October 1963): 89; Ennis, "14 Major

Postwar Buildings Rise from 46th to 57th Street": 1, 12; "The Hilton Controversy (Continued)," letters to the editor, *Interiors* 123 (November 1963): 8; "'Grand Hotel,' New Version," *Architectural Record* 134 (November 1963): 153–60; Anne E. Ferebee, "Trademark Becomes Landmark," *Industrial Design* 11 (February 1964): 70–71; "William Pahlmann, F.A.I.D.," *Interior Design* 35 (March 1964): 158–63; "William Pahlmann Associates: One Thousand Dollars Per Day at the New York Hilton," *Interiors* 124 (March 1965): 132–38; Wolf Von Eckardt, *A Place to Live: The Crisis of the Cities* (New York: Delacorte Press, 1967), 40; White and Willensky, *AIA Guide* (1967), 134; "New York's Selective Hotel Boom," *Business Week* (February 9, 1976): 29, 32, 34; Balfour, *Rockefeller Center*, 230; Krinsky, *Rockefeller Center*, 114; Morris Lapidus, *An Architecture of Joy* (Miami, Fla.: E. A. Seemann, 1979), 196–98, 200; Karp, *The Center*, 121; James Trager, *West of Fifth: The Rise and Fall and Rise of Manhattan's West Side* (New York: Atheneum, 1987), 111.

45. "Doing Over the Town": 56.

46. For the Waldorf-Astoria, see Stern, Gilmartin and Mellins, *New York 1930*, 222–25.

47. Quoted in "'Grand Hotel,' New Version": 156.

48. Huxtable, "Architecture Stumbles On": 23.

49. Huxtable, "The New York Hilton's Two Faces": 13.

50. McQuade, "Architecture" (July 6, 1963): 20.

51. "Appropriate Hotel for New York": 49.

52. Lynes, "New York Hotels (with Reservations)": 61.

53. Gueft, "After 2 Years and 75 Millions, the Colossus Opens: The New York Hilton at Rockefeller Center": 82.

54. Huxtable, "The New York Hilton's Two Faces": 13.

55. Huxtable, "The New York Hilton's Two Faces": 13.

56. Gueft, "After 2 Years and 75 Millions, the Colossus Opens: The New York Hilton at Rockefeller Center": 71.

57. Lynes, "New York Hotels (with Reservations)": 61.

58. "New Buildings in New York Follow New Codes": 70; "Designs for New Skyscraper Show Zoning Impact": 1, 11; "New York Offices: Midtown," *Architectural Forum* 115 (October 1961): 65; "New York Nears Completion—Almost": 12–17; Ennis, "14 Major Postwar Buildings Rise from 46th to 57th Street": 1, 12; White and Willensky, *AIA Guide* (1967), 134; Ballard, *Directory of Manhattan Office Buildings*, 189; David W. Dunlap, "Commercial Property: The Old J. C. Penney Building," *New York Times* (August 19, 1990), X: 13.

59. Glenn Fowler, "C.B.S. Skyscraper Planned on 6th Ave.," *New York Times* (July 26, 1960): 1, 16; "Huge Buildings Planned on Former Zeckendorf Sites": 9, 11; "Personalities," *Progressive Architecture* 41 (September 1960): 58; "C.B.S. Site Assembled," *New York Times* (July 18, 1961): 45; Ennis, "6th Ave. Altered by Building Boom": 1, 6; "Eero Saarinen Dies at 51, Leaving a Striking Legacy of Finished and Unfinished Structures," *Architectural Forum* 115 (October 1961): 5; "Saarinen's Sophisticated Skyscraper for CBS," *Progressive Architecture* 42 (October 1961): 53–54; Aline B. Saarinen, ed., *Eero Saarinen on His Work* (New Haven, Conn.: Yale University Press, 1962), 16–17, rev. ed. (1968), 16–21; Allan Temko, *Eero Saarinen* (New York: George Braziller, 1962), 26, 118–22, plates 125, 128; "New C.B.S. Tower to Include Plaza," *New York Times* (February 18, 1962): 67; "Saarinen's CBS Skyscraper," *Architectural Forum* 116 (March 1962): 13; Walter McQuade, "Eero Saarinen: A Complete Architect," *Architectural Forum* 116 (April 1962): 102–19; "Saarinen's CBS Design," *Architectural Record* 131 (April 1962): 149–50; "Transparent Fence Is Up at 6th Ave. C.B.S. Building," *New York Times* (July 27, 1962): 21; "Doing Over the Town": 56, 64–65, 69; "New York Nears Completion—Almost": 16–17; Huxtable, "Architecture Stumbles On": 6; "A Black Facade Planned by C.B.S.," *New York Times* (September 1, 1963), VIII: 1, 4; Ennis, "14 Major Postwar Buildings Rise from 46th to 57th Street": 1, 12; "Construction: Sidewalk History," *Newsweek* 62 (October 14, 1963): 98–99; Peter Franklin, "Reinforced Concrete Building for C.B.S. Gets Rave Reviews," *New York Times* (March 15, 1964), VIII: 1, 6; "C.B.S. Undertakes 8 Building Projects," *New York Times* (June 7, 1964), VIII: 1, 10; Eric Larrabee, "Saarinen's Dark Tower: The CBS Building and How It Grew," *Harper's* 229 (December 1964): 55–61; "À New York: Le Nouveau Siège de Columbia Broadcasting System," *La Construction Moderne* 81, no. 1 (1965): 28–31; "Eero Saarinens letztes grosses Bauwerk," *Deutsche Architektur* 14 (April 1965): 248; Peter Blake, "Slaughter on 6th Avenue," *Architectural Forum* 122 (June 1965): 13–19; "Saarinen's Skyscraper," *Architectural Record* 138 (July 1965): cover, 111–18; "Il graticello della CBS a New York di Eero Saarinen," *L'Architettura cronache e storia* 11 (July 1965): 182; Bethami Probst, "CBS: Somber Power on Sixth Avenue," *Progressive Architecture* 46 (July 1965): 187–92; Val Adams, "C.B.S. Josephines Are Joes," *New York Times* (July 28, 1965): 71; "Quotes/Corporate Medicis," *Journal of the American Institute of Architects* 44 (August 1965): 22; David Rockefeller, "Commending CBS," letter to the editor, *Progressive Architecture* 46 (September 1965): 20; "C.B.S. Officials Receive Award for Move to Sixth Av.," *Real Estate Record and Guide* 196 (November 1965): 3; Walter McQuade, "Manhattan's Highest Paid Headwaiter," *Architectural Forum* 123 (September 1965): 76; "C.B.S. 'Eye' Zooms In on New Home," *New York Times* (September 12, 1965), VIII: 1, 6; Rafael E. J. Iglesia, *Eero Saarinen* (Buenos Aires: Instituto de Arte American e Investigaciones Estéticas, 1966), 50–54, plates 44–45; "À New York: Le Nouveau Siège de C.B.S.," *La Construction Moderne* 82, nos. 4–5 (1966): 66–70; Olga Gueft, "Deep in CBS's Granite Grove, a Glittering Haven for Hungry Gourmets," *Interiors* 125 (January 1966): 86–95; Patricia L. Conway, "Design at CBS," *Industrial Design* 13 (February 1966): 48–57; C. H. McBride, "The Ground Floor," *Esquire* 65 (March 1966): 94–95; "For Formal Dining: Black Granite?" *Progressive Architecture* 47 (March 1966): 180–83; Ada Louise Huxtable, "Eero Saarinen's Somber Skyscraper," *New York Times* (March 13, 1966), II: 27–28, reprinted in Huxtable, *Will They Ever Finish Bruckner Boulevard?*, 98–102; "A Tale of Two Towers," *Architectural Forum* 124 (April 1966): 28–37; "Total Design on a Grand Scale," *Life* 60 (April 29, 1966): 50–53; Vladimir Kagan, "Uplifted by Ground Floor," letter to the editor, *Interiors* 125 (May 1966): 8; Anne Landsman, "Let Down by Ground Floor," letter to the editor, *Interiors* 125 (May 1966): 8; "Distinguished Interior Architecture for CBS," *Architectural Record* 139 (June 1966): cover, 129–34; David Jacobs, "Saarinen's CBS Skyscraper," *Holiday* 39 (June 1966): 122, 124–26; "Immeuble de la C.B.S. à New-York," *L'Architecture d'Aujourd'hui* 36 (June 1966): 72–73; "Interior Design of C.B.S. Building, 51 W 52, New York," *Architect and Builder* (South Africa) 16 (July 1966): 12–15; "Do-It-Yourself: Fun with Words and Objects," *House and Garden* 130 (July 1966): 102–3; "First Honor: Eero Saarinen & Associates," *Journal of the American Institute of Architects* 46 (July 1966): 26–29; Virginia Lee Warren, "The Men Whose Offices Are Their Castles," *New York Times* (October 3, 1966): 59; Paul Heyer, *Architects on Architecture* (London: Penguin, 1967), 353; Von Eckardt, *A Place to Live: The Crisis of the Cities*, 210–11;

White and Willensky, *AIA Guide* (1967), 134–35; "A Man's Home Away from Home: It's the Detailing that Counts," *House and Garden* 131 (February 1967): 132–35; Robert A. M. Stern, *New Directions in American Architecture* (New York: George Braziller, 1969), 22–23; Vincent Scully, *American Architecture and Urbanism* (New York: Frederick A. Praeger, 1969), 200; "Putting a New Face on the Office," *Business Week* (September 13, 1969): 152–53, 156, 158; Peter Blake, "Slaughter on Sixth Avenue," *New York* 2 (May 12, 1969): 48–49; Crane, "Tabletops": 134; Rupert Spade, *Eero Saarinen* (New York: Simon & Schuster, 1971), 16, 124, plates 91–96; William H. Jordy, *American Buildings and Their Architects: The Impact of European Modernism in the Mid-Twentieth Century*, vol. 4 (Garden City, N.Y.: Doubleday & Co., 1972), 25–26; Goldberger, *The City Observed*, 174–75; William S. Paley, *As It Happened: A Memoir* (Garden City, N.Y.: Doubleday & Co., 1979), 342–45, unnumbered plates; Manfredo Tafuri and Francesco Dal Co, *Modern Architecture*, trans. Robert Erich Wolf (New York: Harry N. Abrams, 1979), 378; Tauranac, *Essential New York*, 218–19; Paul Goldberger, *The Skyscraper* (New York: Alfred A. Knopf, 1981), 114–16; Ada Louise Huxtable, *The Tall Building Artistically Reconsidered* (New York: Pantheon Books, 1982), 72; "Eero Saarinen," *A + U*, extra edition (April 1984): 22, 32, 176–83; Francesco Dal Co, *Kevin Roche* (New York: Rizzoli International Publications, 1985), 23, 27; Dick Hess and Marion Muller, *Dorfsman & CBS* (New York: American Showcase, 1987), 32–44; Lewis J. Paper, *Empire: William S. Paley and the Making of CBS* (New York: St. Martin's Press, 1987), 247–49, 357–58, unnumbered plates; Krinsky, "Architecture in New York City," in Wallock, ed., *New York: Culture Capital of the World, 1940–1965*, 108–9; Sally Bedell Smith, *In All His Glory: The Life of William S. Paley* (New York: Simon & Schuster, 1990), 442–45.

60. Stern, Gilmartin and Mellins, *New York 1930*, 267–69.

61. William Paley quoted in Larrabee, "Saarinen's Dark Tower: The CBS Building and How It Grew": 56.

62. Huxtable, "Eero Saarinen's Somber Skyscraper": 27.

63. Eero Saarinen quoted in Saarinen, ed., *Eero Saarinen on His Work*, 16.

64. Eero Saarinen quoted in "Saarinen's Skyscraper," *Architectural Record*: 113.

65. "Saarinen's CBS Skyscraper," *Architectural Forum*: 13.

66. John Dinkeloo quoted in "Saarinen's Sophisticated Skyscraper for CBS": 53. Joseph N. Lacy is credited with the same quotation in "Eero Saarinen Dies at 51, Leaving a Striking Legacy of Finished and Unfinished Structures": 5.

67. Larrabee, "Saarinen's Dark Tower: The CBS Building and How It Grew": 58.

68. Aline B. Saarinen quoted in Larrabee, "Saarinen's Dark Tower: The CBS Building and How It Grew": 58.

69. Larrabee, "Saarinen's Dark Tower: The CBS Building and How It Grew": 58.

70. For the American Radiator Building, see Stern, Gilmartin and Mellins, *New York 1930*, 575–77, 581–83. For the Monadnock Building, see Carl W. Condit, *The Chicago School of Architecture: A History of Commercial and Public Building in the Chicago Area, 1875–1925* (Chicago and London: University of Chicago Press, 1964), 65–69, figs. 28–30.

71. Larrabee, "Saarinen's Dark Tower: The CBS Building and How It Grew": 55.

72. Eero Saarinen quoted in Larrabee, "Saarinen's Dark Tower: The CBS Building and How It Grew": 55.

73. Huxtable, "Eero Saarinen's Somber Skyscraper": 27–28.

74. Probst, "CBS: Somber Power on Sixth Avenue": 189–90.

75. Blake, "Slaughter on 6th Avenue," *Architectural Forum*: 18.

76. Jacobs, "Saarinen's CBS Skyscraper": 125–26.

77. Lou Dorfsman quoted in Hess and Muller, *Dorfsman & CBS*, 35.

78. William S. Paley quoted in Larrabee, "Saarinen's Dark Tower: The CBS Building and How It Grew": 61.

79. Frank Stanton quoted in Larrabee, "Saarinen's Dark Tower: The CBS Building and How It Grew": 61.

80. "Distinguished Interior Architecture for CBS": 129.

81. Florence Knoll Bassett quoted in "Distinguished Interior Architecture for CBS": 130.

82. Conway, "Design at CBS": 54.

83. Jacobs, "Saarinen's CBS Skyscraper": 122.

84. Huxtable, "Eero Saarinen's Somber Skyscraper": 28.

85. Conway, "Design at CBS": 49.

86. Robert Frost, "Sixth Avenue: Midtown Bank Mecca Is Emerging," *New York Times* (March 16, 1965): 53, 58.

87. McQuade, "Manhattan's Highest Paid Headwaiter": 76; Gueft, "Deep in CBS's Granite Grove, a Glittering Haven for Hungry Gourmets": 86–95; McBride, "The Ground Floor": 94–95; "For Formal Dining: Black Granite?": 180–83; Kagan, "Uplifted by Ground Floor": 8; Landsman, "Let Down by Ground Floor": 8; Crane, "Tabletops": 134; Paper, *Empire: William S. Paley and the Making of CBS*, 248–49. For other projects by Warren Platner, see *Ten by Warren Platner* (New York: McGraw-Hill, 1975).

88. Gueft, "Deep in CBS's Granite Grove, a Glittering Haven for Hungry Gourmets": 86.

89. Gueft, "Deep in CBS's Granite Grove, a Glittering Haven for Hungry Gourmets": 94.

90. "For Formal Dining: Black Granite?": 183.

91. Thomas W. Ennis, "Boom on 6th Ave. Gets New Impetus," *New York Times* (November 6, 1966), VIII: 1; Balfour, *Rockefeller Center*, 231–32; Krinsky, *Rockefeller Center*, 116–18; Karp, *The Center*, 34–35; Newhouse, *Wallace K. Harrison, Architect*, 160.

92. Ada Louise Huxtable, "In This Corner, New York City," *New York Times* (May 5, 1968), II: 32; Peter Blake, "Somebody Up There Likes This City," *New York* 2 (February 2, 1969): 48–49; Jonathan Barnett, *Urban Design as Public Policy* (New York: Architectural Record Books, 1974), 177; Krinsky, *Rockefeller Center*, 121–24.

93. Huxtable, "In This Corner, New York City": 32.

94. Glenn Fowler, "Rockefeller Center Growing Down," *New York Times* (March 21, 1971), VIII: 1, 6; Murray Schumach, "Touches of Sidewalk Splendor Planned for Midtown," *New York Times* (August 6, 1971): 1, 28; "Plazas, Concourses, and Mid-Block Malls Highlight Rockefeller Center Expansion," *Architectural Record* 150 (September 1971): 37; "New Rockefeller Center Complex Will Improve Environment," *Real Estate Record and Guide* 208 (September 18, 1971): 2–3.

95. Glenn Fowler, "Rockefeller Center to Add Skyscraper," *New York Times* (August 30, 1967): 1, 66; Maurice Carroll, "Expansion of Rockefeller Center Unappetizing to Restaurateurs," *New York Times* (September 12, 1967): 49; "Rockefeller Center to Add 18th Office Building," *Progressive Architecture* 48 (October 1967): 57; "Buildings in the News," *Architectural Record* 142 (November 1967): 41; "News of the Realty Trade: Tower Rented Year Before Completion," *New York Times* (September 7, 1969), VIII: 10; "Rockefeller Center Expands Again," *Engineering News-Record* 185 (December 24, 1970): 22–24; John Anderson, "The Many Facets of Exxon's New Domain," *Interiors* 132 (January 1973): 74–85; Balfour, *Rockefeller Center*, 231–32; Ballard, *Directory of Manhattan Office Buildings*, 188; Krinsky, *Rockefeller Center*, 116–17, 119, 125–26, 161–63; White and Willensky, *AIA Guide* (1978), 170; Goldberger, *The City Observed*, 171–72; Karp, *The Center*, 34–35, 76–77.

96. For the Plymouth Hotel, see "New Hotel Project," *New York Times* (August 19, 1928), X: 1; W. Parker Chase, *New York: The Wonder City* (New York: Wonder City Publishing Co., 1932; New York: New York Bound, 1983), 148.

97. Glenn Fowler, "McGraw-Hill Plans a 48-Story Tower," *New York Times* (November 28, 1967): 58; "Buildings in the News," *Architectural Record* 142 (December 1967): 40; "Rockefeller Center and McGraw-Hill Announce Plans for 48-Story Building," *Real Estate Record and Guide* 200 (December 2, 1967): 2–3; "No. 20 for Rockefeller Center," *Progressive Architecture* 49 (January 1968): 32; "Building Din Makers Are Given Matinees Off," *New York Times* (February 5, 1969): 36; "Tall Office Buildings: The Process of Development," *Architectural Record* 145 (April 1969): 181–91; "Rockefeller Center Expands Again": 22–24; "Grace Amid the Concrete," editorial, *New York Times* (August 7, 1971): 22; "Retailing: McGraw Hill Move to Sixth Avenue Includes Plans for Mammoth Bookstore," *Publishers' Weekly* 200 (September 13, 1971): 52–54; James D. Morgan, "A Tale of Two Towers," *Architecture Plus* 1 (October 1973): 42–53, 82–83; Don Campbell, letter to the editor, *Architecture Plus* 2 (January–February 1974): 8; John Anderson, "Georgian Medley atop a Gotham Skyscraper," *Interiors* 133 (March 1974): 76–85; "McGraw-Hill Headquarters," *Interior Design* 45 (July 1974): 100–111; Frederick Fried and Edmund V. Gillon, Jr., *New York Civic Sculpture* (New York: Dover, 1976), 60–61; Balfour, *Rockefeller Center*, 231–32; Ballard, *Directory of Manhattan Office Buildings*, 187; Krinsky, *Rockefeller Center*, 117–19, 122, 124–27; White and Willensky, *AIA Guide* (1978), 170; Goldberger, *The City Observed*, 171–72; Karp, *The Center*, 34–35, 76–77; Donald Martin Reynolds, *The Architecture of New York* (New York: Macmillan, 1984), 254, 261, 265; Newhouse, *Wallace K. Harrison, Architect*, 160.

98. Glenn Fowler, "Bus Terminal Planning Annex, with McGraw-Hill Office Space," *New York Times* (January 22, 1965): 16.

99. Shelton Fisher quoted in "Rockefeller Center and McGraw-Hill Announce Plans for 48-Story Building": 2.

100. For Raymond Hood's McGraw-Hill Building, see Stern, Gilmartin and Mellins, *New York 1930*, 574–75, 579–80, 584–85.

101. McCandlish Phillips, "New Effects Theater Designed to Dazzle Senses," *New York Times* (June 26, 1973): 53.

102. Morgan, "A Tale of Two Towers": 42–53, 82–83.

103. Morgan, "A Tale of Two Towers": 49–50.

104. Morgan, "A Tale of Two Towers": 82–83.

105. Glenn Fowler, "Celanese to Build Skyscraper in Rockefeller Center Complex," *New York Times* (September 16, 1970): 47; "Rockefeller Center Expands Again": 22–24; "News of the Realty Trade: Rockefeller Center Shift," *New York Times* (March 5, 1972), VIII: 9; Balfour, *Rockefeller Center*, 231–32; Ballard, *Directory of Manhattan Office Buildings*, 187; Krinsky, *Rockefeller Center*, 117, 119, 122–26; White and Willensky, *AIA Guide* (1978), 170; Goldberger, *The City Observed*, 171–72; Karp, *The Center*, 77; Alpern and Durst, *Holdouts!*, 41–42.

106. William A. Reuben quoted in Alpern and Durst, *Holdouts!*, 41–42.

107. Charles Dun Leavey quoted in Alpern and Durst, *Holdouts!*, 42.

108. Gerald Allen, "High Rise Office Buildings—The Public Spaces They Make. Rockefeller Center: Second Campaign," *Architectural Record* 153 (March 1974): 134–42. Also see Glenn Fowler, "Rockefeller Center Reaching Its Final Form," *New York Times* (October 4, 1970), VIII: 1, 9; Tafuri and Dal Co, *Modern Architecture*, 340–41.

109. Balfour, *Rockefeller Center*, 232.

110. See Newhouse, *Wallace K. Harrison, Architect*, 281.

111. Herbert Koshetz, "Burlington Moving Northward to a Skyscraper at 54th Street," *New York Times* (February 9, 1967): 49, 53; Ballard, *Directory of Manhattan Office Buildings*, 189. For Joseph Urban's Ziegfeld Theater, see Stern, Gilmartin and Mellins, *New York 1930*, 235–37, 239.

112. "Ziegfeld Museum Planned," *New York Times* (April 9, 1969): 50; A. H. Weiler, "It's All Automated at New Ziegfeld Theater," *New York Times* (December 17, 1969): 60.

113. Philip H. Dougherty, "Advertising: Textile Exhibition Hall Opens," *New York Times* (September 10, 1970): 69; White and Willensky, *AIA Guide* (1978), 171.

114. "News of the Realty Trade: Capitol Leases," *New York Times* (June 28, 1970), VIII: 10; Ballard, *Directory of Manhattan Office Buildings*, 145.

115. Ballard, *Directory of Manhattan Office Buildings*, 186.

116. Ballard, *Directory of Manhattan Office Buildings*, 186.

117. "Tishman Realty, Gramco, Arlen Join to Develop Huge Midtown Office Building Project," *Real Estate Record and Guide* 206 (July 4, 1970): 2; Eleanore Carruth, "New York Hangs Out the For-Rent Sign," *Fortune* 83 (February 1971): 86–90, 114–15, 118; Franklin Whitehouse, "Tishman to Build Around Stand-Patter," *New York Times* (February 14, 1971), VIII: 1, 6; Clark Whelton, "The Excavation of Tombstone Alley," *Village Voice* 19 (June 13, 1974): 1, 24–26; Eleanore Carruth, "The Skyscraping Losses in Manhattan Office Buildings," *Fortune* 91 (February 1975): 78–83, 162, 164, 166; "New York City's Real Estate Mismatch," *Business Week* (October 13, 1975): 108, 110, 113; Ballard, *Directory of Manhattan Office Buildings*, 7; Alpern and Durst, *Holdouts!*, 87–89.

MADISON AVENUE

1. For Starrett & Van Vleck's Canadian Pacific Building and A. D. Pickering's Fifth Church of Christ Scientist, see Stern, Gilmartin and Mellins, *New York 1930*, 150, 532. For LaFarge & Morris's Brooks Brothers, see Stern, Gilmartin and Massengale, *New York 1900*, 196. For George B. Post's Roosevelt Hotel, see Stern, Gilmartin and Mellins, *New York 1930*, 203.

2. "Manhattan Avenues Ranked by Corporation Preferences," *Real Estate Record and Guide* 187 (April 8, 1961): 4.

3. Ada Louise Huxtable, "Elegance Clinging to Avenue, but It Too May Pass," *New York Times* (November 8, 1970), VIII: 1, 7. Also see Christopher Gray, "The Rise and Fall of Midtown's Most Civilized Avenue," *Avenue* 10 (November 1985): 93–103.

4. For Cross & Cross's Knapp Building, see Stern, Gilmartin and Mellins, *New York 1930*, 526–27.

5. "William Zeckendorf's Office," *Fortune* 46 (June 1952): 112–16. Also see Lewis Mumford, "The Sky Line: Big Buildings and Tremendous Trifles," *New Yorker* 27 (December 22, 1951): 60–65; "Lobby of Light," *Architectural Forum* 96 (January 1952): 118–20, 184, 187; William Zeckendorf with Edward McCreary, *The Autobiography of William Zeckendorf* (New York: Holt, Rinehart and Winston, 1970), 98–99.

6. Mumford, "The Sky Line: Big Buildings and Tremendous Trifles": 63.
7. "Lobby of Light": 118.
8. "Office Building Features Strip Windows," *Architectural Forum* 90 (April 1949): 66, 70; "Work Speeded on Three Skyscrapers," *New York Times* (September 18, 1949), VIII: 1; "New York Skyscrapers Are Changing Manhattan's Profile," *Architectural Forum* 91 (December 1949): 10; "Faceless Warrens," *Time* 55 (January 23, 1950): 13; Lewis Mumford, "The Sky Line: The Mud Wasps of Manhattan," *New Yorker* 26 (March 25, 1950): 64, 66, 69–72; "Esquire Bars 'New Look,'" *New York Times* (June 7, 1950): 31; "New Thinking on the Effect of Office Windows on Design," *Architectural Forum* 99 (September 1953): 118–23; Jane Jacobs, "New York's Office Boom," *Architectural Forum* 106 (March 1957): 104–13; Richard Roth, "High-Rise Down to Earth," *Progressive Architecture* 38 (June 1957): 196–200; Robert F. R. Ballard, *Directory of Manhattan Office Buildings* (New York: McGraw-Hill, 1978), 156; John Tauranac, *Essential New York* (New York: Holt, Rinehart and Winston, 1979), 192–93; Steven Ruttenbaum, *Mansions in the Clouds: The Skyscraper Palazzi of Emery Roth* (New York: Balsam Press, 1986), 200–202.
9. "Office Building Features Strip Windows": 66, 70.
10. Mumford, "The Sky Line: The Mud Wasps of Manhattan": 64, 69.
11. "New York Skyscrapers Are Changing Manhattan's Profile": 10; "Improved Designs in Offices Noted," *New York Times* (May 7, 1950), VIII: 9; "New Thinking on the Effect of Office Windows on Design": 118–23; Jacobs, "New York's Office Boom": 106; Roth, "High-Rise Down to Earth": 198–99; Ballard, *Directory of Manhattan Office Buildings*, 158.
12. For J. D. Leland & Company's American Art Association and Gallery, see Stern, Gilmartin and Mellins, *New York 1930*, 360, 362.
13. Lee E. Cooper, "$20,000,000 Offices Will Replace Ritz-Carlton Hotel on Madison Ave.," *New York Times* (January 5, 1950): 1, 3; "Adieu to the Ritz," editorial, *New York Times* (January 7, 1950): 16; "Uris Bros. File Ritz Site Plans," *New York Times* (February 18, 1950): 23; Mumford, "The Sky Line: The Mud Wasps of Manhattan": 72; "Revised Plan for Offices on the Ritz Site," *New York Times* (June 8, 1952), VIII: 1; "Midtown Skyscraper 'Topped Out,'" *New York Times* (February 8, 1953), VIII: 1; "New Office Building Nears Completion," *New York Times* (April 26, 1953), VIII: 8; "Additions to City Skyline—Products of Latest Real Estate Boom," *New York Times* (August 23, 1954): 19; Jacobs, "New York's Office Boom": 107; Roth, "High-Rise Down to Earth": 198; Ballard, *Directory of Manhattan Office Buildings*, 29. For Warren & Wetmore's Ritz-Carlton, see Stern, Gilmartin and Massengale, *New York 1900*, 262–63, 267.
14. "Offices Planned for Madison Ave.," *New York Times* (September 12, 1954), VIII: 1; "Modern Air-Conditioned Office Building to Occupy Madison Ave. Corner Plot," *Real Estate Record and Guide* 174 (September 18, 1954): 3; Jacobs, "New York's Office Boom": 109; Roth, "High-Rise Down to Earth": 198–99; Ballard, *Directory of Manhattan Office Buildings*, 30.
15. "Blitz Starts Work on Three Major East Side Projects," *Real Estate Record and Guide* 177 (May 5, 1956): 3; Roth, "High-Rise Down to Earth": 198; Ballard, *Directory of Manhattan Office Buildings*, 180.
16. Jacobs, "New York's Office Boom": 109; Ballard, *Directory of Manhattan Office Buildings*, 157.
17. Roth, "High–Rise Down to Earth": 198; "New Office Building to Be Linked to Hotel," *New York Times* (July 7, 1957), VIII: 1, 2; "New York-Cleveland Axis," *Architectural Forum* 107 (August 1957): 38; White and Willensky, *AIA Guide* (1967), 158; Ballard, *Directory of Manhattan Office Buildings*, 161.
18. "Office Building to Rise at 600 Madison Avenue," *New York Times* (October 17, 1961): 64; Ballard, *Directory of Manhattan Office Buildings*, 159.
19. Glenn Fowler, "New Weston Hotel to Be Razed to Make Way for Office Building," *New York Times* (August 25, 1964): 35; "437 Madison Av. Opens Fully Rented," *Real Estate Record and Guide* 201 (January 6, 1968): 4; Ballard, *Directory of Manhattan Office Buildings*, 30.
20. For the Hotel New Weston, see W. Parker Chase, *New York: The Wonder City* (New York: Wonder City Publishing Co., 1932; New York: New York Bound, 1983), 132.
21. "News of Realty: Offices Planned," *New York Times* (October 18, 1968): 80; "Oil Co. in New Building," *New York Times* (July 5, 1970), VIII: 4; "Pan Ocean Oil Leases Four Floors in 645 Madison Avenue," *Real Estate Record and Guide* 206 (July 25, 1970): 3; Ballard, *Directory of Manhattan Office Buildings*, 160.
22. "Offices Planned for Madison Ave." (September 12, 1954): 1; "17-Story Offices for Madison Ave.," *New York Times* (October 3, 1954), VIII: 1; "New 17-Story Fully Air-Conditioned Office Building to Be Erected on Madison Avenue, 58th–59th Streets," *Real Estate Record and Guide* 174 (October 23, 1954): 3; "Landmarks Fall on 5th Ave. Block," *New York Times* (April 17, 1955), VIII: 1; "Steel Framing Begun on 625 Madison Ave. Building," *Real Estate Record and Guide* 176 (July 2, 1955): 3; "Standard Brands Building . . . New York," *Empire State Architect* 16 (November–December 1956): 19; Jacobs, "New York's Office Boom": 110; Ballard, *Directory of Manhattan Office Buildings*, 160.
23. "Tall Offices Mark Northward Movement of Business in Madison Avenue District," *New York Times* (September 17, 1950), VIII: 1; Ballard, *Directory of Manhattan Office Buildings*, 161.
24. "Offices Planned on Madison Ave.," *New York Times* (August 15, 1950): 43; "Bomb Refuge Here for 4,000 Planned," *New York Times* (August 20, 1950): 23; "New Building for Madison Avenue," *New York Times* (August 20, 1950), VIII: 1; "Offices Planned for Madison Ave." (September 12, 1954): 1; Jacobs, "New York's Office Boom": 107–8; Ballard, *Directory of Manhattan Office Buildings*, 25–26.
25. "The Many Different Lives of an Office Building," *Life* 42 (February 11, 1957): 89–96.
26. Lee E. Cooper, "Wreckers Take Over Site for Tall Offices at Madison Avenue and Fifty-first Street," *New York Times* (September 7, 1950): 53; "Building Plans Filed," *New York Times* (September 9, 1950): 24; "Simon Bros. Postpone Offices on Madison Ave.," *New York Times* (July 3, 1951): 34; Lee E. Cooper, "East Side to Get Office Buildings of Modern Design," *New York Times* (August 3, 1952), VIII: 1; "Madison Ave. Sets Pace for Offices," *New York Times* (March 15, 1953), VIII: 1; "Cardinal Gets Union Card," *New York Times* (March 31, 1953): 33; "Claim Speed Record for 477 Madison Ave.," *New York Times* (July 5, 1953), VIII: 2; "Offices Dedicated," *New York Times* (April 27, 1954): 50; Ballard, *Directory of Manhattan Office Buildings*, 155.
27. "Mass. Mutual Life Leases 3 Floors in New Building at 540 Madison," *Real Estate Record and Guide* 205 (March 7, 1970): 5; Ballard, *Directory of Manhattan Office Buildings*, 157.
28. "New Skyscraper for Madison Ave.," *New York Times* (June 17, 1960): 50; "Coates Brothers Buy Skyscraper," *New York Times* (June 14, 1963): 47; Ballard, *Directory of Manhattan Office Buildings*, 158.
29. Martin Arnold, "Permanent Mall Planned on Madison by Lindsay," *New York Times* (May 1, 1971): 1, 30; " . . . Depolluting Madison Avenue," editorial, *New York Times* (May 5, 1971): 46; "New York Plans Permanent Madison Avenue Mall," *Progressive Architecture* 52 (June 1971): 42, 44; "The Talk of the Town: Traffic," *New Yorker* 47 (September 18, 1971): 29–30; Michael Stern, "Pedestrian Mall Is Proposed for Madison Ave.," *New York Times* (December 7, 1971): 49, 93; "A Plan and a Policy," editorial, *New York Times* (December 14, 1971): 44; Glenn Fowler, "Showdown Looms on Madison Mall," *New York Times* (February 10, 1972): 44; David Gurin, "New York Regained," *Village Voice* 17 (March 2, 1972): 3, 24; Peter Kihss, "Madison Ave. Mall Test Due to Begin Next March," *New York Times* (September 17, 1972): 1, 58; Barbara Rose, "Why No One Is Making New York Understandable," *New York* 5 (September 25, 1972): 84–85; "The Madison Ave. Mall," editorial, *New York Times* (February 26, 1973): 30; C. Gerald Fraser, "Judge Rules Against Madison Ave. Mall," *New York Times* (March 6, 1973): 1, 35; William H. Whyte and Thomas F. Galvin, "Madison Avenue Mall: Worth Fighting For," letters to the editor, *New York Times* (March 17, 1973): 30; Marguerite Villecco, "City Streets for People," *Architecture Plus* 1 (April 1973): 22–43; Joseph P. Fried, "Appellate Court Bars a Mall on Madison," *New York Times* (April 16, 1973): 1, 11; Frank J. Prial, "Lindsay Offers a New Plan to Get the Madison Mall," *New York Times* (June 7, 1973): 1, 54; "The Talk of the Town: A Street without Cars," *New Yorker* 49 (July 2, 1973): 23–24; Frank Lynn, "Lindsay and Beame Clash over Madison Ave. Mall," *New York Times* (July 11, 1973): 1, 27; Frank Lynn, "Madison Ave. Mall Is Defeated by Estimate Unit," *New York Times* (July 12, 1973): 1, 54; "Planning for the City," editorial, *New York Times* (July 14, 1973): 24; Jaquelin Robertson, "Rediscovering the Street," *Architectural Forum* 139 (November 1973): 24–31; Jonathan Barnett, *Urban Design as Public Policy* (New York: Architectural Record Books, 1974), 134–39; Jonathan Barnett, "Helping Downtown Compete with the Suburbs," *Architectural Record* 155 (January 1974): 127–32; Rebecca Read Shanor, *The City that Never Was* (New York: Viking, 1988), 31–34.
30. "Model of Proposed Midtown 'Pedestrian Mall' Is on Display," *Real Estate Record and Guide* 190 (September 22, 1962): 3. For another proposal of 1961, sponsored by the New York Chapter of the American Institute of Architects and the firm of Pomerance & Breines, which advocated the creation of a new north-south pedestrian street leading from Forty-fifth Street to Rockefeller Plaza and continuing on to Fifty-ninth Street, see Bernard Stengren, "Architect Urges Building a Mall from 45th to 59th West of 5th," *New York Times* (November 15, 1961): 45; "Architects Propose Plan to Aerate New York," *Progressive Architecture* 42 (December 1961): 56.
31. Joseph Lelyveld, "Millions Join Earth Day Observances Across the Nation; Mood Is Joyful as City Gives Support," *New York Times* (April 23, 1970): 1, 30; David Bird, "In the Aftermath of Earth Day: City Gains New Leverage," *New York Times* (April 24, 1970): 28; "Fifth Avenue Turns into a Mall," *Business Week* (July 18, 1970): 22.
32. "Madison Ave. Auto Ban Will Mark Earth Week," *New York Times* (April 9, 1971): 14.
33. "New York Plans Permanent Madison Avenue Mall": 44.
34. John V. Lindsay quoted in Arnold, "Permanent Mall Planned on Madison by Lindsay": 1, also quoted in "New York Plans Permanent Madison Avenue Mall": 44.
35. Van Ginkel Associates, *Movement in Midtown* (Montreal: Van Ginkel Associates, 1970). Also see Van Ginkel Associates, "Movement in Midtown," *Architects' Yearbook* 14 (1974): 54–67.
36. Van Ginkel Associates, "Movement in Midtown": 54.
37. " . . . Depolluting Madison Avenue": 46.
38. "A Plan and a Policy": 44.
39. Fowler, "Showdown Looms on Madison Mall": 44.
40. Quoted in Fowler, "Showdown Looms on Madison Mall": 44.
41. "The Talk of the Town: A Street without Cars": 24.
42. John V. Lindsay quoted in "The Talk of the Town: A Street without Cars": 24.
43. "Planning for the City": 24.

THIRD AVENUE

1. "The New Third Avenue," special advertising section, *New York Times* (December 9, 1962), XI: 5, 7. Also see "Upper East 50's: Area of Diversity," *New York Times* (September 23, 1962), VIII: 1, 15.
2. "The Talk of the Town: Present and Past," *New Yorker* 28 (October 25, 1952): 23–24; "Reported 'El' Demolition Spurs East Side Activity—Bound to Enhance Realty Values, According to Realty Firm Head," *Real Estate Record and Guide* 172 (August 15, 1953): 3; "At the End of the Line: A Pot of Gold," *Business Week* (August 20, 1953): 30–32; Richard T. Baker, "City Hall 'El' Spur at End of the Line," *New York Times* (January 1, 1954): 25; "Nearing the End of the Line," *Newsweek* 43 (January 18, 1954): 31; "End of the 'El,'" editorial, *New York Times* (June 4, 1954): 22.
3. John Pile, "The El Comes Down," *Industrial Design* 2 (April 1955): 29–31; Ralph Katz, "Last Train Rumbles on Third Ave. 'El,'" *New York Times* (May 13, 1955): 1, 16; Harrison Salisbury, "Cars Are Packed for Last 'El' Trip," *New York Times* (May 13, 1955): 16; "3d Ave. 'El' Ends Days in 11 Blazes of Glory," *New York Times* (May 13, 1955): 16; "Farewell, 'El,' Farewell," *New York Times* (May 14, 1955): 18; Meyer Berger, "About New York: 'El' Relics Vanish as Bids Await Opening—New Phone Book Is Bigger than Ever," *New York Times* (May 16, 1955): 25; "The Talk of the Town: Notes and Comment," *New Yorker* 31 (May 21, 1955): 27; "Farewell to the El," *Newsweek* 45 (May 23, 1955): 75; "Industrial Drama: Ring Out the Old, Ring in the New," *New York Times* (January 3, 1956): 53; "On Third Avenue: A Toast . . . to the New," *Newsweek* 49 (January 7, 1957): 56–58; "The Talk of the Town: L," *New Yorker* 49 (May 12, 1973): 33; Stan Fischler, *Uptown, Downtown: A Trip Through Time on New York's Subways* (New York: Hawthorn Books, 1976), 259–60; Norval White, *New York: A Physical History* (New York: Atheneum, 1987), 221.
4. Salisbury, "Cars Are Packed for Last 'El' Trip": 16.
5. "On Third Avenue: A Toast . . . to the New": 56.
6. "The Talk of the Town: Notes and Comment": 27.
7. Charles G. Bennett, "3d Ave. Must Pay for Light and Air," *New York Times* (June 2, 1955): 31.
8. Charles Grutzner, "New Name Urged for Third Avenue," *New York Times* (February 7, 1956): 33, 38.
9. Stephen G. Thompson, "3d Ave. to Get a $20,000,000 Office Building," *New York Herald Tribune* (July 2, 1952): 19; "Lescaze Designs Manhattan Skyscraper," *Architectural Record* 112 (August 1952): 22; "Midtown Move in New York," *Architectural Forum* 101 (September 1954): 48–49; "First Lease Signed for Floor in New Grand Central Build-

ing," *Real Estate Record and Guide* 174 (December 4, 1954): 3; "$9,250,000 Long-Term Mortgage Authorized in Grand Central Building Now Under Construction," *Real Estate Record and Guide* 175 (February 19, 1955): 3; "Current Office Projects Designed for the New Era of US Business Expansion," *Architectural Record* 118 (December 1955): 10–11; "News Bulletins," *Progressive Architecture* 36 (December 1955): 70; "Art for Architecture," *Architectural Record* 119 (February 1956): 18; Dore Ashton, "About Art and Artists," *New York Times* (February 16, 1956): 38; Ennis, "Rezoning Planned for Third Avenue": 1; "New Buildings," *Interiors* 115 (June 1956): 10; "Color and Art Help an Office Building," *Architectural Forum* 105 (October 1956): 154–55; Mr. Harper, "Better Building," *Harper's* 213 (November 1956): 82–83; "711 Third Avenue Building," *Architectural Record* 121 (March 1957): 246; Henry Hope Reed, *The Golden City* (New York: Doubleday, 1959), 29; Ada Louise Huxtable, *Four Walking Tours of Modern Architecture in New York City* (New York: Museum of Modern Art and Municipal Art Society of New York, 1961), 51; "Doing Over the Town," *Time* 80 (September 28, 1962): 56–69; White and Willensky, *AIA Guide* (1967), 121; Robert F. R. Ballard, *Directory of Manhattan Office Buildings* (New York: McGraw-Hill, 1978), 45; Paul Goldberger, *The City Observed: New York* (New York: Random House, 1979), 129; Christian Hubert, "The Late Work: 1939–1969," in Christian Hubert and Lindsay Stamm Shapiro, *William Lescaze* (New York: Institute for Architecture and Urban Studies; New York: Rizzoli International Publications, 1982), 109, 112–13; Lorraine Welling Lanmon, *William Lescaze, Architect* (Philadelphia: Art Alliance Press; London: Associated University Presses, 1987), 128; Margot Gayle and Michele Cohen, *The Art Commission and the Municipal Art Society Guide to Manhattan's Outdoor Sculpture* (New York: Prentice Hall Press, 1988), 134.

10. For the Philadelphia Saving Fund Society Building, see Robert A. M. Stern, *George Howe: Toward a Modern American Architecture* (New Haven, Conn.: Yale University Press, 1975), 108–30, figs. 83–97. For the proposed CBS headquarters, see Stern, Gilmartin and Mellins, *New York 1930*, 267–69.

11. José de Rivera quoted in Reed, *The Golden City*, 29.

12. Hans Hofmann quoted in Ashton, "About Art and Artists": 38.

13. Ennis, "Rezoning Planned for Third Avenue": 16; Ada Louise Huxtable, "Maximum Efficiency/Minimum Cost," *Progressive Architecture* 40 (September 1959): 148–54; Huxtable, *Four Walking Tours of Modern Architecture in New York City*, 51; Barbara Goldsmith, "The Agile Eye of I. M. Pei," *Town and Country* 119 (August 1965): 62, 101–3, 105; Ballard, *Directory of Manhattan Office Buildings*, 180.

14. Ballard, *Directory of Manhattan Office Buildings*, 43.

15. Huxtable, *Four Walking Tours of Modern Architecture in New York City*, 49–50; Ballard, *Directory of Manhattan Office Buildings*, 47.

16. Ballard, *Directory of Manhattan Office Buildings*, 46.

17. "Manhattan Avenues Ranked by Corporation Preferences," *Real Estate Record and Guide* 187 (April 8, 1961): 4. Also see Edmond J. Bartnett, "3d Ave. Sets Pace in New Buildings," *New York Times* (October 21, 1962), VIII: 1, 6.

18. Thomas W. Ennis, "New Offices Open along 3d Avenue," *New York Times* (July 30, 1961), VIII: 1; "Four New Office Towers Open on Third Avenue: Total of 1,810,000 Square Feet of Space Fully Rented upon Completion," *Real Estate Record and Guide* 188 (October 7, 1961): 2–3; "Brick Facade Makes Comeback in New Third Ave. Skyscraper," *New York Times* (March 4, 1962), VIII: 1, 6; Ballard, *Directory of Manhattan Office Buildings*, 44.

19. "Brick Facade Makes Comeback in New Third Ave. Skyscraper": 1.

20. Ennis, "New Offices Open along 3d Avenue": 1; "Four New Office Towers Open on Third Avenue: Total of 1,810,000 Square Feet of Space Fully Rented upon Completion": 2; Ballard, *Directory of Manhattan Office Buildings*, 45.

21. "New 22-Story Building to Rise at Third Ave. and 46th Street," *Real Estate Record and Guide* 185 (February 13, 1960): 3–4; "Manhattan Office Tower," *Architectural Forum* 112 (March 1960): 53; Ennis, "New Offices Open along 3d Avenue": 1; "Four New Office Towers Open on Third Avenue: Total of 1,810,000 Square Feet of Space Fully Rented upon Completion": 3; Ballard, *Directory of Manhattan Office Buildings*, 46.

22. Ennis, "New Offices Open along 3d Avenue": 1; "Four New Office Towers Open on Third Avenue: Total of 1,810,000 Square Feet of Space Fully Rented upon Completion": 2; Ballard, *Directory of Manhattan Office Buildings*, 169.

23. "Four New Office Towers Open on Third Avenue: Total of 1,810,000 Square Feet of Space Fully Rented upon Completion": 3.

24. Thomas W. Ennis, "Airy Skyscraper to Rise on 3d Ave.," *New York Times* (April 15, 1962), VIII: 1, 12; "Sculpture in Manhattan," *Architectural Forum* 120 (February 1964): 16; "18-Foot Abstract Sculpture," *New York Herald Tribune* (March 15, 1964), III: 10; "Owner Controls Office Lobby Art," *New York Herald Tribune* (April 12, 1964), III: 11; Ballard, *Directory of Manhattan Office Buildings*, 48; Hubert, "The Late Work: 1939–1969," in Hubert and Shapiro, *William Lescaze*, 109, 116–17; Lanmon, *William Lescaze, Architect*, 130–31; Gayle and Cohen, *The Art Commission and the Municipal Art Society Guide to Manhattan's Outdoor Sculpture*, 133.

25. For Hidden House, see Stern, Gilmartin and Mellins, *New York 1930*, 472, 474–75.

26. Stern, Gilmartin and Mellins, *New York 1930*, 428–29.

27. William Kaufman quoted in "Owner Controls Office Lobby Art": 11.

28. Ballard, *Directory of Manhattan Office Buildings*, 169.

29. Ballard, *Directory of Manhattan Office Buildings*, 172; White and Willensky, *AIA Guide* (1978), 153.

30. White and Willensky, *AIA Guide* (1978), 153.

31. "Manhattan Post Office," *Architectural Forum* 120 (February 1964): 27; Ballard, *Directory of Manhattan Office Buildings*, 170; White and Willensky, *AIA Guide* (1978), 162.

32. Ballard, *Directory of Manhattan Office Buildings*, 48.

33. Ballard, *Directory of Manhattan Office Buildings*, 170.

34. "News of Realty: A Publisher Moves," *New York Times* (September 14, 1967): 78; Ballard, *Directory of Manhattan Office Buildings*, 49; Andrew Alpern and Seymour Durst, *Holdouts!* (New York: McGraw-Hill, 1984), 94–95.

35. "Front Porch on Third Avenue," *Progressive Architecture* 53 (June 1972): 107; Carter B. Horsley, "Caution, Undulating Sidewalks," *New York Times* (July 16, 1972), VIII: 1, 8; Melvyn Kaufman, "On Sidewalks," letter to the editor, *New York Times* (July 26, 1972), VIII: 10; "New York Architect-Developer Adding to the Fun in Fun City," *Architectural Record* 154 (September 1973): 35; "Fun on Third Avenue," *Architecture Plus* 1 (September 1973): 72; James Murphy, "A Celebration of Systems," *Progressive Architecture* 54 (November 1973): 104–6; Ballard, *Directory of Manhattan Office Buildings*, 47; White and Willensky, *AIA Guide* (1978), 161; Goldberger, *The City Observed*, 129; Alpern and Durst, *Holdouts!*, 68–69.

36. Pamela Waters quoted in Horsley, "Caution, Undulating Sidewalks": 1.

37. "New 39-Story Tower Under Way at 964 Third Avenue," *Real Estate Record and Guide* 202 (August 10, 1968): 2; Catherine C. Crane, "919 Third—What Does It Mean?" *Interiors* 130 (September 1970): 154–55; Ada Louise Huxtable, "Open-Space Designs Breathing New Life into Smothered Blocks," *New York Times* (July 6, 1972): 39; Ballard, *Directory of Manhattan Office Buildings*, 172.

38. "The Talk of the Town: P. J.'s," *New Yorker* 41 (March 13, 1965): 35–36; Thomas W. Ennis, "New Skyscraper Will Preserve P. J. Clarke's on Third Avenue," *New York Times* (September 9, 1967): 48; Franklin Whitehouse, "News of Realty: Garage Acquired," *New York Times* (February 21, 1968): 77; "Fire Report Scores Skyscraper Construction: Two More Fires Occur," *Architectural Record* 149 (January 1971): 37; "New Theater at 919 3rd Ave.," *Real Estate Record and Guide* 210 (September 16, 1972): 3; Ballard, *Directory of Manhattan Office Buildings*, 171; White and Willensky, *AIA Guide* (1978), 162; Goldberger, *The City Observed*, 153; Alpern and Durst, *Holdouts!*, 136–37; James MacQuire, "Letter from P. J. Clarke's," *NY: The City Journal* 1 (spring 1991): 75–82.

39. Goldberger, *The City Observed*, 153.

40. Glenn Fowler, "Vacancies Rise, but Third Ave. Keeps Growing," *New York Times* (October 3, 1971), VIII: 1, 9.

41. Ballard, *Directory of Manhattan Office Buildings*, 171.

42. Ballard, *Directory of Manhattan Office Buildings*, 42.

43. Ballard, *Directory of Manhattan Office Buildings*, 49.

44. "Commissions," *Interiors* 129 (February 1970): 14; "Tishman Breaks Ground for New 38-Story Office Tower on Third Ave.," *Real Estate Record and Guide* 205 (June 27, 1970): 3; Ballard, *Directory of Manhattan Office Buildings*, 43.

45. Goldberger, *The City Observed*, 129.

46. Eugene Archer, "Film House atop Baronet Slated," *New York Times* (July 26, 1961): 36; "3d Ave. Theater to Double Deck," *New York Times* (July 30, 1961), VIII: 1–2; "Piggyback Theaters in Manhattan," *Architectural Forum* 115 (September 1961): 55; White and Willensky, *AIA Guide* (1967), 163.

47. "Piggy-back Movie House on 3rd Avenue," *Progressive Architecture* 43 (March 1962): 84; "Building Housing Two Theaters Nears Completion on the East Side," *New York Times* (June 17, 1962), VIII: 6; "Twin Cinema: Flexible Showcases for Films," *Architectural Forum* 117 (September 1962): 120–23; Olga Gueft, "Two-in-One Art Movie," *Interiors* 122 (November 1962): 124–27; White and Willensky, *AIA Guide* (1967), 163; Christopher Gray, "Schlock of Ages," *Avenue* 17 (December 1992): 31–32, 34, 36, 38.

48. White and Willensky, *AIA Guide* (1967), 163.

49. "La Bonne Soupe East," *Interior Design* 47 (April 1976): 142–43.

50. "Alexander's Unveils Model of Its Windowless Store," *New York Times* (November 12, 1964): 51, 59; McCandlish Phillips, "Cash-and-Carry Palace Rising on East Side," *New York Times* (June 17, 1965): 35; "Bargain House Invades Silk-Stocking District," *Business Week* (August 7, 1965): 112–14; Angela Taylor, "Here's a Look at the New Alexander's," *New York Times* (August 27, 1965): 33; White and Willensky, *AIA Guide* (1967), 162.

51. George Farkas quoted in "Bargain House Invades Silk-Stocking District": 114.

52. "Bargain House Invades Silk-Stocking District": 112.

53. Taylor, "Here's a Look at the New Alexander's": 33.

54. Thomas W. Ennis, "East Side Siring a Shopping Mecca," *New York Times* (November 1, 1964), VIII: 1, 10; Arnold H. Lubasch, "Footbridge Rises above E. 60th St.," *New York Times* (June 18, 1967), VIII: 1, 6; Isadore Barmash, "Economic Tempo Quickening at Lexington and 59th," *New York Times* (July 25, 1967): 43, 54; "Where 'Beautiful People' Find Fashion," *Business Week* (September 2, 1972): 44–45; "The Talk of the Town: Consumption," *New Yorker* 48 (September 16, 1972): 23; "An Expanded Men's Store Opened by Bloomingdale's," *New York Times* (September 28, 1972): 79; Rita Reif, "Will the Crowds Still Come to Look at the Model Rooms?" *New York Times* (February 2, 1973): 36; James Brady, "Meet Me under the Clocks," *New York* 6 (June 4, 1973): 62; Marilyn Bender, "Bloomingdale's and Its Customers—Dancing Chic to Chic," *New York Times* (September 8, 1974), III: 1–2; Jill Robinson, "When I Say I'm Going to the City, I Mean I'm Going to Bloomingdale's," *Vogue* 166 (August 1976): 141, 178–80, 182; Liz Smith, "I Could Trust My Own Taste—But Because of Bloomingdale's—I Don't Have To," *Vogue* 166 (August 1976): 140, 182.

55. Bender, "Bloomingdale's and Its Customers—Dancing Chic to Chic": 2.

56. Stern, Gilmartin and Mellins, *New York 1930*, 317.

57. "Where 'Beautiful People' Find Fashion": 44–45.

58. Bender, "Bloomingdale's and Its Customers—Dancing Chic to Chic": 1.

59. Robinson, "When I Say I'm Going to the City, I Mean I'm Going to Bloomingdale's": 178.

60. Reif, "Will the Crowds Still Come to Look at the Model Rooms?": 36. Also see "Symphony in B," *Interior Design* 36 (November 1965): 154–57; "Cocoon Complex," *Interior Design* 41 (January 1970): 106–7; "New Design: Put-On or Pertinent?" *House Beautiful* 112 (February 1970): 76–79, 110; "Bloomingdale's Designers Create for Themselves and 'the Creators' in Vibrating Model Rooms," *Interiors* 130 (November 1970): 16.

61. Goldberger, *The City Observed*, 154.

TIMES SQUARE

1. Claim of the Broadway Association quoted in Jill Stone, *Times Square: A Pictorial History* (New York: Collier Books, 1982), xi. Also see Meyer Berger, "Times Square Diary," *New York Times* (September 13, 1944), VI: 16–17, 45–46.

2. Ely Jacques Kahn, "Theaters and the Interior Designer," *Interior Design and Decoration* 14 (June 1940): 44–45, 62.

3. "A Preview of the Pix," *New York Times* (December 17, 1939), IX: 6; Kahn, "Theaters and the Interior Designer": 44–45, 62; "Pix Theater: Functionalism Expressed through Lighting," *Interiors* 100 (December 1940): 24–26; "Pix Theater—By Ely Jacques Kahn, Architect, of New York," *Pencil Points* 22 (March 1941): 163–69, 175–76. For Ely Jacques Kahn and Winold Reiss's Longchamps work, see Stern, Gilmartin and Mellins, *New York 1930*, 283–85, 287.

4. Lee E. Cooper, "Times Square Will Get a New Restaurant; Large Space Leased on Fitzgerald Corner," *New York Times* (January 4, 1940): 39; "Toffenetti's Is Opened," *New York Times* (August 7, 1940): 21; Mary Henderson, *The City and the Theater* (Clifton, N.J.: James T. White & Co., 1973), 239; David W. Dunlap, *On Broadway: A Journey Uptown Over Time* (New York: Rizzoli International Publications, 1990), 167–68.

5. Fiorello La Guardia and Toots Shor quoted in Stone, *Times Square: A Pictorial History*, 120.

6. "Blackout Wiring for Big Signs Ordered, with Discontinuance Only Alternative," *New York Times* (March 2, 1942): 3; "Aurora of Lights Dims Out in City for the Duration," *New York Times* (April 29, 1942): 1, 10; "As Manhattan Appeared During Dimout—And Before," *New York Times* (April 29, 1942): 10; "Great Signs Dark as Gay White Way Obeys Army Edict," *New York Times* (April 30, 1942): 1, 10; "Blackout Tonight to Affect 1,000,000," *New York Times* (April 30, 1942): 10; Meyer Berger, "All Midtown Blacked Out; Throngs Watch in Times Sq.; Army Will Enforce Dim-Out," *New York Times* (May 1, 1942): 1, 10; "Crowd in Blackout Angers La Guardia," *New York Times* (May 1, 1942): 1, 10; "War Comes to Broadway," editorial, *New York Times* (May 1, 1942): 18.

7. "Victory Arch for Times Square Proposed, with Permanent Memorial After the War," *New York Times* (May 11, 1943): 23; "Design of 'Victory Arch' for Times Square Shows Two Palm Leaves Spanning Streets," *New York Times* (June 24, 1943): 23; Elvira Black and Joseph M. Robinson, "No Victory Arches Wanted," letters to the editor, *New York Times* (June 28, 1943): 20; Edward Alden Jewell, "Memorials: Post-War Symbols Raise an Issue," *New York Times* (July 4, 1943), II: 6; Percival Goodman, "Architects Not Perturbed," letter to the editor, *New York Times* (July 8, 1943): 18; Ralph Pearson, A. L. Baron, L. G. Collins, Gertrude Zurrer and Robert Epstein, "On Victory Memorials," letters to the editor, *New York Times* (July 11, 1943), II: 6; Albert S. Bard, "Move to Protect City's Art," letter to the editor, *New York Times* (July 12, 1943): 14; John Shayn, "Opinion Under Postage," letter to the editor, *New York Times* (July 25, 1943), II: 6; Rebecca Read Shanor, *The City that Never Was* (New York: Viking, 1988), 217–19.

8. Robinson, "No Victory Arches Wanted": 20.

9. Jewell, "Memorials: Post-War Symbols Raise an Issue": 6.

10. Alexander Feinberg, "All City 'Lets Go,'" *New York Times* (August 15, 1945): 1, 5, quoted in Stone, *Times Square: A Pictorial History*, 125, 127. Also see "V-J Revelry Erupts Again with Times Sq. Its Focus," *New York Times* (August 16, 1945): 1, 6.

11. Meyer Berger, "Noisiest Throngs Since '41 Welcome New Year in City," *New York Times* (January 1, 1946): 1, 3.

12. For further discussion of the history of Times Square and its decline in the postwar period, see Margaret Knapp, "Introductory Essay," in William R. Taylor, ed., *Inventing Times Square* (New York: Russell Sage Foundation, 1991), 120–32; Laurence Senelick, "Private Parts in Public Places," in Taylor, ed., *Inventing Times Square*, 329–53.

13. For Eidlitz & MacKenzie's Times Tower, see Stern, Gilmartin and Massengale, *New York 1900*, 167.

14. For Thomas Lamb's Loew's State and Rapp & Rapp's Paramount, see Stern, Gilmartin and Mellins, *New York 1930*, 248–49, 256, 513, 532–34.

15. For CBS's conversion of theaters to broadcasting studios in the 1930s, see Stern, Gilmartin and Mellins, *New York 1930*, 265–67.

16. Lee E. Cooper, "$6,000,000 Theater, Office Unit Planned for Fringe of Times Sq.," *New York Times* (January 16, 1948): 1, 37; "Square Block Fronting on Broadway to Be Improved with New Building as Result of $15,000,000 Leasing Deal," *Real Estate Record and Guide* 161 (January 24, 1948): 3; "Building Previews," *Architectural Forum* 88 (March 1948): 60.

17. For Goodwin and Stone's Museum of Modern Art, see Stern, Gilmartin and Mellins, *New York 1930*, 141–45.

18. "New Home Office for Mutual Life," *New York Times* (May 18, 1948): 38; "To Build for Mutual Life," *New York Times* (July 30, 1948): 31; "Mutual Life Files Plans for Broadway Offices," *New York Times* (September 18, 1948): 25; "Insurance Tower Praised by Mayor," *New York Times* (October 5, 1948): 23; "Mutual Life Insurance Building," *Architectural Record* 104 (December 1948): 166; "90 Sidewalk 'Supers' Double-Up at Opening," *New York Times* (February 22, 1949): 13; "Hotel Man Hails Broadway Offices," *New York Times* (July 24, 1949), VIII: 1; "Heated Sidewalks Planned by Mutual Life Around Its New Offices in Broadway Block," *New York Times* (October 16, 1949), VIII: 1; "New York Skyscrapers Are Changing Manhattan's Profile," *Architectural Forum* 91 (December 1949): 10; "Stone Work Finished on Skyscraper," *New York Times* (December 25, 1949), VIII: 1; "Uses Fluorescent Lighting," *New York Times* (January 1, 1950), VIII: 2; "Available Space in Mutual Life's New Building Seventy-five Per Cent Leased," *Real Estate Record and Guide* 165 (March 25, 1950): 3; "50-Year Forecasts Put into Building," *New York Times* (April 13, 1950): 13; "The Record Reports," *Architectural Record* 108 (July 1950): 11; "Great White Way to Get Star Tower," *New York Times* (July 26, 1950): 27; "New Weather Star Joins Lights of City," *New York Times* (August 31, 1950): 19; Lewis Mumford, "The Sky Line: More Pelion, More Ossa," *New Yorker* 26 (February 3, 1951): 76, 79–82.

19. Mumford, "The Sky Line: More Pelion, More Ossa": 79–80.

20. "The Record Reports," *Architectural Record* 106 (September 1949): 162; "New York Skyscrapers Are Changing Manhattan's Profile": 10; "Failure of Builders to Provide Off-Street Parking Facilities in New Commercial Building Called False Economy," *Real Estate Record and Guide* 165 (June 3, 1950): 3; Mumford, "The Sky Line: More Pelion, More Ossa": 76, 79, 82; Lewis Mumford, "The Sky Line: Artful Blight," *New Yorker* 27 (May 5, 1951): 84–90; William Zeckendorf with Edward McCreary, *The Autobiography of William Zeckendorf* (New York: Holt, Rinehart and Winston, 1970), 83–88; Robert F. R. Ballard, *Directory of Manhattan Office Buildings* (New York: McGraw-Hill, 1978), 190; Carol Herselle Krinsky, "Architecture in New York City," in Leonard Wallock, ed., *New York: Culture Capital of the World, 1940–1965* (New York: Rizzoli International Publications, 1988), 98; Dunlap, *On Broadway*, 157–58; Christopher Gray, "Neighborhood: Nifties from the Fifties," *Avenue* 14 (January 1990): 117–23.

21. Mumford, "The Sky Line: More Pelion, More Ossa": 82. For Raymond Hood's McGraw-Hill Building, see Stern, Gilmartin and Mellins, *New York 1930*, 574–75, 579–80, 584–85.

22. For Corbett's scheme, see Stern, Gilmartin and Mellins, *New York 1930*, 525–26.

23. "Seeks Fashion Center," *New York Times* (June 28, 1943): 23; "Style Experts Aid Fashion Center," *New York Times* (August 23, 1943): 18; Grover A. Whalen, "'We've Got Style All the While,'" letter to the editor, *New York Times* (September 4, 1943): 12; Grover A. Whalen, "New York—Fashion Capital," *New York Times* (September 12, 1943), VI: 29; "City Must 'Fight' as Fashion Leader," *New York Times* (November 13, 1943): 21, 24; *The Mayor's Committee Report on a World Fashion Center* (New York, 1944); "Report Ready Soon on Fashion Center," *New York Times* (January 12, 1944): 31, 36; "$88,000,000 Style Center and War Memorial Asked," *New York Times* (January 24, 1944): 1, 10; "'Fashion Center,'" editorial, *New York Times* (January 25, 1944): 18; "Whalen Plan Commended," *New York Times* (January 26, 1944): 24; "New York Plans Fashion Center," *Architectural Record* 95 (February 1944): 44; Robert C. Weinberg, "Fashion Center Location Questioned," *Citizens' Housing Council Housing News* 2 (February 1944): 3, 6; "A World Fashion Center," *Interiors* 103 (February 1944): 10; "New York's Proposed Fashion Center—The Report of the Mayor's Committee," *Pencil Points* 25 (February 1944): 14–15.

24. "25-Story Office Building to Replace Old Broadway Landmarks," *Real Estate Record and Guide* 170 (November 29, 1952): 4.

25. "New York Hotel," *Architectural Forum* 117 (November 1962): 55; "The Talk of the Town: New Rooms," *New Yorker* 39 (October 5, 1963): 39–40; Dunlap, *On Broadway*, 187.

26. "Lapidus to Design Two New York Hotels," *Interiors* 120 (August 1960): 22; "Americana Architect Skyline Changer," press release issued by Americana West of New York, August 10, 1960, in *New York Herald Tribune* clipping file, Queens Borough Public Library; "Tallest Hotel to Rise at 7th Ave. and 52d," *New York Times* (August 10, 1960): 1, 10; "The West Side's Rebirth," editorial, *New York Times* (August 11, 1960): 26; "World's Tallest Hotel to Rise at 7th Ave. and 52nd St.," *Real Estate Record and Guide* 186 (August 13, 1960): 2; "Huge Buildings Planned on Former Zeckendorf Sites," *Architectural Forum* 113 (September 1960): 9; "World's Tallest Hotel for N. Y.," *Progressive Architecture* 41 (September 1960): 52; "Name Hotel Engineers," *New York Times* (September 13, 1960): 60; "Baron Sees Upsurge in West Side," *Real Estate Record and Guide* 186 (October 15, 1960): 2; "Good Grief! They're at It Again," *Progressive Architecture* 41 (December 1960): 61; Edmond J. Bartnett, "12 New Hotels Rise in Midtown," *New York Times* (January 14, 1962), VIII: 1, 4; "Tall Hotel Posed Knotty Problems," *New York Times* (April 29, 1962), VIII: 17; "New York Hotels: Boom or Bust?" *Architectural Forum* 116 (May 1962): 11; "Tree Lifted 50 Floors to Top-Out New Hotel," *New York Times* (May 9, 1962): 19; Morris Lapidus, "Reaching New Heights," letter to the editor, *Progressive Architecture* 43 (September 1962): 180; "Fifty-Story Americana Hotel Ready for Debut in Two Weeks," *New York Times* (September 9, 1962), VIII: 1, 14; "Now Bring on the Customers," *Business Week* (September 22, 1962): 42–43; "The Talk of the Town: Marble Halls," *New Yorker* 38 (September 22, 1962): 32–33; Robert Berkvist, "A Taller West Side Story," *New York Times* (September 23, 1962), X: 1, 4; McCandlish Phillips, "Americana Hotel Will Open Today," *New York Times* (September 24, 1962): 31, 57; Joseph Wershba, "Americana's Designer," *New York Post* (September 25, 1962): 37; "Lapidus' Latest," *Architectural Forum* 117 (October 1962): 13, 15; "New York Nears Completion—Almost," *Architectural Forum* 117 (October 1962): 16; "The Supercolossals," *Newsweek* 60 (October 1, 1962): 67; "Americana of New York: World's Tallest Hotel Opens," special advertising section, *New York Times* (October 7, 1962), XI: 1–20; "Two New Hotels," *Architectural Record* 132 (November 1962): 15; Albert E. Kudrle, "Hotels and Motels," *Americana Annual (1963)* (New York and Chicago: Encyclopedia Americana Corporation, 1963): 308–9; "The Americana of New York," *Interior Design* 34 (January 1963): 78–85, 124; Russell Lynes, "New York Hotels (with Reservations)," *Art in America* 51 (April 1963): 58–61; "The Talk of the Town: Higher and Lower," *New Yorker* 39 (December 7, 1963): 46–47; White and Willensky, *AIA Guide* (1967), 114; White and Willensky, *AIA Guide* (1978), 143; Morris Lapidus, *An Architecture of Joy* (Miami, Fla.: E. A. Seemann, 1979), 198–200.

27. Morris Lapidus quoted in Wershba, "Americana's Designer": 37.

28. Morris Lapidus quoted in Wershba, "Americana's Designer": 37.

29. "The Americana of New York," *Interior Design*: 78.

30. "The Talk of the Town: Marble Halls": 32–33.

31. Lynes, "New York Hotels (with Reservations)": 60.

32. Morris Lapidus quoted in "Lapidus' Latest": 13.

33. "400-Room Motel Is Planned for West Side," *New York Times* (May 21, 1958): 1, 40; Mark Freeman, "Motel Plans Protested," letter to the editor, *New York Times* (May 26, 1958): 28; Bartnett, "12 New Hotels Rise in Midtown": 1, 4.

34. Freeman, "Motel Plans Protested": 28.

35. "Steel Finished for Manhattan's First Motel," *Real Estate Record and Guide* 183 (May 23, 1959): 3; "Motor Inn, First of Its Kind in Manhattan, Opens Tuesday," *New York Times* (December 6, 1959), VIII: 1, 6; "The Talk of the Town: Independence," *New Yorker* 35 (January 2, 1960): 17–18; Olga Gueft, "Manhattan's First Motel," *Interiors* 119 (May 1960): 112–13; Bartnett, "12 New Hotels Rise in Midtown": 1, 4.

36. "Steel Finished for Manhattan's First Motel": 3.

37. "Motor Inn, First of Its Kind in Manhattan, Opens Tuesday": 1.

38. "The Talk of the Town: Independence": 18.

39. Harold Steinberg quoted in "Motor Inn, First of Its Kind in Manhattan, Opens Tuesday": 1.

40. "Manhattan Dock Area Motor Hotel," *Architectural Forum* 112 (June 1960): 11; Bartnett, "12 New Hotels Rise in Midtown": 4; "The Talk of the Town: Big Motel," *New Yorker* 38 (July 21, 1962): 18–19; "Manhattan Motor Court," *Architectural Forum* 117 (September 1962): 17; "Another New York Hostelry," *Progressive Architecture* 43 (September 1962): 68; "Three New Hotels and a Motor Inn," *Architectural Record* 132 (October 1962): 13; Ralph William Ernst, "Hotels," *Britannica Book of the Year* (Chicago: Encyclopaedia Britannica, 1964): 414.

41. "The Talk of the Town: Big Motel": 18.

42. "Another New York Hostelry": 68.

43. Bartnett, "12 New Hotels Rise in Midtown": 4; "Riviera Congress Motor Inn Opens on West 41st Street," *Real Estate Record and Guide* 189 (February 3, 1962): 4.

44. "Riviera Congress Motor Inn Opens on West 41st Street": 4.

45. Bartnett, "12 New Hotels Rise in Midtown": 4; "The Talk of the Town: New Rooms": 39–40.

46. Bartnett, "12 New Hotels Rise in Midtown": 4.

47. Bartnett, "12 New Hotels Rise in Midtown": 4.

48. "$10,000,000 Motor Hotel-Apartment House to Rise on Eighth Avenue," *Real Estate Record and Guide* 188 (July 15, 1961): 3; "20-Story Apartment House Now Planned for Stillman's Gym Site," *Real Estate Record and Guide* 188 (November 18, 1961): 4.

49. Gay Talese, "Motel Row on West Side Is Atlantic City-on-Hudson," *New York Times* (August 26, 1963): 29.

50. "The Talk of the Town: Tiger!" *New Yorker* 39 (February 23, 1963): 23–24; Brendan Gill, "Department of Amplification," letter to the editor, *New Yorker* 39 (March 9, 1963): 136, 138; "There's a Small Hotel," *Time* 81 (March 22, 1963): 55; St. Clair McKelway, "Princeton Pond," *New Yorker* 41 (January 1, 1966): 48, 50–51.

51. Stern, Gilmartin and Massengale, *New York 1900*, 264, 267, 275, 278, 382, 385.

52. Stern, Gilmartin and Massengale, *New York 1900*, 27, 42, 231–32, 237, 267.

53. White and Willensky, *AIA Guide* (1967), 110.

54. Stern, Gilmartin and Massengale, *New York 1900*, 101, 237–38, 240, 290.

55. Stern, Gilmartin and Massengale, *New York 1900*, 37, 231, 238–40.

56. For both buildings, see Stern, Gilmartin and Mellins, *New York 1930*, 188–94.
57. "Competitive Design for the N.Y. Academy of Medicine," *American Architect and Building News* 26 (August 31, 1889): plate 714.
58. Quoted in "The Talk of the Town: Tiger!": 24.
59. Quoted in "There's a Small Hotel": 55.
60. "There's a Small Hotel": 55.
61. "Of Local Origin," *New York Times* (July 31, 1952): 14; Bosley Crowther, "New Movie Projection Shown Here; Giant Wide Angle Screen Utilized," *New York Times* (October 1, 1952): 1, 40; Bosley Crowther, "Looking at Cinerama," *New York Times* (October 5, 1952), II: 1; Waldemar Kaempffert, "Science in Review," *New York Times* (October 5, 1952), IV: 9; "Cinerama," *Architectural Forum* 97 (November 1952): 128–29; Henderson, *The City and the Theater*, 217; Dunlap, *On Broadway*, 188.
62. "Cinerama": 128–29.
63. Press release quoted in "Facelifting for the Astor," *Interiors* 119 (January 1960): 14. Also see "Theater Will Change," *New York Times* (August 11, 1959): 21; Richard Nason, "Astor Film House Being Renovated," *New York Times* (September 9, 1959): 50; Howard Thompson, "Work of Buffie Johnson," *New York Times* (November 21, 1959): 26; Anita Ventura, "Buffie Johnson," *Arts* 34 (March 1960): 65; Henderson, *The City and the Theater*, 207; Dunlap, *On Broadway*, 170–71.
64. Milton Z. Esterow, "New Garb for Old Globe," *New York Times* (February 23, 1958), II: 3; Stuart Preston, "Collector's Treasures—Other Art Events," *New York Times* (April 27, 1958), II: 17; Meyer Berger, "About New York: Bit of 18th Century Transplanted to Rialto in Decor of New Lunt-Fontanne Theater," *New York Times* (April 28, 1958): 16; Brooks Atkinson, "The Theater: An Unforgettable 'Visit,'" *New York Times* (May 6, 1958): 40; Louis Calta, "Broadway Agog as Theater Opens," *New York Times* (May 6, 1958): 40; Marya Mannes, "Theater: The View from Row P," *Reporter* 18 (June 12, 1958): 27–28; "Lunt-Fontanne Theater," *Interior Design* 29 (July 1958): 86–89, 113–14; Henderson, *The City and the Theater*, 251; Dunlap, *On Broadway*, 171. For Carrère & Hastings's Globe Theater, see Stern, Gilmartin and Massengale, *New York 1900*, 219. For a more typical cosmetic renovation, Frederick Fox's redecoration of the St. James Theater, see "Theaters," *Interior Design* 30 (April 1959): 166–67.
65. Robert W. Dowling quoted in Mannes, "Theater: The View from Row P": 27.
66. Mannes, "Theater: The View from Row P": 27.
67. "New 22-Story Office Building to Rise on Site Occupied by Empire Theater," *Real Estate Record and Guide* 171 (May 9, 1953): 3; Ballard, *Directory of Manhattan Office Buildings*, 191; Dunlap, *On Broadway*, 158.
68. Dunlap, *On Broadway*, 188. For the Paramount Theater, see Stern, Gilmartin and Mellins, *New York 1930*, 248–49, 256.
69. "Office Boom Is Moving to Broadway," *Real Estate Record and Guide* 199 (February 25, 1967): 2; "Broad Plazas Planned for 40-Story Office Building on 'Old Met' Site," *Real Estate Record and Guide* 199 (May 13, 1967): 3; Ballard, *Directory of Manhattan Office Buildings*, 191; Dunlap, *On Broadway*, 157.
70. "Office Building to Replace Astor," *Real Estate Record and Guide* 197 (February 5, 1966): 4; "Kahn & Jacobs Will Design New Times Square Office Building," *Real Estate Record and Guide* 197 (May 14, 1966): 3; Harold L. Dunn, "Building on Astor Site," letter to the editor, *New York Times* (July 16, 1966): 24; "Office Boom Is Moving to Broadway": 2; Milton Esterow, "City Proposes More Theaters to Revitalize Midtown District," *New York Times* (October 1, 1967): 1, 78; Ada Louise Huxtable, "Faith, Hope and Muscle," *New York Times* (October 2, 1967): 37; "New Life for Broadway?" editorial, *New York Times* (October 2, 1967): 46; Lewis Funke, "New Theaters, New Hopes," *New York Times* (October 15, 1967), II: 1, 5, 11; "Planning Body Acts to Spur Theater Construction," *New York Times* (November 2, 1967): 61; Joseph P. Fried, "New Footlights May Brighten Rialto," *New York Times* (November 12, 1967), VIII: 1; "The Changing Face of Times Square," *Progressive Architecture* 48 (December 1967): 31–32; Lewis Funke, "Test for New Theaters," *New York Times* (December 3, 1967), II: 1, 34; " . . . and Housing Theaters," editorial, *New York Times* (December 7, 1967): 46; John Sibley, "Board of Estimate Approves Measure to Encourage Theater Construction," *New York Times* (December 8, 1967): 56; Thomas W. Ennis, "Theaters to Rise on Site of Astor," *New York Times* (March 10, 1968): 56; "Lehman Firm Joins Astor Project," *New York Times* (March 22, 1968): 44; Ada Louise Huxtable, "Will Slab City Take Over Times Square?" *New York Times* (March 25, 1968): 40; Robert H. Spohn, "Times Square Piazza," letter to the editor, *New York Times* (April 2, 1968): 46; Charles G. Bennett, "Shuberts Oppose 2 New Theaters," *New York Times* (April 11, 1968): 50; "Permits Approved for 2 Theaters," *New York Times* (April 18, 1968): 47; "Buildings in the News," *Architectural Record* 143 (May 1968): 43; "One Astor Plaza," advertisement, *New York Times* (October 11, 1968): 78; "Mayor Lindsay Breaks Ground for One Astor Plaza," *Real Estate Record and Guide* 202 (October 26, 1968): 2–3; Lewis Funke, "News of the Rialto: Opinion," *New York Times* (October 12, 1969), II: 1, 8; Frank Trotta, "Theater at the Office," *Theater Design and Technology* 21 (May 1970): 16–17; David A. Andelman, "Web of Steel Holds Fate of the Stage," *New York Times* (June 21, 1970), VIII: 1, 7; David A. Andelman, "Glass Crashing from Building Forces Closing of 44th Street," *New York Times* (November 29, 1970): 82; "Zoning Rebuilds the Theaters," *Progressive Architecture* 51 (December 1970): 76–78, 114; "What Made Glass Fall in Times Sq.? Inquirers Puzzled," *New York Times* (December 2, 1970): 59; Glenn Fowler, "Broadway Buildings Fill Slowly in Rent Lag," *New York Times* (December 20, 1970), VIII: 1, 3; Richard Weinstein, "How New York's Zoning Was Changed to Induce the Construction of Legitimate Theaters," in Walter McQuade, ed., *Cities Fit to Live In* (New York: Macmillan, 1971), 85–90; Alden Whitman, "Curtain Goes Up on Minskoff's Times Square Building," *New York Times* (June 6, 1971), VIII: 1, 6; Louis Calta, "4 Office Theaters Are Taking Shape," *New York Times* (August 3, 1971): 22; Laurie Johnston, "One Astor Plaza 87 Per Cent Rented," *New York Times* (November 28, 1971): 72; Louis Calta, "Debut of Reade, Cinema, Delayed," *New York Times* (December 1, 1971): 59; "Young Architects in Firms," *Architectural Record* 152 (December 1972): 124; James A. Murphy, "The Architect as Lighting Designer: Merging the Disciplines," *Progressive Architecture* 54 (September 1973): 104–7; "Five Restaurant Interiors," *Interior Design* 44 (October 1973): 178–79; "The Minskoff Theater—One Astor Plaza," *Theater Design and Technology* 34 (October 1973): 6–11; Jonathan Barnett, *Urban Design as Public Policy* (New York: Architectural Record Books, 1974), 16–22; C. Ray Smith, *Supermannerism: New Attitudes in Post-Modern Architecture* (New York: E. P. Dutton, 1977), 104–5; Ballard, *Directory of Manhattan Office Buildings*, 194; White and Willensky, *AIA Guide* (1978), 140; Goldberger, *The City Observed*, 145; Dunlap, *On Broadway*, 168, 170.
71. Smith, *Supermannerism*, 104.
72. Thomas Connolly quoted in Andelman, "Web of Steel Holds Fate of the Stage": 7.
73. Richard Weinstein quoted in Robert J. Schroeder, "Broadway's Theaters: 'Too Valuable to Keep,'" *New York* 2 (April 21, 1969): 47–48.
74. Weinstein, "How New York's Zoning Was Changed to Induce the Construction of Legitimate Theaters," in McQuade, ed., *Cities Fit to Live In*, 85.
75. "Multi-Use Theater Building Awaits New York Code Changes," *Architectural Forum* 98 (April 1953): 137.
76. Weinstein, "How New York's Zoning Was Changed to Induce the Construction of Legitimate Theaters," in McQuade, ed., *Cities Fit to Live In*, 86.
77. Barnett, *Urban Design as Public Policy*, 21.
78. Donald Elliott quoted in "The Changing Face of Times Square": 31.
79. Ada Louise Huxtable, "American Place Theater Finds a Cozy Home Under New City Code," *New York Times* (December 21, 1971): 39, 51. Also see Trotta, "Theater at the Office": 16–17; Calta, "4 Office Theaters Are Taking Shape": 22; Barbara Leslie Cortesi, "The American Place Theater: A Biography of Broadway's Newest House," *Theater Design and Technology* 27 (December 1971): 4–10, 38; Joan Lang, "The Play's the Thing," *Interiors* 135 (October 1975): 82–83.
80. Franklin Whitehouse, "Broadway to Get a Drama Theater," *New York Times* (September 22, 1967): 56; Esterow, "City Proposes More Theaters to Revitalize Midtown District": 1, 78; Huxtable, "Faith, Hope and Muscle": 37; "Uris to Build at 1633 Broadway," *Real Estate Record and Guide* 200 (October 7, 1967): 2; "Planning Body Acts to Spur Theater Construction": 61; Fried, "New Footlights May Brighten Rialto": 1; Sibley, "Board of Estimate Approves Measure to Encourage Theater Construction": 56; Bennett, "Shuberts Oppose 2 New Theaters": 50; "Permits Approved for 2 Theaters": 47; "Capitol Theater Bows Out; 1633 Broadway Takes Spotlight," *Real Estate Record and Guide* 202 (October 5, 1968): 4–5; Thomas W. Ennis, "News of Realty: Annex Is Planned," *New York Times* (January 31, 1969): 64; Ralph Alswang, "Capitol Building," *Theater Design and Technology* 21 (May 1970): 18; Fowler, "Broadway Buildings Fill Slowly in Rent Lag": 1, 3; Ballard, *Directory of Manhattan Office Buildings*, 194; Dunlap, *On Broadway*, 184, 186.
81. Richard Pilbrow, "The New Uris Theater on Broadway," *Marquee* 5, no. 4 (1973): 19–21. Also see Alswang, "Capitol Building": 18; Calta, "4 Office Theaters Are Taking Shape": 22; Louis Calta, "A Hall of Fame for the Theater to Honor Outstanding Figures," *New York Times* (March 7, 1972): 45; Mel Gussow, "Hall to Stage Musical, 'Galactica,' His First," *New York Times* (September 26, 1972): 42; Deirdre Carmody, "For a New Theater, a Nostalgic Gala," *New York Times* (October 26, 1972): 38; McCandlish Phillips, "Broadway Adds a New Face—The Uris," *New York Times* (November 20, 1972): 45.
82. Tennessee Williams quoted in Martin Bloom, "Toward an Architecture of the Theater as a Human Art," *Journal of the American Institute of Architects* 65 (June 1976): 51–54. Also see Calta, "4 Office Theaters Are Taking Shape": 22; Louis Calta, "Circle in the Square Honors Levine in New Name," *New York Times* (October 6, 1972): 36; Carmody, "For a New Theater, a Nostalgic Gala": 38; "News," *Interiors* 132 (June 1973): 16, 20.
83. Schroeder, "Broadway's Theaters: 'Too Valuable to Keep'": 48.
84. "Office Boom Is Moving to Broadway": 2; "Annual Production of Office Space Will More Than Double in '68," *Real Estate Record and Guide* 201 (January 13, 1968): 2; "Builders Dress Up Their Sidewalk Bridge on Broadway," *Real Estate Record and Guide* 201 (March 23, 1968): 2–3; Fowler, "Broadway Buildings Fill Slowly in Rent Lag": 1, 3; Ballard, *Directory of Manhattan Office Buildings*, 195; Dunlap, *On Broadway*, 192.
85. "Construction Started at 57th St. and 7th Ave. for Office Building," *Real Estate Record and Guide* 202 (September 21, 1968): 5; Ballard, *Directory of Manhattan Office Buildings*, 199. For the Rodin Studio Building, see Stern, Gilmartin and Massengale, *New York 1900*, 298.
86. Heinz Ronner and Sharad Jhaveri, *Louis I. Kahn: Complete Work 1935–1974* (Basel: Birkhäuser Verlag, 1974), 314–17; David B. Brownlee and David G. DeLong, *Louis I. Kahn: In the Realm of Architecture*, with an intro. by Vincent Scully (New York: Rizzoli International Publications, 1991), 116–18.
87. Glenn Fowler, "32-Story Tower on Times Square Will Be 6th New Project in Area," *New York Times* (January 13, 1970): 1, 42; Fowler, "Broadway Buildings Fill Slowly in Rent Lag": 1, 3; Robert Metz, "Partners on Broadway," *New York Times* (February 4, 1971): 48; Joseph Lelyveld, "Painting Adorns Building Frame," *New York Times* (January 5, 1972): 47; Michael T. Kaufman, "Broadway Greets New Movie Theater," *New York Times* (December 13, 1972): 60; Ballard, *Directory of Manhattan Office Buildings*, 193; Dunlap, *On Broadway*, 168. For the Hotel Rector, see Stern, Gilmartin and Massengale, *New York 1900*, 167, 269.
88. Tania and Nassos Daphnis quoted in Lelyveld, "Painting Adorns Building Frame": 47.
89. Robert D. McFadden, "$75-Million, 2,000-Room Hotel Is Being Planned for Times Sq.," *New York Times* (November 3, 1972): 1, 36; "A Plush Hotel for Seedy Times Square," *Business Week* (November 4, 1972): 27; "Portman: A New Force for Rebuilding the Cities," *Business Week* (February 17, 1973): cover, 58–62, 64; Ada Louise Huxtable, "54-Story Hotel Expected to Revitalize Times Square," *New York Times* (July 11, 1973): 43, 50; "Inner Space Featured in New $150-Million Hotel," *Engineering News-Record* 191 (July 12, 1973): 13; "The Portman Style," *Newsweek* 82 (July 23, 1973): 53; "The Talk of the Town: Some Dazzle for the Garden," *New Yorker* 49 (July 23, 1973): 23–24; "John Portman to Build Times Square Hotel," *Architectural Record* 154 (August 1973): 39; Stanley Abercrombie, "Dixie Kid Socko on Great White Way," *Architecture Plus* 1 (August 1973): 15; "Times Square Revival Gains Momentum with Portman's Hotel-Plus," *Interiors* 133 (August 1973): 6, 10; Olga Gueft, "John Portman's Economic Garden," editorial, *Interiors* 133 (August 1973): 73; "Portman Show to Open on B'Way in 1977," *Progressive Architecture* 54 (August 1973): 23–24; Paul Goldberger, "Buck Rogers in Times Square," *New York Times* (August 26, 1973), VI: cover, 10–11, 68, 70–72, 74; "A-Courtin' on Times Square," *Architectural Forum* 139 (September 1973): 16; Michael J. Mooney, "Dare We Dream?" *New York Times* (September 16, 1973), VI: 88; "The Room Boom," *New York* 7 (December 31, 1973): 64; Ada Louise Huxtable, "More Bad News about Times Square," *New York Times* (February 9, 1975), II: 32, reprinted as "New York: Bad News about Times Square," in Ada Louise Huxtable, *Kicked a Building Lately?* (New York: Quadrangle/New York Times Book Co., 1976), 112–15; "USA: Fantalbergo," *Domus* 547 (June 1975): 20–21; John Portman and Jonathan Barnett, *The Architect as Developer* (New York: McGraw-Hill, 1976), 40–41, 124–25, 128; Robert A. M. Stern with Thomas Mellins, "The Fall and Rise of New York: Trends and Travesties in the Service of Community Pride," in *New New York*, exhibition catalogue (Flushing, N.Y.: Queens Museum, 1987), 8–17; James Trager, *West of Fifth: The Rise and Fall and Rise of*

Manhattan's West Side (New York: Atheneum, 1987), 116–18; White and Willensky, *AIA Guide* (1988), 230; Dunlap, *On Broadway*, 170–71. For further discussion of Portman's work in general, see Gurney Breckenfield, "The Architects Want a Voice in Redesigning America," *Fortune* 84 (November 1971): 198–99, 203–6; Bernhard Leitner, "John Portman: Architecture Is Not a Building," *Art in America* 61 (March–April 1973): 80–82; "Architect/Developer John Portman," *Royal Institute of British Architecture Journal* 84 (December 1977): 504–13; Paolo Riani, *John Portman* (Washington, D.C.: American Institute of Architects Press, 1990), 144–47.

90. Stern, Gilmartin and Massengale, *New York 1900*, 216–17.

91. Stern, Gilmartin and Mellins, *New York 1930*, 230.

92. Stern, Gilmartin and Mellins, *New York 1930*, 230.

93. Henderson, *The City and the Theater*, 237; Stern, Gilmartin and Massengale, *New York 1900*, 216.

94. John A. Bradley, "Many Structural Feats Are Accomplished in Remodeling of the Victoria Theater," *New York Times* (October 31, 1948), VIII: 1, 6; "Theater: New York, N.Y.," *Progressive Architecture* 31 (May 1950): 59–62; Edward Durell Stone, *The Evolution of an Architect* (New York: Horizon Press, 1962), 99, 118.

95. Jaquelin Robertson quoted in McFadden, "$75-Million, 2,000-Room Hotel Is Being Planned for Times Sq.": 1.

96. Robert Venturi, Denise Scott Brown and Steven Izenour, *Learning from Las Vegas* (Cambridge, Mass.: MIT Press, 1972), 158. Also see "Venturi, Rauch and Scott Brown," *A + U*, extra edition (December 1981): 145; *Venturi, Rauch and Scott Brown: A Generation of Architecture* (Urbana-Champaign, Ill.: University of Illinois at Urbana-Champaign, 1984), 42–43.

97. For the Regency Hyatt Hotel, see Riani, *John Portman*, 62–77.

98. Jaquelin Robertson quoted in Goldberger, "Buck Rogers in Times Square": 74.

99. Goldberger, "Buck Rogers in Times Square": 11.

100. Goldberger, "Buck Rogers in Times Square": 11, 68.

101. Vincent Scully quoted in Goldberger, "Buck Rogers in Times Square": 68.

102. Philip Johnson quoted in "The Portman Style": 53.

103. Philip Johnson quoted in "Portman: A New Force for Rebuilding the Cities": 60.

104. McFadden, "$75-Million, 2,000-Room Hotel Is Being Planned for Times Sq.": 36.

105. "Times Square Revival Gains Momentum with Portman's Hotel-Plus": 10.

106. John V. Lindsay quoted in Goldberger, "Buck Rogers in Times Square": 68.

107. "The Talk of the Town: Some Dazzle for the Garden": 24.

108. "A-Courtin' on Times Square": 16.

109. "The Talk of the Town: Some Dazzle for the Garden": 24.

110. Ada Louise Huxtable quoted in Goldberger, "Buck Rogers in Times Square": 74.

111. Huxtable, "54-Story Hotel Expected to Revitalize Times Square": 50.

112. Huxtable, "More Bad News about Times Square": 32.

113. Abercrombie, "Dixie Kid Socko on Great White Way": 15.

114. John Portman quoted in "Portman: A New Force in Rebuilding the Cities": 62.

115. John Portman quoted in "The Talk of the Town: Some Dazzle for the Garden": 24.

116. John Portman quoted in Goldberger, "Buck Rogers in Times Square": 74.

117. William Bardel quoted in Goldberger, "Buck Rogers in Times Square": 74.

118. Stern, Gilmartin and Mellins, *New York 1930*, 231.

119. Frank J. Prial, "Times Sq. Vice Persists Despite Patrols," *New York Times* (July 4, 1970): 38; McCandlish Phillips, "Times Square's Quiet Hours When Make-Believe Stops," *New York Times* (August 4, 1970): 33; Alan S. Oser, "Times Square Finds Erotica Has Impact," *New York Times* (August 23, 1970), VIII: 1, 8; Edward Ranzal, "Times Sq. Uplift Urged by Lindsay," *New York Times* (January 23, 1971): 27; Linda Charlton, "The Pilgrims Keep Coming to Times Square, the Tarnished Mecca," *New York Times* (July 23, 1972), X: 1, 21.

120. Huxtable, "Will Slab City Take Over Times Square?": 40.

121. White and Willensky, *AIA Guide* (1978), 142; Goldberger, *The City Observed*, 146.

122. Louis Calta, "Half-Price Tickets Will Go on Sale at Times Sq. Unit," *New York Times* (May 22, 1973): 49; "Ticket Sale at Discount Brisk Here," *New York Times* (June 26, 1973): 52; "Notes on People," *New York Times* (June 27, 1973): 55; Louis Calta, "News of the Stage," *New York Times* (July 8, 1973): 36; "Secretary Wins 'Night Music' Bonus," *New York Times* (September 12, 1973): 43; Sharon L. Fujioka, "Discount Ticket Center Found to Be a Theatergoing Stimulus," *New York Times* (October 11, 1973): 57; Louis Calta, "News of the Stage," *New York Times* (October 28, 1973): 58; Louis Calta, "Discount Center to Get Some Heat," *New York Times* (December 9, 1973): 78; Lewis Funke, "'I Love the Theater, Man, but Those Prices,'" *New York Times* (December 16, 1973), II: 3, 8; White and Willensky, *AIA Guide* (1978), 142; Goldberger, *The City Observed*, 145–46; Richard Saul Wurman, *NYC Access* (New York: Access Press, 1983), 71; Dunlap, *On Broadway*, 172.

FORTY-SECOND STREET

1. "Buses Will Replace Trolley Cars on 42d St. Crosstown Line Nov. 17," *New York Times* (November 4, 1946): 27; "Buses, Street Cars Share 42d St., with One Electric Line Supplanted," *New York Times* (November 18, 1946): 1, 12.

2. "New Annex for Manhattan's Chrysler," *Architectural Forum* 91 (November 1949): 14; "Plan 32-Story Addition for Chrysler Building," *Architectural Record* 108 (September 1950): 188, 192; "Texas Company Leases Floor in New Chrysler Building East," *Real Estate Record and Guide* 168 (July 7, 1951): 3–4; Lewis Mumford, "The Sky Line: Preview of the Past," *New Yorker* 28 (October 11, 1952): 66, 69–76; Robert F. R. Ballard, *Directory of Manhattan Office Buildings* (New York: McGraw-Hill, 1978), 13. For William Van Alen's Chrysler Building, see Stern, Gilmartin and Mellins, *New York 1930*, 603–10.

3. Stan Fischler, *Uptown, Downtown: A Trip Through Time on New York's Subways* (New York: Hawthorn Books, 1976), 258.

4. Mumford, "The Sky Line: Preview of the Past": 66, 69.

5. Lee E. Cooper, "42d St. Skyscraper to Cover a Block," *New York Times* (July 23, 1953): 1. Also see "Socony-Vacuum Tower," *Architectural Forum* 99 (August 1953): 43; Winston Weisman, "The Rise and Rise of the Skyscraper," *New York Times* (September 20, 1953), VI: 14–15; "A Glass Bank and Two New Office Buildings," *Architectural Record* 114 (October 1953): 10–11; "Steel Contract Let," *New York Times* (March 17, 1954): 48; "Ground Is Broken for 42d St. Offices," *New York Times* (March 31, 1954): 48; "Socony-Vacuum Company Signs Leases for 553,600 Sq. Ft. in New Skyscraper," *New York Times* (July 18, 1954), VIII: 1; "New York's Biggest Building in 25 Years," *Architectural Forum* 102 (January 1955): 86–92; Richard Thruelsen, "Big Dip in Manhattan," *Saturday Evening Post* 227 (January 22, 1955): 36–37, 70, 74; John A. Bradley, "Use of New Material Changes Socony-Vacuum Building Design," *New York Times* (February 6, 1955), VIII: 1; "Offices in the Socony-Vacuum Building Are Rented a Year Before Completion," *New York Times* (February 27, 1955), VIII: 1; "8th Floor Is Taller in Socony Skyscraper," *New York Times* (March 29, 1955): 49; "Hurricane Glass for Skyscraper," *New York Times* (April 10, 1955), VIII: 3; "Steel Panel Installed," *New York Times* (May 5, 1955): 17; John A. Bradley, "Stainless Panels Reflect Progress," *New York Times* (May 8, 1955), VIII: 1, 5; "Precision Planning and 'Men of Steel' Set Framework for 42d St. Skyscraper," *New York Times* (August 7, 1955), VIII: 2; "Scaffold Pipes Bend in NY; Coliseum Collapse Blame Fixed," *Architectural Forum* 103 (September 1955): 9; Walter McQuade, "Parentheses," *Architectural Forum* 103 (October 1955): 57, 60, 64, 68; Lewis Mumford, "The Sky Line: The Drab and the Daring," *New Yorker* 32 (February 4, 1956): 82–88, partially excerpted in "They Say," *Journal of the American Institute of Architects* 25 (June 1956): 262–63; "Architectural Tie," *Architectural Record* 119 (April 1956): 24; "The Talk of the Town: Champ," *New Yorker* 32 (May 19, 1956): 23–24; "Owner Doubles as Rental Agent," *New York Times* (May 20, 1956), VIII: 1–2; "Building the New New York," *Newsweek* 48 (July 9, 1956): 89–91; "A Special Report on Manhattan's Newest Landmark: The Socony Mobil Building," special advertising section, *New York Times* (August 19, 1956), X: esp. pp. 5, 10, 17; "New Skyscraper Opened by Socony," *New York Times* (October 4, 1956): 52; "New York: Its Business Is Bigness," *Business Week* (October 13, 1956): 125–34, 136–41; "Prophecy Is Put in Cornerstone," *New York Times* (October 18, 1956): 35; "A Glittering Tower for New York's Skyline," *Architectural Forum* 105 (November 1956): 157; "New York Is the Backdrop for the Lofty Pinnacle Club Designed by Leigh Allen," *Interiors* 116 (November 1956): 74–91; Richard E. Paret, letter to the editor, *Business Week* (November 3, 1956): 5; "Socony-Mobil Building," *Architectural Record* 121 (March 1957): 238; "High Rise Office Buildings," *Progressive Architecture* 38 (June 1957): 160; Louise Sloane, "Office-Building Amenities," *Progressive Architecture* 38 (June 1957): 227–33; Henry Hope Reed, *The Golden City* (New York: Doubleday, 1959), 33, 57; Earle Shultz and Walter Simmons, *Offices in the Sky* (Indianapolis, Ind.: Bobbs-Merrill, 1959), 247; Ada Louise Huxtable, *Four Walking Tours of Modern Architecture in New York City* (New York: Museum of Modern Art and Municipal Art Society of New York, 1961), 52–53; Jürgen Joedicke, *Office Buildings*, trans. C. V. Amerongen (New York: Frederick A. Praeger, 1962), 79; White and Willensky, *AIA Guide* (1967), 121; Ballard, *Directory of Manhattan Office Buildings*, 12; John Tauranac, *Essential New York* (New York: Holt, Rinehart and Winston, 1979), 200–202; Gerard R. Wolfe, *42nd Street: River to River* (New York: 42nd Street E.T.C., Inc., 1984), unpaginated; Carol Herselle Krinsky, "Architecture in New York City," in Leonard Wallock, ed., *New York: Culture Capital of the World, 1940–1965* (New York: Rizzoli International Publications, 1988), 100; Victoria Newhouse, *Wallace K. Harrison, Architect* (New York: Rizzoli International Publications, 1989), 150–51.

6. For 26 Broadway (Standard Oil Building), designed in collaboration with Shreve, Lamb & Blake, see Stern, Gilmartin and Mellins, *New York 1930*, 530, 538–40.

7. "New York's Biggest Building in 25 Years": 86.

8. Mumford, "The Sky Line: The Drab and the Daring": 83.

9. For the Airlines Terminal Building, see Stern, Gilmartin and Mellins, *New York 1930*, 704–5.

10. "New York's Biggest Building in 25 Years": 86.

11. For Starrett & Van Vleck's 205 East Forty-second Street, see Ballard, *Directory of Manhattan Office Buildings*, 54. For Howells & Hood's Daily News Building, see Stern, Gilmartin and Mellins, *New York 1930*, 577–79.

12. John P. Callahan, "18-Story Annex for News Building," *New York Times* (October 27, 1957), VIII: 1, 6; Glenn Fowler, "Buildings Found at Every Stage," *New York Times* (June 15, 1958), VIII: 1, 13; "Frame Completed for News Addition," *New York Times* (September 7, 1958), VIII: 13; White and Willensky, *AIA Guide* (1967), 121–22; Ballard, *Directory of Manhattan Office Buildings*, 14; Paul Goldberger, *The City Observed: New York* (New York: Random House, 1979), 134–35; Newhouse, *Wallace K. Harrison, Architect*, 321.

13. Goldberger, *The City Observed*, 135.

14. "East Side to Get New Skyscraper," *New York Times* (March 3, 1959): 55; "New Pfizer Building Will Rise on 42d St.," *Real Estate Record and Guide* 182 (March 21, 1959): 5; "New East Side Skyscraper Begun," *New York Times* (June 5, 1959): 41; "Ground Broken for New Pfizer Building," *Real Estate Record and Guide* 183 (June 20, 1959): 3; "Big Moving Task Set for Week-End," *New York Times* (April 7, 1961): 49; Marian Page, "Dynamic Conservatism Distinguishes Interiors of Pfizer's World Headquarters Building," *Interiors* 121 (February 1962): 92–103; Ballard, *Directory of Manhattan Office Buildings*, 14.

15. "Builder's Professional Efforts Emulated by His Children in Lesser Version," *New York Times* (October 27, 1957), VIII: 12; Dennis Duggan, "Architectural 'Give and Take' Altering City," *New York Times* (September 30, 1962), VIII: 1, 6. For Hector Hamilton's Foltis-Fischer Building, see Stern, Gilmartin and Mellins, *New York 1930*, 274–75, 279.

16. "Tudor City to Get an Office Building," *New York Times* (August 2, 1962): 41; Thomas W. Ennis, "New Offices Rise at a Record Rate," *New York Times* (April 21, 1963), VIII: 1, 19; "Building Concern to Move Offices," *New York Times* (August 6, 1963): 50; Ballard, *Directory of Manhattan Office Buildings*, 15; Christian Hubert, "The Late Work: 1939–1969," in Christian Hubert and Lindsay Stamm Shapiro, *William Lescaze* (New York: Institute for Architecture and Urban Studies; New York: Rizzoli International Publications, 1982), 109, 116–17.

17. "4th Skyscraper to Be Erected at Intersection of 3d and 42d," *New York Times* (March 12, 1964): 58; "Colorful Tapestries with Symbolic Designs Decorate Lobby of New Office Building," *New York Times* (July 4, 1965), VIII: 5.

18. For the Forty-fifth Street Automat, see Stern, Gilmartin and Mellins, *New York 1930*, 279. For the one on Fifty-seventh Street, see White and Willensky, *AIA Guide* (1988), 279.

19. Goldberger, *The City Observed*, 135.

20. Dudley Dalton, "East 42d Street Home to Industry," *New York Times* (January 24, 1965), VIII: 1, 8.

21. Stern, Gilmartin and Massengale, *New York 1900*, 34, 36–40.

22. For Tudor City, see Stern, Gilmartin and Mellins, *New York 1930*, 437–38.

23. Ada Louise Huxtable, "Bold Plan for Building Unveiled," *New York Times* (September 29, 1964): 45; Walter McQuade, "The Ford Foundation's Mid-Manhattan Greenhouse," *Fortune* 70 (October 1964): 177–78, 180–82; "New York Headquarters Enclosing a Garden," *Architectural Record* 136 (November 1964): 10; "Ford Foundation's New Building Looks In On Itself," *Interiors* 124 (November 1964): 10; James T. Burns, Jr., "A

Great Space Taking Shape in New York," *Progressive Architecture* 45 (November 1964): 192–97; "Kevin Go Bragh," *Progressive Architecture* 46 (May 1965): 190–95; "Siège de la Fondation Ford à New York," *L'Architecture d'Aujourd'hui* 35 (September 1965): 28–29; White and Willensky, *AIA Guide* (1967), 122; Richard J. H. Johnston, "210-Ft. Crane Falls on Bus in 42d St.; 4 Injured Slightly," *New York Times* (April 13, 1967): 1, 39; "Landscaped Lobby," *Architectural Forum* 126 (June 1967): 52–53; "The Ford Foundation Headquarters Building, New York City," *Architectural Record* 142 (September 1967): 41; Steven V. Roberts, "Ford Fund's New Building Has Indoor Woods," *New York Times* (October 26, 1967): 49; Ada Louise Huxtable, "Ford Flies High," *New York Times* (November 26, 1967), II: 23, 25, reprinted in Ada Louise Huxtable, *Will They Ever Finish Bruckner Boulevard?* (New York: Macmillan, 1970), 86–91; "Ford's in Its Heaven," *Newsweek* 70 (November 27, 1967): 68; "The Talk of the Town: A Home to Work In," *New Yorker* 43 (December 30, 1967): 23–25; Alan Dunn, "The Ford Foundation—Right?" cartoon, *Architectural Record* 143 (January 1968): 10; "Ford Foundation Building Is Completed and Dedicated," *Architectural Record* 143 (January 1968): 35; "Architecture: A Core of Light," *Time* 91 (January 5, 1968): 50–51; Jonathan Barnett, "Innovation and Symbolism on 42nd Street," *Architectural Record* 143 (February 1968): cover, 105–12; "Fund Fair," *Architectural Review* 143 (February 1968): 95; "Oasis in Manhattan," *Interior Design* 39 (February 1968): 116–25; "Actualités: Ford Foundation: New York," *L'Architecture d'Aujourd'hui* 39 (February 1968): 106–9; Olga Gueft, "Crusaders' Castle," *Interiors* 127 (March 1968): 95–109; Michael Webb, "Oasis in the New York Desert," *Country Life* 143 (April 11, 1968): 874–76; "Whitney Museum Wins Bard Prize," *New York Times* (April 26, 1968): 39; "Awards," *Architectural Forum* 128 (May 1968): 97; Walter F. Wagner, Jr., "Fresh Forms and New Directions from a Special Kind of Problem Solving," *Architectural Record* 143 (May 1968): 145, 162; "Una Grande Serra per Uffici a New York," *Domus* 462 (May 1968): 1–6; Glenn Fowler, "5th Ave. Group Taps 42d St. Building for a 'Wish You Were Here' Award," *New York Times* (May 5, 1968), VIII: 1, 12; "Oase in Manhattan," *Deutsche Bauzeitung* 102 (June 1968): 419–23; Vincent Scully, *American Architecture and Urbanism* (New York: Frederick A. Praeger, 1969), 200, fig. 430; Robert A. M. Stern, *New Directions in American Architecture* (New York: George Braziller, 1969), 27–29, figs. 24–25; Yukihisa Isobe, "Kevin Roche," *Kenchiku Bunka* 25 (September 1970): 71–90; Wolf Von Eckardt, "You Can't See the Foyer for the Trees," *Horizon* 13 (summer 1971): 40–47; John W. Cook and Heinrich Klotz, *Conversations with Architects* (New York: Praeger, 1973), 23, 66–72; Suzanne Stephens, "Savvy about Steel, Game with Glass," *Progressive Architecture* 55 (September 1974): 78–83; *Kevin Roche, John Dinkeloo and Associates, vol. 1: 1962–1975*, with an intro. by Henry-Russell Hitchcock (Tokyo: A.D.A. Edita, 1975), 56–69, 250; John Pile, *Interiors 3rd Book of Offices* (New York: Whitney Library of Design, 1976), 27; C. Ray Smith, *Supermannerism: New Attitudes in Post-Modern Architecture* (New York: E. P. Dutton, 1977), 231–32; Goldberger, *The City Observed*, 134; Tauranac, *Essential New York*, 222–23; Wolfe, *42nd Street: River to River*, unpaginated; Francesco Dal Co, *Kevin Roche* (New York: Rizzoli International Publications, 1985), 7–8, 11, 36–37, 40–41, 43, 45, 106–9, 265; Krinsky, "Architecture in New York City," in Wallock, ed., *New York: Culture Capital of the World, 1940–1965*, 120–21.
24. Burns, "A Great Space Taking Shape in New York": 196.
25. Barnett, "Innovation and Symbolism on 42nd Street": 107.
26. Huxtable, "Bold Plan for Building Unveiled": 45.
27. Kevin Roche quoted in Huxtable, "Bold Plan for Building Unveiled": 45.
28. Huxtable, "Bold Plan for Building Unveiled": 45.
29. Huxtable, "Ford Flies High": 23, 25.
30. Quoted in Roberts, "Ford Fund's New Building Has Indoor Woods": 49.
31. White and Willensky, *AIA Guide* (1967), 122.
32. Huxtable, "Ford Flies High": 23, 25.
33. Barnett, "Innovation and Symbolism on 42nd Street": 111.
34. "Fund Fair": 95.
35. Scully, *American Architecture and Urbanism*, 200.
36. Stern, *New Directions in American Architecture*, 28–29.
37. Goldberger, *The City Observed*, 134.
38. "News of Realty: 2 Leases Signed for Space in New Bank Building," *New York Times* (November 28, 1968): 82; Ballard, *Directory of Manhattan Office Buildings*, 54.
39. Stern, Gilmartin and Mellins, *New York 1930*, 186.
40. "New Skyscraper for Madison Ave.," *New York Times* (March 17, 1960): 56; "Plans for Building in Midtown Filed," *New York Times* (November 23, 1960): 48; "Early Start Set for Skyscraper," *New York Times* (May 25, 1961): 61; "New Danish Construction Crane Simplifies Job with Rotating Jib," *New York Times* (January 28, 1962), VIII: 1, 12; Ballard, *Directory of Manhattan Office Buildings*, 28.
41. For the Manhattan Hotel, see Stern, Gilmartin and Massengale, *New York 1900*, 267. For the Manhattan Hotel's conversion to office use, see Stern, Gilmartin and Mellins, *New York 1930*, 181.
42. Stern, Gilmartin and Massengale, *New York 1900*, 91, 94–98.
43. Byron Porterfield, "City University Gets a Building on 42d St. for Graduate Center," *New York Times* (February 16, 1966): 45; "Woolworth Unit to Be a Campus," *New York Times* (September 28, 1966): 59; M. A. Farber, "New City College to Open Next Fall," *New York Times* (October 25, 1966): 1, 35; "Graduate Center Dedicates Mall," *New York Times* (June 5, 1970): 39; "Buildings in the News," *Architectural Record* 148 (July 1970): 42; "Mall for City and School," *Architectural Forum* 133 (July–August 1970): 7; Ada Louise Huxtable, "What a Little Taste Can Do," *New York Times* (August 9, 1970), II: 18; "Pedestrian Passageway Offers Relief from Midtown Bustle," *Progressive Architecture* 51 (September 1970): 29; Ellen Stock, "Best Bets: Letting It All Hang Up," *New York* 7 (February 4, 1974): 58; White and Willensky, *AIA Guide* (1978), 135; Goldberger, *The City Observed*, 141; Wolfe, *42nd Street: River to River*, unpaginated. For Warren & Wetmore's Aeolian Hall, see "To Build Skyscraper Near Times Square," *New York Times* (March 31, 1911): 5; "Business Growing Rapidly in Forty-second Street," *New York Times* (June 25, 1911), VIII: 2; "Aeolian Hall Opening," *New York Times* (October 13, 1912), VIII: 2; Ballard, *Directory of Manhattan Office Buildings*, 58.
44. Federal Writers' Project, *New York Panorama* (New York: Random House, 1938; New York: Pantheon Books, 1984), 261. In 1927 Warren & Wetmore completed another building for the Aeolian Company at 689 Fifth Avenue, on the northeast corner of Fifty-fourth Street. See Stern, Gilmartin and Mellins, *New York 1930*, 297–98, 312.
45. Huxtable, "What a Little Taste Can Do": 18.
46. For 500 Fifth Avenue and the Salmon Tower, see Stern, Gilmartin and Mellins, *New York 1930*, 610, 612.
47. Isadore Barmash, "Stern's Will Shut 42d St. Store on May 1 as Result of Losses," *New York Times* (January 25, 1969): 1, 39; Leonard Sloane, "Employees of Store Lament Decision," *New York Times* (January 25, 1969): 39; "Good-by to Stern's," editorial, *New York Times* (January 29, 1969): 40; "Manhattan Store of Stern's Closed," *New York Times* (April 2, 1969): 67. For Stern Brothers' 1913 building, see Stern, Gilmartin and Massengale, *New York 1900*, 192, 194.
48. William Robbins, "Skyscraper Due on Stern's Site," *New York Times* (March 21, 1969): 1, 79; "Office Building," *Progressive Architecture* 50 (December 1969): 33; Paul Goldberger, "New Grace Building Is Flamboyant Pop," *New York Times* (March 12, 1974): 32; "WR Grace Selects Student Design for Headquarters Plaza in New York," *Architectural Record* 158 (August 1975): 34; Ballard, *Directory of Manhattan Office Buildings*, 6; White and Willensky, *AIA Guide* (1978), 136; Goldberger, *The City Observed*, 140; Wolfe, *42nd Street: River to River*, unpaginated; Carol Herselle Krinsky, *Gordon Bunshaft of Skidmore, Owings & Merrill* (New York: Architectural History Foundation; Cambridge, Mass.: MIT Press, 1988), 247–51, 290–91, 338.
49. White and Willensky, *AIA Guide* (1978), 136.
50. Goldberger, "New Grace Building Is Flamboyant Pop": 32.
51. Goldberger, "New Grace Building Is Flamboyant Pop": 32.
52. Carter B. Horsley, "Skyscraper Plazas Feel Pressure to Change," *New York Times* (June 22, 1975), VIII: 1, 14; "A Place for People," editorial, *New York Times* (June 25, 1975): 42.
53. For the Bush Terminal and Wurlitzer buildings, see Stern, Gilmartin and Mellins, *New York 1930*, 545–47.
54. Glenn Fowler, "New Phone Office Set for Midtown," *New York Times* (February 4, 1970): 44; Glenn Fowler, "Saga of a Building Traced," *New York Times* (February 8, 1970), VIII: 4; "New York Telephone Company Will Occupy Most of 1095 Sixth Ave.," *Real Estate Record and Guide* 205 (February 21, 1970): 2; "Steel Falls on 6th Ave.: Man Killed," *New York Times* (May 26, 1971): 45; Paul Goldberger, "When Building for Future Means a Step Backward," *New York Times* (December 6, 1975): 33; Goldberger, *The City Observed*, 140–41; Wolfe, *42nd Street: River to River*, unpaginated; White and Willensky, *AIA Guide* (1988), 238.
55. One building that the developers could not acquire was the nine-story Vim Building, 124 West Forty-second Street, which remained as a holdout. New York Telephone built around the building and in 1974 it was partially demolished and renovated to accommodate a six-story branch office for the County Federal Savings & Loan Association. See Carter B. Horsley, "A Holdout Stands Pat on 42d St.," *New York Times* (July 2, 1972), VIII: 1, 6; Carter B. Horsley, "42d St. Holdout Renovated," *New York Times* (September 1, 1974), VIII: 2.
56. For the Barclay-Vesey Building, see Stern, Gilmartin and Mellins, *New York 1930*, 565–70.
57. Goldberger, "When Building for Future Means a Step Backward": 33.
58. Goldberger, *The City Observed*, 140–41.
59. "White Way Vs. Midway," *Business Week* (January 9, 1954): 88.
60. "Upgrading Times Square," editorial, *New York Times* (January 4, 1954): 18; "Times Square Clean-Up Believed Assured," *New York Times* (January 12, 1954): 20; Charles G. Bennett, "New Honky-Tonks in Times Sq. Barred by Estimate Board Vote," *New York Times* (January 14, 1954): 1, 17; William M. Farrell, "Honky-Tonks Due for a Slow Death," *New York Times* (January 22, 1954): 29; "For a Better Square," editorial, *New York Times* (January 23, 1954): 12.
61. "Theater Owner Hailed," *New York Times* (January 25, 1960): 23; Lewis Funke, "News and Gossip of the Rialto," *New York Times* (January 31, 1960), II: 1; Louis Calta, "Theater: A Revue Opens," *New York Times* (February 8, 1960): 35; "Investor-Builder Gets '61 Realty Man Award," *New York Times* (February 10, 1961): 46; Sam Zolotow, "Maidman Adding Two Playhouses," *New York Times* (August 15, 1961): 25; "Two Playhouses Planned," *New York Times* (August 21, 1961): 19; "Maidman Will Construct Theatrical Center Building at 442 West 42nd Street," *Real Estate Record and Guide* 188 (December 9, 1961): 3–4; Edmond J. Bartnett, "Investor Builds a Theater Chain," *New York Times* (December 10, 1961), VIII: 1–2; Lewis Funke, "News of the Rialto: Mr. Malamud," *New York Times* (January 21, 1962), II: 1; Sam Zolotow, "2 New Maidman Houses," *New York Times* (August 18, 1964): 25; Sam Zolotow, "Maidman Shifts Theaters," *New York Times* (May 20, 1965): 54; "New Facelifting Begun on 42d St.," *New York Times* (June 15, 1965): 43.
62. Calta, "Theater: A Revue Opens": 35.
63. Stern, Gilmartin and Mellins, *New York 1930*, 204.
64. Louis Calta, "Civic Group Asks 42d St. Renewal," *New York Times* (November 14, 1962): 41–42; Rev. Jos. A. McCaffrey, "To Clean Up 42d Street," letter to the editor, *New York Times* (November 23, 1962): 28; "Felt Backs Plans to Revitalize Block in Times Sq. Area," *New York Times* (November 25, 1962): 25; "Snibbe Bids 42nd Street Return to Glory," *Progressive Architecture* 43 (December 1962): 52.
65. "Could This Be Times Square Tomorrow?" *Architectural Forum* 103 (August 1955): 106–13.
66. "New Facelifting Begun on 42d St. ": 43.
67. Peter Blake, "The Eighth Annual Cityscape Awards," *New York* 9 (January 12, 1976): 55–57. Also see White and Willensky, *AIA Guide* (1978), 138.
68. Alfred E. Clark, "Top Film and Shopping Center Is Proposed for West 42d Street," *New York Times* (March 14, 1970): 21; Richard May, Jr., "Plans for 42d Street," letter to the editor, *New York Times* (April 25, 1970): 28.
69. Lewis Rudin quoted in "ABNY Urges Times Sq. Cleanup," *Real Estate Record and Guide* 210 (December 30, 1972): 2.
70. For the Lincoln Tunnel, see Stern, Gilmartin and Mellins, *New York 1930*, 691.
71. Stern, Gilmartin and Mellins, *New York 1930*, 701–2.
72. Stern, Gilmartin and Mellins, *New York 1930*, 824 (n. 129).
73. Stern, Gilmartin and Mellins, *New York 1930*, 700–702.
74. "$225,000 Is Added to Capital Budget," *New York Times* (November 29, 1940): 17; "Huge Bus Terminal to Rise on 42d St. at $4,000,000 Cost," *New York Times* (December 8, 1940): 1, 65; "Central Bus Terminal," editorial, *New York Times* (December 9, 1940): 18; "City Enters Deal for Bus Terminal," *New York Times* (January 24, 1941): 19; "Bus Terminal Approved," *Real Estate Record and Guide* 147 (January 25, 1941): 3; "Midtown Bus Ban Is Voided by Court," *New York Times* (February 19, 1941): 1, 18.
75. For the McGraw-Hill Building, see Stern, Gilmartin and Mellins, *New York 1930*, 574–75, 579–80, 584–85.
76. William R. Conklin, "New Bus Terminal Is Approved Here; to Cost $17,500,000," *New York Times* (January 31, 1947): 1, 25; "A Victory Over Bus Traffic," editorial, *New York Times* (January 31, 1947): 22; "Terminal Model Shown," *New York Times* (April 30,

1948): 46; "Razing for Bus Terminal Starts," *New York Times* (May 7, 1948): 2; "Bus Terminal for Manhattan," *Interiors* 107 (June 1948): 16; "Bus Terminal to Reduce New York City Traffic," *Architectural Forum* 90 (May 1949): 70, 74; "New York's New Union Bus Terminal," *Architectural Record* 106 (August 1949): 104–9; "Steelwork Is Raised for New Bus Station," *New York Times* (November 24, 1949): 35; "New Terminal Set for Newark Field," *New York Times* (September 15, 1950): 27; "Night Crew Speeds 9th Ave. Bus Span," *New York Times* (October 6, 1950): 28; John A. Bradley, "West Side Men See New Bus Terminal Converting Realty in Area to Commerce," *New York Times* (November 26, 1950), VIII: 1; "10,000 Match Books Herald New Bus Terminal," *New York Times* (December 10, 1950): 80; "'Grand Central' for Buses," *New York Times* (December 10, 1950), VI: 14–15; "New Bus Terminal: Boon to Commuters, Balm for Traffic Ills," *Business Week* (December 23, 1950): 24–25; illustrated in *Architectural Record* 109 (January 1951): 12; "World's Biggest Bus Station," *Life* 30 (January 15, 1951): 48–50; "The Talk of the Town: Big Terminal," *New Yorker* 27 (December 1, 1951): 42–43; Robert Rice, "A Reporter at Large: Every Place They Tear the House Down," *New Yorker* 30 (April 17, 1954): 92, 94–107; White and Willensky, *AIA Guide* (1978), 138; Goldberger, *The City Observed*, 146–47.

77. "Bus Terminal to Reduce New York City Traffic": 70.

78. "West Side Airlines Terminal Set; Construction to Begin by Summer," *New York Times* (January 28, 1952): 19; Bliss K. Thorne, "Aviation: New Terminal," *New York Times* (July 12, 1953), II: 30; "West Side Station for Airlines Urged," *New York Times* (August 13, 1953): 27; "Parking Site Acquired at Air Lines Terminal," *New York Times* (September 26, 1954), VIII: 8; John A. Bradley, "$2,500,000 Financing Is Set for West Side Air Terminal," *New York Times* (November 7, 1954), VIII: 1, 9; "All Space Rented in Air Terminal," *New York Times* (June 5, 1955), VIII: 1; "New Air Terminal Will Open Sept. 15," *New York Times* (August 21, 1955), V: 11; Morris Gilbert, "The West Side Gets Its Own Air Terminal," *New York Times* (September 11, 1955), II: 23; "New Air Terminal Opens Today; Bus Trip to Newark 21 Minutes," *New York Times* (September 15, 1955): 35; "A New Air Terminal," editorial, *New York Times* (September 15, 1955): 32; Lewis Mumford, "The Sky Line: The Drab and the Daring," *New Yorker* 32 (February 4, 1956): 82–88.

79. Mumford, "The Sky Line: The Drab and the Daring": 82.

80. "Port Agency Asks Ban on Bus Depot," *New York Times* (April 2, 1959): 33; Bernard Stengren, "Terminal Invites 'All' Buses Here," *New York Times* (January 28, 1960): 33; "Bus Depot Grows as Riders Watch," *New York Times* (November 16, 1960): 43; "Outside Columns Support New Bus Terminal Decks," *Architectural Forum* 114 (February 1961): 89; Gregg MacGregor, "Bus Riders Await New Moving Stair," *New York Times* (March 20, 1961): 31; "Ramp Tests Due at Bus Terminal," *New York Times* (December 2, 1961): 25; Bernard Stengren, "Greyhound to Move to Port Bus Depot," *New York Times* (May 18, 1962): 1, 35; "Passenger Congestion Snarls Bus Terminal Flow," *New York Times* (June 29, 1963): 25.

81. "World's Busiest Bus Terminal Expands," *Engineering News-Record* 193 (May 15, 1975): 38; "New York's Bus Station Expands," *Architectural Record* 158 (August 1975): 41; Edward C. Burns, "Bus Terminal Expansion Is Pushed," *New York Times* (March 31, 1976): 45; "Major Bus Terminal Extension Rises on Crowded City Site," *Engineering News-Record* 198 (January 27, 1977): 16–17; Ralph Blumenthal, "At World's Busiest Bus Terminal, New Space and Old Ills," *New York Times* (November 17, 1977), B: 1, 22; Ari L. Goodman, "Extension at Bus Terminal Celebrated," *New York Times* (May 21, 1981), B: 3; William E. Geist, "Bus Fumes and Salsa," *New York Times* (September 3, 1982), B: 3.

82. Max H. Seigel, "Planners Approve Big Housing Project Near Times Sq.," *New York Times* (January 4, 1973): 41; "The Talk of the Town: High Risk," *New Yorker* 50 (April 1, 1974): 27–29; Glenn Fowler, "Builders Hope to Lure Richer Tenants to Project," *New York Times* (August 19, 1974): 27, 36; Paul Goldberger, "Manhattan Plaza: Quality Housing to Upgrade 42d St.," *New York Times* (August 19, 1974): 27; Joseph P. Fried, "Times Sq. Housing Project Poses a Problem for City," *New York Times* (May 29, 1975): 39; Suzanne Stephens, "The Last Gasp: New York City," *Progressive Architecture* 57 (March 1976): 61–63; "Unhousing the City," editorial, *New York Times* (June 6, 1976): 35; Paul Goldberger, "Performers May Get W. 42d St. Housing," *New York Times* (August 2, 1976): 28; White and Willensky, *AIA Guide* (1978), 144; Michael Winkleman, "The New Frontier: Housing for the Artist Industrialist," *New York Affairs* 4, no. 4 (1978): 49–57; Goldberger, *The City Observed*, 148; Tauranac, *Essential New York*, 245–46; Thomas E. Norton and Jerry E. Patterson, *Living It Up: A Guide to the Named Apartment Houses of New York* (New York: Atheneum, 1984), 221; Wolfe, *42nd Street: River to River*, unpaginated.

83. Richard Ravitch quoted in Goldberger, "Manhattan Plaza: Quality Housing to Upgrade 42d St. ": 27.

84. Richard Ravitch quoted in Fowler, "Builders Hope to Lure Richer Tenants to Project": 27.

85. Goldberger, "Manhattan Plaza: Quality Housing to Upgrade 42d St. ": 27.

86. David Todd quoted in Goldberger, "Manhattan Plaza: Quality Housing to Upgrade 42d St. ": 27.

87. Richard Ravitch quoted in Goldberger, "Manhattan Plaza: Quality Housing to Upgrade 42d St. ": 27.

88. Lynda Simmons quoted in Goldberger, "Performers May Get W. 42d St. Housing": 28.

89. Goldberger, *The City Observed*, 148.

FIFTY-THIRD STREET

1. For 825 Seventh Avenue, see Robert F. R. Ballard, *Directory of Manhattan Office Buildings* (New York: McGraw-Hill, 1978), 208–9. For 810 Seventh Avenue, see "7th Ave. Space Leased," *New York Times* (January 4, 1970), VIII: 2; Glenn Fowler, "Broadway Buildings Fill Slowly in Rent Lag," *New York Times* (December 20, 1970), VIII: 1, 3; Ballard, *Directory of Manhattan Office Buildings*, 199; David W. Dunlap, *On Broadway: A Journey Uptown Over Time* (New York: Rizzoli International Publications, 1990), 188.

2. For Goodwin and Stone's building, see Stern, Gilmartin and Mellins, *New York 1930*, 124–25, 136, 138–39, 141–45. For the Heckscher Building, see Stern, Gilmartin and Mellins, *New York 1930*, 588–90.

3. Illustrated in *Museum of Modern Art Bulletin* 13 (February 1946): 17; "Modern Art Plans to Build New Wing," *New York Times* (February 9, 1947): 24; "Modern Museum Starts Building Campaign," *Art News* 46 (March 1947): 8; "New Wing for Modern Museum," *Interiors* 106 (March 1947): 12, 14; "Announcements," *Architectural Forum* 86 (April 1947): 60; "New Museum Wing," *Architectural Record* 101 (April 1947): 10; "New Wing Planned for Museum," *Interiors* 106 (April 1947): 12.

4. "Building Postponement," *Museum of Modern Art Bulletin* 15 (fall 1947): 20.

5. Peter Blake, *Marcel Breuer: Architect and Designer* (New York: Architectural Record Books, in collaboration with Museum of Modern Art, 1949), 110–11; "The House in the Museum Garden," *Museum of Modern Art Bulletin* 17, no. 1 (1949): unpaginated; "Museum Builds 6-Room House as an Exhibit," *New York Herald Tribune* (January 12, 1949): 18; "The Talk of the Town: American Gift," *New Yorker* 25 (March 5, 1949): 26–27; Ann Pringle, "Breuer Plan for a Modern Home," *New York Herald Tribune* (April 12, 1949): 16; Frederick Gutheim, "Museum House Is Romantic, but Has Its Flaws," *New York Herald Tribune* (April 17, 1949), IV: 1, 4; "Officials Dispute Critical Report on Museum House," *New York Herald Tribune* (April 24, 1949): VI: 1–2; "Poor Butterfly," *Time* 53 (April 25, 1949): 59; "House for the Growing Family," *Architectural Forum* 96 (May 1949): 96–101; "Marcel Breuer's 'House in Museum Garden' Open to the Public," *Architectural Record* 105 (May 1949): 10; "The Modern Museum Builds and Acquires," *Art News* 48 (May 1949): 7; "House in Museum Garden," *Arts and Architecture* 66 (May 1949): 33–35; "Exhibitions: Working Model of the Present," *Interiors* 108 (May 1949): 14, 16; "A Modern Museum-Piece," *Architects Journal* 109 (June 2, 1949): 492, 499–52; "Breuer House Survey," *Architectural Record* 106 (December 1949): 156; Harry V. Anderson, "The Years in Retrospect: 1900–1950," *Interior Design* 21 (January 1950): 26–35; Lewis Mumford, "The Sky Line: Not for Internal Use," *New Yorker* 26 (August 26, 1950): 58–61; Peter Blake, ed., *Marcel Breuer: Sun and Shadow* (New York: Dodd, Mead, 1955), 141–42; Giulio Carlo Argan, *Marcel Breuer: Disegno Industriale e Architettura* (Milan: Gorlich, 1957), 90; Ian McCallum, *Architecture USA* (London: Architectural Press, 1959), 98–99; *Marcel Breuer: Buildings and Projects 1921–1961*, with an intro. by Cranston Jones (London: Thames and Hudson, 1962), 214–15; Peter Blake, *No Place Like Utopia* (New York: Alfred A. Knopf, 1993), 138–39.

6. "House in Museum Garden": 33–35.

7. For Roger Bullard and Clifford Wendehack's house, see Stern, Gilmartin and Mellins, *New York 1930*, 348, 354. For William Van Alen's house, see Stern, Gilmartin and Mellins, *New York 1930*, 354. For Edward Durell Stone's house, see Stern, Gilmartin and Mellins, *New York 1930*, 476–77.

8. Gutheim, "Museum House Is Romantic, but Has Its Flaws": 1.

9. Marcel Breuer quoted in "The Talk of the Town: American Gift": 26–27.

10. Gutheim, "Museum House Is Romantic, but Has Its Flaws": 1, 4.

11. Quoted in "Officials Dispute Critical Report on Museum House": 2.

12. "Second House in the Garden," *Interiors* 109 (April 1950): 12; "Merchant and Mentor," *Interiors* 109 (May 1950): 14; "Newsletter," *Progressive Architecture* 31 (May 1950): 1–2; "Our House with a View—To the Future," *Woman's Home Companion* 77 (June 1950): 65–71; "Designed for Subdivisions," *Architectural Record* 108 (July 1950): 91–95; Eliot Noyes, "The Ain House: Agreeable as a Design but Pointless as a Project," *Consumer Reports* 15 (July 1950): 308–9; Mumford, "The Sky Line: Not for Internal Use": 58–61; David Gebhard, Harriette Von Breton and Lauren Weiss, *The Architecture of Gregory Ain: The Play between the Rational and High Art*, exhibition catalogue (Santa Barbara, Calif.: University of California at Santa Barbara, 1980), 9, 18–19, 22, 24, 31, 90–91.

13. Noyes, "The Ain House: Agreeable as a Design but Pointless as a Project": 308.

14. Mumford, "The Sky Line: Not for Internal Use": 61.

15. "Museum to Begin Work on Addition," *New York Herald Tribune* (July 10, 1950): 8; "Museum to Show Glass-Steel Face," *New York Times* (July 11, 1950): 22; "The Record Reports," *Architectural Record* 108 (August 1950): 12; "Up-to-Date Annex for Modern Museum," *Interiors* 110 (August 1950): 10; "Museum Gets $392,000," *New York Times* (February 10, 1952): 15; "Modern Art Annex Open to Amateurs," *New York Times* (September 25, 1952): 27; "Three Approaches to Architecture: 2. Modern Classicism," *Architectural Forum* 102 (May 1955): 146–49; Ada Louise Huxtable, *Four Walking Tours of Modern Architecture in New York City* (New York: Museum of Modern Art and Municipal Art Society of New York, 1961), 38–39; Henry-Russell Hitchcock, "The Current Work of Philip Johnson," *Zodiac* 8 (1961): 64–81; John M. Jacobus, Jr., *Philip Johnson* (New York: George Braziller, 1962), 41, fig. 67; White and Willensky, *AIA Guide* (1967), 135–36; Paul Goldberger, *The City Observed: New York* (New York: Random House, 1979), 173–74; John Tauranac, *Essential New York* (New York: Holt, Rinehart and Winston, 1979), 189–90; Carol Herselle Krinsky, "Architecture in New York City," in Leonard Wallock, ed., *New York: Culture Capital of the World, 1940–1965* (New York: Rizzoli International Publications, 1988), 112.

16. For discussions of Johnson's early career, see William Marlin, "Philip Johnson," *Architectural Forum* 138 (January–February 1973): 26–31; Calvin Tomkins, "Forms Under Light," *New Yorker* 53 (May 23, 1977): 48–50.

17. Deborah Allen, "Before the Twig Is Bent," *Interiors* 110 (October 1950): 100–106; Victor D'Amico, "Creative Art," *Museum of Modern Art Bulletin* 19, no. 1 (1952): 3–20.

18. Hitchcock, "The Current Work of Philip Johnson": 67.

19. "Three Approaches to Architecture: 2. Modern Classicism": 146–49.

20. "The Year's Work: The Projects," *Interiors* 112 (August 1952): 68–69.

21. "From Lounge to Lunches," *Interiors* 111 (April 1952): 94–95; "Interior Design Products: Members Penthouse at the Museum of Modern Art," *Progressive Architecture* 33 (June 1952): 125; "Public Spaces," *Interiors* 112 (February 1953): 67. For the original lounge, see Stern, Gilmartin and Mellins, *New York 1930*, 144.

22. Alfred M. Frankfurter, "Vernissage: Whitney-Modern," *Art News* 48 (June 1949): 15. Also see Sanka Knox, "Whitney to Leave Village," *New York Times* (May 31, 1949): 25; "A Mid-Town Center of Art," editorial, *New York Times* (June 1, 1949): 30; Aline B. Louchheim, "Midtown Museum Plan Progressive," *New York Times* (June 5, 1949), II: 6; "In a Museum Garden," *Interiors* 108 (July 1949): 20.

23. Lloyd Goodrich, "The Whitney's Battle for U. S. Art," *Art News* 53 (November 1954): 38–40, 70–73; Jonathan Marshall, "The Whitney's New Home," *Art Digest* 29 (November 1, 1954): 9; "The Talk of the Town: Urban Life," *New Yorker* 30 (November 6, 1954): 29–31; Robert M. Coates, "The Art Galleries: Museums, Stationary and in Transit," *New Yorker* 30 (November 6, 1954): 147–50; "Midtown Whitney Museum," *Interiors* 114 (December 1954): 12; "New Museums Coast to Coast," *Architectural Record* 117 (February 1955): 10; Lewis Mumford, "The Sky Line: Museum or Kaleidoscope?" *New Yorker* 31 (October 31, 1955): 166, 168, 170–76.

24. Mumford, "The Sky Line: Museum or Kaleidoscope?": 171, 173–74.

25. Coates, "The Art Galleries: Museums, Stationary and in Transit": 150.

26. Alice [*sic*] B. Louchheim, "Fine Trees Doomed in Museum Garden," *New York Times* (June 11, 1952): 31; Aline B. Louchheim, "Projects for Art," *New York Times* (June 15, 1952), VI: 8; "Reconstruction," *Interiors* 111 (July 1952): 14; "A Transformed Sculpture Garden to Open at Modern Art Museum," *New York Times* (April 18, 1953): 1; "The Talk of the Town: Outdoor Room," *New Yorker* 29 (April 25, 1953): 24–25; "Modern

Museum Opens Its Sculpture Garden," *New York Herald Tribune* (April 29, 1953): 21; "Museum Dedicates Sculpture Garden," *New York Times* (April 29, 1953): 14; "Museum Garden," editorial, *New York Times* (April 30, 1953): 30; "Museum Garden Is an Outdoor Living Room for Sculpture Display," *Architectural Forum* 99 (July 1953): 136–37; "Oasis in Manhattan," *Time* 62 (August 31, 1953): 66; "New Restaurant in Garden of Modern Art Museum to Open Tomorrow," *New York Times* (April 27, 1954): 26; Olga Gueft, "Cafeteria on the Rim of the Museum Garden," *Interiors* 113 (July 1954): 68–69; Lewis Mumford, "The Sky Line: Windows and Gardens," *New Yorker* 30 (October 2, 1954): 121–24, 127–29; "Three Approaches to Architecture: 2. Modern Classicism": 146–49; Olga Gueft, "The Indispensable Splurge," editorial, *Interiors* 115 (June 1956): 91; Victor Gruen and Larry Smith, *Shopping Towns USA* (New York: Van Nostrand Reinhold, 1960), 151; Jacobus, *Philip Johnson*, 27–28, plates 39–42; *Philip Johnson: Architecture 1949–1965*, with an intro. by Henry-Russell Hitchcock (New York: Holt, Rinehart and Winston, 1966), 15–16, 96–97; White and Willensky, *AIA Guide* (1967), 135–36; William H. Jordy, *American Buildings and Their Architects: The Impact of European Modernism in the Mid-Twentieth Century*, vol. 4 (Garden City, N.Y.: Doubleday & Co., 1972), 31–34; Charles Noble, *Philip Johnson* (New York: Simon & Schuster, 1972), 13, 123, plates 55–58; Goldberger, *The City Observed*, 173–74; Sam Hunter, "Introduction," in *The Museum of Modern Art, New York: The History and the Collection* (New York: Harry N. Abrams, in association with Museum of Modern Art, 1984), 20, 25–26; Krinsky, "Architecture in New York City," in Wallock, ed., *New York: Culture Capital of the World, 1940–1965*, 112–13.

27. Philip Johnson quoted in "The Talk of the Town: Outdoor Room": 24–25.

28. Philip Johnson quoted in "The Talk of the Town: Outdoor Room": 24–25.

29. Mumford, "The Sky Line: Windows and Gardens": 128–29.

30. "Museum to Get House of Japan," *New York Times* (January 29, 1954): 24; "Museum 'Crowns' Japanese House," *New York Times* (April 23, 1954): 20; "The Talk of the Town: Pine Breeze," *New Yorker* 30 (June 19, 1954): 20–21; "Japanese House," *Interior Design* 25 (July 1954): 57, 82, 84–85; "House with a Spirit," *Newsweek* 44 (July 5, 1954): 50; "Japanese Hit," *Life* 37 (August 23, 1954): 71–72, 74; Ada Louise Huxtable, "Japanese House," *Art Digest* 28 (September 1954): 14–15; Mumford, "The Sky Line: Windows and Gardens": 121–24, 127–29; "News Bulletins," *Progressive Architecture* 37 (July 1956): 74; "The Talk of the Town: Something Old," *New Yorker* 32 (December 15, 1956): 28–29; Hunter, "Introduction," in *The Museum of Modern Art, New York: The History and the Collection*, 28–29.

31. Mumford, "The Sky Line: Windows and Gardens": 123–24.

32. Peter Kihss, "Fire in Modern Museum; Most Art Safe," *New York Times* (April 16, 1958): 1, 30; Sanka Knox, "Violations Listed in Fire at Museum," *New York Times* (April 17, 1958): 33; "Museum Fire Lessons," editorial, *New York Times* (April 17, 1958): 30; Howard Devree, "Crisis Averted," *New York Times* (April 20, 1958), II: 11; "Light from a Fire," editorial, *New York Times* (April 22, 1958): 32; Edith Hoffmann, "New York," *Burlington Magazine* 100 (June 1958): 222; "Modern Art Museum Puts Up Glass Facade," *New York Times* (September 5, 1958): 18; Sanka Knox, "Modern Museum to Reopen Oct. 8," *New York Times* (September 29, 1958): 29; "The Art that Science Forgot," *Architectural Forum* 112 (January 1960): 133–37; Hunter, "Introduction," in *The Museum of Modern Art, New York: The History and the Collection*, 31.

33. "Light from a Fire": 32.

34. Sanka Knox, "Modern Museum Plans New Wing," *New York Times* (November 17, 1959): 1, 28; "N. Y. 's Museum of Modern Art Plans New Wing," *Architectural Forum* 111 (December 1959): 7; "Buildings in the News," *Architectural Record* 126 (December 1959): 13; Alfred Frankfurter, "Bigger and Better," editorial, *Art News* 58 (December 1959): 25; "Lebensraum for the Modern Museum," *Interiors* 119 (December 1959): 16; "Museum of Modern Art Announces Spacious New Wing," *Progressive Architecture* 40 (December 1959): 74; Ada Louise Huxtable, "What Should a Museum Be?" *New York Times* (May 8, 1960), VI: 42–43, 47.

35. "Wing to Open in '64 at Modern Museum," *New York Times* (February 7, 1961): 31; *The Museum of Modern Art Builds* (New York: Museum of Modern Art, 1962); "New Gallery for MOMA," *Interiors* 121 (August 1962): 8; Sanka Knox, "Museum Displays Expansion Plans," *New York Times* (October 2, 1962): 36; "Modern Museum Builds," *Architectural Forum* 117 (November 1962): 16; "New York's Museum of Modern Art Expands," *Architectural Record* 132 (November 1962): 14; "Museum of Modern Art Grows," *Interiors* 122 (November 1962): 12; "Ground Is Broken for Museum of Modern Art Addition," *Progressive Architecture* 43 (November 1962): 61; John Molleson, "Modern Art Museum—A $7 Million Expansion," *New York Herald Tribune* (November 26, 1962): 1; Mildred F. Schmertz, "Architectural Drawing for Printing by Halftone," *Architectural Record* 133 (June 1963): cover, 133–40; "Expansion and Remodelling Plans for Museum of Modern Art," *Architectural Record* 134 (September 1963): 29; "Museum of Modern Art Additions Proceed," *Progressive Architecture* 44 (September 1963): 68; Frank Getlein, "Modern on the Move," *New Republic* 150 (January 18, 1964): 26, 28–29; "Architectural Details: 3. Philip Johnson," *Architectural Record* 135 (April 1964): 137, 150–51; John Canaday, "No Place Like It . . . ," *New York Times* (May 31, 1964), II: 15; Ada Louise Huxtable, " . . . And It's Big and Beautiful," *New York Times* (May 31, 1964), II: 15; "Thinking of Today . . . and Eternal Things," *Newsweek* 63 (June 1, 1964): 48–52; "The More Modern Modern," *Time* 83 (June 5, 1964): 95; Stuart Preston, "Letter from New York: Modern Art Fiesta in a Changing World," *Apollo* 80 (July 1964): 69–70; "Die Glückliche Insel zur vernissage des Museum of Modern Art, New York," *Das Kunstwerk* 18 (July 1964): 66–70; "Modern," *Interiors* 123 (July 1964): 92–95; Peter T. White, "The World in New York City," *National Geographic* 126 (July 1964): 98; "Museum of Modern Art: A Study in Elegance by Johnson," *Progressive Architecture* 45 (July 1964): 63, 65–66; "New Galleries for Architecture and Design," *Architectural Record* 136 (August 1964): 49; Philip Johnson, "Whence and Whither: The Processional Element in Architecture," *Perspecta* 9/10 (1965): 167–78, reprinted in Peter Eisenman and Robert A. M. Stern, eds., *Philip Johnson: Writings* (New York: Oxford University Press, 1979), 150–55; Ralph Howe Lewis, "Museums and Galleries," *Britannica Book of the Year* (Chicago: Encyclopaedia Britannica, 1965): 571; C. Ray Smith, "Johnson's Interior Details: The Right Thing in the Right Place," *Progressive Architecture* 46 (March 1965): 196–99; René d'Harnoncourt, "The Museum of the Future," *Art in America* 53 (June 1965): 25–26; "Erweiterungsbau des Museum of Modern Art in New York," *Werk* 52 (June 1965): 234; "Tipologia del Museo," *Casabella* 298 (October 1965): 74–79; John Jacobus, *Twentieth-Century Architecture: The Middle Years 1940–65* (New York: Frederick A. Praeger, 1966), 158; *Philip Johnson: Architecture 1949–1965*, 15–16, 96–98; "Lack of Dialogue," *Architectural Forum* 124 (May 1966): 91; "Awards and Competitions," *Interiors* 125 (June 1966): 18; White and Willensky, *AIA Guide* (1967), 135–36; "MOMA's New International Study Center Turns Dead Storage into Live," *Interiors* 127 (July 1967): 6; C. Ray Smith, "Camp Mies," *Progressive Architecture* 48 (December 1967): 128–29; Noble, *Philip Johnson*, 123, plates 55, 58; C. Ray Smith, *Supermannerism: New Attitudes in Post-Modern Architecture* (New York: E. P. Dutton, 1977), 70–71; Peter Eisenman, "Introduction," in Eisenman and Stern, eds., *Philip Johnson: Writings*, 19–20; Goldberger, *The City Observed*, 173–74; Tauranac, *Essential New York*, 189–90; Krinsky, "Architecture in New York City," in Wallock, ed., *New York: Culture Capital of the World, 1940–1965*, 112.

36. "News," *Interiors* 132 (June 1973): 20; Janet Nairn, "Renovation Was Solution to Cost and Space Problems," *Architectural Record* 159 (April 1976): 135; White and Willensky, *AIA Guide* (1978), 166; White and Willensky, *AIA Guide* (1988), 873.

37. Huxtable, " . . . And It's Big and Beautiful": 15.

38. Huxtable, " . . . And It's Big and Beautiful": 15.

39. Smith, "Camp Mies": 128.

40. Grace Glueck, "Modern Museum May Add Condominium," *New York Times* (February 10, 1976): 1, 4; "The 'Vasari' Diary. 6 rms, MOMA vw . . . ," *Art News* 75 (April 1976): 20, 22.

41. Abraham D. Beame quoted in "The 'Vasari' Diary. 6 rms, MOMA vw . . . ": 20.

42. Paul Goldberger, "Art People," *New York Times* (November 19, 1976), II: 19.

43. Mitzi Solomon Cunliffe, "Sculpture for Architecture," *Progressive Architecture* 31 (December 1950): 63–65; "Construction Begins on Donnell Library, NYPL," *Library Journal* 78 (December 15, 1953): 2175–77; Anna L. Glantz, "New York's Donnell Building," *Library Journal* 80 (December 1, 1955): 2686–89; "New Branch Library Opens," *New York Times* (December 13, 1955): 26; "A Handsome New Library," editorial, *New York Times* (December 14, 1955): 38; "Donnell Branch Library," *Interiors* 115 (February 1956): 12; Lewis Mumford, "The Sky Line: The Gift Horse's Mouth," *New Yorker* 32 (September 22, 1956): 137–43; White and Willensky, *AIA Guide* (1967), 167.

44. Stern, Gilmartin and Mellins, *New York 1930*, 660.

45. Quoted in Glantz, "New York's Donnell Building": 2688.

46. "Donnell Branch Library": 12.

47. Mumford, "The Sky Line: The Gift Horse's Mouth": 137–38, 142–43.

48. Mumford, "The Sky Line: The Gift Horse's Mouth": 140.

49. "New York's Midtown Art Center," *Interiors* 115 (February 1956): 12; Herwin Schaefer, "The Museum of Contemporary Crafts," *Craft Horizons* 16 (March 1956): 10–12; "The American Craftsmen's Council: A Look at the Future," *Craft Horizons* 16 (March 1956): 12–13; Thomas S. Tibbs, "Craftsmen in a Changing World," *Craft Horizons* 16 (September–October 1956): 40–41; "A Cousin Arrives," *Time* 68 (October 8, 1956): 58; "The Talk of the Town: Riding the Wave," *New Yorker* 32 (November 10, 1956): 44–46; "Craft Museum Opens," *Craft Horizons* 16 (December 1956): 40–41; "Intimate New Museum: Contemporary Crafts," *Interiors* 116 (December 1956): 82–87; Lucy James, "Dual Role for Public Buildings," letter to the editor, *Interiors* 116 (January 1957): 8; Louise Sloane, "Galleries," *Progressive Architecture* 38 (February 1957): 173–75; Ruth Davidson, "News and Views from New York," *Apollo* 65 (April 1957): 153–54; "The Museum of Contemporary Crafts," *Craft Horizons* 20 (January 1960): 37–38; White and Willensky, *AIA Guide* (1967), 135.

50. "Intimate New Museum: Contemporary Crafts": 83.

51. "Brownstone Becomes New Showroom for Handicrafts," *Architectural Forum* 114 (February 1961): 87; "Crafts Store," *Progressive Architecture* 42 (February 1961): 154–57; White and Willensky, *AIA Guide* (1967), 135.

52. Sanka Knox, "Exhibition of American Folk Art Opens on Friday," *New York Times* (September 29, 1962): 25; "Museum of Early Folk Art Finds Temporary Quarters," *New York Times* (October 5, 1962): 29; Stuart Preston, "Art: Another Museum," *New York Times* (September 27, 1963): 26; Sanka Knox, "Folk Art Museum Starts Fund Drive for Larger Home," *New York Times* (June 13, 1970): 27; David L. Shirey, "Folk Art Museum Offers Reminders of City's Past," *New York Times* (December 6, 1970): 42; Grace Glueck, "Ailing Folk Art Museum Is Under Inquiry by State," *New York Times* (April 30, 1974): 43, 46; "Bruce Johnson, 27, Dead; Led Museum of Folk Art," *New York Times* (June 10, 1976): 40.

53. "Bruce Johnson, 27, Dead; Led Museum of Folk Art": 40.

54. "Four Floors of High-Fashion Selling," *Architectural Record* 103 (April 1948): 128–31; "The Customers Have Rosy Cheeks," *Interiors* 107 (June 1948): 88–90; Morris Ketchum, Jr., *Shops & Stores*, rev. ed. (New York: Reinhold Publishing Corp., 1957), 88.

55. For Paul Chalfin's Lenthéric shop of 1929, see Stern, Gilmartin and Mellins, *New York 1930*, 296–98.

56. "Girard's Air Conditioned Bazaar," *Interiors* 120 (July 1961): 78–85; "Shop Designed Like a Display Case," *Architectural Record* 131 (May 1962): 159–60.

57. "Shop Designed Like a Display Case": 159.

58. "Child's Play," *Industrial Design* 17 (April 1970): 38–39; "Designing for the Real Customer," *Progressive Architecture* 51 (November 1970): 74–78; Smith, *Supermannerism*, 321–22; White and Willensky, *AIA Guide* (1988), 873.

59. Ralph Blumenthal, "Paley Is Donating a Vest-Pocket Park to the City on Stork Club Site," *New York Times* (February 2, 1966): 37, 42; Ada Louise Huxtable, "Experiment in Parks," *New York Times* (February 2, 1966): 37, 42; "Waistcoat Parks," *Time* 87 (February 11, 1966): 57; "Paley's Vest Pocket," *Architectural Forum* 124 (March 1966): 27; "Big Little Memorial," *Journal of the American Institute of Architects* 45 (March 1966): 82; "Look What the Stork Left," *Progressive Architecture* 47 (March 1966): 51; "The Samuel Paley Plaza," *Empire State Architect* 26 (March–April 1966): 16–17; Robert E. Koehler, "Mr. Paley's Park," *Architectural Forum* 127 (July–August 1967): 88; William A. H. Burnie, "Oasis on 53rd Street," *Reader's Digest* 94 (January 1969): 173–74; Mitzi Cunliffe, "Townscape: Pocket Parks," *Royal Town Planning Institute Journal* 58 (November 1972): 403–7; White and Willensky, *AIA Guide* (1978), 165; Goldberger, *The City Observed*, 164–65; William S. Paley, *As It Happened: A Memoir* (Garden City, N.Y.: Doubleday & Co., 1979), 363–64; Tauranac, *Essential New York*, 224–25; Stanley Abercrombie, "Evaluation: A Prototype Left Unreplicated," *Architecture* 74 (December 1985): 54–55; Lewis J. Paper, *Empire: William S. Paley and the Making of CBS* (New York: St. Martin's Press, 1987), 213–14, unnumbered plate; William H. Whyte, *City: Rediscovering the Center* (New York: Doubleday, 1988), 131, 159, 257; Sally Bedell Smith, *In All His Glory: The Life of William S. Paley* (New York: Simon & Schuster, 1990), 460–61.

60. Paley, *As It Happened: A Memoir*, 363.

61. Tauranac, *Essential New York*, 224.

62. Robert L. Zion, "Plea for 'Parklets,'" letter to the editor, *Architectural Forum* 116 (February 1962): 19. Also see Jane Jacobs, "Why Parks Live or Die," *Architectural Forum* 115 (October 1961): 144–45, 196.

63. Robert Zion and Harold Breen, *New Parks for New York*, exhibition catalogue (New York: Architectural League of New York and Park Association, 1963). Also see Robert L. Zion, "Midtown Parks for Busy Cities," *Journal of the American Institute of Architects* 40 (December 1963): 35–42.
64. Zion, "Midtown Parks for Busy Cities": 38–41.
65. "Promising Progress for Public Parks," *Progressive Architecture* 45 (December 1964): 54–55.
66. "5 Rockefeller Brothers Gather as Sister Opens a Vest-Pocket Park," *New York Times* (October 15, 1971): 24; "How Green Is Our Acre," *New York* 4 (October 25, 1971): 70; White and Willensky, *AIA Guide* (1978), 160.
67. Ballard, *Directory of Manhattan Office Buildings*, 146; White and Willensky, *AIA Guide* (1978), 165.
68. Laurie Johnston, "Church Moves in a Procession Up Park," *New York Times* (March 5, 1973): 33; "News of the Realty Trade: Assemblage Complete," *New York Times* (July 8, 1973), VIII: 6; "City Bank to Erect a 54-Story Tower at East 53d Street," *New York Times* (July 22, 1973): 1, 38; "Building Will Rise on Four 112-Ft-High Columns," *Engineering News-Record* 191 (August 2, 1973): 13; "Office, Shopping Complex for New York," *Architectural Record* 154 (September 1973): 38; "A Wedge in the Skyline," *Architecture Plus* 1 (September 1973): 16; "New York City: One for the East Side," *Progressive Architecture* 54 (September 1973): 32; "Manhattan's Fifth Tallest Building Is Designed for Energy Conservation," *Journal of the American Institute of Architects* 60 (October 1973): 11, 61; "The Many Sides of Multipurpose," *New York* 7 (December 31, 1973): 64; Ada Louise Huxtable, "The New Urban Image? Look Down, Not Up," *New York Times* (January 6, 1974), II: 21; Peter Hellman, "How They Assembled the Most Expensive Block in New York's History," *New York* 7 (February 25, 1974): 30–37; Carter B. Horsley, "An Office Tower on Columns Designed for Church Facility," *New York Times* (April 8, 1974): 69; "St. Peter's Blooms in the City," *Progressive Architecture* 55 (August 1974): 21; Jane Holtz Kay, "Architecture," *Nation* 219 (August 3, 1974): 93–94; "Alive in '75," *Buildings* 69 (January 1975): 41; "MIT Team Will Lead Major Solar Study," *Architectural Record* 157 (March 1975): 35; illustrated in *Journal of the American Institute of Architects* 63 (March 1975): 8; Hugh Stubbins, *Architecture: The Design Experience* (New York: John Wiley & Sons, 1976), 18–27, 170–73; "Citiscraper," *New York Times* (March 14, 1976), III: 15; Fred Ferretti, "Lexington Avenue Mall Being Planned as a U. N. of Food," *New York Times* (June 4, 1976), II: 1; "At New York's Citicorp Center, a Structure of Masterly Invention Underlies the Urban Face of a Skyscraper in the Grand Manner," *Architectural Record* 159 (mid-August 1976): 66–71; Carter B. Horsley, "A New Wrinkle on the City's Skyline," *New York Times* (September 19, 1976), VIII: 1, 8; "Executives and Workmen Celebrate Topping Out of the Citicorp Center," *New York Times* (October 7, 1976): 21; Grace Glueck, "White on White: Louise Nevelson's 'Gift to the Universe,'" *New York Times* (October 22, 1976), B: 1; "Louise Nevelson Designs a Chapel for a New York Church," *Architectural Record* 160 (November 1976): 35; Charles Kaiser, "Citibank Buying Buildings to Keep Sex Shops Away from Its Offices," *New York Times* (December 14, 1976): 1, 32; "Le pasteur, le sculpteur et la rénovation urbaine," *Connaissance des Arts* 302 (April 1977): 7–8; Robert Mehlman, "Elevating the Urban Environment," *Industrial Design* 24 (May–June 1977): 42–48; "Cost Cools Citibank's Ardor for Solar Energy Project," *New York Times* (May 9, 1977): 35; Ada Louise Huxtable, "An Acrobatic Act of Architecture," *New York Times* (June 5, 1977), II: 27, 33; "Realty News: Citicorp Tower 96 Percent Rented," *New York Times* (August 21, 1977), VIII: 8; Suzanne Stephens, "The Architectural Artifact," *New York* 10 (September 19, 1977): 46–47; Nadine Brozan, "The Citicorp Center: A Complex Complex," *New York Times* (October 4, 1977): 42; Lisa Hammel, "Conran, the First Kid on Citicorp's Block, Celebrates Opening of His First U.S. Store," *New York Times* (October 4, 1977): 42; Paul Goldberger, "Citicorp's Center Reflects Synthesis of Architecture," *New York Times* (October 12, 1977), B: 1, 4; "Citicorp Center Is Dedicated," *New York Times* (October 13, 1977), B: 2; George Vecsey, "Citicorp Towers over St. Peter's but the Church Is Not in Shadow," *New York Times* (October 16, 1977): 52; Anthony J. Parisi, "Tower Uses Energy Efficiently," *New York Times* (October 29, 1977): 29, 33; "St. Peter's Church," *New York Times* (December 1, 1977), B: 3; Paul Goldberger, "No Taint of Materialism in Church Design at Bank Center," *New York Times* (December 5, 1977): 49; Hilton Kramer, "Nevelsons Enhance Chapel," *New York Times* (December 14, 1977), C: 24; August Heckscher, "Design Notebook: The New Market Elicits a Plea to Revive an Old One," *New York Times* (December 22, 1977), C: 10; Ballard, *Directory of Manhattan Office Buildings*, 153; White and Willensky, *AIA Guide* (1978), 152; "Top of Citicorp Center Poses an Icy Problem," *New York Times* (January 22, 1978): 37; Ada Louise Huxtable, "The Sabotaging of Public Space," *New York Times* (January 26, 1978), C: 1, 8; Rita Reif, "Design Notebook: Feeling at Home in St. Peter's," *New York Times* (February 23, 1978), C: 8; Robert Mehlman, "Skyscraper for People: New York's Citicorp," *Contract Interiors* 137 (May 1978): cover, 126–39; David Pearce, "Shining Example on 3rd Avenue," *Building* 234 (May 5, 1978): 64–67; Mildred F. Schmertz, "Citicorp Center: If You Don't Like Its Crown Look at Its Base," *Architectural Record* 163 (June 1978): 107–16; Carter B. Horsley, "Pylons as a Way to Cut Clutter," *New York Times* (June 18, 1978), VIII: 7; Suzanne Stephens, "At the Core of the Apple," *Progressive Architecture* 59 (December 1978): 54–59; Goldberger, *The City Observed*, 158–60; Tauranac, *Essential New York*, 246–48; "Citicorp Center," *Process Architecture* 10 (1979): 24–41; "Hugh Stubbins and Associates: Citicorp Center," *A + U* (March 1979): 69–73; "A Tower with a Distinctive Top and Base," *Journal of the American Institute of Architects* 68 (mid-May 1979): 172–74; Michael deCourcy Hinds, "The Atrium Comeback Transforms Air Shafts," *New York Times* (October 7, 1979), VIII: 1, 8; Paul Goldberger, *The Skyscraper* (New York: Alfred A. Knopf, 1981), 136–37, 163; Charles K. Hoyt, "The Corporation as a Client," in Lisa Taylor, ed., *Cities* (New York: Rizzoli International Publications, 1982), 89–91; Ada Louise Huxtable, *The Tall Building Artistically Reconsidered: The Search for a Skyscraper Style* (New York: Pantheon Books, 1982), 55; Jean Lipman, *Nevelson's World* (New York: Hudson Hills Press, in association with Whitney Museum of American Art, 1983), 115, 130–33; Andrew Alpern and Seymour Durst, *Holdouts!* (New York: McGraw-Hill, 1984), 112–17; Donald Martin Reynolds, *The Architecture of New York City* (New York: Macmillan, 1984), 156; Diane M. Ludman, *Hugh Stubbins and His Associates: The First Fifty Years*, exhibition catalogue (Cambridge, Mass.: Stubbins Associates and Harvard Graduate School of Design, 1986), 85–93; Steven Ruttenbaum, *Mansions in the Clouds: The Skyscraper Palazzi of Emery Roth* (New York: Balsam Press, 1986), 206–7; Robert A. M. Stern with Thomas Mellins and Raymond Gastil, *Pride of Place: Building the American Dream* (Boston: Houghton Mifflin; New York: American Heritage, 1986), 292–93; White and Willensky, *AIA Guide* (1988), 249; Germano Celant et al., *Design: Vignelli* (New York: Rizzoli International Publications, 1990), 192–95.
69. Ballard, *Directory of Manhattan Office Buildings*, 181.
70. Alpern and Durst, *Holdouts!*, 116.
71. Hugh Stubbins quoted in Schmertz, "Citicorp Center: If You Don't Like Its Crown Look at Its Base": 114.
72. For the Cities Service Building, see Stern, Gilmartin and Mellins, *New York 1930*, 600–603.
73. Stubbins, *Architecture: The Design Experience*, 19.
74. For Skidmore, Owings & Merrill's John Hancock Center, see Carl W. Condit, *Chicago, 1930–70: Building, Planning, and Urban Technology* (Chicago and London: University of Chicago Press, 1974), 102–10, 112.
75. "At New York's Citicorp Center, a Structure of Masterly Invention Underlies the Urban Face of a Skyscraper in the Grand Manner": 70.
76. Alfred E. Driscoll quoted in Ferretti, "Lexington Avenue Mall Being Planned as a U.N. of Food": 1.
77. Huxtable, "The New Urban Image? Look Down, Not Up": 21.
78. Horsley, "A New Wrinkle on the City's Skyline": 1.
79. Ronnie Adams quoted in "Executives and Workmen Celebrate Topping Out of the Citicorp Center": 21.
80. Huxtable, "An Acrobatic Act of Architecture": 27.
81. Huxtable, "An Acrobatic Act of Architecture": 27, 33.
82. Goldberger, "Citicorp's Center Reflects Synthesis of Architecture": 1, 4.
83. Stephens, "The Architectural Artifact": 46.
84. Heckscher, "Design Notebook: The New Market Elicits a Plea to Revive an Old One": 10.
85. Stephens, "The Architectural Artifact": 46.
86. Stephens, "At the Core of the Apple": 54–55, 58.
87. Lipman, *Nevelson's World*, 115.
88. Louise Nevelson quoted in Lipman, *Nevelson's World*, 130, 132.
89. Kramer, "Nevelsons Enhance Chapel": 24.
90. Goldberger, "No Taint of Materialism in Church Design at Bank Center": 49.

PLAZA DISTRICT

1. "Plaza Area Busy in Postwar Boom," *New York Times* (January 9, 1966), VIII: 1, 4; "Plaza District—World's Most Expensive Real Estate," *Real Estate Record and Guide* 197 (January 29, 1966): 2–3.
2. "Theater Planned for 58th Street," *New York Times* (May 30, 1948), VIII: 1; "New Paris Theater Ready to Open," *New York Times* (September 5, 1948), II: 3; "Paris Theater Opens," *New York Times* (September 14, 1948): 34; "Cinema in New York," *Architectural Forum* 90 (January 1949): 94–96; "City Cinema," *Interiors* 108 (March 1949): 100–103; White and Willensky, *AIA Guide* (1967), 156; Robert F. R. Ballard, *Directory of Manhattan Office Buildings* (New York: McGraw-Hill, 1978), 183.
3. Quoted in "New Paris Theater Ready to Open": 3.
4. "Blind Group Plans $1,000,000 Project," *New York Times* (August 2, 1949): 22; "New Building for Blind," *New York Times* (January 22, 1950), VIII: 2; "The New Lighthouse," editorial, *New York Times* (June 15, 1950): 30; "Model 'Lighthouse' Started for Blind," *New York Times* (June 16, 1950): 50; "Hoover Hails Work of New Lighthouse," *New York Times* (April 26, 1951): 31; "The Lighthouse," editorial, *New York Times* (April 27, 1951): 22; "'Lighthouse' for the Blind," *Progressive Architecture* 34 (April 1953): 92–94.
5. "Society for Blind Plans New Home," *New York Times* (June 20, 1962): 20; "Expanded Lighthouse in New York," *Progressive Architecture* 43 (September 1962): 76, 78; White and Willensky, *AIA Guide* (1967), 163.
6. White and Willensky, *AIA Guide* (1967), 163.
7. "News of Realty: Building Planned," *New York Times* (January 4, 1967): 68; "News of Realty: Publisher Moves," *New York Times* (October 3, 1968): 77; "3-Ton Revolving Bronze Set in Place," *New York Times* (June 25, 1969): 41; "Huge Monolithic Sculpture Is Erected at East Side Building," *Real Estate Record and Guide* 204 (August 9, 1969): 4; Ballard, *Directory of Manhattan Office Buildings*, 146; White and Willensky, *AIA Guide* (1978), 219.
8. John A. Bradley, "Executive Center for Madison Avenue," *New York Times* (January 22, 1956), VIII: 1, 4; "Black Granite and Stainless Steel Offices for Financing Firm," *Architectural Forum* 104 (February 1956): 9; "Polished Black Granite," *Architectural Record* 119 (March 1956): 11; "News Bulletins," *Progressive Architecture* 37 (March 1956): 94; Jane Jacobs, "New York's Office Boom," *Architectural Forum* 106 (March 1957): 104–13; "Two Notable New Office Buildings for Manhattan: 1. A Squat Headquarters for CIT," *Architectural Forum* 108 (January 1958): 91–93; "News Bulletins," *Progressive Architecture* 39 (January 1958): 74; illustrated in *Architectural Record* 123 (February 1958): 11; Lois Wagner Green, "C.I.T. Financial Corporation: Humanistic Solution on a Grand Scale," *Interiors* 118 (October 1958): 122–39; Ada Louise Huxtable, *Four Walking Tours of Modern Architecture in New York City* (New York: Museum of Modern Art and Municipal Art Society of New York, 1961), 64–65; White and Willensky, *AIA Guide* (1967), 157; Ada Louise Huxtable, "Elegance Clinging to Avenue, but It Too May Pass," *New York Times* (November 8, 1970), VIII: 1, 7.
9. For the Daily Express Building, see Dennis J. and Elizabeth R. De Witt, *Modern Architecture in Europe* (New York: E. P. Dutton, 1987), 178.
10. "Bunny Business in New York," *Progressive Architecture* 43 (April 1962): 60; Jane Kramer, "Dreams of a Playboy: Bunnies on the Rabbit Run," *Village Voice* 8 (November 29, 1962): 1, 15–16; "125 Bunnies for New York," *Progressive Architecture* 44 (January 1963): 46; Gloria Steinem, "A Bunny's Tale," *Show* 3 (May 1963): 90–93, 114–15 and (June 1963): 66–68, 110, 112, 114–16, reprinted as "I Was a Playboy Bunny," in Gloria Steinem, *Outrageous Acts and Everyday Rebellions* (New York: Holt, Rinehart and Winston, 1983), 29–69.
11. "125 Bunnies for New York": 46.
12. For a discussion of Fifty-seventh Street during the interwar period, see Stern, Gilmartin and Mellins, *New York 1930*, 356–67. Also see "Changeless 57th Street," *Real Estate Record and Guide* 186 (July 23, 1960): 2–3; "Traffic Congestion Threatens to Downgrade 57th Street," *Real Estate Record and Guide* 190 (September 22, 1962): 2.
13. "7 New Apartments Brighten E. 57th St.," *New York Times* (April 30, 1961), VIII: 1, 8.
14. "New Apartments for East Side Corner," *New York Times* (May 5, 1946): 1; "New Apartment on East Fifty-seventh Street," *New York Herald Tribune* (April 18, 1948), VI: 1; "Emery Roth, A.I.A.," *Architectural Record* 104 (October 1948): 164; Steven Ruttenbaum, *Mansions in the Clouds: The Skyscraper Palazzi of Emery Roth* (New York: Balsam Press, 1986), 187–89.

15. Arnold H. Lubasch, "Apartment House Rising 47 Floors," *New York Times* (March 27, 1966), VIII: 1; "New Heights for Concrete in New York," advertisement, *Architectural Forum* 127 (November 1967): 94; Arnold H. Lubasch, "Skyscraper Setbacks Serve as Play Areas," *New York Times* (January 28, 1968), VIII: 1, 4; Thomas E. Norton and Jerry E. Patterson, *Living It Up: A Guide to the Named Apartment Houses of New York* (New York: Atheneum, 1984), 139.

16. "Buildings on the Way Up," *Progressive Architecture* 53 (April 1972): 30–31; "An Eye-Boggler 52 Floors Tall Is Rising in East Midtown," *New York Times* (November 11, 1973), VIII: 1, 12; David Kenneth Specter, *Urban Spaces* (Greenwich, Conn.: New York Graphic Society, 1974), figs. 272–73; "The Ultimate Terrace," *New York* 7 (March 11, 1974): 56–57; "Big East Side Assemblage Disclosed," *New York Times* (May 12, 1974), VIII: 6; Carter B. Horsley, "Innovations Modify Apartment Design," *New York Times* (February 23, 1975), VIII: 1, 10; Alan S. Oser, "A New Frontier for 57th St.," *New York Times* (July 11, 1975): 45; Paul Goldberger, "Exclusive New Buildings Here Combine Mixed-Use Facilities," *New York Times* (July 21, 1975): 23, 34; Olga Gueft, "Superb Microcity in the Middle of a Block," *Interiors* 135 (November 1975): 76–79; Gerald Allen, "1 + 1 = 3: A New Equation for Counting a New Building's Cost," *Architectural Record* 158 (December 1975): 68–69, 76–79; Suzanne Stephens, "Microcosms of Urbanity," *Progressive Architecture* 56 (December 1975): 37–47; Leslie Maitland, "Quadraplex 57th St. Penthouse—Or Pie in the Sky?" *New York Times* (December 22, 1975): 31; Charles Kaiser, "$3.2 Million Apartment Refused by Stewart Mott," *New York Times* (February 10, 1976): 41; "The Atrium Club," *Interior Design* 47 (April 1976): cover, 122–27; Ada Louise Huxtable, "A New Twist to the Old Awards Game," *New York Times* (May 2, 1976), II: 30, 38; "Selearchitettura," *L'architettura cronache e storia* 22 (June 1976): 100–101; Carter B. Horsley, "Galleria Is Sold to Morgan Guaranty; Reduction of Apartment Prices Is Seen," *New York Times* (August 6, 1976), B: 3; Judy Klemesrud, "Mott Is a Political Host at New Penthouse," *New York Times* (September 22, 1976): 45; Norma Skurka, "Being in the Swim in Your Own Home," *New York Times* (November 10, 1976), III: 18; Francis X. Clines, "About New York: Rich Man, Poor Man: A Study in Housing," *New York Times* (July 7, 1977), B: 7; Ballard, *Directory of Manhattan Office Buildings*, 176; Ada Louise Huxtable, "The Sabotaging of Public Space," *New York Times* (January 26, 1978), C: 1, 8; White and Willensky, *AIA Guide* (1978), 218; Paul Goldberger, *The City Observed: New York* (New York: Random House, 1979), 154; John Tauranac, *Essential New York* (New York: Holt, Rinehart and Winston, 1979), 241–42; Norton and Patterson, *Living It Up*, 147.

17. Goldberger, "Exclusive New Buildings Here Combine Mixed-Use Facilities": 34.

18. Stephens, "Microcosms of Urbanity": 39–40.

19. Susan S. Sheinbaum, "Philanthropy on a Penthouse," *New York Times* (May 23, 1971), II: 41; Linda Charlton, "Political Philanthropist: Stewart Rawlings Mott," *New York Times* (January 7, 1972): 14; Laurie Johnston, "Notes on People: Park Ave. Co-op Sues Mott on Farm," *New York Times* (January 28, 1975): 39; Laurie Johnston, "Notes on People: The Rostropoviches Get Freedom Award," *New York Times* (April 18, 1975): 26.

20. Glenn Fowler, "The Urban Environment: A Metamorphosis for 57th Street," *New York Times* (September 28, 1969), VIII: 1.

21. "An Office Building to Rise 50 Stories on W. 57th Street," *New York Times* (January 30, 1970): 77; "Avon Products Leases 500,000 Feet in New Office Building on West 57th St.," *Real Estate Record and Guide* 205 (February 14, 1970): 2; "Block-Buster Approach to Architecture," *Progressive Architecture* 51 (April 1970): 41; "Graphics Antics," *Architectural Forum* 133 (October 1970): 25; "Buildings on the Way Up," *Progressive Architecture* 52 (June 1971): 28; "New Office Building to Have First Tri-Level Shopping Mall," *Real Estate Record and Guide* 208 (December 18, 1971): 2; Carter B. Horsley, "Sloping Office Buildings Make Provocative Midtown Debut," *New York Times* (March 26, 1972), VIII: 1, 6; Alan Dunn, "Yes, a Hailstorm! Got Any New Ideas, Mr. Architect?" cartoon, *Architectural Record* 151 (June 1972): 10; Ada Louise Huxtable, "Anti-Street, Anti-People," *New York Times* (June 10, 1973), II: 24; Arthur Drexler, "Introduction," in Axel Menges, *Architecture of Skidmore, Owings & Merrill, 1963–1973* (New York: Architectural Book Publishing Co., 1974), 22–23; "Red-Orange Nine," *Architecture Plus* 1 (March–April 1974): 109; Paul Goldberger, "Award-Givers Honor a Few and Slap a Wrist," *New York Times* (June 2, 1974), VIII: 1, 12; Andrea O. Dean, "Graphics in the Environment," *Journal of the American Institute of Architects* 64 (October 1975): 24–25; Ballard, *Directory of Manhattan Office Buildings*, 173; Goldberger, *The City Observed*, 176–77; Tauranac, *Essential New York*, 230–32; Paul Goldberger, *The Skyscraper* (New York: Alfred A. Knopf, 1981), 136; Albert Bush-Brown, *Skidmore, Owings & Merrill: Architecture and Urbanism 1973–1983* (Stuttgart: Verlag Gerd Hatje; New York: Van Nostrand Reinhold, 1983), 233; Carol Herselle Krinsky, *Gordon Bunshaft of Skidmore, Owings & Merrill* (New York: Architectural History Foundation; Cambridge, Mass.: MIT Press, 1988), 146, 247–51, 292–95, 338; White and Willensky, *AIA Guide* (1988), 281.

22. Horsley, "Sloping Office Buildings Make Provocative Midtown Debut": 1.

23. "Block-Buster Approach to Architecture": 41.

24. For C. F. Murphy's First National Bank Building, see "The First National Bank of Chicago," *Architectural Record* 148 (September 1970): 137–40; Carl W. Condit, *Chicago, 1930–70: Building, Planning, and Urban Technology* (Chicago and London: University of Chicago Press, 1974), 99–102.

25. Drexler, "Introduction," in Menges, *Architecture of Skidmore, Owings & Merrill, 1963–1973*, 22.

26. Wallace K. Harrison quoted in Horsley, "Sloping Office Buildings Make Provocative Midtown Debut": 1.

27. Henry Cobb quoted in Horsley, "Sloping Office Buildings Make Provocative Midtown Debut": 6.

28. Jaquelin Robertson quoted in Horsley, "Sloping Office Buildings Make Provocative Midtown Debut": 1.

29. "Lefrak to Build West 57th Street Office Building," *Real Estate Record and Guide* 201 (May 25, 1968): 3; Ballard, *Directory of Manhattan Office Buildings*, 173.

30. Sheldon Solow quoted in Goldberger, "Award-Givers Honor a Few and Slap a Wrist": 1.

31. Huxtable, "Anti-Street, Anti-People": 24.

32. For the Spanish Flats, see Stern, Gilmartin and Massengale, *New York 1900*, 468 (n. 101). For the New York Athletic Club, see Stern, Gilmartin and Mellins, *New York 1930*, 194–95.

33. For 240 Central Park South, see Stern, Gilmartin and Mellins, *New York 1930*, 424–25.

34. "House Facing Park to Have 150 Suites," *New York Times* (March 9, 1941): 1, 3; "Modern, to Tempt Tenants," *Interiors* 100 (June 1941): 26–27; James J. Nagle, "Concrete Walls Going Up Quietly in 22-Story House," *New York Times* (June 15, 1941), XI: 1, 7.

35. "House Facing Park to Have 150 Suites": 1, 3.

36. For the Rockefeller Apartments, see Stern, Gilmartin and Mellins, *New York 1930*, 421–24.

37. "20-Story Apartments Facing Central Park Will Provide 125 Suites in Luxury Class," *New York Times* (January 3, 1954): 1; "Reports Brisk Renting of Suites in New Central Park South Apartments," *Real Estate Record and Guide* 173 (February 20, 1954): 3–4; "New Luxury Apartment Building Rising on Central Park South," *Real Estate Record and Guide* 173 (January 9, 1954): 4.

38. For the Gainsborough Studios, see Stern, Gilmartin and Massengale, *New York 1900*, 296, 298.

39. Arnold H. Lubasch, "'Luxury Lane' Set to Grow 500 Units," *New York Times* (August 6, 1961): 1, 4.

40. "Plaza Section Serves as Setting for New Apartment Buildings," *New York Times* (November 25, 1962), VIII: 1, 6.

41. "Plaza Section Serves as Setting for New Apartment Buildings": 1, 6.

42. "Rarely Used Zoning Clause Key to Design of New 35-Story Apartment House," *Real Estate Record and Guide* 189 (April 28, 1962): 2; Maurice Foley, "Zone Law Puts Tower off Base in Building Facing Central Park," *New York Times* (May 13, 1962), VIII: 1, 10; "City Praises Apartment House as Tenants Meet to Complain," *New York Times* (December 21, 1963): 25; Goldberger, *The City Observed*, 180; Christopher Gray, "Schlock of Ages," *Avenue* 17 (December 1992): 31–32, 34, 36, 38.

43. For Morris Lapidus's Fontainebleau, see Robert A. M. Stern with Thomas Mellins and Raymond Gastil, *Pride of Place: Building the American Dream* (Boston: Houghton Mifflin; New York: American Heritage, 1986), 208–10.

44. Goldberger, *The City Observed*, 180.

45. "Brownstone Tenants Fight Eviction," *New York Times* (March 31, 1965): 41; Thomas A. Johnson, "Tenants Press Fight for Homes along Park," *New York Times* (March 8, 1966): 41; Franklin Whitehouse, "News of Realty: Park Site Sold," *New York Times* (July 28, 1967): 48.

46. Seth S. King, "Owners Oppose City Hotel Plan," *New York Times* (August 12, 1968): 48; Charles G. Bennett, "City Aids District of Luxury Hotels," *New York Times* (August 28, 1968): 53; Charles G. Bennett, "City Acts to Save Midtown Hotels," *New York Times* (October 17, 1968): 47; "City Board Backs Protective Zoning for Plush Hotels," *New York Times* (November 22, 1968): 39; "Plaza Area Is Booming," *Real Estate Record and Guide* 202 (December 28, 1968): 3–4.

47. Thomas W. Ennis, "News of Realty: Helmsley Plan," *New York Times* (January 31, 1967): 60; Paul J. C. Friedlander, "A Hotel Grows on Central Park South," *New York Times* (March 14, 1971), X: 41; Lacey Fosburgh, "The Park Lane, Midtown's Latest Luxury Hotel, to Open Saturday," *New York Times* (April 29, 1971): 52; "A Gamble on Manhattan," *Time* 97 (May 17, 1971): 92; "Park Lane Hotel," *Interior Design* 42 (October 1971): 128–31; Goldberger, *The City Observed*, 179; James Trager, *West of Fifth: The Rise and Fall and Rise of Manhattan's West Side* (New York: Atheneum, 1987), 116.

48. Tom Lee quoted in "Park Lane Hotel": 128.

49. Stern, Gilmartin and Massengale, *New York 1900*, 129–30; Stern, Gilmartin and Mellins, *New York 1930*, 18.

50. For the Metropolitan Club, see Stern, Gilmartin and Massengale, *New York 1900*, 232–33.

51. For the Plaza, see Stern, Gilmartin and Massengale, *New York 1900*, 252, 258–59, 261–62. For the Sherry-Netherland, the Savoy-Plaza and the Pierre, see Stern, Gilmartin and Mellins, *New York 1930*, 200, 217–22.

52. Foster Hailey, "Savoy Plaza to Be Razed for G.M. Offices," *New York Times* (August 21, 1964): 1, 20; "A Gain for Rayne," *Time* 84 (August 24, 1964): 82; William Lescaze, "Architect Backs Plaza Building," letter to the editor, *New York Times* (September 17, 1964): 42; "More Stone on the Park," *Progressive Architecture* 45 (October 1964): 47; Glenn Fowler, "48-Story Tower to Rise on Savoy Plaza Site," *New York Times* (December 16, 1964): 1, 31; Ada Louise Huxtable, "Nothing Inviolate Here," *New York Times* (December 16, 1964): 31; "GM on the Plaza," *Progressive Architecture* 46 (January 1965): 39–40; "Office Building Will Replace Savoy Plaza," *Architectural Record* 137 (February 1965): 13; Ada Louise Huxtable, "More on How to Kill a City," *New York Times* (March 21, 1965), II: 27, reprinted as "Abortive Cafes and Redundant Plazas," in Ada Louise Huxtable, *Will They Ever Finish Bruckner Boulevard?* (New York: Macmillan, 1970), 50–53; "Sunken Plaza Planned for G.M. Building on 5th Ave.," *New York Times* (August 8, 1965), VIII: 1; Ada Louise Huxtable, "Architecture: Fun and Games," *New York Times* (June 19, 1966), II: 21; "Man with a Billion on the Drawing Board," *Business Week* (October 8, 1966): 124–31; Edward Durell Stone, *Recent & Future Architecture* (New York: Horizon Press, 1967), 9–10, 74–77; White and Willensky, *AIA Guide* (1967), 157; McCandlish Phillips, "Bold New Profile Joins City's East Side Skyline," *New York Times* (October 17, 1967): 49; "Architecture without Tears," *Architectural Forum* 127 (November 1967): 91; "GM Restyles Fifth Avenue," *Business Week* (September 28, 1968): 92–94; "General Motors Building Opens on Central Park," *Progressive Architecture* 49 (October 1968): 80; Ada Louise Huxtable, "The Newest Skyscraper in Manhattan: G.M. Building Draws Crowds but Gets Mixed Reviews," *New York Times* (October 1, 1968): 57, reprinted as "The Parthenon Comes to General Motors," in Huxtable, *Will They Ever Finish Bruckner Boulevard?*, 92–95; Peter Blake, "High-Rise Schrafft's," *New York* 1 (November 25, 1968): 46–47; William Zeckendorf with Edward McCreary, *The Autobiography of William Zeckendorf* (New York: Holt, Rinehart and Winston, 1970), 295–98; John Anderson, "Joyride under the G.M. Building," *Interiors* 130 (October 1970): 116–21; Paul Goldberger, "Edward Durell Stone Finds the 'Universal' Pays," *New York Times* (September 10, 1972), VIII: 1, 10; Ballard, *Directory of Manhattan Office Buildings*, 152; White and Willensky, *AIA Guide* (1978), 216–17; Goldberger, *The City Observed*, 166–67; Ruttenbaum, *Mansions in the Clouds: The Skyscraper Palazzi of Emery Roth*, 207.

53. Stern, Gilmartin and Mellins, *New York 1930*, 285, 287.

54. Stern, Gilmartin and Mellins, *New York 1930*, 360, 541, 617.

55. Edward Durell Stone, *The Evolution of an Architect* (New York: Horizon Press, 1962), 156–57, 270.

56. Edward Durell Stone quoted in "Man with a Billion on the Drawing Board": 126.

57. Edward Durell Stone quoted in "Office Building Will Replace Savoy Plaza": 13.

58. Edward Durell Stone quoted in "Architecture without Tears": 91.

59. Huxtable, "Nothing Inviolate Here": 31.

60. "GM on the Plaza": 39–40.

61. Cecilia Benattar quoted in Fowler, "48-Story Tower to Rise on Savoy Plaza Site": 1, 31.

62. Huxtable, "More on How to Kill a City": 27.
63. Blake, "High-Rise Schrafft's": 46–47.
64. Huxtable, "The Newest Skyscraper in Manhattan: G.M. Building Draws Crowds but Gets Mixed Reviews": 57.
65. Edward Durell Stone quoted in Goldberger, "Edward Durell Stone Finds the 'Universal' Pays": 1.
66. Maurice Foley, "Office Skyscraper to Rise on 5th Ave. at 20 Million Cost," *New York Times* (August 3, 1959): 27.
67. "Coop Planned on Fifth at Plaza," *Real Estate Record and Guide* 186 (December 10, 1960): 3; "Pease & Elliman Agent for 785 Fifth," *Real Estate Record and Guide* 189 (February 24, 1962): 6; Sanka Knox, "Co-op 'Mansions' to Be Open Soon," *New York Times* (August 15, 1963): 25; Norton and Patterson, *Living It Up*, 257.
68. Richard Phalon, "La Banque Is Open—For $25,000," *New York Times* (March 23, 1966): 63, 67; William D. Smith, "Sidelights: No Walls," *New York Times* (April 22, 1966): 58; "Glittering Home for Rich Man's Cash," *Business Week* (April 30, 1966): 40–41; "New York: The Swank Bank," *Newsweek* 67 (May 21, 1966): 88–89; "La Banque Continentale," *Interior Design* 37 (June 1966): 121–27; Enid Nemy, "This Bank's Services Are Free if One Has a Checking Account of $25,000," *New York Times* (April 27, 1969): 82; Norton and Patterson, *Living It Up*, 257.
69. For the Knickerbocker Club, see Stern, Gilmartin and Massengale, *New York 1900*, 238.
70. Paul Goldberger, "Dodge Mansion: A Crucial Decision," *New York Times* (April 20, 1976): 37; "New 61st St. Apartments Will Rent for $300 a Room," *New York Times* (April 21, 1976): 40; Carter B. Horsley, "Apartment House on Dodge Site Rejected by Community Board," *New York Times* (May 9, 1976): 36; "The Dodge Site," editorial, *New York Times* (May 12, 1976): 40; Ada Louise Huxtable, "A Building that Looks Like a Loser," *New York Times* (May 30, 1976), II: 23; "Franzen High-Rise Slated for Fifth Avenue," *Architectural Record* 159 (June 1976): 39; "Central Park Apartment Tower," *Progressive Architecture* 57 (June 1976): 44; " . . . Dodge Site," editorial, *New York Times* (June 30, 1976): 36; Paul Goldberger, "Breaking Up the Bulk of a Brick Box," *New York Times* (June 30, 1976): 41; "Apartments to Go on Dodge Mansion Site," *New York Times* (July 16, 1976), B: 3; "Dodge Mansion Makes Way for High-Rise," *New York Times* (February 9, 1977), B: 2; White and Willensky, *AIA Guide* (1978), 220; Dee Wedemeyer, "Luxury Languishes in Era of Cost Cutting," *New York Times* (December 17, 1978), VIII: 1–2; Goldberger, *The City Observed*, 228–29; Ada Louise Huxtable, "The 'Pathetic Fallacy,' or Wishful Thinking at Work," *New York Times* (February 11, 1979), II: 29; Brent C. Brolin, *Architecture in Context: Fitting New Buildings with Old* (New York: Van Nostrand Reinhold, 1980), 71; Christopher Gray, "Follies!" *Avenue* 15 (February 1991): 65–73.
71. Ulrich Franzen quoted in Goldberger, "Dodge Mansion: A Crucial Decision": 37.
72. Goldberger, "Breaking Up the Bulk of a Brick Box": 41.
73. Huxtable, "The 'Pathetic Fallacy,' or Wishful Thinking at Work": 29.
74. Goldberger, *The City Observed*, 229.

Chapter 6
Interiors

1. Truman Capote, *Local Color* (New York: Random House, 1950), 13.

ART GALLERIES

1. "Isms Rampant: Peggy Guggenheim's Dream World Goes Abstract, Cubist, and Generally Non-Real," *Newsweek* 20 (November 2, 1942): 66; "Modern Art Museum to Exhibit Work of Therapeutic Value—Guggenheim Gallery Opens," *New York Times* (October 16, 1942): 24; Edward Alden Jewell, "In the Realm of Art: A Week of Diverse Activities," *New York Times* (October 25, 1942), VIII: 9; "Modern Art in a Modern Setting," *New York Times* (November 1, 1942), VII: 16–17; Manny Farber, "A New Way of Seeing Pictures," *Magazine of Art* 35 (December 1942): 295, 305, 308; "New Display Techniques," *Architectural Forum* 78 (February 1943): 49–53; "The Year's Work," *Interiors* 103 (August 1943): 25; "Retail Story," *Interiors* 104 (February 1945): 70; "Design's Bad Boy," *Architectural Forum* 86 (February 1947): 88–91, 138, 140; Peggy Guggenheim, *Confessions of an Art Addict* (New York: Macmillan, 1960), 99–114; Bryan Robertson, *Jackson Pollock* (New York: Harry N. Abrams, 1960), 143; Thomas H. Creighton, "Kiesler's Pursuit of an Idea," *Progressive Architecture* 41 (July 1961): cover, 104–23; Jeffrey Potter, *To a Violent Grave: An Oral Biography of Jackson Pollock* (New York: G. P. Putnam's Sons, 1985), 70–71, 74–76, 80; Jacqueline Bograd Weld, *Peggy: The Wayward Guggenheim* (New York: E. P. Dutton, 1986), 285–360; Deborah Solomon, *Jackson Pollock: A Biography* (New York: Simon & Schuster, 1987), 129–30; Steven Naifeh and Gregory White Smith, *Jackson Pollock: An American Saga* (New York: Clarkson N. Potter, 1989), 438–46; Lisa Phillips, "Architect of Endless Innovation," in Lisa Phillips, ed., *Frederick Kiesler*, exhibition catalogue (New York: Whitney Museum of American Art, in association with W. W. Norton, 1989), 12–35; Cynthia Goodman, "The Art of Revolutionary Display Techniques," in Phillips, ed., *Frederick Kiesler*, 56–83; Lisa Phillips, "Environmental Artist," in Phillips, ed., *Frederick Kiesler*, 108–37.
2. Stern, Gilmartin and Mellins, *New York 1930*, 328–29, 350–51, 353–54.
3. Peggy Guggenheim quoted in Jewell, "In the Realm of Art": 9.
4. Peggy Guggenheim, letter to Frederick Kiesler, March 4, 1942, Kiesler Estate Archives, quoted in Goodman, "The Art of Revolutionary Display Techniques," in Phillips, ed., *Frederick Kiesler*, 63.
5. Peggy Guggenheim quoted in "Isms Rampant: Peggy Guggenheim's Dream World Goes Abstract, Cubist, and Generally Non-Real": 66.
6. Frederick Kiesler quoted in Goodman, "The Art of Revolutionary Display Techniques," in Phillips, ed., *Frederick Kiesler*, 63–64.
7. "New Display Techniques": 49.
8. Frederick Kiesler quoted in "Isms Rampant: Peggy Guggenheim's Dream World Goes Abstract, Cubist, and Generally Non-Real": 66.
9. "New Display Techniques": 49.
10. Frederick Kiesler, "Notes on Designing the Gallery," unpublished manuscript, Kiesler Estate Archives, quoted in Goodman, "The Art of Revolutionary Display Techniques," in Phillips, ed., *Frederick Kiesler*, 66.
11. "New Display Techniques": 49.
12. Jewell, "In the Realm of Art": 9.
13. Farber, "A New Way of Seeing Pictures": 305.
14. Phillips, "Environmental Artist," in Phillips, ed., *Frederick Kiesler*, 117.
15. Ad Reinhardt, "Neo Surrealists Take Over a Gallery," *PM* (March 11, 1947): 11. Also see Phillips, "Architect of Endless Innovation," in Phillips, ed., *Frederick Kiesler*, 29–30; Phillips, "Environmental Artist," in Phillips, ed., *Frederick Kiesler*, 117.
16. Sanka Knox, "Stairs 'Float' and Walls 'Flow' at the City's Latest Art Gallery," *New York Times* (January 22, 1957): 31; "Flowing Gallery," *Time* 69 (February 4, 1957): 60; Frederick J. Kiesler, "The Art of Architecture for Art," *Art News* 56 (October 1957): 38–43, 50, 52, 54; Fritz Neugass, "World House Galleries, New York," *Werk* 46 (February 1959): 70–72; Goodman, "The Art of Revolutionary Display Techniques," in Phillips, ed., *Frederick Kiesler*, 78–82. For the Carlyle, see Stern, Gilmartin and Mellins, *New York 1930*, 403–5.
17. "Flowing Gallery": 60.
18. Kiesler, "The Art of Architecture for Art": 43, 50.
19. Kiesler, "The Art of Architecture for Art": 52.
20. Milton Bracker, "English Gallery to Expand Here," *New York Times* (May 25, 1963): 22; "Impassive Giant," *Time* 82 (July 19, 1963): 56; Brian O'Doherty, "Art: Marlborough Opens Branch Here," *New York Times* (October 2, 1963): 38; R. W. Apple, Jr., "Gallery Opening Marked by Chaos," *New York Times* (November 13, 1963): 38; John Canaday, "Maecenas and Midas," *New York Times* (November 17, 1963), II: 15; "Going for Baroque," *Time* 82 (November 22, 1963): 72; "Marlborough Country," *Newsweek* 62 (November 25, 1963): 74; "Marlborough-Gerson Gallery, Inc.," *Progressive Architecture* 45 (July 1964): 162–65; "Art Meets Its Buyers," *Business Week* (May 15, 1965): 150–52, 154, 156.
21. Jack Kroll quoted in "Marlborough Country": 74.
22. Quoted in "Marlborough Country": 74.
23. For the Fuller Building, see Stern, Gilmartin and Mellins, *New York 1930*, 366–67.
24. "Marlborough-Gerson Gallery, Inc.": 162.
25. Wilder Green quoted in "Marlborough-Gerson Gallery, Inc.": 162.
26. "Art Meets Its Buyers": 151.
27. "Illusionary Art Gallery," *Progressive Architecture* 47 (February 1966): 174–77; Stanley Abercrombie, *Gwathmey Siegel* (New York: Whitney Library of Design, 1981), 118.
28. Charles Gwathmey quoted in "Illusionary Art Gallery": 174, 177.
29. "Illusionary Art Gallery": 177.
30. John S. Margolies, "Art Machine for the 70's," *Architectural Forum* 132 (January–February 1970): 44–51, 98; "Architectural Fabergé," *Progressive Architecture* 51 (February 1970): 88–95; Kenneth Frampton, "Richard L. Feigen & Co.," *Architectural Design* 40 (March 1970): 129–33; Jeremy Fisher, "Closely Observed Curves," *Design* (Britain) 256 (April 1970): 42–47; "Macchina per l'arte a Manhattan," *L'Architettura cronache e storia* 16 (July 1970): 184–85; White and Willensky, *AIA Guide* (1978), 234; Paul Goldberger, *The City Observed: New York* (New York: Random House, 1979), 247; Gianni Pettena, *Hans Hollein: Opere 1960–1988* (Milan: Idea Books Edizioni, 1988), 29–33.
31. For Loos's Goldman & Salatsch Building, see Benedetto Gravagnuolo, *Adolf Loos: Theory and Works*, trans. C. H. Evans (New York: Rizzoli International Publications, 1982), 125–33.
32. Frampton, "Richard L. Feigen & Co.": 129, 132.
33. George Gent, "Madison Avenue Sidewalk Bears Design by Calder," *New York Times* (September 22, 1970): 38; "The Sidewalk's Potential," *Time* 96 (October 5, 1970): 44; "Art Underfoot," *Newsweek* 76 (October 5, 1970): 90; "Editors' Eye on People and Things," *House and Garden* 138 (December 1970): 80–81.

RESTAURANTS AND NIGHTCLUBS

1. For the Firenze, see Stern, Gilmartin and Mellins, *New York 1930*, 271, 273. For additional coffee shops by MacDougall, see Stern, Gilmartin and Mellins, *New York 1930*, 272–73, 275.
2. "The Year's Work: Seymour R. Joseph, New York City," *Interiors* 107 (August 1947): 94.
3. "Four Remodeled Restaurants," *Architectural Forum* 85 (August 1946): 97–102. This article also includes Seigel's new bar for Solly Krieger's restaurant and George C. Rudolph's new bar for Hector's cafeteria.
4. "Week End Conversion; (Spaghetti, $1.35)," *Interiors* 102 (September 1942): 30–31.
5. "Sculpture as an Integral Part of Design," *Interiors* 103 (June 1944): 56–59; "Seafare Restaurant," *Architectural Forum* 81 (August 1944): 102–5.
6. "Seafare Restaurant": 103.
7. "Background Suitable for Epicures," *Interiors* 106 (September 1946): 86–87. Also see Zareh Sourian, "Notes on Restaurant Design," *Interiors* 106 (September 1946): 97, 130.
8. "Nantucket at Radio City," *Architectural Record* 104 (July 1948): 134–35.
9. "Broadway Steak House," *Architectural Forum* 90 (February 1949): 119–22; "Al and Dick's, a Restaurant: Designed by Nemeny & Geller," *Interiors* 108 (March 1949): 112–15; Abraham W. Geller, "Restaurants," *Progressive Architecture* 33 (June 1952): 117–23; Talbot F. Hamlin, ed., *Forms and Functions of Twentieth-Century Architecture*, vol. 1 (New York: Columbia University Press, 1952), 481; White and Willensky, *AIA Guide* (1967), 114.
10. "Light on Finnish Food," *Interiors* 108 (October 1948): 129–31; "Finnish Restaurant," *Architectural Forum* 90 (February 1949): 115–18; Huson Jackson, *A Guide to New York Architecture 1650–1952* (New York: Reinhold Publishing Corp., 1952), 27. For Aalto's World's Fair exhibit, located in the Hall of Nations, see Stern, Gilmartin and Mellins, *New York 1930*, 735, 740.
11. For Jones Beach, see Stern, Gilmartin and Mellins, *New York 1930*, 718, 720–22.
12. "The Talk of the Town: Papa's Place," *New Yorker* 33 (October 12, 1957): 36–37; White and Willensky, *AIA Guide* (1967), 120.
13. "How High-Tab Restaurant Keeps Customers Coming," *Business Week* (April 20, 1957): 190–91, 193–94, 196–98, 200, 202; Silas Spitzer, "The World's Most Expensive Restaurant?" *Holiday* 24 (October 1958): 71, 108–9, 111.
14. Spitzer, "The World's Most Expensive Restaurant?": 71.
15. See William Wilson Atkin and Joan Adler, *Interiors Book of Restaurants* (New York: Whitney Library of Design, 1960). Also see Tom Lee, "Pith & Vinegar in Restaurant Design," book review, *Interiors* 120 (December 1960): 24.
16. For Murray's Roman Gardens, see Stern, Gilmartin and Massengale, *New York 1900*, 224–25.
17. Minor L. Bishop, "Atmosphere for Gourmets," *Interiors* 125 (March 1966): 125–27.
18. Bishop, "Atmosphere for Gourmets": 127.
19. "Restaurant Wears Its New Look Gracefully," *Architectural Record* 115 (April 1954): 182–85.
20. John Anderson, "Playbill Restaurant by Melanie Kahane Associates," *Interiors* 118 (February 1959): 62–67; Olga Gueft, "The Man Behind the Client," editorial, *Interiors* 118 (February 1959): 61; Grace Ohanian Ellis, "Roses, and a Correction, for Playbill," letter to the editor, *Interiors* 118 (April 1959): 8.

21. Anderson, "Playbill Restaurant by Melanie Kahane Associates": 64.
22. "Food Is Also Served," *Time* 74 (July 27, 1959): 61–62, 65; "The Talk of the Town: Associates Progress," *New Yorker* 36 (September 24, 1960): 33–35; Geoffrey T. Hellman, "Profiles: Directed to the Product," *New Yorker* 40 (October 17, 1964): 59–60, 62, 64, 67–70, 73–76, 79–82, 85, 90–92, 95–96, 100–102, 106–7.
23. "The Talk of the Town: Creative," *New Yorker* 35 (August 1, 1959): 18–19. Also see Madeleine Goodrich, "Ancient Rome Is Recollected in Rockefeller Center," *Interiors* 117 (March 1958): 90–93; "An Old-Fashioned Roman Christmas," *Esquire* 60 (December 1963): 228–31; Hellman, "Profiles: Directed to the Product": 64, 70, 73–74; C. Ray Smith, *Interior Design in 20th-Century America: A History* (New York: Harper & Row, 1987), 241.
24. Olga Gueft, "L'Etoile," *Interiors* 126 (October 1966): 100–105; White and Willensky, *AIA Guide* (1967), 157; "Colours of France in New York," *Domus* 449 (August 1967): 12–16; C. Ray Smith, *Supermannerism: New Attitudes in Post-Modern Architecture* (New York: E. P. Dutton, 1977), 150–51. For the Sherry-Netherland, see Stern, Gilmartin and Mellins, *New York 1930*, 217–21.
25. For the Jetsons, see Jeff Lenburg, *The Encyclopedia of Animated Cartoons* (New York: Facts On File, 1991), 352–53.
26. "Colours of France in New York": 12.
27. Olga Gueft, "Elegant Irish Saloon," *Interiors* 126 (March 1967): 114–17.
28. Gueft, "Elegant Irish Saloon": 115.
29. "To Greece with Love," *Interior Design* 41 (October 1970): 134–39.
30. "The Swiss Idea on Two Levels," *Interiors* 130 (February 1971): 78–85, 137.
31. Ruth Miller Fitzgibbons, "Cousin Ho's," *Interiors* 134 (March 1975): 82–83.
32. "Design Concept in Color," *Interior Design* 37 (April 1966): 194–97.
33. Marian Page, "A Sliver of Oriental Serenity on 48th Street," *Interiors* 133 (March 1974): 86–87; Paul Goldberger, "Design for Dining: Feasts for the Eye, Too," *New York Times* (July 30, 1976), III: 13; "Three Interiors by Gwathmey-Siegel for Difficult Spaces and Complex Programs," *Architectural Record* 160 (September 1976): 103–5; White and Willensky, *AIA Guide* (1978), 170–71; Stanley Abercrombie, *Gwathmey Siegel* (New York: Whitney Library of Design, 1981), 40–43, 68; *Charles Gwathmey and Robert Seigel: Buildings and Projects 1964–1984*, eds. Peter Arnell and Ted Bickford (New York: Harper & Row, 1984), 78–79.
34. Goldberger, "Design for Dining: Feasts for the Eye, Too": 13; Suzanne Slesin, "The New Great-Looking Restaurants," *New York* 9 (December 20, 1976): 51, 59; Linda Wolfe, "Shezan," *New York* 9 (December 20, 1976): 61; "Elegance without Opulence," *Interior Design* 48 (January 1977): 108–11; Paul Goldberger, "A Design for Orderly Living," *New York Times* (December 11, 1977), VI: 147; "Shezan Restaurant, New York, N.Y.," *Process Architecture* 13 (March 1980): 52–55; Abercrombie, *Gwathmey Siegel*, 50–55, 69; *Charles Gwathmey and Robert Seigel: Buildings and Projects 1964–1984*, 192–93.
35. Abercrombie, *Gwathmey Siegel*, 50.
36. Charles Gwathmey quoted in Slesin, "The New Great-Looking Restaurants": 59.
37. Quoted in Goldberger, "Design for Dining: Feasts for the Eye, Too": 13.
38. Goldberger, "Design for Dining: Feasts for the Eye, Too": 13.
39. Julie Baumgold, "The Expanding Plum and Friday's Children," *New York* 1 (November 18, 1968): 41–43; Tisa Farrow, "Checking Out First Avenue," *Holiday* 45 (May 1969): 38–41; Craig Claiborne, "Yes, Some People Actually Go to Maxwell's Plum for the Food," *New York Times* (July 30, 1970): 36; Jon Bradshaw, "The Action at Maxwell's Plum," *New York* 8 (June 16, 1975): 45–56.
40. Quoted in Bradshaw, "The Action at Maxwell's Plum": 51.
41. Stern, Gilmartin and Mellins, *New York 1930*, 272–79.
42. "Mosaic for New Drama," *Architectural Record* 100 (September 1946): 112. Also see "The Year's Work: Daniel Laitin, New York City," *Interiors* 108 (August 1948): 96.
43. "This Year's Work—Autumn Portfolio: Eugene Schoen, New York," *Interiors* 101 (August 1941): 34.
44. Ralph Caplan, "Eating Out the New York Way," *Design* (Britain) 183 (March 1964): 56–57.
45. Lois Wagner, "Interiors Contract Series '56: Restaurants and Bars," *Interiors* 115 (May 1956): 74–79; "Atmosphere for Dining Out," *Architectural Forum* 107 (July 1957): 153–59.
46. Wagner, "Interiors Contract Series '56: Restaurants and Bars": 75.
47. John Anderson, "Soup in a Gotham Garden," *Interiors* 130 (June 1971): 80–83. Also see Sharon Lee Ryder, "A Matter of Taste," *Progressive Architecture* 53 (June 1972): 109.
48. "Pot au Feu," *Interior Design* 45 (April 1974): 142–45.
49. Charles Mount and Judith Stockman quoted in "Pot au Feu": 142.
50. Max Boas and Steve Chain, *Big Mac: The Unauthorized Story of McDonald's* (New York: E. P. Dutton, 1976); John F. Love, *McDonald's: Behind the Arches* (New York: Bantam Books, 1986).
51. Robert McG. Thomas, "86th Street Neighborhood Group Claims Hamburger War Victory," *New York Times* (February 12, 1975): 41; Lucinda Franks, "Issue and Debate: McDonald's Expansion vs. Community Interests," *New York Times* (February 15, 1975): 33; "Battle of the Burger," editorial, *New York Times* (February 20, 1975): 32. Also see Barbara Garson, "Who Deserves a Break Today?" *Village Voice* 19 (April 25, 1974): 9–10; Mimi Sheraton, "The Burger That's Eating New York," *New York* 7 (August 19, 1974): 30–35.
52. John Corry, "About New York: The East Side vs. McDonald's," *New York Times* (May 17, 1974): 33.
53. Marie Brenner, "New York Intelligencer: Burger Tycoon Cooking in New York," *New York* 7 (February 25, 1974): 49. Also see "McDonald's: A Variation on the Formula," *Interior Design* 46 (May 1975): 172–75.
54. George Nelson quoted in "McDonald's: A Variation on the Formula": 172.
55. "Night Clubs," *Life* 14 (May 10, 1943): 68–73; Earl Wilson, "Night Life," *Holiday* 5 (April 1949): 52–55.
56. Maurice Zolotow, "The Night-Club Business," *American Mercury* 55 (October 1942): 411–20.
57. "Uptown Boogie-Woogie," *Time* 36 (October 21, 1940): 54–55; "Night Club," *Architectural Record* 89 (January 1941): 122; Jac Lessman, "Night Clubs," *Interior Design and Decoration* 14 (May 1941): 34–36, 72, 74.
58. Mary Sanders, "Reviews," *Architectural Forum* 84 (June 1946): 140; "Surrealism in the Night Club," *Interiors* 106 (September 1946): 82–87.
59. "Dramatic Decor in New York Supper Clubs," *Interiors* 100 (December 1940): 32–37, 48–49; Janet Flanner, "The Amazing Career of Dorothy Draper," *Harper's Bazaar* 75 (January 1941): 84–86, 90.
60. "Bring the Tropics to Latitude 40°40′ Longitude 73°50′," *Interior Design* 17 (August 1941): 34–37, 54.
61. "Monte Carlo with Crowns," *Interiors* 103 (March 1944): 36–38; E. J. Kahn, Jr., "Profiles: Big Operator—II," *New Yorker* 27 (December 15, 1951): 41–42, 44, 46, 48, 52, 54, 56–58, 61–63, 66–68; William Zeckendorf with Edward McCreary, *The Autobiography of William Zeckendorf* (New York: Holt, Rinehart and Winston, 1970), 88–91. For the House of Morgan, see Stern, Gilmartin and Mellins, *New York 1930*, 283, 288, 291.
62. "Monte Carlo with Crowns": 37.
63. "The Year's Work: Franklin Hughes, New York City," *Interiors* 106 (August 1946): 96.
64. "Dramatic Decor in New York Supper Clubs": 35, 37, 48. Also see Robert D. B. Carlisle, "How Did You Like Larue?" *Princeton Alumni Weekly* (November 7, 1984): 27–29.
65. "1.2.3. Restaurant and Night Spot," *Architectural Forum* 76 (April 1942): 228–29; "A Spot for Smoothies," *Interiors* 101 (April 1942): 26–29.
66. Carleton Varney, *The Draper Touch: The High Life & High Style of Dorothy Draper* (New York: Prentice Hall Press, 1988), 193–95.
67. Priscilla Ginsberg, "A Regilded El Morocco," *Interiors* 121 (October 1961): 148–49. Also see Arthur Gelb, "New El Morocco Opens Tonight," *New York Times* (January 26, 1961): 34.
68. "John Perona Dies; El Morocco Head," *New York Times* (June 11, 1961): 87.
69. "In Old Morocco," *Time* 84 (December 25, 1964): 35.
70. Jacqueline Kennedy Onassis quoted in Charlotte Curtis, "El Morocco Reopens as a Private Club—And Siberia Has Been Banished," *New York Times* (December 17, 1971): 49.
71. "The Talk of the Town: Record Cabinet," *New Yorker* 39 (October 5, 1963): 42–43. Also see José Ramón Medina, *Marisol* (Caracas: Ediciones Armitano, 1968), 112–17.
72. Charles Mohr, "World of Affluent Youth Favors 'In' Dancing at City Hideaways," *New York Times* (March 30, 1964): 31.
73. John Anderson, "How to Create an Instant Heritage," *Interiors* 128 (February 1969): 110–15; "Go-Goville, N.Y.," *Newsweek* 73 (March 3, 1969): 62; Eugenia Sheppard, "In New York, It's Raffles," *Holiday* 47 (April 1970): 38, 68, 98. Also see Hugo Vickers, *Cecil Beaton* (Boston: Little, Brown, 1985), 522.
74. Cecil Beaton quoted in Sheppard, "In New York, It's Raffles": 68.
75. Sheppard, "In New York, It's Raffles": 68.
76. Vincent Canby, "A New Nightclub to Have 3 Stories," *New York Times* (April 1, 1966): 26; Nan Ickeringill, "And Here's . . . Cheetah: A Roar in the Concrete Jungle," *New York Times* (April 28, 1966): 47; "Night Life: The Roar of the Cheetah, the Look of the Crowd," *Time* 87 (May 6, 1966): 52–53; "Wild New Flashing Bedlam of the Discothèque," *Life* 60 (May 27, 1966): 72–76; White and Willensky, *AIA Guide* (1967), 114.
77. "Mattress for the Mind," *Time* 92 (December 13, 1968): 87. Also see Dan Sullivan, "Cerebrum: Club Seeking to Soothe the Mind," *New York Times* (November 23, 1968): 62; John Gruen, "The Underground: Cerebrum, 'Designed to Soothe the Spirit,'" *Vogue* 153 (January 1, 1969): 68; "Go-Goville, N.Y. ": 62.
78. Ruffin Cooper quoted in "Mattress for the Mind": 87.
79. James Wines, *De-architecture* (New York: Rizzoli International Publications, 1987).

APARTMENTS

1. For Eleanor McMillen Brown, see Rita Reif, "Interiors Well-Bred, Not Trendy," *New York Times* (November 5, 1974): 40; Erica Brown, *Sixty Years of Interior Design: The World of McMillen* (New York: Viking, 1982); C. Ray Smith, *Interior Design in 20th-Century America: A History* (New York: Harper & Row, 1987), 100–102, 148; Stern, Gilmartin and Mellins, *New York 1930*, 192, 456–58, 471. For Dorothy Draper, see Smith, *Interior Design in 20th-Century America*, 104–5, 149–52, 190–91, 234; Stern, Gilmartin and Mellins, *New York 1930*, 140, 394, 431; Carleton Varney, *The Draper Touch: The High Life & High Style of Dorothy Draper* (New York: Prentice Hall Press, 1988).
2. "Snapshots: Nancy V. McClelland," *Interiors* 100 (February 1941): 34, 50; "The Year's Work: Nancy McClelland," *Interiors* 111 (August 1951): 74; "The Year's Work: Nancy McClelland," *Interiors* 112 (August 1952): 82; Smith, *Interior Design in 20th-Century America*, 56–57, 96–97, 149.
3. Jane S. Smith, *Elsie de Wolf: A Life in High Style* (New York: Atheneum, 1982), 319. Also see Smith, *Interior Design in 20th-Century America*, 17–27, 53–56, 103–4, 189, 199.
4. "Taste in Our Time," *House and Garden* 91 (April 1947): 72, 78–79. Also see Smith, *Interior Design in 20th-Century America*, 96, 189.
5. "Regency, Formal Favorite," *House and Garden* 77 (May 1940), sec. 2: 23; "Taste in Our Time": 72–73; William W. Baldwin, *Billy Baldwin Remembers* (New York: Harcourt, Brace, Jovanovich, 1974), 33–46, 48–51, 55–56, 63–66, 70–71, 81, 91, 140, 154, 167–69, 193, 201; William W. Baldwin with Michael Gardine, *Billy Baldwin: An Autobiography* (Boston: Little, Brown, 1985), 79–80, 85–95, 121–28, 132–43, 148, 150–51, 165, 172, 182, 184–85, 189–94, 199, 208–11, 222–25, 297–300; Smith, *Interior Design in 20th-Century America*, 56–59, 96, 98–99, 148–49, 193.
6. T. H. Robsjohn-Gibbings, *Good-bye, Mr. Chippendale* (New York: Alfred A. Knopf, 1944); Kenneth Reid, "From Oscar Wilde to Buffalo Bill: T. H. Robsjohn-Gibbings," *Pencil Points* 25 (July 1944): 62–63; T. H. Robsjohn-Gibbings, *Homes of the Brave* (New York: Alfred A. Knopf, 1954); Smith, *Interior Design in 20th-Century America*, 155–56, 196–97, 235–36.
7. "Black Plus White Plus Gray," *House and Garden* 99 (April 1951): 83.
8. "The City: Living It Up," *Time* 79 (April 13, 1962): 58–67.
9. "Colors to Live With: Soft Twentieth Century Pastels," *House and Garden* 142 (September 1972): 68–73. Also see Smith, *Interior Design in 20th-Century America*, 153–54, 233–34, 268–69.
10. Olga Gueft, "Perfectionism over Turtle Bay: The Greer-Hess Duplex," *Interiors* 116 (March 1957): 148–53; "A Decorator Decorates for Himself," *Vogue* 129 (March 1, 1957): 164–67; Bodil Wrede Nielsen, "The Old World's Idle: Elegant Illusions Recalled by Michael Greer," *Interiors* 118 (June 1959): 98–103; "Revamped Duplex," *Interior Design* 32 (August 1963): 88–89; Henry Lionel Williams and Ottelie K. Williams, *America's Small Houses and City Apartments: The Personal Homes of Designers and Collectors* (New York: Bonanza Books, 1964), 204–15; "From Mozart to Beethoven: Michael Greer's Revised Duplex," *Interiors* 124 (August 1964): 53–78; "Carte Blanche," *Interior Design* 37 (September 1966): 154–61; "Translated from the French," *Interior Design* 38 (June 1967): 86–95; "Fifth on Fifth," *Interior Design* 40 (November 1969): 144–47; Smith, *Interior Design in 20th-Century America*, 234.
11. Typical early work included the living room of Mrs. Warren Persky's Park Avenue duplex. See "Live as Well as You Look," *House and Garden* 94 (October 1948):

109–22. Also see Smith, *Interior Design in 20th-Century America*, 160, 193–94, 236–37, 269–70.

12. George O'Brien, ed., *The New York Times Book of Interior Design and Decoration* (New York: Farrar, Straus and Giroux, 1965), 59; Baldwin with Gardine, *Billy Baldwin: An Autobiography*, 163, 165, 195–201, 206, 210; Smith, *Interior Design in 20th-Century America*, 269.

13. "Cole Porter's Apartment," *Vogue* 126 (November 1, 1955): 131–33; Rita Reif, "Cole Porter's Bookshelves: They're So Nice to Come Home To," *New York Times* (March 1, 1967), VI: 46; Baldwin, *Billy Baldwin Remembers*, 136, 138–39; Charles Schwartz, *Cole Porter: A Biography* (New York: Dial Press, 1977), 203, 251–52; Baldwin with Gardine, *Billy Baldwin: An Autobiography*, 282–83; Smith, *Interior Design in 20th-Century America*, 237.

14. Billy Baldwin quoted in "Life Inside a Bouquet," *Vogue* 146 (October 15, 1965): 146–49.

15. "Life Inside a Bouquet": 148.

16. For the Lawrence apartment, see "How to Make a Room a Portrait of the Up-to-Date You," *House and Garden* 144 (October 1973): 91–101. For the Hayward apartment, see "How Five Rooms Reflect Five Personalities," *House and Garden* 138 (October 1970): 104–9.

17. "Snapshots: William Pahlmann," *Interiors* 100 (April 1941): 29–31, 60–62; William Pahlmann, *The Pahlmann Book of Interior Design* (New York: Studio-Crowell, 1955); C. Ray Smith, "William Pahlmann at 84," *Interior Design* 55 (December 1984): 192–95; Smith, *Interior Design in 20th-Century America*, 156–59, 194–95, 240–41, 254, 317.

18. For the New York School of Fine and Applied Arts, which changed its name to the Parsons School of Design in 1940, see Smith, *Interior Design in 20th-Century America*, 25, 94, 189–90; Stern, Gilmartin and Mellins, *New York 1930*, 456–57.

19. "Regency Revels in Color and Mellow Texture," *House and Garden* 77 (March 1940): 30; "American Art and William Pahlmann," *Interiors* 100 (May 1941): 24–25, 54–55.

20. "Pahlmann Peruvian," *Interiors* 101 (December 1941): 34–35; "Pahlmann Rooms Become Proverbial," *Decorative Furnisher* 82 (June 1942): 10–13; Smith, *Interior Design in 20th-Century America*, 194.

21. "Pahlmann's Private Practice," *Interiors* 102 (September 1942): 44–45. Also see "William Pahlmann, F.A.I.D.," *Interior Design* 35 (March 1964): 158–63.

22. "The Year's Work: William Pahlmann, New York," *Interiors* 103 (August 1943): 45.

23. "Pahlmann's Own Home," *Interiors* 115 (September 1955): 108–9. For an earlier brownstone apartment, see "Blended to Taste," *House and Garden* 94 (September 1948): 102–5.

24. "Pahlmann's Mixture," *Interiors* 108 (November 1948): 106–9.

25. "William Pahlmann," *Interior Design* 36 (March 1965): 206.

26. "Defying Architectural Handicaps in Manhattan," *Interiors* 116 (March 1957): 146–47.

27. "Live as Well as You Look": 113.

28. "The City: Living It Up": 66.

29. "William Pahlmann," *House and Garden* 129 (February 1966): 110–13.

30. Walter Gropius, *Scope of Total Architecture* (New York: Harper, 1955). Also see Nancy J. Troy, *Modernism and the Decorative Arts: Art Nouveau to Le Corbusier* (New Haven, Conn.: Yale University Press, 1991).

31. Stern, Gilmartin and Mellins, *New York 1930*, 468–75.

32. Stern, Gilmartin and Mellins, *New York 1930*, 735, 740.

33. Smith, *Interior Design in 20th-Century America*, 86–87, 182.

34. "Twin Apartments: Individual Designs," *Interiors* 103 (March 1944): 39–43; "Two Identical New York Apartments Have Their Faces Lifted," *Pencil Points* 25 (December 1944): 63–67.

35. "Park Avenue Penthouse: An Apartment Designed by Felix Augenfeld," *Interiors* 108 (June 1949): 98–103.

36. S. G. Weiner, "Park Avenue Butcher Shop," letter to the editor, *Interiors* 108 (July 1949): 8.

37. Louise Sloane, "Apartment Interiors," *Progressive Architecture* 36 (August 1955): 131–35.

38. Arthur Drexler, "Pei's Planned Surprises, or the Subtleties of Goldfish," *Interiors* 109 (March 1950): 98–101.

39. "The Year's Work: Design Unit, New York City," *Interiors* 108 (August 1948): 172; "Hearth and Drafting Table," *Interiors* 108 (November 1948): 102–3. Also see Smith, *Interior Design in 20th-Century America*, 228–29, 266–67, 310–11.

40. Baldwin would repeat this formula with equal success in a later apartment for himself at 70 Central Park West. See O'Brien, ed., *The New York Times Book of Interior Design and Decoration*, 40–41, 68; Barbara Plumb, *Young Designs in Living* (New York: Viking Press, 1969), 48–49; Barbara Plumb, "Livability Lives Here," *New York Times* (October 5, 1969), VI: 118–19.

41. Smith, *Interior Design in 20th-Century America*, 229–30, 265–66, 311–12.

42. Jane Fiske, "Ward Bennett's Rebuttal: Color, Comfort and Comity," *Interiors* 112 (October 1952): 114–17, 140. Also see "The Year's Work: Ward Bennett, New York," *Interiors* 111 (August 1951): 83.

43. Olga Gueft, "Above the City," *Interiors* 114 (May 1955): 76–85.

44. "What Is a Decorator?" *House and Garden* 113 (May 1958): 78–79; Wendy Buehr, "Ward Bennett's Bachelor Digs: An Artful Solution," *Interiors* 117 (June 1958): 96–99.

45. "How to Make the Space You Have More Flexible," *House and Garden* 117 (April 1960): 134–35; "Living with Sculpture," *House and Garden* 119 (March 1961): 120–21.

46. O'Brien, ed., *The New York Times Book of Interior Design and Decoration*, 82–83.

47. "How to Put New Life in Your Living Room," *House and Garden* 117 (April 1960): 130–35.

48. Olga Gueft, "Perfectionism on Park Avenue," *Interiors* 122 (December 1962): 64–71.

49. O'Brien, ed., *The New York Times Book of Interior Design and Decoration*, 38–39, 57, 82; "A Rooftop Eyrie Gives a Modern Designer Exactly the Home He Wants," *House and Garden* 127 (February 1965): 116–21; "Un Attico a New York," *Domus* 429 (August 1965): 36–42. For the Dakota, see Stern, Gilmartin and Massengale, *New York 1900*, 283–85, 364–65.

50. "A Rooftop Eyrie Gives a Modern Designer Exactly the Home He Wants": 116.

51. "Open-End Rooms," *House and Garden* 138 (October 1970): 138–41.

52. Smith, *Interior Design in 20th-Century America*, 321–23.

53. "Decorating that Comes Naturally—Natural Colors, Natural Materials," *House and Garden* 136 (October 1969): 111.

54. "How to Stretch Your Decorating Dollars," *House and Garden* 137 (April 1970): 78–79.

55. For a discussion of supergraphics, see C. Ray Smith, *Supermannerism: New Attitudes in Post-Modern Architecture* (New York: E. P. Dutton, 1977), 269–97.

56. "One Continuous Room," *House and Garden* 138 (October 1970): 130–33. For other work by Saladino, see "Compact and Contemporary," *Interior Design* 47 (September 1976): 116–21.

57. It could also be seen in the work of Robert Bray and Michael Schaible, who teamed up with Bennett's sometime collaborator Poppy Wolff in the design of Mrs. Dutton Herbert's apartment at 88 Central Park West. See "City Statement in White," *Architectural Digest* 31 (January–February 1975): 112–15.

58. Joseph Paul D'Urso quoted in Peter Carlsen, "A Minimalist's Paradigm," *Interiors* 135 (October 1975): 120R–22R. Also see Smith, *Interior Design in 20th-Century America*, 313–14.

59. "Calvin Klein: Modern Classic in America," *Vogue* 165 (November 1975): 198–99; "Expanding the View," *Interior Design* 47 (February 1976): 144–49.

60. Calvin Klein quoted in "Calvin Klein: Modern Classic in America": 198.

61. Walter Rendell Storey, "Interior Decoration," *Americana Annual for 1948* (New York and Chicago: Encyclopedia Americana Corporation, 1949): 331–32.

62. Olga Gueft, "Case of Ambidexterity: Bertha Schaeffer," *Interiors* 116 (April 1957): 94–101, 179. Also see Louise Sloane, "Apartment Interiors," *Progressive Architecture* 36 (August 1956): 131, 137.

63. Cleve Gray, "Bold Words to the Timid," *House and Garden* 121 (March 1961): 198–201, 230–32.

64. Arthur Drexler, "East Side Basement: An Art Gallery to Live In," *Interiors* 109 (May 1950): 72–83. For the Campanile, see Stern, Gilmartin and Mellins, *New York 1930*, 413, 432–33.

65. Drexler, "East Side Basement: An Art Gallery to Live In": 72, 74.

66. "Good Decoration Begins with a Plan," *House and Garden* 106 (October 1954): 132–33.

67. *Philip Johnson: Architecture 1949–1965*, with an intro. by Henry-Russell Hitchcock (New York: Holt, Rinehart and Winston, 1966), 13–14.

68. "Brilliant Sea Mirage in Gotham: Apartment for an Art Collector by Arthur Drexler," *Interiors* 119 (March 1960): 106–11; "Spacemaking—1960," *Vogue* 135 (March 1, 1960): 175–79.

69. "Brilliant Sea Mirage in Gotham: Apartment for an Art Collector by Arthur Drexler": 106.

70. For Wolff's own apartment, see "A Beautiful Party in One Room," *House and Garden* 125 (May 1964): 162–65. For Robert Loggia's apartment, see John Anderson, "All-Purpose Living Area," *Interiors* 129 (March 1970): 106–7. Also see a small entry foyer by Wolff in Betty Raymond, "Private Art Gallery," *Interiors* 126 (July 1967): 110.

71. "Collectors' Co-Op," *Interior Design* 36 (March 1965): 164–69.

72. "The Year's Work: Albert Herbert, New York," *Interiors* 116 (August 1956): 82–83; "Chiaroscuro in Design," *Interior Design* 30 (February 1959): 104–6.

73. "The Contemporary Idiom," *Interior Design* 34 (June 1963): 96–99.

74. "Six Stories in Four," *Interiors* 125 (August 1965): 52–57. For Johnson's apartment, see Stern, Gilmartin and Mellins, *New York 1930*, 472, 474–75.

75. "How Young Collectors Live with Art," *House and Garden* 122 (November 1962): 216–17.

76. "Space-and-Light: The New York Apartment of Fred Mueller," *Vogue* 157 (February 1, 1971): 174–77.

77. Betsy Darrach, "For Epicureans: Fine Art, Immaculate Forms," *Interiors* 117 (May 1957): 124–27; "The City: Living It Up": 63; Carol Herselle Krinsky, *Gordon Bunshaft of Skidmore, Owings & Merrill* (New York: Architectural History Foundation; Cambridge, Mass.: MIT Press, 1988), 134.

78. "Apartment of a Beaux-Arts Gentleman," *Architectural Forum* 117 (August 1962): 114–17. For discussion of Levi's New York work, see Stern, Gilmartin and Massengale, *New York 1900*, 161; Stern, Gilmartin and Mellins, *New York 1930*, 331. For the Osborne, see Stern, Gilmartin and Massengale, *New York 1900*, 282.

79. "Personal Taste—The Great Blender," *House and Garden* 124 (November 1963): 218–23.

80. "Duplex on Park," *Interior Design* 31 (August 1960): 82–87; John Anderson, "Park Avenue Penthouse," *Interiors* 120 (August 1960): 60–65; Edward Durell Stone, *The Evolution of an Architect* (New York: Horizon Press, 1962), 220–21; "The City: Living It Up": 61.

81. "Spectacular Art in the Comfortable Apartment of S. I. Newhouse, Jr.," *House and Garden* 136 (November 1969): 84–91. Baldwin's design of Mr. and Mrs. Lee V. Eastman's living room was intended to highlight a collection of contemporary art. See "Rooms that Say Welcome," *House and Garden* 142 (November 1972): 96–99.

82. Olga Gueft, "Crystallization of Lustig's Style," *Interiors* 114 (July 1955): 82–89. Also see "Two Adjacent Rooms by Alvin Lustig," *Interiors* 116 (January 1957): 116–17; "The Apartment—An Artful Place for Living," *Architectural Forum* 106 (May 1957): 146–47.

83. In 1966 she was to collaborate with the architects Oppenheimer, Brady & Lehrecke on the renovation of the house at 160 East Seventieth Street she shared with her second husband, Arthur Cohen, the novelist and publisher. See "A Knowing Designer Transforms an Ordinary House," *House and Garden* 131 (April 1967): 160–67.

84. C. Ray Smith, "The Designers," *Progressive Architecture* 48 (May 1967): 149.

85. Bodil Wrede Nielsen, "Artful Updating of a Rare Flat," *Interiors* 119 (June 1960): 110–15; "Chameleon Serenity for an Inexhaustible Designer," *Interiors* 122 (November 1962): 92–99; "An Apartment Where Change Is the Rule," *House and Garden* 123 (April 1963): 146–51; Plumb, *Young Designs in Living*, 20–21.

86. Jack Lenor Larson quoted in "Under One Roof: A String of Many Moods," *House and Garden* 133 (September 1968): 110–17. Also see Olga Gueft, "Chameleon Apartment—Phase 2," *Interiors* 127 (April 1968): 132–36; Barbara Plumb, "Sculptured Moods," *New York Times* (August 18, 1968), VI: 56–57. In 1968 Larson furthered his experiments with stretch fabric and special lighting in a room he designed with Earl Reiback and installed at his showroom. See "How to Paint a Room with Light," *House and Garden* 135 (January 1969): 78–83.

87. Aleksandra Kasuba quoted in "Space Shelters for Senses," *Interiors* 130 (July 1971): 22, 26. Also see "Artist Creates a 'Space Shelter for the Senses,'" *Architectural Record* 149 (April 1971): 37; Rita Reif, "From Stretch Fabric and Yak Hair, a 'Background for Living,'" *New York Times* (May 11, 1971): 34; James D. Morgan, "Interiors," *Architectural Record* 150 (August 1971): 93–95; Janet Malcolm, "On and Off the Avenue: About the House," *New Yorker* 47 (September 25, 1971): 115–17; Susan Grant Lewin, "A Truly Sensuous House," *House Beautiful* 113 (November 1971): 118–21; Norma Skurka and Oberto Gili, *Underground Interiors: Decorating for Alternate Life Styles* (New York: Quadrangle Books, 1972), 30–31.

88. Aleksandra Kasuba quoted in "Artist Creates a 'Space Shelter for the Senses'": 37.

89. Aleksandra Kasuba quoted in Malcolm, "On and Off the Avenue: About the House": 115–16.

90. Aleksandra Kasuba quoted in "Space Shelters for Senses": 22, 26.

91. Tiziana and Hugh Hardy quoted in "Implications of Giants," *Progressive Architecture* 48 (May 1967): 156–57. The Hardy's nursery—a corner of their master bedroom denoted by supergraphics—was published in Plumb, *Young Designs in Living*, 136; Smith, *Supermannerism*, 276–78. Also see Barbara Plumb, "Full of Tricks," *New York Times* (April 9, 1967), VI: 114–15; Skurka and Gili, *Underground Interiors*, 94.

92. Smith, *Supermannerism*, 122.

93. Peter Hoppner quoted in "White-and-Silver Orbit," *Progressive Architecture* 48 (May 1967): 152–53. Also see Smith, *Supermannerism*, 151, color plate 16.

94. Frederick Romley quoted in "Portable Silver Capsules," *Progressive Architecture* 48 (May 1967): 154–55. Also see Barbara Plumb, "Making a Scene," *New York Times* (July 9, 1967), VI: 40–41; Smith, *Supermannerism*, 151–52, 311.

95. Sim Van Der Ryn, "A First in the Architectural Press," letter to the editor, *Progressive Architecture* 48 (July 1967): 6.

96. David Bourdon, *Warhol* (New York: Harry N. Abrams, 1989), 170–71, 179.

97. Skurka and Gili, *Underground Interiors*, 84–85; David A. Morton, "Superpainting," *Progressive Architecture* 53 (May 1972): 120–23.

98. "Mini Rooms as Super Furniture," *Progressive Architecture* 49 (February 1969): 136–37; Plumb, *Young Designs in Living*, 140–41; Smith, *Supermannerism*, color plate 17.

99. "Graphics that Make Space Respond," *House and Garden* 136 (October 1969): 113; Smith, *Supermannerism*, 313–14; Karen Fisher, *Living for Today* (New York: Viking Press, 1979), 40–41.

100. "New-Think Furniture: One, Two, Three—Change," *House Beautiful* 113 (July 1971): 50–51.

101. Plumb, *Young Designs in Living*, 150–51.

102. "Room within a Room Storage," *House and Garden* 139 (March 1971): 102.

103. "Two by George Ranalli," *Interior Design* 47 (January 1976): 142–45.

104. Michael Hollander quoted in Smith, *Supermannerism*, 314–15.

105. C. Ray Smith, "Kinetic Kit Environment," *Progressive Architecture* 50 (September 1969): 138–43. Also see Barbara Plumb, "Instant Apartment," *New York Times* (September 7, 1969), VI: 114–15; Barbara Plumb, *Young Designs in Color* (New York: Viking Press, 1972), 162–69; Smith, *Supermannerism*, 317–21.

106. "Color + Carpet for a Big Look in a Small Space," *House and Garden* 146 (September 1974): 92–95. For their apartment for Fern Mallis, see "How to Make a Room with Carpet and Color," *House and Garden* 145 (April 1974): 80–81; Jeanne G. Weeks, "Interior Design," *Americana Annual for 1974* (New York and Chicago: Encyclopedia Americana Corporation, 1975): 297.

107. "Space as Live-In Sculpture," *House Beautiful* 113 (July 1971): 44–49. Also see Barbara Plumb, "Space Find," *New York Times* (June 12, 1969), VI: 44–45; Plumb, *Young Designs in Living*, 24–25; "Mirrors, Sculptural Forms and a Disciplined Palette of Colors and Materials Give this Manhattan Apartment an Emphatically Abstract Vigor," *Architectural Record* 155 (January 1974): 108–9.

108. Gamal El-Zoghby quoted in Jane Geniesse, "The New Art of Uncluttering," *New York* 5 (April 17, 1972): 42.

109. "Space as Live-In Sculpture": 44–46; Skurka and Gili, *Underground Interiors*, 42–45.

110. Skurka and Gili, *Underground Interiors*, 45.

111. "How the Other Half Sleeps: Notable New York Bedrooms," *New York* 6 (April 30, 1973): 51–57.

112. Gamal El-Zoghby quoted in "Space as Live-In Sculpture": 47.

113. "Projection: The New Turned-On Décor," *House Beautiful* 109 (September 1967): 138–39. Also see Skurka and Gili, *Underground Interiors*, 119–20; Smith, *Supermannerism*, 297–98, color plates 23–24.

114. "Floating Platform," *Progressive Architecture* 48 (May 1967): 150–51; Barbara Plumb, "Paul's Pacesetter," *New York Times* (July 23, 1967), VI: 42–43; Plumb, *Young Designs in Living*, 126–27; Smith, *Supermannerism*, 149, color plate 13. In 1954 Philip Johnson designed a geometrically intricate river-facing platform for Mr. and Mrs. Thomas B. Hess's Beekman Place townhouse. See Philip Johnson, "Whence and Whither: The Processional Element in Architecture," *Perspecta* 9/10 (1965): 167–78, fig. 12, reprinted in Peter Eisenman and Robert A. M. Stern, eds., *Philip Johnson: Writings* (New York: Oxford University Press, 1979), 150–55.

115. Paul Rudolph quoted in Plumb, *Young Designs in Living*, 126–27.

116. Paul Rudolph quoted in "A Spectacular Apartment by Paul Rudolph," *House and Garden* 148 (October 1976): 116–23.

117. Paul Rudolph quoted in "Remodeling a Small New York City Apartment," *Architectural Record* 158 (August 1975): 74–75.

118. "Space Design," *Vogue* 165 (September 1975): 294–97.

119. "White, Silver, Hot Color," *House and Garden* 138 (September 1970): 82–83; "Spectacular New Storage Strategies," *House and Garden* 139 (March 1971): 100; Skurka and Gili, *Underground Interiors*, 32–33.

120. "The Talk of the Town: Three Gatherings," *New Yorker* 46 (January 30, 1971): 22–23. Also see Valentine Lawford, "A Reflection of Now," *Vogue* 158 (October 1971): 180–81, 191.

121. Plumb, *Young Designs in Living*, 148–49; *Robert A. M. Stern: Buildings and Projects 1965–1980*, eds. Peter Arnell and Ted Bickford (New York: Rizzoli International Publications, 1981), 240.

122. Barbara Plumb, "Modern Updated," *New York Times* (December 31, 1967), VI: 120–21; "The Daring Never-Before," *House Beautiful* 110 (October 1968): 120–21; Plumb, *Young Designs in Living*, 18–19; "Architect's Apartment, New York City: Der Scutt, Architect," *Architectural Record* 148 (August 1970): 90–91.

123. "Unger Apartment: New Volumes, New Finishes, New Lifestyle," *Architectural Record* 160 (September 1976): 108–10; *Charles Gwathmey and Robert Siegel: Buildings and Projects 1964–1984*, eds. Peter Arnell and Ted Bickford (New York: Harper & Row, 1984), 124–25.

124. Nancy Craig, "An Architect Mixes Landmark Drama with a Casual Lifestyle," *House Beautiful* 112 (July 1970): 31–34; "Architect's Apartment, New York City: David Beer, Architect," *Architectural Record* 148 (August 1970): 94.

125. For 131–135 East Sixty-sixth Street, see Stern, Gilmartin and Massengale, *New York 1900*, 298–99.

126. "The End of the Box," *House Beautiful* 113 (July 1971): cover, 24–27.

127. "Entertaining Environment," *House and Garden* 140 (November 1971): 80–81; Skurka and Gili, *Underground Interiors*, 114–15.

128. "Nonstop Brilliance," *House and Garden* 142 (September 1972): 74–79.

129. Barbara Plumb, "Fighting Space Boredom," *New York Times* (April 21, 1968), VI: 104–5; Elizabeth Sverbeyeff, "New York Grande Dame Puts on a New Face," *House Beautiful* 110 (July 1968): 38–41; Plumb, *Young Designs in Living*, 22–23; *Robert A. M. Stern: Buildings and Projects 1965–1980*, 240. Another early Stern apartment was renovated in 1968 for Mr. and Mrs. Robert Gimbel at 4 East Seventy-second Street. See *Robert A. M. Stern: Buildings and Projects 1965–1980*, 240–41. For his 1971 apartment for Mr. and Mrs. Barrie Sommerfield at 829 Park Avenue, see "Structural Revamping," *Interior Design* 42 (November 1971): cover, 88–89.

130. Norma Skurka, "Spaced Out," *New York Times* (September 24, 1972), VI: 73–74; Nancy Craig, "When the Plan's Redrawn," *House Beautiful* 115 (March 1973): 112–17; *Robert A. M. Stern: Buildings and Projects 1965–1980*, 240–41.

131. Melissa Sutphen, "Remodeling within the Box Sparks a Grand Dialogue between Architecture and Art," *House Beautiful* 114 (May 1972): 115–21; Sharon Lee Ryder, "Breaking out of the Box," *Progressive Architecture* 54 (December 1973): 50–55; *Robert A. M. Stern: Buildings and Projects 1965–1980*, 240–41.

132. Robert Stern quoted in Sutphen, "Remodeling within the Box Sparks a Grand Dialogue between Architecture and Art": 115.

133. Ryder, "Breaking out of the Box": 50, 54–55; "Renovated Duplex Preserves Clues to Its Past," *Architectural Record* 132 (October 1975): 87, 92–94; *Robert A. M. Stern: Buildings and Projects 1965–1980*, 44–47.

134. Ryder, "Breaking out of the Box": 50–51; "Adding the New; Keeping the Best," *Interior Design* 45 (July 1974): 96–99; *Robert A. M. Stern: Buildings and Projects 1965–1980*, 40–43.

135. O'Brien, ed., *The New York Times Book of Interior Design and Decoration*, 49.

136. "Beauty All Around You in a Spa Bath," *House and Garden* 139 (May 1971): 90–91, 146; "Classic Modern Setting for a Fascinating Woman," *House and Garden* 140 (July 1971): 60–63; Paul Goldberger, "A Design for Orderly Living," *New York Times* (December 11, 1971): 147; Richard Henry Tollerton, "The Cool World of Faye Dunaway," *House and Garden* 141 (February 1972): 52–53; Fisher, *Living for Today*, 22–24; *Charles Gwathmey and Robert Siegel: Buildings and Projects 1964–1984*, 44–45.

137. Tom Yee, "Make-Over for Modern Living: Apartment Designed for Books and Art," *House and Garden* 147 (March 1975): 68–73; Ruth Miller Fitzgibbons, "Mini-Building within a Shell," *Interiors* 135 (October 1975): 132R–35R, 164R; *Charles Gwathmey and Robert Siegel: Buildings and Projects 1964–1984*, 60–61.

OFFICES

1. For the Larkin Building, see Jack Quinan, *Frank Lloyd Wright's Larkin Building: Myth and Fact* (New York: Architectural History Foundation; Cambridge, Mass.: MIT Press, 1987). For S. C. Johnson & Son's headquarters, see Jonathan Lipman, *Frank Lloyd Wright and the Johnson Wax Buildings* (New York: Rizzoli International Publications, 1986).

2. See Lois Wagner Green, ed., *Interiors Book of Offices* (New York: Whitney Library of Design, 1959), 1–3; Michael Saphier, *Office Planning and Design* (New York: McGraw-Hill, 1968), 1–3; Maurice Mogulescu, *Profit through Design* (New York: American Management Association, 1970), 9–15; John Pile, *Interiors 3rd Book of Offices* (New York: Whitney Library of Design, 1976), 19–21; Lila Shoshkes, *Space Planning: Designing the Office Environment* (New York: Architectural Record Books, 1976), 1–10; John Pile, *Open Office Planning* (New York: Whitney Library of Design, 1978), 14–16.

3. "Portfolio of Rockefeller Center Interiors," *Interiors* 100 (May 1941): 14–21.

4. "Bulova Watch Co. Rockefeller Center, New York City," *Architectural Forum* 72 (February 1940): 86–88.

5. For all of these offices, see "Portfolio of Rockefeller Center Interiors": 16–17, 19. For Stone's work for Simon & Schuster, also see Maxine Block, ed., *Current Biography 1941* (New York: H. W. Wilson Co., 1941), 797; Edward Durell Stone, *The Evolution of an Architect* (New York: Horizon Press, 1962), 79.

6. "Beryl S. Austrian," *Interiors* 102 (August 1942): 80; "Women Executives and Their Offices," *Interiors* 102 (October 1942): 22–27.

7. "The Year's Work—Autumn Portfolio," *Interiors* 101 (August 1941): 29.

8. "The Year's Work," *Interiors* 103 (August 1943): 34.

9. "Mademoiselle Marches On," *Interiors* 103 (June 1944): 44–47.

10. See Betsy Darrach, "Prime Mover without Pretenses," *Interiors* 116 (May 1957): 118–24. For Lemaire's work in the 1930s, see Stern, Gilmartin and Mellins, *New York 1930*, 326, 363–64, 366. For her large-scale work in New York, see the discussion of the Manufacturers Trust Company branch bank at 510 Fifth Avenue of 1954 in chapter 5 of this volume. For her Manufacturers Trust Company branch bank at 44 Wall Street, see "Banks," *Interior Design* 29 (April 1958): 186–89; "Manufacturers Trust Company: New York, New York," *Progressive Architecture* 39 (August 1958): 154–55.

11. "The Year's Work," *Interiors* 104 (August 1944): 53.

12. For all of these offices, see "Nine to Five: A Portfolio of Offices," *Interior Design and Decoration* 21 (January 1950): 48–53.

13. L. Andrew Reinhard and Henry Hofmeister, "New Trends in Office Design," *Architectural Record* 97 (March 1945): 99–103.

14. "Success Story with Illustrative Notes," *Interiors* 105 (October 1945): 54–61.

15. "Experimental Office," *Architectural Forum* 82 (January 1945): 124–28; "Designed Both for Work and for Display," *Interiors* 104 (June 1945): 62–66; "About the Career of a Young Man with an Inquiring Mind: Alvin Lustig, Designer," *Interiors* 106 (September 1946): 68–75; Jane Fiske Mitarachi, "The Lustig Portfolio '53," *Interiors* 112 (June 1953): 90–97.

16. "Alvin Lustig Designs Offices for: Reporter Publications," *Architectural Forum* 84 (May 1946): cover, 109–13; "Claustrophobia Conquered by Unorthodox Design," *Interiors* 105 (June 1946): 60–69.

17. "Publisher's Reception Room," *Architectural Forum* 83 (October 1945): 98–101; "Work and Play Space for Publishers," *Interiors* 105 (June 1946): 82–83.

18. For Starrett & Van Vleck's 1915 office building, see W. Parker Chase, *New York: The Wonder City* (New York: Wonder City Publishing Co., 1932; New York: New York Bound, 1983), 222.

19. "Dial Press. New York, New York," *Progressive Architecture* 29 (May 1948): 97; "Dial Press. New York, New York," *Progressive Architecture* 29 (November 1948): 97.
20. For Louis Hatkoff Associates' offices for the Sterling Advertising Agency, see "New Offices Emphasize Coordination," *Architectural Record* 111 (March 1952): 168–71. For Ketchum, Giná & Sharp's offices for the H. B. Humphrey Company, see "Three-In-One Office for Advertising Agency," *Architectural Record* 111 (June 1952): 140–41. Carson & Lundin's offices for Cunningham & Walsh are illustrated in "Color Enlivens Offices," *Architectural Record* 114 (October 1953): 173–77; for their offices for the Marschalk & Pratt Division of McCann-Erickson, see Louise Sloane, "Advertising Agency and Architects' Office," *Progressive Architecture* 37 (September 1956): 159–61. Goldstone & Dearborn's offices for Erwin, Wasey & Co. are illustrated in "Agency Offices," *Progressive Architecture* 38 (September 1957): 162–63.
21. Norman Bel Geddes, *Horizons* (Boston: Little, Brown, 1932), 244, 246–47.
22. "Some Redesigned Interiors Add Sparkle to J. Walter Thompson's Home Office," *Architectural Forum* 83 (December 1945): 124–26; "Advertising Offices by Lescaze Facilitate Activities, Express the Mood of an Extrovert Profession," *Interiors* 105 (June 1946): 74–79.
23. Stern, Gilmartin and Mellins, *New York 1930*, 472–73.
24. "Remodeled Offices Yield Pleasant and Flexible Conference Areas," *Architectural Forum* 83 (December 1945): 122–23.
25. Olga Gueft, "Gerald Luss: The Designer Who Thinks of Everything," *Interiors* 116 (January 1957): 106–11, 115; Olga Gueft, "Third Design Firm Case Study: Designs for Business, Inc.," *Interiors* 119 (January 1960): 72–99, 141; Walter McQuade, "The Booming Office Planners," *Architectural Forum* 116 (January 1962): 82–87; Shoshkes, *Space Planning*, 3–4.
26. Jane Fiske, "Room Enough for Copy or Reinforced Concrete," *Interiors* 111 (April 1952): 90–93; "Offices for a Publishing Firm," *Architectural Record* 111 (June 1952): 116–17.
27. Olga Gueft, "Rich Vistas among the Cinder Blocks," *Interiors* 113 (July 1954): 50–57; Green, ed., *Interiors Book of Offices*, 106–7.
28. "Offices," *Progressive Architecture* 35 (December 1956): 134–37.
29. Gerald Luss, "The Module Within," *Progressive Architecture* 38 (November 1957): 185–91.
30. Olga Gueft, "Knock-down Luxury for Olin Mathieson," *Interiors* 114 (July 1955): 62–73; Green, ed., *Interiors Book of Offices*, 18, 133–45.
31. Green, ed., *Interiors Book of Offices*, 85.
32. Luss, "The Module Within": 185–91.
33. Gueft, "Gerald Luss: The Designer Who Thinks of Everything": 106–8, 115.
34. Gueft, "Gerald Luss: The Designer Who Thinks of Everything": 109–11.
35. "Corporate Offices for Diverse Operations," *Progressive Architecture* 44 (July 1963): 138–44. Designs for Business also designed new offices for the classified advertising department of the New York Times. See "Goodbye, Times' Flatiron," *Interiors* 122 (January 1963): 84–87.
36. "Offices for Green Stamps," *Progressive Architecture* 46 (August 1965): 156–61; Mogulescu, *Profit through Design*, 20–36, Exhibit II: 15, Exhibit III: 3–5, 10–14, Exhibit IV: 2.
37. "Partitioning Systems," *Progressive Architecture* 42 (July 1961): 124–26; "A Designs for Business Inc. Showcase: Their Own New York Offices, by Gerald Luss," *Interiors* 122 (September 1962): 126–29.
38. John Anderson, "Luss/Kaplan and Associates Limited," *Interiors* 129 (October 1969): 114–37.
39. "The Minskoff Offices by Gerald Luss," *Interiors* 127 (September 1967): 96–101.
40. Olga Gueft, "Grotto for High Finance," *Interiors* 130 (September 1970): 136–41.
41. Gueft, "Grotto for High Finance": 136.
42. Ada Louise Huxtable, "For Those Who Sit and Wait," *New York Times* (April 13, 1975), VI: 74–76.
43. "Who Gets What Office?" *Architectural Forum* 106 (February 1957): 118–21.
44. "Black-Framed Offices for a Designer's Own Promotion," *Interiors* 114 (January 1955): 64–65; "Office of Merit," *Architectural Forum* 103 (July 1955): 166–67.
45. Barbara Allen, "The Big Business: Saphier, Lerner, Schindler, Inc.," *Industrial Design* 13 (February 1966): 27; Olga Gueft, "A Design Firm Case Study," *Interiors* 129 (February 1970): 87–91.
46. "Partitions with a Purpose," *Architectural Forum* 101 (December 1954): 138–40.
47. "Offices: Functional and Decorative," *Interior Design* 27 (May 1956): 88–93; "Art and Flexibility for an Executive Suite," *Architectural Forum* 105 (November 1956): 156.
48. "Space Planning," *Interior Design* 35 (April 1964): 170–78, 194, 210, 213.
49. Olga Gueft, "Smartly Organized Operation," *Interiors* 116 (March 1957): 144–45.
50. Olga Gueft, "Setting for Securities and Art," *Interiors* 128 (January 1969): 108–11.
51. John Anderson, "Michael Saphier Associates," *Interiors* 120 (January 1961): 84–101, 128–29.
52. Anderson, "Michael Saphier Associates": 90–91.
53. Anderson, "Michael Saphier Associates": 98–100.
54. "Three Reception Lobbies in New York," *Interiors* 123 (January 1964): 96–97.
55. Olga Gueft, "Latest Move by Saphier, Lerner, Schindler, Inc.," *Interiors* 126 (September 1966): 118–25.
56. John Anderson, "Mechanization and Expansion at SLS," *Interiors* 130 (January 1971): 72–79.
57. "Mood Muzak," *Interior Design* 43 (December 1972): 78–79; Huxtable, "For Those Who Sit and Wait": 74–76.
58. "Hot Ad Agency: Leber Katz Paccione's 31,000 Square Feet in New York's General Motors Building Are Laid Out for Hot-Line Efficiency and a Democratic Distribution of Daylight," *Interiors* 129 (February 1970): 99–100.
59. Sharon Lee Ryder, "Off on a Tangent," *Progressive Architecture* 56 (December 1975): 62–65.
60. E. J. Kahn, Jr., "Profiles: Big Operator—I," *New Yorker* 27 (December 8, 1951): 46–48, 50, 52–61; E. J. Kahn, Jr., "Profiles: Big Operator—II," *New Yorker* 27 (December 15, 1951): 41–42, 44, 46, 48, 50, 52, 54, 56–58, 61–63, 66–68; Huson Jackson, *A Guide to New York Architecture 1650–1952* (New York: Reinhold Publishing Corp., 1952), 22–23; "William Zeckendorf's Office," *Fortune* 46 (June 1952): 112–16; "Penthouse Offices: Rooftop Showboat Produces Drama and Income for Realtor Zeckendorf," *Architectural Forum* 97 (July 1952): cover, 105–13; Astragal, "Notes & Topics: Pei in the Sky," *Architects' Journal* 116 (August 28, 1952): 241, 243, reprinted in *Architectural Forum* 97 (October 1952): 90, 92, 96, and *Journal of the American Institute of Architects* 18 (December 1952): 268–69; "Office in the Sky," *Interior Design* 23 (September 1952): 46–55, 111; O'Neil Ford, "Astragal on Zeckendorf," letter to the editor, *Architectural Forum* 97 (October 1952): 90; "Bureaux d'une Agence Immobilière, New York," *L'Architecture d'Aujourd'hui* 24 (December 1953): 92–93; Ian McCallum, *Architecture USA* (London: Architectural Press, 1959), 191, 196; Arthur Herzog, "He Loves Things to Be Beautiful," *New York Times* (March 14, 1965), VI: 34–35, 98–100; Barbara Goldsmith, "The Agile Eye of I. M. Pei," *Town & Country* 119 (August 1965): 62, 101–3, 105; Elliott Bernstein, "Real Estate's Humpty-Dumpty: Bill Zeckendorf After the Fall," *New York* 1 (September 23, 1968): 28–31; William Zeckendorf with Edward McCreary, *The Autobiography of William Zeckendorf* (New York: Holt, Rinehart and Winston, 1970), 98–99, plates; Judith Graf Klein, *The Office Book* (New York: Facts On File, 1982), 33.
61. For Cross & Cross's Knapp Building, see Stern, Gilmartin and Mellins, *New York 1930*, 526–27.
62. For the Barcelona Pavilion, see Arthur Drexler, *Ludwig Mies Van Der Rohe* (New York: George Braziller, 1960), 19–20, figs. 20–25. For the Count Charles de Beistegui apartment, see W. Boesiger, ed., *Le Corbusier: Oeuvre complète 1929–1934*, vol. 2 (Zurich: Les Editions d'Architecture, 1934), 53–57.
63. "Penthouse Offices: Rooftop Showboat Produces Drama and Income for Realtor Zeckendorf": 112.
64. Zeckendorf with McCreary, *The Autobiography of William Zeckendorf*, 98.
65. Kahn, "Profiles: Big Operator—I": 59.
66. I. M. Pei quoted in Kahn, "Profiles: Big Operator—I": 59–60.
67. "Penthouse Offices: Rooftop Showboat Produces Drama and Income for Realtor Zeckendorf": 105.
68. Zeckendorf with McCreary, *The Autobiography of William Zeckendorf*, 99.
69. "Penthouse Offices: Rooftop Showboat Produces Drama and Income for Realtor Zeckendorf": 112.
70. "Achieving Individuality," *Progressive Architecture* 43 (October 1962): 194–98.
71. Elaine Kendall, "A Man's Office Is His Castle," *New York Times* (March 15, 1964), VI: 52, 56, 58, 60.
72. John Morris Dixon, "Madison Avenue Was Never Like This," *Architectural Forum* 126 (January–February 1967): 90–95; C. Ray Smith, "Minimal Interiors," *Progressive Architecture* 48 (March 1967): 148–51; C. Ray Smith, *Supermannerism: New Attitudes in Post-Modern Architecture* (New York: E. P. Dutton, 1977), 67–68.
73. "Trim Advertising Office," *Architectural Forum* 117 (December 1962): 120–23.
74. Dixon, "Madison Avenue Was Never Like This": 95.
75. Michael Korda, "Office Power—You Are Where You Sit," *New York* 8 (January 13, 1975): 36–44.
76. Olga Gueft, "Florence Knoll and the Avant Garde," *Interiors* 116 (July 1957): 58–66; McQuade, "The Booming Office Planners": 82, 86; Christine Rae, *Knoll au Louvre*, exhibition catalogue (New York: Knoll International, 1971), unpaginated.
77. "Special Experience, Skills," *Progressive Architecture* 43 (October 1962): 176–77.
78. "CBS Offices by the Same Designer," *Architectural Forum* 102 (January 1955): 134–39.
79. Olga Gueft, "Knoll without Knolls?" *Interiors* 126 (August 1966): 150–57; C. Ray Smith, *Interior Design in 20th-Century America: A History* (New York: Harper & Row, 1987), 316.
80. "Contemporary at Its Best: A Renovation of a Renovation, by Houston Architect Howard Barnstone, A.I.A.," *Interiors* 122 (April 1963): 98–101. For Johnson's building of 1952, see John Jacobus, Jr., *Philip Johnson* (New York: George Braziller, 1962), figs. 29–32.
81. C. Ray Smith, "Wiggle Walls," *Progressive Architecture* 47 (August 1966): 160–63; Bodil W. Nielsen, "Angling the Rectangle," *Interiors* 126 (September 1966): 132–33; Smith, *Supermannerism*, 103.
82. Smith, "Wiggle Walls": 161.
83. Quoted in Smith, "Wiggle Walls": 162.
84. "Office for W. A. Di Giacomo Associates, New York City," *Architectural Record* 147 (January 1970): 118–20.
85. Barclay F. Gordon, "Record Interiors of 1971," *Architectural Record* 149 (January 1971): 85–104.
86. John Anderson, "Living with Art in a Real-Estate Office," *Interiors* 133 (May 1974): 144–47.
87. Olga Gueft, "Fabergé," *Interiors* 130 (March 1971): 94–105; Sharon Lee Ryder, "Super-Facial," *Progressive Architecture* 52 (June 1971): 78–83.
88. "Office Design Called Factor in Recruitment," *Real Estate Record and Guide* 187 (April 1, 1961): 3.
89. Gueft, "Fabergé": 95–96.
90. Gordon, "Record Interiors of 1971": 102–3.
91. "Law Offices, New York City," *Architectural Record* 157 (January 1975): 108–9.
92. Barclay F. Gordon, "Record Interiors of 1974," *Architectural Record* 155 (January 1974): 105–20; "Reception Areas," *Interiors* 134 (August 1974): 90–91.
93. Gordon, "Record Interiors of 1974": 117; "Joseph E. Seagram & Sons, Inc.," *Interiors* 135 (September 1975): 97.
94. Ruth Miller Fitzgibbons, "Resurrecting the Erector Set," *Interiors* 130 (February 1975): 66–69.
95. Ruth Miller Fitzgibbons, "Partitioning with Awnings," *Interiors* 134 (June 1975): 90–93.
96. "Globik Tankers' Executive Offices," *Interior Design* 46 (September 1975): 150–55.
97. For Bower and Gardner, see Sharon Lee Ryder, "Other Spatial Realms," *Progressive Architecture* 58 (February 1977): 72–83; Roger Yee, "Gwathmey Siegel: Law Office of Bower & Gardner," *Interiors* 136 (March 1977): 90–93; Stanley Abercrombie, *Gwathmey Siegel* (New York: Whitney Library of Design, 1981), 118; *Charles Gwathmey and Robert Siegel: Buildings and Projects 1964–1984*, eds. Peter Arnell and Ted Bickford (New York: Harper & Row, 1984), 118–19. For Barber Oil, see Abercrombie, *Gwathmey Siegel*, 119; Klein, *The Office Book*, 133; *Charles Gwathmey and Robert Siegel: Buildings and Projects 1964–1984*, 128–29.
98. Sharon Lee Ryder, "Two by Four," *Progressive Architecture* 56 (June 1975): 66–73; David Dunster, ed., *Michael Graves* (New York: Rizzoli International Publications, 1979), 50; Abercrombie, *Gwathmey Siegel*, 118; *Charles Gwathmey and Robert Siegel: Buildings and Projects 1964–1984*, 88–89.
99. "When the Designers Design for Themselves," *Architectural Forum* 117 (July 1962): 104–9.
100. Richard M. Bennett, "Architecture," *Britannica Book of the Year* (Chicago: Encyclopaedia Britannica, 1947): 69–72; "Design Offices," *Architectural Forum* 86 (May 1947): 89–91; "The Year's Work: Morris Lapidus, New York City," *Interiors* 107 (August

1947): 90; "Architect's Office," advertisement, *Architectural Record* 112 (January 1953): 2–3; Morris Lapidus, *An Architecture of Joy* (Miami, Fla.: E. A. Seemann, 1979), 117–20. For Lapidus's previous office, see "Success Story with Illustrative Notes," *Interiors* 105 (October 1945): 54–61.

101. For Lescaze's and Sanders's buildings, see Stern, Gilmartin and Mellins, *New York 1930*, 378–83.

102. "Rudolph's Dare-Devil Office Destroyed," *Progressive Architecture* 50 (April 1969): 98–105; Sibyl Moholy-Nagy and Gerhard Schwab, *The Architecture of Paul Rudolph* (New York: Praeger, 1970), 26–27; Paul Rudolph, *Drawings* (Tokyo: A.D.A. Edita, 1972), 140–41; Smith, *Supermannerism*, 147–49.

103. "Rudolph's Dare-Devil Office Destroyed": 98.

104. Paul Rudolph quoted in "Rudolph's Dare-Devil Office Destroyed": 98.

105. "Rudolph's Dare-Devil Office Destroyed": 98.

106. Paul Rudolph quoted in "Rudolph's Dare-Devil Office Destroyed": 98.

107. Paul Rudolph quoted in "Rudolph's Dare-Devil Office Destroyed": 102, 104.

108. Priscilla Dunhill, "Life in a Water Tank Room," *Interiors* 125 (September 1965): 118–21; "A New York, Studio di Architettura al Quarantasettesimo Piano," *Domus* 435 (February 1966): 17–19; Ellen Perry, "The Architect's Own Office: Showplace and Workspace," *Progressive Architecture* 47 (September 1966): cover, 126–39; Paul Goldberger, "Art People," *New York Times* (November 19, 1976), II: 19; "James Stewart Polshek and Associates Office," *Space Design* 166 (July 1978): 52–53; *James Stewart Polshek: Context and Responsibility* (New York: Rizzoli International Publications, 1988), 27, 30–31.

109. For the Knox Building, see Stern, Gilmartin and Mellins, *New York 1930*, 546.

110. For Moyer's 295 Madison Avenue (Lefcourt Colonial Building), see Stern, Gilmartin and Mellins, *New York 1930*, 604–5.

111. Mary Jean Kempner, "Young Architects in the Spotlight," *House Beautiful* 108 (July 1966): 67; Perry, "The Architect's Own Office: Showplace and Workspace": 128–29; *Richard Meier Architect: Buildings and Projects 1966–1976* (New York: Oxford University Press, 1976), 18; *Richard Meier Architect: 1964/1984* (New York: Rizzoli International Publications, 1984), 382.

112. *Richard Meier Architect: Buildings and Projects 1966–1976*, 110; *Richard Meier Architect: 1964/1984*, 388.

113. "Economy and Flair Highlight Six Architects' Own Offices," *Architectural Record* 146 (December 1969): 111–18. For the Fuller Building, see Stern, Gilmartin and Mellins, *New York 1930*, 366–67.

114. "Economy and Flair Highlight Six Architects' Own Offices": 115.

115. Smith, *Supermannerism*, 283. Also see C. Ray Smith, "Supergraphics," *Progressive Architecture* 48 (November 1967): 132–33.

116. John Morris Dixon, "Having Fun with Harsh Reality," *Architectural Forum* 132 (May 1970): 66–69.

117. *Robert A. M. Stern: Buildings and Projects 1965–1980*, eds. Peter Arnell and Ted Bickford (New York: Rizzoli International Publications, 1981), 240.

118. Betty Raymond, "The Problem Solvers: Gwathmey and Siegel," *Interiors* 131 (July 1972): 74–77; Abercrombie, *Gwathmey Siegel*, 11–12; *Charles Gwathmey and Robert Siegel: Buildings and Projects 1964–1984*, 50.

119. "Design for Living," *New York* 1 (January 3, 1972): 49. Also see Sharon Lee Ryder, "Renovation: Blueprint Storefront," *Progressive Architecture* 53 (April 1972): 92–93.

STORES

1. See Ketchum's autobiography, *Blazing a Trail* (New York: Vantage Press, 1982).

2. Stern, Gilmartin and Mellins, *New York 1930*, 734.

3. Morris Ketchum, Jr., *Shops & Stores* (New York: Reinhold Publishing Corp., 1948), 111; Stern, Gilmartin and Mellins, *New York 1930*, 312.

4. Stern, Gilmartin and Mellins, *New York 1930*, 310.

5. Stern, Gilmartin and Mellins, *New York 1930*, 310, 312.

6. "Furniture Shop," *Architectural Forum* 77 (August 1942): 86–88; "Artek Exposed," *Interiors* 102 (August 1942): 58–59; Ketchum, *Shops & Stores*, 61, 108, 149, 153.

7. "Three Small Shops: 1. Women's Accessories," *Architectural Record* 91 (March 1942): 47.

8. Morris Ketchum, Jr., "The Open Faced Shop," *Interiors* 101 (July 1942): 44–47; "Display Case," *Progressive Architecture* 27 (April 1946): 105–6; Ketchum, *Shops & Stores*, 153, 158. Also see Morris Ketchum, Jr., "The Retail Shop," *Interiors* 103 (August 1943): 47–51, 55.

9. Kenneth Reid, "Perspectives: The Modernist from Wainscott: Morris Ketchum, Jr.," *Pencil Points* 25 (August 1944): 65–66.

10. Reid, "Perspectives: The Modernist from Wainscott: Morris Ketchum, Jr. ": 65–66; "Store for American Crafts, New York City," *Pencil Points* 25 (August 1944): 67–69; Ketchum, *Shops & Stores*, 26–28.

11. For the first America House, at 7 East Fifty-fourth Street, see "Three Small Shops: 2. Handcraft Shop," *Architectural Record* 91 (March 1942): 48; Ketchum, *Shops & Stores*, 54, 109.

12. "Three Small Shops. 3. Gift Shop," *Architectural Record* 91 (March 1942): 49; Ketchum, "The Open Faced Shop": 46; Reid, "Perspectives: The Modernist from Wainscott: Morris Ketchum, Jr. ": 65.

13. "Store Designers Don't Suffer from Tradition Fixations—Thank God," *Pencil Points* 25 (August 1944): 40–41. For Carpenter's building, the Hotel & Institute Mart, see Stern, Gilmartin and Mellins, *New York 1930*, 210–11.

14. "Shoe Store," *Architectural Forum* 81 (October 1944): 126–28; Ketchum, *Shops & Stores*, 72.

15. "Shoe Salon on New York's Fifth Avenue Is Designed to Exploit the Possibilities of the Open Front," *Architectural Forum* 85 (October 1946): 138–39; "Ketchum, Giná & Sharp Shoe the Ladies," *Interiors* 106 (November 1946): 98–101; Ketchum, *Shops & Stores*, 56, 73, 90–91, 109, 133, 148, 159, 163; Huson Jackson, *A Guide to New York Architecture 1650–1952* (New York: Reinhold Publishing Corp., 1952), 21–22.

16. "Wide Store Space with Open Front," *Architectural Record* 97 (February 1945): 104–6.

17. Ketchum, *Shops & Stores*, 30, 107, 150, 163; "Specialty Shop: New York, N.Y.," *Progressive Architecture* 29 (September 1948): 52–55; "Selected Details: Plymouth Specialty Shop," *Progressive Architecture* 29 (September 1948): 97.

18. Ketchum, *Shops & Stores*, 153; "Specialty Shop: New York, N.Y.," *Progressive Architecture* 29 (September 1948): 68–69.

19. "Wallachs Opening New Store," *New York Times* (March 7, 1955): 36; "Men's Wear Chain Opening Big Shop," *New York Times* (March 14, 1955): 37; "The New Wallachs, with Something for Everybody," *New York Times* (March 15, 1955): 39; "On Upper 5th Avenue, Something for the Men: The New Wallachs," *Architectural Record* 118 (August 1955): 163–68; Louise Sloane, "Selling Areas," *Progressive Architecture* 36 (September 1955): 141–47; Morris Ketchum, Jr., *Shops & Stores*, rev. ed. (New York: Reinhold Publishing Corp., 1957), 25, 45, 140; James S. Hornbeck, ed., *Stores and Shopping Centers* (New York: McGraw-Hill, 1962), 74–75.

20. For Brooks Brothers, see Stern, Gilmartin and Massengale, *New York 1900*, 196.

21. For Howe & Lescaze's building, see Robert A. M. Stern, *George Howe: Toward a Modern American Architecture* (New Haven, Conn.: Yale University Press, 1975), 108–30, figs. 83–97.

22. Morris Lapidus, *Architecture: A Profession & Business* (New York: Reinhold Publishing Corp., 1967); Morris Lapidus, *An Architecture of Joy* (Miami, Fla.: E. A. Seemann, 1979), 71–108; Stern, Gilmartin and Mellins, *New York 1930*, 302; Martina Düttmann and Friederike Schneider, eds., *Morris Lapidus: Architect of the American Dream* (Basel, Berlin and Boston: Birkhäuser Verlag, 1992), 23–70.

23. See Henry-Russell Hitchcock, *Latin American Architecture Since 1945*, exhibition catalogue (New York: Museum of Modern Art, 1955).

24. Morris Lapidus quoted in John W. Cook and Heinrich Klotz, *Conversations with Architects* (New York: Praeger, 1973), 174.

25. Morris Lapidus, "Business Needs the Interior Designer," *Interior Design and Decoration* 17 (September 1941): 40–45, 68; Düttmann and Schneider, eds., *Morris Lapidus: Architect of the American Dream*, 29–30. Also illustrated in this article are Lapidus's Postman's specialty shop and Mangel's clothing store. Also see "Accessories," *Architectural Record* 89 (January 1941): 118; Morris Lapidus, "Store Design: A Merchandising Problem," *Architectural Record* 89 (February 1941): 113–36; Morris Lapidus, "Store Modernizing without Metals," *Architectural Record* 92 (October 1942): 71–72; Morris Lapidus, "The Retail Store and Its Design Problems," *Architectural Record* 97 (February 1945): 96–102; Morris Lapidus, "Lapidus' Alphabet," letter to the editor, *Interiors* 106 (April 1947): 8; Morris Lapidus, "Let's Beautify the Selling Machine: One of the Functions of the Functional Store Is to Attract," *Interiors* 106 (June 1947): 98–99, 142.

26. Lapidus, "The Retail Store and Its Design Problems": 96, 99.

27. "Shop for Popular Shoes," *Interiors* 105 (October 1945): 59–61; "Baroque for Shoe Selling," *Architectural Record* 100 (August 1946): 89–91; Ketchum, *Shops & Stores*, 69; Lapidus, *An Architecture of Joy*, 105.

28. Ketchum, *Shops & Stores*, 39.

29. "Showplace for Character Shoes," *Architectural Record* 100 (August 1946): 92–94.

30. Lapidus, *An Architecture of Joy*, 124; Düttmann and Schneider, eds., *Morris Lapidus: Architect of the American Dream*, 51.

31. "Designing a Jewel Shop that Beckons," *Interiors* 101 (March 1942): 38–39; "Rebajes Jewelry and Gift Shop, New York," *New Pencil Points* 24 (February 1943): 50–51; "The Year's Work: Joseph A. Fernandez," *Interiors* 103 (August 1943): 32; Ketchum, *Shops & Stores*, 72, 154.

32. "Designing a Jewel Shop that Beckons": 39.

33. "The Talk of the Town: Kitty Kelly Airborne," *New Yorker* 35 (October 17, 1959): 33–34; Marian Page, "Manhattan Shoe Shop," *Interiors* 119 (June 1960): 123.

34. "Corsetorium, Rego Park, Long Island, New York," *New Pencil Points* 24 (February 1943): 54–55; Ketchum, *Shops & Stores*, 163. Ketchum also designed another shop for the Corsetorium chain. See "Corsetorium, New York, N.Y.," *Architectural Record* 112 (July 1952): 177. For the Lucy Lynne shop, see "Dramatizing the Bon Bon," *Interiors* 104 (April 1945): 68–71.

35. "Women's Apparel," *Architectural Forum* 82 (May 1945): 117–18.

36. "Jewelry Shop," *Architectural Forum* 84 (February 1946): 122; Ketchum, *Shops & Stores*, 53.

37. "For a 12-Foot Front," *Architectural Record* 127 (February 1945): 103.

38. "Ten Overtures," *Interiors* 102 (February 1943): 31–38; "Paris Shop: Furniture and Interior Decoration, New York," *New Pencil Points* 24 (February 1943): 58–59.

39. "Interiors to Come: Merchandising Modern," *Interiors* 104 (January 1945): 86–87; "Furniture Store Is Opened to Sidewalk by a Recessed Wall of Glass," *Architectural Forum* 85 (October 1946): 136.

40. For Kiesler's Space House, see Stern, Gilmartin and Mellins, *New York 1930*, 328–29, 350–51, 353–54. For McCobb's house, see "Modernage House Ready for Guests," *New York Times* (June 28, 1948): 16.

41. For Altman & Kuhn's candy shop, see Stern, Gilmartin and Mellins, *New York 1930*, 310, 312.

42. "Recent Work by Gruenbaum, Krummeck & Auer," *Architectural Forum* 75 (September 1941): 191–93, 195, 198–200; Ketchum, *Shops & Stores*, 109.

43. "Barton's Bonbonnière," *Architectural Forum* 84 (February 1946): 119.

44. Düttmann and Schneider, eds., *Morris Lapidus: Architect of the American Dream*, 34–37.

45. "Old Candy Chain Modernizes," *Interiors* 105 (November 1945): 76–79; "Pace-Setter for a Candy Chain," *Architectural Record* 99 (February 1946): 114–17.

46. "Recent Work by Gruenbaum, Krummeck & Auer": 200; Ketchum, *Shops & Stores*, 7–8.

47. "Recent Work by Gruenbaum, Krummeck & Auer": 195.

48. "Men's Shop Uses Art in Its Polite Sales Pitch," *Architectural Forum* 105 (August 1956): 140–41. Also see "The Year's Work: Victor Gruen, A. I. A.," *Interiors* 116 (August 1956): 78; Ian McCallum, *Architecture USA* (London: Architectural Press, 1959), 104–5.

49. Victor Gruen quoted in "Playful Chocolate Shop," *Architectural Forum* 97 (August 1952): cover, 100–103.

50. "This Year's Work: Beauty Salon," *Interiors* 101 (August 1941): 32. Also see "Beauty, a Complement to Design," *Interior Design* 17 (September 1941): 36–39, 58; Carleton Varney, *The Draper Touch: The High Life & High Style of Dorothy Draper* (New York: Prentice Hall Press, 1988), 144–45, unnumbered plate between pp. 174–75.

51. Varney, *The Draper Touch*, 144–45.

52. "American Setting for British Woolens," *Interiors* 101 (February 1942): 30–31; "Selected Details: Display Case," *New Pencil Points* 24 (February 1943): 69; Jackson, *A Guide to New York Architecture 1650–1952*, 30; Edward Durell Stone, *The Evolution of an Architect* (New York: Horizon Press, 1962), 86.

53. Stern, Gilmartin and Mellins, *New York 1930*, 324, 326–27.

54. "Shop for John-Frederics—By Rene C. Brugnoni, Architect, and T. H. Robsjohn-Gibbings, Interior Designer, New York," *Pencil Points* 22 (January 1941): 16–20.

55. Olga Gueft, "All that Glitters Is Gold: An Unostentatious Jewelry Shop," *Interiors* 109 (November 1949): 102–5.

56. "Specialty Shop," *Architectural Record* 91 (February 1942): 47.

57. "The Specialty Store Must Be Specially Designed," *Interiors* 104 (December 1944): 52–55. For other designs by Bry, see "The Year's Work," *Interiors* 107 (August 1947): 93; "The Year's Work," *Interiors* 109 (August 1949): 110.

58. Stern, Gilmartin and Mellins, *New York 1930*, 312.
59. "Gotham Hosiery Shop," *Architectural Forum* 81 (August 1944): 99–101; Ketchum, *Shops & Stores*, rev. ed., 13, 34.
60. "Gotham Hosiery Shop," *Architectural Forum* 84 (February 1946): 121; Ketchum, *Shops & Stores*, rev. ed., 36.
61. Olga Gueft, "The Flooded Cathedral," editorial, *Interiors* 121 (April 1962): 89; "Rebuilding: New Wave of Wood," *Architectural Forum* 116 (June 1962): cover, 123–27; White and Willensky, *AIA Guide* (1967), 132. In 1964 I. Miller opened a boutique on the second floor that was a near duplicate of the street-level space. See "Shops and Stores," *Interior Design* 35 (April 1964): 188–89. For the Heckscher Building, see Stern, Gilmartin and Mellins, *New York 1930*, 588–90.
62. Gueft, "The Flooded Cathedral": 89.
63. Olga Gueft, "Magic Architecture for the Singer Center," *Interiors* 125 (August 1965): 88–93; White and Willensky, *AIA Guide* (1967), 132; "Singer Company Showroom, New York City," *Architectural Record* 147 (January 1970): 116–17.
64. Gueft, "Magic Architecture for the Singer Center": 89.
65. "New Designs," *Architectural Forum* 89 (July 1948): 104–6.
66. "Book Store," *Architectural Forum* 90 (March 1949): 107–11; "Scandinavia in New York," *Interiors* 108 (June 1949): 78–87; "Bonniers, New York, N.Y.," *Progressive Architecture* 30 (June 1949): 59; Jackson, *A Guide to New York Architecture 1650–1952*, 32–33; Ketchum, *Shops & Stores*, rev. ed., 29; White and Willensky, *AIA Guide* (1967), 161.
67. "Book Store": 107.
68. "Glowing Self-Effacement for Gift Shop," *Architectural Forum* 106 (April 1957): 130.
69. Marian Page, "The Cepelia Shop," *Interiors* 119 (June 1960): 116–17.
70. Wilburt and Miriam Feinberg quoted in "Wilburt's, Inc.," *Interiors* 121 (June 1961): 94–95. Also see "An Elegant Opening on Third Avenue," *Architectural Forum* 117 (October 1962): 140; White and Willensky, *AIA Guide* (1967), 93.
71. "The Talk of the Town: New Store," *New Yorker* 39 (December 28, 1963): 26; "Rebuilding: A Split-Level Showcase in Manhattan," *Architectural Forum* 120 (April 1964): 118–21; Priscilla Ginsberg Dunhill, "High Spirits on Fifty-seventh Street," *Interiors* 123 (June 1964): 88–91; White and Willensky, *AIA Guide* (1967), 161.
72. Benjamin Thompson quoted in Dunhill, "High Spirits on Fifty-seventh Street": 89–90.
73. Dunhill, "High Spirits on Fifty-seventh Street": 89.
74. Olga Gueft, "Sona the Golden One," *Interiors* 125 (September 1965): 150–53; White and Willensky, *AIA Guide* (1967), 131; *Richard Meier Architect: Buildings and Projects 1966–1976* (New York: Oxford University Press, 1976), 234; *Richard Meier Architect: 1964/1984* (New York: Rizzoli International Publications, 1984), 384–85.
75. Lois Wagner, "A Stately Tradition Is Given a Smart New Up-Lifting," *Interiors* 116 (April 1957): 86–89; "Retail Shops: Georg Jensen, Inc.," *Progressive Architecture* 38 (April 1957): 164–65.
76. "G. J. Is Coming!" *Architectural Forum* 132 (May 1970): 29; Olga Gueft, "New Heroes and Old Pros," editorial, *Interiors* 130 (August 1970): 63; "New Image for Jensen's," *Progressive Architecture* 51 (September 1970): 32; James D. Morgan, "Design for Merchandising," *Architectural Record* 149 (February 1971): 89–104; White and Willensky, *AIA Guide* (1978), 217; James Stewart Polshek, "Notes on My Life and Work," in *James Stewart Polshek: Context and Responsibility* (New York: Rizzoli International Publications, 1988), 32, 127.
77. Gueft, "New Heroes and Old Pros": 63.
78. "New Image for Jensen's": 32.
79. Polshek, "Notes on My Life and Work," in *James Stewart Polshek: Context and Responsibility*, 32.
80. For Scribner's, see Stern, Gilmartin and Massengale, *New York 1900*, 201. For Brentano's, see Stern, Gilmartin and Mellins, *New York 1930*, 296.
81. "The Shop as Window Display," *Interiors* 112 (December 1952): 16; "Tiny Book Store," *Architectural Forum* 98 (January 1953): 136.
82. John Anderson, "Michael Saphier Associates," *Interiors* 120 (January 1961): 84–101, 128–29.
83. For both showrooms, see Stern, Gilmartin and Mellins, *New York 1930*, 321–22, 327.
84. "Fiberglas Building," *Architectural Record* 103 (February 1948): 140–41; "The Year's Work," *Interiors* 108 (August 1948): 87; "Fiberglas House: A Depression-Born Industry Demonstrates Its Wares in a Remodeled Brownstone," *Interiors* 108 (October 1948): 112–17; Jackson, *A Guide to New York Architecture 1650–1952*, 31.
85. For Lescaze's townhouse, see Stern, Gilmartin and Mellins, *New York 1930*, 378–82.
86. "Blithe Showcase," *Interiors* 118 (June 1959): 104–5.
87. White and Willensky, *AIA Guide* (1967), 162; Thomas J. Watson, Jr., and Peter Petre, *Father, Son & Co.: My Life at IBM and Beyond* (New York: Bantam, 1990), 258–60, unnumbered plate between pp. 308–9.
88. Priscilla Ginsberg Dunhill, "Stark Forms and Colors for Xerox," *Interiors* 123 (May 1964): 104–9; Eliot Noyes, "Architectural Details," *Architectural Record* 139 (January 1966): 121–32; Scott Kelly, "Eliot Noyes and Associates," *Industrial Design* 13 (June 1966): 38–43.
89. "Setting for Machines," *Architectural Forum* 117 (July 1962): 112–15.
90. "Dennison Copier: Standing Up to One of the Most Intimidating Street Scenes in New York, a Sculptural, Bold, Compelling and Very Inexpensive Display Showroom," *Interiors* 129 (February 1970): 101.
91. Stern, Gilmartin and Mellins, *New York 1930*, 303–5.
92. Stern, Gilmartin and Mellins, *New York 1930*, 305.
93. "Buildings on the Way Up," *Progressive Architecture* 53 (February 1972): 24–25.
94. "Frank Lloyd Wright Designs a Small Commercial Installation: A Showroom in New York for Sports Cars," *Architectural Forum* 103 (July 1955): 132–33; William Allin Storrer, *The Architecture of Frank Lloyd Wright* (Cambridge, Mass.: MIT Press, 1974), 380; Herbert Muschamp, *Man About Town: Frank Lloyd Wright in New York City* (Cambridge, Mass.: MIT Press, 1982), 88, 127; Brendan Gill, *Many Masks: A Life of Frank Lloyd Wright* (New York: G. P. Putnam's Sons, 1987), 475; Bruce Brooks Pfeiffer, *Frank Lloyd Wright, vol. 8: Monograph 1951–1959* (Tokyo: A.D.A. Edita, 1988), 148.
95. Stern, Gilmartin and Mellins, *New York 1930*, 299–301.
96. "The Crown Room, Prince Matchabelli, Inc., Designed by William Pahlmann," *Interiors* 106 (December 1946): 96–97.
97. "Pompeii on Fifth Avenue," *Time* 77 (May 26, 1961): 55; "House of Revlon," *Interior Design* 32 (July 1961): 50–57.
98. For the Gotham Hotel, see Stern, Gilmartin and Massengale, *New York 1900*, 278–79.
99. Charles Revson quoted in "House of Revlon": 50.
100. Barbara Dorn quoted in "House of Revlon": 50.
101. "Pompeii on Fifth Avenue": 55.
102. Marian Page, "Charles of the Ritz–Vidal Sassoon—Sleek New Madison Avenue Salon," *Interiors* 124 (July 1965): 64–68; White and Willensky, *AIA Guide* (1967), 160.
103. Vidal Sassoon quoted in Page, "Charles of the Ritz–Vidal Sassoon—Sleek New Madison Avenue Salon": 65.
104. "Boutiques: A New World of Color," *Progressive Architecture* 48 (December 1967): cover, 120–27.
105. White and Willensky, *AIA Guide* (1967), 160.
106. Judy Klemesrud, "Designer Adapts Nuns' Garb for Public," *New York Times* (June 27, 1968): 38; Isadore Barmash, "Now It's Paraphernalia for Men," *New York Times* (December 20, 1968): 71, 82.
107. White and Willensky, *AIA Guide* (1967), 58.
108. C. Ray Smith, "Kinetic Boutiques and Campopop Shops," *Progressive Architecture* 50 (April 1969): 106–21; Daniel Solomon, "Easy Come, Easy Go: Notes on Ephemera," *Design Quarterly* 76 (1970): unpaginated; C. Ray Smith, *Supermannerism: New Attitudes in Post-Modern Architecture* (New York: E. P Dutton, 1977), 206–7.
109. Smith, "Kinetic Boutiques and Campopop Shops": 118.
110. Ulrich Franzen quoted in Smith, "Kinetic Boutiques and Campopop Shops": 118, 120.
111. Solomon, "Easy Come, Easy Go: Notes on Ephemera": unpaginated.
112. Marvin Gelman quoted in "Boutiques: A New World of Color": 127. Also see Smith, *Supermannerism*, 139.
113. Smith, *Supermannerism*, 180.
114. For the Paper Poppy, see Smith, "Kinetic Boutiques and Campopop Shops": 117. For Lucidity, see Smith, "Kinetic Boutiques and Campopop Shops": 116; Harriet Morrison, "Public Places, Private Taste," *House Beautiful* 111 (October 1969): 142–43.
115. Rita Reif, "You Go Past the 'O' and Under the 'N' . . . ," *New York Times* (November 15, 1968): 51; Julie Baumgold, "New Action On First: The Superstore," *New York* 1 (November 18, 1968): cover, 36–40; Smith, "Kinetic Boutiques and Campopop Shops": 108–10; Morrison, "Public Places, Private Taste": 142.
116. Thomas W. Ennis, "Condominium Up; First in the City," *New York Times* (January 24, 1965), VIII: 1, 7; Glenn Fowler, "News of Realty: St. Tropez Sold," *New York Times* (August 3, 1966): 55; Thomas E. Norton and Jerry E. Patterson, *Living It Up: A Guide to the Named Apartment Houses of New York* (New York: Atheneum, 1984), 302.
117. Smith, "Kinetic Boutiques and Campopop Shops": 108.
118. Smith, "Kinetic Boutiques and Campopop Shops": 110.
119. "New on 57th Street," *Interior Design* 43 (March 1972): 102–3; "Quinta Strada," *Time* 107 (May 31, 1976): 57.
120. Morrison, "Public Places, Private Taste": 143.
121. Bernadine Morris, "Valentino for the Masses—Well, Almost," *New York Times* (June 5, 1970): 42; "High Fashion," *Architectural Forum* 134 (May 1971): 6; "In Madison Avenue," *Domus* 500 (July 1971): 20.
122. "A New York: Bianco e Nero," *Domus* 546 (May 1975): 33–35; Angela Taylor, "Along Fifth Ave., the Signs Have an Italian Accent," *New York Times* (December 1, 1975): 42.
123. For Chapman's building, see Christopher Gray, "Neighborhood/West Fifty-seventh Street," *Avenue* 9 (March 1985): 79–91.
124. Geraldine Stutz quoted in Priscilla Dunhill, "Bendel's Great Big Garden Gazebo," *Interiors* 124 (July 1965): 69–73. Also see Sheila John Daly, "A Female Bearcat Named Stutz," *Saturday Evening Post* 236 (April 13, 1963): 60–62.
125. "Pour Madame," *Interior Design* 38 (February 1967): 116–25.
126. Dunhill, "Bendel's Great Big Garden Gazebo": 69–73.
127. Geraldine Stutz quoted in Dunhill, "Bendel's Great Big Garden Gazebo": 69, 71.
128. "2 Boutiques," *Interior Design* 40 (January 1969): 130–33. For Warren & Wetmore's Stewart & Company Building, and Kahn's remodeling, see Stern, Gilmartin and Mellins, *New York 1930*, 316, 319, 321.
129. "Vidal Sassoon's Barber Shop," *Interior Design* 42 (October 1971): 144–45.
130. "Bonwit's Turns Up the Heat," *Business Week* (October 11, 1976): 120, 122; Paul Goldberger, "Design Notebook: Department Store Face Lifts Succeed, but Not Entirely," *New York Times* (July 28, 1977), C: 12.
131. "The 'Biz' of Merchandising Design," *Interiors* 134 (January 1975): 58–63.
132. Goldberger, "Design Notebook: Department Store Face Lifts Succeed, but Not Entirely": 12.
133. Dee Wedemeyer, "Bonwit Teller Building to Be Sold," *New York Times* (January 26, 1979): 1, D: 11; "Allied Seeks Bonwit Stores," *New York Times* (January 31, 1979): 21; Isadore Barmash, "Bonwit Woes: Shifts in Managers Cited," *New York Times* (February 10, 1979): 25.
134. "Farewell to Bonwit's," editorial, *New York Times* (January 31, 1979): 22.
135. "The New Miss Bergdorf Shop," *Interior Design* 27 (January 1956): 72–77. Also see "Fifth Avenue's Finest," *Time* 58 (October 29, 1951): 94–96; "Bergdorf Pins Its Future on the Rich," *Business Week* (November 17, 1951): 46–48. For Buchman & Kahn's building, see Stern, Gilmartin and Mellins, *New York 1930*, 310–11, 318–19.
136. Melissa Hattersley, "Bigi in Black and White," *Interiors* 125 (July 1966): 76–77.
137. Marilyn Bender, "Where's the Party? Over at Bergdorf's," *New York Times* (August 20, 1965): 33.
138. "It's Go-Go for Bigi," *Interior Design* 40 (June 1969): 142–45.
139. Leonard Sloane, "Tailored Woman to Quit Business," *New York Times* (November 13, 1967): 50; Arnold H. Lubasch, "Bergdorf's Expands Through Walls of Its Citadel of Fashion," *New York Times* (February 25, 1968): 6; Isadore Barmash, "Male Comes Into His Own in Bergdorf's Expansion," *New York Times* (November 20, 1968): 59, 70.
140. Stern, Gilmartin and Massengale, *New York 1900*, 195–96.
141. Ron Pavlik quoted in "Lord & Taylor's Manhattan Store Gets a Facelift," *Interiors* 136 (January 1976): 8.
142. Goldberger, "Design Notebook: Department Store Face Lifts Succeed, but Not Entirely": 12.
143. Stern, Gilmartin and Mellins, *New York 1930*, 318.
144. Rosemary Kent, "Drama Department: Comedy, Sex, and Violence in Store Windows," *New York* 9 (May 24, 1976): 82–86.
145. Kent, "Drama Department: Comedy, Sex, and Violence in Store Windows": 82–83, 85; Ruth Miller Fitzgibbons, "Windows of the World: The New Display Art," *Interiors* 136 (January 1977): 92–95.
146. Geraldine Stutz quoted in Kent, "Drama Department: Comedy, Sex, and Violence in Store Windows": 85.

147. Kent, "Drama Department: Comedy, Sex, and Violence in Store Windows": 84–85; Fitzgibbons, "Windows of the World: The New Display Art": 92, 94–95.

148. Grace Glueck, "Art People," *New York Times* (October 22, 1976), C: 16; Ellen Stern, "Through a Glass Starkly," *New York* 9 (November 11, 1976): 66.

Chapter 7
United Nations

1. E. B. White, "Here Is New York," *Holiday* 5 (April 1949): 34–41.

2. See Evan Luard, *A History of the United Nations* (New York: St. Martin's Press, 1982); *United Nations: Press Feature No. 217* (United Nations, N.Y.: Department of Public Information, Press Section, September 1986).

3. "Moses Directed to Prepare Plans for Site of UNO Home in Queens," *New York Times* (December 3, 1945): 5; Edward Allen, "Program Preview: Capital for the United Nations," *Architectural Record* 99 (March 1946): 82–85; "The Record Reports: Architects for the UNO," *Architectural Record* 99 (April 1946): 16; Thomas H. Locraft, "A Capital for the U.N.O.," *Journal of the American Institute of Architects* 5 (April 1946): 178–84; Robert Moses, *Public Works: A Dangerous Trade* (New York: McGraw-Hill, 1970), 483–85.

4. "1,100 UNO Aides Seek Quarters in Overtaxed Facilities of City," *New York Times* (March 22, 1946): 2; "Housing Our UNO Visitors," editorial, *New York Times* (March 23, 1946): 12.

5. "News: United Nations Chambers," *Architectural Forum* 85 (October 1946): 16. For the New York City Building, see Stern, Gilmartin and Mellins, *New York 1930*, 734, 736.

6. "Headquarters Guard Checks All Visitors," *New York Times* (March 24, 1946): 36; "News: UNO in the Bronx," *Architectural Forum* 84 (April 1946): 6; Francis de N. Schroeder, "Cooperation," editorial, *Interiors* 105 (May 1946): 59.

7. "News: United Nations Move," *Architectural Forum* 84 (May 1946): 16.

8. "A Home for the U.N.O.," *Progressive Architecture* 27 (April 1946): 98–100. Also see "News: UNO Headquarters," *Architectural Forum* 84 (February 1946): 12; Kenneth K. Stowell, "A Competition for the World's Capital," editorial, *Architectural Record* 99 (March 1946): 65; Kenneth Reid, "A Home for the U.N.O.," editorial, *Progressive Architecture* 27 (March 1946): 51; "Views," *Progressive Architecture* 27 (July 1946): 8; Thomas H. Creighton, "Observations," editorial, *Progressive Architecture* 28 (August 1947): 118.

9. Lewis Mumford, "Stop and Think," *Progressive Architecture* 27 (April 1946): 10.

10. Frederick Gutheim, "The U.N.O. Capital," excerpt from a letter published in the *New York Herald Tribune* on March 5, 1946, in *Journal of the American Institute of Architects* 5 (April 1946): 218–19.

11. Lewis Mumford, "A World Center for the United Nations," *Progressive Architecture* 27 (August 1946): 70–72. A transcript of Mumford's speech before the Royal Institute of British Architects was published in the *Journal of the Royal Institute of British Architects* (August 1946), with excerpts reprinted as "A Center for United Nations," in the *Journal of the American Institute of Architects* 6 (December 1946): 252–62.

12. Mumford, "A World Center for the United Nations": 72.

13. Mumford, "A Center for United Nations": 261–62.

14. Meyer Berger, "Proposed Plans to Make New York the Permanent Home of the United Nations," *New York Times* (October 19, 1946): 3–4; Robert Moses, "'Natural and Proper Home of the U.N.,'" *New York Times* (October 20, 1946), VI: cover, 9–11, 57–58; "UN Center," *Architectural Forum* 85 (November 1946): 116–20; Hugh Ferriss, *Power in Buildings* (New York: Columbia University Press, 1953), plates 33–35; Rebecca Read Shanor, *The City that Never Was* (New York: Viking, 1988), 65–69.

15. For the Federal Building, see Stern, Gilmartin and Mellins, *New York 1930*, 732, 736.

16. For the Trylon and Perisphere, see Stern, Gilmartin and Mellins, *New York 1930*, 728–30, 750–52.

17. "UN Center," *Architectural Forum*: 119.

18. Le Corbusier, "Annex I: Report of the French Delegate," in *Report of the Headquarters Commission to the Second Part of the First Session of the General Assembly of the United Nations* (Lake Success, N.Y.: United Nations, October 1946), 23. Also see Frederick P. Clark, "Report of the Headquarters Commission," book review, *Journal of the American Institute of Planners* 12 (fall 1946): 35; The Joint Advisory Committee on Planning and Development of the United Nations Headquarters, "Statement on the Report of the Headquarters Commission," *Journal of the American Institute of Planners* 12 (fall 1946): 27–30; Howard K. Menhinick, "United Nations Headquarters Planning," *Landscape Architecture* 37 (October 1946): 19.

19. "Nassau Sees Snag to UNO Housing; County Head Denies Consultation," *New York Times* (February 4, 1946): 1; "Metropolitan Area Unimpeded by Site," *New York Times* (February 5, 1946): 3; "News: Second Chance: Will UNO Design Repeat Geneva Fiasco," *Architectural Forum* 84 (March 1946): 10; "The New Capital: Will UNO's Home Be a Better Design than the League's," *Interiors* 105 (March 1946): 76–77, 102; Frederick P. Clark, "Planning a World Headquarters," *Journal of the American Institute of Planners* 12 (spring 1946): 10–15.

20. Trygve Lie, *In the Cause of Peace* (New York: Macmillan, 1954), 108.

21. Talbot Hamlin, J. Marshall Miller, Leopold Arnaud, Albert Halse, W. H. Hayes, Eugene Raskin, Don Hatch and Charles Rieger, "World Capital Discussed," letter to the editor, *New York Times* (October 31, 1946): 24, cited in Henry H. Saylor, "The Editor's Asides," *Journal of the American Institute of Architects* 6 (December 1946): 289. Also see Robert Moses, "New York Site for U.N.," letter to the editor, *New York Times* (November 2, 1946): 14.

22. E. J. Kahn, Jr., "Profiles: Big Operator—I," *New Yorker* 27 (December 8, 1951): 46–48, 50, 52–61; Eugene Rachlis and John E. Marqusee, *The Land Lords* (New York: Random House, 1963), 259–66; William Zeckendorf with Edward McCreary, *The Autobiography of William Zeckendorf* (New York: Holt, Rinehart and Winston, 1970), 63–78; Shanor, *The City that Never Was*, 67, 70, 72.

23. For Tudor City, see Stern, Gilmartin and Mellins, *New York 1930*, 437–38.

24. Zeckendorf with McCreary, *The Autobiography of William Zeckendorf*, 66.

25. Stern, Gilmartin and Massengale, *New York 1900*, 34, 36, 40–41; Stern, Gilmartin and Mellins, *New York 1930*, 202–3, 417, 515, 530–31, 592, 594–95.

26. Victoria Newhouse, *Wallace K. Harrison, Architect* (New York: Rizzoli International Publications, 1989), 105.

27. "$100,000,000 Plan for Housing Here," *New York Times* (September 19, 1946): 33; "News: Zeckendorf City," *Architectural Forum* 85 (October 1946): 9; "New Zeckendorf Project," *Interiors* 106 (November 1946): 14; Ferriss, *Power in Buildings*, plates 36–38; Shanor, *The City that Never Was*, 67–72.

28. Robert Sellmer, "The Man Who Wants to Build New York Over," *Life* 21 (October 28, 1946): 67–70, 72.

29. Newhouse, *Wallace K. Harrison, Architect*, 106.

30. Howard Myers, "A Letter from the Publisher," *Architectural Forum* 86 (February 1947): 50.

31. George Barrett, "U.N. Body to Renew Site Debate Today," *New York Times* (December 11, 1946): 1, 14; George Barrett, "Rockefeller Offers U.N. $8,500,000 Site on East River for Skyscraper Center; Molotov Clears Snag on German Pact," *New York Times* (December 12, 1946): 1, 3; Warren Moscow, "U.N. Committee Impressed on Tour of East Side Site," *New York Times* (December 12, 1946): 1, 3; "East Side Site Cost $25,000,000 to Buy," *New York Times* (December 12, 1946): 3; "Rockefeller and O'Dwyer Letters on East Side Site for U.N.," *New York Times* (December 12, 1946): 4; "Mr. Rockefeller's Offer," editorial, *New York Times* (December 12, 1946): 28; George Barrett, "Decision Is Final: Skyscraper Parliament of World to Rise on Mid-Island Tract," *New York Times* (December 15, 1946): 1, 5; "U.N. Takes Manhattan," *Architectural Forum* 86 (January 1947): 11–12; Lie, *In the Cause of Peace*, 107–24; Moses, *Public Works: A Dangerous Trade*, 485–91; Zeckendorf with McCreary, *The Autobiography of William Zeckendorf*, 7, 63–78; Robert A. Caro, *The Power Broker: Robert Moses and the Fall of New York* (New York: Alfred A. Knopf, 1974), 771–75; Samuel E. Bleecker, *The Politics of Architecture: A Perspective on Nelson A. Rockefeller* (New York: Rutledge Press, 1981), 51–93.

32. "Truman Proposes Tax Aid on U.N. Gift," *New York Times* (February 8, 1947): 3.

33. Ferriss, *Power in Buildings*, plate 39.

34. "Staten Island Site Suggested to U.N.," *New York Times* (December 15, 1946): 5; Mardges Bacon, *Ernest Flagg: Beaux-Arts Architect and Urban Reformer* (New York: Architectural History Foundation; Cambridge, Mass.: MIT Press, 1986), 271. Also see Ernest Flagg, letter to the editor, *Architectural Forum* 86 (April 1947): 24, 26. Except for a few words of introduction, the letter is a copy of one sent to Trygve Lie, dated December 14, 1946.

35. George Barrett, "Top U.N. Site Post to W. K. Harrison," *New York Times* (January 7, 1947): 6; "Harrison Named to Plan U.N. Site," *Architectural Record* 101 (February 1947): 10; Kenneth K. Stowell, "The Capital of the World," editorial, *Architectural Record* 101 (February 1947): 65.

36. "U.N. Scours World for 10 Architects," *New York Times* (January 12, 1947): 43; "Architects Nominated to U.N. Design Board," *Architectural Record* 101 (March 1947): 14; "United Nations City," *Landscape Architecture* 37 (April 1947): 87; Moses, *Public Works: A Dangerous Trade*, 491–94.

37. Ferriss, *Power in Buildings*, plates 40–44.

38. "United Nations: Men for the Job," *Architectural Forum* 86 (February 1947): 11; "The Record Reports," *Architectural Record* 102 (August 1947): 10.

39. Le Corbusier, *United Nations Headquarters Report* (New York: Reinhold Publishing Corp., 1947), 18. Also see Robert C. Weinberg, "UN Headquarters," book review, *Journal of the American Institute of Planners* 13 (summer–fall 1947): 34–36; Mary Sanders, "Books: UN Headquarters," book review, *Architectural Forum* 87 (August 1947): 124, 128, 132; José Luis Sert, "U.N. Headquarters," book review, *Progressive Architecture* 28 (October 1947): 96, 98, 100, 102; Le Corbusier, *The Modulor*, trans. Peter de Francia and Anna Bostock (London: Faber & Faber, 1954), 62, 130–31, 165–66, 174, 183; W. Boesiger, ed., *Le Corbusier: Oeuvre complète 1946–1952*, vol. 5 (Zurich: Editions Girsberger, 1955), 37–39; Peter Blake, *The Master Builders: Le Corbusier, Mies van der Rohe, Frank Lloyd Wright* (New York: Alfred A. Knopf, 1960), 97, 125–32; Robert Furneaux Jordan, *Le Corbusier* (New York: Lawrence Hill & Co., 1972), 92–102, figs. 11–12; Reyner Banham, "La Maison des hommes and La Misère des villes: Le Corbusier and the Architecture of Mass Housing," in H. Allen Brooks, ed., *Le Corbusier* (Princeton, N.J.: Princeton University Press, 1987), 111–12; Jerzy Soltan, "Working with Le Corbusier," in Brooks, ed., *Le Corbusier*, 11–12; Deborah Gans, *The Le Corbusier Guide* (Princeton, N.J.: Princeton Architectural Press, 1987), 134–35; Brendan Gill, "The Sky Line: Corbu," *New Yorker* 64 (May 9, 1988): 103–9.

40. Le Corbusier, *United Nations Headquarters Report*, 20.

41. Le Corbusier, speech delivered at the closing session of the Permanent Headquarters Committee (December 1946), quoted in Sanders, "Books: UN Headquarters": 128.

42. Le Corbusier, "Architecture & Urbanism," *Progressive Architecture* 28 (February 1947): 67–68.

43. "Discarding of Skyscrapers Denied," *New York Times* (February 8, 1947): 3.

44. Quoted in George Barrett, "Planners See U.N. Home Ready for 1948 Meeting," *New York Times* (February 23, 1947): 1, 43. Even as late as May, the American Institute of Architects was still actively advocating an international competition. See Lee E. Cooper, "Architects Weigh Plan for Contest on a U.N. Design," *New York Times* (May 4, 1947), VIII: 1.

45. "News: United Nations: Men at Work," *Architectural Forum* 86 (March 1947): 11.

46. Thomas J. Hamilton, "Buildings Plotted in U.N. Site Here," *New York Times* (March 24, 1947): 1–2; "'Doodle' Gives Glimpse of World Capital," *New York Times* (March 24, 1947): 2; George Barrett, "3 Tall Buildings in U.N. Plan for a Mechanized Capital," *New York Times* (March 27, 1947): 1, 21; "U.N. Building Plan Approved by City," *New York Times* (March 28, 1947): 1, 12; "U.N.'s Capital," editorial, *New York Times* (March 29, 1947): 14; "Topics of The Times: Something New Under the Sun," *New York Times* (March 31, 1947): 22; "News: United Nations: Five Basic Buildings Located," *Architectural Forum* 86 (April 1947): 11; "Planning for Peace," *Architectural Record* 101 (April 1947): 72–81; Gertrude Samuels, "What Kind of Capitol for the U.N.?" *New York Times* (April 20, 1947), VI: 9, 55–59; Frank Lloyd Wright, "'We Must Shape True Inspiration,'" *New York Times* (April 20, 1947), VI: 59; Francis de N. Schroeder, "For the Parliament of Man and the Federation of the World," *Interiors* 106 (May 1947): 105, 178, 180–81.

47. Wallace K. Harrison quoted in Newhouse, *Wallace K. Harrison, Architect*, 123. Also see Fendall Yerxa, "Design of U.N. 'Workshop for Peace' Revealed," *New York Herald Tribune* (May 22, 1947): 1, 13; "Famed Architects Unveil U.N. Home," *Life* 22 (May 26, 1947): 31–35. The same drawing also appeared in the *New York Times*. See George Barrett, "U.N. Capital Plans Stress Function," *New York Times* (May 22, 1947): 19.

48. Le Corbusier, letter to Wallace K. Harrison, November 7, 1947, quoted in Newhouse, *Wallace K. Harrison, Architect*, 125.

49. W. Boesiger, ed., *Le Corbusier and Pierre Jeanneret: Oeuvre complète 1929–1934*, vol. 2 (Zurich: Editions Girsberger, 1935), 97–109.

50. "News: United Nations," *Architectural Forum* 86 (June 1947): 12–14; Kenneth K. Stowell, "Poor Relations—Public, That Is," *Architectural Record* 102 (July 1947): 69; "The Record Reports: What the United Nations Headquarters May Look Like," *Architectural Record* 102 (July 1947): 10; "Basic Design for U.N. Capital Unveiled," *Interiors* 106 (July 1947): 12, 14.

51. "An Artist's Conception and Location of United Nations' Home," *New York Times* (August 10, 1947): 21; Moses, *Public Works: A Dangerous Trade*, 494–96.
52. "Bronx Descendant Gives Own Plan for U.N. Site," *New York Times* (December 28, 1946): 4.
53. "Rezoning Is Urged Around U.N. Site," *New York Times* (December 28, 1946): 4.
54. Barrett, "Top U.N. Site Post to W. K. Harrison": 6.
55. Zeckendorf with McCreary, *The Autobiography of William Zeckendorf*, 72.
56. "City Plans to Improve Area around United Nations Site," *New York Herald Tribune* (May 22, 1947): 13; "The Basic Design for the United Nations Capital to Be Erected Here," *New York Times* (May 22, 1947): 19. Also see "U.N. Approach to Be Beautified by Redevelopment of 42d Street," *New York Times* (December 22, 1949): 1, 15.
57. "First Ave. Widening for U.N. Is Opposed," *New York Times* (May 1, 1947): 3.
58. "Council Gets Bill to Curb Fund Units," *New York Times* (April 2, 1952): 35; "New Top Hat Area May Be U.N. Plaza," *New York Times* (May 7, 1952): 29; "Jury Fee Rise Now Law: Mayor Also Approves Sunday Car Racing, United Nations Plaza," *New York Times* (May 13, 1952): 13.
59. A. M. Rosenthal, "Plan to Tear Down Church for U.N. Stirs People of 47th Street Area," *New York Times* (March 28, 1947): 12; "Rezoning Mapped Near U.N. Site Here," *New York Times* (April 3, 1947): 7; "Disruptions Follow U.N. Building Plans," *Interiors* 106 (May 1947): 16, 18; "Zoning Change Voted to Protect U.N. Site," *New York Times* (May 2, 1947): 4; Yerxa, "Design of U.N. 'Workshop for Peace' Revealed": 13; "The Basic Design for the United Nations Capital to Be Erected Here": 19; George Barrett, "2,000 Fight Demolition of Church on U.N. Site," *New York Times* (July 11, 1947): 6.
60. "State Gives Plans to Build Hammarskjold Memorial," *New York Times* (October 29, 1964): 11; "Hammarskjold Memorial Dedicated," *New York Times* (October 26, 1965): 5.
61. "U.N. Site Approach Proposed to City," *New York Times* (July 25, 1947): 7.
62. "U.N. Site Under Study," *New York Times* (December 27, 1946): 8; "Architects Offer Plan for U.N. Area," *New York Times* (August 25, 1947): 19; "Moses and Critics Facing Showdown on U.N. Area Plans," *New York Times* (August 26, 1947): 1, 16. Also see Robert C. Weinberg, "A Comprehensive Plan for East Midtown Manhattan," *Journal of the American Institute of Architects* 12 (July 1949): 13–19.
63. Frederick J. Woodbridge quoted in "Architects Offer Plan for U.N. Area": 19. Also see Henry H. Saylor, "The Editor's Asides," *Journal of the American Institute of Architects* 8 (October 1947): 189–90.
64. "Moses and Critics Facing Showdown on U.N. Area Plans": 1, 16; Newhouse, *Wallace K. Harrison, Architect*, 136–37, 288–89.
65. For William Lawrence Bottomley and Edward C. Dean's Turtle Bay Gardens (1920), see Stern, Gilmartin and Mellins, *New York 1930*, 428–29.
66. Dorothy Thompson, "Proposed U.N. Concourse: Plan Protested for Expropriation of Property for Site Approach," letter to the editor, *New York Times* (August 4, 1947): 16. Also see Kahn, "Profiles: Big Operator—I": 54–55.
67. William Zeckendorf, "Proposed U.N. Concourse: Realtor Explains Motives for Offer in Reply to Letter of Criticism," letter to the editor, *New York Times* (August 12, 1947): 22.
68. "U.N. and the East Side," editorial, *New York Times* (August 26, 1947): 22.
69. "News: This Typical Rock," *Architectural Forum* 87 (September 1947): 16.
70. Zeckendorf with McCreary, *The Autobiography of William Zeckendorf*, 73–75.
71. William Zeckendorf quoted in "News: This Typical Rock": 16.
72. "City's U.N. Plan Is Approved in Stormy Board Session," *New York Times* (August 29, 1947): 1, 6.
73. Zeckendorf with McCreary, *The Autobiography of William Zeckendorf*, 72.
74. "News: This Typical Rock": 16.
75. Quoted in Newhouse, *Wallace K. Harrison, Architect*, 289.
76. Zeckendorf with McCreary, *The Autobiography of William Zeckendorf*, 72–73, 76.
77. "City Housing Body Plans Own Building After War," *New York Times* (August 17, 1944): 26; "Offices for Housing Unit," *New York Times* (December 6, 1945): 25; William Farrell, "Housing Authority Joins Rest of Us," *New York Times* (April 19, 1947): 3; "U.N. Offices to Move to Headquarters," *New York Times* (August 16, 1947): 4; "Topics of The Times: Doing Their Homework," *New York Times* (December 25, 1947): 20; "U.N. May Convert a Building on Site," *New York Times* (January 7, 1948): 6; "The Talk of the Town: Topped Out," *New Yorker* 25 (October 15, 1949): 24–25; Newhouse, *Wallace K. Harrison, Architect*, 139.
78. "New U.N. Library Planned," *New York Times* (October 30, 1952): 9; "U.N. Planning New Library on Site at 42d Street," *New York Times* (September 30, 1959): 1, 12; "U.N. Building Partly Collapses during Demolition," *New York Times* (April 30, 1960): 10; "United Nations Library," *Architectural Record* 130 (July 1961): 14; "U.N. Library Name Proposed," *New York Times* (October 5, 1961): 3; "Hammarskjold Library Dedicated," *New York Times* (November 17, 1961): 5; "For the UN's Dag Hammarskjold Library," *Interiors* 122 (April 1963): 102–7; Newhouse, *Wallace K. Harrison, Architect*, 139.
79. "Report on U.N. Headquarters," *Interiors* 107 (September 1947): 8, 10; "News: United Nations: Agreement!" *Architectural Forum* 87 (October 1947): 13; "Report on United Nations Center," *Landscape Architecture* 38 (October 1947): 31–32; George Barrett, "U.N. Clears Path for U.S. Loan Bid," *New York Times* (October 3, 1947): 16; "UN Headquarters Revised for Economy," *Architectural Record* 102 (November 1947): 68–73; "A Model for United Nations," *Interiors* 107 (November 1947): 12; Henry H. Saylor, "The Editor's Asides," *Journal of the American Institute of Architects* 8 (November 1947): 238; "Assembly Accepts Design for Home," *New York Times* (November 21, 1947): 12; Thomas H. Creighton, "U.N. Architects' Work," book review, *Progressive Architecture* 28 (December 1947): 84.
80. Philip Johnson, Henry Wright, the editors of the *Washington Star*, and Frank Lloyd Wright quoted in "Published Comment on the United Nations Headquarters," *Journal of the American Institute of Architects* 8 (October 1947): 158–59.
81. Lewis Mumford, "The Sky Line: United Nations Headquarters: The Ground Plan," *New Yorker* 23 (October 25, 1947): 56, 58, 61–62, reprinted as "UN Model and Model UN," in Lewis Mumford, *From the Ground Up: Observations on Contemporary Architecture, Housing, Highway Building and Civic Design* (New York: Harcourt, Brace, 1956), 20–26. Also see Lewis Mumford, "The Sky Line: United Nations Headquarters: Buildings as Symbols," *New Yorker* 23 (November 15, 1947): 102, 104–9, reprinted as "Buildings as Symbols," in Mumford, *From the Ground Up*, 27–35.
82. "Capital Loan Pact Signed by U.S., U.N.," *New York Times* (March 24, 1948): 12; George Barrett, "U.N. Forced to Plan Building Cuts by Congressional Delay on Loan," *New York Times* (June 13, 1948): 1, 17; "World Capital Loan Shelved; U.N. Officials Are

Dismayed," *New York Times* (June 21, 1948): 1, 9; George Barrett, "U.N. Officials Dismayed," *New York Times* (June 21, 1948): 9; "U.N. without a Home," editorial, *New York Times* (June 24, 1948): 24; "No Loan—No World Capital," *Interiors* 108 (August 1948): 14. Also see George Barrett, "Truman for Loan for Capital of U.N.," *New York Times* (October 31, 1947): 1, 12.
83. Leo Egan, "Dewey Backs $65,000,000 Loan for United Nations Headquarters," *New York Times* (July 3, 1948): 6; "East Side West Side," *Commonweal* 48 (July 16, 1948): 319–20.
84. George Barrett, "U.N. Breaks Ground for Home Tuesday," *New York Times* (September 12, 1948): 21; "Work Begins Today on U.N. Skyscraper," *New York Times* (September 14, 1948): 3; "An Act of Faith," editorial, *New York Times* (September 14, 1948): 28; Morris Kaplan, "U.N. Breaks Ground for Its Capital; O'Dwyer Welcomes 'Plan for Peace,'" *New York Times* (September 15, 1948): 1, 3; "Ground-Breaking for U.N.," editorial, *New York Times* (September 15, 1948): 30; "UN Begins Construction on Secretariat Building," *Engineering News-Record* 41 (September 23, 1948): 6; John M. Willig, "Building a Great Workshop of Peace," *New York Times* (October 10, 1948), VI: 24–25.
85. Le Corbusier and Wallace K. Harrison quoted in "News: United Nations," *Architectural Forum* 90 (January 1949): 15–16. Also see "Battling Architect," *Interiors* 108 (February 1949): 12.
86. "United Nations Builds a Vast Marble Frame for Two Enormous Windows," *Architectural Forum* 90 (June 1949): 81–85; "Simple Geometry," *Time* 53 (June 13, 1949): 51; "Topics of The Times: Betwixt Land and Water," *New York Times* (June 15, 1949): 28; "Workshop for Peace," *Interior Design and Decoration* 20 (July 1949): 30–35; "News: UN Grows in Marble and Glass," *Architectural Forum* 91 (October 1949): 10; R. B. Cutler, "U.N.'s Secretariat," letter to the editor, *Architectural Forum* 91 (October 1949): 46; "The World Capitol: Four Stages," *New York Times* (October 16, 1949), VI: 10; "Topics of The Times: Right Here at Home," *New York Times* (December 16, 1949): 30.
87. "Mayor Proclaims Tomorrow U.N. Day," *New York Times* (October 23, 1949): 11; "The Day Made Visible," editorial, *New York Times* (October 25, 1949): 26; "United Nations Headquarters," *Interiors* 109 (November 1949): 12, 14; "U.N. Dedicates a World Capital," *Life* 27 (November 7, 1949): 33–35.
88. Le Corbusier quoted in "Le Corbusier Irked at UN," *New York Times* (December 8, 1949): 24.
89. "The Talk of the Town: Topped Out": 24–25; "First U.N. Building to Open This Year," *New York Times* (January 20, 1950): 6; Roger Pryor Dodge, "Toward the Cube," letter to the editor, *Progressive Architecture* 31 (May 1950): 9; "U.N. Headquarters Progress Report," *Progressive Architecture* 31 (June 1950): cover, 57–68; "U.N. Soon to Open Part of New Unit," *New York Times* (June 25, 1950): 12; "U.N. Starts Move to New York Home," *New York Times* (August 19, 1950): 8; "450 of U.N. Staff Occupy New Site," *New York Times* (August 22, 1950): 10; "The Talk of the Town: Camping Out," *New Yorker* 26 (September 2, 1950): 19; "United Nations: New York, Center of Peace—Or War?" *Newsweek* 36 (September 18, 1950): cover, 25–26; George Barrett, "Too Few Windows, U.N. Staff Cries," *New York Times* (October 5, 1950): 15; "The Secretariat: A Campanile, a Cliff of Glass, a Great Debate," *Architectural Forum* 93 (November 1950): cover, 93–112; "Spot Check on the UN Influences," *Interiors* 110 (January 1951): 12; Alan Dunn, "O.K., Men, Hop to It! The Sooner We Start, the Sooner We Finish," cartoon, *New Yorker* 26 (January 13, 1951): 21; "The Talk of the Town: Awe-Struck," *New Yorker* 26 (January 20, 1951): 20; "Leaky U.N. Windows Proving a Headache," *New York Times* (March 15, 1951): 31; "New Lights in New York," *Life* 30 (March 26, 1951): 62–64, 67; Lewis Mumford, "The Sky Line: Magic with Mirrors—I," *New Yorker* 27 (September 15, 1951): 84, 86, 89–93, reprinted as "Magic with Mirrors," in Mumford, *From the Ground Up*, 36–44; Lewis Mumford, "The Sky Line: Magic with Mirrors—II," *New Yorker* 27 (September 22, 1951): 99–100, 103–6, reprinted as "A Disoriented Symbol," in Mumford, *From the Ground Up*, 45–52; Arthur Drexler, "Post-War Architecture," in Henry-Russell Hitchcock and Arthur Drexler, eds., *Built in USA: Post-War Architecture* (New York: Museum of Modern Art, 1952), 22–24, 68–69; "Building Reporter: Window Leaks Overcome," *Architectural Forum* 96 (January 1952): 134; Suzanne Sekey, "Design and Furnishing of Offices," *Progressive Architecture* 33 (January 1952): 110–11; Henry Stern Churchill, "United Nations Headquarters: A Description and Appraisal," *Architectural Record* 112 (July 1952): cover, 103–24; "Cheops' Architect," *Time* 60 (September 22, 1952): cover, 78–82, 84, 87; "UN Completed," *Architectural Forum* 97 (October 1952): 140–49; Lewis Mumford, "The Sky Line: Preview of the Past," *New Yorker* 28 (October 11, 1952): 66, 69–76; Talbot F. Hamlin, *Architecture through the Ages* (New York: G. P. Putnam's Sons, 1953), 653–54; "Chemical Bank & Trust Co., UN Secretariat, New York, New York," *Progressive Architecture* 34 (June 1953): 131; Henry-Russell Hitchcock, *Architecture: Nineteenth and Twentieth Centuries* (Baltimore, Md.: Penguin, 1958), 415; Ian McCallum, *Architecture USA* (London: Architectural Press, 1959), 22, 24–26; Henry Hope Reed, *The Golden City* (New York: Doubleday & Co., 1959), 45; Earle Shultz and Walter Simmons, *Offices in the Sky* (Indianapolis, Ind.: Bobbs-Merrill, 1959), 250; Ada Louise Huxtable, "Buildings that Are Symbols, Too," *New York Times* (April 5, 1959), VI: 18–19, 103; Reyner Banham, *Age of the Masters* (New York: Harper & Row, 1962), 108; Martin Meyerson, *Face of the Metropolis* (New York: Random House, 1963), 56–57; White and Willensky, *AIA Guide* (1967), 122; Vincent Scully, *American Architecture and Urbanism* (New York: Frederick A. Praeger, 1969), 186–87; Leonardo Benevolo, *History of Modern Architecture: The Modern Movement*, vol. 2, trans. H. J. Landry (Cambridge, Mass.: MIT Press, 1971), 674–78; William H. Jordy, *American Buildings and Their Architects: The Impact of European Modernism in the Mid-Twentieth Century*, vol. 4 (Garden City, N.Y.: Doubleday & Co., 1972), 59, 233, 235, 237; Paul Goldberger, *The City Observed: New York* (New York: Random House, 1979), 131–33; John Tauranac, *Essential New York* (New York: Holt, Rinehart and Winston, 1979), 196–97; Paul Goldberger, *The Skyscraper* (New York: Alfred A. Knopf, 1981), 105–6; Donald Martin Reynolds, *The Architecture of New York City* (New York: Macmillan, 1984), 155; Carol Herselle Krinsky, "Architecture in New York City," in Leonard Wallock, ed., *New York: Culture Capital of the World, 1940–1965* (New York: Rizzoli International Publications, 1988), 101–2; Newhouse, *Wallace K. Harrison, Architect*, 138–43.
90. Mumford, "The Sky Line: Magic with Mirrors—I": 86, 90.
91. Mumford, "The Sky Line: Magic with Mirrors—I": 90.
92. Mumford, "The Sky Line: Magic with Mirrors—I": 90, 92–93.
93. Mumford, "The Sky Line: Magic with Mirrors—II": 99, 106.
94. Churchill, "United Nations Headquarters: A Description and Appraisal": 111, 113.
95. "The Secretariat: A Campanile, a Cliff of Glass, a Great Debate": 95–97.
96. For Mies van der Rohe's glass skyscraper projects, see Philip C. Johnson, *Mies van der Rohe*, 3rd rev. ed. (New York: Museum of Modern Art, 1978), 21–29, 187. For the

Hallidie Building, see William H. Jordy, *American Buildings and Their Architects: Progressive and Academic Ideals at the Turn of the Twentieth Century*, vol. 3 (Garden City, N.Y.: Doubleday & Co., 1972), 67, 69–70.
97. "The Secretariat: A Campanile, a Cliff of Glass, a Great Debate": 98.
98. George Howe quoted in "The Secretariat: A Campanile, a Cliff of Glass, a Great Debate": 103.
99. "The Secretariat: A Campanile, a Cliff of Glass, a Great Debate": 103–4.
100. George Howe quoted in "The Secretariat: A Campanile, a Cliff of Glass, a Great Debate": 107.
101. Henry-Russell Hitchcock quoted in "The Secretariat: A Campanile, a Cliff of Glass, a Great Debate": 107.
102. Rudolph Schindler quoted in "The Secretariat: A Campanile, a Cliff of Glass, a Great Debate": 107.
103. "The Secretariat: A Campanile, a Cliff of Glass, a Great Debate": 112.
104. Walter Sullivan, "Paris Is Dropped as Assembly Site," *New York Times* (January 25, 1951): 8; Kathleen Teltsch, "New Council Hall Is Ready at U.N.," *New York Times* (July 22, 1951): 6; "Topics of The Times: The U.N. on Tour," *New York Times* (December 2, 1951), IV: 10; Kathleen McLaughlin, "New U.N. Building Will Open Feb. 27," *New York Times* (February 14, 1952): 7; "Steel, Concrete and Faith," editorial, *New York Times* (February 15, 1952): 24; "UN Conference Building," *Architectural Forum* 96 (April 1952): cover, 103–11; "United Nations Conference Building Opens," *Architectural Record* 111 (April 1952): 26; Churchill, "United Nations Headquarters: A Description and Appraisal": 103–24; Olga Gueft, "An Unodious Comparison: The Three Council Chambers of the United Nations," *Interiors* 111 (July 1952): 46–67; "Cheops' Architect": 78–79, 81; "Employee Facilities," *Progressive Architecture* 33 (October 1952): 124–25; Lewis Mumford, "The Sky Line: Workshop Invisible," *New Yorker* 28 (January 17, 1953): 83–88, reprinted in Mumford, *From the Ground Up*, 62–70; Page Beauchamp, "Bars," *Progressive Architecture* 34 (April 1953): 130–31; "A Look at Dining Rooms," *Architectural Forum* 104 (February 1956): 137; White and Willensky, *AIA Guide* (1967), 122; Goldberger, *The City Observed*, 131–33; Newhouse, *Wallace K. Harrison, Architect*, 138–43.
105. "UN Conference Building," *Architectural Forum*: 104.
106. Gueft, "An Unodious Comparison: The Three Council Chambers of the United Nations": 49.
107. Churchill, "United Nations Headquarters: A Description and Appraisal": 118.
108. Churchill, "United Nations Headquarters: A Description and Appraisal": 118.
109. Gueft, "An Unodious Comparison: The Three Council Chambers of the United Nations": 50.
110. Churchill, "United Nations Headquarters: A Description and Appraisal": 118.
111. Churchill, "United Nations Headquarters: A Description and Appraisal": 118–19.
112. "UN General Assembly," *Architectural Forum* 92 (May 1950): 96–101; "Big Tent," *Time* 55 (May 29, 1950): 68; "Work Is Under Way on Final U.N. Building," *New York Times* (February 16, 1951): 6; "UN Assembly Readied for Fall Occupancy," *Architectural Forum* 96 (January 1952): 64; "'52 U.N. Assembly May Be Delayed," *New York Times* (January 3, 1952): 3; Churchill, "United Nations Headquarters: A Description and Appraisal": 103–24; "Cheops' Architect": 78–79, 81; "UN General Assembly," *Architectural Forum* 97 (October 1952): 140–49; Thomas J. Hamilton, "Work Completed on U.N. Buildings," *New York Times* (October 10, 1952): 1, 5; "Aladdin's Tower," editorial, *New York Times* (October 11, 1952): 18; Kathleen Teltsch, "U.N. Housewarming Is Shining Success," *New York Times* (October 15, 1952): 8; "U.N. General Assembly Opens Its 'Capitol of Peace,'" *Newsweek* 40 (October 27, 1952): 47; "Fine Arts," *Interiors* 112 (November 1952): 8; "The U.N.'s New Assembly Building," *Life* 33 (November 3, 1952): cover, 113–19; "UN Assembly. How Do Architects Like It? First Reaction: Most of Them Don't," *Architectural Forum* 97 (December 1952): 114–15; Mumford, "The Sky Line: Workshop Invisible": 83–88; "UN Design Criticism," letters to the editor, *Architectural Forum* 98 (February 1953): 82, 88; "UN Design Symposium, Cont'd," letters to the editor, *Architectural Forum* 98 (March 1953): 76, 80, 84, 88; Lewis Mumford, "The Sky Line: United Nations Assembly," *New Yorker* 29 (March 14, 1953): 72, 74, 76, 79–81, reprinted in Mumford, *From the Ground Up*, 53–61; Reed, *The Golden City*, 37, 57–58; White and Willensky, *AIA Guide* (1967), 122; Goldberger, *The City Observed*, 131–33; Tauranac, *Essential New York*, 196–97; Newhouse, *Wallace K. Harrison, Architect*, 138–43.
113. Mumford, "The Sky Line: United Nations Assembly": 72. For Radio City Music Hall, see Stern, Gilmartin and Mellins, *New York 1930*, 652, 654–57.
114. "UN General Assembly," (May 1950): 97.
115. Mumford, "The Sky Line: United Nations Assembly": 76, 79.
116. Mumford, "The Sky Line: United Nations Assembly": 79.
117. Paul Rudolph quoted in "UN General Assembly" (October 1952): 144.
118. Paul Rudolph quoted in "UN General Assembly" (October 1952): 145.
119. "UN General Assembly" (October 1952): 147–48.
120. George Howe quoted in "UN Assembly. How Do Architects Like It? First Reaction: Most of Them Don't": 114.
121. Pietro Belluschi quoted in "UN Assembly. How Do Architects Like It? First Reaction: Most of Them Don't": 114.
122. Robert Woods Kennedy quoted in "UN Assembly. How Do Architects Like It? First Reaction: Most of Them Don't": 114.
123. Landis Gores, "UN Design Symposium, Cont'd": 88.
124. George Barrett, "Moses Wants Acre of Land in U.N. Site for Playground," *New York Times* (December 16, 1949): 1, 7; "Moses Faces Rebuff on U.N. Playground," *New York Times* (December 17, 1949): 6; Aline B. Louchheim, "U.N. Rejects 'Model' Playground; Moses' Project Is Accepted Instead," *New York Times* (October 7, 1951): 1, 39; Aline B. Louchheim, "Playground Unit Shown at Museum," *New York Times* (March 25, 1952): 25; Thomas B. Hess, "Vernissage: The Rejected Playground," *Art News* 51 (April 1952): 15; "Playground for the UN," *Interiors* 111 (April 1952): 14; "New York Notes," *Art Digest* 26 (April 15, 1952): 14; Dorothy Barclay, "Playgrounds that Are Something More," *New York Times* (April 20, 1952), VI: 52; "Approve Final Plan for Disputed U.N. Playground," *Architectural Record* 112 (October 1952): 22, 366; Isamu Noguchi, *A Sculptor's World* (New York: Harper & Row, 1968), 176–77, figs. 242–43; Moses, *Public Works: A Dangerous Trade*, 499–500; Sam Hunter, *Isamu Noguchi* (New York: Abbeville Press, 1978), 76–77; Nancy Grove, *Isamu Noguchi: A Study of the Sculpture* (New York: Garland Publishing, 1985), 165, fig. 190.
125. Louchheim, "U.N. Rejects 'Model' Playground; Moses' Project Is Accepted Instead": 39.
126. Quoted in Louchheim, "U.N. Rejects 'Model' Playground; Moses' Project Is Accepted Instead": 39.
127. Robert Moses quoted in Louchheim, "U.N. Rejects 'Model' Playground; Moses' Project Is Accepted Instead": 39.
128. Hess, "Vernissage: The Rejected Playground": 15.
129. John P. Callahan, "City Building Tide Surges Eastward," *New York Times* (November 24, 1957): 1, 7.
130. "18-Story Office Building to Go Up on Second Avenue," *Real Estate Record and Guide* 176 (September 17, 1955): 3–4; "Rejuvenation of the East Side Stimulated by U.N. Plaza," *New York Times* (January 24, 1965), VIII: 1, 6; Robert F. R. Ballard, *Directory of Manhattan Office Buildings* (New York: McGraw-Hill, 1978), 41; David W. Dunlap, "Primping Up at a Time When the Best Goes Begging," *New York Times* (June 23, 1991), VIII: 15.
131. "Once-Shabby Building Now an Area Delight," *New York Times* (November 24, 1957), VIII: 7; "Rejuvenation of the East Side Stimulated by U.N. Plaza": 1.
132. "Across from the World Capitol," *Interiors* 109 (February 1950): 12; "'Off-Campus U.N.' Will Cost $2,600,000," *New York Times* (June 19, 1951): 31; "International Group Gets Quarters Here," *New York Times* (May 18, 1952): 53; "Carnegie Endowment for International Peace," *Architectural Record* 111 (June 1952): 122–29; "International Center," *New York Times* (August 16, 1952): 10; "Stone Is Laid Here for World Center," *New York Times* (December 8, 1952): 15; "Mayor Opens Exhibit by Filipino Artists," *New York Times* (September 2, 1953): 27; "World Peace Unit Dedicates Center," *New York Times* (October 20, 1953): 31; Callahan, "City Building Tide Surges Eastward": 1, 7; "The Opportunity of Maintaining the Headquarters of the Carnegie Endowment," *Interiors* 117 (July 1958): 54–59, 114, 116–17; "Rejuvenation of the East Side Stimulated by U.N. Plaza": 1; White and Willensky, *AIA Guide* (1967), 122–23; Newhouse, *Wallace K. Harrison, Architect*, 136.
133. "IBM World Trade Unit Plans Offices on United Nations Plaza," *New York Times* (March 11, 1956), VIII: 1; Callahan, "City Building Tide Surges Eastward": 1, 7; "Rejuvenation of the East Side Stimulated by U.N. Plaza": 1, 6; Newhouse, *Wallace K. Harrison, Architect*, 136.
134. "NYC Leading as Engineers Consider New Headquarters," *Architectural Forum* 102 (February 1955): 21, 25; Charles Grutzner, "Engineer Center Likely to Remain," *New York Times* (June 28, 1956): 31; "The Engineers Stay Here," editorial, *New York Times* (June 29, 1956): 20; "Engineer Center Gains," *New York Times* (July 12, 1956): 26; "News Bulletins," *Progressive Architecture* 37 (August 1956): 86; "Engineers Studying Joint Center Here," *New York Times* (November 14, 1956): 21; Jack R. Ryan, "Engineers' Home Will Remain Here," *New York Times* (November 18, 1956), III: 1, 4; "News Bulletins," *Progressive Architecture* 37 (December 1956): 80; "Engineer Group Gets East Side Blockfront as Site for a New Headquarters Building," *New York Times* (August 1, 1957): 40; "Engineer Center Gains," *New York Times* (August 31, 1957): 26; John P. Callahan, "Hoover Prods U.S. on Engineer Lag," *New York Times* (November 22, 1957): 1, 17; "Engineers' Building to Harmonize with U.N.," *Architectural Forum* 107 (December 1957): 39; "News Bulletins," *Progressive Architecture* 39 (January 1958): 75; "Meetings and Miscellany," *Architectural Record* 123 (January 1958): 24; "Hoover Salutes Engineer Groups," *New York Times* (October 2, 1959): 11; "Foundations Being Set for Engineers' Center," *New York Times* (April 1, 1960): 56; "Engineers Get Building on U.N. Plaza," *Progressive Architecture* 41 (June 1960): 74; "Freedom of Mind Urged by Hoover," *New York Times* (June 17, 1960): 33; "Two New Towers in New York City," *Architectural Record* 130 (November 1961): 14; "Curtain Wall of Stainless Steel Distinguishes New Engineering Center," *New York Times* (November 19, 1961), VIII: 1, 6; "Rejuvenation of the East Side Stimulated by U.N. Plaza": 1; White and Willensky, *AIA Guide* (1967), 122–23.
135. For Whitfield & King's building, see Stern, Gilmartin and Massengale, *New York 1900*, 240, 243–45.
136. "U.S. Delegates' Home," *New York Times* (January 14, 1958): 23; "New U.N. Center for U.S. Blocked," *New York Times* (March 22, 1958): 19; "Fund Bill Is Passed," *New York Times* (June 26, 1958): 18; Wayne Phillips, "U.S. Set to Build for U.N. Mission," *New York Times* (August 30, 1958): 15; "Offices Planned for U.S. Mission to U.N.," *Progressive Architecture* 39 (October 1958): 29; "Buildings in the News," *Architectural Record* 124 (October 1958): 13; "Honeycomb for U.S. Mission to U.N.," *Interiors* 118 (October 1958): 14, 16; "Lodge Breaks Ground for U.S. Mission Offices at U.N.," *New York Times* (December 2, 1958): 3; "We Dig In at the U.N.," editorial, *New York Times* (December 2, 1958): 36; John P. Callahan, "60-Story Skyscraper Is 'Topped Out' via TV," *New York Times* (September 10, 1959): 37; "U.S. Erects Headquarters at U.N.," *New York Times* (August 28, 1960), VIII: 1, 6; "New Headquarters for Mission of U.S. at U.N. Dedicated," *New York Times* (January 7, 1961): 2; "U.S. Moves into New U.N. Home," *New York Times* (May 16, 1961): 3; "Rejuvenation of the East Side Stimulated by U.N. Plaza": 1; White and Willensky, *AIA Guide* (1967), 122–23.
137. "Church Planning 17-Story Building," *New York Herald Tribune* (November 10, 1961): 15; "UN Plaza to Get Church Center," *Progressive Architecture* 43 (February 1962): 46; "Church Peace Center Is Started on the East Side," *New York Times* (August 2, 1962): 41; "Rejuvenation of the East Side Stimulated by U.N. Plaza": 1; Christian Hubert, "The Late Work: 1939–1969," in Christian Hubert and Lindsay Stamm Shapiro, *William Lescaze* (New York: Institute for Architecture and Urban Studies; New York: Rizzoli International Publications, 1982), 109, 116.
138. "Lodge Gets New Post," *New York Times* (February 12, 1961): 13; Edmond J. Bartnett, "Education Group Plans New Home," *New York Times* (January 10, 1962): 2; "Buildings in the News," *Architectural Record* 131 (February 1962): 12; "Rusk Would Extend Student Exchanges," *New York Times* (October 25, 1963): 28; "Rejuvenation of the East Side Stimulated by U.N. Plaza": 1; White and Willensky, *AIA Guide* (1967), 122–23; Newhouse, *Wallace K. Harrison, Architect*, 136.
139. Ada Louise Huxtable, "Architecture: Alvar Aalto, Finnish Master, Represented Here," *New York Times* (November 30, 1964): 38, reprinted as "The Seductive Virtues of Alvar Aalto," in Ada Louise Huxtable, *Will They Ever Finish Bruckner Boulevard?* (New York: Macmillan, 1970), 201–4; "Interviewing Aalto," *Progressive Architecture* 46 (January 1965): 48, 50; "Aalto in New York," *Progressive Architecture* 46 (February 1965): 180–85; "Softener," *Architectural Review* 138 (October 1965): 50; Karl Fleig, ed., *Alvar Aalto, 1963–1970* (New York: Praeger, 1971), 84–87; C. Ray Smith, *Supermannerism: New Attitudes in Post-Modern Architecture* (New York: E. P. Dutton, 1977), 101–2; Malcolm Quantrill, *Alvar Aalto: A Critical Study* (London: Secker & Warburg, 1983), 227–29. For the Baker House dormitory, see Frederick Gutheim, *Alvar Aalto* (New York: George Braziller, 1960), 23, figs. 46–49.
140. Huxtable, "Architecture: Alvar Aalto, Finnish Master, Represented Here": 38.

141. Huxtable, "Architecture: Alvar Aalto, Finnish Master, Represented Here": 38.
142. "$40-Million Development Planned North of U.N.," *Real Estate Record and Guide* 186 (October 22, 1960): 2; "New Neighbor for the U.N.," *Architectural Forum* 115 (September 1961): 53; "Alcoa to Develop 2.3 Acre Site North of U.N.," *Real Estate Record and Guide* 192 (August 3, 1963): 2; "Two-Use Project to Face U.N.," *Progressive Architecture* 44 (November 1963): 84; "Apartments Going Up Next to U.N.," *New York Times* (May 24, 1964), VIII: 1, 10; "Rejuvenation of the East Side Stimulated by U.N. Plaza": 1, 6; "The Co-operators," *Newsweek* 66 (August 23, 1965): 74; Vincent Lee Warren, "Home—Up to $166,000—Sweet Home," *New York Times* (February 16, 1966): 38; Byron Porterfield, "Aluminum Sheathes Tall Buildings Here with Tones of Black, Silver and Gold," *New York Times* (March 13, 1966), VIII: 1, 8; "Apartment Sales in U.N. Plaza Reach $12 Million," *Real Estate Record and Guide* 198 (July 2, 1966): 3–4; Sarah Tomerlin Lee, "Forecast!" *House Beautiful* 107 (September 1966): 149–59; White and Willensky, *AIA Guide* (1967), 123; Arnold H. Lubasch, "Skyscraper Setbacks Serve as Play Areas," *New York Times* (January 28, 1968), VIII: 1, 4; "Instant Manhattan," *Interior Design* 39 (February 1968): 102–9; Murray Schumach, "Presidential Politics Yields to Privacy at Apartments of 3 Candidates Here," *New York Times* (March 18, 1968): 47, 54; Olga Gueft, "Grotto on the 37th Floor," *Interiors* 128 (February 1969): 74–81; "The Home: People Who Live in Glass Houses," *Time* 93 (April 25, 1969): 75; Zeckendorf with McCreary, *The Autobiography of William Zeckendorf*, 293; "High Tension at Walls and Ceilings," *House Beautiful* 112 (March 1970): 76–77; Andrew Alpern, *Apartments for the Affluent* (New York: McGraw-Hill, 1975), 148–49; Ballard, *Directory of Manhattan Office Buildings*, 74; Goldberger, *The City Observed*, 130; Newhouse, *Wallace K. Harrison, Architect*, 136.
143. Lee, "Forecast!": 149–59.
144. Gueft, "Grotto on the 37th Floor": 75.
145. "High Tension at Walls and Ceilings": 77.
146. "The Home: People Who Live in Glass Houses": 75.
147. "Rockefeller 3d Gift Will Provide a Site for Japan Society," *New York Times* (May 11, 1967): 54; "John Rockefeller Purchases Four Parcels for Japan Society," *Real Estate Record and Guide* 199 (June 24, 1967): 2–3; "Work on New Home for Japan Society Begun Near the U.N.," *New York Times* (September 17, 1969): 4; "Japanese Center Here to Blend Styles," *New York Times* (September 28, 1969), VIII: 12; "Buildings in the News," *Architectural Record* 146 (October 1969): 40; Leah Gordon, "Art Notes: 'School of Gems,'" *New York Times* (September 5, 1971), II: 20; Carter B. Horsley, "An Authentic Bit of Japan Rises to House Society on East 47th St.," *New York Times* (September 9, 1971): 45; "Japan House Here Opens with a Call for More Contact," *New York Times* (September 14, 1971): 9; "Buildings in the News," *Architectural Record* 150 (November 1971): 45; "Japan House," *Japan Architect* 47 (August 1972): 77–86; "New Delights for Hammarskjold Plaza," *Architectural Record* 153 (April 1973): cover, 105–10; White and Willensky, *AIA Guide* (1978), 160.
148. Alan S. Oser, "Builder Finds the Times Are Trying," *New York Times* (November 15, 1970), VIII: 1, 4; "Developer Leases Half of Dag Hammarskjold Park for Use as a Plaza," *New York Times* (November 17, 1970): 90; Grace Glueck, "Art Notes: East Side, West Side," *New York Times* (November 29, 1970), II: 24; "Sculpture Garden for New York City," *Progressive Architecture* 52 (January 1971): 29; "News of the Realty Trade: 2d Ave. Lease," *New York Times* (June 13, 1971), VIII: 6; "New Delights for Hammarskjold Plaza": cover, 105–7; Ballard, *Directory of Manhattan Office Buildings*, 73; White and Willensky, *AIA Guide* (1978), 160.
149. Kathleen Teltsch, "Civic Group Urges Expansion of U.N. to Tract on South," *New York Times* (December 6, 1966): 1, 16; Moses, *Public Works: A Dangerous Trade*, 502–5. Also see Kathleen McLaughlin, "Thant Proposes Big Annex at U.N.," *New York Times* (October 6, 1966): 22; "Thant Holds Talks Here on More Space for U.N.," *New York Times* (March 6, 1968): 7.
150. Charles G. Bennett, "2-Block U.N. Expansion Is Planned for East Side," *New York Times* (April 12, 1968): 1, 51; Kathleen Teltsch, "Towers, Parks and Walkways Are Included in Proposal for U.N. 'Campus,'" *New York Times* (April 21, 1968): 78; Maurice Carroll, "Council Delays Project for U.N.," *New York Times* (May 23, 1968): 43; "Rockefeller Signs Home Loan Rise," *New York Times* (June 4, 1968): 34; Kathleen Teltsch, "Park and New Offices Planned in Expansion of U.N. Enclave," *New York Times* (November 4, 1968): 1, 27; Kathleen Teltsch, "McCloy Heads Board to Develop 2 Blocks for U.N. Expansion," *New York Times* (January 7, 1969): 63; "Planners Propose Tudor City Zoning," *New York Times* (April 17, 1969): 26.
151. "Buildings in the News: United Nations Expansion," *Architectural Record* 145 (February 1969): 41; Kathleen Teltsch, "Park Plan Shown at United Nations," *New York Times* (November 29, 1969): 33; "Rx for Tense U.N. Aide: Sauna in Proposed Park," *New York Times* (December 12, 1969): 55; Kathleen Teltsch, "U.N. Funds Are Voted to Build Here," *New York Times* (December 16, 1969): 2.
152. "Alternative Site for United Nations School Proposed by Fund," *New York Times* (May 25, 1967): 14; Teltsch, "Park and New Offices Planned in Expansion of U.N. Enclave": 1, 27; Kathleen Teltsch, "U.N. School's Site to Be at 25th St.," *New York Times* (May 18, 1969): 37; *Mitchell/Giurgola Associates, Architects* (Philadelphia: Mitchell/Giurgola Associates, 1973), unpaginated; *Mitchell/Giurgola Architects*, foreword by Kenneth Frampton (New York: Rizzoli International Publications, 1983), 254.
153. Arnold H. Lubasch, "Loft Building Will Serve as Interim U.N. School," *New York Times* (August 20, 1967), VIII: 1, 8; "UN School in a Loft Building," *Interiors* 130 (November 1970): 126–28; *Mitchell/Giurgola Associates, Architects*, unpaginated; *Mitchell/Giurgola Architects*, 254.
154. For the Beaux-Arts Apartments, see Stern, Gilmartin and Mellins, *New York 1930*, 396–99.
155. "Bridge to the U.N.," *Architectural Forum* 128 (June 1968): 98–99; "United Nations Development District Proposal, New York, N.Y.," *Progressive Architecture* 49 (July 1968): 120.
156. Rudy Johnson, "Tenants Near U.N. Fight Expansion," *New York Times* (December 8, 1968): 36; Ada Louise Huxtable, "Proposed Monument Under Glass at the U.N.," *New York Times* (November 12, 1969): 37; Kathleen Teltsch, "Massive Complex Proposed for U.N.," *New York Times* (November 12, 1969): 1, 17; "Plan on U.N. Development Draws Officials' Criticism," *New York Times* (November 15, 1969): 25; "Towers Proposed for the UN," *Engineering News-Record* 183 (November 20, 1969): 33; "Climatic Complex," *Architectural Forum* 131 (December 1969): 84, 86; "U.N. Mission Offices in New York Grow to 1-Million-Plus Square Feet," *Real Estate Record and Guide* 204 (December 13, 1969): 2; "U.N. Expansion Plan Protested Here," *New York Times* (December 20, 1969): 37; "The U.N. Center," *Architectural Record* 147 (January 1970): 41; "A Crystal Palace for the UN," *Progressive Architecture* 51 (January 1970): 24–25; Pete Hamill, "UN Land Grab," *New York Post* (January 19, 1970): 37; Iver Peterson, "City Panel Backs Project Near U.N.," *New York Times* (January 22, 1970): 60; Ada Louise Huxtable, "Sugar Coating a Bitter Pill," *New York Times* (February 15, 1970), II: 25; "The Future Today—UN in New York," *Housing and Planning News* 28 (March 1970): 1–2; "Goldberg Urges Modifications in Plans for Site Opposite the U.N.," *New York Times* (March 20, 1970): 15; Maurice Carroll, "Action Is Delayed on U.N.-Area Plan," *New York Times* (March 21, 1970): 29; Maurice Carroll, "U.N. Development Approved by City," *New York Times* (April 17, 1970): 64; "Housing on River Backed on Funds," *New York Times* (June 25, 1970): 23; "Murtagh Upholds Proposal for Expanding U.N. Complex," *New York Times* (August 7, 1970): 30; Yukihisa Isobe, "Kevin Roche," *Kenchiku Bunka* 25 (September 1970): 71–90; Wolf Von Eckardt, "You Can't See the Foyer for the Trees," *Horizon* 13 (summer 1971): 40–47; "Projet d'Extension Nations Unis," *L'Architecture d'Aujourd'hui* 43 (August 1971): 23; Kathleen Teltsch, "In Hard Times, U.N. Is a Boon to City," *New York Times* (November 22, 1971): 1, 14; Vincent Scully, "Thruway and Crystal Palace," *Architectural Forum* 140 (March 1974): 18–25; *Kevin Roche, John Dinkeloo and Associates, vol. 1: 1962–1975*, with an intro. by Henry-Russell Hitchcock (Tokyo: A.D.A. Edita, 1975), 192–97; Francesco Dal Co, *Kevin Roche* (New York: Rizzoli International Publications, 1985), 160–63.
157. Hamill, "UN Land Grab": 37.
158. Andrew Stein quoted in Hamill, "UN Land Grab": 37.
159. Huxtable, "Proposed Monument Under Glass at the U.N.": 37.
160. Huxtable, "Sugar Coating a Bitter Pill": 25.
161. Huxtable, "Sugar Coating a Bitter Pill": 25.
162. "Offices Slow but Developments Go," *Housing and Planning News* 29 (summer 1971): 3–4.
163. Kathleen Teltsch, "New Building for U.N. Aims at Security Fears," *New York Times* (August 26, 1972): 27; "Building 55 Stories High Will Have 42 Floors," *Engineering News-Record* 189 (September 14, 1972): 21; Suzanne Stephens, "Savvy about Steel, Game with Glass," *Progressive Architecture* 55 (September 1974): 78–83; *Kevin Roche, John Dinkeloo and Associates, vol. 1: 1962–1975*, 192–97; Robert E. Tomasson, "Office Building-Hotel for U.N. Is Opened," *New York Times* (November 21, 1975): 1, 26; Carter B. Horsley, "In Glass Walls, a Reflected City Stands Beside the Real One," *New York Times* (November 30, 1975), VIII: 1, 4; Henry Lefer, "Through a Glass," *Progressive Architecture* 57 (June 1976): 49–59; Paul Goldberger, "1 United Nations Plaza: A Serious Cause for Rejoicing," *New York Times* (June 8, 1976): 35; "U.N. Plaza Hotel Opens; Many Luxuries Offered," *New York Times* (June 9, 1976): 43; "Downtown Is Looking Up," *Time* 108 (July 5, 1976): 54–62; Paul Goldberger, "Design for Dining: Feasts for the Eye, Too," *New York Times* (July 30, 1976), III: 13; "Roche's UN Plaza Opens in New York," *Progressive Architecture* 57 (August 1976): 17; Angela Taylor, "Newest Hotel in New York: Elegant, Meticulous, Secure," *New York Times* (August 3, 1976): 34; William Marlin, "Beautiful, Friendly Skyscraper," *Christian Science Monitor* (August 27, 1976): 22; William Marlin, "A Friendly Neighborhood Skyscraper," *Architectural Record* 160 (October 1976): cover, 117–24; Betty Raymond, "It's a Grand Hotel," *Interiors* 136 (October 1976): 72–77; Ada Louise Huxtable, "Grand Hotel," *New York Times* (October 3, 1976), VI: 68–70; Nathan Silver, "The First Avenue School," *Harper's* 177 (January 1977): 91–92; Douglas Davis, "Rise of the Come-Hither Look," *Newsweek* 89 (January 17, 1977): 86–87; "'One United Nations Plaza,' New York," *Baumeister* 74 (May 1977): 429–31; "Une chambre à Manhattan," *Architecture Intérieure* 162 (October–November 1977): 60–61; Robert Jensen, "Corporate Slick," *Horizon* 20 (November 1977): 70–73; White and Willensky, *AIA Guide* (1978), 158–59; Goldberger, *The City Observed*, 131–32; Leland M. Roth, *A Concise History of American Architecture* (New York: Harper & Row, 1979), 338–39; Tauranac, *Essential New York*, 243–44; "One United Nations Plaza a New York," *Casabella* 44 (April–May 1980): 49–55; Walter McQuade, "A Sleek and Lofty New York Hotel," *Fortune* 102 (November 17, 1980): 27, 30; Goldberger, *The Skyscraper*, 117–18, 120, 142; Ada Louise Huxtable, *The Tall Building Artistically Reconsidered: The Search for a Skyscraper Style* (New York: Pantheon Books, 1982), 56–58, 70, 72; Philip Jodidio, "L'architecte Doit S'engager," *Connaissance des arts* 369 (November 1982): 62–69; Reynolds, *The Architecture of New York City*, 157; Dal Co, *Kevin Roche*, 12–14, 16–17, 33–38, 41, 43, 160–65.
164. See Hugh Ferriss, *The Metropolis of Tomorrow* (New York: Ives Washburn, 1929); Stern, Gilmartin and Mellins, *New York 1930*, 39, 507–11.
165. Goldberger, "1 United Nations Plaza: A Serious Cause for Rejoicing": 35.
166. Goldberger, *The City Observed*, 131–32.
167. Tauranac, *Essential New York*, 233–34.
168. McQuade, "A Sleek and Lofty New York Hotel": 30.
169. Huxtable, "Grand Hotel": 70.
170. Huxtable, "Grand Hotel": 70.

Chapter 8
Roosevelt Island

1. Peter Blake, "The Island Nobody Knows," *New York* 2 (November 10, 1969): 62–63.
2. For early histories of the island, see James D. McCabe, Jr., *Lights and Shadows of New York Life; Or, the Sights and Sensations of the Great City* (Philadelphia: National, 1872; New York: Farrar, Straus and Giroux, 1970), 631–47; I. N. Phelps Stokes, *The Iconography of Manhattan Island, 1498–1909* (New York: Robert H. Dodd, 1915–28; New York: Arno Press, 1967), II: 207, III: 666. Also see Anthony Bailey, "Manhattan's Other Island," *New York Times* (December 1, 1974), VI: 32–34, 36, 38, 40, 42, 44, 46, 49–50, 52, 54, 56; White and Willensky, *AIA Guide* (1978), 301–6; White and Willensky, *AIA Guide* (1988), 471–74; Paul Goldberger, *The City Observed: New York* (New York: Random House, 1979), 331–37; John Tauranac, *Essential New York* (New York: Holt, Rinehart and Winston, 1979), 242–43; Barbaralee Diamonstein, *The Landmarks of New York* (New York: Harry N. Abrams, 1988), 52–53; Andrew S. Dolkart, *Guide to New York City Landmarks* (Washington, D.C.: Preservation Press, 1992), 241.
3. Charles Dickens quoted in William Robbins, "Proposed Subway on Welfare Island Revives a Dream," *New York Times* (February 21, 1965), VIII: 1, 10.
4. Stern, Gilmartin and Massengale, *New York 1900*, 31. Also see Frank N. Jones, "Topics: A Backward Glance at Welfare Island," *New York Times* (June 11, 1966): 30.
5. "New York Builds a Bridge to Save Money," *Engineering News-Record* 153 (October 7, 1954): 77; "Welfare Island Gets Own Bridge," *New York Times* (May 19, 1955): 33; John M. Hayes, "Bridges," *New International Yearbook (1955)* (New York: Dodd, Mead,

1956): 63; Sharon Reier, *The Bridges of New York* (New York: Quadrant Press, 1977), 149.

6. McCandlish Phillips, "City's Last Trolley at End of Line," *New York Times* (April 7, 1957): 1, 80; Warren James Tanssig, "Trolley Car Nostalgia," letter to the editor, *New York Times* (April 11, 1957): 30.

7. Isadore Rosenfield, "The Fruit of Research: Welfare Hospital on Welfare Island, New York City," *The Modern Hospital* (March 1937): 58–64; Isadore Rosenfield, "Planning of Postwar Hospitals," *Architectural Record* 93 (May 1943): 61–62; White and Willensky, *AIA Guide* (1978), 305.

8. Robbins, "Proposed Subway on Welfare Island Revives a Dream": 10.

9. Victor Gruen, *East Island: A Proposal for the Conversion of Welfare Island* (New York: East Island Development Corporation, 1961); John Sibley, "Welfare Island Town of 70,000 Proposed at 450 Million Cost," *New York Times* (May 17, 1961): 1, 31; "Plan Announced to Transform Welfare Island into East Island Community," *Real Estate Record and Guide* 187 (May 20, 1961): 2–3; "Flesh V. Machine," *Time* 77 (May 26, 1961): 54; John Sibley, "Welfare Island Awaits Its Fate," *New York Times* (June 28, 1961): 37; Joseph R. Tamsky, "Crowded Island," letter to the editor, *Architectural Forum* 115 (July 1961): 200; "Gruen's Chinese Wall and Columbia's Terraces for Welfare Island," *Progressive Architecture* 42 (July 1961): 46–47; "Welfare Island Sought as Park," *New York Times* (July 17, 1961): 25; Philip Langley, "Welfareless Island," letter to the editor, *Architectural Forum* 115 (August 1961): 178; John Sibley, "Davies Appraises Welfare Island," *New York Times* (August 15, 1961): 31; Victor Gruen, "Rebuttal: Welfare Island," letter to the editor, *Architectural Forum* 115 (October 1961): 182–83; Alison Sky and Michelle Stone, *Unbuilt America* (New York: McGraw-Hill, 1976), 118; Rebecca Read Shanor, *The City that Never Was* (New York: Viking, 1988), 183–85.

10. Victor Gruen quoted in "Flesh V. Machine": 54.

11. "A Welfare Island Park," editorial, *New York Times* (August 18, 1961): 20.

12. Simon Breines, Luther Gulick, August Heckscher, Stanley Isaacs, Albert Mayer, Lewis Mumford, Clarence Stein, Ralph Walker, Frederick Woodbridge, "Holiday Islands in the City," letter to the editor, *New York Herald Tribune* (July 28, 1961): 22; Arthur X. Tirohy, "Letter to a Philanthropist: Tivoli-in-Manhattan," *Village Voice* 10 (October 7, 1965): 1, 13–19.

13. Sibley, "Welfare Island Town of 70,000 Proposed at 450 Million Cost": 1, 31; John Sibley, "Older Plan Cited for Welfare Isle," *New York Times* (May 18, 1961): 37; Robbins, "Proposed Subway on Welfare Island Revives a Dream": 1, 10.

14. Francis J. Kleban quoted in Sibley, "Older Plan Cited for Welfare Isle": 37.

15. "Gruen's Chinese Wall and Columbia's Terraces for Welfare Island": 47. Also see Jan C. Rowan, "New Blues and New Trends," *Progressive Architecture* 42 (October 1961): 134–47.

16. Kathleen Teltsch, "Southern Tip of Welfare Island Proposed as Site of U.N. School," *New York Times* (April 2, 1965): 1, 23; Kathleen Teltsch, "U.N. School Bars a Site on Island," *New York Times* (May 29, 1965): 28; "Congress Is Given East River Plan," *New York Times* (August 26, 1965): 35.

17. Paul Hofmann, "City Moves to Restore Desolate Welfare Island," *New York Times* (June 5, 1966): 1, 47.

18. "Panel on Welfare I. Appointed by Mayor," *New York Times* (February 14, 1968): 30; "New Lease," *Architectural Forum* 128 (March 1968): 85.

19. Quoted in "Moderation Wins Out": 85.

20. Seth S. King, "Mayor Discloses Welfare Island Plan," *New York Times* (February 13, 1969): 27; "Moderation Wins Out," *Architectural Forum* 130 (April 1969): 26, 85.

21. Blake, "The Island Nobody Knows": 62–63.

22. Blake, "The Island Nobody Knows": 62–63.

23. Shanor, *The City that Never Was*, 157, 185–88.

24. Philip Johnson and John Burgee, *The Island Nobody Knows* (New York: New York State Urban Development Corporation, 1969). Also see Ada Louise Huxtable, "A Plan for Welfare Island Is Unveiled," *New York Times* (October 10, 1969): 49; Murray Schumach, "Rising Public Interest in City's Parks Stimulates Increased Private Donations," *New York Times* (October 12, 1969): 49; "Satellite Island for Manhattan," *Business Week* (October 18, 1969): 146; Ada Louise Huxtable, "This Time They Mean It," *New York Times* (October 19, 1969): II: 32; "A New Community in New York's East River," *Architectural Record* 146 (November 1969): 40; "Welfare Island Plan," *Industrial Design* 16 (November 1969): 12; "New York Combats Urban Crisis," *Engineering News-Record* 183 (November 6, 1969): 32; Blake, "The Island Nobody Knows": 62–63; "The Master Rebuilder," *Newsweek* 74 (November 17, 1969): 76; "The Development of Welfare Island: The State Steps In," *Progressive Architecture* 50 (December 1969): 42; Shanor, *The City that Never Was*, 188.

25. Johnson and Burgee, *The Island Nobody Knows*, 1.

26. Johnson and Burgee, *The Island Nobody Knows*, 15.

27. Huxtable, "This Time They Mean It": 32.

28. Blake, "The Island Nobody Knows": 63.

29. Philip Johnson quoted in Blake, "The Island Nobody Knows": 63.

30. Blake, "The Island Nobody Knows": 63.

31. Edward C. Burks, "Board Votes Plan for Welfare Isle," *New York Times* (October 30, 1969): 1, 50.

32. "Vision of a New Town Is Unveiled Here," *New York Times* (October 7, 1970): 49; Ada Louise Huxtable, "Quality Design with Amenities," *New York Times* (October 7, 1970): 49, 59; Ada Louise Huxtable, "How Doth Welfare Island Fare?" *New York Times* (November 15, 1970): II: 27; "Welfare Island Work in Progress Revealed," *Architectural Record* 148 (December 1970): 24.

33. Huxtable, "Quality Design with Amenities": 49.

34. Huxtable, "How Doth Welfare Island Fare?": 27.

35. Ada Louise Huxtable, "Too Bad about the Mall," *New York Times* (May 23, 1971), II: 29.

36. Philip Johnson quoted in Bailey, "Manhattan's Other Island": 49.

37. Bailey, "Manhattan's Other Island": 38, 40.

38. "New York City New Town Ready to Start," *Engineering News-Record* 186 (June 3, 1971): 14; "A New Town in Town," *Newsweek* 78 (July 19, 1971): 40–41. Also see "Projekt 'Welfare Island,' New York," *Baumeister* 69 (February 1972): 166–68, 170.

39. *Annual Report to the New York State Urban Development Corporation* (New York, 1972), 18; "Welfare Island Update," *Architectural Record* 152 (July 1972): 38.

40. Steven R. Weisman, "Doubts Linger, but Welfare Island Venture Moves Ahead," *New York Times* (June 4, 1972), VIII: 1, 12.

41. "Welfare Island Plans Becoming Reality," *Progressive Architecture* 54 (June 1973): 65–66; Joanna Mermey, "Does $75,000 Sound Like Middle-Income?" *Village Voice* 18 (Sep-

tember 10, 1973): 7, 62. Also see "A Plea for Planned Communities . . . New Towns in America—With Lessons from Europe," *Architectural Record* 154 (December 1973): 85–144.

42. "Welfare Is. May Be Roosevelt Is.," *New York Times* (January 21, 1973): 60; "FDR Goes on Welfare," *Architecture Plus* 1 (May 1973): 87; "Roosevelt Island," editorial, *New York Times* (July 19, 1973): 34; "Welfare Island Name Changed to Roosevelt," *New York Times* (August 21, 1973): 36; Joanna Mermey, "The Clan Gathers on Roosevelt Island," *Village Voice* 18 (September 27, 1973): 1; "The Talk of the Town: Out of History," *New Yorker* 49 (October 8, 1973): 36.

43. Laurie Johnston, "Plans for Memorial at Roosevelt Island Announced During Dedication Ceremony at Site," *New York Times* (September 25, 1973): 25; Heinz Ronner and Sharad Jhaveri, *Louis I. Kahn: Complete Work 1935–1974* (Basel: Birkhäuser Verlag, 1974), 161; Wolf Von Eckardt, "Famed Architect Louis Kahn Dies," *Washington Post* (March 21, 1974), C: 13; Paul Goldberger, "Design by Kahn Picked for Roosevelt Memorial Here," *New York Times* (April 25, 1974): 1, 45; Thomas B. Hess, "Monumental Bust," *New York* 7 (May 20, 1974): 92, 95; "'Frightening Track' Meets UDC Schedule," *Progressive Architecture* 55 (October 1974): 22–23; Bailey, "Manhattan's Other Island": 52; Romaldo Giurgola and Jaimini Mehta, *Louis I. Kahn* (Zurich: Artemis, 1975), 178–79; *Louis I. Kahn* (Tokyo: Architecture + Urbanism, 1975), 38–39; Martin Waldron, "City's Cash Shortage Imperils Plan for a Roosevelt Memorial," *New York Times* (October 9, 1975): 45; Priscilla Tucker, "Roosevelt Island: A New Deal for Living," *New York* 9 (November 8, 1976): cover, 54–63; Christian Norberg-Schulz, "Kahn, Heidegger and the Language of Architecture," *Oppositions* 18 (fall 1979): 28–47; David B. Brownlee and David G. DeLong, *Louis I. Kahn: In the Realm of Architecture*, with an intro. by Vincent Scully (New York: Rizzoli International Publications, 1991), 138–39.

44. "Cosmetic Spectacular," editorial, *New York Times* (January 8, 1969): 46. Also see "Giving a Geyser," *Time* 93 (June 27, 1969): 54; "Thar She Blows!" *Architectural Forum* 131 (October 1969): 32.

45. Louis I. Kahn quoted in Von Eckardt, "Famed Architect Louis Kahn Dies": 13.

46. Theodore Liebman quoted in Goldberger, "Design by Kahn Picked for Roosevelt Memorial Here": 45.

47. Hess, "Monumental Bust": 92.

48. Waldron, "City's Cash Shortage Imperils Plan for a Roosevelt Memorial": 45.

49. Tucker, "Roosevelt Island: A New Deal for Living": 63.

50. "Roosevelt Island Opens Next Year," *Housing and Planning News* 32 (September 1974): 12.

51. "'Frightening Track' Meets UDC Schedule": 22–23.

52. Ulrich Franzen, "New Forms of the Evolving City Project," *A + U* (August 1975): 101.

53. Joseph P. Fried, "Roosevelt Island Hailed by First New Residents," *New York Times* (June 24, 1975): 37; "O Pioneers!" *Newsweek* 86 (July 14, 1975): 55–56; Richard F. Shepard, "About New York: Roosevelt Island Pilgrims Give Thanks," *New York Times* (November 26, 1975): 14; White and Willensky, *AIA Guide* (1978), 304.

54. Fried, "Roosevelt Island Hailed by First New Residents": 37.

55. Shepard, "About New York: Roosevelt Island Pilgrims Give Thanks": 14.

56. "'Frightening Track' Meets UDC Schedule": 22–23; Bailey, "Manhattan's Other Island": 49–50; "Public Corporation Housing, Roosevelt Island, New York," *International Asbestos-Cement Review* 81 (January 1976): 4–7; Paul Goldberger, "New Urban Environment," *New York Times* (May 18, 1976): 65; "The Little Apple," *Time* 107 (May 24, 1976): 42; Tucker, "Roosevelt Island: A New Deal for Living": 56, 61–62; White and Willensky, *AIA Guide* (1978), 303–4; Stanley Abercrombie, "Roosevelt Island Housing," *A + U* (February 1978): 91–103; Goldberger, *The City Observed*, 334–36; Tauranac, *Essential New York*, 243.

57. John Johansen and Ashok M. Bhavnani quoted in "'Frightening Track' Meets UDC Schedule": 22.

58. Goldberger, "New Urban Environment": 65.

59. Abercrombie, "Roosevelt Island Housing": 103.

60. Bailey, "Manhattan's Other Island": 50. Also see "'Frightening Track' Meets UDC Schedule": 22–23; Jonathan Hale, "Ten Years Past at Peabody Terrace," *Progressive Architecture* 55 (October 1974): 72–77; Goldberger, "New Urban Environment": 65; "The Little Apple": 42; Diana Agrest and Alessandra LaTour, "Roosevelt Island Housing Competition," *L'Architecture d'Aujourd'hui* 186 (August–September 1976): 22–35; Mildred F. Schmertz, "Design Alternatives for Low- to Moderate-Income Urban Housing," *Architectural Record* 160 (August 1976): cover, 100–109; Tucker, "Roosevelt Island: A New Deal for Living": 56–57; Sam Davis, "The House Versus Housing," in Sam Davis, ed., *The Form of Housing* (New York: Van Nostrand Reinhold, 1977), 29, 31; Andrea O. Dean, "The Urbane and Varied Buildings of Sert, Jackson & Associates," *Journal of the American Institute of Architects* 66 (May 1977): 50–57; White and Willensky, *AIA Guide* (1978), 303–4; Goldberger, *The City Observed*, 334–36; Tauranac, *Essential New York*, 243; Josep Lluís Sert: Arquitectura; desseny urbé, exhibition catalogue (Barcelona: Fundació Joan Miró, 1979), 69–71; Edgardo Mannino and Ignacio Paricio, *J. Ll. Sert: Construcción y Arquitectura* (Barcelona: Gustavo Gili, 1983), 135–96; Norval White, *New York: A Physical History* (New York: Atheneum, 1987), 128–29, 179–80.

61. Goldberger, "New Urban Environment": 65.

62. Bailey, "Manhattan's Other Island": 50; White and Willensky, *AIA Guide* (1978), 304; Goldberger, *The City Observed*, 334, 337; Alex Krieger, ed., *The Architecture of Kallmann, McKinnell & Wood* (Cambridge, Mass.: Harvard University Graduate School of Design; New York: Rizzoli International Publications, 1988), 144.

63. Goldberger, *The City Observed*, 334.

64. "Island New Town Plans Cable Car Link with Manhattan," *Engineering News-Record* 190 (March 29, 1973): 13; Glenn Fowler, "Welfare Island-Manhattan Cable-Car Plan Disclosed," *New York Times* (March 30, 1973): 43; Michael Winkleman, "Cable Vision," *New York* 8 (September 15, 1975): 34–35; Peter Blake, "The Eighth Annual Cityscape Awards," *New York* 9 (January 12, 1976): 56; "Aerial Tram's Trial Run Hits Snag," *New York Times* (February 17, 1976): 35; Fred Ferretti, "Aerial Tram Ride to Roosevelt Island Is Opened with a Splash—On O'Dwyer," *New York Times* (May 18, 1976): 65; Goldberger, "New Urban Environment": 65; "The Little Apple": 42; "Airborne Commuters Take a Disneyland Ride to Work," *Popular Mechanics* 146 (July 1976): 52–53, 112, 114; "Engineering for Architecture," *Architectural Record* 160 (mid-August 1976): 65–91; White and Willensky, *AIA Guide* (1978), 155.

65. Goldberger, "New Urban Environment": 65.

66. Winkleman, "Cable Vision": 35.

67. "The Little Apple": 42.

68. Michael Demarest quoted in "The Little Apple": 42.

69. Goldberger, *The City Observed*, 337.

70. Goldberger, *The City Observed*, 336. Also see Diamonstein, *The Landmarks of New York*, 52; Dolkart, *Guide to New York City Landmarks*, 241.

71. Goldberger, *The City Observed*, 336. Also see "1889 Chapel Is Restored in Rite on Roosevelt I.," *New York Times* (October 20, 1975): 37; Gerald Allen, "Religious Buildings," *Architectural Record* 161 (July 1977): 101–16; White and Willensky, *AIA Guide* (1978), 304; Diamonstein, *The Landmarks of New York*, 52; Dolkart, *Guide to New York City Landmarks*, 241.

72. *Roosevelt Island Housing Competition* (New York: New York State Urban Development Corporation, 1974); "New York UDC Holds National Competition for 1,000 Units of Housing," *Journal of the American Institute of Architects* 62 (December 1974): 4; Deborah Nevins, ed., *The Roosevelt Island Housing Competition: The Architectural League of New York*, exhibition catalogue (New York: Architectural League of New York, 1975); "Architects Are Asked to Participate in Major Housing Design Competition," *Architectural Record* 157 (January 1975): 35; Paul Goldberger, "4 Architects Win U.D.C. Competition for Housing Designs for Roosevelt I.," *New York Times* (April 29, 1975): 37; Beth Dunlop, "Competition On an Island New Town," *Journal of the American Institute of Architects* 64 (July 1975): 27–35; Suzanne Stephens, "This Side of Habitat," *Progressive Architecture* 56 (July 1975): 58–63; Gerald Allen, "Roosevelt Island Competition—Was It Really a Flop?" *Architectural Record* 158 (October 1975): 111–20; Charles K. Hoyt, "What Did the New Super-Agency Mean for the Architect?" *Architectural Record* 158 (October 1975): 107–10; William Marlin, "After the Pratfall: UDC Dusts Off the Debris of Default," *Architectural Record* 158 (October 1975): 121–24; Barbara Goldstein, "Roosevelt Island Housing," *Architectural Design* 45 (November 1975): 693–96; "Correction," *Progressive Architecture* 56 (November 1975): 9; Sky and Stone, *Unbuilt America*, 88; Agrest and LaTour, "Roosevelt Island Housing Competition": 22–35; Davis, "The House Versus Housing," in Davis, ed., *The Form of Housing*, 34–38; *Robert A. M. Stern: Buildings and Projects 1965–1980*, eds. Peter Arnell and Ted Bickford (New York: Rizzoli International Publications, 1981), 98–103; Richard Plunz, *A History of Housing in New York City* (New York: Columbia University Press, 1990), 302–3.

73. Edward J. Logue, "Statement by Edward J. Logue, President and Chief Executive Officer," in *Roosevelt Island Housing Competition*, 3.

74. Sharon Lee Ryder, "UDC Financial Woes a Political Ploy?" *Progressive Architecture* 56 (April 1975): 32, 37–38.

75. Joseph Wasserman quoted in Dunlop, "Competition On an Island New Town": 28.

76. Goldberger, "4 Architects Win U.D.C. Competition for Housing Designs for Roosevelt I.": 37.

77. Robert Stern quoted in Allen, "Roosevelt Island Competition—Was It Really a Flop?": 118.

78. Paul Rudolph quoted in Stephens, "This Side of Habitat": 59.

79. Joseph Wasserman quoted in Stephens, "This Side of Habitat": 61.

80. Nevins, ed., *The Roosevelt Island Housing Competition*, entry 32.

81. Nevins, ed., *The Roosevelt Island Housing Competition*, entry 30; Rem Koolhaas, *Delirious New York: A Retroactive Manifesto for Manhattan* (New York: Oxford University Press, 1978), 247–52.

82. Nevins, ed., *The Roosevelt Island Housing Competition*, entry 34; O. M. Ungers, *Architecture as Theme* (Milan: Electa, 1982), 114–17; *O. M. Ungers, 1951–1984: Bauten und Projekte* (Braunschweig, Germany: Vieweg & Sohn, 1985), 110–11; Plunz, *A History of Housing in New York*, 302–3.

83. Nevins, ed., *The Roosevelt Island Housing Competition*, entry 7.

84. Robin Herman, "Metropolitan Baedeker: Across the River to Roosevelt Island," *New York Times* (August 4, 1978), C: 24.

85. Goldstein, "Roosevelt Island Housing": 693.

86. Ron Aaron Eisenberg, "A Not-So-Fond Farewell to Roosevelt Island," *New York Times* (February 22, 1978): 23.

Chapter 9
Upper West Side

1. Lawrence Van Gelder, "Across Central Park, Hostile Worlds Cry 'En Garde!'" *New York Times* (November 30, 1969), VIII: 1, 4.

THE FALL

1. Charles Y. Paterno quoted in "Says River Assures Future of West Side," *New York Times* (July 24, 1940): 37.

2. Stern, Gilmartin and Mellins, *New York 1930*, 451, 453.

3. Warren J. Cox et al., *A Guide to the Architecture of Washington, D.C.*, 2nd rev. ed. (New York: McGraw-Hill, 1974), 135.

4. Edward Teitelman and Richard Longstreth, *Architecture in Philadelphia: A Guide* (Cambridge, Mass.: MIT Press, 1974), 229.

5. Harold M. Mayer and Richard C. Wade, *Chicago: Growth of a Metropolis* (Chicago: University of Chicago Press, 1969), 399; Dominic A. Pacyga and Ellen Skerrett, *Chicago: City of Neighborhoods* (Chicago: Loyola University Press, 1986), 148.

6. Donlyn Lyndon, *The City Observed: Boston* (New York: Random House, 1982), 299; Michael and Susan Southworth, *AIA Guide to Boston* (Chester, Conn.: Globe Pequot, 1984), 455.

7. See Stern, Gilmartin and Massengale, *New York 1900*, 360–95.

8. E. Idell Zeisloft, ed., *The New Metropolis* (New York: D. Appleton, 1899), 633–34, quoted in James Trager, *West of Fifth: The Rise and Fall and Rise of Manhattan's West Side* (New York: Atheneum, 1987), 5.

9. Stern, Gilmartin and Massengale, *New York 1900*, 230–31, 390.

10. For both the Harmonie and Metropolitan clubs, see Stern, Gilmartin and Massengale, *New York 1900*, 232–33, 239–40.

11. Trager, *West of Fifth*, 5.

12. "The Metropolitanites," *Fortune* 20 (July 1939): 84–85.

13. Andrew Alpern, *Apartments for the Affluent* (New York: McGraw-Hill, 1975), 128–29; Stern, Gilmartin and Mellins, *New York 1930*, 403, 410–11, 416.

14. For William Randolph Hearst's triplex in the Clarendon Apartments, see Stern, Gilmartin and Mellins, *New York 1930*, 454–55.

15. Lee E. Cooper, "Ninth Ave. Awaits Revival in Reality," *New York Times* (June 9, 1940), XI: 1, 3; "Two 'El' Lines End Transit Service," *New York Times* (June 12, 1940): 27; "Columbus Avenue Tenements Altered at Cost of $135,000 Following Elevated Line Removal," *Real Estate Record and Guide* 147 (February 22, 1941): 5.

16. Nicholas Pileggi, "Renaissance of the Upper West Side," *New York* 2 (June 30, 1969): 28–39.

17. Frank W. Crane, "Old Apartment on the West Side Being Torn Down," *New York Times* (August 1, 1943), VIII and IX: 1–2.

18. Building permit NB-139, 1950.

19. Frank W. Crane, "West Side Tenants Rent Small Units," *New York Times* (January 26, 1941), XI: 1, 8. For the Eldorado, see Stern, Gilmartin and Mellins, *New York 1930*, 403, 406.

20. White and Willensky, *AIA Guide* (1988), 333.

21. For Kebbon's building, see Stern, Gilmartin and Mellins, *New York 1930*, 120, 122.

22. Thomas E. Norton and Jerry E. Patterson, *Living It Up: A Guide to the Named Apartment Houses of New York* (New York: Atheneum, 1984), 183; Trager, *West of Fifth*, 92.

23. "Renaissance at Riker's," *Architectural Record* 102 (July 1947): 117.

24. American Museum of Natural History, *Extract from the Minutes of the Management Board* (November 19, 1942); A. Perry Osborn, letter to the members of the Management Board of the American Museum of Natural History (November 30, 1942); Eliel Saarinen, letter to Aymar Embury II (December 1, 1942); American Museum of Natural History, *Memorandum of Understanding between the American Museum of Natural History and Department of Parks, City of New York with Respect to Post-War Reconstruction Project* (January 11, 1943); "Museum of Natural History Here Will Be Modernized After the War," *New York Times* (January 12, 1943): 25; "Angles for Curves," editorial, *New York Times* (January 13, 1943): 22; Doris G. Tobias, "Museum Plans Disapproved," letter to the editor, *New York Times* (January 15, 1943): 16; Eva Platt, "New Museum Plans Approved," letter to the editor, *New York Times* (January 19, 1943): 18; Robert Moses, letter to Albert E. Parr (January 21, 1943); Rufus Graves Mather, "Museum Plans Opposed," letter to the editor, *New York Times* (January 27, 1943): 20; A. Perry Osborn, letter to Eliel Saarinen (February 10, 1943); Eliel Saarinen, letter to Albert E. Parr (February 13, 1943); Aymar Embury II, letter to Eliel Saarinen (April 5, 1943); American Museum of Natural History, *Extract from Minutes of Meeting of Management Board of the American Museum of Natural History* (April 23, 1943); Wayne M. Faunce, letter to Aymar Embury II (December 21, 1943); "Model of Proposed Reconstruction and Addition for American Museum of Natural History," *Interiors* 103 (June 1944): 13; New York City Department of Parks, *12 Years of Park Progress* (New York, 1945), 59–60; Karrie Jacobs, "Plans of Extinction," *Metropolis* 7 (November 1987): 28; Barbaralee Diamonstein, *The Landmarks of New York* (New York: Harry N. Abrams, 1988), 164–65. All correspondence and memoranda in the archives of the American Museum of Natural History.

25. "Museums Too Musty for Moses; He Says They Intimidate Visitors," *New York Times* (March 3, 1941): 1, 9; "Moses Feels Sting of 'Dead' Museum," *New York Times* (March 4, 1941): 1; "Mr. Moses Explodes Again," editorial, *New York Times* (March 5, 1941): 20.

26. For Cady, Berg & See's building, see Stern, Gilmartin and Massengale, *New York 1900*, 370–72.

27. Osborn, letter to the members of the Management Board of the American Museum of Natural History (November 30, 1942).

28. Saarinen, letter to Embury (December 1, 1942).

29. Stern, Gilmartin and Mellins, *New York 1930*, 129, 135–36.

30. Moses, letter to Parr (January 21, 1943).

31. Saarinen, letter to Parr (February 13, 1943).

32. White and Willensky, *AIA Guide* (1988), 306; Christopher Gray, "Streetscapes: The Chemists' Club and the Godmothers League," *New York Times* (November 28, 1993), X: 5.

33. Lewis Mumford, "The Sky Line: Schools for Human Beings—II," *New Yorker* 28 (April 26, 1952): 68–74.

34. "New High School for New York City," *Architectural Record* 133 (February 1963): 15.

35. Lucy Greenbaum, "Passing of the Marble Front," *New York Times* (December 1, 1946): 68; "Schwab Home on Drive Sold Its Site for Apartment Center," *New York Times* (May 11, 1947): 1, 42; Lee E. Cooper, "$12,000,000 Apartments to Rise on Schwab 'Castle' Riverside Site," *New York Times* (April 10, 1949): 1, 48; "West Side Square Blocks for Schwab Mansion Site, to Be Improved with Ultra Modern 17–Story Apartment Building," *Real Estate Record and Guide* 163 (April 16, 1949): 3; "Plan 651 Suites for Schwab Site," *New York Times* (August 4, 1949): 37; "Work Soon to Start on Erection of Large Apartment Project on Site of Former Schwab Mansion," *Real Estate Record and Guide* 164 (September 24, 1949): 4; "How to Stretch a View," *Interiors* 110 (January 1951): 10, 12; "Schwab House Uses Porters as Occupancy Nears a Peak Rate of 20 Families a Day," *New York Times* (March 11, 1951), VIII: 1, 4; Nathan Silver, *Lost New York* (Boston: Houghton Mifflin, 1967), 126; White and Willensky, *AIA Guide* (1978), 182; Lewis Mumford, *Sketches from Life* (New York: Dial Press, 1982), 7; Stern, Gilmartin and Massengale, *New York 1900*, 376–77; Norton and Patterson, *Living It Up*, 307–8; Trager, *West of Fifth*, 47, 49, 92; Peter Salwen, *Upper West Side Story: A History and Guide* (New York: Abbeville Press, 1989), 101, 251.

36. For examples of Thomas's work, see Stern, Gilmartin and Mellins, *New York 1930*, 478–86.

37. "H & G Help Decorate a First Apartment," *House and Garden* 109 (May 1956): 102–13.

38. "New Luxury Apartment Building Under Construction on West End Avenue," *Real Estate Record and Guide* 167 (June 2, 1951): 3.

39. "Something New in Air Terminals," *Interiors* 105 (January 1946): 10, 12.

40. William Zeckendorf quoted in "Something New in Air Terminals": 10, 12.

41. Russell Porter, "Our Changing City: Along Manhattan's West Side," *New York Times* (July 4, 1955): 13.

42. Theodore H. White, *In Search of History: A Personal Adventure* (New York: Harper & Row, 1978), 368–69, 371.

43. Marya Mannes, "The New York I Know: I. The West Seventies," *Reporter* 21 (December 24, 1959): 16–19.

44. Trager, *West of Fifth*, 99–100.

45. Don Ross, "Upper West Side—Squalor, Culture Side by Side," *New York Herald Tribune* (June 25, 1961): 1, 17. Also see Don Ross, "West Side Soon Has to Relocate 5,000 Families," *New York Herald Tribune* (June 26, 1961): 9; Don Ross, "West Side Slum Pioneers: Will Their Gamble Pay Off?" *New York Herald Tribune* (June 27, 1961): 25; Don Ross, "Giant Funds Stepping Up Fight on Morningside Heights Blight," *New York Herald Tribune* (June 28, 1961): 11; Don Ross, "What Money, Work Can Do: An Example on West Side," *New York Herald Tribune* (June 29, 1961): 21.

46. Ross, "What Money, Work Can Do: An Example on West Side": 21. For the Hendrik Hudson, see Stern, Gilmartin and Massengale, *New York 1900*, 418.

COLUMBUS CIRCLE

1. For the Cosmopolitan Theater, see Stern, Gilmartin and Mellins, *New York 1930*, 238.
2. Leo Egan, "New Sports Arena Will Seat 25,000," *New York Times* (November 15, 1946): 19; "New Sports Arena," *Engineering News-Record* 137 (November 21, 1946): 10; William R. Conklin, "Moses Loses Plea for Favored Plans," *New York Times* (December 3, 1946): 33.
3. "Albany GOP Group Kills Bill to Build Sports Arena Here," *New York Times* (March 6, 1947): 1, 3; "Moses Criticizes Ban on New Arena," *New York Times* (March 7, 1947): 44; "A New 'Garden,'" editorial, *New York Times* (April 14, 1948): 26.
4. New York City Committee on Slum Clearance, *Columbus Circle* (New York, 1952); Morris Kaplan, "Moses Says Work on Coliseum Here Will Start Soon," *New York Times* (October 23, 1952): 1, 34; "City Speeds Plan for New Coliseum," *New York Times* (November 27, 1952): 33; "Vast Coliseum Plan Goes to Mayor," *New York Times* (December 1, 1952): 1, 13; "The Coliseum Plans," editorial, *New York Times* (December 5, 1952): 26; "Vast Housing Plan Set for Brooklyn," *New York Times* (December 11, 1952): 39; Charles G. Bennett, "City Planners Approve Coliseum and 2 Other Projects for Action," *New York Times* (December 13, 1952): 1, 16; "Two Plans—A Plus and a Minus," *Citizens' Housing News* 11 (January 1953): 1; "Coliseum Project Adopted by Board," *New York Times* (December 19, 1952): 33; "Says Proposed Columbus Circle Development Should Receive Support of All Civic-Minded Citizens and Property Owners in the Vicinity," *Real Estate Record and Guide* 171 (January 3, 1953): 3; "HHFA Approves New York Redevelopment Where Site Costs $35,536 Per Family Unit," *Architectural Forum* 98 (February 1953): 47.
5. Robert Moses, *Public Works: A Dangerous Trade* (New York: McGraw-Hill, 1970), 443. For the Grand Central Palace, see Stern, Gilmartin and Massengale, *New York 1900*, 40.
6. Robert C. Weinberg quoted in "HHFA Approves New York Redevelopment Where Site Costs $35,536 Per Family Unit": 47.
7. "Nation's Costliest Redevelopment Project, New York Coliseum Gets Legal Green Light," *Architectural Forum* 99 (November 1953): 123; Norman Williams, Jr., "Zoning and Planning Notes: Recent Redevelopment Cases," *American City* 68 (December 1953): 13, 153; "HHFA Bows to New York in Coliseum Site Dispute," *Architectural Forum* 102 (May 1955): 17.
8. "Important Commissions," *Architectural Forum* 100 (January 1954): 45; Joseph C. Ingraham, "City Coliseum Plan Revised to Stress Vast Exhibit Area," *New York Times* (March 17, 1954): 1, 22; "New 'Hearts' for Our Cities," *Newsweek* 43 (March 29, 1954): 74–75; "Art News Assails Coliseum Plans but Moses Declines to 'Get Mad,'" *New York Times* (March 31, 1954): 1, 25; Alfred M. Frankfurter, "Where'll Moses Be When the Lights Go On?" editorial, *Art News* 53 (April 1954): 15, reprinted in part in "Excerpts," *Architectural Forum* 100 (June 1954): 178–79; "Threat to Urban Redevelopment," *Architectural Forum* 100 (May 1954): 37, 39; "First Huge Truss Up for Coliseum," *New York Times* (January 4, 1955): 46; "Triborough Bridge & Tunnel Authority Appoints Noyes Company Agent for the Coliseum and Coliseum Tower Building," *Real Estate Record and Guide* 175 (March 12, 1955): 3; "When an Acre of Floor Gave Way," *Business Week* (May 14, 1955): 31; "Falsework of NY Coliseum Floor Collapses," *Architectural Forum* 102 (June 1955): 21; Alan Dunn, "Too Bad Vespasian Couldn't Have Lived to See the One We're Building Back Home in Columbus Circle," cartoon, *Architectural Forum* 118 (October 1955): 15; "Topics of The Times," *New York Times* (April 22, 1956), IV: 8; "New York's Bid for Expositions," *Business Week* (April 28, 1956): 86–88, 90, 92, 98; Charles Grutzner, "Coliseum to Open in Fanfare Today," *New York Times* (April 28, 1956): 1, 19; Clayton Knowles, "Bridge Revenues Built New Center," *New York Times* (April 28, 1956): 19; "Engineer at Coliseum Honored by Professor," *New York Times* (April 28, 1956): 19; "Coliseum's Facade Is Simple in Decor; 4 Medallions Its Principal Adornment," *New York Times* (April 28, 1956): 19; "Visitors Are in a Spending Mood, Dealers Wink at War and Fear," *New York Times* (April 29, 1956): 75; C. B. Palmer, "Coliseum: Showcase of Showcases," *New York Times* (April 29, 1956), VI, part 2: 14, 67; "A Temple for Mecca," *New York Times* 67 (April 30, 1956): 100, 102; Olga Gueft, "The Indispensable Splurge," editorial, *Interiors* 115 (June 1956): 91; "News Bulletins," *Progressive Architecture* 37 (June 1956): 96; Mr. Harper, "After Hours," *Harper's* 213 (July 1956): 85–86; "New New York," *Newsweek* 48 (July 9, 1956): 91; "Redevelopment Today," *Architectural Forum* 108 (April 1958): 110; Moses, *Public Works: A Dangerous Trade*, 443–48; Paul Goldberger, *The City Observed: New York* (New York: Random House, 1979), 180–81; Christopher Gray, "Streetscapes: The Coliseum," *New York Times* (April 26, 1987): 14, reprinted in Christopher Gray, *Changing New York: The Architectural Scene* (New York: Dover, 1992), 7; David W. Dunlap, *On Broadway: A Journey Uptown Over Time* (New York: Rizzoli International Publications, 1990), 215–16.
9. Joseph Addonizio and Albert S. Bard quoted in "Vast Housing Plan Set for Brooklyn": 39.
10. Robert Moses quoted in "Art News Assails Coliseum Plans but Moses Declines to 'Get Mad'": 1.
11. Frankfurter, "Where'll Moses Be When the Lights Go On?": 15.
12. Alfred M. Frankfurter quoted in "Art News Assails Coliseum Plans but Moses Declines to 'Get Mad'": 25.
13. Robert Moses quoted in "Art News Assails Coliseum Plans but Moses Declines to 'Get Mad'": 1.
14. Frank Lloyd Wright quoted in "Visitors Are in a Spending Mood, Dealers Wink at War and Fear": 75.
15. Quoted in Harper, "After Hours": 85.
16. Charles Grutzner, "Coliseum Draws Many Expositions," *New York Times* (February 20, 1956): 14.
17. "Columbus Apartments," *New York Times* (September 30, 1955): 43; "Coliseum Apartments Plans Two Acre Garden on Stilts," *Real Estate Record and Guide* 180 (September 28, 1957): 4; Anthony Jackson, *A Place Called Home: A History of Low-Cost Housing in Manhattan* (Cambridge, Mass.: MIT Press, 1976), 253; Thomas E. Norton and Jerry E. Patterson, *Living It Up: A Guide to the Named Apartment Houses of New York* (New York: Atheneum, 1984), 107.
18. Lewis Mumford, "The Life, the Teaching and the Architecture of Matthew Nowicki, part II: Matthew Nowicki as an Educator," *Architectural Record* 116 (July 1954): 28–136; Bruce Harold Schafer, *The Writings and Sketches of Matthew Nowicki* (Charlottesville, Va.: University Press of Virginia, 1973), 47–51.
19. Henry Hope Reed, Jr., "The Modern Is Dead—Long Live the Modern," with drawings by John Barrington Bayley, *New World Writing* 11 (New York: New American Library, 1957): 134–51. Also see Henry Hope Reed, "Visual Criteria," letter to the editor, *Progressive Architecture* 39 (February 1958): 27, 32; Henry Hope Reed, *The Golden City* (New York: W. W. Norton, 1959), 108–11; Thomas H. Creighton, "The New Sensualism II," *Progressive Architecture* 40 (October 1959): 180–87; Alison Sky and Michelle Stone, *Unbuilt America* (New York: McGraw-Hill, 1976), 34.
20. "City to Get Fountains for Statue," *New York Times* (October 12, 1960): 41; "The Roman Spring of Mr. Leigh," *Progressive Architecture* 42 (January 1961): 58. For Gaetano Russo's statue, see Margot Gayle and Michele Cohen, *The Art Commission and the Municipal Art Society Guide to Manhattan's Outdoor Sculpture* (New York: Prentice Hall Press, 1988), 263–64.
21. Ada Louise Huxtable, "Slab City Marches On," *New York Times* (March 3, 1968), II: 22.
22. Sanka Knox, "Art Museum at Columbus Circle Planned by Huntington Hartford," *New York Times* (June 11, 1956): 1, 32; "A New Art Museum," editorial, *New York Times* (June 12, 1956): 34; illustrated in *Village Voice* 1 (June 13, 1956): 10; Ian McCallum, *Architecture USA* (London: Architectural Press, 1959), 90; "Buildings in the News," *Architectural Record* 126 (July 1959): 14; "Architectural Bulletins," *Progressive Architecture* 40 (July 1959): 81; Creighton, "The New Sensualism II": 184; Edward Durell Stone, *The Evolution of an Architect* (New York: Horizon Press, 1962), 204–5; Sanka Knox, "Huntington Hartford's Gallery Still a Year from Completion," *New York Times* (January 31, 1962): 33; "Healthy New Force," *Newsweek* 82 (September 9, 1962): 89; "Doing Over the Town," *Time* 80 (September 28, 1962): 56–69; "New York Nears Completion—Almost," *Architectural Forum* 117 (October 1962): 16–17; "Splendor in the Skies," *Life* 53 (November 9, 1962): 85; Olga Gueft, "A Designers' Tour of New York in the Spring," *Interiors* 123 (March 1963): 74–77; Ada Louise Huxtable, "Architecture: Huntington Hartford's Palatial Midtown Museum," *New York Times* (February 25, 1964): 33; Stuart Preston, "Letter from New York: More Space for Modern Art," *Apollo* 79 (March 1964): 244–45; Philip M. Herrera, "Huntington Hartford: A Most Unusual Client," *Architectural Forum* 120 (March 1964): 112–13; Alfred Frankfurter, "Caviare?—New York's Newest Museum," *Art News* 63 (March 1964): 32–34, 59–61; Huntington Hartford, "New Museum in Manhattan: A Sneak Preview," *Show* 4 (March 1964): 48–52; Carl J. Weinhardt, Jr., "Why Manhattan Needs Another Museum," *Show* 4 (March 1964): 52–53, 86; "New York's Newest Museum," *Architectural Record* 135 (April 1964): 13; Ellen Perry, "Stone's New Gallery of Art Opens," *Progressive Architecture* 45 (April 1964): 69, 71; Vivien Raynor, "New York Exhibitions: In the Galleries: Pavel Tchelitchew," *Arts* 38 (May–June 1964): 32; "Art in New Setting," *Interior Design* 35 (June 1964): 102–7; Olga Gueft, "Non-Conformity on Columbus Circle," *Interiors* 123 (June 1964): 92–96; Peter White, "The World in New York City," *National Geographic* 126 (July 1964): 99; Frank Getlein, "A New Wing for the Modern," *New Republic* 151 (August 8, 1964): 32; "Gallery Lighting," *Progressive Architecture* 45 (September 1964): 195; Anna Marchi, "Notizario: Antichita," *Domus* 420 (November 1964): 55–56; "Art Gallery," *Architecture International* 1 (1965): 78–83; Thomas W. Ennis, "Marble-Glass Buildings Brighten Midtown," *New York Times* (January 31, 1965), VIII: 1, 4; Nelson Lansdale, "A New Museum in New York," *American Artist* 29 (February 1965): 55–57, 66–69; Wolf Von Eckardt, *A Place to Live* (New York: Delacorte Press, 1967), 215; White and Willensky, *AIA Guide* (1967), 136; "Ivory Tower," *Art in America* 55 (July 1967): 103–4; John Canaday, "Days Are Numbered for a White Elephant," *New York Times* (March 23, 1975), II: 1, 31; "For Sale," *Progressive Architecture* 56 (August 1975): 21; David Bourdon, "N.Y. Museum Crisis: Two Bite Dust," *Art in America* 63 (September–October 1975): 37–39; Grace Glueck, "Cultural Center to Close After 11 Years," *New York Times* (September 10, 1975): 32; Hilton Kramer, ". . . While the Cultural Center Closes Its Doors," *New York Times* (September 15, 1975): 13; "Collage," *Art News* 74 (November 1975): 126; Goldberger, *The City Observed*, 180–81; James Trager, *West of Fifth: The Rise and Fall and Rise of Manhattan's West Side* (New York: Atheneum, 1987), 111; Dunlap, *On Broadway*, 223; Christopher Gray, "Schlock of Ages," *Avenue* 17 (December 1992): 31–32, 34, 36, 38. For Huntington Hartford's views on contemporary art, see his book, initially written under the title *Armageddon of Art* but published as *Art or Anarchy? How the Extremists and Exploiters Have Reduced the Fine Arts to Chaos and Commercialism* (Garden City, N.Y.: Doubleday, 1964). Also see Olga Gueft, "Sorry Spectacle," editorial, *Interiors* 114 (June 1955): 69; "Hartford on Art," *Progressive Architecture* 45 (September 1964): 92.
23. "Museum for Huntington Hartford," *Baukunst und Werkform* 12 (January 1959): 21; "Projet Pour un Musée à New York," *L'Architecture d'Aujourd'hui* 31 (September 1960): 77; Herrera, "Huntington Hartford: A Most Unusual Client": 112–13.
24. For the United States Rubber Building, see Stern, Gilmartin and Massengale, *New York 1900*, 156.
25. Lansdale, "A New Museum in New York": 55.
26. Huxtable, "Architecture: Huntington Hartford's Palatial Midtown Museum": 33.
27. Gueft, "Non-Conformity on Columbus Circle": 95.
28. Preston, "Letter from New York: More Space for Modern Art": 244.
29. Frankfurter, "Caviare?—New York's Newest Museum": 32.
30. "Buildings in the News": 14.
31. Stern, Gilmartin and Mellins, *New York 1930*, 138, 142, 144.
32. Perry, "Stone's New Gallery of Art Opens": 71.
33. Frankfurter, "Caviare?—New York's Newest Museum": 61.
34. Kramer, ". . . While the Cultural Center Closes Its Doors": 13.
35. Canaday, "Days Are Numbered for a White Elephant": 1, 31.
36. Bourdon, "N.Y. Museum Crisis: Two Bite Dust": 37–38.
37. Kramer, ". . . While the Cultural Center Closes Its Doors": 13.

LINCOLN SQUARE

1. Peter Salwen, *Upper West Side Story: A History and Guide* (New York: Abbeville Press, 1989), 121.
2. Salwen, *Upper West Side Story*, 121.
3. "Changing New York," *Newsweek* 52 (July 14, 1958): 75–77; Margot Gayle and Michele Cohen, *The Art Commission and the Municipal Art Society Guide to Manhattan's Outdoor Sculpture* (New York: Prentice Hall Press, 1988), 265; Salwen, *Upper West Side Story*, 121.
4. "French Plan Centre on the Century Site," *New York Times* (August 13, 1929): 1; David W. Dunlap, *On Broadway: A Journey Uptown Over Time* (New York: Rizzoli International Publications, 1990), 214.
5. Salwen, *Upper West Side Story*, 93–94. Also see Nathaniel Shephard, Jr., "Neighborhood: San Juan Hill, 'Eden' to the Eyes of a Playwright," *New York Times* (April 12, 1976): 33.
6. White and Willensky, *AIA Guide* (1978), 180; Salwen, *Upper West Side Story*, 93.

7. Robert A. M. Stern, "With Rhetoric: The New York Apartment House," *Via* 4 (1980): 78–111; Stern, Gilmartin and Massengale, *New York 1900*, 287; Salwen, *Upper West Side Story*, 94.
8. Frederick Gutheim, "Athens on the Subway," *Harper's* 217 (October 1958): 66–71.
9. Lewis Mumford, *Sketches from Life* (New York: Dial Press, 1982), 3; James Trager, *West of Fifth: The Rise and Fall and Rise of Manhattan's West Side* (New York: Atheneum, 1987), 106; Dunlap, *On Broadway*, 208, 210.
10. Raphael Soyer quoted in Salwen, *Upper West Side Story*, 272. Also see Abram Lerner, ed., *The Hirshhorn Museum and Sculpture Garden* (New York: Harry N. Abrams, 1974), plate 748.
11. "Developments in New York," *Housing and Planning News* 5 (November–December 1946): 3; Division of Housing and Business Administration, *Community Study No. 15: The Lower West End Area and Its Neighborhood Schools* (New York, 1947); "Amsterdam Houses," *New York Times* (August 31, 1947), VIII: 1; Talbot F. Hamlin, ed., *Forms and Functions of Twentieth-Century Architecture*, vol. 1 (New York: Columbia University Press, 1952), 292.
12. "Kelly & Gruzen Design Gym for Power Academy," *Architectural Record* 113 (January 1953): 286. Also see Sara Rimer, "The Closing of Power Memorial Is Mourned as a Death in Family," *New York Times* (June 8, 1984), II: 1, 10.
13. "12 New Schools Ready for Pupils," *New York Times* (September 11, 1955): 128. For C. B. J. Snyder's DeWitt Clinton High School, see Stern, Gilmartin and Massengale, *New York 1900*, 80, 82–83.
14. For useful overviews of the development and realization of Lincoln Center, see Ralph G. Martin, *Lincoln Center for the Performing Arts* (Englewood Cliffs, N.J.: Prentice Hall Press, 1971); Edgar B. Young, *Lincoln Center: The Building of an Institution* (New York: New York University Press, 1980); Alan Rich, *The Lincoln Center Story* (New York: American Heritage, 1984). Also see Ellen Manfredonia, "The Politically Viable Plan" (Master's thesis, Graduate School of Architecture and Planning, Columbia University, 1967); White and Willensky, *AIA Guide* (1967), 139–40; Robert Moses, *Public Works: A Dangerous Trade* (New York: McGraw-Hill, 1970), 513–33; Robert A. Caro, *The Power Broker: Robert Moses and the Fall of New York* (New York: Alfred A. Knopf, 1974), 1013–16; Paul Goldberger, *The City Observed: New York* (New York: Random House, 1979), 195, 197–200; John Tauranac, *Essential New York* (New York: Holt, Rinehart and Winston, 1979), 212–14; Trager, *West of Fifth*, 106, 108–10, 174, 177, 179; Carol Herselle Krinsky, "Architecture in New York City," in Leonard Wallock, ed., *New York: Culture Capital of the World, 1940–1965* (New York: Rizzoli International Publications, 1988), 116–18; Victoria Newhouse, *Wallace K. Harrison, Architect* (New York: Rizzoli International Publications, 1989), 186–234; Salwen, *Upper West Side Story*, 270–75; Dunlap, *On Broadway*, 216–23; Kathleen Randall, "Lincoln Center for the Performing Arts: Cultural Visibility and Postwar Urbanism" (Master's thesis, Graduate School of Architecture, Planning and Preservation, Columbia University, 1992).
15. For Rockefeller Center, see Stern, Gilmartin and Mellins, *New York 1930*, 617–71.
16. Howard Taubman, "New Cultural Vista for the City," *New York Times* (April 22, 1956), VI: 14, 76. Also see Howard Taubman, "Civic Pride: City Officials Should Work for Lincoln Center as a Municipal Necessity," *New York Times* (June 2, 1957), II: 7.
17. Stern, Gilmartin and Massengale, *New York 1900*, 14–15.
18. "City Offers Land for Music Center," *New York Times* (May 9, 1951): 1, 57. Also see "$900,000 Now Available for New Metropolitan Site," *Musical America* 72 (January 15, 1952): 3.
19. Rich, *The Lincoln Center Story*, 16.
20. Robert Moses quoted in Caro, *The Power Broker*, 1013.
21. Benjamin Boretz, "Lincoln Center: Tomb of the Future," *Nation* 200 (March 22, 1965): 299–304, 319–20.
22. "New Home for 'Met' Is Under Discussion," *New York Times* (June 9, 1954): 39.
23. Young, *Lincoln Center: The Building of an Institution*, 37. Also see "New York's Bid for Expositions," *Business Week* (April 28, 1956): 86–90, 92, 97–98.
24. "Proposed Cultural Center," *Citizens' Housing News* 13 (May 1955): 3; "News Bulletins," *Progressive Architecture* 36 (November 1955): 94; New York City Committee on Slum Clearance, *Lincoln Square* (New York, 1956); "News Bulletins," *Progressive Architecture* 37 (February 1956): 93.
25. Newhouse, *Wallace K. Harrison, Architect*, 187.
26. Joe Alex Morris, "Colossus on Broadway," *Saturday Evening Post* 237 (July 19, 1958): 28, 75–78.
27. John D. Rockefeller III quoted in Morris, "Colossus on Broadway": 77.
28. Morris, "Colossus on Broadway": 77.
29. John D. Rockefeller III quoted in Morris, "Colossus on Broadway": 77.
30. John D. Rockefeller III quoted in "The Rockefeller Touch in Building," *Architectural Forum* 108 (March 1958): 86–91.
31. Charles Grutzner, "Moses Outlines City Within a City for Lincoln Square," *New York Times* (May 28, 1956): 1, 21.
32. Lewis Funke, "Lincoln Square Plans Theatergoers' Utopia," *New York Times* (January 23, 1957): 1, 31; "Five-in-One Circular Theater Building," *Architectural Forum* 106 (February 1957): 37; "Six-Theater Plan," *Newsweek* 49 (February 4, 1957): 78; "Roger Stevens Promotes Dream Theaters for Lincoln Square," *Architectural Record* 121 (March 1957): 11.
33. "Lincoln Square: Grandest Redevelopment Project; Outstanding Case of Title I Complexities," *Architectural Forum* 107 (October 1957): 9, 12, 14, 16.
34. Robert Moses quoted in Grutzner, "Moses Outlines City Within a City for Lincoln Square": 21.
35. Quoted in "Noted Architects Study New York Opera-Theater Plans," *Architectural Forum* 105 (November 1956): 13.
36. "Lincoln Square Wins Two Cases," *Citizens' Housing News* 15 (March–April 1957): 2; New York City Planning Commission, "In the Matter of Lincoln Square Urban Renewal Plan and Project," transcript of public hearing, September 11, 1957; "Lincoln Square: Grandest Redevelopment Project; Outstanding Case of Title I Complexities": 9; "Moving Ahead—Maybe," *Engineering News-Record* 159 (December 5, 1957): 167–68; "Snags Hit Two Big Urban Renewal Jobs," *Architectural Forum* 108 (January 1958): 8; "N.Y. Project Boosted," *Engineering News-Record* 160 (January 9, 1958): 102; "Lincoln Square Project to Proceed February 28th," *Housing and Planning News* 16 (January–February 1958): 1; "Court Clears Lincoln Square Obstacles," *Architectural Forum* 108 (February 1958): 9, 11.
37. Owen McGivern quoted in "Court Clears Lincoln Square Obstacle": 9, 11. Complaint dismissed, 64th St. Residences, Inc., et al. v. City of New York et al. and Fordham University et al., New York State Supreme Court Appellate Division 170 N.Y.S. 2d 993 (1957); motion for a stay denied, New York State Court of Appeals 972 N.Y.S. 2d 819 (1958); decision upheld, New York State Court of Appeals 4 N.Y.S. 2d 268–77 (1958).
38. Certiorari denied, United States Supreme Court, Harris et al. v. City of New York et al., 357 U.S. 907 (1958).
39. "In Favor of Lincoln Square," editorial, *Citizens' Housing News* 15 (September 1956): 2. Also see "Citizens' Housing Urges Planning of Area around Lincoln Square," *Citizens' Housing News* 15 (November 1956): 1.
40. Harold C. Schonberg, "Progress Report on the New Arts Center," *New York Times* (May 25, 1958), VI: 38–45.
41. Young, *Lincoln Center: The Building of an Institution*, 44. Also see Hope MacLeod, "Nowhere to Go—And 30 Days to Get There," *New York Post* (March 26, 1959): 2, 36.
42. "Lincoln Square: Grandest Redevelopment Project; Outstanding Case of Title I Complexities": 14, 16.
43. Harold C. Schonberg, "Architects Join on Center Plans," *New York Times* (October 11, 1956): 41; "Noted Architects Study New York Opera-Theater Plans," *Architectural Forum* 105 (November 1956): 13; "News Bulletins," *Progressive Architecture* 37 (November 1956): 96; Goran Schildt, *Alvar Aalto: The Mature Years* (New York: Rizzoli International Publications, 1991), 240–41.
44. Newhouse, *Wallace K. Harrison, Architect*, 190.
45. "Lincoln Square Cultural Center," *Interiors* 116 (September 1956): 10; G. M. Kallmann, "Interiors Contract Series 156: Theaters," *Interiors* 116 (September 1956): 108–19; "News Bulletins," *Progressive Architecture* 37 (December 1956): 80; "HHFA Studies New York's Lincoln Square Proposal," *Architectural Record* 121 (March 1957): 10.
46. Schonberg, "Progress Report on the New Arts Center": 38.
47. "Arts Center Picks Last 2 Architects," *New York Times* (November 17, 1958): 33.
48. "P/A News Bulletins," *Progressive Architecture* 39 (December 1958): 34; "Meetings and Miscellany," *Architectural Record* 125 (February 1959): 28.
49. Lincoln Kirstein, *Quarry: A Collection in Lieu of Memoirs* (Pasadena, Calif.: Twelvetrees, 1986), 82.
50. "Man in the News: Realistic Architect Wallace Kirkman Harrison," *New York Times* (November 17, 1958): 33.
51. Harold C. Schonberg, "Six Architects in Search of a Center," *New York Times* (February 8, 1959), VI: 22–25.
52. Wallace K. Harrison quoted in Schonberg, "Six Architects in Search of a Center": 24.
53. Newhouse, *Wallace K. Harrison, Architect*, 195–96.
54. Schonberg, "Six Architects in Search of a Center": 25.
55. Philip Johnson quoted in John W. Cook and Heinrich Klotz, *Conversations with Architects* (New York: Praeger, 1973), 32–33.
56. "Lincoln Center Aids Ancient Spa," *New York Times* (August 27, 1963): 33, 63.
57. Young, *Lincoln Center: The Building of an Institution*, 90.
58. Philip Johnson quoted in "Lincoln Center Aids Ancient Spa": 63.
59. Lincoln Kirstein, "Lincoln Shelter," *New York Review of Books* 28 (August 13, 1981): 8, 10, 12–13.
60. "Buildings in the News," *Architectural Record* 126 (November 1959): 10; Ada Louise Huxtable, *Four Walking Tours of Modern Architecture in New York City* (New York: Museum of Modern Art and Municipal Art Society of New York, 1961), 69.
61. Morris, "Colossus on Broadway": 75.
62. "Business Backs an Art Center," *Business Week* (May 23, 1959): 62, 65, 68. Also see "Eisenhower Breaks Ground for New York's Lincoln Center," *Progressive Architecture* 40 (June 1959): 68.
63. "President Launches Lincoln Square," *New York Herald Tribune* (May 15, 1959): 1–2, quoted in Young, *Lincoln Center: The Building of an Institution*, 101.
64. Dwight D. Eisenhower quoted in Young, *Lincoln Center: The Building of an Institution*, 99.
65. "Lincoln Center Begins," editorial, *New York Times* (May 14, 1959): 32, quoted in Young, *Lincoln Center: The Building of an Institution*, 101.
66. For a profile of Otto L. Nelson, Jr., see Russell Bourne, "Building's Two-Star General," *Architectural Forum* 108 (June 1958): 118–19, 190.
67. "People," *Architectural Forum* 114 (June 1961): 11.
68. Peter D. Franklin, "Lincoln Center Discloses Philharmonic Hall Design," *New York Herald Tribune* (May 10, 1959): 26; Ross Parmenter, "2,400-Seat Philharmonic Hall Set for Lincoln Sq.," *New York Times* (May 10, 1959): 1, 73; "Eisenhower Breaks Ground for New York's Lincoln Center": 58; "Philharmonic Hall Design Made Public at Luncheon," *New York Herald Tribune* (December 2, 1959): 19; Harold C. Schonberg, "Work to Begin This Week on New Philharmonic Hall," *New York Times* (December 2, 1959): 1, 52; "Designer for Listening: Max Abramovitz," *New York Times* (December 2, 1959): 52; "Lincoln Center's Philharmonic," *Architectural Forum* 112 (January 1960): 10; "Buildings in the News," *Architectural Record* 127 (January 1960): 13; "Seek to Put More Seats in New Philharmonic Hall," *New York Herald Tribune* (January 7, 1960): 12; Joseph W. Lovelace, "Architects and Designers," letter to the editor, *Architectural Forum* 112 (June 1960): 217; Douglas Haskell, "Jazz in Architecture," *Architectural Forum* 113 (September 1960): 110–15; "Philharmonic Nears Completion," *Architectural Forum* 115 (July 1961): 9; Leo Beranek, *Music, Acoustics and Architecture* (New York: John Wiley & Sons, 1962), 511–40; "Philharmonic Hall, Lincoln Center for the Performing Arts," *Saturday Review*, special issue (1962); "Lincoln Center, New York, Salle de Concerts de l'Orchestre Philharmonique," *L'Architecture d'Aujourd'hui* 7 (February 1962): 699; "La Filarmonica del Lincoln Center a New York," *L'Archittetura cronache e storia* 34 (February 1962): 34–37; John Molleson, "Art Center Sculpture: It Floats," *New York Herald Tribune* (March 15, 1962): 25; "The Talk of the Town: Hall," *New Yorker* 38 (March 24, 1962): 31–33; Ada Louise Huxtable, "Our New Buildings: Hits and Misses," *New York Times* (April 29, 1962): 16–17, 105–6; Hedy Backlin, "Collaboration: Artist and Architect," *Craft Horizons* 22 (May 1962): 28–41; John Molleson, "Toward 'Intimacy' for 2,612 Who'll Listen," *New York Herald Tribune* (May 28, 1962): 24; "All Ears," *Newsweek* 59 (June 11, 1962): 58–59; Richard Lippold, "Projects for Pan Am and Philharmonic," *Art in America* 50 (summer 1962): 50–55; Leo L. Beranek, "Acoustics of Philharmonic Hall," *Architectural Record* 132 (September 1962): 196–204; "Now Bring On the Customers," *Business Week* (September 22, 1962): 42–43; Harriet Morrison, "Green Room Is Green in Philharmonic," *New York Herald Tribune* (September 24, 1962): 34; Earl G. Talbott, "Nobody Came the Hard Way," *New York Herald Tribune* (September 24, 1962): 14; Harold C. Schonberg, "Music: The Occasion," *New York Times* (September 24, 1962): 34; Ada Louise Huxtable, "Concertgoers Give Building Life," *New York Times* (September 24, 1962): 35; "Concern for Detail: Max Abramovitz," *New York*

Times (September 24, 1962): 34; Paul Henry Lang, "There Was Sparkle, There Was Music in the Air," *New York Herald Tribune* (September 24, 1962): 1, 14; Arthur Gelb, "Acoustical Remedies Set for Philharmonic Hall," *New York Times* (September 25, 1962): 32; Harold C. Schonberg, "Music: Barber Concerto," *New York Times* (September 25, 1962): 32; "New York Nears Completion—Almost," *Architectural Forum* 117 (October 1962): 16–17; "First Lady Attends Opening of First Lincoln Center Element," *Progressive Architecture* 43 (October 1962): 73; "The Interior Design of Philharmonic Hall," *Progressive Architecture* 43 (October 1962): 172; "The Talk of the Town: Beginning," *New Yorker* 38 (October 6, 1962): 41–42; "Scenario for Inexactness," *Time* 86 (October 15, 1962): 83–84; Ada Louise Huxtable, "Balancing Up: A Highbrow Ideal, Lincoln Center Is a Likely Middlebrow Monument," *New York Times* (October 28, 1962), II: 15; Roland Gelatt, "Art, Science, or Just Plain Luck?" *Reporter* 27 (December 20, 1962): 35–36, 38–40; Joseph Papin, "Opening Night at Philharmonic Hall, Lincoln Center," *Reporter* 27 (December 20, 1962): 37; Stuart Preston, "Art: 'Orpheus and Apollo,'" *New York Times* (December 21, 1962): 5; "Better for Talk than Music," *Time* 80 (December 21, 1962): 34; Martin Meyerson, *Face of the Metropolis* (New York: Random House, 1963), 114–15; "Tale of Two Cities," *Architectural Forum* 118 (February 1963): 94–99; Calvin Tomkins, "Profiles: A Thing among Things," *New Yorker* 40 (March 30, 1963): 47–50, 52, 54, 57–58, 60, 63–64, 66, 69–71, 74–76, 79–80, 82, 85–86, 88, 93–96, 99–102, 105–7; John Molleson, "Hear! Hear!" *New York Herald Tribune* (April 14, 1963): 3; Alan Rich, "Center Is Given Acoustical Plan," *New York Times* (April 14, 1963): 77; "Sound of Words," *Newsweek* 61 (April 15, 1963): 92; "Childe Harold in New York," *Time* 81 (September 6, 1963): 36, 41; R. S. Lanier, "Acoustics: What Happened at Philharmonic Hall?" *Architectural Forum* 119 (December 1963): 118–23; "Sound and Fury," *Newsweek* 63 (January 6, 1964): 47; "Acoustics: Philharmonic Hall," letters to the editor, *Architectural Forum* 120 (February 1964): 42, 44; Peter T. White, "The World in New York City," *National Geographic* 26 (July 1964): 52–107; "Art Movies Pack the House," *Business Week* (September 19, 1964): 34; "'Happy Piece,'" *Progressive Architecture* 45 (December 1964): 50–51; Walter McQuade, "Lincoln Center," *Nation* 200 (February 22, 1965): 204, 206; Laymon N. Miller, "Isolation of Railroad/Subway Noise and Vibration," *Progressive Architecture* 46 (April 1965): 263–68; Mina Hamilton, "Developing the Product; 9: Auditorium Seating," *Industrial Design* 12 (June 1965): 64–69; "Reverberations at Lincoln Center," *Progressive Architecture* 46 (July 1965): 62; Hilton Kramer, "Another Sculptural Nullity for New York's Lincoln Center," *New York Times* (July 31, 1966), II: 17; White and Willensky, *AIA Guide* (1967), 140; Clive Barnes, "Lincoln Center," *Holiday* 44 (September 1968): 36–44, 92–96; David Hamilton, "Music," *Nation* 209 (September 29, 1969): 325–26; James Marston Fitch, *American Building: The Environmental Forces that Shape It*, vol. 2, 2nd rev. ed. (Boston: Houghton Mifflin, 1972), 147, 150–51; Alan Rich, "Lincoln Center Strikes Again!!!" *New York* 5 (October 30, 1972): 66–67; "Starting Over," *Time* 105 (April 7, 1975): 67; "Acoustical Renovations Underway for New York Philharmonic's Auditorium," *Architectural Record* 160 (June 1976): 39; Hans Fantel, "Back to Square One for Avery Fisher Hall," *Hi Fi* 26 (October 1976): 70–80; Ada Louise Huxtable, "Fisher Hall Is Alive with Grace," *New York Times* (October 20, 1976): 56; Ada Louise Huxtable, "This Time Avery Fisher Looks Beautiful," *New York Times* (October 24, 1976), II: 29–30; Hubert Saal, "Brave New Hall," *Newsweek* 88 (November 1, 1976): 59; "A Bright New Version," *Time* 106 (November 1, 1976): 75–76; Bruce Bliven, Jr., "Annals of Architecture: A Better Sound," *New Yorker* 52 (November 8, 1976): 51–54, 57–58, 60, 63–64, 66, 68, 70, 72, 74, 77–78, 80–84, 87–88, 90, 95–96, 98, 100, 102, 107–13, 120–22, 124–35; "Philharmonic Hall's Fourth Debut," *Progressive Architecture* 57 (December 1976): 32; White and Willensky, *AIA Guide* (1978), 178–79; Goldberger, *The City Observed*, 195–98; Nory Miller and Richard Payne, *Johnson/Burgee: Architecture* (New York: Random House, 1979), 68–69; Tauranac, *Essential New York*, 212–14; Bernard Taper, *Balanchine* (New York: New York Times Book Co., 1984), 262, 309–10.

69. "Concern for Detail: Max Abramovitz": 34.
70. Max Abramovitz quoted in "The Talk of the Town: Hall": 33.
71. Huxtable, "Concertgoers Give Building Life": 35.
72. Huxtable, "Our New Buildings: Hits and Misses": 105.
73. Huxtable, "Concertgoers Give Building Life": 35.
74. Huxtable, "Balancing Up: A Highbrow Ideal, Lincoln Center Is a Likely Middlebrow Monument": 15.
75. McQuade, "Lincoln Center": 204.
76. Max Abramovitz quoted in Tomkins, "Profiles: A Thing among Things": 48.
77. Marian Willard quoted in Tomkins, "Profiles: A Thing among Things": 49.
78. Richard Lippold quoted in Tomkins, "Profiles: A Thing among Things": 49.
79. Lippold, "Projects for Pan Am and Philharmonic": 55.
80. Kramer, "Another Sculptural Nullity for New York's Lincoln Center": 17.
81. Barnes, "Lincoln Center": 38.
82. Beranek, *Music, Acoustics and Architecture*, 540. Also see Bolt, Beranek and Newman, Inc., *Noise Environment of Urban and Suburban Areas* (Washington, D.C.: United States Department of Housing and Urban Development, 1967); Robert B. Newman with T. J. Schultz, B. G. Watters and R. L. Kirkegaard, "Adjustable Acoustics for the Multiple-Use Auditorium," in George C. Izenour, *Theater Design* (New York: McGraw-Hill, 1977), 479–93; Robert S. Jones, *Noise and Vibration Control in Buildings* (New York: McGraw-Hill, 1984).
83. Schonberg, "Music: The Occasion": 34.
84. Molleson, "Hear! Hear!": 3.
85. Virgil Thomson quoted in Gelatt, "Art, Science, or Just Plain Luck?": 38.
86. "Scenario for Inexactness": 83.
87. "Better for Talk than Music": 34.
88. "Better for Talk than Music": 34.
89. Leo Beranek quoted in Gelatt, "Art, Science, or Just Plain Luck?": 38.
90. Max Abramovitz quoted in Rich, "Center Is Given Acoustical Plan": 77.
91. George Szell quoted in "Scenario for Inexactness": 84.
92. "Scenario for Inexactness": 84.
93. George Szell quoted in "Starting Over": 67.
94. Philip Johnson quoted in Bliven, "Annals of Architecture: A Better Sound": 70.
95. Saal, "Brave New Hall": 59.
96. Cyril M. Harris quoted in Saal, "Brave New Hall": 59.
97. "Aids Design of Theater for Dance," *New York Herald Tribune* (January 2, 1959): 12; "Architectural Bulletins," *Progressive Architecture* 40 (February 1959): 78; Philip Johnson, "Whither Away—Non-Miesian Directions," speech delivered at Yale University, February 5, 1959, published in Peter Eisenman and Robert A. M. Stern, eds., *Philip Johnson: Writings* (New York: Oxford University Press, 1979), 226–40; William H. Jordy, "The Mies-less Johnson," *Architectural Forum* 111 (September 1959): 114–23; Haskell, "Jazz in Architecture": 110; Philip Johnson, "Informal Talk, Architectural Association," lecture delivered at the Architectural Association, School of Architecture, London, November 28, 1960, published in Eisenman and Stern, eds., *Philip Johnson: Writings*, 106–16; Vincent Scully, Jr., *Modern Architecture: The Architecture of Democracy* (New York: George Braziller, 1961), 35, plate 105; John Molleson, "5–Balcony Theater for Lincoln Center," *New York Herald Tribune* (June 27, 1961): 23; Sam Zolotow, "State Gives Plans for Theater Here," *New York Times* (June 27, 1961): 35; "New York State Theater at Lincoln Center," *Architectural Record* 130 (August 1961): 13; John M. Jacobus, Jr., *Philip Johnson* (New York: George Braziller, 1962), 40–41, plates 92–97; Louis Calta, "State Theater Plan Calls for No Aisles in Orchestra Floor," *New York Times* (November 22, 1962): 46; "House of Balanchine," *Newsweek* 61 (April 8, 1963): 88; Emerson Globe, "A Bad Bad World?" editorial, *Architectural Record* 134 (October 1963): 9; Milton Esterow, "New State Theater at Lincoln Center Ready in a Month," *New York Times* (March 23, 1964): 1, 26; John Canaday, "Nadelman Sculpture Is a Deft Adjunct to Architecture," *New York Times* (March 23, 1964): 26; Ada Louise Huxtable, "Glass-Fronted Room Glinting with Gold Lends Regal Air," *New York Times* (March 23, 1964): 26; "Theater Glamour Again," *Architectural Record* 130 (May 1964): 137–44; Russell Lynes, "A Parlor for New York," *Harper's* 228 (May 1964): 28, 30, 32; Jay S. Harrison, "New York State Theater: The Building," *Musical America* 84 (May 1964): 6–9; Ilse M. Reese, John M. Dixon and James T. Burns, "Critical Trialogue on Johnson's Lincoln Center Theater," *Progressive Architecture* 45 (May 1964): 58–59; "Jewel in Its Proper Setting," *Time* 83 (May 1, 1964): 58–62; Winthrop Sargeant, "Musical Events: Housewarming," *New Yorker* 40 (May 9, 1964): 146, 148–49; "'Lear' Raises Acoustical Crisis at Lincoln Center," *New York Herald Tribune* (May 20, 1964): 146, 148–49; Barbara B. Jameson, "Debate on Aisles," *New York Herald Tribune* (June 28, 1964): 25; Olga Gueft, "Philip Johnson Neo-Classic and Philip Johnson Modern," *Interiors* 123 (July 1964): 85–86, 92–95; Forrest Wilson, "Some Details of Elegance," *Interiors* 123 (July 1964): 87–91; Philip Johnson, "Young Artists at the Fair and at Lincoln Center," *Art in America* 52 (August 1964): 112–27; Philip Johnson, "Whence and Whither: The Processional Element in Architecture," *Perspecta* 9/10 (1965): 167–78, reprinted in Eisenman and Stern, eds., *Philip Johnson: Writings*, 150–55; C. Ray Smith, "Johnson's Interior Details: The Right Thing in the Right Place," *Progressive Architecture* 46 (March 1965): 196–99; "Cornell at Lincoln Center," *Interiors* 124 (July 1965): 10, 132; *Philip Johnson: Architecture 1949–1965*, with an intro. by Henry-Russell Hitchcock (New York: Holt, Rinehart and Winston, 1966), 8–27, 100–104; Harold Schonberg, "The House that Roared," *New York Times* (November 20, 1966): 34; Paul Heyer, *Architects on Architecture* (London: Penguin, 1967), 282–90; Ervin Gallantay, "Architecture," *Nation* 204 (April 10, 1967): 473–74, 476; Barnes, "Lincoln Center": 92; Robert A. M. Stern, *New Directions in American Architecture* (New York: George Braziller, 1969), 44, 48; Fitch, *American Building: The Environmental Forces that Shape It*, vol. 2, 148–49; *Philip Johnson*, with an intro. and notes by Charles Noble (London: Thames and Hudson, 1972), 16, plates 59–64; Cook and Klotz, *Conversations with Architects*, 32–34; Lincoln Kirstein, *Elie Nadelman* (New York: Eakins, 1973), 31–32; Lincoln Kirstein, *The New York City Ballet* (New York: Alfred A. Knopf, 1973), 160, 165–66; Roberta Bernstein, *Jasper Johns' Paintings and Sculptures 1954–1974: "The Changing Focus of the Eye"* (Ann Arbor, Mich.: UMI Research Press, 1975), 25; plates 164–66; Izenour, *Theater Design*, 297, 457–58; C. Ray Smith, *Supermannerism: New Attitudes in Post-Modern Architecture* (New York: E. P. Dutton, 1977), 170–71; White and Willensky, *AIA Guide* (1978), 177; *Reminiscences of Philip Cortelyou Johnson*, Columbia University Oral History Collection (February 1978): 10; Goldberger, *The City Observed*, 194–98; Tauranac, *Essential New York*, 212–14; Jeanne L. Wasserman, *Three American Sculptors and the Female Nude*, exhibition catalogue (Cambridge, Mass.: Fogg Art Museum, 1980), 51; Joseph E. Persico, *The Imperial Rockefeller* (New York: Simon & Schuster, 1982), 90; Kirstein, *Quarry: A Collection in Lieu of Memoirs*, 78, 117–18; Moira Shearer, *Balletmaster: A Dancer's View of George Balanchine* (New York: G. P. Putnam's Sons, 1987), 154; Tim Page and Vanessa Weeks Page, eds., *Selected Letters of Virgil Thomson* (New York: Summit, 1988), 369; Robert A. M. Stern with Raymond W. Gastil, *Modern Classicism* (New York: Rizzoli International Publications, 1988), 54.
98. Scully, *Modern Architecture: The Architecture of Democracy*, 35.
99. Jordy, "The Mies-less Johnson": 117.
100. Smith, "Johnson's Interior Details: The Right Thing in the Right Place": 199.
101. "Jewel in Its Proper Setting": 59.
102. Sargeant, "Musical Events: Housewarming": 146.
103. John Morris Dixon quoted in Reese, Dixon and Burns, "Critical Trialogue on Johnson's Lincoln Center Theater": 58.
104. Ilse M. Reese quoted in Reese, Dixon and Burns, "Critical Trialogue on Johnson's Lincoln Center Theater": 58.
105. James T. Burns quoted in Reese, Dixon and Burns, "Critical Trialogue on Johnson's Lincoln Center Theater": 58.
106. Philip Johnson quoted in Heyer, *Architects on Architecture*, 290.
107. Philip Johnson quoted in Cook and Klotz, *Conversations with Architects*, 33–34.
108. Wilson, "Some Details of Elegance": 91.
109. Johnson, "Young Artists at the Fair and at Lincoln Center": 123.
110. Hitchcock, "Introduction," in *Philip Johnson: Architecture 1949–1965*, 24.
111. Canaday, "Nadelman Sculpture Is a Deft Adjunct to Architecture": 26.
112. Johnson, "At Lincoln Center": 123.
113. Philip Johnson quoted in Lynes, "A Parlor for New York": 30.
114. Lynes, "A Parlor for New York": 30.
115. Kirstein, "Lincoln Shelter": 10.
116. Kirstein, *The New York City Ballet*, 166.
117. Hitchcock, "Introduction," in *Philip Johnson: Architecture 1949–1965*, 24.
118. Wilson, "Some Details of Elegance": 89.
119. Kirstein, *Quarry: A Collection in Lieu of Memoirs*, 117–18.
120. Sargeant, "Musical Events: Housewarming": 146, quoted in Young, *Lincoln Center: The Building of an Institution*, 207.
121. Canaday, "Nadelman Sculpture Is a Deft Adjunct to Architecture": 26.
122. Hitchcock, "Introduction," in *Philip Johnson: Architecture 1949–1965*, 18.
123. "Jewel in Its Proper Setting": 58.
124. Huxtable, "Glass-Fronted Room Glinting with Gold Lends Regal Air": 26.
125. Virgil Thomson quoted in Page and Page, eds., *Selected Letters of Virgil Thomson*, 369.

126. Barnes, "Lincoln Center": 92.
127. Izenour, *Theater Design*, 458.
128. Smith, *Supermannerism*, 170.
129. John M. Dixon quoted in Reese, Dixon and Burns, "Critical Trialogue on Johnson's Lincoln Center Theater": 58.
130. James T. Burns quoted in Reese, Dixon and Burns, "Critical Trialogue on Johnson's Lincoln Center Theater": 58.
131. Kirstein, "Lincoln Shelter": 10.
132. Philip Johnson quoted in Molleson, "5–Balcony Theater for Lincoln Center": 23.
133. Johnson, "Whither Away—Non-Miesian Directions," in Eisenman and Stern, eds., *Philip Johnson: Writings*, 234.
134. Molleson, "5-Balcony Theater for Lincoln Center": 23.
135. Philip Johnson quoted in Calta, "State Theater Plan Calls for No Aisles on Orchestra Floor": 46.
136. Quoted in Jamison, "Debate on Aisles": 25.
137. James T. Burns quoted in Reese, Dixon and Burns, "Critical Trialogue on Johnson's Lincoln Center Theater": 58.
138. Izenour, *Theater Design*, 458.
139. Huxtable, "Glass-Fronted Room Glinting with Gold Lends Regal Air": 26.
140. John M. Dixon quoted in Reese, Dixon and Burns, "Critical Trialogue on Johnson's Lincoln Center Theater": 58.
141. Wilson, "Some Details of Elegance": 87.
142. James T. Dixon quoted in Reese, Dixon and Burns, "Critical Trialogue on Johnson's Lincoln Center Theater": 59.
143. James T. Dixon quoted in Reese, Dixon and Burns, "Critical Trialogue on Johnson's Lincoln Center Theater": 59.
144. Ilse M. Reese quoted in Reese, Dixon and Burns, "Critical Trialogue on Johnson's Lincoln Center": 58.
145. Gueft, "Philip Johnson Neo-Classic and Philip Johnson Modern": 86.
146. "Jewel in Its Proper Setting": 58.
147. James T. Dixon quoted in Reese, Dixon and Burns, "Critical Trialogue on Johnson's Lincoln Center Theater": 59.
148. Johnson, "The Processional Element in Architecture," in Eisenman and Stern, eds., *Philip Johnson: Writings*, 154.
149. Lewis Funke, "Rialto Gossip: Saarinen and Mielziner Plan Unusual Theater for Lincoln Center—Items," *New York Times* (November 23, 1958), II: 1; Ben Bagley, "Appeal for Better Theaters," letter to the editor, *Interiors* 120 (August 1960): 8; Arthur Gelb, "New Plans for Lincoln Center Theater," *New York Times* (November 19, 1961), II: 3; "Saarinen Design for Lincoln Center Repertory Theater," *Architectural Record* 130 (December 1961): 13; Allan Temko, *Eero Saarinen* (New York: George Braziller, 1962), 26, plates 121–22; Richard A. Miller, "Eight Concepts for the Ideal Theater," *Architectural Forum* 116 (January 1962): 112–19; Walter McQuade, "Eero Saarinen: A Complete Architect," *Architectural Forum* 116 (April 1962): 102–19; Ernst Danz, *Architecture of Skidmore, Owings & Merrill, 1950–1962*, with an intro. by Henry-Russell Hitchcock (New York: Frederick A. Praeger, 1963), 229–31; Richard Gilman, "Epitaph for Lincoln Center," *Commonweal* 80 (April 10, 1964): 89; McQuade, "Lincoln Center": 206; Ada Louise Huxtable, "Adding Up the Score," *New York Times* (September 25, 1965), II: 29, reprinted in Ada Louise Huxtable, *Will They Ever Finish Bruckner Boulevard?* (New York: Macmillan, 1970), 24–27; "All the Marbles," *Newsweek* 66 (September 27, 1965): 100; "Theater-Library-Museum Is Completed at Lincoln Center," *Architectural Record* 138 (October 1965): 40; "Repertory Theater Opens at Lincoln Center," *Progressive Architecture* 46 (October 1965): 57–58; "The Collaborators," *Time* 86 (October 29, 1965): 60–63; C. Ray Smith, "A Thrust Forward for the Theater," *Progressive Architecture* 46 (November 1965): 189–94; Olga Gueft, "Good Works," editorial, *Interiors* 125 (December 1965): 67; Olga Gueft, "Lincoln Center's Masterpiece: Or What Happens When Two Distinguished Firms Decide to Team Up," *Interiors* 125 (December 1965): 84–91; "NYPL's Performing Arts Library Opens in New Lincoln Center Home," *Library Journal* 90 (December 1965): 5224–25; "Lack of Dialogue," *Architectural Forum* 124 (May 1966): 91; "The Library and Museum of the Performing Arts in Lincoln Center," *Library Journal* 91 (June 15, 1966): 3109; Fitch, *American Building: The Environmental Forces that Shape It*, vol. 2, 149–51; White and Willensky, *AIA Guide* (1978), 178; Goldberger, *The City Observed*, 195–98; Tauranac, *Essential New York*, 212–14; Carol Herselle Krinsky, *Gordon Bunshaft of Skidmore, Owings & Merrill* (Cambridge, Mass.: MIT Press, 1988), 150–52, 212–15.
150. Gueft, "Lincoln Center's Masterpiece: Or What Happens When Two Distinguished Firms Decide to Team Up": 84.
151. Smith, "A Thrust Forward for the Theater": 191.
152. Eero Saarinen quoted in "The Collaborators": 60.
153. Barnes, "Lincoln Center": 38.
154. "The Heroic Bather," *Time* 86 (September 3, 1965): 60; "Calder and Moore at Lincoln Center," *Progressive Architecture* 46 (December 1965): 43; "Awards and Competitions," *Interiors* 125 (June 1966): 18; Kramer, "Another Sculptural Nullity for New York's Lincoln Center": 17; Ionel Jianou, *Henry Moore* (Paris: Arted, 1968), plates 103–7; Robert Melville, *Henry Moore: Sculptures and Drawings 1921–1969* (New York: Harry N. Abrams, 1970), plates 671–75; Frederick Fried and Edmund V. Gillon, Jr., *New York Civic Sculpture* (New York: Dover, 1976), 70–71; Alan Bowness, ed., *Henry Moore: Sculpture and Drawings, vol. 4: Sculpture 1964–73* (London: Lund Humphries, 1977), 38–39, plates 8–13; David Mitchinson, ed., *Henry Moore Sculpture*, with comments by Henry Moore and an intro. by Franco Russoli (London: Macmillan London Limited, 1981), 173; Suzanne Weber, *Henry Moore* (San Francisco: Chronicle Books, 1986), 205; Gayle and Cohen, *The Art Commission and the Municipal Art Society Guide to Manhattan's Outdoor Sculpture*, 272.
155. "The Heroic Bather": 60.
156. Henry Moore quoted in "The Heroic Bather": 60.
157. Kramer, "Another Sculptural Nullity for New York's Lincoln Center": 17.
158. Huxtable, "Adding Up the Score": 24.
159. "Calder and Moore at Lincoln Center": 43; Kramer, "Another Sculptural Nullity for New York's Lincoln Center": 17; H. H. Arnason, *Calder* (Princeton, N.J.: Van Nostrand, 1966), 128–29; H. Harvard Arnason, *Calder*, with comments by Alexander Calder (New York: Viking, 1971), plate 61; Fried and Gillon, *New York Civic Sculpture*, 70; Jean Lipman, *Calder's Universe*, exhibition catalogue (New York: Viking, in cooperation with the Whitney Museum of American Art, 1976), 324; Dorothy Seiberling, "Calder City," *New York* 9 (October 18, 1976): 82–83; Gayle and Cohen, *The Art Commission and the Municipal Art Society Guide to Manhattan's Outdoor Sculpture*, 271.
160. Newbold Morris quoted in Young, *Lincoln Center: The Building of an Institution*, 213.
161. Newbold Morris quoted in Young, *Lincoln Center: The Building of an Institution*, 213.
162. Newbold Morris quoted in "Calder and Moore at Lincoln Center": 43.
163. Kramer, "Another Sculptural Nullity for New York's Lincoln Center": 17.
164. Jo Mielziner also collaborated with the architect Edward Larrabee Barnes on a similar hypothetical design calling for a theater that could be converted from a proscenium to a nonproscenium format as part of a Ford Foundation–sponsored project. See *The Ideal Theater: Eight Concepts*, exhibition catalogue (New York: American Federation of Arts, 1962).
165. "Up & Coming," *Village Voice* 9 (November 7, 1963): 1.
166. "ANTA Repertory Theater Opens Temporary Quarters," *Progressive Architecture* 45 (March 1964): 68.
167. Otto Preminger quoted in "The Collaborators": 60.
168. Alan Jay Lerner quoted in "The Collaborators": 60.
169. Smith, "A Thrust Forward for the Theater": 194.
170. Barnes, "Lincoln Center": 92.
171. Smith, "The Library-Museum at Lincoln Center": 163.
172. Gueft, "Good Works": 67.
173. "$900,000 Now Available for New Metropolitan Site," *Musical America* 72 (January 15, 1952): 3; "New Home for 'Met' Is Under Discussion," *New York Times* (June 9, 1954): 39; Joseph Watterson, "The Editor's Asides," *Journal of the American Institute of Architects* 29 (February 1958): 88; Peter D. Franklin, "Lincoln Center Design: 'A New U.S. Landmark,'" *New York Herald Tribune* (May 25, 1958): 1; Charles Grutzner, "New Opera House Will Be Imposing," *New York Times* (May 25, 1958): 78; "New Metropolitan Opera House," *Architectural Forum* 108 (June 1958): 7; "A Strong Sign of Recovery," *Life* 45 (August 25, 1958): 11–19; "Building for Song—An Idea Grows Up," *Newsweek* 55 (January 25, 1960): 88–89; "Opera in Lincoln Center to Cost $8,400 Per Seat," *Architectural Forum* 113 (September 1960): 5, 8; "Lincoln Center's Opera House Redesigned," *Architectural Forum* 112 (February 1960): 9; "Harrison Reveals Latest Model of Met," *Progressive Architecture* 41 (March 1960): 68; Haskell, "Jazz in Architecture": 110; "The Talk of the Town: Indignant," *New Yorker* 37 (August 19, 1961): 18; Alan Rich, "Met Will Retain Its 80-Year Decor," *New York Times* (April 29, 1963): 24; Raymond Ericson, "New Met Opera House to Have Some Limited Views of Stage," *New York Times* (June 28, 1963): 26; "Interior for the Met," *Architectural Record* 134 (July 1963): 13; "Mets Still Lag in New York," *Progressive Architecture* 44 (July 1963): 54; Walter McQuade, "Architecture," *Nation* 198 (January 13, 1964): 59–60; Herbert Kupferberg, "The Metropolitan's New House," *Atlantic Monthly* 216 (October 1965): 158, 160; "The New Met," *Newsweek* 66 (November 8, 1965): 98; "You Pays Your Money . . . ," *Architectural Forum* 124 (April 1966): 22; "The New Metropolitan Opera House," *Architectural Record* 139 (May 1966): 4; Kramer, "Another Sculptural Nullity for New York's Lincoln Center": 17; "The Met Sets the Stage for Opening Night," *Business Week* (August 20, 1966): 143–44, 146; Josh Greenfeld, "Curtain Going Up for Wallace Harrison," *New York Times* (August 21, 1966), VI: 36–39, 82, 84, 86, 89; Donald Canty and Charles Moore, "The Establishment Invites You to Join in Hushed and Sumptuous Appreciation of the Several Arts—Lincoln Center—Most Evenings Arrival Optional but Difficult," *Architectural Forum* 125 (September 1966): 71–79; "A House for Grand Opera," *Architectural Record* 140 (September 1966): 149–60; Olga Gueft, "Lincoln Center Realized," *Interiors* 126 (September 1966): 93–99; "Look Previews the New Met," *Look* 30 (September 6, 1966): 22–28; "Met Backstage—A Bigger Show," *New York Times* (September 11, 1966), VI, part 2: 14–15; Harold Schonberg, "Good Acoustics," *New York Times* (September 12, 1966): 36; "Exploring Planet Met," *Time* 88 (September 16, 1966): 92; John Canaday, "The List of Art," *New York Times* (September 17, 1966): 17; Ada Louise Huxtable, "Met as Architecture," *New York Times* (September 17, 1966): 17; "The New Met and Its Old Master," *Newsweek* 68 (September 19, 1966): 70–76, 78–79; "The New Opera House—A Triumph of Technology," *Newsweek* 68 (September 19, 1966): 77; "The Talk of the Town: Grand Opening," *New Yorker* 42 (September 24, 1966): 114, 116, 118, 123–24; Harold Schonberg, "After It Was All Over," *New York Times* (September 25, 1966), II: 17; "A Night at the Opera," *Newsweek* 68 (September 26, 1966): 40–41; "The Met Opens in the Blaze of Its New Home," *Life* 61 (September 30, 1966): 32–42; Olga Gueft, "Breuer's Whitney Museum," *Interiors* 126 (October 1966): 98–107; "Chagall Murals Steal Show at Met," *Progressive Architecture* 47 (October 1966): 71; "A Night at the Opera," *Progressive Architecture* 47 (October 1966): 251–53; "The New Met," *Interior Design* 37 (November 1966): 180–91; Robert Kotlowitz, "On the Midway at Lincoln Center," *Harper's* 233 (December 1966): 136–37; Bodil W. Nielsen, "More of the Met Restaurants and Clubs," *Interiors* 126 (December 1966): 124–27; Creighton Peet, "The Giant Stage that Shifts for Itself," *Popular Mechanics* 126 (December 1966): 110–13, 204; "Visitors Trip on Steps Outside the New Met," *Architectural Record* 141 (January 1967): 167; "Eavesdroppings," *Progressive Architecture* 48 (February 1967): 38; "Steps in Front of the Met Will Get Railings, Lights," *Architectural Record* 141 (May 1967): 188; Fitch, *American Building: The Environmental Forces that Shape It*, vol. 2, 148–49; "The Talk of the Town: Preservation," *New Yorker* 50 (September 16, 1974): 32; Izenour, *Theater Design*, 119–21; White and Willensky, *AIA Guide* (1978), 178; Goldberger, *The City Observed*, 195–98; Tauranac, *Essential New York*, 212–14; "Parks, Plazas and Other Outdoor Spaces at Lincoln Center Are to Be Renovated," *New York Times* (September 11, 1981), II: 1; Newhouse, *Wallace K. Harrison, Architect*, 52–55; 198–235; Edmund Wilson, *The Sixties* (New York: Farrar, Straus & Giroux, 1993), 570–71.
174. Newhouse, *Wallace K. Harrison, Architect*, 204.
175. Newhouse, *Wallace K. Harrison, Architect*, 204.
176. Rudolph Bing quoted in "The New Met and Its Old Master": 78, also quoted in Newhouse, *Wallace K. Harrison, Architect*, 209. For a profile of Bing, see Joseph Wechsberg, "The General Manager," *New Yorker* 42 (September 17, 1966): 65–66, 68, 71–72, 74, 77–78, 80, 85–86, 88, 92, 95–96, 98, 101–2, 104, 107–8, 110, 112, 114, 119–20, 122, 124. Also see Bing's autobiography, *5,000 Nights at the Opera* (New York: Doubleday, 1972).
177. For the San Francisco War Memorial Opera House, see David Gebhard et al., *A Guide to Architecture in San Francisco and Northern California* (Santa Barbara, Calif.: Peregrine Smith, 1973), 80. For the Fox Theater, see John Linley, *The Georgia Catalog: Historic American Buildings Survey* (Athens, Ga.: University of Georgia Press, 1982), 221–23, 271. For the Indiana University Auditorium and the Elliott Hall of Music, see Writers' Program of the Works Progress Administration in the State of Indiana, *Indiana: A Guide to the Hoosier State* (New York: Oxford University Press, 1941), 159.
178. Wallace K. Harrison quoted in Newhouse, *Wallace K. Harrison, Architect*, 210.

179. Grutzner, "New Opera Home Will Be Imposing": 78.
180. "New Metropolitan Opera House," *Architectural Forum*: 7.
181. "Lincoln Center's Opera House Redesigned": 9.
182. Marcel Breuer quoted in Newhouse, *Wallace K. Harrison, Architect*, 214.
183. Philip Johnson quoted in Newhouse, *Wallace K. Harrison, Architect*, 214.
184. Herman Krawitz, letter to Anthony A. Bliss, November 1958, Metropolitan Opera Archive, quoted in Newhouse, *Wallace K. Harrison, Architect*, 214.
185. Herman Krawitz quoted in minutes of the meeting with representatives of the Metropolitan Opera, Wallace K. Harrison and Max Abramovitz, February 18, 1959, Metropolitan Opera Archive, quoted in Newhouse, *Wallace K. Harrison, Architect*, 214.
186. Rudolph Bing quoted in minutes of the meeting with representatives of the Metropolitan Opera, Wallace K. Harrison and Max Abramovitz, February 18, 1959, Metropolitan Opera Archive, quoted in Newhouse, *Wallace K. Harrison, Architect*, 214.
187. Newhouse, *Wallace K. Harrison, Architect*, 217.
188. Newhouse, *Wallace K. Harrison, Architect*, 220.
189. Newhouse, *Wallace K. Harrison, Architect*, 221.
190. Canaday, "The List of Art": 17.
191. Wilson, *The Sixties*, 570–71.
192. "The New Met," *Interior Design*: 181.
193. Canaday, "The List of Art": 17.
194. Sargeant, "Grand Opening": 114.
195. Kramer, "Another Sculptural Nullity for New York's Lincoln Center": 17.
196. "The New Opera House—A Triumph of Technology": 77.
197. Barnes, "Lincoln Center": 92.
198. Wallace K. Harrison quoted in Newhouse, *Wallace K. Harrison, Architect*, 228.
199. Huxtable, "Met as Architecture": 17.
200. Wilson, *The Sixties*, 570.
201. Kirstein, "Lincoln Shelter": 8.
202. Canaday, "The List of Art": 17.
203. Sargeant, "Grand Opening": 114.
204. Barnes, "Lincoln Center": 38.
205. "The Opera House—A Triumph of Technology": 77.
206. Sargeant, "Grand Opening": 114.
207. James Marston Fitch quoted in "The Talk of the Town: Preservation": 32.
208. "The New Opera House—A Triumph of Technology": 77.
209. Wallace K. Harrison quoted in "Building for Song—An Idea Grows Up": 88–89.
210. "A House for Grand Opera": 149.
211. Gueft, "Lincoln Center Realized": 96, 98.
212. "Look Previews the New Met": 24.
213. Izenour, *Theater Design*, 458.
214. Gueft, "Breuer's Whitney Museum": 103.
215. Huxtable, "Met as Architecture": 17.
216. Huxtable, "Met as Architecture": 17.
217. "A Night at the Opera": 40.
218. Wilson, *The Sixties*, 571.
219. Fitch, *American Building: The Environmental Forces that Shape It*, vol. 2, 148.
220. Franco Zeffirelli quoted in "Exploring Planet Met": 92.
221. "The New Opera House—A Triumph of Technology": 77.
222. Schonberg, "After It Was All Over": 17.
223. Huxtable, "Met as Architecture": 17.
224. Robert C. Doty, "Lincoln Plaza Fountain to Dance to Computer Tune," *New York Times* (March 7, 1964): 25; "The Talk of the Town: Fountains," *New Yorker* 42 (July 9, 1966): 17–19.
225. Barnes, "Lincoln Center": 38.
226. Huxtable, "Adding Up the Score": 29.
227. William H. Whyte, *City: Rediscovering the Center* (New York: Doubleday, 1988), 137.
228. Henry Raymont, "Lincoln Center Mall to Central Park Is Proposed," *New York Times* (December 6, 1966): 1, 58; Henry Raymont, "Science Academy Fights City Mall," *New York Times* (December 7, 1966): 63; Henry Raymont, "New Lincoln Center Plan Offers Buildings Rather than a Mall," *New York Times* (December 12, 1966): 49; Ada Louise Huxtable, "A Planning Happening," *New York Times* (December 18, 1966), II: 35, 37; Thomas P. F. Hoving, "No Official Mall Plan," letter to the editor, *New York Times* (December 22, 1966): 32; Roy R. Neuberger, "Lincoln Center Park Project Opposed," letter to the editor, *New York Times* (December 23, 1966): 24; "The Greater Glory," *Architectural Forum* (January–February 1967): 48; William Schuman, "Center No Sponsor of Mall," *New York Times* (January 13, 1967): 22; Robert A. M. Stern with Raymond W. Gastil, "A Temenos for Democracy," in Richard Longstreth, ed., *The Mall in Washington, 1791–1991* (Washington, D.C.: National Gallery of Art, 1991), 262–77.
229. Stern, Gilmartin and Massengale, *New York 1900*, 392–93.
230. Stern, Gilmartin and Massengale, *New York 1900*, 392–93.
231. Stern, Gilmartin and Mellins, *New York 1930*, 196–97.
232. Algernon D. Black quoted in Raymont, "Lincoln Center Mall to Central Park Is Proposed": 58.
233. Huxtable, "A Planning Happening": 35, 37.
234. Hoving, "No Official Mall Plan": 32.
235. Schuman, "Center No Sponsor of Mall": 22.
236. Michael Kramer and Sam Roberts, *I Never Wanted to Be Vice-President of Anything* (New York: Basic Books, 1976), 13–14. Also see Newhouse, *Wallace K. Harrison, Architect*, 190.
237. "The Greater Glory": 48.
238. Charles G. Bennett, "Lincoln Sq. to Get a Damrosch Park," *New York Times* (October 13, 1959): 1, 25; "P/A News Report: Bulletins," *Progressive Architecture* 40 (November 1959): 89; "Lincoln Center, New York," *Architectural Record* 132 (September 1962): cover, 133–48; "White Fever in Lincoln Square," *Progressive Architecture* 46 (December 1965): 44; Moses, *Public Works: A Dangerous Trade*, 532–33.
239. "White Fever in Lincoln Square": 44.
240. "Juilliard to Join Lincoln Square Center," *Musical America* 77 (March 1957): 51; John Molleson, "Italy to Juilliard: Gift of $500,000 for Travertine," *New York Herald Tribune* (March 16, 1966): 16; Ada Louise Huxtable, "Juilliard's New Building: Esthetic Reality," *New York Times* (October 8, 1969): 59; "Juilliard at Home," *Newsweek* 74 (October 13, 1969): 127; "A Jewel of a Juilliard," *Time* 94 (October 31, 1969): 46; "Lincoln Center Finale," *Architectural Forum* 131 (December 1969): 78; Mildred F. Schmertz, "The Juilliard School," *Architectural Record* 147 (January 1970): cover, 121–30; Ada Louise Huxtable, "Dissimilar Buildings, Similar Awards," *New York Times* (May 24, 1970), VIII: 1, 7; "1970 Bard Awards for Excellence in Architecture and Design in New York City," *Interiors* 129 (June 1970): 10; "Eighth Annual Bard Awards Presented by City Club of New York," *Architectural Record* 148 (July 1970): 40; Fitch, *American Building: The Environmental Forces that Shape It*, vol. 2, 149; Barclay F. Gordon, ed., *Interior Spaces Designed by Architects* (New York: McGraw-Hill, 1974), 68–75; Frank Popper, *Agam* (New York: Harry N. Abrams, 1976), 277, plates 301–5, 358–59; White and Willensky, *AIA Guide* (1978), 179; Goldberger, *The City Observed*, 197; Gayle and Cohen, *The Art Commission and the Municipal Art Society Guide to Manhattan's Outdoor Sculpture*, 273.
241. "Juilliard at Home": 127.
242. Yaacov Agam quoted in Gayle and Cohen, *The Art Commission and the Municipal Art Society Guide to Manhattan's Outdoor Sculpture*, 273.
243. Schmertz, "The Juilliard School": 121.
244. Schmertz, "The Juilliard School": 121.
245. Huxtable, "Juilliard's New Building: Esthetic Reality": 59.
246. Huxtable, "Dissimilar Buildings, Similar Awards": 7.
247. Goldberger, *The City Observed*, 197.
248. Huxtable, "Adding Up the Score": 29.
249. McQuade, "Architecture": 206.
250. Paul Goldberger, "Architecture: Lincoln Center and Changes Wrought by 20 Years," *New York Times* (May 21, 1979), III: 21. Also see Martin Bloom, "Cultural Colossi: Lincoln Center at 19," *Journal of the American Institute of Architects* 70 (August 1981): 35; Roberta Brandes Gratz, "Lincoln Center at 20: Bringing Down the House," *Metropolis* 2 (October 1982): 13; Sharon Lee Ryder, "Lincoln Center at 20: Cultural Complexes," *Metropolis* 2 (October 1982): 9; Brendan Gill, "The Sky Line: Improving Lincoln Center," *New Yorker* 67 (August 19, 1991): 57–61.
251. Barnes, "Lincoln Center": 38. Also see Jacques Barzun, "Lincoln Center: Centering the Arts," *Columbia University Forum* 3 (winter 1960): 18–19; Percival Goodman, "Lincoln Center: Emporium for the Arts," *Dissent* 8 (summer 1961): 333–37.
252. Gueft, "Lincoln Center's Masterpiece: Or What Happens When Two Distinguished Firms Decide to Team Up": 84.
253. Alan Rich, "The Lincoln Center Condition," *New York* 2 (October 10, 1969): 58. Also see William E. Farrell, "Real Finale at Lincoln Center—Race for Cabs," *New York Times* (January 6, 1969): 36.
254. Barnes, "Lincoln Center": 44, 92.
255. James Marston Fitch, *Architecture and the Esthetics of Plenty* (New York: Columbia University Press, 1961), 226.
256. Barnes, "Lincoln Center": 44.
257. Gutheim, "Athens on the Subway": 71.
258. "New Housing Tied to Lincoln Sq. Site," *New York Times* (November 10, 1956): 1, 40; "Title I Apartments in New York City," *Architectural Forum* 113 (September 1960): 60; "Middle Income Apartment Boom Predicted for West Side," *Real Estate Record and Guide* 187 (March 11, 1961): 4; "Today's Apartment Seekers Are Offered Top Value," *Real Estate Record and Guide* 189 (March 10, 1962): 4–5; "Small City Rising in Lincoln Square," *New York Times* (January 3, 1965), VIII: 1; Thomas E. Norton and Jerry E. Patterson, *Living It Up: A Guide to the Named Apartment Houses of New York* (New York: Atheneum, 1984), 208; Trager, *West of Fifth*, 109.
259. "F.H.A. Office Acts on Lincoln Project," *New York Times* (May 1, 1960), VIII: 1, 18; "Small City Rising in Lincoln Square": 1; Bernard Weinraub, "A Neighborhood Grows at Lincoln Square," *New York Times* (January 22, 1965): 15.
260. Claude Sitton, "F.B.I. Finds 3 Bodies Believed to Be Rights Workers'," *New York Times* (August 5, 1964): 1, 37; Philip Benjamin, "Families of Rights Workers Voice Grief and Hope," *New York Times* (August 6, 1964): 16.
261. Weinraub, "A Neighborhood Grows at Lincoln Square": 15.
262. "New York City Elementary School by Stone," *Architectural Forum* 114 (March 1961): 49; "The School in the Urban Environment," *Progressive Architecture* 42 (May 1961): 142–45; "Urban Redevelopment School," *Architectural Forum* 119 (November 1963): 81; White and Willensky, *AIA Guide* (1978), 181.
263. "Urban Redevelopment School": 81.
264. Russell Porter, "Fordham Starts Work in Spring on 25-Million Lincoln Square Plan," *New York Times* (January 21, 1959): 1, 33; "P/A News Report: Bulletins," *Progressive Architecture* 40 (March 1959): 161; "South of Lincoln Center," *Progressive Architecture* 48 (November 1967): 56; Caro, *The Power Broker*, 1155–56; White and Willensky, *AIA Guide* (1978), 176.
265. "South of Lincoln Center": 56.
266. "Housing in New York City," *Architectural Forum* 115 (October 1961): 61; "Buildings in the News," *Architectural Record* 130 (November 1961): 13–15; Edmond J. Bartnett, "Air-Rights Plans Increasing Here," *New York Times* (October 29, 1962), VIII: 1, 12; Martin Arnold, "Crowding Feared Near Lincoln Sq.," *New York Times* (January 5, 1962): 18; Ada Louise Huxtable, "Litho City: Hit or Flop? Union Housing Plan Meets Snag in Bid for 'Greatness,'" *New York Times* (June 21, 1963): 16; "Litho City: A Civic Contribution," *Progressive Architecture* 44 (December 1963): 51, 53; "Litho City Scheme Protested," letters to the editor, *Progressive Architecture* 45 (March 1964): 10, 16, 22; Charles Thomsen, "Where Are Some Signs of Progress," *Journal of the American Institute of Architects* 44 (September 1965): 38–40; Peter Blake, "New York: Towards a New Venice," *New York* 4 (July 19, 1971): 24–33; Trager, *West of Fifth*, 192; Jonathan Kuhn, "A Tale of Two (or More) Cities," *Metropolis* 6 (June 1987): 18–19; Peter Blake, *No Place Like Utopia* (New York: Alfred A. Knopf, 1993), 195–96.
267. Blake, *No Place Like Utopia*, 196.
268. Edward Swayduck quoted in Kuhn, "A Tale of Two (or More) Cities": 18.
269. Sibyl Moholy-Nagy and Gerhard Schwab, *The Architecture of Paul Rudolph* (New York: Praeger, 1970), 196–205; Paul Rudolph, *Drawings* (Tokyo: A.D.A. Edita, 1971), 66–69.
270. Joseph P. Fried, "2 West-Side Rail Yards Are Sought for Housing," *New York Times* (July 30, 1974): 1, 40; Joseph P. Fried, "West Side Leaders Skeptical of Plan to Develop Rail Yards," *New York Times* (March 12, 1975): 43; Kuhn, "A Tale of Two (or More) Cities": 18–19; Donald J. Trump with Tony Schwartz, *Trump: The Art of the Deal* (New York: Random House, 1988), 229–34.
271. Charles Grutzner, "Work Is Speeded on Red Cross Site," *New York Times* (February 18, 1959): 26; "Eisenhower Hails Red Cross Work," *New York Times* (June 7, 1963): 33; White and Willensky, *AIA Guide* (1978), 181.
272. White and Willensky, *AIA Guide* (1978), 181.
273. White and Willensky, *AIA Guide* (1978), 181.

274. White and Willensky, *AIA Guide* (1978), 181; Goldberger, *The City Observed*, 200.

275. "Memorial Sculpture Hides Air Intakes, Exhausts," *Progressive Architecture* 53 (August 1972): 25, 28; Fried and Gillon, *New York Civic Sculpture*, 72–73; Andrea O. Dean, "Sculpture in Public Spaces: A Portfolio," *Journal of the American Institute of Architects* 66 (October 1976): 47–51; Gayle and Cohen, *The Art Commission and the Municipal Art Society Guide to Manhattan's Outdoor Sculpture*, 276–77.

276. Don Raney, "Urban Housing: A Comprehensive Approach to Quality," *Architectural Record* 145 (January 1969): cover, 97–118.

277. White and Willensky, *AIA Guide* (1988), 296–97.

278. Robert E. Tomasson, "Housing Projects Break Mold," *New York Times* (December 9, 1973), VIII: 1, 6; White and Willensky, *AIA Guide* (1978), 180; Norton and Patterson, *Living It Up*, 43.

279. White and Willensky, *AIA Guide* (1978), 180.

280. Clementine Paddleford, "Around the World in Manhattan," *Library Journal* 91 (June 15, 1966): 3089–96. Also see "Restaurants Are Flocking to West Side," *Real Estate Record and Guide* 204 (November 8, 1969): 2.

281. Paddleford, "Around the World in Manhattan": 3089.

282. Melissa Hattersley, "Gaslit Garden Near Lincoln Center: Veteran Restaurateur Herb Evans and Architect Samuel Arlen Transform Supermarket into a Romantic Restaurant for Theatergoers," *Interiors* 126 (March 1967): 106–9.

283. "Hotels and Motels," *Interior Design* 35 (April 1964): 124–42.

284. Kathleen Teltsch, "Chinese Mission Buys a Motel on West Side," *New York Times* (March 17, 1972): 1, 28.

285. Franklin Whitehouse, "Lincoln Square Undergoes Revival," *New York Times* (May 23, 1972), VIII: 1, 13; Goldberger, *The City Observed*, 211, 213; Norton and Patterson, *Living It Up*, 122; Dunlap, *On Broadway*, 223, 226; Elaine Louie, "Currents: Studying the 'White Boxes,'" *New York Times* (February 17, 1994), C: 3.

286. White and Willensky, *AIA Guide* (1978), 178; Goldberger, *The City Observed*, 199.

287. Dudley Dalton, "Lincoln Sq. Area Will Get Offices," *New York Times* (March 22, 1964), VIII: 1, 12.

288. Stern, Gilmartin and Massengale, *New York 1900*, 381–82.

289. "Structure for Scriptures," *Progressive Architecture* 46 (February 1966): 58; "Some Theater Arts Organizations Are Moving to Lincoln Center," *Real Estate Record and Guide* 198 (October 15, 1966): 4; White and Willensky, *AIA Guide* (1978), 175–76; Dunlap, *On Broadway*, 226.

290. Oliver Carlson and Ernest Sutherland Bates, *Hearst, Lord of San Simeon* (New York: Viking, 1936), 296–97; W. A. Swanberg, *Citizen Hearst* (New York: Charles Scribner's Sons, 1961), 426; Glenn Fowler, "Wreckers Find a Hearst 'Chapel,'" *New York Times* (March 12, 1966): 29; Stern, Gilmartin and Mellins, *New York 1930*, 619, 621; Dunlap, *On Broadway*, 210, 212.

291. Steven Ruttenbaum, *Mansions in the Clouds: The Skyscraper Palazzi of Emery Roth* (New York: Balsam Press, 1986), 192.

292. For Burnham's building, see Stern, Gilmartin and Massengale, *New York 1900*, 164–67.

293. "Tower in New York," *Architectural Record* 137 (May 1965): 12; William Robbins, "Columbus Circle Enters New Era," *New York Times* (June 13, 1965), VIII: 1, 10.

294. Glenn Fowler, "A Circular Tower to Rise in Triangle at Columbus Circle," *New York Times* (June 5, 1966), VIII: 1, 10; Ada Louise Huxtable, "Architecture: Fun and Games," *New York Times* (June 19, 1966), II: 21.

295. Huxtable, "Architecture: Fun and Games": 21.

296. Joseph P. Fried, "Columbus Circle to Get 44-Story Building," *New York Times* (October 27, 1967): 56; "Gulf & Western Industries to Occupy New Columbus Circle Skyscraper," *Real Estate Record and Guide* 200 (November 4, 1967): 2; "Snorkel Theater," *Architectural Forum* 133 (October 1970): 54–55; "Paramount Theater," *Interior Design* 42 (September 1971): 106–7; "Top of the Park," *Interior Design* 43 (April 1972): 144–45; White and Willensky, *AIA Guide* (1978), 174; Goldberger, *The City Observed*, 181; Richard David Story, "The Buildings New Yorkers Love to Hate," *New York* 20 (June 15, 1987): cover, 30–35; Dunlap, *On Broadway*, 226.

297. Ada Louise Huxtable, "How to Keep the Status Quo," *New York Times* (April 16, 1969), II: 23; William Robbins, "Din of Construction Resounds in Lincoln Center," *New York Times* (April 20, 1969), VIII: 1, 9; Maurice Carroll, "Lincoln Center Expansion Is Backed," *New York Times* (April 25, 1969): 32; Walter McQuade, "I Vote Yes," editorial, *Architectural Forum* 130 (May 1969): 96; Jonathan Barnett, "Urban Design as Part of the Government Process," *Architectural Record* 147 (January 1970): 131–50; Jonathan Barnett, *Urban Design as Public Policy* (New York: Architectural Record Books, 1974), 51–52.

298. Barnett, *Urban Design as Public Policy*, 51.

299. McQuade, "I Vote Yes": 96.

300. Paul Goldberger, "Architects of Luxury Towers Shape New Manhattan Skyline," *New York Times* (November 1, 1974): 41; Goldberger, *The City Observed*, 198–99; Andrew Alpern and Seymour Durst, *Holdouts!* (New York: McGraw-Hill, 1984), 84–86; White and Willensky, *AIA Guide* (1988), 293; Dunlap, *On Broadway*, 226.

301. Barnett, *Urban Design as Public Policy*, 51–52.

302. Jack Newfield, "Will the Milstein Monster Eclipse the Sun?" *Village Voice* 19 (July 25, 1974): 1, 77, 79–80.

303. Alpern and Durst, *Holdouts!*, 84–86.

304. White and Willensky, *AIA Guide* (1988), 292–93.

305. Goldberger, *The City Observed*, 199.

306. Goldberger, "Architecture: Lincoln Center and Changes Wrought by 20 Years": 21.

307. Goldberger, "Architecture: Lincoln Center and Changes Wrought by 20 Years": 21.

308. For the Century Apartments, see Stern, Gilmartin and Mellins, *New York 1930*, 403, 410, 416.

309. "Tower for the Mormon Church Is Being Erected at Lincoln Sq.," *New York Times* (April 22, 1973): 34; White and Willensky, *AIA Guide* (1978), 179.

310. Goldberger, "Architects of Luxury Towers Shape New Manhattan Skyline": 41.

311. Goldberger, "Architects of Luxury Towers Shape New Manhattan Skyline": 41; Goldberger, *The City Observed*, 213; Dunlap, *On Broadway*, 227.

312. "New Neighbor," *Progressive Architecture* 53 (January 1972): 28–29; "New 33-Story Apartment Building to Expand Role of Lincoln Center," *Real Estate Record and Guide* 209 (January 15, 1972): 2; Goldberger, "Architects of Luxury Towers Shape New Manhattan Skyline": 41; White and Willensky, *AIA Guide* (1978), 176; Goldberger, *The City Observed*, 199; Norton and Patterson, *Living It Up*, 208.

313. Goldberger, *The City Observed*, 199.

MANHATTANTOWN AND THE WEST SIDE URBAN RENEWAL AREA

1. New York City Committee on Slum Clearance, *Manhattantown* (New York, 1951); "Project Proposed to Clear Slums," *New York Times* (September 21, 1951): 25; "Four Redevelopment Projects Under Way," *Citizens' Housing News* 11 (September 1952): 3; Margaret Boulton Bartlett, "Morningside-Manhattanville: A Pioneer Urban Redevelopment Program," *American City* 44 (May 1953): 94–96; "Urban Redevelopment in New York Gets Going," *Citizens' Housing News* 12 (November 1953): 3; Women's City Club of New York, *Tenant Relocation at West Park* (New York, March 1954); Women's City Club of New York, *Manhattantown Two Years Later* (New York, April 1956); Charles G. Bennett, "Report Shows Tenney Chided City on Manhattantown in 1956," *New York Times* (July 3, 1957): 1, 15; "New Sponsor for an Old Job," *Engineering News-Record* 159 (July 4, 1957): 24; "Park West Nears Half-Way Stage," *New York Times* (September 28, 1958), VIII: 1, 13; "New York Title I Controversy Spotlights Architect Kessler—A Combination of Know-How and Know-Who," *Architectural Forum* 111 (August 1959): 13–14, 16; Stephen G. Thompson, "The Future of Title I," *Architectural Forum* 111 (September 1959): 107–9, 194, 198; Fred J. Cook and Gene Gleason, "The Shame of New York," *Nation*, special issue (October 31, 1959): 284–300; Jerry Miller, "Small Town in a Big City: 100th Street Block on Manhattan's West Side," *New York Times* (January 15, 1961), VIII: 1, 6; White and Willensky, *AIA Guide* (1967), 146; Robert Moses, *Public Works: A Dangerous Trade* (New York: McGraw-Hill, 1970), 449–53; Robert A. Caro, *The Power Broker: Robert Moses and the Fall of New York* (New York: Alfred A. Knopf, 1974), 962–63, 970–76, 978–83, 1010–13; Anthony Jackson, *A Place Called Home: A History of Low-Cost Housing in Manhattan* (Cambridge, Mass.: MIT Press, 1977), 248–52; James Trager, *West of Fifth: The Rise and Fall and Rise of Manhattan's West Side* (New York: Atheneum, 1987), 102–3; Peter Salwen, *Upper West Side Story: A History and Guide* (New York: Abbeville Press, 1989), 274; Richard Plunz, *A History of Housing in New York City* (New York: Columbia University Press, 1990), 282–83, 289.

2. Mary Perot Nichols, "Architect Mayor Banned Is Back on Title I Again," *Village Voice* 8 (January 24, 1963): 3.

3. Thompson, "The Future of Title I": 107.

4. "Plan Board Backs Douglass Houses," *New York Times* (February 7, 1952): 17; "State Lends the City $59,180,000 for 2 Low-Rent Housing Projects," *New York Times* (March 2, 1952): 1, 69; Trager, *West of Fifth*, 103–4.

5. Jerry Miller, "Block on 100th Street Is Given All Facilities of a Small Town," *New York Times* (January 15, 1961), VIII: 1.

6. Grosvenor Neighborhood House, Inc., *Grosvenor Neighborhood House: Where the Need Is Greatest* (New York, 1961).

7. White and Willensky, *AIA Guide* (1988), 334.

8. "West Side Area Needs Conservation Measures," *Housing and Planning News* 12 (January 1954): 1, 4. Also see "Neighborhood Conservation Plan Sent to Mayor," *Housing and Planning News* 12 (February 1954): 1, 4.

9. Robert Wagner quoted in "Mayor's Remarks at Housing Hearing," *New York Times* (October 6, 1955): 22. Also see "Redevelopment of Area on West Side Proposed by Mayor," *Housing and Planning News* 14 (October 1955): 1; Charles Grutzner, "City Gives Plan to Rehabilitate Upper West Side," *New York Times* (October 6, 1955): 1, 22; "Manhattan's West Side In for a Beauty Treatment," *Business Week* (October 15, 1955): 41; "More Than Housing Is Involved," editorial, *Housing and Planning News* 14 (November 1955): 2; Charles Grutzner, "Compromise Seen on Housing by City," *New York Times* (December 27, 1955): 1, 21; Charles G. Bennett, "City Seeks to Bar Spread of Slums with State Law," *New York Times* (February 25, 1957): 1, 17; Emily Goldblat, "Image and Reality in Patterns of Change on Manhattan's Upper West Side" (Master's thesis, Graduate School of Architecture and Planning, Columbia University, 1969); Robert E. Selsam, "The Upper West Side Urban Renewal Area: An Evaluation with Special Emphasis on Implications for New York City and the Urban Renewal Program" (Master's thesis, Graduate School of Architecture and Planning, Columbia University, 1970); Jackson, *A Place Called Home: A History of Low-Cost Housing in Manhattan*, 250–51, 269.

10. "Neighborhood Conservation Plan Sent to Mayor," editorial, *Housing and Planning News* 12 (February 1954): 1, 4.

11. "West Side Urban Renewal Report Presented by Planning Commission," *Housing and Planning News* 16 (June 1958): 1, 4.

12. New York Urban Renewal Board, *West Side Urban Renewal Area Preliminary Plan* (New York, 1959). Also see New York City Planning Commission, *A Report on the West Side Urban Renewal Study to Mayor Robert F. Wagner and the Board of Estimate of the City of New York and to the Urban Renewal Administration* (New York, April 1958); Charles Grutzner, "$150 Million Rebuilding Planned in West 87th to 97th St. Area," *New York Times* (April 23, 1958): 1, 20; Edith Evans Asbury, "City to Preserve," *New York Times* (May 24, 1959): 1, 47; Charles G. Bennett, "Changes Adopted in West Side Plan," *New York Times* (July 16, 1959): 1, 24.

13. Grutzner, "$150 Million Rebuilding Planned in West 87th to 97th St. Area": 20.

14. "Mayor Sets Up Unit for Urban Renewal," *New York Times* (May 28, 1958): 14; "City in Fast Motion," editorial, *New York Times* (May 29, 1958): 26.

15. "Ratensky to Direct Urban Renewal Unit," *New York Times* (June 23, 1958): 44. For an overview of Samuel Ratensky's career, see "Samuel Ratensky of Housing Unit. City Planner Here, 62, Dies—Aided West Side Project," *New York Times* (December 30, 1972): 24.

16. Samuel Ratensky, "Some Observations in European Housing Design," *Journal of the American Institute of Architects* 31 (June 1959): 23–27.

17. "Ratensky Describes West Side Progress," *Housing and Planning News* 17 (October 1958): 1.

18. "West Side Renewal Described in Plan," *Housing and Planning News* 17 (May 1959): 3–4; "City Releases Report Showing Effects of Neighborhood Decline," *Real Estate Record and Guide* 183 (May 2, 1959): 2–3.

19. Chester Rapkin, *The Real Estate Market in an Urban Renewal Area* (New York: New York City Planning Commission and Housing and Home Finance Agency, Urban Renewal Administration, February 1959). For a review of Rapkin's book, see Walter Thabit's article in *Journal of the American Institute of Planners* 26 (May 1960): 150–51.

20. "Many Speakers Discuss Preliminary Approval of West Side Renewal," *Housing and Planning News* 18 (September 1959): 1.

21. Joseph P. Lyford, *The Airtight Cage: A Study of New York's West Side* (New York: Harper & Row, 1966), 315–16. Also see Landmarks Preservation Commission of the City of New York, *Central Park West Historic District Designation Report* (New York, 1990).

22. New York City Urban Renewal Board, *Final Plan for the Rehabilitation Demonstration Pilot Project in the West Side Urban Renewal Plan* (New York, 1959). Also see New

York City Housing and Redevelopment Board, *West Side Urban Renewal Area: A Summary of the Final Plan* (New York, 1959); James S. Ottenberg, *The West Side Urban Renewal Project: An Interim Report* (New York, 1960); "Urban Renewal Board Sets Brick and Mortar Plans for West Side," *Housing and Planning News* 18 (March–April 1960): 1, 4; Thomas W. Ennis, "10-Year Renewal Stirs West Side," *New York Times* (October 13, 1963), VIII: 1, 9.

23. "West Side Renewal Poses Questions," *Housing and Planning News* 19 (May–June 1961): 4.

24. "Private Lending Pool Created for Urban Renewal," *Real Estate Record and Guide* 187 (January 21, 1961): 2–3.

25. "West Side Renewal Poses Questions": 4.

26. Thomas W. Ennis, "West Side Plan Ready to Start," *New York Times* (March 18, 1962), VIII: 1, 9.

27. Robert F. Wagner quoted in "Wagner Details Plan for West Side Urban Renewal Area," *Real Estate Record and Guide* 187 (March 11, 1961): 2–3.

28. Robert F. Wagner quoted in Charles G. Bennett, "Clean-Up of Slums in West Side Area Begun by Wagner," *New York Times* (July 1, 1961): 1, 24.

29. J. Clarence Davies quoted in "Wagner Details Plan for West Side Urban Renewal Area": 3.

30. Jackie Robinson quoted in Trager, *West of Fifth*, 105.

31. Trager, *West of Fifth*, 105.

32. Jack E. Wood and Aramis Gomez quoted in Trager, *West of Fifth*, 105.

33. Stryker's Bay Neighborhood Council, *Annual Report 1967–1968* (New York, 1968); Selsam, "The Upper West Side Urban Renewal Area": 22, 35–37.

34. Martin Arnold, "More Low-Cost Housing Added to Plan for West Side Renewal," *New York Times* (June 22, 1962): 11.

35. Joseph Monserrat quoted in "Board Hears Pleas on West Side Plan," *New York Times* (June 24, 1962): 37.

36. Patrick Rafferty quoted in Martin Arnold, "Renewal Fought by Puerto Ricans," *New York Times* (June 23, 1962): 24.

37. Quoted in Trager, *West of Fifth*, 105–6.

38. Martin Arnold, "2 Slum Projects Approved by City," *New York Times* (June 27, 1962): 37; David B. Carlson, "Rehabilitation: Stepchild of Urban Renewal," *Architectural Forum* 117 (August 1962): 130–33, 181; Greenleigh Associates, Inc., *Report of the Diagnostic Survey of Tenant Households in the Upper West Side Urban Renewal Area of New York City* (New York: Greenleigh Associates, Inc., 1965).

39. "Final Restoration Operation Is Started in West Side Urban Renewal Area," *Real Estate Record and Guide* 196 (November 6, 1965): 2.

40. Charles Thompson, "Where Are Some Signs of Progress?" *Journal of the American Institute of Architects* 44 (September 1965): 38–40. Also see "West Side Urban Renewal Area," *Casabella* 294/295 (December 1964–January 1965): 23–31.

41. Emanuel Perlmutter, "Wagner Appoints Mollen to New City Housing Job," *New York Times* (January 17, 1965): 1, 36.

42. Charles G. Bennett, "Council Approves City Superagency," *New York Times* (July 12, 1967): 1, 31; Charles G. Bennett, "Lindsay Signs Bill for a Superagency," *New York Times* (July 29, 1967): 1, 22.

43. "Commissioner Nathan Offers Program to Speed Up Construction in West Side Area," *Real Estate Record and Guide* 198 (October 1, 1966): 2.

44. New York City Housing and Redevelopment Board, *West Side Urban Renewal Area: A Summary of the Final Plan*, 13; "Middle Income Housing Plans Submitted to Planning Commission," *Real Estate Record and Guide* 192 (July 13, 1963): 2; White and Willensky, *AIA Guide* (1978), 207. For 74 West Ninety-second Street, a housing project completed in 1965 and built by the New York City Housing Authority within the renewal area, see White and Willensky, *AIA Guide* (1978), 207.

45. White and Willensky, *AIA Guide* (1978), 207.

46. White and Willensky, *AIA Guide* (1978), 206.

47. White and Willensky, *AIA Guide* (1978), 206.

48. "Proposed Middle Income Apartment Development Including Neighborhood Shopping and a Public Plaza," *Empire State Architect* 26 (January–February 1966): 13; "$5.5 Million Loan Granted for West Side Urban Renewal Project," *Real Estate Record and Guide* 198 (October 29, 1966): 3; White and Willensky, *AIA Guide* (1978), 206.

49. White and Willensky, *AIA Guide* (1967), 145; Thomas F. Galvin, "New Dimensions in Air Rights," *Journal of the American Institute of Architects* 50 (July 1968): 39–43; Rita Robison, "Architectural Acrobatics," *Progressive Architecture* 54 (March 1973): 92–95; White and Willensky, *AIA Guide* (1978), 207; Trager, *West of Fifth*, 106, 111. For Charles C. Haight's Trinity School, see Stern, Gilmartin and Massengale, *New York 1900*, 87.

50. "New York City Renewal," *Architectural Forum* 117 (August 1962): 41; "Middle Income Housing Plans Submitted to Planning Commission," *Real Estate Record and Guide* 192 (July 13, 1963): 2; "Individualized Architecture Is Apparent in West Side Renewal," *Real Estate Record and Guide* 202 (July 20, 1968): 2; White and Willensky, *AIA Guide* (1978), 207.

51. White and Willensky, *AIA Guide* (1978), 207.

52. White and Willensky, *AIA Guide* (1978), 207.

53. "Town House West a New Dimension in West Side Renewal," *Real Estate Record and Guide* 210 (September 16, 1972): 2; White and Willensky, *AIA Guide* (1978), 207; Thomas E. Norton and Jerry E. Patterson, *Living It Up: A Guide to the Named Apartment Houses of New York* (New York: Atheneum, 1984), 331.

54. Frederick M. Ginsbern quoted in "Town House West a New Dimension in West Side Renewal": 2.

55. White and Willensky, *AIA Guide* (1978), 207.

56. White and Willensky, *AIA Guide* (1978), 208.

57. "Duplex Apartments: Fresh Look at an Elegant Old Idea," *Architectural Record* 143 (June 1968): 156–57; "West Side Housing Project Gets 37% Mortgage Loan," *Real Estate Record and Guide* 205 (May 2, 1970): 2; White and Willensky, *AIA Guide* (1978), 208; Norton and Patterson, *Living It Up*, 338.

58. "New York City Renewal," *Architectural Forum* 117 (August 1962): 41.

59. White and Willensky, *AIA Guide* (1978), 206.

60. "Permanent Home for Trova Sculpture," *Progressive Architecture* 56 (August 1975): 25; Margot Gayle and Michele Cohen, *The Art Commission and the Municipal Art Society Guide to Manhattan's Outdoor Sculpture* (New York: Prentice Hall Press, 1988), 281.

61. White and Willensky, *AIA Guide* (1978), 208.

62. Lawrence Halprin & Associates, *New York, New York* (New York: City of New York, March 1968), 8–14. Also see Ellen Perry Berkeley, "Inquiry into Open Space," *Architectural Forum* 129 (July–August 1968): 96–101.

63. "West Side Houses Will Honor Rabbi," *New York Times* (July 30, 1959): 15; "Art Forms Will Have Free Play in a City Project's Community Plaza," *New York Times* (May 8, 1964): 35; White and Willensky, *AIA Guide* (1967), 145; Frederick Fried and Edmond V. Gillon, Jr., *New York Civic Sculpture* (New York: Dover, 1976), 74–75; Norton and Patterson, *Living It Up*, 368; Gayle and Cohen, *The Art Commission and the Municipal Art Society Guide to Manhattan's Outdoor Sculpture*, 280.

64. Rita Reif, "For Mrs. Wang, Walls Came Tumbling Down," *New York Times* (October 18, 1966): 38.

65. "Summer Living in the City—Five Stories High," *House Beautiful* 112 (August 1970): 60–61.

66. "Record Interiors of 1975," *Architectural Record* 157 (January 1975): 100–103.

67. Nan Ickeringill, "Architects' Own Brownstones: Ideas Tempered by Finances," *New York Times* (June 3, 1970): 56.

68. Franklin Whitehouse, "West Side Houses Reclaimed with Cash and Ingenuity," *New York Times* (February 4, 1968), VIII: 1, 8; Thomas W. Ennis, "Old Houses Gain Status in Renewal," *New York Times* (August 11, 1968), VIII: 1, 8.

69. Ickeringill, "Architects' Own Brownstones: Ideas Tempered by Finances": 56.

70. Susan Grant Lewin, "Bright New Life the Third Time Around," *House Beautiful* 113 (May 1971): 102–7.

71. "Dedication Held at Renewal Site," *New York Times* (October 10, 1968): 2.

72. Ennis, "10-Year Renewal Stirs West Side": 1, 9; "Whatever Happened to the Little Old New York Brownstone," *Progressive Architecture* 49 (December 1968): 46, 48; Thomas W. Ennis, "Group of Friends Review 9 Brownstones as Co-op," *New York Times* (March 2, 1969), VIII: 1, 8; Peter Hellman, "The Consequences of Brownstone Fever," *New York* 2 (March 31, 1969): 22–31; "Hello New Day," *Architectural Forum* 130 (June 1969): 95; "1969 Bard Awards Stress Urban Relationships," *Interiors* 128 (July 1969): 10–12; "Nine-G Cooperative," *Architectural Forum* 131 (July–August 1969): 78–81; "The Brownstoners," *Newsweek* 74 (September 1, 1969): 56–59; Susana Torre, ed., *Women in Architecture: A Historic and Contemporary Perspective* (New York: Whitney Library of Design, 1977), 153.

73. Stanley M. Isaacs, letter to the editor, *Housing and Planning News* 17 (September 1958): 2, 4.

74. For Sullivan-MacDougal Gardens, Turtle Bay Gardens and Sunnyside Gardens, see Stern, Gilmartin and Mellins, *New York 1930*, 427–29, 486–87, 490–92.

75. Quoted in "1969 Bard Awards Stress Urban Relationships": 10–11.

MORNINGSIDE HEIGHTS

1. For general discussions of the Morningside Heights area in the post–World War II era, see Morningside Heights, Inc., *Some Facts about the Population of Morningside Heights* (New York: Morningside Heights, Inc., 1948); Gertrude Samuels, "Community at Work: A Lesson for Others," *New York Times* (August 6, 1950), VI: 18–19, 36–37; Gertrude Samuels, "Rebirth of a Community," *New York Times* (September 25, 1955), VI: 26, 37; Community Research Associates, Inc., *Morningside-Manhattanville Study: Preliminary Report for Committee* (New York, 1957); Robert Bard, "Morningside: Her Profile and Promise," *Columbia Daily Spectator* (September 17, 1957): 7; Wayne Phillips, "Slums Engulfing Columbia Section," *New York Times* (June 9, 1958): 25, 33; Morningside Heights, Inc., *Morningside Heights* (New York: Morningside Heights, Inc., 1959); Thomas W. Ennis, "Morningside Building Boom Brightens the Area's Future," *New York Times* (March 8, 1959), VIII: 1, 7; Chester Rapkin, *Population and Housing* (New York: Morningside Heights, Inc., 1962); Morningside Heights, Inc., *School Needs and Resources of Morningside Heights* (New York: Morningside Heights, Inc., 1962); Charles Kaiser, "Scaling Morningside Heights," *New York Times* (October 1, 1976), C: 21.

2. New York City Committee on Slum Clearance, *Morningside-Manhattanville: Slum Clearance Plan Under Title I of the Housing Act of 1949* (New York, 1951); "Planners Approve $37,495,755 Housing," *New York Times* (September 27, 1951): 33; "Plan Board Backs Columbia Housing," *New York Times* (October 18, 1951): 31; "Slum Clearance for Morningside Heights Gets Backing of 9 N.Y. Schools, Churches," *Architectural Forum* 96 (February 1952): 49; "Morningside Project Approved," *Citizens' Housing News* 11 (January 1953): 1; "Largest Housing Project Okayed for New York City," *Engineering News-Record* 150 (January 29, 1953): 49; Margaret Boulton Bartlett, "Morningside-Manhattanville," *American City* 68 (May 1953): 94–96; "Urban Redevelopment in New York Gets Going," *Citizens' Housing News* 12 (November 1953): 3; Lee E. Cooper, "Housing Families of Middle Income," *New York Times* (January 3, 1954): 1–2; "Wreckers Attack Morningside Site," *New York Times* (January 12, 1954): 17; "$4,500-a-Unit Subsidy Helps N.Y. Middle-Income Co-ops," *Architectural Forum* 100 (March 1954): 54; "Morningside Gardens Contract Awarded," *Real Estate Record and Guide* 176 (September 24, 1955): 3–4; Florence D. May, "Slum Clearance Successes Noted," letter to the editor, *New York Times* (May 29, 1956): 26; Charles Grutzner, "City's 'Acropolis' Combatting Slums," *New York Times* (May 21, 1957): 37, 46; "Redevelopment Today," *Architectural Forum* 108 (April 1958): 108–13; "Architecture at Columbia," *Columbia College Today* 10 (fall 1962): 10–13; "City Slums Vs. a University," *U.S. News & World Report* 56 (April 6, 1964): 74–77; E. J. Kahn, Jr., "Profiles: Resources and Responsibilities—I," *New Yorker* 40 (January 9, 1965): 37–38, 40, 42, 46–47, 50, 52, 54–56, 59, 62, 64, 66, 68, 72, 75–76, 78, 80–83; Robert Moses, *Public Works: A Dangerous Trade* (New York: McGraw-Hill, 1970), 450; Deirdre Carmody, "After 25 Years, Co-op Endures as Stable Symbol," *New York Times* (October 16, 1982): 29–30; Victoria Newhouse, *Wallace K. Harrison, Architect* (New York: Rizzoli International Publications, 1989), 163–64; David W. Dunlap, *On Broadway: A Journey Uptown Over Time* (New York: Rizzoli International Publications, 1990), 276.

3. Harry Emerson Fosdick, speech at City Planning Commission, December 10, 1952, quoted in Bartlett, "Morningside-Manhattanville": 94.

4. "General Grant Houses," *Empire State Architect* 15 (July–August 1955): 12–13.

5. Henry Hope Reed, *The Golden City* (New York: Doubleday, 1959), 104.

6. Kahn, "Profiles: Resources and Responsibilities—I": 71.

7. For a general description of the area's institutions during the immediate postwar period, see "Morningside Heights: Manhattan's 'Acropolis' Is One of the World's Great Cultural Centers," *Life* 33 (September 1, 1952): 70–77.

8. "Columbia," *Architectural Forum* 74 (May 1941): 68.

9. "Columbia Finishes Its New Theater," *New York Times* (November 3, 1940), II: 7; "Columbia Dedicates Drama Building Today," *New York Times* (December 7, 1940): 12; "Columbia Opens Its New Theater," *New York Times* (December 8, 1940): 67; Arthur L. Levy, "Brander Matthews Was Hub of Experimental Productions," *Columbia Daily Spectator* (October 28, 1960): 5.

10. "Columbia Uses Trailers," *Interiors* 105 (April 1946): 12.
11. "Columbia Names Consulting Architects," *Architectural Record* 104 (July 1948): 170.
12. "New Columbia Property," *Architectural Record* 106 (December 1949): 166.
13. "Mobilization Breeds Corp of Science Laboratories," *Architectural Forum* 95 (November 1951): 50; "Columbia Plans $22,150,000 Engineering Center on Riverside Drive Site; Fund-Raising Drive On," *Architectural Record* 110 (December 1951): 13; "Progressive Architecture for Education—1952," *Progressive Architecture* 33 (January 1952): 72; *Columbia University in the City of New York 1754–1954* (New York: Columbia University, 1953), unpaginated.
14. "Columbia Puts Up New Apartments," *New York Times* (October 13, 1963), VIII: 1, 6; Donald H. Shapiro, "Advisory Planning Council Now Playing Stronger Role," *Columbia Daily Spectator* (October 18, 1963): 1, 3; "City Slums Vs. a University": 77; "Single-Loaded Corridor for Good Outlook," *Architectural Record* 136 (August 1964): 124–25.
15. "Columbia Faculty Get New Housing," *New York Times* (October 22, 1967): 76.
16. "Columbia Announces Arts Center Project," *New York Times* (February 15, 1948): 44; "Columbia Center to Rise 15 Stories," *New York Times* (February 16, 1948): 15; "Columbia Center for Arts Planned," *New York Times* (February 9, 1950): 26; "Columbia Arts Center Planning Group Forms," *Architectural Record* 107 (June 1950): 196; Milton Bracher, "Theater Included on Columbia Plan," *New York Times* (November 14, 1954): 85; "Columbia Art Center Plan Includes Architecture School," *Architectural Forum* 103 (July 1955): 25.
17. "Columbia Campus Extension Will Hurdle Road, Cost $17 Million," *Architectural Forum* 104 (May 1956): 16; "Space for People: Superblock Plan Extends Campus of Midcity University," *Architectural Record* 119 (May 1956): 11; "Superblock Development to Increase Columbia U. Campus," *Progressive Architecture* 37 (May 1956): 82; David Farmer, "Trustees Give Authorization for Superblock Construction," *Columbia Daily Spectator* (April 8, 1958): 1; Fred M. Hechinger, "Columbia Plans Huge Expansion," *New York Times* (April 9, 1961): 1, 80; Doron Gopstein, "Kirk Sees Bright CU Architectural Future," *Columbia Daily Spectator* (December 14, 1962): 3.
18. For the President's House, see Stern, Gilmartin and Massengale, *New York 1900*, 417. For Johnson Hall, the Men's Faculty Club and the Casa Italiana, see Stern, Gilmartin and Mellins, *New York 1930*, 109.
19. Stern, Gilmartin and Massengale, *New York 1900*, 417.
20. Wallace K. Harrison quoted in Russell Porter, "Columbia to Add to Campus and Build New Law School," *New York Times* (March 28, 1956): 1, 33.
21. "Columbia's Fine Plans," editorial, *New York Times* (March 28, 1956): 30.
22. Nathan Glazer, "Columbia Project Criticized," letter to the editor, *New York Times* (March 28, 1956): 30.
23. "Columbia to Get Electronic Music," *New York Times* (July 20, 1959): 27; "Columbia to Get Gift of $150,000," *New York Times* (June 29, 1962): 13.
24. Porter, "Columbia to Add to Campus and Build New Law School": 1, 33; "Columbia's Fine Plans": 30; "New Law School to Rise," *Columbia Law School News* 10 (April 18, 1956): 1; "X-Ray View of New Law School," *Columbia Law School News* 10 (May 17, 1956): 3; "$500,000 Given to Law Building," *Columbia Law School News* 12 (April 8, 1958): 1, 3; "Buildings in the News," *Architectural Record* 124 (July 1958): 12; Russell Porter, "Columbia Starts New Law Building," *New York Times* (November 8, 1958): 23; "New Kent Building to Be Ready for Use October, '60," *Columbia Law School News* 13 (May 6, 1959): 1; Jerry C. Straus, "New School to Open in Fall of '60," *Columbia Law School News* 14 (October 7, 1959): 1; John B. Goodrich, "Price Plans Move to New Library; 400,000 Volumes Must Be Shelved," *Columbia Law School News* 14 (March 2, 1960): 3; John B. Goodrich, "Jan. 1, 1961 Completion Date Planned for New Kent Hall," *Columbia Law School News* 14 (March 16, 1960): 3; Raleigh Johnson, "Law School Moves to New Home; Builders to Leave in November," *Columbia Law School News* 16 (October 11, 1961): 1, 3; Linda Bien, "New Buildings: Fifth Rate?" *Columbia Owl* 2 (November 22, 1961): 1, 7; "Alumni Look at Their School," *Columbia Law School Alumni Bulletin* 7 (summer 1962): 11–17; Allan Temko, "A Brilliant Plan Gone Awry?" *Columbia College Today* 10 (fall 1962): 18–23; "Estimate Board Grants Franchise," *Columbia Law School News* 17 (October 10, 1962): 1; "Artist's Conception of Landscaped Plaza," *New York Times* (December 1, 1963), IV: 9; Ada Louise Huxtable, "Expansion at Columbia: A Restricted Vision and Bureaucracy Seen as Obstacles to Its Development," *New York Times* (November 5, 1966): 33–34.
25. For Kent Hall, see Stern, Gilmartin and Massengale, *New York 1900*, 409–10.
26. Temko, "A Brilliant Plan Gone Awry?": 22. For a discussion of Allan Temko's critique, see Fred M. Hechinger, "Columbia Scored on Architecture," *New York Times* (December 5, 1962): 49, 71.
27. Huxtable, "Expansion at Columbia: A Restricted Vision and Bureaucracy Seen as Obstacles to Its Development": 33.
28. "Graduate Dormitory Plans May Face Second Revision," *Columbia Daily Spectator* (November 4, 1963): 1. Drawings in the Drawings Collection, Avery Library, Columbia University.
29. "Int'l. Affairs Design Completed," *Columbia Daily Spectator* (February 3, 1965): 1, 7; Michael Agelasto, "When Columbia Planned for the Future," *Columbia Daily Spectator* (December 19, 1966): 1–2; John Brecher, "$21 Million SIA Building Nears Completion," *Columbia Daily Spectator* (February 18, 1971): 1, 5; Deirdre Carmody, "Columbia Dedicates School of International Affairs," *New York Times* (October 23, 1971): 67.
30. "116th St. Closed," *Columbia Alumni News* 44 (October 1953): 7.
31. "Ornamental Gates Will Adorn Campus," *Columbia Daily Spectator* (July 20, 1967): 1.
32. "News Bulletins," *Progressive Architecture* 38 (January 1957): 80. Also see "Columbia Sets Up Building Council," *New York Times* (December 16, 1956): 118.
33. "Teaching Vs. Practice," editorial, *Architectural Forum* 106 (March 1957): 102.
34. "New Citizenship Center Will Be Built on Campus," *Columbia College Today* 3 (June 1956): 1; Joseph D. Coffee, Jr., "New Gifts Finance Ferris Booth Hall," *Columbia College Today* 4 (January 1957): 1, 3; "Unveil Plans for College Citizenship Center, Federally Financed Dorm at Low Ceremony," *Columbia Daily Spectator* (January 15, 1957): 1, 4; "Columbia Plans Citizenship Hall," *New York Times* (January 15, 1957): 31; "On the Horizon: Booth Hall & New Dorm," *Columbia Alumni News* 48 (February 1957): 16–17, 24; "Columbia Landmark to Be Razed," *New York Times* (November 24, 1957): 126; Robert Burd, "Hold Groundbreaking for Citizenship Center Dormitory," *Columbia Daily Spectator* (November 27, 1957): 1, 4; "The College Breaks Ground: Booth Hall, New Dormitory To Rise on South Campus," *Columbia College Today* 5 (February 1958): 3, 5; "Ferris Booth Hall Takes Shape as Outstanding Center of Student Life," *Columbia College Today* 6 (April 1959): 6–7; Ennis, "Morningside Building Boom Brightens the Area's Future": 1, 7; "Ferris Booth Opening Today, Turns Columbia Dream into Reality," *Columbia Daily Spectator* (April 19, 1960): 1; McCandish Phillips, "Columbia Opens Student Center," *New York Times* (May 4, 1960): 51; "Columbia Dedicating $4 Million Center," *New York Herald Tribune* (May 4, 1960): 12; "Columbia Dedication," *New York Times* (May 6, 1960): 41; John D. Hack, "Student Center Is Culmination of Much Work," *Columbia Daily Spectator* (May 5, 1960): 1, 11; "A Memorable Day for Columbia College," *Columbia College Today* 7 (July 1960): 6–7; "Taylor '21 Views Ferris Booth Hall as Campus Capitol," *Columbia College Today* 7 (July 1960): 3, 11; Bien, "New Buildings: Fifth Rate?": 7; David Binder, "Columbia Is the Latest Target of Protests on Campus Designs," *New York Times* (April 29, 1962), VIII: 1–2; Dunlap, *On Broadway*, 276. For Butler Library, see Stern, Gilmartin and Mellins, *New York 1930*, 109–11.
35. Drawings in the Drawings Collection, Avery Library, Columbia University.
36. For Hartley, Livingston and Hamilton halls, see Stern, Gilmartin and Massengale, *New York 1900*, 410. For John Jay Hall, see Stern, Gilmartin and Mellins, *New York 1930*, 109–11.
37. Dustin Rice quoted in "Columbia Landmark to Be Razed": 126.
38. "Harry Carman at 75," editorial, *New York Times* (January 22, 1959): 40, reprinted in *Columbia College Today* 6 (February 1959): 1; Henry Graff, "A Profile: Harry J. Carman," *Columbia College Today* 6 (February 1959): 2.
39. Temko, "A Brilliant Plan Gone Awry?": 20–21.
40. Voorhees, Walker, Smith, Smith & Haines, *75th Anniversary* (New York, May 1960), 61; "Educators Inspect Columbia Center," *New York Times* (October 26, 1961): 29; Bien, "New Buildings: Fifth Rate?": 1, 7; Binder, "Columbia Is the Latest Target of Protests on Campus Designs": 1; Temko, "A Brilliant Plan Gone Awry?": 21; "Architecture at Columbia," *Columbia College Today*: 12–13.
41. For Pupin Hall, see Stern, Gilmartin and Mellins, *New York 1930*, 109.
42. Alan Lapidus quoted in Binder, "Columbia Is the Latest Target of Protests on Campus Designs": 1.
43. Temko, "A Brilliant Plan Gone Awry?": 21.
44. Drawings in Columbiana, Columbia University.
45. Drawings in the Drawings Collection, Avery Library, Columbia University.
46. Binder, "Columbia Is the Latest Target of Protests on Campus Designs": 10; Marta Gutman and Richard Plunz, "Anatomy of Insurrection," in Richard Oliver, ed., *The Making of an Architect, 1881–1981* (New York: Rizzoli International Publications, 1981), 183–210.
47. George Charles Keller, "Too Many Cooks, Too Few Artists," editorial, *Columbia College Today* 10 (fall 1962): 1.
48. "Ground Breaking Ceremony Set for School of Business," *Columbia Daily Spectator* (April 13, 1962): 3; "Modern Architecture Hit by Reed, Picketers," *Columbia Daily Spectator* (April 18, 1962): 1; "Students Term New Hall Ugly," *New York Times* (April 18, 1962): 18; Joseph Michalak, "Students Protest College Building Designs," *New York Herald Tribune* (April 19, 1962), II: 5; "Professor Joins Design Dispute," *New York Times* (April 19, 1962): 33; "Architecture Protests Bring No Official University Action," *Columbia Daily Spectator* (April 26, 1962): 1; Joseph Michalak, "Students Protest College Building Designs," *New York Herald Tribune* (April 29, 1962), II: 5; Binder, "Columbia Is the Latest Target of Protests on Campus Designs": 1–2; Larry S. Stewart, "The Growing Campus," *Columbia Owl* 3 (May 2, 1962): 1–2; "Columbia Design Under Student Fire," *Architectural Forum* 116 (June 1962): 9; "Top Floor of Columbia Gym Giving Way to Building," *New York Times* (July 25, 1962): 35; Katherine Kuh, "Art in America, 1962: A Balance Sheet," *Saturday Review* 45 (September 8, 1962): 30A-30N; "Architecture at Columbia," *Columbia College Today*: 13; James T. Burns, Jr., "Uris Hall: An Opportunity Missed," *Columbia Daily Spectator* (May 8, 1964): 1–2; "Columbia's Uris Hall Is Formally Dedicated," *New York Times* (May 21, 1964): 17; Gutman and Plunz, "Anatomy of Insurrection," in Oliver, ed., *The Making of an Architect, 1881–1981*, 185, 198.
49. Drawings in the Drawings Collection, Avery Library, Columbia University.
50. Harry Parnass and Alan Lapidus quoted in Binder, "Columbia Is the Latest Target of Protests on Campus Designs": 1.
51. Alan Spector quoted in "Students Term New Hall Ugly": 18.
52. Percy Uris quoted in "Students Term New Hall Ugly": 18.
53. Robert S. Hutchins quoted in "Students Term New Hall Ugly": 18.
54. Peter Blake quoted in Binder, "Columbia Is the Latest Target of Protests on Campus Designs": 10.
55. Burns, "Uris Hall: An Opportunity Missed": 1.
56. William Platt quoted in "Columbia Design Under Fire": 11.
57. Kuh, "Art in America, 1962: A Balance Sheet": 30H.
58. "Tune In, Turn On, Put On: Art 1968," *Progressive Architecture* 49 (December 1968): 43. Also see Margot Gayle and Michele Cohen, *The Art Commission and the Municipal Art Society Guide to Manhattan's Outdoor Sculpture* (New York: Prentice Hall Press, 1988), 301.
59. "Barnard to Seek Dormitory Fund," *New York Times* (June 7, 1957): 21; "2 Millions Sought in Barnard Plan," *New York Times* (February 12, 1958): 70; "Barnard Dormitory," *Architectural Forum* 108 (March 1958): 28; "Barnard Gets Gift of $100,000 for Student Center," *New York Times* (September 29, 1961): 22; Bien, "New Buildings: Fifth Rate?": 7; "Barnard Receives Gift of $500,000," *New York Times* (May 26, 1962): 23; Dunlap, *On Broadway*, 273.
60. "Expanding Barnard to Get Library-Class Building," *Architectural Record* 121 (March 1957): 400; "Barnard to Build Wollman Library," *New York Times* (April 30, 1957): 31; "Barnard to Start on New Building," *New York Times* (April 27, 1958): 70; "A Good Day at Barnard," editorial, *New York Times* (April 28, 1958): 22; "Ceremony Starts Barnard Library," *New York Times* (April 29, 1958): 23; Ennis, "Morningside Building Boom Brightens the Area's Future": 1, 7; "Library Facilities," *Progressive Architecture* 41 (September 1960): 16–63; Bien, "New Buildings: Fifth Rate?": 1, 7. For Brunner & Tryon's Barnard Hall, see Stern, Gilmartin and Massengale, *New York 1900*, 410.
61. Will Lisner, "$1 Million Is Goal in Barnard Drive," *New York Times* (October 2, 1966): 75; "A Science Building and Student Center," *Architectural Record* 140 (November 1966): 40–43.
62. "Planners Approve $37,495,755 Housing," *New York Times* (September 27, 1951): 31; Dunlap, *On Broadway*, 273.
63. "Barnard Acquires Bryn Mawr Hotel as Dormitory Site," *New York Times* (February 19, 1966): 30; "Women's Dormitory Rises in Morningside Heights," *Real Estate Record and Guide* 201 (February 17, 1967): 3; Edith Evans Asbury, "Barnard to Build a New Dormitory," *New York Times* (February 24, 1967): 21; "Barnard College Will Construct 16-Story Dormitory at 121st St.," *Real Estate Record and Guide* 199 (April 8, 1967): 5; Joseph

P. Fried, "Morningside Adds Buildings Other Than 'Gym,'" *New York Times* (May 26, 1968), VIII: 1, 12.

64. John Kifner, "50 Picket Kirk Home to Mourn Buildings 'Killed' by Columbia," *New York Times* (July 9, 1967): 44.

65. "Columbia to Build Sports Center It Will Share with Neighborhood," *New York Times* (January 14, 1960): 20; "Plan to Build New College Gym on Morningside Park Location," *Columbia College Today* 8 (March 1960): 2, 6; "Columbia Gym," *Architectural Forum* 117 (July 1962): 39; "Athletics at Columbia," *Columbia College Today* 11 (fall 1963): 14–18; Robert Alden, "Neighbors Assail Columbia Growth," *New York Times* (January 18, 1964): 25–26; Bernard B. Fishalow, "Columbia Prepares Blueprint for Planned $9 Million Gym," *Columbia Daily Spectator* (March 11, 1965): 5–3; C. Richard Hatch, "No Park Gymnasium," letter to the editor, *New York Times* (February 1, 1966): 34; Ralph Blumenthal, "Columbia Scores Gym Plan Critics," *New York Times* (February 15, 1966): 31; "Columbia Students Ask Reconsideration of Gym," *New York Times* (March 11, 1966): 16; "Negro Architects Get Harlem Job," *New York Times* (April 25, 1966): 27; "Morningside's Late, Late Show," *Columbia College Today* 14 (fall 1966): 55–58; C. Richard Hatch, "Columbia: Pleonexia on the Acropolis," *Architectural Forum* 127 (July–August 1967): 68–75; Huxtable, "Expansion at Columbia: A Restricted Vision and Bureaucracy Seen as Obstacles to Its Development": 34; Rasa Gustaitis, "Columbia's Neighbors: The Slums of Academe," *Reporter* 37 (October 5, 1967): 34–30; Charles G. Bennett, "Columbia Is Given Approval for Gym," *New York Times* (October 26, 1967): 93; Thomas P. F. Hoving, "Slums of Academe," letter to the editor, *Reporter* 37 (November 2, 1967): 10; Jerry L. Avorn and Members of the Staff of the Columbia Daily Spectator, *Up Against the Ivy Wall* (New York: Random House, 1968); Cox Commission, *Crisis at Columbia: Report of the Fact-Finding Commission Appointed to Investigate the Disturbances at Columbia University in April and May 1968* (New York: Vintage, 1968); "Enough Is Enough," editorial, *Columbia Daily Spectator* (March 6, 1968): 2; "Agony on Morningside Heights," *Time* 91 (March 8, 1968): 48; George Keller, "Six Weeks that Shook Morningside," *Columbia College Today* 15 (spring 1968): 2–97; Ada Louise Huxtable, "How Not to Build a Symbol," *New York Times* (March 24, 1968), II: 23; "New Columbia Gym Is Opposed," *Columbia Daily Spectator* (April 18, 1968): 1, 30; "Faculty Recommends Halt to Gym Construction; Campus Closed Down, SDS Holds Kirk's Office," *Columbia Daily Spectator* (April 25, 1968): 1, 3; "Columbia Closes Campus After Disorders," *New York Times* (April 25, 1968): 1, 41; Oren Root, Jr., "Negotiations Are Begun on Discipline of Students After Use of Police Postponed by Administration; Gym Construction Is Halted; University Closed," *Columbia Daily Spectator* (April 26, 1968): 1–2; "Columbia Halting Work on Its Gym; Suspends Classes," *New York Times* (April 26, 1968): 1, 50; Peter Millones, "Gym Controversy Began in Late 50's," *New York Times* (April 26, 1968): 50; Sylvan Fox, "Faculty's Effort Fails to Resolve Columbia Dispute," *New York Times* (April 27, 1968): 1, 18; Murray Schumach, "Columbia Board Scores 'Minority' Crippling Campus," *New York Times* (April 28, 1968): 1, 74; Sylvan Fox, "Pickets Circle Columbia; Class Reopening Delayed; 720 Protesters Arraigned," *New York Times* (May 1, 1968): 1, 34; Kenneth Barry, "Residents March in Protest of Gymnasium Construction," *Columbia Daily Spectator* (May 2, 1968): 1, 3; "Columbia Offers to Meet Leaders of Harlem on Gym," *New York Times* (May 2, 1968): 1, 42; Peter Kihss, "Parks Chief Has Plans for Gym Site," *New York Times* (May 2, 1968): 43; Sylvan Fox, "Columbia Study of Crisis Ordered by Faculty Unit," *New York Times* (May 3, 1968): 1, 32; "The Two Columbias," *Newsweek* 71 (May 20, 1968): 63; Sylvan Fox, "Columbia Trustee Assails Hoving as Foe of Gym," *New York Times* (May 22, 1968): 51; Simon James [James Kunen], "Diary of a Revolutionist, Part I," *New York* 1 (May 27, 1968): 12–17; "Architectural Students Join Columbia Strikes: Out of Chaos, Maturity," *Progressive Architecture* 49 (June 1968): 45; "Colleges Learn Their Urban ABCs," *Business Week* (June 1, 1968): 94–96, 98–99; Murray Schumack, "The Columbia Gymnasium Remains a Problem After 10 Years of Planning," *New York Times* (June 2, 1968): 47; George and Patricia Nash, "Leads Columbia Could Have Followed," *New York* 1 (June 3, 1968): 38–41; Marvin Harris, "Big Bust on Morningside Heights," *Nation* 206 (June 10, 1968): 757–63; Simon James [James Kunen], "Diary of a Revolutionist, Part II," *New York* 1 (June 24, 1968): 34–41; George Nash and Cynthia Epstein, "New York Opinion: Harlem Views Columbia University," *New York* 1 (July 8, 1968): 58–60; David Bird, "Hoving Denies He 'Stimulated' Columbia Unrest," *New York Times* (July 24, 1968): 38; Roger Starr, "Morningside Defense," letter to the editor, *Architectural Forum* 129 (September 1968): 24; "Calm at Columbia?" *Time* 91 (September 27, 1968): 56–57; Victor Crichton, "Morningside Rebuttal," letter to the editor, *Architectural Forum* 129 (October 1968): 16, 22; "The Talk of the Town: Columbia," *New Yorker* 44 (October 5, 1968): 41–44; Sylvan Fox, "Cox Report Finds Columbia Policy 'Invited Mistrust,'" *New York Times* (October 6, 1968): 1, 82; "New Gym Site Plan Presented," *Columbia Daily Spectator* (October 29, 1968): 1, 3; David Bird, "Harlem Architects Urge Amphitheater for Morningside Park," *New York Times* (October 29, 1968): 18; Jack Newfield, "Setting Matters Straight at Columbia," *New York* 1 (November 25, 1968): 68–69; James Kunen, *The Strawberry Statement* (New York: Random House, 1969); Priscilla Tucker, "Poor People's Plan," *Metropolitan Museum of Art Bulletin* 27 (January 1969): 265–69; "Columbia to Decide Whether to Build Gym in Morningside Park on a Poll of Local Leaders," *New York Times* (February 16, 1969): 46; C. Gerald Fraser, "2 Groups Protest Columbia's Move to Revive Plans for Gym," *New York Times* (February 26, 1969): 22; Maurice Carroll, "Columbia Yielding on Its Gym in Park," *New York Times* (February 28, 1969): 1–2; "Columbia's New Approach," editorial, *New York Times* (February 28, 1969): 38; Peter Millones, "Columbia Studies New Site for Gym," *New York Times* (March 1, 1969): 16; "Columbia Trustees Scrap the Gym-in-Park Plan," *New York Times* (March 4, 1969): 28; "Columbia Eats Gym Crow," *Architectural Forum* 130 (April 1969): 85–86; Roger Kahn, *The Battle for Morningside Heights* (New York: William Morrow, 1970); Richard Rosenkrantz, *Across the Barricades* (Philadelphia: Lippincott, 1971); Murray Schumach, "Columbia to Build Its Controversial Gym on Campus," *New York Times* (June 7, 1971): 1, 27; Murrach Schumach, "Once More, Columbia Starts Work on a New Gym," *New York Times* (July 28, 1972): 64; "6 Years After Furor, Columbia Will Get a Gymnasium," *New York Times* (September 23, 1974): 37, 58; Charles Kaiser, "Columbia Opens New Gymnasium," *New York Times* (December 3, 1974): 65; Jamie Katz, "The New Gym Has Something for Everyone," *Columbia College Today* 4 (April 1975): 16–19; Anthony Jackson, *A Place Called Home: A History of Low-Cost Housing in Manhattan* (Cambridge, Mass.: MIT Press, 1976), 269–70; Gutman and Plunz, "Anatomy of Insurrection," in Oliver, ed., *The Making of an Architect, 1881–1981*, 186, 191–98; "1968: The Year that Shaped a Generation," *Time*, special issue (1988): 28–29; Dunlap, *On Broadway*, 276.

66. "$1,000,000 Columbia Gymnasium Burns," *New York Times* (October 10, 1914): 11; "Need of University Hall," *New York Times* (October 16, 1914): 12; Thomas M. Jones, "Columbia's Makeshift 'Eyesore' Started 1896, Famous Fire 1914," *Columbia Alumni News* 32 (February 7, 1941): 5, 11; Clarence Lovejoy, "University Hall to Be Completed: New Gym in Annex," *Columbia Alumni News* 32 (February 7, 1941): 3–4, 11–13.

67. Drawings in the Drawings Collection, Avery Library, Columbia University.

68. Drawings in the Drawings Collection, Avery Library, Columbia University.

69. Drawings for all schemes in the Drawings Collection, Avery Library, Columbia University.

70. "Athletics at Columbia": 17. Also see Bird, "Hoving Denies He 'Stimulated' Columbia Unrest": 38.

71. "City Board Wary of Aid to Parents," *New York Times* (December 16, 1955): 31. Also see "Columbia Plans Public Play Area," *New York Times* (December 30, 1955): 21; "Athletics at Columbia": 14–18.

72. Gutman and Plunz, "Anatomy of Insurrection," in Oliver, ed., *The Making of an Architect, 1881–1981*, 196.

73. "Morningside's Late, Late Show": 56.

74. Alden, "Neighbors Assail Columbia Growth": 26.

75. Basil Patterson quoted in "Morningside's Late, Late Show": 56–57.

76. "School in No-Man's Land," *Progressive Architecture* 46 (October 1965): 68; White and Willensky, *AIA Guide* (1967), 201; "P.S. 36 Is Scaled for Very Small Pupils—And a Highly Urban Setting," *Architectural Record* 144 (November 1968): 152–53; Gayle and Cohen, *The Art Commission and the Municipal Art Society Guide to Manhattan's Outdoor Sculpture*, 328.

77. Quoted in Blumenthal, "Columbia Scores Gym-Plan Critics": 31.

78. Thomas P. F. Hoving quoted in Blumenthal, "Columbia Scores Gym-Plan Critics": 31.

79. Quoted in "Morningside's Late, Late Show": 58.

80. Lawrence Chamberlain quoted in "Morningside's Late, Late Show": 58.

81. Hoving, "Slums of Academe": 10. Also see Cox Commission, *Crisis at Columbia*, 80.

82. Huxtable, "How Not to Build a Symbol": 23.

83. Gutman and Plunz, "Anatomy of Insurrection," in Oliver, ed., *The Making of an Architect, 1881–1981*, 197.

84. "Enough Is Enough": 2.

85. The other members of the Cox Commission were the civil rights lawyer Anthony G. Amsterdam, the psychiatrist Dana Lyda Farnsworth, the sociologist Hylan Garnet Lewis and the trial lawyer and former federal judge Simon Hirsch Rifkind.

86. Harold F. McGuire quoted in Fox, "Columbia Trustee Assails Hoving as Foe of Gym": 51.

87. John Wheeler quoted in Fox, "Columbia Trustee Assails Hoving as Foe of Gym": 51.

88. Thomas P. F. Hoving quoted in Bird, "Hoving Denies He 'Stimulated' Columbia Unrest": 38.

89. "Columbia Seeks Master Planner," *New York Times* (April 15, 1968): 43; Sylvan Fox, "Columbia Hires Pei to Project Its Growth for Decades Ahead," *New York Times* (November 8, 1968): 1, 34; "Columbia's Olive Branch," *Architectural Forum* 129 (December 1968): 26; "Commissions," *Interiors* 128 (December 1968): 26; Marli Weiss, "Pei Reveals Details of Proposed Plans," *Columbia Daily Spectator* (May 8, 1969): 1; "Columbia Considers Gym Under Campus in Expansion Plan," *New York Times* (May 8, 1969): 49; Jerry Kopel, "Pei's Plans: Building and Rebuilding," *Columbia Daily Spectator* (September 29, 1969): 1, 3; Jerry Kopel, "Pei's Plans: The Middle Campus," *Columbia Daily Spectator* (September 30, 1969): 1, 6; Jerry Kopel, "Pei Plans Science Complex to Bolster Ailing Departments," *Columbia Daily Spectator* (October 1, 1969): 1, 4; Jerry Kopel, "Pei Proposes 21-Story Tower for Campus-Community Use," *Columbia Daily Spectator* (October 2, 1969): 1, 6; Jerry Kopel, "Pei Stresses Consultation in Developing Plan," *Columbia Daily Spectator* (October 3, 1969): 1; Ada Louise Huxtable, "Columbia Plan Includes Underground Expansion," *New York Times* (February 18, 1970): 1, 34; I. M. Pei & Partners, *Planning for Columbia University: An Interim Report* (March 1970); "Pei's Campus Plan Is Released," *Columbia University Newsletter* 11 (March 16, 1970): 3; "Columbia Goes Under," *Progressive Architecture* 51 (April 1970): 30; "Petersen: Pei Plan Will Proceed Slowly," *Columbia University Newsletter* 12 (September 23, 1970): 1; John Morris Dixon, "Building Over and Under," editorial, *Progressive Architecture* 54 (March 1973): 71–72; Robert Keating, "Columbia Devours the Upper West Side," *Village Voice* 25 (May 19, 1980): 1, 13–16; Gutman and Plunz, "Anatomy of Insurrection," in Oliver, ed., *The Making of an Architect, 1881–1981*, 210; Tom Robbins and Jack Newfield, "New York's 10 Worst Landlords," *Village Voice* 32 (August 18, 1987): 12–19. For McKim's campus plans of 1893 and 1903, see Stern, Gilmartin and Massengale, *New York 1900*, 405–10.

90. Andrew W. Cordier quoted in Fox, "Columbia Hires Pei to Project Its Growth for Decades Ahead": 1.

91. Cox Commission, *Crisis at Columbia*, 83–86.

92. See Architectural Advisory Council Minutes, May 3, 1966, quoted in Richard Oliver, "History VI: 1959–1968," in Oliver, ed., *The Making of an Architect, 1881–1981*, 180–81.

93. Huxtable, "Expansion at Columbia: A Restricted Vision and Bureaucracy Seen as Obstacles to Its Development": 34. Drawings in the Drawings Collection, Avery Library, Columbia University.

94. Oliver, "History VI: 1959–1968," in Oliver, ed., *The Making of an Architect, 1881–1981*, 181.

95. James Ridgeway, "Columbia's Real Estate Ventures," *New Republic* 158 (May 18, 1968): 15–18. Also see Peter Kihss, "Columbia Spurs Massive Renewal North of 125th St.," *New York Times* (May 14, 1968): 1, 34.

96. Kihss, "Columbia Spurs Massive Renewal North of 125th St.": 1.

97. "Riverside Park Community," *Architectural Record* 144 (November 1968): 41.

98. *The New City: Architecture and Urban Renewal*, exhibition catalogue (New York: Museum of Modern Art, 1967). Also see Ada Louise Huxtable, "Planning the New City," *New York Times* (January 24, 1967): 39, 45.

99. Arnold Beichman, "Where Does Columbia Go from Here?" *New York* 1 (May 27, 1968): 18–23. Also see Percival Goodman, "A Second Campus?" *Columbia Forum* 12 (September 1969): 44–46.

100. I. M. Pei & Partners, *Planning for Columbia University: An Interim Report*, 27.

101. I. M. Pei quoted in "Columbia Goes Under": 30.

102. I. M. Pei & Partners, *Planning for Columbia University: An Interim Report*, 81–86; Robbins and Newfield, "New York's 10 Worst Landlords": 13.

103. I. M. Pei & Partners, *Planning for Columbia University: An Interim Report*, 22. Also see Peter Blake, "I. M. Pei & Partners," *Architecture Plus* 1 (March 1973): 20–25.

104. William J. McGill quoted in "6 Years After Furor, Columbia Will Get a Gymnasium": 37.
105. Drawings in the Drawings Collection, Avery Library, Columbia University.
106. William J. McGill quoted in "6 Years After Furor, Columbia Will Get a Gymnasium": 37.
107. "Buildings in the News," *Architectural Record* 145 (January 1969): 41; "Columbia Omnibuilding Accommodates Community," *Progressive Architecture* 50 (February 1969): 33; Elisabeth K. Thompson, "Teachers College, Columbia," *Architectural Record* 145 (May 1969): 145, 156–57.
108. "Columbia Continues Its Building Boom," *Progressive Architecture* 50 (March 1969): 43, 45.
109. Richard Briffault, "Fairchild Center to Enable Department to Expand Faculty, Research Staff," *Columbia Daily Spectator* (November 2, 1973): 1, 7; Gail Robinson, "Columbia Given $6.5 Million; Biology Tower Plans Released. Grant Will Cover Half of Costs," *Columbia Daily Spectator* (November 2, 1973): 1, 7; "In Context at Columbia," *Architectural Forum* 140 (March 1974): 8; "Buildings on the Way Up," *Progressive Architecture* 55 (March 1974): 20–21; Lou Antonelli, "Fairchild Tower: Close, but . . . ," *Columbia Daily Spectator* (September 30, 1976): 1–2; Paul Goldberger, "Science Building Marks New Day for Architecture at Columbia U.," *New York Times* (October 25, 1977): 41; Ada Louise Huxtable, "A Stylish New Building at Columbia," *New York Times* (December 11, 1977), II: 35–36; Suzanne Stephens, "The New College Try," *Progressive Architecture* 59 (March 1978): 53; Martin Filler, "Hail Columbia," *Progressive Architecture* 59 (March 1978): 54–59; *Mitchell/Giurgola Architects*, foreword by Kenneth Frampton (New York: Rizzoli International Publications, 1983), 8, 152–55.
110. Filler, "Hail Columbia": 54.
111. Goldberger, "Science Building Marks New Day for Architecture at Columbia U.": 41.
112. Huxtable, "A Stylish New Building at Columbia": 35.
113. Stephens, "The New College Try": 53.
114. Filler, "Hail Columbia": 58–59.
115. Jim Shaw, "Art History Struggles for Space," *Columbia Daily Spectator* (March 5, 1969): 1–2; "Art History May Move Underground," *Columbia Daily Spectator* (March 6, 1969): 1; I. M. Pei & Partners, *Planning for Columbia University: An Interim Report*, 36–41; "Avery Grows," *University Record* (September 12, 1974): 4–5; "Avery Library Will Be Enlarged," *Architectural Record* 156 (December 1974): 41; Ted Green, "Completion of Avery Project Threatened by Cost Overruns," *Columbia Daily Spectator* (September 11, 1975): 1, 3; Goldberger, "Science Building Marks New Day for Architecture at Columbia U.": 41; Suzanne Stephens, "Beneath the Halls of Ivy," *Progressive Architecture* 59 (March 1978): 60–61.
116. "News," *Pencil Points* 25 (February 1944): 105.
117. Goldberger, "Science Building Marks New Day for Architecture at Columbia U.": 41.
118. Stephens, "Beneath the Halls of Ivy": 61.
119. Goldberger, "Science Building Marks New Day for Architecture at Columbia U.": 41.
120. Goldberger, "Science Building Marks New Day for Architecture at Columbia U.": 41; Suzanne Stephens, "Saving Traces," *Progressive Architecture* 59 (March 1978): 62–63.
121. "Social Annex to Open Next Month, Law to Gain Berths in New Dorm," *Columbia Law School News* 32 (August 29, 1977): 1, 3; Goldberger, "Science Building Marks New Day for Architecture at Columbia U.": 41; "Greene Hall Dedicated," *Columbia Law School News* 32 (October 31, 1977): 1, 8; Jane Wyatt Strassner, "Greene Hall Dedicated," *Columbia Law Alumni Observer* 7 (February 20, 1978): 1, 5; Martin Filler, "Making It Legal," *Progressive Architecture* 59 (March 1978): 64–65; Brent C. Brolin, *Architecture in Context: Fitting New Buildings with Old* (New York: Van Nostrand Reinhold, 1980), 75; *Robert A. M. Stern: Buildings and Projects 1965–1980*, eds. Peter Arnell and Ted Bickford (New York: Rizzoli International Publications, 1981), 104–5.
122. "Architects Named for $15,000,000 Church Center on Morningside Heights," *Real Estate Record and Guide* 177 (February 25, 1956): 3; "Interchurch Center," *Architectural Forum* 109 (February 1958): 39; Ennis, "Morningside Building Boom Brightens the Area's Future": 1, 7; White and Willensky, *AIA Guide* (1978), 260.
123. For Riverside Church, see Stern, Gilmartin and Mellins, *New York 1930*, 146, 154.
124. Ennis, "Morningside Building Boom Brightens the Area's Future": 1, 7; White and Willensky, *AIA Guide* (1978), 260.
125. White and Willensky, *AIA Guide* (1978), 260.
126. Stern, Gilmartin and Mellins, *New York 1930*, 110.
127. White and Willensky, *AIA Guide* (1978), 287.
128. Stern, Gilmartin and Massengale, *New York 1900*, 402–3.
129. "Hospital Flag Blessed as St. Luke's Opens New Wing," *New York Times* (October 18, 1954): 4; Grutzner, "City's 'Acropolis' Combatting Slums": 32, 46.
130. David M. Alpern, "Reaction to Demolition Mixed," *Columbia Daily Spectator* (April 27, 1961): 1, 4; "First Baby Is Delivered in New Women's Hospital," *New York Times* (August 10, 1965): 26.
131. Fried, "Morningside Adds Buildings Other than 'Gym'": 1, 12.
132. Fried, "Morningside Adds Buildings Other than 'Gym'": 1.
133. "New Home for Aged Planned in Morningside Area," *New York Times* (October 30, 1967): 54; "The Morningside House for the Aged, New York City," *Architectural Record* 142 (December 1967): 43; White and Willensky, *AIA Guide* (1978), 352–53; Nory Miller and Richard Payne, *Johnson/Burgee: Architecture* (New York: Random House, 1979), 52–53.
134. "New Home for Aged Planned in Morningside Area": 54.
135. Stanley Randal, "The City Politic: Operation Move-In," *New York* 3 (July 6, 1970): 8–9; Murray Schumach, "Segregated Slum 'Threat' Fought on West Side," *New York Times* (July 21, 1970): 1, 27; Will Lissner, "Squatters Score Nearby Wrecking," *New York Times* (August 1, 1970): 35; Rudy Johnson, "250 from West Side Area Protest Delays on Renewal Program," *New York Times* (October 26, 1970): 15; Martin Gansberg, "Episcopal Church to Pay for Repairs for Squatters," *New York Times* (November 14, 1970): 33; Bell Gale Chevigny, "Operation Move-In, West Side Demolition: Squatter's Last Stand," *Village Voice* 16 (July 29, 1971): 1, 34; Edward C. Burks, "105 Police Arrive for a Quiet Eviction," *New York Times* (September 4, 1971): 7; "Squatters Carry Protest to Cathedral of St. John," *New York Times* (June 7, 1974): 39.
136. White and Willensky, *AIA Guide* (1978), 254; Goldberger, *The City Observed*, 278.
137. Goldberger, *The City Observed*, 278.
138. Bank Street College of Education, *Proposal for Support of Long-Term Development Program* (New York, 1964–65).
139. Edith Evans Asbury, "Pickets Mar Housing Dedication Here," *New York Times* (July 26, 1972): 8; "The Evolving Urban Architecture of Davis, Brody & Associates," *Architectural Record* 152 (August 1972): 97–106; Ada Louise Huxtable, "Breaking the Mold," *New York Times* (February 10, 1974), II: 22; White and Willensky, *AIA Guide* (1978), 209.
140. For the Woman's Hospital, see Stern, Gilmartin and Massengale, *New York 1900*, 404.
141. David A. Morton, "What General Didn't Know," *Progressive Architecture* 54 (October 1973): cover, 100–101; "Parkitecture Pro and Con," *Progressive Architecture* 54 (December 1973): 6; "Pop Monument," *Architectural Design* 44, no. 3 (1974): 193; Nancy Goldring, "The Greening of Grant's Tomb," *Art News* 75 (February 1974): 56; White and Willensky, *AIA Guide* (1978), 260; Goldberger, *The City Observed*, 284–85.
142. Stern, Gilmartin and Massengale, *New York 1900*, 396–402.
143. Stern, Gilmartin and Mellins, *New York 1930*, 151, 155–57.
144. Frank S. Adams, "10,000 in St. John's See Great Vista to Altar Opened," *New York Times* (December 1, 1941): 1, 3; "Cathedral of Saint John the Divine," *Architectural Forum* 76 (March 1942): 143–46.
145. "Monument for Manhattan," *Architectural Forum* 83 (July 1945): 9. Also see "Manning Delays Cathedral Drive," *New York Times* (October 15, 1945): 12.
146. "St. John the Divine: Started in Gothic. Should It Be Finished in Modern?" *Architectural Forum* 101 (December 1954): 112–17. Also see George Dugan, "Cathedral Faces a Design Problem," *New York Times* (February 26, 1955): 17.
147. James Marston Fitch, *Architecture and the Esthetics of Plenty* (New York: Columbia University Press, 1961), 203–15; "Guarantee Fulfilled," *Architectural Forum* 116 (February 1962): 9; George Collins and F. W. Kervick, "Guastavino's Vaults," letters to the editor, *Architectural Forum* 116 (June 1962): 20; George R. Collins, "The Transfer of Thin Masonry Vaulting from Spain to America," *Journal of the Society of Architectural Historians* 27 (October 1968): 176–201.
148. James Marston Fitch quoted in "St. John the Divine: Started in Gothic. Should It Be Finished in Modern?": 115.
149. Grant La Farge, "St. John the Divine," *Scribner's Magazine* 41 (April 1907): 401, quoted in "St. John the Divine: Started in Gothic. Should It Be Finished in Modern?": 115.
150. Major E. J. Peterson, letter to the editor, *Architectural Forum* 102 (March 1955): 75, 82. Also see "Modern St. John," letters to the editor, *Architectural Forum* 102 (February 1955): 74, 78, 82; Herbert T. Johnson and Rev. Massey H. Shepherd, Jr., letters to the editor, *Architectural Forum* 102 (March 1955): 75.
151. Pietro Belluschi, "The Challenge of St. John's Cathedral," *Architectural Forum* 102 (May 1955): 162–63. Also see Douglas Haskell, "For All Concerned," editorial, *Architectural Forum* 102 (May 1955): 172; Walker O. Cain, "St. John the Divine," letter to the editor, *Architectural Forum* 103 (August 1955): 76, 80; "They Say," *Journal of the American Institute of Architects* 24 (August 1955): 86–88; George Hersey, "St. John the Divine," letter to the editor, *Architectural Forum* 103 (December 1955): 88, 91.
152. "Completing a Cathedral—First Steps," *Architectural Forum* 103 (December 1955): 146–48.
153. Manfredo Nicoletti quoted in "Completing a Cathedral—First Steps": 148.
154. "The United States Air Force Academy," *Architectural Forum* 102 (June 1955): 102–9.
155. "For the Cathedral of St. John the Divine," *Architectural Record* 119 (June 1956): 186–89.
156. "St. John, the Unfinished," *Progressive Architecture* 47 (September 1966): 67. Also see "A Dome for the Divine," *New York Times* 88 (December 2, 1966): 78; Ada Louise Huxtable, "Of Symbolism and Flying Saucers," *New York Times* (December 4, 1966), II: 37, 40, reprinted in Ada Louise Huxtable, *Will They Ever Finish Bruckner Boulevard?* (New York: Macmillan, 1970), 195–98; "'Leave the Copestone to Posterity,'" editorial, *Christian Century* 83 (December 14, 1966): 1528–29; Walter C. Kidney, "St. John the Divine: A History of Happy Accidents?" letter to the editor, *Progressive Architecture* 48 (March 1967): 20.
157. Horace Donegan quoted in "A Dome for the Divine": 78.
158. "St. John, the Unfinished": 67.
159. Kidney, "St. John the Divine: A History of Happy Accidents?": 20.
160. Horace Donegan quoted in "St. John the Divine's Unfinished Symphony," editorial, *Christian Century* 84 (November 22, 1967): 1485–86. Also see Malcolm W. Browne, "St. John's to Remain Unfinished as a Sign of Anguish of Slums," *New York Times* (October 29, 1967): 1, 39; "St. John's to Remain Unfinished," *Progressive Architecture* 48 (December 1967): 29.

THE NEW WEST SIDE STORY

1. John V. Lindsay quoted in Nicholas Pileggi, "Renaissance of the Upper West Side," *New York* 2 (June 30, 1969): 28–39. Also see Murray Schumach, "Neighborhoods: West Side Is Undergoing Renaissance," *New York Times* (May 28, 1970): 41.
2. Pileggi, "Renaissance of the Upper West Side": 28.
3. Lewis Nichols quoted in Pileggi, "Renaissance of the Upper West Side": 32.
4. Lawrence Van Gelder, "Across Central Park, Hostile Worlds Cry 'En Garde!'" *New York Times* (November 30, 1969), VIII: 1, 4.
5. Pileggi, "Renaissance of the Upper West Side": 29–30.
6. "Egyptian Eatery," *Architectural Forum* 133 (September 1970): 5; Olga Gueft, "No Bangles for Cleopatra," *Interiors* 134 (February 1971): 77, 92–95; White and Willensky, *AIA Guide* (1978), 196.
7. Michael T. Kaufman, "New Restaurants Transform Columbus, Amsterdam Aves.," *New York Times* (July 24, 1974): 43, 49; Fred Ferretti, "Rediscovery of Columbus," *New York Times* (May 14, 1976), C: 13; White and Willensky, *AIA Guide* (1978), 180.
8. White and Willensky, *AIA Guide* (1978), 180.
9. William Robbins, "New Mayfair Tower Opens Alongside Venerable Dakota," *New York Times* (October 11, 1964), VIII: 1, 12; "Residential Refuse Disposal Unit First in City to Omit Incinerator," *New York Times* (January 3, 1965), VIII: 1–2; James Trager, *West of Fifth: The Rise and Fall and Rise of Manhattan's West Side* (New York: Atheneum, 1987), 110.
10. "Rounds Out a Site on Riverside Drive," *New York Times* (November 30, 1947), VIII: 1, 3; "New Apartment Being Erected at 70 Riverside Drive, 50% Leased," *Real Estate Record and Guide* 167 (June 30, 1951): 3; "West Side Myth Refuted," *Real Estate Record and Guide* 195 (February 13, 1965): 2–3.

11. Arnold H. Lubasch, "Central Park West Gets New Building," *New York Times* (July 2, 1967), VIII: 1, 6.

12. Robert E. Tomasson, "Luxury Housing Expands on West Side," *New York Times* (October 28, 1973), VIII: 1, 12.

13. Isadore Barmash, "New Alexander's to Rise at W. 96th," *New York Times* (March 19, 1969): 1, 59; Pileggi, "Renaissance of the Upper West Side": 30; Murray Schumach, "Neighborhoods: Alexander's Divides West Side," *New York Times* (January 31, 1970): 33, 38; Isadore Barmash, "Project Dropped by Alexander's," *New York Times* (July 2, 1970): 1, 60.

14. Barmash, "New Alexander's to Rise at W. 96th": 59.

15. Murray Siegel quoted in Schumach, "Neighborhoods: Alexander's Divides West Side": 33.

16. Henry Browne quoted in Schumach, "Neighborhoods: Alexander's Divides West Side": 38.

17. Jeff Brand quoted in Schumach, "Neighborhoods: Alexander's Divides West Side": 38.

18. Carter B. Horsley, "96th Street Development Set," *New York Times* (April 12, 1974), VIII: 1, 10; John L. Hess, "West Siders Seek to Save Theaters," *New York Times* (July 29, 1974): 27; "New York Intelligencer: West Side Ups and Downs," *New York* 7 (September 23, 1974): 72; Ted Wolner, "Christopher Boomis and the Blight of Broadway," *Village Voice* 19 (December 16, 1974): 43–44; Peter Kihss, "Apartment Tower at 96th May Include a Major Store," *New York Times* (February 18, 1975): 1, 35.

19. Christopher Boomis quoted in Kihss, "Apartment Tower at 96th May Include a Major Store": 35.

20. Charles Kaiser, "Developer Is Investigated on Pier-Building Contract," *New York Times* (June 5, 1975): 41.

21. John L. Hess, "Blockfront on Broadway Is Another Casualty of Boomis's Collapse," *New York Times* (March 2, 1976): 22; Nicholas Gage, "Secret Funds for Beame Campaign Reported Tied to Promise of Favor," *New York Times* (December 1, 1976): 1, 15; Charles Kaiser, "Charge by Boomis Found Unsupported," *New York Times* (April 2, 1977): 1, 33; David W. Dunlap, *On Broadway: A Journey Uptown Over Time* (New York: Rizzoli International Publications, 1990), 255.

22. White and Willensky, *AIA Guide* (1978), 183.

23. For Robert W. Gibson's Collegiate Dutch Reformed Church and School, see Stern, Gilmartin and Massengale, *New York 1900*, 87, 366.

24. Irving Stimmler quoted in Pileggi, "Renaissance of the Upper West Side": 30.

25. Judith Cummings, "School without Classrooms Unites Calhoun Students," *New York Times* (May 17, 1975): 31; White and Willensky, *AIA Guide* (1978), 184; Christopher Gray, "Schlock of Ages," *Avenue* 17 (December 1992): 31–32, 34, 36, 38.

26. White and Willensky, *AIA Guide* (1978), 184.

27. "Buildings on the Way Up," *Progressive Architecture* 53 (November 1972): 26; White and Willensky, *AIA Guide* (1978), 203. For the Progress Club, see Stern, Gilmartin and Massengale, *New York 1900*, 230–31.

28. "Child Care with Style," *Architectural Forum* 136 (January–February 1972): 6; White and Willensky, *AIA Guide* (1978), 193; White and Willensky, *AIA Guide* (1988), 313; Christopher Gray, "Streetscapes: West 80th Street Day Care Center," *New York Times* (March 13, 1988), X: 14, reprinted in Christopher Gray, *Changing New York: The Architectural Scene* (New York: Dover, 1992), 43.

29. White and Willensky, *AIA Guide* (1978), 203.

30. John Wicklein, "Crusading Cleric to Brighten Slum," *New York Times* (July 15, 1961): 10.

31. "Jewish Memorial to Rise on Drive," *New York Times* (June 19, 1947): 23; "Memorial Displayed at Jewish Museum," *New York Times* (November 23, 1948): 35.

32. "Memorial Model Shown at Museum," *New York Times* (January 18, 1950): 9.

33. "Plan Monument Here to Jews of Europe," *New York Times* (March 14, 1950): 13; Mitzi Salomon Cunliffe, "Sculpture for Architecture," *Progressive Architecture* 31 (December 1950): 63–65; "Erich Mendelsohn Dies," *Architectural Record* 114 (November 1953): 10–11; Arnold Whittick, *Erich Mendelsohn*, 2nd ed. (London: Leonard Hill, 1956), 169, 174, plates 73–74; Wolf Von Eckardt, *Eric Mendelsohn* (New York: George Braziller, 1960), 30–31, plates 102–3.

34. William E. Farrell, "City Rejects Park Memorials to Slain Jews," *New York Times* (February 11, 1965): 1, 9; William E. Farrell, "2 Jewish Leaders Protest Art Ban," *New York Times* (February 12, 1965): 31, 59; "Memorials in the Parks," editorial, *New York Times* (February 13, 1965): 20; Rebecca Read Shanor, *The City that Never Was* (New York: Viking, 1988), 219–20.

35. Eleanor Platt quoted in Farrell, "City Rejects Park Memorials to Slain Jews": 1.

36. "Memorials in the Parks": 20.

37. Joseph Lelyveld, "Model Play Area for Park Shown," *New York Times* (February 5, 1964): 37; "Out of the Sandbox," *Newsweek* 63 (February 17, 1964): 66; "Kahn-Noguchi Playground Proposed for New York," *Progressive Architecture* 45 (March 1964): 65, 67; Donald C. Mallow, "The Kahn-Noguchi Playground—One Reader's Protest," letter to the editor, *Progressive Architecture* 45 (May 1964): 8, 12, 16; "Giocare con la terra," *L'Architettura cronache e storia* 9 (September 1964): 338; Louis Kahn, "Remarks," *Perspecta* 9/10 (1965): 303–35; Samuel Kaplan, "Mayor Signs Pact for Play Center," *New York Times* (December 30, 1965): 31; Ralph Blumenthal, "Fight over Park Nearing Climax," *New York Times* (February 13, 1966): 63; Ralph Blumenthal, "Mayor Now Backs Levy Playground," *New York Times* (February 19, 1966): 28; Robert E. Tomasson, "City Is Enjoined on a Playground," *New York Times* (April 28, 1966): 45; "Playground Protest Turns to Cheers at Riverside Park," *New York Times* (May 2, 1966): 13; "The Sculptural World of Isamu Noguchi," *Interiors* 127 (May 1967): 6; Isamu Noguchi, *A Sculptor's World* (New York: Harper & Row, 1968), 177–79, plates 244–50; Martin Friedman, *Noguchi's Imaginary Landscapes*, exhibition catalogue (Minneapolis, Minn.: Walker Art Center, 1978), 50–51; Sam Hunter, *Isamu Noguchi* (New York: Abbeville Press, 1978), 51; Isamu Noguchi, *Isamu Noguchi: The Sculpture of Space*, exhibition catalogue (New York: Whitney Museum of American Art, 1980), 16; Nancy Grove, *Isamu Noguchi: A Study of Sculpture* (New York: Garland Publishing, 1985), 165–66, plate 189; Alessandra Latour, *Louis Kahn: Five Unbuilt Projects*, exhibition catalogue (New York: American Institute of Architects, 1986), unnumbered plates; David B. Brownlee and David G. De-Long, *Louis I. Kahn: In the Realm of Architecture*, with an intro. by Vincent Scully (New York: Rizzoli International Publications, 1991), 113–15.

38. Isamu Noguchi quoted in "Out of the Sandbox": 66.

39. Kahn, "Remarks": 330.

40. Lelyveld, "Model Play Area for Park Shown": 37.

41. Louis I. Kahn quoted in "Kahn-Noguchi Playground Proposed for New York": 67.

42. Noguchi, *A Sculptor's World*, 178.

43. Thomas P. F. Hoving quoted in Blumenthal, "Mayor Now Backs Levy Playground": 28.

44. M. Paul Friedberg, "Manhattan Protest," *Landscape Architecture* 59 (October 1968): cover, 43–44; White and Willensky, *AIA Guide* (1978), 195. For Snyder's building, see Stern, Gilmartin and Massengale, *New York 1900*, 447.

Chapter 10
Central Park

1. Marya Mannes, "The New York I Know: II. Central Park," *Reporter* 22 (January 21, 1960): 20–24.

2. Eugene Kinkead and Russell Maloney, "Central Park, Part I: Grass on Manhattan," *New Yorker* 17 (September 13, 1941): 24–28, 30, 32, 34, 36–37; Eugene Kinkead and Russell Maloney, "Central Park, Part II: A 'Nasty Place,'" *New Yorker* 17 (September 20, 1941): 34–38, 40, 42, 44–45; Eugene Kinkead and Russell Maloney, "Central Park, Part III: What a *Nice* Municipal Park!" *New Yorker* 17 (September 27, 1941): 23–26, 28, 31–33. For further general discussions of Central Park, see Henry Hope Reed and Sophia Duckworth, *Central Park: A History and Guide* (New York: Clarkson N. Potter, 1967); Nancy Johnston, *Central Park Country: A Tune Within Us* (San Francisco: Sierra Club, 1968); Elizabeth Barlow, *The Central Park Book* (New York: The Central Park Task Force, 1977); Henry Hope Reed, *Central Park: A Photographic Guide* (New York: Dover, 1979); M. M. Graff, *The Men Who Made Central Park* (New York: Greensward Foundation, 1982); Elizabeth Barlow, *Rebuilding Central Park: A Management and Restoration Plan* (New York: Central Park Conservancy, 1985); M. M. Graff, *Central Park, Prospect Park: A New Perspective* (New York: Greensward Foundation, 1985).

3. Kinkead and Maloney, "Central Park, Part I: Grass on Manhattan": 24.

4. Stern, Gilmartin and Mellins, *New York 1930*, 710–12.

5. Stern, Gilmartin and Mellins, *New York 1930*, 270–71, 280–81, 288, 712.

6. "City Plans Skating Rink," *New York Times* (May 12, 1945): 23; "Rink, Play Area in Central Park Provided in $600,000 Gift to City," *New York Times* (May 17, 1949): 1, 26; Max Stone, "Central Park Plan Opposed," letter to the editor, *New York Times* (May 25, 1949): 28; Ned Goldschmidt, "New Skating Rink Approved," letter to the editor, *New York Times* (June 1, 1949): 30; "Central Park Has a Spring Fling, Runs Up Bills Totaling $1,000,000," *New York Times* (June 7, 1950): 31; "City Has Yule Gift of a Skating Rink," *New York Times* (December 22, 1950): 14; "Thanks to Miss Wollman," editorial, *New York Times* (December 22, 1950): 22; Lewis Mumford, "The Sky Line: Artful Blight," *New Yorker* 27 (May 5, 1951): 84–90; "Roof-top Playground Opened in Central Park," *New York Times* (June 20, 1951): 29; W. A. Powers, "Once Around the Park," *Town & Country* 106 (March 1952): 52–53, 119, 121, 123, 126; Robert Moses, "Gifts to Central Park," *American City* 69 (April 1954): 94–95; Reed and Duckworth, *Central Park: A History and Guide*, 51, 108–10; Robert Moses, *Public Works: A Dangerous Trade* (New York: McGraw-Hill, 1970), 15; Barlow, *The Central Park Book*, 122–23; Barlow, *Rebuilding Central Park*, 13.

7. "Thanks to Miss Wollman": 22.

8. Mumford, "The Sky Line: Artful Blight": 84.

9. Mumford, "The Sky Line: Artful Blight": 85–86.

10. Mumford, "The Sky Line: Artful Blight": 87–88.

11. Moses, *Public Works: A Dangerous Trade*, 14.

12. Richard J. M. Johnston, "Stroll Confirms Neglect of Park," *New York Times* (May 17, 1950): 31.

13. Henry Hope Reed, "The Central Park Memorial Cemetery," *New York Times* (December 3, 1966): 38.

14. Laurie Johnston, "Carrousel Burns in Central Park," *New York Times* (November 9, 1950): 35; "Octagonal Unit to House Central Park Carrousel," *New York Times* (January 3, 1951): 44; "$75,000 for Carrousel," *New York Times* (January 19, 1951): 23; Laurie Johnston, "They're Off at 11, Mayor Riding, in Central Park's New Carrousel," *New York Times* (July 2, 1951): 25; Moses, "Gifts to Central Park": 94–95.

15. "Fixes Burned Carrousel," *New York Times* (September 14, 1951): 27.

16. "Park Checkers Shelter," *New York Times* (December 10, 1951): 31; "Photograph Spur to Chess Shelter," *New York Times* (December 12, 1951): 47; William B. Farrell, "Chess Players Await Vital Move—Into New Central Park Shelter," *New York Times* (August 12, 1952): 21; "The Talk of the Town: Jumping in the Kinderberg," *New Yorker* 28 (January 24, 1953): 19–20; C. B. Palmer, "Checkmating the Weather Man," *New York Times* (February 1, 1953), VI: 8; Moses, "Gifts to Central Park": 95; Stuart E. Jones, "Central Park, Manhattan's Big Outdoors," *National Geographic* 118 (December 1960): 780–811; Reed and Duckworth, *Central Park: A History and Guide*, 107–8.

17. "Park Checkers Shelter": 31.

18. "Park Boat House Is Gift of Couple," *New York Times* (September 2, 1952): 25; "The Talk of the Town: On the Water," *New Yorker* 28 (November 1, 1952): 25; New York City, Department of Parks, *The New Boat House*, opening program (New York, 1953); "Parks Boat House Opened by Mayor," *New York Times* (March 13, 1954): 9; Moses, "Gifts to Central Park": 94–95; "The Talk of the Town: Notes and Comments," *New Yorker* 30 (April 17, 1954): 23; "Honoring the Carl Loebs," editorial, *New York Times* (April 30, 1954): 22; Reed and Duckworth, *Central Park: A History and Guide*, 82–83; White and Willensky, *AIA Guide* (1967), 151.

19. Moses, "Gifts to Central Park": 95. Also see "New Model Yacht Boat House Is Gift of Mrs. J. E. Kerbs to Central Park," *New York Times* (February 2, 1953): 23; Reed and Duckworth, *Central Park: A History and Guide*, 80.

20. New York City, Department of Parks, *Construction Schedule 1946–1947* (New York, 1946), 12–13, 15; "Rowing on 110th St. Lake in Park, Stopped in 1941, Begins Tomorrow," *New York Times* (August 7, 1947): 23; Powers, "Once Around the Park": 52–53, 119, 121, 123; White and Willensky, *AIA Guide* (1967), 153.

21. Barlow, *The Central Park Book*, 37; Graff, *Central Park, Prospect Park: A New Perspective*, 135.

22. "Danes and World Praise Andersen," *New York Times* (April 3, 1955): 30; Jones, "Central Park, Manhattan's Big Outdoors": 795; Margot Gayle and Michele Cohen, *The Art Commission and the Municipal Art Society Guide to Manhattan's Outdoor Sculpture* (New York: Prentice Hall Press, 1988), 221.

23. Richard Morris Hunt, *Designs for the Gateways of the Southern Entrances to the Central Park* (New York, 1866); Paul R. Baker, *Richard Morris Hunt* (Cambridge, Mass.: MIT Press, 1980), 146–61.

24. Stern, Gilmartin and Massengale, *New York 1900,* 129.

25. Lewis Mumford, "The Sky Line: Big Buildings and Tremendous Trifles," *New Yorker* 27 (December 22, 1951): 60–65; Powers, "Once Around the Park": 123; White and Willensky, *AIA Guide* (1967), 136; Paul Goldberger, *The City Observed: New York* (New York: Random House, 1979), 181; Gayle and Cohen, *The Art Commission and the Municipal Art Society Guide to New York,* 235, 237.

26. Mumford, "The Sky Line: Big Buildings and Tremendous Trifles": 64–65.

27. "Venezuela Pays $218,400 to Shift Bolivar Statue," *New York Times* (June 28, 1950): 23; "Topics of The Times," *New York Times* (October 30, 1950): 26; "Statue of Bolivar Put upon Pedestal," *New York Times* (April 12, 1951): 26; "Statue of San Martin Is Dedicated Here as a Symbol of Friendship of the Americas," *New York Times* (May 26, 1951): 5; "Topics of The Times," *New York Times* (June 11, 1951): 24.

28. "Revolt Won't Bar Statue Here Honoring Cuban National Hero," *New York Times* (January 24, 1959): 3; "The Pedestal Is Ready, but Where Is the Statue?" *New York Times* (April 13, 1960): 41; "Disputed Statue of Cuban to Go Up," *New York Times* (January 27, 1965): 37; "Statue of Cuban Hero Out in Open," *New York Times* (April 3, 1965): 31; McCandlish Phillips, "Statue of Cuban Finally Placed," *New York Times* (April 20, 1965): 41; "Marti Statue Unveiled After a 7-Year Wait," *New York Times* (May 19, 1965): 49; Gayle and Cohen, *The Art Commission and the Municipal Art Society Guide to Manhattan's Outdoor Sculpture,* 236.

29. Mumford, "The Sky Line: Big Buildings and Tremendous Trifles": 65.

30. "Park Wonderland Is in Making for Bronze Alice and Friends," *New York Times* (May 23, 1958): 25; "Alice Welcomes Home in Park," *New York Times* (May 8, 1959): 29; "The Talk of the Town: Alice and Her Friends," *New Yorker* 35 (May 23, 1959): 31–32; Jones, "Central Park, Manhattan's Big Outdoors": 795; White and Willensky, *AIA Guide* (1967), 151; Gayle and Cohen, *The Art Commission and the Municipal Art Society Guide to Manhattan's Outdoor Sculpture,* 222.

31. George T. Delacorte quoted in Gayle and Cohen, *The Art Commission and the Municipal Art Society Guide to Manhattan's Outdoor Sculpture,* 222.

32. "Oldsters' Center to Be Built in City," *New York Times* (May 30, 1955): 15; "For the Older People," editorial, *New York Times* (June 1, 1955): 32; Jerome C. O'Brien, "Central Park Plan Opposed," letter to the editor, *New York Times* (June 3, 1955): 23; Kathleen Green Skelton, "To Preserve the Ramble," letter to the editor, *New York Times* (June 7, 1955): 32; Daniel Chase, "Enjoying Central Park," letter to the editor, *New York Times* (June 20, 1955): 20; Robert Cushman Murphy, "Preserving Central Park Area," letter to the editor, *New York Times* (June 22, 1955): 29; Edwin L. Dale, Jr., "Plan for Ramble Upheld by Moses," *New York Times* (September 5, 1955): 13; Murray Illson, "Bird Lovers Balk at Moses Project," *New York Times* (October 2, 1955): 54; William Vogt, "To Preserve the Ramble," letter to the editor, *New York Times* (October 13, 1955): 31; John B. Oakes, "Conservation: A Growing Force," *New York Times* (November 13, 1955), II: 33; "Compromise for the Ramble Is Pressed on Park Tour," *New York Times* (November 27, 1955): 1, 86; "Art Group Fights Ramble Buildings," *New York Times* (November 29, 1955): 26; Amelia G. Hull, "To Preserve the Ramble," letter to the editor, *New York Times* (November 30, 1955): 32; Paul Crowell, "Naturalists Win Battle of Ramble," *New York Times* (December 1, 1955): 37; "Battle of the Ramble," *New York Times* (December 2, 1955): 26; Robert Moses, "The Moses Recipe for Better Parks," *New York Times* (January 8, 1956), VI: 13, 47–48; "The Talk of the Town: Long War," *New Yorker* 32 (July 28, 1956): 16–17.

33. O'Brien, "Central Park Plan Opposed": 23.

34. Crowell, "Naturalists Win Battle of Ramble": 37.

35. "Tavern-On-Green Being Renovated," *New York Times* (January 18, 1956): 33; "37 Fight for a Bit of Central Park," *New York Times* (April 14, 1956): 38; "Central Park Mothers Vanquish Bulldozer Set to Raze Play Area," *New York Times* (April 18, 1956): 33; "Moses Shifts Plans on Siege in Park," *New York Times* (April 20, 1956): 11; "Only a Half Acre—But," editorial, *New York Times* (April 20, 1956): 24; "Battle Renewed over Play Area," *New York Times* (April 21, 1956): 20; Max Frankel, "Moses Fences Off Park Area at Night," *New York Times* (April 24, 1956): 1, 23; Murray Schumach, "Construction of Parking Lot Begun in Central Park," *New York Times* (April 25, 1956): 37; Phyllis Wheelock, "Park Change Protested," letter to the editor, *New York Times* (April 26, 1956): 33; "Isaacs Skeptical on Park Project," *New York Times* (April 26, 1956): 35; "Court Stops Job in Central Park," *New York Times* (April 27, 1956): 29; "Court Adjourned to Lot in the Park," *New York Times* (April 28, 1956): 19; "Moses & the Bulldozer," *New York Times* (April 29, 1956), VI: 2; "Central Park Auto Lot Foes Fear Tavern May Want Airstrip Next," *New York Times* (May 1, 1956): 35; Clarence Kean, "Isaacs Will Seek Tavern Inquiry," *New York Times* (May 2, 1956): 33; "Park-Side Residents Gain Writ to Stay Parking Lot for Tavern," *New York Times* (May 3, 1956): 1, 23; "4-Day Delay Won in Battle of Park," *New York Times* (May 4, 1956): 27; "Moses Attacks 'Noisy Minority' in Battle over Tavern Parking," *New York Times* (May 27, 1956): 1, 71; Charles G. Bennett, "Moses Yields to Mothers; Drops Tavern Parking Lot," *New York Times* (July 18, 1956): 1, 21; "The Talk of the Town: Long War": 16–17; "Central Park Play Site Opens, a Quiet Victory," *New York Times* (April 27, 1957): 21; John B. Keeley, "Moses on the Green," in *Inter-University Case Program: Case Study #45* (Tuscaloosa, Ala.: University of Alabama Press, 1959), 1–7; Reed and Duckworth, *Central Park: A History and Guide,* 65–66; Moses, *Public Works: A Dangerous Trade,* 14–15; Robert A. Caro, *The Power Broker: Robert Moses and the Fall of New York* (New York: Alfred A. Knopf, 1974), 984–1004.

36. Stanley M. Isaacs quoted in Caro, *The Power Broker,* 990.

37. Stanley M. Isaacs quoted in "Central Park Mothers Vanquish Bulldozer Set to Raze Play Area": 33.

38. "Only a Half Acre—But": 24.

39. Caro, *The Power Broker,* 996.

40. Samuel H. Hofstadter quoted in "Park-Side Residents Gain Writ to Stay Parking Lot for Tavern": 1, 23.

41. W. Averell Harriman quoted in "Moses & the Bulldozer": 2.

42. Robert Moses quoted in "Moses Attacks 'Noisy Minority' in Battle over Tavern Parking": 1.

43. "The Talk of the Town: Long War": 16.

44. Louis Calta, "Park Troupe Told to End Free Plays," *New York Times* (April 16, 1959): 35; Judith Crist, "No Free Shakespeare in Park, Moses Rules," *New York Herald Tribune* (April 16, 1959): 1; "Mr. Moses Vs. Free Shakespeare," editorial, *New York Herald Tribune* (April 16, 1959): 18; "City Aides Defend Free Park Plays," *New York Times* (April 17, 1959): 27; Louis Calta, "Bellamy, Lotito Hit Moses Stand," *New York Times* (April 18, 1959): 19; "Shakespeare in the Park," editorial, *New York Times* (April 18, 1959): 22; Brooks Atkinson, "Moses and Shakespeare," *New York Times* (April 20, 1959): 35; "Plays in the Park Get Councilman's Aid," *New York Times* (April 21, 1959): 37; "Park Plays Ruling Scored by Equity," *New York Times* (April 22, 1959): 35; "Isaacs Disputes Moses on Theater," *New York Times* (April 27, 1959): 22; Louis Calta, "Phoenix Begins Subscriber Drive," *New York Times* (April 29, 1959): 28; William Haddad, "Moses Sends Out Unsigned Attack on Park Producer," *New York Post* (April 29, 1959): 4; "The Park—And the Gutter," *New York Post* (April 29, 1959): 45; Arthur Gelb, "Moses Airs Attack on Play Producer," *New York Times* (April 30, 1959): 1; Arthur Gelb, "Papp Supported on Play Festival," *New York Times* (May 1, 1959): 31; Charles G. Bennett, "Wagner Plans Talk with Moses Today," *New York Times* (May 2, 1959): 25; "Tenacious Producer: Joseph Papp," *New York Times* (May 2, 1959): 47; Henry Machirella, "Moses Says Bard Can't Park, He Blames Hoods in the Woods," *New York Daily News* (May 2, 1959): 3; Charles G. Bennett, "Wagner Hopeful on Plays in Park," *New York Times* (May 5, 1959): 35; Judith Crist, "Shakespeare-in-Park Feud Waxes," *New York Herald Tribune* (May 5, 1959): 1; "Park Play Fight Still Unsettled," *New York Times* (May 7, 1959): 17; Charles G. Bennett, "Mayor Backs Moses on Fee for Shakespeare in Park," *New York Times* (May 12, 1959): 1; "Free Shakespeare," editorial, *New York Times* (May 13, 1959): 36; Farnsworth Fowle, "Park Play Talks Break Up in Huff," *New York Times* (May 15, 1959): 31; Henry Machirella and Jack Smee, "Park Shakespeare Down—And Out," *New York Daily News* (May 15, 1959): 10; Brooks Atkinson, "Theater: Sound and Fury," *New York Times* (May 16, 1959): 17; Layhmond Robinson, "Mayor, Irritated, Gives Dispute over Park Plays a Low Priority," *New York Times* (May 16, 1959): 1; Sam Pope Brewer, "Dispute on Plays 'Closed' by Moses," *New York Times* (May 18, 1959): 1; Layhmond Robinson, "Moses Ordered to Court in Dispute on Park Plays," *New York Times* (May 19, 1959): 1; Layhmond Robinson, "Mayor Requests Silence by Moses," *New York Times* (May 20, 1959): 37; "The Talk of the Town: Notes and Comment," *New Yorker* 35 (May 23, 1959): 31; Layhmond Robinson, "Moses Vetoes Bid to Talks on Plays," *New York Times* (May 23, 1959): 1; "Papp Miscasts Him, Moses Complains," *New York Times* (May 29, 1959): 25; Arthur Gelb, "Moses Wins Case on Plays in Park," *New York Times* (June 3, 1959): 1; "Papp Asks Court Speed," *New York Times* (June 10, 1959): 43; "The Law and Mr. Moses," editorial, *New York Post* (June 18, 1959), III: 57; Peter Kihss, "Court Bids Moses Retreat on Bard," *New York Times* (June 18, 1959): 33; Louis Calta, "Show Will Go On if Papp Gets Bond," *New York Times* (June 19, 1959): 1; "As Shakespeare Said," editorial, *New York Times* (June 19, 1959): 24; Charles G. Bennett, "Moses Asks Funds by City for Plays," *New York Times* (June 20, 1959): 23; Charles G. Bennett, "Two Gifts Assure Free Park Plays," *New York Times* (June 24, 1959): 1; Charles G. Bennett, "Papp Is Assailed as Show Is Voted," *New York Times* (June 26, 1959): 27; John Sack, "The Good Earth," *New Yorker* 35 (July 4, 1959): 23–24; Robert Alden, "Papp Troupe Returns to Park," *New York Times* (July 10, 1959): 30; Arthur Gelb, "Papp and Troupe Returns to Park," *New York Times* (August 4, 1959): 30; "Moses Asks City for $250,000 for Park Shakespeare Theater," *New York Times* (August 20, 1959): 1; "Shakespeare in the Park," *New York Times* (August 22, 1959): 16; Jones, "Central Park, Manhattan's Big Outdoors": 804. For an extensive bibliography on the New York Shakespeare Festival, see Christine E. King, *Joseph Papp and the New York Shakespeare Festival: Annotated Bibliography* (New York: Garland Publishing, 1988).

45. Louis Calta, "Theater: Shakespearean Workshop," *New York Times* (October 29, 1955): 12; "Open-Air Theater to Do Bard Here," *New York Times* (March 28, 1956): 26; "Stratford on East River Opens with Julius Caesar under Stars," *New York Times* (June 30, 1956): 19; Arthur Gelb, "Theater: Rained Out," *New York Times* (August 11, 1956): 11; Lewis Funke, "City to Recreate Shakespeare Era," *New York Times* (November 28, 1957): 33.

46. Calta, "Park Troupe Told to End Free Plays": 35.

47. Arthur Gelb, "Broadway Plans for Mrs. Bridge," *New York Times* (May 11, 1959): 30; Louis Calta, "L.I. Site Proposed to Papp for Plays," *New York Times* (May 13, 1959): 39.

48. "The Talk of the Town: Notes and Comment": 31.

49. Quoted in Kihss, "Court Bids Moses Retreat on Bard": 33.

50. "Shakespeare in the Park," editorial, *New York Times* (October 20, 1959): 38.

51. "Trustees Proposed for Park Theater," *New York Times* (October 20, 1959): 45; Charles G. Bennett, "Miss Hayes Plays City Hall's Stage," *New York Times* (November 19, 1959): 41; Brooks Atkinson, "Bard in the Park Plans for Fifth Season of Free Shakespeare," *New York Times* (January 10, 1960), II: 1; "Unit Sought to Aid Park's Shakespeare," *New York Times* (February 2, 1960): 39; Louis Calta, "Wagner Supports Free Park Shows," *New York Times* (March 9, 1960): 39; "Park Association Objects to Cafe," *New York Times* (April 8, 1960): 33.

52. Sam Zolotow, "Shakespeare Tour Planned," *New York Times* (January 2, 1962): 24.

53. "Shakespeare Festival Light Tower Stirs Complaints," *New York Times* (April 6, 1962): 24; ". . . In Central Park, for Instance," editorial, *New York Times* (April 7, 1962): 24; Louis Calta, "Tower Is Shifted at Park Theater," *New York Times* (May 23, 1962): 37; Myron Kandel, "The Bard's New Home in the Park," *New York Times* (May 27, 1962), II: 1; Paul Gardner, "Central Park's Shakespeare Amphitheater Dedicated," *New York Times* (June 19, 1962): 28; "New Theater in Central Park," *Architectural Record* 132 (August 1962): 15; White and Willensky, *AIA Guide* (1967), 151; Goldberger, *The City Observed,* 191.

54. "City, Papp Agree on a Theater," *New York Post* (August 7, 1974): 50; Paul Goldberger, "New Theater in Park as Planned to Replace Delacorte," *New York Times* (August 7, 1974): 1, 22; Paschall Campbell, "Central Park Encroachment," letter to the editor, *New York Times* (August 22, 1974): 32; Paul Goldberger, "Parks Chief Is Now Opposing New Theater to Papp Festival," *New York Times* (September 4, 1974): 1, 54; "Too Solid Concrete," editorial, *New York Times* (September 6, 1974): 32.

55. "Too Solid Concrete": 32.

56. Mark Lieberman, "Peeved Papp May Relocate Shakespeare," *New York Daily News* (September 4, 1974): 38.

57. Louis Calta, "Papp Starts $780,000 Drive for Delacorte," *New York Times* (February 10, 1976): 42; Philip Dougherty, "Aid for Delacorte," *New York Times* (February 10, 1976): 62; "The Shakespeare Free," editorial, *New York Times* (June 16, 1976): 38.

58. "Hartford Gives City a Cafe for Central Park," *New York Times* (March 14, 1960): 1, 23; "In Central Park—No," editorial, *New York Times* (March 17, 1960): 32; David Sher, John A. Ward, Toni Fredella and Gerome C. O'Brien, "Park Cafe Discussed," letters to the editor, *New York Times* (March 24, 1960): 32; "Every Foot of the Park," editorial, *New York Times* (April 19, 1960): 36; Joseph Wechsberg, "'April in Paris' for New York," *New York Times* (April 24, 1960): 42–43, 57; *The Hartford Pavilion in Central Park,* pamphlet (New York: Huntington Hartford Family Fund, Inc., April 26, 1960); "A Sidewalk Cafe in Central Park," *Architectural Forum* 112 (May 1960): 65; "Gift to New York: A $500,000 Cafe in Central Park," *Progressive Architecture* 41 (May 1960): 18;

"Moses Adamant on Cafe in Park," *New York Times* (May 2, 1960): 1, 30; "Up in Central Park," editorial, *New York Times* (May 3, 1960): 38; "Eating Mr. Hartford's Cake," editorial, *New York Times* (May 21, 1960): 22; Ira Henry Freeman, "Gift of Park Cafe May Get Hearing," *New York Times* (May 25, 1960): 41; "Central Park Democracy," editorial, *New York Times* (May 26, 1960): 32; "The Talk of the Town: Notes and Comment," *New Yorker* 36 (June 11, 1960): 25; "Park Pavilion, 71 No, 23 Yes," editorial, *New York Times* (June 17, 1960): 30; Gay Talese, "Tiffany's Sues to Bar Park Cafe Lest Portent of 1928 Come True," *New York Times* (July 8, 1960): 1, 15; "At the Barricades," *Newsweek* 56 (July 18, 1960): 66; Peter Kihss, "Parkland Sliced by City Road Jobs," *New York Times* (July 28, 1960): 29, 54; Paul Crowell, "City Accepts Gift for Cafe in Park," *New York Times* (July 29, 1960): 1, 6; "Central Park Cafe Voted by City Board," *Progressive Architecture* 41 (September 1960): 66; "Tiffany Ends Suit to Bar Park Cafe," *New York Times* (September 2, 1960): 1, 17; Jones, "Central Park, Manhattan's Big Outdoors": 802; Thomas W. Ennis, "Design for Park Cafe Finished; Work Expected to Begin Soon," *New York Times* (February 2, 1961): 17; "Cost of Park Cafe Rises to $1,712,000," *New York Times* (June 10, 1961): 12; John A. Ward, "Proposed Restaurant Questioned on Financial and Other Grounds," letter to the editor, *New York Times* (September 16, 1961): 18; John Sibley, "Suit on Park Cafe Upheld on Appeal," *New York Times* (December 9, 1961): 29; Edward Durell Stone, *The Evolution of an Architect* (New York: Horizon Press, 1962), 226; "$5,000 Brochure Carried New Plea for Cafe in Park," *New York Times* (March 12, 1962): 33; "The Park Cafe Sales Pitch," editorial, *New York Times* (March 14, 1962): 38; Richard G. Blaine, Sidney V. Haas, M.D., Joseph B. Bohan, Dolores B. Lamanna, Alex Saybell and Paul Kver, "Comments on Park Cafe," letters to the editor, *New York Times* (March 22, 1962): 34; "Suit to Block Restaurant in Central Park Is Begun," *New York Times* (June 18, 1963): 26; "Park Cafe Would Damage 5th Avenue Area, Court Told," *New York Times* (June 27, 1963): 19; "Tempers Enliven Park Cafe Trial," *New York Times* (July 3, 1963): 29; John Sibley, "Cafe-Pavilion Plan for Central Park Is Upheld by Court," *New York Times* (August 27, 1963): 1, 19; "It's Only a Park—Build on It," editorial, *New York Times* (August 28, 1963): 32; Giorgio Cavaglieri, "Ruling on Cafe Deplored," letter to the editor, *New York Times* (September 6, 1963): 28; Philip H. Hiss, "Huntington Hartford: A Most Unusual Client," *Architectural Forum* 120 (March 1964): 112–13; "Park Cafe Plan Upheld by Court," *New York Times* (March 27, 1964): 13; "That Unnecessary Cafe," editorial, *New York Times* (March 30, 1964): 28; "City Wins the Right to Build Park Cafe with Hartford Gift," *New York Times* (March 12, 1965): 1, 22; Ada Louise Huxtable, "More on How to Kill a City," *New York Times* (March 21, 1965), II: 17; "That Expendable Park Cafe," editorial, *New York Times* (May 18, 1965): 38; "The Talk of the Town: Escape from Buildings," *New Yorker* 41 (May 29, 1965): 20–21; "A Hartford Saloon for Central Park," *Progressive Architecture* 46 (June 1965): 51–52; John V. Lindsay, "The Hartford Pavilion," letter to the editor, *Progressive Architecture* 46 (September 1965): 12; Joseph Hudak, "The Hartford Pavilion," letter to the editor, *Progressive Architecture* 46 (September 1965): 12, 16; Newbold Morris, "The Hartford Pavilion," letter to the editor, *Progressive Architecture* 46 (September 1965): 16; Thomas P. F. Hoving, *Parks and Recreation*, issued by John V. Lindsay (New York, October 8, 1965), 7, supplement: 12; "New Parks Chief: Hoving to Write 'Finis' to Era of Robert Moses," *Village Voice* 11 (December 2, 1965): 3; Ralph Blumenthal, "Park Cafe Plan Appears Doomed," *New York Times* (February 16, 1966): 1, 24; "Hoving Asks Return of Park Cafe Funds," *New York Times* (March 5, 1966): 8; "The Kiosk & the Curator," *Progressive Architecture* 47 (April 1966): 74; Richard J. H. Johnston, "Hartford Loses in New Cafe Bid," *New York Times* (August 19, 1966): 39; "Offer by Hartford Ends His Dispute with Parks Chief," *New York Times* (August 10, 1966): 22; Theodore J. Strongin, "Old Met Is Given Deposit Deadline," *New York Times* (August 17, 1966): 41; Richard J. H. Johnston, "Much Heat, If Little Light, Shed in Debate on Central Park Cafe," *New York Times* (August 18, 1966): 37.

59. Huntington Hartford quoted in "A Sidewalk Cafe in Central Park": 65.

60. Huntington Hartford quoted in "Hartford Gives City a Cafe for Central Park": 23.

61. "In Central Park—No": 32.

62. Robert Moses quoted in "At the Barricades": 66.

63. Walter Hoving quoted in Talese, "Tiffany's Sues to Bar Cafe Lest Portent of 1928 Come True": 15.

64. Robert Moses, letter to Robert Wagner, quoted in Kihss, "Parkland Sliced by City Road Jobs": 54.

65. Jacob Markowitz quoted in "It's Only a Park—Build on It": 32.

66. Huxtable, "More on How to Kill a City": 17.

67. "That Expendable Park Cafe": 17.

68. Morris, "Hartford Pavilion": 16.

69. John V. Lindsay quoted in Hoving, *Parks and Recreation*, supplement: 12.

70. Thomas P. F. Hoving quoted in Johnston, "Hartford Loses in New Cafe Bid": 39.

71. John C. Devlin, "18-Cubit Noah's Ark Launched Off Central Park Children's Zoo," *New York Times* (June 27, 1961): 35; "Barnyard on Fifth Avenue," *Time* 78 (October 13, 1961): 60–61; "The Talk of the Town: The First One," *New Yorker* 37 (October 28, 1961): 45–46; "The Talk of the Town: Lady in Lavender," *New Yorker* 38 (June 2, 1962): 23–25; White and Willensky, *AIA Guide* (1978), 211; Goldberger, *The City Observed*, 192.

72. "Civic Group Aims to Beautify City," *New York Times* (January 14, 1964): 33; Farnsworth Fowle, "Animal Band Keeps Time at Zoo," *New York Times* (June 25, 1965): 35; White and Willensky, *AIA Guide* (1967), 153; Gayle and Cohen, *The Art Commission and the Municipal Art Society Guide to Manhattan's Outdoor Sculpture*, 198.

73. "Central Park to Get Swimming Pool and Ice Rink," *New York Times* (February 24, 1962): 29; "Pool Skating Rink for Central Park," *Architectural Record* 133 (April 1963): 13; "The Talk of the Town: Escape from Buildings": 20–21; Ada Louise Huxtable, "A New Leaf in the Parks," *New York Times* (October 9, 1966), II: 27–28; White and Willensky, *AIA Guide* (1967), 153.

74. Huxtable, "A New Leaf in the Parks": 27–28.

75. Edith Evans Asbury, "Central Park Proposed as Site for Public Housing," *New York Times* (May 6, 1964): 1, 95; Edith Evans Asbury, "Housing Plan for Central Park Scored as 'Absurd' and 'Outrage,'" *New York Times* (May 7, 1964): 61; "Don't Slice Up Central Park!" editorial, *New York Times* (May 7, 1964): 34; Giorgio Cavaglieri, "Lazarus Plan Opposed," letter to the editor, *New York Times* (May 11, 1964): 30.

76. Terence Smith, "Lindsay, in Alfresco Setting, Names New Commissioner of City Parks," *New York Times* (December 2, 1965): 1, 32; "New Parks Chief: Hoving to Write 'Finis' to Era of Robert Moses": 3; "The Talk of the Town: Two Commissioners," *New Yorker* 42 (March 3, 1966): 35–37; Jack Newfield, "Runnin' Scared," *Village Voice* 12 (December 22, 1966): 1; "Happening at the Met," *Time* 88 (December 23, 1966): 46; "The Metropolitan's Man," *Newsweek* 68 (December 26, 1966): 46; "New York City Loses Hoving to Metropolitan; Names Housing Administrator for New Super-Agency," *Architectural Record* 141 (January 1967): 35–36.

77. Thomas P. F. Hoving quoted in "The Metropolitan's Man": 46.

78. Hoving, *Parks and Recreation*, 11; Ralph Blumenthal, "City Parks Get First Curators," *New York Times* (January 20, 1966): 25; "Curators Named for Parks," *Village Voice* 11 (January 20, 1966): 1; "The Kiosk & the Curator": 74.

79. Reed and Duckworth, *Central Park: A History and Guide*.

80. Hoving, *Parks and Recreation*, supplement: 13.

81. Henry Hope Reed, *The Golden City* (New York: Doubleday, 1959).

82. "The Kiosk & the Curator": 74.

83. "Summer Romance," *Newsweek* 68 (July 18, 1966): 26. Also see "Festivals: Safe with Sound," *Time* 88 (August 19, 1966): 50; "Peopling the Parks," *Time* 88 (September 2, 1966): 48.

84. Taking a cue from Hoving's "happenings," on May 11–13, 1967, the Park Department, together with the New York Chapter of the Industrial Designers Society of America, the Institute for Ecological Studies and New York University's School of the Arts, sponsored a Design-In. See "Design-In," *Architectural Forum* 126 (May 1967): 32; "Environment: Design-In, Central Park, May 11–13," *Interiors* 126 (May 1967): 10; "The Talk of the Town: Games People Play," *New Yorker* 43 (May 27, 1967): 26–28; "The Rites of Spring," *Architectural Forum* 126 (June 1967): 83; "Mayor Announces City Planning Appointment at Design-In in New York," *Interiors* 126 (June 1967): 14.

85. "The Talk of the Town: Kites Restored," *New Yorker* 42 (August 27, 1966): 24–25.

86. Thomas P. F. Hoving quoted in "Peopling the Parks": 48.

87. Thomas P. F. Hoving quoted in "Summer Romance": 26.

88. "$50,000 Pledged for a Small Cafe in Central Park," *New York Times* (April 20, 1966): 49; John C. Devlin, "Fountain Cafe in Central Park Is Dedicated with a Splash," *New York Times* (August 2, 1966): 35; James T. Burns, Jr., "Fun City, Fun Park, Fun Cafe," *Progressive Architecture* 47 (September 1966): 187–89; "The Talk of the Town: The Fountain Cafe," *New Yorker* 42 (September 17, 1966): 50; Huxtable, "A New Leaf in the Parks": 27–28; "New York Park Department Emphasizes Good Design in Implementing Its Programs," *Architectural Record* 140 (October 1966): 36; Betty Raymond, "Fountain Cafe in Central Park," *Interiors* 126 (October 1966): 134–37; White and Willensky, *AIA Guide* (1967), 151.

89. "Roman in the Park," *Architectural Forum* 113 (November 1960): 134–37.

90. "Victorian Fountain in Park to Undergo Its First Restoration," *New York Times* (October 2, 1962): 41.

91. James Lamantia quoted in Raymond, "Fountain Cafe in Central Park": 134.

92. Burns, "Fun City, Fun Park, Fun Cafe": 187.

93. Huxtable, "A New Leaf in the Parks": 27.

94. Hoving, *Parks and Recreation*, supplement: 12.

95. Ralph Blumenthal, "Hoving Planning Park Food Kiosks," *New York Times* (February 10, 1966): 39; Ada Louise Huxtable, "New Era for Parks," *New York Times* (February 10, 1966): 50; "Kiosk Chosen for Central Park," *New York Times* (July 20, 1966): 43; Ada Louise Huxtable, "Credit to Originators," *New York Times* (July 20, 1966): 43; "Building a Better Kiosk," *Progressive Architecture* 47 (September 1966): 58; "Up in Central Park," *Interiors* 126 (September 1966): 10; Scott Kelly, "Good-bye Rinky-dink," *Industrial Design* 13 (October 1966): 58–59; "New York Park Department Emphasizes Good Design in Implementing Its Programs": 36.

96. Thomas P. F. Hoving quoted in "Building a Better Kiosk": 58.

97. William Maurer quoted in Kelly, "Good-bye Rinky-dink": 59.

98. Huxtable, "Credit to Originators": 43.

99. Thomas P. F. Hoving quoted in Kelly, "Good-bye Rinky-dink": 59.

100. Douglas E. Kneeland, "City Accepts 'Adventure' Playground in Central Park," *New York Times* (June 9, 1966): 49; "Adventure in the Park," *Progressive Architecture* 47 (October 1966): 89; White and Willensky, *AIA Guide* (1967), 152; "Central Park Playground Puts Fun Over Asphalt," *New York Times* (May 26, 1967): 31; "Adventures in Play at a Playground Designed as Landscape for Kids," *Architectural Record* 142 (August 1967): 109–24; "Sand Castles," *Industrial Design* 20 (October 1973): 33–37.

101. Leonard Lauder quoted in "City Accepts 'Adventure' Playground in Central Park": 49.

102. "Adventure in the Park": 89.

103. "Buildings in the News," *Architectural Record* 150 (October 1971): 43; "Young Architects on Their Own," *Architectural Record* 152 (December 1972): 89.

104. "A Children's Play Area with Some New Ideas Is Started in Central Park," *New York Times* (September 29, 1972): 47.

105. Jacques Nevard, "Statue of Mary Poppins Planned in Central Park," *New York Times* (October 14, 1966): 45, 86; "Unhappy Happening in Park," editorial, *New York Times* (October 15, 1966): 28.

106. "A 'Revolving World's Fair' in Central Park Proposed," *New York Times* (October 20, 1966): 39. Also see "Revolving Commissioner," editorial, *New York Times* (October 24, 1966): 38; Thomas P. F. Hoving, "Hoving Discusses Central Park Plans," letter to the editor, *New York Times* (November 1, 1966): 40.

107. "Revolving Commissioner": 38.

108. Ada Louise Huxtable, "Five Top Architects Vie on Park Plan," *New York Times* (October 1, 1966): 1, 27; Huxtable, "A New Leaf in the Parks": 27–28; Hoving, "Hoving Discusses Central Park Plans": 40; Reed, "The Central Park Memorial Cemetery": 38; "The Talk of the Town: Friends," *New Yorker* 42 (February 4, 1967): 24–25; "Plan for Riding Complex in Central Park Opposed," *New York Times* (February 13, 1967): 36; "Matching Need and Design," editorial, *New York Times* (February 18, 1967): 28; Ada Louise Huxtable, "Horses, Anyone?" *New York Times* (February 19, 1967), II: 21, 23; "Adding to the Heritage," *Time* 89 (February 24, 1967): 78; "Competitions: Up in Central Park," *Architectural Forum* 126 (March 1967): 28–29; "Design that Respects Landscape Wins Central Park Competition," *Architectural Record* 141 (March 1967): 44; "Underground Police Facilities Win New York City Competition," *Progressive Architecture* 48 (March 1967): 64; Bethuel M. Webster, "Park Stable Opposed," letter to the editor, *New York Times* (March 4, 1967): 26; "Stable Plan Scored by Park Association," *New York Times* (March 6, 1967): 37; Ralph Blumenthal, "Hoving Modifies Plan for Stables," *New York Times* (March 13, 1967): 32; Thomas Hoving, "Stables in Central Park," letter to the editor, *New York Times* (March 13, 1967): 36; "Compromise on Park Stables," editorial, *New York Times* (March 14, 1967): 46; Sheldon Oliensis, "Plans for Central Park Complex," letter to the editor, *New York Times* (March 14, 1967): 46; "$1-Billion Voted for City Projects," *New York Times* (March 15, 1967): 1, 38; Leticia Kent, "Hoving's Hippodrome: It May Be Hippic, but It Will Never Be Hip," *Village Voice* 12 (March 16, 1967): 1, 34; Ada Louise Huxtable, "Up in Central Park," *New York Times* (March 19, 1967), II: 27, 29; "Up in Central Park," *Industrial Design* 14 (April 1967): 14; "Design News of the Environment Around Us: Central Park Bruhaha Follows Competition Award to Kelly & Gruzen," *Interiors* 126 (April 1967): 14; "Horsing Around in Central Park," *Progressive Architecture* 48 (April 1967): 60; James T. Burns, Jr., "A Stable Event," *Progressive Architecture* 48 (May 1967): 166–69; Richard J. H. Johnston, "Heckscher Offers New Riding Plan," *New York Times* (February 18, 1969): 33; "Stable in the Park," editorial, *New York Times* (February 25, 1969): 42; Vivian Akersten, "For Open Park Space," letter to the editor, *New York Times* (February 25, 1969): 42; "The Talk of the Town: Preserving the Greensward," *New Yorker* 45 (March 8, 1969): 28–30; Adele Auchincloss, "Stables in Central Park," letter to the editor, *New York Times* (March 10, 1969): 44; Richard Phalon, "20-Million to City's Budget," *New York Times* (March 15, 1969): 44; John C. Devlin, "Plan for More Stables in Park Is Opposed by Citizens' Group," *New York Times* (November 9, 1969): 78; Maurice Carroll, "Park Stable Plan Is Called 'Dead,'" *New York Times* (March 4, 1970): 41; "Horses Are for People," editorial, *New York Times* (March 31, 1970): 40; Peter Blake, "They Outlaw Horses, Don't They?" *New York* 3 (May 18, 1970): 62–63; Richard Edes Harrison, "Stables for Park," letter to the editor, *New York Times* (May 18, 1970): 28; "Horse Tethers," *New York* 7 (December 31, 1973): 64; Christopher Gray, "Streetscapes: The Central Park Stable," *New York Times* (September 4, 1988), X: 7, reprinted in Christopher Gray, *Changing New York: The Architectural Scene* (New York: Dover, 1992), 61.

109. "Plan for Riding Complex in Central Park Opposed": 36.
110. "Design that Respects Landscape Wins Central Park Competition": 44.
111. For a discussion of Bethuel M. Webster and his influence on John V. Lindsay's career, see John V. Lindsay, *Journey into Politics: Some Informal Observations* (New York: Dodd, Mead, 1976), 11–12.
112. Sheldon Oliensis quoted in "Stable Plan Scored by Park Association": 37.
113. Richard Edes Harrison quoted in Kent, "Hoving's Hippodrome: It May Be Hippic, but It Will Never Be Hip": 36.
114. Huxtable, "A New Leaf in the Parks": 27–28.
115. Thomas P. F. Hoving quoted in Blumenthal, "Hoving Modifies Plan for Stables": 32.
116. Harrison, "Stables for Park": 28.
117. "The Talk of the Town: New Commissioner," *New Yorker* 43 (March 4, 1967): 32–33; "Occurrence," *Architectural Forum* 126 (March 1967): 29. For Heckscher's thoughts on architecture and urbanism, see August Heckscher, "The Architect Today," *Journal of the American Institute of Architects* 28 (November 1957): 408–13; August Heckscher, *The City and the Arts* (Pittsburgh, Pa.: Pittsburgh Institute of Local Government, Graduate School of Public and International Affairs, University of Pittsburgh, 1964); August Heckscher, *Alive in the City: Memoir of an Ex-Commissioner* (New York: Scribner's, 1974); August Heckscher, *Open Spaces: The Life of American Cities* (New York: Harper & Row, 1977); August Heckscher, *When La Guardia Was Mayor: New York's Legendary Years* (New York: W. W. Norton, 1978).
118. August Heckscher quoted in "Occurrence": 29.
119. Claes Oldenburg quoted in "Claes Oldenburg's Invisible Sculpture," *Landscape Architecture* 58 (April 1968): 205–6. Also see "Sculpture Interred," *Architectural Forum* 127 (November 1967): 30.
120. Ronald Maiorana, "Central Park's Curator Assails Hoving on 'Commercial Invasion,'" *New York Times* (June 27, 1967): 1, 27.
121. "Mayor Endorses Park Happenings," *New York Times* (June 28, 1967): 47.
122. "The Road to Central Park," editorial, *New York Times* (June 30, 1967): 36.
123. August Heckscher quoted in Maiorana, "Central Park's Curator Assails Hoving on 'Commercial Invasion'": 27.
124. L. Laurie Johnston, "Central Park Mall May Be Refurbished with Performance Pit and New Lights," *New York Times* (October 4, 1972): 51; "Rus in Urbe?" editorial, *New York Times* (October 9, 1972): 30; August Heckscher, "Proposal to Restore Original Design of the Central Park Mall," letter to the editor, *New York Times* (October 18, 1972): 46; "Foes of Mall Picket at Whitney," *New York Times* (October 19, 1972): 56; Jean McClintock, "Renovating Central Park: A Case of Mallfeasance?" *Village Voice* 17 (December 21, 1972): 23–24; Max H. Seigel, "Planning Agency Accepts Park Bid," *New York Times* (September 6, 1973): 38; "Reviving Central Park," editorial, *New York Times* (December 6, 1973): 46; "Bloomingdale Mall Gifts Will Stay on the Shelf," *New York Times* (December 22, 1973): 49; Heckscher, *Alive in the City: Memoir of an Ex-Commissioner*, 260.
125. "Rus in Urbe?": 30.
126. "The Talk of the Town: Public Spirited," *New Yorker* 48 (November 25, 1972): 41. Also see "Bow Bridge to Be Renovated," *New York Times* (July 26, 1972): 9.
127. "Restored Bow Bridge Reopens to Pedestrians," *New York Times* (September 24, 1974): 45.
128. Richard Edes Harrison quoted in "The Talk of the Town: Friends": 24–25. Also see "The Talk of the Town: Troops," *New Yorker* 44 (November 30, 1968): 54–55.
129. Reed and Duckworth, *Central Park: A History and Guide*.
130. Frederick Law Olmsted, Jr., and Theodora Kimball, *Frederick Law Olmsted: Landscape Architect, 1822–1903* (New York: Benjamin Blom, 1970); S. B. Sutton, ed., *Civilizing American Cities: A Selection of Frederick Law Olmsted's Writing on City Landscapes* (Cambridge, Mass.: MIT Press, 1971); Elizabeth Barlow, *Frederick L. Olmsted's New York*, exhibition catalogue (New York: Praeger with the Whitney Museum of American Art, 1972); Albert Fein, *Frederick Law Olmsted and the Environmental Tradition* (New York: George Braziller, 1972); Frederick Law Olmsted, Jr., and Theodora Kimball, *Forty Years of Landscape Architecture: Central Park; Frederick Law Olmsted, Sr.* (Cambridge, Mass: MIT Press, 1973); Laura Wood Roper, *Frederick Law Olmsted: A Biography of Frederick Law Olmsted* (Baltimore: Johns Hopkins University Press, 1973).
131. Lee Dembart, "Nearly All of Central Park's Trees Suffer from Neglect and Poor Care," *New York Times* (June 4, 1973): 37, 71; Edward Hudson, "Central Park Condition Decried," *New York Times* (June 8, 1973): 43; Lucinda Franks, "An Oasis of Green in Need of Rescue," *New York Times* (March 22, 1974): 41; "Restoring Central Park," editorial, *New York Times* (November 21, 1974): 46; August Heckscher, "Central Park Restoration," letter to the editor, *New York Times* (December 2, 1974): 2.
132. "The Talk of the Town: The Amiability and Conviviality of the Long-Distance Runner," *New Yorker* 44 (May 11, 1968): 34–36; Al Harvin, "Fireman Is First to Finish in Marathon," *New York Times* (September 14, 1970): 54; "Round and Round Central Park, Marathon Runners Provide Show," *New York Times* (September 20, 1971): 37; Laurie

Johnston, "395 Enter, and Most End, Marathon Here," *New York Times* (October 1, 1973): 37; Michael Korda, "Dawn Patrol: Central Park," *New York* 7 (June 10, 1974): 43–46, 51; Steve Cady, "Women Marathon Runners Are Racing to Equality with Men," *New York Times* (September 29, 1975): 33; Ian T. Macauley, "Marathon Men and Women on Their Marks," *New York Times* (October 22, 1976), III: 22; "Columbia Graduate Student Ready for 4th New York City Marathon," *New York Times* (October 24, 1976): 49; Neil Amdur, "New York City's First Citywide Marathon Draws Some of World's Top Runners," *New York Times* (October 25, 1976): 31, 36.
133. Charles G. Bennett, "Subway Tunnel to Queens Voted," *New York Times* (October 18, 1963): 1, 32.
134. Clayton Knowles, "Rockefeller Institute Warns on Subway," *New York Times* (December 19, 1963): 1, 28; Elinor Langer, "Subways and Science: Two N.Y. Institutions Consider Meaning of Coexistence in Crowded Manhattan," *Science* 143 (February 21, 1964): 789–90; "Subway in the Balance," *Newsweek* 63 (March 9, 1964): 57.
135. "5th Ave. Unit Asks for 6lst St. Tunnel," *New York Times* (December 25, 1963): 23. Also see "Engineers Cut Cost of East River Subway Tunnel," *New York Times* (December 15, 1963): 85; Charles G. Bennett, "New Reservoir Called a Waste," *New York Times* (December 17, 1963): 36; Knowles, "Rockefeller Institute Warns on Subway": 1, 28.
136. Martin Arnold, "6 Groups Oppose 64th St. Tunnel," *New York Times* (February 10, 1964): 29.
137. Quoted in Arnold, "6 Groups Oppose 64th St. Tunnel": 29.
138. Quoted in Clayton Knowles, "Proposed Subway Tube Assailed as 'Nowhere-to-Nowhere' Link," *New York Times* (December 16, 1964): 33.
139. Richard J. H. Johnston, "63rd Street Picked for Subway Tunnel," *New York Times* (December 10, 1964): 1, 38. Also see "Architect Scores 64th St. Tunnel," *New York Times* (November 5, 1964): 47.
140. Robert A. Low quoted in Johnston, "63d Street Picked for Subway Tunnel": 38.
141. "Sole Tunnel Bid Tops Estimate by 101%," *Engineering News-Record* 175 (August 12, 1965): 48; "Call for Help," *Engineering News-Record* 175 (September 2, 1965): 22.
142. "Redesign Cuts Tunnel Estimate," *Engineering News-Record* 176 (January 27, 1966): 164; "Tunnel Job Hits Another Snag," *Engineering News-Record* 176 (March 17, 1966): 305–6.
143. "Tunnel Gets Bigger and Richer," *Engineering News-Record* 178 (April 20, 1967): 93; "New York City Leaks Subway Expansion Plan," *Engineering News-Record* 180 (January 11, 1968): 30. For the bond issue, see Richard Witkin, "Bond-Backed Subways to Take at Least 5 Years to Construct," *New York Times* (November 9, 1967): 1, 29. For the state's takeover of the Long Island Railroad, see Emanuel Perlmutter, "State in Accord with the Pensy on Buying L.I.R.R.," *New York Times* (June 3, 1965): 1, 71.
144. Richard Witkin, "M.T.A. Takes Over Transit Network," *New York Times* (March 2, 1968): 36; *Metropolitan Transit Authority Annual Report 1968–1969* (New York, 1969).
145. "New York Transit Tunnel Won by 12%," *Engineering News-Record* 183 (October 23, 1969): 37; "River Tunnel Launched on First Leg of Trip," *Engineering News-Record* 185 (October 15, 1970): 19.
146. Iver Peterson, "Heckscher Will Hold Up Work on 2 Tunnels in Central Park," *New York Times* (May 28, 1970): 49.
147. August Heckscher quoted in Peterson, "Heckscher Will Hold Up Work on 2 Tunnels in Central Park": 49.
148. "The Park: Going, Going . . . ," editorial, *New York Times* (June 1, 1970): 34.
149. Stern, Gilmartin and Mellins, *New York 1930*, 690–92.
150. Heckscher, *Alive in the City: Memoir of an Ex-Commissioner*, 261–63.
151. August Heckscher quoted in Edward Ranzal, "Transit Authority to Modify Central Park Plan," *New York Times* (February 27, 1971): 1, 4. Also see David A. Andelman, "Study Suggests a Big Reduction in Central Park Subway Digging," *New York Times* (January 21, 1971): 69.
152. John V. Lindsay quoted in Ranzal, "Transit Authority to Modify Central Park Plan": 1.
153. "Tunnelers Driving Subway through Rock and under Existing Line," *Engineering News-Record* 192 (March 7, 1974): 18, 23.
154. John C. Devlin, "Shouting Mothers Lead Protest Against Subway Construction in Central Park," *New York Times* (August 20, 1971): 35. Also see "Demonstrators Scrawl Protests Against Excavation in the Park for a Subway Tunnel," *New York Times* (August 21, 1971): 52.
155. Donatella Lorch, "The 'Subway to Nowhere' Now Goes Somewhere," *New York Times* (October 29, 1989): 37.
156. John Corry, "New Parks Director: Richard Michael Clurman," *New York Times* (November 10, 1972): 50; Murray Schumach, "Clurman Will Head Parks Department; Heckscher Resigns," *New York Times* (November 10, 1972): 1.
157. Max H. Seigel, "Plan Announced for Central Park," *New York Times* (September 9, 1973): 37; "Rehabilitation of Central Park Planned," *Progressive Architecture* 54 (October 1973): 23–24; Ada Louise Huxtable, "Just a Little Love, a Little Care," *New York Times* (December 9, 1973), II: 28.
158. Elizabeth Barlow, "32 Ways Your Time or Money Can Rescue Central Park," *New York* 9 (June 14, 1976): 32–99; Elizabeth Barlow, "Readers Respond to Park's Plight," *New York* 9 (August 2, 1976): 6.
159. Laurie Johnston, "Park Gazebo, Rebuilt, Still a 'Ladies Pavilion,'" *New York Times* (September 13, 1973): 49; Huxtable, "Just a Little Love, a Little Care": 28.
160. "Any Sunday," *Newsweek* 74 (June 9, 1969): 90.
161. "Bethesda Fountain Restoration to Mean Closing of Restaurant," *New York Times* (February 10, 1974): 56.
162. "Tavern-on-the-Green," *New York Times* (July 14, 1974): 25; Murray Illson, "Tavern-on-the-Green Closed for 2 Years, to Reopen in August," *New York Times* (June 20, 1976): 40; Mimi Sheraton, "Tavern on the Green—'A Creation to Appeal to All the Senses,'" *New York Times* (July 9, 1976): 14; Judy Klemesrud, "Tavern-on-Green Reopens After $2.5 Million in Work," *New York Times* (September 1, 1976): 37–38; "The Talk of the Town: Splashy," *New Yorker* 52 (September 13, 1976): 30; "Osmosis in Central Park," *Time* 108 (October 4, 1976): 72; Paul Goldberger, "A Stage Set for Dining," *New York Times* (October 8, 1976), II: 14; Mimi Sheraton, "Promise Unfulfilled at Tavern on Green," *New York Times* (October 8, 1976), II: 15; "The Prince of Flash!" *Vogue* 166 (December 1976): 198–201.
163. Warner LeRoy quoted in Sheraton, "Tavern on the Green—'A Creation to Appeal to All the Senses'": 14.
164. Goldberger, "A Stage Set for Dining": 14.
165. Goldberger, "A Stage Set for Dining": 14.
166. Calvin Tomkins, *Merchants and Masterpieces: The Story of the Metropolitan Museum of Art* (New York: E. P. Dutton, 1970), 38–41; Heckscher, *Alive in the City: Memoir*

of an Ex-Commissioner, 263–68; Thomas Hoving, *Making the Mummies Dance: Inside the Metropolitan Museum of Art* (New York: Simon & Schuster, 1993), 128–29, 219–33.
167. Quoted in Tomkins, *Merchants and Masterpieces*, 39.
168. Stern, Gilmartin and Massengale, *New York 1900*, 88, 134, 314.
169. For both wings, see Stern, Gilmartin and Massengale, *New York 1900*, 88.
170. Frederick Law Olmsted quoted in Olmsted and Kimball, *Frederick Law Olmsted: Landscape Architect, 1822–1903*, 472.
171. Stern, Gilmartin and Massengale, *New York 1900*, 88, 90, 92–93, 135.
172. Stern, Gilmartin and Massengale, *New York 1900*, 90–91.
173. Stern, Gilmartin and Mellins, *New York 1930*, 125.
174. Stern, Gilmartin and Mellins, *New York 1930*, 125.
175. "Plans for a Junior Section at the Metropolitan Museum of Art," *New York Times* (September 8, 1941): 5; "Child Art Center Opens Thursday," *New York Times* (October 14, 1941): 25; "Junior Museum Opened," *New York Times* (October 17, 1941): 24.
176. "The Whitney Museum," editorial, *New York Times* (January 19, 1943): 18; "Whitney Art Joins the Metropolitan," *New York Times* (January 19, 1943): 21; Edward Alden Jewell, "Whitney, Metropolitan Merge," *New York Times* (January 24, 1943), II: 9; "The New 'Met,'" *American Artist* 9 (December 1945): 34; "Metropolitan Museum Has Plans," *Interiors* 105 (December 1945): 14; Tomkins, *Merchants and Masterpieces*, 300–301; Avis Berman, *Rebels on Eighth Street: Juliana Force and the Whitney Museum of American Art* (New York: Atheneum, 1990), 439–49.
177. "Post-War City Plan to Include Museum," *New York Times* (January 5, 1943): 22; "Museum Planning Drastic Changes," *New York Times* (January 16, 1945): 21; "$10,240,000 Program Set for Metropolitan Museum," *New York Times* (November 11, 1945): 1, 36; "Expansion Plans of Museum Told," *New York Times* (November 23, 1945): 20; "The New 'Met'": 34; "Metropolitan Museum Has Plans": 14; "Money and the Art Museum," editorial, *New York Times* (May 15, 1946): 20; "Model of Art Museum Being Assembled to Show How It Will Appear When Rebuilt," *New York Times* (August 30, 1946): 36.
178. Francis Henry Taylor quoted in "Museum Planning Drastic Changes": 21.
179. "Museums Abandon Plan for Coalition," *New York Times* (October 1, 1948): 27. Also see Aline B. Louchheim, "A Problem for Our Three Museums," *New York Times* (October 3, 1948), II: 13; Alfred M. Frankfurter, "Vernissage: Whitney-Modern," *Art News* 48 (June 1949): 15; Tomkins, *Merchants and Masterpieces*, 307–9; Alice Goldfarb Marquis, *Alfred H. Barr, Jr.: Missionary for the Modern* (Chicago: Contemporary Books, 1989), 246; Berman, *Rebels on Eighth Street*, 451–53, 485–87, 505.
180. Robert Moses quoted in Tomkins, *Merchants and Masterpieces*, 302–3.
181. Tomkins, *Merchants and Masterpieces*, 303–13; Marquis, *Alfred H. Barr, Jr.: Missionary for the Modern*, 245–46; Berman, *Rebels on Eighth Street*, 485–87.
182. Lee E. Cooper, "New Metropolitan Museum Wing and Changes to Cost $3,000,000," *New York Times* (August 24, 1949): 1, 23; Aline B. Louchheim, "City Votes Funds to Remodel Metropolitan Museum of Art," *New York Times* (December 17, 1949): 1, 32; "Art Unit Approves Plan for Museum," *New York Times* (May 9, 1950): 31; Hugh Ferriss, *Power in Buildings* (New York: Columbia University Press, 1953), plate 26; Aline B. Louchheim, "Museum Curtails Summer Exhibits," *New York Times* (May 25, 1953): 17; "New Galleries at the Metropolitan Museum of Art," *Interior Design* 25 (January 1954): 79–80, 82–83; Francis Henry Taylor, "The Inauguration of the New Galleries," *Metropolitan Museum of Art Bulletin* 12 (January 1954): 106–20; A. L. Chanin, "A New Look at the Metropolitan," *Art Digest* 28 (January 1, 1954): 9, 28; Sanka Knox, "Art Epoch Opens at Metropolitan," *New York Times* (January 9, 1954): 17, 28; Aline B. Louchheim, "As Museum Officials See Tasks," *New York Times* (January 10, 1954), II: 10; Aline B. Louchheim, "The Why and How of Art Museums," *New York Times* (January 10, 1954), VI: 10–11, 52; "The Talk of the Town: Light and Agreeable," *New Yorker* 29 (January 16, 1954): 19–20; Sanka Knox, "Art Museum Gets New Restaurant," *New York Times* (February 24, 1954): 20; John McAndrew, "The Perils of Pompier," *Art Digest* 28 (March 1, 1954): 7–9, 31; "The Talk of the Town: Everything Is Practical," *New Yorker* 30 (March 6, 1954): 22; "Remodeling—A New Version of Museum Expansion," *Architectural Forum* 100 (May 1954): 154–57; John Mason Brown, "The Grace Rainey Rogers Auditorium," *Metropolitan Museum of Art Bulletin* 12 (May 1954): 249–55; Robert B. Newman, "The Acoustics of the New Auditorium," *Metropolitan Museum of Art Bulletin* 12 (May 1954): 256–57; J. Gordon Carr, Gordon Baley Washburn, L. V. Coleman and Thomas C. Colt, Jr., letters to the editor, *Architectural Forum* 101 (August 1954): 62, 68; "Ideas Blend Décor and Sound Conditioning," advertisement, *Architectural Record* 116 (August 1954): 140; "The Year's Work: The Projects," *Interiors* 114 (August 1954): 61; "Decorative Art Galleries Reopened at the Metropolitan," *Antiques* 66 (November 1954): 404; Preston Remington, "The Galleries of European Decorative Art & Period Rooms," *Metropolitan Museum of Art Bulletin* 13 (November 1954): 66–135; Sanka Knox, "Museum to Open Big Gallery Area," *New York Times* (November 10, 1954): 36; Howard Devree, "European Pageant: The Metropolitan Opens Decorative Display," *New York Times* (November 14, 1954), II: 14; "Decorative Arts at the Metropolitan Museum," *Craft Horizons* 15 (January 1955): 44; "Pool at Museum Getting New Art," *New York Times* (November 22, 1955): 21; Carleton Varney, *The Draper Touch: The High Life & High Style of Dorothy Draper* (New York: Prentice Hall Press, 1988), 264–66, 281, unnumbered plate between pp. 174–75.
183. Theodore Rousseau, Jr., quoted in "The Talk of the Town: Light and Agreeable": 19–20.
184. McAndrew, "The Perils of Pompier": 7–9, 31.
185. Brown, "The Grace Rainey Rogers Auditorium": 249–55.
186. Chanin, "A New Look at the Metropolitan": 9, 28.
187. Dorothy Draper quoted in "The Talk of the Town: Everything Is Practical": 22.
188. Alice Frank Merriam, "The New Museum Restaurant," *Metropolitan Museum of Art Bulletin* 36 (October 1941): 194.
189. Tomkins, *Merchants and Masterpieces*, 320.
190. Dorothy Draper quoted in "The Talk of the Town: Everything Is Practical": 22.
191. Varney, *The Draper Touch*, 265.
192. Taylor, "The Inauguration of the New Galleries": 106–20.
193. "Costume Branch for Metropolitan," *New York Times* (December 12, 1944): 20; "Costume Institute Moving," *New York Times* (April 1, 1946): 24; Martha Weinman, "New Dress for the Metropolitan's Costumes," *New York Times* (November 23, 1958), II: 12; "Metropolitan Museum's Costume Institute to Be Redesigned," *Museum News* 36 (December 1, 1958): 1; "Costume Institute Redesigned," *Interiors* 118 (February 1959): 16, 18; "Building Program and New Installations," *Metropolitan Museum of Art Bulletin* 18 (October 1959): 39–42; "The Building Program and Major Installations," *Metropolitan Museum of Art Bulletin* 19 (October 1960): 28–33; Tomkins, *Merchants and Masterpieces*, 292.
194. "Building Program and New Installations": 40–41; "The Building Program and Major Installations": 32–33; Tania Long, "Museum Prepares a Curtain-Raising," *New York Times* (August 29, 1964): 23; Ada Louise Huxtable, "Architecture: Seasoning the Witches' Brew," *New York Times* (January 31, 1965), II: 18; "Winging Away," *Time* 85 (February 5, 1965): 78; James Humphrey III, "Met Museum Turns Modern," *Library Journal* 90 (December 1965): 5028–29.
195. Huxtable, "Architecture: Seasoning the Witches' Brew": 18.
196. Sanka Knox, "Metropolitan Museum Head Chosen," *New York Times* (August 4, 1955): 1, 26; Aline B. Saarinen, "Credo for an Art Museum," *New York Times* (August 14, 1955), VI: 26–27, 65; Tomkins, *Merchants and Masterpieces*, 255–56, 326–33.
197. "Happening at the Met": 46; "The Metropolitan's Man": 46; "New York City Loses Hoving to Met; Names Housing Administrator for New Super-Agency": 35–36; "Hoving the Happening: A Conversation with New York's Former Parks Commissioner and Present Director of the Metropolitan Museum," *Print* 21 (May–June 1967): 30–34; John Peter, "The New Yorker Who Shook Up Central Park," *Look* 31 (May 2, 1967): 80, 82, 84; "Hoving of the Metropolitan," *Newsweek* 71 (April 11, 1968): 54–62; Tomkins, *Merchants and Masterpieces*, 345–47, 350, 352–53, 357–58; Malcolm N. Carter, "The Hoving Years," *Art News* 76 (January 1977): 37–40; Hoving, *Making the Mummies Dance*, 26–43.
198. Tracy Atkinson quoted in "Hoving of the Metropolitan": 54.
199. Richard Randall quoted in "Hoving of the Metropolitan": 55.
200. Katherine Kuh, "What Home for the Temple?" *Saturday Review* 49 (November 26, 1966): 56–57; "U.S. Panel Studies Dendur Temple Bids," *New York Times* (March 2, 1967): 39; Milton Esterow, "Metropolitan Due to Get Temple of Dendur," *New York Times* (April 25, 1967): 1, 40; "Johnson Gives Egyptian Temple to Metropolitan Museum of Art," *New York Times* (April 30, 1967): 81; "A Temple on Fifth Avenue," *Time* 89 (May 12, 1967): 80; "A Temple for Manhattan," *Architectural Forum* 126 (June 1967): 26–27; McCandlish Phillips, "Egyptian Temple Is Delivered Here in 661 Crates," *New York Times* (August 22, 1968): 44; Sophy Burnham, "A Little Bit of Egypt on Fifth," *New York* 1 (November 11, 1968): 46–49; Hoving, *Making the Mummies Dance*, 58–63.
201. Ada Louise Huxtable, "Metropolitan Museum to Expand in Park and Revamp Collections," *New York Times* (September 29, 1967): 1, 23; "Building Program," *Metropolitan Museum of Art Bulletin* 26 (October 1967): 42–43; "Museum News: Master Expansion Plan for Metropolitan Museum," *Interiors* 127 (November 1967): 12, 14; *Kevin Roche, John Dinkeloo and Associates, vol. 1: 1962–1975* (Tokyo: A.D.A. Edita, 1975), 174–83; Francesco Dal Co, *Kevin Roche* (New York: Rizzoli International Publications, 1985), 10, 52–55, 146–53, 265.
202. Thomas P. F. Hoving quoted in Huxtable, "Metropolitan Museum to Expand in Park and Revamp Collections": 1, 23.
203. Robert A. M. Stern, *New Directions in American Architecture* (New York: George Braziller, 1969), 27, fig. 23; Dal Co, *Kevin Roche*, 9, 27, 88–91.
204. Kevin Roche quoted in Huxtable, "Metropolitan Museum to Expand in Park and Revamp Collections": 1, 23.
205. "Metropolitan and Brooklyn Museums Share Architectural Administrator Rosenblatt," *Interiors* 127 (November 1967): 14.
206. Ada Louise Huxtable, "Metropolitan Museum to Get Costly New Facade," *New York Times* (October 22, 1968): 39. Also see "Buildings in the News," *Architectural Record* 144 (November 1968): 40; "Urbane Facade to Help Complete the Metropolitan," *Progressive Architecture* 49 (December 1968): 44; Barbara Goldsmith, "Hoving after 'Harlem,'" *New York* 2 (August 18, 1969): 42–47; "The Talk of the Town: Anniversary," *New Yorker* 45 (October 11, 1969): 43–44; "The Metropolitan Museum in New York Celebrates Its First Hundred Years," *Architectural Record* 146 (November 1969): 37; Bernard Weinraub, "Museum's Facelift Delights Its Chiefs," *New York Times* (November 19, 1969): 44; "A Museum Turns One Hundred," *Architectural Forum* 132 (June 1970): 42–47; Ada Louise Huxtable, "Misgivings at the Metropolitan," *New York Times* (November 8, 1970), II: 27; Hoving, *Making the Mummies Dance*, 162–63, 191.
207. Kevin Roche quoted in Dal Co, *Kevin Roche*, 55.
208. Huxtable, "Metropolitan Museum to Get Costly New Facade": 39.
209. Huxtable, "Misgivings at the Metropolitan": 27.
210. Bernhard Leitner, "A Master Plan: The Met Plans Its Second Century," *Artforum* 9 (October 1970): 64–68.
211. Huxtable, "Misgivings at the Metropolitan": 27.
212. Huxtable, "Misgivings at the Metropolitan": 27.
213. Jonathan Black, "Expansion of a Museum: Hoving Vs. the Metaphobes," *Village Voice* 15 (February 12, 1970): 1, 42, 44–45; Ada Louise Huxtable, "Metropolitan Museum Plans Centennial Expansion," *New York Times* (April 13, 1970): 1, 53; "The Museum's Birthday Cake," editorial, *New York Times* (April 13, 1970): 40; "Growing Pains," *Time* 95 (April 27, 1970): 74; "Art in the Park," *Industrial Design* 17 (May 1970): 6, 10; "Museum Turns One Hundred," *Architectural Forum* 132 (June 1970): 42–47; "The Met and Its Master Plan," *Progressive Architecture* 51 (June 1970): 48; "The Talk of the Town: Meeting," *New Yorker* 46 (June 20, 1970): 25–27; Bryce Walker, "Escalation at the Metropolitan and How I Tried to Stop It," *New York* 3 (June 29, 1970): 45–48; George Gent, "Metropolitan's Expansion into the Park Is Assailed," *New York Times* (August 12, 1970): 30; Leitner, "A Master Plan: The Met Plans Its Second Century": 64–68; Sophy Burnham, "The Arrogance of Culture Power," *New York* 3 (October 26, 1970): 44–46, 49–50, 52; Leon Golub, "Regarding the Lehman and Rockefeller Gifts to the Metropolitan Museum," *Artforum* 9 (November 1970): 40–41; Huxtable, "Misgivings at the Metropolitan": 27; Grace Glueck, "Heckscher Backs Metropolitan Museum's Plan," *New York Times* (January 20, 1971): 25; Joseph James Akston, "Editorial," *Arts* 45 (March 1971): 4–5; Jane Schwarz, "A Comprehensive Architectural Plan for the Second Century," *Metropolitan Museum of Art Bulletin* 29 (June 1971): 444–48; Sophy Burnham, *The Art Crowd* (New York: David McKay Co., 1973), 167–85; Heckscher, *Alive in the City: Memoir of an Ex-Commissioner*, 263–68; "L'Extension du Met," *L'Architecture d'Aujourd'hui* 177 (January 1975): xxi; "Museum Spreads Its Wings to Get Needed Space," *Engineering News-Record* 195 (July 24, 1975): 16–17; Erich Steingräber, "Der Generalbauplan des Metropolitan Museum of Art, New York," *Pantheon* 34 (April 1976): 166–67; Dal Co, *Kevin Roche*, 10, 52, 55, 146–49; Barbaralee Diamonstein, *American Architecture Now II* (New York: Rizzoli International Publications, 1985), 208–10.
214. Kevin Roche quoted in Diamonstein, *American Architecture Now II*, 209.
215. Hoving, *Making the Mummies Dance*, 129.
216. Thomas P. F. Hoving quoted in Black, "Expansion of a Museum: Hoving Vs. the Metaphobes": 1.

217. Thomas P. F. Hoving quoted in Huxtable, "Metropolitan Museum Plans Centennial Expansion": 1, 53.
218. "Growing Pains": 74.
219. Kevin Roche quoted in Dal Co, *Kevin Roche*, 55.
220. "The Talk of the Town: Centennial Ball," *New Yorker* 46 (April 25, 1970): 29–30; "Special Effects for the Met's Birthday Ball," *Interiors* 129 (May 1970): 30; "Spectacular Decoration for a Great Party," *House and Garden* 138 (July 1970): 60–63; Hoving, *Making the Mummies Dance*, 213–14.
221. Walker, "Escalation at the Metropolitan Museum and How I Tried to Stop It": 45.
222. Hoving, *Making the Mummies Dance*, 213.
223. Hoving, *Making the Mummies Dance*, 228.
224. Karl Katz quoted in Hoving, *Making the Mummies Dance*, 233.
225. Hoving, *Making the Mummies Dance*, 233.
226. Gent, "Metropolitan's Expansion into the Park Is Assailed": 30. Also see Edward C. Burks, "Central Park Building Plans Assailed," *New York Times* (October 11, 1970): 43.
227. William J. Diamond quoted in Gent, "Metropolitan's Expansion into the Park Is Assailed": 30.
228. Grace Glueck, "Metropolitan to Begin Wing for Lehman Art," *New York Times* (December 6, 1971): 54.
229. Paul Goldberger, "A Museum Well Met," *Architectural Forum* 139 (March 1974): 42–47.
230. "Treasure Trove," *Newsweek* 94 (October 6, 1969): 96–100; Glueck, "Metropolitan to Begin Wing for Lehman Art": 54; Paul Goldberger, "Grand Design Puts Focus on Court," *New York Times* (May 14, 1975): 47; Hilton Kramer, "Manner of Displaying Works Raises Vital Questions," *New York Times* (May 14, 1975): 47, 90; Ada Louise Huxtable, "The New Lehman Wing—Does the Met Need It?" *New York Times* (May 25, 1975), II: 1, 27, reprinted as "Wrong but Impeccable," in *Progressive Architecture* 56 (August 1975): 60–63, and "The Lehman Wing of the Metropolitan Museum," in Ada Louise Huxtable, *Kicked a Building Lately?* (New York: Quadrangle/New York Times Book Co., 1976), 13–17; Douglas Davis, "$100 Million Speaks for Itself," *Newsweek* 85 (May 26, 1975): 82; Dorothy Seiberling, "And, Behold, It Is Very Good," *New York* 8 (May 26, 1975): 45–52; "The Talk of the Town: Collection," *New Yorker* 51 (June 9, 1975): 31–32; "Lehman Wing Opens at Metropolitan Museum," *Interiors* 134 (July 1975): 8; "Roche, Dinkeloo Museum Wing Opens," *Progressive Architecture* 56 (July 1975): 20; Peter Blake, "The Eighth Annual Cityscape Awards," *New York* 9 (January 12, 1976): 57; "3 Architetture in USA," *Domus* 555 (February 1976): 21; Stephen Kurtz, "Architecture: Nothing Works Best," *Village Voice* 21 (August 2, 1976): 82–83; "Roche Diamond," *Architectural Review* 161 (April 1972): 203–5; White and Willensky, *AIA Guide* (1978), 234; "Metropolitan Museum, Robert-Lehman-Pavillon New York," *Baumeister* 75 (December 1978): 1090; Goldberger, *The City Observed*, 251; Dal Co, *Kevin Roche*, 10, 52–55, 146–49, 153, 265; Diamonstein, *American Architecture Now II*, 209; Hoving, *Making the Mummies Dance*, 130–32, 156–62.
231. Goldberger, "Grand Design Puts Focus on Court": 47.
232. Kramer, "Manner of Displaying Works Raises Vital Questions": 47, 90.
233. Huxtable, "The New Lehman Wing—Does the Met Need It?": 1, 27.
234. Ada Louise Huxtable, "Taking the Wraps Off Egypt," *New York Times* (October 10, 1976), II: 1, 23. Also see Grace Glueck, "Art People," *New York Times* (October 8, 1976), C: 18; Hilton Kramer, "Met Opens Egyptian Galleries," *New York Times* (October 15, 1976), C: 18.
235. John Russell, "The Romance of Egyptology," *New York Times* (October 10, 1976), II: 1, 23. Also see John Russell, "Met Unwraps Egyptian Riches in New Setting," *New York Times* (December 1, 1978), C: 1, 22.

Chapter 11
Upper East Side

1. Joyce Peterson, *The New York I Love* (New York: Tudor, 1964), 97.

THE PLIGHT OF THE PROSPEROUS

1. For Treadwell Farm, see Landmarks Preservation Commission of the City of New York, LP-0536 (December 13, 1967); Barbaralee Diamonstein, *The Landmarks of New York* (New York: Harry N. Abrams, 1988), 385.
2. Lewis Mumford, "The Sky Line: The Plight of the Prosperous," *New Yorker* 26 (March 4, 1950): 68–73.
3. For Frank Lloyd Wright's St. Mark's-in-the-Bouwerie scheme, see Stern, Gilmartin and Mellins, *New York 1930*, 447–49. For his S. C. Johnson Research Tower, see Jonathan Lipman, *Frank Lloyd Wright and the Johnson Wax Buildings* (New York: Rizzoli International Publications, 1986), esp. chapters 9–12.
4. "Apartment Helix," *Architectural Forum* 92 (January 1950): 90–96; E. J. Kahn, Jr., "Profiles: Big Operator—I," *New Yorker* 27 (December 8, 1951): 46–50, 52–56, 58–61; Carter Wiseman, *I. M. Pei: A Profile in American Architecture* (New York: Harry N. Abrams, 1990), 50–52.
5. William Zeckendorf quoted in "Apartment Helix": 90.
6. Thomas H. Creighton, "P.S.: Happy New York," editorial, *Progressive Architecture* 42 (January 1961): 208.
7. Paul Goldberger, *The City Observed: New York* (New York: Random House, 1979), 262.

FIFTH AVENUE

1. Franz K. Winkler (Montgomery Schuyler), "Architecture in the Billionaire District of New York City," *Architectural Review* 11 (October 1901): 679–99. For a discussion of the district, see Stern, Gilmartin and Massengale, *New York 1900*, 306–12.
2. For a discussion of Fifth Avenue's development during the interwar period, see Stern, Gilmartin and Mellins, *New York 1930*, 384–90.
3. For a general description of Fifth Avenue in the early 1950s, see Roul Tunley, "This Is Fifth Avenue," *American Magazine* 153 (June 1952): 32–35, 93–97.
4. Stern, Gilmartin and Mellins, *New York 1930*, 390.
5. "Three More Mansions on Fifth Avenue to Go," *New York Times* (August 14, 1939): 29; "New Fifth Avenue Project," *Real Estate Record and Guide* 146 (November 16, 1940): 7; Landmarks Preservation Commission of the City of New York, *Upper East Side Historic District Designation Report* (New York, 1981), 951–52; Steven Ruttenbaum, *Mansions in the Clouds: The Skyscraper Palazzi of Emery Roth* (New York: Balsam Press, 1986), 179–81; Stern, Gilmartin and Mellins, *New York 1930*, 390.
6. "No. 875 Fifth Avenue," *Empire State Architect* 11 (March–April 1942): 5–6; *Upper East Side Historic District*, 935, 937; Ruttenbaum, *Mansions in the Clouds: The Skyscraper Palazzi of Emery Roth*, 180–82, 184; Stern, Gilmartin, and Mellins, *New York 1930*, 390.
7. For Roth's earlier buildings, see Ruttenbaum, *Mansions in the Clouds: The Skyscraper Palazzi of Emery Roth*, 122–45, 170–77; Stern, Gilmartin and Mellins, *New York 1930*, 403, 406–10.
8. "5th Ave. Mansions to Be Demolished," *New York Times* (September 14, 1941): 36; "Post-War Builders Go for Purchased Steam," advertisement, *Real Estate Record and Guide* 162 (August 7, 1948): 5; *Upper East Side Historic District*, 938–39; Ruttenbaum, *Mansions in the Clouds: The Skyscraper Palazzi of Emery Roth*, 178, 184–86.
9. For the San Remo, see Stern, Gilmartin and Mellins, *New York 1930*, 370, 403, 406–10, 447.
10. "Post-War Builders Go for Purchased Steam": 5; *Upper East Side Historic District*, 957. For Temple Beth-El, see M. Christine Boyer, *Manhattan Manners: Architecture and Style 1850–1900* (New York: Rizzoli International Publications, 1985), 190.
11. For Temple Emanu-El, see Stern, Gilmartin and Mellins, *New York 1930*, 156–57, 160–61.
12. *Upper East Side Historic District*, 931.
13. "Simon Bros. Erecting 19–Story 'Co-op' Corner Fifth Avenue and 68th Street," *Real Estate Record and Guide* 160 (December 13, 1947): 3; "Fifth Avenue Cooperative," *Architectural Record* 104 (July 1948): 162; "Post-War Builders Go for Purchased Steam": 5; "Planners Study Open Area with a Garage Provided with New Fifth Avenue Apartments," *New York Times* (October 1, 1950), VIII: 1; *Upper East Side Historic District*, 936.
14. For a discussion of Hohauser's Miami Beach hotels, see Laura Cerwinske, *Tropical Deco: The Architecture and Design of Old Miami Beach* (New York: Rizzoli International Publications, 1981), 23, 49, 52, 71; Barbara Baer Capitman, *Deco Delights: Preserving the Beauty and Joy of Miami Beach Architecture* (New York: E. P. Dutton, 1988), 29, 32, 34.
15. White and Willensky, *AIA Guide* (1988), 516.
16. "East Side House Will Be a 'Co-op,'" *New York Times* (January 12, 1947), VIII: 1.
17. "'Most Luxurious' Co-op Rising at 900 Fifth Avenue," *Real Estate Record and Guide* 182 (November 1, 1958): 304; *Upper East Side Historic District*, 941–42.
18. "Tishman Realty and Construction Company to Erect Apartment Structure on Recently Acquired Plottage," *Real Estate Record and Guide* 156 (September 8, 1945): 3; "New Apartments on Fifth Avenue Corner Will Have Basement Garage for 60 Cars," *New York Times* (September 17, 1950), VIII: 1; "'Prestige' Emanates from Any Building You Build with Hanley Duraglaze Brick," advertisement, *Architectural Forum* 95 (July 1951): 25; *Upper East Side Historic District*, 946–47.
19. "Tishman Realty and Construction Company to Erect Apartment Structure on Recently Acquired Plottage": 3.
20. "19–Story Housing Will Rise on Site of Ryan Mansion," *New York Times* (January 23, 1949), VIII: 1; "New 'Co-op' Is Rising on Ryan Home Site; 160 Units in Building at 860 Fifth Avenue," *New York Times* (September 4, 1949), VIII: 1; *Upper East Side Historic District*, 933–34. For the Thomas Fortune Ryan house, see Curtis Channing Blake, "The Architecture of Carrère & Hastings" (Ph.D. diss., Columbia University, 1976): 182, plate 138.
21. "Announcements," *Architectural Forum* 89 (November 1948): 70; Lee E. Cooper, "Ground Broken for Tall Apartments on Old Speyer Corner on Fifth Ave.," *New York Times* (January 8, 1950), VIII: 1; "Simon Brothers Improving Fifth Avenue Corner with Deluxe Apartment Building," *Real Estate Record and Guide* 165 (January 14, 1950): 4; "Loan of $1,900,000 Finances Housing," *New York Times* (April 30, 1950), VIII: 1.
22. For both buildings, see Stern, Gilmartin and Mellins, *New York 1930*, 576–84.
23. "Announcements": 70.
24. Beryl Austrian quoted in "Loan of $1,900,000 Finances Housing": 1.
25. Quoted in "Loan of $1,900,000 Finances Housing": 1.
26. "7 Buildings to Get Fifth Ave. Award," *New York Times* (April 27, 1952), VIII: 1; *Upper East Side Historic District*, 927; White and Willensky, *AIA Guide* (1988), 352.
27. "Stained Glass by Robert Pinart Exhibited in New York," *Architectural Record* 127 (January 1960): 20; Percival Goodman, "The Essence of Designing a Synagogue," *Faith & Form* 1 (1967): 16–17; White and Willensky, *AIA Guide* (1978), 220.
28. "New Apartments to Rise on Fifth Avenue Site," *New York Times* (March 21, 1954), VIII: 1; "1025 Fifth Avenue to Be Site of Twin 12-Story Cooperative Apartment Houses," *Real Estate Record and Guide* 173 (May 22, 1954): 3; "1025 Fifth Ave. Entrance and Lobby Nearing Completion," *Real Estate Record and Guide* 175 (April 9, 1955): 3; "Luxury 'Co-op' Buyers Favor Penthouse and Terrace Suites," *Real Estate Record and Guide* 175 (May 7, 1955): 3; "A Look at Lobbies," *Architectural Forum* 104 (January 1956): 122–29; Lois Wagner, "Lobbies," *Interiors* 116 (October 1956): 100–113; Henry Hope Reed, *The Golden City* (New York: Doubleday, 1959), 43; Landmarks Preservation Commission of the City of New York, *Metropolitan Museum Historic District Designation Report* (New York, 1977), 96–97; Andrew Alpern and Seymour Durst, *Holdouts!* (New York: McGraw-Hill, 1984), 26.
29. Herbert Fischbach quoted in "A Look at Lobbies": 127.
30. "Weiler, Glickman Purchase Two Fifth Avenue Mansion Buildings as Site for Air-Conditioned Cooperative Apartment Building; Rogers Peet Building on Lower Broadway Sold, Ends 33-Year Ownership," *Real Estate Record and Guide* 172 (November 7, 1953): 3; "Weiler, Glickman Announce Work Started on Erection of 17-Story Fifth Avenue Co-operative Apartment Building; Wolfson to Erect New Commercial Structure in Downtown Insurance District," *Real Estate Record and Guide* 173 (January 23, 1954): 3; *Upper East Side Historic District*, 951, 954.
31. "End of an Avenue," *Time* 69 (January 21, 1957): 59; "Irving Brodsky Purchased the Rovensky Mansion," *Real Estate Record and Guide* 179 (May 11, 1957): 3; Christopher Gray, "Streetscapes/1050 Fifth Avenue: A Building Ennobled by the Company It Keeps," *New York Times* (June 12, 1994), X: 7. For Lowell's building, see Stern, Gilmartin and Mellins, *New York 1930*, 456–57.
32. Andrew Alpern, *Apartments for the Affluent* (New York: McGraw-Hill, 1975), 94–95; *Upper East Side Historic District*, 941. For Carpenter's building, see Stern, Gilmartin and Mellins, *New York 1930*, 384, 387.
33. "Deluxe Apt. Created at 910 Fifth Ave.," *Real Estate Record and Guide* 182 (March 21, 1959): 4; "18-Room Apartments on 5th Ave. Yield to Smaller Luxury Units," *New York Times* (May 24, 1959), VIII: 1, 10; Alpern, *Apartments for the Affluent*, 96–97; *Upper East Side Historic District*, 943–44; Christopher Gray, "Streetscapes: The Beekman Theater, a French School, Old Initials," *New York Times* (September 5, 1993), X: 6. For French's building, see Stern, Gilmartin and Mellins, *New York 1930*, 384.

34. "Town House/Research Library," *Progressive Architecture* 40 (March 1959): 134–40; White and Willensky, *AIA Guide* (1978), 237.
35. For the Sherman M. Fairchild house, see Stern, Gilmartin, and Mellins, *New York 1930*, 379–80, 383.
36. "Town House/Research Library": 134.
37. "P/A News Report: Bulletins," *Progressive Architecture* 40 (December 1959): 76.
38. *Upper East Side Historic District*, 915, 917.
39. "67th St. Mansion Sold by Institute," *New York Times* (May 8, 1961): 59; Thomas W. Ennis, "Vanderbilts' 5th Ave. Mansion to Be Razed," *New York Times* (July 12, 1961): 19; Alpern, *Apartments for the Affluent*, 144–45; Stern, Gilmartin and Massengale, *New York 1900*, 339.
40. Ennis, "Vanderbilts' 5th Ave. Mansion to Be Razed": 19.
41. Alpern, *Apartments for the Affluent*, 144.
42. *Metropolitan Museum Historic District*, 102–3.
43. "Wide View with Rents to Match," *New York Times* (April 27, 1969), VIII: 9; Alpern, *Apartments for the Affluent*, 152–53; *Metropolitan Museum Historic District*, 86.
44. *Metropolitan Museum Historic District*, 87; Margot Gayle and Michele Cohen, *The Art Commission and the Municipal Art Society Guide to Manhattan's Outdoor Sculpture* (New York: Prentice Hall Press, 1988), 253.
45. Bruce Brooks Pfeiffer, ed., *Frank Lloyd Wright: The Guggenheim Correspondence* (Fresno, Calif.: The Press at California State University; Carbondale, Ill.: Southern Illinois University Press, 1986). Also see Joan M. Lukach, *Hilla Rebay: In Search of the Spirit in Art* (New York: George Braziller, 1983), especially the introduction and chapters 8, 12, 17, 18, 21, 22.
46. Lukach, *Hilla Rebay*, 135, 137–38, fig. 33. Also see Stern, Gilmartin and Mellins, *New York 1930*, 144, 660.
47. Lukach, *Hilla Rebay*, 138–39, figs. 34–35.
48. Rudolf Bauer, letter to Hilla Rebay, October 17, 1936, in Lukach, *Hilla Rebay*, 138.
49. Lukach, *Hilla Rebay*, 139–41, figs. 36–37. For William Muschenheim's work in the 1930s, see Stern, Gilmartin and Mellins, *New York 1930*, 116, 343, 346, 469, 473, 475, 741, 747. Also see *Reminiscences of William Muschenheim*, Columbia University Oral History Collection (1985): 42–43.
50. Hilla Rebay, letter to Frank Lloyd Wright, June 1, 1943, in Pfeiffer, ed., *Frank Lloyd Wright: The Guggenheim Correspondence*, 4.
51. See Robert Moses, *Public Works: A Dangerous Trade* (New York: McGraw-Hill, 1970), 855–72.
52. Frank Lloyd Wright, letter to Solomon R. Guggenheim, July 14, 1943, in Pfeiffer, ed., *Frank Lloyd Wright: The Guggenheim Correspondence*, 9–12.
53. For both houses, see Stern, Gilmartin and Mellins, *New York 1930*, 372–73.
54. Frank Lloyd Wright, letter to Solomon R. Guggenheim, July 14, 1943, in Pfeiffer, ed., *Frank Lloyd Wright: The Guggenheim Correspondence*, 12. Also see Frank Lloyd Wright, letter to Hilla Rebay, July 23, 1943, in Pfeiffer, ed., *Frank Lloyd Wright: The Guggenheim Correspondence*, 13–15.
55. For the J. P. Morgan, Jr., mansion, see Stern, Gilmartin and Massengale, *New York 1900*, 103. For the Parke-Bernet Galleries, see Stern, Gilmartin and Mellins, *New York 1930*, 360, 362.
56. Frank Lloyd Wright, letter to Hilla Rebay, January 20, 1944, in Pfeiffer, ed., *Frank Lloyd Wright: The Guggenheim Correspondence*, 40–41.
57. Frank Lloyd Wright quoted in Sanka Knox, "New Art Museum Opens on 5th Ave.," *New York Times* (October 21, 1959): 1, 38.
58. Frank Lloyd Wright, letter to Hilla Rebay, March 13, 1944, in Pfeiffer, ed., *Frank Lloyd Wright: The Guggenheim Correspondence*, 44–45. Also see "New York Discovers an Architect," *Architectural Forum* 80 (April 1944): 70; "The Editor's Asides," *Journal of the American Institute of Architects* 1 (April 1944): 205; "News," *Pencil Points* 25 (April 1944): 14.
59. Frank Lloyd Wright, letter to Hilla Rebay, ca. March 23, 1944, in Lukach, *Hilla Rebay*, 189.
60. "Museum Building to Rise as Spiral," *New York Times* (July 10, 1945): 11; Howard Devree, "A Summer Cluster of Events," *New York Times* (July 22, 1945), II: 2; "Wright's Spiral," *Architectural Forum* 85 (August 1945): 7; "Post-War Buildings," *Art News* 44 (August 1945): 6–7; "Spiral Museum," *Interiors* 105 (August 1945): 14; Peyton Boswell, "Frank Lloyd Wright's Museum," *Art Digest* 19 (August 1, 1945): 3; "Another Academy?—Devree Views with Alarm," *Art Digest* 19 (August 1, 1945): 14; "Model Is Unveiled of New Museum Here," *New York Times* (September 21, 1945): 38; "Monolithic Masterpiece," *Architectural Forum* 83 (October 1945): 9; "Frank Lloyd Wright's New Museum Plan," *Art News* 44 (October 1945): 29; "Two Views of the Solomon R. Guggenheim Museum of Non-Objective Painting," *Art Digest* 20 (October 15, 1945): 15; "The Modern Gallery," *Architectural Forum* 84 (January 1946): cover, 81–88; Frank Lloyd Wright, "The Modern Gallery for the Solomon R. Guggenheim Foundation," *Magazine of Art* 39 (January 1946): 24–26.
61. Frank Lloyd Wright quoted in Peter Blake, "The Guggenheim: Museum or Monument?" *Architectural Forum* (December 1959): 86–92.
62. Frank Lloyd Wright quoted in Pfeiffer, ed., *Frank Lloyd Wright: The Guggenheim Correspondence*, 111.
63. Bruce Brooks Pfeiffer, *Frank Lloyd Wright, vol. 5: Monograph 1924–1936* (Tokyo: A.D.A. Edita, 1985), 245–64; Jonathan Lipman, *Frank Lloyd Wright and the Johnson Wax Buildings* (New York: Rizzoli International Publications, 1986).
64. Frank Lloyd Wright, letter to Hilla Rebay, March 21, 1944, in Lukach, *Hilla Rebay*, 190.
65. Frank Lloyd Wright, letter to Hilla Rebay, March 23, 1944, in Lukach, *Hilla Rebay*, 191.
66. Frank Lloyd Wright, letter to Hilla Rebay, March 1, 1945, in Pfeiffer, ed., *Frank Lloyd Wright: The Guggenheim Correspondence*, 58–59.
67. Lukach, *Hilla Rebay*, 192–93.
68. Frank Lloyd Wright, letter to Hilla Rebay, August 2, 1945, in Pfeiffer, ed., *Frank Lloyd Wright: The Guggenheim Correspondence*, 65–67.
69. Frank Lloyd Wright, letter to Hilla Rebay, January 1945, in Lukach, *Hilla Rebay*, 195.
70. Hilla Rebay, letter to Frank Lloyd Wright, January 13, 1945, in Lukach, *Hilla Rebay*, 195.
71. Hilla Rebay, letter to Frank Lloyd Wright, October 22, 1949, in Lukach, *Hilla Rebay*, 195.
72. Frank Lloyd Wright, letter to Hilla Rebay, June 2, 1945, in Pfeiffer, ed., *Frank Lloyd Wright: The Guggenheim Correspondence*, 61–62.
73. Frank Lloyd Wright, letter to Solomon R. Guggenheim, September 11, 1947, in Pfeiffer, ed., *Frank Lloyd Wright: The Guggenheim Correspondence*, 101–2. Also see Bruce Brooks Pfeiffer, *Frank Lloyd Wright, vol. 7: Monograph 1941–1950* (Tokyo: A.D.A. Edita, 1988), 170, figs. 318–23.
74. "Typical Plans of Solomon R. Guggenheim Memorial Museum," *Architectural Forum* 88 (January 1948): 136–38.
75. "People," *Architectural Forum* 88 (April 1948): 14.
76. Frank Lloyd Wright, letter to Solomon R. Guggenheim, April 19, 1948, in Lukach, *Hilla Rebay*, 205.
77. "Intermediate Home for Art," *Interiors* 107 (June 1948): 14, 16.
78. Quoted in Pfeiffer, ed., *Frank Lloyd Wright: The Guggenheim Correspondence*, 112.
79. "The Editor's Asides," *Journal of the American Institute of Architects* 16 (September 1951): 142.
80. Frank Lloyd Wright, letter to Hilla Rebay, July 23, 1951, in Pfeiffer, ed., *Frank Lloyd Wright: The Guggenheim Correspondence*, 147–48.
81. Frank Lloyd Wright quoted in Pfeiffer, ed., *Frank Lloyd Wright: The Guggenheim Correspondence*, 179.
82. Frank Lloyd Wright, *60 Years of Living Architecture*, exhibition catalogue (New York: Solomon R. Guggenheim Museum, 1953); Aline B. Louchheim, "Wright Planning Edifice for His Art," *New York Times* (September 3, 1953): 23; "Frank Lloyd Wright Exhibits 60 Years' Work," *Architectural Forum* 99 (October 1953): 45; "Wright Makes New York," *Architectural Record* 114 (October 1953): 20; "Throngs Inspect Wright's Exhibit," *New York Times* (October 23, 1953): 34; "The Talk of the Town: Wright, Continued," *New Yorker* 29 (October 31, 1953): 25–27; "'Sixty Years of Living Architecture'—The Work of Frank Lloyd Wright," *Architectural Forum* 99 (November 1953): 152–55; "5th Avenue at 89th St.," *Citizens' Housing News* 12 (November 1953): 4; "The Talk of the Town: Mr. Wrong," *New Yorker* 29 (November 7, 1953): 33; Lionel Brett, "Wright in New York," *New Republic* 129 (November 16, 1953): 19–20; Lewis Mumford, "The Sky Line: A Phoenix Too Infrequent," *New Yorker* 29 (November 28, 1953): 133–39; Lewis Mumford, "The Sky Line: A Phoenix Too Infrequent—II," *New Yorker* 29 (December 12, 1953): 116–20, 123–27; Herbert Muschamp, *Man About Town: Frank Lloyd Wright in New York City* (Cambridge, Mass.: MIT Press, 1983), 88, 93, 128–29, 154–55; Bruce Brooks Pfeiffer, *Frank Lloyd Wright, vol. 8: Monograph 1951–1959* (Tokyo: A.D.A. Edita, 1988), 106.
83. Frank Lloyd Wright quoted in Louchheim, "Wright Planning Edifice for His Art": 23.
84. Muschamp, *Man About Town*, 88.
85. Frank Lloyd Wright, letter to James Johnson Sweeney, October 5, 1955, in Pfeiffer, ed., *Frank Lloyd Wright: The Guggenheim Correspondence*, 214–15.
86. "News Bulletins," *Progressive Architecture* 36 (December 1955): 70; "Approve Spiral-Ramp Museum," *Engineering News-Record* 155 (December 29, 1955): 24; Sanka Knox, "Museum Designed by Wright to Rise," *New York Times* (May 7, 1956): 29; "Spiral Museum," *Engineering News-Record* 156 (May 10, 1956): 27; "Guggenheim Museum to Rise—Victory for Wright in 12-Year Design Battle," *Architectural Forum* 104 (June 1956): 13; "The Big News Is—It's Under Construction at Last!" *Architectural Record* 119 (July 1956): 28.
87. For the Oliver Gould Jennings house, see Stern, Gilmartin and Massengale, *New York 1900*, 330–31.
88. Hilton Kramer, "The New Guggenheim Museum," editorial, *Arts* 30 (June 1956): 11.
89. "The Hot Cross Bun," editorial, *New York Times* (May 8, 1956): 32. Also see "The Editor's Asides," *Journal of the American Institute of Architects* 26 (September 1956): 134.
90. Sanka Knox, "21 Artists Assail Museum Interior," *New York Times* (December 12, 1956): 46; "The Guggenheim Museum," letter to the editor, *Arts* 31 (January 1957): 4; "News Bulletins," *Progressive Architecture* 38 (January 1957): 80.
91. "The Guggenheim Museum," *Arts*: 4.
92. George Constant quoted in Knox, "21 Artists Assail Museum Interior": 46.
93. Frank Lloyd Wright quoted in "Guggenheim Chides Critics of Museum," *New York Times* (December 22, 1956): 2.
94. Aline B. Saarinen, "Tour with Mr. Wright," *New York Times* (September 22, 1957), VI: 22–23, 69–70. Also see "The Talk of the Town: Lunch Hour," *New Yorker* 33 (August 10, 1957): 17–18; "'The Guggenheim' Progresses," *Progressive Architecture* 39 (January 1958): 77; "Wright's New York Museum," *Architectural Forum* 108 (March 1958): 12.
95. Frank Lloyd Wright quoted in Saarinen, "Tour with Mr. Wright": 22.
96. Frank Lloyd Wright, "The Solomon R. Guggenheim Memorial," *Architectural Record* 123 (May 1958): 182–84. Also see "Guggenheim Museum in Progress," *Architectural Record* 123 (May 1958): 185–90.
97. "Topping Out the Guggenheim," *Architectural Record* 123 (June 1958): 9; "Meetings and Miscellany," *Architectural Record* 124 (October 1958): 28.
98. "The Seven Wonders," *Time* 72 (September 29, 1958): 83; Asher B. Etkes, "Eighteenth Wonder," letter to the editor, *New York Times* (November 2, 1958), VI: 7. Also see Herbert Mitgang, "Sidewalk Views of That Museum," *New York Times* (October 12, 1958), VI: 14, 73.
99. Edgar Kaufmann, Jr., "The Form of Space for Art—Wright's Guggenheim Museum," *Art in America* 46 (winter 1958–59): 74–77.
100. See "The Talk of the Town: Guggenheim's Euclid," *New Yorker* 33 (May 18, 1957): 23–24; George N. Cohen, "Frank Lloyd Wright's Guggenheim Museum," *Concrete Construction* 3 (March 1958): cover, 10–13.
101. Frank Lloyd Wright quoted in Pfeiffer, ed., *Frank Lloyd Wright: The Guggenheim Correspondence*, 248.
102. Frank Lloyd Wright, letter to George Cohen, January 13, 1959, in Pfeiffer, ed., *Frank Lloyd Wright: The Guggenheim Correspondence*, 297.
103. "Only Commission in New York Was Guggenheim Art Museum," *New York Times* (April 10, 1959): 26.
104. Ian McCallum, *Architecture USA* (London: Architectural Press, 1959), 49; Sibyl Moholy-Nagy, "F.Ll.W. and the Ageing of Modern Architecture," *Progressive Architecture* 40 (April 1959): 136–42; Frank Lloyd Wright, "Il Solomon R. Guggenheim Museum nella Fifth Avenue a New York," *Casabella* 227 (May 1959): 19–28; Sanka Knox, "Moses Gets Prize from Art Society," *New York Times* (May 21, 1959), VI: 33; "Frank Lloyd Wright: The Guggenheim Museum," *Architectural Forum* 110 (June 1959): 126–31; "People," *Architectural Forum* 111 (July 1959): 16; "Guggenheim Museum Spirals toward Completion," *Progressive Architecture* 40 (July 1959): 75–77; John Canaday, "Wright Vs. Painting," *New York Times* (October 21, 1959): 1, 38; Knox, "New Art Mu-

seum Opens on 5th Ave.": 1, 38; "The Talk of the Town: Gander at the Guggenheim," *New Yorker* 35 (October 24, 1959): 34–35; Ada Louise Huxtable, "That Museum: Wright or Wrong?" *New York Times* (October 25, 1959), VI: 16–17, 91; "Inside Job," *Newsweek* 54 (October 26, 1959): 120; "Wright's Guggenheim Opens," *Architectural Record* 126 (November 1959): 9; "First View of the Guggenheim," *Art News* 58 (November 1959): 46–47; Russell Lynes, "After Hours: Mr. Wright's Museum," *Harper's* 219 (November 1959): 97–98, 100–101; George McAuliffe, "The Guggenheim: Great Architecture, Difficult Installation," *Industrial Design* 6 (November 1959): 66–69; "Guggenheim Museum Holds Long-Awaited Opening," *Progressive Architecture* 40 (November 1959): 83; Frank Getlein, "A Romp on the Ramp," *New Republic* 141 (November 2, 1959): 21–22; "Last Monument," *Time* 74 (November 2, 1959): 67; John LaFarge, "Opening of the Spiral Museum," *America* 102 (November 7, 1959): 146; Walter McQuade, "Architecture," *Nation* 189 (November 7, 1959): 335–38; Ada Louise Huxtable, "Triple Legacy of Mr. Wright," *New York Times* (November 15, 1959), VI: 18–19; Alan Dunn, "The Guggenheim," cartoons, *New Yorker* 35 (November 28, 1959): 48–51; Alfred Frankenstein, "Critical Opinion," *San Francisco Chronicle* (November 29, 1959), reprinted in *Museum News* 38 (January 1960): 18; Marvin D. Schwartz, "News and Views from New York: The New Solomon R. Guggenheim Museum," *Apollo* 70 (December 1959): 190; Blake, "The Guggenheim: Museum or Monument?": 86–93; Matthew Peters, "Two Domes," *Architectural Forum* 111 (December 1959): 205; Alan Dunn, "Do I Have to Go through Kandinsky to Get to Modigliani?" cartoon, *Architectural Record* 126 (December 1959): 25; "Buildings in the News," *Architectural Record* 126 (December 1959): 12; Hilton Kramer, "Month in Review," *Arts* 34 (December 1959): 48–51; Olga Gueft, "Two Masterpieces: The Guggenheim and the Four Seasons," editorial, *Interiors* 119 (December 1959): 79; "Frank Lloyd Wright's Sole Legacy to New York," *Interiors* 119 (December 1959): 88–95, 172; "Art d'Aujourd'hui Musée de Demain," *L'Oeil* 60 (December 1959): 106–11; "A Westerner Views the Museum," *Pacific Architect and Builder* 65 (December 1959): 50; Betty Kaufman, "Wright's Museum," *Commonweal* 71 (December 4, 1959): 305–7; Lewis Mumford, "The Sky Line: What Wright Hath Wrought," *New Yorker* 35 (December 5, 1959): 105–6, 108, 110, 112, 115–16, 118, 120, 122, 127–28, 130, reprinted in Lewis Mumford, *The Highway and the City* (New York: Harcourt, Brace & World, 1963), 124–38; Henry-Russell Hitchcock, "Notes of a Traveller: Wright and Kahn," *Zodiac* 6 (1960): 14–21; I. D. Robbins, *The Lighting of a Great Museum* (Hackensack, N.J.: American Lighting Corp., 1960); *The Solomon R. Guggenheim Museum, Architect Frank Lloyd Wright* (New York: Solomon R. Guggenheim Foundation; New York: Horizon Press, 1960); "Architecture Vs. Art?" *Architectural Record* 119 (January 1960): 9; Aleksis Rannit, "Das neue Museum der ungegenständlichen Kunst in New York," *Das Kunstwerk* 13 (January 1960): 24, 33; "The Guggenheim Museum," *Journal of the American Institute of Architects* 33 (January 1960): 124; Philip C. Johnson, "Letter to the Museum Director," *Museum News* 38 (January 1960): 22–25; James Johnson Sweeney, "Chambered Nautilus on Fifth Avenue," *Museum News* 38 (January 1960): 14–15; Stephen Raz Auerbach, letter to the editor, *Architectural Forum* 112 (February 1960): 219; Howard Barnstone, letter to the editor, *Architectural Forum* 112 (February 1960): 219–20; "Frank Lloyd Wright," *L'Architecture d'Aujourd'hui* 5 (February 1960): 56–59; Michael Jennings, "The Guggenheim Museum: Frank Lloyd Wright's Legacy to New York," *Light and Lighting* 53 (February 1960): cover, 34–37; "A Word from the Client," *Architectural Record* 127 (March 1960): 9; William Barrett, "Frank Lloyd Wright's Pictorama," *Commentary* 29 (March 1960): 249–52; "Il Museo Guggenheim a New York," *Edilizia Moderna* 69 (April 1960): cover, 39–46; Bruno Zevi, "L'Incessante polemica sul Museo Guggenheim," *L'Architettura cronache e storia* 5 (April 1960): 798–99; Carola Giedion-Welcker, "Zum neuen Guggenheim-Museum in New York," *Werk* 47 (May 1960): 178–81; Ada Louise Huxtable, "What Should a Museum Be?" *New York Times* (May 8, 1960), VI: 42–43, 47; Glenn Fowler, "Wright Museum Is Among Winners," *New York Times* (May 22, 1960): 1, 16; "Visitors to Guggenheim Rate Building Over Art," *Architectural Forum* 112 (June 1960): 7; "The Biggest Hit In Town—The Guggenheim Museum," *Vogue* 135 (June 1960): 108–11, 157; "The Guggenheim Museum," *Architect and Building News* 218 (July 27, 1960): cover, 105–10; Emilio Lavagnin, "Conferma la condanna a Sweeney," *L'Architettura cronache e storia* 6 (August 1960): 262–63; "Man V. Building," *Time* 76 (August 1, 1960): 48; Robert Tennenbaum, letter to the editor, *Architectural Forum* 113 (September 1960): 222; Francis Steegmuller, "Battle of the Guggenheim," *Holiday* 28 (September 1960): 60–61, 105–6; "Carlo Levi e Frank Lloyd Wright," *L'Architettura cronache e storia* 6 (September 1960): 292–93; "Personalities," *Progressive Architecture* 41 (September 1960): 58; Frederick Gutheim, "The Wright Legacy Evaluated," *Architectural Record* 128 (October 1960): 147, 186; Ely Kahn, "Tall Buildings in New York," *Journal of the Royal Institute of British Architects* 67 (October 1960): 451–56; John Portman, "New View on the Guggenheim," letter to the editor, *Interiors* 120 (December 1960): 8; Ada Louise Huxtable, *Four Walking Tours of Modern Architecture in New York City* (New York: Museum of Modern Art and Municipal Art Society of New York, 1961), 69; Ralph H. Lewis, "Museums," *Britannica Book of the Year* (Chicago: Encyclopaedia Britannica, 1961): 465; Vincent Scully, Jr., *Modern Architecture: The Architecture of Democracy* (New York: George Braziller, 1961), 32, 89–91; C. Ray Smith, "Rehousing the Drama," *Progressive Architecture* 43 (February 1962): 98; "Quote . . . Unquote," *Architectural Forum* 116 (March 1962): 75; Douglas Haskell, "Editor's Note: People," *Architectural Forum* 116 (June 1962): 204; John Canaday, "Museum Director Solves Problem," *New York Times* (August 17, 1962): 25; Sherman Emery, "A Sense of Appropriateness," editorial, *Interior Design* 34 (May 1963): 105; Raanan Lurie, "New York," cartoons, *Harper's* 228 (February 1964): 94; "Is Architecture Totalitarian?" *Village Voice* 9 (April 16, 1964): 1; Helen Neville, letter to the editor, *Village Voice* 9 (June 25, 1964): 4; Peter T. White, "The World in New York City," *National Geographic* 126 (July 1964): 98–99; Philip Johnson, "Whence or Whither: The Processional Element in Architecture," *Perspecta* 9/10 (1965): 167–78, reprinted in Peter Eisenman and Robert A. M. Stern, eds., *Philip Johnson: Writings* (New York: Oxford University Press, 1979), 150–55; Stuart Preston, "Letter from New York: Movements and Mobiles," *Apollo* 81 (January 1965): 66–69; "Redressing a Spiral Showcase," *Time* 85 (May 7, 1965): 86; Thomas M. Messer, "Editorial: Past and Future," *Art in America* 53 (June 1965): 25–27; "Evolution of a Museum," *Art in America* 53 (June 1965): 28–32; Olgivanna Lloyd Wright, *Frank Lloyd Wright: His Life, His Work, His Words* (New York: Horizon Press, 1966), 161–68; "The Stamp of Frank Lloyd Wright," *Progressive Architecture* 47 (June 1966): 47; Vincent Scully, *American Architecture and Urbanism* (New York: Frederick A. Praeger, 1969), 176, figs. 365–66; Charles Jencks, *Modern Movements in Architecture* (Garden City, N.Y.: Anchor Press/Doubleday, 1973), 136–37, 372; William Allin Storrer, *The Architecture of Frank Lloyd Wright* (Cambridge, Mass.: MIT Press, 1974), 400; Yukio Futagawa, ed., *Global Architecture* 36 (1975); *The Solomon R. Guggenheim Museum, New York: Frank Lloyd Wright Architect* (New York: Solomon R. Guggenheim Foundation, 1975); Thomas B. Hess, "In the Good Old Guggenheim," *New Yorker* 9 (June 21, 1976): 82–84; Kate Simon, *Fifth Avenue: A Very Social History* (New York: Harcourt Brace Jovanovich, 1978), chapter 13; White and Willensky, *AIA Guide* (1978), 136–37; Paul Goldberger, *The City Observed: New York* (New York: Random House, 1979), 255–56; John Tauranac, *Essential New York* (New York: Holt, Rinehart and Winston, 1979), 203–4; Brent C. Brolin, *Architecture in Context: Fitting New Buildings with Old* (New York: Van Nostrand Reinhold, 1980), 137; Muschamp, *Man About Town*, 58–59, 88, 111–18, 136–38, 142–47; Brendan Gill, *Many Masks: A Life of Frank Lloyd Wright* (New York: G. P. Putnam's Sons, 1987), chapter 25; Bruce Brooks Pfeiffer, *Frank Lloyd Wright, vol. 2: Preliminary Studies* (Tokyo: A.D.A. Edita, 1987), 128–31; Pfeiffer, *Frank Lloyd Wright, vol. 7: Monograph 1941–1950*, viii-ix, 37–43, 170–71; Ezra Stoller, "The Architectural Landscape," *Art News* 86 (November 1987): 163; Carol Herselle Krinsky, "Architecture in New York City," in Leonard Wallock, ed., *New York: Culture Capital of the World, 1940–1965* (New York: Rizzoli International Publications, 1988), 110–12; Landmarks Preservation Commission of the City of New York, LP-1774 (August 14, 1990); Landmarks Preservation Commission of the City of New York, LP-1775 (August 14, 1990).

105. Knox, "New Art Museum Opens on 5th Ave.": 1.
106. Quoted in Knox, "New Art Museum Opens on 5th Ave.": 38.
107. Canaday, "Wright Vs. Painting": 1, 38.
108. Huxtable, "That Museum: Wright or Wrong?": 16, 91.
109. Getlein, "A Romp on the Ramp": 22.
110. McQuade, "Architecture": 335.
111. Mumford, "The Sky Line: What Wright Hath Wrought": 118, 120, 128.
112. Barrett, "Frank Lloyd Wright's Pictorama": 249–51.
113. Portman, "New View on the Guggenheim": 8.
114. Harry Guggenheim quoted in Huxtable, "What Should a Museum Be?": 47.

MADISON AVENUE

1. See Stern, Gilmartin and Massengale, *New York 1900*, 310–12, 315, 326, 329; Stern, Gilmartin and Mellins, *New York 1930*, 392, 394, 399–401.
2. Stern, Gilmartin and Mellins, *New York 1930*, 400–401.
3. "Balcony Units, New York City," *Architectural Record* 101 (March 1947): 104; "Postwar Co-op's," *Architectural Forum* 88 (June 1948): 92–100; Landmarks Preservation Commission of the City of New York, *Upper East Side Historic District Designation Report* (New York, 1981), 702.
4. "102 Fortunate Families Will Enjoy Personalized Heating Control," advertisement, *Real Estate Record and Guide* 159 (February 1, 1947): 7; "Terrace Apartment in Uptown New York," *Architectural Record* 101 (March 1947): 106; "And Now—The Panel-Heated Apartment," *Architectural Record* 102 (September 1947): 117.
5. "Terrace Apartment in Uptown New York": 106.
6. "And Now—The Panel-Heated Apartment": 117; "How Real Radiant Heating Improves Comfort Conditions and Lowers Heating Costs," advertisement, *Architectural Forum* 87 (October 1947): 1; "Postwar Co-op's": 92–93.
7. "Erection of Large East Side Apartment House Development Contemplated," *Real Estate Record and Guide* 164 (October 22, 1949): 3; "Madison Avenue Blockfront to Be Improved with 22-Story Apartment Building Reported to Involve $6,500,000—Occupancy April, 1951," *Real Estate Record and Guide* 165 (March 25, 1950): 3.
8. "Ten Old Trees Saved," *New York Times* (February 9, 1952): 15.
9. "New Apartment Hotel in New York," advertisement, *Architectural Record* 109 (June 1951): 259; *Upper East Side Historic District*, 974; Thomas E. Norton and Jerry E. Patterson, *Living It Up: A Guide to the Named Apartment Houses of New York* (New York: Atheneum, 1984), 82.
10. "New Apartment Structure to Be Erected on Madison Avenue–81st Corner," *Real Estate Record and Guide* 172 (October 10, 1953): 3. For Boak & Raad's fifteen-story apartment building at 26 East Sixty-eighth Street, completed in 1955, see *Upper East Side Historic District*, 367. For H. I. Feldman's fifteen-story Cumberland House, at 30 East Sixty-second Street, on the southwest corner of Madison Avenue, also completed in 1955, see *Upper East Side Historic District*, 56.
11. "East Side Site for New Luxury Suites," *Real Estate Record and Guide* 179 (May 4, 1957): 3; "New Luxury Apartments to Rise on East Side," *Real Estate Record and Guide* 180 (October 5, 1957): 3.
12. "Montclair Features Sumptuous Living," *Real Estate Record and Guide* 182 (November 29, 1958): 3. Also see *Upper East Side Historic District*, 974.
13. For 30 East Sixty-fifth Street, see *Upper East Side Historic District*, 234. For 27 East Sixty-fifth Street, see *Upper East Side Historic District*, 240.
14. *Upper East Side Historic District*, 460.
15. Joseph P. Fried, "A Giant Rises on the Fifth Avenue Skyline," *New York Times* (December 29, 1968), VIII: 1; Paul Goldberger, "Award-Givers Honor a Few and Slap a Wrist," *New York Times* (June 2, 1974), VIII: 1, 12; Andrew Alpern, *Apartments for the Affluent* (New York: McGraw-Hill, 1975), 154–55; White and Willensky, *AIA Guide* (1978), 237; John Tauranac, *Essential New York* (New York: Holt, Rinehart and Winston, 1979), 228–29.
16. Alpern, *Apartments for the Affluent*, 154.
17. Tauranac, *Essential New York*, 228.
18. Fried, "A Giant Rises on the Fifth Avenue Skyline": 1.
19. White and Willensky, *AIA Guide* (1978), 237.
20. "First New Luxury Co-op in Five Years," *Real Estate Record and Guide* 208 (July 3, 1971): 3; Norton and Patterson, *Living It Up*, 92.
21. "Co-op Rises on 89th St.," *New York Times* (February 25, 1973), VIII: 4.
22. White and Willensky, *AIA Guide* (1967), 177; *Adolph Gottlieb*, exhibition catalogue (London: Marlborough, 1971), 5; White and Willensky, *AIA Guide* (1978), 236–37. For the Park Avenue Synagogue, see Stern, Gilmartin and Mellins, *New York 1930*, 160.
23. "Enigmatic Structure," *Architectural Forum* 132 (May 1970): 15.
24. "Auction Gallery to Move Uptown," *New York Times* (August 20, 1948): 7; "New Art Galleries Will Cost $750,000," *New York Times* (August 24, 1948): 39; "New Home Opened by Parke-Bernet," *New York Times* (November 11, 1949): 28; "Dedicating a Building," *Journal of the American Institute of Architects* 13 (January 1950): 16–22; Lewis Mumford, "The Sky Line: Civic Virtue," *New Yorker* 25 (February 4, 1950): 58–63; Thomas E. Norton, *100 Years of Collecting in America: The Story of Sotheby Parke Bernet* (New York: Harry N. Abrams, 1984), 19, 150; Christopher Gray, "Show and Sell," *Avenue* 14 (February 1990): 103–9.

25. Stern, Gilmartin and Mellins, *New York 1930*, 360, 362.
26. William A. Delano quoted in "Dedicating a Building": 17.
27. Mumford, "The Sky Line: Civic Virtue": 58.
28. Mumford, "The Sky Line: Civic Virtue": 60–61.
29. Mumford, "The Sky Line: Civic Virtue": 61.
30. Stern, Gilmartin and Mellins, *New York 1930*, 135, 140–41.
31. "The Whitney Museum," editorial, *New York Times* (January 19, 1943): 18.
32. "Culture Goes North on Madison," *New York Herald Tribune* (June 18, 1963): 17; Sanka Knox, "Whitney Museum Finds a New Home," *New York Times* (June 18, 1963): 39; "Marcel Breuer Designs New Whitney Museum," *Village Voice* 8 (June 27, 1963): 3; Emily Genauer, "Functional 'Sculpture . . . in the Dynamic Jungle,'" *New York Herald Tribune* (December 12, 1963): 23, 26; Ada Louise Huxtable, "Whitney Museum Reveals Design," *New York Times* (December 12, 1963): 41; Ada Louise Huxtable, "Something Awry," *New York Times* (December 22, 1963), II: 15; "Upside-Down Museum in Manhattan," *Architectural Forum* 120 (January 1964): 90–93; "Another New Whitney," *Architectural Record* 135 (January 1964): 13; "Strong Breuer Design for Madison Avenue," *Progressive Architecture* 45 (January 1964): 47, 49; Stuart Preston, "Whitney Museum Seeks $8 Million," *New York Times* (May 8, 1964): 35; "Gradini a rovescio," *L'Architettura cronache e storia* 10 (July 1964): 190; "New Whitney Museum Building Contract Set," *New York Herald Tribune* (September 25, 1964): 16; "Young Building, Young Artists," *New York Herald Tribune* (October 21, 1964): 25; "Whitney Museum of American Art, New York," *Deutsche Bauzeitung* 70 (June 1965): 461–63; John Molleson, "The City: Changing the Skyline," *Time* 88 (August 12, 1966): 46; Gordon Brown, "Museum for Humans," *Arts* 40 (September 1966): 28–29; James R. Mellow, "Culture A-Building," *Industrial Design* 18 (September 1966): 57–65; "Whitney Museum Opens," *Progressive Architecture* 47 (September 1966): 51, 53; Milton Esterow, "Whitney Museum Holds a Preview," *New York Times* (September 8, 1966): 49; Ada Louise Huxtable, "Harsh and Handsome," *New York Times* (September 8, 1966): 49, 57; Emily Genauer, "The Whitney's New Mad Scene," *New York Herald Tribune* (September 18, 1966): 33; Ervin Galantay, "Architecture," *Nation* 103 (September 26, 1966): 292–93; Dan Sullivan, "Whitney Museum Has Gala Opening," *New York Times* (September 28, 1966): 1, 30; "Buildings in the News," *Architectural Record* 140 (October 1966): 40–43; Thomas B. Hess, "Vale Atque Ave Whitney," editorial, *Art News* 65 (October 1966): 29; Olga Gueft, "Breuer's Whitney Museum," *Interiors* 126 (October 1966): 98–107; "People Are Talking About: The New Whitney Museum of American Art and Its Architect, Marcel Breuer," *Vogue* 148 (October 1966): 218–19; John Canaday, "Art: The Whitney Museum Shows What It Can Do . . . in the Right Building," *New York Times* (October 2, 1966), II: 23; Ada Louise Huxtable, "Art: The Whitney Museum Shows What It Can Do . . . in the Right Building," *New York Times* (October 2, 1966), II: 23, 25; "The New Whitney," *Newsweek* 68 (October 3, 1966): 98, 100–104; "Cliff-hanger on Madison Avenue," *Time* 88 (October 7, 1966): 88–91; Frank Getlein, "The New Whitney," *New Republic* 155 (November 5, 1966): 45–46; Alan Dunn, "It Happened during the Night—Pure Vandalism, I Think!" cartoon, *Architectural Record* 140 (December 1966): 10; "Whitney Museum in New York," *Deutsche Bauzeitung* 72 (December 1966): 1059–62; Douglas Haskell, "Ten Buildings that Climax an Era," *Fortune* 74 (December 1966): 156–62; Peter P. Witonski, "The New Whitney," *National Review* 18 (December 27, 1966): 1335–36; "The New Whitney Opens," *Whitney Review* (1967): 3–9; "Das Neue Whitney," *Das Kunstwerk* 20 (February 1967): 20–21; "Un Nouveau Musée à New York," *L'Oeil* 146 (February 1967): 20–25; "Swinging Awards," *Architectural Forum* 126 (May 1967): 89; Alan Dunn, "Watch Where You Toss Your Cigarette, Mac!" cartoon, *Architectural Record* 141 (June 1967): 10; Cranston Jones, "Breuer: The Last 'Modern' Architect," *Horizon* 9 (summer 1967): 32–41; "Bard Program Cites Works of Four Nonprofit Clients," *Journal of the American Institute of Architects* 49 (June 1968): 20, 28; "News Report," *Progressive Architecture* 49 (December 1968): 43; Tician Papachristou, *Marcel Breuer: New Buildings and Projects* (New York: Praeger, 1970), 14–16, 122–31; "Best in the U.S.," *Architectural Forum* 132 (June 1970): 70–71; Ada Louise Huxtable, "Illuminating Show of Breuer's Work," *New York Times* (November 30, 1972): 34, reprinted as "The Work of Marcel Breuer," in Ada Louise Huxtable, *Kicked a Building Lately?* (New York: Quadrangle/New York Times Book Co., 1976), 90–92; C. Ray Smith, *Supermannerism: New Attitudes in Post-Modern Architecture* (New York: E. P. Dutton, 1977), 149–50; White and Willensky, *AIA Guide* (1978), 232–33; Paul Goldberger, *The City Observed: New York* (New York: Random House, 1979), 245–46; Tauranac, *Essential New York*, 219–21; Ezra Stoller, "The Architectural Landscape," *Art News* 86 (November 1987): 165; Carol Herselle Krinsky, "Architecture in New York City," in Leonard Wallock, ed., *New York: Culture Capital of the World, 1940–1965* (New York: Rizzoli International Publications, 1988), 108, 111–12.
33. Marcel Breuer, "Comments at the Presentation of the Whitney Museum Project, November 12, 1963," in Papachristou, *Marcel Breuer: New Buildings and Projects*, 15.
34. Marcel Breuer quoted in "The New Whitney," *Newsweek*: 98.
35. Mellow, "Culture A-Building": 63.
36. Marcel Breuer quoted in "The New Whitney," *Newsweek*: 98.
37. Huxtable, "Whitney Museum Reveals Design": 41.
38. Marcel Breuer quoted in Genauer, "Functional 'Sculpture . . . in the Dynamic Jungle'": 23.
39. Genauer, "Functional 'Sculpture . . . in the Dynamic Jungle'": 23.
40. Huxtable, "Something Awry": 15.
41. Huxtable, "Harsh and Handsome": 49, 57.
42. Huxtable, "Art: The Whitney Museum Shows What It Can Do . . . in the Right Building": 23, 25.
43. Genauer, "The Whitney's New Mad Scene": 33.
44. Hess, "Vale Atque Ave Whitney": 29.
45. Hess, "Vale Atque Ave Whitney": 29.
46. Gueft, "Breuer's Whitney Museum": 103.
47. Goldberger, *The City Observed*, 245–46.

PARK AVENUE

1. For a social chronicle of postwar Park Avenue, see J. Bryan III, "Park Avenue," *Holiday* 14 (December 1953): 42–53, 84, 86, 88–90, 92–93.
2. Stern, Gilmartin and Mellins, *New York 1930*, 395; James Trager, *Park Avenue: Street of Dreams* (New York: Atheneum, 1990), 207.
3. Anthony Campagna quoted in "BWHS Named Managing Agents of 530 Park Avenue," *Real Estate Record and Guide* 147 (January 11, 1941): 8. Also see Lee E. Cooper, "New Ideas for Apartments Used in East Side Houses," *New York Times* (January 19, 1941), XI: 1, 3; "New Apartment Features Attract Tenants," *Real Estate Record and Guide* 148 (August 9, 1941): 6.
4. Stern, Gilmartin and Mellins, *New York 1930*, 20–21.
5. "Park Avenue Co-operative to Be Modernized; Small Units to Replace Twelve-Room Suites," *Real Estate Record and Guide* 147 (May 24, 1941): 5.
6. "Six Suites to Replace Park Ave. Triplex Occupied by the Late Walter P. Chrysler," *New York Times* (October 12, 1941), XI: 1. Also see Stern, Gilmartin and Mellins, *New York 1930*, 371–72, 458–59.
7. "Postwar Project for a Converted Apartment in New York City," *Architectural Forum* 81 (November 1944): 111–13.
8. "East Side Brownstone Gets Modern Features," *New York Times* (February 26, 1950), VIII: 1.
9. "New Housing and Offices in Realty News," *New York Times* (November 24, 1946), VIII: 1; "Park Avenue Apartments, New York: One Compact, One Luxurious," *Architectural Record* 101 (March 1947): 105; "Brisk Demand Seen for Luxury Suites on Park Ave. Sites," *New York Times* (November 27, 1949), VIII: 1; Landmarks Preservation Commission of the City of New York, *Upper East Side Historic District Designation Report* (New York, 1981), 1110; Trager, *Park Avenue*, 208.
10. "Park Ave. House Rising," *New York Times* (November 2, 1947), VIII: 3; "All but Three Apartments Now Leased in 710 Park Avenue," *Real Estate Record and Guide* 162 (August 7, 1948): 3; *Upper East Side Historic District*, 1104; Trager, *Park Avenue*, 208.
11. "Steel Work Started on New Apartments for 70 Families at Park Ave. and 72d St.," *New York Times* (January 28, 1951), VIII: 1; "Ahead of Schedule," *New York Times* (May 1, 1951): 50; "New Park Avenue Apartment Building Receiving First Tenants," *Real Estate Record and Guide* 168 (October 13, 1951): 3–4; "New 17-Story Park Avenue Apartment House Sold by Kleban Interests," *Real Estate Record and Guide* 169 (February 2, 1952): 3; White and Willensky, *AIA Guide* (1978), 231; *Upper East Side Historic District*, 1116; Trager, *Park Avenue*, 208.
12. For Lescaze's proposal, see Stern, Gilmartin and Mellins, *New York 1930*, 393–95.
13. *Upper East Side Historic District*, 1085.
14. Trager, *Park Avenue*, 209.
15. Upper East Side Historic District, *307.*
16. *Upper East Side Historic District*, 557. For a similar twelve-story building designed in 1949 by H. I. Feldman at 65 East Seventy-sixth Street, see *Upper East Side Historic District*, 822.
17. *Upper East Side Historic District*, 627.
18. Maurice Foley, "Apartments Due on Mansion Site," *New York Times* (October 20, 1958): 45; "Tishman Realty Plans Luxury Park Ave. Coop.," *Real Estate Record and Guide* 183 (May 16, 1959): 3; "Lobbies," *Interior Design* 33 (April 1962): 204–7; *Upper East Side Historic District*, 1103. For the Arthur Curtiss James house, see Stern, Gilmartin and Massengale, *New York 1900*, 355.
19. Trager, *Park Avenue*, 209.
20. Trager, *Park Avenue*, 209.
21. "Builders to Raze Sulgrave Hotel," *New York Times* (November 4, 1960): 56; *Upper East Side Historic District*, 1093; Trager, *Park Avenue*, 209. For another white-glazed-brick apartment building on Park Avenue, H. I. Feldman's number 799 (1961), see *Upper East Side Historic District*, 1128; Trager, *Park Avenue*, 209.
22. *Upper East Side Historic District*, 569.
23. Stern, Gilmartin and Mellins, *New York 1930*, 374.
24. "Apartment House Built Under New Zoning Emphasizes Privacy in Design," *New York Times* (March 7, 1965), VIII: 1.
25. "Park Ave. Is Losing a Mansion," *New York Times* (January 26, 1969), VIII: 1, 8; Carter B. Horsley, "Got $190,000? It Will Buy the Cheapest Floor at No. 733," *New York Times* (April 22, 1973), VIII: 1, 6; Andrew Alpern, *Apartments for the Affluent* (New York: McGraw-Hill, 1975), 156–57; Paul Goldberger, *The City Observed: New York* (New York: Random House, 1979), 242–43; *Upper East Side Historic District*, 1114; Trager, *Park Avenue*, 211.
26. For the Hunter College building, see Stern, Gilmartin and Mellins, *New York 1930*, 114–15.
27. Alpern, *Apartments for the Affluent*, 156.
28. "News of the Realty Trade: Park 900," *New York Times* (October 14, 1973), VIII: 8; "The Park 900, New York," *Interior Design* 45 (March 1974): 138–41; "Beame Unveils Park Ave. Sculpture as 'Priceless' Cultural Addition," *New York Times* (March 14, 1974): 41; "Missing Element," editorial, *New York Times* (March 16, 1974): 30; David Finn, *Henry Moore: Sculpture and Environment* (New York: Harry N. Abrams, 1976), 356–59; Goldberger, *The City Observed*, 242; Thomas E. Norton and Jerry E. Patterson, *Living It Up: A Guide to the Named Apartment Houses of New York* (New York: Atheneum, 1984), 259; Trager, *Park Avenue*, 210–11. For another Park Avenue apartment tower set back from the street wall, the thirty-one-story number 1065 (Stephen Lyras, 1974), see Trager, *Park Avenue*, 211.
29. For the John Sherman Hoyt residence, see Stern, Gilmartin and Massengale, *New York 1900*, 356.
30. "The Park 900, New York": 138.
31. Abraham D. Beame quoted in "Beame Unveils Park Ave. Sculpture as 'Priceless' Cultural Addition": 41.
32. "Missing Element": 30.
33. Goldberger, *The City Observed*, 242.
34. "Park Ave. Address for 4½-Ton Nevelson Sculpture," *New York Times* (November 20, 1973): 43; White and Willensky, *AIA Guide* (1978), 239; Jean Lipman, *Nevelson's World* (New York: Hudson Hills Press, in association with the Whitney Museum of American Art, 1983), 224; Margot Gayle and Michele Cohen, *The Art Commission and the Municipal Art Society Guide to Manhattan's Outdoor Sculpture* (New York: Prentice Hall Press, 1988), 247, 255; Laurie Lisle, *Louise Nevelson: A Passionate Life* (New York: Summit, 1990), 10, 282.
35. White and Willensky, *AIA Guide* (1978), 239.
36. Gayle and Cohen, *The Art Commission and the Municipal Art Society Guide to Manhattan's Outdoor Sculpture*, 255.
37. "The Most Talked-About House in New York," *Vogue* 131 (February 1, 1958): 168–77; "More than Modern," *Time* 71 (March 31, 1958): cover, 56–64; Philip Johnson, "Retreat from the International Style to the Present Scene," lecture, Yale University, May 9, 1958, in Peter Eisenman and Robert A. M. Stern, eds., *Philip Johnson: Writings* (New York: Oxford University Press, 1979), 84–97; Wendy Buehr, "In New York's Midst, Edward Stone Turns Brownstone to Castle," *Interiors* 117 (June 1958): 90–95; Ian McCal-

lum, *Architecture USA* (London: Architectural Press, 1959), 91; Winthrop Sargeant, "From Sassafras Branches," *New Yorker* 34 (January 3, 1959): 32–34, 36, 38–49; "Stone's Remodeled Town House," *Architectural Record* 125 (March 1959): 162–64; Ada Louise Huxtable, *Four Walking Tours of Modern Architecture in New York City* (New York: Museum of Modern Art and Municipal Art Society of New York, 1961), 61, 63; Edward Durell Stone, *The Evolution of an Architect* (New York: Horizon Press, 1962), 141–42, 180–83; "A Guide for City Gardeners," *New York* 6 (March 12, 1973): 45–49; White and Willensky, *AIA Guide* (1978), 222; Goldberger, *The City Observed*, 235–36; *Upper East Side Historic District*, 196; Christopher Gray, "Streetscapes: 130 East 64th Street," *New York Times* (June 25, 1989), X: 8, reprinted in Christopher Gray, *Changing New York: The Architectural Scene* (New York: Dover, 1992), 89.

38. Stone, *The Evolution of an Architect*, 141.

39. "The Most Talked-About House in New York": 168.

40. Frank Lloyd Wright quoted in "More than Modern": 64.

41. Goldberger, *The City Observed*, 235.

42. "Manhattan Town Houses: A Rare Breed," *Progressive Architecture* 47 (May 1966): 54; White and Willensky, *AIA Guide* (1978), 230–31; Goldberger, *The City Observed*, 240–41; *Upper East Side Historic District*, 509.

43. Thomas W. Ennis, "Paul Rudolph Plans Modern House Here on Frame of 1870's," *New York Times* (February 19, 1967), VIII: 1, 6; "The Total Town House," *House and Garden* 136 (November 1969): 122–27; Sibyl Moholy-Nagy and Gerhard Schwab, *The Architecture of Paul Rudolph* (New York: Praeger, 1970), 80–83; Herbert L. Smith, Jr., "Private Residence, New York City. Architect: Paul Rudolph," *Architectural Record* 147 (mid-May 1970): 42–45; Paul Rudolph, *Drawings* (Tokyo: A.D.A. Edita, 1972), 40–41; Barclay F. Gordon, ed., *Interior Spaces Designed by Architects* (New York: McGraw-Hill, 1974), 205–7; White and Willensky, *AIA Guide* (1978), 221; Goldberger, *The City Observed*, 234–35.

44. For William Hamby and George Nelson's Sherman M. Fairchild house, see Stern, Gilmartin and Mellins, *New York 1930*, 379–80, 383.

45. "Meet the Architect: Five Houses by Robert A. M. Stern," *GA Houses* 1 (1976): cover, 39–41, 62–69; Sharon Lee Ryder, "Stern Dimensions," *Progressive Architecture* 57 (June 1976): 70–77; "Robert A. M. Stern, John S. Hagmann: Casa a New York," *Domus* 563 (October 1976): 34–35; Paul Goldberger, "Robert A. M. Stern's Two Houses," *A + U* (September 1977): 73–92; "World: Stern Hybrids," *Architectural Review* 162 (December 1977): 331–33; Wolf Von Eckardt, "Architecture's New Rebels," *Washington Post* (December 10, 1977), B: 1–2; Paulhans Peters, "Anpassungsarchitektur," *Baumeister* 75 (December 1978): 1114–21; Goldberger, *The City Observed*, 243–44; Brent C. Brolin, *Architecture in Context: Fitting New Buildings with Old* (New York: Van Nostrand Reinhold, 1980), 128–29; Stanley Abercrombie, "Manhattan Town House Anchored by an Atrium," *Journal of the American Institute of Architects* 69 (mid-May 1980): 234–35; *Robert A. M. Stern: Buildings and Projects 1965–1980*, eds. Peter Arnell and Ted Bickford (New York: Rizzoli International Publications, 1981), 86–97; Toshio Nakamura, ed., "The Residential Works of Robert A. M. Stern," *A + U*, extra edition (July 1982): 18–25, 140; Richard Guy Wilson, "Stern: 'The Enfant Terrible of Postmodernism,'" *Journal of the American Institute of Architects* 72 (March 1983): 105–7, 110; White and Willensky, *AIA Guide* (1988), 374–75; Wendy W. Staebler, *Architectural Detailing in Residential Interiors* (New York: Whitney Library of Design, 1990), 174–75; Ted Kenney, "Marketing the Modern Town House," *New York Times* (May 20, 1990), X: 9; David Dunster, *Key Buildings of the 20th Century, Vol. II: Houses 1945–1989* (New York: Rizzoli International Publications, 1990), 88–89.

46. George O'Brien, ed., *The New York Times Book of Interior Design and Decoration* (New York: Farrar, Straus and Giroux, 1965), 184–89.

47. Abercrombie, "Manhattan Town House Anchored by an Atrium": 234.

48. Ryder, "Stern Dimensions": 70.

49. Goldberger, "Robert A. M. Stern's Two Houses": 84.

50. Goldberger, "Robert A. M. Stern's Two Houses": 84.

51. "Hospital Plans Are Filed," *New York Times* (January 25, 1957): 36; "2,500 Wreckers Leave Jobs Here," *New York Times* (May 2, 1957): 24; Morris Kaplan, "Lenox Hill Goes into 2d Century," *New York Times* (May 11, 1957): 21; "Hospital Group for Park Ave. Corner," *Architectural Forum* 107 (October 1957): 38; "Color and Form with Porcelain Enamel Curtain Walls," advertisement, *Architectural Record* 126 (August 1959): 85; "Hospital Opens Pavilion," *New York Times* (December 11, 1959): 30; "Lenox Hill Hospital Passes Milestone," *New York Times* (December 13, 1959): 126.

52. "Color and Form with Porcelain Enamel Curtain Walls": 85.

53. "Lenox Hill to Get a Health Center," *New York Times* (February 2, 1964), VIII: 1, 8.

54. Carter B. Horsley, "Lenox Hill Hospital Plans a New 12-Story Building," *New York Times* (November 6, 1972): 45; White and Willensky, *AIA Guide* (1978), 233.

55. White and Willensky, *AIA Guide* (1978), 233.

56. White and Willensky, *AIA Guide* (1978), 232; *Upper East Side Historic District*, 664.

57. White and Willensky, *AIA Guide* (1978), 232.

58. "Asia House Viewed," *New York Times* (December 10, 1959): 45; "America Rebuilding," *Architectural Forum* 112 (January 1960): cover; "Asia House Gets Johnson Curtain Wall," *Progressive Architecture* 41 (January 1960): 58; Stuart Preston, "40 Objects from Many Lands on Display at New Building of the Asia Society," *New York Times* (January 7, 1960): 32; Stuart Preston, "Asian and Other Art," *New York Times* (January 10, 1960), II: 11; Huxtable, *Four Walking Tours of Modern Architecture in New York City*, 61, 64; "Three Different Designs for the Facade of Asia House, New York City," *Architectural Review* 129 (February 1961): 81; John M. Jacobus, Jr., *Philip Johnson* (New York: George Braziller, 1962), 41, plates 100–102; *Philip Johnson: Architecture 1949–1965*, with an intro. by Henry-Russell Hitchcock (New York: Holt, Rinehart and Winston, 1966), 29; White and Willensky, *AIA Guide* (1967), 164; Vincent Scully, *American Architecture and Urbanism* (New York: Frederick A. Praeger, 1969), 194; Charles Noble, *Philip Johnson* (New York: Simon & Schuster, 1972), 122; John W. Cook and Heinrich Klotz, *Conversations with Architects* (New York: Praeger, 1973), 30–32; Goldberger, *The City Observed*, 235; *Upper East Side Historic District*, 188; Carol Herselle Krinsky, "Architecture in New York City," in Leonard Wallock, ed., *New York: Culture Capital of the World, 1940–1965* (New York: Rizzoli International Publications, 1988), 112, 114.

59. For the Park Avenue Baptist Church, see Stern, Gilmartin and Mellins, *New York 1930*, 149.

60. Jacobus, *Philip Johnson*, 41.

61. Preston, "Asian and Other Art": 11.

62. Scully, *American Architecture and Urbanism*, 194.

63. Noble, *Philip Johnson*, 122.

64. Goldberger, *The City Observed*, 235.

65. "Remodeling of a City School," *Architectural Forum* 119 (November 1963): 124–27; White and Willensky, *AIA Guide* (1978), 232; *Upper East Side Historic District*, 682. For the Buckley School building on Seventy-fourth Street, see *Upper East Side Historic District*, 732.

66. *Upper East Side Historic District*, 815.

67. "Dickinson Provides Funds for Hunter Scholarships," *New York Times* (May 22, 1966): 72; White and Willensky, *AIA Guide* (1988), 377. For the Vincent Astor residence, see Stern, Gilmartin and Mellins, *New York 1930*, 374–77.

68. "Christian Science Church Opening Today," *New York Times* (December 23, 1954): 12; "Worship Begun in New Edifice," *New York Times* (December 24, 1954): 14.

69. "Christian Science Church Opening Today": 12.

70. "Chapel Is Dedicated," *New York Times* (May 26, 1952): 20; White and Willensky, *AIA Guide* (1978), 239. For the Brick Presbyterian Church, see Stern, Gilmartin and Mellins, *New York 1930*, 164.

71. "Laying Cornerstone for Brick Church Parish House," *New York Times* (November 15, 1948): 17.

72. "Church of Christ Plans to Build," *New York Times* (May 14, 1967), VIII: 4; White and Willensky, *AIA Guide* (1988), 377; Christopher Gray, "Schlock of Ages," *Avenue* 17 (December 1992): 31–32, 34, 36, 38.

73. Thomas W. Ennis, "$2.2-Million Temple Israel Nearing Completion," *New York Times* (November 20, 1966), VIII: 1, 10; White and Willensky, *AIA Guide* (1978), 233; *Upper East Side Historic District*, 786.

THIRD AVENUE

1. "More Insurance Company Housing for New York City," *Architectural Forum* 88 (January 1948): 11; "A Nineteen Story City Apartment," *Architectural Record* 103 (February 1948): 130–31.

2. "More Insurance Company Housing for New York City": 11.

3. "Previews: Manhattan Apartment Is Set Well Back from the Street, and Its Lobby Is Opened to the Outside," *Architectural Forum* 90 (May 1949): 66, 70; "'Manhattan House' Replaces Old Carbarns," *Architectural Record* 105 (May 1949): 106–7, 206; "New York," *Interiors* 108 (June 1949): 12; "Third-Story Park," *Interiors* 109 (November 1949): 14; "Public-Private Corporation to Provide Park-Topped Garage," *American City* 69 (April 1950): 89; Lewis Mumford, "The Sky Line: High, White, and Handsome," *New Yorker* 27 (November 17, 1951): 163–65, 168–70; Talbot F. Hamlin, ed., *Forms and Functions of Twentieth-Century Architecture*, vol. 3 (New York: Columbia University Press, 1952), 73, 80; "Manhattan House Called Outstanding," *New York Times* (May 14, 1952): 46; "Manhattan House," *Architectural Forum* 97 (July 1952): 140–51; Page Beauchamp, "Lobbies," *Progressive Architecture* 33 (November 1952): 124–25; Lois Wagner, "Four Lobbies—All with Views for Manhattan House," *Interiors* 116 (October 1956): 108–9; Ada Louise Huxtable, *Four Walking Tours of Modern Architecture in New York City* (New York: Museum of Modern Art and Municipal Art Society of New York, 1961), 61–63; White and Willensky, *AIA Guide* (1967), 166; Paul Goldberger, *The City Observed: New York* (New York: Random House, 1979), 264–65; John Tauranac, *Essential New York* (New York: Holt, Rinehart and Winston, 1979), 193–94; Thomas E. Norton and Jerry E. Patterson, *Living It Up: A Guide to the Named Apartment Houses of New York* (New York: Atheneum, 1984), 221; Carol Herselle Krinsky, *Gordon Bunshaft of Skidmore, Owings & Merrill* (New York: Architectural History Foundation; Cambridge, Mass.: MIT Press, 1988), 13–14, 30–33, 335; Carol Herselle Krinsky, "Architecture in New York City," in Leonard Wallock, ed., *New York: Culture Capital of the World, 1940–1965* (New York: Rizzoli International Publications, 1988), 96; "White-Brick High Rises," *7 Days* 2 (June 14, 1989): 27, 29; Richard Plunz, *A History of Housing in New York City* (New York: Columbia University Press, 1990), 287–88; Elaine Louie, "Currents: Studying the 'White Boxes,'" *New York Times* (February 17, 1994), C: 3.

4. W. Boesiger, ed., *Le Corbusier: Oeuvre complète 1946–1952*, vol. 5 (Zurich: Editions Girsberger, 1955), 193–227.

5. "A Nineteen Story City Apartment": 131.

6. "A Face-Lifting Job on East Side Block," *New York Times* (March 11, 1951), VIII: 1.

7. "'Manhattan House' Replaces Old Carbarns": 106.

8. Mumford, "The Sky Line: High, White, and Handsome": 163–64.

9. Mumford, "The Sky Line: High, White, and Handsome": 164–65, 168.

10. "New York Life Insurance Co. Taking Applications for Professional Suites in Manhattan House," *Real Estate Record and Guide* 165 (February 4, 1950): 3; Bosley Crowther, "The 'Class Theater': The New Beekman Marks Trend in Film Housing," *New York Times* (May 14, 1952), II: 1; Christopher Gray, "Streetscapes: The Beekman Theater, a French School, Old Initials," *New York Times* (September 5, 1993), X: 6.

11. Crowther, "The 'Class Theater': The New Beekman Marks Trend in Film Housing": 1.

12. "Originality within a Budget," *Progressive Architecture* 43 (October 1962): 192.

13. "Deluxe Apt. Planned for East Side Site," *Real Estate Record and Guide* 182 (November 1, 1958): 4; Olga Gueft, "Downstairs in the Lobby of Imperial House," *Interiors* 123 (February 1964): 83; Norton and Patterson, *Living It Up*, 186.

14. Maurice Foley, "Lenox Hill to Get Housing Project," *New York Times* (August 31, 1958): 58; "City's Largest Luxury Apartment House Started by Rudin at 215 East 68th St.," *Real Estate Record and Guide* 187 (June 3, 1961): 3.

15. Thomas W. Ennis, "High-Rent Houses Will Line 3d Ave.," *New York Times* (March 15, 1959), VIII: 1, 3.

16. Samuel Grafton, "Why You Can Get Stuck Moving into a New Apartment House," *Esquire* 89 (October 1961): 88–89, 187–90.

17. "Tishman to Construct Co-op at 3rd Ave. and 72d St.," *Real Estate Record and Guide* 187 (February 11, 1961): 2; "Manhattan Apartments," *Architectural Forum* 114 (June 1961): 51; "Apartment Projects for New York and Philadelphia," *Architectural Record* 130 (July 1961): 14; "New York Nears Completion—Almost," *Architectural Forum* 117 (October 1962): 16–17; "Apartments in the Context of American Cities," *Progressive Architecture* 44 (July 1963): 106–17; White and Willensky, *AIA Guide* (1967), 168; Andrew Alpern, *Apartments for the Affluent* (New York: McGraw-Hill, 1975), 138–39; Goldberger, *The City Observed*, 266; Norton and Patterson, *Living It Up*, 331; Steven Ruttenbaum, *Mansions in the Clouds: The Skyscraper Palazzi of Emery Roth* (New York: Balsam Press, 1986), 207.

18. For Loew's Seventy-second Street, see Stern, Gilmartin and Mellins, *New York 1930*, 254, 263.

19. "Variation Going Up," *Progressive Architecture* 49 (January 1968): 30; "Twin-Tower Design Makes All Apartments Corner Suites," *Real Estate Record and Guide* 203 (March 22, 1969): 2–3; Norton and Patterson, *Living It Up*, 267.

20. "Lamps Give Old Charm to 3d Ave.," *New York Times* (April 21, 1968), VIII: 6; "Bank Creates Its Own Lamp Posts to Provide 3rd Avenue Blockfront with 'Old New York' Flavor," *Real Estate Record and Guide* 202 (July 27, 1968): 4–5; Norton and Patterson, *Living It Up*, 58.

21. "Coop at 3rd Av. & 86th St.," *Real Estate Record and Guide* 189 (February 10, 1962): 5; "Manhattan's Yorkville Section Gets Taste of Suburbia," *New York Times* (September 3, 1967), VIII: 1; Norton and Patterson, *Living It Up*, 258; Hannah Rubin, "Sturm & Drang Uptown," *On the Avenue* 2 (May 1986): 7.

22. "Manhattan's Yorkville Section Gets Taste of Suburbia": 1.

23. Thomas Buckley, "Ruppert Brewery Is Closed Here," *New York Times* (January 1, 1966): 27.

24. M. A. Farber, "Apartments and School on Old Ruppert Site Studied by City," *New York Times* (April 21, 1967): 25; Seth S. King, "Yorkville Project Is Approved for Housing, School and a Park," *New York Times* (March 21, 1968): 80; Charles G. Bennett, "Park Usage Voted for Steeplechase," *New York Times* (May 23, 1968): 47; Seth S. King, "City Will Build on Ruppert Site," *New York Times* (June 21, 1968): 82.

25. "Ruppert Units May Open in '74," *New York Times* (December 4, 1973): 49; Alan S. Oser, "Ruppert Towers Holds Special East Side Place," *New York Times* (January 10, 1975): 61; Andrea O. Dean, "Profile: Davis, Brody of New York, the 1975 Firm Award Recipient," *Journal of the American Institute of Architects* 63 (May 1975): 44–48; White and Willensky, *AIA Guide* (1978), 245; August Heckscher, "Design Notebook," *New York Times* (June 1, 1978), C: 11; Norton and Patterson, *Living It Up*, 293.

26. Oser, "Ruppert Towers Holds Special East Side Place": 61.

27. Dean, "Profile: Davis, Brody of New York, the 1975 Firm Award Recipient": 48.

28. White and Willensky, *AIA Guide* (1978), 245.

29. Heckscher, "Design Notebook": 11.

30. White and Willensky, *AIA Guide* (1988), 398.

31. "Most New Third Avenue Shops Retain Old Flavor of Street," *Real Estate Record and Guide* 199 (June 17, 1967): 3–4.

32. White and Willensky, *AIA Guide* (1978), 245.

FAR EAST SIDE

1. See Stern, Gilmartin and Mellins, *New York 1930*, 427, 429–35, 437.

2. For a discussion of tenement conversions in the area, see Stern, Gilmartin and Mellins, *New York 1930*, 383.

3. "The Race to Design," *Interiors* 115 (September 1955): 106–7; Thomas W. Ennis, "Architect Becomes Investor, Converts Flat on East Side," *New York Times* (September 2, 1956), VIII: 1; Betsy Darrah, "Metamorphosis on the Upper East Side," *Interiors* 116 (December 1956): 102–3; Thomas E. Norton and Jerry E. Patterson, *Living It Up: A Guide to the Named Apartment Houses of New York* (New York: Atheneum, 1984), 52.

4. "The Race to Design": 106–7.

5. Ennis, "Architect Becomes Investor, Converts Flat on East Side": 1.

6. "From a Rough Old Brownstone, a Calm Religious Building," *Architectural Forum* 100 (May 1954): 162–63.

7. "Fiscal Designs for Two Apartments," *Architectural Forum* 113 (December 1960): 84–89; "Apartments in the Context of American Cities," *Progressive Architecture* 44 (July 1963): 106–17; "FHA Honor Awards for Residential Design," *Architectural Record* 135 (January 1964): 157; White and Willensky, *AIA Guide* (1967), 185; Andrew Alpern, *Apartments for the Affluent* (New York: McGraw-Hill, 1975), 142–43; Paul Goldberger, *The City Observed: New York* (New York: Random House, 1979), 265–66; John Tauranac, *Essential New York* (New York: Holt, Rinehart and Winston, 1979), 215.

8. Stern, Gilmartin and Mellins, *New York 1930*, 207–8.

9. For a discussion of Second Avenue's postwar redevelopment, see "DeLuxe Second Avenue Forecast for 1956," *Real Estate Record and Guide* 177 (January 7, 1956): 3. Also see "Luxury Apartment Building to Occupy 2nd Ave. Blockfront, 66th–67th Streets," *Real Estate Record and Guide* 174 (December 11, 1954): 3; "Estate Sells Second Avenue Blockfront; To Be Improved with Apartment Structure," *Real Estate Record and Guide* 174 (December 25, 1954): 3; "Builders Buy 80,000 Sq. Ft. Plot on Second Ave. for Development," *Real Estate Record and Guide* 177 (February 25, 1956): 4–5; "New East Side Fashionable Residential Center Under Wrap," *Real Estate Record and Guide* 179 (January 19, 1957): 3.

10. White and Willensky, *AIA Guide* (1978), 245.

11. White and Willensky, *AIA Guide* (1988), 409.

12. Goldberger, *The City Observed*, 268–69; White and Willensky, *AIA Guide* (1988), 409.

13. For La Tourette, see Anton Henze, *La Tourette: The Le Corbusier Monastery*, trans. Janet Seligman (New York: George Wittenborn, 1966). For Boston City Hall, see Alex Krieger, ed., *The Architecture of Kallmann, McKinnell & Wood* (Cambridge, Mass.: Harvard University Graduate School of Design; New York: Rizzoli International Publications, 1988), 21–37.

14. Goldberger, *The City Observed*, 268.

15. "New City Housing to Bear Name of Stanley Isaacs," *New York Times* (July 11, 1963): 18; "Mayor Calls Neglect of Aged Society's 'Growing Problem,'" *New York Times* (April 20, 1966): 36; Edith S. Isaacs, *Love Affair with a City: The Story of Stanley M. Isaacs* (New York: Random House, 1967), unnumbered plate; White and Willensky, *AIA Guide* (1978), 242.

16. White and Willensky, *AIA Guide* (1978), 242.

17. For discussion of the Rockefeller Institute for Medical Research, see George W. Corner, *A History of the Rockefeller Institute, 1901–1953, Origins and Growth* (New York: Rockefeller Institute Press, 1964); *Institute to University: A Seventy-fifth Anniversary Colloquium, June 8, 1976* (New York: Rockefeller University, 1977); E. Richard Brown, *Rockefeller Medicine Men: Medicine and Capitalism in America* (Berkeley, Calif.: University of California Press, 1979); John Ensor Harr and Peter J. Johnson, *The Rockefeller Century* (New York: Charles Scribner's Sons, 1988), 62–70. For discussion of the City and Suburban Homes Company's pioneering efforts at housing reform, see Stern, Gilmartin and Massengale, *New York 1900*, 283, 287, 290; Andrew S. Dolkart and Sharon Z. Macosko, *A Dream Fulfilled: City and Suburban's York Avenue Estate*, pamphlet (New York: Coalition to Save City & Suburban Housing, Inc., 1988).

18. For Thomas's housing project, see Stern, Gilmartin and Mellins, *New York 1930*, 419, 421. For the Church of the Epiphany, see Stern, Gilmartin and Mellins, *New York 1930*, 166.

19. "Tishman Realty & Construction Company Adds to York Avenue Housing Plot," *Real Estate Record and Guide* 162 (November 27, 1948): 33; "$10,000,000 Apartments," *Ar-*
chitectural Record 105 (January 1949): 138, 140; "East Side Project Begun by Tishman," *New York Times* (May 3, 1949): 44; "East Side Colony Spreads to North," *New York Times* (May 8, 1949), VIII: 1, 6; "Tishman Realty & Construction Company Starts Work on $12,000,000 Project," *Real Estate Record and Guide* 163 (May 21, 1949): 3; "Comment and Reports to Record and Guide," *Real Estate Record and Guide* 164 (September 24, 1949): 3; "Tishman Realty & Construction Company Providing Elaborate Garage Facilities for Sutton Terrace Tenants," *Real Estate Record and Guide* 164 (December 10, 1949): 3; "Tishman Says Renting Success in Sutton Terrace Partly Due to Landscaped Private Garden," *Real Estate Record and Guide* 168 (August 11, 1951): 3; Lewis Mumford, "The Sky Line: Big Buildings and Tremendous Trifles," *New Yorker* 27 (December 21, 1951): 60–65; Norton and Patterson, *Living It Up*, 327.

20. Norman Tishman quoted in "Tishman Says Renting Success in Sutton Terrace Partly Due to Landscaped Private Garden": 3.

21. Mumford, "The Sky Line: Big Buildings and Tremendous Trifles": 60.

22. "Construction, Renting Underway on Twin Buildings in East Sixties," *Real Estate Record and Guide* 175 (June 4, 1955): 3–4; Norton and Patterson, *Living It Up*, 293.

23. "East Side Colony Spreads to North": 1.

24. "East Side to Get 'Luxury' Housing Overlooking River," *New York Times* (November 19, 1950), VIII: 1; "How to Stretch a View," *Interiors* 110 (January 1951): 10, 12; "Herbert Charles & Company, Inc., Opens Renting Office in 60 Sutton Place South," *Real Estate Record and Guide* 168 (September 1, 1951): 3; "Model Apartments on View at 60 Sutton Place South," *Real Estate Record and Guide* 169 (March 15, 1952): 3.

25. For the Darien Apartments, see Stuart Cohen, *Chicago Architects*, with an intro. by Stanley Tigerman (Chicago: Swallow, 1976), 52–53.

26. Corner, *A History of the Rockefeller Institute, 1901–1953, Origins and Growth*, 63.

27. Ira Henry Freeman, "4 Buildings Added by Institute Here," *New York Times* (January 21, 1958): 31; Victoria Newhouse, *Wallace K. Harrison, Architect* (New York: Rizzoli International Publications, 1989), 176.

28. Freeman, "4 Buildings Added by Institute Here": 31; Newhouse, *Wallace K. Harrison, Architect*, 176.

29. "Medical Center," *Architectural Forum* 106 (April 1957): 39; Morris Kaplan, "Medical Hunters Get Modern Arms," *New York Times* (November 10, 1957): 126; Freeman, "4 Buildings Added by Institute Here": 31; White and Willensky, *AIA Guide* (1967), 185; White and Willensky, *AIA Guide* (1978), 250; Newhouse, *Wallace K. Harrison, Architect*, 177.

30. Freeman, "4 Buildings Added by Institute Here": 31.

31. Newhouse, *Wallace K. Harrison, Architect*, 179–80.

32. Newhouse, *Wallace K. Harrison, Architect*, 179.

33. "Buildings in the News," *Architectural Record* 144 (July 1968): 43.

34. "Faculty Housing on East River," *New York Times* (November 29, 1973): 47; "A 26-Story Faculty Apartment Building for Rockefeller University Is to Be Built on York Avenue between 62d and 63d Streets," *New York Times* (December 16, 1973), VIII: 2; "In New York," *Interiors* 133 (February 1974): 18; White and Willensky, *AIA Guide* (1978), 250.

35. Quoted in "In New York": 18.

36. "Cornerstone Laid at Cancer Center," *New York Times* (May 21, 1938): 17; "Unions Denounced as Hospital Opens," *New York Times* (June 15, 1939): 48; "The Memorial Hospital for the Treatment of Cancer and Allied Diseases, New York City," *Architectural Forum* 71 (November 1939): 379–83; White and Willensky, *AIA Guide* (1988), 403.

37. "New Institute Turns Big Guns of Science on Man's Stubbornest Malady—Cancer," *Architectural Forum* 89 (August 1948): 65–69; White and Willensky, *AIA Guide* (1988), 403.

38. "Projects: Manhattan Nurses' Tower," *Architectural Forum* 113 (July 1960): 50; "Unusual High-Rise Attracts Nurses to Cancer Center," *Architectural Record* 133 (January 1963): 130–39; "Nido per infermiere," *L'Architettura cronache e storia* 9 (June 1963): 108–9; Newhouse, *Wallace K. Harrison, Architect*, 179, 181.

39. Newhouse, *Wallace K. Harrison, Architect*, 179, 181.

40. "Hospital Housing Is Popular in City," *New York Times* (April 17, 1966), VIII: 15; White and Willensky, *AIA Guide* (1988), 404.

41. "Housing Set for Medical Center Units," *New York Times* (April 29, 1972): 35; White and Willensky, *AIA Guide* (1988), 403.

42. "$300-Million Complex May Use Highway Air Rights," *Engineering News-Record* 188 (June 1, 1972): 15; "New Medical Facilities to Rise over East River Drive," *Architectural Record* 152 (September 1972): 36.

43. "Room at the Top," *Newsweek* 64 (August 10, 1964): 65; Norton and Patterson, *Living It Up*, 262.

44. "A.S.P.C.A. Moves Pets into New Quarters," *New York Times* (October 3, 1950): 23; "A.S.P.C.A. Moves Offices Today," *New York Times* (October 25, 1950): 44; "New York A.S.P.C.A. Headquarters," *Architectural Record* 110 (October 1951): 141–43.

45. Stern, Gilmartin and Mellins, *New York 1930*, 434, 437.

46. Stern, Gilmartin and Mellins, *New York 1930*, 433–35.

47. Stern, Gilmartin and Mellins, *New York 1930*, 122, 437.

48. "Political 'Loafers' Berated by Mayor," *New York Times* (May 27, 1939): 17; White and Willensky, *AIA Guide* (1988), 412.

49. "Suites with Terraces Attracting Tenants to New Buildings in Manhattan and Queens," *New York Times* (July 13, 1941), XI: 1; "East End Ave. Suites Nearing Completion," *New York Times* (September 14, 1941), XI: 1–2; "New Apartment Structures for Manhattan and the Bronx," *New York Times* (September 21, 1941), XI: 10.

50. "East End Suites Will Have Garage," *New York Times* (April 30, 1950), VIII: 1; "Steel Work Is Rising on 19-Story House for 150 Families on East End Avenue," *New York Times* (February 18, 1951), VIII: 5.

51. "'Luxury' Suites on East End Avenue Stress Ample Space in Fewer Rooms," *New York Times* (April 22, 1951), VIII: 1.

52. "The Record Reports," *Architectural Record* 111 (June 1952): 330.

53. "New Luxury Co-op Will Feature Roof-Top Pool," *Real Estate Record and Guide* 182 (July 12, 1958): 3–4; "Riviera on the River," *Interior Design* 31 (May 1960): 145–51.

54. "Riviera on the River": 145.

55. "New Luxury Co-op Will Feature Roof-Top Pool": 3.

56. Lee E. Cooper, "Plan Garden Apartments for 575 Families in Long-Vacant Block Facing Schurz Park," *New York Times* (March 27, 1941): 40; Frank W. Crane, "Plan Apartments on Historic Land near Schurz Park," *New York Times* (April 6, 1941), XI: 1–2; Lee E. Cooper, "Apartment Group in Gracie Sq. Area to Cost $2,000,000," *New York Times* (June 15, 1941), XI: 1, 6.

57. William J. Demorest quoted in Cooper, "Plan Garden Apartments for 575 Families in Long-Vacant Block Facing Schurz Park": 40.

58. "Waterfront View from Roof of New East Side Apartment House," *New York Times* (September 7, 1941), XI: 1; "Renting Campaign Stresses Open Areas," *Real Estate Record and Guide* 148 (December 27, 1941): 4; White and Willensky, *AIA Guide* (1978), 243; Norton and Patterson, *Living It Up*, 156–57.

59. "Municipal Asphalt Plant," *Architectural Forum* 80 (March 1944): 109–12; "City Plant Called Ugly by Moses Hailed as a Beauty by Museum," *New York Times* (April 25, 1944): 25; Burton H. Holmes, "Exposed Concrete Today," *Progressive Architecture* 41 (October 1960): 150–57; White and Willensky, *AIA Guide* (1967), 180–81; Goldberger, *The City Observed*, 271; Stern, Gilmartin and Mellins, *New York 1930*, 558.

60. Robert Moses quoted in "Municipal Asphalt Plant": 110.

61. Robert Moses quoted in "City Plant Called Ugly by Moses Hailed as a Beauty by Museum": 25.

62. Quoted in "City Plant Called Ugly by Moses Hailed as a Beauty by Museum": 25.

63. "Municipal Asphalt Plant": 110.

64. White and Willensky, *AIA Guide* (1967), 181.

65. Goldberger, *The City Observed*, 271.

66. "Évolution des modes de construction: Moshe Safdie," *L'Architecture d'Aujourd'hui* 39 (September 1968): 46–52; Moshe Safdie, *For Everyone a Garden* (Cambridge, Mass.: MIT Press, 1974), 88–99.

Chapter 12

Harlem and Upper Manhattan

1. Michael Harrington, "Harlem Today," *Dissent* 8 (summer 1961): 371–77.

BLACK AMERICA'S CAPITAL CITY

1. Fannie Hurst, "The Other, and Unknown, Harlem," *New York Times* (August 4, 1946), VI: 18–19, 38–39.

2. Layhmond Robinson, Jr., "Our Changing City: Harlem Now on the Upsurge," *New York Times* (July 8, 1955): 25. For useful general discussions of Harlem in the postwar period, see Robert C. Weaver, *The Negro Ghetto* (New York: Harcourt, Brace, 1948); Claude Brown, "Harlem, My Harlem," *Dissent* 8 (summer 1961): 378–85; Michael Harrington, "Harlem Today," *Dissent* 8 (summer 1961): 371–77; William A. Glaser, *A Harlem Almanac* (New York: Bureau of Applied Social Research, Columbia University, 1964); Claude Brown, *Manchild in the Promised Land* (New York: New American Library, 1965); Fred Halstead, *Harlem Stirs* (New York: Marzani & Munsell, 1966); Claude McKay, *Harlem, Negro Metropolis* (New York: Harcourt Brace Jovanovich, 1968); Allon Schoener, ed., *Harlem on My Mind: Cultural Capital of Black America 1900–1968*, exhibition catalogue (New York: Random House, 1968); John Henrik Clarke, ed., *Harlem: A Community in Transition* (New York: Citadel Press, 1970); Bennett Harrison and Thomas Vietorisz, *The Economic Development of Harlem* (New York: Praeger, 1970); Harlem Urban Development Corporation, *A Profile of the Harlem Area: Findings of the Harlem Task Force* (New York: Harlem Urban Development Corporation, 1973).

3. For the 1935 riots, see Mayor's Commission on Conditions in Harlem, *The Negro in Harlem: A Report on Social and Economic Conditions Responsible for the Outbreak of March 19, 1935* (New York, 1935); "Police Shoot into Rioters, Kill Negro in Harlem Mob," *New York Times* (March 20, 1935): 1, 35; "Police End Harlem Riot; Mayor Starts Inquiry; Dodge Sees a Red Plot," *New York Times* (March 21, 1935): 1, 16; "Harlem's Stores Ask Soldier Guard," *New York Times* (March 21, 1935): 16; "Mayor Lays Riot to 'Vicious' Group," *New York Times* (March 21, 1935): 16. For the 1943 riots, see "Harlem Disorders Bring Quick Action by City and Army," *New York Times* (August 2, 1943): 1, 16; "Harlem Is Orderly with Heavy Guard Ready for Trouble," *New York Times* (August 3, 1943): 1, 10; "Mayor in Command of Harlem Forces," *New York Times* (August 3, 1943): 9; "Race Bias Denied as Rioting Factor," *New York Times* (August 3, 1943): 9; "Harlem's Tragedy," editorial, *New York Times* (August 3, 1943): 18; Dominic J. Capeci, *The Harlem Riot of 1943* (Philadelphia, Pa.: Temple University Press, 1977).

4. "Harlem's Tragedy": 18.

5. James Felt, "Harlem Riots: Is Bad Housing Responsible?" *Citizens' Housing Committee Housing News and Post-War Planning News Digest* 2 (August–September 1943): 2–3.

6. Felt, "Harlem Riots: Is Bad Housing Responsible?": 3.

7. "The Problem of Harlem," editorial, *New York Times* (June 1, 1945): 14.

8. Robinson, "Our Changing City: Harlem Now on the Upsurge": 25.

9. Theodore Jones, "Negro Boy Killed; 300 Harass Police," *New York Times* (July 17, 1964): 1, 31; Theodore Jones, "Teen-age Parade Protests Killing," *New York Times* (July 18, 1964): 1, 24; Paul L. Montgomery and Francis X. Clines, "Thousands Riot in Harlem Area; Scores Are Hurt," *New York Times* (July 19, 1964): 1, 54; Paul L. Montgomery, "Night of Riots Began with Calm Rally," *New York Times* (July 20, 1964): 1, 16; Junins Griffin, "'Guerrilla War' Urged in Harlem," *New York Times* (July 20 1964): 16; "Harlem Is a Study in Contrasts as Sun Rises on Scene of Riots," *New York Times* (July 20, 1964): 16; Peter Kihss, "City to Increase Negro Policemen on Harlem Duty," *New York Times* (July 21, 1964): 1, 22; David Halberstam, "White Harlem Merchants Tense; Many Would Like to Sell Stores," *New York Times* (July 22, 1964): 18; E. W. Kenworthy, "Johnson Orders Full F.B.I. Inquiry in Harlem Riots," *New York Times* (July 22, 1964): 1, 18; Peter Kihss, "Screvane Links Reds to Rioting," *New York Times* (July 22, 1964): 1, 18; Gay Talese, "A Negro Policeman in Harlem Faces Taunts and Loneliness," *New York Times* (July 22, 1964): 18; "Editorial Comments from Around Nation on Outbreak of Violence in Harlem," *New York Times* (July 22, 1964): 18; Peter Kihss, "Wagner Asserts Disorders Harm Negroes' Cause," *New York Times* (July 23, 1964): 1, 12; Gay Talese, "Puerto Rican Peace Patrol Acts to Keep East Harlem Calm," *New York Times* (July 23, 1964): 13; Will Lissner, "7 Harlem Leaders Agree Time Is Ripe to Cure Slum Evils," *New York Times* (July 27, 1964): 1, 19.

10. Michael Harrington quoted in "Tear the Ghetto Down," *Village Voice* 9 (July 23, 1964): 1.

11. James Baldwin, "Fifth Avenue, Uptown," *Esquire* 54 (July 1960): 70–73, 76, reprinted in James Baldwin, *Nobody Knows My Name: More Notes of a Native Son* (New York: Dial Press, 1961), 56–71.

12. June Meyer, "Instant Slum Clearance," *Esquire* 63 (April 1965): 108–11; Peter Blake, "The World of Buckminster Fuller," *Architectural Forum* 136 (January–February 1972): 49–51; Pier Angelo Cetica, *R. B. Fuller: Uno Spazio Per La Technologia* (Verona: Edam-Padova, 1979), 178, 180.

13. Andrea Lopen, "Harlem's Streetcorner Architects," *Architectural Forum* 123 (December 1965): 50–51; Richard Hatch, "Urban Renewal in Harlem," *Zodiac* 17 (1967): 196–98; "ARCH on the March," *Architectural Forum* 126 (June 1967): 84–85; "Harlem Labeled City's 'Junkyard,'" *New York Times* (August 24, 1968): 30; "ARCH: Black Advocates," *Progressive Architecture* 49 (September 1968): 107–13; "Pilot Apprenticeships," *Architectural Forum* 129 (October 1968): 33–34; Priscilla Tucker, "Poor Peoples' Plan," *Metropolitan Museum of Art Bulletin* 27 (January 1969): 265–69; "Harlem's ARCH Gets Minorities into the Profession," *Architectural Record* 147 (February 1969): 41.

14. Richard Hatch quoted in Lopen, "Harlem's Streetcorner Architects": 50.

15. J. Max Bond quoted in Tucker, "Poor Peoples' Plan": 267.

16. Statement of the Architects Renewal Committee in Harlem quoted in Tucker, "Poor Peoples' Plan": 265.

17. Tucker, "Poor Peoples' Plan": 265.

18. *The New City: Architecture and Urban Renewal*, exhibition catalogue (New York: Museum of Modern Art, 1967); Ada Louise Huxtable, "Planning the New City," *New York Times* (January 24, 1967): 39, 45; C. Richard Hatch, "The Museum of Modern Art Discovers Harlem," *Architectural Forum* 126 (March 1967): 38–47; "Planning Exhibit in New York Hopes to Spur Public Opinion," *Architectural Record* 141 (March 1967): 36; Edward C. Burks, "Tree-Studded Mall to Cover Central's Park Avenue Rail Trestle," *New York Times* (March 5, 1967): 67; Morton Happenfeld, "Artis Amid Chaos," letter to the editor, *Architectural Forum* 126 (April 1967): 16; Giorgio Piccinato, "I problemi delle città americane," *L'Architettura cronache e storia* 13 (June 1967): 120–23; "Urban Design Group: Establishment Advocates," *Progressive Architecture* 49 (September 1968): 111–13; Jonathan Barnett, "New Ways to Practice Urban Design," *Architectural Record* 147 (January 1970): 146–47, 150; Jonathan Barnett, *Urban Design as Public Policy* (New York: Architectural Record Books, 1974), 156–60, 194.

19. Hatch, "The Museum of Modern Art Discovers Harlem": 39, 47.

20. Hatch, "The Museum of Modern Art Discovers Harlem": 40.

21. See Colin Rowe and Fred Koetter, *Collage City* (Cambridge, Mass.: MIT Press, 1978).

22. Hatch, "The Museum of Modern Art Discovers Harlem": 42.

23. Hatch, "The Museum of Modern Art Discovers Harlem": 46.

24. Hatch, "The Museum of Modern Art Discovers Harlem": 44.

25. Barnett, *Urban Design as Public Policy*, 156.

26. Philip Johnson, "Our Ugly Cities," commencement speech, Mount Holyoke College, June 5, 1966, published in *Mount Holyoke Alumnae Quarterly* 1 (summer 1966): 86–88, reprinted in Peter Eisenman and Robert A. M. Stern, eds., *Philip Johnson: Writings* (New York: Oxford University Press, 1979), 156–61. Also see Alison Sky and Michelle Stone, *Unbuilt America* (New York: McGraw-Hill, 1976), 144.

27. Philip Johnson quoted in Sky and Stone, *Unbuilt America*, 144.

28. Quoted in C. Gerald Fraser, "People Are Gloomy on Future of Area," *New York Times* (November 21, 1974): 49, 53. Also see Charlayne Hunter, "Population, Housing and Jobs Declining," *New York Times* (November 21, 1974): 49, 53; Peter Kihss, "Rehabilitation for Harlem: 10-Year Program Is Issued, with New Housing and Jobs," *New York Times* (November 21, 1974): 49.

29. Lena Williams, "Middle-Class Blacks Return to Harlem," *New York Times* (August 21, 1976): 1, 44.

30. Benjamin Grant quoted in Williams, "Middle-Class Blacks Return to Harlem": 1.

EAST HARLEM

1. For a general discussion of life in Italian Harlem, see Robert A. Orsi, *The Madonna of 115th Street: Faith and Community in Italian Harlem, 1880–1950* (New Haven, Conn.: Yale University Press, 1985). For Spanish Harlem, see Dan Wakefield, *Island in the City: The World of Spanish Harlem* (Boston: Houghton Mifflin, 1959); Patricia Cayo Sexton, *Spanish Harlem: An Anatomy of Poverty* (New York: Harper & Row, 1965).

2. Clarence Woodbury, "Our Worst Slum," *American Magazine* 148 (September 1949): 30–31, 128–32.

3. "Women Spur Plan for East Harlem," *New York Times* (April 22, 1942): 27.

4. "The World They Never Made," *Time* 55 (June 12, 1950): 24–26.

5. V. S. Pritchett, "A Stranger in New York, Part II," *Holiday* 36 (August 1964): 48–53, 73–76.

6. Paul Goldberger, *The City Observed: New York* (New York: Random House, 1979), 301.

7. "New Apartments and Civic Developments to Make Harlem a Better Neighborhood," *New York Times* (November 17, 1946): 3; illustrated in *Architectural Forum* 87 (October 1947): cover, 3; "Acquisition of Site at Private Sale for Harlem Housing Project Gets Under Way," *Real Estate Record and Guide* 162 (December 11, 1948): 3; Lewis Mumford, "The Sky Line: The Red-Brick Beehives," *New Yorker* 26 (May 6, 1950): 92, 94–98; Talbot F. Hamlin, ed., *Forms and Functions of Twentieth-Century Architecture*, vol. 3 (New York: Columbia University Press, 1952), 176–77, 194; White and Willensky, *AIA Guide* (1967), 197; White and Willensky, *AIA Guide* (1978), 288; Thomas E. Norton and Jerry E. Patterson, *Living It Up: A Guide to the Named Apartment Houses of New York* (New York: Atheneum, 1984), 189.

8. Mumford, "The Sky Line: The Red-Brick Beehives": 96.

9. "Housing Project Opens," *New York Times* (October 10, 1950): 30; Norton and Patterson, *Living It Up*, 206.

10. "Housing Authority Charts 2 Projects," *New York Times* (November 1, 1951): 31; "Yankees Planning Fans' Parking Lot," *New York Times* (January 3, 1952): 32; "Jack Hopes Congress Will Help on Slums," *New York Times* (June 9, 1954): 25; Norton and Patterson, *Living It Up*, 356.

11. "Housing to Honor Wagner, Sr.," *New York Times* (May 14, 1954): 18; "Mayor Dedicates Housing to Father," *New York Times* (November 6, 1954): 19; "First Tenants Move to Wagner Houses," *New York Times* (August 3, 1956): 10; Norton and Patterson, *Living It Up*, 351.

12. "Housing Contract Let," *New York Times* (June 15, 1954): 55; "Flushing Bus Plan Wins Aid of Moses," *New York Times* (June 17, 1954): 31; Paul Crowell, "City Defers Move on Parking Plan," *New York Times* (October 16, 1954): 19; White and Willensky, *AIA Guide* (1978), 287; Norton and Patterson, *Living It Up*, 145.

13. Walter F. Wagner, Jr., "Franklin Plaza: New Life for an Urban Complex," *Architectural Record* 138 (July 1965): 170.

14. "Units of Four Rooms and Up Planned in New Housing," *New York Times* (June 18, 1958): 35; Norton and Patterson, *Living It Up*, 366.

15. "Housing for City Approved by U.S.," *New York Times* (August 27, 1950): 74; "Harlem Will Get Low Cost Housing," *New York Times* (August 9, 1951): 23; "Harlem's

Playful Playground," *Architectural Forum* 114 (March 1961): 106; Albert Mayer, "Outdoor Recreation Areas for Housing Projects," *Recreation* 55 (May 1962): 253–56; Albert Mayer in consultation with Clarence Stein, "Architecture as Total Community: The Challenge Ahead. II. Public Housing as Community," *Architectural Record* 135 (April 1964): 169–78; Norton and Patterson, *Living It Up*, 190.

16. "East Harlem—A Challenge," *Citizens' Housing and Planning Council Housing News* 8 (July 1950): 1, 4.

17. Thomas W. Ennis, "Harlem Changed by Public Housing," *New York Times* (June 23, 1957), VIII: 1, 12.

18. Gertrude Samuels, "A Walk Along the Worst Block," *New York Times* (September 30, 1962), VI: 18–19, 82.

19. Woody Klein, *Let in the Sun* (New York: Macmillan, 1964). Also see Woody Klein, "Why One of the Worst Slums in New York Hasn't Been Torn Down," *New York* 1 (May 6, 1968): 32–36.

20. "How to Make Easy Money without Really Trying," *Architectural Forum* 116 (January 1962): 9.

21. Quoted in Klein, "Why One of the Worst Slums in New York Hasn't Been Torn Down": 32.

22. Klein, "Why One of the Worst Slums in New York Hasn't Been Torn Down": 35.

23. "Cents and Sensibility," *Progressive Architecture* 47 (January 1966): 45, 57; "Gypsum Begins Work on Rehabilitation of Second Slum," *Real Estate Record and Guide* 197 (April 16, 1966): 2; "The Private Way," *Time* 87 (June 3, 1966): 89; "Rx for Slums?" *Newsweek* 68 (July 25, 1966): 68; "U.S. Gypsum Rehabilitation Project Succeeds," *Progressive Architecture* 48 (February 1967): 28.

24. Zion R. Paige quoted in "The Private Way": 89.

25. *Fifth Ruberoid Architectural Design Competition* (New York: Ruberoid Company, 1963); "$25,000 Ruberoid Competition Uses Manhattan Urban Renewal Project," *Architectural Record* 133 (February 1963): 23; "Ruberoid Award Winners Announced," *Architectural Record* 134 (September 1963): 10; "Minneapolitans Win Ruberoid Competition," *Progressive Architecture* 33 (September 1963): 63, 65–66; "Ruberoid Competition Gives New York Ideas for Urban Renewal," *Architectural Record* 134 (October 1963): 14–15; "City-Planning Brochure," *Progressive Architecture* 46 (February 1965): 58; Richard Plunz, *A History of Housing in New York City* (New York: Columbia University Press, 1990), 290.

26. Quoted in "Minneapolitans Win Ruberoid Competition": 66.

27. Peter Blake, "The Seventh Annual Cityscape Awards: Brownstone-of-the-Year," *New York* 9 (January 13, 1975): 50–51; Suzanne Stephens, "1199 Plaza, New York, N.Y. High-Rise in Harlem," *Progressive Architecture* 57 (March 1976): 64–69; "The Record Reports," *Architectural Record* 160 (September 1976): 33; White and Willensky, *AIA Guide* (1978), 288.

28. Stephens, "1199 Plaza, New York, N.Y. High-Rise in Harlem": 67.

29. Dorothy Kalins Wise, "Dialogue with a Neighborhood," *New York* 1 (June 17, 1968): 28–33; Roger Katan Planning Consultants, *116th Street Renewal Plan* (New York: City of New York and the Manhattan Borough President's Community Planning Board 11, 1969); "Roger Katan: Rénovation de la 116e rue," *L'Architecture d'Aujourd'hui* 157 (August 1971): 82–83.

30. Wise, "Dialogue with a Neighborhood": 28.

31. For the Benjamin Franklin High School, see Stern, Gilmartin and Mellins, *New York 1930*, 120.

32. George Goodman, Jr., "Ground Broken in East Harlem for $33-Million Housing Project," *New York Times* (October 25, 1972): 51; White and Willensky, *AIA Guide* (1978), 286; White and Willensky, *AIA Guide* (1988), 453–54.

33. Robert E. Tomasson, "Ambitious Project in East Harlem at Midpoint," *New York Times* (March 24, 1974), VIII: 1, 8; Robert E. Tomasson, "Four Luxury Towers to House the Poor Opening in Harlem," *New York Times* (October 28, 1975): 35, 64; "Ritzy Towers," *Newsweek* 86 (November 10, 1975): 22; Suzanne Stephens, "The Last Gasp: New York City," *Progressive Architecture* 57 (March 1976): 61–63; Joseph P. Fried, "Construction Projects Running Out of Financial Mortar," *New York Times* (February 11, 1977), B: 1, 5; "Javits Tells of Accord on Taino Towers Work," *New York Times* (March 8, 1977): 26; Joseph P. Fried, "Taino Towers Work Expected to Resume," *New York Times* (May 6, 1977), B: 4; White and Willensky, *AIA Guide* (1978), 290; Goldberger, *The City Observed*, 307–8; Michael Goodwin, "East Harlem's Troubled Taino Towers Set to Open," *New York Times* (February 9, 1979), B: 2; Michael Goodwin, "Opening for Taino Projects Is Still Uncertain," *New York Times* (April 22, 1979): 37; Michael Goodwin, "Project Admits Tenants to End a 3-Year Delay," *New York Times* (August 16, 1979), B: 3; "Low-Income Luxury," *New York Times* (June 8, 1980): 49; Laurie Johnston, "A Pilot Public-Housing Complex in East Harlem Still Unfinished After 10 Years," *New York Times* (June 24, 1981), B: 3; Norton and Patterson, *Living It Up*, 328; Richard Haitch, "Troubled Towers," *New York Times* (April 7, 1985): 25.

34. Goldberger, *The City Observed*, 308.

35. Stephens, "The Last Gasp: New York City": 63.

36. Stephens, "The Last Gasp: New York City": 63.

37. Goldberger, *The City Observed*, 308.

38. Robert Nichol quoted in Tomasson, "Four Luxury Towers to House the Poor Opening in Harlem": 64.

39. Stephens, "The Last Gasp: New York City": 62.

40. Goldberger, *The City Observed*, 308.

41. Talbot F. Hamlin, "The New Schools," *New Pencil Points* 23 (June 1942): 83–89; Hamlin, ed., *Forms and Functions of Twentieth-Century Architecture*, vol. 3, 560.

42. Hamlin, "The New Schools": 87.

43. "New York City Elementary School," *Architectural Forum* 113 (October 1960): 59; White and Willensky, *AIA Guide* (1967), 197.

44. "Parish Church in Harlem," *Architectural Forum* 116 (January 1962): 53; "New Ideas of Victor A. Lundy," *Architectural Record* 131 (February 1962): 105–21; James Bailey, "Neighborhood Church as Focus for Renewal," *Architectural Forum* 124 (January–February 1966): 48–53; "Award of Merit: Victor A. Lundy, AIA," *Journal of the American Institute of Architects* 46 (July 1966): 42–43; White and Willensky, *AIA Guide* (1967), 196; White and Willensky, *AIA Guide* (1978), 286; Goldberger, *The City Observed*, 305.

45. Charles Farrell quoted in Bailey, "Neighborhood Church as Focus for Renewal": 50.

46. Victor Lundy quoted in Bailey, "Neighborhood Church as Focus for Renewal": 50.

47. Victor Lundy quoted in Bailey, "Neighborhood Church as Focus for Renewal": 50.

48. Bailey, "Neighborhood Church as Focus for Renewal": 50.

49. Bailey, "Neighborhood Church as Focus for Renewal": 50.

50. Goldberger, *The City Observed*, 305.

51. White and Willensky, *AIA Guide* (1978), 286.

52. "City Approves Site of General Hospital," *New York Times* (May 25, 1945): 12; "Hospital Land Acquired," *New York Times* (February 5, 1947): 26; "Hospital Greets Neighbor Youths," *New York Times* (June 12, 1955): 37; "Metropolitan Hospital Dedicated on New Site in Upper Manhattan," *New York Times* (October 29, 1955): 21.

53. "Nurses Home, Started 6 Years Ago, Opened at Metropolitan Hospital," *New York Times* (October 24, 1962): 41.

54. Joseph Hirsh and Beka Doherty, *The First Hundred Years of Mount Sinai Hospital of New York* (New York: Random House, 1952); Stern, Gilmartin and Massengale, *New York 1900*, 314.

55. "Dewey Acclaims Mt. Sinai Growth," *New York Times* (May 24, 1952): 40; Page Beauchamp, "Hospital Patients' Rooms," *Progressive Architecture* 34 (November 1953): 129–35; "Maternity Pavilion, Mt. Sinai Hospital, New York, N.Y.," *Journal of the American Institute of Architects* 21 (January 1954): 29; White and Willensky, *AIA Guide* (1978), 241–42.

56. "Dewey Acclaims Mt. Sinai Growth": 40.

57. Emanuel Perlmutter, "Mt. Sinai Center Opened by Mayor," *New York Times* (November 15, 1962): 39.

58. Irving Spiegel, "$6.5 Million Gifts Are Made by List," *New York Times* (October 14, 1965): 49.

59. White and Willensky, *AIA Guide* (1978), 285.

60. "The Mount Sinai Medical Center," special advertising supplement, *New York Times* (May 26, 1974), XI: 1–16; Paul Goldberger, "Building's Role Is Lofty, Its Form Too Much So," *New York Times* (May 27, 1974): 15; Peter Kihss, "Ford Dedicates a Hospital Here," *New York Times* (May 27, 1974): 1, 15; White and Willensky, *AIA Guide* (1978), 241–42; Goldberger, *The City Observed*, 261.

61. *Arnaldo Pomodoro*, exhibition catalogue (New York: Marlborough Gallery, 1976), 58–59; Sam Hunter, *Arnaldo Pomodoro* (New York: Abbeville Press, 1982), 166–71.

62. White and Willensky, *AIA Guide* (1978), 242.

63. Goldberger, *The City Observed*, 261.

64. "Rehabilitation on a City Street," *Architectural Forum* 129 (October 1968): 62–65; "Best in the U.S.," *Architectural Forum* 130 (June 1969): 94–95; "Exodus House, New York, New York," *Architectural Record* 145 (June 1969): 41; "The 1969 Honors Awards," *Journal of the American Institute of Architects* 51 (June 1969): 95–111; "1969 Bard Awards Stress Urban Relationship," *Interiors* 128 (July 1969): 10, 12; White and Willensky, *AIA Guide* (1978), 286–87. Also see Reyner Banham, *The New Brutalism: Ethic or Aesthetic?* (New York: Reinhold, 1966).

65. White and Willensky, *AIA Guide* (1978), 287.

66. White and Willensky, *AIA Guide* (1978), 285–86; Goldberger, *The City Observed*, 303–4.

67. "World's Longest Girder Lift Span," *Engineering News-Record* 144 (February 16, 1950): 42–43; "An Addition to Upper East Side Skyline," *New York Times* (December 31, 1950): 1; "The Talk of the Town: Footbridge," *New Yorker* 27 (May 19, 1951): 28; "Fancy Footbridge Rises 80 Feet," *Popular Science* 159 (September 1951): 123; Anthony Bailey, "Our Footloose Correspondents: All Around the Town," *New Yorker* 42 (April 13, 1966): 142, 144, 146–48, 150–58, 161–64, 167–69; White and Willensky, *AIA Guide* (1978), 286; Goldberger, *The City Observed*, 305. For Moses's park, see Stern, Gilmartin and Mellins, *New York 1930*, 716.

68. "The Talk of the Town: Footbridge": 28.

69. For the George Washington, Bayonne, Triborough and Bronx-Whitestone bridges, see Stern, Gilmartin and Mellins, *New York 1930*, 674–90.

70. White and Willensky, *AIA Guide* (1978), 286.

71. Goldberger, *The City Observed*, 305.

72. "A Rehabilitation Center for Manhattan State Hospital," *Architectural Record* 142 (October 1967): 43; White and Willensky, *AIA Guide* (1978), 306.

73. White and Willensky, *AIA Guide* (1978), 306.

74. Mildred Schmertz, "A Training Center Designed for the Firemen of New York City," *Architectural Record* 151 (April 1972): 109–18; Paul Goldberger, "Crossing Signals," *Progressive Architecture* 57 (February 1976): 64–68; White and Willensky, *AIA Guide* (1978), 306; *Hardy Holzman Pfeiffer Associates: Buildings and Projects 1967–1992* (New York: Rizzoli International Publications, 1992), 50–51, 245.

75. Goldberger, "Crossing Signals": 66–67.

76. White and Willensky, *AIA Guide* (1978), 306.

CENTRAL HARLEM

1. Roi Ottley quoted in "A Plan for Harlem's Redevelopment," *Architectural Forum* 80 (April 1944): 145–52.

2. "A Plan for Harlem's Redevelopment": 145–52.

3. For Williamsburg Houses, see Stern, Gilmartin and Mellins, *New York 1930*, 495, 497–98.

4. "New Apartments and Civic Developments to Make Harlem a Better Neighborhood," *New York Times* (November 17, 1946), VIII: 3; "Model of New Public Housing for the East Side," *New York Times* (March 9, 1947), VIII: 1; "Housing Proposed for City and Suburban Areas," *New York Times* (December 7, 1947), VIII: 1; "Cornerstone Laid at Foster Houses," *New York Times* (December 27, 1951): 31; "New Look on Upper Fifth Avenue Marks Area's Revival," *New York Times* (April 10, 1960), VIII: 1; Kathleen Teltsch, "Negroes Press for Monuments to Race Here," *New York Times* (July 13, 1968): 29; Thomas E. Norton and Jerry E. Patterson, *Living It Up: A Guide to the Named Apartment Houses of New York* (New York: Atheneum, 1984), 320.

5. "Ground Broken for Housing," *New York Times* (March 2, 1961): 13.

6. Paul Crowell, "City Defers Move on Parking Plan," *New York Times* (October 16, 1954): 19; "Wage Limit Eased in Public Housing," *New York Times* (July 5, 1961): 35; Anna Petersen, "4 Old Grads Sing Yale Tunes Dedicating Taft Houses," *New York Times* (October 21, 1961): 1, 24; Daniel Ocasio, Albert Smith and Richard Plunz, "A Prospectus for the Taft and Mitchell Houses, New York City," in Richard Plunz, ed., *Housing Form and Public Policy in the United States* (New York: Praeger Scientific, 1980), 201–32; Norton and Patterson, *Living It Up*, 327; Richard Plunz, *A History of Housing in New York City* (New York: Columbia University Press, 1990), 293–94.

7. Roger Katan, *Pueblos for El Barrio* (New York: United Residents of Milbank–Frawley Circle–East Harlem Association, 1967); Ellen Perry Berkeley, "Vox Populi: Many Voices from a Single Community," *Architectural Forum* 128 (May 1968): 59–63; Ocasio, Smith and Plunz, "A Prospectus for the Taft and Mitchell Houses, New York City," in Plunz, ed., *Housing Form and Public Policy in the United States*, 209–11.

8. Lawrence Halprin and Associates, *New York, New York* (New York: City of New York, 1968).
9. "To Design Housing for Harlem," *New York Times* (July 8, 1950): 22; "159 Slum Acres to Be Condemned," *New York Times* (January 7, 1951): 61; "New Look on Upper Fifth Avenue Marks Area's Revival": 1; "Outdoor Amenity," *Progressive Architecture* 45 (October 1964): 97; "Nurserymen Give Awards on 2 Landscape Jobs Here," *New York Times* (November 27, 1964): 28; "Making Public Housing Human," *Progressive Architecture* 46 (January 1965): 177–78; Charles Thomsen, "Where Are Some Signs of Progress?" *Journal of the American Institute of Architects* 44 (September 1965): 38–40; "Urban Playscapist," *Progressive Architecture* 47 (August 1966): 70–71; Norton and Patterson, *Living It Up*, 86.
10. Mary Perot Nichols, "New York's New Approach: Vest-Pocket Playgrounds," *Village Voice* 11 (December 2, 1965): 5–6.
11. John Emmerling, "How Mad. Ave.'s Insidious Power Built a Small Park in Harlem," *New York* 3 (December 14, 1970): 74–81.
12. Paul Goldberger, *The City Observed: New York* (New York: Random House, 1979), 298; Norton and Patterson, *Living It Up*, 124.
13. "Heckscher Pledges More and Better Parks as He Succeeds Hoving," *New York Times* (March 17, 1967): 46; "Buildings in the News," *Architectural Record* 141 (April 1967): 44; "Mt. Morris Park Will Have a Pool," *New York Times* (July 19, 1967): 25; "U.S. Approves Aid for Harlem Pool," *New York Times* (February 14, 1968): 39; White and Willensky, *AIA Guide* (1978), 274–75.
14. "Housing Project to Rise in Harlem," *New York Times* (September 18, 1944): 21; "Harlem Housing Hearing Oct. 4," *New York Times* (September 21, 1944): 36; "Riverton Contract Signed by the Mayor," *New York Times* (November 19, 1944): 42; "Two Up, Three to Go," *Architectural Forum* 82 (February 1945): 7–8; "New Apartments and Civic Developments to Make Harlem a Better Neighborhood": 3; Lee E. Cooper, "Realty Undergoes Sweeping Changes Along the Harlem," *New York Times* (May 6, 1951), VIII: 1, 9; Plunz, *A History of Housing in New York City*, 256–57.
15. See Stern, Gilmartin and Mellins, *New York 1930*, 478–85.
16. James Baldwin, "Fifth Avenue, Uptown," *Esquire* 54 (July 1960): 70–73, 76, reprinted in James Baldwin, *Nobody Knows My Name: More Notes of a Native Son* (New York: Dial Press, 1961), 56–71.
17. "Architects Picked for Housing Jobs," *New York Times* (July 6, 1943): 3; "New Harlem Housing in City's Post-War Building Program," *New York Times* (March 11, 1945), VIII: 1; "New Apartments and Civic Developments to Make Harlem a Better Neighborhood": 3; "Housing Centers to Receive First Tenants During Holiday Season," *New York Times* (December 21, 1947), VIII: 1; "The New New York," *New York Times* (August 8, 1948), VI: 6; Cooper, "Realty Undergoes Sweeping Changes Along the Harlem": 1, 9; Norton and Patterson, *Living It Up*, 207.
18. "Housing Unit Under Way," *New York Times* (January 4, 1949): 17; "City Housing Bids Opened," *New York Times* (May 12, 1949): 56; "Ground Broken Here for 8 Housing Units," *New York Times* (July 13, 1949): 23; Cooper, "Realty Undergoes Sweeping Changes Along the Harlem": 1, 9.
19. "2 Big Projects Approved," *New York Times* (May 25, 1950): 21; Cooper, "Realty Undergoes Sweeping Changes Along the Harlem": 1, 9; "Housing Project Is Opened," *New York Times* (April 3, 1952): 32; Elizabeth Wood, *Report on the Harlem Welfare Center–St. Nicholas Houses Experiment* (New York: Citizens' Housing and Planning Council, 1958); Anthony Jackson, *A Place Called Home* (Cambridge, Mass.: MIT Press, 1976), 235; Norton and Patterson, *Living It Up*, 302.
20. "Harlem Site Deal Set," *New York Times* (September 14, 1950): 54; "Pioneering in Harlem," editorial, *New York Times* (September 15, 1950): 30; "Cornerstones Laid for 2 Housing Units," *New York Times* (June 7, 1951): 35; "Housing Project in Harlem Lauded," *New York Times* (September 29, 1951): 27; "211 Homes Draw 4,532 in Harlem," *New York Times* (August 12, 1952): 20; "Bank to Start $3,000,000 Harlem Housing; Will Be First Without Subsidy Since 1938," *New York Times* (September 14, 1954): 29; "New Housing in Harlem," *New York Times* (September 15, 1954): 32.
21. James Felt quoted in "Housing Project in Harlem Lauded": 27.
22. "Big Slum Project Insured by F.H.A.," *New York Times* (September 30, 1955): 1, 17; Charles Grutzner, "Harlem Housing Hailed by Moses," *New York Times* (September 12, 1957): 33; "Redevelopment Today," *Architectural Forum* 108 (April 1958): 108–13; Norton and Patterson, *Living It Up*, 119.
23. "Builder to Start Harlem Project," *New York Times* (March 25, 1957): 27; Charles G. Bennett, "Harlem Middle-Income Housing Expedited by Board of Estimate," *New York Times* (March 29, 1957): 23; "Two Savings Banks Assure Funds for Big Harlem Housing Project," *Real Estate Record and Guide* 179 (March 30, 1957): 4; Ernest Dunbar, "The View from Lenox Terrace," *New York Times* (March 3, 1968), VI: 28–29, 106–11; Goldberger, *The City Observed*, 295; Norton and Patterson, *Living It Up*, 204.
24. Dunbar, "The View from Lenox Terrace": 106.
25. Goldberger, *The City Observed*, 295.
26. Thomas W. Ennis, "Harlem Changed by Public Housing," *New York Times* (June 23, 1957): 1, 12; "New Look on Upper Fifth Avenue Marks Area's Revival": 1.
27. "Mission's Apartments and HQ in Central Harlem," *Progressive Architecture* 44 (September 1963): 76; "Mitchell-Lama Project Announced for Site at Lenox and 142d St.," *Real Estate Record and Guide* 198 (September 24, 1966): 3; "Street Art in Harlem," *Architectural Forum* 133 (December 1970): 69–70; Norton and Patterson, *Living It Up*, 66; Margot Gayle and Michele Cohen, *The Art Commission and the Municipal Art Society Guide to Manhattan's Outdoor Sculpture* (New York: Prentice Hall Press, 1988), 315–16. For the Cotton Club, see Earl Caldwell, "Fewer Whites Are Taking 'A' Train to Harlem Nightspots," *New York Times* (November 9, 1967): 49, 59; Jim Haskins, *The Cotton Club* (New York: Random House, 1977).
28. Joseph P. Fried, "In the Shadows of Coogan's Bluff, a New Era Begins," *New York Times* (October 29, 1967), VIII: 1, 8; "Old Polo Grounds Sees a New Opener, Housing," *New York Times* (April 17, 1968): 74.
29. Don Raney, "Urban Housing: A Comprehensive Approach to Quality," *Architectural Record* 145 (January 1969): cover, 97–118; Jason R. Nathan, "Strivers Row," letter to the editor, *Architectural Record* 145 (May 1969): 74; New York City Housing and Development Administration, *St. Nicholas Park Urban Renewal Area* (New York, 1972).
30. Norton and Patterson, *Living It Up*, 209; White and Willensky, *AIA Guide* (1988), 447.
31. David A. Crane, *Planning and Design in New York* (New York: Institute of Public Administration, September 1966), 74; White and Willensky, *AIA Guide* (1967), 194; Robert A. M. Stern, *New Directions in American Architecture* (New York: George Braziller, 1969), 94, 96; "Upbeat in Harlem," *Architectural Forum* 130 (January–February 1969): 65; "1969 Bard Awards Stress Urban Relationship," *Interiors* 128 (July 1969): 10, 12; Peter Blake, "The City Politic: Man or Moon?" *New York* 2 (August 25, 1969): 8–9; Norval C. White, "Art and Architecture for a Vibrant City," *Journal of the American Institute of Architects* 55 (February 1971): 61; "A Riverside Co-op in New York City," *House and Home* 40 (October 1971): 106–7; "The Evolving Urban Architecture of Davis, Brody & Associates," *Architectural Record* 152 (August 1972): 97–106; White and Willensky, *AIA Guide* (1978), 284; Goldberger, *The City Observed*, 296; Plunz, *A History of Housing in New York City*, 294–95.
32. White and Willensky, *AIA Guide* (1978), 396; Robert A. M. Stern, "With Rhetoric: The New York Apartment House," *Via* 4 (1980): 78–111.
33. Quoted in "1969 Bard Awards Stress Urban Relationship": 10.
34. White and Willensky, *AIA Guide* (1978), 284.
35. Blake, "The City Politic: Man or Moon?": 8.
36. Goldberger, *The City Observed*, 296.
37. Peter Wolf, *Another Chance for Cities*, exhibition catalogue (New York: Whitney Museum of American Art, 1970), 44–45; Charlayne Hunter, "Housing Is Dedicated at Schomberg Plaza," *New York Times* (December 14, 1974): 47; Glenn Fowler, "Bard Awards Honor 8 Examples of Good Urban Design," *New York Times* (June 12, 1975): 41; White and Willensky, *AIA Guide* (1978), 273; Goldberger, *The City Observed*, 289.
38. Goldberger, *The City Observed*, 289.
39. Talbot F. Hamlin, "Smaller Public Library Buildings," *Pencil Points* 22 (July 1941): 469–74; "Harlem Branch, N.Y. Public Library," *Progressive Architecture* 27 (August 1946): cover, 56–59; Nat Hentoff, "'Why Forget Who We Are?'" *Reporter* 21 (November 24, 1959): 31–32; White and Willenksy, *AIA Guide* (1967), 194–95.
40. "The Harlem Boy's Club," *Pencil Points* 22 (June 1941): 378–84; Talbot F. Hamlin, ed., *Forms and Functions of Twentieth-Century Architecture*, vol. 4 (New York: Columbia University Press, 1952), 676–77.
41. Superintendent of Schools, City of New York, *All the Children, 1944–45* (New York, 1945), 76; Lewis Mumford, "The Sky Line: Schools for Human Beings—II," *New Yorker* 28 (April 26, 1952): 68–74.
42. Mumford, "The Sky Line: Schools for Human Beings—II": 68.
43. Superintendent of Schools, City of New York, *All the Children, 1944–45*, 80; "New Look on Upper Fifth Avenue Marks Area's Revival": 1.
44. "Mayor Is Acclaimed for Building Schools," *New York Times* (February 27, 1953): 19.
45. "John Hancock School," *Journal of the Board of Education of the City of New York* (January 25, 1962): 147. For further discussion of Paul Williams's work, see Anita Morris, "Recent Work of Paul Williams," *Architect and Engineer* 141 (June 1940): 12–42; Walter H. Waggoner, "Paul Williams Dies; Architect on Coast," *New York Times* (January 26, 1980): 26; Karen Grigsby Bates, "He Was (and Is) the Architect to the Stars," *New York Times* (July 26, 1990), C: 1, 6; Karen E. Hudson, *Paul R. Williams, Architect: A Legacy of Style* (New York: Rizzoli International Publications, 1993).
46. "Mary McLeod Bethune School," *Journal of the Board of Education of the City of New York* (October 11, 1962): 1563; "Mary McLeod Bethune School," *Journal of the Board of Education of the City of New York* (January 8, 1964): 113; White and Willensky, *AIA Guide* (1988), 448.
47. White and Willensky, *AIA Guide* (1978), 272.
48. Leonard Buder, "Showcase School Sets Off Dispute," *New York Times* (September 2, 1966): 33–38; "Harlem's Besieged Showpiece," *Architectural Forum* 125 (November 1966): 48–50; White and Willensky, *AIA Guide* (1967), 193; Carol Doty, "High Schools," letter to the editor, *Architectural Forum* 126 (January–February 1967): 22; Bodil W. Nielsen, "New York Schools: The Work of Curtis & Davis," *Interiors* 126 (February 1967): 127; "The Talk of the Town: I.S. 201 Complex," *New Yorker* 44 (October 5, 1968): 44–45; White and Willensky, *AIA Guide* (1978), 276–77.
49. "Health Care: Narcotics Halfway House," *Progressive Architecture* 50 (February 1969): 134–35; "Centre de Post-cure de Désintoxication, Harlem," *L'Architecture d'Aujourd'hui* 150 (June 1970): 82–83; Charlayne Hunter, "Historic District Is a Harlem Issue," *New York Times* (October 24, 1976): 96.
50. Landmarks Preservation Commission of the City of New York, LP-0452 (November 3, 1971).
51. White and Willensky, *AIA Guide* (1978), 272.

WEST HARLEM

1. Carson Anthony Anderson, "The Architectural Practice of Vertner W. Tandy: An Evaluation of the Professional and Social Position of a Black Architect" (Master's thesis, University of Virginia, 1982): 142–59.
2. Charles Grutzner, "City's 'Acropolis' Combating Slums," *New York Times* (May 21, 1957): 37, 40; Charles Grutzner, "City Begins Work on New Housing," *New York Times* (July 30, 1958): 30; Christian Hubert, "The Late Work: 1939–1969," in Christian Hubert and Lindsay Stamm Shapiro, *William Lescaze* (New York: Institute for Architecture and Urban Studies; New York: Rizzoli International Publications, 1982), 108; Thomas E. Norton and Jerry E. Patterson, *Living It Up: A Guide to the Named Apartment Houses of New York* (New York: Atheneum, 1984), 222; David W. Dunlap, *On Broadway: A Journey Uptown Over Time* (New York: Rizzoli International Publications, 1990), 281.
3. Lawrence O'Kane, "Housing Projects to Hit Peak Here," *New York Times* (December 26, 1960): 21; Charles G. Bennett, "Project to House Nazi Victims Here," *New York Times* (January 19, 1961): 31; Edmond J. Bartnett, "Riverside Drive to Get 2 Co-ops," *New York Times* (January 28, 1962), VIII: 1, 4.
4. "City Speeds Riverside Drive Plan for a Mid-Income Cooperative," *New York Times* (December 1, 1961): 18; Bartnett, "Riverside Drive to Get 2 Co-ops": 1, 4; Norton and Patterson, *Living It Up*, 285.
5. "Riverside Park Community," *Architectural Record* 144 (November 1968): 41; "Buildings on the Way Up," *Progressive Architecture* 53 (March 1972): 28; Paul Goldberger, *The City Observed: New York* (New York: Random House, 1979), 311–12; White and Willensky, *AIA Guide* (1988), 429; Dunlap, *On Broadway*, 284.
6. Goldberger, *The City Observed*, 311.
7. "Architect Hired for Sewage Plant," *New York Times* (August 17, 1967): 39, 42; Sydney H. Schanberg, "State Gives $130-Million to City for Sewage Project on Hudson," *New York Times* (September 19, 1967): 54; "Fountains to Mask NYC Public Works Plant on the River," *Progressive Architecture* 48 (October 1967): 52; "A Sewage Treatment Plant Designed to Enhance a Riverfront," *Architectural Record* 142 (December 1967): 108–9; David Bird, "New Sewage Plant to Rise on Hudson," *New York Times* (January 5, 1968): 1, 20; Richard E. Mooney, "Ryan Scores Site on Sewage Plant," *New York Times* (January 6, 1968): 59; David Bird, "Beauty Loses Out to Efficiency in Design for Sewage Plant," *New York Times* (November 11, 1968): 43.

8. "Fountains to Mask NYC Public Works Plant on the River": 52.
9. Philip Johnson quoted in "A Sewage Treatment Plant Designed to Enhance a Riverfront": 109.
10. "Superscale and Comprehensive Care," *Progressive Architecture* 50 (February 1969): 100; "Citation: Max O. Urbahn Associates, Inc., Architects & Planners and Lucas & Edwards, Urban Planners," *Progressive Architecture* 54 (January 1973): 84–85.
11. John Anderson, "Medical Center Around a Courtyard," *Interiors* 113 (July 1954): 42–49; Page Beauchamp, "P/A Interior Design Data," *Progressive Architecture* 35 (July 1954): 125–29; Frederick Gutheim, "Critique: Health Insurance Plan Clinic," *Progressive Architecture* 35 (July 1954): 120; "Health Insurance Plan Clinic," *Progressive Architecture* 35 (July 1954): 115–19; "Selected Details: Upper Manhattan Medical Group Center," *Progressive Architecture* 35 (July 1954): 121–23; White and Willensky, *AIA Guide* (1967), 204.
12. Gutheim, "Critique: Health Insurance Plan Clinic": 120.
13. White and Willensky, *AIA Guide* (1978), 267.
14. White and Willensky, *AIA Guide* (1988), 434. Also see Christopher Gray, "Schlock of Ages," *Avenue* 17 (December 1992): 31–32, 34, 36, 38.
15. "Adam Powell Recalled at Dedication of School," *New York Times* (March 1, 1976): 27; White and Willensky, *AIA Guide* (1978), 267.
16. "City College to Get a New Library," *New York Times* (October 16, 1955): 120; "College Plans Blast," *New York Times* (October 20, 1955): 58; White and Willensky, *AIA Guide* (1978), 265; White and Willensky, *AIA Guide* (1988), 432.
17. For Post's buildings, see Stern, Gilmartin and Massengale, *New York 1900*, 108–9.
18. Leonard Buder, "City College Envisions New Technology Building," *New York Times* (January 26, 1958), VIII: 1–2; "Functional Invasion of the City's Campus," *New York Times* (August 28, 1960), IV: 9; "City College Opens Technology Center Costing $9,000,000," *New York Times* (September 18, 1962): 41; "Unveiling of a Mural Planned at City College Today," *New York Times* (May 11, 1963): 7; White and Willensky, *AIA Guide* (1978), 264; White and Willensky, *AIA Guide* (1988), 431.
19. Murray Schumach, "City College Plans $40 Million Expansion," *New York Times* (January 29, 1965): 1, 34.
20. Ada Louise Huxtable, "A Creative Truce," *New York Times* (January 29, 1965): 34.
21. Boyce Rensberger, "C.C.N.Y. Dedicates Science Building," *New York Times* (October 8, 1972): 96; "The New Science and Physical Education Building of City College," *New York Times* (November 5, 1972), VIII: 10; White and Willensky, *AIA Guide* (1978), 264; Goldberger, *The City Observed*, 312.
22. Huxtable, "A Creative Truce": 34.
23. Goldberger, *The City Observed*, 312.
24. "Plan Is Revised by City College," *New York Times* (November 7, 1971): 84; Joseph G. Herzberg, "Farewell to Lewisohn: It Gave New Yorkers a Lot of Night Music," *New York Times* (April 5, 1973): 47; Carter Horsley, "Lewisohn Stadium, Center for Culture, to Be Razed," *New York Times* (April 5, 1973): 47, 55; White and Willensky, *AIA Guide* (1988), 431–32.
25. Horsley, "Lewisohn Stadium, Center for Culture, to Be Razed": 47.
26. Huxtable, "A Creative Truce": 34.

125th STREET

1. "The Talk of the Town: Lull," *New Yorker* 43 (November 11, 1967): 51–53; Ada Louise Huxtable, "Hard Questions for Harlem," *New York Times* (February 11, 1968), II: 24; "A State Office Building in Harlem," *Architectural Record* 143 (March 1968): 41; "Rocky's 125th Street War," *Architectural Forum* 132 (January–February 1970): 42; "NYC to Have First All Electric Building," *Progressive Architecture* 53 (December 1972): 23, 32; John W. Cook and Heinrich Klotz, *Conversations with Architects* (New York: Praeger, 1973), 37; Philip Johnson, "Beyond Monuments," *Architectural Forum* 138 (January–February 1973): 63; Charlayne Hunter, "Hopes and Fears on Rise with New Harlem Skyline," *New York Times* (November 20, 1973): 41, 50; White and Willensky, *AIA Guide* (1978), 278–79; Paul Goldberger, *The City Observed: New York* (New York: Random House, 1979), 291.
2. Philip Johnson quoted in Cook and Klotz, *Conversations with Architects*, 37.
3. Huxtable, "Hard Questions for Harlem": 24.
4. Nelson A. Rockefeller quoted in "Rocky's 125th Street War": 42.
5. "Rocky's 125th Street War": 42.
6. For the South Mall complex in Albany, see Victoria Newhouse, *Wallace K. Harrison, Architect* (New York: Rizzoli International Publications, 1989), 244–73.
7. Goldberger, *The City Observed*, 291.
8. Huxtable, "Hard Questions for Harlem": 24.
9. Joseph P. Fried, "Investors Plan Business Center on Harlem Block," *New York Times* (August 20, 1968): 1, 44; Joseph P. Fried, "Skyscraper for Harlem Is Protested," *New York Times* (August 22, 1968): 39.
10. Charlayne Hunter, "Plans for a $30-Million Complex in Harlem at 125th St. Disclosed," *New York Times* (October 8, 1971): 46.
11. Huxtable, "Hard Questions for Harlem": 24.
12. "East Harlem Unit to Plan Renewal," *New York Times* (June 30, 1967): 18; Architects Renewal Committee in Harlem, *East Harlem Triangle Plan* (New York: Community Association of the East Harlem Triangle and the New York City Housing and Development Administration, August 1968); "Roger Katan: East Harlem Triangle," *L'Architecture d'Aujourd'hui* 157 (August 1971): 84; "Recherche théorique pour une restructuration de Harlem," *L'Architecture d'Aujourd'hui* 158 (October 1971): 37–38; "Planning with People: Advocacy in East Harlem," *Forum* (Amsterdam) 23, no. 4 (1972).
13. Architects Renewal Committee in Harlem, *East Harlem Triangle Plan*, 1–2.
14. Architects Renewal Committee in Harlem, *East Harlem Triangle Plan*, 69.
15. Alison Sky and Michelle Stone, *Unbuilt America* (New York: McGraw-Hill, 1976), 142.
16. See Stern, Gilmartin and Mellins, *New York 1930*, 32–39.
17. John Johansen quoted in Sky and Stone, *Unbuilt America*, 142.
18. White and Willensky, *AIA Guide* (1978), 278.
19. "An Office Tower to Rise in Harlem," *New York Times* (October 24, 1971): 52; "Groundbreaking Held in Harlem for $10-Million Office Building," *New York Times* (May 31, 1972): 26; Barbara Campbell, "Nixon Sends Aide to Harlem Ceremony for Black-Owned Building," *New York Times* (March 23, 1973): 39; Hunter, "Hopes and Fears on Rise with New Harlem Skyline": 41, 50; Charlayne Hunter, "$15-Million Black-Owned Building Opens in Harlem," *New York Times* (December 13, 1973): 51; "15-Story Office Tower Opens in Harlem," *Real Estate Record and Guide* 213 (January 5, 1974): 3; Robert F. R. Ballard, *Directory of Manhattan Office Buildings* (New York: McGraw-Hill, 1978), 217.
20. Charles A. Vincent quoted in "Groundbreaking Held in Harlem for $10-Million Office Building": 26.
21. David Dinkins quoted in Hunter, "$15-Million Black-Owned Building Opens in Harlem": 51.

UPPER MANHATTAN

1. Rebecca Read Shanor, *The City that Never Was* (New York: Viking, 1988), 58–64. Also see Stern, Gilmartin and Mellins, *New York 1930*, 148–49, 152.
2. Stern, Gilmartin and Mellins, *New York 1930*, 112–13.
3. "Columbia-Presbyterian to Expand," *New York Times* (January 28, 1962): 60; "Medical Building Is Topped-Out," *New York Times* (August 27, 1963): 63.
4. "Apartments for Medical Center," *New York Times* (March 3, 1968), VIII: 6; White and Willensky, *AIA Guide* (1978), 294; White and Willensky, *AIA Guide* (1988), 462–63.
5. "Columbia Medical School Plans $20-Million Facility," *New York Times* (February 18, 1973): 50; "Columbia Breaks Ground," *New York Times* (April 12, 1973): 49; "Columbia's Medical College Dedicates Sciences Center," *New York Times* (October 7, 1976): 92; White and Willensky, *AIA Guide* (1978), 294; White and Willensky, *AIA Guide* (1988), 462.
6. White and Willensky, *AIA Guide* (1988), 462.
7. Stern, Gilmartin and Mellins, *New York 1930*, 112.
8. White and Willensky, *AIA Guide* (1978), 297.
9. "Yeshiva University Achieves a Washington Heights Campus," *New York Times* (February 16, 1969), VIII: 1.
10. White and Willensky, *AIA Guide* (1967), 211; "Yeshiva University Achieves a Washington Heights Campus": 1; "Articulated Library," *Architectural Forum* 133 (November 1970): 56–59; "Buildings in the News," *Architectural Record* 149 (January 1971): 42; Paul Goldberger, *The City Observed: New York* (New York: Random House, 1979), 322–23.
11. Goldberger, *The City Observed*, 323.
12. "Library to Be Started," *New York Times* (February 4, 1966): 49; White and Willensky, *AIA Guide* (1967), 211; "New Yeshiva Library to House Rare Books Nearing Completion," *New York Times* (November 12, 1967): 126; "Buildings in the News," *Architectural Record* 144 (December 1968): 41; "Yeshiva University Achieves a Washington Heights Campus": 1; White and Willensky, *AIA Guide* (1978), 297; Goldberger, *The City Observed*, 322. For Kahn's Richards Medical Research Building, see Vincent Scully, Jr., *Louis I. Kahn* (New York: George Braziller, 1962), 11, 27–30, figs. 64–74.
13. For Hudson View Gardens and Castle Village, see Stern, Gilmartin and Mellins, *New York 1930*, 436–37, 450–51, 453.
14. "New Apartments Rent Rapidly on Drive," *Real Estate Record and Guide* 148 (October 11, 1941): 7.
15. "City Housing Agency Starts 3 Projects," *New York Times* (March 2, 1940): 3; "New York City Gets Action on Housing with Huge 'Unsubsidized' Program," *American City* 64 (August 1949): 82–83; "Dyckman Houses Open," *New York Times* (September 26, 1950): 33; Thomas E. Norton and Jerry E. Patterson, *Living It Up: A Guide to the Named Apartment Houses of New York* (New York: Atheneum, 1984), 127.
16. "Enlarged Bridge Will Bring City More Traffic Questions," *Architectural Forum* 112 (June 1960): 9; "The Talk of the Town: A New Deck," *New Yorker* 37 (April 29, 1961): 29–30; Bernard Stengren, "'31 Bridge Design Near Realization," *New York Times* (October 26, 1961): 18; "New Patterns Along the Hudson," *New York Times* (November 19, 1961), VI: 76–77; "New Expressway Used," *New York Times* (February 16, 1962): 59; "The Talk of the Town: On Deck," *New Yorker* 38 (September 1, 1962): 24–25; "The Talk of the Town: Organizing Man," *New Yorker* 38 (September 8, 1962): 28; "New Level for George Washington Bridge," *Progressive Architecture* 43 (October 1962): 86; "Second Deck Added to Make Bridge World's Largest," *Popular Science* 181 (December 1962): 90–91; "2d Deck on Bridge Sets Traffic Mark for Port Authority," *New York Times* (April 23, 1964): 16. For Ammann's original design, see Stern, Gilmartin and Mellins, *New York 1930*, 677–82.
17. "Ramps Emerging into Interchange," *New York Times* (February 16, 1964): 69; White and Willensky, *AIA Guide* (1967), 211, 414–15; Sharon Reier, *The Bridges of New York* (New York: Quadrant Press, 1977), 76.
18. "Aluminum Curtain Wall Apartment Buildings to Be Constructed Over Approach to George Washington Bridge," *Real Estate Record and Guide* 188 (August 26, 1961): 2–3; "New York State Middle-Income Housing," *Architectural Forum* 115 (October 1961): 63; "Apartments Over Expressway Are Getting 'Skin' of Aluminum," *New York Times* (April 11, 1963): 35; White and Willensky, *AIA Guide* (1967), 210; Thomas F. Galvin, "New Dimensions in Air Rights," *Journal of the American Institute of Architects* 50 (July 1968): 39–43; Goldberger, *The City Observed*, 326–27.
19. "Washington Heights Terminal Planned," *Real Estate Record and Guide* 179 (March 2, 1957): 3–4; "Nervi's First U.S. Work: A New York City Bus Terminal," *Architectural Forum* 112 (May 1960): 61; "Nervi Designs Bus Station for New York," *Progressive Architecture* 39 (May 1960): 78; Winthrop Sargeant, "Profile: Maestro di Costruzione," *New Yorker* 36 (June 11, 1960): 40–42, 44, 47, 50, 52, 54, 59–60, 62, 64; "Buildings in the News," *Architectural Record* 128 (August 1960): 13; Ada Louise Huxtable, "Nervi in—and on—New York," *New York Times* (June 3, 1962), II: 10; "E Fatto Molto Bene," *Architectural Forum* 117 (July 1962): 13; "Concrete: A Special Report," *Architectural Forum* 117 (September 1962): 78–96; "Doing Over the Town," *Time* 80 (September 28, 1962): 56–69; Clarence Dean, "Jersey Bus Lines Growing Rapidly," *New York Times* (November 12, 1962): 31, 33; P. L. Nervi, *Neue Strucken* (Stuttgart: Verlag Gerd Hatje, 1963), 156–63; "Nervi's Bus Station Opens in New York," *Architectural Record* 133 (February 1963): 14; "New York's Uptown Bus Terminal Dedicated," *Progressive Architecture* 44 (February 1963): 61; "Nervi a New York," *Domus* 400 (March 1963): 1–6; "Pier Luigi Nervi à New York," *L'Architecture d'Aujourd'hui* 34 (October 1963): 20–25; Pier Luigi Nervi, *Aesthetics and Technology in Building* (Cambridge, Mass.: Harvard University Press, 1965), 84–89; White and Willensky, *AIA Guide* (1967), 210; Donald Canty, "Nervi's Gilded Gateway," *Architectural Forum* 126 (March 1967): 68–73; William D. Morgan, "Nervi's First," letter to the editor, *Architectural Forum* 126 (April 1967): 16; Goldberger, *The City Observed*, 326–27; Ada Louise Huxtable, "Master Builder of the Modern Age," *New York Times* (January 21, 1979), II: 25; David W. Dunlap, *On Broadway: A Journey Uptown Over Time* (New York: Rizzoli International Publications, 1990), 312–13, 315.
20. Huxtable, "Nervi in—and on—New York": 10. Also see Ada Louise Huxtable, *Pier Luigi Nervi* (New York: George Braziller, 1960).
21. Huxtable, "Master Builder of the Modern Age": 25.
22. Canty, "Nervi's Gilded Gateway": 71–72.
23. Canty, "Nervi's Gilded Gateway": 72.

Chapter 13
Outer Boroughs

BROOKLYN

1. Thomas Wolfe, "Only the Dead Know Brooklyn," *New Yorker* 11 (June 15, 1935): 13–14.
2. "Brooklyn: Waves from Manhattan Break Over City in a City," *Business Week* (October 3, 1953): 126–29, 132.
3. "Take the 'A' Train," Billy Strayhorn (New York: Tempo Music, 1941).
4. See Truman Capote, "Brooklyn Heights: A Personal Memoir," *Holiday* 25 (February 1959): 64–68, 112–15. Also see Irwin Shaw, "Brooklyn," *Holiday* 7 (June 1950): 34–37, 40–41, 44–45, 48–51, 54–55, 58–59.
5. "Whatever Happened to Brooklyn?" *Time* 87 (March 11, 1966): 29.
6. Frank Leurs, "This Is Brooklyn?" *American Magazine* 161 (February 1956): 38–40, 83–86.
7. Christopher Morley, *Parnassus on Wheels* (New York and Philadelphia: J. B. Lippincott Co., 1917), 64.
8. "Secession by Brooklyn Is Asked in Assembly," *New York Times* (February 23, 1943): 23.
9. Pete Hamill, "Let's Break Up the City . . . Starting with Brooklyn!" *New York* 4 (June 21, 1971): 30–33.
10. "Berle Named Head of City Plan Board," *New York Times* (December 31, 1937): 17.
11. "Cashmore Backed on Bridge Changes," *New York Times* (February 27, 1941): 21; "Brooklyn's Civic Center," editorial, *New York Times* (March 3, 1941): 14; Mayor's Committee on Property Improvement, *Downtown Brooklyn Neighborhood Study* (New York, June 17, 1941); "Dressing Up Brooklyn," editorial, *New York Times* (June 23, 1941): 16; "New Zones Asked in Brooklyn Area," *New York Times* (November 18, 1941): 28.
12. "Brooklyn's Civic Center": 14.
13. George M. Mathieu, "New Road Links Two Boroughs," *New York Times* (August 20, 1939), XI: 1. Also see *Downtown Brooklyn: An Architectural and Urban History*, Preservation Working Paper No. 2 (New York: Graduate School of Architecture, Planning and Preservation, Columbia University, 1993), 98–99.
14. "$65,000,000 Roads Proposed by Moses for City's Defense," *New York Times* (November 11, 1940): 1, 21.
15. "Highway Hearing Ends," *New York Times* (March 11, 1943): 24; "Planning to Give the City a Clearer View of Its Famed Brooklyn Bridge," *New York Times* (June 5, 1944): 21.
16. "Brooklyn Highway to Get Under Way," *New York Times* (August 17, 1946): 15; "Connecting Highway," editorial, *New York Times* (August 20, 1946): 26.
17. Montgomery Schuyler and Liam Dunne, "The Highway's Homeless," letter to the editor, *Architectural Forum* 85 (September 1946): 46, 50, 54, 58, 62; "'Club Sandwich' Road Amazes Residents on Heights Expressway," *Brooklyn Eagle* (October 19, 1947): 3; Jessie Phelps Kahles, "Doorstep to Manhattan," *Interiors* 107 (April 1948): 114–15, 174; Joseph C. Ingraham, "New Highway Link Speeded in Kings," *New York Times* (December 18, 1948): 32; "Triple Decker," *Brooklyn Eagle* (October 11, 1949): 6; "Brooklyn's Stalled Highway," *Brooklyn Eagle* (December 5, 1949): 2; "Brooklyn Heights Trims Its Hem," *Interiors* 109 (February 1950): 12; "Brooklyn to Open New Roadtop Park," *New York Times* (October 1, 1950): 75; "Civic Works Go On, Impellitteri Says," *New York Times* (October 8, 1950): 89; Henrik Krogius, "Promenade: An Endangered Monument," *Brooklyn Heights Press & Cobble Hill News* (October 10, 1991): 1, 10–11; Henrik Krogius, "The Story Behind the Promenade," *Brooklyn Heights Press & Cobble Hill News* (October 17, 1991): 1, 10–11; Henrik Krogius, "The Perilous History of the Promenade," *Brooklyn Heights Press & Cobble Hill News* (October 24, 1991): 1, 10–11; "Review & Comment: Last of the Promenade's Creators," *Brooklyn Heights Press & Cobble Hill News* (April 2, 1992): 4. Also see "How the Esplanade Was Obtained for the Heights," *Brooklyn Heights Press* (April 9, 1953), Clippings Collection, Brooklyn Historical Society.
18. Lewis Mumford, "The Sky Line: From Blight to Beauty—II," *New Yorker* 29 (May 9, 1953): 91–97.
19. "Plaza Improvement," editorial, *New York Times* (February 14, 1941): 16; "Plans 'El' Removal on Brooklyn Span," *New York Times* (February 15, 1941): 17; "Isaacs Offers Plan for Bridge Traffic," *New York Times* (February 17, 1941): 17; "Significant News of the Week in Review," *Real Estate Record and Guide* 147 (February 22, 1941): 2.
20. "Plaza Improvement," editorial, *New York Times* (January 31, 1942): 16; "Brooklyn Bridge 'El' to Go," *New York Times* (April 30, 1942): 21; "Brooklyn Bridge 'El' Goes Out of Service on Sunday," *New York Times* (March 2, 1944): 4; "Last 'El' Train Over Brooklyn Bridge Carries Few to Mourn Over Time's Changes," *New York Times* (March 6, 1944): 21; E. C. McDowell, "Bridges," *Americana Annual for 1944* (New York and Chicago: Encyclopedia Americana Corp., 1945): 112.
21. "Artist in Bridges to Realize Dream by Modernizing Old Brooklyn Span," *New York Times* (September 20, 1948): 27; E. C. McDowell, "Bridges," *Americana Annual for 1948* (New York and Chicago: Encyclopedia Americana Corp., 1949): 84.
22. D. B. Steinman, *The Builders of the Bridge: The Story of John Roebling and His Son* (New York: Harcourt, Brace and Co., 1945).
23. Stanley Edgar Hyman, "The Alluring Roadway," *New Yorker* 28 (May 17, 1952): 39–40, 42, 44, 46–50, 52, 55–58, 60–62, 65–72, 77–79, 81–84.
24. Hyman, "The Alluring Roadway": 50. Also see E. C. McDowell, "Bridges," *Americana Annual for 1949* (New York and Chicago: Encyclopedia Americana Corp., 1950): 85–86.
25. David Steinman quoted in "Artist in Bridges to Realize Dream by Modernizing Old Brooklyn Span": 27.
26. "Last Trolley Crosses Brooklyn Span as Modernization of Bridge Begins," *New York Times* (March 6, 1950): 1, 36; *Downtown Brooklyn: An Architectural and Urban History*, 105.
27. "Brooklyn Bridge," *Life* 36 (May 24, 1954): 130–35; "The Talk of the Town: Notes and Comment," *New Yorker* 30 (August 7, 1954): 15; Morton Dan Morris, "The Wonders of New York," *Collier's* 134 (December 10, 1954): 126–29; E. C. McDowell, "Bridges," *Americana Annual for 1954* (New York and Chicago: Encyclopedia Americana Corp., 1955): 87; David Barnard Steinman, "Bridges," *Britannica Book of the Year* (Chicago: Encyclopaedia Britannica, 1955): 178; "What Happened to the Brooklyn Bridge," *Architectural Forum* 102 (April 1955): cover, 122–24, 176, 180, 184; "What Happened to the Brooklyn Bridge Cont'd.," *Architectural Forum* 103 (August 1955): 140–41.
28. "What Happened to the Brooklyn Bridge": 122, 124.
29. Frederick H. Zermuhlen quoted in "What Happened to the Brooklyn Bridge Cont'd.": 140.
30. "Significant News of the Week in Review," *Real Estate Record and Guide* 147 (February 15, 1941): 2; "With Record Readers," *Architectural Record* 90 (October 1941): 10; Talbot F. Hamlin, "The Frustrated Monument Complex," *Pencil Points* 22 (October 1941): 651–55; "The Curious Story of the Ventilating Tower," *Architectural Forum* 75 (November 1941): 10, 12, 14; E. C. McDowell, "Tunnels," *Americana Annual for 1941* (New York and Chicago: Encyclopedia Americana Corp., 1942): 698–99; James Forgie, "Tunnels," *Britannica Book of the Year* (Chicago: Encyclopaedia Britannica, 1942): 664; "Brooklyn-Battery Tunnel in New York City," *Engineering News-Record* 138 (June 12, 1947): 96–103; Alden P. Armagnac, "Sandhogs' Toughest Job," *Popular Science* 151 (September 1947): 82–90; "The Talk of the Town: Tubes," *New Yorker* 23 (September 13, 1947): 25–26; Ira Henry Freeman, "Battery Tunnel Now 70% Complete After Struggle Against Handicaps," *New York Times* (July 24, 1948): 17; "Huge Volume of Public-Works Projects Proposed for New York City," *Engineering News-Record* 141 (September 23, 1948): 6; "Tunnel 'Holed Through,'" *Architectural Record* 104 (October 1948): 172, 174; Harold W. Richardson, "Tunnels," *Britannica Book of the Year* (Chicago: Encyclopaedia Britannica, 1949): 710; "Fluorescent Lighting for Brooklyn-Battery Tunnel," *American City* 64 (March 1949): 127; George A. Fox, "Hangers Swing Steel Under Caisson for Brooklyn-Battery Shaft Bracing," *Engineering News-Record* 143 (July 28, 1949): 42–43; "The Talk of the Town: Under the Floor," *New Yorker* 25 (September 10, 1949): 20; Richard Thruelsen, "New York's Deepest Tunnel," *Saturday Evening Post* 222 (March 25, 1950): 32–33, 125–27; "New York Dedicates Its New Tunnel This Week," *Engineering News-Record* 144 (May 25, 1950): 30; "The Talk of the Town: Soap and Rats," *New Yorker* 26 (June 3, 1950): 19–20; "Longest Lighted Submarine Highway," *American City* 65 (July 1950): 119, 121; Morris, "The Wonders of New York": 126–29; White and Willensky, *AIA Guide* (1967), 411–12, 414–15; Robert Moses, *Public Works: A Dangerous Trade* (New York: McGraw-Hill, 1970), 197–220. Also see Stern, Gilmartin and Mellins, *New York 1930*, 689–90.
31. Hamlin, "The Frustrated Monument Complex": 651.
32. Hamlin, "The Frustrated Monument Complex": 655.
33. "Ground Broken for Battery Park Underpass Linking East and West Side Highways," *New York Times* (February 1, 1949): 52.
34. Robert Moses quoted in "Moses Asks Unity in Fight on Slums," *New York Times* (October 20, 1941): 19. Also see Triborough Bridge Authority, *Vital Arterial Gaps and the Navy Yard Neighborhood* (New York, October 20, 1941); "Moses Report Calls for Housing Reform," *Real Estate Record and Guide* 148 (October 25, 1941): 3–4.
35. "Housing Project Gets Name," *New York Times* (October 27, 1941): 32; "Housing for Defense Workers Opened in Brooklyn," *New York Times* (November 25, 1941): 22; "U.S. Not 'Bluffing,' La Guardia Says," *New York Times* (December 4, 1941): 16; Richard Plunz, *A History of Housing in New York City* (New York: Columbia University Press, 1990), 247–48.
36. "State's First Loan for Housing Is Set," *New York Times* (February 27, 1941): 32; "Clearing Housing Site," *New York Times* (February 28, 1941): 35; Catherine Bauer, "Planned Large Scale Housing. A Building Types Study. A Balance Sheet of Progress," *Architectural Record* 89 (May 1941): 96; "Lehman and La Guardia to Speak on Tuesday at Ground-Breaking for Fort Greene Houses," *New York Times* (May 4, 1941), XI: 1; "Fort Greene Houses," editorial, *New York Times* (May 6, 1941): 20; "Governor Starts Ft. Greene Housing," *New York Times* (May 7, 1941): 27; "One-Room Suites for Fort Greene," *New York Times* (July 20, 1941), XI: 1; "Large-Scale Housing and Modernization Work Are Features of City Architecture," *New York Times* (January 25, 1942), XI: 1; "Largest Public Housing Project Taking Form in Brooklyn," *New York Times* (June 21, 1942), XI: 1; "War Housing," *Architectural Forum* 77 (October 1942): 33–34; White and Willensky, *AIA Guide* (1967), 277; Victoria Newhouse, *Wallace K. Harrison, Architect* (New York: Rizzoli International Publications, 1989), 76–77; Plunz, *A History of Housing in New York City*, 248.
37. "Metropolis in a Mess," *Newsweek* 54 (July 27, 1959): 29–31.
38. Robert F. Wagner quoted in "Mayor Wagner Says," *Newsweek* 54 (September 14, 1959): 55.
39. "Ft. Greene Houses Will Be Renovated," *New York Times* (February 10, 1957): 71; "Ft. Greene Houses Refitted by City," *New York Times* (February 4, 1958): 23.
40. "Equitable to Build Big Home Project," *New York Times* (January 27, 1942): 23; "No More Towers?" editorial, *New York Times* (January 28, 1942): 18; "Clinton Hill," editorial, *New York Times* (January 29, 1942): 18; "Equitable to Construct Brooklyn Housing," *Real Estate Record and Guide* 149 (January 31, 1942): 4–5; Lee E. Cooper, "Brooklyn Losing Large Mansions on Housing Site," *New York Times* (February 1, 1942), XI: 1–2; "File for First Units of Brooklyn Housing," *New York Times* (February 19, 1942): 33; Talbot Hamlin, "There *Is* Something to Fight For," *Pencil Points* 23 (March 1942): 147–50; Charles Abrams, *Clinton Hill Project of the Equitable Life Assurance Society*, memorandum to the Members of the Subcommittee of the National Committee on the Housing Emergency (May 6, 1942); Lee E. Cooper, "Tenants to Rent New War Housing without Leases," *New York Times* (May 24, 1942), XI: 1, 6; White and Willensky, *AIA Guide* (1978), 416; Newhouse, *Wallace K. Harrison, Architect*, 76–77.
41. For East River Houses, London Terrace and Knickerbocker Village, see Stern, Gilmartin and Mellins, *New York 1930*, 417–19, 450, 452.
42. Hamlin, "There *Is* Something to Fight For": 148–49.
43. "Pentagonal Apartment Building," *Architectural Forum* 86 (January 1947): 63–66; "City Houses, Office Building and Taxpayer Planned," *New York Times* (January 19, 1947), VIII: 1; "Revolutionary City Housing," *Interiors* 106 (March 1947): 14, 16; "Housing Project," *Architectural Record* 102 (September 1947): 132; Carl Vollmer, "A Plan for Middle Income Rental Housing," *Architectural Record* 102 (November 1947): 80–85; Plunz, *A History of Housing in New York City*, 268–69.
44. "Pentagonal Apartment Building": 64.
45. Plunz, *A History of Housing in New York City*, 269.
46. "$15,000,000 Is Voted for City Projects," *New York Times* (February 20, 1952): 21; "City Speeds Plan for New Coliseum," *New York Times* (November 27, 1952): 33; "Vast Housing Plan Set for Brooklyn," *New York Times* (December 11, 1952): 39; Charles G. Bennett, "City Planners Approve Coliseum and 2 Other Projects for Action," *New York Times* (December 13, 1952): 1, 16; "Coliseum Project Adopted by Board," *New York Times* (December 19, 1952): 33; "New City Housing," editorial, *New York Times* (December 25, 1952): 28; "Two Plans—A Plus and a Minus," *Housing and Planning News* 11 (January 1953): 1; *Downtown Brooklyn: An Architectural and Urban History*, 107, 109.

47. White and Willensky, *AIA Guide* (1978), 411.
48. Charles G. Bennett, "Slum Clearance at Pratt Voted," *New York Times* (January 29, 1954): 21; L. J. Davis, "The Happy Reawakening of Clinton Hill," *New York* 3 (February 2, 1970): 38–41.
49. "Delayed Housing to Start Tuesday," *New York Times* (June 16, 1957): 57; "Salvage Job Begins on Building Project," *New York Times* (June 19, 1957): 25; White and Willensky, *AIA Guide* (1967), 269.
50. White and Willensky, *AIA Guide* (1967), 277.
51. Henry Hope Reed, Jr., "The Modern Is Dead—Long Live the Modern," with drawings by John Barrington Bayley, *New World Writing* 11 (New York: New American Library, 1957): 134–51. Also see Thomas Creighton, "P.S.: The Intellectual Fringes," editorial, *Progressive Architecture* 38 (June 1957): 366.
52. Douglas Robinson, "Navy Yard Here Eligible for Aid as Industry Park," *New York Times* (February 18, 1966): 1, 20; Charles G. Bennett, "City Is Negotiating to Take Over Navy Yard for Industrial Center," *New York Times* (July 7, 1966): 1, 33; Martin Gansberg, "Navy Yard Area Will Get U.S. Aid to Spur Job Rise," *New York Times* (August 21, 1966): 1, 34; Seth S. King, "U.S. Plans to Sell Navy Yard to City for $24-Million," *New York Times* (May 21, 1967): 1; "Anchors Away," *Architectural Forum* 127 (July–August 1967): 108; Institute for Urban Studies (Fordham University) and Tippetts-Abbett-McCarthy-Stratton, *The Brooklyn Navy Yard: A Plan for Redevelopment* (Washington, D.C.: United States Department of Commerce, Economic Development Administration, May 1968); Edward C. Burks, "Navy Yard Marks Time, Looking Ahead to Better Days," *New York Times* (January 25, 1969): 16; Martin Tolchin, "Navy Yard to City for $22.5-Million," *New York Times* (January 25, 1969): 1, 16; "Navy Yard Occupied," *Architectural Forum* 130 (March 1969): 30, 87; Edward Ranzal, "Mayor Accepts U.S. Gift with Complaint," *New York Times* (November 11, 1972): 6.
53. "Redeveloper Bonan Depends on Design for Investment Safety," *Architectural Forum* 112 (June 1960): 13; "Brooklyn Civic Groups Battle Cadman Plan," *Housing and Planning News* 18 (summer 1960): 1–2; "Cadman Plaza Debate: Three Ideas—One Site," *Housing and Planning News* 19 (May–June 1961): 2; William J. Conklin, "Clouds Over Radiant City," *Architectural Record* 131 (January 1962): 98–104; "Brooklyn Housing," *Architectural Forum* 120 (March 1964): 41; "Brooklyn Serial Play," *Housing and Planning News* 22 (summer 1964): 1, 4; Maud Dorr, "Scaling the Heights," *Progressive Architecture* 46 (November 1965): 54, 56; "Residential Complex Will Blend Older Urban Neighborhood," *Architectural Record* 140 (July 1966): 398; White and Willensky, *AIA Guide* (1978), 390; *Downtown Brooklyn: An Architectural and Urban History*, 109–10.
54. "Brooklyn Serial Play": 1.
55. Dorr, "Scaling the Heights": 54.
56. New York Chapter, American Institute of Architects, *The State of the City* (New York: New York Chapter, American Institute of Architects, June 1964), unpaginated; White and Willensky, *AIA Guide* (1978), 386–87.
57. Joseph D. McGoldrick, "Downtown Brooklyn: Test Case for Rehabilitation," *Housing and Planning News* 3 (December 1944): 2–3.
58. "M'Goldrick Offers a $20,000,000 Plan," *New York Times* (October 13, 1944): 11; "More Study Urged on Zone Proposals," *New York Times* (October 18, 1944): 23; "M'Goldrick Pushes His Brooklyn Plan," *New York Times* (November 7, 1944): 29; "Board Blocks Plan for Brooklyn Aid," *New York Times* (November 10, 1944): 36; "Brooklyn Project Cut," *New York Times* (November 23, 1944): 34; "M'Goldrick Halted on 45-Acre Purchase," *New York Times* (November 28, 1944): 35; "$196,459,226 Voted as Capital Budget," *New York Times* (December 1, 1944): 20; "Brooklyn Center Has Official Start," *New York Times* (March 2, 1945): 21; "Plans for Huge Terminal Market to Cost $42,000,000 Disclosed," *New York Times* (March 19, 1945): 25; "New Post-War Civic Center Proposed for the Borough of Brooklyn," *New York Times* (March 22, 1945): 25; "Vote Bill to Clear Brooklyn's Slums," *New York Times* (March 24, 1945): 19; New York City Planning Commission, *Master Plan of Brooklyn Civic Center & Downtown Area* (New York, May 9, 1945); "Center Sites Approved," *New York Times* (August 18, 1945): 8; "Brooklyn Center Advanced by City," *New York Times* (November 1, 1945): 25; "Brooklyn's New Center," editorial, *New York Times* (November 3, 1945): 14; "Brooklyn Center Acquired by City," *New York Times* (November 27, 1945): 40; "FWA Approves Funds for Brooklyn Center," *New York Times* (November 9, 1946): 30; Robert Moses, "'It's Going to Be Quite a Town,'" *New York Times* (February 16, 1947), VI: 7, 57–59; "Kings Civic Center Approved by Board," *New York Times* (April 17, 1947): 29; "Civic Center Progress," editorial, *New York Times* (April 22, 1947): 26; William R. Conklin, "'Face-Lifting' Plan Ordered for City," *New York Times* (May 14, 1948): 25, 28; "Start of Center in Brooklyn Nears," *New York Times* (September 25, 1949): 49; "Property Owners Reimbursed for Brooklyn Center Land," *New York Times* (December 20, 1949): 49; "Park, 2 Trolley Lines Planned in Brooklyn," *New York Times* (March 24, 1950): 27; "Civic Center Exhibition," *New York Times* (December 16, 1952): 31; "Brooklyn Booms, Cashmore Says," *New York Times* (August 1, 1954): 65; "Brooklyn Center Causes a Dispute," *New York Times* (November 26, 1954): 50; "Civic Center," editorial, *New York Times* (November 9, 1955): 32; McCandlish Phillips, "Brooklyn Center Now at Mid-Point," *New York Times* (November 5, 1955): 21, 40; Charles Grutzner, "Brooklyn Pushes 200 Million Area," *New York Times* (May 7, 1958): 37; "Civic Center Gain Cited in Brooklyn," *New York Times* (August 16, 1961): 64; "Brooklyn Progress," editorial, *New York Times* (August 17, 1961): 26; Olindo Grossi, *Downtown Brooklyn Civic Center Report* (New York: Pratt Institute, 1962); *Downtown Brooklyn: An Architectural and Urban History*, 100–107.
59. For Cleveland's Group Plan (1903), see Eric Johannesen, *Cleveland Architecture, 1876–1976* (Cleveland: Western Reserve Historical Society, 1979), 70–77.
60. Robert Moses quoted in Charles Grutzner, "Our Changing City: Downtown Brooklyn Glistens," *New York Times* (July 18, 1955): 23.
61. "Brooklyn War Memorial Competition," *Pencil Points* 26 (July 1945): 22; "Agrees on War Memorial," *New York Times* (September 18, 1947): 10; "Brooklyn Asks Aid on War Memorial," *New York Times* (August 19, 1951): 29; "Brooklyn to Try Dedication Today," *New York Times* (November 12, 1951): 11; "Mayor Dedicates $500,000 Memorial Honoring Brooklyn's 7,000 War Dead," *New York Times* (November 13, 1951): 16; "War Memorial to Open," *New York Times* (October 5, 1952): 27; Leslie Katz, "Letter from Brooklyn," *Nation* 195 (December 8, 1962): 410–11; White and Willensky, *AIA Guide* (1967), 251; Moses, *Public Works: A Dangerous Trade*, 65.
62. Mumford, "The Sky Line: From Blight to Beauty—II": 94.
63. Katz, "Letter from Brooklyn": 410–11.
64. Lewis Mumford, "The Sky Line: From Blight to Beauty—I," *New Yorker* 29 (April 25, 1953): 102–7.
65. Mumford, "The Sky Line: From Blight to Beauty—II": 91–92, 94.
66. "City Transit Body Seeks New Home," *New York Times* (August 29, 1938): 15; "City Transit Board May Erect Building," *New York Times* (September 18, 1938), XII: 1, 5; "City Subway Board to Get New Home," *New York Times* (January 26, 1939): 23; "New Home Ready for Transit Board," *New York Times* (March 25, 1951): 44; "City Board Rushes Move to New Site," *New York Times* (March 31, 1951): 30; Mumford, "The Sky Line: From Blight to Beauty—I": 102–7; White and Willensky, *AIA Guide* (1967), 252; *Downtown Brooklyn: An Architectural and Urban History*, 105, 107.
67. For the Aetna Building, see Stern, Gilmartin and Mellins, *New York 1930*, 526–27.
68. Mumford, "The Sky Line: From Blight to Beauty—I": 105–6.
69. "Housing Project Hearing Sept. 26," *New York Times* (September 13, 1945): 34; "Plan Group Votes Bus Terminal Curb," *New York Times* (September 27, 1945): 23; "Seizure of Hotel at Resort Upheld," *New York Times* (June 29, 1946): 29; "Plaza Changes Backed," *New York Times* (July 19, 1946): 21; "Brooklyn Tenants March on Court and Win Delay in Mass Eviction," *New York Times* (August 7, 1946): 29; "137 Tenants Fight Ouster," *New York Times* (September 26, 1947): 17; "Supporters Push Concord Village," *New York Times* (January 22, 1949): 28; "Start of Center in Brooklyn Nears": 49; "Cornerstone Is Laid at Brooklyn Project," *New York Times* (June 8, 1950): 22; "Housing Will Get Stores," *New York Times* (June 3, 1951), VIII: 4; "New Apartment Trio in Brooklyn," advertisement, *Architectural Record* 111 (February 1952): 281; Charles Grutzner, "Housing Is Sought for Middle Group," *New York Times* (May 12, 1952): 31; "Brooklyn Center Causes a Dispute": 50; *Downtown Brooklyn: An Architectural and Urban History*, 107.
70. Mumford, "The Sky Line: From Blight to Beauty—II": 92.
71. "Welfare Unit Plan Ready in Brooklyn," *New York Times* (May 8, 1949): 66; "Mayor to Receive amid New 'Decor,'" *New York Times* (June 14, 1949): 25; "Area Welfare Unit Opened in Brooklyn," *New York Times* (October 19, 1955): 35; *Downtown Brooklyn: An Architectural and Urban History*, 111–13.
72. "Designs Approved for Brooklyn Jail," *New York Times* (July 12, 1949): 29; "Kings Prison Bids Above Estimates," *New York Times* (July 13, 1950): 27; "Exit Raymond Street Jail," editorial, *New York Times* (August 24, 1953): 22; Grutzner, "Our Changing City: Downtown Brooklyn Glistens": 23; Emanuel Perlmutter, "New Jail to Open in Brooklyn Soon," *New York Times* (August 15, 1956): 31; "Mayor Dedicates Brooklyn Prison," *New York Times* (December 5, 1956): 26; White and Willensky, *AIA Guide* (1967), 253.
73. "Mayor Dedicates Brooklyn Prison": 26.
74. "Plans Submitted for Court in Kings," *New York Times* (February 8, 1949): 50; "First Plans Drawn for a New Court," *New York Times* (September 14, 1949): 47; "New Court Building," editorial, *New York Times* (September 19, 1949): 22; "Demolition Due Soon for Court Building," *New York Times* (March 28, 1954): 80; "Sculptor Wins Contest," *New York Times* (April 30, 1957): 17; "Brooklyn Dedicates New Court Building," *New York Times* (October 26, 1957): 14; "Brooklyn to Open New Courthouse," *New York Times* (January 4, 1959): 64; "To Be Dedicated Today," *New York Times* (January 5, 1959): 31; Katz, "Letter from Brooklyn": 410–11; White and Willensky, *AIA Guide* (1967), 251; *Downtown Brooklyn: An Architectural and Urban History*, 112–14.
75. Katz, "Letter from Brooklyn": 410.
76. "New Courthouse in Civic Center of Brooklyn Gets U.S. Approval," *New York Times* (September 24, 1956): 19; "Cashmore Urges U.S. Building," *New York Times* (January 2, 1958): 35; "Courthouse Design Will Cost $110,000," *New York Times* (February 13, 1958): 34; "Brooklyn Court to Break Ground," *New York Times* (March 27, 1960): 63; "Ground Is Broken in Brooklyn for U.S. Courthouse," *New York Times* (March 29, 1960): 42; White and Willensky, *AIA Guide* (1967), 251; *Downtown Brooklyn: An Architectural and Urban History*, 115–16.
77. Joseph C. Ingraham, "Garage Overlaid by Park Sought," *New York Times* (August 18, 1955): 25; "Hearing Dec. 7 Set for Garage Plan," *New York Times* (November 10, 1955): 24; "Brooklyn Plan Urged," *New York Times* (December 5, 1955): 37; Charles G. Bennett, "Brooklyn Garage under Park Voted," *New York Times* (December 22, 1955): 1, 19; "Estimate Board Backs Underground Garage," *New York Times* (December 30, 1955): 12; "53 Bid on City Jobs; Big Saving Is Seen," *New York Times* (July 10, 1958): 29; "Brooklyn to Get Garage in a Hill," *New York Times* (March 16, 1960): 38; Bernard Stengren, "Brooklyn Garage Dedicated by City," *New York Times* (April 13, 1960): 41; *Downtown Brooklyn: An Architectural and Urban History*, 115.
78. "Octagon Observer," *Journal of the American Institute of Architects* 44 (August 1964): 10; "Winners Announced in Brooklyn Competition," *Architectural Record* 138 (September 1965): 62.
79. "Architectural Metals," advertisement, *Architectural Record* 125 (January 1959): 52; *Downtown Brooklyn: An Architectural and Urban History*, 166.
80. "Mayor Assails Fees in Any City College," *New York Times* (May 24, 1962): 36.
81. Stern, Gilmartin and Mellins, *New York 1930*, 114; White and Willensky, *AIA Guide* (1988), 568.
82. "Schrafft's Altering Eight Restaurants," *New York Times* (August 11, 1940), XI: 1; "Schrafft's Stores—Bloch & Hesse, Architects, New York," *Pencil Points* 22 (January 1941): 23.
83. "Brooklyn Jewelers Move," *New York Times* (April 6, 1941), XI: 2; "Fulton Street—1942," *Pencil Points* 22 (October 1941): 673–76.
84. "Fulton Street—1942": 673–76.
85. "Men's Store Remodeled for Modern Merchandising," *Architectural Record* 92 (July 1942): 60–61; "Men's Store, Brooklyn, N.Y.," *Architectural Forum* 79 (September 1943): 73; Morris Ketchum, Jr., *Shops & Stores*, rev. ed. (New York: Reinhold Publishing Corp., 1957), 135, 138.
86. "José A. Fernandez, New York," *Interiors* 104 (August 1944): 53; "Fur-Bearing Store Habitat: Brooklyn," *Interiors* 104 (September 1944): 48–51; "Department Store: Balch Price, Brooklyn, N.Y.," *Architectural Forum* 81 (October 1944): 86–87.
87. "Open Display behind an Open Front," *Architectural Record* 96 (November 1944): 100–101; Thomas H. Creighton, "Observations," *Progressive Architecture* 28 (June 1947): 144; Martina Düttmann and Friederike Schneider, eds., *Morris Lapidus: Architect of the American Dream* (Basel, Berlin and Boston: Birkhäuser Verlag, 1992), 52–54, 60.
88. "Young Shoppers Get Their Own Quarters," *New York Times* (October 11, 1945): 27. Also see "Symphonized Children's Store," *Architectural Record* 100 (August 1946): 81–88; Ketchum, *Shops & Stores*, rev. ed., 51, 53.
89. "Bond Stores Plan New Brooklyn Unit," *New York Times* (May 6, 1944): 27; "New Brooklyn Store for Bond Clothes to Cost $450,000," *New York Times* (March 24, 1945): 29; "Bond's New Store Opens in Brooklyn," *New York Times* (March 24, 1949): 32.
90. "Mays to Expand Brooklyn Store," *New York Times* (January 3, 1954), VIII: 2; "Mays to Open New Addition," *New York Times* (August 26, 1954): 40.

91. Grutzner, "Our Changing City: Downtown Brooklyn Glistens": 23; "Fulton Savings Bank," *Progressive Architecture* 36 (October 1955): 142.
92. For Starrett & Van Vleck's 1929 addition to Abraham & Straus, see Stern, Gilmartin and Mellins, *New York 1930*, 317.
93. "Died: Aged 92," *Business Week* (February 16, 1952): 24; "What the Whiff of a Bargain Can Do," *Business Week* (February 23, 1952): 21; "Namm Acquires Loeser's Name, Its Trade-Marks and Goodwill," *New York Times* (March 7, 1952): 31, 34; "Mays Stores Buys the Loeser Block," *New York Times* (April 11, 1952): 36; *Downtown Brooklyn: An Architectural and Urban History*, 78–79.
94. Joe Weinstein quoted in "Mays Stores Buys the Loeser Block": 36.
95. Carl Spielvogel, "Namm-Loeser's to Close Store, Brooklyn Landmark Since 1886," *New York Times* (February 13, 1957): 1, 51; Carl Spielvogel, "Closing of Namm Saddens Borough," *New York Times* (February 14, 1957): 37, 41; "Namm's Silent," *New York Times* (February 15, 1957): 34; Carl Spielvogel, "Namm's Draws a Crowd at Last; Thousands at Liquidation Sale," *New York Times* (February 19, 1957): 43, 46; "Namm's Rebuked by Stockholders," *New York Times* (February 27, 1957): 35.
96. Isadore Barmash, "Brooklyn's Fulton Street Stores Face Rivals Calmly," *New York Times* (January 5, 1968): 49, 51.
97. "Brooklynites Bid a Nostalgic Farewell to the Fox," *New York Times* (January 4, 1971): 38; David Naylor, *Great American Movie Theaters* (Washington, D.C.: Preservation Press, 1987), 19, 251.
98. Jonathan Barnett, *Urban Design as Public Policy* (New York: Architectural Record Books, 1974), 120.
99. "A Ghirardelli Square in Brooklyn? Why Not?" *Progressive Architecture* 49 (November 1968): 52, 56.
100. For Ghirardelli Square, see David Gebhard et al., *A Guide to Architecture in San Francisco & Northern California* (Santa Barbara, Calif., and Salt Lake City, Utah: Peregrine Smith, Inc., 1973), 51–52.
101. David K. Shipler, "$500-Million Development Plan for Brooklyn Shown by Mayor," *New York Times* (October 17, 1969): 1, 52; Jonathan Barnett, "New Ways to Practice Urban Design as Part of the Governmental Process," *Architectural Record* 147 (January 1970): 142–45, 150; Robert E. Tomasson, "City Plans Fulton St. Mall in Brooklyn," *New York Times* (October 29, 1973): 1, 21; "Small Merchants Hail Brooklyn Mall," *New York Times* (October 30, 1973): 47; "Fulton Mall Plan Lauded by Mayor," *New York Times* (November 2, 1973): 45; "New York's Future Malls," editorial, *New York Times* (November 24, 1973): 30; Barnett, *Urban Design as Public Policy*, 123, 125.
102. "Hearing Called on Brooklyn Renewal," *New York Times* (June 28, 1970): 27; Maurice Carroll, "Renewal Project Nears Approval," *New York Times* (July 16, 1970): 23; Edward C. Burks, "40-Acre Renewal in Brooklyn Approved," *New York Times* (September 18, 1970): 39; Edward C. Burks, "Biggest Building in Brooklyn Set," *New York Times* (April 17, 1971): 1, 26; Steven R. Weisman, "Brooklyn Renewal: Urban Cinderella?" *New York Times* (April 25, 1971): 83, 106; Robert E. Tomasson, "City Signs a Lease to Redevelop Downtown Brooklyn," *New York Times* (October 7, 1972): 1, 66; David C. Berliner, "Barton's Sweetens Downtown Plan," *New York Times* (January 7, 1973): 118; Robert E. Tomasson, "Brooklyn Renewal Slowly Advances," *New York Times* (June 17, 1973), VIII: 1, 10.
103. Burks, "Biggest Building in Brooklyn Set": 1, 26; Weisman, "Brooklyn Renewal: Urban Cinderella?": 83, 106; Tomasson, "City Signs a Lease to Redevelop Downtown Brooklyn": 1, 66; Berliner, "Barton's Sweetens Downtown Plan": 118; Tomasson, "Brooklyn Renewal Slowly Advances": 1, 10; White and Willensky, *AIA Guide* (1978), 371.
104. Burks, "Biggest Building in Brooklyn Set": 1, 26; Weisman, "Brooklyn Renewal: Urban Cinderella?": 83, 106; Tomasson, "City Signs a Lease to Redevelop Downtown Brooklyn": 1, 66; Berliner, "Barton's Sweetens Downtown Plan": 118; Tomasson, "Brooklyn Renewal Slowly Advances": 1, 10; Peter Kihss, "$20-Million Telephone Building Latest in Brooklyn Renaissance," *New York Times* (March 5, 1975): 1, 44; White and Willensky, *AIA Guide* (1978), 371; *Downtown Brooklyn: An Architectural and Urban History*, 153.
105. Weisman, "Brooklyn Renewal: Urban Cinderella?": 83, 106; Tomasson, "Brooklyn Renewal Slowly Advances": 1, 10; John Darnton, "A Housing Project Gains in Brooklyn," *New York Times* (July 20, 1973): 28; Glenn R. Singer, "New Housing for Brooklyn," *New York Times* (May 12, 1974): 90; "Rising Costs Force U.D.C. to Reconsider Project in Brooklyn," *New York Times* (November 26, 1974): 41; Peter Kihss, "City Seeks to Take Over U.D.C. Project in Brooklyn," *New York Times* (March 9, 1975): 89, 104; Alan S. Oser, "About Real Estate: Urban Development Plan Near Downtown Brooklyn," *New York Times* (November 24, 1976): 55; Glenn Fowler, "Housing Development in Brooklyn Is Approved by Board of Estimate," *New York Times* (December 17, 1976), II: 19; Alan S. Oser, "About Real Estate: Schermerhorn Pacific," *New York Times* (January 7, 1977): 11.
106. "The Office of Downtown Brooklyn Development," *Progressive Architecture* 54 (January 1973): 66–69; "Brooklyn Center Shares Award," *New York Times* (January 20, 1973): 37.
107. Charles G. Bennett, "City Spurs Fulton Restoration with Urban-Renewal Action," *New York Times* (May 16, 1968): 94; "5,800 Housing Units Are Given Approval by City's Planners," *New York Times* (June 13, 1968): 78; "Renewal Raises Brooklyn Hopes," *New York Times* (June 24, 1968): 26; Charles G. Bennett, "Metered Water Faces Rate Rise," *New York Times* (July 26, 1968): 66; Charles G. Bennett, "Ft. Greene Market to Be Moved to the Waterfront in Brooklyn," *New York Times* (October 24, 1968): 24; "Brooklyn Heights Fights a Market," *New York Times* (November 17, 1968): 55; Norval C. White, "Waterfront Meat Mart," letter to the editor, *New York Times* (December 3, 1968): 46; "Good-by to the Waterfront," editorial, *New York Times* (December 13, 1968): 46; Don Raney, "Atlantic Terminal: Replanning of a Dense and Complex Core Area," *Architectural Record* 145 (January 1969): 114–16; Gerald Richey, "Meat Market Site," letter to the editor, *New York Times* (January 11, 1969): 32; Ada Louise Huxtable, "New York, Life's Loser, Does It Again," *New York Times* (March 9, 1969), II: 28; Seth S. King, "Sponsor Is Named for Brooklyn Hub," *New York Times* (April 6, 1969): 50; "City Picks Site in Sunset Park for Fort Greene Meat Market," *New York Times* (August 19, 1969): 30; Edward C. Burks, "Rebuilding to Start at L.I.R. Area in Brooklyn," *New York Times* (October 31, 1971), XV: 2; Max H. Seigel, "Housing Is Voted for Fort Greene," *New York Times* (January 27, 1973): 33; Pranay Gupte, "City Wants College at Renewal Site," *New York Times* (February 4, 1973): 93; Max H. Seigel, "Estimate Board Approves Several Projects of Interest to Brooklyn and Queens," *New York Times* (February 11, 1973): 111; Tomasson, "Brooklyn Renewal Slowly Advances": 1, 10; White and Willensky, *AIA Guide* (1978), 410; *James Stewart Polshek: Context and Responsibility* (New York: Rizzoli International Publications, 1988), 35, 209.
108. James Stewart Polshek, "Notes on My Life and Work," in *James Stewart Polshek: Context and Responsibility*, 35.
109. Ada Louise Huxtable, "The Blooming of Downtown Brooklyn," *New York Times* (March 30, 1975), II: 1, 32, reprinted in Ada Louise Huxtable, *Kicked a Building Lately?* (New York: Quadrangle/New York Times Book Co., 1976), 115–18. Also see Edward C. Burks, "A Touch of Frisco in Brooklyn Is Proposed," *New York Times* (December 19, 1971), XV: 12.
110. Michael T. Kaufman, "Brooklyn Acting to Set Up a Fulton St. Artists' Colony," *New York Times* (November 25, 1972): 33, 61; Sally Helgesen, "The Coming Place," *Village Voice* 18 (February 22, 1973): 1, 79; David Gordon, "Fulton Ferry Shaping Up as a Landmark," *New York Times* (July 29, 1973): 90; Alan S. Oser, "Architect Waiting for His Brooklyn Gamble to Pay Off," *New York Times* (May 23, 1975): 60.
111. Paul Goldberger, "Design Notebook: A Natural: Dining in a Barge at the Water's Edge," *New York Times* (July 21, 1977), C: 10.
112. "The Year's Work: Sam J. Glaberson, New York," *Interiors* 109 (August 1949): 72–73; Arthur Drexler, "Transformed Stable: The Horses Never Had It So Good," *Interiors* 109 (October 1949): 108–11.
113. "Citation: Residential Design," *Progressive Architecture* 44 (January 1963): 94–95; White and Willensky, *AIA Guide* (1978), 390.
114. White and Willensky, *AIA Guide* (1978), 376.
115. "Garment House, Brooklyn, New York," *Architectural Record* 145 (mid-May 1969): 70–73.
116. "Houses Bloom in Brooklyn," *Progressive Architecture* 49 (July 1968): 54, 56; Peter Blake, "In the Beginning, There Was the Heights . . . ," *New York* 2 (July 14, 1969): 41–45; H. Dickson McKenna, *A House in the City* (New York: Van Nostrand Reinhold, 1971), 71.
117. McKenna, *A House in the City*, 74–75; L. J. Davis, "Boom at Boerum Hill," *New York* 2 (July 14, 1969): 37–40; David Gelber, "Edging Out the Poor in Boerum Hill," *Village Voice* 17 (March 2, 1972): 9–10, 13.
118. Landmarks Preservation Commission of the City of New York, LP-0767 (November 20, 1973).
119. Davis, "Boom at Boerum Hill": 40.
120. George Herzog quoted in Gelber, "Edging Out the Poor in Boerum Hill": 10.
121. Landmarks Preservation Commission of the City of New York, LP-0320 (December 30, 1969); White and Willensky, *AIA Guide* (1978), 394.
122. "Nursing Home Is Set for Brooklyn Hospital," *New York Times* (July 2, 1972): 57; Ira D. Guberman, "Hospital Cuts Back Expansion," *New York Times* (September 30, 1973): 103, 118; White and Willensky, *AIA Guide* (1978), 394, 396.
123. "A Surprising Victorian," *Architectural Forum* 133 (September 1970): 36–39; "New York Chapter AIA Residential Design Awards," *Architectural Record* 150 (September 1971): 43.
124. "Neighborhoods: The Mood Is Changing Along the Gowanus Canal," *New York Times* (September 20, 1969): 17; Landmarks Preservation Commission of the City of New York, LP-0696 (September 25, 1973); White and Willensky, *AIA Guide* (1978), 400–402.
125. "To Welcome the Merchant Marine," *Architectural Record* 95 (February 1944): 55–59; White and Willensky, *AIA Guide* (1988), 609.
126. Quoted in "To Welcome the Merchant Marine": 59.
127. "Modern Movie Trend," *Interiors* 103 (April 1945): 60–61.
128. For Red Hook Houses, see Stern, Gilmartin and Mellins, *New York 1930*, 496, 498–99.
129. "Neighborhoods: The Mood Is Changing Along the Gowanus Canal": 17.
130. Monica Surfaro, "Dredgers Begin Cleanup of Gowanus Canal in Brooklyn," *New York Times* (February 2, 1975): 82; Robert E. Tomasson, "Upgrading Moves Ahead in Red Hook," *New York Times* (March 2, 1975), VIII: 1, 10.
131. For the Brooklyn Museum, see Stern, Gilmartin and Massengale, *New York 1900*, 87–91. For the Brooklyn Public Library, see Stern, Gilmartin and Mellins, *New York 1930*, 132–33, 139–40.
132. Joseph M. Sheehan, "City Officials to Help Dodgers Get New Stadium and Stay Here," *New York Times* (August 18, 1955): 1, 26; "Fans Are Frantic Over Game Shifts," *New York Times* (August 18, 1955): 26; Ralph Katz, "Subways to Lose by Teams' Moves," *New York Times* (October 9, 1957): 37; Emanuel Perlmutter, "Dodgers Accept Los Angeles Bid to Move to Coast," *New York Times* (October 9, 1957): 1, 37; White and Willensky, *AIA Guide* (1967), 412; Donald Honig, *The Brooklyn Dodgers: An Illustrated Tribute* (New York: St. Martin's Press, 1981); Gene Schoor, *The Complete Dodgers Record Book* (New York: Facts On File, 1984); Elliot Willensky, *When Brooklyn Was the World, 1920–1957* (New York: Harmony Books, 1986), 12–13, 32–37; Duke Snider and Bill Gilbert, *The Duke of Flatbush* (New York: Zebra, 1988).
133. Roscoe McGowen, "Dodgers Sublet Brooklyn Home," *New York Times* (March 5, 1958): 41; "Ebbets Field in Action," *New York Times* (May 31, 1958): 32.
134. "Packing Them in at Ebbets Field," *Housing and Planning News* 18 (January–February 1960): 1, 4. Also see Joseph M. Sheehan, "Realty Firm Takes Control of Baseball Park in Brooklyn," *New York Times* (January 1, 1960): 24; Foster Hailey, "State Funds Back Ebbets Housing," *New York Times* (January 4, 1960): 31, 35; Charles G. Bennett, "11 Million Levy on Trucks Voted," *New York Times* (June 11, 1960): 1, 22; "Kratter Files Plans for Ebbets Project," *New York Times* (June 14, 1960): 60; "New Chapter for Ebbets Field: Apartments Open This Month," *New York Times* (September 2, 1962), VIII: 1; "Ebbets Field Apartment Tenants Charge Newcomers Are Favored," *New York Times* (October 20, 1963): 81.
135. "A Geodesic Dome for Brooklyn Dodgers," *Progressive Architecture* 36 (November 1955): 95.
136. "Sports Center for Brooklyn," *American City* 71 (August 1956): 24.
137. Charles G. Bennett, "Big Dodger Stadium Outlined to Mayor," *New York Times* (July 25, 1956): 1, 22; "News Bulletins," *Progressive Architecture* 37 (September 1956): 100.
138. "News Bulletins," *Progressive Architecture* 38 (February 1957): 98–99.
139. Maurice Carroll, "Now Mr. Mayor, If I Were You . . . ," *New York Times* (December 9, 1973): 151, 168.
140. "Side Streets: The Brooklyn Whats?" *New York Affairs* 2, no. 2 (1974): 116–17.
141. "The Brownstoners," *Newsweek* 74 (September 1, 1969): 56–59; Jan Rosenberg, "Park Slope's Notes on a Middle-Class 'Utopia,'" *Dissent* 34 (fall 1987): 564–67. Also see "Tishman Will Rehabilitate 17 Park Slope Brownstones," *Real Estate Record and Guide* 200 (July 8, 1967): 4; "First Phase of Park Slope Rehabilitation Project Is Completed," *Real Estate Record and Guide* 201 (June 1, 1968): 2; "Flight to the City," *Fortune* 79 (March 1969): 100–103; McKenna, *A House in the City*, 78–79; Ruth Miller Fitzgibbons, "A Trend Grows in Brooklyn," *Residential Interiors* 2 (January 1977): 68–69.

142. Mildred F. Schmertz, "Comprehensive District Planning: Private Sponsored Rehabilitation of Six Blocks in Brooklyn," *Architectural Record* 142 (July 1967): 142–49.
143. White and Willensky, *AIA Guide* (1978), 432.
144. "The Talk of the Town: Prospect Park," *New Yorker* 43 (October 28, 1967): 48–50. For Moses's 1934 construction boom, see Caro, *The Power Broker*, 368–85.
145. "Proposed New Carrousel for Brooklyn's Prospect Park," *New York Times* (April 15, 1952): 29; "Tuesday Post Time of New Carrousel," *New York Times* (October 19, 1952): 59; "Carrousel Is Dedicated," *New York Times* (October 22, 1952): 29; "Carrousel Congests Traffic in Brooklyn," *New York Times* (November 2, 1952): 27; Robert Moses, "Gifts to Central Park," *American City* 69 (April 1954): 94–95; Clay Lancaster, *Prospect Park Handbook* (New York: Walton H. Rawls, 1967), 97–98.
146. Murray Illson, "Pruning and Cleaning Begun in Prospect Park," *New York Times* (October 17, 1959): 25.
147. "Wollman Donates Fund to Brooklyn Ice Rink," *New York Times* (October 23, 1959): 16; "Prospect Park Rink Approved; Wollman Fund Gives $300,000," *New York Times* (October 7, 1960): 37; "Wollman Memorial Rink to Open in Brooklyn," *New York Times* (December 20, 1961): 30; "New Wollman Rink Is Dedicated in Brooklyn," *New York Times* (December 23, 1961): 42; Lancaster, *Prospect Park Handbook*, 98–99; White and Willensky, *AIA Guide* (1967), 291.
148. Martin Tolchin, "A Gaslight Relic Awaits Verdict," *New York Times* (September 19, 1964): 29; "A Pier Is Planned in Prospect Park," *New York Times* (November 14, 1964): 30; Joseph Mathieu, "Prospect Park's Boathouse," letter to the editor, *New York Times* (December 9, 1964): 46; Martin Tolchin, "Boathouse Saved at Prospect Park," *New York Times* (December 11, 1964): 57; Martin Tolchin, "Restoration Due in Prospect Park," *New York Times* (January 1, 1965): 20; "City Will Spruce Up Brooklyn's Prospect Park in a $450,000 Project," *New York Times* (August 8, 1965): 1, 33. For Helmle & Huberty's Boathouse, see Stern, Gilmartin and Massengale, *New York 1900*, 134–35.
149. See Clay Lancaster, *Old Brooklyn Heights* (Rutland, Vt.: Charles E. Tuttle, 1961).
150. "Hoving to Name Curators to Beautify City Parks," *New York Times* (December 12, 1965): 1, 38; Ralph Blumenthal, "2 City Parks Get First Curators," *New York Times* (January 20, 1966): 25; "'Curators' Named for Parks," *Village Voice* 11 (January 20, 1966): 1.
151. Jonathan Randal, "Prospect Park Peristyle to Be Restored," *New York Times* (August 4, 1966): 35; Clay Lancaster, "Plans for Prospect Park," letter to the editor, *New York Times* (August 27, 1966): 28. For the original Croquet Shelter, see Stern, Gilmartin and Massengale, *New York 1900*, 134.
152. "On-Again, Off-Again Restoration Plans On Again in Prospect Park," *New York Times* (September 8, 1967): 41; Bayard Webster, "City to Open 2 Restored Prospect Park Areas Today Amid Criticism," *New York Times* (September 29, 1969): 49.
153. "Quiet Milestone in Prospect Park," *New York Times* (May 30, 1966): 21; "On-Again, Off-Again Restoration Plans On Again in Prospect Park": 41; "Restoration of Old Boathouse in Prospect Park Has Begun," *New York Times* (April 18, 1971): 84; "Restoration of Boathouse in Prospect Park Pushed," *New York Times* (April 9, 1972), XV: 14; "Lindsay Assails Graffiti Vandals," *New York Times* (August 25, 1972): 30; "Prospect Park Boathouse Is Reopened," *New York Times* (July 7, 1974): 63, 75; "Repair Delays Bar Use of Prospect Park Boathouse," *New York Times* (August 14, 1975): 35.
154. "A Real Farmyard in Prospect Park Delights Children," *New York Times* (January 26, 1965): 31; "City Will Spruce Up Brooklyn's Prospect Park in a $450,000 Project": 1, 33; Ralph Blumenthal, "Children's Farm in Park Opposed," *New York Times* (February 23, 1966): 80; "Children's Farm for Prospect Park," *New York Times* (March 2, 1966): 43; F. David Anderson, "Taxpayers' Suit Seeks to Block Children's Farm as Ad for A.& S.," *New York Times* (December 13, 1966): 38; "Children's Farm in Park Blocked," *New York Times* (July 1, 1967): 21; Maurice Carroll, "City Aiming to Proceed on Its Farm," *New York Times* (January 17, 1968): 49; Robert M. Makla, "Ruin in Prospect Park," letter to the editor, *New York Times* (April 28, 1969): 40; "The Sheep Baa, and the Children Squeal as a Farmyard Zoo Is Dedicated in Prospect Park," *New York Times* (August 7, 1971): 27.
155. Clay Lancaster quoted in Carroll, "City Aiming to Proceed on Its Farm": 49.
156. For Weeksville, see Barbaralee Diamonstein, *The Landmarks of New York* (New York: Harry N. Abrams, 1988), 68; Andrew S. Dolkart, *Guide to New York City Landmarks* (Washington, D.C.: Preservation Press, 1992), 187.
157. "Moses Denies Lack of Bedford Parks," *New York Times* (November 28, 1943): 24.
158. "The Talk of the Town: Tour," *New Yorker* 44 (October 12, 1968): 48–51.
159. Jack Newfield, "Robert Kennedy's Bedford-Stuyvesant Legacy," *New York* 1 (December 16, 1968): 25–34.
160. "The Talk of the Town: Bedford-Stuyvesant," *New Yorker* 40 (August 1, 1964): 23–26.
161. Newfield, "Robert Kennedy's Bedford-Stuyvesant Legacy": 27.
162. Ralph Blumenthal, "Brooklyn Negroes Harass Kennedy," *New York Times* (February 5, 1966): 17.
163. "Kennedy Seeking Money for Slums," *New York Times* (October 17, 1966): 61; Steven V. Roberts, "Redevelopment Plan Set for Bedford-Stuyvesant," *New York Times* (December 11, 1966): 1, 88; John Kifner, "Split Generates New Kennedy Corporation to Revitalize Bedford-Stuyvesant," *New York Times* (April 2, 1967): 62; Maurice Carroll, "Mortgage Funds Pledged to Slum," *New York Times* (April 2, 1968): 1, 19; William Borders, "Mrs. Edward Kennedy Tours Slum Project," *New York Times* (April 11, 1969): 32; William Borders, "Mrs. Kennedy Tours 'Superblocks' Renovated in Bedford-Stuyvesant," *New York Times* (October 31, 1969): 47. Also see Kilvert Dun Gifford, "Neighborhood Development Corporations: The Bedford-Stuyvesant Experiment," in Lyle C. Fitch and Annmarie Hauck Walsh, eds., *Agenda for a City: Issues Confronting New York* (Beverly Hills, Calif.: Sage Publications, 1970), 421–50.
164. Steven V. Roberts, "Bedford-Stuyvesant Given Grant to Plan a Network of Parks," *New York Times* (March 26, 1967): 1, 26; Steven V. Roberts, "Brooklyn Ghetto Given $7 Million," *New York Times* (June 25, 1967): 1, 50; "Crane, Pei to Design for Brooklyn Ghetto," *Progressive Architecture* 48 (August 1967): 45; James Bailey, "RFK's Favorite Ghetto," *Architectural Forum* 128 (April 1968): 46–53; "Bits of Brooklyn's Dream," *Architectural Forum* 131 (December 1969): 23–24; "Making Cities Better Places to Live," *Business Week* (August 22, 1970): 36–39; Dalton James, "Restoration in Bed-Stuy: Greening of the Ghetto?" *Village Voice* 16 (July 1, 1971): 61–62; Oscar Newman, *Defensible Space: Crime Prevention Through Urban Design* (New York: Macmillan, 1972), 60–62; "Designing the Urban Landscape: New Projects by M. Paul Friedberg and Associates," *Architectural Record* 151 (March 1972): 97–104; Peter Blake, "I. M. Pei & Partners," *Architecture Plus* 1 (March 1973): 20–25; Peter Wolf, *The Future of the City: New Directions in Urban Planning* (New York: Whitney Library of Design, 1974), 43; White and Willensky, *AIA Guide* (1978), 455; Carter Wiseman, *I. M. Pei: A Profile in American Architecture* (New York: Harry N. Abrams, 1990), 146, 308.
165. I. M. Pei quoted in "Making Cities Better Places to Live": 39.
166. I. M. Pei quoted in "Making Cities Better Places to Live": 38.
167. Martin Tolchin, "City Planner's Call for Hearing Blocks $3.6-Million for 2 Pools," *New York Times* (July 23, 1969): 28; Emanuel Perlmutter, "Pool Opens in Bedford-Stuyvesant," *New York Times* (July 11, 1971): 33; Muriel Fischer, "'If It Worked for the Rich, Why Not for the Poor?'" *New York Times* (November 28, 1971), XV: 17; Ada Louise Huxtable, "How a Pool Grew in Brooklyn," *New York Times* (August 13, 1972), II: 18; "Bedford Stuyvesant Community Pool," *Architectural Record* 153 (June 1974): 98–99; White and Willensky, *AIA Guide* (1978), 447.
168. Huxtable, "How a Pool Grew in Brooklyn": 18.
169. Huxtable, "How a Pool Grew in Brooklyn": 18.
170. Charles Hoyt, "Three Projects by Hoberman and Wasserman: Architecture in Context," *Architectural Record* 156 (September 1974): 125–34; White and Willensky, *AIA Guide* (1978), 447.
171. Norman Hoberman quoted in Hoyt, "Three Projects by Hoberman and Wasserman: Architecture in Context": 132.
172. Kifner, "Split Generates New Kennedy Corporation to Revitalize Bedford-Stuyvesant": 62; Bailey, "RFK's Favorite Ghetto": 48; Rudy Johnson, "Rebuilt Plant Is a Symbol of Hope in Brooklyn," *New York Times* (May 2, 1971): 104; Thomas A. Johnson, "Senators, in Bedford-Stuyvesant, Hear Praise for Development Unit," *New York Times* (June 12, 1971): 1, 15; Frank E. Emerson, "A Man Who Keeps Faith in Bed-Stuy," *New York Times* (May 14, 1972), XV: 14.
173. William E. Farrell, "Bedford-Stuyvesant Group to Build $6-Million Center," *New York Times* (June 29, 1972): 1, 30; Mary E. Osman, "Arthur Cotton Moore/Associates of Washington," *Journal of the American Institute of Architects* 61 (May 1974): 58–61; Judith Cummings, "An Urban Shopping Center," *New York Times* (September 29, 1974): 91, 109; Charlayne Hunter, "Bedford-Stuyvesant Complex Is Opened," *New York Times* (October 3, 1975): 37; "Good News in Brooklyn," editorial, *New York Times* (October 18, 1975): 28; Calvin Trillin, "U.S. Journal: Brooklyn," *New Yorker* 51 (November 10, 1975): 161–63, 165–66, 168; James A. Murphy, "A Lesson from Bedford-Stuyvesant," *Progressive Architecture* 57 (January 1976): 23–24; William I. Clark, "Recognition for Bed-Stuy," letter to the editor, *Progressive Architecture* 57 (April 1976): 8, 12; Fred Powledge, "New York's Bedford-Stuyvesant: Rare Urban Success Story," *Journal of the American Institute of Architects* 65 (May 1976): 40–49; White and Willensky, *AIA Guide* (1978), 450–51.
174. Murphy, "A Lesson from Bedford-Stuyvesant": 24.
175. Olga Gueft, "Caribbean Courtyard in Bedford-Stuyvesant," *Interiors* 136 (December 1976): 68–71; White and Willensky, *AIA Guide* (1978), 447.
176. Edward C. Burks, "Estimate Board Expands Brooklyn Housing Plans," *New York Times* (April 17, 1970): 64; White and Willensky, *AIA Guide* (1978), 451.
177. Burks, "Estimate Board Expands Brooklyn Housing Plans": 64; White and Willensky, *AIA Guide* (1978), 452.
178. John Goldman, "Good News for Bed-Stuy," *New York* 3 (September 7, 1970): 6; Grace Lichtenstein, "Worries Mar Restoration Group's Birthday," *New York Times* (May 7, 1973): 43; Donald Canty, "Editorial," *Journal of the American Institute of Architects* 65 (May 1976): 39; Powledge, "New York's Bedford-Stuyvesant: Rare Urban Success Story": 40–49; Charlayne Hunter-Gault, "The Restoration Corporation Shifts Gears in Bedford-Stuyvesant," *New York Times* (December 16, 1976): 49, 56.
179. Ruth Rejnis, "Young People Coming Home to 'Bed-Stuy,'" *New York Times* (October 20, 1974), VIII: 1, 12. Also see Clifford T. Weller, "A Brooklyn Augury," letter to the editor, *New York Times* (November 7, 1974): 44.
180. "City to Get School Shaped Like a Banjo," *New York Times* (July 18, 1952): 21; "News: Banjo-Shaped School," *Architectural Forum* 97 (August 1952): 57; "Building: Classrooms in a Circle," *Interiors* 112 (September 1952): 10; "Banjo-Plan School," *Architectural Forum* 97 (November 1952): 122–25; Dennis Duggan, "Circular Layout Has Varied Uses," *New York Times* (October 28, 1962), VIII: 1, 8.
181. Don Raney, "Urban Housing: A Comprehensive Approach to Quality," *Architectural Record* 145 (January 1969): 104–5; Thomas W. Ennis, "Nonprofit Co-op in Crown Heights," *New York Times* (February 2, 1969), VIII: 1; Charles G. Bennett, "City Hearing Is Set for Cluster Housing on S.I.," *New York Times* (May 1, 1969): 37; "City Plans Co-op in Crown Heights," *New York Times* (May 4, 1969): 55; "Crown Heights Gets a 239-Unit Co-op," *New York Times* (July 1, 1973), VIII: 8; Glenn Fowler, "Bard Awards Honors 8 Examples of Good Urban Design," *New York Times* (June 12, 1975): 41; White and Willensky, *AIA Guide* (1978), 456.
182. For Turtle Bay Gardens, see Stern, Gilmartin and Mellins, *New York 1930*, 428–29.
183. Stern, Gilmartin and Mellins, *New York 1930*, 139.
184. Sanka Knox, "Museum Beckons: 'Please Do Touch,'" *New York Times* (May 28, 1968): 36; "Art in the Neighborhoods," editorial, *New York Times* (May 30, 1968): 24; "Muse," *Newsweek* 71 (June 24, 1968): 96, 98; Ellen Perry Berkeley, "MUSE . . . ," *Architectural Forum* 129 (September 1968): 86–89; "Spirit of the Muse," letters to the editor, *Architectural Forum* 129 (November 1968): 20; Suzanne Wiedel, "Bed-Stuy's Own MUSE," *New York* 2 (July 14, 1969): 46–47; "Muse," *L'Architecture d'Aujourd'hui* 145 (September 1969): 87–90; Hugh Hardy, "Exhibit of Goodwill," *Journal of the American Institute of Architects* 52 (October 1969): 28; "Spaced in Brooklyn," *New York* 3 (March 2, 1970): 38; "Award Given Museum, Ex-Pool Hall," *New York Times* (May 20, 1970): 83; Ada Louise Huxtable, "Dissimilar Buildings, Similar Awards," *New York Times* (May 24, 1970), VIII: 1, 7; "1970 Bard Awards for Excellence in Architecture and Design in New York City," *Interiors* 129 (June 1970): 10; "Eighth Annual Awards Presented by City Club of New York," *Architectural Record* 149 (July 1970): 40–42; David C. Berliner, "Community Hopes to Keep MUSE," *New York Times* (March 25, 1973): 118; Andrea O. Dean, "An Evocative Approach to Adaptive Use," *Journal of the American Institute of Architects* 65 (June 1976): 38–40; C. Ray Smith, *Supermannerism: New Attitudes in Post-Modern Architecture* (New York: E. P. Dutton, 1977), 252–53, color plate 1.
185. "Children's Museum Gets Room to Grow," *New York Times* (January 6, 1967): 33; C. Ray Smith, "The Great Museum Debate," *Progressive Architecture* 50 (December 1969): 76–85; "The Brooklyn Children's Museum," *Architectural Record* 147 (February 1970): 45; Grace Glueck, "Brooklyn Unveils Plans for a Museum," *New York Times* (May 19, 1971): 38; Mildred F. Schmertz, "Design for Learning: Work of Hardy Holzman Pfeiffer Associates," *Architectural Record* 151 (April 1972): 109–18; George Gent, "A Museum for Children Will Rise in Brooklyn," *New York Times* (June 14, 1972): 40; Phyllis Funke, "Children's Museum Shows New Ideas," *New York Times* (March 24, 1974): 97, 112; Grace Glueck, "Child's World of Wonder in Brooklyn," *New York Times* (May 17, 1977): 35; Paul Goldberger, "A Funhouse Built in a Fun Structure," *New York Times*

(May 29, 1977), II: 23; White and Willensky, *AIA Guide* (1978), 454–55; Michael Sorkin, *Hardy Holzman Pfeiffer* (New York: Whitney Library of Design, 1981), 90–93; *Hardy Holzman Pfeiffer Associates: Buildings and Projects 1967–1992* (New York: Rizzoli International Publications, 1992), 56–59.

186. Goldberger, "A Funhouse Built in a Fun Structure": 23.

187. Stern, Gilmartin and Mellins, *New York 1930*, 717, 720.

188. "Vast Housing Unit Approved for City," *New York Times* (February 1, 1940): 1, 15; "New Housing Adventures," editorial, *New York Times* (February 2, 1940): 16; "Housing Project Named," *New York Times* (February 3, 1940): 26; "Housing Office Opens," *New York Times* (February 14, 1940): 39; "Moving Almost Gets Back to Normal," *New York Times* (August 19, 1941): 11; "Mayor Dedicates Kingsborough Houses, City's 10th Home Project, 3d for Brooklyn," *New York Times* (September 10, 1941): 17; "Kingsborough Houses," editorial, *New York Times* (December 8, 1941): 22.

189. "Moving Almost Gets Back to Normal": 11.

190. *NYC Postwar Program* (New York: City of New York, May 1, 1944), 40; "Brooklyn Housing Project," *Architectural Record* 94 (August 1944): 10; "Brooklyn Housing Project and Manhattan Deals Attract Interest," *New York Times* (September 16, 1945), VIII: 1; "Work Starts on Brooklyn Low-Rent Housing Project," *New York Times* (June 4, 1946): 46; "No Dignitaries to Place Housing Project's Stone," *New York Times* (March 6, 1947): 27; "At Cornerstone Laying of Brownsville Houses," *New York Times* (March 7, 1947): 27; "Housing Project to Open," *New York Times* (June 27, 1947): 18; "Toward Better Standards of City Living," *Progressive Architecture* 30 (October 1949): 14, 16, 18; Newman, *Defensible Space*, 38–49, 239–51; Plunz, *A History of Housing in New York City*, 262–63, 272–73, 294.

191. Quoted in "Toward Better Standards of City Living": 14, 16, 18.

192. Alfred Kazin, *A Walker in the City* (New York: Harcourt, Brace, 1951), 12–14.

193. Murray Schumach, "Our Changing City: Southeastern Brooklyn Area," *New York Times* (July 29, 1953): 19.

194. "Housing Architects Chosen," *New York Times* (June 27, 1950): 18; "Housing for City Approved by U.S.," *New York Times* (August 27, 1950): 76; "159 Slum Acres to Be Condemned," *New York Times* (January 7, 1951): 61; Charles G. Bennett, "Clang! Go 10 More Trolley Lines; Only 3 to Be Left, All in Brooklyn," *New York Times* (January 12, 1951): 29; "1,453 Low-Rent Suites for Brownsville Houses," *New York Times* (March 23, 1951): 36; "Income Rule Eased in Low-Rent Homes," *New York Times* (June 30, 1953): 25; Newman, *Defensible Space*, 38–49, 239–51; Plunz, *A History of Housing in New York City*, 272–73, 294.

195. "City Files Plans for Its Boulevard Houses in Brooklyn Estimated to Cost $14,392,000," *New York Times* (January 15, 1949): 25; "Home Units Occupied," *New York Times* (May 24, 1950): 31.

196. "$75,685,000 in Housing," editorial, *New York Times* (February 5, 1951): 22; "State Aid Approved for New City House," *New York Times* (February 5, 1951): 32; "Housing Bids Opened," *New York Times* (May 12, 1954): 55; "New Project Opening," *New York Times* (August 21, 1955): 52.

197. "Planned for the Good Life in Brooklyn," *Architectural Record* 120 (August 1956): 178–81; "Work Progresses on Linden Houses," *New York Times* (December 20, 1956): 26.

198. "Plans Revamped on Cathay Houses," *New York Times* (February 21, 1957): 20; "Ground Is Broken for Tilden Houses," *New York Times* (April 22, 1959): 22; "Rent Formula Changed," *New York Times* (July 29, 1960): 16.

199. Schumach, "Our Changing City: Southeastern Brooklyn Area": 19.

200. "Fine New Project in Brownsville," *Housing and Planning News* 27 (January 1969): 3–4. Also see David K. Shipler, "Low-Rent Project Shines in Slum," *New York Times* (October 5, 1969), VIII: 1, 12.

201. "Fine New Project in Brownsville": 4.

202. "Model Cities: From Hassle into Concrete," *Progressive Architecture* 50 (February 1969): 31.

203. Roger D. Glasgow quoted in "Model Cities: From Hassle into Concrete": 31.

204. Elaine Weiss and Roger D. Glasgow quoted in "Model Cities: From Hassle into Concrete": 31.

205. *Another Chance for Housing: Low-Rise Alternatives*, exhibition catalogue (New York: Museum of Modern Art, 1973); Joseph P. Fried, "Low-Rise Development Project Begun in Brownsville by U.D.C.," *New York Times* (June 12, 1973): 49; Ada Louise Huxtable, "Another Chance for Housing," *New York Times* (June 24, 1973), II: 23; James D. Morgan, "MOMA on Housing: Nothing New," *Architecture Plus* 1 (August 1973): 68; David A. Morton, "Low-Rise, High-Density," *Progressive Architecture* 54 (December 1973): 56–63; Wolf, *The Future of the City: New Directions in Urban Planning*, 112–16; Theodore Liebman, J. Michael Kirkland and Anthony Pangaro, "Housing Criteria Drawn from Human Response," *Journal of the American Institute of Architects* 61 (March 1974): 46–49; Theodore Liebman and Alan Melting, "Learning from Experience," *Progressive Architecture* 55 (November 1974): 70–77; Robert F. Borg, "'Low-Rise' Priority in Housing Premature," *New York Times* (December 15, 1974), VIII: 1, 6; John Ciardullo, David F. M. Todd and Theodore Liebman, "Low-Rise Housing Priority Defended," letters to the editor, *New York Times* (January 5, 1975), VIII: 4; Sharon Lee Ryder, "Upstairs, Downstairs," *Progressive Architecture* 57 (March 1976): 40–41; Kenneth Frampton, "U.D.C. Low Rise High Density Housing Prototype," *L'Architecture d'Aujourd'hui* 186 (August–September 1976): 15–21; White and Willensky, *AIA Guide* (1978), 496; Suzanne Stephens, "Compromised Ideal," *Progressive Architecture* 60 (October 1979): 50–53.

206. Edward J. Logue, "Introduction," in *Another Chance for Housing: Low-Rise Alternatives*, 5.

207. Kenneth Frampton, "The Evolution of Housing Concepts: 1870–1970," in *Another Chance for Housing: Low-Rise Alternatives*, 6–11.

208. Anthony Pangaro and Kenneth Frampton, "Low Rise High Density: Issues and Criteria," in *Another Chance for Housing: Low-Rise Alternatives*, 13.

209. Logue, "Introduction," in *Another Chance for Housing: Low-Rise Alternatives*, 5.

210. Stephens, "Compromised Ideal": 52–53.

211. Grace Lichtenstein, "Poverty-Stricken Brownsville Has History of Despair," *New York Times* (September 24, 1974): 48; White and Willensky, *AIA Guide* (1978), 497.

212. Barbara Radice and Franco Raggi, eds., *La Biennale di Venezia* (Venice: Alfieri Edizioni d'Arte, 1976), II: 262–66; Robert A. M. Stern, "The Suburban Alternative for the 'Middle City,'" *Architectural Record* 164 (August 1978): 93–100; Robert A. M. Stern with John Montague Massengale, *The Anglo-American Suburb* (London: Architectural Design, 1981), 92; *Robert A. M. Stern: Buildings and Projects 1965–1980*, eds. Peter Arnell and Ted Bickford (New York: Rizzoli International Publications, 1981), 118–21; Aaron A. Betsky, "The Big Boys from the Big Time: Suburbs in the City," *Metropolis* 1 (October 1981): 7–8; Stan Pinkwas, "Suburbia's Cutting Edge," *Metropolis* 2 (June 1983): cover, 10–14, 26; Gavin Macrae-Gibson, "Robert Stern and the Tradition of the Picturesque," *A + U* (August 1985): 83–90; Vincent Scully, *American Architecture and Urbanism*, new rev. ed. (New York: Henry Holt and Co., 1988), 279; Osamu Nakasuji, "Comment: The Architect's Revenge," *A + U* (May 1988): 144–45.

213. Robert Stern quoted in *Robert A. M. Stern: Buildings and Projects 1965–1980*, 118.

214. Stern with Massengale, *The Anglo-American Suburb*, 92.

215. Charles G. Bennett, "Capital Budget Approved by City," *New York Times* (March 16, 1966): 30; White and Willensky, *AIA Guide* (1978), 498.

216. "P.S. 398 in Brooklyn Designed by Perkins & Will," *Architectural Record* 155 (July 1974): 40; "In Progress," *Progressive Architecture* 56 (December 1975): 30; David Morton, "Brooklyn's Blakeslee," *Progressive Architecture* 57 (March 1976): 70–73; White and Willensky, *AIA Guide* (1978), 494–95.

217. "Newest Thing in Playgrounds Opens in Brooklyn," *New York Times* (May 19, 1967): 35; "The Ignoble Experiment," *Progressive Architecture* 48 (August 1967): 47; Asher Etkes, "Children's Playgrounds," letter to the editor, *Progressive Architecture* 49 (January 1968): 16; Robert A. M. Stern, *New Directions in American Architecture* (New York: George Braziller, 1969), 103, fig. 109.

218. "The Ignoble Experiment": 47.

219. "19th Annual *P/A* Design Awards Program: Citation, Works (East)," *Progressive Architecture* 53 (January 1972): 94–95; James A. Murphy, "Street Level 747," *Progressive Architecture* 54 (November 1973): 107–9; "Per bambini, centro pedagogico in Brooklyn," *Domus* 548 (July 1975): 36–39.

220. White and Willensky, *AIA Guide* (1978), 495.

221. White and Willensky, *AIA Guide* (1978), 498.

222. "East New York Savings Bank," *New York Times* (November 21, 1962): 48; White and Willensky, *AIA Guide* (1978), 495.

223. "Brooklyn School Design Wins Commendation," *New York Herald Tribune* (November 17, 1963): 48; "P.S. 45," *Progressive Architecture* 48 (March 1967): 122–29; George Early, "Prejudging the Venerable Board," letter to the editor, and reply, *Progressive Architecture* 48 (May 1967): 6; Morris Ketchum, Jr., *Blazing a Trail* (New York: Vantage Press, 1982), 22–23.

224. Ketchum, *Blazing a Trail*, 22–23.

225. White and Willensky, *AIA Guide* (1988), 688–89. Also see Lesley Oelsner, "35 Try to Halt Hospital Project," *New York Times* (September 10, 1971): 38; David Morton, "Toward the Minimal Shell," *Progressive Architecture* 53 (July 1972): cover, 52–63; Francis X. Clines, "City Plans a Rise in Capital Budget," *New York Times* (December 3, 1972): 31; Glenn Fowler, "New Facilities to Open in Brooklyn and Queens," *New York Times* (May 19, 1974): 97, 114; Max H. Seigel, "City Hospital Built to Be Altered," *New York Times* (July 8, 1974): 33; G. M. Kallmann and N. M. McKinnell, "Movement Systems as Generators of Built Form," *Architectural Record* 158 (November 1975): 105, 114–15; Ronald Sullivan, "State Asks Reorganization of Hospitals in Brooklyn," *New York Times* (June 15, 1978), II: 18; Ronald Sullivan, "The Best Hospital Money Could Buy," *New York Times* (July 19, 1978), II: 1; Ronald Sullivan, "A $150 Million Trim in Hospitals Is Seen," *New York Times* (December 14, 1978): 1, II: 5; Ronald Sullivan, "New York Seeks a U.S. Takeover of New Hospital," *New York Times* (January 20, 1979): 26; Ronald Sullivan, "City Hospital's Revival Is Possible," *New York Times* (May 6, 1979): 61; Ronald Sullivan, "New Delays for $200 Million Hospital, Empty 3 Years," *New York Times* (June 21, 1981): 1, 24; Sydney H. Schanberg, "New York: Waking a Mothballed Elephant," *New York Times* (November 14, 1981): 23; Paul Goldberger, "Woodhull Hospital, a Controversial Giant, Cast in a 60's Mold," *New York Times* (November 5, 1982), II: 1, 11; Ronald Sullivan, "New Hospital Opens Doors, 6 Years Late," *New York Times* (November 5, 1982), II: 1; Alex Krieger, ed., *The Architecture of Kallmann, McKinnell & Wood* (Cambridge, Mass.: Harvard University Graduate School of Design; New York: Rizzoli International Publications, 1988), 113.

226. Goldberger, "Woodhull Hospital, a Controversial Giant, Cast in a 60's Mold": 1, 11.

227. Seth S. King, "Linear City Asked in Brooklyn Plan," *New York Times* (February 26, 1967): 1, 69; Emanuel Perlmutter, "City Seeks 25,000 Parking Meters," *New York Times* (February 27, 1967): 19; Ada Louise Huxtable, "How to Build a City, If You Can," *New York Times* (March 12, 1967), II: 31, reprinted in *Forum* (Amsterdam) 20 (March 1968): 27; "The Process Is the Product," *Architectural Forum* 126 (April 1967): 29–30; "Development in Deepest Brooklyn," *Progressive Architecture* 48 (April 1967): 194–97; Rogers, Taliaferro, Kostritsky, Lamb, *Linear City and Cross Brooklyn Expressway* (Baltimore, Md., September 1967); "Wall-to-Wall Concrete—II," editorial, *New York Times* (November 28, 1967): 46; "Preplanning the Linear City," *Progressive Architecture* 48 (December 1967): 29; "Stadterneuerung in Brooklyn: Bandstadt über Bahnkörper," *Baumeister* 65 (January 1968): 25–56; Ervin Galantay, "Architecture," *Nation* 206 (February 12, 1968): 217–18, 220; "Linear City," *Forum* (Amsterdam) 20 (March 1968): 28–34; "The School as a Generator of Urban Form," *Progressive Architecture* 49 (April 1968): 162–64; "Brooklyn Schools Started It," *Progressive Architecture* 49 (April 1968): 165–67; "Way Paved for Linear City," *Progressive Architecture* 49 (October 1968): 75–76; Richard L. Madden, "U.S. Agrees to Aid Lindsay Proposal for a Linear City," *New York Times* (June 29, 1968): 1, 59; William K. Stevens, "Road Builders Now Face Detours," *New York Times* (November 17, 1968): 84; David K. Shipler, "Mayor Asks School Site Change Because of Linear City 'Delays,'" *New York Times* (February 7, 1969): 26; Maurice Carroll, "Brooklyn Road Plan Halted by Lindsay," *New York Times* (May 4, 1969): 1, 37; Maurice Carroll, "Mayor Drops Plans for Express Roads Across 2 Boroughs," *New York Times* (July 17, 1969): 1, 51; Ada Louise Huxtable, "Politics of Expressways," *New York Times* (July 17, 1969): 51; "Three Urban Expressways Do Not Slash Through Cities," *Architectural Record* 146 (September 1969): 36; "Linear City," *L'Architecture d'Aujourd'hui* 146 (October–November 1969): 78–79; Moses, *Public Works: A Dangerous Trade*, 303–5; Wolf, *The Future of the City: New Directions in Urban Planning*, 55.

228. "Moses Urges 3d Queens Tunnel, with Condition," *New York Times* (June 10, 1963): 24; "Road in Brooklyn Called Essential," *New York Times* (July 2, 1965): 31.

229. John V. Lindsay quoted in Madden, "U.S. Agrees to Aid Lindsay Proposal for a Linear City": 59.

230. "Two Housing Units Approved for City," *New York Times* (March 20, 1952): 31; "Prospect Ave. Close Is Set for Tomorrow," *New York Times* (October 18, 1953): 70; "Brooklyn Opens Expressway Link," *New York Times* (November 30, 1954): 25.

231. "House Remodeling," *Architectural Record* 91 (February 1942): 38–39. For Ocean Parkway's redevelopment, see Edmond J. Bartnett, "Fine Homes Yield to Apartments on Brooklyn's Ocean Parkway," *New York Times* (May 21, 1961), VIII: 1, 14; "Law on Parkways Limits Architect," *New York Times* (August 2, 1964), VIII: 1, 8; William Robbins, "Ocean Parkway Absorbs Change," *New York Times* (November 7, 1965), VIII: 1, 10.

232. "Synagogue Is Started," *New York Times* (September 26, 1954), VIII: 10.

233. "Congregation Beth Torah, Brooklyn, New York. Architect: Richard Foster," *Architectural Record* 147 (January 1970): 98–99.

234. For Kahn's unrealized designs for the Mikveh Israel synagogue, see Heinz Ronner and Sharad Jhaveri, *Louis I. Kahn: Complete Work 1935–1974* (Basel: Birkhäuser Verlag, 1974), 188–97.

235. Stan Fischler, *Uptown, Downtown: A Trip Through Time on New York's Subways* (New York: Hawthorn Books, 1976), 48–56, 240–42.

236. For Flagg Court, see Stern, Gilmartin and Mellins, *New York 1930*, 494. Also see "New Apartments along Shore Road," *New York Times* (October 11, 1931), XI: 2.

237. "State to Back Brooklyn Housing," *New York Times* (June 10, 1972): 35; John G. Taylor, "Housing for Aged in Brooklyn Advances," *New York Times* (June 18, 1972): 90; Kenneth P. Nolan, "Shore Hill Protests Housing for Aged," *New York Times* (January 28, 1973): 90; Max Seigel, "Planners Approve Housing for Aged," *New York Times* (October 14, 1973): 119; Max H. Seigel, "Bay Ridge Renews Its Efforts to Bar Housing for Aged," *New York Times* (April 2, 1975): 41; White and Willensky, *AIA Guide* (1978), 480.

238. "Hospital Forecast," *Architectural Forum* 85 (November 1946): 8–9; "Fort Hamilton Veterans' Hospital, Brooklyn, New York," *Architectural Record* 99 (June 1947): 114–23; "Skyscraper Hospital," *Interiors* 108 (February 1949): 10; Huson Jackson, *A Guide to New York Architecture 1650–1952* (New York: Reinhold Publishing Corp., 1952), 46–47; "City Planning," *Interiors* 111 (June 1952): 12; "VA Hospital," *Progressive Architecture* 33 (July 1952): cover, 63–74; White and Willensky, *AIA Guide* (1967), 336; White and Willensky, *AIA Guide* (1978), 480; Carol Herselle Krinsky, *Gordon Bunshaft of Skidmore, Owings & Merrill* (New York: Architectural History Foundation; Cambridge, Mass.: MIT Press, 1988), 15–16, 34–35, 335.

239. "Half of Luna Park Destroyed by Fire as 750,000 Watch," *New York Times* (August 13, 1944): 1, 34.

240. Michael T. Kaufman, "2 Coney Islands Awaiting Influx," *New York Times* (March 19, 1964): 35.

241. David Binder, "It's Not All Fun at Coney Island," *New York Times* (August 6, 1961), VIII: 1, 4.

242. "Coney Housing Open," *New York Times* (November 12, 1953): 34; "Housing Notes Sold," *New York Times* (August 18, 1954): 36. For Sea Gate, see Stern, Gilmartin and Massengale, *New York 1900*, 421–22. Also see Joseph P. Fried, "Sea Gate Remains Untouched by Coney Island's Clamor," *New York Times* (May 19, 1963), VIII: 1, 17; "Sea Gate Is a Well-Policed Upper Bohemia," *New York Times* (June 13, 1971): 110.

243. "Plan Board Backs Big Coney Project," *New York Times* (May 7, 1953): 33; "11,000 Apartments Scheduled by City," *New York Times* (December 20, 1953): 41; "Colors Featured at City Project," *New York Times* (September 26, 1954), VIII: 1; "New Homes Open Today," *New York Times* (October 15, 1956): 29; Binder, "It's Not All Fun at Coney Island": 4.

244. Martin Tolchin, "Coney Landmark Is Sold to Trump," *New York Times* (July 2, 1965): 60; Bernard Weinraub, "Park Stands Empty Following Its Sale to a Developer," *New York Times* (July 5, 1965): 19; "6 Bikinied Beauties Attend Demolishing of Coney Landmark," *New York Times* (September 22, 1966): 49; Jeanette Bruce, "Where the Fun Was," *Sports Illustrated* 27 (August 28, 1967): 68–76; William Alfred, "The Roller-Coaster History of Coney Island," *New York* 1 (September 9, 1968): 27–33; Susan Poole, "Another New Face for Coney Island," *New York* 1 (September 9, 1968): 34–35. For Steeplechase Park, see Stern, Gilmartin and Massengale, *New York 1900*, 249.

245. "City Revises Plan for Luna Housing," *New York Times* (January 13, 1956): 21; "Revision Is Made of Luna Park Site," *New York Times* (January 19, 1956): 35; "Middle-Income Housing Will Rise on Coney's Luna Park Site Next Year," *New York Times* (November 26, 1956): 29; John P. Callahan, "3 New Designs in Public Housing Are Proffered by Architect Here," *New York Times* (March 31, 1957), VIII: 1, 8; "New Coney Island Is Seen Emerging as Start Is Made on Housing Project," *New York Times* (July 10, 1958): 19; Binder, "It's Not All Fun at Coney Island": 1, 4.

246. Charles Grutzner, "Big Housing Co-op Nears Showdown," *New York Times* (July 4, 1958): 21; Charles G. Bennett, "City Gets Report on Coney Housing," *New York Times* (February 5, 1959): 24; Charles Grutzner, "Showdown Is Due on Housing Taxes," *New York Times* (April 13, 1959): 22; Thomas W. Ennis, "Compromise Ends Coney Tug of War," *New York Times* (November 22, 1959), VIII: 1, 4; A. H. Raskin, "Potofsky's Union Will Build Co-ops," *New York Times* (December 19, 1959): 49; Binder, "It's Not All Fun at Coney Island": 4; Thomas W. Ennis, "2 Large Projects Advance in Coney," *New York Times* (September 29, 1963), VIII: 1, 9.

247. Ennis, "Compromise Ends Coney Tug of War": 1, 4; "Part of Warbasse Site Named Trump Village," *New York Times* (June 14, 1960): 60; "New Method Used in Concrete Work," *New York Times* (May 19, 1963), VIII: 1, 18; Ennis, "2 Large Projects Advance in Coney": 1, 9; "Development in Coney Is Peak of a 40-Year Building Career," *New York Times* (January 5, 1964), VIII: 1–2; Glenn Fowler, "Major Project Is Ahead of Time," *New York Times* (May 17, 1964), VIII: 1, 16. Fred Trump also developed two other large-scale housing projects in Brooklyn. For Shore Haven (Seelig & Finkelstein, 1947), facing the Belt Parkway, between Twentieth and Twenty-first avenues and extending inland as far as Cropsey Avenue, see Lee E. Cooper, "Brooklyn, Astoria Get New Housing with 2682 Units," *New York Times* (June 22, 1947), VIII: 1. For Beach Haven (1950), at 2611 West Second Street, see "Beach Haven Housing Gets $2,058,400 Loan," *New York Times* (February 17, 1950): 41; "Plans Social Program: Trump Offers Lectures as Part of Beach Haven Recreation," *New York Times* (September 10, 1950), VIII: 8; "Rental Housing for 1,860 Families in Brooklyn," *New York Times* (September 17, 1950), VIII: 4. For general discussion of Trump's role as a developer in Brooklyn and Queens, see Lee E. Cooper, "Builder Expects High Home Prices to Be Maintained," *New York Times* (November 10, 1946), VIII: 1; Alden Whitman, "A Builder Looks Back—And Moves Forward," *New York Times* (January 28, 1973), VIII: 1, 9; Donald J. Trump with Tony Schwartz, *Trump: The Art of the Deal* (New York: Random House, 1987), 45–55.

248. "A 160-Foot-High Pleasure Dome Is Proposed for Coney Island," *New York Times* (July 24, 1966), VIII: 1, 6.

249. White and Willensky, *AIA Guide* (1978), 489. Also see Peter Wolf, *Another Chance for Cities*, exhibition catalogue (New York: Whitney Museum of American Art, 1970), 34, 42–43, 48–49; Wolfgang H. Rosenberg, "New York State Urban Development Corporation Is an Action Agency," *Journal of Housing* 27 (December 1970): 584–89; Edward C. Burks, "Housing Gains in Southeast Brooklyn," *New York Times* (September 24, 1972):

130; Glenn Fowler, "Razing Plan Stirs Coney Residents," *New York Times* (April 4, 1974): 45; Glenn Fowler, "2 Zoning Plans in Brooklyn Provoke Community Debates," *New York Times* (April 7, 1974): 108; Joseph P. Fried, "City Seeks More Land in Renewal Area," *New York Times* (August 11, 1974): 83, 86; Glenn Fowler, "Desperate Battle Against Growing Urban Blight," *New York Times* (August 11, 1974): 86; Louis W. Powsner, "Coney Island Development," letter to the editor, *New York Times* (August 18, 1974): 82; "Homeowners Keep Coney Island Property," *New York Times* (September 15, 1974): 107.

250. William Marlin, "Homing in on Housing," *Architectural Forum* 137 (November 1972): 42–55; White and Willensky, *AIA Guide* (1978), 488–89.

251. Hoyt, "Three Projects by Hoberman and Wasserman: Architecture in Context": 128–31.

252. Marlin, "Homing in on Housing": 52–53; White and Willensky, *AIA Guide* (1978), 490.

253. Marlin, "Homing in on Housing": 54–55; Hoyt, "Three Projects by Hoberman and Wasserman: Architecture in Context": 125–27; Nan Robertson, "Helping the Elderly to Flee from Fear," *New York Times* (June 13, 1977): 34; White and Willensky, *AIA Guide* (1978), 489.

254. White and Willensky, *AIA Guide* (1978), 489.

255. White and Willensky, *AIA Guide* (1978), 489.

256. White and Willensky, *AIA Guide* (1978), 489.

257. White and Willensky, *AIA Guide* (1978), 489.

258. White and Willensky, *AIA Guide* (1978), 489.

259. White and Willensky, *AIA Guide* (1978), 490.

260. White and Willensky, *AIA Guide* (1978), 490.

261. New York City Planning Commission, *Coney Island: Neighborhood Improvement Area* (New York, December 1974), 26; White and Willensky, *AIA Guide* (1978), 489.

262. "Design Awards Program: Education," *Progressive Architecture* 36 (January 1955): 87; "Vocational High School to Do a Social Job," *Architectural Record* 118 (July 1955): 168–72; "The Architect and His Community: Architects Associated," *Progressive Architecture* 39 (February 1958): 99–115; White and Willensky, *AIA Guide* (1967), 339–40.

263. "Progressive Architecture for Health—1952," *Progressive Architecture* 33 (January 1952): 76; "City Planning," *Interiors* 112 (June 1952): 12; "Record Reports," *Architectural Record* 112 (July 1952): 304; "The New Coney Island Hospital," *Empire State Architect* 14 (March–April 1954): 8–11; "The Architect and His Community: Architects Associated": 99–115; "General Hospital," *Progressive Architecture* 39 (April 1958): 118–27, 258–59; White and Willensky, *AIA Guide* (1967), 339.

264. "News for Coney Island," *Interiors* 105 (August 1945): 104; "New Aquarium Plan Gains," *New York Times* (August 27, 1953): 27; "Plan of Aquarium at Coney Approved," *New York Times* (October 23, 1953): 34; New York City Department of Parks, *Coney Island Improvement: Aquarium, Ground Breaking Ceremony* (New York, October 24, 1954); "Aquarium Opening Promised by June 1," *New York Times* (January 18, 1956): 27; Emanuel Perlmutter, "Shortages Delay Aquarium Work," *New York Times* (February 4, 1956): 10; "Topics of The Times," *New York Times* (June 5, 1957): 34; Murray Schumach, "City Welcomes Coney Aquarium," *New York Times* (June 6, 1957): 33; "New Aquarium Opens," *New York Times* (June 7, 1957): 25; "Crowds Tax Aquarium's Capacity on Its First Sunday," *New York Times* (June 10, 1957): 1, 35; White and Willensky, *AIA Guide* (1967), 340; Newhouse, *Wallace K. Harrison, Architect*, 73–75.

265. "$350,000 Grant Is Made for Aquarium Laboratory," *New York Times* (July 9, 1964): 30; "Lab Cornerstone Placed," *New York Times* (June 30, 1965): 45; "Zoological Fund Nears $8-Million," *New York Times* (January 13, 1966): 17; White and Willensky, *AIA Guide* (1967), 340; John C. Devlin, "Marine Research May Result in Cures for Man," *New York Times* (February 11, 1969): 17.

266. "New York City Aquarium," *Life* 11 (November 17, 1941): 138–41.

267. For Harrison's African Plains installation, see Stern, Gilmartin and Mellins, *New York 1930*, 713.

268. *Record of Submissions and Awards Competition for Middle-Income Housing at Brighton Beach, Brooklyn. 1968* (New York: City of New York, 1968); "Interconnected Complex Wins Housing Competition for Brooklyn Waterfront Site," *Architectural Record* 143 (April 1968): 40; "Development on a Brooklyn Beach," *Progressive Architecture* 49 (May 1968): 62, 64; Stern, *New Directions in American Architecture*, 8–10; Stanislaus von Moos, *Venturi and Rauch: Architektur im alltag Amerikas* (Zurich: Kunstgewerbemuseum, 1979), 88–89; "Venturi, Rauch and Scott Brown," *A + U*, extra edition (December 1981): 150; Gianni Pettena and Maurizio Vogliazzo, *Venturi, Rauch and Scott Brown* (Milan: Electa Editrice, 1985), 105.

269. See Frank Lloyd Wright, *Letters to Apprentices*, selected and with commentary by Bruce Brooks Pfeiffer (Fresno, Calif.: The Press at California State University, 1982), 24, 81–82.

270. Philip Johnson quoted in "Interconnected Complex Wins Housing Competition for Brooklyn Waterfront Site": 40.

271. José Luis Sert, letter to Jason R. Nathan, October 31, 1968, in *Record of Submissions and Awards Competition for Middle-Income Housing at Brighton Beach, Brooklyn. 1968*, unpaginated.

272. Philip Johnson, letter to Jason R. Nathan, March 12, 1968, in *Record of Submissions and Awards Competition for Middle-Income Housing at Brighton Beach, Brooklyn. 1968*, unpaginated, also quoted in Stern, *New Directions in American Architecture*, 10.

273. Romaldo Giurgola, letter to Jason R. Nathan, March 15, 1968, in *Record of Submissions and Awards Competition for Middle-Income Housing at Brighton Beach, Brooklyn. 1968*, unpaginated.

274. Donlyn Lyndon, letter to Jason R. Nathan, March 15, 1968, in *Record of Submissions and Awards Competition for Middle-Income Housing at Brighton Beach, Brooklyn. 1968*, unpaginated, also quoted in Stern, *New Directions in American Architecture*, 10.

275. "Oasis in Brooklyn," *Architectural Forum* 95 (October 1951): 190–94; Jackson, *A Guide to New York Architecture 1650–1952*, 46.

276. "Kingsborough Community College: Gesamtplan," *Baumeister* 68 (February 1971): 133–37; White and Willensky, *AIA Guide* (1978), 486.

277. *James Stewart Polshek: Context and Responsibility*, 32–33, 124–26.

278. Polshek, "Notes on My Life and Work," in *James Stewart Polshek: Context and Responsibility*, 33.

279. "Sanitation Department Garage," *Pencil Points* 26 (July 1945): 79–81; Antonin Raymond, *Antonin Raymond: An Autobiography* (Rutland, Vt.: Charles E. Tuttle, 1973), 190.

280. "Sanitation Department Garage": 79.

281. Raymond, *Antonin Raymond: An Autobiography*, 190.

282. Schumach, "Our Changing City: Southeastern Brooklyn Area": 19.
283. "Flushing Project Gets State Funds," *New York Times* (September 11, 1949): 56; "Canarsie to Get Housing," *New York Times* (November 6, 1949): 21; "Federal Aid Homes to Open Tomorrow," *New York Times* (December 26, 1951): 27; "First Tenants in Breukelen," *New York Times* (December 28, 1951): 23; "One of the Federal Subsidized Housing Projects in New York," *New York Times* (May 11, 1952): 79; William M. Farrell, "Housing Projects Etch City with Odd Geometric Designs," *New York Times* (November 10, 1952): 27; Newman, *Defensible Space*, 54–56, 67–69, 91–93.
284. "Brooklyn Will Get $20,325,000 Housing," *New York Times* (August 18, 1953): 25; Schumach, "Our Changing City: Southeastern Brooklyn Area": 19; "Wagner Inspects Bay View Houses," *New York Times* (September 8, 1955): 26; "Middle Income Housing," *Progressive Architecture* 39 (February 1958): 106–8; White and Willensky, *AIA Guide* (1967), 343–44.
285. "New Apartments Set for Brooklyn, Queens and Bronx," *New York Times* (March 23, 1952), VIII: 1, 8; Schumach, "Our Changing City: Southeastern Brooklyn Area": 19.
286. Steven V. Roberts, "Project for 6,000 Families Approved for Canarsie Site," *New York Times* (June 28, 1967): 1, 26; Carter B. Horsley, "Housing for 24,000 Begun in Brooklyn," *New York Times* (July 16, 1972): 46; Joseph P. Fried, "Marshes Give Way to Housing Project," *New York Times* (March 21, 1974): 43; "Occupancy Is Expected to Begin in October at Starrett City," *New York Times* (September 1, 1974), VIII: 2; Joseph P. Fried, "Planners Preparing for Starrett City's Tenants," *New York Times* (October 13, 1974): 129, 152; Grace Lichtenstein, "5,881 Unit Project Is Dedicated Here," *New York Times* (October 14, 1974): 1, 23; "News of the Realty Trade," *New York Times* (August 17, 1975), VIII: 6; Joseph P. Fried, "People Move In, and Starrett City Is Homey at Last," *New York Times* (May 23, 1976), VIII; 1, 10; White and Willensky, *AIA Guide* (1978), 498; Michael Goodwin, "Starrett City Lone Concern: Rent," *New York Times* (September 18, 1979), II: 1, 6.
287. White and Willensky, *AIA Guide* (1978), 492–93.

THE BRONX

1. Peter S. Beagle, "Good-by to the Bronx," *Holiday* 36 (December 1964): 96–97, 141, 150–55, 157.
2. Donald G. Sullivan and Brian J. Danforth, *Bronx Art Deco Architecture: An Exposition* (New York: Hunter College Graduate Program in Urban Planning, City University of New York, 1976); Timothy Rub, ed., *Building a Borough: Architecture and Planning in the Bronx, 1890–1940* (New York: Bronx Museum of the Arts, 1986), plates 1, 25–29; White and Willensky, *AIA Guide* (1988), 509–16. For earlier residential development along the Grand Concourse, see Stern, Gilmartin and Mellins, *New York 1930*, 482–83, 485. For discussion of the architecture of Miami Beach, see Laura Cerwinske, *Tropical Deco: The Architecture and Design of Old Miami Beach* (New York: Rizzoli International Publications, 1981); Barbara Baer Capitman, *Deco Delights: Preserving the Beauty and Joy of Miami Beach Architecture* (New York: E. P. Dutton, 1988).
3. "1,500 Unit Housing Planned in Bronx by Equitable Life," *New York Times* (April 21, 1946): 1; "Fordham Hill Apartments," *Architectural Record* 108 (September 1950): 132–36; White and Willensky, *AIA Guide* (1988), 522.
4. For Castle Village, see Stern, Gilmartin and Mellins, *New York 1930*, 450–51, 453.
5. "First Mortgage, of $2,100,000, Arranged on New Apartment House Being Erected at 800 Grand Concourse," *Real Estate Record and Guide* 173 (May 8, 1954): 3; "New Apartment Building Will Rise in Bronx," *Real Estate Record and Guide* 183 (May 9, 1959): 5; Edmond J. Bartnett, "Grand Concourse in Bronx Is Still the Grand Boulevard," *New York Times* (March 4, 1962): 1, 6.
6. Don Raney, "Urban Housing: A Comprehensive Approach to Quality," *Architectural Record* 145 (January 1969): cover, 100–101; "No Drabness in Rudolphian Twins," *Progressive Architecture* 50 (January 1969): 39; Sibyl Moholy-Nagy and Gerhard Schwab, *The Architecture of Paul Rudolph* (New York: Praeger, 1970), 220–23; White and Willensky, *AIA Guide* (1978), 338.
7. For Marina City, see Arthur Siegel, ed., *Chicago's Famous Buildings* (Chicago: University of Chicago Press, 1965), 208–9.
8. For Rudolph's Art and Architecture Building, see Moholy-Nagy and Schwab, *The Architecture of Paul Rudolph*, 120–37.
9. Peter Wolf, *Another Chance for Cities*, exhibition catalogue (New York: Whitney Museum of American Art, 1970), 16–17; "Harlem River Park Housing," *Progressive Architecture* 51 (February 1970): 31; "Life Along the Harlem," *Architectural Forum* 132 (March 1970): 13; Barbara Allen Guilfoyle, "Room for a View," *Industrial Design* 17 (November 1970): 24–25; "High-Density Park Planned for Narrow Riverbank Site," *Architectural Record* 149 (May 1971): 36; "NYC's Harlem River to Get Parks, Housing," *Progressive Architecture* 52 (June 1971): 44; Mildred F. Schmertz, "Designing the Urban Landscape: New Projects by M. Paul Friedberg and Associates," *Architectural Record* 151 (March 1972): 97–104; White and Willensky, *AIA Guide* (1978), 334.
10. "Harlem River Park Housing": 31; "Life Along the Harlem": 13; "NYC's Harlem River to Get Parks, Housing": 44; "The Evolving Urban Architecture of Davis, Brody & Associates," *Architectural Record* 152 (August 1972): 97–106; Ada Louise Huxtable, "Breaking the Mold," *New York Times* (February 10, 1974), II: 22; White and Willensky, *AIA Guide* (1978), 334–35.
11. "Research Center by Johnson," *Progressive Architecture* 45 (November 1964): 47; John Jacobus, *Twentieth-Century Architecture: The Middle Years 1940–65* (New York: Frederick A. Praeger, 1966), 194, 196; *Philip Johnson: Architecture 1949–1965*, with an intro. by Henry-Russell Hitchcock (New York: Holt, Rinehart and Winston, 1966), 21–23, 112–13; "Buildings in the News," *Architectural Record* 139 (June 1966): 42; White and Willensky, *AIA Guide* (1967), 234.
12. Hitchcock, "Introduction," in *Philip Johnson: Architecture 1949–1965*, 21–22.
13. David Bird, "New North Central Bronx Hospital Finally Gets to Admit First Patient," *New York Times* (October 26, 1976): 75; White and Willensky, *AIA Guide* (1988), 527.
14. White and Willensky, *AIA Guide* (1988), 527.
15. "Bulletins," *Progressive Architecture* 40 (February 1959): 80; "New York University Expands to the North," *Architectural Forum* 111 (August 1959): 50; William B. Foxhall, "Design Elements of Food Services for Colleges and Universities," *Architectural Record* 131 (April 1962): 184–88; "Flying Bridges Link N.Y.U. Campus Group," *Architectural Record* 131 (April 1962): 139–43; "Manhattan Malady," *Time* 81 (May 24, 1963): 64; "Bard Awards Presented," *Progressive Architecture* 45 (April 1964): 84; Jacobus, *Twentieth-Century Architecture: The Middle Years 1940–65*, 180; "Buildings in the News," *Architectural Record* 140 (July 1966): 40; White and Willensky, *AIA Guide* (1967), 231; New York City Planning Commission, *Plan for New York City, 1969: A Proposal* (New York, 1969), II: 68, 72; Tician Papachristou, *Marcel Breuer: New Buildings and Projects* (New York: Praeger, 1970), 110–18; *Marcel Breuer at the Metropolitan Museum of Art*, exhibition catalogue (New York: Metropolitan Museum of Art, 1972), 8–9, plate 9. For McKim, Mead & White's campus plan, see Stern, Gilmartin and Massengale, *New York 1900*, 107–8.
16. Ian McCallum, *Architecture USA* (London: Architectural Press, 1959), 101; "Dr. Shuster Finds Hunter Building Named for Him," *New York Herald Tribune* (October 27, 1959): 5; "Architectural Bulletins," *Progressive Architecture* 40 (November 1959): 88; "The Talk of the Town: Airy Architect," *New Yorker* 35 (February 13, 1960): 24; "Gothic Campus Gets a Contemporary Building," *Progressive Architecture* 41 (April 1960): 178–87; "Non si è corretto," *L'Architettura cronache e storia* 6 (August 1960): 263; White and Willensky, *AIA Guide* (1967), 232–33.
17. For Hunter's original buildings, see Stern, Gilmartin and Mellins, *New York 1930*, 114.
18. For Rudolph's Jewett Arts Center, see Moholy-Nagy and Schwab, *The Architecture of Paul Rudolph*, 50–55.
19. "Gothic Campus Gets a Contemporary Building": 178.
20. "Rooftop Greenhouses on Science High School," *Architectural Forum* 105 (November 1956): 24. For Bronx Science's earlier building, on East 189th Street between Creston and Morris avenues, see White and Willensky, *AIA Guide* (1988), 524.
21. David Norflus, "Side Streets: Did New York Really Need the Yankees?" *New York Affairs* 3, no. 3 (1976): 97–101; Nicholas Pileggi, "Was the Stadium Worth It?" *New York* 9 (April 19, 1976): 36–39. Also see "Multi-Level Garage Suggested for Yankee Stadium Area," *Real Estate Record and Guide* 185 (March 5, 1960): 2–3. For Yankee Stadium of 1922–23, see Stern, Gilmartin and Mellins, *New York 1930*, 825 (n. 48).
22. Pileggi, "Was the Stadium Worth It?": 37.
23. For the development of Riverdale prior to World War II, see Stern, Gilmartin and Massengale, *New York 1900*, 432–33; Stern, Gilmartin and Mellins, *New York 1930*, 500–503. For the Riverdale historic district, roughly bounded by Independence Avenue, West 242nd Street, Riverdale Park and the Wave Hill estate, see Landmarks Preservation Commission of the City of New York, *Riverdale Historic District Designation Report* (New York, 1990). For a general discussion of the area, see William A. Tieck, *Riverdale, Kingsbridge, Spuyten Duyvil* (Old Tappan, N.J.: Fleming H. Revell, 1968).
24. Rub, ed., *Building a Borough: Architecture and Planning in the Bronx, 1890–1940*, 62; White and Willensky, *AIA Guide* (1988), 529.
25. White and Willensky, *AIA Guide* (1988), 534.
26. Stern, Gilmartin and Mellins, *New York 1930*, 503.
27. Richard Amper, "Our Changing City: Conflicts in the Upper Bronx," *New York Times* (July 15, 1955): 23. Also see Lee E. Cooper, "Riverdale Area Built Up Rapidly," *New York Times* (February 21, 1954), VIII: 1, 11. For general discussion of Riverdale's evolution during the 1960s and early 1970s, see George McNickle, "Riverdale Is a Contrast in Mansions and Skyscraper Apartment Houses," *New York Times* (October 1, 1961), VIII: 1, 16; McCandlish Phillips, "A Lost Era of Quiet Luxury," *New York Times* (April 15, 1965): 35; Stephen R. Conn, "Riverdale: Woods, Spacious Lawns and 28 Minutes to Grand Central," *New York Times* (October 16, 1966): 90; Deirdre Carmody, "Quiet Cool of Riverdale Belies Nearness of the City's Frenzy," *New York Times* (September 27, 1970): 52; Jack Luria, "A Pox on You, Riverdale," *New York Times* (June 21, 1972): 43.
28. "1,000-Family Apartment Center Planned in Historic Bronx Site," *New York Times* (February 24, 1946), VIII: 1; "Large Privately-Built Housing Project to Be Erected in Riverdale Section," *Real Estate Record and Guide* 157 (March 2, 1946): 4–5.
29. "Campagna Plans Riverdale Houses," *New York Times* (April 20, 1947), VIII: 1; "Designed for Good Living," advertisement, *Architectural Record* 105 (June 1949): 197.
30. Stern, Gilmartin and Mellins, *New York 1930*, 500–503.
31. "Eighteen-Acre Riverdale Tract to Be Improved with Housing Project," *Real Estate Record and Guide* 170 (October 11, 1952): 3.
32. For a history of the Horace Mann School and the development of its Riverdale campus, see R. A. McCardell, ed., *The Country Day School: History, Curriculum, Philosophy of Horace Mann School* (Dobbs Ferry, N.Y.: Oceana, 1962); Harold J. Bauld and Jerome B. Kisslinger, *Horace Mann–Barnard: The First One Hundred Years* (New York, 1987).
33. "School Building Dedicated," *New York Times* (December 19, 1966): 27; White and Willensky, *AIA Guide* (1967), 235; Frost Associates, *Master Plan for the Riverdale Campus of the Horace Mann School* (New York, 1970), II: 9; Bauld and Kisslinger, *Horace Mann–Barnard: The First One Hundred Years*, 52, 99. For Gross Hall (1962), see Frost Associates, *Master Plan for the Riverdale Campus of the Horace Mann School*, II: 9; Bauld and Kisslinger, *Horace Mann–Barnard: The First One Hundred Years*, 52, 99.
34. Frost Associates, *Master Plan for the Riverdale Campus of the Horace Mann School*, II: 10; White and Willensky, *AIA Guide* (1978), 342.
35. Frost Associates, *Master Plan for the Riverdale Campus of the Horace Mann School.*
36. White and Willensky, *AIA Guide* (1978), 342; Bauld and Kisslinger, *Horace Mann–Barnard: The First One Hundred Years*, 90–91.
37. White and Willensky, *AIA Guide* (1978), 345.
38. George McCue and Mary E. Osman, "Eugene Mackey: Translator of Ideals into Images," *Journal of the American Institute of Architects* 54 (August 1970): 23–30; "$1.25-Million Library Building," *New York Times* (August 30, 1970), VIII: 7; "1972 Library Buildings Award Program," *Journal of the American Institute of Architects* 57 (April 1972): 45; White and Willensky, *AIA Guide* (1978), 342. For Stein and Kohn's campus, see Stern, Gilmartin and Mellins, *New York 1930*, 122–23.
39. Tieck, *Riverdale, Kingsbridge, Spuyten Duyvil*, 176–77; White and Willensky, *AIA Guide* (1978), 342.
40. Tieck, *Riverdale, Kingsbridge, Spuyten Duyvil*, 179; White and Willensky, *AIA Guide* (1978), 342.
41. White and Willensky, *AIA Guide* (1978), 346.
42. Glenn Fowler, "Bard Awards Honor 8 Examples of Good Urban Design," *New York Times* (June 12, 1975): 41; James A. Murphy, "Tilt to the River," *Progressive Architecture* 56 (December 1975): 66–69; White and Willensky, *AIA Guide* (1978), 346.
43. For Gund Hall, see Robert Jensen, "Gund Hall: Harvard's Graduate School of Design Under One Roof," *Architectural Record* 152 (November 1972): 95–104; Michael and Susan Southworth, *A.I.A. Guide to Boston* (Chester, Conn.: Globe Pequot, 1984), 217–22.
44. Tieck, *Riverdale, Kingsbridge, Spuyten Duyvil*, 73–74; New York City Planning Commission, *Plan for New York City, 1969: A Proposal*, II: 147, 152; White and Willensky, *AIA Guide* (1988), 536–37.

45. Tieck, *Riverdale, Kingsbridge, Spuyten Duyvil*, 74; White and Willensky, *AIA Guide* (1978), 343.
46. White and Willensky, *AIA Guide* (1967), 235.
47. Betty Raymond, "Life Extension at Hebrew Home for the Aged," *Interiors* 128 (March 1969): 98–99. Also see White and Willensky, *AIA Guide* (1978), 236.
48. White and Willensky, *AIA Guide* (1978), 347.
49. White and Willensky, *AIA Guide* (1978), 344.
50. White and Willensky, *AIA Guide* (1978), 344–45.
51. "Hobart D. Betts: Cinq projets," *L'Architecture d'Aujourd'hui* 44 (August–September 1972): 54–55; White and Willensky, *AIA Guide* (1978), 346.
52. Max H. Seigel, "Russians Ask Variances for Riverdale Housing," *New York Times* (July 12, 1972): 12; "Metropolitan Briefs: Soviet Mission Granted Variance," *New York Times* (July 19, 1972): 41; Robert E. Tomasson, "A Residence for Russians to Go 'Down' in Riverdale," *New York Times* (January 13, 1974), VIII: 1, 4; "Russian Mission Being Built from Top Down," *Journal of the American Institute of Architects* 62 (September 1974): 14; Anne M. Montero, "Faraday Wood—The Reds or the Blacks?" *New York Affairs* 2, no. 3 (1975): 42–51; "Dall'alto al basso," *Domus* 557 (April 1976): 13–15; White and Willensky, *AIA Guide* (1978), 347.
53. Landmarks Preservation Commission of the City of New York, LP-1075 (July 8, 1980); Landmarks Preservation Commission of the City of New York, LP-1286 (February 8, 1983); Barbaralee Diamonstein, *The Landmarks of New York* (New York: Harry N. Abrams, 1988), 401.
54. "Bronx Is Planning Post-War Housing," *New York Times* (September 13, 1942): 10.
55. "Dewey Drops In," *Architectural Forum* 83 (November 1945): 16, 20. Also see "Dewey Views Site for Bronx Housing," *New York Times* (October 11, 1945): 25; New York City Housing Authority, *Project Data* (New York, 1972), 26.
56. New York City Housing Authority, *Project Statistics* (New York, 1960), 6.
57. New York City Housing Authority, *Project Statistics*, 8.
58. Voorhees, Walker, Smith, Smith & Haines, *75th Anniversary* (New York, May 1960), 53; New York City Housing Authority, *Project Statistics*, 13.
59. New York City Housing Authority, *Project Statistics*, 7.
60. New York City Housing Authority, *Project Statistics*, 14.
61. New York City Housing Authority, *Project Statistics*, 14.
62. New York City Housing Authority, *Project Data*, 25.
63. "News Bulletins," *Progressive Architecture* 39 (June 1958): 41; "Skip-Floor Access Saves Cubage," *Architectural Record* 124 (July 1958): 187; New York City Housing Authority, *Project Statistics*, 19.
64. New York City Housing Authority, *Project Statistics*, 18.
65. New York City Housing Authority, *Project Statistics*, 18.
66. New York City Housing Authority, *Project Statistics*, 18.
67. New York City Housing Authority, *Project Statistics*, 18.
68. New York City Housing Authority, *Project Statistics*, 14.
69. White and Willensky, *AIA Guide* (1988), 493.
70. Samuel Kaplan, "The City Politic: The Bronx Arrangement," *New York* 3 (December 14, 1970): 10, 12.
71. New York City Planning Commission, *Plan for New York City, 1969: A Proposal*, II: 36, quoted in Michael Stern, "City Seeks to End Decline of Bronx," *New York Times* (October 3, 1970): 1, 49.
72. New York City Planning Commission, *Plan for New York City, 1969: A Proposal*, II: 18.
73. Quoted in Kaplan, "The City Politic: The Bronx Arrangement": 10.
74. Sydney Gruson, "Our Changing City: New Faces in the Lower Bronx," *New York Times* (July 11, 1955): 25.
75. Herschel Post, "The City Politic: Moving in on the Parks," *New York* 4 (March 15, 1971): 6–9.
76. James Brady, "New York Intelligencer: A Man of Many Parks," *New York* 6 (April 23, 1973): 60.
77. Morris Renek, "Community Hospital in the Ghetto," *New Republic* 155 (December 10, 1966): 9.
78. "Replacement for Lincoln Hospital," *Progressive Architecture* 52 (May 1971): 30; David Bird, "An Emergency Birth Marks First Day for New Lincoln Hospital in Bronx," *New York Times* (March 29, 1976): 33; White and Willensky, *AIA Guide* (1988), 487–88.
79. Bird, "An Emergency Birth Marks First Day for New Lincoln Hospital in Bronx": 33.
80. Stewart Alsop, "The City Disease," *Newsweek* 79 (February 28, 1972): 96. Also see Stewart Alsop, "The Road to Hell," *Newsweek* 79 (March 6, 1972): 84.
81. Martin Tolchin, "South Bronx: A Jungle Stalked by Fear, Seized by Rage," *New York Times* (January 15, 1973): 1, 19. Also see Martin Tolchin, "Gangs Spread Terror in the South Bronx," *New York Times* (January 16, 1973): 1–2, 8; Martin Tolchin, "Rage Permeates All Facets of Life in the South Bronx," *New York Times* (January 17, 1973): 1, 13; Martin Tolchin, "Future Looks Bleak for the South Bronx," *New York Times* (January 18, 1973): 1, 50; "The Bronx Is Burning," *Newsweek* 85 (June 16, 1975): 30.
82. Tolchin, "Rage Permeates All Facets of Life in the South Bronx": 1.
83. William Marlin, "Homing in on Housing," *Architectural Forum* 137 (November 1972): 42–55; Sharon Lee Ryder, "Picking Up the Pieces," *Progressive Architecture* 57 (March 1976): 52–53.
84. *Annual Report to the New York State Urban Development Corporation* (New York, 1972).
85. For a discussion of Father Louis Gigante and his brother, Vincent ("the Chin") Gigante, a reputed member of organized crime, see William Bastone, "The Priest and the Mob," *Village Voice* 34 (March 7, 1989): 1, 25–26.
86. Jonathan Barnett, *Urban Design as Public Policy* (New York: Architectural Record Books, 1974), 91, 95.
87. Barnett, *Urban Design as Public Policy*, 97.
88. Clayton Knowles, "Governor Speaks on Bronx Housing," *New York Times* (October 1, 1970): 35.
89. Wolf, *Another Chance for Cities*, 36–37; "Twin Parks Northwest," *Architectural Record* 152 (September 1972): 154–57; Paul Goldberger, "Twin Parks, an Effort to Alter the Pattern of Public Housing," *New York Times* (December 27, 1973): 39, 43; Barnett, *Urban Design as Public Policy*, 100–101; White and Willensky, *AIA Guide* (1978), 329.
90. White and Willensky, *AIA Guide* (1978), 329.
91. White and Willensky, *AIA Guide* (1978), 327–28. Also see Wolf, *Another Chance for Cities*, 38–39; Richard Severo, "Bronx Buildings Novel in Design," *New York Times* (August 8, 1971), VIII: 1, 10; "'Vest Pocket' Housing Brings a New Scale to the Bronx," *Architectural Record* 153 (June 1973): 121–28; "Split-Level Apartments," *New York Times* (July 22, 1973), VIII: 6; Goldberger, "Twin Parks, an Effort to Alter the Pattern of Public Housing": 39, 43; Alessandra Latour, ed., *Pasanella + Klein: Public and Private Interventions in the Residential Field*, with a preface by Vincent Scully (Rome: Kappa, 1983), 7–8, 29–33, 35–60; Richard Plunz, *A History of Housing in New York City* (New York: Columbia University Press, 1990), 297.
92. Severo, "Bronx Buildings Novel in Design": 1.
93. Giovanni Pasanella quoted in Severo, "Bronx Buildings Novel in Design": 1.
94. Scully, "Preface," in Latour, ed., *Pasanella + Klein: Public and Private Interventions in the Residential Field*, 7.
95. White and Willensky, *AIA Guide* (1978), 327.
96. Scully, "Preface," in Latour, ed., *Pasanella + Klein: Public and Private Interventions in the Residential Field*, 7.
97. Scully, "Preface," in Latour, ed., *Pasanella + Klein: Public and Private Interventions in the Residential Field*, 7.
98. Quoted in "'Vest Pocket' Housing Brings a New Scale to the Bronx": 121.
99. Giovanni Pasanella quoted in "'Vest Pocket' Housing Brings a New Scale to the Bronx": 127.
100. Scully, "Preface," in Latour, ed., *Pasanella + Klein: Public and Private Interventions in the Residential Field*, 7.
101. Goldberger, "Twin Parks, an Effort to Alter the Pattern of Public Housing": 39.
102. Goldberger, "Twin Parks, an Effort to Alter the Pattern of Public Housing": 39, 43; White and Willensky, *AIA Guide* (1978), 328; Latour, ed., *Pasanella + Klein: Public and Private Interventions in the Residential Field*, 28, 30–34, 61–72; Plunz, *A History of Housing in New York City*, 297–98.
103. Mildred F. Schmertz, "Design Alternatives for Low- to Moderate-Income Urban Housing," *Architectural Record* 160 (August 1976): cover, 100–116; White and Willensky, *AIA Guide* (1978), 326; Latour, ed., *Pasanella + Klein: Public and Private Interventions in the Residential Field*, 74–98; Plunz, *A History of Housing in New York City*, 297–98.
104. Wolf, *Another Chance for Cities*, 40–41; "Twin Parks East," *Journal of the American Institute of Architects* 54 (November 1970): cover, 5; Goldberger, "Twin Parks, an Effort to Alter the Pattern of Public Housing": 39, 43; Schmertz, "Design Alternatives for Low- to Moderate-Income Urban Housing": 101, 110–13; *James Stewart Polshek: Context and Responsibility* (New York: Rizzoli International Publications, 1988), 12, 166–69.
105. Helen Searing, "James Stewart Polshek as Form-Giver," in *James Stewart Polshek: Context and Responsibility*, 12.
106. Wolf, *Another Chance for Cities*, 40–41; "Realpolitik and Architecture," *Progressive Architecture* 51 (November 1970): 34; Ursula Cliff, "U.D.C. Scorecard," *Design and Environment* 3 (September 1972): 54–63; Kenneth Frampton, "Twin Parks as Typology," *Architectural Forum* 138 (June 1973): 56–61; Suzanne Stephens, "Learning from Twin Parks," *Architectural Forum* 138 (June 1973): 62–64; Myles Weintraub and Mario Zicarelli, "Tale of Twin Parks," *Architectural Forum* 138 (June 1973): 54–56; "Twin Parks Northeast," *A + U* (June 1973): 55–68; Charles Hoyt, "Richard Meier: Public Space and Private Space," *Architectural Record* 154 (July 1973): 89–98; Goldberger, "Twin Parks, an Effort to Alter the Problem of Public Housing": 39, 43; Stuart Cohen, "Physical Context/Cultural Context: Including It All," *Oppositions* 2 (1974): 14–21, 30–37; David Mackay and Roger Sherwood, "La Obra de Richard Meier en Bronx," *Arquitecturas Bis* 1 (May 1974): 1–7; "Twin Parks Northeast, Housing, Bronx, N.Y., Architects: Richard Meier and Associates," *Journal of the American Institute of Architects* 61 (May 1974): 48; Paul Goldberger, "Two Cheers for Eight Winners," *New York Times* (June 2, 1974), VI: 62–64; "Uno dei 'Five': dall'unicum al tessuto," *L'Architettura cronache e storia* 20 (July 1974): 190–91; Paul Goldberger, "U.D.C.'s Architecture Has Raised Public Standard," *New York Times* (March 5, 1975): 43; *Richard Meier Architect: Buildings and Projects 1966–1976* (New York: Oxford University Press, 1976), 11–12, 128–37; Herbert McLaughlin, "Density: The Architect's Urban Choices and Attitudes," *Architectural Record* 159 (February 1976): 95–100; "U.D.C. Twin Parks Northeast," *L'Architecture d'Aujourd'hui* 186 (August–September 1976): 4–7; Jeanne Davern, *Architecture 1970–1980: A Decade of Change* (New York: McGraw-Hill, 1980), 92–93; *Richard Meier Architect: 1964/1984* (New York: Rizzoli International Publications, 1984), 15–16, 116–23; Plunz, *A History of Housing in New York City*, 296–97.
107. Richard Meier quoted in *Richard Meier Architect: 1964/1984*, 121.
108. Frampton, "Twin Parks as Typology": 58.
109. Frampton, "Twin Parks as Typology": 58.
110. Goldberger, "Twin Parks, an Effort to Alter the Pattern of Public Housing": 43.
111. Stephens, "Learning from Twin Parks": 62, 64.
112. Charles Hoyt, "Lambert Houses: Urban Renewal with a Conscience," *Architectural Record* 153 (January 1974): 133–40; White and Willensky, *AIA Guide* (1978), 323; Plunz, *A History of Housing in New York City*, 304.
113. For a discussion of Andrew J. Thomas's work, see Stern, Gilmartin and Mellins, *New York 1930*, 419–21, 482–86.
114. Stern, Gilmartin and Massengale, *New York 1900*, 141–43. For a general discussion of the zoo's history, see William Bridges, *Gathering of Animals: An Unconventional History of the New York Zoological Society* (New York: Harper & Row, 1974).
115. Stern, Gilmartin and Mellins, *New York 1930*, 712–13.
116. Stern, Gilmartin and Mellins, *New York 1930*, 713; Victoria Newhouse, *Wallace K. Harrison, Architect* (New York: Rizzoli International Publications, 1989), 70, 73.
117. Ada Louise Huxtable, "New Bronx Zoo Building a Rara Avis," *New York Times* (June 14, 1972): 40.
118. "Zoo Modernized at $2,006,873 Cost," *New York Times* (January 27, 1954): 51; "Bronx Zoo Puts Up Top Snake House," *New York Times* (January 29, 1954): 21; James A. Oliver, "The Most Beautiful Reptile House in the World," *Animal Kingdom* 57 (August 1954): 98–109; "Reptiles at Bronx Zoo Move into New Quarters," *Architectural Record* 116 (September 1954): 330.
119. Oliver, "The Most Beautiful Reptile House in the World": 99.
120. "Dark World for Nocturnal Creatures," *Progressive Architecture* 44 (September 1963): 68; William G. Conway, "A World of Darkness in the Zoo," *Animal Kingdom* 72 (June 1969): 4–11; John S. Margolies, "Multimedia Zoo: 1," *Architectural Forum* 130 (June 1969): 86–89; "Hello New Day," *Architectural Forum* 130 (June 1969): 95; "Awards," *Interiors* 128 (July 1969): 10, 12; "Bard Jury Sees 'New Day' in Making Four Awards," *Journal of the American Institute of Architects* 52 (July 1969): 12; Erik Sanberg-Diment, "The Urban Strategist: The Zoo Story," *New York* 3 (September 9, 1970): 56–59; White and Willensky, *AIA Guide* (1978), 323; Morris Ketchum, Jr., *Blazing a Trail* (New York: Vantage Press, 1982), 36–40.

121. William G. Conway quoted in Margolies, "Multimedia Zoo: 1": 86.
122. Margolies, "Multimedia Zoo: 1": 87.
123. Ketchum, *Blazing a Trail*, 39.
124. Quoted in "Awards": 12.
125. Ketchum, *Blazing a Trail*, 42–43. Also see "Watch the Birdies," *Progressive Architecture* 48 (December 1967): 35; John S. Margolies, "Multimedia Zoo: 2," *Architectural Forum* 130 (June 1969): 90–91; Carter B. Horsley, "Bronx Zoo Birds Get a Palace," *New York Times* (June 11, 1972), VIII: 1, 8; Huxtable, "New Bronx Zoo Building a Rara Avis": 40; Jane E. Brody, "Bronx Zoo Opens World of Birds," *New York Times* (June 17, 1972): 32; "World of Birds," *Architectural Record* 152 (July 1972): 39; "For the Birds," *Progressive Architecture* 53 (July 1972): 23; "Focus on Light—Lumen Awards for 1972," *Interiors* 132 (June 1973): 16, 20; White and Willensky, *AIA Guide* (1978), 323.
126. Ketchum, *Blazing a Trail*, 43.
127. "Watch the Birdies": 35.
128. Horsley, "Bronx Zoo Birds Get a Palace": 1.
129. Ketchum, *Blazing a Trail*, 43.
130. Huxtable, "New Bronx Zoo Building a Rara Avis": 40.
131. Stern, Gilmartin and Massengale, *New York 1900*, 141.
132. "To Convert Snuff Mill," *New York Times* (August 22, 1952): 8; "Restaurant Opened in Old Snuff Mill," *New York Times* (April 11, 1954): 82; Landmarks Preservation Commission of the City of New York, LP-0121 (April 19, 1966): 246.
133. "New Research Laboratory Planned for New York Botanical Garden," *Architectural Record* 112 (August 1952): 26. Also see "A Model for New Scientific Research Laboratory," *New York Times* (May 20, 1952): 27; "Botanical Garden Opens a Unit to Aid Mankind by Plant Study," *New York Times* (October 25, 1956): 35; White and Willensky, *AIA Guide* (1978), 321.
134. "Re-cycling a Great Conservatory and Its Botanical Garden," *Architectural Record* 158 (August 1975): 76–82.
135. Alison Sky and Michelle Stone, *Unbuilt America* (New York: McGraw-Hill, 1976), 30–31; Susana Torre, ed., *Women in Architecture: A Historic and Contemporary Perspective* (New York: Whitney Library of Design, 1977), 172.
136. Stern, Gilmartin and Mellins, *New York 1930*, 496–97, 499–500. Also see Walter McQuade, "How Harry Helmsley Speared Parkchester," *Architectural Forum* 130 (January–February 1969): 10; Linda Greenhouse, "Parkchester: Trouble in Paradise," *New York* 2 (February 17, 1969): 36–43; Roger Starr, *Housing and the Money Market* (New York: Basic Books, 1975), 128–30; Richard Plunz, "Reading Bronx Housing, 1890–1940," in Rub, ed., *Building a Borough: Architecture and Planning in the Bronx, 1890–1940*, 30–37; Plunz, *A History of Housing in New York City*, 253–54, 258, 282–84.
137. Kathryn Close, "New Homes with Insurance Dollars," *Survey Graphic* 37 (November 1948): 450–54, 487–88.
138. New York City Housing Authority, *Project Statistics*, 9; "Center for Aging and Children Serves Public Housing," *Architectural Record* 132 (December 1962): 120–24.
139. "Center for Aging and Children Serves Public Housing": 120.
140. "For the Burgher," *Interiors* 109 (December 1949): 10, 12; "Long Range Hospital Center," *Architectural Forum* 98 (June 1953): 162–67; White and Willensky, *AIA Guide* (1978), 352.
141. See Karl Fleig, *Alvar Aalto* (Zurich: Verlag für Architektur, 1963), 30–43.
142. For Yeshiva's upper Manhattan campus, see Stern, Gilmartin and Mellins, *New York 1930*, 112. For a history of the medical school, see *Ten Brave Years: 1955–1965* (New York: Albert Einstein College of Medicine of Yeshiva University, 1966).
143. "Good Medicine," *Interiors* 113 (November 1953): 12, 14; Harry M. Zimmerman, Abraham White and Joseph Blumenkrantz, "New Curriculum: New Structure," *Progressive Architecture* 34 (November 1953): 114–17; "We Still Need Hospitals," *Progressive Architecture* 34 (November 1953): 77–78; "Health: Award Citation," *Progressive Architecture* 35 (January 1954): 102; White and Willensky, *AIA Guide* (1978), 351.
144. "New Angle in Hospital Planning," *Architectural Forum* 114 (February 1961): 124–25.
145. "Yeshiva Research Tower," *Architectural Forum* 117 (December 1972): 53; White and Willensky, *AIA Guide* (1978), 351.
146. "70 Million State Mental Hospital," *Architectural Forum* 106 (June 1957): 37.
147. "A Great House for Children Copes with the Urban Scene," *Architectural Record* 147 (January 1970): 162–63; White and Willensky, *AIA Guide* (1978), 351.
148. "Health Care: The Bronx," *Progressive Architecture* 50 (February 1969): 139–40; "Six Public Projects in New York Win Awards for Urban Design Excellence," *Architectural Record* 154 (August 1973): 40; White and Willensky, *AIA Guide* (1978), 350–51.
149. Joseph Rykwert, "The Very Personal Work of Richard Meier & Associates," *Architectural Forum* 136 (March 1972): 30–37; "Buildings in the News," *Architectural Record* 152 (December 1972): 43; "New Center for Disabled Is Focus of Philosophical Controversy," *Industrial Design* 24 (July–August 1974): 14; *Richard Meier Architect: Buildings and Projects 1966–1976*, 12–17, 110–11, 204–33, 238; Rosemarie H. Bletter, "Recent Work by Richard Meier," *A + U* (April 1976): 96–103; "The Bronx Developmental Center," *A + U* (April 1976): 112–15, 120; David Gebhard and Deborah Nevins, *200 Years of American Architectural Drawing* (New York: Whitney Library of Design, 1977), 272–73; "Bronx Developmental Center, New York City. Richard Meier & Associates," *Journal of the American Institute of Architects* 66 (May 1977): 36; Paul Goldberger, "Masterwork or Nightmare?" *New York Times* (May 3, 1977): 43, 46; Molly Ivins, "New Center for Retarded Opposed as 'Obsolete,'" *New York Times* (May 3, 1977): 43, 46; Ada Louise Huxtable, "'A Landmark Before Its Doors Open,'" *New York Times* (May 8, 1977), II: 25; Mark Stevens, "Living in a Work of Art," *Newsweek* 77 (May 30, 1977): 59; John Morris Dixon, "Awards at a Watershed," editorial, *Progressive Architecture* 58 (June 1977): 8; "Meier Building Wins 1977 Reynolds Award," *Progressive Architecture* 58 (June 1977): 22; Suzanne Stephens, "Architecture Cross-Examined," *Progressive Architecture* 58 (July 1977): 43–54; "Judge Rules on Bronx State Facility," *Progressive Architecture* 58 (July 1977): 30, 34; Francesco Dal Co, "The Modern Language of Architecture and Richard Meier," *A + U* (November 1977): 18–29; Paul Goldberger, "Bronx Developmental Center by R. Meier," *A + U* (November 1977): 11–16; Arata Isozaki, "A Comparative Study—Bronx Developmental Center and Gumma Prefectural Museum of Modern Art," *A + U* (November 1977): 17; "Bronx Developmental Center by Richard Meier and Associates, Architects," *A + U* (November 1977): 3–10; White and Willensky, *AIA Guide* (1978), 351; "Bronx Developmental Centre," *Architectural Review* 163 (January 1978): 95–98; Barbaralee Diamonstein, *American Architecture Now* (New York: Rizzoli International Publications, 1980), 103–22; Michael Winkelman, "Institutional Retreat," *New York Affairs* 6, no. 3 (1980): 80–83; Martin Filler, "Modernism Lives: Richard Meier," *Art in America* 68 (May 1980): 123–31; Barbaralee Diamonstein, "Richard Meier: Frankly Speaking," *Interiors* 140 (October 1980): 84–86, 90; "Bronx Developmental Center," *L'Architecture d'Aujourd'hui* 213 (February 1981): 22–24; *Richard Meier Architect: 1964/1984*, 18–19, 130–51, 388–89.
150. Richard Meier quoted in *Richard Meier Architect: Buildings and Projects 1966–1976*, 218.
151. Huxtable, "'A Landmark Before Its Doors Open'": 25.
152. Huxtable, "'A Landmark Before Its Doors Open'": 25.
153. John Hejduk, "Postscript," in *Richard Meier Architect: Buildings and Projects 1966–1976*, 238.
154. Stevens, "Living in a Work of Art": 59.
155. Richard Meier quoted in Stevens, "Living in a Work of Art": 59.
156. Stevens, "Living in a Work of Art": 59.
157. Anthony Pitto quoted in Goldberger, "Masterwork or Nightmare?": 43.
158. Stephens, "Architecture Cross-Examined": 53–54.
159. Vincent Canby, "'Out of Space' Capers," *New York Times* (February 29, 1980), C: 5.
160. "Huge Play Project Planned in Bronx," *New York Times* (May 1, 1959): 57; Farnsworth Fowle, "Big Exhibit Park Planned in Bronx," *New York Times* (May 26, 1959): 71; Gay Talese, "Bulldozer Frolic Ballyhoos Park," *New York Times* (August 27, 1959): 24; "Sidelights: Not Just for Fun," *New York Times* (May 11, 1960): 54; Morris Gilbert, "Freedomland in the Bronx," *New York Times* (June 12, 1960): II: 1, 3; Thomas Buckley, "25,000 See Freedomland Dedicated in the Bronx," *New York Times* (June 19, 1960): 1, 41; "Freedomland Park Slates Refinancing," *New York Times* (May 24, 1961): 64; Dan Wakefield, "The Final Festivalization of New York City," *Reporter* 27 (September 27, 1962): 40, 42; "Freedomland Asks Court Help in Solving Its Financial Troubles," *New York Times* (September 16, 1964): 33; Thomas W. Ennis, "15,500 Apartment Co-op to Rise in Bronx," *New York Times* (February 10, 1965): 1, 32; William Zeckendorf with Edward McCreary, *The Autobiography of William Zeckendorf* (New York: Holt, Rinehart and Winston, 1970), 151, 291–92, 296.
161. Gilbert, "Freedomland in the Bronx": 1.
162. "Sidelights: Not Just for Fun": 54.
163. Gilbert, "Freedomland in the Bronx": 3.
164. Zeckendorf with McCreary, *The Autobiography of William Zeckendorf*, 292.
165. Thomas W. Ennis, "15,500-Apartment Co-op to Rise in Bronx," *New York Times* (February 10, 1965): 1, 32; "55,000 Neighbors," *Newsweek* 65 (February 22, 1965): 92; "Planners Accept Bronx Co-op City," *New York Times* (May 13, 1965): 38; "A 'City' Is Not a Home," *Progressive Architecture* 46 (June 1965): 52–53; William E. Farrell, "Groups Lose Plea on Commerce High," *New York Times* (June 12, 1965): 15; "Architect Makes Recommendations for Co-op City," *Real Estate Record and Guide* 195 (June 12, 1965): 2; "Bronx Brigadoon," *Progressive Architecture* 46 (September 1965): 154–59; William R. Ginsberg, letter to the editor, *Housing and Planning News* 23 (November–December 1965): 2–3; White and Willensky, *AIA Guide* (1967), 242; Joseph P. Fried, "Debate Still Swirls Around Co-op City," *New York Times* (March 17, 1968): 1, 6; Walter McQuade, "God, Motherhood, and Mass Housing," *Architectural Forum* 129 (November 1968): 96; William E. Farrell, "Vast Co-op City Is Dedicated in Bronx," *New York Times* (November 25, 1968): 1, 43; Ada Louise Huxtable, "A Singularly New York Product," *New York Times* (November 25, 1968): 43; Steven V. Roberts, "Impact on Old Neighborhoods Worries the City," *New York Times* (November 25, 1968): 43; "Housing: Pride of the Bronx," *Newsweek* 72 (December 2, 1968): 78; "In Dubious Rebuttal," *Architectural Forum* 130 (January–February 1969): 107; "The Lessons of Co-op City," *Time* 93 (January 24, 1969): 30; Guy G. Rotheste, "It Can Be Done," letter to the editor, *Architectural Forum* 130 (March 1969): 10; Robert Moses, *Public Works: A Dangerous Trade* (New York: McGraw-Hill, 1970), 470–72; Denise Scott Brown and Robert Venturi, "Co-op City: Learning to Like It," *Progressive Architecture* 51 (February 1970): 64–73; Stephen A. Kurtz, "Toward an Urban Vernacular," *Progressive Architecture* 51 (July 1970): 100–105; "Kibbutz in the Bronx," *Newsweek* 76 (October 5, 1970): 90, 93–94; Robert Goodman, *After the Planners* (New York: Simon & Schuster, 1971), 61; Ada Louise Huxtable, "Co-op City's Grounds: After 3 Years, a Success," *New York Times* (October 26, 1971): 43; "Co-op City," *Architecture Plus* 1 (June 1973): 12; Robert A. Caro, *The Power Broker: Robert Moses and the Fall of New York* (New York: Alfred A. Knopf, 1974), 1145; Allan M. Siegal, "In Parkchester, Old Tenants Fear Condominium Plan . . . ," *New York Times* (June 6, 1974): 39; Peter Blake, *Form Follows Fiasco: Why Modern Architecture Hasn't Worked* (Boston: Little, Brown, 1977), 71; Samuel E. Bleecker, *The Politics of Architecture* (New York: Rutledge, 1981), 64–73; Michael Winkelman, "The Bronx: Co-op City," *Metropolis* 4 (April 1985): 26, 28, 36; Plunz, *A History of Housing in New York City*, 258, 286–87.
166. Herman Jessor quoted in McQuade, "God, Motherhood, and Mass Housing": 96.
167. McQuade, "God, Motherhood, and Mass Housing": 96.
168. Maurice W. Kley quoted in "Architect Makes Recommendations for Co-op City": 2.
169. Quoted in Ginsberg, letter to the editor, *Housing and Planning News*: 2–3.
170. Herman Jessor quoted in "A 'City' Is Not a Home": 52.
171. Fried, "Debate Still Swirls Around Co-op City": 1.
172. Roger Starr quoted in Roberts, "Impact on Old Neighborhoods Worries the City": 43.
173. Quoted in "Kibbutz in the Bronx": 90.
174. Huxtable, "A Singularly New York Product": 43.
175. "The Lessons of Co-op City": 30.
176. See Robert Venturi, *Complexity and Contradiction in Architecture* (New York: Museum of Modern Art, 1966); Robert Venturi, Denise Scott Brown and Steven Izenour, *Learning from Las Vegas* (Cambridge, Mass.: MIT Press, 1972).
177. Scott Brown and Venturi, "Co-op City: Learning to Like It": 70–72.
178. Huxtable, "Co-op City's Grounds: After 3 Years, a Success": 43.
179. For Radburn, see Stern, Gilmartin and Mellins, *New York 1930*, 42–43, 45, 48.
180. Huxtable, "Co-op City's Grounds: After 3 Years, a Success": 43.
181. "Tenant Relocation Part of Road Plan," *New York Times* (February 1, 1946): 35; "2 New Expressways to Oust Few Families from Their Homes This Year, Moses Reports," *New York Times* (May 1, 1946): 29; "Housing Data Disputed," *New York Times* (May 14, 1946): 19; "Planners of America's Largest Port," *Architectural Record* 106 (July 1949): 84–95; Charles G. Bennett, "Bronx Expressway Route Approved to 'Demagogue,' 'Blackmail' Cries," *New York Times* (April 15, 1953): 1, 14; "State to Spend 26 Millions on Highways in City in Year," *New York Times* (March 25, 1954): 1, 10; Warren Weaver, Jr., "Governor Signs Ballot Reforms; Independents in City Are Helped," *New York Times* (April 20, 1954): 1, 23; Joseph C. Ingraham, "Cross Bronx Road Is Merely 2 Ends," *New*

York Times (November 15, 1954): 29; Joseph C. Ingraham, "3 Highway Links Open Tomorrow," *New York Times* (November 4, 1955): 32; Joseph C. Ingraham, "Moses Hails City on Improvements," *New York Times* (April 23 1956): 1, 16; "Eight-Tenths Mile of City Expressway for $9.5 Million," *Engineering News-Record* 158 (May 16, 1957): 48–50; "$105,000 Won in Suit Against the State," *New York Times* (March 23, 1958): 74; Joseph C. Ingraham, "Cross-Bronx Road Gets Revised Plan," *New York Times* (November 27, 1958): 31; "Cross-Bronx Route to Add Section," *New York Times* (April 25, 1960): 32; *Remarks of Robert Moses at the Opening of Alexander Hamilton Bridge, George Washington Bridge Bus Station, and Sections of the Cross-Bronx Expressway* (New York: Triborough Bridge and Tunnel Authority, in cooperation with the Port of New York Authority, Federal and State Highway Agencies and the City of New York, 1963); Moses, *Public Works: A Dangerous Trade,* 210–11; Caro, *The Power Broker,* 850–94; Marshall Berman, "Buildings Are Judgement," *Ramparts* 13 (March 1975): 33–39, 50–57; Marshall Berman, *All That Is Solid Melts Into Air* (New York: Simon & Schuster, 1982), 295–96, 324–29.
182. Caro, *The Power Broker,* 850.
183. Quoted in Bennett, "Bronx Expressway Route Approved to 'Demagogue,' 'Blackmail' Cries": 14.
184. Caro, *The Power Broker,* 878.
185. *Remarks of Robert Moses at the Opening of Alexander Hamilton Bridge, George Washington Bridge Bus Station, and Sections of the Cross-Bronx Expressway,* 1, 3.
186. Robert Moses quoted in Caro, *The Power Broker,* 876.
187. Caro, *The Power Broker,* 893–94.
188. Berman, "Buildings Are Judgement": 56.
189. Berman, *All That Is Solid Melts Into Air,* 324–26.
190. Berman, *All That Is Solid Melts Into Air,* 295–96.

STATEN ISLAND

1. Quentin Reynolds, *I, Willie Sutton* (New York: Farrar, Straus & Young, 1953), 194. In 1947 the famed bank robber hid from the police on Staten Island.
2. See Walter B. Hayward, "Father Knickerbocker's Other Island," *New York Times* (February 2, 1947), VII: 22–23, 59; "Topics of The Times," *New York Times* (March 3, 1948): 22.
3. White and Willensky, *AIA Guide* (1988), 896–97.
4. "To House Ship Workers," *New York Times* (December 10, 1941): 46; "Housing Project Passed," *New York Times* (January 29, 1942): 23; "City Agencies Row Over New Housing," *New York Times* (January 30, 1942): 21; "Wingate Is Retired on $12,409 Pension," *New York Times* (February 6, 1942): 8; "Low Rent Housing on Staten Island Planned by the City," *New York Times* (March 4, 1942): 34; "Clearing City Housing Site," *New York Times* (March 6, 1942): 34; "To Start Housing on Staten Island," *New York Times* (April 2, 1942): 40; "Housing Contract Let," *New York Times* (April 18, 1942): 28; "Completing Markham Houses," *New York Times* (October 22, 1942): 38; "War Housing Nears Completion," *New York Times* (December 18, 1942): 51; Maxwell H. Tretter, "New York's Public Housing Not All Tenements," *American City* 58 (August 1943): 61, 63; "4 Housing Units Merged," *New York Times* (November 3, 1952): 29.
5. "$4,995,000 Plans Filed," *New York Times* (June 30, 1948): 27; "Public Housing to Start," *New York Times* (August 3, 1948): 35; "Housing Project Begun," *New York Times* (August 19, 1948): 23; "Bids Scheduled on New Housing," *New York Times* (September 19, 1948): 20; "Rents Are Raised in Woodside Units," *New York Times* (March 25, 1949): 44; "Housing Forms Ready," *New York Times* (May 15, 1949): 38; "Calls for Housing by Private Capital," *New York Times* (May 17, 1949): 28; "Richmond Housing Visited by Mayor," *New York Times* (September 20, 1949): 25; "4 Housing Units Merged": 29.
6. "5 Housing Projects Approved by Board," *New York Times* (May 28, 1948): 25; "Bids Scheduled on New Housing": 20; "$48,256,000 Lent for City Housing," *New York Times* (October 19, 1948): 39; "New Housing Unit Started by Mayor," *New York Times* (October 26, 1948): 33; "Housing Forms Available," *New York Times* (July 24, 1949): 35; "Richmond Housing Visited by Mayor": 25; "4 Housing Units Merged": 29.
7. "Richmond Housing Visited by Mayor": 25; "4 Housing Units Merged": 29.
8. "New Housing Approved," *New York Times* (June 13, 1951): 33; "Richmond Home Unit to Start Tomorrow," *New York Times* (April 14, 1952): 21; "Housing Agencies Obtain Financing," *New York Times* (May 6, 1953): 52; "Income Rule Eased in Low-Rent Homes," *New York Times* (June 30, 1953): 25; "Housing Authority Sells Note Issues," *New York Times* (November 11, 1953): 46; "11,000 Apartments Scheduled by City," *New York Times* (December 20, 1953): 41; "Housing Project Opens," *New York Times* (January 26, 1954): 17.
9. Robert Conley, "New City Housing to Cost 83 Million," *New York Times* (April 26, 1961): 1, 31; Robert Conley, "New City Housing Reshapes Lives," *New York Times* (April 30, 1961): 81.
10. "New York City Public Housing, with Balconies," *Architectural Forum* 108 (May 1958): 37; "Housing Started on Staten Island," *New York Times* (September 29, 1959): 41; "S.I. Housing Is Opened," *New York Times* (January 24, 1962): 10; "Stapleton: A Look Back," in *Discover Stapleton: A Community Documentation and Marker Program* (Staten Island, N.Y.: High Rock Park Conservation Center, 1976). Also see Jack Reycraft, "New Skyline," *Staten Island Advance* (February 8, 1962) and Julia Martin, "Changing Stapleton: The Decline and Rise," *Staten Island Advance* (January 23, 1972), Clippings Collection, Staten Island Historical Society.
11. Steven J. Roberts, "Estimate Board Approves 5 Low-Rent Housing Projects Over Middle-Class Neighborhood Protests," *New York Times* (January 17, 1968): 17; John Herbers, "City Program Defended," *New York Times* (November 4, 1971): 22; Jonathan Kandell, "Opposition to Scatter-Site Housing Transcends Racial and Economic Lines," *New York Times* (February 6, 1972): 60.
12. Olga Gueft, "Living Up to a Gilt-Edged Site," *Interiors* 121 (October 1961): 108–13.
13. Cynthia Kellogg, "First Frank Lloyd Wright House in City to Go On View on Staten Island," *New York Times* (July 3, 1959): 20; "Prefabricated House Bears Unmistakable Stamp of Frank Lloyd Wright," *New York Times* (July 5, 1959), VIII: 1–2; "Architectural Bulletins," *Progressive Architecture* 40 (August 1959): 79; White and Willensky, *AIA Guide* (1967), 386–87; William Allin Storrer, *The Architecture of Frank Lloyd Wright* (Cambridge, Mass.: MIT Press, 1974), plate 410; Herbert Muschamp, *Man About Town: Frank Lloyd Wright in New York City* (Cambridge, Mass.: MIT Press, 1983), 88–89, 92–93, 131; Eve M. Kalin, "One Wright Dream on Staten Island," *New York Times* (March 24, 1988): 26; Andrew S. Dolkart, *Guide to New York City Landmarks* (Washington, D.C.: Preservation Press, 1992), 222.
14. White and Willensky, *AIA Guide* (1967), 386.
15. Alexander Feinberg, "Staten Island Fire Wrecks Ferry Terminal, Kills 3; Damage Put at $2,000,000," *New York Times* (June 26, 1946): 1–2; "City Hopes to Operate the Ferry to St. George Slip within 48 Hours," *New York Times* (June 28, 1946): 23; "Ferry House Demolition Starting," *New York Times* (August 5, 1946): 12. For Carrère & Hastings's terminal, see Stern, Gilmartin and Massengale, *New York 1900,* 49.
16. "Fund to Be Asked for Studies for $7,500,000 Terminal for St. George Ferry," *New York Times* (June 5, 1944): 21; "$75,000 Set Aside for Ferry Project," *New York Times* (July 21, 1944): 21; "Tunnel Plan Out for Staten Island," *New York Times* (November 17, 1945): 19; "Mayor Helps Hail New Ferry Service," *New York Times* (April 16, 1946): 52; "Transportation Coordinated," *Architectural Record* 101 (April 1947): 194–97; "A Staten Island Event," editorial, *New York Times* (May 16, 1947): 22.
17. "Big Ferry Project in Its Final Stages," *New York Times* (March 7, 1950): 29; "4 New Platforms to Aid Bus Riders," *New York Times* (July 23, 1950): 45; "Ferry Travelers Use New Terminal," *New York Times* (September 14, 1950): 34; "New Ferry Depot Will 'Open' Today," *New York Times* (June 8, 1951): 55; "St. George Terminal," editorial, *New York Times* (June 9, 1951): 18.
18. Ernest Flagg, "Floating Bridge Proposed," letter to the editor, *New York Times* (February 3, 1940): 12. Also see A. N. Parmelee, "Bridge Plan Disapproved," letter to the editor, *New York Times* (February 6, 1940): 20; Frank J. Smith, "Suggested Staten Island Connection Is Regarded as Good Investment," letter to the editor, *New York Times* (February 10, 1940): 14. For Flagg's response to Parmalee's letter, see *New York Times* (February 10, 1940): 14.
19. Paul Crowell, "Tunnel Authority Asks Army for Narrows Bridge Permit," *New York Times* (July 19, 1948): 1; E. C. McDowell, "Bridges," *Americana Annual for 1948* (New York and Chicago: Encyclopedia Americana Corp., 1949): 84.
20. "Realty Fraud Seen in Narrows Bridge," *New York Times* (January 13, 1949): 46.
21. "Army Approves Narrows Bridge, World's Longest Suspension Span," *New York Times* (May 25, 1949): 1, 15; E. C. McDowell, "Bridges," *Americana Annual for 1949* (New York and Chicago: Encyclopedia Americana Corp., 1950): 85.
22. Joseph C. Ingraham, "Vast Bridge-Highway Plan Is Set for City and Jersey; Includes a Narrows Span," *New York Times* (January 17, 1955): 1, 19; George Cable Wright, "Super-Road, 2 Extensions in North Jersey Proposed," *New York Times* (January 17, 1955): 1, 18; "New York Plans Bridges on Grand Scale," *Engineering News-Record* 154 (January 20, 1955): 28; "Bridge to Nowhere," *Engineering News-Record* 156 (March 29, 1956): 22–23; Arthur J. Fox, Jr., "Bridges," *Americana Annual for 1956* (New York and Chicago: Encyclopedia Americana Corp., 1957): 100; "Moses Sees Close of Big-Bridge Era," *New York Times* (June 24, 1957): 1, 26; Paul Crowell, "City Hall Favors Bay Ridge Route," *New York Times* (October 24, 1958): 35.
23. Quoted in "Name Protested on Narrows Span," *New York Times* (August 3, 1959): 27.
24. Lewis Mumford, "The Sky Line: The Skyway's the Limit," *New Yorker* 35 (November 14, 1959): 181–82, 185–91.
25. Mumford, "The Sky Line: The Skyway's the Limit": 188.
26. Gardner Soule, "Biggest Bridge to Span Busiest Harbor," *Popular Science* 166 (June 1955): 90–93, 264, 268; John M. Hayes, "Bridges," *New International Yearbook (1959)* (New York: Funk and Wagnalls, 1960): 60; "Tallest Tale for Bridge Builders," *Business Week* (September 29, 1962): 29; Roger Vaughan, "Furor Rises with Brooklyn Bridge," *Saturday Evening Post* 236 (June 29, 1963): 80–81; "The Biggest Span," *Life* 55 (July 12, 1963): 81–86; "Bridges of New York," *Look* 28 (February 11, 1964): 86–88; "Bridge and Doom: New York's Long Reach," *Newsweek* 54 (August 24, 1959): 62–63; Alden P. Armagnac, "The Biggest Bridge in the World," *Popular Science* 185 (September 19, 1964): 46–49; John W. Frazier, "Biggest Bridge Ever," *Reader's Digest* 85 (November 1964): 266–70; Mary Jean Kempner, "The Greatest Bridge of Them All," *Harper's* 229 (November 1964): 69–76.
27. David Steinman quoted in "Narrows Span a Dream," *New York Times* (February 26, 1950), VIII: 5.
28. For the George Washington Bridge, see Stern, Gilmartin and Mellins, *New York 1930,* 678–79, 681–82.
29. "Floor Truss Erection Begins at the Narrows," *Engineering News-Record* 171 (November 14, 1963): 64–66, 68.
30. Othmar Hermann Ammann quoted in Kempner, "The Greatest Bridge of Them All": 69. Also see Gay Talese, "City Bridge Creator, 85, Keeps Watchful Eye on His Landmarks," *New York Times* (March 26, 1964): 37.
31. Joseph C. Ingraham, "New York Bypass," *New York Times* (November 15, 1964), X: 1, 17; William Federici and Henry Lee, "World's Largest Beauty Is Open for Traffic," *New York Daily News* (November 22, 1964): 3, 66; Gay Talese, "Verrazano Bridge Opened to Traffic," *New York Times* (November 22, 1964): 1, 80; "Web Across the Narrows Was 5 Years in Spinning," *New York Times* (November 22, 1964): 80; "New Jewel in the Harbor," editorial, *New York Times* (November 22, 1964), IV: 8; "New Bridge," *Newsweek* 64 (November 23, 1964): 88–91; "The Talk of the Town: Across the Narrows," *New Yorker* 40 (November 28, 1964): 47–48; "A Bridge to Ease New York Traffic," *U.S. News & World Report* 57 (December 7, 1964): 14; William W. Jacobus, Jr., "Bridges," *Americana Annual for 1964* (New York and Chicago: Encyclopedia Americana Corp., 1965): 100; Robert Michael Echols, "Engineering Projects," *Britannica Book of the Year* (Chicago: Encyclopaedia Britannica, 1965): 345; "Narrows Span Opened," *Progressive Architecture* 40 (January 1965): 42–43; "Eavesdroppings," *Progressive Architecture* 40 (April 1965): 74; William W. Jacobus, Jr., "Bridges," *Americana Annual for 1965* (New York and Chicago: Encyclopedia Americana Corp., 1966): 258; Robert Michael Echols, "Engineering Projects," *Britannica Book of the Year* (Chicago: Encyclopaedia Britannica, 1966): 336; William W. Jacobus, Jr., "Bridges," *Americana Annual for 1966* (New York and Chicago: Encyclopedia Americana Corp., 1967): 125; Robert Moses, *Public Works: A Dangerous Trade* (New York: Macmillan, 1970), 224–35; Robert A. Caro, *The Power Broker: Robert Moses and the Fall of New York* (New York: Alfred A. Knopf, 1974), 736, 843–44; Sharon Reier, *The Bridges of New York* (New York: Quadrant Press, 1977), 140–47. Also see "8th Wonder of the World: It Went Up, Then Across," *Staten Island Advance* (November 4, 1964) and "Dignitaries and Crowd Hop Our New Bridge," *Staten Island Advance* (November 21, 1964), Clippings Collection, Staten Island Historical Society. For a colorful description documenting the construction of the bridge and its impact on Staten Island and the Bay Ridge section of Brooklyn, see Gay Talese, *The Bridge* (New York: Harper & Row, 1964).
32. William H. Quirk, "Bridges," *Americana Annual for 1968* (New York and Chicago: Encyclopedia Americana Corp., 1969): 133; William H. Quirk, "Bridges," *Americana Annual for 1969* (New York and Chicago: Encyclopedia Americana Corp., 1970): 136.

33. George Horne, "Our Changing City: Staten Island Awaits Bridge," *New York Times* (August 12, 1955): 21.
34. Robert Moses quoted in "Moses Sees Close of Big-Bridge Era": 26.
35. John P. Callahan, "Big Growth Seen by Staten Island," *New York Times* (April 19, 1959), VIII: 1, 6.
36. "Undergraduate Planning Projects at Pratt Institute," *Progressive Architecture* 41 (December 1960): 134–39; "Cooper Union Studies Staten Island," *Progressive Architecture* 46 (July 1965): 64.
37. Bernard Stengren, "Bridge Brings Boom and Problems," *New York Times* (October 2, 1963): 43, 82. Also see Dawn Powell, "Staten Island, I Love You," *Esquire* 64 (October 1965): 120–25; Archie Robertson, "The Island in the Bay," *American Heritage* 17 (August 1966): 24–26, 78–81.
38. Quoted in Stengren, "Bridge Brings Boom and Problems": 43.
39. Ada Louise Huxtable, "Staten Island's Beauty Losing to Builders," *New York Times* (August 9, 1965): 1, 28.
40. Huxtable, "Staten Island's Beauty Losing to Builders": 1, 28.
41. Richard J. Whalen, *A City Destroying Itself: An Angry View of New York* (New York: William Morrow, 1965), 91–95; William Robbins, "S.I. Groups Ask Orderly Growth," *New York Times* (January 23, 1965): 27, 50; Charles G. Bennett, "Renewal Dispute Annoys Officials," *New York Times* (March 17, 1965): 46; "Staten Island Down the Drain?" editorial, *New York Times* (March 20, 1965): 26; Samuel Kaplan, "Renewal Backed for Staten Island," *New York Times* (April 29, 1965): 37; Eric Pace, "Builders Balked on Staten Island," *New York Times* (August 29, 1965): 48; Bernard J. Albin, "Open Land Redevelopment in Staten Island," *Landscape Architecture* 56 (October 1965): 56–57. Also see Mark Wiesner, "Planner Outlines 'Ideal' Community on South Shore," *Staten Island Advance* (October 2, 1962), "South Shore Renewal Awaits Federal Approval," *Staten Island Advance* (January 5, 1963), S. S. McSheehy, "It's More 'No' than 'Yes' at Urban Renewal Airing," *Staten Island Advance* (February 26, 1963), "Action Expected on S.I. Renewal," *Staten Island Advance* (March 3, 1963), Clippings Collection, Staten Island Historical Society.
42. For Radburn, see Stern, Gilmartin and Mellins, *New York 1930*, 42–43, 45, 48. For Greenbelt, see Clarence S. Stein, *Toward New Towns for America* (Cambridge, Mass.: MIT Press, 1957), 118–77.
43. Albin, "Open Land Redevelopment in Staten Island": 56.
44. "Staten Island Down the Drain?": 26.
45. Steven V. Roberts, "City Revises Renewals to Give Priority to Housing in 3 Slums," *New York Times* (March 26, 1966): 24; "Planning for Staten Island," editorial, *New York Times* (October 27, 1966): 46; "Open Season on Staten Island," editorial, *New York Times* (December 19, 1966): 36.
46. "Lindsay Orders S.I. Plan Started," *New York Times* (February 18, 1967): 31; Steven V. Roberts, "The Development of Staten Island: Will It Become Another Queens?" *New York Times* (April 23, 1967): 1, 78; Charles G. Bennett, "Clusters Backed by Planning Unit," *New York Times* (July 20, 1967): 19; Raymond & May Associates, in association with Shankland, Cox & Associates, *Annadale-Huguenot: Planning for a New Residential Community on Staten Island* (New York, October 1967); Steven V. Roberts, "'New Town' Urged on Staten Island," *New York Times* (November 9, 1967): 53; "Plans Would Shift Highway from Staten Island Shore and Install a Community," *Journal of the American Institute of Architects* 48 (December 1967): 16; Steven V. Roberts, "Staten Islanders Fighting to Reduce Density Urged in Development Plans," *New York Times* (December 17, 1967), VIII: 1, 6; Charles G. Bennett, "Lindsay Revises Model Area Plan," *New York Times* (February 20, 1968): 76; "Alternative to Suburban Blight," editorial, *New York Times* (January 6, 1969): 46; Joseph P. Fried, "City Offers a 'Model' Plan for S.I. Area," *New York Times* (January 22, 1969): 19; "Staten Island's New Community," editorial, *New York Times* (January 28, 1969): 42; "Planning for Staten Island," editorial, *New York Times* (March 8, 1969): 28; "Staten Island Urban Renewal Project Is Backed," *New York Times* (March 27, 1969): 39; "Vision into Reality," editorial, *New York Times* (August 28, 1969): 38; Arnold H. Lubasch, "Estimate Board Postpones Vote on West Side Housing Project," *New York Times* (September 19, 1969): 66. Also see Charles Hall, "Four Paths to Urban Renewal," *Staten Island Advance* (September 10, 1967), Leonard Novarro, "' . . . We Have Nothing to Say About It,'" *Staten Island Advance* (September 10, 1967), Richard H. Amberg, "Annadale Plan OK Sought," *Staten Island Advance* (January 21, 1969), Clippings Collection, Staten Island Historical Society.
47. "Alternative to Suburban Blight": 46.
48. *South Richmond—A New City within the City* (Columbia, Md.: Rouse Company, 1970); Edward Ranzal, "12-Area 'City' of 300,000 Proposed for Staten Island," *New York Times* (May 14, 1970): 1, 40; "Moses Says Plan for Staten Island Is a Trial Balloon," *New York Times* (May 21, 1970): 37; "Staten Island City," editorial, *New York Times* (May 25, 1970): 32; Edward C. Burks, "City Hall Dominance of S.I. Plan Is Fought," *New York Times* (April 27, 1971): 45, 57; Fred Powledge, "The City Politic: The Urbanization of Staten Island," *New York* 4 (May 24, 1971): 8–9; "New 'City' Is Seen for Staten Island," *New York Times* (September 21, 1971): 73; Alfred E. Clark, "'City within City' Plan Supported on S.I.," *New York Times* (September 23, 1971): 57; Alfred E. Clark, "Connor Opposes S.I. 'City in City,'" *New York Times* (September 29, 1971): 37; "'New City' for Staten Island," editorial, *New York Times* (October 9, 1971): 30; Fred Ferretti, "Two S.I. Officials Differ on a Plan for 'New City,'" *New York Times* (October 25, 1971): 35, 65. Also see "Planned 'City' to Be Unveiled," *Staten Island Advance* (February 1, 1970), William Huus, "South Richmond: Time for Evaluation," *Staten Island Advance* (May 17, 1970), William Huus, "South Richmond? Planner Says It's Up to the People," *Staten Island Advance* (June 16, 1970), William Huus, "Proposal Is Pummeled," *Staten Island Advance* (September 28, 1971), "The Town that Never Arrived," *Staten Island Advance* (March 27, 1986), Clippings Collection, Staten Island Historical Society.
49. Charles G. Bennett, "City Hearing Is Set for Cluster Housing on S.I.," *New York Times* (May 1, 1969): 37; Glenn Fowler, "A Village of 2,000 Town Houses Will Rise in S.I.'s Arden Heights," *New York Times* (March 5, 1970): 1, 30; "Village Greens," *New York Times* (March 8, 1970), VIII: 6; "News of the Realty Trade: Village Greens," *New York Times* (December 19, 1971), VIII: 2; "Large-Scale Condominium Housing," *Architectural Record* 153 (January 1973): 131; Jonathan Barnett, *Urban Design as Public Policy* (New York: Architectural Record Books, 1974), 38–39; Carter B. Horsley, "Out-of-Town Builders Falter in City," *New York Times* (September 15, 1974), VIII: 1, 12; Paul D. Lazarus and Kenneth S. Scanlon, "The Successes of Cluster Development," letters to the editor, *New York Times* (October 6, 1974), VIII: 10; Thomas Michalski and Frances D. Gallogly, "Cluster Concept Must Not Be Destroyed," letters to the editor, *New York Times* (October 13, 1974), VIII: 13; "Unbuilding the Dream," editorial, *New York Times* (October 14, 1974): 32; Glenn Fowler, "O'Dwyer Assails Clinton Zoning Plan," *New York Times* (October 17, 1974): 45; White and Willensky, *AIA Guide* (1978), 552.
50. White and Willensky, *AIA Guide* (1978), 552.
51. "Unbuilding the Dream": 32.
52. "$65,000,000 Housing Project Planned by Zeckendorf on S.I.," *New York Times* (November 8, 1962): 50; "The Twelfth Annual P/A Design Awards Program: Residential," *Progressive Architecture* 46 (January 1965): 166–67.
53. Glenn Fowler, "Westinghouse Co. to Erect Housing," *New York Times* (May 22, 1972): 38; "St. George Place," *New York Times* (May 28, 1972), VIII: 4; Carter Wiseman, *I. M. Pei: A Profile in American Architecture* (New York: Harry N. Abrams, 1990), 311.
54. Wiseman, *I. M. Pei: A Profile in American Architecture*, 68, 308.
55. *Another Chance for Housing: Low-Rise Alternatives*, exhibition catalogue (New York: Museum of Modern Art, 1973); Ada Louise Huxtable, "Another Chance for Housing," *New York Times* (June 24, 1973), II: 23; James D. Morgan, "MOMA on Housing: Nothing New," *Architecture Plus* 1 (August 1973): 68; David A. Morton, "Low-Rise, High-Density," *Progressive Architecture* 54 (December 1973): 56–63; Peter Wolf, *The Future of the City: New Directions in Urban Planning* (New York: Whitney Library of Design, 1974), 112–16; Theodore Liebman, J. Michael Kirkland and Anthony Pangaro, "Housing Criteria Drawn from Human Response," *Journal of the American Institute of Architects* 61 (March 1974): 46–49; Theodore Liebman and Alan Melting, "Learning from Experience," *Progressive Architecture* 55 (November 1974): 70–77; Robert F. Borg, "'Low-Rise' Priority in Housing Premature," *New York Times* (December 15, 1974), VIII: 1, 6; John Ciardullo, David F. M. Todd and Theodore Liebman, "Low-Rise Housing Priority Defended," letters to the editor, *New York Times* (January 5, 1975), VIII: 4; Kenneth Frampton, "U.D.C. Low Rise High Density Housing Prototype," *L'Architecture d'Aujourd'hui* 186 (August–September 1976): 15–21.
56. Huxtable, "Another Chance for Housing": 23.
57. Charles G. Bennett, "Zoning to Guard Richmond Woods," *New York Times* (December 10, 1964): 49; Philip Benjamin, "Governor Offers Aid to Buy Camp," *New York Times* (December 14, 1964): 38; "Renewal Voted in Columbia Area," *New York Times* (January 21, 1965): 39; "Staten Island Camp Sold by Girl Scouts; City May Intervene," *New York Times* (February 27, 1965): 11; "Buyer of Girl Scout Tract on Staten Island Identified," *New York Times* (February 28, 1965): 33; "City Opens Park on Staten Island," *New York Times* (July 8, 1965): 33; John Sibley, "Rockefeller Orders Expansion at Willowbrook," *New York Times* (November 9, 1965): 38. Also see James Whitford, "Woods Called Future 'Must,'" *Staten Island Advance* (January 21, 1965), Clippings Collection, Staten Island Historical Society.
58. S. S. McSheehy, "2nd Thruway Starts in '65," *Staten Island Advance* (January 29, 1964), Clippings Collection, Staten Island Historical Society.
59. "Best Yet to Come," editorial, *Staten Island Advance* (February 3, 1964), Clippings Collection, Staten Island Historical Society.
60. "S.I. Group Seeking Shift of Parkway," *New York Times* (January 16, 1966): 80; "Staten Island Down the Drain," editorial, *New York Times* (January 22, 1966): 28; "Park Group Protests Plan for Staten Island Highway," *New York Times* (January 24, 1966): 32.
61. Robert Moses quoted in "S.I. Group Seeking Shift of Parkway": 80. Also see Moses, *Public Works: A Dangerous Trade*, 310–12.
62. "Farewell to Staten Island?" editorial, *New York Times* (February 17, 1966): 32; "New Route Urged on Staten Island," *New York Times* (February 19, 1966): 29; Robert T. Connor, "Connor Denies Staten Island Despoliation," letter to the editor, *New York Times* (March 2, 1966): 40; Richard Witkin, "City Urges Delay on S.I. Parkway," *New York Times* (March 3, 1966): 1, 23; "Staten Island Parkway Delay," editorial, *New York Times* (March 5, 1966): 26; Richard Witkin, "Lindsay Granted Delay on S.I. Road," *New York Times* (March 5, 1966): 29; Peter Kihss, "Mayor Disagrees on Road Threat," *New York Times* (April 6, 1966): 30.
63. Terence Smith, "Mayor and Moses Exchange Smiles," *New York Times* (April 28, 1966): 33.
64. Edith Evans Asbury, "Park Is Sought on Land Mapped for S.I. Highway," *New York Times* (August 11, 1966): 24; "12 Nature Groups Urge S.I. Havens," *New York Times* (September 9, 1966): 40; Richard B. Irwin, "Memorial to Olmstead [*sic*]," letter to the editor, *New York Times* (September 9, 1966): 44; Eleanor F. Francke, "Staten Island Parkway," letter to the editor, *New York Times* (September 14, 1966): 46. Also see Mark Wiesner, "Green Belt Trailway Proposed," *Staten Island Advance* (August 10, 1966), Mark Wiesner, "Hoving Pushes Trail Plan; Calls Moses a Poor Guide," *Staten Island Advance* (August 11, 1966), Clippings Collection, Staten Island Historical Society.
65. Charles G. Bennett, "Lindsay Bypasses Moses Plan in Picking Parkway Route," *New York Times* (December 15, 1966): 94; "Saving the Green Belt," editorial, *New York Times* (December 16, 1966): 46.
66. Steven V. Roberts, "U.S. Rejects Plan for S.I. Parkway," *New York Times* (January 7, 1967): 29; "City Asks Backing on S.I. Parkway," *New York Times* (January 14, 1967): 28; "Udall Backs City on S.I. Hiking Trail," *New York Times* (January 17, 1967): 76; "The Richmond Parkway," editorial, *New York Times* (January 24, 1967): 36; John Kifner, "Lindsay Leads a Protest on Staten Island Route," *New York Times* (January 30, 1967): 31; Martin A. Dembitz, "Richmond Parkway," letter to the editor, *New York Times* (February 20, 1967): 36; Steven V. Roberts, "Report to U.S. Agency Backs Road in Staten Island Greenbelt," *New York Times* (May 27, 1967): 33; "Parkway vs. People," editorial, *New York Times* (May 30, 1967): 20; Steven V. Roberts, "S.I. Citizen Group Fights Road Plan," *New York Times* (June 30, 1967): 39; Frederick H. Zurmuhlen, "Staten Island Parkway," letter to the editor, *New York Times* (August 2, 1967): 36; Terence H. Benbow, "Staten Island Greenbelt," letter to the editor, *New York Times* (August 25, 1967): 34; Charles G. Bennett, "Mayor Is Seeking to Reroute Road," *New York Times* (May 9, 1968): 48; "Will the Greenbelt Be Saved?" editorial, *New York Times* (May 9, 1968): 46; Morris Kaplan, "Civic Groups Back Mayor on S.I. Road," *New York Times* (July 16, 1968): 41; "Staten Island's Greenbelt," editorial, *New York Times* (September 25, 1968): 46; John A. Scullin, Jr., "Trees vs. People," letter to the editor, *New York Times* (November 11, 1968): 46; Caro, *The Power Broker*, 1121.
67. Wallace, McHarg, Roberts and Todd, *The Least Social Cost Corridor for Richmond Parkway* (New York: Department of Parks, Recreation and Cultural Affairs, 1968).
68. "Road Will Bypass Greenbelt in S.I.," *New York Times* (November 15, 1968): 93; "Richmond Parkway," editorial, *New York Times* (November 16, 1968): 36; "S.I. Route Called 'Lindsay's Folly,'" *New York Times* (November 16, 1968): 74; "Greenbelt Backers Take a Victory Hike," *New York Times* (November 24, 1968): 30; Charles G. Bennett, "Smith Sharply Assails Mayor Over S.I. Parkway," *New York Times* (February 25, 1969):

46; "Slowdown on S.I.'s Greenbelt," editorial, *New York Times* (December 17, 1969): 54; "Governor Spurns City S.I. Road Plan," *New York Times* (February 12, 1970): 25; Iver Peterson, "Richmond Parkway Plan Is Accepted by Lindsay," *New York Times* (February 27, 1970): 72; Robert D. McFadden, "Conservationists' Suit Assails Staten Island Road," *New York Times* (March 1, 1970): 66; "Four Is Better than Six," editorial, *New York Times* (March 3, 1970): 40; "Need for Greenbelt Action," editorial, *New York Times* (November 5, 1970): 46; Terence H. Benbow, "Staten Island's Greenbelt," letter to the editor, *New York Times* (November 19, 1970): 46; "Panel Approves Greenbelt Route," *New York Times* (November 20, 1970): 82; Edward C. Burks, "Citizen Groups Unite to Fight S.I. Road," *New York Times* (December 11, 1971): 33; Edward C. Burks, "City Maps $2-Billion Plan Based on State Bond Issue," *New York Times* (September 28, 1973): 37. Also see John G. Mitchell, ed., *Here's What's at Stake Along the Greenbelt—The Corridor to Knowledge*, pamphlet (Staten Island: Greenbelt Emergency Conference, 1970), S. S. McSheehy, "Alternate 6 Now Seen as Three Years Away," *Staten Island Advance* (October 28, 1970), Clippings Collection, Staten Island Historical Society.

69. Lee Dembart, "Richmond Parkway," *New York Times* (March 17, 1974): 33. Also see "BP Urges Action on Richmond Parkway's Original Route," *Staten Island Advance* (March 6, 1975), Clippings Collection, Staten Island Historical Society.

70. Robert Miraldi, "But Is It Enough?" *Greenbelt Clarion* (fall 1983), Mary Beth Pfeiffer, "Greenbelt: On the Threshold," *Greenbelt Clarion* (fall 1983), "Only the Parkway Pollutes City Plan," editorial, *Greenbelt Clarion* (fall 1983), Clippings Collection, Staten Island Historical Society.

71. "News," *Architectural Forum* 89 (October 1948): 18; Lorraine Welling Lanmon, *William Lescaze, Architect* (Philadelphia: Art Alliance Press; London and Toronto: Associated University Presses, 1987), 149.

72. For Lescaze's Ansonia High School, see Lanmon, *William Lescaze, Architect*, 118–19.

73. "News": 18. For Kebbon's building, see "Mayor Will Break Ground for School," *New York Times* (September 16, 1948): 31; "Mayor Starts Work on Richmond School," *New York Times* (September 18, 1948): 18.

74. "$8,000,000 for New Catholic Schools," *New York Times* (November 14, 1960): 17; "Catholic Schools Open Here Sept. 10," *New York Times* (August 30, 1962): 27; White and Willensky, *AIA Guide* (1978), 560.

75. Robert H. Terte, "Sharp Rise Looms in School Budget," *New York Times* (March 9, 1962): 26; White and Willensky, *AIA Guide* (1978), 548–49.

76. "Buildings in the News," *Architectural Record* 143 (May 1968): 44; Leonard Buder, "Strikes to Delay I.S. 53 in Queens," *New York Times* (August 27, 1972): 41; White and Willensky, *AIA Guide* (1978), 549.

77. "2 Honored in S.I. School Names," *New York Times* (March 8, 1977): 35; White and Willensky, *AIA Guide* (1988), 837.

78. "Government to Give the City a Part of Miller Field on S.I.," *New York Times* (May 29, 1971): 47; "U.S. to Give City 26 Acres for School on Staten Island," *New York Times* (November 26, 1971): 74; Edward Ranzal, "Mayor Accepts U.S. Gift with Complaint," *New York Times* (November 11, 1972): 6; Max H. Seigel, "4 Harlem Students Urge Funds for School for Disadvantaged," *New York Times* (February 23, 1973): 17; Maurice Carroll, "Beame Offers 1.7-Billion Capital Budget," *New York Times* (February 1, 1974): 1, 44; Glenn Fowler, "Board of Estimate Votes Tunnel-Work Compromise," *New York Times* (March 7, 1975): 58; "The Eggers Partnership Announces Construction of a Staten Island High School," *Architectural Record* 158 (November 1975): 42; Fred Ferretti, "Budget Cuts Go Deep into Quality of Life," *New York Times* (November 3, 1975): 1, 40; "Rezoning for S.I. High Schools Is Argued at Hearing by Board," *New York Times* (December 13, 1975): 54; Charles Kaiser, "Beame's Budget Includes Money for Design of Convention Center," *New York Times* (April 23, 1977): 24; Edward A. Gargan, "Rebuilding Plan for City Property Offered by Koch," *New York Times* (May 13, 1981), B: 2.

79. "Wagner College Plans," *New York Times* (February 25, 1959): 33.

80. "Wagner College Plans": 33; "Glass Enclosed Library on Staten Island," *Architectural Forum* 112 (May 1960): 63; "Library to Honor Brewer," *New York Times* (May 7, 1960): 47; "3 Publishers Honored," *New York Times* (October 1, 1961): 70; "Bastion for Books," *Progressive Architecture* 44 (March 1963): 138–41; White and Willensky, *AIA Guide* (1978), 553.

81. "New Buildings Set by Wagner College," *New York Times* (October 28, 1962): 81; "Wagner College Will Start 3-Building Science Center," *New York Times* (October 16, 1966), VIII: 14; "The Wagner College Student Union," *Architectural Record* 148 (July 1970): 40; "A Student Union Activities Building," *New York Times* (January 17, 1971), VIII: 2; White and Willensky, *AIA Guide* (1978), 553.

82. White and Willensky, *AIA Guide* (1978), 553.

83. "State to Help City on Air Raid Victims," *New York Times* (March 25, 1942): 11; "Text of Mayor La Guardia's Budget Message," *New York Times* (April 2, 1942): 24; "Quickly Converted for Casualties," *Architectural Record* 95 (January 1944): 71–78; White and Willensky, *AIA Guide* (1988), 838.

84. "Report Released on Willowbrook," *New York Times* (September 22, 1966): 49.

85. William B. Foxhall, "Retardation Research Lab Has Total Flexibility for Basic Sciences," *Architectural Record* 147 (January 1970): 157–59; White and Willensky, *AIA Guide* (1988), 838.

86. See David J. and Sheila M. Rothman, *The Willowbrook Wars* (New York: Harper & Row, 1984).

87. "Institutional," *Architectural Record* 152 (August 1972): 106; White and Willensky, *AIA Guide* (1978), 555.

88. "Hospital for the Mentally Ill," *Progressive Architecture* 50 (February 1969): 136–37; "Levitt Praises State Psychiatric Center," *New York Times* (April 5, 1976): 35; White and Willensky, *AIA Guide* (1978), 560.

QUEENS

1. Hal Burton, "The City Nobody Knows," *Saturday Evening Post* 225 (August 21, 1952): 36–37, 59–60.

2. "Study Shows Queens Vacant Land Ripe for a Vast Building Boom," *New York Times* (March 3, 1946), VIII: 1.

3. Burton, "The City Nobody Knows": 37.

4. Charles Grutzner, "Slum Work Urged to Spur Economy," *New York Times* (April 18, 1958): 12; "Jamaica Project Pleases Moses," *New York Times* (May 18, 1959): 29.

5. Murray Schumach, "Planners Advise 'Substantial' Aid to Better Queens," *New York Times* (April 6, 1970): 1, 28.

6. For an overview in 1955, see Ira Henry Freeman, "Our Changing City: The Long Island City Area," *New York Times* (August 1, 1955): 21.

7. For the Steinway-built workers' housing, see Richard Plunz, *A History of Housing in New York City* (New York: Columbia University Press, 1990), 114–16. For the Steinway factory in Manhattan, see James Trager, *Park Avenue: Street of Dreams* (New York: Atheneum, 1990), 21–22.

8. Stern, Gilmartin and Mellins, *New York 1930*, 496, 498–99.

9. "City Housing Authority Selects Astoria Site," *New York Times* (March 23, 1944): 30; "Homes Conserved by Building Plan," *New York Times* (January 30, 1947): 11; "Farrell Reports Housing Activity," *New York Times* (July 23, 1947): 21; "Laying Cornerstone for Astoria Housing Project," *New York Times* (December 1, 1948): 32; "Low-Rent Housing Opened in Queens," *New York Times* (December 30, 1948): 14; Victoria Newhouse, *Wallace K. Harrison, Architect* (New York: Rizzoli International Publications, 1989), 163–64.

10. "3 Low-Rent Projects Approved by Board," *New York Times* (July 23, 1948): 11; "Court Fight Looms on Housing Project," *New York Times* (September 25, 1948): 30; Paul Crowell, "City Collector Out, Mayor Announces," *New York Times* (December 2, 1948): 31; "Calls for Housing by Private Capital," *New York Times* (May 17, 1949): 28; "Housing Authority Files Plans for Ravenswood," *New York Times* (June 25, 1949): 24; "Queens Project Finished," *New York Times* (May 12, 1950): 25.

11. Lee E. Cooper, "$8,000,000 Private Project to Offer Non-Profit Homes," *New York Times* (September 19, 1948): 1, 67; "A Non-Profit Housing Project," editorial, *New York Times* (September 21, 1948): 26; "Building Previews," *Architectural Forum* 89 (November 1948): 68, 70; "Cooperative Housing," *Architectural Forum* 90 (March 1949): 20; "Closets Feature Plan for Housing," *New York Times* (April 17, 1949), VIII: 4; "Design for Queensview Omits Basements; Other Innovations to Cut Housing Costs," *New York Times* (May 15, 1949), VIII: 1; "July Start Seen for Queensview," *New York Times* (May 31, 1949): 34; "Queensview Tenants See Model of Home," *New York Times* (July 21, 1949): 22; Lee E. Cooper, "3 'Co-op' Projects to House Families of Medium Income," *New York Times* (August 28, 1949), VIII: 1; "$5,800,000 Plans Filed for Queensview Housing," *New York Times* (September 14, 1949): 47; "Queensview Plans for Fall Opening," *New York Times* (February 19, 1950), VIII: 6; "Queensview Adds 104 'Co-op' Units," *New York Times* (May 26, 1950): 40; "Stone Laid for Project," *New York Times* (July 15, 1950): 17; "Pre-Cast Blocks Used in Housing," *New York Times* (November 12, 1950), VIII: 1, 7; "A New Housing Development in Long Island City," *New York Times* (November 15, 1950): 38; "Queensview Honored," *Housing and Planning News* 11 (December 1952): 2; "Architects Hail Redeveloping Idea," *New York Times* (December 21, 1952), VIII: 3.

12. "Moses Recommends $4,275,000 Housing," *New York Times* (November 20, 1952): 55; Thomas W. Ennis, "Co-op Buyers Get Tenant Training," *New York Times* (January 19, 1958), VIII: 1; "Queensview Housing Opened," *New York Times* (January 21, 1958): 31.

13. Lee E. Cooper, "Brooklyn, Astoria Get New Housing with 2,682 Units," *New York Times* (June 22, 1947), VIII: 1; "$4,406,000 Financing," *New York Times* (July 31, 1947): 34; "New Apartments for Veterans in New York Area," *New York Times* (December 14, 1947), VIII: 1; "New Housing Occupied," *New York Times* (January 18, 1948), VIII: 1; "Occupy Astoria Suites," *New York Times* (January 28, 1948): 40.

14. White and Willensky, *AIA Guide* (1988), 730–31.

15. "Doing Over the Town," *Time* 80 (September 28, 1962): 56–69. For the Queensboro Bridge, see Stern, Gilmartin and Massengale, *New York 1900*, 51–52, 54–55.

16. For the Brewster and American Chicle buildings, see Stern, Gilmartin and Mellins, *New York 1930*, 523–24.

17. "New Integrated Garment Plant Starts Output Today," *New York Times* (November 7, 1958): 37, 41; Ian McCallum, *Architecture USA* (London: Architectural Press, 1959), 206; "Bulletins," *Progressive Architecture* 40 (January 1959): 73; White and Willensky, *AIA Guide* (1967), 355.

18. "Pepsi-Cola Warehouse, Long Island City, N.Y.," *Architectural Forum* 79 (December 1943): 65–66; Newhouse, *Wallace K. Harrison, Architect*, 97.

19. "Proposed City Redevelopment," *Architectural Forum* 84 (February 1946): 113–15; "Riverview Housing—A Planned Community," *Citizens' Housing Council Housing News* 4 (February–March 1946): 4.

20. Henry Hope Reed, Jr., "The Modern Is Dead—Long Live the Modern," with drawings by John Barrington Bayley, *New World Writing* 11 (New York: New American Library, 1957): 134–51.

21. Reed, "The Modern Is Dead—Long Live the Modern": 150.

22. Peter Wolf, *Another Chance for Cities*, exhibition catalogue (New York: Whitney Museum of American Art, 1970), 20–23; Edith Evans Asbury, "Logue Proposes a Town Over Sunnyside Rail Yards," *New York Times* (July 22, 1971): 1, 55; Peter Wolf, *The Future of the City: New Directions in Urban Planning* (New York: Whitney Library of Design, 1974), 170, figs. 133–35.

23. Emanuel Perlmutter, "Queens Sports Center Proposed," *New York Times* (October 7, 1973): 1, 49; Richard J. H. Johnston, "Jets Interested in Queens Arena," *New York Times* (October 8, 1973): 37; Frank Lynn, "Rival Stadium Plans Stir a Bistate Furor," *New York Times* (October 13, 1973): 1, 24; "Sunnyside Surprise," editorial, *New York Times* (October 29, 1973): 34; "'Big A' Regulars Oppose Sale," *New York Times* (November 25, 1973): 146; Frank Lynn, "Two of Wilson's Most Experienced Aides Are Emerging as Top Political Strategists in His Bid for Full Term," *New York Times* (February 4, 1974): 19; Frank Lynn, "Rockefeller Supporters Fear Backlash from Nursing Home and U.D.C. Crises," *New York Times* (March 10, 1975): 22; "Plans for Queens Track Dropped," *New York Times* (March 10, 1975): 38.

24. "U.S. Airports," *Architectural Forum* 73 (August 1940): 73–77. Also see Stern, Gilmartin and Mellins, *New York 1930*, 703–5.

25. Marc Thompson, "What's Wrong with Our Air Terminals?" *Architectural Forum* 84 (January 1946): 122–28, 130, 132, 134.

26. "A Snack Between Landing and Take-Off," *Architectural Record* 104 (July 1948): 140–42.

27. Joseph C. Ingraham, "La Guardia Field to Be Made Over," *New York Times* (June 19, 1957): 1, 20; "La Guardia Airport's Outmoded Terminal . . . Will Become $32 Million Facility by 1965," *Engineering News-Record* 159 (July 4, 1957): 25; "Terminal Replacement," *Architectural Forum* 107 (August 1957): 38; "News Bulletins," *Progressive Architecture* 38 (August 1957): 99.

28. "Buildings in the News," *Architectural Record* 126 (October 1959): 12.

29. "New York Airport," *Architectural Forum* 120 (January 1964): 14; Evert Clark, "La Guardia Terminal Dedicated for Jet Era on Wings of Oratory," *New York Times* (April 17, 1964): 70; "La Guardia Airport Gets New Terminal," *Progressive Architecture* 45 (June 1964): 83; "Bard Awards Honor Five Projects," *Architectural Record* 137 (April 1965): 16; "Awards and Competitions," *Interiors* 124 (April 1965): 14; "New York's Bard Awards," *Progressive Architecture* 46 (April 1965): 63–64; White and Willensky, *AIA Guide* (1967), 364; Newhouse, *Wallace K. Harrison, Architect,* 240–43.
30. "La Guardia Airport Gets New Terminal": 83.
31. Olga Gueft, "The Air-Conditioned Hanging Garden," *Interiors* 124 (February 1965): 101; Mary Simons, "The Transformation of a Cavernous Space," *Interiors* 124 (February 1965): 106–13.
32. George Horne, "Hydrofoil Line to Expand Runs to Include Stops at La Guardia," *New York Times* (July 12, 1964): 70; "Hydrofoils Start Runs to La Guardia," *New York Times* (August 29, 1964): 44; "8 Fair Hydrofoils Seized Over Debt," *New York Times* (October 17, 1964): 58; "Hydrofoil Lines Seeking Capital," *New York Times* (March 18, 1965): 65.
33. Paul J. C. Friedlander, "Design by Decibels," *New York Times* (October 18, 1953), II: 19; "New Hotel at La Guardia Airport Is 'Deaf' to Noise," *New York Times* (December 14, 1954): 42.
34. A. N. Sirof quoted in Friedlander, "Design by Decibels": 19.
35. "New Hotel Is Rising at La Guardia Field," *New York Times* (May 21, 1956): 27; "First Unit of 156-Room Hotel Opens at La Guardia," *New York Times* (July 17, 1956): 25.
36. "Hotel to Rise at La Guardia Airport," *New York Times* (May 5, 1957), VIII: 6.
37. "Airport Hotel Begun," *New York Times* (September 14, 1961): 49; "Motor Inn Completed at La Guardia Airport," *New York Times* (August 17, 1962): 34.
38. "A Complete Reworking of a Popular Novelist's House on Long Island," *Architectural Forum* 90 (January 1949): 109–10; "House Remodeled by Reisner and Urbahn," *Interiors* 108 (February 1949): 86–91.
39. Daniel Karatzas, *Jackson Heights: A Garden in the City,* with an intro. by Robert A. M. Stern (New York: J. M. Kaplan Fund and Jackson Heights Beautification Group, 1990), 156–57.
40. "'Co-op' in Queens for 144 Families," *New York Times* (May 11, 1947), VIII: 1; Karatzas, *Jackson Heights: A Garden in the City,* 157.
41. See Stern, Gilmartin and Mellins, *New York 1930,* 493, 497.
42. "Jackson Heights Plans New 'Co-op,'" *New York Times* (February 1, 1948), VIII: 1, 3; Lee E. Cooper, "Upturn in Building Gives Long Island More Apartments," *New York Times* (August 7, 1949), VIII: 1, 8; Karatzas, *Jackson Heights: A Garden in the City,* 157–58.
43. For a complete list of Birnbaum's work in Jackson Heights, see Karatzas, *Jackson Heights: A Garden in the City,* 186.
44. "Rezoning Is Urged for Light Industry," *New York Times* (July 20, 1950): 23; "Queens Group Fights Watch Factory Plan," *New York Times* (July 22, 1950): 30; "City's Planning Agency Sanctions Factory for a Home Area in Queens," *New York Times* (September 28, 1950): 33; "Factory Promised with Raid Shelter," *New York Times* (December 7, 1950): 42; "Planners Approve Bulova Plant Site," *New York Times* (December 28, 1950): 39; "Community of Interest," *Interiors* 110 (January 1951): 14; Charles G. Bennett, "Clang! Go 10 More Trolley Lines; Only 3 to Be Left, All in Brooklyn," *New York Times* (January 12, 1951): 29; "Big Bulova Plant Started in Queens," *New York Times* (January 28, 1952): 7; "Bulova Sales Set New High Record; Earnings Fall to $4.07 a Share," *New York Times* (June 26, 1952): 41; William M. Freeman, "Bradley Takes Over Tomorrow as Head of Bulova Research in $10,000,000 Plant," *New York Times* (August 16, 1953), III: 1, 6; "Plant of Bulova Wins Top Award," *New York Times* (November 29, 1953), VIII: 1, 6.
45. See Robert A. M. Stern with Raymond W. Gastil, *Modern Classicism* (New York: Rizzoli International Publications, 1988), 44.
46. "3rd-League Stadium Plans Ok'd by Moses," *Progressive Architecture* 41 (May 1960): 82; Paul Crowell, "The Stadium Investment," *New York Times* (August 8, 1960): 18; Charles G. Bennett, "Gerosa Says City Can Extend Debt 286 Million in '61," *New York Times* (August 16, 1960): 1, 19; Paul Crowell, "Mayor Presses National League; Says City Can Build Field by '62," *New York Times* (October 15, 1960): 1, 18; Wayne Phillips, "City Stadium Cost Tops Expectation," *New York Times* (January 25, 1961): 41; Warren Weaver, Jr., "City Stadium Bill Signed in Albany," *New York Times* (April 23, 1961), V: 1–2; Emanuel Perlmutter, "Ground Is Broken for Municipal Stadium in Queens," *New York Times* (October 29, 1961): 1, 46; Charles G. Bennett, "Met Stadium Opening Put Off to '64," *New York Times* (July 12, 1963): 17; Will Lissner, "City Improves Facilities for Shea Stadium Fans," *New York Times* (March 15, 1964), V: 1–2; R. W. Apple, Jr., "New Queens Park Still Needs Work," *New York Times* (April 17, 1964): 39; Leonard Koppett, "Shea Stadium Opens with Big Traffic Jam," *New York Times* (April 18, 1964): 1, 20; Robert Lipsyte, "'Fabulous' Stadium Delights Fans," *New York Times* (April 18, 1964): 20; Bernard Stengren, "Traffic Battle Lost by Barnes," *New York Times* (April 18, 1964): 20.
47. Murray Schumach, "Shrieks of 55,000 Accompany Beatles," *New York Times* (August 16, 1965): 29, 49.
48. Joseph C. Ingraham, "New Expressway to Nassau Slated," *New York Times* (March 11, 1951): 63; "Plan Board Adopts Expressway Route," *New York Times* (May 24, 1951): 36; "Nassau Road Route Set," *New York Times* (July 26, 1952): 15; "Queens Expressway Bids," *New York Times* (July 31, 1953): 7; "State to Spend 26 Millions on Highways in City in Year," *New York Times* (March 25, 1954): 1, 10; "Road Opening in Queens Today Is First Link in New Expressway," *New York Times* (February 25, 1955): 23; "3 Highway Links Open Tomorrow," *New York Times* (November 4, 1955): 32; "Building of Expressway Cuts Off Queens Stores from Customers," *New York Times* (August 26, 1957): 25; Bernard Stengren, "Highways Linked in Three Counties," *New York Times* (October 1, 1958): 27; Joseph C. Ingraham, "L.I. Expressway: A Dilemma," *New York Times* (August 4, 1963), X: 1, 5.
49. George Barrett, "Our Changing City: North Shore-Central Queens," *New York Times* (August 5, 1955): 21; Stan Fischler, *Uptown, Downtown: A Trip Through Time on New York's Subways* (New York: Hawthorn Books, 1976), 244–45.
50. "Horse Sense Planning," *Architectural Forum* 79 (November 1943): 59–74.
51. "Says Borough of Queens Changing to Area of Apartment Dwellings," *Real Estate Record and Guide* 162 (August 21, 1948): 3–4; "Apartment Development," *Architectural Forum* 89 (September 1948): 15; White and Willensky, *AIA Guide* (1967), 367.
52. "Dramatic Designs Are Characteristic of Award-Winning Buildings in Queens," *New York Times* (December 4, 1960), VIII: 1, 9.
53. Maurice Foley, "Plan Apartments for 4,000 Families," *New York Times* (March 27, 1955), VIII: 1; Barrett, "Our Changing City: North Shore-Central Queens": 21; "Dramatic Designs Are Characteristic of Award Winning Buildings in Queens": 1, 9.
54. John A. Bradley, "Lefrak Starts Queens Housing," *New York Times* (November 20, 1955): 1, 4; "Big Development Due in Elmhurst," *New York Times* (May 11, 1960): 63; "New York City Apartments," *Architectural Forum* 113 (July 1960): 50; "Housing Concern Nearing Role of Landlord to 500,000 People," *New York Times* (June 11, 1961), VIII: 1, 18; "Lefrak City," special advertising section, *New York Times* (June 17, 1962), XI; David B. Carlson, "Sam Lefrak: He Builds Them Cheaper by the Dozen," *Architectural Forum* 118 (April 1963): 102–5; "Instant Neighborhoods," *Look* 27 (March 26, 1963): 41–43; "This Is Total Living?" *Newsweek* 66 (November 8, 1965): 101–2; Plunz, *A History of Housing in New York City,* 285.
55. "Instant Neighborhoods": 41–43.
56. Samuel Lefrak quoted in "This Is Total Living?": 101–2.
57. Samuel Lefrak quoted in "Construction Begins on Queens' Largest Office Building," *Real Estate Record and Guide* 201 (June 1, 1968): 4.
58. Samuel Lefrak quoted in Alan S. Oser, "Lefrak Wants to Go on Building in City," *New York Times* (January 25, 1970), VIII: 1, 4. Also see Glenn Fowler, "Sam Lefrak: He Loves Long and Active Workdays," *New York Times* (October 24, 1971), XV: 15.
59. John P. Callahan, "Two New Office Units to Share Building Boom in Forest Hills," *New York Times* (August 2, 1959), VIII: 1–2; "Dramatic Designs Are Characteristic of Award-Winning Buildings in Queens": 1, 9.
60. "News of Realty: Queens Building," *New York Times* (May 20, 1968): 77; "Construction Begins on Queens' Largest Office Building": 4; "Lefrak Builds Queens Office Tower," *New York Times* (June 2, 1968), VIII: 9.
61. Carter B. Horsley, "Buildings Already Rising and Projected May Make Rego Park Center of Queens," *New York Times* (August 24, 1974): 29.
62. Callahan, "Two New Office Units to Share Building Boom in Forest Hills": 1–2; White and Willensky, *AIA Guide* (1967), 366–67.
63. Charles Friedman, "Deposits in Savings Bank Will Be Protected Under Concrete Wings," *New York Times* (June 11, 1967), VIII: 13; White and Willensky, *AIA Guide* (1978), 520.
64. "Doctors' Partnership," *Progressive Architecture* 41 (July 1960): 156–63; White and Willensky, *AIA Guide* (1967), 366.
65. Horsley, "Buildings Already Rising and Projected May Make Rego Park Center of Queens": 29; White and Willensky, *AIA Guide* (1978), 520–21.
66. "A Problem of Pressures in Planning," *Architectural Record* 95 (January 1944): 87–92. For P.S. 101, see Stern, Gilmartin and Mellins, *New York 1930,* 120–21.
67. Carter B. Horsley, "Queens Project Given Tax Relief," *New York Times* (July 23, 1980), B: 3; Alan S. Oser, "Muss Building 16-Story Office Building in Queens," *New York Times* (October 29, 1980), B: 6; White and Willensky, *AIA Guide* (1988), 758.
68. Mario Matthew Cuomo, *Forest Hills Diary: The Crisis of Low-Income Housing,* with a preface by Jimmy Breslin (New York: Random House, 1974; New York: Vintage Books, 1983), 3–4. Also see Steven R. Weisman, "A Housing Crisis Compromise," book review, *New York Times* (July 16, 1974): 33.
69. Steven V. Roberts, "2 Housing Plans Draw Protests," *New York Times* (May 12, 1966): 48; Steven V. Roberts, "Public Housing in Middle-Class Areas Assailed," *New York Times* (June 2, 1966): 25; Steven V. Roberts, "Housing Projects in Queens Scored," *New York Times* (June 16, 1966): 47; Steven V. Roberts, "Mayor Defeated by Borough Heads," *New York Times* (October 28, 1966): 45.
70. Cuomo, *Forest Hills Diary,* 11.
71. Cuomo, *Forest Hills Diary,* 12.
72. Quoted in "Panel Approves Housing in Queens," *New York Times* (December 3, 1966): 46. Also see "Battle Is Renewed on Queens Housing," *New York Times* (December 1, 1966): 54.
73. Francis X. Clines, "New Corona Plan Spares 59 Homes," *New York Times* (December 2, 1970): 1, 43; "Council Unit Acts to End Long Fight Over Corona Homes," *New York Times* (March 10, 1972): 74; Francis X. Clines, "Assembly Votes Lindsay Plan to Save Corona Homes," *New York Times* (April 18, 1972): 41; Glenn Singer, "Voters Hold the Key in 'Battle of Corona,'" *New York Times* (June 11, 1972), XV: 1, 6; Murray Schumach, "Corona Praises Mayor, Forest Hills Pickets Him," *New York Times* (July 7, 1972): 35; "Local Unit in Corona Approves School," *New York Times* (October 7, 1973): 141; Murray Schumach, "Doubt Lingers in Corona on Housing Compromise," *New York Times* (July 16, 1974): 37, 44.
74. Roger Starr quoted in Walter Goodman, "The Battle of Forest Hills—Who's Ahead?" *New York Times* (November 21, 1971), VI: 8–9, 60–65.
75. Ada Louise Huxtable, "Forest Hills: Innovation vs. Red Tape," *New York Times* (February 8, 1972): 35, 66.
76. Steven R. Weisman, "Public Housing Is Fought in Forest Hills," *New York Times* (February 21, 1971): 81; "Despite Protests in Forest Hills, Housing Project Plan Proceeds," *New York Times* (May 2, 1971): 88.
77. "Housing Approved for Forest Hills," *New York Times* (October 30, 1971): 19.
78. Murray Schumach, "Angry Crowd in Forest Hills Protests Housing Project," *New York Times* (November 19, 1971): 1, 49.
79. Murray Schumach, "Housing Protest in Forest Hills Termed 'Deplorable' by Mayor," *New York Times* (November 20, 1971): 1, 20; Richard L. Madden, "Forest Hills Dispute and Politics," *New York Times* (November 20, 1971): 20; "Rosenthal Irked by Housing Plan," *New York Times* (November 20, 1971): 20.
80. Herbert Kahn, "For Forest Hills Cooperation," letter to the editor, *New York Times* (November 22, 1971): 38; Michael T. Kaufman, "'Bigot' and 'Liar' Mark TV Clash on Forest Hills Project," *New York Times* (November 22, 1971): 1, 43. For a description of Jerry Birbach, see Goodman, "The Battle of Forest Hills—Who's Ahead?": 61–62. For a profile of Simeon Golar, see Joseph P. Fried, "Simeon Golar's City-Within-A-City," *New York Times* (April 30, 1972), VI: 16–17, 49–50, 52, 54, 58, 60, 63.
81. George Romney quoted in Murray Schumach, "Romney Affirms Forest Hills Site," *New York Times* (November 23, 1971): 1, 36. Also see "Clash at Forest Hills," editorial, *New York Times* (November 23, 1971): 40.
82. Murray Schumach, "Forest Hills Plan May Be Reduced," *New York Times* (November 24, 1971): 1, 18.
83. "Rage in Forest Hills," *Newsweek* 78 (November 29, 1971): 82; "Fear in Forest Hills," *Time* 98 (November 29, 1971): 25.
84. Clark Whelton, "Battle of Forest Hills," *Village Voice* 16 (November 25, 1971): 1, 92–93.

85. Herman Badillo, "The Forest Hills Affair: Beyond Stereotypes," *Village Voice* 16 (December 2, 1971): 5–6. Also see Ernest Mortuzans, "Queens & Kinks," letter to the editor, *Village Voice* 16 (December 9, 1971): 97; Eleanor Holmes Norton, "Battle of Forest Hills: Tragic Stereotyping," letter to the editor, *Village Voice* 16 (December 9, 1971): 97.
86. Edward I. Koch, "Act of Compromise," letter to the editor, *Village Voice* 16 (December 9, 1971): 97. Also see Jack Newfield and Wayne Barrett, *City for Sale: Ed Koch and the Betrayal of New York* (New York: Harper & Row, 1988), 116–23.
87. "Realities in Forest Hills," editorial, *New York Times* (December 6, 1971): 38.
88. "Romney on Forest Hills," *Time* 98 (December 6, 1971): 20–21; Richard L. Madden, "White House Says It Won't Intervene on Queens Project," *New York Times* (December 9, 1971): 41; Murray Schumach, "Racial Hostility Denied," *New York Times* (December 9, 1971): 41.
89. Murray Schumach, "Lindsay Asserts a Compromise at Forest Hills Is Impossible," *New York Times* (December 18, 1971): 32.
90. "Court Orders Halt in Work on Housing in Forest Hills," *New York Times* (February 15, 1972): 1, 63; Murray Schumach, "Aides of Lindsay Evolve a Compromise Proposal Taking in Lindenwood," *New York Times* (February 17, 1972): 1, 63; David K. Shipler, "And Still the Bitter Dispute Goes On," *New York Times* (February 20, 1972), IV: 4.
91. Quoted in Murray Schumach, "Forest Hills Project Is Upheld on Appeal," *New York Times* (May 5, 1972): 1, 28.
92. Alfonso A. Narvaez, "Bill to Stop Forest Hills Project Gets Final Passage in Assembly," *New York Times* (May 3, 1972): 1, 17.
93. Alfonso A. Narvaez, "Rockefeller Vetoes a Bill to Kill Forest Hills Plan," *New York Times* (May 14, 1972): 1, 62; "Rockefeller Vetoes . . . ," editorial, *New York Times* (May 15, 1972): 34.
94. Quoted in Cuomo, *Forest Hills Diary*, 153. Also see N. Polinsky, "Forest Hills 'Arbitrator,'" letter to the editor, *New York Times* (June 2, 1972): 36.
95. Mario Cuomo quoted in Martin Tolchin, "Forest Hills Site May Be Cut 50%," *New York Times* (July 15, 1972): 1, 30.
96. "Report to Honorable John V. Lindsay Concerning the Proposed Low-Income Housing Project at 108th Street, Forest Hills, Queens," in Cuomo, *Forest Hills Diary*, 175.
97. Simeon Golar and Jerry Birbach quoted in Martin Tolchin, "Forest Hills Compromise Is Assailed by Both Sides," *New York Times* (July 27, 1972): 35.
98. "Halving Forest Hills," editorial, *New York Times* (July 29, 1972): 24.
99. Peter Kihss, "Golar Gives Plan for Forest Hills," *New York Times* (August 13, 1972): 1, 29.
100. Francis X. Clines, "Lindsay Accepts Compromise Plan for Forest Hills," *New York Times* (August 10, 1972): 1, 32.
101. Vernon E. Jordan, Jr., "Forest Hills Compromise Deemed a Failure," letter to the editor, *New York Times* (September 6, 1972): 44.
102. Donald Manes quoted in Peter Kihss, "Manes Calls for 'Innovative' Low-Income Co-op at Controversial Forest Hills Site," *New York Times* (September 6, 1972): 23.
103. Simeon Golar quoted in Kihss, "Manes Calls for 'Innovative' Low-Income Co-op at Controversial Forest Hills Site": 23.
104. Donald Elliott quoted in Francis X. Clines, "Planning Unit Approves Forest Hills Compromise," *New York Times* (October 5, 1972): 51.
105. Murray Schumach, "City Approves a Low-Income Co-op for Forest Hills," *New York Times* (October 27, 1972): 45; Andy Logan, "Around City Hall: Not You, Not You," *New Yorker* 48 (November 11, 1972): 169–72, 175–79, 181–82; Irving Spiegel, "Veterans Demanding Flats in Forest Hills Housing Project," *New York Times* (January 31, 1973): 105.
106. Murray Schumach, " . . . But in Forest Hills, Some See Co-op as a Stabilizer," *New York Times* (June 6, 1974): 39.
107. Newfield and Barrett, *City for Sale*, 122–23.
108. Barry Jacobs, "13 Years After the 'Project' Furor: Forest Hills Has Changed Its Mind," *Village Voice* 29 (December 11, 1984): 28, 30, quoted in Newfield and Barrett, *City for Sale*, 123.
109. "Ground Broken for Church," *New York Times* (September 11, 1939): 19; "Church Auditorium Dedicated," *New York Times* (June 10, 1940): 19; White and Willensky, *AIA Guide* (1988), 772–73.
110. White and Willensky, *AIA Guide* (1978), 515.
111. White and Willensky, *AIA Guide* (1978), 516.
112. White and Willensky, *AIA Guide* (1978), 516–17.
113. "Alfred Levitt, with New Ideas, Methods, Tackles Middle-Income Apartment Field," *Architectural Forum* 104 (February 1956): 16–17; "Apartment Colony Is Built on Principles of Light, Air and Space," *New York Times* (February 24, 1957): 1, 5; White and Willensky, *AIA Guide* (1967), 361.
114. Barbaralee Diamonstein, *The Landmarks of New York* (New York: Harry N. Abrams, 1988), 344; Andrew S. Dolkart, *Guide to New York City Landmarks* (Washington, D.C.: Preservation Press, 1992), 194.
115. Alfred Levitt quoted in "Alfred Levitt, with New Ideas, Methods, Tackles Middle-Income Apartment Field": 16–17.
116. "College Site Weighed," *New York Times* (October 8, 1959): 32; "College Breaks Ground," *New York Times* (February 10, 1962): 21; "New Campus Sought for Queensborough," *New York Times* (July 2, 1962): 23; "Building Plans Advanced at Queensborough College," *New York Times* (December 15, 1963): 70; "Green Light Given for College Plan," *New York Times* (August 5, 1965): 29; White and Willensky, *AIA Guide* (1967), 363; Franklin Whitehouse, "Queens Students to Get Center Overlooking Bay," *New York Times* (December 3, 1967), VIII: 1; "New Campus Facilities, Queensborough College," *Progressive Architecture* 49 (March 1968): 56; "Preview," *Architectural Forum* 131 (July–August 1969): 120; Mildred F. Schmertz, "Design for a Variety of Campus Life Styles," *Architectural Record* 151 (January 1972): 115–19; White and Willensky, *AIA Guide* (1978), 516–17.
117. Lee E. Cooper, "Housing Planned with 3,800 Units on Queens Tract," *New York Times* (May 25, 1947), VIII: 1; "8,300 Garden Apartments by House-Builder Gross-Morton of New York Spotlight the Industry's Shift from Sale to Rent," *Architectural Forum* 87 (August 1947): 70–71; "New Homes and Apartments Going Up in the New York Metropolitan District," *New York Times* (October 26, 1947), VIII: 1; "Glen Oaks Expanding," *New York Times* (November 26, 1947): 52; "Builders to Spend $500,000 to Landscape Glen Oaks Apartment Project in Queens," *New York Times* (December 21, 1947), VIII: 1; "Glen Oaks Village Will Have Stores," *New York Times* (February 3, 1948): 43; "Start the Second Group of 111 Buildings in Glen Oaks Housing Project in Queens," *New York Times* (March 7, 1948), VIII: 1; "Apartment Village," *Architectural Record* 103 (June 1948): 174, 176; "Glen Oaks to Get Shopping Center," *New York Times* (August 15, 1948), VIII: 1, 4; "Garden Apartments," *House and Garden* 94 (October 1948): 134–35, 205; "Builder Acquires Long Beach Tract for 2-Family Home," *New York Times* (October 17, 1948), VIII: 1, 7; "Roslyn Site Sold for Jewish Center in Brisk Dealings," *New York Times* (January 16, 1949), VIII: 1; "Provide Recreation for Housing Center," *New York Times* (May 22, 1949), VIII: 1.
118. "Glen Oak Towers to Open in January," *New York Times* (September 8, 1974): 107; Carter B. Horsley, "Big Queens Project to Open in January," *New York Times* (November 10, 1974), VIII: 8; Alan S. Oser, "About Real Estate: North Shore's Monument to Superluxury," *New York Times* (June 11, 1976): 21; Diana Shaman, "Resentment of High Rise amid Homes Is Still High," *New York Times* (August 28, 1977), VIII: 1, 6; White and Willensky, *AIA Guide* (1988), 786.
119. "Plan-Type Study Precedes Building of Large General Hospital," *Architectural Record* 117 (March 1955): 185–96; John Anderson, "The Race to Design: Hospitals," *Interiors* 114 (June 1955): 78–82.
120. Olga Gueft, "Two Anti-Institutional Institutions for the Aged and the Sick," *Interiors* 128 (March 1969): 100; "Institute for Geriatric Care Will Open on Island," *New York Times* (April 4, 1971): 88; White and Willensky, *AIA Guide* (1988), 787.
121. "A Hebrew Utopia," *New York Times* (June 7, 1905): 16.
122. "Builders Acquire Queens Golf Club for Home Center," *New York Times* (February 3, 1946), VIII: 1; "Housing Project," *Architectural Record* 100 (August 1946): 18, 134; "New Suites Open at Fresh Meadow," *New York Times* (September 2, 1947): 36; "Housing Development Opened in Queens," *New York Times* (September 3, 1947): 28; "Housing Project to Have New Store," *New York Times* (September 14, 1947): 53; "Fresh Meadow Gets Six-Acre Tree Grove," *New York Times* (November 16, 1947), VIII: 1; James Dahie, "Fresh Meadows—New York Life's Big Rental Development in the Borough of Queens, N.Y.," *American City* 63 (July 1948): 80–82; "N.Y. Life's Colony with 3,000 Suites Is 50% Completed," *New York Times* (August 29, 1948), VIII: 1; Kathryn Close, "New Homes with Insurance Dollars," *Survey Graphic* 37 (November 1948): 450–54, 487–88; Otto L. Nelson, "Fresh Meadows: An Equity Investment by a Life Insurance Company," *Journal of the American Institute of Architects* 10 (December 1948): 254–61; "First Units Open in Shopping Area Near Apartments," *New York Times* (February 13, 1949), VIII: 1, 4; "Store Is Opening in Queens Tuesday," *New York Times* (May 22, 1949): 35; Lewis Mumford, "The Sky Line: From Utopia Parkway Turn East," *New Yorker* 25 (October 22, 1949): 102–6; Lewis Mumford, "The Sky Line: The Great Good Place," *New Yorker* 25 (November 12, 1949): 73–78; "Fresh Meadows," *Architectural Record* 106 (December 1949): 85–97; "Fresh Meadows, Queens, New York City," *L'Architecture d'Aujourd'hui* 20 (September 1950): 48–51; Talbot F. Hamlin, ed., *Forms and Functions of Twentieth-Century Architecture*, vol. 3 (New York: Columbia University Press, 1952), 188, 190, 195; Voorhees, Walker, Smith, Smith & Haines, *75th Anniversary* (New York, May 1960), 39, 53; Martin Meyerson, *Face of the Metropolis* (New York: Random House, 1963), 144–47; White and Willensky, *AIA Guide* (1967), 363; Plunz, *A History of Housing in New York City*, 282–84.
123. Nelson, "Fresh Meadows: An Equity Investment by a Life Insurance Company": 254–61.
124. Stern, Gilmartin and Massengale, *New York 1900*, 427–30.
125. Stern, Gilmartin and Mellins, *New York 1930*, 42–43, 45, 48.
126. "Fresh Meadows," *Architectural Record*: 85–97.
127. Mumford, "The Sky Line: From Utopia Parkway Turn East": 102–3.
128. For Sunnyside Gardens, see Stern, Gilmartin and Mellins, *New York 1930*, 486–87, 490–92. For the Greenbelt towns, see Albert Mayer, "Greenbelt Towns Revisited," *Journal of Housing* 24 (January 1967): 12–26.
129. Mumford, "The Sky Line: From Utopia Parkway Turn East": 106.
130. "Mayor Asks Action on College in Queens," *New York Times* (February 25, 1937): 25; "Big School Center in Queens Spurred," *New York Times* (March 9, 1937): 18; "College Site Given to City in Queens," *New York Times* (April 1, 1937): 25; Stern, Gilmartin and Mellins, *New York 1930*, 114.
131. "Queens College to Build Speech and Music Center," *Architectural Record* 119 (April 1956): 394; Leonard Buder, "Queens College to Get Arts Unit," *New York Times* (April 29, 1958): 31; "Queens College Music and Arts Center," *Architectural Forum* 108 (May 1958): 38; "Queens Presents Diplomas to 590," *New York Times* (June 11, 1958): 31; "Queens Stone Laid," *New York Times* (November 11, 1959): 58; "College Center Cited on Design," *New York Times* (December 3, 1961), VIII: 6; "Buildings in the News," *Architectural Record* 131 (February 1962): 14–15; White and Willensky, *AIA Guide* (1988), 774.
132. Leonard Buder, "Special School to Rise in Queens," *New York Times* (April 10, 1963): 28; "Experimental School in New York," *Architectural Record* 134 (August 1963): 13; McCandlish Phillips, "A 'School without Walls' Is Opened in Flushing," *New York Times* (September 21, 1966): 49; Betty Raymond, "Under the Dome—P.S. 219," *Interiors* 126 (December 1966): 113–17; White and Willensky, *AIA Guide* (1988), 774.
133. Milton Bracker, "Our Changing City: Gaps in Queens Are Filling Up," *New York Times* (August 8, 1955): 23.
134. Franklin Whitehouse, "Queens Enclave Struggles to Keep Suburban Flavor," *New York Times* (July 13, 1969), VIII: 1, 4.
135. "U.N. Housing Site Set for Jamaica," *New York Times* (April 23, 1946): 3; "Parkway Village, U.N. Town, Is Near," *New York Times* (May 24, 1946): 11; "U.N. Housing," *Interiors* 105 (June 1946): 12; "U.N. Housing Inspected," *New York Times* (November 24, 1946): 5; "Investing Funds in New Housing," *New York Times* (January 26, 1947), VIII: 1–2; "Last Unit Filled at U.N. 'Village,'" *New York Times* (August 1, 1948), VIII: 1; "Unique Parkway Village," editorial, *New York Times* (August 25, 1952): 16.
136. "Architect Is Selected," *New York Times* (February 10, 1946): 44; "Queens Map Changes Adopted," *New York Times* (September 29, 1949): 38; "St. John's Plans Science Building," *New York Times* (June 26, 1953): 40; "Goal of St. John's Set at $7,100,000," *New York Times* (January 26, 1954): 25; "St. John's Campus in Queens Is Begun," *New York Times* (February 12, 1954): 18; "St. John's Opens Building," *New York Times* (September 29, 1955): 14; "St. John's Begins 86th Year Today," *New York Times* (October 2, 1955): 70; "College Building Dedicated," *New York Times* (December 8, 1955): 34; "St. John's Plans 2 New Buildings," *New York Times* (June 10, 1956): 82; "Twelve Structures in Queens Cited for Excellence in Design," *New York Times* (December 2, 1956), VIII: 1, 4; "St. John's Campus Grows in Queens," *New York Times* (November 7, 1958): 14.
137. "Buildings in the News," *Architectural Record* 148 (October 1970): 42; "Ground Broken in Queens for St. John's Law School," *New York Times* (November 22, 1970): 72; "Standing Four Square," *Progressive Architecture* 52 (April 1971): 33; "A Seven-Story Law School Is Dedicated at St. John's," *New York Times* (October 22, 1972): 83; "St.

John's University School of Law," *New York Times* (December 17, 1972), VIII: 4; White and Willensky, *AIA Guide* (1988), 773–74.

138. Glenn Singer, "Asian Studies to Be Stressed at New Center at St. John's," *New York Times* (October 10, 1971), XV: 20; Kim Lem, "St. John's Is Given Flavor of China," *New York Times* (September 30, 1973): 104; White and Willensky, *AIA Guide* (1988), 773–74.

139. "State Sets Loans for Queens Co-op," *New York Times* (February 17, 1960): 25; Thomas W. Ennis, "Housing Spurred by City and State," *New York Times* (February 21, 1960), VIII: 1, 8; Charles G. Bennett, "Jamaica Housing Meets Opposition," *New York Times* (April 14, 1960): 33, 35; "Rochdale Co-op Sets Aside Park," *New York Times* (July 17, 1960), VIII: 7; "Din of Destruction at Jamaica Replaces Thunder of Hoofbeats," *New York Times* (September 24, 1960): 25; "Hearing on Addition for Lincoln Center to Be Held June 19," *New York Times* (June 6, 1963): 40; "Co-op to Include Classroom Space," *New York Times* (November 24, 1963), VIII: 1, 6; "Rochdale Village Opens," *New York Times* (December 11, 1963): 29; Harvey Swados, "When Black and White Live Together," *New York Times* (November 13, 1966), VI: 47, 102, 104, 106, 109–10, 112, 114, 116, 119–20; Robert Moses, *Public Works: A Dangerous Trade* (New York: Macmillan, 1970), 465–69.

140. "Earthworks for Fun," *Architectural Forum* 132 (April 1970): 5; Suzanne Slesin, "High Relief," *Industrial Design* 17 (November 1970): 30–31; Richard G. Stein, "Space-Framing on the Queens Flats," *Landscape Architecture* 61 (July 1971): 304–6; Michael T. Kaufman, "Residents Avoid Prize-Winning Park," *New York Times* (January 2, 1972), XV: 11; "Buildings in the News," *Architectural Record* 151 (February 1972): 42.

141. "News Bulletins," *Progressive Architecture* 38 (April 1957): 99; Deane McGowen, "$12,930,550 Contract Let for Erection of Grandstand at Aqueduct Park," *New York Times* (January 3, 1958): 18; "$32,000,000 Track: Officials Take a Look at Aqueduct Construction," *New York Times* (June 12, 1958): 42; "Where Horseplayers Will Be Hunting Winners Next Fall: The New $34,000,000 Aqueduct Track," *New York Times* (November 23, 1958), V: 7; "A New Aqueduct," special advertising section, *New York Times* (September 6, 1959), X; Arthur Daley, "Sports of The Times: Baghdad on the Subway," *New York Times* (September 11, 1959): 33; Joseph C. Nichols, "New Aqueduct Track Is Opened; 42,473 Fans Wager $3,430,765," *New York Times* (September 15, 1959): 1, 46; Gay Talese, "Even at a New Racing Course, Every Fan Is an Old Customer," *New York Times* (September 15, 1959): 46; "Buildings in the News," *Architectural Record* 126 (October 1959): 15.

142. Daley, "Sports of The Times: Baghdad on the Subway": 33.

143. Lawrence O'Kane, "Jamaica Seeking a Better Future," *New York Times* (October 2, 1966), VIII: 1, 18; Regional Plan Association, *Regional Plan Bulletin* 108 (April 1968): 9–11, 15, 33–34; F. Carlisle Towery with Arthur Zabarkes, *Jamaica Center* (New York: Regional Plan Association, April 1968); Emanuel Perlmutter, "50,000 Jobs by '85 Seen in Jamaica Renewal Plan," *New York Times* (April 22, 1968): 1, 31; Richard Phalon, "Planners Urging 23 Urban Centers in New York Area," *New York Times* (November 18, 1968): 1, 42; David K. Shipler, "City Offers $380-Million Jamaica Plan," *New York Times* (October 25, 1969): 19; Greater Jamaica Development Corporation, *Jamaica Center* (New York, 1971); Glenn Fowler, "Jamaica Found Making Strides as a Business Center," *New York Times* (March 21, 1971): 83; Deirdre Carmody, "A Bright New 'Downtown' Is Taking Shape in Queens," *New York Times* (June 2, 1972): 39, 46; "Jamaica, Queens, Gains Title of 'All-America City,'" *New York Times* (February 28, 1972): 24; "Recognition Buoys Jamaica Leaders," *New York Times* (March 5, 1972), XV: 13; John Darnton, "Jamaica Renewal Supported," *New York Times* (May 6, 1973): 141; Barnett, *Urban Design as Public Policy*, 130–31; Barry Jacobs, "Jamaica Center: The Long Road Back," *New York Affairs* 7, no. 2 (1982): 50–58.

144. "Unitarian Church for a Tiny Site in New York City," *Architectural Forum* 111 (September 1959): 51; "Church in New York," *Architectural Forum* 120 (February 1964): 17; White and Willensky, *AIA Guide* (1978), 525.

145. "Idlewild Airport Wins Council Test," *New York Times* (December 6, 1941): 33; "New Airport Site Acquired by City," *New York Times* (December 31, 1941): 19; "$994,793 Awarded for Airport Site," *New York Times* (February 17, 1942): 29; "La Guardia Field Marks Birthday," *New York Times* (December 3, 1942): 15; "Sky Harbors," *Architectural Forum* 79 (August 1943): 50; "World's Greatest Airport to Serve Skyways of Tomorrow," *Popular Science* 143 (August 1943): 74–77; "Idlewild: Airport of Tomorrow," *Christian Science Monitor* (January 8, 1944): 6; "Airplanes, Airports Make the Great Age," *Architectural Record* 96 (December 1944): 78–83, 128; Robert Bellaire, "Battle of the Airports," *Collier's* 115 (March 31, 1945): 22–25, 63–65; "Biggest Airport in the World," *Fortune* 31 (April 1945): 142–45; "New York's Airport for World Commerce, Part I—Plan, Layout, Access, and Financing," *Engineering News-Record* 136 (January 24, 1946): 75–78.

146. Thomas Lessner, *Fiorello H. La Guardia and the Making of Modern New York* (New York: McGraw-Hill, 1989), 435.

147. "New York's Airport for World Commerce, Part 1—Plan, Layout, Access, and Financing": 75–78.

148. "An Authority for Airports," editorial, *New York Times* (January 29, 1946): 24; "The Airport Authority Offer," editorial, *New York Times* (January 13, 1947): 20; Robert A. Caro, *The Power Broker: Robert Moses and the Fall of New York* (New York: Alfred A. Knopf, 1974), 766–67.

149. "New Support Won by Port Authority," *New York Times* (January 29, 1947): 27; "Plan for New York's Airports," *Business Week* (April 26, 1947): 39–40.

150. "Two Variations on a Theme," *Architectural Record* 101 (February 1947): 22–23.

151. "The Talk of the Town: Dust Bowl," *New Yorker* 23 (July 26, 1947): 16–17; Wesley Price, "What an Airport!" *Saturday Evening Post* 220 (May 22, 1948): 20–21, 71, 74, 76, 78; "First Flight Activity Initiated at the Idlewild Airport," *New York Times* (June 2, 1948): 31; "Planners of America's Largest Port," *Architectural Record* 106 (July 1949): 84–95; "A Great Airport Opens," editorial, *New York Times* (July 2, 1948): 20; "World Airport," *New York Times* (July 2, 1948), VI: 8–9; "Hub of the World," *Time* 52 (July 12, 1948): 73; "78 Weekly Flights at Idlewild Seen," *New York Times* (July 13, 1948): 47; "East Side West Side," *Commonweal* 48 (July 16, 1948): 319; "The Talk of the Town: New Airport," *New Yorker* 24 (July 24, 1948): 19; Meyer Berger, "Late Jobs Rushed for the Dedication of Idlewild Today," *New York Times* (July 31, 1948): 1, 17; "City's Big Airport an Aerial Harbor," *New York Times* (July 31, 1948): 17; "400 Buses to Aid Air Show Visitors," *New York Times* (July 31, 1948): 17; "Vast Field Result of Years of Work," *New York Times* (July 31, 1948): 17; Meyer Berger, "Truman Dedicates Idlewild Airport; Hails It as 'Front Door' for the U.N.; 900 Planes Stage Parade of Air Might," *New York Times* (August 1, 1948): 1, 29; "Fine Air Show," editorial, *New York Times* (August 2, 1948): 20.

152. "The Record Reports," *Architectural Record* 106 (September 1949): 166; "Idlewild Airport Gets Ready for 10-Million People a Year," *Business Week* (September 10, 1949): 22–23.

153. "World's Largest Steel Arched Hangars," *Architectural Record* 107 (April 1950): 161–64.

154. "Hangar: Idlewild Airport, New York," *Progressive Architecture* 35 (June 1954): 96–98.

155. "Federal Building, New York International Airport: New York, N.Y.," *Progressive Architecture* 32 (March 1951): 67–70.

156. Carlton Bucher, "Supertower to Direct New York Air Traffic," *Popular Science* 160 (June 1952): 96–99; "Idlewild Airport Dedicates Tower," *New York Times* (September 17, 1952): 63; "All-Seeing Tower," *Time* 60 (September 22, 1952): 65.

157. Walter Prokosch, "Airport Design: Its Architectural Aspects," *Architectural Record* 109 (January 1951): 117.

158. Joseph C. Ingraham, "Vast Airport City Set for Idlewild within Five Years," *New York Times* (February 21, 1955): 1, 10; "N.Y. Air Terminal," *Engineering News-Record* 154 (February 24, 1955): 25; "Idlewild to Get New Concept in Terminals," *Aviation Week* 62 (February 28, 1955): 87–88; "Idlewild Airport Plan: Eight Separate Terminals—Parking for 6,000 Automobiles," *Architectural Forum* 102 (March 1955): 17, 21; "Idlewild: Unlimited Airport," *Architectural Forum* 102 (April 1955): 152–57; John Walter Wood, "Unlimited Airport," letter to the editor, *Architectural Forum* 102 (June 1955): 68, 72; "Terminal City Rises at Idlewild," *Business Week* (July 9, 1960): 86–90, 92.

159. "Terminal City Rises at Idlewild": 89.

160. Ingraham, "Vast Airport City Set for Idlewild within Five Years": 1. Also see Newhouse, *Wallace K. Harrison, Architect*, 240–41.

161. "Idlewild: Unlimited Airport": 152–53.

162. "Floodlighting Idlewild's Terminal City," *American City* 72 (September 1957): 141–42. Also see "Lyre Lamp Standards Featured at Idlewild," *American City* 72 (December 1957): 137, 141; "Outdoor Light," *Architectural Forum* 107 (December 1957): 149.

163. "A Big Airport's Big Future," editorial, *New York Times* (February 21, 1955): 20; Edward Hudson, "New Structures Rise at Idlewild," *New York Times* (December 6, 1955): 39.

164. "Building Today—For the Airport of Tomorrow," *Engineering News-Record* 157 (May 2, 1957): 30–34.

165. "The Talk of the Town: New and Old," *New Yorker* 33 (September 7, 1957): 24–25.

166. "New York's Idlewild Gets Some Glamor," *Business Week* (September 21, 1957): 28–30.

167. "Airport 'Terminal City,'" *Interiors* 114 (April 1955): 16; "Three New Giants," *Architectural Forum* 104 (June 1956): 124–25; "Parabolic Span in Revised Idlewild Plans," *Architectural Forum* 105 (September 1956): 16; "Modular Architecture," *Progressive Architecture* 38 (November 1957): 158–61; "Selected Detail: International Airline Wing Buildings, New York International Airport," *Progressive Architecture* 38 (November 1957): 162–63; "Gateway for Overseas Travelers," *Progressive Architecture* 38 (December 1957): 86–95; "NYIA," *Progressive Architecture* 38 (December 1957): 75–79; "A Great Air Terminal," editorial, *New York Times* (December 5, 1957): 34; "Central Heating and Refrigeration Plant," *Progressive Architecture* 38 (December 1957): 80–81; "New International Air Terminal Opens," *Engineering News-Record* 159 (December 5, 1957): 29; Harrison E. Salisbury, "Idlewild Dedicates Central Unit of Mammoth Jet-Age Terminal City," *New York Times* (December 6, 1957): 1, 18; Paul J. C. Friedlander, "Idlewild Transformed," *New York Times* (December 8, 1957), XI: 3–4; "Jet-Age Future—World Airports," *Newsweek* 50 (December 9, 1957): 83–86; "Idlewild Goes Modern," *U.S. News & World Report* 43 (December 13, 1957): 15; "New York International Airport Opens Major Buildings of Its Terminal City," *Architectural Record* 123 (January 1958): 10–11; "New Aerial Gateway to America," *Architectural Forum* 108 (February 1958): 79–87; "Aéroport International de New-York-Idlewild," *L'Architecture d'Aujourd'hui* 29 (April 1958): 2–13; Betsy Darrach, "Idlewild International Arrivals Building," *Interiors* 117 (April 1958): 108–17; "The Jet-Age Idlewild," *Fortune* 57 (June 1958): 125–28; "Airport Cities," *Time* 76 (August 15, 1960): 68–77; "New York's Idlewild—The New Look," *Vogue* 136 (October 1, 1960): 194–95, 217; Dudley Hunt, "How Idlewild Was Planned in the Jet Age," *Architectural Record* 130 (September 1961): cover, 152–56; "International Arrival and Airline Wing Buildings," *Architectural Record* 130 (September 1961): 151, 157–61; Ernst Danz, *Architecture of Skidmore, Owings & Merrill, 1950–1962*, with an intro. by Henry-Russell Hitchcock (New York: Frederick A. Praeger, 1963), 92–97; White and Willensky, *AIA Guide* (1967), 371.

168. "Airline Terminal," *Interior Design* 29 (April 1958): 146–47; Darrach, "Idlewild International Arrivals Building": 108–17.

169. Darrach, "Idlewild International Arrivals Building": 113–14.

170. Marian Page, "Architectural Angles, Abstract Patterns, and Spatial Contrasts Distinguish LAV Departure Terminal at Idlewild," *Interiors* 119 (September 1959): 144–46.

171. Darrach, "Idlewild International Arrivals Building": 117.

172. Darrach, "Idlewild International Arrivals Building": 115.

173. Darrach, "Idlewild International Arrivals Building": 116.

174. Darrach, "Idlewild International Arrivals Building": 111.

175. Barbara J. Melnick, "Restaurant," *Progressive Architecture* 40 (September 1959): 211–17.

176. "4th Jet Terminal Due for Idlewild," *New York Times* (December 3, 1957): 37; "American Plans New Idlewild Terminal," *Aviation Week* 67 (December 23, 1957): 79; "Planes and Passengers in Proximity," *Architectural Forum* 108 (January 1958): 37; "Buildings in the News," *Architectural Record* 125 (March 1959): 13; "The Talk of the Town: Idlewild Art," *New Yorker* 36 (July 2, 1960): 18–20; "American Airlines Terminal," *Interiors* 120 (September 1960): 140–47; "Sky Chef Coffee Shop, Restaurant and Cocktail Lounge at Idlewild," *Interiors* 120 (December 1960): 84–85; "American Airlines," *Architectural Record* 130 (September 1961): 170–71; "The Dazzle of Idlewild," *Life* 51 (September 22, 1961): 70–71, 74–76; Ada Louise Huxtable, "Idlewild: Distressing Monument to Air Age," *New York Times* (November 25, 1962), II: 25; White and Willensky, *AIA Guide* (1967), 372.

177. "Saucer Terminal," *Time* 69 (April 15, 1957): 105; George L. Christian, "Pan Am Plans 'Umbrella' Terminal," *Aviation Week* 66 (April 22, 1957): 117–19; "Pan-Am to Build Radial Air Terminal," *Progressive Architecture* 38 (May 1957): 101; "Umbrella for a Terminal," *Progressive Architecture* 38 (December 1957): 82–85; "New York International Airport Opens Major Buildings of Its 'Terminal City,'" *Architectural Record* 123

(January 1958): 10–11; "Aéroport de New York—Pavillion de la Pan Am Airways," *L'Architecture d'Aujourd'hui* 29 (April 1958): 8–9; "Umbrella for Airplanes," *Time* 75 (June 13, 1960): 103; "Pan American's New Terminal in New York Puts Umbrella Over Planes," *Architectural Forum* 113 (July 1960): 5; "New York's Idlewild—The New Look": 194–95, 217; George Horne, "Airlines' Modern Buildings Ease Tie-Ups and Attract Business," *New York Times* (November 13, 1960), X: 17; "Pan Am Terminal Cited in Queens," *New York Times* (December 4, 1960), VIII: 1, 9; "Pan American World Airways," *Architectural Record* 130 (September 1961): 165–67; "The Dazzle of Idlewild": 70–71, 74–76; Huxtable, "Idlewild: Distressing Monument to Air Age": 25; White and Willensky, *AIA Guide* (1967), 370–71.

178. "Pan American World Airways," *Architectural Record*: 165.

179. "Pan American Starts Giant Jet Terminal," *Aviation Week* 89 (November 20, 1968): 40–42; Charles K. Hoyt, "Big Expansion for a Little Site," *Architectural Record* 160 (October 1976): 132–33, 136.

180. "United Airlines," *Architectural Record* 130 (September 1961): 172–74; Huxtable, "Idlewild: Distressing Monument to Air Age": 25; Danz, *Architecture of Skidmore, Owings & Merrill, 1950–1962*, 99–101; White and Willensky, *AIA Guide* (1967), 372.

181. Huxtable, "Idlewild: Distressing Monument to Air Age": 25. Also see "Architectural Bulletins," *Progressive Architecture* 40 (May 1959): 93; Albert F. Kerss, "Why Colossi?" letter to the editor, *Architectural Forum* 112 (February 1960): 220; "Eastern Airlines," *Architectural Record* 130 (September 1961): 175–77; White and Willensky, *AIA Guide* (1967), 371.

182. "BOAC Plans $19.6 Million JFK Terminal," *Aviation Week* 82 (April 5, 1965): 43; "Air Terminals Planned," *Architectural Record* 137 (May 1965): 14; "BOAC to Build Terminal at Kennedy International Airport," *Progressive Architecture* 46 (May 1965): 55, 57; William B. Foxhall, "BOAC's New York Terminal," *Architectural Record* 148 (August 1970): 126–27; "BOAC Bridgehead," *Architects' Journal* 152 (August 12, 1970): 336–38; "British Air Terminal," *Architectural Forum* 133 (September 1970): 6; Michael Manser, "BOAC's Stake at Kennedy," *Architect & Building News* 7 (October 1, 1970): 33–35; "Aérogare de la B.O.A.C.," *Techniques & Architecture* 32 (December 1970–January 1971): 79; "BOAC Terminal," *L'Architecture d'Aujourd'hui* 56 (June 1971): 80–83; White and Willensky, *AIA Guide* (1978), 527.

183. Edward F. Ward quoted in "BOAC to Build Terminal at Kennedy International Airport": 57.

184. Glenn Garrison, "TWA Picks Futuristic Terminal Design," *Aviation Week* 67 (November 18, 1957): 40; "Jet-Age Umbrella," *Architectural Forum* 107 (December 1957): 37; "Saarinen Designs Terminal for TWA," *Progressive Architecture* 38 (December 1957): 66–67; "TWA's Graceful New Terminal," *Architectural Forum* 108 (January 1958): 78–85; "New York International Airport Opens Major Buildings of its 'Terminal City'": 10–11; "Aéroport International de New-York-Idlewild. Bâtiment de la TWA," *L'Architecture d'Aujourd'hui* 29 (April 1958): 10–13; Philip Johnson, "Retreat from the International Style to the Present Scene," lecture delivered at Yale University, May 9, 1958, in Peter Eisenman and Robert A. M. Stern, eds., *Philip Johnson: Writings* (New York: Oxford University Press, 1979), 95–96; Thomas B. Hess, "A Bevy of Buildings," *Art News* 57 (October 1958): 25, 58–59; McCallum, *Architecture USA*, 150–51; Arthur Drexler and Wilder Green, "Architecture and Imagery: Four New Buildings," *Museum of Modern Art Bulletin* 26, no. 2 (1959): 1, 17–18, 20–21; "Architecture and Imagery: Trend Toward 'Functional' Expression Theme of Exhibit," *Architectural Record* 125 (February 1959): 20; "Architectural Bulletins," *Progressive Architecture* 40 (February 1959): 78; "A New Architecture?" *Interiors* 118 (March 1959): 10; Benedikt Huber, "Projekt für den TWA Terminal in Idlewild, New York," *Werk* 47 (February 1960): 53–54; "Shaping a Two-Acre Sculpture," *Architectural Forum* 113 (August 1960): 118–23; "New York's Idlewild—The New Look": 194–95, 217; "The Concrete Bird Stands Free," *Architectural Forum* 113 (December 1960): 114–15; "Saarinen," *Perspecta* 7 (1961): 29–32; Sybil Moholy-Nagy, "The Future of the Past," *Perspecta* 7 (1961): 60–76; Edgar Kaufmann, Jr., "Inside Eero Saarinen's TWA Building," *Interiors* 121 (July 1961): 86–93; "A Great Architect's Memorial," *Life* 51 (September 22, 1961): 80; Douglas Haskell, "Unrecognized Architects," editorial, *Architectural Forum* 115 (November 1961): 236; "Aérogare de la TWA à l'Aéroport de New York Idlewild," *L'Architecture d'Aujourd'hui* 32 (December 1961): 24–25; Reyner Banham, *Age of the Masters* (New York: Harper & Row, 1962), 122–25; Aline B. Saarinen, ed., *Eero Saarinen on His Work* (New Haven, Conn.: Yale University Press, 1962), 60–67, rev. ed. (1968), 68–75; Allan Temko, *Eero Saarinen* (New York: George Braziller, 1962), 44–48, 92–102; Henry-Russell Hitchcock, "American Architecture in the Early Sixties," *Zodiac* 10 (1962): 5–17; "Progress Reports: TWA and Dulles," *Progressive Architecture* 43 (March 1962): 74; "Javits Asks More to Lure Tourists," *New York Times* (May 29, 1962): 61; "Saarinen's TWA Terminal: An Experience in Space," *Architectural Forum* 117 (July 1962): 72–79; "Saarinen's TWA Flight Center," *Architectural Record* 132 (July 1962): 129–34; "Banchonik," *Werk* 48 (August 1962): 170; Frank Stanton, letter to the editor, *Architectural Forum* 117 (September 1962): 19; Newton D. Angier, letter to the editor, *Architectural Forum* 117 (September 1962): 19; "One Family of Forms," *Progressive Architecture* 43 (October 1962): 158–65; Remmert W. Huygens, "Coventry and TWA," letter to the editor, *Architectural Forum* 117 (November 1962): 19; Olga Gueft, "A Problem in Adaptation at Saarinen's TWA Terminal," *Interiors* 122 (November 1962): 128–33; Huxtable, "Idlewild: Distressing Monument to Air Age": 25; "TWA Terminal Gets First Award of Concrete Industry Board," *Architectural Record* 132 (December 1962): 12–13; Edmond J. Bartnett, "Queens Chamber Cites Air Center," *New York Times* (December 2, 1962), VIII: 1, 4; Aline B. Saarinen, "TWA Ambiguity," letter to the editor, *Interiors* 122 (February 1963): 12; Mrs. Albert C. Brevetti, "Saarinen Defender Protests," letter to the editor, *Interiors* 122 (March 1963): 8; Thomas Johnson, "Student Reacts to Flaps," letter to the editor, *Interiors* 122 (March 1963): 8; Wolf Von Eckardt, "Father and Son," *New Republic* 150 (February 15, 1964): 32–34; John Jacobus, *Twentieth-Century Architecture: The Middle Years 1940–65* (New York: Frederick A. Praeger, 1966), 159–61; "Verifica di una struttura di Saarinen," *Casabella* 303 (March 1966): 34–39; White and Willensky, *AIA Guide* (1967), 370–71; Vincent Scully, *American Architecture and Urbanism* (New York: Frederick A. Praeger, 1969), 198, fig. 421; John Morris Dixon, "Inside Architecture," editorial, *Progressive Architecture* 54 (November 1973): 83; Barclay F. Gordon, "Record Interiors of 1971," *Architectural Record* 149 (January 1971): 85–87; "Le Monde Restaurant," *Interior Design* 42 (April 1971): 134–37; Barbara Allen Guilfoyle, "Sparkle Plenty," *Industrial Design* 18 (November 1971): 32–33; Manfredo Tafuri and Francesco Dal Co, *Modern Architecture*, trans. Robert Erich Wolf (New York: Harry N. Abrams, 1979), 378, fig. 612; Peter Papademetriou, "Coming of Age: Eero Saarinen and Modern Architecture," *Perspecta* 21 (1984): 116–43; Paul Goldberger, "The Statue of Liberty: Transcending the Trivial," *New York Times* (July 17, 1986), C: 18; Thomas Fisher, "Landmarks: TWA Terminal," *Progressive Architecture* 73 (May 1992): cover, 96–101; "TWA's Influence," interview of Peter

Papademetriou by Thomas Fisher, *Progressive Architecture* 73 (May 1992): 102–4; Christopher Hart Leubkeman, "Form Swallows Function," *Progressive Architecture* 73 (May 1992): 105–9.

185. Jacobus, *Twentieth-Century Architecture: The Middle Years 1940–65*, 160.

186. Eero Saarinen quoted in "Saarinen's TWA Flight Center": 129.

187. Eero Saarinen quoted in "Saarinen's TWA Flight Center": 133.

188. "TWA's Graceful New Terminal": 79.

189. "TWA's Graceful New Terminal": 79.

190. Eero Saarinen quoted in "TWA's Graceful New Terminal": 84.

191. "Shaping a Two-Acre Sculpture": 119.

192. Eero Saarinen quoted in Saarinen, ed., *Eero Saarinen on His Work*, 60.

193. "Saarinen's TWA Terminal: An Experience in Space": 72.

194. Huygens, "Coventry and TWA": 19.

195. Scully, *American Architecture and Urbanism*, 198.

196. Kaufmann, "Inside Eero Saarinen's TWA Building": 86.

197. Kaufmann, "Inside Eero Saarinen's TWA Building": 87.

198. Eero Saarinen quoted in "Saarinen's TWA Flight Center": 129.

199. Gueft, "A Problem in Adaptation at Saarinen's TWA Terminal": 129.

200. Dixon, "Inside Architecture": 83.

201. "Three-Airline Terminal at Idlewild Airport," *Progressive Architecture* 42 (May 1961): 54; "Northwest, Northeast, Braniff," *Architectural Record* 130 (September 1961): 178–79; Huxtable, "Idlewild: Distressing Monument to Air Age": 25; White and Willensky, *AIA Guide* (1967), 371.

202. Huxtable, "Idlewild: Distressing Monument to Air Age": 25.

203. "Competitions for Idlewild, Century 21," *Progressive Architecture* 41 (August 1960): 64; "Simplicity Picked for Air Terminal," *New York Times* (August 19, 1960): 47; "Buildings in the News," *Architectural Record* 140 (September 1960): 40–43; "Pei Wins Competition for Design of Idlewild Terminal," *Architectural Record* 128 (October 1960): 12–13; "I. M. Pei Wins Idlewild Terminal Competition," *Progressive Architecture* 41 (October 1960): 72–73; "Idlewild Multi-Airline Terminal," *Journal of the American Institute of Architects* 35 (May 1961): 82–83; "Pei's Terminal to Proceed," *Progressive Architecture* 45 (September 1964): 98; White and Willensky, *AIA Guide* (1967), 371; "Buildings in the News," *Architectural Record* 147 (January 1970): 41; "Airlines Race to Build Terminals," *Engineering News-Record* 184 (March 26, 1970): 24–25; "Pavilion at Kennedy," *Architectural Forum* 135 (October 1971): 18–25; Ada Louise Huxtable, "Two Buildings Win Design Awards," *New York Times* (May 19, 1972): 18; "Buildings in the News," *Architectural Record* 152 (August 1972): 45; White and Willensky, *AIA Guide* (1978), 527; Carter Wiseman, *I. M. Pei: A Profile in American Architecture* (New York: Harry N. Abrams, 1990), 94, 307.

204. Quoted in "Pei Wins Competition for Design of Idlewild Terminal": 12.

205. I. M. Pei quoted in "Pavilion at Kennedy": 22.

206. "Idlewild Chapels Set," *New York Times* (May 17, 1960): 60; "Lagoon Site Set for Idlewild Chapels," *Progressive Architecture* 41 (July 1960): 56.

207. "Model of Chapel of Our Lady of the Skies," *Liturgical Arts* 22 (February 1954): 59; "Chapel at Idlewild Is Dedicated," *New York Times* (October 30, 1955): 50.

208. "Airfield Chapel Designed for New York's Idlewild," *Progressive Architecture* 40 (March 1959): 156; "Buildings in the News," *Architectural Record* 125 (April 1959): 12.

209. "Protestants Map Idlewild Chapel," *New York Times* (February 18, 1959): 60; "Dispute Delaying Idlewild Chapels," *New York Times* (September 10, 1961): 3; "New York Port Authority Hits Snag in Chapel Design," *Architectural Forum* 115 (October 1961): 8; "Design Is Approved for Chapel Complex at Idlewild," *New York Times* (March 14, 1962): 30; "Plans Discussed for Protestant Chapel at Idlewild," *New York Times* (April 11, 1962): 22. For Sole's chapel, see George Dugan, "Catholics Dedicate New Chapel at Kennedy Amid Biting Winds," *New York Times* (November 7, 1966): 47. For Bloch & Hesse's synagogue, see "Board of Rabbis Will Build Synagogue at Idlewild," *New York Times* (April 21, 1959): 39; "Idlewild Will Get a Jewish Museum," *New York Times* (November 26, 1959): 38; "Idlewild Synagogue to Rise in June," *New York Times* (April 29, 1962): 114; Irving Spiegel, "3 Faiths Join in Dedicating Airport Synagogue," *New York Times* (September 11, 1967): 45.

210. "Tri-Faith Ground Breaking Held for 3 Chapels at Idlewild Airport," *New York Times* (June 24, 1963): 55; John Cogley, "Airport Chapels," *New York Times* (October 16, 1966), X: 1, 21; White and Willensky, *AIA Guide* (1967), 371; Dr. W. Schweisheuner, "Airport Chapels," *Architect & Builder* 17 (March 1967): 31.

211. "Bill Tabler's Hotel Boom," *Architectural Forum* 107 (July 1957): 115–21. Also see "Airport Hotel," *Architectural Forum* 105 (July 1956): 16; "Idlewild Hotel Opens," *Architectural Forum* 105 (June 1958): 9; "Hotels and Motels," *Interior Design* 29 (October 1958): 126–28; "Earth-borne Comforts for Airborne Travelers: The International Hotel Near Idlewild," *Interiors* 118 (November 1958): 94–99.

212. "Airport Hotel," *Architectural Forum* 117 (December 1962): 49.

213. "Stone Designs Idlewild Gas Station," *Architectural Forum* 112 (February 1960): 6; "Buildings in the News," *Architectural Record* 127 (February 1960): 10; "Auxiliary Buildings," *Architectural Record* 130 (September 1961): 190; White and Willensky, *AIA Guide* (1967), 372.

214. Huxtable, "Idlewild: Distressing Monument to Air Age": 25.

215. "Auxiliary Buildings": 190; Danz, *Architecture of Skidmore, Owings & Merrill, 1950–1962*, 122–23.

216. Huxtable, "Idlewild: Distressing Monument to Air Age": 25. Also see Robert A. Frosch, "Idlewild," letter to the editor, *New York Times* (December 9, 1962), II: 17, with Huxtable's reply.

217. Philip Benjamin, "Idlewild Is Rededicated as John F. Kennedy Airport," *New York Times* (December 25, 1963): 1, 54.

218. "No Way Out, No Way Back," *Time* 93 (February 21, 1969): 47. Also see Emerson Goble, "Perspectives," *Architectural Record* 140 (December 1966): 10; "Can Airports Cope with the Jet Age?" *Business Week* (July 22, 1967): 54–57, 61–65, 68, 73; William E. Barrows, "Time Runs Out at JFK," *New York* 1 (July 29, 1968): 14–21.

219. William E. Barrows, "Are We Ready for Jumbo?" *New York* 2 (March 10, 1969): 28–32.

220. George Horne, "Kennedy Grows Despite Talk of 4th Jetport," *New York Times* (June 4, 1967): 88; "T.W.A. Terminal for Jumbo Jets Near Completion," *New York Times* (December 15, 1968), V: 24; "Air Terminal Expansion for the Second Jet Revolution," *Progressive Architecture* 50 (January 1969): 43; Edward Hudson, "Mishap on T.W.A. 747 Inaugural: Film Projector Fails," *New York Times* (February 26, 1970): 78; Edward Hudson, "T.W.A. Dedicates Huge Terminal at Kennedy," *New York Times* (March 20, 1970): 93.

221. "Architect Proposes Updating of Airport Runways," *Progressive Architecture* 41 (June 1960): 3; "Proposed Runways for Idlewild," *Aero News* (April 14, 1961): 19.
222. "One Airport in Place of Four," *Progressive Architecture* 50 (September 1969): 104–7; "Ocean Airport, New York," *L'Architecture d'Aujourd'hui* 156 (June 1971): 89.
223. David A. Brown, "New York Airport Developments Keyed to Political Scene," *Aviation Week* 91 (October 20, 1969): 118–20, 122, 127, 129.
224. Jamaica Bay Environmental Study Group, *Jamaica Bay and Kennedy Airport: A Multidisciplinary Environmental Study* (Washington, D.C.: National Academy of Sciences; Washington, D.C.: National Academy of Engineering, 1971). Also see Dorn C. McGrath, Jr., "Multidisciplinary Environmental Analysis: Jamaica Bay and Kennedy Airport," *Journal of the American Institute of Planners* 37 (July 1971): 243–52.
225. "New Jersey Protests Plans for Giant Jet-Age Airport," *Architectural Forum* 112 (January 1960): 10; "New York Authorities Suffer Two Setbacks," *Architectural Forum* 112 (February 1960): 6; "Airline Revolt Looms in New York City," *Engineering News-Record* 173 (November 12, 1964): 56; Jeffrey M. Zupan, "Do We Need Another Airport?" *New York Affairs* 1, no. 2 (1973): 4–19.
226. "70 Miles from Town?" *Newsweek* 69 (March 27, 1967): 84; "Fourth Jetport in New York Is Proposed for Existing Airport," *Engineering News-Record* 190 (May 3, 1973): 12–13.
227. "Air Mail Will Use Newark Port Today," *New York Times* (February 17, 1929): 9; "New 'Air Pattern' on Nov. 1 to Re-allocate Traffic Here," *New York Times* (October 23, 1947): 1, 21; "Good Air News," editorial, *New York Times* (October 24, 1947): 22.
228. "New Terminal Set for Newark Field," *New York Times* (September 15, 1950): 27; "New Terminal Under Way for Newark Airport," *Architectural Record* 112 (November 1952): 26, 342; "Terminal Building Space," *Progressive Architecture* 54 (May 1953): 76–77.
229. "Airliner Carrying 62 Crashes in Elizabeth; 20 Survive Third Wreck There in 2 Months; 5 Die in Apartments; Newark Airport Closed," *New York Times* (February 11, 1952): 1, 7; "Near-Airport Land Values Unaffected by N.Y. Crashes as Homes Encircle Runways," *Architectural Forum* 96 (April 1952): 51, 53; "Newark Field Due to Reopen Nov. 1 If New Runway Is Completed Then," *New York Times* (May 11, 1952): 1, 54; Joseph C. Ingraham, "Air Terminal Set to Open in Newark," *New York Times* (April 22, 1953): 31; Bliss K. Thorne, "Newark Opens Luxurious Terminal," *New York Times* (July 26, 1953), II: 13; Bliss K. Thorne, "New Air Terminal Opened in Newark," *New York Times* (July 30, 1953): 45.
230. "Mid-Airport Control Tower," *Architectural Forum* 106 (May 1957): 41; "Control Tower Opened at Newark," *New York Times* (January 19, 1960): 29.
231. "New Jet-Age Terminal Planned for Newark," *Progressive Architecture* 46 (January 1965): 45; "Terminal Expansion," *Progressive Architecture* 48 (November 1967): 64; "Newark Airport Redevelopment Program Combines Layered Operation with Close-Coupled Parking," *Architectural Record* 144 (August 1968): 142–44; "Engineers Develop Lighting Design from Model Tests," *Architectural Record* 147 (February 1970): 147–52; "Newark: Where a Sophisticated Owner Mustered Talent from All Sources," *Architectural Record* 156 (November 1974): 138–41.
232. See Stern, Gilmartin and Massengale, *New York 1900*, 426.
233. Stern, Gilmartin and Mellins, *New York 1930*, 688–89.
234. "Rockaways Demand Long Island Action," *New York Times* (May 17, 1950): 38; Charles G. Bennett, "$134,500,000 Asked for Queens Transit," *New York Times* (June 22, 1950): 1, 20; "Subway Is Adding 2 Islands to City," *New York Times* (June 30, 1955): 27; "Subway Line Goes to Sea," *Engineering News-Record* 155 (August 11, 1955): 44–45, 48, 51; "Rockaway Line to Open on Time," *New York Times* (February 10, 1956): 13; Ralph Katz, "Rockaways Fare Set at 40 Cents in Revival of Transit Zone Rates," *New York Times* (February 17, 1956): 1, 8; Ralph Katz, "Rockaway Fare Reduced to 30C," *New York Times* (March 30, 1956): 1, 9; Ira Henry Freeman, "Free Ride Opens Rockaways Line," *New York Times* (June 29, 1956): 23; "A New Transit Frontier," editorial, *New York Times* (June 29, 1956): 20; Meyer Berger, "About New York," *New York Times* (July 4, 1950): 16; Fischler, *Uptown, Downtown*, 168–72.
235. Stern, Gilmartin and Mellins, *New York 1930*, 722–23.
236. "Veteran Project Set for Sept. 14," *New York Times* (September 5, 1948): 14; "Rents Cut in City Projects," *New York Times* (May 2, 1950): 21; "No Green Light for Tenants," *New York Times* (January 30, 1951): 19.
237. "New Master Plan on Housing Held Up," *New York Times* (October 20, 1949): 31; Charles G. Bennett, "Commission Votes Housing Program," *New York Times* (November 3, 1949): 32; "Way Now Cleared for 3 Housing Units," *New York Times* (March 10, 1950): 17; "2 Housing Projects Are Begun in Queens," *New York Times* (July 28, 1951): 12; "Redfern Houses Open," *New York Times* (September 17, 1952): 33.
238. "Rockaways to Get 1,656-Unit Housing," *New York Times* (June 7, 1950): 51; "Far Rockaway Housing for 1,656 Families Will Receive Its First Tenants This Week," *New York Times* (August 12, 1951), VIII: 1, 6; "Housing Gets Stores," *New York Times* (July 6, 1952), VIII: 2; "Ocean-Front Apartment Project in Queens," advertisement, *Architectural Record* 112 (August 1952): 317.
239. "News of the Realty Trade: Big Firms Open on Broadway," *New York Times* (August 3, 1969), VIII: 6; White and Willensky, *AIA Guide* (1978), 530.
240. Joseph P. Fried, "Rockaways Hearing Set for Tomorrow," *New York Times* (October 26, 1975): 110; Joseph P. Fried, "Hearings Focus on Rockaway," *New York Times* (November 2, 1975): 131; White and Willensky, *AIA Guide* (1988), 795.
241. John Margolies, "New Projects by Victor Lundy," *Architectural Forum* 131 (November 1969): 78–85; "Queens School," *New York Times* (July 24, 1970): 28; White and Willensky, *AIA Guide* (1978), 530.
242. "Breezy Point Offer Made by Colonists," *New York Times* (August 17, 1960): 49; Maurice Foley, "2,650 Queens Tenants Purchase Land Under Houses They Own," *New York Times* (November 18, 1960): 20; "$12 Million Sale at Rockaway Point Is Closed," *Real Estate Record and Guide* 186 (December 17, 1960): 2; "Breezy Point Acquired," *New York Times* (January 6, 1961): 44. For Sea Gate, see Stern, Gilmartin and Massengale, *New York 1900*, 421–22.
243. Charles G. Bennett, "Site in Rockaway Is Urged as Park," *New York Times* (August 15, 1962): 33, 36; "A Last-Hour Park Battle," editorial, *New York Times* (September 18, 1962): 38; E. Funck, "Against Breezy Point Plan," letter to the editor, *New York Times* (September 25, 1962): 36; Martin Arnold, "Mayor Gives Hope for Breezy Point," *New York Times* (October 5, 1962): 35–36; Martin Arnold, "City Board Split by Breezy Point," *New York Times* (November 12, 1962): 31, 59; Committee for a Park at Breezy Point, *Breezy Point Park* (New York, 1963); "Rockefeller Undermines Plans for 'Poor Man's Beach,'" *Village Voice* 8 (January 24, 1963): 1–2; Sydney H. Schanberg, "Proposed Park at Breezy Point Hotly Supported and Derided," *New York Times* (April 20, 1963): 55; Leonard Ingalls, "Wagner Decides to Build a Park at Breezy Point," *New York Times* (June 3, 1963): 1, 21; "Breezy Point Park: Major Decision for Planners and Public," *Housing and Planning News* 21 (summer 1963): 1–4; Philip Benjamin, "On Breezy Point: A Dispute Ripens," *New York Times* (September 16, 1963): 37, 41; Clayton Knowles, "344 Acres Taken for Breezy Point," *New York Times* (September 3, 1964): 31; Will Lissner, "Stark Urges that U.S. Develop Breezy Point Park," *New York Times* (March 7, 1966): 18.
244. Richard L. Madden, "National Park Urged for Harbor," *New York Times* (December 12, 1969): 1, 48; Douglas Robinson, "Gateway Still Just an Idea," *New York Times* (April 14, 1970): 49; "Moses, the Park Builder, Opposes Gateway Recreation Project," *New York Times* (May 23, 1971): 33; Alan S. Oser, "Issue of Award for Breezy Point Revived by Court," *New York Times* (June 20, 1971), VIII: 1, 6; "Two Unique Close-to-the-City National Parks Underway . . . and a Private Park Planned," *Architectural Record* 150 (July 1971): 35.
245. Les Ledbetter, "Breezy Point Awaits Action on Park," *New York Times* (October 1, 1972): 128; Richard L. Madden, "Four-Year Gateway Effort Ends as Nixon Signs the Bill into Law," *New York Times* (October 29, 1972): 29; Laurie Johnston, "Beach Clubs Fear Gateway Park Means End of Haven," *New York Times* (September 3, 1973): 17; Glenn R. Singer, "Towers May Be Used by Park," *New York Times* (October 7, 1973): 130; "Fort Tilden Preparing for Closing," *New York Times* (February 10, 1974): 93; Peter Kihss, "Work on Gateway Project Awaits Final Legal Approval," *New York Times* (May 30, 1976): 36; Frank J. Prial, "$300 Million Development Plan Disclosed for Gateway Park Area," *New York Times* (September 23, 1976): 45.

Chapter 14
1964–65 New York World's Fair

1. Ogden Nash, "The Promised Land of Mr. Moses," *New York Times* (April 19, 1964), VI, part 2: 30.
2. For a discussion of the 1939–40 New York World's Fair, see Stern, Gilmartin and Mellins, *New York 1930*, 726–55. Also see Martin B. Vinokur, "'The World of Tomorrow' or 'Peace through Understanding'?: A Comparison of the Impact of the 1939–1940 and 1964–1965 New York World's Fairs on New York City" (Master's thesis, Columbia University, 1966).
3. For a profile of Thomas Deegan, Jr., see "He Thumps the Tub for the Fair," *Business Week* (January 25, 1964): 120–22, 126.
4. Edmund Bacon, "P/A at the New York World's Fair," letter to the editor, *Progressive Architecture* 45 (December 1964): 28.
5. Martin Mayer, "Ho Hum, Come to the Fair," *Esquire* 60 (October 1963): 117, 124, 179–83.
6. "L'Esposizione Mondiale 1964 negli Stati Uniti: New York Batte Washington," *L'Architettura cronache e storia* 5 (March 1960): 728.
7. Ira Henry Freeman, "World's Fair Planned Here in '64 at Half Billion Cost," *New York Times* (August 10, 1959): 1, 19; "Plans for 1964 World's Fair," *Architectural Record* 126 (September 1959): 25. A proposal was made by the Los Angeles realtor and industrialist J. A. Smith on behalf of his city, but it lacked official backing and was in fact opposed by the Los Angeles Chamber of Commerce. See "How New York Won the World's Fair," *Business Week* (November 7, 1959): 70, 72.
8. "Nations Invited to Participate in 1964 New York World's Fair," *Department of State Bulletin* 42 (February 15, 1960): 244–45.
9. "Anyone for $100,000?" *Newsweek* (December 28, 1959): 54; "Personalities," *Progressive Architecture* 41 (April 1960): 83. Among the fair corporation's published documents were Robert Moses, *Implications of the New York World's Fair, Remarks to Students at Brandeis University, Waltham, Massachusetts, March 23, 1961* (New York: New York World's Fair 1964–1965 Corporation, 1961); *The Economic Benefits of the New York World's Fair 1964–65* (New York: New York World's Fair 1964–1965 Corporation, 1961); *Fair News: Official Bulletin of the New York World's Fair 1964–1965* (New York: New York World's Fair 1964–1965 Corporation, 1962); Robert Moses, *The Anatomy of a Fair: Remarks of Robert Moses, President of New York World's Fair 1964–1965, at the Yale University School of Art and Architecture, March 13, 1963* (New York: New York World's Fair 1964–1965 Corporation, 1963); Robert Moses, *Remarks of Robert Moses at the Dedication of the Press Building, Flushing Meadows, May 4, 1963* (New York: New York World's Fair 1964–1965 Corporation, 1963); *Interim Report* (New York: New York World's Fair 1964–1965 Corporation, 1963); *The Fair, the City and the Critics: Remarks of Robert Moses, October 13, 1964* (New York: New York World's Fair 1964–1965 Corporation, 1964); *The Fair in 1965* (New York: New York World's Fair 1964–1965 Corporation, 1965).
10. John Skow, "Who Needs the World's Fair?" *Saturday Evening Post* 237 (May 23, 1964): 12, 14; Robert Moses, *Public Works: A Dangerous Trade* (New York: McGraw-Hill, 1970), 535–638; Robert A. Caro, *The Power Broker: Robert Moses and the Fall of New York* (New York: Alfred A. Knopf, 1974), 1082–114; Marc H. Miller, "Something for Everyone: Robert Moses and the Fair," in *Remembering the Future: The New York World's Fair from 1939 to 1964* (New York: Queens Museum; New York: Rizzoli International Publications, 1989), 44–73.
11. Mary Perot Nichols, "Private Opinion: The World's Fair: A Garden of Apples," *Village Voice* 8 (October 17, 1963): 1, 6–7.
12. Douglas Haskell quoted in Nichols, "Private Opinion: The World's Fair: A Garden of Apples": 1.
13. "Personalities": 83.
14. Robert Moses quoted in "Moses Dismisses Criticism of Fair," *New York Times* (September 11, 1963): 88. Also see "1964: Who'll Be Away at the Fair?" *Newsweek* 57 (February 27, 1961): 73; "Moses Builds a Fair," *Architectural Forum* 120 (January 1964): 64–75; "World's Fair '64: A Preview," *Newsweek* 63 (January 13, 1964): 43–47; Caro, *The Power Broker*, 1094.
15. "Fair and Festival Designers," *Architectural Forum* 112 (May 1960): 14–15; Victoria Newhouse, *Wallace K. Harrison, Architect* (New York: Rizzoli International Publications, 1989), 236–37.
16. "Again a Trylon and Perisphere?" *Architectural Forum* 112 (February 1960): 91; "World's Fair—Return to 1939?" *Progressive Architecture* 41 (June 1960): 66; "Chief of Design Discusses Fair," *Progressive Architecture* 41 (September 1960): 56. For a detailed isometric drawing of the fairgrounds, see "Preview: *Look*'s Map of the New York World's Fair," *Look* 28 (February 11, 1964): 84–85.

17. "The World of Already," *Time* 83 (June 5, 1964): cover, 40–52.
18. Gordon Bunshaft quoted in Edith Evans Asbury, "Designers Quit Fair in a Dispute on Plan," *New York Times* (December 5, 1960): 1, 21. Also see "1939 Plan for 1964 Fair? Design Board Schemes Rejected," *Architectural Record* 129 (January 1961): 23.
19. "The Arrested Development of the New York Fair," editorial, *Architectural Forum* 113 (December 1960): 63. Also see James J. Montalto, G. W. Tuttle and Daniel M. Saunders, "Fantasies in Flushing," letters to the editor, *Architectural Forum* 116 (January 1962): 16; Philip Johnson, "The Seven Shibboleths of Our Profession," speech, Eleventh Annual Northeast Regional American Institute of Architects Conference, Oceanlake, Oregon, October 12, 1962, in Peter Eisenman and Robert A. M. Stern, eds., *Philip Johnson: Writings* (New York: Oxford University Press, 1979), 142–49.
20. George Nelson, "New York World's Fair—A Fiasco?" *Art in America* 50 (fall 1962): 32.
21. "Where Was Moses When the Lights Went On? (World's Fair Frolics, Cont'd.)," *Progressive Architecture* 42 (June 1961): 82. Also see Thomas H. Creighton, "The New York World's Fair," editorial, *Progressive Architecture* 42 (July 1961): 206.
22. Moses, *Implications of the New York World's Fair, Remarks to Students at Brandeis University, Waltham, Massachusetts, March 23, 1961*, unpaginated.
23. Robert Moses quoted in "Where Was Moses When the Lights Went On? (World's Fair Frolics, Cont'd.)": 82. Also see "Fairs Start Beating Their Drums," *Business Week* (April 22, 1961): 92–96, 98.
24. Robert Moses quoted in Wolf Von Eckardt, "As the Hucksters See Us," *New Republic* 150 (May 30, 1964): 14–16. Also see W. Bernard Richland, "Correspondence: The Fair," *New Republic* 150 (June 20, 1964): 29–30; Wolf Von Eckardt, *A Place to Live: The Crisis of the Cities* (New York: Delacorte Press, 1967), 219–23.
25. Robert Moses quoted on title page, *Progressive Architecture* 49 (June 1967): 123.
26. Vincent Scully, Jr., "If This Is Architecture, God Help Us," *Life* 57 (July 31, 1964): 9.
27. Mayer, "Ho Hum, Come to the Fair": 183.
28. Von Eckardt, "As the Hucksters See Us": 14.
29. Robert Hughes, "The Golden Grin," *Nation* 199 (October 5, 1964): 189–91.
30. Nelson, "New York World's Fair—A Fiasco?": 32.
31. Bruce Bliven, "To Make It the Fairest of the Fairs," *New York Times* (November 1, 1959), VI: 16–17, 92–93.
32. Martin Stone quoted in Mayer, "Ho Hum, Come to the Fair": 183.
33. "World's Fair Opens Today," *New York Times* (April 22, 1964): 1, 21; "Fair Opens, Rights Stall-In Fails: Protestors Drown Out Johnson: 300 Arrested in Demonstrations," *New York Times* (April 23, 1964): 1, 26; Stephanie Gervis Harrington, "Official CORE Makes Its Point," *Village Voice* 9 (April 30, 1964): 1, 9; Mary Perot Nichols, "It Was Wet, but Was It Worth It?" *Village Voice* 9 (April 30, 1964): 1, 9; "The Talk of the Town: The Fair," *New Yorker* 40 (May 2, 1964): 35–39; Morris Dickstein, "From the Thirties to the Sixties: The New York World's Fair in Its Own Time," in *Remembering the Future*, 32–34.
34. James Farmer quoted in Harrington, "Official CORE Makes Its Point": 1.
35. "The Talk of the Town: Promises," *New Yorker* 37 (May 6, 1961): 34–35; William Whipple, Jr., "World's Fair Construction: Tight Schedules for Complex Program," *Engineering News-Record* 169 (September 13, 1962): 30–32; "Final Push for New York Fair," *Business Week* (April 27, 1963): 31; "All's Fair in Flushing Meadow," *New York Times* (April 28, 1963), VI: 54–55; "The Talk of the Town: Preview," *New Yorker* 39 (May 4, 1963): 34; Joseph C. Ingraham, "State Warns Contractors to End Lag in World's Fair Road Jobs," *New York Times* (May 13, 1963): 31, 42; Robert C. Doty, "World's Fair Gains Impetus Despite Snubs," *New York Times* (September 9, 1963): 1, 21; Frederick P. Pittera, "Fairs, Exhibitions and Shows," *Britannica Book of the Year* (Chicago: Encyclopaedia Britannica, 1964): 355; "City Succumbs to 'Fair Fever,'" *Business Week* (March 21, 1964): 120, 122, 124, 126; "Ready to Swing Open the Gates," *Business Week* (April 18, 1964): 30–31; "The Man Who Gets Things Done," *Engineering News-Record* 172 (April 23, 1964): 49–50, 53; "World's Fair Arrives in a Rush," *Engineering News-Record* 172 (April 23, 1964): 19–21; *The Mighty Fair: New York World's Fair 1964–1965: A Retrospective* (New York: Flushing Gallery, 1985).
36. "The 1964 Fair Slogs Ahead," *Business Week* (January 12, 1963): 102–4.
37. Robert Moses quoted in Bill Davidson, "The Old S.O.B. Does It Again," *Saturday Evening Post* 237 (May 23, 1964): 36, 38, 41.
38. Robert Moses quoted in Davidson, "The Old S.O.B. Does It Again": 36.
39. Mary Perot Nichols, "Private Opinion: Moses, Let Thy City Go!" *Village Voice* 9 (November 14, 1963): 3, 19–20.
40. Robert Moses quoted in Davidson, "The Old S.O.B. Does It Again": 36. Also see "Fair Restrained on Blocking Sign," *New York Times* (March 13, 1964): 21; "World's Fair Goes into Home Stretch," *Architectural Forum* 120 (April 1964): 10.
41. Skow, "Who Needs the World's Fair?": 14.
42. Peter Lyon, "A Glorious Nightmare," *Holiday* 36 (July 1964): 48–67.
43. "The World of Already": 40.
44. Ada Louise Huxtable, "Architecture: Chaos of Good, Bad and Joyful," *New York Times* (April 22, 1964): 25.
45. Emerson Goble, "Why Good Design?" editorial, *Architectural Record* 134 (June 1964): 9.
46. "120-Foot Steel 'Unisphere' Will Be Symbol of the '64 Fair," *New York Times* (February 15, 1961): 37; Ralph Caplan, "Fair Is (So Far) Foul," editorial, *Industrial Design* 8 (March 1961): 27; "Plus Ça Change . . . ," *Progressive Architecture* 42 (March 1961): 64; Walter McQuade, "Architecture," *Nation* 192 (April 22, 1961): 357–58; Bruno Zevi, "'The New Frontier' and the Unisphere," *L'Architettura cronache e storia* 7 (September 1961): 290–91; "Unisphere at 1964 World's Fair to Be 12 Stories High," *New York Times* (April 24, 1962): 20; Daniel Victor Bienko, "Space Needle or Unisphere?—A Fair Question," letter to the editor, *Progressive Architecture* 43 (August 1962): 158; "Moses' Orb Holds Sway Over Fair," *Village Voice* 8 (March 14, 1963): 7; Mildred Constantine, "Visit New York," *Art in America*, special issue (1964): 124–29; "Out of the Bull Rushes," *Time* 83 (January 17, 1964): 52–57; Mary A. MacNeil, "All's Fair," *Industrial Design* 11 (March 1964): 46–51; "Fair Outlook," *Newsweek* 63 (April 20, 1964): 68; "The New York World's Fair," *Ebony* 19 (June 1964): 166–70; William Robbins, "Doodle Grew Into the Unisphere, with Help from a Rubber Ball," *New York Times* (August 16, 1964), VIII: 1, 6; "Design Ideas: 1964," advertisement, *Journal of the American Institute of Architects* 42 (September 1964): 119–21; Ellen Perry and James T. Burns, Jr., "The Busy Architect's Guide to the World's Fair," *Progressive Architecture* 45 (October 1964): 223–38; Robert Alden, "New York World's Fair: The First Year," *Britannica Book of the Year* (Chicago: Encyclopaedia Britannica, 1965): 347; Frederick Fried and Edmund V. Gillon, *New York Civic Sculpture* (New York: Dover, 1976), 144.
47. Walter Dorwin Teague, letter to Robert Moses, May 19, 1960; Robert Moses, memorandum to Stuart Constable, July 21, 1960; Robert Moses, letter to Gilmore D. Clarke, August 21, 1960; Walter Dorwin Teague, letter to John S. Young, December 2, 1960; all in Theme Committee Folder, Container 58, New York World's Fair 1964–1965 Corporation Records, New York Public Library Rare Books and Manuscripts Division. Also see Miller, "Something for Everyone: Robert Moses and the Fair," in *Remembering the Future*, 62–63.
48. Robert Moses, letter to Gilmore D. Clarke, August 12, 1960, Theme Committee Folder, Container 58, New York World's Fair 1964–1965 Corporation Records, New York Public Library Rare Books and Manuscripts Division.
49. "Presentation Book of Portland Cement Association Exhibit at World's Fair," Working Drawings and Models Folder, Container 109, New York World's Fair 1964–1965 Corporation Records, New York Public Library Rare Books and Manuscripts Division. Also see "Rudolph Designs for the New York Fair," *Architectural Record* 43 (July 1961): 12; "Moon-Viewing Platform Shows Concrete," *Progressive Architecture* 42 (July 1961): 43, 45; "Vertigini in fiera e contorsioni in chiesa," *L'Architettura cronache e storia* 7 (November 1961): 47. For an earlier proposed science center and planetarium, see "Astronarium–Science Center Proposed for World's Fair," *Progressive Architecture* 42 (May 1961): 47. For other unbuilt structures at the fair, see "These Won't Be Built," *Industrial Design* 10 (September 1963): 54–59.
50. Robert Moses quoted in "120-Foot Steel 'Unisphere' Will Be Symbol of the '64 Fair": 37.
51. Robert Moses quoted in "120-Foot Steel 'Unisphere' Will Be Symbol of the '64 Fair": 37.
52. Caplan, "Fair Is (So Far) Foul": 27.
53. "Plus Ça Change . . . ": 64.
54. McQuade, "Architecture": 357–58.
55. Caplan, "Fair Is (So Far) Foul": 27.
56. Zevi, "'The New Frontier' and the Unisphere": 290–91. In addition to Zevi's essay, an editorial comment is translated into English, German and Spanish.
57. Austin J. Paddock quoted in "Moses' Orb Holds Sway Over Fair": 7.
58. Quoted in *Official Guide, New York World's Fair 1964–1965* (New York: Time, Inc., 1964), 90.
59. Bienko, "Space Needle or Unisphere?—A Fair Question": 158.
60. "World's Fair Frolics (cont'd.): Federal Proposal," *Progressive Architecture* 42 (January 1961): 54; "World's Fair Follies: Word from Washington," *Progressive Architecture* 42 (October 1961): 64, 66; "U.S. Picks Designers for Pavilion at Fair," *New York Times* (August 9, 1962): 23; "U.S. Architecture and the 1964 Fair," editorial, *Architectural Forum* 117 (September 1962): 77; "Luckman Is U.S. Choice for New York Fair," *Architectural Record* 132 (September 1962): 10; Ada Louise Huxtable, "Federal Pavilion for New York World's Fair Is Nearing a Decision," *New York Times* (November 11, 1962): 79.
61. "U.S. Architecture and the 1964 Fair": 77.
62. "U.S. Architecture and the 1964 Fair": 77.
63. Arthur Drexler, "U.S. Architecture at the Fair," letter to the editor, *Architectural Forum* 117 (November 1962): 19. Also see Charles Luckman, Edmund Bacon, Percival Goodman, Fred Bassetti and Leon Gordon Miller, "U.S. Architecture at the Fair," letters to the editor, *Architectural Forum* 117 (November 1962): 19.
64. "Latest Word on the Federal Pavilion," *Architectural Forum* 117 (November 1962): 7; "The Government Architect," editorial, *New York Times* (November 24, 1962): 22; "U.S. Approves Design for New York Fair Pavilion," *Architectural Record* 132 (December 1962): 10; "Johnson's Fair Pavilion, U.S. Design Set," *Progressive Architecture* 43 (December 1962): 52; Ada Louise Huxtable, "A Fair U.S. Pavilion," *New York Times* (January 26, 1963): 7; "Preview: New York World's Fair 1964–1965," *Architectural Record* 135 (February 1963): 137–44; "The Fair: Progress Report," *Time* 81 (February 8, 1963): 36; "Der Bauplatz der Weltausstellung 1964," *Werk* (June 1963): 121–22; Mina Hamilton, "Rides at the Fair," *Industrial Design* 10 (September 1963): 42–47; "Fun in New York," *Time* 83 (May 1, 1964): 40–41; Von Eckardt, "As the Hucksters See Us": 14–16; "The World of Already": 50; "Art Hunting in Darkest World's Fair," *Art News* 63 (summer 1964): 34–36, 65; Ralph Caplan, "Letter from Flushing Meadow," *Design* 187 (July 1964): 54–57; Scully, "If This Is Architecture, God Help Us": 9; "Challenge to Design," *Landscape Architecture* 55 (October 1964): 33–37; Perry and Burns, "The Busy Architect's Guide to the World's Fair": 232.
65. Huxtable, "A Fair U.S. Pavilion": 7.
66. "Fun in New York": 40.
67. Perry and Burns, "The Busy Architect's Guide to the World's Fair": 232.
68. Scully, "If This Is Architecture, God Help Us": 9.
69. Caplan, "Letter from Flushing Meadow": 57.
70. "The World of Already": 50.
71. George W. S. Trow, Jr., "World's Fair," *New Yorker* 65 (November 17, 1980): 151–52, 154–55, 158–60, 162–70, reprinted in George W. S. Trow, Jr., *Within the Context of No Context* (New York: Little, Brown, 1981), 72–95.
72. Ralph Chapman, "Fair's Tallest—State's Observation Tower," *New York Herald Tribune* (October 10, 1962): 23; "Moses in the Wilderness," *Time* 80 (October 19, 1962): 70; "New York's Fair: Gas In—Russia Out?" *Architectural Forum* 117 (November 1962): 11; "Johnson's Fair Pavilion, U.S. Design Set": 32; "Come to the Fair—In New York," *Newsweek* 61 (March 11, 1963): 82–83; "Sketch of New York State Pavilion," *New York Herald Tribune* (June 23, 1963): 25; Hedy Backlin, "The Laissez-Fair," *Craft Horizons* 23 (September 1963): 40–41; Henry B. Comstock, "They Built the Roof on the Ground," *Popular Science* 184 (March 1964): 98–101; Emily Genauer, "Fair Mural Taken Off; Artist to Do Another," *New York Herald Tribune* (April 18, 1964): 18; Huxtable, "Architecture: Chaos of Good, Bad and Joyful": 25; Stuart Preston, "Letter from New York: The 'Czar's' Veto," *Apollo* 79 (May 1964): 343; "New York: The City and the Fair," *Arts* 38 (May–June 1964): 54–57; George Nelson, "Prime del apertura, una vista alla Fiera di New York," *Domus* 414 (May 1964): 36–38; Von Eckardt, "As the Hucksters See Us": 15; "Una mattina alla Fiera di New York," *Domus* 415 (June 1964): 11–13; "Art Hunting in Darkest World's Fair": 35; "World's Fair Products," *Progressive Architecture* 45 (July 1964): 91–93, 95–96, 100; Max Kozloff, "Pop on the Meadow," *Nation* 199 (July 13, 1964): 16–18; Scully, "If This Is Architecture, God Help Us": 9; Philip Johnson, "Young Artists at the Fair and at Lincoln Center," *Art in America* 52 (August 1964): 112–21; "New York World's Fair," *Interior Design* 35 (August 1964): cover, 75–83; "P.C.I. Honors Eleven Structures in Awards Program," *Architectural Record* 136 (September 1964): 12–13; Perry and Burns, "The Busy Architect's Guide to the World's Fair": 232–33; "Foire Exposition de New York 1964," *L'Architecture d'Aujourd'hui* 34 (November 1964):

18–22; "World's Fair Buildings Honored," *Progressive Architecture* 45 (December 1964): 51; Philip Johnson, "Whence and Whither: The Processional Element in Architecture," *Perspecta* 9/10 (1965): 167–78, reprinted in Eisenman and Stern, eds., *Philip Johnson: Writings*, 150–55; "New York: Gallery Notes," *Art in America* 53 (June 1965): 144–45; *Philip Johnson: Architecture 1949–1965*, with an intro. by Henry-Russell Hitchcock (New York: Holt, Rinehart and Winston, 1966), 23–24, 106–9; White and Willensky, *AIA Guide* (1967), 366; C. Ray Smith, *Supermannerism: New Attitudes in Post-Modern Architecture* (New York: E. P. Dutton, 1977), 170–71; Carter Ratcliff, *Andy Warhol* (New York: Abbeville Press, 1983), 38; Patrick S. Smith, *Andy Warhol's Art and Films* (Ann Arbor, Mich.: UMI Research Press, 1986), 92, 323; Rosemarie Haag Bletter, "The 'Laissez-Fair,' Good Taste, and Money Trees: Architecture at the Fair," in *Remembering the Future*, 112–14; Helen A. Harrison, "Art for the Millions, or Art for the Market?" in *Remembering the Future*, 136, 155–63; David Bourdon, *Warhol* (New York: Harry N. Abrams, 1989), 181–82, plate 169; Christopher Gray, "A Windswept, Gaudy Ghost in Search of a New Role," *New York Times* (April 22, 1990), X: 12.

73. Kozloff, "Pop on the Meadow": 17.

74. Perry and Burns, "The Busy Architect's Guide to the World's Fair": 232–33.

75. Scully, "If This Is Architecture, God Help Us": 9.

76. Huxtable, "Architecture: Chaos of Good, Bad and Joyful": 25.

77. Johnson, "Young Artists at the Fair and at Lincoln Center": 112.

78. Bourdon, *Warhol*, 182.

79. Robert Rosenblum, "Introduction: Remembrance of Fairs Past," in *Remembering the Future*, 18.

80. Kozloff, "Pop on the Meadow": 17.

81. Von Eckardt, "As the Hucksters See Us": 15.

82. "4 Designs for Fair Selected by Jersey," *New York Times* (March 4, 1961): 17; "Philip Collins, 32, Wins in New Jersey," *Architectural Record* 131 (April 1962): 18; "NYWF Designs Gain Strength," *Progressive Architecture* 43 (April 1962): 70; Perry and Burns, "The Busy Architect's Guide to the Fair": 232.

83. "The Talk of the Town: 366," *New Yorker* 38 (November 10, 1962): 43–44; "Into Stride," *Time* 83 (May 8, 1964): 42; "The World of Already": 49; Perry and Burns, "The Busy Architect's Guide to the World's Fair": 232; Trow, "World's Fair": 154–55.

84. "The Talk of the Town: 366": 43.

85. "Into Stride": 42.

86. Trow, "World's Fair": 154–55.

87. Scully, "If This Is Architecture, God Help Us": 9.

88. Perry and Burns, "The Busy Architect's Guide to the World's Fair": 232.

89. Perry and Burns, "The Busy Architect's Guide to the World's Fair": 232; Terence Ross, "P/A at the New York World's Fair," letter to the editor, *Progressive Architecture* 45 (December 1964): 28.

90. Perry and Burns, "The Busy Architect's Guide to the World's Fair": 232; Richard F. Shepard, "Flushing: Where the World Twice Met and Newcomers Dwell," *New York Times* (April 28, 1989), C: 1, 34.

91. Perry and Burns, "The Busy Architect's Guide to the World's Fair": 232.

92. Perry and Burns, "The Busy Architect's Guide to the World's Fair": 233.

93. "Construction's Artist Goes to the Fair," *Engineering News-Record* 173 (July 2, 1964): 74–75; Perry and Burns, "The Busy Architect's Guide to the World's Fair": 232; Vinokur, "'The World of Tomorrow' or 'Peace through Understanding'?: A Comparison of the Impact of the 1939–1940 and 1964–1965 New York World's Fairs on New York City": 83–102. Also see John Tauranac, "The Little Apple," *New York* 8 (May 12, 1975): 75; Bill Barol, "New York City Gets Small," *Newsweek* 109 (June 29, 1987): 54; "The Talk of the Town: Small Town," *New Yorker* 65 (May 8, 1989): 33–34; "Model Donations," *Oculus* 52 (June 1990): 4. For Embury's building, see Stern, Gilmartin and Mellins, *New York 1930*, 734, 736.

94. "The Talk of the Town: Hollywood Pavilion," *New Yorker* 39 (December 28, 1963): 26–27; Perry and Burns, "The Busy Architect's Guide to the World's Fair": 232.

95. "Grauman Theater, Hollywood, Cal.," *American Architect and Architectural Review* 123 (January 31, 1923), unnumbered plates; David Gebhard and Robert Winter, *A Guide to Architecture in Los Angeles and Southern California* (Salt Lake City, Utah: Peregrine Smith, 1982), 146.

96. John Brooks, "Onward and Upward with the Arts: Diplomacy at Flushing Meadows," *New Yorker* 39 (June 1, 1963): 41–42, 44, 47, 48, 50, 53–54, 56–59. For an overview of the international pavilions, see Ada Louise Huxtable, "World's Fair: International Scope," *New York Times* (May 10, 1964), II: 19.

97. "Gems of the Fair," *Industrial Design* 11 (May 1964): 12; Huxtable, "World's Fair: International Scope": 19; "Fair Hits and Misses," *Newsweek* 63 (June 1, 1964): 79; "The World of Already": 50–51; "The Jewel of the Fair," *Architectural Record* 36 (July 1964): 143–50; Caplan, "Letter from Flushing Meadow": 56; Eleanor Graves, "How to Eat and Stay Solvent," *Life* 57 (July 10, 1964): 12; C. J. McNapsy, "Save the Spanish Pavilion," *America* 111 (July 11, 1964): 31; "Spanish Pavilion Is a Beauty, but a Beast to Build," *Engineering News-Record* 173 (July 30, 1964): 22–24; Mildred F. Schmertz, "Architecture at the New York World's Fair," *Life* 57 (August 7, 1964): 80–83, 85, 146; Perry and Burns, "The Busy Architect's Guide to the World's Fair": 229; "Queen of the Fair," *Progressive Architecture* 45 (December 1964): 160–67; "World's Fair Buildings Honored": 51; Bletter, "The 'Laissez-Fair,' Good Taste, and Money Trees: Architecture at the Fair," in *Remembering the Future*, 106–9; Harrison, "Art for the Millions, or Art for the Market?" in *Remembering the Future*, 151.

98. "Queen of the Fair": 160.

99. "Queen of the Fair": 160.

100. Olga Gueft, "Best of the Fair: 4 Distinguished Statements," *Interiors* 124 (October 1964): 122–30.

101. Perry and Burns, "The Busy Architect's Guide to the World's Fair": 229.

102. Caplan, "Letter from Flushing Meadow": 57.

103. Huxtable, "World's Fair: International Scope": 19.

104. "The World of Already": 50.

105. McNapsy, "Save the Spanish Pavilion": 31.

106. "Flushing Meadows Communiqué," *Progressive Architecture* 33 (October 1963): 80–81; Caplan, "Letter from Flushing Meadow": 56; "Display Cases at the New York World's Fair," *Industrial Design* 11 (July 1964): 72–77; Gueft, "Best of the Fair: 4 Distinguished Statements": 130; Perry and Burns, "The Busy Architect's Guide to the World's Fair": 229.

107. See Frank Lloyd Wright, *Letters to Apprentices*, selected and with commentary by Bruce Brooks Pfeiffer (Fresno, Calif.: The Press at California State University, Fresno, 1982), 120, 199.

108. Caplan, "Letter from Flushing Meadow": 56.

109. Huxtable, "Architecture: Chaos of Good, Bad and Joyful": 25; "Gems of the Fair": 12; Huxtable, "World's Fair: International Scope": 19; "Fair Hits and Misses": 79; "The World of Already": 51; Schmertz, "Architecture at the New York World's Fair": 146; Perry and Burns, "The Busy Architect's Guide to the World's Fair": 229; "World's Fair Buildings Honored": 51.

110. Schmertz, "Architecture at the New York World's Fair": 146.

111. For a profile of one of the Danish child-care workers and her impressions of the fair, see Gereon Zimmermann, "Baby-sitter at the Fair," *Look* 28 (July 28, 1964): 74–84.

112. Von Eckardt, "As the Hucksters See Us": 15; "The World of Already": 52; Perry and Burns, "The Busy Architect's Guide to the World's Fair": 229; "Fairs: Second Time Around," *Time* 84 (April 30, 1965): 76, 80.

113. Yves Bottineau, *The Wonders of Spain* (London: Thames and Hudson, 1962), 140, plate 57. For an extensive discussion of the architect's life and work, see Enric Jardí, *Puig i Cadafalch: Arquitecte, polític i historiador de l'art* (Barcelona: Ariel, 1975).

114. Von Eckardt, "As the Hucksters See Us": 15.

115. Perry and Burns, "The Busy Architect's Guide to the World's Fair": 229.

116. "Project pour le Pavillon d'Israel à l'Esposition de New York en 1964," *L'Architecture d'Aujourd'hui* 34 (February 1963): 100–101; "Citation," *Progressive Architecture* 45 (January 1964): 130–31; Perry and Burns, "The Busy Architect's Guide to the World's Fair": 230.

117. "Art Hunting in Darkest World's Fair": 35. Also see Thomas Hine, *Populuxe* (New York: Alfred A. Knopf, 1986), 166.

118. "The Talk of the Town: Meeting," *New Yorker* 40 (July 4, 1964): 24–25; Perry and Burns, "The Busy Architect's Guide to the World's Fair": 230; Moses, *Public Works: A Dangerous Trade*, 579–82; Harrison, "Art for the Millions, or Art for the Market?" in *Remembering the Future*, 164–66.

119. "Things Look Up at the Fair," *Progressive Architecture* 44 (July 1963): 52–53; Huxtable, "World's Fair: International Scope": 19; Gueft, "Best of the Fair: 4 Distinguished Statements": 128; Perry and Burns, "The Busy Architect's Guide to the World's Fair": 229.

120. "The Great Fair," *Saturday Evening Post* 237 (May 23, 1964): 27–35; "The World of Already": 42; Mary Simons, "A Serene Oasis at the World's Fair," *Interiors* 123 (July 1964): 74–77; Perry and Burns, "The Busy Architect's Guide to the World's Fair": 230.

121. Simons, "A Serene Oasis at the World's Fair": 74–77.

122. Perry and Burns, "The Busy Architect's Guide to the World's Fair": 230.

123. "World's Fair '64: A Preview": 44; Huxtable, "Architecture: Chaos of Good, Bad and Joyful": 25; "Gems of the Fair": 12; David Nevin, "A Smasheroo of a World's Fair," *Life* 56 (May 1, 1964): 26–35; Huxtable, "World's Fair: International Scope": 19; Von Eckardt, "As the Hucksters See Us": 15; "The World of Already": 46; "Art Hunting in Darkest World's Fair": 34; Caplan, "Letter from Flushing Meadow": 187; Perry and Burns, "The Busy Architect's Guide to the World's Fair": 229; Bletter, "The 'Laissez-Fair,' Good Taste, and Money Trees: Architecture at the Fair," in *Remembering the Future*, 108–9.

124. "Art Hunting in Darkest World's Fair": 34.

125. Von Eckardt, "As the Hucksters See Us": 15.

126. "The World of Already": 46.

127. "World's Fair '64: A Preview": 44.

128. "1939 Echoes, 'Pietà, Folies Bergère for NYWF," *Progressive Architecture* 44 (May 1963): 74; "For Everybody from Everywhere," *Newsweek* 63 (April 27, 1964): 60–65; "The World of Already": 42; "Art Hunting in Darkest World's Fair": 36; Perry and Burns, "The Busy Architect's Guide to the World's Fair": 230.

129. "Triumph for the Fair," *Business Week* (March 21, 1964): 111–24; "For Everybody from Everywhere": 62; "The World of Already": 43; Perry and Burns, "The Busy Architect's Guide to the World's Fair": 229, 231.

130. Perry and Burns, "The Busy Architect's Guide to the World's Fair": 229.

131. "Ground Is Broken for Bell System Pavilion at Fair," *New York Times* (June 22, 1962): 2; "New York World's Fair," *Industrial Design* 62 (August 1962): 12, 14; "Freedom of Choice at Flushing Meadow," *Progressive Architecture* 43 (October 1962): 76; Edward Carpenter, "Exhibit Techniques at the Fair," *Industrial Design* 11 (May 1964): 43–47; "The World of Already": 49; Perry and Burns, "The Busy Architect's Guide to the World's Fair": 226.

132. "New York World's Fair," *Industrial Design*: 12.

133. "The World of Already": 49.

134. "Come to the Fair—In N.Y.": 82–83; Perry and Burns, "The Busy Architect's Guide to the World's Fair": 226.

135. Hamilton, "Rides at the Fair": 43; "Flushing Meadows Communiqué": 81; "A Billion-Dollar Fair Takes Shape": 48; Nevin, "A Smasheroo of a World's Fair": 32–33; Perry and Burns, "The Busy Architect's Guide to the World's Fair": 226, 228; Bacon, "P/A at the New York World's Fair": 28; Sheldon J. Reaven, "New Frontiers: Science and Technology at the Fair," in *Remembering the Future*, 90–91.

136. "World's Fair Products": 95.

137. "Light on Flushing Meadow," *Industrial Design* 9 (August 1962): 52–57; Von Eckardt, "As the Hucksters See Us": 14; "World's Fair Products": 95; "Kodak Pavilion at Fair Wins Concrete Group's Award," *New York Times* (August 23, 1964), VII: 9; Perry and Burns, "The Busy Architect's Guide to the World's Fair": 228; Hine, *Populuxe*, 166; Reaven, "New Frontiers: Science and Technology at the Fair," in *Remembering the Past*, 78–79.

138. Carpenter, "Exhibit Techniques at the Fair": 43; "The World of Already": 45, 49; Caplan, "Letter from Flushing Meadow": 56; Perry and Burns, "The Busy Architect's Guide to the World's Fair": 228; Richard Schickel, *The Disney Version* (New York: Simon & Schuster, 1985), 32.

139. Carpenter, "Exhibit Techniques at the Fair": 43.

140. "The World of Already": 49.

141. Caplan, "Letter from Flushing Meadow": 187.

142. "Flushing Meadows Communiqué": 81; Perry and Burns, "The Busy Architect's Guide to the World's Fair": 228.

143. "Gas Industry Pavilion," *Architectural Forum* 115 (November 1961): 10; "World's Fair, '64: A Preview": 44; "Gems of the Fair": 12; Carpenter, "Exhibit Techniques at the Fair": 46–47; "World's Fair Products": 95; Perry and Burns, "The Busy Architect's Guide to the World's Fair": 226.

144. "World's Fair '64: A Preview": 44.

145. "Power & Light Exhibit," *Architectural Forum* 115 (November 1961): 10; Huxtable, "Architecture: Chaos of Good, Bad and Joyful": 25; Von Eckardt, "As the Hucksters See Us": 15; Harrison, "Art for the Millions, or Art for the Market?" in *Remembering the Future*, 154–55.

146. Von Eckardt, "As the Hucksters See Us": 15.
147. Perry and Burns, "The Busy Architect's Guide to the World's Fair": 228; Hine, *Populuxe*, 167; Bletter, "The 'Laissez-Fair,' Good Taste, and Money Trees: Architecture at the Fair," in *Remembering the Future*, 124.
148. Jonathan Lipman, *Frank Lloyd Wright and the Johnson Wax Buildings* (New York: Rizzoli International Publications, 1986).
149. "Progetto per la Esposizione Mondiale di New York 1964," *Domus* 402 (May 1963): 38–42; Mayer, "Ho Hum, Come to the Fair": 117; "The Thinking Man's Exhibit," *Esquire* 60 (October 1963): 118–19; Huxtable, "Architecture: Chaos of Good, Bad and Joyful": 25; "For Everybody from Everywhere": 64; "Gems of the Fair": 12; Von Eckardt, "As the Hucksters See Us": 15; "The World of Already": 49; Caplan, "Letter from Flushing Meadow": 56; Scully, "If This Is Architecture, God Help Us": 9; Perry and Burns, "The Busy Architect's Guide to the World's Fair": 226; "Line Derivation Photos Give New View of IBM Pavilion," *Architectural Record* 136 (November 1964): 26; Henry B. Comstock, "Inside IBM's World's Fair 'Egg,'" *Popular Science* 185 (July 1965): 58–59, 179; Walter F. Wagner, Jr., "Fresh Forms and New Directions from a Special Kind of Problem Solving," *Architectural Record* 143 (May 1968): 145–68; Francesco Dal Co, *Kevin Roche* (New York: Rizzoli International Publications, 1985), 92–93; Dickstein, "From the Thirties to the Sixties: The New York World's Fair in Its Own Time," in *Remembering the Future*, 38; Reaven, "New Frontiers: Science and Technology at the Fair," in *Remembering the Future*, 84–88.
150. Scully, "If This Is Architecture, God Help Us": 9.
151. Caplan, "Letter from Flushing Meadow": 56.
152. Perry and Burns, "The Busy Architect's Guide to the World's Fair": 226.
153. Huxtable, "Architecture: Chaos of Good, Bad and Joyful": 25.
154. "For Everybody from Everywhere": 64.
155. Mayer, "Ho Hum, Come to the Fair": 117.
156. "The Thinking Man's Exhibit": 119.
157. Von Eckardt, "As the Hucksters See Us": 15.
158. "Better Living Center," *Interior Design* 35 (August 1964): 92. Also see "Better Living Pavilion," *Architectural Forum* 115 (November 1961): 10; "Resources Council," *Interiors* 122 (February 1963): 12.
159. "New York World's Fair: Pavilion of American Interiors," *Interiors* 122 (September 1962): 10; "Building News: Pavilion of American Interiors," *Interiors* 122 (November 1962): 12; "New York World's Fair," *Interiors* 123 (September 1963): 12; "Contract Interiors: The Home Furnishings Industry at the 1964 World's Fair," *Interiors* 123 (March 1964): 97–107; "The Pavilion of American Interiors," *Interior Design* 35 (August 1964): 84–88; Perry and Burns, "The Busy Architect's Guide to the World's Fair": 226.
160. Ellen Lehman McCluskey quoted in Patricia Leigh Brown, "Fifty Years After the Fair, Where Is Tomorrow?" *New York Times* (March 2, 1989), C: 1, 6.
161. "House of Good Taste," *Interiors* 123 (September 1963): 12; "Contract Interiors: The Home Furnishings Industry at the 1964 World's Fair": 97–101; "The House of Good Taste," *Interior Design* 35 (August 1964): 89–90; Perry and Burns, "The Busy Architect's Guide to the World's Fair": 226.
162. "House of Good Taste," *Interiors*: 12.
163. Lady Malcolm Douglas Hamilton quoted in "House of Good Taste," *Interiors*: 12.
164. "Contract Interiors: The Home Furnishings Industry at the 1964 World's Fair": 99; Brown, "Fifty Years After the World's Fair, Where Is Tomorrow?": 6.
165. "Contract Interiors: The Home Furnishings Industry at the 1964 World's Fair": 99.
166. Edward Durell Stone quoted in Brown, "Fifty Years After the World's Fair, Where Is Tomorrow?": 6.
167. "Contract Interiors: The Home Furnishings Industry at the 1964 World's Fair": 99.
168. "The House of Good Taste," *Interior Design*: 89–90.
169. Perry and Burns, "The Busy Architect's Guide to the World's Fair": 226.
170. "Contract Interiors: The Home Furnishings Industry at the 1964 World's Fair": 106; "Formica House," *Interior Design* 35 (August 1964): 93; Perry and Burns, "The Busy Architect's Guide to the World's Fair": 226; Brown, "Fifty Years After the Fair, Where Is Tomorrow?": 6.
171. "Mole Home at Fair," *Progressive Architecture* 45 (February 1964): 65; "Contract Interiors: The Home Furnishings Industry at the 1964 World's Fair": 107; "The Talk of the Town: Notes and Comment," *New Yorker* 40 (July 1964): 19; Perry and Burns, "The Busy Architect's Guide to the World's Fair": 233; Brown, "Fifty Years After the Fair, Where Is Tomorrow?": 6.
172. Perry and Burns, "The Busy Architect's Guide to the World's Fair": 233.
173. "The Talk of the Town: Notes and Comment": 19.
174. "Flushing Meadows Communiqué": 81; Von Eckardt, "As the Hucksters See Us": 16; Perry and Burns, "The Busy Architect's Guide to the World's Fair": 228.
175. Perry and Burns, "The Busy Architect's Guide to the World's Fair": 226.
176. Von Eckardt, "As the Hucksters See Us": 16.
177. Edward Durell Stone, *The Evolution of an Architect* (New York: Horizon Press, 1962), 259; "Christian Science at Fair," *New York Times* (July 21 1962): 9; Perry and Burns, "The Busy Architect's Guide to the World's Fair": 229.
178. Perry and Burns, "The Busy Architect's Guide to the World's Fair": 229.
179. "Michelangelo at the 1964–65 New York Fair," *Architectural Forum* 116 (May 1962): 11; Alfred Frankfurter, "The Michelangelo Scandal," editorial, *Art News* 61 (May 1962): 23; "1939 Echoes, 'Pietà,' Folies Bergère for NYWF": 74; John Leo, "A Pious Disaster," *Commonweal* 80 (May 15, 1964): 225–26; Skow, "Who Needs the World's Fair?": 12; Von Eckardt, "As the Hucksters See Us": 14; Nanine Bilski and Rev. Donald F. Pugliese, "Correspondence: 'A Pious Disaster,'" letters to the editor, *Commonweal* 80 (June 13, 1964): 370–71; Perry and Burns, "The Busy Architect's Guide to the World's Fair": 230; Hughes, "The Golden Grin": 190; Dickstein, "From the Thirties to the Sixties: The New York World's Fair in Its Own Time," in *Remembering the Future*, 38–39; Harrison, "Art for the Millions, or Art for the Market?" in *Remembering the Future*, 147–49.
180. Perry and Burns, "The Busy Architect's Guide to the World's Fair": 230.
181. Frankfurter, "The Michelangelo Scandal": 23.
182. Scully, "If This Is Architecture, God Help Us": 9.
183. Hughes, "The Golden Grin": 190.
184. Leo, "A Pious Disaster": 226.
185. Scully, "If This Is Architecture, God Help Us": 9; Perry and Burns, "The Busy Architect's Guide to the World's Fair": 235.
186. Scully, "If This Is Architecture, God Help Us": 9.
187. "World's Fair '64: A Preview": 44; "For Everybody from Everywhere": 65; Robert Malone, "Whose Tomorrow?" *Industrial Design* 11 (May 1964): 34–35; "The World of Already": 44–45, 49; Caplan, "Letter from Flushing Meadow": 187; Scully, "If This Is Architecture, God Help Us": 9; Perry and Burns, "The Busy Architect's Guide to the World's Fair": 233.
188. Perry and Burns, "The Busy Architect's Guide to the World's Fair": 233.
189. "World's Fair '64: A Preview": 44.
190. Malone, "Whose Tomorrow?": 34.
191. "For Everybody from Everywhere": 65.
192. Scully, "If This Is Architecture, God Help Us": 9.
193. "The World of Already": 49.
194. Gay Talese, "G.M. Unveils Futurama, 1965, but Crystal Ball Stays Covered," *New York Times* (May 9, 1962): 45; "World's Fair '64: A Preview": 44; Malone, "Whose Tomorrow?": 34–35; "The World of Already": 49; Caplan, "Letter from Flushing Meadow": 56; Scully, "If This Is Architecture, God Help Us": 9; Perry and Burns, "The Busy Architect's Guide to the World's Fair": 235; Hine, *Populuxe*, 167; Dickstein, "From the Thirties to the Sixties: The New York World's Fair in Its Own Time," in *Remembering the Future*, 30–32; Reaven, "New Frontiers: Science and Technology at the Fair," in *Remembering the Future*, 96–99.
195. For Kahn's General Motors Pavilion at the 1939–40 World's Fair, see Stern, Gilmartin and Mellins, *New York 1930*, 742, 747–48.
196. Francesco Tontori, "Ordine e Forma nell'Opera di Louis Kahn," *Casabella* 241 (July 1960): 2–17; Vincent Scully, Jr., *Louis I. Kahn* (New York: George Braziller, 1962), 39–40, fig. 119; Richard Saul Wurman and Eugene Feldman, eds., *The Notebooks and Drawings of Louis I. Kahn* (Philadelphia: Falcon, 1962), fig. 38; Heinz Ronner and Sharad Jhaveri, *Louis I. Kahn: Complete Work 1935–1974* (Basel: Birkhäuser Verlag, 1974), 174–75; David B. Brownlee and David G. Delong, *Louis I. Kahn: In the Realm of Architecture*, with an intro. by Vincent Scully (New York: Rizzoli International Publications, 1991), 60–61.
197. Caplan, "Letter from Flushing Meadow": 56.
198. "The World of Already": 49.
199. Caplan, "Letter from Flushing Meadow": 56.
200. Perry and Burns, "The Busy Architect's Guide to the World's Fair": 230.
201. Scully, "If This Is Architecture, God Help Us": 9.
202. Malone, "Whose Tomorrow?": 34–35.
203. "For Everybody from Everywhere": 63; Perry and Burns, "The Busy Architect's Guide to the World's Fair": 235.
204. Perry and Burns, "The Busy Architect's Guide to the World's Fair": 235.
205. "Port of New York Authority Building," *Architectural Forum* 115 (November 1961): 10; Olga Gueft, "Top of the Fair and Terrace Club," *Interiors* 123 (February 1963): 84–87; "First at the Fair," *Architectural Record* 134 (December 1963): 14; R. H. Havard, "Exploitation at the Fair?" letter to the editor, *Interiors* 123 (April 1964): 8; M. J. Hofflin, "Verdict," letter to the editor, *Interiors* 123 (June 1964): 8; Perry and Burns, "The Busy Architect's Guide to the World's Fair": 235; Mary Perot Nichols, "Private Opinion: Vision of Things to Come: Whirlybirds in Our Parks," *Village Voice* 10 (March 11, 1965): 3, 8; Reaven, "New Frontiers: Science and Technology at the Fair," in *Remembering the Future*, 100–101.
206. "First at the Fair": 14.
207. Mary Perot Nichols, "Private Opinion: Out of Incinerator Ashes a New Museum Emerges," *Village Voice* 8 (April 4, 1963): 3, 9; *Permanent Hall of Science, Dedicated September 9, 1964: Ceremony Excerpts* (New York: New York World's Fair 1964–1965 Corporation, 1964); *Post Fair Expansion: Hall of Science* (New York: New York World's Fair 1964–1965 Corporation, February 24, 1964); Ada Louise Huxtable, "Romantic Science Hall," *New York Times* (September 10, 1964): 27; "Pavilion des sciences à la foire internationale de New York," *L'Architecture d'Aujourd'hui* 35 (September 1965): 30–31; "A $7.5-Million Education Complex," *Architectural Record* 140 (September 1966): 42; "The Talk of the Town: The Existing Structure," *New Yorker* 41 (October 1, 1966): 43; Charles G. Bennett, "Science Museum Called Unworkable," *New York Times* (November 2, 1967): 55; Newhouse, *Wallace K. Harrison, Architect*, 236–40.
208. Huxtable, "Romantic Science Hall": 27.
209. Huxtable, "Romantic Science Hall": 27.
210. Quoted in Bennett, "Science Museum Called Unworkable": 55.
211. Stern, Gilmartin and Mellins, *New York 1930*, 752–55.
212. Robert Fontaine, "No Fair," *Atlantic Monthly* 205 (May 1960): 90–91.
213. "Out of the Bull Rushes": 57.
214. Samuel I. Rosenman quoted in "Out of the Bull Rushes": 57.
215. "The Talk of the Town: Wonderworld," *New Yorker* 39 (September 28, 1963): 36–37.
216. "The Talk of the Town: Preliminaries," *New Yorker* 40 (March 28, 1964): 33–34.
217. "Out of the Bull Rushes": 52.
218. "New York World's Fair," *Interior Design*: 83; "Fair Flowers," *Architectural Forum* 120 (April 1964): 40; Huxtable, "Architecture: Chaos of Good, Bad and Joyful": 25; Caplan, "Letter from Flushing Meadow": 54–55, 57; "World's Fair Products": 93; Perry and Burns, "The Busy Architect's Guide to the World's Fair": 236; "U.S. Progress on Preassembly: Victor Lundy," *Progressive Architecture* 45 (October 1964): 216–17.
219. Huxtable, "Architecture: Chaos of Good, Bad and Joyful": 25.
220. Perry and Burns, "The Busy Architect's Guide to the World's Fair": 236.
221. "The Word from Moses," *Time* 84 (September 25, 1964): 42–43; "More Plus than Minus," *Business Week* (September 26, 1964): 39; Robert Alden, "The Fair Closes Its First Season; 200,000 On Hand," *New York Times* (October 19, 1964): 1, 35; "Fair Enough," *Newsweek* 63 (October 26, 1964): 108, 110; "Can the Fair Make a Comeback?" *U.S. News & World Report* 57 (October 26, 1964): 15.
222. Robert Moses quoted in "Moses vs. the Bankers," *Newsweek* 65 (February 1, 1965): 61. Also see "The Talk of the Town: Well-Rounded," *New Yorker* 40 (February 6, 1965): 26–27; Chris Welles, "The Big Bash that Is Running Short of Cash," *Life* 58 (May 14, 1965): 136–50.
223. Gereon Zimmermann, "The Fair: New York's Spectacle Opens Again," *Look* 29 (April 20, 1965): 27–31; "The Talk of the Town: Salute," *New Yorker* 41 (April 24, 1965): 36–38; "Upbeat Fair," *Newsweek* 65 (April 26, 1965): 88–90; "The Talk of the Town: Summer Festival," *New Yorker* 41 (June 19, 1965): 24.
224. "Upbeat Fair": 88.
225. "The Fair: Low on Customers . . . and Cash," *U.S. News & World Report* 58 (May 31, 1965): 12; "What the Matter Can Be," *Time* 86 (July 16, 1965): 78; "Fair Draws to an End—The Last of Its Kind?" *Business Week* (October 16, 1965): 32–34.
226. Robert Moses quoted in Zimmermann, "The Fair: New York's Spectacle Opens Again": 29.
227. Quoted in "Upbeat Fair": 89.

228. "To the Bitter End," *Time* 86 (October 29, 1965): 52. Also see "World's Fair Postlude: The Demolition Crews Take Over," *Engineering News-Record* 175 (October 21, 1965): 18–19; "Farewell to the Fair," *Newsweek* 66 (October 25, 1965): 34; Byron Porterfield, "Fairs Come and Go but Growth They Spawned Goes On in Queens," *New York Times* (May 1, 1966), VIII: 1.
229. Robert Moses quoted in "What the Matter Can Be": 78.
230. "What the Matter Can Be": 78.
231. Russell Lynes, "Goodbye to World's Fairs," *Harper's* 231 (October 1965): 28–31.
232. Von Eckardt, *A Place to Live: The Crisis of the Cities*, 217–18.
233. "Legislator Blasts Park Department for 'Colossus' Complex," *Village Voice* 8 (February 14, 1963): 3; Mary Perot Nichols, "Private Opinion: You Can't Keep a Good Man Out of the Park," *Village Voice* 9 (March 19, 1964): 3; Mary Perot Nichols, "The $51,000,000 Misunderstanding," *Village Voice* 10 (December 17, 1964): 1, 25.
234. *Flushing Meadows and Beyond* (New York: New York World's Fair 1964–1965 Corporation, 1964). Also see Robert Alden, "Fair Says Pledge Has No Standing," *New York Times* (May 21, 1965): 22; Robert Moses, *The Saga of Flushing Meadows* (New York: Triborough Bridge and Tunnel Authority, 1966); Byron Porterfield, "Wreckers Press Fairgrounds Job," *New York Times* (February 20, 1966), VIII: 1, 8; "Park on Fair Site Due in December," *New York Times* (April 4, 1966): 33; "Foul Lot to Fair: A Saga by Moses," *New York Times* (April 11, 1966): 36; "World's Fair Site Transformed into $330-Million Park," *Engineering News-Record* 178 (June 1, 1967): 24–25.
235. Perry and Burns, "The Busy Architect's Guide to the World's Fair": 228.
236. Will Lissner, "City Considering a Sports Park Over Most of World's Fair Site," *New York Times* (August 22, 1966): 1, 38; Henry Raymont, "2 Top Architects Get a Hoving Bid," *New York Times* (October 6, 1966): 49; Martin Gansberg, "City Gets Details of Fair-Site Plan," *New York Times* (April 12, 1967): 35; "The Conversion of Flushing Meadows," *Progressive Architecture* 48 (May 1967): 54–55; Fred Ferretti, "Flushing in the Mush," *New York* 1 (August 5, 1968): 20–23; Tician Papachristou, *Marcel Breuer: New Buildings and Projects* (New York: Praeger, 1970), 177–81; Kenzo Tange, "New York Sports Park," *Japan Architect* 46 (January 1971): 69–75; Alison Sky and Michelle Stone, *Unbuilt America* (New York: McGraw-Hill, 1976), 124–25; *Kenzo Tange* (Zurich: Artemis, 1978), 158–59.
237. Thomas P. F. Hoving quoted in Raymont, "2 Top Architects Get Hoving Bid": 49.
238. Tange, "New York Sports Park": 71.
239. W. Boesiger, ed., *Le Corbusier: Oeuvre complète 1929–1934*, vol. 2 (Zurich: Les Editions d'Architecture, 1934), 123–37.
240. Ada Louise Huxtable, "Flushing Meadows Park Plan Delayed by Auditing," *New York Times* (August 12, 1967): 27, 53.
241. Huxtable, "Flushing Meadows Park Plan Delayed by Auditing": 53. Also see "Architectural Obstructionism," editorial, *New York Times* (August 11, 1967): 30; John J. Carty, "Plans for Flushing Meadows," letter to the editor, *New York Times* (August 25, 1967): 34.
242. Steven Roberts, "Federal Pavilion Will Be Retained," *New York Times* (January 21, 1966): 20; Howard Taubman, "Queens Arts Council Busy Despite Shortage of Funds," *New York Times* (April 4, 1971): 82; "U.S. Pavilion's Use Is Issue in Queens," *New York Times* (April 25, 1971): 101; Charles Friedman, "New Plan for U.S. Pavilion," *New York Times* (December 14, 1975): 154; Wolfgang Saxen, "Last Round for U.S. World's Fair Pavilion?" *New York Times* (July 29, 1976): 33; "Metropolitan Briefs," *New York Times* (August 25, 1976): 39.
243. Robert Moses quoted in Roberts, "Federal Pavilion Will Be Retained": 20.
244. Charles Grutzner, "Life Stirs Anew at Fairgrounds," *New York Times* (April 11, 1967): 44.
245. Murray Schumach, "Moses Gives City Fair Site as Park," *New York Times* (June 4, 1967): 1, 35.
246. Edith Evans Asbury, "Another Opening, Another Closing for Moses," *New York Times* (February 29, 1968): 39.
247. Edith Evans Asbury, "Moses Helps to Open First Queens Zoo," *New York Times* (October 27, 1968): 81; "The Talk of the Town: New Zoo," *New Yorker* 44 (November 6, 1968): 53–54; Christopher Gray, "Streetscapes: The Queens Aviary," *New York Times* (January 3, 1993), X: 3.

Chapter 15
Beyond the Boroughs

1. David K. Shipler, "New Highways Shaping Future of City's Suburbs," *New York Times* (August 19, 1971): 1, 26.
2. "Llewellyn Park: Country Homes for City People," undated promotional pamphlet. Also see Robert A. M. Stern with John Montague Massengale, *The Anglo-American Suburb* (London: Architectural Design, 1981), 21; Robert A. M. Stern with Thomas Mellins and Raymond Gastil, *Pride of Place: Building the American Dream* (Boston: Houghton Mifflin; New York: American Heritage, 1986), 129, 132–33.
3. *Suburban Long Island, the Sunrise Homeland* (New York: Long Island Railroad Company and Long Island Real Estate Board, 1922), 119–20; Federal Writers' Project, *The WPA Guide to New York City* (New York: Random House, 1939; New York: Pantheon Books, 1982), 572–73.
4. Mildred H. Smith, *The History of Garden City* (Manhasset, N.Y.: Channel Press, 1963).
5. Stern with Massengale, *The Anglo-American Suburb*, 31.
6. Stern with Massengale, *The Anglo-American Suburb*, 40.
7. "A Beauty Spot," *Architecture and Building* 46 (May 1914): 179–207; "The Architect's Scrap Book—Houses at Kensington, Great Neck, L.I.," *Architecture* 33 (February 1916): 44–46; *This Is Great Neck* (Great Neck, N.Y.: League of Women Voters of Great Neck, New York, 1975).
8. Stern with Massengale, *The Anglo-American Suburb*, 32–34; Stern, Gilmartin and Massengale, *New York 1900*, 427–29.
9. Stern, Gilmartin and Massengale, *New York 1900*, 432–33; Stern, Gilmartin and Mellins, *New York 1930*, 500–503.
10. Stern, Gilmartin and Mellins, *New York 1930*, 87, 490–92.
11. Stern, Gilmartin and Mellins, *New York 1930*, 42–43, 45, 48.
12. Edward Whiting Clark, "Large Residential Tract to Be Undisturbed by Through Traffic," *American City* 37 (September 1927): 366–67.
13. "Green Acres: A Residential Park Community," *Architectural Record* 80 (October 1936): 285–86; Diana Agrest, ed., *A Romance with the City: Irwin S. Chanin* (New York: Cooper Union Press, 1983), 86–89, 98–99.
14. See Stern, Gilmartin and Mellins, *New York 1930*, 691, 694–95.
15. Thomas Adams, *The Building of the City* (New York: Regional Plan Association, 1931), 586.
16. Adams, *The Building of the City*, 587.
17. Regional Plan Association, *From Plan to Reality* (New York: Regional Plan Association, 1933), 42.
18. Regional Plan Association, *From Plan to Reality*, vol. 2 (New York: Regional Plan Association, 1938), 2.
19. O'Brien Boldt, "Area Lacks 'Web' Roads," *New York Times* (February 1, 1942), X: 3.
20. Charles G. Bennett, "Automobile News—Motorists on the Road: More Moses 'Loops' Form," *New York Times* (June 29, 1941), X: 10; "New York's Main Highways," editorial, *New York Times* (December 29, 1941): 14; Stern, Gilmartin and Mellins, *New York 1930*, 41, 44, 691, 694–95.
21. "Moses Is Honored as 'Man of Month,'" *New York Times* (January 10, 1941): 21. Also see "Road System Pays Dividends in War," *New York Times* (December 28, 1941), III: 5; "Strategic Links in Highways Urged," *New York Times* (December 29, 1941): 9.
22. John E. Booth, "New Roads to Speed Travel," *New York Times* (August 21, 1949), II: 13.
23. Joseph C. Ingraham, "Controversial Westchester Route Linking Thruways Set," *New York Times* (May 12, 1954): 1, 36; "Highways a Boon," *New York Times* (January 11, 1960): 137; Merrill Folsom, "Westchester Link to Thruway Open," *New York Times* (December 28, 1960): 46; Joseph C. Ingraham, "Around the Town: New York City's System of Bypass Is Beginning to Take Shape," *New York Times* (January 1, 1961), II: 17. For further discussion of highway development in Westchester during the postwar period, see "New Highway Pushed," *New York Times* (October 20, 1945): 25; Merrill Folsom, "Road Plans Fixed by Westchester," *New York Times* (April 25, 1947): 16; "Westchester Parkways," editorial, *New York Times* (May 19, 1947): 20; Merrill Folsom, "New Saw Mill Link to Join Parkways," *New York Times* (January 18, 1949): 25; "New England Route," editorial, *New York Times* (January 26, 1949): 24; Richard H. Parker, "Highway Problems Vex Westchester," *New York Times* (August 10, 1950): 15.
24. Ingraham, "Controversial Westchester Route Linking Thruways Set": 36.
25. Ingraham, "Controversial Westchester Route Linking Thruways Set": 36.
26. Bernard Stengren, "More Belt Roads Urged in Report," *New York Times* (June 9, 1963): 44.
27. Douglas Dales, "Bridge from Westchester to L.I. Studied to Ease Traffic in City," *New York Times* (August 19, 1964): 1, 47; Madigan-Hyland, Inc. and the Triboro Bridge and Tunnel Authority, *Traffic, Earnings and Feasibility of the Long Island Sound Crossing* (New York, 1965); Joseph C. Ingraham, "Moses Is Seeking Bridge from L.I. to Port Chester," *New York Times* (February 15, 1965): 1, 24; Roy R. Silver, "Bridge Authority Split on L.I. Plan," *New York Times* (March 11, 1965): 1, 34; Joseph C. Ingraham, "Moses Revises Plan on L.I. Sound Bridge," *New York Times* (July 17, 1965): 1, 11; Ronald Maiorana, "Governor Urges Bridge from Oyster Bay to Rye," *New York Times* (March 23, 1967): 1, 24; "To Ease the Traffic Flow," editorial, *New York Times* (March 24, 1967): 30; Ronald Maiorana, "Transit Program Sent to Governor; L.I. Bridges Voted," *New York Times* (April 1, 1967): 1, 15; "Controversy Is Stirred by Proposals for Some Long Island Sound Bridges," *New York Times* (February 11, 1968), XIII: 2; Joseph C. Ingraham, "State Approves Rye-Nassau Span," *New York Times* (December 13, 1968): 1, 35; Robert Lindsey, "Plan for Bridge Across Sound Blocked by State Court Ruling," *New York Times* (February 4, 1969): 1, 31; Robert Moses, *Public Works: A Dangerous Trade* (New York: McGraw-Hill, 1970), 262–70; Harvey Aronson, "The Fury Over the Sound," *New York* 3 (October 19, 1970): 32–34; "Famous Homes Threatened by Long Island Bridge," *Architectural Record* 152 (December 1972): 37; Bartle Bull, "Rocky at the Bridge: Avalanches of Cement," *Village Voice* 18 (May 17, 1973): 1, 35; Francis X. Clines, "Rockefeller Halts Efforts to Build L.I. Sound Bridge," *New York Times* (June 21, 1973): 1, 30; "A Bill to Preserve the Tidal Wetlands Signed by Governor," *New York Times* (June 23, 1973): 20; "Not a Bridge but . . . Better Mass Transit," editorial, *New York Times* (June 23, 1973): 30; Robert A. Caro, *The Power Broker: Robert Moses and the Fall of New York* (New York: Alfred A. Knopf, 1974), 1139–49; Marilyn Wood, "Bridging Long Island Sound," *New York Affairs* 2, no. 3 (1975): 52–65.
28. Robert Moses quoted in Ingraham, "Moses Is Seeking Bridge from L.I. to Port Chester": 1.
29. Robert Moses quoted in "Controversy Is Stirred by Proposals for Some Long Island Sound Bridges": 2.
30. Shipler, "New Highways Shaping Future of City's Suburbs": 26.
31. Keith Rosser quoted in Shipler, "New Highways Shaping Future of City's Suburbs": 26.
32. William B. Shore quoted in Shipler, "New Highways Shaping Future of City's Suburbs": 26.
33. "Parkway System Will Be Extended," *New York Times* (November 29, 1947): 28; "Parkway Extensions," editorial, *New York Times* (December 6, 1947): 14; "Parkway Addition in Nassau to Open," *New York Times* (April 11, 1949): 27; "Fund for Parkway to Speed Last Link," *New York Times* (March 25, 1950): 28.
34. Joseph C. Ingraham, "40 Years of Parkways," *New York Times* (August 4, 1963), X: 1, 5.
35. "Dewey Proposes Four Superroads to Speed Traffic," *New York Times* (February 10, 1954): 1, 18; Douglas Dales, "Superhighways: Governor Dewey Outlines Master Plan to Speed Traffic Throughout State," *New York Times* (February 14, 1954), II: 21; Joseph C. Ingraham, "L.I. Expressway: A Dilemma," *New York Times* (August 4, 1963), X: 1, 5; Ronald Maiorana, "Nassau Proposes New L.I.R.R. Hubs," *New York Times* (August 21, 1965): 23; Joseph C. Ingraham, "L.I. Expressway to Be Snarled for Years," *New York Times* (August 21, 1967): 1, 63; David A. Andelman, "L.I. Expressway Nears End of 32-Year Construction," *New York Times* (June 24, 1972): 33; Caro, *The Power Broker*, 940–50.
36. Quoted in Ingraham, "L.I. Expressway to Be Snarled for Years": 1.
37. Ingraham, "L.I. Expressway: A Dilemma": 1.
38. "A Complete House for $6,990," *Architectural Forum* 86 (May 1947): 70–72; "Levitts Deliver $6,990 House," *American Builder* 69 (June 1947): 96–97; "Community Takes Name of Levitts," *New York Times* (January 4, 1948), VIII: 1, 3; "Nation's Biggest Housebuilder," *Life* 25 (August 23, 1948): 75–78; Joseph M. Guilfoyle and J. Howard Ruttledge, "Levitt Licks the Housing Shortage," *Coronet* 24 (September 1948): 112–16; Eric Larrabee, "The Six Thousand Houses that Levitt Built," *Harper's* 197 (September 1948): 79–88; "Line

Forms Early in Sale of Houses," *New York Times* (March 7, 1949): 21; "157 Veterans Buy Houses," *New York Times* (March 8, 1949): 23; "Houses: The Line at Levitt's," *Newsweek* 33 (March 21, 1949): 66, 71; "4,000 Houses per Year," *Architectural Forum* 90 (April 1949): 84–93; "Levitt's 1950 House," *Architectural Forum* 92 (April 1950): 136–37; "Housing: Up from the Potato Fields," *Time* 56 (July 3, 1950): cover, 67–72; Alfred S. Levitt, "A Community Builder Looks at Community Planning," *Journal of the American Institute of Planners* 17 (spring 1951): 80–88; Charles E. Redfield, "The Impact of Levittown on Local Government," *Journal of the American Institute of Planners* 17 (summer 1951): 130–41; John T. Liell, "Levittown: A Study in Community Development and Planning" (Ph.D. diss., Yale University, 1952); Harold L. Wattel, "Levittown: A Suburban Community," in William M. Dobriner, ed., *The Suburban Community* (New York: G. P. Putnam's Sons, 1958), 287–313; William J. Levitt, "What! Live in Levittown?" *Good Housekeeping* 147 (July 1958): 47, 175–76; "Levittown Revisited," *Progressive Architecture* 48 (October 1967): 55–56; Angela Taylor, "25 Years Ago, Levittown Was a Joke, but Today It's Thriving," *New York Times* (April 18, 1972): 52; Alice Murray, "A Tale of Two Levittowns: On Long Island," *New York Times* (June 18, 1972): 81, 100; Paul Goldberger, "Design Notebook," *New York Times* (April 2, 1981), C: 10; Dolores Hayden, *Redesigning the American Dream: The Future of Housing, Work and Family Life* (New York: W. W. Norton, 1984), 6–9; Kenneth T. Jackson, *Crabgrass Frontier: The Suburbanization of the United States* (New York: Oxford University Press, 1985), 234–38; Stern with Mellins and Gastil, *Pride of Place: Building the American Dream*, 151, 154, 156–57; "Goodbye Levittown: 40 Years Later, It's Just Another Suburb," *Newsday Magazine*, special issue (October 4, 1987); Richard Plunz, *A History of Housing in New York City* (New York: Columbia University Press, 1990), 275–77; Georgia Dullea, "The Tract as Landmark," *New York Times* (October 17, 1991), C: 1, 8; Murray Polner, "At 45, Levittown's Legacy Is Unclear," *New York Times* (June 28, 1992), XIII: 1, 8; Peter Blake, *No Place Like Utopia* (New York: Alfred A. Knopf, 1993), 139; David Halberstam, *The Fifties* (New York: Villard Books, 1993), 131–43.

39. "Housing: Up from the Potato Fields": 67.

40. "Nation's Biggest Housebuilder": 77.

41. William Levitt quoted in "Nation's Biggest Housebuilder": 75.

42. See John Sargeant, *Frank Lloyd Wright's Usonian Houses* (New York: Whitney Library of Design, 1976).

43. "Housing: Up from the Potato Fields": 69.

44. Lewis Mumford, *The City in History: Its Origins, Its Transformations, and Its Prospects* (New York: Harcourt, Brace, 1961), 486.

45. "Housing: Up from the Potato Fields": 69.

46. Taylor, "25 Years Ago, Levittown Was a Joke, but Today It's Thriving": 52.

47. Goldberger, "Design Notebook": 10.

48. Levitt, "A Community Builder Looks at Community Planning": 80–88.

49. "Best's to Open New Store," *New York Times* (January 17, 1930): 17; "Shopping in Westchester," *New York Times* (March 2, 1930), II: 8; "Best's Gets East Orange Site," *New York Times* (March 14, 1930): 39. For B. Altman's and Arnold Constable, see Frank E. Sanchis, *American Architecture: Westchester County, New York: Colonial to Contemporary* (Croton-on-Hudson, N.Y.: North River Press, 1977), 344–46.

50. "Macy's Parkchester," *Architectural Forum* 76 (February 1942): 126–28; "Suburban Department Store Branches," *Interiors* 107 (October 1947): 14; Geoffrey Baker and Bruno Funaro, *Shopping Centers: Design and Operation* (New York: Reinhold Publishing Corp., 1951), 246–47.

51. "Unfinished Business," *Interiors* 104 (December 1944): 10, 12; "Retail Rush," *Architectural Forum* 85 (October 1946): 10–11; "A New Store in Jamaica," editorial, *New York Times* (September 3, 1947): 24; "70,000 Crowd New Macy's in Jamaica; Roof-Parking Successful on Opening Day," *New York Times* (September 3, 1947): 36; "New Stores," *Architectural Record* 102 (October 1947): 16; Morris Ketchum, Jr., *Shops & Stores* (New York: Reinhold Publishing Corp., 1948), 67, 75, 79, 87, 102, 220–21; Louis Parnes, *Planning Stores that Pay* (New York: F. W. Dodge Corp., 1948), 67, 79, 128; "Macy's Jamaica Is Designed around Merchandising Methods," *Architectural Forum* 88 (February 1948): 100–104; Baker and Funaro, *Shopping Centers*, 161; Morris Ketchum, Jr., *Shops & Stores*, rev. ed. (New York: Reinhold Publishing Corp., 1957), 20–21.

52. "Macy's Jamaica Is Designed around Merchandising Methods": 100.

53. "A New Store in Jamaica": 24.

54. Baker and Funaro, *Shopping Centers*, 161.

55. Ketchum, *Shops & Stores*, rev. ed., 20.

56. "Building Notes: Suburban Store," *Architectural Record* 104 (August 1948): 24; "Modern Design and Canvas," advertisement, *Architectural Record* 112 (November 1952): 71.

57. "Macy's New Branch Is Opened to 30,000," *New York Times* (March 22, 1949): 29; Baker and Funaro, *Shopping Centers*, 161; Sanchis, *American Architecture: Westchester County, New York: Colonial to Contemporary*, 345–46.

58. Baker and Funaro, *Shopping Centers*, 161.

59. "Bonwit-Teller White Plains: A Suburban Specialty Shop," *Pencil Points* 23 (February 1942): 72–77; Ketchum, *Shops & Stores*, 166–67; Ketchum, *Shops & Stores*, rev. ed., 139.

60. "New Suburban Shop on Long Island," *New York Times* (May 27, 1941): 42; "Lord and Taylor: Suburban Apparel Shop," *Architectural Record* 89 (June 1941): 41–48; "Contemporary Design in the Suburbs," *Interior Design and Decoration* 17 (July 1941): 40–43, 52; "Shopping Made Fun," *Interiors* 100 (July 1941): 30–33; "Does Modern Architecture Pay?" *Architectural Forum* 79 (September 1943): 69–76; Ketchum, *Shops & Stores*, 110–11; Parnes, *Planning Stores that Pay*, 54–55, 65, 186; Baker and Funaro, *Shopping Centers*, 162–63; Raymond Loewy, *Never Leave Well Enough Alone* (New York: Simon & Schuster, 1951), 198–200; Dero A. Saunders, "Department Stores: Race for the Suburbs," *Fortune* 44 (December 1951): 98–102, 164, 166, 168, 170, 173; Ketchum, *Shops & Stores*, rev. ed., 229. Raymond Loewy Associates designed other branch stores for Lord & Taylor, including one in Millburn, New Jersey (1949). See "Building Previews," *Architectural Forum* 88 (February 1948): 56; "Lord & Taylor's New Suburban Department Store," *Architectural Forum* 90 (March 1949): 13; "Raymond Loewy Associates, New York," *Interiors* 109 (August 1949): 113.

61. Loewy, *Never Leave Well Enough Alone*, 198.

62. "Shopping Made Fun": 30.

63. Loewy, *Never Leave Well Enough Alone*, 200.

64. "Shopping Made Fun": 31.

65. "Contemporary Design in the Suburbs": 40.

66. "Shopping Made Fun": 31.

67. See Stern, Gilmartin and Mellins, *New York 1930*, 299–300, 318.

68. Baker and Funaro, *Shopping Centers*, 162–63; Ketchum, *Shops & Stores*, rev. ed., 229.

69. Stern with Massengale, *The Anglo-American Suburb*, 72–74; Stern with Mellins and Gastil, *Pride of Place: Building the American Dream*, 161–63.

70. Charles W. Moore, Peter Becker and Regula Campbell, *The City Observed: Los Angeles* (New York: Random House, 1984), 151–54.

71. "Munsey Park Business Center, Manhasset, Long Island, N.Y.," *American Architect* 144 (July 1934): 67–70.

72. Ketchum, *Shops & Stores*, rev. ed., 229.

73. Ketchum, *Shops & Stores*, 38–39, 62–63, 72–73, 105; "Three Stores," *Progressive Architecture* 29 (February 1948): 55–69.

74. "Dividing 75 Acres Near East Chester," *New York Times* (October 26, 1947), VIII: 1, 4; Ketchum, *Shops & Stores*, 227, 229; Parnes, *Planning Stores that Pay*, 117; Morris Ketchum, Jr., "Lord and Taylor's Westchester Store," *Architectural Record* 103 (April 1948): 111–22; "Fashion Center in the Suburbs," *Interiors* 107 (June 1948): 91–93; "Suburban Branch Department Stores," *Architectural Record* 115 (May 1954): 178–97; Ketchum, *Shops & Stores*, rev. ed., 185, 192–94; Sanchis, *American Architecture: Westchester County, New York: Colonial to Contemporary*, 346.

75. Ketchum, "Lord and Taylor's Westchester Store": 119.

76. Meredeth Clausen, "Northgate Regional Shopping Center—Paradigm from the Provinces," *Journal of the Society of Architectural Historians* 43 (May 1984): 144–61.

77. For Lederer's, see Stern, Gilmartin and Mellins, *New York 1930*, 310.

78. Morris Ketchum, Jr., *Blazing a Trail* (New York: Vantage Press, 1982), 3.

79. "Triangular Site Suggests Circular Mall," *Architectural Record* 106 (August 1949): 129; Baker and Funaro, *Shopping Centers*, 30.

80. "Where the City Meets the Suburbs," *Architectural Record* 106 (August 1949): 128–29.

81. Baker and Funaro, *Shopping Centers*, 172–73; "Shopping Center Opens in Westchester County," *Architectural Record* 118 (January 1955): 280; "Pahlmann in Westchester," *Interiors* 114 (June 1955): 18; "Gimbels Westchester," *Interiors* 115 (October 1955): 20; Ketchum, *Shops & Stores*, rev. ed., 34, 36, 38, 45, 226, 231–33; Lathrop Douglass, "Shopping Center Design," *Traffic Quarterly* 12 (July 1958): 409–24; Victor Gruen and Larry Smith, *Shopping Towns USA: The Planning of Shopping Centers* (New York: Van Nostrand Reinhold, 1960), 160–61; Victor Gruen, "Retailing and the Automobile: A Romance Based upon a Case of Mistaken Identity," *Architectural Record* 127 (March 1960): 191–210; Sanchis, *American Architecture: Westchester County, New York: Colonial to Contemporary*, 347–49.

82. Ketchum, *Shops & Stores*, rev. ed., 216.

83. Ketchum, *Shops & Stores*, rev. ed., 216.

84. Quoted in Joan Didion, "The Shopping Center," *Esquire* 84 (December 1975): 98–99, 234, reprinted as "On the Mall," in Joan Didion, *The White Album* (New York: Simon & Schuster, 1979), 180–86.

85. "Roosevelt Field Shopping Center," *Architectural Record* 117 (June 1955): 16; "Roosevelt Field Shopping Center," *Progressive Architecture* 36 (September 1955): 91–97; "Shopping Centers Receiving Unusual Decorative Notes," *Architectural Forum* 103 (October 1955): 17; "New History for Old," *Time* 68 (July 16, 1956): 80–81; "News Bulletins: International Flight Mall," *Progressive Architecture* 37 (September 1956): 101; "Macy's Opens Doors in 2 New Shopping Centers," *Progressive Architecture* 37 (October 1956): 93; Ketchum, *Shops & Stores*, rev. ed., 231–34, 236–39; "Roosevelt Field Shopping Center, Nassau County, L.I.," *Architectural Record* 122 (September 1957): 206–16; Robert L. Zion, "The Landscape Architect and the Shopping Center: An Unusual Opportunity at Roosevelt Field, New York," *Landscape Architecture* 48 (October 1957): 6–12; "Roosevelt Field Shopping Center, Nassau County, Long Island," *Bauen + Wohnen* 12 (August 1958): 270–80; Morris Ketchum, Jr., "Shops and the Market Place," *Architectural Record* 124 (October 1958): 193–218; Ian McCallum, *Architecture USA* (London: Architectural Press, 1959), 195; Gruen and Smith, *Shopping Towns USA*, 150, 166, 244–45; James S. Hornbeck, ed., *Stores and Shopping Centers* (New York: McGraw-Hill, 1962), 121–30; William Zeckendorf with Edward McCreary, *The Autobiography of William Zeckendorf* (New York: Holt, Rinehart and Winston, 1970), 121, 141, 296; William Severini Kowinski, *The Malling of America: An Inside Look at the Great Consumer Paradise* (New York: William Morrow, 1985), 131–39; Carter Wiseman, *I. M. Pei: A Profile in American Architecture* (New York: Harry N. Abrams, 1990), 53–54.

86. "New History for Old": 80.

87. Hornbeck, ed., *Stores and Shopping Centers*, 121.

88. Hornbeck, ed., *Stores and Shopping Centers*, 127.

89. For Mid-Island Plaza, see Douglass, "Shopping Center Design": 413; Gruen and Smith, *Shopping Towns USA*, 246–47; Kowinski, *The Malling of America*, 133.

90. "New Shopping Centers Show Two Development Approaches," *Architectural Forum* 102 (February 1955): 21.

91. "New Macy Outlet Slated in Suburb," *New York Times* (January 19, 1958): 56; "Center Outlined in New Rochelle," *New York Times* (May 14, 1958): 25; "Milan Center Gave Idea for Plaza Here," *New York Times* (May 25, 1958), VIII: 1; "Gruen Designs $41 Million Shopping Center, Office Building for New Rochelle, N.Y.," *Architectural Forum* 108 (June 1958): 6; Gruen and Smith, *Shopping Towns USA*, 82, 84–85, 89, 96, 131, 180.

92. Merrill Folsom, "New Rochelle Getting Covered Mart," *New York Times* (January 19, 1967): 25; Sanchis, *American Architecture: Westchester County, New York: Colonial to Contemporary*, 348–49.

93. Hornbeck, ed., *Stores and Shopping Centers*, 160–63. Also see "Elegance and Restraint for 'Class' Tenants," *Architectural Record* 131 (June 1962): 170–73.

94. See John Elber Bebout and Ronald J. Grele, *Where Cities Meet: The Urbanization of New Jersey* (Princeton, N.J.: Van Nostrand, 1964); Bergen County Planning Board, *Survey of Business in Bergen County* (Hackensack, N.J.: Bergen County Planning Board, 1966); Joel Garreau, *Edge City: Life on the New Frontier* (New York: Doubleday, 1991), 17–68.

95. "Macy Forms Subsidiary: Garden State Plaza Corp. Will Run New Jersey Center," *New York Times* (May 5, 1954): 49; "Paramus Center to Be Expanded," *New York Times* (September 7, 1958): 61; Gruen and Smith, *Shopping Towns USA*, 84, 116, 119, 238–39; Regional Plan Association, *The Future of Bergen and Passaic Counties: A Supplement to the Second Regional Plan* (New York: Regional Plan Association, 1969), 18.

96. Regional Plan Association, *The Future of Bergen and Passaic Counties: A Supplement to the Second Regional Plan*, 18.

97. Regional Plan Association, *The Future of Bergen and Passaic Counties: A Supplement to the Second Regional Plan*, 18.

98. White and Wilensky, *AIA Guide* (1988), 753.

99. "Macy's Park-and-Shop," *Architectural Forum* 120 (April 1964): 37; "SOM Designs First-of-a-Kind Macy's," *Progressive Architecture* 45 (April 1964): 75; William Robbins, "Woman and Her Dog Put Notch in Macy's Big Circle in Queens," *New York Times* (June 9, 1965): 49; Isadore Barmash, "New Departure Set for Macy's," *New York Times* (July 11, 1965), III: 1, 13; Paul L. Montgomery, "Macy's Opens Big Drive-In Store in Elmhurst," *New York Times* (October 12, 1965): 49, 79; "New Macy's in Queens," *Architectural Record* 138 (November 1965): 41; "The New Macy's Store Gets Good Marks in Traffic Flow . . . but Fails Geometry," *Progressive Architecture* 45 (November 1965): 45; Walter McQuade and Philip Herrera, "The Well-Rounded Shopping Center," *Fortune* 72 (December 1965): 189–90; "A Multi-level Store with Wrap-around Parking," *Architectural Record* 139 (April 1966): 168–70; Axel Menges, *Architecture of Skidmore, Owings & Merrill, 1963–1973* (New York: Architectural Book Publishing Co., 1974), 42–45; White and Willensky, *AIA Guide* (1978), 520; Andrew Alpern and Seymour Durst, *Holdouts!* (New York: McGraw-Hill, 1984), 22–23.
100. "SOM Designs First-of-a-Kind Macy's": 75.
101. Robbins, "Woman and Her Dog Put Notch in Macy's Big Circle in Queens": 49.
102. "The New Macy's Store Gets Good Marks in Traffic Flow . . . but Fails Geometry": 45.
103. Louis G. Redstone, *New Dimensions in Shopping Centers and Stores* (New York: McGraw-Hill, 1973), 33, 38–39.
104. White and Willensky, *AIA Guide* (1988), 752.
105. "Master Plan for Staten Island Mall," *Progressive Architecture* 53 (April 1972): 32–33; "The Talk of the Town: Bee's Knees," *New Yorker* 49 (September 3, 1973): 23–24; "Awards: Winning Store Interiors," *Interiors* 133 (March 1974): 10. For an earlier proposal to develop the site as a shopping and office complex, see Gruen and Smith, *Shopping Towns USA*, 112–13.
106. White and Willensky, *AIA Guide* (1988), 757–58.
107. White and Willensky, *AIA Guide* (1988), 757.
108. Jackson, *Crabgrass Frontier: The Suburbanization of the United States*, 268.
109. Caroline Seebohm, *The Man Who Was Vogue: The Life and Times of Condé Nast* (New York: Viking, 1982), 246–47.
110. "Large Corporation Builds a Research Campus in New Jersey," *Architectural Record* 106 (October 1949): 108–14; Clifford F. Rassweiler, "The Johns-Manville Research Center Six Years Later," *Architectural Record* 118 (September 1955): 222–24.
111. Rassweiler, "The Johns-Manville Research Center Six Years Later": 223.
112. Richard H. Parks, "Trend of Industry to Suburbs Found; Jersey Is Favored," *New York Times* (August 11, 1952): 1, 22.
113. Quoted in Parks, "Trend of Industry to Suburbs Found; Jersey Is Favored": 22.
114. John Bainbridge, *Little Wonder or, the Reader's Digest and How It Grew* (New York: Reynal & Hitchcock, 1945), 76–111; James Playsted Wood, *Of Lasting Interest: The Story of the Reader's Digest* (Garden City, N.Y.: Doubleday, 1967), 61–70; Sanchis, *American Architecture: Westchester County, New York: Colonial to Contemporary*, 305–6; Samuel A. Schreiner, Jr., *The Condensed World of the Reader's Digest* (New York: Stein and Day, 1977), 99–128.
115. Sanchis, *American Architecture: Westchester County, New York: Colonial to Contemporary*, 308.
116. "Esso Starts New Building," *New York Times* (October 29, 1952): 50; "New Plan Creates 'Packaged' Offices," *New York Times* (November 1, 1953), VIII: 1.
117. "General Foods Headquarters Building Started in White Plains," *New York Times* (June 5, 1953): 30; Richard F. Crandell, *This Is Westchester* (New York: Sterling, 1954), 182–83; "General Foods Begins Moving Offices to New Headquarters in White Plains," *New York Times* (March 15, 1954): 15; "General Foods Moves Home Offices from New York City to White Plains," *New York Times* (March 16, 1954): 15; "Food Company Flees Madding Crowd," *Business Week* (March 27, 1954): 52–54, 56; Ralph Walker, *Ralph Walker, Architect* (New York: Henahan House, 1957), 206–11; Sanchis, *American Architecture: Westchester County, New York: Colonial to Contemporary*, 308–9; Jackson, *Crabgrass Frontier: Suburbanization in the United States*, 268, unnumbered plate.
118. "Food Company Flees Madding Crowd": 53–54.
119. Crandell, *This Is Westchester*, 182–83.
120. Quoted in "General Foods Begins Moving Offices to New Headquarters in White Plains": 15.
121. "Trend of Offices to Suburbs Poses Problems for New York's Ritzy Westchester County," *Architectural Forum* 98 (January 1958): 43, 45.
122. "Trend of Offices to Suburbs Poses Problems for New York's Ritzy Westchester County": 43.
123. "Trend of Offices to Suburbs Poses Problems for New York's Ritzy Westchester County": 43.
124. James Felt quoted in "Trend of Offices to Suburbs Poses Problems for New York's Ritzy Westchester County": 45.
125. Herman T. Stichman quoted in "City Urged to Act on Suburban Shift," *New York Times* (February 11, 1953): 31.
126. "City and Suburbs," editorial, *New York Times* (July 9, 1953): 24.
127. "The City Whose Business Is Bigness," *Business Week* (October 13, 1956): 125–34, 137–41.
128. John Morris Dixon, "IBM Thinks Twice," *Architectural Forum* 124 (March 1966): 32–39. Also see "IBM's New Corporate Face," *Architectural Forum* 106 (February 1957): 106–14.
129. "IBM Engineering & Development Laboratory," *Architectural Record* 118 (September 1955): 210–11; "IBM's New Corporate Face": 106–7, 110–11; "IBM Aerospace Headquarters by Eliot Noyes & Associates, Architects," *Arts and Architecture* 81 (October 1964): 15–17; Dixon, "IBM Thinks Twice": 34–35. For another building designed by Eliot Noyes as part of the IBM complex in Poughkeepsie and completed in 1959, see "Clarity, Cohesiveness, Good Detail," *Architectural Record* 126 (September 1959): 199–204.
130. "IBM's New Corporate Face": 110; "Research in the Round," *Architectural Forum* 114 (June 1961): 80–85; Allan Temko, *Eero Saarinen* (New York: George Braziller, 1962), 37–40, plates 61–69; "Centre de recherches I.B.M. Yorktown Heights, États-Unis," *L'Architecture d'Aujourd'hui* 33 (February–March 1962): 40–53; "Research Centre, Yorktown, N.Y.," *Architect and Building News* 221 (June 27, 1962): 923–26; "Centre de recherches I.B.M. Yorktown Heights, N.Y.," *L'Architecture d'Aujourd'hui* 34 (December 1963–January 1964): 45, 50; Rafael E. J. Iglesia, *Eero Saarinen* (Buenos Aires: Instituto de Arte Americano e Investigaciones Estéticas, 1966), 27–31, plates 24–29; Dixon, "IBM Thinks Twice": 34–35; Aline B. Saarinen, ed., *Eero Saarinen on His Work*, rev. ed. (New

Haven, Conn.: Yale University Press, 1968), 76–81; Rupert Spade, *Eero Saarinen* (New York: Simon & Schuster, 1971), 15, plates 32–35; Sanchis, *American Architecture: Westchester County, New York: Colonial to Contemporary*, 311; Thomas J. Watson, Jr., and Peter Petre, *Father, Son & Co.: My Life at IBM and Beyond* (New York: Bantam, 1990), unnumbered plate between pp. 308–9.
131. "The Maturing Modern," *Time* 68 (July 2, 1956): cover, 50–57.
132. Temko, *Eero Saarinen*, 38.
133. Temko, *Eero Saarinen*, 38.
134. "Research in the Round": 81.
135. "Research in the Round": 82. Also see *Seymour Lipton* (Milwaukee, Wis.: Milwaukee Art Center and the University of Wisconsin at Milwaukee, 1969), unpaginated.
136. Temko, *Eero Saarinen*, 39.
137. Eero Saarinen quoted in Saarinen, ed., *Eero Saarinen on His Work*, rev. ed., 76.
138. Sanchis, *American Architecture: Westchester County, New York: Colonial to Contemporary*, 311.
139. Merrill Folsom, "Companies Grow in Westchester," *New York Times* (October 1, 1963): 47; "IBM Headquarters on East Coast and Space Building in West," *Progressive Architecture* 45 (December 1964): 52; "IBM Headquarters Building," *Arts and Architecture* 82 (February 1965): 34–35; Sanchis, *American Architecture: Westchester County, New York: Colonial to Contemporary*, 311; Carol Herselle Krinsky, *Gordon Bunshaft of Skidmore, Owings & Merrill* (New York: Architectural History Foundation; Cambridge, Mass.: MIT Press, 1988), 146–47, 200–203.
140. Sam Hunter, *Isamu Noguchi* (New York: Abbeville Press, 1978), 266–67.
141. "IBM in Jersey," *Architectural Forum* 119 (December 1963): 31; John Morris Dixon, "From Uxmal to IBM," *Architectural Forum* 122 (June 1965): 37–43; Dixon, "IBM Thinks Twice": 37.
142. Dixon, "IBM Thinks Twice": 33.
143. Dixon, "From Uxmal to IBM": 39, 42.
144. "New Laboratory at IBM," *Architectural Forum* 120 (February 1964): 86–87; Dixon, "IBM Thinks Twice": 37; Paul Rudolph, *Drawings* (Tokyo: A.D.A. Edita, 1972), 122–25.
145. "A Continuing Study of the Window Wall by Eliot Noyes," *Architectural Record* 141 (April 1967): 173–75.
146. "A Continuing Study of the Window Wall by Eliot Noyes": 173.
147. John Morris Dixon, "Fortress for Pharmaceuticals," *Progressive Architecture* 45 (November 1964): 168–75. Also see Ronald Maiorana, "L.I. Plant Scores Parkway Screen," *New York Times* (April 4, 1964): 29; Ada Louise Huxtable, "Design of Garden City Plant Stirs Extreme Reactions," *New York Times* (September 20, 1964), VIII: 1, 14; Walter McQuade, "Structure & Design," *Fortune* 70 (November 1964): 205–6, 211–12; "Château Endo," *Architectural Review* 137 (February 1965): 96; Mary Simons, "Sculptured Factory in Suburbia Designed by Paul Rudolph, A.I.A.," *Interiors* 124 (April 1965): 118–22; "Paul Rudolph per medicinali," *L'Architettura cronache e storia* 10 (April 1965): 816–17; "Pharmazeutische Fabrik (Endo Laboratories), Garden City, New York," *Deutsche Bauzeitung* 100 (May 1966): 356–59; Sibyl Moholy-Nagy and Gerhard Schwab, *The Architecture of Paul Rudolph* (New York: Praeger, 1970), 142–51; Rupert Spade, *Paul Rudolph* (New York: Simon & Schuster, 1971), 126, plates 47–53; Rudolph, *Drawings*, 114–15.
148. For Rudolph's Art and Architecture Building, see Moholy-Nagy and Schwab, *The Architecture of Paul Rudolph*, 120–37.
149. Paul Rudolph quoted in Simons, "Sculptured Factory in Suburbia Designed by Paul Rudolph, A.I.A.": 118.
150. Huxtable, "Design of Garden City Plant Stirs Extreme Reactions": 14.
151. "Château Endo": 96. For the Carpenter Center for Visual Arts, see W. Boesiger, ed., *Le Corbusier, Oeuvre complète 1957–1965*, vol. 7 (Zurich: Verlag für Architektur, 1965), 54–67.
152. Huxtable, "Design of Garden City Plant Stirs Extreme Reactions": 14.
153. Spade, *Paul Rudolph*, 126.
154. Quoted in Maiorana, "L.I. Plant Scores Parkway Screen": 29.
155. Paul Rudolph quoted in Maiorana, "L.I. Plant Scores Parkway Screen": 29.
156. Huxtable, "Design of Garden City Plant Stirs Extreme Reactions": 1, 14.
157. Temko, *Eero Saarinen*, 37, 40–41, plates 70–73; "Bell Labs' Mirrored Superblock," *Architectural Forum* 132 (October 1962): 145–52; Iglesia, *Eero Saarinen*, 27–31, plates 30–34; "The Biggest Mirror Ever," *Architectural Forum* 126 (April 1967): 33–41; "Bell Telephone Laboratories Holmdel," *Architectural Design* 37 (August 1967): 356–59; Cesar Pelli and Diana Pelli, "Eero Saarinen: Bell Telephone Corporation Research Laboratories, New Jersey, 1957–1962," *Global Architecture* 6 (1971): 2–21; Spade, *Eero Saarinen*, 15, plates 36–40.
158. Temko, *Eero Saarinen*, 40.
159. Spade, *Eero Saarinen*, 15.
160. Temko, *Eero Saarinen*, 40.
161. Temko, *Eero Saarinen*, 40.
162. Temko, *Eero Saarinen*, 40.
163. "The Biggest Mirror Ever": 35, 37.
164. Temko, *Eero Saarinen*, 40.
165. "Headquarters: Exodus from Fun City," *Time* 89 (February 24, 1967): 83–84; "New York: Nice Place to Visit," *Newsweek* 69 (February 27, 1967): 69; "Why the Growing Flight of Business from New York City," *U.S. News & World Report* 62 (March 6, 1967): 45; "Recent Moves of Big Firms from New York Were Prompted by Space Shortage," *Real Estate Record and Guide* 199 (March 18, 1967): 2–3.
166. "Headquarters: Exodus from Fun City": 83. Also see Merrill Folsom, "Pepsi-Cola Planning to Leave City for Westchester: New Use for Club Fought," *New York Times* (February 11, 1967): 1, 19; Richard Reeves, "Pepsi-Cola Planning to Leave City for Westchester: Mayor Tried to Halt Move," *New York Times* (February 11, 1967): 1, 19; "Not a Ghost Town," editorial, *New York Times* (February 14, 1967): 42; Merrill Folsom, "Companies Tell Why They Leave," *New York Times* (February 16, 1967): 25; Seth S. King, "American Can Co. Will Leave City," *New York Times* (February 16, 1967): 1, 25; "Move Inevitable, Greenwich Feels," *New York Times* (February 16, 1967): 25.
167. "Survey of Former Manhattan Firms Pinpoints Five Reasons for Exodus," *Real Estate Record and Guide* 202 (September 14, 1968): 2–5.
168. Folsom, "Companies Tell Why They Leave": 25.
169. Folsom, "Companies Grow in Westchester": 47.
170. Elizabeth Kendall Thompson, "Suburban Office Buildings," *Architectural Record* 151 (February 1972): 113–28; Sanchis, *American Architecture: Westchester County, New York: Colonial to Contemporary*, 314–15; G. E. Kidder Smith, *The Architecture of*

the United States, vol. 1: New England and the Mid-Atlantic States (Garden City, N.Y.: Anchor/Doubleday, 1981), 452–53.

171. "Greenwich, Conn. Headquarters Offices for American Can Are a Model of Restraint," Architectural Forum 134 (January–February 1971): 28–35; Ada Louise Huxtable, "It's So Peaceful in the Country," New York Times (January 17, 1971), II: 29, reprinted in Ada Louise Huxtable, Kicked a Building Lately? (New York: Quadrangle/New York Times Book Co., 1976), 71–74; "Pastoral Palazzo," Architectural Review 149 (March 1971): 137–46; "American Can Company, Greenwich, Connecticut," Journal of the American Institute of Architects 59 (May 1973): 50–51; Arthur Drexler, "Introduction," in Menges, Architecture of Skidmore, Owings & Merrill, 1963–1973, 34, 36, 84–93; Sanchis, American Architecture: Westchester County, New York: Colonial to Contemporary, 315; Krinsky, Gordon Bunshaft of Skidmore, Owings & Merrill, 239–42, 274–83.

172. Huxtable, "It's So Peaceful in the Country": 29.

173. Gordon Bunshaft quoted in Krinsky, Gordon Bunshaft of Skidmore, Owings & Merrill, 241.

174. Huxtable, "It's So Peaceful in the Country": 29.

175. Charles Hoyt, "Office Buildings in the Suburbs," Architectural Record 156 (October 1974): 125–40.

176. Sanchis, American Architecture: Westchester County, New York: Colonial to Contemporary, 311–12.

177. "The Heart of Technicon," Interior Design 41 (October 1970): 140–45; Sanchis, American Architecture: Westchester County, New York: Colonial to Contemporary, 313–14.

178. William B. Foxhall, "Architecture for Industry," Architectural Record 143 (May 1968): 185–202; John Anderson, "Design Firm Case Study: Vincent G. Kling & Partners," Interiors 131 (February 1972): 58–79; Sanchis, American Architecture: Westchester County, New York: Colonial to Contemporary, 314.

179. Sanchis, American Architecture: Westchester County, New York: Colonial to Contemporary, 315–16; Mildred F. Schmertz, "A Low Profile for IBM," Architectural Record 161 (January 1977): 141–46; Olga Gueft, "IBM Headquarters," Contract Interiors 137 (September 1977): 114–16.

180. Schmertz, "A Low Profile for IBM": 141.

181. Lewis Rudin quoted in "School Prefers City to Suburb," Real Estate Record and Guide 211 (May 26, 1973): 3.

182. William H. Whyte, "End of the Exodus: The Logic of Headquarters City," New York 9 (September 20, 1976): 88–99. Also see William H. Whyte, The Organization Man (Garden City, N.Y.: Doubleday, 1956).

183. Edgar Bronfman quoted in Whyte, "End of the Exodus: The Logic of Headquarters City": 95.

184. Whyte, "End of the Exodus: The Logic of Headquarters City": 99.

185. "Topics of The Times," New York Times (August 8, 1946): 20.

186. Jack Raymond, "$50,000,000 Dream Center Is Projected for Flushing," New York Times (August 7, 1946): 1, 17; "'Dream City,'" New York Times (August 11, 1946), IV: 2; "Zeckendorf City," Architectural Forum 85 (October 1946): 9; Robert Sellmer, "The Man Who Wants to Build New York Over," Life 21 (October 28, 1946): 67–70, 72; "$50,000,000 Retail Center," Architectural Forum 85 (November 1946): 100–105; "Unfavorable Report on 'Dream City' Approved," New York Times (December 5, 1947): 27; "Anti-Queens Bias on Parking Is Seen," New York Times (December 26, 1947): 32.

187. Raymond, "$50,000,000 Dream Center Is Projected for Flushing": 1.

188. "$50,000,000 Retail Center": 104.

189. Quoted in Raymond, "$50,000,000 Dream Center Is Projected for Flushing": 17.

190. "$50,000,000 Retail Center": 104.

191. James A. Burke quoted in "Anti-Queens Bias on Parking Is Seen": 32.

192. Nicholas N. Ryshkoff-Karr, "Redevelopment of Business Center, Main Street, Flushing, N.Y." (Master's thesis, Columbia University, 1957): 4.

193. Ketchum, Shops & Stores, 281, 284–85. Also see "Shopping Center," Architectural Forum 85 (August 1946): 76–79.

194. John W. Stevens, "Mount Kisco Gets Plan for Growth," New York Times (October 14, 1958): 39. Also see William Borders, "Decision in Westchester," New York Times (June 6, 1966): 48; Doris Faber, "Progress in Mt. Kisco Marches into Traffic Snarl," New York Times (September 13, 1970), VIII: 1, 6.

195. Faber, "Progress in Mt. Kisco Marches into Traffic Snarl": 1.

196. Ketchum, "Lord and Taylor's Westchester Store": 111–22.

197. Sanchis, American Architecture: Westchester County, New York: Colonial to Contemporary, 346–47.

198. "Split-level Suburban Store," Architectural Forum 102 (May 1955): 134–37; Ketchum, Shops & Stores, rev. ed., 89, 216–17, 227; Sanchis, American Architecture: Westchester County, New York: Colonial to Contemporary, 346–47.

199. "Split-level Suburban Store": 136.

200. Robert A. Beauregard, "Urban Form and the Redevelopment of Central Business Districts," Journal of Architectural and Planning Research 3 (August 1986): 183–98. Also see Arthur C. Holden, A Plan for the Central Business Area, City of White Plains (White Plains, N.Y.: Holden, McLaughlin and Associates, 1945); Thomas L. Hansen, "A Planning Study of the City of White Plains, New York" (Master's thesis, Columbia University, 1950).

201. City of White Plains, New York, Urban Renewal Plan, Central Renewal Project, U.R.N.Y. R-37, April 11, 1963 (White Plains, N.Y.: City of White Plains, 1963); White Plains Urban Renewal Agency, Annual Report, July 1, 1966–June 30, 1967 (White Plains, N.Y.: White Plains Urban Renewal Agency, 1967).

202. James Feron, "New Malls Spur 2 Suburbs' Recovery," New York Times (January 12, 1980): 21; Barry Maitland, Shopping Malls: Planning and Design (Harlow, England: Construction Press, 1985), 106–7, 112–13, 163, 175; Beauregard, "Urban Form and the Redevelopment of Central Business Districts": 188.

203. Sanchis, American Architecture: Westchester County, New York: Colonial to Contemporary, 347.

204. "Stores and Shops," Architectural Record 157 (April 1975): 107–22; "Two Stores," Interior Design 46 (April 1975): 150–61; Sanchis, American Architecture: Westchester County, New York: Colonial to Contemporary, 347.

205. For Bergdorf Goodman in New York City, see Stern, Gilmartin and Mellins, New York 1930, 310–11, 318–19.

206. "Stores and Shops": 108.

207. See Estelle F. Feinstein and Joyce C. Pendery, Stamford: An Illustrated History (Woodland Hills, Calif.: Windsor, 1984).

208. Herbert S. Swan, Plan of a Metropolitan Suburb (Stamford, Conn.: Stamford Town Planning Commission, 1929), quoted in Feinstein and Pendery, Stamford: An Illustrated History, 111.

209. "Suburban Department Store with Cantilevered Balconies," Architectural Forum 160 (March 1954): 50; William Snaith, "Stores, Shops and Restaurants," Interior Design 25 (October 1954): 89–99; "Bloomingdale's New Stamford Branch," Architectural Record 117 (May 1955): 203–5; Ketchum, Shops & Stores, rev. ed., 228.

210. "Stamford Maps Urban Renewal," New York Times (January 30, 1960): 23; "$65,000,000 Redevelopment Proposed for Stamford," New York Times (March 29, 1961): 35; "Stamford Project Gets Federal Aid," New York Times (November 27, 1962): 26.

211. "Stamford Rejects Plans for Branch of Lord & Taylor," New York Times (January 22, 1965): 23.

212. "Three Oval Apartment Towers Will Start Renewal of Stamford," New York Times (September 25, 1966), VIII: 1, 6; "Stamford Renewal Project Under Way," New York Times (January 19, 1969), VIII: 1, 6.

213. "Tall Tower Is Planned in Stamford," New York Times (February 23, 1969), VIII: 1, 6; "Optical Illusions," Progressive Architecture 52 (February 1971): 28; Carter B. Horsley, "Stamford Renewal Chugging Along," New York Times (April 9, 1972), VIII: 1, 12; "Stamford Renewal Is Finally Taking Shape," New York Times (November 20, 1972): 41.

214. See Schwartz, Fichtner, Bick and Associates, Basic Policies for the Master Plan of Stamford, Connecticut (Stamford, Conn.: Schwartz, Fichtner, Bick and Associates, 1970).

215. Michael Knight, "Stamford: A Small Hub of Wealth and Power," New York Times (June 13, 1976): 1, 8.

216. Michael Knight, "Once-Sleepy Stamford Awakening to New Eminence," New York Times (June 22, 1974): 1, 58.

217. Salem Shapiro quoted in "Stamford Renewal Is Finally Taking Shape": 41.

218. Julius M. Willensky quoted in "Stamford Renewal Is Finally Taking Shape": 41.

219. Victor Bisharat quoted in Andree Brooks, "The 'Stamford Lesson' Influences Architecture," New York Times (October 19, 1980), VIII: 1, 10.

220. Ada Louise Huxtable, "It's Stylish, but Is It Art—Or Spinach?" New York Times (January 25, 1981), II: 1, 25.

221. Victor H. Bisharat, letter to the editor, New York Times (March 15, 1981), II: 29. Replies from Andree Brooks and Ada Louise Huxtable follow Bisharat's letter.

222. Robert E. Tomasson, "Stamford's New Mall Heightens Planning Worries," New York Times (March 12, 1982), B: 1, 4.

Chapter 16
Historic Preservation

1. James Merrill, "An Urban Convalescence," in Water Street (New York: Atheneum, 1962), 3.

2. For useful overviews of historic preservation in New York, see Nathan Silver, Lost New York (Boston: Houghton Mifflin, 1967), 1–21; Harmon H. Goldstone and Martha Dalrymple, History Preserved: A Guide to New York City Landmarks and Historic Districts (New York: Simon & Schuster, 1974), 17–31; Barbaralee Diamonstein, The Landmarks of New York (New York: Harry N. Abrams, 1988), 9–20.

3. "Old 76," New-York Mirror 8 (March 19, 1831): 289, quoted in Diamonstein, The Landmarks of New York, 9.

4. Allan Nevins, ed., The Diary of Philip Hone, 1828–1851 (New York: Dodd, Mead and Co., 1927), 730, quoted in Diamonstein, The Landmarks of New York, 10.

5. Quoted in Diamonstein, The Landmarks of New York, 10.

6. "Early Doom Fixed for Old Postoffice," New York Times (May 21, 1938): 1, 3; "$1 Bid by the City on the Old Postoffice," New York Times (July 16, 1938): 15; "Farewell to an Eyesore," editorial, New York Times (July 18, 1938): 12; "Treasury Accepts $1 Bid of City for Postoffice," New York Times (August 4, 1938): 1; "Topics of The Times," New York Times (August 7, 1938): 8; Frederic Cyrus Leubuscher, "The Old Postoffice Passes," letter to the editor, New York Times (February 22, 1939): 20; "Old Postoffice Is Down at Last," New York Times (March 12, 1939), XIII: 1, 4; "A New New York Appears as Old Landmarks Vanish," New York Times (May 30, 1939): 25; Stern, Gilmartin and Mellins, New York 1930, 94, 96, 713; "The Talk of the Town: Witnesses," New Yorker 68 (April 6, 1992): 25–26.

7. "Farewell to an Eyesore": 12.

8. For Madison Square Presbyterian Church, see Silver, Lost New York, 148; Leland M. Roth, McKim, Mead & White, Architects (New York: Harper & Row, 1983), 275–79; Stern, Gilmartin and Massengale, New York 1900, 110, 112; Stern, Gilmartin and Mellins, New York 1930, 19; Paul R. Baker, Stanny: The Gilded Life of Stanford White (New York: The Free Press, 1989), 149–66. For Madison Square Garden, see Silver, Lost New York, 50–53; Roth, McKim, Mead & White, Architects, 158–65; Stern, Gilmartin and Massengale, New York 1900, 202–9; Stern, Gilmartin and Mellins, New York 1930, 19–20; Baker, Stanny: The Gilded Life of Stanford White, 363–64.

9. R. W. Haddon, "The Threatened Demolition of St. John's Chapel in New York," American Architect and Building News 102 (July 31, 1912): 33–35; "Old St. John's Gets a Stay," New York Times (March 31, 1917): 7; Edward Hagman Hall, "A Plea for Old St. John's," letter to the editor, New York Times (April 6, 1917): 12; C. Lewis Hind, "Old St. John's in Varick Street," letter to the editor, New York Times (May 9, 1918): 12; "St. John's Chapel Razed," New York Times (October 6, 1918), IV: 4; "Sell St. John Site," New York Times (November 24, 1918), VIII: 9; Silver, Lost New York, 151–53; Stern, Gilmartin and Mellins, New York 1930, 167.

10. "Sell St. John Site": 9.

11. Marshall B. Davidson, "Foreword," Art in America 45 (summer 1957): 12–13.

12. For general discussions of house-museums in New York, see Kenneth Holcomb Dunshee, As You Pass By (New York: Hastings House, 1952); Fred W. McDarrah, Museums in New York (New York: E. P. Dutton, 1967); The Heritage of New York, with a preface by Whitney North Seymour (New York: Fordham University Press, 1970).

13. Charles G. Shaw, "A Metropolitan Antique," Antiques 46 (October 1944): 217; "History in Houses: The Van Cortlandt House in New York," Antiques 56 (August 1949): 98–99, 104–7; Huson Jackson, A Guide to New York Architecture 1650–1952 (New York: Reinhold Publishing Corp., 1952), 40; Kenneth Bates, "A Great American Idea: Van Cortlandt House Museum," House and Garden 144 (September 1973): 20; Diamonstein, The Landmarks of New York, 40–41; Andrew S. Dolkart, Guide to New York City Landmarks (Washington, D.C.: Preservation Press, 1992), 216.

14. Helen Comstock, "History in Houses: The Morris-Jumel Mansion in New York," *Antiques* 59 (March 1951): 214–19; Jackson, *A Guide to New York Architecture 1650–1952*, 37–38; Ada Louise Huxtable, *Classic New York: Georgian Gentility to Greek Elegance* (Garden City, N.Y.: Anchor, 1964), 9–10; Stern, Gilmartin and Mellins, *New York 1930*, 131–32; Diamonstein, *The Landmarks of New York*, 44; Dolkart, *Guide to New York City Landmarks*, 147–48.

15. Jackson, *A Guide to New York Architecture 1650–1952*, 40; Diamonstein, *The Landmarks of New York*, 61; Dolkart, *Guide to New York City Landmarks*, 212.

16. Jackson, *A Guide to New York Architecture 1650–1952*, 39; Huxtable, *Classic New York*, 8–9; Diamonstein, *The Landmarks of New York*, 47; Dolkart, *Guide to New York City Landmarks*, 141.

17. Jackson, *A Guide to New York Architecture 1650–1952*, 55; Stern, Gilmartin and Mellins, *New York 1930*, 132; Diamonstein, *The Landmarks of New York*, 27; Dolkart, *Guide to New York City Landmarks*, 222.

18. Jackson, *A Guide to New York Architecture 1650–1952*, 34; Huxtable, *Classic New York*, 12–13; Kenneth Bates, "A Great American Idea: The Abigail Adams Smith House," *House and Garden* 145 (April 1974): 46; Stern, Gilmartin and Mellins, *New York 1930*, 132; Diamonstein, *The Landmarks of New York*, 55; Dolkart, *Guide to New York City Landmarks*, 116.

19. Landmarks Preservation Commission of the City of New York, LP-0397 (August 26, 1969); Diamonstein, *The Landmarks of New York*, 24–26.

20. "The Old Merchant's House," *Antiques* 47 (May 1945): 291; Jackson, *A Guide to New York Architecture 1650–1952*, 11; Huxtable, *Classic New York*, 97–98; "Preserving the Antique," *Village Voice* 10 (April 15, 1965): 1; "The Village's Landmarks," *Village Voice* 10 (September 30, 1965): 1; Landmarks Preservation Commission of the City of New York, LP-0006 (October 14, 1965); "Sandwiched between Two Garages," *Village Voice* 11 (December 2, 1965): 1; Roger Starr, "Must Landmarks Go?" *Horizon* 8 (summer 1966): 48–59; "NYC Greek Revival Classic Being Restored," *Progressive Architecture* 53 (May 1972): 34, 37; Ada Louise Huxtable, "The Old Lady of 29 East Fourth St.," *New York Times* (June 18, 1972), II: 22; White and Willensky, *AIA Guide* (1978), 97; Paul Goldberger, *The City Observed: New York* (New York: Random House, 1979), 67, 69; John Tauranac, *Essential New York* (New York: Holt, Rinehart and Winston, 1979), 17–18; Landmarks Preservation Commission of the City of New York, LP-1244 (December 22, 1981); Donald Martin Reynolds, *The Architecture of New York City* (New York: Macmillan, 1984), 73–75; William F. Buckley, Jr., "A Family Tree's Trimmings," *Art & Antiques* (December 1987): 78–85; Diamonstein, *The Landmarks of New York*, 69; Dolkart, *Guide to New York City Landmarks*, 49–50.

21. Huxtable, "The Old Lady of 29 East Fourth St.": 22.

22. "Official Residence Set Up for Mayor," *New York Times* (January 9, 1942): 15; "Mayor's House," *New York Times* (January 10, 1942): 14; "Repairing Gracie Mansion," *New York Times* (January 23, 1942): 13; "New York City's 'White House,'" *Architectural Forum* 76 (March 1942): 12; "La Guardia May Go to Mansion in May," *New York Times* (April 6, 1942): 17; "Gracie Mansion Ready for Mayor," *New York Times* (May 22, 1942): 23; "La Guardias Begin Moving into the Gracie Mansion," *New York Times* (May 27, 1942): 19; Jackson, *A Guide to New York Architecture 1650–1952*, 36; Huxtable, *Classic New York*, 10–12; Ada Louise Huxtable, "A Plan of Taste: Design for Wing at Gracie Mansion Overcomes Some Awkward Problems," *New York Times* (January 12, 1965): 24; Landmarks Preservation Commission of the City of New York, LP-0179 (September 20, 1966); Ada Louise Huxtable, "A Worthwhile Addition: The Reception Wing of Gracie Mansion Viewed as Object Lesson in Excellence," *New York Times* (September 28, 1966): 49; Marian Page, "Gracie Mansion's New 18th Century Reception Wing," *Interiors* 126 (November 1966): 96–101; White and Willensky, *AIA Guide* (1967), 181–82; Goldberger, *The City Observed*, 270; Tauranac, *Essential New York*, 6–7; Mary C. Black, *New York City's Gracie Mansion: A History of the Mayor's House* (New York: J. M. Kaplan Fund, 1984); David Morton, "Gracie Mansion Refurbished," *Progressive Architecture* 65 (December 1984): 23–24; Landmarks Preservation Commission of the City of New York, *Gracie Mansion Historic Structure Report* (New York, 1985); Diane Cox, "Gracie Mansion—5 Years and $6 Million Later," *Historic Preservation* 37 (April 1985): 20–25; Stern, Gilmartin and Mellins, *New York 1930*, 133, 716; Diamonstein, *The Landmarks of New York*, 56; Mark Alan Hewitt, *The Architecture of Mott B. Schmidt*, with an intro. by Robert A. M. Stern (New York: Rizzoli International Publications, 1991), 26–28, 147–53; Dolkart, *Guide to New York City Landmarks*, 105.

23. Huxtable, "A Plan of Taste: Design for Wing at Gracie Mansion Overcomes Some Awkward Problems": 24.

24. Huxtable, "A Worthwhile Addition: The Reception Wing of Gracie Mansion Viewed as Object Lesson in Excellence": 49.

25. Robert Moses quoted in "Work on Monuments Reported by Moses," *New York Times* (October 30, 1941): 25. Also see Robert Moses, "The Changing City," *Architectural Forum* 72 (March 1940): 142–56.

26. "Significant News of the Week in Review," *Real Estate Record and Guide* 147 (February 15, 1941): 2; "Moses Writes to 'Stuffed Shirts' Who Weep for the Aquarium," *New York Herald Tribune* (February 25, 1941): 1, 18; "Arsenal vs. Castle," editorial, *New York Herald Tribune* (February 25, 1941): 22; "Shall the Aquarium Move Uptown?" letters to the editor, *New York Herald Tribune* (March 1, 1941): 10; "Aquarium Gone," *New York Times* (October 6, 1941): 21; "Moses v. the Architects," *Interiors* 102 (September 1942): 10, 56–57; "Letters from Readers," *Pencil Points* 23 (September 1942): 8; "A Good Thing," letter to the editor, *Pencil Points* 23 (October 1942): 8; Talbot F. Hamlin, "The Battery Park Competition," *Pencil Points* 23 (November 1942): 71–74; "Aquarium Plans," editorial, *New York Times* (July 29, 1943): 18; "Visitor Misses the Aquarium," letter to the editor, *New York Times* (August 7, 1943): 10; "Meditation at Coney Island," *New York Times* (August 11, 1943): 18; Robert Moses, "Parks, Parkways, Express Arteries, and Related Plans for New York City after the War," *American City* 58 (December 1943): 53–58; "News from Coney Island," *Interiors* 105 (August 1945): 104; "M'Aneny Is Pleased: Hails Approval of Restoration Funds for Fort Clinton," *New York Times* (October 8, 1949): 8; Robert A. Caro, *The Power Broker: Robert Moses and the Fall of New York* (New York: Alfred A. Knopf, 1974), 678–88; Diamonstein, *The Landmarks of New York*, 60; Dolkart, *Guide to New York City Landmarks*, 15.

27. Robert Moses quoted in Caro, *The Power Broker*, 679.

28. Caro, *The Power Broker*, 680–81.

29. Robert Moses quoted in "Moses Writes to 'Stuffed Shirts' Who Weep for the Aquarium": 1.

30. Robert Moses quoted in "Moses Writes to 'Stuffed Shirts' Who Weep for the Aquarium": 1.

31. "Arsenal vs. Castle": 22.

32. J.O.G., "To Preserve Historic Sites," letter to the editor, *New York Times* (December 24, 1948): 16.

33. Robert Moses, "Preserving Historic Sites," letter to the editor, *New York Times* (December 31, 1948): 14.

34. Andreas Feininger and Susan Lyman, *The Face of New York: The City as It Was and as It Is* (New York: Crown, 1954).

35. John Kouwenhoven, *Columbia Historical Portrait of New York* (New York: Columbia University Press, 1954).

36. Talbot Hamlin, "Historical Heritage vs. the March of 'Progress,'" *Journal of the American Institute of Architects* 17 (June 1952): 286–89.

37. "New York's Architectural Heritage," *Journal of the American Institute of Architects* 17 (June 1952): 261–62. Also see "City's Landmarks Subject of Study," *New York Times* (January 24, 1954): 69; Municipal Art Society of New York, *Buildings in Manhattan Built before World War I Designated as Worthy of Protection* (New York: Municipal Art Society of New York, 1955); "News Bulletins," *Progressive Architecture* 37 (August 1956): 87; "News Bulletins," *Progressive Architecture* 38 (April 1957): 99.

38. "The Editor's Asides," *Journal of the American Institute of Architects* 20 (November 1953): 249.

39. Alan Burnham, ed., *New York Landmarks: A Study and Index of Architecturally Notable Structures in Greater New York* (Middletown, Conn.: Wesleyan University Press, 1963).

40. "Wall St. Area Cheered by Plans for New Skyscraper," *Architectural Forum* 99 (October 1953): 74; Ada Louise Huxtable, "New York Revisited: The Produce Exchange," *Art Digest* 28 (July 1, 1954): 15; "Another Victorian Vanishes," *Architectural Forum* 106 (June 1957): 142–49; Silver, *Lost New York*, 102–3; "New York's Changing Scene," *New York Daily News Sunday News Magazine* (May 14, 1972): 23; Ada Louise Huxtable, "Farewell, Old New York," *New York Times* (November 18, 1974), VI: 102–5; Stern, Gilmartin and Massengale, *New York 1900*, 146, 150.

41. "Wall St. Area Cheered by Plans for New Skyscraper": 74.

42. Talbot Hamlin quoted in "Wall St. Area Cheered by Plans for New Skyscraper": 74.

43. Silver, *Lost New York*, 102.

44. John P. Callahan, "Ornate Facades Lose Appeal in Era When Less is More," *New York Times* (July 13, 1958), VIII: 1, 6.

45. See Henry H. Reed, Jr., "Monumental Architecture or the Art of Pleasing in Civic Design," lecture, Civic Art Conference, Yale University, April 1952, in *Perspecta* 1 (summer 1952): 51–54, 56.

46. Christopher Tunnard and John N. Pearce, eds., *City Planning at Yale* (New Haven, Conn.: Graduate Program in City Planning, Department of Architecture, Yale University, 1954).

47. Christopher Tunnard and Henry Hope Reed, *American Skyline* (Boston: Houghton Mifflin, 1955). The first paperback edition was published by New American Library in 1956.

48. Henry Hope Reed, "For the 'Superfluous' in Buildings," *New York Times* (March 4, 1956), VI: 26–27, 47–48.

49. Henry Hope Reed, *The Golden City* (New York: Doubleday, 1959).

50. "The Talk of the Town: Lovers," *New Yorker* 33 (October 1957): 33–34.

51. "The Talk of the Town: Griffons for Delight," *New Yorker* 32 (October 13, 1956): 35–36.

52. Reed, *The Golden City*, 108–10. Bayley also conducted walking tours. See "The Talk of the Town: Classical Walk," *New Yorker* 47 (November 20, 1971): 47–48.

53. Edith Evans Asbury, "Landmark Signs Dedicated Here," *New York Times* (November 22, 1957): 23; "Landmark Signs," editorial, *New York Times* (November 26, 1957): 32.

54. For the Daily News Building, see Stern, Gilmartin and Mellins, *New York 1930*, 577–79.

55. Leslie Katz, "The Forgotten Faces," with photographs by Ivan Karp, *Arts* 34 (June 1960): 34–39; Ann Ferebee, "Statement: Doing Good in New York," *Industrial Design* 11 (January 1964): 74–76; Ada Louise Huxtable, "Arts Group Saves Bit of Landmark," *New York Times* (October 6, 1964): 41; "The Talk of the Town: Anonymous Art," *New Yorker* 40 (November 14, 1964): 49–51; "The Gargoyle Snatchers," *Time* 85 (March 5, 1965): 74; "The Man from AARS," *Newsweek* 65 (May 31, 1965): 75.

56. "The Gargoyle Snatchers": 74. Also see Frederick Fried, *The Frieda Schiff Warburg Memorial Sculpture Garden* (New York: Brooklyn Museum, 1966); "Architectural Memorabilia in Brooklyn," *Interiors* 125 (June 1966): 16; "The Talk of the Town: City Fragments," *New Yorker* 42 (June 11, 1966): 28–31; Robert S. Gallagher, "Wrecker, Spare That Frieze!" *American Heritage* 18 (August 1967): 60–64.

57. Ivan Karp quoted in "The Talk of the Town: Anonymous Art": 49.

58. Ivan Karp quoted in "The Talk of the Town: Anonymous Art": 50.

59. Thomas S. Beuchner quoted in "Architectural Memorabilia in Brooklyn": 16.

60. "'Blitz' in New York," *Architectural Forum* 82 (February 1945): 6; David Garrard Lowe, *Stanford White's New York* (New York: Doubleday, 1992), 229–39.

61. Francis Henry Taylor, "The Blumenthal Collection," *Metropolitan Museum of Art Bulletin* 36 (October 1941): 193, 195–98; Frank W. Crane, "Renewal of Park Ave. Building Seen in Blumenthal House Demolition," *New York Times* (August 19, 1945), VIII: 1; Robert Moses, "The City's Museums: Some Prescriptions," *New York Times* (November 20, 1949), VI: 14–15, 64, 66–69; Sanka Knox, "Patio Dedicated in Museum of Art," *New York Times* (April 15, 1964): 78; "Peripatetic Patio," *Time* 83 (April 24, 1964): 76; Tania Long, "Museum Prepares a Curtain-Raising," *New York Times* (August 29, 1964): 23; John Canaday, "Spanish Castle on Fifth Avenue," *New York Times* (November 22, 1964), VI: 106–7; Henry A. LaFarge, "The Metropolitan's New Marble Hall," *Art News* 63 (December 1964): 40–41; Olga Raggio, "The Velez Blanco Patio: An Italian Renaissance Monument from Spain," *Metropolitan Museum of Art Bulletin* 23 (December 1964): 141–76; James J. Rorimer, "Prefatory Note," *Metropolitan Museum of Art Bulletin* 23 (December 1964): 141; Stuart Preston, "Letter from New York: Movements and Mobiles," *Apollo* 81 (January 1965): 66–69; "The Talk of the Town: Wandering Patio," *New Yorker* 40 (February 6, 1965): 23–24; "The Muses' Marble Acres," *Time* 85 (March 19, 1965): 80–85; Calvin Tomkins, *Merchants and Masterpieces: The Story of the Metropolitan Museum of Art* (New York: E. P. Dutton, 1970), 218–24, 281–82; Landmarks Preservation Commission of the City of New York, *Upper East Side Historic District Designation Report* (New York, 1981), 1104; Stern, Gilmartin and Massengale, *New York 1900*, 351; James Trager, *Park Avenue: Street of Dreams* (New York: Atheneum, 1990), 66.

62. George Blumenthal quoted in Rorimer, "Prefatory Note": 141.

63. Taylor, "The Blumenthal Collection": 198.

64. Canaday, "Spanish Castle on Fifth Avenue": 106.
65. "Last Vanderbilt Leaves 5th Avenue," *Architectural Forum* 75 (September 1941): 12; "Death and Taxes," *Architectural Forum* 84 (January 1946): 12; Silver, *Lost New York*, 121–22; Stern, Gilmartin and Massengale, *New York 1900*, 309; "Q and A," *New York Times* (November 25, 1984), VIII: 9; Arnold Lewis, James Turner and Steve McQuillin, *The Opulent Interiors of the Gilded Age* (New York: Dover, 1987), 114–21. Vanderbilt's own twin house at 650 Fifth Avenue had been demolished in 1926 to make way for the DePinna Building. For an extensive discussion of the Vanderbilt family and their social milieu, see Louis Auchincloss, *The Vanderbilt Era: Profiles of a Gilded Age* (New York: Charles Scribner's Sons, 1989).
66. "'Blitz' in New York": 6; Stern, Gilmartin and Massengale, *New York 1900*, 233, 236–37.
67. *Upper East Side Historic District*, 936.
68. *Upper East Side Historic District*, 936.
69. "Going Up," *Interiors* 104 (October 1944): 11; *Upper East Side Historic District*, 934.
70. *Upper East Side Historic District*, 934.
71. *Upper East Side Historic District*, 947.
72. Stern, Gilmartin and Mellins, *New York 1930*, 360, 362.
73. *Upper East Side Historic District*, 927.
74. "Century Old Home Yields to Progress," *New York Times* (March 19, 1953): 31; Landmarks Preservation Commission of the City of New York, *Metropolitan Museum Historic District Designation Report* (New York, 1977), 96–97.
75. Reed, *The Golden City*, 40–41. Also see "Fifth Ave. Corner Will Be Improved," *New York Times* (December 14, 1952), VIII: 1; "Duveen Gallery on Fifth Avenue to Be Replaced by Large Office Building," *Real Estate Record and Guide* 171 (January 24, 1953): 3–4; Stern, Gilmartin and Massengale, *New York 1900*, 200.
76. Jeffrey Karl Ochsner, *H. H. Richardson: Complete Architectural Works* (Cambridge, Mass.: MIT Press, 1982), 62–63.
77. *Upper East Side Historic District*, 942.
78. "New York Discovers an Architect," *Architectural Forum* 80 (April 1944): 70; "Museum in Query," *Art Digest* 24 (May 1, 1951): 4.
79. "Apartment to Replace Noted Park Ave. House," *New York Times* (May 7, 1959): 55; "Treasure Hunters Find a Prize in James Mansion," *New York Times* (May 12, 1959): 37; *Upper East Side Historic District*, 1103; Stern, Gilmartin and Massengale, *New York 1900*, 355.
80. *Upper East Side Historic District*, 325; Stern, Gilmartin and Massengale, *New York 1900*, 339.
81. "Remodeling for a City School," *Architectural Forum* 119 (November 1963): 124–27; *Upper East Side Historic District*, 682.
82. Stern, Gilmartin and Mellins, *New York 1930*, 191.
83. Ada Louise Huxtable, "Despair of Demolition: Plans to Raze 79th Street Mansions in Line with City's Destructive Trend," *New York Times* (September 17, 1964): 39; "The Destruction of New York (Cont'd.)," *Progressive Architecture* 45 (October 1964): 95; Alan Dunn, "Darling, I'd Join You," cartoon, *Architectural Record* 137 (January 1965): 23; "Can Anyone Save the Old Meeting House?" *Housing and Planning News* 23 (February–March 1965): 1, 4; Ada Louise Huxtable, "New York's Architectural Follies," *New York Times* (February 14, 1965), II: 19; Silver, *Lost New York*, 127; Ada Louise Huxtable, "New York City's Growing Architectural Poverty," *New York Times* (February 12, 1968): 38; Ada Louise Huxtable, "Barbarism Notes from All Over," *New York Times* (July 27, 1969), II: 20; Ada Louise Huxtable, "You Win Some, You Lose Some," *New York Times* (October 8, 1972), II: 29; Stern, Gilmartin and Massengale, *New York 1900*, 321.
84. "The Destruction of New York (Cont'd.)": 95.
85. Huxtable, "New York's Architectural Follies": 19.
86. Lucy Greenbaum, "Passing of the Marble Front," *New York Times* (December 1, 1946): 68; "Schwab Home on Drive Sold as Site for Apartment Center," *New York Times* (May 11, 1947): 1, 42; Silver, *Lost New York*, 126; Stern, Gilmartin and Massengale, *New York 1900*, 315, 376–77.
87. "Landmark of City Now Being Razed," *New York Times* (February 12, 1950): 73.
88. "Harriman Speaks at Jewish Center's Unveiling Rite," *New York Times* (May 5, 1958): 32; White and Willensky, *AIA Guide* (1978), 192.
89. "5-Alarm Fire Destroys W. 84th St. Church," *New York Times* (December 2, 1956): 1, 31; White and Willensky, *AIA Guide* (1978), 203.
90. Landmarks Preservation Commission of the City of New York, LP-2017 (April 19, 1973); White and Willensky, *AIA Guide* (1978), 188.
91. Mary Henderson, *The City and the Theater* (Clifton, N.J.: James T. White & Co., 1973), 235; Stern, Gilmartin and Mellins, *New York 1930*, 235.
92. Henderson, *The City and the Theater*, 225.
93. Henderson, *The City and the Theater*, 234.
94. Henderson, *The City and the Theater*, 210.
95. "New 22-Story Office Building to Rise on Site Occupied by Empire Theater," *Real Estate Record and Guide* 171 (May 9, 1953): 3; Henderson, *The City and the Theater*, 229; Stern, Gilmartin and Massengale, *New York 1900*, 206.
96. Henderson, *The City and the Theater*, 208.
97. Silver, *Lost New York*, 72–74; Walter Karp, *The Center: A History and Guide to Rockefeller Center* (New York: American Heritage, 1982), 96–97; Stern, Gilmartin and Mellins, *New York 1930*, 656, 658–59, 661–62.
98. Henderson, *The City and the Theater*, 246.
99. See Stern, Gilmartin and Mellins, *New York 1930*, 238–39.
100. For both theaters, see Henderson, *The City and the Theater*, 233, 269.
101. Henderson, *The City and the Theater*, 258; Stern, Gilmartin and Massengale, *New York 1900*, 219.
102. "The Talk of the Town: Memories," *New Yorker* 31 (September 3, 1956): 22–23; "Swan Song for a Famous Theater: Ruins of the Roxy," *Life* 49 (November 7, 1960): 46; Ben M. Hall, *The Golden Age of the Movie Palace: The Best Remaining Seats* (New York: Clarkson N. Potter, 1961), 254–55; "Roxy Theater Lobby Area Leased to Restaurant," *Real Estate Record and Guide* 187 (June 3, 1961): 3; Silver, *Lost New York*, 81, 83; Stern, Gilmartin and Mellins, *New York 1930*, 250–51, 256–59.
103. Hall, *The Golden Age of the Movie Palace*, 254.
104. "Swan Song for a Famous Theater: Ruins of the Roxy": 46.
105. "The Talk of the Town: Timeless Tower," *New Yorker* 31 (June 17, 1961): 23–24; "A la Recherche du TIMES, Perdu," *Progressive Architecture* 44 (May 1963): 82; "Cosmetic Architecture," *Time* 81 (June 7, 1963): 44–45; "The Changing Times Tower," *Architectural Record* 134 (July 1963): 12; "Denuded Landmark," *Architectural Forum* 120 (March 1964): 16; Thomas W. Ennis, "Marble Facades Lend Distinction," *New York Times* (January 31, 1965), VIII: 1, 4; "Many of City's 'New' Buildings Are Just Old Ones Redressed," *New York Times* (November 21, 1965), VIII: 1, 10; "Showcase on the Square," *Newsweek* 66 (December 13, 1965): 79; Bodil W. Nielsen, "New Tower on Times Square," *Interiors* 125 (April 1966): 120–25; David W. Dunlap, *On Broadway: A Journey Uptown Over Time* (New York: Rizzoli International Publications, 1990), 188–89.
106. "A la Recherche du TIMES, Perdu": 82.
107. "New Face for Times Square Landmark," *Engineering News-Record* 193 (May 22, 1975): 14; *Charles Gwathmey and Robert Siegel: Buildings and Projects 1964–1984*, eds. Peter Arnell and Ted Bickford (New York: Harper & Row, 1984), 114–15.
108. Philip H. Dougherty, "Advertising: An Addition to Times Square," *New York Times* (October 11, 1976): 44.
109. Stern, Gilmartin and Mellins, *New York 1930*, 254, 263.
110. Stern, Gilmartin and Mellins, *New York 1930*, 263.
111. "Footnote: Coming Destructions," *Architectural Forum* 131 (October 1969): 86–87; White and Willensky, *AIA Guide* (1988), 121.
112. "Casino Into Cinema Into Church," *Progressive Architecture* 47 (September 1966): 182–84.
113. "Theater for Harlem," *Architectural Forum* 130 (June 1969): 74–75; C. Ray Smith, *Supermannerism: New Attitudes in Post-Modern Architecture* (New York: E. P. Dutton, 1977), 102; *Hardy Holzman Pfeiffer Associates: Buildings and Projects 1967–1992* (New York: Rizzoli International Publications, 1992), 238.
114. "Another Route to Learning," *Progressive Architecture* 54 (September 1973): 56–62; Andrea O. Dean, "An Evocative Approach to Adaptive Use," *Journal of the American Institute of Architects* 65 (June 1976): 38–40; Michael Sorkin, *Hardy Holzman Pfeiffer* (New York: Whitney Library of Design, 1981), 24, 45; *Hardy Holzman Pfeiffer Associates: Buildings and Projects 1967–1992*, 241.
115. Smith, *Supermannerism*, 50–51; White and Willensky, *AIA Guide* (1978), 371; Elliot Willensky, *When Brooklyn Was the World, 1920–1957* (New York: Harmony Books, 1986), 225–26. For Rapp & Rapp's theater, see Stern, Gilmartin and Mellins, *New York 1930*, 254, 263. In 1968 Davis, Brody & Associates and Horowitz & Chun completed another project for Long Island University, renovating an eight-story reinforced-concrete loft building (1925) to serve as a classroom and office building. See John Morris Dixon, "New Forms on an Old Frame," *Architectural Forum* 128 (June 1968): 82–89; "Davis, Brody & Associates, Horowitz & Chun," *Journal of the American Institute of Architects* 49 (June 1968): 97.
116. Emanuel Perlmutter, "Dodgers Accept Los Angeles Bid to Move to Coast," *New York Times* (October 9, 1957): 1, 37.
117. "Polo Grounds," *Architecture and Building* 44 (November 1912): 457; W. Parker Chase, *New York: The Wonder City* (New York: Wonder City Publishing Co., 1932; New York: New York Bound, 1983), 33; Robert Lipsyte, "Polo Grounds Goes Down Reluctantly Before Wreckers," *New York Times* (May 31, 1964), V: 3; White and Willensky, *AIA Guide* (1978), 333; Michael Gershman, "1963," *Avenue* 17 (April 1993): 20–21.
118. "End of the Old Lady," *Time* 41 (March 29, 1943): 12.
119. Francis de N. Schroeder, "The Setting of the Sun and the Passing of the Ritz," editorial, *Interiors* 109 (February 1950): 67; Lewis Mumford, "The Sky Line: The Mud Wasps of Manhattan," *New Yorker* 26 (March 25, 1950): 64, 66, 69–72; "Last Days of the Ritz," *Time* 57 (May 14, 1951): 27; "Mementos of the Ritz Carlton," *Interiors* 115 (December 1955): 20; Silver, *Lost New York*, 69–71; Stern, Gilmartin and Massengale, *New York 1900*, 262–63, 267.
120. Stern, Gilmartin and Massengale, *New York 1900*, 264, 267.
121. "Apartment to Rise on Brevoort's Site," *New York Times* (January 11, 1952): 23.
122. Stern, Gilmartin and Massengale, *New York 1900*, 267; Stern, Gilmartin and Mellins, *New York 1930*, 181.
123. Dudley Dalton, "Lincoln Sq. Area Will Get Offices," *New York Times* (March 22, 1964), VIII: 1, 12.
124. Peter Blake, "This Way Up," *New York* 8 (December 30, 1974): 45, 48–49.
125. Henry J. Saylor, "The Editor's Diary," *Architectural Forum* 73 (August 1940): 106; Stern, Gilmartin and Massengale, *New York 1900*, 190.
126. Christopher Gray, "Follies!" *Avenue* 15 (February 1991): 65–73.
127. Gray, "Follies!": 67, 69.
128. Stern, Gilmartin and Massengale, *New York 1900*, 136–37.
129. "Plan to Sell St. Nicholas Church for $3,000,000 Stirs Conflict," *New York Times* (January 28, 1946): 1, 22; "Opposition Grows to Sale of Church," *New York Times* (January 29, 1946): 26; "Sizoo Scores Church Sale Plan; Sets Thursday as Day of Prayer," *New York Times* (February 4, 1946): 1–3; Lee E. Cooper, "40-Story Skyscraper Is Planned for Site of St. Nicholas Church," *New York Times* (February 6, 1946): 1, 17; "Split from Collegiate Fold Sought by St. Nicholas as Dr. Sizoo Resigns," *New York Times* (November 11, 1946): 1, 20; Lee E. Cooper, "St. Nicholas Church Again Plans Sale," *New York Times* (February 5, 1949): 1, 16; John A. Bradley, "St. Nicholas Church to Be Razed to Make Way for Office Building," *New York Times* (April 1, 1949): 1, 29; "End of St. Nicholas," *Newsweek* 33 (April 11, 1949): 76; "A Tale of Two Churches," *Christian Century* 66 (April 20, 1949): 486–87; "New York," *Interiors* 108 (June 1949): 12; Austin Stevens, "Old St. Nicholas Goes to Wrecker," *New York Times* (September 16, 1949): 29; "Peak Performance," *Life* 27 (November 14, 1949): 48; Stern, Gilmartin and Massengale, *New York 1900*, 308.
130. Bradley, "St. Nicholas Church to Be Razed to Make Way for Office Building": 29.
131. Joseph R. Sizoo quoted in "Sizoo Scores Church Sale Plan; Sets Thursday as Day of Prayer": 23.
132. Lewis Mumford, "The Sky Line: Artful Blight," *New Yorker* 27 (May 5, 1951): 84–90; "The Money in Modernization," *Architectural Forum* 112 (January 1960): 115–18; Goldberger, *The City Observed*, 119–20; Stern, Gilmartin and Massengale, *New York 1900*, 195–96; Christopher Gray, "Streetscapes: The Old Tiffany Building," *New York Times* (March 25, 1990), X: 8.
133. Mumford, "The Sky Line: Artful Blight": 88.
134. Robert Alden, "Flames Put Finish to Claremont Inn," *New York Times* (March 15, 1951): 42; "Newest City Playground on the Site of the Old Claremont Inn," *New York Times* (March 20, 1952): 32; Silver, *Lost New York*, 57, 59.
135. "Mark Twain House," *Village Voice* 4 (April 29, 1959): 1.
136. Jackson, *A Guide to New York Architecture 1650–1952*, 13; "Rhinelander Gardens," *Village Voice* 1 (February 22, 1956): 1; "Past and Present: Rhinelander Gardens,"

Village Voice 2 (January 2, 1957): 1; Terry Miller, *Greenwich Village and How It Got That Way* (New York: Crown, 1990), 136.

137. Montgomery Schuyler, "The Works of the Late Richard M. Hunt," *Architectural Record* 5 (October–December 1895): 99; Jackson, *A Guide to New York Architecture 1650–1952*, 14; Alan Burnham, "The New York Architecture of Richard Morris Hunt," *Journal of the Society of Architectural Historians* 11 (May 1952): 11; "Famous 10th St. Studio Building to Be Razed to Make Way for Apartments," *Real Estate Record and Guide* 174 (July 24, 1954): 3; Walter McQuade, "Books," *Village Voice* 1 (January 18, 1956): 8; Silver, *Lost New York*, 142; Paul R. Baker, *Richard Morris Hunt* (Cambridge, Mass.: MIT Press, 1980), 93–107; Paul R. Baker, "Richard Morris Hunt: An Introduction," in Susan R. Stein, ed., *The Architecture of Richard Morris Hunt* (Chicago: University of Chicago Press, 1986), 4–5; Sarah Bradford Landau, "Richard Morris Hunt: Architectural Innovator and Father of a 'Distinctive' American School," in Stein, ed., *The Architecture of Richard Morris Hunt*, 49–50. For the Peter Warren apartment house, see Thomas E. Norton and Jerry E. Patterson, *Living It Up: A Guide to the Named Apartment Houses of New York* (New York: Atheneum, 1984), 265; Miller, *Greenwich Village and How It Got That Way*, 131–33.

138. Meyer Berger, "Our Changing City," *New York Times* (June 20, 1955): 1, 23; Stern, Gilmartin and Massengale, *New York 1900*, 145–48.

139. Meyer Berger, "About New York: Old Morgan Chimneys Resist Hammering of Wreckers—Applause for Police," *New York Times* (June 20, 1955): 23; Ada Louise Huxtable, "Landmarks Are in Trouble with the Law," *New York Times* (December 22, 1974), II: 36.

140. "The Talk of the Town: No Return," *New Yorker* 27 (November 3, 1951): 28–29; "The Talk of the Town: Homesick," *New Yorker* 31 (March 12, 1955): 25–27.

141. Stern, Gilmartin and Massengale, *New York 1900*, 459 (n. 160).

142. "Stuyvesant Estate Site for Apartments," *Real Estate Record and Guide* 180 (November 2, 1957): 3; Andrew Alpern, *Apartments for the Affluent* (New York: McGraw-Hill, 1975), 12–13; Baker, *Richard Morris Hunt*, 204–7, 500, 540–41; Robert A. M. Stern, "With Rhetoric: The New York Apartment House," *Via* 4 (1980): 78–111; Landau, "Richard Morris Hunt: Architectural Innovator and Father of a 'Distinctive' American School," in Stein, ed., *The Architecture of Richard Morris Hunt*, 61–64. For Gramercy Green, see Norton and Patterson, *Living It Up*, 161.

143. Baker, *Richard Morris Hunt*, 276–88; Baker, "Richard Morris Hunt: An Introduction," in Stein, ed., *The Architecture of Richard Morris Hunt*, 6–7; David Chase, "Superb Privacies: The Later Domestic Commissions of Richard Morris Hunt, 1878–1895," in Stein, ed., *The Architecture of Richard Morris Hunt*, 150–51, 153, 162–64, 167–68; Landau, "Richard Morris Hunt: Architectural Innovator and Father of a 'Distinctive' American School," in Stein, ed., *The Architecture of Richard Morris Hunt*, 48–49, 58, 71–72.

144. Roth, *McKim, Mead & White, Architects*, 264–65; Stern, Gilmartin and Massengale, *New York 1900*, 321.

145. Stern, Gilmartin and Mellins, *New York 1930*, 274–75, 279.

146. "Russeks Building to Become Office Building," *Real Estate Record and Guide* 184 (November 7, 1959): 4; Stern, Gilmartin and Massengale, *New York 1900*, 196, 198.

147. Stern, Gilmartin and Massengale, *New York 1900*, 180–83.

148. Stern, Gilmartin and Massengale, *New York 1900*, 146, 156, 165, 168.

149. Gerard R. Wolfe, *42nd Street: River to River* (New York: 42nd Street E.T.C., Inc., 1984), unpaginated.

150. Aaron Cohen, "Architectural Oasis," letter to the editor, *Village Voice* 8 (April 15, 1963): 4; "Metropolitan Will Replace Home Office, Except Tower," *Architectural Forum* 100 (January 1964): 45; "New Building vs. Modernization," *Architectural Forum* 100 (May 1964): 130–31; White and Willensky, *AIA Guide* (1978), 116; Stern, Gilmartin and Massengale, *New York 1900*, 171–73; Stern, Gilmartin and Mellins, *New York 1930*, 506, 535–37.

151. Sherman R. Emery, "Now or Never," editorial, *Interior Design* 35 (October 1964): 141; "Many of City's 'New' Buildings Are Just Old Ones Redressed": 10; Ada Louise Huxtable, "A Matter of Urban Delight," *New York Times* (January 28, 1968): II: 31, 33; Ada Louise Huxtable, "The Trashing of Fifth Avenue," *New York Times* (December 5, 1976), II: 33–34; White and Willensky, *AIA Guide* (1978), 163; Stern, Gilmartin and Massengale, *New York 1900*, 200.

152. "Many of City's 'New' Buildings Are Just Old Ones Redressed": 10.

153. Huxtable, "A Matter of Urban Delight": 33.

154. "A Look at Lobbies," *Architectural Forum* 104 (January 1956): 122–29.

155. Lewis Mumford, "The Sky Line: The Genteel and the Genuine," *New Yorker* 25 (July 9, 1949): 42–46.

156. Stern, Gilmartin and Mellins, *New York 1930*, 403, 410–11, 416.

157. "Inside Story: Miss Miller Modernizes," *Interiors* 111 (June 1952): 12.

158. Herbert Tannenbaum quoted in Christopher Gray, "Restoring Luster to a 1912 Lady," *New York Times* (November 26, 1989), X: 4.

159. Glenn Fowler, "Distinctive New Buildings Win Fifth Avenue Plaudits," *New York Times* (May 22, 1960), VIII: 1, 16; White and Willensky, *AIA Guide* (1967), 131; Stern, Gilmartin and Mellins, *New York 1930*, 306–7.

160. Stan Fischler, *Uptown, Downtown: A Trip Through Time on New York's Subways* (New York: Hawthorn Books, 1976), 259. Also see Ella M. Foshay, Barbara Finney and Mishoe Brennecke, *Jasper F. Cropsey: Artist and Architect*, exhibition catalogue (New York: New-York Historical Society, 1987), 144–46, 150.

161. "Two 'El' Lines End Transit Service," *New York Times* (June 12, 1940): 27; "Topics of the Times," *New York Times* (June 13, 1940): 22; Fischler, *Uptown, Downtown*, 259.

162. "Two 'El' Lines End Transit Service": 27; "Topics of The Times": 22; Fischler, *Uptown, Downtown*, 259; Norval White, *New York: A Physical History* (New York: Atheneum, 1987), 221.

163. Fischler, *Uptown, Downtown*, 259–60; White, *New York: A Physical History*, 221.

164. "The Talk of the Town: Old Myrt," *New Yorker* 45 (October 18, 1969): 48–49.

165. "'Manhattan House' Replaces Old Carbarns," *Architectural Record* 105 (May 1949): 106–7, 206.

166. "Aged Powerhouse Being Torn Down," *New York Times* (August 14, 1953): 34.

167. Lee E. Cooper, "Warburg Mansion Sold to Provide Site for 18-Story Apartment House on Fifth Avenue," *New York Times* (May 24, 1941): 29; "Warburg Mansion Goes to Seminary," *New York Times* (January 25, 1944): 21; Heinz Politzer, "The Opportunity of the Jewish Museum," *Commentary* 7 (January–June 1949): 589–93; White and Willensky, *AIA Guide* (1978), 239; Stern, Gilmartin and Massengale, *New York 1900*, 321; Diamonstein, *The Landmarks of New York*, 284; Dolkart, *Guide to New York City Landmarks*, 118, 120.

168. "News," *Architectural Forum* 90 (March 1949): 28; "New Cooper-Hewitt Museum in Carnegie Mansion," *Interiors* 129 (October 1969): 40; "NSID at the Cooper-Hewitt Museum," *Interiors* 130 (April 1971): 6, 8; Ada Louise Huxtable, "Carnegie House Given to Cooper-Hewitt Museum," *New York Times* (April 1, 1972): 1, 11; "The Cooper-Hewitt Museum Acquires Andrew Carnegie's Turn-of-the-Century Fifth Avenue Mansion," *Interiors* 131 (June 1972): 16; Landmarks Preservation Commission of the City of New York, LP-0674 (February 9, 1974); Ada Louise Huxtable, "The New Lehman Wing—Does the Met Need It?" *New York Times* (May 25, 1975), II: 1, 27, reprinted as "The Monumental Muddle: The Lehman Wing of the Metropolitan Museum," in Ada Louise Huxtable, *Kicked a Building Lately?* (New York: Quadrangle/New York Times Book Co., 1976), 13–17; "A New Splendor," *New York* 9 (September 1976): 50–51; "The Talk of the Town: Cooper-Hewitt Transformed," *New Yorker* 52 (October 15, 1976): 31–32; Douglas Davis, "Grand Designs," *Newsweek* 88 (October 18, 1976): 104; Martin Filler, "Cooper-Hewitt Museum Moves into the Carnegie Mansion," *Architectural Record* 160 (November 1976): 37; S. Dillon Ripley, "The View from the Castle," *Smithsonian* 7 (November 1976): 6; Thomas B. Hess, "Design Neglect," *New York* 9 (November 11, 1976): 112, 114–15; Hugh Hardy, Malcolm Holzman and Norman Pfeiffer, "Recycling Architectural Masterpieces—And Other Buildings Not So Great," *Architectural Record* 161 (August 1977): 81–82; White and Willensky, *AIA Guide* (1978), 238; Mary E. Osman, "Honor Awards: Cooper-Hewitt Museum," *Journal of the American Institute of Architectural Historians* 37 (mid-May 1978): 139; Goldberger, *The City Observed*, 256; Tauranac, *Essential New York*, 96–97; Russell Lynes, *More Than Meets the Eye: The History and Collections of the Cooper-Hewitt Museum, the Smithsonian Institution's National Museum of Design* (New York: Cooper-Hewitt Museum, 1981); Sorkin, *Hardy Holzman Pfeiffer*, 76, 82–85; Stern, Gilmartin and Massengale, *New York 1900*, 242–43; Diamonstein, *The Landmarks of New York*, 243; Dolkart, *Guide to New York City Landmarks*, 99; *Hardy Holzman Pfeiffer Associates: Buildings and Projects 1967–1992*, 20, 52–55, 239, 246.

169. Huxtable, "The New Lehman Wing—Does the Met Need It?": 27.

170. Hess, "Design Neglect": 114.

171. "From Repainting to Redesign," *Architectural Forum* 112 (January 1960): 122–30; "Rhythmic Play between Tradition and Modern Converts Fifth Avenue Mansion to Scholastic Institution," *Interiors* 119 (March 1960): 120–25; Robert Venturi, *Complexity and Contradiction in Architecture* (New York: Museum of Modern Art, 1966), 107; Landmarks Preservation Commission of the City of New York, LP-0668 (September 15, 1970); "Venturi," *Architecture Plus* 2 (March–April 1974): 80; "James B. Duke House," *Werk-Archithese* 64 (July–August 1977): 10–11; White and Willensky, *AIA Guide* (1978), 233; Gianni Pettena and Maurizio Vogliazzo, eds., *Venturi, Rauch and Scott Brown* (Milan: Electa, 1981), 111; "Venturi, Rauch and Scott Brown," *A + U*, extra edition (December 1981): 156; *Venturi, Rauch and Scott Brown: A Generation of Architecture* (Urbana-Champaign, Ill.: University of Illinois at Urbana-Champaign, 1984), 20; Stanislaus von Moos, *Venturi, Rauch & Scott Brown: Buildings and Projects* (New York: Rizzoli International Publications, 1987), 296–97; Diamonstein, *The Landmarks of New York*, 301; Dolkart, *Guide to New York City Landmarks*, 101.

172. Quoted in "Rhythmic Play between Tradition and Modern Converts Fifth Avenue Mansion to Scholastic Institution": 125.

173. Stern, Gilmartin and Massengale, *New York 1900*, 354–55; Stern, Gilmartin and Mellins, *New York 1930*, 372–73.

174. Ada Louise Huxtable, "Low Bid Gets Park Ave. Home on Promise Not to Rip It Down," *New York Times* (February 28, 1965): 31; Landmarks Preservation Commission of the City of New York, LP-0705 (November 10, 1970); Diamonstein, *The Landmarks of New York*, 303; Dolkart, *Guide to New York City Landmarks*, 104–5.

175. Huxtable, "Low Bid Gets Park Ave. Home on Promise Not to Rip It Down": 31.

176. Thomas W. Ennis, "Marquesa Saved 2 Landmarks," *New York Times* (January 14, 1965): 1, 32; "The Case of the Munificent Marquesa," *Progressive Architecture* 46 (February 1965): 54; "A Noble Past," *Nation* 200 (February 1, 1965): 98–99; "Bard Awards," *Interiors* 124 (April 1965): 14, 16; "New York's Bard Awards," *Progressive Architecture* 46 (April 1965): 63–64; Grace Glueck, "Latins for Manhattan," *New York Times* (July 30, 1967), II: 25; "Reclaimed Landmark," *Interior Design* 38 (December 1967): 116–21; Marian Page, "A Case of Creative Landmark Preservation in Manhattan," *Interiors* 127 (December 1967): 82–89; Landmarks Preservation Commission of the City of New York, LP-0704 (November 10, 1970); Diamonstein, *The Landmarks of New York*, 303; Dolkart, *Guide to New York City Landmarks*, 113–14.

177. Marquesa de Cuevas quoted in Page, "A Case of Creative Landmark Preservation in Manhattan": 82.

178. Olga Gueft, "Automation House: Confronting Tomorrow's Problems behind Yesterday's Facade," *Interiors* 128 (November 1968): 114–21; "Humanizing Automation," *Architectural Forum* 133 (July–August 1970): 74–75; Landmarks Preservation Commission of the City of New York, LP-0703 (November 10, 1970); White and Willensky, *AIA Guide* (1978), 226; Diamonstein, *The Landmarks of New York*, 321; Dolkart, *Guide to New York City Landmarks*, 99–100.

179. "The Talk of the Town: Wave Hill," *New Yorker* 45 (November 8, 1969): 47–50; White and Willensky, *AIA Guide* (1978), 345; Diamonstein, *The Landmarks of New York*, 90; Dolkart, *Guide to New York City Landmarks*, 216–17.

180. For Baum's armor hall, see Stern, Gilmartin and Mellins, *New York 1930*, 502–3.

181. White and Willensky, *AIA Guide* (1967), 180; Landmarks Preservation Commission of the City of New York, LP-0440 (May 15, 1968); "The Talk of the Town: Being Present," *New Yorker* 50 (January 13, 1975): 26–28, 30; Goldberger, *The City Observed*, 260–61; Stern, Gilmartin and Massengale, *New York 1900*, 344, 346; Diamonstein, *The Landmarks of New York*, 323; Dolkart, *Guide to New York City Landmarks*, 117.

182. "A Residence Transformed for Research," *Architectural Forum* 115 (September 1961): 134–37.

183. "Preservation Solution: Find a Use," *Progressive Architecture* 46 (May 1965): 63–64; White and Willensky, *AIA Guide* (1967), 97; Stern, Gilmartin and Mellins, *New York 1930*, 454; Diamonstein, *The Landmarks of New York*, 279; Baker, *Stanny: The Gilded Life of Stanford White*, 146–48; Dolkart, *Guide to New York City Landmarks*, 54.

184. Stern, Gilmartin and Mellins, *New York 1930*, 384.

185. "The Philistines Win Again," *Progressive Architecture* 42 (March 1961): 66; "Dakota Saved," *Progressive Architecture* 43 (May 1962): 51; "At Home in the Dakota," *Interiors* 123 (June 1964): 58–64; "The Great Dakota," *Look* 28 (July 28, 1964): 93–98; White and Willensky, *AIA Guide* (1967), 142; Carter B. Horsley, "Air-Conditioners Disturb Facades and Tempers," *New York Times* (July 27, 1975), VIII: 1, 6; Stephen Birmingham, *Life at the Dakota: New York's Most Unusual Address* (New York: Random House, 1979),

83–114; Goldberger, *The City Observed*, 204–5; Tauranac, *Essential New York*, 57–58; Stern, Gilmartin and Massengale, *New York 1900*, 283–85; Reynolds, *The Architecture of New York City*, 181–83; Paul Goldberger, "The Dakota," *Antiques* 126 (October 1984): 842–51; James Trager, *West of Fifth: The Rise and Fall and Rise of Manhattan's West Side* (New York: Atheneum, 1987), 110; Jennifer Stern, "Landmarked Districts," *7 Days* 2 (July 19, 1989): 27.

186. "The Philistines Win Again": 66.
187. "Dakota Saved": 51.
188. Lauren Bacall quoted in Horsley, "Air-Conditioners Disturb Facades and Tempers": 6, also quoted in Birmingham, *Life at the Dakota*, 132.
189. Quoted in Birmingham, *Life at the Dakota*, 133.
190. Birmingham, *Life at the Dakota*, 133.
191. "After Carnegie Hall—What?" editorial, *Musical America* 75 (March 1955): 4; Howard Taubman, "Orchestra to Bid on Carnegie Hall," *New York Times* (April 28, 1955): 1, 24; Olin Downes, "Saving a Hall," *New York Times* (June 19, 1955), II: 9; "Landmark in Jeopardy," editorial, *Musical America* 75 (July 1955): 4; "Carnegie Hall Appeal," letters to the editor, *Musical America* 75 (July 1955): 16; "Carnegie Hall Sold to Glickman Firm," *Musical America* 76 (August 1956): 7; "Glickman Buys Carnegie Hall," *Real Estate Record and Guide* 178 (August 4, 1956): 3; "Largest Office Building Planned at Carnegie Hall Site After '59," *New York Times* (November 26, 1956): 29; "A Red Skyscraper to Replace Carnegie Hall," *Real Estate Record and Guide* 180 (August 17, 1957): 4; "Red and Gold Checks," *Architectural Forum* 107 (September 1957): 43; "P/A News Bulletins," *Progressive Architecture* 38 (September 1957): 100; "A Red Tower Replacing Carnegie Hall," *Life* 43 (September 9, 1957): 91; Richard Schickel, *The World of Carnegie Hall* (New York: Julian Messner, 1960), 412–17; "A Hopeful Reprise for Historic Hall," *Life* 48 (April 25, 1960): 116–23; "Carnegie: First Steps toward Salvation," *Musical America* 80 (May 1960): 19–21; "Carnegie Saved," *Progressive Architecture* 41 (August 1960): 64; "Personalities," *Progressive Architecture* 41 (September 1960): 58; Theodore O. Cron, *Portrait of Carnegie Hall* (New York: Macmillan, 1966); White and Willensky, *AIA Guide* (1967), 137; Landmarks Preservation Commission of the City of New York, LP-0278 (June 20, 1967); Ada Louise Huxtable, "Culture Is as Culture Does," *New York Times* (June 2, 1968), II: 25, reprinted in Ada Louise Huxtable, *Will They Ever Finish Bruckner Boulevard?* (New York: Macmillan, 1970), 228–32; Goldberger, *The City Observed*, 184; Tauranac, *Essential New York*, 71; Stern, Gilmartin and Massengale, *New York 1900*, 13, 15, 87; Richard Schickel and Michael Walsh, *Carnegie Hall: The First One Hundred Years* (New York: Harry N. Abrams, 1987); Elkhonon Yoffe, ed., *Tchaikovsky in America: The Composer's Visit in 1891*, trans. Lydia Yoffe (New York: Oxford University Press, 1987); Richard Alleman, *The Movie Lover's Guide to New York* (New York: Harper & Row, 1988), 61–62; Diamonstein, *The Landmarks of New York*, 202–3; Rebecca Read Shanor, *The City that Never Was* (New York: Viking, 1988), 73–80; Dolkart, *Guide to New York City Landmarks*, 70.
192. "A Hopeful Reprise for Historic Hall": 117.
193. For the McGraw-Hill Building, see Stern, Gilmartin and Mellins, *New York 1930*, 574–75, 579–80, 584–85.
194. Louis J. Glickman quoted in "A Red Skyscraper to Replace Carnegie Hall": 4.
195. "A Red Skyscraper to Replace Carnegie Hall": 4.
196. Lewis Mumford, "The Sky Line: Terminals and Monuments," *New Yorker* 30 (March 20, 1954): 99–100, 104–7; "Zeckendorf Signs Up Air Over Pensy Station," *Business Week* (December 4, 1954): 27; Lewis Mumford, "The Sky Line: The Roaring Traffic's Boom—I," *New Yorker* 31 (March 19, 1955): 115–21; "Zeckendorf Promoting World's Most Massive Building," *Architectural Forum* 103 (July 1955): 9; "News Bulletins," *Progressive Architecture* 36 (September 1955): 86; "The Editor's Asides," *Journal of the American Institute of Architects* 24 (October 1955): 189; "World's Largest Building to Top R.R. Station," *Popular Science* 167 (December 1955): 102; "'Palace' Plan Out, Bigger One Urged," *New York Times* (January 6, 1956): 37; "Railroad's Own Changes Will Give Penn Station New Look," *Architectural Forum* 104 (February 1956): 16; "Zeckendorf Switches Palace Project into Bigger Scheme," *Architectural Forum* 104 (February 1956): 16; Walter C. Kidney, "Penn Station," letter to the editor, *Architectural Forum* 104 (April 1956): 72, 78; "Editor's Comment," *Architectural Forum* 104 (April 1956): 78; "Classic Station, Modern Improvement," *Architectural Forum* 104 (June 1956): 113–15; "Old Setting, New Gleam," *Architectural Forum* (August 1957): cover, 104–9; "Architecture Worth Saving," *Architectural Forum* 108 (June 1958): 93–100; Lewis Mumford, "The Sky Line: The Disappearance of Pennsylvania Station," *New Yorker* 34 (June 7, 1958): 106–13, reprinted in *Journal of the American Institute of Architects* 30 (October 1958): 40–43; Reed, *The Golden City*, 50, 83; Glenn Fowler, "Plan for Giant Office Building on West Side Barred in Mix-Up," *New York Times* (February 19, 1959): 33; Glenn Fowler, "Zeckendorf Maps Big Building Plan," *New York Times* (February 27, 1959): 14; "P/A News Report: Bulletins," *Progressive Architecture* 40 (March 1959): 161; "Buildings in the News," *Architectural Record* 125 (April 1959): 12; "With Progress Aforethought: New York's Penn Station, Present and Future," *Architectural Forum* 115 (September 1961): 8; "Penn Station: Site for New Madison Square Garden," *Architectural Record* 130 (September 1961): 12; "Penn Station to Give Way to Madison Square Garden," *Progressive Architecture* 42 (September 1961): 63, 65; Percival Goodman, J. J. P. Oud and Aline B. Saarinen, "Reactions to Pennsylvania Station Demolition," letters to the editor, *Progressive Architecture* 42 (September 1961): 78, 82, 84; "La Pennsylvania Station de New York sará distrutta?" *Casabella* 61 (November 1961): 52–53; "Down with Architecture! Up with Columns!" *Architectural Forum* 116 (April 1962): 9; "Barbarians and Buildings," *America* 107 (May 12, 1962): 223; Alan Dunn, "I Can't Worry Over the Rising Waters of the Nile," cartoon, *Architectural Record* 131 (June 1962): 23; "Quote . . . Unquote," *Architectural Forum* 117 (August 1962): 79; "New Group to Fight for Better Architecture," *Progressive Architecture* 43 (August 1962): 56; "Save Our City," advertisement, *New York Times* (August 2, 1962): 14; Jerome Zukosky, "50 Pickets in March to Save Penn Station," *New York Herald Tribune* (August 3, 1962): 5; Jane Kramer, "Picket Penn Station in Fight for Style," *Village Voice* 7 (August 9, 1962): 1, 9; "Penn Pals," *Time* 80 (August 10, 1962): 42; "Saving Fine Architecture," editorial, *New York Times* (August 11, 1962): 16; A. J. Greenough, "Redeveloping Penn Station," letter to the editor, *New York Times* (August 23, 1962): 28; "AGBANY vs. Apathy at Penn Station," *Architectural Forum* 117 (September 1962): 5; "Architects Want Penn Station Saved, Their Picket Lines Have Proved It: What Does Public Interest Require?" editorial, *Architectural Record* 132 (September 1962): 23; "Penn Pals Protest Penn Plot," *Progressive Architecture* 43 (September 1962): 61, 63; Ken Macrorie, "Arriving and Departing," *Reporter* 27 (September 13, 1962): 52–55; "Editorials without Words," cartoons, *Architectural Forum* 117 (October 1962): 87; Walter McQuade, "Architecture," *Nation* 195 (November 10, 1962): 313–14;

"AGBANY Proposes Plan to Save Penn Station," *Progressive Architecture* 41 (January 1963): 48; "Terminals In and Out," *Village Voice* 8 (January 31, 1963): 1; Robert L. Zion, "Every City a Four-Season Festival," *Journal of the American Institute of Architects* 39 (February 1963): 40–44; Norman Mailer, "The Big Bite," *Esquire* 59 (May 1963): 37, 40; Ada Louise Huxtable, "Architecture: How to Kill a City," *New York Times* (May 5, 1963), II: 15, reprinted as "The Impoverished City," in Huxtable, *Will They Ever Finish Bruckner Boulevard?*, 44–46, and as "The Impoverished Society," in Ada Louise Huxtable, *Goodbye History, Hello Hamburger* (Washington, D.C.: Preservation Press, 1986), 46–49; George McCue, "What (and Who) Determines Quality?" *Journal of the American Institute of Architects* 40 (July 1963): 69–78; "America's Heritage of Great Architecture Is Doomed . . . It Must Be Saved," *Life* 55 (July 5, 1963): 52–60; "Vanishing Glory in Business Buildings," *Fortune* 68 (September 1963): 119–26; Martin Tolchin, "Demolition Starts at Penn Station; Architects Picket," *New York Times* (October 29, 1963): 1, 24; "Farewell to Penn Station," editorial, *New York Times* (October 30, 1963): 38, reprinted in *Journal of the American Institute of Architects* 41 (January–June 1964): 53; "Going & Gone," *Village Voice* 9 (November 7, 1963): 1; "The Talk of the Town: Notes and Comment," *New Yorker* 39 (November 23, 1963): 45; "Pennsylvania Station: Finis," *Progressive Architecture* 44 (December 1963): 54–55; Peter Blake, *God's Own Junkyard* (New York: Holt, Rinehart and Winston, 1964), 9; "The Lipsett Brothers: Biggest Wreckers in the Building World," *Architectural Forum* 120 (January 1964): 76–77; "Editorial," *Progressive Architecture* 45 (March 1964): 125; "The Penn Station Obituary," letters to the editor, *Progressive Architecture* 45 (May 1964): 8; "Penn Station Winds Up as Land Fill," *Progressive Architecture* 45 (November 1964): 49; "The Major Space," *Progressive Architecture* 46 (June 1965): cover, 2, 8, 140–200; "Penn Station Knocked Down and Shored Up for New Sports Arena," *Engineering News-Record* 175 (August 26, 1965): 38–40; Starr, "Must Landmarks Go?": 50–51; Ada Louise Huxtable, "A Vision of Rome Dies: Shorn of Its Proud Eagles, Last Facade of Penn Station Yielding to Modernity," *New York Times* (July 14, 1966): 37, reprinted as "A Vision of Rome Dies," in Huxtable, *Will They Ever Finish Bruckner Boulevard?*, 212–16, and in Huxtable, *Goodbye History, Hello Hamburger*, 49–51; "Eavesdroppings," *Progressive Architecture* 47 (October 1966): 96; Ada Louise Huxtable, "The Art of Destruction," *New York Times* (May 26, 1968), II: 40, reprinted as "The Art of Expediency," in Huxtable, *Will They Ever Finish Bruckner Boulevard?*, 143–47, and in Huxtable, *Goodbye History, Hello Hamburger*, 51–54; "Letters," letters to the editor, *Architectural Record* 144 (October 1968): 46; Vincent Scully, *American Architecture and Urbanism* (New York: Frederick A. Praeger, 1969), 142–43; Ada Louise Huxtable, "Lessons in the Death of Style," *New York Times* (December 21, 1969), II: 36; Nicholas Schneider, "The Grandeur that Was Penn Station," *Architectural Forum* 133 (December 1970): 60–62; Leland Roth, "The Urban Architecture of McKim, Mead & White, 1870–1910" (Ph.D. diss., Yale University, 1973): 699–700; Jonathan Barnett, *Urban Design as Public Policy* (New York: Architectural Record Books, 1974), 70; Jonathan Barnett, "Wanted: Not-for-Profit Entrepreneurs," *Architectural Record* 156 (December 1974): 122–25; Roth, *McKim, Mead & White, Architects*, 316–27; Stern, Gilmartin and Massengale, *New York 1900*, 26, 40–43; Lorraine B. Diehl, *The Late, Great Pennsylvania Station* (New York: American Heritage; Boston: Houghton Mifflin, 1985); David Masello, "The Kinetics of Space," *Metropolis* 7 (November 1987): 64–69, 99–101.
197. Goldstone and Dalrymple, *History Preserved: A Guide to New York City Landmarks and Historic Districts*, 20.
198. "Railroad Terminal Shops," *Pencil Points* 23 (April 1942): 201.
199. Mumford, "The Sky Line: Terminals and Monuments": 105–6.
200. "Zeckendorf Signs Up Air Over Pensy Station": 27.
201. "Zeckendorf Promoting World's Most Massive Building": 9.
202. Diehl, *The Late, Great Pennsylvania Station*, 144.
203. "Railroad's Own Changes Will Give Penn Station New Look": 16; "Zeckendorf Switches Palace Project into Bigger Scheme": 16; "Classic Station, Modern Improvement": 113–15; "Old Setting, New Gleam": cover, 104–9.
204. Kidney, "Penn Station": 72, 78.
205. "Editor's Comment," *Architectural Forum*: 78.
206. "Old Setting, New Gleam": 104.
207. Mumford, "The Sky Line: The Disappearance of Pennsylvania Station": 106–8, 111.
208. "Buildings in the News," *Architectural Record* 128 (December 1960): 13.
209. "With Progress Aforethought: New York's Penn Station, Present and Future": 8.
210. Saarinen, "Reactions to Pennsylvania Station Demolition": 84.
211. Oud, "Reactions to Pennsylvania Station Demolition": 84.
212. "La Pennsylvania Station di New York sará distrutta?": 52–53, quoted in "Down with Architecture! Up with Columns!": 9.
213. Goodman, "Reactions to Pennsylvania Station Demolition": 78.
214. Mailer, "The Big Bite": 37.
215. August Heckscher quoted in "Quote . . . Unquote": 79.
216. Norval White quoted in Zukosky, "50 Pickets in March to Save Penn Station": 5.
217. Arthur Drexler quoted in Zukosky, "50 Pickets in March to Save Penn Station": 5.
218. Philip Johnson quoted in "Penn Pals Protest Penn Plot": 63.
219. Philip Johnson quoted in "Penn Pals": 42.
220. Irving Felt quoted in "Penn Pals": 42.
221. "Saving Fine Architecture": 16.
222. "Architects Want Penn Station Saved, Their Picket Lines Have Proved It: What Does Public Interest Require?": 23.
223. McQuade, "Architecture": 313–14.
224. Greenough, "Redeveloping Penn Station": 28.
225. Barnett, *Urban Design as Public Policy*, 70.
226. "Pennsylvania Station: Finis": 55.
227. Silver, *Lost New York*, 38.
228. "America's Heritage of Great Architecture Is Doomed . . . It Must Be Saved": 54.
229. Huxtable, "Architecture: How to Kill a City": 15.
230. Morris Lipsett quoted in "Penn Station Winds Up as Land Fill": 49.
231. "The Lipsett Brothers: Biggest Wreckers in the Building World": 77.
232. Huxtable, "A Vision of Rome Dies: Shorn of Its Proud Eagles, Last Facade of Penn Station Yielding to Modernity": 37.
233. Huxtable, "Architecture: How to Kill a City": 15.
234. "Farewell to Penn Station": 38.
235. "Down with Architecture! Up with Columns!": 9.
236. "The Talk of the Town: Notes and Comment": 45.
237. "AGBANY vs. Apathy at Penn Station": 5.

238. Goldberger, *The City Observed,* 181.
239. Huxtable, "The Art of Destruction": 40.
240. Christopher Gray, "Streetscapes: The Penn Station Service Building," *New York Times* (August 20, 1989), X: 4, reprinted in Christopher Gray, *Changing New York: The Architectural Scene* (New York: Dover, 1992), 97.
241. "Down with the Twentieth Century!" editorial, *Architectural Forum* 115 (November 1961): 107, 109; "Madison Square Garden Center to Be New AMF Headquarters," *Real Estate Record and Guide* 189 (February 17, 1962): 2; Ada Louise Huxtable, "Penn Station Giving Way to New Sports Arena: Model for Madison Square Garden Is Put on Display," *New York Times* (April 7, 1964): 37; "Heir to Penn Station," *Architectural Record* 135 (May 1964): 12; "Arena Rises Atop Buried Rail Terminal," *Popular Science* 188 (May 1966): 80–81; White and Willensky, *AIA Guide* (1967), 102; "Cabled Coliseum," *Architectural Forum* 126 (January–February 1967): 81; Henry Comstock, "How the Garden Grew," *Popular Mechanics* 128 (November 1967): 140–43, 212; "Better Break for the Fans," *Time* 91 (January 5, 1968): 68; "From Great Roman Hippodrome to . . . Boing! The Latest in Madison Square Gardens," *Progressive Architecture* 49 (February 1968): 48–49; Deirdre Carmody, "New Madison Square Garden, Colorful and Comfortable," *New York Times* (February 10, 1968): 25; "A Dazzling Palace for a New Generation of Thrills," *Life* 64 (February 16, 1968): 60–61; "Blocked Views Plague New Arena," *Engineering News-Record* 180 (February 29, 1968): 12; "The New Madison Square Garden Center: She's Changed Her Style and She May Change Yours," advertisement, *Architectural Forum* 129 (December 1968): 6–7; Scully, *American Architecture and Urbanism,* 142–43; "High 'T' in the Garden," advertisement, *Progressive Architecture* 51 (January 1970): 139; Goldberger, *The City Observed,* 181; Richard David Story, "The Buildings New Yorkers Love to Hate," *New York* 20 (June 15, 1987): cover, 30–35. For the original Madison Square Garden, see Stern, Gilmartin and Massengale, *New York 1900,* 202–6.
242. "'Garden' to Grow a Film Center," *Engineering News-Record* 176 (March 17, 1966): 83; "Cinema Center," *Architectural Forum* 124 (April 1966): 23; "TV Scores TKO on Garden Site," *Progressive Architecture* 47 (April 1966): 59. In 1947 the architects Leon and Lionel Levy proposed to expand the existing Madison Square Garden. See "Three Times Bigger," *Architectural Forum* 88 (April 1948): 13.
243. "Big Deal on 34th Street," *Progressive Architecture* 47 (August 1966): 74.
244. Soon after the arena's opening, hockey fans complained of obstructed views due to seating partitions, railings and a wall enclosing the rink. Charles Luckman Associates redesigned those features. See "Blocked Views Plague New Arena": 12.
245. "Down with the 20th Century!": 109.
246. John Guare quoted in Story, "The Buildings New Yorkers Love to Hate": 33.
247. Huxtable, "A Vision of Rome Dies: Shorn of Its Proud Eagles, Last Facade of Penn Station Yielding to Modernity": 37.
248. Goldberger, *The City Observed,* 117.
249. Goldberger, *The City Observed,* 117.
250. Mailer, "The Big Bite": 37.
251. Scully, *American Architecture and Urbanism,* 142–43.
252. Thomas W. Ennis, "Landmarks Bill Signed by Mayor," *New York Times* (April 20, 1965): 28; "Landmarks Bill Becomes Law," *Village Voice* 10 (April 22, 1965): 3; "Mayor Appoints City's Landmarks Preservation Commission," *Real Estate Record and Guide* 196 (July 10, 1965): 2–3; Robert C. Weinberg, "Preservation, at Long Last," *Journal of the American Institute of Architects* 47 (May 1967): 114–15.
253. In 1968 Platt was followed by the architect Harmon Goldstone, who served as chairman until 1973. The urban planner Beverly Moss Spatt filled the post from 1974 to 1978. For a profile of Goldstone, see "Landmarks Guardian: Harmon Hendricks Goldstone," *New York Times* (August 27, 1969): 46. For an extensive discussion of the commission's structure and procedures, see Diamonstein, *The Landmarks of New York,* 12–14.
254. Local Laws of the City of New York, Title 25, Chapter 3 of the Administrative Code.
255. "NYC Landmarks Law," *Architectural Forum* 139 (December 1973): 19; "Lindsay Signs Landmarks Bill," *New York Times* (December 18, 1973): 45; "The Talk of the Town: Facades Protected," *New Yorker* 49 (January 14, 1974): 24–25; Maurice Carroll, "3 New Sorts of Landmarks Designated in City," *New York Times* (November 14, 1974): 49, 94; Elizabeth G. Miller, "Interior Preservation: Issues and (Some) Answers," *Progressive Architecture* 57 (November 1976): 76–79.
256. "Architectural Historians' Meeting Features Tour of Historic New York Buildings," *Architectural Record* 111 (March 1952): 12–13; Huxtable, *Classic New York,* 68–70; Landmarks Preservation Commission of the City of New York, LP-0047 (December 21, 1965); Landmarks Preservation Commission of the City of New York, LP-0807 (May 27, 1975); Diamonstein, *The Landmarks of New York,* 76–77; Dolkart, *Guide to New York City Landmarks,* 23.
257. "Pacing the Tribune," *Progressive Architecture* 47 (July 1966): 57.
258. Stern, Gilmartin and Massengale, *New York 1900,* 185.
259. "Changing the Skyline," *Time* 88 (August 12, 1966): 46; "Thanks for Memory," *Progressive Architecture* 47 (November 1966): 59; Silver, *Lost New York,* 215; Stern, Gilmartin and Mellins, *New York 1930,* 236–39; Paul Goldberger, "At the Cooper-Hewitt, Designs of Joseph Urban," *New York Times* (December 20, 1987): 75.
260. Thomas W. Ennis, "Office Boom Seen for Times Square," *New York Times* (January 30, 1966), VIII: 1, 4; Sanka Knox, "Paramount's Fixtures Sold at Auction," *New York Times* (July 9, 1966): 17; Thomas W. Ennis, "News of Realty: End of a Theater," *New York Times* (January 17, 1967): 60; Thomas W. Ennis, "Hollow Shell Hides Remnants of Glory of Old Paramount," *New York Times* (June 25, 1967), VIII: 1, 12; "Paramount Theater Being Rebuilt as Building within a Building," *Real Estate Record and Guide* 200 (July 29, 1967): 2–3.
261. Ennis, "Hollow Shell Hides Remnants of Glory of Old Paramount": 1.
262. Knox, "Paramount's Fixtures Sold at Auction": 17.
263. White and Willensky, *AIA Guide* (1978), 377; Stern, Gilmartin and Mellins, *New York 1930,* 374–76.
264. "Kiosk at 116th St. Is Demolished," *Real Estate Record and Guide* 201 (January 6, 1968): 5.
265. "Capitol Theater Bows Out; 1633 Broadway Takes Spotlight," *Real Estate Record and Guide* 202 (October 5, 1968): 4–5; Stern, Gilmartin and Mellins, *New York 1930,* 247, 254, 256.
266. Stern, Gilmartin and Massengale, *New York 1900,* 115–16.
267. Thomas W. Ennis, "Astor Hotel to Be Razed for Office Building," *New York Times* (January 22, 1966): 1, 32; "George Washington Would Have Slept Here," *Progressive Architecture* 47 (March 1966): 56–57; Stern, Gilmartin and Massengale, *New York 1900,* 222–23, 266–67, 269.
268. "Closing a Hotel—At a Profit," *Business Week* (July 23, 1966): 64–66; Stern, Gilmartin and Mellins, *New York 1930,* 202–3.
269. Stern, Gilmartin and Massengale, *New York 1900,* 265, 267; Robert F. R. Ballard, *Directory of Manhattan Office Buildings* (New York: McGraw-Hill, 1978), 214.
270. *Upper East Side Historic District,* 1114; Stern, Gilmartin and Massengale, *New York 1900,* 342, 344.
271. Michael Knight, "Frick Planning to Raze Widener Town House," *New York Times* (March 15, 1973): 45; Michael Knight, "Widener Mansion Given a Reprieve," *New York Times* (March 21, 1973): 54; "More Space for the Frick?" *Architectural Forum* 139 (July–August 1973): 25.
272. Carter B. Horsley, "3 Notable Buildings Face Wrecker's Ball," *New York Times* (May 11, 1974): 35.
273. Horsley, "3 Notable Buildings Face Wrecker's Ball": 35.
274. Horsley, "3 Notable Buildings Face Wrecker's Ball": 35.
275. Stern, Gilmartin and Mellins, *New York 1930,* 545–46.
276. Foster Hailey, "Savoy Plaza to Be Razed for G.M. Offices," *New York Times* (August 21, 1964): 1, 20; "Doom of Savoy Hotel Endangers Plaza Site," *Housing and Planning News* 23 (September 1964): 2–3; William Lescaze, "Architect Backs Plaza Building," letter to the editor, *New York Times* (September 17, 1964): 42; Glenn Fowler, "48-Story Tower to Rise on Savoy Plaza Site," *New York Times* (December 16, 1964): 1, 31; Ada Louise Huxtable, "Nothing Inviolate Here: Plan for Tower on Savoy Plaza Site Raises Some Questions of Esthetics," *New York Times* (December 16, 1964): 31; "Sunken Plaza Planned for G.M. Building on 5th Ave.," *New York Times* (August 8, 1965), VIII: 1; "Eavesdroppings," *Progressive Architecture* 46 (December 1965): 46; Starr, "Must Landmarks Go?": 56; Silver, *Lost New York,* 24–25; McCandlish Phillips, "Bold New Profile Joins City's East Side Skyline," *New York Times* (October 17, 1967): 49; "GM Restyles Fifth Avenue," *Business Week* (September 28, 1968): 92–94; Stern, Gilmartin and Mellins, *New York 1930,* 200, 217–22.
277. Glenn Fowler, "Fifth Avenue, City's Grande Dame, Graciously Suffers Changes," *New York Times* (August 5, 1965): 32–33. Also see Thomas W. Ennis, "Women Score G.M. Building Plan," *New York Times* (January 20, 1965): 41, 77.
278. Starr, "Must Landmarks Go?": 56.
279. Peter Blake, "Somebody Up There Likes This City," *New York* 2 (February 2, 1969): 48–49.
280. Landmarks Preservation Commission of the City of New York, LP-0265 (December 9, 1969); Stern, Gilmartin and Massengale, *New York 1900,* 252, 256, 258–59, 261–62; Diamonstein, *The Landmarks of New York,* 280–81; Dolkart, *Guide to New York City Landmarks,* 88.
281. Landmarks Preservation Commission of the City of New York, LP-0860 (July 23, 1974); Diamonstein, *The Landmarks of New York,* 318; Dolkart, *Guide to New York City Landmarks,* 105.
282. Jean Ann Vincent, "Souvenir of a Golden Age," *Interiors* 114 (August 1954): 20.
283. Philip Clucas, Ted Smart and David Gibbon, *The Plaza* (Secaucus, N.J.: Poplar, 1981), 38.
284. Quoted in "Vanishing New York," *Progressive Architecture* 46 (June 1965): 58.
285. "The Talk of the Town: Outside the Profession," *New Yorker* 29 (September 26, 1953): 26–27; Olgivanna Lloyd Wright, *Our House* (New York: Horizon Press, 1959), 287–89; Olgivanna Lloyd Wright, *The Shining Brow—Frank Lloyd Wright* (New York: Horizon Press, 1960), 172–74; Herbert Muschamp, *Man About Town: Frank Lloyd Wright in New York City* (Cambridge, Mass.: MIT Press, 1982), 98–100, 108, 132–35; Bruce Brooks Pfeiffer, ed., *Frank Lloyd Wright: The Guggenheim Correspondence* (Fresno, Calif.: The Press at California State University; Carbondale, Ill.: Southern Illinois University Press, 1986), 195–96; Brendan Gill, *Many Masks: A Life of Frank Lloyd Wright* (New York: G. P. Putnam's Sons, 1987), 486–87, 490.
286. Wright, *The Shining Brow—Frank Lloyd Wright,* 172.
287. Frank Lloyd Wright quoted in "The Talk of the Town: Outside the Profession": 26, also quoted in Gill, *Many Masks: A Life of Frank Lloyd Wright,* 486.
288. Frank Lloyd Wright quoted in Muschamp, *Man About Town,* 99.
289. Wright, *The Shining Brow—Frank Lloyd Wright,* 173.
290. Muschamp, *Man About Town,* 100.
291. "Vanishing New York": 58; "The Plaza Fights to Stay Elegant—And Profitable," *Business Week* (December 1, 1965): 32–33; Regional Plan Association, *Urban Design Manhattan* (New York: Viking Press, 1969), 112; "Protecting the Plaza," *Architectural Forum* 132 (March 1970): 71–72; Ada Louise Huxtable, "If It's Good, Leave It Alone," *New York Times* (October 31, 1971), II: 22; Ada Louise Huxtable, "An Edwardian Splendor or Green Tulip Modern?" *New York Times* (November 5, 1971): 45, 47; "The Pleasures of the Plaza," *Interior Design* 42 (December 1971): 66–69; Ada Louise Huxtable, "The Needless Sacrifice of the Villard Houses," *New York Times* (June 22, 1975), II: 31, reprinted as "Dilemmas: . . . With the Other Foot," in Huxtable, *Kicked a Building Lately?,* 272–75; "The Talk of the Town: Turn Backward, O Time!" *New Yorker* 52 (February 23, 1976): 27; Clucas, Smart and Gibbon, *The Plaza,* 40–47.
292. Huxtable, "An Edwardian Splendor or Green Tulip Modern?": 45, 47.
293. "The Pleasures of the Plaza": 66.
294. Huxtable, "The Needless Sacrifice of the Villard Houses": 31.
295. Betty Raymond, "Preservation at the Plaza," *Interiors* 135 (February 1976): 72–73.
296. Federal Writers' Project, *The WPA Guide to New York City* (New York: Random House, 1939; New York: Pantheon Books, 1982), 206; "'Manhattan Club' Property Is Sold," *Real Estate Record and Guide* 197 (April 2, 1966): 3; White and Willensky, *AIA Guide* (1978), 564.
297. "Opinion by Justice Marks," *New York Law Journal* (September 9, 1966): 15.
298. Ballard, *Directory of Manhattan Office Buildings,* 215; Goldberger, *The City Observed,* 97.
299. Charles Magruder, "Met's Last Days," *Progressive Architecture* 41 (January 1960): 55; "Committee Dedicated to Saving the Metropolitan," *Musical America* 81 (December 1961): 19; "Last Stand at the Met," *Newsweek* 68 (October 11, 1965): 99–100; Irving Kolodin, *The Metropolitan Opera 1883–1966: A Candid History* (New York: Alfred A. Knopf, 1966); Stuart Preston, ed., *Farewell to the Old House: The Metropolitan Opera House 1883–1966* (Garden City, N.Y.: Doubleday, 1966); The Editors of *Opera News, The Golden Horseshoe: The Life and Times of the Metropolitan Opera House* (New York: Viking, 1966); "New York Landmarks Threatened," *Progressive Architecture* 47 (January 1966): 60; "The Talk of the Town: Mementos," *New Yorker* 41 (January 15, 1966): 35; "The

Talk of the Town: Notes and Comment," *New Yorker* 41 (April 9, 1966): 31–32; Henry Butler, "A Glad Good-bye to the Old Met," *Look* 30 (April 19, 1966): 41–44; "Finale," *Newsweek* 67 (April 25, 1966): 84; "After 83 Years, 'the Queen Is Dead, Long Live the Queen,'" *Life* 60 (April 29, 1966): 24–33; "Save the Real Met," editorial, *New York Times* (May 17, 1966): 46; Theodore Strongin, "Old Met Is Given Deposit Deadline," *New York Times* (August 17, 1966): 41; Silver, *Lost New York*, 226–27; "Smashing Swan Song," *Architectural Forum* 126 (January–February 1967): 109; Theodore Strongin, "Wreckers Begin Demolishing Met," *New York Times* (January 18, 1967): 1, 50; Quaintance Eaton, *The Miracle of the Met: An Informal History of the Metropolitan Opera 1883–1967* (New York: Meredith Press, 1968), 407–11; John Briggs, *Requiem for a Yellow Brick Brewery: A History of the Metropolitan Opera* (Boston: Little, Brown, 1969), 327–40; Paul Seligman, *Debuts and Farewells: A Two-Decade Photographic Chronicle of the Metropolitan Opera* (New York: Alfred A. Knopf, 1972), 80–81, 92–95; Lincoln Kirstein, *The New York City Ballet* (New York: Alfred A. Knopf, 1973), 162–63; Stern, Gilmartin and Massengale, *New York 1900*, 14–15; Jan Morris, *Manhattan '45* (New York: Oxford University Press, 1987), 202–3.

300. Huntington Hartford quoted in Strongin, "Wreckers Begin Demolishing Met": 1.

301. Strongin, "Wreckers Begin Demolishing Met": 1.

302. "Save the Real Met": 46.

303. "The Talk of the Town: Golden," *New Yorker* 30 (February 5, 1955): 24–25; "Too Good to Last," *Architectural Forum* 107 (July–August 1967): 107–8; Joseph P. Fried, "End Near for Singer Building, a Forerunner of Skyscrapers," *New York Times* (August 22, 1967): 41; Jean Progner, "As Ye Sew, So Shall They Reap," *Progressive Architecture* 48 (September 1967): 170–71; "The Talk of the Town: Tallest," *New Yorker* 43 (September 9, 1967): 37–38; Huxtable, "A Matter of Urban Delight": 31; Alan Dunn, "I Keep Asking Myself Why I Go On—," cartoon, *Architectural Record* 143 (February 1968): 10; Joseph P. Fried, "End of a Skyscraper," *New York Times* (March 27, 1968): 49; Seymour Toll, *Zoned America* (New York: Grossman, 1969), 290; William Zeckendorf with Edward McCreary, *The Autobiography of William Zeckendorf* (New York: Holt, Rinehart and Winston, 1970), 274–83; White and Willensky, *AIA Guide* (1978), 21, 417, 562; Tauranac, *Essential New York*, 232–33; Stern, Gilmartin and Massengale, *New York 1900*, 170–71; Mardges Bacon, *Ernest Flagg: Beaux-Arts Architect and Urban Reformer* (New York: Architectural History Foundation; Cambridge, Mass.: MIT Press, 1986), 209–33; Robert A. M. Stern with Thomas Mellins and Raymond Gastil, *Pride of Place: Building the American Dream* (Boston: Houghton Mifflin; New York: American Heritage, 1986), 257–59, 283. Another complex that had added significantly to the lower Manhattan skyline, the Hudson Terminal (Clinton & Russell, 1908), was demolished to make way for the World Trade Center. See Stern, Gilmartin and Massengale, *New York 1900*, 45.

304. "Too Good to Last": 107.

305. For George B. Post's New York Stock Exchange Building, see Stern, Gilmartin and Massengale, *New York 1900*, 144–45, 187–89. For Trowbridge & Livingston's addition, see Stern, Gilmartin and Mellins, *New York 1930*, 535.

306. "New York Stock Exchange," *Architectural Forum* 101 (November 1954): 40, 42; "Two of Manhattan's Oldest Structures Being Razed to Make Way for Erection of General Realty's New Office Building at 20 Broad Street," *Real Estate Record and Guide* 175 (January 1, 1955): 3; "Site Clearance Finished for New Structure at 20 Broad Street," *Real Estate Record and Guide* 175 (June 25, 1955): 3; Stern, Gilmartin and Massengale, *New York 1900*, 144, 152, 155–56.

307. "Too Good to Last": 107.

308. Alan Burnham quoted in Fried, "End Near for Singer Building, a Forerunner of Skyscrapers": 41.

309. Huxtable, "A Matter of Urban Delight": 31.

310. Stern, Gilmartin and Massengale, *New York 1900*, 164, 168, 170–71, 173–74, 176.

311. David Bourdon, "Stacking the Deco," *New York* 7 (November 11, 1974): 64–65. Also see "Art Deco Room at the Brooklyn Museum," *Interiors* 131 (September 1971): 12; Anne Hollander, "Art Deco's Back and New York's Got It," *New York* 7 (November 11, 1974): 54–57; Dorothy Seiberling, "New York Is a Deco Spectacle," *New York* 7 (November 11, 1974): 58–63. For efforts to save the Art Deco apartment buildings of the Bronx, see "Swan Song," *New York* 9 (January 19, 1976): 52.

312. Cervin Robinson and Rosemarie Haag Bletter, *Skyscraper Style: Art Deco New York* (New York: Oxford University Press, 1975). For a discussion of Cervin Robinson's photography, see Paul Goldberger, "Photos Capture Richness of Art Deco Streetscape," *New York Times* (February 18, 1973): 19.

313. Landmarks Preservation Commission of the City of New York, LP-0992 (September 12, 1978); Landmarks Preservation Commission of the City of New York, LP-0996 (September 12, 1978). Also see Daniel S. Levy, "Outracing the Bulldozers," *Time* 136 (August 6, 1990): 80.

314. Landmarks Preservation Commission of the City of New York, LP-2000 (May 19, 1981); Landmarks Preservation Commission of the City of New York, LP-2001 (May 19, 1981).

315. "Video Tower Atop Empire State Will Raise It 199 Feet to 1,499," *New York Times* (January 24, 1950): 1, 52; "TV Tower to Raise Skyscraper 222 Feet," *New York Times* (October 19, 1950): 62; "Radio-TV Notes," *New York Times* (December 19, 1951): 48; "The Talk of the Town: Multiple," *New Yorker* 29 (April 11, 1953): 19–20; "Empire State Building Gets Own TV Antenna," *Real Estate Record and Guide* 177 (March 17, 1956): 3.

316. "Intrusion in the Sky?" *Newsweek* 47 (March 26, 1956): 92–93; "So Symbolic," *Architectural Record* 119 (April 1956): 24; "The Editor's Asides," *Journal of the American Institute of Architects* 25 (May 1956): 229–30; Geoffrey T. Hellman, "Eighty-Six-Storied Pomp," *New Yorker* 32 (May 12, 1956): 95–98.

317. "Empire State Building Could Grow Up," *Engineering News-Record* 189 (October 14, 1972): 13; "Island of the Apes," *Architecture Plus* 1 (October 1973): 19.

318. "The Talk of the Town: Backstage," *New Yorker* 40 (December 26, 1964): 22–25; "Music Hall: Still the No. 1 Hit," *Business Week* (December 25, 1965): 46–49; Gordon Cotler, "The One and Only Radio City Music Hall," *Holiday* 49 (December 1970): 78–79, 98; Lawrence Alloway, "Art," *Nation* 214 (June 19, 1972): 797–98; "Tune-Out for Radio City?" *Time* 100 (October 23, 1972): 98; "Art Deco Exposition," *Progressive Architecture* 55 (March 1974): 40; Michael Ruby with Pamela Lynn Abraham, "Radio City's Last Kick?" *Newsweek* 88 (August 30, 1976): 67–68; Ada Louise Huxtable, "Is It Curtains for the Music Hall?" *New York Times* (March 19, 1978), II: 1, 31; Ada Louise Huxtable, "Update on the Music Hall," *New York Times* (April 22, 1979), II: 33, 36; Stern, Gilmartin and Mellins, *New York 1930*, 652–56.

319. Landmarks Preservation Commission of the City of New York, LP-0995 (March 28, 1978); Diamonstein, *The Landmarks of New York*, 368–70; Dolkart, *Guide to New York City Landmarks*, 89–90.

320. Landmarks Preservation Commission of the City of New York, LP-1446 (April 23, 1985); Diamonstein, *The Landmarks of New York*, 368–70; Dolkart, *Guide to New York City Landmarks*, 89–90.

321. Starr, "Must Landmarks Go?": 53; "Another New York Landmark Faces Demolition," *Interiors* 128 (June 1968): 14; Ada Louise Huxtable, "How to Impoverish City at $400 a Square Foot," *New York Times* (September 29, 1968), II: 31, 33, reprinted as "How to Bankrupt a City at $400 a Square Foot," in Huxtable, *Will They Ever Finish Bruckner Boulevard?*, 60–64; Landmarks Preservation Commission of the City of New York, LP-0268, LP-0269, LP-0270 (September 30, 1968); Thomas W. Ennis, "Archdiocese Headquarters Buildings Designated as Landmarks," *New York Times* (October 3, 1968): 94; "Too Valuable to Keep," *Architectural Forum* 129 (November 1968): 35; Regional Plan Association, *Urban Design Manhattan*, 112; Ada Louise Huxtable, "The Plot Thickens," *New York Times* (February 14, 1971), II: 25; Paul Goldberger, "Landmarks Unit Backs Hotel at Villard Houses," *New York Times* (January 3, 1975): 37; Ada Louise Huxtable, "They Call This 'Saving' a Landmark?" *New York Times* (January 5, 1975), II: 29, reprinted as "Dilemmas: Kicking a Landmark," in Huxtable, *Kicked a Building Lately?*, 269–72; Ada Louise Huxtable, "New York Can Learn a Lot from St. Louis," *New York Times* (January 26, 1975), II: 30; Huxtable, "The Needless Sacrifice of the Villard Houses": 31; "A Reuse Opportunity Endangered by the Development Rote," *Architectural Record* 58 (August 1975): 36; Suzanne Stephens, "Procrustean Preservation," *Progressive Architecture* 56 (August 1975): 27; "Art Loses Again," *Commonweal* 102 (August 29, 1975): 354; Paul Goldberger, "New Villard Houses Plan Preserves the Gold Room," *New York Times* (September 6, 1975): 23; Ada Louise Huxtable, "Another Chapter in the Urban Saga—How Three Lost Causes Were Saved," *New York Times* (September 21, 1975), II: 31, reprinted as "Dilemmas: A Hopeful Toast," in Huxtable, *Kicked a Building Lately?*, 275–77; "Villard Houses," letter to the editor, *Commonweal* 102 (September 26, 1975): 447; "Saving the Past," *Commonweal* 102 (November 21, 1975): 546; "New Plan to Save Villard's Gold Room," *Progressive Architecture* 56 (December 1975): 18; "Villard Houses . . .," editorial, *New York Times* (June 30, 1976): 36; "Planners Reduce Landmark Zoning," *New York Times* (July 15, 1976): 33; Nikolaus Pevsner, "The Villard Houses," letter to the editor, *New York Times* (July 27, 1976): 28; Glenn Fowler, "City Planning Commission Approves the Construction of a Hotel Incorporating Landmark Villard House," *New York Times* (September 23, 1976): 13; Barbaralee Diamonstein, *Buildings Reborn: New Uses, Old Places* (New York: Harper & Row, 1978), 160–61; White and Willensky, *AIA Guide* (1978), 164; Ada Louise Huxtable, "Potted Palms and Wilted Roses," *New York Times* (February 3, 1978): 22; Goldberger, *The City Observed*, 163; Tauranac, *Essential New York*, 63–64; William C. Shopsin and Mosette Glaser Broderick, *The Villard Houses: Life Story of a Landmark* (New York: Viking Press, in cooperation with the Municipal Art Society of New York, 1980); Dudley Clendinen, "Palace Opens, with a Few Reservations," *New York Times* (September 12, 1980), B: 1, 6; Paul Goldberger, "Palace Hotel: A Landmark Opening," *New York Times* (September 12, 1980), B: 1, 3; Ada Louise Huxtable, "Two Triumphant New Hotels for New York," *New York Times* (October 19, 1980), II: 33, 36; Reynolds, *The Architecture of New York City*, 188–92; Diamonstein, *The Landmarks of New York*, 180–81; Dolkart, *Guide to New York City Landmarks*, 96.

322. Bennett Cerf quoted in Huxtable, "How to Impoverish City at $400 a Square Foot": 31.

323. Monsignor James Rigney quoted in Huxtable, "How to Impoverish City at $400 a Square Foot": 31.

324. Huxtable, "How to Impoverish City at $400 a Square Foot": 31.

325. Huxtable, "They Call This 'Saving' a Landmark?": 29.

326. Goldberger, "Landmarks Unit Backs Hotel at Villard Houses": 37.

327. Huxtable, "The Needless Sacrifice of the Villard Houses": 31.

328. *James Stewart Polshek: Context and Responsibility* (New York: Rizzoli International Publications, 1988), 40–41, 84–85.

329. Huxtable, "Another Chapter in the Urban Saga—How Three Lost Causes Were Saved": 31.

330. Landmarks Preservation Commission of the City of New York, LP-0398 (October 19, 1966); "Wails and Walls, Schools and Skulls," *Housing and Planning News* 25 (September–October 1967): 4; "Armory Wall Blocks School Progress," *Housing and Planning News* 26 (fall 1967): 4; "Citadel of Learning," *Architectural Forum* 127 (November 1967): 95; "Intermediate School 29," *Architectural Record* 142 (December 1967): 41; "From Armory to Schoolhouse," *Progressive Architecture* 49 (October 1968): 86, 88; Harmon H. Goldstone, "The Marriage of New Buildings with Old," *Historic Preservation* 23 (January 1971): 19–23; White and Willensky, *AIA Guide* (1978), 240–41; Morris Ketchum, Jr., *Blazing a Trail* (New York: Vantage Press, 1982), 28–33; Diamonstein, *The Landmarks of New York*, 227; Trager, *Park Avenue*, 2, 34–46, 152; Dolkart, *Guide to New York City Landmarks*, 116.

331. "Wails and Walls, Schools and Skulls": 4.

332. "Armory Wall Blocks School Progress": 4.

333. "Wails and Walls, Schools and Skulls": 4.

334. "Office Tower atop High School to Rise on Armory Site," *Real Estate Record and Guide* 209 (April 1, 1972): 2; "Demolition," *Progressive Architecture* 53 (May 1972): 33; "Mixed Use Building Replaces Old Armory, School and Offices to Share One Unit," *Journal of the American Institute of Architects* 57 (June 1972): 12.

335. "Library Renovation for Maritime Cadets," *Progressive Architecture* 46 (September 1965): 160–65; White and Willensky, *AIA Guide* (1978), 354–55; Diamonstein, *The Landmarks of New York*, 71; Dolkart, *Guide to New York City Landmarks*, 205.

336. White and Willensky, *AIA Guide* (1978), 354.

337. Landmarks Preservation Commission of the City of New York, LP-0417 (June 9, 1967); White and Willensky, *AIA Guide* (1978), 224; Goldberger, *The City Observed*, 237; Diamonstein, *The Landmarks of New York*, 173; Trager, *Park Avenue*, 30–31; Dolkart, *Guide to New York City Landmarks*, 115.

338. Landmarks Preservation Commission of the City of New York, LP-0823 (September 24, 1974); White and Willensky, *AIA Guide* (1978), 337; Diamonstein, *The Landmarks of New York*, 317; Dolkart, *Guide to New York City Landmarks*, 204.

339. White and Willensky, *AIA Guide* (1978), 468.

340. White and Willensky, *AIA Guide* (1978), 451.

341. White and Willensky, *AIA Guide* (1978), 433.

342. Landmarks Preservation Commission of the City of New York, LP-0960 (March 8, 1977).

343. Landmarks Preservation Commission of the City of New York, LP-1228 (April 12, 1983).

344. Landmarks Preservation Commission of the City of New York, LP-1390 (May 14, 1985).
345. Kathleen Curran, "The German Rundbogenstil and Reflections on the American Round-Arched Style," *Journal of the Society of Architectural Historians* 47 (December 1988): 351–73.
346. Landmarks Preservation Commission of the City of New York, LP-0016 (October 26, 1965); Ada Louise Huxtable, "A Landmark Is Saved: Historic Building Scheduled for Razing Is Rescued with Aid of City's New Law," *New York Times* (January 6, 1966): 29, 52; Ervin Galanty, "Architecture," *Nation* 22 (April 25, 1966): 500–502; White and Willensky, *AIA Guide* (1967), 75; Ada Louise Huxtable, "The Theater: 'Hair,' a Love-Rock Musical, Inaugurates Shakespeare Festival's Anspacher Playhouse—Structure Is the First Saved as Landmark," *New York Times* (October 30, 1967): 55, reprinted as "Anatomy of a Success," in Huxtable, *Will They Ever Finish Bruckner Boulevard?*, 237–40; Jack Kroll, "Making of a Theater," *Newsweek* 70 (November 13, 1967): 124–25; "Bard Program Cites Works of Four Nonprofit Clients," *Journal of the American Institute of Architects* 49 (June 1968): 20–21; Stuart W. Little, "Joe Papp's Biggest Real-Estate Deal," *New York* 2 (April 21, 1969): 54–55; "New Theater for Landmark Building," *Progressive Architecture* 51 (December 1970): 21; Ada Louise Huxtable, "Missing the Point (and Boat) at City Hall," *New York Times* (January 3, 1971), II: 22; Diamonstein, *Buildings Reborn: New Uses, Old Places*, 136–37; White and Willensky, *AIA Guide* (1978), 94, 97–98; Goldberger, *The City Observed*, 60–61; Tauranac, *Essential New York*, 36–38; Diamonstein, *The Landmarks of New York*, 107; Miller, *Greenwich Village and How It Got That Way*, 81–82; Dolkart, *Guide to New York City Landmarks*, 42.
347. Kroll, "Making of a Theater": 124.
348. Huxtable, "The Theater: 'Hair,' a Love-Rock Musical, Inaugurates Shakespeare Festival's Anspacher Playhouse—Structure Is the First Saved as Landmark": 55.
349. "The Talk of the Town: Landmark," *New Yorker* 32 (March 24, 1956): 24; "Old Jeff's Clock," *Village Voice* 3 (July 2, 1958): 3; "City Puts Jeff Market Courthouse on Block," *Village Voice* 5 (November 25, 1959): 1; "'Old Jeff,' 82, Still Has a Life Left, Official Indicates," *Village Voice* 5 (December 9, 1959): 1; "Publisher Bids for Jeff Mkt.," *Village Voice* 5 (April 13, 1960): 1; "Village Oddity May Become New Library," *Village Voice* 5 (August 18, 1960): 1; "DeSapio Pledges Aid in Fight to Make 'Old Jeff' a Library," *Village Voice* 6 (April 13, 1961): 1; "A Landmark in Search of a Function," *Village Voice* 6 (April 20, 1961): 1; "Wagner Backs Jeff Market as a Library," *Village Voice* 6 (August 24, 1961): 1; "The Talk of the Town: Birdland," *New Yorker* 37 (September 16, 1961): 34–35; "The Crowds Persist, but the Scene Changes," *Village Voice* 7 (March 29, 1962): 3; "City Pushes Plan for Jeff Market," *Village Voice* 7 (May 17, 1962): 3; "Final Victory for Villagers—Courthouse Will Be Library," *Village Voice* 8 (January 31, 1963): 3; "Disregarding Ugly Rumors," *Village Voice* 8 (April 11, 1963): 1; Ada Louise Huxtable, "The Salvage of the Old Jeff: Determination of 'Villagers' to Save Historic Courthouse Proves Effective," *New York Times* (September 23, 1964): 38; "Cantabrigian Is the Word," *Village Voice* 9 (October 1, 1964): 1; "Greenwich Village Salvation Saga," *Progressive Architecture* 45 (November 1964): 49; "Preservation Solution: Find a Use," *Progressive Architecture* 46 (May 1965): 63; "'Old Jeff' to Be NYPL's Newest Branch," *Library Journal* 88 (July 1965): 2658; "A Face Job Is Being Done on the Jefferson Market Courthouse," *Village Voice* 10 (July 15, 1965): 1; White and Willensky, *AIA Guide* (1967), 57–58; "The Return of Old Jeff," *Progressive Architecture* 48 (October 1967): 175–79; Ada Louise Huxtable, "Old Jeff's Conversion: Preservation of 'Village' Courthouse Marks Triumph of Will Over Realty," *New York Times* (November 28, 1967): 49, 94; "Jeff Market Makes It into 20th Century as Library," *Village Voice* 13 (November 30, 1967): 31; "A.I.A. Cites 20 Buildings in Annual Honor Awards Program," *Architectural Record* 143 (June 1968): 40–43; "The 1968 Honor Awards," *Journal of the American Institute of Architects* 49 (June 1968): 84–104; Landmarks Preservation Commission of the City of New York, *Greenwich Village Historic District Designation Report* (New York, 1969), 184; "AIA Honors an Eccentric Victorian Cinderella in Manhattan," *Interiors* 128 (February 1969): 6; Frank B. Gilbert, "Real Estate Values," *Historic Preservation* 23 (April 1971): 21–24; Diamonstein, *Buildings Reborn: New Uses, Old Places*, 150–51; Goldberger, *The City Observed*, 80–81; Tauranac, *Essential New York*, 51–52; Miller, *Greenwich Village and How It Got That Way*, 46–49; Christopher Gray, "Streetscapes/The Jefferson Market Courthouse: A Stopped Clock Sired the Preservation Movement," *New York Times* (April 3, 1994), X: 5; Margot Gayle, "The Jefferson Market Courthouse," letter to the editor, *New York Times* (June 5, 1994), X: 13.
350. Francis R. Kowsky, *The Architecture of Frederick Clarke Withers and the Progress of the Gothic Revival in America after 1850* (Middletown, Conn.: Wesleyan University Press, 1980), 138–44. Also see Silver, *Lost New York*, 105.
351. "The Return of Old Jeff": 175–79.
352. "The Talk of the Town: Landmark": 24.
353. "AIA Honors an Eccentric Victorian Cinderella in Manhattan": 6.
354. Huxtable, "Old Jeff's Conversion: Preservation of 'Village' Courthouse Marks Triumph of Will Over Realty": 49.
355. Ada Louise Huxtable, "Recycling a Landmark for Today," *New York Times* (June 15, 1975), D: 29; White and Willensky, *AIA Guide* (1978), 120; Goldberger, *The City Observed*, 101; Stephen Garmey, *Gramercy Park: An Illustrated History of a New York Neighborhood* (New York: Balsam Press, 1984), 90–91, 174; Diamonstein, *The Landmarks of New York*, 128; *James Stewart Polshek: Context and Responsibility*, 37, 80–83; Dolkart, *Guide to New York City Landmarks*, 55.
356. James Stewart Polshek, "Notes on My Life and Work," in *James Stewart Polshek: Context and Responsibility*, 37.
357. White and Willensky, *AIA Guide* (1978), 8–9. Also see Landmarks Preservation Commission of the City of New York, LP-0020 (October 14, 1965); "I. M. Pei Proposal Suggests New Life for Landmark," *Architectural Record* 155 (March 1974): 34; Landmarks Preservation Commission of the City of New York, LP-1022 (January 9, 1979); Diamonstein, *The Landmarks of New York*, 288–89; *James Stewart Polshek: Context and Responsibility*, 41, 96; Dolkart, *Guide to New York City Landmarks*, 23–24.
358. Ada Louise Huxtable, "Sprucing Up the Bank of Tokyo," *New York Times* (December 28, 1975), II: 28, reprinted in Huxtable, *Kicked a Building Lately?*, 236–38; Charles King Hoyt, "The Bank of Tokyo: New Image with Old Roots," *Architectural Record* 160 (June 1976): cover, 89–94; Sam Hunter, *Isamu Noguchi* (New York: Abbeville Press, 1978), 160–61; Stern, Gilmartin and Massengale, *New York 1900*, 158–59.
359. Huxtable, "Sprucing Up the Bank of Tokyo": 28.
360. Janet Nairn, "Renovation for Art Shop Saved Move Out of Area," *Architectural Record* 159 (April 1976): 130–31, 135; Stern, Gilmartin and Massengale, *New York 1900*, 103–4.
361. Stanley Abercrombie, "Art and Building," *Architecture Plus* 1 (March 1973): 60–61; August Matzdorf, "Cinematheque," letter to the editor, *Architectural Forum* 139 (October 1973): 4.
362. "Ellis Island," editorial, *New York Times* (April 7, 1954): 22; "Ellis Island to Go as Alien Station," *New York Times* (June 3, 1954): 55; "Ellis Island Ends Alien Processing," *New York Times* (November 13, 1954): 20; "End of Ellis Island," *New York Times* (November 14, 1954), IV: 2; "Last Man Off Ellis Island," editorial, *New York Times* (November 14, 1954), IV: 8.
363. "End of Ellis Island": 2.
364. Murray Illson, "Ellis Island 'Raided' by Jersey Claimants," *New York Times* (January 5, 1956): 1, 10.
365. Charles Grutzner, "U.S. Shops for Court Site Here; Would Like to Trade Ellis Island," *New York Times* (May 3, 1956): 1, 20.
366. Victor H. Lawn, "U.S. Selling Haven of Migration Days for Private Use," *New York Times* (September 14, 1956): 1, 8.
367. John P. Callahan, "High Bidder Offers $201,000 for Ellis Island for Use as Resort Area," *New York Times* (February 15, 1958): 1, 15.
368. Sol G. Atlas quoted in Callahan, "High Bidder Offers $201,000 for Ellis Island for Use as Resort Area": 15.
369. "U.S. Rejects Offers to Buy Ellis Island; Inquiry Is Sought," *New York Times* (April 3, 1958): 33.
370. Quoted in Milton Bracker, "$2,100,000 Bid for Ellis Island as Site of Wright 'Dream City,'" *New York Times* (May 11, 1962): 39. Also see Arthur Drexler, *The Drawings of Frank Lloyd Wright* (New York: Horizon Press, 1962), plate 301; Muschamp, *Man About Town*, 139.
371. Paul Douglas Roller, "An Ecumenical Council Center for the Christian Churches," *Liturgical Arts* 32 (May 1964): 75–86.
372. "Mayor Proposes Ellis Island Park," *New York Times* (October 30, 1963): 50.
373. Ada Louise Huxtable, "Architect Named for Ellis Island," *New York Times* (June 8, 1965): 24; "Johnson to Redesign Ellis Island," *Progressive Architecture* 46 (August 1965): 49; "Dog's Domain," *Travel* (January 1966): 60; "Ellis Island Honor Roll: 16 Million Immigrants," *New York Herald Tribune* (February 25, 1966): 16; Alfred Friendly, Jr., "Design Unveiled for National Shrine on Ellis Island," *New York Times* (February 25, 1966): 1, 28; Ada Louise Huxtable, "The Uses of the Past," *New York Times* (February 25, 1966): 28; "'The Wall' at Ellis Island," editorial, *New York Times* (February 26, 1966), IV: 24; "Stabilizing the Ruins," *Time* 87 (March 4, 1966): 78; Conrad L. Wirth, "To Restore Ellis Island," letter to the editor, *New York Times* (March 27, 1966), IV: 11; "'Parkitecture,'" *Architectural Forum* 124 (April 1966): 24; "Ellis Island," *Architectural Review* 139 (April 1966): 305–7; "Ellis Island Shrine: A Babel Tower and Gothic Ruins," *Progressive Architecture* 47 (April 1966): 214–16; "Johnson's Ellis Island Plan Announced," *Progressive Architecture* 47 (April 1966): 57; "How to Lose Money and Space," *America* 114 (April 16, 1966): 540; "Una torre di Babele alla porta d'America," *L'Architettura cronache e storia* 12 (October 1966): 387; Alison Sky and Michelle Stone, *Unbuilt America* (New York: McGraw-Hill, 1976), 143.
374. "Stabilizing the Ruins": 78.
375. Philip Johnson quoted in Huxtable, "Architect Named for Ellis Island": 24.
376. Philip Johnson quoted in "Stabilizing the Ruins": 78.
377. Stewart L. Udall quoted in "Stabilizing the Ruins": 78.
378. "Ellis Island," *Architectural Review*: 305.
379. Huxtable, "The Uses of the Past": 28.
380. "'The Wall' at Ellis Island": 24.
381. Inez Robb quoted in "'Parkitecture'": 24.
382. Wirth, "To Restore Ellis Island": 11.
383. "How to Lose Money and Space": 540.
384. Lester McClanahan quoted in William K. Stevens, "Ellis Island at Low Point in Its History," *New York Times* (March 5, 1968): 43.
385. Deirdre Carmody, "Ellis Island Squatters Get Permit to Develop Center," *New York Times* (August 19, 1970): 1, 17.
386. "Follow-up on the News: Ellis Island," *New York Times* (May 26, 1974): 27.
387. "Main Building on Ellis Island, Dedicated December 1900, Near Ruin," *Architectural Record* 156 (December 1974): 40.
388. Damon Stetson, "World's Loftiest Tower May Rise on Site of Grand Central Terminal," *New York Times* (September 8, 1954): 1, 36; "A New Grand Central?" editorial, *New York Times* (September 9, 1954): 30; "Plan to Update Grand Central Station," *Architectural Forum* 101 (October 1954): 41; Douglas Haskell, "History without Fake," editorial, *Architectural Forum* 101 (November 1954): 170; "Can the Grand Central Concourse Be Saved?" *Architectural Forum* 101 (November 1954): 134–39; "Is Grand Central Terminal 'Outmoded?' Owners Consider Replacement Schemes," *Architectural Record* 116 (November 1954): 20; "Support Grows for Saving Grand Central Concourse," *Architectural Forum* 101 (December 1954): 37; Philip H. Goldman, "Grand Central," letter to the editor, *Architectural Forum* 102 (January 1955): 78; "Save the Concourse," letters to the editor, *Architectural Forum* 102 (February 1955): 116–19; "The Record Reports: Meetings and Miscellany," *Architectural Record* 117 (February 1955): 15; "New Plan Studied on Grand Central," *New York Times* (February 8, 1955): 20; Edmund N. Bacon, "Outdoor Spaces," letter to the editor, *Architectural Forum* 102 (April 1955): 74; "Zeckendorf and Stevens Given Grand Central Agency Job," *Architectural Forum* 102 (April 1955): 25; Carroll V. Hill, Dennis O'Harrow and Robert C. Weinberg, "Grand Central," letters to the editor, *Architectural Forum* 102 (June 1955): 76, 80, 84, 88; "Winning Architectural Battles," editorial, *Architectural Forum* 108 (April 1958): 87; "News Bulletins," *Progressive Architecture* 39 (June 1958): 41; "The Record Reports: Meetings and Miscellany," *Architectural Record* 124 (October 1958): 28; Reed, *The Golden City*, 18, 55–56; "Design of 'Grand Central City' Accepted," *Progressive Architecture* 40 (March 1959): 157; Richard H. Howland, "Architecture Worth Saving," *Journal of the American Institute of Architects* 31 (May 1959): 29–31; "The Talk of the Town: Kitty Kelly Airborne," *New Yorker* 35 (October 17, 1959): 33–34; "Everything—And Trains," *Newsweek* 55 (April 11, 1960): 99–100; "Architects Hit Plans for Grand Central Bowling," *Architectural Forum* 114 (January 1961): 9; "New York Is a Crowded Festival," *Progressive Architecture* 42 (January 1961): 50; "Of Parks and Terminals," editorial, *New York Times* (January 6, 1961): 40; "Bowling Over Grand Central," editorial, *New York Times* (January 10, 1961): 46; "Architects Beat Plan for Grand Central Bowling," *Architectural Forum* 114 (February 1961): 9; Olga Gueft, "A Time for New Brooms," editorial, *Interiors* 120 (February 1961): 87; "Bowling Blackballed," *Progressive Architecture* 42 (February 1961): 54; Joseph Watterson,

"A Correction—And Grand Central Station," *Journal of the American Institute of Architects* 36 (October 1961): 80; "The City's Architecture," editorial, *New York Times* 32 (January 17, 1962): 2; White and Willensky, *AIA Guide* (1967), 114–16; Landmarks Preservation Commission of the City of New York, LP-0266 (September 21, 1967); Glenn Fowler, "Grand Central Proposal Scored," *New York Times* (September 22, 1967): 41; "A Grand Central Proposal," *Progressive Architecture* 48 (November 1967): 56; Ada Louise Huxtable, "Slab City Marches On," *New York Times* (March 3, 1968), II: 22; "Grand Central Bauhaus," *Progressive Architecture* 49 (April 1968): 52–53; Glenn Fowler, "Grand Central Tower Will Top Pan Am Building," *New York Times* (June 20, 1968): 1, 36; Ada Louise Huxtable, "Architecture: Grotesquerie Astride a Palace," *New York Times* (June 20, 1968): 37, reprinted as "Grand Central Tower Grotesquerie," in Huxtable, *Will They Ever Finish Bruckner Boulevard?*, 82–86; "Jumbo atop Grand Central," editorial, *New York Times* (June 20, 1968): 44; Ada Louise Huxtable, "Grand Central: Its Heart Belongs to Dada," *New York Times* (June 23, 1968), IV: 10; "Tower Revives Old Controversy," *Engineering News-Record* 180 (June 27, 1968): 16; "Breuer's Blockbuster," *Time* 91 (June 28, 1968): 48; "The Talk of the Town: Notes and Comment," *New Yorker* 44 (June 29, 1968): 23; "52 Story Office Building Will 'Float' above Grand Central Terminal," *Real Estate Record and Guide* 201 (June 29, 1968): 2–3; Douglas Haskell, "Handstand Operation," letter to the editor, *Architectural Forum* 129 (July-August 1968): 10; Walter McQuade, "A Dissenting Opinion on Grand Central," editorial, *Architectural Forum* 129 (July–August 1968): 112; "Grand Central City," *Architectural Forum* 129 (July–August 1968): 72–73; "55-Story Office Building Will Float over Grand Central," *Architectural Record* 144 (July 1968): 36; Leticia Kent, "An Architect of the 'Inevitable,'" *Village Voice* 13 (July 25, 1968): 3; Walter F. Wagner, Jr., "The Wrong Criticism, in the Wrong Place, at the Wrong Time," editorial, *Architectural Record* 144 (August 1968): 9–10; Frederic A. Birmingham, "Grand Central Station," *Holiday* 44 (August 1968): 26–29, 75–76; "Put It Over Here, Mac," *Progressive Architecture* 49 (August 1968): 46, 48; Peter Blake, "In Defense of an 'Outrage,'" *New York* 1 (August 12, 1968): 50–52; Howard Smith, "Scenes," *Village Voice* 13 (August 22, 1968): 11; Howard Smith, "Scenes," *Village Voice* 13 (August 29, 1968): 10; Sibyl Moholy-Nagy, "Hitler's Revenge," *Art in America* 56 (September 1968): 42–43; Jan C. Rowan, "Editorial," *Progressive Architecture* 49 (September 1968): 101; Howard Smith, "Scenes," *Village Voice* 13 (September 5, 1968): 6; Howard Smith, "Scenes," *Village Voice* 13 (September 12, 1968): 35; Howard Smith, "Scenes," *Village Voice* 13 (September 19, 1968): 20; "Traffic at Grand Central," letter to the editor, *Architectural Forum* 129 (October 1968): 12; Alan Dunn, "O.K.—We Sent Them the Temple of Dendur," cartoon, *Architectural Record* 144 (October 1968): 10; Russell Lynes, "Stacked-Up," *Harper's* 237 (October 1968): 38–42; "Tower above Grand Central Lacks Landmark Certification," *Progressive Architecture* 49 (November 1968): 48; Ada Louise Huxtable, "The Stakes Are High for All in Grand Central Battle," *New York Times* (April 11, 1969): 28; David K. Shipler, "New Tower Sought for Grand Central," *New York Times* (April 11, 1969): 1, 28; "Tower Threatens New York Landmark," *Engineering News-Record* 182 (April 17, 1969): 31; Douglas Haskell, "Grand Central Controversy," letter to the editor, *Architectural Forum* 130 (May 1969): 16, 18; "Breuer Two," *Architectural Forum* 130 (May 1969): 35; "Scheme II for Grand Central Site," *Architectural Record* 145 (May 1969): 43; "N.Y. Real Estate Board Supports Proposed Grand Central Building," *Real Estate Record and Guide* 203 (May 3, 1969): 4; David K. Shipler, "Grand Central Building Plan Revised," *New York Times* (June 27, 1969): 20; Robert Franz, "Haskell on Grand Central," *Architectural Forum* 131 (July–August 1969): 12, 16; David K. Shipler, "Landmarks Panel Bars Office Tower over Grand Central," *New York Times* (August 27, 1969): 1, 46; Martin R. Fisher, "Developing Landmarks," letter to the editor, *New York Times* (September 3, 1969): 46; "$8-Million a Year Asked of City for Denying Grand Central Plan," *New York Times* (September 5, 1969): 40; "Needle in the Sky," *Time* 94 (September 5, 1969): 54; "Saving a Face," *Architectural Forum* 131 (October 1969): 88; "New York City's Landmark Gives Grand Central Station a Reprieve," *Architectural Record* 146 (October 1969): 37; "Suit Prepared for Client in Penn Central Matter," *Journal of the American Institute of Architects* 52 (October 1969): 28; David K. Shipler, "Landmarks Zoning Change Proposed," *New York Times* (October 7, 1969): 34; Robert E. Tomasson, "Penn Central Sues City in Fight to Build Grand Central Tower," *New York Times* (October 8, 1969): 51; Tician Papachristou, *Marcel Breuer: New Buildings and Projects* (New York: Praeger, 1970), 186–89; Peter Blake, "Forum," *Architectural Forum* 133 (October 1970): 23; "Landmarks Preservation Commission's Constitutionality Challenged," *Oculus* 33 (June 1972): 3; "Battle Station," *New York* 5 (November 6, 1972): 80; Barnett, *Urban Design as Public Policy*, 70–74; "The Talk of the Town: Renaissance," *New Yorker* 50 (November 18, 1974): 47–48; Huxtable, "Landmarks Are in Trouble with the Law": 36; *Penn Central Transportation Company et al. v. City of New York et al.*, 50 App. Div. 2d 265-89 (1975); Diane Henry, "Jackie Onassis Fights for Cause," *New York Times* (January 31, 1975): 37; "The Talk of the Town: Grand Central," *New Yorker* 50 (February 10, 1975): 27–29; Ada Louise Huxtable, "Why Did We Lose Grand Central as a Landmark?" *New York Times* (March 2, 1975), II: 33; "Battle Station," *New York* 8 (August 4, 1975): 47; Carter B. Horsley, "City Appeal a Key Test of Policy on Landmarks," *New York Times* (October 12, 1975), VIII: 1, 8; Ada Louise Huxtable, "How Great Buildings Shape a City's Soul," *New York Times* (October 19, 1975), II: 32, reprinted as "Perspective on the City: Three Buildings," in Huxtable, *Kicked a Building Lately?*, 129–33; Ada Louise Huxtable, "Growing Up in a Beaux Arts World," *New York Times* (November 9, 1975), II: 1, 33, reprinted as "Beaux Arts Buildings I Have Known," in Huxtable, *Kicked a Building Lately?*, 217–21; Paul Goldberger, "Grand Central Reinstated as a Landmark by Court," *New York Times* (December 17, 1975): 49; Peter Blake, "The Eighth Annual Cityscape Awards," *New York* 9 (January 12, 1976): 55–57; "Grand Central Wins a Court Victory," *Progressive Architecture* 2 (February 1976): 32; *Penn Central Transportation Company et al. v. City of New York et al.*, 42 N.Y. 2d 324-37 (1977); *Penn Central Transportation Co. et al. v. City of New York et al.*, 438 U.S. 104-53 (1978); Ada Louise Huxtable, "Grand Central at a Crossroads," *New York Times* (January 29, 1978), II: 25, 28; Warren Weaver, Jr., "Justice Dept. Files Brief Backing Grand Central's Landmark Status," *New York Times* (April 14, 1978), B: 4; Wylie F. Tuttle, "To Top Grand Central," letter to the editor, *New York Times* (April 28, 1978): 26; Ada Louise Huxtable, "A 'Landmark' Decision on Landmarks," *New York Times* (July 9, 1978), II: 21, 24; Goldberger, *The City Observed*, 123–25; Tauranac, *Essential New York*, 134–35; Landmarks Preservation Commission of the City of New York, LP–1099 (September 23, 1980); Deborah Nevins, ed., *Grand Central Terminal: City within the City* (New York: Municipal Art Society of New York, 1982); Stern, Gilmartin and Massengale, *New York 1900*, 34, 36–40; Reynolds, *The Architecture of New York City*, 218–27; Steven Ruttenbaum, *Mansions in the Clouds: The Skyscraper Palazzi of Emery Roth* (New York: Balsam Press, 1986), 204–5, 207; Geoffrey Brown, "Preservation, Private Property and the Law," *Village Views* 4 (spring 1987): 12–40; Tony Hiss, "Reflections: Experiencing Places—I," *New Yorker* 63 (June 22, 1987): 45–46, 48–49, 51–60, 62–65, 67–68; Diamonstein, *The Landmarks of New York*, 320–21; Shanor, *The City that Never Was*, xvii, 36; William H. Whyte, *City: Rediscovering the Center* (New York: Doubleday, 1988), 278; Michele Herman, "Yet Another Breuer Controversy," *Metropolis* 8 (May 1988): 24–25; Charles M. Haar and Jerold S. Kayden, *Landmark Justice: The Influence of William J. Brennan on America's Communities* (Washington, D.C.: Preservation Press, in cooperation with the Lincoln Institute of Land Policy, 1989), 12–13, 154–68; Trager, *Park Avenue*, 219–34.

389. "The Talk of the Town: The Giant," *New Yorker* 26 (May 27, 1950): 21; Christopher Gray, "The End of the Line for Grand Central's Big Picture," *New York Times* (June 18, 1989), X: 8.

390. Adolph Stuber quoted in "The Talk of the Town: The Giant": 21.

391. "A New Grand Central?": 30.

392. "Can the Grand Central Concourse Be Saved?": 135.

393. Alfred Fellheimer quoted in "Can the Grand Central Concourse Be Saved?": 137.

394. Marcel Breuer quoted in "Can the Grand Central Concourse Be Saved?": 136. Also see Suzanne Burrey, "Noticed the New Haven?" *Industrial Design* 3 (February 1956): 52–70; "New Operations, New Face," *Architectural Forum* 104 (June 1956): 106–12. For Breuer's design of a railroad station in New London, Connecticut, see Papachristou, *Marcel Breuer: New Buildings and Projects*, 232.

395. Burrey, "Noticed the New Haven?": 53, 69–70.

396. Minoru Yamasaki quoted in "Can the Grand Central Concourse Be Saved?": 136.

397. George Howe quoted in "Can the Grand Central Concourse Be Saved?": 136.

398. Haskell, "History without Fake": 170.

399. Drawings in the archives of Pei Cobb Freed & Partners, New York, New York.

400. "New York Is a Crowded Festival": 50.

401. Gueft, "A Time for New Brooms": 87.

402. Philip Johnson quoted in Fowler, "Grand Central Proposal Scored": 41.

403. Philip Johnson quoted in Huxtable, "Slab City Marches On": 22.

404. Richard Roth quoted in Fowler, "Grand Central Proposal Scored": 41.

405. "Grand Central Bauhaus": 52.

406. Lynes, "Stacked-Up": 42.

407. Marcel Breuer quoted in Kent, "An Architect of the 'Inevitable'": 3.

408. Donald Elliott quoted in Fowler, "Grand Central Tower Will Top Pan Am Building": 1.

409. "Jumbo atop Grand Central": 44.

410. Huxtable, "Architecture: Grotesquerie Astride a Palace": 37.

411. Wagner, "The Wrong Criticism, in the Wrong Place, at the Wrong Time": 9–10.

412. Blake, "In Defense of an 'Outrage'": 52.

413. Smith, "Scenes" (August 22, 1968): 11.

414. Smith, "Scenes" (August 29, 1968): 10.

415. Smith, "Scenes" (September 5, 1968): 6.

416. Smith, "Scenes" (September 19, 1968): 20.

417. Haskell, "Handstand Operation": 10.

418. "The Talk of the Town: Notes and Comment": 23.

419. "Tower above Grand Central Lacks Landmark Certification": 48.

420. Marcel Breuer quoted in Papachristou, *Marcel Breuer: New Buildings and Projects*, 186, 189.

421. Jaquelin T. Robertson quoted in Shipler, "New Tower Sought for Grand Central": 28.

422. Huxtable, "Landmarks Are in Trouble with the Law": 36.

423. Irving H. Saypol quoted in Blake, "The Eighth Annual Cityscape Awards": 55.

424. Irving H. Saypol quoted in Henry, "Jackie Onassis Fights for Cause": 37.

425. Philip Johnson quoted in Henry, "Jackie Onassis Fights for Cause": 37.

426. Francis T. Murphy quoted in Brown, "Preservation, Private Property and the Law": 32–33.

427. *Penn Central Transportation Company et al. v. City of New York et al.*, 42 N.Y. 2d 324-37 (1977).

428. William Rehnquist quoted in Joseph B. Rose, "Landmarks Preservation in New York," *Public Interest* 74 (winter 1984): 132–45, reprinted in Nathan Glazer and Mark Lilla, eds., *The Public Face of Architecture: Civic Culture and Public Spaces* (New York: Macmillan, 1987), 428–42.

429. *Armstrong v. United States*, 364 U.S. 40, 49 (1960).

430. *Pennsylvania Coal Co. v. Mahon*, 260 U.S. 393, 415 (1922).

431. Landmarks Preservation Commission of the City of New York, LP-0249 (June 21, 1966); Stern, Gilmartin and Mellins, *New York 1930*, 429; Diamonstein, *The Landmarks of New York*, 382; Dolkart, *Guide to New York City Landmarks*, 93–94.

432. Landmarks Preservation Commission of the City of New York, LP-0279 (June 21, 1966); Stern, Gilmartin and Mellins, *New York 1930*, 428–29; Diamonstein, *The Landmarks of New York*, 383; Dolkart, *Guide to New York City Landmarks*, 94–95.

433. Landmarks Preservation Commission of the City of New York, LP-0224 (August 16, 1966); Diamonstein, *The Landmarks of New York*, 383; Dolkart, *Guide to New York City Landmarks*, 26–27.

434. Landmarks Preservation Commission of the City of New York, LP-0251 (September 20, 1966); Stern, Gilmartin and Massengale, *New York 1900*, 298, 300, 303; Diamonstein, *The Landmarks of New York*, 384; Landmarks Preservation Commission of the City of New York, LP-1559 (July 12, 1988); Dolkart, *Guide to New York City Landmarks*, 56–57.

435. Landmarks Preservation Commission of the City of New York, LP-0322 (March 16, 1967); Diamonstein, *The Landmarks of New York*, 384; Dolkart, *Guide to New York City Landmarks*, 150.

436. Landmarks Preservation Commission of the City of New York, LP-0225 (August 2, 1967); Stern, Gilmartin and Mellins, *New York 1930*, 427–28; Diamonstein, *The Landmarks of New York*, 385; Dolkart, *Guide to New York City Landmarks*, 48.

437. Landmarks Preservation Commission of the City of New York, LP-0536 (December 13, 1967); Diamonstein, *The Landmarks of New York*, 385; Dolkart, *Guide to New York City Landmarks*, 117.

438. Landmarks Preservation Commission of the City of New York, LP-0450 (May 15, 1968); Diamonstein, *The Landmarks of New York*, 386; Dolkart, *Guide to New York City Landmarks*, 192, 194.

439. Landmarks Preservation Commission of the City of New York, LP-0250 (January 14, 1969); Landmarks Preservation Commission of the City of New York, LP-1420 (June 19,

1984); Diamonstein, *The Landmarks of New York*, 386; Dolkart, *Guide to New York City Landmarks*, 50–51.

440. Landmarks Preservation Commission of the City of New York, LP-0454 (February 11, 1969); Stern, Gilmartin and Mellins, *New York 1930*, 433, 437; Diamonstein, *The Landmarks of New York*, 388; Dolkart, *Guide to New York City Landmarks*, 107.

441. Landmarks Preservation Commission of the City of New York, LP-0451 (July 29, 1969); Stern, Gilmartin and Massengale, *New York 1900*, 101; Diamonstein, *The Landmarks of New York*, 388; Dolkart, *Guide to New York City Landmarks*, 209.

442. Landmarks Preservation Commission of the City of New York, LP-0320 (December 30, 1969); Diamonstein, *The Landmarks of New York*, 389; Dolkart, *Guide to New York City Landmarks*, 163–64.

443. Landmarks Preservation Commission of the City of New York, LP-0638 (August 18, 1970); Diamonstein, *The Landmarks of New York*, 389; Dolkart, *Guide to New York City Landmarks*, 146–47.

444. Landmarks Preservation Commission of the City of New York, LP-0666 (September 15, 1970); Landmarks Preservation Commission of the City of New York, LP-1088 (February 3, 1981); Diamonstein, *The Landmarks of New York*, 390; Dolkart, *Guide to New York City Landmarks*, 53.

445. Landmarks Preservation Commission of the City of New York, LP-0695 (September 14, 1971); Diamonstein, *The Landmarks of New York*, 390–91; Dolkart, *Guide to New York City Landmarks*, 185.

446. "The Talk of the Town: Preservation," *New Yorker* 43 (February 25, 1967): 31–33; Landmarks Preservation Commission of the City of New York, LP-0452 (November 3, 1971); Diamonstein, *The Landmarks of New York*, 391; Dolkart, *Guide to New York City Landmarks*, 148.

447. Landmarks Preservation Commission of the City of New York, LP-0323 (April 19, 1973); Stern, Gilmartin and Massengale, *New York 1900*, 373; Diamonstein, *The Landmarks of New York*, 392; Dolkart, *Guide to New York City Landmarks*, 129–30.

448. Landmarks Preservation Commission of the City of New York, LP-0713 (April 19, 1973); Diamonstein, *The Landmarks of New York*, 391; Dolkart, *Guide to New York City Landmarks*, 123–24. For the American Museum of Natural History, see Stern, Gilmartin and Massengale, *New York 1900*, 370–73; Stern, Gilmartin and Mellins, *New York 1930*, 129, 135–36; Diamonstein, *The Landmarks of New York*, 164–65; Dolkart, *Guide to New York City Landmarks*, 120.

449. Landmarks Preservation Commission of the City of New York, LP-0709 (July 17, 1973); Pranay Gupte, "Park Slope Wins a Landmark Status," *New York Times* (July 22, 1973): 75, 78; Diamonstein, *The Landmarks of New York*, 392; Dolkart, *Guide to New York City Landmarks*, 175–77.

450. Landmarks Preservation Commission of the City of New York, LP-0768 (August 14, 1973); Diamonstein, *The Landmarks of New York*, 393; Dolkart, *Guide to New York City Landmarks*, 37–38.

451. Landmarks Preservation Commission of the City of New York, LP-0696 (September 25, 1973); Diamonstein, *The Landmarks of New York*, 393; Dolkart, *Guide to New York City Landmarks*, 161.

452. Landmarks Preservation Commission of the City of New York, LP-0767 (November 20, 1973); Diamonstein, *The Landmarks of New York*, 394; Dolkart, *Guide to New York City Landmarks*, 155.

453. Landmarks Preservation Commission of the City of New York, LP-0861 (July 23, 1974); Diamonstein, *The Landmarks of New York*, 394; Dolkart, *Guide to New York City Landmarks*, 98.

454. Landmarks Preservation Commission of the City of New York, LP-0872 (November 26, 1974); Diamonstein, *The Landmarks of New York*, 395; Dolkart, *Guide to New York City Landmarks*, 143–44.

455. Landmarks Preservation Commission of the City of New York, LP-0893 (September 23, 1975); Diamonstein, *The Landmarks of New York*, 395; Dolkart, *Guide to New York City Landmarks*, 63–64.

456. Peter Helman, "The Consequences of Brownstone Fever," *New York* 2 (March 31, 1969): 22–26, 30–31; D. K. Patton, "New York City," *Historic Preservation* 21 (October 1969): 15–18; H. Dickson McKenna, *A House in the City: A Guide to Buying and Renovating Old Row Houses* (New York: Van Nostrand Reinhold, 1971); Shalmon Bernstein and Angela Wilson, "Neighborhoods in Transition," *New York Affairs* 1, no. 3 (1974): 78–120.

457. Landmarks Preservation Commission of the City of New York, LP-0973 (September 26, 1978); Stern, Gilmartin and Massengale, *New York 1900*, 125; Diamonstein, *The Landmarks of New York*, 399; Dolkart, *Guide to New York City Landmarks*, 168–69.

458. Landmarks Preservation Commission of the City of New York, LP-1003 (September 26, 1978); Stern, Gilmartin and Massengale, *New York 1900*, 212, 214–16; Diamonstein, *The Landmarks of New York*, 398; Dolkart, *Guide to New York City Landmarks*, 156.

459. Landmarks Preservation Commission of the City of New York, LP-0979 (February 8, 1979); Stern, Gilmartin and Massengale, *New York 1900*, 424–25; Diamonstein, *The Landmarks of New York*, 400; Dolkart, *Guide to New York City Landmarks*, 179–81.

460. Landmarks Preservation Commission of the City of New York, LP-1024 (October 9, 1979); Diamonstein, *The Landmarks of New York*, 401; Dolkart, *Guide to New York City Landmarks*, 177–78.

461. Landmarks Preservation Commission of the City of New York, LP-1236 (August 29, 1981); Stern, Gilmartin and Massengale, *New York 1900*, 425; Diamonstein, *The Landmarks of New York*, 402; Dolkart, *Guide to New York City Landmarks*, 165–66.

462. Landmarks Preservation Commission of the City of New York, LP-2017 (November 10, 1981); Diamonstein, *The Landmarks of New York*, 403; Dolkart, *Guide to New York City Landmarks*, 162–63.

463. Landmarks Preservation Commission of the City of New York, LP-1248 (September 14, 1982); Diamonstein, *The Landmarks of New York*, 403; Dolkart, *Guide to New York City Landmarks*, 171–72.

464. Clay Lancaster, *Old Brooklyn Heights* (Rutland, Vt.: Charles E. Tuttle, 1961); "Area in Brooklyn to Be Landmark," *New York Times* (April 25, 1965), VIII: 1, 14; Thomas W. Ennis, "Landmark Plan Draws Support," *New York Times* (November 18, 1965): 34; Landmarks Preservation Commission of the City of New York, LP-0099 (November 23, 1965); "Brooklyn Heights Now a Landmark," *New York Times* (December 2, 1965): 32; "Bard Awards," *Architectural Forum* 126 (June 1967): 83; Diamonstein, *The Landmarks of New York*, 382; Dolkart, *Guide to New York City Landmarks*, 158–60.

465. Stern, Gilmartin and Massengale, *New York 1900*, 283.

466. Jacob Landy, *The Architecture of Minard Lafever* (New York: Columbia University Press, 1970), 165–69.

467. Margot Gayle, "Changing Scene," *New York Daily News Sunday Magazine* (December 9, 1979): 34; Willensky, *When Brooklyn Was the World, 1920–1957*, 226.

468. Olindo Grossi, *Downtown Brooklyn Civic Center Report* (New York: Pratt Institute, 1962), 19; Stern, Gilmartin and Massengale, *New York 1900*, 178; Margot Gayle, "Changing Scene: Break the Bank," *New York Daily News Sunday Magazine* (May 20, 1990): 23.

469. Grossi, *Downtown Brooklyn Civic Center Report*, 19.

470. Landmarks Preservation Commission of the City of New York, LP-0147 (April 19, 1966); Diamonstein, *The Landmarks of New York*, 96–97; Dolkart, *Guide to New York City Landmarks*, 157.

471. Landmarks Preservation Commission of the City of New York, LP-0146 (July 19, 1966); Diamonstein, *The Landmarks of New York*, 192; Dolkart, *Guide to New York City Landmarks*, 186.

472. Landmarks Preservation Commission of the City of New York, LP-0148 (April 19, 1966); Diamonstein, *The Landmarks of New York*, 214; Dolkart, *Guide to New York City Landmarks*, 158.

473. "Jehovah's Witnesses to Begin Construction of Ten-Story Addition to Brooklyn Home," *New York Times* (January 17, 1947): 12; Barbara Grizzuti Harrison, *Visions of Glory: A History and a Memory of Jehovah's Witnesses* (New York: Simon & Schuster, 1978), 67–72.

474. Bancel LaFarge quoted in Goldstone, "The Marriage of New Buildings with Old": 22.

475. Goldstone, "The Marriage of New Buildings with Old": 22.

476. Goldstone, "The Marriage of New Buildings with Old": 22.

477. "An Architecture of Place that Unites Past and Present," *Architectural Record* 142 (October 1967): 133–44; Thomas W. Ennis, "Modern Building for Historic Brooklyn Heights," *New York Times* (July 20, 1969), VIII: 1, 6; "Watchtower on Brooklyn Heights," *Architectural Forum* 132 (March 1970): 40–41; White and Willensky, *AIA Guide* (1978), 386–87; Brent C. Brolin, *Architecture in Context: Fitting New Buildings with Old* (New York: Van Nostrand Reinhold, 1980), 63–64.

478. Brolin, *Architecture in Context: Fitting New Buildings with Old*, 63.

479. Greenwich Village Historic District," *Village Voice* 11 (November 18, 1965): 3; Mary Perot Nichols, "Fight 'Historic' Village," *Village Voice* 11 (December 9, 1965): 1; Mary Perot Nichols, "Lindsay, Villagers Back Village as 'Historic,'" *Village Voice* 11 (December 16, 1965): 1, 3; Leticia Kent, "Saving Greenwich Village: In Pieces or as a Whole?" *Village Voice* 12 (December 29, 1966): 1, 20; Greenwich Village Historic District; "'Village' Is Named a Landmark," *New York Times* (April 30, 1969): 44; "A Sense of History," *Village Voice* 14 (May 1, 1969): 1; Peter Wolf, *The Future of the City: New Directions in Urban Planning* (New York: Whitney Library of Design, 1974), 140, 142; Diamonstein, *The Landmarks of New York*, 387; Dolkart, *Guide to New York City Landmarks*, 45–47.

480. Frank W. Crane, "Landmarks Pass in the Minettas," *New York Times* (October 13, 1940), XII: 1, 6.

481. McQuade, "Books": 8.

482. "Village May Be 'Historic' Zone to Preserve It," *Village Voice* 4 (April 29, 1959): 1. Also see "Zoning for Survival," editorial, *Village Voice* 4 (April 29, 1959): 4.

483. "Zoning Revision May Save Old Houses in Village," *Village Voice* 5 (December 23, 1959): 1–2; "'Big Building' Plague in Village May Be Thwarted," *Village Voice* 5 (December 30, 1959): 1; "City to Hear Plea to Save the Village," *Village Voice* 5 (February 3, 1960): 1; "Trek to City Hall Wins Support," *Village Voice* 5 (February 24, 1960): 1; "Save-Village Zoning on Way to Final Test," *Village Voice* 5 (March 23, 1960): 1; "'Save the Village' Wins at City Hall," *Village Voice* 5 (March 30, 1960): 1; "Save All! Villagers Tell Mayor," *Village Voice* 5 (June 30, 1960): 1; "Lindsay in Fight to Save Village," *Village Voice* 5 (November 15, 1962): 2; "Villagers Make 'Last Ditch' Protest Against High-Risers," *Village Voice* 8 (February 21, 1963): 1.

484. "What Next?" *Village Voice* 1 (April 25, 1956): 1; "Site and Foresight," editorial, *Village Voice* 1 (May 9, 1956): 4; "Push Plans for Civic, Arts Center," *Village Voice* 1 (June 20, 1956): 3; "Village Jail: Will It Stay or Go?" *Village Voice* 1 (June 29, 1956): 1; "Will the House of Detention Do for a Community Center?" *Village Voice* 1 (October 17, 1956): 1; "Women's Prison Won't Do for Civic Center, Architect Says," *Village Voice* 1 (October 31, 1956): 3; "Women's House of Detention," *Village Voice* 2 (January 21, 1957): 3; "Urge Demolition of Jail for Apt., Off-B'Way Theater," *Village Voice* 3 (June 4, 1958): 20; "Plan Offered for Arts Center to Replace Jail," *Village Voice* 4 (September 2, 1959): 3; "To Go or Not to Go," *Village Voice* 9 (February 13, 1964): 1; Greenwich Village Historic District, 175, 184; "Village Fights Bulldozers," *Village Voice* 14 (August 7, 1969): 1, 31; Mary Perot Nichols, "Women's House: Case for Demolition," *Village Voice* 18 (August 9, 1973): 3, 59; Mary Perot Nichols, "What Next for the WHD?" *Village Voice* 18 (August 23, 1973): 3, 12, 14; James D. Morgan, "No Interest in Recycling," *Architecture Plus* 1 (October 1973): 18; David Bourdon, "Artes Perditae: The Women's House of Detention," *Arts* 48 (November 1973): 6–7; Clark Whelton, "Village Square Garden," *Village Voice* 19 (March 21, 1974): 1, 21; White and Willensky, *AIA Guide* (1978), 73, 563; Stern, Gilmartin and Mellins, *New York 1930*, 99, 101.

485. "Urge Demolition of Jail for Apt., Off-B'Way Theater": 20.

486. "Plan Offered for Arts Center to Replace Jail": 3.

487. Ralph Blumenthal, "School Plan Backed at 'Village' Jail Site," *New York Times* (November 22, 1971): 1, 61; Nichols, "Women's House: Case for Demolition": 59.

488. Bourdon, "Artes Perditae: The Women's House of Detention": 7.

489. Nichols, "Women's House: Case for Demolition": 59.

490. Quoted in Nichols, "Women's House: Case for Demolition": 59.

491. Douglas Robinson, "Townhouse Razed by Blast and Fire; Man's Body Found," *New York Times* (March 7, 1970): 1, 16; Douglas Robinson, "Bombs, Dynamite and Woman's Body Found in Ruins of 11th St. Townhouse," *New York Times* (March 11, 1970): 1, 37; Lawrence Van Gelder, "Two Figures in 'Village' Blast Linked to Politics of New Left," *New York Times* (March 11, 1970): 37; "The House on 11th St.: Digging Up the Debris," *Village Voice* 15 (March 12, 1970): 1, 18; "The House on 11th Street," *Newsweek* 75 (March 23, 1970): 29–30; "Bombing: A Way of Protest and Death," *Time* 95 (March 23, 1970): 8–10; John Neary, "The Two Girls from No. 18," *Life* 68 (March 27, 1970): 26–29; "The Bomb Jitters," *Newsweek* 75 (March 30, 1970): 23; J. Kirk Sale, "Ted Gold: Education for Violence," *Nation* 210 (April 13, 1970): 423–29; Mel Gussow, "West 11th Street: An End to Innocence," *New York* 4 (March 8, 1971): 35–43; Edith Evans Asbury, "Architect Pleads for a 'Village' Design," *New York Times* (March 10, 1971): 45, 86; Ada Louise Huxtable, "Compatibility Called Key to Building Plan," *New York Times* (March 10, 1971): 45; Edward Ranzal, "Design Approved for Town House on Bombing

Site," *New York Times* (May 20, 1971): 24; Ada Louise Huxtable, "The Landmark Hole in the Ground," *New York Times* (January 9, 1972), II: 25; Carleton Knight III, "A Disruption in Greenwich Village," *Historic Preservation* 24 (July–September 1972): 36–42; Smith, *Supermannerism*, 254–55; Paul Goldberger, "Taste in Replacing the House on 11th St.," *New York Times* (April 27, 1977), B: 2; Paul Goldberger, "Design Notebook: A Townhouse Saga Comes to a Close," *New York Times* (May 19, 1977), C: 11; Brolin, *Architecture in Context: Fitting New Buildings with Old*, 72–73; Sorkin, *Hardy Holzman Pfeiffer*, 117; "Modernism Exploding onto the Streets," *Building Design* 629 (February 25, 1983): 16–17; Miller, *Greenwich Village and How It Got That Way*, 137; *Hardy Holzman Pfeiffer Associates: Buildings and Projects 1967–1992*, 70–71, 249.

492. For an extensive discussion of the group, see Kirkpatrick Sale, *SDS* (New York: Random House, 1973).

493. Huxtable, "The Landmark Hole in the Ground": 25.

494. Hugh Hardy quoted in Knight, "A Disruption in Greenwich Village": 42.

495. Smith, *Supermannerism*, 254.

496. Hugh Hardy quoted in Knight, "A Disruption in Greenwich Village": 38.

497. Hugh Hardy quoted in Huxtable, "Compatibility Called Key to Building Plan": 45.

498. Hugh Hardy quoted in Knight, "A Disruption in Greenwich Village": 39.

499. Huxtable, "Compatibility Called Key to Building Plan": 45.

500. Hugh Hardy quoted in Knight, "A Disruption in Greenwich Village": 41.

501. Hugh Hardy quoted in Knight, "A Disruption in Greenwich Village": 41–42.

502. "State of the Union," *Architectural Forum* 137 (October 1972): 22–23; "The Foundation Building," *Architectural Record* 152 (November 1972): 41; "Yesterday's Grace, Today's Usable Space," *Progressive Architecture* 53 (November 1972): 93; "Cooper Union's 19th-Century Centerpiece to Be Renovated by John Hejduk," *Interiors* 132 (February 1973): 10; "Ready for Renovation," *Progressive Architecture* 54 (November 1973): 22; Joel G. Cahn, "Redesigning Cooper Union," *Print* 28 (September 1974): 86–89; "New York Landmark Opens after Major Renovation," *Architectural Record* 156 (October 1974): 34; Ada Louise Huxtable, "The New Cooper Union Still Evokes the Past," *New York Times* (December 8, 1974), II: 36; David Morton, "A Re-Presentation," *Progressive Architecture* 56 (July 1975): 50–57; David Hirsch, "Cooper Question," letter to the editor, *Progressive Architecture* 56 (September 1975): 12; Blake, "The Eighth Annual Cityscape Awards": 55; Beverly Russell, "Color: Architectural Search for Joy," *House and Garden* 148 (March 1976): 90–91; White and Willensky, *AIA Guide* (1978), 101; Goldberger, *The City Observed*, 69–70; Tauranac, *Essential New York*, 39–40; Barbaralee Diamonstein, *American Architecture Now II* (New York: Rizzoli International Publications, 1985), 131–32; Diamonstein, *The Landmarks of New York*, 114–15; Dolkart, *Guide to New York City Landmarks*, 43.

503. Goldberger, *The City Observed*, 69–70.

504. Morton, "A Re-Presentation": 50.

505. Huxtable, "The New Cooper Union Still Evokes the Past": 36.

506. Jackson, *A Guide to New York Architecture 1650–1952*, 15–16; "Grace Church," *Village Voice* 2 (March 6, 1957): 1; "Grace Church," *Village Voice* 4 (December 24, 1957): 1; Landmarks Preservation Commission of the City of New York, LP-0203, LP-0204 (March 15, 1966); White and Willensky, *AIA Guide* (1967), 76; Ada Louise Huxtable, "There but for the Grace . . . ," *New York Times* (February 17, 1974), II: 29; "Church Picketed over Demolition Plan," *New York Times* (March 4, 1974): 33; Paul Goldberger, "Meeting Planned on Grace Church," *New York Times* (March 23, 1974): 34; Ada Louise Huxtable, "A Few Signs of Spring and Other Good News," *New York Times* (May 12, 1974), II: 23; "Saving Grace," *Architecture Plus* 2 (July–August 1974): 106; Goldberger, *The City Observed*, 70–71; Tauranac, *Essential New York*, 30–31; Reynolds, *The Architecture of New York City*, 193, 293; Diamonstein, *The Landmarks of New York*, 88–89; Dolkart, *Guide to New York City Landmarks*, 45.

507. Huxtable, "There but for the Grace . . .": 29.

508. Landmarks Preservation Commission of the City of New York, LP-0852, LP-0853, LP-0854 (February 22, 1977).

509. Ada Louise Huxtable, "Landmark Plans Stir Wall St. Controversy: City Requested to Aid One of Projects," *New York Times* (December 17, 1966): 35, 66; "The Talk of the Town: Washington Market," *New Yorker* 44 (March 16, 1968): 37; Ada Louise Huxtable, "Where Ghosts Can Be at Home," *New York Times* (April 7, 1968), II: 25, reprinted in Huxtable, *Will They Ever Finish Bruckner Boulevard?*, 216–21; Charles G. Bennett, "City Spurs Fulton Restoration with Urban-Renewal Action," *New York Times* (May 6, 1968): 24; Ada Louise Huxtable, "Where Did We Go Wrong?" *New York Times* (July 14, 1968), II: 24; "Downtown Manhattan Is Experiencing Tremendous Construction Boom," *Real Estate Record and Guide* 202 (October 19, 1968): 2–3; H. M. Frankel, "Seaport Project Keys on Heritage," *New York Times* (January 23, 1969): 29, 32; "Markets: Fish Story," *Newsweek* 73 (May 5, 1969): 92; Robert S. Gallagher, "South Street Seaport," *American Heritage* 20 (October 1969): 36–42, 76–77; Jakob Isbrandtsen, "The South Street Seaport Museum," *Historic Preservation* 21 (October 1969): 7–8; Max H. Seigel, "Plan Unit Backs South St. Seaport," *New York Times* (June 1, 1972): 44; "Seaport Museum Plans Big Expansion," *New York Times* (October 20, 1973): 35; Ada Louise Huxtable, "Farewell, Old New York," *New York Times* (November 18, 1973), VI: 102–4, 106; Barnett, *Urban Design as Public Policy*, 74–78; "South St. Seaport Seeking $5-Million for a Tourist Area," *New York Times* (March 14, 1975): 41; William W. Warner, "At the Fulton Market," *Atlantic Monthly* 236 (November 1975): 56–64; Diamonstein, *The Landmarks of New York*, 396; Dolkart, *Guide to New York City Landmarks*, 21–22.

510. Bennett, "City Spurs Fulton Restoration with Urban-Renewal Action": 24.

511. Huxtable, "Where Did We Go Wrong?": 24.

512. For a colorful description of Washington Market in its final years of operation, see "The Talk of the Town: Hey Leach!" *New Yorker* 41 (June 19, 1965): 24–27. Also see "Art Center Planned for Washington Market," *Real Estate Record and Guide* 181 (May 10, 1958): 5–6; "Lower Manhattan Title I Project," *Architectural Forum* 113 (October 1960): 11.

513. Huxtable, "Where Ghosts Can Be at Home": 25; "Federal Houses Restored amidst High-Rise Housing," *Architectural Record* 48 (July 1970): 37; Rita Reif, "A New Incarnation for Old City Houses," *New York Times* (June 20, 1975), VIII: 1, 8; White and Willensky, *AIA Guide* (1978), 26–27; Goldberger, *The City Observed*, 41–42; Diamonstein, *The Landmarks of New York*, 54; Dolkart, *Guide to New York City Landmarks*, 29.

514. Goldberger, *The City Observed*, 42.

515. Jackson, *A Guide to the Architecture of New York 1650–1952*, 7; White and Willensky, *AIA Guide* (1967), 27; Ada Louise Huxtable, "The Case of the Stolen Landmarks," *New York Times* (July 11, 1974): 24; Peter Blake, "The Bogardus Heist," *New York* 7 (August 5, 1974): 58–59; White and Willensky, *AIA Guide* (1978), 563; White and Willensky, *AIA Guide* (1988), 31–32, 51.

516. Blake, "The Bogardus Heist": 58–59.

517. Huxtable, "The Case of the Stolen Landmarks": 24.

518. Landmarks Preservation Commission of the City of New York, LP-0030 (November 23, 1965); "Restoration: Fraunces Tavern, Manhattan's Oldest Landmark," *Interiors* 130 (May 1971): 34, 38; Ada Louise Huxtable, "The Bulldozer Approaches a Historic Block," *New York Times* (July 14, 1974), II: 21; Nory Miller, "Big Business Preservation," *Architectural Record* 171 (October 1983): 91–110; Stern, Gilmartin and Mellins, *New York 1930*, 132; Diamonstein, *The Landmarks of New York*, 34, 399; Dolkart, *Guide to New York City Landmarks*, 17–18.

519. Huxtable, "The Bulldozer Approaches a Historic Block": 21.

520. Laurie Beckelman quoted in Miller, "Big Business Preservation": 92.

521. Brendan Gill quoted in Miller, "Big Business Preservation": 92.

522. Landmarks Preservation Commission of the City of New York, LP-0994 (November 14, 1978).

523. See "Manhattan Now and Then," *Interiors* 133 (June 1974): 8; "New York Through the Lens," *Architecture Plus* 2 (July–August 1974): 35; Ellen Stern, "An Immovable Feast," *New York* 8 (June 23, 1975): 62; "Architectural Embellishments on View at N.Y. AIA Headquarters," *Interiors* 136 (December 1976): 10.

524. "Architectural Buildings Are Sold," *Real Estate Record and Guide* 190 (December 22, 1962): 2; Bernard Rothzeid, "A.I.A. Goes with a Bang," letter to the editor, *Architectural Forum* 132 (May 1970): 18; White and Willensky, *AIA Guide* (1978), 565; Stern, Gilmartin and Mellins, *New York 1930*, 190.

525. Stern, Gilmartin and Massengale, *New York 1900*, 58; White and Willensky, *AIA Guide* (1988), 870.

526. Alan S. Oser, "A Tower Is Born on Park Ave.," *New York Times* (September 17, 1980), D: 21; Christopher Gray, "Fabled Racers, a Brearley Purchase and a Church," *New York Times* (December 3, 1989), X: 9.

527. Ada Louise Huxtable, "Can a Symbol of Graft Be an Architectural Landmark?" *New York Times* (July 7, 1974), II: 19, reprinted as "Can Anyone Use a Nice Anglo-Italianate Symbol of Graft?" in Huxtable, *Kicked a Building Lately?*, 266–69. Also see Paul Goldberger, "Beame Group's Proposal to Raze Tweed Courthouse Expected to Evoke Objections," *New York Times* (June 14, 1974): 35; Maurice Carroll, "Demolition Urged of Tweed Courthouse," *New York Times* (August 11, 1974): 60; Diamonstein, *The Landmarks of New York*, 138–39; Dolkart, *Guide to New York City Landmarks*, 33.

528. Huxtable, "Can a Symbol of Graft Be an Architectural Landmark?": 19.

529. Landmarks Preservation Commission of the City of New York, LP-1122 (October 16, 1984).

530. Ada Louise Huxtable, "What's Best for Business Can Ravage Cities," *New York Times* (April 5, 1975), II: 29–30. Also see Paul Goldberger, "Franklin Savings Bank to Raze Building," *New York Times* (August 5, 1974): 25; "The Bank on 42nd Street," editorial, *New York Times* (August 14, 1974): 32; Alexis Greene, "Doomed Bank Building," letter to the editor, *New York Times* (August 15, 1974): 32; White and Willensky, *AIA Guide* (1978), 565; Stern, Gilmartin and Massengale, *New York 1900*, 178.

531. Edward Rollins quoted in Goldberger, "Franklin Savings Bank to Raze Building": 25.

532. Herbert J. Gans, "Preserving Everyone's Noo Yawk," *New York Times* (January 28, 1975): 33.

533. Ada Louise Huxtable, "Preserving Noo Yawk Landmarks," *New York Times* (February 4, 1975): 33.

534. Herbert J. Gans, "Of City Landmarks and Elitism," letter to the editor, *New York Times* (February 25, 1975): 34.

535. See Richard I. Ortega, "Unwanted: Historic District Designation," *Historic Preservation* 28 (January 1976): 41–43; Christopher Gray, "Landmarks Preservation Comes of Age," *New York Affairs* 6, no. 3 (1980): 46–54; Arthur Zabarkes, "Landmarks: What Price Designation?" *New York Affairs* 6, no. 3 (1980): 56–58; "New York: Wheeling and Dealing," *Architectural Record* 171 (October 1983): 92.

536. Hamlin, "Historical Heritage vs. the March of 'Progress'": 286–87.

537. "The Talk of the Town: Lovers": 34.

538. Alexander Garvin, "New York's J-51: The Program that Restored 700,000 Apartments," in *Tax Incentives for Historic Preservation* (Washington, D.C.: Preservation Press, 1980), 137–43.

539. Ada Louise Huxtable, "From Sentiment to Social Force," *New York Times* (February 3, 1974), II: 26.

Chapter 17
New York and the Arts

1. Andy Warhol and Pat Hackett, *POPism: The Warhol Sixties* (New York: Harcourt Brace Jovanovich, 1980), 3.

NEW YORK IN PAINTING AND SCULPTURE

1. Janet Flint, *The Prints of Louis Lozowick* (New York: Hudson Hills Press, 1982). For Lozowick's interwar work, also see Stern, Gilmartin and Mellins, *New York 1930*, 60.

2. For the Sherry-Netherland Hotel, see Stern, Gilmartin and Mellins, *New York 1930*, 217–21. For the Plaza Hotel, see Stern, Gilmartin and Massengale, *New York 1900*, 256, 258–59, 261–62. For the RCA Building, see Stern, Gilmartin and Mellins, *New York 1930*, 616, 650–53.

3. Grace Glueck, *New York: The Painted City* (Salt Lake City, Utah: Peregrine Smith, 1992), 8–9.

4. Martin Friedman, Bartlett Hayes and Charles Millard, *Charles Sheeler* (Washington, D.C.: Smithsonian Institution Press, 1968); Martin Friedman, *Charles Sheeler* (New York: Watson-Guptill, 1975); William Sharpe, "Living on the Edge: New York in Literature," in Leonard Wallock, ed., *New York: Culture Capital of the World, 1940–1965* (New York: Rizzoli International Publications, 1988), 76–77. For Sheeler's interwar work, see Stern, Gilmartin and Mellins, *New York 1930*, 51, 60.

5. Douglas Dreishpoon and James L. Reinish, *New York Cubists: Works by A. E. Gallatin, George L. K. Morris, and Charles G. Shaw from the Thirties and Forties*, exhibition catalogue (New York: Hirschl & Adler Galleries, 1988).

6. Gail Levin, *Edward Hopper: The Art and the Artist* (New York: W. W. Norton, 1980), 44–46; Seymour Chwast and Steven Heller, *The Art of New York* (New York: Harry N. Abrams, 1983), 110–11; Robert Hobbs, *Edward Hopper* (New York: Harry N. Abrams, 1987). For Hopper's interwar work, also see Stern, Gilmartin and Mellins, *New York 1930*, 55, 62.

7. Abram Lerner, ed., *The Hirshhorn Museum and Sculpture Garden* (New York: Harry N. Abrams, 1974), 368. Also see Katherine S. Drier, *Burliuk* (New York: Société Anonyme and Color and Rhyme, 1944).
8. For the Consolidated Gas Company Building, see Stern, Gilmartin and Mellins, *New York 1930*, 587, 590–92. For the Metropolitan Life Tower, see Stern, Gilmartin and Massengale, *New York 1900*, 171–73. For the Empire State Building, see Stern, Gilmartin and Mellins, *New York 1930*, 610–15.
9. Henry McBride, *Florine Stettheimer*, exhibition catalogue (New York: Museum of Modern Art, 1946); Parker Tyler, *Florine Stettheimer: A Life in Art* (New York: Farrar, Straus, 1963); *Florine Stettheimer*, exhibition catalogue (New York: Columbia University, 1973); *Florine Stettheimer: Still Lifes, Portraits and Pageants, 1910 to 1942*, exhibition catalogue (Boston: Institute of Contemporary Art, 1980).
10. William Seitz quoted in "Vanity Fair: The New York Art Scene," *Newsweek* 65 (January 4, 1965): 54–59.
11. O. Louis Guglielmi, "I Hope to Sing Again," *Magazine of Art* 37 (May 1944): 173–77. Also see "Guglielmi's 'First,'" *Art Digest* 13 (November 15, 1938): 20; Lewis Kachur, "The Bridge as Icon," in *The Great East River Bridge 1883–1983*, exhibition catalogue (New York: Brooklyn Museum, 1983), 166–67; Glueck, *New York: The Painted City*, 32–33.
12. Guglielmi, "I Hope to Sing Again": 175.
13. Irving Hershel Sandler, "New York Letter," *Quadrum* 14 (1962–63): 115–24; Morton Feldman, "Give My Regards to Eighth Street," *Art in America* 59 (March 1971): 96–99; Serge Guilbaut, *How New York Stole the Idea of Modern Art*, trans. Arthur Goldhammer (Chicago: University of Chicago Press, 1983); John Bernard Myers, *Tracking the Marvelous: A Life in the New York Art World* (New York: Random House, 1983); Peter Conrad, *The Art of the City: Views and Versions of New York* (New York: Oxford University Press, 1984); Diana Crane, *The Transformation of the Avant-Garde: The New York Art World, 1940–1985* (Chicago: University of Chicago Press, 1987).
14. For Bonwit Teller, see Stern, Gilmartin and Mellins, *New York 1930*, 64, 318. For the Dream of Venus pavilion, see Stern, Gilmartin and Mellins, *New York 1930*, 753–55.
15. Hans Hess, *Lyonel Feininger* (New York: Harry N. Abrams, 1961); John Gordon and L. Rust Hills, eds., *New York, New York* (New York: Shorecrest, 1965), 362; *Lyonel Feininger*, exhibition catalogue (New York: Marlborough-Gerson Gallery, 1969); Chwast and Heller, eds., *The Art of New York*, 36–37; Ulrich Luckhardt, *Lyonel Feininger* (Munich: Prestel Verlag, 1989).
16. Lyonel Feininger, letter to Alois Schardt, February 3, 1942, quoted in Luckhardt, *Lyonel Feininger*, 156. Also see Hess, *Lyonel Feininger*, 148.
17. Harry Holtzman, "Piet Mondrian's Last Work: Rare Photographs of the Painter's New York Studio," *Interior Design* 55 (May 1984): 320–25.
18. Piet Mondrian quoted in Sharpe, "Living on the Edge: New York in Literature," in Wallock, ed., *New York: Culture Capital of the World, 1940–1965*, 82. Also see Stern, Gilmartin and Mellins, *New York 1930*, 58, 64; Glueck, *New York: The Painted City*, 60–61.
19. Robert Motherwell quoted in Dore Ashton, "The City and the Visual Arts," in Wallock, ed., *New York: Culture Capital of the World, 1940–1965*, 127.
20. Holtzman, "Piet Mondrian's Last Work": 323.
21. Thomas Bender, *New York Intellect* (New York: Alfred A. Knopf, 1987), 334.
22. Clement Greenberg, "The Decline of Cubism," *Partisan Review* 3 (1948): 369, quoted in Guilbaut, *How New York Stole the Idea of Modern Art*, 172.
23. Thomas B. Hess, *Abstract Painting* (New York: Viking, 1951), 97–98, quoted in Bender, *New York Intellect*, 334.
24. Thomas Hess quoted in "Vanity Fair: The New York Art Scene": 56.
25. For discussion of the WPA, see Jo Ann Wahl, "Art under the New Deal" (Master's thesis, Columbia University, 1966); John Franklin White, ed., *American Art Centers and the New Deal* (Metuchen, N.J.: Scarecrow Press, 1987).
26. "Manhattan: Art's Avid New Capital," *Time* 64 (November 29, 1954): 48–49.
27. Arnold Glimcher, *Louise Nevelson* (New York: Praeger, 1972); Jean Lipman, *Nevelson's World* (New York: Hudson Hills Press, in association with the Whitney Museum of American Art, 1983); Laurie Lisle, *Louise Nevelson: A Passionate Life* (New York: Summit, 1990).
28. Louise Nevelson quoted in Lipman, *Nevelson's World*, 213.
29. Louise Nevelson quoted in Glimcher, *Louise Nevelson*, 21.
30. Fielding Dawson, *An Emotional Memoir of Franz Kline* (New York: Pantheon, 1967); John Gordon, *Franz Kline 1910–1962*, exhibition catalogue (New York: Whitney Museum of American Art, 1968); Harry F. Gaugh, *The Vital Gesture: Franz Kline* (New York: Abbeville Press, 1985), 34–53; Sharpe, "Living on the Edge: New York in Literature," in Wallock, ed., *New York: Culture Capital of the World, 1940–1965*, 84.
31. Franz Kline quoted in Gerald Nordland, *Earl Kerkam, Memorial Exhibition*, exhibition catalogue (Washington, D.C.: Washington Gallery of Modern Art, 1966), 9, also quoted in Gaugh, *The Vital Gesture: Franz Kline*, 48.
32. Edward Bryant, *Jack Tworkov* (New York: Whitney Museum of American Art, 1964); Richard Armstrong and Kenneth Baker, *Jack Tworkov: Paintings, 1928–1982* (Philadelphia: Pennsylvania Academy of the Fine Arts; Seattle, Wash.: University of Washington Press, 1987).
33. William C. Seitz, *Mark Tobey* (Garden City, N.Y.: Doubleday, 1962); Joshua C. Taylor, *Tribute to Mark Tobey* (Washington, D.C.: Smithsonian Institution Press, 1974).
34. Annalee Newman quoted in John P. O'Neill, ed., *Barnett Newman: Selected Writings and Interviews* (New York: Alfred A. Knopf, 1990), 30. Also see Thomas B. Hess, "Not There—Here," in *Barnett Newman* (New York: Museum of Modern Art, 1971), 19–31.
35. Barnett Newman quoted in O'Neill, ed., *Barnett Newman: Selected Writings and Interviews*, 30.
36. Thomas B. Hess quoted in "Vanity Fair: The New York Art Scene": 54, 56.
37. Alexander Watt, "Paris Commentary," *The Studio* 157 (May 1959): 153. Also see "P/A News Report: Bulletins," *Progressive Architecture* 40 (July 1959): 81; Yann le Pichon, *Bernard Buffet: 1943–1961* (Paris: Maurice Garnier, 1986), 425–35.
38. Calvin Tomkins, "Profiles: Not Seen and/or Less Seen," *New Yorker* 41 (February 6, 1965): 37–40, 42, 44, 47–48, 50, 55–56, 58, 62, 65–66, 68, 70, 72, 75–76, 78, 80–82, 87–90, 93, reprinted in Calvin Tomkins, *The Bride and the Bachelors: Five Masters of the Avant-Garde*, rev. ed. (New York: Viking, 1968), 9–68.
39. Alan R. Solomon, *Robert Rauschenberg* (New York: Jewish Museum, 1963); Calvin Tomkins, "Profiles: Moving Out," *New Yorker* 40 (February 29, 1964): 39–40, 42, 45, 48, 51–52, 54, 59–60, 62, 64, 66, 71–72, 74, 76, 78, 83–84, 86, 89–90, 92, 95–96, 98, 100, 102, 104–5, reprinted in Tomkins, *The Bride and the Bachelors: Five Masters of the Avant-Garde*, 189–237; Elizabeth Novick, "Happenings in New York," *The Studio* 172 (September 1966): 154–55; Feldman, "Give My Regards to Eighth Street": 96–99; Andrew Forge, *Rauschenberg* (New York: Harry N. Abrams, 1972); Lawrence Alloway, *Robert Rauschenberg* (Washington, D.C.: National Collection of Fine Arts, Smithsonian Institution, 1976); Ashton, "The City and the Visual Arts," in Wallock, ed., *New York: Culture Capital of the World, 1940–1965*, 147–49; Lynn Garafola, "Toward an American Dance: Dance in the City," in Wallock, ed., *New York: Culture Capital of the World, 1940–1965*, 157, 178–80, 182, 185; Mary Lynn Kotz, *Rauschenberg, Art and Life* (New York: Harry N. Abrams, 1990); Walter Hopps, *Robert Rauschenberg: The Early 1950s* (Houston: Menil Collection and Houston Fine Art Press, 1991).
40. Conrad, *The Art of the City*, 301.
41. Robert Rauschenberg quoted in Conrad, *The Art of the City*, 301.
42. Calvin Tomkins, "Profiles: An Appetite for Motion," *New Yorker* 44 (May 4, 1968): 52–56, 58, 60, 63, 66, 69, 70, 72, 75–76, 78, 83, 86, 89–90, 92, 97–98, 100, 103–4, 106, 111–12, 114, 117–20, 123–26, reprinted in Tomkins, *The Bride and the Bachelors: Five Masters of the Avant-Garde*, 239–96.
43. Allan Kaprow quoted in Roselee Goldberg, *Performance: Live Art 1909 to the Present* (New York: Harry N. Abrams, 1979), 83.
44. Allan Kaprow, "The Legacy of Jackson Pollock," *Art News* 57 (October 1958): 24–26, 54–57.
45. Quoted in Al Hansen, *A Primer of Happenings and Time/Space Art* (New York: Something Else, 1965), 61. Also see Barbara Haskell, *Blam! The Explosion of Pop, Minimalism and Performance, 1958–1964* (New York: Whitney Museum of American Art, in association with W. W. Norton, 1984), 32.
46. Goldberg, *Performance: Live Art 1909 to the Present*, 84–85; Haskell, *Blam! The Explosion of Pop, Minimalism and Performance, 1958–1964*, 33–34. For the Mills Hotel, see Mardges Bacon, *Ernest Flagg: Beaux-Arts Architect and Urban Reformer* (New York: Architectural History Foundation; Cambridge, Mass.: MIT Press, 1986), 258–61.
47. Theo Kneubühler, "The Happening: History, Theory and Practice," *Werk* 58 (February 1971): 116–24, 141–43; Grace Glueck, "Red Grooms, the Ruckus Kid," *Art News* (December 1973): 23–27; Douglas Davis, "What's in the Galleries," *Newsweek* 86 (December 8, 1975): 106; Ada Louise Huxtable, "Grooms's Zany 'Manhattan' Puts the City in Focus," *New York Times* (December 21, 1975), II: 1, 41, reprinted as "The Near Past: Through the Artist's Eye," in Ada Louise Huxtable, *Kicked a Building Lately?* (New York: Quadrangle/New York Times Book Co., 1976), 285–87; Robert Hughes, "Gorgeous Parody," *Time* (January 19, 1976): 72–73; Michael Andre, "New York Reviews: Ruckus Manhattan," *Art News* 75 (April 1976): 118–19; Thomas B. Hess, "Grooms, Goya, and the Grotesque," *New York* 9 (June 28, 1976): 76–78; Barbara Rose, "Raucous, Ruckus World of Red Grooms," *Vogue* 166 (July 1976): 54; Richard Lorber, "Arts Reviews," *Arts* 51 (September 1976): 30; Judd Tully, *Red Grooms and Ruckus Manhattan* (New York: George Braziller, 1977); Chwast and Heller, eds., *The Art of New York*, 180; Kachur, "The Bridge as Icon" in *The Great East River Bridge 1883–1983*, 170–71; Conrad, *The Art of the City*, 321–22; Haskell, *Blam! The Explosion of Pop, Minimalism, and Performance, 1958–1964*, 20, 35–36; Carter Ratcliff, *Red Grooms* (New York: Abbeville Press, 1984); Judith E. Stein, John Ashbery and Janet K. Cutler, *Red Grooms: A Retrospective 1956–1984* (Philadelphia: Pennsylvania Academy of the Fine Arts, 1985); Leonard Wallock, "New York City: Capital of the Twentieth Century," in Wallock, ed., *New York: Culture Capital of the World, 1940–1965*, 42.
48. Hess, "Grooms, Goya, and the Grotesque": 76.
49. *Immovable Objects Exhibition*, exhibition catalogue (New York: Cooper-Hewitt Museum, 1975); "A Fashion Show of Manhattan Buildings," *Progressive Architecture* 56 (August 1975): 19; "Collage," *Art News* 74 (September 1975): 118; "Immovable Objects," *Domus* 558 (May 1976): 31–34.
50. Rem Koolhaas later documented the 1931 Beaux-Arts Ball in his *Delirious New York: A Retroactive Manifesto for Manhattan* (New York: Oxford University Press, 1978), 106–8.
51. Quoted in "Collage": 118.
52. Huxtable, "Grooms's Zany 'Manhattan' Puts the City in Focus": 41.
53. Lorber, "Arts Reviews": 30.
54. Hess, "Grooms, Goya and the Grotesque": 76–77.
55. Claes Oldenburg quoted in Ashton, "The City and the Visual Arts," in Wallock, ed., *New York: Culture Capital of the World, 1940–1965*, 149.
56. Claes Oldenburg quoted in Conrad, *The Art of the City*, 314.
57. Quoted in Haskell, *Blam! The Explosion of Pop, Minimalism and Performance, 1958–1964*, 37, 40. Also see Hansen, *A Primer of Happenings and Time/Space Art*, 62–67; Goldberg, *Performance: Live Art 1909 to the Present*, 84.
58. Hansen, *A Primer of Happenings and Time/Space Art*, 64.
59. For the Ansonia Hotel, see Stern, Gilmartin and Massengale, *New York 1900*, 384–86.
60. Claes Oldenburg quoted in Marshall Berman, *All That Is Solid Melts into Air* (New York: Simon & Schuster, 1982), 318, 320.
61. "New York Exhibitions: Month in Review," *Arts* 36 (February 1962): 35–37; Claes Oldenburg and Emmett Williams, *Store Days* (New York: Something Else, 1967); Wallock, "New York: Capital of the Twentieth Century," in Wallock, ed., *New York: Culture Capital of the World, 1940–1965*, 41.
62. Stern, Gilmartin and Mellins, *New York 1930*, 49, 51–52, 59–60.
63. Claes Oldenburg, *Proposals for Monuments and Buildings 1965–69* (Chicago: Big Table, 1969). Also see Jasia Reichardt, "Bridges and Oldenburgs," *Studio International* 173 (January 1967): 2–3; Claes Oldenburg, "Take a Cigarette Butt and Make It Heroic," *Art News* 66 (May 1967): 30–31, 77; Herbert Marcuse, comment on Oldenburg's *Proposed Monuments of New York City*, excerpted from informal discussions with Stuart Wrede, June 1968, printed with photographic montage by Joel Katz, in *Perspecta* 12 (1969): 75–76; Jeanne Siegel, "Oldenburg's Places and Borrowings," *Arts* 44 (November 1969): 48–49.
64. Conrad, *The Art of the City*, 316.
65. Claes Oldenburg, interview with Paul Carroll, in *Proposals for Monuments and Buildings*, 16.
66. Claes Oldenburg, interview with Paul Carroll, in *Proposals for Monuments and Buildings*, 25.
67. Herbert Marcuse, in conversation with Stuart Wrede in June 1968, published in *Perspecta* 12 (1969): 75.

68. Walter Thabit, "The Tinguely Machine," *Village Voice* 4 (March 30, 1960): 4, 12. Also see Calvin Tomkins, "Profiles: Beyond the Machine," *New Yorker* 38 (February 10, 1962): 44–46, 48, 51, 54, 56–58, 61, 63, 66–68, 73–74, 76, 78–80, 83, 85–86, 88–90, 93, reprinted in Tomkins, *The Bride and the Bachelors: Five Masters of the Avant-Garde,* 145–87; *Jean Tinguely: Catalogue Raisonné, Sculptures and Reliefs 1954–1968* (Zurich: Galerie Bruno Bischofberger, 1982); Conrad, *The Art of the City,* 309–10, 312, 322; Pontus Hulten, *Tinguely* (Paris: Centre Georges Pompidou, 1989).

69. Conrad, *The Art of the City,* 309.

70. Sam Hunter, *Chryssa* (New York: Harry N. Abrams, 1974); Douglas G. Schultz, *Chryssa: Urban Icons,* exhibition catalogue (Buffalo, N.Y.: Albright-Knox Gallery, 1983); Chryssa, *Chryssa Citiscapes* (New York: Thames and Hudson, 1990).

71. Chryssa quoted in Schultz, *Chryssa: Urban Icons,* 4.

72. Chryssa quoted in Hunter, *Chryssa,* 10.

73. Richard Armstrong, *Artschwager, Richard,* exhibition catalogue (New York: Whitney Museum of American Art in association with W. W. Norton, 1988); *Artschwager, Richard,* exhibition catalogue (Paris: Centre Georges Pompidou, 1989).

74. "Vanity Fair: The New York Art Scene": 54–59.

75. Irving Sandler, *Alex Katz* (New York: Harry N. Abrams, 1979), 48, fig. 93.

76. David Bourdon, *Christo* (New York: Harry N. Abrams, 1970); Pamela Allara and Stephen Prokopoff, *Christo Urban Projects: A Survey,* exhibition catalogue (Boston: Institute of Contemporary Art, 1979); Per Hovdenakt, *Christo Complete Editions 1964–1982* (New York: New York University Press, 1982); Chwast and Heller, eds., *The Art of New York,* 130–31.

77. For the City Bank Farmers Trust Company Building, see Stern, Gilmartin and Mellins, *New York 1930,* 599–602.

78. For the Times Tower, see Stern, Gilmartin and Massengale, *New York 1900,* 167.

79. Goldberg, *Performance: Live Art 1909 to the Present,* 100; Vito Acconci, *Vito Acconci: A Retrospective, 1969 to 1980* (Chicago: Museum of Contemporary Art, 1980); Vito Acconci, *Vito Acconci* (Prato, Italy: Museo d'arte contemporanea, 1991).

80. Vito Acconci quoted in Goldberg, *Performance: Live Art 1909 to the Present,* 100.

81. Nicholas Pileggi, "Portrait of the Artist as a Garage Attendant in the Bronx," *New York* 5 (October 30, 1972): 37–45. Also see Patrick Watson, *Fasanella's City: The Painting of Ralph Fasanella with the Story of His Life and Art* (New York: Alfred A. Knopf, 1973).

82. Gordon and Hills, eds., *New York, New York,* 396; Lincoln Kirstein, *Paul Cadmus* (New York: Imago Imprint, 1984), 72–74.

83. Kirstein, *Paul Cadmus,* 74.

84. Paul Cadmus quoted in Kirstein, *Paul Cadmus,* 102.

85. Thomas H. Garver, *George Tooker* (New York: C. H. Potter, 1985); Sharpe, "Living on the Edge: New York in Literature," in Wallock, ed., *New York: Culture Capital of the World, 1940–1965,* 76; John L. Ward, *American Realist Painting, 1945–1980* (Ann Arbor, Mich.: UMI Research Press, 1989), 44–48.

86. George Tooker quoted in Garver, *George Tooker,* 30.

87. Karl Lunde, *Isabel Bishop* (New York: Harry N. Abrams, 1973); Gordon and Hills, eds., *New York, New York,* 401.

88. Thomas Hess, *Herman Rose,* exhibition catalogue (New York: ACA Gallery, 1956), quoted in Laurence Campbell, "The City Rises," *Art News* 68 (November 1969): 42–44, 68. Also see "Herman Rose's Skyscraper and Chimney," *Art News* 47 (December 1948): 53; "Herman Rose," *Magazine of Art* 42 (February 1949): 63; Lerner, ed., *The Hirshhorn Museum and Sculpture Garden,* 429, 741.

89. Campbell, "The City Rises": 43.

90. Herman Rose quoted in Lerner, ed., *The Hirshhorn Museum and Sculpture Garden,* 721.

91. Glueck, *New York: The Painted City,* 52–53.

92. Patricia Hills, *Alice Neel* (New York: Harry N. Abrams, 1983).

93. Gordon and Hills, eds., *New York, New York,* 397; John I. H. Bauer, *Philip Evergood* (New York: Harry N. Abrams, 1975); Chwast and Heller, eds., *The Art of New York,* 147; Kendall Taylor, *Philip Evergood: Never Separate from the Heart* (Lewisburg, Pa.: Bucknell University Press; London: Associated University Presses, 1987).

94. "Sunny Side of the Street," words by Dorothy Fields and music by Jimmy McHugh (New York: Shapiro, Bernstein, 1930).

95. Stern, Gilmartin and Massengale, *New York 1900,* 51–53.

96. Philip Evergood, letter to Henry B. Caldwell, undated, Evergood File, Corcoran Gallery of Art, Washington, D.C., quoted in Taylor, *Philip Evergood: Never Separate from the Heart,* 160–61.

97. Wallock, "New York City: Capital of the Twentieth Century," in Wallock, ed., *New York: Culture Capital of the World, 1940–1965,* 44–45; Sharpe, "Living on the Edge: New York in Literature," in Wallock, ed., *New York: Culture Capital of the World, 1940–1965,* 57; Myron Schwartzman, *Romare Bearden: The Life and Art* (New York: Harry N. Abrams, 1990); Glueck, *New York: The Painted City,* 10–11.

98. Milton W. Brown, *Jacob Lawrence* (New York: Whitney Museum of American Art, 1974); Ellen Harkins Wheat, *Jacob Lawrence: American Painter* (Seattle, Wash.: University of Washington Press, 1986); Glueck, *New York: The Painted City,* 54–55.

99. Roberta Smith, "Beauford Delaney," *New York Times* (May 20, 1994), C: 16.

100. Lawrence Campbell, "Jane Wilson," *Art News* 62 (summer 1963): 13; "Sold Out Art," *Life* 55 (September 20, 1963): 126; Lerner, ed., *The Hirshhorn Museum and Sculpture Garden,* 579, 758–59.

101. Fairfield Porter quoted in Glueck, *New York: The Painted City,* 66–67.

102. James Schuyler, "The View from 210 Riverside Drive," *Art News* 67 (May 1968): 36–37, 73–74.

103. Peter Schjeldahl, "Urban Pastorals," *Art News* 69 (February 1971): 32–33, 60; Mark Strand, ed., *The Art of the Real* (New York: Clarkson N. Potter, 1983), 60–87.

104. Schjeldahl, "Urban Pastorals": 62.

105. Mario Amaya, *John Koch,* exhibition catalogue (New York: New York Cultural Center, 1973).

106. Linda Chase et al., "The Photo–Realists: Twelve Interviews," *Art in America* 60 (November–December 1972): 73–89; Barbara Rose, "Treacle and Trash," *New York* 7 (May 27, 1974): 80; John Arthur, *Richard Estes: The Urban Landscape,* rev. ed., with an intro. by John Canaday (Boston: Museum of Fine Arts; New York: New York Graphic Society, 1978); Louis K. Meisel, *Richard Estes: The Complete Paintings 1966–1985,* with an essay by John Perrault (New York: Harry N. Abrams, 1986); Ward, *American Realist Painting, 1945–1980,* 298, 309.

107. Conrad, *The Art of the City,* 313.

108. Richard Estes quoted in John Perrault, "Richard Estes," in Meisel, *Richard Estes: The Complete Paintings 1966–1985,* 11.

109. Stern, Gilmartin and Massengale, *New York 1900,* 384–85.

110. Canaday, "Introduction," in Arthur, *Richard Estes: The Urban Landscape,* 18.

111. Rose, "Treacle and Trash": 80.

112. Lowell Nesbitt, *An Autobiography,* exhibition catalogue, with an intro. by Andrew Crispo (New York: Andrew Crispo Gallery, 1976), unpaginated; "Impressions of New York City," *Arts* 51 (September 1976): 31.

113. Nesbitt, *An Autobiography,* unpaginated.

114. "Impressions of New York City": 31.

115. Jesse Reichek, ed., "Steinberg on the City," *Journal of the American Institute of Planners* 27 (August 1961): 245–93; Harold Rosenberg, *Saul Steinberg* (New York: Alfred A. Knopf, 1978); Sharpe, "Living on the Edge: New York in Literature," in Wallock, ed., *New York: Culture Capital of the World, 1940–1965,* 85–86; Saul Steinberg, *The Discovery of America* (New York: Alfred A. Knopf, 1992).

116. Melvin M. Webber, "Preface," in Reichek, ed., "Steinberg on the City": 246.

117. Grace Glueck, "Art Notes: Tomorrow, the World," *New York Times* (May 11, 1969), II: 23–24. Also see "Footnote," *Architectural Forum* 127 (September 1967): 88–89; *Allan D'Arcangelo,* exhibition catalogue (New York: Marlborough Gallery, 1971).

118. Harold C. Schonberg, "Someone There Is Who Loves a Wall," *New York Times* (May 31, 1970), VIII: 1–2.

119. "New York Artists Paint the City's Walls," *Architectural Record* 148 (July 1970): 36; "Spotlighting the Wall," *Architectural Forum* 133 (July–August 1970): 84; "Painting the Town," *Life* 69 (July 17, 1970): 60–63; Lawrence Alloway, "Art," *Nation* 211 (September 21, 1970): 253–54; "Urban Renewal with Paint," *Progressive Architecture* 51 (November 1970): 98–107; C. Ray Smith, "Outside In," *New York* 4 (November 29, 1971): 61; Lawrence Alloway, "Art," *Nation* 215 (September 25, 1972): 252–53; Ingrid Wiegand, "Painted Walls," *Graphics* 28 (1972/1973): 388–97; Andrea O. Dean, "Graphics in the Environment," *Journal of the American Institute of Architects* 64 (October 1975): 30–32; C. Ray Smith, *Supermannerism: New Attitudes in Post-Modern Architecture* (New York: E. P. Dutton, 1977), 200; Louis G. Redstone with Ruth R. Redstone, *Public Art: New Directions* (New York: McGraw-Hill, 1981), plates 31–33; Alan W. Barnett, *Community Murals: The People's Art* (Philadelphia: Art Alliance Press; New York: Cornwall, 1984), 35–38.

120. Annie Damaz quoted in "New York Artists Paint the City's Walls": 36.

121. Doris Freedman quoted in Redstone with Redstone, *Public Art: New Directions,* text accompanying plates 31–33.

122. Doris Freedman quoted in "New York Artists Paint the City's Walls": 36.

123. Alloway, "Art" (September 21, 1970): 254. Also see "New York Artists Paint the City's Walls": 36; Grace Glueck, "Park Ave. Area Gets Outdoor Mural," *New York Times* (October 20, 1970): 47; Wiegand, "Painted Walls": 394.

124. Suzanne Slesin, "Urban Kaleidoscope," *Industrial Design* 16 (May 1969): 36–41; Harriet Morrison, "Mural for a Parking Lot," *House Beautiful* 111 (October 1969): 142.

125. Slesin, "Urban Kaleidoscope": 37; Glueck, "Art News: Tomorrow, the World": 24.

126. Alloway, "Art" (September 21, 1970): 254. Also see Glueck, "Park Ave. Area Gets Outdoor Mural": 47; Wiegand, "Painted Walls": 390.

127. Alloway, "Art" (September 21, 1970): 254. Also see Glueck, "Park Ave. Area Gets Outdoor Mural": 47; Wiegand, "Painted Walls": 392; Dean, "Graphics in the Environment": 31.

128. Alloway, "Art" (September 21, 1970): 254; Wiegand, "Painted Walls": 390; Redstone with Redstone, *Public Art: New Directions,* plate 32.

129. Dean, "Graphics in the Environment": 32, 31.

130. Tania quoted in "Painting the Town": 62. Also see "Spotlighting the Wall": 84; Smith, *Supermannerism,* 200–201, plate 5.

131. Alloway, "Art" (September 21, 1970): 254.

132. Jason Crum quoted in Barnett, *Community Murals: The People's Art,* 37.

133. John Canaday, "A Mighty Big Hair of the Dog," *New York Times* (September 12, 1971), II: 33.

134. Doris C. Freedman, letter to the editor, *New York Times* (November 14, 1971): 40.

135. Lawrence Alloway, "Art" (September 25, 1972): 252–53. Also see Wiegand, "Painted Walls": 390; Karl Lunde, *Richard Anuszkiewicz* (New York: Harry N. Abrams, 1977); Redstone with Redstone, *Public Art: New Directions,* plate 31.

136. Alloway, "Art" (September 25, 1972): 252.

137. Smith, *Supermannerism,* 200–202; Barnett, *Community Murals: The People's Art,* 98–101.

138. Susan Shapiro-Kiok quoted in Barnett, *Community Murals: The People's Art,* 98.

139. Smith, *Supermannerism,* 200–201.

140. Alloway, "Art" (September 25, 1972): 253. Also see Barnett, *Community Murals: The People's Art,* 98.

141. Alloway, "Art" (September 25, 1972): 253. Also see Barnett, *Community Murals: The People's Art,* 98–99.

142. Barnett, *Community Murals: The People's Art,* 99–100.

143. Barnett, *Community Murals: The People's Art,* 215, 217–18; Volker Barthelmeh, *Street Murals* (New York: Alfred A. Knopf, 1982), 14–15.

144. Alloway, "Art" (September 25, 1972): 252–53. Also see Barnett, *Community Murals: The People's Art,* 100–101.

145. Alloway, "Art" (September 25, 1972): 253.

146. Barnett, *Community Murals: The People's Art,* 214–15.

147. "Trompe l'Oeil Painting Spruces up Soho Wall," *Interiors* 134 (June 1975): 8; "Fake Facade Turns Heads in Soho," *Progressive Architecture* 56 (July 1975): 20; Peter Blake, "The Eighth Annual Cityscape Awards," *New York* 9 (January 12, 1976): 57; C. Ray Smith, "Muralist Richard Haas Paints the Town," *Village Voice* 22 (May 24, 1976): 83–84; Richard Haas, *An Architecture of Illusion,* with an intro. by Paul Goldberger (New York: Rizzoli International Publications, 1981), 18, 66–71.

148. Blake, "The Eighth Annual Cityscape Awards": 57.

149. Goldberger, "Introduction," in Haas, *An Architecture of Illusion,* 18.

150. Richard Haas quoted in Smith, "Muralist Richard Haas Paints the Town": 83.

151. Hilton Kramer, "The Studio vs. the Street," *New York Times* (October 15, 1967), II: 23. Also see Grace Glueck, "Art Notes: Sculptfest," *New York Times* (June 25, 1967), II: 23–24; Sanka Knox, "Two Stabiles May Stay Put After Move to Harlem," *New York Times* (September 3, 1967): 22; "Sites Are Chosen for 19 Sculptures in Parks' Display," *New York Times* (September 14, 1967): 55; Edwin Bolwell, "Sculpture on the City's Sidewalks Sparks Interest and Irreverence," *New York Times* (September 26, 1967): 1, 94; "Sculpture Invasion," editorial, *New York Times* (October 7, 1967): 28; "New Man in Town," *Art News* 66 (November 1967): 27; "Astor Place Cube Will Stay in Place," *New York Times* (November 23, 1967): 33; "Observing the Arts: Manhattan, '67," *Progressive Architecture* 49 (January 1968): 34, 36.

152. Kramer, "The Studio vs. the Street": 23.

153. "Outdoor Sculptures for New York City," *Architectural Record* 150 (November 1971): 37.

154. Robert Moses quoted in Murray Schumach, "Moses Warns Against 'Hideous' Sculpture," *New York Times* (April 12, 1972): 36.

155. Doris C. Freedman, "Moses and the Arts," letter to the editor, *New York Times* (April 27, 1972): 42.

156. James K. Monte, *Mark diSuvero* (New York: Whitney Museum of American Art, 1975); "The Talk of the Town: It Must Be Something," *New Yorker* 51 (November 3, 1975): 34–37; John Russell, "Gallery View: All of New York Is diSuvero's Gallery," *New York Times* (November 11, 1975), II: 1, 25.

157. "The Talk of the Town: It Must Be Something": 37.

158. Russell, "Gallery View: All of New York Is diSuvero's Gallery": 25.

NEW YORK IN PHOTOGRAPHY

1. The Gottscho-Schleisner architectural photographs are located primarily at the Library of Congress, the Museum of the City of New York and the Avery Library, Columbia University.

2. Ezra Stoller, "Photography and the Language of Architecture," *Perspecta* 8 (1963): 43; Ezra Stoller, *Ezra Stoller: Photographs of Architecture, 1939–1980*, with an intro. by Arthur Drexler, exhibition catalogue (New York: Max Protetch Gallery, 1980), intro. reprinted in *Architectural Design* 51 (January–February 1981): 2–3; "Photographer Ezra Stoller Is the Subject of an Exhibition at New York's Max Protetch Gallery," *Architectural Record* 168 (December 1980): 35; Andy Grundberg, "Lies for the Eyes," *Soho Weekly News* (December 17, 1980): 28; Michael Sorkin, "Pretty as a Building," *Village Voice* 25 (December 17, 1980): 112; Paul Goldberger, "Architecture: Portraits by Ezra Stoller," *New York Times* (December 26, 1980), C: 20; Ezra Stoller, "Ezra Stoller's Architectural Photography, with Personal Observations," *Architecture Minnesota* 7 (June–July 1981): 65–79; Akiko Busch, *The Photography of Architecture: Twelve Views* (New York: Van Nostrand Reinhold, 1987), 11–16; Cervin Robinson and Joel Herschman, *Architecture Transformed: A History of Buildings from 1839 to the Present* (New York: Architectural League of New York; Cambridge, Mass.: MIT Press, 1987), 123–24; Ezra Stoller, "The Architectural Landscape," *Art News* 86 (November 1987): 160–66; William S. Saunders, *Modern Architecture: Photographs by Ezra Stoller* (New York: Harry N. Abrams, 1990).

3. Saunders, *Modern Architecture: Photographs by Ezra Stoller*, 8.

4. Sorkin, "Pretty as a Building": 112.

5. Goldberger, "Architecture: Portraits by Ezra Stoller": 20.

6. Stern, Gilmartin and Mellins, *New York 1930*, 222–23.

7. Ezra Stoller quoted in Saunders, *Modern Architecture: Photographs by Ezra Stoller*, 82.

8. Stern, Gilmartin and Mellins, *New York 1930*, 591–92, 593–94.

9. Ezra Stoller quoted in Saunders, *Modern Architecture: Photographs by Ezra Stoller*, 145.

10. Drexler, "Introduction," in Stoller, *Ezra Stoller: Photographs of Architecture, 1939–1980*, 1.

11. Saunders, *Modern Architecture: Photographs by Ezra Stoller*, 8.

12. Drexler, "Introduction," in Stoller, *Ezra Stoller: Photographs of Architecture, 1939–1980*, 2.

13. André Kertész, *View from My Window* (Boston: New York Graphic Society, 1981); André Kertész, *Kertész on Kertész: A Self Portrait* (New York: Abbeville Press, 1983); Peter Conrad, *The Art of the City: Views and Versions of New York* (New York: Oxford University Press, 1984), 173–77; Sandra S. Phillips, David Travis and Weston J. Naef, *André Kertész: Of Paris and New York* (Chicago: Art Institute of Chicago; New York: Metropolitan Museum of Art; London: Thames and Hudson, 1985); *Master Photographs*, with an intro. by Cornell Capa and essays by Norman Cousins, Evan H. Turner, Miles Barth, Nathan Lyons and Naomi N. Rosenblum (New York: International Center of Photography, 1988), 149.

14. Stern, Gilmartin and Mellins, *New York 1930*, 616, 650–53.

15. Conrad, *The Art of the City*, 174–75.

16. Kertész, *Kertész on Kertész: A Self Portrait*, 100.

17. Beaumont Newhall, "City Lens: Todd Webb's New York on Exhibition," *Art News* 45 (October 1946): 46–47, 73–74.

18. Helen Levitt, *In the Street: Chalk Drawings and Messages, New York 1938–1948*, with an essay by Robert Coles (Durham, N.C.: Duke University Press, 1987). Also see Helen Levitt, *A Way of Seeing*, with an essay by James Agee (Durham, N.C.: Duke University Press in association with The Center for Documentary Studies at Duke University, 1989); Sandra S. Phillips and Maria Morris Hambourg, *Helen Levitt*, exhibition catalogue (San Francisco: San Francisco Museum of Modern Art, 1991).

19. Conrad, *The Art of the City*, 252–53; *Weegee*, with an intro. by André Laude (New York: Pantheon Books; Paris: Centre National de la Photographie, 1986); *The Village by Weegee* (New York: Da Capo Press, 1989).

20. Diane Arbus, "The Vertical Journey: Six Movements within the Heart of the City," *Esquire* 54 (July 1960): 102–7, reprinted in Diane Arbus, *Diane Arbus, Magazine Works* (New York: Aperture, 1984); Diane Arbus, *Diane Arbus*, exhibition catalogue (Millerton, N.Y.: Aperture, 1972); Patricia Bosworth, *Diane Arbus* (New York: Alfred A. Knopf, 1984).

21. Arbus, *Diane Arbus*, 10.

22. John Szarkowski, *Winogrand: Figments from the Real World* (New York: Museum of Modern Art, 1988).

23. Ruth Orkin, *A World through My Window* (New York: Harper & Row, 1978); Ruth Orkin, *More Pictures from My Window* (New York: Rizzoli International Publications, 1983).

24. Orkin, *More Pictures from My Window*, 13.

25. Orkin, *More Pictures from My Window*, 16.

26. John Szarkowski, *Callahan* (New York: Aperture, in association with the Museum of Modern Art, 1976).

27. L. Fritz Gruber, Rüdiger Joppien and Julia Scully, *Duane Michals: Photographien 1958–1988* (Hamburg, Germany: Museum für Kunst und Gewerbe, 1989).

28. Gene Thornton, "New York: Photographing the Fabulous Beast," *Art News* 75 (November 1976): 48–53.

29. Andreas Feininger, *New York*, with an intro. by John Erskine and text by Jacquelyn Judge (Chicago: Ziff Davis, 1945).

30. Feininger, *New York*, 23.

31. Feininger, *New York*, 97.

32. Conrad, *The Art of the City*, 252.

33. Andreas Feininger, *The Face of New York: The City as It Was and as It Is*, with a text by Susan E. Lyman (New York: Crown Publishers, 1954).

34. Andreas Feininger and Kate Simon, *New York* (New York: Viking, 1964).

35. Andreas Feininger, *New York in the Forties*, with intro. and text by John von Hartz (New York: Dover, 1978).

36. Von Hartz, "Introduction," in Feininger, *New York in the Forties*, unpaginated.

37. Alfred Eisenstaedt, *Remembrances* (Boston: Little, Brown, 1990).

38. Margaret Bourke-White, "A New Way to Look at the U.S.," *Life* 32 (April 14, 1952): 128–40. Also see Sean Callahan, ed., *The Photographs of Margaret Bourke-White*, with an intro. by Theodore M. Brown (Boston: New York Graphic Society, 1972), 132–33, 196–97; Conrad, *The Art of the City*, 211, 255; Vicki Goldberg, *Margaret Bourke-White* (New York: Harper & Row, 1986), 327.

39. Ingrid Molchin, *New York: Glanz und Schönheit* (Baden-Baden, Germany: Woldemar Klein, 1955).

40. For Erich Mendelsohn's photographs of New York, see Stern, Gilmartin and Mellins, *New York 1930*, 66, 70, 74.

41. William Klein, *New York* (London: Photography Magazine, 1956).

42. Dmitri Kessel, *On Assignment: Dmitri Kessel, Life Photographer* (New York: Harry N. Abrams, 1985).

43. *Master Photographs*, 64.

44. Stern, Gilmartin and Mellins, *New York 1930*, 72–73, 76, 78.

NEW YORK ON FILM

1. For the role of the film industry in New York prior to World War I and during the interwar period, see Stern, Gilmartin and Mellins, *New York 1930*, 78–79.

2. Stern, Gilmartin and Mellins, *New York 1930*, 81, 85.

3. Tom Dardis, *Harold Lloyd: The Man on the Clock* (New York: Viking, 1983), 117–28.

4. "New York—The Big Set," *Newsweek* 69 (May 29, 1967): 86–87. Also see Elodie Osborn, "New York on Screen," *Art in America* 52 (October 1964): 80–89; "40 Films and More to Be Made in New York This Year," *Making Films in New York* 3 (August 1969): 19; Ellen Stern, "How to Make a Movie in New York," *New York* 9 (December 29, 1975–January 5, 1976): 55–60.

5. John V. Lindsay quoted in "New York—The Big Set": 86.

6. Sidney Lumet quoted in "New York—The Big Set": 87.

7. Mel Brooks quoted in "New York—The Big Set": 87.

8. Stern, Gilmartin and Mellins, *New York 1930*, 78–79; Richard Koszarski, *The Astoria Studio and Its Fabulous Films* (New York: Dover, 1983), 9, 107–9, 118.

9. Vincent Canby, "'Next Man' Plays on Paranoia," *New York Times* (November 11, 1976): 52; Vincent Canby, "Cynical Cinema Is Chic," *New York Times* (November 17, 1976), II: 13. Also see Albin Krebs, "Notes on People," *New York Times* (December 15, 1977), C: 2; "Proposal for Astoria Film Center Approved by State Arts Council," *New York Times* (December 18, 1977): 61.

10. Steven Kesten quoted in Stern, "How to Make a Movie in New York": 60.

11. Federal Writers' Project, *New York Panorama* (New York: Random House, 1938; Pantheon, 1984), 286.

12. Bosley Crowther, "Back Street," review, *New York Times* (February 12, 1941): 25.

13. Theodore Strauss, "Broadway," review, *New York Times* (June 5, 1942): 23.

14. Bosley Crowther, "Coney Island," review, *New York Times* (June 17, 1943): 17.

15. Bosley Crowther, "Mr. Skeffington," review, *New York Times* (May 26, 1944): 23.

16. Bosley Crowther, "Greenwich Village," review, *New York Times* (September 28, 1944): 26.

17. Bosley Crowther, "Mrs. Parkington," review, *New York Times* (October 13, 1944): 16.

18. Thomas M. Pryor, "Up in Central Park," review, *New York Times* (May 27, 1948): 29.

19. Bosley Crowther, "The Heiress," review, *New York Times* (October 7, 1949): 35.

20. Bosley Crowther, "Citizen Kane," review, *New York Times* (May 2, 1941): 25.

21. Bosley Crowther, "My Sister Eileen," review, *New York Times* (October 23, 1942): 25; Terry Miller, *Greenwich Village and How It Got That Way* (New York: Crown, 1990), 45.

22. Bosley Crowther, "My Sister Eileen," review, *New York Times* (September 23, 1955): 21; Miller, *Greenwich Village and How It Got That Way*, 45–46.

23. Bosley Crowther, "The Belle of New York," review, *New York Times* (March 6, 1952): 25; Michael Pye, *Maximum City: The Biography of New York* (London: Silver-Stevenson, 1991), 25.

24. Renata Adler, "The Night They Raided Minsky's," review, *New York Times* (December 23, 1968): 43.

25. Renata Adler, "Funny Girl," review, *New York Times* (September 20, 1958): 42.

26. Vincent Canby, "Hello, Dolly!" review, *New York Times* (December 18, 1969): 62.

27. Richard Eder, "Pathos and Wit Light Up 'Hester Street,'" review, *New York Times* (October 20, 1975): 44.

28. B. R. Crisler, "Broadway Melody of 1940," review, *New York Times* (March 29, 1940): 25; Stanley Green and Burt Goldblatt, *Starring Fred Astaire* (New York: Dodd, Mead, 1973), 200–211; Michael Freedland, *Fred Astaire* (New York: Grosset & Dunlap, 1976), 84–86, 88–89; Bob Thomas, *Astaire: The Man, The Dancer* (New York: St. Martin's Press, 1984): 162–67; Tim Satchell, *Astaire* (London: Hutchinson, 1987), 162; Fred Astaire, *Steps in Time* (New York: Harper & Row, 1987), 56, 240–41. For the first *Broadway Melody* (1929), see Stern, Gilmartin and Mellins, *New York 1930*, 80.

29. Crisler, "Broadway Melody of 1940": 25.

30. Thomas M. Pryor, "Babes on Broadway," review, *New York Times* (January 1, 1942): 37. Also see John Mosher, "The Current Cinema: Babes and Adults," review, *New Yorker* 17 (January 10, 1947): 53; Joe Morella and Edward Z. Epstein, *Judy* (New York: Citadel, 1969), 96–99.

31. Theodore Strauss, "Angels over Broadway," review, *New York Times* (November 18, 1940): 23; John Mosher, "The Current Cinema: Mr. Hecht All Alone," *New Yorker* 16 (November 16, 1940): 93–94.

32. Strauss, "Angels Over Broadway": 23.

33. Bosley Crowther, "Copacabana," review, *New York Times* (July 12, 1947): 7.

34. A. H. Weiler, "Lullaby of Broadway," review, *New York Times* (March 27, 1951): 35.

35. Thomas M. Pryor, "Young Man with a Horn," review, *New York Times* (February 10, 1950): 18.

36. Bosley Crowther, "The Band Wagon," review, *New York Times* (July 11, 1953): 8; John McCarten, "The Current Cinema: A Slit in the Oral Curtain," review, *New Yorker* 29 (July 18, 1953): 63; Green and Goldblatt, *Starring Fred Astaire*, 380–95; Freedland, *Fred Astaire*, 135–37; Peter Conrad, *The Art of the City: Views and Versions of New York* (New York: Oxford University Press, 1984), 299; Thomas, *Astaire: The Man, The Dancer*, 221–22, 224–27; Astaire, *Steps in Time*, 66, 300–304; Satchell, *Astaire*, 188–90; Richard Alleman, *The Movie Lover's Guide to New York* (New York: Harper & Row, 1988): 67.

37. For the Eltinge Theater, see Nicholas van Hoogstraten, *Lost Broadway Theaters* (New York: Princeton Architectural Press, 1991), 146–49.

38. Bosley Crowther, "Guys and Dolls," review, *New York Times* (November 4, 1955): 26; Bernard F. Dick, *Joseph L. Mankiewicz* (Boston: Twayne, 1983), 120–26; Conrad, *The Art of the City: Views and Versions of New York*, 297.

39. Bosley Crowther, "A Double Life," review, *New York Times* (February 21, 1948): 19; John McCarten, "The Current Cinema: Steinbeck and a Pseudo-Documentary," review, *New Yorker* 24 (February 28, 1948): 62–63; Gary Carey, *Cukor & Co.: The Films of George Cukor and His Collaborators* (New York: Museum of Modern Art, 1971), 111–12; Alleman, *The Movie Lover's Guide to New York*, 88. For the Lyceum and Empire theaters, see Stern, Gilmartin and Massengale, *New York 1900*, 206, 211–13.

40. Bosley Crowther, "All About Eve," review, *New York Times* (October 14, 1950): 13; John McCarten, "The Current Cinema: Bonanza for Bette," review, *New Yorker* 26 (October 21, 1950): 128–29; Alleman, *The Movie Lover's Guide to New York*, 84.

41. A. H. Weiler, "Sweet Smell of Success," review, *New York Times* (June 27, 1957): 29; Pye, *Maximum City: The Biography of New York*, 23.

42. Weiler, "Sweet Smell of Success": 29.

43. Pye, *Maximum City: The Biography of New York*, 23.

44. A. H. Weiler, "Stage Struck," review, *New York Times* (April 23, 1958): 40; "Minetta Lane and MacDougal Street," *Village Voice* 2 (February 13, 1967): 1; John McCarten, "The Current Cinema: Growing Pain," review, *New Yorker* 34 (May 3, 1958): 60, 62.

45. Renata Adler, "The Producers," review, *New York Times* (March 19, 1968): 38; Pauline Kael, "The Current Cinema: O Pioneer!" review, *New Yorker* 44 (March 23, 1968): 140; William Holtzman, *Seesaw: A Dual Biography of Anne Bancroft and Mel Brooks* (Garden City, N.Y.: Doubleday, 1979), 230–37; Maurice Yacowar, *Method in Madness: The Comic Art of Mel Brooks* (New York: St. Martin's Press, 1981), 71–85; Alleman, *The Movie Lover's Guide to New York*, 213.

46. Bosley Crowther, "Saboteur," review, *New York Times* (May 8, 1942): 27; John Mosher, "The Current Cinema: Hitchcock on Sabotage," review, *New Yorker* 18 (May 9, 1942): 67–68; Donald Spoto, *The Art of Alfred Hitchcock*, rev. ed. (New York: Doubleday, 1979), 109–14; François Truffaut with Helen G. Scott, *Hitchcock*, rev. ed. (New York: Simon & Schuster, 1983), 145, 150–51, 357; Alleman, *The Movie Lover's Guide to New York*, 36, 203.

47. Thomas M. Pryor, "Lucky Jordan," review, *New York Times* (January 25, 1943): 10.

48. Bosley Crowther, "All Through the Night," review, *New York Times* (January 24, 1942): 13.

49. Thomas M. Pryor, "The House on Ninety-second Street," review, *New York Times* (September 27, 1945): 24; John McCarten, "The Current Cinema: Cloak, Dagger, and J. Edgar Hoover," review, *New Yorker* 21 (September 29, 1945): 56; Conrad, *The Art of the City: Views and Versions of New York*, 277; Alleman, *The Movie Lover's Guide to New York*, 143, 156.

50. Thomas M. Pryor, "The Clock," review, *New York Times* (May 4, 1945): 23; Wolcott Gibbs, "The Current Cinema: The Royal Nonesuch," review, *New Yorker* 21 (May 12, 1945): 77–78; "Cinema: The New Pictures," review, *Time* 45 (May 14, 1945): 93–94; Morella and Epstein, *Judy*, 123–26; Anne Edwards, *Judy Garland* (New York: Simon & Schuster, 1974), 99–101; Richard Schickel, *The Men Who Made the Movies* (New York: Atheneum, 1975), 249–50; Alleman, *The Movie Lover's Guide to New York*, 67, 138; Howard Mandelbaum and Eric Myers, *Forties Screen Style: A Celebration of High Pastiche in Hollywood* (New York: St. Martin's Press, 1989), 127.

51. Gibbs, "The Current Cinema: The Royal Nonesuch": 78.

52. Vincente Minnelli quoted in Schickel, *The Men Who Made the Movies*, 250.

53. Pryor, "The Clock": 23.

54. Bosley Crowther, "On the Town," review, *New York Times* (December 9, 1949): 37; John McCarten, "The Current Cinema: None Better," *New Yorker* 25 (December 10, 1949): 140; Clive Hirschhorn, *Gene Kelly* (Chicago: Henry Regnery, 1974), 180–84; Tony Thomas, *The Films of Gene Kelly, Song and Dance Man* (Secaucus, N.J.: Citadel, 1974), 99–111; John B. Manbeck, *Brooklyn on Film* (Brooklyn, N.Y.: The Alliance, 1979), 15, 40; Joan Peyser, *Bernstein* (New York: William Morrow, 1987), 139–42; Conrad, *The Art of the City: Views and Versions of New York*, 298; Michael Webb, "The City in Film," *Design Quarterly* (spring 1987): 1–32; Alleman, *The Movie Lover's Guide to New York*, 38, 66, 192, 202–3, 251; William Sharpe, "Living on the Edge: New York in Literature," in Leonard Wallock, ed., *New York: Culture Capital of the World, 1940–1965* (New York: Rizzoli International Publications, 1988), 66; Pye, *Maximum City: The Biography of New York*, 22.

55. Bosley Crowther, "It's Always Fair Weather," review, *New York Times* (September 16, 1955): 19; Brigid Murnaghan, "Movies," *Village Voice* 1 (November 2, 1955): 6; Hirschhorn, *Gene Kelly*, 242–45; Thomas, *The Films of Gene Kelly, Song and Dance Man*, 159–62; Conrad, *The Art of the City: Views and Versions of New York*, 299.

56. Thomas M. Pryor, "I Can Get It for You Wholesale," review, *New York Times* (April 5, 1951): 34; John McCarten, "The Current Cinema: Culture by the Carload," review, *New Yorker* 27 (April 14, 1951): 127–28.

57. Howard Thompson, "The Garment Jungle," review, *New York Times* (May 16, 1957): 28.

58. Bosley Crowther, "How to Succeed in Business without Really Trying," review, *New York Times* (March 10, 1967): 30.

59. Bosley Crowther, "Funny Face," review, *New York Times* (March 29, 1957): 16. Also see John McCarten, "The Current Cinema: Jokes," review, *New Yorker* 33 (April 6, 1957): 76.

60. Howard Thompson, "Offices Romances," review, *New York Times* (October 9, 1959): 24. Also see Rona Jaffee, *The Best of Everything* (New York: Simon & Schuster, 1958).

61. Bosley Crowther, "A Face in the Crowd," review, *New York Times* (May 29, 1957): 33.

62. Bosley Crowther, "The Hucksters," review, *New York Times* (July 18, 1947): 21.

63. Vincent Canby, "Network," review, *New York Times* (November 15, 1976): 39; Canby, "Cynical Cinema is Chic": 13; Richard Eder, "Hollywood Is Having an Affair with the Anti-Hero," *New York Times* (January 2, 1977), II: 1, 8; Allan Hunter, *Faye Dunaway* (New York: St. Martin's Press, 1986), 141–52; Pauline Kael, "The Current Cinema: Hot Air," review, *New Yorker* 52 (December 6, 1976): 177–80, 182, 185; Frank R. Cunningham, *Sidney Lumet: Film and Literary Vision* (Lexington, Ky.: University Press of Kentucky, 1991), 221–24.

64. Kael, "The Current Cinema: Hot Air": 177.

65. Bosley Crowther, "The Man in the Gray Flannel Suit," review, *New York Times* (April 13, 1956): 21. Also see Sloan Wilson, *The Man in the Gray Flannel Suit* (New York: Simon & Schuster, 1955).

66. Vincent Canby, "Mad Ad Shop Brought to Life at Cinema II," review, *New York Times* (July 11, 1969): 19; Penelope Gilliatt, "The Current Cinema: Mukel Swink," review, *New Yorker* 45 (August 2, 1969): 46, 48.

67. Bosley Crowther, "Taxi," review, *New York Times* (January 22, 1953): 20.

68. A. H. Weiler, "On the Waterfront," review, *New York Times* (July 29, 1954): 18; Alleman, *The Movie Lover's Guide to New York*, 10–11, 104, 297. Also see Malcolm Johnson, *Crime on the Labor Front* (New York: McGraw-Hill, 1950).

69. Bosley Crowther, "Slaughter on Tenth Avenue," review, *New York Times* (November 6, 1957): 43.

70. George Nelson, "Mr. Roark Goes to Hollywood," *Interiors* 109 (April 1949): 106–11; Bosley Crowther, "The Fountainhead," review, *New York Times* (July 9, 1949): 8; John McCarten, "The Current Cinema: Down with Beaux-Arts," review, *New Yorker* 25 (July 16, 1949): 46–47; Stuart M. Kaminsky, *Coop: The Life and Legend of Gary Cooper* (New York: St. Martin's Press, 1980), 154–58; Raymond Durgnat and Scott Simmon, *King Vidor, American* (Berkeley: University of California Press, 1988), 257–69; Mandelbaum and Myers, *Forties Screen Style: A Celebration of High Pastiche in Hollywood*, 18–19, 56, 84; "FLLW: The Hollywood Version," *Interior Design* 65 (August 1994): 64, 66–69. For a discussion of Rand's life, see James T. Baker, *Ayn Rand* (Boston: Twayne, 1987). Also see Ayn Rand, *The Fountainhead* (Indianapolis, Ind.: Bobbs-Merrill, 1943); Orville Prescott, "Books of the Times," review, *New York Times* (May 12, 1943): 23; Lorine Pruette, "Battle Against Evil," review, *New York Times* (May 16, 1943), VII: 7, 18.

71. For the Fifth Avenue Estates Building, see "Apartment-Houses," *American Architect* 91 (January 5, 1907), plates 13–14. For the Hotel Pierre, see Stern, Gilmartin and Mellins, *New York 1930*, 217, 220–21. For the Sherry-Netherland Hotel, see Stern, Gilmartin and Mellins, *New York 1930*, 217–21.

72. Crowther, "The Fountainhead": 8.

73. McCarten, "The Current Cinema: Down with Beaux-Arts": 46.

74. Nelson, "Mr. Roark Goes to Hollywood,": 111.

75. Theodore Strauss, "Mr. and Mrs. Smith," review, *New York Times* (February 21, 1941): 16; John Russell Taylor, *Hitch: The Life and Work of Alfred Hitchcock* (London: Faber & Faber, 1978), 171–73; Michael Haley, *The Alfred Hitchcock Album* (Englewood Cliffs, N.J.: Prentice Hall Press, 1981), 50; Jane E. Sloan, *Alfred Hitchcock: A Guide to References and Resources* (New York: G. K. Hall, 1993), 171–75.

76. Stern, Gilmartin and Mellins, *New York 1930*, 752.

77. Bosley Crowther, "'Tales of Manhattan,' Starring Charles Boyer, Henry Fonda, Edward G. Robinson, Charles Laughton, at the Music Hall," review, *New York Times* (September 25, 1942): 25.

78. Alleman, *The Movie Lover's Guide to New York*, 41–42; Mandelbaum and Myers, *Forties Screen Style: A Celebration of High Pastiche in Hollywood*, 106. For the Waldorf-Astoria Hotel, see Stern Gilmartin, and Mellins, *New York 1930*, 222–23.

79. Bosley Crowther, "Adam's Rib," review, *New York Times* (December 26, 1948): 33; Carey, *Cukor & Co.: The Films of George Cukor and His Collaborators*, 111–12; Carlos Clarens, *George Cukor* (London: Secker & Warburg, in association with the British Film Institute, 1976), 89–91; Patrick McGilligan, *George Cukor: A Double Life* (New York: St. Martin's Press, 1991), 201.

80. Bosley Crowther, "The Marrying Kind," review, *New York Times* (March 14, 1952): 27; Carey, *Cukor & Co.: The Films of George Cukor and His Collaborators*, 113–15; Clarens, *George Cukor*, 95–97; McGilligan, *George Cukor: A Double Life*, 208.

81. Carey, *Cukor & Co.: The Films of George Cukor and His Collaborators*, 135. Also see Bosley Crowther, "Let's Make Love," review, *New York Times* (September 9, 1960): 36; Clarens, *George Cukor*, 105–6.

82. Bosley Crowther, "The Girl from Jones Beach," review, *New York Times* (July 30, 1949): 9.

83. Bosley Crowther, "East Side, West Side," review, *New York Times* (December 23, 1949): 17; Homer Dickens, *The Films of Barbara Stanwyck* (Secaucus, N.J.: Citadel, 1984), 196–99.

84. Bosley Crowther, "Selznick's 'Portrait of Jennie,' with Cotten and Jennifer Jones, Opens at Rivoli," review, *New York Times* (March 30, 1949): 31; John McCarten, "The Current Cinema: Culture with a Capital 'K,'" review, *New Yorker* 25 (April 2, 1949): 95; Alleman, *The Movie Lover's Guide to New York*, 66–67, 97, 120, 216–17; Pye, *Maximum City: The Biography of New York*, 25.

85. A. H. Weiler, "Miracle in the Rain," review, *New York Times* (April 2, 1956): 18.

86. Weiler, "Miracle in the Rain": 18.

87. Bosley Crowther, "Bell, Book, and Candle," review, *New York Times* (December 27, 1958): 22; Alleman, *The Movie Lover's Guide to New York* , 159.

88. Stern, Gilmartin and Massengale, *New York 1900*, 164–67.

89. Bosley Crowther, "How to Marry a Millionaire," review, *New York Times* (November 11, 1953): 37; John McCarten, "The Current Cinema: Curves in Space," review, *New Yorker* 29 (November 21, 1953): 133–34; Laurence J. Quirk, *Lauren Bacall: Her Films and Career* (Secaucus, N.J.: Citadel, 1986), 110–19; Pye, *Maximum City: The Biography of New York*, 26.

90. Bosley Crowther, "The Seven Year Itch," review, *New York Times* (July 4, 1955): 9; Axel Madsen, *Billy Wilder* (Bloomington, Ind.: Indiana University Press, 1969), 101–2; Anthony Summers, *Goddess: The Secret Lives of Marilyn Monroe* (Ann Arbor, Mich.: UMI Research Press, 1986), 76–82; Randall Riese and Neal Hitchens, *The Unabridged Marilyn: Her Life from A to Z* (New York: Congdon & Weed, 1987), 474–76; Alleman, *The Movie Lover's Guide to New York*, 43–44.

91. Bosley Crowther, "The Tender Trap," review, *New York Times* (November 11, 1955): 29.

92. Bosley Crowther, "An Affair to Remember," *New York Times* (July 20, 1957): 8; Eric Braun, *Deborah Kerr* (New York: St. Martin's Press, 1977), 162–64.
93. A. H. Weiler, "Teacher's Pet," review, *New York Times* (March 20, 1958): 33.
94. Bosley Crowther, "Pillow Talk," review, *New York Times* (October 7, 1959): 47; John McCarten, "The Current Cinema: Standard Brands," review, *New Yorker* 35 (October 17, 1959): 197–98.
95. Bosley Crowther, "Butterfield 8," review, *New York Times* (November 17, 1960): 46. Also see Brendan Gill, "The Current Cinema: Yukon 6," review, *New Yorker* 36 (November 19, 1960): 152.
96. Bosley Crowther, "The Apartment," review, *New York Times* (June 16, 1960): 37; John McCarten, "The Current Cinema: Merriment to Murder," review, *New Yorker* 36 (June 25, 1960): 70; Madsen, *Billy Wilder*, 120–23; Christopher Paul Denis, *The Films of Shirley MacLaine* (Secaucus, N.J.: Citadel, 1980), 94–98; Robert A. M. Stern with Thomas Mellins and Raymond Gastil, *Pride of Place: Building the American Dream* (Boston: Houghton Mifflin; New York: American Heritage, 1986), 282–83.
97. Bosley Crowther, "Sunday in New York," review, *New York Times* (February 12, 1964): 30.
98. Bosley Crowther, "Barefoot in the Park," review, *New York Times* (May 26, 1967): 51; Brendan Gill, "The Current Cinema: Love in a Warm Climate," review, *New Yorker* 43 (June 10, 1967): 72; Alleman, *The Movie Lover's Guide to New York*, 170, 178–79; Christopher Anderson, *Citizen Jane: The Turbulent Life of Jane Fonda* (New York: Henry Holt, 1990), 155–56.
99. Vincent Canby, "Sweet Charity," review, *New York Times* (April 2, 1969): 38; Vincent Canby, "Is the Cost of 'Charity' Too High?" *New York Times* (April 6, 1969), II: 1; Denis, *The Films of Shirley MacLaine*, 155–59; Martin Gottfried, *All His Jazz: The Life and Death of Bob Fosse* (New York: Bantam, 1990), 190–98.
100. Peter Stone quoted in Gottfried, *All His Jazz: The Life and Death of Bob Fosse*, 192.
101. Canby, "Sweet Charity": 38.
102. Vincent Canby, "The Owl and the Pussycat," review, *New York Times* (November 4, 1970): 46.
103. Canby, "What Makes a Movie Immoral?" 19.
104. Vincent Canby, "The April Fools," review, *New York Times* (May 29, 1969): 43; Alleman, *The Movie Lover's Guide to New York*, 173.
105. Quoted in Canby, "The April Fools": 43.
106. Vincent Canby, "Plaza Suite," review, *New York Times* (May 14, 1971): 46; Alleman, *The Movie Lover's Guide to New York*, 56. For the Plaza Hotel, see Stern, Gilmartin and Massengale, *New York 1900*, 257–59, 261–62.
107. Thomas M. Pryor, "Port of New York," review, *New York Times* (February 3, 1950): 29.
108. Joseph Wood Krutch, "Beside the Point," *Nation* 171 (August 5, 1950): 129; Bosley Crowther, "The Sleeping City," review, *New York Times* (September 21, 1950): 20; Alleman, *The Movie Lover's Guide to New York*, 32, 164, 198.
109. Crowther, "The Sleeping City": 20.
110. Leland M. Roth, *McKim, Mead & White, Architects* (New York: Harper & Row, 1983), 294–95.
111. For the Williamsburg Bridge, see Stern, Gilmartin and Massengale, *New York 1900*, 50–51.
112. Vincent Canby, "The Hospital," review, *New York Times* (December 15, 1971): 66; Walter Kerr, "I Hate Paddy Chayefsky," *New York Times* (April 2, 1972), II: 1, 3; Alleman, *The Movie Lover's Guide to New York*, 235.
113. Milton Lehman, "Smallpox, the Killer that Stalked New York," *Cosmopolitan* 124 (April 1948), 68–70, 176–83; Bosley Crowther, "'Killer that Stalked New York,' about a Diamond Smuggler, Opens at Palace Theater," review, *New York Times* (January 5, 1951): 17.
114. Bosley Crowther, "Blackboard Jungle," review, *New York Times* (March 21, 1955): 21. Also see Evan Hunter, *Blackboard Jungle* (New York: Simon & Schuster, 1954); Leonard Buder, "2 Reports Clear School in Bronx," *New York Times* (July 17, 1955): 39; "Delinquency Plan of U.S. Supported," *New York Times* (November 17, 1955): 37.
115. "Delinquency Plan of U.S. Supported": 37.
116. Crowther, "Blackboard Jungle": 21.
117. Bel Kaufman, *Up the Down Staircase* (Englewood Cliffs, N.J.: Prentice Hall Press, 1965); Bosley Crowther, "Up the Down Staircase," review, *New York Times* (August 18, 1967): 36; Penelope Gilliatt, "The Current Cinema: Film Flammery," review, *New Yorker* 43 (August 26, 1967): 76–77; Alleman, *The Movie Lover's Guide to New York*, 107.
118. Stern, Gilmartin and Massengale, *New York 1900*, 80–83.
119. Renata Adler, "Where Were You When the Lights Went Out?" review, *New York Times* (August 9, 1968): 30.
120. David W. Dunlap, *On Broadway: A Journey Uptown Over Time* (New York: Rizzoli International Publications, 1990), 250.
121. Roger Greenspun, "The French Connection," review, *New York Times* (October 8, 1971): 35; Garrett Epps, "Does Popeye Doyle Teach Us How to Be Fascist?" *New York Times* (May 21, 1972), II: 15; Manbeck, *Brooklyn on Film*, 38.
122. Greenspun, "The French Connection": 35.
123. Vincent Canby, "Film: Desperate Couple," review, *New York Times* (September 23, 1971): 74; Betty Friedan, "What Makes These Characters Desperate?" *New York Times* (December 19, 1971), II: 15; Denis, *The Films of Shirley MacLaine*, 164–67.
124. Friedan, "What Makes These Characters Desperate?": 15.
125. Canby, "Film: Desperate Couple": 74.
126. Roger Greenspun, "Hiller 'Out-of-Towners' Opens at Music Hall," review, *New York Times* (May 29, 1971): 14; Alleman, *The Movie Lover's Guide to New York*, 42, 67, 173.
127. Greenspun, "Hiller 'Out-of-Towners' Opens at Music Hall": 14.
128. A. H. Weiler, "The Prisoner of Second Avenue," review, *New York Times* (March 15, 1975): 18; Pauline Kael, "The Current Cinema: New York Self-Hatred for Fun and Profit: Notes on 'The Prisoner of Second Avenue,'" review, *New Yorker* 51 (March 10, 1975): 68, 70–71. Also see Thomas Meehan, "The Unreal, Hilarious World of Neil Simon," *Horizon* 21 (January 1978): 70–74; Pye, *Maximum City: The Biography of New York*, 25.
129. Kael, "The Current Cinema: New York Self-Hatred for Fun and Profit: 'Notes on 'The Prisoner of Second Avenue'": 70.
130. Nora Sayre, "The Taking of Pelham One Two Three," review, *New York Times* (October 3, 1974): 50; Edward C. Burks, "It Looks Like Walter Matthau . . . It Could Be Walter Matthau . . . It . . .," *New York Times* (January 28, 1974): 28; Manbeck, *Brooklyn on Film*, 42.
131. Sayre, "The Taking of Pelham One Two Three": 50.
132. Vincent Canby, "New York's Woes Are Good Box Office," *New York Times* (November 10, 1974), II: 1.
133. Bosley Crowther, "The Lost Weekend," review, *New York Times* (December 3, 1945): 17. Also see John McCarten, "The Current Cinema: Very Rare Vintage," review, *New Yorker* 21 (December 1, 1945): 112–13; Madsen, *Billy Wilder*, 66, 68–71, Alleman, *The Movie Lover's Guide to New York City*, 118–19, 164.
134. Bosley Crowther, "A Hatful of Rain," review, *New York Times* (July 18, 1957): 19.
135. Crowther, "A Hatful of Rain": 19.
136. Bosley Crowther, "Rope," review, *New York Times* (August 27, 1948): 12; John McCarten, "The Current Cinema: Still Life," review, *New Yorker* 24 (September 4, 1948): 61; Spoto, *The Art of Alfred Hitchcock*, 165–72; Donald Spoto, *The Dark Side of Genius: The Life of Alfred Hitchcock* (Boston: Little, Brown, 1983), 304–7; Truffaut with Scott, *Hitchcock*, 179–80, 182–84, 358; Theodore Price, *Hitchcock and Homosexuality* (Metuchen, N. J.: Scarecrow, 1992), 28–32.
137. Bosley Crowther, "The Manchurian Candidate," review, *New York Times* (October 25, 1962): 48.
138. A. H. Weiler, "The Screen: Gregory Peck in 'Mirage,'" review, *New York Times* (May 27, 1965): 28.
139. "Is the Housewife Mad?" *New York* 3 (July 20, 1970): 48; Roger Greenspun, "Perrys Present View of Emotional Crisis," review, *New York Times* (August 11, 1970): 27; Penelope Gilliatt, "The Current Cinema: God Save the Language at Least," review, *New Yorker* 46 (August 15, 1970): 68–69; Grace Glueck, "A Funny and Incisively Human 'Housewife,'" *New York Times* (August 23, 1970), II: 11; Russell Baker, "That Was No Housewife; That Was . . . ," *New York Times* (November 5, 1970): 47.
140. Glueck, "A Funny and Incisively Human 'Housewife'": 11.
141. Gilliatt, "The Current Cinema: God Save the Language at Least": 69.
142. Vincent Canby, "Dog Day Afternoon," review, *New York Times* (September 22, 1975): 41; Penelope Gilliatt, "The Current Cinema: Vivid Doldrums," review, *New Yorker* 51 (September 22, 1975): 95; Vincent Canby, "Quintessential New York Film," *New York Times* (September 28, 1975), II: 13, Jack Kroll, "Movies: Bank Shot," review, *Newsweek* 86 (September 29, 1975): 84; Manbeck, *Brooklyn on Film*, 19; Cunningham, *Sidney Lumet: Film and Literary Vision*, 218–21.
143. Kroll, "Movies: Bank Shot": 84.
144. Canby, "Dog Day Afternoon": 41.
145. Canby, "Quintessential New York Film": 13.
146. Vincent Canby, "The Gambler," review, *New York Times* (October 3, 1974): 50.
147. Vincent Canby, "Taxi Driver," review, *New York Times* (February 8, 1976): 36; Pauline Kael, "The Current Cinema: Underground Man," review, *New Yorker* 51 (February 9, 1976): 82, 84–85; Vincent Canby, "Disturbing 'Taxi Driver,'" review, *New York Times* (February 12, 1976), II: 1; Walter Goodman, "Movie Madness," *New York Times* (March 14, 1976), II: 1; Conrad, *The Art of the City: Views and Versions of New York*, 289; Alleman, *The Movie Lover's Guide to New York*, 51, 96, 196; Pye, *Maximum City: The Biography of New York*, 26.
148. Canby, "Disturbing 'Taxi Driver'": 1.
149. Canby, "Taxi Driver": 36.
150. Kael, "The Current Cinema: Underground Man": 82.
151. Kael, "The Current Cinema: Underground Man": 85.
152. Bosley Crowther, "It Should Happen to You," review, *New York Times* (January 16, 1954): 10; Carey, *Cukor & Co.: The Films of George Cukor and His Collaborators*, 135; McGilligan, *George Cukor: A Double Life*, 201.
153. Bosley Crowther, "Marty," review, *New York Times* (April 12, 1955): 25.
154. Bosley Crowther, "The Pawnbroker," review, *New York Times* (April 21, 1965): 51; Brendan Gill, "The Current Cinema: Breaking Free," review, *New Yorker* 41 (April 24, 1965): 164–65; Cunningham, *Sidney Lumet: Film and Literary Vision*, 157–85.
155. Crowther, "The Pawnbroker": 51.
156. Vincent Canby, "Dustin Hoffman and Jon Voight Are Starred," review, *New York Times* (May 26, 1969): 54; Douglas Brode, *Dustin Hoffman* (Seacus, N.J.: Citadel, 1983), 78–89; Alleman, *The Movie Lover's Guide to New York*, 136.
157. Canby, "Dustin Hoffman and Jon Voight Are Starred": 54.
158. Bosley Crowther, "Gentleman's Agreement," review, *New York Times* (November 12, 1974): 36; John McCarten, "The Current Cinema: Just a Slap on the Wrist," review, *New Yorker* 23 (November 15, 1947): 117–18.
159. Bosley Crowther, "House of Strangers," review, *New York Times* (July 2, 1949): 8. Also see Alleman, *The Movie Lover's Guide to New York*, 220. For the Dakota, see Stern, Gilmartin and Massengale, *New York 1900*, 283–85.
160. Bosley Crowther, "A View from the Bridge," review, *New York Times* (January 23, 1962): 36; Brendan Gill, "The Current Cinema: Lower Class, Upper Class," review, *New Yorker* 37 (January 27, 1962): 82–83; Manbeck, *Brooklyn on Film*, 33; Cunningham, *Sidney Lumet: Film and Literary Vision*, 49–68.
161. Crowther, "A View from the Bridge": 36.
162. Bosley Crowther, "West Side Story," review, *New York Times* (October 19, 1961): 39. Also see Leonard Bernstein, *Findings* (New York: Simon & Schuster, 1982), 144–47; Craig Zadan, *Sondheim & Co.*, 2nd ed. (New York: Harper & Row, 1986), 10–31; Michael Freedland, *Leonard Bernstein* (London: Harrap, 1987), 254–64; Peyser, *Bernstein*, 255–71; Alleman, *The Movie Lover's Guide to New York*, 213; Peter Salwen, *Upper West Side Story* (New York: Abbeville Press, 1989), 253–54.
163. Crowther, "West Side Story": 39; Brendan Gill, "The Current Cinema: Outsize," review, *New Yorker* 37 (October 21, 1961): 196.
164. Howard Thompson, "Popi," review, *New York Times* (May 28, 1969): 34; Susan Lardner, "The Current Cinema: Life, Love, Death, Etc.," review, *New Yorker* 45 (May 31, 1969): 81–82; Vincent Canby, "'Popi'—Poverty Played for Laughs and Pathos," *New York Times* (June 15, 1969), II: 1, 20.
165. Thompson, "Popi": 34.
166. Canby, "'Popi'—Poverty Played for Laughs and Pathos": 1.
167. Renata Adler, "Bye Bye Braverman," review, *New York Times* (February 22, 1968): 36; Manbeck, *Brooklyn on Film*, 36; Cunningham, *Sidney Lumet: Film and Literary Vision*, 196–207.
168. Adler, "Bye Bye Braverman": 36.
169. Vincent Canby, "Portnoy's Complaint," review, *New York Times* (June 20, 1972): 35. Also see Fred M. Hechinger, "An Anti-Jewish Joke?" *New York Times* (July 16, 1972), II: 1.
170. For in-depth discussion of the black film industry, see G. William Jones, *Black Cinema Treasures: Lost and Found* (Denton, Tex.: University of North Texas Press, 1991).
171. John McCarten, "The Current Cinema: Home-Grown," review, *New Yorker* 24 (February 12, 1949): 69; Bosley Crowther, "The Quiet One," review, *New York Times* (February 14, 1949): 15.

172. Crowther, "The Quiet One": 15.
173. McCarten, "The Current Cinema: Home-Grown": 69.
174. Bosley Crowther, "Dutchman," review, *New York Times* (February 28, 1967): 32.
175. Roger Greenspun, "Hi, Mom!" review, *New York Times* (April 28, 1970): 50; Vincent Canby, "Ah, Youth! Ah, Sex! Ah, Revolution!" *New York Times* (June 14, 1970), II: 1.
176. "40 Films and More to Be Made in New York This Year": 19; Howard Thompson, "'Landlord,' a Comedy, Opens at Coronet," review, *New York Times* (May 21, 1970): 44; Clayton Riley, "When the All-American Boy Meets Miss Sepia of 1957," *New York Times* (August 2, 1970), II: 9; Manbeck, *Brooklyn on Film*, 24.
177. Riley, "When the All-American Boy Meets Miss Sepia of 1957": 9.
178. "40 Films and More to Be Made in New York This Year": 19; Vincent Canby, "Ossie Davis' 'Cotton Comes to Harlem,'" *New York Times* (June 11, 1970): 50.
179. Canby, "Ossie Davis' 'Cotton Comes to Harlem'": 50.
180. Roger Greenspun, "Gordon Parks' 'Shaft' Begins at 2 Theaters," review, *New York Times* (July 3, 1971): 20; Vincent Canby, "'Shaft'—At Last a Good Saturday Night Movie," *New York Times* (July 11, 1971): 19; Clayton Riley, "A Black Critic's View of 'Shaft': A Black Movie for White Audiences?" *New York Times* (July 29, 1971): 42; Clayton Riley, "'Shaft Can Do Everything . . . I Can Do Nothing," *New York Times* (August 13, 1972), II: 9; Gordon Parks, *To Smile in Autumn* (New York: W. W. Norton, 1979), 227–29; Gordon Parks, *Voices in the Mirror* (New York: Doubleday, 1990), 305–8.
181. For a discussion of "Blaxploitation" films, see Sidney Poitier, *This Life* (New York: Alfred A. Knopf, 1980), 339–53.
182. Parks, *Voices in the Mirror*, 306.
183. Canby, "'Shaft'—At Last, a Good Saturday Night Movie": 1.
184. Greenspun, "Gordon Parks' 'Shaft' Begins at 2 Theaters": 20.
185. Riley, "A Black Critic's View of 'Shaft:' A Black Movie for White Audiences?": 13.
186. Roger Greenspun, "Shaft's Big Score," review, *New York Times* (June 22, 1972): 42.
187. Vincent Canby, "Film Depicts Real Life 'Batman' and 'Robin,'" review, *New York Times* (March 21, 1974): 51; Manbeck, *Brooklyn on Film*, 30.
188. A. H. Weiler, "Black Caesar," review, *New York Times* (February 8, 1973): 36. For Larry Cohen's *Hell Up In Harlem*, see Howard Thompson, "'Hell Up in Harlem' Tracks Crime Czar," review, *New York Times* (December 24, 1973): 21.
189. Roger Greenspun, "Across 110th Street," review, *New York Times* (December 20, 1972): 53.
190. Howard Thompson, "Gordon's War," review, *New York Times* (August 10, 1973): 26. Also see Mary E. Mebane ("Liza"), "Brother Caring for Brother," *New York Times* (September 23, 1973), II: 5.
191. Lawrence Van Gelder, "Compelling 'Education of Sonny Carson,'" review, *New York Times* (July 18, 1974): 32; Manbeck, *Brooklyn on Film*, 20.
192. Van Gelder, "Compelling 'Education of Sonny Carson'": 32.
193. Bosley Crowther, "Lower Level, on Time: Grand Central Murder," review, *New York Times* (May 23, 1942): 8.
194. Lewis B. Funke, "Murder in Times Square," review, *New York Times* (May 31, 1943): 13.
195. Thomas M. Pryor, "Laura," review, *New York Times* (October 12, 1944): 24; Gerald Pratley, *The Cinema of Otto Preminger* (London: A. Zwemmer; New York: A. S. Barnes, 1971), 55, 61, 80–81; Wille Frischauer, *Behind the Scenes of Otto Preminger* (London: Michael Joseph, 1973), 102–12; Otto Preminger, *Preminger* (Garden City, N.Y.: Doubleday, 1977), 71–78; Conrad, *The Art of the City: Views and Versions of New York*, 291.
196. Thomas M. Pryor, "Kiss of Death," review, *New York Times* (August 28, 1947): 28; John McNulty, "The Current Cinema: Three Cases for the Cops," review, *New Yorker* 23 (September 6, 1947): 68.
197. Bosley Crowther, "The Naked City," review, *New York Times* (March 5, 1948): 17; John McCarten, "The Current Cinema: Crime, Foreign and Domestic," review, *New Yorker* 24 (March 13, 1948): 80–81; Jim Bishop, *The Mark Hellinger Story: A Biography of Broadway and Hollywood* (New York: Appleton-Century-Crofts, 1952), 330–67; Manbeck, *Brooklyn on Film*, 40; Conrad, *The Art of the City: Views and Versions of the City*, 274–79, 283; Webb, "The City in Film": 7; Morris Dickstein, "Neighborhoods," *Dissent* 34 (fall 1987): 602–7; Alleman, *The Movie Lover's Guide to New York*, 99, 156, 198; Pye, *Maximum City: The Biography of New York*, 24.
198. Stern, Gilmartin and Mellins, *New York 1930*, 250–51, 256–59.
199. Mark Hellinger, quoted in Crowther, "The Naked City": 17.
200. Bosley Crowther, "Detective Story," review, *New York Times* (November 7, 1951): 35.
201. McCarten, "The Current Cinema: Crime, Foreign and Domestic": 80.
202. "Neighborhoods": 602.
203. Vincent Terrace, *The Complete Encyclopedia of Television Programs 1947–1979*, rev. ed. (New York: A. S. Barnes, 1979), 696; James Wolcott, "On Television: Funky Town," *New Yorker* 69 (May 3, 1993): 103–4.
204. Bosley Crowther, "Force of Evil," review, *New York Times* (December 27, 1948): 16; Conrad, *The Art of the City: Views and Versions of New York*, 289; Alleman, *The Movie Lover's Guide to New York*, 19, 202.
205. Crowther, "Force of Evil": 1.
206. Stern, Gilmartin and Mellins, *New York 1930*, 677–79, 681–82.
207. Bosley Crowther, "Sorry, Wrong Number," review, *New York Times* (September 2, 1948): 18; Conrad, *The Art of the City: Views and Versions of New York*, 289; Dickens, *The Films of Barbara Stanwyck*, 190–96.
208. Bosley Crowther, "Side Street," review, *New York Times* (March 24, 1950): 29.
209. Howard Thompson, "Where the Sidewalk Ends," review, *New York Times* (July 8, 1950): 7.
210. Bosley Crowther, "Detective Story," review, *New York Times* (November 7, 1951): 35. Also see John McCarten, "The Current Cinema: Where Is Everybody Going?" review, *New Yorker* 27 (November 17, 1951): 120–21.
211. Bosley Crowther, "Pickup on South Street," review, *New York Times* (June 18, 1953): 38; John McCarten, "The Current Cinema: Fantasy, Ltd.," review, *New Yorker* 29 (June 27, 1953): 59; Pye, *Maximum City: The Biography of New York*, 23.
212. Bosley Crowther, "Rear Window," review, *New York Times* (August 5, 1954): 18; Truffaut with Scott, *Hitchcock*, 11, 73, 213–19, 317–19, 359–60; John McCarten, "The Current Cinema: Hitchcock Confined Again," review, *New Yorker* 30 (August 7, 1954): 50–51; Spoto, *The Art of Alfred Hitchcock*, 213–24; Sanford Levine, *The 247 Best Movie Scenes in Film History* (Jefferson, N.C.: McFarland, 1992), 176–78; Price, *Hitchcock and Homosexuality*, 76–80, Conrad, *The Art of the City: Views and Versions of New York*, 293–94.
213. Crowther, "Rear Window": 18. For *Street Scene*, see Stern, Gilmartin and Mellins, *New York 1930*, 81.
214. A. H. Weiler, "The Wrong Man," review, *New York Times* (December 24, 1956): 8; John McCarten, "The Current Cinema: Hitchcock, Documentary Style," review, *New Yorker* 32 (January 5, 1957): 61–62; Spoto, *The Art of Alfred Hitchcock*, 283–89.
215. A. H. Weiler, "12 Angry Men," review, *New York Times* (April 15, 1957): 24; Cunningham, *Sidney Lumet: Film and Literary Vision*, 109–22; John McCarten, "The Current Cinema: Surcharged Veniremen," review, *New Yorker* 33 (April 27, 1957): 66; Henry Fonda with Howard Teichman, *My Life* (New York: New American Library, 1981), 248–50; Alleman, *The Movie Lover's Guide to New York*, 200–201.
216. Stern, Gilmartin and Mellins, *New York 1930*, 92–93, 97.
217. A. H. Weiler, "North by Northwest," review, *New York Times* (August 7, 1959): 28; Schickel, *The Men Who Made the Movies*, 294–95; Spoto, *The Art of Alfred Hitchcock*, 300–311; Spoto, *The Dark Side of Genius: The Life of Alfred Hitchcock*, 406; Truffaut with Scott, *Hitchcock*, 11, 19, 102, 250, 254, 262, 265; Alleman, *The Movie Lover's Guide to New York*, 200–201. For the New York County Courthouse, see Stern, Gilmartin and Mellins, *New York 1930*, 92–93, 97–99.
218. Bosley Crowther, "Wait until Dark," review, *New York Times* (October 27, 1967): 48.
219. A. H. Weiler, "Blindfold," review, *New York Times* (May 26, 1966): 55.
220. Howard Thompson, "Madigan," review, *New York Times* (March 30, 1968): 22.
221. Vincent Canby, "Coogan's Bluff," review, *New York Times* (October 3, 1968): 56.
222. Stern, Gilmartin and Mellins, *New York 1930*, 126–29, 131.
223. Canby, "Coogan's Bluff": 56.
224. Vincent Canby, "Serpico," review, *New York Times* (December 6, 1973): 61. Also see "Up Against the Cops," *Time* 97 (May 31, 1971): 52, 55–56; Martin Arnold, "Knapp Witness to Tell of Lindsay Officials' Apathy," *New York Times* (October 30, 1971): 1, 18; "Serpico Tells of Delay of Police Inquiry," *New York Times* (December 15, 1971): 1, 57; Martin Arnold, "Serpico's Lonely Journey to Knapp Witness Stand," *New York Times* (December 15, 1971): 57; Peter Maas, *Serpico* (New York: Viking, 1973).
225. Vincent Canby, "Mean Streets," review, *New York Times* (October 3, 1973): 38; Vincent Canby, "Down 'Mean Streets,'" *New York Times* (October 14, 1973), II: 1; Conrad, *The Art of the City: Views and Versions of New York*, 289.
226. Vincent Canby, "The Godfather," review, *New York Times* (March 16, 1972): 56; Pauline Kael, "The Current Cinema: Alchemy," review, *New Yorker* 48 (March 18, 1972): 132–38; Alleman, *The Movie Lover's Guide to New York*, 205–6.
227. Vincent Canby, "The Godfather, Part II," review, *New York Times* (December 13, 1974): 58; Vincent Canby, "'The Godfather, Part II': One Godfather Too Many," *New York Times* (December 22, 1974), II: 19; Pauline Kael, "The Current Cinema: Fathers and Sons," review, *New Yorker* 50 (December 23, 1974): 63–66.
228. Vincent Canby, "Story of Gunman Takes Dim View of City: Death Wish," review, *New York Times* (July 25, 1974): 27. Also see Penelope Gilliatt, "The Current Cinema: New York, New York," review, *New Yorker* 50 (August 26, 1974): 48, 50; Jerry Vermilye, *The Films of Charles Bronson* (Secaucus, N.J.: Citadel, 1980), 213–16.
229. Stern, Gilmartin, and Mellins, *New York 1930*, 170–71, 174.
230. Stern, Gilmartin and Mellins, *New York 1930*, 155, 160.
231. Canby, "Story of Gunman Takes Dim View of City: Death Wish": 27.
232. Gilliatt, "The Current Cinema: New York, New York": 48, 50.
233. Vincent Canby, "Farce Slides Between Humor and Despair," review, *New York Times* (October 10, 1974): 62. Also see Canby, "New York's Woes Are Good Box Office": 1.
234. Canby, "Farce Slides Between Humor and Despair": 62.
235. Canby, "New York's Woes Are Good Box Office": 1.
236. Vincent Canby, "Three Days of the Condor," review, *New York Times* (September 25, 1975): 60; William F. Buckley, Jr., "Redford vs. the C.I.A.," *New York Times* (September 28, 1975), II: 1; Canby, "Cynical Cinema Is Chic": 13; Pauline Kael, "The Current Cinema: The Visceral Poetry of Pop," review, *New Yorker* 51 (October 6, 1975): 98; Manbeck, *Brooklyn on Film*, 43; Alleman, *The Movie Lover's Guide to New York*, 193, 225, 252.
237. Vincent Canby, "Marathon Man," review, *New York Times* (October 7, 1976): 62; Pauline Kael, "The Current Cinema: Running into Trouble," *New Yorker* 52 (October 11, 1976): 138–40; Vincent Canby, "Explicit Violence Overwhelms Every Other Value on the Screen," *New York Times* (October 17, 1976), II: 1; Vincent Canby, "Who Says There Aren't Any Good Movies Around?" *New York Times* (October 24, 1976), II: 15; Canby, "Cynical Cinema Is Chic": 13; Manbeck, *Brooklyn on Film*, 39; Alleman, *The Movie Lover's Guide to New York*, 67, 142.
238. Stern, Gilmartin and Massengale, *New York 1900*, 342–44.
239. Canby, "Explicit Violence Overwhelms Every Other Value on Screen": 1.
240. Vincent Canby, "No Way to Treat a Lady," review, *New York Times* (March 21, 1968): 56.
241. Roger Greenspun, "Little Murders," review, *New York Times* (February 10, 1971): 34; Vincent Canby, "What's So Funny? 'Murders,'" *New York Times* (February 21, 1971), II: 1; Pauline Kael, "The Current Cinema: Varieties of Paranoia," review, *New Yorker* 47 (March 6, 1971): 92, 94–95.
242. Canby, "What's So Funny? 'Murders'": 1.
243. Kael, "The Current Cinema: Varieties of Paranoia": 92.
244. Howard Thompson, "'Gang that Couldn't' Opens Here," review, *New York Times* (December 23, 1971): 20.
245. Roger Greenspun, "Screen: 'X, Y & Zee' and 'Hot Rock' Begin Runs," review, *New York Times* (January 27, 1972): 42; Manbeck, *Brooklyn on Film*, 21. For the Brooklyn Museum, see Stern, Gilmartin and Massengale, *New York 1900*, 87–91.
246. Roger Greenspun, "Cops and Robbers," review, *New York Times* (August 16, 1973): 40; Penelope Gilliatt, "The Current Cinema: Time Out for the Underdog," review, *New Yorker* 49 (August 27, 1973): 49.
247. See Vincent Canby, "Mame," review, *New York Times* (March 8, 1974): 18; Pauline Kael, "The Current Cinema: A Brash Young Man," review, *New Yorker* 50 (March 11, 1974): 122–24.
248. Bosley Crowther, "Auntie Mame," review, *New York Times* (December 5, 1958): 39.
249. A. H. Weiler, "Breakfast at Tiffany's," review, *New York Times* (October 6, 1961): 28; Charles Higham, *Audrey* (New York: Macmillan, 1984), 148. Also see Truman Capote, *Breakfast at Tiffany's* (New York: Random House, 1958); Pye, *Maximum City: The Biography of New York*, 25.
250. Weiler, "Breakfast at Tiffany's": 28.
251. Bosley Crowther, "Two for the Seesaw," review, *New York Times* (November 24, 1962): 203–4; Denis, *The Films of Shirley MacLaine*, 118–21.

252. Bosley Crowther, "Two for the Seesaw": 43.
253. A. H. Weiler, "Greenwich Village," review, *New York Times* (July 12, 1963): 14; Miller, *Greenwich Village and How It Got That Way*, 228.
254. Weiler, "Greenwich Village Story": 14.
255. Bosley Crowther, "Across the River," review, *New York Times* (April 27, 1965): 27.
256. Bosley Crowther, "A Thousand Clowns," review, *New York Times* (December 14, 1965): 54; Brendan Gill, "The Current Cinema: Mavericks," review, *New Yorker* 41 (December 18, 1965): 162.
257. Crowther, "A Thousand Clowns": 54.
258. Gill, "The Current Cinema: Mavericks": 162.
259. Renata Adler, "The Odd Couple," review, *New York Times* (May 3, 1968): 42.
260. Terrace, *The Complete Encyclopedia of Television Programs 1947–1979*, 732–33.
261. Stern, Gilmartin and Massengale, *New York 1900*, 283–85.
262. Renata Adler, "Rosemary's Baby," review, *New York Times* (June 13, 1968): 57; Barbara Leaming, *Polanski: The Filmmaker as Voyeur* (New York: Simon & Schuster, 1981), 86–87; Roman Polanski, *Roman* (New York: William Morrow, 1984), 267–73; Virginia Wright Wexman, *Roman Polanski* (Boston: Twayne, 1985), 63–65; Alleman, *The Movie Lover's Guide to New York*, 65, 220.
263. Bosley Crowther, "At the Capital," review, *New York Times* (April 8, 1949): 31; Manbeck, *Brooklyn on Film*, 18.
264. Crowther, "At the Capital": 31.
265. Bosley Crowther, "Little Fugitive," review, *New York Times* (October 7, 1953): 35; John McCarten, "The Current Cinema: Small Marvel," review, *New Yorker* 29 (October 10, 1953): 126–27; Manbeck, *Brooklyn on Film*, 25; Ruth Orkin, *A Photo Journal* (New York: Viking, 1981), 11.
266. Bosley Crowther, "The World of Henry Orient," review, *New York Times* (March 20, 1964): 27; Brendan Gill, "The Current Cinema: No Tampering," review, *New Yorker* 40 (March 28, 1964): 144, 147; Nora Johnson, *Flashback: Nora Johnson on Nunnally Johnson* (Garden City, N. Y.: Doubleday, 1979), 287–89, 295–301; Andrew Horton, *The Films of George Roy Hill* (New York: Columbia University Press, 1984), 41–52; Alleman, *The Movie Lover's Guide to New York*, 62, 66, 173.
267. Gill, "The Current Cinema: No Tampering": 144.
268. Howard Thompson, "You're a Big Boy Now," review, *New York Times* (March 21, 1967): 35.
269. Thompson, "You're a Big Boy Now": 35.
270. Howard Thompson, "Greetings," review, *New York Times* (December 16, 1968): 61; Pauline Kael, "The Current Cinema: Frightening the Horses," review, *New Yorker* 44 (December 21, 1968): 91.
271. Vincent Canby, "Patty Duke Plays Ugly Teenager in Coe Film: 'Me, Natalie,'" review, *New York Times* (July 14, 1969): 27. Also see Manbeck, *Brooklyn on Film*, 40.
272. Vincent Canby, "The Magic Garden of Stanley Sweetheart," review, *New York Times* (May 27, 1970): 38; Canby, "Ah, Youth! Ah, Sex! Ah, Revolution!": 1.
273. Canby, "Ah, Youth! Ah, Sex! Ah, Revolution!": 1; Vincent Canby, "Horowitz Adapts Diary of Columbia Student," review, *New York Times* (June 16, 1970): 54; Dotson Rader, "A Razzberry for 'Strawberry,'" *New York Times* (July 19, 1970), II: 9.
274. Rader, "A Razzberry for 'Strawberry'": 9.
275. Roger Greenspun, "Jeremy," review, *New York Times* (August 2, 1973): 28; Rosalyn Drexler, "'Jeremy—A Big 'Little' Movie," *New York Times* (August 12, 1973), II: 1.
276. Greenspun, "Jeremy": 28.
277. A. H. Weiler, "The Lords of Flatbush," review, *New York Times* (May 2, 1974): 61; Manbeck, *Brooklyn on Film*, 26.
278. Vincent Canby, "From the Mixed-Up Files of Mrs. Basil E. Frankweiler," review, *New York Times* (September 28, 1973): 25.
279. Pauline Kael, "The Current Cinema: The Artist as a Young Comedian," review, *New Yorker* 52 (February 2, 1976): 79–81; Vincent Canby, "Next Stop, Greenwich Village," review, *New York Times* (February 5, 1976): 24; Vincent Canby, "Paul Mazursky's Profoundly Superficial Film," *New York Times* (February 5, 1976), II: 19; Manbeck, *Brooklyn on Film*, 40; Miller, *Greenwich Village and How It Got That Way*, 229.
280. Kael, "The Current Cinema: The Artist as a Young Comedian": 79.
281. Thomas M. Pryor, "Christmas in Connecticut," review, *New York Times* (July 28, 1945): 7.
282. Bosley Crowther, "Mr. Blandings Builds His Dream House," review, *New York Times* (March 27, 1948): 10; John McCarten, "The Current Cinema: The Disinherited," review, *New Yorker* 24 (April 3, 1948): 58. Also see Eric Hodgins, *Mr. Blandings Builds His Dream House* (New York: Simon & Schuster, 1946).
283. Stern, Gilmartin and Mellins, *New York 1930*, 591–92, 594.
284. Bosley Crowther, "Please Don't Eat the Daisies," review, *New York Times* (April 1, 1960): 37; John McCarten, "The Current Cinema: Strained Whimsey," review, *New Yorker* 36 (April 9, 1960): 107–8.
285. Vincent Canby, "The Swimmer," review, *New York Times* (May 16, 1968): 53; Penelope Gilliatt, "The Current Cinema: How to Mangle an Idea and Stay Radiant," review, *New Yorker* 44 (May 25, 1968): 84, 87.
286. Canby, "The Swimmer": 53.
287. Theodore Strauss, "Tarzan's New York Adventure," review, *New York Times* (August 7, 1942): 13; Pye, *Maximum City: The Biography of New York*, 26.
288. Strauss, "Tarzan's New York Adventure": 13.
289. Bosley Crowther, "Miracle on 34th Street," review, *New York Times* (June 5, 1947): 32; John McCarten, "The Current Cinema: Santa Out of Season," review, *New Yorker* 23 (June 14, 1947): 88.
290. Thomas M. Pryor, "The Secret Life of Walter Mitty," review, *New York Times* (August 14, 1947): 29.
291. Thomas F. Brady, "Dark Days for Independents," *New York Times* (January 21, 1951), II: 5; Helen Gould, "The Trick Men Take Over," *New York Times* (March 25, 1951), II: 5.
292. Bosley Crowther, "The World, the Flesh and the Devil," review, *New York Times* (May 21, 1959): 35; McCarten, "The Current Cinema: Beating the Heat": 91.
293. Crowther, "The World, the Flesh and the Devil": 35.
294. Nora Sayre, "A King in New York," review, *New York Times* (December 22, 1973): 11; Roger Manvell, *Chaplin* (Boston: Little, Brown, 1974), 215–17; Vincent Canby, "Chaplin—Once a King, Always a 'King,'" *New York Times* (January 20, 1974), II: 1; Dan Kamin, *Charlie Chaplin's One-Man Show* (Metuchen, N.J.: Scarecrow, 1984), 158–59; David Robinson, *Chaplin: His Life and Art* (London: Collins, 1985), 584–93; Charles J. Maland, *Chaplin and American Culture: The Evolution of a Star Image* (Princeton, N.J.: Princeton University Press, 1989), 320–25.
295. Bosley Crowther, "The Mouse that Roared," review, *New York Times* (October 27, 1959): 40; John McCarten, "The Current Cinema: Love at a Glance," review, *New Yorker* 35 (November 7, 1959): 205; George Vecsey, "One on One with New York," *New York Times* (March 15, 1991), C: 1–2.
296. Vincent Canby, "What's So Bad about Feeling Good?" review, *New York Times* (May 25, 1968): 27.
297. A. H. Weiler, "Soylent Green," review, *New York Times* (April 20, 1973): 21.
298. Vincent Canby, "Godspell," review, *New York Times* (March 22, 1973): 52.
299. Roger Greenspun, "Heavy Traffic," review, *New York Times* (August 9, 1973): 30.
300. Vincent Canby, "Sleeper," review, *New York Times* (December 18, 1973): 52; Pauline Kael, "The Current Cinema: Survivor," *New Yorker* 49 (December 31, 1973): 47–49; Douglas Brode, *Woody Allen: His Films and Career* (Secaucus, N.J.: Citadel, 1985), 134–45.
301. *Richard Meier Architect: 1964/1984* (New York: Rizzoli International Publications, 1984), 54–63.
302. "Manufacturers Go Ape Over 'Kong,'" *New York* 9 (October 18, 1976): 87; Wallace Markfield, "The Kong and I," *New York Times* (December 12, 1976), VI: 36–37, 78; Vincent Canby, "King Kong Bigger, Not Better, in a Return to Screen of Crime," review, *New York Times* (December 18, 1976): 16; Vincent Canby, "Kong Speaks: Thoughts of a Private Ape," *New York Times* (December 19, 1976), II: 1, 15; John Simon, "Ape Rape," *New York* 9 (December 27, 1976), 79–82; Eder, "Hollywood Is Having an Affair with the Anti-Hero": 1, 8; Vincent Canby, "What Are We to Make of Remakes?" *New York Times* (January 16, 1977), II: 1, 11; Carolyn See, "Hollywood's Secret Star Is the Special-Effects Man," *New York Times* (May 1, 1977), II: 1, 15; Alleman, *The Movie Lover's Guide to New York*, 194–95. For Ernest B. Schoedash and Merian C. Cooper's *King Kong* (1933), see Stern, Gilmartin and Mellins, *New York 1930*, 81, 85.
303. Canby, "King Kong Bigger, Not Better, in a Return to Screen of Crime": 16.
304. For *Manahatta* and *The City*, see Stern, Gilmartin and Mellins, *New York 1930*, 86–87.
305. A. H. Weiler, "Rudy Burckhardt's New York," review, *New York Times* (March 2, 1974): 22. For further discussion of Burckhardt's life and work, see his autobiographical *Mobile Homes* (Calais, Vt.: Z Press, 1979).
306. "Four Films by Rudy Burckhardt," review, *Village Voice* 8 (February 1, 1962): 11; Weiler, "Rudy Burckhardt's New York": 22.
307. For Reginald Marsh's interwar-period paintings of New York, see Stern, Gilmartin and Mellins, *New York 1930*, 61–62.
308. "Four Films by Rudy Burckhardt": 11.
309. "Four Films by Rudy Burckhardt": 11. Also see Weiler, "Rudy Burckhardt's New York": 22.
310. Weiler, "Rudy Burckhardt's New York": 22.
311. Weiler, "Rudy Burckhardt's New York": 22.
312. Elodie Osborn, "New York on Screen," *Art in America* 52 (October 1964): 80–89; Alfred T. Barson, *A Way of Seeing: A Critical Study of James Agee* (Amherst, Mass.: University of Massachusetts Press, 1972), 111–12; Geneviève Moreau, *The Restless Journey of James Agee*, trans. Miriam Kleiger with Morty Schiff (New York: William Morrow, 1977): 252; Laurence Bergreen, *James Agee: A Life* (New York: E. P. Dutton, 1984), 292–93.
313. James Agee and Walker Evans, *Let Us Now Praise Famous Men* (Boston: Houghton Mifflin, 1941).
314. Helen Levitt, *A Way of Seeing*, with an essay by James Agee (New York: Viking Press, 1965).
315. James Agee quoted in Osborn, "New York on Screen": 84. Also see Bergreen, *James Agee: A Life*, 293.
316. Osborn, "New York on Screen": 86.
317. Francis Thompson, "More Optic Nerve for the Film Maker," *Art in America* 67 (April 1959): 59; Osborn, "New York on Screen": 60, 68; Loren Cocking, "Francis Thompson's Optic Nerve," *Journal of the University Film Association* 21 (1969): 25–28; Lewis Jacobs, *The Documentary Tradition* (New York: W. W. Norton, 1971), 277–78; Flora Rheta Schreiber, "New York—A Cinema Capital," *Quarterly of Film, Radio and Television* 7 (spring 1973): 264–73; George Rehrauer, *The Short Film* (New York: Macmillan, 1975), 110.
318. Thompson, "More Optic Nerve for the Film Maker": 59.
319. Schreiber, "New York—A Cinema Capital": 268.
320. Osborn, "New York on Screen": 86.
321. Osborn, "New York on Screen": 86.
322. Osborn, "New York on Screen": 86.
323. Osborn, "New York on Screen": 86.
324. Jacobs, *The Documentary Tradition*, 277; Rehrauer, *The Short Film*, 40.
325. Osborn, "New York on Screen": 88; Rehrauer, *The Short Film*, 142.
326. For the Bayard and Little Singer buildings, see Stern, Gilmartin and Massengale, *New York 1900*, 153–55.
327. Jacobs, *The Documentary Tradition*, 277–78.
328. Osborn, "New York on Screen": 88.
329. Osborn, "New York on Screen": 88.
330. "On the Bowery," review, *Film Culture* 12 (1957): 16–17; Don Ross, "'On the Bowery': Authentic Face of Skid Row," *New York Herald Tribune* (March 17, 1957): 1, 4; Bosley Crowther, "Screen: 'On the Bowery,'" review, *New York Times* (March 19, 1957): 44; Joe Pihodna, "On the Screen: 'On the Bowery,'" review, *New York Herald Tribune* (March 19, 1957): 17; Bosley Crowther, "Down-and-Outers: 'On the Bowery' Looks Candidly at Drunks," *New York Times* (March 31, 1957), II: 1; Jacobs, *The Documentary Tradition*, 278.
331. Crowther, "Screen: 'On the Bowery'": 44.
332. Crowther, "Down-and-Outers: 'On the Bowery' Looks Candidly at Drunks": 1. For in-depth discussion of documentary films by the movie critic and filmmaker John Grierson, see his *Grierson on Documentary* (London: Faber, 1966).
333. Jonas Mekas, "Movie Journal," *Village Voice* 10 (June 30, 1964): 13; James Stoller, "Beyond Cinema: Notes on Some Films by Andy Warhol," *Film Quarterly* 20 (fall 1968): 35–38; Stephen Koch, *Stargazer—Andy Warhol's World and His Films* (New York: Praeger, 1973), 19, 34, 59; Richard Henshaw, "Stargazer—Andy Warhol's World and His Films," review, *American Film Institute Report* 4 (winter 1973): 51; John Coplans with Jonas Mekas and Calvin Tomkins, *Andy Warhol* (New York: New York Graphic Society, 1969), 147; Peter Gidal, *Andy Warhol: Films and Paintings* (New York: E. P. Dutton, 1971), 90; Victor Bockris, *The Life and Death of Andy Warhol* (New York: Bantam, 1989), 154–55; Jesse Kornbluth, "Andy," *New York* 20 (March 9, 1987): cover, 39–45, 48–49; Jack Kroll, "The Most Famous Artist," *Newsweek* 109 (March 9, 1987): 64–66. For the Empire State Building, see Stern, Gilmartin and Mellins, *New York 1930*, 610–15.

334. Andy Warhol quoted in Bockris, *The Life and Death of Andy Warhol*, 154.
335. Gerard Malanga quoted in Bockris, *The Life and Death of Andy Warhol*, 155.
336. Gidal, *Andy Warhol: Films and Paintings*, 90.
337. Jonas Mekas, "Movie Journal," *Village Voice* 12 (September 29, 1966): 27; Jack Kroll, "Underground in Hell," review, *Newsweek* 48 (November 14, 1966): 109; Dan Sullivan, "Andy Warhol's 'Chelsea Girls' at the Cinema Rendezvous," review, *New York Times* (December 2, 1966): 46; Elenore Lester, "So He Stopped Painting Brillo Boxes and Bought a Movie Camera," *New York Times* (December 11, 1966), II: 3; Andrew Sarris, "Films," review, *Village Voice* 12 (December 15, 1966): 33, "Nuts from Underground," review, *Time* 88 (December 30, 1966): 37; Brian O'Doherty, "Narcissus in Hades," review, *Art & Artists* 2 (February 15, 1967): 15; Vincent Canby, "Cannes Will See Warhol Picture," *New York Times* (April 25, 1967): 37; Rosalyn Regelson, "Where are the 'Chelsea Girls' Taking Us?" *New York Times* (September 24, 1967), II: 15; Coplans with Mekas and Tomkins, *Andy Warhol*, 153; Gidal, *Andy Warhol: Films and Paintings*, 110–18; Henshaw, "Stargazer—Andy Warhol's World and His Films": 51; Kroll, "The Most Famous Artist": 66; Kornbluth, "Andy": 44; Bockris, *The Life and Death of Andy Warhol*, 191–96; David Bourdon, *Warhol* (New York: Harry N. Abrams, 1989), 238–52; Fred Lawrence Guiles, *Loner at the Ball: The Life of Andy Warhol* (London: Bantam, 1989), 255–61.
338. Kroll, "Underground in Hell": 109.
339. O'Doherty, "Narcissus in Hades": 15. Also see Hubert Selby, Jr., *Last Exit to Brooklyn* (New York: Grove Press, 1964).
340. Sullivan, "Andy Warhol's 'Chelsea Girls' at the Cinema Rendezvous": 46.
341. Stephen Holden, "Beauty Amid the Beastliness in Portraits of Manhattan," *New York Times* (July 11, 1989), C: 16.
342. Holden, "Beauty Amid the Beastliness in Portraits of Manhattan": 16.
343. Howard Thompson, "'Street Scenes 1970,'" review, *New York Times* (September 15, 1970): 52.
344. Francis Herridge, "Experiencing New York on Screen," review, *New York Times* (September 29, 1973): 21; Patricia O'Haire, "'New York Experience' on Film," review, *New York Daily News* (September 29, 1973): 23; Paul Gardner, "City Is Star of Multimedia Show," review, *New York Times* (October 2, 1973): 54; Burt Supree, "Hopped-up Hardsell for a City," review, *Village Voice* 20 (February 7, 1974): 25.
345. Gardner, "City Is Star of Multimedia Show": 54.
346. Supree, "Hopped-up Hardsell for a City": 25.
347. O'Haire, "'New York Experience' on Film": 23.
348. Rusty Russell quoted in Gardner, "City Is Star of Multimedia Show": 54.

NEW YORK IN MUSIC AND DANCE

1. Brooks Atkinson, "Knickerbocker Holiday," review, *New York Times* (October 20, 1938): 26.
2. Lewis Nichols, "Up in Central Park," review, *New York Times* (January 29, 1945): 17. For the film version, see Thomas M. Pryor, "Up in Central Park," review, *New York Times* (May 27, 1948): 29.
3. Brooks Atkinson, "Miss Liberty," review, *New York Times* (July 16, 1945): 6.
4. Howard Taubman, "'Hello, Dolly!' Has Premiere," review, *New York Times* (January 17, 1964): 20.
5. Howard Taubman, "Funny Girl," review, *New York Times* (March 27, 1964): 15.
6. Brooks Atkinson, "Little Flower Blooms Again," review, *New York Times* (November 24, 1959): 45.
7. Brooks Atkinson, "Wonderful Town," review, *New York Times* (February 26, 1953): 22; Terry Miller, *Greenwich Village and How It Got That Way* (New York: Crown, 1990), 45–46.
8. Brooks Atkinson, "The Play: 'My Sister Eileen,' a Comedy of the Village," *New York Times* (December 27, 1940): 23; Miller, *Greenwich Village and How It Got That Way*, 45.
9. Brooks Atkinson, "Guys and Dolls," review, *New York Times* (November 25, 1950): 10.
10. Lewis Nichols, "On the Town," review, *New York Times* (December 29, 1944): 11.
11. Brooks Atkinson, "The Jungles of the City," review, *New York Times* (September 27, 1957): 14.
12. "America," words by Stephen Sondheim and music by Leonard Bernstein (New York: G. Schirmer and Chappell, 1957).
13. Atkinson, "The Jungles of the City": 14.
14. Brooks Atkinson, "Helen Gallagher in the Title Part of a Musical Comedy about New York City," review, *New York Times* (February 12, 1953): 22.
15. Frank S. Nugent, "A Witty and Impudent Comedy, 'Nothing Sacred,'" review, *New York Times* (November 26, 1937): 27.
16. "Ev'ry Street's a Boulevard (in Old New York)," words by Bob Hilliard, music by Jule Styne (New York: Stratford Music, 1953).
17. Howard Taubman, "'How to Succeed' a Success," review, *New York Times* (October 16, 1961): 34.
18. Howard Taubman, "Premiere for 'Subways Are for Sleeping,'" review, *New York Times* (December 28, 1961): 22. Also see Edmund G. Love, *Subways Are for Sleeping* (New York: Harcourt, Brace, 1957).
19. "Ride through the Night," words by Betty Comden and Adolph Green, music by Jule Styne (New York: Stratford Music, 1961).
20. Howard Taubman, "Sammy Davis in a Musical 'Golden Boy': Show Based on Odets' Play at the Majestic," review, *New York Times* (October 2, 1964): 56.
21. "Don't Forget 127th Street," words by Lee Adams, music by Charles Strouse (New York: Strada Music, 1964).
22. Stanley Kauffmann, "Show that Wants to Be Loved," review, *New York Times* (January 31, 1966): 22.
23. Clive Barnes, "Simon-Bacharach 'Promises, Promises' Begins Run at the Shubert," review, *New York Times* (December 2, 1968): 59.
24. Howard Taubman, "'Skyscraper' Has Livelier Dream Girl," review, *New York Times* (November 15, 1965): 48; John McCarten, "The Theater: No Firm Foundation," review, *New Yorker* 41 (November 20, 1965): 149; "Pie in the Sky," review, *Newsweek* 56 (November 29, 1965): 91; Andrew Alpern and Seymour Durst, *Holdouts!* (New York: McGraw-Hill, 1984): 6.
25. McCarten, "The Theater: No Firm Foundation": 149.
26. "Pie in the Sky": 91.
27. Taubman, "'Skyscraper' Has Livelier Dream Girl": 48.
28. "Frank Mills," words by James Rado and Gerome Ragni, music by Galt MacDermot (New York: United Artists Music, 1967).
29. "Broadway Baby," words and music by Stephen Sondheim (New York: Valando Music and Beautiful Music, 1971).
30. Clive Barnes, "A Tremendous 'Chorus Line' Arrives," review, *New York Times* (May 22, 1975): 32; Clive Barnes, "'A Chorus Line,' a Musical to Sing about for Years," review, *New York Times* (October 20, 1975): 44.
31. Barnes, "A Tremendous 'Chorus Line' Arrives": 32.
32. *Company: A Musical Comedy* [libretto], book by George Furth, music and lyrics by Stephen Sondheim, originally produced and directed on Broadway by Harold Prince (New York: Random House, 1970). Also see "Another Hundred People," words and music by Stephen Sondheim (New York: Valando Music and Beautiful Music, 1970).
33. *Street Scene* [libretto], music by Kurt Weill, book by Elmer Rice, lyrics by Langston Hughes (New York: Chappell, 1947). Also see Hans F. Redlich, "Kurt Weill," *Music Review* 11 (August 1950): 208.
34. *The Saint of Bleecker Street* [libretto], words and music by Gian-Carlo Menotti (New York: G. Schirmer, 1954). Also see Lincoln Kirstein, "Menotti: The Giants in Bleecker Street," *Center* 1 (December 1954): 3–8; John Gruen, *Menotti* (New York: Macmillan, 1978), 119–24; John Ardoin, *The Stages of Menotti* (Garden City, N.Y.: Doubleday, 1985), 70–82.
35. Kirstein, "Menotti: The Giants in Bleecker Street": 6, 8.
36. "Fancy Free," review, *New York Times* (April 19, 1944): 27.
37. Jane Jacobs quoted in Marshall Berman, *All That Is Solid Melts into Air* (New York: Simon & Schuster, 1982), 318.
38. Berman, *All That Is Solid Melts Into Air*, 318.
39. Meredith Monk quoted in Roselee Goldberg, *Performance: Live Art 1909 to the Present* (New York: Harry N. Abrams, 1979), 93.
40. Goldberg, *Performance: Live Art 1909 to the Present*, 104.
41. Goldberg, *Performance: Live Art 1909 to the Present*, 104.
42. Frances Herridge, "Tharp and Beach Boys as Guests," review, *New York Post* (March 2, 1973): 32; Anna Kisselgoff, "Twyla Tharp's 'Deuce Coupe' Is a Vividly American Dance," review, *New York Times* (March 3, 1973): 17; Deborah Jowitt, "Dancing to Beat the Band," review, *Village Voice* 19 (March 8, 1973): 35–36; "Underground Artists," *Newsweek* 82 (October 1, 1973): 69–70; Deborah Jowitt, "Twyla Tharp's New Kick," *New York Times* (January 4, 1976), VI: cover, 10–12, 18–21.
43. Jowitt, "Dancing to Beat the Band": 35.
44. Kisselgoff, "Twyla Tharp's 'Deuce Coupe' Is a Vivdly American Dance": 17.
45. "The Sidewalks of New York," words and music by Charles B. Lawlor and James W. Blake (New York: Howley, Haviland, 1894).
46. "Autumn in New York," words and music by Vernon Duke (New York: Warren Brothers, 1934). For discussion of interwar-period songs about New York, see Stern, Gilmartin and Mellins, *New York 1930*, 87–89.
47. "How About You," words and music by Ralph Freed and Burton Lane (New York: Leo Feist, 1941).
48. "New York's My Home," words and music by Gordon Jenkins (New York: MCA Music, 1946).
49. "New York's Not My Home," words and music by Jim Croce (New York: Blending Well Music, 1971).
50. "The Brooklyn Bridge," words by Sammy Cahn, music by Jule Styne (New York: Sinatra Songs, 1947).
51. "Brooklyn, U.S.A.," words and music by Abe Burrows, in *The Abe Burrows Songbook* (Garden City, N.Y.: Doubleday, 1955).
52. "Brooklyn Roads," words and music by Neil Diamond (Philadelphia: Stonebridge Music, 1968).
53. "Harlem Nocturne," words by Dick Rogers, music by Earle Hagen (New York: Shapiro, Bernstein, 1940).
54. "Spanish Harlem," words and music by Phil Spector and Jerry Leiber (New York: Unichappell Music/Trio Music, 1960).
55. "On Broadway," words and music by Barry Mann, Cynthia Weil, Mike Stoller and Jerry Leiber (Hollywood, Calif.: Screen Gems–EMI Music, 1962).
56. "Funky Broadway," words and music by Arlester Christian (Hollywood, Calif.: Drive-In Music, 1967).
57. John Rockwell, "A Drop-Out Sings of Her Tangled Life," *New York Times* (February 29, 1976), II: 1, 17.
58. Maggie Paley, "Laura Nyro: Funky Madonna of New York Soul," *Life* 68 (January 30, 1970): 44–47. Also see Irwin Stambler, *Encyclopedia of Pop, Rock, and Soul* (New York: St. Martin's Press, 1974), 381–83.
59. "Mercy on Broadway," words and music by Laura Nyro (New York: Tuna Fish Music, 1969).
60. "Map to Treasure," words and music by Laura Nyro (New York: Tuna Fish Music, 1971).
61. "New York Tendaberry," words and music by Laura Nyro (New York: Tuna Fish Music, 1969).
62. "Does this Bus Stop at 82nd Street," words and music by Bruce Springsteen (New York: Bruce Springsteen Music, 1972).
63. "Incident on 57th Street," words and music by Bruce Springsteen (New York: Bruce Springsteen Music, 1973).
64. "New York City Serenade," words and music by Bruce Springsteen (New York: Bruce Springsteen Music, 1973).
65. "Tenth Avenue Freeze-Out," words and music by Bruce Springsteen (New York: Bruce Springsteen Music, 1975).
66. O. B. Hardison, Jr., *Disappearing through the Skylight* (New York: Viking, 1989), 235; Lisa Peppercorn, *Villa-Lobos* (London: Omnibus Press, 1989), 107.
67. Avenir de Monfred, *Manhattan Sketches: Suite New Yorkaise* (Paris: Editions Musicales des Cinéastes Associés, 1956).
68. "New York City Blues," music by Duke Ellington (New York: Tempo Music, 1952). For discussion of Duke Ellington's life and work, see Stanley Dance, *The World of Duke Ellington* (New York: Charles Scribner's Sons, 1970); Ken Rattenbury, *Duke Ellington, Jazz Composer* (New Haven, Conn.: Yale University Press, 1990).
69. Dave Brubeck, text accompanying "Jazz Impressions of New York," music by Dave Brubeck (New York: Edward B. Marks Music, by arrangement with Groton Music, 1964).
70. "New York State of Mind," words and music by Billy Joel (New York: Homegrown Music and Tin Pan Tunes, 1975).
71. "New York City Rhythm," words and music by Barry Manilow and Marty Panzer (New York: Kamakazi Music and Martin Panzer, 1975).

ARCHITECTURAL CULTURE: DISCOURSE

1. Charles Edouard Jeanneret-Gris, *Quand les cathédrals étaient blanches* (Paris: Plon, 1937), *When the Cathedrals Were White*, trans. Francis E. Hyslop, Jr. (New York: Reynal and Hitchcock, 1947).

2. Stern, Gilmartin and Mellins, *New York 1930*, 344.

3. Stern, Gilmartin and Mellins, *New York 1930*, 330.

4. For further discussion of the "Useful Objects" exhibitions, see Russell Lynes, *Good Old Modern: An Intimate Portrait of the Museum of Modern Art* (New York: Atheneum, 1973), 181.

5. "Industrial Design Competitions," *Bulletin of the Museum of Modern Art* 8 (February–March 1941): 13–14; "Industrial Design Competition," *Bulletin of the Museum of Modern Art* 8 (June–July 1941): 16; "Organic Design in Home Furnishings," *Bulletin of the Museum of Modern Art* 8 (September 1941): 9; "Organic Design in Home Furnishings," *Pencil Points* 22 (October 1941): 633–36; "Organic Design at the Museum of Modern Art," *Interiors* 101 (October 1941): 38–39, 68.

6. Robert Goldwater in collaboration with René d'Harnoncourt, "Modern Art in Your Life," *Bulletin of the Museum of Modern Art* 17, no. 1 (1949): 1–48; "René d'Harnoncourt's 'Modern Art in Your Life,'" *Interiors* 109 (November 1949): 94–97, 168, 170.

7. Betty Pepis, "Designs for Today," *New York Times* (November 19, 1950), VI: 48–49; Betty Pepis, "For the Home: 250 Good Designs for All Purposes," *New York Times* (November 22, 1950): 29; "The Museum of Modern Art Presents 'Good Design,'" *Interior Design and Decoration* 21 (December 1950): 46–47, 84.

8. "Good Design 1952: Paul Rudolph's Installation Gets Raves," *Architectural Record* 111 (March 1952): 26; Olga Gueft, "'Good Design' in Chiaroscuro: Paul Rudolph Designs the Mart's Third Exhibition," *Interiors* 111 (March 1952): 130–37, 186, 189–90; "A Different Light on Good Design: The New York Version," *Interiors* 112 (November 1952): 130–31.

9. Edward Steichen, *The Family of Man*, exhibition catalogue (New York: Published for the Museum of Modern Art by the Maco Magazine Corp., 1955); "The Family of Man," *Interiors* 114 (April 1955): 114–17; Paul Rudolph, *Drawings* (Tokyo: A.D.A. Edita, 1972), 206.

10. Elizabeth Mock, ed., *Built in USA, 1932–1944*, exhibition catalogue (New York: Museum of Modern Art, 1944); "Built in U.S.A. 1932–44," *Architectural Forum* 80 (May 1944): 81–82; Edward Alden Jewell, "Activities in the Art World: Modern Architects and Post-war Building," *New York Times* (August 13, 1944), II: 2.

11. Henry-Russell Hitchcock and Arthur Drexler, eds., *Built in USA: Post-war Architecture*, exhibition catalogue (New York: Museum of Modern Art, 1952); "Built in USA: Post-war Architecture," *Architectural Record* 113 (February 1953): 10–12; Charles Magruder, "Postwar Sobriety: Built in U.S.A.: Postwar Architecture," *Progressive Architecture* 34 (February 1953): 172, 174; "Built Since V/J Day: Recent Architecture in America on Record and in Review," *Interiors* 112 (April 1953): 100–103.

12. Mock, ed., *Built in USA: 1932–1944*, 102–3; Stern, Gilmartin and Mellins, *New York 1930*, 616–71.

13. Mock, ed., *Built in USA: 1932–1944*, 88–89; Stern, Gilmartin and Mellins, *New York 1930*, 141–45.

14. Mock, ed., *Built in USA: 1932–1944*, 114; Stern, Gilmartin and Mellins, *New York 1930*, 694–95.

15. Mock, ed., *Built in USA: 1932–1944*, 50–51; Stern, Gilmartin and Mellins, *New York 1930*, 379.

16. Philip Johnson, "Preface" in Hitchcock and Drexler, eds., *Built in USA: Post-war Architecture*, 8–9.

17. Arthur Drexler quoted in Lynes, *Good Old Modern*, 319. Also see Richard Schickel, *The Museum* (New York: Museum of Modern Art, 1970), unpaginated.

18. Henry-Russell Hitchcock, *Gaudí*, exhibition catalogue (New York: Museum of Modern Art, 1957); "Exhibitions: Fantastic Architecture in Stern Setting," *Interiors* 117 (March 1958): 10, 12.

19. *The Drawings of Frank Lloyd Wright*, exhibition catalogue (New York: Horizon Press, 1962); "Wright Retrospect," *Architectural Forum* 116 (February 1962): 11; Ada Louise Huxtable, "Drawings and Dreams of Frank Lloyd Wright," *New York Times* (March 11, 1962), VI: 24–25; Ada Louise Huxtable, "The Facts of Wright's Greatness," *New York Times* (March 18, 1962), II: 21.

20. F. Lanier Graham, *Hector Guimard*, exhibition catalogue (New York: Museum of Modern Art, 1970); John Gruen, "Back to Nature," *New York* 3 (March 16, 1970): 55; "New Look at Nouveau," *Architectural Forum* 132 (April 1970): 76–77; "Guimard Exhibition Opens in New York," *Progressive Architecture* 51 (April 1970): 39.

21. Ada Louise Huxtable, "Worlds They Never Made," *New York Times* (September 25, 1960), VI: 30–31; "Museum Shows Visionary Design," *Progressive Architecture* 40 (October 1960): 78; Ada Louise Huxtable, "The Architect as a Prophet," *New York Times* (October 2, 1960), II: 21; Walter McQuade, "Architecture," *Nation* 191 (October 29, 1960): 333–34; "Visionary Architecture's Forecast for Future?" *Architectural Record* 128 (November 1960): 14–15.

22. *Twentieth Century Engineering*, exhibition catalogue (New York: Museum of Modern Art, 1964); James T. Burns, Jr., "20th Century Engineering—Where Is the Architect?" *Progressive Architecture* 45 (August 1964): 61.

23. Bernard Rudofsky, *Architecture without Architects: An Introduction to Nonpedigreed Architecture*, exhibition catalogue (New York: Museum of Modern Art, 1964); Ada Louise Huxtable, "Architectless Architecture—Sermons in Stone," *New York Times* (November 15, 1964), II: 23; "MOMA Continues Attack on Architects," *Progressive Architecture* 45 (December 1964): 45, 47; Jan C. Rowan, "Editorial," *Progressive Architecture* 45 (December 1964): 121; C. J. McNaspy, "Three Great Retrospectives," *America* 111 (December 5, 1964): 759–60; Bernard Rudofsky, Arthur Drexler, Peter W. Gygax, Leonard K. Eaton, David E. Coldoff and Henrik Bull, letters to the editor, *Progressive Architecture* 46 (March 1965): 8, 14, 18, 26.

24. *Louis I. Kahn, Architect, Richards Medical Research Building*, exhibition catalogue (New York: Museum of Modern Art, 1961); Ada Louise Huxtable, "In Philadelphia, an Architect," *New York Times* (June 11, 1961), II: 4. For a subsequent Museum of Modern Art exhibition on Kahn's work, see "The Architecture of Louis Kahn," *Interiors* 125 (May 1966): 10, 12; "Kahn at MOMA," *Progressive Architecture* 47 (June 1966): 47, 49.

25. Ada Louise Huxtable, "Planning the New City," *New York Times* (January 24, 1967): 39, 45; *The New City: Architecture and Urban Renewal*, exhibition catalogue (New York: Museum of Modern Art, 1967).

26. Ada Louise Huxtable, "When Life Is Stranger than Art," *New York Times* (July 30, 1967), II: 25–26; "Past and Present," *Architectural Forum* 127 (September 1967): 90.

27. "Neon City," *Architectural Forum* 130 (April 1969): cover, 1, 68–73; "Function without Form," *Progressive Architecture* 50 (April 1969): 46.

28. Ada Louise Huxtable, "Not for City Planners," *New York Times* (April 18, 1971), II: 22.

29. "MOMA Holds Tent Show," *Progressive Architecture* 52 (July 1971): 37; *The Work of Frei Otto*, exhibition catalogue (New York: Museum of Modern Art, 1972).

30. Ada Louise Huxtable, "Poetic Visions of Design for the Future," *New York Times* (April 27, 1975), II: 32; Barbara Rose, "Fantasy Vs. Reality," *Vogue* 166 (May 1975): 166. For a general discussion of Emilio Ambasz's curatorial efforts at the Museum of Modern Art, see Sharon Lee Ryder, "The Art of High Art," *Progressive Architecture* 56 (March 1975): 62–67.

31. Ada Louise Huxtable, "Beaux-Arts—The Latest Avant Garde," *New York Times* (October 26, 1975), VI: 76–82, reprinted as "Art and Theory: Rediscovering the Beaux Arts" in Ada Louise Huxtable, *Kicked a Building Lately?* (New York: Quadrangle/New York Times Book Co., 1976), 58–66; John Lobell, "The Beaux-Arts: A Reconsideration of Meaning in Architecture," *Journal of the American Institute of Architects* 64 (November 1975): 32–37; John Morris Dixon, "Blessing the Beaux-Arts," editorial, *Progressive Architecture* 56 (November 1975): 7; Ada Louise Huxtable, "Growing Up in a Beaux Arts World," *New York Times* (November 9, 1975), II: 1, 33, reprinted as "Pleasures: Beaux Arts Buildings I Have Known" in Huxtable, *Kicked a Building Lately?*, 217–21; "Beaux-Arts: A Major Exhibition at the Museum of Modern Art," *Interior Design* 46 (December 1975): 140–41; "MOMA Beaux-Arts Exhibition a Must," *Progressive Architecture* 56 (December 1975): 17–18; Jean Paul Carlhian, "Beaux Arts or 'Bozarts'?" *Architectural Record* 159 (January 1976): 131–34; Beverly Russell, "The École des Beaux-Arts Show at the Museum of Modern Art: A Shot in the Arm for Architecture," *House and Garden* 148 (February 1976): 106–9; Arthur Drexler, ed., *The Architecture of the Ecole des Beaux-Arts*, exhibition catalogue (New York: Museum of Modern Art, 1977).

32. Drexler, ed., *The Architecture of the Ecole des Beaux-Arts*, 6, 8.

33. Dixon, "Blessing the Beaux-Arts": 7.

34. Huxtable, "Planning the New City": 39, 45.

35. "Architects Induct Ketchum," *New York Times* (April 11, 1958): 39. Also see "Architect League Sets 20 Programs," *New York Times* (August 24, 1958), VIII: 10; Morris Ketchum, Jr., *Blazing a Trail* (New York: Vantage Press, 1982).

36. "Architectural League Exhibit, Recast by Ketchum, Regains Prestige; Scheuer Seeks Congress Seat," *Architectural Forum* 112 (April 1960): 13–14; "Architectural Show Stresses Chords That Make Harmony," *New York Times* (April 17, 1960), VIII: 1, 6; "The Architectural League; Not For Architects Alone," *Interiors* 119 (June 1960): 128–35.

37. "Architecture—Fitting and Befitting," *Architectural Forum* 114 (June 1961): 86–89. Also see "Architectural League of New York: Lively Forum on Art Presented," *Interiors* 120 (March 1961): 22–23; "Personalities," *Progressive Architecture* 42 (May 1961): 48.

38. "Making the Scene at the League," *Progressive Architecture* 46 (December 1965): 42.

39. Ada Louise Huxtable, "Staten Island's Beauty Losing to Builders," *New York Times* (August 9, 1965): 1, 28.

40. *40 Under 40*, exhibition catalogue (New York: Architectural League of New York, 1941).

41. Robert A. M. Stern, *40 under 40: An Exhibition of Young Talent in Architecture*, exhibition catalogue (New York: Architectural League of New York, 1966); "Introverted League Exhibit," *Progressive Architecture* 47 (June 1966): 52–53; Barbara Plumb, "'40 under 40'—Young Design in Living," *New York Times* (April 24, 1966), II: 96–97, 99; "40 under 40," *Interiors* 125 (May 1966): 10, 12; "40 under 40: Young American Trends," *Building* 211 (December 1966): 24.

42. Stern, Gilmartin and Mellins, *New York 1930*, 190.

43. "Uncontrolled Environment," *Architectural Forum* 126 (January–February 1967): 109–10.

44. "Uncontrolled Environment": 110.

45. John Samuel Margolies, "Slipcover, A Place by Les Levine," *Arts* 41 (May 1967): 57–58; William D. Gordy, "Slipcover by Les Levine," *Craft Horizons* 27 (May–June 1967): 67; "Levine Leavens the League," *Progressive Architecture* 48 (June 1967): 62; Anne Tabachnick, "Les Levine," *Art News* 66 (summer 1967): 23; *Public Mind: Les Levine's Media Sculpture and Mass Ad Campaigns 1969–1990*, exhibition catalogue (Syracuse, N.Y.: Everson Museum of Art, 1990), 19, 99.

46. Les Levine quoted in "Levine Leavens the League": 62.

47. Tabachnick, "Les Levine": 23.

48. Gordy, "Slipcover by Les Levine": 67.

49. Barbara Stauffacher quoted in "Budget Subway Esthetics," *Interiors* 127 (June 1967): 24.

50. John Lobell and Michael Steiner quoted in Dore Ashton, "New York," *Studio* 174 (November 1967): 215–17.

51. Ashton, "New York": 216.

52. "Architectural League Exhibits Continue Experimental Program," *Architectural Record* 142 (December 1967): 36; N. J. Loftis, "Environment V: Vibrations," *Craft Horizons* 28 (March–April 1968): 53–54.

53. Loftis, "Environment V: Vibrations": 53.

54. Jacqueline Barnitz, "Six One Word Plays: Byars Presents a Series of Events," *Arts* 43 (September–October 1968), 17, 19; Grace Glueck, "A Mile of Red Acetate Parades Up 65th Street," *New York Times* (September 13, 1968): 38; Grace Glueck, "Arts Notes: Next Year—Or So—In Jerusalem," *New York Times* (September 22, 1968), II: 36; "Psychosculpture," *Time* 92 (September 27, 1968): 77; "The Pink Silk Airplane and Other Events," *Progressive Architecture* 49 (November 1968): 52; David L. Shirey, "Impossible Art—What It Is," *Art in America* 57 (May–June 1969): 32–47; Blair Sabol, "Outside Fashion," *Village Voice* 15 (June 18, 1970): 18, 32; John and Mimi Lobell, *John and Mimi: A Free Marriage* (New York: St. Martin's Press, 1972): 47.

55. James Lee Byars quoted in Shirey, "Impossible Art—What It Is": 38.

56. Glueck, "A Mile of Red Acetate Parades Up 65th Street": 38.

57. Glueck, "Arts Notes: Next Year—Or So—In Jerusalem": 36.

58. "Psychosculpture": 77.

59. Alan Sonfist quoted in "Studied and Stricken: The Survival of the Army Ant," *Craft Horizons* 32 (April 1972): 5. Also see "Obit," *Architectural Forum* 136 (April 1972): 23, 69; William D. Case, "Army Ants: Patterns and Structures," *Arts* 46 (April 1972): 71.

60. "Obit": 69.

61. "Architectural League Exhibits Continue Experimental Program": 36; "The Diamond in Architecture and Painting—Space Experiments," *Interiors* 127 (December 1967): 12.

62. Ada Louise Huxtable, "Peacock Feathers and Pink Plastic," *New York Times* (February 8, 1970), II: 25; "Bruce Goff Exhibition at League," *Progressive Architecture* 51 (March 1970): 47.
63. *Morris Lapidus: Architecture of Joy*, exhibition catalogue (New York: Architectural League of New York and American Federation of Arts, 1970); John Samuel Margolies, "'Now, Once and for All, Know Why I Did It'—Morris Lapidus: The 'Give 'Em What They Want' School of Architecture," *Progressive Architecture* 51 (September 1970): 118–23; Ulrich Franzen, "The Joy Boy," *Architectural Forum* 133 (October 1970): 67; "Show a Success, but the Barkers Walked Out," *Progressive Architecture* 51 (October 1970): 28; Ada Louise Huxtable, "Show Offers 'Joy' of Hotel Architecture," *New York Times* (October 15, 1970): 50; "Johnson, Roche, Rudolph and Lapidus, Subject of Two Exhibitions," *Architectural Record* 148 (November 1970): 37; "The Morris Lapidus Phenomenon at the Architectural League," *Interiors* 130 (November 1970): 10; "Monuments to Showmanship: Morris Lapidus, Architectural League, New York, Exhibit," *Interior Design* 41 (November 1970): 25; Morris Lapidus, *An Architecture of Joy* (Miami, Fla.: E. A. Seemann, 1979), 211–21; Martina Duttmann and Friederike Schneider, eds., *Morris Lapidus: Architect of the American Dream* (Basel: Birkhäuser Verlag, 1992), 8.
64. Franzen, "The Joy Boy": 67.
65. Huxtable, "Show Offers 'Joy' of Hotel Architecture": 50.
66. "Cornell Students Study 'Abroad': Semester Program in New York City," *Architectural Record* 134 (November 1963): 33.
67. Steven V. Roberts, "School Is Formed for Urban Design," *New York Times* (October 15, 1967): 52.
68. Peter Eisenman quoted in Roberts, "School Is Formed for Urban Design": 52.
69. Peter Eisenman quoted in Roberts, "School Is Formed for Urban Design": 52.
70. See *Five Architects: Eisenman, Graves, Gwathmey, Hejduk, Meier*, with an intro. by Colin Rowe (New York: Wittenborn, 1972) and "Five on Five," *Architectural Forum* 138 (May 1973): 46–57. Also see Paul Goldberger, "Architecture's '5' Make Their Ideas Felt," *New York Times* (November 26, 1973): 33, 52; Paul Goldberger, "Should Anyone Care About the 'New York Five'? . . . or About Their Critics the 'Five on Five'?" *Architectural Record* 155 (February 1974): 113–16. Rosemarie Haag Bletter's unpublished talk, "The Grey and White Architects: False Polarizations in Recent Architectural Criticism," delivered at the twenty-ninth annual meeting of the Society of Architectural Historians, Philadelphia, May 19–24, 1976, offered another critique; see *Journal of the Society of Architectural Historians* 35 (December 1976): 292.
71. Goldberger, "Architecture's '5' Make Their Ideas Felt": 52.
72. "Putting the Art before the Course," *New York* 7 (September 9, 1974): 59; Paul Goldberger, "Midtown Architecture Institute Flowering as a Student Mecca," *New York Times* (October 30, 1974): 41, 77.
73. "Goodbye Five: Work by Young Architects," *Progressive Architecture* 56 (November 1975): 20–21.
74. *Oppositions* 1–26 (Cambridge, Mass.: MIT Press, September 1973–April 1984).
75. Goldberger, "Midtown Architecture Institute Flowering as a Student Mecca": 41.
76. For discussions of Lewis Mumford's life and work, see Leif Sjöberg, "An Interview with Lewis Mumford," *Structuralist* 25/26 (1985–86): 1–15; Stern, Gilmartin and Mellins, *New York 1930*, 8–9; Thomas P. Hughes and Agatha C. Hughes, eds., *Lewis Mumford: Public Intellectual* (New York: Oxford University Press, 1990); "Lewis Mumford, a Visionary Social Critic, Dies at 94," *New York Times* (January 28, 1990): 30; Paul Goldberger, "Lewis Mumford: Preacher, Prophet, Romantic," *New York Times* (February 4, 1990), II: 38, 40; Kirkpatrick Sale, "Lewis Mumford," *Nation* 250 (February 19, 1990): 225; Colin Ward, "Obituary: Lewis Mumford," *Architectural Review* 187 (March 1990): 9; Michael J. Crosbie, "Lewis Mumford, 1895–1990," *Architecture* 79 (March 1990): 38; "Lewis Mumford 1895–1990," *Progressive Architecture* 71 (March 1990): 24; Selden Rodman, "Memories of Mumford," *National Review* 42 (March 5, 1990): 58–59; Perry Norton, "Lewis Mumford (1895–1990)," *Journal of the American Planning Association* 56 (spring 1990): 160; Joseph Abram, "Lewis Mumford, Casandre du Moderne," *L'Architecture d'Aujourd'hui* 268 (April 1990): 58, 60; "Lewis Mumford: A Memorial Note," *Town Planning Review* 61 (April 1990): 207–8; Brendan Gill, "The Sky Line: Homage to Mumford," *New Yorker* 66 (April 2, 1990): 90, 92–93; Russell Lynes, "New York: Lewis Mumford," *Architectural Digest* 47 (November 1990): 110, 114; Kenneth Frampton, "Lewis Mumford: Ecologist, 1895–1990," *A + U* (November 1990): 3–4.
77. Letter from Harold Ross to Lewis Mumford, January 13, 1947, in the Lewis Mumford Collection, Charles Patterson Van Pelt Library, Department of Special Collections, University of Pennsylvania, quoted in Donald L. Miller, *Lewis Mumford: A Life* (New York: Weidenfeld & Nicolson, 1989), 445.
78. Books by Lewis Mumford published after 1940 include *The Social Functions of Post-War Building* (London: Faber & Faber, 1943); *The Conditions of Man* (New York: Harcourt, Brace, 1944); *City Development: Studies in Urban Disintegration and Renewal* (New York: Harcourt, Brace, 1945); *The Plan of London County* (London: Faber & Faber, 1945); *Values for Survival: Essays, Addresses, and Letters on Politics and Education* (New York: Harcourt, Brace, 1946); *Green Memories: The Story of Geddes Mumford* (New York: Harcourt, Brace, 1947); *The Conduct of Life* (New York: Harcourt, Brace, 1951); *Art and Technics* (New York: Columbia University Press, 1952); *The Transformations of Man* (New York: Harper & Brothers, 1956); *The City in History: Its Origins, Its Transformations and Its Prospects* (New York: Harcourt, Brace & World, 1961); *The Myth of the Machine: I. Technics and Human Development* (New York: Harcourt, Brace & World, 1967); *The Urban Prospect* (New York: Harcourt, Brace & World, 1968); *The Myth of the Machine: II. The Pentagon of Power* (New York: Harcourt Brace Jovanovich, 1970); *Findings and Keepings: Analects for an Autobiography* (New York: Harcourt Brace Jovanovich, 1975); *My Works and Days: A Personal Chronicle* (New York: Harcourt Brace Jovanovich, 1979); *Sketches from Life: The Autobiography of Lewis Mumford* (New York: Dial Press, 1982). Also see Donald L. Miller, ed., *The Lewis Mumford Reader* (New York: Pantheon, 1986).
79. "Aline Saarinen Resigns," *New York Times* (December 1, 1959): 46; "Programming: Intelluptuously Speaking," *Time* 90 (November 3, 1967): 86; Alden Whitman, "Aline Saarinen, Art Critic, Dies at 58," *New York Times* (July 15, 1972): 26; John Canaday, "Aline Saarinen 1914–1972," *New York Times* (July 23, 1972), II: 15; "Aline Saarinen Memorial," *New York Times* (September 13, 1972): 50; "Governor Eulogizes Mrs. Saarinen Here," *New York Times* (September 15, 1972): 40; Barbara Delatiner, "Library of Art Critic Donated," *New York Times* (November 25, 1973): 149.
80. Aline B. Louchheim, "Now Saarinen the Son," *New York Times* (April 26, 1953), VI: 26–27, 44–45. Louchheim had previously written about Eero Saarinen's father, Eliel; see Aline B. Louchheim, "Architect, Artist, Finn, American," *New York Times* (August 28, 1948), VI: 16–17, 38, 40. Among the critic's other writings on architecture are Aline B. Louchheim, "'No Marbleomania—No Spinach,'" *New York Times* (July 13, 1949), VI: 20–22, 24, 26–27; Aline B. Louchheim, "Blueprint of a Working Architect," *New York Times* (September 10, 1950), VI: 25, 36, 38; Aline B. Louchheim, "To Save the Houses of Our Heritage," *New York Times* (June 28, 1953), VI: 16–17, 22–23; Aline B. Saarinen, "Pioneer of Modern Architecture," *New York Times* (October 28, 1956), VI: 26–27, 37, 39, 42, 44; Aline B. Saarinen, "Tour with Mr. Wright," *New York Times* (September 22, 1957), VI: 22–23, 69–70; Aline Saarinen, "He Saw Architecture as the Permanent Stage Set of an Age," *Life* 61 (September 16, 1966): 103–4, 106, 108.
81. Aline B. Saarinen, "Four Architects Helping to Change the Look of America," *Vogue* 12 (August 1, 1955): 118–21, 149–50, 152.
82. Aline B. Saarinen, ed., *Eero Saarinen on His Work* (New Haven, Conn.: Yale University Press, 1962).
83. "Programming: Intelluptuously Speaking": 86.
84. For an overview of Ada Louise Huxtable's criticism, see Suzanne Stephens, "Voices of Consequence: Four Architectural Critics," in Susana Torre, ed., *Women in Architecture: A Historic and Contemporary Perspective* (New York: Whitney Library of Design, 1977), 136–43. Also see "Newspapers: 'Civic Consciences,'" *Time* 89 (March 31, 1967): 66.
85. Ada Louise Huxtable, *Pier Luigi Nervi* (New York: George Braziller, 1960).
86. Ada Louise Huxtable, "Progressive Architecture in America: Grand Central Depot—1869–71," *Progressive Architecture* 37 (October 1956): 135–38; Ada Louise Huxtable, "Progressive Architecture in America: Harper and Brothers Building—1854," *Progressive Architecture* 38 (February 1957): 153–54; Ada Louise Huxtable, "Progressive Architecture in America: Store for E. V. Haughwout and Company—1857," *Progressive Architecture* 39 (February 1958): 133–36; Ada Louise Huxtable, "Progressive Architecture in America: Brooklyn Bridge—1867–83," *Progressive Architecture* 39 (October 1958): 157–60.
87. Ada Louise Huxtable, *Four Walking Tours of Modern Architecture in New York City*, with an intro. by Arthur Drexler (New York: Museum of Modern Art and Municipal Art Society of New York, 1961).
88. Huson Jackson, *A Guide to New York Architecture 1650–1952* (New York: Reinhold Publishing Corp., 1952).
89. Ada Louise Huxtable, *Classic New York: Georgian Gentility to Greek Elegance* (Garden City, N.Y.: Doubleday, 1964). Also see Alan Burnham, ed., *New York Landmarks: A Study and Index of Architecturally Notable Structures in Greater New York* (Middletown, Conn.: Wesleyan University Press, 1963).
90. Ada Louise Huxtable, "The Art We Cannot Afford to Ignore (But Do)," *New York Times* (May 4, 1958), VI: 14–15, 86.
91. Clifton Daniel quoted in "Eye on the Environment," *Newsweek* 66 (August 23, 1965): 70–71.
92. Huxtable, "Staten Island's Beauty Losing to Builders": 1, 28. Also see "Personalities," *Progressive Architecture* 47 (January 1966): 52; "Civic Consciences": 66.
93. Peter Kihss, "Report of Songmy Incident Wins a Pulitzer for Hersh," *New York Times* (May 5, 1970): 1, 48; "Critics Choice," *Architectural Forum* 132 (June 1970): 71.
94. "Eye on the Environment": 70.
95. Alan Dunn, "Ada Louise Huxtable Already Doesn't Like It!" cartoon, *New Yorker* 44 (June 5, 1968): 33, reprinted in Stephen Grover, "Heeded Words: Ada Louise Huxtable Has Formidable Power as Architecture Critic," *Wall Street Journal* (November 7, 1972): 1, 12.
96. Donald Reilly, "I'd Give Anything to Be There When Ada Louise Huxtable Gets a Load of This," cartoon, *New Yorker* 47 (April 24, 1971): 37, reprinted in Grover, "Heeded Words: Ada Louise Huxtable Has Formidable Power as Architecture Critic": 1.
97. Grover, "Heeded Words: Ada Louise Huxtable Has Formidable Power as Architecture Critic": 1, 12. Also see William Marlin, "Forum," editorial, *Architectural Forum* 137 (December 1972): 17.
98. Ada Louise Huxtable, "Architecture: Huntington Hartford's Palatial Midtown Museum," *New York Times* (February 25, 1964): 33.
99. Lewis Mumford quoted in Grover, "Heeded Words: Ada Louise Huxtable Has Formidable Power as Architecture Critic": 12.
100. Vincent Scully, "Inattention," letter to the editor, *New York Times* (April 26, 1970): 26. Also see Ada Louise Huxtable, "American Architecture and Urbanism," book review, *New York Times* (November 23, 1969), VII: 6–7, 52, 54.
101. Ada Louise Huxtable quoted in "Eye on the Environment": 71.
102. Ada Louise Huxtable quoted in "Eye on the Environment": 71.
103. Harold Uris quoted in "Eye on the Environment": 71.
104. Richard Roth, Sr., quoted in "Eye on the Environment": 71.
105. "Mrs. Huxtable on Editorial Board," *New York Times* (September 26, 1973): 27; "People," *Architecture Plus* 1 (November 1973): 82.
106. Paul Goldberger, "Less Is More—Mies van der Rohe, Less Is a Bore—Robert Venturi," *New York Times* (October 17, 1971), VI: 34–37, 102–5.

Afterword

1. James B. Lindheim, "A New Class," *Harper's* 251 (August 1975): 6.
2. "Tall Ships, Ahoy!" *Newsweek* 88 (July 4, 1976): 95–99; Frank J. Prial, "The Forrestal's Bell Tolls 13 Times for 13 Colonies," *New York Times* (July 5, 1976): 20; Murray Schumach, "Fireworks Emblazon Sky Around Statue of Liberty," *New York Times* (July 5, 1976): 20; Richard F. Shephard, "Nation and Millions in City Joyously Hail Bicentennial," *New York Times* (July 5, 1976): 1, 20; "The Big 200th Bash," *Time* 108 (July 5, 1976): 8–14; "The Talk of the Town: The Fourth," *New Yorker* 52 (July 19, 1976): 19–23; "Oh, What a Lovely Party!" *Time* 108 (July 19, 1976): 8–13; "NYC: A New Spirit," *New York* 9 (September 20, 1976): 46–51; Kenneth Garrett, "Square Rigger," *National Geographic* 150 (December 1976): 824–57.
3. Pete Hamill, "New York Has Its Best Summer," *Village Voice* 21 (August 23, 1976): 11.
4. Walter F. Wagner, Jr., "Some Random Thoughts on Celebrations, Sailboats, and Cities," editorial, *Architectural Record* 160 (August 1976): 13.
5. "Carter & Co. Meet New York," *Time* 108 (July 19, 1976): 14–17. Also see "The Talk of the Town: Prepared," *New Yorker* 52 (July 12, 1976): 27–29; "Polishing the Apple," *Newsweek* 88 (July 19, 1976): 33–35; "When the 'Big Apple' Polished Its Image," *U.S. News & World Report* 81 (July 26, 1976): 28.
6. William Reel quoted in "Carter & Co. Meet New York": 17.
7. Hamill, "New York Has Its Best Summer": 11.
8. Andrew Hacker, *The New Yorkers: A Profile of an American Metropolis* (New York: Mason/Charter, 1975), 148.

1352

1361